The New York Times

CROSSWORD PUZZLE

DICTIONARY

The New York Times
CROSSWORD PUZZLE DICTIONARY

• Second Edition •

By

Tom Pulliam and Clare Grundman

A HUDSON GROUP BOOK

TIMES
BOOKS

Produced in association with Morningside Editorial Associates, Inc.
Designed by Martin Connell

Copyright © 1974, 1977, 1984 by Thomas Pulliam and Clare Grundman

Library of Congress Cataloging in Publication Data

Pulliam, Tom.
  The New York Times crossword puzzle dictionary.

  "A Hudson Group book."
  1. Crossword puzzles—Glossaries, vocabularies, etc.
I. Grundman, Clare, 1913-   . II. New York Times.
III. Title.
GV1507.C7P83   1984   793.73'2'03   84-40108
ISBN: 0-8129-1131-8

Manufactured in the United States of America

B98765432

PREFACE to the First Edition

THE NEW YORK TIMES CROSSWORD PUZZLE DICTIONARY exceeds in completeness and scope all other puzzle dictionaries. No useful word has been omitted. Not only have puzzles themselves been combed for synonyms that are used over and over, but also a word-for-word reading of major unabridged dictionaries, both current and old, has produced a thoroughly complete and extensive checklist.

Each of us has been solving and compiling puzzles for many years, and our chief purpose has been to design a practical and easy-to-use dictionary, in the belief that your needs and requirements for such a volume closely reflect our own. For example, the synonyms are arranged by the number of letters, and then alphabetized so you can quickly find the very word that fills the spaces in the puzzle. Another feature, one that seems obvious for a crossword puzzle dictionary but is not found in most of them, is that all words are printed in easy-to-read capital letters. The type has been chosen with great care for its legibility, and the three-column format not only provides a short line of type to scan but also enables us to get a very large number of words on each page.

Synonyms of great length have been omitted to give room for the shorter, more useful words. The puzzler can always "fill in" the very long words provided he has a good supply of short common synonyms. We have placed, therefore, an arbitrary ceiling of eight-letter word-lengths, knowing this will satisfy almost all needs. Here and there, however, you will find occasional exceptions to this rule. These are synonyms of such frequent, interesting, and normal usage that their omission might handicap the puzzler.

The "shaded boxes" scattered through the book are a notable and unique feature of THE NEW YORK TIMES CROSSWORD PUZZLE DICTIONARY. They collect under one heading a variety of categories and synonyms that you would have a hard time finding in other dictionaries. For example, when you are confronted by the clue "Brazilian river" merely turn to the shaded area marked BRAZIL, where you will find several excellent possibilities. Similarly, look for a "Philippine native" under PHILIPPINES, or a "Scottish measure" under SCOT-LAND.

Another useful feature is the lavish listing of phrases. For instance, instead of being confronted by the simple clue "Sword," you may run up against "Double-edged sword." Under the entry word SWORD in this dictionary you will find ample phrases that qualify the entry word or more sharply specify its meaning. Also, given the definition "Turn aside," simply look under TURN and find that phrase, along with many others.

THE NEW YORK TIMES CROSSWORD PUZZLE DICTIONARY is a versatile reference book that you will want to keep on your desk or next to your chair for help, not only with crossword puzzles, but also for a large variety of other puzzles and contests. In addition, it will be invaluable for writers, speakers, and the like, for (with more than one-half million words) it is one of the largest books of synonyms ever published. Its simple arrangement makes it far easier to use than the standard thesauri.

Our hope is that you will come to use this new word book as we might. Get to know it and be adventuresome! If the first entry you consult does not corner the exact word you are seeking, let any listing at that spot lead you to a cross-reference. Follow this track until you have the right word "treed."

A project of this scope may well have been beyond the ability of only two to accomplish. We have required and welcomed top-flight support during our work. Although many might be named, special note must be given to the efforts of Richard Martz and David House of Dartmouth College, who were responsible for much of the computerization; also, to Gorton Carruth and Robert O'Brien of Morningside Associates. Each made his individual contributions, which we gratefully acknowledge.

Happy word hunting!

Tom Pulliam
Clare Grundman

1974

PREFACE to the Second Edition

This Second Edition of THE NEW YORK TIMES CROSSWORD PUZZLE DIC-TIONARY greatly augments the First Edition. We have added approximately 100,000 new entry words and synonyms into a new four-column format, which maintains the same easy-to-read features and the large numbers of words per page, including many new longer words. An outstanding innovation of this Second Edition is the inclusion of the titles of major works of literature and music, as well as their authors and composers, and the names of characters in books, plays, operas, etc. Another very important addition is the listing of famous people from various walks of life—painters, physicians, playwrights, botanists, etc.—as well as those men and women who have won Nobel Prizes and who have been inducted into the Hall of Fame. We have also assembled what we believe to be the most comprehensive listing of prefixes, suffixes, and combining forms, which are *listed by meaning,* and the largest list of biblical, mythological, and literary relationships ever to appear in a crossword puzzle dictionary. And, of course, we have retained from the First Edition the unique "shaded boxes" that feature pertinent facts about geographical locations.

We would like to acknowledge once more the excellent assistance of Gorton Carruth and Robert O'Brien of Morningside Editorial Associates and to thank the many puzzlers who have sent us their compliments and suggestions.

Again, we wish you happy word hunting!

T. P.
C. G.

1984

The New York Times

CROSSWORD PUZZLE

DICTIONARY

A AY HA AIR ARY PER ALFA EACH
ALPHA
(EVER —) ARROW
AA LAVA
AAL AL MULBERRY
AARDVARK ANTEATER EDENTATE
AARDWOLF HYAENID
AARON (BROTHER OF —) MOSES
(BURIAL PLACE OF —) HOR
(FATHER OF —) AMRAM
(MOTHER OF —) JOCHEBED
(SISTER OF —) MIRIAM
(SON OF —) ABIHU NADAB
ELEAZAR ITHAMAR
(WIFE OF —) ELISHEBA
AARONIC LEVITIC LEVITICAL
AB HATI
ABA ABAYAH
ABACA HEMP FIBER LUPIS LINAGA
MANILA
ABACK SHORT
ABACUS SOROBAN SHWANPAN
ABADDON PIT HELL ABYSS SATAN
APOLLYON
ABAFT AFT BACK BAFT ABAFF
ASTERN BEHIND REARWARD
(— THE BEAM) LARGE
ABALONE EAR PAUA AWABI
NACRE ORMER UHLLO ASSEIR
MOLLUSK
ABANDON EGO CAST DROP FLEE
JUNK QUIT SINK ABAND ALLAY
CHUCK DITCH EXPEL LEAVE
PLANT REMIT SCRAP WAIVE
YIELD ABJURE BANISH BETRAY
DESERT DEVEST DISUSE DIVEST
EXPOSE FOREGO FORHOO FORLET
MAROON RECANT REFUSE
REJECT RELENT RESIGN SLOUGH
VACATE DEPLORE DISCARD
FORFEIT FORSAKE SCUTTLE
ABDICATE FORHOOIE FORSWEAR
JETTISON RASHNESS RENOUNCE
SURCEASE RELINQUISH
(WITH —) DESPERATELY
ABANDONED BAD LEFT LORN
LOST VACANT WICKED CORRUPT
FORLORN PROJECT DEPRAVED
DERELICT DESERTED DESOLATE
FLAGRANT FORSAKEN
ABANDONING
(PREF.) LIPO
ABANDONMENT BURIAL
APOSTASY ABATEMENT
(— OF RESTRAINT) LETUP
ABANGA ADY
ABAS (FATHER OF —) CELEUS
LYNCEUS
(MOTHER OF —) METANIRA
HYPERMNESTRA
(SON OF —) PROETUS ACRISIUS
ABASE SINK VAIL AVALE AVILE
BLAME DEMIT DIMIT LOWER

SHAME ABJECT BEMEAN DEBASE
DEFAME DEJECT DEMEAN
DEPOSE GROVEL HUMBLE LESSEN
MEEKEN REDUCE DEGRADE
DEPRESS MORTIFY DIMINISH
DISGRACE DISHONOR
ABASED ABAISSE DEJECTED
ABASH AWE COW BASH BAZE
DASH AVALE ESBAY SHAME
HUMBLE AFFRONT CONFUSE
MORTIFY BEWILDER BROWBEAT
CONFOUND
ABASHED BLANK CHEAP SHAMED
ASHAMED FOOLISH SHEEPISH
ABASHMENT VERGOYNE
ABATE EBB END LOW CALM CURB
FAIK FALL MEND OMIT SLOW
SOFT VAIL VOID WANE ALLAY
ALLOW ANNUL APPAL BREAK
CHECK LOWER QUASH RELAX
REMIT SLAKE SWAGE ASLAKE
DEDUCT LESSEN PACIFY REBATE
REDUCE RELENT ABOLISH
ASSUAGE CASSARE CHANCER
NULLIFY QUALIFY SLACKEN
SUBSIDE DECREASE DIMINISH
MITIGATE MODERATE OVERBLOW
PALLIATE
ABATEMENT DELF FALL ALLAY
DELFT DELPH LETUP GUSSET
MIOSIS RABATE DECREASE
DISCOUNT PROSTRATION
(— OF DISEASE) LYSIS
ABATIS OBSTACLE SLASHING
ABAXIAL DORSAL
ABBA FATHER
ABBAY ABBACY
ABBE MONK CLERIC CURATE
PRIEST
ABBESS AMMA VICARESS
ABBEY ABADIA ABBAYE PRIORY
CONVENT NUNNERY CLOISTER
ABBOT ABBAS COARB
ARCHIMANDRITE
(— OF MISRULE) BISHOP
ABBREVIATE CUT CLIP DOCK
PRUNE DIGEST ABRIDGE BOBTAIL
CURTAIL SHORTEN CONDENSE
CONTRACT TRUNCATE
ABBREVIATED SHORT BOBTAIL
CRYPTIC MUTILATE
ABBREVIATION LAPSE SIGLUM
SYMBOL
(PL.) SIGLA
ABC ALPHABET
ABDA (FATHER OF —) SHAMMUA
(SON OF) ADONIRAM
ABDEEL (SON OF —) SHELEMIAH
ABDERITE FOOL SCOFFER
SIMPLETON
ABDI (SON OF —) KISHI
ABDICATE CEDE QUIT DEMIT
EXPEL LEAVE REMIT DEPOSE

DISOWN FOREGO RESIGN RETIRE
VACATE ABANDON DISCLAIM
RENOUNCE
ABDICATION DRIFT
ABDIEL (FATHER OF —) GUNI
(SON OF —) AHI
ABDOMEN BOUK WOMB ALVUS
APRON BELLY MELON MIRAC
PLEON THARM PAUNCH VENTER
STOMACH
(PREF.) CELI COELI VENTR(I)(O)
ABDOMINAL BELLY HEMAL CELIAC
COELIAC VENTRAL VISCERAL
ABDON (FATHER OF —) MICAH
HILLEL JEHIEL SHASHAK
ABDUCT LURE TAKE STEAL
ABDUCE KIDNAP RAVISH SPIRIT
CAPTURE
ABDUCTION APAGOGE RAPTURE
ABDUCTION FROM THE
SERAGLIO (CHARACTER IN —)
OSMIN PASHA BLONDE
BELMONTE PEDRILLO CONSTANZE
(COMPOSER OF —) MOZART
ABDUCTOR SPIRIT
ABEAM ABREAST
ABECEDARIAN TYRO NOVICE
LEARNER BEGINNER
ABECEDARIUS ABC
ABED SICK RESTING RETIRED
SLEEPING
ABEL (BROTHER OF —) CAIN SETH
(FATHER OF —) ADAM
(MOTHER OF —) EVE
(PARENT OF —) ADAM
ABE LINCOLN IN ILLINOIS
(AUTHOR OF —) SHERWOOD
(CHARACTER IN —) ABE ANN GALE
MARY SETH TODD GREEN SPEED
GRAHAM JIMMIE MENTOR NINIAN
BOWLING DOUGLAS EDWARDS
HERNDON RUTLEDGE
ABELMOSK MUSK MALLOW
ABENCERAGES (CHARACTER IN —)
ALMANSOR
(COMPOSER OF —) CHERUBINI
ABENCERRAJE (AUTHOR OF —)
VILLEGAS
(CHARACTER IN —) JARIFA
NARVAEZ RODRIGO ABINDARRAEZ
ABERDEEN ANGUS BLACK DODDY
DODDIE
ABERRANT WILD CLAMMY
DEVIANT ABNORMAL STRAYING
VARIABLE
ABERRATION SLIP WARP ERROR
FAULT LAPSE MANIA DELIRIUM
DELUSION INSANITY
ABESSIVE CARITIVE
ABET AID EGG BACK HELP BOOST
COACH ASSIST FOMENT INCITE
SECOND SUCCOR UPHOLD
COMFORT CONNIVE ESPOUSE

FORWARD FURTHER SUPPORT
SUSTAIN ADVOCATE BEFRIEND
ABETO ACXOYATL
ABETTING CONFEDERATE
ABETTOR FAUTOR ADVOCATE
PROMOTER
ABEYANCE ABEYANCY DORMANCY
ABEYANT LATENT
ABHIMANYU (FATHER OF —)
ARJUNA
(VICTIM OF —) LAKSHMANA
ABHOR UG IRK HATE SHUN AGRISE
DETEST LOATHE DESPISE DISLIKE
EXECRATE ABOMINATE
ABHORRENCE HATE ODIUM
HATRED HORROR DISGUST
DISLIKE SCUNNER AVERSION
LOATHING
ABHORRENT ODIOUS UGSOME
HATEFUL ABSONANT INFAMOUS
REPUGNANT
ABI (SON OF —) HEZEKIAH
ABIA (FATHER OF —) BECHER
SAMUEL JEROBOAM REHOBOAM
(HUSBAND OF —) HEZRON
ABIATHAR (FATHER OF —)
AHIMELECH
ABIDA (FATHER OF —) MIDIAN
ABIDE BE WIN WON BEAR BIDE
KEEP LAST LEND LENG LIVE REST
STAY WAIT ABEAR AWAIT DELAY
EXIST HABIT PAUSE STAND
SWELL TARRY ENDURE HARBOR
LINGER REMAIN RESIDE SUBMIT
INHABIT SOJOURN SUBSIST
SUSTAIN CONTINUE TOLERATE
(— BY) HOLD
ABIDING ABY FAST STABLE
LASTING
ABIDINGNESS PERMANENCE
ABIEL (SON OF —) KISH
ABIES FIRS CONIFERS
ABIETATE SYLVATE
ABIEZER (FATHER OF —) GILEAD
ABIGAIL MAID
(HUSBAND OF —) DAVID NABAL
JETHER
(SON OF —) AMASA DANIEL
CHILEAB
ABIGEUS ABACTOR
ABIHAIL (DAUGHTER OF —) ESTHER
(FATHER OF —) HURI ELIAB
(HUSBAND OF —) ABISHUR
REHOBOAM
(SON OF —) ZURIEL
ABIHU (BROTHER OF —) NADAB
(FATHER OF —) AARON
(MOTHER OF —) ELISHEBA
ABIHUD (FATHER OF —) BELA
ABIJAH (FATHER OF —) DAVID
SAMUEL JEROBOAM REHOBOAM
(SON OF —) ASA HEZEKIAH
ABILITY G CAN MAY CLAY EASE

FORM HAND CLASS FLAIR FORCE MIGHT POWER SKILL STUFF VERVE ENERGY ENGINE INGINE MAUGHT STROKE TALENT CALIBER CUNNING FACULTY POTENCY APTITUDE CAPACITY STRENGTH
(— TO ENTER) ACCESS
(— TO THROW) ARM
(BATTING —) STICKWORK
(CREATIVE —) IMAGINATION
(INVENTIVE —) CONTRIVANCE
(MENTAL —) INGENY BRAINPOWER
ABIMELECH (BROTHER OF —) JOTHAM
(FATHER OF —) GIDEON ABIATHA
ABINADAB (FATHER OF —) SAUL JESSE
ABINOAM (SON OF —) BARAK
ABIPON CORONADO
ABIRAM (FATHER OF —) HIEL ELIAB
ABISHAI (BROTHER OF —) JOAB ASAHEL
(MOTHER OF —) ZERUIAH
ABISHALOM (DAUGHTER OF —) MAACHAH
ABISHUA (FATHER OF —) BELA PHINEHAS
(SON OF —) BUKKI
ABISHUR (FATHER OF —) SHAMMAI
ABITAL (HUSBAND OF —) DAVID
ABITUB (FATHER OF —) SHAHARAIM
(MOTHER OF —) HUSHIM
ABJECT LOW BASE MEAN POOR SUNK VILE HELOT PRONE SORRY CRAVEN MENIAL PALTRY SORDID SUPINE FAWNING FORLORN IGNOBLE SERVILE SLAVISH BEGGARLY CRINGING DEGRADED DOWNCAST LISTLESS WRETCHED
ABJOINT ABSTRICT
ABJURE DENY NITTE SPURN ESCHEW RECALL RECANT REJECT RESIGN REVOKE ABANDON DISAVOW EJURATE RETRACT ABNEGATE DISCLAIM FORSWEAR RENOUNCE
ABLAUT APOPHONY
ABLAZE ALOW AFIRE ALOWE ABLEEZE BURNING GLOWING RADIANT GLEAMING INFLAMED
ABLE APT BIG CAN FIT FERE ADEPT HABIL SMART THERE CLEVER EXPERT FACILE FITTED HABILE POTENT STRONG BASTANT CAPABLE DOUGHTY DEXTROUS POSSIBLE POWERFUL SKILLFUL SUITABLE TALENTED VIGOROUS
(— TO WALK) FEERIE FEIRIE
(SUFF.) (— TO) FUL
ABLE-BODIED YAL YALD YAULD
ABLENESS
(SUFF.) ABILITY IBILITY
ABLUTION BATH WIDU WUDU WUZU LOTION BAPTISM BATHING WASHING
ABNAKI WABANAKI
ABNEGATE DENY ABJURE FOREGO REFUSE REJECT DISAVOW DISCLAIM FORSWEAR IMMOLATE RENOUNCE
ABNER (BROTHER OF —) KISH
(FATHER OF —) NER

(SLAYER OF —) JOAB
(SON OF —) JAASIEL
(WIFE OF —) RIZPAH
ABNORMAL ENORM QUEER UTTER ERRATIC UNUSUAL VICIOUS ABERRANT ATYPICAL FREAKISH TERATOID ANOMALOUS MONSTROUS
(PREF.) ANOM(O) DYS MAL PARA POLY PSEUD(O)
ABNORMALITY ATAXY ATAXIA LETHAL ANOMALY BROWNING DEMENTIA ENORMITY
(CATTLE —) SAWDUST
ABOARD ON ONTO ACROSS ATHWART
ABODE COT DAR HUT INN WON BODE CELL FLAT HALL HOME NEST OMEN REST SEAT TENT WOON BEING BOWER DELAY HAUNT HOUSE MANOR PITCH RESET SIEGE SUITE ABIDAL BIDING ESTATE ADDRESS COTTAGE HABITAT LODGING MANSION SITTING CUNABULA DOMICILE DWELLING RESIANCE TENEMENT
(— OF DEAD) DAR AARU HELL ARALU HADES ORCUS SHEOL HEAVEN SHADES XIBALBA
(— OF DELIGHT) ELYSIUM
(— OF EVIL POWERS) ABYSS
(— OF GIANTS) UTGARD
(— OF GODS) MERU ASGARD OLYMPUS
(— OF LOST SOULS) ABADDON
(— OF SOULS) LIMBO
(ANIMAL —) ZOO MENAGERIE
(CELESTIAL —) HEAVEN
(FILTHY —) STY STYE
(MISERABLE —) DOGHOLE
(SHELTERED —) SHADE
ABOLISH END BLOT KILL ABATE ANNUL ERASE FORDO QUASH CANCEL EFFACE FOREDO RECALL REPEAL REVOKE VACATE DESTROY NULLIFY RESCIND REVERSE ABROGATE
ABOLITION EXTINCTION
ABOMA BOA BOM BOMA
ABOMASUM READ REED
ABOMINABLE VILE RUSTY CURSED ODIOUS ROTTEN BEASTLY HATEFUL HEINOUS MALEDICT NEFANDOUS
ABOMINABLY BEASTLY
ABOMINATE HATE ABHOR DETEST LOATHE EXECRATE
ABOMINATION EVIL CRIME CURSE HORROR PLAGUE DISGUST AVERSION
ABONGO BABONGO
ABORAL DORSAL ABACTINAL
ABORIGINAL ABO YAO FIRST NATAL BINGHI NATIVE SAVAGE NATURAL PRIMARY ORIGINAL
(— WOMAN) GIN
ABORIGINE KA KHA TODA ALFUR BAIGA BLACK BOONG DASYU MAORI MYALL ALFURO ARANDA ARANTA ARUNTA BINGHI INDIAN KIPPER KODAGA NATIVE SAVAGE

ADIBASI CHINHWAN WARRAGAL WARRIGAL
ABORT SLIP
ABORTION ABORT FAILURE CASTLING FETICIDE MISBIRTH
ABORTIVE IDLE VAIN BLIND FUTILE BOOTLESS
ABOUND SNY FLOW SNEE TEEM COVER FLEET SWARM REDOUND OVERFLOW
(SUFF.) ULENT
ABOUNDING RIFE FLUSH ROUTH COPIOUS REPLETE TEEMING UBEROUS ABUNDANT AFFLUENT PROLIFIC
(SUFF.) IOUS OSE OUS
ABOUT BY IN OF ON RE SAY AWAY NEAR SOME UMBE UPON ANENT ASTIR CIRCA ABROAD ACTIVE ALMOST ANENST AROUND CIRCUM TOWARD ENVIRON CIRCITER
(PREF.) AMB(I) AMPH(I)(O) CIRCUM HYPER PERI
ABOUT-FACE FLOP
ABOVE ON UP OER SUP ATOP OVER PAST UPON ABEEN ABOON ABUNE ALOFT SUPRA BEFORE BEYOND HIGHER THEREUP OVERHEAD SUPERIOR
(— GENERAL LEVEL) APART
(PREF.) EP EPH EPI HYPER OVER SUPER SUPRA SUR
ABRADE RAW RUB BARK FILE FRET GALL RASP SAND WEAR CHAFE ERASE GRATE GRAZE GRIND SCORE SCUFF TOUCH SCOTCH SCRAPE IRRITATE
ABRADER FILE RASP EMERY SANDER ABRASER GRINDER SCRAPER
ABRAHAM (BIRTHPLACE OF —) UR
(BROTHER OF —) HARAN NAHOR
(CONCUBINE OF —) HAGAR
(FATHER OF —) TERAH
(GRANDFATHER OF —) NAHOR
(GRANDSON OF —) ESAU
(NEPHEW OF —) LOT
(SON OF —) ISAAC MEDAN SHUAH MIDIAN ZIMRAN ISHMAEL JOKSHAN
(WIFE OF —) SARAH KETURAH
ABRASION BURN GALL OUCH SCAR SORE GRAZE BRUISE BLASTING
ABRASIVE SAND EMERY PUMICE QUARTZ SILICA ALUNDUM ERODENT ABRADANT CORUNDUM PUMICITE SCRUBBER
ABRAXAS GEM STONE AMULET ABRASAX
ABREAST EVEN AFRONT BESIDE HANGING
ABRET BREAD WAFER
ABRI SHED COVER DUGOUT SHELTER
ABRIDGE CUT DOCK LASK BRIEF ELIDE LIMIT RASEE RAZEE BRIDGE REDUCE SHRINK CURTAIL DEPRIVE REWRITE SHORTEN ABSTRACT BREVIATE COMPRESS CONDENSE CONTRACT DIMINISH RETRENCH SIMPLIFY ABBREVIATE

ABRIDGED TAIL
ABRIDGEMENT BRIEF ABREGE DIGEST PRECIS RESUME SKETCH COMPEND EPITOME PANDECT SUMMARY SUMMULA ABSTRACT BOILDOWN BREVIARY SYNOPSIS ABBREVIATION ABBREVIATURE
ABROAD OFF ASEA AWAY ABOUT ASTIR FORTH ABREED AFIELD ASTRAY WIDELY DISTANT OUTWARD OVERSEA OFFSHORE
ABROGATE ANNUL QUASH REMIT CANCEL REPEAL REVOKE VACATE ABOLISH NULLIFY RESCIND DISSOLVE OVERRULE
ABRUPT BOLD CURT DEAD FAST RUDE BLUFF BLUNT BRIEF BRUSK HASTY ICTIC PLUMP QUICK ROUGH SHARP SHEER SHORT STEEP STUNT SURLY TERSE TOTAL CHOPPY CRAGGY CRUSTY PROMPT RUGGED SUDDEN ANGULAR BRUSQUE PRERUPT VIOLENT HEADLONG VERTICAL PRECIPITATE
(NOT —) SOFT
ABRUPTLY BANG SHARP SHORT STEEPLY SUDDENLY
ABSALOM (FATHER OF —) DAVID
(MOTHER OF —) MAACHAH
(SISTER OF —) TAMAR
(SLAYER OF —) JOAB
ABSALOM, ABSALOM (AUTHOR OF —) FAULKNER
(CHARACTER IN —) BON ROSA ELLEN HENRY JUDITH SHREVE SUTPEN THOMAS CHARLES COMPSON GOODHUE QUENTIN MCCANNON COLDFIELD
ABSAROKA CROW
ABSCESS BOIL MORO SORE ULCER FESTER INCOME LESION QUINSY VOMICA EXITURE GUMBOIL PARULIS APOSTEME SQUINACY
ABSCISIC ACID DORMIN
ABSCISSA X COSINE
ABSCISSION APOCOPE
ABSCOND GO FLY RUN BOLT FLEE HIDE QUIT ELOPE SCRAM SMOKE DECAMP DEPART DESERT ELOINE ESCAPE LEVANT WITHDRAW
ABSENCE CUT LACK VOID WANT BLANK LEAVE DEFECT REMOVE VACUUM DEFAULT FAILURE VACANCY FURLOUGH
(— FROM DUTY) LIBERTY
(— FROM ONE'S COUNTRY) EXILE
(— OF AN ORGAN) AGENESIA AGENESIS
(— OF BIAS) DETACHMENT
(— OF CEREMONY) FAMILIARITY
(— OF FAMILIARITY) DISTANCE
(— OF FEELING) APATHY
(— OF FEVER) APYREXY APYREXIA
(— OF FORM) ENTROPY
(— OF GOVERNMENT) ANARCHY
(— OF INHIBITIONS) ANIMALITY
(— OF LIGHT) BLACK DARKNESS
(— OF MARRIAGE) AGAMY
(— OF MIND) ABSTRACTION
(— OF NAILS) ANONYCHIA
(— OF PAIN) ANODYNIA

(— OF PIGMENTATION) ACHROMA
ACHROMIA
(— OF SKULL) ACRANIA
(— OF TAIL) ANURY
(— OF TASTE) AGEUSIA
(— OF TRUMPS) CHICANE
(— OF TRUTH) FALSEHOOD
(PREF.) DYS ECTRO NON
ABSENT CUT OFF OUT AWAY
AWOL GONE LOST WANE DESERT
MUSING LACKING MISSING
WANTING ABSORBED DREAMING
(— IN MIND) ABSTRACT
(PREF.) ECTRO
ABSENTMINDED MUSED MUSING
DISTRAIT DREAMING
ABSTRACTED
ABSENTMINDEDNESS
STARGAZING
ABSINTHE AJENJO GENIPI
ABSOLUTE GOD ONE TAO TAT
DEAD DOWN FAIR FINE FREE
MEAR MEER MERE PLAT PLUM
PURE RANK REAL SELF TRUE
VERY BLANK CLEAR FIXED PLUMB
SHEER STARK TOTAL UTTER
WHOLE ENTIRE PROPER SEVERE
SIMPLE SQUARE BRAHMAN
CERTAIN PERFECT PLENARY
ABSTRACT COMPLETE DESPOTIC
EVENDOWN EXPLICIT IMPLICIT
POSITIVE
(— TEMPERATURE) T
(NOT —) NISI FINITE CONDITIONAL
ABSOLUTELY YEA YES AMEN
BONE COLD DEAD FAIR JUST
PLAT SLAP PLAIN PLUMB STARK
BARELY FAIRLY FLATLY SIMPLY
WHOLLY SHEERLY ENTIRELY
EVENDOWN
ABSOLUTION EXCUSE PARDON
SHRIFT LOOSING SHRIVING
ABSOLUTISM CAESARISM
DESPOTISM
ABSOLVE FREE QUIT CLEAR LOOSE
REMIT ACQUIT ASSOIL EXCUSE
EXEMPT FINISH PARDON SHRIVE
UNBIND CLEANSE FORGIVE
JUSTIFY RELEASE DISPENSE
LIBERATE OVERLOOK
ABSORB EAT FIX SOP SUP BLOT
SOAK SUCK TAKE AMUSE DRINK
MERGE RIVET UNITE DEVOUR
ENGAGE ENGULF ENWRAP IMBIBE
INGEST INSORB INWRAP OCCUPY
SPONGE STIFLE COMBINE
CONSUME ENGROSS IMMERSE
INVOLVE OCCLUDE SWALLOW
ABSORBED DEEP GONE LOST
RAPT SUNK FIXED ABSENT
BURIED ENRAPT HIPPED INTENT
PLUNGED RIVETED WRAPPED
IMMERSED ABSTRACTED
(— BY) ALL
ABSORBENT BASE DOPE FOMES
BARYTA SPONGY ANTACID
SORBENT ANTIACID BIBULOUS
DRINKING
ABSORBER SNUBBER
(— OF MONEY) LICKPENNY
(SHOCK —) BUFFER DAMPER
ABSORPTION AUTISM
PREOCCUPATION

(— UNIT) SABIN
ABSQUATULATE DECAMP
ABSCOND
ABSTAIN DENY FAST KEEP STAY
AVOID CEASE SPARE SPURN
WAIVE DESIST DISUSE ESCHEW
FOREGO REFUSE REJECT
FORBEAR REFRAIN RESTRAIN
TEETOTAL WITHHOLD
(— FROM) FAST FORGO LEAVE
ABJURE ESCHEW FOREGO
REFRAIN
ABSTAINER TOTE RECHABITE
ABSTEMIOUS SOBER ACETIC
SLENDER MODERATE
ABSTENTION CELIBACY CHASTITY
ABSTERGE WIPE BATHE CLEAN
PURGE RINSE
ABSTINENCE ENCRATY
ABSTINENT SOBER ABSTEMIOUS
ABSTRACT CULL DEED DRAW
NOTE PART PURE TAKE BRIEF
IDEAL STEAL ABSORB DEDUCT
DETACH DIGEST DIVERT DOCKET
NOETIC PRECIS REMOVE ABRIDGE
COMPEND EXCERPT ISOLATE
PURLOIN SECRETE SUMMARY
VIDIMUS ABSTRUSE ACADEMIC
ARGUMENT BREVIATE DISCRETE
PRESCIND SEPARATE SYLLABUS
SYNOPSIS TABLEITY WITHDRAW
METAPHYSICAL
(NOT —) CONCRETE
(PL.) PARATITLA PARATITLES
ABSTRACTED REMOTE
ABSTRACTION STUDY ENTITY
ABSENCE REVERIE ABSTRACT
QUODDITY
ABSTRUSE DARK DEEP HIGH
HIDDEN MYSTIC REMOTE SECRET
SUBTLE CURIOUS OBSCURE
RETIRED ABSTRACT ACROATIC
ESOTERIC PROFOUND
METAPHYSICAL
ABSURD HOT RICH WILD DOTTY
DROLL FALSE INANE INEPT SILLY
SCREWY STUPID ASININE
FATUOUS FOOLISH LAPUTAN
ABSONANT DOGGEREL FABULOUS
COCKAMANY MONSTROUS
RIDICULOUS PREPOSTEROUS
ABSURDITY BETISE FATUITY
FOOLERY FOPPERY WALTROT
MAGGOTRY NONSENSE
UNREASON
ABUNA METRAN
ABUNDANCE WON COPY FLOW
MORT SONS WONE CHEAP DEPTH
FLUSH FOUTH POWER RIVER
ROUTH ROWTH SCADS SONSE
STORE WRECK BOUNTY FOISON
GALORE LAVISH OODLES PLENTY
POWDER RICHES TALENT UBERTY
WEALTH FLUENCY LASHINS
PLEROMA SATIETY BELLYFUL
FULLNESS LASHINGS OPULENCE
PLEURISY RIMPTION PLENITUDE
REDUNDANCY
(IN —) APLENTY
ABUNDANT FAT OLD FREE LUSH
MUCH RANK RICH RIFE AMPLE
FLUSH HEFTY LARGE OPIME
ROUTH ROWTH STORE DEMOID

GALORE HEARTY ROUTHY
APLENTY COPIOUS FERTILE
FULSOME LIBERAL OPULENT
PROFUSE REPLETE TEEMING
UBERANT UBEROUS WEALTHY
AFFLUENT FRUITFUL GENEROUS
NUMEROUS PLENTIFUL
(NOT —) LIGHT SPARE
(PREF.) HADR(O) LARGI
ABUNDANTLY RIFE WELL FREELY
PLENTY LARGELY HEARTILY
ABUSE MAR MOB TAX BUSE CALL
DRUB FLAY GAFF HARM HURT
LACK MAUL RAIL RUIN SLAM
TEEN VAIN BASTE BLAST CRIME
CURSE FAULT GRIEF SCOLD
SLANG SNASH SPOIL BERATE
DEFILE INJURE INSULT MALIGN
MISSAY MISUSE MUMBLE PUNISH
RAVISH REVILE TANCEL TANSEL
VILIFY YATTER AFFRONT
BACKJAW BEDEVIL DECEIVE
DESPITE FALSIFY MISBEDE
MISCALL MISNAME OBLOQUY
OUTRAGE PERVERT PROFANE
SLANDER TRADUCE UPBRAID
VIOLATE BALLARAG BUSINESS
DISHONOR FRUMPERY LANGUAGE
MALTREAT MISAPPLY MISTREAT
REPROACH SLAPDASH
ABUSED DOWNTROD
DOWNTRODDEN
ABUSIVE FOUL DIRTY SHREWD
CORRUPT SATIRIC CHEATING
INSOLENT LIBELOUS
ABUT BUTT JOIN REST TOUCH
ADJOIN BORDER BUTTAL
PROJECT
ABUTILON MALLOW
ABUTMENT CRIB PIER ALETTE
BUTTRESS
ABUTTING FLUSH ADJACENT
ABY ABIDING
ABYSM ABIME BISME DOWNFALL
ABYSMAL DEEP DREARY
PROFOUND UNENDING
WRETCHED
ABYSS PIT POT DEEP GULF HELL
VOID ABYSM CHAOS CHASM
DEPTH GORGE ABRUPT BOTTOM
VORAGO ABADDON AVERNUS
GEHENNA SWALLOW DOWNFALL
INTERVAL
ABYSSAL ABYSMAL BASSALIAN
ABYSSINIA (SEE ETHIOPIA)
ABYSSINIAN SIDI ABASSIN
(— BANANA) ENSETE
ACACALLIS (FATHER OF) MINOS
(MOTHER OF —) PASIPHAE
(SON OF —) GARAMAS
AMPHITHEMIS
ACACIA GUM JAM KOA WELD
WOLD BABUL GIDYA MULGA
MYALL SIRIS THORN TIMBE VEREK
WOALD WOULD ARABIC BABLAH
BINDER GIDGEA GIDGEE GIDYEA
HASHAB LEGUME LOCUST
MIMOSA SALLEE WATTLE YARRAN
BLUEBUSH BRIGALOW CHAPARRO
IRONWOOD ROSEWOOD
ACADEMIC IVY RIGID FORMAL
ACADEME CLASSIC DONNISH
ERUDITE LEARNED POMPIER

PEDANTIC PLATONIC
ACADEMY LYCEE CRUSCA LYCEUM
MANEGE SCHOOL ACADEME
COLLEGE SOCIETY YESHIVA
SEMINARY
(RIDING —) MANAGE MANEGE
ACADIAN CAJUN
ACAJOU CAJU CAJOO CAJOU
ACALEPH MEDUSA MEDUSAN
ACAMAS (BROTHER OF —)
ARCHELOCHUS
(FATHER OF —) ANTENOR THESEUS
EUSSORUS
(MOTHER OF —) THEANO PHAEDRA
(SLAYER OF —) AJAX MERIONES
(SON OF —) MUNITUS
ACANA ALMIQUE
ACANTHA FIN SPINE THORN
PRICKLE ACANTHON
ACAPU WALNUT WACAPOU
CHAPERNO
ACARID MITE NYMPH NYMPHA
OCTOPOD DIBRANCH
PROTONYMPH
ACARNAN (BROTHER OF —)
AMPHOTERUS
(FATHER OF —) ALCMAEON
(MOTHER OF —) CALLIRRHOE
ACASTUS (FATHER OF —) PELIAS
(SLAYER OF —) PELEUS
(WIFE OF —) HIPPOLYTE
ACAUDAL BOBBED ANUROUS
ECAUDATE TAILLESS
ACAULESCENT STEMLESS
ACCEDE LET AGREE ALLOW ENTER
GRANT YIELD ACCORD ASSENT
ATTAIN COMPLY CONCUR
CONCEDE CONFORM CONSENT
ACCELERATE GUN REV RUN HYPO
JAZZ RACE URGE DRIVE FAVOR
FORCE HURRY SPEED HASTEN
ADVANCE FORWARD FURTHER
QUICKEN ANTEDATE DISPATCH
EXPEDITE INCREASE THROTTLE
ACCELERATING
(PREF.) AUXO
ACCELERATION PICKUP SPEEDUP
(— OF REACTION) CATALYSIS
(— UNIT) STAPP
ACCELERATOR GAS GUN SPEEDER
BETATRON BEVATRON THROTTLE
(LINEAR —) LINAC
ACCENT BEAT BIRR BLAS BURR
MARK TONE ACUTE GRAVE ICTUS
PITCH PULSE SOUND THROB
VERGE BROGUE LENGTH RHYTHM
STRESS THESIS EMPHASIS
(DORIC —) PLATEASM
(IRISH —) BROGUE
(MUSICAL —) BEAT
(WITHOUT AN —) ATONIC
ACCENTED FZ SFZ TONIC STRONG
MARCATO MARCANDO SFORZATO
ACCENTUATE ACCENT
ACCENTUATION DECLAMATION
ENHANCEMENT
ACCEPT BUY EAT BEAR FANG
HAVE HOLD JUMP TAKE ADMIT
ADOPT AGREE ALLOW HONOR
INFER MARRY ASSENT ASSUME
AVOUCH POCKET APPROVE
BELIEVE CONCEDE EMBRACE
ESPOUSE RECEIVE

(— AS ONE'S OWN) NOSTRIFICATE
(— AS TRUE) ACCREDIT
(— AT RANDOM) DRAW
(— BETS) BOOK
(— EAGERLY) LEAP
(— INHERITANCE) ADIATE
(— READILY) SWALLOW
(— WITHOUT QUESTION) ABIDE
ACCEPTABLE LIEF VALID SIGHTLY
WELCOME GRACIOUS PASSABLE
PLEASANT
ACCEPTANCE PASS SNAFF ADITIO
TAQLID PASSAGE CREDENCE
CURRENCY
(— OF INHERITANCE) CERNITURE
(— OF ORDER) ALLOTMENT
ACCEPTATION MEANING
ACCEPTANCE
ACCEPTED GOING VULGAR
POPULAR APPROVED CREDITED
ORTHODOX STANDARD
(NOT —) OUT
(WIDELY —) INVETERATE
ACCEPTOR BASE
ACCESS FIT WAY ADIT DOOR GATE
PATH ROAD ENTRY GOING ROUTE
ACCOST AVENUE COMING
ENTREE PORTAL STREET
ADVANCE APPROACH ENTRANCE
PAROXYSM RECOURSE
(— OF DISEASE) ATTACK
ACCESSIBILITY EXPOSURE
ACCESSIBLE NEAR OPEN HANDY
PATENT AFFABLE PRESENT
FAMILIAR PERVIOUS SOCIABLE
ACCESSION ENTER ACCESS
AFFLUX ALLUVIO ILLAPSE
ADDITION ALLUVION ENTRANCE
INCREASE
ACCESSORY HAT AIDE ALLY
DOME TOOL EXTRA SCARF
HELPER ABETTOR ADAPTER
ADAPTOR ADJUNCT ANCILLA
ENCLAVE FITTING FIXTURE
ADDITIVE HATSTAND ORNAMENT
(PL.) ADDENDA FIXINGS
STAFFAGE
ACCIACCATURA MORDENT
ACCIDENT HAP CASE LUCK EVENT
GRIEF PRANG SHUNT CHANCE
HAZARD INJURY MISHAP
FORTUNE QUALITY CALAMITY
CASUALTY DISASTER FORTUITY
INCIDENT
(— IN CAR RACING) SHUNT
(AUTOMOBILE —) FATAL
(EUCHARISTIC —S) SPECIES
ACCIDENTAL ODD CASUAL
CHANCE RANDOM EXTERNAL
ACCIPITER HAWK
ACCLAIM CRY CLAP FAME HAIL
LAUD ROOT CHEER CLAIM ECLAT
EXTOL SHOUT PRAISE APPLAUD
HOSANNA OVATION PLAUDIT
RECLAME WELCOME APPLAUSE
(NOISY —) RIOT
ACCLAMATION CRY VOTE CHEER
SHOUT ACCLAIM HOSANNA
PLAUDIT APPLAUSE
ACCLIMATE ENURE INURE
HARDEN SEASON ACCUSTOM
ACCLIMATIZE SALT ADAPT
HARDEN SEASON

ACCLIVITY BANK BROW HILL RISE
GRADE PITCH SLANT SLOPE
TALUS ASCENT HEIGHT INCLINE
ACCOLADE EMMY KISS RITE SIGN
AWARD HONOR KUDOS MEDAL
OSCAR TOKEN SYMBOL EMBRACE
GARLAND CEREMONY
ACCOMMODATE AID BED BOW
FIT CAMP GIVE HELP HOLD LEND
SORT SUIT ADAPT BOARD DEFER
FAVOR HOUSE LODGE SERVE
YIELD ADJUST COMPLY FAVOUR
OBLIGE SETTLE CONFORM
CONTAIN FASHION ATTEMPER
GARRISON
ACCOMMODATING OBLIGING
ACCOMMODATION LOAN BERTH
CLASS BERTHAGE GIFFGAFF
(— BILL) KITE
(PL.) PASSAGE
ACCOMPANIED FRAUGHT
ACCOMPANIMENT SON ALBA
BURDEN ESCORT OOMPAH
ADJUNCT DESCANT SUPPORT
OBLIGATO
(PLAY JAZZ —) COMP
(PL.) FIXINGS
ACCOMPANIST JONGLEUR
ACCOMPANY SEE FARE FERE JOIN
LEAD TEND WAIT BRING PILOT
ASSIST ATTEND CONCUR CONVEY
CONVOY ESCORT FOLLOW
SECOND SQUIRE COEXIST
CONDUCT CONSORT SUPPORT
CHAPERON
ACCOMPANYING FELLOW
ADJUNCT
(PREF.) SYMPHORI
ACCOMPLICE PAL AIDE ALLY
CHUM BUDDY CRONY LOUKE
SHILL TILER BONNET COHORT
FELLOW HELPER ABETTOR
FEODARY FEUDARY HUSTLER
PARTNER STEERER
ACCOMPLISH DO GO END WIN
CHAR FILL WORK ENACT EQUIP
FETCH FORTH SWING AFFORD
ATTAIN EFFECT FINISH FULFIL
MANAGE VIRTUE ABSOLVE
ACHIEVE CHEVISE COMPASS
EXECUTE EXPLETE FULFILL
FURNISH OPERATE PERFECT
PERFORM REALIZE SUCCEED
COMPLETE CONTRIVE DISPATCH
ENGINEER OUTCARRY NEGOTIATE
ACCOMPLISHED APT ABLE ARCH
DONE ADEPT ENDED GREAT
TERSE BESEEN EXPERT
HANDSOME TALENTED
ACCOMPLISHMENT ART END
DEED FEAT PASS CRAFT SKILL
EFFECT TALENT EARNING
QUALITY FRUITION LEARNING
(PRIOR —) ANTICIPATION
ACCORD GIVE JIBE JUMP SUIT
UNIT AGREE ALLOW ATONE
AWARD BEFIT CHIME CHORD
CORDE GRANT LEVEL STAND
TALLY UNITY ACCEDE ADJUST
ASSENT BESTOW BEGREE
COMPLY CONCUR SETTLE UNISON
COMPORT COMPOSE CONCEDE
CONCERT CONCORD CONGREE

CONSENT CONSORT HARMONY
RAPPORT RESPOND UNANIME
DIAPASON SYMPATHY
(— WITH) SUIT
(IN —) ALONG
ACCORDANCE CONCERT
CONSENT
(IN —) ALONG
ACCORDANT EVEN ATTUNED
AGREEING COHERENT SUITABLE
ACCORDING **(— TO)** AD BY AUX
SEC EMFORTH ENFORTH
PURSUANT SECUNDUM
(— TO ART) SA
(— TO LAW) SL
ACCORDINGLY SO THEN THUS
HENCE IGITUR
ACCORDION LANTUM FLUTINA
FLAUTINO
ACCOST BAIL HAIL MASH MEET
ABORD ASSAY BOARD GREET
SPEAK ACCESS BROACH HALLOO
SALUTE ACCOAST ADDRESS
SOLICIT APPROACH GREETING
ACCOUCHEUR OBSTETRICIAN
ACCOUCHEUSE MIDWIFE
ACCOUNT TAB BILL BOOK DEEM
DRAW ITEM NICK NOTE RATE
REDE SAKE TAIL TALE TELL TEXT
WORD AUDIT BLAME CHALK
COUNT JUDGE SCORE STATE
STORY VALUE WORTH BATTEL
CREDIT DETAIL ESTEEM HORARY
LEGEND NOTICE PROFIT REASON
RECKON RECORD REGARD RELATE
RENDER REPORT REPUTE TREATY
ACCOMPT COMPOST COMPUTE
EXPLAIN JOURNAL LEXICON
NARRATE PROCESS RECITAL
TAILZIE BREVIARY CONSIDER
ESTIMATE RELATION TREATISE
BORDEREAU MONOGRAPH
RECKONING PRESENTATION
(— FOR) SAVE EXPLAIN
(ACCURATE —) GRIFF GRIFFIN
(CREDIT —) TICK
(LONG —) ILIAD MEGILLAH
(LONG, INVOLVED —) MEGILLA
MEGILLAH
(TRAVEL —) ITINERARY
(PL.) BATTELS
ACCOUNTABILITY DETAIL
LIABILITY
ACCOUNTABLE LIABLE AMENABLE
ACCOUNTANT CLERK SIRCAR
SIRKAR AUDITOR PESHKAR
PUTWARI KULKARNI MUTSUDDY
RECKONER
ACCOUNTANT-GENERAL
DAFTARDAR DEFTERDAR
ACCOUNTING TASK REASON
COSTING
ACCOUTER ARM RIG GIRD ARRAY
DRESS EQUIP ATTIRE CLOTHE
OUTFIT BEDIGHT FURNISH
HARNESS PROVIDE
ACCOUTERMENTS GEAR TIRE
DRESS ATTIRE GRAITH
ACCREDIT ALLOT VOUCH CREDIT
DEPUTE APPOINT APPROVE
ASCRIBE BELIEVE CERTIFY
CONFIRM ENDORSE LICENSE
SANCTION

ACCRETION SUM GAIN GROWTH
DEPOSIT EXUDATE ADDITION
ADHESION INCREASE
(INJURIOUS —) RUST
ACCRUAL ACCRUE DEMERIT
ACCRUE ADD WIN EARN GAIN
GROW PILE ARISE ENSUE ENURE
INCUR INURE ISSUE MATURE
RESULT SPRING ACQUIRE
COLLECT REDOUND ACCRESCE
CUMULATE INCREASE
ACCUMULATE DRAW FUND GROW
HEAP HIVE MASS PILE SAVE
AMASS DRIFT HOARD STACK
STORE TOTAL ACCRUE GARNER
GATHER MUSTER SCRAPE
COLLECT CONGEST HARVEST
INCREASE
ACCUMULATION DRIP DUMP
FUND GAIN HEAP MASS PILE
LODGE STACK STORE ANLAGE
BACKUP BUDGET COLUMN
DEBRIS GARNER BACKLOG
CUMULUS DEPOSIT DOSSIER
MORAINE DIVIDEND INTEREST
(— OF FLUID) EDEMA OEDEMA
ASCITES
(— OF FORCE) CHARGE
(— OF SNOW) ALIMENTATION
(— OF TRIFLES) FLOTSAM
(— ON CONCRETE) LAITANCE
ACCURACY NICETY FIDELITY
JUSTNESS PRECISION
(— OF ADJUSTMENT) TRAM
(HISTORICAL —) SYNCHRONISM
ACCURATE JUST LEAL NICE TRUE
CLOSE EXACT FLUSH RIGHT
NARROW PROPER SEVERE STRICT
CAREFUL CORRECT CURIOUS
PRECISE FAITHFUL PERQUEER
PUNCTUAL RIGOROUS TRUTHFUL
(NOT —) IMPURE
(UNPLEASANTLY —) BRUTAL
ACCURATELY JUST FAIRLY
JUSTLY CLOSELY EXACTLY
INSOOTH
ACCURSED FEY CURSED DAMNED
DOOMED FORBID SACRED
WARIED BLASTED MALEDICT
ACCUSATION BEEF WITE BLAME
CAUSE CRIME POINT WHITE
APPEAL ATTACK CHARGE THREAP
THREEP ACCUSAL SCANDAL
DELATION
(FALSE —) SUGGESTION
ACCUSATORY WRAYFUL
ACCUSE TAX WRY CALL FILE NOTE
SHOW STAIN TASK WITE WRAY
ACOUP ARGUE BLAME PEACH
TAINT TOUCH WHITE APPEAL
ATTACH ATTACK BECALL BEWRAY
CHARGE DEFAME DELATE DETECT
INDICT INTENT MURMUR
APPEACH ARRAIGN ATTAINT
CENSURE IMPEACH IMPLEAD
TRADUCE CHASTISE COMPLAIN
DENOUNCE QUESTION REDARGUE
REPROACH
(— UNJUSTLY) SLANDER
ACCUSER CHARGER DELATOR
LIBELANT
ACCUSING CULPATORY
DENUNCIATORY

ACCUSTOM URE USE WIN WON
HAFT WONT ADAPT BREAK DRILL
ENURE FLESH HABIT HAUNT
INURE TRAIN ADDICT ADJUST
CUSTOM INDUCE SEASON
CONSORT EDUCATE TOUGHEN
ACQUAINT
(**— HORSE TO BIT**) MOUTH
(**— TO PASTURE**) HAFT
ACCUSTOMED TAME USED WONE
WONT USANT USUAL INURED
CHRONIC CURRENT HABITED
CONSUETE
ACE AS ALS JOT ONE PIP TIB ATOM
CARD HERO MARK TOPS UNIT
ADEPT BASTO FLYER POINT
BULLET EXPERT AVIATOR
BRISQUE PARTICLE
(**— OF CLUBS**) BASTA BASTO
(**— OF SPADES**) SPADILLE
SPADILLO
(**— OF TRUMPS**) TIB HONOR
PUNTO
(**THREE —S**) GLEEK
ACEDIA SLOTH ACCIDIA ACCIDIE
ACEPHALOUS HEADLESS
ACER NEGUNDO
ACERB ACID HARD SOUR TART
ACRID HARSH SHARP BITTER
SEVERE
ACERBAS (**WIFE OF —**) ELISSA
ACERBATE EMBITTER IRRITATE
ACERBITY ACRIMONY ASPERITY
SEVERITY TARTNESS
ACESTES (**FATHER OF —**) CRIMISUS
(**MOTHER OF —**) EGESTA
(**WIFE OF —**) ENTELLA
ACETABULUM PAN PYXIS CUPULE
ACETABLE HOLDFAST
ACETAL KETAL FORMAL KETATE
BUTYRAL
ACETALDEHYDE ETHYL ETHANAL
ALDEHYDE
ACETIC SOUR SHARP ZOONIC
ACETOPHENETIDIN PHENACETIN
ACETYLENE TOLAN ALKINE
ALKYNE ETHINE ETHYNE TOLANE
ACHAEMENES (**BROTHER OF —**)
XERXES
(**FATHER OF —**) DARIUS
(**SLAYER OF —**) INARUS
ACHAEUS (**FATHER OF —**) XUTHUS
(**MOTHER OF —**) CREUSA
ACHBOR (**FATHER OF —**) MICHAIAH
(**SON OF —**) BAALHANAN
ACHE AKE NAG NIP ECHE GELL
HURT LONG PAIN PANG PINE
RACK WARK WERK HACHE SMART
STANG STOUN THROB THROE
WARCH YEARN DESIRE MISERY
STITCH STOUND TWINGE TWITCH
ANGUISH EARACHE SORENESS
ACHENE CYPSELA UTRICLE
ACHIEVE DO END GET WIN EARN
GAIN HACK HAVE MAKE FETCH
FORCE NOTCH REACH SCORE
AFFORD ARRIVE ATTAIN EFFECT
FINISH OBTAIN CHEVISE
COMPASS EXPLOIT FULFILL
PERFORM PROCURE PRODUCE
REALIZE SUCCEED TRIUMPH
COMPLETE CONCLUDE CONTRIVE
ACCOMPLISH

(**— HARMONY**) AGREE
(**— ORIENTATION**) ADJUST
ACHIEVEMENT ACT JOB DEED
FEAT WORK ACTION CAREER
RESULT EXPLOIT HARVEST
PROWESS FELICITY
ACHILLEA PTARMICA
ACHILLES PELIDES
(**COMPANION OF —**) PATROCLUS
(**FATHER OF —**) PELEUS
(**FRIEND OF —**) PATROCLUS
(**HORSE OF —**) XANTHUS
(**MOTHER OF —**) THETIS
(**SLAYER OF —**) PARIS
ACHIM (**FATHER OF —**) SADOC
(**SON OF —**) ELIUD
ACHIOTE OLEANA ACHUETE
ANNATTO ARNATTA ARNATTO
ACHRAS SAPOTA
ACHROMACYTE SHADOW
ACHROMATIC GRAY GREY
NEUTRAL
ACHSAH (**FATHER OF —**) CALEB
(**HUSBAND OF —**) OTHNIEL
ACICULAR SPLINTERY
ACID DRY YAR DIAL DOPA KEEN
PABA SOUR TART ACERB ACRID
ALGIN AMINO CERIN EAGER
HARSH LYSIN MALIC OLEUM
RHEIN SHARP ULMIC ABRINE
ALLIIN BITING BITTER GLYCIN
LYSINE NIACIN PROLIN SERINE
TWEAKY VALINE ACERBIC
ACETOSE CERASIN FILICIN
GLYCINE PROLINE STEARIN
VINEGAR ORNITHINE PENICILLIN
(**NITRIC —**) AQUAFORTIS
(**PREF.**) ACETO OXY
(**SUFF.**) (**— RADICAL**) OYL
ACID HYDROGEN
(**SUFF.**) HYDRIC
ACIDITY ACOR VERDURE ACERBITY
SOURNESS VERJUICE
ACIS (**FATHER OF —**) FAUNUS
(**LOVER OF —**) GALATEA
(**MOTHER OF —**) SYMAETHIS
(**SLAYER OF —**) POLYPHEMUS
ACIS & GALATEA (**CHARACTER IN**
—) ACIS GALATEA POLYPHEMUS
(**COMPOSER OF —**) HANDEL
ACKNOWLEDGE NOD OWN AVER
AVOW SIGN ADMIT ADOPT
ALLOW GRANT KITHE KYTHE
THANK YIELD ACCEDE ACCEPT
AGNIZE ANSWER ASSENT
AVOUCH BEKNOW COUTHE
FATHER REWARD CONCEDE
CONFESS DECLARE OBSERVE
PROFESS DISCLOSE RECOGNIZE
ACKNOWLEDGEMENT GRANT
THANK AVOWAL CREDIT SHRIFT
APOLOGY AGNITION COGNOVIT
COGNISANCE COGNIZANCE
RECOGNITION
(**— OF MISTAKE**) JEOFAIL
(**— OF SIN**) PECCAVI
ACLE AKLE IRUL JAMBA
IRONWOOD PYENGADU
ACLYS HURLBAT
ACME IT ACE CAP TOP APEX CULM
HIGH PEAK CREST PITCH POINT
STATE APOGEE CLIMAX COMBLE
CRISIS CULMEN HEIGHT HEYDAY

SUMMIT ZENITH CUMULUS
SUBLIME CAPSHEAF CAPSTONE
PINNACLE
ACNE WHELK ROSACEA
ACOLYTE BOY HELPER NOVICE
SERVER LEARNER PATENER
THURIFER
ACOMIA BALDNESS
ACONITE BIKH ACONITUM
NAPELLUS
ACORN NUT MAST GLAND OVEST
BALANUS BELLOTA BELLOTE
(**— CUPS**) VALONIA
(**PL.**) MAST CAMATA PANNAGE
CAMATINA
(**PREF.**) BALAN(I)(O) GLANDI
GLANDULI
ACORN-SHAPED BALANOID
ACOUSTICS SONICS PHONICS
ACQUAINT KNOW TELL TEACH
VERSE ADVISE INFORM NOTIFY
SCHOOL APPRISE APPRIZE
POSSESS RESOLVE
ACQUAINTANCE KITH HABIT
COUSIN FRIEND GOSSIP PICKUP
AFFINITY FAMILIAR INTIMATE
(**CLOSE —**) HABIT INWARDNESS
(**PRACTICAL —**) PRACTICE
PRACTISE
(**PL.**) KITH SOCIETY
ACQUAINTED ACQUENT VERSANT
ACQUIESCE BOW ABIDE AGREE
CHIME YIELD ACCEDE ACCEPT
ASSENT COMPLY CONCUR
SUBMIT CONCEDE CONFIRM
CONFORM CONSENT
ACQUIRABLE
(**PREF.**) CTETO
ACQUIRE ADD BAG BUY GET WIN
EARN FORM GAIN GRAB HAVE
MAKE REAP ADOPT AMASS
ANNEX BEGET CHEVY CHIVY
GLEAN LEARN REACH SEIZE
STEAL ATTAIN CHIVEY CHIVVY
DERIVE EFFECT GARNER OBTAIN
SECURE SNATCH COLLECT
CONQUER DEVELOP PROCURE
RECEIVE CONTRACT
(**— DESIRABLE QUALITY**) AGE
(**— KNOWLEDGE**) LERE
ACQUISITION WIN GAIN LUCRE
ACQUEST ACQUIST GETTING
CONQUEST ACCESSION
(**DISHONEST —**) GRAFT
ACQUIT PAY FREE QUIT CLEAR
QUIET ASSOIL BEHAVE BESTOW
EXCUSE PARDON ABSOLVE
COMPORT CONDUCT RELEASE
REQUITE LIBERATE OVERLOOK
UNCHARGE ASSOILZIE
ACQUITTAL EXCUSE ABSOLUTION
ACQUITTANCE QUIETUS RELEASE
ACRE AKER LAND ACKER FIELD
STANG ARPENT COLLOP
FARMHOLD
(**QUARTER —**) ROOD
(**120 —S**) HIDE
(**2-3RDS —**) COVER
(**PL.**) ACREAGE
ACREMAN CARUCARIUS
ACRID HOT ACID BASK KEEN SOUR
HARSH ROUGH SHARP SURLY
BITING BITTER CAUSTIC PUNGENT

REEKING UNSAVORY VIRULENT
ACRIMONIOUS MAD ACID KEEN
ACRID ANGRY GRUFF HARSH
IRATE SHARP SNELL SURLY
BITTER CAUSTIC STINGING
VIRULENT
ACRIMONY VIRUS ACERBITY
ASPERITY PUNGENCY SOURNESS
ANIMOSITY
ACRISIUS (**BROTHER OF —**)
PROETUS
(**DAUGHTER OF —**) DANAE
(**FATHER OF —**) ABAS
(**MOTHER OF —**) AGLAIA
(**SLAYER OF —**) PERSEUS
(**WIFE OF —**) AGANIPPE EURYDICE
ACROBAT ZANY KINKER GYMNAST
TOPPLER TUMBLER BALANCER
AERIALIST ROPEWALKER
ACROPOLIS FORT HILL POLIS
CADMEA CITADEL LARISSA
ACROSOME IDIOSOME IDIOZOME
ACROSS OVER SPAN YOND CROSS
ABOARD THWART ATHWART
OPPOSITE TRAVERSE
(**CLEAN —**) SHORT
(**PREF.**) DIA OVER TRANS
ACROSTIC ABC AGLA DORA GAME
POEM TANAK PHRASE PUZZLE
TANACH
ACRYLIC PROPENOIC
ACT BE DO GO APE LAW LET ACTU
AUTO BILL COME DEAL DEED
DORA FACT FEAT HOCK JEST
MAKE MOVE PART PASS PLAY
SKIT SLIM TAKE TURN WORK
ACTUS DRAMA EDICT EMOTE
ENTRY EXERT FEIGN GRACE
KARMA MODEL SCENE SHIFT
STUNT ACTION BEHAVE BESTIR
DECREE DEMEAN FACTUM
MANAGE RAGMAN COMPORT
EXECUTE EXPLOIT PERFORM
PORTRAY PRETEND STATUTE
FUNCTION PRETENSE SIMULATE
(**— AFFECTEDLY**) MIMP
(**— AS WANTON**) RIG
(**— AWKWARDLY**) HOCKER
(**— BEFORE**) ANTICIPATE
(**— BLUNDERINGLY**) BULL
(**— DECEITFULLY**) DOUBLE
(**— DISHONESTLY**) FUDGE
(**— FOOLISHLY**) FON FONNE
FOLEYE FOOTER FOOTLE
(**— FRIVOLOUSLY**) FRIVOL FRIBBLE
(**— IN THEATER**) GAFF
(**— INDECISIVELY**) DITHER
(**— INDEPENDENTLY**) SEVER
(**— OF APPROVAL**) EUGE
(**— OF BEGGING**) CADGE
(**— OF CIVILITY**) CURTSY DEVOIR
CURTSEY
(**— OF KINDNESS**) CARESS BENEFIT
(**— OF LABOR**) DILIGENCE
(**— OF PRAYER**) DEVOTION
(**— OF STUPIDITY**) BETISE
(**— OF TRICKERY**) COG
(**— OUT**) ENACT DRAMATIZE
(**— PLAYFULLY**) DALLY BANTER
(**— QUICKLY**) GIRD
(**— RASHLY**) RACKLE
(**— SPORTIVELY**) DAFF
(**— SUDDENLY**) FLASH

(— TIMIDLY) NESH
(— TOGETHER) AGREE COACT CONCUR CONCORD
(— TRIFLINGLY) JANK
(— UP TO) EVEN
(— UPON) TOUCH AFFECT HANDLE
(— VIGOROUSLY) TWIG
(COMICAL —) JIG
(CONVENTIONAL —) AMENITY
(CORRUPT —) DEPRAVITY
(CRIMINAL —) INFAMY
(DARING —) ESCAPADE
(DECEITFUL —) ABUSE
(DECEPTIVE —) FEINT
(ECCENTRIC —) CANTRIP
(EVIL —) MALEFICENCE
(FAULTY —) PARAPRAXIS
(FOOLISH —) DIDO IDIOTISM
(FORBIDDEN —) CRIME
(FORMAL —) CEREMONY
(HABITUAL—) EXERCISE
(HASTY —) FLING
(HOSTILE —) BLOW
(INJURIOUS —) SPOIL
(LAUDATORY —) COUP
(LITURGICAL —) LAVABO
(LIVELY —) JIG
(MERITORIOUS —) MITZVAH
(MISCHIEVOUS —) DIDO CANTRAP CANTRIP
(OFFENSIVE —) AFFRONT
(OFFICIAL —S) ACTA
(PLAYFUL —) RALLERY RAILLERY
(PRAISEWORTHY —) DEMERIT
(RUDE —) INCIVILITY
(SUDDEN VIOLENT —) BENSEL BENSIL
(THOUGHTLESS —) FOLLY
(UNMANNERLY —) SOLECISM
(UNUSUAL —) STUNT
(VALOROUS —) WORSHIP
(VARIETY —) SKETCH
(WRONG —) DERELICT DERELICTUM
(PL.) DOINGS
(SUFF.) ADE ATE CY ICE ION ISM TH
ACTAEON (FATHER OF —) ARISTAEUS
(MOTHER OF —) AUTONOE
ACTINAL ORAL
ACTING AGENT SERVING
(— AGAINST) ADVERSE
(— BY TURN) ALTERN
(— ODDLY) HAYWIRE
(— RAPIDLY) DRASTIC
(UNSKILLFUL —) BUNGLING
ACTINIAN OPELET VESTLET
ACTINOST RADIAL RADIALE
ACTINOZOAN SEAFLOWER
ACTION ACT AIR DAP JOB PAS ACTO CASE DEED FACT FRAY GEST PLAY PLOY PUSH SHOW STEP SUIT WORK ACTIO DOING EDICT FIGHT FLING GESTE ISSUE THING TREAD VENUE AFFAIR AGENCY BATTLE BEFOOT COMBAT PRAXIS CONDUCT FACTION GESTURE PROCESS TANQUAM ACTIVITY BEHAVIOR BUSINESS CONFLICT FUNCTION PRACTICE PRACTISE

(— BETWEEN HORSE AND RIDER) APPUI
(— OF DRAMA) EPITASIS
(— OF WIND) EOLATION
(— PAINTING) TACHISM
(ABSURD —S) BOSH
(ANTAGONISTIC —) ATOMISM
(BLAMEWORTHY —) WITE
(CAPRICIOUS —) FREAK
(CHEMICAL —) ACTINISM
(COARSE —) HARLOTRY
(COOPERATIVE —) SYNERGISM
(COURT —) LAW SUIT ASSIZE LAWSUIT QUERELA QUERELE
(CRUEL —) RUTH
(CUSTOMARY —) COURSE
(EXAGGERATED —) PRODUCTION
(EXTEMPORE —) SCHEDIASM
(FANTASTIC —) ABTIC
(FINAL —) CATASTROPHE
(FOOLISH —) FOPPERY INEPTITUDE
(FRISKY —) FRISKIN
(FRIVOLOUS —) DALLIANCE
(HOSTILE —) OPPOSITION
(IMPULSIVE —) STAMPEDE
(INDIRECT —) WINDLASS
(INITIAL —) LEADOFF INDUCTION
(JOINT —) COACTION
(LEGAL —) DEBT SUIT ACCOUNT DETINET DETINUE PROCEEDING
(MEAN —S) DOGGERY
(MILITARY —) SWEEP OPERATION
(ODD —S) JIMJAMS
(PLAYFUL —) FUN FROLIC
(RASH —) HASTE
(REPEATED —) DRUM DOUBLE
(SUDDEN —) FLISK
(SYMBOLIC —) CHARADE
(TACTLESS —) GAUCHERIE
(UNAVOIDABLE —) FORCEPUT
(UNINTERMITTED —) HEAT
(VIOLENT —) AFFRAY
(WHIMSICAL —S) HUMORS HUMOURS
(WILY —) WRINKLE
(PREF.) CIN(O) CINET(O) KIN(O) KINESI KINET(O)
(SUFF.) ADE AL ANCE ANT ARD ATION CY ENCE ESIS ING ISATION IVE IZATION MENT OSIS PRACTIC PRAXIA PRAXIS SIS
(CHARACTERIZED BY —) SOME
(SMALL —) LE LING
ACTIS (FATHER OF —) RHODE
(MOTHER OF —) HELIUS
ACTIVATE SPARK ACTIFY ELICIT
ACTIVATION
(SUFF.) KINESIS
ACTIVATOR GOAD
ACTIVE UP YAL YAP YEP BUSY GAIN LISH LIST PERT RASH SPRY TRIG WHAT YALD YARE YEPE YERN ABOUT AGILE ALERT ALIVE ASTIR BRISK DEEDY FRESH LIGHT LINGY LUSTY NIPPY PEART QUICK READY SMART SNELL SPICY SPRIG STOUT SWANK VIVID WIGHT YAULD YERNE ACTUAL BOUNCY CLEVER DIRECT FEERIE FEIRIE FIERCE HEARTY LIVELY LIVING MOVING NIMBLE PROMPT QUIVER SEMMIT SPEEDY SPRACK SPROIL SPRUCE SPRUNT SWANKY

WIMBLE DASHING DEEDFUL DELIVER DYNAMIC HOPPING HUMMING KINETIC STHENIC THRODDY YANKING ANIMATED ATHLETIC BRAWLING DILIGENT SPIRITED VIGOROUS
(NORMALLY —) ABOUT
ACTIVELY DOWN BUSILY DEEDILY HEARTILY
ACTIVITY ACT ADO GOG VIR FIZZ LIFE PLAY PUSH STIR BLAST CAPER EVENT HEART RAJAS RALLY TRADE VIGOR ACTION AGENCY BUSTLE ENERGY HUSTLE SATTVA SPROIL AGILITY CALLING BUSINESS EXERCISE FUNCTION MOVEMENT PARERGON STIRRING OCCUPATION
(— OF INTELLECT) NOESIS
(CHOICE OF —) THING
(FUNCTIONAL —) SHOP
(GAY —) MERRYMAKING
(MENTAL —) CONCEIT BRAINWORK MENTATION
(SHARED —) COMMUNITY
(SPHERE OF —) SCENE
(TROUBLESOME —) COIL
(SUFF.) OR
(OUTBURST OF —) FEST
ACTON HOGTON HAQUETON
ACTOR HAM DOER HERO LEAD MIME STAR AGENT BUFFO COMIC DROLL EXTRA HEAVY MIMIC PLANT SERIO SUPER ARTIST BUSKER COWBOY DISEUR FEEDER FIDDLE MUMMER PLAYER PUPPET STAGER TOMMER ARTISTE CABOTIN DISEUSE HISTRIO PRIMOMO ROSCIUS STORMER TROUPER AISTEOIR COMEDIAN HISTRION JUVENILE STROLLER THESPIAN
(BROTHER OF —) AUGEAS
(DAUGHTER OF —) POLYMELA
(FATHER OF —) DIOMEDES MYRMIDON
(INDIFFERENT —) JAY
(INEPT —) HAM
(INFERIOR —) SHINE
(MOTHER OF —) DEION PASIDICE
(SON OF —) CTEATUS EURYTUS MENOETIUS
(PREF.) HISTRIO
ACTRESS DIVA STAR INGENUE STARLET FARCEUSE PREMIERE THESPIAN
ACTUAL GOOD HARD REAL TRUE VERY POSIT RIGHT BODILY FACTUAL GENUINE CONCRETE DEFINITE EXISTING MATERIAL POSITIVE TANGIBLE
ACTUALITY ACT FACT BEING VERITY REALITY ENERGEIA REALNESS
ACTUALLY BUT DONE TRULY FAIRLY ITSELF REALLY
(NOT —) NOMINALLY
ACTUATE ACT EGG RUN DRAW MOVE URGE ENACT IMPEL ROUSE START AROUSE COMPEL EXCITE INCITE INDUCE AGITATE ANIMATE ENLIVEN INSPIRE POINTED SHARPEN MOTIVATE PERSUADE

ACUITY FINENESS
ACUMEN WIT INSIGHT CAPACITY KEENNESS SAGACITY
ACUTE ACID FINE HIGH KEEN TART HEAVY QUICK SHARP SMART SNACK SNELL ARGUTE ASTUTE CRYING SHREWD SHRILL SUBTLE TREBLE URGENT CRUCIAL FEELING INTENSE POINTED VIOLENT CRITICAL INCISIVE POIGNANT ACUMINATE PENETRATING PENETRATIVE
(MOST —) DIRE
(NOT —) SLOW GRAVE CHRONIC
(PREF.) OXY
ACUTENESS DEPTH SENSE ACUITY ACUMEN NOSTRIL INCISION SAGACITY SUBTLETY
(— OF SMELL) HYPEROSMIA
ACYCLIC SPIRAL ALIPHATIC
ACYLOIN
(SUFF.) OIN
ADA (BROTHER OF —) PIXODARUS
(HUSBAND & BROTHER OF —) IDRIEUS
ADAD RAMMAN
ADAGE SAW DICT REDE TEXT WORD AXIOM MAXIM MOTTO HOMILY SAYING TRUISM WHEEZE BROMIDE PRECEPT PROVERB APHORISM APOTHEGM PAROEMIA
ADAGIO ADAGE ADAGIETTO
ADAH (HUSBAND OF —) ESAU LAMECH
(SON OF —) JABAL JUBAL ELIPHAZ
ADAIAH (FATHER OF —) SHIMHI JEROHAM
ADALIA (FATHER OF —) HAMAN
ADAM ADE EDIE ADKIN
(GRANDSON OF —) ENOS ENOCH
(SON OF —) ABEL CAIN SETH
(TEACHER OF —) RAISEL
(WIFE OF —) EVE LILITH
ADAM-AND-EVE CRAWFOOT
ADAMANT FIRM GRIM HARD SOLID STONY ADAMAS DIAMOND UNMOVED OBDURATE SOLIDITY STUBBORN
ADAMANTINE FIRM BORON STONE VAJRA ADAMANT
ADAM BEDE (AUTHOR OF —) ELIOT
(CHARACTER IN —) ADAM SETH DINAH HETTY ARTHUR BARTLE IRVINE MARTIN MASSEY MORRIS POYSER SORREL DONNITHORNE
ADAMITE PICARD
ADAM'S APPLE GUZZLE THROATBOLL
ADAM'S NEEDLE YUCCA
ADAPT APT FIT PLY PUT EDIT MOLD SORT SUIT AGREE HUMOR INURE SHAPE TALLY ADJUST CHANGE COMPLY DERIVE DOCTOR HUMOUR TEMPER ARRANGE CONFORM CONVERT FASHION PREPARE QUALIFY ATTEMPER CONTRIVE EQUALIZE MODULATE REGULATE ACCOMMODATE
ADAPTABILITY FLUIDITY ELASTICITY
ADAPTABLE LABILE ELASTIC PLASTIC PLIABLE FLEXUOUS

ADAPTATION CONSERTION
ADAPTED FIT FOR FITTED SUITED CONGENIAL
ADAPTER KIT ARRANGER
ADAXIAL SUPERIOR POSTERIOR
ADBEEL (FATHER OF —) ISHMAEL
ADD AD EIK EKE SAY SUM TOT CAST FOOT GAIN JOIN LEND PLUS TOTE AFFIX ANNEX GIVEN TOTAL UNITE ACCRUE ADJECT APPEND ATTACH CONFER FIGURE RECKON SUPPLY ACCRETE AUGMENT COMBINE COMPILE COMPUTE ENLARGE SUBJOIN SUMMATE INCREASE
(**— ALCOHOL**) SPIKE
(**— FUEL**) BEET
(**— IN WRITING**) ASCRIBE
(**— TO**) ADORN ENRICH AUGMENT
(**— UP**) SUM TOT COUNT TOTAL AMOUNT
(**— WORT TO BEER**) KRAUSEN
ADDA SCINK SKINK LIZARD
ADDAR (FATHER OF —) BELA
ADDAX PYGARG PYGARGUS
ADDED AND EKE PLUS ADJUNCT
(**— SOMETHING**) TILLY
ADDEND SUMMAND
ADDER ATHER KRAIT VIPER ELAPID NADDER NEDDER ELAPOID HAGWORM HYPNALE
ADDER'S-TONGUE LILY LILIUM COXCOMB ROOSTERS
ADDERWORT BISTORT
ADDI (FATHER OF —) COSAM
(**SON OF —**) MELCHI
ADDICT FAN BUFF DOPE DOPY HYPE USER COKEY COKIE FIEND HOPPY HOUND JUNKY SLAVE BOTARY DEVOTE JUNKER JUNKIE DELIVER DEVOTEE HABITUE HOPHEAD SNIFTER ACCUSTOM DOPEHEAD SNOWBIRD
ADDICTED GIVEN PRONE HOOKED BIBULOUS
ADDICTION HABIT MONKEY BIBACITY
ADDITION AND EIK EKE ELL TAB TOO ALSO ELSE GAIN PLUS AFFIX RIDER ACCESS ACCRUE AUGEND ENCORE GANSEL INCOME PREFIX ADJUNCT ADVANCE AUCTARY CODICIL JOINING PENDANT UNITING ADDENDUM INCREASE MANTISSA ACCESSION
(**— TO ARTICLE**) SHIRTTAIL
(**— TO BEEHIVE**) IMP
(**— TO MASS**) FARCE FARSE
(**— TO PRICE**) ADVANCE
(**— TO WORD**) PARAGOGE
(**EXTRANEOUS —**) ACCRETION
(**TRIVIAL —**) FILIP FILLIP
(**PREF.**) (**IN —**) SUPER
ADDITIONAL NEW ELSE MORE ADDED EXTRA FRESH OTHER TIDDER TOTHER ANOTHER BESIDES FURTHER ACCESSORY
ADDITIVE CUMOL CUMENE PRESERVATIVE
ADDLE EARN HOME IDLE MIRE AMAZE FILTH RIPEN SPOIL CURDLE MUDDLE THRIVE

AGITATE CONFUSE BEFUDDLE BEWILDER
ADDLED ASEA EMPTY PUTRID MUDDLED UNSOUND
ADDRA DAMA NANGER
ADDRESS AIM SUE WOO BACK CALL EASE HAIL HOME MINT PRAY TACT TALK TULK TURN ABODE APPLY BOARD COURT DRESS ELOGE GREET POISE SKILL SPEAK TREAT ACCOST ADJUST APPEAL BOUNCE CHARGE DEVOTE DIRECT EULOGY MANNER PARLEY SALUTE SERMON SPEECH BEHIGHT CONDUCT CONSIGN ENTRUST LECTURE ORATION TUTOYER APPROACH DEDICATE DELIVERY DISPATCH FACILITY HARANGUE INSCRIBE PETITION
(**— FAMILIARLY**) TOM TUTOYER
(**— SAUCILY**) CHYAK CHYACK
(**METHOD OF —**) TONE
(**PULPIT —**) KHUTBA KHUTBAH
ADDUCE BEAR CITE GIVE NAME ALLAY ARGUE BRING INFER OFFER QUOTE ALLEGE ASSIGN OBJECT ADVANCE COUNTER MENTION PRESENT
ADE SQUASH
ADEPS FAT LARD
ADEPT ACE APT DON ABLE HANDY ADROIT ARTIST CRAFTY DEACON EXPERT MASTER VERSED ANCIENT ARTISTE CAPABLE DABSTER MAHATMA DEXTROUS SKILLFUL PROFICIENT
ADEQUATE DUE FIT ABLE FAIR FULL GOOD MEET WELL AMPLE DIGNE EQUAL COMMON DECENT ENOUGH PROPER CONDIGN SUITABLE COMMENSURATE SATISFACTORY
ADER (FATHER OF —) BERIAH
ADHERE HEW HUG CLAG CLAM CLOG GLUE HOLD JOIN KEEP LINK ABIDE AFFIX APPLY CLEAM CLING STICK UNITE ATTACH CEMENT CLEAVE COHERE FREEZE ACCRETE ANNERRE PERSIST
ADHERENCE CLING ABIDANCE ADHESION ARIANISM FIDELITY
ADHERENT IST ITE AIDE ALLY JAIN SIKH ADEPT BAHAI BLACK BONPA DEIST JAINA SIDER SPIKE STOOP FACTOR KIRKER VOTARY APRISTA BAHAIST CHANIST FASCIST FLACIAN GNOSTIC NICAEAN OWENIAN SECTARY SEQUELA THOMIST AGATHIST BELIEVER BUDDHIST CABALIST DISCIPLE FAITHFUL FATALIST FOLLOWER HUMANIST HYLICIST IMPERIAL PARTISAN RETAINER SERVITOR SOCINIAN UPHOLDER MONTANIST
(**PL.**) FOLD FOLLOWING
(**SUFF.**) ITE
ADHERING PERTINACIOUS
ADHESION BLOCKING STICKAGE SYNECHIA
ADHESIVE GUM WAX BOND CLAM GLUE SIZE TAPE DABBY DAUBY PASTE TACKY BINDER CEMENT CLINGY GLUTEN MASTIC PLUCKY

SMEARY STICKY HOTMELT MOUNTANT MUCILAGE TENACIOUS
(**PREF.**) GLUT
ADHIBIT USE ADMIT AFFIX APPLY ATTACH
ADIANTUM MAIDENHAIR
ADIEL (SON OF —) AZMAVETH
ADIEU ADEW ADDIO ADIOS LEAVE FAREWELL
ADIPOSE FAT HARD SUET FATTY OBESE PURSY SQUAT TALLOW
ADIT DOOK DOOR ENTRY SOUGH STULM ACCESS TUNNEL PASSAGE APPROACH ENTRANCE
ADJACENT NEAR NIGH CLOSE FLUSH HANDY BESIDE NEARBY MEETING VICINAL ABUTTING TOUCHING CONTIGUOUS
(**PREF.**) (**— TO**) AC AD AF AG AL AP AS AT
ADJECTIVE ADNOUN DIPTOTE EPITHET NOMINAL MODIFIER
ADJOIN ADD ABUT BUTT JOIN LINE TACK COAST MARCH TOUCH UNITE ACCOST APPEND ATTACH BORDER CONTACT NEIGHBOR
ADJOINING VICINAL
ADJOURN END MOVE RISE STAY ARISE CLOSE DEFER DELAY RECESS SUSPEND DISSOLVE POSTPONE PROROGUE
ADJUDGE TRY ARET DEEM FIND GIVE HOLD RATE ALLOT AREAD AREED ARETT AWARD GRANT JUDGE ORDER ADDEEM ADDICT ADDOOM ASSIGN DECERN DECIDE DECREE ORDAIN REGARD BEHIGHT CONDEMN SENTENCE
(**— GUILTY**) DAMN
(**— NOT GUILTY**) ABSOLVE
ADJUDICATE ACT TRY HEAR PASS RULE JUDGE DECIDE ESTEEM RECKON REGARD SETTLE ADJUDGE CONSIDER SENTENCE
ADJUNCT AID HELP PART WORD ANNEX DEVICE PHRASE ADJOINT ANCILLA EPITHET FITTING GARNISH PERTAIN TEACHER ADDITION ADDITIVE APPANAGE APPENDIX ORNAMENT
ADJURATION OATH APPEAL SWEARING
ADJURE ASK BEG BID BIND ETHE PRAY CRAVE PLEAD SWEAR APPEAL CHARGE OBTEST BESEECH COMMAND CONJURE CONTEST ENTREAT REQUEST UNSWEAR
ADJUST FIT FIX SET CAST EASE FORM FREE GEAR JUST LINE PARE RATE SIZE SORT SUIT TRAM TRIM TRUE ADAPT ADMIT ALIGN ALINE ANGLE COAPT EQUAL FRAME PATCH RANGE RIGHT SHAPE ACCORD ATTUNE HAMMER JUSTEN ORIENT SETTLE SQUARE TEMPER WANGLE ADDRESS ARRANGE BALANCE CHANCER COMPOSE CONCERT CONFORM CORRECT DISPOSE JUSTIFY PREPARE RECTIFY

COMPOUND REGULATE ACCOMMODATE
(**— A LOOM**) GATE
(**— DULY**) CONCENT
(**— SAIL**) FLATTEN
(**PREF.**) CO
ADJUSTED KEYED
ADJUSTER FIXER FITTER ASSESSOR
ADJUSTMENT FIT GEAR MISE TRIM FITNESS FITTING CHANCERY
ADJUTANT AIDE ALLY STORK ARGALA HELPER HURGILA MARABOU OFFICER
ADJUVANT AIDE HELPER ADJUNCT HELPFUL
ADLAI (SON OF —) SHAPHAT
AD-LIB FAKE
ADMAN HUCKSTER
ADMEASURE METE
ADMETUS (FATHER OF —) PHERES
(**WIFE OF —**) ALCESTIS
ADMINISTER DO RUN DEAL DEEM DOSE GIVE MOVE RULE APPLY SERVE TREAT DIRECT GOVERN MANAGE SETTLE SUPPLY TENDER ADHIBIT CONDUCE CONDUCT CONTROL EXECUTE EXHIBIT FURNISH HUSBAND DISPENSE MINISTER
(**— FORCIBLY**) HAND
(**— SACRAMENT**) BISHOP HOUSEL
ADMINISTRATION HELM RULE SWAY POLICY TAHSIL CONDUCT DIOCESE ECONOMY RECTORY REGIMEN CARRIAGE DISPOSAL MINISTRY
(**— OF OATH**) JURATION
(**CORRUPT —**) MALVERSATION
(**REVENUE —**) HACIENDA
ADMINISTRATOR CAID HELM QAID GABBAI MANAGER TRUSTEE DIRECTOR EXECUTOR MINISTER PROVICAR PROCONSUL
(**INCA —**) CURACA
(**MORMON —**) APOSTLE
ADMIRABLE FINE GOOD HIGH GRAND GREAT LUMMY PROUD DIVINE AMIABLE CAPITAL ELEGANT MIRANDA RIPPING
ADMIRAL (**ALSO SEE NAVAL OFFICER**) FLAG AMREL AMRELLE CAPITAN FLAGMAN GENERAL NAVARCH
ADMIRATION CULT FUROR GLORY ESTEEM LIKING WONDER CONCEIT WORSHIP
(**— FOR BIGNESS**) JUMBOISM
ADMIRE DIG LIKE LOVE ADORE EXTOL HONOR PRIZE VALUE ESTEEM MARVEL REGARD REVERE WONDER ADULATE APPROVE DELIGHT IDOLIZE RESPECT VENERATE
ADMIRER FAN BEAU LOVER SWAIN AMATEUR DEVOTEE FOLLOWER IDOLATER
(**PL.**) FOLLOWING
ADMISSION FEE ADIT CALL ENTRY ACCESS CHARGE ENTREE TICKET APOLOGY CONSENT INGRESS ENTRANCE RECEPTION CONCESSION

(— TO BAR) CALL

ADMIT KEN LET OWN AVER AVOW BEAR TAKE AGREE ALLOW ENTER GRANT IMMIT INLET ACCEDE ACCEPT ADJUST ASSENT AVOUCH ENROLL INDUCT PERMIT SUFFER ADHIBIT CONCEDE CONFESS INCLUDE PROFESS RECEIVE SUFFICE INITIATE

(— AS MEMBER) INDUCT

(— AS VALID) SUSTAIN

ADMITTANCE ACCESS ADMITTY ENTRANCE

ADMITTING THOUGH

ADMIX DALLOP DOLLOP

ADMIXTURE DASH ALLOY BLEND SHADE SPICE TINGE DALLOP DOLLOP FLAVOR LEAVEN STREAK MIXTURE SOUPCON COMPOUND INFUSION

ADMONISH WARN CHIDE SCOLD ADVISE ENJOIN EXHORT NOTIFY REBUKE REMIND SCHOOL CAUTION COUNSEL MONITOR REPROVE

ADMONITION ITEM ADVICE CAVEAT HOMILY CAUTION LECTURE REPROOF WARNING DOCUMENT REMINDER

ADNATE ADHERENT EPIGYNOUS

(— TO CALYX) INFERIOR

ADO DO COIL DEED FUSS ROUT STIR WORK HURRY TOUSE TOWSE BOTHER BUSTLE EFFORT FLURRY HUBBUB POTHER RUCKUS BLATHER BLETHER SPUTTER TROUBLE TURMOIL BUSINESS

ADOBE MUD CLAY DOBE DOBY SILT BRICK DOBIE TAPIA MUDCAP

ADOLESCENCE TEENS YOUTH NONAGE PUBERTY MINORITY

ADOLESCENT LAD TEEN YOUNG YOUTH TEENER IMMATURE TEENAGER

ADONIJAH (BROTHER OF —) AMNON ABSALOM CHILEAB

(FATHER OF —) DAVID

(MOTHER OF —) HAGGITH

(SLAYER OF —) BENAIAH

ADONIS ADON

(FATHER OF —) CINYRAS

(MOTHER OF —) MYRRH MYRRHA

ADOPT TAKE STEAL ACCEPT ASSUME ATTACH BORROW CHOOSE FATHER FOLLOW FOSTER MOTHER ACQUIRE EMBRACE ESPOUSE RECEIVE WELCOME ADVOCATE ARROGATE MAINTAIN

ADOPTION ESPOUSAL

(— OF DEBTS) ASSUMPTION

ADORABLE LOVELY LOVABLE CHARMING

ADORATION HOMAGE WORSHIP DEVOTION

(— OF GOD) LOVE

ADORE DOTE LAUD LOVE EXALT EXTOL HONOR WURTH ADMIRE ESTEEM PRAISE REVERE GLORIFY IDOLIZE WORSHIP VENERATE

ADORN DUB FIG GEM ORN SET BEAD BUSK DECK DILL DINK FOIL GAUD GILD LACE OUCH PICK PINK POSH STUD SWAG TRIM ADORE ANORN ARRAY BEDUB BEGEM BELAY BESEE BRAVE CROWN DIGHT DRAPE DRESS FRONT GRACE HIGHT INLAY JEWEL MENSK PRANK PRICK PRIDE PRIMP PRINK ROUGE SPLAY SPRIG TRICK AGUISE ATTIRE ATTRAP BECOME BEDECK BETRIM BLAZON BROOCH CLOTHE COLLAR DAMASK DIADEM EMBOSS ENAMEL ENRICH ENROBE FIGURE FINIFY FRIEZE FRINGE GRAITH INSTAL INVEST ORNIFY POUNCE PURFLE QUAINT STATUE SUBORN TASSEL ADONISE APPAREL BEDIGHT BEDIZEN COMMEND CORONET DEPAINT DIGNIFY EMPEARL FEATHER FOLIAGE FURNISH GARNISH GLORIFY GRATIFY IMPLUME SPANGLE VARNISH BEAUTIFY DECORATE EMBLAZON FLOURISH ORNAMENT SPLENDOR

ADORNED CLAD BESEEN DAEDAL ORNATE PICKED BRAIDED CLOTHED COLORED DAISIED FIGURED

(SHOWILY —) BEPRANKED

ADORNMENT TIRE ADORN DRESS PRIDE BEAUTY DECORE TAHALI TINSEL DECKING OUNDING PRANKING TIREMENT

ADRAMMELECH (BROTHER OF —) SHAREZER

(FATHER OF —) SENNACHERIB

ADRASTUS (BROTHER OF —) MECISTEUS

(DAUGHTER OF —) AEGIA DEIPYLE

(FATHER OF —) TALAUS GORDIUS

(MOTHER OF —) LYSIMACHE

(SISTER OF —) ERIPHYLE

ADRESTUS (BROTHER OF —) AMPHIUS

(FATHER OF —) MENOPS

(SLAYER OF —) DIOMEDES

ADRIANA LECOUVREUR

(CHARACTER IN —) ADRIANA MAURICE BOUILLON MICHONNET

(COMPOSER OF —) CILEA

ADRIEL (FATHER OF —) BARZILLAI

(WIFE OF —) MERAB

ADRIFT ASEA LOST AWAFT LIGAN LOOSE AFLOAT DERELICT FLOATING UNMOORED

ADROIT DEFT EASY FEAT GOOD NEAT SLIM ADEPT HANDY READY SMART SNACK TIGHT TRICK ARTFUL CLEVER EXPERT HABILE NIMBLE CUNNING DEXTROUS HANDSOME SKILLFUL

ADROITNESS ART EASE TACT KNACK SKILL ADDRESS FACILITY

ADSORBENT BASE EARTH SILICA

ADULATE FAWN LAUD GLOSS GLOZE PRAISE FLATTER

ADULATION GLOSE GLOZE PRAISE INCENSE FLATTERY

ADULT MAN FULL MANLY MATURE EPHEBIC GROWNUP THRIVEN

ADULTERANT DOPE MULTUM ALMEIDINA

ADULTERATE CUT MIX CARD DASH LOAD ABUSE ALLOY HOCUS TAINT DEACON DEBASE DEFILE DILUTE EXTEND MANAGE WEAKEN BASTARD CORRUPT FALSIFY VITIATE DENATURE IMPURIFY SPURIOUS

ADULTERATED CUT SHAM IMPURE CORRUPT SPURIOUS

ADULTEROUS ERRING

ADULTERY AVOUTRY CUCKOLDOM CUCKOLDRY MISCONDUCT

ADUMBRATE IMAGE SHADE VAGUE OBSCURE SUGGEST INTIMATE

ADUMBRATION SHADE SHADOW PHANTASM

ADUNCOUS BENT HOOKED

ADUST BURNT FIERY GLOOMY SALLOW PARCHED SCORCHED SUNBURNT

ADVANCE GO AID PAY SOP WAY BULL CITE COME DASH GAIN HELP INCH LAUD LEND LIFT LOAN MARK MOVE NEAR NOSE PASS PUSH RISE SHOW STEP WORM AVANT BOOST BRING CREEP ENTER EXALT EXTOL FAVOR FORGE MARCH OFFER PLACE PREST RAISE SERVE SPEED STAIR STAKE THROW ADDUCE ADMOVE ALLEGE AMOUNT ASSIGN ASSIST AVAUNT BETTER DEGREE EXTEND FAVOUR GROWTH HASTEN INCEDE INROAD PREFER PREPAY SCHOOL STRIDE STRIKE THRIVE TRAVEL VAUNCE BENEFIT DEVELOP ELEVATE ENHANCE FORTHGO FORWARD FURTHER HEADWAY IMPREST IMPROVE PROCEED PROCESS PROMOTE PROMOVE PROPOSE PROSPER PROVECT SUCCEED ADDITION DEVELOPE HEIGHTEN INCREASE PROGRESS PROGRESSION

(— BY CUTTING) DRIVE

(— BY LEAPS) SALTATION

(— IN LIFE) WAY

(— LABORIOUSLY) STRIVE

(— OBLIQUELY) SIDLE

(— ONE'S POINT) TAKE

(— SLOWLY) INCH WORM CRAWL CREEP

(— WAVERINGLY) HOBBLE

(— WITH EFFORT) DRAG

(DIFFICULT —) SLOG

(GRADUAL —) ILLAPSE

(STEADY —) SWING

(SUDDEN —) SHOOT

(VIGOROUS —) SWING

(PL.) APPROACHES

ADVANCED FAR DEEP GONE HIGH LATE AHEAD OUTER FORWARD IMPREST LIBERAL VANWARD FOREMOST

(— IN AGE) DEEP ANTIQUATED

(— IN YEARS) SENIOR AGEABLE ELDERLY

(MOST —) EXTREME FARTHEST FOREMOST HEADMOST

(WELL —) AGED

ADVANCEMENT UP GOOD ASCENT INCREASE

ADVANTAGE AD BOT USE VAN BEST BOOT BOTE DRAW DROP EDGE GAIN GOOD HANK JUMP MEND NOTE ODDS PULL SAKE VAIL AVAIL BULGE BUNCE FAVOR FRAME FRUIT KINCH LAUGH POINT SPEED START STEAD USAGE BEHALF BEHOOF BETTER CARROT EFFECT PROFIT ACCOUNT BENEFIT CAPITAL EXPLOIT FORDEAL FURTHER PROMOTE PURPOSE UTILITY VANTAGE HANDICAP INTEREST LEVERAGE OVERHAND OVERPLUS PERCENTAGE

(ACCIDENTAL —) FLUKE

(UNDUE —) ABUSE

ADVANTAGEOUS GOOD JOLI WELL JOLIE GOLDEN PLUMMY SPEEDY USEFUL ELIGIBLE BEHOVEFUL PROPITIOUS

(PREF.) EU

ADVENT COMING INCOME ARRIVAL APPROACH PAROUSIA

ADVENTITIOUS CASUAL FOREIGN STRANGE ACQUIRED EPISODIC ACCESSORY

ADVENTURE GEST LARK RISK SEEK WAGE EVENT GESTE PERIL QUEST AUNTER AUNTRE CHANCE DANGER HAZARD EMPRISE EMPRIZE FORTUNE VENTURE ESCAPADE JEOPARDY

ADVENTURER ROUTIER ARGONAUT PICAROON

ADVENTURESS DEMIREP DEMIMONDAINE

ADVENTUROUS BOLD RASH DARING ERRANT AUNTROUS RECKLESS

ADVERSARY FOE ENEMY RIVAL SATAN FOEMAN OPPONENT

(— OF GOD) DEVIL

(PREF.) ENSTATO

ADVERSE FOE ILL EVIL CROSS LOATH THRAW AVERSE INFEST WITHER AWKWARD COUNTER DIVERSE FROWARD HOSTILE OPPOSED CONTRARY INIMICAL OPPOSING OPPOSITE OVERWART THRAWARD

(PREF.) COUNTER

ADVERSITY ILL WOE CROSS DECAY NIGHT MISERY SORROW WITHER ILLNESS TROUBLE CALAMITY DISTRESS MISFORTUNE

ADVERT HEED AVERT RECUR REFER ALLUDE ATTEND RETURN REVERT OBSERVE CONSIDER

ADVERTISE CRY BARK BILL CALL PLUG PUFF STAR WARN BLURB INFORM NOTIFY PARADE DECLARE DISPLAY OBSERVE PLACARD PUBLISH ANNOUNCE PROCLAIM

ADVERTISED AFFICHE

ADVERTISEMENT AD BILL SIGN BLURB CHANT PITCH PROMO ADVERT CACHET DODGER NOTICE POSTER TEASER AFFICHE PLACARD STUFFER CIRCULAR HANDBILL

ADVERTISING BUSH BILLING PUFFERY

(EXTRAVAGANT —) HYPE

ADVICE AVIS AVYS LORE NEWS REDE AVYSE STEER ADVISO DEVICE NOTICE CAUTION CONSEIL COUNSEL OPINION TIDINGS GUIDANCE MONITION (PL.) INFORMATION

ADVISABLE BOOK PROPER PRUDENT

ADVISE SAY READ REDE TELL VISE WARN WISE AREAD AREED COACH GUIDE WEISE WEIZE ADJURE ADVISO BEREDE CONFER DEVISE EXHORT INFORM PONDER REVEAL APPRISE APPRIZE COUNSEL ACQUAINT ADMONISH CONSIDER RECOMMEND (— AGAINST) DISSUADE

ADVISED DELIBERATE

ADVISER AIDE TOUT COACH COMES TUTOR DOCTOR EGERIA LAWYER NESTOR ADVISOR MONITOR STARETS TEACHER ATTORNEY CROUPIER DIRECTOR FIELDMAN PREACHER

ADVISORY URGING PRUDENT

ADVOCACY BOOM FAVOR AVOWRY FAVOUR ARIANISM

ADVOCATE PRO ABET BACK PUSH URGE VOGT ACTOR ADOPT FAVOR PLEAD ASSERT AVOWRY BACKER DEFEND IDEIST LAWYER PATRON SYNDIC ABETTOR APOSTLE DECLAIM ENDORSE ESPOUSE EXPOUND FASCIST GOLDBUG PATRIOT PLEADER PROCTOR PROMOTE SCHOLAR SUPPORT ATTORNEY CHAMPION CLUBBIST DEFENSOR HUMANIST PARTISAN PREACHER PARACLETE PROPONENT (— FAVORED BY JUDGE) PEAT (— OF REVOLT) ANARCH (SUFF.) ARIAN CRAT

ADVOWSON ADVOCACY TENEMENT PATRONAGE

ADZ AX AXE ADZE EDGE ADDIS ADDICE EATCHE THIXLE HATCHET

AEACUS (FATHER OF —) ZEUS JUPITER (MOTHER OF —) AEGINA (SON OF —) PELEUS PHOCUS TELAMON (WIFE OF —) ENDEIS

AECHMAGORAS (FATHER OF —) HERCULES (MOTHER OF —) PHIALO

AECIUM CAEOMA

AEDON (BROTHER OF —) AMPHION (FATHER OF —) PANDAREUS (HUSBAND OF —) ZETHUS POLYTECHNUS (MOTHER OF —) HARMOTHOE (SON OF —) ITYLUS

AEETES (DAUGHTER OF —) MEDEA (FATHER OF —) HELIOS (MOTHER OF —) PERSA PERSEIS (SON OF —) APSYRTUS

AEGAEON (BROTHER OF —) GYGES COTTUS (FATHER OF —) URANUS (MOTHER OF —) GE GAEA (WIFE OF —) AEMILIA

AEGEAN SEA (ANCIENT PEOPLE

OF —) PSARA PSYRA SAMIAN LELEGES SAMIOTE (GULF OF —) SAROS (ISLAND OF —) COS IOS KEOS NIOS RODI SCIO CHIOS LEROS MELOS NAXOS PAROS PATMO SAMOS SIROS TENOS THERA ANDROS IKARIA IMBROS LEMNOS LESBOS RHODES SKYROS (RIVER INTO —) STRUMA VARDAR MARISTA (TOWN ON —) CHIOS VATHY MYTILENE

AEGEON (WIFE OF —) AEMILIA

AEGEUS (BROTHER OF —) LYCUS NISUS PALLAS (FATHER OF —) PANDION (SON OF —) THESEUS (WIFE OF —) PYLIA

AEGIA (FATHER OF —) ADRASTUS (HUSBAND OF —) POLYNICES (SON OF —) THERSANDER

AEGINA (FATHER OF —) ASOPUS (MOTHER OF —) METOPE (SON OF —) AEACUS

AEGIR HLER GYMIR (WIFE OF —) RAN

AEGIRITE ACMITE

AEGIS EGIS SHIELD AUSPICE DEFENCE DEFENSE

AEGISTHUS (FATHER OF —) THYESTES (MOTHER OF —) PELOPIA (SLAYER OF —) ORESTES

AEGLE (BROTHER OF —) PHAETHON (FATHER OF —) HELIUS (MOTHER OF —) CLYMENE

AEGYPTUS (BROTHER OF —) DANAUS (FATHER OF —) BELUS (MOTHER OF —) ANCHINOE (SON OF —) LYNCEUS

AENEAS (COMPANION OF —) ACHATES (FATHER OF —) ANCHISES (GREAT-GRANDSON OF —) BRUT (MOTHER OF —) VENUS APHRODITE (SON OF —) IULUS ASCANIUS (WIFE OF —) CREUSA LAVINIA

AENEID (AUTHOR OF —) VIRGIL (CHARACTER IN —) ANNA DIDO JUNO VENUS AENEAS PALLAS TURNUS EVANDER LATINUS LAVINIA ANCHISES ASCANIUS

AENGUS (MOTHER OF —) BOANN

AEOLUS (BROTHER OF —) DORUS XUTHUS (DAUGHTER OF —) ARNE CANACE ALCYONE HALCYONE (FATHER OF —) HELLEN HIPPOTES (MOTHER OF —) ORSEIS (SON OF —) ATHAMAS CRETHEUS SISYPHUS SALMONEUS

AEON AGE EON ERA AION AEVUM CYCLE KALPA PERIOD (PAIR OF —S) SYZYGY

AEPYTUS (FATHER OF —) CRESPHONTES (MOTHER OF —) MEROPE

AERATE AERIFY CHARGE INFLATE

AERIAL AERY AIRY TWIN AERIE LOFTY DIPOLE UNREAL AEOLIAN

ANTENNA ETHEREAL

AERIALIST FLIER FLYER

AERIE AERY AIRE AYRE EYRY NEST AIERY BROOD EYRIE

AERIFORM UNREAL GASEOUS

AEROBE BACTERIUM

AERODROME AIRPORT AIRFIELD

AEROEMBOLISM BENDS

AEROFOIL SLAT ROTOR

AEROLITE AEROLITH

AERONAUT PILOT SKYMAN

AERONAUTICS AVIATION

AEROPE (DAUGHTER OF —) ANAXIBIA (FATHER OF —) CATREUS CERHEUS (HUSBAND OF —) ATREUS PLISTHENES (LOVER OF —) THYRESTES (SISTER OF —) CLYMENE (SON OF —) MENELAUS AGAMEMNON

AEROPLANE (SEE AIRPLANE)

AEROSE BRASSY

AEROSTAT AIRSHIP BALLOON AIRCRAFT

AERUGO RUST PATINA

AESACUS (FATHER OF —) PRIAM (LOVER OF —) HESPERIA (MOTHER OF —) ARISBE ALEXIRRHOE

AESEPUS (BROTHER OF —) PEDASUS (FATHER OF —) BUCOLION (MOTHER OF —) ABARBAREA (SLAYER OF —) EURYALUS

AESON (BROTHER OF —) PELIAS (FATHER OF —) CRETHEUS (MOTHER OF —) TYRO (SON OF —) JASON (WIFE OF —) ALCIMEDA

AESTHETIC ARTISTIC ESTHETIC TASTEFUL

AETA ITA

AETHALIDES (FATHER OF —) HERMES MERCURY (MOTHER OF —) EUPOLEMIA

AETHRA (FATHER OF —) OCEANUS PITTHEUS (MOTHER OF —) TETHYS (SON OF —) HYAS THESEUS

AETOLUS (FATHER OF —) ENDYMION (SON OF —) CALYDON PLEURON (WIFE OF —) PRONOE

AFAR OFF AWAY SAHO FERNE FERREN REMOTE YFERRE DANAKIL DANKALI DISTANT

AFARA LIMBA

AFFABLE FAIR OPEN BLAND CIVIL FRANK SUAVE BENIGN FACILE FORTHY GENIAL SOCIAL URBANE AMIABLE CORDIAL GENERAL LIKABLE CHARMING FAMILIAR FRIENDLY GRACIOUS PLEASANT SOCIABLE TOWARDLY CONVERSABLE

AFFAIR DO JOB PIE BLOW CASE DUEL GEAR PLOY BRAWL CAUSE EVENT FIGHT LEVEE PARTY THING ACTION BATTLE BEHALF DOMENT EFFEIR MATTER SETOUT SHAURI BLOWOUT CONCERN FUNERAL HOEDOWN JOURNEY

LIAISON PALAVER SHEBANG BUSINESS COMETHER ENDEAVOR HYPOTHEC INTRIGUE OCCASION PROCEEDING (CONFUSED —) SCHEMOZZLE (CRITICAL —) KANKEDORT (LOVE —) LOVE AMOUR INTRIGUE (SOCIAL —) FORMAL JUNKET SUPPER (STATE —S) ESTATE (PL.) SQUARES OCCASIONS

AFFECT AIL AIR HIT BEAR MELT MOVE POSE RINE SHAM STIR SWAY ALLOT ALTER ANNOY ASSAY COLOR DRIVE FANCY FEIGN HAUNT IMPEL MINCE SHOCK TOUCH ASPIRE ASSIGN ASSUME CHANGE DESIRE MOLEST SOFTEN STRIKE THRILL ATTAINT ATTINGE BEWITCH CONCERN EMOTION FEELING IMPRESS OPERATE PASSION PRETEND PROFESS ALLOCATE DISPOSED FREQUENT INTEREST SIMULATE (— BY HANDLING) TOUCH (— FAVORABLY) LIKE (— INJURIOUSLY) INTERESS (— STRONGLY) HIT HOLD SURPRISE (— WITH EXCITEMENT) BLOW

AFFECTATION AIR AIRS POSE SHAM FRILL GRACE MINCE CHICHI CONCEIT DISPLAY FOPPERY FROUNCE GRIMACE PIETISM FONDNESS PRETENSE PUPPYISM (PL.) LUGS

AFFECTED MOY AIRY CAMP FEAT AILED APISH MOVED POSEY CHICHI FALLAL FEISTY FORMAL PRETTY QUAINT SEIZED FEIGNED MINIKIN MISSISH REACHED SMITTEN STILTED TAFFETA TAFFETY TOUCHED INVOLVED PRECIEUX PRECIOUS RECHERCHE (— BY DECAY) DOTY (— WITH RABIES) MAD (SOMETHING —) CAMP (SUFF.) IC ICAL PATH(IA)(IC)(Y)

AFFECTING AIRIFIED FRAPPANT POIGNANT TOUCHING

AFFECTION LOVE WAFF ALOHA AMOUR BOTCH FLAME HEART CHERTE DOTAGE ESTEEM HYDROA MALADY REGARD THRUSH AILMENT CHARITY EMOTION FEELING PASSION SYMPTOM CHLOASMA DEARNESS DEVOTION FONDNESS KINDNESS MELICERA TENDENCY (PARENTAL —) STORGE (PL.) HEART HEARTSTRINGS (SUFF.) OMA PATHY

AFFECTIONATE DEAR FOND WARM ARDENT DOTING LOVING TENDER AMOROUS CORDIAL DEVOTED EARNEST ZEALOUS ATTACHED PARENTAL SISTERLY

AFFECTIVE SENSIBLE

AFFERENT BEAR ESODIC SENSORY ADVEHENT INFERENT

AFFIANCE AFFY FAITH TRUST ASSURE ENGAGE ENSURE FIANCE PLEDGE PLIGHT SPOUSE BETROTH

PROMISE CONTRACT RELIANCE
AFFIANCED INTENDED
AFFIANT DEPONENT AFFIDAVIT
AFFIDAVIT DAVY OATH AFFIANT
　AFFIDAVY AFFYDAVY
AFFILIATE ALLY UNIT ADOPT
　MERGE UNITE ATTACH BRANCH
　RELATE ASCRIBE CHAPTER
　CONNECT FILIATE
AFFINITY KIN TELE FAMILY LIKING
　AVIDITY CHEMISM KINDRED
　KINSHIP RAPPORT ALLIANCE
　GOSSIPRY HOMOLOGY RELATION
　SYMPATHY COGNATION
　(PREF.) (— FOR) TROP(IDO)(O)
　(SUFF.) (— FOR) PHIL(A)(AE)(E)
　(IA)(ISM)(IST)(OUS)(US)(Y) TROPE
　TROPISM
AFFIRM PUT AFFY AVER AVOW
　TAKE POSIT STATE SWEAR TRUTH
　VOUCH ADHERE ALLEGE ASSERT
　ATTEST AVOUCH DEPOSE RATIFY
　SUBMIT THREAP THREEP VERIFY
　ASSEVER CONFIRM DECLARE
　PROFESS PROTEST TESTIFY
　MAINTAIN PREDICATE
AFFIRMATION SAY VOW YES
　AMEN OATH WORD DIXIT
　PONENT THESIS AVERRAL
　AVERMENT
AFFIRMATIVE AY AYE NOD YAH
　YEA YEP YES AMEN ATEN YEAH
　PONENT DOGMATIC POSITIVE
AFFIX ADD FIX PEN PIN SET CASE
　CLIP FAST JOIN NAIL SEAL SIGN
　ANNEX INFIX STAMP UNITE
　ANCHOR APPEND ATTACH
　FASTEN SETTLE STAPLE ADHIBIT
　CONNECT ENTITLE FORMANT
　IMPRESS PLASTER SUBJOIN
AFFLATUS FURY FUROR FRENZY
　VISION IMPULSE
AFFLICT AIL RUE TRY VEX COMB
　FIRE HOLD HURT PAIN PINE RACK
　TUKE ARRAY ASSAY BESET CURSE
　GRILL GRIPE HARRY PINCH PRESS
　SEIZE SMITE TRYST VISIT WOUND
　WRING BURDEN GRIEVE HARASS
　HUMBLE INFECT MOLEST PESTER
　REMORD SCORCH STRAIN STRESS
　STRIKE CHASTEN INFLICT
　OPPRESS SCOURGE TORMENT
　TROUBLE DISTRESS LACERATE
　STRAITEN
AFFLICTED JOB SAD SORRY AILING
　WOEFUL GRIEVED HAUNTED
　SMITTEN IMPAIRED STRICKEN
　TROUBLED
AFFLICTION WOE EVIL LOSS PAIN
　SORE TEEN TINE TRAY ASSAY
　CROSS GRIEF PRESS SMART
　STOUR BUFFET DURESS MISERY
　PATHOS PLAGUE SORROW
　STRESS THRONG AILMENT
　DISEASE ILLNESS PASSION
　PURSUIT SCOURGE TORTURE
　TROUBLE CALAMITY DISTRESS
　HARDSHIP SEVERITY SICKNESS
　VEXATION MARTYRDOM
　(PL.) ,CUP
　(SUFF.) (— WITH) ITIS
AFFLICTIVE SAD DIRE SORE SOUR
　HEAVY SEVERE

AFFLUENCE EASE AFFLUX INFLUX
　PLENTY RICHES WEALTH
　FORTUNE OPULENCE
AFFLUENT FAT RICH FLUSH RIVER
　STREAM BRANCH SPRUIT COPIOUS
　FLOWING HALCYON OPULENT
　WEALTHY ABUNDANT
　INFLUENT
AFFORD GO BEAR GIVE LEND
　GRANT INCUR OFFER STAND
　THOLE YIELD CONFER ENDURE
　MANAGE SUPPLY ACHIEVE
　FORWARD FURNISH FURTHER
　PRODUCE PROVIDE MINISTER
AFFRAY FEUD FRAY RIOT ALARM
　BRAWL BROIL CLASH FIGHT
　MELEE SCARE SPURN ATTACK
　BATTLE COMBAT EFFRAY ENFRAI
　FRIGHT STRIFE TERROR TUMULT
　ASSAULT CONTEST QUARREL
　SCUFFLE STARTLE FRIGHTEN
　STRUGGLE
AFFRIGHT COW FEAR AGAST
　ALARM DAUNT DOUBT DREAD
　SCARE AGRISE APPALL DISMAY
　CONFUSE STARTLE TERRIFY
　FRIGHTEN
AFFRONT CUT DEFY SLAP ABUSE
　BEARD PEEVE HARASS INJURE
　INSULT NETTLE OFFEND SLIGHT
　STRUNT ASSAULT OFFENCE
　OFFENSE OUTRAGE PROVOKE
　CONFRONT DISGRACE ILLTREAT
　IRRITATE CONTUMELY
AFFUSION POURING INFUSION
AFGHAN RUG GHAN COVER
　DURANI HASARA HAZARA
　PATHAN BLANKET PAKHTUN
　PUKHTUN ACHAKZAI COVERLET
AFGHAN FOX CORSAC CORSAK

AFGHANISTAN
CAPITAL: KABUL
COIN: PUL ABBASI AMANIA
　AFGHANI
LAKE: HELMAND
LANGUAGE: DARI PASHTO PUSHTU
　BALOCHI BALUCHI
MEASURE: JERIB KAROH
MOUNTAIN: KOH SAFEO CHAGAI
　PAMIRS SULAIMAN HIMALAYAS
NATIVE: SISTANI
PARLIAMENT: SHURA
PROVINCE: GHOR FARAH HERAT
　KABUL KUNAR KUNUZ LOGAR
　MAZAR ZABUL GHAZNI KAPISA
　PARWAN WARDAK
RIVER: LORA OXUS CABUL FARAH
　HARUT INDUS KABUL KHASH
　KUNAR KOKCHA KUNDUZ
　HELMAND MURGHAB
　AMUDARYA
SEA: DARYA
TOWN: RUI JURM NANI WAMA
　ASMAR BALKH DOSHI HERAT
　KABUL KUNAR MARUF MATUN
　MUKUR PAHRA TULAK URGAN
　CHAMAN GHAZNI KUNDUZ
　NAUZAD PANJAO RUSTAK
　SANGAN SAROBI TUKZAR
　WASHIR BAGHLAN BAMIYAN
　DILARAM KANDAHAR
　MAZARESHARIF

TRIBE: SAFI TURK ULUS KAFIR
　TAJIK UZBEK BALOCH BALUCH
　HAZARA KIRGIZ PATHAN
WEIGHT: PAU PAW SER SIR
　KARWAR KHURDS

AFICIONADO FAN AMATEUR
　DEVOTEE FOLLOWER
AFIELD ABROAD ASTRAY
AFIRE ALOW ALOWE EAGER
　ABLAZE AFLAME ARDENT
　BURNING FLAMING
A-FLAT AS AIS
AFLOAT ASEA ASWIM AWAFT
　AWASH ADRIFT BUOYED NATANT
　ABROACH FLOODED UNFIXED
　FLOATING
AFOOT ABOUT AGATE ASTIR
　ABROAD TOWARD WALKING
AFOREMENTIONED SAID SUCH
AFORESAID SAME DITTO NAMED
　PRIOR PREVIOUS
AFORETIME ERE FORMER
　FORMERLY
AFRAID RAD REDE ADRAD FRAID
　PAVID REDDE TIMID AGHAST
　CRAVEN FEARED SCARED
　WROTHE AFEARED ALARMED
　ANXIOUS ASCARED CHICKEN
　FEARFUL GASTFUL COWARDLY
　GHASTFUL TIMOROUS
AFREET JINN AFRIT DEMON GIANT
　IFRIT JINNI AFRITE EFREET
AFRESH ANEW ANON OVER AGAIN
　NEWLY DENOVO ENCORE
　REPEATED

AFRICA
(ALSO SEE SPECIFIC COUNTRIES)
DESERT: NAMIB NEFUD NUBIAN
　SAHARA ARABIAN KALAHARI
LAKE: CHAD CONGO NYASA
　VOLTA ALBERT KARIBA MALAWI
　RUDOLF TURKANA VICTORIA
　TANGANYIKA
MOUNTAIN: MERU ATLAS ELGON
　KENYA TEIDE TOUBKAL
　KARISIMBI RASDASHAN
　RUWENZORI DRAKENSBERG
　KILIMANJARO
NATION: CHAD MALI TOGO BENIN
　CONGO EGYPT GABON GHANA
　KENYA LIBYA NIGER SUDAN
　ZAIRE ANGOLA GAMBIA GUINEA
　MALAWI RWANDA UGANDA
　ZAMBIA ALGERIA BURUNDI
　LESOTHO LIBERIA MOROCCO
　NIGERIA SOMALIA TUNISIA
　BOTSWANA CAMEROON
　DJIBOUTI ETHIOPIA TANZANIA
　ZIMBABWE SWAZILAND
　IVORYCOAST MADAGASCAR
　MAURITANIA MOZAMBIQUE
　UPPERVOLTA SIERRALEONE
　SOUTHAFRICA GUINEABISSAU
　EQUATORIALGUINEA
　CENTRALAFRICANREPUBLIC
RIVER: NILE ORANGE LIMPOPO
　SENEGAL ZAMBEZI
WATERFALL: FINCHA TUGELA
　KALAMBO RUACANA TESSISAT
　VICTORIA

AFRICAINE, L' (CHARACTER IN —)
　INEZ DAGAMA SELIKA NELUSKO
　(COMPOSER OF —) MEYERBEER
AFRICAN BOER AFRIC
AFRICAN MARIGOLD KHAKIBOS
AFRIKAANS TAAL DUTCH
AFRO NATURAL
AFT BACK REAR ABAFT AFTER
　ASTERN BEHIND
　(FARTHEST —) AFTERMOST
AFTER A AB BY TO AFT EFT FOR
　SIN ANON NEXT PAST POST SYNE
　ABAFT APRES ARTER EFTER
　INFRA LATER SINCE ASTERN
　BEHIND BEYOND FOLLOW HINDER
　(— MEALS) PC
　(PREF.) EPH EPI INFRA META
　POST
AFTERBIRTH HEAM SECUNDINE
　SOOTERKIN
AFTERBODY TONNEAU
AFTERBURNER AUGMENTER
AFTEREFFECT SEQUEL SEQUELA
　(PL.) HANGOVER
AFTERGRASS FOG AFTERFEED
AFTERIMAGE SPECTRUM
　PHOTOGENE SENSATION
　(KIND OF —) PURKINJE
AFTERMATH FOG ETCH LOSS
　ISSUE ROWEN ROWET TRAIL
　TRAIN ARRISH EDDISH EDGREW
　EDGROW EFFECT PROFIT RESULT
　SEQUEL UPSHOT EAGRASS
　STUBBLE BACKWASH
AFTERMOST LAST HINDMOST
AFTERNOON AFTER TARDE
　UNDERN EVENING TEATIME
AFTERPIECE JIG EPODE EXODE
　EXODIUM POSTLUDE
AFTERSONG EPODE
AFTERSWARM CAST SPEW SPUE
　CASTLING
AFTERTASTE TWANG FAREWELL
AFTERTHOUGHT FOOTNOTE
AFTERWARD EFT POST SITH THEN
　APRES LATER EFTSOON
　EFTSOONS
AGA AGHA LORD CHIEF
　(WIFE OF —) BEGUM
AGAIN OR TO BIS EFT YET AGIN
　ANEW ANON AYEN AYIN BACK
　MORE OVER NEWLY AFRESH
　DENOVO ENCORE ITERUM
　EFTSOON FRESHLY FURTHER
　EFTSOONS MOREOVER
　(— AND AGAIN) AND
　(PREF.) ANA OVER PALI RE
AGAINST BY IN UP CON GIN NON
　AGIN ANTI GAIN INTO WITH
　AGAIN ANENT AYENS UNTIL
　ANENST AVERSE AYENST CONTRA
　GAINST UPTILL VERSUS FERNENT
　FORNENT OPPOSED ADVERSUS
　CONTRAIR FORENENT FORNENST
　FORNINST
　(— HOPE) AGLEE AGLEY
　(PREF.) ANTH ANTI CAT(A) CATH
　CONTRA ENANTIO GAIN OB
AGAL HEADROPE
AGALLOCH AGGUR ALOES GAROO
　GARROO GARROW TAMBAC
　LINALOE AGALWOOD CALAMBAC
AGAMA AGA AGHA GUANA

AGAMID IGUANA LIZARD
AGAMIAN
AGAMEDE (FATHER OF —) AUGEAS
(HUSBAND OF —) MULIUS
AGAMEMNON (BROTHER OF —)
MENELAUS
(DAUGHTER OF —) ELECTRA
IPHIGENIA
(FATHER OF —) PLISTHENES
(GRANDFATHER OF —) ATREUS
(SON OF —) ORESTES
(WIFE OF —) CLYTEMNESTRA
AGAMID AGA AGHA BALETE BALITI
AGAPANTHUS TULBAGHIA
LOVEFLOWER
AGAPE LOVE OPEN FEAST GAPING
YAWNING
AGAR MOSS GELOSE KANTEN
GELOSIN GELOSINE
AGARIC BLEWITS BLUSHER
FLYBANE LEPIOTA
AGASP EAGER GASPING
AGATE TAW ONYX RUBY SARD
ACHATE GAGATE MARBLE PEBBLE
QUARTZ
AGATI SESBANIA
AGAVE ALOE LILY AGAUE AMOLE
DATIL SISAL LILIUM MAGUEY
MESCAL PULQUE ZAPUPE
CANTALA KARATTO KERATTO
TEQUILA HENEQUEN HENIQUEN
JINIQUEN SOAPWEED
(BROTHER OF —) POLYDORUS
(FATHER OF —) CADMUS
(HUSBAND OF —) ECHION
(MOTHER OF —) HARMONIA
(SISTER OF —) INO SEMELE
AUTONOE
(SON OF —) PENTHEUS
AGE ALD BIN DAY ELD EON ERA
AEON EDGE OLAM TIME YUGA
AETAT CYCLE EPOCH OLDEN
RIPEN SECLE WORLD YEARS
MATURE MELLOW PERIOD SIECLE
WITHER CENTURY DEVELOP
GLACIAL OLDNESS SECULUM
SENESCE VORHAND ANCIENTY
DURATION ETERNITY LIFETIME
MAJORITY MATURITY
(— OF MOON) EPACT
(— OF 100 YEARS) CENTENARY
(ADVANCED —) DOTAGE
(BEING UNDER 13 YEARS OF —)
PRETEEN
(EARLY MIDDLE —) SUMMER
(GREAT —) ANTIQUITY
GRANDEVITY
(OLD —) CRUTCH SENIUM
VETUSTY SENILITY
(PREF.) **(OLD —)** GERONT(O)
PRESBY(O)
(SUFF.) AEVAL EVAL
(HAVING APPROXIMATE — OF) ISH
ISTIC
AGED AE AET AGY OLD RIPE ANILE
HOARY OLDEN PASSE FEEBLE
INFIRM MATURE SENILE WINTRY
YEARED ANCIENT ELDERLY
OGYGIAN WINTERED
(NOT —) GREEN
(WELL —) STALE
AGEE AJEE AWRY AGLEY ASKEW
(SON OF —) SHAMMAH

AGELESS ETERNAL TIMELESS
AGELONG SECULAR SAECULAR
AGENCY DINT HAND CHECK FORCE
LEVER MEANS MOYEN ORGAN
PROXY ACTION BUREAU MEDIUM
OFFICE ARBITER BENEFIT
BROKERY FACULTY LIBRARY
MACHINE ACTIVITY COMPTOIR
COURTESY MINISTRY
(PUBLIC —) AUTHORITY
(RESTORATIVE —) BALM
(SUPPOSITITIOUS —) ENTELECHY
(THERAPEUTIC —) MODALITY
AGENDUM SLATE DOCKET RECORD
RITUAL PROGRAM
AGENOR (BROTHER OF —) BELUS
(DAUGHTER OF —) EUROPA
(FATHER OF —) ANTENOR
NEPTUNE
(MOTHER OF —) LIBYA
(SON OF —) CILIX CADMUS
PHOENIX
(WIFE OF —) TELEPHASSA
AGENT SPY AMIN DOER ETCH
GENE ACTOR AMEEN BUYER
CAUSE ENVOY MEANS ORGAN
PROXY REEVE RIDER VAKIL
WALLA ADUROL ASSIGN ATOPEN
BROKER BURSAR COMMIS DEALER
DEPUTY ENGINE FACTOR FITTER
KEHAYA LEDGER MEDIUM MINION
MUKTAR PESKAR SELLER SYNDIC
VAKEEL WALLAH BAILIFF BLISTER
CHANNEL COUCHER DRASTIC
FACIENT FEDERAL HUSBAND
LEAGUER MOOKTAR MOUNTAR
MUKTEAR MUTAGEN OFFICER
PESHKAR PROCTOR SCALPER
APPROVER ATTORNEY AUMILDAR
CATALYST EMISSARY EXECUTOR
GOMASHTA GOMASTAH
IMPROVER INCITANT INSTITOR
MINISTER MOOKHTAR OPERATOR
PROMOTER QUAESTOR RESIDENT
SALESMAN VIRUCIDE MIDDLEMAN
OPERATIVE SATELLITE
SENESCHAL MAINSPRING
PROCURATOR PLENIPOTENTIARY
(— AGAINST LEPROSY) DAPSONE
**(— INVESTIGATING DRUG
VIOLATIONS)** NARC NARK
(— OF CROMWELL) AGITATOR
(ANTIKNOCK —) ADDITIVE
ALKYLATE
(CLEANSING —) SOAP
(CONFIDENTIAL —) AMIN AMEEN
(DESTRUCTIVE —) DEVOURER
(EMPLOYMENT —) PADRONE
(ENFORCEMENT —) LAW
(ESPIONAGE —) COURIER
(FISCAL —) STEWARD
(HEALING —) BALSAM
(MEDICINAL —) DRASTIC
(NARCOTIC —) NARC NARK GAZER
(OXIDIZING —) NINHYDRIN
(PRESS —) FLACK
(PUBLICITY —) BEATER
(PURCHASING —) CIRCAR SIRCAR
SIRKAR
(SECRET —) SBIRRO
(STIMULATING —) FILIP FILLIP
(SUBVERSIVE —) STOOGE
(SWEETENING —) DULCIN

(UNDERCOVER —) SPOOK
(VOLATILE —) SPIRIT
(WETTING —) SPREADER
(SUFF.) ANT FIER STAT(IC)(ICS)
AGESILAUS (BROTHER OF —) AGIS
(FATHER OF —) ARCHIDAMUS
(MOTHER OF —) EUPOLIA
AGGLOMERATE HEAP LUMP MASS
PILE SELF SLAG WIND CHAOS
GATHER CLUSTER COLLECT
AGGLOMERATION HORDE
CONGERY FAVELLA CONGERIE
AGGRANDIZE LIFT BOOST EXALT
RAISE ADVANCE AUGMENT
DIGNIFY ELEVATE ENLARGE
MAGNIFY PROMOTE INCREASE
AGGRAVATE IRK NAG VEX FEED
LOAD TWIT ANGER ANNOY
TAUNT TEASE BURDEN PESTER
WORSEN AGGREGE BEDEVIL
ENHANCE ENLARGE MAGNIFY
PROVOKE AGGRIEVE HEIGHTEN
INCREASE IRRITATE
AGGRAVATED ACUTE
AGGREEABLE ACCEPTABLE
AGGREGATE ADD ALL SET SUM
AUGE BAND BULK CLON CLUB
COMB DEME FLOC GOUT LATH
MASS BLOCK BUNCH CLASS
CLONE COVER CROWD FIELD
GROSS SHOOT TOTAL UNITE
WHOLE AMOUNT BALLAS
DOMAIN PLUREL VOLUME
ASBOLAN COLLECT ARCULITE
ASBOLANE ASBOLITE AXIOLITE
COMPOUND COVERAGE
CUMULITE ENSEMBLE
MANIFOLD MULTEITY
TOTALITY
(— OF MICA) BOOK
(— OF MINERALS) EYE
(— OF ORE) KIDNEY
(— OF POINTS) CELL
(— OF RELATED THINGS) SHMEAR
SCHMEAR
(— OF STATEMENTS) AUTHORITY
(— OF TISSUES) BODY
(MATHEMATICAL —) FIELD
SEQUENCE
(MOLECULAR —) MICELLE
(SOIL —) PED
(SUFF.) ERY
AGGREGATION HEAD HERD NEST
CLUMP CUTIN FLOCK GORGE
GROUP LURRY SWARM COLONY
FAMILY NATION SYSTEM CLUSTER
CONGERY GALLERY SORITES
CONGERIE EUMERISM
AGGRESSION WAR RAID ATTACK
INJURY ASSAULT OFFENSE
INVASION
AGGRESSIVE BUTCH PUSHY
PUSHING AGONISTIC
AGGRESSIVENESS CRUST
DEFIANCE BELLICOSITY
AGGRIEVE TRY HARM HURT PAIN
HARRY WRONG INJURE AFFLICT
OPPRESS TROUBLE DISTRESS
AGGRIEVED SORE OFFENDED
AGHAST AGAST AFRAID
AGHRERATH (FATHER OF —)
PESHENG
(SLAYER OF —) AFRASIAB

AGILAWOOD AGALLOCH
AGALLOCHUM
AGILE DEFT FAST LISH SPRY WIRY
ADEPT ALERT BRISK CATTY ELFIN
FLEET LITHE NIFTY NIPPY QUICK
WANLE WITHY ACTIVE ADROIT
FEERIE FEIRIE LIMBER LISSOM
LITHER LIVELY LUTHER NIMBLE
QUIVER SUPPLE WANDLE
LISSOME SALIENT SPRINGE
SPRINGY ATHLETIC
AGILITY LEVITY SPROIL SLEIGHT
ACTIVITY LEGERITY SALIENCE
AGING BINNING
(PREMATURE —) GERODERMA
GERODERMIA
AGIO BATTA DISAGIO PREMIUM
DISCOUNT EXCHANGE
AGIST TAX FEED RATE GRAZE
PASTURE
AGITATE FAN IRK JAR VEX WEY
FRET FUSS MOVE PLOT RILE
ROCK SEEK STIR TEEM ALARM
ALTER BREAK BROIL CHURN
DRIVE HARRY IMPEL QUAKE
ROUSE SHAKE AROUSE BETOSS
BUSKLE DEBATE DEVISE EXCITE
FOMENT HARASS INCITE JABBLE
JOSTLE JUMBLE JUSTLE LATHER
MANAGE RATTLE RUFFLE SEETHE
ACTUATE CANVASS COMMOVE
CONCUSS DISCUSS DISTURB
PERTURB REVOLVE TEMPEST
TORMENT TROUBLE ACTIVATE
CONTRIVE CONVULSE DISQUIET
DISTRACT TRANSACT
(— A LIQUID) SPARGE
AGITATED WILD HECTIC STEWED
STORMY YEASTY AGITATO
ESTUOUS UNQUIET AESTUOUS
FEVERISH FLURRIED SEETHING
OVERWROUGHT
AGITATION GOG JAR JOG BOIL
FEAR FLAP FRET FURY GUST
HEAT ITCH JERK JOLT SNIT
ALARM DANCE HURRY QUAKE
SHAKE STORM STOUR TWEAK
YEAST BREEZE BUSTLE DITHER
ENERGY FIZZLE FLIGHT FLURRY
FRENZY JABBLE MOTION PUCKER
QUIVER RIPPLE SHAKES TAKING
TREMOR TUMULT WELTER
EMOTION FERMENT FLUSTER
FLUTTER MADNESS RAMPAGE
STICKLE SWITHER TEMPEST
TURMOIL DISQUIET PAROXYSM
UPHEAVAL COMMOTION
(— AND PROPAGANDA) AGITPROP
AGITATOR HOG TREATER
AGLAIA (FATHER OF —) JUPITER
(MOTHER OF —) EURYNOME
(SISTER OF —) THALIA
EUPHROSYNE
AGLET TAB TAG LACE STUD PLATE
AIGLET PENDANT SPANGLE
HAWTHORN STAYLACE
AGLEY AWRY AGLEE ASIDE ASKEW
WRONG
AGLYCON GENIN NONSUGAR
SAPOGENIN
AGNATE AKIN ALLIED COGNATE
KINDRED
AGNEL MOUTON

AGNOETE THEMISTIAN
AGNOMEN NAME ALIAS EPITHET SURNAME COGNOMEN NICKNAME
AGNOSTIC ATHEIST DOUBTER SKEPTIC NESCIENT
AGO BY SIN BACK ERST GONE PAST SENS SYNE YGOE YORE ABACK AGONE SINCE YGONE SINSYNE BACKWARD
(LONG —) ANCIENTLY
AGOG AVID KEEN ASTIR EAGER LIVELY EXCITED VIGILANT
AGONIZE BEAR RACK STRAIN WRITHE
AGONIZING GRINDING HARROWING
AGONY ACHE PAIN PANG DOLOR GRIEF GRIPE PANIC STOUR THRAW THROE TRIAL ACHING ANGUISH ANXIETY EMOTION TORMENT TORTURE TRAVAIL DISTRESS PAROXYSM
AGOUTI CAPA CAVY PACA ACUCHI AGOUTY ACOUCHI ACOUCHY
AGRARIAN RURAL PASTORAL PRAEDIAL
AGRAULOS (DAUGHTER OF —) HERSE PANDROSOS
(FATHER OF —) ACTAEUS
(HUSBAND OF —) CECROPS
AGREE FAY FIT GEE HIT PAN YES GIBE GREE JIBE JUMP MEET SIDE SORT SUIT ADMIT ALLOW ATONE BLEND CHECK CLICK CLOSE FADGE GRANT HITCH JUTTY LEVEL MATCH PIECE STAND TALLY UNITE YIELD ACCEDE ACCEPT ACCORD ADHERE ASSENT ASSORT COMPLY CONCUR CONDOG COTTON ENGAGE REWARD SETTLE SQUARE SUBMIT ARRANGE BARGAIN COMPORT CONCEDE CONFORM CONGREE CONGRUE CONSENT CONSIGN DARESAY PACTION PROMISE COINCIDE COMPOUND CONTRACT COVENANT QUADRATE
(— MUTUALLY) STIPULATE
(— TO) ACCEPT
(— TO JOIN) ADHERE
(— UPON) TAILYE TAILZEE TAILZIE
(— WITH) SIT LIKE SIDE TAIL ANSWER
AGREEABLE AMEN EASY FAIR FINE GOOD KIND LIEF NICE SOFT WEME AMENE CANNY DULCE GRATE JOLIE JOLLY LITHE LUSTY QUEME READY SAPID SMIRK SUANT SUAVE SUENT SWEET COMELY COWDIE DAINTY DULCET KINDLY LIKELY MELLOW SAVORY SMOOTH SUITED ADAPTED AMABILE AMIABLE COUTHIE DOUCEUR TUNABLE WELCOME WILLING WINSOME AMENABLE CHARMING DELICATE GRATEFUL LIKESOME LOVESOME OBLIGING PLACABLE PLAUSIVE PLEASANT PLEASING PURSUANT SOCIABLE SUITABLE THANKFUL CONGENIAL PALATABLE

(NOT —) ABHORRENT
(UNPLEASANTLY —) SACCHARINE
AGREEING CONNATE CONTENT ACCORDANT ACCORDING
AGREEMENT GO FIT NOD AXIS BOND DEAL FINE LINE MISE PACT TACK TAIL TRUE ATONE COVIN LEASE MATCH TERMS TOUCH TRUTH TRYST UNITY ACCORD ACTION ASSENT CARTEL CAUTIO COMART COMITY COVINE DICKER LEAGUE PACTUM PLEDGE TREATY UNISON ANALOGY BARGAIN CLOSING CLOSURE COMPACT CONCERT CONSENT CONSORT CONSULT ENTENTE HARMONY ONENESS PACTION RAPPORT CONTRACT DIAPASON SANCTION SORTANCE SYMPATHY ACCEPTANCE ACCORDANCE
(— TO JOIN) ADHESION
(GRAMMATICAL —) ATTRACTION
(SECRET —) CAHOOT CAHOOTS COLLUSION
AGRICANE (SLAYER OF —) ORLANDO
AGRICULTURAL ARABLE GEOPONIC GEOPONICAL
AGRICULTURE FARMING GAINAGE TILLAGE AGRONOMY
(— SYSTEM) KOLKHOZ
(PREF.) AGRO
AGRICULTURIST THO FARMER GROWER SANTAL PLANTER RANCHER
AMERICAN REID MORTON RUFFIN TAYLOR THOMAS WATSON BORLAUG
CANADIAN MACKAY SAUNDERS
ENGLISH TULL YOUNG
GERMAN NAUMANN
SWISS SAUSSURE
AGRIMONY CLIVE BONESET BORWORT HEMPWEED
AGRITO AGARITA MAHONIA ALGERITO ASHBERRY
AGRIUS (BROTHER OF —) LATINUS TELEGONUS
(FATHER OF —) ULYSSES ODYSSEUS PORTHAON
(MOTHER OF —) GAEA CIRCE EURYTE
(SON OF —) THERSITES
AGRONOMIST (ALSO SEE AGRICULTURIST)
AGROUND SEWED ASHORE BEACHED STRANDED
AGRYPHA LOGION
AGRYPNIA INSOMNIA SLEEPLESSNESS
AGUACATE AHUACA AVOCADO
AGUAMAS PINGUIN
AGUE CHILL EXIES FEVER MALARIA QUARTAN SHAKING SHIVERS
AGUE TREE SASSAFRAS
AGUEWEED BONESET
AGUR (FATHER OF —) JAKEH
AH AY ACH
AHAB (FATHER OF —) OMRI
(NEIGHBOR OF —) NABOTH
(WIFE OF —) JEZEBEL
AHAR AGEE AJEE

AHARAH (FATHER OF —) BENJAMIN
AHARTALAV YARROW MILFOIL
AHASBAI (SON OF —) ELIPHELET
AHAZ (FATHER OF —) MICAH JOTHAM
AHAZIAH (FATHER OF —) AHAB JEHORAM
(MOTHER OF —) JEZEBEL ATHALIAH
AHBAN (FATHER OF —) ABISUR
(MOTHER OF —) ABIHAIL
AHEAD ON UP ALEE FORE AFORE ALONG DORMY BEFORE DORMIE ONWARD ALREADY ENDWAYS ENDWISE FORWARD LEADING ADELANTE ADVANCED ANTERIOR
(— OF TIME) FAST
(STRAIGHT —) FORERIGHT
AHEM HUM
AHIAH (FATHER OF —) AHITUB JERAHMEEL
(SON OF —) BAASHA
AHIAM (FATHER OF —) SHARAR
AHIEZER (FATHER OF —) AMMISHADDAI
AHIHUD (FATHER OF —) SHELOMI
AHIKAM (FATHER OF —) SHAPHAN
(SON OF —) GEDALIAH
AHILUD (SON OF —) BAANA JEHOSHAPHAT
AHIMAAZ (DAUGHTER OF —) AHINOAM
(FATHER OF —) ZADOK
AHIMELECH (FATHER OF —) AHITUB
AHINADAB (FATHER OF —) IDDO
AHINOAM (FATHER OF —) AHIMAAZ
(HUSBAND OF —) SAUL DAVID
(SON OF —) AMNON
AHIO (FATHER OF —) BERIAH JEHIEL ABINADAB
AHIRAM (FATHER OF —) BENJAMIN
AHISAMACH (SON OF —) AHOLIAB
AHISHAHAR (FATHER OF —) BILHAN
AHITUB (FATHER OF —) AMARIAH PHINEHAS
(SON OF —) ZADOK AHIJAH AHIMELECH
AHLAI (FATHER OF —) SHESHAN
(HUSBAND OF —) JARHA
(SON OF —) ZABAD
AHOAH (FATHER OF —) BENJAMIN
AHOLIBAMAH (FATHER OF —) ANAH
(HUSBAND OF —) ESAU
AHOY AVAST
AHUEHUETE CEDAR SABINO CYPRESS
AHURA MAZDA ORMAZD
AHUZAM (FATHER OF —) ASHUR
(MOTHER OF —) NAARAH
AH WILDERNESS (AUTHOR OF —) ONEILL
(CHARACTER IN —) BELLE DAVID MILLER MURIEL RICHARD MCCOMBER
AIAH (BROTHER OF —) ANAH
(DAUGHTER OF —) RIZPAH
(FATHER OF —) ZIBEON
AID KEY ABET BACK BEET HAND HELP PONY REDE ALLAY BOOST COACH FAVOR GRANT SERVE SPEED TREAT ASSIST CRUTCH FAVOUR FRIEND PROFIT RELIEF

REMEDY RESCUE SECOND SUCCOR SUPPLY UPHOLD ADVANCE AIDANCE ANCILLA BACKING BENEFIT COMFORT ENDORSE FORWARD FURTHER INDORSE RELIEVE SECOURS SERVICE SUBSIDY SUPPORT ADJUVATE AUXILIUM BEFRIEND SUFFRAGE
(— A VESSEL) HOVEL
(— SECRETLY) SUBAID
(COMPLEXION —) FUCUS
(MORMON —) COUNSELOR COUNSELLOR
AIDA (CHARACTER IN —) AIDA AMNERIS RADAMES AMONASRO
(COMPOSER OF —) VERDI
AIDAN (FATHER OF —) GABRAN
AIDE AID BEAGLE DEPUTY SECOND OFFICER ORDERLY ADJUTANT GALLOPER PARAPROFESSIONAL
(BULLFIGHTER'S —) CAPEADOR
AIGRETTE EGRET HERON PLUME SPRAY AIGRET FEATHERS
AIL ILE AILD EILE EYLE FAIL PAIN PINE AFFECT BOTHER FALTER SUFFER AFFLICT DECLINE TROUBLE COMPLAIN DISTRESS
AILANTHUS SUMAC SUMACH
AILING SICK CRAZY CRONK DONCY DONSY SOBER DONSIE SICKLY UNWELL CRAICHY CREACHY
AILMENT AIL ILL PIP COUGH MALADY DISEASE ILLNESS DISORDER SICKNESS WEAKNESS
(SUDDEN —) WAFF
AIM END LAY TRY BEAD BEAM BEND BENT BUTT FINE GLEE GOAL HEAD HOLD LEAD MARK MINT PLAN SAKE SEEK TEMP VIEW VIZY WINK ACIES BLANK DRIVE ESSAY ETTLE GUESS LEVEL POINT PRICK SCOPE SIGHT TRAIN VISIE VIZZY ASPIRE DESIGN DIRECT ESTEEM INTEND INTENT OBJECT SCHEME STRIVE ADDRESS ATTEMPT CHIMERA MEANING PRETEND PURPOSE RESPECT STAGGER CHIMAERA CONSIDER ENDEAVOR ESTIMATE PRETENSE STEERING TENTAMEN
(— A KICK) FLING
(— AT) EYE AFFECT
(— FURTIVELY) STEAL
(— INDIRECTLY) GLANCE
AIMED FAST
(— AT) AFFECTED
AIMING LEVEL GUNLAYING
AIMLESS IDLE BLIND CHANCE RANDOM DRIFTING
AIMLESSNESS FLANERIE
AIR AER PEW SKY AERE ARIA AURA AYRE BROW DIRT FEEL LILT LOFT MIEN PORT POSE SONG TELL TUNE VENT WIND ETHER FRILL OZONE UTTER VOICE AERATE AETHER ALLURE ASPECT BROACH CACHET MANNER MELODY OSTENT PIAFFE REGARD REGION STRAIN VANITY WELKIN WITHER BEARING DISPLAY EXHIBIT EXPRESS FANFARE MALARIA

NEPHELE PIAFFER ATTITUDE BEHAVIOR CARRIAGE PRESENCE
(— COOLED) WATERLESS
(— EXHALED) BLAST
(— IN MOTION) BREATH
(— PLANT) LIFELEAF
(BOASTFUL —) PARADO
(CONFIDENT —) BRAVURA
(COOL —) FRESCO
(COQUETTISH —) MINAUDERIE
(FETID —) REEK
(FOUL —) DIRT
(HAUGHTY —S) ALTITUDES
(MUSICAL —) ARIA SOLO TUNE BRAWL MELODY ARIETTA ARIETTE BRAVURA CANZONE MUSETTE CAVATINE
(POMPOUS —) SWELL
(PUT ON —S) PROSS
(STALE —) STEAM
(STIFLING —) SMORE
(THE —) GATE
(WARM —) OAM
(PL.) LUGS FRONT
(PREF.) AER(O) ATM(O) PNEO PNEUM(A)(ATA)(O)(ON)(ONO) PNEUSTA
AIRCRAFT KITE ABORT BLIMP CRAFT FLYER PLANE GLIDER AEROBUS AERONEF AIRSHIP BALLOON AEROBOAT AERODYNE AEROSTAT AIRLINER AIRPLANE AUTOGIRO AUTOGYRO GYRODYNE ROTORCRAFT ORNITHOPTER
(UNIDENTIFIED —) UFO BOGY BOGEY BOGIE
AIRCRAFTSMAN ERK
AIRCREWMAN KICKER AIREDALE
AIRFIELD AERODROME SATELLITE
AIRFOIL FIN FLAP SLAT BLADE SURFACE AEROFOIL ELEVATOR
AIRILY JAUNTILY
AIRLESS STUFFY STIFLING
AIRLINE FEEDER SKYWAY NONSKED
AIRMAN ACE FLIER FLYER BIRDMAN WARBIRD AERONAUT WASTEMAN
AIRPLANE BUS CUB JET MIG SST BAKA GYRO KILL KITE SHIP ZERO AVION CAMEL CRATE FLIER FLYER FRITZ GOTHA HEINE JENNY LINER PLANE SCOUT SNOOP BOMBER CANARD CHASER COPTER FERRET FESSEL FOKKER GLIDER JENNIE PUSHER SMOKER TANDEM VESSEL VIMANA AERONEF AVIATIK AVIETTE BIPLANE CLIPPER FIGHTER FLIVVER FLYAWAY HOTSHOT PENGUIN SNOOPER SPOTTER TRACTOR WARBIRD AEROSTAT ALBATROS KAMIKAZE SEAPLANE SKYCOACH SKYCRAFT SOCIABLE STRUTTER TRIPLANE TURBOJET WARPLANE AEROPLANE MONOPLANE
(PART OF —) FIN POD TAB FLAP WING BLADE CABIN PYLON RADAR ENGINE RUDDER AILERON COCKPIT COWLING SPOILER ELEVATOR REVERSER STABILIZER SUPPRESSOR

(REMOTE-CONTROLLED —) DRONE
(TYPE OF —) TRIJET
AIR PLANT LIFELEAF LIVELEAF
AIRPORT DROME AIRPARK JETPORT SCUTTLE AIRDROME AIRFIELD
AIRSHIP (SEE ALSO AIRPLANE AND AIRCRAFT) SHIP BLIMP GASBAG AERONAT AEROSTAT PARSEVAL ZEPPELIN
AIRSTREAM PEW DOWNWASH
AIRSTRIP LILY
AIRTIGHT SEALED AIRPROOF HERMETIC
AIRWAY MONKEY RETURN SKYWAY AIRWAVE WINDWAY WINDROAD
AIRY GAY COOL RARE THIN EMPTY HUFFY LIGHT MERRY WINDY AERIAL BLITHE BREEZY FLUFFY JAUNTY JOCUND LIVELY STARRY AIRLIKE AIRSOME HAUGHTY JOCULAR SFOGATO AFFECTED ANIMATED DEBONAIR DELICATE ETHEREAL FLIPPANT GRACEFUL SPARKISH TRIFLING VOLATILE
AISLE WAY YLE AILE LANE NAVE WALK ALLEE ALLEY FEEDWAY GANGWAY PASSAGE CORRIDOR
AIT OAT EYOT HOLM ILOT ISLE EIGHT ISLET ISLOT
AITCHBONE ICEBONE EDGEBONE
AJA (FATHER OF —) RAGHU DILIPA
AJAR OPEN DISCORDANT
AJAX AIAS
(FATHER OF —) OILEUS TELAMON
(MOTHER OF —) ERIBOEA PERIBOEA
AJIGARTA (SON OF —) SUNAHSEPA
AJONJOLI SESAME
AJOWAN AJAVA AIWAIN
AKALI SHAHIDI
AKAN (FATHER OF —) EZER
AKEAKE AKE HOPBUSH IRONWOOD
AKHA KAW
AKIMBO ANGLED AKEMBOLL AKENBOLD
AKIN SIB LIKE NEAR NIGH ALIKE CLOSE AGNATE ALLIED COUSIN SIBBED TENDER COGNATE CONNATE GERMANE RELATED SIMILAR
(— ON MALE SIDE) AGNATIC
(NOT —) UNSIB
AKKUB (FATHER OF —) ELIOENAI
AKRA ACCRA INKRA
AKU VICTORFISH
AL AAL AWL MULBERRY
ALA AXIL DRUM WING AXILLA RECESS NOSEWING

LAKE: MARTIN
MOUNTAIN: CHEAHA LOOKOUT RACCOON
NATIVE: LIZARD
RIVER: PEA COOSA CAHABA MOBILE SIPSEY TENSAW CONECUH PERDIDO SEPULGA WARRIOR TOMBIGBEE TALLAPOOSA
STATE BIRD: YELLOWHAMMER
STATE FISH: TARPON
STATE FLOWER: CAMELLIA
STATE TREE: PINE LONGLEAF
TOWN: OPP PIPER SELMA ATHENS CORONA HEFLIN JASPER LANETT LINDEN MARION MOBILE SAMSON BREWTON FLORALA GADSDEN ANNISTON SYLACAUGA TUSCALOOSA

ALABASTER GYPSUM TECALI ONYCHITE
ALACK ALAS ALAKE
ALACRITY HASTE SPEED CELERITY RAPIDITY
ALAMEDA MALL WALK
ALAMETH (FATHER OF —) BECHER
ALAN ALAND ALANT ALAUNT
ALANG-ALANG COGON KOGON
ALANS GHUZ OGHUZ
ALANTIN INULIN
ALAR PTERIC WINGED AXILLARY WINGLIKE
ALARBUS (MOTHER OF —) TAMORA
ALARDO (BROTHER OF —) BRADAMANT
ALARM COW DIN BELL FEAR FRAY GAST LARM ALERT BROIL CLOCK DAUNT FEEZE LARUM NOISE PANIC ROUSE SCARE SIREN START STILL UPSET AFFRAY ALARUM APPALL AROUSE ATTACK BUZZER DISMAY EXCITE FRIGHT OUTCRY SIGNAL TERROR TOCSIN DISTURB GLOPNEN GLOPPEN MOUNTEE STARTLE TERRIFY TORPEDO WARNING AFFRIGHT DISQUIET FRIGHTEN SURPRISE CONSTERNATION
(FIRE —) STILL FIREBOX
ALARMED SCARY SCAREY FEARFUL GASTFUL AFFRAYED GHASTFUL SCAREFUL STREAKED
ALARMER HUER
ALARMING SCARY SCAREY FEARFUL SCAREFUL
ALAS AY ACH HEU LAS OCH VAE WOE EHEU HECH OIME WALY ALACK HALAS HELAS OIMEE HARROW OCHONE OTOTOI WAESUCK ULLAGONE WAESUCKS WELLADAY WELLAWAY

FORAKER MCKINLEY
MOUNTAIN RANGE: CRAZY BROOKS KAIYUH CHUGACH KILBUCK WRANGELL
NATIVE: ALEUT AHTENA ESKIMO INGALIK KOYUKON TLINGIT
PENINSULA: KENAI SEWARD
RIVER: CHENA KOBUK YUKON COPPER NOATAK TANANA KOYUKUK SUSITNA CHULITNA COLVILLE KUSKOKWIM PORCUPINE
STATE BIRD: PTARMIGAN
STATE FLOWER: FORGETMENOT
STATE TREE: SPRUCE
TOWN: EEK NOME RUBY KENAI SITKA BARROW JUNEAU KODIAK NENANA SKAGWAY KOTZEBUE ANCHORAGE FAIRBANKS KETCHIKAN
VOLCANO: KUKAK SPURR GRIGGS KATMAI MAGEIK MARTIN PAVLOF DOUGLAS ILIAMNA REDOUBT TORBERT TRIDENT WRANGELL

ALASTRIM AMAAS
ALB ALBE AUBE CAMISIA CHRISOM VESTMENT
ALBACORE TUNA TUNNY GERMAN GERMON LONGFIN ALALONGA ALALUNGA MACKEREL SCOMBRID

ALBANIAN GEG GHEG GUEG ARNAUT SKIPETAR
ALBATROSS GONY GOON GONEY GOONY NELLY FABRIC GOONEY GOONIE QUAKER SEABIRD ALCATRAS BLUEBIRD STINKPOT
ALBEIT ALL ALBE ALBEE ALLBE THOUGH HOWBEIT
ALBERIC (WIFE OF —) MAROZIA
ALBERTA (CAPITAL OF —) EDMONTON
(LAKE OF —) BANFF JASPER WATERTON
(RIVER OF —) BOW OLDMAN WAPITI ATHABASCA

(TOWN OF —) CALGARY REDDEER LETHBRIDGE MEDICINEHAT
ALBIGENSIANS CATHARI
ALBINISM ALPHOSIS
ALBINO LEUCAETHIOP
ALBITE PERICLINE
ALBIZZIA SIRIS
ALBOIN (FATHER OF —) ALDUIN
(SLAYER OF —) HELMICHIS
(WIFE OF —) ROSAMUNDA
ALBUM ALBE BOOK RECORD VOLUME REGISTER
ALBUMEN WHITE
ALBUMIN ALBUMEN PHASELIN SYNTONIN
ALBUMINOID ELASTIN FIBROIN KERATIN PROTEIN SERICIN COLLAGEN GORGONIN
ALBURNUM SAP BLEA SPLINT SAPWOOD
ALBUS BLANCO
ALCAEUS (DAUGHTER OF —) ANAXO
(FATHER OF —) PERSEUS ANDROGEUS
(MOTHER OF —) ANDROMEDA
(SON OF —) AMPHITRYON
ALCAIDE CADE CAID QAID JUDGE ALCADE
ALCATHOUS (FATHER OF —) PELOPS
(MOTHER OF —) HIPPODAMIA
(SLAYER OF —) OENOMAUS IDOMENEUS
(WIFE OF —) EUACHME
ALCESTIS (AUTHOR OF —) EURIPIDES
(CHARACTER IN —) APOLLO ADMETUS ALCESTIS HERCULES THANATOS
(FATHER OF —) PELIAS
(HUSBAND OF —) ADMETUS
ALCHEMIST ADEPT ARTIST CHEMIC CHEMICK CHEMIST HERMETIC
(AUTHOR OF —) JONSON
(CHARACTER IN —) DOL ABEL FACE SURLY COMMON DAPPER MAMMON PLIANT SUBTLE ANANIAS DRUGGER EPICURE KASTRIL LOVEWIT WHOLESOME TRIBULATION
ALCHEMY ART MAGIC ALCUMY CHYMIA SPAGYRIC
(GOD OF —) HERMES
ALCHFRITH (FATHER OF —) OSWIU
(MOTHER OF —) EANFLAED
(WIFE OF —) CYNEBURH
ALCHORNEA DOVEWOOD
ALCIBIADES (FATHER OF —) CLINIAS
(MOTHER OF —) DINOMACHE
ALCIMEDE (FATHER OF —) PHYLACUS
(HUSBAND OF —) AESON
(MOTHER OF —) CLYMENE
(SON OF —) JASON
ALCIMEDES (BROTHER OF —) ARGUS MEDEUS PHERES MERMERUS TISANDER THESSALUS
(FATHER OF —) JASON
(MOTHER OF —) MEDEA

ALCINA (SISTER OF —) MORGANA LOGISTILLA
(VICTIM OF —) RUGGIERO
ALCINOUS (DAUGHTER OF —) NAUSICAA
(FATHER OF —) NAUSITHOUS
(MOTHER OF —) PERIBOEA
(WIFE OF —) ARETE
ALCIPPE (DAUGHTER OF —) MARPESSA
(HUSBAND OF —) EVENUS METION
(SON OF —) DAEDALUS
ALCIS (FATHER OF —) ANTIPOENUS
(SISTER OF —) ANDROCLEA
ALCITHOE (FATHER OF —) MINYAS
(SISTER OF —) ARSIPPE LEUCIPPE
ALCMAEON (FATHER OF —) AMPHIARAUS
(MOTHER OF —) ERIPHYLE
(WIFE OF —) CALLIRRHOE ALPHESIBOEA
ALCMENE (FATHER OF —) ELECTRYON
(HUSBAND OF —) AMPHITRYON
(SON OF —) HERCULES IPHICLES
ALCOHOL ALKY ETHAL ETHYL IDITE LEDOL NEROL VINYL AMYROL ANDROL CEDROL ELEMOL GLYCOL GUAIOL HYDROL IDITOL LUPEOL LUTEIN METHYL PHYTOL SPIRIT STERIN STERNO STEROL TALITE ACRITOL ADONITE ALDITOL ALKANOL ANISOIN BORNEOL BUTANOL CAROTOL DECANOL ETHANOL FENCHOL HEPTITE HEXITOL INOSITE MANNITE MENTHOL PULEGOL QUINITE SCOPINE SORBITE STETHAL STYRONE TAGETOL TALITOL TROPINE XYLITOL CATECHOL LINALOOL MANNITOL METHANOL GLYCERINE PYRIDOXINE
(ETHYL —) METHS
ALCOHOLATE SPIRIT ESSENCE
ALCOHOLIC ALKY
(NOT —) SOFT
ALCOHOLOMETER GENOMETER VINOMETER
ALCOVE BAY NOOK BOWER NICHE ORIEL STALL CARREL RECESS CARRELL CUBICLE DINETTE RETREAT SERVERY ALHACENA SNUGGERY TABLINUM
ALCYONE (BROTHER OF —) EURYSTHEUS
(FATHER OF —) ATLAS AEOLUS
(HUSBAND OF —) CEYX
(MOTHER OF —) ENARETE PLEIONE
(SON OF —) ANTHAS HYRIEUS
ALDABELLA (BROTHER OF —) OLIVIERO BRANDIMARTE
(FATHER OF —) MONODANTES
(HUSBAND OF —) ORLANDO
ALDEHYDE ALDOL CITRAL ALKANAL CHLORAL COGENER DECANAL GLYOXAL HEXANAL RETINAL ACROLEIN CONGENER FURFURAL PIPERONAL PYRIDOXINE
ALDER ARN OLER ALNUS ELDER OWLER SAGEROSE

(PREF.) ALNI
ALDERMAN BAILIE SENIOR HEADMAN
ALDFRITH (BROTHER OF —) ECGFRITH
(FATHER OF —) OSWIU
ALE MUM NOG BASS BEER BOCK BREW FLIP MILD NOGG PURL SCUD YELL AUDIT CLINK DARBY JOUGH LAGER NAPPY STOUT ALEGAR PORTER STINGO SWANKY BITTERS MOROCCO OCTOBER PHARAOH HUGMATEE
(— BREWED WITH BRACKISH WATER) TIPPER
(— MIXED WITH SWEETENER) BRAGGET
(INFERIOR —) SWANKY SWANKEY
(NEW —) SWATS
(SOUR —) ALEGAR
(SPICED —) SWIG
(STRONG —) MUM HUFF BURTON STINGO HUFFCAP
(WEAK —) TWOPENNY
ALEATORY HAZARDOUS
ALEBION (BROTHER OF —) BERGION DERCYNUS
(FATHER OF —) NEPTUNE POSEIDON
(SLAYER OF —) HERCULES
ALECOST COSTMARY
ALECTRYON TITOKI
ALEE AHEAD LEEWARD
ALEHOUSE PUB TAVERN BARROOM MUGHOUSE POTHOUSE
ALEKO (CHARACTER IN —) ALEKO ARENSKY ZEMFIRA
(COMPOSER OF —) RACHMANINOFF
ALEMBIC LIMBEC LIMBECK CUCURBIT
(PART OF —) HEAD LAMP CUCURBIT RECEIVER
ALERT APT GAY HEP HIP YAL YEP FOXY GLEG KEEN LIVE PERT SNAP TRIG WAKE WARN WARY YALD YEPE ACUTE AGILE ALARM ALIVE AWAKE AWARE BREME BRISK EAGER ERECT LEERY MERRY NIPPY PEART PEERT QUICK READY SHACK SHARP SIREN SLICK SWIFT TIGHT WAKER YAULD ACTIVE ALARUM ARRECT BRIGHT DAPPER LIVELY NIMBLE PROMPT SLIPPY SPRACK SUDDEN TIPTOE TOCSIN WACKER CAREFUL KNOWING WAKEFUL WORKING PREPARED THOUGHTY VIGILANT WAKERIFE WATCHFUL
ALERTNESS NOUS SNAP APTNESS APTITUDE
(MENTAL —) WIT
ALETES (FATHER OF —) HIPPOTES AEGISTHUS
(MOTHER OF —) CLYTEMNESTRA
(SLAYER OF —) ORESTES
ALETTE WING ABUTMENT
ALEUT ATKA ORARIAN UNALASKA
ALEUTIANS (ISLANDS AND ISLAND GROUPS OF —) FOX RAT ADAK ATKA ATTU NEAR KISKA UMNAK KODIAK
(TOWN OF —) UNALASKA

(VOLCANO ON —) SHISHALDIN
ALEWIFE BANG ALLICE ALOOFE BUCKIE ALEWHAP HERRING OLDWIFE POMPANO WALLEYE GRAYBACK GREYBACK SAWBELLY SKIPJACK
ALEXANDER ALEX PARIS SAWNY ELLICK SAWNEY SAWNIE ISKANDER
(BIRTHPLACE OF —) PELLA
(FATHER OF —) SIMON
(HORSE OF —) BUCEPHALUS
ALEXIARES (FATHER OF —) HERCULES
(MOTHER OF —) HEBE
ALFA HALFA ESPARTO
ALFALFA HAY MEDIC FODDER LEGUME LUCERN LUCERNE
ALFILARIA ERODIUM FILAREE FILARIA PINWEED PINGRASS
ALFORJA BAG POUCH WALLET ALFARGA ALFORGE
ALGA NORI ALGAL BROWN FUCUS JELLY SLAKE SLOAK SLOKE DESMID DIATOM FUNORI NOSTOC AMANORI GULAMAN HAITSAI OARWEED SEAWEED ANABAENA FERNLEAF GELIDIUM HAIRWEED ROCKWEED SEABEARD SILKWEED SPOROGEN WHIPCORD ZOOGLOEA
ALGAE
(PREF.) PHYC(O)
(SUFF.) PHYCEAE
ALGARROBA CAROB CALDEN
ALGEBRA LOGISTIC
ALGEBRAIC COSSIC
ALGENIB MIRFAK

ALGERIA

BERBER: KABYLE SHAWIA TUAREG
BERBER DIALECT: ZENATA SENHAJA
CAPITAL: ALGIERS
CAVALRYMAN: SPAHI SPAHEE
DEPARTMENT: ORAN ALGER ALGIERS CONSTANTINE
GRASS: ESPARTO
HILL: TELL
HOLY MAN: MARABOUT
MEASURE: PIK REBIS TARRI TERMIN
MONASTERY: RIBAT
MOUNTAIN: AISSA ATLAS AURES DAHRA TAHAT CHELIA AHAGGAR MOUYDIR DJURJURA
NAME: ALGERIE NUMIDIA
NATIVE: BERBER KABYLE
PIRATE: CORSAIR
RIVER: SHELIF CHELIFF MEDJERDA
RULER: BEY DEY BEVLERBEY
SECT: SUNNITE
SETTLER: COLON PIEDNOIR
SHIP: XEBEC
TERRITORY: AINSEFRA GHARDAIA TOUGGOURT
TOWN: BONE ORAN AFLOU ARZEW BATNA BLIDA MEDEA SAIDA SETIF TENES ABADLA ANNABA AUMALE BARIKA BECHAR BEJAIA BENOUD BISKRA BOUGIE DELLYS DJANET

DJELFA DZIOUA FRENDA GUELMA SKIKDA BOGHARI MASCARA MILIANA NEGRINE NEMOURS OUARGLA TEBESSA TLEMCEN
WEIGHT: ROTL

ALGERINE COOLOOLY KOOLOOLY
ALGID COLD COOL CHILLY CLAMMY
ALGOLOGY VERATRIN PHYCOLOGY
ALGONKIAN CREE EOZOIC
 (— ROCKS) UNKAR
ALIAS ELSE OTHER AYLESS
 ASSUMED EPITHET
ALIBI PLEA EXCUSE APOLOGY
 PRETEXT
ALIDADE INDEX DIOPTER
ALIEN GER DEED FREMD METIC
 ALAUNT ALLTUD AUBAIN CONVEY
 EXOTIC INMATE REMOTE
 ADVERSE DENIZEN FOREIGN
 FRAMMIT INVADER OUTLAND
 STRANGE DETAINEE STRANGER
 TRANSFER
ALIENATE PART WEAN ALIEN
 AVERT ANNALY CONVEY DEMISE
 DEVEST FREEZE FORFEIT
 SUBVERT AMORTIZE DISUNITE
 ESTRANGE MORTMAIN SEPARATE
 STRANGER TRANSFER WITHDRAW
ALIENATION GIFT DISTASTE
 DISUNION DISUNITY DIVISION
 DONATION INSANITY
ALIENIST PSYCHOPATH
 PSYCHIATRIST
ALIGHT DROP LAND LEND REST
 STOP AVALE LATCH LIGHT LODGE
 PERCH ROOST STOOP SWOOP
 ARRIVE SETTLE BURNING
 DESCEND
ALIGN LINE TRAM TRUE ALINE
 ARRAY DRESS RANGE ADJUST
 ARRANGE MARSHAL
 (— PAPER) JOG
ALIGNED FAIR COLORED
 COLLINEAR
ALIGNMENT KELTER KILTER
 GROUPING ORIENTATION
ALII ARIKI
ALIKE AKIN BOTH LIKE SAME
 EQUAL INLIKE SQUARE YLICHE
 EQUALLY SIMILAR UNIFORM
 (PREF.) HOM(O) ISO
ALIMENT PAP FOOD FUEL BROMA
 MANNA VIANDS ALIMONY
 PABULUM RATIONS
ALIMONY ALIMENT
ALINDA (FATHER OF —) ALPHONSO
ALIPHATIC FATTY ACYCLIC
ALIVE VIF BUSY KEEN SPRY VIVE
 AGILE ALERT ALIFE ASTIR AWARE
 BEING BRISK FRESH GREEN QUICK
 VITAL AROUND EXTANT LIVING
 SLIPPY ANIMATE VIBRANT
 ANIMATED EXISTENT SENSIBLE
 SWARMING
 (PREF.) VIVI
ALKALI LYE REH BASE BRAK KALI
 SALT SODA USAR BRACK CAUSTIC
 (PREF.) KALI
ALKALOID BASE ERGOT ESERE
 ARICIN BRUCIN CEVINE CODEIN
 CONINE CURINE ESERIN QUINIA

QUININ ACONINE ARABINE
ARICINE ATROPIA BOGAINE
BOLDINE BRUCINE CAFFEIN
COCAINE CODEINE CONIINE
EMETINE HARMINE HYGRINE
JERVINE KAIRINE NARCEIN
NEOPINE OUABAIN PTOMAIN
QUININE SCOPINE SINAPIN
SOLANIN SOPHORA VIOLINE
CURARINE CYTISINE PIPERINE
MESCALINE QUINIDINE
YOHIMBINE PAPAVERINE
PILOCARPINE
ALKANE PARAFFIN
ALKANET BUGLOSS PUCCOON
 REDROOT
ALKANNIN ORCANET ANCHUSIN
 ORCHANET
ALKENE OLEFIN
ALKYD GLYPTAL
ALL A AL ANY SUM EACH FULL
 TOTE AUGHT EVERY GROSS
 OMNES OUGHT QUITE TOTAL
 TOTUM TUTTA TUTTO WHOLE
 ENTIRE SOLELY WHOLLY PLENARY
 ENTIRELY EVERYONE TOTALITY
 (— BUT ABSOLUTELY) ALMOST
 (— IN) ALTOGETHER
 (— TOGETHER) COLLECTEDLY
 (AND —) ANA
 (AT —) AVA ANYWISE ANYTHING
 ANYWHERE
 (OF —) AVA
 (PREF.) CUNCTI OMN(I) PAM PAN
 PANT(A)(O) PASI
ALLANITE CERINE CERITE ORTHITE
ALLAY AID LAY CALM CITE COOL
 EASE HELP HUSH STAY ABATE
 AGATE ALLY CHARM CHECK
 DELAY QUELL QUIET SALVE SLAKE
 STILL ADDUCE LESSEN PACIFY
 QUENCH REDUCE SOFTEN
 SOLACE SOOTHE STANCH
 SUBDUE TEMPER APPEASE
 ASSUAGE COMFORT COMPOSE
 LIGHTEN MOLLIFY RELIEVE
 REPRESS STAUNCH MITIGATE
 PALLIATE
ALLAYED DEFERRED
ALLEGATION PLEA COUNT VOUCH
 CHARGE ESSOIN AVERRAL
 FICTION PROFERT SCANDAL
 SURMISE AVERMENT SCIENTER
 PRETENSION
ALLEGE LAY SAY AVER AVOW CITE
 SHOW URGE ALLAY CLAIM FEIGN
 INFER LEDGE OFFER PLEAD
 QUOTE STATE SWEAR TRUMP
 VOUCH ADDUCE AFFIRM ASSERT
 ASSIGN CHARGE DEPOSE ESSOIN
 OBTEND RECITE ADVANCE
 ASCRIBE DECLARE LIGHTEN
 PRESENT PROFESS PROPOSE
 MAINTAIN
ALLEGED SUPPOSED SURMISED
ALLEGIANCE FOY TIE DUTY FAITH
 HONOR FEALTY HOMAGE LYANCE
 LOYALTY SERVAGE SERVICE
 TRIBUTE CIVILITY DEVOTION
 FIDELITY LIGEANCE
ALLEGORICAL PARABOLIC
 SYMBOLICAL
ALLEGORICALLY SECRETLY

ALLEGORIZE TALMUDIZE
ALLEGORY MYTH TALE FABLE
 STORY EMBLEM PARABLE
 APOLOGUE METAPHOR
ALLELUIA AEVIA LAUDS
ALL-EMBRACING INFINITE
 SWEEPING
ALLERGEN INHALANT
ALLERGY ATOPY IDIOBLAPSIS
ALLEVIATE AID BALM CALM CURE
 EASE HELP ABATE ALLAY QUIET
 ALIGHT ALLEGE LENIFY LESSEN
 PACIFY SOFTEN SOLACE SOOTHE
 SUCCOR SUPPLE TEMPER
 ASSUAGE COMPOSE CONSOLE
 CORRECT LENIATE LIGHTEN
 MOLLIFY RELEASE RELIEVE
 DIMINISH MITIGATE MODERATE
 PALLIATE
ALLEVIATION ALAY SOLACE
ALLEY MIG ROW WAY CHAR LANE
 LEAD MALL MEWS PASS PATH
 VENT WALK WENT WIND WYND
 AISLE ALLEE BLIND BYWAY
 CHARE ENTRY TEWER WEENT
 ALLEGE PEEWEE SMOOTH
 TRANCE VENNEL PASSAGE
 (BLIND —) LOKE STOP CLOSE
 POCKET IMPASSE
ALL FOR LOVE (AUTHOR OF —)
 DRYDEN
 (CHARACTER IN —) ANTONY
 OCTAVIA OCTAVIUS CLEOPATRA
 DOLABELLA VENTIDIUS
ALLHALLOWTIDE HOLLANTIDE
ALLHEAL PANACEA VALERIAN
 WOUNDWORT
ALLIANCE AXIS PACT UNION
 ACCORD FUSION LEAGUE LYANCE
 TREATY COMPACT ENTENTE
 SOCIETY AFFINITY AGNATION
 CACTALES COVENANT DREIBUND
 FEDERACY FUNGALES LILIALES
 TRIPLICE CONSOCIATION
 (— IN WAR) SYMMACHY
ALLICE SHAD ALEWIFE POMPANO
ALLIED SIB AKIN AGNATE COUSIN
 JOINED LINKED UNITED COGNATE
 CONNATE FEDERAL GERMANE
 KINDRED RELATED SIMILAR
 RELATIVE
ALLIGATOR GATOR NIGER CAIMAN
 CAYMAN CROTCH JACARE LIZARD
 TRAVOY YACARE CRAWLER
 CREEPER LAGARTO TRAVOIS
 ALAGARTO LORICATE
 (— PEAR) ZABOCA AVOCADO
 AGUACATE
 (— TURTLE) LOGGERHEAD
 (MALE —) BULL
ALLIGATORING WEBBING
ALL-INCLUSIVE GLOBAL
ALLITERATION RHYME LETTER
ALLITERATIVE LITERAL
ALLIUM LILY ONION GARLIC
ALLNESS OMNEITY OMNITUDE
ALLOCATE DEAL DOLE METE RATE
 ALLOT AWARD SHARE AFFECT
 ASSIGN OUTPLACE
ALLOCATION DRAW DESIGNATION
ALLODIAL UDAL
ALLOT FIX SET ARET BILL CAST
 DEAL DOLE GIVE MARK METE

PART RATE SORT ALLOW ARETT
AWARD CAVEL GRANT SHARE
ACCORD AFFECT ASSIGN BESTOW
DEPUTE DESIGN DIRECT INTEND
ORDAIN RATION ACCOUNT
APPOINT DESTINE PRORATE
QUARTER SPECIFY TRIBUTE
ALLOCATE PROPORTION
(— QUARTERS) CANTON
ALLOTMENT CUT LOT DOLE CAVEL
 SHARE RATION SIZING LOTMENT
 LOTTERY PORTION DIVISION
 PITTANCE
ALLOW LET LOW BEAR GIVE HAVE
 LEND LOAN ADMIT DEFER GRANT
 LEAVE STAND THOLE YIELD
 ACCEPT ACCORD ASSIGN BESTOW
 BETEEM ENABLE ENDURE PERMIT
 SUFFER APPROVE CONCEDE
 CONFESS LICENCE LICENSE
 SUFFICE SUPPOSE SUSTAIN
 CONSIDER DISPENSE SANCTION
 TOLERATE
ALLOWABLE FREE LICIT LAWFUL
 PERMISSIBLE
ALLOWANCE BOT FEE ICE AGIO
 BOTE DOLE EASE EDGE GIFT HIRE
 ODDS RATE SALT SIZE ARRAS
 BATTA CLOFF GRANT LEAVE
 RATIO SHARE STENT STINT
 BOUCHE BOUNTY CORODY
 FODDER MARGIN RATING REGAIN
 SALARY SEQUEL TANTUM
 ALIMENT ALIMONY CORRODY
 DIETARY DIOBELY LEAKAGE
 LOWANCE PENSION PORTION
 PREBEND SCALAGE STIPEND
 TEARAGE APPENAGE APPROVAL
 BREAKAGE DISCOUNT DRAFTAGE
 ORDINARY QUANTITY SANCTION
 SOLATIUM VIATICUM
 (— FOR EXPENSES) DIET
 (— FOR MAINTENANCE) ALIMENT
 (— FOR THICKNESS) BOXING
 (— FOR WASTE) TRET
 (— FOR WEIGHT) BUG TARE DRAFT
 DRAUGHT
 (— OF ARROWS) SHEAF
 (— OF FOOD) DIET BOUCHE
 DIETARY
 (— OF TIME OR DISTANCE) LAW

 (CLOTHING —) INLAY
 (CORRECTIVE —) SALT
 (EXTRA —) BUCKSHEE
 (NEGATIVE —) INTERFERENCE
ALLOWED VENIAL LICENTIATE
 (NOT —) ILLICIT FORBIDDEN
ALLOWING THOUGH
ALLOY LAY LOY MIX AICH ASEM
 ALPAX BIDRI BIDRY BRASS CALIN
 DURAL FLINT INVAR MOKUM
 MONEL TERNE ALBATA ALNICO
 ALUMEL BIDREE BILLON BRONZE
 CERMET GARBLE ILLIUM LATTEN
 LEAVEN NEOGEN NIELLO OCCAMY
 OREIDE OROIDE PEWTER SOLDER
 TAMBAC TOMBAC TOMBAK
 ACIERAL ALCHEMY AMALGAM
 BABBITT BIDDERY ELINVAR
 INCONEL MIXTURE PAKTONG
 PERLITE RHEOTAN RHODITE

SEMILOR SIMILOR TAENITE TUTANIA TUTENAG ALFENIDE ARGENTON ARSEDINE AWARUITE CALAMINE CARACOLI CARACOLY DORALIUM ELECTRUM EUTECTIC GUNMETAL HARDENER KAMACITE METALINE NICHROME ORICHALC ROMANIUM STELLITE PINCHBECK PORPORINO

ALL-PERVADING UNIVERSAL

ALL QUIET ON WESTERN FRONT
(AUTHOR OF —) REMARQUE
(CHARACTER IN —) PAUL KROPP ALBERT BAUMER MULLER TJADENS KEMMERICH STANILAUS KATCYINSKY

ALL RIGHT OK YES OKAY AGREED OKEYDOKE

ALLSEED FLAXSEED BURSTWORT

ALL SOULS' DAY SOULMASS

ALLSPICE BUBBY PIMENTO

ALL'S WELL THAT ENDS WELL
(AUTHOR OF —) SHAKESPEARE
(CHARACTER IN —) DIANA LAFEU HELENA BERTRAM LAVACHE MARIANA PAROLLES VIOLENTA

ALLTHORN JUNCO

ALLUDE HINT IMPLY POINT REFER ADVERT GLANCE RELATE CONNOTE MENTION SUGGEST INDICATE INTIMATE

ALLURE IT AIR COY WIN WOO BAIT DRAW LEAD LURE MOVE SWAY WILE ANGLE BRIBE CHARM COURT DECOY SNARE TEMPT ALLECT ENTICE ENTRAP ILLURE INDUCE INVITE SEDUCE ATTRACT BEGUILE ENSNARE BLANDISH INESCATE INVEIGLE PERSUADE SIRENING

ALLUREMENT BAIT CORD LURE ALLURE GLAMOR GUDGEON AGACERIE SOLICITATION

ALLURING GREEN TAKING AGACANT SIRENIC SUGARED TAKEFUL CATCHING CHARMING ENTICING FETCHING TEMPTING

ALLUSION HINT TWIT TOUCH GLANCE REFLEX INKLING MENTION INNUENDO INSTANCE REFERENCE

ALLUSIVE CANTING

ALLUVIUM WASH

ALLY PAL AIDE JOIN RANGE UNION UNITE BACKER COXCOX FRIEND HELPER LEAGUE ALLIANT CONNECT PARTNER ADHERENT CONFEDER FEDERATE
(PL.) FOEDERATI

ALMANAC ORDO PADDY CALENDAR

ALMEMAR BEMA BIMA BIMAH

ALMIGHTY GOD GREAT CREATOR EXTREME JEHOVAH INFINITE POWERFUL PUISSANT OMNIPOTENT

ALMOND DOE PILI BADAM CHUFA JORDAN KAMANI KANARI AMYGDAL BISCUIT TALISAY ALMANDER ALMENDRO AMYGDALA ROSACEAN VALENCIA
(— BROWN) WOOD

(— SHAPED OBJECT) MANDORLA
(PREF.) AMYGDAL(O) MANDEL(O)

ALMONRY AMBRY

ALMOST JUST LIKE MOST MUCH NEAR NIGH ABOUT ANEAR CLOSE AMAIST FECKLY MOSTLY NEARLY NIGHLY MUCHWHAT WELLMOST WELLNEAR PRACTICALLY
(PREF.) PARA PEN(E)

ALMS DOLE GIFT ALMOIN AUMOUS AWMOUS BOUNTY CORBAN MAUNDY RELIEF ALMOIGN CHARITY HANDOUT PASSADE DEVOTION DONATION GRATUITY OFFERING PITTANCE BENEFACTION

ALMSHOUSE POORHOUSE WORKHOUSE

ALMSMAN BLUECOAT

ALMUCE HOOD AMICE VAGAS TIPPET VAKASS VARKAS

ALODIUM ODAL ODEL ODHAL ESTATE PROPERTY

ALOE PITA AGAVE

ALOEUS (FATHER OF —) NEPTUNE POSEIDON
(MOTHER OF —) CANACE
(SON OF —) OTUS EPHIALTES
(WIFE OF —) IPHIMEDIA

ALOFT UP HIGH ABOVE AHIGH UPWARD AHEIGHT SKYWARD OVERHEAD
(PREF.) HYPS(I)(O)

ALONE ALL ONE BARE LANE LORN ONLY SOLE SOLO ALOOF APART SOLUS SIMPLY SINGLE SOLEIN SOLELY SULLEN UNIQUE ALONELY FORLORN UNAIDED DESOLATE DETACHED ISOLATED SEPARATE SOLITARY
(ALL —) LEELANE LEELONE
(PREF.) MANI MON(O) SOLI
(SUFF.) MONAS

ALONG ON UP VIA AWAY LANG WITH YOND AHEAD LONGS BESIDE FORBYE FOREBY ONWARD ALONGST ENDLONG FORWARD PARALLEL TOGETHER
(— THE MARGIN) DOWN
(— WITH) AND
(WELL —) ENDWAYS ENDWISE
(PREF.) (— WITH) SYM

ALONGSIDE AT BY ASIDE CLOSE ABOARD BESIDE ABREAST FORNENT SIDLINS FORNENST PARALLEL
(PREF.) PAR(A)

ALONSOA MASKFLOWER

ALOOF DRY ICY SHY COLD COOL ABACK ALONE APART PROUD ABEIGH FROSTY OTIOSE REMOTE SILENT SKEIGH DISTANT REMOVED RESERVED

ALOPECIA PELADE ATRICHIA BALDNESS

ALOPECURUS FOXTAIL

ALOUD OUT

ALPACA PACO

ALPENGLOW AFTERGLOW

ALPENSTOCK STOCK BERGSTOCK

ALPHABET ABC ABCEE ABSEY CUFIC KUFIC LATIN ONMUN ORDER BISAYA BRAHMI CIPHER

GLAGOL HANGUL HANKUL KAITHI NAGARI PRIMER ROMAJI SARADA SCRIPT TAGALA VISAYA ALJAMIA FUTHARK KALEKAH LETTERS PESHITO ALJAMIAH CROSSROW GUJARATI GURMUKHI
(— SQUARE) TABLEAU
(ARABIC —) BA FA HA RA TA YA ZA AYN DAD DAL JIM KAF KHA LAM MIM NUN QAF SAD SIN SHIN WAW ZAY ALIF DHAL SHIN GHAYN
(GREEK —) MU NU PI XI CHI ETA PHI PSI RHO TAU BETA IOTA ZETA ALPHA DELTA GAMMA KAPPA OMEGA SIGMA THETA LAMBDA EPSILON OMICRON UPSILON
(HEBREW —) HE PE MEM NUN SIN TAW WAW AYIN BETH HETH KAPH QOPH RESH SHIN TETH YODH ALEPH GIMEL SADHE ZAYIN DALETH LAMEDH SAMEKH

ALPHAEUS (SON OF —) JAMES MATTHEW

ALPHESIBOEA (FATHER OF —) BIAS PHEGEUS
(HUSBAND OF —) ALCMAEON
(SON OF —) ADONIS

ALPS (LAKE IN —) ZUG COMO ISEO THUN GARDA BRIENZ GENEVA ZURICH LUCERNE MAGGIORE CONSTANCE
(PASS IN —) SPLUGA ARLBERG BRENNER SIMPLON SPLUGEN SEMPIONE
(PEAK IN —) ROSA VISO BLANC LEONE TRIGLAV VOLJNAC EISENHUT PARADISO HOCHSTUHL MARMOLADA MONTBLANC KELLERWAND SACCARELLO
(VALLEY IN —) ZERMATT CHAMONIX ENGADINE INTERLAKEN GRINDELWALD LAUTERBRUNNEN

ALREADY EEN NOW DONE EVEN SINCE BEFORE

ALSACE-LORRAINE REICHSLAND

ALSINE ALLBONE

ALSO SO ALS AND EKE TOO YET ERST ITEM MORE PLUS ALONG DITTO BESIDES FURTHER THERETO LIKEWISE MOREOVER
(— KNOWN AS) AKA

ALTAMONT (WIFE OF —) CALISTA

ALTAR ARA BEMA BOMOS TABLE WEVED ACERRA AUTERE HAIKAL SHRINE TRIPOD VEDIKA CHANCEL CHANTRY ESCHARA SCROBIS THYMELE OMPHALOS REPOSOIR REPOSITORY
(— BACK) TABLE
(— TOP) MENSA

ALTARPIECE ANCONA DIPTYCH TRIPTYCH

ALTAZIMUTH ABA

ALTER COOK DRAW EDIT GELD MOVE RASE TURN VARY VEER WEND ADAPT AMEND BREAK ELIDE EMEND FORGE RESET SHAPE SHIFT ADJUST BUSHEL CENSOR CHANGE DEFORM IMMUTE JIGGER MODIFY MUTATE NEUTER REVISE TEMPER UNSAME

CHAFFER COMMUTE CONVERT CORRECT CORRUPT DISTORT FASHION QUALIFY STRANGE ACTIVATE EXCHANGE
(— APPEARANCE) WRY
(— BOUNDARIES) DEACON
(— BRANDS) DUFF
(— DIRECTION) BREAK
(— STANCE) CLOSE

ALTERATION DOWN CROSS ACTION CHANGE JANGLE DISEASE HEMIOLA MUTATION UPHEAVAL
(— OF BOUNDARY) ERUB ERUV

ALTERATIVE LAPPA FUMARIA

ALTERCATE JANGLE STICKLE WRANGLE

ALTERCATION SPAT TIFF TILT BRAWL BROIL CROSS FIGHT BARNEY BICKER FRACAS JANGLE STRIFE BRABBLE CONTEST DISPUTE PASSAGE QUARREL WRANGLE SQUABBLE

ALTERED BURNT BROKEN VARIED ANOTHER FEIGNED ADJUSTED
(PREF.) EPH EPI

ALTERNATE ELSE SWAY VARY OTHER RECUR SHIFT ALTERN CHANGE RINGER ROTATE SECOND SEESAW SPIRAL EXCHANGE INTERMIT TRAVERSE
(— LEAPS AND DIVES) GREYHOUND
(PREF.) CO COUNTER

ALTERNATELY ABOUT RECIPROCALLY

ALTERNATION ADDITION
(— OF GENERATIONS) METAGENESIS

ALTERNATIVE OR FORK HORN BACKUP CHOICE EITHER OPTION DISJUNCT ELECTION
(PREF.) ALLELO

ALTERNATOR MAGNETO

ALTHAEA MALLOW
(FATHER OF —) THESTIUS
(HUSBAND OF —) OENEUS
(SON OF —) MELEAGER

ALTHAEMENES (FATHER OF —) CATREUS
(SISTER OF —) AEROPE CLYMENE APEMOSYNE

ALTHORN SAX ALTO ALTUS SAXHORN

ALTHOUGH ALL EEN SET ALBE ALIF EVEN THAT WHEN WHILE ALBEIT THOUGH WHENAS DESPITE HOWBEIT WHEREAS

ALTITUDE APEX PEAK HIGHT LEVEL PITCH HEIGHT STATURE

ALTO MEAN ALTUS ALTHORN SAXHORN

ALTOGETHER ALL NUDE QUITE SHEER STICK AGREAT ALGATE BODILY FREELY WHOLLY EXACTLY TOTALLY UTTERLY ALLTHING ENTIRELY

ALTRUISM OTHERISM

ALTRUISTIC HEROIC HEROICAL

ALUDEL POT LUDEL UDELL

ALULA LOBE WING ALULET SQUAMA TEGULA LOBULUS WINGLET CALYPTER

ALULIM ALOROS

ALUM AUM ALME ALUMEN MIGITE

TSCHER STYPTIC HARDENER KALINITE

(FEATHER —) ALUNOGEN

ALUMINA ARGIL ALOXITE

ALUMNUS GRAD PUPIL GRADUATE

ALUMROOT HEUCHERA

ALUR LUR LURI

ALVAN (FATHER OF —) SHOBAL

ALVEARY HIVE BEEHIVE

ALVEOLA FAVEOLUS

ALVEOLAR SPUMOID GINGIVAL

ALVEOLATE FAVOSE FAVOUS PITTED

ALWAYS O AY AYE EEN EER EVER SIMLE STILL ALWISE SEMPRE ALGATES FOREVER EVERMORE

ALYSSUM ALISON MADWORT

ALZIRA (CHARACTER IN —) ALZIRA GUSMAN ZAMORO

(COMPOSER OF —) VERDI

AM M AME HAM

(— NOT) NAM AINT AMNT

(I —) CHAM CHYM

AMA CUP AMULA CRUET DIVER VESSEL CHALICE

AMABILE GENTLE TENDER

AMACRATIC AMASTHENIC

AMADAVAT WAXBILL TIGERBIRD

AMADIS (COMPOSER OF —) LULLY

AMADOU PUNK TINDER

AMAH NURSE SERVANT

AMAHL AND THE NIGHT VISITORS (COMPOSER OF —) MENOTTI

AMAIN GREATLY FORCIBLY

AMAL (FATHER OF —) HELEM

AMALA AMLAH

AMALASONTHA (FATHER OF —) THEODORIC

AMALEK (FATHER OF —) ELIPHAZ

(MOTHER OF —) TIMNAH

AMALGAM ALLOY MAGNESIA ARQUERITE

AMALGAMATE MIX FUSE JOIN ALLOY BLEND MARRY MERGE UNITE BLUNGE MINGLE COMBINE COALESCE COMPOUND

AMALGAMATION MERGER ADDITION

AMALGAMATOR PLATEMAN

AMANORI NORI LAVER

AMANUENSIS PENMAN SCRIBE TYPIST RECORDER

AMARANTA (HUSBAND OF —) BARTOLUS

AMARANTH JATACO PIGWEED FLORAMOR

(PL.) LIGHTHOUSES

AMARIAH (FATHER OF —) BANI MERAIOTH

(SON OF —) AHITUB

AMARILLO FUSTIC

AMARYLLIS LILY AGAVE CRINUM SNOWFLAKE

AMASA (FATHER OF —) ITHRA HADLAI JETHER

(MOTHER OF —) ABIGAIL

AMASAI (SON OF —) MAHATH

AMASHAI (FATHER OF —) AZAREEL

AMASIAH (FATHER OF —) ZICHRI

AMASS HEAP HILL MASS PILE SAVE GROSS HOARD STACK STORE GATHER COLLECT

COMPILE CONGEST ENGROSS ASSEMBLE OVERHEAP ACCUMULATE

AMATA (DAUGHTER OF —) LAVINIA

(HUSBAND OF —) LATINUS

AMATEUR HAM TIRO TYRO NOVICE SUNDAY VOTARY ADMIRER DABBLER DEVOTEE FANCIER JACKLEG PATRIOT VARMENT VARMINT BEGINNER

AMATEURISH BUSH TYRONIC

AMATORY EROTIC LOVING TENDER AMOROUS GALLANT ANACREONTIC

AMAZE AWE MAZE STAM STUN ALARM FERLY ASTONY AWHAPE WONDER ASTOUND CONFUSE IMPRESS PERPLEX STAGGER STUPEFY ASTONISH BEWILDER CONFOUND DUMFOUND FRIGHTEN SURPRISE

AMAZED AGAZED BUSHED ASTONIED

AMAZEMENT STAM AMAZE FERLY GHAST FERLIE FRENZY WONDER MADNESS SURPRISE CONSTERNATION

AMAZIAH (FATHER OF —) JOASH

AMAZON VIRAGO

AMBARI KANAF KENAF KANAFF

AMBASSADOR AGENT ELCHI ENVOY VAKIL DEPUTY ELCHEE LEDGER LEGATE NUNCIO VAKEEL EMBASSY LEAGUER CAPUCIUS DIPLOMAT MINISTER

AMBASSADORIAL FETIAL

AMBASSADORS (AUTHOR OF —) JAMES

(CHARACTER IN —) JIM MAMIE MARIA SARAH JEANNE POCOCK GOSTREY LAMBERT NEWSOME CHADWICK STRETHER WAYMARSH

AMBER GRIS LIME AWMER RESIN FUSTIC LAMMER SUCCIN YELLOW BURMITE AMBEROID ELECTRUM SUNSTONE

(PREF.) ELECTRO SUCCIN(I)(O)

AMBERFISH JUREL CARANX KAHALA RUNNER CARANGID CARANGIN KINGFISH MACKEREL MEDREGAL

AMBERGRIS AMBER AMBRACAN

AMBERJACK ALMICORE CORONADO

AMBIENCE MILIEU AMBIANCE

AMBIGUITY AMBAGE PARADOX

AMBIGUOUS DARK VAGUE DOUBLE FORKED LOUCHE CRYPTIC DUBIOUS DOUBTFUL SLIPPERY SPURIOUS

(NOT —) EXPRESS

AMBIT LIMIT SCOPE SPACE BOUNDS EXTENT SPHERE CIRCUIT COMPASS BOUNDARY PRECINCT

AMBITION ATE GOAL HOPE WISH GLORY DESIRE PURPOSE PRETENSION

AMBITIONLESS DRIFTING

AMBITIOUS AVID BOLD HIGH KEEN EAGER ETTLE SHOWY EMULOUS ASPIRANT ASPIRING

AMBITUS TENOR

AMBIVALENCE BIPOLARITY

AMBIVALENT EQUIVOCAL

AMBLE FOOL GAIT MOOCH PADNAG MEANDER SAUNTER TRIPPLE

AMBLING TOLUTATION

AMBO DESK PULPIT

AMBOCEPTOR COPULA MEDIATOR

AMBOYNA LINGOA KIABOOCA

AMBROSIA AMRITA AMBROSE KINGWEED

AMBROSIAL DIVINE FRAGRANT

AMBRY SAFE CHEST NICHE AUMRIE CLOSET PANTRY RECESS ALMONRY ARMOIRE ARMARIUM CUPBOARD

AMBULANCE PANNIER AUXILIUM BRANCARD

AMBULATE GAD HIKE MOVE WALK

AMBULATORY ALURE GALLERY PORTICO CLOISTER PERAMBLE

AMBUSCADE WATCH WAYLAY BUSHMENT

AMBUSH NAB LURE LURK TRAP WAIT AWAIT BLIND BUSSE CATCH COVER LURCH SHOMA SNARE STALE TRAIN WATCH INBUSH THREAT WAYLAY FORELAY SCUPPER DISGUISE ENBUSSHE

(SUFF.) (ONE IN —) DOLOPS

AMCHOOR AMHAR

AMELIA (AUTHOR OF —) FIELDING

(CHARACTER IN —) BOOTH JAMES TRENT AMELIA HARRIS ATKINSON HARRISON MATTHEWS ELIZABETH

AMELIORATE EASE HELP MEND AMEND EMEND BETTER REFORM IMPROVE PROMOTE

AMEN YEA TRULY ASSENT SOBEIT VERILY APPROVAL SANCTION

AMENABLE OPEN LIABLE PLIANT SUBJECT OBEDIENT MALLEABLE

AMEND END BEET HEAL MEND ALTER ATONE BEETE EMEND REDUB BETTER CHANGE DOCTOR REFORM REMEDY REPAIR REPEAL REVISE CONVERT CORRECT ENLARGE IMPROVE RECOVER RECTIFY REDRESS RESTORE CHASTISE

AMENDING COMPENSATION

AMENDMENT RIDER AMENDS REFORM SLEEPER

AMENDS BOOT MEND ASSETH ASSYTH REWARD APOLOGY REDRESS

AMENITY JOY COMITY FEATURE SUAVITY CIVILITY COURTESY MILDNESS

(PL.) AGREMENS FROUFROU NICETIES

AMENT JUL CHAT IDIOT IULUS MORON CATKIN CACHRYS CATTAIL GOSLING IMBECILE NUCAMENT

AMERCE FINE MERCE MULCT TREAT AFFEER PUNISH SCONCE CONDEMN FORFEIT

AMERCEMENT MULCT UNLAW BLOODWIT

AMERICA INDIA

AMERICAN YANK GRINGO YANKEE YANQUI AMERICA WESTERN

JONATHAN COLUMBIAN

(— OF EUROPEAN STOCK) WASP

(AUTHOR OF —) JAMES

(CHARACTER IN —) BREAD CINTRE CLAIRE NEWMAN NIOCHE TRISTRAM VALENTIN BELLEGARDE CHRISTOPHER

AMERICAN GRAY JAKO

AMERICANISM HECKERISM

AMERICAN TRAGEDY (AUTHOR OF —) DREISER

(CHARACTER IN —) ALDEN CLYDE SAMUEL SONDRA ROBERTA FINCHLEY GRIFFITHS

AMESTRIS (FATHER OF —) OTANES ONOPHAS

(WIFE OF —) XERXES

AMETHYST ONEGITE CORUNDUM

AMIABILITY DOUCEUR

AMIABLE GOOD KIND WARM SWEET CLEVER GENIAL GENTLE LOVING MELLOW SMOOTH TENDER AFFABLE LOVABLE WINSOME CHARMING ENGAGING FRIENDLY OBLIGING PLEASING

AMICABLE KIND FRIENDLY NEIGHBORLY

AMICE AMIT AMYS CAPE COWL HOOD EPHOD ALMUCE DOMINO TIPPET VAKASS AMICTUS VESTMENT

AMID IN OMEL AMELL AMONG AMIDST DURING IMELLE AMONGST BETWEEN

AMIDAS (BROTHER OF —) BRACIDAS

AMIDE LACTAM SULTAM ANILIDE ARYLIDE PEPTIDE

AMILDAR AUMIL

AMINE ANILIN ANILINE

AMISS ILL MIS AWRY BIAS AGATE AGLEY ASKEW WONKY WRONG ACROSS AGRIEF ASTRAY FAULTY MISTAKE IMPROPER

(PREF.) MIS PAR(A)

AMITTAI (SON OF —) JONAH

AMITY PEACE ACCORD CONCORD HARMONY

AMMA ABBESS MOTHER

AMMIEL (DAUGHTER OF —) BATHSHEBA

(FATHER OF —) OBEDEDOM

(SON OF —) MACHIR

AMMIHUD (SON OF —) TALMAI PEDAHEL SHEMUEL ELISHAMA

AMMINADAB (FATHER OF —) RAM ARAM KOHATH UZZIEL

(SON OF —) NAASSON

AMMISHADDAI (SON OF —) AHIEZER

AMMIZABAD (FATHER OF —) BENAIAH

AMMONIA HARTSHORN

AMMONIUM CARBONATE HARTSHORN

AMMONITE POLYPOD AMMONOID BACULITE CACULOID CERATITE SALIGRAM

AMMUNITION AMMO AMMU ARMS SHOT BOMBS FODDER POWDER SHELLS BULLETS GRENADES MATERIAL MATERIEL ORDNANCE SHRAPNEL

AMNESIA LAPSE FORGETFULNESS

AMNESTY COWLE PARDON OBLIVION

AMNION SAC CAUL SEROSA INDUSIUM MEMBRANE

AMNON (FATHER OF —) DAVID
(HALF-SISTER OF —) TAMAR

AMOBARBITAL AMYTAL

AMOEBA AMEBA AMEBULA PROTEUS AMOEBULA RHIZOPOD

AMOK MAD AMUCK CRAZY CRAZED VIOLENT FRENZIED

AMOLE EMOL AMOULI AMOLILLA MANFREDA

AMON (FATHER OF —) MANASSEH
(SON OF —) JOSIAH

AMONG IN MID AMID INTO MANG MONG OMEL WITH AMANG AMELL MIDST AMIDST BIMONG IMELLE WITHIN BETWEEN
(— OTHER THINGS) IA
(PREF.) EPH EPI INTER

AMOR EROS LOVE CUPID AMOROSO

AMORAL NEUTRAL NONMORAL

AMORET (HUSBAND OF —) SCUDAMORE
(SISTER OF —) BELPHOEBE

AMORITE CANAANITE

AMOROUS FOND GAMY SOFT WARM CADGY JOLLY MUSHY NUTTY ARDENT COQUET EROTIC LOVELY LOVING SPOONY TENDER WANTON AMATIVE AMATORY AMIABLE FERVENT GALLANT JEALOUS SMICKER LOVESOME VENEREAN

AMORPHOUS VAGUE ATELENE HYALINE DEFORMED FORMLESS RESINOUS

AMORT ALAMORT DEJECTED LIFELESS

AMORTIZE DESTROY MORTISE ALIENATE

AMOUNT GO GOB LOT SUM SUP TOT ANTE BODY COME DOSE DRAW FECK KIND LEVY MESS REAM RISE SOUD SOWD TALE UNIT WARE CHUNK COUNT GROSS MOUNT PRICE REACH STACK STORE STUFF TOTAL WHOLE BUDGET DEGREE DOSAGE EFFECT EXTENT FIGURE MATTER NUMBER SUPPLY ADVANCE FOOTING QUANTUM SCRUPLE SIGNIFY SLATHER TODDICK INCREASE QUANTITY SPOONFUL SURMOUNT VALLIDOM
(— BORNE BY BEAST) SEAM
(— CARRIED AT ONE TIME) GANG
(— DUE) BILL SCORE
(— HELD) CAPACITY
(— OF BASS) BOOMINESS
(— OF CONCRETE) LIFT
(— OF DYE) STRIKE
(— OF FLOW) STRENGTH
(— OF FREIGHT) CARLOAD
(— OF GAS) BREATH
(— OF HERRINGS) CRANNAGE
(— OF LEAKAGE) SLIP
(— OF LIQUOR) SLUG
(— OF MEDICINE) DOSAGE
(— OF MONEY) BEAN BOND CASH SCOT

(— OF OIL) ALLOWABLE
(— OF PAYMENT) FOOTAGE
(— OF POWDER) INCREMENT
(— OF SOIL) INTHROW
(— OF WATER) CATCHMENT
(— OF WORK) ASSIGNMENT
(— OWED) LIABILITY OBLIGATION
(— PAID) COST
(— TURNED BY SPADE) GRAFT
(APPRECIABLE —) BEANS
(COMPLETE —) FULL
(CONSIDERABLE —) MIGHT HANTLE HATFUL
(EXACT —) NICK
(EXTRA —) BONUS
(GREAT —) MICKLE INFINITY MOUNTAIN
(GROSS —) SLUMP
(INADEQUATE —) DEFICIENCY
(INDEFINITE —) BAIT SNAG SOME
(INFINITESIMAL —) IOTA
(INSIGNIFICANT —) SCRAT PEANUTS
(LARGE —) GOB LOB JUNT LUMP MINT RAFT SNAG SWAG SIEGE SLASH SPATE BOODLE SOMDEL BONANZA SOMDIEL CARTLOAD MUCHNESS SOMDEAL
(LAVISH —) SLATHER
(LEAST POSSIBLE —) GRAIN AMBSACE
(LIMITED —) SPRINKLING
(MINUTE —) HAIR FLEABITE
(RENT —) GALE
(SIZABLE —) CHUNK SMART
(SLIGHT —) ADDED SNACK TILLY TINGE
(SMALL —) ACE BIT DAB TAD DITE DOIT DRAM DRIB FLOW HINT HOOT INCH LICK MITE SNAP SONG SPOT SPECK SPURT TRACE DRAPPY PICKLE SMIDGE TICKET CAPSULE DRAPPIE GLIMMER KENNING SMIDGEN SMIDGIN THOUGHT
(SMALLEST —) JOT STIVER STEEVER STUIVER
(TENFOLD —) DECUPLE
(USUAL —) GRIST
(WHOLE —) ALL SUBSTANCE
(YEARLY —) ANNUITY
(SUFF.) ANCE ANT ENCE

AMOUR DRURY DRUERY AMOURET INTRIGUE PARAMOUR

AMOZ (SON OF —) ISAIAH

AMPERSAND AND ALSO PLUS AMPASSY IPSEAND

AMPHETAMINE UPPER BENZEDRINE

AMPHIALUS (MOTHER OF —) CECROPIA

AMPHIARAUS (DAUGHTER OF —) EURYDICE DEMONASSA
(FATHER OF —) OICLES
(MOTHER OF —) HYPERMNESTRA
(SON OF —) ALCMAEON AMPHILOCHUS
(WIFE OF —) ERIPHYLE

AMPHIBIA BATRACHIA

AMPHIBIAN EFT OLM FROG HYLA NEWT RANA TOAD ANURA SIREN SNAKE AMPHIB AXOLOTL CAUDATE ERYOPID PROTEUS

TADPOLE AISTOPOD SALAMANDER

AMPHIBOLE EDENITE ORALITE URALITE ASBESTOS CROSSITE TREMOLITE SMARAGDITE

AMPHICARPA FALCATA

AMPHICTYON (FATHER OF —) DEUCALION
(MOTHER OF —) PYRRHA

AMPHIGASTRIUM UNDERLEAF

AMPHILOCHUS (FATHER OF —) AMPHIARAUS
(MOTHER OF —) ERIPHYLE

AMPHION (BROTHER OF —) ZETHUS
(FATHER OF —) ZEUS IASUS JUPITER
(MOTHER OF —) ANTIOPE
(WIFE OF —) NIOBE

AMPHIOXUS LANCELET

AMPHIPOD SHRIMP

AMPHISSA (FATHER OF —) ECHETUS MACAREUS
(MOTHER OF —) CANACHE

AMPHISSUS (FATHER OF —) APOLLO
(MOTHER OF —) DRYOPE

AMPHITHEA (DAUGHTER OF —) ANTICLEA
(HUSBAND OF —) AUTOLYCUS

AMPHITHEATER BOWL OVAL ARENA CAVEA CIRCUS CIRQUE STADIUM THEATER

AMPHITRITE (FATHER OF —) NEREUS OCEANUS
(HUSBAND OF —) NEPTUNE POSEIDON
(MOTHER OF —) TETHYS
(SON OF —) TRITON

AMPHITRYON (AUTHOR OF —) PLAUTUS
(CHARACTER IN —) SOSIA ALCMENA JUPITER MERCURY AMPHITRYON
(DOG OF —) LAELAPS
(FATHER OF —) ALCAEUS
(MOTHER OF —) HIPPONOME
(WIFE OF —) ALCMENE

AMPHORA JUG URN VASE CADUS DIOTA PELIKE

AMPHOTERUS (BROTHER OF —) ACARNAN
(FATHER OF —) ALCMAEON
(MOTHER OF —) CALLIRRHOE

AMPLE BIG FAIR FULL GOOD MUCH RICH SIDE WIDE BROAD GREAT LARGE LUCKY PLUMP ROOMY ROUND SONSY WALLY ENOUGH HEARTY PLENTY PROLIX COPIOUS LIBERAL OPULENT WEALTHY ABUNDANT ADEQUATE BARONIAL GENEROUS HANDSOME SPACIOUS PLENTIFUL

AMPLIFICATION GAIN

AMPLIFIED EXTENDED

AMPLIFIER BOOSTER REPEATER

AMPLIFY PAD FARCE FARSE SWELL WIDEN DILATE EXPAND EXTEND STRESS AUGMENT ENLARGE STRETCH AMPLIATE HEIGHTEN INCREASE LENGTHEN MULTIPLY

AMPLITUDE BULK

LATITUDE OPULENCE

AMPLY LARGE

AMPUTATE CUT LOP PRUNE SEVER CURTAIL

AMPUTATION APOCOPE ABLATION

AMPYCUS (FATHER OF —) PELIAS
(MOTHER OF —) CHLORIS
(SON OF —) MOPSUS

AMRAM (FATHER OF —) BANI DISHON
(SON OF —) MOSES

AMRITA RASA

AMULA AMA VESSEL

AMULET GEM MET HAND JUJU MOJO PLUM CHARM IMAGE MENAT SAFFI SAFIE TOKEN FETISH GRIGRI MASCOT SAPHIE SCROLL TABLET ABRAXAS AMALETT ICHTHUS ICHTHYS PERIAPT CHURINGA GREEGREE HAGSTONE LIGATURE ORNAMENT TALISMAN PHYLACTERY

AMULIUS (BROTHER OF —) NUMITOR
(FATHER OF —) PROCAS
(NEPHEW OF —) LAUSUS

AMURRU MARTU

AMUSE GAME LAKE ENJOY MIRTH SHORT SPORT ABSORB DELUDE DIVERT ENGAGE FROLIC PLEASE POPJOY SOLACE TICKLE BEGUILE DISPORT GRATIFY PASTIME BEWILDER DISTRACT RECREATE

AMUSEMENT FAD FUN JEU GAME JEST LAKE PLAY MIRTH SPORT LAKING MUSERY PASTIME COTTABUS LAUGHTER PLEASURE (PL.) MIDWAY

AMUSING RICH COMIC DROLL FUNNY MERRY WITTY COMICAL FOOLISH KILLING RISIBLE FARCICAL HUMOROUS PLEASANT SPORTFUL

AMYCLAS (FATHER OF —) LACEDAEMON
(MOTHER OF —) SPARTE
(SON OF —) HYACINTHUS

AMYCUS (FATHER OF —) NEPTUNE POSEIDON
(MOTHER OF —) MELIA
(SLAYER OF —) POLLUX

AMYGDALA TONSIL

AMYL AMYDON PENTYL ISOAMYL

AMYLASE PTYALIN DIASTASE

AMYMONE (FATHER OF —) DANAUS
(HUSBAND OF —) ENCELADUS
(SON OF —) NAUPLIUS

AMYNTOR (FATHER OF —) ORMENUS
(SON OF —) PHOENIX
(WIFE OF —) CLEOBULE

AMYTHAON (BROTHER OF —) AESON PHERES
(FATHER OF —) CRETHEUS
(MOTHER OF —) TYRO
(SON OF —) BIAS MELAMPUS
(WIFE OF —) IDOMENE

AN ONE ARTICLE

ANA EVENTS OMNIANA SAYINGS

ANABAPTIST DIPPER ABECEDARIAN

ANABAS MARTINICO

ANABATIC DESCENDING

ANABO NABO ANABONG
ANABRANCH BRANCH
TALLYWALKA
ANACAONA (BROTHER OF —)
BEHECHIO
(HUSBAND OF —) CAONABO
ANACHARSIS (BROTHER OF —)
SAULIUS
ANACHRONISM SOLECISM
ANACONDA BOA ABOLLA SUCURI
SUCURY CAMOUDIE SUCURUJU
ANACREONTIC TEIAN
ANACRUSIS UPBEAT
ANADEM CROWN DIADEM FILLET
WREATH CHAPLET CORONET
GARLAND
ANAGNOST LECTOR READER
ANAGOGICAL MYSTICAL
ANAGRAM REBUS PUZZLE
METAGRAM LOGOGRIPH
(PL.) VERBARIUM
ANAGUA KNACKAWAY
KNOCKAWAY
ANAH (DAUGHTER OF —)
AHOLIBAMAH
(FATHER OF —) ZIBEON
ANAL PODICAL
ANALABOS CLOAK
ANALGESIC ANODYNE CODEINE
ANTIPYRIN PHENALGIN
ANALOGICAL NORMAL
ANALOGOUS LIKE SIMILAR
ANALOGUE DFDT ANALOG
ANALOGY QIYAS PARALLEL
PREDISONE
(CLOSE —) PARITY
ANALYSIS TEST INDEX STUDY
ANATOMY AUTOPSY SCANSION
SOLUTION
(BLOWPIPE —) PYROLOGY
(CHARACTER —) PSYCHOGRAPH
(ECONOMIC —) DYNAMICS
(LOGICAL —) SYLLOGISM
ANALYTIC SUBTLE REGULAR
(NOT —) SYNTHETIC SYNTHETICAL
ANALYTICAL CLINICAL DIVISIVE
ANALYZE RUN PART SIFT ASSAY
BREAK PARSE SENSE STUDY
WEIGH ASSESS DIVIDE REDUCE
DISSECT EXAMINE ITEMIZE
RESOLVE TITRATE UNPIECE
APPRAISE CONSTRUE DIAGNOSE
SEPARATE
(— ACCOUNT) AGE
(— VERSE) SCAN
ANAMITE TWINE
ANANAS ANANA PINGUIN
ANANI (FATHER OF —) ELIOENAI
ANANIAS LIAR SIDRACH
(FATHER OF —) NEDEBAEUS
(WIFE OF —) SAPPHIRA
ANANSI NANCY
ANAPEST ANTIDACTYL
ANARCHIST RED PROVO REBEL
ANARCH NIHILIST REDSHIRT
ANARCHY RIOT CHAOS REVOLT
LICENSE MISRULE
DISORDER
ANASARCA DROPSY
ANASAZI PUEBLO PLATEAU
ANASCHISTIC EUMITOTIC
ANASTOMOSIS GLOMUS
ANASTROPHE INVERSION

ANATASE OCTAHEDRITE
ANATH (SON OF —) SHAMGAR
ANATHEMA WO BAN MUD WOE
OATH CURSE CENSURE
ANATHEMATIZE BAN CURSE
ACCURSE EXECRATE
ANATHOTH (FATHER OF —) BECHER
ANATOMIST AMERICAN TODD
ALLEN EVANS SABIN WYMAN
DWIGHT KNOWER
COGHILL HERRICK
STOCKARD
AUSTRIAN HYRTL
BELGIAN VESALIUS
DANISH STENO
DUTCH TULP GRAAF CAMPER
COITER DUBOIS
ENGLISH GRAY OWEN JONES
QUAIN COWPER HARVEY HAVERS
HILTON HUNTER WILLIS
FRENCH ROBIN DUVERNEY
DUPUYTREN POISEUILLE
CRUVEILHIER
GERMAN HIS FICK ROUX HENLE
MEYER BRAUNE EBERTH KRAUSE
MECKEL MULLER RATHKE
WAGNER FRORIEP SIEBOLD
ANDERSCH BISCHOFF HARTMANN
MEISSNER SCHULTZE SCHWALBE
WRISBERG GEGENBAUR
HELMHOLTZ LIEBERKUHN
SOEMMERRING WEIDENREICH
GREEK RUFUS HEROPHILUS
ERASISTRATUS
ITALIAN CORTI ASELLI PACINI
SCARPA VAROLI CALDANI
COLOMBO COTUGNO ROLANDO
MALPIGHI EUSTACHIO FALLOPIUS
PACCHIONI
SCOTTISH BELL MONRO FERRIER
GOODSIR PETTIGREW
MACALISTER
SWEDISH KEY
SWISS BAUHIN HALLER HARDER
BRUNNER
ANATOMIZE ANALYZE DISSECT
ANATOMY TOPOLOGY
(— OF HORSE) HIPPOTOMY
(MICROSCOPIC —) HISTOLOGY
(VEGETABLE —) PHYTOTOMY
ANAX (FATHER OF —) URANUS
(MOTHER OF —) GE GAEA
(SON OF —) ASTERIUS
ANAXARETE (LOVER OF —) IPHIS
ANAXIBIA (DAUGHTER OF —)
PELOPEA ALCESTIS PISIDICE
(FATHER OF —) BIAS
(HUSBAND OF —) PELIAS
(SON OF —) ACASTUS
ANAXO (BROTHER OF —)
AMPHITRYON
(DAUGHTER OF —) ALCMENE
(FATHER OF —) ALCAEUS
(HUSBAND OF —) ELECTRYON
ANCAEUS (FATHER OF —) ALEUS
NEPTUNE LYCURGUS POSEIDON
(MOTHER OF —) ASTYPALAEA
(SON OF —) AGAPENOR
ANCESTOR ION MIL ADAM EBER
HETH ROOT SIRE DORUS ELDER
STOCK APETUS ATAVUS AUTHOR
BELDAM EPONYM FATHER
MANNUS MILEDH PARENT STIPES

ANCIENT BELDAME BELSIRE
EPAPHUS FLEANCE FORBEAR
IAPETUS ISHMAEL KACHINA
SAKULYA DARDANUS FOREBEAR
FOREGOER MILESIUS MYRMIDON
RELATIVE PREDECESSOR
PRIMOGENITOR
(— CULT) MANISM
(—S OF GOTLANDERS) GEAT
(MAORI —) TIKI TUPUNA
(PL.) OLDERS ANCESTRY
ANCESTRAL AVAL AVITAL AVITIC
LINEAL FAMILIAL
ANCESTRY KIN RACE SEED ATHEL
FAMILY ORIGIN PEOPLE SOURCE
STRAIN DESCENT KINDRED
LINEAGE BREEDING PEDIGREE
ANCHINOE (FATHER OF —) NILUS
(HUSBAND OF —) BELUS
(SON OF —) DANAUS AEGYPTUS
ANCHISES (FATHER OF —) CAPYS
(MOTHER OF —) THEMIS
(SON OF —) AENEAS
ANCHOR FIX BIND DRAG DRUG
HOOK MOOR REST SLUG SPUD
STOP AFFIX BERTH BOWER
KEDGE RIVET SHEET STOCK
ATTACH DROGUE FASTEN HERMIT
KEDGER KELLEG SECURE STREAM
CHAPLET CONNECT DEADMAN
GRAPNEL GROUSER
KILLICK MUDHOOK
SUPPORT COCKBILL
(— IN PLACE) ACOCKBILL
(— RING) TORUS
(AT —) ASTAY
(BEAM —) WALL
(PART OF —) ARM EYE KEY PEE
PIN BALL BILL HEAD HOOP PALM
RING CROWN FLUKE STOCK
TREND THROAT
ANCHORAGE DOCK STAY HARBOR
REFUGE RIDING MOORAGE
ABUTMENT BERTHAGE
ROOTHOLD
ANCHORITE MONK HERMIT
ANCHORET ASCETIC EREMITE
RECLUSE STYLITE
ANCHOVY NEHU BOCON SPRAT
HERRING SARDINE
(PL.) ALICI
ANCHUSA OXTONGUE
ANCHUSIN ALKANET
ANCIENT ELD OLD AGED AULD
FERN HIGH HOAR IAGO YORE
EARLY ELDER HOARY OLDEN
BYGONE ENSIGN FORMER NOETIC
PISTOL PRIMAL VETUST ANTIENT
ANTIQUE ARCHAIC ARCHEAN
CLASSIC OGYGEAN OGYGIAN
HISTORIC NOACHIAN OBSOLETE
PRIMEVAL PRISTINE
(MOST —) ELDEST
(PREF.) ARCHAE PALAE(O)
PALE(O)
(— ORIGIN) PALE
ANCIENTLY OLD HIGH
ANCILLA HELPER ADJUNCT
SERVANT
ANCON ELBOW CORBEL CONSOLE
AND N U AN ET SO ANT TOO ALSO
PLUS BESIDES FURTHER
MOREOVER

(— SO FORTH) ETC USW
ANDAMAN MINCOPI MINKOPI
MINCOPIE
ANDESITE BONINITE TIMAZITE
PROPYLITE
ANDHAKA (FATHER OF —) KASYAPA
(MOTHER OF —) DITI
(SLAYER OF —) SHIVA
ANDIRON DOG CHENET COBIRON
FIREDOG HESSIAN HANDIRON
LANDIRON
ANDORRA (LANGUAGE OF —)
CATALAN
(NATIVE OF —) ANDOSIAN
(RIVER OF —) VALIRA
ANDRADITE APLOME GARNET
ANDRAEMON (FATHER OF —)
OXYLUS
(MOTHER OF —) GORGE DRYOPE
(SON OF —) THOAS
**ANDREA CHENIER (CHARACTER IN
—)** ANDREA COIGNY GERARD
CHENIER MADELEINE
(COMPOSER OF —) GIORDANO
**ANDROCLES AND THE LION
(AUTHOR OF —)** SHAW
(CHARACTER IN —) LAVINIA
MEGAERA ANDROCLES
FERROVIUS
ANDROCONIUM STIGMA PLUMULE
ANDROGEUS (FATHER OF —) MINOS
(MOTHER OF —) PASIPHAE
ANDROID ROBOT AUTOMATON
ANDROMACHE (AUTHOR OF —)
EURIPIDES
(CHARACTER IN —) PELEUS THETIS
ORESTES PYRRHUS HERMIONE
MENELAUS MOLOSSUS
ANDROMACHE NEOPTOLEMUS
(FATHER OF —) EETION
(HUSBAND OF —) HECTOR
HELENUS NEOPTOLEMUS
(SON OF —) PIELUS ASTYANAX
MOLOSSUS PERGAMUS
ANDROMEDA (FATHER OF —)
CEPHEUS
(MOTHER OF —) CASSIOPEA
(RESCUER OF —) PERSEUS
ANDROMEDE BIELID
ANDRON (FATHER OF —) ANIUS
(SISTER OF —) OENO ELAIS
SPERMO
ANECDOTAL LITERARY
ANECDOTE GAG TOY JOKE TALE
YARN EVENT STORY SKETCH
HAGGADA EXEMPLUM
HAGGADAH
ANECHOIC DEAD
ANEMIA SURRA SURRAH ANAEMIA
HYPAEMA HYPHEMA HYPHEMIA
ISCHEMIA SPANEMIA CHLOROSIS
ANEMIC LOW PALE WEAK MEALY
WATERY LIFELESS
(PREF.) CHLOR(O)
ANEMONE LILY CRASS EMONY
POLYP OPELET BOWBELLS
SNOWDROP
ANENT ON RE ABOUT ANENST
BESIDE TOWARD AGAINST
OPPOSITE
ANESTHESIA BLOCK CORYL
SPINAL

ANESTHETIC GAS ETHER ACOINE
EVIPAN OBTUSE OPIATE COCAINE
DULLING MENTHOL METOPRYL
PARAFORM PROCAINE SEDATIVE
PHENOCAIN METHOXYFLURANE
(SUFF.) CAINE
ANESTHETIZE FREEZE ETHERIZE
ANEW OVER AGAIN NEWLY
AFRESH ITERUM NEWLINS
NEWLINGS RECENTLY
(PREF.) RE
ANFRACTUOUS SPIRAL BENDING
SINUOUS WINDING TORTUOUS
ANGEL MAH DEVA EBUS ANGLE
ARDOR ARIEL DAEVA DULIA
NAKIR YAKSA ABDIEL ARIOCH
BACKER BELIAL CHERUB MONKIR
MUNKAR NEKKAR SERAPH SPIRIT
THRONE UZZIEL YAKSHA
ANGELET EGREGOR ISRAFEL
RAPHAEL SPONSOR WATCHER
ZADKIEL ZOPHIEL APOLLYON
GUARDIAN ITHURIEL SUPERNAL
(— OF DEATH) AZRAEL SAMMAEL
(DESTROYING —) ABADDON
(FALLEN —S) HELL
(GUARDIAN —) YAKSA YAKSHA
YAKSHI
(RECORDING —) SIJIL SIJILL
(PL.) HOST FRAVASHI SERAPHIM
ANGELFISH MONK MUNK ANGEL
QUOTT RHINA SQUAT MONACH
CICHLID FLATFISH KINGSTON
MONKFISH SQUATINA
ANGELIC SAINTLY BEATIFIC
CHERUBIC HEAVENLY SERAPHIC
ANGELICA JELLICA ARCHANGEL
(FATHER OF —) GALAPHRON
(LOVER OF —) ORLANDO
ANGELIN PACAY ANGELEEN
ANGELIQUE (CHARACTER IN —)
CHARLOT BONIFACE ANGELIQUE
(COMPOSER OF —) IBERT
ANGER ARR IRE IRK MAD VEX
BATE BILE BURN CRAB FELL
FUME FURY GALL GRIM HUFF
MOOD RAGE RILE ROIL RUFF
TEEN TIFF ANNOY BIRSE GRAME
GRIPE HATEL IRISH PIQUE SPONK
SPUNK STURT THRAW WRATH
BOTHER CHOLER DANDER
ENRAGE EXCITE GRIEVE MONKEY
NETTLE OFFEND RANCOR SPLEEN
TALENT TEMPER WARMTH
BURNING DESPITE DUDGEON
EMOTION INCENSE INFLAME
PASSION PROVOKE STOMACH
ACRIMONY DISTRESS EBENEZER
IRRITATE VEXATION
ANGERED SORE AGRAMED
PELTISH INCENSED
ANGICO CURUPAY
ANGINA PRUNELLA
ANGIOSPERM HARDWOOD
METASPERM
ANGLE IN BOB DIP ELL OUT TEE
WRO CANT COIN COOK DRAW
FISH FORK HADE KEEN KNEE
LEAD NOOK PEAK SITE WICK
ANCON ARRIS AXIAL BEVEL BIGHT
CHOIL COIGN DRAFT DRIFT
ELBOW FLEAM GROIN GUISE
INGLE PHASE POINT QUOIN

SLANT SLOPE ALLURE ANGULE
ASPECT CANTON CORNEL
CORNER DIRECT ENGHLE EPAULE
HADING LAGGEN LAGGIN OCTANT
SCHEME SQUARE TORNUS
ANGLIAN ANGULUS ANOMALY
AZIMUTH BASTION DRAUGHT
GIMMICK KNUCKLE PERIGON
RAVELIN SALIENT ARGUMENT
DECALAGE DIHEDRAL FISHHOOK
INTRIGUE SHOULDER OBLIQUITY
(— OF BEVEL) FLEAM FLEEM
(— OF BOWSPRIT) STEEVE
STEEVING
(— OF CLUB HEAD) LIE
(— OF EYELIDS) CANTHUS
(— OF HAT BRIM) BREAK
(— OF HIPBONE) HOOK
(— OF LEAF) AXIL
(— OF RAFTER) HEEL
(— OF TIMBER KNEE) BREECH
(DRIFT —) LEEWAY
(OBTUSE —) HEEL BULLNOSE
(ROCK —) DIEDRE
(ROOF —) HIP FASTIGIUM
(ROUND —) PERIGON
(SALIENT —) ARIS ARRIS PIEND
(PREF.) ANGULO GON(I)(IO)(Y)(YO)
(SUFF.) GON
ANGLED CANTED NOOKED
ANGULATE
(PREF.) ACUTI
ANGLER MONK FRIAR THIEF
SLIMER LOPHIID RODSTER
SPINNER WIDEGAB WIDEGAP
ALLMOUTH FROGFISH MONKFISH
PISCATOR TOADFISH WALTONIAN
ANGLESMITH SLABMAN
ANGLEWORM ESS WORM
FISHWORM
ANGLICAN EPISCOPAL
ANGLO CAUCASIAN

ANGOLA

CAPITAL: LUANDA
COIN: MACUTA MACUTE
DISTRICT: CABINDA
KINGDOM: BAKONGO
LANGUAGE: BANTU KIMBUNDU
MOUNTAIN: LOVITI
PLATEAU: PLANALTO
PORT: LOBITO LUANDA
RIVER: CONGO CUITO KASAI
CUANDO CUANZA CUNENE
KUNENE KWANDO KWANZA
CUBANGO
TOWN: LOBITO LUANDA LUBANGO
BENGUELA MOSSAMEDES
NOVALISBOA
TRIBE: BANTU KIKONGO
WATERFALL: RUACANA

ANGORA CAT GOAT ANGOLA
RABBIT
ANGRILY ANGERLY IRATELY
FUMINGLY
ANGRY MAD ASHY EVIL GRIM
GRUM HIGH RILY ROID ROSY
SORE WARM WAXY WILD WRAW
CROOK CROSS GRAME HUFFY
IRATE IROUS MOODY RATTY
RILEY SNAKY STUNT VEXED
WEMOD WROTH BIRSIT CHAFED

CROUSE FRENZY FUMING
FUMOUS HEATED IREFUL LOADED
SHIRTY SNAKEY STUFFY FRETFUL
FURIOUS HOPPING IRACUND
PAINFUL ROPABLE SNAKISH
SPLEENY UPTIGHT CHOLERIC
INFLAMED RIGOROUS SPITFIRE
TEMPERED VEHEMENT
WREAKFUL PASSIONATE
(BE —) STEAM
ANGRY-LOOKING THUNDERY
ANGUISH WOE ACHE HARM HURT
PAIN PANG RACK TRAY AGONY
ANGST ANGUS DOLOR GRIEF
THROE MISERY REGRET SORROW
ANGOISE ANGWICH REMORSE
TORMENT TORTURE TRAVAIL
DISTRESS
ANGUISHED GRIEFFUL
ANGULAR BONE BONY EDGY LEAN
SLIM THIN GAUNT SHARP
ABRUPT POINTED SCRAWNY
CORNERED
(NOT —) SOFT
(PREF.) ANG
ANGULARITY EDGINESS
ANGUS FORFAR FORFARSHIRE
ANHYDRIDE LACTAM SULTAM
FULGIDE LACTIDE SULTONE
GLUCOSAN MANNITAN SORBITAN
ANHYDRITE VULPINITE
ANHYDROUS DRY DESICCATED
ANI WITCH CUCKOO JEWBIRD
KEELBILL KEELBIRD TICKBIRD
ANIAM (FATHER OF —) SHEMIDAH
ANIARA (COMPOSER OF —)
BLOMDAHL
ANIMADVERSION BLAME REMARK
CENSURE COMMENT REPROOF
WARNING MONITION REPROACH
REFLECTION
ANIMAL (ALSO SEE UNDER
SPECIFIC HEADINGS) DEER BEAST
BIPED BLACK BRUTE GRADE
GROSS LUSTY STORE STRAY
BRUTAL CARNAL DAPPLE DESPOT
FLESHY KICKER MAMMAL RODENT
SILVAN SORREL SPONGE SYLVAN
BEASTIE BREEDER CARRION
CRITTER SENSUAL BURROWER
CREATURE EMIGRANT ORGANISM
PREDATOR
(— COLLECTION) LARDER
(— FOR MARKET) STOCKER
(— INHABITED BY SPIRIT) GUACA
HUACA
(— LIVING IN CAVES) TROGLOBITE
(— OF LITTLE VALUE) SCALAWAG
SKALAWAG
(— RESEMBLING MAN) HOMINOID
(— SHOT) KILL
(— WITH BLACK COAT AND
MARKINGS) PARSON
(— WITH DOCKED TAIL) CURTAL
(—S AS RENT) CAIN
(BEEF —) BONER GRASSER
(BOVINE —) BOSS BRUTE
(BROKEN-DOWN —) CROCK
(CARNIVOROUS —) SARCOPHILE
(CASTRATED —) SEG SEGG SPAY
SPADO GELDING
(COLD-BLOODED —) ECTOTHERM

(CREATED —) BARAMIN
(DECOY —) COACH
(DOMESTIC —) DOER SCRUB
BESTIAL FOLLOWER SCRUBBER
(DRAFT —) AVER AIVER
(EMACIATED —) FRAME SKELETON
(FABULOUS —) KYLIN BUNYIP
DRAGON ACEPHAL GRIFFIN
GRIFFON GRYPHON UNICORN
SEMITAUR TRAGELAPH
(FEMALE —) HEN SHE LADY JENNY
SHEDER
(FERAL —) CIMAROON CIMARRON
CIMMARON
(FLEA-RIDDEN —) FLEABAG
(FOOTLESS —) APOD APODE
(FOSSIL —) ZOOLITE
(FREAKISH —) FERLY FERLIE
(GRASSHOPPER-EATING —)
WHANGAM
(GRAY —) GRIZZLE
(GRAZING —) HERBAGER
(GREEDY —) GORB
(HORNED —) HORN REEM
(HYPOTHETICAL —) PROAVIS
(IMAGINARY —) WHANGAM
CATAWAMPUS
(LOWER —) BEAST CREATURE
(LUSTY OR PLUMP —) BILCH BILSH
(MALE —) HE TOM BUCK BULL
JACK STAG JOHNNY BACHELOR
(MARINE —) LANCELET
(MATURE —) SENIOR
(MEAT —) CHOPPER
(MISCHIEVOUS —) ELF
(MYTHICAL —) HODAG KYLIN
MOONACK
(ODD —) SPLACKNUCK
(PACK —) HUNIA SUMPTER
(PET —) CADE
(PURSUED —S) GAME
(ROASTED —) BARBECUE
BARBEQUE
(SADDLE —) LOPER
(SCRAWNY —) SCRAG
(SHORN —) SHEAR
(SKINNY —) SCRAE
(SLUGGISH —) DRUMBLE
(SOLID-HOOFED —) SOLIPED
(SPOTTED —) CALICO
(STOCKY —) BLOCK
(STUNTED —) SHARGAR SHARGER
(THICKSET —) NUGGET
(TOTEM —) EPONYM
(UNBRANDED —) SLICK
(UNCASTRATED —) ENTIRE
(UNDERSIZED —) DURGAN DURGEN
(UNHOUSED —) OUTLER OUTLIER
(UNWEANED —) SUCKER
(WANDERING —) STRAY ESTRAY
(WARM-BLOODED —) ENDOTHERM
HAEMATHERM
(WATER —) AQUATIC AQUATILE
(WEAK —) DRAG DOWNER
(WILD —) SAVAGE WILDLING
(WING-FOOTED —) ALIPED
(WORNOUT —) KANCKER
(WORTHLESS —) CARRION
(YOUNG —) HOG BIRD HOGG JOEY
SHOT TOTO STORE JUNIOR
PULLUS FATLING LITTLIN
KINDLING LITTLING SUCKLING
YOUNGLET

(2-HORNED —) BICORN BICORNE
(PL.) ZOA FAUNA NECTON
NEKTON
(PREF.) ZO(E)(IDIO)(IDO)(O)
ZOOLOGICO
(RUMINATING —) MERYC(O)
(SUFF.) ACEA AD THERE THERIA
THERIUM ZOA ZOIC ZOON
ANIMALCULISM SPERMISM
ANIMALITY HOGGERY
ANIMALS
(SUFF.) ATA IDA IDEA INI
ANIMA MUNDI WELTGEIST
ANIMATE ACT PEP FIRE MOVE
PERK STIR URGE ALIVE BRISK
CHEER DRIVE FLUSH IMBUE
IMPEL LIGHT LIVEN QUICK ROUSE
VITAL AROUSE BRIGHT ENSOUL
EXCITE INCITE INDUCE INFORM
KINDLE LIVING PROMPT SPIRIT
VIVIFY ACTUATE COMFORT
ENLIVEN INSPIRE QUICKEN
ACTIVATE ENERGIZE INSPIRIT
VITALIZE
(NOT —) BRUTE
ANIMATED UP GAY VIF GLAD VIVE
ALIVE ANIME BRISK QUICK VITAL
VIVID ACTIVE ARDENT BLITHE
BOUNCY BRISKY LIVELY LIVING
SPARKY SPUNKY BUOYANT
JOCULAR STHENIC BOUNCING
INSTINCT LIFESOME SPIRITED
VIGOROUS
ANIMATION BRIO VERVE
ANIME COPAL ELEMI RESIN ROSIN
ANIMATO
ANIMIKEAN LAWSON
ANIMISM NATURISM
ANIMOSITY HATE PIQUE SPITE
ANIMUS ENMITY HATRED MALICE
RANCOR DISLIKE ACRIMONY
ANIMUS MIND ONDE WILL EFFORT
ENMITY SPIRIT TEMPER ATTITUDE
ANIRUDDHA (FATHER OF —)
PRADYUMNA
ANISE ANET DILL CUMEN UMBEL
FENNEL SIKIMI SHIKIMI
ANIUS (DAUGHTER OF —) OENO
ELAIS SPERMO
(FATHER OF —) APOLLO
(MOTHER OF —) RHOEO CREUSA
(SON OF —) ANDRON
(WIFE OF —) DORIPPE
ANKH TAU
ANKLE COOT CUIT HOCK QUIT
ANCLE QUEET TALUS WRIST
TARSUS SHACKLE
(COCKED —S) KNUCKLING
(PREF.) TAL(I)(O) TARS(I)(O)
ANKLEBONE TALUS ASTRAGAL
ANKLET SHOE SOCK BANGLE
FETTER SHACKLE
ANLAGE INCEPT PROTON INITIAL
BLASTEMA
ANNA (FATHER OF —) BELUS
(SISTER OF —) DIDO
ANNA BOLENA (CHARACTER IN —)
ANNE JANE HENRY PERCY
BOLEYN SEYMOUR
(COMPOSER OF —) DONIZETTI
ANNA KARENINA (AUTHOR OF —)
TOLSTOY

(CHARACTER IN —) ANNA KITTY
LEVIN ALEXEI STEPAN KARENIN
VRONSKY OBLONSKY
KONSTANTINE SHTCHERBATSKY
ANNALIST WRITER RECORDER
ANNALS FASTI NIHONGI REGISTER
ANNAM (ALSO SEE VIETNAM)
VIETNAM
(BOAT OF —) GAYYOU GAYDIANG
(MEASURE OF —) LY GON NGU
QUO SAO TAT PHAN THAT SHITA
THUOC TRUONG
(TOWN OF —) HUE VINH TOURANE
QUANGTRI
(WEIGHT OF —) CAN BINH DONG
ANNAS (FATHER OF —) SETHI
ANNATTO OTTER URUCU ORLEAN
ROUCOU SALMON ACHIOTE
ACHUETE ANNOTTO ARNATTO
ORLEANS
ANNEAL BAKE FUSE HEAT SMELT
TEMPER INFLAME TOUGHEN
GRAPHITE
ANNEALER TUBER HEATER
ANNEALING LIGHTING
ANNELID NAID WORM LUGWORM
SERPULA ANNULATE SANDWORM
SERPULAN OLIGOCHAETE
ANNEX ADD ELL LAY JOIN AFFIX
SEIZE UNITE ADJECT ANNECT
APPEND ATTACH FASTEN
ACQUIRE CONNECT FIXTURE
POSTFIX SUBJOIN ADDITION
ANNEXURE DOCUMENT
PENTHOUSE
ANNIHILATE END OUT KILL RAZE
RUIN SLAY ABATE ANNUL ERASE
WRECK DELETE DEVOUR NOUGHT
QUENCH REDUCE ABOLISH
DESTROY EXPUNGE DECIMATE
UNCREATE DISCREATE PULVERIZE
ANNIHILATION FANA NEGATION
ANNIVERSARY FETE MASS EMBER
FEAST ANNUAL JUBILEE YEARDAY
BIRTHDAY FESTIVAL YAHRZEIT
(100TH —) CENTENNIAL
(1000TH —) MILLENIUM
(150TH —) SESQUICENTENNIAL
(200TH —) BIMILLENARY
BIMILLENIUM
(25TH —) SEMIJUBILEE
(50TH —) SEMICENTENNIAL
ANNONA ATIS ATTA ATEES
ANNOTATE EDIT NOTE STET
GLOSS BENOTE NOTIFY POSTIL
REMARK APOSTIL COMMENT
EXPLAIN FOOTNOTE
ANNOTATION APOSTIL COMMENT
SCHOLION SCHOLIUM
ANNOTATOR NOTIST SCHOLIAST
ANNOUNCE BID CRY BODE CALL
DEEM MAKE SCRY SHOW SING
TELL BRUIT CLAIM KNELL STATE
VOICE ASSERT BLAZON BROACH
DENOTE HERALD INFORM
PREACH REPORT REVEAL SIGNAL
SPRING STEVEN DECLARE
DIVULGE FORERUN GAZETTE
PUBLISH SIGNIFY DENOUNCE
FORETELL INTIMATE PROCLAIM
RENOUNCE SENTENCE
ANNOUNCEMENT BID CRY HAT
BILL CALL LEAD ALARM BANCO

BANNS BLURB EDICT ALARUM
DECREE DICTUM NOTICE
GAZETTE SENSING BULLETIN
CIRCULAR DECISION RESCRIPT
PROCLAMATION
(— OF DAWN) AUBADE
ANNOUNCER NEBO PAGE CRIER
EMCEE CALLER HERALD NUNCIO
GONGMAN GRINDER SPIELER
NUNCIATE SPRUIKER
ANNOY ARR BUG DUN EAT EGG
GET GIG HOX IRE IRK NAG NOY
NYE TRY VEX BAIT BORE BURN
FASH FRET FUSS GALL GRIG HALE
HARM HAZE HUFF HUMP NARK
PAIN RILE ROIL CHAFE CHASE
CHEVY CHIVY DEVIL GRAMY
GRATE HARRY PEEVE PIQUE
SPITE STURT TEASE THORN
UPSET WEARY WORRY BADGER
BOTHER CADDLE CHIVEY CHIVVY
EARWIG ENRAGE GRAVEL
HAGGLE HARASS HATTER HECKLE
HECTOR INFEST INJURE MADDEN
MOLEST NEEDLE NETTLE OFFEND
PESTER POTTER RATTLE REHETE
RUFFLE TICKLE BEDEVIL DISTURB
HOTFOOT JACKSON TERRIFY
TROUBLE ACERBATE CONTRARY
DISTRESS IRRITATE PERSECUTE
ANNOYANCE VEX FASH PEST
WEED CROSS GRIEF LOATH SPITE
STALL THORN INSECT PESTER
DISGUST FASHERY NOYANCE
TROUBLE UMBRAGE FASHERIE
FLEABITE NOISANCE NUISANCE
PINPRICK
ANNOYED SORE INSULTED
ANNOYING TARE PESKY NOYOUS
DISEASY HATEFUL IRKSOME
NOISOME PAINFUL TARSOME
FASHIOUS FRETSOME NIGGLING
SPITEFUL TIRESOME PROVOKING
PESTIFEROUS
ANNOYINGLY CONFOUNDED
CONFOUNDEDLY
ANNUAL BOOK BUGLE PLANT
FLOWER YEARLY ANNUARY
BUGSEED BUGWEED ETESIAN
GIFTBOOK PERIODIC YEARBOOK
(OLD WORLD —) WELD
ANNUITY CENSO CONSOL INCOME
PENSION TONTINE PERPETUITY
ANNUL TOL CASS NULL TOLL
UNDO VOID ADNUL AVOID BLANK
ELIDE ERASE QUASH REMIT
RETEX UNLAW CANCEL FRIVOL
NEGATE RECALL REPEAL REVERT
REVOKE UNLIVE VACATE ABOLISH
CASHIER CASSARE CASSATE
DESTROY NULLIFY RESCIND
RETRACT REVERSE VACUATE
ABROGATE ARROGATE DEROGATE
DISANNUL DISSOLVE IMBECILE
OVERRIDE OVERRULE
ANNULAR BANDED CYCLIC RINGED
ANNULATE CINGULAR CIRCULAR
ANNULARLY RINGWISE
ANNULET RING RIDGE FILLET
ANNULUS MOLDING
ANNULMENT UNDOING
ABATEMENT
ANNULUS RING ANNULE

COLLAR GYROMA
INDUSIUM
ANNUNCIATION MARYMASS
ANNUNCIATOR TELLER
INDICATOR
ANOA BUFFALO SAPIUTAN
ANODE PLATE ZINCOID
ANODIC ASCENDING
ANODYNE BALM ACOPON BROMAL
OPIATE REMEDY EUGENOL
SOOTHER NARCOTIC SEDATIVE
CHLORODYNE
ANOINT FAT OIL RUB BALM BEAT
CERE NARD ANELE ANOIL CREAM
CROWN ENOIL LATCH NUNCT
PRUNE SALVE SMARM SMEAR
SMERL CHRISM GREASE INUNCT
SPREAD THRASH MOISTEN
UNGUENT
ANOINTMENT CHRISMATORY
ANOMALOUS ODD DIFFORM
STRANGE UNUSUAL ABERRANT
ABNORMAL ATYPICAL PECULIAR
ANOMALY CREEPER CYCLOPY
EPILOIA PARADOX CYCLOPIA
ANON NAN ANEW ONCE SOON
AGAIN LATER AFRESH BEDEEN
BEDENE THENCE SHORTLY
ANONYMITY NOBODYNESS
ANONYMOUS UNKNOWN
NAMELESS UNAVOWED
UNSIGNED
ANOPLURA PARASITA PEDICULINA
ANOTHER NEW THAT ALIAS FRESH
SECOND TIDDER TOTHER
ANITHER FURTHER
(PREF.) ALTERO
(ONE —) ALLELO
ANOXIA ASPHYXIA
ANSHUMANT (FATHER OF —)
ASAMANJAS
(GRANDFATHER OF —) SAGARA
ANSWER DO IT SAY SIT ECHO
MEET PLEA REIN SUIT ATONE
AVAIL COMES COVER JAWAB
REACT REPLY SERVE LETTER
REJOIN RESULT RETORT RETURN
RIPOST ACCOUNT COUNTER
DEFENCE DEFENSE FULFILL
RESPOND SATISFY ANTIPHON
COMEBACK PLEADING REBUTTAL
REPARTEE RESPONSE SOLUTION
(— BACK) CHOP
(— FOR) FORM VANG
(— IN FUGUE) COMES
(— THE PURPOSE) DO FIT SUIT
AVAIL SERVE
(DECISIVE —) SOCKDOLAGER
SOCKDOLOGER
(LEGAL —) DUPLY
ANSWERABLE EQUAL LIABLE
FITTING ADEQUATE AMENABLE
ANSWERER USHABTI
ANSWERING
(PREF.) ANTIPHON
ANT ANAI ANAY ANER ATTA GYNE
MIRE AMPTE EMMET KELEP
MAXIM MINIM NURSE SAUBA
SIAFU SLAVE AMAZON DRIVER
ERGATE NASUTE NEUTER
WORKER BULLDOG FORAGER
FORMICE OUVRIER PISMIRE
PISSANT PONERID REPLETE

SOLDIER TERMITE ACULEATA DORYLINE FORMICID GYNECOID HONEYPOT MACRANER MICRANER MYRMICID TAPINOMA
(— LION) DOODLEBUG
(— SHRIKE) BATARA
(— STUDY) MYRMECOLOGY
(— THRUSH) PITTA
(— TREE) WORMIGO
(PART OF —) EYE WAIST GASTER ANTENNA MANDIBLE
(WORKER —) ERGATE
(PREF.) FORMI(CI) MYRMECO MYRMO TERMITO
(SUFF.) MYRMEX

ANTA PIER PARASTAS PEDESTAL PILASTER

ANTACID SATURANT

ANTAEUS (FATHER OF —) NEPTUNE POSEIDON
(MOTHER OF —) GE GAEA

ANTAGONISM WAR ANIMUS ENMITY QUARREL AVERSION CONFLICT
(IN —) COUNTER

ANTAGONIST FOE ENEMY PARTY RIVAL FOEMAN BATTLER WARRIOR COPEMATE OPPONENT OPPOSITE WRANGLER
(— OF DRUGS) NALAXONE NALOXONE

ANTAGONISTIC ADVERSE COUNTER HOSTILE ANTERGIC CONTRARY INIMICAL OPPONENT OPPOSITE
(— TO GROWTH) ANTIBLASTIC
(NOT —) SYMPATHETIC
(PREF.) ENANTIO

ANTAGONIZE OPPOSE CONTEST

ANTARCTICA (MOUNTAIN ON —) TYREE GARDNER KIRKPATRICK
(VOLCANO ON —) EREBUS MELBOURNE

ANT BEAR BEAR ERDVARK AARDVARK ANTEATER EDENTATE TAMANOIR

ANTE PAY STAKE

ANTEATER TAPIR NUMBAT ECHIDNA TAMANDU AARDVARK AARDWOLF DASYURID EDENTATE PANGOLIN TAMANDUA TAMANOIR

ANTEBRACHIUM CUBIT CUBITAL CUBITUS FOREARM

ANTECEDENT FORE CAUSE PRIOR FORMER REASON WHENCE PREMISE ANTERIOR PREVIOUS PRECEDING PRECEDENCE PREVENIENT
(— OF CANON) GUIDA

ANTECHAMBER LIWAN

ANTEDATE PRECEDE PREDATE FOREDATE PREEXIST

ANTEDATED FORETIMED

ANTELOPE GNU KID KOB RAM SUS ASTE BISA BUCK DODA DUST GUIB IBEX KOBA KUDU ORYX PUKU ROAN SUNI TOPI TORA ADDAX BAIRA BEIRA BEISA BEKRA BOHOR BONGO BOVID BUBAL CHIRU ELAND GORAL GUIBA IPETE LICHI NAGOR NYALA ORIBI PEELE PERON SABLE SAIGA SASIN

SEROW TAKIN YAKIN BAGWYN BHOKRA BUBALE CABREE CABRET CABRIE CABRIT CHOUKA DIKDIK DUIKER DUYKER DZEREN DZERIN DZERON GOORAL GRIMME HEROLA IMPALA INYALA KOODOO LECHWE LELWEL NAKONG NILGAI NILGAU PALLAH POOKOO PYGARG RHEBOK ALGAZEL BLAUBOK BLESBOK BUBALIS CHAMOIS CHIKARA DEFASSA GAZELLE GEMSBOK GERENUK GREENUK GRYSBOK MADOQUA REDBUCK RHEEBOK SASSABY STEMBOK AGACELLA BLEEKBOK BLESBUCK BONTEBOK BOSCHBOK BUSHBUCK KORRIGUM LEUCORYX REEDBUCK STEENBOK PRONGHORN
(YOUNG —) KID LAMB

ANTENNA DISH HORN LOOP PALP TIER YAGI AERIAL DIPOLE FEELER TACTOR DOUBLET WHISKER MONOPOLE PARABOLA RADIATOR

ANTENNATA INSECTA

ANTENOR (FATHER OF —) AESYETES
(MOTHER OF —) CLEOMESTRA
(WIFE OF —) THEANO

ANTERIOR FORNE FRONT PRIOR ATLOID BEFORE FORMER ANTICUS PRORSAL VENTRAL ATLANTAL INFERIOR PREVIOUS PRECEDING
(PREF.) ANTER(O) EPH EPI PRE PRO

ANTEROOM HALL FOYER LOBBY ENTRANCE

ANTEROS (BROTHER OF —) EROS
(FATHER OF —) ARES MARS
(MOTHER OF —) APHRODITE

ANTEWAR PREBELLUM

ANTHAS (FATHER OF —) NEPTUNE POSEIDON
(MOTHER OF —) ALCYONE

ANTHELION HALO NIMBUS ANTISUN AUREOLE

ANTHELMINTIC CUNIC BRAYERA EMBELIN PINKROOT SCAMMONY SANTONICA PIPERAZINE PHENOTHIAZINE

ANTHEM HYMN SONG AGNUS MOTET PSALM INTROIT RESPOND ASPERGES ISODICON
(JAPANESE —) KIMIGAYO

ANTHEMIUS (FATHER OF —) PROCOPIUS

ANTHER TIP AGLET CHIVE THECA

ANTHESIS BLOOM BLOSSOM

ANTHILL BANK TUMP

ANTHOCYANIN ENIN OENIN BETANIN PUNICIN VIOLANIN

ANTHOLOGIST RHAPSODE RHAPSODIST

ANTHOLOGY ANA POSY ALBUM SYLVA CORPUS READER GARLAND SYNTAGMA CHRESTOMATHY

ANTHOZOAN CORAL POLYP ANEMONE GULINULA

ANTHRACITE CULM

ANTHRACONITE STINKSTONE SWINESTONE

ANTHRAX SANG

CHARBON BLACKLEG

ANTHROPOLOGIST TOTEMIST CULTURALIST
AMERICAN BOAS MEAD DIXON HOUGH JENKS SAPIR STARR BUTLER DORSEY HOLMES HOOTON LAUFER PUTNAM BRINTON FOLKMAR KROEBER SPINDEN WISSLER BENEDICT HRDLICKA MACCURDY MACDONALD HERSKOVITS GOLDENWEISER
AUSTRIAN LUSCHAN
ENGLISH KEITH PERRY SMITH TYLOR BEDDOE HADDON HOWITT LEAKEY MARETT RIVERS
FINNISH WESTERMARCK
FRENCH HAMY BROCA DENIKER LAPOUGE TOPINARD MORTILLET HOVELACQUE MANOUVRIER
GERMAN WAITZ GUNTHER HARTMANN SCHWALBE BLUMENBACH WEIDENREICH SCHOETENSACK
ITALIAN SERGI MANTEGAZZA
SCOTTISH FRAZER MONBODDO

ANTHROPOPHAGITE CANNIBAL

ANTIA (BELOVED OF —) BELLEROPHON
(FATHER OF —) IOBATES
(HUSBAND OF —) PROETUS

ANTIAIRCRAFT ARCHIE

ANTIANEIRA (FATHER OF —) MENETES
(SON OF —) ECHION ERYTUS

ANTIBALLOONER SEPARATOR

ANTIBIOTIC BIOTIC ABIOTIC HUMULON TYLOSIN CIRCULIN CITRININ CLAVACIN CLAVATIN COLISTIN FRADICIN HUMULONE NEOMYCIN NYSTATIN SUBTILIN POLYMYCIN PUROMYCIN OLIGOMYCIN PENICILLIN RIFAMPICIN

ANTIBODY LYSIN REAGIN BLOCKER GLUTININ PRECIPITIN

ANTIC TOY DIDO FOOL WILD CAPER CLOWN COMIC DROLL MERRY PRANK STUNT GAMBOL BUFFOON CAPRICE GAMBADE GAMBADO

ANTICIPATE BALK BEAT HOPE JUMP WISH ALLOT AUGUR AWAIT DREAD PSYCH SENSE STALL DIVINE EXPECT PSYCHE THWART DEVANCE FORERUN FORESEE OBVIATE PORTEND PREPARE PREVENE PREVENT PROPOSE RESPECT SUPPOSE ANTEDATE FORECAST FOREFEEL FORETAKE PROSPECT

ANTICIPATION TYPE ODIUM AUGURY OPINION THOUGHT PROSPECT PROLEPSIS PRESCIENCE PREMONITION

ANTICIPATORY PREVENIENT

ANTICLEA (FATHER OF —) AUTOLYCUS
(HUSBAND OF —) LAERTES
(SON OF —) ULYSSES ODYSSEUS

ANTICLIMAX BATHOS

ANTICLINE ARCH DOME NAPPE ISOCLINE OVERFOLD

ANTICYCLONE HIGH

ANTIDEPRESSANT PARGYLINE NORTRIPTYLINE

ANTIDOTE GUACO BEZOAR EMETIC GALENA REMEDY THERIAC DELETERY THERIACA BEZOARDIC MITHRIDATE BLEXIPHARMIC

ANTIGEN N LYSOGEN BIOLOGIC PRECIPITINOGEN

ANTIGERMANISM VANSITTARTISM

ANTIGONE (AUTHOR OF —) SOPHOCLES
(BROTHER OF —) POLYNICES
(CHARACTER IN —) CREON HAEMON ISMENE ANTIGONE TIRESIAS
(FATHER OF —) OEDIPUS
(MOTHER OF —) JOCASTA

ANTIGORITE SERPENTINE

ANTILOCHUS (FATHER OF —) NESTOR
(MOTHER OF —) ANAXIBIA
(SLAYER OF —) MEMNON

ANTIMALARIAL PENTAQUIN PENTAQUINE

ANTIMASK ANTIC ANTICK

ANTIMONIAL STIBIAL

ANTIMONY SB KOHL REGULUS STIBIUM
(PREF.) STIB(IO)

ANTIMONY SULFIDE SURMA SOORMA

ANTINOMIAN FIDUCIARY

ANTINOMY PARADOX

ANTIOPE (FATHER OF —) NYCTEUS
(HUSBAND OF —) LYCUS THESEUS
(SISTER OF —) HIPPOLYTE
(SON OF —) ZETHUS AMPHION HIPPOLYTUS

ANTIOXIDANT SESAMOL

ANTIPATHY HATE ODIUM ENMITY NAUSEA RANCOR ALLERGY DISGUST DISLIKE AVERSION DISTASTE DYSPATHY LOATHING

ANTIPHON SALVE GRADUAL PLACEBO GRADUALE

ANTIPHONALLY CHOIRWISE ANTHEMWISE

ANTIPHONARY LEDGER

ANTIPHUS (BROTHER OF —) MESTHLES
(FATHER OF —) PRIAM TALAEMENES
(HALF-BROTHER OF —) ISUS
(MOTHER OF —) HECUBA

ANTIPODAL ANTARCTIC

ANTIPYRETIC SALOL MALARIN THALLIN THALLINE

ANTIQUARY ARCHAIST ANTIQUARIAN

ANTIQUATED OLD AGED FUSTY MOSSY PASSE FOGRAM FOSSIL VOIDED ANCIENT ARCHAIC FOGYISH NOACHIAN OBSOLETE OUTDATED OUTMODED TIMEWORN

ANTIQUE ANTIC RELIC SIRUP SYRUP VIRTU ANTICK NOETIC ANCIENT ARCHAIC NOACHIC NOACHIAN OUTMODED ARCHAICAL

ANTIQUITY ELD OLD PAST YORE

RELIC OLDNESS ANCIENCE
ANCIENCY
(PL.) ARCHEOLOGY
ARCHAEOLOGY
ANTIRED WHITE
ANTI-SEMITISM JUDOPHOBIA
ANTISEPTIC CAVA EGOL KAVA
SALT AMIDO AMINE EUPAD
EUSOL IODOL SALOL AMADOL
IATROL IODINE KRELOS PHENOL
PICROL ALCOHOL ALUMNOL
ARBUTIN ASEPTIC COLYTIC
LORETIN STERILE TACHIOL
TEUCRIN THALLIN CREOSOTE
ICHTHYOL KAVAKAVA METAPHEN
TEREBENE THALLINE MERBROMIN
ACRIFLAVINE
ANTISOCIAL HOSTILE ANARCHIST
ANTISPASMODIC KELLIN SAMBUL
SUMBAL SUMBUL KHELLIN
PAPAVERINE STRAMONIUM
PENTOBARBITAL
ANTISTROPHE REVERT
COUNTERTURN
ANTITHESIS AND CONTRAST
ANTITHETICAL OPPOSITE
ANTITOXIN SERUM BIOLOGIC
ANTIVIVISECTIONIST BESTIARIAN
ANTLER DAG HORN KNOB RIAL
TRAY DAGUE RIGHT ROYAL
SHOOT SPIKE BOSSET SHOVEL
TROCHE SPELLER DEERHORN
SURROYAL TROCHING
(— POINT) TROCHING
(PL.) HEAD ATTIRE
ANT LION DOODLEBUG
NEUROPTERAN
ANTONINA (HUSBAND OF —)
BELISARIUS
ANTONY AND CLEOPATRA
(AUTHOR OF —) SHAKESPEARE
(CHARACTER IN —) EROS IRAS
MENAS PHILO ALEXAS ANTONY
GALLUS SCARUS SEXTUS SILIUS
TAURUS AGRIPPA LEPIDUS
MARDIAN OCTAVIA THYREUS
VARRIUS CANIDIUS CHARMIAN
DERCETAS DIOMEDES DOMITIUS
MECAENAS OCTAVIUS SELEUCUS
CLEOPATRA DEMETRIUS
DOLABELLA VENTIDIUS
EUPHRONIUS MENECRATES
PROCULEIUS
ANTONYM OPPOSITE
ANTOTHIJAH (FATHER OF —)
JEROHAM
ANTSHRIKE BATARA
ANT THRUSH PITTA
ANT TREE HORMIGO
ANUB (FATHER OF —) COZ
ANUS ASS ARSE BUNG VENT SIEGE
TEWEL
(PREF.) ANO PROCT(O)
(SUFF.) PROCTA
ANVIL BLOCK INCUS SNARL STAKE
STITH TEEST STETHY STITHY
ANDVILE ANFEELD BICKERN
BEAKIRON
(— SUPPORT) STOCK
(MINIATURE —) STAKE STUMP
(PREF.) INCUD(O)
ANXIETY HOW CARE CARK FEAR
FRAY PAIN ALARM ANGOR ANGST

DOUBT DREAD PANIC WORRY
KIAUGH PUCKER ANGUISH
CAUTION CHAGRIN CONCERN
SCRUPLE TENSION THOUGHT
TROUBLE DISQUIET SUSPENSE
SOLICITUDE
ANXIOUS AGOG BUSY FOND TOEY
EAGER FIRST UPSET AFRAID
UNEASY ANGUISH CAREFUL
CARKING EARNFUL FORWARD
TIDIOSE UNQUIET DESIROUS
RESTLESS THOUGHTY WATCHFUL
CONCERNED
ANY A AN AY AIR ALL ARY ONI
ONY AIRY EVER PART SOME
WHAT
(— WHATEVER) ALL
ANYBODY ANY ONE ANYONE
SOMEONE
ANYHOW HOW NOHOW NOWAY
ALWAYS ANYWAY
ANYONE HE MAN ANYBODY
ANYTHING THAT AUGHT OUGHT
ANYWAY NOHOW ALWAYS
ANYWHERE EIHWER OWHERE
UBIQUE ANYPLACE
ANYWISE ANYHOW ANYWAY
ANYWAYS
AOUDAD ARUI UDAD AUDAD
SHEEP CHAMOIS
APACE FAST QUICK QUICKLY
RAPIDLY SPEEDILY
APACHE YUMA PADUCA CIBECUE
VAQUERO QUERECHO
MESCALERO
APAGOGE ABDUCTION
APAP EPIPHI
APAR APARA BOLITA MATACO
APART BY OFF AWAY BOUT ELSE
ALONE ALOOF AROOM ASIDE
RIVEN SOLUS SPLIT YTWYN
ABREID ATWAIN LONELY SUNDRY
ASUNDER ENISLED REMOVED
SEVERAL SEVERED SEPARATE
PIECEMEAL
(— FROM) BARRING
(WIDE —) ASPAR
(WIDELY —) ABROAD
(PREF.) CHORI DI DICH
APARTMENT BUT PAD WON DIGS
FLAT HALL ROOM STEW WENE
WONE WOON ABODE BOWER
OECUS ORIEL ROOMS SALON
SOLAR SUITE ANDRON CLOSET
DECKER DINGLE DUPLEX GROTTO
LYCEUM SALOON SINGLE SOLLAR
SPENCE STANZA BUTTERY
CHAMBER COCKPIT GALLERY
MANSION PRIVACY BUILDING
EPHEBEUM SHOWROOM
SOLARIUM TENEMENT THALAMUS
MAISONETTE
(— FOR IDOL) TING
(— IN CASTLE) BOWER
(— IN CHURCH) SACRISTY
(— OF WARSHIP) COCKPIT
(BACHELOR —) GARCONNIERE
(OUTER —) BUT
(PRIVATE —) MAHAL PARADISE
(RENTED —) LET
(PL.) GYNAECEUM
APATHETIC CALM COLD COOL
DEAD DOWF DULL BLASE DOWFF

INERT STOIC GLASSY SUPINE
TORPID ADENOID PASSIVE
UNMOVED LISTLESS SLUGGISH
LETHARGIC PERFUNCTORY
APATHY SLOTH ACEDIA CAFARD
PHLEGM TORPOR LANGUOR
DOLDRUMS DULLNESS LETHARGY
OMISSION STOICISM STOLIDITY
APATITE IJOLITE MOROXITE
PHOSPHORITE
APAYAO ISNEG
APE KRA LAR PAN BOOR COPY
DUPE FOOL MAHA MIME MOCK
SHAM BEROK CLOWN MAGOT
MIMIC ORANG PONGO PYGMY
APELET BABOON GELADA GIBBON
LANGUR MARTEN MARTIN
MONKEY OURANG PARROT
PONGID SIMIAN SIMIID BUFFOON
COPYCAT EMULATE GORILLA
IMITATE PORTRAY PRIMATE
SATYRUS SIAMANG DURUKULI
IMITATOR MANTEGAR SIMULATE
ORANGUTAN
(— STUDY) PITHECOLOGY
(PREF.) PITHEC(O)
(SUFF.) PITHECUS
APEAK VERTICAL
APEIRON MATTER
APER BOAR MIME SNOB CLOWN
MOCKER BUFFOON COPYCAT
APERCU DIGEST GLANCE PRECIS
SKETCH INSIGHT OUTLINE
APERIENT LAX OPENER CASCARA
APERIODIC DEADBEAT
APERITIF WHET CINZANO
DUBONNET
APERTURE F EYE GAP OPE VUE
BOLE BORE HOLE LEAK PASS
PORE RIMA SLIT SLOT VENT
BREAK CHASM CLEFT CRACK
LIGHT MOUTH PUPIL STOMA
CUTOUT HIATUS KEYWAY
LOUVER WINDOW FISSURE
KEYHOLE OPENING ORIFICE
OSTIOLE PINHOLE PUNCTUM
SWALLOW TROMPIL APERTION
FENESTRA LOOPHOLE OVERTURE
SPIRACLE
APEX EPI PIN TIP TOP ACME AUGE
CONE CUSP NOON PEAK RUFF
CREST HIGHT PITCH POINT SPIRE
APOGEE CLIMAX CRISIS CUPULA
GENION HEIGHT SUMMIT TITTLE
VERTEX ZENITH CACUMEN
EVEREST PAPILLA PUNCTUM
PINNACLE
(— OF HELMET) CREST
(PREF.) APIC(O)
(SUFF.) ACE
APHAREUS (BROTHER OF —)
LEUCIPPUS
(FATHER OF —) PERIERES
(MOTHER OF —) GORGOPHONE
(SON OF —) IDAS LYNCEUS
(WIFE OF —) ARENE
APHASIA ALALIA ALEXIA JARGON
APHEMIA ASYMBOLIA
APHID APHIS LOUSE APTERA
BLIGHT COLLIER DIMERAN
MIGRANS PUCERON BLACKFLY
GREENFLY GYNOPARA HOMOPTER
APHIDAS (DAUGHTER OF —) ANTIA

(FATHER OF —) ARCAS
(MOTHER OF —) ERATO MEGANIRA
CHRYSOPELIA
(SON OF —) ALEUS
APHORISM SAW ADAGE AXIOM
GNOME MAXIM MOTTO SUTRA
SUTTA DICTUM SAYING WISDOM
EPIGRAM PRECEPT PROVERB
APOTHEGM PISHOGUE
APHORISTIC GNOMIC
APHRODISIAC DEWTRY DAMIANA
VENEREAL VENEREOUS
APHRODITE VENUS CYPRIS
URANIA ANTHEIA MYLITTA
CYTHEREA PANDEMOS
(FATHER OF —) ZEUS JUPITER
(HUSBAND OF —) VULCAN
(MOTHER OF —) DIONE
(SON OF —) EROS CUPID AENEAS
APIARIST SKEPPIST
APIARY HIVE SKEP BEEYARD
BEEHOUSE
APICULTURE BEEKEEPING
APIECE UP ALL PER EACH
SERIATIM
APIKORES BECORESH
APIO ARRACACH ARRACACHA
APIOS SOIA SOJA GLYCINE
APIS HAPI
(FATHER OF —) APOLLO
PHORONEUS
(MOTHER OF —) LAODICE
APISH SILLY FOPPISH AFFECTED
APITONG BAGAC HAPITON
KERUING
APIUM UMBEL
APLITE HAPLITE
APLOMB TACT NERVE POISE
SURETY COOLNESS
APOCALYPSE SHOWING
REVELATION
APOCRYPHA PSEUDEPIGRAPHA
APOCRISIARY RESPONSAL
APOCRYPHAL SHAM FALSE
UNREAL DOUBTFUL FABULOUS
FICTIOUS
APODAL FOOTLESS
APOGEE ACME APEX AUGE PEAK
CLIMAX ZENITH
APOGON AMIA CARDINAL
APOLLO SUN PAEAN DELIUS
AGYIEUS APOLLON LYKEIOS
PATROUS PHOEBUS PYTHIUS
CYNTHIUS PYTHAEUS
(FATHER OF —) ZEUS JUPITER
(MOTHER OF —) LETO LATONA
(SISTER OF —) DIANA ARTEMIS
APOLLYON DEVIL SATAN
ABADDON
APOLOGETIC SORRY
APOLOGUE MYTH FABLE STORY
APOLOGY PARABLE ALLEGORY
APOLOGY PLEA ALIBI AMENDS
EXCUSE PARDON REGRET
PRETEXT SCRUPLE APOLOGIA
APOPHYGE SCAPE ESCAPE
APOPLEXY ESCA SHOCK STROKE
POPLESIE
APOSTASY FALL LAPSE
APOSTATE RAT LAPSED CONVERT
HERETIC PERVERT SECEDER
DESERTER DISLOYAL RECREANT
RENEGADE TURNCOAT

APOSTLE ESCAPE TEACHER DISCIPLE FOLLOWER PREACHER **(BIBLICAL —)** JOHN JUDE LEVI PAUL DENIS JAMES JUDAS PETER SIMON ANDREW PHILIP THOMAS DIDYMUS MATTHEW BARNABAS MATTHIAS

APOSTLE BIRD CATBIRD

APOSTROPHE TUISM TURNWAY TURNTALE

APOTHECARY CHEMIC SPICER CHEMICK DRUGGIST

APOTHECIUM CUP PELTA TRICA SHIELD ARDELLA LIRELLA PATELLA

APOTHEGM SAW DICT ADAGE AXIOM GNOME MAXIM SUTRA DICTUM SAYING SUTTAH PROVERB APHORISM SENTENCE

APOTHEOSIS DEIFICATION CONSECRATION

APOTHEOSIZE DEIFY EXALT ELEVATE GLORIFY CANONIZE

APPAIM (FATHER OF —) NADAB

APPALL STUN APPAL DAUNT SHOCK DISMAY REDUCE REVOLT WEAKEN ASTOUND DEPRESS DISGUST DISMISS HORRIFY TERRIFY AFFRIGHT ASTONISH ENFEEBLE FRIGHTEN OVERCOME

APPALLING AWFUL AWESOME FEARFUL TERRIBLE TERRIFIC

APPANAGE GRANT ADJUNCT APANAGE

APPARATUS AID BOX GUN LOG SET ADON DRAG ETNA FAKE GEAR GRIP HECK HELM LAMP LIFT STOW TIRE TOOL BURET GANCH HOIST HORSE LEECH RELAY SCUBA SHEAR SIREN SONAR STILL STOVE SWING BUDDLE BUFFER COILER COOKER DEVICE DINGUS ENGINE FEEDER FILTER FOGGER GADGET GEYSER GRAITH LADDER LIFTER MILKER ORRERY OUTFIT REFLUX SEESAW SHEARS SMOKER SMUDGE TACKLE TIPPLE TREMIE TROMPE AERATOR ALEMBIC APPAREL AUTOMAT BAGGAGE BALANCE BASCULE BURETTE DERRICK ECHELON FURNACE GASOGEN GRILLER HOISTER INHALER ISOTRON MACHINE MEGAFOG PINCERS PRESSER SOXHLET SPRAYER STIRRER TELEPIX TREMOLO TRIMMER UTENSIL AGITATOR AQUALUNG BLOWDOWN CALUTRON CONVEYER CONVEYOR CRYOSTAT DIALYZER DIAPHOTE DIGESTER DRENCHER DUMBBELL EOLIPILE EQUIPAGE ERGOSTAT GASIFIER GAZOGENE INJECTOR ISOSCOPE JACQUARD OSMOGENE OZONIZER PULMOTOR PURIFIER RECORDER REDUCTOR REHEATER SCRUBBER SOFTENER STRIPPER ABSORPTIOMETER **(— IN STOMACH OF LOBSTER)** LADY **(SEGMENTAL —)** BRAINSTEM **(SUFF.)** STAT(IC)(ICS)

APPAREL DECK FARE GARB GEAR ROBE SECT TIRE WEAR WEDE ADORN ARRAY BESEE CLOTH DRESS EQUIP HABIT TUNIC ATTIRE CLOTHE GRAITH OUTFIT PARURE ROBING CLOBBER COSTUME FURNISH GARMENT HARNESS PREPARE RAIMENT VESTURE CLOTHING FOOTWEAR HEADWEAR WARDROBE **(HEAD —)** MILLINERY **(MILITARY —)** WARENTMENT **(RICH —)** ARRAY

APPARENT OPEN BREEM BREME CLEAR OVERT PLAIN FORMAL PARENT PATENT PHANIC CERTAIN EVIDENT GLARING OBVIOUS SEEMING SHALLOW VISIBLE DISTINCT ILLUSORY MANIFEST PALPABLE PROBABLE SEMBLANT SEMBLABLE OSTENSIBLE

APPARENTLY (PREF.) QUASI

APPARITION HUE HANT SHOW DREAM FANCY FETCH GHOST HAUNT IMAGE LARVA PHASM SHADE SHAPE SPOOK ASPECT DOUBLE IDOLUM SOWLTH SPIRIT SPRITE STOUND SWARTH TAISCH THURSE VISION WRAITH DISPLAY EIDOLON FANTASY FEATURE PHANTOM SPECTER SPECTRE EPIPHANY ILLUSION PHANTASM PRESENCE REVENANT SPECTRUM SEMBLANCE

APPARITOR BEADLE PARURE PARITOR SUMMONER

APPEAL ASK BEG BID CRY CALL CASE PLEA SEEK SUIT APPLY CHARM CLEPE REFER SPEAK ACCUSE ADJURE AVOUCH INVOKE PRAYER SUMMON ADDRESS CONJURE ENTREAT IMPLORE REQUEST SOLICIT APPROACH ENTREATY PETITION ADJURATION **(— TO)** APPLY AVOUCH INVOKE ARRAIGN **(SEX —)** IT OOMPH

APPEALING CUTE NICE CATCHY CLEVER CUNNING SUGARED PLEASANT **(STRIKINGLY —)** ZINGY

APPEAR BID CAR EYE GET COME DAWN FARE LOOK LOOM MAKE MEET PEER REAR RISE SEEM WALK ARISE ENTER ISSUE KITHE KYTHE OCCUR SOUND THINK ARRIVE BESEEM EMERGE INFORM REGARD SPRING BLOSSOM COMPEAR DEVELOP OUTCROP RESEMBLE **(— AND DISAPPEAR)** COOK **(— BRIEFLY)** GLINT **(— DIRECTLY BEFORE)** AFFRONT **(— SUDDENLY)** BURST **(— UNEXPECTEDLY)** BLOOM IRRUPT (PREF.) PHANER(O) PHANTA PHANTO

APPEARANCE AIR CUT HUE CAST FARE FORM GARB IDEA LATE LEEN LOOK MIEN SHOW VIEW BLUSH COLOR EIDOS FAVOR FRONT GUISE HABIT PHASE PHASM SHAPE SIGHT SOUND SPICE ASPECT EFFECT FACIES FAVOUR MANNER OBJECT OSTENT REGARD VISAGE ARRIVAL DISPLAY FARRAND FASHION FEATURE GLIMPSE OUTSIDE RESPECT SHOWING SPECIES ARTEFACT ARTIFACT EPIPHANY ILLUSION LIKENESS PRESENCE PRETENSE SEMBLANCE **(— OF LIGHT ON HAIR)** HAG **(CLOUDED —)** HAZE CHILL **(CONSPICUOUS —)** FIGURE **(DISTINCTIVE —)** AURA **(FIRST —)** DAWN DEBUT SPRING **(IMPOVERISHED —)** BEGGARY **(MERE —)** INTENTIONAL **(MOCK —)** SIMULACRUM **(MOTTLED —)** ROE DAPPLE **(MOTTLED SKY —)** BLINK **(OUTWARD —)** FACE SEEM SHOW FACADE APPAREL BALLOON SEEMING SURFACE **(PERSONAL —)** PRESENCE **(STRIPED —)** ROE **(SUPERNATURAL —)** APPARITION **(SURFACE —)** TOUR BLOOM **(UNGAINLY —)** ANGULARITY **(VAGUE —)** BLUR (PREF.) SPECTRO (SUFF.) OPSIA OPSIO OPSIS OPSY PHANE PHANOUS PHANT PHANY

APPEASE LAY PAY CALM EASE HUSH SATE ALLAY ALONE ATONE MEASE PEACE PEASE QUIET SLAKE STILL DEFRAY GENTLE MEEKEN MODIFY PACIFY PLEASE SOFTEN SOOTHE ASSUAGE CONTENT DULCIFY GRATIFY MOLLIFY PLACATE SATISFY STICKLE SUFFICE SWEETEN MITIGATE PROPITIATE **(— APPETITE)** STAY

APPEASEMENT MUNICHISM

APPELLATION NAME TERM GODDY STYLE TITLE APPEAL CALLING EPITHET GOODMAN SURNAME COGNOMEN METRONYM NICKNAME

APPEND ADD PIN TAG CLIP HANG JOIN TACK AFFIX ANNEX ADJOIN ATTACH FASTEN AUGMENT SUBJOIN

APPENDAGE ARM AWN FIN LEG TAB TAG ARIL BARB CAUD FLAP HOOK HORN LIMB LOBE SPUR TAIL AFFIX BEARD CAUDA CERAS EXITE RIDER SCALE TROLL WHISK CERCUS CIRRUS CORONA ELATER ENDITE LAGENA LIGULE PALPUS PAPPUS STIPEL STYLET SUFFIX UROPOD ADJUNCT ANTENNA AURICLE CODICIL EARLOBE EMBLAST FIXTURE FURCULA GONOPOD HOUSING MALELLA PENDANT STIPULE SWIMMER THIMBLE TRAILER WINGLET ADDITION ADHERENT ASCIDIUM BRACHIUM EMPODIUM FILAMENT GNATHITE PEDIPALP PENDICLE PHYLLOID PREDELLA RHABDITE SYNTROPE MAXILLIPED

(— ON MOCCASIN) TRAILER **(EAR-SHAPED —)** AURICLE (PL.) ADNEXA ANNEXA FORCEPS

APPENDIX EKE ANNEX LABEL APPEND VERMIX AURICLE CODICIL PENDANT ADDENDUM AURICULA EPILOGUE

APPERCEPTION RECOGNITION

APPERTAIN LIE FALL REFER BELONG EFFEIR RELATE CONCERN PERTAIN

APPETITE MAW YEN LUST PICA TUCK URGE WILL ZEST BELLY BLOOD GORGE GREED GUSTO TASTE TWIST BULIMY DESIRE FAMINE GENIUS GODOWN HUNGER LIKING OREXIS RELISH STROKE TALENT BULIMIA CRAVING EDACITY LONGING PASSION STOMACH SWALLOW WANTING CUPIDITY FONDNESS GULOSITY TENDENCY **(— LOSS)** ANOREXIA **(ANIMAL —)** BLOOD **(CANINE —)** PHAGEDENA **(EXCESSIVE —)** LIMOSIS GULOSITY POLYPHAGIA **(PERVERTED —)** MALACIA (SUFF.) OREXIA **(— FOR)** PHIL(A)(AE)(E)(IA)(ISM) (IST)(OUS)(US)(Y)

APPETIZER WET WHET SAUCE CANAPE RELISH SAVORY CEVICHE SASHIMI APERITIF COCKTAIL DUBONNET

APPETIZING NICE GUSTY SAVORY GUSTFUL GUSTABLE PALATABLE

APPLAUD HUM CLAP LAUD RISE ROOT RUFF CHEER EXTOL HUZZA PRAISE ACCLAIM APPROVE COMMENT ENDORSE HOSANNA PLAUDIT

APPLAUSE CLAP HAND BRAVO CHEER ECLAT HUZZA SALVO HURRAH PRAISE ACCLAIM OVATION CLAPPING

APPLE PIP CRAB OHIA POME COPEI JAMBO BEEFIN BIFFIN CODLIN DOUCIN ESOPUS GOLDIN KARELA KAVIKA MACUPA MAKOPA PIPPIN PUFFIN RENNET RUSSET BALDWIN BEAUFIN CODLING COSTARD FAMEUSE GOLDING PEELING POMEROY RAMBURE RIBSTON RUDDOCK WAGENER WEALTHY WINESAP AMPALAYA COCCAGEE CORTLAND GREENING JONATHAN MCINTOSH NONESUCH PARADISE PEARMAIN POMANDER POROPORO QUEENING REINETTE ROSACEAN SWEETING WHITSOUR QUARENDEN **(— OF PERU)** JIMSON JIMPSON SHOOFLY **(BITTER —)** COLOCYNTH **(CRAB —)** CRAB SCRAB WHARRE POWITCH **(EMU —)** COLANE **(GOLDEN —)** BEL BAEL **(LIKE AN —)** POMACEOUS **(PEELED —)** DUMPLING **(SHRIVELED —)** CRUMPLING

(SLICED DRIED —S) SNITS SNITZ SCHNITZ
(SMALL —) CODLIN CODLING
(SMALL —S) GRIGGLES
(THORN —) MAD METEL
(PREF.) POMI POMO
APPLEBERRY DUMPLING
APPLEJOHN DEUSAN DEUZAN
APPLE-POLISH BROWNNOSE
APPLIANCE GEAR GRAB IRON TOOL BRACE CLAMP DEVIL FLIER FLYER GLODE SHADE BONNET BREWER DEVICE ENGINE FABRIC GADGET GAITER JUICER SPLINT WINDLE CHARGER MACHINE SCRAPER STOPPER UTENSIL BALANCER DEVIATOR
APPLICABLE APT FIT MEET PROPER USEFUL FITTING PLIABLE APPOSITE RELATIVE RELEVANT SUITABLE
(UNIVERSALLY —) CATHOLIC
(WIDELY —) BROAD
APPLICANT PROSPECT
APPLICATION USE DAUB FORM BLANK TOPIC APPEAL EFFORT ADDRESS EPITHEM REQUEST EPITHEME LENITIVE PETITION PRACTICE SEDULITY
(— OF KNOWLEDGE) PRACTICE PRACTISE
(— TO WRONG PURPOSE) ABUSE
(MEDICINAL —) PLASTER DRESSING FRONTING LENITIVE
(MENTAL —) INTENTION
APPLICATOR COLPOSTAT
APPLIED (CLOSELY —) ACCUMBENT
(PREF.) TECHNO
APPLIQUE DAG DAGGE ATTACH DESIGN ORNAMENT
APPLY ASK LAY PLY PUT RUB SET USE BEAR BEND CLAP DAUB GIVE HOLD MOVE SEEK TOIL TURN WORK ADAPT GRIND IMPLY LABOR LIKEN REFER SMEAR ADDICT APPEAL APPOSE BESTOW BETAKE BUCKLE COMPLY DEVOTE DIRECT EMPLOY EXTEND RESORT ADHIBIT COMPARE CONFORM IMPRESS OVERLAY PERTAIN REQUEST SOLICIT UTILIZE DEDICATE DISPENSE MINISTER PETITION
(— BRAKE) BUR
(— COSMETICS) DO POP
(— GRAPHITE) BLACKLEAD
(— GREASE) ARM
(— HOT CLOTHS) FOMENT
(— IMPROPERLY) ABUSE
(— ONESELF) ATTEND INTEND MUCKLE ADDRESS
(— PIGMENT) DRAG
(— TO) CONSULT CONTACT
APPOGGIATURA BACKFALL ACCIACCATURA
(DOUBLE —) FALL
APPOINT ARM FIX SET CALL DECK GIVE MAKE NAME ALLOT ARRAY AWARD COOPT CREST DIGHT ELECT ENACT EQUIP INSET PITCH PLACE POINT SHAPE SLATE ASSIGN ASSIZE ATTACH CREATE DECREE DEPUTE DETAIL DEVISE

DIRECT ENTAIL ORDAIN OUTFIT SETTLE STEVEN TAILYE ARRAIGN CONFIRM DESTINE DISPOSE FURNISH GAZETTE RESOLVE TAILZIE DELEGATE DEPUTIZE INDICATE NOMINATE ORDINATE
(— A CLERIC) COLLATE
(— BEFOREHAND) STALL
APPOINTEE PLACEMAN
APPOINTMENT SET DATE BERTH ORDER TRYST BILLET OFFICE STEVEN COMMAND STATION CREATION DELEGACY POSITION
(— OF HEIR) INSTITUTION
APPORTION LOT DEAL DOLE MARK METE PART RATE ALLOT AWARD CAVEL GRANT PARAL SHARE SHIFT WEIGH APPLOT ASSESS ASSIGN DIVIDE PARCEL RATION TAVERN ARRANGE BALANCE QUARTER ALLOCATE DESCRIBE ADMEASURE PROPORTION
APPORTIONMENT DIVISION
APPOSITE APT PAT COGENT TIMELY GERMANE INCIDENT RELATIVE RELEVANT SUITABLE
APPRAISAL APPRIZAL
APPRAISE GAGE LOVE METE RATE ASSAY GAUGE JUDGE PRICE PRIZE VALUE ASSESS ESTEEM EVALUE PONDER PRAISE SURVEY ADJUDGE ANALYZE COMMEND ESTIMATE EVALUATE
APPRECIABLE ANY SENSIBLE PERCEPTIBLE
APPRECIATE DIG FEEL LOVE JUDGE PRIZE RAISE SAVOR TASTE VALUE ADMIRE ESTEEM SAVOUR ADVANCE APPRIZE APPROVE CHERISH REALIZE INCREASE TREASURE
APPRECIATION EYE GUSTO SENSE CONCEIT PERCEPTION
APPRECIATIVE AWAKE GRATEFUL
(— OF BEAUTY) ESTHETIC AESTHETIC
APPREHEND COP GET LAG NAB SEE FEAR HEAR KNOW NOTE SCAN TAKE VIEW CATCH DREAD GRASP GRIPE INTUE SEIZE ARREST BEHOLD DETAIN INTEND INTUIT BELIEVE CAPTURE CONCEIT ENDOUTE FORESEE IMAGINE REALIZE RECEIVE SENSATE SUPPOSE CONCEIVE DISCOVER OVERTAKE PERCEIVE
APPREHENDED GRIPPIT
APPREHENSIBLE NOETIC SENSATE SENSIBLE
APPREHENSION FEAR FRAY PAIN PANG SCAN WERE ALARM DOUBT DREAD FANCY WORRY ARREST DISMAY NOESIS ANXIETY CAPTURE CONCERN PRESAGE SUSPECT DISTRUST MISTRUST SUSPENSE COGNITION PREHENSION
APPREHENSIVE APT JUMPY FEARED MORBID ANXIOUS FEARFUL JEALOUS NERVOUS STREAKY UPTIGHT DOUBTFUL SOLICITOUS
APPRENTICE CUB BIND BOOT

SNOB TYRO CADET DEVIL BURSCH HELPER JOCKEY NOVICE BANKMAN GROMMET LEARNER TRAINEE WAISTER APRENDIZ BEGINNER JACKAROO PRENTICE SERVITOR TURNOVER
APPRENTICESHIP SERVITUDE
APPRISE WARN LEARN TEACH ADVISE INFORM NOTIFY REVEAL APPRIZE ACQUAINT DISCLOSE INSTRUCT
APPROACH TRY ADIT BUMP BURN CHAT COME COST DRAW NEAR NERE NIGH ROAD ABORD BOARD CLOSE COAST ESSAY STALK VERGE ACCEDE ACCESS ACCOST ADVENT ANIMUS APPEAL BORDER BREAST BROACH COMING GATHER IMPEND PROACH TRENCH ADVANCE AGGRESS APPULSE CONTACT PREFACE SEAGATE SUCCEED CONVERGE NEIGHBOR ONCOMING
(— FROM WINDWARD) BEAR
(— GAME) DRAW
(— HOSTILELY) SWAY
(— NEAR) TOUCH
(— OF NIGHT) FALL
(— TENDENCY) ADIENCE
(INVITING —) PASS
APPROACHABLE COMMON AFFABLE ACCESSIBLE
APPROACHING LIKE COMING TOWARD ONCOMING
APPROBATION TEST FAVOR PROOF TRIAL ASSENT FAVOUR LOANGE PRAISE REGARD REPUTE PLAUDIT APPLAUSE APPROVAL SANCTION
APPROPRIATE ADD APT DUE FIT LAY PAT AKIN CRIB FEAT GOOD GRAB GRIP HELP JUST MEET SINK SUIT TAKE ALLOT ANNEX FITTY HAPPY RIGHT STEAL USURP ASSELF ASSIGN ASSUME BORROW DECENT DEVOTE DEVOUR DIGEST GATHER GENTIL KINDLY PILFER PIRATE PROPER TIMELY WORTHY APPROVE APROPOS CABBAGE CONDIGN CONVERT FITTING GERMANE GRABBLE GRADELY IMPOUND PREEMPT PURLOIN RELATED SECRETE SWALLOW ACCROACH APPOSITE ARROGATE BECOMING DESERVED EMBEZZLE GRACEFUL HANDSOME IDONEOUS PECULIAR PROPERTY RELEVANT RIGHTFUL SUITABLE
(— UNLAWFULLY) HEIST STEAL
(MOST —) CHOICE
APPROPRIATENESS APTNESS DECENCY FITNESS APTITUDE
(NICE —) ELEGANCE
APPROPRIATION FUND VOTE DEVOTION
(FRAUDULENT —) CON EMBEZZLEMENT
APPROVAL AMEN ECLAT ASSENT ESTEEM APPROOF CONSENT PLAUDIT SUPPORT APPLAUSE BLESSING SANCTION SUFFRAGE AGREEMENT
APPROVE DO OK BUY DIG TRY

AMEN HAVE LIKE OKAY OKEH PASS TEST VOTE ALLOW BLESS CLEAR FAVOR PROVE VALUE ACCEPT ADMIRE BISHOP CONCUR RATIFY APPLAUD CERTIFY COMMEND CONFIRM CONSENT ENDORSE EXHIBIT INDORSE SUPPORT ACCREDIT MANIFEST SANCTION
APPROVED TRYE EXPERT PROBAL ACCEPTED ORTHODOX
(NOT —) OUT
APPROVING HEARTY
APPROXIMATE NEAR ABOUT CIRCA CLOSE COAST ROUGH COARSE GENERAL NOMINAL APPROACH ESTIMATE
APPROXIMATELY SAY AWAY GAIN MUCH NIGH SOME ABOUT CIRCA ALMOST AROUND NEARLY TOWARD CRUDELY ROUGHLY
APPROXIMATING COMPARATIVE
APPROXIMATION CIRCA COUNTERFEIT
APPURTENANCE GEAR ANNEX ASSIGN EFFEIR ADJUNCT COMFORT APPANAGE PENDICLE
(PL.) ADDENDA
APRICOT COT UME ANSU MUME ABRICOCK BLENHEIM
(DRIED —S) MEBOS MEEBOS
A PRIORI PURE
APRON BIB CAP BASE BOOT BRAT DICK RAMP SLOP TAYO TIER COVER EPHOD BARVEL BISHOP CANVAS DAIDLE DICKEY NAPRON RUNWAY SHIELD TARMAC TOUSER BRATTLE CANVASS DAIDLIE GREMIAL TABLIER LAMBSKIN PINAFORE PRASKEEN
(— OF FURNITURE) PETTICOAT
(— OF SEAT) FALL
(CHILD'S —) TIER BISWOP SLIPPER
(LEATHER —) DICK DICKY BARVEL DICKEY BARMFEL BARVELL BARMSKIN
(MASON'S —) LAMBSKIN
(SILKEN —) GREMIAL
(PL.) ARMITAS
APROPOS APT FIT PAT MEET TIMELY RELEVANT SUITABLE
APSE BEMA APSIS NICHE CONCHA EXEDRA RECESS
APSIS APSE AUGE
APSYRTUS (FATHER OF —) AEETES
(MOTHER OF —) IDYIA ASTERODIA
(SISTER OF —) MEDEA
APT FIT PAT YAP ABLE DEFT FAIN FEAT GLEG KEEN VAIN WONT ADEPT ALERT HAPPY PRONE QUICK READY ASPERT CLEVER DOCILE KITTLE LIABLE LIKELY PRETTY SUITED TOWARD APROPOS CAPABLE FITTING IDONEAL WILLING APPOSITE DEXTROUS DISPOSED HANDSOME IDONEOUS INCLINED POIGNANT PRACTIVE PREPARED SKILLFUL SUITABLE
(— TO TURN) WALT
APTERYX KIWI RATITE KIVIKIVI KIWIKIWI
APTITUDE ART BENT GIFT HEAD

TURN CRAFT FLAIR HABIT KNACK
SKILL VERVE GENIUS TALENT
ABILITY CONDUCT FACULTY
FITNESS LEANING CAPACITY
INSTINCT TENDENCY
APTLY PAT
APTNESS GIFT KNACK SKILL
APTITUDE FELICITY
APUS CYPSELUS MICROPUS
AQUARIUS SKINKER
AQUEDUCT AQUA DUCT CANAL
AQUAGE SPECUS CHANNEL
CONDUIT PASSAGE
(— OF SILVIUS) ITER
AQUEOUS HYDATOID WATERISH
AQUILA (WIFE OF —) PRISCILLA
AQUILANT (BROTHER OF —)
GRYPHON
ARA MACAW
(FATHER OF —) JETHER
ARAB AHL AUS IBAD OMAN SLEB
WAIF ARABY GAMIN NOMAD
SAUDI TATAR SEMITE SLUBBI
URCHIN ARABIAN BEDOUIN
SARACEN SOLUBBI AZZAZAME
KABABISH LARRIKIN SLOUBBIE
YEMENITE
ARABELLA (CHARACTER IN —)
MATTEO ZDENKA WALDNER
ARABELLA MANDRYKA
(COMPOSER OF —) STRAUSS
ARABESQUE ORNATE

ARABIA
COIN: LARI CARAT DINAR KABIK
RIYAL
DESERT: NYD ANKAF DEHNA
NAFUD NEFUD
GARMENT: ABA HAIK CABAAN
BURNOUS
GODDESS: ALLAT
HOLY CITY: MECCA MEDINA
HOLY LAND: HEJAZ
ISLAND: SOCOTRA
JUDGE: CADI
KINGDOM: NEJD
MEASURE: DEN SAA FERK KIST
ACHIR BARID CABDA CAFIZ
COVID CUDDY MAKUK QASAB
TEMAN WOIBE ZUDDA ARTABA
ASSBAA COVIDO FEDDAN
GARIBA GHALVA CAPHITE
FARSAKH FARSANG KILADJA
MARHALE NUSFIAH
MOUNTAIN: NEBO HOREB SINAI
PORT: ADEN
RULER: AMIR EMIR AMEER EMEER
STATE: ASIR OMAN YEMEN
KUWAIT
TOWN: ABHA ADEN BEDA BERA
HAIL RIAD SANA TAIF DUBAI
HAUTA HOFUF JIDDA MECCA
MOCHA QATIF TAIZZ YENBO
ANAIZA MANAMA MATRAH
MEDINA RIYADH SALALA
SHAQRA BURAIDA HODEIDA
MUKALLA ONEIZAH SHARJAH
TRIBE: AUS ASIR IRAD TEMA
KEDAR DIENDEL SHUKRIA
WEIGHT: ROTL BAHAR CHEKI
KELLA MAUND NASCH NEVAT
OCQUE OUKIA RATEL TOMAN
VAKIA BOKARD DIRHEM

MISKAL FARSALAH

ARABIC CARSHUNI GARSHUNI
KARSHUNI THAMUDIC
(— ALPHABET) BA FA HA RA TA YA
ZA AYN DAD DAL JIM KAF KHA
LAM MIM NUN QAF SAD SIN THA
WAW ZAY ALIF DHAL SHIN
GHAYN
ARABLE FERTILE PLOWABLE
TILLABLE
ARACHNID CRAB MITE TICK TAINT
ACARID ACARUS CARTER SPIDER
CARTARE OCTOPOD PEDIPALP
SCORPION SOLPUGID
PSEUDOSCORPION
ARAD (FATHER OF —) BERIAH
ARAGONITE ALABASTER
ARAIN ARRAND
ARAKANESE MAGHI
ARAM (FATHER OF —) ESROM
HEZRON KEMUEL SHAMER
ARAMAIC SYRIAC MANDAEAN
(— TRANSLATION) TARGUM
ARAN (BROTHER OF —) UZ
(FATHER OF —) DISHAN
ARANEA EPEIRA
ARAPAIMA PIRARUCU
ARAPONGA BELLBIRD
ARAROBA ZEBRAWOOD
ARAROS (FATHER OF —)
ARISTOPHANES
ARAUCANIAN AUCA PAMPA
MAPOCHE MOLUCHE PAMPERO
PICUNCHE
ARAWA AOTEA MATATUA
ARAWAK ARUA BARE URAN
ARAUA BAURE CAMPA CHANE
GUANA INERI SIUSI BAINOA
BANIVA GUINAU IGNERI GOAJIRO
IPURINA CAQUETIO CUSTENAU
ARBALEST BALISTER CROSSBOW
ARBITER JUDGE CRITIC ODDMAN
UMPIRE ADVISER DAYSMAN
ODDSMAN OVERMAN REFEREE
DICTATOR STICKLER
ARBITRAGE SHUNTING
ARBITRARY SEVERE THETIC
WILLFUL ABSOLUTE DESPOTIC
MASTERLY
(NOT —) FREE
ARBITRATE DECIDE MEDIATE
ARBITRATION DAYMENT
ARBITRATOR REF JUDGE UMPIRE
ARBITER MUNSIFF REFEREE
MEDIATOR
ARBOR BAR AXLE BEAM ABODE
BOWER SHAFT STAFF STALK
TRAIL ARBOUR BOWERY GARDEN
HERBER PANDAL RAMADA
VOIDER BERCEAU HARBOUR
MANDREL MANDRIL ORCHARD
PERGOLA RETREAT SPINDLE
TRELLIS FRESCADE TONNELLE
ARBORVITAE AKEKI ALERCE
ARBUTUS IVY MAYFLOWER
ARC BOW ARCH BEND FOIL HALO
CURVE HANCE ORBIT SPARK
SWING FOGBOW FOLIUM OCTANT
RADIAN COMPASS RAINBOW
FROSTBOW
(— OF HORIZON) AZIMUTH
AMPLITUDE

(ELECTRIC —) SPARK
ARCA BOX CHEST PATEN ARCULA
ARCADE ORB AVENUE LOGGIA
STREET GALLERY PORTICO
ARCATURE CLOISTER
ARCANE RUNIC HIDDEN SECRET
MYSTERIOUS
ARCAS (FATHER OF —) ZEUS
JUPITER
(MOTHER OF —) CALLISTO
ARCESIUS (FATHER OF —) ZEUS
JUPITER CEPHALUS
(MOTHER OF —) PROCRIS
EURYODIA
(SON OF —) LAERTES
ARCH ARC BOW COY SET SLY BACK
BEND COPE COVE DOME HARP
HOOP IRIS LEER OGEE PASS PEND
PERT SPAN ARCUS CHIEF CURVE
FAULD GREAT HANCE HUNCH
INBOW JOWEL OGIVE PAUKY
PAWKY POKEY PRIME ROACH
SAUCY SWEEP VAULT ARCADE
BRIDGE CALCAR CAMBER CLEVER
DIADEM FOGBOW FORNIX GIRDLE
IMPISH INVERT LANCET MANTEL
SPRING SUNBOW WICKET
ZYGOMA ARCHWAY CONCAVE
CUNNING EMINENT GATEWAY
ROGUISH SEGMENT SQUINCH
SUPPORT TESTUDO TRIUMPH
WAGGISH ALVEOLAR ESPIEGLE
FOGEATER OVERCAST
SCUNCHEON
(— OF SKY) FIRMAMENT
(DENTAL —) ARCADE
(LOGGING —) SULKY
(PART OF —) PIER CHORD IMPOST
PILLAR ABUTMENT EXTRADOS
INTRADOS KEYSTONE SKEWBACK
SPANDREL SPRINGER VOUSSOIR
(PL.) SUBARCUATION
ARCHAEOCYTE SORITE
ARCHAEOLOGIST POTHUNTER
PREHISTORIAN
AMERICAN CLAY DAVIS SHEAR
BARBER BUTLER GORDON
HAYNES HEWETT HOLMES
MORELY PARKER PORTER SNYDER
SQUIER MERRIAM NUTTALL
SAVILLE SPEISER BREASTED
CUMMINGS ROBINSON STERRETT
THOMPSON CARPENTER
MOOREHEAD RICHARDSON
FROTHINGHAM
AUSTRIAN ARNETH STUDNICZKA
CANADIAN CURRELLY
CZECH HROZNY
DANISH ZOEGA MULLER POULSEN
WORSAAE BRONDSTED
MATHIASSEN STEENSTRUP
DUTCH GRUYTERE
ENGLISH BELL COOK GANN GELL
HALL BUDGE EVANS RYMER
STEIN CARTER CHILDE LAYARD
MURRAY NEWTON WARREN
BEAZLEY BRAYLEY BURROWS
DAWKINS DODWELL FELLOWS
GARDNER HOGARTH PENROSE
WOOLLEY GARSTANG HAMILTON
LAWRENCE RIDGEWAY STEPHENS
THOMPSON BABINGTON
FRENCH LEBAS MAURY PUGIN

VOGUE BREUIL CAGNAT CHOISY
CLARAC COCHET FORBIN GAIDOZ
LARTET MORGAN PERROT
SAULCY BABELON CHANTRE
CHARNAY DELATRE HOMOLLE
LEBLANT POTTIER BERTRAND
DIEULAFOY LENORMANT
DECHELETTE QUATREMERE
WADDINGTON LECHEVALIER
GERMAN MAU ROSS TREU ADLER
BRAUN BRUNN CONZE SARRE
ANDRAE BECKER HELBIG HILLER
MULLER NISSEN SCHOLL CURTIUS
GERHARD LASAULX WELCKER
WIEGAND BENNDORF BOTTIGER
ESSENWEIN KOLDEWEY
KOSSINNA PETERSEN LOESCHCKE
MICHAELIS SCHLIEMANN
FURTWANGLER WINCKELMANN
GREEK TSOUNTAS
ICELANDIC MAGNUSSON
IRISH STOKES ODONOVAN
MACALISTER
ITALIAN BONI LANZI ROSSI
CANINA FIORELLI LANCIANI
MARUCCHI VISCONTI
RUSSIAN KOPPEN POGODIN
CHWOLSON
SCOTTISH RAMSAY BURGESS
SWEDISH BRENNER MONTELIUS
SWISS KELLER
ARCHAIC OLD ANCIENT ANTIQUE
HISTORIC OBSOLETE
(PREF.) PALE
ARCHANGEL SATAN URIEL
GABRIEL MICHAEL RAPHAEL
HIERARCH
ARCHBISHOP HATTO PRELATE
PRIMATE ORDINARY
ARCHDEMON BELFAGOR
BELFAZOR
ARCHDIOCESE EPARCHY
ARCHDUKE ERZHERZOG
ARCHEAN EOZOIC
ARCHED ARCHY CONVEX ARCUATE
EMBOWED VAULTED HOOPLIKE
CAMERATED
(— IN) CONCAVE
(PREF.) TOX(I)(O) TOXIC(O)
ARCHEGONIUM CALYPTRA
OOANGIUM
ARCHELAUS (BROTHER OF —)
PHILIP ANTIPAS
(FATHER OF —) HEROD
(MOTHER OF —) MALTHAKE
ARCHEMORUS (FATHER OF —)
LYCURGUS
(MOTHER OF —) EURYDICE
(NURSE OF —) HYPSIPYLE
ARCHER BOW CLIM CLYM BOWER
BUTTY CUPID ROVER BOWBOY
BOWMAN BOWYER SHOOTER
PANDARUS
(EQUIPMENT OF —) TACKLE
ARCHERY TOXOLOGY ARTILLERY
(— SPACE) PETTICOAT
(PREF.) TOX(I)(O) TOXIC(O)
ARCHETYPE IDEA MODEL FIGURE
SAMPLE ESSENCE EXAMPLE
PARAGON PATTERN EXEMPLAR
FRAVASHI ORIGINAL PROTOTYPE
ARCHIL CORKE CORCIR CORKER
PERSIS CUDBEAR LECANORA

ORCHILLA ORSEILLE
ARCHING CAMBER
ARCHITECT MAKER ARTIST
ARTISAN BUILDER CREATOR
PLANNER BEZALEEL DESIGNER
SURVEYOR
AMERICAN DAY COBB COPE CRAM
CRET HOOD HOWE HUNT KAHN
PELZ POPE POST TOWN WARE
ALLEN BACON CASEY DAVIS
FLAGG GOULD HEINS HOBAN
MCKIM MILLS PRICE WAUGH
WHITE BARBER GEDDES GILMAN
GRAHAM HAIGHT HOWARD
JENNEY ROGERS WALKER
WALTER WARREN WRIGHT
BRAGDON BRUNNER BURNHAM
CARRERE CORBETT EIDLITZ
GILBERT GOODHUE GRIFFIN
HOWELLS KENDALL KIESLER
KIMBALL LAFARGE LESCAZE
PARSONS PEABODY PLOWMAN
RAYMOND STURGIS TUTHILL
BENJAMIN BOSWORTH BULFINCH
COOLIDGE HARRISON HASTINGS
HOLABIRD MCINTIRE SULLIVAN
THOMPSON THORNTON
VANBRUNT MAGONIGLE
RICHARDSON STEWARDSON
STRICKLAND HARDENBERGH
WHEELWRIGHT
AUSTRIAN NULL WAGNER
FERSTEL HASENAUER
HOLZMEISTER
BELGIAN VELDE POELAERT
CZECH ZITEK
DANISH NYROP HANSEN
DUTCH OUD KEYSER BERLAGE
CUYPERS LOMBARD MOREELSE
EGYPTIAN CALLINICUS
ENGLISH KENT NASH SHAW TITE
WEBB WREN ADAMS BAKER
BARRY BLORE DANCE GLOAG
GOTCH GWILT JONES SCOTT
SOANE STONE WYATT BODLEY
CLARKE COOPER HANSOM
PAXTON STREET STUART
BECKETT BENTLEY JACKSON
KNOWLES LUTYENS PEARSON
PENROSE RICKMAN ATKINSON
CHAMBERS COCKERAM FLETCHER
NESFIELD VANBRUGH
CHAMPNEYS HAWKSMOOR
NICHOLSON WILKINSON
LANCHESTER WATERHOUSE
ABERCROMBIE BUTTERFIELD
PENNETHORNE
FINNISH AALTO SAARINEN
GESELLIUS
FRENCH DUC ETEX COTTE DUBAN
LEVAU MAROT PUGET BENARD
BERAIN BROSSE LEFUEL LESCOT
NEPVEU ANTOINE BALTARD
BLONDEL BULLANT DAVIOUD
DELORME FORMIGE GABRIEL
GARNIER MANSART PERCIER
ANDROUET CHALGRIN CUVILLES
FELIBIEN FONTAINE HITTORFF
LEPAUTRE SOUFFLOT LEMERCIER
LECORBUSIER
GERMAN HOLL LENZ ADLER
ERWIN GEDON LENNE KLENZE
MESSEL MOLLER SEMPER STULER

BEHRENS FRIESEN GROPIUS
NEUMANN OLBRICH POELZIG
HEGEMANN LANGHANS SCHINKEL
SCHLUTER ESSENWEIN
POPPELMANN KNOBELSDORFF
GREEK ICTINUS DOXIADIS
MNESICLES SOSTRATUS
DINOCRATES HIPPODAMUS
POLYCLITUS CALLICRATES
HUNGARIAN STEINDL
ITALIAN BONI DANTI GENGA
NERVI PORTA POZZO VINCI
AGNOLO ALESSI BONOMI CIGOLI
GIOTTO IUVARA ROMANO SERING
SOLARI SUARDI VASARI ALBERTI
ALGARDI BERNINI BIBIENA
CAGNOLA CONTINO CORTONA
FONTANA GUARINI LAURANA
MADERNA PERUZZI TIBALDI
TRIBOLO VIGNOLA AGOSTINO
AMMANATI BRAMANTE CIVITALI
GIOCONDO LOMBARDO PALLADIO
PIRANESI SCAMOZZI BORROMINI
PIERMARINI SANMICHELI
SERVANDONI VANVITELLI
PRIMATICCIO BRUNELLESCHI
MICHELANGELO
ROMAN COSMATI COSSUTIUS
RUSSIAN BRYULOV
SCOTTISH ADAM MACKINTOSH
SPANISH CANO HERRERA
VILLANUEVA
SWEDISH TESSIN OSTBERG
TENGBOM
TURKISH SINAN
ARCHITECTURAL TECTONIC
OECODOMIC
ARCHITECTURE DRAVIDA
ARCHITRAVE EPISTYLE PLATBAND
ARCHIVES TABULARY
TABULARIUM
ARCHIVOLT RING ARCHBAND
HEADBAND
ARCHLUTE THEORBO
ARCHON RULER DIRECTOR
OFFICIAL THESMOTHETE
ARCHWAY ARCH PEND ARCUS
PAILOO PAILOU
ARC LAMP MONOPHOTE
ARCOGRAPH BOW
ARCO SALTANDO SPICCATO
ARCTIC ICY COLD COOL GELID
POLAR BOREAL CHILLY FRIGID
GALOSH NORTHERN OVERSHOE
ARCTIUM LAPPA
ARCTOID URSINE
ARD (FATHER OF —) BELA
ARDENT HOT AVID FOND KEEN
LIVE WARM EAGER FIERY GLEDY
RETHE SHARP ABLAZE FERVID
FIERCE IGNITE STRONG TORRID
AMOROUS BURNING CORDIAL
DEVOTED EARNEST FEELING
FERVENT FLAMING FORWARD
GLOWING INTENSE SHINING
ZEALOUS DESIROUS EMPRESSE
FEVERISH FLAGRANT ROMANTIC
SANGUINE SCALDING SPORTIVE
VEHEMENT PERFERVID
ARDON (FATHER OF —) CALEB
(MOTHER OF —) AZUBAH
ARDOR DASH EDGE ELAN FIRE
GLOW HEAT LOVE ZEST ESTRO

FLAME GUSTO HEART TAPAS
VERVE WRATH DESIRE FERVOR
FOUGUE METTLE SPIRIT SPLEEN
WARMTH ARDENCY EARNEST
ENTRAIN PASSION DEVOTION
FEROCITY VIOLENCE VIVACITY
ARDUOUS HARD LOFTY STEEP
STIFF SEVERE TRYING ONEROUS
EXACTING TIRESOME TOILSOME
ARDYS (FATHER OF —) GYGES
ARE MU RE AIR ARN ARUN HARE
AREA BELT PALE SIZE TREF ZONE
BASIN COAST COURT FIELD
PLACE RANGE REALM SCENE
SCOPE SPACE TRACT ACCENT
AREOLA EXTENT GROUND
LOCALE MOARIA REGION SECTOR
SPHERE SPREAD VOLUME
ACREAGE AMENITY AREAWAY
CIRCUIT COMPASS CONTENT
COUNTRY ENVIRON EXPANSE
KINGDOM PURLIEU SURFACE
CAPACITY DISTRICT
ENCEINTE PLOTTAGE
PROVINCE
(— AT INTERSECTION) CIRCUS
(— BETWEEN FILLETS) CANALIS
(— IN BACTERIAL CULTURE)
PLAQUE
(— IN CARTOON) BALLOON
(— IN HOSTILE TERRITORY)
AIRHEAD
(— OF ACTIVITY) METIER
(— OF EXPERIENCE) BOOK
(— OF FLAG) CANTON
(— OF OLDER LAND) KIPUKA
(— OF OPEN WATER AMID ICE)
POLYNYA
(— OF RIDGES) BILO
(— OF TIMBERLAND) CHENA
(— ON MOON) MARE WANE TERRA
(— UNIT) TAN YOKE LABOR
VIRGATE PLETHRON PLOWGANG
PLOWGATE
(BLANK —) BITE HOLE
(COMBAT —) GLACIS
(CONTINENTAL —) MOARIA
(CULTURAL —) HORIZON
(CURLING —) PARISH
(DARK — OF MOON) MARE MARIA
(DENUDED —) BURN
(DIKED —) SLUSHPIT
(ELONGATED —) BELT
(ENCLOSED —) FOLD SEPT
(EXTRAMURAL —) BANLIEUE
(FENCED —) CAGE COMPOUND
(FERTILE —) HAMMOCK
(FLOORING —) SQUARE
(FORTIFIED —) BASTION ENCEINTE
(GATHERING —) MANDAPA
(HUNTING —) SURROUND
(INFESTED —) FLYBELT
(LOW-LYING —) GLADE SWALE
COULEE COULIE GUTTER
(LUMINOUS —) AUREOLA AUREOLE
(MINE —) SQUEEZE
(NUCLEAR —) HEARTH ECUMENE
(OPEN —) COURT LAUND CAMPUS
SQUARE HAGGARD
(OVERGROWN —) COGONAL
(PASTURE —) SOUM
(PAVED —) CAUSEY
(PLOWED —) BREAK

(RESIDENTIAL —) BANLIEU
BANLIEUE
(SHOPPING —) MALL
(SLUM —) STEW
(SMALL —) AREOLA
(SMOKING —) BULLPEN
(STERN —) AFTERPART
(SUBURBAN —) ADDITION
FAUBOURG
(SUNKEN —) SAG
(SWAMPY —) SLASH
(TEST —) MILACRE
(TIDAL —) CLAMFLAT
(TRANSITION —) ECOTONE
(TREELESS —) SLICK
(TUMID —) CERE
(UNCLEARED —) BUSH
(UPLAND —) COTEAU
(VOLCANIC —) SOLFATARA
(WASTE —) FOREST
(WOODED —) HAG BOSK BOSQUE
(SUFF.) (GEOGRAPHIC —) GAEA
GEA
ARECA ARAK ARCHA BETEL
ARELI (FATHER OF —) GAD
ARENA AREA LIST OVAL RING RINK
COURT FIELD SCENE SCOPE
SPACE STAGE CIRCUS CIRQUE
REGION SPHERE COCKPIT
STADIUM TERRAIN THEATER
BULLRING
ARENACEOUS SANDY GRITTY
SABULOUS
AREOLA PIT AREA RING SPOT
SPACE
ARES MARS ENYALIUS GRADIVUS
QUIRINUS
(FATHER OF —) ZEUS JUPITER
(MOTHER OF —) ENYO HERA JUNO
(SON OF —) REMUS CYCNUS
ROMULUS
ARETE (FATHER OF —) DIONYSIUS
(HUSBAND OF —) DION ALCINOUS
(MOTHER OF —) ARISTOMACHE
AREUS (BROTHER OF —) TALAUS
LEODOCUS
(FATHER OF —) BIAS
(MOTHER OF —) PERO
ARGALA STORK MARABOU
ARGALI AMMON ARKAR AOUDAD
ARGAN IRONWOOD
ARGANTE (DAUGHTER OF —)
OCTAVIA ZERBINETTE
ARGENT LUNA MOON PEARL
WHITE BLANCH SILVER CRYSTAL
SHINING SILVERY

ARGENTINA
CAPITAL: BUENOSAIRES
COIN: PESO CENTAVO ARGENTINO
DANCE: TANGO CUANDO GAUCHO
FALLS: GRANDE IGUAZU
INDIAN: LULE GUARANI
LAKE: VIEDMA CARDIEL FAGNANO
MUSTERS
MEASURE: SINO VARA LEGUA
CUADRA FANEGA LASTRE
MANZANA
MOUNTAIN: TORO ANDES CHATO
LAUDO MAIPU POTRO CONICO
PISSIS RINCON FAMATINA
MURALLON OLIVARES
TRONADOR ZAPALERI

ACONCAGUA INCAHUASI
TUPUNGATO MERCEDARIO
LLULLAILLACO
PLAIN: PAMPA PAMPAS
PORT: ROSARIO
PROVINCE: CHACO JUJUY SALTA
CHUBUT CORDOBA FORMOSA
LARIOJA MENDOZA NEUQUEN
TUCUMAN MISIONES
PATAGONIA
REGION: CHACO PATAGONIA
RIVER: SALI ATUEL CHICO COYLE
DULCE LIMAY NEGRO PLATA
TEUCO BLANCO CHUBUT
CUARTO FLORES GRANDE
PARANA QUINTO SALADO
BERMEJO DESEADO MENDOZA
TERCERO TUNUYAN SENGUERR

TOWN: AZUL GOYA ORAN PUAN
BAHIA JUNIN LANUS LUJAN
METAN SALTA PARANA
RAWSON RUFINO VIEDMA
ZARATE BOLIVAR CORDOBA
DOLORES FORMOSA LABANDA
MENDOZA NEUQUEN POSADAS
RAFAELA ROSARIO TUCUMAN
USHUAIA GALLEGOS
CATAMARCA
VOLCANO: LANIN MAIPU DOMUYO
PETEROA TUPUNGATO
WATERFALL: IGUAZU
WEIGHT: LAST GRANO LIBRA
QUINTAL TONELADA

ARGES (BROTHER OF —) BRONTES
STEROPES
(FATHER OF —) URANUS
(MOTHER OF —) GE GAEA
ARGIA (FATHER OF —) OCEANUS
ADRASTUS
(HUSBAND OF —) INACHUS
POLYBUS POLYNICES
ARISTODEMUS
(MOTHER OF —) TETHYS
AMPHITHEA
(SON OF —) ARGUS PROCLES
EURYSTHENES
ARGIL CLAY ALUMINA
ARGIOPE (DAUGHTER OF —)
EUROPA
(HUSBAND OF —) AGENOR
(SON OF —) CILIX CADMUS
THASUS CERCYON PHINEUS
PHOENIX
ARGOL TARTAR
ARGOSY SHIP FLEET GALLEON
RAGUSYE
ARGOT CANT FLASH LINGO SLANG
JARGON PATOIS DIALECT
ARGUE JAW ARGY CHOP FUSS
MEAN MOOT MOVE SPAR WORD
ARGIE CAVIL ORATE PLEAD
PROVE TREAT ACCUSE ADDUCE
CAFFLE DEBATE EVINCE HASSLE
REASON ARRAIGN CONTEND
CONTEST COUNTER DISCUSS
DISPUTE WRANGLE ERGOTIZE
INDICATE MAINTAIN PERSUADE
QUESTION TRAVERSE
(— DEDUCTIVELY) SYLLOGIZE
(— SUBTLY) DISTINGUISH

ARGUER JAW
ARGUMENT ROW AGON BEEF
BLUE CASE FUSS MOOT PLEA
SPAR TEXT CLASH DEBAT INDEX
KNIFE LEMMA PROOF THEME
TOPIC BARNEY COMBAT CORKER
DEBATE DUSTUP ELENCH HASSLE
MATTER TUSSLE APAGOGE
CLAMPER DEFENCE DEFENSE
DILEMMA DISPUTE ESSENCE
FLUBDUB POLEMIC RHUBARB
SOPHISM SORITES SUMMARY
ABSTRACT CLINCHER COURSING
EVIDENCE SPARRING TRILEMMA
REASONING PARALOGISM
PERSUASION
(INVALID —) SOPHISM
(THEORETICAL —) ACADEMICS
ARGUMENTATION DEBATE
DISPUTE ERGOTISM
ARGUMENTATIVE ERISTIC
FRATCHY FORENSIC
ARGUS (FATHER OF —) ZEUS
JUPITER PHRIXUS
(MOTHER OF —) ARGIA NIOBE
CHALCIOPE
(SLAYER OF —) HERMES MERCURY
ARGUSFISH SCAT
ARHAT MONK LOHAN RAKAN
SAINT ARAHANT
ARIA AIR SOLO SONG TUNE
MELODY SORTIE ARIETTA
ARIETTE SORTITA
ARIADNE (FATHER OF —) MINOS
(HUSBAND OF —) THESEUS
(MOTHER OF —) PASIPHAE
ARIADNE AUF NAXOS
(CHARACTER IN —) ARIADNE
BACCHUS ZERBINETTA
(COMPOSER OF —) STRAUSS
ARIAN AGNOETE AGNOITE
HOMOEAN ANOMOIAN EUSEBIAN
ARID DRY BALD BARE DULL LEAN
BARREN DESERT JEJUNE MEAGER
DROUTHY PARCHED STERILE
THIRSTY DROUGHTY WITHERED
ARIDAI (FATHER OF —) HAMAN
ARIDATHA (FATHER OF —) HAMAN
ARIDITY DROUTH DROUGHT
SICCITY
ARIKARA REE
ARIL POD ARILLUS COATING
ARILLODE
ARIODANTE (COMPOSER OF —)
HANDEL
ARIODANTES (LOVER OF —)
GENEURA
ARISAI (FATHER OF —) HAMAN
ARISBE (FATHER OF —) MEROPS
(HUSBAND OF —) PRIAM
DARDANUS HYRTACUS
(SON OF —) ASIUS NISUS AESACUS
ARISE WAX COME FLOW FORM
GROW LIFT REAR RISE SOAR
STEM AWAKE BEGIN BUILD EXIST
ISSUE MOUNT RAISE SPRAY
STAND START SURGE TOWER
WAKEN ACCRUE AMOUNT
APPEAR ASCEND ATTAIN DERIVE
EMERGE HAPPEN KITTLE SPRING
DEVELOP EMANATE
EXSURGE PROCEED
REDOUND SOURDRE

ARISING LEVEE EMERGENT
(PREF.) (— WITHIN) IDIO
ARISTAEUS (DAUGHTER OF —)
MACRIS
(FATHER OF —) APOLLO
(MOTHER OF —) CYRENE
(SON OF —) ACTAEON
(WIFE OF —) AUTONOE
ARISTE (BROTHER OF —) CHRYSALE
ARISTO (BROTHER OF —)
SGANARELLE
ARISTOCRACY CLASS ELITE
GENTRY ARISTOI SAMURAI
NOBILITY OPTIMACY
ARISTOCRAT LORD NOBLE ARISTO
JUNKER GRANDEE PARVENU
EUPATRID OPTIMATE PATRICIAN
(RUSSIAN —) BOIAR BOYAR
BOYARD
(PL.) ARISTOI
ARISTOCRATIC HIGH TONY NOBLE
QUALITY CAVALIER BELGRAVIAN
ARISTODEMUS (BROTHER OF —)
TEMENUS CRESPHONTES
(FATHER OF —) ARISTOMACHUS
(SON OF —) PROCLES
EURYSTHENES
(WIFE OF —) ARGEIA
ARISTOTELIAN PERIPATETIC
ARITHMETIC SUM AUGRIM
ALGORISM
ARITHMOMETER MULTIPLIER

ARIZONA

CAPITAL: PHOENIX
COUNTY: GILA PIMA YUMA PINAL
APACHE MOHAVE NAVAJO
COCHISE YAVAPAI COCONINO
GREENLEE MARICOPA
SANTACRUZ
INDIAN: HOPI PIMA YUMA
NAVAHO NAVAJO PAPAGO
HUALAPAI
MOUNTAIN: BANGS GROOM
LEMMON TURRET HUALPAI
PASTORA MERIDIAN
MOUNTAIN RANGE: GILA KOFA
MOHAWK GALIURO HUALPAI
AQUARIUS BUCKSKIN
PEAK: HUMPHREYS
RIVER: GILA SALT ZUNI VERDE
PUERCO COLORADO
STATE BIRD: CACTUSWREN
STATE FLOWER: SAGUARO
STATE NICKNAME: OCOTILLO
STATE TREE: PALOVERDE
TOWN: AJO ELOY MESA NACO
YUMA GLOBE LEUPP TEMPE
BISBEE JEROME MCNARY
SALOME TOLTEC TUCSON
CLIFTON CORTARO KINGMAN
MORENCI NOGALES PHOENIX
SAFFORD FREDONIA PRESCOTT
FLAGSTAFF TOMBSTONE

ARJUN KUMBUK
ARJUNA (FATHER OF —) PANDU
(SON OF —) ABHIMANYU
ARK BIN BOX BOAT SHIP BARGE
CHEST HUTCH BASKET COFFER
REFUGE WANGAN RETREAT
SHELTER WANIGAN FLATBOAT
ARKANSAN ARKANSAWYER

ARKANSAS

CAPITAL: LITTLEROCK
COUNTY: LEE CLAY DREW PIKE
POLK POPE YELL BOONE CROSS
DESHA IZARD LOGAN SHARP
STONE BAXTER CHICOT LONOKE
SEARCY CALHOUN PRAIRIE
PULASKI OUACHITA
INDIAN: CADDO OSAGE QUAPAW
CHOCTAW CHEROKEE
LAKE: CONWAY NIMROD GREESON
NORFORK OUACHITA
MOUNTAIN: RICH GAYLOR
MAGAZINE
MOUNTAIN RANGE: OZARK
OUACHITA
NATIVE: TOOTHPICK
NICKNAME: WONDER
RIVER: RED WHITE SALINE
BUFFALO CURRENT COSSATOT
OUACHITA
STATE BIRD: MOCKINGBIRD
STATE FLOWER: APPLE BLOSSOM
STATE TREE: SHORTLEAFPINE
TOWN: COY CUY KEO OLA ROE
ULM ALMA BONO CASA DELL
DIAZ MORO ENOLA PERLA
RISON RONDO WYNNE ALICIA
JASPER PIGGOTT

ARKOSE ARENITE SANDSTONE
ARLECCHINO (CHARACTER IN —)
LEANDRO BOMBASTO COLUMBINE
HARLEQUIN
(COMPOSER OF —) BUSONI
ARLESIANA, L' (CHARACTER IN —)
ROSA MAMMAI METIFIO VIVETTE
FEDERICO
(COMPOSER OF —) CILEA
ARM FIN OAR TOE BOOM HEEL
LIMB WING BLADE BOUGH CRANE
EQUIP FENCE FIORD FIRTH FJORD
FORCE GARDY INLET MIGHT
OXTER POWER RIFLE SNORD
STOCK BRANCH CRUTCH ENERGY
FRETUM GIBBET MEMBER OUTFIT
PINION RADIAL SLEEVE TAPPET
WEAPON CATCHER DERRICK
DRAWARM FLIPPER FOREARM
FORTIFY FURNISH GARNISH
HARNESS OCKSTER PREPARE
PROTECT PROVIDE QUILLON
SUPPORT ARMORIAL CROSSARM
FOLLOWER FORELIMB PULLDOWN
SOUPBONE STRENGTH TRANSEPT
(— HOLDING FLINT) HAMMER
(— OF BARNACLE) CIRRUS CIRRHUS
(— OF CHAIR) ELBOW
(— OF CRANE) JIB GIBBET
RAMHEAD
(— OF GIN) START
(— OF PROPELLER) BLADE
(— OF RECORD PLAYER) PICKUP
(— OF SEA) COVE FLOW MEER
MERE BRACE CANAL FIRTH FRITH
GRAIN FRETUM ESTUARY
EURIPUS
(— OF SPINNING MULE) SICKLE
(— OF WINDMILL) VANE WHIP
(— WITH GAFF) HEEL
(INDEX —) DIOPTER
(IRON —) CRANE

(LEVER —) SWEEP NIGGER
(PITCHING —) SOUPBONE
(PL.) ARMORY ARMAMENT
(PREF.) BRACHI
ARMADA NAVY FLEET FLOTILLA
ARMADILLO APAR PEBA TATU
APARA POYOU TATOU BOLITA
MATACO MATICO MULITA
PELUDO DASYPOD TATOUAY
TATUASU EDENTATE KABASSOU
LORICATE PANGOLIN
ARMAMENT ARMADA BATTERY
ARMATURE ARMING KEEPER
LIFTER
ARMBAND BRASSARD
ARMCHAIR BERGERE FAUTEUIL
ARMED FLUTE HEELED DAGGERED
WEAPONED

ARMENIA
ANCIENT CAPITAL: ANI ARTASHAT
ARTAXATA
ANCIENT NAME: MINNI
CAPITAL: ERIVAN
FORTRESS: EREBUNI
HERO: ARA ARAM HAIK ARAME
VARTAN
KING: ASHOT GAGIK TRDAT ZAREH
DIKRAN ARTAKIAS ARTASHES
TIGRANES ZARIADES
KINGDOM: URARTU VANNIC
CILICIA SOPHENE ARDSRUNI
LAKE: VAN SEVAN URMIA
MOUNTAIN: ARA ALAGEZ ARARAT
TAURUS ALADAGH ARAGATS
KARABAKH
NATIVE: ARMEN GOMER
RIVER: KUR ARAS KURA ARAKS
CYRUS HALYS ZANGA ARAXES
RAZDAN TIGRIS EUPHRATES
SAINT: SAHAK MESROP
TOWN: VAN SIVAS BITLIS EREVAN
ERIVAN ERZURUM TRABZON
YEREVAN

ARMENIAN ERMYN HADJI HAIKH
ARMFUL LOCK YAFFLE
ARMHOLE MAIL SCYE OXTER
ARMSCYE ARMSEYE ARMSIZE
ARMIDE (CHARACTER IN —) ARMIDA
RINALDO
(COMPOSER OF —) GLUCK
ARMINIO (COMPOSER OF —)
HANDEL
ARMISTICE LULL PEACE TRUCE
INDUCIAE
ARMLET BANGLE TABLET TORQUE
ARMHOOP
ARMONI (FATHER OF —) SAUL
(MOTHER OF —) RIZPAH
**ARMOR (AND SPECIFIC PIECES
THEREOF)** ARMS BACK BOOT
EGIS JAMB MAIL TACE WEED
ACTON AMURE BARDS BRACE
CUISH CULET DORON GUARD
GUIGE JAMBE PIECE PLATE
PROOF SCALE STEEL TAPUL
TASSE TRUSS ARMLET ARMOUR
BEAVER BRINIE BRUNIE BYRNIE
CAMAIL CORIUM COUTER CRANET
CUISSE GORGET GRAITH GREAVE
JAMBER POLEYN RONDEL SECRET
SHIELD TASSET THORAX TONLET

TUILLE VOIDER AILETTE
ARMHOOP BESAGNE BROIGNE
CORSLET CUIRASS DEFENSE
EPAULET HARNESS HAUBERK
JAZERAN KNEELET LAMBOYS
PALETTE PANOPLY PLACATE
POITREL REREDOS ROUNDEL
SABATON VENTAIL BRASSARD
PAULDRON RAMENTUM
VAMBRACE BAINBERGS
RONDACHEPALLETTE
(— ON TREE) TROPHY
(— PLATE) TUILLE
(ELBOW —) CUBITIERE
(FOOT —) SABATON SABBATON
SOLLERET
(HEAD —) CASQUE HELMET
PALLET SCONCE
(HORSE —) BARB BARD BARDE
CRINET CHAMFRON CRINIERE
CHAMFRAIN
(LEATHER —) CORIUM
(LEG —) BOOT JAMB CUISH JAMBE
CUISSE GREAVE JAMBER TUILLE
JAMBEAU CHAUSSES
(NECK —) COLLAR GORGET
(PADDED —) GAMBESON
(SUIT OF —) CAST STAND
(PREF.) HOPL(O)
ARMOR-BEARER SQUIRE ARMIGER
CUSTREL
ARMORED PANZER
ARMORER GUNSMITH ARTIFICER
ARMORICAN BRETON
ARMORY ARSENAL HERALDRY
ARMPIT ALA OXTER AXILLA
ARMHOLE
ARMS TACKLE
(PREF.) HOPL(O)
**ARMS AND THE MAN (AUTHOR OF
—)** SHAW
(CHARACTER IN —) LOUKA RAINA
NICOLA PETKOFF SERGIUS
CATHERINE BLUNTSCHLI
ARMY FERD HERE HOST IMPI LEVY
MAIN ARRAY CROWD FORCE
HERSE HORDE POWER RANKS
ZOMBI COHORT HONVED LEGION
NUMBER THRONG TROOPS
MILITIA BATTALIA CHIVALRY
MILITARY
(HOSTILE —) FOE
(VOLUNTEER —) VOLAR
(PL.) SABAOTH
(PREF.) STRATO
**ARMY OFFICER (ALSO SEE
SOLDIER)**
ARMYWORM GRASSWORM
ARNE (FATHER OF —) AEOLUS
(HUSBAND OF —) METAPONTUS
(MOTHER OF —) THEA
(SON OF —) AELOUS BOEOTUS
ARNOTTO ROUCOU
AROD (FATHER OF —) GAD
AROID APII ARAD TARO APIUM
KRUBI TANIA KONJAK TANIER
YAUTIA PINUELA CALADIUM
CUNJEVOI MOCOMOCO
AROMA NOSE ODOR NIDOR SAVOR
SCENT SMELL SNUFF SPICE
FLAVOR BOUQUET PERFUME
REDOLENCE
(— OF WINE) BLOOM

AROMATIC BALMY SPICY SWEET
MASTIC ODOROUS PIQUANT
PUNGENT FRAGRANT REDOLENT
SPICEFUL
AROUND NEAR UMBE ABOUT
CIRCA CIRCUM ENVIRON
(PREF.) AMBI AMPHI CIRCUM
PERI
AROUSAL INDUCTION
AROUSE SOW CALL CITE FIRE GAIN
HEAT MOVE REAR SPUR STIR
WAKE WHET ADAWE ALARM
ALERT AWAKE EVOKE FLESH
PIQUE RAISE RALLY ROUSE
ROUST SHAKE STEER WAKEN
ABRAID AWAKEN ELICIT EXCITE
FOMENT INCITE INDUCE KINDLE
REVIVE SUMMON THRILL
ACTUATE AGITATE CONNOTE
INCENSE INFLAME INSPIRE
PROVOKE SUGGEST INSPIRIT
(— DISPLEASURE) AGGRAVATE
(— ENMITY) ESTRANGE
(— WRATH) SPLEEN
ARPEGGIATE BREAK
ARPEGGIO SWEEP ROULADE
FLOURISH
(— EFFECT) RASGADO
ARPHAXAD (FATHER OF —) SHEM
ARRACACHA APIO ARRA
ARRACK ARAK RACK ARAKI
RACKAPEE
ARRAIGN TRY CITE ARGUE PEACH
ACCUSE CHARGE IMPUTE INDICT
INDITE SUMMON APPOINT
IMPEACH DENOUNCE
ARRANGE DO FIX LAY RAY SET
CAST COMB EDIT FILE FORM
PLAN PLAT RAIL RULE SIDE SIZE
SORT TIER TIFT WORK ADAPT
AGREE ALIGN ALINE ARRAY BESEE
CURRY DRAPE DRESS ETTLE
FANCY FRAME GRADE ORDER
PITCH RANGE SCORE SHAPE
SHIFT SPACE STALL TRICK
ADJUST BRANCH CODIFY DAIKER
DESIGN DEVISE FETTLE INFORM
ORDAIN SETTLE SOLUTE TAILYE
ADDRESS APPOINT BESPEAK
CATALOG COLLATE COMPONE
COMPOSE CONCERT DISPOSE
ENRANGE GRADATE MARSHAL
PERMUTE PREPARE REDRESS
SERIATE TAILZEE TAILZIE
ALPHABET CLASSIFY CONCLUDE
ORGANIZE REGULATE TABULATE
COLLOCATE CONJOBBLE
NEGOTIATE STIPULATE
ORCHESTRATE
(— BEFOREHAND) FORLAY
FORELAY
(— FANTASTICALLY) HARLEQUINIZE
(— FASTIDIOUSLY) PREEN
(— HAIR) SET TED COIF TRUSS
COIFFE
(— HARMONIOUSLY) GRADATE
(— IN FLOCKS) HIRSEL HIRSLE
(— IN FOLDS) DRAPE
(— IN LAYERS) DESS TIER
(— IN ROW) RACE
(— STRAW) HAULM
(— SYSTEMATICALLY) DIGEST
(— WITH BEST AT TOP) DEACON

ARRANGEMENT FIX FLY LAY RAY
DEAL FLOW PLAT RANK TIFF
ARRAY BUILD DRAPE INDEX
ORDER SETUP BORDER DESIGN
HOOKUP LAYOUT SCHEME
SETOUT SYNTAX SYSTEM TREATY
BLEEDER INTERIM POSTURE
TONTINE ATTITUDE CONTRACT
DISPOSAL GROUPING POSITURE
SEQUENCE ORDONNANCE
ORIENTATION BANDSTRATION
ORCHESTRATION
(— IN LOCK) DETECTOR
(— OF BRISTLES) CHAETOTAXY
(— OF CHESS PAWNS) CHAIN
(— OF COMPUTER ELEMENTS)
ARRAY
(— OF DRAPERIES) CAST
(— OF FLOWERS) CASCADE
CORSAGE IKEBANA PARTERRE
(— OF GRADES) CURVE
(— OF GUNS) ARMADA
(— OF HAIRDO) FORETOP
(— OF HAIRS) SCOPA
(— OF HOOKS) GIG
(— OF LOOM BARS) GRIFF GRIFFE
(— OF ROCKS) BEDDING
(— OF TACKLE) BURTON
(— OF TIMBER) ANCHOR
(— OF TROOPS) ECHELON
(CIRCULAR —) CYCLE
(DISHONEST —) CROSS
(GEOMETRICAL —) LATTICE
(ORDERED —) PERMUTATION
(SECRET —) PACK
(TRADITIONAL —) AKOLUTHIA
AKOLOUTHIA
(PREF.) TAX(EO)(I)(O)
(LACK OF —) ATAXO
(SUFF.) OSIS TACTIC TAXIS TAXY
ARRANGING ORDONNANT
(JAPANESE ART OF FLOWER —)
IKEBANA
ARRANT BAD THIEF OUTLAW
ROBBER VAGRANT OUTRIGHT
PRECIOUS RASCALLY
ARRAS ORRIS ARISTE DRAPERY
TAPESTRY
ARRASTRA TAHONA
ARRAU JURARA
ARRAY DON DUB FIG ARMY BUSK
DECK DOLL FYRD GALA GARB
HOST POMP RAIL RANK ROBE
VEST ADORN ALIGN ALINE ATOUR
DRESS EQUIP HABIT HARKA
HEDGE ORDER ADIGHT AGUISE
ATTIRE ATTRAP BEDECK CLOTHE
DEVISE FETTLE FINERY GRAITH
INVEST MUSTER PLIGHT SERIES
SETOUT SHROUD ADDRESS
AFFAITE AFFLICT APPAREL
ARRANGE BATTERY BEDIGHT
COMPANY DISPLAY DISPOSE
ENVELOP FURNISH FYRDUNG
MARSHAL PANOPLY REPAREL
ACCOUTER
(— OF CHEMICALS) ARA
(— OF GUNS) BROADSIDE
(— OF TROOPS) PAREL
(— OF WEAPONS) ARMORY
(— TASTELESSLY) DAUB
(BATTLE —) ACIES HERSE
BATTALIA

ARRAYED HABITED ABULYEIT
ARREAR DEBT BEHIND UNPAID
ARRIERE
(IN —S) BACK BEHIND
ARREST CAP COP FIX FOB LAG
NAB NIP VAG BALK CURB FALL
GLOM GRAB HALT HOLD JAIL
KEEP NAIL NICK PULL REST SHOP
SIST STAY STOP ARRET CATCH
CHECK DELAY PINCH REEST SEIZE
STILL STUNT ATTACH BRIDLE
COLLAR DECREE DETAIN ENGAGE
FINGER HINDER PLEDGE RETARD
SLOUGH SNEEZE THWART
CAPTION CAPTURE CUSTODY
SUSPEND IMPRISON OBSTRUCT
RESTRAIN
(— OF BLEEDING) HEMOSTASIS
(— OF DEVELOPMENT) ABORTION
(PUT UNDER —) BUST
ARRESTER (SPARK —) BONNET
ARRESTING BOLD SEIZING
MAGNETIC PLEASING STRIKING
ARRET EDICT ARREST DECREE
DECISION JUDGMENT
ARRHA HANDGELD
ARRIS PIEN ANGLE PIEND ARRIDGE
ARRIVAL COMER IKBAL VENUE
ADVENT COMING INCOMING
REACHING
(— TIME RECORD) OS
(NEW —) ROOINEK
ARRIVE GO SEY COME FALL FLOW
GAIN LAND LEND RIVE LIGHT
OCCUR REACH WORTH ACCEDE
APPEAR ATTAIN HAPPEN OBTAIN
UPCOME COMPASS
(— AT) GET HIT FIND GAIN HENT
MAKE BRING EDUCE FETCH
GUESS SEIZE ATTAIN DERIVE
ESTIMATE
ARRIVED-IN DONE
ARROBA ROVE
ARROGANCE PRIDE SWANK
TUMOR BOWWOW HUBRIS
BOBANCE CONCEIT DISDAIN
EGOTISM HAUTEUR STOMACH
BOLDNESS SUCCUDRY SURQUIDY
ARROGANT BOLD COXY HIGH
MOOD COBBY COCKY GREAT
HUFFY JOLLY LOFTY PROUD
STOUT SURLY WLONK ASSUME
CHESTY FIERCE LORDLY UPPISH
UPPITY WANTON FORWARD
FROSTED HAUGHTY HAUTAIN
HUFFISH POMPOUS STATELY
TOPPING AFFECTED ASSUMING
CAVALIER FASTUOUS IMPUDENT
SNUFFING SUPERIOR TUMOROUS
OVERBEARING OVERWEENING
ARROGATE GRAB TAKE CLAIM
SEIZE USURP ASSUME ADROGATE
ARROW FLO PIN ROD SEL BOLT
DART REED SELF SELL SHOT VIRE
BLUNT DEATH FLANE ROVER
SHAFT ARCHER FLIGHT GANYIE
GARROT QUARRY STRIX TACKLE
WEAPON BOBTAIL DOGBOLT
MISSILE POINTER PROJECT
QUARREL SAGITTA SPINNER
FISHTAIL FORKHEAD
(— ARUM) TUCKAHOE
(— IN GRASS) GREEN SNAKE

(— IN LEG OF STAND) FOOT
(FIRE —) MALLEOLUS
(PART OF —) TIP BUTT HEAD NOCK
PILE POINT SHAFT FEATHER
FLETCHING
(POISONED —) DERRID SUMPIT
(WOBBLING —) FISHTAIL
(PREF.) BELO(NO) HASTATO
SAGITTI SAGITTO TOX(I)(ICO)(O)
ARROWHEAD BUNT FORK HEAD
PILE FLUKE POINT NEOLITH
ARTIFACT CROWBILL FORKHEAD
SPICULUM
ARROWROOT PIA ARUM MUSA
SAGU ARARU CANNA TACCA
TIKOR ARARAO CURCUMA
ARROWSMITH (AUTHOR OF —)
LEWIS
(CHARACTER IN —) MAX ALMUS
JOYCE LEORA SILVA TERRY
LANYON MARTIN GUSTAVE
WICKETT GOTTLIEB SONDELIUS
ARROWSMITH PICKERBAUGH
ARROWWORM SAGITTA
CHAETOGNATH
ARROYO DRAW BROOK CREEK
GULCH GULLY HONDO ZANJA
RAVINE STREAM CHANNEL
BARRANCA BARRANCO
ARSENAL ARMORY SUPPLY
MAGAZINE
ARSENOPYRITE MISPICKEL
ARSHIN ARCHIN ALTSCHIN
(ONE-24TH OF —) PARMAK
PARMACK
ARSINOE (DAUGHTER OF —) ERIOPIS
(FATHER OF —) PHEGEUS
LEUCIPPUS
(HUSBAND OF —) ALCMAEON
(MOTHER OF —) PHILODICE
(SISTER OF —) PHOEBE HILAIRA
ARSIS BEAT ICTUS ACCENT
RHYTHM UPBEAT DOWNBEAT
ARSON FIRE CRIME FELONY
BURNING
ARSONIST ARSONITE
ARSPHENAMINE SIX SALVARSAN
ART WILE CRAFT KNACK KUNST
MAGIC SKILL TRADE MISTER
TECHNE ARTWORK CALLING
CUNNING DESCANT DISCANT
FACULTY FINESSE MYSTERY
SCIENCE APTITUDE ARTIFICE
BUSINESS LEARNING PRACTICE
PRACTISE
(— OF APPLYING TESTS) DOCIMASY
(— OF BLAZONING) ARMORY
(— OF CALCULATING) ALGORISM
ALGORITHM
(— OF DEFENSE) SKIRMISH
(— OF FLOWER ARRANGEMENT)
IKEBANA
(— OF HEALING) LEECHCRAFT
(— OF HORSEMANSHIP) MANEGE
(— OF PREPARING COLORS)
GUMPTION
(— OF SPEECH) RHETORIC
(— OF TYING KNOTS IN PATTERN)
MACRAME
(DIABOLIC —) DEVILRY DEVILTRY
(DRAMATIC —) STAGE
(JAPANESE — MOVEMENT) YAMATO
YAMATOE

(JUNK —) NEODADA
(LEG —) CHEESECAKE
(MAGIC —) WITHERCRAFT
(MYSTERIOUS —) CABALA KABALA
CABBALA KABBALA QABBALA
CABBALAH KABBALAH QABBALAH
(OCCULT —) THEURGY
(SHODDY —) BONDIEUSERIE
(TYPE OF —) STREETSCAPE
(PREF.) TECHNI TECHNO TYP(I)(O)
(SUFF.) ERY SHIP TECHNICS
TECHNY TYPAL TYPE TYPIC TYPY
(RELATING TO —) METRIC
ARTAXERXES (COMPOSER OF —)
ARNE
ARTEMIS UPIS DELIA DIANA
PHOEBE CYNTHIA AMARYSIA
ARTERY WAY PATH ROAD AORTA
PULSE ROUTE COURSE DENTAL
FACIAL RADIAL STREET VESSEL
ANONYMA CAROTID COELIAC
CONDUIT HIGHWAY SCIATIC
VAGINAL CEREBRAL CERVICAL
CORONARY DORSALIS EMULGENT
PROFUNDA
ARTFUL APT FLY SLY FOXY WILY
AGILE DOWNY PAWKY SUAVE
ADROIT CLEVER CRAFTY FACILE
PRETTY QUAINT SCHEMY
SHREWD SMOOTH TRICKY
CROOKED CUNNING KNOWING
PLAITED POLITIC PRACTIC
SUBTILE VULPINE
DEXTROUS SCHEMING
STEALTHY
ARTFULNESS CUNNING ARTIFICE
SUBTLETY
ART GRAY QUAKER SEAMIST
ARTHRITIS GOUT CARPITIS
ARTHROPOD GOLACH GOLOCH
SPIDER CHILOPOD DIPLOPOD
PERIPATUS
ARTICHOKE BUR CANADA CYNARA
CARDOON CHOROGI CROSNES
KNOTROOT
ARTICLE A AN YE LOT ONE THE
BOOK ITEM TERM BRIEF CHEAT
ESSAY GEANE PAPER PIECE
PLANK POINT STORY THEME
THING CLAUSE DETAIL LEADER
NOTICE OBJECT REPORT FEATURE
BROCHURE CAUSERIE DOCTRINE
PARTICLE POSTFACE TREATISE
(— CLOTHING) DUD DIKO
APRON CLOUT DICKY FANCY
THING CASUAL DICKEY GARMENT
COINTISE CREATION
(— OF FOOD) CATE KNACK
(— OF FURNITURE) STICK
(— OF LITTLE WORTH) DIDO
(— OF SILK) SQUEEZE
(— OF TRADE) PADNAG
(— OF UNUSUAL SIZE) IMPERIAL
(—S OF FAITH) CREDENDA
(—S OF MERCHANDISE) CHAFFER
(CAST-IRON —S) KENTLEDGE
(CHEAP —) CAMELOT
(DECORATIVE —) LACKER LACQUER
(FANCY —) CONCEIT
(FIVE —S) HAND
(GENUINE —) GOODS
(HANDICRAFT —) BOONDOGGLE
(INFERIOR —S) SHODDY

(METAL —S) BATTERY
(MISCELLANEOUS —S) SUNDRIES
(NONDESCRIPT —) DODAD
DOODAB DOODAD WHATNOT
(SECONDHAND —) JUNK
(SHOWY —) FRIPPERY
(VALUABLE —S) SWAG
(WORTHLESS —) TRANGAM
ARTICULATE BACK JOIN CLEAR
FRAME JOINT SPEAK UNITE
UTTER VOCAL ACCENT FLUENT
VERBAL EXPRESS JOINTED
PHONATE DISTINCT SYLLABLE
ARTICULATED BACK BLADE
DENTAL DORSAL LABIAL JOINTED
ALVEOLAR CEREBRAL
VERTEBRATE
ARTICULATION NODE JOINT
VOICE SUTURE ARTHRON
JUNCTURE SYNTAXIS
(DEFECTIVE —) LALLATION
LAMBDACISM
ARTIFACT CELT DISC DISK BATON
GUACA HUACA AMGARN BRONZE
EOLITH FABRIC GORGET REJECT
RONDEL SAGAIE SKEWER
ABRADER ARTEFAC DISCOID
RACLOIR SCRAPER ARTEFACT
DATEMARK RONDELLE TRANCHET
(PL.) CACHE CERAUNIA
ARTIFICE ART GIN JET GAUD
HOAX JOUK PLAN PLOT RUSE
TURN WILE BLIND CHEAT COVIN
CRAFT CROCK CROOK DODGE
DRAFT FEINT FETCH FRAUD
GUILE SHIFT SKILL STALL TRAIN
TRICK CAUTEL DECEIT DEVICE
DOUBLE ENGINE CHICANE
COMPASS CUNNING DODGERY
DRAUGHT EVASION FINESSE
SHUFFLE SLEIGHT COZENAGE
DISGUISE DOUBLING INTRIGUE
MANAGERY MANEUVER PRACTICE
PRACTISE PRETENSE STRATEGY
TRICKERY WINDLASS
(PL.) CABAL CRANS
ARTIFICER WRIGHT ARTIFEX
WORKMAN DAEDALUS LAPIDARY
MECHANIC OPIFICER TVASHTAR
TVASHTRI
ARTIFICIAL CUTE SHAM BOGUS
DUMMY FAKED FALSE ARTFUL
ERSATZ FORCED FORGED UNREAL
ASSUMED BASTARD FEIGNED
PLASTIC AFFECTED FABULOUS
FALSETTO POSTICHE POSTIQUE
SPURIOUS
(NOT —) REAL NATURAL
(OVERLY —) ALEXANDRIAN
(SOMETHING —) CAMP
ARTIFICIALITY MANNERISM
ARTILLERY (OR PIECE THEREOF)
ARMS GUNS DRAKE SAKER
CANNON MINION HEAVIES
LANTACA LANTAKA CANNONRY
ORDNANCE
(— FIRE) STONK RAFALE
ARTILLERYMAN GUN GUNNER
LASCAR REDLEG LASHKAR
ENGINEER TOPECHEE
ARTISAN FEVER SMITH ARTIST
COOPER ARTIFEX TARKHAN
WORKMAN KAMMALAN LETTERER

MECHANIC OPIFICER OPERATIVE
SILVERSMITH
ARTISANSHIP FOLKCRAFT
ARTIST (ALSO SEE PAINTER) DAB
NABI POET ACTOR ADEPT BRUSH
HILDA RAPIN DANCER ETCHER
EXPERT FICTOR MASTER SINGER
WIZARD ARTISAN ARTISTE
ARTSMAN FAUVIST OPERANT
PAINTER PONTIST SCHEMER
ANIMATOR COLORIST FUSINIST
IDEALIST LADISLAW LETTERER
MAGICIAN MUSICIAN SCULPTOR
SKETCHER STIPPLER PASTELIST
PRIMITIVE MINIMALIST
PASTELLIST
(— SCHOOL) LUMINISM
(SIDEWALK —) SCREEVER
(PL.) SCHOOL
ARTISTIC ARTLY DAEDAL EXPERT
ESTHETIC PAINTERLY
(— MATERIAL) KITSCH
(— QUALITY) VERTU VIRTU
ARTISTRY FOLKCRAFT
ARTLESS NAIF OPEN FRANK NAIVE
PLAIN SEELY CANDID RUSTIC
SIMPLE GIRLISH NATURAL
INNOCENT
ARTS TRIVIUM
ARTY CHICHI
ARUM ARAD TARO AROID CALALU
DRAGON TAWKEE WAMPEE
MANDRAKE TUCKAHOE
ARVIRAGUS CADWAL
(FATHER OF —) CYMBELINE
(WIFE OF —) DORIGEN
ARYAN MEDE SLAV OSSET NORDIC
OSSETE
(NOT —) ANARYA
ARZA (SLAYER OF —) ZIMRI
AS S SO ALS FOR HOW QUA ALSO
INTO LIKE SOME THAT THUS TILL
WHEN EQUAL QUOAD SINCE
WHILE BRONZE WHENAS
BECAUSE EQUALLY SIMILAR
QUATENUS
(— FAR AS) TO INTO QUATENUS
(— IT WERE) FAIRLY
(— LONG AS) SOBEIT
(— MUCH) ALSMEKILL
(— SOON) ALSOON ASTITE
ALSWITH DIRECTLY
(— TO) QUOAD
(— WELL) EVEN
(— WELL AS) FORBY FORBYE
(— YET) HITHERTO
ASA (FATHER OF —) ABIJAH
ASAFETIDA HING LASER
FERULA
ASAHEL (BROTHER OF —) JOAB
(MOTHER OF —) ZERUIAH
(SLAYER OF —) ABNER
(SON OF —) JONATHAN
(UNCLE OF —) DAVID
ASANDER (BROTHER OF —)
PARMENION
(FATHER OF —) PHILOTAS
ASAPH (FATHER OF —) BECHERIAH
(SON OF —) JOAH ASARELAH
ASARABACCA HAZEL FOALFOOT
ASAREEL (FATHER OF —)
JEHALELEEL
ASARELAH (FATHER OF —) ASAPH

ASBESTOS ABBEST XYLITE
AMIANTH ABSISTOS ALBESTON
AMIANTUS WOODROCK
(BLUE —) CROCIDOLITE
ASCALAPHUS (BROTHER OF —)
IALMENUS
(FATHER OF —) ARES MARS
ACHERON
(MOTHER OF —) ORPHNE GORGYRA
ASTYOCHE
(SLAYER OF —) DEIPHOBUS
ASCEND UP STY RISE SOAR STYE
UPGO ARISE CLIMB MOUNT
SCALE STAIR TOWER AMOUNT
ASPIRE BREAST CLIMAX UPRISE
CLAMBER UPCLIMB ESCALATE
PROGRESS
ASCENDANCY SWAY POWER
CONTROL MASTERY SUCCESS
DOMINION OWERANCE
PRESTIGE
ASCENDANT MOUNTANT
ASSURGENT
ASCENDING ANODAL ANODIC
ORIENT UPHILL UPWARD
ANABATIC ASPIRANT
SUBERECT
(— WITHOUT A TURN) FLYING
ASCENSION APOTHEOSIS
ASCENT STY HILL RAMP RISE RIST
UPGO CLIMB GLORY GRADE
MOUNT RAISE SCEND SLOPE
STEEP STEPS STILL UPWAY
SOURCE STAIRS UPCOME
UPGANG UPHILL UPRISE UPWITH
INCLINE SCALING UPGRADE
UPSWING EMINENCE GRADIENT
ASCERTAIN GET SEE SET TRY FEEL
FIND TELL COUNT GLEAN LEARN
PITCH PROVE ASSURE ATTAIN
FIGURE ANALYSE ANALYZE
APPRISE APPRIZE COMPUTE
MEASURE UNEARTH DISCOVER
ASCETIC NUN MONK SOFI SUFI
YATI YOGI DANDY FAKIR FRIAR
SADHU SOFEE STOIC YOGIN
CHASTE ESSENE HERMIT SADDHU
SEVERE SOOFEE STRICT ADAMITE
AUSTERE BHIKSHU DEVOTEE
EREMITE RECLUSE SRAMANA
STYLITE TAPASVI AVADHUTA
MARABOUT NAZARITE SANNYASI
(PL.) THERAPEUTAE
ASCIDIAN POLYP CUNGEBOI
CUNGEVOI TETHYDAN TUNICATE
ASCIDIUM PITCHER VASCULUM
ASCOCARP ASCOMA
ASCOGONIUM ARCHICARP
ASCOMA CUPULE
ASCRIBABLE DUE
ASCRIBE LAY ARET EVEN GIVE
APPLY BLAME COUNT GUESS
IMPLY INFER PLACE REFER TITLE
ACCUSE ALLEGE ARETTE ASSIGN
ATTACH CHARGE CREDIT IMPUTE
PREFER RECKON RELATE ASCRIVE
ENTITLE ACCREDIT ARROGATE
DEDICATE INSCRIBE
INTITULE
ASCRIPTION LAUD CREDIT
ADDITION
ASCUS BAG SAC THECA ASCELLUS
ASEA LOST ADDLED ADRIFT

PUZZLED SAILING CONFUSED
ASEMIA ASYMBOLIA
ASENATH (FATHER OF —)
POTIPHERAH
(HUSBAND OF —) JOSEPH
(SON OF —) EPHRAIM MANASSEH
ASEXUAL AGAMIC AGAMOUS
(PREF.) AGAM(O)
ASH AS ALS ASE ASS FIG RON
COKE SORB ARTAR ASHEN EMBER
FRAIN ROWAN CINDER CORPSE
DOTTEL DOTTLE WICKEN CLINKER
RESIDUE DOGBERRY FRAXINUS
HOOPWOOD WINETREE
(SILKY —) CEDAR
(PL.) ASE AXAN KELP SOIL ASHEN
VAREC WASTE BREEZE CINDERS
PULVERIN
ASHAMED MEAN NACE NAIS
ABASHED HANGDOG HONTOUS
SHAMEFACED
ASHBEL (FATHER OF —) BENJAMIN
ASH-BLOND CENDRE
ASH-COLORED CINEREAL
CINEREOUS
ASHEN WAN GRAY GREY PALE
WAXEN WHITE PALLID GHASTLY
BLANCHED CINEREAL
ASHER (FATHER OF —) JACOB
(MOTHER OF —) ZILPAH
ASHES (— OF CREMATED BODY)
CREMAINS
(PREF.) CINE SPODO TEPHRA
TEPHRO
ASHKENAZ (FATHER OF —) GOMER
ASHKOKO CONY DAMAN HYRAX
ASHLAR ASELAR RANGEWORK
ASHORE ACOST ALAND AGROUND
BEACHED STRANDED
ASHTAVAKRA (FATHER OF —)
KAHODA
ASHTRAY SPITKID SPITKIT
ASHUR FEROHER
(FATHER OF —) HEZRON
(MOTHER OF —) ABIAH
(WIFE OF —) HELAH
ASHVATH (FATHER OF —) JAPHLET
ASHWEED GOUTWEED
ASIA (FATHER OF —) OCEANUS
(HUSBAND OF —) IAPETUS
(MOTHER OF —) TETHYS
(SON OF —) ATLAS EPIMETHEUS
PROMETHEUS

ASIA
(ALSO SEE SPECIFIC COUNTRIES)
DESERT: GOBI TAKLAMAKAN
LAKE: ARAL URMIA BAYKAL
CASPIAN BALKHASH
MOUNTAIN: FUJI DJAJA JANNU
KAMET PAMIR ARARAT
KUNGUR KUNLUN LHOTSE
MAKALU MUZTAG NOSHAQ
NUPTSE SEMERU TRIVOR
EVEREST RATHONG
ANNAPURNA
NATION: IRAN IRAQ LAOS BURMA
CHINA INDIA JAPAN NEPAL
QATAR SYRIA YEMEN BHUTAN
ISRAEL JORDAN RUSSIA
TAIWAN TURKEY BAHRAIN
LEBANON SENEGAL VIETNAM
CAMBODIA MALAYSIA

MONGOLIA PAKISTAN
THAILAND INDONESIA
KAMPUCHEA SINGAPORE
BANGLADESH NORTHKOREA
SOUTHKOREA AFGHANISTAN
SAUDIARABIA SOVIETUNION
UNITEDARABEMIRATES
RANGE: ALTAI KOLYMA HIMALAYA
RIVER: OB SI AMUR LENA URAL
INDUS GANGES MEKONG TIGRIS
HWANGHO SALWEEN TANGTZE
YENISEI EUPHRATES
IRRAWADDY
VOLCANO: APO USU FUGI GEDE
TAAL AGUNG ALAID DEMPO
MAYON RAUNG MARAPI
MERAPI SEMERU SINILA
SLAMET ULAWUN BULOSAN

SUNDORO TAMBORA TJAREME
GAMALAMA KERINTJE
RINDJANI TOLBACHIK
WATERFALL: JOG GOKAK KEGON
MEKONG CAUVERY

ASIDE BY BYE OFF AGEE AWAY
GONE NEAR PAST AGLEY ALOOF
APART ASKEW FORBY ASLANT
ASTRAY BESIDE BEYOND BYHAND
FORBYE FORTHBY LATERAL
PRIVATE WHISPER OVERHAND
RESERVED SECRETLY SEPARATE
SIDEWISE OVERBOARD
ASININE DULL CRASS DENSE INEPT
SILLY ABSURD ASSISH OBTUSE
SIMPLE STUPID DOLTISH
FATUOUS FOOLISH IDIOTIC
ASIUS (FATHER OF —) DYMAS
HYRTACUS
(SISTER OF —) HECUBA
(SLAYER OF —) AJAX IDOMENUS
ASK BEG SPY SUE FAND PRAY QUIZ
CLAIM CRAVE EXACT FRAYN
PLEAD QUERY SPEAK SPEER
SPEIR SPELL SPERE ADJURE
DEMAND DESIRE EXAMIN EXPECT
FRAIST FRAYNE INVITE BESEECH
BESPEAK CONSULT ENTREAT
IMPLORE INQUIRE REQUEST
REQUIRE SOLICIT PETITION
QUESTION
(— ALMS) CANT THIG
(— FOR) BEG BID CRY DUN LAIT
SEEK BESPEAK INQUIRE REQUEST
(— PAYMENT) CHARGE
ASKANCE AWRY ASKEW ASKILE
CROOKED SIDEWAYS
ASKEW CAM AGEE ALOP AWRY
AZEW AGLEE AGLEY AMISS ATILT
CRAZY GLEED TIPSY ASKANT
ASLANT ATWIST FLOOEY SKEWED
SKIVIE ASQUINT CROOKED
OBLIQUE BIASWISE COCKEYED
SIDELING
ASKING ROGATION
ASLANT ASIDE SLOPE
(PREF.) PLAGI(O)
ASLEEP DEAD FAST IDLE LATENT
NUMBED DORMANT NAPPING
ASOCIAL EGREGIOUS
ASOKA (FATHER OF —) BINDUSARA
ASOPUS (DAUGHTER OF —) ORNIA

THEBE AEGINA ASOPIS CLEONE
PIRENE SINOPE CHALCIS
CORCYRA SALAMIS TANAGRA
THESPEIA
(SON OF —) ISMENUS PELASGUS
(WIFE OF —) METOPE
ASP ESP ASPIC ASPIDE URAEUS
ASPAR (FATHER OF —) ARDABURIUS
ASPARAGUS LILY GRASS SPRUE
ASPERGE SPARAGE SPERAGE
(— GARNISH) PRINCESS
ASPATHA (FATHER OF —) HAMAN
ASPECT AIR HUE WAY AURA
BROW FACE HAND KIND LEER
LOOK MIEN SIDE VIEW VULT
ANGLE COLOR DECIL FACET
GUISE IMAGE NORMA PHASE
SIGHT STAGE TRINE VISOR VIZOR
DECILE FACIES FIGURE GLANCE
MANNER PHASIS REGARD VISAGE
APPAREL BEARING ESSENCE
FEATURE MALEFIC OUTLOOK
RESPECT RETRAIT SEXTILE
SHOWING SPECIES CARRIAGE
CONSPECT FOREHEAD OUTSIGHT
PROSPECT QUINTILE CHARACTER
SEMBLANCE
(— OF CURVE) INSIDE
(— OF EMOTION) AFFECT
(— OF MOON) CRESCENT
(— OF MUSICAL NUANCES)
AGOGICS
(BALEFUL —) DISASTER
(CULTURAL —) EMANATION
(DETERMINING —) HEART
(EXTERNAL —) PHYSIOGNOMY
(FACIAL —) EXPRESSION
(LANGUAGE —) DURATIVE
(PRIMARY —) HIGHWAY
(QUARTILE —) SQUARE
(SECONDARY —) BYWAY
ASPEN APS ASP ALAMO NITHER
POPLAR POPPLE QUAKER
QUAKING TREMBLE
ASPER AKCHA AKCHEH OTHMANY
ASPERGILLUM HYSSOP SPRINKLE
STRINKLE
ASPERITY IRE RIGOR ACERBITY
ACRIMONY TARTNESS ANIMOSITY
ASPERSE SKIT SLUR SPOT ABUSE
DECRY LIBEL SPRAY DEFAME
DEFILE MALIGN REVILE SHOWER
VILIFY APPEACH BLACKEN
DETRACT LAMPOON SLANDER
TARNISH TRADUCE BESMIRCH
FORSPEAK SPRINKLE
ASPERSION SLUR BAPTISM
CALUMNY INNUENDO
ASPHALT BREA PITCH SLIME
FILLER MANJAK BITUMEN
CUTBACK MANJACK BYERLITE
UINTAITE
ASPHALTUM CONGO
ASPHODEL KNAVERY AFFODILL
ASPHYXIA APNEA APNOEA
ACROTISM
ASPIC JELLY GELATIN GELATINE
LAVENDER
ASPIRATE ROUGH SPIRITUS
ASPIRATION GOAL IDEAL DESIRE
RECOIL SIGHTS AMBITION
PRETENSION
ASPIRE AIM STY HOPE LONG MINT

RISE SEEK SOAR WISH ETTLE
MOUNT TOWER YEARN ASCEND
ATTAIN DESIRE PRETEND
ASPIRIN FEBRIFUGE
ASPIRING ASPIRANT
ASRIEL (FATHER OF —) GILEAD
ASS DOLT FOOL JADE KHUR MOKE
BURRO CHUMP CUDDY DICKY
DUNCE EQUID GUDDA HINNY
CUDDIE DAPPLE DICKEY DONKEY
ONAGER ASINEGO ASSHEAD
JACKASS LONGEAR MALTESE
SOLIPED IMBECILE
(FEMALE —) JENNY JENNET
(MALE —S) JACKSTOCK
(WILD —) KIANG KULAN KYANG
KIYANG KOULAN ONAGER
HEMIPPE CHIGETAI GHORKHAR
HEMIONUS
(PL.) JACKSTOCK
(PREF.) ONISCI ONO
ASSAI MANICOLE
ASSAIL WOO BEAT FRAY HOOT
JUMP PELT SAIL ASSAY BESET
PRESS SHOCK STONE WHACK
WHANG ACCUSE ATTACK BATTER
BICKER BULLET HURTLE IMPUGN
INFEST INSULT INVADE MALIGN
MOLEST OFFEND OPPUGN
RATTLE SAILYE SCATHE STRIKE
ASSAULT ATTEMPT BELABOR
BESEIGE BOMBARD CATCALL
ENFORCE ASSEMBLE BLUDGEON
TOMAHAWK
ASSAILANT ONSETTER
ASSAM (MOUNTAIN OF —) JAPVO
(STATE OF —) KHASI MANIPUR
(TOWN OF —) IMPHAL SADIYA
GAUHATI SHILLONG
(TRIBE OF —) AO AKA AOR AHOM
GARO NAGA
ASSARACUS (BROTHER OF —) ILUS
GANYMEDE
(FATHER OF —) TROS
(MOTHER OF —) CALLIRRHOE
(SISTER OF —) CLEOPATRA
(SON OF —) CAPYS
ASSART SART THWAITE
ASSASSIN THAG THUG BRAVE
BRAVO FEDAI FIDAI CUTTLE
FIDAWI KILLER SLAYER RUFFIAN
STABBER TORPEDO HACKSTER
MURDERER SICARIUS
ASSASSINATE KILL SLAY MURDER
REMOVE
ASSASSINATION THUGGEE
ASSAULT MUG BEAT BLOW COSH
FRAY RAID SLUG ABUSE ALARM
ASSAY BRUNT HARRY ONSET
POISE POUND SHOCK SMITE
STORM STOUR VENUE AFFRAY
ALARUM ASSAIL ATTACK BREACH
BUFFET CHARGE ENGINE EXTENT
HOLDUP INSULT INVADE NAPALM
ONFALL STOUND STOUSH
THRUST YOKING ATTEMPT
BOMBARD DESCENT LAMBAST
PURSUIT RUNNING VIOLATE
INVASION OUTBURST
ASSAY RUN SAY TRY TEST ESSAY
PROOF PROVE TOUCH TRIAL
ASSAIL ATTACK EFFORT ANALYZE
ATTEMPT EXAMINE TASTING

ANALYSIS APPRAISE ENDEAVOR
ESTIMATE HARDSHIP
ASSAYER POTDAR TESTER
ASSAYING DOCIMASY
ASSEMBLAGE ARMY BODY CAMP
CLOT COMA CREW HERD HOST
MASS PACK RUCK BUNCH CHOIR
COURT CROWD DRIFT DROVE
FLOCK GROUP LEVEE POSSE
QUIRE SALON SHOCK SWARM
CONVOY GALAXY HOOKUP
RESORT SPREAD SYSTEM THRONG
CIRCUIT CLUSTER COLLEGE
COMPANY COMPLEX CONVENT
CULTURE SOCIETY STATION
STATUTE TABAGIE ASSEMBLY
AUDITORY CONGRESS MULTIPLE
PARLIAMENT
(— OF FOSSILS) COLONY
(— OF INTEGERS) IDEAL
(CONFUSED —) FARRAGO
ASSEMBLE FIT LAY POD SAM BULK
CALL HERD HOST KNOT MASS
MEET ROUT SAMM AMASS ASAME
FLOCK PIECE RALLY TROOP UNITE
COUPLE GATHER HUDDLE
MUSTER SUMMON COLLATE
COLLECT COMPILE CONDUCE
CONVENE CONVOKE RECRUIT
CONGRESS CONGREGATE
(— CARDS) BUNCH
ASSEMBLED ACCOYLD
ASSEMBLER BONDER
ASSEMBLY HUI SUM BAUD BEVY
BOGY DIET DRUM DUMA FEIS
HOEY MALL MOOT RAAD ROUT
SEJM SEYM TING AGORA BOGEY
BOULE COURT COVEN CURIA
DOUMA FORUM GROUP JUNTA
LEVEE PARTY PRESS SABHA
SETUP SOBOR SYNOD THING
TROOP AENACH AONACH ASSIZE
BOBBIN BUSING CHAPEL COETUS
COVINE GEMOTE MAJLIS PARADE
PLENUM POWWOW SEIMAS
SENATE STEVEN CHAMBER
CHAPTER COLLEGE COMITIA
COMMAND COMPANY CONCION
CONSORT CONVENT COUNCIL
DIETINE EOTATES FOLKMOT
HUSTING LANDTAG MEETING
PENSION SERVICE SESSION
SOCIETY SYNAGOG SYNAXIS
TEMPEST TYNWALD ZEMSTVO
AUDIENCE CONCLAVE CONGRESS
ECCLESIA FOLKMOOT PLACITUM
PORTMOTE PRESENCE SEDERUNT
SOBRANJE TINEWALD TRIBUNAL
VOLKSTAG WARDMOTE
CONCOURSE
(— HOUSE) KASHIM
(— OF BLESSED) HEAVEN
(— OF CONDUCTORS) BUS
(— OF DEPUTIES) AMPHICTYONA
(— OF ELDERS) KGOTLA
(— OF WITCHES) COVEN SABBAT
SABBATH
(AFTERNOON —) LEVEE
(BOY SCOUT —) JAMBOREE
(CLOSED —) CONCLAVE
(FASTENER —) SEMS
(GRENADE —) BOUCHON
(PL.) COMITIA

ASSENT AYE BOW NOD YEA YES
AMEN SEAL SENT ADMIT AGREE
GRANT YIELD ACCEDE ACCEPT
ACCORD BELIEF CHORUS COMPLY
CONCUR SUBMIT UNISON
APPROVE CONCEDE CONFESS
CONFORM CONSENT ADHESION
CONSTATE OKEYDOKE SANCTION
SUFFRAGE ACCESSION
OKEYDOKEY
ASSERT LAY BRAG SHOW VOICE
AFFIRM ALLEGE ASSURE AVOUCH
DEFEND DEPONE DEPOSE INTEND
INTENT THREAP UPHOLD
ADVANCE BETOKEN CONFIRM
CONTEND DECLARE PROTEST
SUPPORT ADVOCATE CHAMPION
CONSTATE MAINTAIN OUTSTAND
POSITIVE PREDICATE
ASSERTION VOW FACT HOTI
CLAIM VOUCH AVERMENT
(— OF MASCULINITY) MACHISMO
(BOASTFUL —) JACTATION
(DUBIOUS —) PLINYISM
ASSERTIVE BRASH DOGMATIC
POSITIVE
ASSESS LAY TAX CESS DOOM LEVY
MISE RATE SCOT TOLL AGIST
CENSE PRICE STENT TEIND VALUE
AFFEER ASSIZE CHARGE EXTEND
IMPOSE SAMPLE MEASURE
APPRAISE ESTIMATE
ASSESSMENT FEE LUG TAX CESS
DUTY LEVY SCOT TOLL CULET
JUMMA PRICE RATAL STENT
TITHE WORTH EXTENT IMPOST
PURVEY SURTAX TARIFF
SCUTAGE BRIGBOTE TAXATION
ASSESSOR JUDGE MUFTI RATER
CESSOR LISTER TASKER AUDITOR
STENTOR TAXATOR
(PL.) FINTADORES
ASSET PLUS HONOR GETPENNY
PROPERTY RESOURCE STRENGTH
ASSETS GOODS MEANS MONEY
STOCK CREDIT WEALTH CAPITAL
EFFECTS ACCOUNTS PROPERTY
RESOURCE
ASSEVERATE SAY VOW AVER
AVOW STATE SWEAR AFFIRM
ALLEGE ASSERT ASSURE DECLARE
PROTEST
ASSEVERATION VOW OATH
ASSHUR (FATHER OF —) SHEM
ASSIDUOUS BUSY GREAT ACTIVE
DEVOTED PENIBLE STUDIED
DILIGENT FREQUENT SEDULOUS
STUDIOUS
ASSIGN FIX LET PUT SET ARET
CAST CEDE DEAL DOLE DRAW
GIVE METE RATE SEAL SHOW
SIGN ALLOT ALLOW APPLY ARETT
AWARD DIGHT ENDOW REFER
SHIFT TITLE ADDUCE AFFECT
ALLEGE ATTACH CHARGE CONVEY
DESIGN DIRECT ENTAIL ORDAIN
ACCOUNT ADJUDGE APPOINT
ASCRIBE CONSIGN DISPOSE
ENTITLE SPECIFY STATION
TRIBUTE ALLOCATE ANTEDATE
ARROGATE DELEGATE INSCRIBE
TRANSFER
(— QUARTERS) BILLET

(— TASK) STINT
ASSIGNATION DATE MEET TRYST
MEETING
ASSIGNMENT DECK DUTY TASK
CHORE GRIND STENT STINT
TUNCA CESSIO LESSON CESSION
BUSINESS HOMEWORK
PLACEMENT
ASSIGNOR CEDOR CEDENS
CEDENT
ASSIMILATE MIX ONE FUSE
ADAPT ALTER BLEND LEARN
MERGE ABSORB DIGEST IMBIBE
COMPARE CONCOCT RESEMBLE
ASSIMILATION ECHOISM
HOMEOSIS RECOGNITION
(— OF FOOD) CONCOCTION
ASSINIBOIN HOHE
ASSIR (FATHER OF —) KORAH
EBIASAPH JECONIAH
ASSIST AID ABET BACK HELP JOIN
AVAIL BOOST COACH FAVOR
NURSE SERVE SPEED STEAD
ATTEND ESCORT PROMPT
SECOND SQUIRE SUCCOR BENEFIT
COMFORT FURTHER RELIEVE
SUPPORT SUSTAIN ADJUVATE
BEFRIEND
(— A READER) FESCUE
(— AT) STAY
ASSISTANCE AID ALMS CAST GIFT
HAND HELP LIFT BOOST FAVOR
HEEZE RELIEF REMEDY SUCCOR
SUPPLY ADJUTOR COMFORT
SECOURS SUBSIDY SUPPORT
AUXILIUM EASEMENT GIFFGAFF
LARGESSE
ASSISTANT CAD AIDE ALLY HAND
HELP MAID MATE PUNK SOUS
ZANY CLERK GROOM USHER
VALET AIDANT BUMPER COMMIS
CURATE DEPUTY FLUNKY HELPER
LEGATE NIPPER SECOND TULTUL
YEOMAN ABETTOR ACOLYTE
ADJOINT ADJUNCT DOORMAN
DRESSER HOGGLER PADRINO
PARTNER PROVOST RUBBLER
SHIFTER STRIKER SWAMPER
ADJUTANT ADJUVANT FELDSHER
GOMASHTA LECTURER MINISTER
OFFSIDER PARASITE SERVITOR
SIDESMAN SUBPRIOR
(— TO ANIMAL SHOW JUDGE)
STEWARD
(AUCTIONEER'S —) SPOTTER
(DYEING —) CARRIER
(GUNNER'S —) MATROSS
(MASON'S —) GOUJAT
(MATADOR'S —) CHULO
(POLICE —) CORPORAL
(SURVEYOR'S —) CHAINMAN
(WAITER'S —) BUSBOY OMNIBUS
ASSOCIATE MIX PAL AIDE ALLY
BAND CHUM HERD JOIN LINK
MATE MOOP MOUP PEER WALK
WIFE YOKE BLEND BUDDY CRONY
HABER MATCH TRAIN TROOP
ASSORT ATTACH ATTEND
CHABER COHORT COUSIN FASTEN
FELLOW FRIEND HELPER HOBNOB
MARROW MEDDLE MEMBER
MINGLE PUISNE PUISNY RELATE
SOCIUS SPOUSE TRAVEL

ADJUNCT ASSOCIE BRACKET
COALITE COMMUNE COMPANY
COMPEER COMRADE CONNECT
CONSORT HUSBAND PARTNER
PEWMATE SOCIATE COMPLICE
CONFRERE CONJOINT CONVERSE
COPEMATE FAMILIAR FEDERATE
FOLLOWER FREQUENT GADSHILL
IDENTIFY INTIMATE PARTAKER
ACCOMPANY ACCOMPLICE
(— WITH) FRAT MOOP MOUP
(DEMON —) FLY
(PL.) ENTOURAGE
ASSOCIATED
(PREF.) SYM
(SUFF.) IC(AL)
ASSOCIATION HUI BODY BOND
BUND CLUB GILD HONG HUNT
TONG ARTEL BOARD GUILD
HANSA HANSE SANGH TRUCK
UNION CARTEL CERCLE CHAPEL
COMITY CONGER GRANGE
LEAGUE LEGION LYCEUM PLEDGE
SANGHA SCHOLA VEREIN CIRCUIT
COMBINE COMPANY CONSORT
CONTACT CONVENT COUNCIL
SOCIETY SOROSIS SYNOECY
AFFINITY ALLIANCE ASSEMBLY
ATHENEUM CONVERSE HABITUDE
INTIMACY SODALITY SYNOMOSY
TAALBOND ORGANIZATION
(— OF FOSSILS) FAUNULA
FAUNULE
(ANTAGONISTIC —) ANTIBIOSIS
(BOOK-SELLERS' —) CONGER
(CLOSE —) HARNESS INTIMACY
(EMPLOYERS' —) GREMIO
(FARMERS' —) GRANGE
(IN —) ALONG
(LABOR —) ARTEL UNION
(RELIGIOUS —) SAMAJ
(SECRET —) CABAL
(STUDENTS' —) CORPS
(SYMBIOTIC —) ACAROPHILY
ASSOIL RID SOIL ATONE CLEAR
SOLVE ACQUIT PARDON REFUTE
ABSOLVE DELIVER EXPIATE
FORGIVE RELEASE RESOLVE
ASSONANCE PUN RHYME
PARAGRAM
ASSORT BOLT CULL SUIT WINNOW
(— COINS) SHROFF
ASSORTED CHOW CHOWCHOW
ASSORTER FEEDER LOOKER
ASSORTMENT BAG LOT SET OLIO
BATCH BUNCH GROUP SUITE
RAGBAG MIXTURE
(— OF TYPE) BILL FONT
(COMPLETE —) STANDARD
ASSUAGE BEET CALM EASE LIOS
LISS ABATE ALLAY CHARM DELAY
LISSE MEASE SALVE SLAKE STILL
SWAGE LENIFY LESSEN MODIFY
PACIFY QUENCH REDUCE SOFTEN
SOLACE SOOTHE TEMPER
APPEASE COMFORT MOLLIFY
QUALIFY RELIEVE SATISFY
DIMINISH MITIGATE MODERATE
ASSUASIVE MILD LENIENT
LENITIVE SOOTHING
ASSUME DON PUT SAY SET BEAR
DARE FANG GIVE MASK PULL
SHAM SHIP TAKE ADOPT ANNEX

CLOAK ELECT FEIGN GUESS
INDUE INFER RAISE USURP
ACCEPT AFFECT BETAKE CLOTHE
FIGURE ASSUMPT BELIEVE
PREMISE PRESUME PRETEND
RECEIVE SUBSUME SUPPOSE
SURMISE ACCROACH ARROGATE
SIMULATE PERSONATE
POSTULATE
(— CHARACTER) ACT AFFECT
(— FORM) ENGENDER
(— OFFICE) ACCEDE
(— PAINTING STANCE) BACK
ASSUMED ALIAS FALSE GIVEN
FEIGNED AFFECTED BORROWED
ASSUMING LOFTY UPPISH UPPITY
AFFECTED ARROGANT SUPERIOR
ASSUMPTION DONNEE THESIS
BALLOON FICTION SURMISE
HOMEOSIS MARYMASS PRETENCE
PRETENSE PRESUMPTION
(BASIC —) BEGINNING
(EMPTY —) IMAGINATION
ASSURANCE FACE GALL SEAL
BRASS CHEEK FAITH NERVE
TRUST APLOMB AVOUCH BELIEF
CAUTIO CREDIT PLEVIN PLIGHT
SAFETY COURAGE PROMISE
WARRANT AUDACITY BOLDNESS
COOLNESS FIRMANCE FOREHEAD
SECURITY SUREMENT
ASSURE AFFY AVER SURE TELL
CINCH HIGHT VOUCH AFFEER
ASSERT AVOUCH ENSURE INSURE
PLEDGE SECURE SEKERE SICCAR
SICKER WITTER BETROTH CERTIFY
CONFIRM DECLARE HEARTEN
PROMISE PROTEST RESOLVE
WARRANT AFFIANCE CONVINCE
EMBOLDEN PERSUADE
ASSURED BOLD CALM COLD FIRM
PERT SURE BOUND SIKER SLUSH
FACILE PROBAL SECURE SICCAR
SICKER CERTAIN POSITIVE
(— OF SUCCESS) MADE
(BLUNTLY —) KNOCKDOWN
ASSUREDLY AMEN SOON INDEED
PERDIE REDELY SICCAR SICKER
SURELY VERILY HARDILY
WITTERLY
ASSYRIA ASHUR ASSUR ASSHUR
(CAPITAL OF —) CALAH NINEVEH
ASSYRIAN NESTORIAN
(— PLUM) SEBESTEN
ASTER ARNICA COCASH AMELLUS
BEEWEED BONESET EUASTER
ASTROFEL COMPOSIT CYTASTER
MONASTER STARWORT STOKESIA
ASTERIA (DAUGHTER OF —) HECATE
(FATHER OF —) COEUS
(HUSBAND OF —) PERSES
(MOTHER OF —) PHOEBE
(SISTER OF —) LETO LATONA
ASTERISK MARK STAR ASTER
ASTERISM WINDMILL
(THREE —S) ASTERISM
ASTERIUS (BROTHER OF —)
AMPHION
(FATHER OF —) ANAX HYPERASIUS
(SLAYER OF —) MILETUS
ASTERN AFT BAFT HIND REAR
ABAFT APOOP BEHIND

OCCIPUT BACKWARD
ASTEROID EROS HEBE IRIS JUNO
CERES DIONE FLORA IRENE METIS
VESTA AURORA EGERIA EUROPA
HYGEIA PALLAS PLANET PSYCHE
THALIA THEMIS THETIS ELECTRA
EUNOMIA FORTUNA LUTETIA
CALLIOPE MASSALIA PLANTOID
STARFISH STARLIKE VICTORIA
ASTHMA PHTHISIC
ASTHMATIC POUCY PURSY
POUCEY WHEEZY PANTING
PUFFING
ASTIR UP AGOG ABOUT AFOOT
AGATE ALERT GOING ACTIVE
AROUND ASTEER MOVING
ROUSED ABROACH EXCITED
STIRRING VIGILANT
ASTONISH AWE DAZE STAM
AMAZE KNOCK SHOCK DAMMER
MARVEL STOUND ASTOUND
GLOPPEN IMPRESS STARTLE
AMERVEIL BEWILDER CONFOUND
SURPRISE
ASTONISHING AMAZING
FABULOUS MARVELOUS
MARVELLOUS
ASTONISHMENT MUSE FERLY
DISMAY FARLEY MARVEL STOUND
WONDER SURPRISE
ASTOUND BEAT STUN ABASH
AMAZE APPAL SHOCK STOUN
APPALL STOUND STAGGER
STUPEFY STUPEND TERRIFY
ASTONISH CONFOUND SURPRISE
ASTOUNDING STUNNING
ASTRAEA (FATHER OF —) ZEUS
JUPITER
(MOTHER OF —) THEMIS
(SISTER OF —) PUDICITIA
ASTRAEUS (BROTHER OF —) PALLAS
PERSES
(FATHER OF —) CRIUS
(MOTHER OF —) EURYBIA
ASTRAGAL TALUS CHAPLET
CORNICE BAGUETTE
ASTRAGALAR
(PREF.) TALO
ASTRAGALUS TALUS VETCH
ASTRAKHAN BOKHARA
ASTRAL REMOTE STARRY STELLAR
ASTRAEAN SIDEREAL STARLIKE
ASTRAY AWRY LOST WILL ABORD
AGATE AGLEE AGLEY AMISS
ASIDE GLEED WRONG ABROAD
AFIELD ERRANT ERRING FAULTY
DEPAYSE DEVIOUS FORLORN
SINNING WILSOME MISTAKEN
STRAYING
ASTRIDE ATOP ABOARD ACHEVAL
SPANNING
ASTRINGENCY ACERBITY
ACRIMONY
ASTRINGENT ACID ALUM COTO
SOUR TART ACERB HARSH
ROUGH SAPAN STERN CORNUS
MASTIC PONTIC SEVERE TANNIN
ALUMNOL AUSTERE BINDING
CATECHU PUCKERY RHATANY
STYPTIC GERANIUM TRILLIUM
(NOT —) SOFT
ASTROLOGER JOTI JOSHI ARTIST
JOTISI MERLIN ZADKIEL SCHEMIST

ASTROLOGY STARCRAFT
MATHEMATICALS
ASTRONOMER JOTI JOSHI JOTISI
AMERICAN SEE BOND BOSS HALE
HALL HILL POOR REES TODD
VERY ADAMS BAADE BAUER
BOWEN CHASE ELKIN FROST
HOUGH PEASE SWIFT YOUNG
AITKEN BAILEY CANNON DRAPER
HOLDEN HUBBLE HUSSEY JACOBY
KEELER LOOMIS LOWELL PETERS
PORTER ROGERS SEARES WALKER
WATSON WILSON BARNARD
BURNHAM EASTMAN FLEMING
GILLIES LANGLEY LITTELL
MERRILL MITCHEL MOULTON
NEWCOMB PERRINE RITCHEY
RUSSELL SAFFORD SHAPLEY
SLIPHER WHITNEY BOWDITCH
CAMPBELL CHANDLER COMSTOCK
DOUGLASS HARKNESS STEBBINS
TOMBAUGH WINTHROP
WOODWARD ALEXANDER
DOOLITTLE LEUSCHNER
MOREHOUSE PRITCHETT
HARRINGTON RUTHERFURD
SCHAEBERLE RITTENHOUSE
SCHLESINGER EICHELBERGER
AUSTRIAN FALB HAGEN LITTROW
PURBACH
BELGIAN QUETELET
CANADIAN KLOTZ PLASKETT
DANISH BRAHE DREYER HANSEN
ROEMER SCHUMACHER
LONGOMONTANUS
DUTCH BLAEU SITTER HUYGENS
KAPTEYN
EGYPTIAN PTOLEMY
ENGLISH AIRY HIND POND RYLE
TODD WARD ADAMS BAILY
DYSON INNES JEANS JONES
MASON MILNE MURIS WALES
CLERKE DARWIN HALLEY LOVELL
BRADLEY CHALLIS CLAXTON
GREGORY HUGGINS LOCKYER
LUBBOCK MICHELL PARSONS
PENROSE PROCTOR BRISBANE
COPELAND EDDINTON GLAISHER
GOMPERTZ HERSCHEL HORROCKS
FLAMSTEED MASKELYNE
PRITCHARD CARRINGTON
GELLIBRAND GROOMBRIDGE
SHEEPSHANKS
FINNISH STONE
FRENCH BIOT FAYE LYOT PONS
WOLF HENRY LOEWY RAYET
FERNEL MOREUX PICARD VALLOT
BORELLY BOUVARD CASSINI
DELISLE JANSSEN LALANDE
LAPLACE MARALDI MESSIER
MOUCHEZ PUISEUX DELAMBRE
DELAUNAY LACAILLE LAGRANGE
BIGOURDAN CHACORNAC
LEMONNIER LEVERRIER
TISSERAND BURCKHARDT
FLAMMARION MAUPERTUIS
GERMAN BEER BODE WOLF ZACH
BAYER BIELA ENCKE GALLE
GAUSS GRAFF KEMPF KNOPF
MAYER ARNOLD ARREST AUWERS
BRUHNS HARZER IDELER KEPLER
LAMONT MADLER MARIUS
MOBIUS MULLER OLBERS PETERS

RUMKER SPORER STRUVE TEMPEL
AMBRONN APIANUS BRENDEL
BRUNNOW LAMBERT SCHONER
SCHWABE FOERSTER GUTHNICK
HARTMANN LINDENAU
MERCATOR RHATICUS SCHEINER
WINNECKE FABRICIUS PALITZSCH
SCHONFELD
GREEK CONON METON
AUTOLYCUS CALLIPPUS
CLEOMEDES OENOPIDES
SOSIGENES HIPPARCHUS
THEODOSIUS ANAXIMANDER
ARISTARCHUS CLEOSTRATUS
ERATOSTHENES
INDIAN ARYABHATA
BRAHMAGUPTA
IRISH BALL MOLYNEUX
ITALIAN AMICI FRISI DONATI
ORIANI PIAZZI SECCHI BORELLI
GALILEI RICCIOLI TACCHINI
BIANCHINI BOSCOVICH
FRACASTORO SCHIAPARELLI
NORWEGIAN HANSTEEN
POLISH COPERNICUS
RUSSIAN BREDICHIN
SCOTTISH GILL NICHOL WILSON
GREGORY ANDERSON FERGUSON
HENDERSON
SWEDISH DUNER BOHLIN GYLDEN
CELSIUS ANGSTROM BACKLUND
STROMGREN
ASTRONOMICAL FAR HUGE
GREAT URANIC DISTANT
IMMENSE URANIAN COLOSSAL
INFINITE
(— INSTRUMENT) ARMILL
ASTRONOMY WAGON WAGONER
WAGGONER
ASTUTE SLY FOXY KEEN WILY
ACUTE CANNY QUICK SHARP
SMART CLEVER CRAFTY NASUTE
SHREWD CUNNING KNOWING
SKILLED
ASTYAGES (FATHER OF —)
CYAXARES
ASTYANAX (FATHER OF —) HECTOR
(MOTHER OF —) ANDROMACHE
ASTYDAMIA (FATHER OF —)
PELOPS
(MOTHER OF —) HIPPODAMIA
(SON OF —) AMPHITRYON
ASTYOCHE (DAUGHTER OF —)
PHYLEUS
(LOVER OF —) HERCULES
(SON OF —) TLEPOLEMUS
ASUNDER ATWO APART SPLIT
ATWAIN SUNDER SUNDRY
DIVIDED DIVORCED YSOWNDIR
(PREF.) AP(H) DI DICH(O)
ASURA VARUNA
ASVATTHAMAN (FATHER OF —)
DRONA
(MOTHER OF —) KRIPA
ASYLUM ARK HOME JAIL ALTAR
COVER GRITH HAVEN BEDLAM
HARBOR REFUGE ALSATIA
COLLEGE HOSPICE RETREAT
SHELTER BUGHOUSE MADHOUSE
NUTHOUSE
ASYMMETRIC PEDIAL
AS YOU LIKE IT (AUTHOR OF —)
SHAKESPEARE

(CHARACTER IN —) ADAM CELIA
CORIN PHEBE AMIENS AUDREY
DENNIS JAQUES LEBEAU OLIVER
CHARLES MARTEXT ORLANDO
SILVIUS WILLIAM ROSALIND
FREDERICK TOUCHSTONE
AT A AL AU BY IN TO ALS TIL TILL
UNTO ATTEN THERE HEREAT
(— ALL) ANY AVA EER EVER HALF
OUGHT SOEVER HOWEVER
ATABAL DRUM TABOR ATTABAL
ATALANTA (CHARACTER IN —)
MERCURY ATALANTA MELEAGER
(COMPOSER OF —) HANDEL
(FATHER OF —) IASUS
(HUSBAND OF —) MELANION
HIPPOMENES
(MOTHER OF —) CLYMENE
ATAMAN CHIEF JUDGE HETMAN
HEADMAN
ATARAH (HUSBAND OF —)
JERAHMEEL
(SON OF —) ONAM
ATAVISM REVERSION
ATELIER SHOP STUDIO BOTTEGA
WORKSHOP
ATEO WAKEA
ATES SWEETSOP
ATHALARIC (FATHER OF —)
EUTHELRIC
(MOTHER OF —) AMALASUINTHA
ATHALIAH (FATHER OF —) AHAB
(HUSBAND OF —) JEHORAM
(MOTHER OF —) JEZEBEL
ATHAMAS (DAUGHTER OF —) HELLE
(FATHER OF —) AEOLUS
(MOTHER OF —) ENARETE
(SON OF —) PHRIXUS LEARCHUS
PALAEMON
(WIFE OF —) INO NEPHELE
ATHANAGILD (DAUGHTER OF —)
BRUNEHILDE GALESWINTHA
ATHANOR OVEN ATHENOR
FURNACE
ATHAPASKAN HAW HARE HUPA
KATO KASKA AHTENA BEAVER
CHETCO GILENO LASSIK SARCEE
SEKANI CARRIER CHILULA
KOYUKON KUTCHIN
ATHEIST ZENDIK DOUBTER INFIDEL
NASTIKA AGNOSTIC APIKOROS
NETHEIST
ATHENA ALEA AUGE NIKE ALERA
AREIA ERGANE HIPPIA HYGEIA
ITONIA PALLAS POLIAS AIANTIS
MINERVA APATURIA
ATHENIAN ATTIC CHORAGUS
CHOREGUS
ATHLAI (FATHER OF —) BEBAI
ATHLETE PRO BLUE JOCK KEMP
STAR BOXER COLOR CRACK
CUTEY CUTIE TURNER ACROBAT
AMATEUR GYMNAST STICKER
TUMBLER VARMINT GAMESTER
REPEATER WRESTLER
PENTATHLETE
(COLLEGE —) REDSHIRT
ATHLETIC AGILE BURLY LUSTY
VITAL BRAWNY GYMNIC ROBUST
SINEWY STRONG BOARDLY
BOORDLY MUSCULAR POWERFUL
VIGOROUS
ATHLETICS GAMES

SPORT EXERCISE
AT-HOME ASSEMBLY
ATHWART CROSS ABOARD
ACROSS ASLANT OBLIQUE
SIDEWISE TRAVERSE
ATLAS BOOK LIST MAPS TOME
TITAN TELAMON MAINSTAY
(DAUGHTERS OF —) ATLANTIDES
(FATHER OF —) IAPETUS
(MOTHER OF —) CLYMENE
(WIFE OF —) PLEIONE
ATLE ETHEL
ATMAN ATMA ATTA SELF
ATMOSPHERE AIR SKY AURA FEEL
LIFT MOOD TONE AROMA CLIME
DECOR ETHER PLACE SMELL
FROWST MIASMA NIMBUS
SPHERE WELKIN FEELING
HYALINE QUALIFY AMBIANCE
AMBIENCE
(— OF DISCOURAGEMENT) CHILL
(CHARACTERISTIC —) VIBE
(NOXIOUS —) MIASMA
(SECTION OF —) SOLENOID
(SENSED —) KARMA
(STALE —) FROUST FROWST
(STUFFY —) FUG
(SUFFOCATING —) STIFLE
ATMOSPHERIC AERIAL
ATMOSPHERICS STATIC STRAYS
SFERICS SPHERICS
ATOM ACE BIT ION JOT DIAD
DYAD HAET HATE IOTA MITE
MOTE WHIT ATOMY HENAD
LABEL MONAD SHADE SPECK
TINGE ADATOM BRIDGE CARBYL
HEPTAD ISOBAR TETRAD
ATOMIZE BODIKIN IONOGEN
ISOTOPE NUCLIDE RADICAL
SPECIES FUNCTION ISOSTERE
MOLECULE PARTICLE PERISSAD
QUANTITY CORPUSCLE SCINTILLA
(— TOTALITY) MATTER
(COMBINING —) ACCEPTOR
(TAGGED —) TRACER
(PL.) SMITHERS SMITHEREENS
ATOMIC TINY MINUTE NUCLEAR
ATOMIZE PULVERIZE
ATOMIZER SPRAY SPARGE
SCENTER SPRAYER AIRBRUSH
ODORATOR PERFUMER
ATOMS
(PREF.) (CONTAINING 20 —) EICOS
(CONTAINING 4 CARBON —) BUT
(HAVING ARRANGEMENT OF —)
GALA GALACTO
(PRESENCE OF 2 NITROGEN —) DIAZ
ATONE AGREE AMEND ACCORD
ANSWER ASSOIL RANSOM
REDEEM REPENT APPEASE
EXPIATE RESTORE SATISFY
(— FOR) ABY BYE ABYE MEND
ABIDE ABEGGE
ATONEMENT MEND RANSOM
MICHTAM PENANCE
SATISFACTION ACCEPTILATION
ATOP ACOR
ATORAI DAURI
ATOSSA (FATHER OF —) CYRUS
(HUSBAND OF —) DARIUS SMERDIS
CAMBYSES
ATRABILIOUS GLUM ADUST
GLOOMY MOROSE SULLEN

ATRAMENTOUS INKY
ATRAX (DAUGHTER OF —) CAENIS
  HIPPODAMIA
  (FATHER OF —) PENEUS
  (MOTHER OF —) BURA
ATREUS (BROTHER OF —) THYESTES
  (FATHER OF —) PELOPS
  (HALF-BROTHER OF —) THYESTES
  (MOTHER OF —) HIPPODAMIA
  (SON OF —) MENELAUS
  (WIFE OF —) AEROPE
ATRIP AWEIGH
ATRIUM HALL ATRIO COURT
  CAVITY AURICLE CHAMBER
  PASSAGE
ATROCIOUS BAD DARK RANK VILE
  AWFUL BLACK CRUEL GROSS
  ATROCE BRUTAL ODIOUS SAVAGE
  WICKED HEINOUS UNGODLY
  VIOLENT FLAGRANT GRIEVOUS
  HORRIBLE TERRIBLE MONSTROUS
ATROPHIC AUANTIC
ATROPHY RUST STUNT TABES
  MACIES MOLDER SHRINK STARVE
  SWEENY WITHER SWINNEY
  WASTING STULTIFY
  (PREF.) NECR(O)
ATROPINE DATURINE
ATTACH ADD FIX PUT SET SEW
  TAG TIE BIND BOLT GLUE HANG
  JOIN LINK SPAN TAKE VEST WELD
  ADOPT AFFIX ANNEX BEWED
  CLING FOUND HINGE HITCH
  LATCH PASTE SCREW SEIZE
  SPEND STICK TACHE TATCH
  UNITE ACCUSE ADDICT ADHERE
  ADJOIN APPEND ARREST CEMENT
  DEVOTE ENGAGE ENTAIL ENTIRE
  FASTEN FATHER INDICT SPLINE
  ADHIBIT APPOINT ASCRIBE
  CONNECT ESPOUSE SUBJOIN
  (— TEMPORARILY) SECOND
ATTACHED FAST FOND ADNATE
  DOTING ADJUNCT BIGOTED
  SESSILE ADSCRIPT INSERTED
ATTACHING INCIDENT ALLIGATION
ATTACHMENT ARM GAG BAIL
  BALE DRUM FLAY HEAD HECK
  LOVE MOTE SHIM SHOE AMOUR
  CHUCK CRUSH DOBBY DODAD
  FENCE GUARD STRIG AFFAIR
  BEATER BINDER BUMPER DAMSEL
  DOBBIE DOCTOR DOODAD
  DREDGE FELLER FETICH FETISH
  HEMMER HILLER LAPPET LAYBOY
  MARKER PACKER PICKUP SECTOR
  SHIELD SIDING ADAPTOR AFFAIRE
  BIGOTRY BRAIDER CREASER
  DROPPER FAGOTER FITTING
  GIGBACK HEADSET HOLDING
  JOINTER KNOCKUP LEVELER
  SPANNER SPRAYER DEVOTION
  DINGDONG FASTNESS FIXATION
  FONDNESS GOVERNOR HEADREST
ATTACK FIT HIT HOP MUG SIC
  BAIT BOMB BOUT CLAW COSH
  DINT FAKE FANG FORK FRAY
  GANG GIVE HOOK JUMP PAIL
  PANG RAID RISE RUSH SAIL SICK
  SLOW TACK TURN WADE YOKE
  ABUSE ALARM ASSAY BEGIN
  BESET BLAST BLITZ BOARD
  BRASH BRUNT CATCH CHECK

DRIVE FIGHT FLUSH FORAY
FORCE GLIDE HARRY ICTUS
ONSET POISE PULSE SALLY SCUFF
SMITE SOUSE SPASM SPELL
STORM ACCESS ACCUSE ACTION
AFFRAY AFFRET ASSAIL ATTAME
BATTLE BICKER BODRAG CHARGE
CRISIS DOUBLE ENVAYE EXPUGN
EXTENT GRUDGE INDICT INFEST
INSULT INVADE OFFEND ONFALL
ONRUSH POUNCE RUFFLE
SAVAGE SHOWER SORTIE
STOUND STRIKE STROKE TACKLE
TAKING THRUST AGGRESS
ASPERSE ASSAULT ATTEMPT
BARRAGE BELABOR BELIBEL
BESEIGE BOMBARD CENSURE
CRUSADE DESCENT OFFENSE
PICKOUT POTSHOT RUNNING
SCALING SEIZURE STACKER
CAMISADE CAMISADO ENDEAVOR
ESCALADE PAROXYSM SKIRMISH
SURPRISE TOMAHAWK OFFENSIVE
ONSLAUGHT PENETRATION
(— IN COCKFIGHT) SHUFFLE
(— OF ILLNESS) GO DWAM DWALM
  ACCESS
(— OF SICKNESS) WHIP SEIZURE
(— TO ROB) THUG
(— WITH SHOUTS) HUE
(— WITH WORDS) STOUSH
(— ZEALOUSLY) CRUSADE
(BOMBING —) PRANG
(CHESS —) FORK
(CRITICAL —) SLATING
(FENCING —) GLIDE
(LIGHT —) TOUCH
(NIGHT —) CAMISADO
(SLIGHT —) WAFF
(SUDDEN —) ICTUS RAPTUS
  SURPRISE
(SUICIDAL —) KAMIKAZE
(SURPRISE —) ALARM ALARUM
(VERBAL —) FIRE BLUDGEON
(SUFF.) LEPSIA LEPSIS LEPSY
  LEPT(IC)
ATTACKER AGGRESSOR
  OFFENDANT
  (SUFF.) MASTIX
ATTACK ON THE MILL
  (CHARACTER IN —) MERLIER
  DOMINIQUE FRANCOISE
  MARCELLINE
  (COMPOSER OF —) BRUNEAU
ATTAI (FATHER OF —) REHOBOAM
  (MOTHER OF —) AHLAI MAACHAH
ATTAIN GO GET HIT WIN BUMP
  COME EARN GAIN RISE SORT
  ARISE CATCH COVER CROSS
  FETCH PROVE REACH TOUCH
  ACCEDE AMOUNT ARRIVE ASPIRE
  EFFECT OBTAIN SECURE STRIKE
  ACHIEVE ACQUIRE COMPASS
  PROCURE SUCCEED OVERTAKE
  (— TO ACCOMPLISH) FIND FORCE
ATTAINMENT ARRIVAL ADEPTION
  ENERGEIA PURCHASE
  (— OF NIRVANA) MOKSHA
  (SCHOLARLY —) LETTERS
ATTAR ITR OIL ATAR OTTO ATHAK
  OTTAR ESSENCE PERFUME
ATTEMPT GO PUT SAY SHY TRY
  BOUT BURL DARE DASH FAND

FIST FOND HACK JUMP MIND
MINT MIRD OSSE SEEK SHOT
SLAP STAB WAGE WORK ASSAY
BEGIN ESSAY ETTLE FLING FRAME
OFFER ONSET PRESS PROOF
PROVE START TEMPT TRIAL
WHACK ASSAIL ATTACK EFFORT
FRAIST STRIVE ENFORCE IMITATE
PRETEND PROFFER STAGGER
VENTURE CONATION ENDEAVOR
EXERTION PURCHASE TENTAMEN
(— TO AROUSE) AGITATE
(— TO BRIBE) APPROACH
(— TO INFLUENCE) AGITATION
(ABORTIVE —) FUTILITY
(PREF.) PEIRA
ATTEND GO HO HOA HOO SEE
  FAND HEAR HEED LIST MIND
  OYES OYEZ STAY TEND WAIT
  WALK APPLY AUDIT AWAIT
  GUARD LACKEY NURSE SERVE
  TREAT VISIT WATCH ASSIST
  CONVEY ESCORT FOLLOW
  HARKEN INTEND LISTEN SECOND
  SHADOW SQUIRE CONDUCT
  CONSORT ESQUIRE HEARKEN
  LACQUEY PERPEND RETINUE
  ACCOMPANY
  (— A LADY) WAIT
  (— FUNERAL) FOLLOW
  (— REGULARLY) KEEP
  (— TO) MIND TREAT FETTLE
  INTEND
  (— UPON) TENT CHASE CHAPERON
ATTENDANCE GATE SUIT CHAPEL
  NUMBER OFFICE REGARD
  SERVICE PRESENCE
ATTENDANT BOY FLY LAD JACK
  MAID MUTE PAGE PEON SYCE
  ZANY CADDY COMES GILLY
  GROOM GUIDE JAGER USHER
  VALET ALEXAS CADDIE DACTYL
  DAMSEL EMILIA ESCORT FRIEND
  GESITH GILLIE HAIDUK HOGMAN
  JAEGER KAVASS MINION PORTER
  SQUIRE STOCAH TUBMAN VARLET
  VERGER WAITER YEOMAN
  ALIPTES ARMORER BULLDOG
  CHOBDAR COURIER CROSSER
  DAMOSEL FAMULUS FENELLA
  FOOTBOY GHILLIE HALLMAN
  HOSTESS JACKMAN LINKMAN
  ORDERLY PAGEBOY PIQUEUR
  PRESSER SEQUENT SERVANT
  SHIPBOY SPOUTER TRABANT
  TRESSEL ATTENDEE BEACHBOY
  CHASSEUR CORYBANT CRUTCHER
  FEWTERER FOLLOWER GATHERER
  HANDMAID HENCHBOY
  HENCHMAN HOUSEMAN
  MINISTER MYRMIDON OBSERVER
  OUTRIDER ROSALINE SERGEANT
  SERJEANT STAFFIER TIPSTAFF
  WATERMAN OBSERVANT
  PURSUIVANT
  (— OF CYBELE) CORYBANT
  (CROSSING —) GATEMAN
  (KNIGHT'S —) SWAIN CUSTREL
  ESQUIRE
  (PALACE —S) BOSTANGI
  (PROCTOR'S —) BULLDOG
  (YOUNG —) BOY LAD JACK PAGE
  KNIGHT

(PL.) MEINY STAFF CORTEGE
  RETINUE
ATTENDED FRAUGHT
ATTENTION EAR CARE GAUM
  HEED HIST MARK MIND NOTE
  RUSH SHUN TENT COURT FLOOR
  GUARD STUDY TASTE DETAIL
  FAVORS NOTICE REGARD
  ACCOUNT ACHTUNG ADDRESS
  EARNEST HEARING RESPECT
  THOUGHT AUDIENCE
  (— FROM SUPERIOR) TASHRIF
  TASHREEF
  (— TO PETTY ITEMS) MICROLOGY
  (AMOROUS —) GALLANTRY
  (FIXED —) DHARANA
  (FLATTERING —) HOMAGE
  (PLEASING —) INCENSE
  (SPECIAL —) ACCENT
ATTENTIVE WARY ALERT AWAKE
  CIVIL CLOSE SHARP TENTY
  ARRECT INTENT POLITE CAREFUL
  GALLANT HEEDFUL LISTFUL
  MINDFUL PRESENT DILIGENT
  OBEDIENT STUDIOUS THOUGHTY
  VIGILANT WATCHFUL
  (— TO) IMMINENT
ATTENUATE SAP DRAW FINE THIN
  WATER DILUTE LESSEN RAREFY
  REDUCE WEAKEN SLENDER
  AVIANIZE DECREASE DIMINISH
  EMACIATE ENFEEBLE TAPERING
ATTENUATED GAUNT AERIAL
  DILUTED SPINDLY FINESPUN
  SMORZATO
ATTENUATION LOSS
ATTENUATOR PAD
ATTEST CHOP SEAL SIGN PROVE
  STATE SWEAR VOUCH ADJURE
  AFFIRM INVOKE RECORD WITTEN
  CERTIFY CONFESS CONFIRM
  CONSIGN TESTIFY WARRANT
  WITNESS EVIDENCE INDICATE
  MANIFEST
ATTESTATION VOUCH DOCKET
  RECORD
ATTESTED SWORN CERTIFIED
ATTIC LOFT CELER SOLAR SOLER
  GARRET TALLET GRENIER
  COCKLOFT
  (— SIDE) SKEELING
ATTILA (BROTHER OF —) BLEDA
  (CHARACTER IN —) LEO EZIO
  ATTILA FORESTO ODABELLA
  (COMPOSER OF —) VERDI
  (FATHER OF —) MUNDZUK
  (WIFE OF —) HILDA ILDICO
ATTIRE (ALSO SEE DRESS) BEGO
  BUSK SUIT TIRE ADORN ARRAY
  BIGAN DRESS HABIT AGUISE
  ENROBE PLIGHT REVEST TOILET
  ADDRESS APPAREL DUBBING
  PANOPLY ACCOUTER CLEADING
  EQUIPAGE FEATHERS
  (EPISCOPAL —) PONTIFICAL
  (FORMAL —) BALLDRESS
  (SHINING —) SHEEN
ATTIRED TRICKSY
ATTITUDE AIR CUE SET BIAS MIEN
  MOOD POSE SIDE ANGLE FRAME
  HEART PHASE SHAPE SHELL
  SIGHT SLANT STAND ACTION
  ANIMUS ASPECT MANNER SPIRIT

STANCE BEARING FEELING
GESTURE POSTURE STATION
STOMACH BEHAVIOR CARAPACE
CROTCHET HABITUDE
POSITION PREPOSSESSION
(— OF HUNTING DOG) POINT
(PREVAILING —) STREAM
ATTORNEY DOER AGENT AVOUE
PROXY VAKIL DEPUTY FACTOR
FISCAL LAWYER LEGIST MUKTAR
SYNDIC VAKEEL PROCTOR
ADVOCATE PROSECUTOR
ATTRACT BAIT CALL DRAW LURE
PULL TILL WIND BRING CATCH
CHARM COURT FETCH TEMPT
ALLURE ATTACH ENGAGE ENLIST
ENTICE GATHER INVITE SEDUCE
STRIKE BEWITCH PROCURE
INTEREST MAGNETIZE
(— FISH) CHUM
ATTRACTANT (MOTH SEX —)
GYPLURE
ATTRACTION BAIT CALL CARD
CLOU DRAW PULL CHARM DRAFT
FAVOR SPELL TRACT APPEAL
DESIRE FAVOUR MAGNET
BLOWOFF COITION DRAUGHT
GRAVITY INDRAFT ADHESION
AFFINITY COHESION CONTRACT
PENCHANT SIDESHOW WITCHERY
ATTRACTIVE BRAW CHIC CUTE
FAIR FOXY GOOD NICE BONNY
DISHY FATAL JOLLY NIFTY QUEME
SWEET COMELY FLASHY FRUITY
HEPPEN LOVELY PRETTY SAVORY
SNAZZY TAKING TRICKY AMIABLE
CIRCEAN CUNNING EYEABLE
EYESOME GRADELY LIKABLE
WINNING WINSOME ALLURING
CHARMING ENGAGING ENTICING
FEATURED FETCHING GRACEFUL
GRACIOUS HANDSOME INVITING
SPECIOUS TEMPTING VENEREAN
PERSONABLE PREPOSSESSING
(— TO OPPOSITE SEX) EPIGAMIC
(FALSELY —) MERETRICIOUS
(NOT —) FOUL INCURIOUS
(STRIKINGLY —) ZINGY
ATTRACTIVENESS CHARM GRACE
LOOKS BEAUTY GLAMOR
AMENITY GLITTER AFFINITY
HARLOTRY
ATTRIBUTABLE DUE
ATTRIBUTE FOX OWE PUT GIVE
MARK SIGN TYPE ALLOT BADGE
BLAME CHARM PLACE POWER
REFER ALLEGE ALLUE ARRECT
ASSERT ASSIGN BESTOW CHARGE
CREDIT IMPUTE PREFER REPUTE
SYMBOL ADJUNCT APANAGE
ASCRIBE COUNTER ESSENCE
PERTAIN QUALITY ACCREDIT
APPANAGE ARROGATE GRANDITY
INTITULE PROPERTY PROPRIUM
STRENGTH
(— WRONGFULLY) FOIST
(—S OF ROCKS) GEOLOGY
(PL.) SARIRA SHARIRA
ATTRIBUTION ACCENT THEORY
ANIMISM ETIOLOGY
ATTRITION WEAR GRIEF REGRET
SORROW ANGUISH ABRASION
BLASTING FRICTION

ATTUNE KEY TUNE ADAPT AGREE
ACCORD ADJUST TEMPER
PREPARE
ATUA AKUA DEMON SPIRIT
ATYPICAL BIZARRE ABERRANT
GROTESQUE
AUBADE ALBA
AUBERGE INN ALBERGO
AUBERGINE EGGPLANT
AUBURN ABRAM BLOND CACHA
CUTCH BLONDE CACHOU
CATECHU GOREVAN TULIPWOOD
AU COURANT CONTEMPORARY
AUCTION CANT ROUP SALE SELL
VEND COKER TRADE BARTER
BRIDGE HAMMER OUTCRY
TROVER VENDUE OUTROOP
UNCTION DISPOSAL KNOCKOUT
PORTSALE
AUCTIONEER CRIER CRYER
OUTCRIER
AUDACIOUS BOLD BRASH BRAVE
FRACK HARDY SAUCY AUDACE
BRAZEN CHEEKY DARING
FORWARD ARROGANT FEARLESS
IMPUDENT INSOLENT INTREPID
SPIRITED BAREFACED
(NOT —) CIVIL
AUDACITY CHEEK NERVE
COURAGE BOLDNESS TEMERITY
PRESUMPTION
AUDIBLE RIFE ALOUD CLEAR
HEARD AUTOMATIC
AUDIENCE EAR PIT FANS AUDIT
COURT FLOOR HOUSE PUBLIC
GALLERY HEARING ASSEMBLY
AUDITORY TRIBUNAL
AUDIT SCAN CHECK PROBE
APPOSE RECKON VERIFY
ACCOUNT EXAMINE INQUIRE
INSPECT ESTIMATE
AUDITION HEARING
AUDITOR CENSOR HEARER
APPOSER AUDIENT PITTITE
COUNTOUR DISCIPLE LISTENER
AUDITORIUM HALL ROOM CAVEA
FRONT ODEUM THEATER
AUDITORY
AUDITORY ORAL OTIC AURAL
AUDILE ACOUSTIC AUDITIVE
AUGE (FATHER OF —) ALEUS
(HUSBAND OF —) TEUTHRAS
(MOTHER OF —) NAERA
(SON OF —) TELEPHUS
AUGER BIT POD BORE BORAL
BORER GRILL BORING GIMLET
NAUGER WIMBLE PIERCER
TEREBRA
(PREF.) TRYPAN(O)
AUGHT ACHT EAWT AUCHT
OWNED CIPHER NAUGHT
WORTHY NOTHING VALIANT
ANYTHING
AUGMENT ADD EKE FEED GROW
HELP URGE BOOST SWELL SWELL
APPEND DILATE EXPAND EXTEND
AMPLIFY BALLOON ENHANCE
ENLARGE IMPROVE INFLAME
MAGNIFY COMPOUND HEIGHTEN
INCREASE MAJORATE MULTIPLY
(— IN STRENGTH) INGROSS
AUGMENTATION RISE EKING
SWELL GROWTH

AUCTARY ADDITION
AUGMENTED SHARP EXTREME
AUGUR BODE OMEN SEER SPEAK
AUSPEX DIVINE BETOKEN
CONJECT FORESEE OMINATE
PORTEND PREDICT PRESAGE
PROMISE PROPHET SIGNIFY
DENOUNCE FOREBODE
FORESHOW FORETELL
FOREWARN INDICATE
PROPHESY
AUGURY ORE OMEN RITE SIGN
SOOTH TOKEN HANSEL RITUAL
AUSPICE HANDSEL PRESAGE
CEREMONY
AUGUST AWFUL GRAND NOBLE
KINGLY SERENE SOLEMN
EXALTED STATELY IMPOSING
MAJESTIC
(FIRST DAY OF —) LAMMAS
LUGNAS LUGHNAS LUGNASAD
(PREF.) SEBASTO
AUGUSTINIAN AUSTIN
ASSUMPTIONIST
AUHUHU HOLA
AUK FALK LOOM ARRIE DIVER
LEMOT MURRE NODDY SCOOT
SCOUT SKOUT MARROT PUFFIN
ROTCHE STARIK TINKER DOVEKEY
DOVEKIE PENGUIN PYGOPOD
SEAFOWL WILLOCK GAIRFOWL
GAREFOWL ROCKBIRD
RAZORBILL
AULA HALL COURT EMBLIC
AUNT TIA BAWD AUNTY NAUNT
TANTA TANTE AUNTIE GOSSIP
(— SALLY) STICKS
AURA AIR HALO ODOR PUFF
AROMA SAVOR SMELL BREEZE
BUZZARD ESSENCE
FEELING
(CHARACTERISTIC —) VIBE
(SENSED —) KARMA
AURAL OTIC
AUREATE GOLDEN ORNATE
ROCOCO YELLOW
AUREOLE HALO CROWN GLORY
LIGHT AREOLA CORONA GLORIA
NIMBUS VESICA GLORIOLE
MANDORLA
AUREUS (HALF —) SEMIS
AURICLE EAR PINNA ATRIUM
EARLET TRUMPET PAVILION
AURICULATE EARED
AURIGA WAGONER WAGGONER
AURIST OTOLOGIST
AUROCHS TUR UROX URUS BISON
WISENT BONASUS
AURORA EOS DAWN DRAPERY
MORNING
AURORA BOREALIS DANCERS
STREAMERS
AUSPICE CARE OMEN SIGN
AUGURY PORTENT GUIDANCE
(PL.) EGIS AEGIS
AUSPICIOUS FAIR GOOD TWINE
WHITE BRIGHT CHANCY DEXTER
CHANCEY FAVORING PROPITIOUS
PROSPEROUS
AUSTERE BARE COLD HARD SOUR
BLEAK BUDGE GRAVE GRUFF
HARSH RIGID ROUGH SHARP
STERN STIFF STOUR BITTER

CHASTE FORMAL RUGGED
SEVERE SIMPLE SOMBER STRICT
SULLEN TETRIC ASCETIC
CRABBED DANTEAN EARNEST
SERIOUS GRANITIC RIGOROUS
TETRICAL ASTRINGENT
PURITANICAL
AUSTERITY RIGOR CATOISM
RIGORISM SIMPLICITY
AUSTRAL SOUTHERN

AUSTRALIA

ABORIGINE: MYALL
CAPE: HOWE
CAPITAL: CANBERRA
COIN: DUMP POUND SHILLING
DESERT: STURT GIBSON TANAMI
SIMPSON
HARBOR: DARWIN BRISBANE
FREMANTLE MELBOURNE
NEWCASTLE
ISLAND: CATO COCOS FRASER
KOOLAN CORINGA KANGAROO
LACEPEDE MELVILLE ROTTNEST
TASMANIA
LAKE: EYRE COWAN FROME
BARLEE BULLOO LEFROY
AMADEUS BLANCHE EVERARD
GREGORY TORRENS GAIRDNER
NABBEROO DISAPPOINTMENT
LANGUAGE: YABBER
MEASURE: SAUM
MOUNTAIN: OLGA BRUCE LEGGE
CRADLE GARNET GAWLER
MAGNET STUART BONGONG
GREGORY WILHELM CUTHBERT
JUSGRAVE MULLIGAN
KOSCIUSKO
MOUNTAIN RANGE: DARLING
FLINDERS
NATIVE: ABO MARA BINGE AUSSIE
DIGGER BILLIJIM KANGAROO
WARRAGAL WARRIGAL
JINDYWOROBAK
PENINSULA: EYRE
RIVER: DALY SWAN BULLO COMET
FINKE ISAAC PAROO ROPER
SNOWY YARRA BARCOO
BARWON CULGOA DAWSON
DEGREY DARLING FITZROY
LACHLAN STAATEN WARREGO
BURDEKIN FLINDERS GEORGINA
VICTORIA
SEA: CORAL TIMOR TASMAN
ARAFURA
SOLDIER: DIGGER SWADDY
BILLIJIM
STATE: TASMANIA VICTORIA
QUEENSLAND
STRAIT: TORRES
TOWN: AYR YASS DUBBO PERTH
WAGGA ALBURY AUBURN
CAIRNS CASINO COBURG
DARWIN HOBART MACKAY
SYDNEY BENDIGO GEELONG
KOGARAH MILDURA MITCHAM
ADELAIDE BRISBANE ESSENDON
RANDWICK RINGWOOD
MELBOURNE TOOWOOMBA
VALLEY: GROSE JAMIESON
MEGALONG
WATER HOLE BILLABONG
WATERFALL: TULLY COOMERA

WALLAMAN WENTWORTH WOLLOMOMBI
WOMAN: LUBRA

AUSTRALIAN ANZAC AUSSIE DIGGER AUSTRAL CURRENCY KANGAROO WARRAGAL WARRIGAL
(— GIRL) LUBRA

AUSTRIA

ANCIENT PEOPLE: HUNS AVARS RAETIANS SLOVENES BAVARIANS
CAPITAL: WIEN VIENNA
CELTIC KINGDOM: NORICUM
COIN: DUCAT KRONE FLORIN HELLER ZEHNER GROSCHEN SCHILLING
DUCHY: STYRIA CARNIOLA CARINTHIA
EMPEROR: CHARLES FRANCIS FERDINAND
LAKE: ALMSEE FERTOTO MONDSEE BODENSEE TRAUNSEE CONSTANCE NEUSIEDLER
MEASURE: FASS FUSS JOCH MASS MUTH YOKE HALBE LINIE MEILE METZE PFIFF PUNKT ACHTEL BECHER SEIDEL DLAFTER VIERTEL DREILING
MOUNTAIN: STUBAI EISENERZ RHATIKON KITZBUHEL
NATIVE: STYRIAN TYROLEAN
NOBILITY: RITTER
PASS: LOIBL ARLBERG BRENNER PLOCKEN
PROVINCE: TIROL TYROL STYRIA VIENNA SALZBURG CARINTHIA VORARLBERG
RIVER: INN MUR DRAU ENNS KAMP LECH MURZ RAAB DONAU MARCH SALZA THAYA TRAUN DANUBE SALZACH
RIVER PORT: LINZ KREMS VIENNA
ROMAN PROVINCE: RAETIA NORICUM PANNONIA
TOWN: ENNS GRAZ LECH LINZ RIED WELS WIEN GMUND LIENZ STEYR TRAUN LEOBEN VIENNA BREGENZ MODLING SPITTAL VILLACH DORNBIRN SALZBURG INNSBRUCK
WATERFALL: KRIMML GASTEIN GOLLING
WEIGHT: MARC SAUM UNZE DENAT KARCH PFUND STEIN CENTNER PFENNIG VIERLING

AUTACOID HORMONE INCRETION
AUTARCHIC FREE
AUTHENTIC ECHT PURE REAL SURE TRUE EXACT PUCCA PUCKA PUKKA RIGHT VALID ACTUAL DINKUM PROPER CORRECT CURRENT GENUINE SINCERE CREDIBLE OFFICIAL ORIGINAL RELIABLE
AUTHENTICATE SEAL PROVE VOUCH ATTEST SIGNET VERIFY APPROVE CONFIRM LEGALIZE

AUTHOR DOER JUDE SIRE JUDAS MAKER RULER AUCTOR FACTOR FORGER LOKMAN PARENT PENMAN SCRIBE SOURCE WRITER ANCIENT CLASSIC CREATOR ELOHIST FOUNDER LOLLIUS ANCESTOR BEGETTER COMPILER COMPOSER IDEALIST IMMORTAL INVENTOR JEHOVIST ORIGINAL PAYYETAN PRODUCER
(BAD —) BLOTTER
(PL.) SS
AMERICAN LEA LEE POE AGEE BAUM BEER BELL BOYD BUCK COOK DANA GALE GREY HALL HUME HUNT KEMP KREY KYNE LANE LONG LOOS MACY MAYO NASH PAUL POST RAND SHAW WARD WOOD ADAMS ADLER AIKEN ALGER ALSOP BACON BASSO BATES BEACH BENET BINNS BOYLE BROWN BRUSH CABLE CAHAN CANBY CHILD COOKE CRANE DAVIS DIETZ DODGE EARLE EATON ELLIS EVANS FOOTE GATES GREEN HECHT HURST KELLY KEYES LEWIS LODGE MAJOR MARCH MASON OGDEN OHARA PAINE POOLE QUEEN REESE REEVE RIVES SIMMS SMITH STEIN STONE STONG STOUT STOWE THANE TRINE TWAIN TUDOR TULLY VANCE VORSE WALSH WATTS WEEMS WELLS WHITE WILEY WOLFE WYLIE ADAMIC ALCOTT ARTHUR AUSTIN BAILEY BARNES BECKER BELLOW BESSIE BISHOP BRALEY BRINIG BROWNE BURMAN BURNET CABELL CAPOTE CARMER CARSON CATHER CATLIN CATTON CLARKE COLTON COOPER CORBIN CORLEY CROUSE DARGAN DAVIES DELAND DEVOTO DILLON DOWNEY EVARTS FARSON FERBER FIELDS FINLEY FISHER FLEBBE FORBES FULLER GILMAN GORMAN GUNTER HALPER HARRIS HERBST HOBART HOLMES HOOKER HORGAN HOSMER HOWARD HUGHES IRVING JEWETT KELLER KESTER KUMMER LARCOM LIBBEY LONDON LOVETT LUMMIS MAILER MARTIN MCEVOY MILLAY MILLER MORLEY MORROW NATHAN NORRIS PARKER PITKIN PORTER POWELL PROUTY RHODES ROURKE RUNYON SALTUS STEELE STREET STRONG SUCKOW TAYLOR THAYER THOMAS TUTTLE UPDIKE VEBLEN WARNER WATKIN WERNER WILDER WILLIS WILSON WINTER WISTER WRIGHT YERKES ALDRICH ANDREWS BANNING BELLAMY BENNETT BIGELOW BOYESEN BOYNTON BURGESS BURNETT CALKINS CARROLL CHILTON CLEMENS COMFORT COURNOS COZZENS CUMMINS CURWOOD DERLETH DREISER EDMONDS ELLIOTT ELLISON ERSKINE

FARRELL FAWCETT FERNALD FINEMAN FOLLETT FRANKEN FREEMAN GARLAND GIFFORD GLASGOW GRATTAN HAMMETT HEYWARD HOLDING HOPKINS JOHNSON KELLAND KILVERT KOMROFF LAFARGE LARDNER LINCOLN MASTERS MULFORD MUMFORD MURFREE NABOKOV OSTENSO PARROTT PEATTIE PRESTON PRUETTE ROBERTS ROLVAAG SAMPSON SAROYAN TARBELL TERHUNE THOREAU THURBER TRAUBEL VANDYKE VANLOON VOLLMER WEBSTER WESCOTT WHARTON WHITNEY WOOLSON YOUMANS ATHERTON ATKINSON AYSCOUGH BAKELESS BARRETTO BILLINGS BRADFORD BURDETTE CALDWELL CANTWELL CHAMBERS CLEGHORN COLLISON CONNOLLY CONVERSE CRAWFORD DONNELLY FAULKNER FERGUSON FREDERIC GELLHORN GLASPELL GOODRICH HAGEDORN HARRISON JOHNSTON KIRKLAND LATHBURY MACAULAY MACGRATH MARQUAND MELVILLE MICHENER MITCHELL NORDHOFF PERELMAN PETERKIN PHILLIPS PROKOSCH RAWLINGS REPPLIER RICHARDS RINEHART SALINGER SEDGWICK SPINGARN SPOFFORD STANFORD STARRETT STEPHENS STOCKTON STODDARD TIETJENS TORRENCE TURNBULL VANDOREN WESTCOTT WIDDEMER WILLIAMS ALTSHELER BACHELLER BERCOVICI BODENHEIM BROMFIELD BURROUGHS DOSPASSOS CARPENTER CHURCHILL EGGLESTON GRANBERRY HAWTHORNE HEMINGWAY KORZYBSKI LANCASTER MCCULLERS NICHOLSON OSULLIVAN SIGOURNEY STALLINGS STEINBECK STEVENSON STRIBLING CLENDENING FITZGERALD MCCUTCHEON SOUTHWORTH TARKINGTON TROWBRIDGE UNTERMEYER VANVECHTEN CANTACUZENE CHAMBERLAIN GERSTENBERG MINNIGERODE STRATEMEYER HERGESHEIMER
ARGENTINIAN GALVEZ MARMOL CANDIOTI CAPDEVILA
AUSTRALIAN BECKE WHITE BROWNE CLARKE LAWSON CALVERT COLLINS EGERTON TRAVERS PRICHARD VILLIERS CAMBRIDGE RICHARDSON
AUSTRIAN BAYER KAFKA PRAED ZWEIG WERFEL BARTSCH COLERUS NEUMANN PICHLER ROSEGGER SCHREKER ALTENBERG BURCKHARD SCHNITZLER
BELGIAN COSTER HYMANS PICARD EEKHOUD LEMONNIER
BRAZILIAN TAUNAY GUIMARAES VERISSIMO
BULGARIAN VAZOV

CANADIAN SETON SULTE PARKER MCLUHAN SERVICE CHAMBERS MCDOWELL STRINGER SULLIVAN CALLAGHAN MACDONALD MACLENNAN PICKTHALL
CHILEAN CORTES
COLOMBIAN CARO REYES CUERVO CARRASQUILLA
CZECH LANGER HOLECEK JIRASEK VANCURRA
DANISH BANG NEXO HERTZ KIDDE SKRAM LARSEN RORDAM BAUDITZ CLAUSEN DINESEN TANDRUP ANDERSEN INGEMANN BUCHHOLTZ DRACHMANN JORGENSEN MICHAELIS BREGENDAHL
DUTCH LOOY BEKKER CREMER EMANTS LENNEP MAARTENS
ENGLISH DAY LEE BECK BEHN BELL BRAY COLE DANE ERTZ FENN FORD GLYN HULL HUME LAMB LEVY LONG LYLY MORE MUIR PAUL PAYN REED REID RICE SHAW WARD WEBB WEST WOOD WREN ADAMS AMORY AYRES BARRY BATES BAYLY BERRY BLOOM CRABB BURKE CAINE CRAIK CROWE DEFOE DIGBY DIXON DOYLE ELIOT ELLIS GIBBS HARDY HEARD HEVER JEANS KEOWN LEVER LEWIS LOCKE LUCAS MASON MAYNE MCFEE MOORE MUNRO MURRY ORCZY POWYS RAMEE READE ROPES SCOTT SHARP SHIEL SHUTE SMITH STEEL STERN SWIFT WELLS WYLIE YONGE YOUNG ANGELL ASCHAM ASHTON ASTELL AUSTEN AUSTIN BELLOC BENSON BESANT BORROW BRIDGE BRONTE BROPHY BULLEN BURGIN BURTON CANNAN CASTLE CHURCH CONRAD CRONIN FARNOL FELKIN FOSTER GODWIN GOUDGE GRAVES GREENE HILTON HOLTBY HORLER HOWELL HUDSON HUGHES HUXLEY LANDON LANDOR LYTTON MACHEN MORGAN MORTON MURRAY NESBIT NORTON ONIONS ORMSBY PALMER PORTER POWELL REEVES SANDYS SAYERS SEWELL SHANKS SOUTAR SPRING STERNE TAYLOR WALTON WARNER WARREN WATSON WEYMAN AGUILAR ASHFORD BAGNOLD BALDWIN BARCLAY BENNETT BENTLEY BERNERS BOLITHO BOTTOME BULLETT BUNBURY CHAMIER COCKTON COLLINS CORELLI DEEPING DICKENS DODGSON DOUGLAS DUDENEY EDWARDS FARJEON FIRBANK FORSTER FREEMAN GARNETT GASKELL GISSING GOLDING GUTHRIE HAGGARD HASSALL HAWKINS HEWLETT HICHENS HORNUNG JACKSON JOHNSON KENNEDY KIPLING LAMBURN LEHMANN MARRYAT MAUGHAM MAXWELL MCKENNA MITFORD MONTAGU MORISON

NICHOLS OXENHAM PEACOCK
PERTWEE RANSOME RITCHIE
ROBERTS SASSOON SHELLEY
SITWELL SMEDLEY SOWERBY
SPENDER TOLKIEN VACHELL
WADDELL WALLACE WALPOLE
ZIMMERN BARBAULD BARTLETT
CHRISTIE DASHWOOD FIELDING
FLETCHER FORESTER HAMILTON
HARRADEN KERNAHAN KINGSLEY
KNOBLOCK KOESTLER LAWRENCE
MACAULAY MARRIOTT MEREDITH
MORDAUNT OLLIVANT PATTISON
SINCLAIR SMOLLETT STANNARD
STRETTON THIRKELL TROLLOPE
WALMSLEY ZANGWILL
AINSWORTH ALDINGTON
BERESFORD BLACKMORE
BLACKWOOD BROUGHTON
CARPENTER CHURCHILL
DEQUINCEY DUMAURIER
GERHARDIE GOLDSMITH
GREENWELL GREENWOOD
HENRIQUES KINGSMILL
LINKLATER LLEWELLYN
MANSFIELD MITCHISON
MONKHOUSE OPPENHEIM
PEMBERTON PHILLPOTS
PICKTHALL PRIESTLEY RADCLIFFE
ROBERTSON SCHREINER
SOUTHWOLD STACPOOLE
THACKERAY TREVELYAN
WHITEHEAD WILKINSON
WILLCOCKS WODEHOUSE
FOTHERGILL GALSWORTHY
HUTCHINSON MEYERSTEIN
RICHARDSON SHORTHOUSE
SWINNERTON WILLIAMSON
YOUNGHUSBAND
ESTONIAN TAMMSAARE
FINNISH AHO KIVI CANTH KALLAS
CYGNAUS SALMINEN SILLANPAA
TAVASTSTJERNA
FRENCH FOA GAY NAU SUE AIDE
HUGO KARR KOCKLOTI MAEL
SAND UZES ZOLA BAZIN BEDEL
BLOCH BOVET CAMUS CARCO
CEARD COLET DUMAS FABRE
HEMON LOUYS OHNET PEYRE
ROSNY VERNE ACHARD AGOULT
ARAGON ARGENS ARLAND
AULNOY AVENEL BALZAC BEDIER
BENOIT BERAUD BISSON BLOUET
BRUEYS CLADEL CRAVEN DAUDET
DONIOL EPINAY FAYARD FRANCE
HUZARD IMBERT LESAGE MOULIE
PROUST REBOUX SARTRE SCHURE
TROYAT VERCEL ANCELOT
ARNAULT BAUMANN BEHAINE
BERNARD BERQUIN BONNARD
BOURGET BOUVIER CAZOTTE
COCTEAU COLETTE DEBERLY
DELTEIL DURTAIN FEYDEAU
FONTANE HERMANT HERVIEU
HOFFMAN LAVEDAN LEBLANC
LERMINA MALRAUX MAURIAC
MERIMEE MONNIER PREVOST
REGNIER ROLLAND ROMAINS
SANDEAU SIMENON TENDRON
ASSOLANT BANVILLE BARBUSSE
BEAUVOIR BENJAMIN BERENGER
BERNANOS BERTRAND BONVALOT
BORDEAUX BOYLESVE BRUNHOFF

CENDRARS CHARTIER CLARETIE
DORGELES DUFRESNY ESTAUNIE
FEUILLET FLAUBERT GENEVOIX
GONCOURT GREVILLE HOUSSAYE
HUYSMANS LATAILLE MALHERBE
MARIETON MARIVAUX MONTEPIN
MONTFORT ROUSSEAU SAVIGNON
SCHOPFER SOUPAULT STENDHAL
VALLETTE VOLTAIRE BEAUCHAMP
BOUHELIER CHERVILLE
COULEVAIN DESCHANEL
FONTAINAS MARMONTEL
MIOMANDRE POURTALES
SENANCOUR BAZANCOURT
DESJARDINS FAUCONNIER
MAUPASSANT MARGUERITTE
GERMAN APEL BALL BAUM BOLL
BURG HOLZ KURZ MANN ARNDT
BULOW BUSSE GRASS GROTH
HAGEN HALBE HAUFF HESSE
HUBER KUHNE LANGE LAUBE
MUGGE MUNDT RAABE UNRUH
ZESEN ZWEIG BECKER BEREND
BINZER BLUNCK BUICKE CONRAD
DAUMER DREYER HAUSER
HEYDEN JENSEN JOHNST KNIGGE
LEWALD LUDWIG MILLER MORIKE
MUSAUS REUTER VIEBIG WERNER
BERTUCH BRONNEN CONRADI
DAUBLER FALLADA FREYTAG
GLAESER GUTZKOW HEIBERG
KRETZER LAROCHE NEUMANN
OSTWALD REDWITZ SEGHERS
VULPIUS AUERBACH BORKENAU
BRENTANO ECKSTEIN HAUSMANN
HOFFMANN KOTZEBUE LIENHARD
MEISSNER REMARQUE ROQUETTE
WOLZOGEN ZSCHOKKE BEYERLEIN
GANGHOFER IMMERMANN
SCHUCKING SUDERMANN
UECHTRITZ WILBRANDT
WITZLEBEN ZERKAULEN
ZOBELTITZ FLAISCHLEN
GERSTACKER KELLERMANN
SPIELHAGEN WASSERMANN
WILDERMUTH HASENCLEVER
FEUCHTWANGER
GREEK IOPHON PLUTARCH
ONOSANDER
GUATEMALAN ASTRUIAS
HUNGARIAN FAY BIRO JOKAI
FOLDES JOSIKA KARMAN SALTEN
HEGEDUS VAMBERY HARSANYI
KORMENDI
ICELANDIC KAMBAN ARNASON
LAXNESS SAEMUND
GUNNARSSON THORODDSEN
GUDMUNDSSON
INDIAN ANAND SORABJI
CHATTERJI SHRIDHARANI
IRISH BEHAN BOWEN COYLE
CROLY DOYLE GWYNN JOYCE
LETTS LOVER MOORE TYNAN
BARLOW BROOKE ERVINE GRAVES
LESLIE MARTIN OGRADY OKELLY
PEARSE BECKETT CARELTON
CORKERY LAWLESS MACGILL
MATURIN MAXWELL KAVANAGH
OFAOLAIN ORIORDAN STEPHENS
OFLAHERTY TODHUNTER
WARBURTON BARRINGTON
MCALLISTER SOMERVILLE
ISRAELI AGNON

ITALIAN VARE SERAO FARINA
MAFFEI PAPINI BARRILI CARCANO
DELEDDA GIACOMO MANZONI
ALBRIZZI BERSEZIO BOCCACCIO
CHIARELLI CORRADINI
DANNUNZIO FOGAZZARO
GUERRAZZI BELGIOIOSO
BERTINELLI PREZZOLINI
CASTELNUOVO
JAPANESE BAKIN TAMAI
FUKUZAWA KAWABATA
LATVIAN RAINIS
MEXICAN GAMBOA
NEW ZEALAND ADAMS MARSH
LYTTLETON
NORWEGIAN LIE BULL FONHUS
HAMSUN UNDSET COLLETT
GARBORG ELVESTAD KIELLAND
ASBJORNSEN
PERUVIAN PALMA URETA ALEGRIA
CACERES
POLISH REJ PRUS STRUG ANCZYC
BERENT GOETEL BALUCKI
REYMONT WITTLIN ZAPOLSKA
ZELENSKI ZEROMSKI ZULAWSKI
MILKOWSKI NALKOWSKA
DANILOWSKI KONOPNICKA
KRASZEWSKI CHMIELOWSKI
OSSENDOWSKI SIENKIEWICZ
KORZENIOWSKI
PORTUGUESE LOBO BRAGA SOUSA
DANTAS MORAES
ROMAN VELLEIUS
RUMANIAN GOGA NEGRUZZI
CARAGIALE RADULESCU
RUSSIAN BUNIN FEDIN GOGOL
GORKI FADEEV GLINKA LEONOV
LESKOV AKSAKOV ALDANOV
ANDREEV GARSHIN GLADKOV
PILNYAK ROMANOV TOLSTOI
KARAMZIN BULGAKOV POTEKHIN
TURGENEV USPENSKI VERESAEY
BESTUZHEV EHRENBURG
GONCHAROV KOROLENKO
LERMONTOV PASTERNAK
SHOLOKHOV SUMAROKOV
DOSTOEVSKI YUSHKEVICH
ZOSHCHENKO AMFITEATROV
ARTSYBASHEV GRIGOROVICH
LAZHECHNIKOV SOLZHENITSYN
SCOTTISH GUNN BEITH BROWN
JACOB MUNRO SCOTT BARRIE
BUCHAN SHAIRP WATSON
BALFOUR FERRIER MACLEOD
BUCHANAN CRAUFURD
CROCKETT LOCKHART MAITLAND
MARSHALL OLIPHANT URQUHART
FINDLATER MACDONALD
MACKENZIE MOLESWORTH
SOUTH AFRICA CLOETE PLOMER
MILLIN
SPANISH ALAS RIVAS ROJAS
TRIGO ALEMAN BAROJA PEREDA
ESPINEL CABALLERO CERVANTES
SWEDISH CARLEN EDGREN
MOBERG AHLGREN ALMQVIST
LAGERLOF SCHWARTZ
BACKSTROM LUNDEGARD
LAGERKVIST STREINDBERG
WETTERBERGH
SWISS ROD FREY HEER SPYRI
KAISER BITZIUS FEDERER
OLIVIER

WELSH MAP EVANS PRYCE
WYNNE DAVIES
AUTHORITATIVE GRAVE CLASSIC
OFFICIAL ORACULAR POSITIVE
TEXTUARY MAGISTERIAL
(PREF.) CURIO
AUTHORITY LAW ROD SEE BALL
RULE SWAY ADEPT BOARD FAITH
POWER RICHE RIGHT STAMP
SWING TITLE ARTIST AUTHOR
CREDIT DANGER EMPERY EXPERT
FASCES PUNDIT REGENT REGIME
SWINGE WEIGHT AMITATE
COMMAND CONTROL DYNASTY
FACULTY LEADING LICENCE
LICENSE POTENCY SCEPTER
WARRANT DISPOSAL DOMINION
DOMINIUM HEGEMONY LORDSHIP
PRESTIGE SANCTION STRENGTH
PROCURATION
(— OF SWITZERLAND) BUNDESRAT
(ARBITRARY —) ABOVE
(MORAL —) MANA
(ONE HIGHEST IN —) SUPREMO
(ROYAL —) SCEPTRE SOVRANTY
(SPIRITUAL —) KEYS KHILAFAT
(SUPREME —) SAY SIRCAR SIRKAR
(TEACHING —) MAGISTERIUM
(UNLIMITED —) AUTOCRACY
(PL.) ISNAD SIRCAR
(SUFF.) CRACY CRAT(IC)
AUTHORIZATION FIAT BARAT
BERAT PASSPORT SANCTION
WARRANTY PERMISSION
AUTHORIZE LET LEAL VEST ALLOW
CLEAR CLOTHE PERMIT RATIFY
APPROVE EMPOWER ENDORSE
ENTITLE INDORSE JUSTIFY
LICENSE WARRANT ACCREDIT
DELEGATE LEGALIZE SANCTION
AUTHORIZED LEGAL OFFICIAL
AUTHORSHIP PENCRAFT
PATERNITY
AUTO (ALSO SEE AUTOMOBILE)
CRATE CHUMMY LIZZIE
AUTOBIOGRAPHY VITA MEMOIR
AUTOCHTHONOUS NATIVE
EDAPHIC ENDEMIC
AUTOCLAVE DIGESTER DIGESTOR
AUTOCRACY MONARCHY
AUTOCRAT CHAM CZAR TSAR
TZAR MOGUL CAESAR DESPOT
AUTARCH MONARCH DICTATOR
MONOCRAT
AUTOCRATIC ABSOLUTE
AUTO-DA-FE AUTO SERMO
AUTOGRAPH NAME SIGN MANUAL
INSCRIBE
AUTOLYCUS (DAUGHTER OF —)
ANTICLEA
(FATHER OF —) HERMES MERCURY
(HALF-BROTHER OF —) PHILAMMON
(MOTHER OF —) CHIONE
AUTOMATIC REFLEX MACHINE
MECHANICAL
(PREF.) SELF
AUTOMATON GOLEM ROBOT
AUTOMA ANDROID MACHINE
AUTOMOBILE BUG BUS CAR SIX
AUTO FOUR HEAP JEEP PONY
TRAP BUGGY COACH COUPE
CRATE EIGHT PONEY RACER
SEDAN BUCKET CHUMMY

CUSTOM JALOPY JUNKER SALOON WHEELS AUTOCAR COMPACT FLIVVER HACKNEY HARDTOP MACHINE MINICAR PHAETON STEAMER TORPEDO VOITURE CARRYALL DRAGSTER ELECTRIC ROADSTER SQUADROL SUBURBAN VICTORIA HATCHBACK NOTCHBACK
(CONVERTIBLE —) DROPHEAD
(DEMONSTRATOR —) DEMO
(MIDGET —) DOODLEBUG
(NOISY —) BANGER
(SMALL —) MINI

AUTONOE (FATHER OF —) CADMUS
(HUSBAND OF —) ARISTAEUS
(MOTHER OF —) HARMONIA
(SISTER OF —) AGAVE
(SON OF —) ACTAEON

AUTONOMOUS FREE SEPARATE

AUTONOMY SOVEREIGNTY SEPARATENESS
(— OF GOD) ASEITY ASEITAS

AUTOPSY NECROPSY

AUTUMN FALL KHARIF AUTOMPNE FALLTIME MATURITY

AUXILIARY AID SUB AIDE ALLY ANSAR AIDING BRANCH DONKEY HELPER ABETTER ABETTOR ADJUNCT HELPING PARTNER ADJUTANT ANCILLARY PERIPHERAL
(PL.) FOEDERATI

AVAIL DO AID DOW USE BOOT HELP FADGE SERVE SKILL STEAD VALUE MOMENT PROFIT BENEFIT BESTEAD PREVAIL SERVICE SUCCEED SUFFICE UTILIZE SUBSERVE
(— ONESELF) EMBRACE IMPROVE SUBSERVE

AVAILABLE FIT FREE OPEN FLUSH HANDY LOOSE READY PATENT USABLE PRESENT VISIBLE

AVALANCHE SLIDE LAWINE VOLLEGE

AVANT-COURIER HERALD SCURRIER

AVANT-GARDE LITERATI

AVARICE GREED MAMMON MISERY AVIDITY CUPIDITY RAPACITY

AVARICIOUS CLOSE SLOAN GREEDY HAVING HUNGRY SORDID STINGY GRIPING GRIPPLE ITCHING MISERLY COVETOUS GRASPING

AVATAR BALARAMA EPIPHANY

AVELLANEOUS HAZEL

AVENGE REPAY RIGHT VISIT WRACK WREAK AWREAK PUNISH BEWREAK REQUITE REVENGE SATISFY CHASTISE

AVENGER KANAIMA NEMESIS WREAKER

AVENS GEUM BENNET BAREFOOT

AVENTURINE SUNSTONE GOLDSTONE

AVENUE RUE WAY GATE MALL PIKE ROAD ALLEE ALLEY DRIVE ENTRY ACCESS ARCADE ARTERY DROMOS RIDING STREET AVENIDA OPENING PASSAGE

AVER SAY AIVER CLAIM PROVE STATE SWEAR AFFIRM ALLEGE

ASSERT ASSURE AVOUCH DEPOSE VERIFY DECLARE JUSTIFY PROFESS PROTEST

AVERAGE PAR SUM DUTY FAIR MEAN NORM RULE SOSO RATIO USUAL VALUE CHARGE MEDIAL MEDIAN MEDIUM MIDDLE NORMAL TARIFF ARRIAGE ESTIMATE MEDIOCRE MIDDLING MODERATE ORDINARY OVERHEAD QUANTITY STANDARD
(NOT —) BORDERLINE

AVERSE LOTH BALKY LOATH AFRAID ADVERSE AGAINST OPPOSED BACKWARD INIMICAL OPPOSITE PERVERSE RELUCTANT
(— TO) ABOVE

AVERSION TOY HATE DERRY ODIUM ENMITY HATRED HORROR PHOBIA REGRET DESPITE DISDAIN DISGUST DISLIKE MISLIKE DISTASTE ABOMINATION
(— TO FOOD) APOSITIA
(— TO WORK) ERGOPHOBIA

AVERT WRY BEND FEND MOVE SHUN TURN WARD AVOID DETER DODGE EVADE PARRY SHEER TWIST DEFRAY DIVERT RETARD SHIELD DECLINE DEFLECT EXPIATE PREVENT ALIENATE ESTRANGE FOREFEND WITHTURN

AVIARY CAGE HOUSE VOLARY ORNITHON

AVIATOR ACE FLIER FLYER PILOT AIRMAN FLYING ICARUS BIRDMAN LOOPIST LUFBERY MANBIRD SOLOIST

AVID AGOG KEEN WARM EAGER ARDENT GREEDY HUNGRY JEJUNE ANXIOUS ATHIRST CRAVING LONGING THIRSTY DESIROUS GRASPING

AVIDITY AVARICE CUPIDITY

AVIFAUNA BIRDS ORNIS BIRDLIFE

AVIKOM JACKS

AVOCADO COYO PEAR PALTA AHUACA CHININ MARROW PERSEA ZABOCA ABACATE ABBOGADA AGUACATE ALLIGATO

AVOCET BARKER TILTER YELPER SCOOPER

AVOID FLY SHY BALK FLEE HELP MISS PASS QUIT SAVE SHUN VOID WARE ABHOR ANNUL AVERT BURKE DITCH DODGE ELUDE EVADE EVITE FEIGN HEDGE PARRY SHIFT SHIRK SKIRT SKULK SLACK SPAIR SPARE START WANDE WONDE ABJURE BLENCH BYPASS DETOUR ESCAPE ESCHEW REFUTE REMOVE VACATE ABSTAIN DECLINE EVITATE FORBEAR FORSAKE REFRAIN
(— A PUNCH) SLIP
(— COMMITMENT) FUDGE
(— EXPENSE) HELP MISS SKIVE
(— OVERWORKING) FAVOR
(— RESPONSIBILITY) BLUDGE
(— SUPERHIGHWAY) SHUNPIKE
(PREF.) PHYGO

AVOIDANCE DODGE OUTLET EVASION ESCHEWAL
(— OF RISK) CAUTION

(PREF.) PHOB(O)

AVOUCH AVER ASSERT

AVOW OWN BIND WARE ADMIT STATE AFFIRM ASSERT AVOUCH DEPONE DEPOSE DEVOTE CONFESS DECLARE JUSTIFY PROFESS MAINTAIN

AVOWAL OATH WORD AVOURE PROTEST

AVOWED FRANK SWORN STATED DECLARED

AWAIT BIDE HEED KEEP PEND STAY TEND WAIT ABIDE TARRY WATCH ATTEND EXPECT IMPEND REMAIN WAYLAY
(— PAYMENT) CARRY

AWAITING BEFORE BIDING

AWAKE DAW STIR WAKE ADAWE ALERT ALIVE AWARE ROUSE ABRADE ABRAID ACTIVE AROUSE AWAKEN EXCITE CAREFUL HEEDFUL STARTLE VIGILANT

AWAKEN DAW STIR ABET AROUSE BESTIR EXCITE KINDLE

AWAKENING REVIVAL WAKEFUL

AWARD LAW ARET GIVE KUDO MARK MEED METE WARD ALLOT ARETT GRANT MEDAL PRICE PRIZE ACCORD ACTION ADDEEM ADDOOM ADWARD ASSIGN BESTOW BOUNTY CONFER DECIDE MODIFY ADJUDGE APPOINT CONSIGN CUSTODY KEEPING ACCOLADE SENTENCE
(MOVIE —) OSCAR
(RADIO OR TELEVISION —) CLIO
(RECORDING —) GRAMMIE
(STATUETTE —) GRAMMY
(THEATER —) OBIE
(THEATRICAL —) TONY
(WRITING —) HUGO
(PL.) DESERTS

AWARE HEP RECK SURE WARE WARY WISE ALERT ALIVE AWAKE JERRY BEWARE KNOWING MINDFUL APPRISED INFORMED SENSIBLE SENTIENT VIGILANT WATCHFUL

AWARENESS EAR FEEL SENSE FEELING INSIGHT COGNITION SENSATION PERCEPTION
(— OF WORTH) APPRECIATION

AWAY BY TO AWA FRO OFF OUT VIA WAY AFAR GONE PAST SCAT YOND ALONG APART ASIDE FORTH HENCE ABROAD ABSENT BEGONE ONWARD THENCE DISTANT FROWARD FAREWELL
(— FROM) DOWN WITH ALONE ALOOF APART BESIDE
(— FROM HOME) AFIELD OUTLAND
(— FROM PORT) AFLOAT
(FARTHER —) BEYOND
(PREF.) DE E
(— FROM) APH APO

AWE COW FEAR AMAZE DAUNT DREAD SCARE FRIGHT HORROR REGARD TERROR WONDER BUFFALO RESPECT ASTONISH BEWILDER OVERCOME RELIGION

AWE-INSPIRING GODFUL SOLEMN AWESOME RELIGIO FEARSOME OLYMPIAN

AWESOME EERY FELL HOLY AWFUL EERIE WEIRD SOLEMN DREADED GHOSTLY

AWESTRUCK SILENT

AWETO WERI

AWFUL DIRE FINE UGLY DREAD GHAST AUGUST HORRID AWESOME FEARFUL HIDEOUS SATANIC DREADFUL SHOCKING TERRIBLE

AWFULLY AWFUL FIERCE

AWKWARD AWK CAR GAUM UNCO BLATE CRANK FALSE FUDGY GAUMY GAWKY GOATY INAPT INEPT SPLAY STIFF UNCOW UNKED UNKID CLUMSY GAUCHE RUSTIC STICKY THUMBY UNEASY WOODEN ADVERSE BOORISH CUBBISH FROWARD HALTING LOUTISH LUMPISH STILTED UNCANNY UNCOUTH UNHANDY UNREADY BUNGLING CLOWNISH FECKLESS LUBBERLY PERVERSE UNGAINLY UNTOWARD UNWIELDY CLOUTERLY MALADROIT
(— PERSON) TAWPY TUMFIE
(NOT —) FACILE

AWL BROD BROG NAIL NALL PROD PROG BRODE ELSEN NALLE BROACH DRIVER ELSHIN FIBULA GIMLET BRADAWL SCRIBER STABBER

AWN AIL EAR JAG BARB BEAK JAGG PILE ARISTA BRISTLE
(— OF BARLEY) HORN
(— OF OATS) JAG JAGG
(PL.) BEARD

AWNED BARBATE

AWNING TILT BLIND SHADE VELUM CANOPY SEMIAN SHADER TIENDA TENTORY SEMIANNA SUNBLIND SUNSHADE VELARIUM

AWNLESS NOT NOTT HUMBLE HUMMEL POLLARD MUTICOUS

AWRY CAM WRY AGEE BIAS SKEW AGLEY AMISS ASKEW GLEED GLEYD SNAFU WONKY WRONG ACROSS ASIDEN BLOOEY BLOOIE CAMMED FLOOEY SKIVIE THRAWN ASKANCE ASQUINT ATHWART CROOKED OBLIQUE PERVERSE

AX ADZ AXE ADZE EAWT HACHE MATAX BIFACE PICKEL PIOLET POLEAX THIXLE TWIBIL BESAGUE BOUCHER BROADAX CHOPPER CLEAVER HATCHET JEDDING PULASKI TWIBILL FRANCISC PALSTAVE SUNDERER TOMAHAWK
(DOUBLE —) LABRYS
(HEADSMAN'S —) MANNAIA
(MASON'S —) CAVEL
(PART OF —) EAR EYE BUTT FACE HAFT HEAD POLL BLADE HELVE HANDLE
(WOODEN —) MACANA
(PREF.) SECURI

AXHAMMER CAVEL CAVIL KEVEL KNAPPER

AXIAL VENTRAL

AXIL ALA

AXILLA AXIS ARMPIT SHOULDER

AXIOM SAW ADAGE MAXIM MOTTO BYWORD DICTUM SAYING TRUISM DIGNITY PRECEPT PROVERB APHORISM APOTHEGM DIGNITAS PETITION SENTENCE POSTULATE

AXIOMATIC PRIMITIVE

AXIS AXE NUT AXLE STEM ARBOR HINGE STALK ARBOUR CAUDEX CENTER CHITRA RACHIS CAULOME CORNCOB DENTATA POLAXIS SPINDLE SUCCULA SYMPODE TENDRIL AXLETREE MONOPODE
(— OF COCHLEA) MODIOLUS
(PREF.) AX(I)(IO)(O)(ONO)

AXLE EX BAR COD PIN AXIS BOGY ARBOR BOGEY BOGIE EXTRE SHAFT AXTREE SLEEVE MANDREL SPINDLE SUCCULA

AXOLOTL SIREDON

AXON PROCESS

AYAH IYA CHAY EYAH MAID NURSE

AYE I AY EY EYE PRO YEA YES EVER ALWAYS ASSENT FOREVER

AYESHA (HUSBAND OF —) MOHAMMED

AYU AI SWEETFISH

AZALEA ERICA MINERVA CARDINAL

AZALIAH (SON OF —) SHAPHAN

AZANIAH (SON OF —) JESHUA

AZAREEL (FATHER OF —) BANI JEROHAM
(SON OF —) AMASHAI MAASIAI

AZARIAH (FATHER OF —) JEHU ODED ETHAN NATHAN AHIMAAZ JEROHAM JOHANAN MAASEIAH JEHALELEL ZEPHANIAH JEHOSHAPHAT
(SON OF —) JOEL

AZAZ (SON OF —) BELA

AZAZEL EBLIS

AZAZIAH (SON OF —) HOSHEA

AZIMUTH ZN ARC BEARING

AZMAVETH (SON OF —) PELET JEZIEL

AZOLE PYRROLE

AZOR (FATHER OF —) ELIAKIM

AZRIEL (SON OF —) SERAIAH

AZRIKAM (FATHER OF —) AZEL NEARIAH
(SLAYER OF —) ZICHRI

AZTEC AZTECA MEXICA MEXICAN TENOCHCA

AZUBAH (HUSBAND OF —) CALEB
(SON OF —) JEHOSHAPHAT

AZUR (SON OF —) HANANIAH JAAZANIAH

AZURE BICE BLUE HURT JOVE COBALT JOVIAL JUPITER CERULEAN SAPPHIRE

AZZAN (SON OF —) PALTIEL

B

B SI BEE BAKER BRAVO
(— FLAT) ZA BEMOL
BA TRIPOS
BAA MAA MAE BLEAT
BAANA (FATHER OF —) AHILUD
(SON OF —) ZADOK
BAANAH (BROTHER OF —) RECHAB
(FATHER OF —) HUSHAI RIMMON
(SLAYER OF —) DAVID
(SON OF —) HELEB HELED
BAARA (HUSBAND OF —)
SHAHARAIM
BAASHA (FATHER OF —) AHIJAH
BABBAR UTU UTUO
BABBITT PHILISTINE
(AUTHOR OF —) LEWIS
(CHARACTER IN —) TED MYRA
PAUL TANIS ZILLA GEORGE
VERONA BABBITT JUDIQUE
REISLING
BABBLE CHAT GASH KNAP PURL
TOVE BABIL BLATE CLACK CLYDE
GLOCK HAVER PRATE TAVER
WLAFF CACKLE DITHER GABBLE
GAGGLE GLAVER GOSSIP JANGLE
MURMUR PALTER PIFFLE RABBLE
TAIVER TUMULT BLABBER
BLATHER BLETHER BLUSTER
BRABBLE CHATTER CHIPPER
CLATTER PRATTLE SMATTER
TWADDLE TWATTLE GLAISTER
BABBLER CACKLER BLATEROON
STIPITURE
BABBLING LALLATION
(PREF.) LALO
BABEL DIN MEDLEY TUMULT
CHARIVARI CONFUSION
BABESIA APIOSOMA NUTTALIA
PIROPLASMA
BABOON APE PAP PAPA DRILL
ADONIS BAVIAN CHACMA GIRRIT
PAPION SPHINX BABUINA
MANDRILL HAMADRYAD
BABUL SANT SUNT ACACIA
BABOOT GARRAT GONAKE
NEBNEB ATTALEH GONAKIE
BABUSHKA SCARF KERCHIEF
BABY MOP BABA BABE CHAP DOLL
JOEY TOTO WEAN BAIRN CHILD
HUMOR SPOIL WAYNE CHRISM
CODDLE FONDLE INFANT MOPPET
PAMPER PUPPET SQUALL WEANIE
BAMBINO CHRISOM INDULGE
PAPOOSE PREEMIE WADDLER
BABY CARRIAGE PRAM BUGGY
WAGON GOCART STROLLER
PERAMBULATOR
BABYISH TIDDY PULING SIMPLE
PUERILE CHILDISH
BABYLONIA CHALDEA
BABYLONIAN (— CYCLE) SAROS
BABY'S BREATH GYP GYPSOPHILA
BACALAO MURRE SCAMP

ABADEJO CODFISH GROUPER
GUILLEMOT
BACCATE BERRIED
BACCHANAL DEVOTEE REVELER
CAROUSER
BACCHANTE FROW MAENAD
BACCHUS LIBER LYAEUS BROMIUS
DIONYSUS
(AUNT OF —) INO
(FATHER OF —) ZEUS JUPITER
(MOTHER OF —) SEMELE
BACHELOR BACH SEAL BATCH
GARCON WANTER BACULERE
BENEDICT CELIBATE
BACILLUS GERM VIRUS MICROBE
BACK AID FRO TUB VAT ABET
BAKE BECK FULL HIND HINT NAPE
NATA REAR TAIL ABACK AGAIN
ANGEL BROAD CHINE DORSE
NOTUM SPINE SPLAT STERN
VOUCH ASSIST DORSUM HINDER
RETRAL SECOND SOOTHE
TERGUM TROUGH UPHOLD
VERIFY CISTERN ENDORSE
FINANCE POSTERN RIGGING
SPONSOR SUPPORT SUSTAIN
BACKWARD FULLBACK HALFBACK
MAINTAIN
(— A ROWBOAT) STERN
(— OF ANIMAL) RIG TERGUM
(— OF ARCHERY TARGET) BOSS
(— OF AWNING) RIDGEROPE
(— OF BOOK) DORSE SPINE
(— OF BULL) ROOF
(— OF HAND) OPISTHENAR
(— OF HEAD) NODDLE NIDDICK
OCCIPUT
(— OF INSECT) NOTUM
(— OF NECK) NAPE NUQUE
SCRUFF
(— OF PAGE) FV
(— OUT) BEG JIB DUCK FLUNK
CRAWFISH
(— TO BACK) ADDORSED
(— UP) ABET VERIFY
(— WATER) STERN SHEAVE
(SHOWING —) TERGANT
(PREF.) ANA DORSI DORSO
NOT(O) OPISTH(O) POST RE RETRO
TERGI TERGO
(AT THE — OF) OPISTH(O) POSTERO
(BENT —) RECURVI RECURVO
(SUFF.) NOTUS
BACKACHE NOTALGIA
BACKBITING CATTY DETRACTION
BACKBOARD BANK MONITOR
BACKBONE BACK GRIT GUTS
CHINE NERVE PLUCK RIDGE
SPINA SPINE LADDER METTLE
SPIRIT GRISTLE RIGBANE SPINULE
STAMINA VERTEBRA
(— OF FISH) GRATE
BACKCOUNTRY BUSH STICKS

BOONIES BACKLAND BACKVELD
BOONDOCKS
BACKDROP OLEO
BACKER ANGEL
BACKFIELD SECONDARY
BACKFIRE BOOMERANG
BACKFLASH GUTTER
BACKGAMMON IRISH LURCH
TABLE FAYLES GAMMON TABLES
BACKGAME TICKTACK VERQUERE
(— MAN) BLOT TABLEMAN
BACKGROUND FOND REAR
GROUND OFFING LINEAGE
SETTING BACKDROP DISTANCE
EXTERIOR OFFSCAPE TRAINING
EDUCATION
(— OF FLOWERS) BOCAGE
(MUSICAL —) SUPPORT
BACKHANDED AWKWARD
BACKHOE PULLSHOVEL
BACKHOUSE PRIVY OUTHOUSE
BACKING AID EGIS AEGIS BACKUP
BEHIND LINING MUSLIN REFUSE
SUPPORT HEARTING FINANCING
(LEGAL —) STRENGTH
BACKLASH LASH SHAKE SLACK
BACKLOG RESERVE SURPLUS
BACKBRAND
BACKPACK GEAR LOAD
BACKPIECE DOSSIERE
BACKPLATE REREDOS
BACKREST LAZYBACK
BACKROPE GOBLINE
BACKSEY SEY SIRLOIN
BACKSLIDE FALL LAPSE DESERT
REVERT RELAPSE
BACKSPIN DRAG UNDERCUT
UNDERSPIN
BACKSTITCH PURL PEARL
BACKSTOP BUTT
BACK TALK LIP SASS
BACKWARD FRO JAY LAX YON
BACK CRAB DARK DULL LOTH
ABACK AREAR BLATE INAPT
LOATH THRAW UNAPT ARREAR
ASTERN AVERSE BYGONE POSTIC
RETRAD RETRAL STUPID ARRIERE
BASHFUL LAGGARD LAGGING
REVERSE UPSTAGE DILATORY
IGNORANT LATEWARD PERVERSE
REARWARD RINKYDINK TAILFIRST
(PREF.) OPISTH(O) RE RETRO
BACKWARDNESS DARKNESS
BARBARISM
BACKWARDS YON ABACK
AROUND
(PREF.) OPISO PALI(M)(N)
BACKWATER EBB COVE SLEW
SLUE BAYOU BOGAN SHEAVE
SLOUGH RETRACT RETREAT
BACKWASH BILLABONG
BACKWOODSMAN HICK WOODSY
BUCKSKIN HILLBILLY

BACKWORT COMFREY
BACON PIG BARD MEAT PORK
BARDE JAMON PRIZE SPECK
FLITCH GAMMON RUSTIC
SAWNEY GAMBONE SOWBELLY
BACOPA BRAMIA
BACTERIOLOGIST AMERICAN GAY
KAHN NOVY PARK BURKE CRAIG
ERNST MOORE PLOTZ BERGEY
ENDERS JORDAN FRANCIS
KENDALL NOGUCHI THEILER
ZINSSER
BELGIAN BORDET
BRAZILIAN CHAGAS
CANADIAN WESBROOK
CUBAN AGRAMONTE
ENGLISH TWORT FLEMING
FRENCH ROUX RAMON MARTIN
LAVERAN NICOLLE
CHAMBERLAND
GERMAN KOCH FLUGGE GAFFKY
GRUBER HUEPPE BEHRING
EHRLICH GARTNER LOFFLER
FRAENKEL PFEIFFER UHLENHUTH
WASSERMANN
JAPANESE HATA SHIGA KITAZATO
RUMANIAN BABES
RUSSIAN METCHNIKOFF
SPANISH FERRAN
SWISS YERSIN
BACTERIUM ROD COLI GERM
AEROBE COCCUS CYTODE
ANTHRAX CHOLERA MICROBE
PROTEUS SARCINA VIBRION
BACILLUS LISTERIA PATHOGEN
BOTULINUS CYTOPHAGA
HEMOPHILE INFECTANT
INFECTION SPIRILLUM
MICROCOCCUS PNEUMOCOCCUS
SCHIZOMYCETE
PNEUMOBACILLUS
BAD BIG DUD ILL SAD EVIL FULL
HARD LEWD POOR PUNK QUED
SICK SOUR VILE WICK ADDLE
GAMMY LOUSY NASTY SORRY
WEARY WORST WRONG ARRANT
FAULTY LITHER LUTHER NOUGHT
ROTTEN SEVERE SHREWD SINFUL
UNGOOD UNKIND WICKED
BALEFUL BANEFUL CHRONIC
CORRUPT FEARFUL HARMFUL
HEINOUS HURTFUL IMMORAL
INUTILE NAUGHTY SPOILED
TAINTED UNLUCKY UNMORAL
UNSOUND VICIOUS ANNOYING
CRIMINAL DEPRAVED DOGGEREL
FIENDISH FLAGRANT INFERIOR
PRECIOUS SINISTER UNSUITED
(— MANNERS) TROLLOPE
(OUTRAGEOUSLY —) GRIEVOUS
(OUTSTANDINGLY —) ARRANT
PIACULAR
(RATHER —) INDIFFERENT

43

(VERY —) ALMIGHTY EXECRABLE
(PREF.) CAC(O) CACH DYS KAK(O)
MAL(E) MIS
(SUFF.) CACE
BADDERLOCKS MURLIN PURSES
HENWARE SEAWEED
HONEYWARE
BADEBEC (HUSBAND OF —)
GARGANTUA
(SON OF —) PANTAGRUEL
BADGE PIN BLUE MARK SIGN STAR
COLOR CREST CROSS FAVOR
HONOR ORDER PATCH TOKEN
WINGS BUTTON BUZZER COLLAR
EMBLEM ENSIGN FASCES GARTER
GIGLIO PLAQUE SHIELD SYMBOL
TIPONI WEEPER CHEVRON
EPAULET FEATHER BRASSARD
EPISEMON INSIGNIA SCAPULAR
VERNICLE EPAULETTE
COGNISANCE
(JAPANESE —) MON KIRIMON
(RUSSIAN —) ZNAK
BADGER NAG PAT BAIT GRAY
GREY GRIS MELE PATE ANNOY
BRACE BROCK BRUSH CHEVY
CHIVY HURON MELES PAHMI
RATED RATEL TAXEL TAXUS
TEASE WORRY BAUSON BAWSON
BOTHER BRAROW CHIVVY
HAGGLE HARASS HAWKER
HECKLE KIDDER MELINE PESTER
TELEDU WOMBAT BAUSOND
GRISARD TORMENT BRAIREAU
BULLYRAG CARCAJOU HUCKSTER
IRRITATE STINKARD MISTONUSK
(— STATE) WISCONSIN
(AUSTRALIAN —) WOMBAT
(COMPANY OF —S) CETE
(LIKE A —) MELINE
BADINAGE FOOL CHAFF JOKER
BANTER RAILLERY TRIFLING
BADLANDS MALPAIS
BADLY BAD ILL EVIL HARD ILLY
SICK SADLY EVILLY HARDLY
POORLY UNWELL FAULTILY
WICKEDLY VICIOUSLY
(PREF.) MAL
BADMINTON POONA
BADNESS MALICE PRAVITY
UNVALUE EVILNESS
(SUFF.) CACE
**BADROULBOUDOUR (HUSBAND OF
—)** ALADDIN
BAD-TEMPERED FOUL ANGRY
STINGY CRABBED GROUCHY
BAFFLE FOX GET BALK BEAT FOIL
LICK MATE POSE STOP UNDO
CHEAT CHECK ELUDE EVADE
FLING STICK STUMP BLENCH
BOGGLE DEFEAT DELUDE FICKLE
INFAMY OUTWIT PUZZLE RESIST
THWART BUFFALO CONFUSE
DECEIVE QUIBBLE STONKER
BEWILDER CONFOUND DISGRACE
JUGGLING
BAFFLED BEATEN
BAFFLING SHREWD ELUSIVE
BAG COD KIT MAT NET PAD POD
POT SAC CELL DRAG GRIP LOBE
MAIL POCK POKE SACK TOOT
TRAP WOMB BELLY BOUGE BULSE
CATCH DILLI DILLY EMERY FLOAT

HUSSY PETER POUCH PURSE
SCRIP SEIZE SNARE STEAL
BLOUSE BUDGET CAVITY ENTRAP
FOLLIS GASBAG MATAPI PAGGLE
POCKET POUNCE SACHET SEABAG
VALISE WALLET ALFORJA
BALLOON BEANBAG BLISTER
BUCKRAM CANTINA CAPCASE
CAPTURE CUSHION GAMEBAG
GOMUKHI HANDBAG HOLDALL
RETICLE SANDBAG SARPLER
SATCHEL TRAVOIS BALLONET
CARRYALL CORNSACK ENTRAILS
ENVELOPE FOLLICLE KNAPSACK
MONEYBAG OVERSLIP POCHETTE
RETICULE RUCKSACK SUITCASE
WINESKIN MULTIWALL
WEEKENDER PORTMANTEAU
(— BULGING) SWAG
(— FOR LETTERS) MAIL POUCH
KAREETA MAILBAG POSTBAG
(— FOR TOOLS) WALLET
(— OF ANISEED) DRAG
(— WITH POCKETS) TIDE TIDY
(AUSTRALIAN —) SWAG DILLI
SHIRT SHAMMY
(GAS —) CELL
(GRAB —) FISHPOND
(HAWSE —) JACKASS
(LEATHER —) JAG JAGG ASKOS
BUDGE BOUGET MUSSUK
(NET —) SNOOD GARLAND
(SEWING —) HUSSY
(SLEEPING —) FUMBA FLEABAG
SLEEPER
(WATER —) CHAGAL CHAGEN
CHAGUL
(PREF.) UTRI
(SUFF.) SACCATE SACCI SACCO
BAGASSE BEGASS LINAGA MEGASS
BAGATELLE CANON TRUNK VERSE
CANNON TRIFLE NOTHING
BAGEL ROLL BIALY
BAGGAGE ARMS GEAR MINX
SWAG CUTTY HUZZY NASTY
SAMAN STUFF TENTS TRASH
WENCH HARLOT REFUSE TRASHY
TRUNKS CLOTHES DUNNAGE
EFFECTS FARDAGE PLUNDER
RUBBISH SALMARY SUMPTER
VALISES CARRIAGE HARLOTRY
RUBBISHY UTENSILS
BAGGAGE CAR WAGON FOURGON
BAGGER SACKER BATCHER
BAGGING SOUTAGE
BAGGY LOOSE POCKY PURSY
FLABBY PUFFED PURSIVE
SACCATE
BAGNIO BAIN BATH BAGNE
PRISON BROTHEL HOTHOUSE
BAGPIPE MUSE PIPE PIVA DRONE
TITTY BIGNOU BINIOU CHORUS
GEWGAW MUSETTE PIFFERO
SAMBUKE DULCIMER SYMPHONY
ZAMPOGNA CORNAMUTE
CORNEMUSE SYMPHONIA
(PART OF —) BAG CORD PIPE
DRONE MOUNT STOCK TASSEL
CHANTER WINDBAG BLOWPIPE
BAGUETTE CHAPLET
BAH PO FOH PAH POH ROT RATS
FAUGH PSHAW NONSENSE
BAHAMAS (CAPITAL OF —) NASSAU

(ISLAND OF —) ABACO EXUMA
ANDROS BIMINI
(TOWN IN —) FREEPORT
BAHRAIN (CAPITAL OF —) MANAMA
(MONEY OF —) FILS DINAR
(TOWN OF —) RIFAA JIDHAFS
BAIL BOW DIP ANDI BALE BOND
HOOP LADE LAVE RING RYND
YOKE LADLE SCOOP THROW
VOUCH BUCKET HANDLE PLEDGE
SECURE SURETY VADIUM
CAUTION CUSTODY DELIVER
RELEASE REPLEVY BAILSMAN
BULWARKS SECURITY
GUARANTEE
(— OUT) ABANDON
BAILEE LESSEE POSITOR
CONDUCTOR
BAILER SPOUCHER
BAILIFF FOUD GRAB HIND AGENT
REEVE SAFFO SCULT STAFF
BAILIE BAILLI BEADLE BEAGLE
DEPUTY FACTOR GRIEVE LOOKER
OFFICE PORTER PREVOT SCHOUT
VARLET BUMTRAP GRIPPER
PROVOST PUTTOCK SHERIFF
STEWARD APPROVER HUISSIER
OVERSEER TIPSTAFF CATCHPOLE
CATCHPOLL CONSTABLE
HUNDREDER PORTREEVE
SENESCHAL WAPENTAKE
BAILIWICK AREA FIELD DOMAIN
OFFICE PROVINCE
BAILMENT MUTUUM
BAILOR LESSOR
BAIN NEAR LITHE READY SHORT
DIRECT LIMBER SUPPLE
FORWARD WILLING
BAIT BAD BOB COG DAP LUG BITE
CAST CHUM FEED HALT HANK
LURE PLUG TAIL DECOY HOUND
LEGER SHACK SLATE SQUID
STALE TEMPT TRAIN WORRY
ALLURE APPAST ATTACK BADGER
BERLEY ENTICE HARASS HECKLE
HECTOR KILLER LEDGER REPAST
SHRAPE SLIVER FULCRUM
GUDGEON PROVOKE TAGTAIL
TOLLING TORMENT BRANLING
CUNGEBOI BRANDLING
(— FOR BIRDS) SHRAP SHRAPE
(— FOR COD) CAPELIN
(GREASY —) ROGUE
(GROUND —) BERLEY
(MAGGOT —) GENTLE
(SCENTED —) DRAG
BAITING HANK
BAIZE BAY BAYES BAYETA DOMETT
BOCKING
BAKE DRY BURN COCT COOK FIRE
BATCH BROIL GRILL PARCH
ROAST ANNEAL HARDEN BISCUIT
PISTATE SCALLOP CLAMBAKE
ESCALLOP
(— EGGS) SHIRR
(— THOROUGHLY) SOAK
BAKED COCTILE
(— IN EARTH OVEN) KALUA
(— PRODUCT) KICHEL
BAKER OVEN FIRER BAXTER
BURNER FURNER PISTOR
FURNACE OVENMAN ROASTER
BAKER BIRD HORNERO

BAKING CUIT BATCH COCTION
FURNAGE ASSATION
BAKONGO FIOT
BALAAM (FATHER OF —) BEOR
BALACHONG NGAPI
BALAK (FATHER OF —) ZIPPOR
BALANCE BEAM EVEN PEIS REST
SWAY TRIM COVER ERASE PEISE
POISE SCALE TRONE WEIGH
WEIHE ADJUST AUNCEL CANCEL
EMBLEM EQUATE KELTER KELVIN
KILTER LAUNCE OFFSET SANITY
SQUARE STRIKE DESEMER
LIBRATE OVERRUN RESIDUE
TRABUCH TRUTINE EQUALITY
EQUALIZE EQUATION SERENITY
WESTPHAL TREBUCHET
PROPORTION
(— DUE) ARREAR
(— IN ACCOUNT) CREDIT
(— OF SAILS) ATRY
(MENTAL —) HEAD
(PREF.) STATO
BALANCED EVEN EQUAL LEVEL
APOISE KITTLE WEIGHED
COMPLETE QUADRATE TOGETHER
(PREF.) SYM
BALANCER HALTER ACROBAT
GYMNAST HALTERE
BALATA ICICA BULLACE
BEEFWOOD BORRACHA
BALCONY POY ORIEL PORCH
STOOP CIRCLE GAZEBO PIAZZA
PODIUM SOLLAR BALAGAN
GALLERY MIRADOR PERGOLA
TERRACE BRATTICE CANTORIA
VERANDAH MEZZANINE
BALD RAW BARE BASE BOLD
CRUDE DODDY NAKED PLAIN
CALLOW PALTRY PEELED PILLED
SIMPLE CALVOUS EPILOSE
LITERAL POLLARD GLABROUS
HAIRLESS TONSURED
(— HEAD) PILGARLIC
(— SPOT) TONSURE
(PREF.) PHALACRO
BALDACHIN CANOPY CIBORIUM
BALDER BALDR BALDUR
BAELDAEG
(CHILD OF —) FORSETE FORSETI
(FATHER OF —) ODIN
(SLAYER OF —) HOTH LOKE LOKI
HOTHR
(WIFE OF —) NANNA
BALDERDASH ROT GUFF PUNK
TRASH TRIPE DRIVEL JARGON
FLUBDUB NONSENSE
BALDUCTUM RIGMAROLE
BALDMONEY MEU
BALDNESS ACOMIA CALVITY
ALOPECIA ATRICHIA OPHIASIS
CALVITIES
BALDPATE ZUISIN POACHER
BALDRIC BELT LACE GIRDLE
ZODIAC BALTEUS SUPPORT
NECKLACE
BALE NO GIB NOT WOE EVIL FIRE
HARM LAVE PACK PYRE BLOCK
CRATE DEATH FARDO SERON
BALLOT BUNDLE EMBALE SEROON
SORROW PACKAGE SARPLER
BALEARIC ISLANDS (ISLAND OF —)
IBIZA CABRERA MAJORCA

MINORCA CONEJERA
(MEASURE OF —) PALMO MISURA
QUARTA QUARTIN BARCELLA
(TOWN OF —) IBIZA MAHON
PALMA
(WEIGHT OF —) CARGO CORTA
QUARTANO
BALEEN WHALEBONE
BALEFUL BAD EVIL DEADLY
MALIGN SACRED SULLEN MALEFIC
NOXIOUS RUINOUS SIDERAL
SINISTER WRETCHED
MALEFICENT
BALI (CAPITAL OF —) DENPASAR
(DANCE OF —) ARDJA BARIS KRISS
BARONG KETJAK MONKEY
DJANGER
(MOUNTAIN OF —) AGOENG
(MUSICAL INSTRUMENT OF —)
GAMELAN
(RICE FIELD OF —) SAWAII
(STRAIT OF —) LOMBOK
(TOWN OF —) SINGARADJA
BALIN (BROTHER OF —) SUGRIVA
(SLAYER OF —) RAMA
BALINGHASAY ANAM ANAN
BALK GAG HEN HUE JIB JUB SHY
BEAM BILK BUCK BULL COND FOIL
GORM HADE HEAP LICK LOFT
MISS OMIT PROP SHUN SKIP SLIP
STAY STOP AVOID BAULK BLOCK
CHECK CLAMP DEMUR HUNCH
MOUND REBEL REEST RIDGE
STAKE STICK WAVER BAFFLE
DEFEAT FALTER HINDER IMPEDE
OUTWIT RAFTER REFUSE STRAIN
THWART BLUNDER CODLING
GALLOWS ISTHMUS MISTAKE
(— IN FISHING) HUE COND
(HALF —) FLITCH
(PL.) MIDDLES
BALKAN (— COIN) NOVCIC
(— COUNTRY) GREECE SERBIA
ALBANIA RUMANIA BULGARIA
(— INSTRUMENT) GUSLA
(— RIVER) JIU OLT IBAR JIUL SAVA
TISA OLTUL DANUBE MORAVA
(— SEA) BLACK AEGEAN IONIAN
ADRIATIC
BALKER HUER CONNER
BALKY NAPPY STICK MULISH
REESTY RESTIVE CONTRARY
STUBBORN OBSTINATE
BALL IN BAL BOB FLY HOP NOB
ORB PEA TOY BEAD BOWL CLEW
CLUE KNOB KNOP KNUR PICK PILL
POME PROM TRAP DANCE EDGER
FAULT FLOAT GLOBE GLOME
HURLY ORBIT PEARL PUPPY
SHAPE SNACK SPORT TRUCK
BULLET BUTTON HOOKER HURLEY
MOONIE MUDDLE PEELEE PELLET
PELOTA POMMEL POMPON
RONDEL RUNDLE SPHERE
SQUASH BALLOON CONFUSE
FLOATER GLOBULE INCURVE
INSHOOT KNAPPAN LEATHER
MANDREL PELOTON RIDOTTO
SLITTER ASSEMBLY BASEBALL
BISCAYEN FANDANGO FOOTBALL
GROUNDER HANDBALL QUENELLE
SOFTBALL SPHEROID TRAPBALL
(— AS SHIP'S SIGNAL) SHAPE

(— FOR MUSKET) GOLI SLUG
(— OF CLAY) KNICKER
(— OF RICE OR MEAT) PINDA
(— OF THREAD) COP CLEW CLUE
GOME BOTTOM COPPIN
WHARROW
(— OF THUMB) THENAR CUSHION
(— OF WASTE IRON) COBBLE
(— USED IN SHINTY) PEG
(—S OF MEDICI FAMILY) PALLE
(BILLIARD —) SPOT IVORY
SNOOKER
(BOWLED —) TICE CURVE SKYER
BAILER BUMPER FIZZER GOOGLY
KICKER POODLE SEAMER YORKER
CREEPER SNORTER SPINNER
BREAKBACK CROSSOVER
INSWINGER
(BOWLING —) DODO JACK
(CORK —) PLUMBER
(CRICKET —) SNICK SHOOTER
(DECORATIVE —) DRAGEE
(FIVES —) SNACK
(GOLF —) PUTTY
(HARD —) SNUG
(HOCKEY —) NUN NUR ORR
(INK —) PUMPET
(MEAT —S) CECILS
(SKITTLE —) CHEESE
(TENNIS —) PALM
(WOODEN —) KNUR
(PREF.) GLOBI GLOBO SPHAER(O)
SPHER(O)
(SUFF.) SPHAERA SPHERE
SPHERIC(AL)
BALLAD JIG LAI LAY LILT MELE
POEM SONG CAROL DERRY
FANCY BALLET BYLINA CARVAL
SONNET BALLANT CANZONE
CORRIDO GWERZIOU SINGSONG
BALLAST BED CRIB LOAD TRIM
METAL POISE STONE BOTTOM
BURDEN GRAVEL WEIGHT
BALANCE LASTAGE SANDBAG
DRAGROPE KENTLEDGE
SABURRATE
BALLET BALLAD MASQUE BOURREE
PANTOMIME
(— MOVEMENT) VOLE TEMPS
APLOMB OUVERT POINTE RELEVE
RETIRE ALLONGE ARRONDI
ASSEMBLE ATTITUDE ARABESQUE
BALLHOOTER BRUTTER
BALLISTA SWEEP MANGONEL
BALLOON BAG BALL BLIMP
EXPAND GASBAG AIRSHIP
DISTEND DRACHEN INFLATE
SAUSAGE SKYHOOK AEROSTAT
ENVELOPE DIRIGIBLE
(TRIAL —) KITE
BALLOONING BOSOMY
BALLOONIST AERONAUT
BALLOON VINE FAROLITO
HEARTPEA HEARTSEED
BALLOT BALE POLL PROX VOTE
ELECT PROXY VOICE BILLET
CHOICE POLICY TICKET SUFFRAGE
BALLROOM SALOON
BALLYHOO BALLY HOOPLA
BALM OIL BEEB BITO DAUB SALVE
ANOINT BALSAM EMBALM LOTION
RELIEF SOLACE SOOTHE
ANODYNE BESMEAR COMFORT

PERFUME UNGUENT OINTMENT
(— OF GILEAD) CANADA
OPOBALSAM
BALMORAL CAP BOOT SHOE
BALMY MILD SOFT BLAND DAFFY
MOONY SPICY SUNNY SWEET
GENTLE INSANE SERENE HEALING
LENIENT AROMATIC BALSAMIC
DRESSING FRAGRANT SOOTHING
BALONEY BUNK HOOEY BUSHWA
BUSHWAH
BALSA RAFT FLOAT GUANO POLAK
POLACK BOBWOOD CORKWOOD
BALSAM BALM RIGA TOLU UMIRI
COPALM GURJAN GURJUN
STORAX AMPALEA COPAIBA
CREEPER AMPALAYA BDELLIUM
BENJAMIN OINTMENT
BALSAM APPLE KARELA
AMARGOSA AMPALAYA
BALSAMINE
BALSAM FIR SAPIN BAUMIER
BALSAM POPLAR TACAMAHAC
BALSAMROOT SUNFLOWER
BALSAMWEED MOONSHINE
FEATHERWEED
BALT YOD ESTH LETT ESTONIAN
BALTIC (— GULF) RIGA DANZIG
BOTHNIA FINLAND
(— ISLAND) AERO DAGO FARO
OSEL ALAND ALSEN OESEL
OLAND GOTLAND HIIUMAA
BORNHOLM
(— PORT) KIEL RIGA MEMEL REVAL
DANZIG GDANSK TALINN LEIPAJA
(— RIVER) ODER ODRA DVINA
VIADUA
(— TOWN) MEMEL DANZIG
GDANSK LEIPAJA
BALUCHISTAN (— CULTURE)
QUETTA
BALUSTER SPOKE COLUMEL
BANISTER COLUMELLA
BALUSTRADE BARRER PARAPET
RAILING BALCONET BANISTER
BAMBOO DHA CANE REED BATAK
GLUMAL GUADUA TONKIN
BATAKAN WANGHEE WHANGEE
(SACRED —) NANDIN
(WOVEN —) SAWALI
BAMBOOZLE DUPE HAVE CHEAT
COZEN GRILL CAJOLE HUMBUG
BUFFALO BUMBAZE DECEIVE
DEFRAUD MYSTIFY PERPLEX
BAN BAR WOE TABU VETO BANAL
BANUS BLOCK CURSE EDICT
ORDER TABOO BANISH CENSOR
ENJOIN FORBID HINDER INVOKE
NOTICE OUTLAW CONDEMN
EXCLUDE ANATHEMA DENOUNCE
EXECRATE PROHIBIT
(— ON NEWS) BLACKOUT
BANA (DAUGHTER OF —) USHA
BANAK UCUUBA
BANAL FLAT CORNY INANE SILLY
STALE TRITE VAPID JEJUNE
INSIPID MUNDANE TRIVIAL
BANANA FEI FIG MUSA SABA
BERRY ENSETE FINGER SAGING
LACATAN PLATANO SAGUING
SUNBEAM PLANTAIN
BAND BAR GAD HUB TIE TUB ZON
BEAD BELT BEND BOND CAME

CASH CORD CREW CUFF FALL
FERD FESS GANG GATE GIRT
HOOD HOOP KNOT LACE LIST
RING SASH SHOE TAPE WISP
ZONA ZONE AMPYX BANDY BRAID
CHOIR CLAMP CORSE COVEY
COVIN CRAPE CROWN FEMUR
FLOCK FRAME GIRTH GORGE
GUARD JATHA LABEL MEINY
NOISE PANEL PATTE PRIDE QUIRE
SABOT SNOOD STRAP STRIP
STROP TAPIS TORSE TRACK TRIBE
UNITE WERED WITHE ARMLET
BENDEL BINDER BORDER BOYANG
BRIDGE BUNDLE CIMBIA CLAVUS
COHORT COLLAR COLLET COPULA
COVINE CRANCE CRAVAT DECKLE
FASCIA FETTER FILLET FRIEZE
FRINGE FUNNEL GAMMON
GARTER GASKET GIRDLE HYPHEN
LEGLET MATRIX NIPPER NORSEL
PLEDGE RADULA REGULA ROLLER
SCREED STRAKE STRING STRIPE
SWATHE TAENIA TETHER TISSUE
WEEPER BINDING BLANKET
CHAMBUL CIRCLET COMPANY
ENOMOTY FERRULE FRONTAL
GARLAND HATBAND HEADING
NECKTIE ORPHREY PALLIUM
PIGTAIL PROMISE SEQUELA
SHACKLE SHOEING SWADDLE
VINCULUM
(— ACROSS SUNSPOT) BRIDGE
(— AROUND MAST) PARREL
(— IN BRAIN) LIGULA FRENULUM
FUNICULUS
(— IN ROCKS) FAHLBAND
(— OF CLAY) COTTLE
(— OF COLOR) SOCK SLASH STRIA
LACING FASCIOLE
(— OF CRAPE) WEED SCARF
(— OF INDIANS) SHIVWITS
(— OF PILLAGERS) SKINNERS
(— OF PIPERS) POVERTY
(— OF PURPLE) CLAVUS
(— OF STRAW) GAD SIMMON
(— OF TISSUE) TISSUE
(— OF 13 WITCHES) COVEN
(— ON SHIELD) ENDORSE
(— TO COMPRESS CHEEKS)
CAPISTRUM
(— TOGETHER) BANDY
(ARMED —) JATHA POSSE
(ARMOR —) TONLET
(CIRCULAR —) HOOP RING ANNULE
WREATH
(DANCE —) CHORO COMBO
(DECORATIVE —) PATTE LEGLET
CORNICE ARCHIVOLT
(DIVIDING —) CLOISON
(EUCHARISTIC —) MANIPLE
(FOREHEAD —) INFULA
(IRON —) FRET GATE TRUSS
FUNNEL STRAKE
(LACE —) SCALLOP
(MUSICIANS —) CONCERT
(RADIO —) CHANNEL
(RESONANCE —) FORMANT
(STREET —) MARIACHI
(TRIBAL —) AIMAK
(PL.) GRIPES INTERLACERY
(PREF.) TAENI(A)(O) ZON(I)(O)

(SUFF.) (CILIATED —) TROCH(A)(AL)(OUS)(US)

BANDAGE BAND BELT BIND TAPE BLIND BRACE CLOUT DRESS GALEA LINEN SLING SPICA SWARF SWATH TRUSS BINDER COLLAR CRAVAT FASCIA FETTLE FILLET LIGATE NIPPER ROLLER SWARTH SWATHE SWEATH REVERSE ROLLING SWADDLE TRUSSER ACCIPTER CAPELINE CINCTURE GAUNTLET LIGAMENT LIGATURE SCAPULAR STOCKING CAPISTRUM **(— FOR NOSE)** ACCIPITER **(EYE —)** MUFFLER **(FINGER —)** HOVEL **(JAW —)** FUNDA **(PL.)** SWADDLING

BANDALORE QUIZ

BANDANNA WEB TURBAN BANDANA PULICAT PULICATE PULLICAT

BANDEAU BAND STRIP FILLET BRASSIERE

BANDICOOT RAT MARL BILBI BILBY BADGER BIELBY PINKIE QUENDA

BANDIT CACA TORY BRAVO THIEF BANISH HAIDUK HEYDUK OUTLAW ROBBER BANDIDO BRIGAND LADRONE TULISAN BUSHWACK MARAUDER MIQUELET PICAROON RAPPAREE BANDOLERO **(PL.)** MANZAS

BANDLEADER MASTER MAESTRO CHORAGUS CONDUCTOR

BANDORE PANDORA PANDURA **(PREF.)** PANDURI

BANDSMAN WINDJAMMER

BANDSTAND KIOSK STAND

BANDY VIE BAND CART CHOP SWAP TRADE LEAGUE RACKET STRIVE CHAFFER CONTEND DISCUSS CARRIAGE EXCHANGE SHUTTLECOCK **(— WORDS)** REVIE GIFFGAFF

BANE BAN WOE BONE EVIL HARM KILL PEST RUIN CURSE DEATH VENOM INJURY MURDER POISON SLAYER NEMESIS SCOURGE MISCHIEF MURDERER NUISANCE

BANEBERRY COHOSH REDBERRY TOADROOT GRAPEWORT

BANEFUL BAD ILL EVIL VILE SWART HARMFUL HURTFUL NOXIOUS RUINOUS VENOMOUS SINISTRAL PERNICIOUS

BANG POM RAP BAFF BEAT BLOW BOOT DASH DOCK DRUB POUF SCAT SLAM SWAP SWOP TANK BLAFF CLASH CRACK DRIVE EXCEL FORCE IMPEL POUND SLAKE SLUMP SOUND SPANG STRAM THUMP WHACK WHANG WHUMP BOUNCE CUDGEL ENERGY FRINGE STRIKE THRASH THUNGE THWACK SARDINE SURPASS THUNDER FORELOCK **(— ON HEAD)** BRAIN

BANGLADESH (CAPITAL OF —) DACCA **(COIN OF —TH)** TAKA

(MONEY OF —) TAKA **(NATIVE OF —)** BENGALI **(RIVER OF —)** GANGES **(TOWN IN —)** KHULNA CHITTAGONG

BANGLE ORNAMENT

BANG-UP SLAP CRACK TIPTOP

BANISH BAN FREE ABAND EJECT EXILE EXPEL FLEME WAIVE WREAK BANDIT DEPORT DISPEL DISTER FORSAY OUTLAW ABANDON CONDEMN CONFINE DISMISS DIVORCE EXCLUDE DISPLACE RELEGATE

BANISHED FUGITIVE

BANISHMENT EXILE BANNIMUS OUTLAWRY XENELASY OSTRACISM XENELASIA

BANISTER RAILING BALUSTER

BANJO BOX BANJORE BANJORINE

BANK BAR BAY COP JUG RIM ROW BINK BRAE BREW BUTT CAJA DIKE DUNE DYKE EDGE HEAD HILL LINK MASS PILE RAKE RAMP RIPA RIVE SAND SCAR SEAT SIDE TIER WEIR BANCO BENCH BLUFF BRINK COAST DITCH EARTH FENCE HOVER HURST LEVEE MARGE MOUND MOUNT RIDGE SAVER SHARE SHELF SHOAL SHORE SLOPE STACK STAGE TRUST HAGGLE BORROW CAISSE CAUSEY CRADGE DEGREE DEPEND DOUBLE MARGIN RANDOM RECKON RIVAGE STRAND ANTHILL BANKING CUSHION DEPOSIT LOMBARD POTTERY SANDBAG SHALLOW WINDROW BARRANCA PLATFORM TRAVERSE **(— A FIRE)** REST **(— FOR DRYING BRICKS)** HACK **(— OF CANAL)** BERM BERME HEELPATH **(— OF EARTH)** COP DAM DITCH **(— OF RIVER)** RIPA WHARF STRAND **(— OF SAND OR MUD)** BAR SCALP **(— OF SNOW)** WREATH SNOWDRIFT **(— OF TURF)** SUNK **(OVERHANGING —)** BREW HOVER **(RUSSIAN —)** CRAPETTE **(STEEP —)** HEUCH HEUGH WOUGH BARRANCA BARRANCO **(PREF.)** RIPI

BANKER BOOK SETH SETT FACTOR FINDER SAHKAR SHROFF SOUCAR SOWCAR LOMBARD MARWARI MONEYER SPONSOR TAILLEUR BANQUETER FINANCIER

BANKNOTE CRISP FLIMSY SCREEN **(FORGED —)** STUMER

BANKRUPT SAP BONG BUNG BUST DUCK RUMP BREAK BROKE DRAIN SMASH STRIP BROKEN BUSTED DYVOUR QUISBY CRACKED DEPLETE

BANKRUPTCY SMASH FAILURE SMASHUP

BANKSMAN LANDER HILLMAN

BANLIEUE LOWY ENVIRONS

BANNER FANE FLAG JACK SIGN

COLOR ENSIGN FANNON PENNON LABARUM LEADING PENNANT SALIENT BANDEROL BRATTACH FOREMOST GONFALON ORIFLAMB STANDARD STREAMER VEXILLUM BEAUSEANT ORIFLAMME **(— ON TRUMPET)** TABARD **(FUNERAL —)** BANNEROL GUMPHEON GUMPHION **(PL.)** ENSIGNRY

BANNOCK PANAK DIGGER JANNOCK

BANNS CRY BANS CRIES NOTICE SIBRET SIBRIT SIBREDE SPURRINGS

BANQUET FETE MEAL DIFFA FEAST DINNER JUNKET MANGER REGALE REGALO REPAST SEUDAH SPREAD AHAAINA CONVITO CONVIVE NAMGERY REGALIO CAROUSAL FESTIVAL SYMPOSIUM SYSSITION

BANQUETER CONVIVE SYMPOSIAST

BANQUETING EPULATION TRENCHERING

BANSHEE BOW SIDHE

BANTAM COCK GRIG BANTY DANDY SAUCY CHICKEN SEBRIGHT COMBATIVE

BANTENG OX TSINE BANTIN TEMADAU

BANTER COD KID RAG ROT CHIP FOOL JEST JOKE JOSH MOCK QUIZ RAIL RAZZ BORAK CHAFF DRAPE JOLLY QUEER RALLY ROAST TAUNT TRICK DELUDE DERIDE HAGGLE SATIRE BADINER STASHIE BADINAGE CHAFFING GIFFGAFF RAILLERY RIDICULE

BANTU ILA BULU GOGO GUHA HEHE YAKA ZULU DUALA KAFIR KAMBA KIOKO KONDE KONGO LAMBA SHONA SWAZI BANYAI BASUTO DAMARA HERERO KAFFIR NATIVE THONGA WAGUHA YAKALA CABINDA MASHONA SWAHILI WACHAGA **(— LANGUAGE)** ILA RONGA NYANJA THONGA NYAMWEZI

BANYAN BUR BURR BANIYA BUNNIA JAGUEY

BAOBAB MOWANA IMBONDO TEBELDI CALABASH ADANSONIA

BAPTISM CLEANSING IMMERSION PALINGENY PERFUSION

BAPTISMAL FONTAL

BAPTIST DIPPER DOPPER DIDAPPER SEPARATE TRASKITE

BAPTIZE DIP DEPE FULL NAME HEAVE VOLOW PLUNGE PURIFY ASPERSE CLEANSE IMMERSE CHRISTEN SPRINKLE

BAPTIZED ILLUMINATE

BAR BAN DAM FID FOX GAD LAW LEG RIB ROD TAP AXLE BALK BAND BAUN BAUR BEAM BOLT BOOM BULL CAKE CHAR CORE CROW DRAG FLAT GATE HIDE JOKE LOCK MAKE OUST POLE RACK RAIL REEF SAVE SETT SHUT SKID SLAB SLAT SLIP SLOT SNIB STOP TREE YARD ARBOR BAULK BENCH BETTY BILBO BLOCK

BLOOM BRACE CATCH CLASP CLOSE COURT CRAMP CREEL DEBAR DETER DOLLY EASER EMBAR ESTOP FENCE FORCE GEMEL HEDGE HORSE HUMET LEVER PERCH PILOT PINCH PITCH RANCE RATCH SHADE SHAFT SHAPE SIGHT SLOTE SNEEK SPELL SPOON SPRAG STAFF STANG STAVE STEEK STRAP STRIP STRUT SWIPE TRACE YAIRD ANCONY BARRET BATTEN BILLET BISTRO BODEGA BROOCH BUMPER CRUTCH DOFFER DOLLEY DOLLIE EVENER EXCEPT EYEBAR FASTEN FORBAR FORBID FORCER FORSET GRILLE HEAVER HINDER LADDER MEAGRE NORMAN PEELER RABBLE RADIAL RETURN RIFFLE SALOON SHADES SHANTY STOWER STRIPE TABLET TANGLE TILLER TOGGLE BARRACE BARRAGE BARRIER BOBSTAY BOLSTER BUVETTE CHANNEL CHARIOT CONFINE COUNTER DRAWBAR EXCLUDE GALLOWS MANDREL MANDRIL OVERARM PREVENT SCRATCH SIDEBAR SNIBBLE SPINDLE STEMMER TOMBOLO TOPRAIL TRUNDLE WIREBAR ASTRAGAL KNIFEWAY MURDERER PESSULUS **(— FOR TAPPING FURNACE)** LANCET **(— IN FABRIC)** BARRE **(— IN RIVER)** CHAR SANDBAR **(— IN SEA)** SWASH **(— OF CULTIVATOR)** ARCH **(— OF DOOR)** SLOT STANG **(— OF ELECTRIC SWITCH)** BLADE **(— OF GATE)** SPAR LEDGE **(— OF HARROW)** BULL **(— OF LOOM)** EASER SWORD BATTEN BACKSTAY **(— OF RAYS)** SHOOT **(— OF STEEL)** BLOOM BILLET STIRRUP **(— OF WAGON)** SHETH **(— ON SIDE OF BOWSPRIT)** WHISKER **(— ON WINDMILL)** UPLONG **(— SUPPORTING MILLSTONE)** MOLINE **(— WITH SHACKLES)** BILBOES **(— WITH SPIKES)** HERISSON **(CAST IRON —)** SOW **(CONNECTING —)** ZYGON **(HERALDIC —)** FESS FESSE HUMET LABEL **(JOINTED —)** CHILL **(MINING —)** MOIL **(NOTCHED —)** RISP SKEY **(PAIR OF —S)** GEMEL GEMMEL **(REFRESHMENT —)** BUFFET CANTEEN **(SOAP FRAME —)** SESS **(STIRRING —)** CRUTCH **(TAMPING —)** STEMMER **(TYPEWRITER —)** BAIL BALE SPACER SHUTTLE **(WEAVING —)** TEMPLE **(WHEEL —)** AXLE SPOKE

BARACHEL (SON OF —) ELIHU

BARAK (FATHER OF —) ABINOAM

BARANI BRANDY
BARB AWN BUR JAG MOW BURR
CLIP FILE FLUE HAIR HERL HOOK
JAGG BEARD HORSE POINT RIDGE
SHAFT SPEAR PIGEON STRAIN
TIPPET WITTER BARBARY
BARBULE BRISTLE FILAMENT
KINGFISH
(— OF ARROW) HOOK WING BEARD
WITTER
(— OF FEATHER) HARL HERL
RAMUS PINNULA FILAMENT
(— OF HARPOON) FLUE FLUKE
(PREF.) ONC(O)
BARBADOS (CAPITAL OF —)
BRIDGETOWN
(MOUNTAIN OF —) HILLABY
(NATIVE OF —) BIM
BARBADOS CHERRY ACEROLA
BARBAREA CAMPE
BARBARIAN HUN BOOR GOTH
RUDE WILD ALIEN BRUTE SAVAGE
VANDAL RUFFIAN FOREIGNER
UNTUTORED TRAMONTANE
BARBARIC GROSS ATROCIOUS
BARBARISM CANT DATISM
SAVAGISM SOLECISM
BARBARITY FERITY CRUELTY
FELLNESS FEROCITY RUDENESS
SAVAGERY BRUTALITY
BARBAROUS FELL RUDE WILD
CRUEL BRUTAL FIERCE GOTHIC
BESTIAL FOREIGN HUNNISH
INHUMAN SLAVISH UNCIVIL
IGNORANT CUTTHROAT
FEROCIOUS PRIMITIVE
BARBARY MAGOT MAGHRIB
MOGHRIB
(— STATE) TUNIS ALGIERS
MOROCCO TRIPOLI
BARBASCO CUBE JOEWOOD
BARBECUE ASADO BOCAN
BUCCAN
BARBEL BEARD CIRRUS WATTLE
BARBLET CYPRINID
BARBER NAI FIGARO POLLER
SHAVER TONSOR SCRAPER
TONSURE
(— FISH) TANG
BARBER OF BAGDAD (CHARACTER
IN —) ABUL BEKAR CALIPH
MARGIANA NUREDDIN
(COMPOSER OF —) CORNELIUS
BARBER OF SEVILLE (CHARACTER
IN —) BERTHA FIGARO ROSINA
BARTOLO LINDORO ALMAVIVA
(COMPOSER OF —) ROSSINI
BARBERRY MAHONIA
BARBET BARBION BARMKIN
DREAMER BARBICAN PUFFBIRD
WATERRUG IRONSMITH
PEARLBIRD THICKHEAD
TIGERBIRD
BARBITAL VERONAL
BARBITURATE DOWNER SECONAL
PENTOBARBITAL PHENOBARBITAL
BARBULE RADIUS RADIOLUS
BARCHESTER TOWERS (AUTHOR
OF —) TROLLOPE
(CHARACTER IN —) BOLD SLOPE
ARABIN BERTIE NERONI ELEANOR
GRANTLY HARDING OBADIAH
PROUDIE SEPTIMUS STANHOPE

CHARLOTTE ETHELBERT
QUIVERFUL
BARD BHAT MUSE POET SCOP
SWAN DRUID OVATE RUNER
SCALD SKALD OSSIAN SHAPER
SINGER BARDING PENBARD
MINSTREL MUSICIAN TALIESEN
DEMODOCUS SEANNACHIE
BARE DRY BALD LEAN MERE NUDE
POOR THIN ALONE BLEAK CRUDE
EMPTY NAKED PLAIN PLUME
SCANT STARK STRIP WASTE
BARISH BARREN CALLOW
DENUDE DIVERT DIVEST EXPOSE
HISTIE MARGIN MEAGER MEAGRE
PALTRY PILLED REVEAL SCARRY
SIMPLE DIVULGE EXPOSED
UNARMED UNCOVER DENUDATE
DESOLATE DISCLOSE STRIPPED
DESTITUTE
(— TEETH) TUCK
(NOT —) COOL
(PREF.) GYMN NUDI PSIL(O)
BAREFACED GLARING IMPUDENT
AUDACIOUS SHAMELESS
BARELY JIMP JUST ONLY FANIT
HARDLY MERELY POORLY SIMPLY
UNEATH UNNETH NAKEDLY
UNNETHE EDGEWAYS SCANTILY
SCARCELY SLIGHTLY
BARER NAVVY DELVER FEIGHER
MUCKMAN CALLOWER
BARFISH DORAB
BARGAIN GO BUY RUG WOD COPE
DEAL HUCK KOOP MART MISE
PACT PICK RUGG SALE SELL SNIP
SONG TROG WHIZ CHEAP FIGHT
PRICE STEAL TROKE TRUCK
WHACK WHIZZ BARTER DICKER
HAGGLE HIGGLE INDENT NIFFER
PALTER CHAFFER CHEAPEN
COMPACT CONTEND CONTEST
DISPOSE PACTION TRAFFIC
CONTRACT COVENANT
PENNORTH PURCHASE STRUGGLE
WANWORTH PENNYWORTH
(— HARD) PRIG
(— IN MINING) STURT
BARGAINER NIP KITE COPER
COWPER CHAFFERER
(SHARP —) SCREW
BARGAINING MART ACHATE
CHAFFER CHEAPING HUCKSTERY
BARGE ARK BOX BOY HOY TOW
TUB BARK BOAT FUST LUMP
PRAM RAFT SCOW TROW BARCA
CASCO DUMMY FOIST LUNGE
LURCH PRAAM SCOLD SHREW
VIXEN BARQUE BERATE BUGERO
DREDGE GALLEY GYASSA
PRAHAM REBUKE STUMPY
TENDER THRUST WHERRY
BALLOON BIRLING BIRLINN
CHALANA DROGHER GABBARD
GABBART GONDOLA LIGHTER
OMNIBUS TOWBOAT TUMBLER
TUMBRIL BILLYBOY BUDGEROW
CARRIAGE BUCENTAUR
MOORPUNKY
(COAL —) KEEL
(TOWED —) BUTTY
BARGEMAN PUG BARGEE BARGER
HOYMAN HUFFLER

BARGHEST PADFOOT
BARITE CAUK CAWK TIFF CAULK
BARYTES BARYTINE HEPATITE
BARK AGO BAG BAY OUF RUB TAN
WAP YAP YIP BAFF BOAT BOOF
COAT COTO DITA HOWL HUSK
OPEN PEEL PELT PILL REND RIND
ROSS SKIN SNAP TAPA WAFF
YAFF YAWP YELP YIPE AABEC
BALAT BARCA BARGE COUGH
MOCHA NIEPA SHELL SHOUT
SPEAK STRIP TIMBE YAMPH
YOUFF ABRADE AGAMID AVARAM
BARKEY BOWWOW CASSIA
CORNUS CORTEX GIRDLE MASSOY
SINTOC TRANKY WAFFLE YAFFLE
CASCARA MALAMBO MESENNA
PEREIRA PHLOEUM SOLICIT
TANBARK DOUNDAKE EUONYMUS
FRANGULA GRANATUM
MEZEREUM WOODSKIN
RHYTIDOME QUERCITEON
(AROMATIC —) CANELLA
CULILAWAN
(EXTERIOR OF —) ROSS
(INNER —) BAST
(LAYER OF —) HAT
(PREF.) CORTICI CORTICO PHELLO
PHLO(E)(EO) QUIN(O)
BARKER BUFFER DOORMAN
GRINDER SPIELER SPUDDER
SPRUIKER CHARLATAN
BARKING BAY SPUD QUEST
LATRANT LATRATION
BARLEY BIG BEAR BENT BERE BIGG
GRAIN SPRAT LICORN HORDEUM
WHITECORN
(AWN OF —) HORN
(GROUND —) TSAMBA
(HULLED —) PTISAN
(REFUSE —) SHAG FLINTS
(PREF.) ALPHITO CRITHO
BARLEY CAKE
(PREF.) MAZO
BARN BYRE AMBAR LATHE STALL
GRANGE STABLE SKIPPER
COWHOUSE
(— OWL) LULU MADGE
(COW —) SAUR SHIPPON
(PART OF —) BAY HIP DOOR EAVE
APRON GABLE RIDGE VERGE
AWNING CUPOLA DORMER
PENTHOUSE VENTILATOR
WEATHERVANE
BARNACLE BRAY BREY ACORN
LEPAS CYPRIS ANATIFA BALANID
LEPADID CIRRIPED GNATHOPOD
SACCULINA
BARNBURNER SOFT
BARNSTORM TOUR
BARNYARD PIGHTLE BACKSIDE
FARMYARD STRAWYARD
BAROMETER GLASS ANEROID
OROMETER STATOSCOPE
BARON THANE DAIMIO BARONET
FREEMAN FREIHERR
(COURT —) HALLMOOT
BARONY HAN DOMAIN
BAROQUE GOTHIC ORNATE
ROCOCO GROTESQUE IRREGULAR
BAROTO VINTA
BARRACK CAMP BOTHY CASERN
CANNABA CUARTEL

BARRACKS HOOCH HOOTCH
BARRACUDA CUDA KAKU SPET
BARRY PELON SNAKE SNOOK
SNOOK BECUNA PICUDA SCOOTS
SENNET VICUDA KATONKEL
SCOOTERS
BARRAGE BAR ATTACK VOLLEY
BARRIER DRUMFIRE UMBRELLA
CANNONADE FUSILLADE
BARRAMUNDA SALMON CYCLOID
DIPNOAN FLATHEAD CERATODUS
BARRED CUCKOO RIBBED STRIPED
BARREL FAT HUB KEG TUN VAT
BUTT CADE CASK DRUM KANG
TREE WOOD BOWIE QUILL SHELL
STAND UNION FESSEL GIRNAL
GIRNEL HOGGET RUMBLE RUNLET
TIERCE TUMBLE VESSEL CALAMUS
CISTERN PACKAGE RATTLER
RUNDLET TUMBLER CYLINDER
HOGSHEAD KILDERKIN
(— OF FEATHER) CALAMUS
(— OF REVOLVER) CHAMBER
(— ROW) LONGER
(— WITH CRANKS) VANGEE
(CAPSTAN —) SPOOL
(CORE —) LANTERN
(HERRING —) CADE CRAN
(PART OF —) HEAD HOOP CHIME
STAVE BOTTOM
(SMALL —) KEG KIT CADE KNAG
RUNLET BARRICO RUNDLET
(TAR —) CLAVIE
BARRELHOUSE GUTBUCKET
BARREN DRY ARID BARE BOWY
DEAD DEAF DOUR DULL EILD
GAST GELD LEAN NUDE POOR
SALT SECK YELD YELL ADDLE
BLEAK BLUNT BOWEY DRAPE
DUSTY EMPTY GAUNT GHAST
GUESS NAKED STARK STERN
WASTE YEILD DESERT EFFETE
FALLOW HISTIE HUNGRY JEJUNE
MEAGER STUPID SAPLESS
STERILE DESOLATE IMPOTENT
TEEMLESS TREELESS
(NOT —) FACILE FECUND
(PL.) LANDES
(PREF.) STEIRO
BARREN GROUND (AUTHOR OF —)
GLASGOW
(CHARACTER IN —) JASON RUFUS
GENEVA JOSIAH NATHAN OAKLEY
PEDLAR DORINDA ELLGOOD
GREYLOCK
BARRENNESS DEARTH VACANCY
EMPTINESS
BARRICADE BAR STOP BLOCK
CLOSE FENCE ABATIS PRISON
BARRAGE BARRIER DEFENSE
FORTIFY OBSTRUCT RAMFORCE
REVETMENT ROADBLOCK
(— OF TREES) ABATIS
BARRIER ALP BAR DAM BALK
BOMA CRIB CROY DIKE DOOR
DYKE FOSS GATE LINE LOCK PALE
STOP WALL WEIR BAULK BOUND
CHAIN FENCE FOSSE GRILL
HEDGE LIMIT STILE STUMP
CORDON GLACIS GRILLE HURDLE
SCREEN TREBLE BARRAGE
CEILING CHICANE CURTAIN
GALLERY PARAPET RAILING

RAMPART BOUNDARY FORTRESS FRONTIER STOCKADE STRENGTH TRAVERSE (— **ACROSS RIVER**) STILL KIDDLE (— **IN TRUCK**) HEADER (— **OF TREES**) SHELTERBELT (**ARTIFICIAL** —) FOSS FOSSE (**PROTECTIVE** —) REDOUBT (**TRAFFIC** —) SEPARATOR (PL.) BAIL (PREF.) HERCO

BARRING BUT SAVE CLOSED

BARRISTER COLT BARMAN JUNIOR LAWYER TUBMAN COUNSEL POSTMAN TEMPLAR ADVOCATE ATTORNEY SERJEANT (PL.) BAR

BARROOM PUB CAFE HOUSE SALOON CANTINA DOGGERY GROCERY TAPROOM DRAMSHOP DRINKERY EXCHANGE GROGGERY GROGSHOP

BARROW HOD HOG BANK BIER DUNE GALT HILL MOTE TUMP CARRY GRAVE GURRY HURLY MOUND SEDAN TRUCK BURROW GALGAL KURGAN NAVETA HILLOCK TROLLEY TUMULUS MOUNTAIN PUSHCART

BARRULET VIVRE

BARTENDER MIXER BARMAN BARMAID SKINKER TAPSTER

BARTER CHAP CHOP COPE COUP HAWK MANG MONG SELL SWAP TROG VEND CORSE TRADE TROKE TRUCK DICKER NIFFER SCORSE BARGAIN CAMBIUM CHAFFER PERMUTE TRAFFIC TRUCKLE COMMERCE EXCHANGE TRUCKAGE

BARTERED BRIDE (**CHARACTER IN** —) JASEK JENIK KECAL MICHA TOBIAS MARENKA ESMERALDA (**COMPOSER OF** —) SMETANA

BARTERER COPER COWPER TRUCKER

BARUCH (**FATHER OF** —) NERIAH ZABBAI COLHOZEH

BARYTES CAUK CAWK HEPATITE

BARZILLAI (**SON OF** —) ADRIEL

BASAL BASIC BASILAR RADICAL

BASALT MARBLE NAVITE DIABASE GHIZITE KULAITE POTTERY AUGANITE BANDAITE BASANITE DOLERITE ANAMESITE ARAPAHITE MELAPHYRE SUDBURITE VARIOLITE (**DECOMPOSED** —) WACKE

BASE BED DEN HUB LOW TUT ANIL CLAM EVIL FOOT FOUL HUBB HUNK LEWD MEAN POOR RELY REST ROOT SACK STAY STEM STEP VILE BASIS BLOCK CHEAP DIRTY FIRST FLOOR FOUND LACHE MUDDY PETTY SNIDE SOCLE STAND STOOL WORSE ABJECT BOTTOM BRASSY COARSE COMMON DEMISS GROUND GRUBBY HARLOT HUMBLE MENIAL NOUGHT PALTRY PATAND PATTEN PERRON PODIUM RASCAL SECOND SHABBY SORDID VULGAR BASTARD

CAITIFF COMICAL CURRISH DEBASED FOOTING HANGDOG HILDING HOUSING IGNOBLE OUTPOST PEASANT ROINISH SERVILE SLAVISH STADDLE STANDER SUBBASE SUPPORT CHURLISH COISTREL COISTRIL DEGRADED DRAWHEAD HARLOTRY HOLDFAST INFAMOUS INFERIOR MECHANIC MESCHANT PEDESTAL PEDIMENT RASCALLY SCULLION SHAMEFUL STANDARD STEPPING SUBSTRAT UNWORTHY WRETCHED NIDDERING (— **IN QUALITY**) LEADEN (— **OF CANNON**) SOUL (— **OF OPERATIONS**) BOOK HOME (— **OF OVULE**) CHALAZA (— **OF PETAL**) CLAW (— **OF PLANT**) CAUDEX (— **OF POLLINIUM**) DISC DISK (— **OF ROCK**) MAGMA (— **OF TUBER**) HEEL (**CHEMICAL** —) ACRIDAN ADENINE ANSERIN CHOLINE GUANINE ACRIDANE ACTININE AGMATINE ALDIMINE ALKALOID ANSERINE CONYRINE GALEGINE KETIMINE LEPIDINE SEMIDINE (**HIDDEN** —) LAIR (**HOME** —) DEN (**LEAF** —) FOVEA (**LOGARITHM** —) E RADIX (**SECOND** —) KEYSTONE (**STALKLIKE** —) CNIDOPOD (PREF.) BASI TAPIN(O) (SUFF.) HEDRAL

BASEBALL PILL APPLE DUSTER FLOATER INSHOOT LEATHER BEANBALL HARDBALL HORSEHIDE STICKBALL (— **PLAYER**) YANNIGAN

BASEBOARD GRIN SKIRT PLINTH EASEMENT MOPBOARD SKIRTING WASHBOARD

BASE-DEALING BROKING

BASELESS IDLE UNFOUNDED

BASEMAN SACKER

BASEMENT BASE CELLAR TAHKHANA

BASENESS FELONY VILITY BEGGARY SQUALOR TURPITUDE

BASH BAT LAM BEAT BLOW DENT MASH SWAT WHAM WHOP ABASH SLOSH SMASH BRUISE STRIKE

BASHEMATH (**FATHER OF** —) ISHMAEL (**HUSBAND OF** —) ESAU

BASHFUL COY SHY HELO SHAN BLATE HELOE TIMID MODEST PUDENT ASHAMED DAUNTED BACKWARD BLUSHING DAPHNEAN DISMAYED LOATHFUL PUDIBUND RETIRING SACKLESS SHAMEFUL SHEEPISH SKITTISH VERECUND SHAMEFACED

BASHFULNESS PUDOR SHYNESS

BASIC NET BASE BASAL VITAL BOTTOM BEDROCK CANONIC CENTRAL CLASSIC PRIMARY ZINCOUS CARDINAL ULTIMATE

ELEMENTAL ESSENTIAL SUBSTRATE

BASIL TULASI

BASILICA (**PART OF** —) APSE BEMA NAVE AISLE ALTAR NARTHEX TRANSEPT

BASIN DOP PAN BOWL COMB COVE DISH DOCK EWER FLOW FONT GULF LAKE PARK SINK SLAD TALA TANK COMBE LAVER SLAKE STOUP BASSON BULLAN CHAFER CIRQUE HOLLOW LAVABO LEKANE LOUTER MARINA VALLEY VESSEL CUVETTE PISCINA RECEIPT URCEOLE BIRDBATH CESSPOOL LAVATORY RECEPTOR VANITORY WASHBOWL GEMELLION (**DESERT** —) PLAYA (**GEOLOGICAL** —) BOLSON (**MOUNTAIN** —) HOYA PUNA (**ROCK** —) KEEVE KIEVE (PREF.) LECAN(O)

BASIS BASE FOND FOOT FORM FUND ROOT SILL AXIOM RADIX STOCK ANLAGE BOTTOM GROUND ACCOUNT BEDROCK FOOTING PREMISE SUPPORT GRAVAMEN STRENGTH AUTHORITY CRITERION FUNDAMENT GROUNDSEL SUBSTANCE

BASK SUN BEEK LAZE WARM ACRID BATHE ENJOY REVEL BITTER REJOICE APRICATE

BASKET IE ARK COB FAN HOT KIT LUG PAD PED PEG POT RIP TAP TOP BUCK CAUL COBB COOP CORB CORF CRIB FLAT GOAL HOTT IEIE KIPE KISH KIST KITT LEAP MAND MAUN SKEP TAPE TILL TOUR TRUG WEEL CABAS CASSY CESTA CHEST CRAIL CRASH CRATE CREEL DEVIL DILLI DILLY FRAIL GRATE MAUND MOLLY NATTE RUSKY SCULL SWILL WILLY BEACON BOKARK CASSIE CLEAVE COFFIN COURGE CRADLE DORSEL DORSER DOSSER FANNER FASCET GABION HAMPER HOBBET HOBBIT HOPPET JICARA JUNKET KIBSEY KIPSEY MOCOCK MOLLIE MURLIN PEGALL PETARA POTTLE PUNNET SEQUIN SERPET TAPPET TEANAL TOPNET VOIDER WINDEL WINDLE WISKET ZEQUIN CANASTA CORBEIL CRESSET FLASKET HANAPER MURLAIN PANNIER PATTARA PITARAH PRICKLE SCUTTLE SEEDLIP SHALLOW SKEOUGH SKIPPET WATTAPE WHISKET CALATHUS CANISTER CHEQUEEN ZECCHINO (— **BOTTOM**) SLATH (— **FOR CRUMBS**) VOIDER (— **FOR EELS**) BUCK COURGE (— **FOR FIGS**) TAP CABAS FRAIL TAPNET (— **FOR FRUIT**) CALA MOLLY CALATHOS (**FISH** —) CRAN HASK (**PART OF** —) RIB RIM FOOT JOIN RAND SLEW WALE FITCH STAKE

UPSET BORDER HANDLE

BASKET MAKER ANASAZI

BASKETRY UPSET

BASKETWORK TEE SLEW WALE SLATH STAKE SLATHE STROKE SLEWING

BASMATH (**FATHER OF** —) SOLOMON (**HUSBAND OF** —) AHIMAAZ

BASQUE VASCON EUSCARA EUSCARO IBERIAN BISCAYAN (— **DIALECT**) LABOURDIN (PL.) VASCONA VASCONES

BAS-RELIEF PLAQUETTE

BASS LOW PES CHUB DEEP DRUM FOOT ROCK BASSO DRONE HURON ROCHE SWEGO VOICE BORDUN BRASSE BURDEN CHERNA GROUND JUMPER REDEYE SINGER STRIPE ACHIGAN BARFISH BOURDON BROWNIE GROWLER JEWFISH STRIPER BACHELOR BIGMOUTH BLUEFISH CABRILLA CONTINUO ROCKFISH SPOTTAIL STREAKER TALLYWAG WELSHMAN LINESIDES (— **DRUM**) TAMBURONE (— **PART**) ALBERTI (**GROUND** —) OSTINATO (**LEADING** —) SUCCENTOR (**THOROUGH** —) BC

BASSOON CURTAL FAGOTT BOMBARD FAGOTTE FAGOTTO (**PART OF** —) BELL BOOT BUTT WING CROOK JOINT

BASSWOOD LIN BASS WAHOO LINDEN WICOPY DADDYNUT WHITEWOOD

BAST LIBER RAMIE PHLOEM NOSEBURN

BASTARD GET SOB BASE FALSE CANNON COWSON GALLEY HYBRID IMPURE MAMZER BYSPELL GETLING LOWBRED MONGREL WOSBIRD BANTLING BASEBORN MISBEGET NAMELESS SPURIOUS WHORESON (PREF.) NOTH(O)

BASTE SEW BEAT CANE COOK DRUB LARD TACK FLAMB SAUCE CUDGEL JIPPER PUNISH STITCH THRASH

BASTION JETTY BULWARK LUNETTE MOINEAU (**PART OF** —) FACE RAMP ANGLE FLANK GORGE CURTAIN BANQUETTE

BAT CAT HIT WAD BACK BAKE BATE BEAT CLUB FOWL GAIT JACK LUMP MASS SWAT TRAP WINK BANDY BATON BRICK CHUCK FUNGO HARPY PIECE SPREE STICK ALIPED BACKIE BASTON BEETLE CUDGEL DRIVER KALONG PADDLE POMMEL RACKET STRIKE STROKE WILLOW BAUCKIE FLUTTER JAVELIN MORMOPS NOCTULE VAMPIRE BLUDGEON ROUSETTE SEROTINE BARBASTEL REREMOUSE CHEIROPTER (**PART OF** —) KNOB MEAT LABEL BARREL HANDLE SIGNATURE

(PREF.) NYCTERI
(SUFF.) NYCTERIS
BATAK (— DIALECT) TOBA
BATCH LOT BAKE BREW CAST
CROP FINE MASS MESS SORT
BUNCH FLOOR GROUP BAKING
CHEESE MAKING BOILING
BREWING FORMULA MIXTURE
RAISING QUANTITY
(— OF EGGS) SETTING
(— OF GRAIN) GRIST
(— OF MAIL) SEPARATION
BATCHER BAGGER
BATE BAIT BEET PUER PURE GRAIN
BATELEUR BERGHAAN
BATEMAN DRENCHER
BATFISH ANGLER DIABLO MALTHE
DEVILFISH
BATH DIP TUB BAIN BATE PERT
TOSH BATHE LAVER STEEP
THERM BAGNIO DOUCHE LIQUOR
MIKVAH PICKLE PLUNGE SHOWER
SPONGE BALNEUM LAVACRE
ABLUTION BALNEARY
(FOOT —) PEDILUVIUM
(HOT —) STEW SCALD STUFE
THERM STUPHE THERME
(MUD —) ILLUTATION
(PHOTOGRAPHIC —) FIXER
(SITZ —) BIDET SITZBAD SEMICUPE
INSESSION
(SPINNING —) DOPE
(STEAM —) SAUNA
(TANNING —) BATE SOAK
(TURKISH —) HAMMAM HUMMUM
HOTHOUSE
(PREF.) BALNE(O)
BATHE BAY TUB BAIN BASK DOOK
LAVE STEW WASH CLEAN DOUSE
DOWSE EMBAY SOUSE STEEP
ENWRAP FOMENT SHOWER
SPLASH EMBATHE IMMERSE
PERVADE SUFFUSE PERMEATE
BATHHOUSE SEW STEW SAUNA
STUFE BAGNIO CABANA
HAMMAM STUPHE BALNEARY
BATHING LAVACRE LAVEMENT
(— SUIT) SLIP TOGS MAILLOT
(SAND —) SABURRATION
BATHROBE PEIGNOIR
BATHROOM BIFFY BALNEARY
BATHSHEBA (FATHER OF —) ELIAM
AMMIEL
(HUSBAND OF —) DAVID URIAH
(SON OF —) NATHAN SHIMEA
SHOBAB SOLOMON
BATHTUB TUB TOSH LAVACRE
BATIA (FATHER OF —) TEUCER
(HUSBAND OF —) DARDANUS
(SON OF —) HIPPOCOON
ERICHTHONIUS
BATON ROD BEND BURN WAND
STAFF STICK BAGUET BASTON
CUDGEL BOURDON SCEPTER
SCEPTRE BAGUETTE CROSSBAR
TRUNCHEON
BATSMAN BAT BATTER HITTER
SLOGGER SLUGGER STRIKER
BATTALION WARD CONREY
BATTEN END LAY RIB SLEY CLEAT
LEDGE BATTON BEATER ENRICH
FATTEN REEPER THRIVE
FERTILIZE

(PL.) SPARRING
BATTER RAM BEAT DENT MAIM
MAUL CLOUR DINGE FRUSH
PASTE POUND SMASH BALLER
BRUISE BUFFET HAMMER HATTER
HITTER PUMMEL THRING TUMBLE
BATSMAN BOMBARD CRIPPLE
DESTROY FRITTER SHATTER
SLUGGER STRIKER DEMOLISH
BATTERCAKE WAFFLE CRUMPET
BATTERING BLAST LACING
BATTERY PILE SINK TIRE TROOP
RADEAU EXCITER SINKBOX
SINKBOAT ACCUMULATOR
(GUN —) SWINGER
BATTLE WAR CAMP DUEL FEUD
FRAY MART MEET TILT TOIL
UNDO BRUSH FIELD FIGHT JOUST
STOUR ACTION AFFAIR AFFRAY
CAMLAN COMBAT SHOWER
STRIVE CONTEND CONTEST
HOSTING JOURNAL JOURNEY
WARFARE CONFLICT SKIRMISH
STRUGGLE ENCOUNTER
NAUMACHIA THEOMACHY
(PREF.) MACHO
(SUFF.) MACHIA MACHY
BATTLE-AX WIFLE POLEAX SPARTH
TWIBIL BROADAX HALBERD
TWIBILL WHIFFLE FAUCHARD
FRANCISC
BATTLE CRY CRY BANZAI ENSIGN
GERONIMO SLUGHORN
BEAUSEANT
BATTLEFIELD ARENA BLAIR
CHAMP TAHUA CHAMPAIGN
BATTLEGROUND COCKPIT
TERRAIN
BATTLEMENT KERNEL MERION
PINION BARMKIN CORNELLE
MURDRESS
(PART OF —) CRENEL MERLON
MACHIOLATION
BATTLE OF LEGNANO
(CHARACTER IN —) LIDA ARRIGO
ROLANDO FREDERICK
BARBAROSSA
(COMPOSER OF —) VERDI
BATTLESHIP MAINE CARRIER
BATTUS (FATHER OF —)
POLYMNESTUS
(MOTHER OF —) PHRONIMA
BATTY BATS BUGGY CRAZY SILLY
BATLIKE FOOLISH
BAUBLE BOW TOY BEAD GAUD
BUTTON GEWGAW TRIFLE
MAROTTE TRINKET GIMCRACK
PLAYTHING
BAWD AUNT HARE DIRTY MADAM
DEFILE MADAME PANDER
COMMODE MACKEREL PROCURER
PURVEYOR
BAWDINESS RAUNCH
BAWDRY SCULDUDDERY
BAWDY LEWD DIRTY SCARLET
BAWL CRY HOWL ROAR ROUT
YAUP YAWP BLORE GOLLY SHOUT
BELLOW BOOHOO GOLLAR
OUTCRY GLAISTER
(— OUT) JUMP CRACK SCOLD
BAY ARM COD DAM RIA VOE BANK
BARK CHOP COVE GULF HOLE
HOPE HOWL LOCH ROAN TREE

WICK YAUP YAWP BAHIA BASIN
BAYOU BERRY BIGHT COLOR
CREEK FIORD FJORD FLEET
HAVEN HORSE INLET LOUGH
MOUTH ORIEL QUEST SINUS
SPEAK TRAVE BABBLE HARBOR
LAUREL RECESS SEVERY TONGUE
WINDOW BADIOUS BAYGALL
ENCLOSE ESTUARY MALABAR
SILANGA ULULATE BREWSTER
CHESTNUT
(— OF BARN) GOAF SKEELING
SKILLING SKILLION
(— OF LIBRARY) CLASSIS
(— STATE) MASSACHUSETTS
(SWEET —) BREWSTER
BEAVERWOOD
BAYBERRY AUSU PIMIENTA
WAXBERRY
BAYOU SLEW SLOO SLUE BROOK
CREEK INLET RIVER OUTLET
SLOUGH STREAM RIVULET
BACKWATER
BAY WINDOW ORIEL MIRADOR
BAZAAR FAIR FETE SALE AGORA
BURSE CHAWK CHOWK MARKET
ALCAZAR CANTEEN BOOKFAIR
EMPORIUM BEZESTEEN
BDELLIUM GUGAL GUGUL GOOGUL
BE ABE ARE BES BEEN BETH BIST
LIVE ABIDE EXIST OCCUR WORTH
REMAIN BREATHE CONSIST
SUBSIST CONTINUE
BEACH AIR BANK CHIP MOOR
NARD RIPA SAND SLIP COAST
PLAGE PLAYA PRAYA SHORE
GROUND SHILLA STRAND
HARDWAY SEASIDE SHINGLE
LAKESHORE
(— RIDGE) FULL
(PROJECTING —) CUSP
(SANDY —) MACHAIR
(PREF.) THIN(O)
BEACH APPLE CANAJONG
BEACHCOMBER SEASONER
STRANDLOOPER
BEACHED AGROUND
BEACH FLEA SCUD SCREW
SANDBOY
BEACH GRASS STAR SPIRE
MARRAM BENTSTAR
BEACON MARK PIKE SIGN BAKEN
FANAL GUIDE PHARE RACON
ENSIGN PHAROS RAMARK SIGNAL
CRESSET SEAMARK WARNING
BALEFIRE NEEDFIRE SIGNPOST
STANDARD
BEAD NIB POT DROP FOAM GAUD
AGGRI AGGRY BUGLE FILET GRAIN
KNURL PEARL QUIRK SIGHT
STAFF ARANGO BAGUET BAUBLE
BICONE BUBBLE CORNET FILLET
PELLET PIPPER POPPET PRAYER
RONDEL WAMPUM CABLING
DEWDROP GLOBULE MOLDING
SPARKLE TRINKET AVEMARIA
CABOCHON
(ROSARY —) GAUD PATERNOSTER
(SHELL —S) SEWAN
BEADING VEINING
(PL.) TASBIH
BEADLE CRIER MACER POKER
USHER BEDRAL BUMBLE HARMAN

HERALD BAILIFF NUTHOOK
OFFICER SERVITOR SUMMONER
APPARITOR MESSENGER
BEADSMAN BEGGAR HERMIT
BLUEGOWN GOWNSMAN
BEAK NEB NIB BECK BILL CLAP
NOSE PIKE PROW LORUM SNOUT
SWORD TUTEL MASTER NOZZLE
SPERON WEAPON EMBOLON
EMBOLUM FOREBOW MOLDING
ROSTRUM BEAKHEAD MANDIBLE
CAPITULUM
(— OF SHELL) UMBO
(— OF SHIP) SPERON
(— OF SWORDFISH) SWORD
(PREF.) RHAMPH(O) RHYNCH(O)
ROSTR(I)(O)
(SUFF.) RHYNCHUS RHYNCUS
ROSTRAL
BEAKED NASUTE
BEAKER CUP HORN TASS BIKER
BOCAL BOUSE GLASS BARECA
BEAM BAR LEG RAY TIE BALK BEAK
BOOM EMIT GLOW PLAT SILE SILL
SKID SPAR STUD ARBOR BAULK
CABER FLASH GLEAM GLEED
JOIST LIGHT RAYON SHAPE SHINE
SHOOT SMILE SPEAR STANG
STOCK TRAVE BINDER BULKER
CAMBER CHEESE COLLAR FLITCH
GIRDER GLANCE HEADER MANTEL
NEEDLE RAFTER SUMMER TIMBER
TRABES TREVIS WALKER
BALANCE BUMPKIN CATHEAD
CHANNEL CHEVRON DORMANT
DRAWBAR FRIJOLE MADRIER
PINRAIL RADIATE SLEEPER
SUPPORT TRANSOM TRIMMER
TYNDALL AXLETREE BROWPOST
HERISSON PADSTONE PLOWHEAD
ROOFTREE STENTREL TEMPLATE
BRESSUMER
(— OF LIGHT) CHINK GLEED RAYON
SHAFT PENCIL SIGNAL STREAM
SUNBEAM STRICTURE
(HIGH —) BRIGHTS
(LARGE —) BALK LACE BAULK
SUMMER
(LOW —) DIM
(SANIO'S —) CRASSULA
(WEAVER'S —) TRAM TAVIL
(PL.) CRANEWAY
(PREF.) DOCO
BEAMER SCUDDER
BEAMING GAY ROSY BRIGHT
LUCENT MASSIVE RADIANT
SHINING
BEAMY BROAD BRIGHT JOYOUS
LUCENT MASSIVE RADIANT
MIRTHFUL
BEAN BON NIB URD CHAP FABA
FAVA GRAM HABA HEAD LIMA
POLE SNAP TEKE TICK BRAIN
CARAT PULSE SIEVA SKULL
CACOON CASTER COLLAR
FELLOW KIDNEY LABLAB LENTIL
NIPPLE NOGGIN RUNNER RUTTEE
SEEWEE STRIKE TEPARY THRASH
TRIFLE CALABAR FRIJOLE
MAZAGAN PHASEMY SNAPPER
WINDSOR BONAVIST BONNYVIS
RAMBUTAN TICKBEAN TORNILLO
(— CURD) TOFU

(LOCUST —) CAROB
(MESCAL —) SOPHORA
(PL.) NIBS FASELS FESELS
PODDER PODWARE
(PREF.) FABI
BEANIE DINK
BEAN-SHAPED FABIFORM
BEANSHOOTER TRUNK
PEASHOOTER
BEAN TREE BOGUM
BEAN TREFOIL LABURNUM
BEAR GO CUB LUG BALU BERN
BORN CAST DREE DUBB FURE
GEST GIVE HAVE HOLD LIFT TEEM
TOTE URSA WEAR ABEAR ABIDE
ALLOW BALOO BEGET BHALU
BREED BRING BROOK BROWN
BRUIN CARRY DREIE DRIVE GESTE
ISSUE KOALA POLAR PRESS
SPARE STAND STICK THOLE
THROW WEIGH WIELD YIELD
AFFORD BEHAVE BRUANG
CONVEY ENDURE IMPORT INFANT
KADIAK KINDLE KODIAK PIERCE
RENDER SUFFER THRUST UPHOLD
URSULA WOMBAT WOOBUT
ABROOKE ARCTOID BROWNIE
COMPORT CONDUCT EPHRAIM
FORBEAR GRIZZLY MUSQUAW
PRODUCE STOMACH SUPPORT
SUSTAIN UNDERGO FISSIPED
SILVERTIP
(— EXPENSES) DEFRAY
(— FLOWERS) FLOURISH
(— FRUIT) FRUCTIFY
(— INVESTIGATION) WASH
(— ON) CONCERN
(— OUT) PROPORT
(— PATIENTLY) DIGEST
(— UP) CAPE ENDURE SUSTAIN
(— WITH CREDIT) TEEM SPEAK ATTEST
DEPOSE
(— WITNESS) TEEM SPEAK ATTEST
DEPOSE
(— YOUNG) FIND CALVE CHILD
(MALE —) BOAR
(SLOTH —) ASWAIL
(PREF.) ARCT(O) URSI
(SUFF.) FER(ENCE)(ENT)(OUS)
GEN(E)(ESIA)(ESIS)(ETIC)(IC)
(IN)(OUS)(Y) GER(ENCE)(ENT)(OUS)
BEARBERRY LARB WHORTLE
BILBERRY DOGBERRY FOXBERRY
CREASHAKS
BEARD ANE AWN AVEL BARB DEFY
FACE FUZZ NECK NOSE PEAK
TUFT ZIFFS ARISTA BEAVER
GOATEE TASSEL AFFRONT
BARBULE CHARLEY CHARLIE
VANDYKE IMPERIAL STILETTO
WHISKERS BILLYGOAT
(— OF GRAIN) AIL AWN
(— TREATISE) POGONOLOGY
(SMALL —) BARBET
(PREF.) ATHERO POGON(O)
(SUFF.) POGON
BEARDED AWNIE HAIRY BARBED
BARBATE HIRSUTE POGONIATE
WHISKERED
BEARDLESS NOT NOTT IMBERBE
POLLARD
BEARDTONGUE PENSTEMON
BEARER NEWS HAMAL MACER
BEADLE HAMMAL HOLDER

PACKER PORTER ANCIENT
CARRIER JAMPANI PINCERN
CHAPRASI ESCUDERO PORTATOR
STANDARD MESSENGER
SUPPORTER
(— OF GREAT BURDEN) ATLAS
(ARMOR —) ESQUIRE
(BURDEN —) HAMAL HAMMAL
(CROZIER —) CROCIARY
(CUP —) SAKI COPPER
(PALANQUIN —) BOY SIRDAR
MUSAHAR
(SHIELD —) SQUIRE ESCUDERO
(STANDARD —) ANCIENT
(STRETCHER —) BRANCARDIER
(SWORD —) PORTGLAVE
PORTGLAIVE
(PREF.) PORTE
BEARING AIM AIR COD BALL DUCT
GEST MIEN ORLE PORT RUBY
BIRTH FRONT GESTE HABIT
JEWEL POISE SETUP TENUE
TREND ALLURE APPORT ASPECT
BILLET CHARGE COURSE DEPORT
GERENT GIGLIO MANNER ORIENT
SADDLE THRUST VOIDER
ADDRESS AZIMUTH CONDUCT
FASHION GESTURE MEANING
POSTURE PURPORT RHODING
SUPPORT AMENANCE ATTITUDE
BEHAVIOR BIRTHING CARRIAGE
DELIVERY DEMEANOR FOOTSTEP
PEDESTAL PRESENCE PRESSURE
RELATION STANDARD TENDENCY
TOURNURE YIELDING REFERENCE
(— FRUIT) FRUCTED
(— OUTWARD) EFFERENT
(ARROGANT —) HUFF
(HERALDIC —) GAD DELF ENTE
GORE MARK ORLE PALL WEEL
CROWN DELFT DELPH FUSIL
LAVER PHEON BILLET DEVICE
ENSIGN GOUTTE CHAPLET
CLARION DEMIVOL PLASQUE
QUARTER ORDINARY QUENTISE
TRESSURE
(PERSONAL —) GARB
(PREF.) PHOR(O)
(SUFF.) GEROUS IGEROUS PARA
PAROUS PHORA PHORE(SIS)
PHORIA PHOROUS PHORUS
BEARLIKE URSINE
BEAR'S-EAR AURICULA
BEAR'S-FOOT OXHEAL PEGROOTS
BEARSKIN BUSBY
BEAR STATE ARKANSAS
BEAST BETE HOOF BRUTE VACHE
ANIMAL JUMENT MONSTER
MUSIMON VENISON BEHEMOTH
BLIGHTER OPINICUS
(— OF BURDEN) JUMENT SUMPTER
(CASTRATED —) SPADO
(DEAD —) MORKIN
(FABULOUS —) YALE THRIS
BAGWYN TRICORN DINGMAUL
EPIMACUS OPINICUS GYASCUTUS
(HORNED —) RETHER ROTHER
(STURDY —) NUGGET
(WILD —) FERIN FERINE OUTLAW
UNBEAST
(WILD —S) ZIIM
(3-HORNED —) TRICORN
(PREF.) THER(A)(IO)(O)

(SUFF.) THERE THERIA THERIUM
BEASTLY GROSS PRONE ANIMAL
BRUTAL WICKED BESTIAL
BRUTISH INHUMAN SWINISH
OFFENSIVE
BEAT BAT BUM COB DAD FAN FIB
LAM PIP PLY PUG PUN RUN TAN
TAP TAW TEW TIE WAX BAFF
BAIT BANG BASH BATE BELT BEST
BLOW BOLT BRAY BUFF CANE
CAST CHAP CLAP CLUB COIL
COLT COMB CRAB DAUD DING
DINT DRUB DUMP DUNT FELL
FIRK FLAP FLAX FLOG FRAM FRAP
FRAT GROW HAZE JOWL KILL
LACE LAMP LASH LICK LOUK
LUMP LUSH MAUL MELL MEND
MILL PAIK PALE PANT PELT POLT
POSS PRAT ROUT SCAT SLAM
SLAT SLOG SOCK SOLE SOWL
STUB SWAP SWOP TACK TAKD
TICK TRIM TUCK TUND TWIG
WALK WARP WELT WHIP WHOP
WIPE BANDY BASTE BATON
BEPAT BERRY BIRCH BLESS
CHURN CLINK CREAM CURRY
DOUSE DRASH DRESS DRIVE
FEEZE FIGHT FILCH FLAIL FLANK
FORGE ICTUS INLAY KNOCK
LABOR NEVEL NOINT POUND
PULSE PUNCH ROUGH ROUND
SCATT SCOOP SCOUR SKELP
STAMP STRAP SWACK SWING
TARGE THREP THROB THUMP
TREAD TRUMP UPEND WADDY
WHACK WHANG WORST ACCENT
ANOINT BAMBOO BATTER BENSEL
BETTLE BOUNCE BUFFET COTTON
CUDGEL DEFEAT DOWSEL
FEAGUE FETTLE HAMMER
HAMPER JACKET KNEVEL LARRUP
LATHER NEAVIL NODDLE OUTRUN
PUMMEL RADDLE REBUKE REESLE
RHYTHM SCUTCH SQUASH
STOUND STOUSH STRIKE STRIPE
STROKE SUGGIL SWINGE SWITCH
TANSEL TEWTAW TEWTER
THRASH THREAP THREIP THREPE
THRESH TICKLE WAGGLE WALLOP
WATTLE WUTHER ASSAULT
BATTUTA BELABOR BLATTER
BLISTER CADENCE CANVASS
CONQUER CONTUSE EXHAUST
FATIGUE FLYFLAP KNUCKLE
LAMBACK LAMBAST LOBTAIL
LOUNDER PULSATE REESHIE
SHELLAC SURPASS SWABBLE
SWADDLE TROLLOP TROUNCE
VIBRATE MALLEATE PALPITATE
SPIFLICATE
(— ABOUT) BUSK BANGLE
(— AGAINST) BLAD
(— AGAINST THE WIND) LAVEER
(— BACK) REBUFF
(— BARLEY) PAIL WARM
(— CLOTHES) BATTLE
(— COVERT) TUFT
(— DOWN) LAY FELL FULL ABATE
FLASH
(— EGGS) CAST
(— FIBERS) BRUSH
(— HIGH) LEAP
(— IT) LAM

(— OF DRUM) RUFF RAPPEL
RATTAN
(— OF HEART) DUNT STROKE
(— ON BUTTOCKS) COB
(— SEVERELY) DRUB LUMP SOAK
BASTE SOUSE LATHER
(— SMALL) CHAP
(— TO AND FRO) BANDY
(— TO WINDWARD) LAVEER
(— WINGS) BATE FLAP
(— WITH HAMMER) DOLLY
(— WITH WHIP) SJAMBOK
(— WOODS) TUSK
(MUSICAL —) BOUNCE BATTUTA
(WEAK —) ARSIS
(PREF.) TYPTO
BEATEN BEAT BETE BATTU PARTY
TRITE TRADED
BEATER RAB MAUL SEAL CANER
LACER STOCK DASHER DRIVER
MALLET TRIMMER SCUTCHER
THRESHER
BEATIFIC DEIFIC ELYSIAN
BEATIFY SAINT HALLOW HEAVEN
ENCHANT GLORIFY SANCTIFY
BEATING COB COBB LICK TUND
BEANS DOUSE JESSE PULSE STICK
HAZING HIDING ROPAND TATTOO
BASHING BATTERY BELTING
CLANKER DASHING DUSTING
LICKING SKELPIN WELTING
WHALING BIRCHING DRESSING
DRUBBING RIBROAST SLOSHING
WHIPPING JACKETING
STRAPPADO PERCUSSION
BEATITUDE JOY BLISS BENISON
MACARISM HAPPINESS
**BEATRICE DI TENDA (CHARACTER
IN —)** AGNESE FILIPPO BEATRICE
VISCONTI OROMBELLO
(COMPOSER OF —) BELLINI
**BEATRICE ET BENEDICT
(CHARACTER IN —)** HERO CLAUDIO
BEATRICE BENEDICT SOMARONE
(COMPOSER OF —) BERLIOZ
BEAU BEW BOY CHAP BLADE
DANDY FLAME LOVER SPARK
SWELL ADONIS ESCORT FELLOW
GARCON STEADY SUITOR TATTLE
ADMIRER AIMWELL BRAVERY
COURTER COXCOMB CUPIDON
GALLANT SPARKER FOLLOWER
BEAU GREGORY COCKEYE
BEAUTIFUL FAIR FINE GLAD GOOD
MEAR MEER MERE WALY BELLE
BONNY KALON LUSTY SHEEN
WLITY WLONK BLITHE BONNIE
COMELY DECORE FREELY LOVELY
POETIC PRETTY VENUST ANGELIC
ELEGANT FORMOSE FORMOUS
TEMPEAN TOKALON CHARMING
DELICATE ESTHETIC FAIRSOME
GORGEOUS GRACEFUL
HANDSOME LUCULENT SPECIOUS
MAGNIFICENT
(PREF.) CALI CALLI CALLO CALO
PULCHRI
BEAUTIFY FAIR GILD ADORN
GRACE HIGHT PREEN PRIMP
PRUNE BEAUTY BEDECK DECORE
ENAMEL QUAINT ADONIZE
ENHANCE GARNISH GLORIFY
DECORATE FAIRHEAD

EMBELLISH PULCHRIFY
BEAUTY FACE FAIR FORM GLEE
BEAUT BELLE CHARM FAVOR
GLORY GRACE PRIDE WLITE
FINERY LOOKER LOVELY POLISH
DECORUM FEATURE TOKALON
SPLENDOR FORMOSITY
(— OF FORM) SYMMETRY
(— OF STYLE) ELEGANCE
(PREF.) CALI CALLI CALLO CALO
PULCHRI
BEAVER BOOMER CASTOR RODENT
PRALINE MUSHROOM SEWELLEL
STARLING
(— SKIN) PLEW
(— STATE) OREGON
(DARK —) NUTMEG
BEBAI (SON OF —) ZECHARIAH
BEBEERINE CURINE
BEBEERU SWEETWOOD
GREENHEART
BECAUSE AS SO FOR THAT BEING
CAUSE SINCE THERE FORWHY
THROUGH INASMUCH
BECCAFICO FIGEATER FIGPECKER
BECHE-DE-MER PIDGIN TREPANG
BECHER (FATHER OF —) EPHRAIM
BENJAMIN
BECHORATH (FATHER OF —)
APHIAH
BECK RUN VAT BECON BROOK
(— AND CALL) DEVOTION
BECKEN CYMBALS
BECKET SQUILGEE SQUILLGEE
BECKON BOW NOD WAG BECK
WAFT WAVE CURTSY SUMMON
BIDDING COMMAND CURTSEY
GESTURE
BECKONING WAFTURE
BECLOUD HIDE MASK BEDIM
DARKEN MUDDLE MYSTIFY
OBSCURE OBNUBILATE
BECLOUDED FOGGY
BECOME GO FIT GET RAX SET SIT
WAX COME FALL GROW LIKE
PASS SUIT TAKE TILL WEAR
ADORN BEFIT GRACE PROVE
WORTH ACCORD BEFALL BESEEM
BETIDE CHANGE IWORTH
BEHOOVE FLATTER PROCEED
(— A PARTY) ACCEDE
(— AUDIBLE) ARISE
(— DAMP) EVE
(— DAZED) DWAM DWALM
(— DIM) DASWEN
(— DROWSY) DOW
(— FAT) GRAZE
(— FLUID) FLOW FLUX LEACH
(— KNOWN) GO KITHE KYTHE
SPUNK
(— MOLDY) FUST MOUL FINEW
(— MOROSE) SOUR
(— ROUND) GLOBE
(— SOUR) FOX BLINK CARVE
(SUFF.) IZE
BECOMING FIT FEAT GOOD BHAVA
FITTY RIGHT COMELY DUEFUL
GAINLY PROPER DECORUM
FARRAND FARRANT DECOROUS
HANDSOME SUITABLE WISELIKE
(SUFF.) ESCENT
(PROCESS OF —) ESCENCE
(STATE OF —) ESCENCE

BECOMINGLY TALLY
BED COT HAY KIP PAD PAN TYE
BAND BASE BODY BUNK DOSS
DOWN FLOP FORM LAIR PLOT
SACK VEIN WADI WADY BERTH
BOIST COUCH FLASK FLOCK
GRATE GROVE LAYER ROOST
THORE BORDER BOTTOM COUCHE
CRADLE GIRDLE HOTBED LIBKEN
LIBKIN LITTER MATRIX OSIERY
PALLET STRATA CHANNEL
CHARPOY FLEABAG HAMMOCK
LODGING QUARTER REPOSAL
SEEDBED SETTING STRATUM
SUBSOIL TRUCKLE TRUNDLE
BASSINET CAPSTONE LENTICLE
PLANCHER SHAKEDOWN
(— DOWN) DOSS
(— IN WAGON) KATEL
(— OF ANIMAL) LAIR KENNEL
(— OF CLAY) CLOD
(— OF COAL) BRAT DELF SEAM
(— OF EMBERS) GRIESHOCH
(— OF FIRE CLAY) THILL
(— OF FURNACE) HEARTH
(— OF GUN-CARRIAGE) FLASK
(— OF HAND PRESS) COFFIN
(— OF OYSTERS) PLANT
(— OF REFUSE) NITRIARY
(— OF ROCK) CAP PLUM
(— OF ROSES) ROSARY
(— OF SEDIMENT) WARP
(— OF SHELLFISH) BANK
(— OF STONES) SHINGLE
(— OF STREAM) DRAW WASH
NULLAH BILLABONG STREAMWAY
(CREEK —) COULEE COULIE
(DRIED LAKE —) CHOTT SEBKA
SHOTT
(FEATHER —) TIE TYE
(FOLDING —) SLAWBANK
(LOW —) LOWBOY
(OYSTER —) STEW LAYER SCALP
CLAIRE LAYING OYSTERAGE
(RUBBLE —) CALLOW
(SEED —) SEMINARY
(WATER-BEARING —) AQUAFER
AQUIFER
(WOODEN —) RUSTBANK
(PREF.) CLIN(O) STRATI STROMATI
STROMATO
(SUFF.) STROMA
BEDAD (SON OF —) HADAD
BEDAN (FATHER OF —) GILEAD
BEDAUB CLAG CLAT DAUB MOIL
SOIL SLAKE SMEAR PARGET
SLUBBER SLAISTER BEPLASTER
BEDBUG BUG CHINK CIMEX
CHINCH CHINTZ COREID PUNESE
VERMIN CIMICID PUNAISE
REDCOAT CONENOSE HEMIPTER
HOUSEBUG
BEDCHAMBER RUELLE BEDROOM
CUBICLE
BEDCLOTHES COVER BEDDING
CLOTHES
BEDCOVER COMFORTER
PALAMPORE
BEDDING BEDROLL DOMESTICS
BEDECK GEM BEDO LARD TRAP
ADORN ARRAY DIGHT GRACE
PRINK ORNAMENT EMBELLISH
BEDECKED PRINKY

BEDEIAH (FATHER OF —) BANI
BEDEVIL ABUSE ANNOY BESET
WORRY HARASS MUDDLE PESTER
BEWITCH CONFUSE TORMENT
BEDEW DEW SHOWER EMBATHE
IRRORATE
BEDIZEN DAUB ADORN ARRAY
DIZEN DEDAUB
BEDLAM RIOT NOISE RUDAS
ASYLUM TUMULT UPROAR
MADNESS MADHOUSE
BETHLEHEM
BEDOUIN ABSI ARAB BEDU MOOR
NOMAD BADAWI BEDAWEE
SHAMMAR HOWEITAT
BEDQUILT POURPOINT
BEDRAGGLE DAG TRACHLE
BEDRAGGLED FORLORN
SHOPWORN
BEDRAIL RAVE RATHE
BEDRIDDEN ILL AILING BEDFAST
(NOT —) AFOOT
BEDROCK LEDGE NADIR SHELF
BOTTOM HARDPAN STONEHEAD
BEDROLL BINDLE
BEDROOM FLAT BERTH CABIN
BEDDER DORMER BOUDOIR
CHAMBER CUBICULO WARDROBE
GARDEROBE
BEDSORE ANACLISIS DECUBITUS
BEDSPREAD ALEZE STRAIL
BEDCOVER COVERLET COVERLID
BEDSTEAD BED COT CRIB HATCH
STEAD STAPLE ANGAREP
CHARPOY
BEDSTRAW CRUDWORT
CURDWORT FLEAWEED
BEDFLOWER CROSSWORT
SCRAMBLER
BED TESTER SPARVER
BEDWARMER CURATE
BEE DOR FLY APIS BEVY KING RING
KARBI MASON NOMIA NURSE
PARTY DINGAR DRONEL DRONER
FROLIC INSECT NOTION TORQUE
TSETSE WORKER ANDRENA
DEBORAH KOOTCHA MELISSA
RAISING SERPENT STINGER
SWERVER TRIGONA ANDRENID
ANGELITO HONEYBEE QUILTING
SCOPIPED SHUCKING WAXMAKER
GATHERING
(QUEEN —) KING
(PL.) BEEN BONE HIVE SPEW
SOCIALES
(PREF.) API
BEEBREAD CERAGO AMBROSIA
BEECH BUCK BIRCH MYRTLE
FLINDOSA FLINDOSY
(PREF.) FAGI FAGO
BEECHNUT SPLITNUT
(PL.) BUCK MAST PANNAGE
BEEF JERK BEEVE BULLY GRIPE
JERKY VIFDA VIVDA CASSON
CUTTER CHARQUI TOPSIDE
COMPLAIN COMPOUND PASTRAMI
PIPIKAULA
(— FOR SLAUGHTER) MART
(BOILED —) BOUILLI
(BROILED —) CHURRASCO
(CORN —) BULLY
(CUT OF —) SEY LOIN RUMP SIDE
BARON CHINE CHUCK FLANK

ROAST ROUND SHANK STEAK
ALOYAU CUTLET SADDLE BRISKET
KNUCKLE QUARTER SIRLOIN
EDGEBONE SHOULDER
AITCHBONE NINEHOLES
RATTLERAN
(GROUND —) HAMBURGER
(INFERIOR —) COMPOUND
(JERKED —) TASAJO BILTONG
CHARQUE CHARQUI
(LEAN —) LIRE
(SALTED —) JUNK VIFDA
BEEF BREAD SWEETBREAD
BEEFEATER OXBIRD BUPHAGA
OXBITER OXPECKER TICKBIRD
BEEFWOOD TOA BELAH BELAR
FILAO
BEEFY HEAVY HEFTY SOLID
BRAWNY FLESHY
BEE GLUE PROPOLIS
BEEHIVE GUM BUTT GUME HIVE
SKEP PYCHE STAND STATE STOCK
SWARM APIARY HOPPET
ALVEARY SWARMER BEEHOUSE
PRAESEPE
(— STATE) UTAH
(— TOMB) TREASURY
BEEKEEPER HIVER BEEMAN
BEEHERD APIARIST SKEPPIST
BEELIADA (FATHER OF —) DAVID
BEELZEBUB DEVIL
BEEN BE BON SEE BONE
BEE PLANT GUACO STINKWEED
BEER ALE MUM BIER BOCK BREW
FARO GAIL GROG GYLE HOPS
KVAS MALT MILD QUAS SCUD
SUDS BELCH CHANG CHICA
GROUT KVASS LAGER POMBE
QUASS SCUDS STOUT WEISS
CHICHA DOUBLE GATTER LIQUOR
PORTER SPRUCE STINGO SWANKY
SWIPES WALLOP ZYTHUM
CERVEZA PANGASI PHARAOH
PILSNER TANKARD TAPLASH
TAPWORT CERVISIA PILSENER
(ADD TO —) KRAUSEN
(BAD —) TACK TAPLASH
(HOT — AND GIN) PURL
(INFERIOR —) BELCH SWANKY
(SMALL —) TIFF GROUT
(SOUR —) BEEREGAR
(STRONG —) HUFF NAPPY DOUBLE
STINGO
(THIN —) PRITCH SWIPES
(TIBETAN —) CHANG
(WARM — AND OATMEAL) STORRY
(WEAK —) BEVERAGE
BEERA (FATHER OF —) ZOPHAH
BEERHOUSE KNEIPE TIDDLYWINK
BEERI (DAUGHTER OF —) JUDITH
(SON OF —) HOSEA
BEESWAX CAPPING
BEET CHARD MANGEL MANGOLD
STECHLING
(SUGAR —) BOLTER
BEETLE BAT BOB BUG JUT RAM
BEAT BUZZ FLEA FOWL GOGA
GOGO IPID MAUL MELL STAG
TROX TURK UANG AMARA ATLAS
BORER BULGE CAROB CHUCK
CLOCK DRIVE FIDIA GOGGA HISPA
LYCID MELOE SAGRA TIGER
BATLET CHAFER CLERID COCUYO

CUCUYO ELATER GOLACH
GOLOCH HISTER JUTOUT KHAPRA
LICTUS MALLET MELOID PESTLE
PRUNER PTINID SAWYER SCARAB
WEAVER WEEVIL ADELOPS
BRUCHID BUZZARD CADELLE
CARABID CARABUS CLOCKER
CUCUJID FIDDLER FIREFLY
GIRDLER GOLDBUG HORNBUG
LADYBUG LUCANID PAUSSID
PRIONID PROJECT SILPHID
SKIPPER SNAPPER SOLDIER
TANBARK TICKLER ATEUCHUS
CALOSOMA CETONIAN COCKTAIL
CURCULIO DYTISCID ENGRAVER
EROTYLID FIGEATER GLOWWORM
HARDBACK LADYBIRD LAMPYRID
LOWERING OVERHANG RUTELIAN
SCOLYTID SEARCHER SHARNBUD
SHARNBUG SKIPJACK SPHINDID
SQUASHER SQUEAKER SYMPHILE
TOKTOKJE WHIRLWIG
DEDEMERID LONGICORN
OSTOMATID TUMBLEBUG
TWIRLIGIG WHIRLIGIG
SCAPHIDIUM RHYNCHOPHORAN
(PL.) XYLOPHAGA
BEEWEED TONGUE
BEFALL HAP COME LIMP SORT
TIDE TIME CHEFE CHIVE OCCUR
SHAPE ASTART BECOME BETIDE
HAPPEN PERTAIN
BEFIT DOW SIT COME LONG SEEM
SORT SUIT BESET SERVE BECOME
BEHOVE BESEEM BETIDE
BEHOOVE
BEFITTING FIT AFTER DECENT
PROPER WORTHY SEEMING
THRIFTY BECOMING DECOROUS
SORTABLE
(PROFESSIONALLY —) ETHICAL
(SUFF.) LY
BEFOG GAUM CLOUD OBSANE
CONFUSE MYSTIFY
BEFOOL BOB FON SOT BURN COLT
CRAP DOLT DUPE FODE JADE
POOP ASSOT ELUDE FONNE
BEFLUM DIDDLE TRIFLE FOOLIFY
BEFORE OR TO AIR BUT ERE FOR
GIN TIL ANTE FORE SAID TILL
YORE AFORE AHEAD ANENT
AVANT CORAM FIRST FORBY
FORNE FRONT PRIOR SOPRA
UNTIL FORBYE FORMER RATHER
SOONER TOFORE WITHIN
AGAINST ALREADY EARLIER
FORTHBY FORWARD
(— LONG) SOON ERELONG
(JUST —) TOWARD FORMERLY
(PREF.) FORE OB PRAE PRE PRO
PROTER(O)
BEFOREHAND AFORE
BEFOUL FILE SLUT SOIL BERAY
DIRTY GRUFT BEMIRE DAGGLE
DARKEN DEFILE DRABBLE
FEWMAND POLLUTE SLUTTER
BESQUIRT ENTANGLE
BEFOULED SHARNY
BEFRIEND AID ABET HELP FAVOR
ASSIST BENEFIT FOSTER FRIEND
SUCCOR SUPPORT SUSTAIN
BEFUDDLE BOX GAS ADDLE BESOT
MUDDLE BECLOUD CONFUSE

FLUSTER MYSTIFY STUPEFY
BEFUDDLED REE MUSED
BEG ASK BID CRY SUE WOO CANT
COAX KICK MOVE MUMP PRAY
PRIG SEEK SORN SUIT THIG TRAM
CADGE CRAVE MAUND MOOCH
PLEAD SCAFF SHOOL TEASE
YEARN ADJURE FLEECH BESEECH
ENTREAT IMPLORE MAUNDER
REQUEST SKELDER SOLICIT
PETITION OBSECRATE
PANHANDLE
BEGET GET WIN BEAR HAVE KIND
SIRE BREED YIELD BIGATE
CREATE FATHER ACQUIRE
ENGRAFF CONCEIVE ENGENDER
GENERATE PROCREATE
(PREF.) GON(O) GONIDIO GONIMO
GONIO
BEGETTER SIRE AUTHOR FATHER
MOTHER PARENT
BEGETTING
(SUFF.)
GON(E)(IDIUM)(IMO)(IUM)(Y)
BEGGAR BLOB PROG RUIN ASKER
HALFY LAZAR RANDY ROGUE
THRUM TRAMP ARMINE BACACH
BIDDER CADGER CANTER
DYVOUR MUMPER PARIAH
PAUPER SORNER WRETCH
ABRAHAM ALMSMAN BAIRAGI
BEGSTER JARKMAN LAZARUS
MAUNDER PARDHAN PROCTOR
RUFFLER SCAFFER SORNARI
STEMMER THIGGER ABRAMMAN
BADGEMAN BEADSMAN
BESOGNIO BEZONIAN BLUEGOWN
DUMMERER GLASSMAN PALLIARD
STROLLER WHIPJACK MENDICANT
SCHNORRER
(— DESCRIPTION) PASS
(PL.) GUEUX
BEGGARED PEELED
BEGGARLY MEAN POOR CHEAP
PETTY SORRY ABJECT PALTRY
PILLED PEGRALL BANKRUPT
INDIGENT HUNGARIAN
BEGGAR'S-LICE STICKWEED
BEGGARS' OPERA (AUTHOR OF —)
GAY
(CHARACTER IN —) LUCY POLLY
LOCKIT PEACHUM MACHEATH
BEGGAR-TICK CUCKOLD
(PL.) BOOTJACKS
BEGGARY THIG WANT INDIGENCE
PAUPERISM
BEGGING MAUND CRAVING
OPENERS MENDICANT
THOMASING
(— FOR FOOD) SCRANNING
(FRAUDULENT —) TRUANDISE
BEGHARD PICARD
BEGIN GIN GYN HIT FALL FANG
HEAD JUMP LEAD OPEN RISE
TAME YOKE ARISE ENTER FRONT
START ATTACK ATTAME INCEPT
SPRING STREAK COMMENCE
INCHOATE INITIATE
BEGINNER BOOT PUNK TIRO TYRO
ROOKY SOFTA GINNER NOVICE
ROOKIE SOPHTA AMATEUR
ENTRANT RECRUIT RUBBLER
STUDENT TRAINEE FRESHMAN

INCEPTOR NEOPHYTE NEWCOMER
NOVELIST ABECEDARIAN
BEGINNING EGG ORD DAWN EDGE
GERM HEAD RISE ROOT SEED
ALPHA BIRTH DEBUT ENTRY
FIRST FRONT ONSET START
VAUNT AURORA INCOME INSTIL
ONCOME ORIGIN OUTSET SETOUT
SOURCE SPRING CALENDS
DAWNING GENESIS HANDSEL
INCIPIT INFANCY INITIAL INITION
KALENDS NASCENT OPENING
SUNRISE ENTRANCE EXORDIUM
INCHOATE OUTSTART RUDIMENT
(NEW —) EPOCH
(PL.) INCUNABULA
(PREF.) ACR(O)
(SUFF.) ARCH ARCHIC ARCHY
ESCENT
BEGONE OFF OUT VIA AWAY SCAT
SHOO SCOOT SCRAM AROINT
AVAUNT DEPART SKIDOO
SKIDDOO VAMOOSE
BEGONIA GAIETY GAYETY
BEGRIME COOM SOIL COLLY DITCH
GRIME BECOOM SMIRCH SMUDGE
BRUCKLE
BEGRIMED DIRTY GRIMY SMUDGY
CINDERY SMIRCHY
BEGRUDGE ENVY GRUDGE MALIGN
JALOUSE
BEGTI NAIR COCKUP
BEGUILE FOX COAX FODE FOIL
FOND GULL LURE VAMP WILE
WISE AMUSE CHARM CHEAT
COZEN ELUDE EVADE GUILE
TEMPT TRICK TROLL TRYST WEIZE
BRIGUE BUTTER DELUDE DIVERT
ENTRAP JUGGLE VAMPEY
DECEIVE ENSNARE FLATTER
FLUMMER MISLEAD
MOUNTEBANK
BEHALF HALF PART SAKE SIDE
FAVOR SCORE STEAD AFFAIR
MATTER PROFIT BENEFIT
DEFENCE SUPPORT INTEREST
BEHAVE DO ACT LET BEAR FARE
HAVE KEEP MAKE PLAY WALK
WORK ABEAR CARRY REACT
TREAT ACQUIT DEMEAN DEPORT
HANDLE COMPORT CONDUCT
CONTAIN DISPORT GESTURE
MANAGER FUNCTION REGULATE
RESTRAIN
(— AFFECTEDLY) MOP
(— AWKWARDLY) GAUM HOCKER
(— BOLDLY) GAUSTER
(— BRASHLY) HOOK
(— CHURLISHLY) CARL
(— EVASIVELY) DODGE
(— FOOLISHLY) DOLT
(— MISCHIEVOUSLY) LARK
(— NOISILY) HELL REHAYTE
(— OSTENTATIOUSLY) SWANK
(— VULGARLY) RAMP
BEHAVING
(SUFF.) ANT ENT
BEHAVIOR AIR MIEN PORT RULE
THEW WALK FRONT GUISE HABIT
LATES USAGE ACTION COURSE
GOINGS MANNER ACTIONS
BEARING BIGOTRY COMPORT
CONDUCT DECORUM ERGASIA

FACTION FASHION HAVANCE
HAVINGS AMENANCE ATTITUDE
BLINDISM BREEDING BYRONICS
CARRIAGE FUNCTION MAINTAIN
PERFORMANCE
(ARROGANT —) SIDE SWAGGER
(COURTEOUS —) COMITY
COURTESY
(DECENT —) CIVILITY
(FOOLISH —) SIMPLES SOTTISE
(GOAL-DIRECTED —) HORME
(IMPROPER —) MISCONDUCT
(LIVELY —) TITTUP
(LOUTISH —) BUFFOONERY
(RIOTOUS —) RAMPAGE
(SILLY —) SPOONISM
(STUDIED —) ART
(UNDERHANDED —)
SKULLDUGGERY
BEHEAD NECK
BEHEST BID LAW HEST RULE
ORDER DEMAND BIDDING
COMMAND MANDATE
BEHIND AFT HINT PAST RUMP
ABACK ABAFF ABAFT AFTER
AHIND AREAR LATER PASSE
TARDY ARREAR ASTERN DERERE
BACKWARD DILATORY
(PREF.) META POST POSTERO
RETRO
BEHINDHAND TARDY LAGGARD
DILATORY HINDERLY
BEHOLD LA LO EYE SEE SPY ECCE
ESPY GAZE HOLD KEEP LOOK
SCAN STOP TOOT VIEW VISE
WAIT HOLDE OCULE SIGHT VOILA
WATCH ASPECT DESCRY MIRROR
REGARD RETAIN DISCERN
OBSERVE SURVISE WITNESS
BEHOLDEN OWING AFFINED
BOUNDEN OBLIGED INDEBTED
BEHOOVE DOW FIT NEED SUIT
THAR BEFIT OUGHT THARF
BELONG PROPER REQUIRE
BEIGE HOP TAN ECRU HOPI GREGE
DORADO GREIGE STRING
SUNBURN
BEING ENS ESSE FEAL SELF ENTIA
GNOME HUMAN SHAPE TROLL
ANIMAL ENTITY EXTANT LIVING
MORTAL PERSON SYSTEM
ESSENCE PRESENT REALITY
VIVENCY CREATURE EXISTENT
ONTOLOGY PRESENCE STANDING
(ANIMATE —) LIFE JAGAT
(CELESTIAL —) ANGEL CHERUB
SERAPH WATCHER DIVINITY
(DIMINUTIVE —) ELF GNOME
(DIVINE —) DEV DEVA DEMIGOD
(ESSENCE OF —) SAT
(ETERNAL —) EON AEON
(EVIL —) DEVIL GHOUL
(FABULOUS —) TENGU TORNIT
(HUMAN —) BODY BUCK JACK
SOUL BLADE HUMAN SLIME
ANIMAL ADAMITE CREATURE
RATIONAL CHRISTIAN
(IDEAL —) IMMORTAL
(ILL-FAVORED —) BLASTIE
(IMAGINARY —) SYLPH
TERMAGANT
(INNER —) INWARD SPRITE
INBEING

(INNERMOST —) HEART
(INTRINSIC —) ESSENCE
(LEGENDARY —) GIANT
(LIVING —) BLOOD WIGHT
(MATERIAL —) HYLIC
(PERFECT —) GOD
(PHYSICAL —) FLESH
(SEMIDIVINE —) SHEDU LAMASSU
(SMALL —) INCHLING
(SO —) SAEBEINS
(SUPERNATURAL —) DEV MAN
AKUA ATUA DEVA JANN ZEMI
ADARO BALAM DAEVA DEMON
FAIRY TROLL WIGHT DAEMON
GARUDA GODKIN SPIRIT GODLING
FOLLETTO HAMINGJA
(SUPREME —) DEITY MONAD
NYAMBE NZAMBI CREATOR
(TRUE —) OUSIA
(PREF.) ONT(O) ZO(E)(IDIO)(IDO)(O)
ZOOLOGICO
(HUMAN —) ANTHROP(O)
(SUFF.) IC(AL) ZOA ZOIC ZOON

BELA (FATHER OF —) AZAZ BEOR
BENJAMIN

BELABOR PLY BEAT DRUB LASH
WORK ASSAIL BOUNCE CUDGEL
HAMMER HAMPER THRASH
THWACK

BELAY BESET BELAGE INVEST
WAYLAY BESEIGE

BELCH YEX BOCK BOKE BOLK BURP
GALP RASP RIFT ERUCT FRUCT
REBOKE ERUCTATE

BELCHING BRASH

BELDAM HAG FURY TROT CRONE
RUDAS ALECTO ERINYS RUDOUS
VIRAGO BELDAME JEZEBEL
TISIPHONE

BELEAGUER BELAY BESET INVEST
ASSAULT BESEIGE LEAGUER
BLOCKADE SURROUND

BELEM PARA

BELEMNITE ARTIFACT KERAUNION

BELFRY SHED TOWER BEFFROY
CLOCHER CLOGHEAD BELLHOUSE

BELGIAN CONGO (CAPITAL OF —)
LEOPOLDVILLE
(LAKE IN —) KIVU MWERU ALBERT
(PROVINCE OF —) KIVA KASAI
EQUATOR KATANGA ORIENTAL
(RIVER IN —) RUKI KASAI LINDI
LOMAMI LUKUGA UBANGI
ARUWIMI LULONGA
(TOWN IN —) BOMA LULUABOURG

BELGIUM
CANAL: YSER UNION ALBERT
CAMPINE
CAPITAL: BRUSSELS BRUXELLES
GAUL TRIBE: REMI BELGAE NERVII
MEASURE: VAT AUNE LAST PIED
CARAT PERCHE BOISSEAU
MOUNTAIN: BOTRANGE
NAME: BELGIE BELGIQUE
PLATEAU: ARDENNES HOHEVENN
PORT: OSTEND ANTWERP
PROVINCE: LIEGE NAMUR
ANTWERP BRABANT
HAINAUT LIMBURG
FLANDERS HAINAULT
RIVER: LYS DYLE LEIE MAAS MARK
YSER BOUCQ DEMER LESSE

MEUSE NETHE RUPEL SENNE
DENDER ESCAUT MANJEL
OURTHE SAMBRE SEMOIS
VESDRE WARCHE AMBLEVE
SCHELDT
TOWN: AS AAT ANS ATH HAL HUY
MOL SPA AATH AMAY ASSE
BOOM BREE DOEL GAND GEEL
GENK GENT HOEI LIER LOOZ
MONS VISE WAHA ZELE AALST
ALOST ARLON CINEY EEKLO
ESSEN EUPEN EVERE GENCK
GHENT HEIST IEPER JETTE
JUMET LIEGE NAMUR RONSE
TIELT UCCLE VORST WEZET
YNOIR YPRES AARLEN ANVERS
BERGEN BILZEN BRUGES
DEURNE ELSENE IZEGEM
LEUVEN LIERRE MERXEM
OPWIJK OSTEND ANTWERP
ARDOOIE BERCHEM DOORWIK
HERSTAL HOBOKEN IXELLES
LOUVAIN MECHLIN ROULERS
SERAING TONGRES TOURNAI
BRUSSELS COURTRAI KORTRIJK
MECHELEN MOUSCRON
TONGEREN TURNHOUT
VERVIERS WATERLOO
WEIGHT: LAST CARAT LIVRE
POUND CHARGE CHARIOT
ESTERLIN

BELIE BELONG DEFAME BESEIGE
FALSIFY PERTAIN SLANDER
TRADUCE DISGUISE STRUMPET
SURROUND MISREPRESENT

BELIEF CRY FAY ISM LEVE MIND
SECT TAKE TROW VIEW VOTE
WEEN CAUSE CREDO CREED
DOGMA FAITH OBEAH TENET
TROTH TRUST CREDIT GROUND
CRIANCE FEELING HOLDING
OPINION TROWING ARYANISM
BITHEISM CREDENCE
DOCTRINE FINALISM
HUMANISM RELIANCE
PREPOSSESSION
(— IN DEVILS) DIABOLISM
(— IN GHOSTS) EIDOLISM
(CONVENTIONAL —) PIETY
(FALSE —) DELUSION
(GROUNDLESS —) CANARD
(MORTAL —) HALL
(READY —) ACCEPTATION
(SHALLOW —) BALLOON
(SUPERSTITIOUS —) FREET
(TRADITIONAL —) ICON IKON
EIKON
(UNFOUNDED —) FICTION

BELIEVABLE PLAUSIBLE

BELIEVE BUY WIS DEEM FEEL
HOLD TAKE TREW TROW WEEN
CREED FAITH FANCY GUESS
JUDGE SEPAD THINK TRUST
ACCEPT CREDIT ESTEEM EXPECT
DARESAY SUPPOSE ACCREDIT
CONSIDER CREDENCE
(— ERRONEOUSLY) FEIGN
(— NAIVELY) SWALLOW
(— UNCRITICALLY) EAT

BELIEVER IST LEVER BOTARY
KITABI CREDENS
ADHERENT ARMINIAN

(SUFF.) ARIAN

BELISARIO (CHARACTER IN —)
ANTONIA EUTRIPIO BELISARIUS
(COMPOSER OF —) DONIZETTI

BELISE (BROTHER OF —)
PHILAMINTE

BELITTLE DECRY DWARF SNEER
BEMEAN MINISH SLIGHT DETRACT
DIMINUE LIGHTLY MINIMIZE
VILIPEND DENIGRATE DISCREDIT
DISPARAGE

BELITTLER ZOILUS

BELIZE (CAPITAL OF —) BELMOPAN

BELL HUB TOM CALL FAIR GONG
HUBB RING ROAR CHIME CLOAK
CLOCK CODON FLARE KNELL
SWELL TENOR BASKET BELLOW
BUBBLE CLOCHE CROTAL
CURFEW PHONIC SOCKET TAPPER
TOCSIN TOLLER TREBLE TRIPLE
VESPER ANGELUS BLOSSOM
CAMPANA CAMPANE COROLLA
COWBELL JANGLER JINGLER
LOWBELL SKELLAT SKILLET
TAMBOUR TANTONY TINKLER
CASCABEL COCKBELL DINGDONG
DOORBELL HANDBELL HAWKBELL
MORTBELL PAVILLON STARTLER
TINGTANG
(ALARM —) TOCSIN
(CLOSED —) CROTAL
(EVENING —) CURFEW
(FUNERAL —) TELLER
(HAND —) CLAG
(LARGE —) SIGNUM
(LOWEST —) BORDON BOURDON
(PART OF —) BOW LIP HEAD
CROWN MOUTH WAIST CLAPPER
SHOULDER
(PASSING —) KNELL
(SACRING —) SQUILLA
(SLEIGH —) GRELOT CROTALUM
(PREF.) CAMPANI CAMPANO

BELLABELLA HAELTZUK HEILTSUK

BELLADONNA DWALE MANICON
BANEWORT DAFTBERRY
DWAYBERRY MYDRIATIC
NIGHTSHADE

BELLARIA (HUSBAND OF —)
PANDOSTO

BELLARMINE GRAYBEARD
GREYBEARD LONGBEARD

BELLBIRD MAKO SHRIKE COTINGA
ARAPUNGA KORIMAKO
MAKOMAKO CAMPANERO

BELLBOY BUTTONS

BELLE SPARK TOAST
(SPANISH —) MAJA

BELLEEK POTTERY CHAMPAGNE

**BELLE HELENE, LE (COMPOSER OF
—)** OFFENBACH

BELLEROPHON (FATHER OF —)
GLAUCUS
(MOTHER OF —) EURYMEDE

BELLFLOWER RAMPION
BELLWORT HASKWORT IVYBELLS
MILKWORT

BELLHOP BELLBOY HALLBOY
CHASSEUR

BELLICOSE MAD IRATE WARFUL
HOSTILE WARLIKE MILITANT

BELLIGERENT BRISTLY HOSTILE
WARLIKE CHOLERIC FIGHTING

JINGOIST COMBATIVE IRASCIBLE
LITIGIOUS WRANGLING
PUGNACIOUS

BELLISANT (HUSBAND OF —)
ALEXANDER
(SON OF —) ORSON VALENTINE

BELLOW CRY LOW MOO YAP BAWL
BEAL BELL GAPE ROAR ROME
ROUT YAUP YAWP BELVE BLART
BLORE CROON ROUST SHOUT
TROAT BULLER CLAMOR
RUMMES BLUSTER
RUMMISH ULULATE

BELLOWING ROUT ROUST BELLING
BLATANT BOATION MUGIENT

BELLOWS BELY LUNGS BULIES
FEEDER SANDER WINKER
SYLPHON WINDBAG
EXPELLER
(SMALL —) PLUFF
(STORAGE —) RESERVOIR
(PREF.) PHYSA PHYSALLO PHYSO

BELLOWS FISH BUGLER SNIPEFISH

BELL RINGER TOLL YOUTH TOLLER
CLINKUM

BELLWETHER MASTER

BELLY BAG COD GIE GUT MAW
POD BOUK BUNT FILL KYTE MARY
WAME WEAM WOMB BINGY
BOSOM BULGE FRONT GORGE
PLEON TABLE THARM THERM
TRIPE BAGGIE BINGEE HUNGER
PAUNCH VENTER ABDOMEN
BALLOON STOMACH TUMBREL
APPETITE
(PREF.) CELI COELI(O) GASTER(O)
GASTR(I)(O) VENTRI VENTRO
(SUFF.) GASTER GASTRIA

BELLYACHE COMPLAIN
COLLYWOBBLES

BELLYBAND WANTY

BELLYING BUNTING PREGNANT

BELONG BE GO FIT LIE BEAR FALL
RELY APPLY BELIE GROUP AFFEIR
INHERE RELATE RETAIN
BEHOOVE PERTAIN
APPERTAIN SUBSCRIBE

BELONGING
(SUFF.) EAE
(— TO) AR ARY EAN INE ISE
ORIUM

BELONGINGS ALLS DUDS FARE
GEAR GOODS TRAPS ASSETS
DUFFEL DUFFLE ESTATE USINGS
BAGGAGE EFFECTS CHATTELS
PROPERTY PURPRISE FURNITURE
HOUSEHOLD PARAPHERNALIA

BELOVED DEAR IDOL LIEF AIMEE
BOSOM CHERI SWEET ADORED
CHERIE MINION DARLING
PRECIOUS
(MOST —) ALDERLIEFEST

BELOW ALOW BAJO DOWN ABLOW
AFTER INFRA NEATH SOTTO
UNDER BEHIND BENEATH
(PREF.) INFERO INFRA SUB

BELT LAS AREA BAND BEAT BLOW
CEST FELT GIRD LACE LIST MARK
RING SASH SLUG ZONE GIRTH
MITER MITRE PATTE STRAP STRIP
SWATH TRACT WAIST WHACK
ZONAR ZONIC BODICE CENTER
CESTUS CINGLE FETTLE GIRDLE

INVEST LUNGER REGION STRAIT
STRIPE SWATHE ZONNAR ZONULE
BALDRIC BALTEUS CIRCUIT
PASSAGE BALTHEUS CEINTURE
CINCTURE CINGULUM ELEVATOR
ENCIRCLE MECHANIC SURROUND
(— OF FOG) BLANKET
(ASTROLOGICAL —) CLIMATE
(CONVEYOR —) HAUL
(ENDLESS —) APRON CREEPER
(GREEK —) ZOSTER
(HINDU SWAMP —) TERAI
(MACHINE —) SWIFTER
(MINERAL —) RANGE
(PART OF —) TIP HOLE FRAME
PANEL PRONG BUCKLE FILLER
KEEPER LINING PIPING TONGUE
STITCHING
(TREE —) BERM BERME
(PL.) BALTEI
(PREF.) ZON(O)
BELTED ZONATE GIRDLED
CINCTURED
(— WITH WHITE) SHEETED
BELUGA HUSE HUSO HAUSEN
MARSOON WHITEFISH
BELUS (BROTHER OF —) AGENOR
(FATHER OF —) NEPTUNE
POSEIDON
(MOTHER OF —) LIBYA EURYNOME
(SON OF —) DANAUS CEPHEUS
AEGYPTUS
BELVEDERE GAZEBO LOOKOUT
BELVIDERA (FATHER OF —) PRIULI
(HUSBAND OF —) JAFFIER
BELVIDERE MIRADOR
BEMIRE DAG SOIL JARBLE
BEMOAN RUE MEAN MOAN SIGH
MOURN PLAIN BEWAIL LAMENT
DEPLORE
BEMUSE SOT BULL DAZE AMUSE
BEMUSED DOPY DOPEY PIXILATED
MOONSTRUCK
BENAIAH (FATHER OF —) JEHOIADA
(SON OF —) PELATIAH
BENCH PEW BANC BANK BENK
BERM BINK DAIS DEAS FORM
MESA SEAT SILL STEP TRAM
BASIN BASON BERME BREAK
CABIN CHAIR FORME JUDGE
PLANK STALL STOOL BANCUS
BANKER SCONCE SEDILE SETTEE
SETTLE SITTER COUNTER
DRESSER REPOSAL SHAMBLE
SITTING TRESTLE TRIBUNE
ALEBENCH
(— FOR DAIRY TUBS) TRAM
(— FOR KNEADING DOUGH) BREAK
(OUTDOOR —) EXEDRA EXHEDRA
(PLAYER'S —) WOOD
(ROWER'S —) BANK THOFT ZYGON
THWART
(SHOEMAKER'S —) FORME
(WORKMAN'S —) SIEGE
BEND BOW NID NIP PLY SAG SET
WIN WRY ABOW ARCH BENT
BOOL BUCK COPE CURB DOME
FAUD FLEX FOLD GENU HOOK
KINK LEAN LOUT PLOY RUMP
TURN VERT WEEP ANGLE BATON
BIGHT BREAK COUCH COUDE
COURB CRANK CRIMP CRINK
CROOK CULGE CURVE DROOP

FLECT FRESE HINGE HUNCH
INBOW KNEEL PLASH PLICA
QUIRL ROUND SCRAG SKELP
SLANT STOOP TREND TWINE
TWIST BOUGHT BUCKLE CAMBER
CONVEX COTICE CROUCH
COMPASS
(SUFF.) FLECT(ION) FLEX(ION)
BENDER BUM JAG LEG BUST
DRUNK SPREE BRIDGE WHOPPER
GUZZLING SIXPENCE BRANNIGAN
INFLECTOR
BENDING BOW SAG KNEE KNOT
PLIE CROOK CURVE LITHE TWIST
PLIANT SUPPLE TWISTY ANFRACT
FLEXION HOGGING SINUOUS
BUCKLING FLECTION
(— OF ROCK) DRAG
(BALLET —) PLIE
(PREF.) SPHINGO
BENDY TREE MIRO MAHOE
BENEATH ALOW ANETH BELOW
LOWER UNDER ANEATH
(PREF.) HYPO INFRA SUB
BENEDICITE BENISON CANTICLE
BENEDICT NEOGAMIST
BENEDICTINE CLUNIAC
CAMALDOLESE TIRONENSIAN
BENEDICTION ABOT AMEN ABOTH
NANDI AMIDAH BROCHO PRAYER
BENISON BERAKAH BLESSING
BENEFACTION ALMS BOON GIFT
PRESENT DONATION GRATUITY
BENEFACTOR AGENT ANGEL
DONOR FRIEND HELPER PATRON
SAVIOR MAECENAS PROMOTER
BENEFICE FEE FEU FEUD FIEF
FAVOR SCARF CURACY LIVING
BENEFIT CANONRY PRELACY
RECTORY TOTQUOT DONATIVE
KINDNESS SINECURE VICARAGE
PLURALITY
BENEFICENCE BOON GIFT GRACE
BOUNTY CHARITY GOODNESS
KINDNESS
BENEFICENT KINDLY AMIABLE
BENEFIC GRACIOUS
BENEFICIAL GOOD USEFUL
HEALTHY HELPFUL BONITARY
SALUTARY SANATIVE SINGULAR
AVAILABLE BENIGNANT
DESIRABLE ENJOYABLE
HEALTHFUL LUCRATIVE
REWARDING WHOLESOME
PROFITABLE
BENEFICIARY HEIR USER DONEE
CESTUI CESTUY USUARY VASSAL
LEGATEE FEUDATORY
(SUFF.) EE
BENEFIT AID USE BOON BOOT
GAIN GIFT GOOD HELP PROW
SAKE AVAIL BOOST FRUIT SELTH
STEAD VISIT ASSIST BEHALF
BEHOOF BETTER FRINGE PROFIT
SALUTE USANCE ADVANCE
BESPEAK CONCERT DESERVE
IMPROVE SERVICE UTILITY
BEFRIEND INTEREST
BENEVOLENCE JEN BOUNTY
GOODNESS GOODWILL HUMANITY
BENEVOLENT GOOD KIND BENIGN
KINDLY LOVING AMIABLE LIBERAL
GENEROUS AVUNCULAR

BENIGNANT ALTRUISTIC
PROPITIOUS
BENHANAN (FATHER OF —) SHIMON
BEN HUR (AUTHOR OF —) WALLACE
(CHARACTER IN —) HUR IRAS
JUDAH ESTHER TIRZAH MESSALA
BALTHASAR SIMONIDES
BENIGN BOON GOOD KIND MILD
BLAND SWEET TRINE GENIAL
GENTLE AFFABLE BENEFIC
BENEDICT GRACIOUS INNOCENT
SALUTARY FAVORABLE
WHOLESOME
BENIGNANT KIND BLAND GENIAL
LIBERAL GRACIOUS MERCIFUL
BENIN (CAPITAL OF —) PORTONOVO
(TOWN IN —) COTONOU
BENISON BENEDICTION
BENJAMIN (FATHER OF —) HARIM
JACOB BILHAN
(MOTHER OF —) RACHEL
(SON OF —) ARD EHI BELA GERA
ROSH ASHBEL BECHER HUPPIM
MUPPIM NAAMAN
BENNET CLOVEWORT
BENNISEED SESAME
BENO TUBA
BENT AIM BOW SET BIAS CAST
CURB GIFT TURN BANDY BOUND
BOWED BOWLY COUDE COURB
CRANK CRUMP FLAIR HUMOR
KNACK LURCH PRONE SQUAT
SWING TASTE TREND AKIMBO
ANLAGE BENNET BIASED BRACED
COURBE COURSE CURVED
DOGLEG ENERGH GENIUS
HOOKED INTENT LIKING NECKED
SQUINT SWAYED TALENT
ADUNCAL ARCUATE BUCKLED
CROOKED CURVANT EMBOWED
FLEXION FLEXURE IMPETUS
INTENSE LEANING LEVELED
PRONATE PURPOSE STOOPED
TENSION ADUNCOUS APTITUDE
ARCUATED CRUMPLED DECLINED
FLECTION IMMINENT INFLEXED
PENCHANT REFLEXED TENDENCY
(— AT THE END) HAMATE HOGGED
GRYPANIAN
(— DOWNWARD) BOWED
DECURVED INCUMBENT
RECLINATE
(— IN) INCAVATE
(— INWARD) ADUNC
(— OF MIND) GEME AFFECTION
(EASILY —) LITHY
(NATURAL —) SWING
(SPECIAL —) VERVE
(PREF.) ANKYL(O) CAMPTO CURVI
CYPH(O) CYRT(O) SCOLIO
BEN-TEAK NANDI NANAWOOD
BENUMB NIP DAZE DUNT NUMB
STUN CHILL DAVER DOZEN
SCRAM SHRAM CUMBER DEADEN
PERISH STOUND BINOMEN
FRETISH FRETIZE STIFFEN
STUPEFY TORPEDO TORPEFY
BENUMBED CHILL SCRAM ASLEEP
CLUMSE CLUMSY FROZEN TORPID
CLUMPST SHRAMMED
BENUMBING LEADEN
**BENVENUTO CELLINI (CHARACTER
IN —)** POMPEO TERESA ASCANIO

CELLINI BALDUCCI SALVIATA
BENVENUTO FIERAMOSCA
(COMPOSER OF —) BERLIOZ
BENZAYDA (LOVER OF —) OZWY
BENZENE PHENE BENZIN BENZOL
PHENENE
(SUFF.) PHEN(E)
BENZINE
(PREF.) PHEN(O)
BENZOIN BENJOIN LINDERA
BENJAMIN FIXATIVE
(SUFF.) OIN
BEOR (SON OF —) BELA BALAAM
BEOWULF (AUTHOR OF —)
UNKNOWN
(CHARACTER IN —) WIGLAF
BEOWULF GRENDEL HIGELAC
UNFERTH AESCHERE HONDSCIO
HROTHGAR
BEQUEATH GIVE WILL ENDOW
LEAVE OFFER BESTOW COMMIT
DEMISE DEVISE LEGATE QUETHE
BEQUEST COMMEND TRANSMIT
BEQUEST GIFT WILL LEGACY
BEQUEATH HERITAGE PITTANCE
ENDOWMENT BENEFACTION
BERACHIAH (SON OF —) ASAPH
BERAIAH (FATHER OF —) SHIMHI
BERATE JAW NAG DRUB LASH
RAIL ABUSE BASTE CHIDE SCOLD
SCORE SLATE REVILE CENSURE
REPROVE UPBRAID CHASTISE
BERBER RIF RIFF KABYL SHLUH
KABYLE SHILHA HARATIN
MZABITE SHILLUH HARRATIN
MOZABITE
(— CHIEF) CAID
BERCEUSE CRADLESONG
WIEGENLIED
BEREAVE ROB STRIP WIDOW
DIVEST SADDEN DEPRIVE
DESPOIL
BEREAVED ORB BEREFT VIDUOUS
WIDOWED DESOLATE
BEREAVEMENT ORBITY ORBITUDE
VIDUATION
BERECHIAH (SON OF —) ASAPH
MESHULLAM ZECHARIAH
BEREFT ORB LORN LOST POOR
QUIT WIDOW ORBATE FORLORN
FORFAIRN DESTITUTE
BERG FLOE BARROW ICEBERG
FLOEBERG
BERGAMOT BOSE BERGAMA
BURGAMOT
BERI (FATHER OF —) ZOPHAH
BERIAH (FATHER OF —) ASHER
EPHRAIM
BERIBERI KAKKE
BERITH BRIS BRISS BRITH
BERM BERME LISIERE HEELPATH
BERNICE (FATHER OF —) HEROD
BERRY BAY DEW HAW ALEY BEAT
CRAN POHA RASP BACCA BLACK
CUBEB FRUIT GRAIN GRAPE
LANSA MOUND SALAL SAVIN
BURROW LANSAT LANSEH
SABINE THRESH CURRANT
ETAERIO HILLOCK ACROSARC
ALLSPICE COWBERRY
DEWBERRY HAWEBAKE
PERSIMMON POKEBERRY
SASKATOON PEPPERCORN

SHEEPBERRY POMEGRANATE
(ACID —) CURRANT
(COFFEE —) CHERRY
(DRIED —) PASA
(JUMPER —) ABHAL
(LAUREL —) BAY
(POISONOUS —) BANEBERRY
(PREF.) BACCI COCC(I)(O)
BERTH BED JOB BUNK DOCK SLIP
SOPT CABIN PLACE UPPER BILLET
OFFICE SECURE LODGING
MOORING SLIPWAY POSITION
ANCHORAGE
BERTHA (FATHER OF —) CARIBERT
(HUSBAND OF —) PEPIN
HEREWARD
(SON OF —) CHARLES
BERYL EMERALD AEROIDES
HELIODOR GOSHENITE
MORGANITE AQUAMARINE
BERYLLIA GLUCINA GLUCINE
BERYLLIUM GLUCINUM
BESEECH ASK BEG BID CRY SUE
WOO PRAY CRAVE HALSE PLEAD
PRESS ADJURE APPEAL OBTEST
CONJURE ENTREAT IMPLORE
SOLICIT IMPETRATE OBSECRATE
BESET PLY SET SIT BEGO SAIL
STUD ALLOT BELAY BIGAN HARRY
PRESS SIEGE SPEND STEAD
ASSAIL ATTACK HARASS INFEST
OBSESS WAYLAY ARRANGE
BESIEGE OVERSET PERPLEX
BLOCKADE ENCUMBER
ENTHRONG OBSTRUCT
SURROUND BELEAGUER
BESHOW SKIL CUDDY CUDDEN
CUDDIE BADDOCK COALFISH
SKILFISH
BESIDE BY HEAR INBY ALONG
ANENT ASIDE FORBY ABREAST
AGAINST FORNENT ADJACENT
FORNENST
(— ONE ANOTHER) ABREAST
(— ONESELF) FEY
(PREF.) EPH EPI PAR(A)
BESIDES BY TO AND BUT TOO YET
ALSO ELSE MORE OVER THEN
UNTO WITH ABOVE AGAIN FORBY
SUPRA WITHAL THERETO
FORBYE WITHAL THERETO
WITHOUT LIKEWISE MOREOVER
(PREF.) EPH EPI PROS
BESIEGE GIRD GIRT BELAY BELIE
BESET SIEGE STORM ATTACK
OBSESS OBSIDE PESTER PLAGUE
COMPASS SOLICIT SURROUND
BELEAGUER
BESMEAR RAY BALM DAUB SOIL
APPLY COVER GRIME GRUFT
MUDDY SLAKE SMEAR SULLY
TAINT BEDAUB PLATCH BESLIME
SMOTHER BESMIRCH BESLUBBER
BESMIRCH TAR DASH SLUR SOIL
SMEAR SULLY SLURRY SMIRCH
ASPERSE BLACKEN DRAGGLE
TURPIFY DISCOLOR
BESMIRCHED MACULATE
MACULATED
BESMUT CROCK
BESOM COW MAP DRAB BISME
BROOM SWEEP SLOVEN HEATHER
BESOT DULL ASOTE ASSOT

MUDDLE STUPID STUPEFY
BEFUDDLE
BESPANGLE DOT STAR STUD
ADORN JEWEL INVENT SPRINKLE
BESPATTER BLOT DASH JAUP SOIL
SPOT MUDDY PLASH STAIN SULLY
BEGARY SPARGE ASPERSE
SCATTER SMOTTER REPROACH
SPRINKLE
BESPEAK CITE HINT SHOW ARGUE
IMPLY ORDER SPEAK TRYST
ACCOST ATTEST ENGAGE STEVEN
ADDRESS ARRANGE BENEFIT
BETOKEN DISCUSS EXCLAIM
RESERVE FORETELL INDICATE
BESPECKLE DASH
BESPRINKLE DROP SHED POWDER
ASPERSE BESTREW BESPRING
SPRINKLE BEQUIRTLE
BEST O ACE BEAT GOOD LACE
MOST PICK TOPS WALE ELITE
EXCEL WORST CHOICE DEFEAT
FINEST FLOWER OUTWIT SUNDAY
TIPTOP UTMOST ARISTOS
CONQUER GARLAND LARGEST
OPTIMUM PALMARY DAMNDEST
GREATEST KOHINOOR OUTMATCH
OUTSTRIP POSSIBLE TOPNOTCH
VANQUISH
(SUNDAY —) BRAWS
(PREF.) ARIST(O)
BESTIAL LOW VILE WILD BRUTE
FERAL PRONE BRUTAL FILTHY
BEASTLY BRUTISH INHUMAN
SENSUAL BELLUINE DEPRAVED
BESTIR STIR AWAKE SHIFT STEER
AROUSE HUSTLE
(— ONESELF) LEG
BEST MAN PARANYMPH
BESTOW ADD PUT USE CAST DEAL
DOTE GIVE SEND STOW TAKE
WARE ALLOT ALLOW APPLY
AWARD BESET GRANT INFER
LODGE PLACE SPEND THOLE
WREAK ACCORD BETEEM CONFER
DEMISE DEVOTE DIVIDE DONATE
DOTATE EMPLOY ENTAIL ESTATE
EXTEND IMPART IMPOSE RENDER
SHOWER COLLATE COMMEND
DISPOSE ENLARGE EROGATE
INDULGE INSTATE PARTAKE
PRESENT QUARTER TRIBUTE
BEQUEATH
(— LAVISHLY) HEAP
(— UPON) GIFT
BESTOWAL DOLE DISPOSAL
COLLATION LARGITION
(— OF PRAISE) ACCOLADE
BESTRIDE HORSE STRIDE
STRADDLE OVERSTRIDE
BET GO UP BAS BOX LAY PUT SET
VIE WAD ANTE BACK BRAG CHIP
GAGE HOLD JACK NOIR PAIR
PLAY PLOT PUNT RISK WAGE
BOUND CARRE HEDGE ROUGE
SAVER SPORT STAKE WAGER
GAMBLE HAZARD IMPAIR
MANQUE MILIEU PLEDGE
DERNIER PREMIER
ACCUMULATOR
(— AGAINST) MILK COPPER
(— AT LONG ODDS) SKINNER
(— BOLDLY) BLUFF

(— CHIP) CHECK
(FARO —) SLEEPER
(HEDGING —) SAVER
(POKER —) BLIND
BETA AND GAMMA GUARDS
BETAKE GO GET HIE MOVE TAKE
APPLY CATCH GRANT ASSUME
COMMIT REMOVE REPAIR RESORT
COMMEND JOURNEY WITHDRAW
(— ONESELF) BUN HIT BOUN MARK
PIKE TEEM AVOID FOUND HAUNT
REFER TRUSS YIELD
(— ONESELF TO MILL) SUE
BETEL PAN IKMO ITMO SERI SIRI
SIRIH PINANG PUPULO
BETEL LEAF PAN BUYO PAUN
PAWNE
BETEL NUT BONGA BONYA BUNGA
SUPARI
BETHABARA NOIBWOOD
GREENHEART
BETHEL BETHESDA
BETHINK TAKE THINK ADVISE
DEVISE RECALL REFLECT
CONSIDER REMEMBER RECOLLECT
(— ONE'S SELF) MIN MINE
UMBETHINK
BETHLEHEM BEDLAM
BETHROOT TRILLIUM
BETHUEL (DAUGHTER OF —)
REBEKAH
(FATHER OF —) NAHOR
(MOTHER OF —) MILCAH
(UNCLE OF —) ABRAHAM
BETIDE HAP TIDE BEFIT OCCUR
TRITE WORTH BECOME BEFALL
CHANCE HAPPEN BETOKEN
PRESAGE
BETIMES ANON RATH SOON EARLY
RATHE TIMEOUS SPEEDILY
FORTHWITH
BETOKEN MARK NOTE SHOW SIGN
AUGUR TOKEN ASSERT BETIDE
DENOTE EVINCE IMPORT
SHADOW BESPEAK EXPRESS
OBLIQUE PORTEND PRESAGE
SIGNIFY FOREBODE FORESHOW
INDICATE
BETONY BROOMWORT
BETRAY BLAB BLOW BOIL GULL
SELL SHOP SILE SING SPOT TELL
TRAY UNDO WRAY ABUSE CROSS
FALSE PEACH ROUND SPILL SPLIT
SWICK SWIKE ACCUSE BEWRAY
DELUDE DESCRY DESERT QUATCH
REVEAL SEDUCE SNITCH SQUEAL
BEGUILE DECEIVE FALSIFY
MISLEAD PROMOTE TRAITOR
DISCLOSE DISCOVER
(— CONFIDENCES) SPILL
BETRAYAL RAP ABUSE ACCUSE
TREASON GIVEAWAY PRODITION
BETRAYER RAT JUDAS SKUNK
SEDUCER TRAITOR DERELICT
RECREANT SQUEALER
BETRAYING TELLTALE
BETROTH AFFY EARL TOKEN
TROTH TRUTH ASSURE ENGAGE
ENSURE PLEDGE PLIGHT ESPOUSE
PROMISE AFFIANCE CONTRACT
DESPOUSE HANDFAST
BETROTHED SURE VOWED
ASSURED ENGAGED HANDFAST

INTENDED COMBINATE
(AUTHOR OF —) MANZONI
(CHARACTER IN —) LUCIA RENZO
RODRIGO ABBONDIO BORROMEO
CRISTOFORO
BETTA PLAKAT
BETTER AID TOP BEET MEND
AMEND AMEND EXCEL SAFER
WISER BIGGER EXCEED REFORM
ADVANCE CHOICER CORRECT
GREATER IMPROVE PROMOTE
RECTIFY RELIEVE SUPPORT
SURPASS EMINENCE INCREASE
SUPERIOR
(— A SCORE) BREAK
(— THAN ORDINARY) EXTRA
BETTING ACTION GAMBLING
(— SYSTEM) PAROLI ALEMBERT
BETTOR ORALER
BETTY JENNY COTBETTY JOCRISSE
MOLLYCOT WIFECARL
BETWEEN AMID EMEL AMELL
AMONG ENTRE TWEEN YTWYN
ATWEEN ATWIXT TWEESH
AVERAGE BETWIXT
(PREF.) DI INTER INTRA
BEUDANITE CORKITE
BEVEL BLOW CANT CONE EDGE
PUSH REAM ANGLE BEARD BEZEL
MITER MITRE SLANT SLOPE
SNAPE SPLAY ASLANT CIPHER
RHYMER CHAMFER INCLINE
OBLIQUE
(— EDGES) BEARD
(WITHOUT —) FLAT
BEVERAGE ADE ALE AVA CUP NOG
POP RUM SAP TEA BEER BREW
CHIA GROG MABI MATE MEAD
MILK NIPA SODA WHIG WINE
CHOCA CIDER CLARY COCOA
DRAFT DRINK JULEP LAGER
LEBAN MORAT MULSE NEGUS
PUNCH SHRUB SMASH TREAT
TWIST WATER BISHOP COFFEE
EGGNOG LIQUID LIQUOR NECTAR
PORTER SPRUCE TISWIN
BUNNELL CASSINA CORDIAL
LIMEADE OENOMEL POTABLE
STEPONY TULAPAI ALEBERRY
COCKTAIL LEMONADE PIQUETTE
POTATION SANGAREE SWITCHEL
BADMINTON CALIBOGUS
CHOCOLATE GINGERADE
ORANGEADE POMPERKIN
SOMETHING
(— FROM COW'S MILK) KEFIR
KEPHIR
(— FROM PEPPERS) KAVA
KAVAKAVA
(— FROM SAP) TUBA
(— OF BUTTERMILK AND WATER)
BLAND
(— OF CHAMPAGNE) POPE
(— OF HONEY AND WATER)
METHEGLIN
(— OF HOT MILK) POSSET
(— OF PORT WINE) BISHOP
(— OF VINEGAR AND WATER)
POSCA
(ALCOHOLIC —) DEW ARAK SAKE
SAKI ARRAK BASIG SHRUB
SNAPS STUFF ARRACK

FIREWATER STIMULANT
(COLA —) DOPE
(EFFERVESCENT —) FIZZ
(FERMENTED —) BASI KAVA KUMYS
KUMISS
(FRUIT —) BEVERAGE
(INSIPID —) WASH
(MEXICAN —) TEPACHE
(POLYNESIAN —) AVA KAVA
(WEAK —) LAP
(PL.) WAIPIRO
BEVY HERD PACK COVEY DROVE
FLOCK GROUP SWARM FLIGHT
SCHOOL COMPANY
BEWAIL CRY RUE WEY KEEN
MOAN RAME SIGH WAIL WEEP
MOURN PLAIN BEMOAN GRIEVE
LAMENT PLAINT SORROW
THROPE DEPLORE COMPLAIN
BEWARE WAR CAVE GARE HEED
SHUN TENT WARD AVOID SPEND
ESCHEW WARNING
BEWILDER FOG FOX MAR BEAT
DAZE FOIL GAUM MAZE STUN
ABASH ADDLE AMAZE AMUSE
DEAVE DIZZY BAFFLE BEMIST
BEMUSE BOTHER DAZZLE
DUDDER MOIDER MOMBLE
MUDDLE PUZZLE WANDER
WILDER BUFFALO BUMBAZE
CONFUSE FLASKER MYSTIFY
NONPLUS PERPLEX STAGGER
STUPEFY ASTONISH CONFOUND
DISTRACT ENTANGLE OVERMUSE
SQUATTER SURPRISE
(PREF.) PLAZO
BEWILDERED MAR ASEA LOST
MANG WILL AGAPE DAZED
MAZED MUZZY BUSHED MAPPED
BEMAZED STUPENT WILSOME
CONFUSED HELPLESS WILLYARD
PERPLEXED
BEWILDERMENT AWE FOG DAZE
MISMAZE STICKLE AMAZEMENT
CONFUSION PERPLEXITY
BEWITCH HEX WISH BLINK CHARM
MAGIC OBEAH SPELL WITCH
ENAMOR ENTICE GLAMOR GRIGRI
HOODOO STRIKE THRILL ATTRACT
BEDEVIL DELIGHT ENCHANT
GLAMOUR ENSORCEL FORSPEAK
GREEGREE OVERLOOK
BEWITCHED HAGGED
BEWITCHING SIREN
BEYOND BY FREE OVER YOND
ABOVE ASIDE AYOND FORBY
ULTRA BEHIND BEYANT YONDER
BENEATH BESIDES FORTHBY
FURTHER OUTGATE PASSING
WITHOUT OVERMORE SUPERIOR
HEREAFTER
(— DOUBT) ASSURED
(— ORDINARY METHODS) AFIELD
(— THE MARK) GONE
(— THE SEA) ULTRAMARINE
(— THIS) STILL
(GO —) OVERSHOOT
(PREF.) EXTRA HYPER META
OVER PARA PERI PRETER SUPER
TRANS ULTRA
BEYOND HUMAN POWER
(AUTHOR OF —) BJORNSON
(CHARACTER IN —) SANG CLARA

ELIAS HANNA ADOLPH RACHAEL
ROBERTS
BEZALEEL (FATHER OF —) URI
BEZEL RIM TOP EDGE OUCH SEAL
BEVIL BEZIL CROWN FACET
CHATON FLANGE MARQUISE
TEMPLATE
BEZER (FATHER OF —) ZOPHAH
BEZIQUE PENCHANT
BEZOAR GOATSTONE HIPPOLITH
B-GIRL SITTER
BHAKTA BHAGAVATA
BHANG BANG BENG BENJ HEMP
HASHISH
BHARAL TUR HALL NAHOOR
BURRHEL
BHARTRIHARI (BROTHER OF —)
VIKRAMADITYA
BHIKSHU GELONG
BHIMA (FATHER OF —) VAYU
PANDU
(MOTHER OF —) KUNTI PRITHA
BHUTAN (ASSEMBLY OF —)
TSONGDU
(CAPITAL OF —) THIMPHU
(CURRENCY OF —) PAISA RUPEE
(LANGUAGE OF —) DZONGKHA
(RIVER OF —) MACHU MANAS
AMOCHU
BHUTAN PINE KAIL
BIANCA (HUSBAND OF —) FAZIO
LEONTIO
(SISTER OF —) KATHERINE
BIANNUAL BIYEARLY
BIANOR (FATHER OF —) TIBERIS
(MOTHER OF —) MANTO
BIAS PLY WRY AWRY BENT CANT
SWAY WARP AMISS COLOR
FAVOR POISE SLANT SLOPE
SWING TWIST BIGOTRY INCLINE
OBLIQUE SUGGEST CLINAMEN
COLORING DIAGONAL TENDENCY
PREJUDICE PROCEDURE
SPECTACLE
(— IN NEWS REPORTING) PLUGOLA
(BROTHER OF —) MELAMPUS
(FATHER OF —) AMYTHAON
(MOTHER OF —) IDOMENE
(WIFE OF —) PERO IPHIANASSA
BIASED SLANT ANGLED COLORED
PARTIAL
BIB SIP BRAT POUT APRON BLAIN
DRINK BRASSY FEEDER TIPPLE
TUCKER BAVETTE
(CHILD'S —) BISHOP
(LEATHER —) DICK
BIBLE BOOK VULGATE SCRIPTURE
(— TEXT) MIKRA MIQRA
(BOOK OF —) EX CHR COL COR
DAN EPH GAL GEN HAB HAG HEB
HOS JER JOB KIN LAM LEV MAL
MIC NAH NEH NUM PET REV ROM
SAM TIM ACTS AMOS CANT DEUT
EZEK EZRA JOEL JOHN JUDE
JUDG LUKE MARK MATT OBAD
PHIL PROV RUTH SONG ZECH
ZEPH HOSEA JAMES JONAH
KINGS MICAH NAHUM PETER
THESS TITUS DANIEL ECCLES
ESTHER EXODUS HAGGAI ISAIAH
JOSHUA JUDGES PHILEM PSALMS
ROMANS SAMUEL EZEKIEL
GENESIS HEBREWS MALACHI

MATTHEW NUMBERS OBADIAH
TIMOTHY JEREMIAH NEHEMIAH
PHILEMON PROVERBS CANTICLES
EPHESIANS GALATIANS LEVITICUS
ZECHARIAH ZEPHANIAH
CHRONICLES COLOSSIANS
REVELATION CORINTHIANS
DEUTERONOMY PHILIPPIANS
ECCLESIASTES LAMENTATIONS
THESSALONIANS
(SYRIAC VERSION OF —) PESHITO
BIBLE LEAF COSTMARY
BIBULOUS DRINKING BIBACIOUS
BICKER JAR WAR BOWL SPAR TIFF
ARGUE BRAWL CAVIL FIGHT
ASSAIL ATTACK BATTLE
CONTEND DISPUTE PICKEER
QUARREL QUIBBLE WRANGLE
PETTIFOG SKIRMISH SQUABBLE
BICKERN ANVIL BEAKIRON
BICUSPID PREMOLAR
BICYCLE BIKE QUAD CORGI CORGY
CYCLE HOBBY MOUNT STEED
WHEEL JIGGER ORNARY SAFETY
TANDEM ORDINAR TRIPLET
ORDINARY ROADSTER
(PART OF —) ARM LUG RIM CLIP
FORK POST RACK RING SEAT
STAY STEM TIRE CHAIN GUARD
PEDAL SHIFT SPOKE FENDER
HANGER SADDLE DOWNTUBE
SPROCKET CHAINWHEEL
DERAILLEUR
(PLACE WHERE —S ARE SERVICED)
CYCLERY
BID GO BEG NAP BEDE BODE CALL
GIVE HEST HIST PRAY TELL WISH
CHEAP CLEPE FRAGE OFFER
ORDER ADJURE CHARGE DIRECT
ENJOIN INVITE REVEAL SIMPLE
SUMMON TENDER BALANCE
CHEAPEN COMMAND DECLARE
DROPVIE ENTREAT PROFFER
ANNOUNCE PROCLAIM PROPOSAL
(— ADIEU) TEACH
(— AT AUCTION) CRY
(— IN CARDS) CUE FROG JUMP
PASS SKIP SOLO FRAGE GRAND
NULLO SHIFT BOSTON DEFEND
DEMAND DENIAL DOUBLE
SMUDGE BLUCHER COMMAND
SHUTOUT SUPPORT CONTRACT
REDOUBLE SCHMEISS
(SEALED —) TICKET
BIDDING BEHEST AUCTION
BIDDANCE DIRECTIVE
BIDE FACE STAY WAIT ABIDE
AWAIT DWELL TARRY WATCH
ENDURE REMAIN SUFFER
SOJOURN CONTINUE TOLERATE
BIDENS CUCKOLD MANZANILLA
BIDET SITZBAD INSESSION
BIDRI VIDRY BIDDERY TUTENAG
BIENNIAL TRIETERIC
BIER BEAR PYRE FRAME GRAVE
HANDY HORSE TABUT COFFIN
HEARSE LITTER SUPPORT
FERETORY FERETRUM
BIFURCATION WYE FORK SPLIT
BRANCH CROTCH CRUTCH
FORKING DIVISION DICHOTOMY
BIG FAT BARO BOLD HUGE MUCH
VAST BULKY CHIEF GAUCY

GRAND GREAT GROSS HUSKY
LARGE GAUCIE MIGHTY BIGGISH
BUMPING EMINENT HUMMING
LEADING MASSIVE POMPOUS
UPRIGHT VIOLENT BOASTFUL
BOUNCING ENORMOUS
GENEROUS GIGANTIC IMPOSING
PLUMPING PREGNANT SLAPPING
SWANKING SWAPPING THUMPING
(— WITH YOUNG) FULL GRAVID
(MARVELOUSLY —) TREMENDOUS
(PREF.) MAGNI
BIGFOOT SASQUATCH
BIGHORN ARGAL AOUDAD ARGALI
CIMARRON
BIGHT BAY BEND BITE COIL GULF
LOOP ROVE ANGLE CURVE INLET
NOOSE BOUGHT CORNER
HOLLOW POCKET
BIGNESS BULK
BIGOT CAFARD ZEALOT FANATIC
MUMPSIMUS
BIGOTED BIASED NARROW
HIDEBOUND ILLIBERAL
SECTARIAN
BIGOTRY INTOLERANCE
BIGROOT MANROOT BITTERROOT
BIG SHOT HEAVY MUCKAMUCK
BIG SKY COUNTRY MONTANA
BIKINI (TOPLESS —) MONOKINI
BILE BOIL GALL HUMP VENOM
CHOLER GROWTH ATRABILE
MELANCHOLY
(PREF.) BILI CHOL(E)(O)
(SUFF.) CHOLIA CHOLY
BILGE PUMP SCUM BOUGE BULGE
BILLAGE THURROCK
BILHAH (SON OF —) DAN NAPHTALI
BILHAN (FATHER OF —) JEDIAEL
BILIMBI CAMIAS KAMIAS
CUCUMBER
BILINGUAL DIGLOT
BILIOUS GALLISH LIVERISH
BILIOUSNESS LIVER CHOLER
BILK DO GYP BALK HOAX CHEAT
COZEN TRICK DELUDE FLEECE
SWEDGE DECEIVE DEFRAUD
SWINDLE
BILL ACT DUN GET LAW NEB NIB
TAB BEAK CHIT CLAP KITE
NOTE PECK SHOT CHECK ENTRY
LIBEL SCORE CARESS CHARGE
DOCKET INDICT LAWING PECKER
PICKAX POSTER STRIKE DERTRUM
INVOICE LAMPOON MATTOCK
PLACARD PROGRAM REMANET
STATUTE BILLHOOK DOCUMENT
HEADLAND INNOCENT PETITION
TREASURY RECKONING
ACCEPTANCE
(— OF ANCHOR) PEE PEAK
(— OF COMPLAINT) QUERELA
(— OF CREDIT) ANGEL
(— OF DIVORCE) GET GETT
(— OF EXCHANGE) SOLA HUNDI
DEVISE
(— OF FARE) MENU CARTE
(— OF PARCELS) FACTURE
(COUNTERFEIT —S) STIFF
(DOLLAR —) BUCK SPOT SINGLE
FROGSKIN
(REVOLUTIONARY —) ASSIGNAT
(10-DOLLAR —) TEN

TENNER SAWBUCK
(100-DOLLAR —) CENTURY
(2-DOLLAR —) DEUCE
(5-DOLLAR —) FIN VEE FIVE FIVER
BILLET BAR GAD HUT LAY LOG
LOOP NOTE PASS POST SPOT
BERTH ENROL HOUSE LODGE
ORDER SHIDE SPRAG STICK
STRAP BALLOT BULLET COUPON
ENROLL HARBOR LETTER LIBBET
NOTICE TICKET BEARING EPISTLE
MISSIVE POLLACK COALFISH
DOCUMENT FIREWOOD
ORNAMENT POSITION QUARTERS
(— SOLDIERS) CESS
BILLET-DOUX CAPON
BILLETING LIVERY
BILLFISH GAR LONGJAWS SAILFISH
SPEARFISH
BILLFOLD WALLET NOTECASE
BILLHOOK BILL DHAW HOOK
PAWPAW SLASHER SNAGGER
SCIMITAR
BILLIARD BALL IVORY
BILLIARD CUE MACE MAST
(TIP OF —) LEATHER
BILLIARDS PILLS TRUCKS
(LAWN —) TROCO
BILLINGSGATE ABUSE SLAPDASH
BILLION MILLIARD
(PREF.) GIGA
BILLIONTH
(PREF.) BICRO NANO
**BILL OF MARRIAGE (CHARACTER
IN —)** MILL FANNY SLOOK TOBIAS
EDOARDO
(COMPOSER OF —) ROSSINI
BILLON BAIOC VELLON BAJOCCO
BILLOW SEA BLOW WAVE BULGE
CLOUD FLOAT SURGE SWELL
RESACA RIPPLE ROLLER WALLOW
BREAKER UNDULATE
BILLY CAW CHAP CLUB GOAT
MACE MATE BATON FANNY
NEDDY CUDGEL FANNIE FELLOW
BROTHER COMRADE BILLIKIN
BILLYCAN BLUDGEON JACKSHAY
BLACKJACK TRUNCHEON
BILLY BUDD (CHARACTER IN —)
BUDD VERE BILLY CLAGGART
(COMPOSER OF —) BRITTEN
BILSHAN (COMPANION OF —)
ZERUBBABEL
BIMAH ALMEMAR ALMEMOR
BIMHAL (FATHER OF —) JAPHLET
BIN ARK BOX CUB GUM BING BONE
CART CRIB VINA FRAME HUTCH
KENCH PUNGI STALL STORE
WAGON BASKET BUNKER GARNER
HAMPER MANGER POCKET
TROUGH WITHIN BLEACHER
(— FOR CEMENT) SILO
(— FOR FISH) KENCH
(— FOR GRAIN) ARK
BINARY HYDRIDE
BINATE DUAL DOUBLE PAIRED
COUPLED TWOFOLD GEMINATE
BINAURAL DIOTIC
BIND JAM LAP TIE WAP EARL FAST
FRAP GIRD GYVE HOLD HOOP
KNIT KNOT LASH MAIL NAIL TAPE
YERK BRACE CADGE CHAIN CINCH
EDDER GIRTH SNAKE STICK

STRAP TRUSS ATTACH BUNDLE
COMMIT EMBIND ENGAGE FETTER
FREEZE GARTER GIRDLE LIGATE
OBLIGE STRAIN SWATHE TETHER
WRITHE ARTICLE ASTRAIN
BANDAGE CONFINE EMBOUND
ENCHAIN GRAPPLE SHACKLE
SWADDLE ASTRINGE CONCLUDE
FLIGHTER HANDFAST INNODATE
LIGATURE OBLIGATE RESTRAIN
(— A FALCON) MAIL
(— BY LEASE) THIRL
(— BY PLEDGE) GAGE SWEAR
(— IN BUNDLE) KID BAVIN
(— INTO SHEAVES) GAVEL THRAVE
(— ONESELF) ADHERE
(— TO SECRECY) TILE
(— TOGETHER) LIME FAGOT SEIZE
CEMENT FAGGOT ASTRINGE
RELIGATE COLLIGATE
(— UP) KILT BAVIN TRUSS
UPBAND ASTRICT REVOLVE
(— WINGS) PINION
(— WITH THREAD) OOP
(PREF.) SPHINGO
(SUFF.) SPHINX
BINDER BAND BEAM BOND CORD
ROPE BALER COVER FRAME
LEVER FILLET FOLDER GIRDER
HEADER LIGNIN TARMAC
HAYBAND BONDSTONE
BOOKMAKER
BINDING TAG BAND CORD GARD
HARD TEAR ROPE TAPE YAPP
COVER VALID CADDIS EDGING
RIBBON BOUNDEN CADDICE
GALLOON LAPPING MOUSING
WEBBING FAITHFUL LIGATIVE
LIGATORY STRINGENT
OBLIGATORY
(— FAST) IRON
(— OF BOOK) BOCK FACE YAPP
(— OF GOLD) BISSET
(— ON DRESS) FENT
(SUFF.) DESIS
BINDLESTIFF BUM
BINDWEED BINE WIRE CREEPER
TIEVINE BEARBIND BEARBINE
BELLBINE BINEWEED CORNBIND
HELLWEED MILKMAID WOODBINE
WITHYWIND
BINE WIRE
BINGE BAT BOW HIT BLOW BUST
SOAK TEAR TOOT BEANO PARTY
SOUSE SPRAY SPREE CRINGE
BLOWOFF CAROUSAL
BINGO KENO BEANO LOTTO
BRANDY SCREENO TOMBOLA
BINNACLE PYX BITTACLE
BINNUI (FATHER OF —) HENADAD
(SON OF —) NOADIAH
BINOCULARS GLASS
BINOMIAL DIONYM BINOMEN
BIOCHEMIST **AMERICAN** CORI
BLOCH MOORE OCHOA ALSBERG
AXELROD LIPMANN OSBORNE
SHAFFER KORNBERG NIRENBERG
ARGENTINIAN LELOIR
CANADIAN COLLIP
ENGLISH KREBS PERUTZ PORTER
SANGER MITCHELL
FRENCH MONOD DUCLAUX
GERMAN LYNEN

BIODEGRADABLE SOFT
BIOGEOGRAPHY CHOROLOGY
BIOGRAPHER PLUTARCH
SCOTTISH BOSWELL
BIOGRAPHY BIO LIFE VITA
MEMOIR ACCOUNT HISTORY
RECOUNT PSYCHOGRAPH
(— OF SAINTS) HAGIOGRAPHA
HAGIOGRAPHY
BIOLOGIST NATURALIST
AMERICAN EAST JUST LUTZ WALD
CHILD CLARK LURIA MINOT
PEARL SHULL TYLER WOODS
BAILEY BEADLE BUMPUS FISHER
JORDAN LITTLE OSBORN PALADE
WELLER CONKLIN HERRICK
HERSHEY WETMORE CHAMBERS
DELBRUCK HARRISON SEDGWICK
STOCKARD
AUSTRIAN STEINACH
BELGIAN CLAUDE
CUBAN FINLAY
ENGLISH CRICK HUXLEY MIVART
BATESON COBBOLD KENDREW
MEDAWAR ROMANES CUMMINGS
NICHOLSON
FRENCH GIARD CARREL NOCARD
BOUCHARD LEDANTEC
GERMAN WOLFF DRIESCH
HAECKEL UEXKULL WEISMANN
MUCKERMANN
IRISH ALLMAN
NORWEGIAN MJOEN
RUSSIAN GURVICH LYSENKO
SCOTTISH GEDDES THOMSON
BIOPHORE BIOGEN PLASOME
BIOPLAST MICELLA MICELLE
BIOTITE MICA ANOMITE
MEROXENE RUBELLAN
BIOTOPE STATION
BIPARTITE
(PREF.) DIPHY
BIPED DIPODE HINDQUARTERS
BIRCH COW BIRK CANE FLOG WHIP
ALDER ALNUS CANOE SWISH
BETULA BIRKEN TAWHAI HICKORY
BIRD ANI DAW DOG JAY NUN PIE
TIT TUI CHAT COOT CROW DOVE
FOWL IBIS JACK KAGU KITE KNOT
LARK QUIT RUFF TERN TODY
WING WREN BAKER BRANT
CHUCK CLEAR COVEY EGRET
FINCH FLIER FLYER GOOSE HOBBY
JUNCO LARID LIVER PEWEE
PEWIT RAVEN ROBIN SNIPE STILT
SWIFT TEREK TURCO TWITE
VIREO BULBUL DICKEY DIPPER
DRIVER DRONGO DUCKER DUNLIN
FALCON FINGER GROUSE GUINEA
HOOPOE HOOTER JACANA
JAEGER LINNET MARTEN MOCKER
NESTER ORIOLE OSCINE PHOEBE
PLOVER SHRIKE SILVAN SINGER
SITTER SYLVAN THRUSH TROGON
TURNIX VERDIN YAWPER
ANTBIRD BABBLER BLUEJAY
BUNTING BUSTARD BUZZARD
CATBIRD CHIRPER COTINGA
COURLAN FEATHER FLAPPER
FLICKER FLIGGER FLOPPER
GRACKLE HALCYON HORNERO
HURGILA INCOMER IRRISOR
JACAMAR JACKDAW KINGLET

MINIVET MOULTER ORTOLAN
PEACOCK PERCHER QUILLER
REDWING SCRAPER SKINNER
SKYLARK SPARROW SUNBIRD
SWALLOW TANAGER TINAMOU
TITLARK TOMFOOL WARBLER
WAXWING WAYBUNG ACCENTOR
AIRPLANE AMADAVAT ANNOTINE
BLACKCAP BLACKNEB BLUEBIRD
BOATBILL BOBOLINK BOBWHITE
BUBBLING CAGELING CARINATE
COCKBIRD COCORICO DREPANID
FERNBIRD FIREBIRD FIRETAIL
GROSBEAK GRUIFORM IBISBILL
JUVENILE KILLDEER KINGBIRD
LOBEFOOT LONGSPUR OXPECKER
PALMIPED PHEASANT PLUMIPED
POORWILL PREACHER REDSTART
SALTATOR SONGBIRD STARLING
SURFBIRD SWAMPHEN TAPACOLO
THRASHER THROSTLE TITMOUSE
TREMBLER UMBRETTE WHINCHAT
WOODCHAT WOODCOCK
YEARBIRD COCKYOLLY CROSSBILL
ROADRUNNER MOCKINGBIRD
(— OF BRILLIANT PLUMAGE) TODY
JALAP BARBET ORIOLE TROGON
JACAMAR KIROMBO MINIVET
TANAGER
(— OF INDIA) BAYA KALA SHAMA
(— OF OMEN) WAYBIRD
(— OF PREY) OWL HAWK KITE
EAGLE ELANT GLEAD GLEDE
STOOP EAGLET ELANET BUZZARD
GOSHAWK STOOPER VULTURE
ACCIPITER
(AFRICAN —) TAHA QUELEA
TOURACO UMBRETTE NAPECREST
(AUSTRALIAN —) EMU ROA LORY
ARARA LEIPOA BOOBOOK
BUSTARD FIGBIRD WAYBUNG
BELLBIRD LORIKEET LYREBIRD
MANUCODE
(BIG-BEAKED —) BECARD HORNBILL
(CRESTED —) KAGU COPPY
HOATZIN TOPKNOT
(CROCODILE —) TROCHIL
(DECOY —) CALL STOOL
(DIVING —) AUK LOON GREBE
DARTER DOPPER DUCKER
GRAYLING PLUNGEON
(EUROPEAN —) ANI DAW MEW
QUA CIRL DARR KITE MALL MORO
QUIS ROOK STAG WHIM YITE
AMSEL BOONK GLEDE MAVIS
MERLE OUSEL OUZEL SACER
SAKER SERIN TARIN TEREK TERIN
WHAUP AVOCET CUCKOO
CUSHAT GAYLAG GODWIT
MARTEN MERLIN MISSEL REDCAP
WHEVER WINDLE WINNEL
WRANNY BITTERN BUSTARD
HAYBIRD KESTREL MOTACIL
ORTOLAN SAKERET STARNEL
WHISKEY WINNARD WITWALL
BARGOOSE CHEPSTER DOTTEREL
GARGANEY REDSTART
WHEATEAR WHEYBIRD
WHIMBREL WRANNOCK
YOLDRING
(EXTINCT —) MOA DODO JIBI KIWI
MAMO RUKH OFFBIRD
(FABULOUS —) FUM ROC FUNG

HALCYON OOFBIRD WHISTLER
(FEMALE —) HEN JENNY
(FICTITIOUS —) JAYHAWK PHOENIX
(FISH-CATCHING —) OSPREY
CRABIER
(FLEDGLING —) SQUAB
(FLIGHTLESS —) EMU GOR MOA
DODO EYAS GORB GULL KAGU
KIWI CALLOW GORLIN APTERYX
GORLING NESTLER OSTRICH
PENGUIN BUBBLING NESTLING
(FRIGATE —) IOA IWA
(FRUIT-EATING —) COLY
(GALLOWS —) HEMPY HEMPIE
(GAME —) QUAIL SNIPE COLIMA
GROUSE INCOME FLAPPER
INCOMER
(GREEN —) SIRGANG
(HAWAIIAN —) IO OO AVA IOA IWA
OOA IIWI JIBI KOAE MAMO MOHO
OMAO OOAA KAMAO PALILA
(HORN-HEADED —) KAMICHI
(INJURED —) CRIPPLE
(LARGEST —) LAMMERGEIER
(LIMICOLINE —) PRATINCOLE
(MADAGASCAR —) KIROMBO
(MECHANICAL —) ORTHOPTER
(MYTHICAL —) FUM ROC GANZA
SIMURG SIMURGH
(NEW ZEALAND —) KEA MOA OII
ROA HUIA KAKA KIWI KOKO KUKU
KULU PEHO RURU TITI WEKA
POAKA KAKAPO KOKAKO KUKUPA
APTERYX KORIMAKO MOREPORK
NOTORNIS
(PASSERINE —) QUIT FINCH
SPARROW STARNEL SWALLOW
SYLVIID DREPANID FALCONET
FERNBIRD GRALLINA JACKBIRD
OVENBIRD
(PERTAINING TO —S) OSCINE
(RAPACIOUS —) SKUA JAEGER
(RASORIAL —) SCRATCHER
(RUNNING —) COURSER
(SAMOAN —) IAO
(SEA —) AUK ERN ERNE GONY
GULL PINK SMEW TERN EIDER
SOLAN FULMAR GANNET
HAGDON OSPREY PETREL PUFFIN
PELICAN SEAFOWL MURRELET
MALLEMUCK
(SHORE —) REE RAIL SORA SNIPE
STILT WADER AVOCET CURLEW
PLOVER WILLET WRYBILL
SHEATHBILL
(SHORT-TAILED —) BREVE
(SINGING —) LARK WREN PIPIT
ROBIN VEERY VIREO CANARY
LINNET MOCKER ORIOLE OSCINE
SINGER THRUSH WARBLER
FAUVETTE REDSTART
NIGHTINGALE
(SMALL —) TIT TODY WREN DICKY
PEGGY PIPIT TYDIE VIREO DICKEY
LINNET SISKIN TOMTIT CREEPER
SPARROW TITLARK COCORICO
GNATSNAP PERCOLIN STARLING
WHEATEAR
(SOUTH AMERICAN —) GUAN MINA
MITU MYNA RARA TOCA BAKER
CHAJA JOPIM TURCO BARBET
BECARD CHUNGA TOUCAN
CARIAMA OILBIRD BELLBIRD

BOATBILL CARACARA GUACHARO
HOACTZIN PUFFBIRD SCREAMER
TAPACOLO TAPACULO TERUTERO
(STYLIZED —) DISTELFINK
(TROPICAL —) ANI GUAN KOAE
TODY BOS'N BOSUN JALAP
BARBET BECARD MOTMOT
TROGON JACAMAR MANAKIN
WIGTAIL LONGTAIL SALTATOR
(WADING —) HERN IBIS RAIL SORA
CRANE HERON SNIPE STILT
STORK ARGALA AVOCET GODWIT
JACANA LIMPKIN BOATBILL
FLAMINGO SHOEBILL SHOEBIRD
SANDERLING
(WILD —S) GALLINAE
(YEAR-OLD —) ANNOTINE
(YOUNG —) EYA GULL PIPER
CHEEPER FLAPPER NESTLER
BIRDIKIN NESTLING
(PL.) AVIFAUNA POLYMYODI
PRAECOCES
(PREF.) AVI ORNIS ORNITH(I)(O)
(SUFF.) ORNIS ORNITHES
BIRD BOLT BURBOLT QUARREL
BIRD CAGE AVIARY PINJRA
VOLARY VOLERY PADDOCK
BIRDCATCHER FOWLER
BIRD CHERRY DOGWOOD
EGGBERRY HACKWOOD
HAGBERRY
BIRDLIFE ORNIS
BIRDLIME GLUE LIME BELIME
VISCUM BIRDGLUE
BIRD OF PARADISE APUS
MANUCODE RIFLEBIRD
BIRDS (AUTHOR OF —)
ARISTOPHANES
(CHARACTER IN —) EPOPS TEREUS
BASILEIA EUELPIDES
PISTHETAERUS
BIRD'S-FOOT FOWLFOOT
SERRADELLA
BIRD'S KNEE SUFFRAGO
BIRD'S MANTLE STRAGULUM
BIRENO (WIFE OF —) OLIMPIA
BIRI BIDI
BIRTH KIN BEAR FALL BLOOD
BURDEN GENTRY ORIGIN
BEARING BORNING DESCENT
GENESIS LINEAGE DELIVERY
GENITURE NASCENCY NATALITY
NATIVITY
(FALSE —) SOOTERKIN
(GENTLE —) GENTILITY
(HIGH —) PARAGE
(HONORABLE —) BLOOD
(OF LOW —) CRESTLESS
(OF NOBLE —) CORONETED
(PREF.) NATI
(SUFF.) (GIVING —) PARA PAROUS
BIRTHMARK MOLE IMAGE NAEVE
NEVUS BLEMISH SPILOMA
SIGNATURE
BIRTHRATE NATALITY FERTILITY
BIRTHRIGHT KIND BIRTHDOM
HERITAGE
BIRTHROOT BATHROOT
BATHWORT DEATHROOT
DISHCLOTH SQUAWROOT
BIRTHWORT GUACO ASARUM
BATHROOT
BISAYAN AKLAN CEBUAN

AKLANON CEBUANO
BISCUIT BUN NUT BAKE ROLL
RUSK SNAP WOOD BREAD COOKY
SCONE WAFER BISQUE COOKIE
DODGER MALLOW MUFFIN
PARKIN SIMNEL CRACKER
GALETTE PENTILE PRETZEL
RATAFIA RATIFIA CRACKNEL
HARDTACK ZWIEBACK
(BROKEN —S) DUNDERFUNK
(COLOR —) DOE PAWNEE
BISECT FORK CROSS HALVE SPLIT
CLEAVE DIVIDE MIDDLE
SEPARATE
BISECTION MEDIATION
BISEXUAL ACDC
BISHOP EP ABBA EPUS LAWN
PAPA POPE ANGEL COARB DENIS
ARCHER BUSTLE DESPOT EPARCH
EXARCH MAGPIE PRESUL PRIEST
PRIMUS ROCHET ROCKAT
PONTIFF PRELATE PRIMATE
TULCHAN ANTISTES DIOCESAN
DIRECTOR ORDINARY OVERSEER
PONTIFEX PATRIARCH
(— AND MARTYR) EM
(CHESS —) ALFIN ALPHYN ARCHER
BISHOP'S-WEED AMMI AMMEOS
KHELLA WILLIAM BOLEWORT
BULLWORT GOUTWEED
TOOTHPICK
BISKOP BRUSHER STEENBRAS
BISMARK KRAPFE KRAPFEN
BISMUTH WISMUTH TINGLASS
BISON BUGLE BOVINE MITHAN
WISENT AUROCHS BONASUS
BUFFALO
BISTORT PATIENCE ADDERWORT
ASTROLOGE SNAKEWEED
SNAKEWORT
BISTRO BAR CAFE TAVERN
WINESHOP ESTAMINET
NIGHTCLUB
BIT ACE FID FIP GAG JOT NIP ORT
PIP TAD WEE ATOM BITE BITT
CHIP CROP CURB DITE DOIT DRIB
FLAW FOOD GRUE HAET HATE
HOOT IOTA ITEM LEVY MITE
MOTE PART SLUT SNAP SNIP
SPOT TOOL WHIT AUGER BLADE
CHECK CRUMB DRILL GROAT
PATCH PEZZO PIECE POINT
SCRAP SHRED SMACK SNACK
SPECK STEEK TASTE THRUM
WIGHT BITTIE BRIDLE CANNON
EATING MORSEL PELHAM PICKLE
SCATCH SHTICK SIPPET SMIDGE
SPLICE STITCH STIVER THOUGHT
TITTLE TRIFLE BRADOON
BRIDOON CHILENO GLIMMER
MORCEAU PALLION PORTION
SMIDGEN SMIDGIN SNAFFLE
TRANEEN FISHTAIL FRACTION
FRAGMENT QUANTITY SMIDGEON
SMITCHIN TWOPENNY
(— OF GOSSIP) HEARING
(— OF INFORMATION) GRIFF
GRIFFIN WRINKLE
(— OF KEY) WEB
(— OF LAND) CROOK
(— OF METAL) FLITTER
(— OF TOAST) SNIPPET
(— TO EAT) MUNGEY

(—S AND PIECES) GUBBINS
GUBBINGS
(—S OF COKE) BREEZE
(—S OF WRITING) EXCERPTA
(CUTTING —) CHASER
(DRILL —) CROWN
(FANCIFUL —) FLAM
(FIPPENY —) SIXPENCE
(FLORID —) FLOURISH
(HORSE'S —) KEVEL SNODE
CANNON PELHAM SCATCH
SNAFFLE BASTONET
(LEAST —) FIG JOT RAP HANG LICK
GHOST GROAT RIZZOM STITCH
(LITTLE —) PICK TOUCH BITTOCK
REMNANT SOUPCON
(ONE — PER SECOND) BAUD
(ONE BILLION —S) GIGABIT
(ONE-QUARTER —) GILL
(SEQUENCE OF —S) BYTE
(SMALL —) BLEB GLIM SPUNK
(SMALL —S) SMATTER
(THEATRICAL —) SHTICK SCHTICK
(TINY —) SPECK DRIBBLE SCRINCH
TODDICK
(PL.) SMITHERS SMITHEREENS
BITCH DO GYP BICK LAMP SLUT
BRACH BROOD CHEAT GROUSE
COMPLAIN
BITE BIT CUT EAT JAW NIP BAIT
CHAM CHEW ETCH FOOD GASH
GNAP GNAW HOLD KNAP MEAL
RIVE SNAP TAKE CHACK CHAMM
CHAMP CHEAT GNASH PINCH
SEIZE SMART SNACK STING
TOOTH TRICK CRUNCH MORSEL
NIBBLE PIERCE SAVAGE BUGBITE
CHEATER CORRODE FORBITE
IMPRESS MORSURE MUNCHET
PARTAKE SHARPER SLANDER
(— AT) HIT
(— GREEDILY) HANCH
(— REPEATEDLY) CHAMP
BITER
(SUFF.) DECTES
BITHIAH (HUSBAND OF —) MERED
BITING BIT HOT ACID HOAR KEEN
ACRID NIPPY QUICK SHARP SNELL
BITTER RODENT SEVERE SHREWD
STINGY TEETHY TWEAKY CAUSTIC
CUTTING MORDANT MORSURE
NIPPING PUNGENT SUBACID
DRILLING INCISIVE PIERCING
POIGNANT SCALDING SCATHING
STINGING ACIDULOUS
MORDACIOUS
BITIS ECHIDNA
BITO BALM HAJILIJ
BITON (BROTHER OF —) CLEOBIS
(MOTHER OF —) CYDIPPE
BITT BLOCK KNIGHT BOLLARD
(PL.) RANGEHEADS
BITTER AWA GAL ACID ACRE ASIM
BASK KEEN MARA RUDE SALT
SORE SOUR TART ACERB ACRID
AMARA ASPER BLEAK EAGER
HARSH IRATE SHARP SNELL
BITING PICRIC SEVERE AUSTERE
CAUSTIC CRABBED CUTTING
FERVENT GALLING GALLISH
PAINFUL PUNGENT SATIRIC
POIGNANT SARDONIC
STINGING SUBAMARE

VIRULENT ACRIMONIOUS
(PREF.) PICR(O)
(SUFF.) PICRIN
BITTER APPLE COLOCYNTH
BITTER BIT SMALLPOX
BITTERBUSH SNAKEROOT
BITTER CLOVER YELLOWTOP
BITTERLY SOUR FELLY BITTER
ROUNDLY CURSEDLY
BITTERN BUMP SOCO BOONK
BUTOR HERON BITORE BUMBLE
BUMMLE BUTTAL KAKKAK
BLITTER BUMMLER ERICIUS
DUNKADOO GRUIFORM
LONGNECK
(FLOCK OF —) SEDGE SIEGE
BITTERNESS RUE ACOR BILE FELL
GALL ATTER MARAH ENMITY
MALICE RANCOR AMARITY
ACERBITY ACRIDITY ACRIMONY
ASPERITY FERVENCY SEVERITY
WORMWOOD
(EXTREME —) VIRULENCE
(WITH —) AMAREVOLE
BITTER PIT STIPPEN
BITTERROOT LEWISIA
TOBACCOROOT
BITTERS AMER
BITTER SPAR DOLOMITE
BITTERSWEET FELLEN DOGWOOD
LOBSTER SOLANUM WAXWORK
DULCAMARA FELONWOOD
FELONWORT FEVERTWIG
WITHYWIND WOLFBERRY
BITTER VETCH ERS
BITTERWEED RAGWEED
HORSEWEED
BITTERWORT FELWORT
DANDELION
BITUMEN TAR CONGO PITCH SLIME
MALTHA ASPHALT CARBENE
ALKITRAN ALCHITRAN ELATERITE
BIVALENT DIATOMIC
BIVALVE HEN CLAM SPAT PINNA
COCKLE DIATOM MUSSEL OYSTER
MOLLUSK NUCULID PANDORA
SCALLOP TOHEROA
BIVOUAC CAMP ETAPE WATCH
ENCAMP SHELTER
BIZARRE ODD ANTIC DEDAL
OUTRE QUEER QUAINT ANTICAL
BAROQUE CURIOUS FANCIFUL
ECCENTRIC FANTASTIC
GROTESQUE OUTLANDISH
BLAB LAB CHAT BLART BLATE
CHEEP CLACK PEACH BABBLE
BETRAY GOSSIP REVEAL SQUEAL
TATTLE BLABBER CHATTER
CLATTER
BLACK DHU JET WAN CALO CROW
DARK EBON FOUL INKY NOIR PIKY
SOOT BUGLE COLLY DUSKY
DWALE MURKY NEGRO NOIRE
RAVEN SABLE SOOTY TARRY
THICK ATROUS BRUNET DISMAL
ETHIOP GLOOMY MURREY PITCHY
SULLEN ABAISER AFRICAN
BLACKEN DIAMOND MELANIC
NEGRITO NIGRINE NIGROUS
PICEOUS SWARTHY UNCLEAN
MOURNFUL
(— AND BLUE) LIVID
(— OUT) CONK

(BONE —) SPODIUM
(BROWNISH —) LAVA
(GREENISH —) CORBEAU
(IVORY —) ABAISER
(LIGHT-SKINNED —) BROWN
(RATHER —) DUSKISH
(VIOLET —) CROW
(PREF.) ATRO MAVRO MEL(A)
MELAN(O) NIGRI
(SUFF.) MELANE
BLACKAMOOR BLECK NEGRO
MORIAN NEGRESS ETHIOPIAN
BLACK ARROW (AUTHOR OF —)
STEVENSON
(CHARACTER IN —) DICK ELLIS
OATES DANIEL JOANNA OLIVER
SEDLEY LAWLESS RICHARD
SHELTON BRACKLEY DUCKWORTH
BLACK ASH HOOPWOOD
BLACKBALL PIP PILL BALLOT
EXCLUDE HEEBALL OSTRACIZE
BLACK BASS HURON TROUT
ACHIGAN GROWLER OCHIGAN
BLACKBERRY AGAWAM LAWTON
BRAMBLE DEWBERRY MULBERRY
ROSACEAN
(— BUSH) MORE
BLACKBIRD ANI DAW PIE CROW
MERL AMSEL COLLY MERLE
OUSEL OUZEL RAVEN BLACKY
COLLEY MAIZER BLACKIE
COWBIRD GRACKLE JACKDAW
REDWING WOOFELL TROOPIAL
BLACKBOARD CHALKBOARD
GREENBOARD
BLACKBREAM TARWHINE
BLACK-BROWED GLOOMY
BLACK BRYONY LILY LILIUM
OXBERRY BINDWEED MANDRAKE
BLACK BUCK SASIN
BLACKCAP GULL JACK PEGGY
HAYBIRD WARBLER MOCKBIRD
TITMOUSE JACKSTRAW
RASPBERRY
BLACKDAMP STYTH STYTHE
CHOKEDAMP
BLACKDRINK YAPON YAUPON
BLACKEN INK TAR CHAR CORK
SMUT SOIL SOOT BLECK CLOUD
COLLY JAPAN SMOKE SULLY
BEFOUL BLATCH DARKEN
DEFAME MALIGN SMEETH SMIRCH
SMUTCH VILIFY ASPERSE
BENEGRO NIGRIFY SLANDER
SMOLDER TRADUCE BESMIRCH
BLACKENED REECHY
BLACKEYE COWPEA
BLACKFELLOW BLACKBOY
YAMMADJI
BLACKFIN CISCO SESIS
BLACKFISH GRIND TAUTOG
BORLASE DOGFISH GRAMPUS
POTHEAD HARDHEAD
BLACKFLY GNAT SIMULIID
BLACKFOOT BLOOD KAINAH
PIEGAN SIKSIKA SIHASAPA
BLACK GROUPER MERO AGUAJI
WARSAW GARRUPA
BLACKGUARD SHAG BLECK CATSO
GAMIN GUARD SNUFF SWEEP
ROTTER LADRONE SKELLUM
VAGRANT BLAGGARD CRIMINAL
LARRIKIN VAGABOND SCOUNDREL

BLACK GUILLEMOT CUTTY TYSTE
SCRABE DOVEKEY DOVEKIE
SCRABER PUFFINET
BLACK GUM TUPELO HORNPIPE
STINKWOOD
BLACK HAW SLOE BOOTS ALISIER
STAGBUSH VIBURNUM
BLACKHEAD COMEDO
BLACK HOLE COLLAPSAR
BLACK HOREHOUND HENBIT
ARCHANGEL
BLACK HORSE SUCKER SUCKEREL
BLACKING LINK BLECK BLATCH
BLEACH ATRAMENT
BLACK IRONWOOD AXMASTER
AXEMASTER
BLACKISH DUSKY MOREL SWART
BLACKY
BLACKJACK OAK SAP CLUB COSH
DUCK FLAG JACK BEETLE BILLY
BLENDE JERKIN BOMBARD
NATURAL BLUDGEON
BLACKLEG LEG FIRE SCAB SNOB
ANTHRAX GAMBLER JACKLEG
APOSTATE BLACKNEB BLACKNOB
SWINDLER KNOBSTICK
BLACK LETTER GOTHIC
BLACKLY SABLY
BLACK MAGIC DIABLERIE
BLACKMAIL BRIBE CHOUT COERCE
EXTORT RANSOM TRIBUTE
CHANTAGE
BLACKMAILER GHOUL BRIBER
LEECHER
BLACK MANGROVE COURIDA
BLACK MEDIC HOP TREFOIL
NONESUCH SHAMROCK
BLACKNESS GRIME DARKNESS
NIGRITUDE
BLACK NIGHTSHADE MOREL
DUSCLE SOLANUM BLUEBERRY
MOONSHADE TROMPILLO
BLACK OLIVE OXHORN
BLACK PEPPER PIMENTA
BLACK PINE MATAI
BLACK POISON WALNUT
BLACK RHINOCEROS BORELE
KEITLOA UPEYGAN
BLACK SALLY SALLEE
MUZZLEWOOD
BLACK SANICLE LUNGWORT
MASTERWORT
BLACK SHANK LANAS
BLACK SKIMMER CUTWATER
SHEARBILL
BLACKSMITH GOW SMUG LOHAR
SHOER SMITH PLOVER SMITHY
VULCAN BROOKIE FARRIER
STRIKER BURNEWIN IRONSMITH
BLACKSNAKE WHIP QUIRT RACER
ELAPID RUNNER COLUBRID
BLACK SPECK DARTROSE
BLACK SPURGE FLUXWEED
BLACKTAIL DASSY DASSIE
BLACK TERN DARR STARN
BLACKTHORN HAW SLOE SNAG
SCROG GRIBBLE SLOEBUSH
SLOETREE SNAGBUSH
BLACK-VARNISH TREE THEETSEE
BLACK VULTURE URUBU CORBIE
ZOPILOTE
BLACK WALNUT NOGAL
BLACKWATER STATE NEBRASKA

BLACK WIDOW POKOMOO
BLACK WOLF KARAKURT
BLACKWOOD BITI LIGHTWOOD
BLACKWORT COMFREY
BLADDER SAC VES VESICA
AMPULLA BLATHER BLISTER
INFLATE UROCYST UTRICLE
VESICLE
(AIR —) POKE SWIM SOUND
SINGALLY
(PREF.) ASC(I)(IDI)(IDIO)(O)
CYST(I)(O) PHYSO VESICO
(SUFF.) CYST(IS)
BLADDER-AND-STRING BUMBASS
BLADDER CAMPION BEHN BEHEN
SILENE COWBELL SNAPPER
RATTLEBOX
BLADDER KETMIE MODESTY
BLADDERNUT BAGNUT
BLADDERWORT POPWEED
BLADDER WRACK CUTWEED
KELPWARE
BLADE BIT FIN FOP OAR SAW WEB
BLOW BONE BOWL EDGE FLAG
HEAD LEAF LIMB TANG WEAK
BLOOD BRAND DANDY FLUKE
GRAIN GUIDE HEALD KNIFE
LANCE SHEAR SPARK SPEAR
SPIRE SWORD BLUNGE BUCKET
BUSTER CUTTER DOCTOR FOIBLE
HEDDLE LAMINA PAGINA RIPPER
ROARER SCYTHE SICKLE TOLEDO
BAYONET CHIPPER GALLANT
POLESAW SCALPEL SCAPULA
SCRAPER SPINNER MOLDBOARD
PROPELLER
(— OF FAN) VANE
(— OF GRASS) PILE CHIRE SPEAR
SPIRE STRAP TRANEEN
(— OF KNIFE) TANG GRAIN
(— OF LEAF) LIMB LAMINA
(— OF MORION) COMB
(— OF OAR) PALM PEEL PELL
WASH
(— OF SCISSORS) BILL
(— OF YOUNG GRAIN) SORAGE
(CULTIVATOR —) SWEEP
DUCKFOOT
(SKATE —) RUNNER
(SURGICAL —) LEUCOTOME
(SUFF.) SPATH
BLAES CAM
BLAFFERT PLAPPERT
BLAIN RUBY SORÉ BULLA BLISTER
INFLAME PUSTULE
BLAKE MCKAY
BLAMABLE FAULTY CULPABLE
BLAME CALL CHOP HURT LACK
ONUS SAKE SPOT TWIT WITE
CHIDE FAULT GUILT ODIUM
PINCH SHEND SNAPE SWICK
SWIKE THANK TOUCH WHITE
ACCUSE ATTASK BUMBLE
BURDEN CHARGE DIRDUM PLIGHT
REBUKE REVILE SCANCE APPOINT
ASCRIBE CENSURE CONDEMN
CULPATE OBLOQUY REPROOF
REPROVE SLANDER UPBRAID
WITHNIM REPROACH
BLAMED BLINDING BLISTERING
BLAMELESS PURE ENTIRE
PERFECT INNOCENT SACKLESS
SPOTLESS WITELESS RIGHTEOUS

BLAMEWORTHY GUILTY CRIMINAL CULPABLE REPROBATE

BLANCH FADE PALE BLENK CHALK SCALD WHITE APPALL ARGENT BIANCA BLEACH BLENCH FALLOW WHITEN ETIOLATE

BLANCHED ASHEN MEALY ETIOLATE BLOODLESS COLORLESS

BLANCMANGE FLUMMERY

BLAND COLD KIND MILD OILY OPEN SOFT SLEEK SUAVE BENIGN BREEZY GENIAL GENTLE SMOOTH URBANE AFFABLE AMIABLE LENIENT VANILLA FAVONIAN GRACIOUS UNCTUOUS

BLANDISH COAX CHARM ALLURE BLANCH CAJOLE FONDLE SMOOTH FLATTER WHEEDLE HONEYFUGLE

BLANDLY CREAMILY

BLANK BARE BURR FLAN FORM SHOT VOID ANNUL BLIND BREAK CHASM CLEAN EMPTY FALSE RANGE SPACE WASTE WHITE COUPON VACANT ANTIQUE BRINDLE NONPLUS UNMIXED VACUOUS UNFILLED

BLANKED BLIND

BLANKET RUG BROT MAUD WRAP BLUEY COTTA COVER CUMLY LAYER MANTA PATTU QUILT SHEET SUGAN THROW AFGHAN COOLER CUMBLY GLOBAL KAMBAL MANTLE PALLET PONCHO PUTTOO SERAPE SOOGAN STIFLE STROUD TILPAH CHIRIPA DOUBLER SMOTHER WHITTLE COVERLET MACKINAW
(— A VESSEL) WRONG
(— OF SKINS) KAROSS
(— WITH BOMBS) SATURATE
(BUSHMAN'S —) BLUEY
(QUILTED —) BROT
(SADDLE —) CORONA
(PREF.) REGO

BLANKETING DUFFEL DUFFLE

BLANKNESS VACUITY NEGATION

BLARE PEAL BLART BLAST BLEAR NOISE BLAZON SCREAM FANFARE TANTARA TRUMPET

BLARNEY CON TAFFY BUTTER CAJOLE SAWDER FLATTER WHEEDLE

BLAS GIL RUY

BLASPHEME ABUSE CURSE DEFAME REVILE PROFANE

BLASPHEMOUS BAD RIBALD IMPIOUS PROFANE

BLASPHEMY CALUMNY CURSING IMPIETY ANATHEMA SWEARING

BLAST BUB NIP WAP BANG BLOW FRAP GALE GUST RUIN RUST SHOT TOOT WAFF WIND BLAME BLIST BLORE SPLIT STUNT TRUMP ATTACK BLIGHT BUGGER FORBID NIDDER NITHER REBUFF VOLLEY WITHER BLUSTER DESPOIL EXPLODE SHATTER SHRIVEL DYNAMITE OUTBURST PROCLAIM WHIRLPUFF
(— OF WIND) GUST RISE PERRY PIRRIE VENTOSITY
(— ON HORN) TOOT PRYSE

(— WITH COLD) SNEAP
(FURIOUS —) SNIFTER
(RAINY —) BLATTER

BLASTED BLAME BLAMED BLIGHTED BLINDING BLINKING

BLASTER FROSTER SHOOTER SHOTMAN

BLASTING SCATHING SHOOTING STELLATION
(— METHOD) MUDCAP

BLASTOMERE MESOMERE MACROMERE MICROMERE

BLASTULA PLACULA PLANULA PLANULAN

BLATANT GLIB LOUD BRASH GROSS NOISY SILLY VOCAL COARSE GARISH TONANT VULGAR BRAWLING STRIDENT

BLATHER STIR BLEAT BABBLE WAFFLE BLITHER PRATTLE NONSENSE

BLAUBOK ETAAC BLUEBUCK

BLAZE LOW BURN FIRE GLOW HACK LEAM LOWE LUNT MARK SHOT SPOT FLAME FLARE FLASH GLARE GLEAM GLORY INGLE RATCH SHINE STARE STEAM TORCH BLAZON BLEEZE BONFIRE PIONEER SPLENDOR
(— OUT) FLAP

BLAZING AFIRE FIERY FLAMY LIGHT FLAMING FLARING

BLAZING STAR LIATRIS GRUBROOT SNAKEROOT

BLAZON DECK SHOW ADORN BLARE BLAZE BOAST DEPICT SHIELD DECLARE DISPLAY EXHIBIT PUBLISH EMBLAZON INSCRIBE

BLAZONED ARMED BANNERED

BLEACH SUN WASH BLEAK CHALK CROFT POACH BLANCH BLENCH CHLORE PURIFY WHITEN DECOLOR LIGHTEN BLONDINE ETIOLATE PEROXIDE
(— PULP) POTCH

BLEACHER WHITSTER

BLEACHERS SCAFFOLD

BLEAK DIM RAW BLAE BLAY COLD DOUR GRAY PALE ABLET OURIE SPRAT STARK SWALE ALBURN BITTER BLEACH DISMAL DREARY FRIGID PALLID CUTTING DESOLATE CHEERLESS

BLEAK HOUSE (AUTHOR OF —) DICKENS
(CHARACTER IN —) JO ADA JOHN ALLAN CLARE FLITE GUPPY KROOK BUCKET ESTHER RAWDON DEDLOCK JELLYBY RICHARD WILLIAM CARSTONE CHADBAND JARNDYCE SKIMPOLE LEICESTER SUMMERSON WOODCOURT TULKINGHORN

BLEAT BAA BLAT BLEA YARM BLART BLATE BLATHER BLUSTER WHICKER

BLEATING BALANT

BLEB BLOB BULLA BUBBLE BLISTER PUSTULE VESICLE SWELLING

BLEED FLUX MILK WEEP BLOOD LEECH MULCT SWEAT SWINDLE

TEICHER PHLEBOTOMIZE

BLEEDER STICKER

BLEEDING BLOODY SANGLANT

BLEEDING HEART EARDROP DICENTRA

BLEMISH MAR BLOT BLUR DENT FLAW GALL LACK MAIM MARK MOIL MOLE RIFT SAKE SCAR SLUR SPOT TASH VICE WANT AMPER BLAME BOTCH BRECK CLOUD CRACK FAULT FLECK MULCT NAEVE SPECK STAIN SULLY TACHE TAINT TOUCH BLOTCH BREACH DEFAME DEFECT IMPAIR INJURE MACULA MACULE MAYHEM SMIRCH STIGMA BUBKLE CATFACE DEFAULT FAILING FISSURE SUNSPOT MACULATION
(— IN CLOTH) AMPER SULLY
(— IN PAPER) FISHEYE
(PRINTING —) MACKLE

BLEMISHED BAD WEMMY

BLENCH FOIL SHUN WILE AVOID ELUDE EVADE QUAIL SHAKE SHIRK TRICK BAFFLE BLANCH BLEACH FLINCH RECOIL SHRINK DECEIVE

BLEND MIX RUN BLOT FADE FUSE JOIN MELT MENG MOLD ADMIX BLIND CREAM GRADE MERGE MOULD PUREE SHADE SMEAR SPOIL STAIN TINGE UNITE BLUNGE COMMIX CRASIS DAZZLE MINGLE TEMPER COMBINE CONFUSE CORRUPT DECEIVE GRADATE MIXTURE POLLUTE COALESCE CONCRETE IMMINGLE TINCTURE CONTEMPER
(— OF NOISES) CHARM
(— OF SHERRY) SOLERA
(— OF WINES) CUVEE

BLENDE JACK SPHALERITE

BLENDED FONDU FUSED MIXED MERGED MINGLED CONFLATE CONFLUENT

BLENDING FUSION HOTCHPOT

BLENNY GUNNEL SHANNY EELPOUT JUGULAR KELPFISH SENORITA WOLFFISH WRYMOUTH QUILLFISH ROCKSKIPPER

BLESBOK NUNNI BLESBUCK

BLESS KEEP SAIN WAVE ADORE ANELE BENSH CROSS EXTOL FAVOR GUARD THANK VISIT WOUND CROUCH FAVOUR HALLOW PRAISE THRASH APPROVE BEATIFY EMBLISS GLORIFY PROTECT MACARIZE PRESERVE SANCTIFY

BLESSED HOLY BLEST HAPPY SEELY DIVINE JOYFUL SACRED SEELFUL BENEDICT BHAGAVAT BLISSFUL BLOOMING HALLOWED HEAVENLY CELESTIAL

BLESSEDNESS BLISS FELICITY BEATITUDE HAPPINESS

BLESSING BOON GIFT SAIN BLISS DUKAN GRACE SORRA BARAKA DUCHAN PRAISE BENISON DARSHAN WORSHIP BERACHAH FELICITY MACARISM BEATITUDE
(PL.) CUP

BLEU DE ROI SEVRES

BLIGHT NIP FIRE RUIN RUST SMUT SOKA BLAST BRANT FROST SNEAP MILDEW NITHER TAKING WITHER DESTROY
(PREF.) UREDO

BLIND BET POT ANTE BOMA DARK DEAD DULL HIDE HOOD SEEL BISME BLANK BLEND CHICK CLOAK DUNCH SHADE STAKE STALL WAGER AMBUSH BISSON BLENDE DARKEN DAZZLE SCREEN SECRET AIMLESS ANTIQUE BANDAGE BATTERY BENIGHT ECLIPSE EYELESS OBSCURE PRETEXT RAYLESS SHUTTER ABORTIVE ARTIFICE BAYARDLY BLINDING EXCECATE HOODWINK IGNORANT INVOLVED JALOUSIE OUTSHINE PURBLIND UMBRELLA VENETIAN
(— IN ONE EYE) PEED GLEED GLEYD
(— MAN) MOLE
(HALF —) STARBLIND
(PL.) PERSIENNES
(PREF.) CECO TYPHL(O)

BLIND ALLEY LOKE STOP POCKET IMPASSE

BLINDER FLAP HOOD BLIND BLUFF LUNET WINKER BLINKER EYEFLAP LUNETTE HOODWINK BLINDFOLD

BLINDFOLD MOP DARK BLINK BLUFF SCARF MUFFLE BANDAGE BLINDER OBSCURE ENCLOSER HEEDLESS HOODWINK RECKLESS CONCEALED

BLINDING BISME BISSON

BLINDMAN'S BLUFF POST HOODWINK

BLINDNESS BISSON CECITY MYOPSY ABLEPSY ANOPSIA MEROPIA ABLEPSIA DARKNESS IGNORANCE
(— TO TRUTH) AVIDYA AVIJJA
(COLOR —) ACHROBIA MONOCHROMATISM
(DAY —) HEMERALOPIA
(NIGHT —) NYCTALOPIA
(PARTIAL —) MEROPIA HEMIOPSIA
(RED-GREEN —) DALTONISM
(SNOW —) CHIONABLEPSIA
(STUDY OF —) TYPHLOLOGY
(TEMPORARY —) MOONBLINK

BLINDSTITCH FELL

BLINDWORM SLOW ORVET ANGUID HAGWORM SLOWWORM

BLIND-YOUR-EYES GANGWA ALIPATA

BLINK BAT PINK SHUN WINK BLUSH CHEAT FLASH GLEAM SHINE TRICK GLANCE IGNORE OBTUSE WAPPER BLINTER CONDONE GLIMMER GLIMPSE NEGLECT NICTATE SPARKLE TWINKLE

BLINKER EYE BLINK BLUFF LIGHT SIGNAL WAPPER WINKER BLINDER FLASHER GOGGLES COQUETTE HOODWINK MACKEREL

BLINTZE BLIN BLINTZ PANCAKE

BLIP PIP ECHO

BLISS JOY·EDEN KAIF SEEL SEIL
BLESS GLORY ANANDA HEAVEN
DELIGHT ECSTASY GLADDEN
NIRVANA RAPTURE FELICITY
GLADNESS PARADISE PLEASURE

BLISSFUL HOLY SEELY BLITHE
BLESSED ELYSIAN UTOPIAN
BEATIFIED GLORIFIED

BLISTER BEAT BLAB BLEB BLOB
BLOW BOIL BURN LASH QUAT
APTHA BLAIN BLIBE BULGE BULLA
TOPIC VESIC APHTHA BUBBLE
CUPOLA SCORCH SOTTER TETTER
BLADDER BLUSTER SCALDER
SKELLER VESICLE VESICATE
(PREF.) PUSTULI VESICUL(O)

BLISTERED BULLATE

BLITHE GAY GLAD BONNY BUXOM
HAPPY JOLLY MERRY BONNIE
JOVIAL JOYOUS LIVELY GAYSOME
JOCULAR WINSOME CHEERFUL
GLADSOME SPRIGHTLY

BLIZZARD BLOW GALE WIND
BURAN PURGA RETORT SNIFTER
SQUELCHER
(— **STATE**) SD SDAK

BLOAT BLOW BLAST BLOWN
FLOAT HOOVE HOVEN PUFFY
SWELL BOWDEN EXPAND
TUMEFY DISTEND FERMENT
INFLATE

BLOATED FOZY BLOAT BROSY
CURED FOGGY HOVEN PUFFY
TUMID GOTCHY SODDEN TURGID
POMPOUS REPLETE

BLOATER MOONEYE

BLOB LIP WEN BEAD BLEB BLOT
BOIL CLOT DAUB DROP GLOB
GOUT LUMP MARK MASS BUBBLE
DALLOP DOLLOP PIMPLE SPLASH
BLEMISH BLISTER BLOSSOM
GLOBULE PUSTULE SPLOTCH

BLOC RING BLOCK CABAL PARTY
UNION CLIQUE BENELUX FACTION

BLOCK AME BAR COB COG DAM
DIE DIT DOG FID HOB HUB JAM
KEY NOG ROW TOP VOL BALK
BASE BEAR BILK BLOC BUCK
BUNT CAKE CLOG CUBE DRUM
FOIL FOUL FROG GLUT HEAD
JAMB LEAD MASK MASS MOCK
QUAR STAY STEP STOP TRIG
BAULK BRICK CHAIR CHECK
CHEEK CHUMP CLAMP CLEAT
CLOSE COVER DETER DOLLY
DUMMY EMBAR FLOAT HEART
HORST JUMBO NUDGE PARRY
PATCH SHAPE SLUMP SPIKE
SPOKE STOCK STUFF STUMP
ASSIZE DENTIL DOLLEY DOMINO
FIPPLE FORMER HAMPER HINDER
IMPEDE KIBOSH MONKEY MUFFLE
MUTULE OPPOSE OUTWIT
QUERRE RIPPER SADDLE SCOTCH
SNATCH SQUARE STREET STYMIE
TAPLET THWART TROLLY
WAYLAY BOLLOCK BOLSTER
BUCKLER CONDEMN DEADEYE
ERRATIC INHIBIT OUTLINE
PREVENT QUADREL RAMHEAD
STONKER TRIGGER TROLLEY
BLOCKADE DEADHEAD ELECTRET
FOLLOWER KEYSTONE MONOLITH

OBSTACLE OBSTRUCT STOPPAGE
WITHSPAR BRIQUETTE
(— **A WHEEL**) SCOTE
(— **AT SPAR END**) STEEVE
(— **FOR SKIDDING LOGS**) BICYCLE
(— **FOR SLAVE SALES**) CATASTA
(— **IN SPEAKING**) STAMMER
(— **OF BUILDINGS**) INSULA
(— **OF COAL**) JUD JUDD
(— **OF EARTH'S CRUST**) HORST
(— **OF GRANITE**) SET
(— **OF ICE**) SERAC
(— **OF LAND**) FORTY
(— **OF SEATS**) CUNEUS
(— **OF TIMBER**) BOLT JUGGLE
(— **SUPPORTING MAST**) STEP
(— **THE WAY**) SCOAT
(— **UP**) BAR DAM CLOY QUIRT
CONDEMN OPPILATE FORECLOSE
(— **WITH HOLE IN IT**) WAPP
EUPHROE
(— **WITH PROJECTING CORE**)
SETTLE
(—**S OF STONE**) DIMENSION
(**ARCHITECTURAL —**) DRUM STONE
DENTIL IMPOST MUTULE PLINTH
DOSSERET
(**CHOPPING —**) HACKLOG
(**CLAY —**) DRAWBAR
(**FAULT —**) MASSIF
(**FELTED —**) DAMPER
(**FOOTBALL —**) CRACKBACK
(**FULCRUM —**) GLUT
(**FUSE —**) CUTOUT
(**HOSPITAL —**) PAVILION
(**IRON —**) USE VOL BITT ANVIL
CHAIR
(**LOGGING —**) LEAD JUMBO
(**NAUTICAL —**) CHOCK HEART
STOCK SADDLE DEADEYE
FAIRLEAD
(**ORNAMENTAL —**) BOSS
MODILLION
(**PAVING —**) SET CUBE SETT STONE
WHEELER
(**PLASTER —**) BATTER
(**POLISHING —**) BUFF FLOAT RABOT
(**PRINTING —**) CUT QUAD RISER
QUADRAT
(**PULLEY —**) CRAWL
(**SANDSTONE —**) SARSEN
(**SQUARED —**) MITCHEL
(**STUMBLING —**) HURTING
(**TACKLE —**) CALO TONGUE
(**VAULTING —**) BUCK HORSE

BLOCKADE DAM FERM BESET
BLOCK EMBAR SIEGE WHISKY
BESIEGE EMBARGO BLOCKAGE
OBSTRUCT BARRICADE
BELEAGUER

BLOCKAGE LOGJAM

BLOCKER CASER BRACER

BLOCKHEAD ASS LUG OAF BUST
CLOT COOF COOT DAFF DOLT
FOOL MOME NOWT STUB BLOCK
BOOBY CHUMP CUDDY GOLEM
GOOSY IDIOT NINNY SNIPE
SUMPH DIMWIT DISARD NITWIT
NOODLE TUMPHY TURNIP
ASSHEAD BUZZARD DIZZARD
DULBERT JACKASS LACKWIT
MUDHEAD NOGHEAD TOMFOOL
BEEFHEAD BONEHEAD CLODPATE

CLODPOLL CODSHEAD DULLHEAD
DULLPATE DUMBHEAD
DUMMKOPF GAMPHREL
HARDHEAD JOLTHEAD
LUNKHEAD

BLOCKHOUSE SPUR PUNTAL
GARRISON

BLOCKING JAM JAMB DUNNAGE
BLOCKADE CROSSING

BLOKE MAN CHAP COVE TOFF
BLOAK JOKER FELLOW

BLOLLY BEEFWOOD CORKWOOD
PORKWOOD

BLOND BAN FAIR LIGHT BLONDE
FLAXEN GOLDEN YELLOW
LEUCOUS BLONDINE
(**AUTUMN —**) FAWN

BLOOD KIN SAP GORE LIFE MASS
MOOD RACE SANG SANK BLADE
BLUDE BLUID CRUOR FLESH
FLUID SERUM STOCK CLARET
INDRED KAINAH SLUDGE
GALLANT KINSHIP KINSMAN
LINEAGE RELATION TROPHEMA
(**CORRUPT —**) YOUSTIR
(**HALF —**) DEMISANG
(PREF.) HAEM(A)(O) HAEMAT(O)
HEM(A)(O) HEMAT(O) SANGUI
SANGUINO SANO
(SUFF.) AEMIA EMIA HAEMIA
HEMIA

BLOOD CLOT
(PREF.) THROMB(O)

BLOODCURDLING GORY HORROR

BLOODFLOWER HIPPO REDHEAD
BLOODWEED

BLOODHOUND LYM LYAM LYME
HOUND LIMER SLOTH BANDOG
LEAMER SLEUTH TIEDOG
LYAMHOUND SLEUTHHOUND

BLOODIED BEBLED

BLOODLESS DEAD ANEMIC
ANAEMIC INHUMAN TURNIPY
LIFELESS UNFEELING

BLOODLETTER BLEEDER

BLOOD PHEASANT ITHAGINE

BLOODROOT PUCCOON REDROOT
BOLOROOT COONROOT
CORNROOT TURMERIC
SANGUINARIA

BLOODSHED DEATH CARNAGE
VIOLENCE SLAUGHTER

BLOODSHOT RED INFLAMED

BLOODSTAINED GORY

BLOODSTONE SANGUINE
HEMACHATE

BLOODSUCKER LEECH SPONGER
VAMPIRE

BLOODTHIRSTINESS
ACHARNEMENT

BLOODTHIRSTY BLOODY CARNAL
SANGUINE TIGERISH FEROCIOUS
MURDEROUS SANGUINARY

BLOOD VESSEL VEIN COMES
HEMAD ARTERY CAPILLARY
(PREF.) ANGIO

BLOODWOOD AJHAR JAROOL

BLOODY GORY RUDE BALLY BLODE
CRUEL RUDDY BLUGGY CRUENT
PLUCKY CRIMSON BLEEDING
DEATHFUL HEMATOSE INFAMOUS
SANGLANT BUTCHERLY
CRUENTOUS FEROCIOUS

MERCILESS MURDEROUS
SANGUIARY

BLOODY BARK LANCEPOD

BLOOM DEW BLOW CAST HAZE
KNOT BLURT BLUSH CHILL
BLOOTH BLOWTH BLOSSOM
BLOWING ANTHESIS BLOOMING
FLOREATE FLOURISH
(— **OF WILLOW**) GULL
(— **ON INSECT**) POLLEN
(— **ON SHELL**) CUTICLE
(— **ON TREE**) GOSLING
(**METAL —S**) HEAT
(**POWDERY —**) PRUINA

BLOOMER ERROR BLOWER
BLUNDER FAILURE

BLOOMERS KNICKERS PANTALETS

BLOOMERY FORGE HEARTH
FURNACE

BLOOMING PERT ROSY FLUSH
FRESH GREEN PRIME ABLOOM
FLORID BLOWING FLAMING
ROSEATE BLINKING

BLOOPER BLOOMER

BLOSSOM BUD BELL BLOB BLOW
CHIP SILK BLOOM LEHUA FLOWER
BLOWING BURGEON PROSPER
BOURGEON FLOURISH
(**BLIGHTED —**) BLAST
(**HERALDIC —**) FRASE FRAISE
(PL.) SET BLOSSOMRY

BLOSSOMING BLOWTH
FLORAISON FLORULENT
(— **AFTER NOON**) POMERIDIAN

BLOT MAR BLOB BLUR DAUB SOIL
SPOT BLACK BLANK BLEND BLOTE
ERASE SMEAR SPECK STAIN
SULLY BLOTCH CANCEL DAMAGE
EFFACE IMPAIR MACULA
SHADOW SMIRCH SMOUCH
SMUDGE SMUTCH STIGMA
BLEMISH ECLIPSE EXPUNGE
INKBLOT OBSCURE SPLOTCH
TARNISH DISGRACE REPROACH
(— **OUT**) OUT BURY ANNUL ERASE
CANCEL DELETE EXPUNGE

BLOTCH DAB BLOT DASH GOUT
MONK SPOT AMPER PATCH
SMEAR SPLAT STAIN MACULA
MOTTLE PLOTCH PURPLE SMIRCH
SPLASH STIGMA BLEMISH
PUSTULE SPLOTCH ERUPTION
MACULATE
(PL.) BLIBE
(PREF.) MACUL(I)(O)

BLOTCHED SCABBY PIEBALD
MACULATE SCABROUS SPLASHED
MACULATED
(SUFF.) MACULATE

BLOTCHY SCOVY

BLOTTER BLAD

BLOUSE CHOLI MIDDY SHIRT
SMOCK TUNIC CAMISA GUIMPE
JUMPER CASAQUE VAREUSE
CAMISOLE CASAQUIN JIRKINET
(**BUSHMAN'S —**) BLUEY

BLOW BOB COB COP CUT DAB DAD
DUB FAN FIB HIT JAB JAR NAP
ONE PAT PEG POP RAP TAP TIP
TIT WAP ANDE BAFF BANG BASH
BEAT BELT BIFF BIRR BLAD BLAW
BRAG BUFF BULL BUMP BUTT
CHAP CHOP CONK COUP CRIG

CUFF DASH DAUD DENT DING
DINT DIRD DOLE DRAW DRUB
DUNT DUSH FLAP FLEG FLIG
FUFF FUNK GALE GOWF GUST
HACK HUFF HURT JOLT KNAP
KNEE LASH LEAD LEFT LICK LOUK
LUSH MINT ONER PAIK PALT
PANT PASS PICK PIRR PLUG POLT
PUCK PUFF PUSH SCAT SCUD
SLAM SLAP SLAT SLUG SOCK
SPAT STOP SWAP SWAT SWOP
SWOT THUD WELT WHAP WHOP
WIND WIPE YANK BINGE BLADE
BLAST BLIZZ BLOOM BOAST
BRUNT BURST CLAUT CLINK
CLOUR CLOUT CLUMP CLUNK
CRUMP CRUNT CURSE DEVEL
DOUSE DOWSE DUNCH FACER
FILIP FLACK FLICK FLIRT GOWFF
ICTUS IMPEL KNOCK OUTER
PALMY PANDY PASTE PEISE
PLUMP PLUNK PUNCH RIGHT
SHAKE SHOCK SKELP SKIRL SKITE
SLASH SLIPE SLOSH SMACK
SMASH SMITE SNICK SOUND
SOUSE SPANK SPEND STORM
STRIP SURGE SWACK SWEEP
SWIPE THROW THUMP TOUCH
TRICE WHACK WHANG WHIFF
WHOOF WHUFF BELTER BENSEL
BENSIL BETRAY BOUNCE BUFFET
CONKER DEPART DIRDUM
DUNDER EXPAND FILLIP FISTER
FLOWER FROLIC HANDER HUFFLE
LARRUP REBUKE SIFFLE STOUSH
STRIPE STROKE SWITCH THUNGE
THWACK WALLOP WINDER
AFFLATE ASSAULT ATTAINT
BELLOWS BENSAIL BLOSSOM
BLOWOUT BLUSTER BOASTER
COUNTER CRUSHER DESTROY
INFLATE KNOCKER LAMBACK
LOUNDER MOUTHER PUBLISH
SHATTER SMACKER SPANKER
SQUELCH WHAMPLE WHIFFLE
WHIRRET WHITHER CALAMITY
DISASTER KNOCKOUT PASHWAFF
SASARARA SICKENER
SIDEWINDER
(**— ABRASIVES**) BLAST
(**— CEMENT**) KIBOSH
(**— GUSTILY**) FLAW TUCK WINNOW
(**— IN PUFFS**) FAFF
(**— NOSE**) SNITE
(**— OFF STEAM**) SNIFT
(**— ON CHEEK**) ALAPA
(**— ON HEAD**) NOB CONK CLOUR
CONKER NOBBER TOPPER
NOBBLER
(**— ON NOSE**) NOSER CANKER
NOZZLER SMELLER
(**— SMOKE**) NOSE
(**— SOFTLY**) BREATHE
(**— UP**) BOMB BLAST DYNAMITE
SUFFLATE
(**— VIOLENTLY**) STORM
(**— WITH CUDGEL**) DUB DRUB
CRUNT
(**— WITH FIST**) BOP BOX PEG BELT
HOOK CLOUT BUFFET
ROUNDHOUSE
(**— WITH FOOT**) BOOT KICK SPURN

(**DECISIVE —**) SOCKDOLAGER
SOCKDOLOGER
(**FENCING —**) MONTANT
(**GENTLE —**) CHUCK
(**GLANCING —**) SCUFF
(**HARD —**) SLOG STOT YANK BEVEL
SWACK TWITCHER
(**HEAVY —**) DAD DONG DRUB
DUNT ONER SLAM SLUG CLOUT
KNOCK POISE SOUSE SQUAT
STAVE SWASH STOUND PLUMPER
REEMISH
(**MOCK —**) FEINT
(**NOISY —**) DUNDER DUNNER
(**RESOUNDING —**) CLAP CRACK
(**SHARP —**) BAT NAP CLIP KNAP
SLAP SPAT CLICK FLICK FLEWIT
STINGER
(**SLIGHT —**) SCLAFF
(**SMART —**) CLIP FLIP SKELP SKITE
YANKER
BLOWCASE EGG
BLOWER PAN DRIER DRYER
WHALE FANNER PUFFER
BELLOWS BLOOMER BOOSTER
MUMBLER BRAGGART OUTBURST
(**GLASS —**) GAFFER
BLOWGUN SUMPIT SUMPITAN
SARBACANE PEASHOOTER
BLOWHOLE BLOW GLOUP SPOUT
SPIRACLE
(**— IN STEEL**) ROAK
BLOWING ABLOW BLAST BLORE
GUSTY BLUSTER BLUSTERY
(**— AT LOW SPEED**) SLACK
(**— AT RIGHT ANGLES**) SIDE
(**— OF WHALE**) SPOUT
BLOWN STALE TIRED OPENED
WINDED BLOSSOM SWOLLEN
TAINTED BETRAYED FLYBLOWN
INFLATED
BLOWOUT BLOW FEED MEAL
BURST VALLEY FLAMEOUT
BLOWPIPE HOD
BLOWSY DOWDY BLOUSY BLOWZY
FROWZY
BLOWY DUSTY
BLUBBER CRY FAT SOB BLUB
FOAM WAIL WEEP BIBLE MELON
PIECE SPECK SPICK SWELL THICK
WHINE BUBBLE FLITCH LIPPER
LUBBER MEDUSA NETTLE SEETHE
BLABBER BLUSTER SLOBBER
SWOLLEN WHIMPER
(**— AT WHALE'S NECK**) CANT
(**CUT WHALE —**) FLENSE
(**REFUSE —**) FENKS FOOTING
FRITTERS
BLUDGEON BAT HIT SAP CLUB
COSH MACE BILLY STICK TOWEL
COERCE COURSE BLACKJACK
TRUNCHEON
BLUE (**ALSO SEE COLOR**) HAW LOW
SAD SKY AQUA BICE BLAE GLUM
SAXE TEAL WOAD AZURE BERYL
LIVID NIKKO PERSE SMALL
WAGET COBALT GLOOMY INDIGO
LUPINE ORIENT PEWTER SEVERE
TRYPAN CELESTE CYANINE
GENTIAN GOBELIN HYPPISH
LEARNED LIBERTY LOBELIA
MATELOT MISTBLU MURILLO
NATTIER PEACOCK QUIMPER

REGATTA WATCHET CERULEAN
DEJECTED LABRADOR LARKSPUR
LITERARY MAZARINE MIDNIGHT
NATIONAL SAPPHIRE
WEDGWOOD POMPADOUR
(**BLACKISH —**) BLO BLOO
(**DULL —**) HAW
(**ROYAL —**) HATHOR
(**SHADE OF —**) INDE
(**PREF.**) CYAN(O) IND(I)(O) INDICO
(**SUFF.**) (**— PIGMENT**) CYAN(IC)
BLUEBELL CROWBELL HAREBELL
BLUEBERRY OHELO STONER
PALBERRY RABBITEYE VACCINIUM
BLUEBIRD (**— GUIDE**) LEADER
BLUE-BLACK BLO
BLUEBLOSSOM LILAC
BLUEBONNET CAP SCOT BLUECAP
BLUEBOTTLE BLUET BLAVER
BARBEAU BLAWORT BLOWFLY
BLUECAP BLUECUP BRUSHES
HARDOCK BLUEBLAW HYACINTH
CORNBINKS
BLUE CREEPER LOVE
BLUE CURLS FLEASEED FLEAWEED
BLUE-EYED GRASS PIGROOT
SATINFLOWER
BLUEFIN TUNNY
BLUEFISH ELF BASS ELFT SHAD
TUNA HORSE SAURY DARZEE
TAILER TAILOR FATBACK
SKIPJACK WEAKFISH
(**YOUNG OF —**) SNAPPER
WHITEFISH
BLUEGILL BREAM SUNFISH
PONDFISH PUMPKINSEED
BLUE GOOSE BALDHEAD
BLUEGRASS STATE KENTUCKY
BLUE GREEN VENICE
BLUE GUM FEVERGUM
EUCALYPTUS
BLUE HEN STATE DELAWARE
BLUE HERON CRANE NAILROD
BLUEJACKET SAILOR DRAGMAN
BLUEJOINT REDTOP BLUETOPS
BLUENESS (**— OF SKIN**) CYANOSIS
BLUE PETER ASK
BLUE PINE LIM
BLUE POINTER MAKO
BLUEPRINT MAP PLAN PLOT
DRAFT TRACE SKETCH DIAGRAM
PROJECT CYANOTYPE
BLUE RUNNER JUREL
BLUES MARE DUMPS CAFARD
DISMAL GLOOMS DISMALS
HORRORS HUMDRUM MEGRIMS
SADNESS DOLDRUMS DOLEFULS
MULLIGRUBS
BLUE SHEEP BURHEL
BLUE SLATE SKAILLIE
BLUESTOCKING BASBLEU
BLUE SUCCORY CATNACHE
CUPIDONE
BLUET PISSABED EYEBRIGHT
INNOCENCE
BLUE TIT NUN STONECHAT
BLUE TITMOUSE YAUP TYDIE
TIDIFE BLUECAP
BLUETONGUE THICKHEAD
BLUE VERVAIN IRONWEED
BLUE VINNY DORSET
BLUEWEED ECHIUM IRONWEED
ADDERWORT

BLUFF ALTO BANK BRAG CURT
FOOL RUDE BLUNT BRAVE BURLY
CLIFF FRANK GRUFF SHORT
SURLY SWANK WINDY ABRUPT
BOUNCE CRUSTY BLINDER
BLINKER BLUFFER BRUSQUE
DECEIVE UNCIVIL BARRANCA
BARRANCO CHURLISH HOODWINK
IMPOLITE
BLUISH-GRAY MERLE
BLUMEA PLACUS
BLUNDER ERR MIX BALK BONE
BOOB BUBU BULL DOLT FLUB
GAFF ROIL SKEW SLIP STIR TRIP
BEVUE BONER BOTCH BREAK
ERROR FAULT FLUFF GAFFE
LAPSE MISDO BOGGLE BOOBOO
BUMBLE BUMMLE BUNGLE
ESCAPE FUMBLE GAZEBO
HOWLER MAFFLE MINGLE
MUDDLE BLOOMER BLOOPER
CLANGER CONFUSE DERANGE
FAILURE FLOATER MISTAKE
OVERSEE SOTTISE STUMBLE
PRATFALL SOLECISM
(**— IN LANGUAGE**) BULL
(**— IN SPEECH**) SOLECISM
(**VERBAL —**) SLIPSLAP SLIPSLOP
BLUNDERBUSS TRABU TRABUCO
TRABUCHO TROMBONE
ESPINGOLE
BLUNDERER BUMBLER BUMMLER
KNOTHEAD LUMBERER
BLUNDERING AWKWARD
BUMBLING
BLUNT BALD BATE BULL CURT
DAMP DULL FLAT MULL SNUB
ABATE BLATE BLUFF BRUSK
DUBBY INERT MORNE PLAIN
PLUMP STUNT CANDID CLUMSY
DEADEN DIRECT OBTUND OBTUSE
REBATE RETUND SHEATH STUBBY
STUPID BRUSQUE DISEDGE
HACKNEY SHEATHE SNUBBED
SPADISH STUBBED STUPEFY
HEBETATE
BLUNTED
(**PREF.**) OBTUSI
BLUNTLY PLAT PLUMP FLATLY
CRUDELY FRANKLY
BLUR DIM FOG HUM BLOB BLOT
FADE FUZZ MIST SLUR SOIL SPOT
BLEAR CLOUD FUDGE SHAKE
SMEAR STAIN SULLY MACKLE
MACULE SMUDGE STIGMA
BLEMISH CONFUSE FEATHER
OBSCURE TAILING
BLURB AD BOLT PUFF RAVE BRIEF
NOTICE
BLURRED FAINT FUZZY MUZZY
VAGUE WOOZY BLEARY BLURRY
CLOUDY SMEARY SMUDGY
SWIMMY WOOLLY CLOUDED
COMATIC EDGELESS FLANNELLY
BLURT BLAT BOLT PLUMP
BLUNDER EXCLAIM
BLUSH BLUE GLOW BLINK COLOR
FLUSH GLEAM PAINT ROUGE
TINGE CHANGE GLANCE MANTLE
REDDEN CRIMSON FLICKER
SCARLET LIKENESS JOSEPHINE
BLUSHING RED ROSY ABLUSH
ROSEATE FLUSHING ROSACEOUS

BLUSTER BEEF BLOW DING HUFF RAGE RAIL RANT BLAST BLEAT BLORE BOAST BRACE BULLY NOISE STORM SWANK BABBLE BELLOW BOUNCE FRAPLE HECTOR HUFFLE TUMULT WUTHER BLUBBER BRAVADO FLUSTER GAUSTER ROISTER SWAGGER WHITHER BOASTING BULLYING THREATEN RODOMONTADE

BLUSTERER SWAG FLASH HECTOR HUFFER FRAPLER HUFFCAP TEARCAT CACAFOGO FANFARON

BLUSTERING BOG LOUD BLUFF BRASH BULLY VAPORS HUFFCAP VAPOURS ARROGANT BULLYING

BOA BOM BOID BOMA ABOMA JIBOA SCARF THROW ABOLLA ADJIGA GIBOIA JOBOYA PYTHON ADJIGER CAMOODI EMPEROR PEROPOD ANACONDA CORALLUS

BOADICEA (HUSBAND OF —) PRASUTAGUS

BOAR HOG APER SUID BRAWN SWINE BARROW HOGGET TUSKER BRAWNER SOUNDER SUIDIAN VENISON WILRONE BRISTLER SANGLIER HOGGASTER
(— CRY) FREAM
(— HEAD) HURE
(— IN 2ND YEAR) HOGGET
(— IN 3RD YEAR) HOGSTEER HOGGASTER
(— STY) FRANK
(YOUNG —) GRISE SOUNDER
(PREF.) SUI

BOARD EAT LAG PAX TOE DAIL DEAL DECK DIET EATS FARE FLIP HACK JOIN KEEP LATH MEAT SHIP SIGN SLAT TRAY TRIP ASTEL BUIRD CHESE CLEAR COARD COUCH COURT ENTER FOUND HOUSE LODGE MEALS PANEL PLANK RATCH SHIDE STAGE STALL SWALE TABLE THEAL ABACUS ACCOST ASTYLL COMMON PALLET PLANCH RANDOM RIBBON SHIELD SIDING TUCKER CABINET CHAMBER COUNCIL CRIMPER DUOVIRI ENPLANE ENTRAIN KNEELER PALETTE PENSION PLANCHE SCRAPER TABLING TRANSOM WHATMAN APPROACH ASSEMBLY BOXBOARD CUPBOARD EXCLUDER FETIALES KEYBOARD LAPBOARD PEGBOARD TRIBUNAL PRESSBOARD MORTARBOARD
(— FOR FALCON'S MEAT) HACK
(— OF BRIDGE) CHESS
(— OF LOOM) CARD
(— OF MILL WHEEL) AWE
(— ON CALF'S NOSE) BLAB
(— OVER) BERTH
(— WITH GROOVE) COULISSE
(— WITH HANDLE) CLAPPER
(— WITH NUMBER) SLATE
(— WITH PINS) RIDDLE
(— WITH TEETH) HACKLE RUFFER
(BLOCKHEAD —) DOLL
(CHANNEL —) PAN
(CHESS —) TABLER

(DRAWING —) COQUILLE
(EXHIBITION —) FRAME
(FLOOR —) KEY
(GAME —) HALMA
(HEART-SHAPED —) PLANCHET
(MORTAR —) HAWK
(NOTCHED —) HORSE
(OTTER —) DOOR
(POLING —) RUNNER
(PRESSED —S) FELT
(PULP-PRESSING —) COUCH
(RABBETED —S) SHIPLAP
(SHEATHING —S) SARKING
(STRIKE —) SCREED
(TANNING —) BEAM
(THIN —) SHIDE SARKING
(THIN —S) SLITWORK
(WARPING —) BARTREE

BOARDER MEALER TABLER GRAINER PENSIONER SOJOURNER TRANSIENT

BOARDING LIVERY

BOARDINGHOUSE FONDA HOUSE PENSION

BOARDWALK MARINA DUCKBOARD

BOARWOOD CHEWSTICK

BOAST BOG GAB JET BEEF BLAW BLOW BRAG CROW POMP PUFF RAVE VANT WIND WOST YELP BLAST BRAVE CRACK CRAKE EXTOL EXULT GLORY PRATE QUACK ROOSE SCOLD SKITE VAPOR VAUNT VOUST YOLPE AVAUNT BLAZON BLEEZE BOUNCE CLAMOR FLAUNT INSULT MENACE OUTCRY SPLORE BLUSTER BRAVING CLAMOUR DEVAUNT DISPLAY GLORIFY SWAGGER FLOURISH THREATEN VANTERIE VAUNTERY

BOASTER BLOW HUFF GALAH SKITE BLOWER CROWER GASCON PEDANT PRATER SHAKER BLOWOFF BOUNCER BRAGGER BRAVADO CRACKER RUFFLER BLOWHARD BRAGGART CACAFUGO FANFARON GLORIOSO JINGOIST RODOMONT TARTARIN WOUSTOUR

BOASTFUL BIG BRAG HIGH COCKY LARGE BRAGGY PARADO BOBADIL JACTANT VAUNTIE FANFARON GLORIOUS GASCONADE THRASONIC

BOASTFULLY SIDE LARGE

BOASTFULNESS GLORY EGOTISM WINDINESS

BOASTING BLOW HUFF YELP BOAST CRACK PRATE ROOSE QUACKY BOBANCE GASSING JACTANCE JACTANCY QUACKISH VAPORING VAUNTAGE VENTOSITY RODOMONTADE
(EMPTY —) GAS

BOAT ARK BUM BUN CAT COG COT DOW GIG MON TUB ACON BAIT BARK BOOT BRIG CARV CHOP COCK DHOW DINK DORY DUMP FLAT FOUZ JUNK PAIR PLAT PRAM PUNT RAFT SCOW SHIP SKAG TACK TODE TOPO TROW WAKA YAWL YOLE ACCON AVISO

BANCA BARCA BARGE BARIS BATEL BIDAR BOLIA BOYER BULLY BUYER CANOE COBLE CRAFT DHONI DINGY FERRY FOIST FORTY FUNNY JOLLY KETCH LAKER LINER NADIR OOLAK PIECE PILOT PRAAM RACER SHELL SHOUT SIKAR SKIFF SKIFT SMACK TOPPO UMIAK WAAPA WHIFF XEBEC ZEBEC BAIDAK BANGKA BATEAU BAWLEY BELLUM BILALO BORLEY BOTTOM BOUTRE CAIQUE CARVEL CAYUCO CHEBEC COCKLE CRUISE CUTTER DINGHY DREDGE DRIVER DROVER DUGOUT FLATTY GALLEY GARVEY GAYYOU GLIDER HOOKER JAGGER JIGGER KEELER KICKER KUPHAR LERRET MAILER NAGGAR NUGGAR PACKET PEAPOD PEDULE PICARD PINKIE PLAYTE PULWAR RANDAN ROCKER SANDAL SCAPHE SCHOUW SCHUYT SETTEE SINGLE SKERRY STRUSE TANKER TENDER TIMBER TOGGER TORPID TRANKY TROUGH VESSEL WAFTER WHERRY ZEBECK AIRBOAT ALMADIA ANGEYOK BALLOEN BALLOON BAULEAH BUMBOAT CAISSON CARRIER CATCHER CORACLE COROLAN CRUISER CURRACH DOGBODY DRIFTER DROGHER FLATTIE FLEETER FLYBOAT FOYBOAT FRIGATE GAIASSA GASBOAT GEORDIE GONDOLA HOVELER HUFFLER KELLECK LIGHTER MACHINE MASOOLA NACELLE PEARLER PEDIWAK PINNACE PIRAGUA POOKAWN PUTELEE SCOOTER SCULLER SHALLOP SHARPIE SHIKARA SIKHARA SKAFFIE SKIPPET SPONGER SPYBOAT STEAMER TRAWLER TUCKNER TUMBREL TUMBRIL VEDETTE WHIRREY BALANGAY BARANGAY BILLYBOY BOOMBOAT BULLBOAT BUMBARGE CANALLER CHALOUPE CHEBACCO CHELINGA CHELINGO COCKBOAT COROCORE DAHABEAH DUCKBOAT FIREBOAT FLAGBOAT KEELBOAT LIFEBOAT MACKINAW MONOXYLE NEWSBOAT OYSTERER PALANDER PANCHWAY PESSONER PESSULUS PULLBOAT SAILBOAT SCHOKKER SCHOONER SURFBOAT TONGKANG TRANSFER OUTRIGGER
(— OF MALTA) DGHAISA
(— WITH SAILS AND OARS) LYMPHIAD
(ABANDONED —) DERELICT
(CHEMICAL —) CAPSULE
(CHINESE —) JUNK SAMPAN
(CLUMSY —) HOOKER DROGHER
(COLLEGE —) TORPID
(DISPATCH —) AVISO PACKET
(ESKIMO —) KAMIK UMIAK OOMIAC UMIACK
(FERRY —) BAC CUTT
(FISHING —) COG BOVO BUSS DONI CANOA COBLE DHONI NOBBY

PYKAR SMACK VINTA BALDIE BAWLEY BORLEY DOGGER DROVER FISHER KUPHAR NICKEY SANDAL SCAFFY SEINER SEXERN TOSHER VOLYER CARAVEL CRABBER DRAGGER FOLLYER POOKAUN SHARPIE SKAFFIE TRAWLER DRAGBOAT GAROOKUH SHRIMPER
(FLAT-BOTTOM —) ARK BAC BUN DORY FLAT PLAT PRAM PUNT SCOW BARGE COBLE DOREY FLOAT MOSES PRAAM SHOUT BATEAU BUGEYE GAYYOU PUTELI GONDOLA LIGHTER FLATBOAT GUNDELOW JOHNBOAT
(FLY —) BUSS FLUTE FLIGHT
(GANGES —) PUTELI
(HIGHLAND —) BIRLINN
(INCENSE —) NEF SHIP NAVICULA
(MALAY —) COROCORE GALLIVAT
(MORTAR —) PALANDER
(OPEN —) WHIFF LERRET SHALLOP
(PATROL —) SPITKID SPITKIT
(RACING —) SIX FOUR EIGHT SCULL SHELL SINGLE TORPID SCULLER
(SHIP'S —) GIG MOSES DINGEY DINGHY LAUNCH TENDER PINNACE
(SKIN —) BIDAR BAIDAR ANGEYOK BIDARKA BULLBOAT
(SMALL —) CARTOPPER
(WICKER —) KUFA GOOFA GOOFAH CORACLE
(3-OAR —) RANDAN
(6-OAR —) SEXERN
(8-OAR —) SHIP
(PL.) LIGHTERAGE
(PREF.) CYMBI CYMBO
(SUFF.) SCAPH

BOATBUILDING SETWORK
BOATHOOK STOWER HITCHER
BOATMAN DANDI DANDY PHAON BARGER BOWMAN CHARON YAWLER HOBBLER HOVELER HUFFLER COBLEMAN VOYAGEUR WATERMAN GONDOLIER
BOAT SEAT TAFT
BOAT-SHAPED
(PREF.) SCAPH(O)
BOAT SHELL YET SWEETMEAT
BOATSWAIN BOSN BOSUN SERANG TINDAL
BOAZ (FATHER OF —) SALMA SALMON
(SON OF —) OBED
(WIFE OF —) RUTH
BOB BAB BOW CUT DAB DIP HOD JOG POP RAP TAP BALL BLOW BUFF CALF CLIP CLOD COIN CORK DUCK GRUB JEER JERK JEST KNOB MOCK WORM BUNCH CHEAT DANCE FILCH FLOAT FLOUT SHAKE TAUNT TRICK BINGLE BOBBER BOBBLE BUFFET CURTSY DELUDE HOBBLE POMMEL POPPLE STRIKE WEIGHT BOBSLED BOBTAIL CLUSTER HAIRCUT PAGEBOY PENDANT PLUMMET REFRAIN SHINGLE SHILLING
(— UP) LOLLOP

BOBAC PAHMI TARBAGAN
BOBBER CORK DUCK FLOAT
BOBFLY
BOBBIN PIN CONE CORD PIRN
REEL BRAID QUILL SPOOL
BROCHE HANGER SKREEL TAVELL
WORKER RATCHET SPINDLE
TARELLE TORCHON
(PL.) BONES
BOBBINET ILLUSION
BOBBLE ERROR
BOBOLINK DEER REED SUCKER
BUNTING MAYBIRD ORTOLAN
REEDBIRD RICEBIRD
BOBSLED BOB DRAY BOBLET
RIPPER TRAVERSE
BOBWHITE COLIN QUAIL
PARTRIDGE
BOCACCIO JACK TOMCOD
BOCCACCIO TRECENTIST
BOCCARELLA NOSEHOLE
BOCCARO YIHSING
BOCE BOGUE OXEYE
BOCHERU (FATHER OF —) AZEL
BODE OMEN SIGN STOP AUGUR
OFFER HERALD MESSAGE
PORTEND PRESAGE FOREBODE
FORECAST FORESHOW FORETELL
INDICATE
BODHISATTVA KWANNON
MAITREYA AVALOKITA
PADMAPANI
BODICE JUPE CHOLI GILET JUMPS
WAIST BASQUE BOLERO CORSET
JELICK LYFKIE CORSAGE
OVERBODY SLIPBODY
BODIERON BOREGAT
BODILY SOLID SOMAL ACTUAL
CARNAL FLESHLY SOMATIC
CORPORAL ENTIRELY EXTERNAL
MATERIAL PERSONAL PHYSICAL
SARKICAL VISCERAL CORPOREAL
(NOT —) INTERIOR
BODKIN AWL PIN POINT BROACH
DAGGER NEEDLE POPPER
HAIRPIN PONIARD STILETTO
EYELETEER
BODLE TURNER
BODO CACHARI
BODY BAND BELL BOLE BOOK
BOUK BUCK BULK CREW DEHA
FORM HEAD LICH MASS MOLD
NAVE RIND RUPA SOMA STEM
ATOMY FLESH FRAME HABIT
MOULD SHANK STIFF TORSO
TRUNK CORMUS CORPSE CORPUS
CUERPO EXTENT FUSEAU LICHAM
PERSON SARIRA AIRFOIL
ANATOMY CADAVER CARCASS
COMPANY ECONOMY QUANTUM
SKINFUL SUPTION TEXTURE
CORSAINT DEMARCHY EXTENSUM
MAJORITY QUARROME TENEMENT
PERSONNEL
(— OF ARROW) SHAFT STELE
(— OF BELIEVERS) FAITH
(— OF CANONS) CHAPTER
(— OF CARDINALS) CONCLAVE
(— OF CHILDREN) INFANTRY
(— OF CHRISTIANS) KOINONIA
COMMUNION
(— OF DOCTRINES) DOGMA

(— OF ECHINODERM) DISC DISK
(— OF EVIDENCE) CASE CORPUS
(— OF FIBERS) FORNIX
(— OF HELMET) BELL
(— OF ISLAMIC CUSTOM) SUNNA
SUNNAH
(— OF KNOWLEDGE) STUFF
(— OF LAW) CODE SHAR HALAKA
SHARIA PANDECT SHARIAT
HALACHAH
(— OF MANKIND) HERD
(— OF MUSCLE) BELLY
(— OF NOTIONS) FOLKLORE
(— OF OFFICERS) BUREAU
(— OF ORE) BUNCH MANTO
(— OF PIGMENT) EYESPOT
IMPASTO
(— OF POETRY) EPOS
(— OF PRINCIPLES) ORGANON
(— OF ROCK) DIKE DYKE HORSE
STOCK BIOHERM MUDFLOW
INTRUSION
(— OF SINGERS) CHORUS
(— OF STUDENTS) CLASS
(— OF TEN) DECURY
(— OF TENANTS) GAVEL HOMAGE
(— OF THIEVES) SCHOOL
(— OF TRADITIONS) HADIT HADITH
(— OF TROOPS) FORCE TAXIS
AMBUSH BATTLE CONREY
SCREEN SQUARE BRIGADE
LASHKAR SUPPORT BATTALIA
GARRISON
(— OF TYPE) SHANK
(— OF VASSALS) BAN MANRED
(— OF WARRIORS) IMPI
(— OF WATER) BAY RIP SEA BAHR
FORD HEAD LAKE LAVE POND
POOL WAVE ABYSS BAYOU DRINK
FLOOD OCEAN SHARD SHERD
SWASH LAGOON NYANZA
STREAM FLOWAGE SWALLOW
(— OF WELLBORN MEN)
COMITATUS
(— OF WRITINGS) SMRTI SMRITI
(— OF 12 MEN) DOUZAINE
(— POLITIC) ESTATE
(— RIDDLED BY BULLETS) SIEVE
(CAROTID —) GLOMUS
(CART —) SIRPEA
(CELESTIAL —) SUN BALL COMET
PLANET SPHERE ELEMENT
ASTEROID PLANETOID SATELLITE
PLANETESIMAL
(COMPACT —) GLOBE
(CONDUCTING —) GROUND
(CORPORATE —) SOCIETY
(DEAD —) LICH MORT CADAVER
CARCASS CARRION SUBJECT
(ECCLESIASTICAL —) CLASSIS
(ELASTIC —) CUSHION
(EXTENDED) LENGTH
(FAT —) EPIPLOON
(FRUITING —) CONK CLAVA
ASCOCARP MAZAEDIUM
(GLOBULAR —) NOB KNOB
(GOVERNING —) KAHAL SYNOD
DURBAR SENATE DECARCHY
DIRECTORY
(HAT —) HOOD
(HEAVENLY —) SUN LAMP STAR
COMET LIGHT CANDLE
(HYALINE —) DRUSE

(IMMUNE —) DESMON
(JUDICIAL —) FORUM
(LEGISLATIVE —) CHAMBER
ASSEMBLY CONGRESS LAGTHING
PARLIAMENT
(MAIN — OF ARMY) BATTLE
(MATHEMATICAL —) FILAMENT
(MORMON —) BISHOPRIC
(MORTAL —) KHET
(POROUS —) MADREPORITE
(PRESBYTERIAN —) SESSION
JUDICATORY
(RELIGIOUS —) SECT CONVENT
(REPRODUCTIVE —) EGG GEMMA
SPORE GEMMULA
(SONOROUS —) PHONIC
(SPIRITUAL —) SAHU
(SWELLING —) BOSS
(WAGON —) BED BUCK PUNT
(PREF.) CORPORI SOMAT(O)
SOMATICO SOMO
(SUFF.) CY DEMA
SOMA(TO)(TOUS) SOME SOMIA
SOMIC SOMOUS SOMUS
(— OF A KIND) ID
BODYGUARD THANE ESCORT
INWARD HUSCARL RETINUE
TRABANT THINGMAN WARDCORS
BOER TAKHAAR AFRIKANER
BOG BUG CAR DUB FEN GOG HAG
BOLD CARR CESS FLOW MIRE
MOOR MOSS OOZE QUAG SINK
SLEW SLUE SPEW STOG SUDS
SYRT WASH LETCH MARSH MIZZY
SAUCY SLADE SLOCK SWAMP
MORASS MUSKEG POLDER
SLOUGH CRIPPLE FORWARD
PEATERY TURBARY QUAGMIRE
(PEAT —) CESS MOSS PETARY
YARPHA
(PREF.) HELO
BOG ASPHODEL KNAVERY
BOGEY BUG COW HAG BOGIE
BOGLE DEVIL GNOME TRUCK
BOGGLE BOOGER GOBLIN
BOGGARD BOGGART BUGABOO
BUGBEAR SPECTER SPECTRE
BOGGLE JIB SHY BALK FOIL STOP
ALARM BOTCH DEMUR SCARE
START STICK BAFFLE BUNGLE
GOBLIN SHRINK BAUCHLE
BLUNDER PERPLEX SCRUPLE
STUMBLE FRIGHTEN HESITATE
BOGGY WET DEEP MIRY SOFT
FENNY FOGGY GOUTY HAGGY
MOSSY SNAPY SPEWY MARISH
MARSHY QUAGGY SLOBBY
SWAMPY WAUGHY BOGGISH
QUEACHY SQUASHY
BOGIER RIDER GEARMAN
BOGLAND SLADE
BOG MANGANESE WAD
LAMPADITE
BOGO ABILO ABILAO
BOGOMILE PATARIN PATARINE
BOGUS FAKE SHAM FALSE PHONY
SPURIOUS
BOHEME, LA (CHARACTER IN —)
MIMI COLLINE MUSETTA
RODOLFO MARCELLO
SCHAUNARD
(COMPOSER OF —) PUCCINI
BOHEMIAN ARTY PICARA PICARD

PICARO ARTISTIC
(— RIVER) ELBE VLTAVA LUZNICE
BEROUNKA
(— TOWN) PISEK PLZEN PRAHA
TABOR PILSEN PRAGUE
BOHEMIAN GIRL (COMPOSER OF —)
BALFE
BOHOR REEDBUCK
BOIL FRY PET STY BILE BLOB BOLL
BRAN BUCK BUMP COCT COOK
COWL LEEP PLAY PUSH QUAT
RAGE SEED SORE STEW STYE
TEEM WALL WALM WELL BLAIN
BOTCH BREDE STEAM BETRAY
BUBBLE BULDER BULLER BURBLE
DECOCT GALLOP PIMPLE RISING
SEETHE SIMMER TOTTLE WABBLE
WOBBLE ANTHRAX BEALING
BREEDER CATHAIR ELIXATE
ESTUATE INFLAME AESTUATE
EBULLATE FURUNCLE PHLEGMON
CARBUNCLE
(— IN LYE) BUCK
(— SYRUP) PEARL
(SAND —) BLOWOUT
(PREF.) COCTO DOTHI(EN)(O) ZEO
BOILED SOD SODDEN
(— WITHOUT SAUCE) ANGLAISE
BOILER YET REEF STILL COPPER
KETTLE RETORT TEACHE ALEMBIC
CALDRON FURNACE
(SALT —) WELLER
BOILING WALM ABOIL FERVID
COCTION FERVENT SCALDING
SEETHING ELIXATION
BOILING POINT
(PREF.) COCTO
BOISTERER (MASTER OF —)
FORTUNIO
BOISTEROUS GURL HIGH LOUD
RUDE WILD BURLY GURLY NOISY
RANDY ROARY ROUGH WINDY
COARSE RUGGED SHANDY
STOCKY STORMY STRONG
UNRULY FURIOUS MASSIVE
ROARING VIOLENT BIGMOUTH
CUMBROUS LARRIKIN STRIDENT
VEHEMENT ROBUSTIOUS
BOLD BIG BOG MOD YEP DERF
HARD KEEN PERT RASH RUDE
TALL WHAT YEPE APERT BARDY
BIELD BRASH BRAVE BRENT
FRACK FREAK FRECK GALLY
HARDY JOLLY LARGE MANLY
NERVY PAWKY PEART POKEY
RUDAS SAUCY STEEP STOUT
WLONK ABRUPT AUDACE BRASSY
BRAZEN CROUSE DARING FIERCE
HEROIC PLUCKY PRETTY STRONG
ASSURED DASHING DEFIANT
FORWARD GRIVOIS HAUGHTY
MASSIVE VALIANT ARROGANT
FAMILIAR FEARLESS IMMODEST
IMPUDENT INTREPID MALAPERT
POWERFUL RESOLUTE TEMEROUS
(NOT —) GENTEEL
BOLDFACE BOLD BLACK FULLFACE
BOLDLY CRANK BARELY CROUSE
HARDLY HARDILY ROUNDLY
STRONGLY
BOLDNESS BROW DARE FACE
GALL BIELD CHEEK NERVE PLUCK
VIGOR DARING BRAVERY

COURAGE FREEDOM AUDACITY
TEMERITY
(— OF SPEECH) PARRHESIA
BOLDO NUTMEG
BOLE CLAY DOSE STEM BOLUS
CRYPT TRUNK RUDDLE TIMBER
BOLETUS CEPE
BOLIDE FIREBALL
BOLIVIA PILE

BOLIVIA

CAPITAL: LAPAZ SUCRE
COIN: TOMIN CENTAVO
DEPARTMENT: LAPAZ ORURO
PANDO ELBENI POTOSI TARIJA
INDIAN: URO INCA ITEN MOXO
URAN ARAWAK AYMARA
CHARCA CHICHA IXIAMA
TACANA PUQUINA QUECHUA
SIRIONE TUMUPASA
LAKE: POOPO COIPASA ROGAGUA
AULLAGAS TITICACA
MEASURE: LEAGUE CELEMIN
MOUNTAIN: JARA CUSCO CUZCO
PUPUYA SAJAMA SORATA
ILLAMPU ANCOHUMA ILLIMANI
ZAPALERI
MOUNTAINS: ANDES SUNSAS
SANSIMON SANTIAGO
PANPIPE: SICU SIKU
PLATEAU: ALTIPLANO
RIVER: BENI YATA ABUNA APERE
BOOPI LAUCA ORTON BAURES
GRANDE ICHILO ITENEZ MADIDI
MAMORE MIZQUE TARIJA
YACUMA GUAPORE ITONAMA
MACHUPO BENECITO INAMBARI
PARAGUAY PARAPETI
SALT DEPOSIT: UYUNI EMPEXA
SWAMP: IZOZOG
TOWN: IVO ICLA ITAU MOJO POJO
SAYA YACO YATA YURA CLIZA
LAPAZ LLICA ORURO QUIME
SUCRE UNCIA UYUNI ZONGO
GUAQUI POTOSI TARIJA
VOLCANO: OLLAGUE
WEIGHT: LIBRA MARCO

BOLL BOW POD BULB KNOB SNAP
ONION BUBBLE CAPSULE
BOLLARD BITT KEVEL DOLPHIN
DEADHEAD
(—S AND BITTS) APOSTLES
BOLLER STRIPPER
BOLL WEEVIL PICUDO
BOLO MACHETE SUNDANG
BOLSHEVISM COMMUNISM
SOVIETISM
BOLSHEVIST BOLO
BOLSTER AID PAD JACK PILLOW
CUSHION HEADING STIFFEN
SUPPORT BACKSTOP BALUSTER
COMPRESS MAINTAIN
BOLT BAR JAG KEY LUE PEN PIN
ROD RUN BEAT BURR CRAM
DART DUMP FLEE GULP LOCK
PAWL SHUT SIFT SLOT SNIB SPAR
STUD ARROW BILBO CLOSE
ELOPE FLASH FLOUR GORGE
LATCH RIVET SETUP SHAFT
STOCK ASSORT DECAMP DESERT
FASTEN FLIGHT GANYIE GARBLE
MOOTER PINTLE PURIFY QUARRY

REFINE SAFETY SEARCE SECURE
SNIBEL STREAK STRONG TOGGLE
WINNOW BAYBOLT DOGBOLT
EYEBOLT MISSILE QUARREL
SETBOLT SHACKLE SLABBER
THUNDER DRAWBOLT FASTENER
FISHBOLT FLATHEAD KINGBOLT
RINGBOLT SEPARATE SLUMMOCK
STAMPEDE
(— FOOD) SKOFF
(DOOR —) DRAWBOLT
(FIERY —) RESHEPH
(LIGHTNING —) SHAFT
(THUNDER —) FULMEN
(PREF.) GOMPHO
BOLTER BOLT DRESSER
MUGWUMP
BOLTHEAD MATRASS
BOMB DUD EGG ROC AZON BOOM
FRAG BLARE CRUMP PRANG
RAZON SHELL SQUIB ASHCAN
SALUTE AEROSOL BALLOON
BOMBARD GRENADE MARMITE
AEROBOMB FIREBALL WHIZBANG
PINEAPPLE
(— RELEASE) TOGGLE
(TRENCH —) MINNIE
(PL.) STICK
BOMBARD BOMB CRUMP SHELL
ATTACK BATTER BOTTLE STRAFE
BOMBARDMENT BLITZ SIEGE
ATTACK RAFALE STRAFE BATTERY
SHELLING
BOMBARDON TUBA NICOLO
POMMER BRUMMER
BOMBAST GAS PAD PUFF RAGE
RANT RAVE STUFF TUMOR
BLUSTER FUSTIAN TYMPANY
BALLYHOO BOASTING RHAPSODY
TURGIDITY
BOMBASTIC PUFFY TUMID VOCAL
WINDY FLUENT HEROIC MOUTHY
TURGID BLOATED BOMBAST
FLOWERY FUSTIAN OROTUND
POMPOUS RANTING STILTED
SWOLLEN INFLATED SWELLING
(— STYLE) TYMPANY
BOMBAY DUCK BUMMALO
BONACE TREE NOSEBURN
BONACI AGUAJI
BONA FIDE LEVEL GENUINE
AUTHENTIC
BONANZA BUNCH
BONANZA STATE MONTANA
BONBON CANDY CREAM GOODY
DAINTY CARAMEL COSAQUE
SNAPPER CONFETTO
(PL.) CONFETTI
BOND BON DOG TIE VOW ANDI
BAIL BAND DUTY FIVE FOUR
GLUE GYVE HOLD KNOT LINK
NOTE YOKE BOUND CHAIN NEXUS
SWATH BINDER CEDULA CEMENT
CONNEX COPULA COUPLE
ENGAGE ESCROW FETTER
LEAGUE PLEDGE SOLDER SWATHE
FOREIGN HUSBAND LIAISON
LIBERTY LINKAGE MANACLE
SHACKLE STATUTE ADHESIVE
CONTRACT COVENANT LIGAMENT
LIGATION LIGATURE MORTGAGE
SECURITY VADIMONY VINCULUM
(EMOTIONAL —) RAPPORT

(PL.) IRON KHAKIS SHORTS
(PREF.) DESM(A)(IDI)(IDIO)(O)
ETHMO OSSE(O) OSSI OST(E)(EO)
(SUFF.) **(CONTAINING TRIPLE —)**
OLIC
BONDAGE YOKE THRALL HELOTRY
SERFDOM SLAVERY BONDSHIP
THIRLING CAPTIVITY SERVITUDE
BONDED CATTED ENGAGED
BONDMAN CARL ESNE PEON SERF
CHURL HELOT SLAVE STOOGE
SURETY THRALL VASSAL CHATTEL
PEASANT SERVANT VILLEIN
BONDSMAN
BONDSTONE BINDER BONDER
KEYSTONE
BONE OS DIB HIP LUZ RIB TOT
BANE ULNA BLADE FEMUR HYOID
ILIUM INCUS JUGAL SLATE STONE
TALUS TIBIA UNION VOMER
CANNON COCCYX CONCHA
COPULA CUBOID EPURAL FIBULA
FILLET HAMATE NUCHAL PECTEN
RADIAL SPLINT STAPES TRIPOD
UNGUIS ZYGOMA DENTARY
PALATAL PROOTIC CORACOID
PALATINE PERIOTIC PISIFORM
QUADRATE NAVICULAR
OPERCULAR METACARPAL
(ANKLE —) TALUS
(HIP —) HUGGIN
(PUBIC —) PECTEN
(SHIN —) CNEMIS
(THIGH —) FEMUR
(PREF.) ETHMO OSSE(O) OSSI
OST(E)(EO)
(SUFF.) OST(EON)(EUS)(OSIS)
BONED
(SUFF.) OSTEUS
BONEFISH OIO MACABI GRUBBER
BONYFISH LADYFISH
BONER BUBU FLUB ROCK ERROR
BRODIE STAYER STUMER
BLOOMER BLOOPER BLUNDER
MISTAKE STEELER STUMOUR
BONES
(PREF.) **(— OF HAND OR FOOT)**
PHALANGI(A)
BONESET COMFREY AGUEWEED
EUPATORY HEMPWEEK
BONEYARD STOCK
BONFIRE BLAZE TANDLE TAWNIE
BALEFIRE BURNFIRE NEEDFIRE
BONGO DOR
BONING SAP
BONITO AKU ATU NICE COBIA
SARDA BONITA ROBALO
ALBACORE KATONKEL MACKEREL
SCOMBRID SKIPJACK
BONNET CAP HAT COWL HOOD
POKE POXY SCON COVER DECOY
SCONE SHAPE TOQUE CAPOTE
MOBCAP SLOUCH CHAPEAU
COMMODE CORONET LEGHORN
SOWBACK VOLUPER BALMORAL
BONGRACE HEADGEAR
BONNET MONKEY ZATI MUNGA
TOQUE MACACO RILAWA
MACAQUE
BONNY GAY FINE MERRY PLUMP
BLITHE BONNIE PRETTY STRONG
HEALTHY BUDGEREE HANDSOME
BEAUTIFUL

BONTOK IGOROT
BONUS GIN TIP GIFT MEED AWARD
BRIBE BUNCE BUNTS PILON PRIZE
SPIFF REGALO REWARD
CUMSHAW DOUCEUR PREMIUM
SUBSIDY BOUNTITH DIVIDEND
TANTIEME LAGNIAPPE
BON VIVANT SPORT EPICURE
BON VIVEUR FLANEUR
BONY HARD LANK THIN LANKY
STIFF TOUGH OSTEAL SKINNY
ANGULAR OSSEOUS SCRAGGY
SKELETAL
BONYFISH MENHADEN
BOOB ASS OAF FOOL GOON
GOOP DUNCE GOONY NEDDY
NITWIT
BOOBOOK OWL PEHO RURU
CUCKOO MOPOKE MOPEHAWK
MOREPORK
BOOB TUBE BOX
BOOBY GAWK GONY SULA DUNCE
IDIOT LOSER PATCH PRIZE SILLY
SLEIGH STUPID CAMANAY
PIQUERO GOOSECAP
BOOBYALLA DOGWOOD
WATERBUSH
BOODLE LOOT SWAG CROWD
GRAFT BUDDLE NOODLE
PLUNDER CABOODLE
BOOGEYMAN PADFOOT
TANKERABOGUS
BOOJUM SNARK
BOOK MO LIL LOG CHAP CODE
FORM HEFT OPUS PAGE TEXT
TOME ALBUM ALDUS BIBLE
CANON CANTO CODEX DETUR
DIARY DIVAN ENTER FLETA FOLIO
FROST GUIDE KITAB LIBEL LIBER
QUAIR QUIRE RAZEE ZOHAR
ALDINE ANONYM BODONI
CURSUS DOCKET HERBAL LEDGER
MAHZOR MANUAL MISSAL
NUMBER REBIND RECORD RITUAL
SCHOOL TICKET TROPER VOLUME
BLOTTER CATALOG COUCHER
DIETARY DISCARD FEODARY
GARLAND GRAMMAR JOURNAL
LAWBOOK LEXICON MANDALA
OCTAPLA OMNIBUS ORDINAL
OUTBOOK PEERAGE RECITER
SAMHITA SERVICE SLEEPER
SPEAKER SPELLER SYNAXAR
TERRIER TICKLER TRAVAIL
TRIGLOT TYPICON TYPICUM
WRITING BANKBOOK BROCHURE
CALCULUS CASEBOOK CASHBOOK
CHAPBOOK COOKBOOK
COPYBOOK DECRETAL
DOCUMENT FESTIVAL GIFTBOOK
GOSPELER HANDBOOK HARDBACK
HERDBOOK JESTBOOK JUVENILE
LIBRETTO PASTORAL POMANDER
POSTBOOK REGISTER SONGBOOK
STUDBOOK SYNAXARY TALEBOOK
TRIODION TWENTYMO VESPERAL
PAPERBACK PONTIFICAL
NOMENCLATOR PROCESSIONAL
PHARMACOPOEIA
(— BACK) DORSE
(— FOR HARVARD GRADUATE)
DETUR

(— OF CHARTS) WAGONER PORTOLAN

(— OF HERALDRY) ARMORY ARMORIAL

(— OF MAPS) ATLAS

(— OF PSALMS) PSALTER TEHILLIM

(— OF RULES) HOYLE

(— OF SERVICES) PIE

(— OF SOLUTIONS) KEY

(— OF THE MASS) ORDO

(—S KEPT IN PRINT) BACKLIST

(CHEAP —) BLOOD

(CHINESE —) CHING

(COMMONPLACE —) ADVERSARIA

(ELEMENTARY —) PRIMER

(FOLDED —) ORIHON

(JOKE —) JOE JESTBOOK

(MEMORANDUM —) AGENDA JOTTER TICKLER

(MINIATURE —) BIBELOT

(PART OF —) CASE FLAP COVER HINGE JOINT SPINE TITLE JACKET LINING ENDLEAF BACKBONE ENDPAPER HEADBAND BACKSTRIP SHELFBACK

(PRAYER —) PORTAS SIDDUR PORTASS PORTHORS

(READING —) ABC ABCEE ABSEY

(RECORD —) LIBER TICKLER

(RELIGIOUS —) KITAB KORAN QURAN GOSPEL HORARY KYRIAL PROSAR GRADUAL KYRIALE BREVIARY MEGILLAH ORDINARY SYNAXARY

(SERVICE —) COMES GRAIL TEXTUS

(SLOW-SELLING —) PLUG

(STRANGE —S) CURIOSA

(UNBOUND —) CAHIER

(PL.) LIBRI SHELF STUDY EROTICA SCRIPTURE

(PREF.) BIBLIO LIBRI

BOOKBINDING STUB YAPP STRING

BOOKCASE DESK STAGE STALL SCRINE PLUTEUS CREDENZA

BOOK COVER LID SIDE FOREL RECTO VERSO FORREL REVERSE REVERSO

BOOKISH BOOKY ERUDITE INKHORN PEDANTIC STUDIOUS

BOOKLET FOLDER NOVELET BROCHURE

BOOK LOUSE PSOCID

BOOKMAKER LAYER BOOKER BOOKIE

BOOKMARK MARKER TASSEL REGISTER

BOOK PALM TARA TALIERA

BOOKSHELF DESK PLUTEUS

(PL.) CLASSIS

BOOKWORM GOME GRUB NERD TOOL WONK CEREB GNURD GRIND SQUID SPIDER WEENIE

BOOM JIB BEAM BOMB BUMP CRIB POLE ROAR SPAR BRAIL CHAIN CRANE CROON PROBE BUMPKIN CATHEAD CURTAIN RESOUND SUPPORT BOWSPRIT FLOURISH

(CRANE —) ARM GIB JIB

BOOMERANG KALIE KILEY KYLIE WANGO ATLATL BOUNCE RECOIL LEEWILL REBOUND WOMERAH WOOMERA BACKFIRE HORNERAH

LEEANGLE RICOCHET TROMBASH

BOOMING HUMMING ROARING

BOOM IRON WITHE CRANCE

BOON GAY BENE GIFT GOOD KIND BOUND FAVOR GRANT MERRY ORDER BENIGN BOUNTY GOODLY JOVIAL PRAYER BENEFIT COMMAND PRESENT BLESSING INTIMATE PETITION BENEFACTION

BOOR CAD OAF BOER BORE CARL HICK JACK KERN LOUT PILL RUNT SLOB CHUFF CHURL CLOWN KERNE SLAVE BUMKIN CARLOT CLUNCH HOBLOB JOBSON JOSKIN LUBBER LUMMOX RUSTIC BUMPKIN CAUBOGE GROBIAN PEASANT VILLAIN BOEOTIAN BOSTHOON CLODHOPPER

BOORISH ILL RUDE GAWKY ROUGH RUNTY SURLY CLUMSY RUSTIC SAVAGE SULLEN VULGAR WOOLEN AWKWARD CRABBED HIRSUTE HOBLIKE KERNISH LOUTISH PEAKISH ROISTER UNCOUTH VILLAIN WOOLLEN BOEOTIAN CARTERLY CHURLISH CLODDISH CLOWNISH LUBBERLY SWAINISH UNGAINLY

BOORISHNESS VILLAINY GROBIANISM

BOOST AID LEG ABET BACK BOOM HELP LIFT PLUG PUSH COACH EXALT HOIST HOOSH RAISE ASSIST ADVANCE COMMEND ELEVATE ENDORSE PROMOTE INCREASE

BOOT PAC PAD USE CURE GAIN HALF HELP HOOF KICK PUNT SHOE SOCK AVAIL BOOTY DERBY EJECT JEMMY KAMIK PEWEE SPOIL BOOTEE BUDGET BUSKIN CASING CHUKKA CRAKOW ENRICH FUMBLE GAITER GALOSH INSHOE JEMIMA JOCKEY MUKLUK PEDULE SHEATH BENEFIT BOTTINE COTHURN COWHIDE CRUISER HESSIAN HIGHLOW SEABOOT SHOEPAC VANTAGE BALMORAL BOTTEKIN CHASSURE COVERING FINNESKO JACKBOOT LARRIGAN NAPOLEON COTHURNUS

(— OF CARRIAGE) FOREBOOT

(— ON SADDLE) GAMBADE GAMBADO

(HALF —) PAC BUSKIN COCKER SKILTY BRODEKIN

(HOB-NAILED —) BAT

(HORSE'S —) SCALPER

(LUMBERMAN'S —) CRUISER

(MARINE —) SKINHEAD

(RIDING —) JEMMY JIMMY JODHPUR

(SEALSKIN —) KAMIK

(STOUT —) STOGA STOGY

(TORTURE —) SQUEEZER

(PL.) OVERS FINNESKO HESSIANS

BOOTBLACK SHINER BLACKER SHOEBOY

BOOTED OCREATE

BOOTES WAINMAN HERDSMAN

BOOTH BOX BULK COOP DESK

LOGE SHED SHOP SOOK BOTHY CABIN CRAME HOUSE KIOSK LIWAN LODGE PITCH SLANG STALL STAND BOTHAN PAGODA PANDAL PAYBOX SUCCAH SUKKAH TIENDA BALAGAN COCKSHY TABERNA

BOOTLACE LACET THONG

BOOTLEG SHY SLY ILLEGAL ILLICIT

BOOTY BOOT FANG GAIN LOOT PELF PREY SACK SWAG BUTIN CHEAT FORAY GRAFT PRIZE CREAGH FLEECE SPOILS DESPOIL PILLAGE PLUNDER SPREAGH SPREATH STEALTH PURCHASE SPUILZIE STEALAGE

BOOZE BOLL BOUT BUDGE DRINK HOOCH SPREE FUDDLE LIQUOR

BOOZY TIPPLE LIQUORY

BOPHUTHATSWANA (CAPITAL OF —) MMABATHO

(TOWN OF —) TEMBA MABOPANE GARANKUWA

BORAGE ANCHUSA

BORAX FLUX TINCAL

(— SOURCE) KERNITE

BORDER CUT HEM RIM TAB ABUT BABK BRIM CURB DADO EAVE EDGE LIMB LINE LIST LOVE MARK NARK ORLE RAND ROON RUND SIDE TRIM WELL WELT BOARD BOUND BRAID BRINK CHEEK COAST COSTA DRAFT FILET FLANK FOREL FRAME FRILL GUARD LIMIT MARCH MARGE MARLI PLAIT SHORE SKIRT STRIP SWAGE TOUCH VERGE ACCOST ADJOIN COTISE EDGING FILLET FORREL FRINGE IMPALE LACING LIMBUS LISERE MARGIN ORFRAY PURFLE QUADRA SCREED STRIPE TANIKO WEEPER CONFINE DRAUGHT FIMBRIA FLOROON MARGENT SELVAGE VALANCE BOUNDARY DOUBLING FRONTIER MARCHESE NEIGHBOR OUTSKIRT PLATBAND SKIRTING SURROUND TERMINUS TRESSOUR TRESSURE

(— OF EXTERNAL EAR) HELIX

(— OF LACE) PICOT

(— OF ROCK) SALBAND

(— OF SAIL) DOUBLING

(— OF SHIELD) BORDURE

(— OF STREAM) ROND

(— ON) ABUT ACCOST AFFRONT NEIGHBOR

(FLOWERED —) FLOROON

(ORNAMENTAL —) PURL WAGE FRAME FRINGE MATTING DENTELLE TRESSURE

(RIBBON —) FRILAL

(PL.) CONFINE PURLIEU CONFINES

(PREF.) CRASPEDO LIMBI

BORDERED ORLE LIMBATE

BORDERING MARGENT FRONTIER

BORE BIT CUT EAT IRK JET TAP DRAG FLAT HOLE JUMP PALL PILL POKE REAM RUSH SINK SIZE TIDE TIRE TOOL ANNOY CHINK DRILL EAGRE ENNUI GAUGE GOUGE OUGHT PLONK PRICK PUNCH SUGUR TEWEL THIRL TRICK

VAPOR WEARY BEFOOL CANNON GIMLET PIERCE THRILL THRUST TUNNEL WIMBLE BROMIDE CALIBER CALIBRE CONCAVE CREVICE HUMDRUM NUDNICK OPENING AIGUILLE CAPILLUS DIAMETER DRAWBORE GRATIANO POROROCA

(— OF CANNON) SOUL CHASE

(PREF.) FORAMINI

BOREAL NORTHERN

BOREAS AQUILO AQUILON

(BROTHER OF —) NOTUS HESPERUS ZEPHYRUS

(DAUGHTER OF —) CLEOPATRA

(FATHER OF —) ASTRAEUS

(MOTHER OF —) EOS AURORA

(SON OF —) ZETES CALAIS

BORED BLASE WEARY ENNUYEE TEDIOUS SATIATED

BOREDOM YAWN ENNUI ACEDIA TEDIUM

(FEELING OF —) BLAHS

BORELE KEITLOA UPEYGAN

BORER MOLE BARDEE WIMBLE HAGFISH TANBARK TERMITE TERRIER FLATHEAD SHIPWORM WOODWORM

(PREF.) TRYPAN(O)

BORING DIM DRY FLAT SLOW BROACH STODGY STUPID TIRING LUMPISH TEDIOUS PIERCING TIRESOME TEREBRANT

(— TOOL) AIGUILLE

(SOMETHING —) DRAG

BORIS GODUNOV (CHARACTER IN —) BORIS PIMEN DMITRY GRIGORY MISSAIL RANGONI SHUISKY VARLAAM

(COMPOSER OF —) MUSSORGSKY

BORN N NEE NATE INNATE NASCENT NATURAL UTERINE ORIGINAL

(PREMATURELY —) SLINK ABORTIVE

(WELL —) FREE EUGENIC

(SUFF.) GEN(E)(ESIA)(ESIS)(ETIC)(IC)(IN)(OUS)(Y)

BORNE RODE NARROW CARRIED ENDURED

(— AFFRONTEE) CABOCHED

(— LOWER THAN USUAL) ABASED

(— ON WATER) AFLOAT

BORNEO

BAY: ADANG KUMAI SAMPIT

CAPE: ARU DATU LOJAR PUTING SAMBAR SELATAN

MOUNTAIN: RAJA SARAN NIJAAN TEBANG

MOUNTAINS: IRAN MULLER SCHWANER

NAME: KALIMANTAN

NATIVE: DYAK DAJAK

RIVER: ARUT IWAN BAHAU BERAU KAJAN PADAS PAWAN BARITO KAPUAS SEBUKU KAHAJAN MAHAKAM MENDAWI PEMBUANG

TOWN: KUMAI SAMBAS SAMPIT MALINAU PAGATAN SANGGAU SINTANG TARAKAN KETAPANG

TREE: KAPOR KAPUR

WEIGHT: PARA CHAPAH

BORO MARIANA
BORON BORAX ULEXITE
BORORO COROADO
BOROUGH BURG CITY PORT TOWN
WICK BORGO BRUSH BURGH
CASTLE COUNTY CITADEL
FORTESS VILLAGE TOWNSHIP
(SUFF.) BURG
BORROW BOT BITE COPY HIRE
KICK LOAN SHIN TAKE THIG
ADOPT STEAL TOUCH DESUME
DUPLEX PLEDGE STRIKE SURETY
CHEVISE HOSTAGE MUTUATE
TITHING
BORROWED SECONDHAND
BORROWER BOT CRIB MUTUARY
BORS (BROTHER OF —) BAN
(UNCLE OF —) LANCELOT
BOS OX NEAT TAURUS
BOSH END ROT JOKE SHOW TALK
TOSH FUDGE TRASH BUSHWA
FIGURE FLAUNT HUMBUG TRIVIA
TOSHERY GALBANUM NONSENSE
POPPYCOCK
BOSKY BUSHY TIPSY WOODY
FUDDLED
BOSNIA-HERZEGOVINA (RIVER OF
—) BOSNA DRINA NERETVA
(TOWN OF —) TUZLA MAGLAJ
MOSTAR VISOKO SARAJEVO
BOSOM LAP BARM BUST CLOSE
DICKY HEART SINUS BREAST
CAVITY DESIRE DICKEY RECESS
BELOVED EMBRACE GREMIAL
INCLOSE INTIMATE POITRINE
(— OF DRESS) SQUARE
(FALSE —) PLUMPER
BOSS BUR HUB MOP NOB ORB PAD
POP BAAS BEAD BOCE BUHR
BURR COCK CZAR KNOB KNOP
KNOT NAIL NAVE NULL STUD
TSAR BULLA BULLY BWANA CHIEF
EMPTY JEWEL KNOSP ORDER
OWNER PEARL ANCHOR BROOCH
BUCKRA BUTTON CHEESE DIRECT
HOLLOW HONCHO MANAGE
MASTER OCULUS PATERA PELLET
SHIELD BULLION CACIQUE
CAPATAZ CAPTAIN CUSHION
FOREMAN HASSOCK HEADMAN
HOBNAIL MANAGER PADRONE
PHALERA SPANGLE SPONSON
DIRECTOR DOMINEER MISERERE
OMPHALOS OVERSEER UMBILICUS
(— OF LOGGING CAMP) BULLY
(— OF SHIELD) UMBO
(FIRE —) GASMAN
(LEATHER —) BUTTON
(MINE —) SHIFTER SHIFTMAN
(POLITICAL —) CACIQUE CAUDILLO
(STRAW —) BULL LEADER
(PREF.) UMBO
BOSSY PUSHY
BOSTONIAN HUBBITE
BOTANIST **AMERICAN** AMES BEAL
COOK GRAY HOWE ROSE BROWN
CLUTE GAGER HEALD JAMES
JONES LOGAN MOORE PURSH
SEARS SHULL SMALL VASEY
BAILEY BESSEY CANNON CARVER

CUTLER DUDLEY DUGGAR
FARLOW HARRIS HOWELL JEPSON
LEMMON PEIRCE SHANTZ TAYLOR
TORREY WATSON BARTRAM
BIGELOW BRITTON COULTER
CROCKER ELLIOTT FERNALD
GOODALE HOLLICK JOHNSON
MERRILL PEATTIE POLLARD
RYDBERG SWINGLE THURBER
CALDWELL CAMPBELL COPELAND
KNOWLTON MARSHALL TRELEASE
BLAKESLEE FAIRCHILD
LONGWORTH NIEUWLAND
OSTERHOUT SULLIVANT
UNDERWOOD CHAMBERLAIN
AUSTRIAN UNGER KERNER
MENDEL JACQUIN HABERLANDT
BELGIAN LINDEN
CANADIAN SAUNDERS
DANISH HANSEN WARMING
JOHANNSEN RAUNKIAER
DUTCH TREUB DODOENS
ENGLISH WARD BOWER BUDDLE
CLARKE DARWIN GERARD
HOOKER HUDSON MARTYN
PAXTON TURNER BENNETT
FORSYTH HAWORTH HENSLOW
JACKSON LINDLEY DRYANDER
SIBTHORP BABINGTON
FRENCH BORNET MAGNOL MIRBEL
THURET TRECUL BONNIER
JUSSIEU LECLUSE MICHAUX
TULASNE DECAISNE MILLARDET
JACQUEMONT TOURNEFORT
VANTIEGHEM DESFONTAINES
GERMAN BOCK COHN KOCH LINK
MOHL ZINN BLUME DRUDE
FUCHS KUNTH SACHS ENGLER
GLOXIN GMELIN GOEBEL HEDWIG
KUNTZE MIGULA REINKE
CORRENS EICHLER FITTING
GARTNER JUNGIUS KARSTEN
KUTZING MOLISCH PFEFFER
RIVINUS WARBURG BRUNFELS
LEDEBOUR LONITZER SPRENGEL
DILLENIUS GRISEBACH
KOLREUTER CAMERARIUS
HOFMEISTER PRINGSHEIM
REICHENBACH STRASBURGER
HUNGARIAN ENDLICHER
IRISH HARVEY
ITALIAN TONI CORTI ALPINI
BECCARI CESALPINO
JAPANESE IKENO
NORWEGIAN GUNNERUS
RUSSIAN BUNGE FAMINTSYN
SCOTTISH AITON BROWN
DOUGLAS FORTUNE MORISON
FALCONER
SPANISH CAVANILLES
SWEDISH DAHL KALM FRIES
RETZIUS ACHARIUS AFZELIUS
LINNAEUS THUNBERG
ANDERSSON BROMELIUS
SWISS BAUHIN VAUCHER
CANDOLLE
BOTANY HERBARISM PHYTOLOGY
BOTCH MAR MUX BOIL BOSS FLUB
MEND MESS MULL SORE BITCH
BODGE BUTCH FLUFF FUDGE
SPOIL STICK BOGGLE BOLLIX
BUMBLE BUNGLE COBBLE JUMBLE

MUCKER REPAIR TINKER
BLUNDER BUTCHER CLAMPER
SCAMBLE SCLATCH SLUBBER
SWELLING
BOTCHER GRILSE SALMON TINKER
BUNGLER BUTCHER CLOUTER
COBBLER
BOTCHERY PATCHERY
BOTE KINBOT MAGBOTE CARTBOTE
FRITHBOT PLOWBOTE WAINBOTE
BOTFLY BOTT BREEZE GADBEE
GADFLY NITTER CANOPID
OESTRID TORSALO DIPTERAN
OESTRIAN
BOTH BO ALL TWO BAITH EQUALLY
(PREF.) AMBI AMBO AMPH(I)(O)
BIS
(— SIDES) AMPHI
BOTHER ADO AIL BUG IRK NAG
VEX FASH FAZE FUSS JADE WORK
ANNOY DEAVE KNOCK PHASE
TEASE TRADE WORRY BADGER
BUSTLE CUMBER DITHER FLURRY
GRAVEL HARASS MEDDLE MITHER
MOIDER MOLEST MUCKLE PESTER
PLAGUE POTHER POTTER PUTTER
PUZZLE TAMPER CONFUSE
DISTURB FASHERY GRIZZLE
PERPLEX TERRIFY TRACHLE
TROUBLE BEWILDER DISTRESS
IRRITATE NUISANCE
BOTOCUDO BORUN AIMORE
AYMORO
BOTONEE TREFLEE FLEURONE
BO TREE PIPAL

BOTSWANA
CAPITAL: GABORONE GABERONES
COIN: RAND
DESERT: KALAHARI
LAKE: DOW NGAMI
LANGUAGE: BANTU CLICK
KHOISAN SETSWANA
MOUNTAIN: TSODILO
NATIVE: BANTU TSWANA
BUSHMAN
RIVER: NATA OKWA CHOBE
NOSOB CUANDO MOLOPO
SHASHI CUBANGO LIMPOPO
OKAVANGO
TOWN: KANYE ORAPA TSANE
SEROWE LOBOTSI MOCHUDI
PALAPYE THAMAGA
GABERONES

BOTTLE JUG BOSS SKIN VIAL VIOL
AMPUL ASKOS BETTY BOCAL
BUIRE BURET CADUS COOJA
CROFT CRUET CRUSE FIFTH
FLASK GIRBA GLASS GOURD
HOUSE PHIAL SPLIT VERRE
ALUDEL BACBUC BUNDLE CARAFE
CARBOY CASTER CASTOR CHAGUL
CHATTY CREWET DORUCK
DUBBER FESSEL FIASCO FLACON
FLAGON GOGLET GUTTUS
JORDAN LAGENA MAGNUM
MARINE MATARA NURSER
PACKER SIPHON VESSEL WOULFF
BALLOON BIBERON BOMBARD
BOMBOLA BURETTE CANTEEN
CARAFON COSTREL DEADMAN

FLACKET FLOATER GRENADE
INKHORN BOMBONNE BORACHIO
BUILDING CALABASH DECANTER
DEMIJOHN GARDEVIN JEROBOAM
MARIOTTE PRESERVE REHOBOAM
PEPPERBOX
(— IN WICKER) CARBOY DEMIJOHN
(EGYPTIAN —) DORUCK
(EMPTY —) MARINE
(HOT-WATER —) PIG
(LARGE —) KIT JEROBOAM
(LEATHER —) BOOT JACK DUBBA
BUDGET DUBBER DUPPER
MATARA BOMBARD BORACHIO
WHINNOCK WINESKIN
(OVERSIZED —) BALTHAZAR
(PAIR OF —S) GEMEL GEMMEL
(PART OF —) LIP CORK KICK NECK
PUNT MOUTH MUZZLE CAPSULE
SHOULDER
(PILGRIM'S —) AMPULLA
(SMALL —) VIAL AMPUL PHIAL
SPLIT FLACON AMPOULE TICKLER
CRUISKEN CRUISKEEN
(18 —S OF WINE) RIDDLE
(40 —S) KEMPLE
(PREF.) UTRI
BOTTLE CAP CAPSULE
BOTTLE CARRIER FASCET
BOTTLE CASE CELLAR
BOTTLEHEAD DOEGLING
BOTTLER COOPER
BOTTOM ASS BED ARSE BASE
DALE DOUP FLAT FOND FOOT
FUND HOLM LEES REAR ROOT
ABYSS BASIS DREGS FLOOR LAIGH
NADIR BATHOS FOUNCE FUNDUS
GROUND GUTTER LAAGTE LEEGTE
BEDROCK LOWLAND SUPPORT
SURFACE BUTTOCKS INTERVAL
SEDIMENT TETRAPOD
(— OF BENCH) TOE
(— OF CUPOLA) HEARTH
(— OF FURROW) SOLE
(— OF PAGE) TAIL
(— OF PISTOL GRIP) BUTT
(— OF POT) POTSTONE
(— OF PRINTER'S GALLEY) SLICE
(— OF PULLEY BLOCK) BREECH
(— OF SEA) GROUND BENTHOS
(— OF SOLE) NAUMK NAUMKEAG
(MARSHY —) SIKE
(ROCK —) HARDPAN
(PL.) HOLM HOLME
BOTTOM-DWELLING DEMERSAL
BOTTOMER FOOTMAN
STATIONMAN
BOTTOMLAND STRATH
BOTTOMLESS ABYSMAL
BOTULISM LAMSIEKTE LAMZIEKTE
BOUDOIR ROOM BOWER CABIN
BEDROOM CABINET
BOUGH ARM LEG LIMB TWIG
CHUCK SHOOT SPRAY SPRIG
BRANCH RAMAGE SHROUD
GALLOWS PHYLLIS OFFSHOOT
SHOULDER
(— ON TAVERN) BUSH
(— USED AS TORCH) ROUGHIE
(PL.) RAMAGE DUNNAGE
RAMMAGE
BOUGHT KEFT

STORE ZEBINA
BOUGIE CANDLE COLLYRIE
FILIFORM
BOULDER NOB KELK KNOB ROCK
STONE GIBBER BOOTHER
DORNICK ERRATIC GRAYBACK
HARDHEAD MEGALITH POTSTONE
BOULE BIRNE
BOULEVARD DRIVE PRADO
AVENUE STREET ALAMEDA
HIGHWAY TERRACE CORNICHE
BOULTER TRAWL SPILLER SPILLET
BOUNCE DAP HOP BANG BLOW
BRAG BUMP DING DIRD FIRE
GATE JUMP LEAP SACK STOT
BOAST BOUND BULLY CAROM
CHUCK EJECT KNOCK SCOLD
THUMP VERVE BLAGUE MORGAY
SPIRIT SPRING STRIKE ADDRESS
BLUSTER CHOUNCE DISMISS
REBOUND SWAGGER PROCLAIM
RICOCHET
BOUNCER CHUCKER SCROUGER
BOUNCING BIG BUXOM LUSTY
STOUT BOUNCY HEALTHY
WALLOPING
(— OF TONGUE) FLAP
BOUNCING BET SOAPWORT
BOUND DAP END HOP LOP BENT
BIND BOND BONE BROW BUTT
DART GIRT JUMP LEAP LIST MERE
RAMP RISE SCUD SKIP STEM STOT
SURE TERM WALL AMBIT BORNE
BOURN FIXED GOING LIMIT
READY SALLY SCOUP SKELP
START STEND STING TILED VAULT
VERGE BORDER BOUNCE BOURNE
BUTTAL CAVORT CURVET DEFINE
DOMAIN FINISH GAMBOL GIRDED
HURDLE JETTED LIABLE LOLLOP
OBLIGE PRANCE SPRING AFFINED
BARRIER CERTAIN CHAINED
CLOSURE CONFINE CONTAIN
COSTIVE DELIMIT DRESSED
GAMBADO INCLUDE REBOUND
SALTATE SECURED SUBSULT
TERMINE TRUSSED BOUNDARY
CONFINED DESTINED ENCLOSED
FASCIATE FRONTIER HANDFAST
LANDMARK LIMITATE OBLIGATE
PINIONED PRECINCT PREPARED
RESTRICT SHACKLED
(— BY OATH) SWORN
(— BY OBLIGATION) AFFINED
(NOT —) SOLUTE
(RIGIDLY —) STATIC STATICAL
(PL.) PALE AMBIT MOUND
CLOSURE COMPASS CONFINE
PURLIEUS PERIPHERY
BOUNDARY AHU END RIM DOLE
DOOL EDGE FINE FORM LINE LIST
MARK MEAR MEER MERE META
METE PALE SURF TERM TRIG
WALL AMBIT BOURN CLOSE
FENCE FRAME FRONT HEDGE
LIMES LIMIT MARCH MEITH
MOUND SHORE VERGE BORDER
COLLET DEFINE OCTROI OCTROY
TROPIC BARRIER BOUNDER
BUTTING COMPASS FURLONG
OUTLINE CURBLINE FRONTIER
LANDLINE LIMITARY PRECINCT
TERMINUS UMSTROKE PERIMETER

PERIPHERY MAGNETOPAUSE
(PL.) ABUTTALS ENVIRONS
(PREF.) HORO LIMI ORI TERMINO
(— OF AIR MASS) FRONTO
BOUNDER ROUE
BOUNDLESS VAST UNTOLD
ENDLESS ETERNAL INFINITE
UNLIMITED
BOUNTEOUS BOON CROWNED
LIBERAL PLENTEOUS
BOUNTIFUL GOOD LUSH RICH
AMPLE FREELY LAVISH LIBERAL
PROFUSE ABUNDANT GENEROUS
BOUNTY BOON GIFT MEED AWARD
BONUS GRANT LARGE VALOR
WORTH BONTEE REWARD VIRTUE
LARGESS PREMIUM PRESENT
PROWESS SUBSIDY DONATIVE
GOODNESS GRATUITY KINDNESS
BOUQUET BOB AURA ODOR POSY
AROMA BLOOM CIGAR POSEY
SHEAF SPRAY BOWPOT BUSKET
SHOWER CORSAGE NOSEGAY
BOUGHPOT
(— GARNI) FAGOT FAGGOT
BOURGEOIS ORGON COMMON
POOTER STUPID BOORISH
BURGHER
BOURGEOIS GENTILHOMME
(AUTHOR OF —) MOLIERE
(CHARACTER IN —) CLEANTE
LUCILLE COVIELLE JOURDAIN
BOURSE BOLSA BORSE CAMBIO
BOURTREE ELDER
BOUT GO JOB BOOT FALL PULL
TURN BOOZE BRASH CRASH
ESSAY FIGHT MATCH PLUCK
ROUND TRIAL VENNY VENUE
ATTACK COURSE FRACAS YOKING
ASSAULT ATTEMPT CAROUSE
CIRCUIT CONTEST DEBAUCH
OUTSIDE WITHOUT CONFLICT
(DRINKING —) BAT BEND BUST
TIRL BOOZE SPRAY SPREE
RANDAN SCREED SPLORE
CAROUSE GAEDOWN WASSAIL
POTATION
BOUTONNIERE BOUQUET
BUTTONHOLE
BOUW BAHU BAHOE
BOVATE OSKEN OXGANG OXGATE
OXLAND
(TWO —S) HUSBANDLAND
BOVINE OX BOS COW BOSS BULL
CALF DULL NEAT SLOW ZEBU
BEAST BISON STEER ANIMAL
COWISH HUMLIE HUMMEL OXLIKE
ROTHER BULLOCK TAURINE
BANGTAIL LEPTOBOS
BOW ARC LEG LUG NOD SAW TIE
YEW ARCH BAIL BEAK BECK BEND
BENT CURB DUCK FOLD FORE
GORA JOUK KNEE KNOT LATH
LOUT MOVE PROW SELF STEM
SWIM TRUE TURN WEND BINGE
CLINE CONGE COQUE COUCH
CROOK CRUSH CURVE DEFER
GOURA HONOR KNEEL NOEUD
SHIKO STICK STOOP VENIE YIELD
ARCHER ASSENT BAUBLE BUCKLE
CONGEE CRINGE CROUCH CURTSY
FIDDLE FOGBOW RIBBON SALAAM
SALUTE SCRAPE SUBMIT SWERVE

TOURTE WEAPON DEPRESS
FOREBOW FORMBOW HANDBOW
INCLINE INFLECT LONGBOW
NECKTIE RAINBOW ARBALEST
COURTESY CRESCENT ENTRANCE
FOGEATER GREETING
STONEBOW TRUELOVE
OBEISANCE
(— DOWN) ALOUT HUMBLE
(— IN ONE PIECE) SELF
(— LOW) BINGE
(— OF PLOW) DRAIL
(— OF VESSEL) HEAD PROW STEM
ENTRANCE
(— ON SCRAPER) BAIL BALE
(— ON SEA) ATRY
(— OUTWARD) CONVEX
(— SLIGHTLY) ADDRESS
(OVERHANGING —) SWIM
(PART OF —) DIP TIP BACK FACE
GRIP LIMB LOOP NOCK BELLY
BRIDGE HANDLE RECURVE
SERVING BOWSTRING
(PART OF VIOLIN —) NUT TIP FROG
HAIR HEAD POINT SCREW STICK
(PREF.) ARCI ARCO TOX(I)(ICO)(O)
BOWED ARCO BENT BANDY KNEED
ARCATE ARCATO CURVED
BULGING CURVANT SHAMBLE
DOWNBENT
(PREF.) TOX(I)(O)
BOWELS GUT GUTS WOMB BELLY
COLON ROPES VISCERA ENTRAILS
(PREF.) VISCER(I)(O)
BOWER RUN BOOR JACK NOOK
SALE ABODE ARBOR JOKER
KNAVE ANCHOR BOWERY LEFSEL
PANDAL BERCEAU CABINET
CHAMBER COTTAGE EMBOWER
ENCLOSE LEVESEL PERGOLA
RETREAT SHELTER TRELLIS
THALAMUS
(— FOR SNAKES) KISI
(GARDEN —) ALCOVE
BOWERBIRD CATBIRD
COLLARBIRD
BOWFIN AMIA GANOID LAWYER
MORGAY SAWYER CHOUPIC
DOGFISH GRINDAL GRINDLE
GRINNEL MUDFISH
BOWIE STATE ARKANSAS
BOWING CERNUOUS FEATHERING
BOWL CAP CUP PAN TUN COUP
ROLL TASS TRAY WOOD ARENA
BASIN BOWIE DEPAS GUARD
JORUM KITTY LAVER MAZER
PHIAL PITCH ROGAN SCALE
TANOA TAZZA TREEN TROLL
BEAKER BICKER CHAWAN CLOSET
COOTIE CRATER FESSEL JICARA
KETTLE LEKANE MAZARD
MORTAR PIGGIN TROUGH
TUREEN VESSEL BRIMMER
DITCHER DOUBLER DUGGLER
SCYPHUS SKYPHOS SPILLER
STADIUM TOUCHER TRINDLE
TRUNDLE WHISKIN AQUARIUM
BRIDECUP FISHBOWL JEROBOAM
LAVATORY MONTEITH REHOBOAM
PORRINGER
(— ILLEGALLY) JERK
(— OF PIPE) CHILLUM STUMMEL
(— ON PEDESTAL) TAZZA SALVER

(— OUT) YORK
(— THAT TOUCHED JACK) TOUCHER
(— WITH TWO HANDLES) CAP
DEPAS
(DRINKING —) TUN TASS
(MARBLE CUTTER'S —) SEBILLA
(OBLONG —) PITCHI
(PUNCH —) SNEAKER
(SHALLOW —) CAP COUPE
WHISKIN
(SMALL —) JACK
(SOUP —) ECUELLE
(SUGAR —) SUGAR SUCRIER
(TOILET —) HOPPER
(WOODEN —) CAP BOWIE COGIE
KITTY ROGAN BASSIE BICKER
COGGIE COOTIE
BOWLEG OUTKNEE
BOWLEGGED BANDY VALGUS
BOWLER HAT POT DERBY KEGLER
PINMAN SPINNER TRUNDLER
(CRICKET —S) ATTACK
BOWLINE BOWLIN FARGOOD
BOWLING BOWLS ATTACK
KEGLING TENPINS
BOWLS RINK BOCCE BOCCIE
BOWMAN ARCHER
BOW-SHAPED ARCATE
BOWSTRING SERVING
BOWYER BOWER ARTILLER
BOX BED BIN CAR EAR FUR GIG KIT
LOB LUG PIX PYX TYE ARCA BARK
BODY BOOT CAGE CAJA CASE
CIST CRIB CUFF CYST DRAB FLAT
HEAD LOGE MILL PACK PUNG
SCOB SEAT SLAP SLUG SPAR
STOW TILL TRAY ARBOR BARGE
BIJOU BOIST BUIST BUXUS
CADDY CAPSA CHEST CLOUT
CRATE FIGHT FRAME HUTCH
LADLE POUCH PUNCH SHRUB
STALL TRUNK ASCHAM BRUISE
BUFFET BUNKER CARTON CASKET
COFFER COFFIN DRAWER GRILLE
HAMPER HATBOX HAYBOX
HOPPER ICEBOX MAROON
MOCUCK PATRON PETARA PILLAR
SAGGER SHRINE STRIKE TARBOX
VANITY ARCANUM BANDBOX
BATTERY BOXTREE BOXWOOD
CABINET CAISSON CARRIER
CASHBOX CASQUET CASSONE
COFFRET CONFINE COREBOX
DICEBOX DREDGER DUSTBOX
ENCLOSE EXHAUST FOSTELL
FREEZER HANAPER JACKBOX
PACKAGE PILLBOX PITARAH
PRINTER SANDBOX SCATULA
SHELTER TRUMMEL WHERRET
BOXTHORN DOVECOTE DRAGEOIR
JUNCTION LAVARIUM MATCHBOX
POMANDER SHOWCASE SLIPCASE
SOLANDER SWEATBOX
PEPPERBOX PHYLACTERY
(— FOR CARRYING COAL) DAN
(— FOR CUTLERY) CANTEEN
(— FOR FIRE) CHAUFFER
(— FOR FISH) CAR NID
(— FOR MONEY OFFERING) ARCA
LADLE
(— FOR SALT) DRAB
(— FOR SEAL) SKIPPET
(— FOR SEED) LEAP

(— FOR TOBACCO) BUTT DOSS CADDY SARATOGA
(— IN TIMEPIECE) BARREL
(— IN WHEEL HUB) FUR
(— OF BIRCHBARK) MOCUCK
(— OF CYLINDER) BUSH
(— OF FIRE CLAY) SAGGAR SAGGER
(— OF ORGAN) BOOT SWELL
(— TO SHELTER BELL) SCONCE
(— USED AS DARKROOM) TENT
(BERRY —) HALLOCK
(BREAD —) BARGE
(CANDLE —) BARK
(CIRCULAR —) THIMBLE
(COLLECTION —) BROD
(COMPASS —) KETTLE BINNACLE
(FANCY —) ETUI ETWEE
(FLOATING —) CAISSON
(FOUNDRY —) FRAME
(IRON —) HANGER
(JUGGLER'S —) TRANKA
(MONEY —) CASH SAFE PIRLIE
(PERFUME —) CASSOLETTE
(PIVOTING —) TOUR
(PRINTING —) TURTLE
(REFRIGERATOR —) COOLER
(SHALLOW —) FLAT BACKET HARBOR
(SNUFF —) MILL MULL
(TEA —) CADDY
(TIN —) TRUMMEL VASCULUM
(PREF.) CAPSULI CAPSULO CISTO PYXID(O)
BOX BRIER INDIGO INKBERRY
BOXCAR LOWRY STOCKCAR
BOX ELDER MAPLE NEGUNDO
BOXER PUG CHAMP DARES BANTAM MILLER NOBBER TANKER WELTER BRUISER CRUISER FIGHTER SLUGGER SPARRER BUFFETER PUGILIST SOUTHPAW
BOXFISH CHAPIN COWFISH SHELLFISH TRUNKFISH
BOXING PLUG RING SAVATE PARINGS SCIENCE SPARRING
(— GLOVE) MUFFLE
BOX TORTOISE COOTER
BOXWOOD KNYSNA DUDGEON
BOXY BLOCKY
BOY BO BUB FAG GUY HIM LAD PUR TAD BOYO CHAP LOON NINO PAGE PUER BILLY BUBBY BUDDY CHABO CHILD CRACK GAMIN GILPY GROOM KNAVE PUTTO ROGUE SWAIN VALET YOUTH BIRKIE BUTTON CALLAN CHOKRA GAFFER GARCON MANNIE MASTER NIPPER RASCAL SHAVER STIRRA UMFAAN URCHIN BOUCHAL CALLANT DRAWBOY GLEANER GOSSOON GRUMMET JACKBOY RUBBLER SERVANT SPADGER TRAPPER CLERGION HENCHBOY MUCHACHO SPALPEEN
(— DRESSED AS WOMAN) MALINCHE
(— OF FREE BIRTH) CAMILLUS
(ALTAR —) ACOLYTE THURIFER
(AWKWARD —) CUB CALF GRUMMET
(BOLD —) SPALPEEN
(CHIMNEY SWEEPER'S —) CHUMMY

(CHOIR —) CHILD
(CLEANING —) BUSBOY
(COLLIER'S —) HODDER
(EFFEMINATE —) SISSY MOLLYCODDLE
(ERRAND —) GALOPIN
(FIRST-YEAR —) GYTE
(HEAD —) SENIOR CAPTAIN
(ILL-MANNERED —) CUB
(MISCHIEVOUS —) NICKUM
(MY —) AVICK
(NATIVE —) MOWGLI
(NON-JEWISH —) SHEGETZ
(OFFICE —) DUFTRY DUFTERY
(PERT —) CRACK
(POOR —) HERO
(ROGUISH —) CRACK GAMIN URCHIN
(SAUCY —) NACKET
(SERVING —) KNAVE PEDEE CHOKRA MOUSSE FOOTBOY GOSSOON
(SILLY —) CALF
(SMALL —) BO BUDDY UMFAAN SPADGER
(SPRIGHTLY —) CRACK
(STABLE —) MAFU MAFOO MEHTAR
(TOWN —) CAD
(YOUNG —) LAD SONNY YOUTH NIPPER
(PL.) BOYHOOD
(PREF.) PAED(O) PAID(O) PED(O)
BOYCOTT MITE SHUN AVOID DEBAR BLACKBALL
BOYFRIEND BEAU STEADY
BRABANTIO (DAUGHTER OF —) DESDEMONA
BRACE LEG MAN TIE TWO BEND BIND CASE FRAP GIRD JACK KNEE LACE MARK PAIR PROP SPUR STAY STEM STUD CLAMP CRANK DWANG GIRTH HOUND NERVE POISE RIDER SHORE STOCK STRUT ANKLET BINDER BRACHE CLENCH COLLAR COUPLE CRUTCH FASTEN FATHOM HURTER SPLINT STRING WIMBLE BOTTINE BRACKET EMBRACE REFRESH SPANNER STIFFEN SUPPORT ACCOLADE BITBRACE BITSTALK BITSTOCK BUTTRESS CROSSBAR ENCIRCLE
(— A YARD) TRAVERSE
(— ACROSS CABLE) STUD
(— AND HALF) LEASH
(— BETWEEN FRAMES) TOM
(— FOR POST) SPUR
(— UP) ACCINGE SHARPEN
(PART OF —) BOW HEAD JAWS PAWL RING CHUCK CRANK QUILL SHELL HANDLE RATCHET
(PL.) BRIDGING
BRACED BENT
(— ABACK) ABOX
BRACELET BAND RING ARMIL CHAIN ARMLET BANGLE GRIVNA ARMILLA CIRCLET MANACLE POIGNET RACETTE WRISTER BARRULET HANDCUFF MUFFETEE WRISTLET
(— USED AS MONEY) MANILLA
(SHELL —) SANKHA

BRACER TONIC SHORER BLOCKER ARMGUARD STIFFENER STIMULANT
BRACHIAL HUMERAL
BRACHIOPOD ATREMATE ATRYPOID SPIRIFER
BRACHIUM ARM
BRACHYCEPHALIC ROUNDHEADED
BRACING CRISP QUICK TONIC DUNNAGE
BRACKEN FERN TARA BRAKE PLAID
BRACKET BIBB COCK CONK FORK GATE PUNK ANCON BELOW BRACE CLASS CONCH COUCH CRANE CRANK CROOK LEVEL SHELF STRUT TRUSS ANCONE BECKET BRIDGE CORBEL COUPLE GUSSET HANGER LADDER MUTULE SADDLE SCONCE BECKETT CONSOLE DERRICK FEATHER FIXTURE GATELEG LOOKOUT POTENCE SPONSON SPOTTED BRAGWORT CATEGORY CROTCHET MISERERE SPECKLED STRADDLE MODILLION CANTILEVER
(PL.) HOOKS CROOKS
BRACKISH YAR FOIST SALTY BRACKY SALINE BREACHY SALTISH NAUSEOUS
BRACT HUSK LEAF GLUME LEMMA PALEA PALET SCALE SPADIX SPATHE BRACTLET PHYLLARY
BRACTEOLE PROPHYLL
BRAD PIN NAIL PRIG RIVET SPRIG
BRADAMANT (BROTHER OF —) RINALDO
(HUSBAND OF —) ROGERO
BRAE BANK BRAY BROW HILL CLEVE SLOPE WOUGH CLEEVE VALLEY
BRAG GAB JET BLAH BLAW BLOW CROW DEFY FACE HUFF PUFF WIND WOST YELP BLUFF BOAST CRACK FLIRD PREEN SKITE STRUT VAUNT BLEEZE BOUNCE INSULT SPLORE SPROSE SQUIRT DISPLAY GAUSTER ROISTER SWAGGER BRAGGART FLOURISH PRETENSE THREATEN
BRAGGART BRAG PUFF BOAST FACER BLOWER CROWER GASCON HECTOR POTGUN SKITER THRASO BLOWOFF BOASTER BOBADIL BOUNCER CRACKER RUFFLER SHALLOW VAPORER BANGSTER BLOWHARD CACAFUGO FANFARON PAROLLES PUCKFIST RENOWNER RODOMONT SKIPJACK
BRAGGARTISM COCKALORUM
BRAGGING ROOSE JACTANCE RODOMONT THRASONIC
BRAHMA KA SELF BRAMAH
BRAHMAN ARYAN HINDU PUNDIT SMARTA BRAHMIN
BRAID CUE BRAY GIMP JERK LACE PLAT TAIL TRIM BREDE FANCY FREAK JIFFY LACET MILAN ONSET ORRIS PLAIT PLEAT QUEUE START TAGAL TRACE TRADE TRESS

TRICK TWINE VOMIT WEAVE BOBBIN BORDER CORDON EDGING GALLON LACING MOMENT PLIGHT RIBBON RICRAC SENNET SNATCH STRING BANDING BULLION CAPRICE ENTWINE UPBRAID BRANDISH ORNAMENT REPROACH RICKRACK SOUTACHE TRIMMING
(— FOR HATS) SENNET SINNET
(— OF WIG) SNAKE
(LINEN —) INKLE
BRAIDER RATCHER
BRAIDING FROG BREDE
BRAIN MAD BEAN HARN MIND PATE UTAC WITS AXION HAIRN HAURN SKULL NODDLE PSYCHE FURIOUS SENSORY THINKER CEREBRUM
(PL.) HARN PATE SCONCE HEADPIECE
(PREF.) CEREBELLI CEREBELLO CEREBR(I)(O) ENCEPHAL(O)
(SUFF.) ENCEPHALIA ENCEPHALUS ENCEPHALY
BRAINLESS SILLY STUPID FOOLISH WITLESS
BRAINPAN PAN HARNPAN PANNICLE
BRAIN SAND SABULUM
BRAIZE BECKER
BRAKE COW BULL BURR CAGE CLOG CURB DRAG FERN LOCK RACK SKID SLOW STAY TARA TRAP TRIG BLOCK CHECK COPSE DELAY DETER GRIPE SNARE SPOKE SPRAG VOMIT BRIDLE CONVOY HARROW HINDER REMORA RETARD STAYER WARABI BRACKEN DEADMAN DILEMMA SLIPPER STOPPER THICKET TRIGGER DRAGROPE RETARDER
BRAKEMAN GUARD SHACK SHAKE BRAKIE NIPPER DILLIER SNAPPER SWAMPER DILLYMAN INCLINER TRAINMAN
BRAKES ANCHORS
BRAMBLE WHIN BRIER RHAMN THIEF THORN BUMBLE JAGGER LAWYER STICKER DEWBERRY MAYBERRY NESSBERRY
(PREF.) BATO
BRAMBLE BUSH TUTU GRANJENO
BRAMBLING KATE SNOWHAMMER
BRAMBLY DUMAL SPINY THORNY PRICKLY
BRAN GRIT SEED DARAK TREAT CEREAL CHESIL CHISEL POLLARD TOPPING BEESWING
(— AND MEAL) SHORTS
(CORNMEAL —) HUSK
(FINE —) POLLEN
(UNSORTED —) RUBBLES
(PREF.) PITYRO
BRANCH ARM BOW COW KOW LAP LEG LOP RAY RUN BARB BROG BUSH CHAT FANG FORK LIMB PALM PART RAME RICE RISE SNAG SNUG SPUR STEM STUD TANG TWIG YARD AXITE BAYOU BOUGH BREAK BRIAR BRIER CREEK DRUPA GRAIN LAYER LULOV PLASH PRONG RAMUS

REISE SCROG SHOOT SHRAG SPRAY SPRIG STICK TWIST VIMEN WITHE BUREAU CLADUS DIVIDE DRUKPA EXOPOD GERMEN GREAVE GROWTH LEADER MEMBER OFFSET OUTLET PHYLUM PORTIO RADDLE RAMAGE RAMIFY RUNNER SHROUD SPRANG STOLON STREAM TAPOUN CHAPTER CLADODE DIALECT DIVERGE ENDOPOD FURCATE LATERAL PHYLLIS RAMULUS TENDRIL TORRENT ANAPHYTE BRONCHUS DISTRICT EFFLUENT OFFSHOOT PEASTICK SCAFFOLD SPRANGLE TRAILING PHYLLOCLADE RAMIFICATION
(— OF ANTLER) SPELLER ADVANCER
(— OF COLONY) STIPE
(— OF CRAFT) INDUSTRY
(— OF FAMILY) SEPT
(— OF FEATHER) BARB
(— OF HORN) RIAL ANTLER
(— OF IVY) BUSH
(— OF LEARNING) ART STUDY FACULTY KNOWLEDGE
(— OF MATHEMATICS) ALGEBRA CALCULUS
(— OF THALLUS) STICHID
(— OF TREASURY) FISCUS
(DEAD —) FLAG
(EVERGREEN —S) GREENS
(LANGUAGE —) INDIC
(LOCAL —) COURT
(MINE —) LEADER
(PALM —) LULAB
(RAILWAY —) LYE
(SMALL —) RICE
(YOUNGER —) CADET
(PL.) LOFT RAMI SKIRT SPRAY RAMAGE CYPRESS DEADWOOD
(PREF.) CLON(O) FRONDI RAMI RAMOSO RAMULI
(SUFF.) RAMOSE
BRANCHED FORKY FORKED RAMATE RAMOSE CLADOSE TROCHED RAMIFORM
(SUFF.) CLADOUS
BRANCHES
(SUFF.) (HAVING —) CLEMA
BRANCHIA GILL
BRANCHING ARMY RAMOSE FURCATE DICHOTOMY
BRANCHIOPOD SHRIMP
BRANCHLET RAMULUS SPILLER
BRAND BIRN BLOT BURN CHOP FLAW KIND MARK NOTE SEAR SMIT SMOT SORT VENT WIPE BUIST INURE LABEL SCEAR STAIN STAMP SWORD TAINT TORCH BARREL MARQUE STIGMA FLAMBEAU NAMEPLATE
BRANDIMART (SLAYER OF —) GRADASSO
(WIFE OF —) FLORDELIS
BRANDING IRON BRAND CAUTER SEARER CAUTERY
BRANDISH WAG DART STIR WAVE WIND BLESS BRAID SHAKE SWING WIELD FLAUNT HURTLE QUAVER RUFFLE STRAIN WINNOW

FLUTTER GLITTER SWAGGER VIBRATE WAMPISH FLOURISH VAMBRASH
BRANDY DOP VSO BOOF FINE JACK MARC VSOP BINGO MOBBY NANTS NANTZ PEACH RAKIA VVSOP CINDER COGNAC GRAPPA KIRSCH PUPELO RAKIJA VISNEY ANISADO AQUAVIT QUETSCH ARMAGNAC CALVADOS SLIVOVIC SLIVOVITZ AGUARDIENTE
BRANK MUMPS BRIDLE PILLORY
BRANLE BRAWL
BRANT ROUT ERECT PROUD QUINK SHEER STEEP ROUGHT
BRASH GAY BOLD FACY RASH HASTY NERVY SAUCY STORM ATTACK RUBBLE BRITTLE FORWARD IMPUDENT TACTLESS BALDFACED
BRASQUE STEEP
BRASS CASH ALLOY MONEY NERVE BRAZEN BRONZE MASLIN ORMOLU OFFICER ORICHALC
(— PLAYER) WINDJAMMER
(PREF.) CHALC(O) CHALK(O)
BRASSARD ARMBAND
BRASSEY BIB
BRASSIERE BANDEAU
BRASSY LOUD RUDE BRAZEN COARSE SHRILL IMPUDENT STRIDENT OVERBLOWN
BRAT BIB GET IMP BROT FILM SCUM APRON BAIRN BILSH BROLL CHILD CLOAK GAITT INFANT MANTLE TERROR URCHIN GARMENT BANTLING
BRATTICER AIRMAN CANVASMAN
BRAVADO POMP BRAVE PRIDE STORM HECTOR BLUSTER BOMBAST BRAVERY SWAGGER VAUNTERY GASCONISM
BRAVE BOLD BRAW DARE DEFY FACE FINE GAME GOOD PROW TALL WILD ADORN BOAST BRAVO BULLY FELON HARDY JOLLY MANLY MOODY ORPED ROMAN STIFF STOUT VAUNT WIGHT BRAWLY BREAST DARING HEROIC MANFUL PLUCKY SANNUP STURDY BRAVADO DOUGHTY GALLANT HAUTAIN SOLDIER SWAGGER VALIANT VENTURE WARRIOR CAVALIER DEFIANCE EMBOLDEN FEARLESS INTREPID LIONLIKE STALWART SUPERIOR VALOROUS VIRTUOUS
BRAVELY BIG FINELY
BRAVE NEW WORLD (AUTHOR OF —) HUXLEY
(CHARACTER IN —) JOHN MARX MOND CROWNE LENINA WATSON BERNARD MUSTAPHA HELMHOLTZ
BRAVERY GRIT VALOR SPIRIT VIRTUE BRAVADO BRAVURA COURAGE HEROISM JOLLITY MANHEAD MANHOOD PROWESS BOLDNESS CHIVALRY
BRAVO OLE RAH EUGE THUG BRAVE BULLY BANDIT CUTTER BRAVADO SHABASH VILLAIN APPLAUSE ASSASSIN

BRAWL DIN ROW BEEF CLEM DUST FRAY RIOT BLIND BROIL CHIDE CLASH FIGHT FLYTE MELEE REVEL SCOLD SCRAP AFFRAY BICKER FRACAS FRATCH HABBLE REVILE RUFFLE RUMPUS SHINDY STOUSH STRIFE TUMULT UPROAR YATTER BAGARRE BOBBERY BRABBLE BRANGLE DISCORD DISPUTE QUARREL SCUFFLE TUILYIE WRANGLE COMPLAIN RIXATION SQUABBLE STRAMASH
BRAWLER FRATCH NICKER SQUARER FRAMPLER NIGHTCAP OUTCRIER
BRAWLING NOISY BLATANT FLITING SCAMBLING SHEMOZZLE
BRAWN BEEF BOAR LIRE PORK FLESH SINEW FATTEN MUSCLE MANPOWER STRENGTH
(MOCK —) HEADCHEESE
BRAWNY BEEFY FLESHY ROBUST SINEWY SQUARE STRONG STURDY CALLOUS MUSCULAR POWERFUL STALWART
BRAXY BRADSOT
BRAY CRY MIX RUB BEAT ROUT TOOL CRUSH GRIND NOISE POUND STAMP BRUISE HEEHAW OUTCRY PESTLE THRASH WHINNY
BRAYERA KOSO CUSSO KOSSO
BRAZEN BOLD CALM HARD PERT BRASS HARDY HARSH SASSY AENEAN BRASSY BLATANT CALLOUS FORWARD IMMODEST IMPUDENT INSOLENT METALLIC
BRAZENFACED CHEEKY
BRAZIER HEARTH MANGAL BRASERO HIBACHI REREDOS SCALDINO
BRAZIL ROSET

BRAZIL
BAY: MARAJO IGRANDE SEPETIBA GUANABARA
BIRD: MITU MITUA
CAPE: FRIO BLANCO BUZIOS GURUPY ORANGE SAOTOME SAOROQUE
CAPITAL: BRASILIA
COIN: JOE REIS CONTO DOBRA HALFJOE MILREIS CRUZEIRO
DAM: FURNAS ITAIPU PEIXOTO
DANCE: SAMBA MAXIXE
ESTUARY: PARA
FALLS: IGUACU IGUASSU
INDIAN: ANTA ACROA ARARA ARAUA BRAVO CARIB GUANA ARAWAK CARAJA CARAYAN JAVAHAI TARIANA BOTOCUDO CHAMBIOA
ISLAND: MARACA MARAJO BANANAL CARDOSO CAVIANA MEXIANA COMPRIDA
LAKE: AIMA FEIA MIRIM
MEASURE: PE MOIO PIPA SACK VARA BRACA FANGA LEGOA MILHA PALMO PASSO TONEL CANADA COVADO CUARTA LEAGUE QUARTO TAREFA ALQUIER GARRAFA ALQUEIRE
MOUNTAIN: URUCUM BANDEIRA ITATIAIA

MOUNTAINS: MAR GERAL ORGAN PIAUI ACARAI GURUPI ORGAOS PARIMA AMAMBAI CARAJAS GRADAUS RONCADOR TOMBADOR
NATIVE: CABOCLO CURIBOCA MAMELUCO PAULISTA
PORT: RIO PARA BAHIA BELEM NATAL SANTOS PELOTAS SALVADOR
PRESIDENT: BRAS DUTRA FILHO VARGAS
RIVER: APA ICA DOCE GEIO IVAI JARI PARA PARU SONO TEFE ABUNA ANAUA APORE CAPIM CLARO CORUA ICANA IRIRI ITAPI JURUA JUTAI MANSO NEGRO PARDO PIAUI PRETO TIETE TURVO URUBU VERDE XINGU AJUANA AMAZON ARINOS BALSAS BRANCO CANUMA CONTAS CUIABA DEMINI GRAJAU GRANDE GURUPI IBICUI IGUACU JAPURA JAVARI MEARIM MORTES MUCURI PARANA PURPUS RONURO SANGUE TACUTU TIBAGI UATUMA UAUPES VELHAS CORUMBA IGUASSU MADEIRA PARAIBA SUCURIU TAPAJOS TAQUARI TEODORO URUGUAI ARAGUAIA PADAUIRI PARACATU PARAGUAI PARNAIBA SOLIMOES TARAUACA
STATE: ACRE PARA AMAPA BAHIA CEARA GOIAS GOYAZ PIAUI PARANA PIAUHY ALAGOAS GUAPORE PARAIBA RORAIMA SERGIPE AMAZONAS MARANHAO PARAHIBA PARAHYBA RONDONIA SAOPAULO
TOWN: ACU EXU ICO IPU ITU JAU LUZ RIO UBA BAGE FARO IBIA IJUI ITAI LAPA LINS PARA PIUI TUPA UNAI BAHIA BAIAO BAURU BELEM CEARA NATAL NEVES CAMPOS CUIABA ILHEUS MACEIO MANAOS MANAUS OLINDA RECIFE SANTOS ARACAJU CARUARU CITORIA GOIANIA ITABUNA JUNDIAI NITEROI PELOTAS TAUBATE UBERABA ANAPOLIS BRASILIA CAMPINAS CURITIBA LONDRINA SALVADOR SOROCABA TERESINA
TREE: APA ICICA UCUUBA ARARIBA WALLABA
WATERFALL: GLASS IGUAZU
WEIGHT: BAG ONCA LIBRA ARROBA OITAVA ARRATEL QUILATE QUINTAL TONELADA

BRAZIL NUT JUVIA CASTANA
BRAZILWOOD SAPPAN VERZINO HYPERNIC PEACHWOOD SAPPANWOOD
BREACH GAP CHAP FLAW GOOL RENT RIFT SLAP BRACK BRECK BURST CHASM CLEFT CRACK PAUSE SPLIT WOUND BRUISE

HARBOR HERNIA HIATUS INROAD
SCHISM SCREED SLUICE ASSAULT
BLEMISH DISPUTE FISSURE
OPENING QUARREL RUPTURE
BREAKING CREVASSE FRACTION
FRACTURE INTERVAL OUTBREAK
SOLUTION TRESPASS
(— IN DIKE) GOOL
(— IN SEAWAY)
(— OF CONTINUITY) SALTUS
(— OF DUTY) BARRATRY
(— OF ETIQUETTE) SOLECISM
(— OF FAITH) TREASON
(— OF GRAMMAR) SOLECISM
(— OF MORALITY) SCAPE VAGARY
(— OF PEACE) AFFRAY FRACTION
(— OF UNITY) SOHISM
BREAD BAP BUN PAN BODY BRAD
DIET FARE FOOD LOAF PAIN
PONE RIMA ROLL RUSH RUSK
TOKE AZYME BATCH BATON
BOXTY CAPER CHEAT KISRA
LIMPA MICHE ROOTY TOMMY
CHAPON COCKET DAMPER
DODGER ENZYME HALLAH KANKIE
MASLIN MATZOS PANNAM
SIMNEL TAMMIE WASTEL
YANNAM ALIMENT BANNOCK
EULOGIA MANCHET POPOVER
STOLLEN TOASTER CORNCAKE
HARDTACK SOFTTACK TORTILLA
ZWIEBACK PUMPERNICKEL
(— AND MILK) POBS PANADA
POBBIES
(— BOX) PANETIERE
(— QUALITY) PANEITY
(BATCH OF —) CAST
(BUTTERED —) CAPER
(DRY —) TOKE
(EUCHARISTIC —) BODY HOST
AZYME
(FANCY —) BRAID
(MAIZE —) PIKI
(OATMEAL —) ANACK JANNOCK
(POTATO —) FADGE
(QUICK —) SCONE
(S. AFRICAN —) DIKA
(SLICE OF —) TARTINE TRENCHER
(SMALL LOAF OF —) COB
(SMALL PIECE OF —) SIPPET
MEALOCK
(SOPPED —) MISER BREWIS
BROWIS
(SWEET —) BUN BROWNIE
STOLLEN
(TOASTED —) SIPPET
(UNLEAVENED —) AZYM AZYME
BANNOCK CHAPATTI
(WHEAT —) CHEAT HOVIS COCKET
MANCHET
(PREF.) ARTO PANI
BREADBOARD PANEL
BREADED ANGLAISE
BREADFRUIT MASI RIMA RIMAS
DUGDUG NANGCA CAMANSI
CASTANA ANTIPOLO BREADNUT
CHESTNUT
BREADNUT RAM
BREADROOT PSORALEA
BREADTH BEAM
BREADWINNING GAP BOON BUST
DASH HINT KNAP PICK PLOW
REND RENT RIFT RIVE

BREAK GO CUT JAR LOP TEN ABRA
BUST CHIP DRAG FALL FLAW
KNAP PART RUIN RUSH SLIP
SNAP STEP STOP TEAR TURN
UNDO WASH WORK ALTER BLANK
BRACK BURST CHECK CHINK
CLEFT COMMA CRACK CRAZE
DAUNT FALSE FRACT FRUSH
LAPSE PAUSE PLUCK ROUGH
SEVER SMASH SOLVE SPAWN
SPELT STAVE SWING WOUND
BRUISE CABBLE CHANGE CLEAVE
CRANNY CUTOUT DEFEAT HIATUS
IMPAIR LACUNA PIERCE SALTUS
SHREND SPRING TEWTAW
TEWTER BLUNDER CAESURA
CRACKLE CRANKLE CREVICE
CRUMBLE DESTROY DISABLE
DISPART DISRUPT EXHAUST
FISSURE GRITTLE INFRACT
INTERIM OPENING RESPITE
RUPTURE SHATTER TAILING
VARIATE BREATHER CREVASSE
DIERESIS DIFFRACT FRACTION
FRACTURE FRAGMENT INFRINGE
INTERVAL SEPARATE SOLUTION
STRAMASH
(— APART) SUNDER DISRUPT
SHATTER
(— AWAY) BOLT ESCAPE
(— BOULDERS) BULLDOZE
(— DOWN) CONK FAIL GIVE CRAZE
CROCK PLASH TRAIK BRUISE
TUMBLE ANALYZE FOUNDER
REFRACT COLLAPSE INFRINGE
(— FORCE) BAFFLE
(— FORTH) BOIL ERUPT EVENT
FLASH EXPLODE
(— FROM ICE MASS) CALVE
(— GLASS) SHREND DRAGADE
(— IN) ENTER
(— IN PIECES) CHAP DICE KNAP
CRASH CRAZE SMASH SMOKE
SHIVER CRUMBLE FRITTER
SMATTER DEMOLISH DIFFRACT
DISJOINT SPLINTER STRAMASH
(— IN WAVES) JABBLE
(— IN YARN) SMASH
(— INTO) BROACH IRRUPT
(— INTO FOAM) COMB
(— INWARD) STAVE
(— LANCE) TAINT
(— OF CONTINUITY) SALTUS
(— OFF) NUB DROP SNAP CEASE
LEAVE ABRUPT DIREMPT
PRETERMIT
(— OFF END) SNUB
(— OPEN) BUST CHOP FORCE
(— ORE) COB SPALL SPAWL
(— OUT) ERUPT START ASSURD
STRIKE
(— RANKS) DISMISS
(— SHARPLY) KNACK
(— SILENCE) QUATCH QUETCH
(— SKIN) GALL
(— SLATE) SCULP
(— STONE) CAVIL KEVEL
(— THE BACK) CHINE
(— THROUGH) BEAT FORCE
BREACH
(— THROUGH SHELL) PIP
(— UP) BUCK FALL MELT FLOUR

SEVER SPALE SPLIT STASH INCIDE
DEGRADE DIFFUSE DISBAND
DISSECT DISTURB REFRACT
SCARIFY SCATTER CROSSCUT
DISJOINT DISPERSE DISSOLVE
DISUNIFY FRAGMENT
(— UP EARTH) HACK FALLOW
(— UP SIEGE) LEVY
(— WATER) FIN
(— WINDOWS) NICK
(STEM —) BROWNING
(SUFF.) CLASE CLASIA CLAST(IC)
BREAKABLE BRITTLE BRUCKLE
FRIABLE DELICATE FRANGIBLE
BREAKAGE GRIEF
BREAKAX IRONWOOD
BREAKDOWN JUBA EDGER
BURNOUT DEBACLE HOEDOWN
COLLAPSE DILUTION
(— OF RIND) ADUSTIOSIS
(ELECTRIC —) AVALANCHE
BREAKER JUMP SURF WAVE
BARECA BEAKER BILLOW COMBER
ROLLER CRACKER SLEDGER
LEDGEMAN SCRAPPER
(— OF WORD) WARLOCK
(CIRCUIT —) CUTOUT
(ROCK —) ALLIGATOR
(PL.) BREACH
(SUFF.) CLASTIC
BREAKFAST BRUNCH DEJEUNE
DISJUNE DEJEUNER DISJEUNE
BREAKING BREACH BREAKUP
FRACTION FRACTURE SOLUTION
(— FORTH) ERUPTIVE
(— OFF) CHIPPING ABRUPTION
(— UP) DEBACLE ANALYSIS
(SUFF.) CLASE CLASIA CLAST(IC)
(— INTO SMALL PIECES) THRIPSIS
BREAKSTONE SAXIFRAGE
BREAKWATER COB DAM COBB
CROY DIKE MOLE PIER PILE QUAY
JETTY GROYNE REFUGE
BULWARK STOCKADE
BREAM TAI BRIM CARP CHAD
SCUP SHAD ZOPE BROOM ROMAN
BALEEN BARWIN BRAISE SARGUS
OLDWIFE SUNFISH WAREHOU
CYPRINID FLATFISH TARWHINE
STEENTJIE
BREAST DUG BUMP CROP FACE
BOOBY BOSOM BRAVE BUBBY
CHEST HEART MAMMA PETTO
STALL PECTUS POMMEL THORAX
BRISKET COUNTER KNOCKER
FOREBOWS
(— OF HORSE) COUNTER
(PHOTOGRAPH OF —S)
MAMMOGRAM
(PL.) BUST
(PREF.) MAMM(I)(ILLI) MAST(O)
MAZ(O) PECTORI STERN(O)
STETH(O)
BREASTBAND HORSE
BREASTBONE BREAST STERNUM
XIPHOID
BREASTHOOK CRUTCH FOREHOOK
BREASTPIECE RABAT RABBI
BREASTPLATE EGIS URIM AEGIS
BREAST BYRNIE GORGET LORICA
ORACLE SHIELD THORAX CUIRASS
PALETTE POITREL PECTORAL
PLASTRON RATIONAL

BREASTS
(SUFF.) MASTIA
BREASTWORK FORT REDAN
SANGAR SCHANZ SCHERM
SCONCE SUNGAR BRATTLE
PARAPET PLUTEUS RAMPART
BARBETTE BRATTICE
BREATH AIR ANDE GASP HUFF
LIFE ONDE PANT PECH PUFF SIGH
WAFT WIND BLAST PAUSE SCENT
SMELL VAPOR WHIFF WHIFT
BREEZE FLATUS PNEUMA
HALITUS INSTANT RESPITE
SUSPIRE SPIRACLE
(— OF WIND) SPIRIT
(BAD —) OZOSTOMIA
(DIVINE —) NEPHESH
(LIFE —) PRANA SPIRIT
(STINKING —) FUMOSITY
(PREF.) PNEO PNEUM(A)(O)
PNEUMATO PNEUMON(O)
RESPIRO SPIRACULI SPIRO
(SUFF.) PNEA PNEUSTA PNOEA
BREATHE ANDE LIVE ONDE PANT
PECH PUFF SIGH VENT EXIST
EXUDE SPEAK SPIRE UTTER
ASPIRE EXHALE INHALE WHEEZE
AFFLATE EMANATE RESPIRE
SUSPIRE
(— HEAVILY) FOB PECH FNESE
SOUGH THROTTLE
(— LABORIOUSLY) GASP
(— NOISILY) SOUGH SNOTTER
(— UPON) FAN
BREATHER PAUSE
BREATHING AIR ALIVE PNEUMA
SPIRIT GASPING AFFLATUS
SPIRITUS SPIRATION
(— HEAVILY) SUSPIRIOUS
(LABORED —) ASTHMA
(ROUGH —) ASPER
(SMOOTH —) LENE LENIS
BREATHLESSNESS TIFT
BREATHY HOLLOW ADENOID
BRECCIA BROCKRAM
BRED **(WELL —)** FREE
BREECH BORE BUTT DOUP BLOCK
BRICK CULOTTE DRODDUM
BUTTOCKS CYLINDER DERRIERE
BREECHBLOCK BLOCK VENTPIECE
BREECHCLOTH HIPPEN HIPPING
BREECHES HOSE CHAPS JEANS
LEVIS SLOPS STOCK TREWS
BRACAE BRAGAS BREEKS GASKIN
SMALLS TIGHTS TROUSE
BOMBARDS BREEKUMS
JODHPURS KICKSIES KNICKERS
LEATHERS TROUSERS
PANTALOON SMALLCLOTHES
BREED GET ILK BEAR KIND RACE
REAR SORT BEGET BROOD CASTE
CAUSE CLASS FANCY HATCH
ISSUE RAISE STOCK STORE TRAIN
CREATE GENDER STRAIN
EDUCATE NOURISH PRODUCE
PROGENY SPECIES VARIETY
ENGENDER GENERATE INSTRUCT
MULTIPLY PULLULATE
(DWARF —) TOY
BREEDER RANCHER AURELIAN
HERDSMAN HORSEMAN
(FISH —) MILTER
BREEDING ORIGIN DESCENT

NURTURE TUPPING BEHAVIOR
CIVILITY PREGNANT TRAINING
(GOOD —) GENTRY
BREEZE AIR AURA BLOW FLAW
GALE GUST PIRR STIR WIND
BLAST RUMOR SLANT WALTZ
BREATH DOCTOR REPORT SLATCH
SPIRIT ZEPHYR FRESHEN
MUZZLER QUARREL VIRASON
WHISPER
(COOL —) DOCTOR
(GENTLE —) AIR AURA ZEPHYR
(LAND —) TERRAL
(STIFF —) STOUR TIFTER
BREEZE FLY WHAME
BREEZY AIRY BRISK FRESH WINDY
AIRISH
BRETHREN IKHWAN
BRETON ARMORICAN
BREVE NOTE WRIT BRIEF MINIM
ORDER SHORT PRECEPT
BREVIARY ORDO CURSUS DIGEST
LEDGER PORTAS COUCHER
EPITOME SUMMARY ABSTRACT
PORTESSE PORTHORS
BREVITY SYNTOMY LACONISM
UNLENGTH BRIEFNESS
SHORTNESS TERSENESS
BRACHYLOGY
BREW ALE MIX BEER BOIL MAKE
PLOT POUR DRINK HATCH STOUT
BROWST DEVISE DILUTE FOMENT
GATHER LIQUOR SEETHE
CONCOCT INCLINE PREPARE
CONTRIVE
(HOME —) SAMOGON
BREWER TUNNER
BREWERY BRASSERIE
BREWING GAIL GYLE BROWST
BUMMOCK
BRIBE BUD BUY FEE FIX OIL ROB
SOP TIP BAIT DASH GIFT HAVE
HIRE MEED MOIL PALM VAIL
WAGE BONUS CUDDY GRAFT
OFFER STEAL SUGAR TEMPT
TOUCH EXTORT GREASE HAMPER
NOBBLE PAYOLA SQUARE
SUBORN CORRUPT DOUCEUR
SWEETEN TICKLER GRATUITY
VENALIZE
(— TO POLICEMAN) NUT
BRIBERY MEED
BRIC-A-BRAC CURIO VERTU VIRTU
BIBELOT TROCKERY TRUMPERY
BRICK BAT BUR BURR GLUT MARL
PAVE TILE BLOCK GAULT QUARL
SLOPE SPLIT STOCK STONE
TOOTH CUTTER FELLOW HEADER
PAMENT PAVIOR BACKING
CLINKER FLETTON GRIZZLE
PERPEND SOLDIER BURNOVER
(— WALL) NECK
(CRACKED —) CHUFF SHUFF
(FINAL HALF —) JACK
(IMPERFECT —) SHIPPER
BURNOVER
(PILE OF —S) HACK CLAMP
(PULVERIZED —) SOORKY SOORKEE
(SECOND QUALITY —S) BRINDLES
(SECOND-RATE —) GRIZZLE
(SOFT —) CUTTER RUBBER
PICKING
(SQUARE —) QUADREL

(STACK OF —) LIFT
(SUN-DRIED —) BAT ADOBE
(UNBURNT —) ADOBE
(WOODEN —) DOOK
(PL.) CLAYWARE
(PREF.) PLINTHI
BRICKLAYER BRICKY MASONER
BRICKMAKER MOLDER
BRICKWORK HOB BRICKING
BRIDAL NUPTIAL BRIDALTY
BRIDE KALLAH SPOUSE SHULAMITE
BRIDE OF LAMMERMOOR
(AUTHOR OF —) SCOTT
(CHARACTER IN —) LUCY CALEB
EDGAR FRANK ASHTON HAYSTON
WILLIAM RAVENSWOOD
BALDERSTONE
BRIDE-PRICE LOBOLD LOBOLO
BRIDESHEAD REVISITED (AUTHOR
OF —) WAUGH
(CHARACTER IN —) BOY REX CARA
KURT BERYL CELIA JULIA RYDER
BRIDEY ANTHONY BLANCHE
CHARLES MOTTRAM CORDELIA
MUSPRATT SAMGRASS
MARCHMAIN MULCASTER
SEBASTIAN BRIDESHEAD
BRIDESMAID PARANYMPH
BRIDEWELL MILLDOLL
BRIDGE WAY BRIG LINK NOSE
PONS PONT REST SPAN WIEN
CROSS SIRAT TOWIE GANTRY
ISLAND JIGGER RUNWAY SANGAR
AUCTION BASCULE BIFROST
CONNECT CULVERT EXOSTRA
PASSAGE PASSING PINNOCK
PONCEAU PONTOON PROPONS
TRAJECT TRESTLE VIADUCT
CONTRACT TRAVERSE DUPLICATE
(— OF MUSICAL INSTRUMENT)
MAGAS CHEVALET CHEVILLE
(— TO PARADISE) ALSIRAT
(ARCADED —) RIALTO
(CONTRACT —) CHICAGO GHOULIE
PLAFOND
(FLUE —) ALTAR
(GATEWAY —) GOUT
(HOSE —) JUMPER
(IMPEDANCE —) DIPLEXER
(NATURAL —) ARCH
(PLANK —) LIGGER
(ROPE SUSPENSION —) JOOLA
(RUDE —) CLAPPER
(PREF.) GEPHYR(O) PONTI PONTO
BRIDGEMAKER PONTIFEX
BRIDGEMAN EBBMAN
BRIDGE OF SAN LUIS REY
(AUTHOR OF —) WILDER
(CHARACTER IN —) PIO JAIME
PILAR MANUEL PEPITA ESTEBAN
JUNIPER PERICHOLE
MONTEMAYOR
BRIDGING ASTRIDE STRUTTING
BRIDLE BIT CURB REIN RULE
BRAKE BRANK BRIDE CHECK
GUARD GUIDE STRUT DIRECT
GOVERN HALTER MASTER SIMPER
SUBDUE BLINDER CONTROL
LORMERY REPRESS SNAFFLE
SWAGGER CAVESSON RESTRAIN
SUPPRESS
BRIDLE PATH SPURWAY
BRIEF FEW CURT LIST RIFE WRIT

BLURB BREVE CHARM PITHY
QUICK SHORT TERSE ABRUPT
COMMON CURTAL FLYING
HOURLY LETTER LITTLE SNIPPY
SUDDEN ABRIDGE CAPSULE
COMPACT COMPOSE CONCISE
CRYPTIC INVOICE LACONIC
MANDATE OUTLINE PRECEPT
SUMMARY BREVIATE CONDENSE
FLEETING FLITTING SNATCHED
SNIPPETY SUCCINCT SYLLABUS
(PREF.) BREVI
BRIEF CASE FOLIO TASHIE
BRIEFLY BRIEF ENFIN SHORTLY
BRIER BARB PIPE BRIAR THORN
SMILAX BRUYERE PRICKER
INKBERRY
BRIER TREE PIPER
BRIG RIG JAIL PRISON GEORDIE
BRIGADE TERZO CAMPOO
BRIGAND THIEF USKOK BANDIT
KLEPHT LATRON PIRATE ROBBER
CATERAN KETTRIN LADRONE
ROUTIER SOLDIER PICAROON
(PL.) TCHETNITSI
BRIGANDINE PLACCATE
BRIGHT APT GAY NET FINE GILD
GLAD GLEG HIGH LIVE ROSY
ACUTE AGLOW ALERT ANIME
BEAMY BRAVE CLEAR CRISP
EAGLE FLARY FRESH GEMMY
JOLLY LIGHT LUCID NITID PRINT
QUICK RIANT SHARP SHEEN
SHEER SHINY SMART SMOLT
STEEP SUNNY TINNY VIVID WHITE
WITTY BERTHA CHEERY CLEVER
FLASHY FLORID GARISH LIMPID
LIVELY LUCENT ORIENT SERENE
SHRILL SILVER BEAMISH
DIAMOND DILUCID FORWARD
FULGENT LAMBENT RADIANT
RINGING SHINING ANIMATED
CHEERFUL FLASHING GLEAMING
LIGHTFUL LUMINOUS LUSTROUS
SPLENDID SPLENDOR STARLIKE
SUNSHINY
(BLINDINGLY —) GLARING
(NOT —) SOFT
(OFFENSIVELY —) GARISH
(SOFTLY —) LAMBENT
(PREF.) AETHIO AGLAO LAMPR(O)
BRIGHTEN GILD LAMP BLOOM
CHEER CLEAR FLAME GLOZE
LIGHT LIVEN SHINE SNUFF
CANTLE ENGILD POLISH ANIMATE
BURNISH EMBRAVE ENLIVEN
FURBISH LIGHTEN REFRESH
SMARTEN ILLUMINE
BRIGHTENER FLUOROL
BRIGHTLY GAY CLEAR LIGHT
SHEEN BRIGHT FRESHLY SHEENLY
BRIGHTNESS SUN BLAZE BLOOM
ECLAT FLAME GLARE GLEAM
GLINT GLORY GLOSS LIGHT NITOR
SHEEN SHINE ACUMEN BRIGHT
CANDOR FULGOR LUSTER
CLARITY GLISTEN GLITTER
LAMBENT NITENCY SPARKLE
RADIANCE SPLENDOR BRILLIANCE
(— OF TOBACCO) FLASH
(— UNIT) STILB
(UNIT OF —) NIT
(PREF.) GANO

BRIGUE BLAT
BRILLIANCE FAME BLARE BLAZE
ECLAT FLAME GLARE GLORY
SHINE VALUE KEENNESS
RADIANCE SPLENDOR VIVACITY
REFULGENCE
BRILLIANCY FIRE BLARE ECLAT
GLORY REFLET CLARITY GLITTER
ORIENCY RADIANCE SPLENDOR
BRILLIANT GAY GOOD KEEN SAGE
WISE BREME QUICK VIVID BRIGHT
CLEVER GIFTED LIVELY PURPLE
SIGNAL BRAVURA BRITTLE
EMINENT FLAMING GLARING
LAMBENT LAMPING LOZENGE
PRISMAL RADIANT SHINING
BLINDING DAZZLING DIZZYING
GLORIOUS INSPIRED LUCULENT
LUMINOUS SLASHING SPLENDID
PRISMATIC
(TRANSIENTLY —) METEORIC
BRIM LIP RIM RUT SEA EDGE TURF
BLUFF BRINK MARGE OCEAN
VERGE WATER BORDER MARGIN
TURNUP COPULATE STRUMPET
(— OF HAT) FLAP LEAF POKE
BRINK TARFE SLOUCH
BRIMFUL TIPFUL TOPFUL
CROWNED
BRIMMING BIG FULL ABRIM
BRIMSTONE SULFUR VIRAGO
SULPHUR BRINSTON SPITFIRE
(PREF.) THI(O)
BRIMSTONY LURID
BRINDLED TABBY TAWNY
BRANDED FLECKED STREAKED
BRINE SEA MAIN SALT BRACK
LEACH OCEAN TEARS PICKLE
MARINADE
BRINER COBBERER
BRING DO LAY TEE WIN BEAR
BUCK CALL FIRK LEAD STOP TAKE
TEEM CARRY DRIVE ENDUE
FETCH INCUR APPORT ARRIVE
CONVEY DEDUCE CONDUCE
CONDUCT EXHIBIT PROCURE
PRODUCE
(— ABOUT) DO SEE BREW MAKE
STAY TEEM CAUSE DIGHT FRAME
INFER MOYEN SHAPE SWING
CREATE EFFECT INVOKE SECURE
SPIRIT COMPASS CONDUCE
INSPIRE OPERATE PROCURE
PRODUCE CATALYZE OCCASION
TRANSACT PERPETRATE
(— ABOUT CAPTURE) ACCOUNT
(— BACK) REFER EFFECT RECALL
REDUCE REDUCT RELATE RETURN
REVIVE REVOKE PRODUCE
RESTORE OCCASION RETRIEVE
TRANSACT
(— BEFORE) HAUL
(— CHARGE) APPEACH
(— DOWN) LAY DROP FALL FELL
STOP ABATE COUCH EMBASE
SOFTEN DECLINE DESCEND
DISMOUNT OVERTHROW
(— DOWN STEER) HOOLIHAN
(— FORTH) CAST FOAL GIVE MAKE
TEEM EDUCE HATCH ISSUE
SPAWN THROW PROFER DELIVER
TRADUCE ENGENDER PROCREATE
(— FORTH YOUNG) EAN KID YEAN

(— **FORWARD**) CITE LEAD INFER ADDUCE ALLEGE ADJOUST ADVANCE PROPOSE
(— **IN**) EARN INFER USHER IMPORT INDUCE INVECT REPORT RETURN ADHIBIT
(— **INTO BATTLE**) COMMIT
(— **INTO COURT**) SIST
(— **INTO DISGRACE**) FOUL
(— **LOW**) AVALE DEGRADE SUPPLANT
(— **ON**) INFER INDUCE
(— **ONESELF**) GET
(— **OUT**) DRAW ACCENT ELICIT DISINTER HEIGHTEN
(— **OVER**) CONVERT
(— **SHIP INTO POSITION**) EASE
(— **TO A HALT**) STICK
(— **TO AN END**) DO END FIT DOCK DRAW REDD CEASE FORDO DECIDE EXPIRE FINISH FOREDO FULFIL DISJOIN INCLUDE COMPLETE CONCLUDE DISSOLVE SURCEASE
(— **TO BAY**) CORNER
(— **TO BEAR**) EXERT
(— **TO HEEL**) FACE
(— **TO LIFE**) EVOKE ANIMATE
(— **TO LIGHT**) GRUB REAP DREDGE ELICIT EXPOSE REVEAL UNEARTH DISCLOSE DISCOVER
(— **TO NAUGHT**) DASH FOIL UNDO NEGATE CONFUTE DESTROY
(— **TO PERFECTION**) RIPEN
(— **TO STOP**) CURB HALT ARREST
(— **TO THE GROUND**) GRASS
(— **TOGETHER**) JOIN AMASS RAISE UNITE ADDUCT CONFER CORRAL ENGAGE ENLINK GATHER SUMMON COLLATE COLLECT COMPILE COMPORT ASSEMBLE CONFLATE ENSEMBLE
(— **UP**) REAR BREED NURSE RAISE TRAIN NURSLE NUZZLE UPREAR EDUCATE NOURISH
(**SUFF.**) FER(ENCE)(ENT)(OUS)
(— **ABOUT**) FIC(AL)(ATE)(ATION) (ATIVE)(ATOR)(ATORY)(E)(ENCE) (ENT)(IAL)(IARY)(IENT) FIQUE

BRINGING-UP BREEDING EDUCATION
BRINJAL EGGPLANT
BRINK END EVE LIP RIM SEA BANK BRIM EDGE FOSS MARGE SHORE VERGE BORDER MARGIN MARGENT PRECIPICE
BRINY BRACK SALTY SALINE BRACKISH MURIATED
BRIOCHE ROLL STICH SAVARIN
BRISE-SOLEIL BLIND SUNBREAK SUNSHADE
BRISK GAY BRAG BUSY CANT FAST KEEN PERK PERT RACY RASH SPRY TRIG VIVE YARE YERN AGILE ALERT ALIVE BUDGE BUXOM CANTY COBBY CRANK CRISP FRESH FRISK KEDGE NIPPY PEART PEPPY PERKY QUICK ROUND ZIPPY ACTIVE BREEZY COCKET CROUSE DAPPER FLICKY LIVELY NIMBLE SNAPPY SPRACK SPRUNT TROTTY VIVACE ALLEGRO CHIPPER HUMMING ROUSING

ANIMATED BRUSHING FRISKFUL GALLIARD RATTLING SMACKING SPANKING SPIRITED
BRISKLY YERN SHARP YERNE BUSILY CROUSE ALLEGRO ROUNDLY
BRISKNESS ALACRITY VIRITOOT
BRISTLE AWN JAG RIB BARB HAIR JAGG SETA TELA BIRSE BRUSH PARCH PREEN STARE STRUT STYLE TOAST CHAETA PALPUS RUFFLE SETULA STIVER STRIGA STYLET GLOCHIS SMELLER STUBBLE WHISKER ACICULUM FRENULUM SPICULUM VIBRISSA VIBRACULUM
(**PREF.**) CHAET(I)(O) CHETO HIRSUTO HORRI SETI SETULI
(**SUFF.**) CHAETA CHAETES CHAETUS
BRISTLED HERISSE HORRENT
BRISTLE-SHAPED STYLOID
BRISTLING ROUGH HISPID HORRID SETOSE THORNY HORRENT SCRUBBY SPINOUS
BRISTLY BIRSY PENNY SETOSE STUBBY SCRUBBY STICKLE
BRITAIN
(**PREF.**) BRITO
BRITISH ENGLISH BRITANNIC WHITEHALL
BRITISH COLUMBIA (**CAPITAL OF —**) VICTORIA
(**MOUNTAINS OF —**) COAST CARIBOO CASCADE PURCELL SELKIRK MONASHEE
(**RIVER OF —**) NASS LIARD PEACE FRASER SKEENA STIKINE
(**TOWN OF —**) KELOWNA KAMLOOPS VANCOUVER
BRITISH HONDURAS (**BAY OF —**) CHETUMAL
(**CAPITAL OF —**) BELMOPAN
(**FORMER CAPITAL OF —**) BELIZE
(**MOUNTAIN RANGE OF —**) MAYA
(**TOWN OF —**) CAYO STANN COROZAL
BRITOMARTIS (**FATHER OF —**) ZEUS JUPITER
(**MOTHER OF —**) CARME
BRITON CELT SCOT BRYTHON
BRITTANY ARMORICA
(**NATIVE OF —**) BRETON
BRITTLE DRY FROW WEAK BRASH CANDY CRIMP CRISP CRUMP EAGER FRAIL FROWY FRUSH SHORT SPALT CRISPY CRUMPY FEEBLE FICKLE FROUGH GINGER INFIRM SLIGHT BRICKLE BRUCKLE CRACKLY FRAGILE FRIABLE REDSEAR SHIVERY SMOPPLE BRITCHEL DELICATE SNAPPISH
BRITTLEBUSH ENCELIA
BRITTLE STAR OPHIUROID
BROACH AIR AWL CUT PIN ROD TAP OPEN OUCH SHED SPIT SPUR STAB TAME VEER VENT BEGIN DRESS DRIFT PRICK RIMER SPOOL START VOICE ATTAME BORING BROOCH DRIVER FIBULA LAUNCH PIERCE REAMER RHYMER STRIKE ENLARGE EXPRESS PUBLISH SPINDLE SQUARER VIOLATE

WIDENER APPROACH DEFLOWER DRIFTPIN INCISION PORPOISE
BROAD DEEP FREE VAST WIDE AMPLE BEAMY BRAID DORIC GROSS LARGE LARGO PLAIN ROOMY SPLAY SQUAB STOUT THICK WOMAN COARSE GLOBAL BELCHER EVIDENT GENERAL GRIVOIS LIBERAL OBVIOUS PLATOID BARNYARD SPACIOUS TOLERANT
(— **AND FLAT**) PLATOID
(**NOT —**) STRAIT
(**PREF.**) EURY LATI PLAT(Y)
BROADBILL GAYA RAYA GAPER SCAUP BOATBILL SHOVELER SWORDFISH
BROADCAST AIR SOW SEED SEND CARRY RADIO STREW AIRING SPREAD DECLARE DIFFUSE PUBLISH SCATTER ANNOUNCE TELEVISE TRANSMIT
BROADCLOTH CASTOR SUCLAT TAUNTON
BROADEN BREDE WIDEN DILATE EXPAND EXTEND SPREAD ENNOBLE
BROADHORN ARK
BROADNESS BIGNESS LIBERALITY
BROADSIDE TIRE BROAD GARLAND
BROADSWORD BILL KRIS GLAIVE HANGER SPATHA CUTLASS FERRARA CLAYMORE MONTANTO SCIMITAR
BROBDINGNAGIAN HUGE
BROCADE ACCA BROCHE KINCOB KINKHAB NISHIKI BAUDEKIN DAMASSIN
BROCADED BROCHE
BROCCOLI ASPARAGUS
BROCCOLI BROWN GOAT LOAM PLOVER RABBIT
BROCHURE TRACT BOOKLET PAMPHLET TREATISE
BROCKET PITA STAG BROCK SPITTER
BRODIAEA GRASSNUT
BROGAN STOGA STOGY BROGUE STOGIE
BROGUE STOGY STOGIE
BROIL ROW BURN CHAR FEUD FRAY GRID HEAT TOIL ALARM BRAWL GRILL MELEE SCRAP SWELT AFFRAY BIRSLE BRAISE GRILLY SPLORE SQUEAL TUMULT BRANDER BRULYIE CARBONE CONTEST DISCORD DISPUTE EMBROIL FRIZZLE GARBOIL QUARREL SIMULTY BARBECUE BLOODWIT CONFLICT GRILLADE STRAMASH
BROILER GRILL SEARER CHICKEN POUSSIN
BROKE HOG LOW BUST STONY STONEY CHICANE UPTIGHT BANKRUPT
BROKEN DOWN DUFF RENT RUDE TORN BLOWN BROKE BURST FRACT GAPPY HAIRY KAPUT ROMPU ROUGH TAMED BRASHY HACKLY RUINED SHAKEN CRACKED CRUSHED FRACTED

REDUCED SUBDUED VICIOUS WHIPPED BANKRUPT CONTRITE OUTLAWED RUPTURED TATTERED WEAKENED
(— **BUT NOT TRAINED**) GREEN
(— **IN**) STOVEN
(— **IN HEALTH**) CRAZY
(— **OFF**) ABRUPT
(**EASILY —**) GINGER
(**PREF.**) FRACTO
BROKEN-DOWN HAYWIRE DISJASKED DISJASKIT
BROKER AGENT CRIMP BANIAN BANYAN CORSER DEALER FACTOR JOBBER BROGGER CHANGER COURSER MONEYER PEDDLER REALTOR SCALPER HUCKSTER INSTITOR MERCHANT
BROKERAGE AGIOTAGE
BROMATIUM KOHLRABI
BROME CHEAT
BROMEGRASS CHESS
BROMIA (**HUSBAND OF —**) SOSIA
BROMO ACID EOSIN EOSINE
BROMUS DRAWK
BRONCHITIS HUSK HOOSE HOOZE
BRONCO PONY PONEY CAYUSE BRONCHO MUSTANG
BRONCOBUSTER BUSTER GINETE BUCKAROO
BRONZE AES TAN BUST ALLOY BROWN COWBOY ORMOLU STATUE ASIATIC GUNMETAL
(— **AGE CULTURE**) UBAID
(**ANTIQUE —**) CACAO
(**GILDED —**) VERMEIL
(**MEDAL —**) CALABASH
(**PREF.**) CHALC(O) CHALK(O)
BRONZEWING SQUATTER
BROOCH BAR PIN BOSS LACE OUCH PRIN PROP CAMEO CLASP MORSE PREEN SLIDE SPRAY SPRIG FIBULA NOUCHE PLAQUE SHIELD FERMAIL PETALON CROTCHET ORNAMENT SUNBURST
BROOD EYE FRY NYE SET SIT MOPE NEST NIDE RACE TEAM TRIP WEEP AERIE BREED CLOCK COVER COVEY FLOCK GLOOM GROUP HATCH HOVER ISSUE SEDGE STOCK WORRY YOUNG CLETCH CLUTCH FAMILY KINDLE LITTER PONDER PROGENY SPECIES CLECKING COGITATE INCUBATE KINDLING MEDITATE
(— **OF BIRDS**) AERY AERIE COVEY EYRIE SEDGE SIEGE
(— **OF PHEASANTS**) EYE NID NYE NIDE
BROODER HOVER MOTHER NURSERY
BROOK RUN BEAR BECK BURN GHYL GILL LAKE RILL RUSH SIKE ABIDE BAYOU BOURN CREEK FLEET GLIDE STAND STELL TCHAI ARROYO BRANCH CANADA DIGEST ENDURE GUTTER RINDLE RIVOSE RUNLET RUNNEL SICKET STREAM SUFFER ABROOKE COMPORT CONCOCT STOMACH QUEBRADA TOLERATE
(**RIPPLING —**) PURL

(SALT —) LICK

BROOKLET BECK DOKE RILL RILLET RUNNEL RILLOCK RIVULET

BROOM COW MOP FRAY SWAB WISP BESOM BISME BREAM BRUSH SCRUB SPART SWEEP UALIS WHISK GENISTA HAGWEED WHISKER HACKWEED SPLINTER

(DYER'S —) GENET DYEWOOD

(NATIVE —) DOGWOOD

(TOPS OF —) SCOPARIUS

(PREF.) SCOPI SCOPULI

BROOMCORN HURL

BROOMCORN MILLET HIRSE PANIC PANICLE KADIKANE

BROOMRAPE HELLROOT HERBBANE

BROOMROOT SACATON ZACATON

BROSE ATHOLE CROWDIE

BROTH SEW BREE BROO FOND KAIL KALE SOUP GLAZE STOCK BREWIS CULLIS JUSSAL JUSSEL LIQUOR SKILLY CALDERA POTTAGE SOUCHIE SUPPING BOUILLON CONSOMME PISHPASH POSSODIE POWSOWDY

BROTHEL KIP CRIB STEW BAGNE HOUSE BAGNIO BORDEL CORINTH LUPANAR SHEBANG BORDELLO CATHOUSE HOOKSHOP HOTHOUSE JOYHOUSE SERAGLIO

BROTHER FR BUB FRA KIN PAL SIB BHAI BRER EGIL FRAY MATE MONK PEER BILLY BUBBY BUDDY CADET FRERE FRIAR FELLOW FRAILE FRATER GERMAN COMRADE SIBLING FOSTERER

(HUSBAND'S —) LEVIR

(LAY —) SCOLOG

(WIFE'S —) AFFINE

(YOUNGER —) CADET

(PL.) FF ADELPHI BRETHREN CURIATII HARLUNGEN

(PREF.) ADELPHO FRATRI

(SUFF.) ADELPHIA ADELPHOUS

BROTHERHOOD GILD GUILD LODGE ORDER PAPEY FRIARY BRATSVO CHISHTI THIASOS THIASUS BRODHULL SODALITY

(— OF FREEMASONS) CRAFT

(LITERARY —) FELIBRIGE

BROTHER-IN-LAW MAUGH

BROTHERS KARAMAZOV

(AUTHOR OF —) DOSTOEVSKI

(CHARACTER IN —) IVAN ALEXEY DMITRI FYODOR ALYOSHA KATRINA ZOSSIMA GRUSHENKA SMERDYAKOV

BROUGHAM PILLBOX CARRIAGE

BROUGHT BROCHT

(— FROM ELSEWHERE) DERIVED

(— TO BAY) CORNERED

(— TOGETHER) CONFLATE

(— UP BY HAND) CADE

BROW TOP BRAE EDGE MIEN SNAB BOUND BRINK CREST EAVES FRONT RIDGE SLOPE BOLDNESS FOREHEAD

BROWBEAT BOSS FACE ABASH BULLY BOUNCE HECTOR DEPRESS DUMBCOW OUTFACE SWAGGER

BROWBEATEN HACKED

BROWN (ALSO SEE COLOR) ART

DUN TAN ARAB COIN COOK DARK GOAT LION SEAR ABRAM ACORN ARGUS BRUNO DUSKY HAZEL KAFFA MOSUL PABLO PENNY QUAIL SEDGE SEPIA TAWNY TENNE TOAST UMBER APACHE BEAVER BRUNET BURNET GLOOMY MALAGA MANILA MASTIC MOHAWK PALOMA PLOVER PONGEE RABBIT RUSSET SENNET TANNED TURTLE WIGWAM ASPHALT FUSCOUS HARVEST LIBERIA MUSCADE OAKWOOD OXBLOOD POMPEII PRAIRIE REDWOOD TANBARK TOBACCO VESUVIN BRUNETTE MOCCASIN MUSHROOM PHEASANT PERSIMMON PYGMALION

(CONDOR —) TIFFIN

(DARK —) BURNET

(GRAYISH —) DUN

(HAIR —) ARGALI

(LIGHT —) ALOMA ALESAN STRING

(OLIVE —) BARK AUTUMN

(REDDISH —) BAY SORE SEPIA AUBURN CROTAL GINGER RUSSET SORREL AMBROSIA

(YELLOWISH —) AZTEC ALMOND BAMBOO BLONDE BEESWAX ALDERNEY

(PREF.) AITHO

BROWNBACK DOWITCH DOWITCHER

BROWNED ADUST

BROWN HEART RAAN

BROWNIE ELF INS COOKY DOBBY NISSE URISK DOBBIE GOBLIN URUISG

BROWNING SCALD SCORCH SUNTAN

BROWNISH UMBER BURNET

(— BLACK) LAVA

BROWNSTONE CHESTNUT

BROWSE BRUT CROP FEED GRAZE FORAGE NIBBLE PASTURE

BRUCITE NEMALITE

BRUISE JAM BASH BRAY BUBU DENT DUNT HURT JAMB MAIM MAUL SORE STUN TUND BLACK BREAK BRIZZ CRUSH CURRY DELVE DINGE FRUSH POUND PUNCH SQUAT BATTER BREACH HATTER INJURY INTUSE MANGLE POUNCE SHINER STOUND SUGGIL BATTERY CONTUND CROWNER DAMMISH DISABLE

(— FLAX) BRAKE

BRUISED HURT LIVID FROISSE

BRUIT DIN FAME RALE ROAR TELL NOISE RUMOR SOUND BLAZON CLAMOR REPORT DECLARE HEARSAY

BRUNEI (— WEIGHT) PARA CHAPAH

(COIN OF —) SEN

(TOWN OF —) SERIA

BRUNET DARK BLACK BROWN GIPSY GYPSY MORENA SWARTHY BRUNETTE MORENITA

BRUNHILD (HUSBAND OF —) GUNTHER

BRUNT JAR BLOW JOLT CLASH FORCE ONSET SHOCK ATTACK

EFFORT IMPACT STRAIN STRESS ASSAULT OUTBURST VIOLENCE

BRUSH DIP DUB PIG TIP BOSH CARD COMB DUST FLAP FLAT FRAY KIYI SKIM SWAB BROOM CHAPE CLEAN COPSE FIGHT FITCH GRAZE LINER SABLE SCOPA SCRUB SCUFF SWEEP SWOOP WHISK BADGER BATTLE BRIGHT BROSSE DABBER DAUBER DUSTER MOGOTE PALLET PENCIL PICKUP PUTOIS RIGGER RUBBER SPONGE STROKE TEASEL CLEANSE FOXTAIL GRAINER GROOMER MOTTLER STIPPLE STRIPER THICKET SCRUBBER SKIRMISH SOFTENER STIPPLER TARBRUSH NAILBRUSH PAINTBRUSH

(— ASIDE) SCUFF

(— IN DANCING) SCUFFLE

(— OF HAIR) PENCIL

(— OF TWIGS) COW

(— TO CLEAN SHIP BOTTOM) HOG

(BLUNT —) BLENDER

(DENSE —) BUNDOCKS BOONDOCKS

(ELECTRIC —) DOCTOR

(EMPHASIZED —) SLAP

(FLESH —) SCRAPER STRIGIL

(GROWTH OF —) SYLVAGE

(POLLEN —) SCOPA SAROTHRUM

(SMALL —) TOOL FITCH FITCHEW

(PREF.) MUSCARI SCOPI

BRUSHER LIMBER LIPPER

BRUSH MAKER FLIRTY FLICKER

BRUSH SHUNT PIGTAIL

BRUSHWOOD HAG RICE RONE RUSH BAVIN BRAKE BRUSH COPSE FRITH REISE SCROG SCRUB SPRAY COPPET GARSIL MALLEE RAMMEL SCRAWL SCRUNT SHROGS TINNET TINSEL COPPICE ROUGHIE TEENAGE THICKET WOODRIS BUSHWOOD OVENWOOD

BRUSQUE CURT RUDE BLUFF BLUNT GRUFF HASTY ROUGH SHORT ABRUPT VIOLENT CAVALIER IMPOLITE

BRUTAL CRUEL FERAL GROSS CARNAL COARSE SAVAGE BEASTLY BESTIAL BRUTISH CADDISH DOGGISH INHUMAN BELLUINE INHUMANE INSOLENT RUTHLESS

BRUTE BETE BEAST GROSS YAHOO ANIMAL BRUTAL SAVAGE BEASTLY BESTIAL BRUTISH GORILLA RUFFIAN

BRUTISH FELL CRUEL BRUTAL CARNAL FIERCE SAVAGE STUPID BESTIAL INHUMAN SENSUAL GADARENE

BRYONY HOP NEP ALRAUN COWBIND MANDRAKE

(— FRUIT) OXBERRY

BRYOPHYTE ANOPHYTE LIVERWORT

BRYOZOAN POLYZOAN

BRYTHONIC CYMRIC KYMRIC BRITTONIC

BUBBLE AIR BUB BEAD BELL BLEB BLOB BOIL BOLL DUPE FOAM

GLOB SCUM SEED CAPER CHEAT EMPTY VAPOR BURBLE DELUDE HOTTER POPPLE SEETHE SOTTER TRIFLE BLISTER BLUBBER DECEIVE GLOBULE DELUSIVE

(— IN GLASS) BOIL REAM SEED BLISTER

(PL.) SUDS

(PREF.) BULLI

BUBBLING GAY BULLER BURBLY BOILING GASSING EFFUSIVE

BUBINGA KEVAZINGO

BUBO EMEROD

BUCCANEER PIRATE RIFLER ROBBER VIKING CORSAIR MARINER SPOILER MAROONER PICAROON

BUCHMANITE GROUPER

BUCHU BUKA DIOSMA

BUCK FOB RAM BOIL BUTT DEER DUDE MALE PRIG REAR SOAK STAG TOFF WASH BLOOD DANDY PITCH SASIN STEEP BASKET DOLLAR OPPOSE RESIST STRIVE SAWBUCK BUCKJUMP BUCKWASH

(— IN 1ST YEAR) FAWN

(— IN 2ND YEAR) PRICKET

(— IN 3RD YEAR) SORREL

(— IN 4TH YEAR) SORE

(— STEADILY) SUNFISH

(— UP) BRACE

BUCKBEAN BOGBEAN THREEFOLD

BUCKER DOLLYMAN

BUCKET SAY TUB BAIL BOOT BOWK CAGE GRAB MEAL PAIL SKIP BOWIE CHEAT SCOOP SKEEL STOOP STOUP BAILER DIPPER DRENCH HOPPET KIBBLE SITULA SUCKER VESSEL FERMAIL GRAPPLE SNAPPER SWINDLE CANNIKIN HEDGEHOG PAINTPOT

(— ON MILL WHEEL) AW AWE EIE

(— ON WHEELS) SKIP

(GLASS-MAKING —) CUVETTE

(GRAVEL —) GRAB

(HOISTING —) HUDGE

(PART OF —) EAR RIM BAIL BODY CURL HANDLE

(TWO —S OF WATER) GAIT

BUCKEYE STATE OHIO

BUCKLAW HAYSTON

BUCKLE BOW BEND CURL KINK OUCH TACH TACK WARP BRACE CLASP MARRY STRAP TACHE TWIST FIBULA CONTEND FERMAIL GRAPPLE FASTENER STRUGGLE

BUCKLER CRAB BLOCK PELTA SCUTE TARGE SHIELD TAIRGE TARGET BUCKLUM BUCKRAM ROTELLA ROUNDEL SHUTTER RONDACHE

BUCKLING KINK UPSET

BUCK RAKE SWEEP

BUCKRAM STIFFENER

BUCKTHORN COMA RHAMN SCROG WAHOO ALATERN CASCARA BEARWOOD FRANGULA LOTEBUSH WAYTHORN STINKWOOD

BUCKTHORN BROWN SUMAC SUMACH

BUCKWHEAT BUCK CRAP BRANK WRIGHT KNOTWEED SARRAZIN

POLYGONUM
(PL.) FAGOPYRUM
BUCOLIC IDYL LOCAL NAIVE
RURAL FARMER RUSTIC SIMPLE
COWHERD ECLOGUE AGRESTIC
HERDSMAN PASTORAL
BUCOLION (FATHER OF —)
LAOMEDON
(SON OF —) AESEPUS PEDASUS
(WIFE OF —) ABARBAREA
BUD BUR EYE GEM IMP PIP BULB
BURR CION FORM GERM GIRL
GROW KNOP KNOT WORK CAPOT
CHILD CLOVE GEMMA GRAFT
SCION SHOOT SPRIT SPURT
YOUTH BUDLET BULBIL BUTTON
FLOWER GERMIN OCULUS OILLET
SPROUT BLOSSOM BROTHER
CABBAGE GEMMULE PLUMULE
ROSEBUD TENDRON BOURGEON
BULBILLA
(BLIGHTED —) BLAST
(BROOD —) SOREDIUM
(UNDEVELOPED —) EYE
(UNOPENED —) KNOSP
(PL.) CAPERS
(PREF.) BLAST(O) GEMMI GEMMO
BUDDENBROOKS (AUTHOR OF —)
MANN
(CHARACTER IN —) TOM JEAN
TONI ERICA GERDA HANNO
JOHANN THOMAS ANTONIE
GRUNLICH CHRISTIAN
PERMANEDER
BUDDHA FO FOH BUTSU JATAKA
GAUTAMA SRAMANA DAIBUTSU
(— STORY) JATAKA
(FATHER OF —) SUDDHODANA
(SON OF —) KAHULA
BUDDHISM DAIJO FOISM KEGON
CHANISM LAMAISM HINAYANA
(— CODE) VINAYA
(BRANCH OF —) MAHAYANA
BUDDHIST (— DOCTRINE) ANATTA
TRIKAYA
(— FESTIVAL) WESAK
(— PATH) VEHICLE
(— SCHOOL) RITSU
(— SECT) SHIN TENDAI
BUDDLE TYE FRAME BODDLE
SLIMER STRIPE TROUGH
BUDDY BO BOY BUD PAL JACK
MATE COBBER DIGGER BROTHER
COMRADE COMPADRE TENTMATE
BUDGE FUR JEE BOGY MOVE STIR
BOOZE BRISK MUDGE STIFF THIEF
JOCUND LIQUOR SOLEMN
AUSTERE POMPOUS MOVEMENT
BUDGET BAG BOGY BOOT PACK
PLAN ROLL BATCH BOGEY BOGIE
BUNCH STOCK STORE BOTTLE
BUNDLE PARCEL SOCKET WALLET
PROGRAM
BUFF ASH BOB FAN TAN BLOW
COAT CURT FIRM SHINE SNUFF
SPARK BUFFET POLISH STURDY
STAMMER STUTTER NAUMKEAG
(TILLEUL —) ALABASTER
BUFFALO OX ANOA ARNA ARNI
BUFF STAG ARNEE BISON BUGLE
BUFFLE HAMPER KERBAU
MURRAH WUNTEE CARABAO
CARIBOU GAZELLE OVERAWE

TIMARAU ZAMOUSE BEWILDER
SAPIUTAN SELADANG
BUFFALO CHIPS BODEWASH
BUFFALO FISH SUCKER BUFFALO
BIGMOUTH GOURDHEAD
BUFFER DOG PAD FROG RACK
BUMPER FENDER HURTER PISTOL
CUSHION
BUFFET BAR BOB BOX BEAT BLAD
BLOW BUFF CUFF GOWF PLAT
SCAT SLAP TOSS YANK FILIP
KNOCK SCUFF SCUFT SMITE
STOOL ABACUS BATTER FILLIP
FLEWIT SERVER SETOUT STRIKE
STRIVE THRASH COLPHEG
CONTEND COUNTER HASSOCK
SMACKER SQUELCH CREDENCE
CREDENZA CUPBOARD
SPANGHEW
BUFFETING DIRD SKITE DUSTING
BUFFLEHEAD DUCK FOOL CLOWN
BUFFLE DIPPER DOPPER
MARIONET WOOLHEAD
MERRYWING
BUFFOON DOR WAG WIT APER
FOOL JAPE MIME MOME VICE
ZANY ACTOR ANTIC BUFFO
CLOWN COMIC DROLE DROLL
HARLOT JESTER MUMMER
STOOGE ANTIQUE BOUFFON
FARCEUR JUGGLER PIERROT
PLAYBOY SCOGGIN TOMFOOL
BALATRON GRACIOSO HUMORIST
MACAROON MERRYMAN
OWLGLASS PLEASANT RIDICULE
PANTALOON SCARAMOUCH
PUNCHINELLO
BUFFOONERY JAPERY ZANYISM
CLOWNERY TOMFOOLERY
BUG (ALSO SEE INSECT) DOR FLAW
GERM IDEA MITE BOGEY BULGE
FIEND LYGUS ROACH ARADID
BEDBUG BEETLE BUGGER CAPSID
CHINCH COREID CORUCO ELATER
INSECT SALDID SCHEME TINGID
BELLIED BOATMAN BUGBEAR
CIMICID CORSAIR FORWARD
POMPOUS STRIDER BARBEIRO
CONENOSE HEMIPTER HOBBYIST
NAUCORID VINCHUCA
(RED —) CHIGGA CHIGGER
(SOW —) SLATER
(PREF.) CIMI(CI)
(SUFF.) CORIS
BUGABOO BOGY FEAR GOGA
GOGO OGRE TURK ALARM BOGEY
BOGIE GOGGA BODACH GOBLIN
BUGBEAR SPECTER SPECTRE
WORRICOW
BUGANDA (— KING) KABAKA
BUGBANE COHOSH BUGWORT
RICHWEED HELLEBORE
BUGBEAR BUG COW BOGY OGRE
BOGEY BOGIE CADDY MORMO
POKER BOGGLE BOGGART
BUGABOO FEARBABE SCAREBUG
BUGGER SOD CHAP BOOGER
FELLOW PERSON RASCAL
HERETIC
BUGGY CART SHAY TRAP NUTTY
CALESA CABOOSE CALESIN
FOOLISH VEHICLE DEMENTED
INFESTED ROADSTER STANHOPE

BUGLE BEAD HORN BLACK
BUFFALO BULLOCK CLARION
HUTCHET TRUMPET KEYBUGLE
(— CALL) WARISON
(PART OF —) CUP RIM BELL BITE
EDGE
(YELLOW —) IVA
BUGLER WINDJAMMER
BUGLOSS ALKANET ANCHUSA
BLUEWEED OXTONGUE
BUILD BIG SET FORM LEVY MAKE
REAR TELD CREATE DRIVE EDIFY
ERECT FOUND FRAME HOUSE
RAISE SHAPE THROW FABRIC
GRAITH TAILLE TIMBER COMPILE
EXTRUCT FASHION ASSEMBLE
PHYSIQUE
(— FIRE) CHUNK
(— HASTILY) CLAP
(— NEST) AERIE NIDIFY
(— UP) AGGRADE
(BODY —) HABITUS
BUILDER EPEUS MAKER BIGGAR
EPEIUS HANGER ERECTOR
ENGINEER TECTONIC
(DAM —) DAMMER
(PREF.) TECTO
(SUFF.) TECT
BUILDING GIN CASA CRIB DOME
FLAT HALL IGLU JAIL LAND PILE
SHED SHOP SLAB SPOT TELD
ABBEY AEDES ARENA BLOCK
COURT FOLLY FRAME HOTEL
HOUSE IGLOO JAWAB STORE
STUDY ARMORY BIGGIN BOTTLE
CASING CHAPEL FABRIC GARAGE
HAMMAM INSULA LYCEUM
PALACE SCHOOL SUCCOR
BREWERY BROODER CARBARN
COLLEGE DIORAMA EDIFICE
FACTORY FLATTOP FOUNDRY
KURHAUS MANSION PALAZZO
SALTERN STATION SYNAGOG
ATHENEUM BAGHOUSE BASILICA
BROLETTO CHANCERY DIPTEROS
DRYHOUSE DWELLING DYEHOUSE
ELEVATOR EPHEBEUM FIRETRAP
GASHOUSE GINHOUSE HOTHOUSE
ICEHOUSE MAGAZINE NYMPHEUM
PANORAMA SERAPEUM
STEMMERY TAXPAYER TENEMENT
VELODROME OBSERVATORY
OUTBUILDING PLANETARIUM
MEETINGHOUSE
(— FOR AIRCRAFT) DOCK
(— GROUPS) HAM
(— OF STONE) KAABA CASHEL
TRUDDO TRULLO
(— ON POSTS) PATAKA
(— WITH TRIANGULAR FRONT)
AFRAME
(BUDDHIST —) TOPE
(CIRCULAR —) THOLE THOLOS
ROTUNDA
(CRUDE —) SHANTY
(DILAPIDATED —) ROOKERY
FIRETRAP
(EXHIBITION —) MUSEUM
(FARM —) BARN STABLE
HACIENDA
(FORTIFIED —) CASTLE
(GLOOMY —) MAUSOLEUM
(GRAIN —) GARNER

(GROUP OF —S) CLUSTER
(JAI ALAI —) FRONTON
(MOVABLE —) TURRET
(ORNAMENTAL —) ALCOVE
(PUBLIC —) CASINO THEATER
THEATRE COLISEUM
(QUADRANGULAR —) TETRAGON
(QUARANTINE —) LAZARET
(ROUND —) THOLUS
(SACRED —) CHURCH MOSQUE
TEMPLE SACRARY PANTHEON
SARAPEUM
(SERIES OF —S) SWEEP
(SLIGHT —) SHED
(SMALL —) HUT COOP HOCK
EDICULE
(SPORTS —) CAGE
(STATELY —) DOME
(STORAGE —) BARN HORREUM
(SUBSIDIARY —) ANNEX
(TALL —) SKYSCRAPER
(TRADE —) HALL
(UNCOMFORTABLE —) ARK
(PL.) FUNDUS
BUILT SET BOUKIT STACKED
TIMBERED
(COMPACTLY —) CORKY
(HEAVILY —) BLOCKY
(LOOSELY —) GANGLING
(STRONGLY —) BURLY GROSS
QUARRY
(WELL —) BUIRDLY
BUKIDNON MONTES BINOKID
BUKKI (FATHER OF —) JOGLI
ABISHUA
(SON OF —) UZZI
BULB BUD SET BLUB CORM IXIA
KNOB LAMP ROOT SEED SEGO
CAMAS CHIVE CLOVE FLOAT
GLOBE ONION SWELL TUBER
BULBIL BULBUS CAMASS CROCUS
GARLIC OFFSET SCILLA BABIANA
GALTONIA SPARAXIS TRITONIA
PHOTOFLASH
(— OF PERCUSSION) CONCHOID
(LIGHT —) HELION
(ONION —) BUTTON
(PL.) SQUILL
(PREF.) BULBI BULBO
BULBIL CHIVE BULBLET
(PL.) SPAWN
BULBLET CHIVE CORMEL BULBULE
NUCLEUS PROPAGO
BULBUL KALA BUHLBUHL
GREENBUL LEAFBIRD

BULGARIA

ASSEMBLY: SOBRANJE SOBRANYE
CAPE: EMINE SABLA KURATAN
CAPITAL: SOFIA
COIN: LEV LEW STOTINKA
COMMUNE: SLIVEN SLIVNO
SISTOVA
GULF: BURGAS
MEASURE: OKA OKE KRINE LEKHE
MOUNTAIN: BOTEV SAPKA
MUSALA VIKHREN
MOUNTAINS: PIRIN BALKAN
RHODOPE
PEOPLE: SLAV TATAR BULGAR
SLAVIC
RIVER: LOM VIT ARDA OSMA ISKER
MESTA DANUBE MARICA

OGOSTA STRUMA YANTRA
MARITSA STRYAMA TUNDZHA
TOWN: RILA RUSE AYTOS BUTAN
BYCLU ELENA ISKRA STARA
VARNA BLEVEN BURGAS
DULOVO LEVSKY PLEVNA
SHUMEN SHUMLA SLIVEN
SLIVNO WIDDIN YAMBOL
ZAGORA GABROVO KARLOVO
PLOVDIV SISTOVA TIRNOVO
RUSTCHUK
WEIGHT: OKA OKE TOVAR

BULGARIAN POMAK
BULGE BAG BUG JUT SAG BIAS
BULB BUMP CASK HUMP KNOB
LUMP PANT BILGE BLOAT BOUGE
FLASK POUCH START STRUT
SWELL BEETLE BILLOW COCKLE
EXTEND PUCKER WALLET BLISTER
PROJECT OVERHANG PROTRUDE
SWELLING PROJECTION
(— OUT) TUT BELLY BOWDEN
STRUNT
(OFFENSIVE —) SALIENT
BULGING FULL BOMBE BOWED
BUGGY GOUTY PUDGY TUMID
BAGGED BUNCHY CONVEX
GOOGLY TOROSE GAMPISH
GIBBOUS GOUTISH SWOLLEN
BOUFFANT PROPTOSIS
BULK BODY BOUK FECK HEAP HEFT
HOLD HULK HULL LUMP MASS
MOLE PILE SIZE BURLY CARGO
GROSS MIGHT POWER SLUMP
STALL SWELL CORPSE AMOUNT
EXTENT FIGURE VOLUME BIGNESS
MAJORITY QUANTITY
(PREF.) ONCO
BULKHEAD CHECK BATTERY
PARTITION
BULKY BIG MAIN BURLY GROSS
LARGE LUSTY PUDGY STOUT
CLUMSY STODGY HULKING
LUMPING MASSIVE VOLUMED
WEIGHTY CUMBROUS UNWIELDY
(PREF.) PYCN(O)
BULL COP SEG APIS BEEF BILL JEST
MALE ROAN SEAL SEGG SLIP
STOT TORO ZEBU BACIS BEEVE
BOBBY BONER BOVID BRUTE
CROCK DRINK EDICT ERROR
ANIMAL BOVINE BUSHWA LETTER
PEELER TAURUS BULLOCK
BUSHWAH CRITTER CRUSADE
NOVILLO TAURINE CAJOLERY
DOCUMENT FLATTERY IRISHISM
(— AREA) QUERENCIA
(— KILLING) VOLAPIE
(HORNLESS —) DODDY DODDIE
(HUMAN-HEADED —) SHEDU
CAMASSU
(YOUNG —) STOT BUGLE MICKY
STIRK STOTT BULLOCK
(PL.) BATTERY
(PREF.) TAUR(I)(O)
BULLA BLEB BULL SEAL BLAIN
BLISTER VESICLE
BULL CELL TORIL
BULLDOG BULL BULLER BULLDOZE
BULLDOZE COW RAM BULLY
FORCE SCOOP COERCE
BROWBEAT BULLYRAG RESTRAIN

BULLDOZER (PART OF —) ARM EYE
SHOE TANK BLADE FRAME IDLER
LEVER LIGHT STRUT TRACK
CANOPY FENDER GRILLE ROLLER
CLEANER HOUSING MUFFLER
CYLINDER
BULLET GUN BALL LEAD PILL SHOT
SLUG TOWEL CONOID DUMDUM
PELLET PICKET SINKER TRACER
DINGBAT MISSILE PELLOCK
PROJECT SPITZER BISCAYAN
MUSHROOM WADCUTTER
(PL.) BALL LEAD STUFF
BULLETIN ITEM MEMO NOTICE
POSTER REPORT SERIAL
PROGRAM NEWSBILL
BULLFIGHT CORRIDA NOVILLADA
BULLFIGHTER TORERO MATADOR
PICADOR CAPEADOR TOREADOR
NOVILLERO
BULLFIGHTING REJONEO
TAUROMACHY
BULLFINCH ALP OLP HOOP MAWP
MONK NOPE OLPH POPE HEDGE
TANNY TAWNY MONACH
REDBIRD REDHOOP SHIRLEY
BLOODALP TONYHOOP
BULLHEAD CUR POUT POGGE'
COTTOID
BULLHORN HAILER
BULLIMONG FARRAGE
BULLION BILLOT
BULLISH STIFF
BULLOCK HOG HOGG NEAT NOWT
STOT BUGLE COACH KNOUT
STEER STIRK BOVINE
(AUSTRALIAN —) SNAIL
(BAD-TEMPERED —) RAGER
(DECOY —) COACH
BULL-ROARER BUZZ BUMMER
BUZZER ROARER TUNDUN
HUMBUZZ TURNDUN WHIZZER
BULL'S-EYE EYE BULL DUMP GOLD
BLANK OXEYE WHITE TARGET
ROUNDEL
BULL SNAKE GOPHER
BULL TROUT TRUFF
BULLY COW NUT BOAT BOSS FACE
FINE GOOD HAZE HUFF MATE
BRAVE BRAVO GREAT JOLLY
SNOOL TIGER VAPOR BOUNCE
CUTTER CUTTLE HARASS HECTOR
HUFFER JOVIAL RUFFLE TYRANT
BLUSTER BOUNCER BULLOCK
DARLING DASHING GALLANT
GAUSTER HUFFCAP ROISTER
RUFFIAN RUFFLER SLASHER
SOLDIER SWAGGER BANGSTER
BARRATER BLUDGEON
BROWBEAT BULLDOZE DOMINEER
FRAMPLER NIGHTCAP RABIATOR
(MASTIC —) ACOMA
BULLY TREE BALATA BULLACE
GAUSTER BEEFWOOD
BULRUSH REED RISP RUSH TULE
SEDGE BUMBLE GLUMAL AKAAKAI
CATTAIL PAPYRUS SCIRPUS
TUSSOCK
BULWARK BAIL FORT WALL FENCE
JETTY MANTA MOUND TOWER
SCONCE WARDER BASTION
DEFENCE DEFENSE PARAPET
PROTECT RAMPART WEREWALL

BUM BEG DIN BOMB BOOM HOBO
DRINK DRONE IDLER MOOCH
SHACK STIFF TRAMP FROLIC
GUZZLE SPONGE SQUEEF
GUZZLER LAYABOUT VAGABOND
BINDLESTIFF
BUMBLE ERR
BUMBLEBEE DOR CLOCK BUMBEE
BUMBLE CARDER BUMBLER
BUMMER SKIDDER
BUMP CRY HIP HIT NOB BANG
BLOW BOOM BUNK DIRD JOLT
JOWL KNOB LUMP WHAP WHOP
BARGE BULGE CLASH CLOUR
CLOUT DUNCH KNOCK ORGAN
THUMP BOUNCE CANNON
IMPACT JOUNCE NODULE STRIKE
BITTERN COLLIDE CONFLICT
SWELLING
(— IN SKI RUN) MOGUL
(— ON WHALE'S HEAD) HOVEL
BUMPER BOWL FINE GOOD FACER
GLASS ROUSE BUFFER CASABE
FENDER GOBLET HURTER KELTIE
BRIMMER DINGMAN CARANGID
(— GUARD) OVERRIDER
BUMPKIN JAY YAP BEAM BOOM
BOOR CHAW CLOD GAWK HICK
LOUT PUTT RUBE SWAB SWAD
TIKE TYKE CHURL CLOWN ROBIN
YAHOO YOKEL FARMER JOSKIN
LUMMOX RUSTIC BUCOLIC
CAUBOGE HAWBUCK
BUMPTIOUS COXY BRASH COCKSY
BUN PUG CHOU BRICK COOKIE
BUNAH (FATHER OF —) JERAHMEEL
BUNCH BOB SET BALE BOSS CHOU
CLEW CLUB CLUE COMA KICK
KNOB KNOT PACK SWAD TUFT
WISP BREAK CLUMP FAGOT
FLOCK KNOLL PAHIL THUMP
CLUTCH GAGGLE HUDDLE
(— OF BANANAS) HAND STEM
(— OF FLAX) HEAD STRICK
(— OF FLOWERS) BOWPOT
BOUQUET BOUGHPOT
(— OF FRUIT) HOG STRAP
(— OF GRAIN) RIP
(— OF GRAPES) RAISIN
(— OF GRASS) WHISK
(— OF HAIR) COB
(— OF HERBS) BOUQUET
(— OF IVY) BUSH
(— OF TOBACCO LEAVES) HAND
BREAK
(— OF TWIGS) COW KOW
(— UP) SHRUG
(SMALL —) WISP
BUNCHER BINDER
BUNCHY TRUSS
BUNCOMBE HOOEY BUNKUM
BUND BAND QUAY PRAYA LEAGUE
SOCIETY
BUNDLE KID LOT PAD TOD WAD
WAP BALE BAND BEAT BOLT
BOOK BUNG DRUG DRUM GARB
HANK HAUL HEAD KNOT LOCK
PACK ROLL SWAG BLUEY BULTO
BUNCH FADGE FAGOT GAVEL
GLEAN GROUP LITCH NICKY
PETER SHEAF SKEIN TARRY
TRACE TRUSS TURSE WADGE
BARSOM BATTEN BINDLE BOTTLE

BUDGET DRIVER DUFTER FAGGOT
FARDEL FASCES FUMBLE GATHER
KNITCH LOGGIN NUMBER PACKET
PARCEL SCROLL THRAVE
DORLACH FASCINE GARBAGE
MATILDA PACKAGE FASCICLE
TROUSSEAU
(— OF BOARDS) BOLT
(— OF CELLULOSE) MICROFIBRIL
(— OF FASCINES) ROULEAU
(— OF FIBRILS) AXONEME
(— OF FILAMENTS) BYSSUS
(— OF FLAX) BEET HEAD
(— OF HAIR) LEECH
(— OF HAY, STRAW, ETC.) WAP
WASE WISP GAVEL SHEAF
BATTEN BOLTIN BOTTLE TIPPLE
WINDLING
(— OF HEATH) KID
(— OF HIDES) KIP
(— OF NERVE FIBERS) TRACT
COLUMN
(— OF PAPERS) SPUR DUFTER
(— OF RODS) FASCES
(— OF SACKS) BADGER
(— OF SACRED TWIGS) BARSOM
(— OF THONGS) KNOUT
(— OF TOBACCO) CARROT
(— OF TWIGS) BIRCH BROOM
FAGGOT
(— OF WOOD) PIMP BAVIN FAGOT
(— OF YARN) HAUL SLIP
(— OF 60 SKINS) TURN
(BUSHMAN'S —) DRUM BLUEY
BUNG CORK DOOK PLUG SHIVE
SPILE STOPPER
BUNGEY KIT
BUNGI-BUNGI STAVEWOOD
BUNGLE ERR BOOB DUFF FLUB
GOOF MESS MUCK MUFF MULL
BLUNK BOTCH FAULT FLUFF
FUDGE MISDO SPOIL STICK
BOGGLE BOLLIX BUMBLE FOOZLE
FUMBLE MANGLE MOMBLE
MUCKER MUDDLE TAILOR
TOGGLE BAUCHLE BLUNDER
BUTCHERY SHAMMOCK
BUNGLER MUFF LUMMOX PUDDLE
TINKER BLUNKER BUMBLER
BUMMLER FOOZLER DAUBSTER
SCHLEMIEL
BUNGLING FLUFF FUDGY INERT
CLUMSY AWKWARD TINKERLY
MUDDLEHEADED
BUNG START FLOGGER
BUNION ONION WYROCK
CARBUNCLE
BUNJI-BUNJI CUDGERIE
BUNK BED CAR BLAA BLAH CASE
JUNK SACK ABIDE BERTH BUNKO
FRAME HOKUM HOOEY LEAVE
LODGE SLEEP TRUCK BUNKUM
TIMBER BALONEY BOLSTER
CHICORY HEMLOCK TWADDLE
BUNCOMBE COBBLERS MALARKEY
NONSENSE
BUNKHOUSE BULLPEN
BUNKUM BLAH BUNK FUDGE
HOKUM HOOPLA BALONEY
BUNCOMBE MALARKEY
BUNTAL BURI BANGKOK
BUNTING EBB POP CIRL FLAG PAPE
POPE CHINK DUMPY FINCH

PLUMP COTTON STOCKY TOWHEE
UNTIDY COWBIRD ETAMINE
GARMENT OATFOWL ORTOLAN
ROUNDED BELLYING BOBOLINK
PRUSIANO RICEBIRD RINGBIRD
SLOVENLY NONPAREIL
BUNTON DIVIDER
BUNUS (FATHER OF —) HERMES
  (MOTHER OF —) ALCIDAMEA
BUOY DAN WAFT BAKEN ELATE
  FLOAT LAGAN RAISE BEACON
  MARKER DOLPHIN SUSTAIN
  DEADHEAD LEVITATE MAKEFAST
  SONOBUOY
BUOYANCY BALON BALLON
  LEVITY SPRING ELATION
BUOYANT GAY CORKY HAPPY
  LIGHT BLITHE BOUNCY FLOATY
  LIVELY ELASTIC HOPEFUL
  JOCULAR LILTING SPRINGY
  ANIMATED CHEERFUL SANGUINE
  SPIRITED VOLATILE
BUPHAGUS (FATHER OF —)
  IAPETUS
  (MOTHER OF —) THORNAX
  (SLAYER OF —) ARTEMIS
BUR BUZZ TEAZEL STICKER
BURBARK AKONGE BOXBUSH
  BURRBARK
BURBOT COD CONY CUSK LING
  LOTA CONEY LOCHE LAWYER
  MORGAY DOGFISH EELPOUT
  GUDGEON BIRDBOLT
BURBUNG BORA
BURDEN TAX VEX BIRN CARE CARK
  CLAG CLOG DRAG DUTY FARE
  FOOT GANG LADE LOAD MUCK
  ONUS PORT SEAM TACK TASK
  BIRTH CARGO CROWD CRUSH
  DRONE HEAVY LABOR MIDST
  CHARGE CUMBER ENTAIL FARDEL
  HAMPER IMPOSE LADING SADDLE
  THRACK WEIGHT BALLAST
  BURTHEN CONVETH FRAUGHT
  FREIGHT HAGRIDE ONERATE
  OPPRESS REFRAIN REPRISE
  SUMPTER TROUBLE CAPACITY
  CARRIAGE ENCUMBER ENGREGGE
  HANDICAP OVERCOME PRESSURE
  QUANTITY RUMBELOW
  MILLSTONE RESPONSIBILITY
  (— OF SONG) WHEEL FADING
  HOLDING OVERTURN OVERWORD
  (FINANCIAL —) EXPENSE
BURDENED HEAVY LADEN GRAVID
  FRAUGHT HARASSED
BURDENER INCUBUS
BURDENSOME HEAVY IRKSOME
  ONEROUS WEIGHTY CUMBROUS
  GRIEVOUS GRINDING LOADSOME
BURDOCK DOCK GOBO CLITE
  CLOTE CLOTS DRAIN LAPPA
  BARDANE BURWEED BUZZIES
  CADILLO CLOTBUR HARDOCK
  HAREBUR CLEAVERS HAULBACK
BUREAU DESK CHEST AGENCY
  EXCISE OFFICE CENTRAL DRESSER
  AGITPROP
BUREAUCRAT MANDARIN
BURFISH ATINGA
BURGEON BUD GROW ERUPT
  SHOOT SPROUT
BURGESS CITIZEN FREEMAN

PORTMAN COMMONER GORGIBUS
  (PL.) BURGWARE
BURG GRASS SANDBUR
  COCKSPUR SANDSPUR
BURGLAR YEGG CRACK THIEF
  GOPHER ROBBER RAFFLES
  YEGGMAN PETERMAN PICKLOCK
BURGLARY BREAK CRACK THEFT
  LARCENY ROBBERY STEALAGE
BURGUNDY MACON POMMARD
  VOUGEOT TONNERRE
BURIAL FUNERARY INTERMENT
  (— MOUND) TOLA HUACA
BURIAL PLACE AHU TOMB GRAVE
  BURIAL GIGUNU LAYSTOW
  PYRAMID CATACOMB CEMETERY
  GOLGOTHA LAYSTALL
BURIED HIDDEN HUMATE SEPULT
  ABSORBED IMBEDDED
  (NOT —) UNRESTED
  (RECENTLY —) GREEN
BURIN GRAVER PLASTIC
BURL BURR KNAR KNOT LUMP
  KNAUR PIMPLE PUSTULE
BURLAP GUNNY CROCUS BAGGING
  HESSIAN SACKING WRAPPING
BURLER LECKER SPILER
BURLESQUE APE ODD COPY JEST
  MIME SKIT BURLY DROLL FARCE
  REVUE COMEDY OVERDO PARODY
  BUFFOON JOCULAR MIMICRY
  MOCKERY OVERACT DOGGEREL
  RIDICULE TRAVESTY
BURLY BIG FAT BLUFF BULKY
  GROSS HEAVY HUSKY LARGE
  LUSTY NOBLE OBESE STOUT
  THICK TRAMP BOWERLY BUIRDLY
  MASTIFF STATELY IMPOSING

BURMA

BAY: BENGAL HUNTER HEANZAY
CAPITAL: RANGOON
DIVISION: PEGU MAGWE ARAKAN
  KARENNI SAGAING MANDALAY
  IRRAWADDY TENASSERIM
GULF: MARTABAN
MEASURE: LY DHA GON LAN MAU
  NGU SAO TAO TAT BYEE DAIN
  PHAN SEIT TAUN TENG THAT
  SALAY SHITA THUOC LAMANY
  PALGAT TRUONG CHAIVAI
  OKTHABAH
MONEY: KYAT
MOUNTAIN: POPA NATTAUNG
  SARAMATI VICTORIA
MOUNTAINS: CHIN NAGA DAWNA
  KACHIN KARENNI PEGUYOMA
NATIVE: AO VU WA LAI LAO MON
  PYU TAI CHIN KADU KUKI LOLO
  MIAO NAGA SEMA SGAU SGAW
  SHAN THAI KAREN KHMER
  LHOTA BIRMAN BURMAN
  KACHIN RENGMA PALAUNG
  ARAKANESE
PLATEAU: SHAN
PORT: AKYAB BASSEIN HENZADA
  MOULMEIN
RIVER: HKA NMAI PEGU MEKONG
  SALWIN SHWELI KALADAN
  MALIKHA MYITNGE SALWEEN
  SITTANG CHINDWIN INDAWGYI
  IRRAWADDY
SEA: ANDAMAN

TOWN: YE AVA PEGU AKYAB
  BHAMO KARBE KATHA MINBU
  PAPUN PROME TAVOY HSENWI
  HSIPAW LASHIO MAYMYO
  MONYWA SHWEBO BASSEIN
  HENZADA PAKOKKU RANGOON
  MANDALAY MOULMEIN
WEIGHT: TA CAN MAT MOO PAI
  VIS BINH DONG KYAT RUAY
  VISS BAHAR BEHAR CANDY
  TICAL TICUL ABUCCO PEIKTHA

BUR MARIGOLD BACLIN CUCKOLD
BURMESE KADU BIRMAN
  ARAKANESE
BURN BREN BREW CHAR FIRE
  GLOW PLOT RAZE RILL SEAR SERE
  TEND TIND ADUST BLAZE BROIL
  BROOK CENSE CHARK CLAMP
  FLAME FLARE PARCH PLOUT
  QUICK ROAST SCALD SCAUM
  SINGE SWEAL WASTE WATER
  CLOZLE IGNIFY NIGGER SCORCH
  SIZZLE STREAM CHARPIT
  COMBURE COMBUST CONSUME
  CREMATE CROZZLE FLICKER
  FRIZZLE INCENSE OXIDIZE
  RIVULET SCOWDER SMOLDER
  FLAGRATE SQUANDER
  AMBUSTION
  (— FEEBLY) GUTTER
  (— FITFULLY) FLICKER
  (— IN) INURE
  (— MIDNIGHT OIL) LUCUBRATE
  (— OUT) GUT
  (— UP) ADUST EXUST
  (— WITH LITTLE FLAME) SMUDGE
  (LET —) BISHOP
  (PREF.) COMBURI
BURNED ADUST COMBUST
  (PREF.) AITHO
BURNER BEAK KORO BAKER PILOT
  ARGAND BUNSEN CENSER
  BATSWING CALCINER GASLIGHT
  THURIBLE WELSBACH
BURNET SELFHEAL BLOODWORT
BURNING HOT FIRE LIVE ADUST
  AFIRE ANGRY BLAZE CALID
  EAGER FIERY FLAME GLEDY
  QUICK SCALD URENT ABLAZE
  ARDENT FERVID FIRING LIVING
  TORRID USTION ADURENT
  CAUSTIC CAUTERY FERVENT
  FLAMING GLARING GLOWING
  INTENSE MORDANT SCOWDER
  SHINING ARDUROUS EXCITING
  FLAGRANT INUSTION MUIRBURN
  PARCHING SCOUTHER
  (— BRIGHTLY) LIGHT
  (— OF FORESTS IN INDIA) JHOOM
  (MALICIOUS —) ARSON
  (NO LONGER —) EXTINCT
  (PREF.) IGNI
BURNING BUSH WAHOO
BURNISH RUB GLAZE GLOSS INLAY
  POLISH FURBISH
BURNISHER AGATE BUFFER
  GLAZER FROTTON POLISHER
BURP BOKE BELCH BUBBLE
BURR NUT PAD RIB BARB BIRR
  BOSS BUZZ HALO KNOB PILE RING
  ROVE SLUG WHIR BRIAR BURGH
  CROUP WHARL WHIRR BANYAN

CIRCLE CORONA TEASEL TUNNEL
WASHER CORONET STICKER
PARASITE
  (— IN WOOD) GNAR KNAR
  (— OF ANTLER) CORONET·
  (— ON TYPE) RAG
BURRO ASS DONKEY
BURROW BED DEN DIG SET BURY
  HEAP HOLE HOWK MINE MOLE
  PIPE ROOT TUBE BERRY COUCH
  EARTH MOUND FURROW ROOTLE
  TUNNEL CLAPPER GALLERY
  PASSAGE SHELTER EXCAVATE
  WORMHOLE
  (— AS EEL) MUD
  (— IN) MOIL
  (— OF BADGER) SET
  (— OF OTTER) COUCH
  (FOSSIL —) SCOLITE
BURROWS TOWN
BURSA SAC SACK POUCH CAVITY
  BURSULA
BURSAR BOWSER PURSER TERRAR
  BOUCHER CASHIER
BURSE CASE SHOP FOREL BAZAAR
  BOURSE POCKET
BURST FIT FLY POP BLOW BUST
  DASH GUSH GUST LOSS LOUP
  REND SCAT TILT BLAST BLOUT
  BREAK CRACK ERUPT FLAFF
  FLASH GRAZE REAVE SALVO
  SCATT SHOUT SPASM SPLIT
  START STAVE BROKEN DAMAGE
  INJURY SPROUT EXPLODE
  IMPLODE RUPTURE SHATTER
  AIRBURST OUTBREAK SUNDERED
  (— ASUNDER) OUTRIVE
  (— FORTH) ERUPT SALLY EXPIRE
  BALLOON
  (— IN) IRRUPT IMPLODE
  (— INTO FRAGMENTS) FLITTER
  (— INTO LAUGHTER) BUFF
  (— OF ACTIVITY) BRASH SPURT
  SPRINT SPLURGE
  (— OF ARTILLERY) GRAZE RAFALE
  (— OF CHEERS) SALVO
  (— OF ENERGY) BANG
  (— OF FIRING) COUGH
  (— OF HARMONIOUS SOUND)
  DIAPASON
  (— OF LIGHT) FLASH GLORY
  (— OF SPEED) KICK FLUTTER
  (— OF TEARS) BLURT
  (— OF TEMPER) FUFF BOUTADE
  (— OF WIND) FLAW
  (— OPEN) DEHISCE UPBRAST
  (— OUT) BUFF PRORUMP
  (— THE HEART) RIVE
  (SUFF.) RRHAGE RRHAGIA
  RRHAGY
BURSTER GALE LUGGER CRACKER
BURSTING TUMID ABURST
  BLOWOUT RUPTION ERUPTING

BURUNDI

CAPITAL: BUJUMBURA
COIN: FRANC
LAKE: RUGWERO TSHOHOHA
NATIVE: TWA HUTU BANTU
  PYGMY TUTSI WATUSI
RIVER: KAGERA RUVUBU RUZIZI
  AKANYARU MALAGARAZI
TOWN: NGOZI BURURI KITEGA

MUYINGA BUJUMBURA

BURY URN CAMP HIDE MOOL RAKE TURF VEIL CLOAK COVER EARTH GRAVE INTER INURN PLANT VAULT WHELM ENTOMB ENWOMB HEARSE INHUME SEPULT SHROUD BEDELVE CONCEAL ENGROSS IMMERSE PITHOLE REPRESS SECRETE FUNERATE INHEARSE SUBMERGE SEPULCHER

BUS CAMION JITNEY JEEPNEY MINIBUS

BUSBOY OMNIBUS PICCOLO

BUSH TOD BUTT BOSCH BURSE CLUMP GROVE PLASH SCRAY SHRUB BOUCHE BRANCH BUSKET MAQUIS TAVERN BOSCAGE BOUCHON CLUSTER OUTBACK THICKET BUSHLAND
(— OF HAIR) GLIB
(— SICKNESS) TAURANGA
(BLACKBERRY —) BRAMBLE
(STUNTED —) SCROG
(PL.) RUFFMANS
(PREF.) THAMN(O)

BUSHBUCK BONGO
BUSH CLOVER HAGI
BUSH COW ZAMOUSE
BUSHEL FOO FOU GOB LOT MET EPHA EPHI EPHAH BUCKET MODIUS STRICK
(1-HALF —) TOVET
(1-HALF TO 3-4THS —) CABOT
(1-4TH —) PECK
(1.6 —) FANEGA
(3 TO 5 —S) SACK
(3-4THS —) SKIPPLE
(4 —S) COMB COOMB
(41.28 —) WEY
(8 —S) SEAM
BUSHER SWAMPER
BUSHGRASS WOODREED
BUSHING BUSH COAK DRILL LINER BOUCHE COLLET LINING SLEEVE BOUCHON FERRULE GROMMET PADDING
(HALF —) STEP
BUSHMAN GUNG BUSHY KHUAI ABATOA ABATWA WHALER BUSHBOY SWAGMAN NEGRILLO
(PL.) SAN SAAN
BUSHMASTER CURUCUCU SURUCUCU
BUSHWHACKER PAPAW PAWPAW
BUSHY BOSKY SHOCK DUMOSE DUMOUS BUSHMAN QUEACHY
BUSIED VERSANT
BUSILY THRANG
BUSINESS ADO ART BIZ FAT JOB PIE CARE FEAT FIRM FUSS GAME GEAR LINE NOTE TASK WORK CAUSE CRAFT ERGON TRADE TRUCK AFFAIR CUSTOM EMPLOY ERRAND MATTER METIER NEGOCE OFFICE PIDGIN PIGEON RACKET TURKEY ACCOUNT CALLING CONCERN JOURNEY PALAVER TRADING TRAFFIC ACTIVITY AGIOTAGE BESOIGNE COMMERCE FOLLOWER INDUSTRY INTEREST VOCATION

OCCASIONS OCCUPATION
(COMIC —) LAZZO
(MONKEY —) JOUKERY PAWKERY
(STAGE —) BYPLAY
BUSINESSMAN TYCOON POACHER BOURGEOIS CONVERTER
BUSKIN BOOT SHOE CALIGA BOTTINE COTHURN BRODEKIN COTHURNUS
BUSSU UBUSSU TROOLIE
BUST BUMP FAIL RUIN TAME BOSOM BREAK BURST BUSTO CHEST EDGAR FLUNK SPREE BRONZE DEMOTE REDUCE STATUE TURKEY DEGRADE DISMISS FAILURE PROTOME PORTRAIT
(— SHAPE) TAILLE
BUSTARD KORI OTIS WATO PAAUW TURKEY BEBILYA HOUBARA KORHAAN FLORICAN GOMPAAUW
(PREF.) OTIDI
BUSTIC AUSUBO CASSADA
BUSTLE ADO TEW BUZZ FIKE FRAY FUSS JUMP STIR WHEW WHIR FRISK HASTE HYPER KNOCK PAVIE STEER WHIRL WHIRR BISHOP BUMBLE ENERGY FISSLE FISTLE FLURRY FUSTLE HUDDLE HUSTLE POTHER PUDDER RACKET ROMAGE RUFFLE TATTER THRONG TUMULT UNREST UPROAR CLATTER CLUTTER CONTEND LOUSTER SCOWDER SCUFFLE SCUFTER SPUFFLE ACTIVITY IMPROVER SPLUTTER STRUGGLE TOURNURE CRINOLETTE
BUSTLING ADO BUSY FUSSY SPOFFISH STIRRING
BUSY FAST FELL APPLY BRISK QUICK ACTIVE EIDENT EMPLOY INTENT LIVELY OCCUPY STEERY THRONG UNIDLE ENGAGED HOPPING HUMMING OPEROSE TROUBLE WORKING DILIGENT EMPLOYED EXERCISE OCCUPIED SEDULOUS TIRELESS UNTIRING PRAGMATIC PRAGMATICAL
(— ONESELF) STRAP
(NOT —) SLACK
BUSYBODY BUSY SNOOP EARWIG SPOFFY ARDELIO MARPLOT MEDDLER SNOOPER FACTOTUM QUIDNUNC PRAGMATIC
BUT AC LO MA BIT SED YEA YET MERE ONLY SAVE ARRAH STILL ALWAYS EXCEPT UNLESS BESIDES HOWBEIT HOWEVER
BUTCHER KILL SLAY BUTCH SPOIL BUNGLE KIDDER LEGGER LEMMER MURDER VENDOR BOTCHER BRAINER BRITTEN FLESHER MEATMAN PORKMAN KILLCALF PIGSTICK SLAUGHTER
BUTCHERBIRD SHRIKE MATAGASSE
BUTCHER'S-BROOM RUSCUS BRUSCUS
BUTCHERY MURDER CARNAGE MASSACRE SHAMBLES SLAUGHTER

BUTEA DHAK
BUTEO BUZZARD
BUTES (BROTHER OF —) ERECHTHEUS
(FATHER OF —) NEPTUNE PANDION POSEIDON
(SISTER OF —) PROCNE PHILOMELA
(WIFE OF —) CHTHONIA
BUTLER SOMLER YEOMAN BOTELER SERVANT SPENCER STEWARD CELLARER CONSUMAH KHANSAMA STEPHANO MAJORDOMO
BUTT JUR JUT MOT PIT PUT RAM RUN TOY TUP BUCK BUNT BURT BUSH CART CASK DISH DOSS FOOL GOAD GOAL GOAT HORN JOLT JURR PIPE POLL PUCK PUSH STUB TANG TOPE TURR BOUND DUNCH HINGE JOINT MOUND ROACH SCOPE STOCK STUMP BREECH TARGET THRUST BEEHIVE BUTTOCK PARAPET PROJECT REVERSE STUMMEL ARIETATE FLATFISH FLOUNDER RIDICULE SACKBUTT
(— FOR RIDICULE) GAME SPORT STALE COCKSHY
(— OF CIGAR) DOCK SNIPE
(— OF HORSEHIDE) SHELL
(— OF JOKE) JEST SCOGGIN JESTWORD
(CIGARETTE —) BUMPER
(HALF —) BEND
BUTTE HILL PICACHO
BUTTER SHEA CLART COCUM BAMBUK BEURRE CAJOLE SPREAD BLARNEY FLATTER
(— MEASURE) SPAN
(ARTIFICIAL —) BOSH OLEO BOSCH MARGARINE
(BROWNED IN —) NOISETTE
(PRUNE —) LEKVAR
(SEMIFLUID —) GHI GHEE
BUTTER-AND-EGGS RANSTEAD TOADFLAX
BUTTERBUR CLEAT CLOTE ELDIN GALON GALLON OXWORT GILTCUP FLEADOCK
BUTTERCUP BOLT CYME CRAZY ANEMONE CRAISEY CROWTOE GILTCUP GOLDCUP KINGCOB KINGCUP CRAWFOOT CROWFOOT FROGWORT PASQUEFLOWER
BUTTERFISH GUNNEL POMPANO WHITING PALOMETA SKIPJACK
BUTTERFLY IO BLUE ARGUS ELFIN GHOST NYMPH QUEEN SATYR SWIFT WHITE ZEBRA ADONIS ALPINE APOLLO CALIGO COPPER DANAID HOPPER IDALIA JUGATE MORPHO PIERID PROGNE PSYCHE SULFUR THECLA URSULA VIOLET YELLOW ADMIRAL BUCKEYE DIURNAL DOLPHIN EMPEROR FRENATE MONARCH PIERINE SATYRID SKIPPER SULPHUR TROILUS TUSSOCK VANESSA VICEROY ARTHEMIS CECROPIA CRESCENT GRAYLING HESPERID ITHOMIID WANDERER METALMARK
(— BREEDER) AURELIAN

BUTTERFLY FISH MOJARRA FLATFISH
BUTTERFLY WEED FLUXROOT MILKWEED WINDROOT
BUTTERMILK WHIG JOCOQUE SOURDOUGH
(— AND WATER) BLAND
BUTTERSCOTCH TOFFY
BUTTERTREE MAHWA
BUTTERWORT BEANWEED ROTGRASS SHEEPWEED
BUTTERY BOTRY LARDER SPENCE BUTLERY SPICERY
BUTTOCKS ASS BUM CAN FUD HAM ARSE BUNS BUTT CULE DOCK DOUP DUFF LEND POOP PRAT SEAT TAIL TOBY CROUP FANNY NATES SLATS STERN TOUTE BEHIND BOTTOM BREECH CURPIN HEINIE HINDER CROUPON CRUPPER DRODDUM HURDIES KEISTER BACKSIDE DERRIERE NATIFORM POSTERIOR
(PRACTICE OF EXPOSING —) MOONING
(PREF.) NATI PYG(O)
(SUFF.) PROCTA PYGAL PYGE PYGIA(N) PYGOUS PYGUS
BUTTON BUD ZIP BOSS CHIN DOME HOOK KNOB KNOP SPUR TUFT BADGE CATCH GLIDE OLIVE PEARL PRILL BARREL BAUBLE BOUTON BUCKLE GLIDER SHINER TOGGLE TROCHE DEWDROP HORNTIP KNICKER NETSUKE PRESSEL REGULUS DOORBELL FASTENER OLIVETTE
BUTTONBUSH BUCKBRUSH SWAMPWOOD
BUTTONHOLE EYE LOOP SLIT
BUTTON SNAKEROOT LIATRIS SAWWORT
BUTTONWOOD COTONIER
BUTTRESS NOSE PIER PILE PROP SPUR STAY BRACE BRICK ALLETTE OUTCAST OUTSHOT SUPPORT TAMBOUR ABUTMENT
(— MEMBER) TIRE
BUTYL TETRYL
BUXOM MILD AMPLE JOLLY PLUMP PRONE SONSY BLITHE CRUMBY CRUMMY FLORID FODGEL HUMBLE PLIANT SONSIE BOWERLY BOUNCING FLEXIBLE OBEDIENT OBLIGING YIELDING JUNOESQUE
BUY CHAP COFF COUP GAIN HAVE SHOP SNIP TAKE BRIBE CLAIM TRADE ABEGGE MARKET RANSOM REDEEM SECURE ACQUIRE CHAFFER PURCHASE
(— BACK) REPRISE
(— OFF) APPEASE
(— UP STOCKS) COVER
BUYER CHAP AGENT CATER BEGGER EMPTOR PATRON VENDEE CHAPMAN SHOPPER ACHATOUR CUSTOMER PROSPECT
(— OF CLOTH) REDUBBER
BUYING ACATE ACHATE EMPTION
(— MANIA) ONIOMANIA
BUZ (FATHER OF —) NAHOR
(MOTHER OF —) MILCAH

BUZI
(SON OF —) EZEKIEL

BUZZ HUM BURR CALL DASH HISS
HUSS HUZZ RING WHIR FANCY
FLING PHONE RUMOR BUMBLE
NOTION WHISPER

BUZZARD AURA FOOL HAWK PERN
BUTEO GLADE GLEDE HARPY
STOOP BEETLE CURLEW PREYER
STUPID PUDDOCK PUTTOCK
VULTURE BROMVOEL

BUZZER BEE BELL ALARM HOWLER
SIGNAL WHIZZER

BY A P X AB AT OF TO AGO BYE
GIN PAR PER TIL ABUT ANON
INTO NEAR PAST TILL APART
ASIDE CLOSE FORBY BESIDE
TOWARD BESIDES THROUGH
(— AND BY) BELIVE BIMEBY
(— FAR) EASILY
(— HEART) PERQUEIR
(— HOOK OR CROOK) HABNAB
(— MEANS OF) PER MOYENANT
(— NO MEANS) NA
(— REASON OF THIS) HEREAT
(— STEALTH) STOWLINS
(— SURPRISE) ABACK
(— THE DAY) PD
(— THE ORDER OF) O
(— THE WAY) APROPOS
(— THIS TIME) ALREADY
(— WAY OF) VIA

(GONE —) AGO PAST
(NEAR —) GIN
(PREF.) PRETER

BY-BIDDER FUNK CAPPER PUFFER

BYBLIS (BROTHER OF —) CAUNUS
(FATHER OF —) MILETUS
(MOTHER OF —) IDOTHEA

BY-CHANNEL BAYOU BRANCH

BYCOKET ABACOT ABOCOCKET

BYGONE PAST YORE OLDEN
BYPAST FORMER ANCIENT
ELAPSED BACKWARD DEPARTED
FOREPAST PRETERIT

BYPASS JUMP SHUN AVOID
BURKE EVADE SHUNT CUTOFF
DETOUR CIRCUIT OUTFLANK

BYPATH LANE BYWAY
UNDERWALK

BY-PRODUCT SCRAP SHORTS
EFFLUVIUM MIDDLINGS
OUTGROWTH

BYRE SHIPPEN COWHOUSE

BYROAD BOREEN

BYWAY LANE PATH ALLEY BYPATH
BYWALK OUTWAY SIDEWAY

BYWORD ADAGE AXIOM MOTTO
BYNAME DIVERB PHRASE SAYING
NAYWORD PROVERB NICKNAME
REPROACH

BY-WORK PARERGON

C

C DO CEE DOH COCA CHARLIE HUNDRED

CAAMA FOX ASSE SILVER

CAB FLY KAB TAXI ARABA ARANA CABIN NODDY GHARRI CRAWLER HACKNEY SHOWFUL TAXICAB VETTURA COUPELET MOTORCAB
(HINDU —) JUDKA
(LOW-HUNG —) HERDIC
(2-PONY —) KOSONG
(4-WHEELED —) BOUNDE BOUNDER DROSHKY GROWLER

CABAL PLOT RING JUNTA PARTY BRIGUE CLIQUE SCHEME SECRET CHATTER CONSULT COUNCIL DISPUTE FACTION TALKING INTRIGUE CAMARILLA

CABALISTIC MYSTIC

CABARET CAFE TAVERN

CABASSOU XENURUS

CABBAGE CAB CHOU CRIB KALE WORT CROUT FILCH SAVOY STEAL STOCK PECHAY PILFER TAILOR BOWKAIL OXHEART PAKCHOI PALMITO PURLOIN BORECOLE COLEWORT CRUCIFER CULTIGEN DRUMHEAD KOHLRABI KERGUELEN
(STUFFED —) HOLISHKES
(PL.) WORTS

CABBAGE BARK ANGELIM ANGELIN

CABBAGE SOUP SHCHI STCHI SHTCHEE

CABBAGE STALK CASTOCK

CABDRIVER HACK MUSH CABBY CABMAN COCHER MUSHER COCHERO HACKMAN

CABIN BOX CAB COT DEN HUT CAVE CELL CREW CRIB SHED TILT BOOTH CHOZA COACH CUDDY FELZE HOVEL LODGE SHACK BOHAWN CABANA CASITA LITTER REFUGE SALOON SHANTY SHELTY WIGWAM BEDROOM BOUDOIR COTTAGE HUDDOCK MUDSILL
(— ON SHIP'S DECK) TEXAS ROUNDHOUSE
(DOUBLE —) SADDLEBAG
(RUSSIAN LOG —) IZBA

CABINET BOX BUHL CASE FILE SINK AMBRY BAHUT BOARD CABIN CHEST BAFFLE BUREAU CLOSET ICEBOX ALMIRAH BOUDOIR COMMODE CONSOLE COUNCIL ETAGERE FREEZER JUKEBOX WHATNOT CELLARET CUPBOARD MINISTRY SHOWCASE VARGUENO MONOCLEID
(FILING —) MORGUE

CABINETMAKER EBENISTE

CABLE GUY TOW BOOM COAX CORD FAST JUNK LINK ROPE STAY WIRE CABLET GANGER STRAND TETHER COAXIAL GUNLINE SKYLINE CATENARY HIGHLINE TELEGRAM UMBILICAL
(— WITH EYE AT EACH END) STRAP
(— WOUND) KECKLING
(CHAIN —) BOOM
(DERRICK —) BACKSTAY
(SPLICED —) SHOT
(SUSPENDED —) ROPEWAY

CABLE CAR TELFER TELPHER

CABLED RUDENTED

CABMAN IZVOZCHIK

CABOCHON CAB SHELL CARBUNCLE

CABOODLE KIT LOT CALABASH

CABOOSE CAB CAR VAN CRIB HACK BUGGY CRUMMY GALLEY PALACE BOUNCER COOKROOM DOGHOUSE

CABRILLA CONY GAPER GROUPER

CABSTAND HASARD HAZARD

CABUYA PITEIRA

CACAO BROMA COCOA ARRIBA COCKER CRIOLLO FORASTERO

CACHARI BODA

CACHE BURY HIDE DEPOT STASH STORE SCREEN CONCEAL DEPOSIT TREASURE

CACHET SEAL STAMP WAFER ESSENCE KONSEAL

CACIQUE BUNYAH CASSICAN HANGNEST

CACKEREL MENDOLE

CACKLE CANK CONK CLACK LAUGH BABBLE GABBLE GAGGLE GIGGLE GOSSIP KECKLE TITTER CHACKLE CHATTER SNICKER TWADDLE LAUGHTER

CACKLING GOOSE GREASER

CACOMISTLE CIVET ARCTOID RINGTAIL BASSARISK

CACOON SEGRA SEQUA

CACOPHONOUS HARSH RAUCOUS JANGLING STRIDENT

CACTUS BLEO DILDO NOPAL BAVOSO CARDON CEREUS CHAUTE CHENDE CHINOA CHOLLA COCHAL MESCAL PEYOTE PEYOTL TASAJO AIRAMPO BISAGRE BISNAGA SAGUARO ALICOCHE CHICHIPE PITAHAYA XEROPHIL
(— FRUIT) MUYUSA

CAD CUR BOOR CHUM HEEL CHURL SWEEP BRAKJE MUCKER RASCAL ROTTER BOUNDER DASTARD BLIGHTER ASSISTANT

CADASTRAL UNIT YOKE

CADAVER BODY STIFF CORPSE CARCASS SUBJECT SKELETON

CADAVEROUS PALE GAUNT LIVID PALLID GHASTLY HAGGARD

CADDIE NACKET

CADDIS FLY DUN CADEW SEDGE CADBIT

CADDISWORM PIPER

CADDO ADAI TEXAS EYEISH HAINAI KICHAI HASINAI

CADE LAMB SOCK

CADENAS NEF

CADENCE BEAT FALL IAMB LILT PACE TONE CLOSE METER METRE SOUND SWING THROB DACTYL IAMBUS JINGLE RHYTHM BACCHIC ANAPAEST CLAUSULA MOVEMENT MEDIATION

CADENZA MELISMA BARIOLAGE

CADET SON DODO GOAT PLEBE YOUTH EMBRYO JUNIOR SERGEANT

CADGE BEG BOT BUM TIE BIND HAWK CARRY MOOCH PEDDLE SPONGE SCROUNGE

CADGER BOT BUM DEALER HAWKER CARRIER PACKMAN SPONGER HUCKSTER SCAMBLER

CADGY KEDGY MERRY WANTON AMOROUS LUSTFUL CHEERFUL MIRTHFUL

CADMUS (DAUGHTER OF —) INO AGAVE SEMELE AUTONOE
(FATHER OF —) AGENOR
(MOTHER OF —) TELEPHASSA
(SISTER OF —) EUROPA
(SON OF —) POLYDORUS
(WIFE OF —) HARMONIA

CADRE CORE FRAME

CADUCEUS WAND STAFF SCEPTER SCEPTRE KERYKEION

CAECUM TYPHLON
(PREF.) ILEO TYPHL(O)

CAESURA REST STOP BREAK PAUSE INTERVAL DIAERESIS

CAFE BARROOM CABARET ESTAMINET
(— AU LAIT) ALESAN
(ROADSIDE —) BUVETTE

CAFE CREME SUEDE

CAFETERIA AUTOMAT

CAFFEINE THEIN THEINE

CAGAYAN IBANAG

CAGE BOX CAR GIG MEW PEN COOP CORF CRIB GOAL BRAKE CAVEA GRATE HUTCH AVIARY BASKET BUCKET CHAPEL ENCAGE FLIGHT PRISON CHANTRY CONFINE ENCLOSE LANTERN SHELTER TUMBREL TUMBRIL CARRIAGE ELEVATOR IMPRISON LAVARIUM RETAINER SCAFFOLD STRAINER
(— FOR HAWKS) MEW
(— FOR HENS) CAVEY CAVIE
(— OF MINE SHAFT) GIG
(— OF TRAM) CABIN
(BIRD —) AVIARY PINJRA VOLARY BIRDCAGE
(FIRE —) CRESSET
(LOBSTER —) CORF CREEL

CAGED PENT CAPTIVE

CAGER ONSETTER

CAGEY CAGY WARY COONY

CAGMAG KEGMEG

CAGOT AGOTE

CAHITA YAQUI

CAHOT PITCHHOLE

CAIMAN CAYMAN JACARE ALLIGATOR

CAIN (BROTHER OF —) ABEL SETH
(FATHER OF —) ADAM
(MOTHER OF —) EVE
(SON OF —) ENOCH

CAINAN (FATHER OF —) ENOS ARPHAXAD
(SON OF —) SALA MAHALALEEL

CAINGANG COROADO AWEIKOMA CORONADO

CAIRN MAN PIKE MOUND RAISE GALGAL CATSTONE STONEMAN

CAIRNGORM MORION SMOKESTONE

CAISSON BOX PONT CAMEL CHEST WAGON COFFER PONTON SAUCER CAMAILE CHAMBER LACUNAR PONTOON
(— DISEASE) BENDS

CAITIFF BASE MEAN VILE COWARD WICKED CAPTIVE COWARDLY PRISONER WRETCHED

CAJOLE COG CON JIG COAX FLAM FLUM PALP WORD CARNY CHEAT CURRY DECOY FRAIK INGLE JOLLY TEASE BEFLUM CARNEY DELUDE DIDDLE ENTICE FRAISE HUMBUG WHILLY BEGUILE BEHONEY CUITTLE FLATTER PALAVER SOOTHER TWEEDLE WHEEDLE BLANDISH

CAJOLERY FRAIK SOOTH TAFFY WILES BUTTER FRAISE WHILLY BLARNEY DAUBERY FLATTERY

CAKE BAR BUN NUT WIG BAKE BALL FLAE FOOL LUMP MASS MOLE PUFF TART ARVAL BATTY BLOCK BOXTY COOKY CRUST CUPID FADGE KYAAK SCONE SHIVE TORTE WAFER WEDGE BARKLE CIMBAL COOKIE DAMPER ECLAIR GATEAU HALLAH HARDEN KICHEL KUCHEN NACKET PARKIN PASTRY POPLIN SIMNEL TABLET WASTEL ASHCAKE BANBURY BANNOCK BRIOCHE BROWNIE CAKETTE CARAWAY CROZZLE CRUMPET CUPCAKE FAIRING GALETTE HOECAKE MANCHET NUTCAKE OATCAKE PANCAKE PLASTER POPADAM CHRIMSEL

CLAPCAKE KUGELHOF MADELINE MARZIPAN SEEDCAKE SOLIDIFY SOULCAKE TORTILLA TURNPIKE
(— OF CLAY) PLATTEN
(— OF COCONUT PULP) POONAC
(— OF MEAL) DODGER
(— OF RUBBER) BISCUIT
(ALMOND —) RATAFIA
(CREOLE RICE —) CALA
(FANCY —) SUNKET
(FLAT —) PLATE BUNUELO GALETTE PLACENT CHRIMSEL
(FOURTH PART OF —) FARL FARLE
(FRIED —) WONDER CRULLER DOUGHNUT
(GINGER —) BOLIVAR
(GRIDDLE —) LATKE FLIPPER FRITTER FLAPJACK
(HOLIDAY —) SIMNEL
(HONEY —) LEKACH
(LAMB AND WHEAT —) KIBBE KIBBEH
(LEAVENED —) BAP
(NEW YEAR'S —) HAGMENA HOGMANAY
(OATEN —) BANNOCK
(OIL —) GRIT POONAC
(PLUM —) SIMNEL
(POTATO —) FADGE
(PRESS —) CACHAZA
(RUM —) BABA
(SEED —) WIG SEEDCAKE
(TEA —) LUNN SCONE PIKELET
(THIN —) WAFER JUMBLE BANNOCK TORTILLA
(UNLEAVENED —) CHAPATI CHAPATTI
(YEAST —) KOJI
(PL.) AMSATH COLYBA
CAKED CLIT
CAKE PULLER KNOCKER
CAKES AND ALE (AUTHOR OF —) MAUGHAM
(CHARACTER IN —) AMY KEAR KEMP ALROY ROSIE EDWARD GEORGE ASHENDEN TRAFFORD DRIFFIELD
CALABA BIRMA GALBA
CALABASH GOURD CURUBA JICARA
CALABASH TREE HIGUERO
CALABOOSE JUG BRIG JAIL STIR POKEY PRISON CABOOSE BASTILLE HOOSEGOW
CALABUR TREE CAPULI CAPULIN SILKWOOD
CALAIS (BROTHER OF —) ZETES
(FATHER OF —) BOREAS
(MOTHER OF —) ORITHYIA
CALAMANCO MANKIE
CALAMINE CADMIA
CALAMITOUS BAD SAD DIRE EVIL BLACK FATAL BITTER DISMAL TRAGIC WOEFUL ADVERSE BALEFUL DIREFUL HAPLESS RUINOUS UNHAPPY UNLUCKY GRIEVOUS TRAGICAL WRETCHED
CALAMITY ILL WOE BLOW DOOM EVIL RUIN RUTH SLAP HYDRA STORM WRACK MISERY ONCOME PLAGUE SORROW EXTREME SCOURGE ACCIDENT DISASTER DISTRESS FATALITY

JUDGMENT MISCHIEF
CALAMONDIN ORANGE CALAMANSI
CALAMUS PEN CANE REED QUILL ACORUS RATTAN ROTANG
CALANGAY ABACAY COCKATOO
CALANTHA (FATHER OF —) AMYCLAS
CALASH CALESA GALECHE
CALCANEUM FIBULARE HYPOTARSUS
CALCAR OVEN SPUR FURNACE CALCARIUM PREHALLUX
CALCEOLARIA FAGELIA IONIDIUM
CALCIFY CRETIFY
CALCINING BURNING
CALCINO MUSCADINE
CALCITE APHRITE CALCSPAR ALABASTER ARAGONITE ARGENTINE HISLOPITE
CALCIUM LIME
CALCIUM CARBONATE WHITING DRIPSTONE
CALCULATE AIM SUM CALK CAST PLAN RATE TELL COUNT FRAME THINK CIPHER DESIGN EXPECT FIGURE NUMBER RECKON ACCOUNT AVERAGE CALLATE COMPUTE PREPARE CONSIDER ESTIMATE FORECAST
(— BY ASTROLOGY) ERECT
CALCULATED COLD MEASURED
CALCULATING COLD WISE BRITTLE CAUTIOUS
CALCULATION CARE SHARE CALCUL ACCOUNT CAUTION WORKING CALCULUS FORECAST HINDCAST PRUDENCE
(PL.) FIGURES
CALCULATOR TABLE ABACUS ABACIST SOROBAN CALCULER COMPUTER ISOGRAPH
CALCULUS STONE UROLITH ANALYSIS
(PREF.) LITH(O)
(SUFF.) LITE LITH(IC) LITIC
CALDRON POT RED VAT LEAD ALFET BOILER KELDER KETTLE TRIPOD VESSEL CALDERA CAULDRON
CALEB (DAUGHTER OF —) ACHSAH
(FATHER OF —) HEZRON JEPHUNNEH
(SON OF —) HUR
CALENDAR ORDO DIARY FASTI ALMANAC CALENDS JOURNAL KALENDS REGISTER SCHEDULE
(— OF MARTYRS) MENOLOGY
(PL.) FASTI
CALENDER TABBY SCHREINER
CALENDERER CANROYER SMOOTHER
CALENDS K KAL
CALF CA BOB BOX BOY LEG BOSS BUSS DOLT VEAL VEAU BOBBY BOSSY BUNCH DOGIE MOGGY PODDY RANNY SOOKY YOUTH MUSCLE VEALER WEANER BULCHIN FATLING SLEEPER CALFLING
(LIKE A —) VITULINE
(PREMATURE —) SLINK

(UNBRANDED —) LONGEAR SLEEPER
(YEARLING —) BUD DAIRT
(YOUNG —) DEACON
(PL.) CAURE
CALF'S-FOOT JELLY SULZE FISNOGA
CALFSKIN OOZE COROVA VELLUM GRASSER TULCHAN VEALSKIN
CALIBER BORE RANK DEGREE TALENT ABILITY BREADTH COMPASS QUALITY CAPACITY DIAMETER MAGNITUDE
(HIGH —) STATURE
CALIBRATED BRIX BEAUME BALLING
CALICHE CALCRETE TEPETATE NITRATINE
CALICO BLAY PINTO SALLO CHINTZ SALLOO CROYDON SPOTTED DUNGAREE GOLDFISH
CALICO ASTER WISEWEED
CALICOBACK STINKBUG
CALICO BASS CRAPPIE BACHELOR
CALICUT KOZHIKODE

CALIFORNIA

CAPITAL: SACRAMENTO
COLLEGE: MILLS POMONA WHITTIER
COUNTY: INYO KERN MONO NAPA YOLO YUBA MARIN MODOC COLUSA LASSEN MERCED PLACER PLUMAS SHASTA SOLANO SONOMA SUTTER TEHAMA TULARE ALAMEDA VENTURA SISKIYOU CALAVERAS
DESERT: MOJAVE COLORADO
INDIAN: HUPA POMO YANA YUKI KAROK MAIDU MIWOK WAPPO WIYOT YUROK PATWIN SHASTA TOLOWA YOKUTS CHUMASH LUISENO SALINAN SERRANO DIEGUENO
LAKE: MONO SODA EAGLE OWENS TAHOE SALTON TULARE ALMANOR BERRYESSA
MOUNTAIN: MUIR LASSEN SHASTA WHITNEY
NAME: ELDORADO
PARK: LASSEN SEQUOIA YOSEMITE
PRESIDENT: NIXON
PRISON: ALCATRAZ
RIVER: EEL MAD PIT KERN OWENS PUTAH STONY FEATHER KLAMATH RUBICON TRINITY SACRAMENTO
STATE BIRD: QUAIL
STATE FLOWER: POPPY
STATE NICKNAME: GOLDEN
STATE TREE: REDWOOD
TOWN: LODI AZUSA CHICO CHINO INDIO BLYTHE CARMEL COVINA EUREKA FRESNO LOMPOC MERCED OXNARD POMONA SONOMA TULARE ALAMEDA BURBANK GARDENA NEEDLES SALINAS VALLEJO VISALIA ALTADENA BERKELEY PASADENA REDLANDS CUCAMONGA

UNIVERSITY: USC UCLA CALTECH STANFORD

CALIPER JENNY ODDLEGS CALIPERS
CALIPH ABU ALI BEKR IMAM OMAR CALIF OTHMAN ABBASID UMAYYAD
CALISTA (HUSBAND OF —) ALTAMONT CLEANDER
(LOVER OF —) LOTHARIO LYSANDER
CALISTO, LA (CHARACTER IN —) PAN JOVE JUNO DIANA LYCAON CALISTO MERCURY ENDYMION
(COMPOSER OF —) CAVALLI
CALIXTINE UTRAQUIST
CALK (ALSO SEE CAULK) JAG NAP PAY COPY CORK FILL STOP CAULK CLOSE HORSE ROUGH CAREEN CALTROP CHINTZE OCCLUDE SILENCE
CALKING OAKUM
CALL HO KA BAN BID CRY CUP DUB HOY SAY SEE CITE COOP HAIL JERK NAME NOTE PAGE PIST ROUP STOP TERM TOOT YELL BEDUB CHUCK CLAIM CLEPE CLOCK ELECT HALLO HIGHT HOLLA PHONE ROUSE SHOUT SPEAK STYLE UTTER VISIT VOUCH WAKEN YODEL ACCUSE APPEAL AROUSE BECALL CHANGE DEMAND HALLOA HALLOO INVITE INVOKE MUSTER QUETHE SUMMON TEKIAH TERUAH YELPER ACCLAIM ADDRESS APPOINT BEHIGHT BETITLE COLLECT COMMAND CONVENE CONVOKE DECLARE ENTITLE IMPEACH INQUIRE INSTYLE MOUNTEE WHISTLE ANNOUNCE APPELATE ASSEMBLE NOMINATE PROCLAIM VOCATION
(— A BET) STAY
(— ALOUD) COUNT
(— BACK) RECALL REVOKE
(— COARSELY) ROOP ROUP
(— DOWN) BRAWL DEVOCATE IMPRECATE
(— FOR) CRY TAKE CLAIM EXACT DEMAND DESIRE COLLECT SOLICIT
(— FOR HELP) SOS
(— FOR HOGS) SOOK SOOEY
(— FOR PARLEY) CHAMADE
(— FORTH) STIR EVOKE ELICIT INDUCE INVOKE ATTRACT PROVOKE SUGGEST
(— HOUNDS) LIFT
(— IN ANGER) GREET
(— IN CHILDRENS' GAMES) FAN FEN FIN VENTS
(— IN MARBLES) DUBS
(— IN WHIST) ABUNDANCE
(— INTO QUESTION) IMPUGN OPPUGN
(— LOUDLY) CRY HAIL ACCLAIM
(— MAN BY MAN) ARRAY
(— ON TELEPHONE) BUZZ
(— OUT) HAIL LURE ASCRY EVOKE

HALLO GOLLAR GOLLER HOLLER
HULLOO
(— TO ACCOUNT) AREASON
CONTROL
(— TO ARMS) ALARM ALARUM
RAPPEL
(— TO BELLBOY) FRONT
(— TO CAT) CHEET
(— TO COURT) ARRAIGN
(— TO COWS) PROO SOOK COBOSS
SOOKIE
(— TO FOOD) SOSS
(— TO HORSE) HIE HUP WAY PROO
(— TO MIND) CITE MING RECORD
BETHINK RECOLLECT
(— TO PRAYER) ADAN AZAN
(— TO READINESS) ALERT
(— TO SPARROW) PHIP PHIPPE
(— TO WITNESS) APPEAL
(— UPON) ASK SEE CITE GREDE
HALSE BECALL DEPOSE ENGAGE
SUMMON ADDRESS BESEECH
IMPLORE
(BIRD'S —) WEET
(BOATSWAIN'S —) WINDING
(BRIDGE —) DOUBLE
(BUGLE —) POST HALLALI STABLES
(CLOSE —) TOUCH
(DUCK —) SQUAWKER
(FRIENDLY —) CEILIDH
(HUNTING —) MOT RECHATE
RECHEAT
(MORNING —) MATIN
(NAUTICAL —) AHOY
(SHEPHERD'S —) OVEY
(SPORTSMAN'S —) HOICKS YOICKS
HALLALI
(SQUARE DANCE —) GEE HAW
(STAGE TRUMPET —) SENNET
SINNET
(TRUMPET —) BERLOQUE
CALLA ARUM LILY DRAGON
MAYFLOWER
CALLBOY FRONT CALLER HALLBOY
CALLED NEMPT
CALLER FLOORMAN
CALLIGRAPHER PENMAN WRITER
COPYIST ENGROSSER
CALLIGRAPHY LETTERING
CHIROGRAPHY
CALLING ART JOB WAY CALL HAIL
RANK TRADE CAREER METIER
NAMING OUTCRY MISSION
MYSTERY PURSUIT STATION
SUMMONS WARNING BUSINESS
FUNCTION POSITION SHOUTING
VOCATION
CALLIOPE (FATHER OF —) ZEUS
JUPITER
(MOTHER OF —) MNEMOSYNE
(SON OF —) ORPHEUS
CALLIRRHOE (FATHER OF —)
OCEANUS
(HUSBAND OF —) TROS ALCMAEON
(SON OF —) ILUS GANYMEDE
ASSARACUS
CALLISTO (FATHER OF —) LYCAON
(SON OF —) ARCAS
CALLITHRIX HAPALE JACCHUS
CALLOP YELLOWBELLY
CALLOSAL TRABAL
CALLOSITY SEG CALLUS SITFAST
TYLOSIS CHESTNUT

CALLOUS HARD HORNY TOUGH
BRAWNY OBTUSE SEARED TORPID
WAUKIT DEDOLENT OBDURATE
CALLOUSED BRAWNY
CALLOW BALD BARE CRUDE
GREEN SQUAB JEJUNE MARSHY
IMMATURE UNFORMED
YOUTHFUL
CALLUS SEG POROMA TYLOMA
CALLOUS
(PREF.) PORA PORO
CALM LAY LEE COOL DILL EASY
EVEN FAIR FLAT HUSH LOWN
LULL MEES MILD REST SOFT STAY
ABATE ALLAY CHARM LEVEL
LITHE LOUND MEASE PEACE
QUELL QUIET SLEEK SMOLT
SOBER STILL STOIC STREW
APLOMB DEFUSE DOCILE GENTLE
GLASSY IRENIC PACIFY PLACID
SEDATE SERENE SETTLE SILENT
SLATCH SLIGHT SMOOTH SOOTHE
STEADY APPEASE ASSUAGE
CALMATO COMPOSE GLACIAL
HALCYON MOLLIFY PACIFIC
PATIENT PLACATE QUALIFY
QUIETEN RESTFUL UNMOVED
CALMNESS COMPOSED
DECOROUS MODERATE PEACEFUL
PLACABLE RESTRAIN SERENITY
TRANQUIL UNRUFFLE POSSESSED
PHILOSOPHIC
(INTERNAL —) HARMONY
(NOT —) BOISTEROUS
CALMLY COOLY COOLLY STILLY
CALMNESS CALM LULL POISE
PHLEGM REPOSE SERENE TEMPER
ATARAXY COOLNESS SERENITY
SOBRIETY STILLNESS
CALNO KULLANI
CALOMEL TURPETH
CALORIC THERMOGEN
CALORIE THERM THERME
CALQUE LOANSHIFT
CALTROP CROWTOE GALTRAP
BULLHEAD CROWFOOT
CALUMNIATE BLOT SLUR TEEN
BELIE LIBEL ACCUSE ATTACK
BEFOUL DEFAME MALIGN REVILE
VILIFY ASPERSE BLACKEN
SLANDER TRADUCE
CALUMNIATION SATIRE
ASPERSION
CALUMNY SLUR DEPRAVE
OBLOQUY ASPERSION
CALVA CALOTTE SINCIPUT
CALVARIA SKULLCAP
CALVARY GOLGOTHA
CALVE FRESHEN
CALVINIST GENEVAN GOMARIAN
CALYCE (FATHER OF —) AEOLUS
(MOTHER OF —) ENARETE
(SON OF —) ENDYMION
CALYCULUS CELL CALYX
CALYPTER ALULA SQUAMA
CALYPTRA CAP VEIL EPIGONIUM
CALYX CUP POP HULL HUSK LEAF
CULOT SEPAL SHUCK
(PREF.) CALYC(I)(O)
CAM COG AWRY LOBE TRIG ASKEW
CATCH SNAIL WIPER LIFTER
TAPPET CROOKED TRIPPET
KNOCKOFF PERVERSE ROLLBACK

CAMACHILE INGA HUAMUCHIL
CAMAGON MABOLO
CAMAS LOBELIA
CAMBER SET ARCH SWEEP
ROUNDUP CROSSFALL

CAMBODIA

CAPE: SAMIT
CAPITAL: PNOMPENH
PHNOMPENH
COIN: RIEL PUTTAN PIASTER
GULF: SIAM
LAKE: TONLESAP
MOUNTAIN: PAN AURAL
MOUNTAINS: DANGREK
CARDAMOM ELEPHANT
NAME: CAMBOJA CAMBODGE
KAMPUCHEA
NATIVE: CHAM KHMER
RIVER: SAN SEN BASSAC MEKONG
PORONG SREPOK SEKHONG
TONLESAP
RUINS: ANGKORWAT
TOWN: REAM TAKEO KAMPOT
KRATIE PURSAT KOHNIEH
KRACHEH ROVIENG SAMRONG
PNOMPENH SISOPHON
WEIGHT: MACE TAEL

CAMBRIC BATISTE PERCALE
CAMBUSCAN (SON OF —) CANACE
CAMBALLO ALGARSIFE
CAME BAND CALM
CAMEL COLT OONT DELOUL
DROMED FENDER HAGEEN
MEHARI CAISSON TYLOPOD
BACTRIAN RUMINANT
DROMEDARY
CAMEL GRASS SCHOENANTH
CAMELLIA JAPONICA
CAMEL LIP CHILOMA
CAMELOPARD GIRAFFE
CAMEO GEM GAMAHE CAMAIEU
CARVING PHALERA RELIEVO
ANAGLYPH
CAMERA KINO KODAK CHAMBER
MINICAM PANORAM ENLARGER
MINIATURE VERASCOPE
(— TUBE) VIDICON
(PART OF —) LUG BODY DOOR
KNOB LENS LOCK CRANK DRIVE
FOCUS LATCH SCALE STRAP
TIMER BUTTON SENSOR SOCKET
WINDOW ADVANCE BELLOWS
LANYARD RELEASE SHUTTER
PHOTOCELL TRANSDUCER
VIEWFINDER
CAMERAMAN LENSMAN
CAMEROON (CAPITAL OF —)
YAOUNDE
(RIVER OF —) DJA NYONG SANAGA
(TOWN OF —) EDEA POLI YOKO
BAFIA KRIBI DOUALA
CAMILLA (FATHER OF —) METABUS
(SLAYER OF —) ARUNS
CAMILLE (AUTHOR OF —) DUMAS
(CHARACTER IN —) DUVAL
ARMAND NANINE CAMILLE
GAUTIER PRUDENCE VARVILLE
CAMIRUS (FATHER OF —)
CERCAPHUS
(MOTHER OF —) CYDIPPE
CAMISOLE WAISTCOAT

CAMLET MOHAIR PARAGON
BARRACAN
CAMOMILE OXEYE MORGAN
MAYWEED
CAMOUFLAGE FAKE HIDE DAZZLE
MUFFLE SCREEN CONCEAL
DISGUISE
CAMOUFLET STIFLER
CAMP TAN PEST TENT DOUAR
ETAPE HORDE SIEGE TABOR
CASTLE LAAGER SUGARY
BIVOUAC HUTMENT LASHKAR
LODGING MAHALLA PALANKA
ZAREEBA QUARTERS
(— OUT) MAROON OUTLIE
(HOBO —) JUNGLE
(LUMBER —) CHANTIER
(PREF.) CASTRA
(SUFF.) CASTER CESTER CHESTER
CAMPA ANDA ANDI ANTI
CAMPAIGN BLITZ DRIVE PLAIN
WHOOP CANVASS CRUSADE
JOURNEY SERVICE SOLICIT
WARFARE
(STUNT —) JIHAD
CAMPANA GUTTA
CAMPANERO COTINGA
ARAPUNGA BELLBIRD COTINGID
CAMPANILE TOWER BELFRY
CLOCHER STEEPLE CARILLON
CAMPANULA BELLWORT
CAMPESTRAL AGRARIAN
CAMPHOL BORNEOL
CAMPHOR ASARONE BORNEOL
MENTHOL
(ANISE —) ANETHOLE
CAMPHOR TREE KADUR KAPOR
CAMPING BIVOUAC
CAMPION ROBIN COWBELL
CAMPUS GATE QUAD YARD FIELD
CAN CUP JUG MAY MOW POT TIN
ABLE FIRE JAIL BILLY CADDY
COULD ESHIN OILER SHALL SKILL
BOTTLE VESSEL ABILITY
BOMBARD CANIKIN CAPABLE
CREAMER DISMISS GROWLER
PIPETTE BILLYCAN CONSERVE
PRESERVE
(— FOR LIQUOR) JACK
(— ON WHEELS) DANDY
(BULGED —) SWELL FLIPPER
(DEFECTIVE —) SPRINGER
(LEAKY —) LEAKER
(MILK —) CHURN
(TIN —) DESTROYER
(TRASH —) DUSTBIN
(PREF.) SCYPH(I)(O)
CANAAN (FATHER OF —) HAM
CANAANITE ARKITE HIVITE
AMORITE HIVVITE JEBUSITE
CANACE (BROTHER OF —)
MACAREUS
(FATHER OF —) AEOLUS
(MOTHER OF —) ENARETE
(SON OF —) TRIOPAS

CANADA

(ALSO SEE SPECIFIC PROVINCES)
BAY: JAMES HUDSON UNGAVA
GEORGIAN
CAPITAL: OTTAWA
INDIAN: CREE COMOX HAIDA
NISKA SARSI STALO MICMAC

NAHANE NOOTKA SARCEE
SEKANE CARRIER NANAIMO
SHUSWAP SONGISH TAHLTAN
ALGONKIN COWICHAN
LILLOOET MALECITE SQUAMISH
TSATTINE
ISLAND: READ BANKS BYLOT
COATS DEVON SABLE BAFFIN
MANSEL VICTORIA ANTICOSTI
VANCOUVER
ISLANDS: PARRY BELCHER
BATHURST MAGDALEN
LAKE: BEAR CREE GARRY RAINY
SLAVE LOUISE SIMCOE ABITIBI
DUBAWNT NIPIGON KOOTENAY
OKANAGAN NIPISSING
MEASURE: MINOT PERCH ARPENT
CHAINON
MOUNTAIN: LOGAN ROYAL
ROBSON TREMBLANT
MOUNTAIN RANGE: SKEENA
CARIBOO PEMBINA STELIAS
COLUMBIA LAURENTIAN
NATIVE: CANUCK
PARK: YOHO BANFF ACADIA
JASPER
PENINSULA: GASPE BOOTHIA
MELVILLE
PROVINCE: BC NB NS MAN ONT
PEI QUE ALTA SASK QUEBEC
ALBERTA ONTARIO MANITOBA
NOVASCOTIA NEWBRUNSWICK
NEWFOUNDLAND
SASKATCHEWAN
PROVINCIAL CAPITAL: QUEBEC
REGINA STJOHN HALIFAX
TORONTO EDMONTON
VICTORIA WINNIPEG
CHARLOTTETOWN
RIVER: HAY RED BACK PEEL PEACE
SLAVE YUKON FRASER NELSON
OTTAWA SKEENA THELON
KOKOSAK PEMBINA PETAWAWA
SAGUENAY MACKENZIE
RICHELIEU
STRAIT: CABOT DEASE HECATE
HUDSON GEORGIA
SYMBOL: MAPLELEAF
TERRITORY: YUKON
TOWN: HULL BANFF LAVAL
GUELPH OSHAWA REGINA
SARNIA CALGARY HALIFAX
MONCTON NANAIMO SUDBURY
TORONTO WELLAND WINDSOR
KINGSTON MONTREAL
VICTORIA WINNIPEG
SASKATOON VANCOUVER
UNIVERSITY: MCGILL DALHOUSIE
WATERFALL: DELLA PANTHER
TAKAKKAW

CANADA BLUEBERRY SOURTOP
CANADA GOOSE HONKER
BUSTARD OUTARDE
CANADA JAY MEATBIRD
MOOSEBIRD
CANADA LYNX PISHU LUCIVEE
CANADA PLUM CHENEY
CANADA VIOLET JUNEFLOWER
CANADIAN CANUCK
CANAILLE MOB FLOUR RABBLE
DOGGERY RIFFRAFF
CANAL CUT CANO DUCT LODE

PIPE SHAT TUBE BAYOU DITCH
DRAIN FOSSA GRAFF KLONG
SCALA ZANJA ESTERO GROOVE
KENNEL STRAIT TRENCH VAGINA
ACEQUIA APHODUS CHANNEL
CONDUIT FOREBAY RACEWAY
SHIPWAY TOWPATH AQUEDUCT
EMISSARY IRRIGANT MILLRACE
PROSODUS VOLKMANN
(— LABORER) NAVIGATOR
(ALIMENTARY —) GUT ENTERON
INTESTINE
(ANATOMICAL —) SCALA MEATUS
(CARINAL —) LACUNA
(PREF.) MEATO
CANARD DUCK HOAX RUMOR
GRAPEVINE
CANARY DICKY FRILL SERIN
LIZARD ROLLER CAYENNE
CHOPPER JONQUIL SQUEALER
(— HYBRID) MULE

CANARY ISLAND
CAPITAL: SANTACRUZ
ISLAND: ROCA CLARA FERRO
LOBOS PALMA ROCCA GOMERA
HIERRO INFERNO GRACIOSA
TENERIFE LANZAROTE
MEASURE: FANEGADA
MOUNTAIN: TEYDE LACRUZ
ELCUMBRE TENERIFE
PROVINCE: LASPALMAS
TOWN: LAGUNA ARRECIFE
VALVERDE
VOLCANO: TENEGUIA

CANARY MOSS CORKIR
CANASTA SAMBA BOLIVIA
CANCEL BLOT DASH DELE OMIT
UNDO VENT WIPE ABORT ADEEM
ANNUL BELAY CROSS ERASE
QUASH REMIT SCORE SCRUB
DELETE EFFACE KILLER RECALL
REMOVE REVOKE STROKE
ABOLISH DESTROY EXPUNGE
NULLIFY RESCIND RETRACT
SCRATCH SUBLATE UNWRITE
ABROGATE OVERRIDE
OBLITERATE
CANCELED OFF
CANCELER BUMPER STAMPER
CANCELLATION GRID CANCEL
REVOKE RECISION SURRENDER
CANCER WOLF KASHYAPA
SCIRRHUS
(PREF.) CARCIN(O)
CANCERWORT FLUELLIN
CANDAREEN FAN FEN
CANDELABRUM PHAROS
MENORAH GIRANDOLE
CANDID FAIR JUST OPEN PURE
BLUNT CLEAR FRANK NAIVE
PLAIN HONEST ARTLESS
JANNOCK SINCERE EVENDOWN
INNOCENT SPLENDID STRAIGHT
PLAINSPOKEN
CANDIDA (AUTHOR OF —) SHAW
(CHARACTER IN —) MORELL
CANDIDA MARCHBANKS
CANDIDATE AGREGE LEGACY
ESQUIRE NOMINEE ASPIRANT
GRADUAND ORDINAND
PROSPECT

(DOCTORAL —) ABD
CANDIDE (AUTHOR OF —) VOLTAIRE
(CHARACTER IN —) CACAMBO
CANDIDE PANGLOSS PAQUETTE
CUNEGONDE
CANDIDIASIS MONILIASIS
CANDIED GLACE
CANDLE DIP WAX GLIM SIZE SLUT
LIGHT SPERM TAPER TOLLY
TORCH BOUGIE CIERGE MORTAR
PLANET SHAMUS SLUSHY
TALLOW TORTIS CANDELA
PERCHER PRICKET SHAMMES
AMANDINE
(IMITATION —) JUDAS
(SQUARE —) QUARRIER
CANDLEFISH SKIL EULACHON
HOOLAKIN OOLACHAN SKILFISH
SABLEFISH
CANDLEHOLDER SPIDER
CANDLEMAKER CHANDLER
TALLOWER
CANDLEMAS TERM MARYMASS
CANDLENUT AMA LAMA BIABO
KUKUI IGUAPE KEMIRI LUMBANG
ABURAGIRI
CANDLESNUFFER DOUTER
CANDLESTAND TORCHERE
CANDLESTICK BUGIA DYKER
JESSE STICK CRUSIE LAMPAD
MORTAR SCONCE PASCHAL
PRICKET CHANDLER DICERION
FLAMBEAU STANDARD TORCHERE
TRIKERION
CANDLEWICK MATCH SNAST
SHROUD
(CHARRED PART OF —) SNOT
SNUFF SNUFFING
CANDLEWOOD CIRIO OCOTILLO
TABANUCO
CANDOR PURITY FAIRNESS
KINDNESS INTEGRITY SIMPLICITY
CANDY DROP DUMP KISS PIPE
ROCK CREAM CRISP DULCE
FUDGE GLACE GUNDY LOLLY
NABIT SPICE SQUIB SWEET TAFFY
BONBON COMFIT HUMBUG
NOGADA NOUGAT PATTIE PENIDE
BRITTLE CANDIEL CARAMEL
CONGEAL FLATTER FONDATE
GUMDROP SWEETEN SWEETIE
TORRONE ALPHENIC LOLLIPOP
STICKJAW PEPPERMINT
(PL.) CUTS CONFETTI
CANDYTUFT CRUCIFER
(PL.) IBERIS
CANE ROD BEAT CRAB DART FLOG
PIPE REED STEM TUBE WAND
WHIP BIRCH GIBBY GUNDY LANCE
STAFF STICK SWISH TOLLY
WADDY BAMBOO JAMBEE KEBBIE
PUNISH RATTAN CALAMUS
HICKORY KIPPEEN MALACCA
SCOURGE STADDLE TICKLER
WHANGEE GIBSTAFF
(BLACK —) JAPAN
(END OF —) FRAZE
(SPLIT —) CANEWORK
CANELLA CINNAMON WHITEWOOD
CANELO CIXO
CANESCENT HOARY
CANE TREE BEJUCO
CANFIELD KLONDIKE

CANICULA SIRIUS
CANINE CUR DOG FOX PUP FISC
TUSH WOLF DOGLY DOGLIKE
LANIARY EYETOOTH
CANING RATTAN BIRCHING
CANISTEL TIES EGGFRUIT
CANNA ACHIRA GOLDBIRD
CANNABIS BHANG GANJA GUAZA
GUNJA HEMPWORT
(— TOPS) TAKROURI
CANNEL BONE FURCULE
CANNEL COAL AMPELITE
CANNER CANMAN TINNER
CANNIBAL WINDIGO LESTRIGON
THYESTEAN
CANNON BIT EAR GUN BASE SHOT
TUBE ASPIC CAROM CRACK
MOYEN PIECE SACRE SACRI
SAKER SHANK SLING THIEF
BARKER BICORN CURTAL FALCON
FOWLER JINGAL LICORN MORTAR
POTGUN BASTARD BOMBARD
BULLDOG CHAMBER HANDGUN
LOMBARD MOYENNE ROBINET
SERPENT STINGER UNICORN
BASILISK CULVERIN HOWITZER
MURDERER OERLIKON ORDNANCE
SPITFIRE CARAMBOLE
CARRONADE ZUMBOORUK
(— OF BELL) EAR
(CARRIAGE OF —) NADRIER
(DISCHARGE OF —) TIRE
(DUMMY —) QUAKER
(PART OF —) BASE BORE FACE
KNOB NECK OGEE RING VENT
CHASE FILET SWELL BREECH
BUTTON FILLET MUZZLE
CHAMBER DOLPHIN GUNLOCK
RIMBASE ASTRAGAL CASCABEL
TRUNNION REINFORCE
CANNONBALL GUN PILL BULLET
GUNSTONE
CANNON BOSS TRUNNION
CANNON PLUG TAMPION
CANNOT CANT CANNA DONNA
DOWNA UNABLE
CANNULA TROCAR
CANNY SLY COZY SNUG WARY
WILY WISE COONY LUCKY PAWKY
QUIET CLEVER FRUGAL GENTLE
SHREWD STEADY CAREFUL
CUNNING KNOWING PRUDENT
QUIETLY THRIFTY CAUTIOUS
SKILLFUL WATCHFUL
CANOE AMA KIAK LISI PAHI PROA
WAKA AOTEA ARAWA BANCA
BIRCH BONGO BUNGO CANKA
KAYAK KOLEK PRAHU SKIFF
TONEE UMIAK VINTA WAAPA
BAIDAR BALLAM BAROTO CORIAL
CUNNER DUGOUT OOMIAK
PAOPAO PITPAN PUNGEY TAINUI
TROUGH ALMADIA BIDARKA
BUCKEYE CANADER CASCARA
CORACLE CURIARA CURRANE
HOROUTA LAKATOI PIRAGUA
PIROGUE BALANGAY BARANGAY
FALTBOAT FOLDBOAT MONOXYLE
MONTARIA TAKITUMU
THAMAKAU TSUKUPIN
WOODSKIN
CANON FEN LAW CODE FUGA
HYMN LAUD LIST ROTA RULE

SONG AXIOM GORGE GULCH
MODEL NODUS ROUND TABLE
TENET ACTION DECREE GNOMON
BROCARD LIBRARY PRECEPT
STATUTE DECISION MATHURIN
STAGIARY STANDARD SACRISTAN
PREBENDARY
PREMONSTRATENSIAN
(BODY OF —S) CHAPTER
CANONICAL CANONIC ACCEPTED
ORTHODOX
(NOT —) APOCRYPHAL
CANOODLE PET CARESS FONDLE
CAN OPENER CHURCHKEY
CANOPY SKY CEIL COPE DAIS
HOOD TILT CHUPA CROWN
HOVEL SHADE STATE VAULT
AWNING BUBBLE CELURE ESTATE
FINIAL GABLET HUPPAH PELMET
SHADOW TESTER CEILING
HEAVENS MARQUEE SHELTER
SPARVER BASILICA CIBORIUM
COVERING OVERWOOD PAVILION
SEMIANNA SHAMIANA
TABERNACLE
(— ABOVE THRONE) STATE
(— FOR LIVESTOCK) HOVEL
(— OF ALTAR) DAIS CIBORIUM
(— OF HEAVEN) VAULT
(— OVER BROODER) HOVER
(BED —) TESTER SPARVER
(HEARSE —) MAJESTY
CANT TIP COAX HEEL LEAN LIST
NOOK SING TILT TURN ARGOT
BEVEL CHANT DRIFT FLASH HIELD
LINGO LUSTY MERRY NICHE
PITCH SHARE SLANG SLANT
SLOPE WHINE CAREEN CASTER
CORNER INTONE JARGON LIVELY
PATOIS PATTER SNIVEL AUCTION
DIALECT INCLINE PORTION
SINGING WHEEDLE CHEERFUL
PRETENSE VIGOROUS
CANTABRIGIAN CANTAB
CAMBRIDGE
CANTALA MAGUEY
CANTALOUPE MELON
MUSKMELON
CANTANKEROUS ILL CURSED
CUSSED ORNERY KICKISH PIGGISH
CANKERED CONTRARY PERVERSE
CANTATA MOTET SERENATA
VILLANCICO
CANTEEN BAR FLASK BAZAAR
CANTINA
CANTER JOG RUN GAIT LOPE PACE
RACK AUBIN ROGUE BEGGAR
WHINER TRIPPLE SNUFFLER
VAGABOND
CANTERBURY BELL MILKWORT
CAMPANULA
**CANTERBURY TALES (AUTHOR OF
—)** CHAUCER
(CHARACTER IN —) NUN COOK
DYER HOST MONK WIFE CLERK
FRIAR REEVE DOCTOR KNIGHT
MILLER PARSON PRIEST SQUIRE
WEAVER YEOMAN CHAUCER
PLOWMAN SHIPMAN FRANKLIN
MANCIPLE MERCHANT PARDONER
PRIORESS SERGEANT SUMMONER
CARPENTER HABERDASHER
CANTICLE ODE HYMN LAUD SONG

CANTO ANTHEM CANTIC HIRMOS
BRAVURA MAGNIFICAT
CANTILEVER LOOKOUT SEMIBEAM
CARTOUCHE
CANTING CANT PIOUS SNUFFLING
CANTO AIR FIT BOOK DUAN PACE
RUNE SONG VERSE MELODY
PASSUS CANTICLE
CANTON ANGLE UNION CORNER
VOLOST PORTION QUARTER
SECTION DISTRICT DIVISION
(HALF —) ESQUIRE
CANTOR HAZAN HAZZAN SINGER
CHANTER CHAZZAN SOLOIST
PSALMIST
CANVAS FLY PAT DUCK GLUT
PATA SAIL TARP TENT TEWK
CLOTH COAST SCRIM TOILE VITRY
BALINE BURLAP CATGUT LINING
MUSLIN PICTURE POLDAVY
SACKING SCUTAGE DRABBLER
PAINTING VANDELAS SAILCLOTH
(— FOR CONVEYING GRAIN) APRON
(OLD CONDEMNED —)
RUMBOWLINE
(RUBBERIZED —) TOSH
(STUFFED —) BOLSTER
(TARRED —) COAT
CANVASBACK CAN DIVER CHEVAL
DUCKER POCHARD BULLNECK
CANVASS BEAT CASE DRUM
HAWK POLL SIFT RANDY STUDY
DEBATE PEDDLE SEARCH
AGITATE DISCUSS EXAMINE
SOLICIT TROUNCE CAMPAIGN
CONSIDER
CANVASSER AGENT POLLER
ROADMAN
CANYON CAJON CHASM COULE
GORGE GULCH ARROYO CANADA
RAVINE
CAOUTCHOUC RUBBER ELATERITE
CAP CUP FEZ HAT LID PAD POT
TAJ TAM TIP TOP ACME CALL
COIF CORK COWL DINK DOME
DOWD ETON GAGE HOOD HURE
JOAN KEEP KEPI MATE SHOE
SHOW TOPI BERET BOINA BUSBY
CHIEF COVER CROWN EXCEL
FANON GALEA HOUVE KULAH
MATCH MUTCH OUTDO PHANO
PUNCH SEIZE SHAKO TOPEE
TRUMP ARREST BARRAD BARRET
BEANIE BIGGIN BIRRUS BONNET
CALPAC CLIMAX COCKUP CORNET
GALERA HELMET HUBCAP JINNAH
MOBCAP PILEUS PINNER PRIMER
PUZZLE SUMMIT TABARD
TURBAN ALOPEKE BIRETTA
CALOTTE CAMAURO CAPITAL
CEREVIS CHAPEAU CHECHIA
CLOSURE COMMODE FERRULE
FLATCAP FORAGER HEADCAP
OVERLIE OVERTOP PERPLEX
PETASOS PILLBOX PILLION
SOWBACK SURPASS THIMBLE
TURNCAP ACROSOME BALMORAL
BEARSKIN BYCOCKET CAPELINE
CHAPERON COONSKIN ELECTRIC
FOLLOWER HEADGEAR PHRYGIUM
SKEWBACK SKULLCAP SURPRISE
TARBOOSH
(— FOR PILEDRIVER) PUNCH

(— OF FLAGSTAFF) TRUCK
(— OF FOAM) HOOD
(— OF PIER) CUSHION
(— OF PYXIDIUM) LID
(— OF WATCH) DOME CROWN
(— ON MAST) TRUCK
(ACADEMIC —) MORTARBOARD
(BISHOP'S —) HURA HURE
(CANADIAN —) TUQUE
(CHIMNEY —) GRANNY
(HORSEMAN'S —) MONTERO
(HUNTER'S —) MONTERA
MONTERO
(ICE —) BRAE CALOTTE
(JESTER'S —) COXCOMB FOOLSCAP
(MILITARY —) KEPI BUSBY SHAKO
(MOUNTAIN —) SCALP
(PERCUSSION —) AMORCE
CAPSULE
(PERUVIAN —) CHULLO
(POPE'S —) CAMAURO
(ROOT —) CALYPTRA
(TRIANGULAR —) KALPAK
(WOMAN'S —) TOY CAUL DOWD
JOAN KELL MUTCH COMMODE
VOLUPER BIGGONET
(WOOLEN —) BOINA TOQUE
TUQUE
(PREF.) PILEI PILEO PILO
CAPABILITY POWER STROIL
ABILITY CONDUCT FACULTY
POTENCY CAPACITY
CAPABLE APT CAN FIT ABLE GOOD
ADEPT CAPAX FENDY TIGHT
EXPERT SKILLED POWERFUL
(— OF BEING DEFENDED) TENABLE
(— OF BEING DRAWN OUT) DUCTILE
(— OF BEING SEVERED) SEVTILE
(— OF BEING THROWN) MISSILE
(— OF BEING UTTERED) EFFABLE
(— OF FLYING) VOLANT
(— OF SUBMISSION) AMENABLE
(NORMALLY —) ABOUT
(SUFF.) ABLE IBLE
(— OF) ILE
CAPACIOUS FULL SIDE WIDE
AMPLE BROAD LARGE ROOMY
WOMBY GOODLY ROOMFUL
CAPTIOUS ROOMSOME SPACIOUS
CAPACITOR CONDENSER
CAPACITY BACK BENT BIND DISH
GIFT GIVE SIZE TURN BLAST
FLAIR FORCE KNACK MODEL
POWER SKILL SPACE AGENCY
BOTTOM BURDEN ENERGY
ENGINE EXTENT GENIUS MODULE
SPREAD TALENT VOLUME ABILITY
CALIBER CALIBRE CONTENT
FACULTY FITNESS QUALITY
APTITUDE INSTINCT STRENGTH
INFLUENCE
(— FOR EATING) STROKE
(— FOR ENDURANCE) STAY
(— FOR HIGHER KNOWLEDGE)
INTELLECT
(— OF LATHE) SWING
(— OF SHIP) BURDEN
(CIVIL —) CAPUT
(INNATE —S) STAMINA
(INTELLECTUAL —) BROW
(LOAD-PULLING —) DRAFT
DRAUGHT
(MENTAL —S) BELFRY

(SPECIAL —) KNACK
(UNIT OF —) MUD MUID LAGEN
KISHEN MEDIMNUS KILDERKIN
(UNLIMITED —) INFINITY
CAPANEUS (FATHER OF —)
HIPPONOUS BELLEROPHON
(SLAYER OF —) JUPITER
(SON OF —) STHENELUS
(WIFE OF —) EVADNE
CAPARISON DECK TRAP HOUSE
COVERING TRAPPING
CAPE RAS COPE GAPE HEAD HOOK
LOOK NAZE NECK NESS SKAW
TANG WRIT AMICE CAPPA CLOAK
FICHU ORALE POINT SAGUM
STARE STOLE TALMA BERTHA
BYRRUS CABAAN CHAPEL
DOLMAN MANTLE SONTAG
TABARD TIPPET CHLAMYS
LEATHER MANTEEL MOZETTA
SALIENT TANJONG VANDYKE
CIRCULAR COLLARET HEADLAND
LAMBSKIN MANTILLA MOZZETTA
PALATINE PELERINE SEALSKIN
RAINPROOF
(— OF SKINS) KAROSS
(— OF STRAW) MINO
(BULLFIGHTER'S —) CAPA
(CLERGICAL —) ALMUCE
(DRESSING —) TOILET
(FEATHER —) AHUULA
(HOODED —) HUKE DOMINO
(LACE OR SILK —) VISITE
(LOW —) TANG
(PAPAL —) FANO FANON FANUM
ORALE PHANO
(RAIN —) CAPOTE
CAPE ANTEATER AARDVARK
CAPE ARMADILLO PANGOLIN
CAPE GOOSEBERRY POHA
CAPE HEN STINKER STINKPOT
CAPELIN SMELT ICEFISH
CAPE PIGEON PINTADO
CAPE POLECAT ZORIL MUISHOND
CAPER HOP JET DIDO HOIT JUMP
LEAP ROMP SKIP SKIT ANTIC
BRANK DANCE FLING FLISK FRISK
PRANK SAUCE SCOUP SHRUB
CAVORT CURVET FRISCO FROLIC
GAMBOL GAMOND PRANCE
SPRING TITTUP VAGARY CORSAIR
COURANT FRISCAL GAMBADO
PRANKLE CAPRIOLE MARIGOLD
(— ABOUT) FLING CAVORT
(SILLY —) SHINE
CAPER SPURGE CATEPUCE
CAPE TOWN BOVENLAND
**CAPE VERDE ISLANDS (CAPITAL
OF —)** PRAIA
(TOWN OF —) MINDELO
(VOLCANO ON —) FOGO
CAPHITE KIST
CAPITAL CAP CASH CITY FUND
GOOD LIMA MAIN RARE SEAT
BASIC CHIEF FATAL GREAT
MAJOR MONEY MUANG STOCK
VITAL DEADLY HEADLY IMPOST
LETTER LISBON MORTAL PRIMAL
UNCIAL WEALTH CENTRAL
CHATTEL DRESDEN LEADING
RADICAL SERIOUS WEIGHTY
CABECERA CATALLUM CHAPTER
CHAPTREL DOSSERET SWINGING

(**— OF HEAVEN**) AMARAVATI
(**— OF HELL**) PANDEMONIUM
(**DIVISION OF —**) ABACUS
(**GAMBLER'S —**) STAKE
(**INADEQUATE —**) SHOESTRING
CAPITATUM MAGNUM
CAPITELLUM KNOP
CAPITOL STATEHOUSE
CAPITOLINE SATURNIAN
CAPITULATION MUNICH TREATY
CAPITULUM HEAD KNOP
ANTHODIUM
CAPOTE HOOD CAPPO CLOAK
BONNET MANTLE TOPPER
CAPPER CORKER SEALER STEERER
CAPPY TALLOWY
CAPRICCIO (**CHARACTER IN —**)
FLAMAND OLIVIER MADELEINE
(**COMPOSER OF —**) STRAUSS
CAPRICE FAD TOY KINK MOOD
WHIM ANTIC BRAID CRANK
FANCY FREAK HUMOR QUIRK
CHANGE MAGGOT NOTION
SPLEEN TEMPER VAGARY
WHIMSY BOUTADE CONCEIT
CROCHET IMPULSE TANTRUM
WHIMSEY
CAPRICIOUS DIZZY DODDY FLUKY
MOODY CHANCY FICKLE FITFUL
KITTLE PLATTY WANTON
COMICAL ERRATIC FLIGHTY
MAGGOTY MOONISH PEEVISH
VAGRANT WAYWARD EPISODAL
FANCIFUL FREAKISH HUMOROUS
PERVERSE SKITTISH UNSTEADY
VARIABLE VOLATILE CROTCHETY
FANTASTIC VAGARIOUS
CAPRICIOUSNESS FREAK
CAPRICORN GOAT
CAPRIPEDE SATYR
CAPRYL RUTYL DECANOYL
CAPSHEAF CAP HOOD
CAPSICUM AJI PEPPER
(**— SAUCE**) TABASCO
CAPSID MIRID
CAPSIZE COUP KEEL PURL UPSET
WRONG WHEMMLE OVERTURN
CAPSTAN CRAB DRUM DANDY
HOIST LEVER NIGGER CYLINDER
WINDLASS
CAPSTONE LECH TOPSTONE
CAPSULE CAP POD URN BOLL
CASE CYST PILL SEED PEARL
PERLE SHELL THECA WAFER
AMPULE BARROW CACHET
COCOON OOCYST SHEATH
AMPOULE EYEBALL OTOCYST
SEEDBOX SILIQUE VANILLA
PERICARP PYXIDIUM
(**SPACE —**) TERRELLA
(**PREF.**) THEC(A)(I)(O)
CAPTAIN BO BOH CID BAAS HEAD
JOAB RAIS REIS BARAK CHIEF
LEADER MASTER NAAMAN
SOTNIK CAPITAN FOREMAN
HEADMAN MANAGER PATROON
SKIPPER FLUELLEN GOVERNOR
SUBAHDAR
(**— OF ARAB VESSEL**) NACODAR
(**— OF CAVALRY**) RESSALDAR
RITMASTER
(**— OF CRICKET TEAM**) SKIPPER
(**— OF CURLING TEAM**) SKIP

(**— OF PRIVATEER**) CAPER
(**— OF SHIP**) WAFTER
(**STRICT —**) SUNDOWNER
CAPTAINS COURAGEOUS
(**AUTHOR OF —**) KIPLING
(**CHARACTER IN —**) DAN JACK
DISKO TROOP CHEYNE HARVEY
MANUEL SALTERS
CAPTAIN'S DAUGHTER (**AUTHOR
OF —**) PUSHKIN
(**CHARACTER IN —**) MARIA PETER
ALEXEI ZOURIN EMELYAN
GRINEFF GRINYEV EGOROVNA
IVANOVNA MIRONOFF PUGACHEV
SHVABRIN VASILISA SAVELITCH
POUGATCHEFF
CAPTION TITLE LEADER LEGEND
CUTLINE HEADING SUBHEAD
CITATION HEADLINE SUBTITLE
CAPTIOUS CRAFY TESTY CRAFTY
SEVERE CARPING CYNICAL
FRETFUL PEEVISH TETTISH
ALLURING CATCHING CAVILING
CONTRARY CRITICAL
CAPTIOUSLY TUTLY
CAPTIVATE WIN TAKE CATCH
CHARM ALLURE ENAMOR PLEASE
RAVISH SUBDUE ATTRACT
BEWITCH CAPTIVE CAPTURE
ENCHANT ENTHRALL OVERTAKE
SURPRISE
CAPTIVATED EPRIS EPRISE
CAPTIVE
CAPTIVATING TAKING KILLING
WINNING WINSOME CATCHING
CAPTIVE SLAVE DANIEL ENAMOR
THRALL BRISEIS CAITIFF CAITIVE
PRISONER
(**— OF HERCULES**) IOLE
CAPTIVITY BOND IRON BONDS
CHAINS DURESS BONDAGE
SERFDOM SLAVERY
CAPTOR TAKER VICTOR CATCHER
CAPTURE BAG COP FIX GET NAB
NET WIN FALL FANG GRAB HOOK
LAND PREY SNIB TAKE TRAP TREE
CARRY CATCH FORCE PINCH
PRIZE PURSE RAVEN SEIZE
SWOOP ARREST COLLAR CORRAL
ENTRAP GOBBLE OBTAIN PIRACY
REDUCE TAKING CAPTIVE
LOWBELL SEIZURE WINNING
EXCHANGE SURPRISE UNDERNIM
(**— BACKGAMMON PIECE**) HIT
(**— BIRDS**) TOODLE
(**— GAME**) SATCHEL
(**— OF ALL PRIZES**) SWEEP
(**— TROUT**) TICKLE
CAPUCHIN MONKEY CAY SAI
CEPID SAJOU WEEPER SAPAJOU
RINGTAIL
CAPULIN CEREZA
CAPYBARA CAVY CARPINCHO
CAPYS (**FATHER OF —**) ASSARACUS
(**SON OF —**) ANCHISES
(**WIFE OF —**) THEMISTE
CAR BOX BUS PIG AUTO BOGY
BUNK DOLL DRAG DUMP GRIP
JEEP RATH TRAM ZULU BOGEY
COACH CRATE DINER DUMMY
GURRY HUTCH JIMMY RATHA
SEDAN STOCK TRAIN TRUCK
WRONG BASKET BOXCAR BUFFET

CHIPPY DINGEY DINGHY DUPLEX
HOPPER JIGGER JINGLE SALOON
SETOFF SMOKER TOURER
AWKWARD CARROCH CHARIOT
COMBINE FLATCAR FREEZER
GIRAFFE GONDOLA HANDCAR
SIDECAR TELPHER TRAILER
TROLLEY VEHICLE VETTURA
AMPHICAR DRAGSTER HORSECAR
OUTSIDER QUADRIGA ROADSTER
SINISTER
(**— FOR TRAIN CREW**) CABOOSE
(**— ON RAIL**) TROLLEY
(**BAGGAGE —**) BLIND
(**CABLE —**) GONDOLA
(**COAL —**) HUTCH JIMMY WAGON
WAGGON
(**ELECTRIC —**) TELFER TELPHER
(**ELEVATOR —**) CAB CAGE
(**EMPTY —**) EMPTY IDLER
(**JAUNTING —**) SIDECAR
(**LOG —**) BUNK
(**LOW-WHEELED —**) HUTCH
TRUCKLE
(**MINE —**) SKIP LARRY BARNEY
GIRAFFE GUNBOAT
(**MONORAIL —**) GYROCAR
(**OBSERVATION —**) BUGGY
(**OLD —**) JUNKER
(**POLICE —**) CRUISER
(**SMALL —**) MINICAB
(**TROLLEY —**) SHORT
(**USED —**) DOG
CARABAO BUFF BUFFALO
CARACAL GORKUN SYAGUSH
CARACARA HAWK CARANCHA
CHIMANGO
CARACOLE FRISK CAREER
CARADOC BALA CRADOCK
CARAFE CROFT BOTTLE
CARAGUATA CHAGUAR
CARAJURA CHICA
CARAMBOLA BLIMBING
BALIMBING
CARAMEL BLACKJACK
CARAPA CRAB CRAPPO
CRABWOOD
CARAPACE CRUST SHELL LORICA
SHIELD CALAPASH
(**SUFF.**) STEGE STEGITE
CARATE PINTA
CARATHIS (**SON OF —**) VATHEK
CARAVAN VAN TREK TRIP FLEET
TRAIN CAFILA COFFLE CONVOY
SAFARI TRAVEL JOURNEY
VEHICLE CONDUCTA
CARAVANSARY INN CHAN KHAN
HOTEL SERAI ZAYAT HOSTEL
IMARET CHOULTRY HOSTELRY
SERAGLIO
CARAWAY CARVY UMBEL
CARBAMATE MEPROBAMATE
CARBINE STEN DRAGON MUSKET
DRAGOON ESCOPET
CARBOHYDRATE SUGAR AMYLAN
GELOSE INULIN STARCH
FUCOSAN GLUCIDE CELLULIN
DEXTRINE DEXTROSE GLYCOGEN
GRAMININ PENTOSAN TRITICIN
CELLULOSE PARAMYLUM
POLYSACCHARIDE
CARBON COAL COKE COPY SOOT
NORIT CRAYON DIAMOND

REPLICA CHARCOAL
GRAPHITE SCHUNGITE
(**PREF.**) ANTHRAC(O)
(**SUFF.**) ANE
CARBONADO BORT BOART BOORT
CARBON
CARBONATE BURN CHAR FIZZ
AERATE ALKALI ENLIVEN
ENERGIZER
CARBONATOR GASMAN
CARBON DIOXIDE
(**SUFF.**) CAPNIA
CARBONIZER PICKLER
CARBORUNDUM EMERY ABRASIVE
SILUNDUM
CARBOXYL
(**SUFF.**) (**CONTAINING —**) OIC ONIC
CARBUNCLE RUBY PYROPE
ANTHRAX CHARBOCLE
(**PREF.**) ANTHRAC(O)
CARBURETOR CARB DIFFUSER
VAPORIZER
CARCASS BEEF BODY BOUK CASE
CULL BLOCK MUMMY CORPSE
CARRION
(**— OF WHALE**) CRANG KRANG
KRENG
CARCERULE SARCOBASIS
CARD ACE MAP PAM WAG CLUB
COMB DRAW FACE FIVE FOUR
JACK KING MENU PLAN ROVE
STOP BALOP BLANK CARTE
CHART CHECK DEUCE DUMMY
EIGHT ENTRY EQUAL FICHE FLATS
GREEN HEART HONOR JOKER
LOSER PIECE QUEEN SPADE
STAMP STIFF TAROT TEASE
BENDER CARTEL CONVEX FILLER
KICKER KNIGHT PIGEON READER
SECOND TICKET TOWSER
BRAGGER BRISQUE DIAMOND
PROGRAM RELEASE STARTER
STOPPER TAROCCO TRIUMPH
BOOKMARK COMOQUER
DECKHEAD DRAWCARD
SCHEDULE SCRIBBLE SQUEEZER
STRIPPER TIMECARD
(**— IN OMBRE**) MANILLE
(**— LAST IN BOX**) HOCK HOCKELTY
(**— WOOL**) TUM ROVE
(**ACE OF CLUBS —**) BASTA BASTO
MATADOR PUPPYFOOT
(**ACE OF SPADES —**) MATADOR
SPADILLE
(**ACE OF TRUMPS —**) TIB
(**AVIATOR'S —**) CARNET
(**CLUB —**) OAK
(**COMPASS —**) FLY ROSE
(**CRIBBAGE —S**) CRIB
(**DEAD —**) SLEEPER
(**DIAMOND —**) PICK CARREAU
(**DISCARDED —S**) CRIB
(**DRAWING —**) BLOWOFF
(**FARO —**) SODA
(**FOUR —**) CATER QUATRE
(**FOURTH —**) CASE
(**HIGHEST UNPLAYED —**) COMMAND
(**JOKER —**) BRAGGER MISTIGRIS
(**KING, QUEEN OR KNAVE —**) COST
FACE
(**KNAVE —**) PAM TOM JACK
BOWER EQUES MAKER NODDY
COQUIN KNIGHT PICARO VARLET

WENZEL CUSTREL PEASANT VILLAIN VARLETTO
(LAYOUT OF —)S TABLEAU
(LOW —) GUARD
(MARKED —) STAMP
(POSTAL —) COVER
(PULLING —)S TIRE
(QUEEN AND KNAVE —)S INTRIGO INTRIGUE
(RUN OF —)S SEQUENCE
(SPADE —) PICK DIGGER
(STOCK —) TALON
(THIRD HIGHEST TRUMP —) BASTA
(THREE —) TREY THREE
(WILD —) FREAK
(3 ACE —)S CORONA
(3 FACE —)S GLEEK
(3 —S IN SEQUENCE) TIERCE FOURCHETTE
(3 —S OF KIND) TRIO TRICON PAIRIAL TRIPLET
(4 OF TRUMPS —) TIDDY
(5 FACE —)S BLAZE
(7, 8 AND 9 —S) VOIDS
CARDAMOM KNOBWOOD
CARDBOARD CARD PALL BLANK BOGUS CARTON BRISTOL TAGBOARD PAPERBOARD
(TWO —S) SPHEROGRAPH
CARDER TOZER TEASER TUMMER
CARDIALGIA HEARTBURN
CARDIGAN CORGI WAMUS FABRIC JACKET WAMPUS SWEATER
CARDINAL MAIN BASIC CHIEF CLOAK VITAL ALEPHA CLERIC DATARY PRINCE RADICAL ALEFNULL ALEFZERO CAMPEIUS PENITENTIARY
CARDINALATE PURPLE
CARDINAL BIRD CARNAL REDBIRD REDLEGS GROSBEAK REDSHANK
CARDINAL FISH FUCINITA ALFONCINO
CARDSHARP TRAMPOSO
CARDSHARPER GREEK SHARPER SPIELER
CARE DO DOW HOW CARK CURE DUTY FASH FRET HEED KEEP KEPE MIND PASS RECK SOIN TEND TENT WISH YEME COUNT GRIEF GUARD NURSE PAINS SORGE TRUST WORRY BURDEN CARIEN CHARGE CUMBER DESIRE GRIEVE KIAUGH LAMENT REGARD SORROW ANXIETY AUSPICE CAUTION CHERISH CONCERN CULTURE CUSTODY KEEPING RESPECT RUNNING SCRUPLE THOUGHT TUITION BUSINESS PERIERGY TENDMENT NURTURANCE PRECAUTION SOLICITUDE
(— FOR) KNOW MIND RECK TEND WARD FORCE NURSE SAVOR FATHER MATTER REGARD CHERISH PROCURE
(— FOR ONESELF) BACH
(— OF HOUSEHOLD) HUSBANDRY
(— OF LIVESTOCK) CHORE
(JUDICIOUS —) LEISURE
(WATCHFUL —) TENDANCE OVERSIGHT
CAREEN GIP CANT HEEL KEEL LIST

TILT VEER LURCH SLOPE SWIFT INCLINE
CAREER RUN WAY LIFE ROAD RUSH TRADE CHARGE COURSE GALLOP CALLING CARIERE PURSUIT
(MILITARY —) ARMS SERVICE
CAREFREE EASY FRANK HAPPY BREEZY DEGAGE HOLIDAY DEBONAIR
CAREFUL BUSY WARY CANNY CHARY CLOSE EXACT HOOLY TENTY CHOICE DAINTY EIDENT EYEFUL FRUGAL NARROW TENDER ANXIOUS CURIOUS ENVIOUS GUARDED HEEDFUL PAINFUL PRUDENT THRIFTY ACCURATE CAUTIOUS CRITICAL DILIGENT DISCREET DREADFUL GINGERLY MOURNFUL PUNCTUAL TROUBLED VIGILANT WATCHFUL OBSERVANT METICULOUS SOLICITOUS PUNCTILIOUS
CAREFULLY HOOLY NARROW CANNILY CHARILY TENTILY CHOICELY GINGERLY
CAREFULNESS CAUTION
CARELESS LAX COOL EASY LASH RASH MESSY SLACK CASUAL OVERLY RAKISH REMISS SECURE SLOPPY SUPINE UNTIDY UNWARY CURSORY LANGUID SLIGHTY UNCANNY HEEDLESS LISTLESS MINDLESS RECKLESS SLATTERN SLIPSHOD SLOVENLY YEMELESS NEGLECTFUL SLATTERNLY
CARELESSLY SLACK OVERLY SLACKLY SLIGHTLY
CARELESSNESS LACHES LAXITY INCAUTION
CARESS COY HUG PAT PET BILL CLAP DAUT DAWT KISS MUCH NECK INGLE NURSE CODDLE COSSET CUDDLE FONDLE PAMPER STROKE CHERISH EMBRACE FLATTER BLANDISH CANOODLE LALLYGAG
CARETAKER KEEPER WARDER JANITOR
CARGO BULK LAST LOAD BURDEN LADING FREIGHT PACKAGE PORTAGE CARGASON PROPERTY SHIPLOAD SHIPMENT TRAFFICS
CARIAMA CHUNGA SERIEMA
CARIB GALIBI CALINAGO
CARIBBEAN (— GULF) DARIEN HONDURAS
(— ISLAND) CUBA SABA ARUBA HAITI NEVIS BEQUIA NASSAU TOBAGO ANTIGUA BARBUDA BONAIRE CURACAO GRENADA JAMAICA TORTOLA ANGUILLA BARBADOS DOMINICA TRINIDAD GUADELOUPE MONTSERRAT
(— ISLAND GROUP) TURKS CAICOS CAYMAN LEEWARD ANTILLES WINDWARD
CARIBE PIRAI PIRANHA CHARACINE
CARIBOU STAG RANGIFER REINDEER
CARICATURE APE COPY MOCK SKIT FARCE LIBEL MIMIC SQUIB

OVERDO PARODY SATIRE CARTOON TRAVESTY BURLESQUE
CARILLONNEUR CAMPANIST BELLMASTER
CARINA KEEL
CARIOUS ROTTEN
CARMELITE EXTERN TERESIAN
CARMEN (CHARACTER IN —) JOSE CARMEN ZUNIGA MICAELA ESCAMILLO
(COMPOSER OF —) BIZET
CARMI (FATHER OF —) REUBEN
(SON OF —) ACHAN
CARMINATIVE GINGER CALAMUS CAMPHOR ANETHOLE VALERIAN
CARMINE RED LAKE CRIMSON SCARLET
CARNAGE WAL MURDER POGROM STRAGE BUTCHERY MASSACRE BLOODSHED SLAUGHTER
CARNAL CROW LEWD GROSS ANIMAL BODILY SEXUAL BESTIAL BRUTISH EARTHLY FLESHLY SECULAR SENSUAL WORLDLY MATERIAL PANDEMIC PHYSICAL TEMPORAL
CARNATION JACK PINK FLAKE BIZARRE PICOTEE DAYBREAK DIANTHUS GRENADINE MALMAISON
CARNELIAN SARD COPPER
(BEAD OF —) ARANGO
CARNIVAL FETE SHOW CARNY CANVAS APOKREA CANVASS REVELRY FASCHING FESTIVAL
CARNIVORE CAT DOG FOX BEAR COON LION LYNX MINK PUMA SEAL WOLF CIVET GENET HYENA OTTER PANDA PEKAN RATEL SABLE STOAT TIGER BADGER COUGAR ERMINE FELINE FERRET FISHER FOUSSA JACKAL JAGUAR MARTEN OCELOT POSSUM SERVAL WEASEL DASYURE GLUTTON LEOPARD MEERKAT POLECAT RACCOON TIGRESS AARDWOLF MONGOOSE OPPOSSUM PREDACEAN ZOOPHAGAN
(FOSSIL —) CREODONT
CARNIVOROUS SARCOPHAGOUS
CAROB HUSK LOCUST ALGAROBA
CAROL LAY NOEL SING SONG DITTY YODEL WARBLE WASSAIL MADRIGAL AGUINALDO
CAROLINA ALLSPICE SHRUB
CAROLINE ISLANDS (— ISLAND GROUP) PALAU
(ISLAND OF —) YAP HALL PALU TRUK PELEW PULAP OROLUK PONAPE WOLEAI PELELIU
(TOWN OF —) LOT NIF RUNU KOROR MUTOK TOMIL PONAPE MALAKAL GARUSUUN
CAROLINGIAN KARLING
CAROM SHOT BOUNCE CANNON GLANCE STRIKE REBOUND BILLIARD CARAMBOLE
CAROUSAL BAT GELL LARK ORGY RIOT ROMP TOOT BINGE FEAST RANDY REVEL ROUSE SPRAY SPREE FROLIC SHINDY SPLORE BANQUET CAROUSE REVELRY

WASSAIL DRINKING FESTIVAL JAMBOREE
CAROUSE JET BOUT HELL RANT TEAR TOOT BINGE BIRLE BOUSE DRINK QUAFF RANDY REVEL ROUSE SPREE TOAST COURANT JOLLIFY WASSAIL CAROUSAL
CAROUSER BACCHANT BACCHANAL
CAROUSING REVEL RAFFING
CARP KOI NAG BITE DRUM SING SNAG TALK YERK CAVIL PINCH PRATE SCOLD SPEAK CENSOR NIBBLE RECITE TWITCH CENSURE CHATTER CRUCIAN QUIBBLE COMPLAIN CYPRINID GOLDFISH
(CRUCIAN —) GIBEL
(LAKE —) DRUM LAKER
(PREF.) CYPRIN(O)
CARPAL ACTINOST
CARPEL ACHENE CARPID COCCUS MERICARP CARPOPHYL
(PL.) CORE
CARPENTER ANT LOHAR FITTER FRAMER HOUSER JOINER PINNER WRIGHT BUILDER HOWSOUR WOODMAN INDENTER TECTONIC TIMBERER PITWRIGHT SHIPWRIGHT
(SHIP'S —) CHIPS
(PREF.) TECTO
CARPENTRY WOODWORK WRIGHTRY
CARPER MOME CRITIC
CARPET MAT RUG AGRA KALI KUBA HERAT KILIM SARUK SCOLD SUMAK TAPET TAPIS TEKKE USHAK AFGHAN FLOSSA FRIEZE KASHAN KIDDER KIRMAN LAVEHR NAMMAD RUNNER SAROUK SAXONY SELJUK SMYRNA TABRIZ VELVET WILTON DHURRIE GIORDES HAMADAN INGRAIN ISFAHAN ISPAHAN SHEMAKA TEHERAN AKHISSAR AMRITSAR BRUSSELS COVERING FOOTPACE KARABAGH MOQUETTE TAPESTRY TURCOMAN VENETIAN AXMINSTER SITRINGEE
(HOLY —) KISWA
(PILELESS —) KILIM GELEEM
CARPETING FILLING
CARPET SHARK WOBBEGONG
CARPET SHELL EEROCK PULLET
CARPETWEED FICOID FICOIDAL MESEMBRYANTHEMUM
CARPING CRAB CAPTIOUS CAVILING CRITICAL
CARPSUCKER QUILLBACK
CARPUS WRIST CARPOPODITE
CARRAGEEN KILLEEN
CARREL STALL CUBICLE
CARRIAGE AIR CAB CAR FLY GIG RIG RUT SET VIS ARBA BIGA CART CHAR DRAG DUKE EKKA GAIT GARB HACK LOAD MIEN PORT RUTH SHAY TEAM TRAP WYNN ARABA BANDY BRAKE BREAK BRETT BUGGY CHAIR COACH COUPE ESSED FRONT JUTKA MIDGE NODDY PANEL POISE SADOO SETUP SULKY TENUE TONGA TRUCK WAGON BURDEN

CALASH CHAISE CHARET CISIUM
CONVOY DENNET FIACRE GHARRY
GOCART HANSOM HERDIC
KOSONG LANDAU MANNER
MOTION PORTER REMISE SADDLE
SPIDER SURREY TANDEM TELEGA
TROIKA BAGGAGE BEARING
BERLINE BOUNDER BRITSKA
CALECHE CALESIN CARAVAN
CARIOLE CAROCHE CHARIOT
COACHEE CONDUCT CROYDON
DOGCART DOSADOS DROSHKY
FORECAR GESTURE HACKMAN
HACKNEY MINIBUS PHAETON
POSCHAY SHANDRY SKYHOOK
TALLYHO TARTANA TILBURY
TRANSIT TROLLEY UNICORN
VECTURE VEHICLE VETTURA
VOITURE VOLANTE WAFTAGE
BAROUCHE BEHAVIOR
BROUGHAM CARRIOLE CARRYALL
CLARENCE CURRICLE DEARBORN
DEMEANOR DORMEUSE
EQUIPAGE PORTANCE PRESENCE
ROCKAWAY SOCIABLE STANHOPE
TARANTAS TOURNURE VICTORIA
(— OF HANDPRESS) COFFIN
(— OF HORSE) AIR
(AMMUNITION —) CAISSON
(CEREMONIAL —) RATH
(ELEVATED —) LIFT
(GUN —) CHASSIS
(INDIAN —) RUT EKKA BANDY
GHARRI GHARRY
(JAVANESE —) SADO SADOO
(LIVERY —) REMISE
(LOG —) DRAG
(PUBLIC —) FLY OMNIBUS
CARRIAGE HOUSE REMISE
CARRIER HOD BASE JEEP SHIP
TRAM BUGGY HAMAL KAHAR
MACER PLANE SABOT TAMEN
TIGER BARKIS BEARER CADGER
COOLIE HAMMAL HODMAN
JAGGER PACKER PORTER
RUNNER TAILER WEASEL
DRAYMAN DROGHER FLATTOP
POSTMAN REMOVER TACULLI
TROTTER VEHICLE CARGADOR
CARRYALL PORTATOR RAILROAD
TEAMSTER SUBSTRATE
(COAL —) FLATIRON
(COLOR —) LURRIER
(ENDLESS —) TAILER
(FIRE —) PORTFIRE
(MAIL —) COURIER POSTMAN
(WATER —) BHISTI BHEESTY
(PREF.) PORTE
CARRION KET VILE OFFAL CORPSE
HOODIE REFUSE ROTTEN
CARCASS CORRUPT DOGMEAT
CROWBAIT
CARRION BIRD SCAVENGER
CARRION CROW DOWP HOODY
URUBU CORBIE HOODIE
GERCROW
CARROT UMBEL CONIUM DAUCUS
CACHRYS SECRETE BUPLEVER
HILLTROT
(DEADLY —) DRIAS
(PERUVIAN —) ARRACACH
(PREPARED WITH —S) CRECY
CARROTING SECRETAGE

CARROUSEL RIDE
WHIRLIGIG QUADRILLE
CARRY CAR HUG JAG LUG BEAR
BUCK CART DRAY FARE GEST
HAVE HOLD HUMP LEAD PACK
PORT SHOW TAKE TOTE TUMP
BRING BROOK CADGE CROSS
FERRY GESTE GUIDE POISE
WALTZ WEIGH BEHAVE CONVEY
CONVOY DELATE DEPORT DERIVE
EXTEND COMPORT CONDUCT
CONTAIN ENTRAIN PORTAGE
PRODUCE SUPPORT SUSTAIN
UNDERGO BAJULATE CONTINUE
TRANSFER TRANSMIT
(— AWAY) FIRK DRAIN REAVE
SWEEP TRUSS ABLATE ASPORT
(— EFFIGY) GUY
(— FORWARD) EXTEND
(— IN OXCART) KURVEY
(— LIQUOR) BOOTLEG
(— OFF) RAP HENT LIFE SACK
FETCH HEAVE RIFLE SCOUR
SWOOP ABDUCT ASPORT BRAZEN
KIDNAP SPIRIT
(— ON) DO RUN WAR HAVE LEAD
LEVY WAGE APPLY DRIVE ENSUE
FIGHT TRAIN CREATE DEMEAN
FOLLOW MANAGE OCCUPY
CONDUCT EXERCISE MAINTAIN
TRANSACT
(— ONESELF) HOLD
(— ONWARD) CONTINUE
(— OUT) DO ACT END GIVE LAST
HONOR AFFORD EFFECT ACHIEVE
EXECUTE FULFILL PERFORM
SATISFY PERPETRATE
(— UPWARD) RAP ESCALATE
(SUFF.) GER(ENCE)(ENT)(OUS)
PHER PHORA PHORE(SIS) PHORIA
PHOROUS PHORUS
(— ON) IZE
CARRYALL BUS CASE WAGON
CARRIAGE
CARRYING BURDEN GERENT
FRAUGHT
(— AWAY) REVEHENT
(— ON) GESTION
(— WEIGHT) EFFECTIVE
(PREF.) (— ON) PHORO
CART CAR JAG POT RUT BUTT
CHAR COOP COUP DRAY HAUL
JANG LEAD LOAD PLOW PUTT
RUTH TOTE WAIN ARABA BANDY
BOGEY BOGIE CADDY CARRY
DANDY DILLY DOLLY SULKY
TONGA TRUCK WAGON BARROW
CADDIE CHAISE CHARET CISIUM
CONVEY DOLLIE DUMPER GHARRI
GHARRY JIGGER JINKER KURUMA
LIMBER PLOUGH SPIDER CARIOLE
CARRETA CHARIOT DOGCART
GUJERAT HACKERY MORFREY
SHALLOW SHANDRY TROLLEY
TRUNDLE TUMBLER TUMBREL
TUMBRIL VEHICLE BUCKCART
DUMPCART HANDCART
PUSHCART
(— WITH TANK) TUMBLER
(BULLOCK —) BANDY HACKERY
(COSTER'S —) TROLL
(COVERED —) JINGLE CARIOLE
(FARMER'S —) PUTT

GAMBO MORPHREY
(FREIGHT —) CARRETON
(LOG —) TUG BUNK
(LUMBER —) GILL BUMMER
(MILKMAN'S —) PRAM
(OX —) RECKLA
(PARCELS —) FLY
(TIMBER —) CUTS
(TIP —) COOP COUP COUPE
(UNDERSLUNG —) FLOAT
(2-PONY —) KOSONG
(2-WHEELED —) BANDY BUGGY
SULKY CARRETA TUMBREL
(3-WHEELED —) PORTER
CARTE MAP CARD LIST MENU
CHART CHARTER DIAGRAM
CARTE BLANCHE BLANK
CARTEL CARD DEFY PACT POOL
SHIP PAPER TRUST CORNER
LETTER TREATY CONTRACT
SYNDICATE
CARTER CARMAN JAGGER LEADER
DRAYMAN LADEMAN TRUCKER
HORSEMAN TEAMSTER
CARTILAGE COPULA TISSUE
CRICOID EPIURAL GRISTLE
RADIALE STERNUM TARSALE
THYROID CHONDRUS EPIPUBIS
HYPOHYAL SESAMOID TURBINAL
(— UNDER DOG'S TONGUE) LYTTA
(PREF.) CHONDR(I)(IO)(O) CRICO
(SUFF.) CHONDRIA CHONDRY
CRINUS
CARTILAGINOUS CHONDRIC
CARTLOAD SEAM
CARTOGRAPH MAP PLAT CHART
CARTOGRAPHER CHARTIST
MAPMAKER
AMERICAN GANNETT HUTCHINS
SOUTHACK STEVENSON
ENGLISH SPEED
GERMAN KIEPERT STIELER
PETERMANN WALDSEEMULLER
RUSSIAN KAULBARS
SWISS SIEGFRIED
CARTON BOX CASE SHELL
CARTOON EPURE ANIMATION
CARTOONIST **AMERICAN** NAST
BLOCK DUFFY KIRBY OPPER
SEGAR YOUNG BRIGGS DORGAN
KEMBLE NEWELL POWERS
DARLING GRUELLE KEPPLER
MCMANUS GOLDBERG OUTCAULT
SCHULTZE WILLIAMS NANKIVELL
FITZPATRICK
AUSTRALIAN LINDSAY
DUTCH RAEMAEKERS
ENGLISH LOW DYSON TENNIEL
ROBINSON
CARTOUCHE MESA OVAL
DURANGO CARTRIDGE
CARTRIDGE BAG CASE HULL
BLANK SHELL SHORT BULLET
MAGNUM PATRON CAPSULE
TORPEDO HANDLOAD SHOTSHELL
(PART OF —) RIM CASE HEAD
NOSE SLUG CRIMP BULLET
JACKET PRIMER
(TAPE —) CASSETTE
CARTULARY COUCHER
CARTWHEEL CLOGWHEEL
CARUCATE CARVE PLOWLAND
CARUNCLE ARIL

COMB STROPHIOLE
CARVE CUT ALAY SIDE BEHEW
BREAK GRAVE KIRVE MINCE
SHEAR SPLAY SPOIL THIGH INCISE
QUINSE SCULPT THWITE TRENCH
UNLACE ENCHASE ENGRAIL
ENGRAVE DISJOINT MALAHACK
SCULLION
(— A BIRD) WING
(— CHICKEN) FRUSH
(— GOOSE) REAR
(— HEN) SPOIL
(— PEACOCK) DISFIGURE
(— PLOVER) MINCE
(— SWAN) LIFT
(PREF.) GLYPHO GLYPT(O)
SCULPTO
(SUFF.) GLYPH
CARVED CARVEN GLYPHIC INCISED
(PREF.) GLYPT(O)
CARVER BODGER KIRVER CROPPER
FROSTER IVORIST CISELEUR
TRENCHER
CARVING CAMEO GLYPH IVORY
ENTAIL SCRIVE GLYPTIC MASKOID
NICKING APLUSTRE INTAGLIO
TRIPTYCH PETROGLYPH
(CIRCULAR —) TONDO
CARYA HICORIA
CARYATID TELAMON CANEPHORA
(PART OF —) GAINE
CARYOCAR SOUARI
CARYOPHYLLUS JAMBOSA
CARYOPSIS SEED
CASCABEL POMMEL POMMELION
CASCADE LIN FALL LINN FORCE
SPOUT CATARACT
CASCARA BUCKTHORN WAHOO
SHITTIM
CASCARILLA CROTON GOATWEED
SWEETWOOD
CASE BAG BOX CUP HAP LEG POD
POT PYX BIND BOOT BUNK BURR
CASK COPE DEED DESK DOCK
DOME FILE PACK PAIR ROLL SUIT
TICK BRACE BRIEF BULLA BURSE
CADDY CASUS CAUSE CHAPE
COVER CRATE EVENT FOLIO
FOREL HUSSY HUTCH PRESS
PYXIS SHELL STATE THECA THING
TRIAL ACTION AFFAIR APPEAL
BARREL BINDER BOXING CARTON
CASING CELLAR CHANCE CHRISM
COFFIN COUPLE LOCKET LORICA
MATTER PATRON PENNER
PETARD POPPET QUIVER RIDDLE
SHEATH SHRINE STATOR SURVEY
TASHIE TWEEZE VALISE VANITY
CABINET CAMISIA CAPCASE
CAPSULE COUNTER CUSHION
DIECASE ENCLOSE ENVELOP
EXAMPLE GEARBOX HOLDALL
HOLSTER HOUSING HUMIDOR
INCLOSE LAWSUIT LUNETTE
PACKAGE REMANET SATCHEL
SHIPPER WARDIAN ACCIDENT
ARGUMENT BOOKCASE CARRYALL
CUPBOARD ENVELOPE EQUIPAGE
EXEMPLAR GARDEVIN INSTANCE
KNAPSACK PACKSACK PORTFIRE
SHOWCASE SITUATED
SOLANDER TANTALUS
PORTFOLIO

(— CONTAINING ELEVATOR BELT)
LEG
(— ENCLOSING CLOCK DIAL) HOOD
(— FOR BOTTLES) CELLARET
(— FOR CARDS) SHOE
(— FOR COMPASS) BINNACLE
(— FOR EXPLOSIVES) TRUNK
(— FOR JEWELS) TYE
(— FOR MAINSPRING) BARILLET
(— FOR MOLD) COPE CHAPE
(— FOR MUMMY) SLEDGE
(— FOR PISTOL) HOLSTER
(— FOR PULLEY) BLOCK
(— FOR RIFLE) BOOT
(— FOR SEWING ITEMS) HUSSY
(— FOR TOOLS) TROUSSE
(— FOR TWEEZERS) BUBBLEBOW
(— FOR WRITING MATERIALS)
STANDISH
(— IN WATCH) DOME BARREL
(— OF) A
(— OF FLOUR BOLTER) HUTCH
(— OF VENETIAN BLIND) HEADBOX
(— WITH COMPARTMENTS) RIDDLE
(BONY —) CARAPACE
(CARTRIDGE —) DOP CARTOUCHE
(COSMETIC —) COMPACT
(COURT —) LAWSUIT
(EGG —) OVISAC OOTHECA
(FIREWORKS —) LANCE
(GRAMMATICAL —) DATIVE ESSIVE
LATIVE ELATIVE FACTIVE
ABLATIVE EQUATIVE ERGATIVE
GENITIVE ILLATIVE LOCATIVE
VOCATIVE ACCUSATIVE
(HOPELESS —) GONER
(LARVA —) INDUSIUM
(LUGGAGE —) IMPERIAL
(ORNAMENTAL —) ETUI
(PAPER —) COFFIN
(PILLOW —) SLIP
(WICKER —) HASK BARROW
HANAPER
(WING —) SHARD
(WRITING —) KALAMDAN
(PREF.) THEC(A)(I)(O)
(EGG —) OOTHEC(O)
(SUFF.) THECA THECIUM
CASED BOUND
CASEMENT SASH LUKET WINDOW
CASE OF SERGEANT GRISCHA
(AUTHOR OF —) ZWEIG
(CHARACTER IN —) BABKA
LYCHOW GRISCHA WILHELMI
WINFRIED BJUSCHEFF
PAPROTKIN PONSANSKI
SCHIEFFENZAHN
CASHEW ACAJOU ANACARD
CASHIER CASS CAST BREAK
DEALER POTDAR PURSER
CHECKER DISMISS
CASHIERED BROKEN DEGOMME
CASHMERE KASHMIR PRUNELL
CASH REGISTER DAMPER REGEST
GREFFIER RECORDER REGISTER
CASING BODY BOOT BUNG CASE
CURB HULL SHOE SKIN TIRE
APRON BELLY DERMA EPHOD
GAINE LINER ROUND STOCK
TRUNK BOXING COFFIN COLLET
JACKET KISHKE LINING SCROLL
SHEATH VOLUTE COWLING
FEEDBOX HOUSING MANHEAD

OUTCASE STAVING THIMBLE
CACHEPOT COVERING PLOWSHOE
SHIRTING WHEELBOX
(— FOR BRAIN) HARNPAN
CASK KEG PIN TUB TUN VAT BOSS
BUTT CADE COWL DRUM KNAG
PIPE RAPE RIER SLIP TREE WOOD
ANKER BOWIE BULGE FOIST
STAND UNION BARECA BARREL
CARDEL CASQUE DOLIUM FIRKIN
FOODER LONGER OCTAVE TIERCE
WINGER BARRICO BREAKER
FOSTELL LEAGUER RUNDLET
SACKBUT CASSETTE HOGSHEAD
PUNCHEON QUARDEEL
ROUNDLET KILDERKIN
(BREWING —) UNION
(LOCKED —) TANTALUS
(PERFORATED —) POT
(SMALL —) KEG TUB KNAG STOOP
STOUP
(WINE —) FAT TUN BOSS BUTT
PIPE TIERCE HOGSHEAD
(PL.) COOPERAGE
CASKET BOX PIX TYE CASE CASK
CIST TILL TOMB BUIST CHEST
ACERRA CHASSE COFFER COFFIN
SHRINE CADENAS FOSTELL
CASSETTE
CASQUE CASK HORN GALEA
HELMET BRASSET
CASSABANANA CURUBA
CASSANDRA (BROTHER OF —)
HELENUS
(FATHER OF —) PRIAM
(HUSBAND OF —) AGAMEMNON
(MOTHER OF —) HECUBA
(SLAYER OF —) CLYTEMNESTRA
CASSAREEP CAXIRI
CASSAVA AIPI YUCA AIPIM YUCCA
CASIRI CAZIBI MANIOC TAPIOCA
CASSEROLE TUREEN COCOTTE
MARMITE TERRINE TZIMMES
CASSIA KEZIA SENNA SICKLEPOD
CASSIA FISTULA AMALTAS
CASSIMERE ZEPHYR
CASSINI OLEG
CASSITERITE TINSTONE
CASSITES KUSHSHU
CASSOCK GOWN SLOP VEST
APRON GIPPO PRIEST PELISSE
SOUTANE ZIMARRA
CASSOWARY EMU MURUP
MOORUP RATITE
CAST MEW PUT SET BILL DART
HURL MOLD MOLT PICK SHED
SLAT SLIP SPEW SWAK TINT TOSS
TREE TURN WHAP WHOP WURP
BLOCK BRAID CHUCK COOST
DEUCE DRIVE EJECT ERECT FLING
FLIRT FOUND FUSIL HEAVE
IMAGE KEIST PITCH SHADE SHAPE
SHOOT SLING STAMP THROW
TINGE COLLAR INJECT NOSING
STRIKE STRIND THRILL AGARWAL
CASHIER DEPOSIT DISCARD
MOULAGE VIBRATE CASTLING
CONSPECT OUTSLING POLYTYPE
TINCTURE
(— A SPELL) TAKE HOODOO
BESPELL BEWITCH FORSPEAK
(— ASIDE) DICE FLING
(— ASPERSIONS) SLUR

SKLENT APPEACH
(— AWAY) DUMP SHOVE DEJECT
REJECT
(— DICE) WHIRL
(— DISCREDIT) GLANCE
(— DOWN) DASH DUMP HURL
SINK ABASE AMATE AMORT
AWARP STREW ABATTU ABJECT
DECAST DEJECT DEMISS THRING
ECLIPSE RUINATE DEJECTED
(— FORTH) SPEW SPUE WARP
BELCH BRAID LAUNCH
(— GLOOM) DUSK CLOUD DARKEN
DEPRESS
(— IN A MOLD) STRIKE
(— LOTS) CAVEL
(— METAL) YET
(— OF DICE) COUP DEUCE
(— OF HERRINGS) WARP
(— OF LANGUAGE) IDIOM
(— OF NET) SHOT SHOOT
(— OFF) DAFF JILT MOLT SHED
DITCH LOSSE SHAKE SLIRT SLUFF
WAIVE CASTEN DEVEST REFUSE
REJECT SLOUGH ABDICATE
RENOUNCE
(— ON GROUND) TERRE
(— OUT) EGEST EJECT EXPEL
BANISH ABANDON EXTRUDE
OSTRACIZE
(— SHADOW) ADUMBRATE
(— UP) SUM LEVY UPBRAID
(FRESHLY —) GREEN
(PLASTER —) CUIRASS
(SUFF.) JECT
CASTANET KNACKER KNOCKER
SNAPPER TCHAPAN CROTALUM
CASTAWAY WAIF WEFT TRAMP
CRUSOE REJECT OUTCAST
DERELICT STRANDED
CASTE (OR CASTE MEMBER) DOM
MEO AHIR BHAR BHAT GOLA JATI
KOLI KORI MALI MINA PASI TELI
BAGDI BANIA DHOBY GOALA
IRAVA KAHAR KUMNI KUNBI
KURMI LADHA LOHAR MAHAR
PALLI PUGGI SAMAR SANSI SINGH
SONAR SUDRA TANTI VARNA
ARORAS BAIDYA BALIJA BANIAN
BHANGI CHAMAR CHETTY
CHUHRA DHANUK DHOBIE
DOSADH DURZEE HOLEYA HOLIYA
ILAVAN JAJMAN KALWAR
KAMBOH KHATRI KUMHAR
KURUBA LOHANA MADIGA
NATION PALLAR PRABHU PULAYA
PULIAN PURVOE RAJPUT VAISYA
AGARWAL BRAHMAN BRAHMIN
DHANGAR GADARIA HARIJAN
KAYASTH KOMATRI KURUMBA
NISHADA VELLALA KAMMALAN
KHANDAIT PARAIYAN POVINDAH
RAJBANSI VAKKALIGA
(LOWER —S) PANCHAMA
CASTER VIAL CRUET CRUSE PHIAL
CASTOR HORRAL HURLER
MASTER ROLLER FOUNDER
PITCHER TRUCKLE TRUNDLE
(SURF —) SQUIDDER
CASTIGATE LASH EMEND SCARE
SCORE BERATE PUNISH REVISE
STRAFE SUBDUE CANVASS
CENSURE CHASTEN CORRECT

LEATHER REPROVE CHASTISE
KEELHAUL LAMBASTE FUSTIGATE
OBJURGATE
CASTIGATION HELL LASHING
DRESSING
CASTILIAN BROWN TANAGRA
CASTING DIE PIG CAST FONT KEEP
MOLD TYMP BLOCK CHOCK
CHUCK FOUND MOULD BILLET
BUMPER MATRIX MISRUN SPIDER
COULAGE DARTING SEGMENT
SEPARATOR SORTILEGE
(— LOTS) SORTITION
(— OF HOROSCOPE) APOTELESM
(— OVERBOARD) JETTISON
(PL.) SPRAY FOUNDRY
CAST IRON YETLING
CASTLE BURY FORT HALL KEEP
ROCK ROOK ABODE BROCH
COURT MORRO PIECE CASBAH
BASTILE BOROUGH CHATEAU
CITADEL SCHLOSS UDOLPHO
BASTILLE CASTELET CASTILLO
FASTNESS FORTRESS STAROSTY
TINTAGEL
(— IN CHESS) JUEZ ROOK TOUR
JUDGE TOWER
(PART OF —) KEEP MOAT WARD
MOUNT TOWER WHARF BAILEY
BRIDGE DONJON TURRET
BASTION BULWARK DUNGEON
OUTWORK RAMPART BARBICAN
CASEMATE GATEHOUSE
BATTLEMENT DRAWBRIDGE
PORTCULLIS
(SMALL —) PEEL TOWER CASTLET
CHATELET
CASTLE OF OTRANTO (AUTHOR OF
—) WALPOLE
(CHARACTER IN —) CONRAD
JEROME MANFRED MATILDA
ISABELLA THEODORE
CASTOR BEAVER LEATHER
TRUCKLE TRUNDLE BARKSTONE
(— AND POLLUX) TWINS GEMINI
DIOSCURI
CASTOR AND POLLUX
(CHARACTER IN —) CASTOR
PHOEBE POLLUX JUPITER
MERCURY TELAIRA
(COMPOSER OF —) RAMEAU
CASTOR-OIL
(PREF.) RICIN(I)
CASTOR-OIL PLANT KIKI MAMONA
PALMCRIST
CASTRATE CUT FIX GIB LIB GELD
GLIB SPAY SWIG TRIM ALTER
CAPON DESEX PRUNE STEER
CHANGE EUNUCH NEUTER
EVIRATE CAPONIZE MUTILATE
SATURNIZE
CASTRATED CUT GIBBED NEUTER
UNPAVED
CASTRATO EUNUCH EVIRATO
TENORINO
CASUAL GLIB ORRA STRAY BLITHE
BYHAND CHANCE FOLKSY
RANDOM CASALTY CURSORY
LEISURE NATURAL OFFHAND
RUNNING GLANCING INFORMAL
PROMISCUOUS
CASUALTY LOSS DEATH CADUAC
CHANCE HAZARD INJURY MISHAP

ACCIDENT DISASTER
CASUARINA BEEFWOOD
CASUIST JESUIT
CAT GIB RAT SOW TAB CHAT EYRA
FLOG LION LYNX MISS PARD
PUMA PUSS CHAUS CIVET FELID
GATOL KITTY MANUL MEWER
MOGGY OUNCE PUSSY SMOKE
TABBY TIGER TILER WHITE ZIBET
ANGORA COUGAR FELINE
JAGUAR KITTEN KODKOD MALKIN
MARGAY MAWKIN MIAUER
MOUSER MUSION NEUTER
OCELOT PAJERO PURRER SERVAL
TIBERT TORTIE BURMESE
CARACAL CATHEAD CATLING
CHEETAH KITLING KUICHUA
LEOPARD LINSANG PANTHER
PERSIAN SIAMESE TIGRESS
WILDCAT WRAWLER BAUDRONS
DASYURID FISSIPED PUSSYCAT
RINGTAIL
(— CRY) WAW
(— GROUP) CLOWDER
(FEMALE —) QUEEN WHEENCAT
(MALE —) GIB TOM TOMCAT
(PART OF —) EAR EYE PAW TOE
HEEL KNEE LIPS LOIN NAPE NECK
RUMP TAIL BELLY BREAK ELBOW
FLANK SHANK THIGH WRIST
FEELER DEWCLAW LEATHER
WHISKER FOREHEAD SHOULDER
VIBRISSA METATARSUS
(ROOF-PROWLING —) TILER
(TAILLESS —) RUMPY
(PREF.) AELUR(O) AILUR(O)
FELIN(O)
CATACHRESIS ABUSION
CATACHRESTICAL ABUSIVE
CATACLYSM FLOOD DELUGE
DEBACLE DISASTER UPHEAVAL
CATACOMB TOMB CRYPT VAULT
CEMETERY HYPOGEUM
(PL.) ARENARIAE
CATADROMOUS SEAGOING
CATALECTIC HEMIAMB
TRUNCATED
CATALEPSY TRANCE SEIZURE
CATATONY
CATALOG PIE PYE BILL BOOK LIST
ROLL ROTA BRIEF CANON FLIER
FLYER INDEX PINAX AUTHOR
RAGGER RAGMAN RECORD
ROSTER ARRANGE BEADROW
DIPTYCH NOTITIA BEADROLL
BULLETIN CALENDAR CLASSIFY
REGISTER SCHEDULE SYLLABUS
CATALOGUE DIDASCALY
INVENTORY
CATALUFA SCAD TORO BIGEYE
CATALYST CARRIER SAUSAGE
ZIEGLER CATALYTE HOPCALITE
(NEGATIVE —) INHIBITER
CATAMARAN RAFT TROW BALSA
FLOAT GUNBOAT JANGADA
MONITOR AUNTSARY
CATAMITE INGLE GUNSEL NINGLE
PATHIC BARDASH GANYMEDE
CATAMOUNT LYNX PUMA
COUGAR
CATAPLASM PELOID POULTICE
CATAPULT GUN BIBLE SLING
SWEEP THROW HURTLE LAUNCH

ONAGER TREPAN ALACRAN
BRICOLE PEDRERO TORMENT
TRABUCH WARWOLF BALLISTA
CROSSBOW DONDAINE
LAUNCHER MANGONEL
MARTINET SCORPION SPRINGAL
STONEBOW
CATARACT LIN FALL LINN FALLS
FLOOD PEARL DELUGE CASCADE
NIAGARA CATADUPE OVERFALL
VICTORIA
CATARRH MUR COLD MURR POSE
RHEUM CORYZA NASITIS
CATASTROPHE ACCIDENT
CALAMITY DISASTER CATACLYSM
CATCH BAG COB COG COP GET GIN
KEP NAB NET NIP DRAW FANG
GLOM HASP HAUL HAWK HENT
HOLD HOOK LAND MAKE MEET
MESS NAIL NICK PAWL SAVE
SEAR SNAG SNAP SNIB STOP
TAKE TRAP TREE VANG BENET
CHAPE CLASP CLEEK CREEL
FETCH GLOVE GRASP HITCH
KETCH KNACK LASSO LATCH
PLANT SEIZE SNARE SNICK
SWOOP TRICK TROLL ARREST
ATTAIN BUTTON CLUTCH CORNER
CORRAL DETECT DETENT ENGAGE
ENMESH ENTRAP IMMESH
LOCKET NOBBLE NOODLE SNATCH
SPRENT TAIGLE TAKING TURNEL
ATTRACT CAPTURE ENSNARE
GIMMICK GRAPNEL RELEASE
SNIGGLE SPRINGE TRIGGER
CONTRACT CRANNAGE ENTANGLE
FASTNESS HOLDBACK HOLDFAST
OVERTAKE SNAPHAAN SURPRISE
(— AT PROPER TIME) NICK
(— ATTENTION) FLAG
(— BIRDS) BATFOWL BIRDLIME
(— EELS) SNIGGLE
(— FIRE) SPUNK IGNITE KINDLE
(— FISH) JAB JIG GILL HANG
GILLNET
(— FISH WITH HANDS) GUDDLE
GRABBLE HANDFAST
(— IN VOICE) FETCH
(— OF DOOR) LATCH SNECK SNICK
(— OF FISH) FARE HAUL SHOT
TACK TRIP SHACK
(— ONE'S BREATH) GASP CHINK
(— SIGHT OF) SPY ESPY SPOT
DESCRY
(CRICKET —) DOLLY
(RATCHET —) CLICK
(SAFETY —) CLEVIS
CATCHER TAKER BIRDER FANGER
LARKER RECEIVER
CATCHFLY SILENE FLYBANE
CATCHING CATCHY TAKING
ALLURING ARRESTING
CATCHPOLE BAILIFF PUTTOCK
CATCHWEED CLEAVERS
CATCHWORD CUE TAG MOTTO
BYWORD PHRASE SLOGAN
STARTER CATCHCRY SHIBBOLETH
CATCHY CATCHING APPEALING
CATECHISM QUIZ GUIDE MANUAL
CARRITCH QUESTIONS
CATECHU COTCH CUTCH KHAIR
GAMBIER
CATECHUMEN PUPIL AUDIENT

AUDITOR CONVERT BEGINNER
NEOPHYTE COMPETENT
CATEGORICAL DIRECT ABSOLUTE
EXPLICIT KNOCKDOWN
CATEGORIZE CODE HAVE
CATEGORY WAY KING RANK TALE
CLASS FIELD GENRE GENUS
ORDER STYLE FAMILY LEAGUE
NUMBER RUBRIC SERIES SPECIES
DIVISION PIGEONHOLE
PREDICAMENT
(— OF TENSES) INFECTUM
(HIGHEST —) IDEA
(PRIMARY —) SUBSTANCE
(TAXONOMIC —) FORM FORMA
GENUS TAXON COHORT LEGION
SUBCLASS SUBGENUS SUBFAMILY
CATER CUT FEED HUMOR SERVE
TREAT PANDER PURVEY SUPPLY
PROVIDE
(PREF.) OPSONI OPSONO
CATERER ACATER MANCIPLE
CATERINA CORNARO (CHARACTER
IN —) ANDREAS GERARDO
CATERINA MOCENIGO LUSIGNANO
(COMPOSER OF —) DONIZETTI
CATERPILLAR CAT MUGA AWETO
ERUCA CANKER LOOPER PALMER
PORINA RISPER TAILOR WOUBIT
CUTWORM TRACTOR WEBWORM
HANGWORM HORNWORM
SILKWORM SKINWORM
WORTWORM PALMERWORM
(PREF.) CAMPO ERUCI
(SUFF.) CAMPA
CATERWAUL CRY HOWL WAIL
MIAUL WRAWL
CATFACE ARR SCAR
CATFISH MUD CUSK ELOD POUT
RAAD SHAL WOOF BAGRE DORAD
RAASH BARBER DOCMAC GLANIS
GOONCH GOUJON HASSAR
MADTOM MUDCAT BARBUDO
CANDIRU COBBLER FIDDLER
PYGIDID SILURID WALLAGO
BULLHEAD BULLPOUT CORYDORA
FLATHEAD MATHEMEG PLOTOSID
SQUEAKER STONECAT
CATGUT THARM THAIRM CATLING
WHIPCORD
CATHARI BULGARI PATARINE
CATHARTIC ALOIN BRYONY
PHYSIC CALOMEL RHUBARB
SCOURER EUONYMUS EVACUANT
HYDRAGOG KALADANA LAPACTIC
LAXATIVE SCAMMONY SOLUTIVE
SOLUTORY PURGATIVE
PODOPHYLLIN
CATHAYAN KITAN
CATHEDRA SEE
CATHEDRAL DOM SEE DUOMO
SOBOR MARTYRY MEMORIA
MINSTER BASILICA
(PART OF —) ARCH ROOF CROSS
GABLE IMAGE LABEL SPIRE
TOWER BELFRY FINIAL LINTEL
LOUVER PORTAL WINDOW
CROCKET GALLERY LOZENGE
MOLDING MULLION TRACERY
TREFOIL PINNACLE TYMPANUM
DRIPSTONE THROATING
TRIFORIUM CINQUEFOIL
CLERESTORY QUATREFOIL

CATHEXIS CHARGE
CATHODE K KA FILAMENT
ELECTRODE HYDROGODE
CATHOLIC BROAD GENERAL
LIBERAL TOLERANT
CATHOLICISM PAPISM POPERY
CATHOLICON PANACEA
CATKIN RAG TAG CHAT GULL
AGLET AMENT IULUS PUSSY
CACHRYS CATTAIL GOSLING
(PREF.) AMENTI
CATMINT NEP
CATNAP NAP DOZE
CATNIP NEP CATARIA CATMINT
CATWORT
CATREUS (DAUGHTER OF —)
AEROPE CLYMENE APEMOSYNE
(FATHER OF —) MINOS
(MOTHER OF —) PASIPHAE
(SON OF —) ALTHAEMENES
CAT'S-CLAW LONGPOD
ESCAMBRON
CAT'S CRADLE HEI
CAT'S-EAR GOSMORE CAPEWEED
FLATWEED
CAT'S EYE CHATOYANT
CAT'S-FOOT PUSSYTOE
CATTAIL DOD DODD FLAG MUSK
RUSH TULE AMENT BAYON BLECK
CLOUD RAUPO REREE WONGA
CATKIN GLADEN TOTORA
BULRUSH GLADDON MATREED
BLACKCAP CARBUNGI FLAXTAIL
CAT THYME HULWORT
CATTLE ZO BOW FEE GIR AVER
DHAN GAUR KINE NEAT NOWT
OXEN ZEBU ZOBO DEVON STOCK
ANKOLI DURHAM GALYAK
ONGOLE ROTHER SINDHI SUSSEX
BESTIAL NELLORE REDPOLL
COMPOUND OUTSIGHT TUBICORN
(— CARRIED OFF) SPREATH
(BREED OF —) ANGUS BORAN
DEVON FJALL KERRY KYLOE
SANGA SANGU ANGONI ANKOLE
ANKOLI DEXTER DURHAM FULANI
JERSEY SUSSEX BAROTSE
BRAFORD BRAHMAN COASTER
CRIOLLA GUZERAT HARIANA
SAHIWAL ALDERNEY AYRSHIRE
CHARBRAY FRIBOURG FRIESIAN
GALLOWAY GUERNSEY HEREFORD
HOLSTEIN KANGAYAM LONGHORN
(DWARF —) NATA NIATA
(WILD YOUNG —) KANGAROO
(PREF.) BOVI
CATTLE-BREEDER AHIR ALUR
CATTLE DEALER DROVER
CATTLEHIDE BUFF CROUPON
CATTLEMAN FAZENDEIRO
CATTLE MARKET SALEYARD
CATTLE PEN KRAAL
CATTLE RAID SPRAITH SPREAGH
CATTLE RUN STATION
CATTLE STEALER ABACTOR
ABIGEUS
CATTLE YARD CANCHA
CATTY KIN KATI
CAUCASIAN WHITE IRANIAN
EUROPEAN JAPHETIC PALEFACE
(— LANGUAGE) UDI UDIC UDIN
(PL.) MELANOI
CAUCHO ULE RUBBER

CAUCUS PRIMARY
CAUDAL POSTERIOR
(PREF.) UR(O)
CAUDATA URODELA
CAUDEX STIPE
CAUGHT GRIPPIT ENTANGLED
CAUL HOW WEB KEEL KELL TRUG
VEIL GALEA HOUVE DORLOT
CREPINE KERCHER NETWORK
OMENTUM MEMBRANE SILLYHOW
TRESSOUR TRESSURE
(PREF.) AMNIO OMENT(O)
CAULDRON KOHUA CALDRON
CAULICLE SCAPEL ROSTELLUM
CAULIFLOWER BROCCOLI
SNOWBALL CHOUFLEUR
CAULK CALK CORK FILL FLAG
CHINSE
CAUNUS (FATHER OF —) MILETUS
(MOTHER OF —) CYANEE
(SISTER OF —) BYBLIS
CAUSAL GENETIC
CAUSE DO AIM GAR ISM KEY LET
WAY CASE CHAT FATE HOTI LEAD
MAKE MOVE ROOT SAKE SPUR
SUIT AGENT ARCHE BASIS BREED
CAUSA FRAME PARTY SKILL
SLAKE WREAK YIELD ADDICT
CREATE EFFECT ELICIT GOSSIP
GROUND INDUCE INVOKE
MALADY MANNER MATTER
MOTIVE OBJECT ORIGIN PARENT
REASON RESORT SOURCE SPEECH
SPRING CHESOUN CONCERN
DISEASE LAWSUIT PROCURE
PRODUCE PROVOKE QUARREL
SUBJECT BUSINESS ENGENDER
GENERATE INSTANCE MOVEMENT
OCCASION WHEREFORE
MAINSPRING
(— A SORE) RANKLE
(— DAMAGE) DAMNIFY
(— FOR COMPLAINT) COMEBACK
(— OF RUIN) BANE
(— OF TERROR) AFFRIGHT
(— OF TROUBLE) TRACHLE
(— PAIN) URN
(— TO ARCH) ROACH
(— TO CONTRACT) PUCKER
(— TO CROUCH) COUCH
(— TO DESERT) DEFECT
(— TO END) ACHIEVE
(— TO MOVE RAPIDLY) GIG
(— TO PROJECT) JET
(— TO RESULT) ISSUE
(— TO STICK) MIRE
(— TO SWELL) BINGE EMBOSS
(— TO THICKEN) CURD
(FINAL —) END
(FORM-GIVING —) IDEA
(IMMEDIATE —) SIGNAL
(PRIMAL —) URGRUND
(PREF.) AETIO AITIO CAUSI ETIO
(SUFF.) FIC(AL)(ATE)(ATIVE)
(ATOR)(ATORY)(E)(ENCE)(ENT)(IAL)
(IARY)(IENT) FIQUE
CAUSED
(SUFF.) **(— BY)** IC(AL)
CAUSEWAY WAY DIKE ROAD
HIGHWAY CHAUSSEE
CAUSING
(SUFF.) ABLE FACIENT
FACT(ION)(IVE)(ORY) IBLE

CAUSTIC LYE ACID TART ACRID
QUICK SALTY SHARP SNELL
ACIDIC BITING BITTER SEVERE
BURNING CAUTERY CUTTING
ERODENT MORDANT NIPPING
PUNGENT PYROTIC SATIRIC
ALKALINE DIERETIC SCATHING
SNAPPISH STINGING ACIDULOUS
SARCASTIC MORDACIOUS
CAUSTICITY ACRIMONY
CAUTERIZATION USTION
INUSTION
CAUTERIZE BURN CHAR FIRE SEAR
BRAND INUST SINGE
CAUTERY MOXA
CAUTION CARE FEAR HEED WARN
GUARD ADVICE CAUTEL CAVEAT
EXHORT ANXIETY COUNSEL
PRECEPT PROVISO WARNING
ADMONISH FORECAST
FOREWARN MONITION PRUDENCE
WARINESS
CAUTIOUS SHY SAFE WARE WARY
ALERT CANNY CHARY SIKER
FABIAN HOOLIE SICKER TENDER
TIPTOE CAREFUL CURIOUS
ENVIOUS FEARFUL FERDFUL
GUARDED PRUDENT DISCREET
SUSPENSE VIGILANT CAUTELOUS
CAUTIOUSLY CANNY CANNILY
CHARILY EASYLIKE GINGERLY
TENDERLY
CAVAL
(PREF.) VEN(I)(O)
CAVALCADE RAID RIDE MARCH
TRAIN PARADE SAFARI COMPANY
JOURNEY PAGEANT
CAVALIER GAY CAVY CURT EASY
FINE BRAVE FRANK MOUNT
RIDER ESCORT KNIGHT BRUSQUE
GALLANT HAUGHTY OFFHAND
SOLDIER CAVALERO ROYALIST
CHAMBERER CHEVALIER
COMMANDER
CAVALLA CERO JACK TORO ULUA
JUREL CARANX CARANGID
CREVALLE SCOMBRID
CAVALLERIA RUSTICANA
(CHARACTER IN —) LOLA ALFIO
TURIDDU SANTUZZA
(COMPOSER OF —) MASCAGNI
CAVALRY HORSE HEAVIES
CHIVALRY HORSEMEN YEOMANRY
CAVALRYMAN SOWAR SPAHI
SUWAR HUSSAR JINETE LANCER
REITER ARGOLET COURIER
DRAGOON PLUNGER SABREUR
TROOPER GENDARME HORSEMAN
SILLADAR STRADIOT
(PL.) FORAGERS
CAVE DEN TIP COVE HOLE LAIR
MINE REAR SINK TOSS WEEM
ANTAR ANTRE CABIN CACHE
CALVE CAVEA CRYPT DELVE
FOGOU SLADE SPEOS STORE
UPSET BEWARE CAVERN CAVITY
CELLAR DUGOUT GROTTO
HOLLOW LARDER LUSTER
PANTRY PLUNGE SHROUD
MANSION RESERVE SPELUNK
CASTILLO COLLAPSE OVERTURN
MITHRAEUM
(— IN) COLT

(ANIMAL LIVING IN —)
TROGLODYTE
(PREF.) SPELEO
CAVEAT BEWARE NOTICE
CAUTION WARNING
CAVE-DWELLER HORITE
TROGLODYTE
CAVE-DWELLING NATUFIAN
(PREF.) TROGLO
CAVEMAN NEANDERTHAL
CAVER SPELUNKER
CAVERN DEN CAVE COVE GROT
HOLE LAIR WEEM CROFT VAULT
ANTRUM CAVITY GROTTO
HOLLOW SPELUNK
(PREF.) ANTR(O)
CAVERNOUS ERECTILE
CAVESSON CHAIN
CAVETTO GULA GORGE
CAVIAR OVA ROE IKRA GARUM
IKARY
CAVIL CARK CARP HAFT HAGGLE
CAPTION CHICANE QUARREL
QUIBBLE PETTIFOG QUIDDITY
FORMALIZE
CAVILER CRITIC GIRDER HAFTER
ZOILUS
CAVILING CAPTIOUS CRITICAL
PICAYUNE
CAVITIED
(SUFF.) COELOUS COELUS
CAVITY BAG CUP PIT SAC ABRI
AXIL CASE CAVE CELL DALK DENT
DUCT HOLE MIND MINE VEIN
VOID WELL WOMB ABYSS BOSOM
BURSA CRYPT DRUSE FOSSA
GEODE GOUGE LUMEN MOUTH
ORBIT SCOOP SINUS ANTRUM
AREOLE ATRIUM AXILLA BORING
CAECUM CAMERA CAVERN
COELIA COELOM COTYLE CRATER
DEBLAI GROTTO HOLLOW
LACUNA POCKET RECESS SCAPHA
SOCKET VACUUM VOMICA
ABDOMEN CHAMBER CISTERN
CYATHUS DIOCOEL KYATHOS
LOCULUS MORTISE VACUITY
VACUOLE VESICLE ALVEOLUS
BROODSAC EPICOELE FOLLICLE
WELLHOLE VESTIBULE
(— IN BONE) LACUNA
(— IN CASTING) PIPE
(— IN HEAD OF WHALE) CASE
(— IN HILLSIDE) ABRI
(— IN LAVA) AMYGDALE
AMYGDULE
(— IN MINE) BAG
(— IN ROCK) KETTLE
(— MADE BY SEALS) IGLOO
(— OF SEA-SHELL) FLUE
(ALTAR —) TOMB
(BODY —) GUT BELLY CLOACA
THORAX ABDOMEN STOMACH
PSEUDOCOEL PERICARDIUM
(CHEST —) THORAX
(CRYSTAL-LINED —) VUGG DRUSE
GEODE
(GUN —) BORE
(NASAL —) CAVUM
(SUBTERRANEAN —) SLUGGA
(PREF.) ALVEOL(I)(O) ANTR(O)
CAEC(I)(O) CEC(I)(O) CEL(I)(O)
COEL(I)(O)

(SUFF.) CELE COELE COELUS
CAVORT PLAY BOUND CAPER
CURVET GAMBOL PRANCE
CAVY PACA PONY AGOUTI APEREA
CAYUSE CAPYBARA
(FEMALE —) SOW
CAW KA CRY CALL CROAK QUARK
QUAWK
CAYMAN JACARE
CAYSTER (DAUGHTER OF —)
SEMIRAMIS
(FATHER OF —) ACHILLES
(MOTHER OF —) PENTHESILEA
CAYUSE CAVY PONY BRONCO
MUSTANG
CEASE HO BOW CUT DIE END LIN
BALK BLIN DROP FINE HALT HOLD
LIFT LISS QUIT REST SACE SHUT
STAY STOP STOW AVAST CLOSE
DOWSE LEAVE PAUSE PETER
STINT SWICK WAIVE DESIST
DEVALL EXPIRE FINISH FORGET
ABSTAIN OUTGIVE REFRAIN
SUSPEND INTERMIT OVERGIVE
SURCEASE
(— MILKING COW) SINE
(— TEMPORARILY) LIFT
(— TO ASSERT) ABANDON
CEASELESS EVER ENDLESS
ETERNAL IMMORTAL UNENDING
CEASING CESSER CESSATION
CEBUS SAI
CECILIA SIS SISSU
CECROPS (DAUGHTER OF —) HERSE
AGLAUROS PANDROSOS
(WIFE OF —) AGLAURUS
CECUM
(PREF.) TYPHL(O)
CEDAR SUGI TOON SAVIN AROLLA
DEODAR SABINA TUMION
CYPRESS JUNIPER WAXWING
CALANTAS PAHAUTEA
CEDAR SWAMP GREENING
CEDAR WAXWING RECOLLET
CEDE CESS GIVE AWARD GRANT
LEAVE WAIVE YIELD ASSIGN
RESIGN SUBMIT CONCEDE
RENOUNCE TRANSFER
CEDILLA TITTLE
CEIBA KAPOK BENTANG POCHOTE
CEIL LINE SYLE OVERLAY
WAINSCOT
CEILING TOP DOME LACE LOFT
CHUTT CUPOLA LINING SCREEN
SOFFIT SYLING CURTAIN
LACUNAR PLAFOND TESTUDO
COVERING DECKHAND OVERHEAD
PANELING PLANCHER SEMIDOME
CELAENO (FATHER OF —) ATLAS
(MOTHER OF —) PLEIONE
(SON OF —) LYCUS NYCTEUS
CELANDINE FICARY KILLWORT
PILEWORT WARTWEED
WARTWORT FELONWORT
JEWELWEED
CELEBES (GULF OF —) BONE TOLO
TOMINI
(ISLAND OF —) MUNA BUTUNG
PELENG SULAWESI
(PEOPLE OF —) TORAJA
(TOWN OF —) BUOL LUWUK
MANADO MAKASAR
CELEBRATE FETE KEEP SING

CHANT DITTY EXTOL HONOR
REVEL SACRE SPEAK BESING
CHAUNT EXTOLL PRAISE ELEGIZE
EXECUTE GLORIFY MAFFICK
OBSERVE EMBLAZON EULOGIZE
PROCLAIM
(— 2 MASSES) BINATE DUPLICATE
CELEBRATED KEPT FAMED NOTED
FAMOUS EMINENT FEASTED
RENOMME STORIED FABULOUS
GLORIOUS NOTIFIED OBSERVED
RENOWNED
CELEBRATION EED FETE GALA
POPE RITE FESTA REVEL COOLIN
CUSTOM DOMENT EASTER FIESTA
POWWWOW RENOWN SIMHAH
BLOWOUT HAGMENA HOLIDAY
JUBILEE PASCHAL SHINDIG
SIMCHAH BINATION BIRTHDAY
HOGMANAY MAKAHIKI OCCASION
OLYMPIAD POTLATCH SHIVAREE
FESTIVITY HOOLAULEA
JUNKETING MERRIMENT
MILLENIUM
CELEBRATOR JUBILIST
CELEBRITY FAME LION NAME
STAR CELEB ECLAT RENOWN
REPUTE
CELERITY HASTE HURRY SPEED
DISPATCH RAPIDITY VELOCITY
SWIFTNESS
CELERY SIT ACHE STICK UMBEL
KARPAS SALARY CELERIAC
SMALLAGE
CELESTIAL HOLY DIVINE HEAVEN
URANIC ANGELIC CHINESE
ETHERED EMPYREAL ETHEREAL
HEAVENLY OLYMPIAN
CELESTITE APOTOME
CELEUS (SON OF —) DEMOPHON
TRIPTOLEMUS
(WIFE OF —) METANIRA
CELIBACY CHASTITY VIRGINITY
CELIBATE CLERK CHASTE SINGLE
BACHELOR SPINSTER
CELL BOX EGG BAND BOOT CAGE
CYTE DISC DISK GERM GONE
HOLE JAIL KILL ASCUS CABIN
CAROL CLINK CRYPT CYTON
FIBER FIBRE GHOST GLAND
GROUP OOTID TMEMA TORIL
VAULT ZOOID ANAXON CEPTOR
COCCUS COOLER CYTODE
GAMETE GONIUM INAXON
NEURON PRISON SHIELD SIPHON
SYPHON WESTON ZYGOTE
AGAMETE AMEBULA APOCYTE
CELLULE CHAMBER CLOCHAN
CLOSTER COCCOID CUBICLE
DIPLOID DUNGEON ELEMENT
EPICYTE EUPLOID HAPLOID
HEMATID INITIAL LOCULUS
MYOCYTE NEURONE OOBLAST
PAPILLA PLASTID RENETTE
SEGMENT SPORONT STEREID
TRISOME UTRICLE VESICLE
AMACRINE BASOCYTE BASOPHIL
BIFORINE BIOPLAST CLOGHAUN
DIKARYON FAVEOLUS GLIOCYTE
GONIDIUM GONOCYTE HEMOCYTE
HOLDOVER IDIOSOME LOCELLUS
MYOBLAST ORGANULE PROSORUS
RECEPTOR SCLEREID SPERMULE

SYNERGID TRACHEID TRIPLOID
ZOOBLAST MACROCYTE
MICROCYTE MYELOCYTE
OSTEOCYTE PHAGOCYTE
PROGAMETE MELANOCYTE
MOTONEURON NEUTROPHIL
OSTEOCLAST MELANOBLAST
MELANOPHORE ODONTOBLAST
(— CONTAINING LATEX) LATICIFER
(— OF LEADERS) CADRE
(BEE —) PIPE
(CLUSTER OF —S) MORULA
(DETENTION —) BULLPEN
(PART OF —) SAP NUCLEUS
PLASTID VACUOLE MEMBRANE
CENTRIOLE ECTOPLASM
ENDOPLASM NUCLEOLUS
RETICULUM CENTROSOME
CHONDRIOSOME
(PHOTOELECTRIC —) EYE PEC
PHOTOCELL
(PRISON —) BING HOLE CABIN
CLINK COOLER JIGGER
(STAB —) BAND
(THIN-WALLED —S) STOMIUM
(VOLTAIC —) BATTERY
(PL.) LAURA POTLINE SWEATBOX
(PREF.) CYT(IO)(O) GAMET(O)
GONIDI ONT(O) THYRE(O) THYRO
(SUFF.) BLAST(IC)(Y) CYTE
PHAG(A)(E)(O)(OUS)(US)(Y) PLASIA
PLASIS PLASM(A)(IA)(IC)
PLAT(I)(IC)(Y) SPONGIA(E)(N)
SPONGIUM THYRIS
CELLA NAOS
CELLAR CAVE VAULT BODEGA
PALACE FAVISSA HYPOGEE
BASEMENT HYPOGEUM
MATAMORO VAULTAGE
CELLARET TANTALUS
CELLARMAN SOMMELIER
CELLULAR
(SUFF.) ENCHYMA ENCHYMATA
CELLULOID XYLONITE
CELLULOSE CRUMB AMYLOID
LIGNOSE TAMIDINE
CELT GAEL GAUL KELT MANX IRISH
WELSH BRETON BRITON EOLITH
GADHEL GOIDEL BRYTHON
CORNISH PALSTAFF PALSTAVE
(PL.) CYMRY KYMRY
CELTIC ERSE GAEL SCOTCH
CEMBALO DULCIMER ZIMBALON
CEMENT FIX KIT TIE GLUE HEAL
JOIN KNIT LIME LUTE SLIP BETON
GROUT IMBED PASTE PUTTY
SIMON STICK TABBY UNITE
BINDER CHUNAM COHERE
FASTEN FILLER GULGUL KIBOSH
MALTHA MASTIC MORTAR
OOGLEA SOLDER ASPHALT
MIXTION ADHESIVE ALBOLITE
ALBOLITH CEMENTUM HADIGEON
SOLIDIFY SOLUTION
(BEES' —) PROPOLIS
(SUFF.) LITE LITH(IC) LITIC
CEMENTER GLUER GLUEMAN
SMEARER
CEMENT MIXER TEMPERER
CEMETERY HOWF KILL LAIR
LITTEN CHARNEL BONEYARD
CATACOMB GOLGOTHA URNFIELD
NECROPOLIS

CENCHRIAS (FATHER OF —)
POSEIDON
(MOTHER OF —) PIRENE
(SLAYER OF —) ARTEMIS
CENCI (AUTHOR OF —) SHELLEY
(CHARACTER IN —) CENCI MARZIO
ORSINO CAMILLO GIACOMO
OLIMPIO SAVELLA BEATRICE
BERNARDO LUCRETIA
**CENERENTOLA, LA (CHARACTER IN
—)** TISBE RAMIRO ALIDORO
DANDINI ANGELINA CLORINDA
MAGNIFICO CINDERELLA
(COMPOSER OF —) ROSSINI
CENOBITE NUN MONK FRIAR
ESSENE RECLUSE MONASTIC
SYNODITE
CENOTAPH TOMB
CENSE THURIFY
CENSER INCENSER THURIBLE
CASSOLETTE
CENSOR CRITIC SCREEN SYNDIC
LAUNDER RESTRICT SUPPRESS
CENSORIOUS SEVERE BLAMING
CARPING BLAMEFUL CAPTIOUS
CRITICAL CULPABLE SLASHING
CENSORSHIP WRAPS ASSIZE
CENSURE
CENSURABLE TAXABLE BLAMABLE
CULPABLE
CENSURE BAN HIT NIP RAP TAP
TAX WIG CALL CARP DEEM DRUB
FLAY HELL LASH RATE SLAP TASK
WITE BEANS BLAME CHIDE CURSE
DECRY FAULT HOKER JUDGE
PINCH SCOLD SLANG SLASH
SLATE TAUNT TOUCH WHITE
ACCUSE ATTACK BERATE CHARGE
REBUFF REBUKE REFORM
REMORD STRAFE TARGUE TIRADE
APPEACH BLISTER CHASTEN
CONDEMN CONTROL DECRIAL
DYSLOGY IMPEACH IMPROVE
INVEIGH REPROOF REPROVE
SCARIFY TRADUCE TROUNCE
UPBRAID BACKBITE CHASTISE
DISALLOW JUDGMENT LANGUAGE
REPROACH SATIRIZE SENTENCE
STRICTURE ADMONITION
CENSUS LIST POLL CENSE COUNT
LUSTER LUSTRUM CAPITATION
CENT RED DUIT SANT BROWNIE
CENTAVO STUIVER
(ODD —S) BREAKAGE
(12 1-2 —S) LEVY
CENTAUR CHIRON NESSUS
HORSEMAN BUCENTAUR
SAGITTARY
CENTAURUS (FATHER OF —) IXION
(MOTHER OF —) NEPHELE
CENTAURY BEHN BEHEN
SABBATIA EARTHGALL
CENTENNIAL STATE COLORADO
CENTER COR EYE GIG HUB MID
AXIS CORE NAVE SEAT SNAP
YOLK FOCUS FOYER GLOME
HEART MIDST PIVOT SPINE
BOTTOM CENTRE MIDDLE PIPPER
STAPLE TEMPLE CENTRUM
ESSENCE LINEMAN NUCLEUS
UMBILIC INCENTER OMPHALOS
SNAPBACK
(— FOR SPINDLE) GIG

(— FOR TARGET) EYE PIN PINHOLE
(— OF ACTIVITY) HUB HIVE
(— OF ARCH) COOM
(— OF ASSURANCE) FORTRESS
(— OF ATTRACTION) FOCUS STAGE
CYNOSURE POLESTAR
(— OF BASKET) SLATHER
(— OF CITY) DOWNTOWN
(— OF CULTIVATION) HOME
(— OF CULTURE) ATHENS
(— OF DIAMOND) WELL
(— OF ESCUTCHEON) NOMBRIL
(— OF FIGURE) CENTROID
(— OF FISHING NET) BUNT
(— OF FLOWER) EYE
(— OF HURRICANE) EYE
(— OF OPERATIONS) SHOP
(— OF POPULATION) CITY
(— OF POWER) SEE SIEGE
(— OF STAGE) LIMELIGHT
(— OF STRENGTH) GANGLION
(BASKETBALL —) PIVOTMAN
(COLLECTION —) ENTREPOT
(COMMERCIAL —) MACHI
EMPORIUM
(HARD —) KNOT
(INTIMATE —) BOSOM
(LATHE —) PIKE
(NERVOUS —) BRAIN NIDUS
(NEURAL —) APPESTAT
(PROPAGANDA —) AGITPUNKT
(REHABILITATION —) HOSTEL
(TRADING —) BEACH EXCHANGE
(VITAL —) HEARTH HEARTBEAT
(PREF.) CENTR(I)(O)
(SUFF.) CENTRIC
CENTERING COOM COOMB
CENTRY FANTAIL
CENTERPIECE ROSACE
DORMANT EPERGNE
DUCHESSE
CENTETES TENREC
CENTIARE LI
CENTIGRADE CELSIUS
CENTIME RAPPEN
CENTIMETER GAL
CENTIPEDE VEI VERI EARWIG
GOLACH GOLOCH POLYPOD
CHILOPOD MULTIPED MYRIAPOD
SANTAPEE SCUTIGER
SCOLOPENDRA
CENTRAL MID AXIAL BASIC CHIEF
FOCAL MIXED PRIME MEDIAN
MIDDLE CAPITAL CENTRIC
LEADING NUCLEAR PIVOTAL
PRIMARY CARDINAL
DOMINANT
(PREF.) CENTR(I)(O)

CENTRAL AFRICAN REPUBLIC
CAPITAL: BANGUI
COIN: FRANC
NATIVE: BAYA SARA BANDA
BWAKA SANGO YAKOMA
BANZIRI MANDJIA
RIVER: BOMU NANA CHARI KOTTO
MBARI MPOKO OUAKA OUHAM
CHINKO LOBAYE SANGHA
UBANGI
TOWN: OBO IPPY BIRAO BOUAR
KEMBE NDELE NGOTO PAOUA
RAFAI ZEMIO BABOUA BAKALA
BANGUI BOZOUM BAMBARI

GRIMARI ZEMONGO
BERBERATI BOSSANGOA

CENTRAL AMERICAN LADINO
NATION: COSTARICA BELIZE
HONDURAS GUATEMALA
ELSALVADOR
(**— TREE**) TUNO TUNU
CENTRANTH SPURFLOWER
CENTRIFUGAL EFFERENT
RADIATING
CENTRIFUGE CYCLONE
SEPARATOR
CENTRIPETAL AFFERENT
CENTROSOME CENTRUM
CENTRIOLE
CENTRUM CORE
CENTURIED SECULAR
CENTURY AGE TON SECLE SIECLE
(**14TH —**) TRECENTO
CENTURY PLANT ALOE PITA
AGAVE MAGUEY CANTALA
TEQUILA MONOCARP
CENWALH (**FATHER OF —**)
CYNEGILS
CEPHALALGIA SODA HEADACHE
CEPHALIC CRANIAL ATLANTAL
CEREBRAL
CEPHALOPOD SQUID CUTTLE
INKFISH OCTOPUS SPIRULA
DIBRANCH SCAPHITE
CEPHALOTHORAX PROSOMA
CEPHALUS (**FATHER OF —**) DEION
(**MOTHER OF —**) DIOMEDE
(**WIFE OF —**) PROCRIS
CEPHEUS (**BROTHER OF —**) DANAUS
AEGYPTUS AMPHIDAMAS
(**DAUGHTER OF —**) ANDROMEDA
(**FATHER OF —**) ALEUS BELUS
(**MOTHER OF —**) ANCHINOE
(**WIFE OF —**) CASSIOPEA
CERAMICS TILES POTTERY
CERAMUS (**FATHER OF —**) BACCHUS
DIONYSUS
(**MOTHER OF —**) ARIADNE
CERATE WAX LARD SALVE
UNGUENT OINTMENT
CERATOBRANCHIAL APOHYAL
CERCYON (**DAUGHTER OF —**) ALOPE
(**FATHER OF —**) NEPTUNE
POSEIDON HEPHAESTUS
(**SLAYER OF —**) THESEUS
CEREAL RYE BEAN BRAN CORN
MUSH OATS RICE SAMP TEFF
ARZUN GRAIN MAIZE SPELT
WHEAT BARLEY BINDER FARINA
HOMINY PABLUM OATMEAL
SOYBEAN PORRIDGE
CEREAL LEAF FLAG
CEREBRAL CEPHALIC INVERTED
(**PREF.**) PSYCH(O)
CEREBRATION THOUGHT
CEREBROSIDE KERASIN
CEREMENT SHROUD
CEREMONIAL FORM PRIM RITE
STIFF FORMAL RIALTY RITUAL
SOLEMN PRECISE STUDIED
TRIUMPH UPANAYA AVERSION
SPLENDOR
CEREMONIOUS GRAND LOFTY
STIFF FORMAL PROPER SOLEMN
PRECISE STATELY STUDIED
CEREMONY BRIS FETE FORM

GAUD HAKO ORGY POMP RITE
SEAL SHOW SIGN SING BERIT
DANCE DOSEH STATE ACTION
AUGURY BERITH BRIDAL BURIAL
EXEQUY GOMBAY HOMAGE
KERIAH MALKAH MAUNDY NIPTER
OFFICE PARADE POWWOW
REVIEW RITUAL SALUTE BAPTISM
DISPLAY KIDDUSH MELAVEH
OVATION PAGEANT PANAGIA
PORTENT PRODIGY TAHARAH
ACCOLADE APOLUSIS ASPERGES
COEMPTIO CRIOBOLY ENCAENIA
EXERCISE FUNCTION HABDALAH
HAKAFOTH HERALDRY MARRIAGE
OCCASION SKEYTING INAUGURAL
INDUCTION ORDINANCE
OBSERVANCE
(**GRADUATION —**) CAPPING
(**HAZING —**) CREELING
(**MARRIAGE —**) ESPOUSAL
(**TEA —**) CHANOYU
(**PL.**) DEGREE HOLIES AGENDUM
FERALIA JUSTMENTS
CERES DEMETER
(**DAUGHTER OF —**) PROSERPINE
PHERREPHATTA
(**FATHER OF —**) SATURN
(**MOTHER OF —**) VESTA
CERINTHE HONEYWORT
CERO SEARER SIERRA CAVALLA
PINTADO KINGFISH
CERTAIN COLD COOL DEAD FAST
FIRM FREE REAL SEAL SURE TRUE
BOUND CLEAR EXACT FIXED
PLAIN SIKER ACTUAL MEMORY
SECURE SICKER STATED WITTER
ASSURED PERFECT PRECISE
SETTLED SRADDHA ABSOLUTE
APPARENT CONSTANT OFFICIAL
PALPABLE POSITIVE RELIABLE
RESOLVED UNERRING CONFIDENT
CERTAINLY AY AYE WIS AMEN
IWIS SOON SURE WHAT YWIS
TRULY CERTES INDEED PERDIE
SICCAR SICKER SURELY VERILY
HARDILY EVERMORE FORSOOTH
SECURELY NATURALLY
(**MOST —**) SO
CERTAINTY YEA CERT PIPE SNIP
CINCH POLICY SURETY SURENESS
CONSTANCY
(**LACK OF —**) SCRUPLE
CERTIFICATE BOND CHIT CHECK
DEMIT JURAT LIBEL SCRIP TALON
TITLE AMPARO ATTEST CEDULA
COUPON INDENT PATENT
POTTAH RETURN TICKET VERIFY
CERTIFY CONSTAT DIPLOMA
VOUCHER WARRANT WAYBILL
AEGROTAT JUDGMENT KABBALAH
NAVICERT REGISTER REGISTRY
SECURITY TESCARIA TESTAMUR
TEZKIRAH NOTARIZATION
(**CUSTOMHOUSE —**) COCKET
(**MARRIAGE —**) LINES
(**MINER'S —**) LICENCE LICENSE
(**PILOT'S —**) BRANCH
(**SERVANT'S —**) CHIT
CERTIFICATION PASS STAMP
APPROVAL HECHSHER
CLEARANCE DISCHARGE
CERTIFIED SWORN

CERTIFY AVOW VISE SWEAR
AFFIRM ASSURE ATTEST DEPOSE
EVINCE VERIFY WITTER APPROVE
ENDORSE LICENSE TESTIFY
ACCREDIT
CERTITUDE CERTAIN CONFIDENCE
CERULEAN BLUE AZURE COELIN
CYANEAN CYANEOUS
CERUMEN WAX EARWAX
CERVIX NECK
CESS BOG TAX CEDE DUTY LEVY
LUCK RATE ABWAB SLOPE YIELD
IMPOST MEASURE SURRENDER
(**BAD —**) SORRA
CESSATION HO END HOO BLIN
HALT HUSH LISS LULL REST STAY
STOP BREAK CEASE CLOSE DEVAL
LETUP LISSE PAUSE SLACK STINT
TRUCE CUTOFF DEMISE DISUSE
OFFSET PERIOD RECESS CEASING
CLOSURE RESPITE ABEYANCE
BLACKOUT DESITION INTERVAL
SHUTDOWN STOPPAGE
SURCEASE SUSPENSE
(**— OF HOSTILITIES**) TRUCE
INDUCIAE ARMISTICE
(**— OF LIFE**) DEATH
(**— OF RESPIRATION**) APNEA
APNOEA
(**— OF WORK**) HARTAL
CESSPOOL SINK SUMP SINKER
CISTERN JAWHOLE SINKHOLE
SUSPIRAL
CESTODE POLYZOAN
CESTRUM POISONBERRY
CESTUS CEST CESTON HURLBAT
GAUNTLET WHIRLBAT
CETACEAN ORC CETE ORCA SUSU
WHALE BELUGA COWFISH
DOLPHIN GRAMPUS NARWHAL
MUTILATE PORPOISE
CETO (**BROTHER OF —**) PHORCYS
(**DAUGHTERS OF —**) GRAEAE
GORGONS HESPERIDES
(**FATHER OF —**) PONTUS
(**MOTHER OF —**) GAEA
CEYLON (**SEE SRI LANKA**)
SERENDIP TAPROBANE
CEYLONESE CEYLON BURGHER
CEYLON MOSS GULAMAN
CGS UNIT STILB STOKE
CHA TSIA CHAIS
CHACMA BAVIAN BOBBEJAAN

CHAD

CAPITAL: NDJAMENA
COIN: FRANC FRANCCFA
LAKE: CHAD
NATIVE: ARAB SARA KREDA
MASSA TOUBOU KAMADJA
MOUNDAN
PLATEAU: ENNEDI
RIVER: CHARI SHARI LOGONE
BAHRAOUK
TOWN: ATI BOL LAI MAO FADA
FAYA MONGO ABECHE BOKORO
BONGOR LARGEAU MOUNDOU
FORTLAMY MOUSSORO

CHADOR PHULKARI
CHAETA UNCINUS
CHAETOCHLOA SETARIA
CHAETOPOD SCALEBACK

CHAETURA DRAB BEAR
CHAFE IRK RUB VEX FRET FRIG
FROT FUME GALD GALL HEAT
JOSH RAGE WARM WEAR ANGER
ANNOY CHAFF GRIND SCOLD
SNUFF WORRY WRING ABRADE
BANTER EXCITE FRIDGE HARASS
INJURY NETTLE RANKLE INCENSE
INFLAME SNUFFLE FRICTION
IRRITATE RAILLERY
CHAFER CRESSET
CHAFF GUY HAY PUG RAG ROT
BRAN CAFF CHIP GRIT GUFF JOSH
PULU QUIZ RAZZ BORAK CHIAK
CHYAK DROSS GLUME HULLS
HUSKS JOLLY RALLY SLACK
STOUR STRAW TEASE TRASH
BANTER BHOOSA REFUSE
CAVINGS TAILING RAILLERY
RIDICULE SHELLING
CHAFFER BANDY SIEVE WARES
BUYING DICKER HAGGLE HIGGLE
MARKET PALTER BARGAIN
CHATTER SELLING TRAFFIC
EXCHANGE
CHAFFINCH PINK CHINK SPINK
TWINK ROBERD SCOBBY SHILFA
SKELLY ROBINET SNABBIE
WETBIRD
CHAFFY SCALY ACEROSE ACEROUS
PALEATE
CHAFING GALLING IMPATIENCE
CHAGRIN ENVY SPITE VEXATION
CHAGRINED SICK ASHAMED
CHAIN FOB GUY NET ROW SET
TEW TIE TOE TOW TUG TYE BIND
BOND CURB FALL FAST FILE GYVE
JOIN LINE LINK SEAL SOAM TEAM
BRAIL CABLE GROUP GUARD
LEASH SHANK SHEET SLANG
SLING SHANK TRACE TRAIN
WRASE CARCAN CATENA COLLAR
CORDON FASTEN FETTER
GANGER HANGER HOBBLE
JACKER JIGGER LINKER RACKAN
SECURE SERIES STRING TETHER
TOGGLE BOBSTAY CATFALL
CHIGNON CONNECT EMBRACE
ENSLAVE LASHING MANACLE
NETWORK PAINTER PENDANT
SAUTOIR SHACKLE TACKLER
BACKROPE BRACELET CARCANET
GLEIPNIR LINKWORK NECKLACE
RECEPTOR RESTRAIN RIGWIDDY
STROBILA WOOLDING
(**— FOR ANCHOR**) CATFALL
PAINTER
(**— FOR BINDING**) JACKER TACKLER
(**— FOR WRAPPING MAST**)
WOOLDING
(**— OF AUTHORITIES**) ISNAD
(**— OF DUNES**) SAIF SEIF
(**— OF MOUNTAINS**) RANGE
(**— OF ROCKS**) REEF
(**— ON CONVICT'S LEG**) SLANG
(**— TO BIND CATTLE**) SEAL
(**DECORATIVE —**) FESTOON
(**ENDLESS —**) CREEPER
(**MAGIC —**) GLEIPNIR
(**SHORT —**) SHANK
(**SUSPENDED —**) CATENARY
(**WATCH —**) FOB ALBERT
(**PL.**) IRONS CONVEYOR

(PREF.) HORMO STREPHO
STREPSI STREPT(O)
CHAIN LINK SHUT COPULA
SWIVEL
CHAINMAN CLASHY CLASHEE
LINEMAN TAPEMAN
CHAIN-SHAPED CATENOID
CHAIR KEEP SEAT SHOP HORSE
SEDAN STOOL ESTATE OFFICE
PULPIT ROCKER SADDLE SITTER
TONJON CACOLET COMMODE
FANBACK GONDOLA SITTING
VOYEUSE WINDSOR ARMCHAIR
CARRIAGE CATHEDRA FAUTEUIL
KANGAROO SGABELLO VOLTAIRE
(— OF STATE) THRONE
(— SLUNG FROM POLE) KAGO
TALABON
(— WITH CANOPY) STATE
(BISHOP'S —) CATHEDRA
FALDSTOOL
(EASY —) COGSWELL
(GREEK —) KLISMOS
(MINING —) DOG
(PART OF —) ARM EAR LEG BACK
POST RUNG SEAT SLAT CREST
STILE STUMP ROCKER ARMREST
SPINDLE BACKRAIL HEADPIECE
(PORTABLE —) SEDAN
(SEDAN —) NORIMONO
(SPRING —) PERCH
(THRONE —) SHINZA
CHAIRMAN HEAD CHAIR EMCEE
PRESES SPEAKER CONVENER
DIRECTOR MODERATOR
PROLOCUTOR
(PREF.) SYMPOSI
CHAISE GIG SHAY CHAIR CALESIN
CARRIAGE CURRICLE
SHANDRYDAN
CHAISE LONGUE DAYBED
DUCHESSE
CHALAZA TREAD TREADLE
GALLATURE
CHALCEDONY ONYX OPAL SARD
AGATE CHERT PRASE CATEYE
JASPER PLASMA QUARTZ
CARNEOL ENHYDROS OPALINE
SARDINE SARDIUS CORNELIAN
CHALCIOPE (FATHER OF —) AEETES
(HUSBAND OF —) PHRIXUS
(MOTHER OF —) ASTERODIA
(SISTER OF —) MEDEA
(SON OF —) ARGUS MELAS
PHRONTIS CYTISSORUS
CHALCIS (CHILDREN OF —)
CURETES CORYBANTES
(FATHER OF —) ASOPUS
(MOTHER OF —) METOPE
CHALCOPYRITE RUN
CHALDEAN KALDANI BABYLONIAN
(— MEASURE) CANE FOOT MAKUK
QASAB ARTABA GARIBA GHALVA
MANSION
(— RIVER) TIGRIS EUPHRATES
(— TOWN) UR
CHALICE AMA CUP BOWL CALIX
GRAIL REGAL GOBLET KRASIS
CHALK CAUK CORK PALE SCAR
TALC TICK CRETA FLOUR SCORE
BLANCH BLEACH CRAYON CREDIT
RUBBLE WHITEN ACCOUNT
WHITING

(GREEN —) PRASINE
(HARD —) HURLOCK
(RED —) RUBRIC
(SURVEYOR'S —) KEEL
(PREF.) CALC(I)(IO)(O) CALCAREO
CHALKBOARD GREENBOARD
CHALKSTONE TOPHUS
CHALKY CRETACIC CRETACEOUS
CHALLENGE HEN VIE BRAG CALL
DARE DEFY FACE GAGE ASSAY
BANCO BLAME BRAVE CLAIM
QUERY STUMP ACCUSE APPEAL
BANTER CARTEL CHARGE DACKER
DAIKER DEMAND DESCRY FORBID
IMPUGN INFIRM INVITE RECUSE
SERDAB ARRAIGN CENSURE
IMPEACH PROVOKE REPROVE
SOLICIT SUMMONS CHAMPION
DARRAIGN DEFIANCE GAUNTLET
QUESTION REPROACH
(— A BULL) CITE
CHALLENGING PIQUANT
BLOODSHOT
CHALONE AUTACOID
CHALYBEATE MARTIAL
CHALYBITE SIDERITE
CHAMBER ODA AGER CELL CIST
DOME FLAT FOLD HALL IWAN
KIVA ROOM SALE TOMB BOWER
CAVUM COURT GOMER HOUSE
SENAT SHAFT SOLAR SOLER
STOVE ATRIUM CAMARA CAMERA
COFFER HEADER HOLLOW
MIHRAB SENADO SENATE SOLLAR
SPRING STANZA WILSON
BEDROOM CAISSON CHALMER
CHANNEL CHAUMER CONCAVE
CUBICLE FAVISSA FIREBOX
GALLERY GEHENNA MANSION
RECEIPT CASEMATE CYLINDER
DIFFUSER FOUNTAIN GROSSRAT
SMOKEBOX SNEMOVNA
THALAMUS
(— FOR MOLTEN GLASS) FONT
(— IN FURNACE) SHAFT DOGHOUSE
(— OF EAR) SACCULE UTRICLE
(— POT) JORDAN JEROBOAM
(AIR —) SPONSON
(AUDIENCE —) DURBAR
(BOMBPROOF —) CASEMATE
(CLIMATE CONTROL —) BIOTRON
(FIRE —) ARCH STOVE COCKLE
FIREBOX
(FORTIFICATION —) BUNKER
(OPEN —) LANTERN
(ORGAN —) SWELL
(PISTON —) BARREL
(PRIVATE —) CLOSET CONCLAVE
(PUEBLO —) KIVA ESTUFA
(SLEEPING —) BEDROOM
WARDROBE
(SMALL —) LOCULUS
(SUPPLY —) MAGAZINE
(UNDERGROUND —) CAVE CRYPT
CAVERN SERDAB HYPOGEE
(WATERTIGHT —) CAISSON
(PREF.) THALAM(I)(O)
(SUFF.) CELE COELE COELUS
CHAMBERLAIN EUNUCH FACTOR
SERVANT STEWARD PALATINE
POLONIUS
CHAMELEON ANOLE ANOLI
LACERT SAURIAN

CHAMFER BEVEL CHIMB CHIME
CHINE FLUTE CIPHER
FURROW GROOVE
CHAMOIS GEMS IZARD AOUDAD
SHAMMY
CHAMOMILE MAYWEED
MARGUERITE
CHAMONT (SISTER OF —) MONIMIA
CHAMP BITE CHAW FIRM HARD
MASH CHANK CHOMP FIELD
GNASH TRAMPLE
CHAMPAGNE AY BUBBLY SIMKIN
BELLEEK SILLERY
CHAMPION ACE AID FAN ABET
BACK BOSS DEFY HERO KEMP
GHAZI ASSERT ATTEND DEFEND
KNIGHT PATRON SQUIRE VICTOR
APOSTLE ESPOUSE FIGHTER
PALADIN PROTECT ADVOCATE
DEFENDER PALMERIN
PROTAGONIST
CHAMPIONING
(PREF.) PRO
CHAMPIONSHIP TITLE LAURELS
ADVOCACY
CHAMPLEVE INLAID
CHANCE DIE HAP LOT CASE CAST
DINT DRAW FATE LINE LUCK
ODDS RISK SHOT SHOW TIDE
BREAK ETTLE STAKE WHACK
BETIDE CASUAL GAMBLE HAPPEN
HAZARD MISHAP RANDOM
SQUEAK TUMBLE AIMLESS
FORTUNE OPENING STUMBLE
VANTAGE VENTURE ACCIDENT
CASUALTY EVENTUAL FORTUITY
QUESTION ALEATORIC
OPPORTUNITY PERADVENTURE
(ADVERSE —) HAZARD
(EVEN —) TOSSUP
(SLIGHT —) PRAYER
(PL.) PROSPECTS
(PREF.) TYCH(O)
CHANCEL BEMA CHOIR ADYTUM
CHANCELLOR LOGOTHETE
CHANDELIER CORONA LUSTER
PHAROS PENDANT CHANDLER
GASELIER
CHANDLER TALLOWER
CHANE OREJON
CHANGE MEW CHOP FLOP MOLT
MOVE ODDS PEAL TURN VARY
VEER WARP WEND ADAPT ALTER
AMEND BREAK COINS EMEND
MOULT SHIFT THROW ADJUST
BECOME DIFFER DIGEST IMMUTE
MODIFY MUANCE MUTATE
REMOVE REVAMP REVISE SWITCH
WISSEL WRIXLE COMMUTE
CONVERT CUTOVER DEVIATE
FLUXION MORTIFY BECOMING
DENATURE EXCHANGE INNOVATE
LENITION MUTATION REVISION
TRANSFER TRANSUME VARIANCE
PERMUTATION METAMORPHOSE
MODIFICATION METAMORPHOSIS
(— APPEARANCE) DISGUISE
(— COLOR) TURN
(— COURSE) GYBE JIBE
(— DIRECTION) CUT CANT CHOP
HAUL KNEE VEER ANGLE BREAK
SHIFT
(— FOR BETTER) HELP

(— FOR WORSE) BEDEVIL
(— FORM) DEVELOP
(— GAIT) BREAK
(— GRADUALLY) PASS GRADUATE
(— IN COURSE) SHEER
(— IN DIRECTION) JOG KNEE STEP
(— IN ELEVATION) FORK
(— IN LAKE LEVEL) SEICHE
(— IN SIZE) ASTOGENY
(— INTO VAPOR) FLASH
(— MONEY) WISSEL
(— OF FORM) SET
(— OF GEAR) KICKDOWN
(— OF MIND) CAPRICE
(— OF MOOD) VARY
(— OF PITCH) MOTION INFLECT
(— OF SEA LEVEL) EUSTACY
(— OF SOUND) BREAKING
(— OF WORD) ANAGRAM
(— ONE'S HEART) REPENT
(— PACE) BREAK
(— POSITION) STIR FLEET HOTCH
(— QUICKLY) FLY
(— RESIDENCE) FLIT
(— SHAPE) DRAW CREEP DEFORM
(ABNORMAL —) LESION
(ABRUPT —) DOGLEG SALTATION
(GEAR —) KICKDOWN
(GRADUAL —) DRIFT
(PRESSURE —) ALLOBAR
(SHORT —) FLUFF
(SMALL —) GROCERY
(UNEXPECTED —) SWITCH
(PL.) DOUBLES PLASTIQUE
(PREF.) ALLAGO ALLASSO AMOEBI
AMOEBO MUTA MUTO
(SUFF.) MUTE
CHANGEABLE EEMIS GIDDY IMMIS
LIGHT WINDY CHOPPY FICKLE
FITFUL GERFUL KETCHY LABILE
MOBILE MOTLEY MUABLE SHIFTY
WANKLE BRUCKLE ERRATIC
MUTABLE PROTEAN UNSTAID
VARIANT VARIOUS VOLUBLE
AMENABLE CATCHING GLIBBERY
MOVEABLE SKITTISH TICKLISH
UNSTABLE VARIABLE VEERABLE
VOLATILE WEATHERY
CHAMELEON VERSATILE
CHANGEABLENESS LEVITY
CAPRICE VIBRATION
CHANGED VARIED ANOTHER
CHANGEFUL FICKLE SHIFTY
MUTABLE RESTLESS
CHANGELESS CONSISTENT
CHANGELING AUF AWF OAF DOLT
FOOL CHILD DUNCE IDIOT
WAVERER IMBECILE KILLCROP
RENEGADE TURNCOAT
CHANGING FLUXIBLE ALTERNATE
(— MONEY) AGIO
(CONTINUALLY —) FLOATING
CHANK SANK CONCH
CHANNEL CUT GAT POD REE RUT
SOW CANO CAVA DEEP DIKE
DUCT DYKE FLUE GATE GOOL
GOTE GOUT GURT KILL KYLE LAKE
LANE PACE PIPE RACE SLEW
SLOO VALE VEIN WADI WADY
BAYOU CANAL CARRY CHASE
COWAL DITCH DRAIN DRILL
FLUME FLUTE GLYPH GUIDE
INSET LATCH QUIRK RIVER SINUS

SLIDE SOUND STOOL STOVE
STRIA SWASH AIRWAY ALVEUS
ARROYO ARTERY BRANCH
COURSE CUTOFF ESTERO
FURROW GROOVE GULLET
GUTTER HOLLOW KENNEL
KEYWAY LAGOON MEDIUM
OFFLET OILWAY RABBET RESACA
RIVOSE RUNWAY SLOUGH SLUICE
SPECUS STRAIT STRAND STREAM
THROAT TROUGH CHAMFER
CONDUCT CONDUIT CULVERT
CUNETTE EURIPUS OFFTAKE
PASSAGE RACEWAY RIVULET
SHIPWAY SILANGA STRIGIL
THALWEG TIDEWAY WASHOUT
AQUEDUCT FLOODWAY
GUIDEWAY GUNKHOLE RACELINE
SCOURWAY SPILLWAY
CANNELURE
(— FOR MOLTEN METAL) SOW GATE
RUNNER
(— IN CLOTH) FLUTE
(— IN ICE FIELD) LEAD
(— IN MOLD) SPRAY
(— OF AQUEDUCT) SPECUS
(— ON A DECK) CHIMB CHIME
(— ON WHALE) SCARF
(ARTIFICIAL —) GAT GOUT
(DRAINAGE —) GAW
(ENGLISH —) SLEEVE
(INCLINED —) SHOOT
(INFORMATION —) PIPELINE
(IRRIGATION —) AUWAI DROVE
(LYMPH —) CISTERNA
(SECONDARY —) BINNACLE
(SLOPING —) CHUTE SHUTE
(PREF.) CANALI RHYN(O) SOLEN(O)
VAS(I)(O)
CHANNELBILL RAINFOWL
CHANNELED FLUTED
CHANT CANT MELE SING SONG
TONE CAROL PSALM SOUGH
ANTHEM CANTUS INTONE LITANY
WARBLE CHORTLE INTROIT
PROSODE REQUIEM WORSHIP
ALLELUIA ANTIPHON CANTICLE
SINGSONG PLAINSONG
CANTILLATE
CHANTER STICK CANTOR SINGER
BAGPIPE SONGSTER CHALUMEAU
(— OF BAGPIPE) OBOE
CHANTERELLE CANTINO
CHANTING CHARM HAZANUT
ANTIPHONY CHAZZANUT
CHANTLATE SPROCKET
CHANTRY CAGE
CHAOS NU NUN PIE APSU GULF
HYLE MESS VOID ABYSS BABEL
CHASM JUMBLE MATTER TOPHET
ANARCHY MIXTURE DISORDER
SHAMBLES TAILSPIN TOHUBOHU
CHAOTIC MUDDLED CONFUSED
FORMLESS TUMULTUARY
CHAP BOY BUY DOG LAD MAN RAP
WAG BEAN BEAT BIRD BLOW
CHIP CHOP COVE DICK DUCK
HIND JOHN KIBE MASH MATE
NABS SNAP BILLY BLOKE BUCKO
BULLY BUYER CHAFT CHINK
CLEFT CRACK FRUIT KNOCK
LOVER RUMMY SCOUT SPLIT
SPORT SPRAY SWIPE TRADE

YOUTH BARTER BOHUNK BREACH
BUGGER CALLAN CHOOSE
CODGER CUFFIN FELLOW FOUTER
FOUTRA GAFFER GEEZER JOSSER
KIPPER SHAVER STRIKE STROKE
TURNIP BASTARD BROTHER
CALLANT FISSURE HUSBAND
ROUGHEN BLIGHTER CUSTOMER
DIVISION MERCHANT
(— HANDS) RACK SPRAY
(— IN SKIN) KIN KIBE
(FINE —) BULLY
(OLD —) BO GEEZER
(PLUCKY —) COCK
(QUEER —) GALOOT
(S.AFRICAN —) KEREL
(YOUNG —) GAFFER
(PL.) CHOPS
CHAPARRAL MONTE CHAMISAL
BUCKTHORN
CHAPARRO YAYA
CHAPBOOK CHAP GARLAND
CHAPE CRAMPET MORDANT
CHAPEL CAGE CAPE COPE COWL
HOOD CLOAK CRYPT PORCH
SALEM BETHEL BEULAH CHARRE
CHURCH HAIKAL MORADA SHRINE
CAPELLA CHANTRY CHAPLET
CHARNEL CHHATRI GALILEE
MARTYRY MEETING MEMORIA
ORATORY SACRARY SERVICE
BETHESDA DEACONRY DIACONIA
FERETORY FERETRUM PARABEMA
SACELLUM SODALITY
(UNDERGROUND —) SHROUDS
CHAPERON HOOD ATTEND
DUENNA ESCORT MATRON
GRIFFIN PROTECT GUARDIAN
TRAPPING
CHAPLAIN PADRE LEVITE
ALMONER CONDUCT ALTARIST
ORDINARY
CHAPLET BEAD ORLE STUD
CROWN ANADEM ANCHOR CIRCLE
FILLET JAMBER JAMMER ROSARY
STAPLE TROPHY WREATH
CORONAL CORONET GARLAND
MOULDING NECKLACE
ORNAMENT
(PREF.) STEMMATI
CHAPMAN CHAP BUYER DEALER
HAWKER TRADER COPEMAN
PEDDLER CUSTOMER MERCHANT
CHAPPIE JOCKEY
CHAPS FLEWS BREECHES
LEGGINGS OVERALLS
CHAPTER BODY CELL PACE POST
CAPUT COURT LODGE BRANCH
CABILDO CAPITAL CORRECT
COUNCIL MEETING SECTION
ASSEMBLY
(— OF BOOK) CAPITAL
(— OF KORAN) SURA SURAH
(— OF SOCIETY) CAMP CIRCLE
CHAR BURN CART COAL SEAR
BROIL CHARK CHORE SHARD
SINGE TROUT SCORCH BLACKEN
CHARIOT TORGOCH REDBELLY
SAIBLING SALMONID SANDBANK
(PL.) SALVELINI
CHARA MUSKGRASS
CHARACIN DORADO DOURADE
BLOODFIN

CHARACTER AURA BALL BENT
CARD CASE CLAY CLEF DASH
ECAD FLAT FOND FORM HAIR
KIND MAKE MARK MOLD NOTE
PART ROLE RUNE SIGN SORT
TONE TRIM TYPE BRAND COLOR
ETHIC ETHOS FIBER HABIT HEART
HUMOR INDEX SAVOR STAMP
TENOR TOKEN TRAIT WRITE
CARACT CIPHER COCKUP DAGGER
DIRECT EMBLEM FIGURE GENIUS
HANGER LETTER MANNER
METTLE NATURE REPUTE SIGLUM
SPIRIT STRIPE SYMBOL CALIBER
CLOTHES EDITION ENGRAVE
ESSENCE IMPRESS QUALITY
CAPACITY FRACTION IDENTITY
INFERIOR INSCRIBE LIGATURE
SELFHOOD SYLLABIC DESCENDER
PARAGRAPH PERSONAGE
(— IN DRAMA) CHORUS
(— IN PLAY) DAME BESSY
(— OF SOIL) LAIR
(ASSUMED —) ROLE FIGURE
INCOGNITO
(BAD —) DROLE BUDMASH
(BASIC —) BOTTOM
(CHIEF —) AGONIST
(CHINESE —) SHOU RADICAL
(COMMON —) COMMUNITY
(ESSENTIAL —) ALLOY
(FIRM —) BACKBONE
(GIVE — TO) TONE
(GREEK —) SAMPI
(JAPANESE —S) HIBUNCI
(MENDELIAN —) ALLEL ALLELE
(PHYSICAL —) ARMENOID
(PRIME —) ESSENCE
(SHIFTLESS —) BEAT
(STOCK —) BESSY MACCUS
(TESTED —) ASSAY
(TRIED —) TOUCH
(VULGAR —S) ONMUN
(PL.) MANA
(SUFF.) ERY
(HAVING — OF) IC(AL)
CHARACTERISTIC CAST COST
MARK MIEN ANGLE AROMA
GRACE POINT TACHE TOKEN
TRAIT TRICK ACCENT BEAUTY
NATURE STIGMA STROKE
ADJUNCT AMENITY FEATURE
IMPRESS QUALITY SPECIES
TYPICAL ACTIVITY HEADMARK
PECULIAR PROPERTY SYMBOLIC
PARAMETER PROPRIETY
PECULIARITY PARTICULARITY
QUALIFICATION
(— OF ANTIBODIES) AVIDITY
(ADVENTITIOUS —) ACCIDENT
(DISTINGUISHING —) SPECIES
HALLMARK BIRTHMARK
(PECULIAR —) IDIOPATHY
(PL.) CORNERS FACULTY
(SUFF.) IC(AL)
(— OF) ISH ISTIC LY
CHARACTERIZATION ELOGY
ELOGIUM
CHARACTERIZE MARK STYLE
DEFINE DEPICT TITLE ENGRAVE
ENTITLE IMPRINT PORTRAY
DESCRIBE INDICATE
INSCRIBE

CHARACTERIZED
(SUFF.) (— BY) AL FUL IAL
IC(AL) LEW
CHARACTERLESS INANE
CHARADES GAME
CHARCOAL COAL CARBO CHARK
CARBON FUSAIN PENCIL BLACKEN
SPODIUM SCRIBBET
CHARGE FEE LAP LAY RAP TAX
BEEF BILL BUCK CALL CARE CARK
CAST COST CURE DUES DUTY
FILL GIBE KEEP LADE LIEN LOAD
NICK NOTE ONUS RACK RATE
REST RUSH SHOT SIZE SOAK SPAR
TASK TOLL WARD WIKE AGIST
BLAME CAUSE CHALK COUNT
CRIME DEBIT EXTRA GYRON
ONSET ORDER PRICE REFER
SCORE SHOCK STICK STING THING
TRUST ACCUSE ADJURE ALLEGE
APPEAL ASSESS ATTACK BEHEST
BURDEN CAREER CENSUS
COURSE CREDIT DAMAGE
DEFAME DEMAND DITTAY ENJOIN
ENURNY EXCESS IMPOSE IMPUTE
METAGE OBJECT OFFICE PIPAGE
REATUS SURMIT SURTAX TARIFF
TOWAGE WEIGHT ACIDIZE
ANNULET ARRAIGN ARTICLE
ASCRIBE ASSAULT AVERAGE
BOATAGE CARTAGE CENSURE
CHEVRON CLAMPER COMMAND
CONCERN CONJURE CORKAGE
CORNAGE CUSTODY DOCKAGE
DRAYAGE EMBASSY EXPENSE
FLOTAGE HAULAGE IGNITER
IMPEACH KEEPING MANDATE
MILEAGE MISSION MIXTURE
MOORAGE PANNAGE QUAYAGE
REPRISE SIDEAGE SLANDER
SLIDAGE SURMISE WARPAGE
BILLBACK BRASSAGE CASUALTY
CHASTISE CRESCENT DELAYAGE
DENOUNCE LEGATION ORDINARY
OVERLOAD PLANKAGE
POUNDAGE PROVINCE QUESTION
SLINGING SPENDING STANDAGE
TUTORAGE VIGORISH COMPLAINT
ACCUSATION ACCUSEMENT
(— AGAINST) TILT
(— BATTERY) SOAK BOOST
(— EXCESSIVELY) FLEECE
(— FALSELY) SURMISE
(— OF FIREARM) LOAD AMORCE
(— OF MENTAL ENERGY) CATHEXIS
(— OF METAL) HEAT
(— OF ORE) POST
(— TO BE PAID) LAW
(— UPON PROPERTY) LIEN
(— WITH CRIME) ACCUSE DELATE
INDICT ARTICLE ATTAINT
IMPEACH
(— WITH GAS) AERATE
(AGGREGATE —S) BOOK
(CANNON —) GRAPE
(COVER —) COUVERT
(DEPTH —) CAN
(EXPLOSIVE —) CAP BLAST SNAKE
SQUIB TULIP BOOSTER BURSTER
IGNITER
(FALSE —) CALUMNY
(HERALDIC —) DELF DROP GIRON
GYRON LABEL BEZANT BILLET

DRAGON GURGES
BEARING ESQUIRE
(MAILING —) FRANKAGE
(POWDER —) GRAIN
(SHAPED —) BEEHIVE
(SPIRITUAL —) CURE
(TEMPORARY —) CARE
(WINE —) CORKAGE
CHARGED UP HOT LADEN BELAST
BILLETY BILLETTE ELECTRIC
INSTINCT
(— WITH EMOTION) SWOLLEN
CHARGEHAND CLICKER
CHARGEMAN BLASTER
CHARGER DISH HORSE MOUNT
STEED ACCUSER COURSER
PLATTER TROOPER
CHARILY FRUGALLY GINGERLY
CHARIOT CAR BIGA CART CHAR
RATH WAIN BUGGY CHAIR ESSED
RATHA TRIGA WAGON CHARET
QUADRIGA
CHARIOTEER AURIGA CARTER
DRIVER IOLAUS LEADER CARTARE
WAGONER MYRTILUS
AUTOMEDON
CHARITABLE KIND BENIGN
HUMANE LENIENT LIBERAL
GENEROUS
CHARITY ALMS DOLE GIFT LOVE
PITY RUTH MERCY BASKET
BOUNTY CARITAS HANDOUT
LARGESS LENIENCE TZEDAKAH
CHARIVARI BABEL SHALLAL
SERENADE SHIVAREE
CHARLATAN FAKE CHEAT FAKER
FRAUD QUACK CABOTIN EMPIRIC
IMPOSTER MAGICIAN SYCOPHANT
MOUNTEBANK QUACKSALVER
CHARLES II DAVID
CHARLIE MCCARTHY STOOGE
CHARLOCK KRAUT RUNCH
HARLOCK KEDLOCK KERLOCK
MUSTARD SINAPIS YELLOWS
CHARDOCK CHEDLOCK SKEDLOCK
SKELLOCH
CHARM IT GBO KEY OBI CALM
CHIC HAND JINX JUJU JYNX
LUCK MOJO PLAY RUNE SNOW
SONG TAKE TILL ZOGO ALLAY
AROMA BRIEF CATCH FAVOR
FREET FREIT GRACE LAMIN
MAGIC OBEAH OOMPH SAFFI
SAFIE SPELL VENUS WANGA
WEIRD ALLURE AMULET BEAUTY
CARACT DEASIL ENAMOR ENGAGE
ENTICE FETISH GLAMOR GRIGRI
INCANT MANTRA MELODY
PLEASE SAPHIE SCARAB SOOTHE
SUBDUE SUMMON VOODOO
ABRAXAS ASSUAGE ATTRACT
BEGUILE BEWITCH CANTION
CANTRIP CONJURE CONTROL
DELIGHT ENCHANT ENTHRALL
FLATTER HEITIKI PERIAPT
PHILTER PHILTRE SINGING
SORCERY BLESSING BRELOQUE
COMETHER COQUETRY ENTHRALL
ENTRANCE GLAUMRIE GREEGREE
PISHOGUE PRACTICE TALISMAN
CAPTIVATE MAGNETIZE
PATERNOSTER
CHARMED CAPTIVE

CHARMER SIREN EXORCIST
MAGICIAN SORCERER
ENCHANTER
CHARMING LEPID SWEET GOLDEN
WIZARD AMIABLE DARLING
EYESOME TEMPEAN WINNING
WINSOME ADORABLE DELICATE
GRACEFUL LOVESOME
PICTURESQUE
CHARNEL GHASTLY CEMETERY
GOLGOTHA
CHARON (FATHER OF —) EREBUS
(MOTHER OF —) NOX
CHARPOY COT
CHARQUI JERKY XARQUE
CHART MAP BILL CARD MARK
PLAN PLAT PLOT ROSE CARTE
GRAPH STILL RECORD SCHEME
DIAGRAM EMAGRAM EXPLORE
ISOTYPE OUTLINE PROJECT
DOCUMENT DOPEBOOK
MERCATOR PLATFORM
(— BOOK) WAGONER
(— FROM AIR) AEROVIEW
(— MARK) VIGIA
(— OF A COURSE) RUTTER
(MARINER'S —) ROSE RUTTER
(WEATHER —) ANALOGUE
NEPHANALYSIS
CHARTER FIX LET BOND BOOK
DEED HIRE RENT CARTE CHART
FUERO GRANT LEASE SANAD
CHARTA PERMIT SUNNUD
DIPLOMA CONTRACT GRUNDLOV
HEIRLOOM LANDBOOK
MONOPOLY PANCHART
CHARTERHOUSE OF PARMA
(AUTHOR OF —) STENDHAL
(CHARACTER IN —) GINA CONTI
DONGO MOSCA CLELIA FAUSTA
GILETTI FABRIZIO FERRANTE
MARIETTA PIETRANERA
CHARWOMAN CHARER CHARLADY
PORTRESS JANITRESS
CHARY SHY DEAR WARY CHERE
SCANT SPARE DAINTY FRUGAL
PRIZED SKIMPY CAREFUL
CURIOUS SPARING CAUTIOUS
HESITANT PRECIOUS RESERVED
SPAREFUL VIGILANT
CHASE FOG SIC SUE FALL HUNT
JERL SHAG SHOO SICK ANNOY
CATCH CHEVY CHIVY DRIVE
HARRY HOUND SCORE SHACK
CACCIA CHIVVY CHOUSE EMBOSS
FOLLOW FRIEZE FURROW GALLOP
GROOVE HALLOO HARASS
HOLLOW INDENT PURSUE
QUARRY SCORSE TRENCH
CHANNEL ENGRAVE HUNTING
PURSUIT ORNAMENT PURCHASE
(— GAME) COURSE
(— HARD) RATTLE
CHASER RAM DRINK HOUND
FROGGER
(WOMAN —) SHEEPBITER
CHASING CISELURE
CHASM GAP KIN PIT GULF RIFT
YAWN ABYSS BLANK CANON
CHAOS CLEFT GORGE BREACH
CANYON HIATUS FISSURE
MEGARON SWALLOW VACANCY
APERTURE CREVASSE

INTERVAL VACATION
CHASSE SLIP GLIDE SASHAY
CHASSEUR HUNTER BELLBOY
DOORMAN FOOTMAN HUNTSMAN
CHASSIS SASH FRAME FIGURE
CHASTE CAST PURE ATTIC CLEAN
ZONED DECENT HONEST MODEST
PROPER SEVERE VESTAL VIRGIN
CLEANLY PUDICAL REFINED
CELIBATE INNOCENT VIRGINLY
VIRTUOUS CONTINENT
CHASTEN RATE ABASE SMITE
SMOTE SNEAP SOBER HUMBLE
PUNISH REBUKE REFINE SUBDUE
TEMPER AFFLICT CENSURE
CORRECT NURTURE CHASTISE
MODERATE RESTRAIN
CHASTISE BEAT FIRK FLOG LASH
SLAP TRIM WHIP AMEND BLAME
FEEZE SCOLD SPANK SPILL STRAP
TAUNT ACCUSE ANOINT BERATE
CHARGE DISPLE PUNISH PURIFY
REBUKE REFINE STRAFE SWINGE
TEMPER THRASH TICKLE
CHASTEN CORRECT REPROVE
SCOURGE SHINGLE SUSPECT
CASTIGATE
CHASTISEMENT ROD HELL TOCO
TOKO CENSURE PAYMENT
FLOGGING
(DIVINE —) WRATH
CHASTITY HONOR PURITY VIRTUE
HONESTY MODESTY PUDENCY
CELIBACY GOODNESS PUDICITY
INNOCENCE
CHASUBLE CASULA DEACON
INFULA PLANET PAENULA
PIANETA VESTMENT
CHAT GAS JAW MAG RAP BIRD
CHIN CONE COZE DISH GIST TALK
TELL TOVE TWIG YARN AMENT
CAUSE COOSE CRACK DALLY
PITCH POINT PRATE PROSE
PROSS SPEAK SPIKE VISIT BABBLE
BRANCH CATKIN CONFAB COURSE
DEVICE GABBLE GIBBER GOSSIP
GOSTER HOBNOB JABBER NATTER
POTATO POTTER SAMARA
CHAFFER CHATTER CAUSERIE
CHATTERY CONVERSE SPIKELET
STROBILE
CHATEAU HOUSE TOWER CASTLE
MANSION SCHLOSS CHATELET
FORTRESS
CHATON BASIL BEZEL BEZIL STONE
COATING SETTING
CHATTEL CATTLE PLEDGE
DEODAND FIXTURE CATALLUM
PERSONAL
(DISTRAINT OF —S) NAAM
(PL.) STUFF FARLEU FARLEY
COMODATO HOUSEHOLD
CHATTER GAB JAW MAG YAP
BLAB CARP CHAT CHIN CLAP
CLAT DISH GASH HACK KNAP
RICK TALK TEAR YIRR CABAL
CLACK CLASH GARRE HAVER
PRATE SHAKE BABBLE BRUDGE
CACKLE CLAVER GABBLE GIBBER
GOSSIP JABBER JANGLE JARGON
PALTER RATTLE SHIVER TATTER
TATTLE TINKLE YAMMER YATTER
BLABBER BRABBLE CHACKLE

CHAFFER CHIPPER CHITTER
CLACKET CLATTER CLITTER
GABNASH NASHGOB PALAVER
PRABBLE PRATING PRATTLE
SHATTER SMATTER TRATTLE
TWATTLE TWITTER TWITTLE
WHITTER BABBLING LOLLYGAG
SCHMOOSE VERBIAGE
(SUFF.) LALIA
CHATTERBOX JAY MAG PIET
BUCCO CLACK CRYSTE GOSSIP
MAGPIE
CHATTERER JAY MAG PIE BLAB
CHUET CHEWET GABBER MAGPIE
RATTLE HAVERER
CHATTERING PIET BABBLY
CHAVISH POPPING TWITTER
BABBLING
CHATTY CHIRRUPY GARRULOUS
CHAUFFEUR DRIVER SHOVER
TESTER
CHAUVINISM JINGOISM
CHAUVINIST JINGO JINGOIST
CHAW JAW VEX CHEW ENVY MULL
GRIND PONDER
CHAYOTE CHOCHO TALLOTE
HUISQUIL MIRLITON
CHEAP LOW BASE GAIN POOR VILE
BORAX CLOSE FLASH GAUDY
GROSS KITCH LIGHT MUCKY
NASTY PRICE SNIDE TATTY TIGHT
TINNY VALUE ABJECT BRUMMY
CHEESY COMMON CRUMBY
CRUMMY JITNEY LEADEN PLENTY
SHODDY SORDID STINGY TAWDRY
TRASHY UNDEAR BARGAIN
CHINTZY POPULAR TINHORN
INFERIOR PENNORTH SIXPENNY
TWOPENNY BRUMMAGEM
PINCHBECK
(— ITEM) TWOFER
(PREF.) VILI
CHEAPEN DOCK STALE VILIFY
SMALLEN
CHEAPSKATE STIFF PIKER
CHEAT DO BAM BOB COG CON FOB
FOP FUB GIP GUM GYP JIG
NIP TOP BEAT BILK BITE BULL
BURN CLIP COLT CRIB DISH DUFF
DUPE FAKE FIRK FLAM FLUM
GECK GULL HAVE HOAX JILT JINK
JOUK KNAP LIAR MACE MUMP
NAIL NICK NOSE POOP PULL
REAM ROOK SELL SHAM SILE SKIN
SLUR SNAP SWAP SWOP TRIM
WEED WIPE BITCH BLINK BOOTY
BUNCO BUNKO COZEN CROOK
CULLY DODGE FAKER FLING FOIST
FOURB FRAUD FUDGE GLEEK
GOUGE GREEK GUILE HOCUS
KNAVE LURCH MULCT PINCH
PLOAT ROGUE SCAMP SCREW
SHARP SHORT SLANG SPOIL STICK
STIFF STING SWICK SWIKE TOUCH
TRICK VERSE WRINK BAFFLE
BLANCH BUBBLE BUCKET CHIAUS
CHISEL CHOUSE CLOYNE COGGER
DADDLE DECEIT DELUDE DERIDE
DIDDLE DOODLE DUFFER
EMUNGE EUCHRE FIDDLE FLEECE
GAZUMP GREASE HUMBUG
HUMMER HUSTLE ILLUDE INTAKE
JOCKEY NIGGLE NOBBLE NUZZLE

OUTWIT RADDLE RENEGE RIPOFF
SHAVER SHICER SNUDGE SUCKER
TWICER ABUSION BEGUILE
BUBBLER CHICANE CULLION
DECEIVE DEFRAUD ESCHEAT
FAITOUR FINAGLE FINESSE
FOISTER GUDGEON JUGGLER
MISLEAD PLUNDER QUIBBLE
SHARPER SHIFTER SKELDER
SLICKER SWINDLE VERNEUK
ARTIFICE BEJUGGLE CHALDESE
CHISELER DELUSION HOODWINK
IMPOSTOR INTRIGUE OUTREACH
OVERTAKE PICAROON
SHAMMOCK SWINDLER
BAMBOOZLE CIRCUMVENT
SHORTCHANGE
CHEATED SOLD
CHEATER BITE GULL KNAVE
BILKER INTAKE TOPPER SHARPER
FINAGLER TREACHER
CHEATING HOCUS BARRAT
ODLING ABUSIVE FUBBERY
MICHERY ROGUERY CHEATERY
JUGGLING TRICKERY
CHECK BIT DAM HAP LID NAB NIP
SAY SET TAB BAIL BALK BEAT
BILK BILL CHIP CHIT COOK CRIB
CURB DAMP FACE FOIL GAGE
HURT ITEM KITE PAWL REIN SKID
SNEB SNIB SNIP SNUB STAY STEM
STOP STUB TAKE TEST TICK TRIG
TURN TWIT WERE ABORT ALLAY
ANNUL BAULK BLOCK BRAKE
CATCH CHIDE CHILL CHING
CHOKE CRACK CROOK DAUNT
DELAY DETER DRAFT EMBAR
FACER FAULT GAUGE LIMIT
MODER PAUSE QUELL REPEL
SNAPE SPOKE STALL STILL STUNT
TALLY TAUNT THROW TOKEN
TRASH WAVER ARAYNE ARREST
ATTACK BAFFLE BOTTLE BRIDLE
CHEQUE COUPON DAMPEN
DEFEAT DETAIN DETENT DURESS
GRAVEL HAFFET HAFFIT HINDER
IMPEDE OPPOSE OUTWIT
QUENCH RABBET REBATE REBUFF
REBUKE RETURN SCOTCH
STANCH STAYER STIFLE STYMIE
TICKET VERIFY ANSTOSS
AWEBAND BACKSET BECLOUD
COMMAND CONTAIN CONTROL
COUNTER CURTAIN DRAUGHT
INHIBIT MONITOR REFRAIN
REPRESS REPROOF REPROVE
REPULSE REVERSE SETBACK
SNAFFLE STAUNCH STOPPER
TRAMMEL TROUBLE BULKHEAD
ENCUMBER HOLDBACK OBSTRUCT
PULLBACK RESTRAIN WITHHOLD
(— ENTHUSIASM) DISMAY
(— GRADUALLY) CUSHION
(— GROWTH) BLAST STINT STUNT
(— IN GLASS) SPLIT
(— IN TIMBER) STARSHAKE
(— MOTION) SPRAG
(— OF HORSE) SACCADE
(— PASSER) PAPERHANGER
(— PROGRESS) DEFEAT
(FORGED —) STIFF STUMER
(HOLD IN —) COMPESCE
(RESTAURANT —) LAWING

(WORTHLESS —) DUD STUMER
(PREF.) ISCH(O)
CHECKED CHECK BEATEN CLOSED
CAPTIVE STOPPED
CHECKER DAM DICE FRET KING
CHECK FREAK FRECK PIECE
WHITE DAMPER DRAUGHT
CHECKERBERRY JINKS
DRUNKARD TEABERRY
CHECKERBOARD TABLE
DAMBROD DAMBOARD
CHECKERED PIED VAIR DICED
PLAID CHECKY MOTLEY
CHECKERS DRAFTS CHEQUERS
DRAUGHTS
CHECKERWORK TESSEL CHECKER
TESSERA
CHECKING REST BLOCK SETBACK
EBRILLADE
(SUFF.) SCHESIS SCHETIC
CHECKMATE LICK MATE STOP
UNDO BAFFLE CORNER DEFEAT
OUTWIT STYMIE THWART
SUIMATE
CHECKSTONE CHUCK
CHEDDAR CHEESE
CHEEK CHAP CHOP GALL GENA
JAMB JOLE JOWL LEER SASS
WANG WANK BUCCA CHOKE
CHYAK CRUST NERVE SAUCE
SHICK CHYACK HAFFET HAFFIT
OXCHEEK AUDACITY TEMERITY
(— OF SPUR) SHANK
(— OF VISE) CHAP
(PREF.) BUCCO MEL PAREI(A)
CHEEKBONE MALAR ZYGOMA
CHEEKY BOLD
CHEEP PIP YAP YIP CHIP HINT
PEEP PULE CHIRP CREAK TWEET
SQUEAK TATTLE
CHEER OLE RAH FARE FOOD MIND
ROOT VIVA YELL BRAVO BRISK
CHIRK ELATE ERECT FEAST
HEART HUZZA JOLLY MIRTH
SHOUT SPORT TIGER WHOOP
CANTLE CHERRY GAIETY HOORAY
HURRAH HUZZAH REHETE
SOLACE VIANDS ACCLAIM
ANIMATE APPLAUD CHERISH
COMFORT CONSOLE ENCHEER
GLADDEN HEARTEN JOLLITY
LIGHTEN REFRESH REJOICE
SUPPORT UPRAISE APPLAUSE
BRIGHTEN HILARITY INSPIRIT
RECREATE VIVACITY
(BURST OF —S) SALVO
(GOOD —) WELFARE
(JAPANESE —) BANZAI
(SORRY —) PENANCE
CHEERFUL GAY CANT GLAD GLEG
GOOD HIGH ROSY BONNY CADGY
CANTY CHIRK DOUCE HAPPY
JOLLY LIGHT MERRY PEART
READY SAPPY SUNNY VAUDY
BLITHE BRIGHT CHEERY CHIRPY
CROUSE GAWSIE GENIAL HEARTY
HILARY JOCUND LIVELY BUOYANT
CHEERLY CHIPPER HOLIDAY
JOCULAR SMILING WINSOME
CHEERING CHIRRUPY EUPEPTIC
FRIENDLY GLADSOME HOMELIKE
SANGUINE SUNBEAMY SUNSHINE
(PREF.) HILARO

CHEERFULLY GLADLY CANTILY
CHEERLY JOLLILY LIGHTLY
CHEERLY GENIALLY
CHEERFULNESS JOY GLEE TAIT
CHEER CHERTE GAIETY GAYETY
LEVITY SPIRIT JOLLITY BUOYANCY
FESTIVAL GLADNESS HILARITY
CHEERING GLAD CORDIAL
CHEERFUL CHIRPING
CHEERLESS SAD BLAE COLD DIRE
DRAB GLUM GRAY BLEAK DREAR
ELYNG WASTE DISMAL DREARY
GLOOMY WINTRY DOLEFUL
FORLORN JOYLESS SUNLESS
DEJECTED DESOLATE LITHLESS
CHEER PINE CHIL
CHEERY BUXOM BRIGHT BOBBISH
GAYSOME
CHEESE OKA BLUE BRIE EDAM
FETA HAND JACK TRIP APPLE
BRICK COLBY CREAM DAISY
DERBY GOUDA GRANA KENNO
MAHON QUESO SWISS WHEEL
ZIEGA ZIGER ASIAGO BARRIE
BONDON BRYNZA BURGOS
CANTAL CASSAN DUNLOP
GLARUS JUNKET MYSOST
ROMANO RONCAL SAANEN
SBRINZ TILSIT ZAMORA ZIEGER
ANGELOT CHEDDAR CHEVRET
COTTAGE CROWDIE FONTINA
FROMAGE GJEDOST GRUYERE
KEBBUCK LASELVA PRIMOST
PROVOLA RICOTTA SAPSAGO
SERRANO STILTON TETILLA
TRUCKLE AMERICAN CABRALES
CHESHIRE EMMENTAL LONGHORN
MUENSTER PARMESAN PECORINO
RACLETTE SANSIMON SLIPCOAT
TRONCHON LEICESTER
MOUSETRAP PROVOLONE
ROQUEFORT WILTSHIRE
MOZZARELLA NEUFCHATEL
SERVILLETA
(— FANCIER) TUROPHILE
(— IN OATMEAL) CABOC
(INFERIOR —) DICK
(LARGE —) KEBBOC
(WELSH —) CAERPHILLY
(PREF.) TURO CASE(O) TYR(O)
CHEESEPARING STINGY
CHEESE VAT CHESSEL CHESSART
CHEESEWOOD BONEWOOD
WHITEWOOD
CHEETAH CAT OUNCE YOUSE
YOUZE GUEPARD
CHEF COOK COMMIS SAUCIER
CUISINIER
CHEFOO YENTAI
CHELA HAND MANUS NIPPER
PINCER
CHELATE COMPLEX
CHELICERA FALX FANG FALCER
MANDIBLE
CHELLIAN ABBEVILLIAN
CHELUBAI (FATHER OF —) HEZRON
CHEMICAL (ALSO SEE SPECIFIC
HEADINGS) ACID BASE SALT
ALKALI BLEACH CHEMIC DODGER
SAFENER ADDITIVE ALGICIDE
CATALYST DEHORNER
(PREF.) ACETO ALCO ALDO
AMIDO AMYL(I)(O) AZ(O) BENZ(O)

BOR(O) BROM(O) BUT(YR)(YRO)
CADM(I)(O) CAPRO CARB(O)
CHAVI(O) CUMO DIAZO DIOL
DUPLO EKA ESTERI FORM(O)
GLY(O) IDO IMIDO IMINO KER(O)
KET(O) LAUR LIP LYSO LYXO
MAL(O) MENTH(O) MERCUR(O)
METH MOLYBD MURIO NAPHTH
NITRATO NITRILO NITROSO NOR
OLEO ORTHO OSMIO OX OXAL(O)
OXIDI OXIDO OXIMIDO OXO OXY
OZO PENT(A) PERI PHLOR(O)
PHTHAL(O) PIPTO PLUMB(I)(O)
POLY PROP PROS PROTE(O)
PYRROL(O) SYN TOL(U)
(SUFF.) AMIN(E)(O) ANE ASE ATE
ENE ID(E) ILE INE INOL INONE ION
ITE ITOL IUM OIC OIN OL OLE
OLIC OLID(E) ON(E) ONIC ONIUM
OSAN OSE OSIDE OUS OYL PHORE
RETIN THIN(E) YL YNE ZYME
CHEMIN-DE-FER SHIMMY
CHEMISE SARK SHIFT SHIRT SIMAR
SMOCK CAMISA SHIMMY LINGERIE
CHEMISETTE SHAM GUIMPE
TUCKER PARTLET
CHEMIST ANALYST ASSAYER
CHEMICK BENCHMAN COLORIST
DRUGGIST
AMERICAN DOW ABEL CADY
DANA HALE HALL HARE HART
HUNT KING LAMB LIND LOEB
LONG REID UREY CLARK COOKE
CROSS DROWN DUMEZ FLORY
GOOCH HAMOR HERTY KRAUS
LEWIS LIBBY MOORE NOYES
POWER SEMON SMITH SNELL
STINE WILEY BROWNE BUCHER
BURTON CALVIN CLARKE CRAFTS
DORSET DUDLEY EGLOFF HOLMES
HOOVER LEVENE MENDEL
MORGAN MUNROE PALMER
ROBLIN ROGERS SHIMER TORREY
WARREN ALDRICH ANDREWS
ATWATER CASTNER CUSHMAN
DUSHMAN GIAUQUE GODLOVE
GOMBERG GUTHRIE HARKINS
KHORANA MIDGLEY ONSAGER
PAULING SEABORG SHERMAN
SLOSSON WHITNEY BANCROFT
BENEDICT CHANDLER COOLIDGE
COTTRELL FRANKLIN HORSFORD
LANGMUIR LIPSCOMB MCCOLLUM
MCMILLAN MULLIKEN RICHARDS
SILLIMAN SPRINGER STODDARD
WILLIAMS WOODWARD
ALEXANDER CAROTHERS
HENDERSON NIEUWLAND
PATTERSON CHITTENDEN
HILLEBRAND
AUSTRIAN KUHN EMICH PREGL
PRECHTL
BELGIAN STAS SOLVAY
BAEKELAND PRIGOGINE
CZECH BRAUNER HEYROVSKY
DANISH THOMSEN BRONSTED
KJELDAHL SORENSEN
DUTCH COHEN MULDER HOMBERG
ENGLISH ABEL BELL DAVY POPE
SWAN TODD ABNEY BOYLE
CROSS DAKIN HENRY MARSH
PROUT SODDY YOUNG BARTON
BRANDE DALTON DONNAN

GREGOR HARDEN MARTIN MILLER PERKIN PORTER RAMSAY THORPE TILDEN WATSON ANDREWS CROOKES DANIELL FARADAY HAWORTH HODGKIN NORRISH TENNANT TRAVERS HATCHETT PLAYFAIR ROBINSON WILLIAMS ARMSTRONG CORNFORTH FRANKLAND GLADSTONE PRIESTLEY WILKINSON HINSHELWOOD **FRENCH** BAUME BEHAL CONTE CURIE DUFAY DUMAS FREMY LEBEL LEBON WURTZ BALARD CLAUDE DARCET GERNEZ GUIMET LEMERY NAQUET ORFILA PERRIN PROUST RAOULT CHAPTAL DAUBENY FRIEDEL GLENARD LAURENT LEBLANC LUMIERE MACQUER MOISSAN PASTEUR PELOUZE THENARD BERTRAND CAVENTOU CHEVREUL COURTOIS DEBIERNE DEMARCAY FOURCROY FOURNEAU GERHARDT GRIGNARD KUHLMANN REGNAULT SABATIER BERTHELOT LAVOISIER LECLANCHE LENORMAND PELLETIER VAUQUELIN BERTHOLLET CHARDONNET DUBRUNFAUT LECHATELIER BOUSSINGAULT SCHUTZENBERGER **GERMAN** CARO HAHN KOPP MOND ALDER BOSCH DIELS EIGEN FRANK HABER KNORR KOLBE LUNGE MEYER STAHL ACHARD BAEYER BECHER BREDIG BUNSEN DOMAGK FITTIG GIESEL GRAEBE KOSSEL LIEBIG MAGNUS NERNST TRAUBE WOHLER BERGIUS BISCHOF BUCHNER CASSIUS CURTIUS ERDMANN FEHLING FISCHER GLAUBER HOFMANN OSTWALD TIEMANN WALLACH WIELAND WINDAUS ZIEGLER KLAPROTH MARGGRAF SPRENGEL BEILSTEIN BUTENANDT FRESENIUS LADENBURG LAMPADIUS SCHEIBLER SCHONBEIN STRASSMAN WIEDEMANN ZSIGMONDY BODENSTEIN DOBEREINER ERLENMEYER LIEBERMANN STAUDINGER STROHMEYER GOLDSCHMIDT UNVERDORBEN WILLSTATTER MITSCHERLICH **HUNGARIAN** HEVESY **IRISH** KIRWAN STEWART **ITALIAN** NATTA COVELLI FABRONI SOBRERO AVOGADRO CIAMICIAN CANNIZZARO BRUGNATELLI **JAPANESE** TAKAMINE **NORWEGIAN** WAAGE HASSEL GULDBERG **POLISH** MOSCICKI **RUSSIAN** BACH WALDEN SEMENOV BUTLEROV MENDELEV ZELINSKI **SCOTTISH** URE BELL BLACK BROWN DEWAR YOUNG BEILBY GRAHAM THOMSON **SPANISH** RODRIGUEZ **SWEDISH** CLEVE BERGMAN

SCHEELE MOSANDER SEFSTROM SVEDBERG ARRHENIUS BERZELIUS CRONSTEDT BLOMSTRAND ABDERHALDEN **SWISS** NEF GLASER KARRER MULLER PRELOG WERNER MARIGNAC SAUSSURE REICHSTEIN **CHEMOSTERILANT** METEPA **CHENAANAH (FATHER OF —)** BILHAN **CHENDE** CHINOA **CHENFISH** KINGFISH **CHENILLE** SNAIL **CHEQUEEN** BASKET SEQUIN ZEQUIN CECCHINE ZECCHINO **CHERAN (FATHER OF —)** DISHON **CHERAW** SARA **CHEREMIS** MARI **CHERISH** AID HUG PET BEAR DOTE HAVE HOPE LIKE LOVE SAVE ADORE BOSOM BROOD CHEER CLING COWER ENJOY NURSE PRIZE VALUE CARESS ESTEEM FADDLE FONDLE FOSTER GRUDGE HARBOR MOTHER NESTLE NUZZLE PAMPER PETTLE REVERE COMFORT EMBOSOM EMBRACE INDULGE NOURISH NURTURE PROTECT SUPPORT SUSTAIN ENSHRINE INSPIRIT PRESERVE TREASURE **CHERISHED** PET DEAR BOSOM DANDILY AFFECTED PRECIOUS **CHEROOT** MANILA TRICHI TRICHY **CHERRY** BING CHOP DUKE FUJI GEAN MERRY MOREL CORNEL MAZARD BURBANK CAPULIN CHAPMAN LAMBERT MAHALEB MARASCA MAYDUKE MORELLO OXHEART PITANGA WINDSOR AMARELLE DURACINE EGGBERRY LUKEWARD NAPOLEON ROSACEAN BIGARREAU MARASCHINO MONTMORENCY **CHERRY BLOSSOM** HEBE **CHERRY-COLORED** CERISE **CHERRY ORCHARD (AUTHOR OF —)** CHEKHOV **(CHARACTER IN —)** ANYA GAYEV VARYA YASHA DUNYASHA LOPAKHIN RANEVSKY TROFIMOV CHARLOTTE **CHERRY PLUM** MYROBALAN **CHERRY STONE** PAIP **CHERT** BOONE WHINSTONE **CHERUB** AMOR EROS ANGEL CUPID SERAPH SPIRIT AMORINO AMORETTO CHERUBIM **CHERVIL** BUN KECK ARFOIL CERFOIL COWWEED HONEWORT MILKWEED RATSBANE **CHESED (FATHER OF —)** NAHOR **CHESS** CHEAT SHOGI CHECKER SKITTLES **(— MOVE)** ZUGZWANG **CHESSBOARD** CHESS TABLE CHECKER **CHESSMAN** PIN KING PIECE CHECKER CHEQUER **(— SET)** MEINY MEINIE **(ANY — BUT PAWN)** OFFICER **(BISHOP —)** ALFIN ALPHIN ARCHER

(CASTLE —) JUEZ ROOK TOUR UDGE JUDGE LEDGE TOWER **(KNIGHT —)** HORSE CHEVALIER **(PAWN —)** PON POUNE **(QUEEN —)** FERS FIERS PHEARSE **CHEST** ARK BOX CUB FIX KIT PIX PYX ARCA BUST CAJA CASH CIST CYST FUND KIST SAFE SCOB AMBRY BAHUT BUIST CADDY FRONT HOARD HUTCH RAZEE SISTA TRUNK ALMOIN BASKET BREAST BUNKER BUREAU CAISSE CAJETA CASKET COFFER COFFIN FORCER GIRNAL GIRNEL HAMPER JORDAN LARNAX LOCKER LOWBOY SCRINE SHRINE SPRUCE STRIPE THORAX WANGAN BRAZIER BRISKET CAISSON CAPCASE CASSONE COMMODE DEPOSIT DRAWERS DRESSER ENCLOSE HIGHBOY TOOLBOX WANIGAN WINDBAG CISTVAEN CUPBOARD FORCELET MANIFOLD STANDARD TREASURE TREASURY **(— FOR CUTLERY)** CANTEEN **(— FOR FISH)** CAUF **(— OF ORES)** CAXON **(FRONT OF —)** BREAST **(MEDICINE —)** INRO **(PREF.)** STERN(O) STETH(O) THORAC(I)(O) **CHESTNUT** JOKE LING RATA BROWN HORSE CASTOR MARRON SATIVA CRENATA DENTATA **(HORSE —)** CONKER **(POLYNESIAN —)** RATA **(WATER —)** LING **(PREF.)** CASTANO **CHESTNUT-COLORED** BAY ROAN BADIOUS **CHEVAL-DE-FRISE** TURNPIKE **CHEVAL GLASS** PSYCHE **CHEVALIER** CADET NOBLE KNIGHT GALLANT CAVALIER HORSEMAN **CHEVIN** CHUB CHEVESNE **CHEVRON** BEAM MARK WOUND RAFTER STRIPE ZIGZAG **CHEVROTAIN** MUSK NAPU DEERLET KANCHIL MEMINNA PLANDOK TRAGULE BOOMORAH PEESOREH RUMINANT **CHEW** CUD EAT GUM TAW BITE CHAM CHAW GNAW NOSH QUID CHAMP CHONK GRIND MUNCH RUMEN CRUNCH MUMBLE CHUMBLE MEDITATE RUMINATE MANDUCATE **(— UP NOISILY)** CHANK GROUZE **CHEWINK** FINCH JOREE TOWHEE GRASSET **CHEYENNE** DOG **CHIAN** SCIAN **CHIANTI** FLORENCE **CHIASTOLITE** MACLE ANDALUSITE **CHIBCHA** MUISCA **CHIC** PERT POSH TRIG TRIM KIPPY NATTY NIFTY SMART CHICHI DAPPER GIGOLO MODISH ELEGANT STYLISH **CHICAGO** PORKOPOLIS **CHICANE** DECEPTION **CHICANERY** DIRT RUSE WILE FEINT TRICK ARTIFICE

INTRIGUE TRICKERY DECEPTION PETTIFOGGERY **CHICHI** TONY **CHICK** BIRD GIRL PEEP TICK CHILD NATTY POULET SCREEN SEQUIN SPROUT CHICKEN CHUCKIE **CHICKADEE** TOMTIT BLACKCAP TITMOUSE **CHICKAREE** BOOMER **CHICKEN** HEN KIP COCK FOWL BIDDY CAPON CHICK CHILD CHOOK CHUCK DEEDY FRYER LAYER MANOC POULT SILKY TIMID AFRAID CHICKY PULLET SULTAN SUSSEX TURKEN ANCOBAR BOARDER BROILER DIBBLER POUSSIN ROASTER ROOSTER SCRATCH ARAUCANA COCKEREL PHASANID SPRINGER **(— SHELTER)** MOTHER **CHICKEN COOP** CAVY CAVIE **CHICKEN POX** SOREHEAD VARICELLA **CHICK-PEA** CHIT GRAM CHICH CICER COWGRAM SOWGRAM GARBANZO GARVANCE **(PL.)** FASELS **CHICKWEED** BLINK BLINKS SPURRY ALLBONE STARWORT **CHICO** SAPODILLA **CHICORY** BUNK CREPIS ENDIVE SUCCORY WITLOOF BLUEWEED COMPOSIT **CHIDE** BAN FUSS RAIL RATE BLAME CHECK FLITE FLYTE SCOLD SNAP BERATE REBUFF REBUKE SCHOOL THREAP THREAT THREEP TONGUE CENSURE REPROVE UPBRAID WRANGLE ADMONISH BETONGUE LAMBASTE REPROACH **CHIEF** (ALSO SEE CHIEFTAIN) BO AGA BIG BOH CAP CID COB DUX MIR MOI TOP AGHA ALII ARCH ARII BOSS CAID CHEF COCK DATO DEAN DOEG DUCE DUKE HEAD HIER HIGH INCA JARL JEFE KAID KHAN KING MAIN MICO MOST NAIK ONLY QAID RAIS RAJA REIS TYEE ALDER ALPHA ARIKI DATTO ELDER FIRST GREAT MAJOR MATAI NAYAK PRIMA PRIME PRIMO RAJAH RULER THANE TITAN VITAL ZAQUE ZIPPA ADALID CABEZA DEPUTY FLAITH HEADLY INKOSI KEHAYA KUBERA KUVERA LEADER LULUAI MASTER MIRDHA NAIQUE PENLOP PRABHU PRIMAL RECTOR SACHEM SAYYID SHAYKH SHEIKH SHERIF STAPLE SUDDER TOPMAN TURNUS CAPITAL CAPTAIN CENTRAL EMINENT FOREMAN GENERAL HEADMAN INGOMAR LEADING LEMPIRA MUGWUMP OVERMAN PADRONE PALMARY POLYGAR PRELATE PREMIER PRIMARY SHEREEF STELLAR SUPREME TOPSMAN TRIBUNE CABOCEER CAPITANO CARDINAL DECURION DIRECTOR DOMINANT ELDORADO ESPECIAL FOREMOST GOVERNOR HEADSMAN HIERARCH INTIMATE MOKADDAM

PREMIERE SAGAMORE STAROSTA
SUBCHIEF PENDRAGON
(— IN INDIA) PRABHU SIRDAR
(— OF ADVOCATES) BATONNIER
(— OF RELIGIOUS ORDER) GENERAL
(— OF TITHING) BORSHOLDING
(— OF 10 MEN) DEAN
(CHINOOK —) TYEE
(CLAN —) TOISECH
(INDIAN —) SUNCK SACHEM
SUNCKE CACIQUE MOCUDDUM
SAGAMORE
(MOHAMMEDAN —) DATO DATTO
SAYID SAYYID
(SCHOOL —) DUX
(SCOTTISH —) MAORMOR
(TIBETAN —) POMBO
(TURKISH —) AGA AGHA
(PREF.) ARCH(I) PROT(O)
CHIEFLY MAINLY LARGELY
CHIEFTAIN BEG CHAM EMIR HEAD
JARL KHAN ASTUR CHIEF EMEER
LEADER SIRDAR CAUDILLO
HIAWATHA
CHIEFTAINCY STOOL CHIEFRY
CHIEFTAINESS QUEEN
CHIFFCHAFF PEGGY CHIPCHAP
CHIPCHOP
CHIFFON SHEER
CHIFFONIER BUREAU CABINET
COMMODE
CHIGGER BICHO PIQUE CHIGGA
CHIGOE GIGGER JIGGER LEPTUS
WHEELWORM
CHIGNON COB KNOT COBBE TWIST
CHIGOE SIKA BICHO NIGUA PIQUE
SCREW CHIGGA ENIGUA JIGGER
SANDBOY SANDWORM
CHIH FU PREFECT
CHILBLAIN KIBE MULE BLAIN
MOOLS MOULS PERNIO
CHILD BEN BOY BUD ELF GET IMP
KID LAD SON SOT TAD TOT WAY
BABA BABE BABY BATA BIRD
BRAT CHIT CION FOOD GIRL GYTE
PAGE PUSS TIKE TINY TOTO TROT
TYKE WEAN BAIRN BIRTH BROLL
BROWL CHICK CHIEL COOKY
ELFIN GAMIN ISSUE KEIKI OLIVE
POULT SCION TIDDY TRICK
WAYNE WENCH WHELP CHERUB
COLLOP COOKIE ENFANT FILIUS
FOSTER INFANT MOPPET NIPPER
PLEDGE PROLES STUMPY TACKER
TODDLE URCHIN BAMBINO
CHOOKIE CHOPPER CHRISOM
COCKNEY DICKENS GANGREL
GYTLING KINCHIN KITLING
LAMBKIN PAPOOSE PRETEEN
PROGENY STICHEL SUBTEEN
TIDDLER TODDLER TROTTIE
WRAWLER YOUNKER BANTLING
CHISELER DAUGHTER EPIGONUS
JUVENILE LITTLING NURSLING
PRATTLER RUNABOUT WEANLING
WHIMLING PRESCHOOLER
(— OF THE WORLD) WELTKIND
(— UNDER 7 YEARS) INFANS
(BAD-MANNERED —) GOOP
(BAPTISMAL —) CHRISOM
(CHUBBY —) CHUNK
(ELF'S —) AUF OAF CHANGELING
(FAVORITE —) BENJAMIN

(FOSTER —) DAULT NORRY NURRY
FOSTER REARLING
(ILLEGITIMATE —) MISHAP
BASTARD
(INNOCENT —) CHRISOM
(LAST-BORN —) DILLING
(LOVED —) JOY
(MERRY —) SUNBEAM
(MISCHIEVOUS —) IMP LIMB TIKE
DICKENS
(NAKED —) SCUDDY
(NEWBORN —) NEONATE
STRANGER
(PAUPER —) MINDER
(PLAYFUL —) ELF WANTON
(PLUMP —) FOB FUB
(PRECOCIOUS —) PRODIGY
(PURE —) DOVE
(ROWDY —) HOODLUM
(SMALL —) TAD TOT MITE SPUD
GAITT KIDDY TIDDY TOTUM
KIDLET PEEWEE TACKER BAIRNIE
(SPOILED —) CADE COSSET
WANTON COCKNEY
(STUNTED —) URF
(TROUBLESOME —) PICKLE STICHEL
(UNMANNERLY —) SMATCHET
(YOUNG —) BABY JOEY INFANT
SQUIRT GANGREL NESTLER
TODDLER BANTLING INNOCENT
LITTLING SUCKLING
(YOUNGEST —) WRIG DILLING
(PREF.) INFANTI PAED(O) PAID(O)
PED(O) TECHNO TECNO TEKNO
CHILDBED JIZZEN
CHILDBIRTH LABOR CRYING
INLYING TRAVAIL OXYTOCIA
(— WOMAN) PUERPERA
(PREF.) LOCHIO LOCHO TOCO
TOKO
(SUFF.) TOCIA TOCO(US) TOKIA
TOKO(US)
CHILDHOOD INFANCY CHILDAGE
(2ND —) DOTAGE TWICHILD
CHILDISH TID WEAK DANSY NAIVE
PETTY SILLY YOUNG CHITTY
PULING SIMPLE WEANLY ASININE
BABYISH CHILDLY FOOLISH
KIDDISH PEEVISH PROGENY
PUERILE UNMANLY BAIRNISH
BRATTISH IMMATURE TOOTLING
CHILDLESS ORBATE
CHILDREN ISSUE PROLES STRAIN
PROGENY OFFSPRING
(NUMBER OF —) PARITY
(SUFF.) PAEDES
CHILE SOCOMPA
(— INDIAN) FUEGIAN

CHILE

BAY: COOK EYRE NENA TARN
LOMAS OTWAY SARCO DARWIN
INUTIL MORENO STOKES
TONGOY DYNELEY INGLESA
SKYRING DESOLATE
CAPE: DYER HORN CHOROS
HORNOS QUILAN TABLAS
DESEADO BASCUNAN
CARRANZA
CAPITAL: SANTIAGO
CHANNEL: ANCHO CHEAP BEAGLE
COCKBURN MORALEDA
COIN: PESO LIBRA

CONDOR ESCUDO
DESERT: ATACAMA
GULF: ANCUD GUAFO PENAS
ARAUCO
INDIAN: ONA AUCA INCA ONAN
ARAUCA CHANGO YAHGAN
FUEGIAN MAPUCHE MOLUCHE
PAMPEAN PATAGON RANQUEL
ALIKULUF PICUNCHE
TSONECAN
ISLAND: LUZ PRAT BYRON GUAFO
HOSTE MOCHA NUEVA NUNEZ
VIDAL CHILOE DAWSON EASTER
LENNOX PIAZZI PICTON QUILAN
RIESCO STOSCH TALCAN
ANGAMOS CAMPANA HANOVER
REFUGIO TRANQUI CLARENCE
HUAMBLIN NALCAYEC
NAVARINO TRAIGUEN
ISLANDS: CHONOS HERMITE
PAJAROS CHAUQUES
ISTHMUS: OFQUI
LAKE: TORO RANCO YELCHO
PUYEHUE RUPANCO
MEASURE: VARA LEGUA LINEA
CUADRA FANEGA
MOUNTAIN: MACA TORO CHATO
MAIPO PAINE POTRO PULAR
TORRE YOGAN APIWAN
BURNEY CONICO JERVIS
POQUIS RINCON CHALTEL
COPIAPO FITZROY PALPANA
VELLUDA COCHRANE
TRONADOR YANTELES
MOUNTAINS: ANDES DARWIN
ALMEIDA DOMEYKO
NATIVE: PATAGONIAN
PENINSULA: HARDY LACUY TAITAO
TUMBES
POINT: TORO GALLO LILES LOBOS
LOROS MORRO TALCA TETAS
VIEJA CACHOS GALERA MOLLES
ANGAMOS LAVAPIE
PORT: LOTA TOME ARICA
COQUIMBO
PROVINCE: AISEN ARICA AYSEN
MAULE NUBLE TALCA ARAUCO
BIOBIO CAUTIN CHILOE CURICO
OSORNO ATACAMA LINARES
MALLECO COQUIMBO OHIGGINS
SANTIAGO TARAPACA VALDIVIA
RIVER: LOA LAJA YALI ALHUE
AZAPA BRAVO BUENO ELQUI
ITATA LAUCA LLUTA MAIPO
MAULE PUELO RAHUE RAPEL
VITOR BIOBIO CAMINA CHOAPA
CHOROS CISNES COLINA
HUASCO LIMARI MORADO
PALENA POSCUA TOLTEN
COPIAPO VALDIVIA
SHRUB: LITRE
STRAIT: NELSON MAGELLAN
TOWN: BOCO CUYA LEBU LOTA
OCOA TOCO TOME ARICA
TALCA ARAUCO CURICO
GATICO OSORNO SERENA
TEMUCO VICUNA YUMBEL
YUNGAY CALDERA CHILLAN
COPIAPO COQUIMBO
RANCAGUA SANTIAGO
VALDIVIA
TREE: RAULI
VOLCANO: LANIN MAIPO ANTUCO

LASCAR LLAIMA OSORNO
OYAHUE TACORA LAUTARO
PETEROA SOCOMAP VILLARICA
GUALLATIRI
WEIGHT: GRANO LIBRA QUINTAL
WIND: SURES

CHILEAB (FATHER OF —) DAVID
(MOTHER OF —) ABIGAIL
CHILE-BELLS COPIHUE LAPAGERIA
CHI-LIN KYLIN UNICORN
CHILION (DAUGHTER OF —) ORPAH
(MOTHER OF —) NAOMI
CHILL ICE RAW AGUE COLD COOL
DAZY ALGID ALGOR DAVER GELID
OURIE RIGOR SCHEL SHAKE
FRAPPE FREEZE FRIGID FROSTY
SHIVER SNELLY DEPRESS FRETISH
FRISSON MALARIA COLDNESS
CHILLED ACOLD CHILL FROZEN
STARVEN
CHILLING ICY COLD EERY BLEAK
EERIE NIPPY CHILLY WINTRY
GLACIAL NIPPING SHIVERY
CHILLY RAW COLD COOL LASH
ALGID BLEAK HUNCH NIPPY
PARKY AGUISH AIRISH ARCTIC
CRIMMY FROSTY FROZEN LEEPIT
CAULDRIFE
CHIMAERA BELUE DRAGON
CATFISH PLACOID RATFISH
RATTAIL DOODSKOP
CHIME DIN RIM BELL EDGE PEAL
RING SUIT TING TINK AGREE
CHIMB CHINE PRATE ACCORD
CLOCHE CYMBAL JINGLE MELODY
CONCORD HARMONY SINGSONG
(PL.) BELL
CHIMER CYMAR SIMAR CHIMAR
TABARD
CHIMERA FANCY MIRAGE MOSAIC
POMATO ILLUSION
CHIMERICAL VAIN WILD INSANE
UTOPIAN DELUSIVE FANCIFUL
ROMANTIC IMAGINARY
CHIMNEY BAG LUM TUN FLUE
LUMM PIPE TUBE VENT GULLY
STACK STALK TEWEL CHIMLA
FUNNEL LOUVER SMOKER
TUNNEL FISSURE OPENING
ORIFICE FUMIDUCT SMOKESTACK
CHIMNEY CAP TURNCAP
CHIMNEY CORNER FIRESIDE
INGLENOOK
CHIMNEY COWL COW
CHIMNEY HOOD JACK
CHIMNEY PIECE PAREL
CHIMNEY PIPE TALLBOY
CHIMNEY POST SPEER
CHIMNEY SEAT SCONCE
CHIMNEY SWEEP SWEEP
CHUMMY FLUEMAN RAMONEUR
CHIMPANZEE APE CHIMP JACKO
JOCKO PIGMY PYGMY NCHEGA
PIGMEW PYGMEAN
CHIN JAW CHAT TSIN MENTUM
CHOLLER
(— POINT) MENTON POGONION
(DOUBLE —) BUCCULA CHOLLER
(PREF.) GENIO MENTI MENTO
CHINA WARE JAPAN LENOX SPODE
CATHAY PARIAN SEVRES
CERAMIC CHEENEY DRESDEN

LIMOGES MEISSEN POTTERY
CINCHONA CROCKERY EGGSHELL

CHINA

ABORIGINE: YAO MANS MIAO
MANTZU YAOMIN MIAOTSE
AREA UNIT: MU MOU MOW
BASIN: TARIM
BAY: LAICHOW HANGCHOW
BUDDHA: FO
CAPE: OLWANPI
CAPITAL: PEKING TAIPEI PEIPING
CHANNEL: BASHI
COIN: PU CASH CENT MACE TAEL
TIAO YUAN CHIAO SYCEE
DOLLAR
DEPRESSION: TURFAN
DESERT: GOBI ORDOS SHAMO
ALASHAN TAKLAMAKAN
DIALECT: WU MIN AMOY HAKKA
CANTON HSIANG SWATOW
FOOCHOW WENCHOW
KANHAKKA MANDARIN
DRY LAKE: LOPNOR
DYNASTY: WU HAN SHU SUI WEI
YIN CHIN CHOU HSIA HSIN
MING SUNG TANG YUAN CHING
SHANG
GULF: POHAI CHIHLI TONKIN
PECHILI LIAOTUNG
ISLAND: AMOY FLAT MACAO
MATSU NAMKI CHUSAN
HAINAN PRATAS QUEMOY
TAIWAN YUHWAN FORMOSA
HUNGTOW TUNGSHA
CHOUCHAN KULANGSU
STAUNTON
ISLANDS: PENGHU TACHEN
CHUSHAN MIAOTAO
LAKE: TAI CHAO KAOYU OLING
TELLI BAMTSO BORNOR EBINOR
ERRHAI KHANKA LOPNOR
NAMTSO POYANG CHALING
HUNGTSE KARANOR KOKONOR
HULUNNOR MONTCALM
TAROKTSO TELLINOR TIENCHIH
TSINGHAI TUNGTING
MEASURE: HO HU KO LI MU PU TO
TU FAN FEN PAU TOU TUN YIN
CHIH FANG KISH PARA QUEI
SHIH TSUN CHANG CHING
SHENG SHING CHUPAK
KUNGHO KUNGLI KUNGMU
KUNGFEN KUNGYIN KUNGCHIH
MOUNTAIN: OMI OMEI SUNG
KAILAS POBEDA EVEREST
MUZTABH SUNGSHAN
MOUNTAINS: ALTAY KUNLUN
ALASHAN KUENLUN MEILING
MINSHAN NANLING NANSHAN
TANGLHA BOGDOULA
HIMALAYA TAPASHAN
TAYULING TIENSHAN
WUYLISHAN
NAME: CATHAY
NATIVE: PAT
PENINSULA: LEICHU LUICHOW
LIAOTUNG
PORT: AMOY WUHU AIGUN SHASI
ANTUNG CANTON CHEFOO
DAIREN ICHANG NINGPO
PAKHOI SWATOW SZEMAO
WUCHOW YOCHOW FOOCHOW

HUNCHUN MENGTSZ NANKING
SAMSHUI SANTUAO SOOCHOW
WENCHOW CHANGSHA
HANGCHOW KIUKIANG
KONGMOON LUNGCHOW
SHANGHAI TENGYUEH TIENTSIN
TSINGTAO WANHSIEN
PROVINCE: HONAN HOPEI HUNAN
HUPEI HUPEN JEHOL KANSU
KIRIN TIBET ANHWEI FUKIEN
SHANSI SHENSI TAIWAN
YUNNAN KIANGSI KWANGSI
NGANHUI CHEKIANG
KWEICHOW LIAONING
MONGOLIA SHANTUNG
SZECHWAN TSINGHAI
MANCHURIA
RELIGION: JU SHINTO TAOISM
BUDDHISM
RESERVOIR: SUNGARI
RIVER: SI HAN ILI MIN NEN PEI
WEI AMUR HUAI LOHO TUNG
YALU YUAN YUEN ARGUN
FENHO MACHU PEIHO TARIM
TUMEN WEIHO CHUMAR
DRECHU DZACHU KHOTAN
KUMARA LIAOHO MANASS
MEKONG OCHINA URUNGU
YELLOW HOANGHO HWANGHO
KERULEN KIALING SALWEEN
SIKIANG SUNGARI TSANGPO
WUKIANG YANGTZE YARKAND
YUKIANG CHERCHEN HANKIANG
HUNGSHUI MINKIANG
RULER: WANG
SEA: ECHINA SCHINA YELLOW
STRAIT: HAINAN TAIWAN
FORMOSA
TOWN: BAI NOH AHPA AMOY ANSI
ANTA AQSU FUYU GUMA HAMI
HUMA HOPE KIAN KISI LINI LOHO
LUTA MOHO MOYU MULI NIYA
NOHO NURA OMIN OWPU RIMA
SAKA SIAN TALI TAYU WUHU
WUSU WUTU YAAN CHIAI
FUSIN HOFEI ICHUN JEHOL
KIRIN KOKLU LHASA MACAO
PENKI SHASI TAIAN TALAI
TUTZE TUYUN TZEPO WUHAN
WUSIH YENKI YULIN YUMEN
ANSHAN ANTUNG CANTON
CHENDU DAIREN FUCHAU
FUSHUN HANKOW HANTAN
HARBIN HOIHOW KALGAN
LOYANG LUSHUN MUKDEN
NINGPO PAOTOW PEKING
PENGPU SUCHOW SWATOW
TAINAN TAIPEI TALIEN TSINAN
YUNNAN CHUNGTU FATSHAN
FOOCHOW HANYANG HUHEHOT
KAIFENG KUNMING KWEISUI
LANCHOW NANKING PAOTING
PEIPING SOOCHOW TAIYUAN
TIANJIN TZEKUNG URUMCHI
WUCHANG YENPING
CHANGSHA CHAOCHOW
CHENGTEH CHINCHOW
HANGCHOW KIAOCHOW
KWEIYANG NANCHANG
QARAQASH SHANGHAI
SHENYANG SIANGTAN
TANGSHAN TENGCHOW
TIENTSIN TSINGTAO

TUNGCHOW CHUNGKING
WEIGHT: LI TA FAN FEN HAO KIN
SSU TAN YIN CHEE CHIN DONG
MACE SHIH TAEL CATTY CHIEN
LIANG PICUL TCHIN HAIKWAN
KUNGFEN KUNGSSU KUNGCHIN

CHINABERRY LILAC AZEDARACH
CHINABALL SOAPBERRY
CHINA BLUE NIKKO
CHINA HAT HAELTZUK HEILTSUK
CHINAMAN CHOW JOHN JOHNNY
CELESTIAL
(PL.) TANKA
CHINA ROSE MANETTI HIBISCUS
CHINA STONE PETUNSE
CHINA TREE LILAC HAGBUSH
CHINCHILLA ABROCOME
VIZCACHA
CHINE BACK IKAT CHINK CRACK
CREST GORGE RIDGE SPINE
CLEAVE RAVINE SPROUT CREVICE
CHINESE PAT BABA CHOW CERAI
CHINK SERES SERIC SINIC
MANZAS MONGOL ASIATIC
CATAIAN CHINOIS PIGTAIL
SANGLEY
(PREF.) CHINO SINICO SINO
CHINESE ARTICHOKE CROSNE
CHOROGI CROSNES STACHYS
KNOTROOT
CHINESE CABBAGE PECHAY
PAKCHOI
CHINESE DATE BER JUJUBE
CHINESE GELATIN AGAR
CHING TSING
CHINGPAW KACHIN SINGPHO
YAWYINS
CHINIOFON YATREN
CHINK GAP BORE CASH CHAP COIN
JINK KINK RENT RIFT RIME SCAR
BOORE CHECK CHINE CHUNK
CLEFT CRACK GRIKE KNACK
MONEY CRANNY RICTUS SPRAIN
CHINKLE CREVICE FISSURE
APERTURE
CHINPIECE BARBEL
CHINQUAPIN OAK BONNET
BONNETS CANDOCK CHESTNUT
WANKAPIN YOCKERNUT
CHINTZ PINTADO SALAMPORE
CHIONE (FATHER OF —) BOREAS
DAEDALION
(HUSBAND OF —) NEPTUNE
(MOTHER OF —) ORITHYIA
DAEDALION
(SLAYER OF —) DIANA
(SON OF —) EUMOLPUS
AUTOLYCUS PHILAMMON
CHIOT SCIOT
CHIP BIT CPU CUT DIB GAG HEW
NIG BONE CHAP CLIP HACK KNAP
KNOP NICK PARE SAND SKIN SNIP
SNUB BEACH CHECK CRACK
FLAKE PIECE SCRAP SKELF SLICE
SPALE SPALL SPALT SPAWL SPELL
SPOON WASTE BORING CHISEL
GALLET MARKER NOODLE
COUNTER SHAVING CHIPPING
COSSETTE FRAGMENT SPLINTER
WHITLING
(— OF SOLDER) LINK
(— OF WOOD) SPOON

(— OUT) DESEAM
(BUFFALO —S) BODEWASH
(CORN —S) FRITOS
(POTATO —) CRISP
(SUPPLY OF —S) STACK
CHIPMAN SCRAPMAN
CHIPMUNK CHIPPY GOPHER
GRINNY HACKEE GRINNIE
SQUIRREL
CHIPPENDALE AFGHAN
CHIPPER GAY SPRY CHIRP PERKY
BABBLE COCKEY FIERCE HACKER
KIPPER LIVELY CHATTER CHIRRUP
TWITTER CHEERFUL
CHIPPINGS SWARF
CHIRO BONYFISH FRANCESCA
CHIROGRAPHY WRITING
CHIRON (— AS CONSTELLATION)
SAGITTARIUS
(FATHER OF —) SATURN
(MOTHER OF —) PHILYRA
CHIROPODIST PEDICURE
CORNCUTTER
CHIRP PEW PIP PEEK PEEP PIPE
PULE TWIT WEAK CHEEP CHELP
CHIRK CHIRL CHIRM CHIRT
TWEET TWINK CHIPPER CHIRRUP
CHITTER REJOICE SHATTER
TWEEDLE TWITTER WHEETLE
WHITTER
CHIRR PITTER
CHIRU SUS
CHISEL BUR CUT GAD CHIP ETCH
FORM MOIL PARE SEAT SETT
TANG TOOL BRUZZ BURIN CARVE
CHEAT DROVE GOUGE HARDY
POINT SCOOP SLICK STIFF
BROACH CHESIL FIRMER FORMER
GRAVEL HAGGLE POMMEL
QUARRY REAMER TOOLER
BARGAIN BOASTER BOLSTER
CHIPPER ENGRAVE GRADINE
GRUBBER POINTER QUARREL
SCOOPER SCORPER SHINGLE
CROSSCUT SPLITTER
(BLACKSMITH'S —) HARDY HARDIE
(FLINT —) TRANCHET
(ICE —) SPUD
(JEWELER'S —) SCAUPER SCORPER
(PREHISTORIC —) CELT
(STONEMASON'S —) TOOL DROVE
POMMEL TOOLER SPLITTER
(TOOTHED —) GRADINE
(TRIANGULAR —) BUR BURR
(WHEELWRIGHT'S —) BRUZZ
(PREF.) CELTI
CHISELER CHEAT CROOK COYOTE
GOUGER
CHISLON (SON OF —) ELIDAD
CHIT DAB TAB BILL NOTE DRAFT
LETTER VOUCHER
CHITARRONE ARCHLUTE
CHITCHAT GAB GASH GUFF TALK
BANTER GOSSIP GOSSIPRY
BAVARDAGE
CHITINOUS SHELLY
CHITON EXOMIS DIPLOIS EXOMION
CHITTAMWOOD IRONWOOD
CHIVALROUS BRAVE CIVIL NOBLE
PREUX GENTLE POLITE GALLANT
GENTEEL VALIANT WARLIKE
KNIGHTLY
CHIVE CIVE SIVE CIVET

SITHE ALLIUM
CHIVY RUN VEX BAIT HUNT RACE CHASE CHEVY TEASE BADGER CHIVVY FLIGHT HARASS PURSUE PURSUIT SCAMPER TORMENT MANEUVER
CHLOASMA MOTH
CHLOR LEMON
CHLORDIAZEPOXIDE LIBRIUM
CHLORIDE BUTTER CALOMEL MURIATE ALEMBROTH
CHLORINE OXYGEN
CHLORION SPHEX
CHLORIS (BROTHER OF —) AMYCLAS
(FATHER OF —) AMPHION
(HUSBAND OF —) NELEUS ZEPHYRUS
(MOTHER OF —) NIOBE
(SON OF —) NESTOR
CHLORITE AMESITE
CHOANA COLLAR
CHOBDAR USHER CHOPDAR
CHOCK COG PAD BLOCK BRACE CHUCK CLEAT SPOKE SPRAG WEDGE SCOTCH
(PL.) STOWWOOD
CHOCOLATE BUD CANDY COCOA NORFOLK JACOLATT
CHOGAK SHOQ
CHOICE BET ODD TRY BEST FINE FORE GOOD MIND PICK RARE WALE WEAL WILL CREAM ELITE PRIME VOICE CHOSEN DAINTY DESIRE FLOWER OPTION PICKED PLUMMY SELECT DILEMMA ELEGANT EXCERPT PERMISS DELICATE ELECTION EXIMIOUS UNCOMMON VOLITION RECHERCHE PREFERENCE
(FAVORITE —) STANDBY
(FREE —) SWING DRUTHERS
CHOICEST PRIMROSE
CHOIR KERE QUIRE CHAPEL CHORUS CHORALE CONCERT KAPELLE PSALMODY
CHOIRBOY CLERGEON CHORISTER
CHOIR LEADER CANTOR CHORAGUS CHORISTER PRECENTOR
CHOIRMASTER CHORAGUS
CHOKE DAM GAG GOB CLOG DAMP PLUG QUAR STOP WARP CHECK CHOCK CLOSE GRAIN GRANE SCRAG WORRY ACCLOY HINDER IMPEDE STIFLE SWARVE CONGEST QUACKLE QUEAZEN QUERKEN REPRESS SILENCE SMOLDER SMOTHER OBSTRUCT QUEASOME SCUMFISH STOPPAGE STRANGLE SUPPRESS THROTTLE
(— OFF) BESET
(— UP) CLOY GORGE STUFF
CHOKEBERRY DOGBERRY SOAPBERRY
CHOKED FOUL WOOLY WOOLLY CLOTTED
CHOKEDAMP STYTHE BLACKDAMP
CHOKERMAN CHAINER CHAINMAN
CHOKWE KIOKO
CHOLER IRE BILE FURY RAGE ANGER WRATH SPLEEN TEMPER DISTEMPER
CHOLERIC MAD ANGRY CROSS

FIERY HUFFY TESTY FUMISH IREFUL TOUCHY BILIOUS ENRAGED IRACUND PEEVISH PEPPERY WASPISH WRATHFUL IMPATIENT
CHOLIAMB SCAZON
CHONDRIOME CYTOME
CHOOSE OPT TRY CHAP CULL LIKE LIST LOVE LUST PICK TAKE VOTE WALE WEAL ADOPT ELECT PRICK ANOINT DECIDE PLEASE PREFER SELECT EMBRACE ESPOUSE EXTRACT SEPARATE
CHOOSY PICKY CHOICY FINICAL
CHOP AX AXE CUT HAG HEW JAW LOP CHAP CHIP DICE GASH HACK HASH HOWL RIVE SLIT CARVE CLEFT CRACK KNOCK MINCE NOTCH SLASH STAMP TRADE TRUCK WHANG BARTER CHANGE CLEAVE INCISE EXCHANGE
(— OFF) SNIG
(— SMALL) DEVIL MINCE
(— UP) HACKLE
(— WITH DULL AX) BUTTE
(DOG'S —) FLEW
(PORK —) GRISKIN
CHOPINE CIOPPINO PANTOFLE
CHOPPED CUT CHAPPED
CHOPPER SAX MINCER CLEAVER SLASHER TRANCHET
CHOPPINESS CHOP JABBLE
CHOPPING BLOCK HACKLOG
CHOPPING TOOL (— CULTURE) SOAN SOHAN
CHOPPY BUMPY LOPPY LUMPY PECKY ROUGH SHORT POPPLY
CHORAL (— SOCIETY) ORPHEON
CHORD CORD DYAD ROLL TONE CORDE NERVE TRIAD TRINE ACCORD STRING TENDON TETRAD CADENCE CONCORD HARMONY ARPEGGIO DIAMETER FILAMENT SFORZANDO
CHORDATA VERTEBRA
CHORE JOB JOT CHAR DUTY TASK CHARE KNACK STINT ERRAND BUSINESS
CHOREA JUMP JERKS
CHOREOGRAPHY TERPSICHORE
CHORION SEROSA
CHORISTER SINGER CHANTER CHOIRBOY
CHORUS SONG CHOIR DRONE QUIRE ACCORD ASSENT BURDEN UNISON CHORALE HOLDING REFRAIN RESPONSE THYMELICI
(— IN PLAY) GREX
CHOSEN ELECT ELITE SORTED ELECTED FANCIED AFFECTED SELECTED
(PREF.) LECTO
CHOUGH COW CHANK CHEWET CORBIE CHOCARD
CHOWRY COWTAIL
CHRISM CREAM CREME MURON MYRON
CHRIST X KING LORD TRUE JUDGE RANSOM VERITY MESSIAH SAVIOUR DRIGHTEN PARAMOUR
(INFANT —) BAMBINO
CHRISTEN NAME KIRSEN BAPTIZE
CHRISTENING GOSSIPING

CHRISTIAN XN XT XTIAN UNIATE GENTILE THOMEAN CHRISTEN EBIONITE GALILEAN MELCHITE NAZARENE ORIENTAL STONEITE TRADITOR COLOSSIAN
(JEWISH —) JUDAIZER
(PL.) FLOCK LAPSED ACEPHALI FAITHFUL
CHRISTIANIA CRISTY
CHRISTIANITY WAY XTY XNTY
CHRISTMAS NOEL YULE HOLIDAY NATIVITY YULETIDE MIDWINTER
CHRISTMAS ROSE BEARFOOT LUNGWORT MELAMPOD PEDELION
CHRISTOPHE COLOMB (COMPOSER OF —) MILHAUD
CHRIST'S-THORN NABK JUJUBE ZIZYPHUS
CHROMA COLOR QUALITY
CHROMATIC HUEFUL FLAMING SEMITONAL
CHROMATOPHORE ALLOPHORE LIPOPHORE UNIVALENT RHODOPLAST
CHROMOLITHOGRAPH OLEOGRAPH
CHROMOSOME DIAD DYAD IDANT HOMOLOG ALLOSOME AUTOSOME IDIOSOME MONOSOME KARYOMERE LEPTONEMA PLANOSOME
(PL.) GEMINI
(SUFF.) (HAVING — NUMBER) PLOID
CHROMOSPHERE SIERRA
CHRONIC FIXED SEVERE INTENSE CONSTANT STUBBORN
CHRONICLE BRUT ANNAL DIARY ENACT RECORD ACCOUNT HISTORY RECITAL CORNICLE REGISTER
(PL.) ANNALS ARCHIVE PARALIPOMENON
CHRONICLER WRITER CHRONIST COMPILER RECORDER HISTORIAN SEANNACHIE
CHRONOLOGICAL TEMPORAL
CHRONOMETER DIAL HACK CLOCK TIMER WATCH
CHRYSAL FRET
CHRYSALIS KELL PUPA AURELIA
CHRYSANTHEMUM MUM KIKU OXEYE SPOON BRUTUS POMPON KIKUMON KIRIMON AZALEAMUM PYRETHRUM MARGUERITE
CHRYSEIS (FATHER OF —) CHRYSES
CHRYSIN FLAVONE
CHRYSIPPUS (FATHER OF —) PELOPS
(MOTHER OF —) ASTYOCHE
(SLAYER OF —) HIPPODAMIA
CHRYSOBERYL CATEYE CHRYSOPAL CYMOPHANE
CHRYSOLITE OLIVINE PERIDOT CHRYSOPAL
CHRYSOTILE ASBESTOS
CHTHONIAN INFERNAL
CHUB DACE DOLT FOOL KIYI LOUT POLL CHOPA CHEVIN SHINER CYPRINID FALLFISH MACKEREL CHAVENDER HORNYHEAD

CHUBBY FAT CHUFF FUBSY PLUMP PUDGY CHOATY CHUFFY PLUMPY ROTUND ROLYPOLY
CHUB MACKEREL TINK TINKER HARDHEAD SCOMBRID
CHUCK HEN LOG PIG CHUG GRUB HURL JERK LUMP TOSS CHOCK CLUCK PITCH THROW BOUNCE CHUCKY COLLET CHUCKLE DISCARD
CHUCK-A-LUCK SWEAT HAZARD BIRDCAGE
CHUCKER CROZER
CHUCK-FARTHING CHUCK KNICKER
CHUCKHOLE CAHOT CHUGHOLE
CHUCKLE CHUCK CLUCK EXULT LAUGH GIGGLE GIZZEN KECKLE SMUDGE TITTER CHORTLE
CHUD VEPS VEPSE
CHUDDAR PHULKARI
CHUFA SEDGE GLUMAL CYPRESS EARTHNUT GALANGAL TIGERNUT GROUNDNUT
CHUM CAD PAL BAIT MATE PARD TOLE TOLL BUDDY BUTTY CRONY SPROG AIKANE CHUMMY COBBER COPAIN FRIEND PARDNER ROOMMATE
(— AROUND) HOBNOB
CHUMMY GREAT MATEY PALLY FAMILIAR
CHUMP ASS DOLT HEAD BLOCK PUMPKIN ENDPIECE SCHLEMIEL
CHUNCHO CHAMA
CHUNK DAB DAD FID GOB PAT WAD JUNK JUNT SLUG CHOCK CHUCK CLAUT PIECE THROW WHANG WHANK GOBBET DORNICK KNUCKLE LUNCHEON
CHUNKY LUMPY PLUMP SQUAT STOUT THICK TRUSS BLOCKY CHUBBY STOCKY CHUNKED
CHURCH DOM SEE DOME FANE FOLD HIGH KILL KIRK KURK TERA ABBEY AUTEM FAITH FLOCK KOVIL SAMAJ TITLE BETHEL CHAPEL CHARGE HIERON SPOUSE TEMPLE EDIFICE FANACLE IGLESIA LATERAN MEMORIA MINSTER ORATORY RECTORY STATION TEMPLET BASILICA EBENEZER ECCLESIA PECULIAR PROCATHEDRAL
(— BOOK) TRIODION
(CHRISTIAN —) BODY ISRAEL HERITAGE
(PREF.) ECCLESI(O) ECCLESIASTICO
CHURCHMAN KIRKMAN
(HIGH —) PUSEYITE PRELATIST
(LOW —) SIM LOWBOY SIMEONITE
CHURCH SERVICE HEARING TENEBRAE
CHURCHWARDEN STRAW WARDEN WARNER
CHURCHYARD HAW LITTEN CEMETERY KIRKYARD
CHURL CAD MAN BOOR CARL GNOF HIND LOUT SERF CARLE CEORL CHUFF GNOFF KNAVE MISER BODACH CARLOT HARLOT LUBBER RUSTIC VASSAL YEOMAN

BONDMAN FREEMAN HASKARD HUSBAND NIGGARD PEASANT VILLAIN VILLEIN CURMUDGEON

CHURLISH MEAN BLUFF GRUFF ROUGH RUNTY SURLY URSAL CRABBY RUSTIC SORDID SULLEN VULGAR BOORISH CARLAGE CARLISH CRABBED CURRISH DOGGISH INCIVIL PEEVISH VIOLENT

CHURN BEAT BOIL KIRN MOIL STIR DRILL SHAKE BUBBLE SEETHE AGITATE BARATTE TRUNDLE

CHUTE RUSH SLIP TUBE FLUME HURRY RAPID SHOOT SLIDE HOPPER TROUGH DECLINE DESCENT DOWNFALL STAMPEDE TELEGRAPH
(— MINING) PASS TELEGRAPH

CHUZA (WIFE OF —) JOANNA

CIBOL SYBO ONION SYBOW SHALLOT

CIBORIUM PIX PYX CANOPY CIVORY COFFER CIMBORIO

CICADA CAD CIGALE JARFLY LOCUST TETTIX LYREMAN HOMOPTER

CICATRICE FESTER

CICATRICLE TREAD GALLATURE

CICATRIX EYE MARK SCAB SCAR SEAM

CICATRIZE FESTER SCARIFY

CICELY MYRRH

CICERO TULLY

CICERONE GUIDE PILOT MENTOR ORATOR COURIER SIGHTSMAN

CICERONIAN TULLIAN

CID HERO CAMPEADOR
(AUTHOR OF —) CORNEILLE
(CHARACTER IN —) GOMES DIEGUE SANCHE CHIMENE FERNAND URRAQUE RODRIGUE

CID, EL (COMPOSER OF —) MASSENET

CIDER PERRY PERKIN SWANKY SYDDIR POMMAGE SCRUMPY BEVERAGE COCCAGEE
(HARD —) APPLEJACK
(INFERIOR —) SWANKY

CIGAR PURO TOBY WEED BREVA CLARO SEGAR SHUCK SMOKE CONCHA CORONA HAVANA MADURA MADURO MANILA STOGIE TWOFER BOUQUET CHEROOT CULEBRA LONDRES REGALIA TRABUCO COLORADO LOCOFOCO PANATELA PERFECTO PICKWICK PURITANO
(PART OF —) BAND FOOT HEAD TUCK FILLER WRAPPER

CIGARETTE CIG FAG BIRI BUTT KING PILL SKAG CUBEB JOINT SHUCK SMOKE GASPER REEFER CIGARITO
(— BUTT) ROACH
(MARIHUANA —) JOINT STICK
(PART OF —) BAND FOOT PAPER FILTER

CIGARFISH SCAD QUIAQUIA

CILIATION
(SUFF.) TRICHA TRICHI(A) TRICHOUS TRICHY

CILIUM HAIR LASH EYELASH UNCINUS BARBICEL CILIOLUM
(PREF.) BLEPHAR(O)

CILIX (BROTHER OF —) CADMUS THANUS PHINEUS PHOENIX
(FATHER OF —) AGENOR
(MOTHER OF —) TELEPHASSA
(SISTER OF —) EUROPA

CILLOSIS LIFEBLOOD

CIMBALOM CEMBALON DULCIMER

CIMEX BEDBUG ACANTHIA

CIMON (FATHER OF —) MILTIADES
(MOTHER OF —) HEGESIPYLE

CINCH BELT GIRD GRIP PIPE SNAP GIRTH GRAVY BREEZE CINCHA FASTEN PIANOLA SINECURE

CINCHONA CHINA QUINA

CINCHONA BARK
(PREF.) QUIN(O)

CINCINNATI PORKOPOLIS

CINCTURE BAND BELT GIRD HALO LIST RING ZONE GIRTH CENTER CESTUS COLLAR FILLET GIRDLE BALDRIC COMPASS ENCIRCLE SURCINGLE

CINDER ASH TAP COAL GRAY SCAR SLAG CHARK DROSS EMBER DANDER SCORIA CLINKER FOXTAIL RESIDUE
(REFUSE —) BREEZE
(VOLCANIC —) LAPILLUS
(PL.) GLEEDS

CINEMATIZE FILMIZE

CINEMATOGRAPH KINO VERISCOPE VITAGRAPH

CINERARIA SENECIO

CINGULUM BAND RIDGE GIRDLE

CINNABAR MINIUM

CINNAMON CANEL SPICE CASSIA SANELA STACTE CANELLA BARBASCO
(WILD —) BAYBERRY

CINNAMONROOT FLYBANE FLEAWORT

CINNAMON STONE GARNET ESSONITE

CINQUEFOIL FRASIER COWBERRY HARDHACK ROSACEAN QUINTFOIL SILVERWEED

CINYRAS (DAUGHTER OF —) MYRRHA
(FATHER OF —) APOLLO
(SON OF —) ADONIS

CION BUD IMP SECT SLIP GRAFT SCION SHOOT UVULA SARMENT GRAFTING

CIPHER KEY NIL CODE NULL ZERO ALBAM AUGHT OUGHT DECODE DEVICE FIGURE LETTER NAUGHT NOUGHT NUMBER SYMBOL ATHBASH NULLITY MONOGRAM VIGENERE NOTHINGLY

CIRCASSIAN ADIGHE KABARD CHERKESS KABARDIN

CIRCE SIREN TEMPTER
(BROTHER OF —) AEETES
(FATHER OF —) SOL
(LOVER OF —) ULYSSES ODYSSEUS
(MOTHER OF —) PERSE
(SON OF —) TELEGONUS

CIRCINATE SCORPIOID

CIRCLE DOT LAP ORB RED SET CLUE CULT DISK GYRE HALO

HOOP IRIS LOOP MARU ORBE RING RINK ROLL TOUR TURN ZONE BLACK CAROL CLASS CROWN CYCLE FETCH FRAME GROUP KREIS MONDE ORBIT PEARL REALM RHOMB RIGOL ROUND ROWEL SWIRL TWIRL BEZANT BROUGH CIRCUS CIRQUE CLIQUE COLLET COLURE CORDON CORONA DIADEM EQUANT GIRDLE RONDEL ROTATE RUNDLE SPIRAL SYSTEM TROPIC AZIMUTH CHUKKAR CHUKKER CIRCLET CIRCUIT COMPANY COMPASS CORONET COTERIE ENCLOSE HORIZON MONTHON REVOLVE RINGLET DEFERENT ECLIPTIC FROSTBOW ROUNDURE SURROUND
(— AROUND ORGAN) ANNULET
(— IN BULL'S-EYE) CARTON
(— OF FRIED DOUGH) POPADUM
(— OF HELL) MALEBOLGE
(— OF MONOLITHS) CROMLECH
(— TRACED BY HORSE) VOLT
(ASTRONOMICAL —) EQUANT EPICYCLE
(DANCE —) GALLEY
(FAIRY —) RINGLET
(GREAT —) EQUATOR ECLIPTIC MERIDIAN
(IMAGINARY —) CYCLE DEFERENT
(INNER —) BOSOM
(MYSTIC —) MANDALA
(PARHELIC —) FROSTBOW
(QUARTER —) ARC
(STONE —) CAROL HURLER GORSEDD CROMLECH
(TRAVERSE —) RACER
(TWO —S) CACHET
(PREF.) CYCL(O) GYRO

CIRCLET BAND HALO HOOP RING CROWN RIGOL VERGE BANGLE CIRQUE CORONA WREATH CIRCUIT CORONET VALLARY BRACELET HEADBAND
(PREF.) STEPHAN(O)

CIRCUIT LAP AREA BOUT EYRE ITER LOOP TOUR WEND ZONE AMBIT CHAIN CYCLE ORBIT ROUND ROUTE VIRON AMBAGE BUFFER CIRCLE DETOUR DOUBLE SPHERE UMGANG ZODIAC ADAPTER ADDRESS COMARCA COMPASS COUNTER DIOCESE ACCEPTER DIPLEXER DISTRICT PERIPLUS PROGRESS
(BRANCH —) LEG
(COMPUTER —) NOR NAND
(ELECTRIC —) LEG LOOP DOUBLER SQUELCH SECONDARY
(ELECTRONIC —) GATE
(INTEGRATED —) CHIP

CIRCUITOUS MAZY CURVED CROOKED DEVIOUS OBLIQUE SINUOUS TWISTED VAGRANT WINDING FLEXUOUS INDIRECT RAMBLING TORTUOUS AMBAGIOUS DECEITFUL DEVIATING WANDERING ROUNDABOUT
(— METHOD) WINDLASS

CIRCULAR O BILL FLIER FLYER LIBEL ORBAL ORBED ROUND DODGER FOLDER RINGED WHEELY ANNULAR COMPASS CYCLOID DISCOID DISLIKE HANDOUT PERFECT RUNDLED COMPLETE DOPEBOOK ENCYCLIC GLOBULAR INFINITE NUMMULAR PAMPHLET DOPESHEET ORBICULAR

CIRCULAR-KNIT SEAMLESS

CIRCULATE GO AIR MIX MOVE PASS RISE TURN WALK WIND BANDY TROLL CANARD PURVEY ROTATE SCURRY SPHERE SPREAD WANDER CANVASS CONVECT DIFFUSE PUBLISH CONVOLVE

CIRCULATING WAIF AFLOAT AMBIENT CURRENT

CIRCULATION ISSUE COURSE COVERAGE CURRENCY

CIRCUMCISER MOHEL

CIRCUMCISION BRITH PERITOMY

CIRCUMFERENCE ARC AUGE AMBIT APSIS GIRTH VERGE BORDER BOUNDS CIRCLE LIMITS COMPASS BOUNDARY SURROUND
(— OF SHELL) LIMBUS

CIRCUMFERENTOR PLANCHETTE

CIRCUMFLEX DOGHOUSE
(INVERTED —) HACEK

CIRCUMLOCUTION AMBAGE CIRCUIT WINDING VERBIAGE

CIRCUMNAVIGATION PERIPLUS

CIRCUMSCRIBE BOUND FENCE LIMIT DEFINE CAPTURE CONFINE ENCLOSE ENVIRON ENCIRCLE RESTRAIN RESTRICT SURROUND CONSCRIBE

CIRCUMSCRIBED NARROW INSULAR LIMITED
(PREF.) CIRCUM

CIRCUMSPECT SHY WARY WISE ALERT CHARY CAREFUL GUARDED PRUDENT CAUTIOUS DISCREET VIGILANT WATCHFUL

CIRCUMSPECTION RESPECT PRUDENCE WARINESS

CIRCUMSTANCE GO FIX CASE FACT ITEM NOTE EVENT PHASE POINT START STATE THING AFFAIR DETAIL FACTOR PICKLE CALLING ELEMENT EPISODE INCIDENT INSTANCE POSITION OCCURRENCE PARTICULAR
(CRITICAL —S) EXTREMES
(EXECRABLE —) ATROCITY
(LUDICROUS —) JEST
(PL.) CIRCS STATE TERMS ESTATE FORTUNE

CIRCUMSTANCED OFF

CIRCUMSTANTIAL EXACT FORMAL MINUTE PRECISE DETAILED ITEMIZED PARTICULAR

CIRCUMSTANTIATE SUPPORT EVIDENCE

CIRCUMVENT BALK BEAT DISH DUPE FOIL CHEAT CHECK COZEN EVADE OUTGO TRICK BAFFLE DELUDE ENTRAP NOBBLE OUTWIT THWART CAPTURE

CIRCUMVENT DECEIVE DEFRAUD ENSNARE PREVENT OUTFLANK SURROUND UNDERFONG

CIRCUS RING SHOW ARENA CANVAS CIRCLE CIRQUE CARNIVAL
(— LOT) TOBER
(— RING) TAN

CIRQUE CWM CIRC BASIN CIRCLE CIRCUS CORRIE RECESS CIRCLET EROSION

CIS SYN NERAL NORMAL

CISCO KIYI BLOAT BLOATER BLUEFIN LONGJAW MOONEYE BLACKFIN GRAYBACK TULLIBEE WHITEFIN

CISKEI (CAPITAL OF —) BISHO
(TOWN OF —) ALICE ZWELITSHA

CISSA SIRGANG

CISSEUS (BROTHER OF —) GYAS
(COMPANION OF —) HERCULES
(FATHER OF —) MELAMPUS
(SLAYER OF —) AENEAS

CISSUS TREEBINE

CIST BOX KIST TOMB CHEST CISTA QUOIT CASKET CHAMBER KISTVAEN

CISTERCIAN TRAPPIST

CISTERN BAC FAT SAC TUB URN VAT BACK PANT SUMP TANK URNA WELL LAVER CAVITY CAISSON CHULTUN CUVETTE STEEPER FEEDHEAD

CITADEL ARX FORT HALL ALAMO BURSA BYRSA TOWER CASTLE BOROUGH CHESTER KREMLIN ALHAMBRA FASTNESS FORTRESS TOOTHILL ACROPOLIS

CITATION CITAL NOTICE MENTION SUMMONS EPIGRAPH MONITION AUTHORITY EVOCATION

CITE CALL NAME SIST TELL ALLAY EVOKE QUOTE REFER ACCITE ACCUSE ADDUCE ALLEGE AROUSE AVOUCH EXCITE INVOKE NOTIFY RECITE REPEAT SUMMON ADVANCE ARRAIGN BESPEAK CONVENT EXCERPT EXTRACT IMPEACH MENTION INDICATE INSTANCE REHEARSE

CITHARA CITHER CITOLE PHORMINX

CITHERN ZITTERN LANGSPEL

CITIZEN CIT ALLY VOTER NATIVE BURGESS BURGHER CITOYEN CLERUCH DENIZEN ELECTOR FLATCAP FREEMAN OPPIDAN SUBJECT TOWNMAN AMERICAN CIVILIAN COMMONER CONSCIVE DOMESTIC NATIONAL OCCUPANT RESIDENT
(— OF SECOND CLASS) KNIGHT HIPPEUS
(—S OF MEDINA) ANSAR
(FOREIGN-BORN —) ALIEN
(PL.) SUBJECT PERIOECI CITIZENRY

CITIZENRY COUNTRY SUBJECT

CITRAL GERANIAL

CITRON LIME CEDRA LEMON CEDRAT ETHROG YELLOW BERGAMOT

CITTERN LAUD CITHERN PENORCON

CITY FU WON BURG DORP TOWN URBS WOON ZION BURGH CALNO EKRON JEBUS LILLE MANOA PIECE PLACE POLIS SETTE STEAD VILLE CALNEH CENTER CIUDAD CUTHAH GILEAD JAMNIA JEBUSI LAGADO NAGARA PITHOM STAPLE BABYLON CAMBALU CHESTER ELLASAR FREEDOM JABNEEL MECHLIN CABECERA ELDORADO MAGAZINE PALENQUE
(— LIFE) ASHCAN
(ANCIENT —) PERGAMUM
(CAPITAL —) SEAT
(CHIEF —) CAPITAL CABECERA MEGAPOLIS
(RICH —) MAGAZINE
(TREASURE —) RAAMSES
(WICKED —) BABYLON
(PREF.) URBI
(SUFF.) GRAD POLE POLIS POLITAN POLITE

CITY-STATE POLIS CIVITAS

CIVET CAT CIT GENET RASSE ZIBET BONDAR FOUSSA MUSANG PAGUMA ZIBETH CIVETTA FOSSANE LINSANG NANDINE POLECAT ZIBETUM ZINSANG FANALOKA MONGOOSE TANGALUNG

CIVIC LAY CIVIL SUAVE URBAN POLITE URBANE CIVICAL SECULAR

CIVIL FAIR HEND HENDE SUAVE POLITE URBANE AFFABLE AMIABLE COURTLY ELEGANT GALLANT POLITIC REFINED SECULAR DISCREET GRACIOUS OBLIGING POLISHED WELLBRED

CIVILIAN CIT CIVIE CIVIL CIVVY PEKIN MOHAIR CITIZEN TEACHER CIVILIST GOWNSMAN NONCOMBATANT
(— ENTERTAINING SOLDIER) PYKE

CIVILITY BONTE COURT COMITY NOTICE AMENITY COURTESY URBANITY GENTILITY
(PL.) HONOURS HONOURS

CIVILIZATION ISLAM KULTUR POLICE CULTURE ECUMENE CIVILITY
(GREEK —) HELLENISM

CIVILIZE TAME TEACH TRAIN POLISH REFINE EDUCATE HUMANIZE URBANIZE

CIVILIZED CHRISTIAN

CLABBER LOP MUD MIRE CURDLE LOPPER CLAUBER

CLACKDISH CLICKET

CLAD DREST ROBED BESEEN CLEDDE DECKED ADORNED ARRAYED ATTIRED CLOTHED COVERED DRESSED SHEATHED
(— IN PURPLE) PORPORATE
(SCANTILY —) SINGLY

CLADOSE RAMOSE CLADINE BRANCHED

CLAIM ASK DUE AVER AVOW CALL CASE DIBS LIEN MINE NAME PLEA COLOR DRAFT EXACT PLEAD RIGHT SHOUT TITLE ASSERT DEMAND DESIRE ELICIT EQUITY

INTEND RECKON ACCLAIM COLLECT DERECHO DRAUGHT PRETEND PRETEXT PROFESS RECLAIM REQUIRE SOLICIT ARROGATE DARRAIGN INTEREST MAINTAIN PRETENCE PRETENSE PROCLAIM SUBCLAIM CHALLENGE POSTULATE PRETENSION PRESCRIPTION
(— IN BUSINESS) CAPITAL
(— TO BE BELIEVED) AUTHORITY
(FALSE —) JACTATION
(FORESTER'S —) PUTURE
(INDIAN LEGAL —) HAK HAKH
(MINING —) SHICER

CLAIMANT CLAIMER USURPER PRETENDER

CLAIRE PARK

CLAIRVOYANCE INSIGHT VOYANCE LUCIDITY SAGACITY TELOPSIS PRECOGNITION

CLAIRVOYANT FEY SEER OMENER PROPHET SEERESS

CLAM MYA BASE CLOG DAUB GLAM HUSH MEAN BLUNT CLAMP CRASH GAPER GLAUM GRASP GROPE PAHUA RAZOR SHELL SMEAR SOLEN SPOUT STICK VENUS ADHERE CLUTCH GWEDUC QUAHOG STICKY BIVALVE CLANGOR COQUINA MOLLUSK STEAMER ADHESIVE BULLNOSE SHIPWORM NANNINOSE
(PART OF —) BEAK FOOT SHELL VALVE MANTLE SIPHON UMBONE ORIFICE

CLAMBAKE BAKE RALLY CLAMAROO SQUANTUM

CLAMBER CLIMB SCALE CLAVER SCRAWM SPRAWL RAMMACK SCRABBLE SCRAMBLE SPRACHLE STRUGGLE

CLAMMY DAMP DANK SOFT WACK MOIST SAMMY STICKY WAUGHY FLACCID SQUIDGY CLAMMISH

CLAMOR CRY DIN HUE BARK BERE BUNK GAFF RANE RERD ROAR ROUP ROUT SONG UTAS WAIL BLARE BOAST BRUIT CHIDE CHIRM NOISE OUTAS RERDE RUMOR SHOUT BELLOW BOWWOW HUBBUB OUTCRY QUETHE RACKET TUMULT UPROAR YATTER CLAMOUR EXCLAIM ORATION STASHIE NORATION PILILLOO PULLALUE SHOUTING
(— AGAINST) DECRY

CLAMOROUS NIP LOUD NOISY VOCAL BLATANT CLAMANT DINSOME YELLING BRAWLING DECRYING OPENMOUTHED OBSTREPEROUS

CLAMP DOG HOG LUG NIP PIN SET BAIL BALE BEND BOLT BURY CLAM GLAM GRIP JACK MUTE NAIL VISE YOKE BLOCK BRACE CLASP CRAMP GLAND GLAUM HORSE CLINCH FASTEN MOPHEAD STIRRUP FASTENER HOLDFAST
(— FOR BASS DRUM) SPUR
(— FOR CORK) AGRAFE AGRAFFE
(— FOR FLASK) GLAND

(— ON TUBE) PINCHCOCK
(STORAGE —) GRAVE

CLAMSHELL CLAM GRAB SHUCK

CLAN ATI HAN KIN SET SIB CULT GENS HAPU NAME RACE SECT SEPT SIOL UNIT AIMAK AYLLU CLASS GENOS GROUP HORDE PARTY TRIBE ABUSUA CLIQUE FAMILY SENAAH ABIEZER KINDRED PHRATRY SATSUMA SOCIETY ZADRUGA CALPULLI DIVISION
(— SUBDIVISION) OBE

CLANDESTINE BYE SLY FOXY HEDGE PRIVY QUIET SNEAK COVERT HIDDEN SECRET BOOTLEG FURTIVE ILLICIT BACKDOOR HIDLINGS STEALTHY

CLANG DIN DING PEAL RING TONK CLANK CLASH NOISE JANGLE TIMBRE

CLANGOR DIN CLAM ROAR CLANG HUBBUB UPROAR

CLANGOROUS BRAZEN PLANGENT

CLANGULA HARELDA

CLANK RING RACKLE

CLAP BANG CHOP FLAP PEAL SLAP SPAT TACK CHEER CLINK CRACK SMITE POSTER STRIKE STROKE APPLAUD CHATTER CLAPPER PLAUDIT HANDCLAP
(— OF THUNDER) DINT
(— ON) CRACK

CLAPBOARD KNAPPLE CLAPHOLT

CLAPNET DAYNET

CLAPPER CLAP CLACK RATTLE TONGUE JINGLET KNACKER KNOCKER CROTALUM
(— OF BELL) TONGUE
(PL.) BONES

CLAPTRAP HOKUM TRASH TRIPE BLAGUE BUNKUM DEVICE EYEWASH FUSTIAN BUNCOMBE NONSENSE TRICKERY

CLARE MINORESS

CLARENCE GROWLER

CLARET TERSE PONTAC LAFITTE BORDEAUX BADMINTON

CLARIAS HARMOOT KARMOUTH

CLARIBEL (HUSBAND OF —) PHAON

CLARICE (BROTHER OF —) HUON
(HUSBAND OF —) RINALDO

CLARIFIED PURED LAUTER

CLARIFY CLAY FINE CLEAN CLEAR PURGE SNUFF PURIFY REFINE RENDER SERENE SETTLE CLEANSE DESPUME EXPLAIN GLORIFY DEFECATE DEPURATE ELIQUATE SIMPLIFY

CLARIN ACOCOTL

CLARINET BEN BIN BON BEEN BONE REED AULOS CLARY PUNGI CLARONE LAUNEDDAS
(PART OF —) KEY PAD BELL CORK REED CLAMP COVER BARREL LIGATURE MOUTHPIECE FINGERPLATE

CLARION REST CLARE CLARY CLEAR CLARINO SUFFLUE TRUMPET

CLARISSA HARLOWE (AUTHOR OF —) RICHARDSON
(CHARACTER IN —) HOWE JOHN

JAMES MORDEN ROBERT SOLMES BELFORD HARLOWE WILLIAM ARABELLA CLARISSA LOVELACE SINCLAIR

CLARITY GLORY SPLENDOR STRENGTH CLEARNESS SIMPLICITY

CLARY ORVAL CLARRE SALVIA

CLASH JAR BANG BOLT BUMP DASH FRAY NEWS SLAM BRAWL BRUNT CHECK CRASH CROSS FIGHT FRUSH KNOCK OCCUR PRATE SHOCK AFFRAY DIFFER GOSSIP HURTLE IMPACT JOSTLE STRIFE STRIKE TATTLE THRUST THWART COLLIDE DISCORD SCANDAL ARGUMENT CONFLICT
(— OF WORDS) BARGE

CLASHING HARSH CONFLICT FRICTION COLLISION

CLASP HUG PIN CLIP DOME FOLD GRAB GRIP HASP HOLD HOOK HOOP KEEP OUCH STAY TACH BRACE CATCH CLING GRASP MORSE PREEN SEIZE SLIDE SPANG TACHE ACCOLL AGRAFE AMPLEX BECLIP BROOCH BUCKLE CLENCH CLUTCH ENFOLD ENWRAP FASTEN FIBULA GIMMER GIMMOR INCLIP INFOLD JIMMER STRAIN TASSEL AGRAFFE AMPLECT EMBRACE ENTWINE FERMAIL HOLDING MOUSING TENDRIL BARRETTE CORSELET FASTENER SURROUND
(— HANDS) SHAKE WRING

CLASPING AMPLECTANT

CLASS ILK BRAN CHOP FORM KIND RACE RANK RATE SECT SORT SUIT TYPE YEAR BREED CASTE GENRE GENUS GRADE GROUP ORDER RANGE TRIBE VARNA VERGE ASSORT CIRCLE CLINIC DECURY FAMILY GENDER LEAGUE MISTER NATION PHYLUM RATING RECKON REMOVE RUBRIC STRAIN STRIPE CATALOG FACTION LECTURE REGIMEN SEMINAR SPECIES VARIETY CATEGORY DESCRIBE DIVISION GENOTYPE GEOMOROI
(— OF BARDS) THULIR
(— OF GOODS) BRAND
(— OF OUTCASTS) ETA
(— OF PEOPLE) FOLK SALARIAT
(— OF SECURITIES) LEGAL
(— OF SHASTRAS) SRUTI SHRUTI
(— OF SOUNDS) ENDING
(— OF TEASELS) KINGS
(ARISTOCRATIC —) ARISTOI
(CHOICEST —) ROBUR
(DEPRESSED —) PANCHAMA
(FIRST —) GAY
(HEREDITARY —) CASTE
(JAPANESE —) HEIMIN KWAZOKU
(LABORING —) PARAIYAN PROLETARIAT
(LEARNED —) VATES CLERISY
(LOWER —) BELOW GENTE
(LOWEST —) LAG SCUM
(PEASANT —) JACQUERIE
(SLAVEHOLDING —) CHIVALRY
(SOCIAL —) ESTATE SHIZOKU

(WORKING —) TOIL
(PREF.) CRATO
(SUFF.) CY OIDA OIDEA OIDEI

CLASSIC VINTAGE AUGUSTAN

CLASSICAL PURE ATTIC GREEK LATIN ROMAN CHASTE CLASSIC ACADEMIC HELLENIC MASTERLY
(NOT —) BASE

CLASSICALLY IDEALLY

CLASSIFICATION FILE RANK RATE SORT CODEN GENRE GENUS GRADE ORDER TAXIS RATING SYSTEM ANALYSIS CATEGORY DIVISION TAXONOMY BREAKDOWN

CLASSIFIED SECRET

CLASSIFIER COUNTER SEPARATOR

CLASSIFY CODE LIST RANK RATE SIZE SORT SUIT TAPE TYPE BREAK CLASS DRAFT GRADE GROUP LABEL RANGE TRIBE ASSORT CODIFY DIGEST DIVIDE IMPOST TICKET ACCOUNT ARRANGE BRACKET BRIGADE CATALOG DISPOSE DRAUGHT GRAMMAR MARSHAL SUBSUME REGISTER PIGEONHOLE
(— TOGETHER) SLUMP

CLASSIS CONFERENCE

CLATHRATE LATTICED

CLATTER DIN JAR CLACK NOISE RUMOR BABBLE GABBLE GOSSIP HOTTER HURTLE RACKLE RATTLE TATTLE BLATTER CHATTER CLUNTER CLUTTER PRATTLE REESHLE SHATTER SLAMBANG

CLATTERING CLATTERY SLITHERING

CLAUSE ITEM PART CLOSE COMMA JOKER PLANK RIDER SALVO TROPE MEMBER PHRASE ADJUNCT ARTICLE COMMATA PASSAGE PROVISO SLEEPER APODOSIS CLAUSULA PARTICLE PETITION REDDENDO SENTENCE TENENDAS TENENDUM NOVODAMUS
(— IN CREED) FILIOQUE
(— IN WRIT) TESTE
(— OF WILL) DEVISE
(ADDITIONAL —) RIDER
(SUBORDINATE —) PROTASIS

CLAVACIN PATULIN

CLAVER PRATE CLOVER GOSSIP CHATTER CLABBER CLAIVER CLAMBER

CLAVICHORD CLAVIER MANICORD UNICHORD CLARIGOLD MONOCHORD

CLAVICLE FURCULE COLLARBONE

CLAVIER MANUAL KLAVIER

CLAVUS CORN BUNION HELOMA

CLAW DIG PEG CLEE CRAB FANG FAWN HAND HOOK NAIL PULL SERE TEAR UNCE CHELA CLAUT CLOOF CLUFE COURT GRASP GRIFF ONGLE SCLAW SEIZE TALON UNCUS CLUNCH CLUTCH CRATCH NIPPER POUNCE SCRAPE SINGLE UNGUAL UNGUIS UNGULA WEAPON CRUBEEN FALCULA FLATTER SCRATCH SHUTTLE WHEEDLE SCRABBLE

(PL.) CLUTCH
(PREF.) CHEL(I)(O) ONYCH(O) UNGUI
(SUFF.) ONYCHA ONYCHES ONYCHIA ONYCHUS ONYX

CLAY BAT COB PUG WAD WAX BASS BEND BODY BOLE BOTT GALT GLEY LOAM LUTE MARL MIRE PAPA SMIT TILL ARGIL BRICK CLOAM EARTH GAULT LOESS OCHRE PASTE RABAT TASCO BINDER CLEDGE CLUNCH KAOLIN PUDDLE SAGGER DAUBING MOULDER RASHING CAMSTANE CAMSTONE CIMOLITE FIRECLAY GUMBOTIL LATERITE LIFELESS SINOPITE SMECTITE
(— FOR MELTING POTS) TASCO
(— IN GLASS) TEAR
(— IRON) BULL
(— LAYER) VARVE
(— USED MEDICALLY) FANGO
(COVERED WITH —) LUTOSE
(HARD —) BEND
(HARDENED —) METAL
(INDURATED —) BASS CLUNCH
(PIECE OF FIRED —) TILE
(PIPE —) CAMSTANE CAMSTONE
(POTTER'S —) SLIP ARGIL PETUNTSE
(REMOVE —) UNLUTE
(SURPLUS —) SPARE
(TOUGH —) LECK
(3-ARMED, HARD-FIRED —) STILT
(PREF.) ARGILL(O) ARGILLACEO PEL(O)

CLAYEY BOLAR HEAVY MALMY MARLY CLEDGY LUTOSE ARGILLIC

CLAYMORE FERRARA MORGLAY

CLAY PIGEON BIRD CLAY

CLAYSTONE LECK

CLAYWARE GLOST

CLEADING CLOTHING

CLEAN DO FAY FEY HOE MOP NET DRUM DUST FAIR NEAT PURE REDD RIPE SIDE SMUG SWAB TRIM WASH WIPE CLEAR CURRY EMPTY FEIGH GRAVE SCOUR SCRUB SMART SWEEP TERSE TOSHY BARREL CHASTE CLEVER KOSHER PURIFY SPANDY APINOID BANDBOX CHAMOIS CLEANLY CLEANSE CLEARLY FURBISH PERFECT SWINGLE ABSTERGE BACKWASH BRIGHTLY DEXTROUS ENTIRELY RENOVATE SCAVENGE SPOTLESS UNSOILED
(— A FUR) DRUM
(— A QUILL) DUTCH
(— BOAT) CAREEN
(— BY SCRAPING) GRAVE
(— BY SMOKE) SMEEK
(— CANNON) SCALE
(— FIREARM) WORM
(— FLAX) SWINGLE
(— IN ACID) BLANCH
(— OUT) USH SPEAR
(— SHIP'S BOTTOM) HOG BREAM GRAVE
(— UP) DISPATCH
(RITUALLY —) KOSHER

CLEAN-CUT CRISP

CLEANED BRIGHT

CLEANER SOAP BORAX PURER FOLDER GUMMER RAMROD FLUEMAN SPOTTER CLEANSER
(AIR —) CAN
(GRAIN —) KICKER

CLEAN-LIMBED CLEVER

CLEAN-LINED SPRUCE

CLEANLY PURE CLEAN ADROIT ARTFUL CHASTE FAIRLY SPANDY CORRECT ELEGANT INNOCENT SKILLFUL

CLEANNESS PURITY

CLEANSE FAY BRAN CARD COMB FARM HEAL PICK SOAP WASH BROOM BRUSH CLEAN CLEAR DIGHT DRESS FEIGH FLAME FLUSH PURGE RINSE SCOUR SCRUB SNUFF BOTTOM CAREEN EMUNGE PICKLE PURIFY REFINE SPONGE WILLOW BAPTIZE CLARIFY DEBRIDE DETERGE EXPIATE LAUNDER MUNDIFY SWEETEN ABSTERGE DEPURATE OFFSCOUR RENOVATE SCAVENGE SPRINKLE

CLEANSER LYE SOAP CLEANER PURIFIER DETERGENT DETERSIVE

CLEANSING BATH FLUSH ABLUENT CLYSMIC WASHING ABLUTION CLEANING LAVATION DETERGENT MENDATORY ABSTERGENT
(CEREMONIAL —) LAVABO PURGATION

CLEANTE (FATHER OF —) HARPAGON
(LOVER OF —) ANGELIQUE
(SISTER OF —) ELMIRE

CLEANTHE (BROTHER OF —) SIPHAX

CLEANTHIS (HUSBAND OF —) SOSIA

CLEANUP KILLING SWEEPUP

CLEAR HOT JAM NET RID WAY CAST EASY FAIR FINE FLAT FREE GAIN GRUB JUMP NEAT OPEN OVER PURE PUTE QUIT REDD RIFE SHUT SLAM VOID ACUTE ATRIP AZURE BREAK BREME BRENT BROAD CHUCK CLEAN CRISP DRIVE LIGHT LUCID NAKED PLAIN PRINT PRUNE SCOUR SHARP SMOLT SUNNY SUTEL SWEEP UNTIE VIVID ACQUIT AERIAL ASSOIL BRIGHT CANDID CLEVER EXCUSE EXEMPT FLUTED LAUTER LIMPID LIQUID LUCENT PATENT PURIFY REMBLE SERENE SETTLE SHRILL SMOOTH UNSTOP ABSOLVE CAPITAL CLARIFY CLARION CRYSTAL DELIVER DILUCID EVIDENT EXPLAIN EXPRESS GLARING GRAPHIC LIGHTEN OBVIOUS PERVIAL RELEASE SILVERY THROUGH ACCREDIT APPARENT BRIGHTEN BULLDOZE DEFINITE DISTINCT EXPLICIT LUCULENT LUMINOUS MANIFEST PELLUCID REVELANT PERSPICUOUS
(— AWAY) FAY FEY FEIGH BANISH DISPEL DISCUSS
(— FROM) ALOOF
(— LAND) CURE BRUSH SLASH DEADEN
(— OF GROUND) ATRIP AWEIGH

(— OF MUD) SLUTCH
(— OF SCUM) SKIM
(— OF TUFTS) HOB
(— OUT) BLOW HOOK SWAMP
SKIDDOO HIGHTAIL DISCHARGE
(— PATH) FRAY HACK BUSHWACK
(— THROAT) HOICK HOUGH
(— UP) SOLVE ASSOIL RESOLVE
DISSOLVE UNSHADOW
(NOT —) DULL DUSKY FOGGY
INEVIDENT
CLEARANCE CHOP ROOM RUNBY
BACKLASH ALLOWANCE
(— FOR SHIP) PRATIQUE
CLEAR-CUT LUCID SHARP DIRECT
CONCISE DECIDED CHISELED
DEFINITE DISTINCT INCISIVE
TRENCHANT
CLEARHEADED LUCID
CLEARING SART FIELD FRITH
GLADE SHADE TRACT ALCOVE
ASSART RIDING RIDDING
SLASHING
CLEARLY FAIR CLEAR LIGHT REDLY
FAIRLY FRANKLY PATENTLY
WITTERLY
CLEAR-MINDEDNESS LUCIDITY
CLEARNESS CLARITY FINESSE
EVIDENCE FINENESS
CLEARWEED RICHWEED
CLEAT BITT STUD BLOCK CHOCK
KEVEL LEDGE RANGE WEDGE
BATTEN RIFFLE BOLLARD
COXCOMB GROUSER SIRMARK
SUPPORT SURMARK
CLEAVAGE RIFT CLEFT WASSIE
FISSION FISSURE WEDGING
DIVISION SCISSION
(PREF.) SCHISTO SCHIZ(O)
(SUFF.) CLASE SCHISIS SCHIST
CLEAVE CUT RIP CHOP HANG
HOLD JOIN LINK PART RELY REND
RIFT RIVE SLIT TEAR BREAK
CARVE CHAWN CHINE CLAVE
CLEFT CLING CLOVE CRACK
SEVER SHALE SHARE SHEAR SLIVE
SPLAT STICK ADHERE BISECT
COHERE DIVIDE FURROW PIERCE
SLEAVE SUNDER DISPART
FISSURE SEPARATE
(— OFF) SCIND
CLEAVER CLIVE CLEAVE FROWER
PARANG CHOPPER PARANGI
CLEAVERS GRIP CLOTE CLOTS
CLITHE HAIRIF HAIRUP BURHEAD
LOVEMAN PIGTAIL BIRDLIME
CLEAVING DYSTOME FISSION
DYSTOMIC
(— READILY) EUTOMOUS
CLECHE URDE URDY URDEE
CLEF KEY CLIVE CHIAVETTA
CLEFT CUT GAP JAG CHAP CHOP
FENT FLAW GASH NOCK REFT
RIFT RILL RIMA RIVE SLIT BIFID
BREAK CHASM CHAWN CHINK
CLOFF CLOVE CRACK CREEK
CRENA GULCH KLOOF RILLE
RIVEN SINUS SPLIT BREACH
CHAPPY CLEAVE CLOUGH CLOVEN
CRANNY CROTCH DIVIDE LISSOM
PARTED RECESS RICTUS STIGMA
BLASTED CHIMNEY CREVICE
DIVIDED FISSURE OPENING

SLIFTER APERTURE CREVASSE
FRACTURE INCISION INCISURA
MULTIFID SCISSURA SCISSURE
PALMATIFID
(— BETWEEN HILLS) SLACK RAVINE
(— IN HOOF) SEAM
(— IN THE POSTERIORS) NOCK
(— OF BUTTOCKS) CREASE
(PREF.) FISSI SCHISTO SCHIZ(O)
(SUFF.) FID FIDATE
CLEMATIS PIPESTEM CURLYHEAD
CLEMENCY ORE PITY GRACE
MERCY LENITY QUARTER
KINDNESS LENIENCY MILDNESS
CLEMENT MILD SOFT WARM
GENTLE LENIENT MERCIFUL
**CLEMENZA DI TITO (CHARACTER
IN —)** TITUS ANNIUS SEXTUS
BERENICE SERVILIA VITELLIA
(COMPOSER OF —) MOZART
CLENCH FIST GRIP GRIT HOLD
NAIL BRACE CLASP CLENK CLINT
CLOSE GRASP CLINCH CLUTCH
DOUBLE
(— FIST) GRIPE
CLEONTE (LOVER OF —) LUCILLE
CLEOPATRA (BROTHER OF —) ILUS
ZETES CALAIS GANYMEDE
ASSARACUS
(FATHER OF —) IDAS TROS BOREAS
PTOLEMY
(HUSBAND OF —) PHILIP PHINEUS
PTOLEMY MELEAGER
(MOTHER OF —) MARPESSA
ORITHYIA CALLIRRHOE
CLEPE CLUPIEN
CLEPSYDRA GURRY GHURRY
CLERGY CLOTH CRAPE CHURCH
CLERISY MINISTRY
(BODY OF —) PULPIT
CLERGYMAN ABBA ABBE DEAN
PAPA CANON CLERK FROCK
PADRE PILOT PRIOR RABBI VICAR
BISHOP CLERIC CURATE DEACON
DIVINE DOMINE PAROCH PARSON
PASTOR PRIEST RECTOR SUPPLY
CASSOCK PRELATE CARDINAL
CHAPLAIN CLERICAL DIOCESAN
EMERITUS LECTURER MINISTER
ORDINARY PREACHER REVEREND
SQUARSON PRESBYTER
PREBENDARY REVIVALIST
CLERIC ABBE CLERK FROCK
DEACON GALLAH LEVITE PRIEST
ACOLYTE GOLIARD ANAGNOST
CLERICAL BLACK CLERIC CLERKISH
PARSONIC PARSONLY
CLERIMOND (BROTHER OF —)
FERRAGUS
(HUSBAND OF —) VALENTINE
CLERIMONT (LOVER OF —)
CLARINDA
CLERK NUN BABU MONK AGENT
AWARD BABOO CLARK FILER
RALPH WRITE BILLER CHASER
CLERIC COMMIS GRADER HERMIT
KITMAN LAYMAN MAPPER
MASTER MUNSHI PANDIT
PENMAN PRIEST PUNDIT RALPHO
SCRIBE SIRCAR TELLER WRITER
YEOMAN ACOLYTE ACTUARY
BOOKMAN CARCOON COMPOSE
DOPSTER GOMASTA PIARIST

SCHOLAR SHIPPER SHOPMAN
STUFFER CLERGEON CLERGION
CLERKESS CURSITOR EMPLOYEE
GREFFIER MUTSUDDY PENCLERK
RECORDER SALESMAN
(— OF ST PAUL) BARNABITE
(CHIEF —) PROTHONOTARY
(HOTEL —) DESKMAN
CLERKLY LEARNED SCRIBAL
CLERGIAL SCHOLARLY
CLEVE BRAE CLIFF CLEEVE
HILLSIDE
CLEVER APT SLY ABLE CUTE DEFT
FEAT FELL FINE FOXY GLEG GNIB
GOOD HEND KEEN NEAT SLIM
SPRY AGILE ALERT CANNY CLEAN
CLEAR CUNNY FALSE FEATY
FENDY HANDY HEADY HENDE
LITHE QUICK SHARP SLICK SMART
SNACK WITTY ACTIVE ADROIT
ARTFUL ASTUTE BRIGHT CRAFTY
EXPERT HABILE HEPPEN KITTLE
KNACKY NEATLY NIMBLE PRETTY
SHREWD SPIFFY STALKY SUBTLE
AMIABLE CUNNING GNOSTIC
PARLISH PARLOUS VARMENT
VARMINT DEXTROUS HANDSOME
OBLIGING SKILLFUL TALENTED
CLEVERLY SLICK FEATLY TIDELY
SMARTLY ASTUTELY
CLEVERNESS CAN CHIC NOUS
TACT KNACK SKILL ESPRIT
INDUSTRY DEXTERITY
CLEVIS COP DEE HAKE CLEVY
COPSE BRIDGE BRIDLE MUZZLE
SHACKLE PLOWHEAD
CLEW BALL CLUE HINT GLOBE
GLOME SKEIN BOTTOM HURDLE
THREAD
CLICHE COMMONPLACE
CLICK DOG DOT DASH PAWL SLAP
TICK AGREE CATCH FORGE SNECK
SNICK DETENT PALLET RATCHET
(HEEL —S) BELLS
(TELEGRAPH —) DASH
CLICK BEETLE ELATER
CLIENT CEILE JAJMAN PATRON
PATIENT CUSTOMER HENCHMAN
RETAINER
CLIENTELE PUBLIC CLIENTRY
CLIFF HOE NIP CRAG HILL KLIP
ROCK SCAR BLUFF CLEVE CLINT
HEUCH HEUGH KRANS SCARP
SHORE SLOPE STEEP CLEEVE
HEIGHT KRANTZ PISKUN
CLOGWYN HILLSIDE PALISADE
TRAVERSE
(BROKEN —) CRAG
(ICE —) ICEBLINK
(LINE OF —S) PALISADE
(PREF.) CREMNO
CLIFFY SCARRY
CLIMATE SKY SUN MOOD CLIME
HEAVEN REGION TEMPER
ATTITUDE
(SCIENCE OF —) PHENOLOGY
(PREF.) METEOR(O)
CLIMAX CAP TOP ACME APEX
HEAD NEAR PEAK SHUT CREST
CROWN MOUNT SCALE TIGHT
APOGEE ASCEND FINISH HEIGHT
PAYOFF SHINNY SUMMIT ZENITH
BLOWOFF EVEREST CAPSHEAF

CAPSTONE EPIPLOCE
CULMINATION
CLIMB GAD STY COON RAMP RISE
SHIN SKIN SOAR STYE CREEP
GRIMP MOUNT SCALE SKLIM
SPEED SPEEL SWARM TWINE
ASCEND ASCENT BREAST SCLIMB
SCRAWM SHINNY SWARVE
SWERVE CLAMBER SCRAMBLE
TRAVERSE
(— ABOARD) HOP
(— DOWN) LIGHT UNSCALE
(— IN MOUNTAINEERING) CHIMNEY
(— OVER) SURMOUNT
CLIMBER CUBE AKALA AKELA
KAIWI TIMBO RIGGER SCALER
COWHAGE CRAMPON CREEPER
(MOUNTAIN —) ALPINIST
CLIMBING RAMPANT SCANDENT
(MOUNTAIN —) ALPINISM
CLIMBING FERN NITO AGSAM
CLIMBING IRON SPUR PRICK
CRAMPET CRAMPIT CRAMPON
CREEPER PRICKER CRAMPBIT
CLIMBING PALM RATTAN
CLIMBING PEPPER BETEL
CLIMBING ROSE SCRAMBLE
CLINCH FIX GET HUG TOE BIND
GRIP LOCK NAIL SEAL CLAMP
CLING CLINK CLINT GRASP RIVET
SEIZE CLENCH CLUTCH FASTEN
SECURE SNATCH CONFIRM
EMBRACE GRAPPLE SCUFFLE
COMPLETE CONCLUDE HOLDFAST
CLING HUG BANK HANG HOLD
RELY CLASP HITCH STICK TRUST
ADHERE CLEAVE CLINCH COHERE
DEPEND FASTEN SHRINK WITHER
CHERISH EMBRACE SHRIVEL
CONTRACT
CLINGER LIMPET
CLINGFISH SUCKER TESTAR
TETARD SUCKFISH
CLINGING CLUNG HUGGING
ADHAMANT ADHERENT
OSCULANT
CLINK ALE JUG PUT RAP BEAT
BLOW BRIG CASH CLAP COIN JAIL
MOVE RING SLAP CHINK KLINK
LATCH MONEY RHYME SEIZE
CLINCH JINGLE LOCKUP MOMENT
PRISON STRIKE TINKLE INSTANT
JINGLING
CLINKER BUR BUHR BURR SCAR
SLAG WASTE HOLLANDER
(PL.) BREEZE
CLINKER-BUILT SHINGLED
LAPSTRAKE
CLINOMETER TRIMMER
CLINTONIA BLUEBEAD DOGBERRY
COWTONGUE
CLIP BAT BOB CUT DOD HUG LIP
LOP MOW NIG NIP BARB BEAK
CHIP COLL CROP DOCK DODD
FLAG HOLD PACE PARE POLL
SNIP TRIM BRUSH CLASP DRESS
FORCE LUNET MINCE PRUNE
SHAVE SHEAR SHRIP SNICK STEEK
CLUPPE CLUTCH CRUTCH FASTEN
GADGET HINDER HOLDER LACING
CALIPER CURTAIL CURTAIN
EMBRACE HICKORY LUNETTE
SCISSOR SHORTEN DIMINISH

ENCIRCLE RETAINER
(— A COIN) SHORTEN
(— OF LEAD) TINGLE
(— WOOL) CRUTCH
(CARTRIDGE —) CHARGER
(HAIR —) BARRETTE
(SPRING —) JACK
CLIPPED TONSURED
CLIPPER BOAT SHIP DOCKER
SLICER CHAINER CLAMMER
CLEANER GRABMAN GRIPPER
SHEARER SNAPPER
CLIPPING BOB SCROW CUTTING
SNIPPING
(—S OF METAL) SCISSEL
(PL.) BRASH SHORTS EXCERPTA
CLIQUE COT MOB SET BLOC CLAN
CLUB GANG KNOT PUSH RING
CABAL CROWD GROUP JUNTO
WRITE CIRCLE CLETCH SCHISM
COTERIE FACTION CONCLAVE
SODALITY CAMARILLA
CLISTHENES (FATHER OF —)
MEGACLES
(MOTHER OF —) AGARISTA
CLITANDRE (LOVER OF —) LUCINDE
CELIMENE ANGELIQUE
CLITELLUM GIRDLE SADDLE
CINGULUM
CLOAK ABA HAP BRAT CAPA CAPE
COPE HIDE HUKE IZAR MANT
MASK PALL RAIL ROBE VEIL
WRAP AMICE BURKA CAPOT
CHOGA COVER GREGO GUISE
JELAB MANTA MANTO PILCH
SAGUM SHUBA TALAR TALMA
TILMA ABOLLA AHUULA ASSUME
BAUTTA CAMAIL CAPOTE CASTER
CHAMMA CHAPEL CHIMER
DOLMAN JOSEPH MANTLE
MANTUA PHAROS PONCHO
RHASON SCREEN SERAPE SHIELD
SHROUD TABARD VISITE ALICULA
BAVAROY CASSOCK CHLAMYS
CHUDDAR CONCEAL COURTBY
GARMENT MANTEAU PAENULA
PALLIUM PELISSE PELLARD
PRETEXT ROKELAY SHELTER
SURCOAT ZIMARRA ALBORNOZ
BURNOOSE CAPUCHIN CARDINAL
DISGUISE INTRIGUE MANTILLA
PALLIATE ROQUELAURE
(— OF FEATHERS) MAMO AHUULA
(— WITH CROSSES) ANALABOS
(CORONATION —) SACCOS
(HOODED —) HUKE CAPOT BAUTTA
BIRRUS BAVAROY CARDINAL
DJELLABA
(INQUISITION —) SANBENITO
(RED —) CAPE
(RUSSIAN —) SARAFAN
(SOLDIER'S —) SAGUM MANTEEL
(WATERPROOF —) GOSSAMER
(PREF.) PALLIO
CLOAKED PALLIATE
CLOAKROOM VESTRY VESTIARY
CLOAM DAUB CLOMB CROCKERY
CLOCHE BELL
CLOCK NEF BELL CALL DIAL GOER
GONG TIME WRAP BUNDY CLUCK
GURRY HATCH HURRY KNOCK
METER QUIRK STYLE VERGE
WATCH BEETLE CROUCH GHURRY

ORLAGE TICKER SKELPER STRIKER
TATTLER HOROLOGE INCUBATE
ORNAMENT RECORDER SOLARIUM
TELLTALE
(— IN FORM OF SHIP) NEF
(— ON STOCKING) QUIRK GUSHET
GUSSET
(— WITH PENDULUM) PENDULE
(PART OF —) BOB ROD BASE DIAL
DOOR FACE FOOT HAND HOOD
RING ROPE CHAIN CREST PLATE
TRUCK FINIAL PLINTH WEIGHT
CHAPTER NUMERAL PENDULUM
SPANDREL
(TIME —) BUNDY
(WATER —) GURRY GHURRY
SOLARIUM CLEPSYDRA
CLOCKER SIZER TIMER RAILBIRD
CLOCKWISE DEASIL DESSIL
SUNWISE POSITIVE
CLOD SOD CLAT CLOT DOLT DULL
LOUT LUMP SLOB TURF CLOUT
CLOWN DIVOT EARTH GLEBE
GROSS KNOLL YOKEL CLATCH
GROUND STUPID BUMPKIN
CLODDISH GROSS STUPID
BOORISH
CLODHOPPER BOOR CLOD SHOE
RUSTIC HOBNAIL PLOWMAN
CLODIA LESBIA
CLODPATE CLOT DOLT FOOL
RAMHEAD CLODPOLE CLODPOLL
IMBECILE
CLODPOLE BOOR BUMPKIN
CLOG FUR GUM JAM LOG BALL
CLAG CLAM CLOY CURB DRAG
GAUM GLUB LEAD LOAD LUMP
SHOE SKID STOP BLIND BLOCK
CHECK CHOKE DANCE SABOT
SPOKE TRASH ACCLOY ADHERE
BURDEN CHOPIN COBCAB
DAGGLE ENCLOG FETTER FREEZE
GALOSH HAMPER HOBBLE
IMPEDE PATINE PATTEN REMORA
SANDAL SECQUE WEIGHT
CONGEST CREEPER ENGLEIM
FETLOCK PERPLEX SHACKLE
SPANCEL TRAMMEL TRIGGER
BEDAGGLE COALESCE ENCUMBER
OBSTRUCT OVERSHOE RESTRAIN
(— A FILE) PIN
(WOODEN —S) GETA GETAS
CLOG ALMANAC STAFF
CLOGGED FOUL FURRY PINNY
FROZEN CLOTTED BEGUMMED
CLOGGING CLOGGY FOULING
CUMBROUS
CLOGGY DULL HEAVY LUMPY
STICKY
CLOISONNE SHIPPO
CLOISTER HALL STOA ABBEY AISLE
ARCADE FRIARY IMMURE PIAZZA
PRIORY CLOSTER CONVENT
NUNNERY MONASTERY
CLOISTER AND THE HEARTH
(AUTHOR OF —) READE
(CHARACTER IN —) KATE DENYS
ELIAS GILES MARIE PETER
BRANDT GERARD MARTIN PIETRO
ELIASON MARGARET
GHYSBRECHT
CLOISTERED RECLUSE

CLONE DESMA SPICULE
CLORINDA (SLAYER OF —)
TANCRED
CLOSE BY IN CAP END GUM HAW
HOT TYE AKIN BUNG CHOP CLAP
CLIT DAUB FAST FILL FINE FIRM
GRIP HARD HIDE LOUK MEET
NEAR NIGH QUIT SEAL SHUT
SLAM SNUG SPAR STOP TINE
WINK WYND ZERO ANEAR BLOCK
BREAK CEASE DENGE FINIS FLIRT
COAPT DENSE FENCE FINIS FLIRT
GARTH GROSS ISSUE MUGGY
SNECK SOLID STEEK STICK STIVY
THICK TIGHT BUCKLE BUTTON
CLAUSE CLENCH CLUTCH DOUBLE
EFFECT EXPIRY FINALE FINISH
INSTOP INWARD NARROW
NEARBY PERIOD SECRET SETTLE
SILENT STANCH STINGY STITCH
STRAIT STRICT STUFFY THRONG
ADJOURN BOROUGH CLOSING
CLOSISH COMPACT CONDEMN
CONTEXT COSTIVE EXTREME
GRAPPLE MISERLY OCCLUDE
POCKETY PUTHERY RAMPIRE
RECLUDE SHUTTER SIMILAR
STAUNCH STOPPER ACCURATE
ADJACENT BLOCKADE CLAUSULA
COMPLETE COMPRESS CONCLUDE
ENCEINTE ESPECIAL FAMILIAR
FINALIZE HAIRLINE IMMINENT
INTIMATE OBTURATE PARCLOSE
PRECLUDE STIFLING PROXIMATE
(— BY) FORBY AROUND BESIDE
FOREBY HEREBY FORTHBY
SISTERING
(— EYES OF HAWK) SEEL
(— IN) BESET ENCLOSE INCLOSE
(— IN ON) TAKE
(— THE MOUTH) STOPPLE
(— TO) BY INBY NEAR NIGH
ANEAR INBYE ALMOST AGAINST
(— TO BATSMAN) SILLY
(— TO COMMUNICATION) CORDON
(— TO QUARRY) HOT
(— TO THE HEART) DEAR
(— TO THE WIND) SHARP
(— TOGETHER) COLLAPSE
(— UP) DIT CORK DITT FILL FOLD
STOP SERRY UPCLOSE
(— WITH) BIND
(— WITH A CLICK) SNECK
(PARTIALLY —) HOOD
(VERY —) CHIEF STINGY
(PREF.) PLESI(O) PYCN(O) STEN(O)
(SUFF.) STENOSIS
CLOSE-COUPLED COMPACT
CLOSED DARK DOWN SHUT CLOSE
LUCKEN UNOPEN BLOCKED
COVERED
(— AT ONE END) BLIND
(PREF.) CLEIST CLIST OCCLUSO
CLOSEFISTED MEAN NEAR FISTY
TIGHT SNIPPY STINGY MISERLY
HANDFAST
CLOSE-FITTING FIT HARD MEET
SNUG THEAT THEET TIGHT
THIGHT PRINCESS SUCCINCT
PRINCESSE
CLOSE-IN SILLY
CLOSE-KNIT TRUSSED
CLOSE-LIPPED SILENT

CLOSELY FAST JUST NEAR WELL
SADLY ALMOST BARELY HARDLY
NARROW NEARLY JUNCTLY
STRICTLY
CLOSEMOUTHED SECRET SILENT
TACITURN
(NOT —) LEAKY
CLOSENESS DENSITY SECRECY
FIDELITY INTIMACY NEARNESS
PARSIMONY
CLOSER VAMPER CLOSURE
CLOSEST NEXT NEAREST
CLOSESTOOL STOLE
CLOSET ARK EWRY ROOM SAFE
ZETA AMBRY CUBBY CUDDY
PRESS LOCKER PANTRY SECRET
CABINET CONCEAL PRIVATE
CONCLAVE CUPBOARD GARDEVIN
WARDROBE
CLOSING FLY SLAM SNAP CLINCH
CLOSURE CLOTURE CLAUDENT
PHASEOUT BUTTONING
(— DOWN OF OPERATIONS)
PHASEOUT
CLOSURE END GAG BOLT SEAL
BOUND LIMIT ATRESIA CLOTURE
FERRULE TENSION CLAUSURE
FINALITY KANGAROO
(SUFF.) CLEISIS CLISIS
CLOT DOT GEL CLAG CLAT GOUT
JELL LUMP MASS MOLE SHED
CLART CLUMP GRUME BALTER
COTTER LAPPER LOPPER
CLODDER EMBOLUS THICKEN
CONCRETE SOLIDIFY THROMBUS
(PREF.) THROMB(O)
CLOTH DAB RAG BLUE COAT DRAB
DRAP ECRU FELT FILE PALL SEAM
WARE WOOF BEIGE BLUET CABAN
CLOUT DITTO FOULE GOODS
GREEN LODEN LUNGI MOORY
PRINT STUPE TAMMY TAWNY
TIBET TOILE TWEED TWILL
WIGAN ALPACA AWNING BENGAL
BYSSUS CANAMO CANVAS
CHADOR CLAITH CLERGY COVERT
DOMETT DORSEL DOSSAL DOSSER
DRAPET DUSTER FABRIC LIVERY
LONGYI LOWELL MELLAY MULETA
NAPKIN RENGUE REXINE SARONG
SURNAP TILLOT WITNEY ACETATE
BAGGING BOULTEL CHADDAR
CHRISOM COATING CRIMSON
DRAPERY DUSTRAG FALDING
GARMENT JACONET ORLEANS
PANUELO RAIMENT SACKING
SURNAPE TEXTILE WATCHET
WORSTED BATSWING CHRISMAL
COMPRESS CORPORAL CRAMOISY
DWELLING FROCKING HOMESPUN
LAMBSKIN MATERIAL PHULKARI
RADEVORE SHAATNEZ SHEETING
THICKSET TOILINET
(— FOR BELT) SHROUD
(— FOR WIPING TABLE) FILE
(— FOR WRAPPING FABRICS) TILLET
(— FOR WRAPPING THE DEAD)
CEREMENT
(— HANGING FROM WAISTBAND)
LANGOOTY
(—OF GOLD) CICLATON SONERI

CHECKLATON
(— OF SINGLE WIDTH) STRAITS
(— REMAINING AFTER CUTTING)
CABBAGE
(— WORN LIKE KILT) LAVALAVA

(ALTAR —) TOWEL PENDLE
PALLIUM VESPERAL CATASARKA
(ARABIAN —) HAIK CABAN
CABAAN
(BAPTISMAL —) CHRISOM
(BARK —) TAPA TAPPA
(BED —) COVER SPREAD
(BLACK —) KISWA KISWAH
(BLUE —) PERSE
(COARSE —) KELT DOZEN DUROY
RUDGE BURREL CANGAN
DOWLAS DOZENS FORFAR FRIEZE
HODDEN KERSEY KHARVA
KHARWA STAMIN STROUD
TAPALO WADMAL CAMBAYE
COTONIA DRUGGET FORFARS
RAPLOCH RUGGING SARPLER
SOUTAGE FLUSHING RADEVORE
SARCILIS
(COMMUNION —) FANON SINDON
ANIMETTA CORPORAL
PURIFICATOR
(COTTON —) BAFT JEAN TOBE
ADATI BLUET CAFFA CRASH
DURRY JEANS KHADI KHAKI
SURAT BEAVER CALICO CANGAN
DOWLAS DURRIE GANZIE
HUMHUM KALMUK NANKIN
PENANG CAMBAYE FUSTIAN
GALATEA GINGHAM JACONET
KHADDAR LASTING NANKEEN
REGATTA BOGOTANA CRETONNE
DOMESTIC MUSLINET
(CRIMSON —) CRAMASIE
CRAMOISY
(DECORATIVE —) SCARF
(EMBROIDERED —) SAMPLER
BAUDEKIN
(FINE —) SINDON
(GLASS —) DORON
(GOAT-WOOL —) ABA ABBA ABAYA
SLING
(GREEN —) KENDAL
(GUNNY —) TAT
(HAIR —) ABA ABBA CILICE
(HEMP —) PINAYUSA
(HOMESPUN —) KELT KHADI
PATTU PUTTOO HEADING
KHADDAR
(INFERIOR —) MOCKADO
(LAP —) GREMIAL
(LINEN —) BRIN LINE GULIX
DOWLAS FORFAR BRABANT
LOCKRAM SILESIA BLANCARD
CORPORAL DRILLING GAMBROON
GHENTING LINCLOTH
(LONG —) LUNGI WHITE LUNGEE
(ORNAMENTAL —) TRAP DOSSAL
DOSSEL
(PACK —) MANTA
(PACKING —) SOUTAGE
(PIECE OF —) APRON CLOUT
GODET LANGOOTY
(PURLOINED —) CABBAGE
(RICH —) SCARLET
(SADDLE —) PANEL NUMNAH
SHABRACK

(SILK —) CAFFA BENGAL PATOLA
LUSTRING
(SOAKED —) BUCK
(SOFT —) RUGINE
(STAGE —) BACKDROP
(STARCHED —) GUIMPE
(STRIPED —) RAY
(STRONG —) CANVAS DURANCE
BARRACAN
(TWILLED —) JANE JEAN
BARATHEA GAMBROON
(UNDYED —) HODDEN
(WASHING —) SHAMMY CHAMOIS
(WAX —) MUMJUMA
(WET —) DAB
(WOOL —) SAY DRAB PUKE BEIGE
BUREL DOZEN DUROY LAINE
STARA TAMIS TAMMY BURNET
DOZENS DUFFEL HODDEN
KENDAL KERSEY MEDLEY MELTON
MUSTER SATARA SAXONY
STAMIN TAMINY TARTAN
BASTARD BLANKET DUNSTER
FLANNEL RAPLOCH ROPLOCH
RUGGING BEARSKIN BOMBAZET
BUCKSKIN FLORENCE SARCILIS
VENETIAN PETERSHAM
BOMBAZETTE
(WORSTED —) RASH SHAG
BOTANY BOMBAZET
(PREF.) HISTI(O)
CLOTHE DON DUB HAP LAP RIG
TOG BUSK COAT DECK GARB GIRD
GOWN ROBE VEST ADORN ARRAY
CLEAD CLEED DRESS ENDOW
ENDUE FLESH FROCK HABIT
INDUE ATTIRE BEWRAP SHRIDE
SHROUD SWATHE ADDRESS
APPAREL FEATHER RAIMENT
VESTURE ACCOUTER ACCOUTRE
CLOTHED CLAD BECLAD HABITED
CLOTHES CASE DUDS GARB GEAR
GORE KAPA SUIT TACK TOGS
WEAR BRAWS CLAES DUCKS
HABIT ATTIRE FARDEL SHROUD
TROGGS APPAREL BAGGAGE
COSTUME IRONING RAIMENT
REGALIA THREADS TOGGERY
VESTURE WEARING CLOTHING
FEATHERS FRIPPERY GARMENTS
INDUMENT
(CASTOFF —) FRIPPERY
(DAINTY —) PRETTIES
(DRESS —) WAMPUM
(FINE —) BRAWS
(HANDSOME —) BRAVERY
(MOURNING —) DOLE
(SHOWY —) LUGS
(SOAKED —) BUCK
CLOTHES DRYER AIRER TUMBLER
CLOTHESPIN PEG
CLOTHESPRESS ARMOIRE
TALLBOY WARDROBE
CLOTH FOLDER CUTTLER
CLOTHING (ALSO SEE CLOTHES)
BACK BLUE BRAT COAT GARB
GEAR SEAM WEAR ARRAY BUREL
CLOTH DRESS GREEN HABIT
JABOT STUFF ATTIRE FARDEL
ROBING VESTRY APPAREL
CLOBBER CLOTHES CRIMSON
DRAPERY OUTWALL RAIMENT
VESTURE WEEDERY INDUMENT

KNITWEAR MENSWEAR
ORNAMENT SLOPWORK VESTIARY
VESTMENT
(BLACK —) SABLE
(COARSE —) BUREL
(INFORMAL —) PLAYWEAR
(LOWER —) LAP
(MUSLIM —) IHRAM
(NAUTICAL —) SLOPS
(SHEER —) FLIMSIES
(SHOWY —) SHEEN FINERY
(WOMEN'S —) FRILLIES
(WORK —) FATIGUES
(SUFF.) ESTHES
CLOTHING DEALER HOSIER
CLOTHWORKER FULLER
CLOTILDA (FATHER OF —)
CHILPERIC
(HUSBAND OF —) CLOVIS
AMALARIC
(UNCLE OF —) GUNDEBALD
CLOTTED GORY CLOTTY CLOUTED
GARGETY GRUMOUS LIVERED
CLOTURE GAG CLOSURE
CLOUD DOG FOG NUE SKY BLUR
DAMP DARK DUST FOOL HAZE
HELM HIDE MIST PUFF REEK
SMUR ARCUS BEDIM BEFOG
BLOOM DRIFT GLOOM MUDDY
NUBIA OXEYE SHADE STAIN
SULLY SWARM TAINT VAPOR
CIRRUS DAMAGE DARKEN
DEEPEN DEFAME FUNNEL
MUDDLE NEBULA NIMBUS PILEUS
POTHER SCREEN SHADOW
STIGMA BLACKEN CONFUSE
CUMULUS ECLIPSE FUMULUS
GRANULE OBSCURE POOTHER
STRATUS SUNSPOT TARNISH
CLOUDCAP CLOUDLET COCKTAIL
NIGHTCAP NUBILATE OVERCAST
WOOLPACK
(— OF DUST OR VAPOR) STEW
SMOTHER
(— OF MIST) SOP
(— OVER MOUNTAIN) HELM
(FLYING —) RACK
(HIGH —) CIRRUS
(HORIZONTAL —) STRATUS
(MASS OF HIGH —S) RACK
(MASSY —) CUMULUS
(NUCLEAR —) FIREBALL
(RAIN —) NIMBUS
(PL.) SCUD SOUP CARRY GASHES
(PREF.) CIRR(I)(O) CIRRH(I)(O)
NEBULI NEPHEL(I)(O) NEPHO
NIMBI NUBI
CLOUDBERRY AKPEK MOLKA
AVERIN
(FRUIT OF —) NOOP
CLOUDED HAZY DIRTY DUSTY
FILMY JASPE MUCKY SHADY
ACLOUD GLOOMY TURBID
INFUMATE NEBULOUS
CLOUDINESS FAIR HAZE GLOOM
MUDDLE NUBECULA
CLOUDING DAPPLE
(— OF EYE) CATARACT
CLOUDLESS AZURE CLEAR BRIGHT
CLOUDY DIM DARK DULL HAZY
BLEAR FILMY FOGGY MISTY
MUDDY MURKY SHADY GLOOMY
LOWERY OPAQUE SMURRY

VEILED BLURRED CLOUDED
NEBULAR OBSCURE CONFUSED
NUBILOUS OVERCAST VAPOROUS
CLOUGH CLUF CLEFT CLOES
CLEUCH CLEUGH RAVINE VALLEY
CLOUT BAT BOX DAB HIT LAP
BEAT BLOW BUMP CLOD CLUB
CUFF JOIN MEND NAIL SLAP
SLUG SWAT PATCH SMITE
WHACK KLOWET STRIKE TACKET
TARGET THRASH WASHER
BANDAGE BOSTHOON
CLOVE GAP NAIL CHIVE CLEFT
GILLY BUTTON CLEAVE RAVINE
SHERRY GILLIVER
CLOVE BROWN EAGLE
CLOVEN CLEFT SPLIT DIVIDED
BISULCATE
CLOVEN-FOOTED SLIT FISSIPED
CLOVE PINK GELOFER GRENAD'N
CLOVER RED HAGI SEED HUBAN
LOTUS MEDIC NARDU PUSSY
ALSIKE BERSIM LADINO LEGUME
LUXURY NARDOO ALFALFA
BERSEEM BERSINE CLAIVER
COMFORT LUCERNE MELILOT
SAPLING TREFOIL TRIFOLY
COWGRASS HAREFOOT
NAPOLEON PUSSYCAT SHAMROCK
SUCKLING YELLOWTOP
CLOVER DODDER AILWEED
EPITHYME HAILWEED HAIRWEED
HALEWEED
CLOWN HOB OAF PUT APER BOOR
FOOL GAUM GOFF JOEY LOUT
MIME MOME SWAD ZANY ANTIC
BUFFO CHUFF CHURL COMIC
FESTE IDIOT MIMER PATCH
PUNCH WAMBA ZANNI AUGUST
BODACH CHOUGH HOBBIL JESTER
JOSKIN LUBBER RUSTIC STOOGE
AUGUSTE BODDAGH BUFFOON
BUMPKIN CHARLEY COSTARD
KOSHARE LAVACHE LOBSTER
MUDHEAD PEASANT PIERROT
PLAYBOY SCOFFER TOMFOOL
COVIELLO KOYEMSHI MERRYMAN
WHITEFACE PUNCHINELLO
CLOWNISH RAW RUDE ZANY
GAWKY ROUGH BORREL CLUMSY
COARSE RUSTIC AWKWARD
BOORISH BORRELL HOBLIKE
KERNISH LOBBISH LOUTISH
UNCIVIL VILLAIN BOEOTIAN
CLUBBISH SWADDISH UNGAINLY
CLOY CLOG GLUT NAIL PALL SATE
GORGE PRICK ACCLOY PIERCE
SATIATE SATISFY SURFEIT
SATURATE
CLOYED BLASE
CLOYER SNAP
CLOYING GOOEY SWEET VANILLA
CLOYSOME LUSCIOUS
SACCHARINE
CLUB BAT DOG HIT HUI SET BEAT
CANE JOIN MACE MALL MAUL
MERE POLT TEAM BAFFY BANDY
BATON BILLY BUNCH CLOUT
HURLY KEBBY LODGE MASHY
ORDER STAFF STICK TOWEL
UNITE YOKEL ZONTA BULGER
CERCLE CIRCLE CLIQUE CUDGEL
HURLEY KEBBIE LIBBET MACANA

MASHIE MENAGE MUCKLE
NULLAH PRIEST STRIKE TAIAHA
VEREIN WEAPON WHITES
BOURDON CAMBUCA COLLEGE
COUNCIL HETAERY HETAIRY
SOROSIS ATHENEUM BLUDGEON
CATSTICK SODALITY SORORITY
SPONTOON TERTULIA
KNOBKERRY
(— IN PLAYING CARDS) OAK
(— OF ANTENNA) CLAVUS
(BASEBALL —) FARM
(GOLF —) IRON WOOD BAFFY
CLEEK MASHY SPOON STICK
BRASSY BULGER DRIVER JIGGER
LOFTER MASHIE PUTTER BLASTER
MIDIRON NIBLICK PITCHER
(MAORI —) MERE MERAI MARREE
(POLICEMAN'S —) SAP BILLY
PANTOON SPONTON SPONTOON
NIGHTSTICK
(POLITICAL —) ROTA FASCIO
HETAERY HETAIRY
(SPIKED —) ALLIDE
(WAR —) WADDY
(WOMEN'S —) SOROSIS SORORITY
(PREF.) CLAVI CORDYL(O)
RHOPAL(O)
(SUFF.) CORYNUS
CLUB CARRIER CLAVIGER
CLUBFOOT TALUS VARUS VALGUS
TALIPES CYLLOSIS POLTFOOT
CLUB, GOLF (PART OF —) TOE FACE
GRIP HEAD HEEL NECK NOSE
SOLE HOSEL SHAFT
CLUB MOSS MOSS FOFEET
LYCOPOD PILIGAN CROWFOOT
FERNWORT
CLUBROOT CLUB ANBURY
ANBERRY HANBURY CLUBBING
CLUBFOOT
CLUB RUSH RUSH SEDGE GLUMAL
DEERHAIR
CLUCK HEN FUSS CHUCK CLACK
CLICK CLOCK CLOOK
CLUE KEY TIP BALL CLEW HINT
IDEA LEAD GUIDE TWINE
BOTTOM CLAVIS THREAD
INNUENDO
CLUMP SOP TOD BLOW BUSH
CLOT HEAP KNOT LUMP MASS
MOSS MOTT TOPE TUFT TUMP
TURB BLUFF BUNCH CLAMP
GROUP GROVE HOUSE PATCH
PLUMP STUMP TREAD WUDGE
CLUNCH DOLLOP LUMPER
BOSCAGE CLUMPER CLUSTER
THICKET
(— OF BRIERS OR ROSES) ROAN
RONE
(— OF CELLS) SLUDGE
(— OF SHRUBS) BUSH
(— OF SPORANGIA) SORUS
(— OF TREES) BLUFF HOUSE
HURST HYRST BOSQUE
CLUMSILY SOUSE GREENLY
GAUCHELY
CLUMSY AWK FLOB LEWD NUMB
RUDE BLUNT BULKY GAUMY
GAWKY HOGGY HULKY INAPT
INEPT SCRAM SPLAY STIFF STOGY
CLUMPY GAUCHE LUBBER
NOGGEN THUMBY WOODEN

AWKWARD BOORISH CHUCKLE
LOUTISH LUMPISH UNHANDY
UNREADY BENUMBED BUNGLING
CLOWNISH FOOTLESS GAUMLESS
HANDLESS LUMBERLY TACTLESS
UNGAINLY UNWIELDY CLOUTERLY
PONDEROUS
(NOT —) FINE
CLUSTER BOB BOG BUSH CLOT
COMA CONE CYME KNOT LUMP
TUFT BUNCH CLUMP DRUSE
GROUP PLUMP SHEAF SORUS
CENTER COLONY GATHER
MORULA PLEIAD REGIME
BOUROCK CLUTHER DOLPHIN
ENVIRON FOLIAGE FASCICLE
NUCLEATE SURROUND
(— AS BEES) BALL KNIT
(— OF BANANAS) HAND
(— OF BRANCHES) SPRAY
(— OF CRYSTALS) DRUSE
(— OF FEATHERS) MUFF
(— OF FIBERS) NEP
(— OF FLOWERS) CYME TRUSS
CORYMB ANTHEMY PANICLE
(— OF HAIRS) MYSTAX
(— OF METAL BALLS) GRAPE
(— OF NODULES) GRAPES
(— OF PILES) DOLPHIN
(— OF PLANTS) BED
(— OF RAYS) AIGRETTE
(— OF SPORES) SORUS
(— OF STARS) PRAESEPE
(— OF TINES) TROCHE
(— OF WOOL) NEP
(CONFUSED —) SPLATTER
(GERM CELL —) MORULA
(SUSPENDED —) SWAG
(PREF.) CORYMBI CYM(I)(O)
KYM(I)(O) RACEMI RACEMO
CLUSTER BEAN GUAR
CLUSTERED TUFTED RACEMOSE
AGGREGATE CONGLOMERATE
CLUTCH HUG NAB SET CLAM
CLAW CLEM CLIP FIST GLAM
GRAB GRIP NEST BROOD CATCH
CLASP CLAUT CLEEK CLICK
GLAUM GRASP GRIPE GRISP
HATCH LEVER POWER SEIZE
TALON CLEACH CLENCH CLETCH
CLINCH CUTOUT FASTEN RETAIN
SNATCH CLAUGHT CONTROL
CRAMPON COUPLING
(— OF EGGS) SET LAWTER LAYING
SETTING SITTING LAUGHTER
CLUTCHING GRIP GRIPING
CLUTTER MESS STUFF BUSTLE
CUMBER LITTER CLATTER
DISORDER CONFUSION
CLUTTERED CLATTY CLOTTED
CLYMENE (DAUGHTER OF —)
ALCIMEDE
(FATHER OF —) MINYAS CATREUS
OCEANUS
(HUSBAND OF —) IAPETUS
NAUPLIUS PHYLACUS
(MOTHER OF —) TETHYS
(SON OF —) OEAX ATLAS IPHICLUS
PHAETHON MENOETIUS
PALAMEDES
CLYPEUS NASUS EPISTOME
PRELABRUM

CLYSTER LAVEMENT INJECTION
CLYTEMNESTRA (BROTHER OF —)
CASTOR POLLUX POLYDEUCES
(DAUGHTER OF —) ELECTRA
LAODICE IPHIGENIA IPHINASSA
CHRYSOTHEMIS
(FATHER OF —) TYNDAREUS
(HUSBAND OF —) TANTALUS
AGAMEMNON
(LOVER OF —) AEGISTHUS
(MOTHER OF —) LEDA
(SISTER OF —) HELENA
(SON OF —) ORESTES
CLYTIUS (BROTHER OF —) PRIAM
(FATHER OF —) EURYTUS
LAOMEDON
(MOTHER OF —) GAEA
(SLAYER OF —) HERCULES
(SON OF —) CALETOR
COACH BUS CAR FLY DRAG HACK
HELP ARABA BOGEY BOGIE BRIEF
CABIN FLIER FLYER PILOT PRIME
STAGE TEACH TRAIN TUTOR
ADVISE DIRECT FIACRE JARVEY
SALOON ADVISER CHARIOT
COACHER CONCORD GONDOLA
PREPARE RATTLER TALLYHO
CARRIAGE DORMEUSE PUPILIZE
(FAST —) FLIER FLYER
(HACKNEY —) FIACRE JARVEY
(HEAVY —) DRAG
(SLOW —) SLOWPOKE
(3-WHEELED —) TRICYCLE
COACHMAN FLY FISH JEHU WHIP
PILOT COACHY DRIVER COACHEE
COACHER YAMSHIK YEMSCHIK
COACTION EXPLOITATION
COADJUTOR PRIOR
COAGULANT CURD RENNET
STYPTIC COAGULUM GELATINE
COAGULATE GEL SET CAKE CLOD
CLOT CURD JELL QUAIL YEARN
COTTER CURDLE LAPPER LOBBER
LOPPER POSSET CLABBER
CLOTTER CONGEAL PECTIZE
THICKEN COAGULUM CONCRETE
SOLIDIFY
COAGULATED CRUDY CURDY
LIVERED
COAGULATION GOUT CLOTTER
COAGULUM CLOT THROMBUS
COAL RIB BASS DUFF FUEL SWAD
BLOCK CHARK EMBER GHOST
GLEED STOKE BARING BRAZIL
BURGEE CANNEL CARBON CINDER
FIRING SPLINT BACKING
BOGHEAD BRIGHTS BYERITE
COBBLES LIGNITE RATTLER
VITRAIN AMPELITE LANDSALE
(— IN PLACE) SOLID
(— PILLAR) STOOK
(— SLAB) SKIP
(BAD —) SMUT
(BED OF —) SEAM
(DIRTY —) RASH
(FINE —) DUFF SCREENINGS
(IMPURE —) SWAD
(LARGE BLOCK OF —) JUD JUDD
(LIVE OR GLOWING —) GLEED
GLEYD
(REFUSE —) BREEZE
(SIZE OF —) EGG NUT PEA LUMP

RICE SLACK STOVE BARLEY
BROKEN CHESTNUT WALLSEND
BUCKWHEAT
(SLATY —) BASS BONE BONY
(SMALL LUMP OF —) NUBBLING
(SMALL PORTION OF UNCUT —)
PANEL
(PREF.) ANTHRAC(O) CARBON(I)
COAL BED SEAM
COALBIN BUNKER
COAL BROKER CRIMP
COAL CAR JIMMY
COAL CHUTE DOCK
COAL DUST COOM CULM SMUT
COOMB
COALESCE MIX CLOG FUSE JOIN
BLEND MERGE UNITE COHERE
EMBODY MINGLE SINTER
COMBINE
COALESCENCE UNION FUSION
LEAGUE CAPTURE SYNANTHY
COALFISH SEY PARR COLEY
CUDDY SEITH BESHOW BILLET
CUDDEN PODLER SAITHE SILLOC
BADDOCK GLASHAN GLASSIN
PILTOCK POLLACK
(YOUNG —) PODLER PODLEY
COMAMIE POODLER SILLOCK
GRAYFISH
COALITION FRONT TRUST UNION
FUSION LEAGUE MERGER
ENTENTE ALLIANCE
COAL OIL KEROSENE
COALRAKE HOE FREGGIN
FRUGGAN SCRAPPLE
COAL WORKER GEORDIE HURRIER
COAL YARD REE
COAMING CURB LEDGE COMBING
COARSE FAT LOW RAW BASE BULL
DANK FOUL HARD HASK LEWD
LOUD RANK RUDE SOUR VILE
BAWDY BRASH BROAD CRASS
CRUDE DIRTY GREAT GROFF
GROSS HARSH HASKY HEAVY
LARGE LOOSE PLAIN RANDY
ROUGH ROUTH ROWTY RUDAS
STOGY STOUR THICK UNORN
BLOWSY BRAZEN BRUTAL
CALLOW CHUFFY COMMON
DUDGEN EARTHY IMPURE INCULT
RANDIE RIBALD ROUDAS RUDOUS
RUGGED RUSSET RUSTIC SULTRY
UNFELE VULGAR BLATANT
CARLAGE CARLISH CRIBBLE
FULSOME GOATISH LOUTISH
LOWBRED OBSCENE PROFANE
RAPLOCH RAUCOUS ROINISH
SENSUAL BARBARIC CLOWNISH
HOMESPUN IMMODEST INDECENT
PLEBEIAN STUBBORN UNCHASTE
COARSE-FIBERED STRONG
COARSE-GRAINED DRY GRUFF
COARSELY BROADLY HARSHLY
COARSEN HACKNEY
COAST BANK LAND RIPA BEACH
BOARD CLIFF SHORE SLIDE
WARTH ADJOIN BORDER RIVAGE
STRAND BOBSLED SEASIDE
APPROACH SEABOARD SEASHORE
COASTAL ORARIAN
COASTER MAT SLED TILE DOLLY
TROUT BARCON CRADLE CREEPER
MISTICO TOBOGGAN

COASTLAND MAREMMA

COAT FUR LAY PEE SAC TOG BARK BLUE BUFF CONY DAUB FOIL FOLD HIDE HUSK JACK JAMA JUPE MIDI PINK RIND SACK SCAB SEAL TOGE ZINC BENNY CLOTH CONEY COVER CRUST FLASH FROCK GLACE GLAZE HABIT JAMAH JEMMY LAYER OILER PAINT PLATE QUYTE SAQUE SHELL TERVE ALPACA BYRNIE COATEE DUSTER ENAMEL EXTIMA GROUND HACKLE INTIMA INVEST JACKET JOSEPH KIRTLE LACKER MANTLE MELOTE PARGET PELAGE RABBIT REEFER SEALER SILVER SLOUGH STUCCO TABARD VENEER BEESWAX BOBTAIL CASSOCK COATING COURTBY CRISPIN CUTAWAY GARMENT GROGRAM INCRUST KARAKUL LACQUER OILCOAT OVERLAY PALETOT PELISSE PLASTER SHELLAC SHOOTER SPENCER STRATUM SUBCOAT SURCOAT SURTOUT SWAGGER TOGEMAN TOPCOAT VESTURE BENJAMIN COURTEPY GRAPHITE INTONACO MACKINAW MEMBRANE OVERCOAT ROCKELAY SEALSKIN SHERWANI SILICATE TEGUMENT TRENCHER OUTERCOAT PETERSHAM REDINGOTE
(— **FOOD**) DREDGE
(— **LENS**) BLOOM
(— **OF ARMS**) CREST BLAZON BEARINGS
(— **OF BIRD SKINS**) TEMIAK
(— **OF BLOOD VESSEL**) MEDIA
(— **OF CARIBOU SKINS**) KOOLETAH
(— **OF DEFENSE**) JACK
(— **OF EYE**) CHOROID
(— **OF EYEBALL**) SCLERA
(— **OF GRAVEL**) BLOTTER
(— **OF INDIA**) ACHKAN
(— **OF MAIL**) FROCK BRINIE BYRNIE SECRET HAUBERK CATAPHRACT
(— **OF ORGAN**) INTIMA
(— **OF OVULE**) PRIMINE
(— **OF PLASTER**) SET ARRICCIO BROWNING INTONACO
(— **OF SEED**) ARIL BRAN EPISPERM
(— **OF WOOL**) FLEECE
(— **WITH ALLOY**) TERNE
(— **WITH PITCH**) PAY
(— **WORN UNDER ARMOR**) GAMBESON
(**DEER'S WINTER —**) BLUE
(**FIRST — OF TIN**) LIST
(**FUR —**) ANARAK ANORAK
(**HAIR —**) MELOTE
(**HOODED —**) GREGO CAPOTE
(**LONG —**) MAXI JIBBA JIBBAH KAPOTE DJIBBAH MAXICOAT NEWMARKET
(**LOOSE —**) CASSOCK PALETOT INVERNESS
(**MILITARY —**) TUNIC BLOUSE BUFFCOAT
(**OLD —**) MUMMOCK
(**RIDING —**) JOSEPH
(**SACKCLOTH —**) SANBENITO
(**SEALSKIN —**) NETCHA

(**SHEEPSKIN —**) ZAMARRA ZAMARRO
(**SHORT —**) PEA JUMP MIDI SACK TERNE JERKIN REEFER PEACOAT
(**THREE-QUARTER LENGTH —**) ACHKAN
(**WATERPROOF —**) BURSATI SLICKER
(**WOMAN'S —**) CARACO DOLMAN
(**WOOLLY —**) LANUGO

COATED GLACE BACKED FURRED LOADED CANDIED

COAT HANGER SHOULDER

COATI NASUA TEJON NARICA PISOTE ARCTOID

COATING (ALSO SEE COAT) FUR GUM ARIL DOPE DRAB FILM FLOR HAIR HOAR SKIN BLOOM FLASH GLACE GLAZE ICING SCALE BEAVER CHATON COVERT CRUSTA FINISH JACKET PATINA VENEER BACKING DIPCOAT FURRING GILDING LACQUER OVERLAY PLATING TINNING ACIERAGE CAMBOUIS CLADDING EMULSION FLOODING MUCILAGE OVERCOAT PERIDIUM PLASTERING
(— **OF BACTERIA**) SLIME
(— **OF GLASS**) MOILES FOLIATION
(— **OF GLUE**) ENAMEL
(— **OF ICE**) GLAZE
(— **OF SEED**) TESTA
(— **OF TONGUE**) ATTER
(**CORROSION —**) RUST
(**POWDERY —**) DOWN
(**PRUINOUS —**) FARINA
(**WALL —**) GROUT

COATLICUE (**HUSBAND OF —**) MIXCOATL
(**SON OF —**) HUITZILOPOCHTLI

COATTAIL LABIE LAPPET

COAX BEG COY PET CANT DUPE FAGE FAWN LURE URGE WILE JOLLY TEASE BANTER CAJOLE CUITLE CUTTER ENTICE FLEECH SEDUCE BEGUILE CROODLE CROWDLE CRUDDLE FLATTER IMPLORE SOOTHER WHEEDLE BLANDISH COLLOGUE INVEIGLE PERSUADE

COAXIAL CONCENTRIC

COB EAR LOB MEW COBB

COBBERER ROARER ROUSER

COBBLE DARN MEND PAVE BOTCH PATCH BUNGLE COGGLE REPAIR

COBBLER PIE SNOB SHEEP SOLER SUTOR ARTIST COZIER SOUTER BOTCHER CATFISH CRISPIN POMPANO SADDLER CHUCKLER SCORPION SNOBSCAT

COBBLERFISH COBBLER SUNFISH SHOEMAKER

COBBY STOUT HEARTY LIVELY STOCKY COMPACT

COBLE MULE KOBIL

COBNUT COB OUABE HOGNUT PIGNUT

COBRA ASP NAG HAJE NAGA NAJA KRAIT VIPER ELAPID URAEUS

COBWEB NET TRAP SNARE WEVET GOSSAMER

COCA CUCA KHOKA TRUXILLO

COCAINE COKE SNOW
(— **MIXED WITH HEROIN**) SPEEDBALL

COCASH ASTER SWANWEED

COCCOID BERRYLIKE

COCCULUS CEBATHA FISHBERRY

COCCYX (PREF.) COCCYG(O) COCCYGEO

COCHE MOCOA

COCHINEAL GRAIN BLANCO COCCUS GRANILLA

COCHINEAL FIG NOPAL

COCHINEAL INSECT VERMIL VERMEIL VERMILION

COCK COX TAP BANK BOOT COIL FOWL HEAP KORA PILE RICK SPAN COCKY COQUE FIGHT FUGIE GALLO SHOCK STACK STRUT VALVE YOWLE CRAVEN FAUCET HAMMER HEELER LEADER CONTEND GORCOCK PETCOCK ROOSTER SWAGGER ASTROLOG COCKBIRD COCKEREL COXBONES GAMECOCK JERMONAL STOPCOCK
(— **GUNLOCK**) NAB
(— **OF HAY**) HIPPLE
(— **OF THE WALK**) KINGFISH
(— **WITHOUT COURAGE**) CRAVEN
(— **WITHOUT SPURS**) MUCKNA
(**FIGHTING —**) FUGIE HEELER TURNPOKE
(**TURKEY —**) STAG
(**WATER —**) KORA
(**WEATHER —**) FANE VANE
(PREF.) ALECTORO ALECTRYO GALLI

COCKADE KNOT BADGE COCKARD ROSETTE TRICOLOR

COCKATIEL QUARRION

COCKATOO ARA ARARA COCKY GALAH MACAW ABACAY COCKIE PARROT CORELLA JACATAO CALANGAY GANGGANG

COCKATOO BUSH BLUEBERRY

COCKBOAT COG COCK SCULL COGBOAT

COCKCHAFER OAKWEB BUZZARD HUMBUZZ

COCKED HAT SCRAPER RAMILLIE

COCKER CODDLE COGGER CUITER QUIVER SPANIEL

COCKEREL COCK SLIP BANTAM

COCKFIGHT MAIN

COCKINESS SWAGGER

COCKLE COCK GALL GITH KILN OAST BULGE KAKEL SHELL STOVE DARNEL NUCULA PALOUR PUCKER RIPPLE WABBLE ZIZANY CUCKOLD WRINKLE HARDHEAD (PREF.) CONCH(O)

COCKLEBUR COTS CLOTE COCKLE BURDOCK BURWEED CADILLO CLOTBUR CUCKOLD CLOTWEED DITCHBUR

COCKNEY ARRY ORTHERIS LONDONESE

COCKPIT PIT RING RINK WELL ARENA CABIN FIELD GALLERA

COCKROACH BUG DRUM ROACH BEETLE BLATTID DRUMMER KNOCKER

COCKSCOMB CREST COXCOMB

COCKSPUR FINGRIGO GARABATO

COCKTAIL SOUR ZOOM BRONX CRUSTA GIBSON MAITAI COBBLER MARTINI NEGRONI SAZERAC SIDECAR STINGER SWIZZLE APERITIF DAIQUIRI MARGARITA

COCKY PERK PERT CRANK PERKY CROUSE FARMER JAUNTY COCKING ARROGANT

COCO KOKO BROMA COCOA COKER YUNTIA

COCOA MAHAL TURTLE PATASHTE

COCOA BROWN PUEBLO

COCONUT COCO COCKER NARGIL COCOANUT

COCONUT FIBER COIR KAIR KYAR CAYAR

COCONUT MEAT COPRA

COCONUT PALM KOKO NIOG

COCOON POD CLEW CLUE KELL SCAB SHED SHELL BOTTOM DOUPION FOLLICLE

COCO PLUM ICACO HICACO

COCOWOOD KOKRA

COCUSWOOD KOKRA

COD BAG BIB COR KID POD AXLE BANK CUSK FOOL GADE HOAX HUSK POOR ROCK BELLY DORSE DROUD GADID POUCH SCROD SHALE SHAUP TORSK BURBOT CODGER CULTUS ESCROD FELLOW MULVEL PILLOW POCKET TOMCOD WACHNA BACALAO CODFISH CODLING CUSHION KEELING KILLING MILWELL MORRHUA SCROTUM CABELIAU DOLEFISH KABBELOW KLIPFISH ROCKLING
(**BUFFALO —**) LING
(**CURED —**) DUNFISH
(**DRIED —**) STOCK
(**PILE OF DRIED —**) YAFFLE
(**SALTED —**) COR KLIPFISH HABERDINE
(**YOUNG —**) SPRAG

CODA CAUDA RONDO EPILOG FINALE CODETTA EPILOGUE POSTLUDE

CODDLE PET BABY CADE COOK MUCH HUMOR NURSE SMALM SPOIL CARESS COCKER COSSET COTTON FONDLE PAMPER PTISAN QUADLE PARBOIL

CODE BCD LAW FLAG CANON CODEX DOGMA FUERO CIPHER DIGEST SECRET SIGNAL MULTEKA PRECEPT DOOMBOOK MICROCODE
(— **OF CHIVALRY**) BUSHIDO
(— **OF LAWS**) ADA ADAT PANDECT SHERIAT DOOMBOOK
(— **OF RULES**) VINAYA
(— **OF WHAT IS FITTING**) DECORUM PROTOCOL
(**COMPUTER —**) ASCII
(**PUNCHCARD —**) HOLLERITH

CODETTA CONDUIT

CODEX ALEF CODE ALEPH ANNAL

CODFISH POOR SPRAG TORSK KEELING

CODGER COD CUFF CHURL CRANK MISER FELLOW NIGGARD

CODICIL ANNEX LABEL SCRIPT
CODIFY INDEX DIGEST CLASSIFY
CODLING HAKE
CODOL RETINOL
COEFFICIENT CUMULANT
  AUSTAUSCH
COELENTERATE POLYP MEDUSA
  ACALEPH RADIATE ACALEPHE
COENOBIUM COLONY
COENOCYTE SYMPLASM
  SYMPLAST SYNCYTIUM
COENZYME NAD NADP COFACTOR
COERCE COW CURB MAKE BULLY
  CHECK DRIVE FORCE ORDER
  COHERT COMPEL HIJACK
  CONCUSS ENFORCE REPRESS
  SANDBAG BLUDGEON BULLDOZE
  DISTRAIN RESTRAIN RESTRICT
  BLACKJACK
COERCION HEAT FORCE DURESS
  COMMAND
COEUR D'ALENE SKITSWISH
COEUS (BROTHER OF —)
  ENCELADUS
  (DAUGHTER OF —) LETO LATONA
  ASTERIA
  (FATHER OF —) URANUS
  (MOTHER OF —) GAEA
  (SISTER OF —) FAMA RUMOR
  (WIFE OF —) PHOEBE
COFFEE JO JOE RIO CAFE COHO
  COHU JAVA MILD MOCHA
  BOGOTA BRAZIL CAUFLE CHAOUA
  JAMOKE SANTOS TRIAGE
  ARABICA BOURBON MELANGE
  SUMATRA ESPRESSO MAZAGRAN
  MEDELLIN TRILLADO
COFFEE BEAN QUAKER
COFFEEBERRY JOJOBA CASCARA
  SOYBEAN PEABERRY
COFFEE CAKE KUCHEN
COFFEEHOUSE INN CAFE
  CAFENEH CAFENER CAFENET
COFFEEMAKER SILEX
COFFEEPOT PERCOLATOR
COFFEE TREE BONDUC CHICOT
  VIRGILIA
COFFER ARK BOX DAM PYX CHEST
  HUTCH TRUNK CASKET FORCER
  FORCET SPRUCE TRENCH
  CAISSON CASHBOX CASSOON
  COFFRET LACUNAR LAQUEAR
  CIBORIUM STANDARD
COFFIN BIER CASE CIST KIST MOLD
  PALL SHELL BASKET CASING
  CASKET COFFER HEARSE TROUGH
  THROUGH
  (LEADEN —) COPE
COG CAM LIE NOG CAUK COCK
  GEAR JEST CATCH CHEAT CHOCK
  CHUCK COGUE COZEN TENON
  TOOTH TRICK WEDGE WHEEL
  CAJOLE COGGING DECEIVE
  PRODUCE QUIBBLE WHEEDLE
COGENT GOOD PITHY VALID
  POTENT STRONG TELLING
  FORCIBLE POWERFUL PREGNANT
COGITATE MULL MUSE PLAN
  THINK PONDER CONNATE
  MEDIATE REFLECT CONSIDER
COGNATE KIN AKIN ALIKE ALLIED
  COGENER KINDRED RELATED

SIMILAR BANDHAVA RELATIVE
  APOPHONIC
COGNITION GNOSIS NOESIS
  KENNING KNOWLEDGE
  PERCEPTION
  (SUFF.) GNOSIA GNOSIS GNOSTIC
  GNOSY
COGNITIVE KNOWING EPISTEMIC
COGNIZANCE KEN WIT HEED
  MARK BADGE CREST EMBLEM
  NOTICE BEARING COCKADE
  KNOWING PRIVITY WITTING
COGNIZANT WARE WISE AWAKE
  AWARE GUILTY KNOWING
  WITTING ACKNOWNE SENSIBLE
  (BE —) DEEM
COGNOMEN NAME BYNAME
  AGNOMEN SURNAME NICKNAME
  PATRONYM
COGON ILLUK KUNAI LALANG
COGWOOD CERILLO
COHABIT BED LIVE DWELL
  ADHERE OCCUPY COMPANY
  ACCUSTOM
CO-HEIR PARCENER
COHERE FIT BOND GLUE SUIT
  AGREE CLING SEIZE STICK UNITE
  ADHERE CEMENT CLEAVE
  CONNECT COINCIDE
COHERENCE UNION CONSENT
  CONTEXT COHESION STRENGTH
COHERENT SERRIED
COHESION BOND ADHESION
  HARDNESS STRENGTH
COHESIVE FATTY TENACIOUS
COHESIVENESS TENACITY
COHOBA PARICA
COHOSH SQUAWROOT
  PAPOOSEROOT
COHUNE COROJO COROZO
COIF CAP HOW HOOD HOUVE
  BEGGIN BIGGIN BURLET HAIRDO
  QUAIFE ARRANGE CALOTTE
  BIGGONET COIFFURE SKULLCAP
COIFFURE COIF HEAD HAIRDO
  TUTULUS TRESSURE
COIL ADO WIN WIP ANSA CLEW
  CURL FAKE FANK FURL FUSS
  HANK LINK LOOP ROLL TUFT
  WIND ENROL FLAKE HELIX QUERL
  QUILE ROUND SPIRE TENSE
  TESLA TWINE TWIRL TWIST
  WHORL WRING BOBBIN BOTTOM
  BOUGHT DIMMER ENROLL
  GLOMUS HEATER RENDER
  RUNDLE SPIRAL TEASER TOROID
  TUMULT UPWIND VOLUME
  WINDUP WREATH ENTRAIL
  HAYCOCK INVOLVE PRIMARY
  RINGLET ROULEAU SNAKING
  TICKLER TROUBLE WREATHE
  COFUSION CONVOLVE ENCIRCLE
  INDUCTOR OVERCOIL
  (— IN STILL) SCROLL
  (— INTO BALL) WIRE
  (— OF CAPILLARIES) TUFT
  (— OF HAIR) BUN PUG
  (— OF SNAKE) FOLD
  (— OF WIRE) BOBBIN SOLENOID
  (INDUCTION —) JIGGER
  (PREF.) SPIR(I)(O) SPIRILLO
COILED GYRATE TORTILE WRITHEN

COILER FLARER
COILING SPIRY
COIN AS BU PU AVO BAN BIT BOO
  COB DAM DIE DUB ECU FIL JOE
  KIP LAT LEK LEU LEV LEY ORI PUL
  SEN SOL TRA WEN WON ZUZ
  ABAS ANNA ATTE BAHT BATZ
  BESA CASH CENT CHIP CHON
  DEMY DIME DOIT DONG DOTT
  DUMP DURO FELS FILS GILL GROS
  GROT HARP HOON HWAN JACK
  JANE KRAN KYAT LEVY LION MAIL
  MAKE MERK MILL MINT MITE
  MULE OBAN ONZA OORD PARA
  PAUL PESA PESO PICE POND
  POUL QUAN RAND RIAL ROCK
  RYAL SCAD SENT SINK SIZE SLUG
  TAEL TARA TARE TARI TARO TIAO
  TREY TYPE UNIT ACKEY AGNEL
  AGORA AKCHA ALBUS ALTIN
  ALTUN AMANI ANGEL ANGLE
  ASPER BAIOC BAIZA BATTE BEKAR
  BELGA BETSO BEZZO BISTI BLANC
  BLANK BODLE BROAD BROWN
  CHINK CLINK COIGN CONTO
  COROA CROSS CROWN CUNYE
  DARIC DINAR DISME DOBLA
  DUCAT EAGLE EYRIR FANAM
  FANON FODDA FRANC GAZET
  GRANO GROAT GROSZ HALER
  HECTE JACOB JULIO JUSTO
  KOBAN KRONA KRONE KROON
  LIARD LIBRA LITRA LIVRE LOUIS
  MEDAL MEDIN MEDIO MILAN
  MOHUR MOPUS NOBLE NOMOS
  OBANG ORKEY ORKYN PAISA
  PAOLO PARDO PENNY PERAU
  PESSA PIECE PLACK PLATE POALI
  POALO PROOF PRUTA QUART
  QUINE RAPPE REBIA RIDER RIYAL
  ROYAL RUBLE RUPIA SAIGA
  SAPEK SCEAT SCUDO SCUTE
  SEMIS SHAHI SICCA SMASH
  SOLDO STAMP STYCA SUCRE
  TALER TANGA TANKA TEMPO
  THRIP TICAL TRIME UNCIA UNITE
  WHITE ABASSI ABBASI AFGHAN
  AHMADI ARGENT ASSARY
  AUREUS AZTECA BALBOA BAUBEE
  BAWBEE BEAVER BEZANT BIANCO
  BLANCO BOGACH BRONZE CARLIN
  CENTAS CHAISE COBANG
  CONDOR COPPER CORONA
  CUARTO CUNZIE DECIME DENARY
  DENIER DERHAM DINDER DIOBOL
  DIRHAM DIXAIN DIZAIN DOBLON
  DODKIN DOLLAR DOPPIA DOUBLE
  ESCUDO FILLER FLORIN FOLLIS
  FORINT GEORGE GIULIO GOURDE
  GRIVNA GROSSO GUINEA GULDEN
  HARPER HELLER ICHIBU ITZEBU
  JUSLIK KLIPPE KOPECK KORONA
  KORUNA LAUREL LEPTON
  MACUTA MAHBUB MAIDEN
  MANCUS MEDINO MISKAL NICKEL
  NORKYN OCHAVO OCTAVE
  ONGARO PADUAN PAGODA
  PARDAO PATACA PATART PHILIP
  PRUTAH QUEZAL ROSARY
  SALUNG SALUTE SATANG SEQUIN
  SESKIN SHEKEL SHIELD SIGLOS
  SINKER SIXAIN SOMALO SOVRAN

STATER STELLA STIVER TALENT
  TARGET TESTAO TESTER TESTON
  THALER THOMAN TOSTON TRIENS
  TUMAIN TUNGAH TURNER
  TURNEY TURTLE UNGARO
  VINTEM XERIFF YUZLIK ZECHIN
  ZEHNER ZEQUIN ALFONSO
  ALTILIK ANGELET ANGELOT
  ANGOLAR ANGSTER BAIOCCO
  BAJOCCO BARBONE BOLIVAR
  CARDECU CARLINE CARLINO
  CAROLIN CAROLUS CENTAVO
  CHALCUS CHALKOS CORDOBA
  COUNTER CRUSADO DAMPANG
  DRACHMA DUCATON DUPLONE
  ESCALAN FANTASY JACOBUS
  JOANNES KASBEKE KREUZER
  LEMPIRA LEONINE LEOPARD
  LUIGINO MANGOUR MARENGO
  MOIDORE MONARCH MUZOONA
  NOUMMOS ONCETTA PAHLAVI
  PARISIS PATACAO PATAGON
  PATAQUE PENNING PFENNIG
  PISTOLE QUADRIN QUARTER
  QUATTIE QUETZAL QUINYIE
  REDDOCK RUDDOCK RUSPONE
  SANTIMS SCRUPLE SEXTANS
  SILIQUA SIZEINE SOLIDUS SPECIES
  STAMPEE STOOTER STUIVER
  SULTANE TALLERO TEECALL
  THRYMSA TORNESE TRIOBOL
  UNICORN XERAFIN ALBERTIN
  AMBROSIN AQUILINO AUGUSTAL
  AUKSINAS BAETZNER BAGATINE
  BECHTLER BLAFFERT BLANKEEL
  BLANKILO BROCKAGE CAVALIER
  CHINKERS CHUCKRAM COLONIAL
  COURONNE CROCKARD CRUZEIRO
  DECUSSIS DENARIUS DIDRACHM
  DIOBOLON DOUBLOON EQUIPAGA
  FARTHING FILIPPIC FREDERIK
  GAZZETTA GENOVINO GIGLIATO
  GIUSTINA GROSCHEN HARDHEAD
  HYPERPER IMPERIAL ISABELLA
  JOHANNES KREUTZER LUSHBURG
  MACARONI MAJIDIEH MARAVEDI
  MARCELLO METALLIK MILESIMA
  PATACOON PAVILION PICAYUNE
  PIEDFORT PISTOLET PLAPPERT
  PORTAGUE QUADRANS
  QUADRINE QUARTINE QUINCUNX
  RESTRIKE RIGMAREE RISDALER
  RIXDALER SCUDDICK SEMUNCIA
  SESTERCE SHILLING SIXPENCE
  SKILLING SLEEPING SOLIDARE
  STERLING STOTINKA SULTANIN
  TENPENNY TETROBOL THIRTEEN
  TWOPENCE ZECCHINO
  BRACTEATE
  (— AROUND NECK) TALI
  (— HAVING MINTING ERROR) FIDO
  (— IMPERFECTLY MINTED)
  BROCKAGE
  (— OF TRIFLING VALUE) RAP
  (BASE —) SHAND SHEEN SINKER
  (COUNTERFEIT —) RAP GRAY GREY
  SLIP SHEEN SHOFUL STUMER
  STUMOR
  (PLUGGED —) PLUG
  (SMALL THICK —) DUMP
  (PL.) AGOROT CHANGE CHINKS
  SERIES COINAGE

(PREF.) NUMISMATO NUMMI
COINAGE FICTION GALUMPH
MINTAGE
COINCIDE FIT GEE JIBE JUMP
AGREE TALLY CONCUR
COINCIDENT EVEN TOGETHER
COINCIDING CONGRUENT
CONSILIENT
COINER MONIER MONEYER
SMASHER
COITION SOIL VENERY MEETING
CONGRESS
COKE ASK COAL COLK CORE DOPE
CHARK COCAINE
(BROKEN —) BREEZE
COL GAP NEK HALS JOCH PASS
HALSE SWIRE SADDLE
COLANDER SIEVE STRAINER
COLAXAIS (BROTHER OF —)
ARPOXAIS LIPOXAIS
(FATHER OF —) TARGITAUS
COLCOTHAR SAFFRON TUSCANY
COLD FLU ICY MUR NIP COOL
DEAD DULL HARD HASK HOAR
MURR ROUP SOUR ACALE ACOLD
AGUED ALGID BLEAK CHILL CRISP
FISHY FRORE GELID GLACE GLARE
OORIE OURIE PARKY POOSE
RHEUM SHARP SNELL STONY
VIRUS ARCTIC BITTER BOREAL
CHILLY CLAMMY CRIMMY FREDDO
FRIGID FRIGOR FROSTY GLASSY
MARBLY STECKY WAIRCH WINTRY
BRITTLE CATARRH CHILLED
COLDISH COSTIVE DISTANT
FROSTED GLACIAL INHUMAN
MORFOND SHIVERY STRANGE
FREEZING MORFOUND PIERCING
RESERVED RHIGOSIS STANDOFF
UNHEATED REPULSIVE
(— IN HEAD) POSE POOSE CORYZA
CATARRH GRAVEDO SNIVELS
SNIFFLES SNIFTERS
(BITTER —) ARCTIC
(VERY —) FRIGID PEEVISH
(PREF.) CRY(O) FRIGO FRIGORI
KRY(O) PSYCHRO
COLD-BLOODED BRUTAL LEEPIT
COLD CUTS ASSIETTE
COLD-HEARTED COLD FROZEN
BLOODLESS
COLDLY DRILY DRYLY
COLDNESS COLD FROST STEEL
PHLEGM ALGIDITY ASPERITY
DISTANCE FROIDEUR
COLDONG FRIARBIRD
COLE CALE KAIL KALE COLZA
FRIGOR COLEWORT
COLESEED NAVEW
COLEUS KOORKA
COLEWORT COLE KALE RIBE
STOCK CABBAGE
(SPROUT OF —) STOVEN
COLIC BATS FRET BATTS GUTTIE
BELLYACHE
COLICROOT UNICORN ALOEROOT
HUSKROOT HUSKWORT
STARWORT
COLIMA TAPA IRONWOOD
COLISEUM HALL STADIUM
THEATER COLOSSEUM
COLL HUG CLIP CULL POLL PRUNE
EMBRACE

COLLABORATE AID ASSIST
COOPERATE
COLLAGEN OSSEIN
COLLAPSE CAVE FALL FLOP FOLD
GIVE SINK CRASH SLUMP WRECK
BUCKLE SHRINK TUMBLE CAPSIZE
CROPPER CRUMBLE CRUMPLE
DEBACLE DEFLATE FAILURE
FLUMMOX FOUNDER SMASHUP
CONTRACT DOWNFALL TAILSPIN
PROSTRATION
COLLAPSED QUAT CLUNG
COLLAPSIBLE FOLDING
COLLAPSING FAILURE COLLABENT
COLLAR CAP FUR NAB BAND BOSS
ETON FALL FANO GILL GRAB
POKE RING RUFF CHAIN DICKY
FANON FANUM FICHU PHANO
RUCHE SEIZE STOCK TRASH
WHISK BERTHA CARCAN CHOKER
COLLET COLLUM DICKEY GORGET
PARRAL PARREL RABATO REBATO
SADDLE SLEEVE TACKLE TORQUE
TUCKER TURNUP BOBACHE
BOBECHE CAPTURE CHIGNON
CIRCLET PANUELO PARTLET
POTHOOK REBATER SHACKLE
STICKUP VANDYKE CARCANET
CINCTURE NECKBAND NECKLACE
RABATINE STARCHER TURNDOWN
(— FOR HORSE) BARGHAM
BRECHAM
(HIGH —) GILLS JAMPOT
(HORSE —) BRECHAM
(IRON —) JOUG JOUGS CARCAN
POTHOOKS
(LACE —) SCALLOP
(MAGISTRATE'S —) GOLILLA
(ROMAN —) RABAT
(WHEEL-SHAPED —) RUFF
(WOODEN —) CANG CANGUE
COLLAR BEAM SPANNER
SPANPIECE
COLLARBONE CLAVICLE
COLL'ARCO ARCATO
COLLARED ACCOLLE ACCOLLEE
TORQUATE
COLLAR PAD AFTERWALE
COLLATE BESTOW CONFER VERIFY
COMPARE
COLLATERAL SIDE MARGIN
OBLIQUE INDIRECT PARALLEL
SECURITY
COLLATION TEA MEAL BEVER
LUNCH REPAST SERMON
ADDRESS READING DEJEUNER
HOTCHPOT TREATISE
COLLEAGUE AIDE ALLY UNITE
DEPUTY SOCIUS ADJUNCT
COLLEGE COMPEER CONSORT
PARTNER CONFRERE CONSPIRE
COLLECT JUG SAM TAX CALL
CARD CULL DRAW HEAP LEVY
LIFT PICK PILE POOL REAR SAMM
SAVE AMASS CROWD GLEAN
GROUP HOARD RAISE STORE
SWEEP ACCOIL ACCRUE CENTER
CONFER GARNER GATHER
MUSTER PRAYER SEMBLE SHEAVE
UPTAKE ARCHIVE CLUSTER
COMPILE CONGEST ENGROSS
IMPOUND RAMMASS RECUEIL
SCAMBLE SYNAPTE ASSEMBLE

CONFLATE CONTRACT CUPBOARD
INGATHER RESEMBLE SCRAMBLE
SCROUNGE
(— AND DRIVE INTO ENCLOSURE)
WEAR
(— FOOD) FORAGE
(— GRAIN) GAVEL
(— INTO COVEY) JUG
(— MONEY) NOB
(— WAGES) UPLIFT
COLLECTED CALM COOL SOBER
SERENE PRESENT COMPOSED
(PREF.) ATHRO
COLLECTION ANA BAG KIT SET
BAND BEVY BOOK CLAN CROP
FILE HEAP HEAP KNOT LEVY OLIO
RAFT SORT ALBUM ANNEX BATCH
BUDGE BUNCH DEPOT FLOCK
GLEAN GROUP HOARD KITTY
SHEAF STORE SUITE SWATH
AFFLUX BUDGET BUNDLE
CONGER CORPUS FARDEL
MISHNA PARCEL RAGBAG RECULE
SORITE SPRING SWATHE TUMBLE
ACCOUNT BOILING BULLARY
CLUSTER COLLECT CONGERY
EXHIBIT FERNERY FISTFUL
FLUTTER GALLERY QUOTITY
RECUEIL SAMHITA SMATTER
SMYTRIE SYLLOGE TERRIER
ASSEMBLY CABOODLE CONGERIE
CUSTOMAL FASCICLE GATHERUM
GLOSSARY JINGBANG ROMESCOT
ROMESHOT SYNTAGMA
(— AT FOX HUNT) CAP
(— OF ANIMALS) ZOO HEAD
(— OF BOOKCASES) STACK
(— OF BOOKS) SET BIBLE CANON
LIBRARY
(— OF CONIFERS) PINETUM
(— OF DATA) GROUND
(— OF FORMULAS) CODEX
(— OF FOUR) TETRAD
(— OF HUTS) BUSTEE
(— OF LAWS) CODE
(— OF MAPS) ATLAS
(— OF OBJECTS) AFFAIR
(— OF OPINIONS) SYMPOSIUM
(— OF PERSONS) BOODLE
(— OF PLANTS) SERTULE
(— OF POEMS) DIVAN DIWAN
SYLVA ANTHOLOGY
(— OF PUS) ABSCESS HYPOPYON
(— OF REVENUES) TAHSIL TEHSIL
(— OF ROCKS) SUITE
(— OF RULES) SUTRA SUTTA
(— OF SAMPLES) SWATCH
(— OF SAYINGS) ANA
(— OF SPECIMENS) CABINET
(— OF STAFFS) SYSTEM
(— OF STORIES) LEGEND
(— OF TIPS) TRONC
(— OF TOOLS) LAYOUT
(— OF TREES) SERINGAL
(— OF UNWANTED ANIMALS)
LARDER
(— OF WRITINGS) CORPUS
(— OF 24 SHEETS) QUIRE
(CONFUSED —) CLUTTER
(MISCELLANEOUS —) OLIO FARDEL
SMYTRIE
(VAST —) CLOUD
(SUFF.) ERY

COLLECTIVE GROUP AGGREGATE
COLLECTIVIST COMMUNIST
SOCIALIST
COLLECTOR COMB CAMEIST
CURIOSO DUSTMAN FURIOSO
UPTAKER ANTIQUER COUNTOUR
GATHERER OOLOGIST STAMPMAN
VIRTUOSO ZAMINDAR
(— ITEMS) RARIORA
(— OF BUTTERFLIES) AURELIAN
(— OF HERBS) SIMPLER
(— OF REVENUE) AUMIL AUMILDAR
TALUKDAR ZAMINDAR
(CUSTOMS —) HOPPO CUSTOMER
(TAX —) CAID QAID GABBAI
PUBLICAN TAHSILDAR
COLLECTORATE TALUK
COLLEEN GIRL LASS MISS BELLE
CAILIN DAMSEL
COLLEGE TOL HALL AGGIE HOUSE
LYCEE CAMPUS COLAGE SCHOOL
SIWASH ACADEMY MADRASA
SEMINARY
COLLEGER TUG
COLLET BAND NECK RING CHUCK
CULET CASING CIRCLE COLLAR
COLLUM FLANGE BUSHING
COLLIDE HIT RAM BUMP DASH
FRAY HURT BARGE CLASH CRASH
KNOCK SHOCK SMITE WRECK
CANNON HURTLE STRIKE THRUST
(— WITH) PRANG IMPINGE

COLLIE KELPIE BEARDIE
COLLIER MINER PLOVER GEORDIE
COILYEAR FLATIRON SCUTCHER
COLLIQUATION SYNTEXIS
COLLISION HIT FOUL CLASH
CRASH PRANG SHOCK HURTLE
IMPACT JOSTLE PILEUP SMASHUP
CLASHING CONFLICT
COLLOCATE SET PLACE ARRANGE
COLLOID GEL
COLLOQUIAL FAMILIAR INFORMAL
COLLOQUIUM INDUCEMENT
COLLOQUY CHAT TALK PARLEY
DIALOGUE
COLLOTYPE ARTOTYPE HELIOTYPE
COLLUDE PLOT SCHEME CONNIVE
COLLOGUE CONSPIRE
COLLUM NECK
COLLUSION DECEIT CAHOOTS
SECRECY PRACTICE PRACTISE
COLLUSIVE COVINOUS COLLUSORY

COLOMBIA
CAPE: VELA AGUJA MARZO
AUGUSTA
CAPITAL: BOGOTA
CAY: VELA VIGIA RONCADOR
COIN: PESO REAL CONDOR
PESETA CENTAVO
FORMER NAME: DARIEN
NEWGRANADA
GULF: URABA CUPICA DARIEN
TIBUGA TORTUGAS
INDIAN: BORO CUNA HOKA MACU
MUZO PAEZ CARIB CATIO
CHOCO COFAN COGUI CUBEO
GUANE PIJAO SEONA ARAWAK
BETOYA CALIMA INGANO
SALIVA TAHAMI TUCANO
TUNEBO YAHUNA ACHAGUA

ANDAQUI CHIBCHA CHIMILA
GUAHIBO GUAJIRO PANCHES
PUINAVE PUITOTO QUECHUA
TAIRONA GUARAUNO
MOTILONE
INLET: TUMACO
ISLAND: BARU NAIPO FUERTE
GORGONA CUSACHON
MEASURE: VARA AZUMBRE
CELEMIN
MOUNTAIN: CHITA HUILA PURACE
TOLIMA
MOUNTAINS: ABIBE ANDES BAUDO
COCUY AYAPEL PERIJA TUNAHI
CHAMUSA ORIENGAL
PLAINS: LLANOS
POINT: CRUCES LACRUZ SOLANO
CARIBANA GALLINAS
PORT: LORICA CARTAGENA
PROVINCE: META CAUCA CHOCO
HUILA VALLE ARAUCA BOYACA
CALDAS NARINO TOLIMA
VAUPES BOLIVAR CAQUETA
GUAJIRE VICHADA AMAZONAS
PUTUMAYO
RIVER: UVA BITA META MUCO
SINU TOMO UPIA YARI BAUDO
CAUCA CESAR ISANA MESAI
NECHI PATIA PAUTO SUCIO
AMAZON ARAUCA ARIARI
ATRATO CAGUAN VAUPES
YAPURA CAQUETA GUAINIA
INIRIDA TRUANDO VICHADA
APAPORIS CASANARE
GUAVIARE PUTUMAYO
MAGDALENA
TOWN: TEN ANZA BUGA CALI
MITU MUZO PAEZ SIPI TADO
TOLU YARI BELLO CHINU GUAPI
NEIVA PASTO TUNJA BOGOTA
CUCUTA IBAGUE QUIBDO
SANGIL CARTAGO LETICIA
PALMIRA PEREIRA POPAYAN
GIRARDOT MEDELLIN
MONTERIA CARTAGENA
TREE: ARBOLOCO
VOLCANO: PURACE
WEIGHT: BAG SACO CARGA LIBRA
QUILATE QUINTAL

COLON CROWN POINT HEMISTICH
MESYMNION
COLONIAL OVERSEA OVERSEAS
COLONIST BOOR COLON FATHER
CUTHEAN PIONEER PLANTER
SETTLER EMIGRANT
(— IN SICILY) SIKELIOT
(AUSTRALIAN —) STERLING
(PL.) DEHAITES DEHAVITES
COLONIZE ECIZE FOUND PLANT
GATHER SETTLE MIGRATE
COLONIZER OECIST OEKIST
COLONNADE ROW STOA PORCH
PARVIS PIAZZA XYSTUS EUSTYLE
GALLERY PARVISE PERGOLA
PORTICO TERRACE CHOULTRY
DIASTYLE PERISTYLE
COLONNETTE COLUMELLA
COLONY STATE STOCK SWARM
CENOBE CORMUS APOIKIA
COLONIA CENOBIUM GANNETRY
PLANTATION POLYZOARIUM
(— OF BEES) HIVE SKEP SWARM

(BRYOZOAN —) ESCHARA
COLOR (ALSO SEE SPECIFIC COLOR)
DIP DYE HUE BLEE CAST FAKE
FLAG PUKE SUIT TINT TONE
BADGE BLUSH GLAZE GLOSS
GRAIN PAINT SHADE STAIN TAINT
TASTE TENNE TINCT TINGE
TOUCH BANNER BLEACH BOTTOM
BRIDGE CHROMA ENSIGN INFECT
LOCKET MANTLE RADDLE
REDDEN STREAK TEMPER
COULEUR DEPAINT DISTORT
ENGRAIN PENNANT PIGMENT
SPECKLE COLORING STANDARD
TERTIARY TINCTURE
(— IMPARTED TO HERRINGS)
GILDING
(— LOSS) POLIOSIS
(— OF BIRD) SMUT
(— OF BODY) HEAT
(— OF EYES OF FOWLS) DAW
(— OF HUMAN FLESH) CARNATION
(— OF REFLECTED LIGHT)
OVERTONE
(— OF ROCK) STONE
(BLUE —) FOG JAY SKY WAD AQUA
BICE CIEL CYAN DELF DUSK IRIS
NAVY PAON SAXE WADE WOAD
ZINC AZURE BERYL BLUET CADET
CAPRI CHING COPEN DELFT
DELPH DIANA DRAKE EMAIL
GRAPE METAL NIKKO ORION
PEARL ROYAL SLATE SMALT
SMOKE VANDA CANTON CENDRE
COELIN ENSIGN GROTTO HATHOR
INDIGO LUPINE MARINE MASCOT
MIGNON ORIENT PENSEE
ROMANY SEVRES VENICE ZENITH
CELESTE CERAMIC CHICORY
DUSTBLU GOBELIN HORIZON
LIBERTY LOBELIA LOGWOOD
MATELOT PEACOCK PETUNIA
RAMESES SISTINE SIXTINE
ABSINTHE BLUEBIRD BLUEWOOD
BRITTANY CAESIOUS CATTLEYA
CERULEAN CERULEUM DUCKLING
ELECTRIC GENDARME HYACINTH
INFANTRY LABRADOR LARKSPUR
MASCOTTE MAZARINE MIDNIGHT
MOONBEAM NATIONAL SAPPHIRE
TWILIGHT WEDGWOOD
(BROWN —) BAY ELK FOX OAK
TAN ARAB BARK BOLE BRAN
BURE CAIN CLAY CORK CUBA
DATE DEER DRAB DUST ECRU
FAON FAWN GOAT GOLD HOPI
IRON LAMA LION MAST MESA
MUSK SEAL SIAM TEAK ACORN
ADUST ALOMA AZTEC BEIGE
BISON BLOND BLUSH BOLUS
BRIAR BRICK BRIER BROWN
BUNNY CACAO CAMEL CANNA
CLOVE COCOA CONGO EAGLE
FRIAR FUDGE GIPSY GRAIN GYPSY
HAZEL HENNA KAFFA KHAKI
LIVER MAHAL MALAY MECCA
MINIM MUMMY NEGRO OTTER
PABLO QUAIL SABEL SEDGE SEPIA
SIENA SIRUP SNUFF SUDAN
SUEDE SUMAC SYRUP TABAC
TAFFY TENNE TOAST TOPAZ
AFGHAN ALESAN ALMOND
APACHE ARGALI AUBURN

BAMBOO BEAVER BISQUE BISTER
BISTRE BLONDE BRONCO BRONZE
BURNET COCHIN COFFEE
CONDOR COOKIE COWBOY
CROTAL DORADO ESKIMO
FALLOW GINGER GRAVEL GROUSE
HAVANA ISABEL LOUTRE
MAROON MERIDA MOHAWK
MUFFIN NUTMEG ORIOLE
PAWNEE PLOVER PUEBLO RABBIT
RACKET RUDDLE RUSSET SAHARA
SANTOS SHERRY SORREL SPHINX
SPONGE STRING STUCCO
SUMACH SUNTAN THRUSH TIFFIN
TURTLE ASPHALT BADIOUS
BEESWAX BITUMEN BRACKEN
BRONCHO CALDRON CATTAIL
CIGARET COCONUT COTRINE
CRACKER DOGWOOD DURANGO
FEUILLE FILBERT GAZELLE
GOREVAN HARVEST LEATHER
LIBERIA MALABAR MIRADOR
MORDORE MOROCCO MUSCADE
MUSTANG NORFOLK OAKWOOD
PERIQUE PRALINE RACQUET
ROSARIO SABELLA SUNBURN
SUNDOWN TALLYHO TANBARK
TOBACCO TUSCANY ALDERNEY
ALGERIAN AMBROSIA BISMARCK
BOBOLINK CALABASH CARTOUCH
CAULDRON CINNAMON
CLAYBANK CORDOVAN
DOUBLOON ETRUSCAN
EUCHROME HAZELNUT ISABELLA
KOLINSKY LEAFMOLD MANDALAY
MOCCASIN MOLESKIN MOROCCAN
MUSHROOM NOISETTE PHEASANT
SAUTERNE SHAGBARK STARLING
TAMARACK TEAKWOOD
TERRAPIN TORTOISE WOODBARK
(DEAD-LEAF —) FILEMOT
(DEEP —) DARK
(FAST —) GRAIN
(GREEN —) BOA FIR IVY ALOE BICE
FERN JADE LEEK MOSS NILE SAGE
ALOES CEDRE CHLOR DRAKE
FAIRY HOLLY KELLY LOVAT OLIVE
SPRAY CANNON EMPIRE HUNTER
JASPER LAUREL LIERRE LIZARD
MEADOW MOUSSE MYRTLE
SPRUCE VERDET CELADON
CITRINE CORBEAU CRESSON
CYPRESS EMERALD INGENUE
JADEITE JUNIPER MESANGE
NEPTUNE OLIVINE PERIDOT
SEAFOAM SERPENT TILLEUL
VERDURE BAYBERRY CHASSEUR
COPPERAS EMERAUDE GLAUCOUS
GLOWWORM PARAKEET
PERRUCHE PISTACHE POPINJAY
SHAMROCK TARRAGON VIRIDIAN
WOODLAND
(GRIZZLED —) AGOUTI AGOUTY
(LACK OF —) PALLOR
(OF A DARKISH —) SUBFUSE
(OTHER —S) OR ASH BAT DOE DUN
JET TEA CHIP CORN CROW DAWN
DOVE GRAY GREY GULL HEMP
LAVA LEAD MODE MOLE NICE
NUDE PLUM PORT PUKE ROAN
RUST SAND SOOT WOOD AMBER
BEACH BLACK CAMEO CERES
CHILE CHILI COPRA CRANE CRASH

CREAM DWALE EBONY FLESH
GRAPE GREBE GREGE MAUVE
MOUSE PANSY PHLOX PLOMB
PRAWN PRUNE PUTTY RIFLE
SABLE SPICE STEEL THYME TWINE
ANATTO AURORA AUTUMN
CASTOR CINDER COLLIE CORCIR
DAHLIA DAMSON DENVER
EVEQUE FIESTA FUSTIC GAMBIA
GRIEGE KASPER MALLOW
MODENA NAVAHO NAVAJO
NIMBUS NUTRIA ONDINE ORCHID
OXFORD OYSTER PEANUT PEBBLE
PIGEON QUAKER RAISIN RESEDA
ROUCOU SEASAN SILVER TUSCAN
VANITY VESTAL VIOLET WALNUT
ADMIRAL ANNATTO ARBUTUS
ARDOISE ARNATTA BEGONIA
BERMUDA BLOSSOM BRINDLE
CARAIBE CARAMEL CORBEAU
COTRINE COWSLIP CRACKER
CRUISER MORELLO MURILLO
NATURAL OPHELIA PELICAN
PONTIFF POPCORN PRELATE
PUMPKIN QUIMPER REGATTA
ROSEBUD SAKKARA SANDUST
SPARROW SUNBEAM THISTLE
TUSSORE VERVAIN VIOLINE
WEIGELA WHEATEN ALUMINUM
AMARANTH AMETHYST BLONDINE
CARMETTA CHARCOAL CLEMATIS
COCOBOLO COQUETTE CREVETTE
CYCLAMEN EGGPLANT EMINENCE
FELDGRAU FLAMINGO GILLIVER
GRAPHITE GUNMETAL
HONEYDEW IMPERIAL JACINTHE
LAVENDER MARATHON MORILLON
MULBERRY PALMETTO
ROSEWOOD SAUTERNE SQUIRREL
SUNBURST WIRELESS WISTARIA
WISTERIA CARNELIAN
(RED —) DAWN FLEA GOLF GOYA
HEBE LAKE MIST PUCE RUBY
TULY WINE AGATE BRASS BRICK
CANNA CANON CEDAR CORAL
CUTCH EMBER FLAME FLASH
GULES LILAC MELON NYMPH
PEACH PEONY POPPY ROSET
SIENA SPARK TOTEM ACAJOU
ARCHIL AURORE AUTUMN
AZALEA BRAZIL CANYON CARROT
CATSUP CERISE CHERRY CHERUB
CLARET COGNAC DAMASK FRAISE
GAIETY GARNET GAYETY GRANET
JOCKEY KERMES MADDER
MALAGA MIKADO MURREY
NECTAR ORCHIL PATISE SALMON
SANDIX SHRIMP SIERRA SULTAN
TITIAN TOMATO AFRICAN
ANAMITE ANEMONE BEGONIA
BISCUIT BOKHARA CARMINE
CASTORY CATAWBA CATCHUP
CATECHU CRIMSON CURRANT
FIREFLY FUCHSIA FUCHSIN
GRANATE GRANITE HEATHER
INDIANA KETCHUP LACQUER
LOBSTER MAGENTA MASCARA
NACARAT OXBLOOD PAPRIKA
POMPEII PONCEAU REDWOOD
ROSETAN ROSETTE RUBELLE
SAFFLOR SARAVAN SCARLET
SINOPLE STAMMEL SULTANA
VERMEIL ALKERMES AMARANTH

ARCHILLA BISMARCK BORDEAUX BURGUNDY CAMELLIA CARDINAL CHAUDRON CHEROKEE CHERUBIM CHESTNUT COCOANUT CONFETTI DAMONICO DIANTHUS DUBONNET EVENGLOW GERANIUM GRENADIN GRIDELIN MAHOGANY MANDARIN MAROCAIN NACARINE TOREADOR
(SOLID —) SOLID
(TONE —) TIMBRE
(YELLOW —) HAY RAT WAX BEAR BUFF CLAY CORN CUIR ECRU FLAX GOLD LARK LIME MOTH WELD WOLD ACIER ALOMA AZTEC BEIGE BLAKE BRASS CRASH CREAM GRAIN HONEY IVORY LEMON MAIZE MAPLE SHELL STRAW TAUPE WOULD ACACIA ALMOND BANANA CANARY CATHAY CHROME CITRON CITRUS CROCUS DORADO FALLOW MANILA MASTIC MIMOSA NANKIN NUGGET OXGALL SULFUR SUNRAY SUNSET ANTIQUE APRICOT BISCUIT CAVALRY CHAMOIS GAMBOGE JASMINE JONQUIL LEGHORN MEXICAN NANKEEN PRAIRIE RHUBARB SAFFRON SULPHUR SUNGLOW ANTELOPE CALABASH CAPUCINE COCKATOO DAFFODIL EGGSHELL GENERALL GOLDMIST MARIGOLD ORPIMENT PRIMROSE SNOWSHOE
(PL.) FLAG
(PREF.) CHROM(AT)(ATO)(I)(IDIO)(O)
(HAVING DARK —) FUSCO
(SUFF.) CHROIA CHROIC CHROID CHROMASIA CHROME CHROMIA CHROMY CHROOUS
COLORABLE SPECIOUS PLAUSIBLE

COLORADO
CAPITAL: DENVER
COLLEGE: REGIS
COUNTY: BACA MESA YUMA OTERO OURAY ROUTT GILPIN CHAFFEE
MOUNTAIN: OSO LONGS PIKES ELBERT
MOUNTAIN RANGE: ROCKY
NATIVE: ROVER
PARK: ESTES
RIVER: YAMPA DOLORES APISHAPA ARIKAREE GUNNISON PURGATOIRE
STATE FLOWER: COLUMBINE
STATE NICKNAME: CENTENNIAL
STATE TREE: SPRUCE
TOWN: ASPEN DELTA LAMAR GOLDEN PUEBLO SALIDA ALAMOSA BOULDER DURANGO GREELEY GUNNISON LOVELAND TRINIDAD

COLORATION BLEE PILE FLASH CLOUDING COLORISM SCHILLER PIGMENTATION
COLORATURA GORGIA SOPRANO
COLOR-BLINDNESS DALTONISM
COLORED FAW HUED MALE BIASED DEPAINT STAINED

(— IN RED) RUBRIC
(— LIKE PIPE BOWL) TROUSERED
(BRILLIANTLY —) SUPERB FLAMING PSYCHEDELIC
(HIGHLY —) CHROMATIC PRISMATIC
(PARTI —) PIED PIEBALD
(UNIFORMLY —) HARD
(PREF.) CHROM(AT)(ATO)(I)(IDIO)(O)
(SUFF.) CHROME CHROOUS
COLORFUL GAY BRAVE JUICY VIVID COLORY GOLDEN FREAKED GORGEOUS
COLORING DYE BLEE TINT PAINT TINGE TINGENT BRONZING PAINTING TINCTURE
(— MATTER) TINCTION
(SUFF.) CHROMY
COLORING MATTER
(SUFF.) PHYLL(A)(OUS)(UM)(Y)
COLORLESS WAN DRAB DULL PALE ASHEN BLAKE BLANK PLAIN MOUSEY PALLID HUELESS NEUTRAL ACHROMIC ACHROOUS BLANCHED ETIOLATE LIFELESS
(PREF.) LEUC(O)
COLOSSAL BIG HUGE VAST GREAT JUMBO LARGE IMMENSE TITANIC ENORMOUS GIGANTIC MONSTROUS
COLOSSUS GIANT TITAN STATUE COLOSSO MONOLITH
COLOSTRUM FOREMILK AFTERINGS
COLT FOAL STAG FILLY POTRO STAIG HOGGET POLEYN STAGGIE EQUULEUS
COLTER LAVER COOTER COULTER FOREIRON
COLTSFOOT DOCK CLOTE HOOFS CLEATS FARFARA LAGWORT SOWFOOT BULLFOOT CLAYWEED FOALFOOT
COLUGO COBEGO
COLUMBATE NIOBATE
COLUMBIA SINKIUSE
COLUMBINE AQUILEGE BLUEBELL CHUCKIES ROCKBELL
COLUMBITE DIANITE NIOBITE
COLUMELLA STALACE
COLUMN COG LAT ROW FILE FUST GOAL LINE POLE POST PROP STUB BAGUE SHAFT STELA STELE TORSO TRUNK WURTZ ASOKAN CORNER GNOMON PILLAR SCAPUS STAPLE STRING TSWETT COLUMEL SUPPORT VIGREUX CYLINDER PILASTER
(— IN EAR) MODIOLUS
(— OF FIGURES) SUM
(— OF FILAMENTS) SYNEMA
(— OF MOLTEN ROCK) PLUME
(BUDDHIST —) LAT
(FIGURE USED AS —) ATLAS TELAMON
(PART OF —) BASE DADO NECK OVOLO SHAFT TORUS ABACUS PLINTH REGLET SCOTIA CAPITAL ECHINUS FLUTING ASTRAGAL CINCTURE COLARENO PEDESTAL
(ROCK —) HOODOO
(ROULETTE —) DERNIER

(SPINAL —) HORN SPINE BACKBONE
(STRUCTURAL —) LALLY
(TWISTED —) TORSO
COLUMNAR TERETE STELENE COLUMNAL VERTICAL
COLUMNIST WRITER ANALYST
COLY MOUSEBIRD
COLZA SARSON
COMA TUFT BUNCH CARUS SLEEP SOPOR STUPOR SUBETH TORPOR TRANCE SEMICOMA CHEVELURE
COMATOSE OUT DROWSY LETHARGIC
COMB CARD GILL KAME LASH RACK RAKE REDD REED SEEK TOZE BREAK BRUSH CAMBE CLEAN CREST CTENE CURRY FLISK RAVEL TEASE HACKLE SMOOTH CUSHION HATCHEL WRAITHE BEATILLE CARUNCLE TORTOISE
(WEAVING —) RADDLE
(PREF.) CTEN(O) LOPH(I)(IO)(O) PECTINATO
COMBAT WAR BLOW BOUT COPE DUEL FRAY MEEK MEET RUSH TILT CLASH FIGHT JOUST REPEL STOUR ACTION AFFRAY BATTLE MEDLEY OPPOSE RESIST SHOWER STRIFE CONTEND CONTEST COUNTER DERAIGN DISPUTE EXPLOIT SCUFFLE SERVICE ARGUMENT CONFLICT STRUGGLE
(— BETWEEN KNIGHTS) JOUST
(FUTILE —) SCIAMACHY
(SHAM —) SCIOMACHY
(SINGLE —) DUOMACHY
COMBATANT DUELER BATTLER FIGHTER CHAMPION GLADIATOR
COMBATIVE BANTAM MILITANT AGONISTIC BELLICOSE DEPENDENT PUGNACIOUS AGONISTICAL
COMBE HOPE
COMBED CRESTED
COMBER WAVE HANDER BREAKER KEMPSTER
COMBINATION KEY BLOC CLUB GANG PACT POOL RING CABAL COMBO GROUP JUNTO PARTY TRUST UNION CARTEL CLIQUE CORNER CRASIS FUSION LEAGUE MEDLEY MERGER AMALGAM BATTERY COMBINE CONSORT COTERIE FACTION HARMONY JOINING MIXTURE ADDITION ALLIANCE ENSEMBLE MONOPOLY GOODLIBET
(— OF CARDS) SET BUILD FLUSH SPREAD STRAIGHT
(— OF CIRCUMSTANCES) ACTION
(— OF COLORS) HARLEQUIN
(— OF FACES) FORM
(— OF FIRMS) TRUST
(— OF INTAGLIO FORMS) GRYLLI
(— OF NUMBERS) GIG SADDLE
(— OF TACKLES) JEERS
(— OF TONES) CHORD
(— OF 10) DECUPLET
(DANCE —) SEQUENCE
(HARMONIOUS —) CONCORD
(NOSE-JAW —) LAYBACK

(SCORING —) IMPERIAL
(PREF.) HAPT(O)
COMBINE ADD FIX MIX WED BIND BLOC CLUB JOIN NICK POOL BLEND GROUP JOINT MARRY MERGE TOTAL UNITE ABSORB CONCUR LEAGUE MEDDLE MERGER MINGLE SPLICE ACCRETE AMALGAM COMPACT CONJOIN CONJURE MACHINE COALESCE COMPOUND CONCRETE CONDENSE CONFLATE CONSTRUE CONTRACT CUMULATE FEDERATE ORCHESTRATE
(— AGAINST) BOYCOTT
(— WITH GAS) AERATE
(— WITH WATER) AQUATE
COMBINED GUM BOUND FIXED JOINT UNITED CONJOINT
COMBUSTIBLE FUEL FIERY ARDENT CINDER PICEOUS BURNABLE
COMBUSTION FIRE HEAT FLAME THERM TUMULT BURNING BACKFIRE
COME BE GET LAY COOP DRAW FALL GROW HAUL PASS WHEN ARISE CHIVE FETCH ISSUE LIGHT OCCUR REACH ACCRUE ADVENE APPEAR ARRIVE BECOME BEFALL EMERGE HAPPEN OBTAIN SPRING ADVANCE DEVELOP EMANATE PROCEED APPROACH PRACTICE
(— ABOUT) ARISE CHANCE
(— AFTER) SUE FOLLOW
(— APART) FRAY SHED BREAK STAVE
(— BACK) REVERSE
(— BEFORE) FORERUN PREVENE ANTECEDE ANTEDATE
(— DOWN) AVALE SWOOP ALIGHT DESCEND SUCCEED DISMOUNT
(— FORTH) EMIT BREAK ISSUE ACCEDE FORTHGO FURNACE
(— FORWARD) ACCEDE
(— IN CONTACT) ATTINGE
(— IN SECOND) PLACE
(— IN THIRD) SHOW
(— INTO BLOOM) BURST BLOSSOM
(— INTO COLLISION) MEET CLASH COLLIDE
(— INTO EXISTENCE) FORM BEGIN ACCRUE HAPPEN SPRING
(— INTO POSSESSION) ACQUIRE INHERIT
(— OF AGE) MAJORIZE
(— OFF) HARL PEEL
(— OUT) ISSUE APPEAR EMERGE EMANATE
(— SUDDENLY) CLAP
(— THROUGH) DELIVER
(— TO) TOUCH ADVENE STRIKE RECOVER REVERSE
(— TO BELIEVE IN) ADOPT
(— TO CONCLUSION) DECIDE
(— TO DIE) DO DIE SET DROP EXPIRE FINISH SURCEASE
(— TO GRIEF) FOUNDER
(— TO HAND) OFFER
(— TO LIGHT) SPUNK DEVELOP
(— TO MIND) OCCUR STRIKE
(— TO NOTHING) ABORT
(— TO PASS) SORT BREAK LIGHT

BEFALL BETIDE HAPPEN
(— TO PERFECTION) RIPEN
(— TO TERMS) AGREE TRYST
ACCORD BARGAIN COMPOSE
COMPOUND ACCOMMODATE
(— TOGETHER) ADD HERD JOIN
MEET AMASS CONCUR COUPLE
GATHER COLLECT COMBINE
CONVENE ASSEMBLE
(— UNDER) SUBVENE
(— UPON) FIND CROSS INVENT
STRIKE OVERTAKE
(FULLY —) EXPIATE
COMEBACK RALLY ANSWER
RETORT RETURN REBOUND
HAULBACK RECOVERY REPARTEE
COMECRUDO CARRIZO
COMEDIAN WAG WIT CARD
ACTOR ANTIC CLOWN COMIC
GAGMAN JESTER BUFFOON
FUNSTER COMOEDUS FUNMAKER
FUNNYMAN PATTERER
COMEDO BLACKHEAD
COMEDOWN BATHOS DESCENT
LETDOWN
COMEDY SOCK DRAMA FARCE
LAZZO REVUE SITCOM COMEDIA
TEMACHA COMOEDIA TRAVESTY
BACCHIDES SLAPSTICK
(HEROIC —) NATAKA
(PREF.) COMICO
COMEDY OF ERRORS (AUTHOR OF
—) SHAKESPEARE
(CHARACTER IN —) LUCE PINCH
AEGEON ANGELO DROMIO
ADRIANA AEMILIA EPHESUS
LUCIANA SOLINUS BALTHAZAR
ANTIPHOLUS
COMELINESS GRACE DECORUM
FEATURE VENUSTY PULCHRITUDE
COMELY FAIR GOOD HEND PERT
TALL TIDY WEME BONNY BUXOM
HENDE QUEME SONCY SONSY
TIGHT DECENT FORMAL GOODLY
LIKELY LIKING LOVELY PRETTY
PROPER SEEMLY SONSIE VENUST
FARRANT FORMFUL SIGHTLY
BECOMING DECOROUS FEATURED
GRACEFUL HANDSOME PLEASING
SUITABLE
COMET STAR METEOR XIPHIAS
(— HEAD) COMA
COMEUPPANCE REBUKE DESERTS
BUSINESS
COMFIT CANDY SUCKLE CONFECT
PRALINE CONSERVE PRESERVE
COMFORT AID EASE REST STAY
BIELD CHEER LIGHT SOOTH VISIT
ENDURE RELIEF REPOSE SOLACE
SOOTHE SUCCOR ANIMATE
ASSUAGE CHERISH CONFIRM
CONSOLE ENLIVEN GLADDEN
REFRESH RELIEVE SUPPORT
SUSTAIN INSPIRIT NEPENTHE
PLEASURE REASSURE
COMFORTABLE RUG BEIN BIEN
COSH COSY COZY EASY FEEL FEIL
LIKE SNUG TOSH TRIG CANNY
COMFY COUTH CUSHY LITHE
QUEME QUILT SCARF SONCY
COUTHY HEPPEN PENTIT SONSIE
RELAXED RESTFUL CHEERFUL
DELICATE EUPHORIC HOMELIKE

WRISTLET GEMUTLICH
COMFORTABLY SWEETLY
COMFORTED CONSOLATE
COMFORTER PUFF COVER EIDER
NAHUM QUILT SCARF TIPPET
CHEERER PACIFIER
COMFORTING TOSY TOSIE
FRIENDLY
COMFORTLESS DREARY FORLORN
UNCOUTH DESOLATE EITHLESS
COMFREY DAISY BONESET
BACKWORT KNITBACK
BRUISEWORT
COMIC DROLL FUNNY STRIP
BUFFONE COMIQUE THALIAN
COMEDIAN FARCICAL
COMICAL LOW BASE BUFFO
DROLL FUNNY MERRY QUEER
STRIP WITTY BOUFFE AMUSING
CARTOON JOCULAR RISIBLE
STRANGE TRIVIAL HUMOROUS
TICKLISH BURLESQUE SPLITTING
COMING DUE ANON COME NEXT
VENUE ADVENT FUTURE
TOWARD ARRIVAL FOOTING
FORWARD BECOMING DESERVED
NAISSANT PAROUSIA
(— AFTER) LATTER
(— AND GOING) FITFUL
(— INTO BEING) BIRTH GENESIS
(— NEAR) ACCESSION
(— OUT) ISSUE EGRESS
(— TO) ADIT
(— TO OFFICE) ACCESS ACCESSION
(— TOGETHER) SEANCE CONGRESS
COUPLING GATHERING
(SECOND —) PAROUSIA
COMMA POINT VIRGULE
(SCRATCH —) DIAGONAL
COMMAND DO BID SAW SOH
BECK BODE BOON CALL COME
EASY FIAT HEST HETE MAND
RATE RULE SWAY WARN WILL
WISH WORD BEKEN CHECK
COVER EDICT EXACT FORCE
HIGHT ORDER POWER SWEEP
UKASE ADJURE BEHEST CHARGE
COMPEL DECREE DEMAND
DEVICE DIRECT ENJOIN GOVERN
HOOKUM IMPOSE MASTER
ORACLE ORDAIN STEVEN
SUMMON APPOINT BEHIGHT
BIDDING CONCERN CONTROL
DICTATE JUSSION JUSSIVE
LEADING MANDATE OFFICER
PRECEPT REQUIRE SKIPPER
WARRANT BIDDANCE DOMINEER
IMPERATE INSTRUCT MANDAMUS
RESTRAIN
(— OF ARMY) CONDUCT
(— TO HORSE) GEE HAW HUP
HUPP WHOA GIDDAP HUDDUP
(— TO TURN LEFT) HAW
(— TO TURN RIGHT) GEE HUP HUPP
(MAGICIAN'S —) PRESTO
COMMANDANT GOVERNOR
KILLADAR
COMMANDED IMPERATE
COMMANDEER PRESS
(— AN AIRPLANE) SKYJACK
COMMANDER CID CIO DUX DUKE
EMIR HEAD JEFE BLOKE CHIEF
EMEER ADALID LEADER MASTER

RAMMER TARTAN ALCALDE
CAPTAIN CROWNER DECARCH
DEKARCH DRUNGAR EMPEROR
GENERAL KHALIFA MARSHAL
NAVARCH OFFICER VAIVODE
HERETOGA HIPPARCH LOCHAGER
LOCHAGUS MYRIARCH PHYLARCH
RISALDAR SERASKER TAXIARCH
TETRARCH VINTENER
PROCONSUL
(— IN CHIEF) SIRDAR TARTAN
TURTAN ADMIRAL GENERAL
COMMANDERY PRECEPTORY
COMMANDING DOMINANT
IMPERANT IMPERIAL IMPOSING
COMMANDMENT LAW RULE
ORDER COMMAND MITZVAH
PRECEPT BODEWORD
(DIVINE —) LAW
(TEN —S) DECALOG DECALOGUE
COMMANDO RAIDER RANGER
CHINDIT FEDAYEE
COMMELINA DEWFLOWER
COMMEMORATE FETE KEEP
FEAST REMENE EPITAPH
MEMORATE MONUMENT
REMEMBER MEMORIALIZE
COMMEMORATION AWARD
MEDAL COMMEM PLAQUE
JUBILEE MEMORIA MENTION
SERVICE EBENEZER ENCAENIA
MEMORIAL REMEMBRANCE
COMMEMORATIVE HONORARY
MEMORIAL
COMMENCE FALL FANG FILE
MOVE OPEN ARISE BEGIN FOUND
START ARRAME EMBARK INCEPT
LAUNCH SPRING STREAK STREEK
INITIATE
COMMENCEMENT ONSET ORIGIN
OUTSET KICKOFF OPENING
ENTRANCE
COMMENCING INITIAL NASCENT
INCIPIENT
COMMEND KEN PAT GIVE LAUD
ADORN ALOSE BEKEN BOOST
EXTOL GRACE OFFER BESTOW
BETAKE COMMIT PRAISE RESIGN
APPLAUD APPROVE BESPEAK
BETEACH DELIVER ENTRUST
INTRUST BEQUEATH
COMMENDABLE GOOD WORTHY
LOVABLE LOWABLE LAUDABLE
COMMENDATION LAUD PRAISE
CITATION
(EFFUSIVE —) SLAVER
(MARKED —) APPLAUSE
COMMENSAL EPIZOON MESSMATE
COMMENSALISM SYNOECY
SYMPHILY COMMUNISM
COMMENSURATE EVEN EQUAL
ENOUGH ADEQUATE RELEVANT
COMMENT BARB BRAG GIBE JIBE
NOTE TALK WORD ASIDE BREAK
DUNCE GLOSS GLOZE CUTTER
DILATE GAMBIT NOTATE POSTIL
REMARK SCANCE CAPTION
DESCANT DISCUSS EXPLAIN
EXPOUND ADDENDUM SCHOLION
SCHOLIUM DISPRAISE
(— DISAPPROVINGLY) HARRUMPH
(CAUSTIC —) SATIRE
(ILL-TIMED —) CLANGER

(MARGINAL —) APOSTIL
COMMENTARY GLOSS GEMARA
MEMOIR SATIRE ACCOUNT
COMMENT MEKILTA POSTILS
FOOTNOTE GLOSSARY TREATISE
COMMENTATOR HAKAM CRITIC
GLOZER ANALYST GLOSSIST
SCHOLIAST
COMMERCE TRADE BARTER
CHANGE TRAFFIC BUSINESS
EXCHANGE MERCATURE
NAVIGATION
COMMERCIAL STORE TRADY
TRADAL MERCHANT TRADEFUL
(— ESTABLISHMENT) HONG
COMMERCIALISM HUCKSTERISM
MERCANTILISM
COMMINGLE MIX FUSE JOIN
BLEND IMMIX MERGE UNITE
MINGLE COMBINE COMINGE
EMBROIL COMEDDLE
COMMINUTE MILL CRUSH GRIND
POUND POUNCE POWDER
COMMINUTED FINE
COMMISERATE PITY
COMMISERATION EMPATHY
SYMPATHY
COMMISSION PLAT SEND TASK
BOARD PRESS TRUST BRANCH
BREVET CHARGE DEMAND
DEPUTE ERRAND LEGACY OFFICE
ORDAIN PERMIT COMMAND
CONSIGN DUOVIRI EMPOWER
FITTAGE GOSPLAN MANDATE
MISSION SQUEEZE WARRANT
CORNETCY DELEGATE ENCHARGE
INTERPOL OVERRIDE POUNDAGE
(— AS CAPTAIN) POST
COMMISSIONAIRE CADDY CADDIE
DUBASH
COMMISSIONER ENVOY TRIER
LEDGER ARRAYER OFFICER
PRISTAW DELEGATE
COMMISSURE VINCULUM
COMMIT DO GIVE PULL STOW
TAKE ALLOT ARRET HIGHT LEAVE
REFER TEACH ARETTE ASSIGN
BETAKE ENGAGE PERMIT
REMAND BEHIGHT BETEACH
COMMAND COMMEND COMMISE
CONFIDE CONSIGN DELIVER
DEPOSIT ENTRUST INTRUSE
INTRUST BEQUEATH DEDICATE
DELEGATE IMPRISON RELEGATE
RECOMMEND PERPETRATE
(— ERROR) SNAPPER
(— MONEY) INVEST
(— TO BATTLE) LAUNCH
(— TO JAIL) JUG
(— TO MEMORY) CON LEARN
MEMORIZE
(— VIOLENCE) TOUCH
COMMITMENT OBLIGATION
COMMITTAL COMPROMISE
COMMITTED (— TO) ENGAGE
COMMITTEE BODY JURY RUMP
BOARD GROUP JUNTA TABLE
BUREAU SOVIET COUNCIL
DELEGACY POLITBURO
PRESIDIUM SYNDICATE
COMMIXTURE MIXTURE
HOTCHPOT CONFUSION
IMMISSION

COMMODE CAP CHEST STOOL TOPKNOT CUPBOARD FONTANGE

COMMODIOUS FIT AMPLE ROOMY PROPER USEFUL SPACIOUS SUITABLE CAVERNOUS

COMMODITY ITEM WARE GOODS STUFF EXPORT FUTURE STAPLE ARTICLE SHIPMENT
(**— SOLD SHORT**) BEAR
(**UNSALABLE —**) DRUG
(PL.) KIND SPOTS CHANDLERY

COMMON LAY LOW NOA TYE BASE MEAN RIFE TOWN VILE BANAL BRIEF CHEAP EJIDO EXIDO GREEN GRIMY GROSS JOINT LEASE OFTEN SLACK STALE TACKY TRITE USUAL COARSE DEMOID FAMOUS MODERN MUTUAL ORNERY PROPIO PUBLIC SIMPLE VULGAR AVERAGE CURRENT DEMOTIC GENERAL GENERIC IGNOBLE NATURAL POPULAR PROFANE RAFFISH REGULAR TRIVIAL UNNOBLE VILLAIN BANAUSIC EPIDEMIC FAMILIAR FREQUENT HABITUAL MECHANIC MEDIOCRE ORDINARY PANDEMIC PLEBEIAN TRIFLING TRITICAL RECIPROCAL
(**— OF ESTOVERS**) BOT BOTE
(**IN —**) ALIKE
(**NOT —**) UNTRADED
(PL.) COMMUNE
(PREF.) CAEN(O) CEN(O) COEN(O) HOM(O)

COMMONER SNOB CEORL PLEBE SIMPLE BURGESS CITIZEN STUDENT ROTURIER

COMMONLY OFTEN VULGO FAMILIARLY

COMMONNESS IDIOTISM COMMUNITY VULGARITY

COMMON PEOPLE VULGUS

COMMONPLACE DULL FADE WORN BANAL DAILY PLAIN PROSE PROSY STALE TOPIC TRIPY TRITE USUAL COMMON GARDEN HOMELY MODERN TRUISM VULGAR FADAISE HUMDRUM INSIPID PROSAIC TEDIOUS TRIVIAL BANALITY BROMIDIC COPYBOOK EVERYDAY ORDINARY RUMTYTOO PEDESTRIAN

COMMONPLACENESS BATHOS HUMDRUM

COMMON SENSE WIT NOUS SALT GUMPTION

COMMONWEAL WEAL REPUBLIC

COMMONWEALTH POLIS STATE ESTATE PUBLIC WEALTH COMONTE COUNTRY COMMONTY
(**IDEAL —**) UTOPIA

COMMOTION DO ADO DIN BREE DUST FLAP FRAY FUSS HEAT HELL RIOT STIR TOSS WHIR ALARM FLARE FUROR HURLY HURRY STORM STOUR WHIRL BUSTLE CATHRO FISSLE FISTLE FLURRY FRACAS FRAISE FURORE GARRAY HOOPLA HOTTER MOTION MUTINY PHRASE POTHER RUFFLE SHINDY SPLORE SQUALL STEERY TUMULT UNREST UPSTIR WELTER BLATHER BLUSTER CATOUSE CLATTER KIPPAGE SHINDIG TAMASHA TEMPEST TURMOIL DISORDER ERUPTION REMOTION STIRRAGE STRAMASH TIRRIVEE UPHEAVAL UPRISING

COMMUNAL EJIDAL

COMMUNE MIR AREA DEME TALK ARGUE REALM SHARE TREAT ADVISE CONFER DEBATE IMPORT PARLEY REVEAL CONSULT DISCUSS DIVULGE COMMERCE CONVERSE DISTRICT STANITZA TOWNSHIP

COMMUNICABLE OPEN FRANK CATCHING SOCIABLE

COMMUNICATE SAY GIVE SHOW SIGN TELL BREAK DRILL SPEAK YIELD BESTOW COMMON CONVEY IMPART INFECT INFORM REVEAL SIGNAL ADDRESS BREATHE DECLARE DICTATE DIVULGE CONVERSE DESCRIBE INTIMATE
(**— BY ALLUSION**) IMPLY

COMMUNICATION CALL NOTE WORD CABLE FAVOR LETTER SPEECH ADDRESS DIVULGE GALLERY MESSAGE COMETHER LANGUAGE TELEGRAM MEMORANDUM
(**— SERVICE**) TELEX

COMMUNICATIVE FREE SOCIABLE EXPANSIVE

COMMUNION CULT HOST MASS SECT TALK CREED FAITH SHARE UNITY CHURCH HOMILY COMMUNE CONCORD NAGMAAL SYNAGOG ANTIPHON COMMERCE CONVERSE KOINONIA VIATICUM
(**— SERVICE**) ACTION

COMMUNISM LENINISM SOVIETISM

COMMUNIST RED COMMIE SOVIET COMRADE

COMMUNITY MIR BODY BURG CITY CLAN DESA MARK MURA DESSA FIRCA STATE THORP CENOBY CLIMAX COLONY FAMILY HAMLET MILLET NATION POLITY PUBLIC SOCIES ANTHILL BOHEMIA COMMUNE COMONTE CONVENT HERONRY KINGDOM PHALANX SOCIETY VILLAGE ZADRUGA AUTONOMY COMMONTY DISTRICT LIKENESS PRIORATE PROVINCE SODALITY SWEEPDOM TOWNSHIP
(**— OF ANCHORITES**) LAURA
(**— OF INTERESTS**) KINSHIP
(**— OF KNIGHTS TEMPLARS**) PRECEPTORY
(**— OF NATURE**) RACE
(**— OF ORGANISMS**) GAMODEME
(**— OF TURKS**) KIZILBASH
(**COOPERATIVE —**) PHALANSTERY
(**ECOLOGICAL —**) PROCLIMAX
(**JEWISH —**) JEWRY KOLEL ALJAMA SHTETL JUDAISM SHTETEL SYNAGOG KEHILLAH
(**MAORI —**) KAIK KAIKA
(**PERUVIAN —**) AYLLU COMUNIDAD
(**PLANT —**) HEATH FOREST ALTERNE ENCLAVE
(**RELIGIOUS —**) CENOBY SAMGHA SANGHA CONVENT CENOBIUM
(**RUSSIAN —**) MIR
(**UTOPIAN —**) PANTISOCRACY
(**VILLAGE —**) IKHWAN

COMMUTATE COMMUTE UNDIRECT

COMMUTATIVE ABELIAN

COMMUTATOR BREAK BREAKER RHEOTROPE

COMMUTE ALTER CHANGE TRAVEL CONVERT EXCHANGE

COMOROS (**CAPITAL OF —**) MORONI
(**ISLAND OF —**) MWALI MOHELI NZWANI ANJOUAN NJAZIDJA
(**VOLCANO OF —**) KARTHALA

COMPACT SAD BALL BOND CASE FAST FIRM HARD KNIT PACK PACT PLOT SNUG TRIM TRUE BRIEF CLOSE COVIN CROWD DENSE GROSS HARDY HORNY MATCH PITHY SOLID SPISS TERSE THICK TIGHT BEETLE COMART HARDEN LEAGUE SHRINK SPISSY STOCKY VANITY BARGAIN CONCISE CONCORD CROWDED NUGGETY PACTION SERRIED TABLOID ALLIANCE CONDENSE CONTRACT COVENANT FLAPJACK HEAVYSET SOLIDIFY SUCCINCT PELLETIZE
(PREF.) GLOMERO GLOMERULO PYCN(O) PYKN(O)

COMPACTED SAD CROWDED
(PREF.) PECTO

COMPACTNESS BODY DENSITY FASTNESS SOLIDITY INTENSITY

COMPANION PAL SOC CHUM FERE MAKE MATE PEER TWIN WIFE BILLY BUDDY BULLY BUTTY CHINA COMES CRONY CULLY DARES GREEK MATCH MATEY MAUGH RIVAL SPORT ATTEND BELAMY BILLIE BROLGA COBBER COHORT COMATE CUMMER CUPMAN DUENNA EGERIA ESCORT FELLOW FRIEND GESITH GOSSIP KIMMER MARROW PANION SHADOW SPOUSE STEADY TROJAN ACHATES COMPANY COMPEER COMRADE CONSORT ELPENOR FRANION HUSBAND PARTNER SOCIATE SOCIETY SPECIAL BARNACLE BEAUPERE COMPADRE CORRIVAL EPHESIAN EPHESINE FAITHFUL FAMILIAR HELPMATE PARALLEL PLAYFERE SYNODITE
(**ARCHER'S —**) BUTTY
(**DRINKING —**) CUPMATE
(**POT —**) ALEKNIGHT
(**READING —**) LECTRICE
(**TABLE —**) CONVICTOR
(PL.) SOCIETY
(PREF.) HETAERO

COMPANIONABLE FERE MATEY SOCIAL CORDIAL FELLOWLY GRACIOUS SOCIABLE

COMPANIONSHIP FERE SHIP HAUNT COMPANY SOCIETY AFFINITY

COMPANY CRY MOB SET BAND BEVY BODY CORE CREW CRUE FARE FERE FIRM GANG GEST GING HERD HOST MANY PUSH ROUT SORT TEAM TURM AERIE COVEN COVEY CROWD FLOCK FLOTE GESTE GROUP GUEST HORDE JATHA MEINY PARTY SQUAD SUITE TROOP TURMA CIRCLE CLIQUE COHORT COVINE CURNEY DECURY LOCHUS OUTFIT RESORT THRAVE THRONG TROUPE TWENTY VOLLEY BATTERY COLLEGE CONDUCT CONSORT HOLDING JIMBANG MANIPLE SOCIETE SOCIETY THIASOS THIASUS VISITOR ASSEMBLY FAISCEAU FOLKMOOT JINGBANG PRESENCE
(**— OF BADGERS**) CETE
(**— OF BIRDS**) BANK
(**— OF BOOKSELLERS**) CONGER
(**— OF DANCERS**) COMPARSA
(**— OF HERDSMEN**) BOOLY BOOLEY
(**— OF HORSEMEN**) TROOP
(**— OF MARTENS**) RICHESSE
(**— OF SINGERS**) CHOIR QUIRE CHORUS
(**— OF THE FAITHFUL**) FOLD
(**— OF TRAVELERS**) CAFILA CAVALCADE
(**— OF WOMEN**) GAGGLE
(**— OF WORSHIPPERS**) THIASUS
(**EXCLUSIVE —**) CROWD
(**FINANCIAL —**) FACTOR
(**FIRE —**) SQUAD
(**MILITARY —**) WATCH DECURY VENLIN PELOTON VEXILLUM
(**RECORDING —**) LABEL
(**SUITABLE —**) BESORT

COMPARABLE LIKE SAME SIMILAR

COMPARATIVE
(SUFF.) ER IOR

COMPARE VIE EVEN LIKE SIZE APPLY EQUAL LIKEN MATCH SCALE TALLY ALLUDE CONFER PARIFY RELATE SEMBLE BALANCE BRACKET COLLATE EXAMINE SENIBLE SIGNIFY ASSEMBLE CONFRONT CONTRAST ESTIMATE PARALLEL RESEMBLE SIMILIZE
(**— WITH**) TO

COMPARISON SIMILE ANALOGY BALANCE COMPARE PARABLE PARAGON DISIMILE LIKENESS LIKENING METAPHOR PARALLEL

COMPARTMENT BAY BIN BOX CAB POD CELL DECK FLUE PANE PART SLOT WELL ABODE CABIN HATCH HUTCH PANEL STALL VOLET ABACUS ALCOVE BUNKER GARAGE HOPPER MUFFLE REGION SEVERY SMOKER ALVEOLE CABINET CAPSULE CELLULE CHAMBER FIREBOX HOUSING KITCHEN LOCULUS MANSION ROTONDE SECTION ALVEOLUS COALHOLE DIVISION FOREPEAK GRINTERN LOCELLUS STEERAGE TRAVERSE PIGEONHOLE
(**— FOR COAL**) BUNKER
(**— FOR TREATING ORE**) KITCHEN
(**— IN BARN**) BAY
(**— IN CAR**) BOOT
(**— IN STOVE**) BROILER
(**— OF COACH**) IMPERIAL

(— OF ROOF) SEVERY

(— OF WINDOW) LIGHT

(— ON GAMEBOARD) STORE

(— ON ROULETTE WHEEL) EAGLE

(— ON TRAIN) COUCHETTE

(CARGO —) HOLD

(DETACHABLE —) POD

(GAS-TIGHT —) BALLONET

(GUNNER'S —) BLISTER

(REFRIGERATOR —) CHILLER

(SLEEPING —) CUBICLE

(STAGECOACH —) COUPE

(STORAGE—) BOOT

COMPASS BOW AREA DIAL GAIN ROOM ROSE SIZE TOUR AMBIT FIELD GAMUT RANGE REACH SCOPE SWEEP TENOR WHEEL ARRIVE ATTAIN BOUNDS CIRCLE DEGREE DEVICE DIACLE EFFECT EXTENT MERIST MODULE SPHERE SPREAD VOLUME ACHIEVE AZIMUTH CALIBER CIRCUIT CONFINE DIVIDER EMBRACE ENCLOSE ENVIRON HORIZON IMAGINE PELORUS PURVIEW TRAMMEL BOUNDARY CINCTURE CIRCUITY DIAPASON PRACTICE PRACTISE SURROUND

(— IN SHIP'S CABIN) TELLTALE

(— NEEDLE END) LILY

(— OF MELODY) AMBITUS

(— OF TONES) DIAPASON

(— OF VOICE) GAMUT SCALE

(— POINT) RHUMB

(BELL-MAKING —) CROOK

(PART OF —) PIN CARD DOME HOOD PIVOT HOUSING BINNACLE

COMPASS BOX KETTLE

COMPASS CARD ROSE PEDRERO PERRIER

COMPASSION RUE PITY RUTH GRACE HEART MERCY PIETY SORRY KARUNA LENITY REMORSE STOMACH CLEMENCY HUMANITY KINDNESS SYMPATHY

COMPASSIONATE MEEK RUTH SOFT HUMAN GENTLE TENDER CLEMENT PIETOSO PITEOUS PITIFUL GRACIOUS MERCIFUL

COMPASS PLANT PILOTWEED ROSINWEED

COMPASS QUARTER PLAGE

COMPASS SIGHT VANE

COMPATIBLE AKIN CIVIL ARTISTIC SUITABLE

COMPATRIOT NATIVE PATRIOT SYNETHNIC

COMPEL GAR MAKE MOVE URGE BRING CAUSE COACT DRIVE EXACT FORCE IMPEL PRESS SHOVE COERCE ENJOIN EXTORT INCITE OBLIGE THREAT ACTUATE AFFORCE ATTRACT COMMAND DRAGOON ENFORCE NECESSE REQUIRE VIOLENCE NECESSITATE

(— TO GO) HALE

(— TO PAY) STICK

COMPELLED HAS FAIN MUST BOUND FORCED ENFORCED

COMPELLING COGENT STRONG TELLING BRUISING FORCEFUL

COMPELLINGLY BADLY

COMPENDIOUS BRIEF SHORT

DIRECT COMPACT CONCISE SUMMARY SUCCINCT

COMPENDIUM LIST BRIEF APERCU DIGEST PRECIS SKETCH SURVEY CATALOG COMPEND EPITOME LEXICON MEDULLA OUTLINE PANDECT SUMMARY SYLLOGE ABSTRACT BREVIARY BREVIATE LANDSKIP SYLLABUS SYNOPSIS ABRIDGEMENT

COMPENSATE PAY JIBE AGREE ATONE COVER REPAY TALLY OFFSET RECOUP REDEEM REWARD SQUARE COMMUTE CORRECT PLASTER REDRESS REPRISE REQUITE RESTORE SATISFY COMPENSE DISPENSE EQUALIZE

COMPENSATION BOT FEE PAY UTU BOOT BOTE HIRE MEND TOLL BONUS LOWER WAGES AMENDS ANGILD GERSUM OFFSET REWARD SALARY SETOFF DAMAGES FREIGHT PAYMENT REDRESS SALVAGE STIPEND BREAKAGE DONATIVE EARNINGS INTEREST OCTOGILD PILOTAGE PITTANCE REQUITAL SOLATIUM

(— FOR INJURY) SATISFACTION

(— FOR KILLING MAN) MANBOT MANBOTE

(MEAGER —) PITTANCE

(WORKER'S —) COMPO

COMPENSATORILY EVEN

COMPETE PIT VIE COPE KEMP TEND CLASH MATCH RIVAL STRIVE CONTEND CONTEST EMULATE CORRIVAL

(— WITH) BUCK

COMPETENCE SKILL ABILITY FACULTY CAPACITY

COMPETENCY MAY CAPACITY

COMPETENT UP APT CAN FIT ABLE GOOD HOME MEET SANE ADEPT CAPAX SMART SWEET TIGHT INTACT LAWFUL WORTHY CAPABLE ENDOWED SKILLED ADEQUATE SUITABLE QUALIFIED

COMPETITION VIE DRAW GAME HEAT JUMP MATCH PRIZE TRIAL WAGER CONTEST PARAGON RIVALRY BIATHLON CONCOURS CONFLICT

(— AMONG REAPERS) KEMP

(VERSE —) TENSON

COMPETITOR FOE ENEMY MATCH RIVAL WAGER COUSIN PLAYER AGONIST ENTRANT CORRIVAL FAVORITE GAMESTER OPPONENT

COMPILATION ANA BOOK CODE CENTO DIGEST CASEBOOK DIRECTORY GATHERING

COMPILE ADD EDIT AMASS GATHER SELECT ARRANGE COLLECT COMPOSE PREPARE

COMPILER AUTHOR EDITOR GATHERER GLOSSIST SCISSORER

COMPLACENT CALM SMUG PLACID FATUOUS PRIGGISH

COMPLACENTLY FATLY

COMPLAIN AIL YIP BEEF CARP CRIB FRET FUSS GREX KEEN KICK KREX MEAN MOAN MOOT MUTE

RULE WAIL YELP YIRN BITCH BLEAT BRAWL CRAKE CROAK CROON GRIPE GROWL GRUMP GRUNT PINGE PLAIN WHINE BEWAIL CHARGE COTTER CREATE GRIEVE GROUSE GRUTCH HOLLER KVETCH MURMUR PEENGE REPINE SQUAWK THREAP THROPE WHINGE YAMMER CHUNNER DEPLORE GRIZZLE GRUMBLE INVEIGH PROTEST BELLYACHE

COMPLAINANT ACTOR ASKER ORATOR ACCUSER PLAINER QUERENT RELATOR

COMPLAINING BRAY PULY LATRANT QUERENT DOLEANCE QUERULOUS

COMPLAINT RAP BEEF FUSS HOWL MEAN MOAN WAIL BITCH GRIPE GROWL WHINE CHESON GROUCH GROUSE GRUDGE GRUTCH HOLLER LAMENT MALADY PLAINT REPINE SQUAWK AILMENT DISEASE GRUMBLE ILLNESS PROTEST QUARREL QUERELE RECLAMA TRAGEDY COMPLAIN DISORDER DOLEANCE GRAVAMEN JEREMIAD

COMPLAISANCE AMENITY SUAVITY FACILITY URBANITY

COMPLAISANT BON ABLE EASY KIND BUXOM CIVIL SUAVE BONAIR POLITE SMOOTH SUPPLE URBANE AFFABLE AMIABLE BOWABLE LENIENT GRACIOUS OBLIGING PLEASING

COMPLEMENT CREW GANG FORCE TALLY ALEXIN AMOUNT COUSIN ADJUNCT OBVERSE PENDANT

(MILITARY —) STRENGTH

COMPLEMENTARY OPPOSITE

(PREF.) COUNTER

COMPLETE DO ALL CAP END BLUE DASH DEAD DEEP FAIR FILL FINE FULL JUST PASS PURE RANK VERY CLEAN CLOSE CROWN EVERY GROSS LARGE PLAIN PLUMB POINT PUCCA PUKKA QUITE RIPEN ROUND SOLID SOUND STARK TOTAL UTTER WHOLE CHOATE DAMPEN DEADLY EFFECT ENTIRE FINISH GLOBAL HOLLOW INTACT MATURE PROPER SINGLE STRICT VESTED ACHIEVE CONFIRM EXECUTE EXPLETE FULFILL GERMANE OUTWORK PERFECT PLENARY REALIZE REPLETE SPHERAL ABSOLUTE BLINKING CIRCULAR CONCLUDE FINALIZE IMPLICIT INTEGRAL OUTRIGHT OVERCOME PRECIOUS PROFOUND THOROUGH BODACIOUS NEGOTIATE ACCOMPLISH

(— CARELESSLY) HUDDLE

(— IN SYLLABLES) ACATHLECTIC

(REMARKABLY —) SPLENDID

(PREF.) HOL(O) TEL(E)(EO)

COMPLETED PAU OVER CLOSED SUMMED COMPLETE FINISHED

(NOT —) DURATIVE

COMPLETELY ALL JAM BARE BUCK

FAIR FLAT GOOD SLAM SLAP SPAN BLACK CLEAN CLOSE FULLY PLUMB QUITE SHEER SMACK SPANG STARK STICK STOCK UTTER BODILY ENTIRE GAINLY HOLLOW PURELY SPANDY WHOLLY ALGATES BLANKLY THROUGH CLEVERLY DIRECTLY ENTIRELY HEARTILY OUTRIGHT

(PREF.) DE DIS OB PAN

COMPLETENESS DEPTH ALLNESS FULLNESS RIPENESS INTEGRITY PLENITUDE

COMPLETION END CROWN FINISH

(PREF.) TELEUT(O)

COMPLEX HARD MAZY BEING ETHOS FIELD HYOID MIXED ADDUCT DESERT KNOTTY SYSTEM CULTURE NETWORK SAMKARA SINUOUS TANGLED TWISTED ABSTRUSE COMPOUND EQUATION EXCHANGE INVOLVED MANIFOLD SAMSKARA SYNDROME MACROCOSM

(— OF CHARACTERISTICS) PERSONALITY

(— OF DIALECTS) HINDI

(— OF HORMONES) CALINE

(— OF IDEAS) EGO SYSTEM

(— OF SHOPS) MALL

(BASEMENT —) FLOOR

(NOT —) SIMPLE

COMPLEXION HUE RUD BLEE CAST LEER LOOK RUDD TINT COLOR HUMOR STATE TENOR TINGE ASPECT TEMPER COLORING

(BAD —) DYSCHROA

COMPLEXITY NODUS SCHEME TANGLE INTRIGUE

COMPLIANCE TRUE ASSENT MUNICH CESSION CONSENT HARMONY OBSEQUY ABIDANCE CIVILITY FACILITY FORMALITY

COMPLIANT EASY MEEK OILY SOFT BUXOM FACILE PLIANT SUPPLE COMMODE DUCTILE DUTIFUL WILLING OBEDIENT TOWARDLY YIELDING

COMPLICATE INTORT PUZZLE TANGLE EMBROIL INVOLVE PERPLEX BEWILDER INTRIGUE INTRICATE

COMPLICATED HARD KNOTTY PROLIX COMPLEX GORDIAN SNARLED TANGLED INVOLVED PLEXIFORM

COMPLICATION KNOT NODE PLOT NODUS SNARL TANGLE INTRIGUE

COMPLIMENT GIFT KUDO LAUD EXTOL EULOGY PRAISE SALAAM SALUTE ADULATE APPLAUD BOUQUET COMMEND DOUCEUR FLATTER TRIBUTE ENCOMIUM FLUMMERY GRATUITY GREETING

COMPLY PLY CEDE OBEY ABIDE ADAPT AGREE APPLY YIELD ACCEDE ACCORD ASSENT ENFOLD SUBMIT CONFORM EMBRACE OBSERVE

(— WITH) OBEY SERVE OBSERVE SATISFY

COMPONE GOBONE GOBONY
COMPONENT KEY DRAG FORM
ITEM PART UNIT GIVEN FACTOR
MEMBER SIMPLE ELEMENT
FORMANT PARTIAL CONJUNCT
INTEGRAL
(**— OF ARMY**) CAVALRY
(**— OF CELL WALLS**) CALLOSE
(**ELECTRIC —S**) CIRCUITRY
(**PHYSICAL —S**) HARDWARE
(**PRINCIPAL —**) BASIS
COMPORT ACT BEAR HAVE HOLD
JIBE KEEP SUIT ABEAR AGREE
BROOK CARRY TALLY ACCORD
ACQUIT BEHAVE DEMEAN
ENDURE SQUARE CONDUCT
COMPORTMENT DEALING
BEHAVIOR DEMEANOR
COMPOSE BAT PEN SET CALM
COMP DITE FORM LULL MAKE
ALLAY BREVE BRIEF CLERK CLINK
COUCH DIGHT DRAFT FRAME
ORDER PATCH PIECE SPELL STICK
WRITE ACCORD ADJUST CREATE
DESIGN GRAITH INDITE RECITE
REDACT SETTLE SOOTHE STEADY
ARRANGE COMPACT COMPILE
COMPONE CONCOCT CONFORM
DICTATE DISPOSE DRAUGHT
FASHION PATIENT PRODUCE
TYPESET COMPOUND COMPRISE
REGULATE
(**— POETRY**) MAKE SING
COMPOSED SET CALM COOL
QUIET SOBER WROTE DEMURE
DIGEST PLACID SEDATE SERENE
COMPACT WRITTEN COMPOUND
DECOROUS TOGETHER TRANQUIL
(**— IN METER**) FOOTED
(**ILL —**) LAME
COMPOSEDNESS SOSSIEGO
COMPOSER BARD POET LYRIC
ODIST AUTHOR LYRIST PENMAN
WRITER CONTEUR ELEGIST
FANTAST MAESTRO COLORIST
ELEGIAST IDYLLIST ILIADIST
MELODIST MONODIST MUSICIAN
PHANTAST TUNESMITH
AMERICAN FRY BIRD BOND CAGE
COLE IVES KERN ROOT BEACH
BLOCH DANKS FOOTE HANDY
HAYDN HOMER NEVIN OHARA
PRATT SCOTT SOUSA WEILL
BARBER CADMAN HARRIS KRENEK
LOOMIS PALMER PARKER PISTON
PORTER SEEGER SPEAKS SUESSE
TAYLOR WINNER ANTHEIL
BRISTOW CHASINS COPLAND
DEKOVEN GILBERT GOLDMAN
HAESCHE HERBERT MENOTTI
PARROTT RODGERS SCHUMAN
THOMSON YOUMANS BARTLETT
BROCKWAY BURLEIGH CHADWICK
CONVERSE GERSHWIN GOODRICH
GRAINGER KREISLER SESSIONS
THOMPSON ARMSTRONG
BERNSTEIN CARPENTER
ELLINGTON MACDOWELL
ARGENTINIAN CASTRO
AUSTRIAN FUX GAL BERG WOLF
BRULL DRDLA MOTTL ZAYTZ
BLEYLE CZERNY EYBLER LANNER
MOZART BITTNER NEUKOMM

STRAUSS BRUCKNER DIABELLI
GYROWETZ KORNGOLD REZNICEK
SCHUBERT HEUBERGER
MILLOCKER SCHONBERG
GANSBACHER ALBRECHTSBERGER
BELGIAN FETIS LEKEU BENOIT
BERIOT BLOCKX BRASIN DUMONT
FRANCK GRISAR JONGEN
GEVAERT HUBERTI LEMMENS
MATHIEU CAMPENHOUT
BRAZILIAN GOMES VILLALOBOS
CANADIAN BRANSCOMB
CZECH BENDL NOVAK DVORAK
FIBICH FORSTER JANACEK
KUBELIK SMETANA DESPAUER
NESWADBA KALLIWODA
KOVAROVIC MYSLIVECEK
DANISH ENNA GADE HAMERIK
NIELSEN HARTMANN
DUTCH FODOR OBRECHT
ARCADELT WAGENAAR
SWEELINCK
ENGLISH BAX TYE ARNE BLOW
BYRD CARR CLAY HOOK MONK
BACHE BLISS BOYCE CAREY
COOKE COWEN CROFT ELGAR
ELVEY FIELD HOLST LAWES
LOCKE PARRY SCOTT TOVEY
ARNOLD ASHTON AUSTIN AVISON
BARNBY BISHOP BRIDGE COATES
COWARD CRAMER CROTCH
CROUCH CUSINS DAVIES DELIUS
DIBDIN GERMAN GLOVER GREENE
HANDEL LAMOND LINLEY
MCEWEN ONEILL PARKER TALLIS
THOMAS WALTON WILSON
ATTWOOD BANTOCK BARNETT
BENNETT CELLIER COLEMAN
DUNHILL FARRANT GIBBONS
HORSLEY IRELAND JACKSON
LATROBE NOVELLO PURCELL
STAINER STORACE BENJAMIN
BOUGHTON SULLIVAN TYRWHITT
ARMSTRONG CALDICOTT
HESELTINE MACFARRNE
MACKENZIE SOMERVELL
GOLDSCHMIDT RAVENSCROFT
FINNISH PACIUS KAJANUS
MADETOJA MELARTIN PALMGREN
SIBELIUS WEGELIUS JARNEFELT
MERIKANTO
FRENCH ERB HUE ADAM INDY
LALO ALARD ALKAN AUBER
AURIC BAZIN BIZET COHEN DAVID
DUKAS FAURE GOUVY HERVE
IBERT LULLY MASSE MEHUL
RAVEL REBER REYER SATIE
WIDOR AUBERT AUDRAN
CAMPRA CHOPIN DANCLA
DAQUIN DUBOIS DUPARC
GODARD GOSSEC GOUNOD
HALEVY HEROLD LECOCQ LEROUX
PIERNE STRAUS THOMAS BERLIOZ
BERTINI BOESSET BRUNEAU
CAMBERT CHELARD COQUARD
DEBUSSY DELIBES DUCASSE
GUIRAUD LACOMBE LAPARRA
LECLAIR LESUEUR MARTINI
MILHAUD POULENC SCHMITT
CHABRIER CHAUSSON COUPERIN
DALAYRAC ERLANGER GOUDIMEL
GUILMANT HONEGGER LEFEBVRE
MAILLART MASSENET MESSAGER

MONSIGNY BOELLMANN
BOIELDIEU CHAMINADE
OFFENBACH WECKERLIN
BURGMULLER DESAUGIERS
DESTOUCHES PLANQUETTE
WALDTEUFEL CHARPENTIER
GERMAN ABT ETT AHLE BACH
BOHM BOTT DORN GOTZ HAAS
KAUN LOBE ORFF RAFF ABERT
BIBER BLECH BOEHE BRUCH
DANZI EBERS FASCH FESCA FINCK
FRANK GENEE GLUCK GRAUN
GRELL KLEIN LOEWE NEEFE
WEBER ALBERT AMBROS BECKER
BERGER BOHNER BRAHMS
COMMER CRUGER ECKERT EITNER
FLOTOW HILLER JENSEN KOHLER
KUCKEN KUHLAU KUHNAU
LINCKE MAHLER WAGNER
WINTER BARGIEL CONRADI
EBERLIN HASSLER JARNACH
MOLIQUE NAUMANN RICHTER
SILCHER STRAUSS WULLNER
ZOLLNER AGRICOLA BENEDICT
BRAMBACH DIETRICH DRAESEKE
EBERWEIN HOFFMANN HOLSTEIN
KAMINSKI KEUSSLER KIRCHNER
KREUTZER PFITZNER REINECKE
SCHUMANN VOLKMANN
AIBLINGER AMBROSIUS
BEETHOVEN BRAUNFELS
BUXTEHUDE CANNABICH
DELLINGER HINDEMITH
KLUGHARDT MARSCHNER
MATTHESON MEYERBEER
NEITHARDT REICHARDT
BELLERMANN BLUMENTHAL
DESTOUCHES PRAETORIUS
SCHARWENKA HUMPERDINCK
MENDELSSOHN FRANCKENSTEIN
LEICHTENTRITT
HUNGARIAN ERKEL HUBAY LEHAR
LISZT BARTOK KODALY KUSSER
JOACHIM ROMBERG DOHNANYI
GOLDMARK
IRISH BALFE OSBORNE WALLACE
ITALIAN LOTI PAER PERI ARAIA
BAINI BOITO BRAGA CESTI CLARI
COSTA VERDI ALFANO ANERIO
ARDITI ARTUSI BUSONI CIAMPI
COCCIA MERULO NANINI PACINI
PEROSI VECCHI ALBERTI ALLEGRI
ANFOSSI ARIOSTI BASSANI
BAZZINI BELLINI BERTONI
BIANCHI CACCINI CALDARA
CAMBINI CASELLA CAVALLI
COLONNA CONCONE CORELLI
DURANTE FERRARI FLORIMO
PICCINI PORPORA PUCCINI
ROSSINI SALIERI TARTINI TOSELLI
VIADANA VIVALDI ZACCONI
ZARLINO AGOSTINI ALBINONI
BERNABEI CLEMENTI FIORILLO
GABRIELI GAGLIANO GIORDANI
GIORDANO JOMMELLI LEGRENZI
MARCELLO MASCAGNI PRATELLA
RAIMONDI RESPIGHI SPONTINI
ANIMUCCIA BANCHIERI
BONONCINI BOTTESINI
BRAMBILLA CARISSIMI CAVALIERI
CHERUBINI DONIZETTI GUGLIELMI
LOCATELLI MALIPIERO
MARCHETTI MORLACCHI

PAISIELLO PERGOLESI SCARLATTI
TOMMASINI VICENTINO
BOCCHERINI CAMPAGNOLI
MERCADANTE MONTEVERDI
PALESTRINA PONCHIELLI
ZINGARELLI LEONCAVALLO
MEXICAN CHAVEZ CARRILLO
NORWEGIAN GRIEG KJERULF
NORDRAAK SVENDSEN
SCHJELDERUP
POLISH KOLBERG FITELBERG
KAMIENSKI KARLOWICZ
MONIUSZKO NOSKOWSKI
SZYMANOWSKI
PORTUGUESE ARNEIRO MACHADO
BOMTEMPO PORTOGALLO
RUMANIAN ENESCO OTESCUA
RUSSIAN LVOV SEROV GLINKA
LIADOV ONEGIN TANEEV ARENSKI
BORODIN REBIKOV GODOWSKY
LIPAUNOV SCRIABIN BALAKIREY
CHEREPNIN GLAZOUNOV
KASHPEROV KASTALSKI
MUSORGSKI PROKOFIEV
KALINNIKOV MOUSORGSKY
STRAVINSKY AZANCHEVSKI
BORTNYANSKI TCHAIKOVSKY
KHACHATURIAN RACHMANINOFF
SHOSTAKOVICH
SCOTTISH GOW SPOTTISWOODE
SPANISH ARBOS FALLA CASALS
ALBENIZ MARTINI PEDRELL
BARBIERI GUERRERO VICTORIA
SWEDISH ALFVEN HALLEN
ATTERBERG HALLSTROM
WENNERBERG
SWISS EGLI HEGAR HUBER
VENEZUELAN CARRENO
WELSH EVANS PARRY
COMPOSITE HYBRID ITALIC
MOTLEY COMPLEX COMPOSED
CONCRETE INTEGRAL
COMPOSITION ANA DITE MASS
OPUS WORK CENTO DITTY
DRAMA FUGUE GETUP MURKY
PIECE POESY STUCK THEME
ACCORD EULOGY FILLER HAIKAI
LESSON MAGGOT MONODY
THESIS THREAD VULGUS ARTICLE
COMPOST CONSIST DISPLAY
EBURINE EPISTLE MIXTURE
PICTURE STOPPER WRITING
ACROSTIC CAUSERIE COMPOUND
DIALOGUE DIAPENTE EXERCISE
FANTASIA FROTTAGE HEELBALL
(**— FOR BILLIARD BALLS**) COMPO
(**— TO BE ACTED**) PLAY DRAMA
(**— TO FILL LEATHER**) STUFF
(**AMOROUS —**) EROTIC
(**ARTISTIC —**) COLLAGE
(**BAGPIPE —**) PORT
(**BANKRUPT'S —**) COMPO
(**BUILDING —**) STAFF
(**CHORAL —**) MOTET CANTATA
ORATORIO
(**GUMMY —**) GROUND
(**HAND —**) CASEWORK
(**HUMOROUS —**) BURLA
(**IMPERFECT —**) SOOTERKIN
(**INSTRUMENTAL —**) AIR GATO
FANCY RONDO GROUND SKETCH
SONATA TIENTO BOURREE
CANZONE BERCEUSE CONCERTO

FANTASIA RHAPSODY SYMPHONY PASSACAGLIA
(LITERARY —) BOOK CENTO DEBAT ESSAY PIECE COMEDY SATIRE SKETCH THESIS TREATISE
(MAGIC —) HELLBROTH
(MUSICAL —) DUET GLEE IDYL OPUS SOLO SONG TRIO BURLA CANON DANCE ELEGY ETUDE GAZEL FUGUE IDYLL MOTET NONET SCORE STUDY ADAGIO ARIOSO AZIONE ENTREE GHAZEL HOCKET HOQUET SEPTET SEXTET BALLADE BOURREE BOUTADE BRAVURA ORGANUM QUARTET SCHERZO TOCCATA CAVATINA CHACONNE CLAUSULA CONCERTO INNOMINE SERENADE SINFONIA STANDARD SYMPHONY ANTIPHONY OFFERTORY PROCESSIONAL
(NARRATIVE —) BALLAD
(PLASTIC —) CEMENT
(POETIC —) GLOSS KAVYA
(RAMBLING —) SATIRE RHAPSODY
(RELIGIOUS —) MOTET ANTHEM HYMNIC CANTATA ORATORIO
(RUBBER —) GUM
(VEDIC —) GAYATRI
(VITREOUS —) ENAMEL
(VOCAL —) ARIA SOLO SONG CANON ANTHEM ELEVATIO CONDUCTUS
(PL.) JUVENILIA LITERATURE
COMPOSITOR COMP TYPO ADMAN SETTER BANKMAN CASEMAN CLICKER PRINTER STONEMAN
COMPOST PELF SOIL MINGLE COMPOTE MIXTURE COMPOUND DRESSING
COMPOSURE BOND MIEN POISE QUIET UNION REPOSE TEMPER BALANCE POSTURE CALMNESS SERENITY
(LOSE —) CHOKE
COMPOTATION SYMPOSIUM
COMPOTE BOWL COMPORT COMPOST
COMPOUND MIX BASE FILL JOIN MIXT SOUR TEPA ALKYL ALLOY AMIDE AMINE BLEND ESTER FURIL UNION ACETAL ADJUST ALKIDE BORANE COMMIX COPULA IODIDE JUMBLE KETONE MEDLEY PHENOL POLYOL PTERIN PYRONE SETTLE TEMPER URACIL URAMIL AGATHIN ALCOHOL ALLICIN ALLOXAN AMALGAM AMIDATE AMIDINE AMINATE AMMONIA COMBINE COMPLEX COMPONE COMPOSE COMPOST DVANDVA KAMPONG KHELLIN PHORBIN PREPARE SPIRANE STEROID AGLUCONE AGLYCONE ALIZARIN ALKOXIDE AMMONATE ANTIPODE APIGENIN BRAZILIN CEROMIDE COMPOSED FUCHSONE GARDENIN GENTISIN GOSSYPOL IODOFORM ISOLOGUE STYRACIN
(ADHESIVE —) SALVE
(COMBINING —) ACCEPTOR
(POISONOUS —) KETENE CACODYL GLYCINE HELENIN STIBINE

(SYNTHETIC —) ANDROGEN SORBITAN
(PREF.) **(PARENT —)** NOR
(SUFF.) GENIN
(CARBON —) ENE
COMPOUNDED CONCRETE COMPOSITE
COMPOUNDER TANKER
COMPOUNDING INTIMACY
COMPREHEND GET SEE KNOW TAKE TWIG COVER GRASP IMPLY LATCH REACH SAVVY SEIZE SENSE SKILL SMOKE SPELL ATTAIN BOTTOM DIGEST EMBODY FATHOM FOLLOW PIERCE UPTAKE COMPASS CONTAIN DISCERN EMBRACE ENCLOSE IMAGINE INCLUDE INVOLVE REALIZE RECEIVE SWALLOW COMPRISE CONCEIVE CONCLUDE PERCEIVE
COMPREHENSIBLE EXOTERIC INCLUDED SENSABLE SCRUTABLE
COMPREHENSION HOLD SABE GRASP SAVVY SENSE ESPRIT FATHOM NOESIS UPTAKE EPITOME INSIGHT KNOWING SUMMARY BEARINGS PREHENSION
COMPREHENSIVE BIG FULL WIDE BROAD GRAND LARGE GLOBAL SCOPIC CAPABLE CONCISE · GENERAL GENERIC CATHOLIC ENCYCLIC SPACIOUS
COMPREHENSIVENESS POWER SCOPE EXTENT BREADTH WIDENESS LARGENESS
COMPRESS NIP TIE BALE BIND FIRM LACE WRAP CLING CRAMP CROWD CRUSH PINCH PRESS SMASH BUNDLE DEFORM DIGEST GATHER SHRINK STRAIN THRONG ABRIDGE ASTRICT BOLSTER CABBAGE COMPACT CURTAIL DEFLATE EMBRACE FLATTEN PLEDGET REPRESS SQUEEZE SQUINCH ASTRINGE CONDENSE CONTRACT LAMINATE PEMMICAN RESTRAIN SUPPRESS
(— WOOL) DUMP
(MEDICAL —) BOLSTER PLEDGET
COMPRESSED STRICT CROWDED SUCCINCT ANGUSTATE COARCTATE
COMPRESSION CRUSH SQUEEZE PRESSURE THLIPSIS
(PREF.) SYMPIESO SYMPIEZO
COMPRESSOR PUMP ROTARY CONDENSER
COMPRISE HOLD COVER IMPLY SEIZE ATTACH CONFER EMBODY EMPLOY MUSTER COMPOSE CONTAIN EMBRACE ENCLOSE INCLUDE INVOLVE CONCEIVE PERCEIVE
COMPROMISE FINE TRIM COMMIT INTERIM COMPOUND ENDANGER PALLIATE
COMPROMISING FALSE
COMPULSION NEED URGE FORCE PRESS DURESS STRESS IMPULSE COACTION COERCION DISTRESS EXACTION PERFORCE NECESSITY
COMPULSORY COERCIVE

FORCIBLE NECESSARY
COMPUNCTION QUALM REGRET SORROW REMORSE SCRUPLE PENITENCE
COMPURGATOR COJUROR COSWEARER
COMPUTATION COMPOT ACCOUNT COMPUTE CALCULUS COMPUTUS ESTIMATE RECKONING
COMPUTE ADD SUM CAST ITEM RATE COUNT TALLY VALUE ASSESS CIPHER FIGURE NUMBER RECKON ACCOUNT BALANCE SUPPUTE ESTIMATE CALCULATE
COMPUTER ADDER ENIAC MANIAC MAINFRAME PROCESSOR MINICOMPUTER
(— LANGUAGE) FORTRAN
(PARTS OF — SYSTEM) HARDWARE
COMRADE PAL ALLY CHUM MATE PEER BILLY BUDDY BUTTY CRONY HABER HAVER TOWNY BURSCH CHABER CHAVER CÒPAIN COUSIN DIGGER ENGIDU FELLOW FRATER FRIEND GOSSIP HEARTY BROTHER COMPEER CONVIVE BEAUPERE CAMARADA CAMARADE COMORADO CONFRERE COPEMATE TOVARICH SKAINSMATE
(— AT TABLE) CONVIVE
(PL.) SOCE
COMRADESHIP CAMARADERIE
CON DO RAP ANTI KNOW LEAD LOOK PORE QUIN READ SCAN CHEAT CUNNE GUIDE KNOCK LEARN STEER STUDY DIRECT PERUSE REGARD VERSUS AGAINST DECEIVE EXAMINE INSPECT OPPOSED SWINDLE
CONCAVE CAVE VOID CAMUS MINUS ARCHED DISHED HOLLOW SIMOUS VAULTY VAULTED CRESCENT INCURVED
(SUFF.) COELOUS COELUS
CONCAVITY COVE DISH CONCHA HOLLOW VENTER KNEEPAN
CONCEAL MEW WRY BURY DERN FEAL HIDE KEEP LENE MASK SCUG SILE VEIL VEST WRAP BLIND BOSOM CACHE CLOAK COUCH COVER FEIGN LAYNE PLANT SHADE BURROW CLOSET DOCTOR ELOIGN EMBOSS HUDDLE HUGGER IMBOSK OCCULT POCKET SCREEN SHADOW SHIELD SHROUD STIFLE VIZARD ABSCOND ENVELOP OPPRESS PLASTER SECRETE SMOTHER BESCREEN DISGUISE ENSCONCE PALLIATE PRETENCE PRETENSE WITHHOLD
(— A FUGITIVE) HARBOR
(— A TRAIL) TRASH
(— INFORMATION) LAYNE
(— TO AVOID TAX) SKIM
CONCEALED DERN SCUG SNUG BLIND PRIVY BURROW COVERT HIDDEN LATENT OCCULT PERDUE SECRET VEILED COVERED LARVATE WRAPPED ABSTRUSE CRYPTOUS

HIDEAWAY RECONDITE
(— BY) BENEATH
(PREF.) ADEL(O)
CONCEALING DESIGNING OBVELATION
CONCEALMENT MEW LAIN COVER FRAUD NIGHT STALE SECRECY CELATION VELATION SECRETION
(— OF TREASURE) MISPRISION
(IN —) DOGGO
CONCEDE OWN CEDE GIVE ADMIT AGREE ALLOW GRANT WAIVE YETTE YIELD ACCORD ASSENT BETEEM CONFESS OTTROYE BEGRUDGE ACKNOWLEDGE
(— AS ADVANTAGE) SPOT
CONCEIT EGO TOY IDEA SIDE WIND CRANK FANCY KNACK POESY PRIDE QUIRK BABERY DEVICE NOTION VAGARY VANITY BIGHEAD CAPRICE EGOTISM OUTRAGE TYMPANY CONCETTO FLIMFLAM
CONCEITED BUG BRAG COXY FESS VAIN CHUFF COCKY FLORY HUFFY PENSY PROUD SAUCY CLEVER BIGGETY BIGGITY ARROGANT DOGMATIC NOSEWISE PENSEFUL PRIGGISH SNOBBISH
CONCEIVABLE EARTHLY POSSIBLE
CONCEIVE FORM HOLD MAKE PLAN TEEM WEEN BEGIN BRAIN CATCH DREAM FANCY FRAME GUESS IMAGE THINK DESIGN DEVISE IDEATE INTEND PONDER SETTLE GESTATE IMAGINE REALIZE SUPPOSE SUSPECT COMPRISE CONTRIVE ENVISAGE
CONCENTRATE AIM FIX MASS PILE BUNCH COACT EXALT FOCUS PURSE UNIFY ARREST ATTEND CENTER CITRIN DECOCT DISTIL FIXATE GATHER SINGLE COMPACT CONGEST DISTILL ENGROSS ESSENCE EXTRACT THICKEN ABSOLUTE APPROACH ASSEMBLE CONDENSE CONTRACT FOCALIZE GRADUATE
(— ORE) STRAKE
CONCENTRATED HARD DENSE FIXED INTENT STRONG EXALTED INTENSE
(NOT —) DIFFUSE
CONCENTRATION BRIX TITER CENTER BALLING SAMADHI ACTIVITY FIXATION PELMANISM
(— OF ARTILLERY FIRE) STONK
(— OF ENERGY) EXCITON
(— OF GRAPE JUICE) BESHMET
(— OF PLANTS) BED
(EXCESS —) MONOMANIA
CONCEPT GUT GUTS IDEA FANCY IMAGE BEGRIFF CONCEIT OPINION THOUGHT ABSOLUTE CATEGORY PLURALISM PERCEPTION
CONCEPTION ENS IDEA VIEW EIDOS FANCY FETUS IMAGE BELIEF DESIGN EMBRYO ENTITY NOTION CONCEIT CONCEPT PROJECT PURPOSE CATEGORY ESTHETIC NOTATION RATIONAL
(— OF IDEA) HENT

(— OF ONESELF) BOVARISM BOVARYSM
(ABSTRACT —) ARCHETYPE
(FALSE —) IDOL DELUSION
(QUICKNESS OF —) PREGNANCY
CONCEPTUAL IDEAL NOTIONAL
CONCEPTUALISM SERMONISM
CONCERN BUG BEAR CARE FEAR FIRM GEAR HAND PART RECK SAKE APPLY CAUSE CERNE DRIVE EVENT GRIEF HEART SORGE STAND TOUCH WORRY AFFAIR AFFECT BEHOLD CHARGE DIRECT EMPLOY FINGER IMPORT MATTER REGARD ANXIETY ARTICLE BOTTLER COMPANY DISTURB FUNERAL INVOLVE PERTAIN RESPECT SHEBANG SOLICIT TROUBLE BUSINESS HYPOTHEC INTEREST JEALOUSY
(— ONESELF) DEAL PASS TOUCH INTERMIT
(INDUSTRIAL —) COLOSSUS
(PRUDISH —) COMSTOCKERY
(SOMETHING CAUSING —) ALBATROSS
(SPECIAL —) ACCENT
(WORLDLY —S) EARTH
(SUFF.) (— FOR) ITIS
CONCERNED INTENT ANXIOUS VERSANT WORRIED ATWITTER BOTHERED
CONCERNING BY OF ON RE TO FOR TIL TILL ABOUT ANENT ANENST APROPOS TOUCHING
CONCERT POP PLAN RECK UNITE ACCORD DEVISE SMOKER ARRANGE BENEFIT CONCENT CONCORD CONSORT CONSULT HARMONY POPULAR RECITAL NEGOTIATE
CONCERTINA ORGAN LANTUM SQUIFFER BANDONION MELOPHONE
CONCESSION BOON FAVOR GRANT LEASE STOOP ASSENT GAMBIT OCTROY CESSION EPITROPE MYNPACHT ADMISSION ALLOWANCE PRIVILEGE
CONCESSIONAIRE GRIFTER
CONCH CONK PUNK SHELL COCKLE MUSSEL STROMB STROMBUS
CONCIERGE PORTER SUISSE WARDEN DVORNIK JANITOR
CONCILIATE GET CALM EASE GAIN ATONE HONEY THING ADJUST PACIFY SOFTEN ACQUIRE APPEASE CONCILE MOLLIFY PLACATE SATISFY PROPITIATE
CONCILIATOR ARBITRATOR
CONCILIATORY MILD SOFT GENTLE GIVING IRENIC LENIENT PACIFIC WINNING IRENICAL LENITIVE TREATABLE
CONCISE CURT NEAT TRIG BRIEF CRISP PITHY SHORT TERSE COGENT CUTTED COMPACT LACONIC POINTED PRECISE SERRIED SUMMARY TABLOID MUTILATE PREGNANT SUCCINCT
CONCISELY PRESSLY ELLIPTICALLY
CONCISENESS BREVITY ECONOMY SYNTOMY FASTNESS

SYNTOMIA BRACHYOLOGY
CONCLAMATION SHOUT
CONCLAVE SOBOR CLOSET CHAMBER MEETING AREOPAGY ASSEMBLY
CONCLUDE BAR END AMEN FINE REST TAKE CLOSE DRIVE ESTOP INFER JUDGE LIMIT CLINCH DECIDE DEDUCE EXPIRE FIGURE FINISH GATHER INDUCE PERIOD REASON RECKON SETTLE ACHIEVE ARRANGE COLLECT CONFINE EMBRACE ENCLOSE RESOLVE SUPPOSE COMPLETE DISPATCH ESTIMATE GRADUATE PARCLOSE RESTRAIN
CONCLUDED OVER COMPLETE
CONCLUDING LAST DESITIVE
CONCLUSION END AMEN CODA ERGO FINE LAST TERM CLOSE ENVOY EVENT FINIS ISSUE LOOSE POINT ENDING FINALE FINISH PERIOD RESULT SEQUEL THIRTY UPSHOT CLOSURE CURTAIN FINDING OUTCOME SEQUELA VERDICT APODOSIS DECISION EPILOGUE FINALITY FRUITION GODSPEED ILLATION ILLATIVE JUDGMENT PARCLOSE SENTENCE
(— OF ARIA) CABALETTA
(FINAL —) ISSUE
(RANDOM —) SURMISE
(PL.) COLLATION
CONCLUSIVE LAST FINAL VALID COGENT CERTAIN EVIDENT EXTREME TELLING DECISIVE DEFINITE ULTIMATE
CONCOCT MIX BREW COOK FAKE PLAN PLOT VAMP FRAME HATCH THINK DECOCT DEVISE DIGEST INVENT MINGLE REFINE SCHEME COMPOSE CONFECT PERFECT PREPARE COMPOUND INTRIGUE
CONCOCTION PLAN PLOT MUMMY DEVICE MUMMIA BREWING MIXTURE SNEEZER BUSINESS COMPOUND
CONCOMITANT SEQUELA INCIDENT ACCESSORY ASSOCIATE ATTENDANT ATTENDING COMPANION CONJOINED COOPERANT SATELLITE
CONCORD PART AGREE AMITY PEACE TERMS UNION UNITY TREATY UNISON COMPACT CONCENT CONCERT HARMONY ONENESS QUARTER COVENANT SYMPATHY COMMUNITY
(— OF SOUNDS) SYMPHONIA
CONCORDANT UNISON TUNABLE TUNEFUL HARMONIC UNISONAL UNISONOUS
CONCOURSE CROWD HAUNT PLACE POINT REPAIR RESORT THRONG COMPANY ASSEMBLY FREQUENCE
(INFERNAL —) HELL
CONCRESCENCE ADHESION
CONCRETE CLOT FIRM HARD REAL BETON GROUT SOLID UNITE ACTUAL CEMENT GUNITE COMBINE CONGEAL SPECIAL COALESCE COMPOUND POSITIVE

TANGIBLE AEROCRETE
CONCRETION CLOT KNOT MESS FLINT FUSIL PEARL STONE BEZOAR DOGGER NODULE TOPHUS LITHITE OTOLITH CALCULUS POTSTONE SEBOLITH
(— IN BAMBOO) TABASHIR TABASHEER
CONCUBINAGE KARAO KAREWA HETAERISM
CONCUBINE DASI MOLL HAGAR RIZPAH BEDMATE HETAIRA ODALISK MISTRESS ODALISQUE
CONCUPISCENCE DESIRE
CONCUPISCENT ANTSY
CONCUR HAND JIBE JOIN AGREE CHECK CHIME UNITE ACCEDE ACCORD ASSENT CONDOG APPROVE COMBINE CONSENT CONVENT COINCIDE CONSPIRE CONVERGE
(— IN) SUBSCRIBE
CONCURRENCE UNION ASSENT BESTOW CONSENT CONSORT MEETING ADHESION SYNDROME ADMISSION
CONCURRENT COEVAL UNITED MEETING COPUNCTAL
CONCUSSION BUMP SHOCK IMPACT ICEQUAKE COMMOTION
CONDEMN BAN CAST DAMN DEEM DOOM FILE FINE HISS BLAME BLESS DECRY JUDGE AMERCE ATTAIN AWREAK BANISH DETEST ADJUDGE CENSURE CONVICT DENOUNCE FORJUDGE REPROACH SENTENCE PROSCRIBE
CONDEMNATION BAN DOOM BLAME CENSURE DECRIAL BRICKBAT
CONDEMNATORY SEVERE ADVERSE
CONDEMNED FATAL DAMNED
CONDENSATION BAN STORY DIGEST CAPSULE BOILDOWN
CONDENSE CUT JIG BRIEF UNITE DECOCT DIGEST HARDEN LESSEN NARROW REDUCE SHRINK ABRIDGE CAPSULE COMBINE COMPACT DEFLATE DENSATE DISTILL SHORTEN SQUEEZE THICKEN COMPRESS CONTRACT DIMINISH PEMMICAN SOLIDIFY
CONDENSED CURT BRIEF CAPSULE COMPACT CONCISE SUMMARY TABLOID ABSORBED
CONDENSER ALUDEL REFLUX BALANCER CAPACITOR
CONDER HUER
CONDESCEND DEIGN FAVOR GRANT STOOP ASSENT OBLIGE SUBMIT CONCEDE DESCEND
CONDESCENDING AVUNCULAR
CONDESCENSION STOOP DISDAIN COURTESY DIGNATION
CONDIGN DUE FIT FAIR JUST SEVERE WORTHY ADEQUATE SUITABLE
CONDIMENT SOY HERB KARI MACE SAGE SALT CAPER CURRY DULCE DULSE SAUCE SPICE THYME AIWAIN AJOWAN CATSUP CLOVES GARLIC PEPPER RELISH

SAMBAL TAMARA BADIANE CANELLA CHUTNEY KETCHUP MUSTARD OREGANO PAPRIKA VINEGAR ALLSPICE BALACHAN BLATJANG DRESSING SEASONER TURMERIC
CONDITION IF AND FIG PLY WAY CASE FORM HOOD MODE PASS RANK ROTE TERM TIFF TRIM ANGLE BIRTH CAUSE CENSE CLASS COLOR COVIN ESTRE FACET JOKER PLACE POINT SHAPE STAGE STATE THEAT WHACK AGENCY DEGREE DONNEE ESTATE FETTLE GENTRY MORALE MUSCLE PLIGHT STATUS STRING ARTICLE CALLING FEATHER FOOTING PLISKIE PREMISE PREPARE PROVISO STATION SUSPEND COVENANT OCCASION POSITION PROTASIS STANDING PREDICAMENT REQUIREMENT
(— OF ANXIETY) CARK
(— OF BODY) HEAT AFFECTION
(— OF FATIGUE) FRAZZLE
(— OF FLUCTUATION) EURIPUS
(— STATED BEFOREHAND) PREMISE
(BEING IN DIRTY —) GRUNGY
(CHANCE —) ACCIDENT
(DEBASED —) CACHEXY CACHEXIA
(DEPRESSED —) DOWNBEAT
(DETERMINING —) GROUND
(DIRTY —) CLAT
(DISEASED —) DIEBACK
(DISGRACEFUL —) IGNOMINY
(DRUNKEN —) BUN
(FLOURISHING —) HEALTH
(GENERAL —) VOGUE
(HABITUAL —) TENOR
(MEAN —) DUST
(MISERABLE —) SQUALOR
(MORBID —) HOLDOVER
(MOST APPROPRIATE —) CHECKER
(NECESSARY —) MEAN
(NEUROTIC —) LATAH
(ORDERLY —) DECENCY
(PAINFUL —) CRICK
(PERMANENT —) HEXIS
(PROPER —) KILTER
(PROTECTIVE —) CALLUS CALLOUS
(SCURFY —) BUCKSKIN
(STATIONARY —) JIB
(SUBLIME —) HEAVEN
(SURROUNDING —) AIR
(TRUE —) SIZE
(UNEQUAL —) ODDS
(UNPROSPEROUS —) ILLTH
(UNWHOLESOME —) MALADY
(WEATHER —S) ELEMENTS
(PL.) HAND TERMS STRINGS
(SUFF.) ACITY ATION DOM ERY ICE ICITY ILITY ION ISM MENT NESS OR OSIS SHIP TH TY
(MORBID —) IASIS
CONDITIONAL EVENTUAL CONNEXIVE PROVISORY QUALIFIED
CONDITIONED FINITE LIMITED
CONDITIONER DEGGER
CONDITIONING EDUCATION HYPOTHESIS
CONDOLENCE PITY RUTH

EMPATHY SYMPATHY
CONDONE BLINK REMIT ACQUIT
EXCUSE FORGET IGNORE PARDON
ABSOLVE FORGIVE OVERLOOK
CONDOR TIFFIN BUZZARD
VULTURE
CONDUCE GO AID HELP HIRE LEAD
TEND BRING GUIDE CONFER
EFFECT ENGAGE ADVANCE
CONDUCT FURTHER REDOUND
CONDUCT ACT CON RUN USE WIN
BEAR CALL COND CONN DEED
FACT FARE FIRK FORM GARB
GEST HAND KEEP LEAD MIEN
PLAY QUIT RULE SHOW TAKE
WAGE WALK BATON CARRY
CHAIR DRESS DRIVE FETCH GESTE
GUARD GUIDE HABIT MAYNE
SITHE TRADE TRAIN USAGE
USHER ACTION ATTEND BEHAVE
COLORS CONVEY CONVOY
COURSE DEDUCE DEMEAN
DEPORT DIRECT ESCORT GOVERN
INDUCT MANAGE MANNER
SQUIRE ACTIONS BEARING
CHANNEL COMPERE COMPORT
CONDITE CONDUCE CONDUIT
CONTAIN CONTROL EXECUTE
GALLANT GESTION OFFICER
OPERATE WIREWAY ARRIVISM
BEHAVIOR CARRIAGE CHAPLAIN
COURTESY DEMEANOR GUIDANCE
REGULATE SHEPHERD TRANSACT
(— ONESELF) DO ACT ACQUIT
BEHAVE BESTOW DEMEAN
DEPORT COMPORT CONTAIN
DISPORT ENTREAT MAINTAIN
(APPROPRIATE —) DHARMA
(BRASH —) FACE
(CONVENTIONAL —) PRAXIS
(DISORDERLY —) RANDAN
(DORMANT —) LATENCY
(ETHICAL —) HONOR
(PROPER —) CRICKET
(RECKLESS —) DEVILRY DEVILTRY
(RIGHT —) TE TAO
(RIOTOUS —) RANDAN
(SAFE —) KOWL COWLE
(SEDITIOUS —) MISPRISION
(SHOWY —) BRAVADO
(SLOPPY —) SWASH
(VAINGLORIOUS —) HEROICS
(WANTON —) RUFF
(WEAK —) FOLLY
CONDUCTANCE G
(UNIT OF —) MHO SIEMENS
CONDUCTION COURSING
CONDUCTOR CON BOND CADE
LEAD MAIN BRUSH GUARD
SHUNT SPOUT TRUNK BRIDGE
BUSMAN CARMAN CONVOY
COPPER ESCORT FEEDER LEADER
OFFSET RETURN CAPTAIN
CATHODE MAESTRO MANAGER
AQUEDUCT BATONIST CICERONE
CONVEYOR DIRECTOR EMPLOYEE
FILAMENT STICKMAN ANELECTRIC
(— OF FESTIVAL) SKUDLER
(ELECTRIC —) FILAMENT
(LIGHTNING —) ROD
(OMNIBUS —) CAD
(WOMAN —) CLIPPIE
(PL.) SERVICE

(SUFF.) EER
CONDUIT BOSS DUCT GOUT MAIN
PIPE SINK TUBE WIRE CABLE
CANAL CUNDY SEWER STACK
HEADER SLUICE TROUGH
CARRIER CHANNEL CHIMNEY
CONDITE CONDUCT CULVERT
CUNDITE EXHAUST FOGGARA
LATERAL LAUNDER PASSAGE
WIREWAY AQUEDUCT OLEODUCT
PENSTOCK WASTEWAY
(PL.) LIMBERS
CONDYLOMA SYCOMA
CONE CAP YOW CHAT KING MOXA
PINA TOOT CONUS CRACK SCREW
SHAPE SPIRE YOWIE BOBBIN
CONOID MONTRE PASTIL
CLUSTER CONELET CONIOLE
FISSURE FRUSTUM PROLONG
PYRAMID STROBIL THIMBLE
CANNELON DUMPLING GALBULUS
PASTILLE PINECONE STROBILE
STROBILUS
(— OF CLOTH) VANE
(— OF FIR) YOW YOWIE STROBIL
STROBILE STROBILUS
(— OF GUNPOWDER) PEEOY
(— OF HOP PLANT) BUR BURR
(— OF SILVER AMALGAM) PINA
(— ON LOG END) CAP
(— ON SHOE) CLEAT
(— STRUCTURE) NURAGHE
(HALF —) FORME NAPPE
(ICE CREAM —) ICE CORNET
(INVERTED —) HOPPER
(PAPER —) SPILL COFFIN
(ROPE-MAKING —) TOP
(TOP CUT FROM —) UNGULA
(VOLCANIC —) PUY MONTICULE
(PL.) HOPS
(PREF.) CON(I)(ICO)(O) STROBILI
CONENOSE BEDBUG BARBEIRO
CONESTOGA WAGON CARAVAN
CONEY CONY HYRAX HYRACID
GUATIBERO
CONFAB CHAT TALK POWWOW
CONFLAB PRATTLE
CONFECTION CHOW MOSS CANDY
DULCE MEBOS SWEET BONBON
COCKLE COMFIT DAINTY DRAGEE
HALVAH JUNKET MAJOON
NOUGAT SWEETY TABLET
CARAMEL CONFECT FONDANT
MIXTURE POMFRET PRALINE
SEATRON SUCCADE ANGELICA
CHOWCHOW CODINIAC
COMPOUND CONSERVE DELICACY
MARZIPAN PRESERVE QUIDDANY
SUBTLETY MARSHMALLOW
CONFECTIONERY CIMBAL
CONFISERIE
CONFEDERACY BUND COVIN
CREEK JUNTA KEDAR UNION
COVINE LEAGUE COMPLOT
ALLIANCE COVENANT FEDERACY
ILLINOIS BLACKFOOT
CONFEDERATE AID PAL REB ALLY
BAND PUFF COVER REBEL STALL
UNITE LEAGUE SANTAR ABETTER
ABETTOR CONJURE FEDARIE
FEDERAL FEODARY PARTNER
STEERER CONSPIRE FEDERARY
FEDERATE

(— SOLDIER) CONFED JOHNNY
GRAYBACK GRAYCOAT GREYBACK
(PICKPOCKET'S —) STALL
CONFEDERATION BODY BUND
ZUPA GUEUX UNION LEAGUE
COMPACT HASINAI SOCIETY
ALLIANCE COVENANT
CONFER DUB GIVE MEET TALK
AWARD ENDOW FEOFF GRANT
INFER PARLE SPEND TREAT
ADVISE BESTOW COMMON
CONFAB DONATE ENTAIL HUDDLE
IMPARL IMPART INVEST PARLEY
POWWOW COLLATE COMMUNE
COMPARE CONDUCE CONSULT
CONTACT COUNSEL DISCUSS
INSTATE PRESENT COLLOGUE
COMPRISE CONVERGE NEGOTIATE
(— DEGREE UPON) CAP
(— KNIGHTHOOD UPON) DUB
CONFERENCE DIET TALK SYNOD
TREAT TRUST CAUCUS CONFAB
HUDDLE INDABA KORERO PARLEY
PARVIS POWWOW SUMMIT
CIRCUIT COUNCIL MEETING
PALAVER PARLING SEMINAR
COLLOQUE COLLOQUY CONCLAVE
CONGRESS PRACTICE PRACTISE
TUTORIAL PARLIAMENT
(SCIENCE —) PUGWASH
CONFERRING GRANT DATION
CONFESS OWN AVOW FESS KNOW
SING ADMIT GRANT KITHE
ACKNOW AGNISE ATTEST
AVOUCH BEKNOW COUTHE
RENDER REVEAL SHRIFT SHRIVE
SQUEAK CONCEDE DIVULGE
PROFESS WHITTLE DISBOSOM
DISCLOSE DISCOVER MANIFEST
ACKNOWLEDGE
CONFESSION ALHET CREDO
CREED GRANT AVOWAL SHRIFT
SHRIVE VIDDUI ASHAMNU
FORMULA PECCAVI COGNOVIT
(MUTUAL —) SHARING
CONFESSIONAL SHRIFT MALCHUS
CONFESSOR FATHER SHRIFT
SHRIVER
CONFIDANT PRIVY FRIEND
INWARD PRIVADO INTIMATE
CONFIDE AFFY RELY TELL TRUST
COMMIT DEPEND LIPPEN BELIEVE
CONSIGN ENTRUST INTRUST
(— IN) VENTURE
CONFIDENCE FACE HARK HOPE
BIELD CHEEK FAITH STOCK TRUST
APLOMB BELIEF CREDIT FIANCE
FIDUCE METTLE MORALE SECRET
SPIRIT SURETY COUNSEL
COURAGE PRIVITY AFFIANCE
BOLDNESS CREDENCE RELIANCE
SECURITY SURENESS
CONFIDENT BOLD SMUG SURE
COCKY CRANK HARDY SIKER
CROUSE SECURE SICKER TRAIST
ASSURED CERTAIN HOPEFUL
RELIANT CONSTANT FEARLESS
FIDUCIAL IMPUDENT POSITIVE
SANGUINE TRUSTFUL
CONFIDENTIAL PACK BOSOM
PRIVY CLOSET COVERT HUSHED
INWARD SECRET PRIVATE
ESOTERIC FAMILIAR INTIMATE

CONFIDING TRUSTY CREDENT
RELIANT TRUSTFUL CONFIDENT
CONFIGURATION FORM SHAPE
FIGURE BANDING CONTOUR
DIAMOND GESTALT OUTLINE
GEOMETRY POSITURE
OPPOSITION PERSPECTIVE
(CELESTIAL —) SYZYGY
CONFINE BAR BOX CUB DAM HEM
MEW NUN PEN PIN STY TIE BAIL
BIND BOOM CAGE COOP CRIB
FOLD HASP JAIL KEEP LACE LOCK
PEND SEAL SHUT SPAN STEW
STOP STOW BOUND CABIN CHAIN
COART CRAMP CROWD DELAY
FENCE HOUSE LIMIT MARCH
PINCH POUND STICK STINT THIRL
BORDER BOTTLE COARCT CORRAL
EMBANK FETTER FORBAR
HAMPER HURDLE IMMURE
IMPALE IMPARK INTERN KENNEL
PINION POCKET PRISON STRAIN
TETHER ASTRICT CHAMBER
COMPASS CONTAIN IMPOUND
INCLUDE MANACLE PINFOLD
POISTER RECLOSE SECLUDE
SHACKLE TRAMMEL BASTILLE
BOUNDARY CLOISTER CONCLUDE
DISTRAIN FOCALIZE
IMPRISON RESTRAIN
STRAITEN
(PL.) AMBIT PURLIEU PERIPHERY
CONFINED ILL FAST PENT BOUND
CAGED CLOSE CRAMP BEDRID
IMPALE IMPENT PENTIT SEALED
CAPTIVE CRAMPED CRIBBED
LIMITED SQUEEZY IMPENDED
IMPLICIT INTERNED
PAROCHIAL
(— TO CERTAIN AREA) ENDEMIC
(— TO SELECT GROUP) ESOTERIC
CONFINEMENT MEW BOND HOLD
JAIL WARD CRYING GATING
DURANCE INLYING JANKERS
WARDING CLAUSURE
FIRMANCE GROANING
SOLITARY
CONFINING NARROW
CONFIRM FIX SET FIRM SEAL
PROVE VOUCH AFFEER AFFIRM
ASSENT ASSURE ATTEST AVOUCH
BISHOP CLINCH FASTEN HARDEN
RATIFY REABLE SECOND SETTLE
STABLE VERIFY APPROVE
COMFORT COMPACT CONSIGN
ENDORSE FORTIFY JUSTIFY
PROPORT SUPPORT SUSTAIN
THICKEN ACCREDIT CONVINCE
CORROBER ENTRENCH INSTRUCT
SANCTION STRENGTH
VALIDATE CORROBORATE
REDETERMINE
CONFIRMATION PROOF CHRISM
SANCTION
CONFIRMED SET FIXED SWORN
ARRANT STABLE CERTAIN
CHRONIC AFFEERED HABITUAL
HARDENED RATIFIED
CONFISCATE GRAB SEIZE USURP
CONDEMN CONFISK ESCHEAT
PUBLISH DISTRAIN
CONFISCATION ESCHEAT
INCENSION

CONFLAGRATION FIRE BLAZE FEVER BURNING INFERNO

CONFLICT JAR WAR AGON BATE BOUT BUMP CAMP DUEL FRAY MEET MUSS RIFT AGONY BROIL BRUSH CLASH FIGHT GRIPS STOUR ACTION BATTLE COMBAT MUTINY OPPOSE SCRAPE SHOWER STRIFE CONTEND CONTEST DISCORD SCUFFLE WARFARE ANTIMONY CLASHING DISAGREE MILITATE SKIRMISH STRIVING STRUGGLE COLLISION COLLUCTATION
(DRAMATIC —) AGON
(FINAL —) ARMAGEDDON

CONFLICTING ADVERSE ABHORRENT

CONFLUENCE FORK CROWD INFALL CONFLUX MEETING JUNCTION

CONFORM DO GO FIT HEW BEND LEAN OBEY SORT SUIT ABIDE ADAPT AGREE APPLY SHAPE YIELD ACCEDE ADJUST ASSENT COMPLY CONFER SETTLE SQUARE SUBMIT COMPOSE CONFIRM
(— TO) KEEP MEET ANSWER BEHAVE SATISFY

CONFORMABLE DONE SUING SUITED CONFORM PURSUANT QUADRANT

CONFORMATION FORM BUILD
(MENTAL —) SAMSKARA

CONFORMING FAIR SAME COMELY DECENT CORRECT CONGRUOUS

CONFORMIST BOY COMPLIER

CONFORMITY FIT ACCORD DHARMA EQUITY HARMONY JUSTICE KEEPING ACCURACY AFFINITY JUSTNESS LIKENESS SYMMETRY CONGRUITY FORMALITY ACCORDANCE CONSERTION
(— TO LAW) DECENCY LEGALITY

CONFOUND MIX BLOW DASH MATE MAZE ROUT STAM STUN WHIP ABASH ADDLE AMAZE APPAL BLAST FOUND SHEND SPOIL STUMP WASTE AWHAPE BAFFLE BUNKER COMMIT DISMAY DUDDER MINGLE MUDDLE RABBIT RATTLE ASTOUND BUMBAZE CONFUSE CONFUTE CORRUPT DESTROY FLUMMOX FORLESE MISTAKE NONPLUS PERPLEX PETRIFY STUMBLE STUPEFY ASTONISH BABELIZE BEWILDER DISTRACT DUMFOUND SURPRISE SPIFLICATE

CONFOUNDED MATE BALLY BLAME RUDDY BLAMED DEUCED POCKED BLASTED BLESSED MURRAIN PEEVISH DUMMERED JIGGERED SWITCHED CONSARNED
(BE —) ABAVE ABAWE

CONFRATERNITY BODY UNION SOCIETY CONFRAIRY

CONFRONT DARE DEFY FACE MEET NOSE BEARD BRACE BRAVE CROSS FRONT STAND ACCOST ASSAIL BREAST OPPOSE RESIST VISAGE AFFRONT COMPARE OUTFACE PROPOSE ENVISAGE THREATEN

CONFRONTING BEFORE ADVERSE ABUTTING CONFRONT

CONFUSE BOX FOX MIX BALL DASH DAZE DOIT DOZE DUST GAUM HARL MAZE MUSS ROIL ROUT ABASH ADDLE AMAZE BEFOG BITCH BLEND CLOUD DEAVE DIZZY MUDDY SHEND SHENT SNARL STEER TWIST UPSET BAFFLE BEDAZE BEMUSE BOTHER BURBLE CADDLE COMMIT CORPSE DUDDER DUDDLE FLURRY FUDDLE GRAVEL JUMBLE MADDLE MAFFLE MAMMER MASKER MIZZLE MOIDER MOMBLE MUDDLE PUZZLE RAFFLE RATTLE TWITCH WIMPLE BECLOUD BEDEVIL BLUNDER BUMBAZE DERANGE DIFFUSE EMBROIL FLUSTER GARBOIL GIDDIFY MISTAKE MYSTIFY NONPLUS PERPLEX PERTURB SCATTER SHUFFLE STUPEFY UNRAVEL BEFUDDLE BEWILDER CONFLATE CONFOUND DISORDER DISTRACT DUMFOUND ENTANGLE MISORDER SQUATTER OBFUSCATE
(— AN ACTOR) CORPSE
(— BY NOISE) DUDDER

CONFUSED ASEA LOST ADDLE DIZZY FOGGY FUZZY HEAVY MISTY MUDDY MUZZY VAGUE WESTY WOOLY BLOTTO CLOUDY DOILED DOITED DRUMLY JUMBLY MEDLEY MOPISH MUSHED SHAGGY TAVERT WOOLLY BEMUSED BLURRED CHAOTIC CLOUDED CONFUSE DIFFUSE MIFFLED OBSCURE RATTLED STUPENT COCKEYED DERANGED FLURRIED INVOLVED MUDDLEHEADED

CONFUSING DIZZY MAZEFUL BAFFLING BLINDING DIZZYING

CONFUSION PI DIN PIE COIL DUST FLAP FUSS HARL MESS MOIL RIOT AMAZE ATAXY BABEL CHAOS CHEVY CHIVY DERAY FRASE HAVOC HURLY LARRY LURRY SNAFU SNARL STROW ATAXIA BABBLE BAFFLE BALLUP BEDLAM BUMBLE CHIVVY DUDDER FRAISE HABBLE HOBBLE HUBBUB HUDDLE JABBLE JUMBLE MASTIC MUCKER MUDDLE POTHER PUCKER RABBLE RUFFLE RUMPUS THRONG TOPHET TUMULT UPROAR WELTER ANARCHY BLUNDER BLUSTER CLUTTER COBWEBS FARRAGE FLUTTER GARBOIL HURLING KIPPAGE LOUSTER MISMAZE MISRULE ROOKERY RUMMAGE SCADDLE SCOWDER TOPHETH TURMOIL WHEMMEL WIDDRIM BABELISM DISARRAY DISORDER EQUIVOKE HOOROOSH SCOUTHER SHAMBLES SPLUTTER STRAMASH TOHUBOHU

CONFUTATION DISPROOF

CONFUTE DENY EVICT REBUT EVINCE EXPOSE REFUTE FALSIFY IMPROVE SILENCE SUBVERT CONCLUDE CONFOUND CONVINCE DISPROVE INFRINGE OVERCOME REDARGUE

CONGEAL GEL ICE SET GEAL JELL CANDY COTTER CURDLE FREEZE HARDEN STIFFEN STORKEN THICKEN CONCRETE SOLIDIFY
(— INTO HOARFROST) RIME

CONGEALED FROZEN

CONGELATION FROST

CONGENER BEAVER DOTTREL DOTTEREL

CONGENIAL SIB BOON HAPPY NATAL NATIVE AMIABLE CONNATE KINDRED

CONGENITAL INNATE CONNATE CONNATAL GENETOUS

CONGERIES CALCULARY COLLECTION

CONGEST STUFF IMPACT

CONGESTED INJECTED

CONGESTION JAM HEAP LAMPAS LAMPERS CROWDING STOPPAGE

CONGLOMERATE HEAP MASS PILE ROCK STACK BANKET PSEPHITE NAGELFLUH
(-S OF JAPAN) ZAIBATSU

CONGLOMERATION HUDDLE GLOMMOX IMBROGLIO

CONGO MUMMY ASPHALTUM

CONGO		
CAPITAL: BRAZZAVILLE		
COIN: FRANC FRANCCFA		
LAKE: MWERU TUMBA UPEMBA LEOPOLD		
NATIVE: SUSA VILI MANTU PYGMY BATEKE MBOCHI WABUMA BAKONGO BANGALA		
PLATEAU: BATEKE		
RIVER: UELE CONGO KWILU LULUA NGOKO NIARI SANGA WAMBA KWENGE LOANGE SANGHA UBANGI KOUILOU LUBILASH		
TOWN: EWO EPENA HOLLE JACOB OKOYO SEMBE MAKOUA OUESSO ZANAGA DOLISIE ENYELLE LOUBOMO SOUANKE DJAMBALA BRAZZAVILLE		
TRIBUTARY: LOMAMI UBANGI ARUWIMA LUALABA LUAPULA ITIMBIRI		

CONGOU KEEMUN

CONGRATULATE HUG JOY LAUD GREET SALUTE FLATTER MACARIZE

CONGRATULATION PARABIEN
(PL.) GRATTERS

CONGREGATE HERD MASS MEET PACK TEEM GROUP SWARM TROOP GATHER MUSTER COLLECT CONVENE ASSEMBLE

CONGREGATION PEW BODY FOLD HERD HOST MASS FLOCK SAMAJ SWARM CHURCH PARISH COMPANY MEETING ORATORY SYNAXIS ASSEMBLY

BRETHREN CHAPELRY
(— OF WITCHES) COVEN
(JEWISH —) KOLEL ALJAMA SYNAGOG
(PL.) CHARGE

CONGRESS MOD DAIL DIET SYNOD UYEZD OBLAST OUYEZD POWWOW COUNCIL GORSEDD MEETING ASSEMBLY CONCLAVE

CONGRESSMAN SENATOR DOUGHFACE

CONGRUITY ACCORD CONCORD FITNESS HARMONY KEEPING SYMMETRY COHERENCE

CONGRUOUS CONGRUE HARMONIC SUITABLE ACCORDING

CONICAL CONIC TAPER COPPED MITRAL COPPLED TAPERING
(PREF.) TURBIN(I)(O) TURBINATO

CONICALLY
(PREF.) TURBINATO

CONIDIUM CIDIUM ARTHROSPORE

CONIFER FIR YEW PINE CEDAR LARCH SPRUCE SOFTWOOD EVERGREEN

CONIFERAE PINALES

CONIUM HEMLOCK

CONJECTURE AIM CAST PLOT ROVE SHOT VIEW AUGUR ETTLE FANCY GUESS OPINE THINK BELIEF DIVINE THEORY CONJECT IMAGINE OPINION PRESUME SUPPOSE SURMISE SUSPECT HINDCAST SUPPOSAL

CONJOIN JOIN KNIT ATTEND EMPALE IMPALE ALLIGATE

CONJOINED JOINED JUGATE LINKED JUGATED CONJUNCT TOUCHING

CONJOINTLY JUNCTLY TOGETHER

CONJUGAL SPOUSAL CONNUBIAL

CONJUGATE YOKED JOINED UNITED COUPLED INFLECT PARONYMOUS

CONJUGATION SYNGAMY ZYGOSIS CYTOGAMY ENDOGAMY SYNOPSIS

CONJUNCTION AS ET IF OR AND BUT NOR TIE THAN JOINT SINCE SYNOD UNION UNITY THOUGH COITION CONSORT JOINDER CONJUNCT RATIONAL
(PREF.) (IN —) CO

CONJUNCTURE SEASON

CONJURATION ART CHARM MAGIC SPELL VOODOO EXORCISM

CONJURE PRAY WISH CHARM HALSE ADJURE ENJOIN INVENT INVOKE SUMMON BESEECH COMBINE ENTREAT IMAGINE CONSPIRE CONTRIVE EXORCIZE
(— UP) RAISE

CONJURE MAN CUNJAH CUNJER GOOFER GUFFER

CONJURER MAGE PELLAR POWWOW SHAMAN WIZARD JUGGLER WARLOCK WIELARE ANGEKKOK JONGLEUR MAGICIAN PYTHONIC SORCERER

CONJURING JADU JADOO CONJURY VOODOOISM

CONK FAIL HEAD KONK NOSE FAINT KNOCK STALL BRACKET

CONNECT COG PUT TIE ALLY BIND

BOND GEAR GLUE JOIN KNIT KNOT LINK AFFIX CHAIN MARRY NITCH UNITE ATTACH BRIDGE CEMENT COHERE COMMIT CONNEX COUPLE ENLINK FASTEN RELATE SPLICE COMBINE ENCHAIN INVOLVE APPARENT CATENATE CONTINUE DOVETAIL INTERTIE
(— TREADLE) CORD
CONNECTED ALLIED CONNEX AFFINED COUPLED HANGING
(— WITH) ABOUT
(ELECTRICALLY —) ALIVE
(NOT —) FOREIGN ASYNARTETE
(SYNTACTICALLY —) ABSOLUTE
(SUFF.) (— WITH) ARIA ARIUM AST ORIAL

CONNECTICUT
CAPITAL: HARTFORD
COLLEGE: TRINITY
COUNTY: TOLLAND WINDHAM
INDIAN: PEQUOT MOHEGAN NIANTIC
STATE BIRD: ROBIN
STATE FLOWER: LAUREL
STATE NICKNAME: NUTMEG
STATE TREE: OAK
TOWN: AVON BETHEL CANAAN COSCOB DARIEN MYSTIC SHARON STORRS WILTON DANBURY MERIDEN NIANTIC NORWALK NORWICH TOLLAND WINDSOR NEWHAVEN SIMSBURY WESTPORT GREENWICH RIDGEFIELD
UNIVERSITY: YALE WESLEYAN

CONNECTING BETWEEN SYNDETIC
CONNECTION Y HUB TAP TIE BOND LINK HITCH NEXUS UNION BUCKLE CLEVIS FAMILY GROUND REPORT SUTURE SWIVEL BEARING BOLSTER CONTACT DESCENT FERRULE HOLDING KINSHIP LIAISON RAPPORT SIAMESE SIBNESS SOCIETY AFFINITY ALLIANCE COMMERCE CONNEXUS INTIMACY JUNCTION LIGATION RELATIVE SYNDETIC RELATIONSHIP
(ELECTRICAL —) GROUND
(FORKED —) BRANCH
(MECHANICAL —S) LEADOUT
CONNECTIVE IZAFAT SUTURAL JUNCTION LIGATIVE SYNDETIC VINCULAR
CONNING TOWER SAIL
CONNIVANCE CAHOOT CAHOOTS
CONNIVE ABET PLOT WINK BLINK CABAL ASSENT FOMENT INCITE COLLUDE
(— AT MEDICAL TREATMENT) COVER
CONNOISSEUR JUDGE CRITIC EXPERT CAMEIST EPICURE GOURMET CIDERIST DILETANT LAPIDARY COGNOSCENTE MEDIEVALIST
CONNOTATION DEPTH INTENT MEANING
CONNUBIAL MARITAL

CONJUGAL DOMESTIC
CONQUER GET WIN BEAT BEST DOWN FIRK GAIN LICK ROUT TAME WHIP CRUSH DAUNT DEBEL EVICT DEBELL DEFEAT EVINCE HUMBLE IMPORT MASTER REDUCE SUBDUE VICTOR ACQUIRE PREVAIL SUBJECT SURPASS TRIUMPH OVERCOME OVERGANG SURMOUNT VANQUISH
CONQUEROR HERO MASTER VICTOR WINNER TRIUMPHER
CONQUEST MASTERY SCALING TRIUMPH VICTORY WINNING
CONSANGUINEOUS AKIN CARNAL KINDRED NATURAL RELATED
CONSANGUINITY BLOOD NASAB KINSHIP AFFINITY
CONSCIENCE WORD DAENA HEART INWIT SENSE SCRUPLE THOUGHT
CONSCIENTIOUS FAIR JUST EXACT RIGID EIDENT HONEST STRICT DUTIFUL UPRIGHT FAITHFUL
CONSCIENTIOUSNESS RELIGION
CONSCIOUS KEEN WARE ALIVE AWAKE AWARE JERRY GUILTY FEELING KNOWING WITTING RATIONAL SENSIBLE SENTIENT CONSCIENT
CONSCIOUSNESS EGO HEART SENSE SPIRIT ANOESIS FEELING THOUGHT SENTIENT AWARENESS PERCEPTION
(HALF —) DOVER
CONSCRIPT LEVY CHOCO DRAFT ENROL ENLIST MUSTER DRAFTEE DRAUGHT RECRUIT JEANJEAN
CONSCRIPTION LEVY
CONSECRATE VOW FAIN HOLY SAIN SEAL BLESS DEIFY HEAVE SACRE ANOINT DEVOTE HALLOW ORDAIN SACRATE CONSACRE DEDICATE SANCTIFY
CONSECRATED BLEST OBLATE SACRED VOTARY VOTIVE BLESSED SACRATE HALLOWED HIERATIC
CONSECRATION IHRAM SACRE SACRY SACRING DEVOTION HOLINESS
CONSECUTIVELY TOGETHER
CONSECUTIVENESS SEQUENCE
CONSENT HEAR AGREE ALLOW GRANT YIELD ACCEDE ACCORD AFFORD ASSENT BETEEM COMPLY CONCUR PERMIT APPROVE GOODWILL PERMISSION
CONSENTIENT UNANIMOUS
CONSEQUENCE AND END BORE EVENT FORCE FRUIT ISSUE SUITE WORTH BROWST CHARGE EFFECT ENTAIL FIGURE GROWTH IMPORT MOMENT REPUTE RESULT SEQUEL WEIGHT CONCERN OUTCOME PRODUCE PURPOSE SEQUELA SEQUENT BACKLASH INTEREST MISCHIEF OCCASION SEQUITUR COROLLARY OUTGROWTH CONSECTARY RAMIFICATION
(DONE IN —) PURSUANT

(HARMFUL —) EVIL
(PERSON OF —) HEAVY
(PL.) AFTERINGS
CONSEQUENT COMES THESIS ADJUNCT
CONSEQUENTIAL HEAVY POMPOUS COROLLARY MOMENTOUS
CONSEQUENTLY SO ERGO THEN THUS HENCE LATER PURSUANT PRESENTLY
CONSERTAL SUTURAL
CONSERVATION HUSBANDRY
CONSERVATISM BOURBONISM
CONSERVATIVE SAFE TORY FUSTY QUIET STAID FABIAN HUNKER STABLE BOURBON DIEHARD HARDHAT MODERATE UNIONIST
CONSERVATORY STOVE SCHOOL ACADEMY
CONSERVE CAN JAM SAVE GUARD GUMBO JELLY DEFEND SECURE SHIELD UPHOLD HUSBAND PROTECT SEATRON SUSTAIN MAINTAIN PRESERVE
(GRAPE —) UVATE
CONSIDER AIM BAT LET SEE CALL CAST DEEM GAUM GIVE HASH HEED HOLD MULL MUSE RATE SEEM TAKE TALE VIEW VISE WISE ALLOW BESEE COUNT ENTER ETTLE JUDGE PANSE POISE SPELL STUDY THINK VERSE VOLVE WEIGH ADVERT ADVISE BEHOLD DEBATE DEVISE DIGEST ESTEEM EXPEND FIGURE IMPUTE PONDER REASON RECKON REGARD REWARD SURVEY ACCOUNT BELIEVE BETHINK CANVASS CONSULT EXAMINE INSPECT PERPEND PREPEND REFLECT RESPECT REVOLVE SUPPOSE COGITATE ESTIMATE MEDITATE PERPENSE RUMINATE
(— FAVORABLY) CREDIT
(— PROS AND CONS) ARGUE
(— SEPARATELY) SPECIALIZE
CONSIDERABLE GAY GEY FAIR GOOD TIDY BONNY CANNY GEYAN GREAT LARGE SMART STARK GOODLY PRETTY GOODISH HEALTHY INTENSE NOTABLE SEVERAL HANDSOME POWERFUL SENSIBLE UNLITTLE
CONSIDERABLY GAY GEY WELL GEYAN PRETTY SMARTLY
CONSIDERATE KIND MILD NICE GENTLE TENDER CAREFUL HEEDFUL PRUDENT SERIOUS TACTFUL DELICATE GRACIOUS ATTENTIVE
CONSIDERATENESS GRACE
(MUTUAL —) SHU
CONSIDERATION GUT GUTS SAKE COUNT PRICE STUDY TOPIC ADVICE ASPECT COMITY DEBATE ESTEEM MOMENT MOTIVE NOTICE REASON REFLEX REGARD SURVEY ACCOUNT INSIGHT PREMIUM RESPECT THOUGHT ALTRUISM COURTESY DELICACY EMINENCE EMPHASIS GRATUITY PROSPECT SANCTION

(BASIC —) BEDROCK
(ETHICAL —) SCRUPLE
(THOUGHTFUL —) THEORIA
CONSIDERED ADVISED DELIBERATE
CONSIDERING IF FOR SINCE SEEING
CONSIGN DOOM GIVE MAIL SEND SHIP ALLOT AWARD CHECK DIGHT REMIT SHIFT YIELD ASSIGN COMMIT DESIGN DEVOTE REMAND RESIGN ADDRESS BETEACH CONFIDE DELIVER DEPOSIT ENTRUST INTRUST BEQUEATH DELEGATE RELEGATE TRANSFER
(— FOR DESTRUCTION) ACCURSE
(— TO OBLIVION) BURY EXPUNGE
(— TO PERDITION) DAMN CONDEMN
CONSIGNEE AGENT FACTOR SHIPPER RECEIVER
CONSIGNMENT INVOICE FOREDOOM SHIPMENT
(— OF TEA) BREAK
CONSIST LIE HOLD RELY REST DWELL EXIST STAND INHERE RESIDE CONTAIN EMBRACE COMPRISE
CONSISTENCY BODY UNION DEGREE CONCENT CONCORD HARMONY KEEPING COMPAGES EVENNESS FIRMNESS SOLIDITY SYMMETRY
CONSISTENT EVEN FIRM STEADY DURABLE LOGICAL REGULAR UNIFORM COHERENT ENDURING SUITABLE COMPATIBLE SEQUACIOUS
(— WITH NATURE) KIND KINDLY
(BE —) ACCORD
(MAKE —) CLEAR
CONSISTING
(PREF.) (— OF) DIA
(SUFF.) (— OF) IC(AL)
CONSOCIES
(SUFF.) ETUM
CONSOLATION SOP FINE RELIEF SOLACE COMFORT SPIRITING
CONSOLE CALM ALLAY ANCON CHEER ORGAN TABLE SOLACE SOOTHE BRACKET CABINET COMFORT RELIEVE SUPPORT SUSTAIN CARTOUCH
CONSOLER PARACLETE
CONSOLIDATE COG MIX KNIT MASS POOL WELD BLEND CLOSE MERGE UNIFY UNITE HARDEN MINGLE SETTLE COMBINE COMPACT ANKYLOSE COALESCE COMPRESS CONDENSE ORGANIZE SOLIDIFY
CONSOLIDATED CONFLATE
CONSOLS GOSCHENS
CONSOMME MADRILENE
CONSONANCE ACCORD UNISON HARMONY DIAPASON DIAPENTE SYMPATHY SYMPHONY
CONSONANT WAW MUTE STOP DENTAL FORTIS LABIAL LETTER LIQUID SONANT UNISON LATERAL MUTABLE PALATAL PLOSIVE SPIRANT UNIFIED ALVEOLAR

ASPIRATA ASPIRATE BILABIAL
EJECTIVE GEMINATE HARMONIC
SUITABLE
(CONSECUTIVE —S) CLUSTER
(SMOOTH —) LENE LENIS
(TENSE AND STRONG —) FORTIS
(VOICELESS —) SURD SPIRATE
CONSORT COT AIDE ALLY JOIN
MATE MOUP WIFE YOKE GROUP
TROOP UNITE ACCORD ATTEND
ESCORT MINGLE SPOUSE
COMPANY COMRADE CONCERT
DAMKINA EMPRESS HUSBAND
PARTNER ACCUSTOM ASSEMBLY
PRINCESS
(VISHNU'S —) LAKSHMI
CONSPECTUS LIST APERCU
SURVEY OUTLINE THEATER
THEORIC SPECTRUM SYNOPSIS
CONSPICUOUS BIG BOLD RANK
CLEAR FAMED PLAIN STARY
EXTANT FAMOUS MARKED
PATENT SIGNAL BLATANT
EMINENT GLARING NOTABLE
OBVIOUS POINTED SALIENT
SIGHTLY STARING VISIBLE
APPARENT EMPHATIC FLAGRANT
KENSPECK MANIFEST STRIKING
PROMINENT NOTICEABLE
OUTSTANDING
CONSPIRACY COUP PLAN PLOT
RING CABAL COVIN JUNTO PARTY
COVINE SCHEME COMPACT
COMPLOT INTRIGUE CATILINISM
CONSPIRATOR PACKER PLOTTER
SCHEMER
CONSPIRE ABET PACK PLOT
CABAL UNITE LEAGUE SCHEME
COLLUDE COMPLOT CONJURE
CONNIVE COLLOGUE CONTRIVE
CONSTABLE COP BULL PEON SLOP
BEADLE BEAGLE HARMAN
KAVASS KEEPER KOTWAL
WARDEN BAILIFF CORONER
DOZENER NUTHOOK OFFICER
STALLER SUBASHI ALGUAZIL
DOGBERRY TIPSTAFF CASTELLAN
CATCHPOLE CATCHPOLL
BORSHOLDER
CONSTANCE (FATHER OF —)
FONDLOVE NONESUCH
(HUSBAND OF —) ALLA
(SON OF —) ARTHUR
CONSTANCY ZEAL ARDOR FAITH
TRUTH FEALTY HONESTY
LOYALTY ONENESS PURPOSE
DEVOTION FIDELITY
CONSTANT K SET EVEN FIRM JUST
LEAL TRUE FIXED LOYAL SOLID
STILL TIGHT TRIED ITHAND
STABLE STEADY CERTAIN
CHRONIC DURABLE FOREVER
LASTING REGULAR STAUNCH
UNIFORM DEFINITE ENDURING
FAITHFUL POSITIVE RESOLUTE
SEDULOUS STANDING PERENNIAL
CONSTANTLY AWAY EVER
ALWAYS THRONG
CONSTANT NYMPH (AUTHOR OF —
) KENNEDY
(CHARACTER IN —) DODD KATE
CARYL LEWIS SUSAN TESSA
ALBERT SANGER TERESA

ANTONIA PAULINA FLORENCE
CHURCHILL SEBASTIAN
CONSTELLATION ARA CUP FLY
FOX LEO APUS ARGO COLT CROW
CRUX DOVE GOAT GRUS HARE
HARP LION LYNX LYRA MAST
PAVO PLOW SIGN SWAN TAUR
URSA VELA WAIN WOLF ALTAR
ARIES CAMEL CETUS CLOCK
CRANE DRACO EAGLE GROUP
HYDRA INDUS LEPUS LIBRA
LUPUS MALUS MENSA MUSCA
NORMA ORION PYXIS RAVEN
TABLE VIRGO WAGON WHALE
ANTLIA AQUILA AURIGA BOOTES
CAELUM CANCER CARINA
CORVUS CRATER CYGNUS DIPPER
DORADO FORNAX GEMINI
HYDRUS INDIAN LIZARD OBELUS
OCTANS OKNARI PICTOR PISCES
PISCIS PLOUGH PUPPIS SCALES
SCUTUM TAURUS TIGRIS TOUCAN
TUCANA VOLANS ALGEBAR
CEPHEUS CLUSTER COLUMBA
COMPASS DOLPHIN FURNACE
GIRAFFE LACERTA MONARCH
OETAEUS PATTERN PEACOCK
PEGASUS PERSEUS PHOENIX
RHOMBUS SAGITTA SCORPIO
SERPENS SERPENT SEXTANS
SEXTANT XIPHIAS AQUARIUS
ASTERISM CHAMPION CIRCINUS
CYNOSURE EQUULEUS ERIDANUS
HERCULES HERDSMAN KASHYAPA
QUADRANS REINDEER RETICULE
SCORPION SCORPIUS SCULPTOR
TRIANGLE
CONSTERNATION FEAR ALARM
PANIC DISMAY FRIGHT HORROR
TERROR TREPIDITY
CONSTIPATE BIND ASTRICT
CONSTIPATED BOUND COSTIVE
STENOTIC
CONSTITUENCY BOROUGH
CONSTITUENT ATOM ITEM PART
PIECE VOTER DETAIL FACTOR
FUSAIN MATTER MEMBER SIMPLE
ELECTOR ELEMENT FEATURE
TAGMEME INTEGRAL
(— OF BLOOD SERUM) OPSONIN
(— OF CLINKER) ALITE CELITE
(— OF COAL) DURAIN FUSAIN
(— OF DURAIN) ATTRITUS
(— OF MUSCLE) CREATINE
(— OF STEEL) PEARLITE
(—S OF BEER) EXTRACT
(NECESSARY —) ESSENCE
(PL.) MATTER BIOSESTON
CONSTITUTE BE FIX SET FORM
MAKE ENACT ERECT FORGE
FOUND SHAPE SPELL CREATE
DEPUTE GRAITH ORDAIN
APPOINT COMPOSE FASHION
STATION COMPOUND COMPRISE
CONSTITUTION LAW SET CODE
SETT BEING CANON FRAME
FUERO HUMOR SETUP STATE
CHARTE CRASIS CUSTOM DESIGN
ESTATE HEALTH NATURE TEMPER
CHARTER HABITUS SYNODAL
GRONDWET GRUNDLOV
HABITUDE PHYSIQUE POLITEIA
(— STATE) CONNECTICUT

(BODILY —) HABIT SPIRITS
(GERMINAL —) HEREDITY
CONSTITUTIONAL WALK HECTIC
INNATE RIKKEN EXERCISE
CONSTITUTIVE FORMAL
CONSTRAIN ART PUT TIE ARCT
BEND BIND CURB DOOM FAIN
HALE HOLD LEAD URGE CHAIN
CHECK CLASP COART CRAMP
DETER DRIVE FORCE IMPEL LIMIT
PRESS COERCE COMPEL EVINCE
OBLIGE RAVISH SECURE STRAIN
THRAST ASTRICT CONFINE
CONJURE ENFORCE MANACLE
OPPRESS REPRESS VIOLATE
COMPRESS CONCLUDE DISTRESS
OBLIGATE PERFORCE POUNDAGE
RELIGATE RESTRAIN
CONSTRAINED FAIN TIED VAIN
BOUND FORCED FORMAL UNEASY
COACTED
CONSTRAINING UNEASY
COMPELLENT
CONSTRAINT BOND CRAMP FORCE
BRIDLE DURESS STRESS RESERVE
STRAINT COERCION DISTRESS
PRESSURE
CONSTRICT TIE BIND CURB GRIP
CHOKE CRAMP LIMIT STRAP
HAMPER SHRINK STRAIN STRAIT
ASTRICT DEFLATE SQUEEZE
STIFFEN TIGHTEN ASTRINGE
COMPRESS CONDENSE CONTRACT
DISTRAIN RESTRICT
CONSTRICTED STRAIT STRICT
ADENOID
(— AT INTERVALS) MONILIFORM
CONSTRICTION KNOT CHOKE
ISTHMUS STENOSIS THLIPSIS
CONSTRICTOR BOA ABOMA
GUAVINA
CONSTRUCT UP BIG ATOM FORM
IDEA LEVY MAKE REAR BUILD
CRAFT DIGHT EDIFY ERECT
FRAME MODEL WEAVE BURROW
DEDUCE DESIGN DEVISE FABRIC
ARRANGE CARPENT COMBINE
COMPILE COMPOSE CONCEPT
CONFECT CONTOUR EXTRUCT
FASHION CONSTRUE ENGINEER
PRACTISE
(— ARCH) TURN
CONSTRUCTED BUILT EDIFICATE
(CAREFULLY —) CLEVER
(HASTILY —) GIMCRACK JIMCRACK
CONSTRUCTION BOOM ALTAR
FRAME FABRIC MONSTER SYNESIS
APPROACH BUILDING DWELLING
ERECTION
(— OF NAME) ABSTRACTION
(ABSTRACT —) STABILE
(GRAMMATICAL —) SYNESIS
APPOSITION
(POINTED —) BEAK
CONSTRUCTIVE PONENT FACTIVE
HELPFUL VIRTUAL CREATIVE
IMPLICIT INFERRED
CONSTRUCTOR ENGINEER
CONSTRUE INFER PARSE STRUE
INTEND RENDER ANALYZE
CONSTER DISSECT EXPLAIN
EXPOUND RESOLVE
CONSUL SUFFECT

CONSULT LOOK SEEK TALK ADVISE
CONFER EMPARL IMPARL
COUNSEL RESOLVE
CONSULTANT EXPERT ADVISER
COUNSEL
CONSULTATION ADVICE COUNCIL
COUNSEL
CONSUL, THE (CHARACTER IN —)
JOHN MAGDA SOREL
(COMPOSER OF —) MENOTTI
CONSUME EAT SUP USE BOLT
BURN CHEW FANG FEED
FRET GULP IDLE KILL RUST TAKE
TUCK WEAR DALLY DRINK FLAME
LURCH RAVEN SHIFT SPEND
TOOTH WASTE ABSORB BEZZLE
BROWSE CANKER DEVOUR
ENGAGE EXPEND FINISH IMBIBE
INHALE PERISH PUNISH VANISH
CORRODE DESTROY DWINDLE
ENGROSS EXHAUST SWALLOW
CONTRIVE SQUANDER
(— TOTALLY) KILL
(— VORACIOUSLY) HOG
CONSUMED ALL PAU DOWN
BURNT SPENT COMBUST
OUTWORN
CONSUMING EATING SACRED
BURNING FLAMING
CONSUMMATE END FINE FULL
RIPE CLOSE IDEAL SHEER ARRANT
EFFECT FINISH FULFIL RATIFY
ACHIEVE CONSUME CROWNED
FULFILL PERFECT PERFORM
ABSOLUTE COMPLETE MERIDIAN
THOROUGH
CONSUMMATION CROWN PERIOD
UPSHOT
CONSUMPTION USE DECAY
WASTE EXPENSE WASTING
PHTHISIS SPENDING
(PREF.) PHTHISIO
CONSUMPTIVE LUNGY HECTIC
PREDATORY
CONTACT ABUT JOIN KISS MEET
SLED CROSS TOUCH TRUCK
UNION ARRIVE IMPACT SYZYGY
EPHAPSE HOLDING MEETING
TACTION JUNCTION TANGENCY
TOUCHING
(— OF TELEGRAPH KEY) ANVIL
(ELECTRICAL —) HUB HUBB POINT
(EVIL —) CONTAGION
(FLEETING —) BRUSH
(FORCIBLE —) IMPACT
(3-POINT —) OSCNODE
(PREF.) HAPT(O) THIGMO
CONTAGION POX TAINT VIRUS
MIASMA POISON
CONTAGIOUS TAKING NOXIOUS
SMITTLE CATCHING EPIDEMIC
CONTAIN RUN HAVE HOLD KEEP
STOW TAKE CARRY CHECK CLOSE
COVER HOUSE EMBODY ENFOLD
ENSEAM HARBOR RETAIN
COMPILE EMBRACE ENCLOSE
INCLUDE INVOLVE RECEIVE
SUBSUME SUSTAIN COMPRISE
RESTRAIN
(PREF.) CHADA
CONTAINED IN
CONTAINER BAG BOX CAN CUP
HAT JAR JUG KEG LUG NIN PAN

POD POT TIN TUB URN VAT BAIL
BOMB CAGE CASE CASK CRIB
DRUM EWER FILE FLAT JACK
SACK SALT SILO SINK SKIP TANK
TUBE VASE ALBUM BASIN BILLY
CADDY CHEST CRATE CRUET
DEWAR EMPTY FLASK GLASS
GOURD POUCH SCOOP SCRAY
STAND STOOP STOUP BARREL
BASKET BOTTLE BUCKET BUSHEL
CARBOY CARTON CASTER
CASTOR COOLER CRADLE DUSTER
HAMPER HATBOX HOLDER
INKPOT MAILER PICNIC RABBIT
RIDDLE SHAKER WITJAR AEROSOL
AMPULLA BANDBOX BLADDER
CAPSULE COASTER COSTREL
CRISPER FEEDBOX HANAPER
HOLDALL INKWELL PACKAGE
SEEDLIP SHIPPER STEEPER
CANISTER DECANTER DEMIJOHN
ENVELOPE HOGSHEAD HONEYPOT
INHOLDER KNAPSACK PUNCHEON
SLIPCASE RELIQUARY
POCKETBOOK
(— FOR BEER) GROWLER
(— FOR BOBBINS) BUFFALO
(— FOR COINS) BANK
(— FOR EXPLOSIVE CHARGE) CAP
(— FOR FISH) BASS
(— FOR GOLD DUST) SHAMMY
(— FOR HOLY OIL) STOCK
(— FOR PLANTS) BAND
(— MADE OF HOLLOW LOG) GUM
(COFFEE —) INSET
(DESSERT —) COUPE
(DRINK —) DOP
(EARTHENWARE —) STEAN
(FIRECLAY —) SETTER
(RAILROAD —S) BUNKER
(SHELVED —) CABIN
(SHIPPING —) KIT
(SNUFF —) WEASAND
(TOBACCO —) SARATOGA
(VENTILATED —) CHIP
(5-GALLON —) JERICAN JERRICAN
(PL.) CONVEYER CONVEYOR
CONTAINING
(SUFF.) IC(AL)
CONTAMINATE FOUL HARM SLUR
SMIT SOIL STAIN SULLY TAINT
BEFOUL DEBASE DEFILE INFECT
INJURE POISON ATTAINT
CORRUPT DEBAUCH FLYBLOW
POLLUTE TARNISH VITIATE
DISHONOR
CONTAMINATED DIRTY
DEGRADED INFECTED
CONTAMINATION INFECTION
TAINTMENT
(— IN GLASS) STONE
CONTE TALE CRAYON
CONTEMN HATE FLOUT SCORN
SPURN REJECT SLIGHT DESPISE
DISDAIN CONTEMPT INDIGNIFY
CONTEMPLATE FACE MUSE PLAN
SCAN VIEW DEIGN STUDY THINK
WEIGH BEHOLD DESIGN PONDER
REGARD SURVEY CHERISH
PROPOSE REFLECT CONSIDER
ENVISAGE ENVISION MEDITATE
CONTEMPLATION MUSE STUDY
DHYANA MUSING PRAYER

REGARD THEORY INSIGHT
MOONING REQUEST THEORIA
PETITION RECOLLECTION
CONTEMPLATIVE BROODY
PENSIVE THEORIC STUDIOUS
CONTEMPORANEOUS COEVAL
LIVING MODERN CURRENT
EXISTING
CONTEMPORARY EQUAL COEVAL
FELLOW CURRENT PRESENT
YEALING EXISTENT
SIMULTANEOUS
CONTEMPT PRUT SCORN SHAME
SNEER SLIGHT CONTEMN
DESPECT DESPITE DISDAIN
HETHING MOCKERY DEFIANCE
DERISION DESPISAL DISGRACE
MISPRIZE MISPRISION
OPPROBRIUM
(ONE HELD IN —) FINK
CONTEMPTIBLE LOW BASE MEAN
POOR VILE BALLY CHEAP DIRTY
DUSTY LOUSY MANGY MUCKY
PETTY POCKY RUDDY SCALD
SORRY ABJECT BLOODY CRUDDY
GRUBBY MEASLY PALTRY SCABBY
SCUMMY SCURVY SHABBY
SNOTTY SORDID YELLOW
BROKING LIGHTLY PEEVISH
PELTING PITIFUL SCALLED
SCORNED SHITTEN SLAVISH
SQUALID BAUBLING BEGGARLY
FRIPPERY INFAMOUS INFERIOR
PICAYUNE PITIABLE PRECIOUS
SNEAKING UNWORTHY
WRETCHED MISBEGOTTEN
(SUFF.) (— ONE) EEN EER
CONTEMPTIBLENESS BEGGARY
CONTEMPTUOUS SLIGHT SNEERY
SNOOTY HAUGHTY LOFTY
SLIGHTY SPITOUS ARROGANT
FLOUTING INSOLENT SCOFFING
SCORNFUL
CONTEND TUG VIE WAR WIN
CAMP COCK COPE DEAL FRAB
KEMP PLEA RACE WAGE ARGUE
BANDY BRAWL CHIDE CLAIM
FIGHT FLITE PRESS ASSERT
BATTLE BICKER BREAST BUCKLE
BUFFET BUSTLE COMBAT DEBATE
DIFFER JOSTLE JUSTLE MEDDLE
OPPOSE PINGLE REASON STRIVE
BARGAIN COMPETE CONTEST
COUNTER DISPUTE PROPUGN
QUARREL SCUFFLE STICKLE
SUSTAIN WRESTLE CONFLICT
CONTRAST CONTRIVE MAINTAIN
MILITATE SQUABBLE STRUGGLE
CONTENT PAY CALM EASE GIST
GLAD PAID RATH APPAY HAPPY
HUMOR RATHE SERVE AMOUNT
CUBAGE PLEASE APPEASE
CONTENU GRATIFY PERFECT
REPLETE SATIATE SATISFY
SUFFICE WILLING BLISSFUL
CAPACITY CONTINEU WILCWEME
(-S OF SACK) BUDGET
(—S OF STOMACH) COOKIES
(ENERGY —) STRENGTH
(HEAT —) ENTHALPY
(SUPERFICIAL —S) AREA
(PL.) LINING

CONTENTED COZY FAIN VAIN
QUIET SATED CONTENT PLEASED
CHEERFUL
CONTENTION WAR BAIT BATE
CASE FEUD PLEA RIOT TIFF TOIL
BROIL CHEST STRUT BICKER
COMBAT DEBATE ESTRIF JANGLE
STRIFE CHIDING CONTEKE
CONTEST DISCORD DISPUTE
OPINION QUARREL RIVALRY
WRANGLE ARGUMENT CONFLICT
SQUABBLE STRUGGLE VARIANCE
COLLUCTATION
CONTENTIOUS CROSS BATEFUL
PEEVISH PERVERSE BELLICOSE
CONTENTMENT EASE BLISS
HEAVEN PLEASURE
SATISFACTION
CONTERMINOUS NEXT ADJACENT
FRONTIER PROXIMAL
CONTEST GO IT BEE FIX RUN SUE
TRY VIE AGON BOUT CAMP COPE
DUEL FEUD FRAY GAME HOLD
KEMP LAKE MART PULL RACE
SHOW SPAR TIFF TILT TURN
YOKE AGONY ARGUE BROIL
CLASH DERBY EVENT FIGHT
MATCH PLATE PRIZE ROLEO
SCRUB SPORT TRIAL WAGER
ACTION ADJURE AFFRAY BATTLE
BISLEY COMBAT DEBATE DEFEND
FLIGHT OPPOSE RESIST RUBBER
SEESAW STRIFE STRIVE TUSSLE
YOKING BARGAIN BRABBLE
CLASSIC COMPETE CONTECK
CONTEND DERAIGN DISPUTE
GRAPPLE PROTEST SHUTOUT
TOURNEY WARFARE ARGUMENT
CONCOURS CONFLICT DOGFIGHT
HANDICAP LITIGATE SKIRMISH
SLUGFEST STRIVING STRUGGLE
WALKAWAY WALKOVER
PANCRATIUM PENTATHLON
(— IN WORDS) SPAR
(— NARROWLY WON) SQUEAKER
(ATHLETIC —) BIATHLON
(AUTOMOBILE — ON FROZEN LAKE)
ICEKHANA
(CLOSE —) DICE
(DRAWN —) TIE DRAW STALEMATE
(MOCK —) SCIAMACHY
(RACING —) DRAG
(REAPING —) KEMP
(PREF.) MACHO
(SUFF.) AGONIST(IC) MACHIA
MACHY
CONTESTANT VIER RIVAL WAGER
PLAYER AGONIST ENTRANT
SCRATCH FINALIST PROSPECT
CONTIGUITY ADJACENCY
CONFINITY IMMEDIACY
CONTIGUOUS NEXT NIGH NEARBY
TANGENT ABUTTING ADJACENT
TOUCHING
CONTINENT ASIA MASS PORE
SOBER AFRICA CHASTE EUROPE
CONTENT CAPACITY MAINLAND
MODERATE ABSTINENT
CONTINGENCY BOOK CASE EVENT
CHANCE ADJUNCT CONTACT
VENTURE ACCIDENT CASUALTY
FORTUITY INCIDENT JUNCTURE
PROSPECT

CONTINGENT CASUAL CHANCE
DOUBTFUL EVENTUAL INCHOATE
TOUCHING
CONTINUAL STILL HOURLY
ABIDING ENDLESS ETERNAL
LASTING REGULAR UNDYING
UNIFORM CONSTANT ENDURING
UNBROKEN
CONTINUALLY AY AYE EVER STILL
ALWAYS EVERLY HOURLY STEADY
ENDLESS ETERNAL FOREVER
MINUTELY
CONTINUANCE STAY WHEN
DELAY LEASE SEQUEL ABIDING
DURANCE LASTING ABIDANCE
DURATION STANDING SURVIVAL
CONTINUANT OPEN LIQUID
DURATIVE
CONTINUATION SEQUEL
CONTANGO DURATION
PROLONGATION PERSEVERATION
(— OF DOUBLET) BASQUE
CONTINUE BE DO ABY SUE ABYE
BIDE DURE HOLD JUMP KEEP
LAST LIVE STAY TIDE ABIDE
CARRY EXIST PERGE STICK UNITE
ABEGGE BELEVE ENDURE EXTEND
PURSUE REMAIN RESUME
BELEAVE CONNECT CONTUNE
PERSIST PROCEED PROLONG
SUBSIST SURVIVE SUSTAIN
PROTRACT
(— UNALTERED) TARRY
CONTINUED STILL SERIAL
CHRONIC CONSTANT
CONTINUING ABIDING DURABLE
LASTING DURATIVE PERPETUAL
PERSISTENT OUTSTANDING
(— FOR LONG TIME) CHRONIC
(— TO BE) YET
CONTINUITY TRACT SCRIPT
COHESION SCENARIO
CONTINUUM
(PREF.) SYNECHIO
CONTINUOUS RUN EVEN ANEND
EIDENT ENTIRE EYDENT STEADY
CHRONIC ENDLESS RUNNING
UNBROKEN PERENNIAL
PERPETUAL
CONTINUOUSLY AWAY EVER FAST
ANEND OUTRIGHT
CONTORT WRY BEND COIL CURL
TURN WARP GNARL SCREW
TWIST WREST CRINGE DEFORM
WRITHE DISTORT PERVERT
SQUINCH WREATHE OBVOLUTE
CONTORTED WRY WRIED KNOTTY
CRISPED KNOTTED SCREWED
WRITHEN OBVOLUTE
CONTORTION SCREW STITCH
WRITHE MURGEON WORKING
CONTOUR FORM LINE CURVE
GRAPH SHAPE SWEEP AMOEBA
FIGURE OUTLINE PROFILE
CARTOUCH CONTORNO
MANDORLA PLANFORM
TOURNURE
(— ON SHIP) HANCE
CONTRA CONTRE AGAINST
COUNTER OPPOSED
CONTRABAND HOT GOODS
ILLEGAL ILLICIT SMUGGLED
UNLAWFUL

CONTRABASS BASS OCTOBASS
CONTRACEPTIVE (ORAL —) PILL
CONTRACT GET BOND DRAW
FARM FORM HALE KNIT PACT
SALE TACK CATCH CLOSE COACT
COUCH CRAMP FEVER INCUR
LEASE LIMIT NEXUM PINCH
SHRUG SNURP CARTEL COCKLE
COMMIT CRINGE ENGAGE FUTURE
GATHER HIRING INDENT LESSEN
MUTUUM NARROW PIGNUS
PLEDGE POLICY PROMPT PUCKER
REDUCE SHRIMP SHRINK SUBLET
TREATY ABRIDGE APPALTO
BARGAIN BUMMERY CHARTER
COMPACT CRIMPLE CRUMPLE
CURTAIL DEFLATE FIDUCIA
MANDATE PROMISE SCRUNCH
SHORTEN SHRIVEL SOCIETY
WRINKLE ASSIENTO BOTTOMRY
CONDENSE COVENANT
HANDFAST HARDNESS LOCATION
RESTRICT STEELBOW STRAITEN
SYNGRAPH ABBREVIATE
OBLIGATION
(— BROW) FROWN
(— INTO WRINKLES) KNIT
(BRIDGE —) SOLO AUCTION
(MARRIAGE —) KETUBA AFFIANCE
HANDFAST BETROTHAL
SPONSALIA
CONTRACTED BOXY CRAMP
BOOKED ASTRICT INGROWN
INSULAR SCREWED CONTRACT
CONTRACTILITY MOTILITY
CONTRACTION HM ANT NIP TIC
TIS AINT CANT ISNT KNIT MAAM
WONT CRAMP HADNT HASNT
NISUS SPASM CRASIS GATHER
INTAKE MUSTNT SHRINK TWITCH
ELISION EPITOME WOULDNT
APNEUSIS TRACTION
ABRIDGMENT ABRIDGEMENT
(— OF HEART) SYSTOLE
(— OF SYLLABLES) SYNIZESIS
(PL.) TREPPE
CONTRACTOR KHOT BUTTY
BUILDER REMOVER SUPPLIER
CONTRADICT DENY BELIE CROSS
REBUT FORBID IMPUGN NEGATE
OPPOSE RECANT REFUTE THREAP
COUNTER GAINSAY REVERSE
WITHSAW CONTRARY DISPROVE
DOWNFACE NEGATIVE
OUTSTAND
CONTRADICTION CLASH DENIAL
DEMENTI PARADOX WITHSAW
ANTILOGY ANTIMONY ANTILOQUY
(LUDICROUS —) BULL
CONTRADICTORY OPPOSE
ANTINOME OPPOSITE
THWARTING
CONTRAPTION RIG TOOL DEVICE
GADGET JIGGER CONCERN
MACHINE
CONTRARILY BACKWARD
CRISSCROSS
CONTRARIWISE CONTRA
CONTRARY
CONTRARY BALKY CROSS KICKY
SNIVY AVERSE CONTRA ORNERY
SNIVEY THRAWN ADVERSE
COUNTER CRABBED FROWARD

HOSTILE INVERSE OPPOSED
PEEVISH RESTIVE REVERSE
WAYWARD ABSONANT ANTIPODE
CAPTIOUS CONTRAIR INIMICAL
OPPOSITE PERVERSE PETULANT
SINGULAR ABHORRENT
(— TO) BESIDE AGAINST
ATHWART
(— TO HAPPINESS) ILL
(— TO REASON) SILLY ABSONANT
(PREF.) CONTRA COUNTER DIS
RETRO
CONTRAST CLASH STRIFE
COMPARE CONTEND DISCORD
ANTIMONY DIVISION DYNAMICS
OPPOSITE
CONTRASTING
(PREF.) CONTRA
CONTRAVENE DEFY DENY HINDER
OPPOSE THWART DISPUTE
VIOLATE INFRINGE OBSTRUCT
CONTRAVENTION SIN VICE CRIME
BREACH OFFENSE
CONTRETEMPS SLIP BONER HITCH
MISHAP SCRAPE ACCIDENT
INCIDENT
CONTRIBUTE AID ANTE FORK GIVE
HELP MAKE TEND CAUSE ENTER
GROUT SERVE ASSIST BESTOW
CONCUR CONFER DONATE
PUNGLE RENDER SUPPLY TENDER
ANIMATE CONDUCE FURNISH
FURTHER PROVIDE
CONTRIBUTING ACCESSORY
CONTRIBUTION BIT SUM TAX
ALMS BOON GIFT SCOT SHOT
ESSAY INPUT SHARE IMPOST
SYMBOL ARTICLE LARGESS
PAYMENT PRESENT RENEWAL
WRITING DONATION EXACTION
OFFERING ROMESHOT
CONTRITE WORN SORRY HUMBLE
RUEFUL PENITENT SORROWFUL
CONTRITION SORE SORROW
PENANCE PENITENCE
CONTRIVANCE (ALSO SEE DEVICE)
ART BOW FLY GIN JET JIG LEG
DROP GEAR HARP JACK KITE
LURE PAGE PLAN PLOT RASP
REED TOOL ALARM BRAKE CARRY
CHECK DOLLY DRAFT FLOAT
FRAME GUIDE HICKY KNACK
MIXER QUIPU SHIFT SNARE
STOCK ANCHOR DAMPER DECEIT
DESIGN DEVICE DOCTOR DOLLIE
ENGINE FABRIC FANGLE GABION
GADGET GIMBAL HANGER
HARROW HEATER HICKEY
HOLDER JIGGER JINKER MARKER
MORTAR MUZZLE POLICY RATTLE
SCHEME SLUICE SPIDER TEASEL
WEIGHT WHEEZE WINDAS
WRENCH BOLSTER CLEANER
CLEARER CONCERN COUPLER
CUNNING DINGBAT DRAUGHT
FICTION FISHWAY HUMIDOR
KNOCKER MACHINE PAGEANT
PROJECT REDUCER ROASTER
SCRAPER SHEBANG SPANNER
STOPPER TOASTER TRIPPER
VOLVELL ADAPTION ARTIFICE
CROTCHET DUTCHMAN EUPYRION
FAKEMENT FORECAST GOVERNOR

INDUSTRY MOLITION OXIDATOR
REGISTER RESOURCE SCISSORS
SQUEEZER SUBTLETY WITCRAFT
CONTRIVE GET LAY BREW CAST
DRAW FIND FIRK MAKE PLAN
PLOT WORK FRAME FUDGE
HATCH SHAPE STAGE WEAVE
AFFORD DESIGN DEVISE DIVINE
ENGINE FIGURE INVENT MANAGE
SCHEME WANGLE ACHIEVE
AGITATE COMMENT COMPASS
CONCOCT CONJURE CONSULT
CONTEND FASHION IMAGINE
MACHINE PROCURE PROJECT
REPAREL CONSPIRE ENGINEER
FORECAST INTRIGUE PURCHASE
CONTRIVED PAT SLICK STAGED
TIMBERED
CONTRIVER DAEDAL DAEDALUS
ENGINEER
CONTRIVING FASHION SCHEMERY
CONTROL BIT LAP LAW MAN POT
RUN CONN CURB EGIS GRIP
HAND HANK HAVE HOLD REDE
REIN RULE STAY SWAY WIND
AEGIS BOOST CHARM CHECK
COACT DAUNT DUMMY GRASP
GUIDE LEASH ORDER POWER
STEER SWING THEAT TREAT
TUTOR VERGE WIELD BANDON
BRIDLE CHARGE CLUTCH COERCE
CORNER DANGER DIRECT EMPERY
GOVERN HANDLE MANAGE
POCKET TEMPER AMENAGE
COMMAND CONDUCT CONTAIN
CUSTODY FORBEAR MASTERY
QUALIFY STRINGS COACTION
DOMINATE DOMINIUM IMPERIUM
MODERATE REGULATE SERVOTAB
POSSESSION
(— A BULL) MANDAR
(— OF RESOURCES) HUSBANDRY
(— OVER WIFE) MANUS
(ABSOLUTE —) BECK
(FIRE —) BLANKET
(GOVERNMENT —) DIRIGISM
SQUADRISM
(MANUAL —) JOYSTICK
(NONCLERICAL —) LAICISM LAICITY
CONTROLLED STEADY SERVILE
CONTAINED
CONTROLLER FENCER GERENT
MASTER STARTER
(SPEED —) GOVERNOR RHEOCRAT
CONTROLLING MASTER LEADING
DOMINANT HEGEMONIC
CONTROVERSIAL ERISTIC
POLEMIC
CONTROVERSIALIST ERISTIC
POLEMIC DISPUTANT GLADIATOR
CONTROVERSY PLEA SPAT SUIT
CHEST FUROR BATTLE COMBAT
DEBATE FURORE HASSEL HASSLE
HOORAH HURRAH STRIFE TUSSLE
DISPUTE POLEMIC QUARREL
WRANGLE ARGUMENT TRAVERSE
CONTENTION
(ART OF —) POLEMICS
CONTROVERT DENY FACE MOOT
ARGUE DEBATE DEFEND OPPOSE
OPPUGN REFUTE CONTEST
DISPUTE GAINSAY DISPROVE
CONTUMACIOUS UNRULY

RIOTOUS CONTUMAX INSOLENT
MUTINOUS PERVERSE STUBBORN
CONTUMELY ABUSE SCORN
INSULT CONTECK DISDAIN
REPROOF UPBRAID CONTEMPT
RUDENESS
CONTUSE BEAT POUND THUMP
BRUISE INJURE SQUEEZE
CONTUSION POUND BRUISE
CONUNDRUM PUN WHIM GUESS
ENIGMA PUZZLE RIDDLE CONCEIT
CROTCHET
CONURE ARATINGA
CONVALESCE MEND GUARISH
RECOVER
CONVENANCE FORM
CONVENE SIT CALL HOLD MEET
UNITE GATHER MUSTER SUMMON
CONVENT CONVOKE ASSEMBLE
CONVERGE
CONVENIENCE GAIN BEHOOF
URINAL LEISURE COMMODITY
CONVENIENT FIT GAIN HEND NIGH
HANDY HENDE READY CLEVER
FITTED PROPER SUITED USEFUL
ADAPTED AVENANT COMMODE
HELPFUL BECOMING EXPEDITE
SUITABLE OPPORTUNE
COMMODIOUS
CONVENIENTLY HANDILY
CLEVERLY
CONVENT ABBEY HOUSE TEKKE
TEKYA CENOBY FRIARY PRIORY
CONVENT MEETING RECLUSE
CLOISTER LAMASERY
MOTHERHOUSE
CONVENTION DIET FEIS FORM
MISE RULE TABU SYNOD TABOO
USAGE CARTEL CAUCUS CUSTOM
TREATY DECORUM MEETING
ASSEMBLY ASSIENTO CONCLAVE
CONGRESS CONTRACT COVENANT
PRACTICE PRECEDENT
(LONG-ESTABLISHED —) TRADITION
(STAGE —) ASIDE
(PL.) DECENCIES
CONVENTIONAL MORE NOMIC
RIGHT TRITE USUAL DECENT
FORMAL MODISH PROPER
CORRECT POMPIER REGULAR
ACADEMIC ACCEPTED COPYBOOK
ORTHODOX CUSTOMARY
(RIGIDLY —) UPTIGHT
CONVENTIONALITY FORM
ACADEMISM FORMALITY
GRUNDYISM
CONVENTIONALIZE STYLIZE
CONVERGE JOIN MEET FOCUS
CONCUR CORNER CONNIVE
DESCEND APPROACH FOCALIZE
CONVERSANT ADEPT BUSIED
EXPERT VERSED SKILLED
FAMILIAR OCCUPIED
CONVERSATION RAP SAY CALL
CHAT CHIN RUNE TALE TALK
BOARD CRACK PROSE CACKLE
CONFAB DEVICE GOSSIP PARLEY
POWWOW SPEECH YABBER
CEILIDH COMMUNE CONDUCT
PALAVER PURPOSE BACKCHAT
BEHAVIOR CAUSERIE CHITCHAT
COLLOGUE COLLOQUY DIALOGUE
GIFFGAFF HARANGUE PARLANCE

QUESTION COLLOCUTION
(— BETWEEN WHALERS) GAM
CONVERSATIONALIST TALKER
CAUSEUR
CONVERSE CHAT CHIN LIVE MOVE
TALK DWELL SPEAK CACKLE
COMMON CONFER DEVISE
HOMILY PARLEY REASON
COMMUNE CONVERT DISCUSS
OBVERSE PROPOSE REVERSE
COLLOQUE EXCHANGE OPPOSITE
QUESTION
CONVERSION CHANGE EXCHANGE
METRICATION PROSELYTISM
(— INTO VAPOR) FLASH
(— OF IRON) FINING
CONVERT TAW TURN WEND
ALTER AMEND APPLY MAULA
RENEW CHANGE DECODE DETECT
DIRECT MAWALI NOVICE SHAIKH
SOUPER COMMUTE CONCOCT
RESOLVE RESTORE REVERSE
ACTIVATE CONVERSE DISCIPLE
NEOPHYTE PERSUADE PROSELYTE
(— COTTON) LAP
(— INTO CASH) NEGOTIATE
(— INTO LEATHER) TAN TAW
(— INTO LIQUID) BREW
(— INTO PELLETS) PRILL
(— INTO SOAP) SAPONIFY
(— INTO STEEL) ACIERATE
(— INTO STONE) LAPIDIFY
(— SOAP) CLOSE
(— TO CARBON) CHAR
CONVERTER ROTARY SELECTOR
CONVERTIBLE AUTO DROPHEAD
CONVEX BOWED ARCHED CAMBER
CURVED BULGING EMBOWED
GIBBOUS ROUNDED
CONVEXITY CAMBER ARCUATION
CONVEY JAG BEAR BOOK CART
CEDE DEED DUCT HAVE LEAD
MEAN PASS SEND SIGN TAKE
TOTE WAIN WILL BRING CARRY
DRIVE FETCH GRANT GUIDE
HURRY STEAL ARRIVE ASSIGN
CONVOY DEDUCE DELATE DEMISE
DEVISE ELOIGN GIGGIT IMPART
IMPORT REMOVE YMMOTE
AUCTION CHANNEL CHARIOT
CHARTER CONDUCT DELIVER
DERRICK DISPONE DISPOSE
LIGHTER RESTORE ALIENATE
BEQUEATH DESCRIBE TRANSFER
TRANSMIT
(— AN ESTATE) DEMISE
(— BY ALLUSION) IMPLY
(— FORCIBLY) HUSTLE
(— LEGALLY) DEED GRANT LEASE
DEMISE ELOIGN DISPONE
(— NEARER) BRING
(— SECRETLY) CRIM
CONVEYANCE BUS CAR AUTO
CART DEED DRAG GIFT LOAD
SLED TAXI TRAM GRANT SEDAN
STAGE TAUGA THEFT TRAIN
WAGON DEMISE JINGLE CHARTER
CONDUCT COURIER MACHINE
RATTLER TRAILER TRAJECT
TRANSIT TROLLEY VECTURE
VEHICLE WAFTAGE CARRIAGE
CARRYING CONVEYAL DELATION
FERRIAGE STEALING TRANSFER

CONVEYOR LIFT WORM DRAPER
LADDER SHAKER CARRIER
CREEPER HURRIER SCRAPER
CAROUSEL CONVEYER ELEVATOR
CONVICT LAG CAST FIND STAR
ARGUE EXILE FELON LIFER PROVE
TAINT ATTAIN FORCAT LAGGER
TERMER TRUSTY APPROVE
ATTAINT CAPTIVE CONDEMN
CULPRIT EXPIREE IMPEACH
REPROVE CRIMINAL JAILBIRD
PRISONER REDARGUE SENTENCE
CONVICT FISH MANINI HINALEA
CONVICTION CREDO CREED
DOGMA FAITH SENSE TAINT
TENET BELIEF CREDIT CONCERN
OPINION SENTENCE
CONVINCE EVICT FETCH ASSURE
EVINCE REPROVE RESOLVE
SATISFY CONCLUDE
(— OF ERROR) CONVICT
CONVINCED FIRM SOLD SURE
CERTAIN ABSOLUTE POSITIVE
CONVINCING SOUND VALID
COGENT POTENT EVIDENT
TELLING FORCIBLE LUCULENT
POWERFUL PREGNANT
CONVIVIAL GAY BOON FESTAL
GENIAL JOVIAL SOCIAL FESTIVE
HOLIDAY JOCULAR REVELING
ANACREONTIC
CONVIVIALITY REVEL FESTIVAL
MERRYMAKING
CONVOCATION DIET SYNOD
CALLING COUNCIL MEETING
SUMMONS ASSEMBLY CONGRESS
VOCATION
CONVOKE CALL HOLD GATHER
SUMMON CONVENE ASSEMBLE
CONVOLUTE COIL ROLL WIND
TWIST TANGLE WRITHE CONTORT
INVOLUTE OBVOLUTE
CONVOLUTED GYRATE
CONVOLUTION COIL CURL FOLD
TURN WRAP GYRUS SWIRL TWINE
TWIRL TWIST WHORL CUNEUS
GYROMA VOLUME VOLUTION
CONVOLVE TURN WIND TWIST
ENFOLD ENWRAP INFOLD
WRITHE
CONVOLVULUS BINDWEED
SCAMMONY
CONVOY LEAD WAFT CARRY
GUARD GUIDE PILOT TRADE
WATCH ATTEND CONVEY ESCORT
MANAGE CONDUCT WAFTAGE
SAFEGUARD
CONVULSE ROCK STIR SHAKE
EXCITE AGITATE DISTURB
CONVULSION FIT SHRUG SPASM
THROE ATTACK TUMULT UPROAR
CONVULSE LAUGHTER PAROXYSM
COMMOTION
CONVULSIVE FITFUL EPILEPTIC
CONY DAS HARE PIKA CONEY
CUNNY DAMAN DASSY GANAM
HUTIA HYRAX BURBOT CONEEN
DASSIE GAZABO GAZEBO RABBIT
WABBER ASHKOKO BOOMDAS
HYRACID KLIPDAS HYRACOID
KLIPDACH
COO CROO CURR WOOT CHIRR
CHIZZ CROOD MURMUR

CROODLE CRUDDLE
COOEE BIRD KOEL
COOK DO FIX FRY BAKE BOIL CHEF
COCT FAKE MAKE SEAR STEW
BROIL CUSIE FRIZZ GRILL POACH
ROAST SCALD SHIRR STEAM
BRAISE CODDLE COOKIE COOPER
DECOCT DIGEST PORTER SAUTEE
SEETHE SIMMER ARTISTE BROILER
FRIZZLE GRIDDLE PASTLER
PERCOCT POTAGER PREPARE
PROCESS SERVANT SMOTHER
SWAMPER BAWARCHI BOBACHEE
COCINERO CUSINERO GRILLADE
MAGIRIST PASTERER
(— TOO LONG) OVERDO
(— UP) BUILD
(BULL —) FLUNKY FLUNKEY
GREASER
(SHIP'S —) DOCTOR SLUSHY
SKILLET SLUSHER
(PREF.) MAGIRO
COOKED DONE FRIED BOILED
(— BY BOILING) AUBLEU
(— WITH SUGAR) CANDIED
(PREF.) COCTO
COOKEE FLUNKY HASHER
FLUNKEY
COOKER CANNER HAYBOX
DIGESTER
COOKERY CURY CUISINE KITCHEN
MAGIRICS
COOKHOUSE GALLEY
COOKIE CAKE ROCK SNAP COOKY
HERMIT KIPFEL BISCUIT BROWNIE
OATCAKE PLACENT CRESCENT
SEEDCAKE
COOKING COCTION
COOKROOM CUDDY
COOL AIR FAN ICE CALM COLD
KEEL AKELE ALGID ALLAY CHILL
EVENT FRESH GELID NERVY
QUEEL SOBER STAID WHOLE
AIRISH CALLER CHILLY PLACID
QUENCH SEDATE SERENE TEMPER
UNWARM COOLISH REFROID
UNMOVED CARELESS CAUTIOUS
COMPOSED MITIGATE MODERATE
TRANQUIL NERVELESS
POSSESSED NONCHALANT
UNFLAPPABLE
(— IN WATER) SLACK SLACKEN
(— OF EVENING) SERENE
COOLED COLD FRAPPE
COOLER COLA ICER JAIL KEEL
OLLA SINK ICEBOX LOCKUP
PRISON SINKER KEELFAT
ALCOGENE
(WINE —) GLACIER
COOLIE CHANGAR MADRASI
MAZDOOR
COOLNESS COOL FROST NERVE
SWALE APLOMB PHLEGM
SERENITY
COOM CULM GAUM SMUT SOOT
COOMB GRIME SLACK
COONTIE SAGO ZAMIA COMPTIE
COOP COT CUB CUP MEW PEN POT
RIP CAGE COOB COTE JAIL
CRAMP HUTCH BASKET CORRAL
CONFINE
(— UP) PEN IMMEW INCOUP
(HEN —) CAVEY CAVIE BARTON

COOPER BUNGS COPER COWPER
HEADER HOOPER TUBBER TUBBIE
TUBMAN
COOPERATE HAND TEND AGREE
COACT UNITE CONCUR COMBINE
CONDUCE CONNIVE COADJUTE
CONSPIRE
COOPERATION SOCIETY
COURTESY TEAMWORK
COOPERATIVE COOP SOCIAL
SYNERGIC
COORDINATE SINE ADAPT EQUAL
ADJUST ARRANGE SYNTONY
ABSCISSA CLASSIFY ENSEMBLE
COORDINATION BOND SKILL
HARMONY LIAISON
COORG KADAGA
COOT CUIT DUCK RAIL QUEET
SMYTH BELTIE GORHEN PELICK
SCOTER HENBILL LOBIPED
PULLDOO LOBEFOOT RAILBIRD
SWAMPHEN
COP BAG NAB ROB BANK BLOW
BULL HEAD HEAP JOHN LIFT PILE
TRAP TUBE CATCH CREST FILCH
MOUNT QUILL SHOCK SNARE
STEAL STOCK SWIPE BOBBIN
COPPIN PEELER SPIDER STRIKE
CAPTURE
COPA YAYA COPITA
COPAL BOEA LOBA ANIME CONGO
KAURI KAURY RESIN COWRIE
DAMMAR CHAKAZI
COPE VIE WAR CAPE DUTY FACE
LIFT MEET CAPPA CLOAK COVER
DRESS EQUAL FIGHT MATCH
NOTCH RIVAL VAULT WIELD
BARTER CANOPY CHAPEL
COMBAT MANTEL MUZZLE
OPPOSE SEMBLE STRIKE STRIVE
ANABATA CHLAMYS CONTEND
CONTEST GRAPPLE MANDYAS
PLUVIAL COMPLETE EXCHANGE
FACTABLE SEMICOPE STRUGGLE
VESTMENT
COPEHAN WINTUN
COPEPOD CALANID CAYENNE
DIAPTOMID
COPIAPITE MISY MISSY IHLEITE
COPIER COPIST SCRIBE
JOHNSONIAN
COPING CAP COPE FLUE SKEW
CORDON CAPSTONE FACTABLE
COPING STONE TABLET TABLING
COPIOUS FREE FULL GOOD LUSH
RANK RICH AMPLE LARGE
FLUENT LAVISH DIFFUSE
FLOWING FULSOME LENGTHY
PROFUSE REPLETE TEEMING
UBEROUS ABUNDANT AFFLUENT
FRUITFUL GENEROUS NUMEROUS
PLENTIFUL
COPIOUSNESS COPY PLENTY
COPPER AES COP BULL CENT
BOBBY METAL PENNY VENUS
CUPRUM PEELER VELLON BLISTER
CARNELIAN
(GILDED —) VERMEIL
(OF —) AEN
(PREF.) CHALC(O) CHALK(O)
CUPR(I)(O)
(SUFF.) CHALCITE
COPPERAS COPEROSE

INKSTONE COQUIMBITE
COPPERHEAD REDEYE MOCCASIN
COPPERSMITH TINKERBIRD
COPPER SULFATE BLUESTONE
COPPER SULFIDE FERRETTO
COVELLINE COVELLITE
COPPERY CUPREOUS
COPPICE COP BROW WOOD COPPY
COPSE FIRTH FRITH GROVE
COVERT FOREST GROWTH
SPROUT THICKET ARBUSTUM
(SUFF.) DRYMIUM
COPREUS (FATHER OF —) PELOPS
(HORSE OF —) ARION
(MOTHER OF —) HIPPODAMIA
COPSE CUT HAG HASP HEWT HOLT
MOTT SHAW TRIM DROKE HURST
CLEVIS SPINNY COPPICE
LOWWOOD SHACKLE SPINNEY
ARBUSTUM COPEWOOD
COPULA BAND LINK UNION
COPY APE CALK CAST ECHO EDIT
MIME MOCK NICK DITTO DUMMY
GROSS IMAGE MIMIC MODEL
PRINT REVIE STICK STUFF TRACE
CALQUE DOUBLE ECTYPE EFFIGY
FILLER FLIMSY FOLLOW MATTER
RECORD REFLEX SAMPLE
SHADOW EDITION EMULATE
ENGROSS ESTREAT EXTRACT
IMITATE PATTERN REDRAFT
REPLICA REPRINT RUBBING
TRACING VIDIMUS APOGRAPH
AUTOTYPE EXEMPLAR EXSCRIBE
EXSCRIPT KNOCKOFF LIKENESS
MANIFOLD POROTYPE PORTRAIT
RESEMBLE SPECIMEN MICROCOPY
MINIATURE PHOTOSTAT
(— EDITOR) SLOT
(— IN COMPUTER) DUMP
(— OF DOCUMENT) EXTRACT
PROTOCOL
(— OF DRESS) FORD
(DUPLICATE — OF PROGRAM)
BACKUP
(EXACT —) TENOR
(PRINTING —) KILL BOGUS
(UNREMUNERATIVE —) LEAN
(WORTHLESS —) BALAAM
COPYING MIMICRY INSINUATION
COPYIST COPIER PENMAN SCRIBE
COPYCAT SCRIVENER
COPYREAD EDIT SUBEDIT
COQUET TOY VAMP COPPY DALLY
FLIRT TRIFLE BLINKER CELIMENE
COQUETRY AGACERIE
COQUILLE SHELL
COQUINA DONAX
CORA NAYARIT
(HUSBAND OF —) ALONZO
CORACIIFORM NONPASSERINE
CORACLE SCOW CURAGH
CURRACH CURRANE
CORAL RED PINK AKORI BLOOD
POLYP ALCYON PALULE PORITE
FUNGIAN OCULINA ACROPORE
ASTRAEAN CORALLUM FAVOSITE
POLYPITE STAGHORN TUBIPORE
ZOOPHYTE MADREPORE
MILLEPORE
CORAL BEAN SOPHORA
FRIJOLILLO
CORAL-BELLS HEUCHERA

CORALBERRY BUCKBUSH
CORALFISH DOLLFISH
CORALROOT ORCHID CRAWLEY
CORAL SNAKE ELAPID ROLLER
ELAPOID SCYTALE
CORAL TREE GABGAB ERYTHRINA
CORBEIL PANNIER
CORBEL KNOT ANCON CORBET
TIMBER BRAGGER RESPOND
CARTOUCH SPRINGER
CORBELING SQUINCH
CORBIESTEP CATSTEP CROWSTEP
CORCIR CORKE ARCHIL CORKER
ORCHIL ARCHILLA
CORD AEA RIB AGAL BAND BIND
BOND FILE LACE LASH LINE ROPE
WELT BRAID CHORD FUNIS
GUARD LEASH LIGNE MATCH
NERVE OLONA TWINE TWIST
BINDER BOBBIN BRIDLE BUNGEE
CATGUT CHORDA CORDON
FIADOR GIRDLE LASHER LISERE
RACHIS SENNET STRING TENDON
TOGGLE AMENTUM BOWYANG
BULLION CORDING FUNICLE
LANIARD LANYARD MACRAME
SEAMING SEIZING SKIRREH
TIEBACK URACHUS BELLPULL
CHENILLE DRAWCORD HAIRLINE
SHOELACE WHIPCORD
(— AROUND BOWSTRING) SERVING
(— FOR PIPING) BOBBIN
(— OF CANDLENUT BARK) AEA
(CROCHETING —) CORDE
(ELECTRIC —) FLEX
(EMBROIDERY —) ARRASENE
(FRINGED —) LLAUTU
(HAMMOCK —S) CLEW
(HAWK'S —) CREANCE
(MASON'S —) SKIRREH
(ORNAMENTED —) AGLET AIGLET
(PARACHUTE —) SHROUD
(SACRED —) KUSTI
(SPINAL —) EON AEON NUKE
(TWISTED —) TORSADE
(PREF.) CHORD(O)
CORDAGE DA COIR ERUC FERU
HEMP IMBE JUTE KYAR ROPE
HAMBER SENNIT RIGGING
(LENGTH OF —) CATENARY
CORDATE HEARTED
CORDED TIED JETTED REPPED
RIBBED WELTED TWILLED
COR-DE-NUIT PASTORITA
CORDER RUFFER
CORDIAL REAL WARM CREAM
ARDENT CASSIS CLOVES DEVOUT
ELIXIR GENIAL HEARTY PASTIS
CORDATE DIAMBER LIQUEUR
PERSICO RATAFIA ROSOLIO
SINCERE ZEALOUS ANISETTE
FRIENDLY GRACIOUS PERSICOT
VIGOROUS BENEDICTINE
(NOT —) DISTANT STANDOFF
(PL.) SWEETS
CORDIERITE IOLITE FAHLUNITE
CORDON BLEU BENGALEE
CORDONNET CRESCENT
CORDWOOD BODYWOOD
CORE AME COB HUB NUT BONE
COKE COLK GIST KNOT NAVE
PITH BLOCK FOCUS HEART
NOWSE RUMPF SPOOL BARREL

CENTER CENTRE HEATER KERNEL
MATRIX MIDDLE NODULE POCKET
STAPLE CENTRUM CHEMISE
COMPANY CORNCOB ESSENCE
NUCLEUS FILAMENT HEARTING
(— OF COAL) STOCK
(— OF COLUMN) BELL HEART
(— OF CRICKET BALL) QUILT
(— OF LOG) PITH
(— OF MOLD) NOWEL
(EARTH'S HYPOTHETICAL —) NIFE
(WATER —) GLASSINESS
CORE ARBOR STALK
COREE CORANINE
CORELIGIONIST BROTHER
COREMIUM SYNEMA SYNNEMA
COREOPSIS TICKSEED TICKWEED
LEPTOSYNE
CORF TUB CAGE CAWF COFF CORB
SKIP CREEL BASKET DOSSER
CORGI CARDIGAN PEMBROKE
CORIANDER (— LEAVES) CILANTRO
CORIOLANUS (AUTHOR OF —)
SHAKESPEARE
(CHARACTER IN —) CAIUS TITUS
BRUTUS JUNIUS TULLUS LARTIUS
MARCIUS VALERIA AUFIDIUS
COMINIUS MENENIUS SICINIUS
VIRGILIA VOLUMNIA
CORIUM CUTIS DERMA LAYER
DERMIS
CORK BUNG PLUG FLOAT SHIVE
SUBER BOBBER BOUCHON
CRINKLE PHELLEM SOBERIN
STOPPER STOPPLE
(PREF.) PHELL(O) SUBERI
CORKED BOUCHE
CORKER WHIZ RAKER WHIZZ
CUTTER HUMDINGER
CORKSCREW WORMER
CORKWING CONNER
CORKWOOD BALSA GUANO
HAREFOOT
CORM SET BULB SEED CORMEL
CORMUS FREESIA UINTJIE
CORMEL BULBLET
(PL.) SPAWN
CORMORANT SHAG CRANE
GORMA NORIE SCARF SCART
DUIKER DUYKER GORMAW
GUANAY SCARFE SCARTH
GLUTTON SHAGLET
CORN ZEA DANA DENT SALT SAMP
GRAIN MAIZE SPIKE WYROK
AGNAIL CALLUS CLAVUS HELOMA
INDIAN KERNEL MEALIE NOCAKE
NUBBIN POWDER WYROCK
FORMITY FRUMENT FRUMENTY
PRESERVE SAUTERNE
(— SPURREY) YARR
(CROW —) COLICROOT
(CRUSHED —) STAMP
(DECORATED EAR OF —) TIPONI
(EAR OF —) ICKER
(GUINEA —) DURRA DHURRA
(INDIAN —) MAIZE INDIAN NOCAKE
(PARCHED —) ROKEE NOCAKE
PINOLE YOKAGE GRADDAN
ROKEAGE YOKEAGE
(STRING OF —) TRACE
(UNRIPE EAR OF —) TUCKET
CORNAGE HORNGELD
CORN BREAD PONE

KANKIE BANNOCK
CORN COCKLE GITH COCKLE
POPPLE COCKWEED HARDHEAD
MELANTHY
CORNCRACKER STATE
KENTUCKY
CORNCRAKE RAIL CORNBIRD
CORN CROWFOOT JOY
GOLDWEED HELLWEED
JACKWEED
CORNEL DOGWOOD REDBRUSH
CORNEOUS HORNLIKE KERASINE
CORNER IN GET OUT WRO BEND
CANT COIN HALK HERN JAMB
NOOK POOL TRAP TREE WICK
ANCON ANGLE BIGHT CATCH
COIGN ELBOW HERNE INGLE
JAMBE NICHE QUOIN TRUST
BOTTLE CANTLE CANTON COLLAR
CORNEL CRANNY RECESS SQUARE
OUTSIDE QUINYIE TURNING
MONOPOLY
(— IN A DRIFT) ARRAGE
(— OF EYE) CANTHUS
(— OF GUNSTOCK) TOE
(— OF MOLDBOARD) SHIN
(— OF SAIL) CLEW CLUE TACK
GOOSEWING
(CHIMNEY —) LUG
(LOWER —) CLEW CLUE
(RE-ENTRANT —) DIEDRE
(ROUNDED —) FILET FILLET
(SECRET —) CREEK
(TIGHT —) BOX
(PREF.) **(— OF EYE)** CANTH(O)
CORNERPIECE BUMPER CANTLE
CORNERSTONE COIN BASIS COIGN
QUOIN HEADSTONE
CORNET CONE HORN ZINK TWIST
ZINKE ZINCKE CORONET
CORNETTO CORNOPEAN
CORNETFISH FLUTEMOUTH
HEMIBRANCH
CORNFIELD MOW
CORN FLAG LEVERS
CORNFLOWER BLUET BLAVER
BARBEAU BLUECAP BLUECUP
BLAEWORT
CORN GROMWELL SALFERN
CORNHUSK CAP
CORNHUSKER STATE NEBRASKA
CORNHUSKING SHUCKING
CORNICE CAP BAND DRIP EAVE
JOPY ANCON CROWN JOWPY
DETAIL GEISON PELMET ANTEFIX
MOLDING SURBASE ASTRAGAL
SWANNECK
(UNDER SIDE OF —) PLANCIER
(PREF.) GEISSO
CORNICLE SIPHON SYPHON
CORNISHMAN CELT KELT
CORN MARIGOLD GOLD GOOLS
BODDLE BOODLE BUDDLE
GOWLAN GOLDING GOLLAND
CORN MEAL MASA SAMP ATOLE
HOECAKE
CORN PARSLEY UMBEL
CORN POPPY BLAVER CANKER
COCKLE COPROSE EARACHE
PONCEAU REDWEED SOLDIER
CORN SALAD FETTICUS
MILKGRASS
CORN SPURREY YARR

CORN STACK HOVEL
CORNSTALKS KARBI
CORNSTARCH BINDER
CORNU HORN THYROHYAL
CORNUCOPIA HORN CORNU
  COFFIN
CORNUS CORNIN REDBRUSH
CORN VIOLET SPECULARIA
CORN WOUNDWORT STACHYS
CORNY BANAL STALE TRITE
  MICKEY BUCKEYE
COROADO BORORO
CORODY CONRED
COROEBUS (FATHER OF —)
  MYGDON
  (SLAYER OF —) DIOMEDES
COROLLA CUP BELL COROL
  CUPULE LIGULE PERIANTH
COROLLARY DOGMA PORISM
  RESULT TRUISM ADJUNCT
  THEOREM CONSECTARY
COROMANDEL COLCOTHAR
CORONA BUR BURR CIGAR CROWN
  GLORY AURORA FILLET ROSARY
  WREATH AUREOLE CIRCLET
  CORONET GARLAND LARMIER
  SCYPHUS
CORONAL CRONET CORONEL
  CROWNAL
CORONATION ABHISEKA
  CROWNMENT
CORONATION OF POPPAEA
  (CHARACTER IN —) NERONE
  OTTONE SENECA OTTAVIA
  POPPAEA DRUSILLA
  (COMPOSER OF —) MONTEVERDI
CORONER ELISOR CROWNER
  EXAMINER SEARCHER
CORONET BAND BURR CROWN
  TIARA ANADEM CIRCLE CRONET
  DIADEM TIMBRE WREATH
  CHAPLET CORONAL CROWNAL
  CROWNET GARLAND CROWNLET
CORONIS (FATHER OF —) PHLEGYAS
  PHORONEUS
  (HUSBAND OF —) BUTES
  (LOVER OF —) APOLLO ISCHYS
  (SON OF —) ASCLEPIUS
CORONOPUS CARARA
CORPORAL NYM FANO NAIG NAIK
  PALL FANON FANUM NAYAK
  PHANO BODILY EXEMPT GUNNER
  NAIGUE NAIQUE SINDON TINDAL
CORPORATE UNITED COMBINED
CORPORATION BODY CITY FIRM
  POUCH TRUST SCHOLA BOROUGH
  COLLEGE COMMUNE FREEDOM
  GUILDRY SOCIETY SPONSOR
CORPOREAL REAL HYLIC SOMAL
  ACTUAL BODILY CARNAL FLESHLY
  SOMATIC MATERIAL PHYSICAL
  TANGIBLE
CORPOSANT HERMO
CORPS CORE ORDU VELITES
  SERAGLIO
  (— DE BALLET) ENSEMBLE
CORPSE BIER BODY CLAY DUST
  LICH MORT GHOST MUMMY RELIC
  STIFF TRUCK ZOMBI CORPUS
  DEADER ZOMBIE ANATOMY
  CADAVER CARCASS CARRION
  CROAKER DEADMAN FLOATER
  (— WASHING) TAHARAH

  (PREF.) NECR(O)
CORPSMAN MEDIC BEARER
CORPULENCE FAT FATNESS
  STOUTNESS
CORPULENT FAT BULKY BURLY
  FATTY GROSS HUSKY OBESE
  PLUMP STOUT TUBBY FLESHY
  GREASY PORTLY ROTUND
  ADIPOSE BELLIED WEIGHTY
CORPUSCLE CELL GHOST
  GLOBULE HEMATID HAEMATID
  HEMOCYTE
CORRAL PEN STY COOP ATAJO
  POUND TAMBO CONFINE
  ENCLOSE STOCKAGE SURROUND
  (ELEPHANT —) KRAAL KEDDAH
CORRECT DUE FIT FIX TIC BEET
  BOOK EDIT JAKE JUST LEAL LEAN
  MARK MEND NICE OKAY SMUG
  TRUE AMEND CHECK CLEAN
  EMEND EXACT ORDER RIGHT
  SOUND SPILL ADJUST BETTER
  CHANGE INFORM PROPER PUNISH
  REBUKE REFORM REMEDY REPAIR
  REVAMP REVISE SEEMLY STRICT
  ADDRESS CHAPTER CHASTEN
  CORRIGE ELEGANT IMPROVE
  PERFECT PRECISE RECLAIM
  RECTIFY REDRESS REGULAR
  REPROVE SINCERE ACCURATE
  CHASTISE DEFINITE EMENDATE
  EQUALIZE REGULATE RIGOROUS
  STRAIGHT TRUTHFUL CASTIGATE
  (APPROXIMATELY —) BALLPARK
  (GRAMMATICALLY —) CONGRUE
  (MATHEMATICALLY —) PURE
  (PREF.) ORTH(O)
CORRECTABLE CORRIGIBLE
CORRECTION YARD REFORM
  CENSURE FLEXURE IMPRINT
  REDRESS SCOURGE FUGACITY
  (— IN COMPUTER PROGRAM)
  PATCH
CORRECTIVE SALT REMEDY
CORRECTLY JUST RIGHT ARIGHT
  RIGHTLY SOUNDLY PROPERLY
CORRECTNESS TRUTH DECORUM
  FITNESS JUSTICE ACCURACY
  JUSTNESS VERACITY
CORREGIDOR, DER (CHARACTER IN
  —) TIO LUCAS MERCEDES
  FRASQUITA CORREGIDOR
  (COMPOSER OF —) WOLF
CORRELATE PARALLEL
  HARMONIZE
CORRELATIVE OR NOR THEN
  EQUAL STILL EITHER MUTUAL
  NEITHER ANALOGUE CONJOINT
  REDDITIVE
CORRESPOND FIT GEE JIBE SUIT
  AGREE MATCH TALLY WRITE
  ACCORD ANSWER CONCUR
  SQUARE COMPORT RESPOND
  COINCIDE PARALLEL QUADRATE
  (— IN SOUND) ASSONATE
  (— TO) ENSUE
CORRESPONDENCE MAIL TALLY
  ANALOGY CONSENT HARMONY
  KEEPING LETTERS
  TRAFFIC FUNCTION
  HOMOGENY HOMOLOGY
  SYMMETRY SYMPATHY
  SIMILARITY SIMILITUDE

  PARALLELISM RESEMBLANCE
  (INCOMPLETE —) ASSONANCE
  (OFFICIAL —) BUMF
CORRESPONDENT NEWSMAN
  QUADRATE RELEVANT STRINGER
  SUITABLE STRINGMAN
CORRESPONDING LIKE SIMILAR
  PARALLEL ACCORDANT
  CONGRUENT
  (PREF.) COUNTER
CORRESPONDINGLY SORTLY
  SIMILARLY
CORRIDA BULLFIGHT
CORRIDOR HALL AISLE ORIEL
  VISTA ARCADE COULOIR GALLERY
  PASSAGE COULISSE HALLCIST
  TRESANCE
CORRIE CIRQUE
CORRIGENDUM ERRATUM
CORROBORATE PROVE SECOND
  APPROVE COMFORT CONFIRM
  SUPPORT SUSTAIN ROBORATE
CORRODE EAT BITE BURN ETCH
  FRET GNAW RUST DECAY ERODE
  EXEDE TOUCH WASTE BEGNAW
  CANKER IMPAIR CONSUME
  GRAPHITE
CORRODING BITE RODENT
  ESURINE
CORROSION EROSION
  EMBAYMENT
CORROSIVE ACID ACRID ARDENT
  BITING CORSIE EATING CAUSTIC
  EROSIVE ESURINE FRETFUL
  MORDANT DIERETIC
CORRUGATE GIMP CRIMP CRISP
  FURROW RUMPLE CRINKLE
  CRUMPLE WRINKLE
CORRUGATED PLAITED WRINKLY
  FURROWED WRINKLED
CORRUGATION BAT FOLD GILL
  REED RUGA CREASE PUCKER
  CRINKLE WRINKLE
CORRUPT BAD ILL LOW ROT WEM
  EVIL RANK SICK SOIL VILE ADDLE
  BLEND BRIBE FALSE SPOIL STAIN
  SULLY TAINT VENAL VENOM
  WEMMY AUGEAN CANKER
  DEBASE DEFILE FESTER IMPURE
  INFECT PALTER POISON PUTRID
  RAVISH ROTTEN SEPTIC ABUSIVE
  ATTAINT BEDEVIL BEGRIME
  BESHREW CARRION CORRUMP
  CROOKED DEBAUCH DEFINED
  DEGRADE DEPRAVE ENVENOM
  FALSIFY IMMORAL PECCANT
  PERVERT POLLUTE PUTREFY
  SUBVERT TRADING VIOLATE
  VITIATE CONFOUND DEPRAVED
  EMPOISON PERVERSE POLLUTED
  PRACTICE PRACTISE SINISTER
  VITIATED PERVERTED
  ADULTERATE CONTAMINATE
  PECKSNIFFIAN
CORRUPTED SICK
CORRUPTION DIRT SOIL VICE
  DECAY SPOIL TAINT JOBBERY
  PRAVITY SQUALOR ADULTERY
  BARRATRY INFECTION
  MALVERSATION PUTREFACTION
CORSAC ADIVE KARAGAN
CORSAGE WAIST BODICE
  BOUQUET CANEZOU

CORSAIR BUG CAPER PIRATE
  ROBBER CURSARO PICAROON
  ROCKFISH
CORSAIR, THE (CHARACTER IN —)
  SEID MEDORA CORRADO
  GULNARA
  (COMPOSER OF —) VERDI
CORSELET LORICA THORAX
  ALLECRET HALECRET
CORSET BELT BUSK STAY STAYS
  GIRDLE SUPPORT
CORSICA (CAPITAL OF —) AJACCIO
  (HARBOR OF —) BASTIA
  (MOUNTAIN OF —) CINTO
  ROTONDO
  (RIVER OF —) GOLO TARAVO
  GRAVONE
  (TOWERLIKE STRUCTURES OF —)
  TORRI
  (TOWN OF —) CALVI CORTE ALERIA
  BASTIA AJACCIO SARTENE
  (VEGETATION OF —) MAQUIS
CORSICAN PINE LARCH
CORTEGE POMP SUITE TRAIN
  PARADE RETINUE
CORTEX BARK PEEL RIND MANTLE
  PALLIUM PERIBLEM PERIDIUM
CORUNDUM RUBY SAND EMERY
  ADAMAS ALUMINA ABRASIVE
  AMETHYST CORINDON SAPPHIRE
  BARKLYITE
  (SYNTHETIC —) EMERALD
CORUSCATE BLAZE FLASH GLEAM
  SHINE GLANCE GLISTEN GLITTER
  RADIATE SPARKLE BRANDISH
CORVEE POLO
CORVINO (WIFE OF —) CELIA
CORYPHENE DORADO
CORYTHUS (FATHER OF —) ZEUS
  PARIS JUPITER
  (SON OF —) DARDANUS
  (WIFE OF —) ELECTRA
CORYZA COLD
COSAM (FATHER OF —) ELMODAM
COSA RARA, UNA (CHARACTER IN
  —) TITA LILLA CORRADO LISARGO
  GIOVANNI
  (COMPOSER OF —) SOLER
COSCET COTTAR COTARIUS
  COTSETLE
COSETTE (MOTHER OF —) FANTINE
COSI FAN TUTTE (CHARACTER IN —
) ALFONSO DESPINA FERRANDO
  DORABELLA GUGLIELMO
  FIORDILIGI
  (COMPOSER OF —) MOZART
COSMETIC KOHL WASH CREAM
  FUCUS HENNA LINER PAINT
  PETER ROUGE BLANCH CERUSE
  CRAYON ENAMEL POMADE
  POWDER BLUSHER MASCARA
  STIBIUM AMANDINE LIPSTICK
  STIBNITE
COSMIC VAST MUNDANE ORDERLY
  CATHOLIC INFINITE
COSMOLABE PANTACOSM
COSMOPOLITAN URBAN
  ECUMENIC PANDEMIC
  AMPHIGEAN
COSMOS EARTH GLOBE ORDER
  REALM WORLD FLOWER HEAVEN
  HARMONY UNIVERSE
COSSACK TURK TATAR ATAMAN

HETMAN TARTAR ZAPOROGUE

COSSET MUD PET LAMB CARESS CODDLE CUDDLE FONDLE PAMPER TIDDLE

COSSETTE CHIP SLICE STRIP SCHNITZEL

COST SIT GAFF LOSS PAIN SOAK BASIS PRICE SPEND STAND VALUE CHARGE DAMAGE OUTLAY SCATHE EXPENSE REPRISE ESTIMATE SPENDING

COSTA RICA
CAPE: ELENA VELAS BLANCO
CAPITAL: SANJOSE
COIN: COLON CENTIMO
DANCE: PUNTO TORITO
GULF: DULCE NICOYA PAPAGAYO
INDIAN: BORUCA GUAYMI
ISLAND: COCO
LAKE: ARENAL
MEASURE: VARA CAFIZ CAHIZ FANEGA TERCIA CAJUELA CANTARO MANZANA
MOUNTAIN: BLANCO CHIRRIPO
PENINSULA: OSA NICOYA
POINT: QUEPOS CAHUITA GALONOS LLERENA
PORT: LIMON PUNTARENAS
RIVER: POAS IRAZU MATINA SIXAOLA TENORIA TARCOLES
TOWN: CANAS LIMON VESTA BORUCA NICOYA BAGACES CARTAGO GOLFITO HEREDIA LIBERIA NEGRITA ALAJUELA COLORADO GUAPILES
VOLCANO: POAS IRAZU
WEIGHT: BAG CAJA LIBRA

COSTERMONGER COSTER HAWKER NIPPER PEARLY PEDDLER BARROWMAN

COSTIVE BOUND EMPLASTIC

COSTLINESS DEARTH DEARNESS

COSTLY DEAR FINE HIGH RICH SALT DAINTY LAVISH SILVER COSTFUL COSTLEW GORGEOUS PLATINUM PRECIOUS PRODIGAL SPLENDID PRICELESS

COSTMARY TANSY ALECOST MAUDLIN ROSEMARY

COSTREL KEG HEAD FLASK BOTTLE COYSTREL

COSTUME RIG GARB ROBE SARI SUIT BURKA DRESS GETUP HABIT SHAPE TRUSS ATTIRE DOMINO FORMAL SETOUT TOILET APPAREL BLOOMER CLOTHES POLLERA RAIMENT SCARLET UNIFORM CHARSHAF CLOTHING ENSEMBLE TOILETTE VENETIAN
(ACADEMIC —) GUISE

COSTUSROOT PACHAK PUTCHOCK

COSY FEEL FEIL SNUG INTIME

COT BED HUT MAT PEN BOAT COOP COTE FOLD ABODE BOTHY CABIN COUCH COVER HOUSE STALL COTEEN CRADLE GURNEY PALLET SHEATH TANGLE CHARPAI CHARPOY COTTAGE SHELTER BEDSTEAD COTHOUSE DWELLING STRETCHER

COTERIE SET RING CABAL JUNTO

MONDE CIRCLE CLIQUE GALAXY SETOUT CENACLE CIRCUIT COLLEGE PLATOON SOCIETY

COTHURNUS BOOT BUSKIN COTHURN

COTILLION GERMAN

COTO OREJON

COTTA KATHA STOLE MANTLE BLANKET SURPLICE VESTMENT

COTTAGE BOX COT HUT BACH BARI COSH CRIB SHED WALK BOTHY BOWER CABIN HOUSE HOVEL LODGE SHACK BOHAWN BOTHIE CABANA CHALET SHELTER BUNGALOW COTHOUSE SHEELING SHIELING THALTHAN

COTTAGE CHEESE SKYR SMEARCASE SMIERCASE

COTTAGER MAILER

COTTER KEY MAT PIN VEX CLOT BOWPIN COTMAN FASTEN MAILER POTTER PUCKER SHRINK TOGGLE WITHER CONGEAL COTTIER PEASANT SHRIVEL VILLEIN COTARIUS COTTAGER COTTEREL ENTANGLE FORELOCK LINCHPIN

COTTON SAK BEAT DRAB FLOG MALO PIMA AGREE BAYAL BOLLY DERRY MATTA SAKEL SURAT BOMBACE BROACH CODDLE COMBER DHURRY FABRIC MAARAD MALLOW NANKIN PEELER STAPLE ALGODON BENDERS CANTOON DHURRIE GARMENT GINNING SILESIA SUCCEED
(— SQUARE) TZUT TZUTE
(BOLL OF —) SNAP
(NAPPED —) LAMBSKIN
(PAINTED —) INDIENNE
(PIECE OF —) SPONGE
(PRINTED —) SARONG
(RAW —) LINT BAYAL
(SILK —) FLOSS
(STRIPED —) BENGAL
(TREE —) MACO
(TWILLED —) JEAN SALLO SALLOO
(WAD OF —) TAMPON
(WASTE —) GRABBOTS
(PREF.) BYSSI BYSSO

COTTON GRASS CANNA CANNACH DRAWLING

COTTON PLANT LAMB
(— FLOWER) SQUARE

COTTON TREEE SIMAL

COTTONWOOD ALAMO

COTYLEDON BUTTON PICHURIM SARCOLOBE

COUCH BED COT KIP LAY LIE HIDE LAIR LURK SOFA SUNK DIVAN INLAY LODGE PRESS SKULK SLINK SNEAK SNOOP SQUAB SQUAT UTTER BURROW CLOTHE DAYBED LITTER PALLET PLINTH SETTEE CONCEAL EXPRESS HAMMOCK OTTOMAN OVERLAY RECLINE TRANSOM
(NUPTIAL —) THORE
(WOODEN —) RUSTBANK
(PREF.) CLIN(O) STROMATI STROMATO
(SUFF.) STROMA

COUCH GRASS CUTCH KUTCH QUACK QUICK TWICH QUITCH SCOTCH SCUTCH STROIL QUICKEN WITHVINE

COUGAR CAT PUMA PAINTER PANTHER CARCAJOU

COUGH YEX YOX BAFF BARK HACK HOST KINK CHINK CROUP HOAST HOOSE HOOZE TISICK TUSSIS

COUGH DROP PASTIL TROCHE LOZENGE PASTILLE

COUGH SYRUP LINCTUS

COULEE DRAW GORGE GULCH COOLEY RAVINE

COULOMB WEBER

COUMA SORVA HYAHYA

COUNCIL BODY BULE DAEL DIET DUMA FONO RAAD REDE YUAN BOARD BOULE BUNGA CABAL CAPUT DIVAN DIWAN DOUMA JIRGA JUNTA JUNTO SABHA SOBOR STATE SYNOD THING JIRGAH LUKIKO MAJLIS POWWOW QUORUM SENATE SOVIET TARYBA CABILDO CABINET CHAMBER CONSULT GERUSIA HUSTING MEETING PENSION WHITLEY ASSEMBLY CONCLAVE CONGRESS FOLKMOOT FOLKMOTE HEEMRAAD HEEMRAAT MINISTRY PLACITUM RIGSRAAD CAMARILLA PARLIAMENT AMPHICTYONS
(MORMON —) PRESIDENCY

COUNCILLOR RAT VIZIR ENDUNA INDUNA VIZIER FAIPULE SENATOR WISEMAN DECURION
(PL.) ANZIANI

COUNSEL RAD LORE REDE RULE RUNE SILK WARD WARN AREED CHIDE DEVIL GUIDE ADVICE ADVISE CONFER LEADER ABOGADO CAUTION COUNCIL LECTURE ADMONISH ADVOCATE PRUDENCE
(JUNIOR LEGAL —) DEVIL
(KING'S —) SILK
(SACRED —) TORAH

COUNSELOR RAT SAGE WITE CONSUL LAWYER MENTOR NESTOR ADVISER ADVISOR COUNSEL ECHEVIN GONZALO PROCTOR STARETS ADVOCATE ATTORNEY REDESMAN UCALEGON

COUNT ADD GAN SUM TOT BANK CAST EARL FOOT GANO GRAF NAME RELY RIME SIZE TALE TELL TOTE COMES COMPT COMTE GRAVE JUDGE RHYME SCORE TALLY WEIGH CENSUS CONSUL COUNTY DEPEND ESTEEM FIGURE IMPUTE NUMBER RECKON TOTTLE ACCOUNT ARTICLE ASCRIBE COMPUTE GANELON ADNUMBER NUMERATE SANCTION CALCULATE PALSGRAVE
(— IN BILLIARDS) DOUBLE
(— OF A FIBER) GRIST
(— OF SHEEP OR CATTLE) BREAK
(— ON) LITE RELY
(— UNIT) WARP

COUNTABLE DISCRETE

COUNTENANCE AID MUG OWN RUD ABET BROW FACE GIZZ LEER MIEN PUSS SHOW VULT CHEER FAVOR FRONT GRACE ASPECT ENDURE UPHOLD VISAGE APPROVE BEARING CONDUCT ENDORSE FEATURE PROFFER SUPPORT BEFRIEND DEMEANOR FOREHEAD SANCTION SEMBLANCE
(PREF.) PROSOP(O)

COUNTER BAR DIB LOT BANK BUCK CENT CHIP DESK DUMP EDDY FISH JACK KIST PAWN STOP CAROM CHECK FORCE HATCH JETON MERIL PIECE SHELF STALL STAND TABLE TOTER BUFFET COMBAT GEIGER ISLAND JETTON MARKER OPPOSE SQUAIL ADVERSE BUTTOCK CONTEND CURRENT FANTAIL SHAMBLE CONTRARY MAHOGANY OPPOSITE TELLTALE
(— TO) AGAINST
(LEADEN —) DUMP
(LUNCH —) PLACE
(PREF.) ANTI GAIN

COUNTERACT CHECK CANCEL OPPOSE RESIST THWART BALANCE CORRECT DESTROY NULLIFY ANTIDOTE NEGATIVE

COUNTERACTION DEADLOCK

COUNTERACTIVE REMEDY ADVERSE

COUNTERBALANCE COVER WEIGH CANCEL SETOFF BALANCE

COUNTERCLOCKWISE DIRECT DIRECTLY

COUNTERCURRENT BACKSET

COUNTEREARTH ANTICHTHON

COUNTERFEIT ACT BASE COIN COPY DAUB DUFF FAKE IDOL MOCK SHAM BELIE BOGUS DUMMY FALSE FEIGN FLASH FORGE FUDGE GAMMY MIMIC PHONY QUEER SNIDE AFFECT ASSUME CHEMIC ERSATZ FORGED PSEUDO TINSEL BASTARD CHEMICK DUFFING FALSIFY FASHION FEIGNED FORGERY IMITANT IMITATE SIMULAR BORROWED DEFORMED PHANTASM POSTICHE POSTIQUE RESEMBLE SIMILIZE SIMULATE SPURIOUS SUPPOSED
(PREF.) PSEUD(O)

COUNTERFEITER COINER JACKMAN JARKMAN SCRATCHER

COUNTERFEITERS (AUTHOR OF —) GIDE
(CHARACTER IN —) LAURA VEDEL ARMAND GEORGE ROBERT BERNARD EDOUARD LILLIAN OLIVIER VINCENT DOUVIERS GRIFFITH MOLINIER PASSAVANT GHERIDANISOL PROFITENDIEU

COUNTERFEITING COINING FICTION POSTICHE POSTIQUE

COUNTERFOIL FOIL STUB CHECK

COUNTERFORT SCONCE BUTTRESS

COUNTERION GEGENION

COUNTERIRRITANT MOXA GINGER
IODINE PEPPER MUSTARD
CANTHARIS
COUNTERMAND STOP ANNUL
CANCEL FORBID RECALL REVOKE
ABOLISH RESCIND REVERSE
UNORDER ABROGATE PROHIBIT
COUNTERMOVE DEMARCHE
COUNTERMOVEMENT BACKFIRE
COUNTERPANE PANE LIGGER
BEDSPREAD
COUNTERPART COPY LIKE MATE
SPIT TWIN FETCH IMAGE MATCH
MORAL SHELL TALLY COUSIN
DOUBLE SHADOW BALANCE
COUNTER OBVERSE PENDANT
SIMILAR ANTIPART PARALLEL
RESCRIPT SIMILITUDE
(SPEECH —) A
COUNTERPOINT FOIL DESCANT
CONTRAST FABURDEN
COUNTERPOISE POISE OFFSET
BALANCE EQUALIZE MAKEWEIGHT
COUNTERPOISON ORVIETAN
COUNTERSIGN BACK MARK SEAL
SIGN SIGNAL CONFIRM
ENDORSE PASSWORD SANCTION
COUNTERSINK DISH REAM BEVEL
CHAMFER
COUNTERSTATEMENT ANSWER
COUNTERSUN ANTHELION
COUNTERWEIGHT TARE
MAKEWEIGHT
COUNTERWORD ANIMAL
COUNTER
COUNTESS OLIVIA COMTESSE
CONTESSA
COUNTING ACCOUNT
COUNTLESS INFINITE
NUMBERLESS
(PREF.) MYRI(A)(O)
COUNT OF MONTE CRISTO
(AUTHOR OF —) DUMAS
(CHARACTER IN —) FARIA ALBERT
DANTES EDMOND HAIDEE
MONDEGO MORREL DANGLARS
MERCEDES FERDINAND
VALENTINE VILLEFORT
CADEROUSSE MAXIMILIAN
COUNTRIFIED JAY BUCOLIC
LOBBISH AGRESTIC HOBNAILED
COUNTRY SOD DESH EARD HICK
HOME KITH LAND PAIS SOIL
ADDLE CLIME EARTH FAIRY FRITH
MARCH PLAGE REALM STATE
TRACT WEALD GROUND KINTRA
KINTRY NATION PEOPLE REGION
STICKS UPLAND IMAMATE
KWINTRA MONKERY MUFASAL
BACKVELD DISTRICT DOMINION
ELDORADO LANDWARD
MAGAZINE MOFUSSIL REGALITY
PRINCIPALITY
(— OF ETHIOPIA) SEBA
(— OF ORIGIN) HOMELAND
(— OF PERFECTION) EUTOPIA
(— ON SEA) SEABOARD
(— STYLE) PAYSANNE
(ANCIENT —) ARAM
(CABIN —) LOBBY
(FRONTIER —) BORDER
(HOME —) BLIGHTY

(IMAGINARY —) EREWHON
LILLIPUT RURITANIA
(LIMESTONE —) KARST
(MARITIME —) MAREMMA
(MYTHICAL —) UTOPIA LEONNOYS
SVITHIOD SWITHIOD TEUTONIA
(OPEN —) BLED VELD FIELD VELDT
WEALD CAMPAIGN
(PETTY —) TOPARCHY
(ROUGH —) BOONDOCK
BUNDOCKS
(RURAL —) OUTBACK
(PREF.) RURI
(SUFF.) STAN
COUNTRYMAN HOB BOOR HIND
KERN TIKE CHURL CLOWN HODGE
KERNE SWAIN YOKEL GAFFER
GIBARO JIBARO GRANGER
HAYSEED LANDMAN PAESANO
PAISANO PEASANT PLOWMAN
LANDSMAN
(PL.) KITH
COUNTRYSIDE BLED BOCAGE
MOFUSSIL
COUNTRY WIFE (AUTHOR OF —)
WYCHERLEY
(CHARACTER IN —) HORNER
ALITHEA HARCOURT SPARKISH
PINCHWIFE
COUNTY AMT LAN SEAT FYLKE
SHIRE DOMAIN PARISH BOROUGH
COMITAT NORFOLK DISTRICT
COUP BUY BLOW DEAL PLAN PLAY
COUPE FAULT SCOOP UPSET
ATTACK BARTER PUTSCH REFAIT
STRIKE STROKE CAPSIZE TRAFFIC
OVERTURN
COUP DE POING BOUCHER
HANDSTONE
COUPE CUT CABRIOLET
LANDAULET
COUPED HUMETTY HUMETTEE
COUPLE DUO TIE TWO BOND CASE
DYAD JOIN LINK MATE PAIR SPAN
TEAM TWIN YOKE BRACE LEASH
MARRY TWAIN UNITE GEMINI
SPLINE SWINGE BRACKET
CONNECT COUPLER COUPLET
DOUBLET SHACKLE TWOSOME
VOLTAIC ACCOUPLE ASSEMBLE
COPULATE ACCOMPANY
(— OF HAWKS) CAST
COUPLED GEMEL YOKED JOINED
WEDDED GEMELED COPULATE
GEMINATE
COUPLER LINK RING BOBBER
COPULA JANNEY LINKER SUTURE
UNITER DRAGBAR DRAWBAR
REDUCER SHACKLE SNAPPER
TIRASSE DRAGBOLT DRAWBOLT
DRAWGEAR SHACKLER
COUPLET BAIT COPLA ELEGIAC
COUPLING HUB HICKY UNION
CLUTCH HICKEY NIPPLE SHACKLE
SHACKLER
COUPON TWOFER
COURAGE BIEL FIRE GRIT GUTS
MIND MOOD PROW SAND SOUL
BIELD CREST HEART HONOR
MOXIE NERVE PLUCK SPUNK
VALOR DARING DAUBER METTLE
PECKER SPIRIT VIRTUE VIRTUS

BRAVERY COJONES CORAGIO
HEROISM MANHEAD MANHOOD
MANSHIP PROWESS STOMACH
VENTURE AUDACITY BOLDNESS
CORRAGIO FIRMNESS TENACITY
(— OF CONVICTION) STAMINA
(MORAL —) STRENGTH
(PREF.) THYM(O)
(SUFF.) THYMIA
COURAGEOUS BOLD GAME GOOD
TALL BRAVE GUTSY HARDY LUSTY
MANLY STOUT WIGHT DARING
HEROIC MANFUL PLUCKY SPUNKY
CORIAUS GALLANT SPARTAN
STAUNCH VALIANT FEARLESS
GENEROUS INTREPID VALOROUS
COURAGEOUSLY BIG BRAVELY
COURANT ROMP CAPER DANCE
LETTER CORANTO CURRENT
GAZETTE RUNNING
COURBARIL JATOBA LOCUST
GUAPINOL CUAPINOLE
COURGETTE ZUCCHINI
COURIER NEWS POST GUIDE
SCOUT KAVASS NEWING POSTER
ESTAFET ORDERLY PATAMAR
POSTBOY POSTMAN SOILAGE
CICERONE CURSITOR DRAGOMAN
HORSEMAN ORDINARY
PATTAMAR
COURLAN LIMPKIN
COURONNE CROWN
COURSE FLY LAP RUN WAY BEAT
BENT FLOW GAGE GAME GANG
GATE HEAT HUNT LANE LINE
LODE MESS MODE PACE PATH
RACE RACK RAIK RAND RILL RING
RINK ROAD ROTA ROTE WENT
CLASS COURS CRUST CURRY
CURVE CYCLE DRAFT DRIFT
DRIVE EMBER GAUGE GREAT
LAPSE LAYER LEDGE MARCH
MOYEN ORBIT PLATE POINT
ROUTE SENSE SITHE SPACE STEPS
SWELT SWING TENOR TRACK
TRACT TRADE TRAIL TREND
WEENT ARTERY CAREER COPING
CURSUS DROMOS FURROW
GALLOP GIRDER GUTTER HONORS
MANNER METHOD MOTION
RESACA SCHOOL SERIES SPHERE
STREAM STREET SYSTEM TRIPOS
ZODIAC AZIMUTH BEELINE
CHANNEL CIRCUIT CONDUCT
DIAULOS DRAUGHT HIGHWAY
LECTURE PASSADE PASSAGE
PATHWAY PROCESS ROUTINE
RUNNING SEMINAR SERVICE
STRETCH SUBJECT SUCCESS
TIDEWAY TRAJECT TRUNDLE
CURRENCY CURRICLE DIADROME
DISTANCE ELECTIVE PROGRESS
RECOURSE SEQUENCE STEERAGE
TENDENCY MOTORDROME
(— OF A ROPE) LEAD
(— OF ACTION) LARK TACK TROD
VEIN DANCE CUSTOM ROUTINE
DEMARCHE
(— OF ACTIVITY) SIDELINE
(— OF BOAT) LEG
(— OF BRICK) BED ROWLOCK
SCINTLE CREASING

(— OF FEEDING) DIET
(— OF KNITTING) BOUT
(— OF LIFE) GOINGS PILGRIMAGE
(— OF LUCK) FORTUNE
(— OF MASONRY) BAHUT STILT
COPING HEADING SKEWBACK
(— OF NATURE) TAO
(— OF PROCEDURE) RULE
(— OF PROCEEDING) FORE
(— OF PURSUIT) SCENT
(— OF ROADBED) SUBCRUST
(— OF STONES) BED PLINTH
(— OF STUDY) DEBATE COLLEGE
LECTURE SEMINAR ELECTIVE
(— OF SUN) JOURNEY
(— OF TREATMENT) CURE
(— OF WALL) CORNICE
(— WITH GREYHOUNDS) GREW
(BELL-RINGING —) HUNT
(CIRCULAR —) SWEEP CHUKKAR
CHUKKER COMPASS
(COLLEGE —) PRECEPTORIAL
(CURVING —) SWING
(CUSTOMARY —) GUISE
(DOWNWARD —) DIP DECLINE
TOBOGGAN
(DUE —) TRAIN
(EASY —) PIPE
(EXACT —) BEAM
(FIRST —) ANTEPAST
(FREE —) FORTH
(IRREGULAR —) ERROR
(LAST —) VOID
(MIDDLE —) MIDS TEMPER
(NATURAL —) RITA
(OBLIQUE —) SKEW
(OVERHANGING —) JET
(PREDETERMINED —) DESTINY
(ROUNDABOUT —) DETOUR
WINDLASS
(SETTLED —) BIAS GROOVE
(SKIING —) SCHUSS
(PREF.) DROM(O)
COURSER HORSE RACER STEED
CUSSER CHARGER
COURSING CURSIVE
COURT BAR BID HOF SEE SUE WOO
AREA BAIL BODY CLAW FUSS
GATE GIRL LEET QUAD ROTA
SEAT SEEK SUIT TOWN WALE
WARD WYND YARD ARENA
BENCH BUREO CURIA CURRY
DAIRI DIVAN FAVOR FORUM
FUERO GARTH JUDGE PATIO
SHIRE SPACE SPARK SPOON
SWEET TEMPT THING THINK
TOURN TRAIN YAMEN ADALAT
ALLURE ATRIUM BAILEY COUNTY
DARGAH DURBAR DURGAH
GEMOTE HOMAGE INVITE PALACE
PARVIS PURSUE SPLUNT SUITOR
TOLSEY ADAWLUT ADDRESS
ASSIZES ATTRACT BARMOTE
DUOVIRI EPHETAE FOREIGN
HELIAEA HUSTING JUSTICE
PARVISE RETINUE SOLICIT
TEMENOS TOURNEL AUDIENCE
BURHMOOT CHANCERY
FOUJDARY LAWCOURT
MARKMOOT MARKMOTE
QUARANTY SERENADE SESSIONS
SWANMOTE TRIBUNAL

WOODMOTE PERIBOLOS
PARLIAMENT
(— **FAVOR**) FAWN
(— **OF A HUNDRED**) MALL MALLUM
MALLUS
(— **OF CIRCUIT JUDGES**) EYRE
(— **OF FORTRESS**) PEEL
(— **OF MIKADO**) DAIRI
(— **ORDER**) VACATUR
(— **THE GREAT**) LEVEE
(**ECCLESIASTICAL** —) ROTA CURIA
SYNOD COLLOQUY AUDIENCIA
(**EXERCISE** —) EPHEBEUM
(**FORTIFIED** —) BAWN
(**GERMAN** —) FEHM VEHM
(**INNER** —) PATIO
(**MUSLIM** —) DIVAN DIWAN
(**REFORMED** —) CLASIS
(**SMALL** —) WIND WYND CORTILE
(**SUPREME** —) SUDDER
(**TURKISH** —) GATE
COURTEOUS FAIR HEND BUXOM
CIVIL GENTY SUAVE BONAIR
GENTLE POLITE SMOOTH URBANE
AFFABLE CORDIAL GALLANT
GENTEEL GENTILE REFINED
DEBONAIR FAMILIAR GRACIOUS
OBLIGING
COURTEOUSLY FAIR FAIRLY
GENTLY KINDLY AFFABLY
COURTEOUSNESS COMITY
COURTESAN MADAM QUAIL THAIS
WHORE COURTY GEISHA LALAGE
MADAME PLOVER AMOROSA
ASPASIA CANIDIA DELILAH
LORETTE PUCELLE DEVADASI
(PL.) DEMIMONDE
COURTESY MENSK COMITY
EXTENT GENTRY MANSHIP
TASHRIF BREEDING CALIDORE
CORTEISE ELEGANCE GENTRICE
GRATUITY URBANITY
(PL.) HONORS
COURTHOUSE CUTCHERY
KACHAHRI
COURTIER CURAN OSRIC WOOER
OSRICK COURTER IACHIMO
COURTMAN POLONIUS
COURTING SUING SPLUNT
COURTLY HEND AULIC CIVIL
HENDE POLITE AULICAL ELEGANT
REFINED STATELY POLISHED
DIGNIFIED
COURT-NOUE RONCET
COURTSHIP SUIT AMOUR DRURY
SPARKING
COURTYARD AREA WYND CLOSE
CURIA PATIO TRANCE BALLIUM
CORTILE TETRAGON CURTILAGE
COUSIN COZ KIN AKIN HERO
ALLIED NEPHEW
COUSIN BETTE (**AUTHOR OF** —)
BALZAC
(**CHARACTER IN** —) HULOT AGATHE
CREVEL MONTES ADELINE
LISBETH HORTENSE MARNEFFE
VICTORIN CELESTINE STEINBOCK
COVE CO BAY DEN CAVE CHAP
FILE GILL HOLE NOOK PASS SUMP
BASIN BAYOU BIGHT CREEK INLET
COVING FELLOW HOLLOW RECESS
VALLEY MOLDING CALANQUE
GUNKHOLE

COVENANT BIND BOND BRIS MISE
PACT TRUE AGREE BERIT BRITH
TOUCH ACCORD BERITH CARTEL
COMART CONAND ENGAGE
INDENT LEAGUE PATISE PLEDGE
TREATY BARGAIN COMPACT
CONCORD PROMISE ALLIANCE
CONTRACT DOCUMENT
HANDFAST TREATISE
COVENANTER HILLMAN TRUEBLUE
COVER DO CAP COT HAP LAP LAY
LID NAP TOP TUP WRY BIND CEIL
CLAD COAT COOM CURE DAUB
DECK FACE FADE FALL FURL
GARB GATE HEAD HEAL HEEL
HIDE HILL HOOD LATH LEAD LEAP
LINE MASK PAVE ROOF SILE SPAN
TELD TICK TIDE TILT VEIL WRAP
APRON BATHE BOARD CLOAK
CLOUT COPSE CROWN DRAPE
DRESS FENCE FLESH FLOOD
GUISE HATCH KIVER MOUNT
RECTO SCARF SERVE SHADE
STREW STUDY THEAK THEEK
TOWEL TREAD VERSO WELME
WHALM AWNING BATTER BINDER
BLAZON CANOPY CHALON
CLOTHE DOUBLE EARLAP ENAMEL
ENCASE ENFOLD ENTIRE ENVEIL
FOLDER HACKLE IMMASK INVEST
JACKET KIRTLE MANTLE OVERGO
POTLID RUNNER SCONCE SCREEN
SHADOW SHEATH SHIELD SLEEVE
SPREAD SPRING SWATHE TOILET
TOPPER WHAUVE APPAREL
ASPHALT BANDAGE BESTREW
BLANKET CAPSULE CONCEAL
CONTECT COUVERT ELYTRON
EMBRACE ENCRUST FASCINE
HEADCAP HOUSING INCRUST
KNEECAP MANHEAD OBSCURE
OMNIBUS OVERLAY PRETEXT
SHEATHE SHELTER SHUTTER
TAMPION THIMBLE BEDCOVER
COMPRISE COVERCLE DEBRUISE
ENCLOTHE ENSCONCE
HOODWINK IMMANTLE OVERHAIL
OVERSILE OVERWEND PALLIATE
PRETENCE PRETENSE SLIPOVER
SURPOOSE
(— **A FIRE**) BANK DAMP
(— **AROUND FLOWER**) CYMBA
(— **BRICKS**) SCOVE
(— **BY EXCUSES**) ALIBI PALLIATE
(— **FOR ALEMBIC**) HEAD
(— **FOR CHALICE**) PALL
(— **FOR DIAPER**) SOAKER
(— **FOR ENGINE**) COWLING
(— **FOR FOOD**) BELL
(— **FOR GUN**) TAMPION
(— **FOR MILITARY CAPE**) HAVELOCK
(— **FOR PISTON**) FOLLOWER
(— **FOR POWDER PAN**) HAMMER
(— **FOR WIRES**) BOOTLEG
(— **GROUND**) HEAT
(— **HEARTH**) FETTLE
(— **OF BALL**) CARCASS
(— **OF BOILER**) VOMIT
(— **OF COFFIN**) COOM
(— **OF HAWSEHOLE**) BUCKLER
(— **OF MINE CAGE**) BONNET
(— **OF RIFLE MAGAZINE**) GATE

(— **OF SPORANGIUM**) EPIGONE
(— **OF VEGETATION**) GROWTH
(— **OPPRESSIVELY**) SMOTHER
(— **OVER**) RAKE WELME WHELM
QUELME SHEUGH BECLOUD
OVERDECK WITHHELE
OVERWHELM
(— **PLANTS**) BAG
(— **PROTECTIVELY**) SHROUD
SHEATHE
(— **ROAD**) BLIND
(— **SOIL WITH CLAY**) GAULT
(— **UP**) HAP BELY FOLD BELIE
SALVE SLEEK HUDDLE
(— **WITH ASHES**) SOIL
(— **WITH BACON**) BARD
(— **WITH CLAY**) CLOAM
(— **WITH COWL**) MOB
(— **WITH CRUMBS**) BREAD
(— **WITH DOTS**) CRIBBLE
(— **WITH DROPS**) DAG
(— **WITH EARTH**) BURY HEAL INTER
(— **WITH FILM**) SKIM
(— **WITH FLESH**) INCARN
(— **WITH FOAM**) EMBOSS
(— **WITH GOLD**) GILD
(— **WITH MEAL**) MELVIE
(— **WITH MUD**) BEMUD BELUTE
(— **WITH OAKUM**) FOTHER
(— **WITH PITCH**) PAY
(— **WITH PLASTER**) PARGET
(— **WITH SHEATH**) GLOVE
(— **WITH SOLDER**) SPLASH
(— **WITH STONE**) ASHLAR
(— **WITH STRAW**) THATCH
(— **WITH TIN**) BLANCH
(— **WITH TOPSOIL**) KELLY
(— **WITH WATER**) DOUSE DOWSE
FLOOD WHELM OVERFLOW
(— **WITH WAX**) CERE
(— **WITH WEAVING**) GRAFT
(— **WITH WINGS**) BROOD
(**BED** —**S**) HEALING
(**BEEHIVE** —) QUILT
(**BOOK** —) CASE SIDE
(**GLASS** —) STRIKE
(**PACK** —) MANTA
(**POSTAL** —) ENTIRE
(**POT** —) BRED
(**SADDLE** —) PILCH HOUSING
(**SLIDING** —) BRIDGE
(**TABLE** —) BAIZE DUCHESSE
(**WING** — **OF BEETLE**) SHARD
(**PREF.**) OPERCULI
COVERAGE PROTECTION
COVERALL GOWN JUMPER
COVERED CLAD FULL SHOD TECT
BLIND MOSSY CLOSED COVERT
HIDDEN ENCASED OBTECTED
SCREENED
(— **WITH CRYSTALS**) DRUSY
(— **WITH FEATHERS**) HIRSUTE
(— **WITH FOREST**) HYLEAN
(— **WITH HAIRS**) COMATE VILLOUS
(— **WITH PROTUBERANCES**) HUMPY
(— **WITH SCALES**) SCUTATE
(— **WITH SEAWEED**) TANGLY
(— **WITH WHITE DUST**) PRUINOSE
(**THINLY** —) BARISH
(**PREF.**) CALYPT(O) CRYPT(O)
KRYPT(O)
COVERED WAGON WHITETOP
BUCKWAGON

COVERER DECKER
COVERING (**ALSO SEE COVER**) BOX
COT FUR HAP KEX LAG ARIL BARB
BARK BOOT CASE CAUL COAT
CUFF DECK FILM HAME HEAD
HOOD HULL HUSK KELL MASK
OVER PALL PUFF ROBE ROOF SLIP
SPAT TARP TILE TILT TRAP VEIL
APRON ARMOR BRAID BURSE
CRUST DRESS GLOBE GLOVE
HATCH QUILT SCALE SHELL SKIRT
STALL SWARD TESTA TUNIC
TWEEL WREIL ARMING ATTIRE
AWNING BANCAL BANKER
CANOPY CANVAS COVERT
DRAPET EMBRYO ENAMEL
FACING FENDER GAITER GANOIN
HACKLE HATCAP HELMET JACKET
MUZZLE PELAGE SADDLE SCREEN
SHEATH SHROUD SINDON
TEGMEN VERNIX BLANKET
BUFFONT CAMISIA CAPPING
CAPSULE CEILING COATING
COWLING EARFLAP ENVELOP
EXCIPLE GRATING HAPPING
HEALING HEELCAP HOUSING
MUFFLER OVERLAY PURPORT
SARPLER SHADING SHELTER
SHOEING SLIPPER TECTURE
TEGMENT VESTURE WRAPPER
ARMGUARD BLAZONRY
BOARDING CASEMENT CLEADING
CLOTHING COMPRESS COVERLET
EGGSHELL EPISPORE INDUMENT
INDUSIUM MANTELET MANTLING
OVERCAST PAVILION PERICARP
SETATION UMBRELLA TECTORIAL
PILLOWCASE
(— **FOR ANTENNA**) RADOME
(— **FOR BENCH**) BANKER
(— **FOR BOXERS' HANDS**) CESTUS
(— **FOR EGG**) COSY
(— **FOR FOREHEAD**) BONGRACE
(— **FOR NECK**) TUCKER PARTLET
(— **FOR ROOF APEX**) EPI
(— **FOR SHOULDERS**) STOLE
(— **FOR SKI**) SKIN
(— **FOR STIRRUP**) HOOD
(— **OF BED**) TIKE
(— **OF BELL ROPE**) GRIP
(— **OF BIRD**) INDUMENT
(— **OF BOW HANDLE**) ARMING
(— **OF CASH SHORTAGE**) LAPPING
(— **OF FEATHERS**) DOWN
(— **OF GILLS**) OPERCULUM
(— **OF NUTMEG**) MACE
(— **OF ROOT**) CALYPTRA
(— **OF ROPE**) SERVICE
(— **OF VEGETATION**) FLEECE
(— **WITH IRON**) ACIERAGE
(—**S FOR NIPPLES**) PASTIES
(**CAST** —**S**) EXUVIAE
(**CHIMNEY** —) COWL
(**CLOTH** —) TOILET
(**COARSE** —) CADDOW TILLET
(**DEFENSIVE** —) ARMOR KICKER
(**EAR** —) EARLAP EARFLAP
EARMUFF OREILET
(**EYE** —**S**) GOGGLES
(**FLOOR** —) RUG TILE CRASH
CARPET LINOLEUM OILCLOTH
(**FOUL** —) SCUM
(**HEAD** —) CAP HAT WIG HAIR HIVE

HOOD CURCH BONNET HELMET
BIRETTA CHAPEAU CHAPERON
HAVELOCK HEADRAIL TROTCOZY
(LEG —) BOOT HOSE STOCK
GAITER LEGGIN PEDULE KNEELET
LEGGING STOCKING
(LIGHT —) GRIMING
(LINEN —) BARB
(OUTER —) BARK HIDE HULL HUSK
CRUST TESTA JACKET CARAPACE
(PLANT —) PERIDERM
(PROTECTIVE —) APRON ARMOR
SHELL COCOON
(SADDLE —) MOCHILA
(SEED —) PERIGONE
(SLIGHT —) CYMAR
(STAGE —) HEAVENS
(STERILE —) DRAPE
(STICKY DAMP —) GLET
(THIN —) FILM SCRUFF WASHING
(PREF.) CALYPT(O) COLE STEG(O)
STRATI STRATO
(— OF EYEBALL) CORNEA
(SUFF.) DERM(A)(ATOUS)(IA)(IS)(Y)
(— PLATE) STEGE
COVERLET PANE HELER HOUSE
QUILT REZAI THROW AFGHAN
CADDOW CHALON COLCHA
LIGGER SPREAD BLANKET
BUFFALO COVERLID DAGSWAIN
COVER-SHAME SAVIN SAVINE
COVERT DEN LAY LIE SLY LAIR
VERT EARTH NICHE PRIVY
ASYLUM HARBOR HIDDEN
LATENT MASKED MYSTIC REFUGE
SECRET COVERED DEFENSE
PRIVATE SHELTER TECTRIX
THICKET DISGUISE INVOLVED
(PL.) CRISSUM
COVERTLY CLOSE CLOSELY
COVET ACHE ENVY PANT WANT
WISH CRAVE YEARN YISSE DESIRE
GRUDGE HANKER
COVETOUS AVID GAIR GARE
EAGER FRUGAL GREEDY SORDID
STINGY ENVIOUS GRIPPLE
MISERLY DESIROUS GRASPING
COVETOUSNESS GREED MISERY
AVARICE YISSING COVETISE
CUPIDITY PLEONEXIA
COVEY BEVY FALL BROOD FLOCK
HATCH COVERT COMPANY
COVIN BAND CREW FRAUD COVINE
COMPANY CONVENE ASSEMBLY
TRICKERY
COW AWE KEY NOT BEEF BOGY
BOSS COWL CUSH FAZE MOIL
MULL NOTT ROAN RUNT VACA
ABASH ALARM BEEVE BOSSY
BROCK BULLY CUSHA DAUNT
DOMPT DRAPE MOGGY QUAIL
SCARE SNOOL VACHA BOVINE
BULLER COLLOP CRUMMY GOBLIN
HAWKEY HAWKIE HEIFER MAILIE
MILKER MULLEY ROTHER SUBDUE
BOARDER BUGBEAR BULLOCK
CRITTER CRUMMIE DEPRESS
MESTENO MILCHER OVERTOP
SQUELCH TERRIFY ALDERNEY
AUDHUMLA BROWBEAT
COWBRUTE DISPIRIT FRIGHTEN
STRIPPER THREATEN
(— ABOUT 3 FEET HIGH) GYNEE

(— BEFORE CALVING) SPRINGER
(BAD-TEMPERED —) RAGER
(BARREN —) DRAPE BARRENER
(DRY —) KEY SEW
(HORNLESS —) NOT MOIL NOTT
DODDY MULEY DODDIE HUMLIE
MAILIE HUMBLIE POLLARD
MOULLEEN
(PART OF —) HIP JAW RIB CROP
HOCK HOOF HORN KNEE LOIN
NECK POLL RUMP TAIL TEAT
CHEST CHINE FLANK GIRTH
PLATE THIGH THURL UDDER
BARREL BRIDGE DEWLAP MUZZLE
SWITCH THROAT BRISKET
DEWCLAW PASTERN PINBONE
WITHERS FOREHEAD
(PREGNANT —) CALVER INCALVER
(WHITE-FACED —) HAWKEY
HAWKIE
(YOUNG —) QUEY STIRK HEIFER
(PL.) KYE KINE DAIRY
(PREF.) VACCI(NI)(NO)
COWARD COW COOF DAFF FUNK
FUGIE LACHE PIKER CRAVEN
FUNKER PIGEON BUZZARD
CAITIFF CHICKEN COUCHER
DASTARD MEACOCK NITHING
PANURGE QUITTER NIDERING
POLTROON RECREANT TURNBACK
TURNTAIL VILLIAGO
COWARDICE DASTARDY
LASHNESS POLTROONERY
COWARDLINESS PUSILLANIMITY
COWARDLY SHY ARGH FAINT
LACHE TIMID AFRAID COWARD
COWISH CRAVEN TURPID YELLOW
CAITIFF CHICKEN GUTLESS
HILDING MEACOCK FACELESS
NIDERING POLTROON RECREANT
SNEAKING POLTROONISH
PIGEONHEARTED
COW BARN BYRE SAUR BARTH
SHIPPON VACCARY
COWBIRD BECCO BUNTING
CUCKOLD OXBITER COKEWOLD
LAZYBIRD
COWBOY HAZER RIDER ROPER
SCREW WADDY CHARRO GAUCHO
GINETE HERDER JINETE WADDIE
COWHAND COWHERD COWPOKE
GRAZIER HERDBOY LLANERO
PANIOLO PUNCHER REFUGEE
VAQUERO BUCKAROO DALLYMAN
JACKAROO NEATHERD
NOWTHERD OUTRIDER PASTORAL
RANCHERO SWINGMAN
WRANGLER
COWCATCHER GUARD LASSO
PILOT FENDER
COWED HANGDOG DOWNCAST
COWER HUG COUR FAWN RUCK
HOVER QUAIL SHRUG SNOOL
SQUAT STOOP TOADY WINCE
COORIE CRINGE CROUCH HURKLE
SHRINK CROODLE CRUDDLE
COWFISH TORO BECCO CUCKOLD
MANATEE SIRENIA
COWHAGE KIWACH
COWHAND PEELER FLANKER
STOCKMAN
COWHERB COCKLE SOAPWORT
COWHERD HERDSMAN NEATHERD

COWHOUSE BYRE SHIPPEN
SHIPPON
COWL CAP COW LID SOE TUB
COUL HOOD MONK MITER
BONNET CUCULE CAPUCHE
SCUTTLE CAPUCHIN
COW PARSNIP MADNEP
CADWEED HOGWEED PIGWEED
BEARWORT BUNDWEED
COWPEA SITAO FRIJOL FRIJOLE
TOWCOCK BLACKEYE BLACKPEA
COWPEN CUPPEN CUPPIN
COW PILOT PINTANO
COWPOX PAPPOX KINEPOX
VACCINA VACCINIA
COWRIE COWRY VENUS ZIMBI
CYPRAEID
COWSLIP PAIGLE PRIMULA
SHOOTER AURICULA CYCLAMEN
MARIGOLD PRIMROSE
COXA HIP HAUNCH
COXCOMB FOP NOB BUCK DUDE
FOOL PRIG TOFF CLEAT DANDY
HINGE PRINCOX POPINJAY
PRINCOCK
COXCOMBRY FOPPERY
COXSWAIN PATROON
COY PAL SHY ARCH COAX NICE
ALOOF CHARY DECOY QUIET
SQUAB STILL ALLURE CARESS
DEMURE MODEST PROPER
SKEIGH BASHFUL DISTANT
PEEVISH STRANGE RESERVED
SKITTISH VERECUND KITTENISH
COYNESS SHYNESS
COYO CHININ
COYOL COROJO COROZO
COYOTE VARMINT
(— STATE) SOUTHDAKOTA
COYPU DEGU NUTRIA
COZBI (FATHER OF —) ZUR
COZEN COG CON BILK GULL POOP
CHEAT TRICK CHISEL GREASE
BEGUILE DECEIVE DEFRAUD
SWINDLE HOODWINK
COZENER SNAP SNECKDRAW
COZENING SIMILATE
COZIER CADGER CODGER COSIER
COZY RUG BEIN BIEN COSY EASY
HOMY SAFE SNUG BIELD CANNY
CUSHY HOMEY CHATTY PENTIT
SECURE TOASTY COVERING
FAMILIAR HOMELIKE SOCIABLE
CPU CHIP
CRAB GIN UCA BOCO JUEY MAJA
ZOEA ANGER ARROW AYUYU
BLUEY MAIAN MAIID MAJID
RACER SANDY THIEF WINCH
BUSTER CANCER GROUSE
HARPER HERMIT KABURI NIPPER
PARTAN PEELER PUNGAR
PUNGER RACING SCRAWL SPRITE
BUCKLER BUCKLUM BURSTER
CABOUCA CANCRID FIDDLER
GRUMBLE INACHID OCYPODE
PANFISH POLYPOD SHEDDER
SOLDIER SPECTER SPECTRE
SURIQUE ARACHNID CRABFISH
DORIPPID GRAPSOID HORSEMAN
IRRITATE LIMULOID LITHODID
OCHIDORE OXYSTOME PAGURIAN
PORTUNID RANINIAN TRAVELER
WINDLASS BRACHYURA

(MATING —) DOUBLER
(PREF.) CANCERI CANCERO
CANCRI CARCIN(I)(O)
CRAB APPLE CRAB SCRAB SCROG
COLING
CRABBED SOUR UGLY CABBY
CRANK CROSS SURLY TESTY
BITTER COPPED CROOSE CROUSE
CRUSTY MOROSE RUGGED
SULLEN TEETHY TRYING BOORISH
CANKERY CRABBIT CRAMPED
CRONISH CROOKED FRABBIT
GNARLED KNOTTED OBSCURE
PEEVISH CANKERED CHURLISH
CONTRARY CRABBISH LIVERISH
PETULANT VINEGARY
CRABBEDNESS ACRIMONY
ASPERITY
CRABCATCHER CRABIER
CRABER VOLE AGOUARA
CRABGRASS DRAWK FONIO PANIC
DARNEL PANICLE CRABWEED
ELEUSINE
CRAB LOUSE CRAB MORPION
MOREPEON
CRAB PLOVER DROME
CRAB TREE GRIBBLE
CRABWOOD ANDIROBA
POISONWOOD
CRACK GAG KIN POP BANG BLOW
CHAP CHIP CHOP CLAP CONE
DOKE FENT FLAW GAIG JEST JIBE
JOKE KIBE LEAK LICK QUIP REND
RIFT RIME RIVE SCAR SLAT SNAP
YERK BRACK BREAK CHARK
CHECK CHICK CHINE CHINK
CLACK CLEFT CRAKE CRAZE
FLAKE FLANK FLASH GRIKE
KNACK KNICK SCORE SHAKE
SLASH SOLVE SPANG SPLIT
CLEAVE CRANNY SLITER SPIDER
SPRING BLEMISH CRACKLE
CREVICE FISSURE SLIFTER
SLITHER FRACTURE HAIRLINE
STRAMASH
(— A WHIP) YERK FLANK
(— IN FLESH) KIN CHAP KIBE
(— IN FLOOR) STRAKE
(— IN INGOT) SPILL
(— IN MAST) SPRING
(— IN ROCK) GRIKE JOINT
(— IN SEA ICE) RIFTER
(— IN STEEL) CHECK SPILL
(— OPEN) SEAM
(— PETROLEUM) BURN
(— WHILE FIRING) DUNT
(PL.) CRAZE
(PREF.) RIMI
CRACKAJACK NAILER NAILING
CRACKBRAINED BATS CRAZY
NUTTY CRACKY ERRATIC
CRACKED BATS FLED NECKED
CHAPPED COMICAL TOUCHED
CRACKERS
CRACKER BAKE LIAR WAFER
BONBON POPPER BISCUIT
BOASTER BREAKER BURSTER
COSAQUE REDNECK SALTINE
SNAPPER
(— STATE) GEORGIA
(BOILED —S) CUSH
(BROKEN —S) DUNDERFUNK
CRACKERJACK TRUMP

CRACKING CRAZE SHIVERING
(PL.) SCRAP
CRACKLE SNAP BREAK CRACK
CRISP BRUSTLE CRINKLE SPARKLE
SPUTTER CREPITATE
CRACKLING CRISP GREAVE
SNAPPY CRACKEL CRACKLE
CREMANT GREAVES CRACKNEL
CRITLING CREPITANT
(PL.) SCRAPS GRIEBEN
CRACKNEL SIMNEL CRACKLING
CRACKPOT CRACK ERRATIC
LUNATIC CRANKISH
CRACKSMAN YEGG BURGLAR
PETEMAN
CRADLE BED COT CRIB REST ROCK
WOMB CRATE FRAME CRECHE
MATRIX ROCKER SADDLE
TROUGH BERCEAU SHELTER
BASSINET CUNABULA
(— FOR SHIP) BED SLEE
(— FOR VATS) STILLING STILLION
(— IN ARCHERY) PURSE
(CERAMICS —) CHUM
(GRAIN —) CADAR CADER
(PL.) CHOCKS
CRADLESONG BERCEUSE
CRADLING BRACK
CRAFT ART BARK BOAT SAIL
FRAUD GUILE SKILL TRADE
BARQUE BATEAU CAUTEL DECEIT
DROGER METIER MISTER POLICE
ROADER STRUSE TALENT VESSEL
ABILITY CUNNING DROGHER
MYSTERY PANURGY SLEIGHT
APTITUDE ARTIFICE BASKETRY
VOCATION
(ANTIQUATED OR CLUMSY —)
HOOKER
(LANDING —) DUCK
(PREF.) TECHNI TECHNO
(SUFF.) TECT
CRAFTILY FOXILY
CRAFTINESS DESIGN SLEIGHT
SLYNESS
CRAFTSMAN CARL HAND CARLE
CRAFT NAVVY ARTIST WRITER
ARTISAN TOHUNGA WORKMAN
LETTERER MECHANIC ARTIFICER
MACHINIST
CRAFTY SLY ARCH DEEP DERN
FINE FOXY NOUP SLIM WILY WISE
ADEPT COONY PAWKY SLAPE
SLEEK ADROIT ARTFUL ASTUTE
CALLID QUAINT SHREWD SOLERT
SUBTLE TRICKY CUNNING POLITIC
SLEEKIT SLEIGHT SUBTILE
VAFROUS VERSUTE VULPINE
CAPTIOUS DEXTROUS ENGINOUS
FETCHING JESUITIC SLEIGHTY
CAUTELOUS
CRAG TOR CRAW KNEE NECK ROCK
SCAR SPUR ARETE BRACK CLIFF
CLINT CRAIG HEUCH HEUGH
THROAT
(PREF.) CREMNO
CRAGGY ROUGH ABRUPT CLIFFY
CLIFTY KNOTTY PAMPER RUGGED
CRAGGED KNAGGED
CRAKE CROW RAIL ROOK RAVEN
CORNBIRD RAILBIRD
CRAKOW BEAKER CRACOWE
POULAINE

CRAM BAG MUG RAM WAD BONE
CRAP FILL GLUT LADE PACK
PANG PORR PURR STOW TRIG
TUCK URGE CROWD CRUSH
DRIVE FARCE FORCE FRANK
GORGE GRIND LEARN PRESS
SCRAM STECH STUDY STUFF
TEACH AGROTE CROMME PESTER
STEEVE STODGE THRACK
(— WITH RICH FOOD) PAMPER
CRAMMED PANG STODGY
CHOCKFUL JAMPACKED
CRAMMER CRAM FEEDER
CRAMMING GAVAGE
CRAMP ART ARCT COOP CRIB KINK
PAIN TUCK CRICK CRIMP CROWD
DOWEL PINCH STUNT TRAMP
AGRAFE DOGTIE HAMPER HINDER
KNOTTY PESTER CONFINE
CRAMPER CRAMPET COMPRESS
CONTRACT RESTRAIN RESTRICT
CRAMPED POKY CRIMP POKEY
BOUNDED CRIMPED SQUEEZY
CRAMPFISH TORPEDO
CRAMPING UNEASY
CRAMPON CRAMP CRAMPET
CRAMPOON
CRANBERRY BERRY CRANE
ERICAD BOGWORT PEMBINA
ACROSARC BILBERRY BOGBERRY
COWBERRY FENBERRY FOXBERRY
CROWBERRY
(— BUSH) PIMBINA
CRANBERRY TREE PEMBINA
SNOWBALL VIBURNUM
CRANE JOB GRUS HOOK SWAY
CYRUS DAVIT HERON HOIST
JENNY RAISE SARUS TITAN
WADER BROLGA COOLEN JIGGER
KULANG SAHRAS COOLUNG
CRAWLER DERRICK GOLIATH
KAIKARA WHOOPER ADJUTANT
GRUIFORM TRAVELER
(— FOR FIREPLACE) COTTREL
COTTEREL
CRANE ARM GIB JIB GIBBET
RAMHEAD COTTEREL
CRANESBILL ALUMROOT
DOVEFOOT FLUXWEED
CRANIUM PAN HEAD CRANE
CRANY SKULL BRAINPAN
CRANK NUT WIT BENT SICK WALT
WEAK WHIM WIND BRACE LOOSE
ROGUE SHAKY THROW WALTY
WINCH AILING BOLDLY CRANKY
EVENER GROUCH HANDLE INFIRM
AWKWARD BRACKET FANATIC
LUSTILY
(SOMEWHAT —) TENDER
CRANKCASE SUMP
CRANKINESS ANGULARITY
CRANKY UGLY CRAZY CRONK
CROSS LUSTY SHAKY TESTY
AILING CRANNY FIFISH INFIRM
SICKLY CROOKED GROUCHY
PERVERSE TORTUOUS
CRANNY HOLE NOOK CHINK CLEFT
CRACK CORNER CRANNEL
CREVICE FISSURE
CRANTARA TARIE
CRANTS WREATH CORANCE
GARLAND
CRAPE BAND CURL FRIZ CREPE

CRIMP DRAPE GAUZE SHROUD
MOURNING
CRAPE MYRTLE JAPONICA
ASTROMEDA
CRAPPIE BACH SHAD BATCH
CALICO CROPPIE BACHELOR
BACULERE NEWLIGHT SACALAIT
TINMOUTH CHINKAPIN
CRAPS CRAP HAZARD
CRASH BASH FAIL FALL RACK
BLAST BURST CLOTH CRUSH
FRUSH PRANG SHOCK SMASH
SOUND FIASCO FRAGOR HURTLE
FAILURE SHATTER STENTER
COLLAPSE ICEQUAKE SPLINTER
STRAMASH
(— OF THUNDER) CLAP
CRASHING ROPAND SMASHING
CRASH-LAND DITCH
CRASS RAW DULL LOUD RUDE
CRUDE DENSE GROSS ROUGH
THICK COARSE OBTUSE STUPID
CRASSNESS SQUALOR
CRATCH CRIB RACK CRITCH
MANGER GRATING
CRATE BOX CAR CASE CRIB FLAT
PLANE SERON BASKET CRADLE
ENCASE HAMPER HURDLE
CACAXTE CANASTA CARRIER
PACKAGE VEHICLE
(EMPTY —) EMPTY
CRATER CUP PIT CONE HOLE
DINOS FOVEA NICHE CELEBE
HOLLOW CALDERA
(— FORMED BY STEAM) MAAR
(LUNAR —) LINNE
(VOLCANIC —) MAAR
CRATUS (FATHER OF —) PALLAS
URANUS
(MOTHER OF —) GAEA STYX
CRAUNCH CRANCH SCRANCH
CRAVAT TIE TECK ASCOT FRONT
SCARF STOCK CHOKER GRAVAT
BANDAGE NECKTIE OVERLAY
SOUBISE CRUMPLER
CRAVE ASK BEG GAPE ITCH LONG
NEED PRAY SEEK WISH COVET
GREED YEARN DESIRE HANKER
HUNGER LINGER THIRST YAMMER
BESEECH ENTREAT IMPLORE
REQUEST REQUIRE SOLICIT
APPETITE
CRAVEN AFRAID COWARD SCARED
DASTARD COWARDLY DEFEATED
OVERCOME POLTROON RECREANT
SNEAKING
CRAVING AVID ITCH WANT LETCH
DESIRE HUNGER THIRST LONGING
APPETITE LIKEROUS TICKLING
APPETENCE
(— FOR LIQUOR) DRY
(— FOR UNNATURAL FOOD) PICA
(ABNORMAL —) BULIMY BULIMIA
BOULIMIA
CRAW MAW CRAG CROP STOMACH
CRAWFISH KREEF
CRAWL LAG COON DRAG FAWN
INCH LOOP RAMP SHUG SWIM
CREEP KRAAL SLIDE SLIME SNAKE
TRAIL BUSTLE CRINGE GROVEL
SCRAWL SCRIDE CLAMBER
SLITHER SNIGGLE TRUDGEN
INCHWORM SCRABBLE

CRAWLING
(SUFF.) (— CREATURE) ERPETON
CRAWLY CREEPY
CRAYFISH DAD CRAB YABBY
YABBIE CAMARON CRAWDAD
LOBSTER CAMBARUS CRABFISH
CRAWFISH
CRAYON KEEL PLAN CHALK CONTE
SAUCE PASTEL PENCIL SKETCH
SANGUINE
CRAZE BUG FAD FLAW MAZE
MODE RAGE BREAK CRACK
CRUSH FEVER FUROR MANIA
VOGUE DEFECT IMPAIR MADDEN
MADDLE WEAKEN WHIMSY
DERANGE DESTROY FASHION
SHATTER WHIMSEY DISTRACT
(PREF.) MANIC
CRAZED MAD REE AMOK LOCO
WILD WOOD WOWF ZANY BALMY
BATTY DAFFY DOTTY GIDDY
MANIC NUTTY POTTY WACKY
COOCOO DOTTLE INSANE LOONEY
BERSERK FANATIC LUNATIC
DATELESS DELEERIT DEMENTED
DERANGED POSSESSED
CRAZINESS CRAZE LUNACY
DEMENTIA
CRAZY (ALSO SEE CRAZED) APE
OFF REE WET BATS BUGS GYTE
HITE LOCO NUTS WILD ZANY
BATTY BEANY BUGGY DAFFY
DIPPY DOILT DOTTY FLAKY
GOOFY KOOKY LOOLY LOONY
POTTY CRANKY CUCKOO DOTTLE
FLAKEY FRUITY INSANE LOCKET
MENTAL SCATTY SCREWY
BANANAS BONKERS CRACKED
LUNATIC PEEVISH SCRANNY
BUGHOUSE COCKEYED CRACKERS
DERANGED HALLICET HALUCKET
MESHUGGA
CREAK CRY GIG GEIG GIRG JARG
RASP YIRR CHARK CHEEP CHIRK
CRAIK CRANK CROAK GRIND
GROAN FRATCH SCREAK SCRIKE
SCROOP SKRAIK SQUEAK
COMPLAIN
CREAKING JARG SCREAK SCRIKE
CREAKY ARTHRITIC
CREAM DIP BEAT BEST FOOL HEAD
REAM CREME ELITE FROTH
REAME SAUCE BONBON CHOICE
TRIFLE COLOGNE FATNESS
EMULSION OINTMENT
CREAMING MANTLING
CREAM PUFF PUFF DUCHESSE
CREAMY RICH REAMY ACREAM
SMOOTH LUSCIOUS
CREASE GAW CLAM FOLD LINE
LIRK RUCK RUGA SEAM BLOCK
CRESS CRIMP PLAIT PLEAT PRESS
SCARF SCORE FURROW SCARPA
SUTURE WREATH CRUMPLE
CRUNKLE WRIMPLE WRINKLE
(SERIES OF —S) BREAK
(PL.) RASCETA
CREASED CRUMPLED ACCORDION
CREATE COIN CREE FORM MAKE
PLAN BUILD CAUSE ERECT FORGE
IMPEL RAISE SHAPE WRITE
AUTHOR DESIGN IMPOSE INVENT
COMPACT COMPOSE CONJURE

FASHION IMAGINE PRODUCE COMPOUND GENERATE CONSTRUCT
(— A DISTURBANCE) RIOT
(— CONFUSION) GARBOIL
CREATION WORLD COSMOS EFFECT NATURE POETRY EDITION FACTURE FASHION POIESIS PRODUCT SHAPING BERESHIT BUSINESS CREATURE UNIVERSE
(MENTAL —) FANTASY PHANTASY
(VISIONARY —) DREAM
CREATIVE FERTILE FORMFUL PLASTIC POIETIC FORGEFUL GERMINAL NATURING POMATIVE PROMETHEAN ORIGINATIVE
CREATOR MAKER AUTHOR FATHER FORMER VARUNA WORKER KHEPERA TAGALOA DESIGNER INVENTOR OPERATOR PRODUCER TANGALOA
CREATURE MAN FOOD TOOL BEAST BEING DABBA JOKER SLAVE THING TRICK WIGHT ANIMAL FELLOW MINION PERSON WRETCH CRITTER GANGREL MINIKIN MINIMUS SHAPING CRAYTHUR CREATION HELLICAT
(— OF LITTLE VALUE) SHOT
(CANNIBALISTIC —) WENDIGO WINDIGO
(DISORDERLY —) ROIT ROYT
(DWARF —) FAIRY GNOME
(ELFLIKE —) PERI
(EVIL —) HELLICAT
(FABLED —) LUNG SIREN MERMAN WIVERN ALBORAK MERMAID
(LITTLE —) MITING
(MANGY —) RONION RONYON
(MANLIKE —) HOMINID HOMONID HOMINIAN
(MEAN —) LEFT
(MECHANICAL —) GOLEM
(MISERABLE —) SNAKE
(NONSENSE —) SNARK
(SILLY —) GOOSE
(SMALL —) ATOM GRIG BEASTIE
(SPRY —) WHIPPET
(STUNTED —) WIRL URLING WIRLING
(SUPERNATURAL —) MAN DRAGON
(TINY —) ELF ATOMY
(UNDERDEVELOPED —) SLINK
(UNDERSIZED —) DURGAN
(USELESS —) HUSHION
(VICIOUS —) DEVIL
(WORTHLESS —) SCULPIN SNIPJACK
(WRETCHED —) ARMINE
(3 —S OF A KIND) LEASH
(PL.) CREATION
CRECHE CRIB PUTZ MANGER NURSERY
CREDENCE FAITH TRUST BELIEF BUFFET CREDIT CREANCE CREDENZA
CREDENTIAL VOUCHER CREDENCE
CREDENZA NICHE SHELF TABLE BUFFET SERVER CREDENCE CUPBOARD
CREDIBILITY FAITH CREDIT
CREDIBLE LIKELY CREDENT FAITHFUL PROBABLE

TROWABLE PLAUSIBLE
CREDIT LOAN TICK ASSET CHALK ENDOW FAITH HONOR IZZAT MENSK MERIT STRAP TENET TRUST BELIEF CHARGE ESTEEM IMPUTE RENOWN REPUTE TICKET WEIGHT ACCOUNT ASCRIBE BELIEVE CREANCE JAWBONE OPINION WORSHIP ACCREDIT CREDENCE HEADMARK PRESTIGE
(HOCKEY —) ASSIST
CREDITABLE HONEST CREDIBLE REPUTABLE
CREDITOR DEBTEE SHYLOCK TRUSTER ADJUDGER APPRIZER CRANSIER CREANCER
(TROUBLESOME —) DUN
CREDO FAITH
CREDULITY EASINESS
CREDULOUS FOND SIMPLE SPOONY SPOONEY BOOBYISH CREDIBLE GULLIBLE
CREED ISM LAY CULT SECT CREDO DOGMA FAITH TENET BELIEF KELIMA SYMBOL CREANCE KALIMAH TROWING DOCTRINE SYMBOLUM
CREEK BAY CUT GEO GIO GUT POW RIA RIO RUN VLY VOE BURN COVE HOPE KILL PILL RILL SLEW SLUE VLEI VLEY WASH WICK BACHE BAYOU BIGHT BOGUE BROOK CRICK DRAFT FLEET INLET ZANJA ARROYO BRANCH BREACH CANADA ESTERO SLOUGH STREAM DRAUGHT ESTUARY RIVULET ZANJONA MUSKOGEE
(AUSTRALIAN —) COWAL
(TIDE —) SLAKE
CREEK SEDGE THATCH
CREEL RIP CAUL CAWL HASK JACK KELL RACK TRAP HARSK BASKET JUNKET
(— FOR BOBBINS) BANK SKEWER
CREELER TUBER LIGGER
CREEP COON FAWN INCH RAMP CRAWL CROPE DRIFT GLIDE PROWL SKULK SLINK SMOOT STEAL TRAIL CRINGE GROVEL SCRIDE SPRAWL CRAMBLE CRAMMEL SNIGGLE TAURANGA
(— AS IVY) RIZZLE
(PL.) WILLIES
(PREF.) HERPETI HERPETO
CREEPER IVY JITI SHOE VINE WORM CREEP CROPE SNAKE COWAGE CRADLE IPECAC REPENT ROMPER TECOMA CLAMPER CLIMBER COWHAGE COWITCH CRAWLER REPTANT REPTILE RUNNING TRAILER FOXGLOVE GUITGUIT PICUCULE WOODBINE PERIWINKLE
CREEPING SLOW REPTANT REPTILE SERVILE SERPIGINOUS
(PREF.) HERPET(I)(O)
(SUFF.) (— CREATURE) ERPETON
CREEPING CROWFOOT SITFAST CRAWFOOT
CREEPING SNOWBERRY MOXA TEABERRY
CREESE KRIS STAB CRESS CRISE SWORD DAGGER

CREMATE BURN
CRENEL LOOP CORNEL KERNEL CRENELET
CREOLE PATOIS CRIOLLO DIALECT HAITIAN MESTIZO
(— STATE) LOUISIANA
CREON (DAUGHTER OF —) GLAUCE
(FATHER OF —) MENOECEUS
(SISTER OF —) JOCASTA HIPPONOME
CREOSOTE BUSH LARREA
CREPE CRAPE FRIZZED NACARAT PANCAKE CHIRIMEN CRINKLED WRINKLED
CREPITATE SNAP GRATE RATTLE CRACKLE
CRESCENT HORN LUNE MOON ROOL CURVE LUNAR LUNOID LUNULE MOONED SICKLE WAXAND LUNETTE DEMILUNE MENISCUS
(END OF —) CUSP HORN
(PREF.) MENISCI MENISCO
CRESCENTLIKE BICORN
CRESCENT-SHAPED MOONY LUNATE LUNATED
(PREF.) SELEN(O)
CRESOL FROTHER
CRESPHONTES (BROTHER OF —) TEMENUS ARISTODEMUS
(FATHER OF —) ARISTOMACHUS
(SON OF —) AEPYTUS
CRESS EKER KERSE CUCKOO MADWORT CRUCIFER WHITETOP PEPPERGRASS
CRESSET TORCH BASKET BEACON SIGNAL CRISSET FLAMBEAU
CREST COP TIP TOP ACME APEX COMB EDGE HOOD KNAP PEAK RUFF SEAL TUFT CHINE CROWN PLUME RIDGE COPPLE CREASE CRISTA CUMBRE FINIAL HEIGHT HELMET SUMMIT TIMBER TIMBRE BEARING FEATHER TOPKNOT CENTROID CRESTING ECTOLOPH METALOPH PINNACLE WHITECAP
(— OF BREAKER) SEEGE
(— OF HELMET) COMB CIMIER
(— OF HILL) KNAP
(— OF MINERAL VEIN) APEX
(— OF MOUNTAIN RANGE) ARETE SAWBACK
(— OF PEACOCK) CHAPLET
(— OF RIDGE) EDGE
(— OF SNOW) CORNICE
(— ON BIRD) CROWN ECKLE COPPLE
(IMPERIAL —) KIKUMON
(WAVE —) FEATHER WHITECAP
(PREF.) CRISTI LOPH(I)(IO)(O)
(SUFF.) LOPH(US)
CRESTED COMBED MUFFED TAPPET TAPPIT COPPLED CRISATE CROWNED CRISTATE PILEATED CRISTATED
CRESTED GREBE CARGOOSE
CRESTED QUAIL COPPY
CRESTFALLEN COWED DEJECTED
CRESTING CHENEAU
CRETACEOUS CHALKY
CRETAN KEFTI MINOAN CANDIOT
CRETAN SPIKENARD PHU

CRETE
BAY: SUDA KANCA KISAMO MESARA
CAPE: BUZA LIANO SALOME SIDERO SPATHA STAVROS LITHINON SIDHEROS
CAPITAL: CANEA
GULF: KHANIA MERABELLO
MOUNTAIN: IDA DIKTE JUKTAS LASITHI THEODORE
NAME: CRETA KRETE CANDIA
TOWN: HAG LATO CANEA KHORA SITIA ZAKRO ANOYIA CANDIA KHANIA KISAMO RETIMO KISAMOS KASTELLI HERAKLION

CRETHEUS (FATHER OF —) AEOLUS
(MOTHER OF —) ENARETE
(SLAYER OF —) TURNUS
(SON OF —) AESON PHERES AMYTHAON
(WIFE OF —) TYRO
CRETIN IDIOT
CREUSA GLAUCE GLAUKE
(FATHER OF —) CREON PRIAM ERECHTHEUS
(HUSBAND OF —) AENEAS XUTHUS
(MOTHER OF —) HECUBA PRAXITHEA
(SLAYER OF —) MEDEA
(SON OF —) ION DORUS ACHAEUS ASCANIUS
CREVALLE JACK JUREL
CREVASSE CHASM SPLIT MOULIN SCHRUND CLEAVAGE BERGSCHRUND
CREVICE KIN BORE LEAK NOOK PEEP SEAM VEIN BREAK CHINE CHINK CLEFT CRACK CREEK CUNNE GRIKE CRANNY STRAKE CRANNEL FISSURE GUNNIES KRAVERS OPENING SLIFTER CREVASSE PEEPHOLE
(VOLCANIC —) SOLFATARA
CREW LOT MEN MOB SET BAND GANG GING HERD OARS SHIP TEAM COVIN EIGHT HANDS MEINY PARTY SQUAD STAFF COVINE MEINIE SEAMEN THRONG AIRCREW COMPANY FACULTY MANNING MEMBERS RETINUE EQUIPAGE
(— OF SHEARERS) BOARD
CREWEL CRUEL CADDIS CADDICE
CRIB BED BIN BOX CAB COT CUB HUT KEY BOOM CRUB CURB DIVE JACK PONY RACK RAFT SKIN TROT BOOSE BOOSY CHEAT CRATE FRAME HOVEL STALL STEAL BUNKER CRATCH CRECHE CRITCH MANGER PIGSTY PILFER CABBAGE ENGLISH PURLOIN BASSINET CORNCRIB CRIBBAGE CRIBBING CRIBWORK
CRIBBER SHORER STUMPSUCKER
CRICK KINK CREEK HITCH SPASM TWIST
CRICKET GRIG MOLE SNOB CHANGA SADDLE GRYLLID TWIDDLER ORTHOPTERAN
(— HIT) SLOG

(— SCORE OF 100 RUNS) TON
(PREF.) GRYLLO
CRICKETER CUT COLT PLAYER
RABBIT GENTLEMAN
CRICKET ON THE HEARTH
(AUTHOR OF —) DICKENS
(CHARACTER IN —) DOT MAY JOHN
CALEB BERTHA EDWARD
PLUMMER FIELDING TACKLETON
PERRYBINGLE
CRIER HUER CRYER BEADLE
HERALD WAILER BELLMAN
MUEZZIN WRAWLER OUTCRIER
CRIME ACT SIN EVIL FACT LACK
ABUSE ARSON BLAME CAPER
FOLLY LIBEL WRONG FALSUM
FELONY INCEST MURDER PIACLE
FORFEIT FORGERY MISDEED
OFFENCE OFFENSE INIQUITY
SABOTAGE VILLAINY
MALEFACTION MISDEMEANOR
(ORGANIZED —) GANGLAND
CRIME AND PUNISHMENT
(AUTHOR OF —) DOSTOEVSKI
(CHARACTER IN —) SONIA DOUNIA
LUZHIN PORFIRY PETROVICH
RAZUMIHIN MARMELADOV
RASKOLNIKOV SVIDRIGAILOV
CRIMINAL BAD SORE YEGG CROOK
FELON TOUGH APACHE BASHER
DACOIT GUILTY GUNMAN INMATE
KILLER NOCENT SLAYER WARGUS
WICKED CONVICT CULPRIT
HEINOUS HOODLUM ILLEGAL
MOBSTER NOXIOUS SEVENER
VAUTRIN CRIMEFUL CULPABLE
GANGSTER GAOLBIRD HABITUAL
HARDCASE JAILBIRD PIACULAR
SCELERAT
(HABITUAL —) RECIDIVIST
(PETTY —) ROUNDER
(VIOLENT —) DESPERADO
(PL.) AMALAITA
CRIMINATE IMPEACH
CRIMP BEND CURL FOLD FRIZ
POKE POTE WAVE WEAK CLAMP
CRISP FLUTE FRILL FRIZZ PINCH
PLAIT BUCKLE GOFFER RUFFLE
CRIMPER CRIMPLE CRINKLE
FRIABLE GAUFFER WRINKLE
OBSTACLE
CRIMSON LAC RED PINK GRAIN
BLOODY JOCKEY MAROON
MODENA CARMINE SCARLET
CRAMOISY CREMOSIN
CRIMSON CLOVER NAPOLEON
CRIMSON LAKE SULTAN
CRINED MANED
CRINGE BOW BEND CURB CURR
DUCK FAWN JOUK BINGE COWER
CRAWL CREEP QUAIL SNEAK
SNOOL STOOP WINCE YIELD
BUCKLE CROUCH GROVEL SHRINK
SUBMIT ADULATE CRINKLE
DISTORT SCRINGE TRUCKLE
CRINGER FLUNKEY
CRINGING ABJECT HANGDOG
SERVILE SPANIEL
CRINKLE BEND CURL KINK TURN
WIND CREPE CRISP PUCKER
RIPPLE RUMPLE RUSTLE CRACKLE
CRANKLE FRIZZLE WRINKLE
CRINKLED CRIMP CURLY BUCKLED

ENCOMIC CRISPATE
CRINKLY CREPY CREPEY
CRINOID POLYP CRINITE
CAMERATE COMATULA
(BODY OF —) CROWN
CRINOLINE CRIN HOOP
CRIPPLE MAR CRIP GIMP HARM
HURT LAME MAIM BACACH
HOBBLE IMPAIR INJURE SCOTCH
WEAKEN CRAPPLE CRUMPET
DISABLE LAMETER LAMIGER
LAMITER HANDICAP LAMESTER
MUTILATE PARALYZE
(PL.) LAMZIEKTE
CRIPPLED GIMPY COUPLED
DISABLED
CRIPPLING MAIM MAYHEM
CRISIS FIT ACME CRUX FLAP HEAD
JUMP PASS TURN BRUNT CARDO
CRISE PANIC PERIL PINCH POINT
STATE STORM TRIAL STRAIT
DUNKIRK DECISION JUNCTURE
MOUNTAIN
(AUTHOR OF —) CHURCHILL
(CHARACTER IN —) BRICE GRANT
CARVEL COLFAX ABRAHAM
LINCOLN STEPHEN WHIPPLE
CLARENCE VIRGINIA
CRISP NEW COLD CURL FRIZ FROW
HARD BRISK CLEAR CRIPS CRUMP
CURLY FRESH FRIZZ NIPPY PITHY
SHARP SHORT SPALT STIFF TERSE
BITING BRIGHT CRISPY LIVELY
SNAPPY BRACING BRITTLE
CONCISE CRACKLY CRUNCHY
CUTTING FRIABLE FRIZZLE
SMOPPLE INCISIVE
CRISPED FUZZY FRIZZLY CRISPATE
CRISPINELLA (SISTER OF —)
BEATRICE
CRISPNESS SNAP
CRISSCROSS AWRY CROSS
NETWORK CONFUSED
CRITERION LAW NORM RULE TEST
TYPE AXIOM CANON CHECK
GAUGE MODEL PROOF TOUCH
CRISIS METRIC INDICIA MEASURE
PLUMMET STANDARD
SHIBBOLETH
CRITIC MOME BOOER JUDGE
MOMUS CARPER CENSOR CORNER
EXPERT PUNDIT SLATER SYNDIC
ZOILUS STYLIST ZOILIST
COLLATOR CRITIQUE DEBUNKER
OVERSEER REVIEWER THONGMAN
ARISTARCH
AMERICAN CARY MORE TATE
AIKEN BROWN ELSON FINCK
FISKE KOBBE MABIE POUND
WHITE BECKER BROOKS CHENEY
DOWNES FULLER GILMAN
HUTTON KRUTCH LEDOUX
LOWELL MANTLE MILLER
MUNSON NATHAN PARKER
PHELPS TAYLOR WILSON ALDRICH
ANDREWS HUNEKER WHIPPLE
ATKINSON HAGEDORN
ROSENFELD WOOLLCOTT
CHOTZINOFF
AUSTRALIAN TURNER
AUSTRIAN KUH KRAUS
DANISH LANGE BRANDES
GERSTENBERG

DUTCH BRINK BILDERDIJK
JONCKBLOET VALCKENAER
ENGLISH BELL LAMB READ SHAW
WEST AGATE DILKE ELWIN
GOULD GREIN PAGET PATER
RYMER SCOTT WAUGH ARNOLD
COLLES COLVIN DENNIS HUXLEY
MORGAN PALMER RUSKIN
SYMONS THOMAS WALKER
WARTON AINSLIE BENTLEY
BRADLEY COLLIER COLLINS
FREEMAN GIFFORD JOHNSON
RALEIGH SHORTER SITWELL
STEPHEN WALKLEY WHIBLEY
BEERBOHM MARRIOTT SECCOMBE
STEPHENS MACCARTHY
PARTRIDGE SAINTSBURY
SWINNERTON
FRENCH BIDOU BLAZE GILLE TAINE
FAGUET FRANCE LANSON
BATTEUX BOURGET BREMOND
GAUTIER REGNIER AUBIGNAC
MEZIERES MONTEGUT VALLETTE
BRUNETIERE
GERMAN BAB EYE KERR MERCK
MUNDT OPITZ MENZEL SCHOLL
WAAGEN LESSING NICOLAI
RIBBECK ZARNCKE ACIDALIUS
GREEK ZOILUS ARISTARCHUS
HUNGARIAN KOLCSEY
ICELANDIC BLONDAL
INDIAN ANAND
IRISH BOYD MARTYN
ITALIAN OJETTI OVIDIO BARETTI
CAPUANA ZANELLA CHIARINI
ALGAROTTI CASTELVETRO
CAVALCASELLE
NORWEGIAN WELHAVEN
POLISH LANGE
PORTUGUESE VASCONCELLOS
RUSSIAN PYPIN STASOV BELINSKI
SCOTTISH ARCHER WILSON
JEFFREY
SPANISH CANETE
SWEDISH SIREN LEOPOLD
KELLGREN LEVERTIN
SWISS BODMER
CRITICAL EDGY HIGH NICE ACERB
ACUTE CHILLY CRITIC NASUTE
SEVERE URGENT ACERBIC
ADVERSE CARPING EXIGENT
NERVOUS PARLOUS CAPTIOUS
CARDINAL CAVILING DECISIVE
EXACTING JUDICIAL PRESSING
SLASHING TICKLISH CLIMACTERIC
CRITICISM RAP FIRE FLAK GAFF
SLAM BLAME KNOCK SLATE
ATTACK CRITIC REVIEW CENSURE
COMMENT DESCANT PANNING
QUIBBLE SLASHER SLATING
ZOILISM BLUDGEON CRITIQUE
DIATRIBE JUDGMENT STRICTURE
(PETTY —) NITPICKING
CRITICIZE HIT PAN RAP RIP CARP
CRAB FLAY FLOG SKIN SLAM
SLUR TIDE YELP BLAME BLAST
CAVIL DECRY GRIPE JUDGE
KNOCK ROAST SCORE SLASH
SLATE BERATE CRITIC REBUKE
REVIEW CENSURE COMMENT
CONDEMN CRITIZE EXAMINE
SCARIFY BADMOUTH CRITIQUE
DENOUNCE TOMAHAWK

(— MINUTELY) NITPICK
(— SEVERELY) FLAY JUMP
(— SLASHINGLY) SLASH SLATE
CRITIQUE CRITIC REVIEW
CRITICISM
CRIUS (FATHER OF —) URANUS
(MOTHER OF —) GAEA
(SON OF —) PALLAS PERSES
ASTRAEUS
CRO CROY PAYMENT
CROAK CAW DIE GASP KILL PORK
ROUP CRAKE CREAK CRONK
PLUNK QUALM QUARK SPEAK
CROAPE GRUMBLE COMPLAIN
FOREBODE
CROAKER SPOT RONCO CROCUS
RONCHO TOMCOD BUBBLER
CABEZON CORBINA CORVINA
CABEZONE HARDHEAD KINGFISH
SCIAENID
CROAKING CROAKY HOARSE
RANARIAN COAXATION
CROAT CHORWAT CHROBAT
SYRMIAN
(PL.) HRVATI HERVATI
CROCARD BRABANT SCALDING
SLEEPING
CROCHET HOOK KNIT BRAID PLAIT
WEAVE CROTCHET
CROCK JAR PIG POT SMUT SOIL
SOOT STEAN STEEN STOOL
CHATTY CRITCH GOOLAH
PANMUG SMUDGE CRAGGAN
TERRINE POTSHERD
CROCKERY CHINA CLOAM DISHES
PIGGERY POTWARE CLAYWARE
CROCODILE GOA CROC GATOR
MAGAR CAYMAN GAVIAL JACARE
LIZARD MUGGER YACARE
CRAWLER CREEPER DIAPSID
REPTILE SAURIAN SERPENT
LORICATE
CROCODILE BIRD SICSAC TROCHIL
MESSMATE
CROCUS IRID LILY SAFFRON
COLCHICUM
CROFT FARM TORP CRAFT CRYPT
FIELD GARTH VAULT BLEACH
CAVERN PARROCK PIGHTLE
CROMLECH QUOIT CIRCLE
DOLMEN CROMMEL GORSEDD
CROMORNA CREMONA
KRUMHORN
CRONE HAG AUNT TROT CRONY
WITCH BELDAM RIBIBE BELDAME
CRONY PAL CHUM BILLY GOSSY
NETOP GIMMER GOSSIP
CROOK BEND HOOK TURN WARP
CHEAT CHINK CLEEK CRANK
CROMB CROOM CRUMP CURVE
HUNCH NIBBY PEDUM STAFF
THIEF TRICK CRUMMY INDENT
TWICER CAMBUCA CROSIER
CROZIER CRUMMIE INCURVE
POTHOOK SLICKER ARTIFICE
CHISELER CRUMMOCK SWINDLER
(— IN BRANCH) KNEE
(— OF HEAD) HEEL
(SHEPHERD'S —) CROTCH KEBBIE
CROOKBACKED CROUCHIE
CROOKED CAM WRY AGEE AWRY
BENT GAME WOGH AGLEY ASKEW
BANDY BOWLY CRANK CRUMP

FALSE GLEED KINKY SNIDE
THRAW TIPSY WRONG ACROOK
AKIMBO ARTFUL ASLANT
CAMMED CAMSHO CRABBY
CRAFTY CRANKY CURVED
DOGLEG HURLED THRAWN
TRICKY WEEWAW WEEWOW
ZIGZAG ASKANCE ASQUINT
CORRUPT CRABBED CURVOUS
OBLIQUE TURNING TWISTED
WINDING CAMSHACH THRAWART
TORTUOUS
(PREF.) ANKYL(O) CROM
CROOKEDNESS PRAVITY
RHEBOSIS
CROOKNECK CASHAW CUSHAW
CROON HUM LOW BOOM LULL
SING WAIL CHIRM CRONY WHINE
LAMENT MURMUR TEEDLE
COMPLAIN
CROP BOB COW CUT MAW SET
TOP CLIP CRAP CRAW KNAP MINE
REAP SETT STOW TRAP TRIM
WHIP FRUIT GRAZE PLANT QUIRT
SHAVE SHEAR SHIFT SWATH
TILTH TRASH BROWSE BURDEN
DECERP GATHER GEBBIE SILAGE
BEARING BURTHEN CRAPPIN
CURTAIL CUTTING HARVEST
MAMMONI MASHLUM TILLAGE
GLEANING PROFICHI TRASHIFY
INGLUVIES
(— CANDLEWICK) SNUFF
(— OF A HAWK) GORGE
(— OF FRUIT) HANG
(— OF GRASS) LEA LEY SWATH
SWARTH SWATHE
(— OF OYSTERS) SET
(— OF POTATOES) GARDEN
(— OUT) BASSET
(GREEN —S) SOILAGE
(INDIAN —) RABI KHARIF
(LARGE —) HIT
(RIDING —) ROP
(SECOND-GROWTH —) ROWEN
AFTERMATH
(PL.) FEED TILLAGE
CROPPED GOTCH SHAVED
GOTCHED
CROPPER CARVER MUCKER
PURLER GRINDER PLUMPER
CROPPING EARMARK
CROQUET ROQUE BOMBARD
CROQUETTE CECIL OYSTER
KROMESKI KROMESKY
CROSIER BAGLE CROCE CROOK
PEDUM STAFF POTENT BACULUS
CAMBUCA CROZIER PASTORAL
CROSS GO CAM CUT MIX TAU
ANKH CRUX FORD FUNK MARK
PASS ROOD SIGN SOUR SPAN
TREE WOOD ANGRY CANGY
CHUFF CORSE GAMMY GURLY
SURLY TEATY TESTY THRAW
TRAVE TRIAL YAPPY BISECT
CHUFFY CRABBY CRANKY
CROUCH DENIAL EMBLEM
FRANZY GIBBET GROUTY GRUMPY
HIPPED OUTWIT PATCHY SIGNUM
SNAGGY SNASTY SNUFFY SULLEN
SYMBOL TEETHY THWART
TOUCHY WICKED WOOLLY
ATHWART BECROSS CALVARY

CRABBED CROSIER CROZIER
CRUSADE CRUSADO FRABOUS
FRETFUL FROWARD OBLIQUE
PASSAGE PATIBLE PEEVISH
PETTISH POTENCE SALTIER
SALTIRE CAMSHACH CRANTARA
CROCIATE CROISADE CROSSLET
CROTCHED CRUCIFIX DEBRUISE
DEMISANG FRAMPOLD FRATCHED
FRUMPISH OVERPASS PECTORAL
PETULANT PHRAMPEL SNAPPISH
SWASTIKA THUNDERY TRAVERSE
VEXILLUM WINDMILL
(— BETWEEN GRAPEFRUIT AND
TANGERINE) UGLI
(— BY PLANE) HOP
(— ONESELF) SAIN
(— OVER) SPAN TRAJECT
(DOUBLE —) BUSINESS
(MALTESE —) FIREBALL
(PREF.) CRUCI STAUR(O)
CROSSARM WISHBONE
CROSSBAR RUNG CROWN JUGUM
DRIVER TRANSOM
(— IN GATE) SWORD
(— IN SHAFT) STEMPEL STEMPLE
(— OF BALANCE) BEAM
(— OF DOOR) SLOAT
(— OF WINDOW) LOCKET
CROSSBEAM BAR BUNK SPUR
TRAVE GIRDER BOLSTER
DORMANT TRANSOM TRAVERSE
CROSSBEARER CRUCIFER
SPREADER
CROSSBILL FINCH
CROSSBOW PROD RODD BRAKE
LATCH PIECE PRODD TILLER
SLURBOW ARBALEST BALISTER
BALLISTA STEELBOW STOCKBOW
STONEBOW
(PART OF —) NUT IRON LOCK
GUARD SIGHT STOCK WEDGE
GROOVE STIRRUP TRIGGER
BOWSTRING
CROSSBREED HUSKY METIS
SANGA SANGU HYBRID
CROSS CARRIER CRUCIFER
CROSSCURRENT SURGING
CROSSCUT DRIFT OFFSET TUNNEL
COUPURE
CROSSCUT SAW BRIAR
CROSSCUTTER BUCKER
CROSSE STICK
CROSSED ACROSS SQUINT
WOOFED CRUCIAL THWARTING
(PREF.) CHIASTO
CROSSER STICKER
CROSSETTE EAR ANCON ELBOW
ANCONE CROSET
CROSSEXAMINE TARGE
CROSS-EYE ESOTROPIA
CROSS-EYED SQUINT
CROSS-FERTILIZATION
ALLOGAMY PHYTOGAMY
CROSS FORM URDE URDY
CROSS-GRAINED UGLY NURLY
GNARLED HICKORY CONTRARY
FRAMPOLD
CROSSHEAD YOKE
CROSSING XG PASS CROSS LACED
MIXTURE PASSAGE TRAJECT
CRUCIATE OPPOSING OVERPASS
TRAVERSE CROSSOVER

(KIND OF —) ZEBRA
CROSSPATCH BEAR CRAB
CRANK GROUCH
CROSSPIECE BAR BAIL SPAR STEP
YOKE BEARD GLAND GRILL
ROUND STOCK PUTLOG THWART
TOGGEL TOGGLE BOLSTER
TRANSOM CROSSARM CROWFOOT
FOOTRAIL HEADRAIL TRAVERSE
CHOPSTICK
(PL.) CROSSTREE
CROSS-QUESTION TARGE TAIRGE
CROSSROAD LEET VENT WENT
WEENT CAREFOX CARFOUR
COMPITUM CROSSWAY
(PL.) TRIVIA
CROSSRUFF SAW SEESAW
CROSS-SHAPED CRUCIAL
CRUCIATE
CROSS-STAFF CROSS RADIUS
CROSIER CROZIER ARBALEST
CROSS STROKE BIND
CROSS-TEMPERED FRUMPISH
CROSSWISE CROSS ACROSS
ATHWART ACROSTIC DIAGONAL
OVERWART TRAVERSE WEFTWISE
CROSSWAYS
CROSSWORT MAYWORT
MUGWEED MUGWORT
CROTALUM CROTAL CYMBAL
CROTCH FORK POLE POST CLEFT
NOTCH STAKE CRATCH CRUTCH
GRAINS CROTCHET
CROTCHET FAD TOY HOOK KINK
WHIM CRANK FANCY FREAK
FIZGIG MAGGOT VAGARY
CORCHAT CRANKUM
CROTCHETY KINKY CRANKY
CROUCH HUG BEND CLAP COOK
CURB DARE DROP FAWN FORM
ROOK RUCK COWER HOVER
SQUAT STOOP COORIE CRINGE
CROOCH HUDDLE HUNKER
HURKLE HURTLE SCOOCH
SCOUCH CROODLE CROWDLE
SCROOCH SCRUNCH SQUATTER
CROUCHING SQUAT CROUCHANT
CROUD SCROUGE
CROUP CRUP HIVES CRUPPER
CROUPIER DEALER TOURNEUR
CROUTON DIABLOTIN
CROW AGA CAW CRY DAW BRAG
BRAN CRAW DOWP ROOK AYLET
BOAST CRAKE CROWD EXULT
HOODY KELLY RAVEN VAUNT
CARNAL CHOUGH CORBIE
CORVUS HOODIE KOKAKO
GORCROW GRAPNEL JACKDAW
SWAGGER ABSAROKA BALDHEAD
BLACKNEB GAVELOCK GRAYBACK
GREYBACK
(PREF.) CORACO CORVI
(SUFF.) CORAX
CROWBAR PRY SET CROW BETTY
JEMMY JIMMY LEVER SETUP
SWAPE FORCER GABLOCK
PITCHER GAVELOCK HANDSPEC
CROWBERRY HEATH HEATHER
CROWD FRY HUG JAM MOB SET
TAG TIP BIKE CRAM CRUT FARE
HEAP HERD HOST JOSS MONG
PACK PAVE PILE PUSH RAFT
ROCK ROTE ROUT RUCK SERR

SKIT SLUE SORT STOW SWAD
TURB WOOD BUNCH CLOUD
COHUE COVEY CRAMP CRUSH
CRWTH DROVE FLOCK GROUP
HORDE HURRY PLUMP POSSE
PRESS ROTTA SERRY SHACK
SHOAL STECH STIVE STUFF
SWARM THREE VOLGE WEDGE
BOODLE CHORUS CLIQUE HUBBLE
HUDDLE HUSTLE IMPACT JOSTLE
MITHER MOIDER OUTFIT PESTER
RABBLE RESORT SCRUZE THRAVE
THREAD THRIMP THRONG
THRUST TOURBE TYMPAN
VOLLEY BOUROCK CHROTTA
CLUSTER COMPANY CONGEST
IMPRESS JIMBANG SCROOGE
SCROUGE SQUEEZE THICKEN
THRUTCH CABOODLE ENTHRONG
FREQUENT JINGBANG SANDWICH
SATURATE VARLETRY
CONCOURSE GATHERING
MULTITUDE CLAMJAMFRY
(— ABOUT) FLOCK
(— AROUND) BESIEGE
(— OUT) DISPLACE
(— TOGETHER) HUG HOTTER
HOWDER HUDDLE CLUTTER
CONTRUDE
(CONFUSED —) HURRY
(MOVING —) DROVE
(NOISY —) ROUT
(PREF.) OCHLO
CROWDED PANG CLOSE DENSE
SPISS STIFF THICK FILLED SPISSY
THRONG BUNCHED COMPACT
OPPLETE POPULAR SERRIED
STIPATE STUFFED TEEMING
NUMEROUS POPULOUS
CROWFOOT JOY PAGLE CREATE
EXOGEN PAIGLE EELWARE
GOLDCUP GOLLAND GOWLAND
BANEWORT CRAWFOOT
GOLDWEED HELLWEED
CROWING COCK
CROWN CAP TAJ TIP TOP BULL
COIN GULL HELM PALE PATE
PEAK POLL RIGO TIAR ADORN
BASIL BEZEL BEZIL CREST MITER
MITRE MURAL POLOS REGAL
ROUND ROYAL TIARA ANADEM
CANTLE CIRCLE CLIMAX CORONA
DIADEM DOLLAR FILLET INVEST
LAUREL POTONG REWARD
SUMMIT TIMBER TROPHY
UPWARD VALLAR VERTEX
WREATH AUREOLE CHAPLET
CORNICE CORONAL CORONET
FORETOP GARLAND INSTALL
PSCHENT STEPHEN TONSURE
CORONATE CORONULE
ENTHRONE PINNACLE SURMOUNT
TURNPIKE
(— OF CHICORY) ENDIVE
(— OF EGYPT) ATEF PSCHENT
(— OF HEAD) NOLL PATE SKULL
CANTLE POMMEL FORETOP
(— OF HILL) KNAP
(— OF LAUREL) BAY
(— OF ROCK) KRANTZ
(HALF —) GEORGE ALDERMAN
(PIECE OF —) BULL
(PLANT —) STOOL

(PREF.) CORONI CORONO STEPHAN(O)

CROWNED CORONATE LAURELED
(— WITH ROSES) ROSATED
CROW SHRIKE MAGPIE SQUEAKER
CROW'S NEST LOOKOUT
CROZER CHUCKER
CRUCIAL KEY ACUTE PIVOT NEEDLE SEVERE TRYING PIVOTAL SUPREME TELLING CRITICAL DECISIVE
CRUCIAN CARP GIBEL
CRUCIBLE POT DISH ETNA SHOE TEST CRUCE FOYER CRUSET HEARTH MONKEY RETORT FURNACE CROSSLET
CRUCIFIX PAX ROOD CROSS
CRUCIFIXION RANSOM
CRUCIFY VEX HANG KILL HARRY MORTIFY TORMENT TORTURE CRUCIATE
CRUDE ILL RAW BALD BARE RUDE BRUTE CRASS GREEN GROSS HAIRY HARSH ROUGH TACKY CALLOW COARSE DOUGHY INCULT KUTCHA SAVAGE UNRIPE VULGAR ARTLESS GLARING SQUALID UNCOUTH AGRESTIC IGNORANT IMMATURE IMPOLITE INDIGEST PRIMITIVE
(NOT —) DELICATE
CRUDELY HARSHLY GAUCHELY
CRUDITY BARBARITY CRASSNESS GAUCHERIE ROUGHNESS
CRUEL ILL FELL GRIL GRIM HARD BLACK BREEM BREME BRUTE FELON HARSH RETHE SADIC STERN WROTH BITTER BLOODY BRUTAL DIVERS DREARY FIERCE IMMANE SAVAGE SEVERE UNJUST UNKIND UNMEEK UNMILD UNRIDE WANTON WICKED BESTIAL BOARISH BRUTISH GRIMFUL INHUMAN NERONIC SCADDLE SPITOUS WILROUN BARBARIC DIABOLIC FELONOUS FIENDISH INHUMANE PITILESS RUTHLESS SADISTIC TYRANNIC TRUCULENT
CRUELLY FELL HARD CRUEL FELLY HARSHLY
CRUELTY RIGOR DURESS SADISM DEVILRY DEVILTRY FELLNESS SEVERITY
CRUET AMA JAR JUG VIAL BURET CRUSE BOTTLE CASTER CREVET CREWET GUTTUS AMPULLA BURETTE URCEOLE
CRUISE SAIL TRIP JUNKET STOOGE
(— AS A PIRATE) BUSK
CRUISER SHIP VALUER VESSEL WARSHIP ESTIMATOR
CRULLER WONDER OLYCOOK OLYKOEK TWISTER DOUGHNUT
CRUMB BIT ORT MURL NIRL PIECE LITTLE MORSEL CRIMBLE CRUMBLE MEALOCK MURLACK REMNANT FRAGMENT
(PL.) PANADA PANURE MOOLINGS
CRUMBLE ROT CRIM MULL MURL MUSH BREAK BROCK CRUSH DECAY RAVEL SLAKE SPALL SPOIL

BUCKLE MOLDER MYRTLE PERISH SLOUGH CORRADE CRIMBLE MOULDER COLLAPSE
(— DOWN) GRUSH
(— UNDER OVERWEIGHT) FLUSH
CRUMBLED UNDURE
(EASILY —) CRIMP BRUCKLE CRUMBLY
CRUMBLING SAMEL SAMMEL POWDERY
CRUMBLY NESH MURLY CRUMBY CRUMMY FRIABLE PULVERULENT
CRUMPET CAKE MUFFIN PIKELET
CRUMPLE FOLD MOOL MUSS ROOL WISP CRUSH SCREW BUCKLE CREASE FURROW RAFFLE RUCKLE RUMPLE CRIZZLE CRUNKLE FRUMPLE SCRUNCH WRINKLE COLLAPSE CONTRACT SCRUMPLE
CRUNCH BITE CHEW MUCH CHOMP CRASH CRUMP CRUSH GNASH GRIND PRESS RUNCH CRANCH CRINCH GRANCH GROWSE CRAUNCH SCRANCH SCRUNCH
CRUPPER CROUP CURPEL CURPIN TAILBAND
CRUSADE WAR JEHAD JIHAD CROISEE CAMPAIGN CROCIATE
CRUSADER PILGRIM TEMPLAR EQUITIST REFORMER
(PL.) CROISES
CRUSADER IN EGYPT (CHARACTER IN —) ADRIANO ALADINO ARMANDO PALMIDE DORVILLE ELMIRENO
(COMPOSER OF —) MEYERBEER
CRUSH BOW HUG JAM BEND BORE BRAY CASE CHEW CRAM DASH MASH MILL MULL PASH RAVE STUB BRAKE BREAK BRIZZ CHAMP CHECK CRASH CRAZE CREEM CROWD FORCE FRUSH GRIND GRUSH PRESS QUASH QUELL SMASH SMUSH SQUAB SQUAT STAMP TREAD UNMAN BRUISE BURDEN CRUNCH DEFOIL DEFOUL KNATCH KNETCH SCOTCH SCRUSH SCRUZE SQUASH SQUISS SUBDUE THRING THRONG THWACK ACCABLE BECRUSH CONQUER CONTUSE CRACKLE CRUMPLE DEPRESS DESTROY OPPRESS OVERRUN REPRESS SCRUNCH SCRUNGE SHATTER SQUEEZE SQUELCH SUCCUMB TRAMPLE COMPRESS FORBREAK OVERCOME SQUABASH SUPPRESS OVERWHELM
(— BEANS) NIB
(— HAT) BONNET
(— IN) STAVE
(— ROCK) DOLLY DOLLEY DOLLIE
(— SPIRIT) BREAK
CRUSHABLE QUASHY
CRUSHED TAME BROKEN ECRASE MUSHED CONTRITE CRUMPLED
CRUSHER NIBBER
CRUSHING FIERCE BRUISING SMASHING SQUABASH
(SUFF.) TRIPSY
CRUST FUR PIP CAKE HULL RIND SCAB SHELL SKULL COFFIN

CRUSTA ESCHAR GRATIN HARDEN RONDLE SCRUFF ABAISSE CALICHE COATING ENCRUST INCRUST CARAPACE PELLICLE SCUTULUM WINEBALL DURICRUST
(— OF DIKE) SALBAND
(— ON WINE) ARGAL ARGOL
(PIE —) HUFF COFFIN
(PL.) SORDES
CRUSTA PES
CRUSTACEAN BUG APUS CRAB FLEA SCUD ZOEA ALIMA CARID KRILL LOUSE PRAWN SCREW SCROW CYPRID ENDITE ISOPOD SHRIMP SLATER SQUILL ARTEMIA COPEPOD CRAYLET DAPHNID DECAPOD GRIBBLE HAYSEED LOBSTER SQUAGGA SQUILLA AMPHIPOD BARNACLE CIRRIPED CRAYFISH GAMMARID LERNAEAN MONOCULE OSTRACOD PAGURIAN SQUILLID BRACHYURA PHYLLOPOD SCHIZOPOD SHELLFISH MALACOSTRACAN RHIZOCEPHALAN
CRUSTADE DARIOLE
CRUSTY CURT BLUFF BLUNT RUSTY TESTY MOROSE SULLEN CRABBED PEEVISH PETTISH STARCHY SNAPPISH
CRUTCH FORK STILT CLUTCH CRATCH CROTCH POTENT SADDLE SCATCH STADDLE
CRUX NUB GIST HALF PITH CROSS POINT PUZZLE RIDDLE PROBLEM
CRUX ANSATA ANKH
CRWTH ROTA ROTE CROWD CRUTH ROTTA ROTTE CROUTH CHROTTA
CRY HO BOO CAW CRI FAD HOA HUE OLE PIP SOB YIP BAWL BELL BUMP CALL COWL CROW EVOE FALL GLAM GOWL HAIL HAWK HOOT HOWL KEEN MEWL NOTE OYES OYEZ PULE RAGE RAME RANE REEM RERD ROOP SCRY SIKE TOOT WAIL WEEP YELL YELP BARLA BLART BLORE CHEVY CLEPE CRAKE CROUP CRUNK GREDE GREET GROAN QUEAK RUMOR SHOUT SOUND TROAT UTTER VOGUE WHEWL WHINE WHULE WRAWL BARLEY BELLOW BOOHOO CHIVVY CLAMOR DEMAND ENSIGN LAMENT OUTCRY QUETHE SCREAM SHRIEK SLOGAN SNIVEL SQUALL SQUAWL SQUEAL TONGUE WIMICK YAMMER EXCLAIM FASHION HOSHANA SCREECH SPRAICH GARDYLOO PROCLAIM SCRONACH
(— ALOUD) BLART GREDE
(— AT SIGHT OF WHALE) FALL
(— DOWN) DOWNCRY BERATTLE
(— FOR TRUCE) BARLA BARLY BARLEY
(— HOARSELY) CROUP
(— LIKE ELEPHANT) BARR TRUMPET
(— LIKE PIG) WRINE
(— OF A BAT) CHIP
(— OF ABORIGINES) COOEE

(— OF BACCHANALS) EVOE
(— OF BIRD) CAW COO PEW BOOM CAWK CLANG BIRDCALL
(— OF BITTERN) BILL
(— OF CAT) MEW MEWL MIAOU MIAOW MIAUL MIAUW CALLING
(— OF CONTEMPT) BOO
(— OF DEER) BELL
(— OF ENTHUSIASM) BANZAI
(— OF GOOSE) HONK YANG
(— OF GUINEA HEN) POTRACK
(— OF HOUND) MUTE MUSIC
(— OF JACKAL) PHEAL PHEALE PHEEAL
(— OF MOURNING) KEEN TANGI
(— OF NEWBORN CHILD) VAGITUS
(— OF RAVEN) QUALM
(— OF SHEEP) BAA BLAT BLEAT
(— OF SNIPE) SCAPE
(— OF SORROW) ULLAGONE
(— OF SURRENDER) KAMERAD
(— OF WATCHMAN) WATCH
(— OUT) BAY BAWL BRAY GALE GAPE HOOT HOWL JERK SCRY BLORE CHIRM CLAIM ESCRY SHOUT HALLOO HOLLER SCREAM SHRIEK THREAP THROPE BREATHE EXCLAIM RECLAIM DISCLAIM PROCLAIM
(— TO CLEAR PASSAGE) HALL
(— TO COMBATANTS) BAILE
(— UP) CRACK
(BATTLE —) CRY ENSIGN MONTJOY GERONIMO MONTJOYE
(DRINKING —) RIVO
(HOARSE —) CROAK
(HUNTING —) TIVY CHEVY CHIVY CHEVVY STABOY YOICKS TALLYHO TANTARA TANTIVY PILILLOO
(PROLONGED —) RANE
(RALLYING —) SLOGAN
(RAUCOUS —) CATCALL
(SHRILL) SKIRL SQUEAK SQUEAL SCREECH YALLOCK
(WAR —) DIN ALALA HAVOC BANZAI SLOGAN
(WORDLESS —) KEEN ULULU
CRYING PIPING URGING CLAMANT HEINOUS VAGIENT PRESSING RECREANT
(— OF HOUND) BELLING
CRYPT PIT CRAFT CROFT CROWD VAULT CAVERN GROTTO RECESS SHROUD CHAMBER FOLLICLE
CRYPTIC DARK VAGUE HIDDEN OCCULT SECRET OBSCURE ELLIPTIC MYSTICAL SIBYLLIC
CRYPTOGAM ACROGEN
CRYPTOGAMOUS AGAMIC AGAMOUS
CRYPTOGRAM CODE CRYPT CIPHER
CRYPTOGRAPH GEMATRIA
CRYPTOGRAPHER VIGENERE
CRYPTORCHID RIDGLING

CRYSTAL XL ICE DIAL DOME HARD IRIS SEED XTAL CLEAR GLASS GRAIN LUCID LUNET NICOL TABLE GLASSY LIMPID MIRROR NEEDLE PEBBLE QUARTZ TABLET ACICULA DIAMOND DIPLOID GLASSIE LUNETTE ORTHITE TWOLING

ULEXITE YAJEINE ZOISITE
FIVELING FOURLING PELLUCID
TRICHITE TRILLING PERIMORPH
PHENOCRYST
(— FOREIGN TO ROCK) XENOCYST
(— OF GREAT STRENGTH) WHISKER
(FINE —) BERYL
(ICE —S IN WATER) FRAZIL
(NEEDLE-SHAPED —S) RAPHIDES
(ROCK —) BRISTOL CITRINE
(TWIN —) TWIN MACLE TWINDLE
TWOLING FOURLING
(PL.) DRUSE GRAIN
(PREF.) CHRYSTO
(SUFF.) BLAST(IC)(Y) HEDRON
CRYSTAL GAZE SCRY
CRYSTAL GAZER SEER SCRYER
SKRYER
CRYSTALLINE PURE CRYSTAL
PELLUCID
CRYSTALLITE BELONITE TRICHITE
BACILLITE SCOPULITE
CRYSTALLIZE FIX FIRM JELL
CANDY SUGAR NEEDLE CONGEAL
SOLIDIFY
CRYSTALLOGRAPHY LEPTOLOGY
C-SHAPED SIGMATE
CTENIDIUM COMB
CTENOPHORE RIB NUDA CESTOID
CYDIPPID JELLYFISH
CUADRA MANZANA
CUB FRY PEN BEAR CHIT COOP
SHED TOTO STALL WHELP LIONET
NOVICE CODLING REPORTER
(— SCOUT) WEBELOS

CUBA

BAY: NIPE PIGS
CAPE: CRUZ MAISI LUCRECIA
CAPITAL: HAVANA
CIGAR: HAVANA
COIN: PESO CENTAVO CUARENTA
DANCE: CONGA RUMBA DANZON
   RHUMBA GUARACHA
   PACHANGA
FALLS: TOA AGABAMA CABURNI
GULF: MEXICO ANAMARIA
   BATABANO
INDIAN: CARIB TAINO ARAWAK
ISLAND: PINES
ISLANDS: SABANA CAMAGUEY
MEASURE: VARA BOCOY TAREA
   CORDEL FANEGA
MOUNTAIN: TURQUINO
MOUNTAINS: CRISTAL MAESTRA
   ORGANOS TRINIDAD
PROVINCE: HAVANA ORIENTE
   CAMAGUEY MATANZAS
RIVER: ZAZA CAUTO
SWAMP: ZAPATA
TOWN: COLON MANES ALAMAR
   BAYAMO GUINES HAVANA
   BARACOA HOLGUIN PALMIRA
   ARTEMISA CAMAGUEY
   GUAYABAL MATANZAS
   SANTIAGO
TREE: JIQUE JIQUI
WEIGHT: LIBRA TERCIO

CUBAN LILY SCILLA
CUBBYHOLE NOOK CUBBY
CUBE CUT DIE NOB KNOB BLOCK
EIGHT SOLID TIMBO BABASCO

CUBELET TESSERA BARBASCO
QUADRATE TESSELLA
(— OF BREAD) CROUTON
(MEAT —S) CABOB KABOB KEBOB
(PL.) DICE
CUBIC SOLID CUBOID CUBICAL
CUBICALLY DIEWISE
CUBIC CENTIMETER FLUIGRAM
CUBICLE BAY CELL ROOM BOOTH
CABIN NICHE STALL ALCOVE
CARREL CARRELL
CUBIC METER STERE
CUBIT ELL CODO HATH COVID
HASTA COUDEE
CUB SHARK LAMIA GALEID
REQUIEM
CUCKING STOOL THEW TUMBLER
TUMBREL TUMBRIL
CUCKOLD TUP HORN BECCO
VULCAN WITTOL ACTAEON
CORNUTE CORNUTO HORNIFY
RAMHEAD COKEWOLD
CUCKOLDED FORKED UNICORN
CUCKOLDRY HORNWORK
CUCKOO ANI COWK CUCK FOOL
GOUK GOWK KOEL KOIL CLOCK
CRAZY KOKIL SILLY COUCAL
DIDRIC HUNTER KOBIRD
BOOBOOK CHATAKA DIEDRIC
KOWBIRD SIRKEER CHOWCHOW
PICARIAN RAINBIRD RAINFOWL
(PREF.) CUCULI
CUCKOOFLOWER HEAD PAGLE
SPINK CUCKOO PAIGLE
HEADACHE MILKMAID
CUCKOOPINT ARUM RAMP AARON
BOBBIN DRAGON BUCKRAM
OXBERRY MANDRAKE
CUCKOO SPIT WOODSERE
CUCULLATE COWLED HOODED
COVERED
CUCUMBER CUKE PEPO GOURD
CONGER CUCURB PEPINO PICKLE
GHERKIN PICKLER CUCURBIT
PEPONIDA PEPONIUM
(BITTER —) COLOCYNTH
(SHRIVELED —) CRUMPLING
(WILD —) SICYOS CREEPER
(PREF.) CUCUMI
CUCURBIT BODY FLASK GOURD
CUCURB ALEMBIC MATRASS
CUD CHEW QUID BOLUS QUEED
RUMEN CUDGEL
CUDBEAR CORK PERSIO PERSIS
CUDWEED
CUDDLE HUG LAP PET CARESS
COSSET FONDLE HUGGLE KIDDLE
KIUTLE NESTLE PETTLE CROODLE
CRUDDLE EMBRACE SMUGGLE
SNOOZLE SNUGGLE CANOODLE
CUDDLESOME HUGGABLE
CUDDY ASS LOUT BRIBE CABIN
DONKEY GALLEY PANTRY
CUDEIGH
(BELOVED OF —) BUXOMA
CUDGEL BAT CUD BEAT CANE
CLUB CRAB DRUB KENT MACE
RACK RUNG TREE BASTE BATON
BILLY DRIVE KEBBY KEVEL LINCH
LINGE SHRUB STAFF STAVE STICK
THUMP TOWEL ALPEEN BALLOW
BASTON BILLET GIBBET KEBBIE
LIBBET THRASH WASTER

BELABOR BOURDON DRUBBER
SWADDLE SWINGLE TROUNCE
BLUDGEON SHILLALA THWACKER
CUDWEED ENAENA CATFOOT
CUE QU NOD TAG TIP HINT MAST
TAIL WINK BRAID CLUFF PLAIT
QUEUE TWIST PROMPT SIGNAL
PIGTAIL
(BILLIARD —) MACE MAST STICK
(MUSICAL —) PRESA
(PART OF —) TIP BUTT HILT JOINT
POINT SHAFT BUMPER FERRULE
(SHUFFLEBOARD —) SHOVEL
(TIP OF —) LEATHER
CUFF BOX BANK BLOW GOWF
SLAM SLAP SLUG SWAT TURF
CLOUT FIGHT GOWFF MISER
SCUFF SCUFT SMITE SOUSE
BUFFET CODGER FENDER MITTEN
STRIKE TURNUP COLPHEG
SCUFFLE WHERRET GAUNTLET
HANDBLOW HANDCUFF
TURNBACK
CUIR DORADO
CUIRASS CURACE CURATE CURIET
LORICA THORAX
CUIRASSIER LOBSTER
CUISINE FOOD MENU TABLE
COOKERY KITCHEN
CUITLATEC TECO
CUL-DE-SAC POCKET STRAIT
IMPASSE
CULL OPT CAST COIL DUPE GULL
PICK PIKE SIFT SORT ELECT
GLEAN PLUCK ASSORT CHOOSE
GARBLE GATHER REMOVE SELECT
CULLING SEPARATE
CULLET SCRAP
CULM COOM HAULM SLACK
COOMBE REFUSE DEPOSIT
(PL.) SIRKI SIRKY
CULMINATION END ACME APEX
AUGE CULM NOON ROOF BLOOM
CREST CROWN HIGHT POINT
APOGEE CLIMAX CULMEN
CUMBLE HEIGHT PERIOD SUMMIT
VERTEX ZENITH BLOWOFF
CULPABILITY BLAME FAULT GUILT
DEMERIT
CULPABLE FAULTY GUILTY
LACHES SINFUL IMMORAL
BLAMABLE CRIMINAL
CULPRIT FELON CONVICT
CRIMINAL OFFENDER
CULT CLAN DADA SECT CREED
KUKSU CHURCH CULTUS DOMNEI
MANISM NUDISM RITUAL SCHOOL
SHINTO AMIDISM DADAISM
ICONISM MYALISM MYSTERY
WORSHIP DEVILISM HUMANISM
SATANISM
(SUFF.) ISM
CULTCH CUTCH STOOL SCULCH
CULTIVATE EAR HOE CROP DISC
DISK FARM GROW PLOW REAR
TEND TILL WORK DRESS EARTH
LABOR NURSE RAISE STUDY
TRAIN AFFECT FOSTER FURROW
HARROW MANAGE MANURE
PLOUGH RATOON SARCLE
SCHOOL ACQUIRE CHERISH
CONTOUR CULTURE EDUCATE
EMBRACE EXPLOIT HUSBAND

IMPROVE NOURISH PREPARE
SCRATCH CIVILIZE
(— FAVOR) BOOTLICK
CULTIVATED ABAD TAME CIVIL
GROWN POLITE SATIVE TOILED
POLITIC REFINED CULTURED
ARTIFICIAL
(ARTIFICIALLY —) HOTHOUSE
CULTIVATION CROP TILTH FINISH
GROWTH CULTURE TILLAGE
TILTURE LABORAGE MANURAGE
REFINEMENT
(— IN MANNERS) FINISH
(MENTAL —) HUMANITY
CULTIVATOR JAT KMET RYOT
ILAVA SULKY FARMER GADABA
HARROW ILAVAN MAMOTY
MILLER RIDGER TILLER FLORIST
GRUBBER HUSBAND MEADOWER
ROSARIAN SCUFFLER
(— GANG) RIG
(PL.) LAETI
CULTURAL HUMANIST
CULTURE ART AGAR STAB KULLI
NASCA NAZCA SHAKE SLANT
SLOPE TAJIN TASTE TILTH
JHUKAR KULTUR POLISH STREAK
WILTON ABASHEV ANANINO
AZILIAN IRANISM JHANGAR
KAYENTA SOCIETY STARTER
TILLAGE HUMANISM LEARNING
(ESKIMO —) DORSET
(MEXICAN —) MAZAPAN
CULTURED CIVIL POLITE LETTERED
CULVERIN SLING CULVER
LANTACA PELICAN SPIROLE
CULVERT FOX GOUT DRAIN SLUIT
BRIDGE CONDUIT CULBERT
PINNOCK PONCEAU OVERPASS
CUMBER BURDEN CUMMER
SHACKLE
CUMBERSOME GOURD HEAVY
CLUMSY UNRIDE AWKWARD
LUGSOME ONEROUS WEIGHTY
CUMBROUS UNWIELDY
CUMMER GIRL LASS WOMAN
KIMMER
CUMMERBUND BAND BELT SASH
CUMULATE HEAP GATHER
COMBINE
CUMULATIVE CHAIN SUMMATIVE
CUNA CUEVA DARIEN
CUNEIFORM ULNARE WEDGED
CUNNER CANOE NIPPER WRASSE
BURGALL CHOGSET GOLDNEY
NIBBLER BERGGYLT
BLUEFISH CORKWING
GILTHEAD
CUNNING ART OLD SHY SLY WIT
ARCH CUTE DEEP FAST FINE
FOXY KEEN SLIM SNOD TRAP
WILY WISE CANNY CRAFT
DOWNY FAVEL GUILE LOOPY
PAUKY PAWKY POKEY SHARP
SMART ADROIT ARTFUL ASTUTE
CALLID CLEVER CRAFTY DAEDAL
DECEIT ENGINE FOXERY PRETTY
QUAINT SHREWD SUBTLE SUPPLE
TRICKY WISDOM COMPASS
CRAFTLY CURIOUS FINESSE
KNOWING PARLISH PARLOUS
POLITIC PRACTIC SLEIGHT
SUBTILE VARMINT VULPINE

CONTOISE DEXTROUS MANAGERY QUENTISE SKILLFUL SLEIGHTY STEALTHY YEPELEIC

CUNNING LITTLE VIXEN
(CHARACTER IN —) LAPAK PRIEST HARASTA TERYNKA FORESTER SHARPEARS GOLDENMANE SCHOOLMASTER
(COMPOSER OF —) JANACEK
CUNNINGLY YEPLY YEPELY
CUP AMA BOX CAN DOP MUG NOG POT TOT TUN TYG CELL DOPP HORN LOTA PECE SHOE SKEW TASS TOSS BOUSE CALIX CHARK COGUE COPPE CRUSE CYLIX DEPAS GLASS GODET GRAIL KITTY PHIAL SCALE STEIN STOOP STOUP TAZZA THECA BEAKER BICKER BUCKET BUMPER CAPPIE CHOANA COTYLA CRATER CUPULA DOBBIN EGGCUP EYECUP FALSIE FESSEL FINJAN GOBLET JICARA KOTYLE MAZARD NAGGIN NOGGIN OXHORN POTION RUMKIN TASSIE VESSEL BRIMMER CAPSULE CHALICE CHEERER CYATHUS GODDARD KYATHOS QUONIAM SCYPHUS SHERBET STIRRUP THIMBLE TRINKET VENTOSE BRIDECUP GRADUATE PANNIKIN STANDARD TJANTING
(— FOR HOLDING DIAMOND) DOP DOPP
(— FOR PERFUMES) CONCH
(— FOR YEAST) SKEP
(— IN SAUCER OF ALCOHOL) ETNA
(— OF FLOWER) BELL
(— OF TEA) DISH SPEED OYSTER
(— ON BULLET) GASCHECK
(— WITH COVER) HANAP
(ASSAYING —) CUPEL
(DRINKING —) CAN MUG NUT TIG TUN TYG CANN HORN TASS TOSS GODET BEAKER GOBLET HOLMOS QUAICH RUMMER CHALICE GODDARD TRINKET
(FAIRY —) COOLWORT
(FILLED —) BUMPER
(IRISH —) MADDER METHER
(IRON —) CULOT MUSHROOM
(LARGE —) FACER BLACKJACK
(LEATHER —) WELL GISPIN
(LONG-HANDLED —) CYATH DIPPER CYATHUS KYATHOS
(MAPLE —) MAZER
(NAUTICAL —) THIEF
(ORNAMENTAL —) TAZZA
(PAPER —) DIXIE
(PASTRY —) DARIOLE
(PRIZE —) PEWTER
(SACRED —) GRAIL
(SHALLOW —) CYLIX TAZZA TASTER CAPSULE
(SMALL —) DOP NOG TOT DOPP TASS DOBBIN NAGGIN NOGGIN TASSIE
(SQUARE —) MADDER METHER
(STIRRUP —) BONAILIE
(WOODEN —) COG COGUE CAPPER CAPPIE METHER QUAICH
(PL.) VALONIA
(PREF.) CALATHI CALICI COTYL(I)(O) CUPULI CYATH(I)(O)

POCILLI SCYPH(I)(O)
(SUFF.) COTYL(LY)(OUS)
CUPBEARER HEBE SAKI CUPPER GANYMEDE
CUPBOARD CUB KAS BOLE CASE COIN SAFE AMBRY CHEST CUBBY CUDDY HUTCH PRESS ABACUS AUMBRY BUFFET CLOSET LARDER LOCKER PANTRY SPENCE ALMIRAH ARMOIRE CABINET DRESSER SKIBBET ALHACENA CREDENCE CREDENZA TROSTERA
(ARCHERY —) ASCHAM
CUPEL TEST
CUPFUL CUP CAROUSE
CUP HOLDER ZARF
CUPID DAN AMOR EROS LOVE PUTTO CHERUB AMORINO AMOURET AMORETTO
(PL.) PUTTI
CUPIDITY LUST GREED DESIRE AVARICE AVIDITY LONGING APPETITE RAPACITY
CUPOLA DOME KILN TYPE VAULT BELFRY TURRET CALOTTE FURNACE LANTERN LOOKOUT CIMBORIO COCKLOFT
(ROUND —) THOLUS
CUPOLAMAN HEATER
CUPPED GLENOID
CUPPING GLASS VENTOSE
CUPSEED NUTSEED
CUP-SHAPED PEZIZOID SCYPHATE
CUPULE CUP BOLSTER CYATHUS THUMBMARK
CUR DOG YAP FICE FIST FYCE MUTT TIKE TYKE FEIST KEOUT BRAKJE MESSAN MESSIN BOBTAIL MONGREL WHAPPET
CURABLE SANABLE
CURARE URARE URARI OORALI WOORALI
CURASSOW MITU COPPY HOCCO MITUA PAUXI
CURATE ABBE CURA AGENT VICAIRE MINISTER
CURATIVE HEALING IATRICAL PHYSICAL REMEDIAL SALUTARY SANATIVE
CURATOR KEEPER STEWARD GUARDIAN OVERSEER
CURB BIT LID CRUB FOIL KERB REIN SKID SNIP SNUB BRAKE CHECK CRIMP CURVE GUARD LIMIT MOUND ARREST BOTTLE BRIDLE COERCE COLLAR DECKLE GOVERN HAMPER STIFLE STRAIN SUBDUE THWART CONTROL CURBING INHIBIT REFRAIN REPRESS SHACKLE ATTEMPER COMPESCE MODERATE RESTRAIN RESTRICT WITHHOLD
(OFFICIAL —) LID
(WELL —) PUTEAL
CURCULIO TURK WEEVIL
CURCUMA ZEDOARY
CURD CRUD DAHI CHEESE CURDLE CASEINE CLABBER CONGEAL COAGULUM
(— IN MILK) ZIEGA
(—S AND WHEY) SLIP PINJANE
(BEAN —) TOFU
(PL.) SKYR FLEETINGS

(PREF.) THROMB(O)
CURDLE CAP LOP RUN SAM SET CRIM CURD EARN LEEP QUAR SAMM SOUR TURN WHIG YERN CARVE QUAIL QUARL SPOIL YEARN CAILLE LAPPER LOBBER LOPPER POSSET QUARLE CLABBER CONGEAL CRIDDLE CRUDDLE THICKEN CONDENSE
CURDLED CURDLY QUARRED SHOTTEN
(NOT —) UNCRUDDED
CURE DIP DRY DUN FIX BEEF BOOT CARE CORN HEAL HEED HELP JERK MEND SALT SANE SAVE AMEND BLOAT BOTEN LEECH REEST SMEEK SMOKE CHARGE CURATE KIPPER PHYSIC PRIEST RECURE REMEDY SEASON SUCCOR TEMPER WARISH BESMOKE RECOVER RESTORE THERAPY TREACLE ANTIDOTE BARBECUE CURATION GUERISON PRESERVE REVOCERY
(— A HABIT) BREAK
(— BY SMOKING) GAMMON SMUDGE
(— FISH) DUN ROUSE
(— GRASS) HAY
(— HAY) WIN
(— HERRINGS) BLOAT
(— IN SUN) RIZZAR
(— SKINS) DRESS
(COUGH —) SAPA SAPE
CURE-ALL BALM AVENS ELIXIR REMEDY PANACEA THERIAC
CURED SALT BLOATED
CURIOSITY CURIO ODDITY INTEREST
(— OF SMALL VALUE) GABION
(—S OF THE CITY) LIONS
(PL.) CURIOSA
CURIOUS ODD NOSY RARE SELI QUEER SELLE SELLY PRYING QUAINT SNOOPY CUNNING STRANGE UNUSUAL FREAKISH MEDDLING PECULIAR SINGULAR
CURL BOB BEND COIL FEAK FURL KINK LOCK PURL ROLL TUBE WAVE WIND ACKER CANON CRIMP CRISP DILDO FRILL FRIZZ QUIRL SPIRE TRESS TWIRE TWIST BERGER BUCKLE CANNON CRUCHE CURDLE FROWSE MULLET RIPPLE SPIRAL TUNNEL WRITHE CRIDDLE CRIMPLE CRINKLE CROCKET CRUDDLE EARLOCK FLEXURE FRIZZLE FROUNCE RINGLET SERPENT TENDRIL WHISKER FAVORITE LOVELOCK SQUIGGLE
(— HAIR) CROOK
(— OF SMOKE) WREATH
(— OF WIG) SNAKE
(— ON FOREHEAD) CRUCHE CROUCHE
(— OVER) BREAK
(— UP) CRUMP HUNCH SNIRL HUDDLE SHRINK SNUGGLE
(FRINGE OF —S) FRISETTE FRIZETTE
(METAL —) CHIP
(SMALL —) CROCK
(PREF.) CIRR(I)(O) CIRRH(I)(O)

CURLED CRISP FUZZY KINKY SPIRY CIRRATE COCKLED CRISPED FRIZZLY SAVOYED WREATHY CRISPATE CRUMPLED GAUFFRED GOFFERED HELICINE SCROLLED
CURLER GOFFER TEASER CRIMPER FRIZZER MULLETS
CURLEW FUTE JACK SPOW KIOEA SNIPE SPOWE WHAAP WHAUP DIKKOP MARLIN SMOKER BANKERA BUSTARD DOEBIRD BLUELEGS WHIMBREL SICKLEBILL
CURLICUE ESS CAPER CURVE CASSIS PARAPH SQUIRL FLOURISH PURLICUE SCRIGGLE SQUIGGLE
CURLING MARK TEE
CURLING MATCH SPIEL
CURLING STONE IRON STONE LOOFIE GRANITE
(— SPIN) RAISE
CURLY WAVY CRISP CRULL OUNDY CRIMPY RIPPLED CRINKLED
(— HAIR) VEDDOID
CURMUDGEON CRAB CHURL HUNKS MISER GLEYDE GROUCH NIGGARD
CURMUDGEONLY STINGY
CURRANT PASA BERRY CASSIS RAISIN RIZZAR RIZZLE CORINTH
(PL.) RIBES SPICE
CURRANT BUN WIG WIGG
CURRAWONG SQUEAKER STREPERA
CURRENCY CASH COIN PASS BILLS CATER MONEY SCRIP SERIES SPECIE PASSAGE WILDCAT
(FRACTIONAL —) SPONDULIX
(SHELL —) UHLLO
CURRENT NOW WAY EDDY FLOW FLUX FORD RACE RIFE TIDE VEIN WAFT ALIVE DRIFT GOING RAPID ROUST SCOUR SWIFT TENOR TESLA TREND USUAL ABROAD ACTUAL COEVAL COMMON COURSE DOUCHE DURANT FLUENT LATEST LIVING MOTION MOVING OFFSET OUTSET RECENT RIZZER RULING SLUICE STRAND STREAM TONGUE VOLANT COUNTER DRAUGHT FLOWING FRESHET GENERAL INDRAFT INSTANT PASSANT PRESENT RUNNING STICKLE THERMAL TORRENT BACKWASH CURRANCE DOWNCAST FREQUENT MILLRACE OCCURENT PASSABLE TIDERACE TODAYISH UNDERTOW
(— IN SPEECH) WAIF
(AIR —) DRAFT SHEET SPLIT BREEZE DRAUGHT DOWNCAST DOWNFLOW
(ELECTRIC —) STRAY
(HOT —) BACK
(JAPAN —) KUROSHIO KUROSIWO
(PREVAILING —) MAINSTREAM
(RAPID —) SWIFT TONGUE
(SOUND —) DISTORTION
(STRONG —) GALE ROOST ROUST
(PREF.) RHEO
CURRENTLY ANYMORE
CURRICULUM STREAM PROGRAM PROGRAMME

CURRISH BASE CYNICAL DOGGISH
IGNOBLE SNARLING
CURRY COMB DRUB KARI CLEAN
DRESS GROOM BRUISE CAJOLE
CARREE POWDER PREPARE
TARKEEAN
(— FAVOR) HUG NUT QUILL
COTTON SMOOGE CUITTLE
SMOODGE
CURSE BAN POX BANE BLOW CUSS
DAMN OATH PIZE WARY BLAST
BLESS CORSE SHREW SPELL
SWEAR WEARY WINZE DETEST
DEVOTE GOOFER GUFFER
MAKUTU MALIGN MAUGER
MAUGRE ACCURSE BESHREW
MALISON ANATHEMA EXECRATE
FORSPEAK MALEDICTION
CURSED DASH CUSSED DAMNED
DASHED ACCURSED
CURSER WARIER
CURSING BLESSING BLASPHEMY
CURSIVE RUNNING
CURSORY FAST BRIEF HASTY
QUICK SHORT FITFUL ROVING
SPEEDY PASSANT PASSING
SHALLOW CARELESS RAMBLING
CURT BUFF RUDE TART BLUFF
BLUNT BRIEF BRUSK NIPPY
SHORT SQUAB TERSE ABRUPT
CURTAL CUTTED SNIPPY
BRUSQUE CONCISE CRYPTIC
LACONIC CAVALIER SNAPPISH
SNIPPETY SUCCINCT
CURTAIL CUT LOP CLIP CROP
DOCK PARE STOP ABATE ELIDE
SHORT SLASH STUNT TRUNK
DECURT LESSEN REDUCE
ABRIDGE BOBTAIL CRACKLE
SHORTEN DIMINISH MINORATE
RETRENCH
CURTAILED TAIL CUTTY SHORT
STUNT CURTAL BOBTAIL CONCISE
ABRIDGED
CURTAIN END BOOM DROP IRIS
MASK VEIL WALL BLIND DRAPE
SCENE SHADE SHEET VELUM
COSTER HANGER PURDAH
SCREEN SHROUD CEILING
CONCEAL CORTINE DRAPERY
HANGING VITRAGE ASBESTOS
PORTIERE TRAVERSE
(CHURCH —) CLOTH RIDDEL
ENDOTYS ENDOTHYS
(THEATER —) IRON SCRIM TEASER
TRAVELER TORMENTER
CURTAIN ROD TRINGLE
CURTAIN STRETCHER SCRAY
STRAINER
CURTAL CRAPE COURTAL
CURTLAX
CURTSY BOB BOW DIP DOP BECK
DROP JOUK KNEE CONGE HONOR
CURCHY
CURUBA CASSA BANANA
CURVATED STUNT HOOKED
CURVATURE ARC PLY ARCH BENT
BOOL CURL CURVE SHEER SINUS
CAMBER CURVITY ADUNCITY
APOPHYGE CYRTOSIS GRYPOSIS
KYPHOSIS LORDOSIS
(— OF BONE) ARCUATION
(— OF DECK) SHEER

(— OF LEGS) RHEBOSIS
(— OF SHOE SOLE) SWING
(— OF SPINE) KYPHOSIS SCOLIOSIS
(— OF STOMACH) FUNDUS
(— OF STRAKE) SPILING
CURVE ARC BOW CUP ESS SAG
ARCH BEND BOUT COME CURB
FADE HOOK KNEE LINE OGEE
TURN VEER WIND AMBIT BIGHT
BREAK CONIC CROOK CRUMP
CUBIC HELIX NONIC OGIVE PEDAL
POLAR QUIRK SLICE SWEEP
SWIRL TARVE TREND TWIST
WITCH BOUGHT CAMBER CIRCLE
DEFLEX JORDAN LITUUS SOLVUS
SPIRAL SPRING TOROID WIMPLE
ADIABAT BRACKET CAUSTIC
CIRCUIT CISSOID COMPASS
CONCAVE CONTOUR COSEISM
CURVITY CYCLOID ELLIPSE
ENVELOP FESTOON FLEXURE
INCURVE INFLECT LIMACON
PHUGOID PROFILE QUARTIC
SCALLOP SINUATE SOLIDUS
CARDIOID CATENARY CONCHOID
DYGOGRAM ELASTICA EXTRADOS
FADEAWAY INTRADOS INVOLUTE
LIGATURE LIQUIDUS OPHIURID
PARABOLA SINUSOID TONOGRAM
TRACTRIX TROCHOID
CATACAUSTIC
(— DESCRIBED BY GRAPH) GRAM
(— IN HANDRAIL) KNEE
(— IN PLANKING) HANG
(— IN SAIL) ROACH
(— OF ARCH) INTRADOS
(— OF BALL) DROP
(— OF BIT) LIBERTY
(— OF COLUMN) APOPHYGE
(— OF FINGERNAIL) GRYPOSIS
(— OF HORSE'S NECK) CREST
(— OF PLANK) SNY
(— OF SHIP'S BOW) FLAIR FLARE
(— OF TIMBER) CUP
(— SATISFYING EQUATION)
BRANCH
(— SPACE) KNOT
(— WHEN DRAWN) COME
(BASEBALL —) SNAKE
(CRICKET —) SWERVE
(DOUBLE —) CIMA CYMA
(PLANE —) ROSE STROPHOID
(PLANE CUBIC —) WITCH
(VERTICAL —) RAMP
CURVED BENT SOFT ADUNC
CORBE CURVE CURVY ROUND
WOUND CONVEX CURVEY
GYRATE HAMATE TURNED
ARCUATE ARRONDI CONCAVE
CROOKED CURVANT EMBOWED
FALCATE SIGMOID ADUNCOUS
ANCHORAL AQUILINE ARCIFORM
CRUMPLED CYGNEOUS
DECURVED EXCURVED SCROLLED
ARCHIFORM
(PREF.) ANCYLO ANKYLO
CAMPTO CAMPYL(O) CURVI
CURVO CYRT(O)
(SUFF.) CLASTIC
CURVET HOP LEAP LOPE SKIP
TURN BOUND CAPER FRISK
PRANK VAULT CAVORT CROUPE
FROLIC GAMBOL PRANCE

PANNADE CORVETTO CROUPADE
CURVING SPIRY SIMOUS TWISTY
AQUILINE DRAWDOWN
(— IN) CONCAVE
(DOWN —) EPINASTY
(SMOOTHLY —) FAIR
CUSH (FATHER OF —) HAM
CUSH-CUSH CARA YAMPEE
CUSHION BAG COD MAT PAD PIG
BALL BANK BOSS PUFF SEAT
SUNK TRIM GADDI GADHI PANEL
SQUAB TRUSH BUFFER INSOLE
JOCKEY MUSNUD PILLOW
SACHET BOLSTER BRIOCHE
COSSHEN HASSOCK KNEELER
MUFFLER PILLION REPOSAL
ROOTCAP CUTIDURE OREILLER
PULVINAR PINCUSHION
(LACE-MAKERS —) BOTT
(PIN —) PRINCOD
(SEAT —) BANKER
(TAILOR'S —) HAM
(PREF.) PULVILLI PULVINI
CUSHIONING DUNNAGE
CUSHIONLIKE PULVINAR
CUSHION PLANT POLSTER
CUSHIONY PADDY
CUSHITIC NUBIAN
CUSK COD TUSK TORSK BURBOT
CATFISH
CUSP APEX CONE HORN PEAK
ANGLE POINT STYLE TOOTH
CORNER SPINODE ENTOCONE
HYPOCONE METACONE
PARACONE
CUSPID CANINE
CUSPIDOR GABOON CRACHOIR
SPITTOON
CUSSO KOSO KOUSSO BRAYERA
BRAZERA
CUSTARD FLAN FOOL CREME
FLAWN DOUCET DOWCET
CHARLET PARFAIT FLUMMERY
DIABLOTIN ZABAGLIONE
CUSTARD APPLE ANONA
ANNONA PAWPAW CORAZON
SWEETSOP
CUSTODIAN HACK GUARD BAILEE
CUSTOS KEEPER SEXTON
WARDEN WARDER CURATOR
JANITOR CERBERUS CLAVIGER
GUARDIAN CONCIERGE
CUSTODY LAP BAIL CARE HOLD
KEEP WARD TRUST ARREST
CHARGE SAFETY YEMSEL
CONTROL DURANCE KEEPING
TUITION COMMENDA CUSTODIA
HANDFAST SECURITY WARDSHIP
CUSTOM FAD LAW MOS PAD TAX
URE USE WON ASAL DUTY FORM
GARB MODE MORE RITE ROTE
RULE THEW TOLL WONE WONT
FUERO GUISE HABIT HAUNT
RITUS STYLE SUNNA TRADE
TREAD TRICK USAGE VOGUE
BYRLAW DASTUR DHARMA
GROOVE IMPOST MANNER
MINHAG MONTEM PRAXIS
SUNNAH USANCE COSTUME
DUSTOOR DUSTOUR FASHION
FORMULA HALAKAH TRIBUTE
USAUNCE WARNOTH BUSINESS
ENDOGAMY HABITUDE PRACTICE

ASSUETUDE CONSUETUDE
PRESCRIPTION
(BINDING —) LAW
(BUSINESS —) TRADE GOODWILL
(CHILDBIRTH —) COUVADE
(CHURCH —) COMITY
(CORRUPT —) ABUSE
(FESTIVAL —) HOCKING
(OUTMODED —) ARCHAISM
(PRIMITIVE —) COUVADE
(RURAL —) HEAVING
(SECRET —) SANDE
(TEMPORARY —) FAD VOGUE
(PL.) MORES MOEURS HAIKWAN
FOLKLORE PROPRIETIES
CUSTOMARILY USUALLY
CUSTOMLY
CUSTOMARY PER RIFE TAME
USED NOMIC USUAL BEATEN
COMMON SOLEMN VULGAR
WONTED CLASSIC GENERAL
REGULAR USITATE EVERYDAY
FAMILIAR HABITUAL ORTHODOX
(NOT —) INSOLENT
CUSTOMER CHAP COVE BUYER
CLIENT PATRON SUCKER
ACCOUNT CALLANT CHAPMAN
PATIENT SHOPPER MERCHANT
PROSPECT
(PRINTER'S —) AUTHOR
(TOUGH —) HARDCASE
(PL.) CUSTOM CLIENTELE
CUSTOMHOUSE ADUANA
DOGANA DOUANE
CUSTOM-MADE BESPOKE
BESPOKEN
CUSTOMS OFFICER SHARK
WAITER
CUT AX ADZ AXE BOB DAG DAP
DIE HAG HEW KIT LOP MOW NIP
RIT SAW SNY TAP ADZE BANG
BITE BOLO BOLT BUZZ CHIP CHOP
CLIP CROP DADO DOCK FACE
FELL FILE GASH GIRD HACK HASH
HEWN JERK KNAP LIMB MAKE
MODE MUSH NICK OCHE PARE
RACE RASH RAZE REAP SIDE SKIN
SLIT SLOT SMIT SNEE SNEG SNIP
SNUB STOW SUMP SWAP SWOP
TAME TRIM VELL VIDE BEVEL
BLOCK BREAK CANAL CANCH
CARVE CHIVE CHYND CLEFT
COPSE COUPE CRIMP DRESS
FLICK FRAZE FRITH GOUGE
GRAVE GRIDE GROOP HOWEL
KITTE KNIFE LANCE LATHE MINCE
NOTCH PLATE PRUNE RAZEE
SABER SABRE SCALP SCARP
SCIND SCORE SEVER SHAPE
SHARE SHEAR SHIVE SHRED SKICE
SKISE SLASH SLICE SLICK SLISH
SLIVE SNICK SPLIT STAMP SWEEP
SWIPE SWISH TOUCH TWITE
VOGUE WHITE ABLATE AJOURE
BARBER BISECT BROACH CAMBER
CHISEL CLEAVE CORNER CUTTED
DIVIDE EXCISE FIGURE FLETCH
FLITCH FRENCH GROOVE GULLET
HACKLE HAGGLE INCISE INCIDE
INCISE INDENT LESSEN MANGLE
OUTPUT RASURE REDUCE RIPPLE
SCORCH SCOTCH SCRIBE SCYTHE
SLIGHT SLIVER SNATHE STRAIT

STREAK SULLET SWINGE TAILYE
THWITE TRENCH AFFRONT
CONVERT CURTAIL CUTTING
DIACOPE DISCIDE DISSECT
DRAWCUT ENGRAVE FASHION
FRITTER HATCHET SCALPEL
SCISSOR SCUTTLE SECTILE
TAILZEE WHITTLE DISSEVER
FRACTION INCISION INCISURE
INTAGLIO LACERATE MALAHACK
RETRENCH THWITTLE
(— A THREAD) CHASE
(— AN OPENING) BREACH
(— AT ANGLE) CANT BEVEL
(— AT RANDOM) SLASH
(— AWAY) COPE SLIT UNDO
ABATE CONCISE
(— BACK) HEAD SPUR
(— BARK) CHIP
(— BEAM) KERF
(— CARS) LIFT
(— CHEESE) HARP
(— CLAY) SLING
(— CORNERS) SKIRT CHAMFER
CHAMPHER
(— CRUST) CHIP
(— DEEPLY) DIG SHANK
(— DIAGONALLY) CATER SLANT
(— DOWN) MOW FELL STAG STUB
RAZEE SCANT SCARP ABRIDGE
SHORTEN RETRENCH
(— FANCY FIGURE) DASH
(— FISH) SOLAY STEAK
(— FOR FODDER) CHAFF
(— GEAR TEETH) RATCH
(— GLASS) SPLIT
(— GRAIN) BAG FAG CRADLE
SWINGE
(— HAIR) DOD
(— IN) INSECT INCISED
(— IN A TREE) FACE
(— IN BARREL STAVE) HOWEL
(— IN EXCAVATIONS) GULLET
(— IN RELIEF) ENCHASE
(— IN SOFT ROCK) CAVATE
(— IN SQUARES) CHECK
(— INTO LARGE SLICES) WHANG
(— INTO SLIPS) ZEST
(— INTO STRIPS) JERK FLETCH
FLITCH JULIENNE
(— INTO TREE) BOX
(— JAGGEDLY) HACK SNAG
(— LEDGES) BENCH
(— LOGS) LUMBER
(— OF FISH) JOWL
(— OF GEM) STAR
(— OF GRAIN) MELL
(— OF MEAT) ARM SEY CROP HOCK
SHIN SIDE CHUCK SHANK STEAK
BRISKET FORESEY ICEBONE
SIRLOIN EDGEBONE FORERIBS
(— OF RIFLING) GROOVE
(— OFF) BOB LOP CLIP CROP DOCK
KILL PARE SHUT SLIT STAG BELEE
CROSS ELIDE PRUNE SCIND
SEVER SHAVE SHEAR SKIVE SLIPE
SPIKE COUPED DECIDE EXEMPT
FORCUT RESECT SHIELD STIFLE
SWATCH ABJOINT ABSCIND
ABSCISE ABSCISS CURTAIL
EXSCIND ISOLATE PRECIDE
RESCIND AMPUTATE CLEIDOIC
DESECATE RESECATE

RETRENCH TRUNCATE
(— OFF BY BITS) DRIB
(— OFF END) BUTT
(— OFF WOOL) DOD DODD
(— OPEN) SPLAY
(— OUT) DESS DINK CLICK
BROACH EXCIDE EXCISE EXSECT
(— PATH) FRAY
(— SALMON) CHINE
(— SHEEP) TOMAHAWK
(— SHORT) BOB COW HOG LOP
BANG CROP DOCK JIMP SNIB
BOBBED CURTAL HOGGED
BOBTAIL CHAPPED CONCISE
SCANTLE PRESCIND
(— TENDONS) ENERVATE
(— THE THROAT) JUGULATE
(— THE WAVES) SNORE
(— THINLY) CURL
(— TO PIECES) CHOP DICE MINCE
BRITTLE FRITTER
(— TO SIZE) TAIL
(— TURF) VELL
(— UNDER) KIRVE
(— UNEVENLY) CHATTER
(— UP) TUSK CARVE CHINE JOINT
PRANK SPOIL TRAIN GOBBET
COLLOPED
(— UP SWAN) LIFT
(— WHALE BLUBBER) LEAN FLENSE
(— WITH BACKWARD SLOPE) COOT
(— WITH DIE) DINK BLANK
(— WITH SHEARS) SHIRL
(— WITH SICKLE) BAG REAP
(COLD —S) ASSIETTE
(CREW —) BUTCH FLATTOP
(DEEP NARROW —) JAD
(FENCING —) STRAMAZON
(LARGE — OF FOOD) DODGE
(NOT —) UNCORVEN
(SHORT —) ATAJO
(SLIGHT —) SNICK SCOTCH
(THIN —) TARGET
(PREF.) SEC(O) TEMNO TOMO
(SUFF.) COPATE COPE SECT
SECTED TOMA TOME TOMIC
TOMOUS TOMY
CUT-AND-DRIED CANNED
CUTANEOUS DERMAL
CUTCH GAMBIR CATECHU
GAMBIER
CUTE COY KEEN COONY DINKY
DUCKY SHARP CLEVER PRETTY
SHREWD CUNNING DARLING
CUTICLE DERM HIDE SKIN SHUCK
THECA MEMBRANE PELLICLE
(— OF EGGSHELL) BLOOM
CUTLASS SWORD CURTAL DUSACK
HANGER TESACK CURTAXE
MACHETE SHABBLE CAMPILAN
CUTLASS FISH HIKU SAVOLA
KALKVIS MACHETE HAIRTAIL
CUTLET SCHNITZEL
CUTOVER COUPE
CUTPURSE NIP BUNG THIEF
HORNTHUMB
CUTTER DIE BEEF BOAT IRON MILL
PONE SLED BRAVO FACER FRAZE
SLOOP SMACK BAYMAN CHERRY
COLTER COTTER DOCKER EDITOR
FRAZER MINCER SLEIGH SLICER
CLIPPER COULTER DROMOND
INCISOR RUFFIAN KNIFEMAN

REVENUER SCHOKKER SHEPSTER
(— OF STONES) LAPIDARY
(BRICK —) RUBBER
(PEAT —) PINER
(WIRE —) SECATEUR
CUTTERHEAD WABBLER WOBBLER
CUTTHROAT THUG BRAVO
CUTTER RUFFIAN SWORDER
CUTTHROAT TROUT MYKISS
CUTTING CUT HAG RAW SET ACID
CARF CURT KEEN KERF SECT
SETT SLIP TART TWIG ACUTE
BLEAK CHECK CRISP EAGER
EDGED GRIDE SCION SCRAP
SCROW SHARP SMART BITING
BITTER BORING ENTAIL GODOWN
GORING JAGGED PHYTON PIPING
SECANT SEVERE SNITHE BURNING
CAUSTIC GRIBBLE INCISAL
MORDANT NICKING OVERCUT
PAINFUL PIQUANT POLLING
SARMENT SATIRIC SECTION
SLICING CHILLING CLEARING
INCISIVE PIERCING POIGNANT
QUICKSET SCATHING SCISSION
SNAPPISH WOUNDING
TRENCHANT
(— FOR DIRT-CAR TRACK) GULLET
(— FOR WATER) TAJO
(— FROM PLANT) SLIP SHROUD
SARMENT PROPAGULE
TRUNCHEON
(— OF DEER) SAY
(— OF TREES) HAG
(— OFF) AVULSION
(— SHORT) ABORTIVE
(DRILL —S) MUD
(OBLIQUE —) BARBING
(SECOND —) ROWEN
(WASTE —) SELVAGE SELVEDGE
(SUFF.) THEMA THESIS TOMA
TOME TOMIC TOMOUS TOMY
(— OUT) ECTOMY
CUTTLEBONE SEPIA SEPION
SEPIUM GLADIUS SEPIARY
CUTTLEFISH SEPIA SHELL SQUID
CUDDLE CUTTLE SCRIBE CATFISH
DECAPOD INKFISH MOLLUSK
OCTOPUS SCUTTLE
(PREF.) TEUTHIS
CUVETTE POT TUB TANK BASIN
BUCKET TRENCH CISTERN
CYANEE (DAUGHTER OF —) BYBLIS
(FATHER OF —) MAEANDER
(HUSBAND OF —) MILETUS
(SON OF —) CAUNUS
CYANIDE NITRILE CYANURET
PRUSSIATE
CYANIPPUS (FATHER OF —)
PHARAX
(WIFE OF —) LEUCONE
CYANITE SAPPARE DISTHENE
CYANOGEN PRUSSIN PRUSSINE
CYBELE RHEA KYBELE AGDISTIS
(DAUGHTER OF —) JUNO
(FATHER OF —) URANUS
(HUSBAND OF —) SATURN
(MOTHER OF —) GAEA
(SON OF —) JUPITER NEPTUNE
CYCAD BANGA CICAD ZAMIA
COONTIE CYCADITE
CYCHREUS (DAUGHTER OF —)
GLAUCE

(FATHER OF —) NEPTUNE
POSEIDON
(MOTHER OF —) SALAMIS
CYCLADES (ISLAND OF —) IOS KEOS
DELOS MELOS NAXOS PAROS
SYROS TENOS ANDROS AMORGOS
KYTHNOS SANTORIN SERIPHOS
CYCLAMEN BACCHAR PRIMWORT
SOWBREAD
CYCLE AGE EON ERA AEON BIKE
EPOCH KALPA PEDAL PRIME
ROUND SAROS SECLE WHEEL
BAKTUN CIRCLE COURSE CYCLUS
PERIOD BICYCLE CIRCUIT DICYCLE
TRICYCLE
(— OF WORK) ROTA JOURNEY
(—S CAUSED BY KARMA) SAMSARA
SANSARA
(BUSINESS —) JUGLAR KITCHIN
(LUNAR —) SAROS
(ONE — PER SECOND) HERTZ
(SECONDARY —) EPICYCLE
CYCLIC CYCLAR ANNULAR
CYCLICAL PERIODIC
CYCLIST CYCLER WHEELER
WHEELMAN
CYCLOLITH CROMLECH
CYCLOMETER ODOGRAPH
VIAMETER
CYCLONE GALE GUST WIND BLAST
STORM BAGUIO TORNADO
TWISTER TYPHOON SECONDARY
NEUTERCANE
CYCLOPARAFFIN NAPHTHENE
CYCLOPEAN HUGE VAST STRONG
MASSIVE COLOSSAL GIGANTIC
CYCLOPS ARGES BRONTES
COPEPOD STEROPES
CYCLORAMA CYKE PANORAMA
CYCLOSIS STREAMING
CYCLOSTOME HAGFISH
CYCNUS (DAUGHTER OF —)
HEMITHEA
(FATHER OF —) ARES MARS
NEPTUNE POSEIDON
(MOTHER OF —) CALYCE PYRENE
PELOPIA
(SON OF —) TENES
(WIFE OF —) PROCLEA
PHYLONOME
CYLINDER CAN EKE GIG TIN BEAM
BOMB BURR CAGE CANE DRUM
LEAD MUFF PIPE PRIM ROLL SLUG
TUBE WELL BLOCK CORER DRAIN
FIBER FIBRE FUDGE SCREW SHELL
SPOOL STELA STELE SWIFT
BARREL BOBBIN BUTTON
COLUMN COPPER DECKER
DOFFER DUSTER FILTER GABION
PISTON PLATEN ROLLER SCREEN
TIPITI TUMBLE URCHIN WORKER
CUTCHER SLEEVER SLUDGER
SUCCULA FOLLOWER GRADUATE
NEURAXIS SPARKLET
(— AROUND MOLD) COTTLE
(— FOR DANCE RHYTHM) CLAVE
(— OF STEAM WHISTLE) BELL
(— OF TISSUE) CORTEX
(— OF YARN) CAKE
(— ON LOOM) BEAM
(— WITH PERFORATIONS) FLUSHER
(—S PULLED THROUGH DUCT)
MANDREL

(ARMORED —) BARBETTE
(GLASS —) MUFF
(HOLLOW —) PIPE TUBE
(MARKING —) LEAD
(NAPPING —) GIG
(RELAY —) BATON
(REVOLVING —) BEATER ROLLER
(TOOTHED —) SPROCKET
(WATERMARK —) DANDY
CYLINDRICAL ROUND TERETE
  TOROSE CENTRIC TUBULAR
  TERETIAL
  (PREF.) TERETI
CYMA GOLA GULA OGEE DOUCINE
  MOLDING CYMATIUM
CYMA REVERSA HEEL
CYMBA YET
CYMBAL ZEL CHIME TARGET
  CROTALUM KYMBALON
  (PL.) TAL BECKEN PIATTI
CYMBELINE (AUTHOR OF —)
  SHAKESPEARE
  (CHARACTER IN —) CAIUS HELEN
  CLOTEN IMOGEN LUCIUS
  MORGAN IACHIMO PISANIO
  BELARIUS LEONATUS PHILARIO
  ARVIRAGUS CORNELIUS
  CYMBELINE GUIDERIUS
  POSTHUMUS
  (SON OF —) ARVIRAGUS
  GUIDERIUS
CYMBIUM MELO
CYME CYMULE BOSTRYX
CYMLING SIMNEL CYMBLIN

SCALLOP PATTYPAN
CYMOSE DEFINITE SYMPODIAL
CYMRY KYMRI WELSH
CYNIC SATYR TIMON DOUBTER
  APEMANTUS
CYNICAL CYNIC SULLEN CURRISH
  DOGGISH DOGLIKE CAPTIOUS
  SARDONIC SNARLING JAQUESIAN
  MISOGYNIC PESSIMISTIC
  MISANTHROPIC
CYNOCEPHALUS AANI
CYNORTES (BROTHER OF —)
  HYACINTHUS
  (FATHER OF —) AMYCLAS
  (MOTHER OF —) DIOMEDE
  (SON OF —) PERIERES
CYNOSURE SHOW LODESTAR
CYPRESS CULL SABINO SIPERS
  FIREBALL AHUEHUETE
  BELVEDERE
CYPRESS SPURGE BALSAM
  NAPOLEON
CYPRIPEDIUM CYP DUCK
  NERVINE

CYPRUS
CAPE: GATA GRECO ANDREAS
  ARNAUTI ZEVGARI
CAPITAL: NICOSIA
COIN: PARA
MEASURE: OKA OKE PIK CASS
  DONUM KOUZA GOMARI
  KARTOS MEDIMNO
MOUNTAIN: TROODOS

RIVER: PEDIAS PEDIEOS
TOWN: POLIS CITIUM PAPHOS
  KYRENIA LARNACA MORPHOU
  NICOSIA LIMASSOL FAMAGUSTA
WEIGHT: OKA OKE MOOSA
  KANTAR

CYRANO DE BERGERAC (AUTHOR
  OF —) ROSTAND
  (CHARACTER IN —) CYRANO
  ROXANE VALVERT DEGUICHE
  CHRISTIAN
CYRENE (FATHER OF) HYPSEUS
  (MOTHER OF —) CHLIDANOPE
  (SON OF —) IDMON DIOMEDES
  ARISTAEUS
CYRILLA TITI
CYRUS KORESH
CYST BAG SAC WEN POUCH
  CYSTUS RANULA DERMOID
  HYDATID HYGROMA SACCULE
  VESICLE ATHEROMA DACRYOPS
  MUCOCELE STEATOMA
CYSTOPTERIS FILIX
CYTOKININ ZEATIN
CYTOLYSIN AMBOCEPTOR
CYTOME SPHEROME
CYTOPLASM MASSULA OOPLASM
  PLASMON DIASTEMA
  (PREF.) PLASTO
CZAR CSAR IVAN TSAR TZAR
  PETER NICHOLAS
CZARDAS CSARDAS
  (SECTION OF —) FRISS

LASSU FRISZKA
CZECH CECH TSECH TSCEKH
  BOHEMIAN

CZECHOSLOVAKIA
BEER: PILSEN
CAPITAL: PRAHA PRAGUE
CASTLE: HRADCANY
COIN: CROWN DUCAT HALER
  HELLER KORUNA
DANCE: POLKA REDOWA FURIANT
MEASURE: LAN SAH MIRA KOREC
  LATRO STOPA MERICE STRYCH
MOUNTAIN: ORE TATRA SUDETEN
PROVINCE: BOHEMIA MORAVIA
  SLOVAKIA
REGION: BOHEMIA MORAVIA
  SLOVAKIA
RIVER: UH MZE VAG VAH DYJE
  EGER ELBE GRAU HRON IPEL
  ISAR ISER LABE NISA ODER
  OHRE OLSE OPPA WAAG BECVA
  DUNAJ MARCH NITRA SLANA
  TISZA DANUBE HORNAD
  MOLDAU MORAVA ONDAVA
  SAZAVA TORYSA VLTAVA
  LABOREC LUZNICE BEROUNKA
TOWN: AS ASCH BRNO CHEB EGER
  MOST BRUNN OPAVA PLZEN
  TABOR TUZLA AUSSIG BILINA
  KLADUS PILSEN PRESOV VSETIN
  ZVOLEN BUDWEIS JIHLAVA
  OSTRAVA TEPLITZ

D

D DE DEE DOG DELTA

DAB DAP DOB DOT DUB HIT PAT BLOW CHIT DAUB LICK LUMP PECK SPOT CLOUT DHABB DIGHT LEMON SMEAR BLOTCH EXPERT STRIKE DABSTER PORTION SPLOTCH FLATFISH FLOUNDER MARYSOLE SANDLING

DABBER BALL PROD TAMPON

DABBING PICKING

DABBLE DAB DIB MESS DALLY DIBBLE MEDDLE MUDDLE PADDLE POTTER SOSSLE SPLASH TAMPER TRIFLE DRABBLE MOISTEN PLOUTER PLUTTER SMATTER SPATTER DELIBATE SPRINKLE (— WITH BLOOD) ENGORE

DABBLER AMATEUR DABSTER

DABCHICK GREBE DIPPER DOBBER DOPPER PUFFER HENBILL DIDAPPER DOPCHICK

DACE CHUB DARE DART CYPRINID GRAYLING

DACHSHUND DACHS TECKEL BADGERER

DACOIT DAKU DAKOO ROBBER CRIMINAL

DACTYL TOE FOOT FINGER

DACTYLOPODITE POLLEX

DACTYLOZOOID PALPON

DACTYLUS DACTYL DIGITUS

DAD BEAT BLOW DAUD HUNK LUMP PAPA KNOCK THUMP FATHER STRIKE

DADDY BABBO DEDDY

DADDY LONGLEGS SPINNER LONGLEGS PHALANGID

DADO DIE GROOVE SOLIDUM

DAEDALUS (ANCESTOR OF —) ERECHTHEUS (NEPHEW OF —) TALUS (SON OF —) ICARUS

DAEMON (ALSO SEE DEMON) GHOST DAIMON PYTHON EUDAEMON MISTRESS (PL.) CURETES

DAFFODIL GLEN LILY DAFFY DILLY JONQUIL ASPHODEL BELLWORT CROWBELL

DAFT GAY WILD BALMY BATTY CRAZY DAFFY GIDDY LOONY POTTY SILLY INSANE FOOLISH IDIOTIC IMBECILE

DAG JAG DAGG STAB SLASH DAGGLE PIERCE DAGGING DAGLOCK PRICKET

DAGAME SALAMO MADRONA LEMONWOOD

DAGGER DAG SAX DIRK ITAC KRIS SAEX SNEE SPUD STAB TANG CRISE DAGUE KATAR KREES POINT PRICK SKEAN STEEL ANLACE BODKIN COUTEL CREESE DIESIS HANGER KIRPAN KUTTAR PANADE PINKER POPPER SKHIAN STYLET BALARAO BAYONET COUTEAU DUDGEON HANDJAR KANDJAR KHANJAR OBELISK PONIARD SLASHER STABBER BASELARD PUNCHEON PUNTILLA STILETTO (— AS CERAMICS COVER) HILLER (— REFERENCE MARK) SPIT (— WITH WAVY BLADE) KRIS CREESE KREESE (DOUBLE —) DIESIS (SACRED —) KIRPAN (PREF.) MACHAIRO

DAGOMBA DAGBANE DAGBANI

DAH DAO DOW DHAO

DAHLIA JICAMA POMPON

DAHOMEY (CAPITAL OF —) PORTONOVO (PEOPLE OF —) FON FONG BARIBA (RIVER OF —) NIGER OUEME (TOWN IN —) KANDI NIKKI ABOMEY OUIDAH COTONOU

DAILY ADAY ADAYS DIARY DIURNAL

DAINCHA NARDOO

DAINTIES EST ESTE SOCK CATES DIABLOTIN

DAINTILY CHOICELY GINGERLY MINIONLY

DAINTINESS FLUTTER DELICACY

DAINTY CATE FINE NICE RARE TEAR ACATE DAINT DENTY FRILL GENTY NAISH BONBON CHOICE COSTLY FRIAND MIGNON MINION PICKED REGALO SCARCE SPICED SUNKET CURIOUS ELEGANT FINICAL FINICKY MINIKIN REGALIA TAFFETA TAFFETY DAINTITH DAINTREL DELICACY DELICATE ETHEREAL LIKEROUS MIGNIARD TRYPHOSA (PREF.) ABRO HABRO

DAIRY TAMBO LACTARY VACCARY CREAMERY DEYHOUSE (— PRODUCTS) MILCHIGS

DAIRYMAID DEE DEY DEYWOMAN MILKMAID

DAIRYMAN AHIR MILKMAN

DAIS PACE SEAT BENCH LEWAN STAGE TABLE CANOPY ESTATE LISSOM PODIUM PULPIT SETTLE ESTRADE TERRACE TRIBUNE CHABUTRA FOOTPACE HALFPACE HATHPACE HUSTINGS PLATFORM

DAISY BULL GOLD DANDY GOWAN OXEYE BENNET MORGAN SHASTA BONESET BOWWORT COMFREY DOGBLOW BACKWORT BONEWORT COMPOSIT HEXAFOIL KNITBACK PISSABED MOONPENNY BRUISEWORT MARGUERITE

DAISY CUTTER GRUB

DAISY FLEABANE ERIGERON SCABIOUS

DAKOTA SIOUX LAKOTA

DALE HAW DELL DENE GLEN VALE SPOUT BOTTOM DINGLE TROUGH VALLEY

DALEA PAROSELA

DALIBOR (CHARACTER IN —) BENES ZDENEK DALIBOR MAILADA (COMPOSER OF —) SMETANA

DALLES DELLS RAPIDS

DALLIANCE TOY CHAT PLAY TALK SPORT GOSSIP TOUSEL TOUSLE TRIFLE COLLING

DALLIER PINGLER

DALLY TOY CHAT DAFF FOOL IDLE JAKE JAUK PLAY SWAN WAIT DELAY FLIRT SPORT TARRY COQUET DABBLE DAWDLE LINGER LOITER PINGLE TRIFLE WANTON DRINGLE SLIDDER

DALLYING COQUETRY SISSETON

DALMATIC TUNICLE

DALPHON (FATHER OF —) HAMAN

DAM BAR BAY PEN REE BUND DAME HEAD POND SADD SPUR STAY STEM STOP SUDD WEIR BLOCK CAULD CHECK CHOKE GARTH MOUND POUND STANK ANICUT CAUSEY HINDER MOTHER PARENT ANNICUT BARRAGE BARRIER BURROCK MILLDAM PENHEAD RAMPIRE TAPPOON ABOIDEAU BLOCKADE GRANDDAM OBSTACLE OBSTRUCT RESTRAIN (PART OF —) GATE PIER POOL SILL WALL BASIN CREST OUTLET SLUICE ROADWAY TAINTOR OVERFLOW SPILLWAY POWERHOUSE

DAMAGE MAR BLOT BURN COST HARM HURT JEEL LOSS RUIN SKIN TEEN BLITZ BURST CLOUD CRACK HAVOC PRANG SPOIL WOUND WRONG BATTER CHARGE DANGER DEFACE DEFECT HINDER IMPAIR INJURE INJURY INSULT LESION SCATHE SORROW AFFLICT DAMNIFY DEGRADE DISTURB EXPENSE FOUNDER OFFENCE OFFENSE PAYMENT SCRATCH SCUTTLE SHATTER ACCIDENT BUSINESS DISSERVE FRACTURE FRETTING MISCHIEF SABOTAGE (PREF.) DAMNI

DAMAGED HURT CRAZY LESED BROKEN CRACKED INJURED

DAMAGES INTEREST HAMESUCKEN

DAMAGING HARMFUL HURTFUL SCATHING

DAMAN DAS CONY CONEY CUNNY DASSY GANAM HYRAX DASSIE WABBER ASHKOKO CHEROGRIL

DAMA PADEMELON TAMMAR WALLABY

DAMASCENED WATERED

DAMASCENE WORK KOFTGARI

DAMASK LINEN DARNEX DORNIC DORNICK VALANCE DAMASSIN DRAWLOOM

DAMAYANTI (HUSBAND OF —) NALA

DAME DINT LADY DAMIE WOMAN MATRON

DAME BLANCHE, LA (CHARACTER IN —) ANNA BROWN JENNY GEORGE DICKSON GAVESTON (COMPOSER OF —) BOIELDIEU

DAME'S VIOLET EVEWEED

DAMKINA (HUSBAND OF —) EA

DAMMARA AGATHIS

DAMN DEE DEM DOG RAT BLOW BURN DANG DARN DASH DING DRAT DUMB DURN BLAME BLANK BLAST BLESS CURSE FETCH TARAL WHOOP BEDAMN BUGGER DEMPNE DEVOTE GODDAM CONDEMN CONSARN DOGGONE GODDAMN GOLDARN GOLDURN CONFOUND EXECRATE

DAMNABLE RUDDY DAMNED ODIOUS ACCURSED INFERNAL

DAMNABLY DEUCED CURSEDLY DEUCEDLY

DAMNATION NATION PERDITION

DAMNATION DE FAUST (CHARACTER IN —) FAUST MARGUERITE MEPHISTOPHELES (COMPOSER OF —) BERLIOZ

DAMNED DEE DAMN DARN DEED DURN LOST BALLY DOOMS BLAMED BLOODY DARNED DASHED DURNED GODDAM GORMED TARNAL BLASTED BLESSED CONSARN DOGGONE ETERNAL GOLDARN GOLDURN MUCKING ACCURSED BLANKETY BLINKING DASHEDLY INFERNAL JIGGERED

DAMO (FATHER OF —) PYTHAGORAS (MOTHER OF —) THEANO

DAMP DEG FOG RAW WAK WET CLAM DANK DEWY DULL MIST ROKY SOFT WACK BLUNT DABBY HUMID JUICY MALMY MOCHY MOIST MOOTH MUGGY MUNGY MUSTY RAFTY RAINY RAWKY SAPPY SEEPY SOBBY SOGGY THONE WAUGH WEAKY BLIGHT CLAMMY DAMPEN DEADEN MUFFLE QUENCH RHEUMY STUPOR BEDEWED DAMPISH DEPRESS MOISTEN SQUIDGY

DEJECTED DISPIRIT HUMIDIFY
HUMIDITY MOISTURE
(— OF EVENING) SERENE
(CHOKE —) STYTHE
(PREF.) HUMI(DI)
DAMPEN DEG DAMP MOIL CHILL
CRAMP FREEZE SPONGE
MOISTURE
DAMPENER MULLER
DAMPER DAMP MUTE BREAD
CHECK CHECKER SORDINE
REGISTER
DAMPNESS CLAM DAMP
HUMIDITY
DAMSEL GIRL WENCH MAIDEN
MOPPET DAMOSEL DAMOZEL
PUCELLE DONZELLA PRINCESS
DAMSELFISH PINTANO
DAMSELFLY NAIAD ODONATE
DAN GI DEN
(MOTHER OF —) BILHAH
DANAKIL AFAR
DANAUS ANOSIA
(BROTHER OF —) AEGYPTUS
(DAUGHTER OF —) AMYMONE
(FATHER OF —) BELUS
(MOTHER OF —) ANCHINOE
DANCE BAL BOB HOP JIG MAI SON
BALL DRAG DUET DUMP FISH
FOOT FRUG HEEL HOOF HORA
JAZZ JIVE JUBA JUKE KOLO LEAP
LOPE LOUP MASK MILL MOVE
PROM REEL SAIL SHAG SKIT STEP
BAILE BAMBA BONGO BRAWL
CANON CAPER CAROL CONGA
DANZA ENTRY FLING FLISK FRIKE
FRISK GOPAK LASYA LIMBO LINDY
MAMBO PAVAN POLKA RINKA
RUMBA SALLY SAMBA STOMP
SWING TANGO TRACE TREAD
TWIST VOLTA WALTZ ALTHEA
AREITO BALLET BALTER BOLERO
BOOGIE BOSTON BRANLE CANARY
CANCAN CEBELL CORDAX
DANZON DIDDLE DREHER FADING
FORMAL FROLIC GERMAN
HORMOS MASQUE MINUET
MOBBLE MONKEY MORRIS NRITTA
PASSAY RACKET RHUMBA
SHIMMY TODDLE TRESCA TUMBLE
VALETA VELETA ANTHEMA
BEGUINE CALINDA CANTICO
COURANT CZARDAS DANSANT
FADDING FARRUCA FOOTING
FOXTROT FURLANA GAVOTTE
MEASURE MORISCO PATTERN
SALTATE SARDANA SHUFFLE
TEMPETE TRESCHE TRIPPLE
VOLTIZE ZIGANKA ANGLAISE
AURRESCU BAMBOULA
BUNNYHUG CACHUCHA
CAKEWALK CHACONNE
COMPARSA COONJINE COTILLON
ENTRACTE ESTAMPIE FANDANGO
FANTASIA FLAMENCO GALLIARD
GALOPADE GUARACHA
HABANERA HEYDEGUY HORNPIPE
KOLATTAM MATELOTE
MERENGUE SALTATION
SHAKEDOWN CARMAGNOLE
SCHOTTISCHE
(— ART) NATYA ORCHESIS

(— ATTENDANCE) LACKEY
LACQUEY
(— CLUMSILY) BALTER
(— DRAMA) NO NOH
(— FACE TO FACE) SET
(— FORM) PIVA
(— IN CIRCLE) JIGGER
(— METHOD) LABAN
(— NIMBLY) CANARY
(— RESEMBLING THE POLKA)
BERLIN
(— STEP) RIFF PICKUP
(— STYLE) ABHINAYA
(— TYPE) TANDAVA
(ACROBATIC —) ADAGIO
(AFRICAN —) SHOUT
(ARGENTINE —) CUANDO
(AUSTRIAN —) LANDLER
(BALINESE —) KEBYAR LEGONG
(BALLROOM —) SON CONGO
COTILLON
(BOHEMIAN —) REDOWA FURIANT
(CARNIVAL —) COOCH FOLIA
COOTCH
(CEREMONIAL —) AREITO CANTICO
DUTUBURI
(COQUETTISH —) PURPOSE
(COUNTRY —) HAY RANT CONFESS
LANDLER MUSETTE ANGLAISE
SARABAND
(COURTSHIP —) CUECA BATUQUE
LEZGINKA
(DANISH —) SEXTUR
(FIESTA —S) AKRIEROS
(FLAMENCO —) ALEGRIAS
(FRENCH —) BAL BOREE BRAWL
GAVOT BRANLE BOURREE
BOUTADE BRANSLE GAVOTTE
LAVOLTA
(GAY —) RANT GAILLARD
GALLIARD
(GESTURE —) SIVA
(GREEK —) CORDAX KORDAX
ROMAIKA SIKINNIS
(GYPSY —) FARRUCA
(HAITIAN —) JUBA
(HOBBYHORSE —) CALUSAR
(HOLIDAY —) PATTERN
(HUNGARIAN —) KOS
(IMPROMPTU —) BOUTADE
(INDIAN —) IRUSKA KATHAK
KANTIKOY
(IRISH —) FADING PLANXTY
(ITALIAN —) FORLANA FURLANA
BERGAMASK SALTARELLO
(JAPANESE —) BUGAKU KAGURA
(JAVANESE —) SERIMPI
(LIVELY —) JIG REEL GALOP GIGUE
POLKA RUMBA BOLERO CANARY
RHUMBA SPRING BOURREE
CORANTO FURLANA HOEDOWN
GALLIARD GALOPADE HORNPIPE
(MAORI —) HAKA
(MARTIAL —) PYRRHIC
(MEXICAN —) JARABE HUAPANGO
SANDUNGA
(MOURNFUL —) DUMP
(NORWEGIAN —) HALLING
(OLD ENGLISH —) CEBELL MORRIS
ARGEERS ANGLAISE
(OLD-FASHIONED —) LOURE
PASSACAGLIA
(PEASANT —) JOTA

DANZON BALITAO
(PERUVIAN —) CUECA KASWA
CACHUA
(POLISH —) POLACCA KUJAWIAK
POLONAISE VARSOVIENNE
(POLYNESIAN —) HULA
(PORTUGUESE —) FADO
(ROMAN —) TRIPUDIUM
(ROUND —) RAY BRAUL CAROL
WALTZ CAROLE MAXIXE
(RUSSIAN —) ZIGANKA
(RUSTIC —) HAY HEY HAYMAKER
(SPANISH —) JOTA POLO JALEO
BOLERO JARABE CHACONNE
FLAMENCO GUARACHA
MALAGUENA ZAPATEADO
SEGUIDILLA
(SPEAR —) BARIS
(SQUARE —) SQUARE ARGEERS
HOEDOWN LANCERS QUADRILLE
(STATELY —) PAVAN PAVANE
EMMELEIA SARABAND POLONAISE
(SWORD —) BACUBERT MATACHIN
(VENEZUELAN —) JOROPO
(WEDDING —) CANACUAS
(WEST INDIAN —) LIMBO
(PREF.) CHORE(I)(O) CHORO
ORCHESO
DANCER PONY CLOWN PONEY
ARTIST CORNER HOOFER HOPPER
MAENAD APSARAS CLOGGER
DANSEUR PASCOLA PRANCER
PRANKER SAILOUR STEPPER
TODDLER BALADINE BAYADERE
DANSEUSE DEVADASI FIGURANT
MORRICER
(BALLET —) ETOILE SOLISTE
CORYPHEE
(EGYPTIAN —S) GHAWAZI
GHAWAZEE
(JAVANESE —) SERIMPI
(JAVANESE —S) BEDOYO
(MASKED —S) GAHE
(SQUARE —S) FLOOR
(SWORD —) MATACHIN
(ZUNI —) SHALAKO
DANCING SWING ADANCE BALLET
CHANGE FROLIC MORRIS
SALTANT SURGING STEPPING
TRIPSOME
(— MANIA) TARANTISM
DANDELION BLOW BLOWER
CANKER DINDLE CHICORY
HAWKBIT BLOWBALL COMPOSIT
PISSABED
(RUSSIAN —) KOKSAGYZ
DANDELION HEAD PUFF CLOCK
BUFFBALL BULLFICE BULLFIST
PUFFBALL
DANDER ANGER DUTCH SCURF
STROLL TEMPER WANDER
HACKLES PASSION SAUNTER
DANDRUFF
DANDIFIED SPRUCE BUCKISH
ADONIZED
DANDIFY ADONIZE DANDYIZE
DANDLE DANCE DIDDLE DOODLE
FADDLE FONDLE PAMPER
DANDRUFF SCURF DANDER
FURFUR PORRIGO
DANDY FOP JAY ADON BEAU BUCK
DAND DUDE FINE JAKE MAJO
PRIG TOFF TRIG YAWL BLOOD

DILDO JEMMY SWELL ADONIS
MIZZEN BUCKEEN CAPSTAN
COXCOMB ELEGANT FOPPISH
JESSAMY MACARONI MUSCADIN
SAILBOAT
DANDY HORSE HOBBY DRAISINE
DANDYISHNESS SPIFF
DANDYISM BUCKISM
DANE DANSKER LOCHLIN
DUBHGALL
DANEWORT EBULUS LOCHLIN
DANEBALL DANEWEED
DEADWORT WALLWORT
DANGER FEAR RISK DOUBT PERIL
WATHE HAZARD PLIGHT
EXTREME PITFALL VENTURE
DISTRESS JEOPARDY
DANGEROUS BAD HOT ILL RUM
DEAR FOUL GRAVE NASTY RISKY
FICKLE KITTLE SCATHY SHREWD
UNSURE AWKWARD FEARFUL
PARLOUS UNCANNY DOUBTFUL
INSECURE PERILOUS UNCHANCY
BREAKNECK WANCHANCY
PRECARIOUS PESTIFEROUS
(MAKE LESS —) DEFUSE
DANGLE BOB LOP HANG LOLL
DROOP SWING DANDLE SHOGGLE
SHOOGLE SUSPEND SWINGLE
TROLLOP
DANGLIN DANLI
DANGLING VERSATILE
DANIEL (FATHER OF —) DAVID
(MOTHER OF —) ABIGAIL
DANK WET DAMP DONK HUMID
MADID MOIST CLAMMY COARSE
DAMPEN DANKISH DRIZZLE
WETNESS MOISTURE
DANSEUSE DANCER BALLERINA
DANZIG GDANSK
(— LIQUEUR) RATAFIA
DAPHNE (CHARACTER IN —) GAEA
APOLLO DAPHNE PENEIOS
LEUKIPPOS
(COMPOSER OF —) STRAUSS
DAPPER NEAT TRIM NATTY
SPRUCE FINICAL FOPPISH
SPARKISH
DAPPLE COVER FLECK FRECK
DAPPLED BLOCKY DOTTED
POMELY FLECKED MOTTLED
SPOTTED FRECKLED
DARBHA KUSA KUSHA
DARDA (FATHER OF —) MAHOL
DARDANUS (CHARACTER IN —)
VENUS IPHISE TEUCER ANTENOR
ISMENOR DARDANUS
(COMPOSER OF —) RAMEAU
(DAUGHTER OF —) IDAEA
(FATHER OF —) ZEUS JUPITER
(MOTHER OF —) ELECTRA
(SON OF —) ILUS DEIMAS IDAEUS
ERICHTHONIUS
DARE OSS DAST DEFY FACE OSSE
RISK BRAVE STUMP ASSUME
BANTER DACKER ATTEMPT
BRAVADE FASHION PRESUME
VENTURE
(— NOT) DASSNT DAURNA
DASSENT
DAREDEVIL MADCAP
HARDYDARDY
DARING BOLD DARE DERF PERT

RASH WILD BRAVE HARDY MANLY
NERVE PREST FELONY HEROIC
COURAGE DAIROUS DAREFUL
BOLDNESS DEVILISH FEARLESS
STALWART
DARIOLE MADELINE
DARK DIM DUN MUM SAD WAN
BASE BLAE DEEP DERK DERN
DUSK EBON HARD MALE MIRK
MURK BLACK BLIND BROWN
CLOUD DINGY DUSKY FAINT
MIRKY MURKY ROOKY SHADY
SOOTY SWART UMBER UNLIT
VAGUE CLOSED CLOUDY CYPRUS
DIMPSY DISMAL DRUMLY
GLOOMY OPAQUE SOMBER
SOMBRE SWARTH WICKED
APHOTIC DARKISH DUSKISH
MELANIC OBSCURE PITMIRK
RAYLESS STYGIAN SUNLESS
SWARTHY THESTER UNCLEAR
ABSTRUSE DARKLING DARKSOME
GLOOMFUL GLOOMING IGNORANT
LOWERING SINISTER CIMMERIAN
CALIGINOUS
(PREF.) AITHO MAVRO MEL(A)
MELAN(O)
(SUFF.) MELANE
DARK BEAVER PRALINE
DARK-COLORED SAD SWART
SOMBER SOMBRE SWARTH
SWARTHY
(PREF.) FUSCO
DARKEN DIM DUN BLUR DULL
DUSK BEDIM BLIND CLOUD
GLOAM GLOOM POCHE SHADE
SULLY SWART UMBER DEEPEN
ENDARK SHADOW BECLOUD
BENIGHT BLACKEN ECLIPSE
EMBROWN OBSCURE OPACATE
PERPLEX SLUBBER TARNISH
OVERCAST OBFUSCATE
OVERSHADOW
(— HAIR) BLEND
DARKENED SABLE CLOUDY
BLINDED LAMPLESS
DARKENING SCURF
DARK HORSE MOREL
DARKISH DIM
DARKLY DARK CLOSE SABLY
MISTILY
DARKNESS DARK DERN DUSK
MIRK MURK BLACK GLOOM NIGHT
SHADE TAMAS SHADOW DIMNESS
PITMIRK PRIVACY SECRECY
TENEBRA GLOAMING INIQUITY
MIDNIGHT TENEBRES TWILIGHT
NIGRITUDE
(PREF.) SCOTO TENEBRI
DARKNESS AT NOON (AUTHOR OF
—) KOESTLER
(CHARACTER IN —) ARLOVA
BOGRAV IVANOV GLETKIN
HARELIP KIEFFER MICHAEL
NICHOLAS RUBASHOV
DARLING JO JOE PET CHOU CONY
DEAR DUCK LIFE LOVE NOBS
PEAT ROON AROON ARUIN BULLY
CHERI DEARY DUCKS LIEVE
SWEET WHITE CHERIE DAUTIE
DAWTIE MINION MOPPET OCHREE
POPPET ACUSHLA ASTHORE
BUNTING CUSHLAM DILLING

MINIKIN PIGSNEY PINKENY
QUERIDA STOREEN DEARLING
DUMPLING FAVORITE LIEBCHEN
LOVELING MACUSHLA PRECIOUS
SWEETING MAVOURNIN
MAVOURNEEN
DARLING PEA INDICO INDIGO
DARN DOG BLOW DERN DURN
MEND PATCH BUGGER RENTER
REPAIR DOGGONE
DARNED BLAME BLAMED DEUCED
DURNED BLESSED BLINDING
DOWNGONE
DARNEL RAY CRAP TARE WEED
CHEAT CHESS DRANK DRAWK
DRUNK EAVER GRASS IVRAY
NEELE COCKLE EGILOPS AEGILOPS
DART JET POP BOLT BUZZ CANE
CHOP COLP FLIT JOUK LEAP LICK
PILE PLAN PLAY ROUT ARROW
BOUND FLAME FLING FLIRT
GLEAM GLINT LANCE SCAMP
SCOOT SHAFT SHOOT SKITE SKIVE
SPEAR SPEED SPRIT START
ANCHOR BULTEN DARTLE ELANCE
GLANCE LANCET LAUNCH
METHOD SCHEME SPRING SQUIRT
STRIKE SUMPIT THRUST JAVELIN
MISSILE STRALET VERUTUM
BRANDISH GAVELOCK JACULATE
SPICULUM BANDERILLA
(— ABOUT) SPRINKLE
(— OF LIGHTNING) STREAK
(— OF MOLDING) ANCHOR
(— REPEATEDLY) DARTLE
(PART OF —) POINT SHAFT BARREL
FLIGHT
(PREF.) JACULI TELI
DARTER SPECK
DARTING SALLY ARROWY
DARTLIKE SPICULAR
DASH DAD DAH PEP ZIP BANG
BOLT CAST DING DIVE ELAN GIFT
HINT HURL LASH LINE LUSH PASH
PELT POSS RACE RASH RUIN
RULE RUSH SHOW SLAM SOSH
TICK VEIN WHAP WHOP ABASH
ARDOR BLANK BREAK CHAFE
CLASH CRASH CRUSH DRIVE
ECLAT FLASH FLING FRUSH
KNOCK PLASH PLOUT SKITE
SLASH SLOSH SMASH SPEED
SPEND SPICE SPURN START
STYLE SWASH SWELL TASTE
THROW TOUCH TRICK BEDASH
DALLOP DASHEE DOLLOP ENERGY
HURTLE HYPHEN JABBLE RELISH
SHIVER SPIRIT SPLASH SPRINT
STRAIN STROKE THRUST
ABANDON BRAVURA BREENGE
COLLIDE DEPRESS DISPLAY
HUNDRED IMPINGE PANACHE
SHATTER SPATTER SPLOTCH
TANTIVY VIRETOT CONFOUND
GRATUITY SPLINTER
(— ABOUT WILDLY) GAD REEL
(— AGAINST) BEAT
(— DOWN) QUELL STRAM
STRAMASH
(— IN PIECES) CRASH
(— OF LIQUID) JAW
(— OF SPIRITS) LACE LACING
(— OUT) QUELL

(— TOGETHER) COLLIDE
(— UP) FLURR
(— WITH WATER) JAW BLASH
SLASH
DASHARATHA (FATHER OF —) AJA
(SON OF —) RAMA BHARATA
LAKSHMANA SHATRUGHNA
(WIFE OF —) KAIKEYI SUMITRA
KAUSHALYA
DASHBOARD DASH FACIA DASHER
FASCIA
DASHED SWITCHED
DASHEEN TARO
DASHER DASH BEATER PLUNGER
DASHING BOLD BULLY DASHY
DOGGY SHOWY SMART SPICY
SWASH JABBLE SPANKY SWANKY
VELOCE DOGGISH GALLOWS
LARKING STYLISH SWAGGER
VARMINT SLASHING SPANKING
SPIRITED
DASTARD CAD SOT DAFF SNEAK
COWARD CRAVEN DULLARD
HILDING WITHING POLTROON
DASTARDLY FOUL VILLAIN
COWARDLY POLTROON SNEAKING
DASYLIRION SOTOL
DASYPUS TATU
DASYURE TIGER YABBI DAPPLE
DATA DOPE FILE FACTS IMPUT
INPUT MATERIAL
(INACCURATE —) GARBAGE
(STORE OF —) PUSHDOWN
(USELESS —) GARBAGE
DATE DAY ERA DRAG FARD FUSS
DATUM EPOCH FARDH FRUIT
SAIDI CUTOFF FRIEND HALAWI
JUJUBE RECKON GALLANT
ANTEDATE ASHARASI DEADLINE
(— FIXED UPON) TERM
(— RIPENING) KIMRI RUTAB
KHALAL
(CHINESE —) BER
DATED GIVEN PASSE OUTMODED
DATE PLUM LOTUS SAPOTE
ZAPOTE
DATHAN (FATHER OF —) ELIAB
DATOLITE BAKERITE
HUMBOLDTITE
DATUM FACT ITEM GIVEN DONNEE
DATURA DUTRA STRAMONY
TOGUACHA
DAUB DAB DOB MUD BALM BLOB
BLOT CLAG CLAM CLAT CLAY
COAT GAUM MOIL SOIL TEER
CLAIK CLART CLEAM COVER
DITCH FLICK PAINT SLAKE SLAUM
SMEAR BEDAUB CLATCH GREASE
LABBER SMUDGE SPLASH
BESMEAR DRIBBLE PLASTER
SCLATCH SLUBBER SPLATCH
SPLOTCH SLAISTER
DAUBED GAUMY
DAUBING DUBBING MOILING
DAUBY BLOTTY
DAUGHTER ANAC BINT DAME GIRL
CHILD FILLE FILLY KIBEI REGAN
ALUMNA CADETTE DOCHTER
GONERIL CORDELIA
(PANTALOON'S —) COLUMBINE
(PREF.) FILI
DAUGHTER OF THE REGIMENT
(CHARACTER IN —) MARIE TONZIO

SULPICE COUNTESS
(COMPOSER OF —) DONIZETTI
DAUNT AWE COW DAW ADAW
DARE DAZE FAZE MATE PALL
STUN TAME ABASH ACCOY
AMATE BREAK CHECK DETER
DOMPT QUAIL DANTON DISMAY
SUBDUE CONQUER CONTROL
OVERAWE REPRESS STUPEFY
TERRIFY DISPIRIT OVERCOME
DAUNTLESS BOLD GOOD BRAVE
AWELESS SPARTAN FEARLESS
INTREPID
DAUNUS (DAUGHTER OF —) EUIPPE
(FATHER OF —) PILUMNUS
(MOTHER OF —) DANAE
(SON OF —) TURNUS
(WIFE OF —) VENILIA
DAVENPORT DESK SOFA COUCH
DIVAN
DAVID TAFFY DAWKIN
(COMPANION OF —) JONATHAN
(DAUGHTER OF —) TAMAR
(FATHER OF —) JESSE
(SON OF —) AMNON ABSALOM
(WIFE OF —) ABIGAIL AHINOAM
DAVID COPPERFIELD (AUTHOR OF
—) DICKENS
(CHARACTER IN —) HAM DICK
DORA HEEP JANE MICK ROSA
AGNES BETSY CLARA DAVID
EMILY JAMES MEALY TOMMY
URIAH BARKIS DARTLE GRINBY
STRONG WALKER CREAKLE
SPENLOW WILKINS MICAWBER
PEGGOTTY TRADDLES
TROTWOOD MURDSTONE
WICKFIELD STEERFORTH
DAVIDIST JORIST
DAVIT CRANE
DAW DA DAWN DRAB DAUNT
MAGPIE DAWPATE JACKDAW
SLATTERN SLUGGARD
DAWDLE LAG IDLE JAUK LOAF
MUCK MULL POKE TOIT DALLY
DELAY DRILL KNOCK DADDLE
DAIDLE DIDDLE DOODLE DRETCH
FADDLE LINGER LOITER MUCKER
PICKLE PIDDLE PINGLE POTTER
PUTTER TANTLE TRIFLE DRIDDLE
FINNICK QUIDDLE SAUNTER
LALLYGAG LOLLYGAG SHAMMOCK
SLUMMOCK
DAWDLER DAWDLE MUSARD
LOUTHER
DAWN DAW ROW EOAN MORN
BREAK CREEK LIGHT PRIME SHINE
SUNUP AURORA MORROW
ORIENT SPRING UPRISE DAWNING
GREKING MORNING SUNRISE
COCKCROW DAYBREAK
(PREF.) EO EOSINO
DAY DA DEI ERA SUN YOM DATE
DIEM DIES DIET TIME EPOCH
LIGHT FRIDAY MONDAY PERIOD
SUNDAY JOURNEY TUESDAY
LIFETIME SATURDAY THURSDAY
WEDNESDAY
(— AND NIGHT) KALPA
(— BEFORE) EVE
(— OF JUDGMENT) INQUEST
DOOMSDAY
(— OF ORIGIN) BIRTHDAY

(— OF REST) SABBATH
(— OF ROMAN MONTH) IDES
NONES CALENDS KALENDS
(DOG —S) CANICULE
(EVERY —) ALDAY
(EVIL —S) DISMAL
(FAST —) ASHURA FASTEN
(FIRST — OF AUGUST) LAMMAS
(FIRST — OF MAY) BELTANE
BEALTINE
(HOLY —) FEAST HOLIDAY
(HOT —) BROILER ROASTER
SCORCHER
(LAST — OF FESTIVAL) APODOSIS
(MARKET —) NUNDINE TIANGUE
(NO FLESH —) MAIGRE
(PATRON SAINT'S —) PATTERN
(QUARTER —) TERM
(TWELFTH —) EPIPHANY
(UNLUCKY —S) DISMAL
(WEEK —) FERIA
(WORK —) WARDAY
(5 NAMELESS —S) UAYEB
(60TH OF —) GHURRY
(8TH — AFTER FEAST) UTAS
(PREF.) HEMER(O)
(LASTING BUT A —) EPHEMERO
DAYAK DYAK IBAN BAHAU DUSUN
KAYAN KENYA KENYAH KELABIT
DAYBOOK BOOK DIURNAL
JOURNAL
DAYBREAK DAWN MORN SUNUP
DAWNING DAYDAWN DAYLIGHT
(PREF.) EO EOSINO
DAYDREAM DWAM MUSE DREAM
DWALM FANCY VISION FANTASY
REVERIE PHANTASY
DAYDREAMER REVEUR
DAYFLOWER COHITRE
DAYLIGHT DAY LIGHT DAYSHINE
(BROAD —) FUIRDAYS
DAYWORKER DILKER
DAZE FOG DAMP DARE MAZE ROCK
STUN DAUNT DAVER DIZZY
DOZEN GALLY SWOON ASTONY
BEDAZE BEMUSE BENUMB
DAZZLE DEAFEN MUDDLE
TRANCE CONFUSE PETRIFY
STUPEFY TORPIFY ASTONISH
BEWILDER DUMFOUND PARALYZE
DAZED MAD ASEA DAMP ASSOT
DIZZY DOYLT MUZZY SILLY TOTTY
WOOZY CUCKOO DOILED GROGGY
ROTTEN BEMUSED DONNERT
SPOILED WITLESS ASTONIED
BESOTTED DITHERED DONNERED
WITHERED
DAZEDLY GROGGILY
DAZZLE DARE DAZE BLEND BLIND
DROWN GLAIK SHINE FULGOR
ECLIPSE BEWILDER OUTSHINE
SURPRISE
DAZZLED BLINDED
DAZZLING FLARE FLASH GLAIK
FLASHY GARISH ADAZZLE
FLARING FULGENT GLARING
RADIANT DIZZYING GORGEOUS
DDT TDE DICOPHANE
DEACON ADEPT CLERIC DOCTOR
LAYMAN LEVITE MASTER PHILIP
MINISTER
DEACONESS WIDOW
DEAD FEY LOW AWAY BONG BUNG

COLD DEAF DOWD DULL FLAT
GONE MORT NUMB POKY SURE
TAME ADEAD AMORT BLIND
DEEDS INERT NAPOO POKEY
QUIET SLAIN STARK VAPID
ASLEEP BYGONE FALLEN LAPSED
NAPOOH PARTED REFUSE
DEADISH DEFUNCT EXACTLY
EXPIRED EXTINCT INSIPID
SAINTED STERILE TEDIOUS
ABSOLUTE COMPLETE DECEASED
DEPARTED INACTIVE LIFELESS
OBSOLETE SCUPPERED
(— AT TOP) RAMPICK
(PREF.) NECR(O)
DEAD-ARM NECROSIS
DEAD-DRUNK BLIND
DEADEN DAMP DULL DUMB KILL
MULL MUTE NUMB SEAR STUN
BLUNT SLAKE BENUMB DAMPEN
MUFFLE OBTUND OPIATE RETARD
STIFLE WEAKEN MORTIFY
PETRIFY REPRESS SLUMBER
SMOTHER AMORTIZE ASTONISH
ENFEEBLE
(— A SCENT) FOIL
DEAD END PLACE
(AUTHOR OF —) KINGSLEY
(CHARACTER IN —) KAY JACK
DRINA TOMMY GIMPTY HILTON
MARTIN BABYFACE
DEADENED DEAD DEAF SEAR SERE
DEADENING PUGGING
DEADHEAD SINK BOBBER SINKER
DEADHOUSE MORGUE MORTUARY
DEAD LETTER NIX
DEADLINE DATELINE
DEADLINESS LETHALITY
DEADLOCK TIE LOGJAM IMPASSE
STANDOFF STOPPAGE
DEADLY WAN DIRE FELL MORT
FATAL FERAL TUANT DEATHY
FUNEST LETHAL MORTAL
CAPITAL DEATHLY FATEFUL
RUINOUS MORTIFIC VENOMOUS
VIRULENT PESTILENT THANATOID
PERNICIOUS
DEADLY CARROT DRIAS THAPSIA
DEAD NETTLE HENBIT
DEADS MULLOCK
DEAD SOULS (AUTHOR OF —)
GOGOL
(CHARACTER IN —) PAVEL ALEXEI
PLATON KLOBUEFF KOPEYKIN
MANILOFF NOZDREFF LYENITZEN
PLATONOFF PLIUSHKIN
SOBAKEVITCH KOSTANZHOGLO
TCHITCHIKOFF TENTETNIKOFF
BETRISHTCHEFF
DEAF SURD DUNCH DUNNY SORDA
SORDO
(PREF.) SURDI SURDO
DEAFEN DIN DORR DEAVE DEADEN
DEAFENING DEEVEY
DEAF-MUTE FENELLA SURDOMUTE
DEAFNESS ASONIA SURDITY
ANACUSIA ANACUSIS COPHOSIS
DEAL GO END JOB DAIL DOLE
LEND PART SALE TALE WHIZ
ALLOT BOARD BROKE FETCH
PLANK SERVE SEVER SHAKE
SHARE SHIFT TRADE TREAT
TROKE TRUCK WIELD YIELD

BATTEN BESTOW DIVIDE HANDLE
MEDDLE NUMBER PARCEL
BARGAIN DELIVER INFLICT
PIANOLA PORTION SCATTER
TRUCKLE WRESTLE DISPENSE
SEPARATE
(— CARDS) DRAW TALLY
(— CLANDESTINELY) TRINKET
(— IN A TRIFLING WAY) PIDDLE
(— IN BRIDGE) BOARD
(— IN GRAIN) SWALE
(— OF CARDS) COUP SPOIL
GOULASH
(— SHREWDLY) JOCKEY
(— WITH) HAND COVER DIGHT
TOUCH TREAT BUCKET CUSTOM
DEMEAN HANDLE ENTREAT
NEGOTIATE
(GREAT —) MORT LOADS MIGHT
SIGHT JUGFUL OODLES SKINFUL
(POLITICAL —) DICKER
DEALER BANK CHAP AGENT COPER
BADGER BANKER BROKER
CADGER EGGLER GROCER JOBBER
JUNIOR MONGER SELLER TRADER
BUTCHER CHAPMAN KEELMAN
YOUNGER CHANDLER MERCHANT
OCCUPIER OPERATOR STICKMAN
TAILLEUR
(— IN CATTLE) COUPER COWPER
DROVER
(— IN CHEMICALS) SALTER
DRYSALTER
(— IN DRY GOODS) DRAPER
(— IN GRAIN) SWALER
(— IN OLD CLOTHES) FRIPPER
(— IN PAINTS) COLORMAN
(— IN TEXTILES) MERCER
(CARDS —) FARMER
(COAL —) COLLIER
(HORSE —) COPER COUPER
COWPER CHANTER SCORSER
(SLAVE —) MANGO
(STOCK —) STAG JOBBER
OUTSIDER
DEALFISH VAAGMAR VAAGMAER
RIBBONFISH
DEALING DOLE PRICE TRUCK
TAFFIC TRADING EXCHANGE
(BUSINESS —S) TROKE
(JUST —) DOOM
(TRICKY —) BROKING
(PL.) DEAL TRAFFIC BUSINESS
COMMERCE PRACTICE PRACTISE
(SUFF.) (—WITH) IC(AL)
DEAN DECAN DOYEN DEANER
SENIOR VERGER PREFECT
PROVOST SUBDEAN ARCHDEAN
PRAEFECT
DEAR JO GRA HON JOE PET AGRA
CARA CHER CHOU CONY FAIR
FOND GOOD HIGH LAMB LIEF
LOVE NEAR NOBS SALT ANGEL
BOSOM CHARY CHERE CHUCK
DEARY HONEY LOVED SWEET
TIGHT COSTLY DAUTIE DAWTIE
DEARIE DEARLY POPPET SCARCE
SEVERE SQUALL TENDER
WORTHY BELOVED DARLING
LOVABLE PIGSNEY QUERIDA
SPECIAL TOOTSIE ESPECIAL
ESTEEMED GLORIOUS PRECIOUS
VALUABLE

(SUFF.) (— ONE) EEN
DEARLY DEAR ALIFE DEEPLY
KEENLY RICHLY HEARTILY
DEARNESS CHERTE DEARTH
DEARTH LACK WANT CHERTE
FAMINE PAUCITY POVERTY
DEARNESS SCARCITY SOLITUDE
(SUFF.) PENIA
DEASPIRATION PSILOSIS
DEATH DEE END BALE BANE DEAD
DOOM EXIT FAIL FATE KILL MORS
MORT OBIT PASS REST WINK
ANKOU DECAY GRAVE GRUEL
LETHE NIGHT SLEEP CHAROS
CHARUS DEMISE DEPART ENDING
EXITUS EXPIRY MURDER PERIOD
REAPER WAGANG ACHERON
CURTAIN DECEASE FUNERAL
PARTING PASSAGE QUIETUS
SILENCE BIOLYSIS CASUALTY
CURTAINS FATALITY NECROSIS
RAWBONES THANATOS
MORTALITY NOTHINGNESS
(— ANGEL) AZRAEL
(— BY HANGING) HALTER
(— OF TISSUE) GANGRENE
(PREF.) LETHI THANAT(O)
(SUFF.) THANASIA
DEATH ADDER ELAPID ELAPOID
DEATH CAMASS LOBELIA
DEATH IN VENICE (CHARACTER IN
—) TADZIO ASCHENBACH
(COMPOSER OF —) BRITTEN
DEATHLESS ETERNAL UNDYING
IMMORTAL
DEATHLESSNESS ATHANASY
DEATHLIKE CHARNEL DEATHLY
GHASTLY MACABRE GHASTFUL
MORIBUND MORTUOUS
DEATHLY DEAD FATAL DEADLY
MORTAL GHASTLY STYGIAN
DEATHFUL GHASTFUL
DEATH OF A SALESMAN (AUTHOR
OF —) MILLER
(CHARACTER IN —) BIFF HAPPY
LINDA LOMAN WILLY
DEATH'S-HEAD SKULL
DEBACLE ROUT STAMPEDE
COLLAPSE
DEBAR DENY TABU CROSS ESTOP
REPEL TABOO DISBAR FORBID
HINDER REFUSE BOYCOTT
DEPRIVE EXCLUDE OUTSHUT
PREVENT SECLUDE SUSPEND
PRECLUDE PROHIBIT
DEBARK LAND
DEBARRED FROZEN OUTSHUT
DEBASE SINK ABASE ALLAY ALLOY
AVILE DIRTY LOWER STOOP
BEMEAN DEFILE DEMEAN DILUTE
EMBASE IMPAIR NIDDER NITHER
REDUCE REVILE VILIFY CORRUPT
DEBAUCH DECLINE DEGRADE
DEPRAVE PERVERT PROFANE
TRADUCE VILLAIN VITIATE
PROSTITUTE
DEBASED BASE VILE HEDGE
BASTARD CORRUPT SQUALID
CANKERED DEGRADED DEROGATE
DEBASEMENT TARNISH
PROSTITUTION
DEBASING DOWNWARD
DEBATABLE MOOT DISPUTABLE

DEBATE AGON BEAT FRAY MOOT ARGUE FIGHT PLEAD STUDY ARGUFY COMBAT HASSEL HASSLE REASON STRIFE AGITATE CANVASS CONTEND CONTEST DISCEPT DISCUSS DISPUTE EXAMINE MOOTING PALAVER QUARREL WRANGLE ARGUMENT COLLOQUY CONSIDER CONTRARY MILITATE PARLANCE QUESTION CONTENTION
DEBATER PICADOR
DEBAUCH BUM BOUT FILE SPREE TAINT WHORE DEBASE DEBOSH DEFILE GUZZLE MISUSE SEDUCE SPLORE VILIFY CORRUPT DEBOISE DEPRAVE MISLEAD POLLUTE VIOLATE DISHONOR SQUANDER STRUMPET STUPRATE
DEBAUCHED LEWD RAKELY RAKISH DEBOIST DEBOSHED RAKEHELL
DEBAUCHEE RIP RAKE ROUE HOLOUR LECHER RAKEHELL
DEBAUCHERY RIOT RAKERY DEBAUCH PRIAPISM
DEBENTURE BOND SECURITY
DEBENZOLIZE STRIP
DEBILITATE SINK
DEBILITATED WEAK SEEDY FEEBLE INFIRM SAPPED ASTHENIC
DEBILITY ATONY ADYNAMY ASTHENY LANGUOR ADYNAMIA ASTHENIA WEAKNESS MYASTHENIA (PREF.) ASTHEN(O) (SUFF.) ASTHENIA
DEBIR (SLAYER OF —) JOSHUA
DEBIT DEBT LOSS CHARGE
DEBONAIR AIRY JAUNTY POLITE CAVALIER GRACEFUL GRACIOUS
DEBORA E JAELE (CHARACTER IN —) JAELE DEBORA SISERA (COMPOSER OF —) PIZZETTI
DEBOUCH FALL MOUTH
DEBOUCHMENT INFLUX INFLUXION
DEBRIS GUCK SLAG DECAY FRUSH TRADE TRASH WASTE RAFFLE REFUSE RUBBLE RUDERA CRUMBLE ELUVIUM RUBBISH SLIDDER DETRITUS (— IN WOOL) BUR BURR (— OF INSECTS) FRASS (— OF ROCKS) HEAD DRIFT SCREE TALUS ELUVIUM (FLUFFY —) FLUE (FOREST —) SLASH
DEBT DUE SIN POST DEBIT FAULT STOCK ARREARS DEBITUM JUDGMENT TRESPASS (PL.) OBLATA WANIGAN ARREARAGE
DEBTOR OWER PEON SKIP DYVOUR DEBITOR YIELDER
DEBUT OPENING ENTRANCE
DEBUTANTE BUD DEB DEBBY INGENUE ROSEBUD
DECADENT EFFETE DECAYED HOTHOUSE OVERRIPE
DECAHYDRATE SODA
DECALOGUE WITNESS
DECAMP GUY PUT BOLT HIKE KITE

ELOPE MOSEY SCOOT SCOUR SLOPE VAMOS DEPART ESCAPE LEVANT MIZZLE MORRIS POWDER VAMOSE ABSCOND DISCAMP VAMOSE ABSQUATULATE
DECAMPING GUY
DECAN DECURION
DECANT EMIT POUR RACK UNLOAD TRANSFER
DECANTER CARAFE CARAFON URCEOLE GARDEVIN INGESTER
DECAPITATE BEHEAD DECOLLATE
DECAPITATION DECOLL HEADING
DECAPOD BUSTER
DECARBONIZE DECOKE
DECATING SPONGING
DECAY EBB ROT ROX BLET CONK DOAT DOTE DOZE FADE RUIN SEED WANE WEAR CROCK DEATH FAIL SHANK SLOOM SLOUM SPOIL WASTE BLIGHT CANKER CARIES FADING MARCOR MILDEW MOLDER MOSKER SICKEN WITHER CRUMBLE DECLINE FAILURE FORFAIR MORTIFY PUTREFY DECREASE FORDWINE (— IN WOOD) CONK DOZE (— OF FRUIT) BLETTING (INCIPIENT —) BLET (PREF.) (TOOTH —) CARIO
DECAYED BAD DEAF DOZY ROXY FRUSH SEEDY DAISED MARCID PUTRID ROTTEN SPAKED CARIOUS RUINOUS SNAGGLED
DECAYING COLD DOTY SHABBY CARIOUS
DECEASE DIE FAIL OBIT PASS DEATH DEMISE PASSAGE
DECEASED DEAD LATE PARTED DEFUNCT EXTINCT UMWHILE DEPARTED UMQUHILE
DECEIT GAB DOLE FLUM GAFF GULL RUSE SHAM TRAP TRAY WILE ABUSE COVIN CRAFT DOLUS FRAUD GUILE SARAB SWICK SWIKE CAUTEL FELONY WOIDRE CUNNING DISSAIT FAITERY FICTION ARTIFICE COZENAGE FALSEDAD INTRIGUE SPOOFERY SUBTLETY TRICKERY TRUMPERY WILINESS
DECEITFUL JIVE BLIND BRAID FALSE GAUDY JANUS LOOPY PUNIC SLAPE SNAKY ARTFUL COVERT CRAFTY DOUBLE FICKLE HOLLOW ROTTEN TRICKY CUNNING EVASIVE FICTIVE SIRENIC SLEEKIT SLIDDER UNWREST WINDING COVINOUS GUILEFUL ILLUSIVE INDIRECT SHAMMISH TORTUOUS MENDACIOUS
DECEITFULLY DOUBLE FALSELY
DECEITFULNESS SHAM DECEIT FALSITY
DECEIVE BOB COG CON DOR FOB FUB GAB GAS GUM KID LIE BILK BRAG BUNK CRAP DUPE FAKE FLAM FOOL GAFF GULL HAVE HOAX HYPE JILT JOUK MOCK SELL SHAM SILE SNOW TURN WILE ABUSE AMUSE BLEAR BLEND BLENK BLIND BLINK BLUFF

CATCH CHEAT COZEN CROSS CULLY DODGE DORRE FEINT GLEEK GLOZE HOCUS LURCH PATCH SHUCK SPOOF SWICK SWIKE TRICK TROIL TRUFF TRUMP TRYST BAFFLE BARRAT BEDOTE BEFLUM BEFOOL BETRAY BLANCH BUBBLE CAJOLE CLOINE CLOYNE DELUDE DIVERT EUCHRE GAMMON HUMBUG ILLUDE JUGGLE MISUSE NIGGLE SUCKER WIMPLE BEGUILE DEFRAUD MISLEAD OVERSEE TRAITOR BEJUGGLE FLIMFLAM HOODWINK OUTREACH
DECEIVER ANGLE CHEAT HOCUS COGGER FAITOR FALSER GUILER MOCKER TRAPAN TREPAN FALSARY ILLUSOR JUGGLER SHARPER SPOOFER TRUMPER WARLOCK WERNARD IMPOSTOR LOSENGER LOTHARIO MAGICIAN TREGETOUR
DECELERATE SLOW
DECENCY GRACE DECORUM HONESTY MODESTY CHASTITY
DECENNIUM DECADE
DECENT FAIR CHASTE COMELY HONEST MODEST PRETTY PROPER SEEMLY FITTING GRADELY JANNOCK SHAPELY SIGHTLY DECOROUS GRAITHLY WISELIKE
DECENTLY WHITE
DECEPTION BAM COG DOR GAG LIE DOLE FLAM FLUM GAFF GULL HOAX HYPE MAZE RIDE RUSE SELL SHAM WILE ABUSE BLIND BLUFF CHEAT COVIN CRAFT CURVE DOLUS DORRE FAVEL FRAUD GLAIK GLEEK GUILE MAGIC SHUCK SNARE SPOOF TRICK BARRAT CAUTEL DECEIT DUPERY HUMBUG JUGGLE ABUSION BLAFLUM CHICANE CUNNING EVASION FALLACY FALSERY FICTION GULLAGE GULLERY KNAVERY PRETEXT SLYNESS ARTIFICE DISGUISE FALSEDAD FLIMFLAM ILLUSION INTRIGUE PHANTASM PRESTIGE SUBTLETY TRICKERY TRUMPERY WILINESS
DECEPTIVE FLAM FALSE ARTFUL BUBBLE SIRENIC TRICKSY DELUSIVE DELUSORY FLIMFLAM ILLUSORY IMPOSING SHAMMISH UNSICKER
DECEPTIVENESS FANTASTRY
DECIBEL (10 —S) BEL
DECIDE FIX CAST DEEM HOLD RULE TELL WILL AWARD JUDGE PATCH PITCH DECERN DECISE DECREE FIGURE REWARD SETTLE ADJUDGE DERAIGN RESOLVE CONCLUDE SENTENCE (— UPON) SET ELECT CHOOSE TERMINE
DECIDED FIRM FLAT MAIN FORMED SETTLED DECISIVE RESOLUTE
DECIDEDLY DIRECTLY DISTINCTLY
DECIDUA CADUCA
DECIGRAM LI

DECIMA TENTH TITHE
DECIMAL DENARY REPEATER (— PART) MANTISSA
DECIMATE TENTH DESTROY
DECIPHER READ SOLVE CIPHER DECODE DETECT REVEAL DECRYPT DISCOVER INDICATE UNPUZZLE
DECIPHERING EPIGRAPHY
DECISION ACT END CALL DOOM FIAT GRIT ARRET AWARD CANON FAITH ISSUE PARTY PLUCK POINT ACTION CHOICE CRISIS DECREE DIKTAT RULING ACUERDO CONSULT INTERIM PRACTIC VERDICT FINALITY JUDGMENT PLACITUM SENTENCE SUFFRAGE UMPIRAGE (— OF COURT) HOLDING ABSOLVITOR (EXISTENTIAL —) LEAP (FINAL —) ISSUE (LEGAL —) FETWA
DECISIVE FATAL FINAL CRISIC PAYOFF VIRILE CRUCIAL DECIDED CRITICAL CRUSHING DECRETAL POSITIVE
DECISIVELY FINALLY
DECK FIG TOG BANK BUSK BUSS DAUB DINK FLAT HEAP PINK POOP PROW TRIG ADORN ARRAY COVER DIZEN DRESS EQUIP FLOOR HATCH PRANK PRINK STORE AWNING BEDECK BETRIM BLAZON CLOTHE ENRICH FETTLE FOCSLE LAUREL APPAREL BEDIGHT BEDIZEN FEATHER FLOUNCE GEMMATE BEAUTIFY DECORATE EMBLAZON PLATFORM (— OF CARDS) BOOK (— OUT) BARB TIFF DIZEN SPICK BEDECK DAIKER FANGLE FINIFY BEDIGHT (HIGH —) POOP (LOWEST —) ORLOP
DECKED CLAD BESEEN ARMORIED LAURELED (— OUT) SPIFFED
DECKHAND BOATMAN TRIMMER BARGEMAN ROUSTABOUT
DECKHOUSE CABOOSE CAMBOOSE PILOTHOUSE
DECKLE DECKEL FEATHEREDGE
DECKMAN TRIPPER LEVERMAN
DECLAIM GALE RANT RAVE ROLL MOUTH ORATE SPEAK SPOUT BLEEZE RECITE ELOCUTE INVEIGH DENOUNCE DISCLAIM HARANGUE PERORATE SINGSONG
DECLAIMER BARD SPEECHIFIER
DECLAMATION FROTHING HARANGUE RHETORIC SPOUTING PHILIPPIC
DECLARATION BILL CALL DICK NARR TALE WORD COUNT FUERO LIBEL PAROL AVOWAL DECEIT MISERE ORACLE PAROLE PLACET SAYING EXPRESS PROMISE RESOLVE MANIFEST PLATFORM (— IN BRIDGE) MAKE AUCTION (— OF HOSTILITIES) DEFIANCE (OFFICIAL —) AUTHORITY
DECLARE BID KEN LAY SAY VOW

AVER AVOW DENY MAKE READ
SHOW SNUM SWAN TROW VOTE
AREAD AREED BRUIT KEETH
KITHE KYTHE POSIT SNORE
SOUND SPEAK STATE TRUTH
VOUCH AFFIRM ALLEGE ASSERT
ASSURE AUTHOR AVOUCH
BLAZON COUTHE DEPONE
DESCRY EXPONE HERALD INDICT
NOTIFY PATEFY RELATE SPRING
UPGIVE ACCLAIM BEHIGHT
DISCUSS EXPRESS OUTTELL
PROFESS PROTEST PUBLISH
SIGNIFY TERMINE TESTIFY
ANNOUNCE DENOUNCE DESCRIBE
INDICATE INTIMATE MAINTAIN
MANIFEST NUNCIATE PROCLAIM
RENOUNCE PREDICATE
(— A SAINT) CANONIZE
(— ARBITRARILY) GAVEL
(— INVALID) ANNUL
(— PUBLICLY) CRY
(— UNTRUE) DENY
(— WAR) DEFY
(SOLEMNLY —) AFFY SWEAR
DECLARED AVOWED STATED
DECLARER LAWMAN VIVANT
DECLINATION BIAS DECAY SLOPE
REGRET DECLINE DESCENT
REFUSAL SOUTHING SWERVING
DECLINE BEG DIP EBB SAG SET
BALK BEND BUST DENY DIVE
DOWN DROP FADE FAIL FALL
FLAG FLOP HELD SINK SLIP TURN
VAIL WANE WELK BAULK CHUTE
DECAY DROLL DROOP DWINE
FAINT HEALD HIELD LAPSE
LOWER QUAIL REPEL SLACK
SLOPE SLUMP SPURN STOOP
STRAY TABES WAIVE DEBASE
DEVALL FALTER REFUSE REJECT
RENEGE SICKEN WEAKEN
ATROPHY DESCEND DESCENT
DETRECT DEVIATE DISAVOW
DWINDLE ECLIPSE FAILURE
FALLOFF FORBEAR INFLECT
LETDOWN SINKAGE DECREASE
DOWNBEAT DOWNTURN
FOREBEAR LANGUISH TOBOGGAN
WITHDRAW REPUDIATE
(— IN MARKET PRICE) SPILL
(— IN POPULATION) CRASH
(PREF.) CLIN
DECLINING DOWN AWANE
BEARISH FALLING WESTERN
DECADENT
DECLIVITY BENT BREW FALL
HANG SIDE SKUG CLIFF COAST
DEVEX PITCH SCARP SLENT
SLOPE CALADE HANGER DECLINE
DESCENT HANGING DOWNHILL
DECLIVOUS PRONE SLOPING
DECOCT BOIL COOK SMELT EXCITE
KINDLE REFINE EXTRACT
DECOCTION BANG OOZE SAVE
BHANG APOZEM CREMOR PTISAN
TISANE APOZEMA DECOCTUM
DECOHERER TAPPER
DECOLLETE LOW
DECOMPOSE ROT FOUL FRIT
DECAY ATTACK DIGEST DEGRADE
DISSOLVE
DECOMPOSED PUTRID

DECOMPOSITION DECAY
BREAKUP BIOLYSIS EXCHANGE
(DOUBLE —) METATHESIS
(SUFF.) LYSE LYSIS LYST LYTE
LYTIC LYZE
DECORATE DO BIND BUSK CHIP
CITE DECK EDGE FRET GAUD PINK
RAIL RULE TIFF TIRE TRIM ADORN
DRESS FLOCK FRILL GRAIN INLAY
MENSE PANEL POKER TRAIL
TRICK BEDECK BUTTON DAIKER
DAMASK DECORE EMBOSS
FLOWER FRESCO PARGET
POUNCE PURFLE SPONGE
SUBORN BECROSS CORONET
ENCHASE FESTOON FURNISH
GADROON GARNISH HISTORY
IMPASTE INWEAVE MINIATE
PERFORM BELETTER FLOURISH
ORNAMENT OVERWORK TITIVATE
DECORATED GIDDY LACED
AJOURE FLAMBE ORNATE
ADORNED DAMASSE FROGGED
INCISED WROUGHT COCKADED
DISTINCT FLORETED
DECORATING LIMNERY
DECORATION KEY BUHL FALL
FUSS IKAT BOULE DECOR DODAD
HONOR MEDAL PRIDE BOULLE
DECKER DECORE DESIGN DOODAB
DOODAD FINERY FLORET FRIEZE
GOTHIC NIELLO PLAQUE SETOFF
TINSEL ARTWORK BARBOLA
DECKING EPERGNE FLUTING
GARNISH TRACERY BAYADERE
DENTELLE DIAMANTE ESCALLOP
FLOURISH FRETTING FRETWORK
INTARSIA ORNAMENT
(— IN GUEST CHAMBER) XENIUM
(— OF LEAVES) VIGNETTE
(— OF MONKEYS) SINGERIE
(— TECHNIQUE) PLANGI
(BOOK-COVER —) DENTELLE
(CUTOUT —) APPLIQUE
(ENAMEL —) WUTSAI
(FESTIVE —) GALA
(INESSENTIAL —) SPINACH
(MURAL —) TOPIA
(MUSICAL —) GRACE
(PORCELAIN —) KAKIEMON
(POTTERY —) BRODERIE
(RICH —) PARAMENT
(SCANDINAVIAN —) ROSEMALING
(WALL —S) TENTURE
(PL.) COLORS BUNTING
GREENERY
DECORATIVE FANCY FIKIE
DECOROUS CALM DONE GOOD
NICE PRIM DOUCE GRAVE QUIET
SOBER STAID CHASTE DECENT
DEMURE MODEST POLITE PROPER
SEDATE SEEMLY SERENE STEADY
BECOMED FITTING ORDERLY
REGULAR SETTLED BECOMING
COMPOSED MANNERLY
DECOROUSLY FITLY
DECOROUSNESS CHASTITY
POLITESSE
DECORTICATE FLAY HULL HUSK
PARE PEEL PILL SKIN STRIP
DENUDE
DECORUM DECENCY DIGNITY
FITNESS HONESTY

MODESTY PROPRIETY
DECOY COY BAIT CALL GOAD LURE
TOLE TOLL COACH CRIMP DRILL
PLANT ROPER SHILL STALE STALL
STOOL TEMPT TRAIN ALLURE
BUTTON CALLER CAPPER ENTICE
ENTRAP PIGEON SEDUCE TOLLER
TREPAN BARNARD BERNARD
DECOYER INVEIGLE SQUAWKER
(— FOR GAMBLERS) CAPPER
(— FOR SWINDLERS) BARNARD
BERNARD
(AUCTIONEER'S —) BONNET
BUTTON
DECREASE EBB BATE DROP FALL
LOSS SINK WANE WELK WILK
ABATE CROCK DECAY LAPSE
SWAGE TAPER WANZE WASTE
CHANGE DECESS DECREW IMPAIR
LESSEN NARROW REDUCE SHRINK
ATROPHY CUTDOWN DECLINE
DWINDLE SHORTEN SLACKEN
SUBSIDE ABLATION DECIMATE
DIMINISH DOWNTURN MODERATE
RETRENCH
(— IN FORCE) LAY
(— IN VOLUME) ABLATION
(— OF EFFICIENCY) FATIGUE
(— STITCHES) FASHION
DECREE ACT DIT LAW SAW SET
DOOM FIAT REDE RULE WILL
WITE AREAD AREED ARRET
CANON EDICT ENACT FIANT
GRACE HATTI IRADE JUDGE
ORDER POINT SHAPE TENET
UKASE WRITE ARREST ASSIZE
DECERN DICTUM FIRMAN INDICT
MODIFY ORDAIN PLACIT RECESS
ADJUDGE APPOINT BESLUIT
COMMAND CONSULT DECREET
DICTATE DIVORCE ESCRIPT
GEZERAH MANDATE SETNESS
STATUTE WORKING DECISION
DECRETUM JUDGMENT PLACITUM
PSEPHISM RESCRIPT ROGATION
SANCTION SENTENCE ORDINANCE
ABSOLVITOR
(— BEFOREHAND) DESTINE
(ECCLESIASTICAL —) CANON
SYNODICAL
(JUDICIAL —) AUTO
(MOHAMMEDAN —) IRADE
(OFFICIAL —) RESCRIPT
(PAPAL —) DECRETAL
DECREPIT LAME WEAK UNORN
BEDRID CREAKY FEEBLE INFIRM
SENILE FAILING INVALID
FORFAIRN
DECRY BOO CRAB SLUR LOWER
ROGUE DESCRY LESSEN ASPERSE
BARRACK CENSURE CONDEMN
DEBAUCH DEGRADE DETRACT
BELITTLE DEROGATE MINIMIZE
DECRYPT BREAK DECODE
DECURRENT DEFLUENT
DECUSSATION CHIASM CHIASMA
DEDAN (FATHER OF —) RAAMAH
JOKSHAN
(MOTHER OF —) KETURAH
DEDANS HAZARD
DEDICATE VOW VOTE DEVOW
SACRE SACRI DEVOTE DEVOVE
DIRECT HALLOW OBLATE ASCRIBE

ENTITLE CHRISTEN INSCRIBE
INTITULE SEPARATE NUNCUPATE
DEDICATED HOLY OBLATE SACRED
VOTIVE
DEDICATION CULT WAKF
DEVOTION
DEDUCE PUT DRAW LEAD TAKE
BRING DRIVE FETCH GUESS INFER
TRACE DEDUCT DERIVE ELICIT
EVOLVE GATHER COLLECT
EXPLAIN EXTRACT SUBSUME
CONCLUDE
DEDUCT BATE DOCK TAKE ABATE
ALLOW SHAVE DEFALK REBATE
RECOUP REDUCT REMOVE
CURTAIL SUBDUCT TRADUCE
ABSTRACT DISCOUNT SEPARATE
SUBTRACT
DEDUCTION AGIO SALT CREDIT
DEDUCT REBATE BEAMAGE
DOCKAGE IMPRESS OFFTAKE
REPRISE DISCOUNT ERGOTISM
ILLATION STOPPAGE ABATEMENT
COROLLARY
DEDUCTIVE DOGMATIC
DEE DUANT
DEED DO ACT BILL BOOK CASE
FACT FAIT FEAT FIAT GEST HARD
JEST TURN WORK ACTUM ACTUS
BROAD CHART DOING GESTE
ISSUE SANAD THING TITLE
ACTION CONVEY ESCROW
FACTUM POTTAH REMISE SASINE
SUNNUD TAILYE CHARTER
EXPLOIT FACTION TAILZIE
CHIVALRY HEIRLOOM PARERGON
PRACTICE PRACTISE TRANSFER
PERFORMANCE
(BRUTAL —) ATROCITY
(CHARITABLE —S) ALMS
(EVIL —) MALEFACTION
(GOOD —) BENEFIT MITZVAH
(HEBREW —) STARR
(PART OF —) HABENDUM
(VALIANT —) VALIANCE
(WICKED —) ILL
(PL.) DOINGS SERVICE
MUNIMENTS
DEEM LET SAY SEE GIVE HOPE
RECK SEEM TELL JUDGE OPINE
THINK ESTEEM EXPECT ORDAIN
RECKON REGARD ACCOUNT
ADJUDGE BELIEVE RECOUNT
RESPECT SURMISE ANNOUNCE
CONSIDER JUDGMENT PROCLAIM
DE-EMPHASIZE DOWNPLAY
DEEMSTER DOOMSMAN
DE-ENERGIZE KILL CLEAR
DEEP LOW SAD SEA BASS BOLD
DUAT HOLL HOWE NEAL RAPT
ABYSS BROAD DEWAT GRAVE
GREAT GRUFF HEAVY OCEAN
SOUND STIFF STOOR STOUR
HOLLOW INTENT STRONG SULLEN
ABYSMAL INTENSE SERIOUS
UNMIXED ABSORBED ABSTRUSE
COMPLETE POWERFUL
PROFOUND THOROUGH
RECONDITE
(PREF.) **(— SEA)** BATH(O)(Y)
DEEP-DYED ENGRAINED
DEEPEN CLOUD DARKEN DREDGE
ENHANCE THICKEN HEIGHTEN

DEEPEST INMOST DEEPMOST
DEEPLY DEEP ADEEP DEARLY
SOUNDLY DEVOUTLY GROUNDLY
INWARDLY
DEEP-SEA DIPSY BATHYL DIPSEY
BATHYAL
DEEP-SEATED DEEP INTIMATE
PROFOUND INGRAINED
DEEP-TONED STOUR
DEER ELK RED ROE AXIS BUCK
DAIM HART HIND MILU MUSK
OLEN PARA PUDU RUSA SHOU
SIKA STAG WILD BROCK GEMUL
MARAL MOOSE SABIR SPADE
STAIG CERVID CHITAL CHITRA
FALLOW GUEMAL HANGUL
HEARST HUEMUL PARRAH
RASCAL SAMBAR SAMBUR
THAMIN VENADA BROCKET
BROWZER CARIBOU CERVINE
CERVOID CHEETAL DEERLET
FANTAIL GUAZUTI KASTURA
MUNTJAC PLANDOK SAMBHAR
THAMENG VENISON BOBOLINK
CARIACOU CARJACOU ELAPHURE
RUMINANT
(— IN 3RD YEAR) SPAY SOREL
SPAYAD SPAYARD
(— UNDER 1 YEAR) KID
(CASTRATED —) HAVIER
(FEMALE —) DOE ROE HIND
(FEMALE — IN 2ND YEAR) TEG
HEARST
(HINDQUARTERS OF —) FOUCH
FOURCHE
(MALE — IN 2ND YEAR) PRICKET
(MALE — IN 4TH YEAR) SORE
STAGGARD STAGGART
(MALE — OVER 5 YEARS) HART
STAG
(RED —) OLEN SPAY MARAL
BROCKET
(RUSINE —) AXIS
(YOUNG —) KID FAWN SPITTER
(2-YEAR OLD —) KNOBBER
(PREF.) CERVI
DEER BUSH SOAPBUSH
DEER FERN HARDFERN
DEERFLY TABANID
DEERHAIR SEDGE BULRUSH
DEERHOUND DEERDOG
BUCKHOUND
DEERSKIN BUCK DEER
DEERSLAYER (AUTHOR OF —)
COOPER
(CHARACTER IN —) HARRY HETTY
NATTY UNCAS BUMPPO HUTTER
JUDITH THOMAS CHINGACHGOOK
DEFACE MAR FOUL RUIN SCAR
ERASE SHAME SPOIL CANCEL
DAMAGE DAMASK DEFAME
DEFOIL DEFORM DEFOUL EFFACE
INJURE INJURY DESTROY
DETRACT DISTORT SLANDER
DISGRACE DISHONOR MALAHACK
MUTILATE OUTSHINE
DEFACED FOUL
DEFACING DIMINUTION
DEFALCATE DRIB DEFALK
DEFAMATION LIBEL DEFAME
DEFAMY DEPRAVE SCANDAL
SLANDER ASPERSION
DEFAMATORY SCANDALOUS

DEFAME FOUL ABASE BELIE
CLOUD LIBEL NOISE SMEAR
ACCUSE CHARGE DEFACE DEFOIL
DEFOUL FORGAB INFAME INJURE
MALIGN REVILE SUGGIL VILIFY
ASPERSE BLACKEN BLEMISH
DEBAUCH DETRACT DIFFAME
PUBLISH SCANDAL SLANDER
SPATTER TRADUCE DISHONOR
INFAMIZE VILIPEND
DEFAMER SYCOPHANT
DEFAULT FAIL FLAW LOSS MORA
ERROR FAULT OFFEND BLEMISH
FAILURE MISTAKE NEGLECT
OFFENSE OMISSION
(— ON DEBT) LEVANT
DEFAULTER DUCK
(PL.) JANKERS
DEFEASANCE DEFEAT UNDOING
DEFEASIBLE IMPERFECT
DEFEAT EAT PIP WIN BALK BEAT
BEST BOWL CAST DING DOWN
DRUB FOIL HAVE JINK KILL LACE
LICK LOSS ROUT RUIN RUSH SINK
SKIN STOP TOLL TOSS TRAP TRIM
UNDO WHAP WHIP WHOP AVOID
BREAK CHECK FACER FALSE
FLING FLOOR OUTDO PASTE
SHEND SKUNK SMITE SWAMP
THROW WASTE WHACK WORSE
WORST WRACK BAFFLE CUMBER
DEROUT EUCHRE LARRUP
MASTER MURDER OUTGUN
REBUFF STOUSH THWACK
THWART WAGGLE WEAKEN
CLOBBER CONQUER DEPRIVE
DESTROY LICKING OVERSET
PEREMPT REVERSE SCOMFIT
SETBACK SHELLAC SNOOKER
SUBVERT TROUNCE INFRINGE
IRRITATE OUTFIGHT OVERCOME
SLOSHING VANQUISH WATERLOO
OVERPOWER OVERTHROW
(— COMPLETELY) SKUNK
(— DECISIVELY) EAT DRUB SACK
BLAST CLEAN FLATTEN SHELLAC
(— IN BRIDGE) SET
(— IN LAWSUIT) CAST
(DECISIVE —) CLEANUP CLEANING
PLASTERING
(INTO —) DOWN
(UTTER —) MATE ROUT DEROUT
DEFEATED DOWN LOST KAPUT
BEATEN CRAVEN WHIPPED
DEFEATIST BOLO FATALIST
DEFECT BUG FLAW LACK MAIM
MOTE TWIT VICE WANE WANT
BOTCH CLOUD CRAZE ERROR
FAULT MINUS MULCT TOUCH
DAMAGE DESERT HIATUS INJURY
LACUNA MALADY MAYHEM
PLIGHT VICETY VITIUM ABSENCE
BLEMISH DEMERIT FAILING
MISPICK PEELING PINHOLE
COLOBOMA CRESCENT
DRAWBACK WEAKNESS
SHORTCOMING
(— IN ARTICULATION) PSELLISM
(— IN CRYSTAL) HOLE
(— IN ENAMEL) SCAB SAGGING
SCUMMING
(— IN FABRIC) GOUT SCOB BARRE
BRACK SMASH

(— IN GLASS) KNOT TEAR STONE
WREATH THREADS
(— IN IRON) SEAM
(— IN MARBLE) TERRAS TERRACE
TERRASSE
(— IN METAL) SNAKE BLOWHOLE
(— IN PRINTING PLATE) HICKY
HICKEY
(— IN STEEL) LAP
(— IN TIMBER) LAG SHAN
COLLAPSE
(— IN YARN) SINGLING
CORKSCREW
(— OF CHARACTER) HOLE SHADE
HAMARTIA
(LINT —) SPOT
(SPEECH —) BALBUTIES
CLUTTERING
(TELEVISION —) FLOPOVER
DEFECTION LETDOWN APOSTASY
DESERTION
DEFECTIVE BAD ILL EVIL FOXY
LACK LAME MANK POOR SICK
BAUCH BAUGH BLIND FALSE
FLAWY PASUL COMMON FAULTY
FLAWED MANGUE MEAGER
MEAGRE RAGGED HALTING
TOMFOOL VICIOUS DISGENIC
DYSGENIC MUTILOUS VITIATED
(PREF.) ATEL(O)
DEFEND FEND HOLD KEEP SAVE
WARD WARN WEAR COVER
GUARD SHEND WATCH ASSERT
FORBID SCREEN SECURE SHIELD
UPHOLD WARISH BUCKLER
BULWARK CONTEST DERAIGN
ESPOUSE EXPOUND FLANKER
JUSTIFY PREVENT PROPUGN
PROTECT SHELTER SUPPORT
WARRANT ADVOCATE CHAMPION
CONSERVE GARRISON MAINTAIN
PRESERVE PROHIBIT SAFEGUARD
DEFENDANT REA REUS ACCUSED
AVOWANT APPELLEE
DEFENDER FENDER PATRON
ADVOCATE ASSERTER ASSERTOR
CHAMPION GUARDIAN UPHOLDER
DEFENSE EGIS FORT PALE ROCK
WALL WARD WEAR AEGIS ALIBI
FENCE GRITH GUARD TOWER
ABATIS ANSWER BEHALF COVERT
FRAISE SCONCE BARRACE
BARRIER BASTION BULWARK
CONTEST COUNTER DEFENCE
DILATOR OUTWORK PARADOS
RAMPART SHELTER WARDING
WARRANT ADVOCACY APOLOGIA
BOUNDARY FRONTIER GALAPAGO
GARRISON MUNITION SECURITY
SEPIMENT
DEFENSELESS BARE COLD NAKED
SILLY UNARMED HELPLESS
DEFENSIBLE TENABLE JUSTIFIABLE
DEFER BOW RISE STAY WAIT
DELAY DRIVE HONOR REFER
REMIT STAVE TARRY TRACK
WAIVE YIELD ESTEEM HUMBLE
RETARD REVERE SUBMIT
ADJOURN SUSPEND CONSIDER
INTERMIT POSTPONE PROROGUE
PROTRACT SUSPENSE
DEFERENCE VAIL COURT HONOR
CRINGE ESTEEM HOMAGE

REGARD RESPECT WORSHIP
CIVILITY OBEISANCE
DEFERENT ECCENTRIC
DEFERENTIAL DUTIFUL OBEISANT
DEFERMENT STAY
DEFERVESCENCE LYSIS DECLINE
DEFIANCE DARE DEFI DEFY GAGE
BRAVE DEFIAL CHALLENGE
DEFIANT BOLD BARDY BRAVE
STOUT DARING STOCKY
INSOLENT STUBBORN
OBSTREPEROUS
DEFIANTLY ACOCK
DEFICIENCY FAIL LACK WANT
ANOIA ERROR FAULT MINUS
DEARTH DEFECT INLAIK ULLAGE
ABSENCE ANOESIA BLEMISH
DEFICIT FAILING FAILURE
POVERTY DELETION SCARCITY
SHORTAGE SHORTFALL
SHORTCOMING
(— OF BLOOD) ISCHEMIA
(— OF NERVOUS ENERGY) ANEURIA
(— OF OXYGEN) ASPHYXIA
(CARBON DIOXIDE —) ACAPNIA
(MENTAL —) IDIOCY AMENTIA
(PL.) SHORTS
(PREF.) ISCH
(SUFF.) PENIA
DEFICIENT BAD LEAN WANE
BLUNT MINUS SCANT BARREN
FEEBLE MEAGER MEAGRE SCARCE
SCRIMP SKIMPY BOBTAIL
DISGENIC DYSGENIC INDIGENT
(— IN TURGOR) FLACCID
(MENTALLY —) SOFT
(SUFF.) PRIVIC
DEFICIT SHORTAGE UNDERAGE
DEFILE GUT RAY ABRA BAWD
BEDO FILE FOIL FOUL GATE GOWL
HALS LIME MOIL MUCK PACE
PASS SLIP SLOT SLUT SMUT SOIL
ABUSE BERAY CLEFT CROCK
DIRTY FILTH GLACK GORGE
HALSE NOTCH SLACK SMEAR
STAIN SULLY TAINT BEWRAY
DEBASE GULLET IMBRUE INFECT
RAVISH SMOUCH SMUTCH
CORRUPT DEBAUCH DEPRAVE
DISTAIN PASSAGE POLLUTE
PROFANE SLOTTER SMATTER
TARNISH VIOLATE DISHONOR
MACULATE
DEFILED DIRTY IMPURE SPOTTY
UNCLEAN MACULATE
DEFILEMENT MOIL SOIL SULLAGE
TAINTURE
(PREF.) MEASMATO MIASMO
MYS(O)
DEFILING PIKY PITCHY
DEFINE END FIX SET MERE TERM
BOUND LIMIT DECIDE CLARIFY
DELIMIT EXPLAIN EXPOUND
DESCRIBE DISCOVER
DEFINED FORMED STRICT
(SHARPLY —) HARD
DEFINITE SET FIRM HARD SURE
CLEAR FINAL FIXED SHARP FINITE
FORMED LIQUID STRAIT CERTAIN
EXPRESS LIMITED POINTED
PRECISE DISTINCT EMPHATIC
EXPLICIT LIMITING POSITIVE
PUNCTUAL SPECIFIC

DEFINITELY BUT WELL FAIRLY
EVERMORE
DEFINITION GLOSS CLARITY
DIORISM
(— OF FORM) SFUMATO
(PREF.) ORISMO
DEFINITIVE LAST FINAL GRAND
ORISTIC DEFINITE
DEFLATE EMPALE IMPALE
CONTRACT
DEFLATED FLAT
DEFLATING SETDOWN
DEFLATION HANGOVER
DEFLECT CUT WRY BEND COCK
SWAY WARP PARRY WREST
WRING BAFFLE DETOUR DIVERT
SWERVE DEVIATE DIVERGE
INFLECT REFLECT REFRACT
DEFLECTION DROOP SWEEP
WINDAGE
(— ON METER) KICK
(PREF.) SPHINGO
DEFLECTOR (AIR —) SPOILER
DEFLOWER FRAY DEFOIL DEFOUL
FORLIE RAVAGE RAVISH DEFLORE
DESPOIL VIOLATE UNMAIDEN
UNVIRGIN
DEFORM MAR FLOW WARP GNARL
DEFACE BLEMISH CONTORT
DISFORM DISTORT DIFFORME
DISGUISE DISHONOR MISSHAPE
SHAUCHLE
DEFORMATION CREEP SPRING
STRAIN FLEXURE FLOWAGE
DEFORMED GAMMY WRONG
INFORM PAULIE CROOKED
HIDEOUS MISBORN FORMLESS
UNMACKLY
(PREF.) CAC(O) CACH
(SUFF.) CACE
DEFORMITY GALL VICE BLEMISH
HARELIP PRAVITY CLUBFOOT
CLUBHAND FLATFOOT
WANSHAPE
DEFRAUD ROB BEAT BILK FAKE
GULL NICK ROOK TRIM WIPE
CHEAT COZEN GOUGE LURCH
MULCT SLICK STICK TRICK
WRONG BOODLE CHOUSE
CHOWSE DECEIVE SKELDER
SWINDLE
DEFRAY PAY BEAR AVERT COVER
ABSORB EXPEND PREPAY
APPEASE REQUITE SATISFY
DISBURSE
DEFT FEAT GAIN NEAT TALL TRIM
AGILE HANDY NATTY QUICK SLICK
ADROIT EXPERT HEPPEN NIMBLE
SPRACK SPRUCE DELIVER
DEXTROUS SKILLFUL
DEFTEST EFTEST
DEFTLY LIGHTLY SLICKLY
DELIVERLY
DEFTNESS SLEIGHT
DEFUNCT DEAD EXTINCT
DECEASED DEPARTED FINISHED
DEFY BRAG DARE DEFI FACE MOCK
BEARD BRAVE STUMP TEMPT
CARTEL FORBID MAUGER
MAUGRE REJECT AFFRONT
BRAVADE DESPISE DISDAIN
OUTDARE OUTFACE CHAMPION
DEFIANCE OUTSCOUT RENOUNCE

CHALLENGE
DEGENERATE ROT SINK DEBADE
EFFETE UNKIND DEGENER
DEGRADE DEPRAVE DESCEND
DEGENDER DEROGATE
(— IN IDLENESS) RUST
(— TOWARD BARBARISM) WILDER
DEGENERATION WALLER
ATROPHY ADIPOSIS PEJORATION
DEGRADATION FALL WOHL
SHAME DEMISS DECLINE
DESCENT ADULTERY COMEDOWN
DEPOSURE IGNOMINY ABJECTION
DEGRADE BUST SINK ABASE
BREAK DECRY LOWER SHAME
SHEND STOOP STRIP UNMAN
DEBASE DEMEAN DEMOTE
DEPOSE EMBASE HUMBLE LESSEN
REDUCE VILIFY CORRUPT
DECLINE DEPRESS IMBRUTE
REGRADE VILLAIN DIMINISH
DISGRACE DISHONOR DISMOUNT
DISPLUME SUPPLANT
DEGRADED BASE BROKE SEAMY
ABJECT DEMISS FALLEN SORDID
DEBASED DEGREED GRIECED
OUTCAST
DEGRADING BASE VILE MENIAL
SHAMEFUL
DEGRAS MOELLON
DEGREE PEG PIP POL BANK CAST
DEAL FORM GREE HEAT PEEP
POLL RANK RATE RUNG STEP
TERM TIER CLASS GRADE GRADO
GRECE GRICE HONOR LEVEL
NOTCH ORDER PITCH PLACE
POINT PRICK SHADE STAGE STAIR
EXTENT GRIECE LENGTH MEDIUM
SOEVER DESCENT DIGNITY
MEASURE SAENGER STATION
ACCURACY AEGROTAT QUANTITY
STANDING STRENGTH
(— OF CLOSENESS) FIT
(— OF COMBINING POWER)
VALENCE
(— OF CONTRAST) GAMMA
(— OF DEVIATION) LEEWAY
(— OF ELEVATION) ASCENT
(— OF ENGAGEMENT) DEPTH
(— OF FLAWLESSNESS) CLARITY
(— OF FORCE) KICK
(— OF HEIGHT) GRADE
(— OF IMPORTANCE) CALIBER
CALIBRE
(— OF INFESTATION) BURDEN
(— OF INTOXICATION) EDGE
(— OF KNOWLEDGE) SCIENTER
(— OF LIGHTNESS) VALUE
(— OF MIXTURE) ALLOY
(— OF OPACITY) DENSITY
(— OF PLENTIFULNESS)
ABUNDANCE
(— OF PRESTIGE) PLACE
(— OF SLOPE) PITCH SPLAY
(— OF STREAMLINING) FAIRNESS
(— OF THE SOUL) RUACH
(— OF WATER HARDNESS) GRAIN
(— OF WHITENESS) BLEACH
(EXCESSIVE —) EXTREME
(GREATEST —) UTMOST OPTIMUM
(HIGHEST —) PINK SUMMIT
SUPREME SUBLIMITY
(INDEFINITE —) SEEM

(MINUTE —) DROP SHADE
(MUSICAL —) SPACE SUBTONIC
(RABBINICAL —) SEMICHA
SEMIKAH SEMICHAH
(SMALL —) ACE TAD HAIR INCH
IOTA SHADOW GLIMMER
(SOME —) BIT
(UTMOST —) SUM ACME HEIGHT
EXTREME EXTREMITY
(10 —S OF LONGITUDE) FACE
(15 —S) HOUR
(PREF.) (OF THE THIRD ALGEBRAIC
—) CUB(I)(O)
(SUFF.) ANCE ANT ENCE ITY NESS
TY
DEGU OCTODONT
DEGUM STRIP
(— SILK) SOUPLE
DEHGAN SWAT SWATI
DEHORN SNUB DISBUD
DEHWAR DEHKAN
DEHYDRATE DRY DESICCATE
DEIANIRA (BROTHER OF —) TYDEUS
MELEAGER
(FATHER OF —) OENEUS
(HUSBAND OF —) HERCULES
(MOTHER OF —) ALTHAEA
DEIDAMIA HIPPODAMIA
(FATHER OF —) LYCOMEDES
(LOVER OF —) ACHILLES
(SON OF —) PYRRHUS
NEOPTOLEMUS
DEIFICATION APOTHEOSIS
DEIFY GOD BEGOD DIVINE
GODDIZE DIVINIFY DIVINIZE
DEIGN STOOP VOUCHSAFE
DEILEON (BROTHER OF —)
PHLOGIUS AUTOLYCUS
(FATHER OF —) DEIMACHUS
DEION (DAUGHTER OF —)
ASTERODIA
(FATHER OF —) AEOLUS
(MOTHER OF —) ENARETE
(SON OF —) ACTOR AENETUS
CEPHALUS PHYLACUS
(WIFE OF —) DIOMEDE
DEIPHOBUS (BROTHER OF —) PARIS
HECTOR
(FATHER OF —) PRIAM
(MOTHER OF —) HECUBA
(WIFE OF —) HELEN
DEIPYLE (FATHER OF —) ADRASTUS
(HUSBAND OF —) TYDEUS
(SISTER OF —) AEGIA ARGIA
(SON OF —) DIOMEDES
DEIPYLUS (FATHER OF —)
POLYMNESTOR
(MOTHER OF —) ILIONE
DEITY (ALSO SEE GOD AND
GODDESS) EA EL KA RA RE SU
ABU BEL GAD GOD RAN SHU SOL
AKAL AMEN AMON BAAL CAGN
DEVA FAUN FURY GWYN MIND
MORS RANA SIVA SOBK ALALA
ALALU AMIDA AMITA AMMON
DAGAN DAGON HAOMA HOBAL
HORUS HUBAL INUUS JANUS
MIDER MITRA MONAD SATYR
SEBEK SHIVA SIRIS SURYA ZOMBI
ASHIMA ATHTAR BATALA
BUNENE CAISSA FATHER FAUNUS
IASION MARDUK MOLOCH NIBHAZ
OANNES ORISHA ORMAZD

ORMUZD RIMMON SOMNUS
SUCHOS SYLVAN VARUNA
ZOMBIE SYLVAN FORSETE
FORSETI GODDESS GODHEAD
GODLING GODSHIP HERSHEF
IAPETUS KHEPERA MANITOU
NINURTA NISROCH PHORCUS
PHORKYS RESHEPH SETEBOS
SILENUS TAGALOA TARANIS
VIRBIUS BAALPEOR BEELPEOR
BELFAGOR DEVARAJA DIVINITY
ELAGABAL GOVERNOR HACHIMAN
MELKARTH MERODACH
PICUMNUS PILUMNUS SEILENOS
SILVANUS TANGALOA
TUTELARY ZEPHYRUS
ZOOMORPH
(AVENGING —) ALASTOR
(HEATHEN —) IDOL
(INFERIOR —) GODKIN GODLING
DEMIURGE PETTYGOD
(SHINTO —) KAMI
(SUPREME —) HANSA
(TUTELARY —) NUMEN GENIUS
(PL.) CABIRI PENATES
DEJECT ABASE LOWER HUMBLE
LESSEN FLATTEN DISPIRIT
DOWNCAST
DEJECTA EGESTA
DEJECTED BAD LOW SAD DAMP
DOWN GLUM POOR SUNK AMORT
MUDDY WAPED ABASED ABATTU
DEJECT DEMISS DROOPY GLOOMY
PINING SOMBER SOMBRE
ALAMORT DUMPISH HANGDOG
HANGING HUMBLED LUMPISH
UNHAPPY DOWNCAST
DOWNWARD REPINING
WOBEGONE WRETCHED
MELANCHOLY
DEJECTEDLY HEAVILY
DEJECTION CRAB DAMP GLOOM
SLOTH DISMAY DISMALS
HUMDRUM SADNESS
MELANCHOLY
DEJEUNER LUNCH BREAKFAST
COLAZIONE COLLATION
DEKASTERE (ABBR.) DAS
DEL NABLA
DELAIAH (FATHER OF —)
MEHETABEEL
(SON OF —) SHEMAIAH

DELAWARE	
CAPITAL: DOVER	
COUNTY: KENT SUSSEX
NEWCASTLE	
INDIAN: LENAPE	
STATE BIRD: BLUEHEN	
STATE FLOWER: PEACH	
STATE NICKNAME: FIRST BLUEHEN
DIAMOND	
STATE TREE: HOLLY	
TOWN: LEWES NEWARK SMYRNA
ELSMERE CLAYMONT	
WILMINGTON	

DELAY LAG LET BLIN BODE HOLD
HONE LENG LING LITE MORA SIST
SLOW SLUG STAY STOP WAIT
ABIDE ABODE ALLAY BLINE
CHECK DALLY DEFER DEMUR
DETER DRIFT DWELL FRIST

PAUSE REPRY SLOTH STALL STENT STICK STINT TARDY TARRY TRACT ARREST ATTEND BACKEN BELATE DAWDLE DETAIN DILATE DILUTE DRETCH ESSOIN FUTURE HINDER HOLDUP IMPEDE LINGER LOITER QUENCH REMORE RETARD TAIGLE TARROW TEMPER WEAKEN ADJOURN ASSUAGE BARRACE CONFINE DRUTTLE FORSLOW PROLONG RESPECT RESPITE SLACKEN SOJOURN DEMURRAL DILATION FORESLOW FOURCHER HANGFIRE HESITATE MACERATE MITIGATE MORATION OBSTRUCT POSTPONE PROTRACT REPRIEVE STOPPAGE CUNCTATION OBSTRUCTION
(— IN COUNTDOWN) HOLD
(— TRIAL) TRAVERSE
(LEGAL —) DILATOR INDUCIAE
(UNDUE —) LACHES
(PL.) AMBAGES
DELAYED LATE TARDY LAGGED BELATED OVERDUE
DELAYING TRAIN DILATORY
DELECTABLE TASTY DESIROUS PLEASING BEAUTIFUL EXQUISITE
DELEGATE NAME SEND ASSIGN COMMIT DELATE DEPUTE DEPUTY LEGATE NUNCIO APPOINT CONSIGN EMPOWER ENTRUST EMISSARY RELEGATE TRANSFER
DELEGATION MISSION DELEGACY
(ATHENIAN —) DELIA
DELETE DELE EDIT OMIT BLACK ERASE PURGE SLASH CANCEL CENSOR DELATE REMOVE STRIKE DESTROY EXPUNGE STONKER CASTRATE
DELETERIOUS BAD PRAVE HARMFUL HURTFUL NOXIOUS PRAVOUS DAMAGING DELETERY PERNICIOUS
DELIBERATE COOL PORE RUNE SLOW STUDY THINK VOULU ADVISE CONFER DEBATE PONDER REGARD ADVISED BALANCE BETHINK CONSULT COUNCIL COUNSEL DELIBER DELIVER REFLECT RESOLVE STUDIED WILLING WITTING CONSIDER DESIGNED MEASURED MEDITATE PERPENSE PREPENSE PROPENSE STUDIOUS
DELIBERATELY COOLY COOLLY APURPOSE ADVISEDLY
DELIBERATENESS MATURITY
DELIBERATION ADVICE COUNCIL COUNSEL LEISURE THOUGHT VISEMENT
DELICACY BIT ROE CATE EASE NORI TACT ACATE FRILL KNACK TASTE CAVIAR DAINTY DELICE JUNKET LUXURY NICETY REGALO FINESSE RAREBIT REGALIA TENUITY TRINKET AIRINESS DAINTITH DAINTREL DELICATE KICKSHAW LEGERETE NICENESS PLEASURE SUBTLETY
(PL.) CATES ACATES
DELICATE SLY AIRY FINE LACY NESH NICE SOFT TEAR ZART

DELIE DORTY ELFIN FAIRY FRAIL LIGHT SILKY TEWLY CASHIE CHOICE DAINTY FLIMSY GENTLE GINGER INCONY KITTLE MINION PASTEL PETITE PULING QUEASY SILKEN SLIGHT SUBTLE TENDER TICKLE TWIGGY ELEGANT EPICENE FINICAL FRAGILE MINIKIN REFINED SLIMMER SUBTILE SUMMERY TAFFETA TAFFETY TENUOUS TIFFANY WILLOWY ARANEOUS CHARMING ETHEREAL FEATHERY GOSSAMER GRACEFUL HOTHOUSE LUSCIOUS MIGNIARD PINDLING PLEASANT SENSIBLE SUMMERLY TICKLISH UNLUSTIE
(— IN APPEARANCE) HUNGRY
(AFFECTEDLY —) ROSEWATER
(PREF.) ABRO HABRO
DELICATELY FINE SMALLY FAIRILY MELTINGLY
DELICATESSEN GASTRONOME CHARCUTERIE
DELICIOUS DAINTY FRIAND DELICATE SCRUMPTIOUS
DELIGHT JOY GLEE GUST LITE LOVE SEND TAKE BLESS BLISS CHARM EXULT FEAST GRACE GUSTO MIRTH REVEL SAVOR SMACK ADMIRE ARRIDE DELICE DIVERT LIKING PLEASE RAVISH REGALE RELISH TICKLE DISPORT ECSTASY ENCHANT GLADDEN GRATIFY JOYANCE JOYANCY LECHERY RAPTURE REJOICE DELICATE ENTRANCE GLADNESS PLEASURE SAVORING
(— IN) LOVE SAVOR
(PL.) DELICIAE
DELIGHTED GLAD
DELIGHTFUL NICE GREAT JAMMY JOLLY MERRY SOOTH DREAMY SAVORY ELYSIAN LEESOME ADORABLE CHARMING DELICATE DELITOUS GLORIOUS GORGEOUS HEAVENLY LUSCIOUS SCRUMPTIOUS
DELIMER DRENCHER
DELIMIT FIX DEFINE SUBTEND
DELIMITATION
(PREF.) HORISMO
DELIMITED MERED MEERED
DELINEATE MAP DRAW ETCH LIMN LINE CHALK CHART FENCE IMAGE PAINT STELL TABLE TOUCH TRACE TRICK BLAZON CIPHER DELINE DEPICT DESIGN DEVISE SKETCH SURVEY DEPAINT EXPRESS LINEATE OUTLINE PICTURE PORTRAY DECIPHER DEFIGURE DESCRIBE TRAVERSE
DELINEATION DRAFT DESIGN SKETCH SURVEY DRAUGHT
(CARELESS —) PERIGRAPH
DELINQUENCY FAULT GUILT FAILURE MISDEED OFFENSE OMISSION
DELINQUENT CRIMINAL
(PL.) KALANG
DELIQUESCE MELT LIQUEFY DISSOLVE
DELIRIOUS FEY MAD OFF REE

GYTE LIGHT MANIC INSANE RAVING FLIGHTY FRANTIC LUNATIC MADDING BRAINISH DELEERIT DELIERET DERANGED FRENETIC FRENZIED
DELIRIUM FURY MAZE MANIA FRENZY LUNACY RAVERY RAVING MADNESS DELIRACY IDLENESS INSANITY
DELIRIUM TREMENS JUMP HORRORS JIMJAMS JIMMIES POTAMANIA
DELIVER DO HIT LAY LET RID BAIL BORN DEAL FREE GIVE LEND REDD SAVE SELL SEND TAKE BEKEN BRING COUGH LIVER SERVE SPEAK UTTER ADDICT ASSIZE ASSOIL BETRAY COMMIT CONVEY EXEMPT PREACH RANSOM REDEEM RENDER RESCUE RESIGN SUCCOR UNBIND BETEACH BITECHE COMMEND CONSIGN DECLAIM DICTATE OUTTAKE PRESENT RECOVER RELEASE RELIEVE DISPATCH EXORCISE EXORCIZE LIBERATE
(— BALL) BOWL
(— BLOW) LEND POKE SEND
(— BLOWS ON HEAD) NOB
(— CHILD) LIGHT
(— FORCEFULLY) FASTEN
(— LOGS) STOCK
(— MERCHANDISE) UTTER
(— OVER) BETAKE CONSIGN
(— RHETORICALLY) DECLAIM
(— SPEECH) ADDRESS
DELIVERANCE BOOT ESCAPE RESCUE SAVING DELIVERY RIDDANCE SOLUTION VOIDANCE SALVATION
DELIVERED LANDED
(— FREE) FRANCO
(PRECISELY —) FLUSH
DELIVERER SOTER DRAYMAN SAOSHYANT
DELIVERY FLY BAIL FLIER FLYER ISSUE LIVERY RESCUE ADDRESS AIRDROP BAILMENT SHIPMENT ACCOUCHEMENT
(— IN SPEAKING) DICTION
(— OF BALL) BOWL
(— WAGON) FLY
(MAIL —) TAPPALL TAPPAUL
(PREF.) TOCO TOKO
(SUFF.) TOCIA TOCO(US) TOKIA TOKO(US) TOKY
DELL DEN HOW DALE DEAN DENE DILL DRAB GLEN VALE SLACK SLADE TRULL WENCH DARGLE DIMBLE DINGLE RAVINE VALLEY
(PL.) DALLES
DELPHINIUM DAUPHIN DOLPHIN LARKSPUR
DELPHUS (FATHER OF —) APOLLO NEPTUNE POSEIDON
(MOTHER OF —) CELAENO MELANTHO
DELUDE BOB JIG BILK DUPE FOOL HOAX MOCK AMUSE CHEAT COZEN ELUDE EVADE GLAIK SPOOF TRICK BAFFLE BANTER BEFOOL BUBBLE CAJOLE DIDDLE ILLUDE BEGUILE DECEIVE

ENCHANT MISLEAD OVERSEE BEJUGGLE HOODWINK INVEIGLE OVERSILE
DELUGE SEA FLOW FLOOD SWAMP DILUVY CATARACT INUNDATE OVERFLOW SATURATE SUBMERGE CATACLYSM
DELUNDUNG LINSANG ZINSANG VIVERRINE
DELUSION MAZE MOHA ABUSE DWALE FRAUD TRICK MIRAGE VISION CHIMERA FALLACY FANTASM PHANTOM WANHOPE ILLUSION NIHILISM PHANTASM
DELUSTER DULL
DELUXE PALACE ELEGANT ELABORATE SUMPTUOUS
DELVE DEN DIG DIP PIT CAVE DINT MINE DITCH PLUMB BRUISE BURROW EXHUME FATHOM INDENT IMPRESS EXCAVATE INSCRIBE
DEMAGNETIZE DEPERM DEPOLARIZE
DEMAGOGUE CLEON LEADER ORATOR ROUSER DEMAGOG JACOBIN SPEAKER TRIBUNE JAWSMITH OCHLOCRAT
DEMAND ASK CRY TAX USE CALL NEED RAME SALE CLAIM CRAVE DRAFT EXACT GAVEL ORDER QUERY SIGHT BEHEST CHARGE DESIRE ELICIT EXPECT SNATCH SUMMON ARRAIGN COMMAND CONSIST DRAUGHT INQUIRE MANDATE REQUEST REQUIRE SOLICIT INSTANCE QUESTION POSTULATE SCISCITATION
(— PAYMENT) DUN CALL
(— RECOGNITION) CLAIM ASSERT
(PL.) EXIGENCE EXIGENCY
DEMANDABLE DUE EXIGIBLE
DEMANDED COMPULSORY
DEMANDING HEFTY EXIGENT
(— ATTENTION) ACUTE
DEMANTOID EMERALD OLIVINE
DEMARCATE DELIMIT SEPARATE
DEMARCATION CELL
DEMEAN ABASE CARRY LOWER BEHAVE DEBASE DEPORT CONTAIN DEGRADE DESCEND MALTREAT
DEMEANOR AIR GARB MIEN PORT FRONT HABIT ACTION HAVIOR BEARING CONDUCT DISPOSE FASHION CARRIAGE PORTANCE
(COLD —) MORGUE
DEMENTED MAD NUTS BUGGY CRAZY LOONY NUTTY INSANE SKEWED FATUOUS
DEMENTIA FATUITY INSANITY
DEMERIT MARK FAULT DESERT BROWNIE
(PL.) GIG
DEMESNE MANOR PLACE REALM DOMAIN ESTATE REGION DISTRICT
DEMETER CERES MISTRESS
DEMETRIUS (BELOVED OF —) CELIA HERMIA
(MOTHER OF —) TAMORA
DEMIGOD AITU HERO KAMI YIMA ADAPA SATYR GARUDA PAGODA

TRITON GODLING
(PL.) NEPHILIM
DEMIGODDESS URD NORN
HEROINE
DEMILUNE RAVELIN
DEMISE WILL DEATH CONVEY
DECEASE BEQUEATH
DEMISED LETTEN
DEMIT LOWER HUMBLE RESIGN
ABDICATE
DEMOCRACY POPULACY
COMMONALTY
DEMOCRAT DEMO DANITE
HUNKER SNAPPER DEMOCRAW
LOCOFOCO POPOCRAT
(CONSERVATIVE —) HARD
DEMODULATE DETECT
DEMOISELLE KULM CRANE
COOLEN KAIKARA
DEMOLISH RASE RAZE RUIN
ABATE BREAK ELIDE LEVEL
WASTE WRECK BATTER SLIGHT
DESTROY RUINATE SHATTER
SUBVERT UNBUILD DOWNCAST
STRAMASH PULVERIZE
DEMOLITION END FALL
DEMON ALP DEV HAG IMP NAT OKI
AITU ATUA BADB BALI BHUT
DEVA DOOK OGRE OKEE PUCK
RAHU SURT WADE ASURA DEVIL
DHOUL FIEND GENIE GHOST
JUMBY LAMIA LESHY LESIY
OTKON SATAN SATYR SHEDU
SURTR TAIPO WITCH ABIGOR
AFREET ARIOCH BILWIS DAEMON
DAIMON DAITYA GENIUS JUMBIE
MAMMON PILWIZ PISACA THURSE
VRITRA YAKSHA YAKSHI ASMADAI
ASMODAY DEMONIO HARPIER
PISACHA VILLAIN WARLOCK
ALICHINO ASHMODAI ASMODEUS
BAALPEOR BEELPEOR CURUPIRA
EUDAEMON OBIDICUT SUCCUBUS
WATERMAN
(— OF WOODS) LESHY LESIY
LESHEY
(ARABIC —) AFRIT AFREET AFRITE
EFREET
(EVIL —) SHEDU
(FEMALE —) HAG LAMIA PISACHI
SUCCUBUS
(NATURE —) GENIUS
(PETTY —) IMP
(WATER —) NICKER
(PL.) DASYUS
DEMONASSA (FATHER OF —)
AMPHIARAUS
(HUSBAND OF —) THERSANDER
(MOTHER OF —) ERIPHYLE
(SON OF —) TISAMENUS
DEMONIAC DEMONIC LUNATIC
SATANIC DEVILISH DIABOLIC
FIENDISH INFERNAL
DEMONIACAL DEMONIAC
INFERNAL
DEMONICE (FATHER OF —) AGENOR
(MOTHER OF —) EPICASTE
(SON OF —) MOLUS EVENUS
PHYLUS THESTIUS
DEMONSTRABLE ACTUAL
DEMONSTRATE GIVE SHOW
CLEAR PROVE SPEAK CONVICT
DISPLAY PORTRAY CONVINCE

INSTANCE MANIFEST
DEMONSTRATION SHOW SIGN
TIME PROOF OVATION APODIXIS
BALLYHOO DARSHANA MANIFEST
(— OF POWER) MANIFESTATION
(OSTENTATIOUS —) SPLURGE
DEMONSTRATIVE THAT THIS
THESE THOSE EFFUSIVE EVINCIVE
DEMOPHON (FATHER OF —) CELEUS
THESEUS
(MOTHER OF —) PHAEDRA
METANIRA
(NURSE OF —) DEMETER
DEMORALIZE WEAKEN CONFUSE
CORRUPT DEPRAVE PERVERT
DEMORALIZING INFECTIOUS
SHATTERING
DEMOTE BUMP BUST REDUCE
UNRANK DEGRADE DISRATE
DEMOTIC POPULAR ENCHORIAL
DEMOTION BUMP
DEMULCENT MANNA SALEB SALEP
BORAGE GINSENG EMULSION
SOOTHING
DEMUR COY GIB JIB SHY BALK
STAY DELAY DOUBT PAUSE
QUALM STICK BOGGLE LINGER
OBJECT STRAIN DEMEORE
SCRUPLE STICKLE STUMBLE
SUSPEND DEMURRER HESITATE
SUSPENSE
DEMURE COY MIM SHY MURE
PRIM GRAVE SPAKE STAID SUANT
SUENT MODEST SEDATE PRENZIE
PRIMSIE COMPOSED DECOROUS
DEN MEW CAVE COVE DEAN DELL
DIVE GLEN HELL HOLE HOLT
HUNK LAIR LAKE NEST ROOM
SHED SINK BIELD CABIN CAVEA
COUCH DELVE HAUNT LODGE
SLADE STUDY BURROW CAVERN
COVERT GROTTO HOLLOW
KENNEL RAVINE SHROUD
RETREAT SPELUNK HIDEAWAY
SNUGGERY WORKROOM
(— OF BEAR) WASH
(— OF INIQUITY) DOMDANIEL
(DRINKING —) BOTHAN
(FOUL —) SPITAL
(GAMBLING —) DEADFALL
DENARIUS DENAR PENNY DINDER
DENATURANT PYRIDINE
DENDRITE PROCESS
DENIAL NO NAY WARN DENAY
DENIER NAYSAY DEFENSE
DEMENTI REFUSAL REPULSE
CONTRARY NEGATION TRAVERSE
(— OF AUTHORITY) ANARCHY
(— OF TRUTH) HERESY
DENIED LOST
DENIER DINERO NEGATOR
DENARIUS DINHEIRO
(HALF —) MAIL MAILLE
DENIGRATE BEFOUL CRUCIFY
DENIM DUNGAREE
DENIZEN CITIZEN RESIDENT
(— BY BIRTH) NATIVE
(— OF HELL) HELLION

DENMARK
CAPITAL: COPENHAGEN
CHEESE: SAMSO
COIN: ORA ORE KRONE

COUNTY: AMT FYN RIBE SORO
VEJLE AARHUS MARIBO
ODENSE TONDER VIBORG
AALBORG RANDERS AABENRAA
BORNHOLM
INLET: ISE LIM FJORD VEJLE
NISSUM ODENSE HORSENS
LOGSTOR MARIAGER
ISLAND: OE ALS FYN MON AARO
AERO FANO FOHR MORS ROMO
BAAGO FAROE LAESO SAMSO
SANDO AMAGER SEJERO
SUDERO FALSTER SEELAND
ZEALAND
MEASURE: ELL FOD MIL POT ALEN
FAVN RODE ALBUM KANDE
LINJE PAEGL TOMME ACHTEL
PAEGL SKEPPE LANDMIL
OLTONDE SKIEPPE VIERTEL
FJERDING
PARLIAMENT: RIGSRAAD
FOLKETING LANDSTING
PENINSULA: JUTLAND
POSSESSION: FAROE ICELAND
GREENLAND
RIVER: ASA HOLM OMME STOR
GUDEN SKIVE SUSAA VARDE
GELSAA STORAA VORGOD
GUDENAA LILLEAA LONBORG
SETTLERS: OSTMEN
STRAIT: KATTEGAT SKAGERRAK
TOWN: ARS HOV HALS KOGE NIBE
SORO VRAA FARUM HOBRO
SKIVE AARHUS DRAGOR
KORSOR NYBORG ODENSE
SKAGEN STRUER VIBORG
AALBORG HERNING HORSENS
KOLDING RANDERS ALSINORE
BALLERUP GENTOFTE
GLOSTRUP ROSKILDE
HELSINGOR COPENHAGEN
TRIBE: DANES JUTES ANGLES
CIMBRI TEUTONS
TRIBUNAL: RIGSRAD RIGSRET
WEIGHT: ES LOD ORT VOG LAST
MARK PUND UNZE CARAT
KVINT POUND QUINT TONDE
CENTNER LISPUND QUINTIN
LISPOUND SKIPPUND

DENOMINATE CALL NAME STYLE
TITLE DENOTE CHRISTEN
INDICATE NOMINATE
DENOMINATION CULT NAME SECT
CLASS FAITH TITLE VALUE
CHURCH SCHOOL SOCIETY
CATEGORY
DENOMINATIONAL SECTARIAN
CONFESSIONAL
DENOTATION SIGN TOKEN EXTENT
NOTION SPHERE AMBITUS
BREADTH REFERENCE
DENOTE GIVE MARK MEAN NAME
NOTE SHOW SOUND IMPORT
NOTIFY BETOKEN CONNOTE
EXPRESS SIGNIFY DENOTATE
DESCRIBE INDICATE
DENOUEMENT END ENVOY ISSUE
PAYOFF OUTCOME SOLUTION
ANAGNOSIS
DENOUNCE BAN DAMN WRAY
ASCRY BASTE BLAST DECRY
TAUNT ACCUSE DELATE DESCRY

DETEST MENACE SCATHE
ARRAIGN CONDEMN DECLAIM
DECLARE UPBRAID EXECRATE
PROCLAIM THREATEN
OBJURGATE
DENOUNCEMENT DELATION
DENSE SAD FAST FIRM CLOSE
CRASS DUNCH FOGGY GROSS
HEAVY MASSY MURKY SILLY
SOLID SOUND SPISS STIFF THEET
THICK TIGHT WOOFY OBTUSE
OPAQUE SPISSY STUPID THICKY
THIGHT COMPACT
CROWDED INTENSE
SERRIED CONDENSE
(NOT —) TENUOUS
(PREF.) PACHY PYCN(O) PYKN(O)
DENSITY FOG CANDY FASTNESS
GAUSSAGE SOLIDITY
(UNIT OF —) TESLA
(PREF.) DASY
DENT BASH BURT DINT DOKE
DUNT FAZE NICK CLOUR DELVE
DINGE NOTCH STOVE TOOTH
BATTER DUNTLE HALLOW INDENT
BLEMISH DEPRESS
(— OF REED) SPLIT
(PL.) BEER
DENTAL POINT
DENTICULATE SERRATE SERRATED
DENTICULATION JAG JAGG
DENTIFRICE WASH
DENTIL DENTEL DENTELLO
DENTICLE
DENTINE IVORY DENTIN
DENTIST ODONTIST OPERATOR
DENTISTRY PROSTHODONTICS
DENTURE PLATE BRIDGE
DENUDE BARE SCALP SHAVE STRIP
DIVEST NUDATE DESPOIL
DENUDATE
DENUNCIATION BAN THREAT
THUNDER ANATHEMA DIATRIBE
DENY NAY NAIT NICK NITE WARN
BELIE DEBAR NITTE RENAY REPEL
WERNE ABJURE DISOWN FORBID
IMPUGN NEGATE REFUSE REFUTE
REJECT RENEGE CONFUTE
DEPRIVE DISAVOW DISPUTE
FORSAKE GAINSAY PROTEST
SUBLATE WITHSAY ABNEGATE
DENEGATE DISALLOW
DISCLAIM FORSWEAR
NEGATIVE RENOUNCE
TRAVERSE WITHHOLD
(— ACCESS) CLOSE
(— RECOGNITION) BLINK
DEOXIDIZE REDUCE
DEOXIDIZED
(PREF.) DESOXY
DEPART GO DIE MOG OFF WAG
BLOW EXIT FLIT HOOK MOVE
PACK PART PASS PIKE QUIT SHED
STEP VADE VARY VOID WALK
WEND WITE AVOID BREAK
FOUND LEAVE MOSEY SEVER
SHAKE SHIFT START TRUSS
AVAUNT BEGONE DECAMP
DECEDE DEMISE DESIST DIVIDE
PERISH RECEDE REMOVE RETIRE
SKIDOO SUNDER SWERVE
WANDER ABSCOND DEVIATE
DISCEDE FORSAKE RETREAT

SKIDDOO VAMOOSE DISCOAST
FAREWELL SEPARATE TRESPASS
WITHDRAW
(— FROM HARBOR) SORTIE
(— FROM LIFE) DECEASE
(— IN HASTE) BREEZE
(— IN HURRY) SKIVE LAMMAS
(— SECRETLY) ABSCOND
ABSQUATULATE
(— SUDDENLY) FLEE DECAMP
MIZZLE
(— WITH SPEED) VAMOOSE
DEPARTED DEAD BYGONE
DEFUNCT DECEASED DECEDENT
DEPARTMENT END PART OKRUG
REALM AGENCY BRANCH BUREAU
EXCISE MEMBER OKROOG SPHERE
FOUNDRY HANAPER PORTION
REVENUE SPICERY AGITPROP
CHANCERY DIVISION INDUSTRY
NOMARCHY PROVINCE SCULLERY
(— IN CHINA) FU
(— OF CHANCERY) HAMPER
(NEWSPAPER —) COLUMN
FEATURE
(TREASURY —) CAMERA
DEPARTURE BUNK EXIT BREAK
DEATH EXODE GOING LEAVE
LUCKY OUTGO CHANGE CONGEE
DEPART EGRESS EXODUS HEGIRA
SETOFF WAGANG WAYING
DECEASE EASTING OUTGANG
PARTING PARTURE RETREAT
SAILING TRUNDLE WAYGATE
DEPARTER FAREWELL OFFGOING
REMOTION
(— FROM CORRECTNESS) ATROCITY
(— FROM SUBJECT) ASIDE
(— FROM THEME) CADENZA
(— OF SHIP) SORTIE
(CHARACTER IN —) LUISE TROTT
GILFEN
(COMPOSER OF —) D'ALBERT
(EMERGENCY —) BAILOUT
(GEOLOGICAL —) ANOMALY
(SECRET —) GUY SLIP
DEPEND BANK HANG LEAN PEND
RELY REST RIDE STAY TURN
BUILD COUNT FOUND HINGE
TRUST LIPPEN CONFIDE
DEPENDABILITY SECURITY
DEPENDABLE GOOD SURE TRIG
SIKER SOLID SOUND THERE
SECURE SICCAR SICKER STANCH
STEADY CERTAIN STAUNCH
RELIABLE SILVENDY SUREFIRE
DEPENDENCE MAINSTAY
RELIANCE SERVILITY
DEPENDENCY TALUK COLONY
APANAGE APPANAGE
DEPENDENT CHILD CLIENT
HANGBY MINION SPONGE VASSAL
FEODARY FEUDARY PRONEUR
RELIANT SERVILE SPONGER
SUBJECT WRAPPED BEHOLDEN
CLINGING CREATURE ENCLITIC
EVENTUAL FOLLOWER RETAINER
(— ON) ILLATIVE
(NOT —) ABSOLUTE
DEPENDING ATTENDANT
(— ON UNCERTAIN EVENTS)
ALEATORY
DEPICT HUE DRAW ETCH LIMN

PICT UNDO ENTER IMAGE PAINT
SPEAK WRITE BLAZON SHADOW
DEPAINT DISPLAY EXPRESS
IMPAINT PICTURE PORTRAY
DESCRIBE EMBLAZON RESEMBLE
DEPICTED DEPAINT
(— AS BROKEN) ROMPU
DEPICTION SCAN SCHEMA
DEPILATION PSILOSIS
DEPILATORY RUSMA EPILATOR
PELADORE PSILATRO
DEPLETE DRAIN EMPTY PUNISH
REDUCE UNLOAD EXHAUST
BANKRUPT DIMINISH
DEPLETED WASTE BANKRUPT
DEPLETION DRAIN EROSION
DEPLORABLE SAD WOFUL
WOFUL DOLOROUS GRIEVOUS
WAILSOME WRETCHED
DEPLORABLY SADLY
DEPLORE RUE MOAN SIGH WAIL
MOURN BEMOAN BEWAIL GRIEVE
LAMENT REGRET COMPLAIN
DEPLOY UNFOLD DISPLAY
DEPLOYMENT FORMATION
DEPOLYMERIZE DEGRADE
DEPONE SWEAR DEPOSE TESTIFY
DEPONENT AFFIANT DEPONER
EXAMINATE
DEPOPULATE RAVAGE DESOLATE
DISPEOPLE
DEPORT BEAR EXILE EXPEL BANISH
BEHAVE DEMEAN BEARING
CONDUCT DISPORT RELEGATE
DEPORTMENT AIR GEST MIEN
PORT GESTE HABIT ACTION
DEPORT HAVING MANNER
ADDRESS BEARING COMPORT
CONDUCT GESTURE HAVANCE
BREEDING CARRIAGE DEMEANOR
MAINTAIN PORTANCE
DEPOSE AVER ABASE PRIVE
SWEAR AFFIRM ASSERT BANISH
DEPONE DIVEST REDUCE REMOVE
DEGRADE DEPOSIT DESTOOL
TESTIFY DETHRONE DISCROWN
DISPLACE
DEPOSIT FUR LAY PUT SET ADHI
BANK CAKE CAST CRUD DROP
DUMP FUND HIDE HOCK PAWN
BLOOM CHEST COUCH COVER
DEPOT LODGE PLACE SCURF
STORE TOSCA BESTOW DEPONE
DEPOSE ENTOMB ESCROW
FLYSCH GARNER IMPOSE INHUME
PLEDGE REPOSE SALINE SCORIA
SCROLL SETTLE SINTER TOPHUS
ASHFALL CONSIGN HORIZON
DILUVIUM FOULNESS SANDBANK
PRECIPITATION
(— BALLOT) CAST
(— DRIFT-SAND) SUD
(— EGGS) BLOW SPAWN
(— FOR COPYRIGHT) ENTER
(— IN CHAMPAGNE) GRIFFE
(— IN EARTH) INTER INHUME
(— IN GUN BORE) FOULING
(— IN WINE CASK) CRUST TARTAR
(— OF DEBRIS) BRECCIA
(— OF LOAM) LOESS
(— OF ORE) BANK FLAT
(— OF PEBBLES AND SAND) BEACH
CASCALHO

(— OF SALT WATER) SOAK
(— ON LEATHER) BLOOM
(— ON LEAVES) HONEYDEW
(— STOLEN ARTICLES) FENCE
(— USED AS FERTILIZER) FALUN
(ALLUVIAL —) APRON DELTA
(ARCHAEOLOGICAL —) LENS LENSE
(BANK —S) CASH
(BLACK —) STUPP
(CORNEA —) ARCUS
(EARTHY —) GUHR MARL
(GEOLOGIC —) BLANKET HORIZON
(GLACIAL —) TILL DRIFT ESKAR
ESKER SHEET PLACER MORAINE
(GRAVEL —) LEAD
(KIDNEY —) GRAVEL
(MASS OF SEDIMENTARY —S) GOBI
(MINERAL —) FLAT LODE CARBONA
(MUDDY —) SLUDGE
SLUMGULLION
(POWDERY —) BERGMEHL
(SEDIMENTARY —) SILT VARVE
(SHELLY —) CRAG
(SHOAL-WATER —) CULM
(SKELETAL —) CORAL
(STOMACH —) SABURRA
(TARRY —) GUM
(WELDING —) TACK
(PREF.) THESO
DEPOSITARY POSITOR SEQUESTER
DEPOSITION PAD BURIAL DEPOSIT
OPINION SILTING DEPOSURE
SEDIMENT
DEPOSITORY BANK DROP SAFE
AMBRY ATTIC VAULT DEPOSIT
OSSUARY SENTINE DEPOSITO
ESCROWEE OSSARIUM
DEPOT BANK BASE GARE AURANG
AURUNG STAPLE STATION
MAGAZINE TERMINAL TERMINUS
DEPRAVE TAINT DEBASE DEFILE
INFECT MALIGN REVILE BESHREW
CORRUPT PERVERT VITIATE
DEPRAVED BAD EVIL UGLY VILE
PRAVE ROTTEN SHREWD WICKED
BESTIAL CORRUPT IMMORAL
PRAVOUS VICIOUS MISCREANT
DEPRAVITY VICE ABYSS ILLNESS
PRAVITY VILLAINY TURPITUDE
DEPRECATE PRAY INVOKE
BESEECH
DEPRECATORY PEJORATIVE
DEPRECIATE FALL LACK SLUR
ABASE AVILE DECRY SLUMP
DEBASE EMBASE LESSEN MINISH
REDUCE SHRINK CHEAPEN
DEBAUCH DEGRADE DEPRAVE
DEPRESS DETRACT DISABLE
SLANDER SMALLEN BELITTLE
DEROGATE DISCOUNT DISPRIZE
DISVALUE MINIMIZE PEJORATE
VILIPEND
DEPRECIATION AGIO DECRIAL
DISCOUNT
DEPREDATION PREY RAPINE
PILLAGE
DEPRESS BOW COW HIP LOW
BATE BEAR BORE DAMP DASH
DENT FALL FLAT SINK SUMP
ABASE APPAL BREAK CHILL
COUCH CRUSH FAINT LOWER
SLUMP VAPOR WEIGH APPALL
DAMPEN DEBOSS DISMAY

HUMBLE INDENT LESSEN
MURDER SADDEN SETTLE SICKEN
SLOUCH STRIKE WEAKEN
DECLINE DEGRADE DESTROY
FLATTEN OPPRESS REPRESS
BROWBEAT DIMINISH DISPIRIT
DOWNBEAR ENFEEBLE
(— STRINGS OF INSTRUMENT) FRET
DEPRESSANT HELLEBORE
DEPRESSED LOW SAD BLUE DAMP
DULL FLAT SICK SUNK COWED
WROTH BROODY DISHED GLOOMY
HIPPED HOLLOW LONELY OBLATE
SOMBER TRISTE ACCABLE
LETDOWN DEJECTED DOWNCAST
DOWNSOME
(— AT THE POLES) OBLATE
(ECONOMICALLY —) HARD
DEPRESSING SAD BLUE COLD
BLEAK CHILL DREAR DUSKY
MUZZY OURIE DISMAL DREARY
GLOOMY SOMBER SOMBRE TRISTE
OPPRESSIVE
DEPRESSION COL DIP EYE GAT
PAN PIT BUST CROP DAMP DELK
DENT DOKE DOWN FALL FOSS
GASH GLEN HOLL HOWE SLEW
SLOT SLUE WELL ATRIO BASIN
BLUES BOSOM CANON COWAL
CRYPT DELVE DINGE FOSSA
FOSSE FOVEA GLOOM GROIN
NADIR NAVEL ORBIT POLJE
SALAR SCOOP SELLA SINUS
SLUMP SWALE AMPHID BLIGHT
BUCKLE CAFARD CANYON CAVITY
CRATER CUPULE DIMPLE DISMAY
FURROW GROOVE GULLEY
GUTTER INDENT LACUNA RAVINE
SAUCER SLOUGH SPLEEN VALLEY
WALLOW ALVEOLA BLOWOUT
BOGHOLE CHAGRIN CLAYPAN
CONCAVE COUNTER FOSSULA
FOSSULE FOVEOLA JIMMIES
SADNESS SALTPAN SINKAGE
SINKING VARIOLE BOTHRIUM
DOLDRUMS DOWNBEND
FAINTING FOLLICLE FOREDEEP
FOSSETTE FOSSULET PUNCTURE
SINKHOLE SOAKAWAY EPHIPPIUM
MELANCHOLY OPPRESSION
(— BEHIND COW'S SHOULDERS)
CROP
(— BETWEEN BREASTS) CLEAVAGE
(— BETWEEN HILLS) SWIRE
(— IN BOARD) SKIP
(— IN BOTTLE BOTTOM) KICK
(— IN DECK) COCKPIT
(— IN DOG'S FACE) STOP
(— IN FRUITS) EYE
(— IN GROUND) DALK DELK SOAK
SWAG WELL SWALE CHARCO
(— IN MILLSTONE) BOSOM
(— IN NILE VALLEY) KORE
(— IN RANGE) PASS
(— IN RIDGE) COL
(— IN SNOW) SITZMARK
(— IN VELD) COMITJE KOMMETJE
(— OF EAR) SCAPHA
(— OF SPIRITS) JAWFALL
(— PRONE) VAPORISH
(ARTICULAR —) GLENE
(OBLONG —) CIRCUS
(SMALL —) DENT DIMPLE

LACUNA FOLLICLE
DEPRIVATION COST LOSS MAIM
WANT MAYHEM AMOTION
MISTURE DEPRIVAL
(— OF SIGHT) DARKNESS
(SUFF.) STERESIS
DEPRIVE BAR ROB BATE DENY
DOCK EASE GELD TWIN ABATE
BENIM BREAK DEBAR EMPTY
EXUTE PREVE SPOIL STRIP
WRONG AMERCE DEFEAT
DENUDE DEPOSE DEVEST DISMAY
DIVEST FAMISH FORBAR HINDER
HUSTLE REMOVE ABRIDGE
BEGUILE BEREAVE CASHIER
CURTAIL DECEIVE DEFORCE
DEPRAVE DESPOIL DESTROY
DISABLE EXHAUST FOREBAR
GUDGEON PRIVATE UNDRESS
BANKRUPT DENATURE DESOLATE
DISANNUL EVACUATE
(— BY TRICKERY) NOSE MULCT
(— FRAUDULENTLY) GUDGEON
(— OF BRILLIANCE) DEADEN
(— OF COURAGE) UNNERVE
(— OF FREEDOM) FETTER
(— OF INDIVIDUALITY) FORDIZE
(— OF LIFE) DEADEN
(— OF OFFICE) DEPOSE
(— OF POSSESSIONS) FLAY
(— OF REASON) DEMENT
(— OF SENSATION) BENUMB
(— OF SENSE) INEBRIATE
(— OF SIGHT) SEEL
(— OF STRENGTH) ENERVATE
(— OF VIRGINITY) DEFLOWER
(PREF.) (— OF) DE DIS
DEPRIVED REFT SANS BANKRUPT
DESOLATE
DEPTH DIP BURY DEEP DROP
MOHO ABYSS MIDST SIDTH
FATHOM HEIGHT ALTITUDE
DEEPNESS PROFOUND SOUNDING
STRENGTH PENETRATION
(— OF NIGHT OR WINTER) HOLL
HOWE
(— OF SAIL) HOIST
(— OF SHIP) GAGE GAUGE
(— OF SIN) SLOUGH
(— OF SPADE) SPIT GRAFT
(— OF WATER) DRAFT DRAUGHT
(-S OF SEA) PROFOUND
(LOWEST —) GROUND
(MORAL —) ABYSS
(PL.) MUD ABYSS HEART
(PREF.) BATH(O)(Y)
DEPUTATION MISSION THEORIA
LEGATION
DEPUTE SEND ALLOT ASSIGN
DEVOTE APPOINT DELEGATE
DEPUTY AIDE VICE AGENT ENVOY
NABOB PROXY VICAR ANGELO
COMMIS CURATE DEPUTE
EXARCH FACTOR KEHAYA LEGATE
MINION ADJOINT BAILIFF
ESCALUS SUBDEAN CAIMACAM
DELEGATE ORDINARY PYLAGORE
QAIMAQAM TENIENTE VICARIAN
(— OF BISHOP) VICAR VIDAME
(PREF.) CO
DERAIL TOAD DERAILER
THROWOFF
DERANGE TURN CRAZE UNWIT

UPSET HAMPER RUFFLE CONFUSE
DERAIGN DISEASE DISTURB
PERTURB UNSHAPE DISORDER
DISPLACE UNSETTLE
DERANGED OUT GYTE CRAZY
CRAZED SKIVIE FRANTIC FURIOUS
BUGHOUSE DEMENTED
DETRAQUE INFORMAL
DERANGEMENT MANIA UPSET
FRENZY LUNACY DISEASE
MADNESS PHRENSY RUMMAGE
DELIRIUM DISORDER INSANITY
DERBY POT CADY KATY RACE
BOXER CADDY DICER KELLY SHIRE
BOWLER
DERBY BLUE ELDERBERRY
DERELICT STREET FAILURE
BETRAYER CASTAWAY
DERELICTION FAILURE RELICTION
DERIDE BOO GECK GIBE HOOT
JAPE JEER JIBE LOUT MOCK TWIT
DRAPE FLEER FLOUT KNACK
LAUGH RALLY SCOFF SCORN
SCOUT TAUNT EXPOSE ILLUDE
IRRIDE CATCALL LOWBELL
RIDICULE
DERIDER IRRISOR
DERISION GECK JEER MOCK
HOKER SCORN SPORT MOWING
ASTEISM MOCKERY CONTEMPT
IRRISION RIDICULE
DERISIVE JEERY SNIDE MOWING
SATANIC DERISORY IRRISORY
SARDONIC SCOFFING
DERIVATION ORIGIN DESCENT
PEDIGREE PARENTAGE
DERIVATIVE FURAN LININ SLOPE
ACOINE ACYLAL BORANE FURANE
INDOLE PHENOL RETENE ALKYLOL
ANALGEN DERIVED ENOLATE
FLAVONE FLUXION FULGIDE
FULVENE GERMANE SUCRATE
ALBUMOSE ANALGENE FLAVONOL
FORMAZAN HEMATINE INDAZOLE
STANNANE SECONDHAND
ADSCITITIOUS
DERIVE GET DRAW STEM TAKE
BRING CARRY DRIVE FETCH INFER
TRACE BORROW CONVEY DEDUCE
DESUME ELICIT EVOLVE GATHER
OBTAIN SPRING DESCEND
EXTRACT PROCEED RECEIVE
TRADUCE
DERIVED
(SUFF.) (— FROM) IC(AL)
DERMA LAYER CORIUM DERMIS
KISHKE
DERMATITIS ICH ICK CASCADO
CUTITIS
DERMATOGEN PROTODERM
DERMIS CUTIS DERMA CORIUM
DERNIER LAST FINAL DARREIN
DERNIER CRI FASHION
DEROGATE ANNUL DECRY LESSEN
REPEAL DETRACT SLANDER
RESTRICT WITHDRAW
DEROGATORY BAD
DERRICK JIB RIG LIFT SPAR CRANE
DAVIT HOIST STEEVE TACKLE
ERECTER ERECTOR GALLOWS
HANGING HANGMAN STIFFLEG
JINNYWINK
DERRIS TUBA DEGUELIA

DERVISH AGIB FAKIR FAKEER
SADITE SANTON DARWESH
WHIRLER CALENDER
DESALT DEIONIZE
DESATURATE SADDEN
DESCANT SING SONG COPULA
MELODY REMARK WARBLE
COMMENT QUINIBLE
DESCEND DIP SYE DIVE DROP
DUCK FALL SHED SINK SKIN VAIL
AVALE LIGHT LOWER SQUAT
STOOP SWOOP ALIGHT DERIVE
DEVALL DEVAUL SETTLE DECLINE
DELAPSE DEVOLVE SUBSIDE
SUCCEED DISMOUNT
PREPONDERATE
(— INTO HELL) HARROW
DESCENDANT SON CION GHUZ
HEIR SEED SLIP CHILD GHUZZ
SCION BRANCH LINEAL DESCENT
AARONITE ASHERITE DAUGHTER
EPIGONUS
(— OF IMMIGRANTS) BRAVA
(— OF JEW) CHUETA
(— OF MOHAMMED) EMIR
(— OF NOAH) AD
(—S OF MOHAMMED) ASHRAF
(INSIGNIFICANT —) TAG
(PL.) SEED DONMEH DUNMEH
STRAIN PROGENY OFFSPRING
POSTERITY
(SUFF.) ITE
DESCENDING FALL CADENT
DOWNWARD
(— FROM COMMON ANCESTOR)
AKIN
DESCENT JET KIN SET DIVE DOWN
DROP FALL KIND VAIL BIRTH
BLOOD CANCH CHINE ISSUE
PITCH SCARP SHUTE SLOPE
STOCK CLEUCH CLEUGH ESCARP
RAPPEL STRAIN ASSAULT
DECLINE DISSENT EXTRACT
FALLOUT INCLINE KINDRED
LINEAGE PROGENY ANCESTRY
BREEDING COMEDOWN
DOWNCOME DOWNFALL
DOWNGATE DOWNHILL GLISSADE
INVASION PEDIGREE PARENTAGE
(— IN MOUNTAINEERING) ABSEIL
(— OF AIRPLANE) LETDOWN
APPROACH
(— OF BIRD) STOOP
(— OF DEITY) AVATAR AVATARA
(— OF LIQUID) DRIBBLE
(— OF MASS) SLIDE
(— OF RIVER) LEAP
(FAMILIAR —) HAVAGE
(OVERWHELMING —) AVALANCHE
(PARACHUTE —) JUMP BAILOUT
(PLUNGING —) SPIN
DESCHAMPSIA AIRA
DESCRIBE GIVE READ TELL BLAZE
IMAGE PAINT POINT STYLE WRITE
DEFINE DENOTE DEPICT DEVISE
DILATE RELATE REPORT SKETCH
TITULE DECLARE DEPAINT
DISPLAY EXPLAIN EXPRESS
NARRATE OUTLINE PICTURE
PORTRAY PRESENT RECOUNT
STORIFY DESCRIVE INSCRIBE
REHEARSE
(— A LINE) CUT

(— AS) CALL
(— BRIEFLY) KODAK
(— GRAMMATICALLY) PARSE
DESCRIPTION KIN IMAGE BLAZON
SKETCH SURVEY ACCOUNT
DICTION DISPLAY PICTURE
LANDSKIP RELATION TREATISE
(— OF A COUNTRY) FACE
(— OF VISION) AISLING
(BRIEF —) LEGEND
(RUSTIC —) IDYL IDYLL
DESCRY SEE SPY ESPY MAKE SCRY
ASCRY SIGHT BEHOLD BETRAY
DETECT REVEAL DISCERN
DISPLAY DENOUNCE DESCRIBE
DISCLOSE DISCOVER PERCEIVE
DESDEMONA (FATHER OF —)
BRABANTIO
(HUSBAND OF —) OTHELLO
DESECRATE ABUSE DEFILE
POLLUTE PROFANE VIOLATE
TEMERATE UNHALLOW
DESECRATION PROFANATION
DESERT DUE ERG RAT RUN AREG
ARID BOLT FAIL FLEE MEED SAND
SERT TURN VAST GUILT LEAVE
LURCH MERIT PLANT SERIR
START WAIVE WASTE WORTH
BARREN BETRAY DEFECT EXPOSE
LONELY RENEGE REWARD SHRINK
THIRST WESTEN ABANDON
ABSCOND CHICKEN DEMERIT
FORSAKE HORNADA OVERRUN
WASTERN WASTINE DESOLATE
RENOUNCE SOLITARY SOLITUDE
WASTABLE
(PL.) GUILT
(PREF.) EREM(O)
DESERTED DEAD LONE WYSTY
LONELY FORLORN DESOLATE
FORSAKEN SOLITARY
(— WOMAN) AGUNAH
DESERTER RAT BOLTER BUGOUT
APOSTATE BUSHWACK FUGITIVE
RECREANT RENEGADE RUNAGATE
TURNTAIL
DESERTION BUGOUT RATTERY
APOSTASY
DESERT LEMON KUMQUAT
DESERVE EARN MEED RATE MERIT
REPAY SERVE ASSERVE BENEFIT
DEMERIT DISSERVE PROMERIT
DESERVED JUST COMING WORTHY
CONDIGN
DESERVING WORTHY CONDIGN
WORTHFUL ADMIRABLE
MERITORIOUS
DESICCATE DRY ARID SEAR SERE
DRAIN DEHYDRATE
DESICCATION XERANSIS
DESIDERATUM NEED DESIRE
DESIGN AIM END MAP CAST DRAW
GOAL IDEA MARK MEAN PLAN
PLAT PLOT TREE WORK ALLOT
CHECK DECAL DECOR DODAD
DRAFT DRIFT ETTLE FANCY
MODEL MOTIF NOTAN QUILT
SHAPE STAMP STUDY STYLE
BOWPOT CACHET CORNER
CREATE DEVICE DEVISE DOODAD
DOODLE EMBLEM FIGURE FLORAL
FLOWER INCUSE INTEND INTENT
INVENT LAYOUT MODULE OBJECT

OBTENT PROJET SCHEME SKETCH SYSTEM VERVER ALLOVER BOSCAGE CARTOON CARVING CHASING COMPOSE CONCERT COUNSEL CROQUIS DESTINE DIAGRAM DRAUGHT ETCHING FANTASY FASHION OUTLINE PATTERN PRETEND PROJECT PROPOSE PURPORT PURPOSE REVERSE SCALLOP SLEIGHT THOUGHT APPLIQUE BAYADERE BOUGHPOT CONTRIVE CYMATION CYMATIUM ENGINEER FILIGREE FLOCKING FORECAST GRAFFITO GROOVING INTAGLIO PHANTASY PLATFORM REMARQUE SINGERIE STRIPING SUNBURST GOFFERING SCHEMATISM
(— AS TITLE PAGE) VIGNETTE
(— ON BOOK) TOOL
(— ON CARPET) MEDALLION
(— ON COIN) BEADING
(— ON FABRIC) BATIK BATTIK
(ARTFUL —) MACHINATION
(BOOK —) FILET FILLET
(CUP-SHAPED —) HUSK
(EMBLEMATIC —) IMPRESS
(ESSENTIAL —) BONES
(FASHION —) FORD
(OUTLINE —) KEYSTONE
(PERFORATED —) POUNCE
(STRIPED —) STRIA STRIE
(TESSELLATED —) MOSAIC
(TEXTILE —) STRIPE HAIRLINE
DESIGNATE SET HAIL MARK MEAN NAME SHOW ELECT LABEL SPEAK STYLE TITLE ANOINT ASSIGN DENOTE DESIGN FINGER INTEND SETTLE APPOINT EARMARK ENTITLE EXPRESS SPECIFY SURNAME ALLOCATE DESCRIBE IDENTIFY INDICATE NOMINATE PRESCRIBE
DESIGNATION NAME TYPE LABEL STYLE TITLE CAPTION HOMONYM ADDITION
(— OF PLACE) ADDRESS
DESIGNED PREPENSE SUPPOSED
(— FOR MALE AND FEMALE) UNISEX
DESIGNER STYLER FANCIER PLANNER PLOTTER SCHEMER STYLIST COLORIST ENGINEER MEDALIST MOSAICIST
(PL.) COUTURE
DESIGNING ARTFUL CUNNING JESUITIC PLANNING PLOTTING SCHEMING
DESIRABLE FAIR GOOD KEEN WORTH PLUMMY AMIABLE GRADELY HEALTHY OPTABLE WELCOME WISHFUL DESIROUS ELIGIBLE ENVIABLE PLEASING SALUTARY
DESIRE YEN ACHE CARE ENVY EROS FAIN HAVE HOPE ITCH KAMA KEEP LEST LIST LOAD LUST MIND NEED PANT URGE WANT WILL WISH WIST ARDOR BOSOM BRAME COVET CRAVE FANCY GIMME GREED GROAN HEART MANGE MANIA NISUS QUEST STUDY TANHA TASTE WILNE YEARN YISSE AFFECT APPETE

ASPIRE BEHEST BESOLN DEMAND DEVICE HANKER HUNGER OREXIS POTHOS PREFER TALENT THIRST UTINAM YAMMER AVARICE AVIDITY CONATUS COURAGE CRAVING EROTISM FANTASY HIMEROS INKLING LONGING PASSION STOMACH VOLUNTY WILLING AMBITION APPETITE COVETISE CUPIDITY PLEASING NECESSITY
(— FOR LIFE) TANHA
(— WITH EAGERNESS) ASPIRE
(ARDENT —) THIRST
(IRRITATING —) ITCH
(SEXUAL —) HOTS PRIDE
(STRONG —) CUPIDITY SLAVERING
(UNCONTROLLABLE —) CACOETHES
(PREF.) **(SEXUAL —)** ERO EROTO
(SUFF.) OREXIA
DESIRE UNDER THE ELMS
(AUTHOR OF —) ONEILL
(CHARACTER IN —) EBEN ABBIE CABOT PUTNAM EPHRAIM
DESIROUS AVID FAIN FOND LIEF VAIN EAGER FRACK FRECK LUSTY ARDENT WILFUL ANXIOUS THIRSTY WILLFUL WILLING WISHING APPETENT COVETOUS LIKEROUS PRURIENT SPIRITED
DESIST HO LIN EASE HALT QUIT REST SIST STOP WHOA CEASE LEAVE SPARE STINT SWICK SWIKE WONDE DEPART ABANDON FORBEAR FORFEIT RESPITE SUBSIST SURCEASE
(— FROM) CUT LEAVE REMIT FORBEAR
DESK PEW AMBO SCOB BOARD DESSE TABLE BUREAU CAISSE PULPIT CONSOLE LECTERN PLUTEUS COPYDESK STANDISH VARGUENO
DESMA CLON CLONE
DESMAN MOLE SQUASH MUSKRAT ONDATRA
DESMANTHUS ACUAN
DESOLATE SAD BARE LORN RUIN SACK SOLE VAST WILD ALONE BLEAK DREAR GAUNT GUBAT OURIE STARK UNKED UNKET UNKID WASTE WASTY WYSTY BARREN DESERT DISMAL DREARY GLOOMY GOUSTY LONELY RAVAGE DESTROY FORLORN GOUSTIE HOWLING LACKING UNCOUTH WIDOWED WILSOME DEPRIVED DESERTED FORSAKEN SOLITARY WASTEFUL WOBEGONE
DESOLATION WOE RUIN GLOOM GRIEF HAVOC WASTE RAVAGE SADNESS
DESPAIR GLOOM UNHOPE WANHOPE
DESPAIRING HOPELESS
DESPERADO BRAVO BADMAN BANDIT RUFFIAN CRIMINAL RESOLUTE
DESPERATE MAD DIRE RASH ACHARNE DESPERT EXTREME FORLORN FRANTIC HEADLONG HOPELESS PERILOUS RECKLESS
DESPERATELY BONE

DESPICABLE BUM BASE MEAN ORRA VILE CHEAP DIRTY FOUTY SCALY ABJECT PALTRY SHABBY SORDID CAITIFF IGNOBLE PITIFUL REPTILE PITIABLE UNWORTHY WRETCHED
DESPICABLY DIRTILY
DESPISE DEFY HATE SCORN SCOUT SPISE SPURN DETEST FORHOO LOATHE SLIGHT VILIFY CONTEMN DESPITE DISDAIN DISPRIZE MISPRIZE VILIPEND
DESPITE BY VEX SPITE MALGRE DESPISE
DESPOIL ROB PELF PILL POLL RAID RAPE RUIN SKIN BOOTY HARRY PLUME RAVEN REAVE RIFLE SPOIL STRIP STRUB TRICE BEZZLE DIVEST FLEECE HESPEL HUSPEL RAVAGE RAVISH REMOVE BEREAVE DEPRIVE DISROBE PILLAGE PLUNDER UNSPOIL DEFLOWER DISARRAY SPOLIATE SPUILZIE UNCLOTHE
DESPOINA KORE PERSEPHONE
DESPONDENCY DUMP HUMP BLUES DUMPS GLOOM ATHYMY MISERY ATHUMIA ATHYMIA DESPAIR DESPOND
DESPONDENT SAD BLUE GLOOMY FORLORN DEJECTED DOWNCAST HOPELESS
DESPOT CZAR TSAR TZAR ANARCH SATRAP TYRANT AUTARCH MONARCH AUTOCRAT
DESPOTIC LORDLY ABSOLUTE DOMINANT
DESPOTISM TYRANNY AUTARCHY SULTANISM
DESQUAMATE PEEL
DESSERT ICE PIE CAKE FOOL SKYR SNOW VOID BETTY BOMBE COUPE DOLCE FRUIT GLACE GRUNT JELLY LACTO SLUMP AFTERS ECLAIR JUNKET MOUSSE PASTRY POSTRE SPONGE SWEETS TRIFLE BAKLAVA BANQUET PARFAIT PUDDING SHERBET SOUFFLE SPUMONE STRUDEL SUPREME DUMPLING FLUMMERY FRUMENTY NAPOLEON PANDOWDY SILLABUB
DESTINATION END GOAL PORT BOURN BILLET BOURNE
DESTINE DOOM EURE FATE MARK ALLOT SHAPE SLATE WEIRD DEPUTE DESIGN DEVOTE INTEND ORDAIN APPOINT PURPOSE SENTENCE
DESTINY LOT DOLE DOOM EURE FATE SORT KARMA MOIRA STARS WEIRD KHARMA KISMET DESTINE FORTUNE PORTION FOREDOOM
DESTITUTE BARE NACE POOR SANS VOID CLEAN EMPTY NAKED NEEDY WASTE BEREFT DEVOID VACANT WASTED FORLORN LACKING NAUGHTY VIDUATE WANTING BANKRUPT BEGGARED DEFEATED DEPRIVED DESOLATE FORSAKEN HELPLESS INDIGENT INNOCENT VIDUATED PENNILESS

(— OF) BUT
(— OF FEATHERS) DEPLUMATE
(— OF LEAVES) APHYLLOUS
(— OF LIGHT) DARK
(— OF TEETH) EDENTATE
(— OF WATER) ANHYDROUS
(SUFF.) **(— OF)** LESS
DESTITUTION NEED WANT FAMINE PENURY BEGGARY DEFAULT POVERTY
DESTROY BAG EAT END GUT MOW RID ZAP BLOW CHEW FRAP FULL KILL NULL RASE RAZE RUIN RUSH SINK SLAY SMIT STRY TINE UNDO VOID BREAK CRACK CRAZE DECAY ELIDE ERASE ERODE FORDO HAVOC MISDO PRANG QUADE QUAIL QUELL SHEND SHOOT SMASH SMITE SPEED SPEND SPILL SPLIT SPOIL STROY SWAMP TOTAL TRASH WASTY WRACK WRECK BLIGHT CANCEL CUMBER DEFACE DEFEAT DELETE DEVOID DEVOUR EFFACE FAMISH FOREDO MURDER PERISH QUENCH RANKLE RAVAGE STARVE STIFLE UNMAKE UNPILE UNWORK UPROOT UPTEAR ABOLISH CONSUME CORRODE DEPRIVE DISTURB ENECATE EXPUNGE FLATTEN FORFARE FORLESE MORTIFY NULLIFY OVERRUN PEREMPT RUINATE SHAMASH SHATTER SMOTHER SUBVERT TERRIFY UNBUILD WHITTLE AMORTIZE CONFOUND DECIMATE DEMOLISH DESOLATE DESTRUCT DISANNUL DISPLANT DISSOLVE FRACTURE FRAGMENT IMMOLATE INFRINGE MUTILATE OVERTURN PARALYZE SABOTAGE STRAMASH OBLITERATE
(— BARK) GIRDLE
(— BY FIRE) CONSUME
(— FERTILITY) EXHAUST
(— SELF-POSSESSION) ABASH
(— TOTALLY) SMASH SWEEP CUMBER SCUTTLE
(SUFF.) CLASE CLASIA CLAST(IC)
DESTROYED FLAT BLOWN KAPUT KAPUTT
DESTROYER CAN HUN DEATH TINCAN UNDOER VANDAL VICTOR FLIVVER STROYER UNMAKER WARSHIP APOLLYON DEVOURER SABOTEUR
(SUFF.) CIDAL CIDE PHTHORA
DESTROYING FELL
(PREF.) ANTI
(SUFF.) CLASTIC
DESTRUCTIBLE FRAIL
DESTRUCTION BAR END HEW BANE DOGS DOOM FIRE LOSS RACK RUIN STRY TALA CRUSH DEATH DECAY GRAVE HAVOC SMASH STRIP STROY WASTE WRACK DEFEAT DISMAY ENDING EXPIRY WONDER ABADDON CARNAGE EROSION UNDOING COLLAPSE DELETION DISPOSAL DOWNFALL EVERSION EXCISION SHAMBLES SMASHERY RUINATION
(— OF BONES) CARIES

(— OF ENVIRONMENT) ECOCIDE
(— OF SHIP'S PAPERS) SPOLIATION
(CELL —) LYSIS
(GRADUAL —) CORROSION
(MALICIOUS —) SABOTAGE
(UTTER —) PERDITION
(SUFF.) LYSE LYSIS LYST LYTE
LYTIC LYZE
DESTRUCTIVE FELL FATAL
DEADLY MORTAL BALEFUL
BANEFUL DEATHLY EXITIAL
FATEFUL HARMFUL HUMLIKE
HURTFUL NOISOME NOXIOUS
RUINOUS ANERETIC DEATHFUL
EXITIOUS WASTEFUL WRACKFUL
WREAKFUL ANAERETIC
PESTILENT
DESUETUDE BREACH DISUSE
DESULTORY IDLE HASTY LOOSE
ROVING AIMLESS CURSORY
RAMBLING UNSTEADY WAVERING
IRREGULAR
DETACH CUT DRAFT LOOSE SEVER
LOOSEN UNBIND UNGLUE
UNWORK CRACKLE DISJOIN
DRAUGHT ISOLATE UNHINGE
UNRIVET UNSEIZE ABSTRACT
DISSOLVE DISUNITE PRESCIND
SEPARATE UNFASTEN WITHDRAW
DETACHABLE SLIP
DETACHED CUT COLD FREE ALONE
ALOOF DEADPAN INSULAR
PORTATO SCIOLTO ABSTRACT
CLINICAL DISCRETE ISOLATED
OUTLYING SEPARATE SPICCATO
UNBIASED
(PREF.) APH APO
DETACHMENT POINT POSSE
ATARAXY OUTPOST ATARAXIA
AVULSION OUTGUARD
(SUFF.) LYSE LYSIS LYST LYTE
LYTIC LYZE
DETAIL CREW ITEM DODAD POINT
ACCENT ASSIGN DOODAB
DOODAD NICETY PARCEL RELATE
RETAIL ACCOUNT APPOINT
ARTICLE ITEMIZE MINUTIA
NARRATE NULLING RESPECT
SEVERAL SPECIFY INSTANCE
REHEARSE SALIENCE PARTICULAR
PARTICULARITY
(—S OF MAP) CULTURE
(CLIMACTIC —) BEAUTY
(PETTY —) CHICKEN
(PL.) DOPE FROUFROU
FURNITURE
DETAILED NARROW PROLIX
CLOSEUP SPECIAL PUNCTUAL
TIRESOME
DETAIN BAIL HOLD KEEP STAY
STOP CHECK DELAY TARRY
ARREST ATHOLD COLLAR HINDER
RETARD TAIGLE IMPRISON
RESTRAIN WITHHOLD
DETECT SEE SPY ESPY FIND NOSE
SPOT CATCH SCENT SENSE
SMOKE TRACE DESCRY DIVINE
EXPOSE REVEAL DEVELOP
DISCERN UNCOVER DECIPHER
DISCOVER OVERTAKE
DETECTIVE EYE TEC BULL BUSY
DICK JACK TRAP PLANT SNOOP
BEAGLE MOUSER RUNNER

SHADOW SHAMUS SLEUTH
TAILER TRACER GUMSHOE
SCENTER SNOOPER SPOTTER
TRAILER DETECTOR FLATFOOT
HAWKSHAW HOUSEMAN
OPERATOR SHERLOCK OPERATIVE
PINKERTON PLAINCLOTHESMAN
DETECTOR ASDIC COHERER
REAGENT SFERICS SPHERICS
(LIE —) POLYGRAPH
DETENT DOG PALL PAWL CATCH
CLICK RATCH PALLET RATCHET
DETENTION DELAY ARREST
CAPTURE DETINUE JANKERS
DETAINER STOPPAGE
DETER BAR FEAR BLOCK BLUFF
CHECK DELAY DEHORT HINDER
RETARD PREVENT TERRIFY
DISSUADE PRECLUDE RESTRAIN
DETERGE PURGE CLEANSE
MUNDIFY
DETERGENT SOAP SYNDET
ABLUENT PURGING RHYPTIC
SMECTIC SOLVENT CLEANSER
GARDINOL
DETERIORATE GO FAIL GIVE SLIP
SOUR WEAR DECAY ERODE SPILL
WORST APPAIR APPERE DEBASE
IMPAIR SICKEN WORSEN DECLINE
PERVERT FIREFANG
DETERIORATING DECADENT
DETERIORATION DECAY IMPAIR
MALADY DECLINE EROSION
FAILURE DOLDRUMS PEJORATION
DETERMINABLE FIXED DEFINITE
DEFINABLE GAUGEABLE
DETERMINANT CYTOGENE
JACOBIAN CIRCULANT
WRONSKIAN PLASTOGENE
DETERMINATE CERTAIN ORISTIC
DEFINITE RESOLUTE RESOLVED
SPECIFIC
DETERMINATION ACT HEST WILL
ASSAY BLANK CAUSE ADVICE
BEARING CONSULT PURPOSE
RESOLVE ANALYSIS BACKBONE
BIOASSAY DECISION DIVISION
FIRMNESS FORECAST JUDGMENT
JUDICIAL SENTENCE VOLITION
DETERMINATIVE FINAL FORMANT
SHAPING LIMITING
(MOST —) DOMINANT
DETERMINE END FIT FIX GET RUN
TEST WILL ASSAY AWARD JUDGE
PITCH WIELD ADJUST ASSESS
ASSIGN ASSOIL CHOOSE DECERN
DECIDE DECREE DEFINE DESCRY
DETECT DETERM DEVISE FIGURE
GOVERN PERFIX SETTLE
ACCOUNT ADJUDGE ANALYZE
APPOINT ARRANGE COMPUTE
DELIMIT DERAIGN DISPOSE
RESOLVE TERMINE COGNOSCE
CONCLUDE DISCOVER PINPOINT
INFLUENCE
(— FINENESS) SET SETT
(— PATERNITY) AFFILIATE
(— RATE) ASSESS
(— ROOT) EXTRACT
DETERMINED SET BENT DERN
FIRM GRIM BOUND GIVEN STOUT
UPSET BITTER DOGGED GRITTY
INTENT MULISH STURDY DECIDED

SETTLED DECISIVE FOREGONE
PERVERSE RESOLUTE RESOLVED
STUBBORN
DETERMINER GENE CHANCE
PLASMAGENE
DETERMINIST JABARITE
DETEST DAMN HATE ABHOR
CURSE LOATHE CONDEMN
DESPISE DISLIKE DENOUNCE
EXECRATE ABOMINATE
DETESTABLE FOUL HORRID
ODIOUS BLASTED HATABLE
HATEFUL HELLISH HIDEOUS
ACCURSED DAMNABLE HATEABLE
INFAMOUS INFERNAL MALEDICT
ABHORRENT ABOMINABLE
DETESTATION ODIUM HATRED
HORROR LOATHING ANTIPATHY
DETHRONE DEPOSE DIVEST
UNCROWN
DETONATE FIRE BELCH BLAST
SHOOT EXPLODE DETONIZE
DETONATION BLAST KNOCK
AMBITUS PINGING PINKING
DETONATOR CAP FUSE FUZE
FUSEE FUZEE SQUIB TORPEDO
INITIATOR
DETOUR BYPASS CIRCUIT
DIVERSION ROUNDABOUT
DETRACT TAKE DECRY DEDUCT
DEFAME DETRAY DIVERT VILIFY
ASPERSE TRADUCE BELITTLE
DEROGATE DIMINISH DISTRACT
MINIMIZE PROTRACT SUBTRACT
WITHDRAW
(— FROM) IMPEDE
DETRACTION CALUMNY SCANDAL
SLANDER ZOILISM
DETRIMENT COST HARM HURT
LOSS SORE WOUND DAMAGE
DAMNUM DENIAL INJURY
BEATING EXPENSE JACTURE
DISFAVOR MISCHIEF
DETRIMENTAL ADVERSE CAPITAL
HARMFUL HURTFUL LOSSFUL
DAMAGING INVIDIOUS
PERNICIOUS PREJUDICIAL
(— TO HEALTH) HARD
DETRITUS OUTWASH SHINGLE
SHEETWASH
DEUCALION (FATHER OF —)
PROMETHEUS
(MOTHER OF —) CLYMENE
(SON OF —) HELLEN ORESTHEUS
AMPHICTYON
(WIFE OF —) PYRRHA
DEUCE DIANTRE DICKENS
(WILD —) FREAK
DEUCEDLY BLAME BLAMED
DEUEL (SON OF —) ELIASAPH
DEUTERIUM DIPLOGEN
DEUTEROGAMY DIGAMY
DEUTOMALA LABIUM
DEUX JOURNEES, LES
(CHARACTER IN —) ARMAND
MIKELI MAZARIN
(COMPOSER OF —) CHERUBINI
DEVA DEV DEWA SURA ANGEL
DEITY
DEVASTATE EXILE HARRY HAVOC
WASTE DEVAST RAVAGE
ATOMIZE DESTROY PILLAGE
PLUNDER SCOURGE DEMOLISH

DEVASTATED WASTE
DEVASTATING DEADLY LETHAL
SAVAGE CRUSHING FEROCIOUS
MURDEROUS
DEVASTATION RUIN SACK EXILE
HAVOC WASTE WRACK HARASS
RAVAGE SACCAGE SACKAGE
SACCADGE
DEVELOP BUD RUN BOOM COOK
FORM GROW STEM TILL ARISE
BREAK BREED BUILD ERECT RIPEN
SHOOT APPEAR BRANCH DETECT
EVOLVE EXPAND FLOWER FULFIL
MATURE REVEAL UNFOLD
UNFURL BURGEON BURNISH
EDUCATE ENLARGE EVOLUTE
EXPOUND FULFILL UNCOVER
DEVELOPE DISCLOSE DISCOVER
DISVELOP ENGENDER GENERATE
INCUBATE MANIFEST
(— A HEAD) HEART
(— BULB) BOTTOM
(— COLOR) AGE
(— CRACKS) ALLIGATOR
(— WELL) COTTON
DEVELOPABLE TORSE
DEVELOPED DEEP FORWARD
(— AFTER BIRTH) ACQUIRED
(FULLY —) BOLD ADULT FLORID
FORMED SUMMED
(GREATLY —) ADVANCED
(IMPERFECTLY —) ABORTIVE
(INCOMPLETELY —) SEED
DEVELOPER ELON SOUP METOL
ORTOL AMIDOL GLYCIN KACHIN
QUINOL BUILDER GLYCINE
RODINAL
DEVELOPING
(SUFF.) PLASTIC
DEVELOPMENT WAX DRIFT EVENT
HATCH ESTATE GROWTH
DESCENT GENESIS PROCESS
STATURE BREEDING INCREASE
ONTOGENY PEDIGREE
UPGROWTH UPSPRING
(— OF SEX) DIOECISM
(FULL —) BLOW MATURITY
(HIGHEST —) BLOOM
(NORMAL —) APHANISIA
(SUBSEQUENT —) SEQUEL
(THEMATIC —) CONTINUITY
(UNEXPECTED —) ACCIDENT
(PREF.) PLASTO
(SUFF.) PLASIA PLASIS
PLASM(A)(IA)(IC) PLAST(IC)(Y)
PLASY
DEVI UMA KALI DURGA GAURI
CHANDI SHAKTI BHAVANI
BHOWANI HIMAVAT MAHADEVI
HAIMAVATI
(FATHER OF —) HIMAVAT
(HUSBAND OF —) SHIVA
DEVIANT KINKY ABERRANT
DIVERGENT
DEVIATE ERR RUN WRY YAW LEAN
MISS VARY VEER BEVEL BREAK
DRIFT LAPSE SHEER SPORT START
STRAY WAIVE CHANGE DEPART
DETOUR DIVERT RECEDE SQUINT
SWERVE WANDER DECLINE
DEFLECT DIGRESS DIVERGE
INCLINE REFLECT ABERRANT
ABERRATE DEROGATE

(— FROM VERTICAL) HADE
DEVIATING SKEW DEVIANT
DEVIOUS ERRATIC SINUOUS
ABERRANT INDIRECT
DEVIATION BOW YAW HELM JUMP
SKEW TURN DRIFT LAPSE QUIRK
SHEER TWIST ABRASH BATTER
CHANGE DETOUR FIGURE SPREAD
ANOMALY BRISURE LICENCE
LICENSE ACCURACY DRIFTAGE
LATITUDE SOLECISM VARIANCE
ABERRATION
(— OF COLOR) ABRASH
(STANDARD —) SIGMA
DEVICE (ALSO SEE INSTRUMENT)
ARM ART DIE DOG DOP EYE FAN
FLY FOB GAG GIN GUN HOG JIG
KEY MOP MOT PEN SET TIP TUP
WAY WIT ARCH BELL BOND
BOOM BUFF COIN COMB COUP
DARE DOPP DRAG DRIP FAKE
FIRE FLAG FORK FROG FUSE FUZE
GAGE GATE GOBO GRAB GRIP
GYRO HASP HAUL HEAD HECK
HORN IRIS IRON JACK KEEP KITE
LAMP LENS LOCK MOVE MULE
MUTE NAIL PACE PAGE PAWK
PLOW POKE PUMP REEL SEAL
SHOE SHUT SIGN SLAY SLEY SLUR
SNAP SPUD STOP STUD SUMP
TOOL TRAP TRIP VICE WEIR
WHIM WHIP WIND WING WOLF
ALARM APRON BADGE BALUN
BITCH BLOCK BREAK BRUSH
CHECK CLAMP CODER COVIN
CRAMP CROSS DODGE DRIER
DRIFT DRYER DUMMY FADER
FANCY FLAIL FLARE FLASH FLIRT
FLOAT GAUGE GLAND GORGE
GRIPE GUARD GUIDE GUILE HICKY
HINGE HOKUM IMAGE KAZOO
KEYER LADLE LASER LATCH LEVEL
MATCH OTTER PARER PLATE
PUNKA SCREW SHADE SHANK
SHIFT SIEVE SIGHT SIGIL SIREN
SIZER SKATE SLAVE SLICK SLIDE
SLING SONDE SPOOL SPOUT
SQUIB STAMP STILL STOOL STOVE
SWEEP SWELL TABLE TABUT
TAMER THIEF TIMER TORCH
TRUER TUNER UNION VERGE
AGRAFE AIRWAY ALARUM ALINER
ANCHOR ARREST BAILER BASTER
BEACON BEATER BECKET BEDDER
BEEPER BINDER BLOWER BOBBIN
BOOMER BRIDLE BROOCH BUCKLE
BUFFER BULLEN BUMPER
BUNGEE BUNTER BURNER
BUTTON CHARGE CIPHER COOKER
DASHER DECEIT DERAIL DESIGN
DIMMER DOFFER DOTTER DRIVER
DROGUE DUMPER EMBLEM
ENGINE EVENER FABRIC FALLER
FEEDER FENDER FILLER FILTER
FINDAL FINDER FORMER GADGET
GLAZER GOFFER GOGGLE GRADER
GRATER GRISLY GUIDER HANGER
HEATER HICKEY HOLDER HOOTER
INVENT JIGGER JOGGER KEEPER
KICKER LAYBOY LETOFF LIFTER
LOOPER MARKER MIRROR
MODULE MORTAR MOTHER
NAVAID NIPPLE NONIUS NOTION

PACKER PEELER PICKUP PLAYER
PLOUGH PORTER POTEYE PULLER
PUNKAH REROLL RINGER ROCKET
ROLLER ROOTER ROTULA ROUTER
SACKER SADDLE SAFETY SANDER
SCALER SCHEME SCREEN SEALER
SEEKER SENSOR SETTER SHAKER
SHIELD SIFTER SIGNAL SINKER
SIPPER SLEIGH SLICER SLIDER
SLIMER SLOPER SLUICE SOCKET
SOLION SORTER SPACER SPRING
STONER STYLUS SUCKER SWITCH
TACTIC TAGGER TAPPER TELLER
TEMPLE TESTER TILLER TRACER
TUCKER TUNNEL TURNER
WARMER WASHER WEANER
WEEDER WHEEZE WINDER
WINNOW WORKER ADAPTER
ADJUNCT AERATOR AGRAFFE
ALIGNER AUTOCUE BALANCE
BECKETT BIMETAL BIMORPH
BINDING BLEEDER BLEEPER
BLENDER BLINKER BLOCKER
BLOWOFF BLOWOUT BOOKEND
BOOSTER BREAKER CALTROP
CHIPPER CLAPPER COMPASS
DASHPOT DISHMOP DIVISOR
DRAWOFF DRESSER DRINKER
EARPICK EDUCTOR EJECTOR
EMPRESA EXCITER FACEBOW
FASHION FETLOCK FICELLE
FICTION FITMENT FIXTURE
FLASHER FLIPPER FLUSHER
FLYFLAP FRISKET GAUFFER
GIMMICK GLASSES GRAINER
GRENADE GRIDDLE GRILLER
GRINDER GRIPPER GRIZZLY
GUDGEON GUZZLER HATCHER
HELIDON IGNITER IMAGINE
IMPRESA IMPRESS INFUSER
INHALER IRONMAN KICKOFF
KNOTTER LIGHTER MACHINE
MUFFLER OOGRAPH PIGTAIL
PLOTTER POINTER PRESSER
RATCHET RATTLER RECEDER
REDUCER RELEASE ROASTER
ROSETTE SAMPLER SCALPER
SCANNER SCOGGAN SCRAPER
SCUPPER SERVANT SETBACK
SETOVER SETWORK SHACKLE
SHEDDER SHIFTER SHIPPER
SHOOFLY SHUTTER SHUTTLE
SINKBOX SKIMMER SLAPPER
SLEEVER SLINGER SLITTER
SLUDGER SLUSHER SNAPPER
SNIFFER SNIGGLE SNORKEL
SNUBBER SNUFFER SNUGGER
SONOVOX SOUNDER SPARGER
SPEEDER SPLICER SPOTTER
SPRAYER SQUEEZE STACKER
STAPLER STARTER STEMMER
STENTER STIRRER STOPPER
STRIKER STRIPER SUCTION
SWATTER SWEEPER SYRINGE
TAMBOUR TENDRIL TENSION
THEORIC THINNER TICKLER
TREADLE TRINDLE TRIPPER
TRIPPET TUMBLER TURNOUT
TWISTER WASHOUT WRINGER
ABSORBER ADJUSTER AQUASTAT
BACKSTAY BAROSTAT BIOMETER
BLOCKING BOOTJACK BRAILLER

BREATHER BRONTEUM BUSINESS
BUSYBODY CATAPULT CATHETER
COLOPHON CONTOISE COUPLING
CROTCHET CRYOTRON
DAMPENER DEHORNER DERAILER
DIFFUSER DIRECTOR DISPOSER
DOORSTOP DROPHEAD DUPLEXER
EARPHONE EPISEMON ESPRESSO
EXPLODER FAIRLEAD FAKEMENT
FASTENER FLASHGUN FLYBRUSH
FUELIZER GASCHECK GATHERER
GIMCRACK GUNSTICK GYROSTAT
HALLMARK HANDTRAP
HEADGEAR HOLDBACK IMPROVER
INKSTAND IRENICON IRISCOPE
ISOLATOR KNOCKOUT LAUNCHER
LEEBOARD LOXOCOSM LUNARIUM
MNEMONIC MOLITION NEOSTYLE
ODOGRAPH OVERLIFT OVERRIDE
PACIFIER PARAVANE PENWIPER
PINWHEEL PULSATOR PYROSTAT
QUADRANT QUENTISE REFILTER
REHEATER REPEATER RETARDER
REVERSER SCORCHER SCOTCHER
SCRAWLER SCUTCHER SELECTOR
SHRINKER SILENCER SILVERER
SINKBOAT SMOOTHER
SNOWPLOW SNOWSHOE
SPLITTER SPREADER SPROUTER
SQUEEGEE SQUEEZER STOPWORK
STRAINER STRINGER STRIPPER
STROPPER SURFACER SWEATBOX
TELETYPE TELLTALE TERMINAL
THROWOFF THROWOUT
TRAVELER TRAVERSE TRIANGLE
NEURISTOR PINSETTER
PROJECTOR STRATAGEM
MARTINGALE PERIPHERAL
PINSPOTTER ACCELERATOR
(— FOR BENDING PIPE) HICKEY
(— FOR BORING WELLS) TIGER
(— FOR CONCENTRATING ORE)
JIGGER
(— FOR PUTTING IN GEAR) STRIKER
(— IN LOOM) FEELER TEMPLE
(— ON FLAG) UNION
(— PLACED OVER CHIMNEY) JACK
(— PROTECTING DENTIST'S HAND)
THIMBLE
(— THAT CONVERTS SIGNALS)
MODEM
(— TO LOCATE AN OBJECT) LIDAR
(— TO RETAIN COFFEE GROUNDS)
GRECQUE
(ARTIFICIAL —) PROSTHESIS
(CENTRIFUGAL —) CYCLONE
(CLEVER —) COUP KNACK
(COMPUTER —) TERMINAL
ACCUMULATOR
(DISTINGUISHING —) SPOT
(ELECTRICAL —) OVONIC
(GAMBLING —) HOLDOUT
(GLASSBLOWER'S —) DUMMY
(HAMPERING —) HOBBLES
(HEATING —) ETNA
(HERALDIC —S) ARMS
(LITERARY —) FRAME
(MAGICIAN'S —) FAKE FEKE CRAFT
(MIXING —) CRUTCHER
(POLISHING —) WAGWAG
(PYROTECHNIC —) FOUNTAIN
(RHETORICAL —) ANAPHORA
(ROTATION —) TACH

(SIGHTING —) ALIDADE
(SIGNALLING —) CRICKET
(SKILLFUL —) ART
(SPEECH —) ITALICS
(THEATRICAL —) SLOAT SLOTE
(TIMEKEEPING —) HOROLOGE
(TOROIDAL —) TOKAMAK
(WATER-RAISING —) JANTU SWEEP
CHURRUS
(WEAVING —) BOAT ENGINERY
(SUFF.) STAT(IC)(ICS)
(MUSICAL —) INA INE
DEVIL DEL IMP BENG BHUT BOGY
DEIL HAZE MAHU NICK PUCK
QUED WOLF WOND ANNOY
BOBBY BOGEY BOGIE CHORT
CLOOT DEMON DEUCE EBLIS
FIEND HARRY SATAN SCRAT
SHEDU TAIPO TEASE AMAMON
BELIAL DAEMON DIABLE DIABLO
HORNIE NICKIE PESTER RAGMAN
SORROW THURSE AMAIMON
ANHANGA CLOOTIE DIANTRE
DICKENS GREMLIN LUCIFER
MAHOUND RUFFIAN SERPENT
SHAITAN TORMENT WARLOCK
WENDIGO WINDIGO APOLLYON
BAALPEOR BEELPEOR BELFAGOR
CAGNAZZO CURUPIRA DEVILING
DEVILKIN DIABOLUS MEPHISTO
MISCHIEF OBIDICUT PLOTCOCK
WIRRICOW WORRICOW
WORRYCOW
(BLUE —S) MARE
(PREF.) DIABOL(O)
DEVILFISH RAY MANTA
DEVILISH DARING DEUCED DEVILY
RAKISH WICKED DEMONIC
EXTREME FIENDLY HELLISH
INHUMAN SATANIC DEMONIAC
DIABOLIC FIENDISH INFERNAL
SATURNINE
DEVILISHLY DEUCED DEUCEDLY
DEVIL'S CLUB FATSIA
DEVIL'S COACHHORSE DARDAOL
DEVIL'S DISCIPLE (AUTHOR OF —)
SHAW
(CHARACTER IN —) DICK ESSIE
JUDITH DUDGEON ANDERSON
BURGOYNE
DEVIL'S-MILK WARTWEED
WARTWORT
DEVIL'S-TREE DITA
DEVIOUS DEEP ERRING LOUCHE
ROVING SHIFTY SUBTLE TRICKY
OBLIQUE PLAITED VAGRANT
WINDING HAVERING INDIRECT
RAMBLING SCHEMING TORTUOUS
AMBAGIOUS MEALYMOUTHED
DEVISE AIM CAST COOK FIND GIVE
PLAN PLOT WARP WILL ARRAY
FANCY FRAME FUDGE IMAGE
LEAVE SHAPE WEAVE ADVISE
CONVEY DECOCT DESIGN DEVICE
DIVIDE DIVINE INVENT SCHEME
AGITATE APPOINT ARRANGE
BETHINK COMMENT COMPASS
CONCERT CONCOCT CONSULT
IMAGINE PREPARE PROJECT
BEQUEATH CONTRIVE
DEVISER FINDER ARTIFICER
DEVISING DEVICE DEVISAL
FORGERY

DEVITALIZE DULL DEADEN
DEVITALIZED DEGENERATE
DEVITRIFIED AMBITTY
DEVOID FREE VAIN VOID EMPTY
BARREN EXPERT VACANT
SINCERE WANTING DESOLATE
(— OF) BOUT EMPTY
(— OF HELP) AIDLESS
(— OF KINDNESS) CRUEL
(— OF MERCY) BRUTAL
(— OF MIND) AMENTAL
(— OF VALUE) HOLLOW
DEVOLUTION DESCENT
DEVOLVE FALL PASS VEST RESULT
BLOSSOM SUCCEED OVERTURN
TRANSFER TRANSMIT
DEVOTE VOW ALLY AVOW DOOM
GIVE LEND TAKE TURN APPLY
DEVOW ADDICT ATTACH BESTOW
DEPUTE DESIGN DEVOVE DIRECT
EMPLOY INTEND RESIGN
ADDRESS APPOINT CONSIGN
DESTINE DEDICATE VENERATE
(— TIME) BOTHER
(— TO MISERY) ACCURSE
DEVOTED MAD HIGH TRUE LIEGE
LOYAL PIOUS ARDENT DEVOUT
DOOMED ENTIRE FERVID LOVING
OBLATE VOTARY VOTIVE
ADORING ARDUOUS JEALOUS
SERIOUS ZEALOUS ADDICTED
ATTACHED CONSTANT FAITHFUL
(— TO COUNTRY) PATRIOTIC
(— TO ENJOYMENT) APOLAUSTIC
(OVERLY —) SUPERSTITIOUS
DEVOTEE CAT FAN NUN BUFF
MONK YATI ADEPT JNANI ADDICT
BHAGAT BHAKTA DEVOTO
DEVOUT HEPCAT VOTARY
VOTEEN ZEALOT ADMIRER
AMATEUR BOPPIST BOPSTER
CINEAST FANATIC HEPSTER
HIPSTER SHAVIAN TARTUFE
AMOURIST BURNSIAN CABALIST
DEVOTARY FOLLOWER IBSENITE
PARTISAN PRIAPIAN SAVOYARD
SIMPLIST TARTUFFE VOTARESS
VOTARIST ALLIGATOR
AFICIONADO
DEVOTION CULT ZEAL ARDOR
PIETY BHAKTI NOVENA ANGELUS
ARABISM CULTISM LOYALTY
PIETISM FIDELITY IDOLATRY
JEALOUSY KAVVANAH
KAWWANAH RELIGION
NATIONALISM
(— OF ONESELF) VOW NARCISSISM
(— TO HUMAN WELFARE)
HUMANISM
(FERVENT —) ADORATION
(PARENTAL —) PROGENITY
(PL.) HOLIES
(SUFF.) LATER LATRIA LATROUS
LATRY
DEVOTIONAL PIOUS SOLEMN
DEVOUR EAT JAW FRET GULP
SWAP SWOP VOUR GORGE
RAVEN SCOFF WASTE AFRETE
ENGULF CONSUME ENGORGE
FRAUNCH SWALLOW
(— GREEDILY) SWILL
(SUFF.) VORA VORE VOROUS
DEVOURING PREY EATING GREEDY

VORANT EDACIOUS
DEVOUT GOOD HOLY WARM
FROOM GODLY GRACY PIOUS
HEARTY INWARD SOLEMN
CORDIAL DEVOTED GODLIKE
PITEOUS SAINTLY SINCERE
REVERENT PIETISTIC PRAYERFUL
RELIGIOUS PIETISTICAL
SANCTIMONIOUS
(NOT —) LINK
DEVOUTNESS PIETY DEVOTION
DEW DAG RIME BLOOM FROST
MOISTEN REFRESH MOISTURE
(— METER) PAGOSCOPE
(NIGHT —) SERENE
(PREF.) DROSO RORI
DEWBERRY MAYES
DEWDROP PEARL
DEWLAP JOWL GULLET JOLLOP
CHOLLER WATTLES
(— OF MALE MOOSE) BELL
DEWY DAMP RORY MOIST RORAL
RORIC RORID GENTLE ROSCID
DEXTERITY ART CHIC CRAFT
KNACK SKILL STROIL ABILITY
ADDRESS AGILITY APTNESS
CUNNING FINESSE SLEIGHT
APTITUDE DEFTNESS FACILITY
(— IN ARMS) CHIVALRY
DEXTEROUS APT FLY DEFT FEAT
HEND NEAT WISE ADEPT CANNY
CLEAN FEATY HANDY HAPPY
HENDE JIMMY QUICK READY
SMART TIGHT ADROIT ARTFUL
CLEVER DRAFTY CUNNING
SLEIGHT DEXTROUS HANDSOME
SKILLFUL SLEIGHTY
DEXTEROUSLY YARELY HANDILY
DEXTRAN GLUCOSAN
DEXTROROTATORY POSITIVE
DEXTRORSE EUTROPIC
DEXTROSE AME CEROLESE
DHAK DAK PALAS PULAS
DHAVA BAKLI
DHOLE KOLSUN
DHOW BUGALA LATEEN SAMBUK
SAMBOUK LATEENER
DHRITARASHTRA (BROTHER OF —)
PANDU
(FATHER OF —) VYASA
VICHITRAVIRYA
(SON OF —) DURYODHANA
(WIFE OF —) GANDHARI
DHYANA JHANA
DIABASE OPHITE DOLERITE
THOLEITE
DIABOLICAL CRUEL WICKED
DEMONIC HELLISH INHUMAN
SATANIC VIOLENT DEMONIAC
DEVILISH DIABOLIC FIENDISH
INFERNAL
DIABOLISM SATANISM
DIACETATE ACETIN
DIACONATE DEACONRY
DIACONICON PARABEMA
DIACRITIC HACEK TILDE UMLAUT
MODIFIER
DIAD DIGONAL TWOFOLD
DIADEM TAJ MIND CROWN TIARA
ANADEM CIRCLE EMBLEM FILLET
CIRCUIT CORONET HEADBAND
DIAERESIS TREMA CESURA
CAESURA DIALYSIS

DIAGNOSE ANALYZE IDENTIFY
KNOWLEDGE
DIAGONAL BIAS SLANT SLASH
COUNTER SOLIDUS VIRGULE
BENDWISE DIAGONIC
DIAGONALLY BIAS ASLOPE
BENDWAYS BENDWISE
DIAGRAM MAP PLAN PLOT TREE
CARTE CHART EPURE GRAPH
DESIGN FIGURE SCHEMA SCHEME
SYMBOL YANTRA ISOGRAM
ISOTYPE SECTION VIAGRAM
PICTOGRAM PICTOGRAPH
DIAGRAMMATIC GRAPHIC
DIAGRAPH OE
DIAL NOB FACE KNOB WATCH
DIACLE JIGGER AZIMUTH
CRYSTAL DECLINER HOROLOGE
INCLINER RECLINER
DIAL BIRD DAYAL DHYAL
DIALECT (ALSO SEE LANGUAGE)
HO KA WU GEG GIZ KHA LAI SAC
TWI AMOY CANI CANT DRAA EFIK
EGBA EPIC GEEZ GHEG GONA
GUEG IOWA ITZA KORA MANX
NAMA NORN OGAM PALI SAUK
SHOR SOGA TALK TCHI TOSK
TUBA ALTAI ARGOT ASURI ATTIC
CONOY DORIC FANTI GHEEZ
GHESE HAKKA IDIOM IONIC
IOWAY IRAQI KANSA KAREL
KOINE LADIN LINGO MAZUR
MOPAN MUKRI NGOKO OGHAM
PARSI PUNIC SABIR SAXON SCOTS
SLANG TIGRE TSCHI VALVE
VOGUL ZMUDZ AEOLIC AGNEAN
ASANTE ATSINA AWADHI
BADAGA BRETON BROGUE
CANTON CREOLE DEBATE
DUNGAN FAEROE FANTEE
FURLAN GASCON GULLAH
GUTNIC HARARI HARAYA IBANAG
ISINAI ITAVES JARGON KABYLE
KANSAS KHAMIR KORANA KVITSH
LADAKI LADINO LAHULI LALLAN
LEDDEN LIBYAN PARSEE PATOIS
PATTER PICARD SANTEE SCOTCH
SHARRA SKAGIT SPEECH SUDANI
SWATOW SYRIAC SZEKEL TAVAST
TONGUE TUSCAN YANKEE
ZENAGA ACADIAN AEOLIAN
AMOYESE ANGLIAN ASHANTI
BHOTANI BHUTANI BUNDELI
CATALAN CHILULA CHUVASH
CLATSOP COCKNEY CORNISH
CUZCENO CYPRIOT FAYUMIC
FOOCHOW GEECHEE GHEGISH
GUTNISH JAIPURI KARAITE
KENTISH KITKSAN KONKANI
LADAKHI LALLAND LEONESE
LESBIAN MALTESE MARSIAN
MARWARI MERCIAN MIDLAND
MULTANI MUNDARI OLONETS
PANAYAN PRAKRIT SAHIDIC
SANROIL SHORTZY SOKOTRI
SPOKANE SQUAXON SWABIAN
SZEKLER TIGRINA VAUDOIS
WALLOON ABANEEME ACHMIMIC
AKHMIMIC ALGERINE ARCADIAN
ASSYRIAN BASILECT BAVARIAN
BHOJPURI BISCAYAN BOEOTIAN
BOHAIRIC CLAKAMAS COLVILLE
CORSICAN CYPRIOTE FALERIAN

FALISCAN FAROEISH FRANCIEN
FRIULIAN GARHWALI HARARESE
IZCATECO KANESIAN KARELIAN
KERMANJI KICKAPOO KINGWANA
LACANDON LANGUAGE
LAWLANTS MAGHREBI MAGHRIBI
MAITHILI MANDAEAN MANDARIN
MANISIAN MAZATECO MAZURIAN
MEMPHITE NABATEAN
NEENGATU PANAYANO PEKINESE
RABBINIC SALTEAUX SOULETIN
SOUTHERN TAUNGTHU TIGRINYA
TIRHUTIA TUNISIAN VENERIAN
VIENNESE NORTHUMBRIAN
(ENGLISH — IN LIVERPOOL) SCOUSE
(STRANGE —) GIBBERISH
(PL.) WU ANGLIAN
DIALECTIC PILPUL
DIALOGUE ION CRITO DIALOG
EPILOG PATTER PHAEDO
TIMAEUS COLLOQUY DUOLOGUE
EPILOGUE EXCHANGE PHAEDRUS
COLLOCUTION
(—S OF BUDDHA) SUTRA SUTTA
(COMIC —) LAZZO
DIAMETER BORE GAGE GEAR
MOOT GAUGE WIDTH MODULE
(— OF BULLET) CALIBER CALIBRE
(— OF PELVIS) CONJUGATA
(— OF PUPIL) APERTURE
(— OF WIRE) GAGE GAUGE
DIAMOND GEM ICE BORT LASK
PICK ROCK ROSE BAHIA BOORT
BORTZ DORJE FANCY FIELD
JAGER JEWEL LOZEN MELEE
POINT RHOMB RIVER SANCY
SPARK TABLE VAJRA ADAMAS
BOARTS CANARY CARBON
JAEGER LASQUE ORLOFF PENCIL
REGENT RONDEL SHINER TABLET
ADAMANT BRIOLET CARREAU
CRYSTAL FISHEYE INFIELD
LOZENGE PREMIER RHOMBUS
SPARKLE CORUNDUM KOHINOOR
RONDELLE SPARKLER BRIOLETTE
(— CUT TOO THIN) FISHEYE
(— MOLDER) DOP
(— STATE) DELAWARE
(— USED FOR ENGRAVING) SHARP
(BLACK —) CARBONADO
(FLAT —) LASQUE
(GLAZIER'S —) QUARREL
(IMITATION —) SCHLENTER
(INFERIOR GRADE OF —) FLAT
(PERFECT —) PARAGON
(PURE WHITE —) RIVER
(ROUGH —) BRAIT
(SINGLE —) SOLITAIRE
(TRANSPARENT —) CRYSTAL
(YELLOW —) CANARY
(PL.) MELANGE
DIAMOND BIRD PARDALOTE
DIAMORPHINE HEROIN
DIANA LUCINA TRIVIA ARTEMIS
(BROTHER OF —) APOLLO
(FATHER OF —) JUPITER
(MOTHER OF —) LATONA
DIANA MONKEY ROLOWAY
DIAPASON MONTRE DIAPASE
DIAPAUSE BLOCK
DIAPER FUR DIDY CLOUT DIDIE
NAPPY HIPPEN HIPPIN NAPKIN
NAPPIE DIAPERY

DIAPHANOUS CLEAR SHEER FRAGILE DIAPHANE VAPOROUS

DIAPHONY ORGANUM TRIPHONY

DIAPHORETIC BUCCO BUCHU BUCKU BORAGE DIAPNOIC HIDROTIC SUDATORY SASSAFRAS PILOCARPINE

DIAPHRAGM IRIS RIFF SLIT APRON PHREN SKIRT WAFER DECKER PLATEN MIDRIFF PHRAGMA SKIRTING TRAVERSE TYMPANUM (PREF.) PHREN(O)

DIAPHRAGMATIC PHRENIC

DIARRHEA LAX FLUX LASK GURRY RELAX SCOUR SPRUE PURGING SQUIRTS LIENTERY

DIARY LOG RECORD DAYBOOK DIURNAL JOURNAL REGISTER EPHEMERIS

DIASKEUAST EDITOR REVISER

DIASPORA GALUT GOLAH GALUTH

DIASPORE MIGRULE

DIASTASE MALT ENZYME AMYLASE

DIATOM BRITTLEWORT ASTERIONELLA

DIATOMITE TRIPOLI

DIATONIC ACHROMATIC

DIATRIBE SATIRE SCREED HARANGUE INVECTIVE

DIB DAP DIP DIBBLE DIBSTONE

DIBBLE DAP DIB DABBLE DIBBER KIPPIN TRIFLE DIBBLER KIPPEEN

DIBRI (SON OF —) SHELOMITH

DIBS COCKAL

DICAST HELIAST JURYMAN

DICE CHOP CUBE DEES BONES CRAPS FLATS LOWMEN REJECT CHECKER IVORIES
(**— GAME)** SET RAPHE MUMCHANCE
(**— HAVING FOUR SPOTS)** QUATRE
(**FALSE —)** GOAD TATS GOURD GRAVIERS SQUARIER STOPDICE
(**HIGHEST THROW AT —)** APHRODITE
(**LOADED —)** TOPS DOCTOR
(**LOWEST THROW AT —)** AMBSACE
(**PAIRED NUMBERS AT —)** DUPLET DOUBLETS
(**2, 3, OR 12 ON 1ST —)** MISSOUT
(PREF.) ASTRAGAL(O)

DICE PLAYER THROWSTER

DICER HAT DERBY GAMBLER GRAINER

DICERION DYKER

DICHASIAL BIPAROUS

DICHLORVOS DDVP

DICHONDRA LAWNLEAF

DICHOTOMY DUALITY

DICHROITE IOLITE

DICKENS HECK DEUCE

DICKER ICRE SWAP DAKER BARTER HAGGLE BARGAIN CHAFFER EXCHANGE

DICKEY POOP WEAK DICKY FRONT GILET SHAKY DONKEY RUMBLE VESTEE HADDOCK PLASTRON

DICKIE SHAM DICKY FRONT SQUARE TUCKER STARCHER

DICLINOUS IMPERFECT

DICTATE SAW SAY DITE TELL UTTER WRITE DECREE DICTUM ENJOIN IMPOSE INDITE OCTROY ORDAIN SCHOOL COMMAND DELIVER REQUIRE SUGGEST WARRANT DICTAMEN PRESCRIBE

DICTATION DICTAMEN

DICTATOR CHAM CZAR DUCE TSAR CAESAR PENDRAGON

DICTATORIAL BOSSY LORDLY CZARIST POMPOUS TSARIST ARROGANT DOGMATIC ORACULAR POSITIVE ARBITRARY MAGISTERIAL

DICTION STYLE TERMS PHRASE IMAGERY LANGUAGE PARLANCE VERBIAGE
(**BAD —)** CACOLOGY
(**SUFF.)** ESE

DICTIONARY GRADUS ALVEARY CALEPIN LEXICON GLOSSARY WORDBOOK THESAURUS
(PREF.) LEXICO

DICTUM SAY ADAGE AXIOM EDICT DECREE SAYING DICTATE EFFATUM OPINION APOTHEGM PRINCIPLE STATEMENT

DID D CAN DED DEDE DYDE
(**— NOT)** DIDNA DIDNT

DIDACTIC DRY PREACHY SERMONIC

DIDO ANTIC CAPER TRICK
(**BROTHER OF —)** PYGMALION
(**FATHER OF —)** BELUS
(**HUSBAND OF —)** SICHAEUS
(**LOVER OF —)** AENEAS

DIDO AND AENEAS (CHARACTER IN —) DIDO AENEAS BELINDA MERCURY
(**COMPOSER OF —)** PURCELL

DIE GO BED DEE DOD END HOB HUB PIP ROT SIX TAT BOSS COIN CONK CUBE DADO DEAD DICE DROP EXIT FADE FAIL FALL FINE FIVE FLIT KICK MARK MOLD PART PASS PIKE PILE SEAL TATT TINE WANE CROAK FORCE FUDGE GHOST IVORY NAPOO PATAY PRINT PUNCH QUAIL SHAPE SNUFF SOUGH SPILL STALL STAMP STOCK SWELT CHANCE DEMISE DEPART DOCTOR EXPIRE FAMISH FINISH FORCER FORMER FULLAM MATRIX MULLAR PATRIX PERISH ROLLER STARVE STRIKE TORFEL TORFLE TRANCE VANISH WITHER BLOCKER DECEASE SUCCUMB TESSERA INTAGLIO LANGUISH MISCARRY PUNCHEON TRESPASS TRUSSELL
(**— AWAY)** FAIL SWOON
(**— BEFORE)** PREDECEASE
(**— BY HANGING)** SWING
(**— DOWN)** FLIT SINK ABATE
(**— FOR DRAWING WIRE)** WHIRTLE WHORTLE
(**— FOR MAKING DRAINPIPE)** DOD
(**— FOR MOLDING BRICK)** KICK
(**— FROM HUNGER)** AFFAMISH
(**— OF COLD)** STARVE
(**— OF PEDESTAL)** SOLIDUM
(**— WITH 4 SPOTS)** QUATRE
(**— WITH 6 SPOTS)** CISE SICE SISE SIZE
(**COINING —)** SICCA

(**FRAUDULENT —)** FULHAM FULLAM FULLOM
(**HOLLOW —)** GOURD
(**IMPROPER —)** FLAT
(**LOADED —)** TAT DOCTOR FULHAM HIGHMAN LANGRET
(**LOWER —)** BED
(**REVOLVING —)** DREIDEL

DIEBACK STAGHEAD EXANTHEMA

DIED DYDE OBIIT WRATE

DIEHARD TORY BLIMP

DIESIS FEINT

DIET BANT FARE FAST FOOD SEIM SEYM BOARD HOFTAG REDUCE SEIMAS VIANDS VICTUS DIETINE LANDTAG REGIMEN RIKSDAG CONGRESS KREISTAG VOLKSTAG

DIETARY (— LAWS) KASHRUTH

DIETETICS SITOLOGY

DIETHER APIOL APIOLE DIOXANE

DIETING BANTING

DIFFER VARY RECEDE SQUARE COMPARE DISCORD DISSENT DIVERGE DISAGREE

DIFFERENCE SHED CHASM CLASH FAVOR BREACH CHANGE DIFFER ANOMALY BRISURE DISCORD DISPUTE QUALITY VARIETY DISTANCE DIVISION IMPARITY VARIANCE
(**— IN ELEVATION)** HEAD
(**— IN EXCHANGE)** AGIO
(**— IN LATITUDE)** SOUTHING
(**— IN LONGITUDE)** EASTING
(**— IN PITCH)** COMMA INTERVAL
(**— IN PRESSURE)** DRAFT DRAUGHT
(**— IN WIDTH)** BILGE
(**— OF OPINION)** DISSENT ARGUMENT
(**— OF VESSEL'S DRAFT)** DRAG
(**ANGULAR —)** EXPLEMENT
(**GRADED —)** GRADIENT
(**MINUTE —)** SHADE
(**PRICE —)** BASIS
(**SMALL —)** HAIRLINE

DIFFERENT FAR MANY SERE FRESH OTHER PARTY DIVERS SCREWY SUNDRY UNLIKE ANOTHER DISTANT DIVERSE SEVERAL STRANGE UNALIKE UNUSUAL VARIANT VARIOUS CONTRARY DISTINCT MANIFOLD SEPARATE OTHERWISE OTHERGUESS NONIDENTICAL
(PREF.) DIVERSI HETER(O)

DIFFERENTIA MARK LIMIT

DIFFERENTIAL FLUXION

DIFFERENTIATE APLITE DIFFER DISCERN HAPLITE CONTRAST SPECIATE

DIFFERENTIATION ANABOLY DEVIATION DICHOTOMY
(PREF.) ALL(O)

DIFFERING DIVERSE SINGULAR DIVERGENT

DIFFICULT ILL HARD WICK CRAMP CRANK GREAT HEAVY SPINY STEEP STIFF AUGEAN CRABBY CRANKY KNOTTY SEVERE STICKY STRAIT STRONG TICKLE TRAPPY UNEASY UNEATH UPHILL WENETH WICKED ARDUOUS AWKWARD BRITTLE COMPLEX

CRABBED DIFFUSE LABORED NERVOUS OBSCURE PAINFUL PERPLEX PRACTIC SERIOUS STICKLE UNNETHE ABSTRACT CUMBROUS FIENDISH PUZZLING SCABROUS STRUGGLE STUBBORN TICKLISH
(**— TO BEAR)** BITTER
(**— TO COMPREHEND)** STRANGE
(**— TO FOLLOW)** DIRTY
(**— TO GRASP)** FUGITIVE
(**— TO HANDLE)** SPINOUS
(**— TO MANAGE)** SURLY STURDY
(**— TO OBTAIN)** CLOSE
(**— TO PLEASE)** CURIOUS
(**— TO RAISE)** DORTY
(**— TO SATISFY)** CHOOSY CHOOSEY
(**— TO UNDERSTAND)** DEEP HIGH SUBTLE CRABBED ABSTRACT ABSTRUSE ESOTERIC
(PREF.) DYS MOGI

DIFFICULTY ADO BAR BOX ILL JAM RUB BUMP CLOG COIL HEAT JAMB KNOT LOCK NODE PAIN PINE SNAG SORE WERE CHECK DOUBT GRIEF NODUS PRESS RIGOR STAND STOUR TRADE APORIA BOGGLE BUNKER HABBLE HOBBLE PLIGHT PLUNGE RUBBER SCRAPE STRAIT TIFTER BARRIER DICKENS GORDIAN PITFALL PROBLEM SQUEEZE ASPERITY DISTRESS HARDNESS HARDSHIP OBSTACLE SEVERITY STRUGGLE
(**UNEXPECTED —)** SNAG
(**WITH —)** SCARCELY
(PREF.) (**WITH —)** DYS MOGI

DIFFIDENCE DOUBT MODESTY RESERVE SHYNESS DISTRUST HUMILITY TIMIDITY

DIFFIDENT SHY BLATE CHARY MODEST BACKWARD RESERVED RETIRING SHEEPISH

DIFFUSE FULL SHED BLEED EXUDE LARGE STREW WORDY DEFUSE DERIVE DILATE DIVIDE EXPAND EXTEND OSMOSE PROLIX SPREAD SPRING COPIOUS DIALYSE DIALYZE DIFFUND PERFUSE PERPLEX PERVADE PUBLISH RADIATE SCATTER SPARKLE SPRAWLY SPRENGE SUFFUSE VERBOSE CONFUSED DIFFUSED DIOSMOSE DISPERSE PATULENT PATULOUS SPRANGLE
(**NOT —)** STRICT COMPACT

DIFFUSION SPREAD OSMOSIS BLEEDING DEFUSION

DIG HOE JOB NIP CLAW DIKE DYKE GIRD GORE GRUB HOWK MINE MOOT PICK PION POKE PROD ROOT SINK SLAM SMUG SPIT SPUD SUMP SWOT DELVE DITCH DWELL GAULT GRAFT GRAVE LODGE POACH PROBE SNOUT SPADE START STOCK BURROW DREDGE EXHUME GRAVEL HOLLOW PLUNGE SHOVEL THRUST TUNNEL BEDELVE COSTEAN SPUDDLE UNEARTH EXCAVATE
(**— OUT)** SCOOP STUMP EXHUME
(**— OUT CREVICES)** FOSSICK

(— PEAT) SHEUGH
(— POTATOES) LIFT
(— TRENCHES) GRIP COSTEAN
COSTEEN
(— UP) CAST GRUB STUB SPADE
STOCK EXHUME UPGRAVE
DISINTER
(— WITH NAILS) SCRAPE
(— WITH SNOUT) GROUT
(— WITH STICK) CROW
DIGAMMA VAU
DIGEST COCT CODE DEFY ENDEW
ENDUE INDUE RIPEN CODIFY
DECOCT DOCKET MATURE
SEETHE CONCOCT EPITOME
PANDECT SUMMARY CONDENSE
SYLLABUS
DIGESTION PEPSIS COCTION
EUPEPSY EUPEPSIA
(SUFF.) PEPSIA PEPTIC
DIGESTIVE PEPSIN PEPTIC
DIGERENT
DIGGER DIG PAL PLOW MINER
BANKER BILDAR DRUDGE
PLOUGH COMRADE PEATMAN
PIONEER PLODDER TRENCHER
(POST HOLE —) LOY
DIGGING DIG DIKAGE DYKAGE
STRIPPING
DIGHT DAB RUB DECK DINK DITE
WIPE ADORN DICHT DRESS EQUIP
ORDER RAISE TREAT MANAGE
REPAIR WINNOW APPOINT
CONSIGN PERFORM PREPARE
DIGIT TOE UNIT DOIGT POINT
THUMB DACTYL FIGURE FINGER
HALLUX MEDIUS NUMBER
DEWCLAW DIGITAL
(BINARY —) BIT BINIT
(EXTRA —) PREPOLLEX
(PREF.) DACTYL(O) DACTYLIO
(SUFF.) DACTYLIA DACTYLOUS
DIGITAL KEY MANUAL
DIGITATE DIGITAL FINGERED
DIGNIFIED GRAND LOFTY MANLY
NOBLE STAID AUGUST LORDLY
SEDATE SOLEMN COURTLY
EXALTED STATELY TOGATED
ELEVATED ENNOBLED MAJESTIC
DIGNIFY DUB ADORN CROWN
EXALT GRACE HONOR RAISE
ELEVATE ENNOBLE PROMOTE
DIGNITARY DON WIG BABA RAJA
CANON RAJAH PRIEST SHERIF
DIGNITY HUTUKTU PRELATE
PROVOST SHEREEF ALDERMAN
HUTUKHTU VESTIARY
DIGNITY DOG CHIC FACE RANK
BENCH DINES HONOR IZZAT
PRIDE STATE AFFAIR BARONY
LAUREL REPOSE BARONRY
BEARING DECORUM DUKEDOM
EARLDOM FITNESS GRAVITY
MAJESTY SHAHDOM STATION
WORSHIP CHIVALRY EARLSHIP
GRANDEUR NOBILITY
(— OF BISHOP) LAWN
(ACCIDENTAL —) JOY HAYZ
(PAPAL —) TIARA
(SUFF.) DOM SHIP
DIGRAPH CH OE PH RH TH RRH
BIGRAM LIGATURE DIPHTHONG
DIGRESS VEER EXCUR DIVERT

SWERVE WANDER DEVIATE
DIVERGE EXCURSE DISGRESS
DIVAGATE
DIGRESSION ASIDE VAGARY
DIGRESS ECBASIS EPISODE
EXCURSE PASSAGE TANGENT
DISGRESS EXCURSUS SIDESLIP
PARENTHESIS
(RHETORICAL —) ECBOLE
DIKE BAR RIB BANK BUND DICE
DICK DYKE GALL POND POOL
DIGUE DITCH LEVEE CAUSEY
CRADGE CHANNEL DIKELET
POWDIKE ABOIDEAU CAUSEWAY
ESTACADE SPREADER
DIKER COWAN COWEN
DIKETONE BENZIL BIACETYL
DIMEDONE
DIKLAH (FATHER OF —) JOKTAN
DILACTONE LACTIDE ANEMONIN
DILAPIDATE DESTROY
DILAPIDATED BAD BEATEN
CREAKY RAGGED RUINED SHABBY
WRECKY CRAICHY CREACHY
RUINOUS DESOLATE TATTERED
WOBEGONE
DILAPIDATION RUIN DECAY
DECREPITY DISREPAIR
DILATATION BULB SINUS VARIX
JARBOT SPREAD AMPULLA
ECTASIA ECTASIS ANEURISM
DILATION MYDRIASIS
(SUFF.) ECTASIA ECTASIS
DILATE TENT DELAY PLUMP SWELL
WIDEN DELATE EXPAND EXTEND
SPREAD AMPLIFY BROADEN
DESCANT DIFFUSE DISTEND
ENLARGE INFLATE PROLONG
STRETCH DISPERSE INCREASE
LENGTHEN PROTRACT DISCOURSE
DILATING
(SUFF.) EURYSIS
DILATOR DIOPTER DIOPTRA
DIOPTRY DIVULSOR SPECULUM
DILATORY LATE SLOW SLACK
SPARE TARDY FABIAN REMISS
DILATOR LAGGARD LATREDE
TEDIOUS BACKWARD DELAYING
INACTIVE SLUGGISH
DILEMMA FIX FORK LOCK NODE
BRIKE CHOICE PLUNGE CORNUTE
SNIFTER JEOPARDY QUANDARY
DILETTANTE LOVER SUNDAY
ADMIRER AMATEUR DABBLER
DABSTER ESTHETE AESTHETE
DILIGENCE HIE CARE HEED DILLY
EFFORT CAUTION HORNING
BUSINESS INDUSTRY SEDULITY
ASSIDUITY
DILIGENT BUSY HARD TIDY ACTIVE
EIDENT ITHAND STEADY CAREFUL
EARNEST HEEDFUL OPEROSE
PAINFUL PATIENT WORKFUL
CAUTIOUS CONSTANT LABOROUS
SEDULOUS STUDIOUS
DILL ANET CALM SOYA ANISE
UMBEL PICKLE SOOTHE DILLWEED
DILLYDALLY LAG TOY LOAF DELAY
DILLY STALL LOITER TRIFLE
DILOGY ECHO
DILUENT CARRIER VEHICLE
DILUTE CUT BREW FUSE LEAN
THIN WEAK ALLAY BLUNT DELAY

WATER RAREFY REDUCE WEAKEN
WHITISH DIMINISH LENGTHEN
WATERISH
(— LIQUOR) BREW SPLIT
(— WINE) GALLIZE
(VERY —) SMALL
DILUTED WASHY DILUTE REMISS
DILUTING ATTENUANT
DIM DIP WAN BLUR DARK DULL
FADE GRAY HAZY MIST PALE
PALL VEIL BEDIM BLEAK BLEAR
BLIND DUSKY DUSTY FAINT
FOGGY MISTY STAIN UNLIT
BEMIST BLEARY CLOUDY DARKEN
DASWEN DIMPSY GLOOMY
OBTUSE SHADOW TWILIT
BECLOUD DARKISH DISLIMN
ECLIPSE OBSCURE OPACATE
SHADOWY TARNISH DARKLING
OVERCAST CALIGINOUS
CREPUSCULAR
(NOT —) FRESH
DIME HOG HOGG DISME TENPENCE
TENPENNY
(HALF —) PICAYUNE
DIMEDON METHONE
DIMENHYDRINATE DRAMAMINE
DIMENSION BODY BULK SIZE
SCOPE WIDTH ASSIZE DEGREE
EXTENT HEIGHT LENGTH MOISON
BREADTH PROPORTION
MEASUREMENT
(COLOR —) CHROMA
(TYPE —) EM EN
(PL.) GAGE SIZE GAUGE GIRTH
EXTENT SIDING MEASURE
DIMENSIONS
(PREF.) (THREE —) STERE(O)
DIMER (— IN EXCITED STATE)
EXCIMER
DIMIDIATE HALVED
DIMINISH GO CUT EBB SAP BATE
BURN CHOP DAMP DROP EASE
FADE FAIL FINE FRET MELT PARE
PINK SINK WANE WEAR ABATE
ALLAY BREAK CLOSE DRAFT
DWARF ELIDE ERODE LOWER
MINCE PETER SLACK SMALL
TAPER DAMPEN DEBATE DECOCT
DEDUCT DILUTE IMPAIR LESSEN
MINISH REBATE REDUCE SLOUGH
VANISH WITHER ABRIDGE
ASSUAGE CORRODE CURTAIL
DEGRADE DEPLETE DEPRESS
DETRACT DIMINUE DRAUGHT
DWINDLE FRITTER INHIBIT
QUALIFY REFRACT RELIEVE
TARNISH ADMINISH AMOINDER
CONDENSE DECREASE DIMINUTE
DISCOUNT MINORATE MITIGATE
MODERATE RETRENCH
(— FRONT) PLOY
DIMINISHED SLACK ABATED
GRAYED DIMINUTE
DIMINISHING TAPER CRITICAL
FLAGGING
(— IN LOUDNESS) CALANDO
DIMINUTION FALL WASTE RABATE
DECREASE PERDITION
DIMINUTIVE TOY WEE BABY TINY
BANTY DWARF PETTY RUNTY
SMALL YOUNG BANTAM LITTLE
MIDGET PETITE POCKET MANIKIN

MIDGETY MINIKIN SHRIMPY
EXIGUOUS
(— OF BAR) SCARP CLOSET
SCARPE
(SUFF.) CLE CULE CULUS EL ET
ETTE KIN OCK SY ULA ULE
DIMLY DULLY DARKLY FEEBLY
SHADOWY
DIMMED BLEARY CLOUDY GRAYED
BLEARED
DIMMING GRAYOUT
DIMNESS DIM HAZE MIST SLUR
GLOOM CALIGO DARKNESS
DIMPLE DOKE AHMADI AHMEDI
RIPPLE GELASIN FOSSETTE
DIM-SIGHTED PURBLIND
DIN BUM DUN REEL RERD RIOT
UTIS ALARM BABEL BRUIT CHIME
CHIRM CLANG DEAVE DEEVE
FRUSH NOISE RERDE ALARUM
BELDER CLAMOR FRAGOR
HUBBUB RACKET RANDAN
RATTLE STEVEN TUMULT
UPROAR CLANGOR CLATTER
DISCORD TURMOIL DINGDONG
TINTAMAR
DINAH (BROTHER OF —) LEVI
SIMEON
(FATHER OF —) JACOB
(MOTHER OF —) LEAH
DINAR DENARE MARAVEDI
DINARZADE (SISTER OF —)
SCHEHERAZADE
DINDLE RING QUIVER THRILL
TINGLE TINKLE TREMOR STAGGER
VIBRATE
DINE EAT SUP FARE FEAST REGALE
DINER EPICURE GOURMAND
DING DIN BEAT DANG DASH KICK
PUSH RING WHIP CLANG DRIVE
EXCEL FLING KNOCK PITCH
POUND PUNCH THUMP STROKE
THRASH THRUST
DINGE DENT DINT BATTER BRUISE
TARNISH
DINGHY PRAM SKIFF DINGEY
ROWBOAT SHALLOP SNOWBIRD
DINGLE DEN DALE DELL GLEN
VALE DIMBLE DUMBLE HOLLOW
VALLEY
DINGMAN BUMPER
DINGO WARRAGAL WARRIGAL
DINGUS GADGET DOOHICKEY
DINGY DUN DARK BLACK DIRTY
DUSKY GRIMY OURIE SMOKY
DINGHY FUSCOUS SUBFUSC
SMIRCHED
DINING CENATION
(PREF.) DEIPNO
DINING ROOM TRICLINIUM
DINKA JANGHEY
DINNER DINE HALL KALE MEAL
MEAT NOON BEANO FEAST
DINING REPAST BANQUET
PUCHERO FUNCTION
(CEREMONIAL —) SEDER
(PERTAINING TO —) PRANDIAL
(PREF.) DEIPNO
DINOSAUR DIAPSID SAURIAN
DUCKBILL NODOSAUR SAUROPOD
TROODONT ORNITHISCHIAN
DINT BEAT BLOW DENT DUNT NICK
CLOUR DELVE DINGE FORCE

NOTCH ONSET POWER PRESS
SHOCK ATTACK CHANCE EFFORT
STRIKE STROKE IMPRINT
EFFICACY STRIKING
DIOCESAN EPISCOPAL
DIOCESE SEE EPARCHY DISTRICT
BISHOPRIC
DIODE KENOTRON
(**— THAT EMITS LIGHT**) LED
(**TYPE OF —**) ZENER
DIOLEFIN DIENE ALLENE
HEXADIENE
DIOMEDES (**FATHER OF —**) MARS
TYDEUS
(**MOTHER OF —**) CYRENE DEIPYLE
(**WIFE OF —**) AEGIALE
DION (**DAUGHTER OF —**) EUPHRASIA
(**FATHER OF —**) HIPPARINUS
(**SISTER OF —**) ARISTOMACHE
(**SLAYER OF —**) CALLIPPUS
(**TEACHER OF —**) PLATO
(**WIFE OF —**) ARETE
DIONYSUS BACCHUS BROMIOS
BROMIUS LENAEUS LIKNITES
DIONYZA (**HUSBAND OF —**) CLEON
DIOPSIDE VIOLAN ALALITE
PYROXENE
DIORITE CORSITE DIABASE
ORNOITE APPINITE TONALITE
DIOSCURI ALCIS ANACES ANAKES
CASTORES
DIOXIDE SILICA BINOXIDE
DIP DAP DIB DOP SOP BAIL DROP
DUCK DUNK LADE LAVE SINK
SOAK BATHE DELVE LADLE
LOWER MERSE PITCH SCOOP
SLOPE SOUSE SWOOP TAINT
CANDLE HOLLOW PLUNGE
BAPTIZE DECLINE IMMERGE
IMMERSE INCLINE MOISTEN
DIPSTICK SUBMERGE GUACAMOLE
(**— AND THROW**) BAIL BALE
(**— IN DANCING**) CORTE
(**— INTO**) SAMPLE
(**— OUT**) KEACH
DIPENTENE CINENE CAJUPUTENE
DIPHTHONG BIVOCAL
DIPHTHONGIZED BROKEN
DIPLOIDIZE SPERMATIZE
DIPLOMA SANAD DEGREE
SUNNUD CHARTER CODICIL
PARCHMENT SHEEPSKIN
DIPLOMACY TACT POLICE TREATY
DIPLOMAT DEAN ENVOY CONSUL
ATTACHE MINISTER
DIPLOMATIC SUAVE FECIAL
FETIAL
DIPLOPIA POLYOBA AMBIOPIA
DIPNOAN DIPNOID MUDFISH
DIPODY METER METRE DIIAMB
SYZYGY
DIPPER BAIL GAWN PIET PLOW
GOURD HANDY LADLE SCOOP
SPOON BUCKET DUNKER PIGGIN
PLOUGH TUNKER DUNKARD
PICKLER CALABASH
(**ASTRONOMICAL —**) WAGON
WAGGON
DIPPING
(**SUFF.**) CLINIC CLINOUS
DIPSOMANIA ENOMANIA
POTOMANIA
DIPTERAN SYRPHID

DIPTEROCARP GURJUN
DIPTERON DIPTER
DIPTEROUS BIALATE
DIRDUM BLOW BLAME DURDUM
OUTCRY REBUKE TUMULT
UPROAR SCOLDING
DIRE DERN EVIL FELL AWFUL
FATAL DEADLY DISMAL DREARY
FUNEST TRAGIC WOEFUL
DIREFUL DOLEFUL DRASTIC
FEARFUL DREADFUL FUNESTAL
HORRIBLE TERRIBLE ULTIMATE
DIRECT AIM BID CON KEN SAY SET
WIS AGYE AIRT BAIN BEAM BEND
BOSS CAST DEAD EDIT EVEN
FLAT FULL GAIN HEAD HELM
HOLD LEAD NEAR NIGH OPEN
REIN SEND SOON SWAY TELL
TURN WAFT WEND WILL WISE
AIRTH APPLY AREAD AREED
BLANK BOUND BURLY COACH
DRESS ETTLE FLUSH FRAME
FRANK GUIDA GUIDE HIGHT
INDEX LEVEL ORDER PLUMP
POINT REFER RIGHT SPEED STEER
TEACH TRAIN UTTER WEISE
WRITE ADVERT ARRECT CUSTOS
DEVOTE ENJOIN ENSIGN FASTEN
GOVERN GRAITH HANDLE
HOMELY HONEST IMPART INDITE
INFORM INTEND LINEAL MANAGE
MASTER MOSTRA REFORM
SQUARE STEADY STRECK TEMPER
WITTER ADDRESS APPOINT
COMMAND CONDUCT CONTROL
CONVERT DEICTIC DESTINE
EXECUTE EXPRESS FRONTAL
GENERAL INSTANT MARSHAL
OFFICER PRESIDE SPADISH
ABSOLUTE ADMONISH CONVERSE
DEDICATE DIRECTOR HOMESPUN
IMMEDIAL INSTRUCT INTIMATE
MANUDUCE MANUDUCT
MINISTER OUTRIGHT REGULATE
STRAIGHT
(**— AGAINST**) LAUNCH
(**— ATTENTION**) ATTEND
(**— BLOW**) MARK
(**— DOGS**) BLOW
(**— FALL OF TREE**) GUN
(**— HELMSMAN**) CON CONN
(**— HORSE**) HUP
(**— ITSELF**) TENT
(**— ONE'S COURSE**) HIT
(**— PROCEEDINGS**) PRESIDE
(**— SECRETLY**) STEAL
(**— SIDEWAYS**) SKLENT
(**— TO GO**) ADDRESS
(**— UPWARD**) MOUNT
DIRECTED FAST COMPULSORY
(**— FORWARD**) ANTRORSE
(**— TOWARD GOAL**) HORMIC
(**— UPWARD**) ERECT
DIRECTING AIM LEADING
PRINCIPAL
DIRECTION (**ALSO SEE MUSICAL
DIRECTION**) AIM RUN WAY AIRT
BENT CARE DUCT EAST EGIS
GATE HAND LEFT PART ROAD
RULE WEST WORD YARD AEGIS
ANGLE COAST DRIFT EAVER
KIBLA NORTH ORDER PARTY
POINT QIBLA RANGE ROUTE

SENSE SOUTH TENOR TREND
ASPECT COURSE DESIGN
ADDRESS BEARING BIDDING
CHANNEL COMMAND CONDUCT
CONTROL COUNSEL DICTATE
HEADING HELMAGE MANDATE
PRECEPT STRETCH BEARINGS
CALENDAR DELEATUR DIAGONAL
GUIDANCE STEERAGE STEERING
TENDENCY ORDINANCE
ORIENTATION PRESCRIPTION
(**— OF CURRENT**) AXIS
(**— OF FLOW**) SET
(**— OF ROCK CLEAVAGE**) GRAIN
(**— OF WIND**) EYE CORNER
(**— OUTWARD**) BEAM
(**—S FOR DELIVERY**) ADDRESS
(**DANCE —**) CALL
(**HORIZONTAL —**) COURSE
AZIMUTH
(**OBLIQUE —**) SKEW
(**OPPOSITE —**) EYE COUNTER
(**SINGING —**) GIMEL GYMEL
(**PREF.**) PHORO
(**SUFF.**) ERLY ERN
(**— TO**) WARD
DIRECTIVE DICTATE CIRCULAR
DIRECTLY DUE BANG BOLT DEAD
FLAT GAIN JUST MEAN PLAT
PLUM SLAP SOON PLAIN PLUMB
PLUNK POINT ROUND SHEER
SMACK SOUSE SPANG STANG
ARIGHT CLEVER SIMPLY SQUARE
RIGHTLY SHEERLY OUTRIGHT
PROMPTLY SLAPDASH STRAIGHT
PRESENTLY
DIRECTNESS CLARITY IMMEDIACY
DIRECTOR BOSS HEAD COACH
GUIDE PILOT STAFF ARCHON
AUTEUR BISHOP LEADER MASTER
RECTOR WARDEN CURATOR
DESKMAN MANAGER PREFECT
STARETS STERNER TRAINER
ACCENTOR DISPOSER GOVERNOR
PRAEFECT PRODUCER TETRARCH
(**FILM —**) AUTEUR
DIRECTORY PIE BOOK
DIRGE KEEN SONG ELEGY KINAH
LINOS LINUS QINAH TANGI
HEARSE LAMENT MONODY
THRENE EPICEDE REQUIEM
CORONACH THRENODY
ULLAGONE
(**PREF.**) THREN(O)
DIRIGIBLE BLIMP AIRSHIP
DIRK SNEE SKEAN SWORD DAGGER
SKHIAN SKIVER WHINGER
WHINIARD
DIRT FEN MUD PAY DUST GORE
GUCK MOOL MUCK NAST SOIL
SUMP CROCK EARTH FILTH GRIME
GROUT SEUCH SEUGH TRASH
FULYIE FULZIE GRAVEL GROUND
REFUSE MULLOCK SLOTTER
MUCKMENT
DIRTINESS GRIME JAKES
DIRTY LOW RAY BASE CLAT DIRT
FOUL MOIL MUSS SOIL WORY
BAWDY BLACK CABBY DINGY
FOGGY GRIMY GUSTY HORRY
MUDDY NASTY POUSY SOILY
SULLY BEMIRE CLARTY CLATTY
DEFILE DIRTEN FILTHY FULYIE

FULZIE GREASY GRUBBY IMPURE
MUSSED POUCEY REECHY SCRIMY
SLASHY SLURRY SMIRCH SMUTTY
SOILED SORDID STORMY BEGRIME
BROOKED BROOKIE BRUCKLE
CLOUDED GRUFTED IMBROIN
MUDDIED PIGGISH ROYNOUS
SCRUFFY SLOTTER SMUTCHY
SQUALID SULLIED TARNISH
UNCLEAN AMURCOUS SLOBBERY
SLOTTERY SOAPLESS
DISABLE OUT HOCK LAME MAIM
BREAK CHINK CROCK GRUEL
UNFIT WRECK BRUISE DISMAY
UNABLE WEAKEN CRIPPLE
(**— CANNON**) SPIKE
(**— HORSE**) NOBBLE
(**— TANK**) BELLY
DISABLED LAME INVALID
DISABLING BUM
DISACCHARIDE BIOSE LACTOSE
MALTOSE SUCROSE
DISACCUSTOM DISUSE
DISACKNOWLEDGE DISCLAIM
DISADVANTAGE HURT MISS RISK
LURCH WORRY DAMAGE DENIAL
INJURY STRIKE DICKENS PENALTY
UNSELTH UNSPEED DISAVAIL
DISFAVOR HANDICAP
DISADVANTAGEOUS HURTFUL
INCONVENIENT
DISAFFECT DEBAUCH ESTRANGE
DISAFFECTED FALSE UNTRUE
DISEASED DISLOYAL FORSWORN
PERJURED RECREANT
DISAFFECTION DECEIT MUTINY
DISEASE DISGUST DISLIKE
DISORDER HOSTILITY
DISAFFIRM DENY ANNUL REVERSE
DISCLAIM
DISAGREE VARY ARGUE CLASH
DIFFER DISCEPT DISCORD
DISSENT QUARREL CONFLICT
DISAGREEABLE BAD ILL ACID EVIL
FOUL PERT SOUR UGLY VILE
AWFUL CROSS HARSH NASTY
STIFF GREASY PUTRID ROTTEN
SNUFFY STICKY UNEASY UNGAIN
BEASTLY CHRONIC COMICAL
GHASTLY HATEFUL INGRATE
IRKSOME NAUGHTY UNLUSTY
CHISELLY KINDLESS TERRIBLE
UNGENIAL UNLIKELY UNLOVELY
UNSAVORY
DISAGREEABLENESS ILLNESS
ASPERITY
DISAGREEABLY HARSHLY
DISAGREEING ODD DISSENTIVE
DISAGREEMENT BREE CLASH
CROSS FIGHT BREACH FRATCH
DISCORD DISGUST DISPUTE
DISSENT FISSURE MISLIKE
QUARREL WRANGLE ARGUMENT
CLASHING DISTANCY DIVISION
FRICTION SQUABBLE VARIANCE
MISUNDERSTANDING
(**IN —**) APART
DISALLOW FORBID REJECT
CENSURE DISCLAIM DISPROVE
PROHIBIT
DISAPPEAR DIE FLY DROP FADE
FALL FLEE LIFT PASS SINK WEND
WHOP BREAK CLEAR FAINT LAPSE

SLIDE SLOPE SNUFF REMOVE
RETIRE VANISH EVANISH
IMMERGE DISSOLVE EVANESCE
(— GRADUALLY) ELY FADE DRAIN
EVANESCE
(— SUDDENLY) COOK DUCK BURST
MIZZLE
(— UNEXPECTEDLY) LEVANT
DISAPPEARANCE ECLIPSE
FADEAWAY
DISAPPOINT BALK BILK FAIL FALL
MOCK SOUR UNDO CHEAT SNAPE
BAFFLE DEFEAT DELUDE OUTWIT
THWART BEGUILE DECEIVE
DESTROY FALSIFY NULLIFY
DISPOINT
DISAPPOINTED OUTED THROWN
SOREHEAD
DISAPPOINTING FIERCE
FALLACIOUS
DISAPPOINTMENT RUE BALK
SUCK BAULK LURCH DENIAL
LETDOWN COMEDOWN
DISAPPROBATION ODIUM DISLIKE
DISAPPROVAL BAN BOOH HISS
VETO CATCALL CENSURE
DISFAVOR DISGRACE
DISAPPROVE NIX GROAN REJECT
RESENT CENSURE CONDEMN
DISLIKE MISTAKE PROTEST
DISALLOW DISPROVE HARRUMPH
DISAPPROVED DISTASTED
DISAPPROVER WOWSER
DISARM SUBDUE UNSTEEL
DISARRANGE MESS MUSS
DEFORM GARBLE RUFFLE TIFFLE
UNTIDY UNTUNE CLUTTER
CONFUSE DERANGE DISTURB
RUMMAGE SLATTER TROUBLE
COCKBILL DISHEVEL DISORDER
UNSETTLE
(— TYPE) SQUABBLE
DISARRANGEMENT DISARRAY
DISARRAY MESS TASH RIFLE
STRIP CADDLE DISRAY FUFFLE
HUDDLE DESPOIL UNDIGHT
DISHEVEL DISORDER
DISARRAYED UNKEMPT
DISASSEMBLE STRIP DEMOUNT
DISMOUNT
(— CASK) SHAKE
DISASSEMBLY TAKEDOWN
TEARDOWN
DISASSOCIATE SEVER SEPARATE
DISASTER ILL WOE BALE BLOW
EVIL FATE RUIN GRIEF MISHAP
STROKE REVERSE ACCIDENT
CALAMITY CASUALTY EXIGENCY
FATALITY
DISASTROUS BAD ILL FATAL
WEARY SINISTER
DISAVOW DENY DEVOW ABJURE
DISOWN RECANT REFUSE
DECLINE RETRACT ABNEGATE
DISCLAIM DISVOUCH RENOUNCE
DISAVOWAL DENIAL
DISBAND BREAK REDUCE REFORM
ADJOURN CASHIER DISMISS
RELEASE SCATTER DISSOLVE
DISBAR EXCLUDE
DISBELIEF ATHEISM SCRUPLE
ACOSMISM
DISBELIEVE DOUBT REJECT

SUSPECT DISCOUNT DISCREDIT
DISBELIEVER ATHEIST HERETIC
INFIDEL
DISBURDEN RID EASE CLEAR
UNLOAD DELIVER DISLOAD
RELIEVE
DISBURSE SPEND DEFRAY EXPEND
OUTLAY DEBURSE
DISC (ALSO SEE DISK) DIAL DISK
BLANK MEDAL PATEN PLATE
QUOIT COLTER RECORD RONDEL
SQUAIL COULTER DISCOID
PLATTER TROCHUS
(— FOR PRESSING HERRINGS)
DAUNT
(FLOPPY —) DISKETTE
DISCANT HOCKET
DISCARD CAST DECK DEFY JILT
JUNK MOLT OMIT OUST SHED
CHUCK DITCH FLING SCRAP
SHUCK SLUFF THROW TRASH
CHANGE DECARD DISUSE DIVEST
EXCUSS REJECT SLOUGH
ABANDON CASHIER DISMISS
EXPUNGE FORSAKE ABDICATE
JETTISON
(— IN BRIDGE) ECHO
DISCARDED DORMANT OFFCAST
DISCARDING DISPOSAL
DISCERN KEN SEE SPY WIT DEEM
ESPY KNOW READ SCAN JUDGE
SIGHT BEHOLD DESCRY DETECT
DEVISE NOTICE PIERCE SCERNE
DIGNOSCE DISCOVER PERCEIVE
DISCERNIBLE EVIDENT VISIBLE
APPARENT MANIFEST
OBSERVABLE
DISCERNING SAGE WISE NASUTE
SHREWD SUBTLE SAPIENT
SAGACIOUS PERCEPTIVE
PERCIPIENT PENETRATING
DISCERNMENT EYE DOOM GOUT
TACT FLAIR SENSE SKILL TASTE
ACUMEN INSIGHT ELECTION
JUDGMENT SAGACITY SAPIENCE
PERCEPTION PENETRATION
DISCHARGE AX DO AXE CAN GUN
LET RUN BOLT BOOT CASS DUMP
EMIT FIRE FLOW FLUX FREE GIVE
KICK PASS POUR QUIT RIFF SACK
SEND SHOT VENT VOID BLAST
BLEED BRUSH CLEAR DRAIN
EJECT EMPTY EXPEL EXUDE
FRUSH GLEET GRASS ICHOR ISSUE
LOOSE OZENA PURGE RHEUM
SHOOT SPEED START VOMIT
WHIFF YIELD ACQUIT ASSOIL
BOUNCE DEFRAY EFFECT EXCERN
EXEMPT EXHALE FEEDER LOCHIA
OZAENA TICKET UNLADE UNLOAD
ABSOLVE CASHIER DEBOUCH
DEFEASE DEHISCE DELIVER
DERAIGN DISBAND DISMISS
EXCRETE EXHAUST MISSION
PAYMENT PERFORM QUIETUS
RELEASE RELIEVE SATISFY
SKITTER SOLUTIO CATAPULT
COMPOUND DEFECATE
DESPATCH DISGORGE DISPATCH
DISPLACE DISPLODE EMISSION
EVACUATE MITTIMUS OUTSHOOT
PERSOLVE SEPARATE SOLUTION
STREAMER

(— ARROW) TWANG
(— BULLET) DRIVE
(— CARGO) STRIKE
(— DEBT) MEET CLEAR ACQUIT
LOOSING
(— DUTY) SERVE
(— FROM HORSE'S FOOT) FRUSH
(— FROM RESERVOIR) HUSHING
(— MATTER) WEEP
(— OF DEBT) SETOFF
(— OF GAS) FEEDER
(— OF STREAM) FALL SPOUT
(— SUDDENLY) HIKE
(BLOODY —) SHOW SANIES
(CANNON —) TIRE CANNON
(CONCENTRATED —) BARRAGE
(DISHONORABLE —) BOBTAIL
(ELECTRIC —) ARC SPARK LEADER
EFFLUVE STREAMER LIGHTNING
(ELECTRIC —S) STATIC
(HEAVY —) STORM
(SIMULTANEOUS —) SALVO
BROADSIDE FUSILLADE
(SUFF.) CENOSIS RRHAGIA RRHEA
RRHOEA
DISCHARGED SPED SATISFIED
DISCHARGER EXCITATOR
DISCHARGING LABILE
DISCIPLE SON JOHN MARK CHELA
JUDAS MURID PETER PUPIL
TEACH TRAIN ANANDA DISPLE
DORCAS HEARER PUNISH
APOSTLE AUDITOR MATTHEW
OVIDIAN SCHOLAR SECTARY
SRAVAKA STUDENT ADHERENT
FOLLOWER GALENIST SECTATOR
DISCIPLINARIAN RAMROD
TRAINER MARTINET
DISCIPLINARY STRICT
DISCIPLINE THEW WHIP BREAK
DRILL INURE TEACH TRAIN
TUTOR CHURCH ETHICS FERULA
FERULE GOVERN INFORM PUNISH
SEASON TAIRGE VIRTUE CHASTEN
CORRECT CULTURE EDUCATE
FURNACE NURTURE SCOURGE
DISCIPLE DOCTRINE EXERCISE
INSTRUCT LEARNING MATHESIS
PEDAGOGY REGULATE RESTRAIN
TEACHING TRAINING TUTORING
PHILOSOPHY CASTIGATION
(MENTAL —) YOGA
(RELIGIOUS —) CHURCH PENANCE
SADHANA
DISCIPLINED INURED STEADY
DISCLAIM DENY DEVOW ABJURE
DISOWN REFUSE DISAVOW
ABDICATE ABNEGATE DISALLOW
RENOUNCE
DISCLOSE OPE RIP BARE BLOW
CALL KNOW OPEN TELL BREAK
COUGH UNRIP UNWRY UTTER
BETRAY BEWRAY DESCRY DIVINE
EVOLVE EXPOSE IMPART REVEAL
SHRIVE UNBURY UNCASE
UNHASP UNHIDE UNLOCK
UNROLL UNSEAL UNSHUT UNVEIL
UNWRAP CONFESS DEVELOP
DISCUSS DISPLAY DIVULGE
EXHIBIT EXPLAIN PROPALE
UNCLOSE UNCOVER DISCOVER
INDICATE MANIFEST UNBUNDLE
UNKENNEL UNSECRET UNTHATCH

(— PARTIALLY) ADUMBRATE
DISCLOSED OUT
DISCLOSURE REVEAL SHRIFT
COLORING DESCRIAL DISCLOSE
OVERTURE APOCALYPSE
DISCOLOR FOX BURN FADE SPOT
BLACK SMOKE STAIN TINGE
SMIRCH STREAK DISTAIN
TARNISH BESMIRCH
DISCOLORATION CORN BLEED
SCALD SPECK STAIN TINGE
FOXING LIVEDO MILDEW ARGYRIA
BURNING MELASMA BRONZING
BROWNING CHLOASMA CYANOSIS
DYSCHROA SCALDING
(— OF FRUIT) SUNBURN
(— OF TURKEYS) BLUEBACK
(— ON CHOCOLATE) BLOOM
(— ON CURED FISH) RUST
(SMALL —) FRECKLE
(SUFF.) CHROIA
DISCOLORED HAW FOUL DINGY
FOXED RUSTY STAINED
SCORCHED USTULATE
(— BY DECAY) DOTY FOXED
DISCOMFIT MATE ROIT ABASH
ABAVE AFLEY SHEND SHENT
UPSET WORST BAFFLE DEFEAT
FEAGUE SQUASH CONFUSE
CONQUER DISTURB
DISCOMFITURE LURCH
DISCOMFORT (FEELING OF —)
BLAHS
DISCOMPOSE FEEZE PERTURB
DISCONCERT BASH BOWL FAZE
FUSS HACK ABASH BLANK DAUNT
FEEZE PHASE UPSET WORRY
BAFFLE BLENCH MISPUT PUZZLE
RATTLE SQUASH CONFUSE
DISTURB FLUMMOX NONPLUS
PERTURB SQUELCH BROWBEAT
DISORDER
DISCONCERTED BLANK ASHAMED
RATTLED CONFUSED
DISCONCERTING BAFFLING
DISCONNECT UNDO SEVER DIVIDE
UNDOCK UNYOKE DISJOIN
DISSOLVE DISUNITE SEPARATE
UNCOUPLE
DISCONNECTED LOOSE ABRUPT
BROKEN CHOPPY CURSORY
DECOUSU RAMBLING STACCATO
ASYNARTETE
DISCONSOLATE SAD GLOOMY
WOEFUL DOLEFUL FORLORN
UNCOUTH DEJECTED DESOLATE
DOWNCAST HOPELESS
DISCONTENT ENVY DISQUIET
SOURNESS
DISCONTENTED DUMPY RESTLESS
MALCONTENT
DISCONTINUANCE BREAK LAPSE
DEMISE CUTBACK DISUNION
SHUTDOWN CESSATION
DISCONTINUE END DROP HALT
QUIT STOP BREAK CEASE CLOSE
LETUP DESIST DISUSE SUNDER
DISRUPT SUSPEND INTERMIT
SURCEASE
DISCONTINUITY JAR BREAK
COMMA BREACH
DISCONTINUOUS BROKEN
DISJUNCT SALTATORY

DISCORD DIN JAR BROIL JANGLE SCHISM STRIFE DISLIKE FACTION FISSURE JARRING MISTONE CONFLICT DISTANCE DIVISION FRACTION MISCHIEF UNSAUGHT VARIANCE CACOPHONY

DISCORDANT AJAR RUDE CRONK HARSH FROWZY HOARSE JANGLY HIDEOUS JARRING SQUAWKY ABSONANT CONTRARY JANGLING SCORDATO

DISCOTHEQUE AGOGO

DISCOUNT AGIO BATTA SHAVE REBATE REDUCE DISCOMPT

DISCOURAGE CARP DAMP CHILL DAUNT DETER FROST DAMPEN DEJECT DISMAY FREEZE STIFLE DEPRESS FLATTEN INHIBIT DISPIRIT DISSUADE

DISCOURAGEMENT COLD DAMP CHILL DAUNT REBUFF LETDOWN PUTBACK

DISCOURAGING CHILL DREARY

DISCOURSE SAW CARP RANT READ TALE TALK TELL WORD DROOL FABLE ORATE PAPER SPEAK SPELL THEME TRACT TREAT COMMON DILATE EULOGY HOMILY PARLEY PREACH REASON SCREED SERMON THESIS TONGUE TREATY ACCOUNT ADDRESS COMMENT CONTEXT DECLAIM DELIVER DESCANT DIETARY DISCANT DISCUSS DISSERT ENTREAT EXPOUND GRAMMAR LECTURE NARRATE ORATION PARABLE PRATING PRELECT PURPOSE RECITAL TALKING ARGUMENT COLLOQUY CONVERSE EXERCISE LOCUTION LOQUENCE PARLANCE SPEAKING SPELLING TRACTATE TREATISE PHILIPPIC PROLUSION
(— OF LITTLE VALUE) STUFF
(LAUDATORY —) PANEGYRIC
(LONG —) SCREED
(PROLONGED —) DIATRIBE
(RAMBLING —) RHAPSODY
(SERIOUS —) HOMILY
(SIMPLE —) PAP
(UNIMAGINATIVE —) PROSE
(PL.) EXOTERICS
(PREF.) LOG(O)
(SUFF.) LOG(ER)(IA)(IAN)(IC)(ICAL)(IST)(UE)(Y)

DISCOURTEOUS RUDE SCURVY UNCIVIL UNHENDE CAVALIER IMPOLITE UNGENTLE

DISCOURTESY CUT SLIGHT

DISCOVER RIP SEE SPY WIT ESPY FEEL FIND PICK TWIG CATCH LEARN SPELL DEFINE DESCRY DETECT DIVINE EXPOSE IMPART INVENT LOCATE OVERGO REVEAL STRIKE UNHIDE CONFESS DESCURE DEVELOP DISCERN DISCURE DISPLAY DIVULGE EXHIBIT EXPLORE UNCOVER UNEARTH CONTRIVE DECIPHER DESCRIBE DISCUREN MANIFEST UNKENNEL

DISCOVERABLE VISIBLE

DISCOVERER SPY SCOUT

COLUMBUS EXPLORER INVENTOR

DISCOVERY FIND TROVE DESCRY ESPIAL STRIKE DESCRIAL

DISCREDIT FOUL SLUT DECRY DOUBT REFEL DEFACE DEFECT ASPERSE BLEMISH DESTROY IMPEACH SCANDAL SUSPECT BELITTLE DISGRACE DISHONOR DISTRUST REPROACH UNCREDIT
(SUFF.) ARD ART

DISCREDITABLE BLACK UNHONEST

DISCREET SAGE WARY WISE CIVIL WITTY HUSHED POLITE SILENT CAREFUL GUARDED POLITIC PRUDENT CAUTIOUS RESERVED RETICENT

DISCREETLY SENSIBLY

DISCREPANCY VARIANCE

DISCREPANT VARIANT CONTRARY DISSONANT

DISCRETE ETERNAL DISTINCT

DISCRETION TACT OPTION WISDOM CONDUCT RETENUE COURTESY JUDGMENT PRUDENCE

DISCRETIONARY ARBITRARY

DISCRIMINATE PART SEVER SECERN DISCERN PERCEIVE SEPARATE

DISCRIMINATED DISTINCT

DISCRIMINATING GOOD NICE ACUTE SHARP ASTUTE CHOICE NASUTE SELECT CHOOSEY CRITICAL EXPLICIT

DISCRIMINATINGLY CHOICE FINELY

DISCRIMINATION EYE DOOM TACT TASTE ACUMEN AGEISM CHOICE SEXISM FINESSE RESPECT DELICACY SAPIENCE
(SYMBOL OF —) HANSA

DISCRIMINATIVE RESPECTIVE

DISCURSIVE ROVING CURSORY RAMBLING DESULTORY

DISCURSIVELY WIDE

DISCUS DISC DISK QUOIT DISKOS DISCOID

DISCUSS AIR MOOT RUNE TALK ARGUE BANDY COVER DANDY TRACT TREAT COMMON CONFER DEBATE DICKER EMPARL EXCUSS IMPARL PARLEY AGITATE BESPEAK CANVASS COMMENT CONSULT DESCANT DISCANT DISCEPT DISCUTE DISPUTE DISSERT EXAMINE NARRATE TRAVERSE CONJOBBLE
(— AT LENGTH) BAT
(— CASUALLY) MENTION
(— EXCITEDLY) AGITATE
(— LIGHTLY) BANDY
(— QUICKLY) SKIP
(— SECRETLY) ROUN
(— TERMS) CHAFFER
(— THOROUGHLY) EXHAUST
(— TO EXCESS) VEX

DISCUSSION MOOT DEBAT FORUM COMMON CONFAB DEBATE HASSEL HOMILY HUDDLE PARLEY TREATY BARGAIN CANVASS COMMENT COUNSEL DISCUSS DISPUTE MOOTING PALAVER PRIBBLE ARGUMENT CAUSERIE

CHINFEST COLLOQUY DIATRIBE ENTREATY EXCURSUS QUESTION
(CONTROVERSIAL —) DISPUTE
(DIDACTIC —) HARANGUE
(HEATED —) FLAK

DISDAIN COY TUT DAIN DEFY PRIDE SCORN SDAIN SPURN SDEIGN SLIGHT CONTEMN DESPISE CONTEMPT

DISDAINFUL COY DIGNE PROUD SAUCY TOSSY SCORNY SLIGHT SNIFFY SNUFFY DAINFUL HAUGHTY ARROGANT DEIGNOUS PROUDFUL SCORNFUL SNIFFISH TOPLOFTY

DISDAINFULLY SMALL SNIFFILY

DISEASE BUG FLU MAL ROT AIDS BATS COTH CRUD EVIL FLAW GOUT GRIP NOMA PEST PHOS SORE AGROM BATTS BEJEL BENDS CAUSE COTHE CROUP DECAY DOLOR FEVER GRIEF LUPUS PHOSS PINTA PINTO SCALL SHAKE SPRUE SURRA AINHUM ANGINA CANCER CARATE CORYZA COURAP DENGUE GRAVEL GRIPPE HERPES MALADY MORBUS PALMUS PIEDRA POPEYE SCURVY SICKEN SURRAH UROSIS ZOOSIS AILMENT CHOLERA COXALGY DECLINE ENDEMIC ENTASIA LANGUOR LEPROSY MALEASE MISLIKE MYCOSIS MYIASIS PATHEMA RAPHANY SCOURGE SEQUELA SERPIGO SIBBENS SORANCE SYCOSIS XERASIA ZYMOTIC ALASTRIM ATHEROMA BERIBERI COXALGIA CRIPPLER CYNANCHE DIAMONDS ENZOOTIC JAUNDICE LEUKEMIA PALUDISM PANDEMIC PELLAGRA RAPHANIA SCABBADO SICKNESS SMALLPOX SORRANCE STAGGERS SYPHILIS UNHEALTH XANTHOMA ZOONOSIS
(— OF ANIMALS, GENERAL) ROT CLAP CORE FIRE GOUT HUSK LICK WEED APTHA CLEFT CLING CLOSH COTHE CROOK DRUSE FARCY FLAPS NENTA NGANA PAINS SPEED SWEAT TAINT APHTHA AVIVES BROSOT CANKER CARNEY CREEPS FARCIN GARGET GRAPES LAMPAS NAGANA ROUGET SPAVIN SURRAH WOBBLE ANTHRAX BIGHEAD CALCINO CALORIS CARCEAG DOURING EARWORM EQUINIA FASHION FISTULA FOUNDER FROUNCE KETOSIS LAMPERS MURRAIN MURRINA QUITTER QUITTOR SLOBBER SOLDIER TAKOSIS BULLNOSE CRATCHES CRIPPLES FERNSICK FOOTHALT HORSEPOX HYSTERIA MAWBOUND SLOBBERS SNUFFLES THWARTER VACCINIA EPIZOOTIC
(— OF APPLES) CORK BLOTCH
(— OF BANANAS) SIGATOKA SQUIRTER
(— OF BARLEY) STRIPE
(— OF BEES) SACBROOD
(— OF BEETS) HEARTROT

(— OF BIRDS) GOUT
(— OF BLUEBERRY) BLUESTEM
(— OF CABBAGE) ANBURY CLUBROOT
(— OF CATERPILLARS) WILT FLACHERY
(— OF CATS) PANLEUCOPENIA
(— OF CATTLE) PUCK TURN BARBS BLAIN CLOSH FARCY HOOVE HOOZE SLOWS COWPOX GARGET GRAPES HAMMER HEAVES ANTHRAX BLACKLEG BLOATING
(— OF CEREALS) BRAND ERGOT
(— OF CHICKEN) PIP CORYZA
(— OF CHILDREN) PROGERIA
(— OF COTTON) HYBOSIS CYRTOSIS STENOSIS
(— OF DUCKLING) KEEL
(— OF EYES) WALL GLAUCOMA SYNECHIA TRACHOMA
(— OF FIGS) SMUT
(— OF FINGERNAILS) FLAW
(— OF FLAX) BROWNING
(— OF FOWLS) PIP CRAY ROUP GAPES SOREHEAD
(— OF GRAIN) ILIAU ICTERUS
(— OF GRAPES) COLEUR ERINOSE ROUGEAU ROUGEOT SHELLING
(— OF HAWKS) RYE CRAY CROAK CROAKS FROUNCE FILANDER
(— OF HORSES) HAW CLAP CURB MOSE MULE WEED FARCY LEUMA VIVES APHTHA SCALMA THRUSH BARBELS DOURINE QUITTOR SARCOID AZOTURIA GLANDERS HORSEPOX STRANGLES
(— OF INSECTS) POLYHEDROSIS
(— OF LAMB) SWAYBACK
(— OF LETTUCE) STUNT
(— OF NARCISSUS) SMOLDER SMOULDER
(— OF ONION) SMUDGE
(— OF ORANGE) LEPROSIS
(— OF PALMS) KOLEROGA
(— OF PLANTS) SCAB NECROSIS
(— OF PLANTS, GENERAL) POX ROT BUNT CORK DROP FIRE GOUT KNOT PULP SMUT BLAST DWARF EDEMA ERGOT FLECK FLOCK GRUBS SCALD SCALE SCURF SEREH SPIKE STUNT TUKRA TWIST AUCUBA BLIGHT BLOTCH BLUING BRAUNE CALICO CANKER COLEUR GIRDLE OEDEMA OIDIUM PETECA SMUDGE STREAK STRIPE VIROSE BLISTER BLUEING BRINDLE CRINKLE DIEBACK ERINOSE EYESPOT FROGEYE HYBOSIS MEASLES PRURIGO ROSETTE SHATTER SMOLDER STIPPEN TIPBURN TOMOSIS VIRUELA WALLOON BLUESTEM BREAKING BROWNING BUCKSKIN CLUBROOT CYRTOSIS DARTROSE EXANTHEM FLYSPECK GUMMOSIS KOLEROGA LEPROSIS MELANOSE MELAXUMA POLEBURN PSOROSIS RAPHANIA SMOULDER STENOSIS VIROSITY WHIPTAIL WILDFIRE CHLOROSIS
(— OF POTATO) CURL HAYWIRE
(— OF RABBITS) SNUFFLES
(— OF RICE) BLAST SPECK

(— OF SHEEP) CAW COE GID MAD RAY ROT BANE BELT CORE HALT SHAB WIND BLAST BLOOD BRAXY GILLAR OVINIA PINING STURDY ANTHRAX BRADSOT DAISING RUBBERS SCRAPIE THWARTER WILDFIRE BREAKSHARE
(— OF SILKWORM) UJI CALCINO GATTINE PEBRINE FLACHERY
(— OF SUGARCANE) ILIAU SEREH EYESPOT
(— OF SWINE) GARGET
(— OF TOBACCO) ETCH CALICO BRINDLE FROGEYE
(— OF TOMATO) FERNLEAF GRAYWALL
(— OF TONGUE) AGROM
(— OF TREES) KNOT CANKER
(— OF TULIPS) SHANKING
(— OF UNKNOWN ORIGIN) AINHUM ACRODYNIA
(CAISSON —) CHOKES
(FATAL — OF NERVOUS SYSTEM) KURU
(FOOT-AND-MOUTH —) AFTOSA
(FUNGUS —) PECK MYCOSIS
(KIDNEY —) RIPPLE
(LUNG —) CON
(MUSHROOM —) FLOCK
(PINK —) ACRODYNIA
(PLANT —) ESCA YAWS
(SKIN —) ACNE SCAB FAVUS HIVES LEPRA MANGE PSORA RUPIA SCALL TINEA ECZEMA LICHEN TETTER EXORMIA PORRIGO PRURIGO PURPURA SERPIGO VERRUGA CHLOASMA IMPETIGO MILIARIA MYCETOMA SHINGLES VERRUGAS VITILIGO PEMPHIGUS
(SWELLING —) EDEMA
(VENEREAL —) BURNING SYPHILIS
(WINE —) GRAISSE
(WOOLSORTER'S —) ANTHRAX
(PREF.) MORBI NOS(O) PATH(O)
(SUFF.) IASIS ITIS NOSUS OMATOSIS OSIS SIS
(FUNGUS —) OSIS
DISEASED BAD EVIL SICKLY MORBOSE PECCANT VICIOUS MORBIFIC
(PREF.) CAC(O) CACH DYS
(SUFF.) CACE
DISEMBARK LAND ALIGHT DEBARK UNBARK UNBOAT DISBOARD
DISEMBARRASS EXTRICATE
DISEMBODIED SEPARATE DISBODIED FLESHLESS
DISEMBODIMENT SOUL SPIRIT
DISEMBOGUE MOUTH
DISEMBOWEL GUT HULK PAUNCH DEBOWEL EMBOWEL GARBAGE UNTRIPE GRALLOCH
DISEMIC DIMORIC DICHRONOUS
DISENCHANT DISMAY
DISENCHANTED SOUR
DISENCUMBER RID FREE REDD UNCUMBER
DISENGAGE FREE CLEAR EDUCE UNTIE DETACH EVOLVE LOOSEN CUTOVER DISGAGE RELEASE UNRAVEL LIBERATE UNCLUTCH
DISENTANGLE CARD COMB FREE

REED TOSE TOZE CLEAR LOOSE RAVEL TEASE EVOLVE SCUTCH SLEAVE UNMAZE UNMESH RESOLVE UNRAVEL UNREAVE UNTWINE UNTWIST OUTTWINE UNTANGLE
DISENTANGLEMENT SOLUTION
DISESTEEM UMBRAGE DISVALUE
DISFAVOR DUTCH ODIUM DISLIKE OFFENCE OFFENSE UMBRAGE MALGRACE
DISFIGURE MAR BLUR FOUL MAIM SCAR TASH AGRISE DEFACE DEFEAT DEFORM INJURE MANGLE BLEMISH DISGRACE DISGUISE MUTILATE
DISFIGURED FOUL DEFET DEFEIT DEFORMED
DISFIGUREMENT SCAR BLEMISH CATFACE DEFORMITY
DISGORGE SPEW VENT EJECT EMPTY VOMIT
DISGRACE BLOT FOIL FOUL HISS LACK SLUR SMIT SOIL SPOT TASH ABASE CRIME ODIUM SCORN SHAME SHEND SPITE STAIN TAINT BAFFLE BEFOUL BISMER HUMBLE INFAMY REBUKE STIGMA VILIFY AFFRONT ATTAINT DEGRADE OBLOQUY OFFENCE OFFENSE REPROOF SCANDAL SLANDER UMBRAGE CONTEMPT DISHONOR IGNOMINY REPROACH SHENDING UNWORTHY VILLAINY OPPROBRIUM
(PUBLIC —) ATIMY
DISGRACEFUL MEAN SOUR FILTHY INDIGN IGNOBLE CRIMINAL DEFAMOUS INHONEST SHAMEFUL
DISGRUNTLED SORE PEEVISH
DISGUISE DAUB FACE HIDE LAIN LEAN MASK VEIL BELIE CLOAK COLOR COUCH COVER FEIGN GLOZE GUISE SHADE VISOR VIZOR COVERT DEFORM IMMASK MANTLE MASQUE VIZARD CONCEAL OBSCURE PRETEND PURPORT COLORING DISLIKEN MISGUISE PALLIATE PRETENCE PRETENSE TRAVESTY UMBRELLA
(— INFORMATION) LAYNE
DISGUISED COVERT FUCATE GILDED LATENT MYSTIC FEIGNED PALLIATE TRAVESTY
DISGUST IRK CLOY PALL LOATH REPEL SHOCK STALL DEGOUT HORROR NAUSEA OFFEND REVOLT SICKEN SCUNNER STOMACH SURFEIT AVERSION DISTASTE KREISTLE LOATHING NAUSEATE SCOMFISH SICKNESS
DISGUSTED IRK SICK IRKSOME
DISGUSTING FOUL PERT VILE LOUSY MUCKY NASTY FILTHY SCRIMY SICKLY BEASTLY CLOYING FULSOME HATEFUL LOATHLY MAWKISH NOISOME OBSCENE SHITTEN FOULSOME LOATHFUL NAUSEOUS SHOCKING
DISH CAP CAUP CUSH DISC DISK FOOL MEAT MOLD PLAT SOLE BASIN BATEA COMAL DEVIL MOULD NAPPY PATEN PINAX

PLATE SHAPE BASQUE BASSIE BICKER BLAZER BUTTER CHAFER CRITCH CUSCUS ENTREE FONDUE LUGGIE OLIVES PADDLE PANADA PATERA PATINA PHIALE RECIPE SAUCER SUNDAE TAMALE TUREEN BALANCE BOBOTEE BOBOTIE CAPSULE CEVICHE CHARGER COCOTTE COMPORT COMPOTE CRESSET DORMANT DOUBLER EPERGNE PAPBOAT PATELLA PLATEAU PLATTER RAMEKIN SCUTTLE SUPREME TERRINE TIMBALE AMATORIO CIOPPINO CLAPDISH COQUILLE COUSCOUS GALATINE KEDGEREE MAZARINE POWSODDY STANDARD ENTREMETS
(— IN PYRAMID STYLE) BUISSON
(— OF MEAT AND EGGPLANT) MOUSSAKA
(BAKING —) SCALLOP SCOLLOP
(BRAISED —) HASLET
(CHAFING —) CHAFER CHOFFER SCALDINO
(CONE-SHAPED —) BOMBE
(EXQUISITE —) AMBROSIA
(FANCY —) SURPRISE
(FLAT —) ASHET COMAL CHARGER
(HIGH-FLAVORED —) HOGO
(JAPANESE —) SUSHI TERIYAKI
(JEWISH —) CHOLENT
(PHILIPPINE —) BURO
(PIE —) COFFIN
(PILE OF —S) BUNG
(ROMAN —) LANX PATERA PATINA
(SAILOR'S —) BURGOO SCOUSE
(SCOTTISH —) BROSE
(SIDE —) OUTWORK
(SWEET —) JUNKET FLUMMERY
(TASTY —) MORSEL
(WOODEN —) CUP CAUP BOWIE GOGGAN LUGGIE KICKSHAW
(PL.) GARNISH BAKEWARE FLATWARE ENTREMETS
(PREF.) LECO
DISHABILLE MOB DISARRAY DISORDER NEGLIGEE
DISHAN (FATHER OF —) SEIR
DISHARMONY SCHISM ADHARMA FRACTION
DISHCLOTH DISHRAG TORCHON
DISHCLOTH GOURD LOOFAH PATOLA DISHRAG
DISHEARTEN AMATE DAUNT FAINT DEJECT DEPRESS FLATTEN UNHEART UNNERVE DISHEART DISPIRIT
DISHEARTENED DULL GLOOMY DOWNCAST DEPRESSED
DISHEARTENING GLOOMY DESOLATE
DISHEVEL MUSS TOWSE RUFFLE TOUSEL TOUSLE TUMBLE TRACHLE DISARRAY DISORDER
DISHEVELED ROOKY BLOUSY BLOWZY FROWZY TUMBLED UNKEMPT FROWZLED SHEVELED SLIPSHOD TATTERED
DISHON (FATHER OF —) ANAH
DISHONEST FOUL LEWD CRONK CROSS FALSE LYING QUEER SNIDE TWISTY UNFAIR UNJUST

CORRUPT CROOKED JACKLEG KNAVISH INDECENT INDIRECT SHAMEFUL SINISTER UNCHASTE UNHONEST MENDACIOUS
DISHONESTLY DOUBLY FALSELY
DISHONESTY IMPROBITY
DISHONOR FILE FOUL ABASE ABUSE ATIMY ODIUM SHAME SPITE STAIN WRONG DEFAME DEFILE DEFORM INFAMY VILIFY DEGRADE DISTAIN OBLOQUY SLANDER VIOLATE DISGLORY DISGRACE DISPLUME IGNOMINY REPROACH VILLAINY ATTAINDER
DISHONORABLE BASE FOUL MEAN BLACK NASTY SHABBY YELLOW DISLEAL IGNOBLE SHAMEFUL UNHONEST UNWORTHY
DISHONORED DEFAMED
DISHPAN KEELER
DISH RACK FIDDLE
DISHWASHER SWILLER
DISILLUSION SOUR DISMAY
DISINCLINATION NILL UNLUST UNWILL DISLIKE QUARREL AVERSION DISTASTE
DISINCLINED LOTH LOATH AFRAID AVERSE HESITANT
(— TO) ABOVE
DISINFECT SCRUB SEASON CLEANSE SWEETEN
DISINFECTANT LYSOL IODINE PHENOL CREOLIN EUGENOL TACHIOL FUMIGANT HALAZONE PARAFORM
DISINGENUOUS FALSE UNFAIR OBLIQUE
DISINHERIT DEPRIVE DISHEIR ABDICATE DISHERIT
DISINTEGRATE BEAT DUST MELT BREAK DECAY ERODE GRUSH SLAKE SPLIT MOLDER CRUMBLE DISBAND RESOLVE SHATTER COLLAPSE DISSOLVE SEPARATE
DISINTEGRATING ROTTEN SCHIZOID
(SUFF.) CLASTIC
DISINTEGRATION DECAY BREAKUP EROSION BIOLYSIS COLLAPSE HEARTROT SOLUTION
(SUFF.) LYSE LYSIS LYST LYTE LYTIC LYZE
DISINTER EXHUME UNBURY UNTOMB UNGRAVE
DISINTERESTED FAIR CANDID APATHETIC IMPARTIAL
DISJOIN PART UNDO SEVER DETACH SUNDER UNTACK UNYOKE DISSOLVE DISUNITE SEPARATE
DISJOINED BITTY SEJOINED DIAZEUTIC
DISK (ALSO SEE DISC) EYE NOB ORB PAN SAW WAX WEB BURR CHAD DIAL DISC FLAN FLAT KNOB PALM PUCK STAR TUFT CAKRA DAUNT MEDAL PATEN PLATE ROUND SABLE SABOT SPILL TOKEN TRUCK WAFER WHEEL WHORL BEZANT BOTTOM BUCKET BUMPER BUTTON CACHET CARTON CHAKRA CONCHA CONCHO CORONA DISCUS

GHURRY HARROW PALLET PELLET
RECORD RIFFLE RONDEL SEQUIN
SHEAVE SQUAIL WASHER WEIGHT
ZEQUIN ACETATE BLOTTER
BOBECHE CHECKER CHIPPER
CLIPEUS DIOPTER DISCOID
GOGGLES KNICKER MEDALET
PHALERA ROSETTE SLITTER
SPINNER SPOTTER TONDINO
DIFFUSER EYEPIECE HOLDFAST
PLANCHET RONDELLE ROUNDLET
ZECCHINO
(— FOR BARRELING HERRING)
DAUNT
(— FOR CHEESE) FOLLOWER
(— FOR STRIKING HOURS) GHURRY
(— OF JELLYFISH) BELL
(— OF WAX) AGNUS
(— ON WOODEN ROD) SPILL
(BULL'S-EYE —) CARTON
(COIN-MAKING —) FLAN PLANCHET
(ECCENTRIC —) SHEAVE
(FLESHY —) SARCOMA
(HANDLED —) RIFFLE
(MEDICATED —) LAMELLA
(METAL —) SLUG MEDAL
(ORNAMENTAL —) BANGLE
SPANGLE
(PADDED IRON —) SPINNER
(PAPER —S) CONFETTI
(POTTER'S —) BAT
(REVOLVING —) WAFTER
(ROTATING —) SCANNER
(SOLAR —) ATEN ATON
(SUN —) CAKRA CHAKRA
(TROCHAL —) CORONA
(WINGED —) FEROHER
(PREF.) DISC(I)(O)
DISLIKE DEFY DOWN HATE LOTH
LUMP MIND DERRY LOATH SPITE
DETEST PHOBIA REGRET SPLEEN
UNLIKE DESPISE MISLIKE
QUARREL SCUNDER SCUNNER
STOMACH AVERSION DESPISAL
DISFAVOR DISTASTE DYSPATHY
(— OF CHILDREN) MISOPEDIA
(FOOLISH —) TOY
DISLOCATE LUX SLIP BREAK
SPLAY UNSET LUXATE DISLOCK
UNWREST DISJOINT DISPLACE
DISLOCATED SHOTTEN DISLOCATE
DISLOCATION BREAK SHIFT SLIDE
THROW
(PL.) SETTLEMENTS
DISLODGE BEAT BOLT BUCK BUMP
EXPEL SHAKE SHIFT SWOOP
REMOVE DISROOT UNHORSE
UNHOUSE UNLODGE DISHABIT
(— BY BLASTING) BRUSH
DISLODGING BULLING
DISLOYAL FALSE FELON UNTRUE
DISLEAL
DISLOYALTY SWICK SWIKE
UNLEWTY UNTRUTH
DISMAL SAD WAN BLUE DARK
DIRE DOWF DREE DULL EERY
GASH GLUM GRAY GREY BLACK
BLEAK DOWFF DREAR EERIE
LURID MORNE OURIE SABLE
SORRY SURLY SWART WASTE
WISHT DREARY DREICH DREIGH
GLOOMY GOUSTY LENTEN
SULLEN TRISTE DIREFUL DOLEFUL

FUNERAL GASHFUL GHASTLY
GOUSTIE JOYLESS OMINOUS
POCOSIN STYGIAN UNCOUTH
UNHAPPY DESOLATE DOLESOME
DOLOROUS FUNEREAL GROANFUL
LONESOME NOVEMBRY SOLITARY
WEARIFUL MELANCHOLY
DISMAL-LOOKING GASH
WOBEGONE
DISMALLY DERNLY DIRELY
DISMANTLE RASE RAZE STRIP
DIVEST STRIKE DEPRIVE DESTROY
UNCLOAK DISMOUNT
DISMAY BOWL FEAR RUIN ALARM
AMATE APPAL DAUNT DREAD
FLUNK APPALL ASTONY CHASSE
FRIGHT SUBDUE TERROR
DEPRESS DEPRIVE FOUNDER
HORRIFY TERRIFY AFFRIGHT
CONFOUND CONSTERNATION
DISMAYED ASTONIED
DISMAYING HIDEOUS
DISMEMBER LIMB MAIM PART
REND SEVER MANGLE UNLIMB
DISCERP DISLIMB DISSECT
QUARTER DISJOINT MUTILATE
DISMISS AX AXE CAN PUT BOOT
BUMP BUST CASH CAST DAFF
DROP DRUM FIRE KICK OUST
QUIT SACK SEND SHAB SWAP
SWOP TURN VAIK VOID AMAND
AMOVE BREAK BRUSH CHUCK
DEMIT DIMIT DITCH EJECT EXPEL
FLIRT FLUNK LOOSE SCOUT
BANISH BOUNCE CHASSE CONGEE
DISMIT DISOWN REJECT REMOVE
SHELVE CASHIER DISBAND
DISCARD LICENCE LICENSE
DISGRACE DISPATCH DISPOINT
RELEGATE WITHDRAW
DISMISSAL AX BOOT SACK BRUSH
CHUCK CONGE SHAKE AVAUNT
BOUNCE KICKAXE REMOVAL
DISPATCH MITTIMUS
REDUNDANCY
(UNCEREMONIOUS —) CONGE
CONGEE
DISMISSED DEGOMME
DISMOUNT AVALE AVOID LIGHT
ALIGHT DEVOID DESCEND
FLYAWAY UNHORSE UNMOUNT
DISHORSE UNSTRIDE
DISOBEDIENCE CONTEMPT
DISOBEDIENT BAD FORWARD
FROWARD NAUGHTY UNBUXOM
UNGODLY WAYWARD MUTINOUS
DISOBEY SIT REJECT
DISOBLIGE OFFEND REFUSE
AFFRONT NEGLECT
DISOBLIGING MEAN UNBAIN
UNBANE
DISORDER ILL MUX PIE CRUD
FLAW MESS MUSS RIOT RUFF
STIR TOUT CHAOS CRACK DERAY
GRIME HAVOC REVEL SNAFU
SPLIT TOUSE TUKRA UPSET
BURBLE CHOREA DEFUSE DESRAY
HUDDLE JUMBLE LITTER MALADY
MASTIC MUCKER MUDDLE
RUFFLE TOUSLE TROPPO TUMULT
UNTIDY WALTER AILMENT
CLUTTER COBWEBS CONFUSE
DERANGE DISEASE DISTURB

EMBROIL FERMENT FLUTTER
GARBOIL ILLNESS MISDEED
MISRULE OUTRAGE PERTURB
SHATTER TROUBLE UNRAVEL
UNSHAPE DISARRAY DISHEVEL
EPILEPSY MILIARIA MISORDER
NEUROSIS ROWDYISM SICKNESS
UNSETTLE COMMOTION
CONFUSION POLLINOSIS
(— OF BIRDS) PIP
(— OF EYES) HIPPUS
(— OF VISION) DIPLOPIA
(— OF WINES) CASSE
(COMPLETE —) CHAOS ANARCHY
(MENTAL —) INSANITY PARANOIA
(SPEECH —) LALOPATHY
(SUFF.) **(SPEECH —)** PHASIA
PHEMIA PHRASIA
DISORDERED ILL SICK WILD CRAZY
GAUMY LIGHT MESSY UNRID
BLOTTO FROUZY FROWSY
FROWZY INCULT INSANE MUSSED
TURBID CHAOTIC CLOUDED
FORLORN TUMBLED UNSIDED
CONFUSED DERANGED DISEASED
FEVERISH FLURRIED INCHOATE
DISORDERING CRIMP
DISORDERLY RAND RANDY
ROWDY RABBLE UNRULY
BUNTING LAWLESS ROARING
CONFUSED FAROUCHE LARRIKIN
SLIPSHOD SLOVENLY SLUTTISH
SLATTERNLY
DISORGANIZE SHOCK UPSET
CONFUSE CONTUSE DERANGE
DISBAND DISRUPT DISORDER
DISSOLVE
DISOWN DENY RENAY UNOWN
REJECT DISAVOW RETRACT
ABDICATE DISALLOW DISCLAIM
RENOUNCE REPUDIATE
DISPARAGE LACK SLUR ABUSE
DECRY LOWER TRASH DEBASE
LESSEN SLIGHT BACKCAP
DEBAUCH DEGRADE DEMERIT
DEPRESS DETRACT DISABLE
DOWNCRY IMPEACH BELITTLE
DEROGATE DIMINISH DISCOUNT
DISHONOR DISPRIZE MINIMIZE
MISLIKEN VILIPEND
DISPARAGEMENT DIASYRM
SNIDERY WASHWAY
DISPARAGING SNIDE SLIGHTING
PEJORATIVE
DISPARATE UNEQUAL SEPARATE
DISPARITY DISSENT DISTANCE
IMPARITY
DISPASSIONATE CALM COOL FAIR
STOIC SEDATE SERENE CLINICAL
COMPOSED MODERATE
DISPATCH RID FREE KILL MAIL
NOTE POST SEND SLAY WING
BRIEF ENVOY FLASH HASTE
HURRY SHOOT SPEED DIRECT
EMPLOY HASTEN ADDRESS
COMMAND DELIVER DISPEED
EXPRESS HATCHET BREVIATE
CELERITY CONCLUDE DESPATCH
EXPEDITE TELEGRAM
DISPATCH BOAT AVISO PACKET
DISPATCHER STARTER
DISPEL FRAY SHOO CHASE ASSOIL
BANISH DISCUSS SATISFY

SCATTER DISPERSE
DISPENSATION LAW LILA GRACE
LIVERY ECONOMY FACULTY
QUIENAL TOTQUOT COVENANT
DISPOSAL
DISPENSE DEAL DOLE HELP SHED
WEIGH EFFUSE EXCUSE EXEMPT
FOREGO MANAGE SPREAD
ABSOLVE ARRANGE DISPEND
DRIBBLE MINISTER
(— WITH) MISS WANT SPARE
SUSPENSE
DISPENSER BOMB MANAGER
STEWARD
DISPERSE DOT SOW FRAY MELT
PART ROUT SHED LOOSE SCALE
SEVER SKAIL STREW BAFFLE
DEFEAT DILATE DISPEL SKIVER
SPARSE SPERSE SPREAD UNKNIT
VANISH WINNOW DIFFUSE
DISBAND DISJECT DISMISS
DRIBBLE FRITTER SCATTER
SHATTER SPARKLE SPARPLE
SPERPLE DISSOLVE DISTRACT
SEPARATE SQUANDER STAMPEDE
DISPERSEDLY PASSIM
DISPERSING SCALE
(— SHADOWS) SCIALYTIC
DISPERSION CUT FOAM STAIN
SPREAD DEBACLE SCATTER
DIASPORA EMULSOID SOLUTION
STAMPEDE
(PREF.) LYO
DISPIRIT COW DAMP MATE MULL
CHILL DAUNT DEJECT DEPRESS
FLATTEN OPPRESS
DISPIRITED DOWY DOWIE ABATTU
ABATTUE LETDOWN SHOTTEN
DOWNCAST DOWNSOME
SACKLESS UNHEARTY WOBEGONE
DISPIRITING COLD CHILL DISMAL
DISPLACE BUMP EDGE MOVE STIR
BANISH DEPOSE LUXATE MISLAY
REMOVE WINKLE DERANGE
SWALLOW UNHINGE UNPLACE
ANTEVERT DISLODGE DISPLANT
MISPLACE SUPPLACE SUPPLANT
UNSETTLE
(— LATERALLY) HEAVE
DISPLACED ATOPIC DEPAYSE
DISPLACEMENT JEE BUMP SLIP
HEAVE SCEND SHIFT START
CUBAGE OFFSET UPSLIP FALLING
EVECTION
(— OF STAR) ABERRATION
(DOWNWARD —) PTOSIS
(OPTICAL —) PARALLAX
DISPLAY ACT AIR BRAG DASH
GAUD ORGY POMP SHOW SIGN
STAR WEAR AGONY ARRAY BINGE
BLAZE BOAST DERAY ECLAT
EMOTE FLASH PRIDE SCENE
SHINE SIGHT SPLAY SPORT STAGE
VAUNT BLAZON DEPLOY DESCRY
ESTATE EVINCE EXPOSE EXTEND
FLAUNT MUSTER OSTENT
OUTLAY PARADE REVEAL RUFFLE
SETOUT SPLASH SPRANK SPREAD
UNCASE APPROVE BALLOON
BRAVERY ETALAGE EXHIBIT
EXPRESS FANFARE FLUTTER
GAUDERY PAGEANT PRESENT
SHOWING SPLURGE TRADUCE

UNCOVER BEEFCAKE BLAZONRY
BOOKFAIR CEREMONY DISCLOSE
DISCOVER EMBLAZON EQUIPAGE
EVIDENCE EXERCISE EXPOSURE
FLOURISH INDICATE MANIFEST
PARAFFLE SPLENDOR TINSELRY
(— EXCITEMENT) FAUNCH
(— OF COMPUTER TASKS) MENU
(— OF EMOTION) GUSH
(— OF SKILL) APPERTISE
(BOASTFUL —) JACTATION
(DARING —) BRAVURA
(EMPTY —) GAUD EYEWASH
(EXCESSIVE —) OSTENTATION
(FLORAL —) BLOW BLANKET
(IMPRESSIVE —) SWELL
(LAVISH —) PROFUSION
(OSTENTATIOUS —) DOG GAUDERY
SWAGGER
(RADAR —) SCAN
DISPLAYED SPLAY EXPANDED
DISPLEASE VEX MIFF ANGER
ANNOY PIQUE MISPAY MISSET
OFFEND DISLIKE DISSUIT MISLIKE
PROVOKE IRRITATE
DISPLEASED MAD GLUM UNEASY
UNFAIN
DISPLEASING BAD DRY PUTRID
IRKSOME TEDIOUS UNLOVELY
DISPLEASURE IRE ANGER MUMPS
PIQUE INJURY STRUNT UNLUST
UNWILL DISLIKE OFFENSE
TROUBLE UMBRAGE UNTHANK
DISFAVOR DISGRACE DISTASTE
DISPORT PLAY AMUSE FRISK
SPORT DIVERT FROLIC GAMBOL
DISPLAY
DISPOSAL SALE BANDON
CLEANUP PROPINE BESTOWAL
DEVOTION DISPATCH
(QUICK —) WASHWAY
DISPOSE APT SET BEND CAST
DUMP GIVE MIND TRIM YARK
ARRAY BRUSH DIGHT ORDER
PLACE POSIT ADJUST ATTIRE
BESTOW DIGEST SETTLE TEMPER
APPOINT ARRANGE DISPONE
GESTURE INCLINE PREPARE
RESOLVE DISPATCH REGULATE
(— OF) JOB SELL SCRAP FINISH
HANDLE
DISPOSED APT FIT SET SIB LIEF
DIGHT GIVEN PRONE READY
WRAST MINDED MINDFUL
SUBJECT WILLING ADDICTED
AFFECTED PREGNANT PROCLIVE
PROPENSE PROTENSE TALENTED
(— AT INTERVALS) ALTERNATE
(— TO ACTION) ACTIVE
(— TO ASSOCIATE WITH ONE
GROUP) CLANNISH
(— TOWARD) AFFECTED
(FAIRLY —) CANDID
(FAVORABLY —) PROPITIOUS
(WELL —) FAIN INCLINED
DISPOSITION BENT BIAS MAKE
MIND MOOD RACE SORT TRIM
TURN DRIVE ETHOS FRAME
GRAIN HABIT HEART HUMOR
SPITE TACHE AFFECT ANIMUS
DESIGN GENIUS HEALTH KIDNEY
NATURE PTYXIS SPIRIT SPRITE
STRIND TALENT TEMPER

CONCEPT COURAGE DISPOSE
FACULTY STOMACH APTITUDE
ATTITUDE DISPOSAL POSITURE
PERSONALITY
(— OF DRAPERIES) CAST
(— OF PAWNS) SKELETON
(— TO ANGER) CHOLER
(— TO RESIST) DEFIANCE
(GENEROUS —) HEART
(GENIAL —) BONHOMIE
(KINDLY —) CHARITY HUMANITY
(NATURAL —) KIND GRAIN TARAGE
INDOLES
(ORNAMENTAL —) DECOR
(ULTIMATE —) FATE
DISPOSSESS OUST EJECT EVICT
EXPEL STRIP WRONG DEPOSE
DIVEST BEREAVE CASHIER
DEPRIVE DISSEIZE SEPARATE
DISPOSSESSED LUMPEN
DISPOSSESSION OUSTER
DISPRAISE BLAME CENSURE
DISPROOF ELENCH REFUTE
IMPROOF REPROOF
DISPROPORTIONATE UNEQUAL
DISPROVE BREAK REBUT REFEL
NEGATE REFUTE CONFUTE
EXPLODE IMPROVE REPROVE
DISALLOW NEGATIVE REDARGUE
DISPUTABLE MOOT VAGUE
UNSURE DUBIOUS FALLIBLE
DISPUTANT FENCER POLEMIC
WRANGLER
DISPUTATION PARVIS PILPUL
POLEMIC PROBLEM WRANGLE
ARGUMENT COURSING DEBATING
EXERCISE QUODLIBET
DISPUTATIOUS POLEMIC
LITIGIOUS POLEMICAL
DISPUTE JAR ROW TAX CALL
CHOP DENY FEUD FRAY FUSS
HOLD MOOT ODDS RIOT SAKE
SPAR SPAT TILT ARGUE BRAWL
BROIL CABAL CHEST FLITE FLYTE
HURRY PLEAD SPUTE SQUIB
ARGUFY BARNEY BICKER CAMPLE
CANGLE DABBER DACKER DAIKER
DEBATE DIFFER FITTER FRATCH
HAGGLE HASSLE IMPUGN
MATTER NAGGLE SHARRY
SQUALL SQUEAL THREAP
BRABBLE CONTEND CONTEST
DERAIGN DISCEPT DISCUSS
DISSERT FACTION GAINSAY
PRIBBLE QUARREL WRANGLE
ARGUMENT CATFIGHT CONTRARY
POLEMIZE QUESTION SKIRMISH
SPARRING SPLUTTER SQUABBLE
(POETICAL —) FLYTING PARTIMEN
DISQUALIFY DEBAR UNFIT
OUTLAW DISABLE
DISQUIET VEX FEAR FRET PAIN
TOSS UNRO EXCITE UNCALM
UNEASE UNREST AGITATE
ANXIETY DISREST DISTURB
INQUIET PERTURB SOLICIT
TROUBLE TURMOIL UNPEACE
UNQUIET
DISQUIETED UNEASY
DISQUIETINGLY UNEASILY
DISQUIETUDE CHAGRIN WANREST
WANRUFE
DISRAELI DIZZY

DISREGARD BY SIT BLOW MOCK
OMIT PASS WANE BELAY FLING
WAIVE FORGET HUBRIS IGNORE
SLIGHT UNHEED CASHIER
DESPISE FORHEED LICENCE
LICENSE NEGLECT OVERSEE
DISCOUNT DISFAVOR DISPENSE
DISVALUE EASINESS OVERHALE
OVERLOOK OVERPASS UNREGARD
DISRELISH DISLIKE DISTASTE
DISREPUTABLE LOW BASE GAMY
HARD WAFF GAMEY SEAMY
SEEDY SHADY TOUGH LOUCHE
SHODDY RAFFISH SHAMEFUL
UNHONEST
DISREPUTABLENESS BEGGARY
DISREPUTE DISFAME DISFAVOR
DISHONOR REPROACH
DISRESPECT AFFRONT CONTEMPT
RUDENESS
DISRESPECTFUL HARM SAUCY
UNCIVIL IMPOLITE IMPUDENT
INSOLENT
DISROBE STRIP CHANGE DIVEST
DESPOIL UNDRESS
DISRUPT GASH REND TEAR BREAK
CROSS HAMPER DISRUMP
DISTRACT
DISRUPTED BROKEN DISRUPT
DISRUPTION BREACH BREAKUP
DEBACLE RUPTURE SOLUTION
DISSATISFACTION PAIN DISTASTE
VEXATION
(FEELING OF —) BLAHS
DISSATISFIED UNEASY
MALCONTENT
DISSATISFY MISPAY
DISSECT BAR ANALYZE DISJOIN
SCALPEL UNPIECE
DISSECTED MATURE
DISSECTION ANATOMY ANALYSIS
DISSEMBLE ACT FOX HIDE MASK
CLOAK FEIGN BOGGLE SEMBLE
CONCEAL DISGUISE SIMULATE
SIMULIZE
DISSEMBLER SIMULAR
DISSEMBLING SLY BRAIDE IRONIC
FICTION AESOPIAN IRONICAL
DISSEMINATE SOW BEAR BLAZE
STREW EFFUSE SPREAD DIFFUSE
PUBLISH SCATTER SPARPLE
DISPERSE SEMINATE
DISSEMINATION PROPAGATION
DISSENSION JAR ODDS DEBATE
STRIFE DISCORD DISLIKE DISSENT
FACTION MISLIKE BROILERY
DISPEACE DISTANCE DISUNION
DISUNITY DIVISION FRACTION
FRICTION SEDITION
DISSENT VARY DIFFER HERESY
CONTEND PROTEST DISAGREE
DISSENTER HERETIC SECTARY
RECUSANT SEPARATE RASKOLNIK
(PL.) SEPARATION
DISSENTING PANTILE
DISSEPIMENT REPLUM SEPTUM
PHRAGMA
DISSERTATION ESSAY THEME
TRACT DEBATE MEMOIR SCREED
THESIS DESCANT LECTURE
MEMOIRS EXCURSUS EXERCISE
TRACTATE TREATISE
(— ON TEA) TSIOLOGY

DISSERVICE HARM DAMAGE
INJURY MISCHIEF
DISSIDENT FRONDEUR
DISSIMILAR UNLIKE DIFFORM
DIVERSE UNLIKEN
DISSIMILATE UNLIKEN
DISSIMULATION IRONY DECEIT
DISSIPATE BURN FRAY SPEND
WASTE BANISH DISPEL EXPEND
CONSUME DIFFUSE DISCUSS
FRITTER RESOLVE SCAMBLE
SCATTER SHATTER SWATTLE
TARNISH DISPERSE DISSOLVE
EMBEZZLE EVANESCE SQUANDER
DISSIPATED FAST HIGH LOST
SPORTY OUTWARD RACKETY
DISSIPATION RAKERY
DISSOLUTE LAX LEWD WILD
LOOSE SLACK RAKELY RAKISH
SUBURB UNTIED WANTON
IMMORAL LAWLESS VICIOUS
DESOLATE RAKEHELL RECKLESS
RESOLUTE SUBURBAN UNCURBED
DISSOLUTION END RUIN DECAY
BREAKUP DECEASE DIVORCE
DIALYSIS
(PREF.) LYS(I)
DISSOLVE CUT END DEFY FADE
FUSE MELT SOLV THAW BREAK
FLEET LOOSE SOLVE UNFIX
DIGEST DISTIL RELENT SOLUTE
UNBIND UNGLUE UNKNIT
ADJOURN DESTROY DISBAND
DISJOIN DISTILL DIVORCE
LIQUEFY RESOLVE DISCANDY
DISUNITE SEPARATE
(— OUT) LEACH
(PREF.) LY(O)
DISSOLVED SOLUT REMISS
SOLUTE RESOLUTE
DISSOLVING
(SUFF.) LYSE LYSIS LYST LYTE
LYTIC LYZE
DISSONANCE WOLF DISCORD
DIAPHONY
DISSONANT HARSH RAGGED
GRATING JARRING JANGLING
DISSUADE BLUFF DETER DEHORT
DIVERT RETIRE
DISTAFF ROCK
DISTAFFINA (LOVER OF —)
BOMBASTES
DISTANCE DX WAY BLUE GAIT
GATE LOOK PIPE SPAN STEP
DEPTH DRAFT RANGE SPACE
GROUND HEIGHT LENGTH
SPREAD STANCE STITCH
BOWSHOT BREADTH DRAUGHT
FARNESS JOURNEY MILEAGE
MILEWAY RESERVE STRETCH
YARDAGE COLDNESS COSECANT
DIAMETER FOOTSTEP HANDSPAN
INTERVAL LATITUDE OFFSCAPE
OUTSTRIP
(— ALONG TRACK) LEAD
(— BETWEEN BATTENS) GAG
(— BETWEEN GEAR TEETH) PITCH
(— BETWEEN MASTS) INTERVAL
(— BETWEEN RAILS) GAGE GAUGE
(— BETWEEN RIVET-HEADS) GRIP
(— FOR PUTTING COAL) RENK
(— FROM BELLY TO BACK) BODY
(— FROM EQUATOR) HEIGHT

(— FROM LOCK FACE) BACKSET
(— FROM THE EYE) DEPTH
(— IN ADVANCE) START
(— OF ARCHERY RANGE) BUTT
(— OF BOW SHOT) CAST
(— OF HAUL) LEAD LEADAGE
(— OF TURNING SHIP) ADVANCE
(— OF VISION) KEN
(— ON FISHHOOK) BITE
(— ON GEAR WHEEL) ADDENDUM
(— OVER WHICH WIND BLOWS)
FETCH
(ANGULAR —) ANOMALY
(AT A —) LARGE
(GREAT —) INFINITY
(INTERVENING —) GAP
(PERPENDICULAR —) DROP
CAMBER ALTITUDE
(SAFE —) BERTH
(SEA —) OUTING STEAMING
(SHOOTING —) SHOOT
(SHORT —) INCH SPIT STEP SPELL
BITTIE FOOTSTEP
(SHORT — AWAY) OUTBYE
(SMALL —) HAIR STEP
(UNIT OF —) LI YOJAN PARASANG
DISTANT DX COY FAR OFF AFAR
AWAY BACK COLD SIDE YOND
ALOOF CHILL FERNE HENCE
FERREN REMOTE YONDER
FARAWAY FOREIGN FROSTED
REMOVED STRANGE RESERVED
(— IN TIME) EARLY
(— PART) OFFSCAPE
(MORE —) YOND YONDER
ULTERIOR
(PREF.) TEL(E)(EO)
DISTASTE HATE DEGOUT UNLUST
DISGUST DISLIKE MISLIKE
AVERSION MISTASTE
(— FOR FOOD) APOSITIA
DISTASTEFUL SOUR AUGEAN
BITTER BEASTLY HATEFUL
BRACKISH NAUSEOUS SHOCKING
UNSAVORY REPUGNANT
DISTEMPER SOAK STEEP CHOLER
DILUTE GARGET GARGIL GARGLE
MALADY PANTAS AILMENT
DISEASE ILLNESS DISORDER
DYSCRASE SICKNESS UNSETTLE
(— OF COLT) STRANGLES
DISTEND BAG BLOW FILL GROW
HEFT BLOAT PLUMP STRUT
SWELL WIDEN DILATE EXPAND
EXTEND INTEND SPREAD
BALLOON ENLARGE INFLATE
STRETCH
DISTENDED BIG FULL PENT TAUT
TRIG WIDE BLOWN POOCH TUMID
ASTRUT GRAVID BLOATED
DISTENT SWOLLEN INFLATED
PATULENT PATULOUS
DISTENDEDLY ASTRUT
DISTENTION BLOAT DISTENT
TYMPANY
DISTHENE CYANITE KYANITE
DISTICH SLOKA PROODE COUPLET
DISTILL DROP ELIX EMIT RATE
STILL DISTIL EXTILL INFUSE
ALEMBIC LIMBECK TRICKLE
DISTILLATE GUNDY ROSIN BENZIN
ALCOHOL BENZINE
DISTILLATION RUN DESCENT

DISTILLER ABKAR STILLER
DISTILLERY STILL JIGGER STILLERY
DISTINCT HOT FAIR FREE VIVE
BREME BRISK CLEAR PLAIN
SHARP VIVID PLUCKY PROPER
SECRET SUNDRY ANOTHER
ASUNDER DIVERSE EVIDENT
LEGIBLE OBVIOUS PRECISE
SCIOLTO SEVERAL SPECIAL
APPARENT DISCRETE DIVIDUAL
PALPABLE PECULIAR SEPARATE
TRENCHANT
(PREF.) CHORI CHORIST(O) IDIO
DISTINCTION MARK NOTE RANK
SHED TEST CLASS GLORY HONOR
FIGURE LAUREL LUSTER LUSTRE
RENOWN DIORISM QUALITY
QUILLET ACCESSIT DIVISION
GRANDEZA SUBTLETY
REFINEMENT
(ACADEMIC —) HONORS HONOURS
(LACKING —) VANILLA
(WITHOUT —) COMMON
DISTINCTIVE JUICY DIRECT
PROPER SIGNAL PECULIAR
PHONEMIC SEPARATE SPANKING
TALENTED
DISTINCTIVENESS EMPHASIS
DISTINCTLY CLEAR REDLY FAIRLY
CLEARLY
DISTINCTNESS PLUCK CLARITY
SEVERALTY
(LACKING —) SMUDGY
DISTINGUISH DEEM KNOW MARK
SORT BADGE JUDGE LABEL SEVER
SKILL STAMP DECERN DEFINE
DESCRY DEVISE DIVIDE ENSIGN
SECERN SINGLE CONCERN
DISCERN DESCRIBE PERCEIVE
SEPARATE
DISTINGUISHED CLEAR GREAT
NOTED SWELL BANNER FAMOUS
GENTLE MARKED SOLEMN
EMINENT INSIGNE NOTABLE
SIGNATE SPECIAL TOPPING
DISTINCT ESPECIAL LAUREATE
RENOWNED SPLENDID
CONSPICUOUS
DISTINGUISHING BETWEEN
DISTORT WRY SKEW WARP CLOUD
COLOR FUDGE SCREW TWIST
WREST WRING CRINGE DEFACE
DEFORM DETORT GARBLE
MANGLE SHEVEL WRENCH
WRITHE BLUBBER CONTORT
FALSIFY GRIMACE PERVERT
SHACHLE SHACKLE SLANDER
OUTIMAGE WIREDRAW
DISTORTED WRY AWRY SKEW
ASKEW CRANK SKEWED WARPED
CROOKED DISTORT GNARLED
LOXOTIC WRITHEN CAMSHACH
DEFORMED DEGRADED STRAINED
TORTIOUS PERVERTED
DISTORTING CONVULSION
DISTORTION FIB HOG SAG WOW
WREST STRAIN FLUTTER
GRIMACE GARBLING SKEWNESS
(— IN WOOD) WARP DIAMONDING
DISTRACT MAD AMUSE CRAZE
STROY BEMUSE DETRAY DIVERT
HARASS INSANE MADDEN MITHER
MOIDER PUZZLE TWITCH AGITATE

CONFUSE DETRACT DISTURB
EMBROIL PERPLEX SCATTER
BEWILDER CONFOUND FORHAILE
DISTRACTED GYTE WILD CRAZY
EPERDU STRACT FRANTIC
SCRANNY FRENETIC
DISTRACTION ALARM BLIND
ALARUM ESCAPE FRENZY
TUMULT ECSTASY
DISTRAIN NAM NAAM DRIVE
POIND STRAIN STRESS DISTRESS
POUNDAGE
DISTRAINT NAM NAAM POIND
DISTRAUGHT MAD CRAZED
FRANTIC DERANGED DISTRACT
DISTRAIT STRAUGHT
DISTRESS AIL ILL MAR VEX BITE
CARK GNAW HURT MOAN NEED
PAIN PORT PUSH TEAR TEEN
AGONY ANGER ANNOY DOLOR
GRATE GRIEF GRILL GRIPE LABOR
PINCH PRESS SMART TRYST
TWEAK WORRY WOUND WRING
BARRAT DANGER DURESS GRIEVE
GRUDGE HARASS HARROW
LAMENT MISERY SORROW STRESS
TAKING THRONG WORRIT
AFFLICT ANGUISH ANXIETY
CHAGRIN DAYMARE DESTROY
DISEASE EXTREME HERSHIP
MISEASE OPPRESS PASSION
PENANCE PERPLEX STURBLE
TORMENT TORTURE TRAVAIL
TROUBLE UNQUERT AGGRIEVE
CALAMITY DARKNESS DISTASTE
DISTRAIN EXIGENCE FORHAILE
PRESSURE SORENESS STRAITEN
WANDRETH GRIEVANCE
DISTRESSED WRUNG DOWNGONE
DISTRESSFUL STRAIT
DISTRESSING BAD HOT SAD GRIM
HARD SORE BLEAK CHARY CRUEL
DIRTY SHARP BITTER SEVERE
SHREWD THORNY CARKING
FEARFUL GRIPING PAINFUL
GRIEVOUS
DISTRIBUTE DOT SOW CAST DEAL
DOLE GRID METE SEED SORT
TAME ALLOT CLASS DIVVY ISSUE
PLACE SHARE SHIFT SPEND
ASSIGN ASSORT DEPART DEVISE
DIGEST DIVIDE EXPEND IMPART
PARCEL REPART SPARSE SPREAD
ARRANGE DISPEND DISPOSE
EROGATE PRORATE SCATTER
ALLOCATE CLASSIFY DESCRIBE
DISBURSE DISPENSE DISPERSE
SEPARATE SPRINKLE
(— GUNFIRE) SEARCH
(— SEED) SOW SEED DRILL
(— TYPE) DISH THROW
DISTRIBUTED BALANCED
DISPERSE
DISTRIBUTION DOLE SALE ARRAY
DIVVY DETAIL DIVIDE PARTING
DISPOSAL DIVIDEND
DISTRIBUTIVELY EACH APIECE
DISTRIBUTOR SOWER SHARER
CARRIER ZANJERO
DISTRICT DO AMT GAU LAN SOC
WAY WON AREA COIL FARM
HUNT LEET LIWA PALE PART SIDE
SLUM SOKE TEMA WARD WENE

WICK WOON AIMAK ANNEX COILA
EXURB HARSH JAGIR JEWRY
MAHAL OKRUG PAGUS PARTY
SHIRE SOKEN TALUK TEMAN
TRACT VICUS AGENCY BARRIO
BOWERY CANTON CERCLE CIRCLE
COUNTY FOREST JAGHIR MARKAZ
MEMBER MERINA OKROOG
PARAMO PARISH POLLAM
REGARD REGION SIRCAR STAPLE
STREET SYSSEL VINTRY ZILLAH
CALABAR CIRCUIT CLASSIS
COMARCA COMMUNE COUNTRY
CURRAGH DEMESNE DIOCESE
ENCLAVE FREEDOM LIBERTY
MAHALLA MALACCA MAYFAIR
MELIZKI MISSION PIMLICO
PURLIEU QUARTER SEASIDE
SLUMDOM THANAGE THEBAID
UPRIVER CHAPELRY CIMARRON
DISTRITO DIVISION FAUBOURG
GILDABLE LEGATION MACASSAR
MAGAZINE MONTANAS PRECINCT
PROVINCE REGIMENT
MAGISTRACY PREFECTURE
(— BORDERING RIVER) WATER
(— OF COURT) LEET
(— OF JAPAN) DO KEN
(BROTHEL —) STEW
(BURNED —) QUEMADO
(CHINESE —) HIEN
(COASTAL —) RIVIERA
(ECCLESIASTICAL —) SYNOD
CLASSIS DIOCESE
(HUNTING —) WALK
(ICELANDIC —) SYSSEL
(JUDICIAL —) CIRCUIT
(OUTWARD —) END
(POOR —) SLUM SLUMS
(POSTAL —) RAYON
(RURAL —) WAYBACK
(RURAL —S) STICKS
(RUSSIAN —) OBLAST STANITSA
STANITZA
(TENANT —) THIRL
(TRIBAL —) GAU
(TURKISH —) ORDU SANJAK
(PL.) GAELTACHT
DISTRUST FEAR DOUBT DREAD
STRIFE DIFFIDE SUSPECT
UNFAITH UNTRUST DEFIANCE
DISFAITH MISFAITH MISTRUST
QUESTION WANTRUST
DISTRUSTFUL SHY LEERY JEALOUS
DISTURB JEE VEX BUSY FAZE FRET
FUSS JOLT RILE ROCK ROIL STIR
TOSS ALARM ANNOY BRASH
DROVE FEEZE KNOCK PHASE
ROUSE SHAKE STEER UPSET
AFFRAY BOTHER HARASS JOSTLE
MOLEST RUFFLE SQUEAK
UNCALM UNEASE AGITATE
COMMOTE COMMOVE CONCUSS
DERANGE DISREST DRUMBLE
FRAZZLE GARBOIL INQUIET
MISMAKE PERTURB SCUFFLE
SOLICIT STURBLE TEMPEST
TROUBLE CONVULSE DISJOINT
DISORDER DISQUIET DISTRACT
DISTRESS FRIGHTEN
(— BY HANDLING) TOUCH
(— SUDDENLY) START
(— THE PEACE) RIOT INQUIET

DISTURBANCE VEX BOIL BREE
CAIN COIL DUST RIOT ROUT STIR
WIND WORK ALARM BEANO
BRAWL BROIL DERAY FUGUE
FUROR HURRY SHINE SHOCK
STEER STORM STROW STURT
TOUSE AFFRAY BOTHER BREEZE
CATHRO DESRAY FRACAS FRAISE
FURORE HUBBUB KICKUP POTHER
RUCKUS RUMBLE RUMPUS
SHINDY SQUALL STATIC TUMULT
TURNUP UPROAR BLUNDER
BOBBERY BRULYIE BRULZIE
CHAGRIN CLATTER CLUTTER
DISTURB EMOTION FERMENT
GRINDER MADNESS ROOKERY
RUCTION TROUBLE TURMOIL
BROILERY BUSINESS DISORDER
FOOFARAW INCIDENT REELRALL
STRAMASH TRAVALLY
RABBLEMENT PERTURBATION
(— OF OCEAN) SEA
(ATMOSPHERIC —) STORM
GRINDER
(DIGESTIVE —) BLOAT
(MENTAL —) FRENZY PHRENSY
DELIRIUM
(SEISMIC —) SEAQUAKE
DISTURBED CRACKED INQUIET
MAKADOO TROUBLE AGITATED
FLURRIED STREAKED
DISTURBING BREAK NASTY
HAUNTING
DISUNION DIVORCE
DISUNITE RIP PART SEVER UNTIE
DETACH DIVIDE SUNDER UNKNIT
UNLIME DISBAND DISJOIN
DISLINK DISSENT DIVORCE
UNRAVEL ALIENATE DISSEVER
DISSOLVE ESTRANGE SEPARATE
UNSOLDER
DISUNITY DISCORD DISUNION
DIVISION
DISUSE MISUSE OUTAGE
ABANDON DISCARD DISUSAGE
MISAPPLY
DISUSED DEAD WASTE DESUETE
EXOLETE OBSOLETE
DITCH GAW RUT SAP SOW DELF
DICK DIKE DYKE FOSS GOOL
GOUT GRIP GURT HOLL LEET
LODE MOAT SEEK SICK SIKE SINK
TRIG CANAL CLAUD DELFT DELVE
FENCE FLEAM FOSSA FOSSE
GRAFF GRAFT GRAVE GRIPE
GROOP GULLY PUDGE RHEEN
RHINE RIGOL SEWER SHORE
SLONK SLUIT SOUGH STANK
STELL ZANJA GUTTER GUZZLE
HOLLOW RELAIS SHEUCH SHEUGH
TRENCH ZANJON ABANDON
ACEQUIA CHANNEL GRINDLE
GRIPPLE LATERAL VANFOSS
ZANJONA WATERING
(MUDDY —) LETCH
(NARROW —) RELAIS
(OPEN —) STELL
(WIDE —) SLOT
(PREF.) FOSSI
DITCH GRASS ENALID
DITCH MILLET HUREEK PASPALUM
DITCH REED SPIRE BENNEL
DITHER SHAKE TIZZY BOTHER

LATHER SHIVER TROUBLE
DITI (FATHER OF —) DAKSHA
(HUSBAND OF —) KASHYAPA
DITROCHEE DIPODY
DITTO SAME REPEAT LIKEWISE
DITTY DIT LAY DITE DYTE POEM
SING SONG THEME VERSE SAYING
DICTATE VINETTA
DIURETIC ZEA CAVA KAVA BUCCO
BUCHU CUBEB LAPPA PICHI
SABAL NASROL DROSERA
EMICTORY PIPSISSEWA
DIVAN SOFA OTTOMAN SOCIABLE
DIVE BAR DEN DASH DUMP JOINT
SOUSE GAINER HEADER PLUNGE
SALOON BROTHEL JACKNIFE
SUBMERGE
(KIND OF —) SWAN TWIST GAINER
JACKKNIFE
(MAKE A NOSE —) PEARL
DIVER AMA LOON DUCKER
PEARLER PLUNGER PLUNGEON
(SCUBA —) AQUANAUT
(SUFF.) DYTA DYTES
DIVERGE LEAVE BRANCH DIFFER
DIVIDE RAMIFY SPREAD SQUARE
SWERVE DEVIATE DIGRESS
DIVERSE DISAGREE DIVAGATE
DIVERGENCE DIP ERROR CHANGE
SPREAD SWERVE VAGARY
CONTRAST OBLIQUITY
DIVERGENT OFF APART REMOTE
TANGENT VARIANT
(MORE —) FARTHER
DIVERS EVIL MANY CRUEL SUNDRY
SEVERAL VARIOUS PERVERSE
DIFFERING
(PREF.) PARTI PARTY
DIVERSE EVIL SERE MOTLEY
SUNDRY UNLIKE VARIED
ADVERSE SEVERAL VARIOUS
DISTINCT PERVERSE SEPARATE
VARIETAL
(PREF.) PARTI PARTY POLY
VARI(O)
DIVERSIFIED MOTLEY EXTENDED
DIVERSIFY DOT FRET VARY CHECK
FRECK BEGARIE CHECKER
VARIATE SPRINKLE
DIVERSION JEU GAME MASK PLAY
ALARM FEINT FRISK HOBBY
SPORT ATTACK DEDUIT DIVERT
LAUGHS SCHEME SOLACE
DISPORT PASTIME ESCAPISM
PLEASURE SIDESHOW VARIORUM
(— OF STREAM) CAPTURE
DIVERSITY CHANGE DISCORD
DISSENT VARIETY CONTRAST
(PREF.) POLY
DIVERT SWAY AMUSE BLANK
RELAX SHUNT SPORT WRING
DERAIL DERIVE DETURN SIPHON
SWITCH SYPHON TICKLE BEGUILE
CELIGHT DECEIVE DEFLECT
DETRACT DISPORT PASTIME
PERVERT REFLECT ABSTRACT
DISSUADE DISTRACT ESTRANGE
RECREATE
(— ATTENTION) COVER
(— HEADWATERS) BEHEAD
(— STREAM) CAPTURE
(— WATER) FLUME
DIVERTED MERRY

AMUSED DISTRACT
DIVERTICULUM UTERUS
OLEOCYST
DIVERTING DROLL AMUSING
FOOLISH PLEASANT SPORTFUL
LAUGHABLE
DIVEST BARE DOFF REFT TIRL
EMPTY EXUTE REAVE SHEAR
SPOIL STRIP DELAWN DENUDE
DEPOSE DEVEST DISMIT UNVEST
BEREAVE DEPRIVE DESPOIL
DISROBE UNCOVER UNDRESS
DENATURE DETHRONE
UNCLOTHE
(— OF) ABDICATE
(— OF ARMOR) DEMAIL
(— OF VALUE) DEVALUE
DIVIDE CUT LOT CAST DEAL FORK
MERE PART RIFT SHED SLIP TEAR
ZONE BREAK CARVE CLASS CLEFT
DIVVY GAVEL JOINT SCALE SCIND
SEVER SHARE SHIFT SLICE SNACK
SPACE SPLIT SPRIT WHACK
BEPART BISECT BRANCH CANTLE
CANTON CLEAVE COTEAU
DEPART DEVISE DIFFER DOMIFY
INDENT PARCEL RAMIFY SECTOR
SEJOIN SLEAVE SUNDER ALIQUOT
ANALYZE ATOMIZE AVERAGE
BRITTEN COMPART DIFFUSE
DIREMPT DISCIDE DISPART
DISSECT DIVERGE FISSURE
FRITTER PARTAKE PRORATE
ALLOCATE CLASSIFY CROSSCUT
DISCRETE DISSEVER DISTRACT
DISUNITE FRACTION FRAGMENT
GRADUATE HEMISECT MEDISECT
SEPARATE STRATIFY UNSEEDER
(— BEEF) BLOCK
(— FILAMENTS) SLEAVE
(— INTO DISTRICTS) CANTON
(— INTO MEASURES) BAR
(— INTO PIECES) GOBBET
(— INTO 2 PARTS) HALVE BISECT
(— INTO 4 PARTS) QUARTER
(— LAND) STINT
(— NATURALLY) FALL
(— SMALL) SCANTLE
DIVIDED ENTE REFT SIDE CLEFT
FORKY SPLIT ATOMIC CLOVEN
PRONGY FISSATE FOURCHE
GYRONNY PARTITE SEPTATE
AEROLATE CAMERATE DIVIDUAL
FOURCHEE
(— IN TWO) FOURCHE DIMIDIATE
(— INTO 4 PARTS) PALY
QUARTERED
(— TWICE) RETAILLE
(NOT —) GLOBAL
(PREF.) CHORI(ST)(STO) FISSI
PARTI PARTY SCHIZ(O)
(SUFF.) FID FIDATE SECT SECTED
TOMOUS
DIVIDEND BONUS SHARE
DIVIDER BUNTON MERIST SHARER
BUNTING COMPASS SEVERER
DIVIDANT
DIVI-DIVI LIBIDIBI
DIVINATION OMEN SORS SORT
AUGURY MANTIC SORTES
AUSPICE SCRYING SORCERY
GEOMANCY TAGHAIRM
(— SCIENCE) MANTIC

(PREF.) MANTO
(SUFF.) MANCER MANCY MANTIC
DIVINE HOLY SORT SPAE TWIG
AREAD AREED ATMAN AUGUR
DIVUS GUESS PIOUS DEIFIC
DETECT DEVISE GODFUL HALSEN
PRIEST SACRED BLESSED
FORESEE GODLIKE PORTEND
PREDICT PRESAGE ARIOLATE
CONTRIVE FOREBODE FOREKNOW
FORETELL HEAVENLY IMMORTAL
MINISTER PERCEIVE UBIQUIST
SPIRITUAL
DIVINER SEER AUGUR SIBYL
ARUSPEX AUGURER PROPHET
HARUSPEX
DIVING BELL NAUTILUS
DIVING BOARD RISE
DIVING SUIT GANGAVA
DIVINING ROD TWIG DOWSER
DIVINITY (ALSO SEE GOD AND
GODDESS) JOSS LLEU LLEW TIEN
AHURA DEITY HYBLA NUADA
NUADU NYMPH POWER ATHTAR
VEDUIS GLAUCUS GODDESS
GODHEAD GODSHIP HYBLAEA
TARANIS VIRBIUS TEUTATES
VEDIOVIS
(— CIRCUIT BINDING) YAPP
(PL.) CABIRI ELOHIM
DIVISIBLE SECABLE DIVIDUAL
PARTIBLE
(— BY 2) AIM
DIVISION BAY BOX CUT DAG FIT
JAG LEG CHAP CLAN DOLE FARM
FAUN FORK GELD GELT GORE
HOLD LITH NEAT PACE PANE
PART RANK RAPE RIFT CAPUT
CHASM CLASS CLEFT CURIA
DIGOR DIVVY DULAN DULAT
FIELD FIGHT GENOS GRANT
GROUP IJORE MURUT PERES
REALM SHARD SHARE SUBAH
TAXIS THEME TOMAN WHEEN
BARONY CANTON COHORT
DECADE DECURY DEGREE DIVIDE
EOGAEA HAWIYA IMAHAL JHURIA
PORTIO SCHISM SEASON SECTOR
SUNDER VOLOST ZILLAH
BREAKUP COMARCA CUSTODY
DIOCESE DUALISM ENOMOTY
FISSURE FURLONG HASHIYA
KINGDOM KITKSAN NATUARY
PARTAGE PARTING ROULADE
SECTION SEGMENT SUBRACE
ARPEGGIO CATEGORY CLEAVAGE
DECANATE DIERESIS DISTRICT
FASCICLE MEROTOMY PARGANNA
PRECINCT SCISSION SCISSURE
SHEDDING SQUADRON SUBCLASS
(— BETWEEN PIERS) BAY
(— BETWEEN STALLS) BAIL
(— FOR TAXATION) GELD
(— IN DENMARK) AMT
(— IN HUNGARY) COMITAT
(— IN MINING BED) CLEAVE
(— OF ANGELS) CHOIR
(— OF ARMY) BATTLE LOCHUS
(— OF BEJA) BISHARIN
(— OF BOOK) CHAPTER FASCICLE
(— OF BUILDING) STORY STOREY
(— OF CHARIOTEERS) FACTION
(— OF CHURCH) AISLE

(— OF CONTEST) HEAT INNING
(— OF COUNTY) RAPE BARONY
HUNDRED
(— OF CROPLAND) FLAT
(— OF DISCOURSE) HEADING
(— OF DRAMA) ACT SCENE
(— OF FAMILY) BRANCH
(— OF FIELD) RIG
(— OF FOOT) SEMEION
(— OF FOREST) WARD
(— OF GEOLOGICAL TIME) ERA
EPOCH PERIOD
(— OF GRASS) SPRIG
(— OF GREAT HORDE) DULAN
DULAT KANGLA KANGLI
(— OF HEADLINE) BANK DECK
(— OF HERALDIC SHIELD) POINT
(— OF ISLE OF MAN) SHEADING
(— OF KENT) LATHE
(— OF LAND) LAINE KONOHIKI
(— OF LEGION) COHORT HASTATI
MANIPLE TRIARII
(— OF LOG LINE) KNOT
(— OF MANCHU ARMY) BANNER
(— OF MANKIND) RACE
(— OF MEAL) COURSE
(— OF NIGHT) WATCH
(— OF ORANGE) LITH
(— OF POEM) FIT DUAN CANTO
STANZA STROPHE
(— OF PROCESS) STAGING
(— OF ROCKS) SYSTEM
(— OF ROSARY) DECADE CHAPLET
(— OF SOCIETY) CASTE ATOMISM
(— OF SONG) FIT
(— OF STOPE) FLOOR
(— OF STRUCTURE) STAGE
(— OF SUSSEX) RAPE
(— OF TREF) RANDIR
(— OF UTTERANCE) COLON
(— OF WINDOW) DAY
(— OF YORKSHIRE) RIDING
(— OF ZILLAH) PARGANA
(— OF ZODIAC) SIGN DECAN
(— OVER ISSUE) BREACH
(ADMINISTRATIVE —) FU LATHE
CHARGE CIRCLE COUNTY EYALET
CUSTODY DIOCESE TOWNSHIP
(ANTHROPOLOGICAL —) STOCK
(ARMY —) MORA
(ASTROLOGICAL —) FACE
(CELL —) MITOSIS AMITOSIS
(ECCLESIASTICAL —) SCHISM
SOCIETY PRECINCT
(GEOLOGICAL —) ERA LIAS MALM
BUNTER KEUPER LUDIAN SERIES
LARAMIE ARNUSIAN RICHMOND
(HINGED —) LEAF
(ISLE OF MAN —) SHEADING
(MUSICAL —) ALLEGRO
(NUCLEAR —) FISSION
(PHILIPPINE —) ATO
(POLICE —) TANA THANA
(POLITICAL —) ATO CITY LATHE
STATE COUNTY PARISH BOROUGH
HUNDRED SURPLUS DISTRICT
PURCHASE WAPENTAKE
(POPULATION —) STRATUM
(SOCIAL —) HORDE
(TRIBAL —) CLAN
(SUFF.) KINESIS
DIVITIACUS (BROTHER OF —)
DUMNORIX

DIVORCE GET GETT AHSAN HASAN
KHULA SEVER TALAK SUNDER
ASUNDER DISBAND DISMISS
MUBARAT UNMARRY DISSOLVE
DISUNION DISUNITE SEPARATE
DIVOT CLOD TURF
DIVULGE BARE CALL SHOW TELL
BLURT BREAK SPILL UTTER VOICE
BABBLE BEWRAY EVULGE IMPART
REVEAL SPREAD UNFOLD
PROPALE PUBLISH UNCOVER
DISCLOSE DISCOVER EVULGATE
PROCLAIM
DIZZINESS HILO SWIM DINUS
TIEGO MEGRIM VANITY MERLIGO
SCOTOMY VERTIGO SWIMMING
WILLNESS
DIZZY DUNT CRAZY FAINT GIDDY
LIGHT TOTTY WESTY WOOZY
FICKLE STUPID FOOLISH
SWIMMING UNSTEADY
DJIBOUTI (GULF OF —) TADJOURA
DNA (— SEGMENT) CISTRON
DO D ACT DIV FAY TRY BILK BURN
CHAR COME DEAL DOST MAKE
PASS SUIT AVAIL BITCH CHEAT
EXERT GUISE SERVE SHIFT TRICK
ANSWER COMMIT NOBBLE
RENDER ACHIEVE EXECUTE
PERFORM PRODUCE SATISFY
SUFFICE TRANSACT
(— AWAY WITH) BURK ABATE
BURKE FORDO BANISH FOREDO
ABOLISH AMOLISH CASHIER
CONSUME ABROGATE DEMOLISH
DISSOLVE IMBOLISH RETRENCH
(— BUSINESS) CHAFFER
(— CARELESSLY) SLIM
(— CASUAL WORK) GRASS
(— FOR) FIX GET JACK POOP SINK
FETCH NAPOO DIDDLE SCUPPER
(— IMPERFECTLY) HUDDLE
(— IN SLOVENLY WAY) SLUBBER
(— INJURY) BANE
(— NOT) DONT DINNA
(— PENANCE) SATISFY
(— PIECEWORK) DACKER
(— SMARTLY) LINK
(— THOROUGHLY) FLOOR
(— WITHOUT) LACK SPARE
FORBEAR DISPENSE
(— WRONG) ERR SIN MISCARRY
(— YE) DEE
DOABLE AGIBLE
DOBLON ISABELLA
DOBRA JO JOE OCTAVE
DOCENT TUTOR TEACHER
LECTURER
DOCILE CALM MEEK TALL TAME
TAWIE FACILE GENTLE DOCIOUS
DUCTILE DUTIFUL BIDDABLE
OBEDIENT TOWARDLY
DOCK BOB CUT PEN BANG CLIP
MOOR PIER QUAY RUMP SCUT
BASIN SHORE WHARF CAMBER
COFFER DOCKEN FIDDLE HAMBLE
MARINA SORREL STRUNT
BOBTAIL CURTAIL PARELLA
PARELLE SHORTEN CANAIGRE
PATIENCE SHIPSIDE
DOCKAGE BERTHAGE
DOCKMACKIE VIBURNUM
DOCKYARD ARSENAL

(— WORKMAN) MATEY
DOCTOR (ALSO SEE PHYSICIAN)
DOC COOK DOPE DOSE FAKE PILL
BRUJO HAKIM LEECH SUGAR
TREAT CROCUS DEACON EXTERN
HAIKUN HEALER INTERN MAULVI
POWWOW CROAKER KORADJI
TEACHER MEDICATE PHYSICIAN
MANIPULATE
(— OF CANON LAW) JCD
(— OF LAWS) JD
(— UP) COOK FAKE EYEWASH
(PLAY —) FIXER
(QUACK —) CROCUS
(WITCH —) BOCOR BOKOR GOOFER
GUFFER WIZARD WITCHMAN
**DOCTOR'S DILEMMA (AUTHOR OF
—)** SHAW
(CHARACTER IN —) LOUIS RALPH
CULLEN COLENSO DUBEDAT
PATRICK RIDGEON WALPOLE
JENNIFER BONINGTON
BLENKINSOP
DOCTRINAIRE ISMY
DOCTRINE ISM DOXY LEAR LORE
RULE CREDO CREED DOGMA
LIGHT MAXIM TABLE TENET
ZOISM AHIMSA BABISM BELIEF
DHARMA EGOISM EROTIC GOSPEL
HOLISM MALISM MONISM NOETIC
THEORY ACROAMA AMIDISM
ANIMISM ARTICLE ATAVISM
ATHEISM ATOMISM BAHAISM
DUALISM EGOTISM EVANGEL
KARAISM KRYPSIS MISHNAH
NEOLOGY NOETICS OPINION
PEELISM PRECEPT PROGRAM
REALISM SENSISM TRIKAYA
ACTIVISM AGATHISM ANALYTIC
ARIANISM ARYANISM BAJANISM
CHILIASM CYNICISM DARBYISM
DEVILISM DOCETISM DYNAMISM
ENERGISM FATALISM FINALISM
GOBINISM HEDONISM HYLOLOGY
IDENTISM IDEOLOGY ISLAMISM
MOLINISM NIHILISM PAJONISM
PAMNESIA PEJORISM POSITION
POSOLOGY PSYCHISM REGALISM
RHEMATIC SIDERISM SOLIDISM
SPHERICS TYPOLOGY UBIQUITY
VITALISM DITHEISM MECHANISM
MUTUALISM PANTHEISM
PESSIMISM PLURALISM
NATURALISM
(BAD —) CACODOXY
(BUDDHIST —) ANATTA ANATMAN
(CONTRARY —) HERESY
(ESOTERIC —) CABALA QABBALA
CABALISM
(EVIL —) MOLOCH
(PL.) ESOTERY SCOTISM
CREDENDA DONATISM LABADISM
SCRIBISM
(SUFF.) ISM LOGER LOGIA(N)
LOGIC(AL) LOGIST LOGUE LOGY
OLOGY
DOCUMENT DOC GET BILL BOND
BOOK CALL CHOP DEED FORM
GETT OLLA SEAL WRIT CHART
DEMIT DIMIT GRIEF LEASE PAPER
PROOF SCRIP SCRIT STIFF TARGE
TEACH TITLE BILLET BREVET
CADJAN CAJANG CEDULA

COCKET DOCKET PATENT
RAGMAN SCHOOL SCRIPT SOURCE
SURVEY TICKET VOLUME ARCHIVE
CONDUCT DIPLOMA ELOHIST
ESCRIPT EXHIBIT INQUEST
LICENSE MISSIVE PLACARD
PRECEPT WARRANT WAYBILL
WHEREAS WRITING CITATION
CONTRACT COVENANT
FURLOUGH INSTRUCT MORTGAGE
SCHEDULE SECURITY TRANSIRE
BORDEREAU
(CONDITIONAL —) SCRIP
(COPY OF —) VIDIMUS
(PL.) BUMF ARCHIVE ARCHIVES
PALAPALA
DODAVAH (SON OF —) ELIEZER
DODDER SCAD SCALD SHAKE
DODDLE DOTHER FIDEOS TOTTER
TREMBLE FLAXDROP HAIRWEED
HALEWEED HELLWEED
MULBERRY
DODDERING OLD ANILE INANE
INFIRM SENILE FOOLISH
DODDER LAUREL WOEVINE
MISTLETOE
DODDIE HUMLIE
DODECANESE (— ISLAND) KOS
SYME KASOS LEROS TELOS
KHALKE LIPSOS PATMOS NISYROS
KALYMNOS
DODGE RIG SHY BILK DUCK GAME
JINK JOUK LURK RUSE AVOID
CHEAT ELUDE EVADE FENCE
FUDGE GLOSS LURCH PARRY
PLANT SHIFT SHIRK SHUNT STALL
TRICK ESCAPE FIDDLE PALTER
RACKET WHEEZE DECEIVE
EVASION PROFFER ARTIFICE
CROTCHET GILENYIE MALINGER
SIDESTEP
DODGER FLIER FLYER SOGER
HAGGLER HANDBILL
(DRAFT —) BUSHWACK
DODGING JINK
DODO (SON OF —) ELEAZAR
ELHANAN
DOE DA ROE TEG FAUN HIND
NANNY ALMOND BISCUIT
(— IN 1ST YEAR) FAWN
(BLUE —) FLIER FLYER
DOER ACTOR AGENT MAKER
AUTHOR FACTOR FEASOR
WORKER FACIENT MANAGER
ATTORNEY EXECUTOR
(— OF ODD JOBS) JACK
(SUFF.) AST ATOR IST OR STER
STRESS
DOES S DOTH DUSE
(— NOT) DONT DISNA DOESNT
DOFF OFF DAFF VAIL AVALE
DOUSE DOWSE STRIP DIVEST
REMOVE UNDRESS
DOFFER DRUM DUFFER
DOFFING CAP
DOG CUR MUT PUG PUP YAP ALAN
ALCO CHOW DANE FAUS GOER
KIYI MONG MUTT PAWL STAG
TIKE TRAY TYKE ALAND ALANT
ARGOS BAWTY BEDOG BESET
BOUCH BOXER CALEB CANID
CORGI DERBY DODGE HOUND
HUSKY LIMER PELON POOCH

PUPPY RACHE RAKER RATCH
SILKY SLING SPITZ STALK WHELP
AFGHAN BANDOG BARBET
BARKER BASSET BAWTIE BEAGLE
BELTON BORZOI BOSTON
BOWWOW BRIARD BUFFER
CANINE COCKER COLLIE COONER
DANCER DETENT DRIVER ESKIMO
FINDER GUNDOG HEADER HEELER
HUNTER JOWLER KELPIE KENNET
MISSET POODLE RANGER RATTER
SALUKI SEIZER SETTER SHOUGH
SIRIUS SUSSEX TALBOT TOLLER
TOWSER VIZSLA YAPPER YAUPER
YELPER BASENJI BOARDER
BULLDOG CARRIER COURSER
CRAMPON CREEPER DOGGESS
DROPPER GRIFFON HARRIER
LURCHER MALTESE MASTIFF
MONGREL OWTCHAH POINTER
SCOTTIE SKIRTER SLEUGHI
SPANIEL SPORTER STARTER
TERRIER TUMBLER WHIPPET
YAPSTER ABERDEEN AIREDALE
ALEUTANT ALSATIAN CERBERUS
COACHDOG CYNHYENA
DEMIWOLF DOBERMAN
ELKHOUND FISSIPED FOXHOUND
KEESHOND LABRADOR LANDSEER
LONGTAIL MALEMUTE MALINOIS
PAPILLON PEKINESE SAMOYEDE
SEALYHAM SHEPHERD SIBERIAN
SPRINGER TURNSPIT VERMINER
WATCHDOG WATERRUG
PEKINGESE POMERANIAN
AFFENPINSCHER
(— OF INDIA) PARIAH
(— OF LATHE) DRIVER
(— TRAINED AS DECOY) TOLLER
(BELGIAN —) SCHIPPERKE
(BIRD —) BOLTER
(CHAINED —) BANDOG
(CHINESE —) SHIHTZU
(DECOY —) PIPER
(ESKIMO —) HUSKY SIWASH
(FARM —) KOMONDOR
(FEMALE —) GYP SLUT BITCH
DOGGESS
(FOXLIKE —) COLPEO
(GERMAN —) ROTTWEILER
(HOUSE —) WAP WAPP
(HUNGARIAN —) PULI KUVASZ
(HUNTING —) ALAN BRACH RACHE
RATCH ALAUND BASSET HUNTER
KENNET LUCERN RACCHE SALUKI
SEIZER SETTER SLOUGH COURSER
DROPPER HARRIER POINTER
STRIKER
(JAPANESE —) AKITA
(LAP —) MESSAN SHOUGH
(LARGE —) DANE TOWSER
MASTIFF KOMONDOR
(LIKE A —) CYNIC
(LONG-HAIRED —) ALCO SHOCK
(MONGREL —) CUR BRAKJE
DEMIWOLF
(NON-BARKING —) BASENJI
(PART OF —) PAD PAW TOE ARCH
BACK DOME HOCK KNEE LOIN
RUMP STOP CHEEK CHEST CREST
CROUP ELBOW FLEWS THIGH
CARPUS DEWLAP MUZZLE STIFLE
BRISKET CUSHION KNUCKLE

LEATHER OCCIPUT PASTERN
WITHERS FOREHEAD HEELKNOB
(PARTI-COLORED —) PIE PYE
(PET —) MINX LAPDOG MOPPET
(PUG —) MOPS
(PUNCH'S —) TOBY
(SHAGGY —) RUG OWTCHAH
(SHEEP —) CUR COLLIE KELPIE
BEARDIE MALINOIS SHEPHERD
(SMALL —) TOY FICE FIST DOGGY
FEIST LAIKA PIPER DOGGIE
AMERTOY SPANIEL PAPILLON
PEKINESE
(VICIOUS —) TAEPO
(WATCH —) CUR GARM GARMR
(WILD —) ADJAG DHOLE DINGO
GUARA JACKAL AGOUARA
CIMARRON
(YELPING —) WAPPET
(PL.) DOGGERY
(PREF.) CYN(O)
DOGBANE KENDIR KENDYR
ECHITES FLYTRAP ALSTONIA
MILKWEED OLEANDER
PERIWINKLE
DOGBOAT PIG
DOGCART GADDER TUMTUM
BOUNDER GADABOUT
DOG COLLAR TRASH
DOG DAYS CANICULE
DOG EAR LEATHER
DOG FENNEL HOGWEED
DOGFIGHT SCRAMBLE
DOGFISH DOG HOE HUSS TOPE
FLAKE HOUND HURSE MANGO
TOPER BOUNCE DAGGAR GALEID
MORGAY BONEDOG GABBACK
SPURDOG TRIAKID GRAYFISH
SEAHOUND
(PREF.) SCYLLIO SQUALI SQUALO
DOGGED DOUR SULLEN DOGGISH
DOGLIKE STUBBORN OBSTINATE
DOGGEREL NOMINY TRIVIA
DOGGREL SINGSONG
DOGGONE BLESSED DOWNGONE
DOGIE LEPPY STRAY
DOG KEEPER FEWTERER
DOGLIKE CYNIC CYNOID DOGGED
DOGMA CREED TENET DICTUM
DOCTRINE DOCUMENT
DOGMATIC THETIC PONTIFIC
POSITIVE ARBITRARY CONFIDENT
PONTIFICAL
DOGMATISM BOWWOW
DOGMATIST BIGOT PHILODOX
DOG POUND GREENYARD
DOG ROSE BUCKY CANKER
BEDEGUAR DOGBERRY
DOG SALMON CHUM KETA
MORGAY DOGFISH
DOGSHORE DOG DAGGER
DOG'S MERCURY SAPWORT
DOG SNAPPER JOCU
DOGSTAIL BENT
DOGWOOD OSIER SUMAC CORNEL
CORNUS GAITER WIDBIN
BARBASCO FISHWOOD
DOILY MAT TIDE TIDY NAPKIN
DOING ACT DEED FACT STIR EVENT
ACTION FUNCTION PRACTIVE
(PL.) FARE GEAR
(SUFF.) ANT ENT PRACTIC PRAXIA
PRAXIS

DOIT DODKIN
DOLE LOT ALMS DEAL DOOL GIFT
GOAL METE PART VAIL ALLOT
FRAUD GRIEF GUILE MOURN
POGEY SHARE DECEIT GRIEVE
RELIEF SORROW CHARITY
DEALING DESTINY HANDOUT
PAYMENT PORTION BOUNDARY
DIMENSUM DISPENSE DIVISION
GRATUITY LANDMARK PITTANCE
DOLEFUL SAD DOWY DOWIE
DREAR HEAVY DISMAL DOOLFU
DREARY FUNEST RUEFUL FLEBILE
DOLESOME DOLOROUS FUNESTAL
MOURNFUL TRAGICAL
DOLERITE DIABASE
DOLL TOY BABE BABY MOLL ARRAY
DOLLY DOLLIE KEWPIE MAIDEN
MAUMET MOPPET MUNECA
POPPET POUPEE PUPPET
KACHINA KATCINA KATCHINA
MISTRESS
(— UP) SWANK
(PASTEBOARD —) PANTINE
(PREF.) PUPI
DOLLAR BALL BEAN BONE BUCK
CASE DURO FISH ROCK SCAD
SKIN SPOT ADOBE BERRY DALER
EAGLE PLONK PLUNK WHEEL
GOURDE PATACA DAALDER
SMACKER FROGSKIN PATACOON
SIMOLEON
(ONE MILLION —S) MEGABUCK
(SILVER —) SINKER
(SPANISH —) COB DURO COBBE
(THOUSAND —S) GEE THOU GRAND
DOLLARFISH SHINER MOONFISH
STARFISH
DOLL'S HOUSE (AUTHOR OF —)
IBSEN
(CHARACTER IN —) NORA RANK
HELMER LINDEN TORVALD
KROGSTAD CHRISTINA
DOLLY DRAB HOBBY PEGGY
PUNCH SWAGE MAIDEN
FOLLOWER MISTRESS SLATTERN
DOLLYMAN BUCKER
DOLLYWAY DOCK
DOLMEN SENAM TOLMEN
CROMMEL CROMLECH MEGALITH
DOLOMITE ANKERITE PEARLSPAR
DOLOR CALOR GRIEF SORROW
ANGUISH SADNESS DISTRESS
MOURNING
DOLOROUS SAD DISMAL DOLEFUL
GRIEVOUS PATHETIC
DOLPHIN INIA SUSU BOUTO
WHALE DORADO KILLER PALACH
TURSIO BOLLARD COWFISH
PELLOCK PULLOCK SNUFFER
CETACEAN MAHIMAHI MUTILATE
PORPOISE
(PREF.) DELPHIN DELPHO
(SUFF.) DELPHIS
DOLPHIN STRIKER MARTINGALE
DOLT ASS OAF PUT ASSE CALF
CHUB CLOD COOF DULT FOOL
GOFF MOKE PEAK POOP STUB
BOOBY CHUMP CLUNK DOBBY
DUMMY DUNCE FUNGE GOLEM
IDIOT NUMPS PATCH THICK
BEFOOL CUDDEN DOODLE DULTIE
HOBBIL OXHEAD BLUNTIE

DAWCOCK DULLARD JACKASS
SAPHEAD SCHNOOK BONEHEAD
BOSTHOON CLODPATE CLODPOLL
DUMBBELL IMBECILE LUNKHEAD
MACAROON MOONCALF
NUMSKULL LAMEBRAIN
DOLTISH DULL STUPID FOOLISH
PEAKISH SOTTISH TOMFOOL
BESOTTED BLOCKISH DOLTLIKE
DOMAIN LAND BOUND BOURN
REALM SCOPE STATE WORLD
BARONY BOURNE COUNTY
DEMAIN EMPERY EMPIRE ESTATE
SPHERE DEMESNE EARLDOM
BIRTHDOM DOMINION LORDSHIP
PROVINCE SEIGNORY STAROSTY
(— OF SULTAN) SOLDAN
(— OF THE UNCONSCIOUS)
SHADOWLAND
(MATHEMATICAL —) FIELD
(NETHER —) HELL
(TRANSCENDENT —) HEAVEN
(WOMAN'S —) DISTAFF
DOMBEYA ASSONIA
DOMBEY AND SON (AUTHOR OF —)
DICKENS
(CHARACTER IN —) GAY PAUL
EDITH CARKER CUTTLE DOMBEY
WALTER GRANGER FLORENCE
DOME CAP CIMA TYPE CROWN
VAULT COCKLE CUPOLA THOLOS
CALOTTE EDIFICE CIMBORIO
HEMIDOME
(— OVER TOMB) WELI
(BUDDHIST —) TOPE
(OBSERVATION —) BLISTER
(ROUND —) THOLUS
(SNOW-CAPPED —) CALOTTE
DOMER CLASPER
DOMESTIC HIND HOME MAID
MOZO DOMAL TABBY FAMILY
HAMEIL HAMLET HEYDUC
HOMELY HOMISH HOUSAL
INLAND INMATE INWARD MENIAL
NATIVE FAMELIC HEYDUCK
ONSHORE SCALDER SERVANT
FAMILIAR HOMEBRED HOMEMADE
INTIMATE
(PL.) FOLK
DOMESTICALLY ONSHORE
DOMESTICATE TAME ENTAME
AMENAGE RECLAIM CIVILIZE
DOMESTICATED CADE TAME
GENTLE INWARD DOMESTIC
FAMILIAR
DOMICILE CRIB HOME SHED
ABODE HOUSE MENAGE
DWELLING RESIDENCE
DOMINANCE SWAY INFLUENCE
DOMINANT BOSSY CHIEF FIFTH
TENOR MASTER RULING SOVRAN
CENTRAL REGNANT SUPREME
DOMINULE SUPERIOR
PARAMOUNT OVERBEARING
PREPONDERANT
DOMINATE TOP HAVE RULE
CHARM REIGN COERCE DIRECT
GOVERN VASSAL BEWITCH
COMMAND CONTROL ENVELOP
POSSESS BESTRIDE DOMINEER
OVERRIDE OVERSWAY OVERTONE
DOMINATING SUPERIOR
BREATHLESS

DOMINATION EMPIRE CONTROL STRINGS BOVARISM BOVARYSM DOMINION POSSESSION
DOMINEER BOSS BRAG LORD RULE BULLY FEAST REVEL TOWER COMPEL COMMAND SWAGGER DOMINATE OVERBEAR OVERLEAD OVERLORD
(— OVER) RIDE HECTOR
DOMINEERING SURLY LORDLY HAUGHTY ARROGANT DESPOTIC MASTERLY MASTERFUL
DOMINICA (CAPITAL OF —) ROSEAU
(MOUNTAIN PEAK IN —) MORNEDIABLOTIN
DOMINICAN JACOBIN JACOBITE PREACHER PREDICANT

DOMINICAN REPUBLIC
BAY: OCOA YUMA NEIBA RINCON SAMANA ISABELA CALDERAS ESCOCESA
CAPE: BEATA FALSO CABRON ENGANO CAUCEDO ISABELA MACORIS
CAPITAL: SANTODOMINGO
COIN: ORO PESO
INDIAN: TAINO
ISLAND: BEATA SAONA ALTOVELO CATALINA HISPANIOLA
LOWLAND: CIBAO
MEASURE: ONA TAREA FANEGA
MOUNTAIN: TINA GALLO DUARTE
MOUNTAINS: NEIBA BAHORUCO ORIENTAL
RIVER: YUNA OZAMA
TOWN: AZUA BANI MOCA PENA POLO BONAO COTUI NAGUA NEIBA NIZAO SOSUA HIGUEY OVIEDO SANCHEZ BARAHONA SANTIAGO
VALLEY: REAL NEYBA

DOMINIE MASTER PASTOR
DOMINION RULE SWAY CROWN REALM REIGN DITION DOMAIN EMPERY EMPIRE REGNUM CONTROL DIOCESE DYNASTY KHANATE MASTERY POUSTIE REGENCY CALIFATE IMPERIUM LORDSHIP SEIGNORY SIGNORIA SOVRANTY OBEDIENCE
(PL.) DUCHY
DOMINO DIE BONE CARD FIVE MASK TILE BLANK JETON STONE DOUBLE JETTON MATADOR VENETIAN
(FIRST — PLAYED) SET
(PL.) MATADOR MUGGINS BONEYARD
DOMINO NOIR, LE (COMPOSER OF —) AUBER
DOMITILLA (DAUGHTER OF —) DOMITILLA
(HUSBAND OF —) VESPASIAN
(SON OF —) TITUS DOMITIAN
DOM PEDRO SNOOZER
DON WEAR ARRAY DRESS ENDUE INDUE THROW ASSUME CLOTHE INVEST ADDRESS NOBLEMAN
DONALBAIN (FATHER OF —) DUNCAN

DONATE GIE GIFT GIVE BESTOW PRESENT
DONATION GIFT GRANT DONATIO PRESENT DONATIVE BENEFACTION
(—S RECEIVED BY SINGERS) CARL
DON CARLOS (CHARACTER IN —) EBOLI CARLOS PHILIP VALOIS CHARLES RODRIGO ELISABETH
(COMPOSER OF —) VERDI
DONE GAR DEEN OVER BAKED ENDED GIVEN COOKED THROUGH FINISHED
(— BY WORD OF MOUTH) PAROL PAROLE
(— CARELESSLY) SCAMBLING
(— FOR) GONE SUNK KAPUT KAPUTT FINISHED
(— IN FAITH) AF
(— IN PLAIN SIGHT) BRAZEN
(— POORLY) BOTCHY
(— TOGETHER) CONCERTED
(— WITH) BY
(— WITHOUT DELIBERATION) SNAP
(— WRONG WAY) AWK
(TO BE —) PASS
DONEE DONATOR HERITOR RECEIVER
DON GIOVANNI (CHARACTER IN —) ANNA ELVIRA MASETTO OTTAVIO ZERLINA GIOVANNI LEPORELLO
(COMPOSER OF —) MOZART
DONJON KEEP ROCCA DUNGEON
DONKEY ASS BUSS DONK FUSS MOKE BURRO CHUMP CUDDY DICKY EQUID GENET GUDDA HINNY HORSE JENNY NEDDY BRAYER CUDDLE DICKEY JENNET ONAGER ASINEGO BUSSOCK FUSSOCK JACKASS LONGEAR CARDOPHAGUS
DONKEY ENGINE DOCTOR DONKEY ROADER YARDER DOLLBEER
DONNA DEL LAGO (CHARACTER IN —) ELENA DOUGLAS GIACOMO MALCOLM RODERICK
(COMPOSER OF —) ROSSINI
DONNA DIANA (COMPOSER OF —) REZNICEK
DONOR GIVER DONATOR
DO-NOTHING DONNOT DONOUGHT FAINEANT
DON PASQUALE (CHARACTER IN —) NORINA ERNESTO PASQUALE SOFRONIA MALATESTA
(COMPOSER OF —) DONIZETTI
DON QUIXOTE (AUTHOR OF —) CERVANTES
(CHARACTER IN —) PANZA PEDRO PEREZ ALONZO DAPPLE SAMSON SANCHO TOBOSO GUINART QUIXOTE CARRASCO DULCINEA NICHOLAS ROSINANTE
DONUM GIVER DEUNAM
DOODAD DODAD DOODAB DOFUNNY GIMCRACK JIMCRACK
DOOM KER LAW LOT DAMN FATE RUIN CURSE DEATH JUDGE ADDEEM DECREE DEVOTE STEVEN CONDEMN DESTINE DESTINY FORTUNE STATUTE DECISION FOREDOOM SENTENCE

DOOMED FEY DEAD DONE LORN FATAL DAMNED FORLORN ACCURSED FINISHED
DOOM PALM DOUM
DOOMSMAN LAWMAN
DOOR LID DROP EXIT FOLD GATE HECK SHUT TRAP ENTRY HATCH JANUA VALVE DAMPER JIGGER PORTAL RADDLE WICKET BARRIER DOORWAY INGRESS OPENING OUTDOOR PASSAGE POSTERN ANTEPORT ENTRANCE FOREDOOR POSTICUM SERVIDOR STOPPING TRAVERSE VOMITORY
(— IN MINE) STOPPING
(— OF ASH PIT) ARCH
(— OF MASONIC LODGE) TILE
(AIRPLANE —) CLAMSHELL
(HALF —) HECK HATCH
(PART OF —) RAIL SILL STILE LINTEL MULLION
(ROMAN —S) FORES
(SLIDING —) SHUT SHOJI FUSUMA TRAVERSE
(STORM —) DINGLE
(STRONG —) OAK
(TRAP —) SLOT SCRUTO VAMPIRE VAMPYRE
(PREF.) THYRE(O) THYRO
(SUFF.) THYRIS
DOORFRAME BUCK
DOORHEAD DERNER
DOORKEEPER TILER TILIA USHER DURWAN PORTER WARDEN DOORMAN JANITOR OSTIARY DOORWARD HUISSIER JANITRIX PORTRESS WISKINKY
DOOR KNOCKER HAMMER RAPPER
DOOR LATCH SNECK HAGGADAY
DOORMAN FOOTMAN HALLMAN DOORWARD
DOORMAT COCOMAT
DOORPOST DURN JAMB PIER POST ALETTE POSTEL
DOORSILL SOIL
DOORSTOP BUMPER HOLDBACK
DOORWAY DOOR EXIT PORTAL OPENING
DOOZER LULU SNORTER HUMDINGER
DOOZY LULU HUMDINGER
DOPATTA UPARNA DOOPUTTY
DOPE HOP LUG BOOB DRUG GOFF GOON GOOP INFO BOOBY OPIUM PASTE STUPE HEROIN INSIDE OPIATE LOWDOWN PREDICT STUPEFY NARCOTIC
DOPED CRONK
DOPER GREASER
DOR BEE DAW JOKE MOCK BONGO CLOCK DORRE JOKER SCOFF TRICK BEETLE DRONER BUFFOON DECEIVE MOCKERY
DORADO CUIR XIPHIAS GOLDFISH
DORALICE (HUSBAND OF —) PHODOPHIL MANDRICARDO
(LOVER OF —) RODOMONT
DORBEETLE DOR CLOCK DRONER BUZZARD BUMCLOCK
DORIGEN (HUSBAND OF —) ARVIRAGUS
(LOVER OF —) AURELIUS

DORIMENE (HUSBAND OF —) SGANARELLE
(LOVER OF —) DORANTE
DORINDA (HUSBAND OF —) AIMWELL
(SISTER OF —) MIRANDA
DORIS (BROTHER AND HUSBAND OF —) NEREUS
(FATHER OF —) OCEANUS
(MOTHER OF —) TETHYS
DORMANCY TORPOR ABEYANCE
DORMANT FIXED INERT ASLEEP LATENT TORPID RESTING SLEEPER INACTIVE LATITANT SLEEPING CONNIVENT
DORMER WINDOW LUCOMB MEMBER DORMANT EYEBROW LUCARNE LUTHERN
DORMITORY DORM HALL HOUSE DORMER DORTER HOSTEL BULLPEN COLLEGE DORTOUR CUBATORY QUARTERS
DORMOUSE LOIR DRYAD LEROT GLIRID SLEEPER
(PREF.) GLIRI
DORNICK DONEY LINEN DARNEX DONACK DONNICK
DORPER DORSIAN
DORSAL NOTAL DORSER DOSSER NEURAL TERGAL ABAXIAL HANGING SUPERIOR POSTERIOR
(PREF.) OPISTH(O)
DORSUM BACK
DORUS (BROTHER OF —) LAODOCUS POLYPOETES
(FATHER OF —) APOLLO HELLEN XUTHUS
(MOTHER OF —) CREUSA ORSEIS PHTHIA
(SLAYER OF —) AETOLUS
DOSAGE (SCIENCE OF —) POSOLOGY
DOSE BOLE DOST SHOT BROMO DATIO DOSIS DRAFT STORE TREAT DATION DOCTOR DOSAGE DRENCH POTION BOOSTER BROMIDE CAPSULE DRAUGHT QUANTITY
(NARCOTIC —) LOCUS BINDLE LOCUST
DOSS BOW DOS KNOT TUFT BUNCH
DOSSERET PULVINO
DOT SET CLOT DOTE LUMP MOTE PECK SPOT STAR TICK COVER DOWER DOWRY POINT PRICK PUNTO SPECK BULLET CENTER CENTRE DOTLET PERIOD STIGME TITTLE TOCHER PUNCTUM PUNCTUS SPECKLE SPOTTLE STIPPLE FLYSPECK PARTICLE SPRINKLE
(— IN CODE) DIT
(— ON FOREHEAD) BOTTU
(— ON PATCH OF DIFFERENT COLOR) ISLET
(BLACK —) DARTROSE
(PL.) LEADERS
DOTAGE DOTE FOLLY DRIVEL SENILITY TWICHILD
DOTARD DOBBY DOTER SILLY DOBBIE DOTANT SENILE DOTTREL DOTTEREL IMBECILE LIRIPIPE LIRIPOOP

DOTCHIN STEELYARD
DOTE ROT DOVE DOZE FOND LIKE LOVE TIRE ADORE DECAY ENDOW BESTOW DOTAGE DOTARD DRIVEL STUPOR IMBECILE
DOTING FON FOND GAGA DOTAGE PAWING
DOTTED SEME CRIBLE SEMEED TICKED TOUCHY SPOTTED PUNCTATE SPECKLED STIPPLED STELLATED
(— SWISS) LAPPET
DOTTER SPOTTER
DOTTEREL DUPE GULL WIND PLOVER DOTTREL MORINEL
DOTTY TOTY CRAZY TOTTY FEEBLE SPOTTY
DOUBLE KA BOW PLY DUAL FOLD SORE TWIN CRACK DUPLE FETCH ROUND SOSIE BIFOLD BINARY BINATE DOPPIO DUPLEX MIDDLE DIPLOID DOUBLET TWOFOLD BIVALENT GEMINATE BIFARIOUS SIMILITUDE
(— IMPRESSION) MACKLE
(— IN POKER) STRADDLE
(— MUSICAL NOTES) AUGMENT
(— UP) BUCK JACKKNIFE
(PHANTOM —) FETCH
(PREF.) BI BIN(I)(O) DI(S) DIPHY DIPL(O) DISS(O) DITTO GEMINI
DOUBLE BASSOON FAGOTTONE
DOUBLE CHIN CHOLLER
DOUBLECROSS BITCH CHEAT BETRAY DECEIVE SWINDLE BUSINESS
DOUBLE-CROSSER RAT HEEL
DOUBLED GEMEL GEMINOUS
(PREF.) BIS
DOUBLE DAGGER DIESIS
DOUBLE-DEALING DECEIT DUPLICITY
DOUBLE FLUTE DIAULOS
DOUBLENESS DUALITY PLENITUDE
DOUBLE-RIPPER BOBSLED BOBSLEIGH
DOUBLE-RUNNER SKATE
DOUBLET SNIFF DOUBLE DUPLET PALTOCK PLACCATE POURPOINT
DOUBLE-TALK NEWSPEAK RAZZMATAZZ
DOUBLETREE EVENER SPREADER
DOUBLING LAP FOLD HEAD LOOP
(— OF THE BLIND) STRADDLE
DOUBLOON ONZA
DOUBLY
(PREF.) BI
DOUBT FEAR WEIR DEMUR DREAD DWERE QUERY WAVER BALANCE DIFFIDE DUBIETY SCRUPLE SKEPSIS SUSPECT SWITHER UMBRAGE DISTRUST DUBITATE HESITATE MISTRUST QUESTION STAGGERS MISLIPPEN
DOUBTER CYNIC SKEPTIC DUBITANTE
DOUBTFUL JUBUS DOUBTY UNSURE DUBIOUS FEARFUL JEALOUS PERHAPS WILSOME BOGGLISH DREADFUL JUBEROUS PERILOUS WAVERING QUESTIONABLE PROBLEMATICAL
DOUBTING DUBIOUS DUBITANT

DOUBTLESS WITTERLY
DOUCEUR BONUS POURBOIRE
DOUCHE RINSE EYEWASH
DOUGH CASH DUFF MASA CRUST DAIGH MONEY PASTE PUPPY CHANGE HALLAH NOODLE SPONGE BRIOCHE MANDLEN TEIGLACH
(BISCUIT —) CAKE
(BREAD —) SPONGE
(FERMENTING —) LEAVEN
(FRIED —) SPUD
(NOODLE —) FARFEL FERFEL
DOUGHNUT NUT SINK DONUT CYMBAL SINKER CRULLER FATCAKE NUTCAKE OLYCOOK OLYKOEK SIMBALL TWISTER BISMARCK FASNACHT
(SHAPED LIKE —) TOROIDAL
DOUGHTY FELL PREU TALL BRAVE VALIANT INTREPID
DOUGHY SAD DUNCH SODDEN
DOUR DERN GLUM GRIM HARD SOUR ROUGH STERN GLOOMY MOROSE SEVERE STRONG SULLEN OMINOUS TACITURN
DOUSE BEAT BLOW DOFF DUCK QUIT STOW CEASE DOWSE RINSE SOUSE DRENCH PLUNGE SLUICE STRIKE STROKE IMMERSE DOWNPOUR
DOUZEPER ANSEIS PALADIN
DOVE DOO DOW DOZE KUKU JONAH CULVER CUSHAT JEMIMA PIGEON COLUMBA DOVELET LAUGHER NAMAQUA SLUMBER DOVELING RINGDOVE
(— SOUND) CURR
(GROUND —) ROLA
(RING —) TOOZOO
(ROCK —) SOD
(SCALE —) INCA
DOVECOTE DOOCOT LOUVER DOVECOT DOWCOTE PIGEONRY COLUMBARY
DOVEKIE AUK ALLE BULL ROTCH ROTGE DOVEKEY BULLBIRD DOVELIKE
DOVETAIL COG JAG JAGG MESH MERGE TENON
DOWDINESS FRUMPERY
DOWDY POKY FRUMP MOPSY POKEY TACKY BLOWZY SHABBY STODGY UNTIDY FRUMPISH SLOVENLY
DOWEL NOG PEG PIN COAK STUD SPRIG JOGGLE PINTLE DULEDGE
DOWER DOS DOWRY ENDOW TOCHER DOARIUM PORTION HERITAGE MARITAGE
DOWITCHER SNIPE DRIVER SLEEPER GRAYBACK GREYBACK LONGBEAK
DOWN HUP OFF BETE CAST DOON DOWL FELL FLIX FLUE FUZZ HILL LINT MOXA PILE SOUR ADOWN BELOW DOWLE EIDER FLOOR FLUFF BEDOWN FRIEZE LANUGO PAPPUS HANDOUT HILLOCK PLUMAGE DOWNLAND
(— AND OUT) QUISBY
(— AT THE HEEL) SLIPSHOD

(— THAT WAY) DOWNBY DOWNBYE
(— THE LINE) ALONG
(FAR —) DEEP DEEPLY
(FARTHEST —) BOTTOMMOST
(STRAIGHT —) DOWNRIGHT
(PREF.) CAT(A)(O) CATH DE HYPO KAT(A) LACHN(O) OB PTIL(O) SUB
DOWNBEAT THESIS
DOWNCAST BAD SAD DOWN ABJECT GLOOMY HANGING DEJECTED HOPELESS
DOWNFALL PIT FALL FATE RUIN TRAP ABYSS DECAY FINISH DESCENT ECLIPSE UNDOING COLLAPSE DOWNCOME
(AUTHOR OF —) ZOLA
(CHARACTER IN —) JEAN WEISS HONORE GOLIATH GUNTHER MAURICE SILVINE FOUCHARD MACQUART HENRIETTE LEVASSEUR DELAHERCHE GARTLAUBEN
DOWNFEED OVERHEAD
DOWNFLOW VAIL DEFLUX
DOWNFOLD SADDLE DOWNWARP
DOWNHILL DOWNDALE
(SKI —) WEDEL
DOWNPOUR POUR RAIN BRASH DOUSE DOWSE FLOOD PLASH SPILL SPOUT DELUGE TORRENT CATARACT AVALANCHE
DOWNRIGHT FAIR FLAT PURE RANK BLANK BLUNT PLAIN PLUMB PLUMP ROUND SHEER STARK ARRANT DIRECT FAIRLY STURDY REGULAR ABSOLUTE EVENDOWN POSITIVE THOROUGH
DOWNSPOUT SPOUT DOWNPIPE DOWNTAKE
DOWNSTAIRS BELOW
DOWNSTROKE DOWNBEAT
DOWNSWING DOLDRUMS
DOWNWARD ADOWN BELOW LOWER PRONE DEORSUM DOWNWITH
(— ON ONE SIDE) SIDEWAYS
(PREF.) BATH(O)(Y) CAT(A)(O) CATH
DOWNWIND LEEWARD
DOWNY SOFT FLUEY MOSSY NAPPY PILAR PLUMY QUIET CALLOW FLEDGY FLOSSY FLUFFY PILARY PLACID COTTONY CUNNING KNOWING SOOTHING
(PREF.) HEBE
DOWRY DOS DOT GIFT DOWER SULKA DOWAGE LOBOLA LOBOLO TALENT PORTION
DOWSE WITCH
DOXOLOGIZE LAUD
DOXOLOGY GLORIA KADDISH
DOXY WENCH HARLOT
DOYEN DEAN DOYENNE
DOZE NAP NOD ROT DARE DORM DOTE DOVE DECAY DOVER SLEEP SLOOM CATNAP DROWSE MUDDLE SNOOZE MEMENTO PERPLEX SLUMBER SNOOZLE STUPEFY
DOZEN DIZZEN DOSAIN
(FIVE —) TALLY
(TWO —) THRAVE

DOZING DOGSLEEP
DRAB BOX DAW FOX SAD DELL DRUG DULL BESOM BLEAK DINGY DOLLY GRAVE GRAZE HEAVY TRULL WENCH WHORE FRUMPY ISABEL MALKIN POISON PUSSEL STODGY PROSAIC PUCELLE SUBFUSC DOLLYMOP EVERYDAY POMPLESS
(CHAETURA —) BEAR
DRABBLE DRAGGLE
DRACHM DRAM
DRACO ANGUIS DRAGON
DRAFT NIP SIP CHIT DOSE DRAG DRAM DRAW GLUT GULF GUST ITEM LEVY PLAN PLOT SUCK SWIG TOOT WORK BLAST CHECK DRINK EPURE SLOCK SWILL SWIPE TAPER WRITE DESIGN DRENCH GODOWN MINUTE POTION PROJET REDACT RETURN SCHEME SCROLL SKETCH WAUCHT WAUGHT ABBOZZO DRAUGHT DRAWING OUTLINE PATTERN PHILTER PROJECT BEVERAGE POTATION PROTOCOL
(— OF A VESSEL) GAGE GAUGE
(— OF AIR) COOKE
(— OF COMPOSITION) SCORE
(— OF LAW) BILL
(— OF PATTERN) STRIP
(— OFF) SHED
(HEAVY —) WHITTER
(LARGE —) SCOUR CAROUSE
(MIDDAY —) NOONING
(ORIGINAL —) PROTOCOL
(ROUGH —) EBAUCHE BROUILLON SCANTLING
(SLEEPING —) DORTER
(SMALL —) NIP SIP SUCK TIFF TIFT
DRAFTER HORSER
DRAFTSMAN DRAWER TRACER TIPPLER
DRAG DOG LAG DRUG HALE HONE HOOK KITE RASH SHOE SKID SLUR TOLE TOLL TUMP CREEP DEVIL DRAWL DRIFT FLOAT LURRY NOWEL PLUCK RALLY SLIDE SNAKE SWEEP TEASE TRAIL TRAIN TRAWL TRICE DAGGLE DROGUE LINGER REMORA SCHOOL TAIGLE TRAYNE DRAGBAR DRAGGLE GRAPNEL GRAPPLE SCHLEPP SKIDPAN ARRASTRA DRAGSHOE
(— ALONG) LUG CRAWL SHOOL TRAYNE TRACHLE TRAUCHLE
(— CARELESSLY) HIKE
(— DOWN) DEGRADE
(— FEET) SLODGE
(— FORCIBLY) SNAKE
(— HOME CARCASS OF GAME) TUMP
(— IN DEEP WATER) CREEP
(— JERKILY) SNIG
(— LOGS) SKID
(— OFF) HARRY
(— OUT) DRAWL
(PLANK —) RUBBER
DRAGGING LEADEN
(— DEAD BULL FROM RING) ARRASTRE
DRAGGLE LAG DRAIL DAGGLE

DRABBLE TRACHLE
DRAGNET FLUE TRAIN TRAWL
DRAWNET TRAINEL
DRAGON AHI LUNG WORM DRAKE
RAHAB NIDHOG VRITRA WYVERN
BASILISK DRAGONET NIDHOGGR
NITHHOGG
(— WITH 7 HEADS) HYDRA
(SEA —) QUAVIVER
(WINGLESS —) LINDWORM
(PREF.) DRACO(NT)(NTO)
DRAGONET FOX ILLECK FOXFISH
GOWDNIE GURNARD JUGULAR
SCULPIN LORICATE QUAVIVER
DRAGONFLY NAIAD ODONATE
SKIMMER LIBELLULA
DRAGON TREE DRACAENA
DRAGROPE DRAG GUSS
DRAGSTER FUELER SLINGSHOT
DRAIN DRY FRY GAN GAW SAP
SEW TOP BUZZ COUP DAIL DALE
DELF DIKE DRAG DRAW GOUT
GRIP GURT LADE LODE MILK SIKE
SINK SOAK SUFF SUMP TEEM TILE
BLEED BUNNY CANAL DELFT
DRAFT DREEN DRILL DROVE
EMPTY FLEET GROOP GULLY
LEECH RHINE SEUCH SEUGH
SEWER SHORE SIVER STANK
STELL EMULGE FILTER FURROW
GUZZLE RIGGOT SHEUCH SHEUGH
SIPHON SPONGE SWOUGH
SYPHON TRENCH TROGUE
TROUGH ZANJON ACEQUIA
ALBERCA CAROUSE CARRIER
CHANNEL CULVERT DEPLETE
DRAUGHT EXHAUST GRINDLE
GRIPPLE SCUPPER ZANJONA
CANALIZE CARRIAGE SINKHOLE
SUBDRAIN THURROCK
(— DRY) JIB
(— IN FEN) LEAM
(— IN MINE) SOUGH
(— IN STABLE) GROOP
(COVERED —) THURROCK
(OPEN —) SIVER STELL
(SMALL —) TRONE
DRAINAGE ADIT SAUR SOCK
SULLAGE SUMPAGE
DRAINAGEWAY DRAW
DRAINING SEEPAGE DRAINAGE
EMULGENT
DRAINPIPE SINK SHELL WHELM
LEADER QUELME
DRAKE STAG STAIG DRAKELET
DRAM GO NIP MITE SLUG TIFF TIFT
DRAFT DRINK SOPIE CALKER
CHASSE DRACHM JIGGER
CAULKER SNIFTER MERIDIAN
POTATION QUANTITY
(— OF LIQUOR) TOT SLUG SNIFTER
(— OF SPIRITS) NOBBLER
DRAMA RAS AUTO MIME PLAY
LEGIT OPERA COMEDY NATAKA
SCENES SOAPER TRAGIC ATELLAN
COMEDIA HISTORY PROVERB
THEATRE TRAGEDY DUODRAMA
MONODRAM OPERETTA
PASTORAL
(DANCE —) KATHAKALI
(JAPANESE —) NO KABUKI
(MUSICAL —) OPERA SAYNETE
OPERETTA

DRAMATIC WILD VIVID SCENIC
THESPIAN
(— REPRESENTATION) WAYANG
(HAVING LYRIC AND — QUALITIES)
SPINTO
DRAMATIST (ALSO SEE
PLAYWRIGHT) OG ACTOR
IBSENITE
DRAMSHOP GROGSHOP
DRAPE HANG PALL VEST ADORN
COVER CRAPE WEAVE CURTAIN
FESTOON HANGING VALANCE
DRAPED BEHUNG
DRAPER TAILOR LINENMAN
DRAPERY SWAG BAIZE DRAPE
SCENE CURTAIN REREDOS
VALANCE MOURNING
(— ON BEDSTEAD) PAND
(PIECE OF —) HANGING
DRAPING BLOUSE DRAPERY
DRASTIC DIRE HARSH EXTREME
RADICAL RIGOROUS
(NOT —) BLAND
DRAT RABBIT DOGGONE
DRATTED BLESSED
DRAUGHT (ALSO SEE DRAFT)
SLUG WAUGHT OENOMEL
DRAUPADI (FATHER OF —)
DRUPADA
DRAVIDIAN GOND KOTA TODA
TULU ARAVA COORG GONDI
KHOND KLING MALTO ORAON
TAMIL ANDHRA BADAGA BIRHOR
BRAHUI KODAGU KURUKH
TELEGU TELUGU COLLERY
DRAVIDA TAMILIC KANARESE
TAMILIAN
DRAW LUG TEE TIE TOW TUG
DRAG DUCT HALE HAUL LADE
LIMN LINE LURE PUFF PULL RAKE
SPAN TILL TIRE TOLL TREK VENT
CATCH DRAFT DRILL EDUCE
ENDUE EXACT HEAVE PAINT
SKINK TRACE TRAIN TRECK
ALLURE BUCKET DEDUCE DEPICT
DERIVE DESIGN DEVISE ELICIT
ENGAGE ENTICE INDUCE INHALE
SELECT SKETCH STRIKE ATTRACT
BEGUILE CONTOUR DETRACT
DOGFALL DRAUGHT EXTRACT
INSPIRE PORTRAY SCREEVE
SCUMBLE INSCRIBE INVEIGLE
OUTBRAID STANDOFF
(— A CARD) CUT
(— AIR) BREATHE
(— ALONG) TRACK TRAIN
(— APART) REAM DIVEL DIDUCE
DIVERGE
(— AT A PIPE) SHOOH SHAUGH
(— AWAY) ARACE DRAFT ABDUCT
ARACHE DRAUGHT ENTRAIN
ABSTRACT DISTRACT
(— AWKWARDLY) SCRAWL
(— BACK) FADE REVEL START
WINCE ARREAR RETIRE REVOKE
SHRINK CRINKLE RECLAIM
WITHTEE
(— BACK FROM) BLENCH FLINCH
RESILE TORFEL TORFLE DETRECT
(— BACK LIPS) GRIN
(— BOLT) SLOT
(— BY SUCTION) ASPIRATE
(— DEEP BREATH) SUSPIRE

(— DRINK) BIRL
(— EARTH AROUND) HILL
(— FIRST FURROW) FEER
(— FORTH) EDUCE EVOKE FETCH
ELICIT DEPROME EXHAUST
(— IN) PINK
(— OFF) BROACH
(— ON) INDUE INDUCE SOLICIT
(— OUT) MILK SLUB EXACT SKINK
TRACT ELICIT EXHALE EXTEND
(— TIGHT) FRAP THRAP STRAIN
(— TOGETHER) COWL LACE COART
GATHER CRIMPLE
(— UP) FORM MAKE HUCKLE
INKNIT UPWALE
DRAWBACK OUT LETDOWN
TAKEOFF DISCOUNT PULLBACK
DRAWBAR DRAGBAR BULLNOSE
DRAWLINK SLIPRAIL
DRAWBRIDGE PONTLEVIS
DRAWEE ACCEPTER
DRAWER TILL LIMNER LOCKER
TILLER ENTERER INTAKER
SHUTTLE
(— OF WATER) GIBEONITE
(COAL —) PUTTER
(TYPEWRITER —) BED
DRAWER-DOWN KNOBBLER
DRAWER-IN ENTERER HEALDER
HEDDLER
DRAWER-OFF RACKER
DRAWERS PANTS SHORTS LININGS
PANTIES SHALWAR CALSOUNS
CALZOONS SHINTYAN PANTELETS
SHULWAURS
DRAWGATE SLACKER
DRAWING DRAW CHALK DRAFT
ENVOI EPURE SEPIA TUSHE
CRAYON DESIGN DETAIL FIGURE
FUSAIN SKETCH CAMAIEU
CARTOON CROQUIS DIAGRAM
DRAUGHT HAULING ISOTYPE
PULLING RETRAIT TOUSCHE
ADDUCENT CHARCOAL CROSSING
DOODLING FREEHAND FROTTAGE
HATCHING LINEWORK SANGUINE
SLUBBING SPECULUM STICKMAN
TRACTION TRANSFER TRICKING
(— BACK) ABDUCENT
(— IN) INDRAFT
(— OF LOTS) BALLOT
(— OUT) BATTUE
(COMIC —) CARTOON DROLLERY
(PREHISTORIC —) PICTOGRAM
PICTOGRAPH
(SIDEWALK —) SCREEVE
(PREF.) GRAMO
(SUFF.) GRAM
DRAWING-IN DRAW ENTERING
DRAWKNIFE SHAVE JIGGER
DRAWL DRANT DRATE DRUNT
TRAIN LOITER PROLATE
DRAWN DRAFT STREIT DRAUGHT
GRAPHIC HAGGARD
(— APART) DISTRACT
(— AWAY) ABSTRACT
(— CLOSE) STRICT
(— OFF) DRAINED
(— OUT) DREE DREICH DREIGH
EXTENDED
DRAWPLATE AGATE FLATTER
DRAWSHEET TYMPAN
DRAWSTRING LATCH STRING

DRAY CART LORRY SCOOT SLOOP
WAGON CAMION JIGGER ROLLEY
RULLEY SLOVEN WHEERY
DREAD AWE DREE FEAR FRAY
FUNK WARD WERE ANGST
AWFUL DOUBT GRISE TIMOR
ADREAD AGRISE DISMAY ESCHEW
HORROR TERROR ANXIETY
DISMISS DRIDDER REDOUBT
AFFRIGHT DREDDOUR GASTNESS
MISDREAD TERRIBLE
(SUFF.) PHOBE PHOBIA(C) PHOBIC
PHOBOUS
DREADED AWESOME BEDREAD
DREADFUL DERN DIRE AWFUL
CRUEL DISMAL GRISLY HORRID
AWESOME CAREFUL DIREFUL
DRIDDER FEARFUL GHASTLY
GRIMFUL HIDEOUS UNCOUTH
DOUBTFUL DOUBTOUS GHASTFUL
HORRIBLE HORRIFIC PERILOUS
SCAREFUL SHOCKING TERRIBLE
TERRIFIC
DREADFULLY DIRELY GRISLY
ABYSMALLY
DREADNOUGHT TANK DAREALL
WARSHIP FEARLESS
DREAM METE MOON MUSE REVE
FANCY SWEVEN VISION AISLING
AVISION CHIMERA FANTASY
IMAGINE NIRVANA REVERIE
ROMANCE CHIMAERA DAYDREAM
PHANTASM SOMNIATE
(FRIGHTENING —) NIGHTMARE
(PREF.) ONEIR(O) ONIR(O)
DREAMER POET METER MUSARD
FANTAST IDEALIST PHANTAST
DREAMINESS LANGUOR
DREAMING ADREAM TRAUMEREI
DREAMTIME ALCHERA
DREAMY KEF SOFT MOONY VAGUE
POETIC FARAWAY LANGUID
MUSEFUL ONEIRIC PENSIVE
DREAMFUL FANCIFUL SOOTHING
DREAR DERN BLEAK DISMAL
GLOOMY DOLEFUL
DREARY SAD DIRE DOWY DREE
DULL FLAT GLUM BLEAK CRUEL
DOWIE DRURY OURIE WASTE
WISHT DISMAL DREICH ELENGE
GLOOMY GOUSTY LONELY
DOLEFUL GOUSTIE HOWLING
WILSOME GRIEVOUS WEARIFUL
DREDGE MOP DRAG DREG SIFT
SCOOP TRAIN DEEPEN DRUDGE
SCRAPE SPONGE TANGLE
GANGAVA SCALLOP EXCAVATE
SPRINKLE
DREDGER DUSTER HEDGEHOG
DREDGING JILLING
DREGS LAG MUD CRAP FAEX LAGS
LEES SCUT SILT SUDS TAIL DRAFF
DREST DROSS DRUGS FECES
FOOTS GROUT JAUPS MAGMA
BOTTOM DRAINS DUNDER
FECULA MOTHER REFUSE SORDES
SORDOR ULLAGE DRIBBLE
GROUNDS GRUMMEL HEELTAP
OUTWALE RESIDUE RINSING
GRUMMELS REMNANTS
SEDIMENT SETTLING
(— OF LIQUOR) TAPLASH
(— OF MOLTEN GLASS) DRIBBLE

(— OF SOCIETY) WASH LEGGE CANAILLE
(— OF TALLOW) GREAVES
DREIBUND TRIPLICE
DREIDEL TRENDEL
DREI PINTOS, DIE (CHARACTER IN —) GOMEZ PINTO GASTON AMBROSIO CLARISSA PANTALEONE
(COMPOSER OF —) MAHLER
DRENCH DOSE HOSE SIND SINK SOAK TOSH BLASH DOUSE DOWSE DRAFT DRINK DROKE DROUK DROWN SLOCK SLUSH SOUSE STEEP SWILL BUCKET DELUGE DOUCHE IMBRUE INFUSE POTION SLUICE DRUNKEN EMBATHE IMMERSE INDRENCH PERMEATE SATURATE SUBMERGE
DRENCHED DRUNKEN
DRENCHER INFUSER
DRENCHING DOUSE DOWSE DOWNPOUR
DRESS AX AXE BED DON DUB FIG FIT HOE KIT RAG RAY RIG TOG BARB BEGO BOWN BUSK BUSS CLAY COAT COMB DESK DILL DINK GALA GARB GEAR GORE GOWN HONE HUKE KNAP MIDI MILL MINI RAIL ROBE SUIT TIFF TIRE TRIM TUBE TUCK VEST WEAR ADORN ARRAY BIGAN BRAWS CLEAN CLOTH CRUMB CRUSH CURRY DIGHT DIZEN EQUIP FLOAT FROCK GUISE HABIT IHRAM MAGMA PREEN PRICK PRIMP PRINK PRUNE SHAPE THING TRICK AGUISE ATTIRE ATTRAP BARBER BETRIM BROACH CLOTHE ENROBE FANGLE FETTLE FRAISE GRAITH INVEST JELICK JUMPER KIRTLE MAGPIE MULLET MUUMUU OUTFIT PLIGHT REVEST SARONG SHEATH SHROUD TOILET ADDRESS AFFAITE APPAREL BANDAGE BEDIZEN CHEMISE CLOTHES COSTUME DALLACK DUBBING GARMENT GARNISH HARNESS HATCHEL RAIMENT TOGGERY VESTURE ACCOUTER ACCOUTRE CLEADING CLOTHING DECORATE FEATHERS HANDMADE ORNAMENT SUNDRESS TAILLEUR VESTMENT EMBELLISH
(— A SKIN) WHEEL
(— DOWN) BRACE
(— ELEGANTLY) DINK
(— FISH) CALVER
(— FLAX) TED
(— FLINT) NAP KNAP
(— FOOD) SAUCE
(— FOR FELTING) CARROT
(— HAIR) TIRE TRUSS BARBER
(— HIDES) BEAM
(— HURRIEDLY) HUDDLE
(— IN FINE CLOTHES) DIKE BRANK
(— MEAT) LARD SHROUD
(— NEGLIGENTLY) MOB
(— ORE) VAN
(— OVER) STOP
(— SHEEPSKINS) TAW
(— SMARTLY) DALLACK
(— STONE) DAB NIG DAUB DRAG

FACE GAGE HACK GAUGE NIDGE POINT SCABBLE SCAPPLE
(— TAWDRILY) BEDIZEN
(— UNTIDILY) MAB
(— UP) BUSK DILL ADORN ARRAY PRANK PRIMP PRINK SPICK WATER FETTLE TOGGLE BECLOUT BEDRESS TITIVATE
(— VULGARLY) DAUB
(— WITH CHISEL) DROVE
(— WITH TROWEL) STRIKE
(— WORN BY MAN) DRAG
(— WOUND) PANSE BANDAGE
(COAT —) SIMAR SYMAR SIMARRE
(EVENING —) FORMAL
(FESTIVE —) GALA
(INCOMPLETE —) DISARRAY
(LONG —) MAXI
(LOOSE —) SACK SACQUE
(MORNING —) PEIGNOIR
(ONE-PIECE —) CAGE
(PECULIAR —) LIVERY
(POPLIN —) TABINET TABBINET
(RUSSIAN NATIONAL —) SARAFAN
(SHOWY —) BRAVERY
(SLEEVELESS —) SKIMMER
(STYLE OF —) GETUP
(SUFF.) ESTHES
DRESSED CLAD DONE BOUND BECLAD COATED COMBED HABITED GOFFERED
(— GAILY) FRESH SPARKISH
(— IN WHITE) CANDIDATE
(LOOSELY —) DISCINCT
(RICHLY —) BROCADED
(ROUGHLY —) HEWN
(SHOWILY —) BEPRANKED
(STYLISHLY —) SMART
(WELL —) BRAW GASH
DRESSER AMBRY ROBER TAWER BUREAU FRAMER MODISTE CUPBOARD
(LEATHER —) LEVANTER
DRESSING CAST GRAVY BEATING BLANKET IODOFORM RAVIGOTE REMOLADE SCOLDING STUFFING MAYONNAISE
(— FOR WOUNDS) LINT SPONGE
(— OF STONE) SKIFFLING
(HAIR —) LACKER LACQUER
DRESSING ROOM SHIFT VESTRY CAMARIN VESTUARY
DRESSMAKER SEWER SEAMER MODISTE STITCHER COUTURIER TIREWOMAN
DRESSMAKING COUTURE
DRESS RACK FRIPPERY
DRESSY SHARP
DRIBBLE DRIB DRIP DROP CARRY DRIVEL DRIBLET DRIPPLE DRIZZLE SLABBER
DRIBLET CLOT PIECE
(PL.) SMALLS
DRIED SEAR SERE ADUST GIZZEN TORRID WIZENED GIZZENED
DRIFT FAN JET SAG DENE DUNE FORD HERD PLOT RACK SILT TIDE TILL DRIVE DROVE FLEET FLOAT FLOCK IOWAN SENSE SLIDE SLOOM SLOUM TENOR TREND BROACH COURSE DESIGN DEVICE DRIVER OFFSET PODGER SCHEME STREAM TUNNEL WINDLE

CURRENT DIPHEAD DRIBBLE GALLERY HEADING IMPETUS IMPULSE LATERAL OUTWASH PASTURE PROCESS PURPORT SETBOLT DILUVIUM DRIFTPIN TENDENCY
(— LANGUIDLY) SWOON
(— OF CLOUDS) CARRY
(— OF SAND OR SNOW) WREATH
(— SIDEWISE) CRAB
(— WITH ANCHOR DOWN) CLUB
(DOWNWARD —) DROOP
(GLACIAL —) CARY TILL IOWAN
(RUBBLE —) HEAD
DRIFTER DROVER
DRIFTING ADRIFT DRIFTAGE
DRIFT PLUG DUMMY
DRIFTWAY DROVE
DRIFTWOOD WAFTURE
DRILL GAD JAR JIG RIG SOW TAP BORE CORE SPUD AUGER BORER CHARK CHURN DECOY DREEL PADDY THIRL TRAIN TUTOR TWIRL WHIRL ALLURE BROACH ENTICE FURROW JUMPER PIERCE SCHOOL SEEDER SINKER STOPER THRILL CHANNEL DRIFTER JANKERS PLUGGER STARTER EXERCISE INSTRUCT
(— SYSTEM) MARTINET
(MASONRY —) AIGUILLE
DRILLMAN STOPER
DRINK GO ADE ALE BIB BUM FIX GIN HUM LAP MOP PEG POT RUM RYE SIP SUP TEA TOT WET BALL BEER BEND BENO BOLL BOSA BOZA BREW BULL BUMP CHIA COKE COLA DRAG DRAM FIZZ FLIP GROG HAVE HORN JAKE LUSH MEAD NIPA NOGG PULL PURL SHOT SIND SLUG SOAK SMACH SOPE SPOT SWIG TIFF TOOT TOPE WHET AIRAH ASSAI BEVER BINGE BLAND BOMBO BOOZE BOUSE BOZAH BUBUD BUMBO CIDER CRUSH DAISY DRAFT FLOAT GLOGG HAOMA JULEP LAGER MORAT NEGUS PAINT POSCA PUNCH QUAFF ROUSE SETUP SKINK SLING SLOCK SMACH SMASH SMILE SMOKE SNIFF SNORT SOPIE SOUSE SWATS SWILL THING TOAST TODDY VODKA WHIFF ZOMBI ABSORB BEZZLE BRACER BRANDY BUMPER BURTON CALKER CASIRI CATLAP CAUDLE CHASER COFFEE COOPER DIBBLE DRENCH EGGHOT EGGNOG FUDDLE GIMLET GODOWN GUGGLE GUZZLE HOOKER IMBIBE MESCAL POSSET POTION PTISAN RICKEY SCREED SHANDY SIPPLE SIRPLE SWANKY SWINGE TACKLE TAMPOY TASTER TIPPLE VELVET WAUCHT WAUGHT ZOMBIE BRAGGET BRIMMER CAROUSE CHEERER CHIRPER COBBLER COLLINS CONSUME CORDIAL DILUENT DRAUGHT EXHAUST FLANNEL GUARANA GUARAPO INHAUST MORNING NOONING PROPOMA SHERBET SIDECAR SNEEZER

SNIFTER SUCTION SUPPAGE SWALLOW TANKARD TRILLIL APERITIF BEVERAGE BRIDECUP COCKTAIL HIGHBALL LIBATION MAHOGANY NIGHTCAP POTATION QUENCHEh REFRESCO RUMBARGE SANGAREE SPRITZER SYLLABUB TEQUILA PHOSPHATE
(— AT DRAFT) TOP
(— EXCESSIVELY) TOPE BIBLE SOUSE BEZZLE BIBBLE SWIZZLE
(— FROM FERMENTED MILK) AIRAN KEFIR
(— GREEDILY) SLOP SWACK SWILL GUTTLE GUZZLE
(— HEAVILY) TOOT SWINK
(— INTOXICATING LIQUOR) IRRIGATE
(— LIQUOR) TIP DRAM SOAK BOOZE PAINT
(— NOISILY) SLURP
(— OF BEER) BUTCHER
(— OF BEER AND BUTTERMILK) BONNY CLABBER
(— OF BEER AND GINGERALE) SHANDYGAFF
(— OF IMMORTALITY) SOMA
(— OF INDIA) SHRAB
(— OF LIQUEUR) FRAPPE
(— OF LIQUOR) WET DRAM JOLT SHOT SPOT TASS WHET SETUP WHIFF CALKER JIGGER TASTER WETTING HIGHBALL NIGHTCAP
(— OF MOLASSES) SWITCHEL
(— OF THE GODS) AMRITA NECTAR
(— OF VINEGAR AND WATER) POSCA
(— OFF) COUP
(— SOCIALLY) BIRL HOBNOB
(— SPARINGLY) BLEB
(— TO LAST DROP) BUZZ
(— UP) CRUSH EPOTE CAROUSE EXHAUST
(— WITHOUT PAUSE) CHUGALUG
(ADDITIONAL —) EIK EKE
(ALCOHOLIC —) BENO BINO MIST NIPA BOMBO BUDGE BUMBO DRAIN JOUGH SHRAB SLING SNORT SNIFTER
(AUSTRALIAN —) BEAL
(BRAZILIAN —) ASSAI ASSAHY
(BUTTERMILK AND WATER —) BLAND
(CURRANT —) CASSIS
(DRUGGED —) HOCUS
(FARINACEOUS —) PTISAN
(FERMENTED —) BOSA MEAD BALCHE MUSHLA PULQUE CASSIRI GUARAPO
(FREE —) SHOUT
(GREAT —) JORUM
(HALF-SIZED —) CHOTAPEG
(HEADY —) HUFFCAP
(HOT —) COPUS SALOP TODDY BISHOP EGGHOT PLOTTY SALOOP CARDINAL
(INCLINED TO —) OUTWARD
(INSIPID —) SLUM
(INTOXICATING —) AVA GROG SUCK BOOZE KUMISS SCOTCH DRAPPIE PAIWARI SWIZZLE SKOKIAAN
(INTOXICATING —S) SAUCE BOTTLE

(LONG —) SWIPE HIGHBALL
(MEAN —) LAP
(MEDICINAL —) ADVOCAAT
(MIDDAY —) NOONING MERIDIAN
(NARCOTIC —) KAVA
(NON-ALCOHOLIC —) GAZOZ
COOLER
(PALM —) ASSAI
(PARTING —) BONAILIE
(POISONOUS —) DRENCH
(RUSSIAN —) OBARNE OBARNI
(SACRED —) HOMA AMRIT HAOMA
AMRITA
(SACRIFICIAL —) HOMA SOMA
(SMALL —) PEG DRAM SOPIE
DALLOP WETTING
(SOUR —) ALEGAR
(STRONG —) BUB HUM BENO
SICER FUDDLE SHICKER
(TASTELESS —) SLOP
(THIN —) SLOSH
(WEAK —) LAP BOOL BULL CATLAP
DRINKER SOT LUSH TANK POTER
TOAST TOPER BARFLY BENDER
CUPMAN LUSHER SOAKER
SPONGE IMBIBER INTAKER
QUAFFER DRUNKARD
(EXCESSIVE — OF TEA) THEIC
(HEAVY —) JUICEHEAD
(WATER —) HYDROPOT
DRINKING BEVER DRAFT DRINKY
GUZZLE DRAUGHT POTTING
CAROUSAL POTATION
(CONTINUOUS —) BOUT
DRIP LIP SIE SYE DROP LEAK SEGE
SILE WEEP CANAL DRILL EAVES
LABEL STILL DRIBBLE DRIPPLE
LARMIER TRICKLE TRINKLE
TRINTLE
(— WITH TINKLING SOUND) PINK
(PREF.) STALACTI(TI) STALAGMO
DRIPPING ADRIP STAXIS WEEPING
DRIPSTONE BAT DING LABEL
HOODMOLD
DRIVE CA CAW COT FOG HOY JOG
AUTO BANG BEAR BEAT BUTT
CALL CRAM DING DRUB DRUM
FIRE FIRK FLOG GOAD HACK
HERD HUNT HURL JASM JEHU
KICK LASH MOVE PICK PILE POSS
PUSH RACK RIDE SEND SERR SINK
SLOG SPUR STAB STUB TOOL
TOUR TURN URGE BRAWL CHASE
CHECK COACT CROWD DRIFT
DROVE FEEZE FLAIL FORCE
HORSE HURRY IMPEL INFER
LODGE MOTOR PEDAL POACH
PRESS PULSE PUNCH REPEL
ROUST SHOVE SLASH SMITE
SPANK SWEEP TEASE ATTACK
BATTER BEETLE BENSEL CHARGE
COMPEL CUDGEL DEDUCE DERIVE
FERRET HAMMER HASTEN
IMPACT JARVEY JOSTLE PLUNGE
PROPEL BLUSTER ENFORCE
IMPULSE OVERTAX SETDOWN
TRAVAIL CATAPULT CONATION
SHEPHERD TENDENCY
MOTIVATION
(— A BALL) LACE SEND
(— A HORSE ONWARD) WHIG
(— AIR) BLOW
(— ANIMALS) HAZE

(— AT TOP SPEED) BARREL CAREER
(— AWAY) RID FIRK HUSH SHOO
BANDY EXILE FEEZE FLEME
HOOSH REPEL SMOKE SWEEP
AROINT BANISH DEFEND DISPEL
ENCHASE DISPLACE EXORCISE
(— BACK) RUSH REBUT REPEL
CULBUT DEFEND REBATE REBUFF
RETUND REPULSE REFRINGE
(— BACK AND FORTH) TENNIS
(— BEFORE STRONG WIND) SPOON
(— BRISKLY) JUNE
(— CLOSE BEHIND WHILE RACING)
DRAFT
(— CRAZY) BUG
(— DISTRACTED) BEDEVIL
(— FORTH) ISH
(— HARD) SWEAT HACKNEY
(— HOME) CLINCH
(— HURRIEDLY) BUM BUCKET
(— IN) CRAM DINT PILE TAMP
INJECT
(— IN A PARK) TOUR
(— INTO THE GROUND) STUB
(— INTO WATER) ENEW
(— LOGS) SPLASH
(— OFF) KEEP LIFT EXCOCT
(— OFF STAGE) EXPLODE
(— OUT) BOLT FIRE DEPEL DROWN
EJECT EXPEL KNOCK WREAK
AROINT EXTURB ABANDON
DISLODGE EXORCISE PROPULSE
(— RECKLESSLY) COWBOY
(— ROUGHLY) CHOUSE
(— SLANTINGLY) TOE
(— TO BAY) EMBOSS
(— TO MADNESS) FRENZY
(— VIOLENTLY) THUD SMASH
HURTLE
(— WITH BLOWS) SKELP COURSE
(— WITH SHOUTS) HOY HUE
(FREE GOLF —) MULLIGAN
DRIVEL BLAH DOTE DRIP MUSH
DROOL SLUSH DOTAGE DRUDGE
FOOTLE HUMBUG MENIAL SLAVER
DRIBBLE EYEWASH MAUNDER
SLABBER TWADDLE NONSENSE
SALIVATE CODSWALLOP
DRIVELING SLAVERY FOOTLING
IMBECILE SLOBBERY BLITHERING
DRIVEPIPE POINT
DRIVER MUG HACK JEHU MUSH
WHIP DRABI URGER CABMAN
CALLER COWBOY DROVER
FLYMAN HAULER JARVEY JOCKEY
MALLET MIZZEN MUSHER PONIER
STAGER VANMAN WAINER
CATCHER COCHERO FLANKER
HACKMAN HOODLUM HURRIER
JITNEUR PHAETON SPANKER
SPEEDER SUMPTER TOPSMAN
TRUCKER WHIPMAN BANDYMAN
BULLOCKY CALESERO CAMELEER
COACHMAN DRAGSMAN
ENGINEER GALLOWAY
GOADSMAN IMPULSOR JITNEUSE
MOTORMAN OVERSEER
REINSMAN TEAMSTER WHIPSTER
(— OF ANIMALS) DROVER SKINNER
(— OF ELEPHANT) MAHOUT
(— OF OMNIBUS) PIRATE
(CAMEL —) SARWAN CAMELEER
(FAST —) JEHU SPEEDER

(FIELD —) HAYWARD
(PACK-HORSE —) SUMPTER
(SKILLFUL —) REINSMAN
(TOWPATH —) HOGGY HOGGEE
(PREF.) ELATRO
DRIVEWAY DRIVE SWEEP AVENUE
DRIFTWAY
DRIVING PELTING COACHING
SLASHING
(— ALONG) SCUD
(— OF GAME) BATTUE
(— OF WIND) GUST
(— TOGETHER) DRIFT
(— TOWARD) APPULSE
DRIZZLE DEG MUG DANK DRIP
DROW HAZE LING RAIN SMUR
STEW DRISK MISLE SMURR
MIZZLE DRISSEL SCOUTHER
SPRINKLE
(— OF RAIN) SKEW
DRIZZLY SOFT DRIPPY MIZZLY
DROGUE DRAG DRUG SLEEVE
DROLL ODD RUM COMIC DROLE
FUNNY MERRY QUEER WITTY
JESTER JOCOSE AMUSING
BUFFOON COMICAL JOCULAR
STRANGE WAGGISH FARCICAL
HUMOROUS
DROLLERY WIT JEST FARCE
HUMOR DROLERIE
DROMEDARY OONT CAMEL DELUL
DELOUL HAGEEN HAGEIN HYGEEN
MEHARI CAMAILE CAMELUS
DROMOND
DRONE BEE BUM HUM DRUM SLUG
SPIV DRANT DROLL IDLER SNAIL
THRUM BUMBLE BURDEN
CHORUS DRAUNT DRONEL
DRONET LUBBER BAGPIPE
BUMBARD BUMBASS HUMMING
SHIRKER SLEEPER SOLDIER
SPEAKER LOITERER SLUGGARD
DRONE BASS FOOT
DRONGO FORKTAIL
DRONING BOURDON HUMDRUM
HUMMING SINGSONG
DRONISH SLOW INDOLENT
SLUGGISH
DROOL FLAT DRIVEL SLAVER
DRIBBLE SLABBER SLOBBER
SALIVATE
DROOP FAG LOB LOP SAG BEND
DROP FADE FLAG HANG LAVE
LOLL PEAK PINE SINK SWAG
WEEP WILT DAVER DREEP
DROWK FLACK HEALD HIELD
MOURN BANGLE BLOUSE DANGLE
DEPEND NUTATE SLOUCH
CURTAIN DECLINE FLITTER
LANGUISH PENDENCY
DROOPING LOP DRAG FLAG LANK
LAZY LIMP GOTCH OURIE
ADROOP DROOPY FLAGGY
NUTANT SLOUCH SOPITE
GOTCHED HANGING LANGUID
NODDING POPPIED CERNUOUS
TRAILING
(— OF EARS) LAVE
(— OF EYELID) PTOSIS
DROOPY DREEPY SLIMPSY
DROP DAP DIP SIE SYE BEAD BEDE
BLOB CAST DRIB DRIP DUMP FALL
GLOB GOUT OMIT SEGE SHED

SILE SINK SPOT STOP TEAR
BREAK CLOTH DROOP FLUMP
GUTTA LAPSE LOWER MINIM
PEARL PLUMP PLUNK SLUMP
STILL SWOOP CANCEL DISTIL
DRAPPY EXTILL FUMBLE GOBBET
GOUTTE PLUNGE SINKER SLOUGH
SPRINK TUMBLE ABANDON
CURTAIN DESCENT DEWDROP
DISCARD DISMISS DISTILL
DRAPPIE DRIBBLE DRIBLET
DROPLET EXPUNGE FORSAKE
GLOBULE GUTTULA GUTTULE
INCURVE LETDOWN MELDROP
PLUMMET RELEASE SPATTER
DECREASE DROPLING
(— ANCHOR) SLIP
(— ARGENT) LARME
(— AS SEEDS FROM A POD) ROSE
(— AWAY) DESERT
(— BAIT IN WATER) DAP
(— BY DROP) DROPWISE
GUTTATIM
(— DOWN) VAIL
(— IN) STOP HAPPEN INSTIL
INSTILL
(— OF GIN) DAFFY
(— OUT) FLOUNCE
(CHOCOLATE —) DRAGEE
(THEATRICAL —) TAB SCRIM
(UNEXPECTED —) DOYST
(PL.) GTT GUTT
(PREF.) GUTTI STAGMO STAGONO
STILLI
DROP-CURTAIN GREENY
DROP ELBOW PIERDROP
DROPLET GLOBULE
(PL.) DEW
DROPLIGHT PENDANT
DROPPER SINK BOBBER SINKER
PIPETTE
DROPPING FALL SCAT SKAT
SHARD COWSHARD
(— ABRUPTLY) BOLD
(— SHARPLY) ABRUPT
(PL.) SOIL SPOOR FLYINGS
DROPSICAL PUFFY EDEMIC
DROPSIED HYDROPIC
DROPSY EDEMA ASCITES
ANASARCA
DROPWORT HORSEBANE
DEADTONGUE
DROSS KISH LEES SCUM SLAG
CHAFF DREGS DRUSH SCOBS
SLACK SPRUE WASTE GARBLE
REFUSE SCORIA SCRUFF SHRUFF
SINTER CINDERS LEAVING
OFFSCUM
DROSSEL SLUT HUSSY DRAZEL
DRAZIL
DROUGHT DRYTH DROUTH THIRST
ARIDITY DRYNESS
DROVE MOB SENT ATAJO CROWD
DRIFT FLOCK MANADA BOASTER
DISTURB TROUBLE DRIFTWAY
DROVER DEALER DRIVER TOPMAN
TOPSMAN WHACKER HERDSMAN
DROWN DEAFEN DRENCH STIFLE
ADRENCH DRUNKEN INDRENCH
INUNDATE OVERTONE
DROWNED ADRENT
DROWNING NOYADE
DROWSE NOD SOG DOZE DOVER

DRONE SLEEP SNOOZE SLUMBER
DROWSINESS COMA DULLNESS
LETHARGY
DROWSING DORMANT
DROWSY DOZY DULL LOGY HEAVY
NODDY SLEEPY SNOOZY SOPITE
STUPID SUPINE SWOONY
DORMANT LULLING NODDING
POPPIED COMATOSE COMATOUS
OSCITANT SLUGGISH LETHARGIC
DRUB TAP WAP BANG BEAT BLOW
DRUM PAIK ARRAY CURRY STAMP
THUMP WHALE ANOINT CUDGEL
SCUTCH THRASH BELABOR
DRYBEAT SHELLAC
DRUBBING PAIK LICKING SACKING
DRUDGE DIG FAG TUG DROY DRUG
GRUB HACK MOIL PLOD SERF
TOIL DROIL GRIND SCRAT SCRUB
SLAVE SWEAT DIGGER DRIVEL
ENDURE JACKAL MOILER SCODGY
SCOGIE SLAVEY SLUDGE SUFFER
GRUBBER HACKNEY PLODDER
SLAVERY SWEATER TRACHLE
DRUDGERY FAG MOIL SLOG TOIL
WORK LABOR SWEAT SWINK
FAGGERY SLAVERY TRACHLE
TURMOIL DRUDGISM
DRUG (ALSO SEE NARCOTIC) HOP
ACID ALOE ALUM BUKU CURE
DOPE DRAB DULL HEMP LOAD
NUMB SINA BUCHU HOCUS JALAP
LOCUS MECON OPIUM RUTIN
SALOL SENNA SPECE SPEED
SULFA TONGA TRUCK COOLER
DEWTRY FINGER HEROIN IPECAC
JAMBUL LOCUST MYOTIC NOBBLE
OPIATE PEYOTE PEYOTL PITURI
POTION SIDDHI SIMPLE SULPHA
ANODYNE ASPIRIN ATEBRIN
BOTANIC CUSHION DAMIANA
DAPSONE DILATER ECBOLIC
ETHICAL HASHISH JAMBOOL
METOPON PHILTER PHILTRE
QUASSIA STUPEFY STYPTIC
SURAMIN ZEDOARY ADJUVANT
AROMATIC ASPIDIUM ATARAXIC
BANTHINE HYPNOTIC KOROMIKO
LAXATIVE MEDICATE MEDICINE
MERSALYL NARCOTIC NEPENTHE
PEMOLINE SALIVANT SEDATIVE
SPECIFIC TOXICANT ZERUMBET
ATARACTIC BARBITONE
COLCHICUM SALURETIC
PAINKILLER
(— DOSE) HIT
(— IN TABLET OF VARIOUS COLORS)
RAINBOW
(— SMUGGLER) MULE
(— USER) ACIDHEAD JOYPOPPER
(BITUMINOUS —) MUMMY
(DEPRESSANT —) DOWNER
(FREE FROM — ADDICTION) CLEAN
(INHALE A —) SNORT
(NONUSER OF —S) STRAIGHT
(ONE WHO USES A —) HEAD
(ONE WHO USES ILLICIT —S) FREAK
(ORAL DIURETIC —) THIAZIDE
(STIMULANT —) UPPER
(STRENGTHENING —) ROBORANT
(TAKE A — THROUGH THE MOUTH)
DROP
(TAKE —S ORALLY) POP

(TO INJECT —) SHOOT
(VEGETABLE —) FINGER
(PL.) DRUGGERY
(PREF.) PHARMACO
DRUGGED POPPIED
DRUGGET BAUGE BOCKING
DRUGGIST CHEMIST DRUGGER
GALLIPOT
DRUGSTORE APOTHEC PHARMACY
DRUID SARONIDE
DRUM GIN GOO BOWL CAGE DRUB
LALI ROUT SKIN SPOT TOPH TRAP
BONGO CONGA CRAWL DRONE
GUMBE GUMBY SHAPE SNARE
SWASH TABOR THRUM TOMBE
ATABAL BARREL CROCUS RIGGER
TABRET TAMBOR TIMBRE TUMBLE
TUMMER TYMPAN ANACARA
BUBBLER CROAKER FRUSTUM
GRUNTER RATTLER REDFISH
SNUBBER TABORIN TAMBOUR
TEMPEST TIMBREL TUMBLER
BAMBOULA BARBUKKA CANISTER
CYLINDER DERBUKKA DRUMFISH
HUEHUETL MOULINET MRIDANGA
TYMPANUM MRIDANGAM
(— AS SHIP'S SIGNAL) SHAPE
(— FOR WINDING ROPE) CAGE
(— IN WINCH) GIPSY GYPSY
(— MADE FROM HOLLOW TREE)
GUMBE GUMBY
(— OF CAPSTAN) RUNDLE
MOULINE
(— OF INDIA) MRIDANGA
MRIDANGAM
(— ON WINDLASS) WILDCAT
(— UP BUSINESS) HUSTLE
(— UP INTEREST) BALLYHOO
(HEATED —) DRIER DRYER
(IGOROT —) GANGSA
(PAIR OF HINDU —S) TABLA
(REVOLVING —) GURDY RATTLER
(SUMERIAN —) ALA ALAL
DRUMBEAT DUB FLAM RUFF TUCK
MARCH RUFFLE ASSEMBLY
BERLOQUE BRELOQUE
(— SOUND) TUCK
DRUMFISH SPOT CROCUS
BUBBLER CROAKER DRUMMER
DRUMSLER SCIAENID
DRUMLIN DRUM SOWBACK
DRUMMER DRUM TABOR STICKS
TABRET ROADMAN SWASHER
TAMBOUR TUMBLER DRUMSLER
SALESMAN
DRUMMING TATTOO
DRUM ROLL DIAN DIANA
DRUMS ALONG THE MOHAWK
(AUTHOR OF —) EDMONDS
(CHARACTER IN —) HON JOHN
LANA MARK YOST BRANT JURRY
NANCY WOLFF ARNOLD GAHOTA
JOSEPH MARTIN DEMOOTH
GILBERT MCLONIS SCHUYLER
MAGDELANA MCKLENNAR
DRUMSTICK LEG STICK BAGUET
TAMPON BAGUETTE
DRUNK CUT FAP FOU REE WET
GONE HIGH LUSH NASE PAID RIPE
SOSH BLIND BOOZE BOSKY CLEAR
DRINK LUMPY LUSHY MALTY
MOPPY OILED QUEER SHICK STIFF
TIGHT TIPSY BAGGED BLOTTO

BOILED BOMBED BUZZED
CANNED FLUFFY GROGGY
JAGGED LOADED LOOPED
MORTAL POTTED SLOPPY
SODDEN SOSHED SOUSED SOZZLY
SPONGY SPRUNG STEWED
STINKO STONED TIDDLY UPPISH
UPPITY ZONKED BLOTTER
BONKERS BOTTLED CROCKED
DRUNKEN JINGLED MAUDLIN
PICKLED SCREWED SHICKER
SLOPPED SMASHED SOZZLED
SQUIFFY SWACKED COCKEYED
GLORIOUS MUCKIBUS PLEASANT
SQUIFFED STINKING BLITHERED
PIXILATED
DRUNKARD SOT LUSH SOAK
BLOAT DIPSO DRUNK GULCH
RUMMY SOUSE TOPER LUSHER
SOAKER SPONGE DRUNKER
FUDDLER POTSHOT SHICKER
STEWBUM TIPPLER TOSSPOT
BORACHIO HABITUAL SWILLTUB
DRUNKEN REE WAT GONE WINY
BLIND BOUSY DROWN DRUNK
BLOTTO FLUFFY SODDEN
BACCHIC DRUCKEN PICKLED
SOTTISH WHIPCAT DRENCHED
SATURATE SQUIFFED VINOLENT
WOODSERE
DRUNKENNESS BUN IVRESSE
POTSHOT METHYSIS
DRUPE TRYMA DRUPEL DRUPELET
DRUPEOLE
DRUPELET GRAIN ACINUS
DRUPE STONE NUTLET
DRUSILLA (BROTHER OF —)
CALIGULA
(FATHER OF —) HEROD CALIGULA
GERMANICUS
(HUSBAND OF —) FELIX AZIZUS
AUGUSTUS
(MOTHER OF —) CYPROS CAESONIA
AGRIPPINA
(SON OF —) AGRIPPA TIBERIUS
DRY EBB KEX SEC TED WIN ADRY
ARID BAKE BLOT BRUT DULL EILD
GELD HASK KEXY KILN PINE SAVE
SERE SOUR WELT WIPE AREFY
CORKY DRAIN FROST GUESS
HASKY JUSKY MEALY PARCH
PROSY SANDY SECCO SMEEK
SWEAT VAPID WIZEN BARKEN
BARREN BIRSLE BORING CHIPPY
ENSEAR GIZZEN HISTIE JEJUNE
SCORCH STARKY AREFACT
BRUSTLE INSIPID SAPLESS
SICCATE SQUALID STERILE
THIRSTY TORREFY XEROTIC
BARBECUE DROUGHTY INFUMATE
TIRESOME WOODSERE
(— HERRINGS) DEESE
(— IN SUN) RIZZAR
(— OF MILK) SEW EILD
(— PARTLY) SAMMY
(— UP) SERE WELK WITHER
AREFACT FORWELK SKELLER
(— WOOD) BEATH SWEAT SEASON
(NOT —) SWEET
(PREF.) DEHYDR(O) JEJUN(O)
SCLER(O) SICCI TORRE XER(O)
(— PLACE OR PROCESS) XER(O)
DRYAD DRYAS NYMPH CAISSA

YAKSHA YAKSHI WOODMAID
DRYER DRIER STOVE SIROCCO
DRY GOODS DRAPERY
DRYING SICCANT
DRYING RACK CRIB
DRYNESS DROUTH ARIDITY
DROUGHT SICCITY XEROSIS
XEROTES HASKNESS AREFACTION
DRYOPE (FATHER OF —) EURYTUS
(HUSBAND OF —) ANDRAEMON
(SISTER OF —) IOLE
(SON OF —) AMPHISSUS
DUAL TWIN BINARY DOUBLE
DUALIST TWOFOLD
DUALISM DVAITA
DUALITY DUAD TWINE TWONESS
DUANT DE DEE
DUB DIB RUB ADUB BLOW CALL
NAME POOL ADORN ARRAY
DRESS STYLE THUMP CLOTHE
KNIGHT PUDDLE SMOOTH STRIKE
ENTITLE BEGINNER DRUMBEAT
ORNAMENT
DUBBIN DAUBING
DUBIOUS DICKY FISHY JUBUS
DOUBTY BEARISH DOUBTFUL
DOUBTING JUBEROUS
PRECARIOUS QUESTIONABLE
(NOT —) EXPRESS
DUCA D'ALBA, IL (CHARACTER
IN —) AMELIA EGMONT MARCELLO
(COMPOSER OF —) DONIZETTI
DUCHY SAVOY DUCATUS DUCHERY
DUKEDOM PARMESAN
DUCK AIX BOB BOW CAN DIG DIP
DOP MIG PET WIO CHAP COLK
COOT DIVE DOGS DOGY DOKE
DUKW JOUK LADY LORD PATO
ROOK SMEE SMEW TEAL TEUK
BOOBY BUNTY CRICK DILLY
DODGE DOUSE DOWSE DUCKY
EIDER HOUND MOMMY NODDY
PADDY POKER RODGE ROUEN
SCAUP SHIRK SOUSE SPIKE SPRIG
STOOL BOBBER CALLOO CALLOW
CANARD CANNET DUCKIE
FELLOW GARROT HARELD PEKING
PERSON PLUNGE QUANDY
RUNNER SCOTER SMETHE
ANATINE BARWING BLACKIE
BOWSSEN BUMMALO CANETTE
CRACKER DABBLER DARLING
DRABBET DUCKING DUCKLET
DUNBIRD FIDDLER FLAPPER
GADWALL GEELBEC GREASER
MALLARD OLDWIFE PENTAIL
PINKEYE PINTAIL POCHARD
REDHEAD REDLEGS REDWING
SCOOTER SLEEPER SPATTER
WADDLER WIDGEON YAGUAZA
BALDPATE BLUEBILL BLUEWING
BOATBILL BULLNECK DUCKLING
DUCKWING GARGANEY
GRAYBACK GREYBACK HARDHEAD
IRONHEAD MOONBILL MORILLON
PIKETAIL REDSHANK RINGBILL
RINGNECK SHOVELER SHUFFLER
SQUEALER WIRETAIL BERGANDER
(— AT CRICKET) BLOB
(— EGGS) PIDAN
(MALE —) DRAKE
(PART OF —) EAR EYE WEB BEAN
BILL CAPE HEAD NECK RUMP TAIL

WING FLUFF SHANK BREAST
SADDLE COVERTS NOSTRIL
SHOULDER PRIMARIES
SECONDARIES
(STUFFED —) DUMPOKE
(YOUNG —) CANETON FLAPPER
FLOPPER
DUCKBILL OOTOCOID PLATYPUS
TAMBREET MONOTREME
DUCKWEED GLIT GRAIN LEMNAD
LENTIL DIGMEAT DUCKMEAT
FROGFOOT
DUCT VAS MAIN PIPE TUBE VEIN
CANAL ALVEUS BUSWAY DUCTUS
MEATUS URETER CHANNEL
CONDUIT DUCTULE DUCTURE
LACTEAL LEADING PASSAGE
TRACHEA AQUEDUCT CALIDUCT
DOWNTAKE EFFERENT EMISSARY
EXHALANT GONADUCT GUIDANCE
OLEODUCT
(PREF.) RHYN(O) VAS(I)(O)
DUCTILE SOFT DOCILE FACILE
PLIANT PLASTIC PLIABLE TENSILE
FLEXIBLE TRACTILE
(PREF.) ELAST(O)
DUD FLOP LEMON STUMER
STUMOR FAILURE
DUDE FOP DANDY DUDINE
JOHNNY COXCOMB JACKEEN
DUDGEON PIQUE OFFENSE
DUE HAK LOT OWE BACK CENS
DEBT FAIR FARM FLAT HAKH
JUST MEED OWED TOLL DROIT
ENDOW ENDUE FATED MERIT
OWING COMING CUSTOM DESERT
EXTENT LAWFUL MATURE
PROPER UNPAID CONDIGN
EXACTLY FALDFEE FITTING
JETTAGE TALLAGE ADEQUATE
DIRECTLY HEREGELD HEREZELD
RIGHTFUL SUITABLE TRUNCAGE
DUEL TILT FENCE FIGHT AFFAIR
COMBAT DUELLO MENSUR
CONTEST MEETING CONFLICT
DUELLIZE HOLMGANG
DUELIST FIGHTER SPADASSIN
DUENNA DRAGON GRIFFIN
CHAPERON
DUES TOLLS DROITS CHIEFRY
INWARDS JETTAGE PAYMENT
PENSION QUAYAGE ALTARAGE
HAVENAGE SOUNDAGE THIRLAGE
WHARFAGE
DUET DUO TWO DUETTO
TWOSOME
(BALLET —) ADAGIO
DUFF ALTER BRAND CHEAT FLOOR
PUDDING
DUFFER DUB MUFF SHAM CHEAT
BUFFER HAWKER RABBIT SHICER
PEDDLER
DUG TEAT
(— UP) HOWKIT
(PREF.) ORYCTO
DUGONG SEACOW YUNGAN
COWFISH HALICORE MUTILATE
SIRENIAN
DUGOUT ABRI BOAT BURY CAVE
BANCA BONGO BUNGO CANOE
DONGA DUNGA SHELL BAROTO
BUNKER CAYUCA CAYUCO CORIAL
TROUGH BANTING PIRAGUA

PIROGUE SHELTER BLINDAGE
LIPALIPA
DUHSHASANA (FATHER OF —)
DHRITARASHTRA
DUIKER IPITI DUYKER BLAUBOK
DUKE DUC DUX KNEZ PEER AYMON
CHIEF KNIAZ HERZOG LEADER
ORSINO AUMERLE GORLOIS
SOLINUS STEENIE HERETOGA
PROSPERO
DUKEDOM DUCHY ALBANY
DUCATUS
DULCET SWEET DULCID SIRUPY
SYRUPY SOOTHING
DULCIAN CURTAL
DULCIMER ROTA CANUN CITOLE
SANTIR CEMBALO MAGADIS
SANTOUR CYMBALOM PANTALON
SAUTERIE ZIMBALON
DULIA ADORATION
DULL DIM DOW DRY FAT LAX MAT
SAD ARID BLAH CLOD COLD
DAMP DEAD DILL DOWD DOWF
DOWY DRAB DREE DRUG DUMB
FLAT GRAY GREY LOGY MOPE
MULL POKY SLOW TAME THIN
TURN BESOT BLACK BLAND
BLATE BLEAR BLIND BLUNT
BRUTE CRASS DENSE DINGY
DOWFF DOWIE DOWLY DREAR
DUBBY DUNCH DUNNY DUSTY
FISHY FOGGY GLAZY GRAVE
GROSS HEAVY INERT LOURD
MATTE MORON MOSSY MUDDY
MUSTY MUZZY NOOSE PLUMP
POKEY PROSE PROSY SHADE
SLACK SOGGY STARY STILL SULKY
TERNE THICK UNAPT VAPID
WASTE BARREN BLEARY BOVINE
CLOUDY DAMPEN DARKEN
DEADEN DISMAL DRAGGY
DREARY DRIECH DRIEGH DROWSY
EARTHY FRIGID FRUMPY GLASSY
HEBETE JEJUNE LEADEN LOURDY
MUFFLE OBTUND OBTUSE
OPAQUE PALLID REBATE RETUND
SLEEPY SLOOMY SODDEN
SOMBER SOMBRE STODGY STOLID
STUFFY STUPID SULLEN TIMBER
TORPID TRISTE TURBID URLUCH
WOODEN ADENOID BLUNTED
CONFUSE DEADISH DISEDGE
DOLTISH DOWFART DRAINED
DULLISH DUMPISH HUMDRUM
INSIPID IRKSOME LANGUID
LUMPISH MUMPISH PEAKISH
PINHEAD PROSAIC SHEATHE
SOTTISH STUPEFY TEDIOUS
UNLUSTY VACUOUS BACKWARD
BANAUSIC BEFUDDLE BLOCKISH
BOEOTIAN BROMIDIC COMATOSE
COMATOUS DIDACTIC DISCOLOR
DULLSOME EDGELESS FRUMPISH
GAUMLESS HEBETATE INFICETE
LIFELESS LISTLESS LOURDISH
OVERCAST PLODDING SLOTTERY
SLUGGISH SOULLESS STAGNANT
TIRESOME PINHEADED
PONDEROUS SATURNINE
(— EDGE OF) ABATE
(— IN MOTION) LOGY
(— SCENT) FOIL
(— WITH LIQUOR) SEETHE

(BECOME —) PALL RUST
(MENTALLY —) DOPY DOPEY
BARREN
(PREF.) AMBLY(O) BRADY
DULLARD DOLT BOOBY DUNCE
IDIOT MORON DODUNK STUPID
BROMIDE DASTARD DOLDRUM
DULBERT POTHEAD BLINKARD
DULLHEAD
DULLED EMPTY HEAVY JADED
BROKEN CLOUDY GRAYED
SODDEN STUPID BLEARED
DULLISH DIRTY
DULLNESS DRAB HAZE YAWN
CLOUD TAMAS FADEUR PHLEGM
TORPOR DIMNESS DOLDRUM
DULLITY DUNCERY FATUITY
LANGUOR OPACITY DUMBNESS
HEBETUDE SLOWNESS SOPITION
VAPIDITY SEGNITUDE STOLIDITY
DULL-SPIRITED MUZZY
DULL-WITTED FOZY WITLESS
BESOTTED DONNERED
(— PERSON) MOREPORK
DULLY FLATLY HEAVILY
DULSE DILLESK DILLISK SEAWEED
DULY DUE FITLY RIGHT RITELY
PROPERLY
DUMAH (FATHER OF —) ISHMAEL
DUMB DULL MUTE STONY SILENT
STONEY STUPID
DUMBBELL DUMMY DUNCE
HALTER KNOTHEAD
DUMBFOUND DAZE STUN AMAZE
CONFUSE CONFOUND SURPRISE
DUMBFOUNDED STUPENT
DUMBNESS SILENCE APHRASIA
DUMBWAITER LIFT DUMMY
DUMMY COPY DOLT MUTE SHAM
DUMBY FAGOT EFFIGY FAGGOT
PONTIC SHADOW SILENT
PHANTOM DUMBBELL
(SWORDSMAN'S —) PEL
DUMNORIX (BROTHER OF —)
DIVITIACUS
DUMP SUM TIP BEAT CASH COIN
COUP FALL HOLE JAIL MUSE NAIL
TOOM EMPTY HOUSE SHOOT
GRIEVE PLUNGE TIPPLE UNLOAD
BOGHOLE COUNTER DEPOSIT
REVERIE SADNESS STORAGE
(MINE —) BURROW
(PL.) SUDS MOPES SADNESS
DUMPCART DUMPER TUMBREL
TUMBRIL
DUMPER TIPMAN
DUMPLING COB CRUST KNODEL
KNAIDEL NOCKERL DOUGHBOY
QUENELLE
(PL.) KLOSSE GNOCCHI
DUMPY DUNCH GROSS PUDGY
SQUAB SQUAT DUMPTY STOCKY
SQUATTY
DUN BUM TAN FORT KICK URGE
ANNOY BROWN CRAVE CROWD
DINGY FAVEL MOUND SEPIA
DUNNER LEADEN PESTER PLAGUE
DUNNISH SWARTHY
DUNCE ASS DOLT DULT GABY
GONY BOBBY BOOBY DOBBY
IDIOT NINNY DULTIE HOBBIL
PEDANT DULLARD SOPHIST
NUMSKULL STUNPOLL

TOMNODDY WISEACRE
DUN-COLORED
(PREF.) PHAEO PHEO
(SUFF.) PHAEIN PHEIN
DUNDERHEAD OAF CLOD DOLT
DUNCE TURNIP GOMERIL
DUNE BAR DENE MEAL MOUND
TOWAN TWINE BARKAN
BARCHAN BARKHAN
(SAND —) DRAB SAIF SEIF
DUNG MIS CACK CHIP DOLL FIME
GORE MERD MUCK MUTE SOIL
TATH ARGAL ARGOL FECES FILTH
FUMET MIXEN SCARN SHARN
BILLET CASSON FIANTS LESSES
MANURE ORDURE SCUMBER
SCUMMER TREDDLE COWSHARD
DROPPING STALLAGE
(— AS FUEL) ARGOL CASSON
CASSONS
(— OF BEAST OF PREY) LESSES
(— OF DEER) FUMET FEWMET
(COW —) MIST UPLA COWSHARD
COWSHARN
(OTTER'S —) SPRAINTS
(SHEEP —) BUTTONS TREDDLE
TROTTERS
(PREF.) COPR(O) FIMI GUANI
GUANO MERDI SCAT(O) SCORI
SPATILO STERCO STERCOR(I)
DUNGEON PIT CELL HELL HOLE
LAKE VAULT CACHOT DONJON
PRISON CONFINE OUBLIET
REVOLVER OUBLIETTE
DUNGHILL MIXEN MIDDEN MIXHILL
DUNGON DONGON SUNDARI
DUNK DIP SOP SOAK STEEP
IMMERSE MOISTEN
DUNKER DIPPER TAUFER TUNKER
DUMPLER DUNKARD TUMBLER
DUNLIN STIB OXEYE PURRE STINT
DORBIE OXBIRD REDBACK
LEADBACK
DUNNAGE FARDAGE
DUODECIMO TWELVEMO
DUPE APE BAM FOB FOP MUG
BOOB COAX CONY CULL DUST
FOOL GECK GULL HOAX LAMB
ROOK TOOL CHEAT CHUMP
COKES CONEY CULLY HEALD
MOOTH MOUTH SLANG STALE
TRICK BEFOOL BUBBLE CHOOSE
CHOUSE COUSIN DELUDE DERIDE
MONKEY PIGEON PLOVER SQUARE
SUCKER VICTIM BECASSE
CATSPAW CHICANE CULLION
DECEIVE GUDGEON MISLEAD
SAPHEAD SWINDLE YOUNKER
DOTTEREL HOODWINK RODERIGO
DUPERY RAMP
DUPLE BINARY DOUBLE TWOFOLD
DUPLEX DOUBLE TWOFOLD
DUPLEXITY EQUIVOKE
DUPLICATE BIS COPY DUPE ALIKE
DITTO SPARE TALLY DOUBLE
FLIMSY REPEAT COUNTER
ESTREAT MISLEAD REPLICA
TWOFOLD LIKENESS
(PREF.) COUNTER
DUPLICATION DISOMATY
DUPLICATOR MIMEOGRAPH
DUPLICITY ART GUILE DECEIT
TRICKERY

DUPONDIUS BRONZE
DURABILITY WEAR FIBER FIBRE
STEEL DURANCE STAMINA
DURABLE FIRM HARD LASTY
STOUT STABLE STAPLE LASTING
SERVICE CONSTANT ENDURING
LIVELONG
DURABLENESS DURATION
DURAMEN HEARTWOOD
DURANCE DURANT DURESS
CUSTODY
DURANGO CARTOUCH
DURATION AGE DATE LAST LIFE
SPAN TERM TIME WHEN DUREE
KALPA SPACE LENGTH PERIOD
DURANCE LASTING INFINITE
LIFETIME STANDING
(— BREEZE) SLATCH
(BOUNDLESS —) INFINITE
(INFINITE —) ETERNITY
DURAZZO (WARD OF —) CALDORO
DURESS FORCE DANGER CRUELTY
DURANCE COERCION HARDNESS
PRESSURE
DURGA KALI CHAMUNDA
(HUSBAND OF —) SHIVA
DURIAN JAK JACK JAKFRUIT
DURING IN ON BIN AMID OVER
TIME AMONG INTRA WHILE
AMIDST WHILST WITHIN
AMONGST DURANTE PENDING
ENDURING
(PREF.) DIA INTRA
DURRA DARI DURA MILO JOWAR
CHOLUM DHURRA JONDLA
SORGHUM FETERITA
DURYODHANA (BROTHER OF —)
PANDU
(FATHER OF —) DHRITARASHTRA
(SON OF —) LAKSHMANA
(WIFE OF —) DRAUPADI
DUSACK TESACK
DUSHYANTA (SON OF —) BHARATA
(WIFE OF —) SHAKUNTALA
DUSK DIM EVE DARK DIMPS
GLOAM GLOOM DIMMET DIMPSY
DIMNESS DUCKISH DARKNESS
GLOAMING OWLLIGHT TWILIGHT
NIGHTFALL
DUSKY DIM DUN SAD WAN DARK
DUSK ADUSK BLACK BROWN
DINGY GRIMY MOORY TAWNY
GLOOMY PHAEIC SMUTTY
SOMBER SOMBRE SWARTH
DARKISH DARLING OBSCURE
SUBFUSC SUBFUSK SWARTHY
BLACKISH
(PREF.) PERCNO PHAEO
DUST ROW COOM DIRT FOGO
MUCK MULL PILM SMUT BRISS
CLEAN COOMB FLOUR POUCE
STIVE STOUR DREDGE FILLER
KITTEN POLLEN POWDER SMEECH
BEFLOUR EBURINE REMAINS
SAWDUST SMEDDUM TURMOIL
ANTELOPE BULLDUST PUMICITE
(— IN FLOUR MILLS) STIVE
(— IN QUARTZ MILL) SLICKENS
(BLOOD —) HEMOCONIA
(CHOKING —) POTHER
(COAL —) COOM CULM DUFF
COOMB
(COKE —) BREEZE

(COSMIC —) STARDUST
(DIAMOND —) SEASONING
(FIBER —) FLOCK
(FLAX —) POUCE POUSE
(THICK —) SMOTHER
(PREF.) CON(I)(ICO)(IDIO)(O)
(SUFF.) CONITE
DUST CLOUD STEW
DUST COVER WRAPPER
DUSTER DEVIL WILLOW ZEPHYR
TORCHON DUSTCOAT
DUSTY ADUST MOTTY MOTTLE
POUCEY STOURY POWDERY
UNDUSTED
DUTCH (SEE NETHERLANDS)
HOGEN HOLLAND
DUTCH FOIL ORSEDE ORSEDUE
DUTCH GOLD CLINQUANT
DUTCHMAN HANS HOGEN
BLANDA DUTCHY BELANDA
DUTCHER MYNHEER BATAVIAN
DUTCHMAN'S-BREECHES
DICENTRA
DUTIFUL PIOUS DOCILE LAWFUL
DEBTFUL DUTEOUS OBEDIENT
OFFICIAL REVERENT OFFICIOUS
DUTIFULNESS PIETY
DUTY DO END JOB LOT TAX CALL
CARE FYRD ONUS PART PROW
ROLE TAIL TASK TOLL WIKE
CHORE DEVER ERMIN LADLE LIKIN
OUGHT PREST RIGHT STINT
WIKEN BLANCH BURDEN CHARGE
COCKET DEVOIR DHARMA EXCISE
EXITUS HERIOT IMPOSE IMPOST
INGATE OFFICE RIVAGE TARIFF
AVERAGE BAILAGE BOOMAGE
FOSSAGE FURDUNG GRANAGE
INDULTO KEELAGE LASTAGE
PONTAGE PRIMAGE ROYALTY
SCAVAGE SERVICE STATION
TONNAGE TRIBUTE TRONAGE
TUNNAGE BALLIAGE BUSINESS
FUNCTION MALIKANA MALTOLTE
REDDENDO WEIGHAGE
OBLIGATION
(— FOR LEAD ORE) COPE
(CUSTOMS —) OCTROI
(FEUDAL —) HERIOT
(IMPORT —) ERMIN INDULTO
(MILITARY —) STABLES
(TIRING —) FATIGUE
(PL.) CUSTOMS INGATES
ACTIVITY
DUX CHIEF LEADER SUBJECT
HERETOGA
DWARF ELF PUG URF AETA CRUT
GRIG GRUB NANA RUNT CRILE
CROWL GALAR GNOME KNURL
MIDGE PIGMY PYGMY SCRUB
STUNT TROLL ABLACH ALVISS
CONJON DROICH DURGAN
DURGEN MIDGET SHRIMP
ANDVARI ANDWARI BLASTIE
CONGEON MANIKIN OVERTOP
PACOLET WRATACK ALBERICH
BELITTLE HOMUNCIO HOMUNCLE
HUCKMUCK KNURLING
MENEHUNE NANANDER
(PL.) CERCOPES NIBLUNGS
NIBELUNGS
(PREF.) NAN(O) NANN(O)
DWARF DANDELION KRIGIA

DWARFED STUNTY STUNTED
DWARF ELDER WALLWORT
DWARFING BRACHYSM
DWARFISH ELFIN PIGMY PYGMY
GRUBBY KNURLY NANOID
RUNTISH STUNTED
DWARFISHNESS NANISM
DWARFISM NANISM ATELIOSIS
DWARF MALLOW CHEESE PELLAS
DWARF RASPBERRY PLUMBOG
DWELL BIG COT DIG SIT WIN WON
BIDE BIGG HAFT HARP LIVE STAY
TELD WINE WONT ABIDE BIELD
BOWER BROOD BUILD DELAY
HOUSE LODGE PAUSE SHACK
STALL TARRY LINGER REMAIN
RESIDE TENANT CLIMATE
COHABIT INHABIT CONVERSE
(— IN) BIG BIGG BEDWELL INHABIT
(— IRRITATINGLY) GRATE
(— ON) HARP BROOD GLOAT
DWELLER TENANT WONNER
DENIZEN PALEMAN DOWNSMAN
HABITANT OCCUPANT RESIDENT
(— BY SEA) PARALIAN
(BUSH —) HATTER
(CAVE —) CAVEMAN TROGLODYTE
(CITY —) SLICKER
(COAST —) BUFFALO ORARIAN
(LAKE —) LACUSTRIAN
(PL.) HUTHOLD
(SUFF.) ITE
DWELLING DAR HUT INN SEE WON
CASA FARM FLAT FORT HAFT
HALL HOME NEST ROOF SLUM
TENT WIKE WONE ABODE BOWER
CABIN DOMUS HOGAN HOOCH
HOTEL HOUSE HOVEL JOINT
MANSE MOTEL PLACE CASTLE
DUGOUT DUPLEX HOMING
HOOTCH MALOCA SHANTY
TEEPEE WIGWAM WONING
COTTAGE LODGING MANSION
SALTBOX TRAILER TRIPLEX
WONNING BUILDING BUNGALOW
DOMICILE TENEMENT PENTHOUSE
RESIDENCE
(— IN UNDERWORLD) CHTHONIC
(— PLACE) HOWF HOWFF
(— WITH ANOTHER) INMATE
(ATTRACTIVE —) BOWER
(CRUDE —) SHED SHEBANG
(LAKE —) CRANNOG PALAFITTE
(MEAN —) SHANTY
(MISERABLE —) BURROW
DOGHOLE
(NAVAJO —) HOGAN
(NEOLITHIC —) TERRAMARA
(ONE-ROOM —) CELL
(PORTABLE —) CAMPER
(RAMSHACKLE —) HUMPY
(RUDE —) BOTHY BOTHIE
(SMALL —) CRIB
(SUBTERRANEAN —) WEEM
(SWISS —) CHALET
(PL.) HOUSING
DWINDLE FADE FAIL FINE MELT
PINE WANE DECAY DRAIN PETER
TAPER TRAIL WASTE MOLDER
SHRINK CONSUME DECLINE
FRITTER MOULDER DECREASE
DIMINISH FORDWINE
DWINDLING DOWN FLAGGING

DYAD PAIR
DYBBUK GILGUL
DYE (ALSO SEE DYESTUFF) AAL DIP
LIT ANIL BLUE COLOR EMBUE
FUCUS IMBUE LOKAO STAIN
SUDAN TINCT VENOM ARCHIL
IMBRUE INFECT MADDER TINGER
ENGRAIN INTINCT LOGWOOD
LOGWOOD PUCCOON ZAMBESI
AMARANTH COLORANT DYESTUFF
FUGITIVE INDIGOID TINCTURE
(— FUR) FEATHER
(— NOT FAST) FUGITIVE
(BLACK —) GUAKO
(BLUE —) RUM ROOM SAXE WOAD
CYANINE DICYANINE
(BROWN —) CACHOU
(GENERAL —S) NIL NILL AZINE
BROWN EOSIN GREEN DIANIL
EOSINE ISAMIN ORANGE PURPLE
VIOLET CYANINE FUCHSIN
METANIL PONCEAU PRIMULA
ALIZARIN AURANTIA CIBACRON
DICYANIN EURHODOL FUCHSINE
HYPERNIC INDULINE NIGROSIN
TURNSOLE VIRIDINE NIGROSINE
SAFRANINE
(HAIR —) RASTIK
(KIND OF —) SRA
(ORANGE —) KAMALA ROUCOU
(PURPLE —) CASSIUS GALLEIN
TURNSOLE
(RED —) AAL ANATO AURIN EOSIN
GRAIN HENNA RUBIN ANATTO
AURINE CERISE EOSINE RELBUN
RUBINE ALKANET ANNATTO
CORINTH CRIMSON MAGENTA
PONCEAU SAFFLOR ALIZARIN
AMARANTH BORDEAUX CORALLIN
CROCEINE
(SCARLET —) TULY GRAIN
(VIOLET —) MAUVE ARCHIL ORCHIL
LACMOID ARCHILLA
(YELLOW —) ARUSA FLAVIN
CHRYSIN FISETIN FLAVINE
LAWSONE WONGSHY AURAMINE
DYED INGRAIN
(PERMANENTLY —) FAST
DYEING TINCTION
DYER LISTER TINGER TINTER
DYESTER FIELDER SKEINER
TAINTOR TINTIST
DYERMA ZARMA ZAREMA
DYERS' MULBERRY FUSTIC
DYERS'-WEED SOLIDAGO
DYESTUFF (ALSO SEE DYE) DYE
LIT WELD WOAD CHICA LOKAO
WOULD ANATTO BRAZIL KAMALA
LITMUS ORCEIN RELBUN
ALKANET ARNATTO CUDBEAR
DYEWARE SAFFRON INDULINE
LUTEOLIN PITTACAL PURPURIN
DYEWEED WOODWAX
DYEWOOD FUSTET FUSTIC
BARWOOD CAMWOOD HYPERNIC
DYING FEY DEATH MORENDO
PARTING MORIBUND
(— AWAY) CALANDO DILUENDO
MANCANDO PERDENDO
SMORZATO
DYNAMIC POTENT DRIVING
KINETIC FORCEFUL
DYNAMITE BLAST DUALIN

SAWDUST RENDROCK GELIGNITE

DYNAMO EXCITER TORNADO

(PART OF —) BRUSH FIELD FRAME
RIGGING ARMATURE COUPLING
COMMUTATOR

DYNASTY (OR MEMBER THEREOF)
KIN SUI WEI YIN CHIN CHOU HSIA
RACE SUNG TANG YUAN BUYID
CHING PIAST REALM RULER
SHANG HAFSID PRINCE SAFAVI
SELJUK ABBASID ALMOHAD
ARSACID ATTALID AYUBITE
AYYUBID BOUIDES FATIMID
HAFSITE IDRISID JAGELLO
LAKHMID MONARCH OMAYYAD
ROMANOV SAADIAN SAFAWID
SAMANID TULUNID ABBASIDE
AGHLABID AGLABITE ASMONEAN
BUWAIHID CAPETIAN CHALUKYA
DOMINION EDRISITE GOVERNOR
IDRISITE JAGIELLO LORDSHIP
SAFFARID SARGONID SASANIAN
SELEUCID SOFFARID SASSANIDE

DYSENTERY FLUX SCOUR
MENISON TOXEMIA DIARRHEA

DYSPEPTIC CACOGASTRIC

DYSPHORIA FIDGET

DYSSODIA BOEBERA

DZIGGETAI HEMIONUS

E

E EASY ECHO
EA HEA ENKI
EACH A EA UP ALL ILK THE UCH
ILKA UCHE EVERY APIECE EITHER
EVERYONE
(OF —) ANA
EAGER HOT RAD YAN ACID AGOG
AVID EDGY FAIN FELL FOND FREE
GAIR HIGH KEEN RATH SOUR
TARE THRO VAIN WARM WAVE
YARE YERN AFIRE AGASP ANTSY
BRIEF FIRST FRACK FRECK HASTY
HIGRE ITCHY PRIME READY
SHARP SNELL YIVER ARDENT
FIERCE GREEDY HETTER INTENT
STRONG TIPTOE ANXIOUS
ATHIRST BRITTLE BURNING
EXCITED FERVENT FORWARD
ITCHING PROVOKE DESIROUS
IRRITATE SPIRITED VIGOROUS
YEARNING SOLICITOUS
(— IN PURSUIT) SHARP
(WILDLY —) CRAZY
EAGERLY FAST FELL YERN HOTLY
BELIVE TIPTOE YARELY YEPELY
PRESTLY HUNGRILY INTENTLY
EAGERNESS GOG ELAN GARE ZEAL
ARDOR DESIRE FERVOR ARDENCY
AVIDITY ALACRITY CUPIDITY
DEVOTION FAINNESS FERVENCY
EAGLE AAR ERN CROW ERNE GIER
TERN HARPY AQUILA BERGUT
EAGLET FALCON FORMAL FORMEL
RAPTOR ALLERION BATALEUR
BATELEUR BEARCOOT BERGHAAN
RINGTAIL
(SEA —) ERN ERNE PYGARG
PYGARGUS
(PREF.) AET(O)
(SUFF.) AETUS
EAGLE OWL KATOGLE
EAGLESTONE AETITES
EAGLET BIRD LAIGLON
EAGLEWOOD AGAR AGILA ALOES
AGALLOCH AQUILARI
EAGRE BORE WAVE AEGIR HYGRE
EANFLED (FATHER OF —) EADWINE
(HUSBAND OF —) OSWIU
EAR LUG NEB CLIP HEAR HEED
HOOK LIST OBEY PLOW TILL
AURIS BRACE PINNA SENSE
SOUSE SOWSE SPIKE CANNON
CONCHA CROSET EARLET LISTEN
AURICLE HEARING SENSORY
AUDIENCE PAVILION RECEPTOR
(— OF BELL) CANON CANNON
(— OF CORN) COB ICKER MEALIE
NUBBIN CORNCOB
(— OF GRAIN) RISOM SPIKE
RIZZOM
(— OF WHEAT) SPICA WHEATEAR
(—S OF GRAIN) CAPES EARHEAD
(PART OF —) LOBE TUBE CANAL

HELIX INCUS PINNA CONCHA
MEATUS SCAPHA STAPES
TRAGUS COCHLEA MALLEUS
MEMBRANE TYMPANUM
ANTIHELIX ANTITRAGUS
(UNRIPE — OF CORN) TUCKET
(PREF.) AUR(I) AURICULO
OT(ICO)(IO)(O) SPICI SPICULI
SPICULO
(— OF CORN) ATHERO STACHY(O)
(SUFF.) OTIC
EARACHE OTALGY OTALGIA
EARCOCKLE PURPLES
EARDRUM TABOR TABOUR
TYMPAN MYRINGA DRUMHEAD
TYMPANUM
(PREF.) TRYPAN(O) TYMPAN(O)
EARFLAP LUG EARLAP EARTAB
EARMUFF
EARINE (LOVER OF —) AEGLAMOUR
EARL EORL GRAF JARL LORD PEER
COMES NOBLE CONSUL SIWARD
(— OF COVENTRY)
SNIPSNAPSNORUM
EARLDOM DERBY COUNTY
EARLIER ERE OLD ERST FORE
ELDER UPPER BEFORE FORMER
HITHER RATHER SOONER FIRSTER
FURTHER PIONEER PREMIER
PREVIOUS
(PREF.) FORE PROTER(O)
(— THAN) PRE PRO
EARLIEST ERST FIRST ELDEST
MAIDEN PIONEER PREMIER
RATHEST FURTHEST PRIMROSE
ABORIGINAL
(PREF.) EO
EAR LOBE LUG EARLAP
(— PEOPLE) OREJON
EARLY AIR ERE OLD GOOD HIGH
RARE RATH SOON FORME PRIMY
RATHE VERTY REARLY SUDDEN
TIMELY ANCIENT BETIMES
ERLICHE FORWARD YOUTHFUL
MATUTINAL
(PREF.) EO PALAE(O) PALE(O)
EARMARK BIT CROP SPLIT
LUGMARK OVERBIT SLEEPER
ALLOCATE OVERCROP UNDERBIT
EAR MUFF OREILET
EARN GET WIN FANG GAIN TILL
VANG ADDLE ETTLE GLEAR MERIT
GARNER HUSTLE OBTAIN
ACHIEVE ACQUIRE CHEVISE
DEMERIT DESERVE
(— BY LABOR) ADDLE SWINK
BESWINK
EARNEST ARRA DEAR DERN HARD
PAWN ARLES EAGER GRAVE
SMART SOBER STAID ARDENT
ENTIRE HANSEL HEARTY INTENT
SEDATE SOLEMN EMULOUS
ENGAGED FERVENT FORWARD

HANDSEL INTENSE SERIOUS
SINCERE ZEALOUS DILIGENT
EMPHATIC STUDIOUS
(IN —) AGOOD
EARNESTLY HARD DEARLY
WISHLY WISTLY EARNEST
DEVOUTLY DINGDONG ENTIRELY
HEARTILY INTENTLY INWARDLY
EARNESTNESS GLOW FERVOR
WARMTH GRAVITY DEVOTION
DILIGENCE
EARNINGS GET MAKING ADDLINS
PICKING ADDLINGS
EARPIECE BUTTON
EARPLUG STOPPLE TEMBETA
EARSPOOL
EARRING DROP GRIP EARBOB
EARLET PENDLE EARCLIP
EARDROP PENDANT EARSCREW
EAR SHELL ORMER ABALONE
EARSHOT SOUND HEARING
EARREACH
EARTH ERD ORB SET BALL BANK
BURY BYON CLAY CLOD DIRT
DUST FLAG FOLD GRIT LAND
LOAM MARL MASS MEAL MOLD
MOOL MUCK ROCK SOIL SORY
STAR VALE YIRD ADOBE CRUMB
FLOSS GLEBE GLOBE GROOT
INTER LOESS MOULD REGUR
TERRA TRASS UMBER WORLD
CENTER CENTRE COARSE
GROUND YACATA KOKOWAI
MIDGARD TERRENE TIERRAS
TOPSOIL TRIPOLI MAGNESIA
MIDGARTH
(— FOR RAMPART) REMBLAI
(— INHABITANT) TERRAN
(— PROVIDING OCHER) KOKOWAI
(— SUITABLE FOR CULTIVATION)
LAYER
(BLACK —) MUCK SORY KILLOW
AMPELITE CHERNOZEM
(BLUE —) KIMBERLITE
(BROWN —) UMBER
(CLAYEY —) LAME LOAM
(DRY —) MOOL GROOT
(FULLER'S —) CRETA CIMOLITE
SMECTITE
(GEM-BEARING —) BYON
(HEAVY —) BARYTA
(LOOSE —) CRUMB GEEST
(MOIST —) SLAB SLIME
(POOR —) RAMMEL
(RAMMED —) PISE
(RED —) RUDDLE
(REFUSE —) MURGEON
(RIVER-BANK —) GREWT
(SMALL —) TERRELLA
(SOAP —) SOAPROCK
(STRAW-YELLOW —) BISMITE
(SUN-DRIED —) SWISH
(VITRIFIED —) FLOSS

(VOLCANIC —) TRASS TARRASS
(PREF.) GE(O) TELLUR(I)
TERR(A)(E)(I)
(SUFF.) GAEA GEA
EARTHEN FICT DIRTEN EARTHLY
YARTHEN
EARTHENWARE PIG POT DELF
CHINA CLOAM CROCK DELFT
CLAYEN JASPER ASTBURY
BISCUIT FAIENCE POTTERY
TICKNEY BUFFWARE CROCKERY
MAJOLICA TALAVERA
(BROKEN PIECE OF —) CROCK
EARTHINESS SALT TERREITY
EARTHKIN TERRELLA
EARTHLY LAIRY CARNAL EARTHY
MORTAL EARTHEN GLEBOUS
MUNDANE SECULAR TERRAIN
TERRENE WORLDLY SUBLUNAR
TELLURIC TEMPORAL
EARTHNUT ARNOT ARNUT CHUFA
HOGNUT JARNUT PEANUT
PIGNUT HARENUT HAWKNUT
TRUFFLE
EARTH PIG ERDVARK AARDVARK
EARTHQUAKE QUAKE SEISM
SHAKE SHOCK TEMBLOR
SEAQUAKE
(PREF.) SEISMO SISMO
(SUFF.) SEISM SEISMAL SEISMIC
EARTHSTAR GEASTER
EARTHWALL TRINCHERA
EARTH WOLF AARDWOLF
EARTHWORK BANK RATH AGGER
CASTLE SCONCE RAMPART
TERRACE
(PL.) PARADOS
EARTHWORM ESS MAD WORM
ANNELID DEWWORM IPOMOEA
MADDOCK ANGLEDOG BRANDLIN
EACEWORM FISHWORM
RAINWORM TWATCHEL
BRANDLING LUMBRICID
OLIGOCHATE
EARTHY GROSS SALTY WORMY
CLODDY VULGAR EARTHLY
TERRENE BARNYARD TERREOUS
VISCERAL
EAR TICK PINOLIA
EAR TRUMPET CORNET
AEROPHONE
EARWAX CERUMEN
(PREF.) CERUMINI
EARWIG GOLACH GOLOCH
TOUCHBELL
EARWORM BOLLWORM
EASE CALM COSY COZY EASY REST
ALLAY KNACK PEACE QUIET
RELAX SLAKE LOOSEN PACIFY
REDUCE RELIEF REPOSE SAUGHT
SMOOTH SOFTEN SOOTHE
APPEASE ASSUAGE COMFORT
CONTENT FACULTY FLUENCY

FREEDOM LEISURE LIBERTY LIGHTEN RELIEVE SLACKEN SUBSIDE DIMINISH FACILITY MITIGATE MODERATE PALLIATE PLEASURE SECURITY UNBURDEN
(— OF A BURDEN) LIGHT
(— OFF) FLOW CHECK START SLOUGH
(APATHETIC —) INDOLENCE
(AT —) OTIOSE
(CAREFREE —) ABANDON

EASEL FRAME SUPPORT SCAFFOLD

EASEMENT EASE EASING RELIEF HERBAGE TURBARY SERVITUS WAYLEAVE

EASE-TAKING PICKTOOTH

EASIEST EFTEST

EASILY EASY EATH WELL LIGHT EATHLY GENTLY GLIBLY HANDILY LIGHTLY READILY SLIGHTLY SMOOTHLY
(PREF.) EU

EASINESS GRACE FACILITY

EASING DETENTE

EAST ASIA MORN LEVANT ORIENT SUNRISE EASTWARD
(— OF) FOLLOWING

EAST AFRICA (— TREE) PODO

EASTER PT PACE PASCH EOSTRE PASCHA PASQUE

EASTERN LEVANT ORTIVE AURORAL ORIENTAL

EASTERNER DUDE

EAST GERMANY
CAPITAL: EASTBERLIN
DISTRICT: GERA SUHL HALLE ERFURT ROSTOCK
RIVER: ELBE ODER HAVEL SAALE SPREE
TOWN: GERA SUHL HALLE ERFURT COTTBUS DRESDEN LEIPZIG POTSDAM ROSTOCK SCHWERIN MAGDEBURG

EAST INDIAN (— TREE) SAL AMLA DHAK TEAK KOKAN LANSA MAHUA MOHWA NIEPA PALAS PULAS ROHAN ROHUN SALAI SIMAL

EASTLAND ESTRICHE

EASTWARD EAST EASEL EASSEL

EASY CALM COZY CRIP EATH EITH GAIN GLIB MILD RIFE SNAP SOFT CUSHY JAMMY LARGE LIGHT PLAIN PRONE ROYAL SUAVE YEZZY CASUAL COMODO FACILE FLUENT FRUITY GENTLE GENTLY SECURE SIMPLE SMOOTH UNHARD ARTLESS GRADUAL LENIENT NATURAL CAREFREE CARELESS CAVALIER EXPEDITE FAMILIAR GRACEFUL HOMELIKE MODERATE TRANQUIL UNFORCED
(— IN MIND) SECURE
(— TO HANDLE) HANDSOME
(— TO UNDERSTAND) PELLUCID
(— TO USE) CLEVER

EASYGOING LAX QUIET DEGAGE

EAT FOG KAI SUP BITE CHOP CHOW DINE FARE FEED FRET GNAW GRUB HAVE HEYT MAKE PECK RUST TUCK ERODE FEAST GRAZE MANGE MUNCH SCOFF STOKE TASTE WASTE ABSORB BEGNAW DEVOUR INGEST NIBBLE RAVAGE CONSUME CORRODE DESTROY SWALLOW VICTUAL
(— A MEAL) GRUB
(— A SNACK) NOSH
(— AS HOGS) SLUICE
(— AWAY) GNAW ERODE RANKLE CORRODE
(— BETWEEN MEALS) NOSH
(— BIG MEAL) STOKE
(— CRUNCHINGLY) GROUZE
(— GLUTTONOUSLY) GUDGE STUFF
(— GREEDILY) GAMP GAWP SLAB SLOP TUCK CHAUM MOOCH SCOFF GOBBLE GOFFLE GUTTLE GUZZLE RAUNGE GLUTTON GOURMAND
(— HEARTILY) THORN
(— IN GULPS) LAB
(— MINCINGLY) PICK PICKLE PIDDLE
(— NOISILY) SLOP GULCH SLURP GUTTLE SLOTTER
(— OUT) EXEDE
(— RUDELY) TROUGH
(— SLOVENLY) SLUP MUMMICK
(— SPARINGLY) DIET
(— TO EXCESS) COLF BEZZLE
(— UP) DEMOLISH
(— VORACIOUSLY) CRAM WORRY
(— WITH GUSTO) SMOUSE
(— WITHOUT CHEWING) BOLT
(SUFF.) ESTES PHAG(A)(E)(IA)(ISM) (IST)(O)(OUS)(US)(Y) VORA VORE VOROUS

EATABLE FOODY COOKER EDIBLE ESCULENT

EATEN CANKERED
(HALF —) SEMESE
(PREF.) BROTO

EATER PECKER DEVOURER
(GREEDY —) GOURMAND

EATING BIT FOOD ESURINE
(— BETWEEN MEALS) TIFFIN
(— COARSE FOOD) FOUL
(— INTO) CANKEROUS
(— OUT) EXESION
(PREF.) PHAG(O)

EAVES EASE EASING

EAVESDROP DARK HARKEN LISTEN HEARKEN

EAVESDROPPER COWAN EARWIG DRAWLATCH

EAVES TROUGH CHENEAU

EBAL (FATHER OF —) SHOBAL

EBB FAIL FALL SINK WANE ABATE DECAY RECEDE REFLOW REFLUX RETIRE TIDING DECLINE REFLOAT SUBSIDE DECREASE DIMINISH
(— AND FLOW) ESTUS AESTUS FLUIDITY

EBBING AWANE REFLUENT REFLUOUS
(— AND FLOWING) TIDAL

EBED (FATHER OF —) JONATHAN
(SON OF —) GAAL

EBER (FATHER OF —) SALAH ELPAAL

EBLIS JANN IBLIS

EBONY EBON BLACK GABON GABOON WAMARA HEBENON IRONWOOD

EBULLIENCE OVERFLOW ELEVATION

EBULLIENT BRASH FERVID BOILING

EBULLIOSCOPE ZEOSCOPE

EBULLITION SEETHE FERMENT OUTBURST

ECAD ECOPHENE

ECCENTRIC FEY ODD OFF CARD DOER NUTS CRANK DOTTY KINKY OUTRE QUEER WIPER CRANKY LOCOED OUTISH PSYCHO SCREWY SHAGGY BIZARRE CURIOUS DEVIOUS ERRATIC STRANGE TOUCHED ABNORMAL FITIFIED PECULIAR SINGULAR
(— PERSON) KOOK

ECCENTRICITY KINK FERLY ODDITY ANOMALY CROTCHET QUIDDITY
(— OF CURVE) E

ECCLESIASTES KOHELETH QOHELETH

ECCLESIASTIC ABBE ABBOT CLERK VICAR ARCHON FATHER LECTOR LEGATE PRIEST KIRKMAN PRELATE SECULAR EPISTLER SUBDEACON

ECCLESIASTICAL CHURCH CANONIC CHURCHLY CHRISTIAN SPIRITUAL

ECHELES (FATHER OF —) ACTOR
(FOSTER SON OF —) EUDORUS
(WIFE OF —) POLYMELA

ECHEVIN SCABINE SCABINUS

ECHIDNA NODIAK ANTEATER EDENTATE MONOTREME PORCUPINE
(CHILD OF —) HYDRA LADON ORTHUS SPHINX CERBERUS CHIMAERA
(FATHER OF —) PHORCYS CHRYSAOR
(MOTHER OF —) CETO CALLIRRHOE
(SLAYER OF —) ARGUS

ECHINODERM CYSTID CRINOID BLASTOID STARFISH

ECHINOPANAX FATSIA

ECHINO-SOREX GYMNURA

ECHION (FATHER OF —) MERCURY
(MOTHER OF —) ANTIANIRA
(SON OF —) PENTHEUS
(WIFE OF —) AGAVE

ECHO ECO RING SING CHORUS REPEAT REVERB SECOND IMITATE ITERATE RESOUND RESPEAK RESPOND REVOICE REDOUBLE RESPONSE
(— EFFECT) REVERB
(RADAR —) ANGEL

ECLAT FAME GLORY RENOWN ACCLAIM SCANDAL APPLAUSE FACILITY PRESTIGE SPLENDOR

ECLECTIC BROAD LIBERAL

ECLIPSE DIM BIND BLOT HIDE BLIND CLOUD SHADE STAIN SULLY DARKEN DAZZLE DEFECT EXCEED OCCULT DEFAULT OBSCURE PRODIGY TRAVAIL OUTRIVAL OCCULTATION

ECLOGUE IDYL IDYLL BUCOLIC

ECOLOGIST BIONOMIST

ECOLOGY BIOLOGY BIONOMY MESOLOGY

ECONOMIC (PREF.) EC(O) OEC(O) OIKO

ECONOMICAL WARY CHARY FENDY FRUGAL SAVING CAREFUL PRUDENT SPARING THRIFTY SCREWING

ECONOMICS PLUTONOMY

ECONOMIST HUSBAND MANAGER PHYSIOCRAT
AMERICAN DAY ELY GRAY POOR ADAMS ARROW BALCH CAREY CLARK DEWEY HANEY HICKS LUBIN MEYER WELLS YOUNG CARVER DUNBAR DURAND ECCLES FISHER FOSTER GEORGE HADLEY HARVEY MILLIS RAGUET RIPLEY SPLAWN SUMNER TUCKER TURNER WALKER WEAVER WILLIS BULLOCK COMMONS CROWELL GARRETT JOHNSON KUZNETS TAUSSIG TUGWELL ANDERSON FRIEDMAN KEMMERER KOOPMANS LAUGHLIN LEONTIEF MITCHELL GALBRAITH HENDERSON HOLLANDER SAMUELSON WILLOUGHBY
AUSTRALIAN DONALD
AUSTRIAN HAYEK MISES SPANN MENGER
BELGIAN ZEELAND LEVELEYE MOLINARI
CANADIAN MAVOR LEACOCK
DUTCH TINBERGEN
ENGLISH COLE MILL WARD WEBB WEST HICKS HIRST JAMES MEADE PAISH PETTY PRICE STAMP ASHLEY BARBON BAXTER COBDEN FARRER GIFFEN HOBSON JEVONS KEYNES KIRKUP LAYTON LESLIE REEVES ROGERS SALTER SENIOR TUCKER WILSON BAGEHOT CHAPMAN CLAPHAM FAWCETT MALTHUS MALYNES RICARDO TOYNBEE BELLERBY MARSHALL BEVERIDGE EDGEWORTH MACMILLAN MARTINEAU NICHOLSON OVERSTONE CUNNINGHAM
FINNISH PROCOPE
FRENCH SAY LEVY RIST BODIN GUYOT CAMBON HAUSER BASTIAT BLANQUI BLONDEL COURNOT FAUCHER GARNIER GOURNAY MONTYON QUESNAY MIRABEAU PECQUEUR ROEDERER WOLOWSKI CHEVALIER LEVASSEUR SIEGFRIED
GERMAN RAU BONN HAHN ENGEL FUCHS HARMS JUSTI KNIES LANGE BRIEFS BUCHER CONRAD ECKERT ERHARD GOSSEN HIRSCH SERING ANDREAE DUHRING EHEBERG GERLOFF HEIMANN JASTROW LEDERER MICHELS ROSCHER HUFELAND SCHAFFLE BAMBERGER RODBERTUS SCHMOLLER FLURSCHEIM HAXTHAUSEN HELFFERICH RAIFFEISEN SCHUMPETER OPPENHEIMER
GREEK ANDREADES
IRISH SMIDDY CAIRNES

BASTABLE CANTILLON
ITALIAN BODIO CARLI GIOJA
LORIA NITTI ROSSI BOTERO
PARETO BECCARIA GENOVESI
LUZZATTI SCIALOIA CERNUSCHI
PANTALEONI
NORWEGIAN FRISCH
POLISH GRABSKI WOJCIECHOWSKI
RUSSIAN BUNGE KANTOROVICH
VOZNESENSKI
SCOTTISH MILL SMITH
MACLEOD ANDERSON
MCCULLOCH
SWEDISH OHLIN CASSEL MYRDAL
SWISS SISMONDI CHERBULIEZ
URUGUAYAN COSIO
ECONOMIZE HAIN SAVE SKIMP
STINT SCRIMP HUSBAND UTILIZE
RETRENCH
ECONOMY SPARE SAVING SYSTEM
THRIFT MANAGERY PARSIMONY
ECOTONE EDGE
ECSTASY JOY BLISS POWER
SWOON TRANCE DELIGHT
EMOTION MADNESS RAPTURE
RHAPSODY
ECSTATIC HOT RAPT PYTHIAN
GLORIOUS
ECTENE IRENICON
ECTODERM EXODERM EPIBLAST
ECTOMORPHIC LINEAR ASTHENIC
LEPTOSOME
ECTROPION EVERSION
ECU CROWN SCUTE SHIELD

ECUADOR
ANCIENT NAME: QUITO
CAPE: ROSA PASADO PUNTILLA
CAPITAL: QUITO
COIN: SUCRE CONDOR CENTAVO
INDIAN: CARA INCA PALTA
   CANELO JIVARO
ISLAND: PUNA WOLF MOCHA
   PINTA BALTRA CHAVES
   DARWIN PINZON WENMAN
   ISABELA
ISLANDS: COLON GALAPAGOS
LANGUAGE: JIBARO QUECHUA
   SPANISH
MEASURE: CUADRA FANEGA
MOUNTAIN: ANDES SANGAY
   CAYAMBE ANTISANA COTOPAXI
NATIVE: MONTUVIO
PROVINCE: LOJA AZUAY CANAR
   COLON ELORO CARCHI GUAYAS
   MANABI BOLIVAR LOSRIOS
   COTOPAXI IMBABURA
RIVER: COCA MIRA NAPO DAULE
   PINDO TIGRE GUAYAS TUMBES
   ZAMORA CURARAY PASTAZA
   AGUARICO BOBONAZA
   CONONACO NARANJAL
   PUTUMAYO
TOWN: JAMA LOJA MERA NAPO
   PUYO TENA CANAR GUANO
   MANTA PAJAN PINAS PIURA
   QUITO YAUPI AMBATO CUENCA
   IBARRA PUJILI TULCAN
   ZARUMA AZOGUES CAYAMBE
   GUAMOTE MACHALA PELILEO
   PILLARO SALINAS BABAHOYO
   GUARANDA RIOBAMBA
WATERFALL: AGOYAN

WEIGHT: LIBRA

ECUMENE HEARTH
ECUMENICAL LIBERAL CATHOLIC
ECZEMA TETTER EARWORM
MALANDERS
EDACITY GREED APPETITE
VORACITY
EDDA SAGA
EDDISH ETCH ARRISH EEGRASS
EDDO TARO COCOYAM
EDDY CURL GULF PURL WASH
WEEL WELL ACKER GURGE SHIFT
SWIRL TWIRL WHIRL SWOOSH
VORTEX WIRBLE BACKSET
WREATHE
(PREF.) DINO
EDDYING WALE
EDEMA BRAXY TUMOR DROPSY
BIGHEAD HYDROPS ANASARCA
SWELLING
EDEMATOUS BLOATED HYDROPIC
EDEN ADEN HEAVEN UTOPIA
ARCADIA ELYSIUM PARADISE
(FATHER OF —) JOAH
EDENTATA BRUTA
EDENTATE SLOTH AARDVARK
ANTEATER
EDGE AGE BIT HEM JAG LIP RIM
BANK BERM BRIM BROW CURB
DRAW FACE KANT LIMB LIST
RAND SIDE TRIM WELL WHET
ARRIS BERME BEVEL BLADE
BOARD BRINK CHIMB CHIME
CREST EAVES FRILL KNIFE LABEL
LEDGE MARGE PEARL RULER
SHARP SIDLE SPLAY VERGE
BORDER CANTLE DECKLE FLANGE
FORAGE IMPALE LABRUM MARGIN
NOSING PLANGE MARGENT
SELVAGE SHARPEN VANDYKE
BOUNDARY EMBORDER KEENNESS
MAJORITY OUTSKIRT SELVEDGE
STICKING UMSTROKE
(— FORWARD) CREEP
(— IN MINING DRIFT) ARRAGE
(— OF BASKET) FOOT
(— OF BED) STOCK
(— OF BIRD'S BILL) TOMIUM
(— OF BOOK) FERRULE BACKBONE
(— OF BOOK COVER) FLAP
(— OF BRILLIANT) GIRDLE
(— OF CASK) CHIME CHINE
(— OF COAL PILE) RUN
(— OF DAM) CREST
(— OF DUMP) TOE
(— OF FLAG) HOIST
(— OF MESA) CEJA
(— OF MINERAL VEIN) APEX
(— OF ROADWAY) SHOULDER
(— OF RUDDER) BEARDING
(— OF RUFFLE) HEADING
(— OF SAIL) FOOT HEAD LEACH
LEECH
(— OF SAW) SAFE
(— OF SHELL) HINGE
(— OF STRATUM) BASSET
(— OF STREAM) HAG
(— OF TOOL) BEZEL BEZIL
(— OF TOOTH) SCALPRUM
(— OF TROUSERS) CREASE
(— OF VAULT) GROIN
(— OF WOOD) WOODRIME

(—S OF COAT) LAP
(BEVELED —) CHAMFER
(CUTTING —) SHOE
(DOUBLE —) FLAT
(EMBROIDERED —) SURFLE
SURPHUL
(EXTERIOR —) AMBITUS
(FRONT — OF BOOK) FACE
(ORNAMENTAL —) FRILL
(RAGGED —) RAG
(ROCKY —) ARETE
(ROUGH —S) FASH
(SHARP —) ARRIS BEARD
(UNPLOWED — OF FIELD) RAND
(UNTRIMMED —) DECKLE
(PREF.) AMBO
EDGED EDGY EROSE SHARP
CRENATE CUTTING
(— BY ARCS) INVECTED
EDGER WHETTER STRANDER
EDGING HEM CURB EDGE LACE
LIST FILET FRILL LEDGE PICOT
BORDER FILLET FRINGE LIMBUS
BEADING BINDING GIMPING
HAMBURG COQUILLE FRILLING
PUNTILLA RICKRACK SKIRTING
SURROUND PASSEMENTERIE
EDGY EAGER SHARP ANGULAR
CRITICAL SNAPPISH
EDIBLE EDULE EATABLE ESCULENT
EDICT ACT BAN LAW BULL FIAT
TYPE ARRET BANDO BULLA IRADE
ORDER SANAD UKASE ASSIZE
DECREE DICTUM NOTICE
COMMAND EMBARGO PLACARD
PROCESS PROGRAM STATUTE
ECTHESIS RESCRIPT
EDIFICE DOME CHURCH TURBEH
BUILDING ERECTION TETRAGON
EDIFY GROW BUILD FAVOR TEACH
BENEFIT IMPROVE PROSPER
CONVINCE INSTRUCT ORGANIZE
EDIFYING HIGH SAVORY ELEVATED
EDIT CUT EMEND DIRECT REDACT
REVIEW REVISE ARRANGE
COMPILE CORRECT PREPARE
PUBLISH REWRITE COPYREAD
EDITION KIND EXTRA FINAL FIRST
ISSUE PRINT STAMP ALDINE
DIGLOT SOURCE AUSGABE
BULLDOG HEXAPLA OCTAPLA
VERSION PRINCEPS VARIORUM
(FIRST —) PRINCEPS
EDITOR AUTHOR OVERSEER
REDACTOR
AMERICAN BOK BURR CARY DANA
DELL DUNN FOSS FUNK HILL
LUCE REID SHAW WARE YUST
ALLEN CANBY CLARK COLBY
DEBOW FENNO GRADY KNOTT
MABIE MOORE NILES PAINE
PRATT RIDER WHITE ABBOTT
AIKENS BARRON BOWKER
BOWLES CAPPER CATTON
CHURCH CLARKE COWLEY DANIEL
DENNIE DUBOIS FINLEY FLOWER
GILDER HANSEN HOOPER LARSEN
LUMMIS MALONE MANTLE
MARTIN MERWIN MONROE
MUNSON NATHAN PALLEN
RASCOE WILLIS ALDRICH
BURNETT COUSINS EASTMAN
FADIMAN FERNALD FREEMAN

GANNETT HAPGOOD HAZLITT
HOFFMAN HOLLAND HUBBARD
JOHNSON LINCOLN LITTELL
MENCKEN STEDMAN VIERECK
WALLACE ALLIBONE ANDERSON
BARSOTTI BENJAMIN CRAWFORD
GRINNELL GRUENING LIPPMANN
PETERSON SEDGWICK STRUNSKY
THOMPSON VANDOREN
WHEELOCK ALTSHELER
BARTHOLDT BLACKWELL
KAEMPFFERT UNTERMEYER
CHAMBERLAIN CROWNINSHIELD
ENGLISH LEE MEE READ RHYS
TODD CRAIG GIBBS WAUGH
ALLOTT BARNES DELANE GARVIN
HUTTON HUXLEY KELTIE SEAMAN
BOWDLER BURNAND CHAPMAN
HYAMSON KNOWLES VERRALL
CHISHOLM GOLDRING MUIRHEAD
PROTHERO SPEDDING
BOTTOMLEY CUSHENDUN
PEMBERTON RAPPOPORT
MONTGOMERY
FRENCH MIGNE MORTIER YRIARTE
CHAUMEIX HACHETTE
GERMAN BARTH HUBER MULLER
HUNGARIAN HARSANYI
SCOTTISH CURRIE HERVEY
ANDERSON HASTINGS LOCKHART
FINDLATER
EDITORIAL LEADER
EDO BENI BINI
EDRED (BROTHER OF —) EDMUND
(FATHER OF —) EDWARD
(MOTHER OF —) EADGIFU
EDUCATE REAR BREED TEACH
TRADE TRAIN EXPAND INFORM
SCHOOL DEVELOP NURTURE
INSTRUCT
EDUCATED BRED CIVIL TAUGHT
TRAINED INFORMED LETTERED
LITERATE
EDUCATION CLERGY NURTURE
BREEDING LEARNING NORTELRY
PEDAGOGY TRAINING
(LIBERAL —) HUMANITY
(PHYSICAL —) GYM
EDUCATOR TEACHER
AMERICAN DAY FEW HAM AMES
BLOW CASE CHEW COLN CONE
FORD FRYE HALL HART HILL HOLT
HOPE HULL HYDE LYON MANN
MOON PAGE RAND ROOT RUGG
TARR TRUE WARD WARE WEST
ADAMS ADLER AVERY AYRES
BAKER BATES BEARD BEERS
BERRY BROWN BRYAN BYRNE
CAPEN CAPPS CHASE CLARK
CROSS CURRY DAMON DENNY
DEWEY DOBIE ELIOT FRANK
FUESS GATES GAUSS GOULD
HEDGE JAMES JENKS JONES
KNOTT KRAPP KRAUS LANGE
LOCKE LOWES MANLY MEYER
MEZES ORTON PATRI PERRY
POUND ROLFE SCOTT SMITH
SMYTH TYLER UPHAM WHITE
YOUNG ANGELL BAGLEY BAILEY
BARNES BASCOM BAXTER
BOVARD BOWMAN BRIGGS
BUMPUS BUTLER CARTER
CONANT COOPER CORSON

COUNTS DABNEY DAVIES
DONHAM DRAPER DUBOIS
DURANT FERRIS FINLEY FINNEY
FOWLER GAYLEY GEDDES GILMAN
GOEBEL GRAVES HADLEY HARPER
HARRIS HAWKES HAZARD HIBBEN
HOWARD JESSUP JEWETT
JUDSON KELLER KEPPEL LANDIS
LERNER LOVETT LOWELL MARTIN
MATHER MCAFEE MEARNS MILLIS
MONROE NORTON PALMER
PARKER PEFFER PEIRCE PHELPS
PORTER SARETT SCOPES SLOANE
SPARKS STRONG STUART
THOMAS THWING WIGGIN
WILDER WRIGHT ANAGNOS
ANDREWS BABBITT BARBOUR
BARNARD BARROWS BENEZET
BETHUNE BRADLEY BRAWLEY
CALKINS CLAXTON COFFMAN
COLBURN COMFORT CONNELY
DENNETT DOHERTY DYKSTRA
ERSKINE FARRAND GARNETT
GILMORE GOODNOW GOODWIN
GOUCHER GUMMERE HASKINS
HERRICK HOPKINS HOUSTON
HUEBNER HULBERT HULBURT
JACKSON JARDINE JOHNSON
KIMBALL KIMPTON LEONARD
LINCOLN LINDSAY MATHEWS
MCMURRY PATRICK PEABODY
RAYMOND RICKERT ROLLINS
SCUDDER SHUSTER TATLOCK
TAUSSIG THACHER VANDYKE
VANHISE WALLACE WHEELER
WILLARD WOOLSEY ZEITLIN
ALDERMAN BANCROFT
BASHFORD BREWSTER BRITTAIN
CALLAHAN CHANDLER
COMMAGER COMSTOCK
COPELAND FLETCHER FOERSTER
GRISWOLD HARRISON HOLLOWAY
HUTCHINS LANGSTON LAWRENCE
MARQUAND MATTHEWS
MCGUFFEY MCKNIGHT PENNIMAN
PHILLIPS ROBINSON SCHURMAN
SEASHORE STODDARD SUZZALLO
TUTWILER WHEELOCK WILLIAMS
WOODBURN WOODWARD
ARMSTRONG AYDELOTTE
CARPENTER CHAUVENET
FAIRBANKS FAIRCHILD
GOODSPEED GRANDGENT
GREENOUGH HENDERSON
KITTREDGE LOUNSBURY
PARTRIDGE PATTERSON
PENDLETON SCHELLING
SHARPLESS SPAULDING
THORNDIKE WENTWORTH
BLOOMFIELD CHADBOURNE
KILPATRICK LONGSTREET
PARRINGTON STURTEVANT
WASHINGTON GILDERSLEEVE
ARGENTINIAN AVELLANEDA
AUSTRALIAN HOLME
CANADIAN GRANT PRATT CAPPON
HUTTON MACKAY MURRAY
MACLEAN
CZECH COMENIUS
DANISH LUND
ECUADORIAN ROCAFUERTE
ENGLISH DENT KING ALLEN BEALE
ELTON FITCH GRANT LUCAS

OGDEN ROUSE SMITH ARNOLD
BARNES COTTON FARMER
HADDON HOGBEN KEYNES
MORANT RIPMAN SADLER
BALFOUR BALLARD STARKIE
CHAMBERS CUNLIFFE SPURGEON
MANSBRIDGE
FRENCH ANDLER BOUTMY
CAMPAN FONCIN WAILLY
BELJAME BIDAULT BUISSON
BOUTROUX COMPAYRE
GERMAN AHN ALER KERN REIN
CAMPE GRAFE LANGE STURM
GEDIKE NATORP ZIMMER
BECKMAN FISCHER FROEBEL
DORPFELD DIESTERWEG
TROTZENDORF
HUNGARIAN BEOTHY
INDIAN HUSAIN GOKHALE
ITALIAN FEDELE VILLARI
GALLENGA MONTESSORI
JAPANESE ASAKAWA NEESIMA
FUKUZAWA
MEXICAN CAMPOS
SCOTTISH BELL DALGARNO
SWEDISH SIREN
SWISS GIRARD TOPFFER
FELLENBERG
EDUCE DRAW EVOKE ELICIT
EVOLVE EXTORT EXTRACT
EEL ELE GRIG LING OPAH SNIG
TUNA ELVER MORAY SIREN
APODAN CARAPO CONGER
FAUSEN MOREIA MURENE
CONGRIO KWATUMA LAMPREY
MURAENA SNIGGLE WRIGGLE
CONGEREE GYMNOTID KINGKLIP
(YOUNG —) ELVER OLIVER YELVER
(25 —S) STICK SWARM
EELGRASS DREW WRACK ENALID
EELPOUT BARD LING POUT QUAB
BURBOT CONGER GUFFER
YOWLER LYCODOID
EELSKIN (10 —S) TIMBER
EELSPEAR PILGER
EELWORM EEL NEMA
EERIE EERY SCARY TIMID WEIRD
WISHT CREEPY DISMAL GLOOMY
GOUSTY SPOOKY AWESOME
GHOSTLY GOUSTIE MACABRE
STRANGE UNCANNY ELDRITCH
GHOULISH POKERISH
EFFACE BLOT DASH DELE RASE
RAZE WEAR ERASE CANCEL
DEFACE SPONGE STRIKE DESTROY
DISLIMN EXPUNGE NULLIFY
UNPAINT
EFFECT DO SEE DENT DOES FECK
HAVE PRAY PREY TEEM WORK
CAUSE CLOSE ECLAT ENACT
ETTLE EVENT FORCE FRUIT ISSUE
STAMP ACTION ENERGY GROWTH
INDUCE INTENT OBTAIN RESULT
SECURE SEQUEL STEREO UPSHOT
ACHIEVE ACQUIRE ARRANGE
COMPASS CONDUCE EMOTION
EXECUTE FULFILL IMPRESS
IMPRINT OPERATE OUTCOME
PERFORM PROCURE PRODUCE
PURPORT REALIZE CAUSATUM
COMPLETE CONCLUDE CONTRIVE
FRUITAGE CONSEQUENT
(— OF PAST EXPERIENCE) MNEME

(BLURRED —) FUZZ
(COUNTERBALANCING —)
STANDOFF
(DAZZLING —) ECLAT
(DECORATIVE —) CHIPPING
(ELECTRICAL —) STRAY
(ESTHETIC —) ATMOSPHERE
(FALSE —) FACADE
(FINAL —) AMOUNT
(ILL —) EVIL
(INTENSE —) STRESS
(MOTTLED —) SPRINKLE
(MUSICAL —) BEND SHADING
(OPTICAL —) PHANTASMAGORIA
(PAINFUL —) JAR
(PAINTING —) STIPPLE
(PENETRATING —) SEARCH
(PERNICIOUS —) BLAST
(PERSONAL —S) DUNNAGE
(SECONDARY —) OVERTONE
(SHATTERING —) BRISANCE
(THEATRICAL —) CURTAIN
(TO HAVE —) MILITATE
(TOTAL —) ENSEMBLE
(TOXIC —S) THEISM
(TREMOLO —) BEBUNG
(VISIBLE —) TOUCH
(SUFF.) ERGATE ERGY
EFFECTIVE ABLE HOME MEAN
REAL ALIVE GREAT HAPPY PITHY
SIKER SOUND VALID ACTIVE
ACTUAL CAUSAL DEADLY DIRECT
FRUITY POTENT SEVERE SICKER
SOVRAN CAPABLE FECKFUL
OPERANT TELLING VIRTUAL
ADEQUATE FORCEFUL POWERFUL
SMASHING STRIKING VIGOROUS
TRENCHANT
EFFECTIVELY NAITLY
EFFECTIVENESS AIM BANG CHIC
EDGE VOLTAGE EFFICACY
LEVERAGE
EFFECTUAL ACTUAL TOOTHY
ADEQUATE POWERFUL
MAGISTRAL
EFFECTUATE FULFIL FULFILL
COMPLETE
EFFEMINATE NICE SOFT MILKY
MISSY SAPPY SISSY BITCHY
FEMALE LYDIAN NIMINY PRISSY
SILKEN TENDER WANTON
WEAKLY CITIZEN EPICENE
MEACOCK WOMANLY FEMINATE
FEMININE LADYLIKE OVERSOFT
WOMANISH
EFFERENT EXODIC
EFFERVESCE FIZZ HUFF KNIT
BUBBLE SPARKLE
EFFERVESCENCE FRET CRACKLE
SPARKLE
EFFERVESCENT UP BRISK FIZZY
QUICK BUBBLY ABUBBLE ELASTIC
BUBBLING
EFFERVESCING BRISK
EFFETE SERE PASSE SPENT
BARREN DECADENT ETIOLATE
MORIBUND
EFFICACIOUS VALID MIGHTY
POTENT FORCIBLE POWERFUL
SINGULAR VIGOROUS VIRTUOUS
OPERATIVE
EFFICACY DINT FECK DEVIL FORCE
GRACE MIGHT POWER DEGREE

VIRTUE POTENCY VALIDITY
OPERATION
EFFICIENCY POWER SKILL AGENCY
ABILITY FACULTY DISPATCH
EFFICACY PERFORMANCE
EFFICIENT ABLE GOOD SMART
VALID POTENT CAPABLE FECKFUL
POWERFUL SPEEDFUL
EFFIGY GUY IDOL POPE SIGN
DUMMY IMAGE LIKENESS
MONUMENT
EFFLORESCE GERMINATE
EFFLORESCENCE RASH BLOOM
BLOSSOM ROSEOLA ANTHESIS
ERUPTION WHITEWASH
EFFLUENCE ISSUE EFFLUX ELAPSE
EMANATE
EFFLUVIA SCENT
EFFLUVIUM AURA MIASMA
FLUXION SPECIES APORRHEA
EMISSION OUTGOING EMANATION
EFFLUX OUTGO OUTFLOW
EFFUSION
EFFORT JOB TRY TUG DINT FIST
HUMP JUMP MINT PASS SHOT
TOIL ASSAY BRUNT BURST CRACK
DRIVE ESSAY FLING LABOR NISUS
PAINS POWER REACH STUDY
THROE TRIAL ANIMUS DEVOIR
FAVORS FIZZLE FUFFLE PINGLE
STRAIN STROKE THRIFT ATTEMPT
CONATUS MOLIMEN NITENCY
SPLURGE STRETCH TENSURE
TROUBLE WORKING ENDEAVOR
EXERTION GOODWILL INDUSTRY
MOLITION REACHING STRIVING
STRUGGLE
(— FOR ONESELF) FEND
(ABORTIVE —) FIZZLE
(AGONIZED —) THROE
(ARTICULATE —) ACCENT
(EARNEST —) STUDY
(EFFECTIVE —) LICK
(FINAL —) CHARETTE
(INITIAL —) ASSAY
(MAXIMUM —) BEST
(SALVATIONIST —) ATTACK
(SINGLE —) HEAT TRICE
(STRENUOUS —) HASSEL HASSLE
(UNSUCCESSFUL —) ATTEMPT
(UTMOST —) DEVOIR BUSINESS
(VIOLENT —) BURST STRAIN
OUTRAGE STRUGGLE
EFFORTLESS EASY
EFFORTLESSNESS EASE
EFFRONTERY BROW FACE GALL
BRASS FRONT BRONZE AUDACITY
BOLDNESS CHUTZPAH FOREHEAD
TEMERITY
EFFULGENCE BLAZE GLORY
RADIANT RADIANCE SPLENDOR
EFFULGENT BRIGHT FULGENT
RADIANT SHINING
EFFUSE GUSH SHED FLING EFFUND
EMANATE DISPENSE
EFFUSION EFFLUX FOISON SCREED
SPILTH STREAM
EFFUSIVE GOOEY GUSHY LAVISH
SLOPPY GUSHING BUBBLING
EFFUSIVENESS SLOP
EFT ASK EVET NEWT LIZARD
TRITON
EGAD ADAD ECOD IGAD SGAD

EGEST VOID EXCRETE ELIMINATE
EGEUS (DAUGHTER OF —) HERMIA
EGG AI ABET GOAD GOOG OVUM
PROD SEED SPUR URGE CHECK
HUEVO OVULE SPORE DARNER
INCITE OOCYTE PEEWEE ZYGOTE
ACTUATE COCKNEY COKENEY
OOPLAST OOSPERM PROTOVUM
(— CASE) POD
(— CLUTCH) LAUGHTER
(— OF FISH OR LOBSTER) BERRY
(— ON) HAG EDGE GOAD URGE
(— PRODUCT) ZOON
(— WITH BACON) COLLOP
(—S OF BEES) BROOD
(—S OF SILKWORM) GRAINE
(ACID —) SLOWCASE
(CRACKED —) CHECK CRACK
LEAKER
(DRIED —S) AHUATLE
(DUCK —S) PIDAN
(FLY'S —) BLOW FLYBLOW
(FOSSIL —) OVULITE
(GOLDEN —S) SUNCUP
(GOOSE —) BLOB
(HUNT BIRDS' —S) OOLOGIZE
(INFERTILE —) CLEAR
(INSECT —) BLOW
(PART OF —) YOLK SHELL WHITE
ALBUMEN CHALAZA MEMBRANE
BLASTODISC
(SMALL —) OVULE OVULUM
(PL.) OVA ROE SEED EYREN
SPAWN CLUTCH ETTING
AHUATLE
(PREF.) OARI(O) OIDIO OO OV(I)(O)
(— CASE) OOTHEC(O)
EGG AND DART ECHINUS
EGGFRUIT LUCUMA CANISTEL
EGGHEAD HIGHBROW
INTELLECTUAL
EGGNOG NOG CAUDLE ADVOCAAT
EGGPLANT BRINJAL SOLANUM
BRINGELA EGGFRUIT
EGG-SHAPED OOID OVAL OVATE
OVOID OOIDAL OBOVOID
OVALOID OVIFORM
EGGSHELL SHARD CASCARON
EGG WHITE GLAIR ALBUMEN
EGG YOLK YELLOW VITELLUS
EGLAH (HUSBAND OF —) DAVID
EGLANTINE (FATHER OF —) PEPIN
(HUSBAND OF —) VALENTINE
EGO I ATTA SELF ATMAN EGOITY
FYLGJA CONCEIT SUBJECT
EGOCENTRIC INSEEING
EGOISM PRIDE ONEISM VANITY
CONCEIT EGOTISM OWNHOOD
SELFNESS NARCISSISM
EGOIST (AUTHOR OF —) MEREDITH
(CHARACTER IN —) DALE LUCY
CLARA HARRY OXFORD VERNON
DECRAYE CROSSJAY DARLETON
LAETITIA PATTERNE WHITFORD
MIDDLETON CONSTANTIA
WILLOUGHBY
EGOTISM EGO PRIDE EGOISM
VANITY CONCEIT EGOMANIA
EGREGIOUS FINE GROSS CAPITAL
EMINENT FLAGRANT PRECIOUS
SHOCKING
EGREGIOUSLY BEASTLY
EGRESS EXIT ISSUE OUTGO

OUTLET EXITURE OUTCOME
OUTGATE PASSAGE REGRESS
OUTGOING
EGRET HERON PLUME GAULIN
KOTUKU AIGRETTE GAULDING
EGYPT MIZRAIM

EGYPT

BAY: FOUL
CALENDAR: AHET APAP TYBI
PAYNI SHEMU THOTH CHOIAK
HATHOR MECHIR MESORE
PAOPHI PACHONS
CANAL: SUEZ
CAPE: BANAS RASBANAS
CAPITAL: CAIRO ELQAHIRA
CHRISTIAN: COPT COPTIC
COIN: FILS DINAR GIRSH POUND
DIRHAM GUINEA JUNAYH
PIASTER MILLIEME
DAM: ASWAN
DESERT: LIBYAN
GOVERNORATE: SUEZ CAIRO
CANAL SINAI BAHARIYA
BAHRIYAH ALEXANDRIA
GULF: AQABA
ISTHMUS: SUEZ
KING: AY IB KA ITI ITY TUT DJER
DJET HUNY PAMI PEPI SETI
TEOS TETI UNIS ARSES BEBTI
FOUAD ITETI KEBEH KHUFU
KNIAN MENES NEBKA NECHO
NEFER UDIMU ZEMTI ZOSER
CHEOPS DARIUS FAROUK
KHAFRE NARMER RANSES
SENEDJ XERXES MENKURE
PHARAOH PTOLEMY RAMESES
SALADIN CHEPHREN THUTMOSE
LAKE: EDKU IDKU MARYUT
MOERIS MANZALA BURULLUS
MAREOTIS
LAKES: BITTER
MEASURE: APT DRA HEN PIK ROB
DRAA KHET ROUB THEB ABDAT
ARDAB CUBIT FARDE KELEH
KILAH SAHME ARTABA AURURE
FEDDAN KEDDAH ROBHAH
SCHENE CHORYOS DARIBAH
MALOUAH ROUBOUH
TOUMNAH KASSABAH
KHAROUBA
MOUNTAIN: SINAI GHARIB
KATHERINA
NAME: UAR
NATIVE: ARAB COPT NILOT
BERBER MUSLIM NUBIAN
OASIS: SIWA DAKHLA KHARGA
FARAFRA BAHARIYA
PENINSULA: SINAI
PORT: TOR SUEZ ATTUR DUMYAT
QUSEIR RASHID SAFAGA
SALLUM ROSETTA DAMIETTA
HURGHADA PORTSAID
ALEXANDRIA
PROVINCE: GIZA QENA QINA
ASWAN ASYUT MINYA SOHAG
DUMYAT FAIYUM SAWHAJ
TAHRIR ALJIZAH BEHEIRA
BENISUEF DAMIETTA GHARBIYA
MINUFIYA SHARQIYA
RESERVOIR: ASWAN
RIVER: NILE
RUINS: ABYDOS THEBES

MEMPHIS PYRAMIDS
SUN GOD: RA RE ATUM
TOWN: NO MUT DUSH GIZA IDFU
ISNA QENA SAIS SIWA SUEZ
ZOAN ASWAN ASYUT BENHA
BULAQ CAIRO ELTUR FAYID
GIRGA GIZEH LUXOR NAKHL
SALUM SOHAG TAHTA TANIS
TANTA ABYDOW AKHMIN
DUMYAT ELQASR HELWAN
RASHID THEBES BURSAID
ROSETTA ZAGAZIG BENISUEF
DAMIETTA ISMAILIA
WEIGHT: KAT KET OKA OKE HEML
KHAR OKIA ROTL ARTAL ARTEL
DEBEN KERAT MINAE MINAS
OKIEH POUND RATEL UCKIA
HAMLAH KANTAR DRACHMA
QUINTAL
WELL: BIRTABA
WIND: KAMSIN SIROCCO
KHAMSEEN

EGYPTIAN ARAB COPT GIPPY
GYPPY TASIAN PHARIAN
BADARIAN MEMPHIAN
EHUD (FATHER OF —) GERA BILHAN
EIDER COLK WAMP DIVER EDDER
DUCKER SHOREYER
EIDOLON ICON GHOST IMAGE
IDOLUM PHANTOM LIKENESS
EIGHT ETA ECHT AUGHT CHETH
OCTAD OCTET OCTAVE OGDOAD
OCTONARY
(PREF.) OCT(A)(O)(U)
EIGHTEENMO OCTODECIMO
EIGHTH AUGHT
EIGHTH NOTE UNCA CROMA
CHROMA QUAVER
EIRE (SEE IRELAND)
EITHER ANY EDDER ITHER OTHER
WHETHER
EJACULATE BELCH BLURT EJECT
FLING EXCLAIM EMISSION
EJACULATION HOW COADS
ZOWIE BEGORRA CRIMINE
UTTERING
(MYSTIC —) OM
EJACULATORY SPUTTERY
EJECT OUT BLOW BOOT CAST EMIT
FIRE HOOF OUST SHED SPAT
SPEW SPIT VOID WARP AVOID
BELCH CHUCK ERUCT ERUPT
EVICT EXPEL SHAKE SHOOT
SPOUT SPURT VOMIT BANISH
BOUNCE REJECT SQUIRT
DEFORCE DISMISS EXCLUDE
EXTRUDE OBTRUDE DISGORGE
OUTBRAID
EJECTION BLOW OUSTER OUTING
EVICTION
EJECTOR LIFTER EDUCTOR
EKE IMP ALSO YEKE AUGMENT
ENLARGE HUSBAND STRETCH
APPENDIX INCREASE LENGTHEN
LIKEWISE UNDERLAY
ELABORATE LUSH FIKIE GREAT
LABOR DELUXE DRESSY ELABOR
ORNATE QUAINT REFINE CURIOUS
DEVELOP ENLARGE LABORED
PERFECT
(OVERLY —) NIGGLING
ELABORATED WROUGHT

ELABORATELY FANCILY
ELABORATENESS FINENESS
CURIOSITY
ELAH (FATHER OF —) UZZI CALEB
BAASHA
(SLAYER OF —) ZIMRI
(SON OF —) HOSHEA
ELAINE (FATHER OF —) PELLES
BRANDEGORIS
(SON OF —) GALAHAD
ELAIS (FATHER OF —) ANIUS
(MOTHER OF —) DORIPPE
(SISTER OF —) OENE SPERMO
ELAMITE SUSIAN ANZANITE
ELAN DASH ARDOR DRIVE GUSTO
VERVE SPIRIT WARMTH POTENCY
ELAND ORYX IMPOFO
ELAN VITAL ZOISM
ELAPS MICRURUS
ELAPSE GO RUN PASS ROLL SLIP
GLIDE SPEND EXPIRE
ELAPSING CURRENT
ELASAH (FATHER OF —) SHAPHAN
ELASMOBRANCH PLACOID
ELASTIC QUICK GARTER RUBATO
SPONGY BUOYANT SPRINGY
STRETCH CHEVEREL CHEVERIL
FLEXIBLE STRETCHY VOLATILE
ELASTICITY GIVE LIFE ELATER
SPRING STRETCH
ELATE BYOU PUFF CHEER EXALT
EXULT FLUSH LOFTY RAISE
ELATED EXCITE PLEASE THRILL
ELEVATE GLADDEN INFLATE
SUBLIME SUCCESS ELEVATED
HEIGHTEN INSPIRIT JUBILATE
ELATED RAD HIGH RADE CHUFF
ELATE HAPPY PROUD VAUDY
VOGIE WLONK CHUFFY JOVIAL
UPPISH UPPITY EXCITED
EXULTED JOCULAR SUBLIME
EXULTANT GLORIOUS INFLATED
JUBILANT PRIDEFUL UPLIFTED
ELATER BEETLE CRINULA SKIPJACK
ELATION JOY GLEE RUFF
BUOYANCY
ELATUS (FATHER OF —) ARCAS
(MOTHER OF —) ERATO
CHRYSOPELIA
(SON OF —) CYLLEN ISCHYS
PEREUS AEPYTUS STYMPHALUS
(WIFE OF —) LAODICE
ELBOW ELL BEND ANCON JOINT
NUDGE SHOVE CROSET ELBUCK
JOSTLE JUSTLE SPRING PIERDROP
(PREF.) CUBITO ULNO
ELCAJA MAFURA
ELDER AIN IVA AINE WITE ELLER
OLDER PRIOR MAHANT PRIMUS
SENIOR ANCIENT NEGUNDO
STAROST TRAMMON ANCESTOR
BOUNTREE BOURTREE CARELESS
DANEWORT ELDERMAN
PRESBYTER
ELDERLY AGED GRAY ALDER
ELDERN SENILE BADGERLY
ELDEST AYNE EIGNE OLDEST
PRIMUS
ELEASAH (FATHER OF —) HELEZ
RAPHA
ELEAZAR (BROTHER OF —) ABIHU
NADAB ITHAMAR
(FATHER OF —) AARON ELIUD

MAHLI PAROSH ABINADAB PHINEHAS
(GRANDFATHER OF —) MERARI
ELECAMPANE INULA CANADA ELFWORT SCABWORT
ELECT CALL PICK VOICE ASSUME CHOOSE CHOSEN DECIDE ISRAEL PREFER SELECT
ELECTION PROXY CHOICE LECTION PRIMARY
ELECTIONEERING HUSTINGS
ELECTIVE OPTION OPTIONAL
ELECTOR VOTER ELISOR CHOOSER ELIGENT INTRANT ELECTANT
ELECTORATE PEOPLE COUNTRY
ELECTRA LAODICE
  (BROTHER OF —) ORESTES
  (DAUGHTER OF —) IRIS AELLO OCYPETE
  (FATHER OF —) ATLAS OCEANUS AGAMEMNON
  (HUSBAND OF —) PYLADES THAUMAS
  (MOTHER OF —) ERATO TETHYS PLEIONE CLYTEMNESTRA
  (SON OF —) IASION DARDANUS
ELECTRIC
  (PREF.) POTAM(O)
  (— RAY) NARC(O)
ELECTRICIAN GAFFER JUICER BOARDMAN
ELECTRICITY JUICE POWER PYROGEN ELECTRIC GALVANISM
ELECTRIFY EXCITE THRILL STARTLE
ELECTROCUTE BURN EXECUTE
ELECTRODE DE DEE GRID ANODE PLATE DYNODE CATHODE IGNITER CROWFOOT REOPHORE
  (PL.) ELEMENT
ELECTRODEPOSIT STRIKE REGULINE
ELECTROLYTE STRIKE IONOGEN
ELECTROMAGNETIC (— UNIT) OERSTED ABAMPERE
ELECTRON ION NEGATON POLARON NEGATRON POSITRON CORPUSCLE
ELECTRONIC RADIONIC
ELECTRONOGRAPHY ONSET
ELECTRON TUBE TRIODE
ELECTROPHONE MARTENOT
ELECTROPLATE SILVER
ELECTROTYPE PATCH CLICHE WORKER ELECTRO
ELECTRUM AMBER ELECTRE ORICHALC
ELECTRYON (DAUGHTER OF —) ALCMENE
  (FATHER OF —) PERSEUS
  (MOTHER OF —) ANDROMEDA
ELECTUARY DISCORD LECTUARY THERIACA MITHRIDATE
ELEGANCE CHIC GARB LUXE TONE CLASP GRACE STYLE SWANK TASTE FINERY GAIETY GAYETY LUXURY NICETY POLISH COURTESY EUPHUISM FINENESS FRIPPERY GRANDEUR SPLENDOR
ELEGANT CHIC DINK FAIR FEAT FINE FIXY GENT JIMP POSH CIVIL COMPT FANCY NOBBY RITZY SHARP SLEEK SWANK SWISH

CHOICE CLASSY DAINTY DELUXE DRESSY FACETE MINION POLITE PRETTY QUAINT SUPERB SWANKY URBANE VENUST CAPITAL CLEANLY COURTLY FEATISH FEATOUS GENTEEL MINIKIN REFINED SMICKER DEBONAIR DELICATE GINGERLY GRACEFUL GRAZIOSO HANDSOME POLISHED TASTEFUL CONCINNOUS
ELEGANTLY FINE TALLY FAIRLY GENTLY GINGERLY
ELEGIAC MOURNFUL EPICEDIAL
ELEGY POEM SONG DIRGE KINAH QINAH LAMENT MONODY EPICEDE
ELEKTRA (CHARACTER IN —) OREST AEGISTH ELEKTRA CHRYSOTHEMIS KLYTEMNESTRA
  (COMPOSER OF —) STRAUSS
ELEMENT AIR ATOM DIAD DYAD RECT WOOF BEARD ETHER FIBER FIBRE METAL MONAD PUNCT STUFF AETHER ARTIAD COSTAL FACTOR HEPTAD LOSSER MATTER MOMENT SIMPLE ACTINON ADAPTER BUNCHER CARRIER CATCHER ESSENCE FEATURE ACTINIDE BACKBONE CEREBRAL EQUATION PERISSAD RUDIMENT SELECTOR THERBLIG
  (— IN GRAPH) SPIKE
  (— IN WAVE) DART
  (— IN WORD GROUP) KOINON
  (— OF ALCHEMIST) AIR FIRE EARTH WATER
  (— OF EXISTENCE) DHARMA
  (— OF MACHINE) HORN SPIDER
  (— OF WEALTH) COMMODITY
  (ALIEN) ALLOY
  (ARCHITECTURAL —) SLAB
  (BINDING —) CEMENT
  (CHARACTERISTIC —) PARAMETER
  (CHEMICAL —) TIN GOLD IRON LEAD NEON ZINC ARGON BORON RADON XENON BARIUM CARBON CERIUM CESIUM COBALT COPPER CURIUM ERBIUM HELIUM INDIUM IODINE MURIUM NICKEL OSMIUM OXYGEN RADIUM SILVER SODIUM SULFUR ARSENIC BISMUTH BROMINE CADMIUM CALCIUM FERMIUM GALLIUM HAFNIUM HOLMIUM IRIDIUM KRYPTON LITHIUM MERCURY NIOBIUM RHENIUM RHODIUM SILICON TERBIUM THORIUM THULIUM URANIUM WOLFRAM YTTRIUM ACTINIDE ACTINIUM ANTIMONY ASTATINE CHLORINE CHROMIUM EUROPIUM FLUORINE FRANCIUM HYDROGEN LUTETIUM MASURIUM NITROGEN NOBELIUM NONMETAL PLATINUM POLONIUM RUBIDIUM SAMARIUM SCANDIUM SELENIUM TANTALUM THALLIUM TITANIUM TUNGSTEN VANADIUM METALLOID PALLADIUM PLUTONIUM
  (COMMUNION —) GIFT
  (CRIMINAL —) GANGLAND
  (DECORATIVE —S) ART
  (DOMINANT —) CAPSHEAF

(ELECTRIC —) IMPEDOR
(ESSENTIAL —) CORPUS
(EUCHARISTIC —S) HAGIA SPECIES
(FATAL —) BANE
(FUNDAMENTAL —) STAMEN KEYSTONE
(GLOOMY —) PALL
(HEATING —) CALANDRIA
(HYPOTHETICAL —) CORONIUM
(INTERFERING —) CRIMP
(LAMP —) GLOWER
(LEADING —) HEAD
(LINGUISTIC—) SERVILE INTENSIVE
(MILITARY —) SUPPORT
(MODIFYING —) LEAVENING
(MORAL —) DAENA
(MOST IMPORTANT —) CAPSTONE
(PRIMAL —) GUNA SALT ARCHE
(PRINCIPAL —) STAPLE
(SKELETAL —) SCLERE
(STRUCTURAL —) ARCUALE
(SUPPOSED —) PROTYLE WELSIUM VICTORIUM
(SUSTAINING —) BREAD STAPLE
(TRACE —) MICRONUTRIENT
(TRANSITORY —S) SKANDHAS
(UNITING —) BOND
(PL.) DETAIL ALPHABET
(PREF.) (FIRST —) STOICHIO
(SUFF.) AD IUM
(CHEMICAL —) ID IDE INE IUM
ELEMENTAL PURE BASIC PRIMAL SIMPLE PRIMARY ULTIMATE PRIMITIVE
ELEMENTARY PRIMAL SIMPLE INITIAL PRIMARY INCHOATE ULTIMATE RUDIMENTARY
ELEMI ANEMI ANIME MATTI RESIN CONIMA
ELEPHANT COW BULL CALF HINE PUNK HATHI HATTY JUMBO ROGUE MUCKNA TUSKER KOOMKIE AIRAVATA LOXODONT MASTODON OLIPHANT PROBOSCIDEAN
ELEPHANT FISH JOSEF JOSUP JOSEPH
ELEPHANTIASIS TYRIASIS
ELEPHANTINE HUGE ENORMOUS
ELEPHANT'S-EAR TARO
ELEPHANT SHREW JUMPER
ELEUT KALMUK KALMYK KALMUCK
ELEVATE HAIN JUMP LIFT REAR RISE EDIFY ELATE ENSKY ERECT EXALT EXTOL GRIMP HEAVE HOIST MOUNT RAISE TOWER REFINE UPLIFT ADVANCE DIGNIFY ENHANCE ENNOBLE GLORIFY PROMOTE SUBLIME UPRAISE HEIGHTEN INSPIRIT
ELEVATED EL FINE HIGH GREAT LOFTY NOBLE RISEN STEEP AERIAL AMOTUS ELATED RAISED RISING WINGED BULLATE ELEVATO EXALTED MOUNTED STILTED SUBLIME MAJESTIC UPLIFTED
  (— IN CHARACTER) HIGH
  (NOT —) COMICAL
ELEVATION UP ARM BAND BANK DOME DRUM GLEE HIGH HILL HUMP LIFT RISE SPUR TOFT TOOT UMBO AGGER BULLA GRADE

KNOLL MOUND PITCH RAISE RIDGE SHOAL SWELL TOWER WHEAL CONULE CRISTA HEIGHT PAPULE UPLIFT DIGNITY FURCULA MAJESTY UPRIGHT ALTITUDE EMINENCE EVECTION HIGHNESS LEVATION MOUNTAIN SWELLING MONTICULE
  (— OF CARTILAGE) ANTHELIX
  (— OF CUTICLE) BLEB
  (— OF SKIN) BLISTER
  (— ON TOOTH) STYLE
  (— SEPARATING CREEKS) BUGOR
  (GUN —) RANDOM
  (TURRET —) HOOD
  (PREF.) ORO
ELEVATOR BIN CAGE LIFT SILO HOIST BRIDGE LIFTER TEAGLE HOISTER STACKER UPTAKER UPLIFTER UPRAISER
ELEVEN
  (PREF.) HENDEC(A) UNDEC(A)
ELEVENTH ELFT
ELF FAY HAG HOB IMP OAF PUG DROW FANE OUPH PERI PIXY PUCK DWARF ELFIN FAIRY GNOME OUPHE PIGMY PIXIE ELFKIN GOBLIN SPIRIT SPRITE URCHIN BLASTIE BROWNIE INCUBUS SUCCUBUS
ELFIN ELF FEY CHILD ELFIC ELFISH URCHIN
ELFISH ELFIN ELVAN ELVISH IMPISH URCHIN ELFLIKE TRICKSY
ELFRIDA (HUSBAND OF —) EDGAR
  (SON OF —) AETHELRED
ELIAB (BROTHER OF —) DAVID
  (DAUGHTER OF —) ABIHAIL
  (FATHER OF —) HELON NAHATH
  (SON OF —) ABIRAM DATHAN
ELIADA (FATHER OF —) DAVID
ELIADAH (SON OF —) REZON
ELIAKIM (FATHER OF —) ABIUD MELEA HILKIAH
  (SON OF —) AZOR JONAN
ELIAM (DAUGHTER OF —) BATHSHEBA
ELIASAPH (FATHER OF —) LAEL
ELIASHIB (FATHER OF —) BANI ZATTU
ELICIT DRAW MILK PUMP CLAIM EDUCE EVOKE EXACT FETCH WREST WRING DEDUCE DEMAND ENTICE EXTORT INDUCE EXTRACT PROVOKE SOLICIT
ELIDE OMIT SKIP ANNUL IGNORE DESTROY NULLIFY DEMOLISH SUPPRESS
ELIEZER (FATHER OF —) JORIM MOSES BECHER ZICHRI DODAVAH
ELIGIBILITY FITNESS
ELIGIBLE FIT ACTIVE WORTHY SUITABLE
  (— IN POKER) ACTIVE
ELIMELECH (SON OF —) MAHLON CHILION
  (WIFE OF —) NAOMI
ELIMINATE FAN COMB EDIT KILL EDUCE EXPEL PURGE SCRUB DELETE EFFACE EXCEPT IGNORE REMOVE SCREEN WINNOW BLANKET BRACKET DIVULGE EXCLUDE EXCRETE RELEASE

SCISSOR SILENCE SUBLATE
SEPARATE
ELIMINATION STRIP
ELIOENAI (FATHER OF —) NEARIAH
ELIPHAL (FATHER OF —) UR
ELIPHAZ (FATHER OF —) ESAU
  (MOTHER OF —) ADAH
  (SON OF —) TEMAN
ELIPHELET (FATHER OF —) DAVID
  ESHEK
ELISABETH (HUSBAND OF —)
  ZACHARIAS
  (SON OF —) JOHN
ELISHA (FATHER OF —) SHAPHAT
ELISHAH (FATHER OF —) JAVAN
ELISHAMA (FATHER OF —) DAVID
  (SON OF —) NETHANIAH
ELISHAPHAT (FATHER OF —) ZICHRI
ELISHEBA (BROTHER OF —)
  NAHSHON
  (FATHER OF —) AMMINADAB
  (HUSBAND OF —) AARON
ELISHUA (FATHER OF —) DAVID
ELISION SYNCOPE
ELISIR D'AMORE (CHARACTER IN —) ADINA BELCORE NEMORINO
  DULCAMARA
  (COMPOSER OF —) DONIZETTI
ELISSA (BROTHER OF —)
  PYGMALION
  (FATHER OF —) BELUS METGEN
  (HUSBAND OF —) ACERBAS
  SYCHAEUS SICHARBAAL
  (SISTER OF —) ANNA
ELITE BEST LITE PINK CREAM
  CHOICE CIRCLE FLOWER GENTRY
  SELECT PERFECTI
ELIUD (FATHER OF —) ACHIM
ELIXIR DAFFY AMRITA SPIRIT
  AMREETA ARCANUM CORDIAL
  CUREALL ESSENCE PANACEA
  MEDICINE
ELIZAPHAN (FATHER OF —) UZZIEL
ELK ALCE DEER LAMA LOSH ALAND
  ALCES ELAND LOSHE MOOSE
  CERVID SAMBAR WAPITI
  SAMBHUR WAMPOOSE
  (— HIDE) LOSH
  (YOUNG —) DEACON
ELKANAH (FATHER OF —) KORAH
  (SON OF —) SAMUEL
  (SLAYER OF —) ZICHRI
ELK BARK BIGBLOOM
ELL ULNA ELBOW ALNAGE
  ADDITION
ELLIPSE OVAL
ELLIPSIS BRING ELLIPSE
ELLIPSOGRAPH TRAMMEL
ELLIPSOID CONOID ELLIPTIC
  SPHEROID
ELLIPTICAL OVAL OVATE OBLONG
ELLOBIUM AURICULA
ELM ULME ELVEN ULMUS WAHOO
  MEZCAL CHEWBARK
  ORHAMWOOD
ELMODAM (FATHER OF —) ER
ELMSEED
  (PREF.) SAMARI
ELNAAM (SON OF —) JERIBAI
  JOSHAVIAH
ELOCUTION SPEECH DICTION
  ORATORY

ELOCUTIONIST READER RECITER
ELOIGN CONVEY REMOVE
  ABSCOND CONCEAL
ELON (FATHER OF —) ZEBULUN
ELONGATE EXTEND REMOVE
  STRETCH LENGTHEN PROTRACT
ELONGATED LANK LONG LINEAR
  OBLONG PROLATE SLENDER
  HAIRLIKE PRODUCED
ELOPE DECAMP ESCAPE ABSCOND
ELOQUENCE FACUND FLUENCY
  ORATORY
ELOQUENT VOCAL DISERT
  FACUND FERVID FLUENT SILVER
  RENABLE SPEAKING ORATORICAL
ELPAAL (BROTHER OF —) ABITUB
  (FATHER OF —) SHAHARAIM
  (MOTHER OF —) HUSHIM
ELPALET (FATHER OF —) DAVID

EL SALVADOR
CAPITAL: SANSALVADOR
COIN: PESO COLON CENTAVO
DANCE: PASILLO
DEPARTMENT: LAPAZ CABANAS
  MORAZAN SONSONATE
GULF: FONSECA
INDIAN: PIPIL
LAKE: GUIJA ILOPANGO
MEASURE: VARA CAFIZ CAHIZ
  FANEGA TERCIA BOTELLA
  CAJUELA CANTARO MANZANA
POINT: REMEDIOS
PORT: CUTUCO ACAJUTLA
RIVER: JIBOA LAPAZ LEMPA
RUINS: TAZUMAL
TOWN: CUTUCO IZALCO CORINTO
  METAPAN ACAJUTLA
  USULUTAN SONSONATE
  AHUACHAPAN
VOLCANO: IZALCO
WEIGHT: BAG CAJA LIBRA

ELSE OR ENS ENSE OTHER BESIDES
  INSTEAD
ELSEWHERE ALIBI EXCEPT THENCE
  (FROM —) ALIUNDE
ELUCIDATE CLEAR LUCID EXPLAIN
  SIMPLIFY
ELUDE BEAT FLEE FOIL JINK MISS
  MOCK SLIP AVOID DODGE EVADE
  BAFFLE BEFOOL DELUDE DOUBLE
  ESCAPE BEGUILE DECEIVE
  HEDGEHOP
ELUSIVE EELY LUBRIC SHIFTY
  SUBTLE TRICKY TWISTY EVASIVE
  BAFFLING FUGITIVE SLIPPERY
ELYSIUM EDEN ANNWFN
  PARADISE
ELYTRON HUSK SCUTE SHARD
  SHERD SHEATH
ELYTRUM SHARD TEGMEN
ELZAPHAN (FATHER OF —) UZZIEL
EM EMMA
  (HALF —) EN
EMACIATED LEAN POOR EMPTY
  GAUNT MEAGER PEAKED SKINNY
  WASTED TABETIC WASTREL
  MARASMIC SKELETAL
  WANTHRIVEN
EMACIATING MARCID
EMACIATION NITON TABES
  MACIES ATROPHY POVERTY

ASTHENIA MARASMUS
EMANATE FLOW ARISE EMANE
  EXUDE ISSUE DERIVE EFFUSE
  EXHALE OUTRAY SPRING
  BREATHE OUTCOME PROCEED
  RADIATE
EMANATING EFFLUENT
EMANATION FUG AURA BEAM
  BLAS GLORY NITON AZILUT
  BREATH EFFLUX ELAPSE EIDOLON
  MOFETTE OUTCOME PROCESS
  SEPHIRA EMISSION PROCESSION
  (— FROM A MEDIUM) ECTOPLASM
  (SENSED —) KARMA
  (PL.) SCENT
EMANCIPATE FREE MANUMIT
  RELEASE LIBERATE UNFETTER
EMANCIPATION FREEDOM
  RELEASE
  (FINAL —) NIRVANA
EMASCULATE GELD SOFTEN
  EVIRATE CASTRATE ENERVATE
EMATHION (BROTHER OF —)
  MEMNON
  (FATHER OF —) TITHONUS
  (MOTHER OF —) EOS
  (SLAYER OF —) HERCULES
EMBALM BALM CERE MUMMY
  SPICE BALSAM SEASON CONDITE
  MUMMIFY
EMBANK BUND
EMBANKMENT BAY BAND BANK
  BUND DIKE DYKE FILL QUAY
  ARGIN DIGUE LEVEE MOUND
  REVET BUNKER STAITH BACKING
  BANKING PARADOS PILAPIL
  RAMPART RAMPIRE SEAWALL
  APPROACH STRENGTH
  REVETMENT
EMBARGO EDICT ORDER IMBARGE
  BLOCKADE STOPPAGE
EMBARK BANK SAIL SHIP ENGAGE
  ENLIST INSHIP INVEST LAUNCH
  IMBARGE
EMBARRASS SET CHAW CLOG
  FAZE HACK LAND POSE ABASH
  ANNOY SHAME UPSET BOGGLE
  CUMBER GRAVEL HAMPER
  HINDER HOBBLE IMPEDE PLUNGE
  PUZZLE RATTLE CONFUSE
  ENTRIKE FLUMMOX INVOLVE
  NONPLUS BEWILDER CONFOUND
  DUMFOUND ENCUMBER
  ENTANGLE HANDICAP IMPESTER
  OBSTRUCT STRAITEN
EMBARRASSED AWKWARD
  FLURRIED SHEEPISH
EMBARRASSING STICKY
  AWKWARD HIDEOUS
EMBARRASSINGLY AWKWARDLY
EMBARRASSMENT FIX GENE
  LURCH SHAME STAND CADDLE
  CUMBER HOBBLE PUZZLE
  NONPLUS CONFUSION
EMBASSY SAND ERRAND
  AMBASSY MESSAGE MISSION
  INBASSAT LEGATION
EMBATTLED BATTLED CRENELE
  BRETESSE CRENELEE
EMBAY BATHE DETAIN ENCLOSE
  SHELTER SUFFUSE ENCIRCLE
  SURROUND
EMBAYMENT FIORD FJORD

EMBED BED SET BOND IMBED
  STAMP CHARGE ENGAGE
  EMBOWEL IMMERSE
  (— IN SAND) DOCK
EMBEDDED INNATE ENGAGED
  IMMERSED
EMBELLISH GEM DECK GILD TRIM
  ADORN DRESS FUDGE GRACE
  BEDECK BETRIM BLAZON EMBOSS
  ENRICH FIGURE FLOWER
  APPAREL BEDRAPE EMBLAZE
  GARNISH MYSTIFY VARNISH
  BEAUTIFY DECORATE FLOURISH
  ORNAMENT
EMBELLISHED FLORID GESTED
  ORNATE COLORED FUCUSED
  BROCADED SPLENDID
EMBELLISHMENT FILIP GRACE
  FILLIP RELISH AGREMEN GARNISH
  GILDING WINDING AGREMENT
  FLOURISH MOUNTING ORNAMENT
  PARERGON TRAPPING TRICKING
  PASSAGGIO
  (MUSICAL —) MELISMA ROULADE
  ARABESQUE
  (PL.) FIXINGS
EMBER ASH COAL AIZLE GLEED
  IMBER CINDER
  (RED-HOT —S) BAGA
EMBEZZLE STEAL PECULATE
  SQUANDER
EMBEZZLEMENT THEFT
  PLUNDERAGE
EMBITTER SOUR BITTER CURDLE
  ACIDIFY ENVENOM ACERBATE
  EMPOISON VERJUICE
EMBITTERED SOURED ACERBATE
  ENFESTED
EMBLAZON LAUD ADORN EXTOL
  BLAZON DISPLAY EMBLAZE
  EXHIBIT GLORIFY
EMBLAZONED CLOUE CLOUEE
  CRINED CRESTED BRISTLED
  (— WITH ANTLERS) ATTIRED
  (— WITH BEARD) BARBED
EMBLAZONMENT HERALDRY
EMBLEM BAR ANKH ATEN LOGO
  MACE ORLE SEAL SIGN STAR
  TYPE AWARD BADGE CREST
  CROSS EAGLE FAVOR IMAGE
  TIARA TOKEN DEVICE DIADEM
  ENSIGN FIGURE KAHILI SABCAT
  SHIELD SIGNAL SYMBOL TRISUL
  CHARACT IMPRESA IMPRESE
  SCEPTER SCEPTRE ALLEGORY
  CADUCEUS COLOPHON INSIGNIA
  (— OF CUCKOLD) HORN
  (— OF IMMORTALITY) AMARANTH
  (— OF IRELAND) SHAMROCK
  (— OF WALES) LEEK
  (AUTOMOBILE —) MARQUE
  (PRINTING —) COLOPHON
  (SACRED —) HIEROGRAM
EMBLEMATIC TYPAL FIGURAL
  TYPICAL SYMBOLIC
EMBLIC AMLA AULA MYROBALAN
EMBODIMENT MAP SON SELF
  AVATAR GENIUS EPITOME
  IMAGERY BODIMENT
EMBODY BODY UNITE INBODY
  CONTAIN EXPRESS COALESCE
  ORGANIZE
EMBOLDEN BOLD BIELD BRAVE

ERECT NERVE ASSURE BOWDEN ENHARDY HEARTEN STOMACH

EMBOLUS CLOT STYLE

EMBOSOM BOSOM FOSTER CHERISH ENCLOSE IMBOSOM SHELTER SURROUND

EMBOSS BOSS HIDE KNOB KNOT ADORN BLOCK CHASE GOFFER INDENT POUNCE ANTIQUE CONCEAL ENCLOSE EXHAUST GAUFFER INFLATE ORNAMENT

EMBOSSED BOSSED RAISED ANTIQUE CHAMPED MATELASSE

EMBOSSING CELATURE

EMBOUCHURE LIP CHOPS LIPPING

EMBOWER BOWER

EMBOWERED ARBORED

EMBRACE ARM HUG CLIP COLL FOLD LOVE NECK PLAT SIDE ZONE ADOPT BOSOM BRACE CHAIN CLASP CLING CRUSH ENARM GRASP HALCH HALSE INARM OXTER PRESS TWINE ABRAZO ACCEPT ACCOLL AMPLEX BECLIP CARESS CLINCH COMPLY CUDDLE ENFOLD FATHOM HUDDLE INCLIP INFOLD PLIGHT SHRINE AMPLECT CHERISH CONTAIN ENCLOSE ESPOUSE INCLUDE INVOLVE ACCOLADE AMPLEXUS CANOODLE COMPLECT COMPRESS COMPRISE CONCLUDE ENCIRCLE

EMBRACING COLLING OSCULANT AMPLECTANT

EMBRASURE LOOP PORT VENT CRENEL CRENELLE PORTHOLE

EMBROCATION ARNICA EMBROCHE LINIMENT

EMBROIDER RUN TAT DARN FRET LACE BROUD COUCH FAGOT PANEL SMOCK BEWORK EMBOSS FAGGOT FRIEZE NEEDLE PURFLE STITCH SURFLE TISSUE BROIDER TAMBOUR ORNAMENT

EMBROIDERED BRODE BRODEE BROWDEN BROCADED

EMBROIDERER SPRIGGER

EMBROIDERY KANT LACE OPUS WORK BREDE ASSISI BONNAZ CREWEL EDGING HEDEBO APPAREL CHICKEN CUTWORK ORPHREY SETWORK TAMBOUR ARRASENE BRODERIE BROIDERY COUCHING FAGOTING LISTWORK PHULKARI SMOCKING TAPESTRY CREWELLERY NEEDLEPOINT

EMBROIL BROIL JUMBLE INVOLVE PERPLEX TROUBLE DISORDER DISTRACT ENTANGLE

EMBRYO GERM CADET FETUS OVULE FOETUS EMBRYON NEURULA PLANULA ACANTHOR BLASTULA GASTRULA PRINCIPE (PREF.) BLAST(O)

EMBRYONIC GERMINAL

EMCEE HOST

EME AUNT YEME UNCLE FRIEND NEIGHBOR

EMEND (ALSO SEE AMEND) EDIT MEND ALTER AMEND BETTER REFORM REPEAL REVISE CORRECT IMPROVE RECTIFY

REDRESS EMENDATE

EMERALD BERYL GREEN EMRAUD EMERANT PRASINE SMARAGD

EMERALD FISH ESMERALDA

EMERGE BOB DIP BOLT LOOM PEER RISE BREAK ERUPT EXUDE ISSUE START APPEAR BECOME PLUNGE SPRING DEBOUCH EXTRUDE

(— FROM EGGSHELL) HATCH ECLOSE

(— FROM SLEEP) AWAKE

(— SLOWLY) PEEK

EMERGENCE NEED BIRTH PINCH EGRESS GROWTH PRICKLE BECOMING DEBOUCHE ECLOSION EMERSION ERUPTION EXIGENCE TENTACLE

(— FROM DARKNESS) BREAK

EMERGENCY NEED PEND PUSH PINCH CRISIS STRAIT SUDDEN EMERGENT EXIGENCY JUNCTURE

EMERGENT RISING ONCOMING

EMERGING EMANANT EMERGENT

EMERITA HIPPA

EMERY EMERIL SMIRIS ABRASIVE CORUNDUM

EMETIC ALUM PICK PUKE PUKER VOMIT EVACUANT VOMITIVE VOMITORY

EMIGRANT EMIGRE EXODIST PATARIN SETTLER COLONIST PATERINE STRANGER

(— FROM MECCA) COMPANION

EMIGRATE MOVE REMOVE MIGRATE

EMIGRATION EXODUS HEGIRA HEJIRA SWARMING

EMILIA (HUSBAND OF —) IAGO PALAMON

EMINENCE DUN NAB BALL BERG CRAG KNOT MONS MOTE NOTE POLE RANK RISE SCAR TOOT CHIEF HOYLE KNOLL PERCH STATE WHEAL WORTH ASCENT HEIGHT KRANTZ RENOWN RIDEAU ALTITUDE GRANDEUR TUBERCLE

(— OF HAND) SUBVOLA

EMINENT BIG ARCH HIGH CHIEF GRAND GREAT LOFTY NOBLE NOTED FAMOUS MARKED SIGNAL EXCELSE SUBLIME TOPPING GLORIOUS RENOWNED SINGULAR TOWERING PROMINENT CONSPICUOUS

EMIR AMIR AMEER NOBLE RULER LEADER PRINCE ADMIRAL GOVERNOR

EMISSARY SPY AGENT SCOUT LEGATE DELEGATE

EMISSION FUME GUST VENT

EMISSIVE EMITTENT EXHALANT

EMIT RUN BARK BEAM CAST DRIP GIVE GUSH HURL LASH MOVE OOZE PASS POUR REEK SEND SHED SPIT VENT VOID WARP AVOID BELCH EJECT ERUCT EXERT EXUDE FLASH FLING ISSUE UTTER YIELD DECANT DONATE EVOLVE EXHALE EXPIRE SPREAD BREATHE DISTILL EMANATE EXHAUST OUTSEND RADIATE

REFLAIR ERUCTATE TRANSMIT

(— COHERENT LIGHT) LASE

(— FOAM) SPURGE

(— FORCEFULLY) FIRE

(— IN PUFFS) PLUFF

(— LIGHT) GLOW

(— ODOR) REEK STEAM

(— OUTCRIES) CHUNNER CHUNTER

(— PLAY OF COLORS) OPALESCE

(— RAYS) RADIATE IRRADIATE

(— SMOKE) SMEECH

(— SOUND) BUFF MOVE

(— SPARKS) SNAP

EMITTING EMISSIVE SOUNDING (SUFF.) (— LIGHT) ESCENT

EMMA (AUTHOR OF —) AUSTEN

(CHARACTER IN —) EMMA JANE BATES ELTON FRANK SMITH GEORGE MARTIN ROBERT WESTON FAIRFAX HARRIET CHURCHILL KNIGHTLEY WOODHOUSE

EMMENAGOGUE ALOE SAFFRON GROUNDSEL

EMMER SPELTZ AMELCORN

EMMET ANT ENEMY PISMIRE FORMICID

EMMOR (SON OF —) SHECHEM

EMOLLIATE SOFTEN

EMOLLIENT LENIENT ICHTHYOL LENITIVE MALACTIC MOLLIENT SUPPLING

EMOLUMENT FEES WAGES INCOME PROFIT SALARY BENEFIT STIPEND

EMOTION IRE LOVE ONDE PANG STIR AGONY ANGER CHORD GRIEF HEART SHAME AFFECT EFFECT MOTION RAPTUS SNIVEL SPLEEN ECSTASY FEELING PASSION VULTURE GRAMERCY MOVEMENT SURPRISE SENTIMENT

(CONTROLLING —) LEITMOTIF LEITMOTIV

(EVIL —) DEMON DAEMON (PREF.) THYM(O) (SUFF.) THYMIA

EMOTIONAL MUSHY DRIPPY EMOTIVE AFFECTIVE

(UNDULY —) SPOONY SPOONEY RHAPSODIC

EMOTIONLESS COLD

EMPATHY SYMPATHY

EMPEROR I IMP CZAR INCA KING TSAR AKBAR RULER TENNO CAESAR DESPOT KABAKA KAISER SULTAN BAGINDA MONARCH VIKRAMA AUGUSTUS IMPERIAL PADISHAH

EMPERY DOMAIN EMPIRE EMPIRY DOMINION

EMPHASIS ANGLE ACCENT STRESS WEIGHT EMPIRISM SALIENCE

EMPHASIZE HIT CLICK PINCH PRESS ACCENT BETONE CHARGE STRESS

EMPHATIC LOUD STRONG EARNEST MARCATO SERIOUS ENFATICO FORCIBLE MARCANDO POSITIVE RESOUNDING

EMPHATICALLY FLATLY STRONGLY POINTEDLY

EMPHYSEMA HEAVES

EMPIRE RULE SWAY POWER REALM REIGN STATE DIADEM DOMAIN EMPERY CONTROL KINGDOM IMPERIUM

(— STATE) NEWYORK

(— STATE OF SOUTH) GEORGIA

(SELJUK —) RUM ROUM

EMPIRIC QUACK IMPOSTOR

EMPIRICAL POSITIVE

EMPIRICIST VIRTUOSO

EMPLACEMENT BATTERY GALLERY PLATFORM

EMPLOY FEE PAY USE BUSK BUSY HIRE PLOY TAKE WAGE WISE ADOPT APPLY BESET IMPLY SPEND BESTOW ENGAGE ENLIST INFOLD INVOKE OCCUPY SUPPLY CONCERN CONDUCT ENCLOSE IMPROVE INVOLVE SERVICE UTILIZE PRACTICE

(— FLATTERY) COLLOGUE

(— ONESELF ABOUT) TOSS

(— SHIFTS) CHICANE

EMPLOYED APPLIED ENGAGED

EMPLOYEE HAND HELP BOOTS CLERK FACTOR LEADER BELLBOY BOOTBOY CALLBOY CARRIER SERVANT CHASSEUR CIVILIAN FLOORMAN IMPROVER

(— WHO RUNS ERRANDS) GOFER GOPHER

EMPLOYER BOSS JOSS BLOKE GAFFER ENGAGER MANAGER PADRONE GOVERNOR

(SMALL —) CORK

EMPLOYMENT FEE JOB USE CALL HIRE NOTE TASK TOIL USER WORK CRAFT TRADE TREAD USAGE MISTER THRIFT CALLING PURPOSE PURSUIT SERVICE USAUNCE BUSINESS EXERCISE POSITION RETAINER VOCATION

(CASUAL —) GRASS

EMPORIUM MART SHOP BAZAR STORE BAZAAR EMPORY MARKET STAPLE MONOPOLE

EMPOWER POWER ENABLE ENTITLE DELEGATE DEPUTIZE

EMPRESS IMPX EMPERESS IMPERIAL KAISERIN

EMPTIED DRAINED

EMPTILY TOOMLY

EMPTINESS VAIN VOID INANE ANEMIA VACUUM VANITY ANAEMIA INANITY VACANCY VACUITY LEERNESS

(— OF SPIRIT) ENNUI

EMPTY DRY FAT RID TIM AIRY BARE BOSS BUZZ CANT DEAF DUMP EMPT FALL FARM FREE GLIB HOWE IDLE LEER NEAR POUR ROOM TEEM TOOM VAIN VIDE VOID ADDLE AVOID BLANK BLEED CLEAN CLEAR DRAIN EQUAL EXPEL HUSKY INANE LEERY MOUTH SCOOP SHOOT SKAIL STARK START STRIP SWAMP TINNY WINDY BARREN BUBBLE CHAFFY DEVOID GOUSTY HOLLOW JEJUNE STRIKE SWASTY UNEMPT UNLOAD VACANT VACATE DELIVER DEPLETE EXHAUST EXPRESS UNTAKEN

VACUATE VACUOUS VIDUOUS
DISGORGE EVACUATE EVANESCE
NEGATION UNFILLED
(— AN EGG) BLOW
(PREF.) CEN(O) JEJUN(O) KEN(O)
EMPTY-HEADED VAIN DOLLISH
EMPTYING EVACUANT
(ACT OF —) KENOSIS
EMPTY-SOUNDING TOOM
EMPUSA MONSTER SPECTER
SPECTRE
EMPYREAN ETHER AETHER
HEAVENS EMPYREUM
EMU EMEU RHEA RATITE
EMU APPLE COLANE
EMU BUSH BERRIGAN
EMULATE APE VIE COPY EMULE
EQUAL EXCEL RIVAL COMPETE
IMITATE
EMULATION STRIFE CONTEST
PARAGON RIVALRY
EMULATOR RIVAL
EMULOUS EMULATE ENVIOUS
CORRIVAL
EMULOUSLY AVIE
EMULSIFIABLE SOLUBLE
EMULSION PAP LATEX
EMU WREN STIPITURE
EN NUT
ENABLE ABLE EMPOWER ENTITLE
QUALIFY INHABILE
ENACT LIVE MAKE PASS ADOPT
DECREE EFFECT ORDAIN
ACTUATE APPOINT PERFORM
PORTRAY
ENACTMENT LAW DOOM ENACT
NOVEL ASSIZE DECREE MEASURE
PASSAGE STATUTE ENACTION
ENACTURE
ENAMEL AMEL FLUX SLIP EMAIL
GLAZE GLOSS PAINT SLUSH
AUMAIL SHIPPO SMALTO
DENTINE LIMOGES SCHMELZ
ENAMOR LOVE CHARM SMITE
CAPTIVE
ENAMORED FOND EPRIS EPRISE
MASHED AMOROUS CHARMED
SMITTEN
(VAINLY —) FOOLISH
ENARCHUS (NEPHEW OF —)
MUSIDORUS
(SON OF —) PYROCLES
ENCAMP TELD TENT LODGE PITCH
INCAMP LAAGER BIVOUAC
LEAGUER
ENCAMPMENT CAMP DOUAR
ETAPE SIEGE LAAGER BIVOUAC
CASTRUM HUTMENT TOLDERIA
ENCASE CASE HOUSE SHELL
INCASE ENCHASE INCLOSE
SURROUND ENCAPSULE
ENCELIA INCIENSO
ENCEPHALON CEREBRUM
ENCHAIN FETTER INCHAIN
ENCHANT CHARM DELUDE
GLAMOR INCANT ATTRACT
BECHARM BESPELL BEWITCH
DELIGHT GLAMOUR BEDAZZLE
ENSORCEL CAPTIVATE
ENCHANTED RAPT HAGGED
CAPTIVE
ENCHANTER MAUGIS CHARMER
MAGICIAN MALAGIGI ARCHIMAGE

ENCHANTING ORPHIC WIZARD
HEAVENLY SPELLFUL
ENCHANTMENT HEX TAKE CHARM
FAIRY MAGIC SPELL SPOKE
CARACT CHANTRY DEVILRY
GRAMARY SORCERY SORTIARY
WITCHERY
ENCHANTRESS CIRCE FAIRY
MEDEA ACRASIA URGANDA
ENCHARGE ENJOIN ENTRUST
ENCHASE INFIX ENRICH ENGRAVE
ENCHIRIDION MANUAL
HANDBOOK TREATISE
ENCHORIAL NATIVE DEMOTIC
DOMESTIC
ENCIPHER CODE CIPHER ENCRYPT
ENCIRCLE ORB BAND BELT BIND
CLIP COIL GIRD GIRT HALO HOOP
PALE RING RINK STEM WIRE
ZONE BELAY BESET BRACE CLASP
CROWN EMBAY EMBOW GIRTH
HEDGE INORB ROUND TWINE
TWIST BECLIP CIRCLE EMBALL
ENGIRT ENLACE ENRING ENWIND
FATHOM GIRDLE IMPALE SWATHE
WRITHE BETREND COMPASS
EMBRACE ENCLAVE ENCLOSE
ENTWINE ENVIRON ENWHEEL
SERPENT WREATHE CINCTURE
CORSELET ENSPHERE IMMANTLE
SURROUND
ENCIRCLED GIRT CINCT BELTED
SUCCINCT
ENCIRCLEMENT EMBRACE
ENCIRCLING AROUND EMBRACE
CORONARY ENCYCLIC
(PREF.) AMPLEXI
ENCLAVE INLIER
(— IN SOUTH AFRICA) BANTUSTAN
ENCLOAK MANTLE
ENCLOSE IN BAY BOX CAN HEM
LAP MEW ORB PAR PEN PIN RIM
BANK BUNG CAGE CASE COOP
FORT GIRD HAIN HOOP PALE
SPAR TINE WALL WARD WOMB
YARD BOSOM BOUND BOWER
BRICK CHEST CLOSE DITCH
EMBAR EMBED EMBOX FENCE
FRAME GARTH GRIPE HEDGE
HOUSE IMBED INURN BOUGHT
CARTON CASTLE CAVERN CIRCLE
CORDON CORRAL EMBANK
EMBOSS EMPALE EMPARK
EMPLOY ENCASE ENCYST ENFOLD
ENGULF ENLOCK FASTEN IMMURE
IMPALE IMPARK INCASE INCLIP
INHOOP INSACK INWALL JACKET
PICKET POCKET TACKLE APPROVE
CAPSULE COMPASS CONFIDE
CONTAIN CURTAIN EMBOSOM
EMBOWEL EMBOWER EMBRACE
ENCHASE ENCLAVE ENGLOBE
ENHEDGE ENVELOP HARNESS
IMBOSOM IMMERSE IMPOUND
INBOUND INCLUDE INFIELD
PARROCK PINFOLD SHEATHE
BULKHEAD COMPRISE COMPRIZE
CONCLUDE CONVOLVE
EMBORDER ENCIRCLE ENSHRINE
ENSPHERE IMPRISON LANDLOCK
PALISADE PARCLOSE SURROUND
(— IN ARMOR) EMPANOPLY
(— LOGS) CRIB

ENCLOSED BOUND CLOSED
OBTECT INGROWN INTERNAL
ENCLOSING LIMITARY
(PREF.) PERI
ENCLOSURE HAG HAW HOK MEW
PAR PEN REE STY TYE BAWN
BOMA BYTH CAGE CAVE CELL
COOP DOCK FOLD HAIN HOCK
HOPE KILN LIST PALE PEEL SEPT
SKIT SLOT TIGH TOWN WALL
WEIR YARD ALTIS ATAJO BASIN
BLIND BOOLY BOOTH BOSOM
CAROL CLOSE COURT CRAWL
CREEP CUBBY FENCE FRANK
GARTH GOTRA HOARD KENCH
KRAAL LOBBY MARAI PLECK
POUND REEVE STALL STELL
AVIARY BOOLEY BOXING CANCHA
CARREL CORRAL COWPEN CRUIVE
DRYLOT GARDEN HURDLE INTAKE
KENNEL OUTSET PALING PRISON
SERAIL TAMBOR TEOPAN TINING
VIVARY WARREN BELLOWS
BOROUGH BULLPEN CLOSURE
COCKPIT EMBRACE GALLERY
GONDOLA HAINING HENNERY
HOUSING HUMIDOR LANTERN
PADDOCK PIGHTLE PUDDOCK
SEVERAL STUFFER TAMBOUR
AEDICULA CASEMATE CHIPYARD
CINCTURE CLAPNEST CLAUSURE
CLOISTER COMPOUND DELUBRUM
ENCEINTE ENCHASER PARADISE
POUNDAGE PRECINCT PURPRISE
SEPIMENT SERAGLIO SKIRTING
STOCKADE VIVARIUM
(— ABOUT ALTAR) BEMA
(— FOR BOWLING) ALLEY
(— FOR COCKPIT) CANOPY
(— FOR FISH) CROY YAIR YARE
KENCH SPILLER SPILLET
(— FOR JURY) BOX
(— FOR KNIGHTLY ENCOUNTERS)
BARRACE
(— FOR LIGHT) LANTERN
(— FOR ROASTING ORE) STALL
(— OF HOUSE) BAWN
(— SURROUNDED BY DITCH) COP
(ELEPHANT —) KEDDAH
(OBLONG —) CIRCUS
(PORTABLE —) PLAYPEN
(POULTRY —) HENNERY
(SACRED —) SECOS SEKOS
(PREF.) CLAUSTRO SEPTATO
(SUFF.) SEPTATE
ENCOLPION PANAGIA
ENCOMIAST EULOGIST
ENCOMIUM ELOGE ENCOMY
EULOGY PRAISE PLAUDIT
TRIBUTE PANEGYRIC
ENCOMPASS BEGO BELT CLIP
GIRD PALE RING SPAN WALL
WRAP BELIE BERUN BESET BIGAN
BRACE CLOSE CROWN ROUND
BEGIRD BEGIRT CIRCLE ENGIRD
BESEIGE COMPASS EMBOWEL
EMBRACE ENCLOSE ENVIRON
INCLUDE SUBSUME UMBESET
CINCTURE ENCIRCLE ENGIRDLE
PURPRISE SURROUND
(— WITH ARMS) FATHOM
ENCOMPASSED AMID BAYED
AMIDST BEGIRT

ENCOMPASSING ROUND AMBIENT
CINCTURE PROFOUND INCLUSIVE
ENCORE BIS AGAIN ANCORA
RECALL REPEAT
ENCOUNTER BIDE BUMP COIL
COPE FACE FIND KEEP MEET
MOOT RINK BRUSH CLOSE FIGHT
FORCE GREET INCUR OCCUR
ONSET SHOCK STOUR VENUE
ACCOST AFFRAY ANSWER ASSAIL
ATTACK BATTLE BREAST CAREER
COMBAT JOSTLE JUSTLE OPPOSE
RUFFLE ADDRESS AFFRONT
CONTEST COUNTER DISPUTE
HOSTING JOINING PASSAGE
CONFLICT CONFRONT CONGRESS
REANSWER RECONTER SKIRMISH
COLLISION
(— HOSTILELY) CROSS
(HOSTILE —) CLOSE
(PUGILISTIC —) MILL
ENCOURAGE DAW EGG ABET
BACK FIRM URGE BOOST CHEER
ERECT FAVOR FLUSH HEART
IMPEL NERVE SERVE STEEL
ADVISE ASSURE EXHORT FOMENT
FOSTER HALLOO HARDEN INCITE
INDUCE INVITE NUZZLE REHETE
SECOND SPIRIT UPHOLD
ADVANCE ANIMATE CHERISH
COMFORT CONFIRM CONSOLE
ENFORCE ENLIVEN FLATTER
FORTIFY FORWARD HEARTEN
INSPIRE PROMOTE STOMACH
UPCHEER UPRAISE EMBOLDEN
INSPIRIT REASSURE
ENCOURAGED BUCKED
CONFIRMED
ENCOURAGEMENT BOOST FLUSH
HURRAH COMFORT FOMENTO
IMPETUS BLESSING SANCTION
ENCOURAGING HELPFUL
FAVORING
ENCRATITE TATIAN AQUARIAN
ENCROACH JET PINCH POACH
IMPOSE INVADE TRENCH IMPINGE
INTRUDE SHINGLE ENTRENCH
INFRINGE INTRENCH TRESPASS
ENCROACHING INVASIVE
ENCROACHMENT BREACH
INROAD ENCROACH INVASION
ENCRUST CAKE CANDY BARKEN
BARKLE INCRUST
ENCRUSTED CAKED SCABROUS
ENCUMBER CLOG LOAD PACK
BESET CHECK CROWD TRASH
ACCLOY BEMOIL BURDEN FELTER
HAMPER HINDER IMPEDE LUMBER
MITHER MOIDER RETARD SADDLE
WEIGHT BEPAPER INVOLVE
OPPRESS ACCUMBER ENTANGLE
HANDICAP OBSTRUCT OVERCOME
OVERLOAD
ENCUMBERED HEAVY CONGESTED
ENCUMBRANCE CLOG LIEN LOAD
CLAIM BURDEN CHARGE CUMBER
TROUBLE MORTGAGE ALBATROSS
ENCYCLICAL PASCENDI
ENCYCLOPEDIA TOME
(GAME —) HOYLE
ENCYSTED CYSTIC SACCATE
SACCATED
END EN AIM DAG EAR FAG TIP

BUTT DATE DOUP FACE FATE
FINE FOOT GOAL HALT HEEL LAST
MAIN MARK SAKE STOP TAIL
TERM VIEW AMEND ARTHA
BLOCK BREAK CAUSE CEASE
CLOSE DEATH ENSUE EVENT
FINIS ISSUE LIMIT LOOSE NAPOO
OMEGA POINT PRICK RAISE
SCOPE SCRAP SHANK START
STASH THULE DECIDE DEFINE
DESIGN DOMINO EFFECT EFFLUX
ENDING EXITUS EXPIRE EXPIRY
FINALE FINISH INTENT NAPOOH
OBJECT PERIOD RESULT THIRTY
UPSHOT UTMOST WINDUP
ABOLISH ACHIEVE CLOSURE
CURTAIN DESTROY FANTAIL
FINANCE LINEMAN MEANING
OUTGIVE PURPOSE REMNANT
BOUNDARY COMPLETE
CONCLUDE DESITION DISSOLVE
FINALITY SURCEASE TERMINAL
TERMINUS ULTIMATE
(— DEBATE) CLOTURE
(— OF ANTENNA) CLAVA
(— OF ANVIL) BICKIRON
(— OF ARCHERY PILE) STOPPING
(— OF ARROW) NOCK
(— OF BEEF LOIN) BUTT
(— OF BLANKET) DAGON
(— OF BONE) EPIPHYSIS
(— OF BOOM) JAW
(— OF BOW) EAR
(— OF BRICK) HEADING
(— OF BRISTLE) FLAG
(— OF BUILDING) GABLE
(— OF CAN) BREAST
(— OF CANE) FRAZE
(— OF CART) TIB
(— OF CRESCENT) HORN
(— OF EAR CANAL) AMPULLA
(— OF EGG) DOUP
(— OF EXISTENCE) DEMISE
(— OF FABRIC) FENT
(— OF FISHHOOK) SPEAR
(— OF FLAG) FLY
(— OF FROG) TOE
(— OF HALTER) CAPITULUM
(— OF HAMMER) CLAW POLL
(— OF HAMMERHEAD) PEEN
(— OF HORSE-COLLAR) GULLET
(— OF INGOT) CROP
(— OF KEEL) GRIPE
(— OF LEVER) FORK
(— OF LOAF) HEEL
(— OF MINE TUNNEL) FACE
(— OF MINERAL LODE) SLOVAN
(— OF MINING LEVEL) DEAN
(— OF MUZZLE) MUFFLE
(— OF NAIL) CLENCH
(— OF ONE'S LIFE) DOOM
(— OF PIER) CUTWATER
(— OF PIPE) TAFT SPIGOT
(— OF POCKETKNIFE HANDLE)
BOLSTER
(— OF RAILROAD CAR) BEND
(— OF ROAD) ROADHEAD
(— OF ROD) FORKHEAD
(— OF SHEEP SHEARING) CUTOUT
(— OF SHIP) STERN
(— OF SPINE) ACRUMION
(— OF TENON) HAUNCH
(— OF TOOL) BUTT

(— OF UTERUS) FUNDUS
(— OF WORLD) PRALAYA
(— OF YARD) ARM YARDARM
(— ON) ABUT
(— ON POND) FOREBAY
(—S OF RIBBONS) FATTRELS
(—S OF SATURN'S RINGS) ANSA
(CANDLE —) DOUP SNUFF
(DOMINO —) ACE
(FAG —) RUMP
(HANGING —) DAG DAGGE
(JAGGED —) SHRAG
(NARROWED —) NEB
(NORTH — OF COMPASS NEEDLE)
LILY
(POINTED —) APEX
(POSTERIOR —) BOTTOM
(REEF —S) DEADMAN
(ROPE'S —) COLT FEAZE PIGTAIL
FEAZINGS
(SPECIAL —) SAKE
(TAPERING —) POINT
(TATTERED —) FRAZZLE
(ULTIMATE —) SUM TELOS
(UNPLEASANT —) GRIEF
(UPPER —) HEAD
(WARP —S) ACCIDENTAL
(PREF.) ACR(O) FINI TEL(IO)
ENDANGER DANGER HAZARD
IMPERIL SCUPPER
ENDANGERED BESTED BESTEAD
FRAUGHT
ENDANGERER MARPLOT
ENDEARMENT LOVE CARESS
ENDEAVOR DO AIM PUT TRY WIN
BEST MINT SEEK WORK ASSAY
ESSAY ETTLE EXERT OFFER
STUDY TEMPT TRIAL AFFAIR
ASSAIL DEVOIR EFFORT INTEND
STRIFE STRIVE AFFORCE
ATTEMPT CONATUS CONTEND
CULTURE EMPRISE EMULATE
IMITATE MOLIMEN NITENCY
WORKING EXERTION PURCHASE
STRUGGLE
(— TO CONCLUSION) STUDY
(BEST —) DEVOIR
(EARNESTLY —) FEND
ENDED DONE OVER PAST FINISHED
(— BY CONSONANT) CHECKED
ENDEMIC LOCAL ENDEMIAL
ENDING END CLOSE DEATH GRAVE
FINALE BREAKUP FINANCE
DESITION
(NERVE —) SPINDLE
ENDIVE CHICORY WITLOOF
ESCAROLE SCARIOLE
ENDLESS ANANTA ETERNE
ETERNAL FOREVER UNDYING
UNENDED UNENDLY DATELESS
FINELESS IMMORTAL INFINITE
UNENDING
ENDMOST TIPMOST FARTHEST
REMOTEST
ENDOCARP STONE PYRENA
PUTAMEN
ENDOGENOUS INNATE
AUTOGENIC
ENDOMORPHIC PYCNIC PYKNIC
ENDOPITE PETASMA
ENDOPLEURA TEGMEN
ENDORSE BACK SIGN ADOPT
BOOST DOCKET ENDOSS SECOND

APPROVE CERTIFY INDORSE
SPONSOR SUPPORT ADVOCATE
SANCTION RECOMMEND
ENDORSEE HOLDER
ENDORSEMENT FIAT FORM VISA
RIDER BACKING APPROVAL
HECHSHER SANCTION
ENDOSPERM FARINA ALBUMEN
ENDOSPORIUM INTINE
ENDOW DOW DUE DOTE GIFT
RENT VEST BLESS CROWN
DOWER ENDUE EQUIP FOUND
INDUE SEIZE STATE STUFF
ASSIGN CLOTHE DOTATE ENABLE
ENRICH ENSOUL ESTATE INVEST
CHARTER ENLARGE FURNISH
INSTATE APPANAGE BENEFICE
BEQUEATH ENTALENT
(— WITH FORCE) DYNAMIZE
ENDOWED ABLE GIFTED FAVORED
ENDOWMENT CLAY FINE GIFT
WAKF WAQF DOWER DOWRY
GRACE CORPSE GENIUS TALENT
APANAGE CHANTRY CHARISM
FACULTY APPANAGE DOTATION
PATRIMONY BENEFACTION
(NATURAL —S) BUMP DOTES
TALENT
(PL.) ALTARAGE
ENDPAPER FLYLEAF
ENDPIECE BRACE CHUMP
(— OF STETHOSCOPE) BELL
ENDUE DUE ENDOW INDUE TEACH
CLOTHE INVEST INSTRUCT
ENDURABLE LIVABLE BEARABLE
LIVEABLE PORTABLE
ENDURANCE GAME LAST TACK
PLUCK BOTTOM BEARING
COMFORT DURANCE GRANITE
LASTING STAMINA BEARANCE
DURATION GAMENESS HARDSHIP
PATIENCE STRENGTH
ENDURE GO ABY SIT VIE ABYE
BEAR BIDE DREE DURE HOLD
KEEP LAST TAKE TIDE WEAR
ABEAR ABIDE ALLOW BROOK
CARRY DRIVE POUCH SPARE
STAND STICK STOUT THOLE
TOUGH WIELD ABROOK ACCEPT
DRUDGE HARDEN REMAIN
SUFFER ABROOKE COMFORT
FORBEAR PERSIST STOMACH
SUPPORT SUSTAIN SWALLOW
TOUGHEN UNDERGO WEARING
CONTINUE FOREBEAR TOLERATE
ENDURING FAST SURE STOUT
BIDING DURING STABLE STURDY
ABIDING DURABLE ETERNAL
LASTING PATIENT IMMORTAL
REMANENT STUBBORN
PERENNIAL
ENDWAYS ANEND ENDWISE
ENDYMION (DAUGHTER OF —)
EURYDICE
(FATHER OF —) ZEUS JUPITER
AETHELIUS
(MOTHER OF —) CALYCE
(SON OF —) EPEUS PAEON
AETOLUS
(WIFE OF —) CROMIA ASTERODIA
HYPARIPPE
ENEMA CLYSMA CLYSTER
LAVEMENT

ENEMY FOE AXIS BOYG FEID DEVIL
FIEND SATAN FOEMAN HOSTILE
CONTRARY OPPONENT
(— OF MANKIND) DEVIL FIEND
SATAN
(PERSONAL —) HATER
ENEMY OF THE PEOPLE (AUTHOR
OF —) IBSEN
(CHARACTER IN —) KIIL PETER
MORTEN HORSTER HOVSTAD
ASLAKSEN STOCKMANN
ENERGETIC BUSY FAST FELL HARD
LIVE RASH BRISK DASHY LUSTY
PITHY STOUT TIGHT VITAL YAULD
ZIPPY ACTIVE HEARTY HUSTLE
LIVELY SPROIL ACTIOUS ANIMOSO
ARDUOUS DASHING DRIVING
DYNAMIC ENERGIC FURIOUS
NERVOUS PUSHFUL PUSHING
VIBRANT EMPHATIC ENERGICO
FORCEFUL FORCIBLE HUSTLING
VIGOROUS
(— PERSON) TOWSER
ENERGETICALLY MANLY
FURIOUSLY
ENERGID PROTOPLAST
ENERGIZE EXCITE ANIMATE
ENERGIZING KINETIC VIRTUAL
ENERGY U W GO PEP VIM ZIP
BANG BENT BIRR DASH EDGE
JASM LIFE SAKT SNAP TUCK ZING
ARDOR ECLAT FORCE INPUT
NERVE POWER STEAM SPICE
EFFORT FOISON INTAKE ORGONE
OUTPUT SPIRIT SPRAWL SPRING
SPROIL STARCH VIRTUE POTENCY
SPIRITS ACTIVITY AMBITION
DYNAMISM ENERGEIA MOTIVITY
PRAKRITI STRENGTH VIVACITY
(— PEAK) NUCLEUS
(EMOTIONAL —) LIBIDO
(LIBINAL —) CATHEXIS
(LIFE —) JIVA SAKTI SHAKTI
(LIGHT —) RAD
(MENTAL —) DOCITY PSYCHURGY
(POTENTIAL —) ERGAL
(QUANTUM OF —) PLASMON
(RADIANT —) SOUND ACTINISM
EINSTEIN
(VITAL —) HORME PANZOISM
(PREF.) (RADIANT —) PENETRO
(SOLAR -) HELI(O)
ENERVATE SAP COOK FLAG MELT
SOFTEN WEAKEN MOLLIFY
UNNERVE UNSINEW ENFEEBLE
ENERVATED BEDRID EFFETE
LANGUID BEDRIDDEN
ENERVATING MUGGY DREARY
ENERVATION COLLAPSE
ENFEEBLE NUMB FAINT SHAKE
APPALL DEADEN FEEBLE IMPAIR
SOFTEN WEAKEN DEPRESS
UNSINEW AFFEEBLE ENERVATE
IMBECILE UNSTRONG
ENFEEBLED FEY NUMB
ENFOLD (ALSO SEE INFOLD) LAP
FURL ROLL WRAP CLASP COVER
DRAPE ENROL IMPLY COMPLY
ENLACE ENROLL ENWIND
ENWRAP INCLIP INFOLD INWIND
SHADOW SWATHE WATTLE
EMBRACE ENCLOSE ENVELOP
ENVIRON INCLUDE INVOLVE

UMBELAP CONVOLVE
ENFORCE BULL LEVY EXACT FORCE
PRESS COERCE COMPEL EFFECT
FOLLOW INVOKE EXECUTE
IMPLANT
ENFORCED COMPULSORY
ENFORCER EXECUTOR
MUSCLEMAN
ENFRAMEMENT CARTOUCH
ENG AGMA
ENGAGE DIP WED BOOK BUSY
GAGE HAVE HIRE JOIN LIST MESH
RENT SIGN TAKE WAGE AGREE
AMUSE CATCH ENTER LEASE
PITCH TRADE TRYST ABSORB
ARREST EMBARK EMPLOY ENLIST
INDUCE OBLIGE OCCUPY PLEDGE
PLIGHT BESPEAK BETROTH
CONCERN CONDUCE CONSUME
ENGROSS IMMERSE INVOLVE
PROMISE AFFIANCE CONTRACT
COVENANT ENTANGLE INTEREST
INTRIGUE PERSUADE PREOCCUPY
(— DEEPLY) DROWN
(— IN) GO CUT SUE HAVE JOIN
LEAD PROSECUTE
(— IN ARGUMENT) BALK BAULK
(— IN COMBAT) DEBATE STRIKE
(— IN DEBATE) STONEWALL
(— IN DISCUSSION) CONTEND
(— IN PRANKS) LARK
(— IN TILT) JUST JOUST
(— WHOLLY) ABSORB CONSUME
IMMERSE
(SUFF.) (— IN) IZE
ENGAGED BENT BUSY FAST GONE
HIRED ACTIVE BONDED BOOKED
MESHED ASSURED BESPOKE
EARNEST ENTERED PLEDGED
TOKENED VERSANT ABSORBED
ATTACHED EMBEDDED
EMPLOYED INSERTED INTEREST
INVOLVED OCCUPIED PROMISED
(— IN) ABOUT
(— IN CONTROVERSY) DISPUTANT
(MENTALLY —) VERSANT
(WARMLY —) ZEALOUS
ENGAGEMENT AVAL DATE COWLE
SPURN ACTION AFFAIR BATTLE
COMBAT ESCROW PLIGHT
STANZA SURETY BARGAIN
BOOKING DUSTING SERVICE
CONFLICT RETAINER SKIRMISH
WARRANTY
(— TO MARRY) TRYST
(MILITARY —) DO SHOW
(SHORT —) SNAP
(SINGLE —) GIG
(THEATRICAL —) SHOP
(WRITTEN —) COWLE
ENGAGING SOFT SAPID SWEET
TAKING
ENGENDER BEGET BREED CAUSE
EXCITE GENDER DEVELOP
PRODUCE GENERATE INGENDER
OCCASION
ENGIDU EABANI
ENGINE GAS JET SIX FOUR GOAT
TANK EIGHT JINNY MOTOR OILE
STEAM BANKER DIESEL DOCTOR
DUDLER DUDLEY INGENE JORDAN
KICKER PUFFER RADIAL ROADER
YARDER MACHINE POACHER

POTCHER SKIDDER STEAMER
TRACTOR TURBINE BULLGINE
COMPOUND DOLLBEER
EXPANDER GASOLINE IMPULSOR
(— FOR HAULING LOGS) DUDLER
DUDLEY
(— FOR THROWING MISSILES) GIN
PETRARY SPRINGAL
(— OF TORTURE) GIN RACK
(— OF WAR) RAM SWEEP
HELEPOLE
(AIRPLANE —) SCRAMJET
(DONKEY —) DOCTOR
(FIRE —) TUB
(JET —) ATHODYD
(MILITARY —) BOAR TOWER
BRICOL FABRIC TREPAN BRICOLE
DONDINE PERRIER PETRARY
TORMENT WARWOLF BALLISTA
DONDAINE MANGONEL MARTINET
SCORPION
(RAILROAD —) HOG GOAT YARDER
SWITCHER
(REACTION —) THRUSTER
THRUSTOR
(ROCKET —) ARCJET VERNIER
(TYPE OF ROTARY —) WANKEL
ENGINEER PLAN GUIDE DRIVER
FANNER HOGGER MANAGE
SAPPER HOGHEAD PLANNER
PLOTTER CONTRIVE DESIGNER
INGENIER INVENTOR MANEUVER
AMERICAN AMY BURR BUSH DORR
DUNN EADS HERR HILL KRUG
LAKE PECK RICE ALLEN CARTY
ELLET GANTT HAUPT LAMME
MILLS MOORE OWENS PRATT
STOUT ARNOLD BOGART CONRAD
COOPER COWLES CRAVEN FERRIS
GREENE HAMMER HOLLEY HOLLIS
HOUDRY HUTTON JACOBY
LAMONT LITTLE MORGAN
NEWELL PARKER PENDER PORTER
RUMSEY WILSON BALDWIN
BARRELL BEHREND CLEMSON
CROCKER FANNING FREEMAN
GODFREY HASWELL KINEALY
KINTNER KNOWLES LATROBE
LEONARD PACKARD PARSONS
PATRICK SERRELL STRAUSS
WHIPPLE AMSTRUTZ EDGERTON
ELLSBERG ERICSSON GOETHALS
HARRISON HARTNESS HUNSAKER
KENNELLY MCALPINE OVINGTON
REYNOLDS RICHARDS ROEBLING
ARMSTRONG CARPENTER
GILLESPIE KETTERING STEINMETZ
TRAUTWINE FARNSWORTH
LINDENTHAL RIESENBERG
STRICKLAND WORTHINGTON
ALEXANDERSON BRECKENRIDGE
AUSTRALIAN CLAPP
AUSTRIAN BIRAGO ENGERTH
MANNLICHER
CANADIAN KLOTZ
CUBAN MENOCAL
CZECH SKODA
DANISH POULSEN
DUTCH MUSSERT
ENGLISH FOX AIRD PAUL BAKER
BOYLE CLARK COOKE GOOCH
GROVE KEMPE MANCE ROYCE
AYRTON BRAMAH BRUNEL

CLARKE CUBITT DONKIN FOWLER
HARRIS HEDGES MCADAM
BERKLEY BOULTON CAUTLEY
DUDDELL FLEMING HARTLEY
MURDOCK SMEATON ANDERSON
BRINDLEY BUCHANAN CRAMPTON
FERRANTI HAWKSHAW
REDMAYNE GREATHEAD
GRIFFITHS HOPKINSON
WILLCOCKS WIMSHURST
HORNBLOWER TREVITHICK
BRAITHWAITE FITZMAURICE
FRENCH LAME ARCON MALUS
PRONY BERTIN CHAPPE CUGNOT
DEPREZ EIFFEL LEPLAY MARTIN
RATEAU RIQUET ALPHAND
BELIDOR BERLIER BERNARD
BIERIOT CLERGET GIFFARD
LEBLANC LENFANT TELLIER
BELGRAND PONCELET
FOURNEYRON HENNEBIQUE
GERMAN BACH BENZ BOSCH
KNORR CRELLE DIESEL GERBER
LANGEN CARNALL CULMANN
DAIMLER SIEMENS FLETTNER
EYTELWEIN LILIENTHAL
BAUERNFEIND GOLDSCHMIDT
HASELWANDER
ITALIAN VINCI CODAZZI FABRONI
MARCONI
POLISH NARUTOWICZ
RUSSIAN THEREMIN
SCOTTISH BARR BELL WATT
CLERK ELDER EWING MURRAY
NAPIER RANKINE TELFORD
BRUNLEES FAIRBAIRN
STEVENSON SYMINGTON
SPANISH CIERVA
SWEDISH LAVAL POLHEM BRINELL
DAHLBERG
SWISS ILG FAVRE
ENGINEMAN HOISTER HOISTMAN
ENGINERY TIRE
ENGIRDLED CINCT
ENGLAND HOME ALBION LOGRIA
BLIGHTY BRITAIN LOEGRIA
HOMELAND

ENGLAND
AIRFORCE: RAF
BAY: TOR LYME WASH START
MOUNTS BIGBURY BIDEFORD
CARDIGAN FALMOUTH
TREMADOC WEYMOUTH
CAPITAL: LONDON
CHANNEL: SOLENT BRISTOL
ENGLISH SPITHEAD
CHANNEL ISLAND: HERM SARK
JERSEY ALDERNEY GUERNSEY
COIN: ORA RIAL RYAL ACKEY
ANGEL CROWN GROAT NOBLE
PENCE PENNY POUND SPRAT
UNITE BAWBEE FLORIN GUINEA
SESKIN TESTON ANGELET
CAROLUS HAPENNY TUPPENY
FARTHING SHILLING SIXPENCE
TUPPENCE
CONSERVATIVE: TORY
COUNTY: KENT DEVON ESSEX
HANTS NOTTS SALOP WIGHT
DORSET DURHAM LONDON
SURREY SUSSEX NORFOLK
RUTLAND SUFFOLK CHESHIRE

CORNWALL SOMERSET
DANCE: MORRIS
FIRTH: SOLWAY
FOREST: ARDEN EXMOOR
DARTMOOR SHERWOOD
HEAD: SPURN BEACHY FORMBY
LIZARD CEMMAES TREVOSE
HILLS: MENDIP BRENDON CHEVIOT
MALVERN CHILTERN
COTSWOLD
INVADER: DANE PICT ROMAN
SAXON NORMAN
ISLAND: HOLY LUNDY WIGHT
COQUET MERSEA THANET
TRESCO WALNEY BARDSEY
HAYLING IRELAND SHEPPEY
ANGLESEA ANGLESEY
FOULNESS HOLYHEAD
ISLANDS: FARNE SCILLY CHANNEL
KING: HAL LUD BRAN BRUT CNUT
COLE KNUT LEAR HENRY JAMES
SWEYN ALFRED BLADUD
BRUTUS CANUTE EDWARD
EGBERT GEORGE ARTEGAL
ELIDURE RICHARD WILLIAM
GORBODUC
LAKE: CONISTON
LIBERAL: WHIG
MEASURE: CUT ELL LEA MIL PIN
ROD RUN TON TUN VAT ACRE
BIND BOLL BUTT CADE COMB
COOM CRAN FOOT GILL GOAD
HAND HANK HEER HIDE INCH
LAST LINE MILE NAIL PACE
PALM PECK PINT PIPE POLE
POOL ROOD ROPE SACK SEAM
SPAN TRUG TYPP WIST YARD
YOKE BODGE CABOT CHAIN
COOMB CUBIT DIGIT FLOAT
FLOOR FLUID HUTCH JUGUM
MINIM OUNCE PERCH POINT
PRIME QUART SKEIN STACK
TRUSS BARREL BOVATE BUSHEL
CRANNE FATHOM FIRKIN
GALLON HOBBET HOBBIT
LEAGUE MANENT OXGANG
POTTLE RUNLET SECOND
SQUARE STRIKE SULUNG
THREAD TIERCE AUCHLET
FURLONG KENNING QUARTER
RUNDLET SEAMILE SPINDLE
TERTIAN VIRGATE CARUCATE
CHALDRON HOGSHEAD
LANDYARD PUNCHEON
QUADRANT QUARTERN
STANDARD
MOUNTAIN: PEAK SCAFELL
SKIDDAW SNOWDON
MOUNTAINS: BLACK PENNINE
SNOWDON CAMBRIAN
CUMBRIAN
NAME: ALBION BRITAIN
BRITANNIA
PENINSULA: PORTLAND
POINT: NAZE LYNAS MORTE SALES
DODMAN LIZARD PRAWLE
HARTLAND LANDSEND
GIBRALTAR
POLICEMAN: BOBBY COPPER
PEELER
RACE TRACK: ASCOT
RESORT: BATH BRIGHTON
BLACKPOOL

RIVER: CAM DEE DON ESK EXE
LEA NEN URE WYE AIRE AVON
EDEN LUNE NENE NIDD OUSE
PENK TAME TEES TILL TYNE
WEAR YARE ANKER COLNE
DEBEN STOUR SWALE TAMAR
TAWAR TRENT TWEED HUMBER
KENNET MERSEY RIBBLE
ROTHER SEVERN THAMES
WENSUM WHARFE WITHAM
DERWENT PARRETT WAVENEY
WELLAND TORRIDGE
ROCKS: MANACLES
ROYAL HOUSE: YORK TUDOR
STUART HANOVER WINDSOR
LANCASTER PLANTAGENET
SCHOOL: ETON RUGBY HARROW
SEA: IRISH NORTH
SETTLER: JUTE PICT ANGLE
SAXON NORMAN
SOLDIER: TOMMY REDCOAT
FUSILEER
STRAIT: DOVER
TOWN: ELY BATH DEAL HULL
RYDE WARE YORK BLYTH
BRENT DERBY DOVER ERITH
FLINT LEEDS RIPON TRURO
WIGAN BARNET BOLTON
BOOTLE CAMDEN DURHAM
EALING EXETER HANLEY
JARROW LEYTON LONDON
OLDHAM OXFORD YEOVIL
BRISTOL BROMLEY BURNLEY
CHELSEA CROYDON ENFIELD
GRIMSBY HALIFAX HORNSEY
IPSWICH LAMBETH NEWPORT
NORWICH PRESTON SALFORD
SEAFORD WESTHAM BRADFORD
BRIGHTON CORNWALL
COVENTRY DEWSBURY
HASTINGS PLYMOUTH
ROCHDALE WALLASEY
WALLSALL GREENWICH
LIVERPOOL SHEFFIELD
BIRMINGHAM MANCHESTER
TRIBE: ICENI
UNIVERSITY: LONDON OXFORD
CAMBRIDGE
VALLEY: COOM EDEN TEES TYNE
COMBE COOMB COQUET
WEIGHT: BAG KIP TOD TON KEEL
LAST MAST MAUN BARGE
FAGOT GRAIN MAUND POUND
SCORE STAND STONE TRUSS
BUSHEL CENTAL FANGOT
FIRKIN FOTHER FOTMAL
POCKET QUARTER QUINTAL
SARPLER

ENGLISH SAXON AUSTRAL BRITISH
ENGLAND SAXONISH SOUTHRON
STANDARD
(**— DIALECT IN LIVERPOOL**) SCOUSE
(**— MIXED WITH SPANISH**)
SPANGLISH
(**IN —**) ANGLICE
(PREF.) ANGLO
ENGLISHMAN SAXON BRITON
BRONCO GODDAM GRINGO
JOHNNY ROOINEK
MACARONI SOUTHRON
ENGLISHER
ENGLISHWOMAN INGLESA

ENGORGE GLUT GORGE DEVOUR
SWALLOW
ENGRAFT INSET
ENGRAM TRACE
(**— PATTERN**) MEANING
ENGRAVE CUT ETCH RIST CARVE
CHASE GRAVE HATCH PRINT
SCULP CHISEL INCISE SCULPT
CRIBBLE ENCHASE EXARATE
IMPRESS IMPRINT INSCULP
STIPPLE INSCRIBE ORNAMENT
ENGRAVED GRAVEN GRAPHIC
INCISED
(PREF.) GRAPTO
ENGRAVER POINT CHASER
ETCHER GRAVER ARTISAN
INSCULP BURINIST MEDALIST
SCULLION WRIGGLER
(**— OF STONES**) LAPIDARY
ENGRAVING CUT PRINT SCULP
STAMP GRAVERY GRAVING
GRAVURE WOODCUT AQUATINT
DRYPOINT HATCHING INTAGLIO
LINEWORK MEZZOTINT
(PREF.) GLYPHO GLYPT(O)
ENGROSS BURY SINK SOAK AMASS
GROSS ABSORB ENGAGE ENROLL
ENWRAP OCCUPY SCROLL
COLLECT CONSUME IMMERSE
INVOLVE PREOCCUPY
ENGROSSED DEEP FULL RAPT
INTENT BEMUSED WRAPPED
ABSORBED IMMERSED
PREOCCUPIED
ENGULF GULF ABYSM ABYSS
SOUSE SWAMP WHELM ABSORB
DEVOUR INVADE QUELME
SLOUGH ENGORGE SWALLOW
SUBMERGE
ENHANCE FOIL LIFT BUILD ENARM
ENDOW EXALT RAISE DEEPEN
AUGMENT ELEVATE ENLARGE
EXHANCE GREATEN IMPROVE
SHARPEN HEIGHTEN INCREASE
ENHANCEMENT SAKE
ENHYDRA LATAX
ENID (HUSBAND OF **—**) GERAINT
ENIGMA WHY EGMA GRIPH REBUS
PUZZLE RIDDLE SPHINX GRIPHUS
MYSTERY PROBLEM PROVERB
ENIGMATIC HUMAN MYSTIC
CRYPTIC OBSCURE ELLIPTIC
MYSTICAL ORACULAR PUZZLING
RIDDLING
ENJAMBMENT OVERFLOW
ENJOIN BID JOIN WILL ENIUN
ORDER CHARGE DECREE DIRECT
FORBID COMMAND DICTATE
REQUIRE ADMONISH PROHIBIT
ENJOY GO JOY FAIN HAVE LIKE
BROOK FANCY PROVE SAVOR
TASTE WIELD ADMIRE DEVOUR
GROOVE RELISH DELIGHT
(**— ONESELF**) FEAST LAUGH
ENJOYABLE GOOD FRUITY
AMIABLE BLESSED CAPITAL
GLORIOUS SAVOROUS SPLENDID
ENJOYING FRUITIVE
ENJOYMENT FUN JOY USE BANG
BASK BOOT EASE GUST KAMA
PLAY ZEST FEAST GUSTO LIKING
RELISH COMFORT DELIGHT
JOLLITY JOYANCE JOYANCY

FELICITY FRUITION PLEASURE
SKITTLES
(**— FROM OTHERS' TROUBLES**)
SCHADENFREUDE
ENKINDLE WARM INCENSE
INFLAME
ENLARGE ADD EKE BORE GROW
HONE HUFF OPEN REAM ROOM
BUILD FARCE LARGE SWELL
WIDEN BIGGEN BRANCH BROACH
DIDUCE DILATE EXPAND EXTEND
FRAISE GATHER LARGEN OMNIFY
SPREAD AMPLIFY AUGMENT
DISTEND ENHANCE GREATEN
IMPROVE INGREAT MAGNIFY
STRETCH AMPLIATE CUMULATE
FLOURISH INCREASE
(**— COAL MINE**) SNUB
ENLARGED TUMID BLOATED
CLUBBED SWELLED SWOLLEN
AMPLIATE CAPITATE EXPANDED
EXTENDED VARICOSE
ACCRESCENT
ENLARGEMENT BULB DISC DISK
KNOP NODE CLAVA SWELL
BLOWUP BUNION GIBBER
GROWTH SCYPHA ENLARGE
FOOTING SCYPHUS STATION
ANEURYSM INCREASE SWELLING
PROPAGATION
(**— IN MINE SHAFT**) STATION
(**— IN MUSCLE**) KNOT
(**— OF GLAND**) GOITER GOITRE
(**— OF GULLET**) CROP
(**— OF MOLD**) RAPPAGE
(**— OF NERVE FIBER**) BOUTON
(**— OF ORGAN**) STRUMA
(**BONY —**) SPAVIN SPAVINE
(PREF.) MACR(O) MEG(A)
MEGAL(O) PLETHYSMO
(SUFF.) AUXE MEGALY
ENLARGING EVASE SWELLING
(PREF.) MICR(O)
ENLIGHTEN OPEN CLEAR EDIFY
TEACH ILLUME INFORM UNSEEL
EDUCATE LIGHTEN CIVILIZE
ENKINDLE INSTRUCT
ENLIGHTENED WISE LUMINOUS
ENLIGHTENMENT BODHI LIGHT
SATORI WISDOM CULTURE
INSIGHT SAMADHI AUFKLARUNG
ENLIST DRUM JOIN LEVY SOUD
ENROL ENTER HITCH PREST
ENGAGE ENROLL INDUCT
IMPRESS RECRUIT REGISTER
ENLISTMENT LEVY HITCH PREST
LISTING
ENLIVEN DASH JAZZ WARM BRACE
BRISK CHEER QUICK RAISE ROUSE
KITTLE REVIVE ANIMATE
COMFORT INSPIRE REFRESH
SMARTEN BRIGHTEN INSPIRIT
RECREATE
ENLIVENING GENIAL LIVELY
VIVIFIC CHIRPING
ENMESH TRAP CATCH SNARL
IMMESH ENSNARE ENTANGLE
ENMITY WAR FEUD SPITE WRAKE
ANIMUS HATRED MALICE
RANCOR STRIFE FOEHOOD
AVERSION
ENNEAGON NONAGON
ENNOBLE LORD EXALT HONOR

NOBLE RAISE GENTLE UPLIFT
DIGNIFY ELEVATE GLORIFY
GREATEN NOBLIFY SUBLIME
ENNUI BORE TEDIUM ACCIDIE
BOREDOM DOLDRUM
ENOCH (FATHER OF **—**) CAIN JARED
(SON OF **—**) METHUSALEH
ENOCH ARDEN (AUTHOR OF **—**)
TENNYSON
(CHARACTER IN **—**) LEE RAY LANE
ANNIE ARDEN ENOCH MIRIAM
PHILIP
ENORMITY GRAVITY
ENORMOUS BIG GOB HUGE REAM
VAST ENORM GREAT HEROIC
MIGHTY UNRIDE IMMENSE
ABNORMAL COLOSSAL FLAGRANT
GIGANTIC WHAPPING WHOPPING
ENOS (FATHER OF **—**) SETH
(GRANDFATHER OF **—**) ADAM
(SON OF **—**) CAINAN
ENOUGH BAS ENOW WELL WHEN
AMPLE ASSAI BASTA BELAY
ANEUCH PLENTY APLENTY
SUFFICE ADEQUATE
(HARDLY **—**) SKIMP
ENOUNCE STATE UTTER AFFIRM
DECLARE PROCLAIM
ENRAGE RAGE ANGER GRIEVE
MADDEN INCENSE INFLAME
STOMACH
ENRAGED MAD ASHY WODE
WOOD ANGRY IRATE LIVID
SAVAGE AGRAMED BERSERK
CHOLERIC INCENSED MADDENED
ENRAPTURE RAVISH TRANCE
ECSTASY ENCHANT ENRAVISH
ENTRANCE
ENRAPTURED RAPT ENRAPT
TRANCED ECSTATIC
ENRICH FAT BOOT FEED FRET
LARD RICH ADORN CROWN
ENDOW GUANO BATTEN FATTEN
INVEST FEATHER FORTIFY
FURNISH GUANIZE INCREASE
ORNAMENT TREASURE
(**— A GAS**) CARBURET
(**— A MINE**) SALT
(**— FUEL MIXTURE**) CHOKE
ENRICHED FLORID
ENRICHMENT DITATION
ENROLL BEAR JOIN LIST POLL
ENROL ENTER WRITE ATTEST
BILLET ENFOLD ENLIST INDUCT
MUSTER RECORD ASCRIBE
IMPANEL INITIATE INSCRIBE
REGISTER
ENROLLMENT LISTING REGISTRY
ENROOT ENRACE IMPLANT
ENSCONCE HIDE COVER SETTLE
CONCEAL SHELTER
ENSEMBLE CORPS DECOR WHOLE
COSTUME PANTSUIT
(**— OF ARMS**) ARMORY
(WOMAN'S **—**) PANTSUIT
ENSHEATHE EMBOSS
ENSHRINE SAINT SHRINE ENCHASE
ENTEMPLE
ENSHROUD WRAP
ENSIFORM ENSATE XIPHOID
GLADIATE
ENSIGN FLAG IAGO SIGN BADGE
COLOR SENYE AQUILA BANNER

BEACON PENNON PISTOL SIGNAL
SYMBOL ALFEREZ ANCIENT
INSIGNE DANEBROG GONFALON
ORIFLAMB PAVILION STANDARD
(—S ARMORIAL) ARMS
(IMPERIAL —) TUT
(JAPANESE —) SUNBURST
(PL.) ENSIGNRY HERALDRY
ENSILE SILO SILAGE
ENSLAVE THEW CHAIN SLAVE
THIRL ENTHRAL NESLAVE
SLAVISH ENTHRALL
ENSLAVED SLAVE THRALL
ENSLAVEMENT DULOSIS SLAVERY
ENSNARE NET WEB GIRN LACE
LIME MESH TOIL TRAP WRAP
BENET CATCH NOOSE SNARE
SNARL ALLURE ATTRAP ENGINE
ENMESH ENTOIL ENTRAP TANGLE
TREPAN BEGUILE DECEIVE
ENGLEIM SNIGGLE SPRINGE
BIRDLIME INVEIGLE OVERTAKE
SURPRISE
ENSNARL ENTANGLE
ENSPHERE INORB SPHERE
ENSTATITE BRONZITE
ENSUE FOLLOW RESULT SUCCEED
(— UPON) SUE
ENSUING NEXT SUING SEQUENT
ENSURE ASSURE INSURE SECURE
BETROTH ESPOUSE WARRANT
AFFIANCE
ENTABLATURE (PART OF —)
CORONA FRIEZE TAENIA CORNICE
CYMATIUM ARCHITRAVE
ENTADA LENS
ENTAIL TAIL INCUR IMPOSE
CONTAIN INVOLVE REQUIRE
TAILZIE
ENTAILED AYNE TAIL EIGNE
ENTAMOEBA LOSCHIA
ENTANGLE ELF LAP MAT TAT WEB
BALL CAST COLL FOUL HARL KNIT
KNOT LIME MESH MIRE TOIL
WRAP BROIL CATCH HALCH
RAVEL SNAFU SNARE SNARL
TWIST BEFOUL COMMIT COTTER
ENGAGE ENLACE ENMESH
ENTRAP ENWRAP FANKLE FELTER
HAMPER HANKLE HATTER
INMAZE INMESH PESTER PUZZLE
RAFFLE RANGLE TACKLE TAIGLE
TANGLE WRAPLE CONFUSE
EMBRAKE EMBROIL ENSNARL
ENTRIKE IMBRIER INVOLVE
PERPLEX TRAMMEL BEWILDER
ENCUMBER IMPESTER INTRIGUE
STRAPPLE
ENTANGLED DEEP FOUL COTTY
TANGLY COMPLEX KNOTTED
IMPLICIT
ENTANGLEMENT FOUL KNOT
TWIT HITCH BUNKER COBWEB
ENTRAIL HEDGEHOG OBSTACLE
PERPLEXITY
ENTASIS SWELL
ENTENTE TREATY ALLIANCE
ENTER BOX DIP SET BEAR BOOK
JOIN POST ADMIT BEGIN BOARD
BREVE ENROL INCUR PROBE
SHARE START ACCEDE APPEAR
BILLET ENGAGE ENLIST ENROLL
ENTRER INCEPT INVADE PIERCE

RECORD SPREAD INGRESS
INTRUDE COMMENCE ENCROACH
INITIATE INSCRIBE NOMINATE
REGISTER PENETRATE
(— BY FORCE) BREAK IRRUPT
INTRUDE
(— DATA) INPUT
(— HASTILY) BULGE
(— IN ATTACK) FORCE
(— IN BOOK) ACCESS
(— IN BOOKS) ACCRUE
(— INFORMATION INTO COMPUTER)
WRITE
(— INTO) JOIN INTERN
(— PROGRAM INTO COMPUTER)
LOAD
(— SLOWLY) SEEP
(— UNNOTICED) CREEP
(— UPON CAREER) INCEPT
(— UPON DUTIES) ASSUME
(— WITHOUT RIGHT) ABATE
ENTERING ENTRY INGOING
INGRESS INTRANT INCOMING
ENTEROTOXEMIA STRUCK
ENTERPRISE FIRM IRON PUSH
TOGT DRIVE ESSAY ACTION
EMPIRE SPIRIT VOYAGE ATTEMPT
EMPRISE HOLDING PROJECT
VENTURE BUSINESS CARNIVAL
GUMPTION VIRITOOT
(CRIMINAL —) JOB
(HARD —) DIFFICULTY
(REMEDIAL —) CRUSADE
(SPECULATIVE —) ADVENTURE
(UNPROFITABLE —) SINKHOLE
ENTERPRISING BOLD FORTHY
PUSHFUL PUSHING
ENTERTAIN INN BEAR BUSK EASE
FETE HAVE HOLD HOST AMUSE
ENJOY FEAST GUEST SPORT
TREAT DIVERT FROLIC GESTEN
HARBOR JUNKET RECULE REGALE
RETAIN SOLACE TICKLE ACCOURT
BEGUILE CHERISH DISPORT
KITCHEN CONSIDER INTEREST
RECREATE
(— WITHOUT CHARGE) DEFRAY
ENTERTAINED OUGHT
ENTERTAINER BHAT HOST ACTOR
AMUSER ARTIST BUSKER DANCER
FIDDLE HARLOT SINGER ACTRESS
ARTISTE DISEUSE GLEEMAN
HETAERA HOSTESS REGALER
SPEAKER BEACHBOY COMEDIAN
HOSTELER MAGICIAN MINSTREL
ENTERTAINING GOOD RICH TREAT
PRETTY AMUSING BEDSIDE
GUESTING SPORTFUL
ENTERTAINMENT BASH BILL FARE
FETE GALA GLEE PLAY SHOW
BOARD CHEER FEAST GAUDY
OPERA REVUE SPORT CIRCUS
DIVERT DOMENT GAIETY GAYETY
HOSTEL INFARE KERMIS NAUTCH
SETOUT SHIVOO WATTLE
BANQUET BENEFIT BUMMACK
BUMMOCK BURLESK CEILIDH
CONCERT COSHERY FESTINE
FESTINO JOLLITY KERMESS
PASTIME RIDOTTO TAMASHA
CAKEWALK CARNIVAL
COMMORTH DROLLERY
EASEMENT ENTREATY ENTREMES

FUNCTION GESTNING GESTONIE
GUESTING HOGMANAY JONGLERY
MUSICALE WAYZGOOSE
(FAREWELL —) FOY
ENTHALPY H
ENTHRALL SEND CHARM THIRL
THRALL ENSLAVE ENTHRAL
CAPTIVATE
ENTHRONE CROWN EXALT STALL
ENSEAT THRONE THRONIZE
ENTHUSIASM BUG ELAN FIRE
FURY ZEAL ZEST ZING ARDOR
ESTRO FEVER FLAME FUROR
HEART MANIA OOMPH VERVE
FERVOR HURRAH SPIRIT WARMTH
ABANDON ARDENCY AVIDITY
MADNESS MUSTARD DEVOTION
LYRICISM
(— IN BATTLE) EARNEST
(CONTAGIOUS —) FUROR FURORE
(EXCESSIVE —) MANIA
(WILD —) DELIRIUM
ENTHUSIAST BUG FAN NUT BUFF
BIGOT FREAK ROOTER VOTARY
ZEALOT DEVOTEE EUCHITE
FANATIC FANCIER FOLLOWER
VOTARESS VOTARIST
(PL.) ARDITI
ENTHUSIASTIC GAGA KEEN NUTS
WARM HAPPY NUTTY RABID
ARDENT HEARTY CRACKED
FERVENT GLOWING CRACKERS
PASSIONATE
(BECOME —) FLIP
(EXCESSIVELY —) FANATIC
(VAINLY —) FOOLISH
ENTICE COG COY PUT WIN BAIT
COAX DRAW DRIB LEAD LOCK
LURE TICE TOLE TOLL WILE
CHARM DECOY DRILL LATHE
SIREN SLOCK STEAL TEMPT TRAIN
TROLL TULLE ALLECT ALLURE
ATTICE CAJOLE ENLURE INCITE
INDUCE INVITE SEDUCE ATTRACT
BEWITCH SOLICIT SUGGEST
INVEIGLE PERSUADE
ENTICEMENT BAIT CORD LURE
TICE
ENTICING SIREN ALLURING
ENTIRE ALL DEAD EVEN FULL HALE
MEAR MERE SOLE FULL EVERY
GROSS PLAIN QUITE ROUND
SOUND STARK TOTAL TUTTO
UTTER WHOLE VERSAL PERFECT
PLENARY ABSOLUTE COMPLETE
ENDURING GLOBULAR INTEGRAL
LIVELONG OUTRIGHT TEETOTAL
UNBROKEN
(PREF.) HOL(O) INTEGRI
ENTIRELY DEAD DEIN FAIR FULL
PURE CLEAN CLEAR FULLY PLAIN
QUITE STARK WHOLE BODILY
WHOLLY EXACTLY QUITELY
THROUGH CLEVERLY ABSOLUTELY
ENTIRETY WHOLE ENTIRE
TOTALITY
(PREF.) PAM PAN
ENTITLE DUB CALL NAME TERM
AFFIX STYLE ENABLE CAPTION
EMPOWER QUALIFY INTITULE
NOMINATE
ENTITLED APPARENT ELIGIBLE
ENTITY ENS BODY FORM UNIT

BEING HABIT OUSIA SPACE THING
ENERGY ESSENCE INTEGER
TOTALITY
ENTOMB BURY TOMB INTER INURN
ENCAVE HEARSE IMMURE
INHUME SHRINE
ENTOMBMENT BURIAL
ENTOMOLOGIST AMERICAN SAY)
DYAR HORN BANKS BRUES RILEY
FORBES HARRIS HOWARD
MORGAN BURGESS PACKARD
POLLARD SCHWARZ COMSTOCK
COQUILLETT
DANISH FABRICIUS
DUTCH LYONNET
ENGLISH SCOTT LEFROY
HAWORTH ORMEROD
WESTWOOD
FRENCH FABRE AUDOUIN
LATREILLE LACORDAIRE
GERMAN BRAUER
SWISS FOREL SAUSSURE
ENTOMOLOGY BUGOLOGY
ENTOMOPHTHORA EMPUSA
ENTOTROPHI DIPLURA
ENTOURAGE TRAIN COMITES
RETINUE
ENTRACTE INTERACT INTERVAL
ENTRAIL BOWEL TRAIL INTRAIL
(PREF.) SPLANCHN(O)
ENTRAILS GUT GUTS DRAFT TRIPE
FIBERS GIBLET HALLOW HASLET
INWARD JAUDIE MUGGET
PAUNCH QUARRY QUERRE
UMBLES INSIDES NUMBLES
CHAWDRON GRALLOCH
PURTENANCE
ENTRANCE ADIT BOCA CUSP
DOOR GATE HALL PEND BOCCA
CHARM DEBUT ENTER ENTRY
FOYER GORGE INLET MOUTH
PORCH STULM THIRL TORAN
ACCESS ATRIUM ENTREE INFAIR
INGANG INGATE INROAD PORTAL
RAVISH TORANA TRANCE
ZAGUAN DELIGHT GATEWAY
HALLWAY INGOING INGRESS
INITIAL INTRADO INTROIT
PASSAGE POSTERN ENTRESSE
FOREGATE VOMITORY
PROPYLAEUM
(— TO SEWER) JAWHOLE
(— TO VALLEY) CHOPS
(ASTROLOGICAL —) CUSP
(CELLAR —) ROLLWAY
(FORCIBLE —) INROAD
(FORMAL —) DEBUT
(HARBOR —) BOCA
(HOSTILE —) INVASION
(HURRIED —) BOUT
(MINE —) EYE ADIT
(PRIVATE —) POSTERN
ENTRANCED RAPT CHARMED
TRANCED ECSTATIC
ENTRANCEMENT SPELL
ENTRANCING ORPHIC
ENTRANT INTRANT STARTER
BEGINNER
ENTRAP BAG EBB NET HOOK SNIB
TOIL TRAP CATCH CRIMP DECOY
NOOSE SNARE ALLURE AMBUSH
ATTRAP CAJOLE ENGAGE ENTOIL
TAIGLE TANGLE TREPAN BEGUILE

ENSNARE PITFALL ENTANGLE INVEIGLE

ENTRAPPED (— IN SEDIMENT) CONNATE

ENTREAT ASK BEG BID SUE WOO PRAY PRIG SEEK URGE CRAVE HALSE PLEAD PRESS TREAT ADJURE APPEAL DESIRE INVOKE BESEECH CONJURE EXORATE IMPLORE PREVAIL PROCURE REQUEST SOLICIT PERSUADE PETITION

ENTREATING TREAT CRAVING

ENTREATY DO CRY PLEA SUIT APPEAL DEESIS PRAYER TREATY BESEECH BIDDING ENTREAT PURSUIT REQUEST URGENCY PETITION PLEADING

ENTREE ENTRY ACCESS BOUDIN OSTIUM ENTRADA INTRADA SOUFFLE ENTRANCE FRICANDO MAZARINE

ENTREMES SAINETE SAYNETE

ENTRENCH INVADE SCONCE TRENCH ENCROACH TRESPASS

ENTRENCHMENT CLOSURE COUPURE LODGMENT

ENTROPY S

ENTRUST ARET FIDE GIVE STOW BEKEN TRUST CHARGE COMMIT CREDIT LIPPEN ADDRESS BEHIGHT COMMEND CONFIDE CONSIGN DEPOSIT INTRUST BEQUEATH DELEGATE ENCHARGE RECOMMEND

(— TO DEPUTY) DEVIL

ENTRY ADIT HALL ITEM STET BREAK CLOSE DEBIT AUTHOR CREDIT DOCKET ENTREE PORTAL POSTEA RECORD RINGER TRANCE ENTRADA INGRESS INTRADO PASSAGE ENTRANCE ENTRESSE ENTRYWAY NOTANDUM REGISTER VOCATION

(— IN CHRONICLE) ANNAL

ENTWINE FOLD LACE WIND BRAID CLASP IMPLY PLASH TWINE TWIST WEAVE ENLACE INWIND ENTWIST INVOLVE SERPENT WREATHE

ENTWINED ACCOLLE BRAIDED INWOVEN ACCOLLEE

ENUMERATE POLL TELL COUNT SCORE DETAIL NUMBER RECITE RECKON RELATE COMPILE COMPUTE ITEMIZE RECOUNT ESTIMATE REHEARSE

ENUMERATION LIST TALE COUNT SCORE CENSUS ACCOUNT CATALOG RECITAL CITATION

ENUNCIATE SAY UTTER DECLARE DELIVER ENOUNCE ANNOUNCE PROCLAIM

ENUNCIATION DICTION DELIVERY

(IMPERFECT —) LALLATION

ENVELOP BUR FOG LAP LOT POD WEB BURR CASE COMA FOLD HUSK MAIL ROLL BRACE CLOUD COVER KNIFE ROUND BEGIRD BEGIRT BEMIST BINDLE CLOTHE COCOON CORONA CUPULE ENFOLD ENGIRT ENTIRE ENWRAP FARDEL FOLDER INFOLD INVEST

JACKET MANTLE MUFFLE POCKET SHEATH SHROUD STIFLE SWATHE WRIXLE CALYMMA CAPSULE CHORION ENCLOSE ENVIRON INVOLVE SWADDLE SWALLOW VESTURE WRAPPER ENSPHERE ENVELOPE MANTLING PERIANTH PERIDIUM POCHETTE SURROUND WRAPPAGE

(— IN SMOKE) ENFUME

(GLASS —) BULB

(LUMINOUS —) CORONA

(NEBULOUS —) CHEVELURE

(OPEN —) JACKET

(PAY —) PACKET

(STAMPED —) ENTIRE

(VEGETABLE —) COD

ENVELOPE

(PREF.) (OUTER —) PERIDI

(SUFF.) LEMMA

ENVELOPED WOMPLIT

ENVELOPING AMBIENT

ENVENOM VENOM CORRUPT VITIATE EMBITTER EMPOISON

ENVIOUS YELLOW EMULOUS JEALOUS ENVIABLE

ENVIRON HEM BEGO GIRD BIGAN LIMIT VIRON ENVIRE GIRDLE SUBURB COMPASS ENVELOP INCLOSE INVOLVE PURLIEU DISTRICT ENCIRCLE SURROUND

(PL.) SKIRT UMLAND BANLIEU SUBURBS PRECINCT

ENVIRONMENT HOTBED MEDIUM MILIEU AMBIENT CONTEXT ELEMENT HABITAT SETTING TERRAIN AMBIANCE CINCTURE PRECINCT

(— OF NURTURE) LAP

(ACADEMIC —) ACADEME

(DOMESTIC —) INTERIEUR

(NORMAL —) HOME

(PREF.) EC(O) OEC(O) OIK(O)

ENVISAGE FACE CONFRONT ENVISION

ENVOY AGENT ELCHI ENVOI DEPUTY ELCHEE LEGATE LENVOY NUNCIO EMBASSY TORNADA ABLEGATE LEGATION METATRON

ENVY CHAW ONDE COVET GRUDGE EMULATE BEGRUDGE GRUDGERY JEALOUSY

ENWRAP FOLD ROLL CLASP IMPLY ENFOLD INFOLD KIRTLE ENGROSS ENVELOP OBVOLVE CONVOLVE ENVELOPE INSWATHE

ENZOOTIC RABIES

ENZU SIN

ENZYME ASE ZYM ZYMO LYASE RENIN CYTASE KINASE LIGASE LIPASE LOTASE MUTASE OLEASE PAPAIN PEPSIN RENNIN UREASE ZYMASE ACYLASE ADENASE AMIDASE AMINASE AMYLASE APYRASE CASEASE EMULSIN ENOLASE EREPSIN FERMENT GUANASE HYDRASE INULASE LACCASE LACTASE MALTASE MYROSIN OXIDASE PECTASE PEPSINE PHYTASE PLASMIN PRUNASE TANNASE TRYPSIN ALDOLASE ARGINASE BROMELIN CATALASE CATALYST CYTOLIST

DIASTASE ELASTASE EREPTASE ESTERASE FUMARASE INVERTIN LYSOZYME NUCLEASE PERMEASE PROTEASE RACEMASE SEMINASE SYNTHASE THROMBIN TRYPTASE

(PREF.) ZYM(O)

(SUFF.) ASE EIN EINE IN INE

EOS MORNING

EPAPHUS (DAUGHTER OF —) LIBYA

(FATHER OF —) ZEUS JUPITER

(MOTHER OF —) IO

(WIFE OF —) MEMPHIS

EPAULET KNOT SWAB SWOB WING SCALE SHELL

EPENDYTES HAPLOMA

EPENTHESIS ANAPTYXIS

EPEUS (BROTHER OF —) AETOLUS

(DAUGHTER OF —) HYRMINA

(FATHER OF —) ENDYMION PANOPEUS

(WIFE OF —) ANAXIROE

EPHAH BATH

(FATHER OF —) JAHDAI MIDIAN

EPHELIS FRECKLE

EPHEMERAL BRIEF VAGUE HORARY DIURNAL FUNGOUS PASSANT PASSING EPISODAL EPISODIC FUGITIVE MUSHROOM STAYLESS MOMENTARY

EPHEMERIS DIARY TABLE RECORD ALMANAC JOURNAL CALENDAR

EPHER (FATHER OF —) EZRA MIDIAN

EPHIPPIUM SADDLE

EPHOD VAKASS

(SON OF —) HANNIEL

EPHRAIM (FATHER OF —) JOSEPH

(MOTHER OF —) ASENATH

EPHRATAH (HUSBAND OF —) CALEB

(SON OF —) HUR

EPHRON (FATHER OF —) ZOAR

EPHTHALITE HAITHAL

EPI PEAK SPIRE FINIAL PINNACLE

EPIBLAST ECTODERM

EPIC EDDA EPOS SAGA GRAND ILIAD NOBLE BYLINA EPOPEE HEROIC LUSIAD BEOWULF EPYLLION KALEVALA RAMAYANA

(SUFF.) AD

EPICALYX CALYCLE

EPICARP HUSK RIND EXOCARP

EPICENE SEXLESS

EPICURE FRIAND FEASTER GLUTTON GOURMET GOURMAND PALATIST

EPICUREAN APICIAN SENSUOUS

EPIDEMIC FLU PLAGUE POPULAR PANDEMIA PANDEMIC

EPIDERMIS SKIN CUTICLE ECDERON VELAMEN

EPIDOTE SCORZA

EPIGLOTTIS FLAP WEEZLE

EPIGRAM POEM ENGLYN EPITAPH

EPIGRAMMATIC LACONIC POINTED

EPIGRAPH EPIGRAM IMPRINT

EPILEPTIC FITIFIED

EPILOGUE CLOSE APPENDIX

EPIMANIKION CUFF

EPINAOS POSTICUM

EPINEPHRINE ADRENINE

EPIPACTIS SERAPIAS

EPIPHANY TWELFTH

EPIPHARYNX PALATE EPIGLOTTIS

EPIPHRAGM TYMPANUM

EPIPHYTE KARO EPIPHYLL

EPIPHYTOTIC EPIDEMIC

EPIRUS (KING OF —) PYRRHUS

EPISCOPACY BISHOPRIC PRELATISM

EPISCOPAL PRELATIC

EPISODE GAG EPOCH EVENT SCENE STORY AFFAIR INCIDENT SEQUENCE OCCURRENCE

(COMIC —) BURLA

(MUSICAL —) COUPLET

EPISPASTIC VESICANT

EPISPERM TESTA

EPISTAXIS NOSEBLEED

EPISTERNUM MANUBRIUM

EPISTLE CANON JAMES LETTER PISTLE MISSIVE WRITING DECRETAL

EPISTLER SUBDEACON

EPISTOLOGRAPHIC DEMOTIC

EPISTROPHE EPODE ABGESANG

EPISTYLE PLATBAND

EPITHELIUM ENDODERM

EPITHET AKAL GOOD NAME TERM LABEL SMEAR TITLE BYWORD MONETA PHRASE AGNOMEN JAPHETIC MULCIBER

(PL.) LANGUAGE

EPITOME MAP SUM FLETA DIGEST PRECIS SCHEME COMPEND PITOMIE SUMMARY SUMMULA ABSTRACT BREVIARY LANDSKIP SYLLABUS SYNOPSIS ABRIDGMENT CONSPECTUS

EPITOMIZE RESUME ABRIDGE CURTAIL ABSTRACT COMPRESS CONDENSE CONTRACT DIMINISH

EPITONIUM SCALA

EPIZOA PARASITA

EPOCH AGE ERA DATE ECCA TIME DWYKA EVENT EOCENE PERIOD CLINTON OLIGOCENE

EPONYM LIMMU ANCIENT

EPOPEUS (BROTHERS OF —) ALOIDAE

(FATHER OF —) ALOEUS POSEIDON

(MOTHER OF —) CANACE IPHIMEDIA

(WIFE OF —) ANTIOPE

EQUABLE EVEN JUST EQUAL SUANT SMOOTH STEADY UNIFORM TRANQUIL

EQUAL AEQ PAR TIE COPE EGAL EVEN FERE JUST LIKE MAKE MATE MEET PEEL PEER SAME ALIKE LEVEL MATCH PARTY RIVAL TOUCH DOUBLE EQUATE EVENLY FELLOW MARROW PAREIL ABREAST BALANCE COMPEER EMULATE EQUABLE IDENTIC PARAGON PAREGAL UNIFORM ADEQUATE EQUALIZE EVENHAND PATCHING TRANQUIL

(— IN MEANING) BE

(— QUANTITY) ANA

(— TO) ANOTHER

(NOT —) UNMEET UNMETE

(PREF.) AEQUI EQUI IS(O) PARI

EQUALING TO

EQUALITY PAR TIE EQUITY OWELTY PARAGE PAREIL PARITY BALANCE EGALITE EGALITY

ISOTELY EQUATION EVENHAND
EVENNESS FAIRNESS
(— BEFORE THE LAW) ISONOMY
(— OF ELEVATION) ISOMETRY
(— OF POWER) ISOCRACY
(— OF RATIOS) ANALOGY
(— STATE) WYOMING
EQUALIZATION EQUATION
DISCHARGE
EQUALIZE EVEN KNOT EQUAL
LEVEL EQUATE BALANCE
ADEQUATE
EQUALIZER EVENER
EQUALLY AS BOTH LIKE ONCE
SAME ALIKE EGALLY EVENLY
JUSTLY EMFORTH
EQUANIMITY POISE PHLEGM
TEMPER BALANCE EGALITY
CALMNESS EVENNESS SERENITY
SANGFROID
EQUATE EQUAL BALANCE
EQUALIZE
EQUATING COMPARISON
EQUATION CUBIC IDENTITY
EQUATOR LINE GIRDLE EQUINOX
(— CROSSER) POLLIWOG
**EQUATORIAL GUINEA (CAPITAL OF
—)** MALABO
(RIVER OF —) MUNI CAMPO BENITO
(TOWN OF —) BATA NSOK
SANTAISABEL
EQUES KNIGHT
EQUIDISTANT CENTRAL HALFWAY
EQUILIBRIUM POISE APLOMB
BALANCE STATION EQUATION
EVENHAND ISOSTASY
(— OF FLUID) LEVEL
(PREF.) STATO
EQUINE COLT FOAL MARE FILLY
HORSE ZEBRA EQUOID EQUINAL
HORSELY
EQUINIA MALLEUS
EQUIP ARM FIT IMP KIT RAY RIG
ABLE BEAM DECK FEAT FIND
GEAR GIRD GIRT HEEL REEK TRIM
ARRAY DIGHT DRESS ENARM
ENDOW POINT SPEED STUFF
AGUISE ATTIRE BUCKLE ORDAIN
OUTFIT SUBORN APPAREL
APPOINT BEDIGHT FORTIFY
FRAUGHT FURNISH GARNISH
HARNESS PLENISH PREPARE
QUALIFY ACCOUTER ACCOUTRE
ACCOMPLISH
(— FOR ACTION) ARM
EQUIPAGE RIG CREW SAMAN
SUITE TRAIN SUPPLY RETINUE
TURNOUT UNICORN CARRIAGE
EQUIPMENT KIT FARE GEAR TIRE
STOCK STUFF ATTIRE CONREY
DUFFEL DUFFLE FITOUT GRAITH
OUTFIT SETOUT TACKLE APPAREL
BAGGAGE FITMENT HARNESS
PANOPLY ARMAMENT EQUIPAGE
MATERIAL MATERIEL MOUNTING
SUPELLEX
(— FOR CATCHING FISH) CRAFT
(— FOR JOURNEY) FARE
EQUIPOISE POISE BALANCE
EQUIPOTENTIAL LEVEL
EQUIPPED SEEN ARMED BODEN
THERE EQUIPT ARMORED
INSTRUCT WEAPONED

(FULLY —) SUMMED
(INADEQUATELY —) HAYWIRE
(LIGHTLY —) EXPEDITE
EQUISETUM CANDOCK
EQUITABLE EVEN FAIR JUST
EQUAL RIGHT EVENLY HONEST
EQUABLE UPRIGHT BONITARY
RATIONAL RIGHTFUL
EQUITY LAW EPIKY MARGIN
EPIKEIA HONESTY JUSTICE
EQUALITY EVENHAND FAIRNESS
EQUIVALENT KIND SAME EQUAL
COUSIN UNISON ANALOGUE
EVENHAND
(— IN MONEY) CHANGE
(— OF TWO BUSHELS) HUTCH
EQUIVOCAL FISHY SHADY DOUBLE
FORKED DUBIOUS EVASIVE
HALFWAY OBSCURE DOUBTFUL
HAVERING PUZZLING SIBYLLIC
EQUIVOCATE LIE DODGE EVADE
SHIFT BOGGLE ESCAPE PALTER
TRIFLE WAFFLE WEASEL QUIBBLE
SHUFFLE SCRAFFLE PREVARICATE
EQUIVOCATION QUIP QUIRK
EVASION QUIBBLE SHUFFLE
EQUIVOKE
EQUULEUS FOAL
ER (FATHER OF —) JOSE
(SON OF —) ELMODAM
ERA AGE AEON DATE TIME EPOCH
STAGE PERIOD CENOZOIC
PROTEROZOIC
(EMPEROR'S —) KIMIGAYO
(HINDU —) SAMVAT
(MUSLIM —) HEGIRA HEJIRA
ERADICATE DELE ROOT SLAY
WEED CROSS ERASE STAMP
DELETE EFFACE REMOVE UNROOT
UPROOT ABOLISH DESTROY
EXPUNGE OUTROOT SUPPLANT
(— HAIR) EPILATE
ERADICATOR ERASER
ERAL MOINE
ERAN (GRANDFATHER OF —)
EPHRAIM
ERASE BLOT DASH DELE RACE
RASE RASH RAZE ANNUL PLANE
CANCEL DEFACE DELETE EFFACE
EXCISE REMOVE SCRAPE SPONGE
DESTROY EXPUNGE OUTRAZE
SCRATCH UNWRITE OBLITERATE
ERASER RASER RUBBER
ERASTE (LOVER OF —) JULIE
LUCILLE ORPHISE
ERASURE RASURE ERASION
DELETION EXCISION
ERD SHREW RANNY
ERE OR AIR SOON EARLY PRIOR
BEFORE EREWHILE FORMERLY
EREBUS (FATHER OF —) CHAOS
(SISTER OF —) NOX
(SON OF —) CHARON
ERECHTHEUS (DAUGHTER OF —)
CREUSA PROCRIS CHTHONIA
ORITHYIA
(FATHER OF —) PANDION
(SLAYER OF —) JUPITER
(SON OF —) MERION CECROPS
PANDORUS
(WIFE OF —) PRAXITHEA
ERECT BIG SET BIGG LEVY REAR
RECT STEP STEY SWAY TELD

AREAR BRANT BUILD DRESS
EXALT FRAME MOUNT RAISE
SETUP STAND ARRECT UPLIFT
UPREAR ADDRESS ATROPAL
BRISTLE ELEVATE STATELY
UPRAISE UPRIGHT UPSTART
STANDING STRAIGHT VERTICAL
(— TENT) PITCH
(NOT —) LAZY COUCHED
ERECTED UPSET
ERECTION DOME HARD FABRIC
CHORDEE MACHINE
ERELONG ANON SOON
EREMITE HERMIT ASCETIC
RECLUSE ANCHORET
EREWHILE ERE WHILOM
EREWHON (AUTHOR OF —) BUTLER
(CHARACTER IN —) HIGGS GEORGE
STRONG ZULORA CHOWBOK
AROWHENA NOSNIBOR
ERG REG EROGON
(PL.) AREG
ERGINUS (FATHER OF —) CLYMENUS
POSEIDON
(SON OF —) AGAMEDES
TROPHONIUS
ERGO SO ARGO ARGAL HENCE
ERGOT SPUR CLAVUS ECBOLIC
(STAGE OF —) SPHACELIA
ERI (FATHER OF —) GAD
ERICHTHONIUS (FATHER OF —)
VULCAN DARDANUS
(MOTHER OF —) ATTHIS
(SON OF —) PANDION
ERIDANUS (FATHER OF —)
OCEANUS
(MOTHER OF —) TETHYS
ERIE WENRO
ERIGONE (FATHER OF —) ICARIUS
AEGISTHUS
(MOTHER OF —) CLYTEMNESTRA
ERINYS FURY ALECTO MEGAERA
(PL.) DIRAE FURIAE SEMNAE
EUMENIDES
ERIOPHORUM DRAWLING
ERIPHYLE (FATHER OF —) TALAUS
(HUSBAND OF —) AMPHIARAUS
(SON & SLAYER OF —) ALCMAEON
ERISTIC DIALECTIC
ERMINE VAIR VARE STOAT WEASEL
ERMELIN FUTERET FUTTRAT
MINIVER CLUBSTER WHITRACK
WHITTRET
ERNANI (CHARACTER IN —) CARLO
GOMEZ SILVA ELVIRA ERNANI
(COMPOSER OF —) VERDI
ERODE EAT COMB ETCH GNAW
GULL WEAR CLIFF GULLY SCOUR
ABRADE DENUDE CORRODE
DESTROY
ERODIUM HERONBILL
EROS AMOR CUPID AENGUS
POTHOS
EROSE ERODED UNEVEN
EROSION PIPING CHIMNEY
NIVATION SCOURING
(MECHANICAL —) PLANATION
ERO THE JOKER (COMPOSER OF —)
GOTOVAC
EROTIC LOVING AMATORY
AMOROUS CURIOUS LESBIAN
THERMAL
EROTICA CURIOSA FACETIAE

ERR MAR SIN BOOT FAIL MISS SLIP
ABERR LAPSE MISGO STRAY
BUNGLE FORVAY WANDER
BLUNDER DEVIATE MISPLAY
MISTAKE SCRITHE STUMBLE
MISCARRY MISJUDGE
ERRAND CHORE ENVOY JOURNEY
MISSION LEGATION
(— BOY) LOBBYGOW
ERRANT STRAY ASTRAY ERRING
DEVIOUS PRICKANT
ERRATIC WILD CRAZY HUMAN
LOONY QUEER WACKY CRANKY
WHACKY STRANGE TANGENT
VAGRANT ACROSTIC ERRABUND
FITIFIED PLANETAL PLANETIC
TRAVELED VAGABOND
PLANETARY
ERRATUM ERROR
ERRING ASTRAY ERRANT DEVIOUS
ERRINGLY FALSE
ERRONEOUS AMISS FALSE WRONG
UNTRUE ERRATIC MISTAKEN
STRAYING WRONGFUL
(PREF.) PSEUD(O)
ERRONEOUSLY AWRY
ERRONEOUSNESS FALLACY
ERROR X HOB SIN BALK BUBU
BULL FLUB HELL MUFF SLIP TRIP
BEARD BEVUE BONER DEVIL
FAULT FLUFF LAPSE SCAPE
BOBBLE BOOBOO FUMBLE GARBLE
HOWLER LAPSUS MISCUE
NAUGHT SPHALM BLOOMER
BLUNDER DEFAULT ERRATUM
FALLACY FALSITY LITERAL
MISPLAY MISSTEP MISTAKE
OFFENSE RHUBARB SNAPPER
STUMBLE DELUSION HAMARTIA
MISPRINT MISSMENT SOLECISM
OVERSIGHT MISPRISION
(— IN PLEADINGS) JEOFAIL
ERS VETCH KERSANNE
ERSE ERSCH IRISH CELTIC GAELIC
SCOTTISH
ERST ONCE FORMERLY RECENTLY
ERSTWHILE ONCE FORMER
FORMERLY
ERUCT RASP BELCH
ERUCTATION BRASH
ERUDITE LEARNED CLERGIAL
DIDACTIC
ERUDITION WIT LORE WISDOM
LETTERS LEARNING
ERUPT BOIL BELCH BURST EJECT
IRRUPT
ERUPTING ACTIVE
ERUPTION ITCH RASH REEF RUSH
AGRIA BLAIN BRASH BURST
RUPIA SALLY SALVO STORM
BLOTCH HYDROA NIRLES ACTERID
BLOWOUT ECTHYMA MORPHEA
MORPHEW PUSTULE SAWFLOM
SUDAMEN SYCOSIS EMPYESIS
ENANTHEM EXANTHEM
MALANDER OUTBREAK
OUTBURST
(— ON CHIN) MENTAGRA
(CUTANEOUS —) HUMOR
(SUFF.) ANTHEMA PHLYSIS
ERVUM LENS LENTILLA
ERYSICHTHON (FATHER OF —)
CECROPS TRIOPAS

(MOTHER OF —) AGRAULOS
(SISTER OF —) IPHIMEDIA
ERYSIPELAS POX ROSE BLAST
WILDFIRE
ERYTHROBLASTOSIS HYDROPSY
ERYX (FATHER OF —) BUTES
(MOTHER OF —) VENUS
(SLAYER OF —) HERCULES
ESAU EDOM
(BROTHER OF —) JACOB
(FATHER OF —) ISAAC
(MOTHER OF —) REBEKAH
(SON OF —) JEUSH KORAH REUEL
JAALAM ELIPHAZ
(WIFE OF —) ADAH BASHEMATH
ESCALADE SCALE SCALADE
SCALADO ESCALADO
ESCAPADE CAPER PRANK SALLY
SCHEME SPLORE RUNAWAY
FREDAINE
ESCAPE FLY GUY LAM RUN BAIL
BALE BEAT BLOW BOLT FLEE
GATE HISS JINK JUMP LEAK MISS
SHUN SKEW SLIP VENT AVOID
BREAK CHAPE DODGE ELOPE
ELUDE EVADE FLANK ISSUE
SCAPE SHIFT SKIRT SMOKE SPILL
ASTERT DECAMP ESCHEW
OUTLET POWDER SQUEAK
ABSCOND AVOLATE BLOWOUT
ELUSION EXHAUST GETAWAY
LEAKAGE MISTAKE OUTFLOW
SCRITHE SQUEEZE WILDING
BLOWBACK ESCAPADE ESCAPAGE
EXSHEATH OUTSCAPE OVERSLIP
RIDDANCE WITHSLIP
(— FROM) FLY SHUN ILLUDE
(— FROM WORK) SNIB
(— LEGAL PROCESS) ABSCOND
(— NOTICE) ELUDE
(— OF FLUID) EFFUSION
(NARROW —) SHAVE
ESCAPEMENT SCAPE CRUTCH
ESCAPE FOLIOT VIRGULE
KARRUSEL
ESCARGOT SNAIL
ESCAROLE ENDIVE SCAROLA
ESCARPMENT EDGE
ESCHAR SCAB CRUST ASCHER
ESCHAROTIC CAUSTIC
ESCHEAT FALL LAPSE REVERT
EXCHEAT FORFEIT
ESCHEW SHUN ABHOR AVOID
FORGO ESCAPE FOREGO ABSTAIN
ESCOLAR PALU ROVET OILFISH
ROVETTO MACKEREL
ESCORT MAN SEE SET TRY BEAR
BEAU COND LEAD SHOW TEND
WAIT BRING CARRY GUARD
USHER ATTEND CONVEY CONVOY
FOLLOW SQUIRE COLLECT
CONDUCT CONSORT ESQUIRE
GALLANT CAVALIER CHAPERON
SHEPHERD SAFEGUARD
(PAID —) GIGOLO
ESCRITOIRE DESK BUREAU
LECTERN
ESCULENT EDIBLE EATABLE
ESCUTCHEON CREST SHIELD
(CENTER OF —) NOMBRIL
ESHBAN (FATHER OF —) DISHON
ESHCOL (BROTHER OF —) ANER
MAMRE

(COMPANION OF —) ABRAHAM
ESKER AS OS OSE KAME ESKAR
HOGBACK
ESKIMO ITA HUSKY INUIT INNUIT
AGOMIUT AMERIND ANGAKOK
KUNMIUT OKOMIUT ORARIAN
AGLEMIUT ESQUIMAU IKOGMIUT
KIDNELIK KINIPETU MAGEMIUT
MALEMIUT NUGUMIUT SINIMIUT
(— ASSEMBLY HOUSE) KASHIM
(— CULTURE) PUNUK
(— TENT) TUPEK TUPIK
ESLI (FATHER OF —) NAGGE
ESOPHAGUS GULLET SWALLOW
WEASAND
(PREF.) LAEMO LEMO
ESOTERIC INNER MYSTIC ORPHIC
SECRET PRIVATE ABSTRUSE
RAREFIED RARIFIED
ESPADON ESPADA SPADON
SPADROON
ESPALIER CORDON LATTICE
RAILING TRELLIS PALISADE
ESPARTO ALFA HALFA SPART
STIPA ATOCHA
ESPAVE CARACOLI
ESPECIAL VERY CHIEF SPECIAL
PECULIAR UNCOMMON
ESPECIALLY SUCH EXTRA RATHER
CHIEFLY OVERALL SPECIAL
ESPIAL SPY ESPY SCOUT NOTICE
ESPINAL MONTE
ESPIONAGE SPYING
ESPLANADE BUND WALK DRIVE
MAIDAN MARINA
ESPOUSAL CEREMONY SPOUSAGE
BETROTHAL
ESPOUSE WED AFFY MATE ADOPT
MARRY DEFEND ENSURE SPOUSE
BETROTH EMBRACE HUSBAND
SUPPORT ADVOCATE MAINTAIN
ESPOUSED HANDFAST
ESPUNDIA UTA
ESPY SEE ASPY SPOT ASCRY SIGHT
WATCH BEHOLD DESCRY DETECT
LOCATE NOTICE DISCERN
OBSERVE DESCRIBE DISCOVER
ESQUIRE RADMAN ARMIGER
ESCUDERO SERGEANT
ESSAY TRY SEEK ASSAY CHRIA
OFFER PAPER PROVE TASTE
THEME TRACT TRAIL CASUAL
EFFORT MEMOIR SAILYE SATIRE
SCREED THESIS ARTICLE
ATTEMPT PROFFER VENTURE
WRITING CAUSERIE ENDEAVOR
EXERCISE EXERTION TRACTATE
TREATISE TURNOVER
ESSAYIST AMERICAN MORE VERY
ADAMS GRANT WHITE YOUNG
BROOKS COFFIN FISHER GUINEY
HOLMES HUTTON KRUTCH
LOWELL EMERSON LAZARUS
WHIPPLE STRUNSKY TUCKERMAN
AUSTRIAN BLEI
BELGIAN MAETERLINCK
CANADIAN MACMECHAN
ENGLISH HUNT LAMB DRAKE
MUNRO MYERS PAGET PATER
GARROD MACHEN MARTIN
SEELEY STEELE TEMPLE ADDISON
BUDGELL CHAPONE HAYWARD
HAZLITT HEWLETT SYMONDS

CONGREVE NEVINSON STERLING
DICKINSON
FRENCH CAMUS ARAGON MOUREY
CHAMSON STAPFER CHARTIER
SCHOPFER MONTAIGNE
GERMAN ZWEIG FONTANE
GREEK XENOPHON
IRISH BOYD LECKY MAGEE
ITALIAN BRACCO
POLISH BELCIKOWSKI
MAKUSZYNSKI
SCOTTISH WILSON CARLYLE
STEVENSON
SWEDISH EKELUND
ESSE BEING
ESSENCE ENS NET ALMA ATAR
BASE BONE CORE CRUX DRAW
ESSE GIST GUTS KIND ODOR
OTTO PITH QUID RASA SOUL
YOLK ATTAR BASIC BASIS BEING
EIDOS FIBER FIBRE FUMET HEART
JUICE OTTAR OUSIA STUFF
BOTTOM EFFECT ENTITY FLOWER
INWARD MARROW NATURE
SPRITE ALCOHOL ELEMENT
EXTRACT FUMETTE GODHEAD
INBEING MEDULLA PERFUME
RATAFIA BERGAMOT CONCRETE
ESSENTIA
(— OF BEING) SAT
(— OF FLOWERS) CONCRETE
(— OF GOD) SPIRIT DIVINITY
(— OF MEAT) BLOND
(— OF TEA) DRAW
(— OF VITAL MATTER) GLAME
(INNERMOST —) ATMAN
(UNIVERSAL —) FORM
(VITAL —) STAMINA
ESSENE ESSEE ASCETIC
ESSENTIAL KEY REAL BASAL BASIC
VITAL ENTIRE FORMAL INWARD
CENTRAL CRUCIAL NEEDFUL
CARDINAL CRITICAL INHERENT
MATERIAL OBLIGATE NECESSARY
(— TO LIFE) BIOGENOUS
(NOT —) ACCIDENTAL
ESSENTIALLY AUFOND
ESSONITE GARNET HYACINTH
ESTABLISH BED FIX PUT SET BASE
FAST FIRM FOOT MAKE REAR
REST ROOT SEAT BUILD DEFIX
EDIFY ENACT ERECT EVICT
FOUND PLANT PROVE RAISE
SEIZE SETUP START STATE STELL
ATTEST AVOUCH BOTTOM
CEMENT CLINCH CREATE ENROOT
FASTEN FICCHE GROUND INVENT
INVEST LOCATE ORDAIN RATIFY
SETTLE STABLE VERIFY ACCOUNT
APPOINT APPROVE CONFIRM
ENSTATE INSTALL INSTATE
INSTORE POSSESS PREEMPT
SUSTAIN COLONIZE CONSTATE
CONTRACT ENSCONCE ENTRENCH
IDENTIFY INITIATE INSTRUCT
RADICATE REGULATE STABLISH
VALIDATE ASCERTAIN
(— FACT) APPROVE
(— FIRMLY) HAFT INDURATE
(— MORALS) ETHIZE
(— TRUMP) PITCH
ESTABLISHED SAD FAST FIRM
SURE LEGAL ROOTED SEATED

SICCAR STABLE STAPLE STATED
STRONG CERTAIN SETTLED
STANDING
ESTABLISHMENT HONG MILL
SHOP STAB DAIRY FORGE JOINT
PLANT POWER SALON STORE
AGENCY CAISSE CENOBY ECESIS
LAYOUT MENAGE SALOON
SCHOOL ARSENAL ATELIER
BROTHEL COENOBY CONCERN
DOWNSET FACTORY FISHERY
FOUNDRY FUNDUCK SHEBANG
AQUARIUM AVERMENT BUSINESS
CHEESERY CREAMERY ERECTION
HACIENDA
(— IN NEW HABITAT) ECESIS
(— OF COLONY) DEDUCTION
(BATHING —) THERM
(DOMESTIC —) MENAGE
(DRINKING —) STUBE SALOON
BARROOM SHEBEEN
(GAMBLING —) HOUSE TRIPOT
(HORSE-BREEDING —) HARAS
(MONASTIC —) CLOISTER
(WHITE —) MAN
ESTAFETTE COURIER STAFETTE
ESTATE FEE ALOD COPY FEOD FIEF
HOME LAND POMP RANK UDAL
ACRES ALLOD DAIRA DOWER
DOWRY ESTER ESTRE ETHEL
FINCA FUNDO HABIT HOUSE
MANOR STATE TALUK ABBACY
BARONY DEMISE DOMAIN ENTAIL
GROUND LIVING MISTER QUINTA
TALUKA ALODIUM CHATEAU
COMMONS DEMESNE DIGNITY
DISPLAY FORTUNE HAVINGS
MAJORAT ALLODIUM BENEFICE
COPYHOLD DOMINION EXECUTRY
FREEHOLD HACIENDA JOINTURE
LIFEHOLD LONGACRE MESNALTY
POSITION PROPERTY SENATORY
STANDING STAROSTY PATRIMONY
PERPETUITY
(— OF REBEL) FISC FISK
(— WITH SERFS) HAM
(CATTLE —) ESTANCIA
(HINDU —) CHAK
(PORTION OF —) LEGITIM
(REAL —) FUNDUS
(PL.) AMANI
ESTEEM AIM LET USE DEEM HOLD
RATE TALE ADORE COUNT FAVOR
HONOR PRICE PRIDE STEEM
THINK VALUE WEIGH WORTH
ADMIRE CREDIT EXTIME REGARD
REPUTE REVERE TENDER
WONDER ACCOUNT CONCEIT
OPINION RESPECT SUSPECT
APPRAISE CONSIDER ESTIMATE
VENERATE
ESTEEMED DEAR PRECIOUS
ESTER FMN BIXIN ETHER OLEIN
SARIN TABUN BORATE CAPRIN
ERUCIN HUMATE LAURIN MALATE
OLEATE ACETATE ADIPATE
ANISATE AZELATE CINERIN
ELAIDIN FORMATE FUROATE
GALLATE HEPARIN INDICAN
LACTATE LACTONE LAURATE
MALEATE MELLATE NITRATE
OCTOATE OXALATE OXAMATE
PECTATE PEPSIDE PICRATE

SORBATE STEARIN SULTONE
ABIETATE ACRYLATE ARSENATE
ARSENITE ARSONATE BEHENATE
BENZOATE CAFFEATE CONGENER
DIPHENAN ESTOLIDE FLUORIDE
FUCOIDIN KETIPATE LINOLATE
LINOLEIN MALONATE MARGARIN
MYRISTIN NUCLEATE PALMITIN
PIMELATE PIPERATE RACEMATE
SEBACATE SELENATE SILICATE
SINAPATE STEARATE SUBERATE
TARTRATE PYRETHRIN
(SUFF.) OATE
ESTHER (COUSIN OF —) MORDECAI
(FATHER OF —) ABIHAIL
(HUSBAND OF —) AHASUERUS
ESTHER WATERS (AUTHOR OF —)
MOORE
(CHARACTER IN —) FRED RICE
LATCH SARAH ESTHER JACKIE
PEGGIE TUCKER WATERS
PARSONS WILLIAM BARFIELD
ESTIMABLE GOOD SOLID WORTH
GENTLE HONEST WORTHY
THRIFTY VALUABLE
ESTIMATE AIM SET CALL CAST
GAGE RANK RATE READ RECK
ASSAY AUDIT CARAT CENSE
COUNT GAUGE GUESS JUDGE
MOUNT PLACE PRIZE SCALE
STOCK TALLY VALUE WEIGH
ASSESS BUDGET ESTEEM RECKON
REGARD SURVEY ACCOUNT
AVERAGE BALANCE CENSURE
COMPUTE CONCEIT MEASURE
APPRAISE CONSIDER CRITIQUE
CALCULATE
(— OF ONE'S SELF) OPINION
(— TOO HIGHLY) OVERRATE
(LOW COST —) LOWBALL
ESTIMATION AIM EYE CESS FAME
NAME ODOR PASS RATE COUNT
HONOR PRICE SIEGE VALUE
CHOICE ESTEEM REGARD REPUTE
ACCOUNT OPINION JUDGMENT
PRESTIGE
(— OF STRAIGHTNESS) BONING
(HIGH —) CONCEIT
(LOW —) DISREPUTE
ESTIMATOR RATER CRUISER
ESTOC STOCK SWORD
ESTOILE STAR ETOILE

ESTONIA
CAPITAL: TALLINN
COIN: SENT KROON ESTMARK
DIALECT: TARTU
ISLAND: DAGO MUHU OESEL
SAARE VORMSI HIIUMAA
SAAREMAA
LAKE: PEIPUS
MEASURE: TUN ELLE LIIN PANG
SUND TOLL TOOP FADEN VERST
SAGENE VERSTA KULIMET
VERCHOC TONNLAND
NATIVE: ESTH AESTI
PROVINCE: SAARE
RIVER: EMA NARVA PARNU
KASARI
TOWN: NARVA PARNU REVAL
TARTU TALLINN
WEIGHT: LOOD NAEL PUUD

ESTONIAN ESTH
ESTOP BAR FILL PLUG STOP DEBAR
PREVENT
ESTRANGE PART WEAN ALIEN
AVERT DIVERT ALIENATE
DISUNITE STRANGER
ESTRANGED ALIEN
ESTRANGEMENT STANCE
DISTASTE
ESTRAY STRAY WANDER
ESTREAT COPY FINE EXACT
RECORD STREET EXTRACT
EXTREAT
ESTREPEMENT STRIP
E STRING QUINT
ESTRIOL THEELOL
ESTROGEN MESTRANOL
ESTRONE THEELIN
ESTRUS HEAT SEASON
ESTUARY PARA WASH CREEK
FIRTH FLEET FRITH INLET LIMAN
ESTERO
ETCETERA ETC KTL
ETCH BITE FROST ENGRAVE
AQUATINT INSCRIBE
ETCHED FROSTED
ETCHER POINT
ETCHING ETCH AQUATINT
ETEOCLES (BROTHER OF —)
POLYNICES
(FATHER OF —) OEDIPUS
(MOTHER OF —) JOCASTA
ETERNAL ETERNE TARNAL
AGELESS ENDLESS LASTING
UNAGING ENDURING IMMORTAL
TIMELESS UNCAUSED
ETERNALLY AKE EER EVER
ALWAYS ETERNE FOREVER
ETERNITY AGE EON AEON OLAM
GLORY ETERNE ETERNAL
EWIGKEIT INFINITY PERPETUITY
ETESIAN ANNUAL PERIODIC
ETHAN (FATHER OF —) KISHI MAHOL
ETHANE DIMETHYL
ETHAN FROME (AUTHOR OF —)
WHARTON
(CHARACTER IN —) ETHAN FROME
ZEENA MATTIE PIERCE SILVER
ZENOBIA
ETHBAAL (DAUGHTER OF —)
JEZEBEL
ETHER AIR SKY APIOL ESTER
PINOLE ANISOLE ASARONE
EPOXIDE ETHYLIN HARMINE
SAFROLE SESAMIN SESAMOL
SOLVENT ACACETIN ELEMICIN
EMPYREAN GUAIACOL
PHENETOLE
ETHEREAL AERY AIRY SKYEY
AERIAL SKYISH AIRLIKE ETHERIC
FRAGILE SLENDER DELICATE
HEAVENLY SUPERNAL VAPOROUS
ETHICAL ETHIC MORAL
HONORABLE
ETHICS HEDONICS PHILOSOPHY

ETHIOPIA
ANCIENT CAPITAL: AXUM AKSUM
CAPITAL: ADDISABABA
COIN: BESA BIRR AMOLE GIRSH
DOLLAR TALARI ASHRAFI
PIASTER
DEPRESSION: DANAKIL

FALLS: TISISAT BLUENILE
ISLANDS: DAHLAK
LAKE: ABE TANA ABAYA SHOLA
ZEWAY RUDOLF STEFANIE
LANGUAGE: GEEZ TIGRE SOMALI
AMHARIC GALLINYA TIGRINYA
MARRIAGE: DAMOZ QURBAN
SEMANYA
MEASURE: TAT KUBA SINJER
SINZER FARSAKH FARSANG
MOUNTAIN: BATUGUGEGUNATALO
MOUNTAINS: AHMAR CHOKE
NAME: ABYSSINIA
NATIVE: AFAR GALLA ABIGAR
AMHARA ANNUAK HAMITE
SEMITE SOMALI TIGRAI CUSHITE
DANAKIL FALASHA
PORT: ASSAB MASSAWA
PRINCE: RAS
PROVINCE: BALE KEFA WELO
ARUSI GOJAM HARER SHEWA
TIGRE SIDAMO ERITREA
RIVER: OMO WEB BARO DAWA
GILA ABBAI AKOBO AWASH
FAFAN TAKKAZE
TOWN: EDD DESE GOBA GORE
JIMA THIO ADOLA ADUWA
AKSUM ASSAB AWASH DIMTU
HARAR HARER JIMMA MOJJO
ASMARA DESSYE DUNKUR
GONDAR MAKALE MEKELE
GARDULA MASSAWA NAKAMTI
NEKEMTE DIREDAWA LALIBALA
MUSTAHIL
VALLEY: RIFT
WATERFALL: FINCHA DALVERME
TESISSAT
WEIGHT: KASM NATR OKET ALADA
NETER WAKEA WOGIET
FARASULA

ETHIOPIAN SIDI HAMITE HARARI
AETHIOP AFRICAN CUSHITE
FALASHA
ETHIOPIC GIZ GEEZ GHEEZ
ETHNAN (FATHER OF —) ASHUR
(MOTHER OF —) HELAH
ETHNIC (— GROUP) ACHANG
ETHNOLOGIST AMERICAN GIBBS
HODGE LOWIE MASON SMITH
FEWKES MOONEY MORGAN
THOMAS BARROWS GODDARD
HENSHAW PILLING FLETCHER
GATSCHET GRINNELL CHURCHILL
SCHOOLCRAFT
AUSTRIAN MULLER LUSCHAN
WINTERNITZ
DANISH RASMUSSEN
DUTCH STEINMETZ NIEUWENHUIS
ENGLISH HADDON LATHAM
PRICHARD
FINNISH CASTREN
GERMAN BOEHM FINSCH GROSSE
KRAUSE BASTIAN GERLAND
STEINEN FROBENIUS FRIEDERICI
RUSSIAN KOPPEN
ETHOS MANNER
ETHYLENE ELAYL ETHENE ETHERIN
ETIQUETTE FORM DECORUM
MANNERS
(— OF DRINKING TEA) CHANOYU
ETRUSCAN TUSCAN RASENNA
ETRURIAN TYRRHENE

(PL.) TURSENOI TYRRHENI
ETUDE STUDY
ETUI CASE ETWEE TWEEZE
TWEEZER EQUIPAGE RETICULE
ETYMOLOGY ORIGIN DERIVATION
ETYMON RADIX
EUAECHME (DAUGHTER OF —)
PERIBOEA
(FATHER OF —) MEGAREUS
(HUSBAND OF —) ALCATHOUS
EUBOEANS ABANTES
EUCALYPT GUM YATE APPLE
BIMBIL CARBUN JARRAH MALLEE
MYRTAL CARBEEN CUTTAIL
MESSMAN COOLABAH IRONBARK
MESSMATE WHITETOP YERTCHUK
EUCALYPTOLE CINEOL CINEOLE
EUCALYPTUS BLUEGUM
EUCALYPT WHIPSTICK
EUCHARIST HOUSEL MAUNDY
SUPPER MYSTERY VIATICUM
EUCHARISTIC (— ELEMENTS) HAGIA
EUCHITE SATANIST ADELPHIAN
MESSALIAN
EUCHRE LOVE
(— HAND) JAMBONE JAMBOREE
EUDAEMONIA HAPPINESS
EUDOCIMUS GUARA
EUDOXIA (FATHER OF —) BAUTO
(HUSBAND OF —) ARCADIUS
(SON OF —) THEODOSIUS
EUGENE ONEGIN (CHARACTER IN —
OLGA GREMIN LARINA ONEGIN
OLENSKY TATYANA TRIQUET
(COMPOSER OF —) TCHAIKOVSKY
EUGENIE GRANDET (AUTHOR OF —)
BALZAC
(CHARACTER IN —) NANON
CHARLES CRUCHOT EUGENIE
GRANDET DEGRASSINS
EULALIA NETI
EULENSPIEGEL OWLGLASS
EULOGIST PRAISER LAUREATE
PANEGYRIST
EULOGISTIC EULOGIC EPENETIC
MAGNIFIC LAUDATORY
EULOGY PRAISE TONGUE ADDRESS
ELOGIUM ORATION ENCOMIUM
PANEGYRE
EUMOLPUS (FATHER OF —)
NEPTUNE
(MOTHER OF —) CHIONE
(SON OF —) ISMARUS
EUNEUS (BROTHER OF —) THOAS
(FATHER OF —) JASON
(MOTHER OF —) HYPSIPYLE
EUNICE (SON OF —) TIMOTHEUS
EUNUCH CAPON SPORUS WETHER
GELDING HALFMAN CASTRATE
EUPHAUSID SHRIMP
EUPHEMISM DEE FIB GEE GOR
DASH GOSH GOLES GOLLY LAWKS
DIANTRE DICKENS GRACIOUS
EUPHEMUS (FATHER OF —)
NEPTUNE POSEIDON
(MOTHER OF —) EUROPA
(SON OF —) BATTUS
EUPHONIOUS TUNEFUL
EUPHORIA ELATION
EUPHROSYNE JOY
EUPHUISM GONGORISM
EURASIAN BURGHER FERINGI
EUREKA RED PUCE

EURO WALLAROO
EUROPA (BROTHER OF —) CILIX
CADMUS THASUS PHINEUS
PHOENIX
(FATHER OF —) AGENOR
(HUSBAND OF —) ASTERIUS
(MOTHER OF —) TELEPHASSA
(SON OF —) MINOS SARPEDON
RHADAMANTHYS
EUROPE BELAIT CONTINENT

EUROPE
(ALSO SEE SPECIFIC COUNTRIES)
LAKE: COMO GARDA ONEGA
VANEM GENEVA LADOGA
LUGANO PEIPUS VANERN
ZURICH BALATON MALAREN
SCUTARI VATTERN MAGGIORE
CONSTANCE NEUCHATEL
MOUNTAIN: DOM ETNA ELBRUS
KAZBEK LYSKAMM SHKHARA
JUNGFRAU NADELHORN
WEISSHORN ZUGSPITZE
MATTERHORN
NATION: ITALY SPAIN FRANCE
GREECE MONACO NORWAY
POLAND RUSSIA SWEDEN
ALBANIA ANDORRA AUSTRIA
BELGIUM DENMARK ENGLAND
FINLAND GERMANY HOLLAND
HUNGARY IRELAND ROMANIA
BULGARIA PORTUGAL
SCOTLAND SANMARINO
LUXEMBOURG YUGOSLAVIA
EASTGERMANY NETHERLANDS
SOVIETUNION SWITZERLAND
VATICANCITY WESTGERMANY
GREATBRITAIN LIECHTENSTEIN
UNITEDKINGDOM
CZECHOSLOVAKIA
RANGE: ALPS URAL BALKAN
KJOLEN RHODOPE SUDETEN
CAUCASUS PYRENEES
APENNINES CARPATHIAN
RIVER: PO AAR DON AARE EBRO
ELBE ODER DOURO DVINA
LOIRE RHINE RHONE SEINE
TAGUS TIBER VOLGA DANUBE
THAMES DNIEPER VISTULA
DNIESTER

EUROPEAN FRANK SAHIB BOHUNK
EUROPE FRINGE INDIAN FERINGI
TOPIWALA
(— IN INDIES) BLIJVER
(WESTERN —) FRANK
EUROPEAN BARRACUDA SPET
EUROPEAN BASS BRASSE
EUROPEAN BISON AUROCHS
EUROPEAN CLOVER ALSIKE
EUROPEAN GULL MEW
EUROPEAN HERRING SPRAT
EUROPEAN JUNIPER CADE
EUROPEAN KITE GLEDE
EUROPEAN LAVENDER ASPIC
EUROPEAN LINDEN TEIL
EUROPEAN MINT HYSSOP
EUROPEAN OAK DURMAST
EUROPEAN PERCH RUFF RUFFE
EUROPEAN POLECAT FITCHEW
EUROPEAN PORGY BESUGO
EUROPEAN RABBIT CONY
EUROPEAN SHARK TOPE

EUROPEAN SPARROW WHITECAP
EUROPEAN STARLING STARNEL
EUROPEAN SWALLOW MARTIN
EUROPEAN THRUSH MAVIS
OUZEL
EUROPEAN WIDGEON WHIM
WHEWER
EUROPEAN WREN STAG
EURYANTHE (CHARACTER IN —)
ADOLAR LYSIART EGLANTINE
EURYANTHE
(COMPOSER OF —) WEBER
EURYBIA (FATHER OF —) PONTUS
(MOTHER OF —) GAEA
(SON OF —) PALLAS PERSES
ASTRAEUS
EURYNOME (DAUGHTERS OF —)
GRACES CHARITES
(FATHER OF —) CHAOS OCEANUS
EURYPTERID SERAPHIM
EURYPYLUS (FATHER OF —)
NEPTUNE TELEPHUS
(MOTHER OF —) ASTYOCHE
(SLAYER OF —) PYRRHUS
HERCULES
EURYSACES (FATHER OF —) AJAX
(MOTHER OF —) TECMESSA
EURYSTHEUS (FATHER OF —)
STHENELUS
(MOTHER OF —) NICIPPE
(SLAYER OF —) HYLLUS
EURYTUS (DAUGHTER OF —) IOLE
(FATHER OF —) ACTOR AUGEAS
MELANEUS
(MOTHER OF —) GAEA
(SLAYER OF —) HERCULES
EUTECTIC STEADITE
EUTERPE (FATHER OF —) JUPITER
(MOTHER OF —) MNEMOSYNE
EUXANTHONE PURRONE
EUXOA AGROTIS
EVACUATE PASS VENT VOID
AVOID EMPTY EXPEL STOOL
VACATE DEPRIVE EXCRETE
EXHAUST NULLIFY VACUATE
PERSPIRE
EVACUATION OFFICE DUNKIRK
EVADE BEG GEE BILK DUCK FLEE
FOIL JOUK JUMP SHUN SLIP VOID
AVERT AVOID BLINK DALLY
DODGE ELUDE FENCE FLANK
PARRY SHIRK SKIRT SKIVE BAFFLE
BLENCH BYPASS COPOUT DELUDE
ESCAPE ILLUDE BEGUILE FINESSE
OUTSLIP QUIBBLE HEDGEHOP
LEAPFROG SIDESTEP
(— LEGAL PROCESS) ABSCOND
(— PAYMENT) BILK
(— WORK) JOUK BLUDGE
EVADNE (FATHER OF —) PELIAS
NEPTUNE POSEIDON
(HUSBAND OF —) CAPANEUS
(MOTHER OF —) IPHIS PITANA
(SON OF —) IAMUS
EVALUATE RATE ASSESS PONDER
RECKON DISSECT APPRAISE
ESTIMATE
EVALUATION STOCK ESTIMATE
EVANDER (FATHER OF —) HERMES
(MOTHER OF —) CARMENTA
EVANESCE FADE VANISH
EVANESCENCE ANICCA
EVANESCENT FLEET EVANID

BRITTLE CURSORY EVASIVE
FRAGILE DELICATE FLEETING
FLITTING FUGITIVE STAYLESS
EVANGELICAL GOSPEL SIMEONITE
(— ACTIVITY) WARFARE
EVANGELIST LUKE MARK EVANGEL
GOSPELER SALVATIONIST
EVAPORATE DRY EXHALE
AVOLATE CONDENSE VAPORIZE
EVAPORATOR BOILER EFFECT
EVASION JINK SLIP DODGE QUIRK
SALVE SHIFT AMBAGE ESCAPE
SNATCH ELUSION OFFCOME
SHUFFLE TWISTER ARTIFICE
ESCAPISM VOIDANCE
EVASIVE SLY EELY DODGY SHIFTY
SUBTLE TWISTY ELUSIVE
ELUSORY TRICKSY SLIPPERY
SLIPSKIN
(TO BE —) STONEWALL
EVE DUSK EREB EREV EVEN VIGIL
SUNSET SUNDOWN
(NEW YEAR'S —) HAGMENA
HOGMANAY
EVELINA (AUTHOR OF —) BURNEY
(CHARACTER IN —) JOHN DUVAL
ARTHUR HOWARD ANVILLE
BELMONT CLEMENT EVELINA
ORVILLE VILLARS WILLOUGHBY
EVEN ALL DEN EEN TIE YET FAIR
HUNK JUST PAIR TIED TILL ALINE
CLEAN EQUAL EVERY EXACT
FLUSH GRADE HUNKY LEVEL
MATCH PLAIN RIVAL STILL SUANT
SUENT SWEET DIRECT ITSELF
PLACID SILKEN SMOOTH SQUARE
STEADY ABREAST BALANCE
EQUABLE FLATTEN REGULAR
UNIFORM UPSIDES EQUALIZE
MODERATE PARALLEL
(— NUMBERS) PAIR
(— OFF) LEVEL
(— THOUGH) IF ALTHO ALBEIT
ALTHOUGH
(MAKE —) WEIGH STEADY
(PREF.) ARTIO HOMAL(O) LEUR(O)
EVENING DEN EVE EREB EVEN
ABEND TARDE SUNSET VESPER
EVENTIDE VESPERAL
(— BEFORE PASSOVER) PARASCEVE
(— OF SONG) CEILIDH
(AT —) TEEN
(YESTERDAY —) STREEN
EVENING PRIMROSE SUNCUP
SCABIOUS
EVENING STAR VENUS HESPER
VESPER EVESTAR HESPERUS
EVENLY FAIR PLAIN FLATLY
EQUALLY
EVENNESS EQUALITY
EVENT HAP CASE FACT FATE FEAT
TILT CASUS DOING EPOCH FRAME
ISSUE THING ACTION EFFECT
FACTUM RESULT TIDING TIMING
EPISODE FIXTURE MIRACLE
PORTENT TRAGEDY INCIDENT
OCCASION OCCURRENCE
(AMUSING —) COMEDY
(CHANCE —) ACCIDENT FORTUITY
(EXTRAORDINARY —) MIRACLE
(FORTUITOUS —) HAZARD
(GRAVE —) CALAMITY
(HAPPY —) GODSEND

(IMPORTANT —) ACE ERA
(PAST —S) HISTORY
(SEISMIC —) STARQUAKE
(SET OF —S) EPISODE
(SIGNIFICANT —) CRISIS
(SKI —) DOWNHILL
(SOCIAL —) BENEFIT
(SPORTING —) STAKE
(THEATRICAL —) DRAW
(TURNING-POINT —) LANDMARK
(UNEXPECTED —) STUNNER
ACCIDENT AFTERCLAP
(UNPLEASANT —) BUMMER
(YEARLY —) ANNUAL
EVENTFUL LIVELY NOTABLE
EVENTIDE VESPER EVENING
EVENTUAL LAST FINAL ULTIMATE
EVENTUALITY EVENT
EVENTUALLY YET FINALLY
EVENTUATE GO LEAD ISSUE
RESULT SUCCEED ULTIMATE
EVENUS (DAUGHTER OF —)
MARPESSA
(FATHER OF —) ARES MARS
EVER O AY SO AYE EER ONCE STILL
ALWAYS ETERNE FOREVER
EVERGLADE STATE FLORIDA
EVERGREEN BOX FIR IVY YEW ASIS
BAGO ILEX PINE TAWA BOLDO
CAROB CEDAR HEATH HOLLY
LARCH SAVIN THUYA TOYON
BAUERA COIGUE DAHOON
LAUREL MASTIC SPRUCE BANKSIA
BARETTA BEBEERU BILIMBI
GOWIDDE HEMLOCK JASMINE
TARATAH BOXTHORN CALFKILL
CARAUNDA IRONWOOD TILESEED
(PL.) CHRISTMAS
EVER-INCREASING ACCRESCENT
EVERLASTING ETERNE AEONIAL
AEONIAN AGELONG DURABLE
ENDLESS ETERNAL FOREVER
LASTING TEDIOUS ENDURING
IMMORTAL INFINITE TIMELESS
PERPETUAL
EVERLASTINGLY ALWAYS
FOREVER
EVERSION BLOWOUT BEARINGS
EVERT UPSET EVERSE SUBVERT
OVERTURN
EVERY ALL ANY ILK PER THE EACH
EVER ILKA ENTIRE EVERICH
COMPLETE
(— DAY) QD QUOTID
(— HOUR) QH
(— NIGHT) QN
(PREF.) PAM PAN
EVERYBODY ALL EACH EVERYMAN
EVERYONE
EVERYDAY USUAL HOMELY
PROSAIC ORDINARY WORKADAY
EVERY MAN IN HIS HUMOUR
(AUTHOR OF —) JONSON
(CHARACTER IN —) EDWARD
KITELY BOBADIL BRIDGET
CLEMENT KNOWELL MATTHEW
WELLBRED BRAINWORM
EVERYTHING ALL ATHING
EVERYWHERE PASSIM UBIQUE
ALGATES AYWHERE OVERALL
ALLWHERE
EVICT OUST EJECT EXPEL
EVIDENCE MARK SHOW SIGN TEST

PROOF SCRIP SMOKE TOKEN
TRACE TRIAL ATTEST AVOUCH
BETOKE RECORD REVEAL
CHARTER EXHIBIT HEARSAY
SHOWING SUPPORT ARGUMENT
DISPROOF DOCUMENT EVICTION
INDICATE MANIFEST MONUMENT
MUNIMENT WARRANTY
ADMINICLE
(— OF DISEASE) SYMPTOM
(— OF FRESHNESS) BLOOM
(— OF WRONGDOING) GOODS
(POSITIVE —) CONSTAT
EVIDENT LOUD OPEN PERT APERT
BROAD CLEAR FRANK GROSS
NAKED PLAIN EXTANT LIQUID
PATENT WITTER EMINENT
GLARING OBVIOUS PROBATE
VISIBLE APPARENT DISTINCT
FLAGRANT LUCULENT MANIFEST
PALPABLE
(PREF.) DELO
EVIL BAD DER ILL SIN BALE BASE
DIRE HARM LEWD PAPA POOR
SORE VICE VILE WICK YELL CRIME
CURSE DEVIL FELON FOLLY
HYDRA MALUM QUEDE SORRY
WATHE WRONG CANCEL DIVERS
INJURY MALIGN MENACE
NAUGHT PLAGUE ROTTEN
SHREWD SINFUL UNFEEL UNFELE
UNGOOD UNWELL WICKED
WONDER ADVERSE BALEFUL
CORRUPT DISEASE DIVERSE
HEINOUS HURTFUL IMMORAL
MISDEED NOXIOUS SATANIC
UNHAPPY UNSOUND VICIOUS
CALAMITY DEPRAVED DEVILISH
DISASTER GANGRENE IMPROPER
INIQUITY MISCHIEF QUEDSHIP
SINISTER NEFARIOUS
(— BEING) MARE
(— OF MANY PHASES) HYDRA
(— SPIRIT) JUMBIE
(IMAGINARY —) WINDMILL
(IMPENDING —) MENACE
IMMINENCE
(SOCIAL —) SCOURGE
(SPIRITUAL —) SCAB
(PREF.) MAL(E) PONERO
EVILDOER BADMASH BUDMASH
SLASHER
EVIL EYE DROCHUIL MALOCCHIO
EVINCE SHOW ARGUE PROVE
SUBDUE BREATHE CONQUER
DISPLAY EXHIBIT EVIDENCE
INDICATE MANIFEST
EVISCERATE GUT DRAW BOWEL
PAUNCH GARBAGE
EVOCATION SADHANA
EVOCATIVE REDOLENT
EVOKE FIT MOVE STIR EDUCE
AROUSE ELICIT SUMMON
EVOCATE PROVOKE SUGGEST
EVOLUTION DRIFT GROWTH
BIOGENY DIOECISM HOROTELY
MANEUVER BRADYTELY
(PL.) AEROBATICS
EVOLUTIONISM DARWINISM
EVOLVE COOK EMIT EDUCE DERIVE
UNFOLD UNROLL BLOSSOM
DEVELOP EVOLUTE CONCEIVE
UNPLIGHT

EWE KEB TEG CROCK CRONE
DRAPE SHEEP GIMMER LAMBER
RACHEL THEAVE CHILVER
(— AND LAMB) COUPLE
(OLD —) BIDDY CROCK CRONE
BIDDIE
(YOUNG —) THEAVE
EWER JUG CREW LAIR BASIN
UDDER PITCHER URCEOLE
EXACERBATE SOUR ENRAGE
FERMENT EMBITTER IRRITATE
EXACERBATION PAROXYSM
EXACT ASK DUE DEAD EVEN FINE
FLAT HAVE JUMP JUST LEVY
NEAT NICE TRUE VERY PRESS
SCREW WREAK WREST COMPEL
DEMAND ELICIT EVINCE EXTORT
FORMAL GRAITH MINUTE
NARROW PROPER SEVERE
SQUARE STRAIT STRICT CAREFUL
CERTAIN COLLECT COMMAND
CORRECT ENFORCE ESTREAT
EXPRESS EXTRACT LITERAL
PARTILE PERFECT POINTED
PRECISE PRECISO REFINED
REGULAR REQUIRE ACCURATE
CRITICAL EXPLICIT FAITHFUL
RIGOROUS SPECIFIC
(— BY FINE) ESTREAT
(— SATISFACTION) AVENGE
(NOT —) PLATIC
(PREF.) ORTH(O)
EXACTING NICE HARSH PICKY
STERN STIFF TIGHT SCREWY
SEVERE STRAIT STRICT ARDUOUS
EXIGENT FINICKY ONEROUS
CRITICAL IMPOSING IRONCLAD
PRESSING SCREWING
PARTICULAR PERSNICKETY
(— EXCLUSIVE DEVOTION) JEALOUS
EXACTION TAX MART GOUGE
GRIPE
(— OF PROVISIONS) CESS COYNE
COIGNY
(UNDUE —) EXTORTION
EXACTLY DUE BANG DEAD EVEN
FLAT FLOP FULL JUMP JUST
VERY PLUMB PLUNK QUITE RIGHT
SHARP SPANG TRULY ARIGHT
EVENLY ITSELF JUSTLY NICELY
PERFECT SLAPDAB DIRECTLY
MINUTELY SMACKDAB
EXACTNESS RIGOR TRUTH NICETY
ACCURACY DELICACY DISPATCH
FIDELITY IDENTITY JUSTNESS
SAPIENCE SEVERITY PRECISION
PARTICULARITY
(FUSSY —) FIKE
EXAGGERATE GAB MORE COLOR
BOUNCE CHARGE COLOUR
EXTEND OVERDO AMPLIFY
ENHANCE ENLARGE MAGNIFY
OUTLASH ROMANCE STRETCH
INCREASE OVERDRAW OVERLASH
OVERPLAY OVERTELL OVERSTATE
OVERCHARGE
(— OPENING OF MOUTH) CHINK
EXAGGERATED CAMP SLAB TALL
COLORED FUSTIAN FABULOUS
INFLATED OVERDONE OVERSHOT
OVERWEENING
EXAGGERATING ARROGANT
EXAGGERATION BLAH

REACHER HYPERBOLE
EXALT HAUT REAR AREAR BUILD
DEIFY ELATE ERECT EXTOL HEAVE
HEEZE HONOR MOUNT RAISE
TOWER ALTIFY ASCEND EXHALE
PREFER REFINE THRONE UPREAR
WORTHY ADVANCE AUGMENT
DIGNIFY ELEVATE ENHANCE
ENNOBLE FEATHER GLORIFY
GREATEN INSPIRE MAGNIFY
PROMOTE SUBLIME DIVINIZE
ENTHRONE GRADUATE HEIGHTEN
INHEAVEN PEDESTAL
EXALTATION LAUD AVATAR
ANAGOGE ANAGOGY ELATION
RAPTURE ERECTION
EXALTED HAUT HIGH ELATE
GRAND LOFTY NOBLE SHEEN
SKYEY SOARY ASTRAL TIPTOE
TOPFUL HAUGHTY SUBLIME
ELEVATED EXALTATE MAGNIFIC
EXALTING HUMAN
EXAM MUG
EXAMINATION EX MAY EXAM
FACE QUIZ TEST ASSAY AUDIT
BOARD CHECK FINAL GREAT
POINT PROBE STUDY TRIAL
BIOPSY EXAMEN NOTICE REVIEW
SCHOOL SEARCH SURVEY TRIPOS
AUTOPSY BEARING CANVASS
CHECKUP DIVVERS EXAMINE
HEARING INQUEST INQUIRY
MIDYEAR OPPOSAL TUGGERY
ANALYSIS CRITIQUE DOCIMASY
EXERCISE NECROPSY PHYSICAL
RESEARCH SCANNING SCRUTINY
PRACTICAL PRELIMINARY
(PL.) HOURS
(SUFF.) SCOPE SCOPIC SCOPUS
SCOPY
EXAMINE ASK CON FAN SEE SPY
TRY BOLT CASE COMB FEEL LAIT
LINE LOOK OGLE QUIZ RIPE SCAN
SEEK SIFT TEST VIEW ASSAY
AUDIT CHECK ENTER GROPE
PROBE QUEST QUOTE SAMEN
SENSE SOUND STUDY VISIT
APPOSE BEHOLD CANDLE DEBATE
PERUSE PONDER REVIEW SCREEN
SEARCH SURVEY ANALYZE
CANVASS COLLATE DISCUSS
EXPLORE INQUIRE INSPECT
OVERSEE PALPATE RUMMAGE
COGNOSCE CONSIDER OVERHAUL
TRAVERSE
(— BY TOUCH) PALPATE
(— CAREFULLY) SCAN SIFT
PONDER
(— LAND) SOUM
EXAMINER POSER TRIER CENSOR
CONNER SABORA ANALYST
APPOSER AUDITOR CORONER
PROBATOR SEARCHER
EXAMPLE A CASE CAST COPY
LEAD NORM TYPE BEAUT BYSEN
ESSAY LIGHT MODEL PIECE
EMBLEM PRAXIS SAMPLE
BOUNCER LEADING LECTURE
PATTERN PURPOSE SAMPLER
THEATER CALENDAR ENSAMPLE
EXEMPLAR EXEMPLUM FORBYSEN
FOREGOER INSTANCE PARADIGM
SPECIMEN

(DISGRACEFUL —) BIZEN BYSEN
BYZEN MONSTROSITY
(EXTREME —) CAUTION
(FINEST —) PEARL
(INFERIOR —) EXCUSE
(INSTRUCTIVE —) LESSON
(OLDEST —) DOYEN
(PERFECT —) APOTHEOSIS
(STANDARD —) PROTOTYPE
(SUPERLATIVE —) BLINGER
EXANTHEMA DIEBACK ERUPTION
EXASPERATE IRE IRK MAD BAIT
GALL HEAT URGE ANNOY BLOOD
ENRAGE EXCITE NETTLE EXASPER
INFLAME PROVOKE ROUGHEN
ACERBATE IRRITATE
EXASPERATED SNAKY WROTH
SNAKEY SNAKISH ACERBATE
EXASPERATION GALL HEAT
WRATH
EXCAVATE CUT DIG PIT HOLE
HOWK MINE MOLE MUCK PION
SINK DELVE DRILL DRIVE GRAVE
NAVVY SCOOP STOPE BURROW
DREDGE EXCAVE GULLET
HOLLOW QUARRY
EXCAVATION CUT DIG PIT HOLE
MINE REDD SINK SUMP BERRY
DELFT DELPH DITCH GRAFT
GRAVE HEUGH PILOT STOPE
BURROW CAVITY DUGOUT
GROOVE TRENCH BREAKUP
CUTTING PADDOCK TUTWORK
WORKING DENEHOLE SLUSHPIT
EXCAVATOR DIG BILDAR CLEOID
DIGGER DIPPER DRIFTER
HATCHET PIONEER
EXCEED COW TOP BEST PASS
EXCEL OUTDO OUTGO BETTER
OUTRUN OUTVIE OVERDO
OVERGO ECLIPSE OUTPASS
OVERRUN OVERTAX PRECEDE
SURPASS OUTRANGE OUTREACH
OUTSTRIP OVERCOME OVERGANG
OVERSTEP OVERWEND
SURMOUNT PREPONDERATE
(— IN IMPORTANCE) OVERSHADOW
(— THE RESOURCES) BEGGAR
EXCEEDING VILE
EXCEEDINGLY ALL DONE PURE
TRES VERY AMAIN BLAME
BLAMED MASTER PROPER
PURELY AWFULLY LICKING
PARLOUS PASSING HEARTILY
HEAVENLY HORRIBLE PROPERLY
(PREF.) PRE ULTRA
EXCEL CAP COB TOP BANG BEAT
BEST DING FLOG MEND PASS
STAR BLECK OUTDO OUTGO
SHINE TRUMP BETTER EXCEED
MASTER OUTRAY OVERDO
OVERGO PRECEL ECLIPSE
EMULATE OUTPEER SURPASS
OUTCLASS OUTRANGE OUTRIVAL
OUTSHINE OUTSTRIP OVERPEER
SUPERATE SURMOUNT
EXCELLENCE ARETE MERIT PRICE
VIRTU WORTH BEAUTY DESERT
HEIGHT VIRTUE DIGNITY
PROWESS GOODNESS SPLENDOR
BRILLIANCE PREROGATIVE
(— OF QUALITY) STRIKE
(MORAL —) GRACE

(PL.) SANCTITIES

EXCELLENT FAB GAY RUM BEST
BOSS BRAW COOL FINE GOOD
HEND HIGH PURE RARE RIAL
SLAP TALL TRIM ATHEL BONNY
BONZA BRAVE BULLY BURLY
CRACK GREAT JAMMY JOLLY
LUMMY PIOUS PRIME SOLID
SUPER SWELL TOUGH TRIED
WALLY BONNIE BONZER BOSKER
BUMPER CHEESY CHOICE CLASSY
FAMOUS FREELY GENTLE GOODLY
PRETTY PROPER SELECT SPIFFY
WICKED WIZARD WORTHY
YANKEE BLIGHTY BOSHTER
CAPITAL CORKING CURIOUS
ELEGANT GALLANT IMMENSE
QUALITY SNIFTER STAVING
TOPPING CLIPPING COLOSSAL
EXIMIOUS GENEROUS KNOCKOUT
SPIFFING STUNNING SUPERIOR
VALUABLE VIRTUOUS WAUREGAN
YNGOODLY
(— IN QUALITY) FRANK
(MOST —) BEST

EXCELLENTLY BRAWLY CLEVER
FINELY FREELY PROUDLY
DIVINELY FAMOUSLY

EXCELLING BEST PASSANT

EXCEPT BAR BUT CEP NOT BATE
BOUT OMIT ONLY SAVE ABATE
FORBY SEVER EXEMPT FORBYE
NOBBUT SAVING SCUSIN UNLESS
BARRING BESIDES EXCLUDE
OUTCEPT OUTSIDE OUTTAKE
OUTWITH RESERVE WITHOUT
FORPRISE OUTTAKEN RESERVED
(PREF.) PRETER

EXCEPTING BATING EXCEPT
SAVING UNLESS BARRING

EXCEPTION DEMUR SALVO SAVING
DISSENT OFFENSE DEMURRER
FALLENCY FORPRISE INSTANCE

EXCEPTIONAL RARE EXEMPT
ROUSING STRANGE UNUSUAL
ABERRANT ABNORMAL ESPECIAL
SINGULAR UNCOMMON

EXCEPTIONALLY AMAZING
SPANKING

EXCERPT CITE PATCH QUOTE
SCRAP EXTRACT OFFPRINT
(— FROM SONG) SNATCH

EXCESS OVER PLUS RIOT FLOOD
INORD LUXUS PRIDE ACRASY
SPILTH ACRASIA BALANCE
DEBAUCH EXTREME MISRULE
NIMIETY OUTRAGE OVERAGE
OVERSET PROFUSE RIOTISE
SURFEIT SURPLUS EXCEDENT
GLUTTONY INTEREST OVERLASH
OVERMUCH OVERPLUS
PLEONASM PLETHORA PLEURISY
SATURNALIA OVERABUNDANCE
(— OF ACTION) OVERKILL
(— OF LOGS) BANK
(— OF METAL) FEEDHEAD
(— OF SOLAR MONTH) EPACT
(— OF VOTES) PLURALITY
(SUFF.) ARD ART

EXCESSIVE TOO OVER RANK
ENORM FANCY STEEP STIFF
THICK UNDUE DEADLY DEUCED
WOUNDY BURNING EXTREME

FURIOUS NIMIOUS OVERDUE
SURFEIT ABNORMAL CRIMINAL
DEVILISH ENORMOUS HORRIBLE
INSOLENT OVERMUCH TERRIBLE
TERRIFIC PLETHORIC
(PREF.) POLY SUR

EXCESSIVELY TOO SUPER DEADLY
OVERLY STRONG UNDULY
PARLISH PARLOUS PASSING
PLAGUEY WOUNDLY DEVILISH
PLAGUILY
(PREF.) HYPER

EXCHANGE RAP SET CASH CAUP
CHOP CODE COPE COUP KULA
MART SELL SWAP SWOP BANDY
BOARD BOLSA CORSE SHIFT
STORE TRADE TROKE TRUCK
BARTER BOURSE CAMBIO
CHANGE DICKER EXCAMB
MARKET NIFFER RESALE RIALTO
SCORSE SHOPPE TOLSEL TOLZEY
VALUTA WISSEL WRIXLE
BARROOM CAMBIUM CHAFFER
COMMUTE CONVERT DEALING
PERMUTE TRAFFIC COMMERCE
TRUCKAGE
(— IN CHECKERS) CUT SHOT
(— OF BLOWS) HANDPLAY
(— OF PRISONERS) CARTEL
(— OF SYLLABLES) ANACLASIS
(— SMALL TALK) CHAFFER
(— THOUGHTS) CONVERSE
(— VISITS) GAM
(DANCE —) CROSSOVER
(FAIR —) GIFFGAFF
(FOREIGN —) DEVISE
(POETICAL —) FLYTING
(POST —) CANTEEN
(TELEPHONE —) CENTRAL
(PREF.) CAMBI(O)

EXCHEQUER FISC PURSE COFFER
KHALSA CHECKER FINANCE
TREASURY

EXCIPIENT OXYMEL

EXCISE CUT TAX CROP DUTY GELD
TOLL SLASH EXCIDE EXSECT
IMPOST RESECT EXSCIND
ALCABALA RETRENCH

EXCISEMAN GAGER GAUGER
EXCISOR

EXCISION CUT ERASURE ABLATION

EXCITABLE NERVY NERVOUS

EXCITATION LASH

EXCITE HOT CITE FIRE HEAT HYPO
SEND SPUR STIR URGE WAKE
WHET WORK YERK ALARM
AMOVE ANGER CHAFE ELATE
ERECT FLAME FLUSH IMPEL
PIQUE RAISE ROUSE SCALD
SPOOK AROUSE AWAKEN BOTHER
DAZZLE DECOCT FLURRY FOMENT
GROOVE IGNITE INCEND INCITE
INVOKE JANGLE KINDLE LATHER
PROMPT SALUTE TICKLE UPREAR
WECCHE AGITATE ANIMATE
COMMOVE ENCHAFE FERMENT
INCENSE INFLAME PHILTER
PROVOKE QUICKEN STARTLE
WHITTLE DISQUIET ENGENDER
EXCITATE IRRITATE
(— MIRTH) DIVERT

EXCITED UP GAY HOT AGOG GYTE
PINK ABOIL AGLOW CADGY

EAGER PROUD RANTY SKEER
BLEEZY ELATED HEATED STEAMY
ATHRILL FEVERED HAYWIRE
SKEERED WAKENED AGITATED
ATWITTER ELEVATED FEVERISH
FLURRIED FRENETIC STARTLED
OVERWROUGHT
(EASILY —) KITTLE
(INTENSELY —) MAD

EXCITEMENT ADO GOG BUZZ
FUME FUSS GLOW HEAT KICK
RUFF STIR TOSS UNCO FEEZE
FEVER FUROR KICKS LARRY
MANIA SETUP STOUR UNCOW
FRENZY SPLASH WARMTH
FERMENT FRISSON NERVISM
TAMASHA WIDDRIM BROUHAHA
DELIRIUM INTEREST RACKETRY
(FILLED WITH —) HECTIC
(GREAT —) FEVER
(MENTAL —) WIDDRIM
(PLEASANT —) SUSPENSE
(VIOLENT —) GARE

EXCITING HOT HIGH ZINGY HECTIC
AGACANT BURNING PARLOUS
RACKETY ROUSING EXCITANT
EXCITIVE PATHETIC STIRRING
TERRIFIC
(— HORROR) DIRE DIREFUL

EXCLAIM CRY HOWL BLURT ESCRY
SNORT CLAMOR OUTCRY
BESPEAK

EXCLAMATION (ALSO SEE
INTERJECTION) O AH AI AY BO
EH EY HA HI HO LA LO MY OH
OW SO ST YO AHA AIE BAH BAM
BOO FEN FIE FOH GEE GIP GRR
GUP HAI HAW HAY HEM HEP HEY
HIC HOY HUH NOW OCH OFF OHO
OUF OUT PAH PEW POH POX ROT
SEE SUZ TCH TCK TUT UGH VOW
WEE WOW YAH YOW AHEM ALAS
AVOY BUFF DEAR DRAT EGAD
EVOE FAST GARN GOOD HAIL
HECH HECK HIST HOLA HUFF
HUNH HUSH HYKE OONS OUGH
PHEW PHOO PHUT PIFF PISH
POOH PRUT PUGH RATS RIVO
SCAT SIRS SOFT SOHO TCHU
TUSH WALY WEEK WEET WELL
WHAM WHAT WHEE WHEW WHIR
WHIT WUGG YOOP YULE ALACK
BRAVO EWHOW FAINS FANCY
FAUGH FEIGH GLORY GOODY
HEIGH HELLO HOLLA HUFFA
HULLO HUMPH HUZZA JOSSA
OHONE PSHAW RIGHT SALVE
SHISH SKOAL SORRY SUGAR
TEREU WAUGH WELOO WHING
WHISK WHIST WHOOP WIRRA
WOONS CARAJO CLAMOR
ENCORE HALLOO HEYDAY
HOOTAY HURRAH INDEED
OUTCRY PERFAY QUOTHA
RATHER RIGHTO SHUCKS STEADY
WALKER WHOOSH CARAMBA
DOGGONE GODSAKE HOSANNA
JEEPERS JIGGERS KERCHOO
KERWHAM NICHEVO PRITHEE
RUBBISH SALAMAT TANTIVY
THUNDER WELCOME WHOOPEE
FAREWELL WAESUCKS
WELLAWAY

(— OF DISGUST) AUH FIE FOH PAH
UGH AUGH AVOY PHEW PISH
POOT PSHA PUGH FAUGH FEICH
FEIGH PSHAW WELOO
(— OF DISTRESS) AI AIE HARO
HARROW
(— OF DOUBT) HUM HUMPH
(— OF IMPATIENCE) GIP PHEW
(— OF INCREDULITY) AHEM INDEED
WALKER
(— OF REPUGNANCE) UGH
(— OF SURPRISE) HA OW GIP LAW
HEIN HUNH LACK LAND LAWK
LORD ODSO BABAI HEUGH LAWKS
MARRY CRIMINE CRIMINY
HEAVENS JUCKIES GORBLIMY
GRAMERCY
(— OF TRIUMPH) AH IO GRIG
HEUCH HOOCH HURRAH
(PROFANE —) BAN

EXCLAMATION POINT BANG
SHOUT SCREAMER

EXCLUDE BAR SHUT SINK CLOSE
DEBAR EJECT EXPEL FENCE
BANISH DISBAR EXCEPT EXEMPT
FORBAR FORBID REJECT BLANKET
DEFAULT EXPUNGE FOREBAR
FOREIGN OUTTAKE OUTWALL
REPULSE SECLUDE SUSPEND
OSTRACIZE
(PREF.) DIS

EXCLUDED EXEMPT FOREIGN

EXCLUDING BAR BUT LESS
BARRING

EXCLUSION OSTRACISM

EXCLUSIVE ALL ONLY RARE SOLE
VERY ALONE ELECT WHOLE
NARROW SELECT CLIQUISH
ENTIRELY RECHERCHE
(— OF) BEFORE

EXCLUSIVELY ALL ONLY ALONE
SINGLY ENTIRELY

EXCOGITATE CONSIDER

EXCOMMUNICATE CURSE
UNCHURCH

EXCOMMUNICATION BAN CURSE
HEREM EXCISION

EX-CONVICT LAG LAGGER

EXCORIATE FLAY GALL SCORE
STRIP ABRADE SCATHE SCORCH
BLISTER LAMBASTE

EXCREMENT LEE CRAP DIRT DREG
DUNG FRASS JAKES SIEGE
HOCKEY ORDURE REFUSE
VOIDING CROTTELS COLLUVIES
(— OF EARTHWORM) CAST
(— OF FOXES) SCUMBER
(— OF HARES) CROTTELS
(— OF INSECTS) FRASS
(PL.) DEJECTA
(PREF.) COPR(O) MERDI

EXCRESCENCE NOB PIN WEN
BURL BURR GALL HORN KNOB
KNOT KNUR LUMP SCAB WART
FUSEE FUZEE KNURL THORN
EXCESS HURTLE MORULA NUBBLE
PIMPLE BOLSTER PUSTULE
RATTAIL SPINACH CARUNCLE
EPITHEMA TUBERCLE
(— ON HORSE'S FOOT) FIG TWITTER
(— ON WHALE'S HEAD) BONNET
(PREF.) GANGLI GANGLO

EXCRETA EGESTA

EXCRETE EGEST SWEAT EXCERN SECERN DEFECATE PERSPIRE

EXCRETION SORDES ECRISIS PERISARC

EXCRUCIATE RACK GRIND AGONIZE TORMENT TORTURE

EXCRUCIATING GRINDING

EXCULPATE FREE CLEAR REMIT ACQUIT EXCUSE PARDON ABSOLVE FORGIVE JUSTIFY RELEASE PALLIATE

EXCULPATION EXCUSE

EXCURSION DIP HOP ROW DIET RIDE SAIL SPIN TOUR TRIP ESSAY JAUNT RANGE SALLY START TRAMP AIRING CANTER CRUISE FLIGHT JUNKET OUTING PASEAR RAMBLE SASHAY VAGARY VOYAGE JOURNEY OUTLOPE OUTRIDE OUTROAD CAMPAIGN ESCAPADE

EXCURSIONIST TRIPPER

EXCUSABLE VENIAL

EXCUSE FAIK PLEA ALIBI COLOR GLOSS PLANE REMIT SALVO SCUSE ACQUIT ESSOIN EXEMPT PARDON REASON REFUGE SCONCE SECURE SUNYIE ABSOLVE APARDON APOLOGY CONDONE ESSOIGN EVASION EXCUSAL FORGIVE OFFCOME PRETEXT DISPENSE OCCASION OVERLOOK PALLIATE PRETENCE (**CONSCIENTIOUSLY —**) SCRUPLE

EXCUSS SHAKE DISCARD DISCUSS

EXECRABLE BAD CURST CURSED DAMNED HEINOUS ACCURSED DAMNABLE WRETCHED

EXECRATE BAN DAMN ABHOR CURSE DEVOTE

EXECRATION CURSE ANATHEMA MALEDICTION

EXECUTE DO ACT CUT TOP BURN DASH FILL GIVE HANG HAVE KILL OBEY PASS PLAY SLAY FRAME GANCH LYNCH SCRAG YIELD DESIGN DIRECT EFFECT FINISH FULFIL GARROT GIBBET MANAGE ACHIEVE CONDUCT ENFORCE FULFILL GAROTTE PERFORM STRETCH COMPLETE DISPATCH EXPEDITE PRACTICE PRACTISE (**— BOW**) WREATHE (**— POORLY**) DUB (**— SUCCESSFULLY**) COMPLETE

EXECUTED GIVEN (**— EXQUISITELY**) CURIOUS (**— WITH CARE**) ACCURATE (**CRUDELY —**) DAUBY

EXECUTION GANCH TOUCH EFFECT FACTURE GARROTE HANGING TECHNIC CARRIAGE GARROTTE PRACTICE PERFORMANCE (**— BY BURNING**) STAKE (**— BY DROWNING**) NOYADE (**— OF WILL**) FACTUM

EXECUTIONER BURRIO HEADER TORTOR BUTCHER HANGMAN HEADMAN LOCKMAN CARNIFEX EXECUTOR HEADSMAN CRUCIFIER

EXECUTIVE BOSS DEAN MAYOR WARDEN CASHIER MANAGER PODESTA PREMIER GOVERNOR OFFICIAL

EXECUTOR DOER AGENT ALBACEA SECUTOR ENFORCER MINISTER

EXEGESIS ANAGOGE ANAGOGY MIDRASH HAGGADAH

EXEMPLAR COPY TYPE MODEL FATHER MIRROR MODULE EIDOLON EXAMPLE PARABLE PATTERN PARADIGM

EXEMPLARY LAUDABLE

EXEMPLIFICATION SOUL SAMPLE CONSTAT EXAMPLE

EXEMPLIFY SAMPLE SATISFY ENSAMPLE MODELIZE

EXEMPT EXON FREE EXEEM EXEME FRANK SEVER SPARE EXPERT FIDATE IMMUNE EXCLUDE RELEASE DISPENSE EXCEPTED PRIVILEGE (**PREF.**) IMMUNO

EXEMPTION GRACE CHARTER FREEDOM LIBERTY SWEATER BLOODWIT IMMUNITY IMPUNITY

EXEQUATUR PLACET

EXERCISE ACT AIR DIP PLY URE USE BEAR HAVE DRILL ETUDE EXERT HALMA LATIN LONGE SWEAT AIRING BREATH CAREER EMPLOY EXERCE LESSON MANUAL PARADE PRAXIS SCHOOL AUFGABE BREATHE DISPLAY ENHAUNT JOGGING PROBLEM ACTIVITY EXERTION FORENSIC PALESTRA PRACTICE PRACTISE (**— CONTROL**) BOSS PRESIDE (**— HORSE**) BREEZE (**—S TO REDUCE WEIGHT**) SLIMNASTICS (**ACADEMIC —**) PRACTICUM (**CAVALRY —**) MELEE (**DEVOTIONAL —**) ANGELUS (**MUSICAL —**) ETUDE SOLFEGE VOCALISE (**PRELIMINARY —**) WARMUP PROLUSION (**PUNISHMENT —**) PENSUM (**STRONG —**) INTENSION (**SYSTEM OF —**) AEROBICS (**UNWARRANTED —**) STRETCH (**PL.**) ALLEGRO ATHLETICS

EXERT DO PLY PUT DRAW EMIT HUMP STIR DRIVE SPEND SWING BESTIR EXTEND REVEAL STRAIN AFFORCE ENFORCE IMPRESS CHARETTE ENDEAVOR EXERCISE (**— A SPELL**) TAKE (**— POWER**) ACT BEAR (**— PRESSURE**) PRESS SQUEEZE (**— TRACTION**) HAUL

EXERTING (**— POWER**) AGENT

EXERTION DINT HEFT BURST ESSAY LABOR TRIAL WHILE ACTION EFFORT MOTION PINGLE STRESS STRIFE ATTEMPT TROUBLE ENDEAVOR EXERCISE STRUGGLE (**EXCESSIVE —**) STRAIN (**STRENUOUS —**) HUMP

EXFOLIATE SCALE SPALL SPAWL

EXFOLIATION FURFUR

EXHALATION AURA FUME REEK STEAM BREATH EXPIRY MIASMA HALITUS MALARIA FUMOSITY MEPHITIS

EXHALE CAST EMIT REEK EXUDE STEAM WHIFF EXPIRE BREATHE FURNACE REFLAIR RESPIRE EXHALATE PERSPIRE

EXHALED SFOGATO

EXHAUST DO FAG SAP BEAT BURN COOK COWL EMIT FAIL FLAG FLOG JADE KILL MATE SOAK TIRE TUCK BLAST BREAK CLEAN DRAFT DRAIN EMPTY FORDO GRUEL LEECH PETER SHOOT SPEND SWINK WASTE WEARY ABRADE BETOIL BOTTOM BUGGER EMBOSS FINISH FOREDO HARASS HATTER OVERDO TAIGLE TUCKER BREATHE CONSUME DEPLETE DEPRIVE DRAUGHT EXTRACT FATIGUE OUTWEAR SCOURGE SURREIN TRACHLE DISTRESS EDUCTION EVACUATE FORSPEND FORSWINK FORWEARY OVERWEAR OVERSPEND

EXHAUSTED TAM BEAT DEAD DONE DUNG GONE WEAK WORN BLOWN EMPTY JADED SPENT STANK TIRED BARREN BEATEN BUSHED EFFETE GROGGY MARCID PLAYED TOILED TRAIKY ATTAINT DRAINED EMPTIED FORDONE FORSUNG FORWORN TEDIOUS WHACKED BANKRUPT CONSUMED FOREDONE FOREWORN FORFAIRN FORSPENT FOUGHTEN HARASSED OUTSPENT OVERWORN (**— OF AIR**) HIGH

EXHAUSTING ARDUOUS IRKSOME PREYING

EXHAUSTION EXHAUST FATIGUE SELLOUT SOOREYN DISTRESS GONENESS PROSTRATION

EXHAUSTIVE FULL MINUTE THOROUGH

EXHIBIT AIR PEN FAIR HAVE SHEW SHOW TURN WEAR CARRY SPORT STAGE BLAZON DEMEAN EVINCE EXPOSE OPPOSE OSTEND PARADE REVEAL APPROVE CONCENE DIORAMA DISPLAY EXPRESS MONSTER PERFORM PRESENT PRODUCE PROJECT PROPOSE TRADUCE BOOKFAIR BRANDISH CONCEIVE DISCLOSE DISCOVER EMBLAZON EVIDENCE FORTHSET MANIFEST SHOWCASE (**— ALARM**) GLOFF (**— DOGS**) BENCH (**— IN SNARLING**) GRIN

EXHIBITION EXPO FAIR SALE SHOW DROLL ENTRY SALON SIGHT ANNUAL PARADE SALARY ACADEMY DISPLAY EXHIBIT PAGEANT PENSION PRESENT SHOWING STAGERY EXERCISE PERFORMANCE (**— OF DOGS**) BENCH (**— ON STAGE**) STAGERY (**PUBLIC —**) SPECIES (**RIDING —**) CAROUSEL

EXHIBITIONER SERVITOR

EXHIBITIONIST HAM HAMFATTER

EXHIBITOR SHOWER

EXHILARATE AMUSE CHEER ELATE ANIMATE ELEVATE ENLIVEN GLADDEN

EXHILARATED RAD GLAD HAPPY HEADY ELEVATED

EXHILARATING SAPID

EXHILARATION GAIETY JOLLITY GLADNESS HILARITY

EXHORT URGE WARN CHARM ADHORT ADVISE CHARGE DEHORT ENGAGE INCITE PREACH CAUTION ADMONISH DISSUADE

EXHORTATION ADVICE EXHORT HOMILY COUNSEL PROPHECY PREACHMENT

EXHORTER HORTATOR PREACHER

EXHUME DIG DELVE UNBURY UNTOMB UNEARTH DISINTER EXHUMATE

EXIGENCY NEED PUSH WANT EXIGENT URGENCY JUNCTURE OCCASION PRESSURE

EXIGENT DIRE VITAL URGENT CRITICAL EXACTING PRESSING

EXIGUITY PAUCITY

EXIGUOUS MEAGER MEAGRE

EXILE EXUL POOR RUIN THIN EXPEL GALUT WREAK BANISH DEPORT GALUTH OUTLAW SCANTY WRETCH EXULATE GERSHOM OUTCAST PILGRIM REFUGEE SLENDER DIASPORA FUGITIVE OUTLAWRY OSTRACIZE

EXILED FOREIGN FUGITIVE

EXIST AM BE IS ARE LIE COME GROW LIVE MOVE PASS DWELL CONSIST SUBSIST (**— IN FULL SUPPLY**) FLOW

EXISTENCE ENS ESSE LIFE SEIN BEING DASEIN ENTITY IDEATE INESSE ESSENCE IDEATUM REALITY ENERGEIA IDENTITY STANDING SURVIVAL PERSONALITY (**— AFTER DEATH**) AFTERLIFE (**DULL —**) DEATH (**ETERNAL —**) SAT (**EVER-CHANGING —**) SAMSARA SANSARA (**IN —**) GOING AROUND EXTANT (**INDEPENDENT —**) ASEITY PERSEITY (**PERMANENT —**) INHERENCE (**WAKING —**) JAGRATA (**PREF.**) ONTO

EXISTENT HARD REAL ALIVE BEING ACTUAL EXTANT EXISTING (**— IN DIFFERENT FORMS**) ALLOTROPIC (**CONTINUALLY —**) STUBBORN

EXISTING GOING ACTUAL EXTANT PRESENT EXISTENT (**— IN NAME ONLY**) DUMMY (**SUFF.**) ANT ENT

EXIT ISH DOOR GATE VENT GOING ISSUE LEAVE EGRESS EXITUS OUTLET OUTWAY EXITION OUTGATE OUTPORT PASSAGE DEBOUCHE (**HURRIED —**) BOUT

EXITE BRACT

EX LIBRIS BOOKPLATE

EXOCYCLIC IRREGULAR
EXODUS EXODY EXITUS HEGIRA HEJIRA EXODIUM
EXON EXEMPT
EXONERATE FREE ALIBI CLEAR ACQUIT EXCUSE EXONER UNLOAD ABSOLVE RELIEVE
EXOPODITE EXOPOD SQUAMA
EXORABLE PRAYABLE
EXORBITANT STEEP UNDUE ABNORMAL
EXORCIST BENET
EXORDIUM PREFACE PRELUDE
EXOSKELETON CORSLET CORSELET
EXOSPORIUM EXINE EXTINE EXOSPERM
EXOSTOSIS POROMA SPLINT OSSELET RINGBONE
EXOTIC ALIEN FOREIGN STRANGE ADVENTIVE RECHERCHE
EXOTOSPORE BLAST
EXOTROPIA WALLEYE
EXPAND OPE WAX BLOW BULK FLAN FLUE FOAM GROW HUFF OPEN FARCE FLASH RETCH SPLAY SWELL WIDEN DIDUCE DILATE EXTEND INTEND SPREAD SPROUT UNFOLD UNFURL AMPLIFY BALLOON BLOSSOM BOLSTER BROADEN BURGEON DEVELOP DIFFUSE DISPAND DISPLAY DISTEND EDUCATE ENLARGE EXPANSE EXPLAIN INFLATE STRETCH DISPREAD INCREASE LENGTHEN OUTREACH
(— AS A VESSEL) FLAN
(— FEATHERS) PRIDE
(— INTO PODS) KID
EXPANDED NOWY OPEN OVERT DILATE PATENT SPREAD DILATED SWOLLEN INFLATED PATULENT PATULOUS
EXPANDER EXTENDER
EXPANDING BOSOMY
EXPANSE AREA ROOM BOSOM BURST FIELD REACH TRACT EXTENT LENGTH SPREAD COUNTRY STRETCH DISTANCE EXPANSUM SEPARATE
(— OF ICE) SHEET
(— OF SEA ICE) FIELD
(BROAD —) ACRE MAIN
(FLAT —) LEVEL
(IMMEASURABLE — OF TIME) ETERNITY
(IMMENSE —) OCEAN
(INDEFINITE —) VAGUE
(VAST —) SEA
(WIDE —) BREADTH
EXPANSIBILITY ELATER
EXPANSION ALA BULB WING FLUSH SPLAY GROWTH SPREAD ECTASIA ECTASIS EXPANSE HASTULA ACROCYST COQUILLE DIASTOLE DILATION INCREASE SWELLING
(— IN SEEDS) ALA WING
(— OF RIVER) BROAD
(FOLIOSE —) LAMINA
(LITURGICAL —) EMBOLISM
EXPANSIVE FREE WIDE BROAD GENIAL ELASTIC LIBERAL GENEROUS SPACIOUS SWELLING

EXPATIATE DWELL DILATE EXPAND SPREAD AMPLIFY BROADEN DESCANT DIFFUSE ENLARGE SATISFY
EXPATRIATE EXILE EXPEL BANISH OUTLAW OUTCAST
EXPATRIATION EXILE
EXPECT ASK DEEM HOPE LITE LOOK STAY TEND TROW WAIT WEEN ABIDE AWAIT THINK ATTEND DEMAND INTEND LIPPEN RECKON PRESUME REQUIRE SUPPOSE SUSPECT CALCULATE
EXPECTANT ATIPTOE CHARGED HOPEFUL INCHOATE
EXPECTANTLY AGOG TIPTOE
EXPECTATION HOPE VIEW WAIT WEEN TRUST EXPECT FUTURE ESPEIRE OPINION SUPPOSE THOUGHT WEENING PROSPECT
EXPECTED DUE NATURAL SUPPOSED
EXPECTORANT CINEOL STORAX CINEOLE EMETINE AMMONIAC CREOSOTE GUAIACOL TEREBENE
EXPECTORATE SPIT
EXPECTORATION EMPTYSIS
EXPEDIENCE ARTIFICE
EXPEDIENT FIT WISE ATAJO CRAFT DODGE JOKER KNACK SALVO SHIFT DEVICE RESORT STRING DODGERY POLITIC STOPGAP ARTIFICE RESOURCE DESIRABLE MAKESHIFT
EXPEDITATE LAW
EXPEDITATION LAWING
EXPEDITE HIE EASY FREE HURRY SPEED EXPEDE GREASE HASTEN QUICKEN DISPATCH
EXPEDITION CAMP FARE PLOY ROAD TREK DRAVE HASTE HURRY RANGE SCOUT TRADE SAFARI VOYAGE CARAVAN CRUSADE ENTRADA JOURNEY OUTLOPE SERVICE WARFARE WARPATH COMMANDO HEADHUNT PROGRESS
(FISHING —) DRAVE
(HUNTING —) SAFARI
(MILITARY —) HARKA CRUSADE HOSTING JOURNEY WARPATH
EXPEDITIOUS FAST HASTY QUICK RAPID READY SHORT PROMPT SPEEDY
EXPEL CAN OUT USH BLOW BOLT DRUM DUMP FIRE OUST VOID WARP AVOID CHASE CHECK DEPEL EJECT ERUPT EVICT EXILE KNOCK SPURT BANISH BOUNCE DEBOUT DEPORT DEVOID DISBAR DISOWN OUTPUT OUTRAY REFUSE ABANDON EXCLUDE EXPULSE EXTRUDE OBTRUDE SCRATCH SECLUDE SUSPEND DISLODGE DISPLACE EVACUATE FORJUDGE
(— AIR) COUGH
(— FROM MEMBERSHIP) HAMMER
(— GAS) BELCH
(— SUDDENLY) SLIRT
(PREF.) DIS
EXPEND USE LEND SPEND SPORT

WASTE WREAK DEFRAY IMPEND OCCUPY OUTLAY PONDER CONSUME DISPEND EROGATE EXHAUST OVERUSE DISBURSE SQUANDER
EXPENDITURE COST MISE OUTGO PENSE CHARGE OUTLAY EXPENSE PENSION SPENDING
(— OF ENERGY) EFFORT
EXPENSE EX COST GAFF LOSS BATTA PRICE SUMPT CHARGE DAMAGE GERSUM ONCOST OUTLAY OUTSET AVERAGE OVERHEAD SUMPTURE
(— OF CARRYING) CARRIAGE
(— OF TREAT) SAM
(PL.) BATTA COSTS MISES
EXPENSIVE DEAR HIGH SALT PRICY STIFF COSTLY LAVISH PRICEY APICIAN LIBERAL THRIFTY
EXPERIENCE SEE TRY FEEL FIND GUST HAVE HENT HOLD KNOW LIVE TEST ASSAY EVENT PROOF PROVE SKILL TASTE TRIAL USAGE BEHOLD EXPERT FRAIST ORDEAL SAMPLE SUFFER APPROVE CALVARY CONTACT FEELING FURNACE KNOWING REALIZE SUSTAIN UNDERGO ESCAPADE
(— GOOD OR ILL FORTUNE) SPEED
(— OF INTENSE SUFFERING) CALVARY
(— WITH BITTERNESS) BEAR
(CALAMITOUS —) ADVERSITY
(DRUG —) TRIP
(ENJOYABLE —) GROOVE
(EXCITING —) TRIP
(FIRST —) TIROCINIUM
(HALLUCINATORY —) TRIP
(ORDINARY —) USE
(PAINFUL —) FIT
(PARTIAL —) GUST
(TRYING —) ORDEAL
EXPERIENCED HAD MET OLD SEEN USED SALTY EXPERT SALTED TRADED ANCIENT PRACTIC THRIVEN VETERAN WEIGHED SEASONED
(— INTENSIVELY) ACUTE
(ACTUALLY —) SPECIOUS
EXPERIENTIAL EMPIRIC
EXPERIMENT SHY TRY TEST ASSAY ESSAY TRIAL ATTEMPT CONTROL
(PREF.) EMPIRICO EMPIRIO
EXPERIMENTAL SAMPLE
(NOT —) STANDARD
EXPERT ACE DAB DEFT FULL GOOD PERT ADEPT CRACK FLASH MAVEN MAVIN READY SHARP SWELL ADROIT ARTIST CLEVER FACILE HABILE KAHUNA MASTER MAYVIN PANDIT PERTLY QUAINT SUBTLE WIZARD ARTISTE ATTACHE CAPABLE DABSTER PERFECT PERITUS SKILLED DEXTROUS GAINSOME SKILLFUL SPEEDFUL VIRTUOSO PROFESSED PROFICIENT
(— IN JEWISH LAW) DAYAN
(— ON DRIVING LOGS) LAKER
(BANK —) SHROFF
(GREAT —) ONER
(SCIENTIFIC —) BOFFIN

(SUFF.) ICIAN
EXPERTNESS SAVVY SKILL FACILITY HABILITY
EXPIATE ABY SKUG ATONE AVERT ASSOIL RANSOM
EXPIATORY PIACULAR
EXPIRATION END DEATH BREATH EFFLUX ELAPSE EXPIRE EXPIRY
(SPASMODIC —) SNEEZE
EXPIRE DIE END EMIT FALL EXPEL GHOST LAPSE ELAPSE EXHALE INLAIK OUTRUN PERISH
EXPIRED UP DEAD EXPIATE
EXPIRING DYING
EXPIRY ISH CLOSE DEATH EFFLUX
EXPLAIN OPEN REDE SAVE SCAN UNDO WISE AREAD AREED CLEAR GLOSS GLOZE PLANE RECHE SOLVE SPEED TOUCH DEFINE EXPAND EXPLAT EXPONE REMENE RIDDLE UNFOLD ABSOLVE ACCOUNT AMPLIFY CLARIFY COMMENT CONTRUE DECLARE DEVELOP DISCUSS EXHIBIT EXPOUND JUSTIFY RESOLVE CONSTRUE DESCRIBE MANIFEST SIMPLIFY UNPLIGHT UNWONDER
EXPLAINER EXPONENT
EXPLAINING EXPONENT
EXPLANATION KEY NOTE FARSE GLOSS SALVE SALVO ANSWER CAVEAT ACCOUNT APOLOGY ADDENDUM EXEGESIS INNUENDO NOTATION SOLUTION
EXPLETIVE AND GEE BOSH EGAD GOSH OATH BEGAD MODAL BEHEAR SDEATH TUNKET DAMMISH MORBLEU GOODYEAR GRACIOUS
EXPLICATE OPEN CLEAR EXPAND UNFOLD ACCOUNT EXPLAIN
EXPLICATION CRIB ANALYSIS
EXPLICIT OPEN CLEAR EXACT FIXED PLAIN EXPRESS PRECISE ABSOLUTE DEFINITE IMPLICIT POSITIVE PUNCTUAL SPECIFIC
EXPLICITLY BARELY DIRECT FORMALLY
EXPLODE POP BLOW FIRE BELCH BLAST BURST CRUMP ERUPT PLUFF SHOOT SQUIB SPRING BACKFIRE DETONATE DISPLODE
EXPLOIT ACT DEED FEAT GEST JEST MILK WORK GESTE GOUGE STUNT PERFORM SUCCESS CHIVALRY PARERGON PROPERTY
(— FINANCIALLY) RIPOFF
(— SUCCESSFULLY) PARLAY
EXPLOITER KULAK
EXPLORATION SPY PROBE SEARCH EXPLORE
EXPLORATORY FRONTIER PROBATIVE PROBATORY
EXPLORE DO DIP MAP SPY DIVE DRAG FEEL VIEW CHART COAST DELVE RANGE SCOUT SOUND SEARCH EXAMINE PALPATE BOTANIZE DISCOVER
(— FOR MINERALS) PROSPECT
EXPLORER CAVEMAN PIONEER COLUMBUS
AMERICAN BYRD COOK GRAY

HALL KANE LONG PIKE BEEBE
CLARK FIALA HAYES JAMES
LEWIS MUSIL NILES PEARY
AKELEY ASHLEY BRYANT CARVER
DELONG GREELY HERVEY RAINEY
ANDREWS BALDWIN BURNHAM
FREMONT STANLEY WELLMAN
WORKMAN BRAINARD BRIDGMAN
LOCKWOOD MELVILLE SCHWATKA
ELLSWORTH MACMILLAN
DANENHOWER HUNTINGTON
HALLIBURTON
AUSTRALIAN WILLS STUART
FORREST KENNEDY LINDSAY
WILKINS BERNACCHI
AUSTRIAN HUGEL PAYER GLASER
BAUMANN PAULITSCHKE
BELGIAN GERLACHE
CANADIAN MACKAY JOLLIET
SIMPSON BARTLETT PALLISER
STEFANSSON
COLOMBIAN REYES
DANISH BOCK HOLM KOCH
MIKKELSEN RASMUSSEN
DUTCH NIEUWENHUIS
ENGLISH BACK BASS BENT COOK
EYRE BAKER BRUCE DAVYS
EVANS GRANT OATES PARRY
SCOTT SPEKE STURT YOUNG
BURTON CONDER GROGAN
HEARNE HOWITT LANDER
MAWSON OSBORN PHILBY SABINE
WILSON CAMERON CHESNEY
DEWINDT GREGORY HOLDICH
JACKSON WICKHAM FRANKLIN
GRENFELL JOHNSTON SCORESBY
ALEXANDER WARBURTON
INGLEFIELD MCCLINTOCK
SCHOMBURGK SHACKLETON
LIVINGSTONE YOUNGHUSBAND
FRENCH BONIN MONTS BINGER
BRAZZA CALLIE DULUTH GENTIL
HAARDT ABBADIE CARTIER
CRAMPEL CREVAUX FOUREAU
GARNIER LASALLE NICOLET
BONVALOT COUDREAU
MARCHAND CAILLIAUD
CHAMPLAIN IBERVILLE
MARQUETTE VINCENNES
GERMAN LENZ BARTH PFEIL
POGGE REISS VOGEL DECKEN
FLEGEL JUNKER PETERS ROHLFS
FISCHER NEUWIED NIEBUHR
OVERWEG DENHARDT FILCHNER
FRANCOIS KOLDEWEY KOTZEBUE
WISSMANN FEDERMANN
GUSSFELDT WEYPRECHT
LEICHHARDT SCHLAGINTWEIT
IRISH BURKE
ITALIAN ZENO CABOT CAGNI
GESSI CASATI NOBILE BELZONI
CODAZZI FILIPPI PIAGGIA
ALBERTIS ANTINORI COLUMBUS
NEW ZEALAND HAAST HILLARY
NORWEGIAN ASTRUP NANSEN
WISTING AMUNDSEN JOHANSEN
SVERDRUP JOHANNESEN
BORCHGREVINK
PORTUGUESE CABRILLO COVILHAO
FERNANDES
RUSSIAN TOLL POTANIN
WRANGEL PRZHEVALSKI
BELLINGSHAUSEN

SCOTTISH RAE PARK ROSS BRUCE
LAING LAIRD CADELL FORBES
THOMSON MITCHELL MACKENZIE
CLAPPERTON·
SPANISH ANZA OJEDA AYLLON
BALBOA CORTES DESOTO
AGUIRRE ALARCON CORDOBA
MENDOZA PIZARRO BASTIDAS
CARDENAS CORONADO GRIJALVA
ORELLANA VIZCAINO ESCALANTE
SWEDISH HEDIN NATHORST
PALANDER ANDERSSON
NORDENSKJOLD
SWISS MUNZINGER
EXPLOSION POP BANG BLOW
BLAST BURST CRUMP SALVO
BLOWUP BOUNCE REPORT
PLOSION INCIDENT OUTBURST
(FUEL —) BACKFIRE
(SLIGHT —) PLUFF
EXPLOSIVE EGG TNT MINE AMVIS
AMATOL JOVITE LIMPET POWDER
TETRYL TONITE TORPEX TOUCHY
TRITON ABELITE AMMONAL
AZOTINE DUNNITE LIGNOSE
LYDDITE PLOSIVE PRIMING
PUDDING SHIMOSE THORITE
AMMONITE CHEDDITE DYNAMITE
ECRASITE ERUPTIVE GELATINE
MAXIMITE MELINITE PYROLITE
ROBURITE SABULITE SAXONITE
SECURITE RACKAROCK
SAMSONITE
(CHARGE OF —) TULIP RESPONDER
EXPONENT INDEX POWER
(SUFF.) ICIAN
EXPORT OUTCARRY
EXPORTATION EXPORT OUTPORT
EXPOSE AIR BARE GIVE OPEN RISK
SHOW STRIP BEWRAY DEBUNK
DETECT EXPONE GIBBET OBJECT
OPPOSE REVEAL UNHUSK
UNMASK DISPLAY EXHIBIT
EXPOUND PILLORY PROPINE
PUBLISH SUBJECT UNCOVER
UNEARTH UNTRUSS BRANDISH
DISCLOSE DISCOVER MUCKRAKE
RIDICULE SATIRIZE UNCLOTHE
UNSHROUD
(— FOR BLEACHING) CROFT
(— ORE) HUSH
(— PLAYING CARD) BURN
(— SELF TO) WAGE
(— SUDDENLY) FLASH
(— TO AIR) AERATE
(— TO DANGER) JUMP COMMIT
SUBMIT
(— TO HEAT) AIR
(— TO INFAMY) GIBBET
(— TO MOISTURE) RET
(— TO SCORN) PILLORY
(— TO SULFUR DIOXIDE) STOVE
(— TO SUN) INSOLATE SOLARIZE
(— TO SUN AND AIR) FIELD
EXPOSED AIRY BARE OPEN BLEAK
LIABLE PUBLIC UNSAFE SUBJECT
VEILLESS
(— TO) AGAINST
(— TO DANGER) INSECURE
EXPOSITION FAIR GECK SHOW
ZEND TRACT APERCU EXPOSE
METHOD SURVEY ACCOUNT
EXPOSAL MIDRASH ANALYSIS

EXEGESIS EXPOSURE EXTHESIS
HAGGADAH TREATISE
(— OF FEAST) SYNAXARY
EXPOSITORY EXEGETIC
EXPOSTULATE ARGUE OBJECT
DISCUSS EXAMINE PROTEST
EXPOSTULATION PROTEST
EXPOSURE ASPECT EXPOSE
EXPOSAL FLASHING FRONTAGE
PROSPECT
(— OF CARDS) SPREAD
(— OF KING) CHECK
(— TO AIR) AERATE AIRING
(BODY —) FLASH
EXPOUND OPEN REDE UNDO
GLOZE SENSE TREAT DEFINE
EXPONE EXPOSE COMMENT
DEVELOP DISCUSS EXPLAIN
EXPOSIT EXPRESS CONSTRUE
SIMPLIFY PHILOSOPHIZE
EXPOUNDER MUFTI MULLAH
EXPRESS EXPONENT HERMETIC
(— OF THEORY) ALFAQUI
PHILOSOPHER
EXPRESS AIR BID PUT SAY CAST
EMIT PASS POST VENT COUCH
EMOTE FRAME OPINE SPEAK
STATE UTTER VOICE WIELD
BROACH DEMEAN DENOTE
DIRECT EVINCE IMPORT PHRASE
ABREACT BREATHE DECLARE
DICTATE EXPOUND EXPREME
TESTIFY DEFINITE DESCRIBE
DISPATCH EXPLICIT INTIMATE
MANIFEST
(— APPROVAL) AGREE ACCEDE
APPLAUD
(— AS LANGUAGE) LAY
(— BY GESTURE) BECK
(— BY LAUGHTER) LAUGH
(— CONCERN) CLUCK
(— DISAPPROVAL) BOO CHIDE
DECRY GROAN CATCALL
(— DISDAIN) TUT
(— EFFERVESCENTLY) CHORTLE
(— FOLLY) EXPAND
(— GRATITUDE) THANK AGGRATE
(— GRIEF) DEPLORE
(— IN WORDS) SAY DRAW SPEAK
PHRASE
(— NUMERICALLY) EVALUATE
(— ONE'S FEELINGS) FLOW
(— SORROW) LAMENT COMPLAIN
(— WILLINGNESS) CONSENT
EXPRESSION DIT HIT SAY CAST
EUGE FACE FORM POSE SHOW
SIGN TERM VULT WORD ADIEU
GLIFF IDIOM SNEER TOKEN VOICE
BYWORD DILOGY DIVERB EFFECT
FACIES ORACLE PHRASE SPEECH
SYMBOL COMMENT DESCANT
EPITHET EXPRESS GRIMACE
ALLEGORY AUSDRUCK DANICISM
FELICITY LACONISM MONOMIAL
(— IN FEW WORDS) BREVITY
(— OF ANNOYANCE) SOH
(— OF APPROVAL) EUGE PLACET
(— OF ASSENT) CONTENT
(— OF BEAUTY) ART
(— OF CHOICE) VOTE
(— OF CONTEMPT) COBLOAF
(— OF DISPLEASURE) FROWN
(— OF DISTASTE) FACE

(— OF HOMAGE) OVATION
(— OF JOY) GREETING
(— OF OPINION) EDITORIAL
(— OF RESPECT) DUTY
(— OF SADNESS) SHADE
(— OF SCORN) GECK
(— OF SINGLE IDEA) RHEME
(APT —) FELICITY
(CHEMICAL —) EQUATION
(COMMONPLACE —) BROMIDE
(CORRECT —) SUMPSIMUS
(CURT —) LACONIC
(FACIAL —) GRIN CHEER SCOWL
SMILE
(INCONGRUOUS —) BULL
(LOUD —) CLAMOR
(MATHEMATICAL —) INDEX SERIES
BINOMIAL EQUATION FUNCTION
INTEGRAL
(MOCKING —) SCOFF
(PECULIAR —) IDIOM
(PET —) CANT
(PUERILE —) BOYISM
(SARCASTIC —) GIBE JIBE
(SERIOUS —) EARNEST
(SINCERE —) CANDOR
(SYMBOLIC —) FORMULA
(TENDER —) LANGUISH
(TRITE —) CLICHE
(UNRESTRAINED —) EFFUSION
(VERBAL —) LETTER
(VULGAR —) SOLECISM
(WISE —) ORACLE
(SUFF.) LOG(ER)(IA)(IAN)(IC)(ICAL)
(IST)(UE)(Y)
EXPRESSIONLESS BLANK STONY
LEADEN SODDEN VACANT
WOODEN TONELESS
EXPRESSIVE POETIC TONGUED
ELOQUENT EMPHATIC SPEAKING
EXPRESSIVENESS DICTION
DELICACY TOURNURE
ELOQUENCE
EXPRESSLY NAMELY EXPRESS
PRESSLY FORMALLY
EXPRESSWAY FREEWAY
SPEEDWAY
EXPROBATE CENSURE UPBRAID
EXPULSION EXILE BOUNCE
OUSTER BANNIMUS EJECTION
EXCISION
(— OF SPORES) ABJECTION
EXPUNGE BLOT DELE ERASE SLASH
CANCEL DELETE EFFACE EXCISE
SCRAPE DESTROY SCRATCH
DISPUNGE
EXPURGATE GELD PURGE
CASTRATE
EXPURGATION BOWDLERISM
EXQUISITE FOP DUDE FINE NICE
PERT PINK RARE DANDY EXACT
CHOICE DAINTY CAREFUL
ELEGANT GEMLIKE PERFECT
REFINED AFFECTED DELICATE
ETHEREAL MACARONI
RECHERCHE
EXQUISITELY CHOICELY
EXSCIND CUT SEVER EXCISE
EXTANT ALIVE BEING LIVING
VISIBLE EXISTING MANIFEST
(PREF.) NEO
EXTEMPORE SUDDEN OFFHAND
IMPROVISO

EXTEND GO EKE LIE RUN BEAR
BUSH COME DATE DRAW GROW
LAST OPEN PASS PUSH RISE ROLL
SPAN SPIN BREDE BULGE CARRY
COVER FARCE REACH RENEW
RETCH SEIZE SHOOT STENT
VERGE WIDEN AMOUNT DEEPEN
DEPLOY DILATE EXPAND INTEND
OUTLIE SPREAD SPRING STRAIN
STREAK THRUST TRENCH
AMPLIFY BROADEN DIFFUSE
DISPLAY DISTEND ENLARGE
OVERLAP OVERRUN PORRECT
PORTEND PRODUCE PROFFER
PROJECT PROLONG PROMOTE
PROTEND RADIATE STRETCH
CONTINUE ELONGATE INCREASE
LENGTHEN OUTREACH
PROROGUE PROTRACT PROTRUDE
OUTSPREAD PROPAGATE
OUTSTRETCH
   (— ACTIVITIES) BRANCH
   (— AROUND) GIRTH
   (— HAND) RAX
   (— IN SPACE) DURE
   (— IRREGULARLY) TRAIL
   (— OVER) SPAN COVER CROSS
   CONTAIN OVERLAP OVERRIDE
   (— SAIL) SHEET
   (— THE FRONT) DEPLOY
   (— TO) LINE REACH
EXTENDED FAT LONG OPEN
BROAD EXTENT SPREAD EXTENSE
LENGTHY PROLATE SPLAYED
EXPANDED INTENDED
   (PREF.) MEG(A) MEGAL(O)
EXTENDER INERT FILLER LIGNIN
EXTENDING BROAD
   (— OVER) ASTRIDE
EXTENSION ARM EKE ELL AREA
CAPE SCOPE POCKET SATTVA
SPHERE SPREAD BREADTH
STRETCH ADDENDUM ADDITION
DURATION INCREASE PROTENSE
   (— OF BUILDING MATERIAL) APRON
   (— OF CREDIT) DATING
   (— OF MINERAL VEIN) FLAT
   (— OF RACE TRACK) CHUTE SHUTE
   (— OF SHELL) LAPPET
   (— OF TIME) RESPITE
   (— OF WAGON FRAME) THRIPPLE
   (BALLET —) BATTEMENT
EXTENSIVE HUGE VAST WIDE
AMPLE BROAD LARGE EXTENSE
IMMENSE EXPANDED INFINITE
SWEEPING
EXTENT DUE RUN TAX AREA BODY
BULK DEAL GAGE LEVY PASS SIZE
WRIT AMBIT DEPTH FIELD GAUGE
LIMIT RANGE REACH SCOPE
SPACE STENT SWEEP TRACK
AMOUNT ASSIZE ATTACK DEGREE
LENGTH SPREAD STREEK
ACREAGE ASSAULT BREADTH
COMPASS CONTENT EXPANSE
PURVIEW SEIZURE STRETCH
VARIETY DISTANCE INCREASE
LATITUDE OUTREACH QUANTITY
STRAIGHT
   (— OF FRONT) FRONTAGE
   (— OF LAND) HEIGHT CONTINENT
   (— OF SPACE) ROOM
   (BROAD —) SWEEP MAGNITUDE

   (RELATIVE —) SCALE
   (SOME —) BIT
   (UNLIMITED —) INFINITY
   (UTMOST —) FULL
   (VAST —) DEEP
   (VERTICAL —) ALTITUDE
EXTENUATE THIN GLOZE MINCE
EXCUSE LESSEN SOOTHE WEAKEN
DIMINISH PALLIATE
EXTERIOR CRUST ECTAD ECTAL
OUTER SHELL EXTERN OUTSIDE
OUTWARD SURFACE EXOTERIC
EXTERNAL OUTLYING
   (PREF.) OUT
EXTERMINATE WIPE EXPEL
UPROOT ABOLISH DESTROY
EXTERNAL OUT OUTER EXTERN
OUTSIDE OUTWARD STRANGE
EXOTERIC EXTERIOR INCIDENT
PHYSICAL PERIPHERAL
   (PREF.) ECT(O) OUT
EXTERNALITY OUTNESS
EXTERNALIZE OBJECTIFY
EXTERNALLY OUTWARD WITHOUT
EXTINCT DEAD BYGONE DEFUNCT
QUENCHED
   (— MAN) KANJERA
   (PREF.) NECR(O)
EXTINCTION DOOM FINE DEATH
EXPIRY DELETION
EXTINGUISH OUT DAMP DOUT
REDD STUB ANNUL CHOKE
CRUSH DOUSE DOWSE DROWN
QUELL REPEL SLAKE SNUFF
STAMP ASLAKE QUENCH STANCH
STIFLE ABOLISH BLANKET
DESTROY ECLIPSE EXPIATE
EXTINCT OBSCURE OPPRESS
SLOCKEN STAUNCH SUPPRESS
   (— BY CRUSHING) DINCH
   (— CIGARETTE) SNUB
EXTINGUISHED OUT DEAD
EXTINCT
EXTINGUISHER DOUTER STAUNCH
BACKPACK QUENCHER STANCHER
EXTIRPATE DELE ROOT STUB
ERASE EXPEL STAMP STOCK
EXCISE EXTIRP UPROOT DESTROY
EXSCIND OUTROOT SUPPLANT
EXTIRPATION ROOTAGE EXCISION
EXTOL CRY FETE HYMN LAUD
BLESS CRACK EXALT KUDOS
ROOSE SPEAK EXTOLL PRAISE
ADVANCE APPLAUD COLLAUD
COMMEND ELEVATE ENHANCE
GLORIFY MAGNIFY RESOUND
UPRAISE EMBLAZON EULOGIZE
PROCLAIM
EXTOLMENT PRECONY
EXTORT PEEL PILL RAMP BLEED
BRIBE EDUCE EXACT FORCE
PINCH WREST WRING COMPEL
ELICIT SPONGE STRAIN WRENCH
WRITHE EXTRACT OUTWREST
EXTORTION CHOUT GOUGE
EXTORT HOLDUP SCOTAL
BRIBERY PILLAGE CHANTAGE
EXACTION RAPACITY
SHAKEDOWN
EXTORTIONATE HARD CRIMINAL
GRINDING
EXTORTIONER BRIBER POLLER
SHAVER BLEEDER VAMPIRE

EXTORTIONIST POLLER
EXTRA ODD GASH MORE ORRA
OVER PLUS ADDED SPARE
SPECIAL SURPLUS SUPERIOR
LAGNIAPPE
   (PREF.) HYPER SUPER
EXTRACT DIG PRY CITE COPY
DRAW KINO KOLA PULL SOAK
ANIMA BLEED CUTCH DRAFT
EDUCE ELUTE EXACT KUTCH
KYPOO QUOTE RENES RUSOT
SCRAP STEEP WRING CORTIN
CURARE DECOCT DEDUCE DERIVE
DEWTRY DISTIL ELICIT ELIXIR
EVULSE EXTORT GOBBET GUACIN
MULIUM OVARIN REMOVE
RENDER RUSWUT TRIPOS
UZARON ABORTIN AMALTAS
ARCANUM CATECHU DESCENT
DISTILL DRAUGHT ERGOTIN
ESSENCE ESTREAT EXCERPT
EXHAUST FUMARIA INTRAIT
LIMBECK MONESIA PASSEWA
SUMMARY VANILLA ACETRACT
AMBRETTE GINGERIN HYPERNIC
INFUSION LICORICE PERICOPE
SEPARATE TIKITIKI TINCTURE
WITHDRAW
   (— BY BOILING) DECOCT ELIXATE
   (— BY DIGGING) GRUB
   (— DATA FROM COMPUTER) READ
   (— FORCIBLY) EVULSE
   (— FROM ACACIA) KATH CASHOO
   CATECHU
   (— FROM BERBERIS) RUSOT
   RUSWUT
   (— OF BARK) EUONYMIN
   (— OF GINGER) JAKE JAKEY
   (— ORE) STOPE
   (TANNING —) AMALTAS
EXTRACTION KIN BIRTH BROOD
STOCK ORIGIN DESCENT EDITION
ESSENCE EXTRACT EXTREAT
BREEDING TINCTURE
   (— OF ROOTS) EVOLUTION
   (— OF STEAM) BLEEDING
EXTRACTIVE AGAR BANG BHANG
AMAROID CARAGEEN
EXTRADITE BANISH
EXTRANEOUS ALIEN OUTER
EXOTIC FOREIGN OUTLYING
SPURIOUS
EXTRAORDINARILY BYOUS
EXTRAORDINARY ODD FREM
ONCO RARE BYOUS ENORM
SMASH DAMNED EXEMPT MIGHTY
RAGING SIGNAL CORKING
CURIOUS HUMMING NOTABLE
SPECIAL STRANGE UNUSUAL
ABNORMAL EXIMIOUS FORINSEC
SINGULAR SMASHING
UNCOMMON PHENOMINAL
PRODIGIOUS
EXTRARETINAL PAROPTIC
EXTRAVAGANCE CAMP FRILL
PRIDE WASTE LUXURY EXPENSE
RAMPANCY SQUANDER UNTHRIFT
WILDNESS PROFUSION
SATURNALIA
   (MENTAL —) MADNESS
EXTRAVAGANT MAD HIGH LUSH
WILD FANCY FISHY FOLLE LARGE
OUTRE COSTLY GOTHIC HEROIC

LAVISH SHRILL WANTON
BAROQUE BIZARRE COSTLEW
FANATIC FLAMING FURIOUS
NIMIOUS PROFUSE RAMPANT
VAGRANT INSOLENT PRODIGAL
RECKLESS ROMANTIC UNTHRIFT
WANDERER WASTEFUL
BOMBASTIC PROFLIGATE
EXTRAVAGANTLY LARGE
EXTRAVAGANZA FEERIE
EXTRAVAGATION VIBEX
EXTRAVASATION EFFUSION
EXTREME NTH BLUE DEEP DIRE
HIGH LAST RANK SORE VILE
ACUTE BLACK CLOSE CRUEL
DENSE DIZZY FINAL GREAT LIMIT
PITCH STEEP ULTRA UNDUE
UTTER ARDENT ARRANT BRAZEN
DEADLY FAROUT FIERCE HEROIC
LENGTH MORTAL SAVAGE SEVERE
STRONG UTMOST WOUNDY
ABYSMAL DRASTIC FEARFUL
FORWARD FRANTIC HOWLING
INTENSE OUTWARD PROFUSE
RADICAL SURFEIT VICIOUS
VIOLENT ALMIGHTY DEVILISH
DREADFUL EGYPTIAN ENORMOUS
FABULOUS FARTHEST GREATEST
MERCIFUL SPENDFUL TERRIBLE
TERRIFIC ULTIMATE EXQUISITE
   (NOT —) SWEET
   (PL.) PASO
   (PREF.) ACR(O) ARCH
EXTREMELY SO BIG DOG TOO
WAY BONE DEAD EVER FULL
MAIN RANK SELI THAT UNCO
VERY AWFUL BLACK BULLY
BYOUS CRAZY CRUEL EXTRA
HEAPS RIGHT SELLE SOWAN
SUPER BITTER DAMNED DEADLY
DEUCED HIGHLY MIGHTY NATION
POISON SORELY SURELY UNCOLY
APLENTY AWFULLY BOILING
CRUELLY EXTREME GALLOWS
HOPPING INNERLY SOPPING
STAVING ALMIGHTY ENORMOUS
MORTALLY PRECIOUS PROPERLY
EXTREMISM JACOBINISM
EXTREMIST JACOBIN RADICAL
SANSCULOTTE
EXTREMITY END TIP HEAD NEED
PUSH TAIL CLOSE LIMIT SHIFT
START VERGE BORDER FINGER
EXIGENT EXTREME ACROSTIC
ALTITUDE DISASTER JUNCTURE
OUTRANCE TERMINAL
   (— OF MOON) HORN
   (— OF TENDRIL) HOLDFAST
   (— OF TOOTH ROOT) APEX
   (REMOTEST —) CORNER
   (PREF.) ACR(O)
EXTRICATE FREE HELP WIND
CLEAR LOOSE RESCUE SQUIRM
OUTWIND EXPEDITE LIBERATE
UNTANGLE
   (— ONESELF) WANGLE
EXTRINSIC ALIEN EVERY FOREIGN
OUTWARD EXTERNAL OUTLYING
EXTROVERT SYNTONIC
EXTRUDE BEAR SPEW EJECT
EXPEL SHOOT PROJECT
PROTRUDE
EXUBERANCE PRICE EXCESS

LUXURY PLENTY ABANDON
LAUGHTER OVERFLOW
RAMPANCY
EXUBERANT RANK BOUNCY
FEISTY LAVISH COPIOUS FERTILE
GLOWING PROFUSE RAMPANT
EFFUSIVE
EXUDATE GUM SPEW SPUE
MANNA DIKAMALI GUAIACUM
HONEYDEW SARCOCOL
EXUDATION DIP GUM LAC SAP
TAR BALM KINO COPAL PITCH
RESIN ROSIN SUDOR ULMIN
CHARAS MASTIC SANIES
CHURRUS GALIPOT MOCHRAS
SPEWING BLEEDING EXUDENCE
LAITANCE MOISTURE
EXUDE GUM DRIP EMIT OOZE REEK
SPEW BLEED STILL SWEAT EXTILL
STRAIN STREAM EXUDATE
GUTTATE SCREEVE SECRETE
SWELTER PERSPIRE
EXULT JOY CROW LEAP BOAST
GLOAT GLORY INSULT SPRING
MAFFICK REJOICE TRIUMPH
EXULTANT PROUD ELATED
PRIDEFUL
EXULTATION JOY PAEAN OVATION
RAPTURE
EXULTING EXULTANT JUBILANT
EYALET VILLAYET
EYAS NESTLING
EYE O EE HE ORB SPY DISC GAZE

GLIM LAMP LOOP MIEN OGLE
SCAN UVEA VIEW GLARE GLASS
GLENE NAVEL OPTIC SENSE
SHANK SIGHT TOISE WATCH
BEHOLD COLLAR EUCONE EYELET
GOGGLE OCULAR OCULUS OILLET
PEEPER POPEYE REGARD ROLLER
SHINER STEMMA VISION WINDOW
WINKER BLINKER EUCONIC
EXOCONE EYEBALL EYEHOLE
OBSERVE OCELLUS PIERCER
PIGSNEY PINKANY PINKENY
SENSORY WITNESS LATCHING
NOISETTE OMMATEUM RECEPTOR
(— AMOROUSLY) OGLE
(— FORMED BY ROPE) TONGUE
(— IN BIGHT) COLLAR
(— IN EGYPTIAN SYMBOLISM) UTA
(— OF BEAN) HILUM
(— OF FRUIT) NOSE
(— OF HINGE) GUDGEON
(— OF INSECT) STEMMA
(— OF RA) SEKHET
(— SORENESS) LIPPITUDE
(BLACK —) KEEK MOUSE SHINER
(EVIL —) DROCHUIL MALOCCHIO
(JERKY — MOVEMENT) SACCADE
(METAL —) HONDA
(PART OF —) IRIS LENS FOVEA
PUPIL CORNEA MACULA SCLERA
CHAMBER CHOROID LIGAMENT
CONJUNCTIVA
(PL.) EEN EES NIE YEN YES EYNE

LAMPS LIGHTS SEEING GOGGLES
KEEKERS GLAZIERS GLIMMERS
(PREF.) OCELLI OCUL(I)(O)
OMMA(TO) OPHTHALM(O)
OPTI(CO) OPTO
(SUFF.) OMMA OPHTHALMA
OPHTHALMUS OPIS OPS
(DEFECT OR CONDITION OF —) OPE
OPIA OPIC OPIS OPS OPY
EYEBALL EYE BALL GLASS GLOBE
(— MOVEMENT) VERGENCE
(PREF.) OPHTHALM(O)
EYEBOLT SPRIG RINGBOLT
(INTERLOCKING —S) SNIBEL
EYEBRIGHT EYEWORT EUPHRASY
EYEBROW BREE BROW EEBREE
WINBROW WRIGGLE
EYE-CATCHING BOLD
EYE-CORNER
(PREF.) CANTH(O)
EYECUP EYEGLASS
EYED
(SUFF.) OPIS OPS
EYEGLASS QUIZ NIPPER MONOCLE
EYEGLASSES GLIMS SPECS LENSES
GLASSES LORGNON NIPPERS
BIFOCALS
EYEHOLE EYELET EYEPIT
EYELASH BREE LASH CILIUM
WINKER EYEBREE
(LOSS OF —S) MADAROSIS
(PL.) CILIA EAVES
(PREF.) CILI(I)(O)

EYELET MAIL PINK OELET AGRAFE
OILLET POUNCE AGRAFFE
CRINGLE GROMMET PEEPHOLE
EYELID HAW LID BREE WINDOW
EYEBREE PALPEBRA
(PL.) EAVES
(PREF.) BLEPHAR(O) CILI(I)(O)
(SUFF.) BLEPHARON CIL
EYEPIECE OCULAR EYEGLASS
(— OF TELESCOPE) POWER
EYESHADE VISOR OPAQUE
EYESHOT RANGE REACH EYESIGHT
EYESIGHT VIEW LIGHT SIGHT
EYE SOCKET ORBIT
EYESORE DESIGHT
EYESPOT EYEDOT STIGMA
EYEHOLE OCELLUS EYEPOINT
EYESTALK STIPES
EYETOOTH CUSPID DOGTOOTH
EYEWASH COLLYRIE EYEWATER
COLLYRIUM
EYOT AIT EIGHT ISLET
EYRE AIR ITER
EZBAI (SON OF —) NAARAI
EZBON (FATHER OF —) GAD BELA
EZEKIEL (FATHER OF —) BUZI
EZER (FATHER OF —) EPHRAIM
(SON OF —) HUSHAH
EZRA (SON OF —) EPHER
EZRI (FATHER OF —) CHELUB

F

F EF FF EFF FOX DIGAMMA
FOXTROT

FABA VICIA

FABLE MYTH TALE FEIGN STORY
LEGEND TRIFLE FICTION PARABLE
POETIZE UNTRUTH ALLEGORY
APOLOGUE FABULATE
FABULIZE
(— OF GOLD COAST) NANCY
(MORAL —) EMBLEM
(PREF.) MYTHO

FABRIC ABA BAN ACCA CORD
DUCK GOLD GROS HAIR HUCK
IKAT SILK SUSI TAPA TARS TUKE
CHECK CREPE DHOTI DOBBY
DYNEL FANCY MOIRE NINOW
PRINT RUMAL SCRIM SPLIT STUFF
SUPER SURAH SURAT TABBY
TAMMY TARSE TERRY TEWKE
TWEED TWILL UNION VICHY
VOILE WEAVE WIGAN AGARIC
ALACHA BENGAL BROCHE BYSSUS
CAFFOY CARPET COTTON
CREPON CYPRUS DACRON
DAMASK DIAPER DOBBIE EPONGE
ESTRON FLEECE HARDEN LAPPET
LUSTER LUSTRE MARBLE MASHRU
MURREY POODLE SENNIT STRIPE
TAMINY TANJIB TARTAN TRICOT
TUSSAH VELURE VELVET
WADMAL WINCEY ZENANA
ACETATE ALEPINE ALLOVER
BANDALA BANDING BELTING
BEWPERS BINDING BUCKRAM
CANILLE CHALLIS CHEKMAK
CHIFFON CYPRESS DAMASSE
DOESKIN DRABBET EDIFICE
ELASTIC EPINGLE FACONNE
FUSTIAN MIXTURE MORELLA
PAISLEY PLUMBET SAYETTE
SEGATHY SILESIA SUITING
TABARET TABINET TAFFETA
TEXTILE TIFFANY VESSETS
AGABANE BARRACAN BOCASINE
BOURETTE BROCATEL CAMELINE
CANNELLE CASEMENT CHAMBRAY
CRETONNE DIAMANTE DUCHESSE
HAIRLINE HANDMADE HARATEEN
JACQUARD KNITTING LUSTRINE
MATERIAL MOLESKIN OSNABURG
SHANTUNG SHIRTING
SICILIAN SKIRTING
SWANSKIN TAPESTRY
TARLATAN VALENCIA
(— CONTAINING GOLD OR SILVER
THREAD) ACCA TASH TASS KINCOB
(— FOR STIFFENING) WIGAN
(— OF TWO OR MORE MATERIALS)
UNION
(— RESEMBLING TOWELING)
AGARIC
(— WITH INWOVEN SCENES) ARRAS
(ABSORBENT —) HUCK

(BROCADED —) LAME LAMPAS
(CARPET —) DURRIE
(COARSE —) TAT BAFT CRASH
HAIRE DUFFEL RATINE STAMIN
BAGGING BOCKING DRABBET
SACKING STAMMEL DAGSWAIN
(CORDED —) REP PIQUE DUCAPE
POPLIN OTTOMAN BENGALINE
(COTTON —) CREA DUCK JEAN
LENO LINO SUSI BAIZE BASIN
DENIM DRILL RUMAL SUPER
SWISS VICHY WIGAN BURRAH
CALICO CANVAS CATGUT CHILLO
CHINTZ COUTIL COVERT DIMITY
MADRAS MUSLIN PENANG
SATEEN BLANKET BUSTIAN
CANTOON DAMASSE ETAMINE
FLANNEL GALATEA GINGHAM
HICKORY HOLLAND JACONET
ORLEANS PERCALE TICKING
BOCASINE BUCKSKIN COTELINE
COUTILLE CRETONNE DRILLING
DUNGAREE INDIENNE SHEETING
SILKALINE MARSEILLES
(DECORATED —) DIAMANTE
(DELICATE —) HUSI JUSI
(DURABLE —) SCRIM SERGE
(ELASTIC —) GORING ELASTIC
(EMBOSSED —) CLOKY CLOQUE
(EMBROIDERED —) BALDAQUIN
(FIGURED —) BROCADE BROCATEL
(FINE —) PIMA SILK SUSI LINEN
DIMITY MERINO MOHAIR BATISTE
PERCALE
(GAUZELIKE —) BAREGE GOSSAMER
(GLAZED —) CIRE
(GLOSSY —) SATIN GLORIA
SATEEN PERCALINE
(GOAT'S-HAIR —) ABA TIBET
(HEAVY —) GROS CRASH DENIM
DRILL BURLAP CATGUT
FRIEZE LINENE TOBINE
WHITNEY
(JUTE —) BALINE BURLAP
(KNITTED —) SUEDE BOUCLE
JERSEY TRICOT CHIFFON
(LIGHTWEIGHT —) GLORIA
BUNTING DELAINE FORTISAN
PARAMATTA SEERSUCKER
(LINEN —) HARN SINDON
BEWPERS BUCKRAM CAMBRIC
DRABBET HOLLAND NACARAT
CRETONNE
(MOTTLED —) CHINE
(MOURNING —) ALMA
(MUSLIN —) TANJIB
(OPENWORK —) LACE SKIPDENT
(ORNAMENTAL —) GIMP LACE
LAMPAS GALLOON
(PEBBLY-SURFACED —) ARMURE
(PILED —) TERRY BOLIVIA
KRIMMER CHENILLE
(PRINTED —) BATIK CALICO

ALLOVER PERCALE TOURNAY
(RAFFIA —) RABANNA
(RIBBED —) CORD GROS PIQUE
COTELE FAILLE SOLEIL DROGUET
CORDUROY MAROCAIN
MOGADORE WHIPCORD
(RICH —) SAMITE
(ROUGH —) TERRY HOPSACK
HOMESPUN
(SATIN —) CAMLET ETOILE
CHARMEUSE
(SHEER —) LAWN NINON SHEER
SWISS BAREGE DIMITY BATISTE
SOUFFLE VALENCE GOSSAMER
MOUSSELINE MARQUISETTE
(SHORT-NAPPED —) RAS
(SILK —) ACCA ALMA FUGI FUJI
GROS IKAT MOFF RASH ATLAS
CARDE NINON PEKIN RAJAH
RUMAL SATIN SHIKH SURAH
TIRAZ ARMURE BROCHE CAMACA
CHAPPE CREPON DIAPER DUCAPE
FAILLE KHAIKI MANTUA PONGEE
SENDAL ALACHAH ALAMODE
BROCADE EPINGLE GROGRAM
SCHAPPE YESTING BARATHEA
DUPPIONI EOLIENNE IMPERIAL
ORMUZINE SHAGREEN SIAMOISE
MARCELINE MESSALINE
BROCATELLE
(SOFT SILK —) KASHA BARATHEA
(SOFT-NAPPED —) PANNE
DUVETYN
(STRIPED —) ABA STRIPE
BAYADERE MERALINE
(THIN —) CRISP GAUZE VOILE
PONGEE TAMISE HERNANI
MARABOU PERSIAN
(TWILLED —) REP SAY DENIM
KASHA SERGE SURAH COUTIL
RUSSEL BOLIVIA ESTAMIN
FLANNEL ZANELLA CAMELINE
CASHMERE CORDUROY DIAGONAL
MARCELLA SHALLOON VENETIAN
(UNBLEACHED —) DRABBET
(UNGLAZED —) CRETONNE
(UPHOLSTERY —) FRISE FRIEZE
BROCATEL MOQUETTE
(VELVETY —) TRIPE DUVETYN
(WATERPROOF —) MACINTOSH
MACKINTOSH
(WOOLEN —) REPP BAIZE DOILY
OSSET SERGE TAMIS TWEED
BUFFIN BURNET COTTON DJERSA
DUFFEL FRISCA MANTLE MOREEN
MOTLEY PERPET SAXONY SHAYAK
SHODDY STAMIN TAMISE VICUNA
WADMAL WITNEY BATISTE
BOCKING BOLIVIA CHEVIOT
CHEYNEY CRYSTAL DELAINE
DRUGGET FRISADO HEATHER
RATTEEN STAMMEL ALGERINE
BATSWING BURBERRY CASHMERE

CATALOON CHIVERET HARATEEN
LAMBSKIN PRUNELLA RATTINET
SHALLOON SHETLAND WOOLENET
ZIBELINE
(WORSTED —) TABBY COBURG
ESTAMIN ETAMINE SAGATHY
BARATHEA
(WOVEN —) LENO TWEED TWILL
SOLBIL TISSUE GROGRAM
TEXTURE VALENCIA

FABRICATE COIN COOK FAKE
FORM MAKE MINT VAMP WARP
BUILD FORGE FRAME FRUMP
WEAVE DEVISE FANGLE INVENT
CONCOCT FASHION IMAGINE
PRODUCE CONTRIVE
(— CLOTH) DRAPE
(— PAPER) CONVERT

FABRICATION LIE WEB TRIFLE
CHIMERA FICTION FINGURE
FORGERY UNTRUTH BASKETRY
PRETENSE
(PL.) INVENTARY

FABRICATOR LIAR COINER
FORGER

FABULIST LIAR AESOP FABLER

FABULOUS FEIGNED MYTHICAL
ROMANTIC

FACADE FACE FRONT FUCUS
FRONTAL FRONTLET

FACE JIB MAP MUG NEB PAN BIDE
CHIV CLAD COPE DARE DEFY DIAL
GIZZ HEAD LEER LINE MASK MEET
MOUE MUNS PHIZ PUSS SIDE
ABIDE BEARD BRAVE BRICK
BRUNT CASTE CHECK CHEER
COVER FACET FAVOR FRONT
GUARD INDEX REVET STAND
STONE VISOR VIZOR ASPECT
BRAZEN FACADE FACIES KISSER
MAZARD MUZZLE OPPOSE PHIZOG
VENEER VISAGE AFFRONT
BAZOOKA COMMAND DIGLYPH
FASHION FEATURE GRIMACE
GRUNTLE PROPOSE RESPECT
REVERSE SURFACE UPRIGHT
CONFRONT ENVISAGE EXTRADOS
FEATURES FROGFACE FRONTAGE
FRONTIER PROSPECT SEMBLANT
PERPENDICULAR
(— DOWN) DEFACE
(— IN DEFIANCE) AFFRONT
(— OF ANIMAL) MASK
(— OF CUBE) SQUARE
(— OF CUTTING TOOL) BEZEL BEZIL
(— OF GLACIER) SNOUT
(— OF STUMP) SCARF SCARPH
(— ON DOOR KNOCKER) MASCARON
(— ONE'S DANCING PARTNER) SET
(— THE EAST) ORIENTATE
(— TO FACE) AFRONT BEFORE
FACIAL DIRECTLY
(— WITH MARBLE) PIN

(— **WITH STONE**) BATCH
(**CLOCK** —) DIAL TABLE WATCH
(**CRYSTAL** —) PINAKOU
(**CURVED** —) EXTRADOS INTRADOS
(**DIE** —) ACE
(**FANTASTIC** —) ANTIC
(**HALF DOMINO** —) END
(**HAVING SHORT BROAD** —)
LATERAL
(**INNER** —) CONCAVE
(**MADE-UP** —) MOP
(**MINING** —) BANK BREAST
FOREHEAD LONGWALL
(**MOCKING** —) MOE MOWE
(**QUARRY** —) HEUGH
(**ROCK** —) CLIFF
(**UPPER** —) BROW
(**WRY** —) MOUTH GRIMACE
(PREF.) FACIO PROSOP(O)
FACE-ARBOR KNIFE
FACED
(SUFF.) PROSOPOUS
FACE GUARD FRONTAL
FACEMAN HAGGER WINNER
FACEPLATE FRONT DOGPLATE
FACER BUMPER DRIFTER TANKARD
FACET PANE STAR BEZEL CULET
PHASE COLLET STEMMA FACETTE
LOZENGE TEMPLET
FACETIAE CURIOSA
FACETIOUS FUNNY MERRY SMART
WITTY FACETE JOCOSE JOCULAR
HUMOROUS POLISHED
FACIAL
(PREF.) FACIO
FACILE PAT ABLE EASY QUICK
READY EXPERT FLUENT GENTLE
AFFABLE DUCTILE LENIENT
FACILITATE AID EASE HELP FAVOR
SPEED ASSIST GREASE EXPEDITE
FACILITY ART EASE FEEL HELP
ECLAT KNACK SKILL ADDRESS
COMMAND FREEDOM PROWESS
EASINESS
(PL.) ADDITIONS
FACING DADO HARL FRONT HARLE
LAPEL LINER PANEL SKIRT
BEFORE TOWARD VENEER
AGAINST FORNENT SURFACE
BLACKING CAMPSHOT CONFRONT
COVERING FACEWORK FORNENST
OPPOSITE PITCHING
(— **AGAINST GLACIER**) STOSS
(— **AHEAD**) FULL
(— **APEX**) ACROSCOPIC
(— **AUDIENCE OBLIQUELY**) EFFACE
(— **EACH OTHER**) AFFRONTE
AFFRONTY
(— **FOR WALLS**) CASE
(— **FROM GLACIER**) STOSS
(— **INWARD**) INTRORSE
(— **OUTWARDS**) EXTRORSE
(PREF.) OB
FACSIMILE FAX COPY MODEL
REPLICA AUTOTYPE
FACT CASE DEED FAIT DATUM
EVENT SOOTH TRUTH DONNEE
EFFECT FACTUM VERITY
COMPERT FORMULA GENERAL
INDICIA KEYNOTE LOWDOWN
REALITY PARTICULAR
(**CONCLUSIVE** —) CRUSHER
(**DECISIVE** —) CLINCHER

(**FUNDAMENTAL** —) KEYNOTE
(**TRUE** —**S**) STRENGTH
(PL.) DATA FEAT
FACTION BLOC NERI PART SECT
SIDE WING CABAL JUNTO PARTY
BRIGUE CLIQUE SCHISM BIANCHI
DISPUTE PINFOLD QUARREL
INTRIGUE SPLINTER
(— **OF SECEDERS**) CAVE
(**PARTY** —) STASIS
FACTITIOUS SHAM WHIPPED
KRITRIMA
FACTOR GEN DOER GENE ITEM
AGENT ALLEL CAUSE MAKER
ALLELE AUTHOR CENTER DETAIL
BAILIFF CONTROL COUCHER
CUSHION ELEMENT ENTROPY
FACTRIX ISOLATE STEWARD
ADHERENT AUMILDAR COFACTOR
DOMINANT EQUATION
GOMASHTA INCIDENT INCITANT
PARAMETER
(—**S IN EVOLUTION**) ANTICHANCE
(**CYTOPLASMIC** —) KAPPA
(**DECISIVE** —) CAPSTONE
(**ECOLOGICAL** —) INFLUENT
(**ENVIRONMENTAL** —) GEOGEN
(**HEREDITY** —) GENE INSTINCT
(**HINDERING** —) CRIMP
(**INTELLIGENCE** —) G
(**PERSONALITY** —) SURGENCY
(**RESTRICTIVE** —) BARRIER
FACTORY HONG MILL SHOP PLANT
USINE AURANG AURUNG FABRIC
SUGARY CANNERY HATTERY
HOSIERY OFICINA SOAPERY
BUILDING COMPTOIR FABRIQUE
FILATURE HACIENDA OFFICINA
STAMPERY WORKSHOP
MANUFACTORY
FACTOTUM SIRCAR FAMULUS
COMPRADOR
FACTUAL HARD REAL TRUE
ACTUAL BEDROCK EARTHLY
EMPIRIC LITERAL PROSAIC
(**INSUFFICIENTLY** —) ABSTRACT
FACTUALLY INSOOTH
FACULTY ART WIT BOOM BUMP
EASE GIFT WILL FANCY POWER
SENSE BREATH BUDDHI GIFTIE
SEEING TALENT ABILITY COLLEGE
COUNSEL HABITUS APTITUDE
CAPACITY FELICITY
(— **OF EXPRESSION**) LANGUAGE
(**CRITICAL** —) JUDGMENT
(**MENTAL** —) HEADPIECE
(**POETIC OR CREATIVE** —) IDEALITY
PRINCIPLE
(**REASONING** —) DISCOURSE
(PL.) INDULTS
FAD BUG CULT FIKE RAGE WHIM
CRAZE FANCU HOBBY FOIBLE
MAGGOT CROCHET FASHION
WRINKLE
FADDIST CRANK
FADE DIE DIM DOW FLY WAN BRIT
CAST FATE FLAT GIVE PALE PEAK
PINE PINK VADE WELK WILK WILT
BLANK DAVER DECAY FLEET
PASSE PETER QUAIL SWING
SWOON DARKLE PERISH VANISH
WITHER DECLINE INSIPID
LIGHTEN DIMINISH DISCOLOR

DISSOLVE EVANESCE LANGUISH
(— **AWAY**) DOW BREAK FLEET
WALLOW
FADED PASSE SHABBY EXOLETE
SHOPWORN
FADGE FAY FIT SUIT
FADING FUGITIVE MANCANDO
SWINGING
FAERIE QUEENE (**AUTHOR OF** —)
SPENSER
(**CHARACTER IN** —) UNA GUYON
IRENE TALUS ACRASY AMORET
ARTHUR DUESSA TIMIAS
ASTRAEA MALEGER ARTEGALL
CALIDORE GLORIANA ORGOGLIO
RADIGUND ARCHIMAGO
BELPHOEBE BRITOMART
FLORIMELL GRANTORTO
SCUDAMOUR
FAFNIR (**FATHER OF** —) HREIDMAR
(**SLAYER OF** —) SIGURD
FAG FLAG JADE TIRE TOIL DROOP
WEARY DRUDGE HARASS MENIAL
EXHAUST FATIGUE FRAZZLE
FAGGED TASKIT
FAGGOT BROSNA CHUMPA
FAGALD
FAGOT KID BUNT PILE PIMP BAVIN
FADGE NICKY NITCH FAGGOT
KNITCH GARBAGE
FAIL GO CUT EBB ERR PIP BANK
BUST CONK FALL FLAG FLOP
FOLD LACK LOSE MISS SINK SKEW
SPIN WANE APPAL BREAK BURST
CRACK FAULT FLUFF FLUKE
FLUNK PETER QUAIL SLAKE
SMASH SPILL VAILE APPALL
BETRAY DEFAIL DEFECT DESERT
FALTER FIZZLE REPINE WINDER
DECLINE DEFAULT EXHAUST
FALSIFY FLICKER FLUMMOX
FOUNDER MISFARE MISGIVE
SCANTLE LANGUISH
(— **AT**) FLUB
(— **IN DUTY**) LAPSE
(— **IN EARLY STAGES**) ABORT
(— **IN HEALTH**) SINK BREAK
(— **IN STUDIES**) BILGE
(— **ON RIFLE RANGE**) BOLO
(— **TO GAIN ALTITUDE**) MUSH
(— **TO GROW**) MISS
FAILING BAD ILL BLOT FAULT
FOIBLE BLEMISH FAILURE FRAILTY
ABORTIVE WEAKNESS
FAILURE DUD BALK BOMB BUST
FAIL FLOP FLUB FOIL LACK LOSS
MISS MUFF TRIP BAULK BILGE
CRASH DECAY ERROR FAULT
FLUKE FLUNK FROST GRIEF GUILT
LAPSE LEMON PLUCK SMASH
BRODIE FIASCO FIZZLE OUTAGE
STUMER STUMOR BLOOMER
CROPPER DEBACLE DECLINE
DEFAULT FLIVVER FLUMMOX
NEGLECT STUMBLE ABORTION
COLLAPSE DISASTER FAILANCE
FLOPEROO OMISSION
(— **OF DAM**) BLOW
(— **OF FIREARM**) STOPPAGE
(— **OF MILK SECRETION**) AGALAXY
AGALAXIA
(— **OF MUSCLE**) ACHALASIA
(— **OF PAVEMENT**) BLOWUP

(— **OF PRIMER**) HANGFIRE
(— **OF VITALITY**) DELIQUIUM
(— **TO RAISE OAR**) CRAB
(**COMPUTER** —) CRASH
(**FLAT** —) DUD
(**RIDICULOUS** —) FIASCO
FAIN FOND GLAD LIEF EAGER
PLEASED WILLING DESIROUS
INCLINED
FAINEANT IDLE LAZY
FAINT GO DIM LOW WAN WAW
COLD CONK COOL DARK PALE
PALL SOFT THIN WEAK LIGHT
QUEAL QUEER SHADY SWELT
SWOON TIMID WAUFF WAUGH
WERSH EVANID FEEBLE REMISS
REMOTE SICKLY WAMBLY
FEIGNED FORGONE LANGUID
OBSCURE SWITHER SYNCOPE
WEARISH COWARDLY DELICATE
LANGUISH LISTLESS SLUGGISH
TIMOROUS
(— **FROM HEAT**) SWELTER
(— **FROM HUNGER**) LEERY
(— **OF SCENT**) COLD WAUGH
FAINTHEARTED TIMID COWARD
CRAVEN COWARDLY UNHEARTY
FAINTHEARTEDNESS QUALM
FAINTING AFAINT SYNCOPE
DELIQUIUM
(— **SPELL**) DROW DWAM DWALM
FAINTLY DIMLY FAINT SMALL
FAINTNESS TENUITY GONENESS
WEAKNESS
FAINT-VOICED INWARD
FAIR GAY GEY MOP BEAU BELL
CALM EVEN FINE GAFF GALA
GOOD HEND JUST MART PLAY
TIDE TIDY BAZAR BLOND CLEAN
CLEAR EQUAL FERIA HENDE
LARGE RIGHT ROUND SHEER
TRYST WHITE AONACH BAZAAR
BLONDE CANDID COMELY
DECENT DINKUM HONEST KERMIS
PRETTY SERENE SQUARE EXHIBIT
JANNOCK KERMESS STATUTE
BOOKFAIR DISTINCT FESTIVAL
HORNFAIR MIDDLING RATIONAL
STRAIGHT UNBIASED OBJECTIVE
REASONABLE
(— **AND CALM**) SETTLED
(— **AND SQUARE**) DINKUM
(**HINDU** —) MELA
(**VILLAGE** —) WALK
FAIRER SHIPWRIGHT
FAIRING SPAT SPINNER FAIRLING
FAIR-LEAD WAPP
FAIRLY WELL GAILY GAYLY GEYAN
EVENLY JUSTLY MEANLY
HANDILY PLAINLY RIGHTLY
MIDDLING PROPERLY SUITABLY
FAIRNESS FAIR CANDOR EQUITY
HONESTY JUSTICE EQUALITY
EVENNESS FAIRHEAD FAIRHOOD
FAIRWAY HOLE WATERWAY
FAIR-WEATHER SUNSHINE
FAIRY ELF FAY FEE HOB IMP FAIN
PERI PIXY PUCK SHEE VILA
OUPHE PECHT PIXIE SIDHE
WIGHT COURIL FAERIE HATHOR
KEWPIE SPIRIT SPRITE YAKSHA
YAKSHI ARGANTE BANSHEE
ORIANDA SHEOGUE SYLPHID

URGANDA FOLLETTO MELUSINA
(IRISH —) SHEE SIDHE
(TRICKSY —) PUCK
(PL.) GENTRY
FAIRY BELL FOXGLOVE
FAIRYFOLK SHEE SIDHE
FAIRYLAND ANNWN ANNWFN
FEERIE ELFLAND
FAITH DIN FAY FOY LAW LAY VAY
FACK FAIX FEGS SLAM TROW
CERTY CREED HAITH STOCK
TOUCH TROTH TRUST TRUTH
BELIEF CERTIE CREDIT GOSPEL
CREANCE FACKINS AFFIANCE
RELIANCE RELIGION
(BAD —) DUPLICITY
(RELIGIOUS —) SRADH SRADDHA
SHRADDHA
(PREF.) FIDE(I) PISTIO PISTO
FAITHFUL FAST FEAL FIRM GOOD
JUST LEAL LIKE REAL TRIG TRUE
FALSE HEMAN LIEGE LOYAL
PIOUS SOOTH SWEER TIGHT
TREST TRIED AEFALD ARDENT
ENTIRE FIDELE HONEST LAWFUL
PISTIC STANCH STEADY TRUSTY
DEVOTED SINCERE STAUNCH
ACCURATE CONSTANT RESOLUTE
SPEAKING RELIGIOUS
FAITHFULNESS HSIN FEALTY
VERITY LOYALTY FIDELITY
TRUENESS
FAITHFUL SHEPHERDESS
(AUTHOR OF —) FLETCHER
(CHARACTER IN —) CHLOE ALEXIS
AMORET CLORIN THENOT
DAPHNIS PERIGOT AMARILLIS
FAITHLESS FALSE PUNIC FICKLE
HOLLOW ROTTEN UNJUST
UNTRUE ATHEIST APOSTATE
DELUSIVE DISLOYAL SHIFTING
UNSTABLE NIDDERING
PERFIDIOUS
FAITHLESSNESS FALSITY PERFIDY
UNTRUTH
FAKE DUD DUFF FEKE HOAX HOKE
SHAM BOGUS CHEAT FALSE
FEIGN FLAKE FRAUD FUDGE
PHONY WANGLE DUFFING
FALSIFY FURBISH GUNDECK
PRETEND SWINDLE SIMULATE
SPURIOUS ADULTERINE
(— OF STOWED ROPE) FLEET
(FOOTBALL —) JUKE
(PREF.) PSEUD(O)
FAKER FAKIR QUACK HUMBUG
CAMELOT PEDDLER
(— OF ART) TRUQUEUR
FAKIR FAKIH FAQUIR DERVISH
FALCHION FALX
FALCON EYAS HAWK SORE BESRA
HOBBY SAKER STOOP GENTLE
JAGGER JUGGER LANNER
LUGGAR LUGGER MERLIN
MUSKET PREYER RAPTOR SHAHIN
TERCEL KESTREL SAKERET
BERIGORA BOCKEREL FALCONET
PEREGRIN SOREHAWK
(— BOARD) HACK
(— IN FIRST YEAR) SORE
SOREHAWK
(FEMALE —) FORMAL FORMEL
LANNER

(MALE —) TASSEL TERCEL
SAKERET
(SMALL —) HOBBY MERLIN
KESTREL
(WHITE —) ICELANDER
FALCONER HAWKER OSTREGER
FALCONRY HAWKING
FALDSTOOL ORATORY
FALL GO EBB SAG SYE TIP BACK
BAND COME COUP DIVE DRIP
DROP DUNT FLOP HANG PICK
PLOP RASH RUIN RUSE SHED SILE
SINK SLIP SWAK SWAP SWAY
SWOP TILT WHAP WHOP ABATE
CHUTE CLOIT CRASH DROOP
HANCE INCUR JABOT LAPSE
LIGHT LODGE PITCH PLUMB
PLUMP RAPID SAULT SHAKE
SHOOT SKITE SLIPE SLUMP SPILL
SQUAB SQUAT THROW TRACE
TWINE ALIGHT AUTUMN BRODIE
DEVALL DOUNCE DRYSNE
FOOTER HAPPEN HEADER
JOUNCE PERISH PLUNGE RECEDE
SEASON SLOUGH STREEK STRIKE
TOPPLE TUMBLE CASCADE
CROPPER CROWNER DECLINE
DEGRADE DEPRESS DESCEND
DEVOLVE DRIBBLE ESCHEAT
ILLAPSE PLUMMET RELAPSE
RETREAT SQUELCH STUMBLE
SUBSIDE CATARACT COLLAPSE
COMMENCE DECREASE
DOWNCOME PRECIPITATE
(— ABRUPTLY) DUMP
(— APART) BREAK SHIVER
COLLAPSE DISUNITE
(— AWAY) DEFECT
(— BACK) RECEDE RESORT
(— BEHIND) LAG
(— DIZZILY) SPIN
(— DOWN) CAVE FLOP SWAP
SLUMP REVERSE SWITHER
(— DUE) ACCRUE BEFALL
(— FAST) HOP
(— FLAT) PLAT FLIVVER
(— FORWARD) PECK PITCH
PROLAPSE
(— FROM A HORSE) PURL
VOLUNTARY
(— FROM SURFBOARD) WIPEOUT
(— FROM UNDERMINING) CALVE
(— FROM VIRTUE) LAPSE
(— GRADUALLY) EBB SAG
(— HEAVILY) DING LUMP SOSS
CLOIT CLYTE GULCH PLOUT
PLUMP SOUSE SWACK THROW
(— ILL) TRAIK
(— IN) CAVE FOUNDER
(— IN DROPS) DRIP STILL DRIBBLE
(— IN FLURRIES) SPIT
(— IN FOLDS) BLOUSE
(— IN RIVER) SAULT
(— IN WITH) INCUR
(— INTO) STRIKE
(— INTO ERROR) SLIP STUMBLE
(— INTO FAINT) DWAM DWALM
(— INTO RUIN) DECAY
(— INTO SLUMBER) DROWSE
(— INTO TRAP) DECOY
(— INTO WATER) DOP
(— OF DEW) SEREIN SERENE
(— OF RAIN) SKIFF SKIFT

ONDING SHOWER
(— OF SNOW) SKIFF SKIFT
ONCOME SCOUTHER SNOWFALL
(— OF WICKETS) ROT
(— OFF) BATE SLIP SLACK
(— ON BACK) BACKER
(— ON SUCCESSIVE DAYS) CONCUR
(— ON THE NOSE) NOSER
(— OUT) BREAK LIGHT FORTUNE
QUARREL
(— PRONE) GRABBLE
(— RAPIDLY) SKID
(— SHORT) DROP FAIL FAULT
(— SLOWLY) SETTLE
(— SUDDENLY) BOLT PLOP SLUMP
(— THROWING HORSE AND RIDER)
CRUMPLER
(— TO NOTHING) DISSOLVE
(— TO PIECES) BUCKLE CRUMBLE
(— UPON) WARP
(— VIOLENTLY) BEAT
(BAD —) BUSTER
(HEAVY —) PASH POUR SWAG
BLASH CLOIT GULCH SKELP
SOUSE SQUAT MUCKER
(INCOMPLETE WRESTLING —) FOIL
(SOFT —) SCLAFF
(SUDDEN —) HANCE SQUAT
SQUASH
FALLACIOUS SLY WILY ABSURD
CRAFTY UNTRUE DELUSIVE
GUILEFUL ILLUSORY
FALLACY IDOL ERROR FALLAX
IDOLUM SOPHISM EQUIVOKE
ILLUSION
(PL.) IDOLA
FALLEN DOWN FAUN FLAT SHED
LAPSED DECLASSE
(— IN) SUNKEN
FALLER GILL FLATHEAD
FALLFISH CHUB DACE CORPORAL
FALL HERRING TAILOR
FALLIBLE HUMAN ERRANT
ERRABLE
FALLING SIT CADENT CAVING
PROLAPSE WINDFALL
(— BACK) ESCHEAT
(— DOWN) RUIN
(— INTO) INFALL
(— OF MINE ROOF) SIT
(— OF RAIN) SPIT
(— OFF) CADUCE LEEWAY
CADUCOUS
(— ON SOMETHING) INCIDENT
(— OUT) DIFFICULTY
(— SHORT) DEFICIT
(PREF.) CADUCI
(SUFF.) PTOMA PTOSIS
FALLOPIAN TUBE TUBAL
(PREF.) FALL(O)
FALLOVER OSTREGER
FALLOW LEA PALE HOBBY BARREN
VALEWE
(PREF.) POLI(O)
FALLOW DEER DAMINE DAPPLE
FALLOWING ARDER
FALSE DEAD FAKE FLAM SHAM
BOGUS FAUSE LYING PASTE
PHONY WRONG FICKLE HOLLOW
LUTHER PSEUDO UNTRUE
ASSUMED BASTARD CROOKED
FEIGNED APOSTATE DISLOYAL
ILLUSIVE RECREANT RENEGADE

SPECTRAL SPURIOUS
MENDACIOUS
(PREF.) PSEUD(O)
FALSE BEACHDROPS PINESAP
FALSE CRAWLEY PINEDROPS
FALSE FOXGLOVE FEVERWEED
FALSE HELLEBORE EARTHGALL
FALSEHOOD COG FIB LIE BUNG
CRAM FLAM TALE CRACK ERROR
FABLE STORY FALSET UNFACT
YANKER CRAMMER CRETISM
FALSAGE FALSERY FALSITY
FIBBERY FICTION LEASING
PERFIDY PHANTOM ROMANCE
UNTRUTH FALSHEDE ROORBACK
STRAPPER
FALSE MERMAID FLOERKEA
LIMNANTH
FALSENESS SHAM DECEIT
FALSE WINTERGREEN PYROLA
FALSEWORK CENTERING
FALSIES CHEATERS
FALSIFIER LIAR FALSER FORGER
FALSARY
FALSIFY LIE COOK FAKE WARP
ABUSE BELIE FEINT FORGE
BETRAY DOCTOR FIDDLE
GUNDECK VIOLATE EMBEZZLE
MISREPRESENT
FALSITY LIE ERROR VANITY
UNTRUTH INVERITY
FALSTAFF (CHARACTER IN —) MEG
FORD JOHN PAGE ALICE BROOK
CAIUS FENTON QUICKLY
FALSTAFF NANNETTA
(COMPOSER OF —) VERDI
FALTER FAIL HALT PAUSE WAVER
BOGGLE FLINCH TOTTER FRIBBLE
STAMMER STUMBLE TREMBLE
HESITATE
FALTERING HINK HALTING
FALX FALCULA
FAME BAY CRY LOSE NAME STAR
WORD BRUIT ECLAT GLORY
HONOR KUDOS PRICE RUMOR
VOICE ESTEEM LAUREL RENOWN
REPORT REPUTE TONGUE
HEARSAY WORSHIP

(HALL OF —) (SEE HALL OF FAME)
(ILL —) OPPROBRIUM
FAMED RIFE KNOWN NOTED
EMINENT RENOMEE RENOWNED
FAMILIAR FLY BAKA BOKO BOLD
COZY EASY FREE FULL HOMY
TAME TOSH CLOSE CONNU
GREAT HOMEY KNOWN PRIVY
THICK USUAL BEATEN CHUMMY
COMMON ENTIRE FOLKSY
GERMAN HOMELY INWARD
KENNED STRAIT THRONG VERSED
AFFABLE FAMULAR FOLKSEY
POPULAR FREQUENT HABITUAL
INTIMATE SOCIABLE
STANDARD
(— WITH) KNOWING
(MAKE —) POST
(PRESUMPTUOUSLY —) INSOLENT
FAMILIARITY HABIT FREEDOM
LIBERTY PRIVACY PRIVITY
TRAFFIC HABITUDE INTIMACY
CONSUETUDE
FAMILIARIZE HAFT VERSE

ACCUSTOM ACQUAINT FREQUENT
FAMILIARLY HOMELY
FAMILY ILK KIN AIGA CLAN GING
KIND LINE NAME RACE TEAM
TRIP CINEL CLASS FLESH GOTRA
GROUP HOUSE MEINY STIRP
STOCK CLETCH FAIMLY PARAGE
STEMMA STIRPS STRAIN ZEGRIS
DYNASTY KINDRED LINEAGE
ORLEANS PROGENY CATEGORY
FIRESIDE
(COSMOPOLITAN —) FELIDAE
FABACEAE
(FIRST —) FF
(LANGUAGE —) CHON BANTU
CLICK COCHE CUNAN KADAI
STOCK AIMARA ATALAN AYMARA
CHOLON GILIAK HUARPE LENCAN
SERIAN BOTOYAN CADDOAN
CARIBAN CATIBAN CHINOOK
CHOLONA CHUMASH COPEHAN
ESSELEN KARTHLI KARTVEL
KERESAN SHASTAN ATAKAPAN
CHANGOAN
(LARGE —) QUIVERFUL
(ONE-PARAMETER —) PENCIL
(SUPER —) APINA APOIDEA
FAMINE LACK PINE WOLF DEARTH
HUNGER SCARCITY
FAMISH KILL STARVE DESTROY
ENFAMISH
FAMOUS MERE BREME FAMED
GRAND NOBLE NOTED FAMOSE
NAMELY EMINENT NAMABLE
NOTABLE RENOWNED
FAMULUS WAGNER SERVANT
FAN ONE RUN VAN BEAT BLOW
BUFF COOL WASH DELTA PUNKA
WHIFF BASKET BLOWER CHAMAR
COLMAR FANNER FLABEL FLIGHT
PUNKAH ROOTER SHOVEL
SPREAD VENTOY WINNOW
ADMIRER DEVOTEE FLABRUM
FLYFLAP MPANGWE PAHOUIN
WHISKER EVENTAIL FOLLOWER
RHIPIDION
(— FOR BLOWER) WAFTER
(ALLUVIAL —) CONE APRON DELTA
(FEMALE — OF ROCK MUSICIAN)
GROUPIE
(FOOTBALL —) GRIDDER
(JAZZ —) CAT
(WINNOWING —) SAIL LIKNON
(PL.) FOLLOWING
(PREF.) FLABELLI RHIPI(D)(DO)
FANALOKA FOSSA FOUSSA
FANATIC MAD BIGOT CRAZY FIEND
RABID ULTRA ZEALOT DEVOTEE
FURIOSO PHANTIC PULAHAN
PULIJAN BABAYLAN FRENETIC
FANATICAL RABID ULTRA
EXTREME FURIOUS
FANCIED UNREAL DREAMED
AFFECTED
FANCIFUL ODD ANTIC FAIRY IDEAL
QUEER VIEWY DREAMY QUAINT
UNREAL BIZARRE CURIOUS
FANCIED LAPUTAN STRANGE
WHIMSIC CHIMERIC FANCICAL
FILIGREE NOTIONAL ROMANTIC
FANCY BEE FAD GIG IDEA ITEM
LIKE LOVE MAZE TROW WEEN
WHIM BRAID BRAIN DREAM

FREAK GUESS HUMOR SHINE
AFFECT BEGUIN FANGLE FIGURE
FLOSSY IDEATE LIKING MAGGOT
MEGRIM NOTION ORNATE SHINDY
VAGARY VISION WHIMSY CAPRICE
CHIMERA CONCEIT CONCEPT
CROCHET FANCIED FANCIFY
FANTASY PROPOSE ROMANCE
SUSPECT THOUGHT WRINKLE
CHIMAERA CONCEIVE CROTCHET
DAYDREAM ILLUSION PHANTASM
PHANTASY
(FOOLISH —) CHIMERA CHIMAERA
(PASSING —) FIKE
(PERVERSE —) CROTCHET
(WILD —) TOY MAZE
(PL.) DREAMERY
FANDANGO MURCIANA
FANE FLAG BANNER FANACLE
FANFARE TUSCH HOORAY
HURRAH TUCKET TANTARA
FANFARON FLOURISH
FANFARONADE BLUSTER
FANFARE SWAGGER BOASTING
FANFLOWER TACCADA
FANG FAN EARN FALX TAKE TANG
TUSK VANG BEGIN PRONG SEIZE
SNARE TOOTH ASSUME OBTAIN
PANGWE CAPTURE PAHOUIN
PROCURE
FANON CAPE ORALE PHANO
FANNEL MANIPLE
FAN PALM YARAY ERYTHEA
FANTREE TALIPOT
FAN-SHAPED ALARY RHIPIDATE
FANTAIL COMET SHAKER WAGTAIL
FAN-TAN PARLIAMENT
FANTASIA FANTASY QUODLIBET
FANTASTIC ODD WILD ANTIC
LUCIO OUTRE QUEER ABSURD
GOTHIC ROCOCO TOYISH UNREAL
ANTICAL BAROQUE BIZARRE
WHIMSIC FANCIFUL FREAKISH
ROMANTIC SINGULAR
(— PERSON) KICKSHAW
FANTASY IDEA DREAM FANCY
DESIRE VISION CAPRICE CHIMERA
PHANTOM ROMANCE CHIMAERA
PHANTASM PHANTASY
FANTINE (DAUGHTER OF —)
COSETTE
FAR AWAY LONG MUCH ROOM
SIDE WELL WIDE CLEAN SIZES
WIDEN REMOTE DISTANT
FARAWAY ROOMWARD
(— AND AWAY) STREETS
(— OFF) OUTBYE
(— ON) ADVANCED
(PREF.) TEL(E) TELOTERO
FARAMONDO (COMPOSER OF —)
HANDEL
FARCE MIME DROLL EXODE FORCE
STUFF COMEDY GARLIC SOTTIE
EXODIUM MOCKERY TEMACHA
BURLETTA DROLLERY FARCETTA
(RELATING TO —) ATELLAN
FARCEUR WAG JOKER FORCER
FARCICAL BUFFO COMIC DROLL
ATELLAN
FARCTATE STUFFED
FARCY FARCIN EQUINIA FASHION
FARE DO GO EAT TRY COME DIET
FEND FOOD PATH RATE TIME

WEND CHEER CHEFE CHIVE
FRAME GOING LIGHT PRICE
SPEED TABLE TOKEN TRACK
VIAND COMMON FARING FETTLE
HAPPEN TRAVEL CARFARE
JOURNEY PASSAGE PROCEED
PROSPER WAFTAGE WAYFARE
FERRYAGE PROGRESS
(— FOR FERRY) NAULUM
FERRYAGE
(— WELL) SPEED
(COARSE —) HAWEBAKE
FAREWELL AVE VALE ADIEU ADIOS
ALOHA CONGE FINAL LEAVE
CHEERO BONALLY CHEERIO
GOODBYE LEAVING LULLABY
PARTING
FAREWELL TO ARMS (AUTHOR OF
—) HEMINGWAY
(CHARACTER IN —) HENRY
BARKLEY RINALDI FREDERIC
CATHERINE
FARFETCHED FARFET FORCED
DEVIOUS STRAINED EXQUISITE
FAR-FLUNG EXTENDED
FAR FROM THE MADDING
CROWD (AUTHOR OF —) HARDY
(CHARACTER IN —) OAK TROY
FANNY ROBIN GABRIEL
BOLDWOOD EVERDENE
BATHSHEBA
FARIDUN (FATHER OF —) ABTIN
(MOTHER OF —) FIRANAK
(SON OF —) TUR IRAJ SALM
FARINA MEAL FLOUR FARINE
POLLEN STARCH
FARKLEBERRY BLUET
FARL PARLY FARREL
FARM FEU PEN CROP TACK TILL
TORP TOWN WALK CROFT DAIRY
EMPTY FIRMA HARAS MAINS
MILPA PLACE RANCH RANGE
STEAD BARTON BOWERY CHACRA
ESTATE FURROW GRANGE
RANCHO TYDDEN TYDDYN
CLEANSE HENNERY KOLKHOZ
MAILING POTRERO POULTRY
SOVKHOS VACCARY ESTANCIA
HACIENDA HATCHERY LABORING
LOCATION STEADING TOWNSHIP
(— OUT) DIMIT ARRENT
(COLLECTIVE —) KIBBUTZ KOLKHOZ
(COMMUNAL —) KVUTZA KVUTZAH
(DAIRY —) WICK
(LARGE —) RANCH BARTON
(RENTED —) MAILING
(SMALL —) CHACRA
(STOCK —) ESTANCIA
(STUD —) STUD HARAS
FARMER HOB CARL FARM HOBB
KHOT KYLE RUBE RYOT TATE
AILLT AUMIL BOWER CARLE CEILE
CLOWN COLON HODGE KISAN
COCKIE GROWER HOGMAN
JIBARO TILLER YEOMAN BUCOLIC
BUSHMAN BYWONER COTTIER
CROFTER GRANGER HAYSEED
HUSBAND LANDMAN METAYER
PLANTER PLOWMAN RANCHER
SCULLOG TILLMAN TRUCKER
COCKATOO PRODUCER PUBLICAN
RURALIST SELECTOR
(AUSTRALIAN —) SELECTOR

(NORWEGIAN —) BONDER
(POOR —) PIKE
(PROSPEROUS —) KULAK
(SMALL —) BOOR COCKIE
(TENANT —) AILLT GEBUR SIRDAR
COLONUS SHAREMAN
SHARECROPPER
FARMHAND HAND HELP
FARMHOLD CROFT
FARMHOUSE FARM TOWN ONSET
GRANGE QUINTA CASERIO
ONSTEAD STEADING
FARMING SOIL FARMERY
HUSBANDRY
(— SYSTEM) METAYAGE
FARMLAND ACREAGE
FARMSTEAD TOWN WICK STEAD
FARMERY ONSTEAD
FARMYARD WERF CLOSE BARTON
RICKYARD
FARO MONTE STUSS TIGER
PHARAOH
(— CARD) SODA
FARO BANK TIGER
FAR-OFF DISTANT
FAR-OUT KINKY
FAR-REACHING GREAT FARGOING
FARRIER SHOER SMITH MARSHAL
FARROW PIG ROW RAKE DRAPE
LITTER
FARSEEING ORACULAR
FARSIGHTED SHREWD SIGHTY
FARTHER YOND AHEAD STILL
LONGER FURTHER REMOTER
THITHER
FARTHEST ULTIMA ENDMOST
EXTREME FARMOST LONGEST
OUTMOST DOWNMOST FURTHEST
REMOTEST ULTIMATE
FARTHING RAG GRIG JACK QUAD
FADGE FERLING QUARTER
QUADRANS QUADRANT
(HALF —) CUE
(THREE —S) GILL
FARTHINGALE FERDEGEW
VERTUGAL
FASCIA BAND SASH FACIA FILLET
BANDAGE MOLDING LIGATURE
PLATBAND
FASCICLE BUNDLE PHALANGE
FASCICULUS HEFT BUNDLE
COLUMN TRACTUS
FASCINATE DARE CHARM SEIZE
WITCH ALLURE ENAMOR
ATTRACT BEWITCH ENCHANT
ENGROSS GLAMOUR PHILTER
PHILTRE ENSORCEL ENTRANCE
INTEREST INTRIGUE SIRENIZE
CAPTIVATE
FASCINATED BESOTTED
FASCINATING NUTTY ORPHIC
TAKING SIRENIC CHARMING
FETCHING MESMERIC
FASCINATION CHARM SPELL
WITCHERY
FASCINE FAGOT FAGGOT
SAUCISSE
FASCIOLA DISTOMA DISTOMUM
FASCIOLE SEMITA
FASCIST BLACK FASCISTA
FASHION GO CRY CUT FAD LAT
TON WAY CHIC FEAT FORM GARB
GATE KICK MAKE MODE MOLD

RAGE RATE SORT TURN TWIG
WEAR WISE BUILD CRAZE FEIGN
FORGE FRAME GUISE MODEL
MOULD SHAPE STYLE VOGUE
WEAVE AGUISE ASSIZE BUSTLE
CAMBER CREATE CUSTOM
DESIGN FANGLE INVENT MANNER
METHOD ALAMODE COMPOSE
IMAGERY PORTRAY QUALITY
CONTRIVE
(LATEST —) KICK
(PREVAILING —) CRY
(SPECIAL —) TOUCH
FASHIONABLE CHIC PINK POSH
TONY DASHY DOGGY DOSSY
NOBBY RITZY SMART SWELL
SWISH VOGUE GIGOLO JAUNTY
MODISH TIMISH TONISH TRENDY
DASHING GALLANT GENTEEL
STYLISH SWAGGER BELGRAVIAN
(NOT —) DEMODE
FASHIONABLY SMARTLY
FASHIONED HUED CARVED
SHAPED WROUGHT FEATURED
FASHIONING FINGENT
FASHION PLATE SWELL
FASSAITE PYRGOM
FAST HOT HUT COLD FIRM HARD
LENT SOON SURE WIDE AGILE
APACE BRISK CHEAP FIXED FLASH
FLEET HASTY QUICK RAPID
ROUND SADLY STUCK SWIFT
TIGHT TOSTO CARENE ESTHER
FASTLY LIVELY SECURE SPEEDY
SPORTY STABLE STARVE ABIDING
EXPRESS HOTSHOT HURRIED
PROVISO RASPING SETTLED
SIKERLY STATION TAANITH
ENDURING FAITHFUL SPINNING
SPORTING WIKIWIKI
(— DAY) ASHURA
(SUFF.) **(MAKING —)** PEXIA PEXIS
PEXY
FAST-DYED INGRAIN
FASTEN BAR DOG FAY FIX GAD GIB
KEY LAG PEN PIN SEW TAG TIE
YOT BELT BEND BIND BITT BOLT
BRAD CLIP FRET GIRD GLUE
GRIP HANG HANK HASP HOOK
HOOP HORN KILT KNIT KNOT
LACE LASH LINK LOCK MOOR
NAIL ROPE SEAL SNIB SOUD SPAN
SPAR STAY WELD WIRE AFFIX
ANNEX BELAY BIGHT BRACE
CABLE CATCH CHAIN CHOCK
CINCH CLAMP CLASP CLING
COPSE CRAMP DEFIX GIRTH
HALSH HITCH INFIX LATCH PASTE
RIVET SCREW SEIZE SLOUR SNECK
STEEK STICK STRAP TRUSS WITHE
ANCHOR ATTACH BATTEN
BUCKLE BUTTON CEMENT CLINCH
COTTER COUPLE ENGAGE ENTAIL
FATHER GARTER HAMPER
HANKLE INKNOT PICKET SECURE
SKEWER SOLDER STAPLE STITCH
STRAIN TETHER BRACKET
CONFINE CONNECT EMBRACE
GRAPPLE GROMMET PADLOCK
BARNACLE FORELOCK INTERTIE
OBLIGATE TRANSFIX
(— A SAIL) CROSS
(— ABOUT) THRAP

(— ANCHOR) SCOW
(— AS SPURS) SPEND
(— IN) EMBAR
(— PROMPTLY) CLAP
(— TO) TAG
(— TOGETHER) COAPT SEIZE
SPLICE CONNECT
(— WINGS ON) IMP
(— WITH A GIRTH) WARRICK
(— WITH NOTCHES) GAIN
(PREF.) HAPT(O)
FASTENED FAST SHUT BOUND
FIXED BOUNDEN
(PREF.) **(— TOGETHER)** SYNAPTO
FASTENER BAR GIB GIN NUT PIN
AGAL BOLT DOME FAST FROG
HASP LOCK NAIL SNAP TACK
CATCH CLAMP CLASP LATCH
RIVET SCREW SPIKE STRAP
TATCH THONG BUCKLE BUTTON
HATPIN STAPLE ZIPPER FIXATOR
LATCHET PADLOCK SNAPPER
TENDRIL FASTNESS STAYLACE
FASTENING TEE TIE FROG HASP
SEAL SNAP SNIB STAY TACK
TACHE BUCKLE CLINCH LACING
MUZZLE STRIKE TINGLE BINDING
CLOSURE LATCHET MOUSING
PINNING SEIZING FORELOCK
KNITTING
(— FOR HAWK'S WING) BRAIL
(— OF COPE) MORSE
(— ON HARPOON IRON) HITCH
(HOOK AND LOOP —) AGRAFE
AGRAFFE
(PL.) GRIPES
(PREF.) DESM(A)(IDI)(IDIO)(O)
(SUFF.) PEXIA PEXIS PEXY
FASTIDIOUS FINE NEAT NICE
CHARY DONCY FEEST FUSSY
NAISH NATTY PAWKY PICKY
CHOICE CHOICY CHOOSY DAINTY
DONSIE MOROSE PICKED QUAINT
QUEASY SPRUCE CHOOSEY
CURIOUS ELEGANT FINICAL
FINICKY HAUGHTY PICKING
REFINED TAFFETA TAFFETY
CRITICAL DELICATE EXACTING
GINGERLY OVERNICE PICKSOME
PRECIOUS SCORNFUL SQUEAMISH
PARTICULAR PERSNICKETY
SCRUMPTIOUS
(NOT —) GROSS
(OVERLY —) SAUCY
FASTIDIOUSNESS DAINTY NICETY
DELICACY
FASTING RAMADAN
(PREF.) NEST(I)
FAST-MOVING SUDDEN
FASTNESS FORT CASTLE CITADEL
RETREAT FORTRESS
FAST-WORKING HOTSHOT
FAT GHI OIL TUB FOZY GHEE LARD
LIPA MORT RICH SAIM SUET
ADEPS BROSY CETIN CHUFF
COCUM ESTER FLECK FLICK
FOGGY GROSS JUICY KEDGE
KOKUM LARDY LIPID LIPIN LUSTY
OBESE PLUMP PODGY PORKY
PUDDY PUDGY PURSY SAAME
SPICK SQUAB STOUT SUMEN
THICK WASTY AXUNGE BLOWSY
CHOATY CHUBBY CHUFFY

DEGRAS FATTED FINISH FLESHY
GREASE LIPIDE LIPOID PLUFFY
PORTLY PUBBLE PUNCHY PYKNIC
ROTUND STOCKY STUFFY
TALLOW UCUUBA ADIPOSE
BLOATED BLUBBER CEROTIN
FATNESS FERTILE FLESHLY
FULSOME LANOLIN OPULENT
PINGUID PURSIVE REPLETE
STEARIN EXTENDED FRUITFUL
MARROWED MURUMURU
PALMITIN UNCTUOUS
(— AROUND WHALE'S NECK) KENT
(— MEAT) SPECK
(— OF HIPPOPOTAMUS) SPECK
(— PERSON) SQUAB
(ANIMAL —) GLOR SAIM SUET
ADEPS GLORE GREASE TALLOW
(FLOATING —) FLOT
(LARD —) FLARE FLECK FLICK
(LUMP OF —) KEECH
(NATURAL —) ESTER
(POULTRY —) SCHMALZ SCHMALTZ
(SOLID —) LARD KIKUEL STEARIN
(PREF.) LIP(O) LIPAR(O) PI(O)
PIA(R)(RO) PINGUE PINGUI SEBI
STEAR(O) STEAT(O)
FATAL FEY DIRE MORT FERAL
VITAL DEADLY DISMAL DOOMED
FUNEST LETHAL MORTAL TRAGIC
CAPITAL DEATHLY EXITIAL
FATEFUL KILLING OMINOUS
RUINOUS UNSONSY BASILISK
DESTINED EXITIOUS FUNESTAL
MORTIFIC
FATALITY DOOM ACCIDENT
CALAMITY DISASTER
FAT-BELLIED GUTTY
FATE DIE END KER LOT CAST DOLE
DOOM EURE NORN RUIN SORT
STAR CAVEL EVENT GRACE
KARMA MOIRA MORTA WEIRD
WHATE WRITE ANANKE CHANCE
KISMET DESTINY FORTUNE
OUTCOME PORTION DOWNFALL
FATALITY
(INEXORABLE —) HEAVEN
(PREF.) FATI
FATED DUE FEY FATAL DOOMED
DECREED DESTINED
FATEFUL FATAL FATED DEADLY
DOOMFUL OMINOUS DOOMLIKE
FATES CLOTHO MOERAE PARCAE
ATROPOS LACHESIS
(ONE OF —) URD NONA PARCA
SKULD CLOTHO DECUMA
ATROPOS LACHESIS VERDANDE
FATHEAD REDFISH
FATHEADED FOZY
FATHEADEDNESS FOZINESS
FATHER BU DA PA ABU AMA DAD
POP TAT ABBA ABOU AMBA
ANBA ATEF BABA BAPU DADA
PAPA PERE SIRE ADOPT BABBO
BEGET DADDY FRIAR PADRE
PATER VADER PARENT PRIEST
SUBORN ELKANAH GENITOR
TATINEK BEAUPERE GENERATE
GOVERNOR PATRIARCH
PATERFAMILIAS
(CHURCH —) APOLOGIST
(SEMIDIVINE —) PITRI
(SIDE OF —) AGNATE

(PL.) PP
(PREF.) PARRI PATR(I)(IO)(O)
FATHER GORIOT (AUTHOR OF —)
BALZAC
(CHARACTER IN —) EUGENE
GORIOT VAUTRIN DELPHINE
ANASTASIE DERESTAUD
TAILLEFER VICTORINE
DENUCINGEN DEBEAUSEANT
DERASTIGNAC
FATHERLAND KITH HOMELAND
FATHER-LASHER GUNDIE COTTOID
SCULPIN BULLHEAD LORICATE
FATHERLESS ORBATE SIRELESS
**FATHERS AND SONS (AUTHOR OF
—)** TURGENEV
(CHARACTER IN —) KATYA PAVEL
ARKADY VASILY NIKOLAI
BAZAROFF FENICHKA KIRSANOFF
ODINTZOFF SITNIKOFF
FATHOM BRACE BRASS DELVE
FADME PLUMB SOLVE SOUND
TOUCH BOTTOM MEASURE
PLUMMET
FATIGUE FAG HAG TEU BEAT BORE
COOK JADE TASH TIRE TRAY
SPEND STALL TARRY THRIE TRAIK
TRASH WEARY HARASS OVERDO
TAIGLE TUCKER EXHAUST
LANGUOR TRACHLE FATIGATE
VEXATION
FATIGUED BEAT GONE JADED
TIRED WEARY TASKIT OUTWORN
WEARIED FATIGATE HARASSED
OVERDONE TUCKERED
FATIGUING HARD IRKSOME
FATLIKE LIPOID
FATNESS BLOOM GREASE
FATTEN FAT BEEF LARD SOIL
BRAWN FARCE FLESH FRANK
PROVE SMEAR STALL BATTEN
BATTLE ENRICH FINISH TALLOW
THRIVE PINGUEFY SAGINATE
FATTENING FRANK BATTEL
BATTABLE
FATTY SUETY BACONY GREASY
ADIPOSE ADIPOUS FATLIKE
PINGUID SEBIFIC LIPAROID
LIPAROUS UNCTUOUS ALIPHATIC
(PREF.) LIPAR(O)
FATUOUS DOPY GAGA DOPEY
INANE SILLY SIMPLE STUPID
UNREAL FATUATE FOOLISH
IDIOTIC WITLESS DEMENTED
ILLUSORY IMBECILE
FAUCES JAWS
FAUCET BIB TAP BIBB COCK QUILL
SPOUT VALVE CUTOFF DOSSIL
DOZZLE OFFLET SPIGOT BIBCOCK
HYDRANT PETCOCK TURNCOCK
(WOODEN —) HORSE
FAUGH BAH FOH VAH
FAUJDAR PHOUSDAR
FAULT BUG RUB SIN BEAM CLAG
COUP DEBT FAIL FLAW FLUB
GALL HOLE LACK LAST MOLE
SAKE SLIP SPOT VICE WANT WITE
ABUSE AMISS BLAME BREAK
CULPA ERROR FLUFF GUILT
LAPSE SCAPE SHIFT SLIDE SWICK
TACHE BLOTCH DEFECT FOIBLE
RUNNER THRUST VICETY VITIUM
BLEMISH BLISTER BLUNDER

DEFAULT DEMERIT EYELAST
FAILING FAILURE FRAILTY
MISTAKE NEGLECT OFFENSE
FAULTING PECCANCY WEAKNESS
(— IN BADMINTON) SLING
(MINING —) COUP LEAP CHECK
HITCH
(PL.) FAULTAGE
FAULTFINDER MOMUS CARPER
CRITIC MOMIST CAPTION
KNOCKER NAGSTER
FAULTFINDING CARPING
CAPTIOUS CRITICAL
FAULTILY BADLY
FAULTLESS PURE CLEAN RIGHT
CORRECT PERFECT PRECISE
FLAWLESS
FAULTY BAD ILL SICK AMISS UNFIT
WRONG FLAWED FAULTED
PECCANT VICIOUS BLAMABLE
CULPABLE SPURIOUS
(PREF.) DYS PARA
FAUN SATYR WOODMAN
WOODWOSE
FAUNA FAUNULA FAUNULE
ZOOLOGY
(FOSSIL —) BIOCHRON
FAUSSEBRAIE VAMURE VAUMURE
FAUST (AUTHOR OF —) GOETHE
(CHARACTER IN —) FAUST HELEN
SIEBEL WAGNER GRETCHEN
VALENTINE HOMUNCULUS
MARGUERITE MEPHISTOPHELES
(COMPOSER OF —) GOUNOD
FAUX PAS GAFF SLIP BONER
ERROR GAFFE BLOOMER FLOATER
MISSTEP MISTAKE SNAPPER
FAVOLA D'ORFEO (CHARACTER IN
—) PLUTO APOLLO CHARON
ORPHEUS MESSENGER
PROSERPINA
(COMPOSER OF —) MONTEVERDI
FAVOR AID FOR ORE PRO BOON
ESTE FACE GREE HEAR HELP LIKE
MAKE BLESS BRIBE GRACE LEAVE
MENSK SERVE SPARE SPEED
THANK TREAT ASSIST ERRAND
ESTEEM FAVOUR LETTER NOTICE
PENCEL UPHOLD ADVANCE
AGGRACE BENEFIT ENFAVOR
FEATURE FORWARD GRATIFY
INDULGE RESPECT SUPPORT
ADVOCACY BEFRIEND COURTESY
FAVORIZE GOODWILL KINDNESS
RESEMBLE SYMPATHY
ACCEPTANCE
(— TO PURCHASER) KEEN
(NOT —) INFAUST
FAVORABLY FAIR WELL HIGHLY
FAVORED WELL FAURD HAPPY
FAURED GIFTED BLESSED

FAVOURED
FAVORER FAUTOR FRIEND
FAVORITE
FAVORING FAVONIAN
(PREF.) PRO
(SUFF.) ABLE IBLE
FAVORITE BOY PET POT PEAT
CHALK GREAT INGLE WHITE
MINION DARLING FANCIED
MINIKIN POPULAR SPECIAL
GRACIOSO WHITEBOY
FAVORITE, LA (CHARACTER IN —)
GUSMAN ALFONSO LEONORA
FERNANDO
(COMPOSER OF —) DONIZETTI
FAVORITISM BIAS FAVOR
NEPOTISM
FAVUS WHITECOMB
FAWN COG BUCK CLAW DEER
FAON JOUK ROOT COWER CRAWL
CREEP GLOZE HONEY SMARM
TOADY WHELP CRINGE CROUCH
GROVEL KOWTOW SHRINK
SLAVER ADULATE CROODLE
CRUDDLE FLATTER FLETHER
HANGDOG SERVILE SPANIEL
TOADEAT TRUCKLE WHEATEN
BOOTLICK
(— UPON) SUCK SMOOGE
ADULATE
FAWNIA (LOVER OF —) DORASTUS
FAWNING SLEEK CRINGE GREASE
MENIAL SLEEKY SMARMY SUPPLE
FLETHER GLOZING HANGDOG
SERVILE SPANIEL FLATTERY
FAWNSKIN NEBRIS
FAY ELF FEY FAIRY FEIGH
FAZE DAUNT FEEZE PHASE WORRY
FEALTY FEE FEWTE HOMAGE
LOYALTY SERVICE TREWAGE
FIDELITY
FEAR UG AWE DREE FLAY FUNK
WARD ALARM DOUBT DREAD
JELLY PANIC AFFRAY ALARUM
DANGER DISMAY FRIGHT HORROR
PHOBIA TERROR ANXIETY
SUSPECT AFFRIGHT DISQUIET
DISTRUST EERINESS MISDOUBT
VENERATE
(PREF.) PHOB(O)
(SUFF.) PHOBE PHOBIA(C) PHOBIC
PHOBOUS
FEARFUL ARGH DIRE AWFUL
FERLY PAVID TIMID WINDY
WROTH AFRAID COWISH FRIGHTY
GHASTLY NERVOUS PANICKY
WORRIED CAUTIOUS DOUBTFUL
DREADFUL GREWSOME
GRUESOME HORRIBLE HORRIFIC
SHOCKING SKITTISH TERRIBLE
TERRIFIC TIMOROUS
(PREF.) DEIN(O) DIN(O)
FEARLESS BOLD BRAVE DARING
HEROIC AWELESS IMPAVID
INTREPID
FEASIBLE FIT LIKELY POSSIBLE
PROBABLE SUITABLE
FEAST (ALSO SEE FESTIVAL) EAT
FOY PIG SUP DINE FARM FETE
LUAU MEAL TUCK UTAS AZYME
CHEER CHOES CITUA DIRGY
FESTA FESTY GAUDY REVEL
TREAT ARTHEL AVERIL BRIDAL

DEVOUR DINNER DOUBLE INFARE
ISODIA JUNKET MAUNDY REGALE
REPAST SIMPLE SMOUSE SPREAD
AHAAINA BANQUET BRIDALE
DELIGHT FESTINO GRATIFY
GREGORY LAMBALE LEMURIA
SHEVUOS SYNAXIS ANALEPSY
CAROUSAL DOMINEER EPIPHANY
FESTIVAL GESTNING GESTONIE
HANUKKAH KOIMESIS PASSOVER
POTLATCH SHABUOTH VESTALIA
(— BEFORE JOURNEY) FOY
(— OF BOOTHS) SUCCOS SUKKOTH
(— OF LANTERNS) HON
(— OF LOTS) PURIM
(— OF WEEKS) SHEVUOS
SHABUOTH
(— PLACE) IDGAH
(DRINKING —) BANQUET
(FUNERAL —) ARVAL ARVEL DIRGY
DIRGIE DREDGIE
(HARVEST —) BUSK
(JEWISH —) SENDAH
(RELIGIOUS —) CANAO KANYAW
PENTECOST
(VILLAGE —) TANSY
(PREF.) DAPI FESTI FESTO
HEORTO
(SUFF.) (— DAY) MAS
FEASTER CONVIVE
FEASTING FEAST CARNIVAL
FEAT ACT KIP DEED FATE GEST
WORK GESTE SPLIT STUNT TRICK
CRADDY CUTOFF EXPLOIT
MASTERY MIRACLE WORSHIP
DEXTROUS PERFORMANCE
(— IN SURFING) SPINNER
QUASIMODO
(CRICKETER'S —) DOUBLE
(TUMBLING —) SCISSORS
(PL.) DAGS
FEATHER BOO PEN TAB DECK
DOWN FLAG HERL SETA STUB
VANE ADORN AXIAL PENNA
PINNA PLUMA PLUME QUILL
REMEX CLOTHE COVERT CRINET
FLEDGE FLETCH FLIGHT HACKLE
MANUAL PINION SARCEL SICKLE
SQUAMA TIPPET TONGUE
AXILLAR BRISTLE FLEMISH
IMPLUME PRIMARY RECTRIX
REMICLE STIPULE TECTRIX
TERTIAL TOPPING AXILLARY
SCAPULAR STREAMER TERTIARY
(BRISTLELIKE —) VIBRISSA
(HAWK'S —S) BRAIL BRAILS
(HORSE —) SPEAR
(NEW —) STIPULE
(OSTRICH TAIL —) BOO
(PINION —) SARCEL
(TAIL —) SICKLE RECTRIX
(YELLOW —S) HULU
(PL.) GIG BOOT CAPE DOWN FLUE
MAIL BRAIL CRISSUM CUSHION
FLIGHTS PLUMAGE REMIGES
SPURIAE
(PREF.) PENNAT(I)(O) PENNI
PENNO PINN(I)(O) PINNAT(I)(O)
PLUMI PTER(O) PTIL(O)
(SUFF.) PENNATE PENNINE PTILE
PTILUS
FEATHER BED TYE
FEATHER CLOAK AHUULA TEMIAK

FEATHERED FLEDGE FLEDGY
PENNATE PINNATE FLIGHTED
(PREF.) PTENO
(SUFF.) PINNATE
FEATHERING STOCKING
FEATHER KEY FIN STOP SPLINE
FEATHER
FEATHER-LEGGED COOTY COOTIE
FEATHERLIKE PINNATE
FEATHERY PLUMY FLEDGY FLUFFY
PLUMOSE PLUMEOUS
FEATLY NEATLY FOOTINGLY
FEATURE WAY FACE ITEM NOTE
STAR BREAK FAVOR GRACE
MOTIF TOKEN TRACT TRAIT
TREAT ASPECT CACHET
FAVOUR SPLASH AMENITY
OUTLINE HALLMARK
SALIENCE
(— OF WORD FORM) ASPECT
(ATTRACTIVE —) AMENITY
(DETERMINING —) LIMIT
(DISTINGUISHING —) TRAIT STROKE
HALLMARK
(ESSENTIAL —) CHARACTER
(FATAL —) BANE
(LINGUISTIC —) ISOGLOSS
SURVIVAL
(MAIN —) CRUX
(MOST COGENT —) BEAUTY
(OBJECTIONABLE —) DISCOUNT
DRAWBACK
(SALIENT —) MOTIF
(TOPOGRAPHIC —) ARC
(TOPOGRAPHIC —S) LIE
(PL.) LAY FACE CONTOUR
FASHION GEOLOGY RETRAIT
FEAZE FRAY FAIZE ROUGHEN
FEBRIFUGE PEREIRA ANGOSTURA
FEBRILE PYRETIC FEVERISH
FECES DRAST HOCKEY ORDURE
(PREF.) COPR(O)
FECKLESS WEAK FEEBLE
FECULENCE DREG
FECULENT DREGGY
FECUND FERTILE FRUITFUL
PROLIFIC
FED FAT MEATED
FEDERATION BUND CROM UNION
LEAGUE NATION
COUNCIL ALLIANCE
FEDERACY TRIALISM
FEDORA (CHARACTER IN —) LORIS
FEDORA IPANOV ROMANOV
(COMPOSER OF —) GIORDANO
FEE FEU DUES DUTY FEAL FEUL
FIEF FIER HIRE RATE WAGE
CAULP EXTRA HANSE PRICE
RIGHT ALNAGE AMOBER BARONY
CHARGE DASTUR EMPLOY EXCISE
REWARD SALARY SHEKEL
BUOYAGE DASTURI DUMPAGE
DUSTOOR FALDAGE FIRNAGE
FURNAGE GAOLAGE GARNISH
GRATIFY GUIDAGE HALLAGE
HOUSAGE JAILAGE MULTURE
PAYMENT PINLOCK PREFINE
STIPEND STORAGE TALLAGE
TRIBUTE VANTAGE BOOTHAGE
BOUNTITH CHUMMAGE EXACTION
FAREWELL GRATUITY MALIKANA
POUNDAGE REREFIEF RETAINER
SHIPPAGE WHARFAGE

(— TO LANDOWNER) TERRAGE
(— TO TEACHER) MINERVAL
(CUSTOMARY —) DASTUR
(CUSTOMS —) LOT
(ENTRANCE —) HANSA HANSE
INCOME
(GRINDING —) THIRLAGE
(INITIATION —) FOOTING
(PHYSICIAN'S —) SOSTRUM
(ROAD —) PIKE
(UNAUTHORIZED —) GARNISH
(PL.) EXHIBITS

FEEBLE LOW WAN FLUE LAME
MEAN PALE POOR PUNY SOFT
WEAK DONCY DOTTY FAINT
SEELY SILLY SOBER UNORN
WANKY WASHY WERSH WONKY
CADUKE DEBILE DONSIE DOTAGE
FAINTY FLABBY FLIMSY FOIBLE
INFIRM PAULIE PUISNE SCANTY
SEMMIT SICKLY SIMPLE TANGLE
UNFIRM WANKLE WEANLY
DWAIBLY DWEEBLE FRAGILE
INVALID LANGUID QUEECHY
RICKETY SAPLESS SHILPIT
SLENDER SLIMPSY THREADY
UNWIELD UNWREST WEARISH
DECREPIT DROGHLIN FEATLESS
IMBECILE IMPOTENT INFERIOR
LUSTLESS MALADIVE RESOLUTE
SACKLESS THEWLESS THOWLESS
UNSTRONG UNWIELDY WATERISH
YIELDING NERVELESS

FEEBLE-MINDED ANILE DOTTY
DOTTLE FOOLISH MORONIC
WANTING IMBECILE

FEEBLENESS DOTAGE FEEBLE
POVERTY CADUCITY DEBILITY
WEAKNESS

FEED EAT HAY BAIT BEET BRAN
CROP DIET DINE FILL FOOD GLUT
GRUB MEAL MEAT OATS SATE
AGIST FLESH FLUSH GORGE
GRASS GRAZE NURSE SERVE
STOKE TABLE BATTLE BROWSE
FODDER FOSTER INFEED NOODLE
REFETE REPAST SUCKLE SUPPLY
BLOWOUT FURNISH GRATIFY
HERBAGE INDULGE KEEPING
NOURISH NURTURE PASTURE
PROVENT SATIATE SATISFY
SUBSIST SURFEIT SUSTAIN
VICTUAL PROVENDER
(— ABUNDANTLY) STOKE
(— ANIMAL) SORT SERVE
(— AT NIGHT) SUP
(— CATTLE) SOIL
(— FOR CATTLE) FODDER STOVER
TACKLE
(— FORCIBLY) CRAM
(— GLUTTONOUSLY) BATTEN
(— GREEN FOOD TO CATTLE) SOIL
(— HIGH) FRANK
(— IN STUBBLE) SHACK
(— ON FLIES) SMUT
(— RAVENOUSLY) FRAUNCH
(— STOCK) FOG SOIL SOILING
(— TO REPLETION) ENGORGE
(— TO THE FULL) SATIATE
(— WELL) BATTLE
(GROUND —) CHOP
(POULTRY —) SCRATCH
(RED —) HAYSEED

(STOCK —) BRAN
(WHALE —) GRIT
(PREF.) THREP(SO)
FEEDBOARD DECK
FEEDER HOGGER HOPPER PECKER
STOCKER
(YARN —) CARRIER
FEEDHEAD RISER FEEDER
SINKHEAD
FEEDING RELIEF FOLDAGE
PANNAGE
(— GROUND FOR FISH) MEADOW
(— THROUGH TUBE) GAVAGE
(FREE-CHOICE —) CAFETERIA
(PREF.) PHAG(O)

FEEL FIND PALP GROPE SENSE
THINK TOUCH FIMBLE FINGER
HANDLE RESENT EXAMINE
EXPLORE FEELING SENSATE
PERCEIVE
(— ACUTELY) SUFFER
(— AVERSION FOR) HATE LOATHE
(— CHILLY) CREEM
(— COMPASSION) PITY YEARN
(— DEJECTION) REPINE
(— FEAR) UG GRUE UGGE
TREMBLE
(— GRIEF) GRIEVE DEPLORE
(— HAPPY OR BETTER) LIGHT
(— NAUSEA) WAMBLE
(— OF CLOTH) HAND
(— ONE'S WAY) GROPE FUMBLE
GRAMMEL
(— OUT) SOUND
(— PAIN) URN
(— REPUGNANCE) ABHOR
(— SHAME) BLUSH
(— WANT OF) MISS
FEELER DRAW KITE PALP SNIFF
PALPUS TACTOR ANTENNA
SMELLER PROPOSAL TENTACLE
(PREF.) ANTENNI
FEELING FEEL PITY TACT VIEW
CHEER HEART HUMOR SENSE
SORGE TOUCH AFFECT CEMENT
MORALE CONSENT EMOTION
OPINION PASSION VELUNGE
ATTITUDE SENTIENT SENSATION
PRESENTIMENT
(— ILL) HOWISH
(— MIRTH) JOCUND
(— OF ACCORD) SYMPATHY
(— OF AMUSEMENT) CHARGE
(— OF ANTIPATHY) ALLERGY
(— OF ANXIETY) ANGST
(— OF CONTEMPT) DISDAIN
(— OF DISGUST) UG
(— OF DOUBT) SCRUPLE
(— OF HORROR) CREEP CREEPS
(— OF HOSTILITY) ANIMUS
(— OF JOY) GLOAT
(— OF OPPOSITION) KICK
(— OF RESENTMENT) GRUDGE
(— OF ROMANCE) STARDUST
(— OF UNEASINESS) MALAISE
(— OF WEARINESS) ENNUI
(— OF WELL-BEING) EUPHORIA
(— PRODUCED BY DRUG) RUSH
(ANGERED —) DUDGEON
(BODILY —) TABET
(CONCEITED —) SWELLING
(ILL —) HARDNESS
(INTUITIVE —) HUNCH

(KINDLY —) GOODWILL
(REPRESSION OF —) STOICISM
(STRONG —) STAB
(STRONG, POSITIVE —) SOUL
(PL.) HEART WITHERS
(PREF.) SENSI
(SUFF.) PATH(IA)(IC)(Y)
FEEN, DIE (CHARACTER IN —) ADA
GROMA ARINDAL
(COMPOSER OF —) WAGNER
FEET DOGS TONGS STAMPS
WALKERS GUNBOATS TRILBIES
PETTITOES
(— WASHING) MAUNDY
(BOARD —) FOOTAGE
(LARGE —) GUFFINS
(PREF.) PED(I)
(SUFF.) PEDE
(MEASURE OF —) METER
FEIGN ACT FAKE MINT MOCK SEEM
SHAM VEYN AVOID FABLE FALSE
FORGE PAINT SHAPE SHIRK
AFFECT ASSUME GAMMON
INVENT POSSUM CONCEAL
FALSIFY FASHION IMAGINE
POETIZE PRETEND ROMANCE
DISGUISE SIMULATE
(— ASSENT) COLLOGUE
(— IGNORANCE) CONNIVE
(— ILLNESS) MALINGER
FEIGNED SHAM FALSE FEINT
POETIC PSEUDO ASSUMED
COLORED FICTIVE FICTIOUS
SIMULATE
(PREF.) PSEUD(O)
FEIGNING FICTION FORGERY
SIMULATION
FEIJOA ANDRE
FEINT FAKE MINT RUSE APPEL
FAINT SHIFT SPOOF TRICK
FALSIFY FEIGNED FEINTER
FINCTURE PRETENSE REVIRADO
FELDSPAR ALBITE AMBITE GNEISS
CELSIAN SYENITE ADULARIA
ANDESINE FELSPATH PERTHITE
PETUNTZE SANIDINE
MOONSTONE
FELICIA AGATHAEA
FELICITATE HUG BLESS MACARIZE
FELICITOUS FIT HAPPY
FELICITOUSLY HAPPILY
FELICITY JOY BLISS SONSE
HEAVEN
FELINE CATTISH
FELL CUR FEN HEW COSH DOWN
DROP FALL HIDE HILL MOOR PELT
RUIN SKIN VERY CRUEL EAGER
FIELD GRASS GREAT SHARP
DEADLY FIERCE FLEECE INTENT
MIGHTY SAVAGE SHREWD
TUMBLE BRUTISH CRASHED
DOUGHTY HIDEOUS INHUMAN
STRETCH TUMBLED MOUNTAIN
SPIRITED VIGOROUS
(— A TREE) HEW LODGE
FELLER GIDEON
FELLING FALL CUTTING
FELLOE BOD FELF FALLY
FELLOW S BO BOY COD DON EGG
FOX GUY JOE LAD MAC MAN
MUN NUT WAG WAT YOB BALL
BEAN BEAU BIRD BOZO BUFF
CARL CHAL CHAP COVE CUSS

DEAN DICK DUCK DUDE DULL
GENT GILL GINK HIND HUSK JACK
JAKE JOHN LOON MATE NABS
PEER PRIG SNAP BILLY BIMBO
BLOKE BROCK BUDDY BULLY
CARLE CHIEL COVEY CULLY FRUIT
GROOM GUEST JOKER MATCH
PARTY SCOUT SKATE SLAVE
SPORT SPRIG SWIPE BEGGAR
BILLIE BIRKIE BOHUNK BOOGER
BUDDIE BUFFER BUGGER BUSTER
CALLAN CHIELD CODGER CUFFIN
CUTTER FELLER FOOTER FOUTER
FOUTRA GALOOT GAZABO
HOMBRE JASPER JOCKEY JOHNNY
JOSSER KIPPER PERSON SHAVER
SINNER SIRRAH SISTER SOCIUS
TURNIP BASTARD BROTHER
CALLANT CHAPPIE COMRADE
CULLIES CULLION CUSTRON
KNOCKER PARTNER SCROYLE
SNOOZER BLIGHTER CONFRERE
DOTTEREL MERCHANT NEIGHBOR
SYNODITE
(AWKWARD —) JAY OAF CLUB
GAWK CLOWN LOOBY GALOOT
SLOUCH
(BASE —) CARL CARLE CULLION
(BASHFUL —) SHEEP
(BOLD —) HEARTY
(BRUTAL —) CLUBFIST
(CLOWNISH —) COOF BAYARD
LOBLOLLY
(CLUMSY —) BOOB FILE CAMEL
FARMER LUBBER PALOOKA
(COMMON —) JACK LOUT
(CONCEITED —) JEMMY DALTEEN
PRINCOX
(CONTEMPTIBLE —) DOG SCUT
SMAIL SNAKE RABBIT SMATCH
PEASANT
(CONTENTIOUS —) SQUARER
(CORPULENT —) POMPION
(COUNTRY —) JAKE JASPER
(CRUDE —) STIFF
(DASHING —) BUCK BLADE
(DASTARDLY —) HOUND
(DESPICABLE —) FOUTER FOUTRA
HANGDOG SMATCHET
(DIRTY —) SCAB BROCK
(DISAGREEABLE —) GLEYDE
(DISSOLUTE —) RAKE ROUE
RAKEHELL
(DROLL —) CARD
(DROWSY —) LUNGIS
(DRUNKEN —) BORACHIO
(DULL —) BUFF DRIP FOGY CHUFF
SUMPH LUNGIS HUMDRUM
(FAT —) HIND GULCH GLUTTON
(FIERCE-LOOKING —) KILLBUCK
(FINE —) BAWCOCK
(FOOLISH —) SOP GABY GOFF
ZANY GANDER JACKSON
WIDGEON
(GAY —) GALLIARD
(GOOD —) BRICK BULLY TRUMP
HEARTY TROJAN
(GOOD-FOR-NOTHING —) JACKEEN
(GREEDY —) SLOTE
(IDLE —) FANION FOOTER STOCAH
LOLLARD SKULKER
(IGNORANT —) GOBBIN
(ILLBRED —) LARRIKIN

(IMPERTINENT —) JACK WHISK
(INSIGNIFICANT —) SQUIB
(JOLLY —) VAVASOR VAVASOUR
(LAZY —) BUM LUSK TOOL LENTO
(LOW —) RAG WAFF SWEEP
LIMMER VARLET MECHANIC
WHORESON
(MEAN —) CAD DOG BOOR BOUCH
BUCKO CAVEL CHURL SCURF
RASCAL CULLION BEZONIAN
COISTREL COISTRIL SNEAKSBY
SPALPEEN STINKARD
(NIGGARDLY —) SNUDGE
(NOISY —) MOUTH
(OLD —) GLYDE GAFFER GEEZER
(OLD-FASHIONED —) FOGY
(OVERBEARING —) GRIMSIR
(PROSAIC —) PRUNE
(PUNY —) SMAIK
(QUARRELSOME —) HECTOR
(QUEER OLD —) CODGER GEEZER
(RESIDENTIAL —) DON
(ROGUISH —) DOG
(RUDE —) BOOR JACK ROUGH
(SHABBY —) SHAB SQUEEF
(SHEEPISH —) SUMPH
(SHIFTLESS —) PROG SHACK
PROGGER
(SHREWD —) COLT
(SILLY —) TOT GUMP ZANY SHEEP
SMAIK BUFFER DOTTEREL
MUSHHEAD
(SIMPLE —) DOODLE
(SLOVENLY —) SLUTE
(SLY —) FOX COON
(SNEAKING —) SNUDGE
(SORDID —) HUNKS
(SOUTH AFRICAN —) KEREL
(SPIRITED —) BRICK
(SPORTY —) PLAYBOY
(STRANGE —) CODGER
(STRAPPING —) SWANKY SWANKIE
(STUPID —) ASS BOOB CLOD COOF
DAFF DOLT GUMP HASH MUFF
SIMP BOOBY CUDDY DUNCE
MORON STIRK BAYARD BUFFER
FARMER FOOZLE GANDER
ASINOCO DOWFART HUMDRUM
CLODPOLL CODSHEAD SOCKHEAD
(SULLEN —) GLUMP
(SURLY —) CHUFF CHOUGH
(TRICKISH —) HUMBUG
(TRICKY —) ROOK GREEK KNAVE
SCAMP DODGER RASCAL
(UNCIVIL —) RUDESBY
(UNCOUTH —) JAKE KEMP TIKE
(VILE —) RAT SKUNK
(VULGAR —) TIGER
(WORTHLESS —) BUM CUR DOG
HASH PROG RAFF WAFF JAVEL
ROGUE SCAMP SHOAT SNAKE
STUMER BROTHEL BUDMASH
PROGGER VAURIEN TARTARET
(WRETCHED —) DEVIL DOGBOLT
(YOUNG —) BILLY BUCKO CADIE
CADDIE
(PREF.) CO
(SUFF.) ENGRO
FELLOWMAN BROTHER NEIGHBOR
FELLOWSHIP GUILD HAUNT
UNION FAMILY COMPANY
ALLIANCE SODALITY
(CHRISTIAN —) KOINONIA

FELLY RIM FELF FELLOE KEENLY
CRUELLY BITTERLY FIERCELY
SAVAGELY TERRIBLY
FELO-DE-SE SUICIDE
FELON WILD CRUEL FETLOW
FIERCE WICKED CONVICT
CULPRIT PANARIS VILLAIN
WHITLOW PHLEGMON
RUNROUND MALEFACTOR
FELONY ARSON CRIME OFFENSE
FELT JIG PLAIT FILTER NUMNAH
SENSED SOLEIL VELOUR DOUBLER
FELTING PANNOSE
(— INTENSIVELY) ACUTE
(— THROUGH SENSES) SENSATE
(DEEPLY —) CORDIAL INTENSE
(PERSONALLY —) CONSCIOUS
(PL.) CLOTHING
(PREF.) PIL(O)
FELTWORK NEUROPIL
FEMALE DOE EWE HEN HER SHE
SOW DAME GIRL GYNE LADY
MORT ADULT JENNY SMOCK
SQUAW WOMAN WAHINE
WEAKLY DISTAFF FEMINAL
WOMANLY DAUGHTER FEMININE
GYNAECIC LADYLIKE WOMANISH
PETTICOAT
(— ANCESTOR) TAPROOT
(IMPERFECT —) FREEMARTIN
(PARTHOGENETIC —) AMAZON
(PREF.) FEMINO GYN(AE)(AECO)
(AEO)(ANDRO)(E)(ECO)(EO)(O)
THELY
(SUFF.) ESS ETTE GYN(E)(IST)(OUS)
INE TRIX
FEMININE FAIR SOFT WEAK
WOMAN FEMALE TENDER
WAHINE FEMINAL WOMANLY
WOMANISH PETTICOAT
(SUFF.) INA INE
FEMININE WILES (CHARACTER IN —
) BELLINA LEONORA FILANDRO
GIAMPOLO ROMUALDO
(COMPOSER OF —) CIMAROSA
FEMININITY MUSLIN FEMINITY
MULIEBRITY
FEMME FATALE SIREN
FEMORAL CRURAL
(PREF.) CRURO
FEMUR THIGH
FEN BOG CARR FAIN FELL FOWL
MERE MOOR WASH BROAD FAINS
MARSH SNIPE SWAMP VENTS
MORASS QUAGMIRE
FENCE BAR HAW HAY BANK DIKE
DUEL DYKE HAHA HAIN PALE
PLAY RAIL STUB WALL WEIR
WIRE BEARD DODGE FRITH
GUARD HEDGE MOUND PALIS
STICK STUMP DETENT FENDER
FRAISE GLANCE HURDLE LEADER
PALING PICKET RADDLE RASPER
SCHERM SCRIME TIMBER BARRIER
BULWARK CYCLONE DEFENSE
ENCLOSE FENCING FENSURE
IMPALER PASSAGE RAILING
SWAGMAN BACKSTOP ENCHASER
ENCLOSER GRAFFAGE HOARDING
PALISADE PALISADO SEPIMENT
SKIRMISH BRANDRETH
BRANDRITH
(— AROUND BULLRING) BARRERA

(— AROUND MACHINERY) BRATTICE
(— CLOSING DITCH) WOLF
(— OF LOCK) STUB
(— OF LOGS) GLANCE
(CATTLE —) OXER WIPE SKERM
SCHERM
(FISH —) WEIR KIDDLE LEADER
(METAL —) RAIL RAILING
(PREF.) HERCO PHRAGMO
SEPTATO
(SUFF.) SEPTATE
FENCER DUELIST IMPALER
PARRIER PROVOST SCRIMER
SWORDER FOILSMAN
BACKSWORD
FENCE RAIL DRAWBAR
FENCE SECTION PANE
FENCE-SITTER MUGWUMP
FENCING WIRE FENCE PALING
ESCRIME PASSAGE SCIENCE
SWORDING
FEND WARD PARRY SHIRK DEFEND
FORBID RESIST SUPPORT
FENDER SKID WING CAMEL GUARD
SKATE BUFFER BUMPER SHIELD
DOLPHIN PUDDING BOWGRACE
MUDGUARD SPLASHER
(— FOR FIREPLACE) CURB KERB
(— NEAR HOLE) TELLTALE
(ROPE —) PUDDENING
FENDER SKID GLANCER
FENESTRA FORAMEN
FENGHUANG FUM PHOENIX
FENKS FRITTERS
FENMAN WEBFOOT
FENNEC ZERDA
FENNEL ANIS DILL HEMP SOYA
FERULE FINKEL COWBANE
HOGWEED SPINGEL FINOCHIO
FLORENCE CAROSELLA
FENNER ZERDA
FENRIS (FATHER OF —) LOKI
(MOTHER OF —) ANGURBODA
(SISTER OF —) HEL
(SLAYER OF —) VIDAR
FENSTER WINDOW
FENUGREEK BAUMIER MELLILOT
(SEEDS OF —) HELBEH
FERAL WILD BRUTAL DEADLY
FERINE SAVAGE BESTIAL
UNTAMED FUNEREAL UNBROKEN
FER-DE-LANCE BONETAIL
JARARACA
FERMATA HOLD PAUSE TENOR
CORONA
FERMENT FRY LOB ZYM BARM
FRET HEAT SOUR TURN WORK
ZYME FEVER SWEAT YEAST
DANDER ENZYME FLOWER
FOMENT SEETHE SIMMER
TUMULT UPROAR AGITATE
QUICKEN TURMOIL DISORDER
(PREF.) ZYM(O)
(SUFF.) ZYME
FERMENTATION SWEAT CUVAGE
FERMENT MOWBURN WORKING
ZYMOSIS
FERMENTED SOD
(IMPROPERLY —) FOXY
FERMENTING BARMY WORKING
FERN HEII NITO PULU TARA WEKI
BRAKE DUGAL EKAHA FROND
NARDO PITAU PONGA ULUHI

WHEKI AMAMAU DOODIA
NARDOO OSMUND PTERIS
ACROGEN ATERACH BOGFERN
BRACKEN OSMUNDA SYNANGE
WOODSIA ADIANTUM ASPIDIUM
BAROMETZ BUCKHORN
BUNGWALL CETERACH DAVALLIA
DENDRITE FERNWORT FILICITE
GOLDBACK HARDFERN KOLOKOLO
MOONWORT MULEWORT
PARARELA PILLWORT POLYPODY
SPOROGEN STAGHORN
MAIDENHAIR
(PART OF —) AXIS CASE LEAF
STEM BLADE FROND PINNA STIPE
TOOTH MIDRIB RACHIS LEAFLET
PETIOLE PINNULE SUBLEAFLET
(PL.) FILICES
(PREF.) PTERID(O)
(SUFF.) PTERIS
FERN LEAF FROND CROSIER
FERNLIKE FERNY PTEROID
FEROCIOUS ILL FELL GRIM RUDE
WILD BRUTE CRUEL FERAL
BLOODY BRUTAL FEROCE FIERCE
GOTHIC RAGING SAVAGE
ACHARNE INHUMAN OMINOUS
VIOLENT WOLFISH PITILESS
RAVENOUS RUTHLESS TARTARLY
FEROCITY FERITY SAVAGERY
VIOLENCE ACHARNEMENT
FERRARA ANDREW
FERRET HOB MONK TAPE PADOU
MONACH WEASEL POLECAT
(— OUT) FOSSICK
(FEMALE —) GIL GILL JILL BITCH
(MALE —) HOB HOBB
FERRIAGE WAFTAGE
FERRIC OXIDE CROCUS
FERROCYANIDE PRUSSIATE
FERROTYPE GLAZE TINTYPE
FERROUS SIDEROUS
FERRULE CAP TIP CUFF RING SHOE
VIRL COLLET PULLEY RUNNER
VERREL VIROLE ARMGARN
BUSHING CRAMPET
FERRY FORD PASS PONT SCOW
PASSAGE TRAJECT TRANECT
TRANSFER
FERRYBOAT BAC PONT SCOW
FERRY
FERRYMAN CHARON FERRIER
WATERMAN
FERTILE FAT GOOD RANK RICH
GLEBY BATFUL BATTLE FECUND
HEARTY STRONG TEEMING
ABUNDANT BATTABLE FRUITFUL
GENEROUS PREGNANT PROLIFIC
SPAWNING
FERTILITY HEART FATNESS
(PATRON OF —) YAKSHA
FERTILIZATION ENDOGAMY
POROGAMY
FERTILIZE FAT DUNG FISH LIME
MARL CHALK BATTEN ENRICH
FRUCTIFY
FERTILIZER FAT MARL GUANO
HUMUS ALINIT FLOATS MANURE
POLLEN POTASH CARRIER
COMPOTE HUMOGEN KAINITE
NITRATE TANKAGE AMMONITE
CINEREAL NITROGEN
FERULA NARTHEX

FERULE ROD RULER COLLET FENNEL FERULA PALMER

FERVENCY WARMTH CANDENCY

FERVENT HOT KEEN WARM EAGER FIERY ARDENT BITTER FERVID FIERCE INWARD RAGING SAVAGE BOILING BURNING GLOWING INTENSE PECTORAL ROMANTIC VEHEMENT RELIGIOUS

FERVID HOT ARDENT TROPIC BOILING BURNING FERVENT GLOWING ZEALOUS UNCTUOUS VEHEMENT

FERVOR FIRE HEAT HWYL RAGE SOUL ZEAL ARDOR WARMTH PASSION CANDENCY DEVOTION STRENGTH VIOLENCE
(— IN PRAYER) KAVVANAH KAWWANAH

FESCUE VESTER

FESS BAR BAND PERT DANCE HUMET
(DIMINUTIVE —) TRANGLE

FESTAL GAY GALA GAUDY FESTIVE FESTUAL FEASTFUL

FESTER ROT BEAL RANK SCAR RANKLE PUSTULE PUTREFY

FESTERING RANK FRETTY

FESTIVAL (ALSO SEE FEAST) ALE BON PWE BUSK FAIR FEIS FETE GALA HOLI MELA PUJA TIDE UTAS WAKE DELIA FEAST FERIA FESTA GAUDY HALOA PURIM REVEL ROUSE SEDAR ADONIA BAIRAM BRIDAL CARNEA DEWALI DIASIA DIPALA FIESTA HOHLEE HUFFLE KERMIS LAMMAS LENAEA OPALIA PONGOL POOJAH POSADA SUCCOS AGONIUM AGRANIA BANQUET BELTANE DASAHRA EQUIRIA FESTIAL HILARIA KERMESS MATSURI PALILIA SUKKOTH THIASOS TOXCATL UPHELYA VINALIA AGRIONIA AIANTEIA APATURIA ATHENAEA BEALTINE BRUMALIA CARNIVAL COTYTTIA DASAHARA DIIPOLIA DIONYSIA DUSSERAH ENCAENIA FASNACHT FLORALIA HANUKKAH HIGHTIDE KALENDAE LUPERCAL MARYMASS MATRALIA MITHRIAC MUHARRAM MUNYCHIA NATIVITY NEOMENIA POTLATCH STAMPEDE TAARGELIA SATURNALIA
(HIGHLAND —) MOD
(MUSICAL —) EISTEDDFOD
(PL.) MOED VOTA
(SUFF.) MAS

FESTIVE GAY GALA JOLLY FESTAL GENIAL JOYOUS FEASTLY HOLIDAY JOCULAR CONVIVAL FEASTFUL MIRTHFUL SPORTIVE CONVIVIAL

FESTIVITY GALA GAUD UTAS UTIS BEANO FEAST MIRTH RANDY REVEL GAIETY GAYETY SPLORE HOLIDAY JOLLITY JOYANCE PATTERN FESTIVAL FUNCTION MERRIMENT MERRYMAKING

FESTOON SWAG WREATH GARLAND DECORATE
(PL.) ENCARPUS

FETCH FET FESH GASP GIVE SHAG TACK TAKE TEEM WAIN BRING SWEEP TRICK DOUBLE STROKE WRAITH ACHIEVE ATTRACT ARTIFICE FETCHING INTEREST

FETCHED FOSH

FETCHING SWEET CRAFTY CUNNING ALLURING PLEASING SCHEMING

FETE FAIR GALA FEAST HONOR BAZAAR FIESTA HOLIDAY

FETID OLID RANK MUSTY PUTID ROTTEN VIROSE NOISOME SANIOUS MALODOROUS

FETIDLY FOULLY

FETISH OBI IDOL JUJU OBIA ZEME ZEMI ZOGO ANITO ASCON CHARM GUACA HUACA OBEAH OBIAH TOTEM AMULET FETICH GRIGRI NAGUAL VOODOO SHINTAI SORCERY FETISHRY GREEGREE TALISMAN

FETLOCK COOT FOOTLOCK

FETTER BAND BEND BOLT BOND FIND GYVE IRON SPAN BASIL BEWET BILBO CHAIN SLANG SWATH ANKLET GARTER HALTER HAMPER HOBBLE HOPPLE IMPEDE LANGEL RACKAN SWATHE CLINKER CONFINE ENCHAIN FETLOCK GARNISH MANACLE SHACKLE SPANCEL TRAMMEL RESTRAIN
(PL.) IRONS LINKS DARBIES GARNISH GARTERS

FETTERBUSH PIPESTEM PIPEWOOD

FETTLE BEAT DECK FUSS MULL TIDY TWIG VEIN DRESS GROOM WHACK YARAK GIRDLE REPAIR SETTLE STRIKE ARRANGE BANDAGE FEATHER HARNESS

FETTLER BILLYER NOBBLER

FETTLING FIX FETTLE FIXING

FETUS BIRTH CHILD YOUNG AMELUS BREECH EMBRYO FOETUS ABORTUS CYCLOPS FEATURE AMORPHUS
(PREF.) EMBRY(O) FETI FETO FOETI FOETO

FEUD FIEF FRAY BROIL AFFRAY ENMITY FEODUM FEUDUM STRIFE CONTEST DISPUTE QUARREL VENDETTA

FEUDATORY FIEF VASSAL ZAMINDAR ZEMINDAR

FEUILLE MORTE PHILAMOT

FEVER AGUE FIRE ARDOR CAUMA DANDY LEUMA OCTAN CAUSUS DENGUE FEBRIS HECTIC SEPTAN SEXTAN SODOKU TYPHIA TYPHUS VOMITO AMAKEBE FERMENT FEVERET HELODES MALARIA PINKEYE PYREXIA QUARTAN TERTIAN TYPHOID SYNOCHUS TERTIANA TYPHINIA CALENTURE
(— OF HORSE) WEED SCALMA
(— OF PERU) VERRUGA
(— OF SHEEP) BRAXY
(BRAIN —) PHRENITIS
(HAY —) RHINITIS
(MALARIAL —) TAP
(MARSH —) HELODES

(TEXAS —) TRISTEZA
(WITHOUT —) APYRETIC
(PREF.) FEBRI PYR(ET)(ETO)
(SUFF.) PYRA

FEVERED DISEASED

FEVERFEW MAYWEED MUGWORT PELLITORY

FEVERISH HOT FIERY FEVERY HECTIC EXCITED FEBRILE FRANTIC RESTLESS

FEVERLESS APYREXIA

FEVERROOT GENSON

FEVER TREE BITTERBARK

FEVERWEED FITWEED

FEVERWORT BONESET

FEW LIT CURN LESS SOME SCANT THREE WHEEN WHONE CURRAN PICKLE LIMITED SEVERAL EXIGUOUS
(PREF.) OLIG(O) PAUCI

FEWER LESS
(PREF.) MI(O)

FEWNESS PAUCITY

FEY DEAD DYING ELFIN FATAL UNLUCKY PIXILATED

FEZ TARBOOSH

FIADOR THEODORE

FIANCE TRUST SPOUSE FIANCEE PROMISE AFFIANCE

FIASCO CRASH FLASK FROST FIZZLE FAILURE DISASTER

FIAT EDICT ORDER UKASE DECREE COMMAND DECISION SANCTION

FIB LIE YED FLAW WHID SLANT STORY FITTEN PUMMEL SKLENT TARADIDDLE

FIBBER LIAR

FIBER TAL ADAD BASS BAST COIR ERUC FERU FLAX HARL HEMP IMBE JUTE LINE PITA SILK SUNN TULA ABACA AGUST AZLON CAJUN CAROA CHOEL ERIZO FIBRE GRAIN HARLE ISOTE ISTLE IXTLE IZOTE KENAF KITUL MURVA OAKUM RAMIE RAPHE SIMAL SISAL STRAW TERAP TOSSA TUCUM VIVER AMIRAY ARGHAN BINDER BUNTAL BURITI CABUYA CATENA DACRON EMBIRA FIBRIL FIMBLE HINOKI KANAFF KENDIR KOHEMP MUCUNA NYTRIL RAFFIA SALAGO STAPLE STRAND STRING SUTURE THREAD TUCUMA TURURI VINYON YACHAN ZAPUPE ACETATE ACRYLIC ANONANG ARAMINA BASSINE CANTALA CASCARA CHANDUL CHINGMA COQUITA ESPARTO FILASSE FUNICLE GEBANGA GRAVATA GUAXIMA GUMIHAN HUARIZO KERATTO KITTOOL MOCMAIN PALMITE PANGANE PAUKPAN POCHOTE SABUTAN CANAPINA CURRATOW FILAMENT HARAKEKE HENEQUEN PIASSAVA TOQUILLA TRONADOR
(— FROM PEACOCK FEATHERS) MARL
(— OF PALM) DOH LIF ERUC COYOL COROZO GOMUTI KITTUL COQUITA GEBANGA
(—S OF FLAX) HARE
(CLUSTER OF —S) NEP

(COARSE —) KEMP
(COCONUT —) COIR KYAR
(COTTON —) LINT STAPLE
(FLAX —) TOW
(KNOT OF —) NOIL
(MANUFACTURED —) DYNEL ORLON ESTRON ACRILAN SPANDEX
(MATTED —) SHAG
(MINERAL —) ASBESTOS
(MUSCLE —) RHABDIUM
(NERVE —) EFFERENT DEPRESSOR
(PULVERIZED —) FLOCK
(SILKY —) PULU KAPOK KUMBI YACHAN CASTULI
(TWISTED —S) STRAND
(WASTE —) FLY GOUT
(WASTE —S) FLOSS
(WOODY —) BAST GRAIN SCUTCH
(PL.) FUZZ KERATTO
(PREF.) FIBRO IN(O)

FIBRIL AXONEME DESMOSE MYONEME MYOPHAN

FIBRILS (SUFF.) (NETWORK —) SPONGIA(E)(N) SPONGIUM

FIBRIN GLUTEN MYOSIN

FIBROCARTILAGE FABELLA MENISCUS

FIBROID DESMOID

FIBROMA INOMA FIBROID

FIBROUS FIBROSE STRINGY NEMALINE

FIBULA LACE CLASP BROOCH BUCKLE PERONE SPLINT
(PREF.) PERONEO PERONO

FICHE FILMCARD

FICKLE GERY DIZZY FALSE GIDDY LIGHT UNSAD HARLOT KITTLE MOBILE PUZZLE SHIFTY VOLAGE WANKLE WANKLY CASALTY CASELTY FLATTER MOONISH MOVABLE MUTABLE VAINFUL VARIANT VOLUBLE GOSSAMER MOVEABLE SKITTISH STIRRING UNSTABLE UNSTEADY VARIABLE VOLATILE WAVERING

FICKLENESS CHANGE LEVITY EASINESS FICKLETY VARIANCE

FICO FIG FIGO TANTI

FICTILE FIGULINE

FICTION BAM TALE FABLE FALSE NOVEL ROMAN STORY DECEIT DEVICE FABULA FITTEN LEGEND COINAGE FANTASY FIGMENT FORGERY MARCHEN NOVELRY ROMANCE ROMANZA KAILYARD PHANTASY PRETENCE PRETENSE

FICTITIOUS MADE BOGUS DUMMY FALSE PHONY FABLED POETIC ASSUMED FEIGNED PHANTOM FABULOUS FICTIOUS MYTHICAL ROMANTIC SIMULATE SPURIOUS LEGENDARY
(PREF.) PSEUD(O)

FICUS PYRULA

FID PRICK NORMAN PRICKER SPLICER

FIDDLE BOW BOX GIG SAW VIOL CHEAT CROWD GEIGE GIGUE GUDOK CHORUS FITHEL POTTER TRIFLE URHEEN VIOLIN CHROTTA SARANGI SWINDLE HUMSTRUM

(— STRING) THAIRM
(— WITH) TWIDDLE
FIDDLER CRAB VIOLER VIOLIN CROWDER SCRAPER SIXPENCE
FIDDLER CRAB RACER FIDDLER OCYPODE SOLDIER
FIDDLESTICKS PSHAW FIDDLE
FIDELIO (CHARACTER IN —) ROCCO FIDELIO LEONORE PIZARRO JACQUINO FLORESTAN MARZELLINE
(COMPOSER OF —) BEETHOVEN
FIDELITY TRUE ARDOR FAITH PIETY TROTH TRUTH FEALTY HONESTY LOYALTY ADHESION DEVOTION RELIGION VERACITY CONSTANCY
FIDGET MOP FIKE FIRK FUSS ROIL FIDGE FITCH HOTCH SHRUB SHRUG WORRY BREVIT FIGGLE FISSLE FISTLE FRIDGE FUSSER HIRSEL JIFFLE JIGGET NESTLE NIBBLE NIGGLE TIDDLE TRIFLE VIGGLE WORRIT NERVOUS RESTLESS TWITCHET
(— ABOUT TRIFLES) SPOFFLE
(STATE OF —) FANTAD FANTOD
(PL.) JUMPS
FIDGETY FIKIE FUSSY ITEMY FEISTY FIGENT FLISKY KITTLE UNEASY RESTIVE TWITCHY RESTLESS
FIDUCIARY TRUSTEE TRUSTFUL
FIE SISS FAUGH
FIEF FEE HAN FEUD FEOFF TIMAR ZIAMET SATSUMA SUBFIEF BENEFICE
(— HOLDER) TIMARIOT
FIELD LEA LOT ACRE AGER AREA BENT CAMP FELL FLAT HADE INAM LAND LIST MEAD PALE PARK RAND TOWN WONG BRECK CAMPO CHAMP CLOUR CROFT EARTH GLEBE INNAM LAYER MILPA NILPA PADDY RANGE ROWEN SAWAH TILTH VELDE ARRISH CAMPUS CAREER CHAMPE DOMAIN FURROW GARDEN GROUND MACHAR MATTER MEADOW PADANG PINGLE SHIELD SPHERE CHARMEL COMPASS CULTURE DIAMOND FERRING GARSTON INFIELD MOWLAND NEWTAKE PADDOCK PARROCK PIGHTLE PURVIEW QUILLET TERRAIN THWAITE TILLAGE CLEARING PROVINCE
(— ADJOINING HOUSE) CROFT
(— AT CRICKET) SCOUT
(— OF ACTIVITY) GAME ARENA BARONY SPHERE TERRAIN
(— OF BATTLE) PLAIN
(— OF BLOODSHED) ACELDAMA AKELDAMA
(— OF CONTROL) DOMAIN
(— OF ENDEAVOR) BUSINESS
(— OF SNOW) NEVE SNOWPACK
(— OF STUDY) GROUND
(— ON WHICH GRASS IS GROWN) MEAD MEADOW
(— SOWN FOR TWO SUCCESSIVE YEARS) HOOK
(ENCLOSED —) AGER TOWN

CLOSE CROFT
(FOOTBALL —) GRIDIRON
(FRUITFUL —) CHARMEL
(GRASSY —) LEA PEN GARSTON
(HOP —) HOPYARD
(LAVA —) PEDREGAL
(LITTLE-KNOWN —) BYWAY
(NEW GOLD —) RUSH
(PLOWED —) FURROW
(RICE —) SAWAH
(SMALL —) HAW CLOSE CROFT PADDOCK
(SPORTS —) ARENA PITCH
(STUBBLE —) HIRSH ROWEN ARRISH GRATTEN GRATTON
(TILTING —) LISTS
(TOBACCO —) VEGA
(UNEXPLOITED —) FRONTIER
(UNPLOWED EDGE OF —) RAND
(PL.) FIELDEN
(PREF.) AGRI AGRO ARVI CAMPI
FIELD BALM SHEEPMINT
FIELD CAMOMILE OXEYE
FIELDER GLOVEMAN
(CRICKET —) SLIP COVER FIELD GULLY POINT SCOUT GULLEY INFIELDER
FIELDFARE FELT JACK REDLEG FELLFARE HILLBIRD JACKBIRD REDSHANK SNOWBIRD VELTFARE
FIELD MADDER SPURWORT
FIELD MOUSE VOLE MIGALE
FIELDPIECE GUN AMUSETTE GALLOPER
FIELD SCABIOUS BLUECAP
FIELDWORK LUNET REDAN LUNETTE
FIEND FEN FOE PUG FEND FYND DEMON DEVIL ENEMY SATAN TRULL WIZARD SHAITAN SUCCUBA TITIVIL BARBASON SUCCUBUS
FIENDISH CRUEL WICKED DEMONIC FIENDLY SATANIC DEMONIAC DEVILISH DIABOLIC INFERNAL
FIERCE ILL BOLD FELL GRIM KEEN RUDE THRO WILD WOOD ASPER BREME CRUEL EAGER FELON HATEL ORPED RETHE SHARP SMART STARK STERN STOUR STOUT WROTH ARDENT FEROCE GOTHIC HETTER IMMANE LUPINE RAGING SAVAGE SAVAGE STURDY UNMEEK UNMILD WICKED BRUTISH FERVENT FURIOSO FURIOUS GRIMFUL INHUMAN MANKIND RABIOUS RAMPANT SCADDLE VICIOUS VIOLENT STERNFUL TIGERISH
(PREF.) LABRO
FIERCE-EYED WALLEYED
FIERCELY FELL HARD FELLY FIERCE
FIERCENESS FURY FEROCITY
FIERY HOT RED ADUST FIRED QUICK SHARP ARDENT FLASHY IGNITE BURNING FERVENT FLAMING FURIOUS GLOWING HOTHEAD IGNEOUS PARCHED PEPPERY VIOLENT ADUSTIVE CHOLERIC FEVERISH FRAMPOLD INFLAMED PHRAMPEL SPIRITED SPITFIRE VEHEMENT

FIERY ANGEL (CHARACTER IN —) RENATA AGRIPPA HEINRICH RUPPRECHT MEPHISTOPHELES
(COMPOSER OF —) PROKOFIEV
FIERY RED SANDIX
FIESTA FETE FERIA PARTY HOLIDAY
(— COSTUME) POLLERA
FIFE STICK PIFERO PIFFERO
FIFTEEN FIVE
(PREF.) PENTADEC(A)
FIFTEENTH DOUBLETE
FIFTH QUINT QUINTIN HEMIOLIA
(PREF.) QUINT(I)
FIFTY (— YEAR ANNIVERSARY) JUBILEE
FIFTY-FIFTY EVEN
FIG RIG FICO ARRAY BREBA DRESS ELEME ELEMI PIPAL SABRA TANTI BALETE BALITI FOUTER FOUTRA GINGER LOBFIG PEEPUL TRIFLE FURBISH GONDANG SICONUS SYCONUS WARINGIN
(— CROP) MAMME
(PREF.) FICI SYCO
FIG BASKET CABAS
FIGHT BOX MIX WAP WAR WIN BEAT BEEF BLUE BOUT CAMP CLEM COCK COPE COWP CRAB CUFF DUEL FLOG FRAY LAKE MEET MELL MILL SHOW SLUG SPAR TILT WAGE YOKE BANDY BRAWL CLASH FIELD FLOLT HURRY JOUST MATCH MELEE RAMMY SCRAP SHINE SPURN STOUR TOUSE AFFRAY AFFRAY BARNEY BATTLE BICKER BLOWUP COMBAT DEBATE FEUCHT FRACAS FRAISE HASSLE IMPUGN MEDDLE OPPOSE RELUCT REPUGN RESIST RIPPIT RUFFLE SHOWER STOUSH STRIFE STRIKE STRIVE TOUSEL TURNUP BARGAIN BRABBLE CONTEND CONTEST COUNTER JOURNEY QUARREL RUCTION SIMULTY TUILYIE WARFARE CONFLICT DOGFIGHT DUOMACHY FINISHER GUNFIGHT MILITATE SKIRMISH SLUGFEST SQUABBLE STRUGGLE TIRRIVEE TIRRWIRR TRAVERSE
(— AGAINST) BUCK OPPUGN
(— BETWEEN TWO) DUEL DUOMACHY
(— FOR) SERVE CHAMPION
(— WITH CLUB) TIMBER
(FIST —) RIPPIT TURNUP
(SEA —) NAUMACHY
(STREET —) HABBLE
(SUFF.) MACHIA MACHY
FIGHTER PUG VAMP BOXER COCKER BATTLER DUELIST SLUGGER SOLDIER WARRIOR ANDABATA BARRATER BARRATOR CHAMPION GUERILLA PUGILIST SCRAPPER
(FIRE —) EXEMPT HOTSHOT
(GUERILLA —) MAQUIS
FIGHTING BLOW ACTION AFFRAY DEBATE WARLIKE CONFLICT MILITANT
(— WITH SHADOW) SCIAMACHY
FIGHTING FISH PLAKAT

FIGLIA DI JORIO, LA (CHARACTER IN —) MILA ALIGI LAZARO
(COMPOSER OF —) PIZZETTI
FIG MARIGOLD SAMH MESEM FICOID FOXCHOP FICOIDAL
FIGMENT IDEA FICTION
FIGPECKER BECCAFICO
FIGURATE FLORID FIGURAL FIGURED FIGURATO
FIGURATION FORM SHAPE DESIGN OUTLINE
FIGURATIVE FLORID FIGURAL FIGURED FLOWERY TYPICAL ALLUSIVE TROPICAL
FIGURE FIG HUE VOL BOSH DOLL FORM IDEA SIGN STAR ANGLE ANTIC DATUM DIGIT FLIRT FRAME IMAGE MAGOT MOTIF SHAPE SPADE SPRIG AUMAIL BABOON CHANGE CIPHER COCKUP CUTOUT DEVICE EFFIGY EMBLEM ENTAIL FIGGER GOOGOL INCUSE NUMBER PERSON SCHEME SYMBOL TAILLE TATTOO CHASSIS CHEVRON CHIFFER CHIFFRE COMPUTE CONTOUR DRAWING GESTALT IMPRESS NUMERAL OUTLINE STATURE DIHEDRAL FIGURATE GRAFFITO HEXAGRAM LIKENESS SEMBLANT MARIONETTE
(— FORMED BY INTERSECTING LINES) KNOT
(— IN PRAYER) ORANT
(— IN WOOD GRAIN) BURL FLAKE
(— MADE OF CORN) KNACK
(— MADE OF 3 LINES) TRIGRAM TRIANGLE
(— OF SPEECH) IMAGE IRONY TROPE APORIA CLIMAX FLOWER SCHEME SIMILE VISION ZEUGMA ANALOGY IMAGERY CHIASMUS DIALLAGE METAPHOR METONYMY OXYMORON SYLLEPSIS ABSCISSION
(— OUT) BOTTOM
(— UP) ITEM
(— USED AS COLUMN) ATLAS TELAMON CARYATID
(— USED AS MAGIC SYMBOL) PENTACLE
(—S OF SPEECH) COLORS
(ANATOMICAL —) ECORCHE
(ARTIFICIAL —) GOLEM
(BIBLICAL —) ANGEL CHERUB
(CARVED —) GLYPH FIGURINE
(CENTRAL —) HERO
(CIRCULAR —) HOOP
(COMIC —) BILLIKEN
(CONSPICUOUS —) MARK
(CRESCENT-SHAPED —) LUNE
(DANCE —) SWING TRACE SQUARE PURPOSE ASSEMBLE PROMENADE
(DOMINANT —) CAPTAIN
(FEMALE —) ORANTE
(FOLDED PAPER —) FLEXAGON
(GEOMETRICAL —) BODY CONE CUBE LUNE PRISM RHOMB SOLID CIRCLE GNOMON ISAGON ISOGON OBLONG SECTOR SQUARE DIAGRAM ELLIPSE LOZENGE PELCOID RHOMBUS SECTION HEXAFOIL SPHEROID

(GREEK —) KOUROS
(GROTESQUE —) MAGOT BABOON MAXIMON
(HAVING FULL ROUNDED —) ZAFTIG ZOFTIG
(IDEAL —) EIDOLON
(IMAGINARY —) BOGEYMAN
(INCISED —) INTAGLIO
(JAPANESE — ON GRAVE) HANIWA
(MUMMYLIKE —) USHABTI
(MUSICAL —) IDEA LICK OSTINATO
(ODD —) MAUMET
(OVAL —) SWASH ELLIPSE
(PREHISTORIC —) CHACMOL CHACMOOL
(QUADRILLE —) POULE
(QUEER —) GIG
(RHETORICAL —) COLOR COLOUR
(RHYTHMIC —) SNAP
(SCULPTURED —) CANEPHOR
(SHADOW —) SKIAGRAM
(SKATING —) SPIRAL BRACKET COUNTER
(SPINDLE-SHAPED —) FUSEE FUZEE
(STUFFED —) DUMMY
(SYLLOGISTIC —) SCHEMA
(SYMBOLIC —) MORAL EMBLEM
(TAILOR'S —) MANNEQ MANNEQUIN
(TRIANGULAR —) TRIQUET
(UNDRAPED —) NUDE
(WINGED —) ANGEL EIDOLON
(PL.) SPILING
(PREF.) EID(O)
(SUFF.) HEDRON
FIGURED FIGURY FACONNE
FIGUREHEAD DUMMY FRONT SCROLL
FIGURINE TANAGRA CRIOPHORE
FIGWORT BARTSIA PILEWORT PAULOWNIA PENSTEMON BLUEHEARTS

FIJI
BAY: MBYA NATEWA NGALOA SAVUSAVU
CAPITAL: SUVA
EASTERN GROUP: LAU
ISLAND: ELD KIA ONO AIWA KIOA KORO MALI NGAU VIWA WAIA AGATA MANGO MOALA NAIAU RAMBI MAMOLO MATUKU MBENGA MBULIA NAIRAI NAVITI NGAMEA OVALAU TOTOYA YASAWA YENDUA KAMBARA KANDAVU LAKEMBA TAVEUNI VITILEVU
MOUNTAIN: NARARU MONAVATU
NIECE OR NEPHEW: VASU
POINT: VUYA
TOWN: BA MAU MBA MOMI NADI REWA SUVA TUVU NANDI THUVU ETUMBA LABASA NALOTO NAMOLI NARATA NASALA NAVOLA SAGARA LAUTOKA VATUKOULA

FIJIAN VITIAN
FILAGO GIFOLA
FILAMENT BRIN DOWL HAIR HARL NEMA PILE SILK CHIVE CHORD FIBER FIBRE FILUM TWIRE CIRRUS ELATER HEATER MANTLE STRAND THREAD CIRRHUS FIMBRIA FLIMMER RHIZOID TEXTILE PARANEMA PHACELLA STERIGMA PARAPHYSIS
(— OF FEATHER) BARB DOWL DOWLE
(— OF MINERAL) STRINGER
(— OF SILK) BRIN
(—S OF FLAX OR HEMP) HARL
(TWISTED —S) STRAND
(PL.) HACKLE
FILAMENTOUS BYSSOID STRINGY HAIRLIKE
FILANDERS BACKWORM
FILARIASIS MUMU
FILBERT HAZEL COBNUT HAZELNUT
(SIEVE OF —S) PRICKLE
FILCH BOB FUB NIM ROB BEAT DRIB FAKE PILK PRIG SMUG SNIP FETCH LURCH PILCH SNAKE SNEAK STEAL CLOYNE PILFER SMOUCH STRIKE CABBAGE PURLOIN
FILE BOX ROW BARB DECK LINE LIST RANK RASP RATE RISP ROLL SLIP STUB EMERY ENTER FLOAT FOUND GRAIL INDEX LABEL RIFLE TRACK TRAIN ACCUSE ANSWER BEFOUL CARLET DEFILE FILACE RASCAL RUBBER STRING TOPPER ARCHIVE ARRANGE CHOILER CONDEMN DOSSIER EXHIBIT GRAILLE QUANNET TICKLER DRAWFILE
(— DOWN SAW TEETH) JOINT
(— OF SIX SOLDIERS) ROT
(— OFF) DEFILE
(— USED BY COMBMAKERS) GRAIL TOPPER GRAILER GRAILLE
(— WITH COURT OF LAW) BOX
(COARSE —) RAPE
(CURVED —) RIFFLER
FILE BOX SOLANDER
FILEFISH LIJA UNIE TURBOT UNICORN BALISTID FOOLFISH PLECTOGNATH
FILIAL PIUS SONLY
FILIBUSTER FLIBUTOR STONEWALL
FILING RASION LIMATION
(PL.) LEMEL SCOBS LIMAIL
FILIPENDULA ULMARIA
FILIPINO KALINGA KANKANAI
FILL EKE HIT PAD BUNG CLOY CRAM FEED GLUT HOLD LADE LINE MEET PANG QUAR SATE STOP TEEM BELLY BLOAT BULGE CHOKE ESTOP FLOCK GORGE KEDGE PITCH PRIME STORE STUFF CHARGE FULFIL INFUSE OCCUPY QUERRE SUPPLY AGGRADE DISTEND ENLARGE EXECUTE FILLING FRAUGHT FULFILL IMPLETE INFLATE INVOLVE PERFECT PERFORM PERVADE PLENISH SATIATE SATISFY SUFFUSE COMPLETE COMPOUND FREQUENT PERMEATE
(— COMPLETELY) SATURATE
(— CUP TO BRIM) BRIM CROWN BUMPER
(— FULL) FARCE STUFF

(— HORSES' TEETH) BISHOP
(— IN) NOG KILL STOP SLUSH INFILL BALLAST
(— IN CHINKS) LIP
(— IN WITH RUBBLE) HEART
(— INTERSTICES) BLIND
(— LEATHER WITH OIL) FAT
(— OUT) BUNCH SWELL
(— TO EXCESS) CROWD FLOOD CONGEST SURFEIT
(— TO OVERFLOWING) FLOW THWACK
(— UP) STOP BRICK CHOKE CLOSE ESTOP STOAK FULFIL IMPACT STODGE PLENISH
(— UP HOLE) STIFLE
(— WITH) SWILL
(— WITH ALE) RACK
(— WITH ANXIETY) ALARM ALARUM
(— WITH CARGO) STOW
(— WITH CLAY) CAT PUG
(— WITH FEAR) APPAL APPALL
(— WITH HORROR) ABHOR
(— WITH LIGHT) GLUT
(— WITH LIQUOR) TUN SKINK
(— WITH METAL) BACK
(— WITH MORTAR) GROUT
(— WITH ODORS) EMBALM
(— WITH RUBBISH) BASH
(— WITH TERROR) AMAZE
(ONE'S —) SLITHERS
FILLED BIG ALIVE FLUSH QUICK SATED SOLID GRAVID LOADED CROWDED HAUNTED IMPLETE OPPLETE REPLETE SWOLLEN FREQUENT INSTINCT POPULOUS
(— OUT) BOLD FULL
(— TO EXCESS) FLOWN
(— WITH EXCITEMENT) ABUZZ
(— WITH FEAR) AFRAID
(— WITH INTERSTICES) AREOLAR
(— WITH MOISTURE) FAT
(— WITH PRIDE) YNPRIDID
FILLER GARA BOGUS SILEX SILKA SQUIB BALAAM LIGNIN FILLING LOADING WRAPPER
FILLET BAND BONE GIRT LIST ORLE ORLO SOLE TAPE AMPYX CROWN FACET FILET GORGE LABEL LEDGE MITER MITRE QUIRK SCROD SNOOD STRAP STRIA TIARA VITTA ANADEM BENDEL BINDER CIMBIA COMBLE CORONA DIADEM FASCIA INFULA LISTEL NORSEL POTONG QUADRA REGLET REGULA RIBBON ROLLER TAENIA TURBAN TURBOT ANNULET BANDAGE BANDEAU CLOISON CORONET EYEBROW FACETTE FRONTAL GARLAND LAMBEAU MOLDING TRESSON TRINGLE BANDELET CINCTURE FRONTLET HAIRLACE HEADBAND PLATBAND TRESSOUR TRESSURE UNDERCUT
(PREF.) TAENI(A)(O)
FILLIFORM CATENOID
FILL-IN MODESTY
FILLING GOB FILL MODE PLUG WEFT WOOF INLAY STUFF FILLER STOPPING STUFFING
(— OF GAPS) CONFAB
(— UP) CLOSURE RIPIENO

(BASKET —) SLEW
(DENTAL —) INLAY
(SILK —) SHIKII
FILLIP BLOW FLIP SNAP SPUR TOSS URGE FILIP FLASH FLIRT FLISK IMPEL BUFFET INCITE MOMENT PROJECT STIMULATE
FILLY COLT FOAL GIRL
FILM H BRAT HAZE HULL KELL MIST SCUM SKIM SKIN VEIL WEFT BLEAR COVER FLAKE FLICK GLAZE LAYER PEARL PLATE SCALE SHOOT SHORT BUBBLE MOTHER PATINA SCRUFF CUTICLE FEATURE PHILOME TAFFETA TOPICAL TRAILER BEESWING FIRECOAT NEGATIVE PELLICLE MICROFILM MONOLAYER
(— OF AIR) PLASTRON
(— OF ICE) VERGLAS
(— OF OIL) SLICK
(— OF TARTAR) SCALE PLAQUE
(— ON COPPER) PATINA
(— ON PORRIDGE) BRAT
(— ON WINE) BEESWING
(— OVER EYE) WEB
(DISCARDED —) OUTTAKE
(POLYESTER —) MYLAR
(X-RAY —) BITEWING
FILMY FINE HAZY GAUZY MISTY SHEER WISPY CLOUDY CLOUDED TIFFANY FILMLIKE GOSSAMER
FILOSOFO DI CAMPAGNA, IL
(CHARACTER IN —) NARDO EUGENIA LESBINA RINALDO TRITEMIO
(COMPOSER OF —) GALUPPI
FILTER CLAY RAPE SIFT SILE DRAIN SEITZ SIEVE BOUGIE CANDLE COLATE CONTEX LAUTER MEDIUM PURIFY REFINE STRAIN BAGHOUSE COLATURE FILTRATE INFILTER STRAINER
FILTERER CLARIFIER
FILTH FEN KET DIRT DUNG GORE MUCK NAST SLUT SOIL SUDS ADDLE BILGE DRECK GLEAM GLEET JAKES POUCE SWILL DEFILE FULYIE FULZIE IMMUND ORDURE SORDES SORDOR VERMIN SLOTTER SQUALOR SULLAGE FOULNESS MUCKMENT SNOTTERY WORTHING COLLUVIES
(PREF.) COPR(O)
FILTHINESS MUCOR SQUALOR SULLAGE CENOSITY
FILTHY LOW FOUL MIRY VILE BAWDY DIRTY DROVY DUNGY GROSS LAIRY MUCKY NASTY AUGEAN BAWDRY CRUMBY CRUMMY CRUSTY DIRTEN IMMUND IMPURE SORDID BEASTLY BESTIAL HOGGISH OBSCENE PIGGISH SQUALID UNCLEAN ORDUROUS SLUTTISH
FILTRATE MALLEIN
FILTRATION BAGGING COLATURE
FIN ARM RAG RIB ANAL BURR FANG HAND KEEL SAIL FLASH PINNA CAUDAL FINLET ACANTHA FEATHER FLIPPER PINNULE VENTRAL FORELIMB PECTORAL
(BOMB —) VANE

(PREF.) PTER(O) PTERYG(O)

FINAGLE CHEAT TRICK REVOKE
DECEIVE FENAGLE

FINAL LAST UTTER FINIAL LATTER
RUNOFF ULTIMA UTMOST
DARREIN DERNIER EXTREME
FINALIS OUTMOST PARTING
SUPREME ABSOLUTE DECISIVE
DECRETAL DEFINITE EVENTUAL
FAREWELL ULTIMATE
(— STANZA) ENVOI
(NOT —) NISI

FINALE END CODA FINIS ENDING
CLOSING

FINALITY END ERGO

FINALLY YET LAST AFINE LASTLY

FINANCE TAX BACK BANK FUND
GOODS REVENUE TAXATION
TREASURE

FINANCIAL FISCAL MONETARY
PECUNIARY

FINANCIER BANIAN BANYAN
MONEYMAN
(AUTHOR OF —) DREISER
(CHARACTER IN —) FRANK HENRY
AILEEN BUTLER EDWARD SEMPLE
STENER LILLIAN WINGATE
COWPERWOOD

FINBACK WHALE FINNER GIBBAR
FINFISH RORQUAL JUBARTAS

FINCH FINK MORO PAPE JUNCO
SERIN TERIN BURION CANARY
CITRIL LINNET PALILA SISKIN
TOWHEE BUNTING CHEWINK
PEEWEEP REDHEAD REDPOLL
SENEGAL SPARROW TANAGER
WAXBILL AMADAVAT COMBASOU
FIRETAIL GOULDIAN GROSBEAK
HAWFINCH LONGSPUR
SNOWBIRD BRAMBLING
SEEDEATER
(— FLOCK) CHARM

FIND GET RUG MEET VAIL CATCH
INVENT LOCATE STRIKE ADJUDGE
FINDING DISCOVER SCROUNGE
(— FAULT) CARP BARGE BLAME
CAVIL GRONT KNOCK PINCH
SCOLD NATTER ARRAIGN
(— GUILTY) ATTAINT CONVICT
(— OUT) AFIND CHECK ESSAY
LEARN SPELL TROVE DETECT
CONTRIVE DECIPHER DISCOVER
(— REFUGE) BIEL BIELD
(— SOLUTION) SOLVE
(— THE SUM) SUMMATE
(— TIME) EEM

FINDER SIGHT SEEKER FOUNDER

FINDING TROVER INQUEST
VERDICT

FINE CRO GAY RUM TAX BEIN BIEN
BOTE BRAW CAIN CROP DIRE
ERIC FAIR GENT GOOD HUNK
JAKE LEVY MOOI NICE PURE RARE
SEPT SLAP TALL TEAR TINE TRIM
ABWAB BONNY BRAVE BULLY
CHECK DAISY DANDY DELIE
DUCKY FRAIL GAUDY GRAND
GREAT HUNKY ISSUE KELTY
MULCT NIFTY NOBLE RORTY
SHARP SHEER SMALL SPALE
SWANK SWEET UNLAW WALLY
WHITE AMENDE AMERCE BONNIE
BONZER BRAWLY BRIGHT CHEESY

CHOICE CLEVER COSTLY CRAFTY
DAINTY FACETE FINISH FLUTED
GERSUM HERIOT HUNGRY
INCONY ORNATE PEACHY PRETTY
PROPER QUAINT RANSOM
SARAAD SCONCE SERENE SILKEN
SLIGHT SPIFFY TENDER CLARIFY
CONDEMN CORKING CREANCE
CUNNING ELEGANT ESTREAT
FERDWIT FINICAL FORFEIT
FRAGILE GALANAS GALLANT
GALLOWS GRADELY GRASSUM
IMMENSE MARCHET MERCHET
MURDRUM ORFGILD PENALTY
PERFECT REFINED SCUTAGE
STAVING TENUOUS TOPPING
VALIANT WERGILD ABSOLUTE
BLOODWIT BUDGEREE CAVALIER
CLINKING DELICATE DUSTLIKE
FLITWITE FOOTGELD HANDSOME
LASHLITE MARITAGE PENALIZE
PESHKASH PINPOINT PLEASANT
SKILLFUL SPLENDID SUPERIOR
WARDWITE WIRESPUN
MAGNIFICENT
(— AGAINST SERVANTS) CHECK
(— FOR KILLING) BOTE
(— IN LIEU OF FLOGGING) HIDE
(BLOOD —) ERIC WITE
(OSTENTATIOUSLY —) GAUDY
(PRINTING OFFICE —) SOLACE
(VERY —) BUNKUM SPLENDID
(PL.) SILT FLOUR
(PREF.) LEPT(O)

FINE-DRAW RANTER

FINE-LOOKING SPICY WALLY
SPIFFY

FINELY FINE GAILY GAYLY WALLY
BRAGLY RARELY SMALLY
BRAVELY SMICKLY SWEETLY

FINENESS ALLOY GRAIN TRICK
DENIER FINERY PURITY THREAD
EXILITY FINESSE DELICACY
(— AS RECKONED BY CARATS)
TITLE
(— OF FABRIC) CUT GAGE GAUGE
(— OF METAL) STANDARD
(— OF PITCH) COUNTS

FINERY GAUD WALY ARRAY
BRAWS WALLY BAUBLE BAWDRY
BEAUTY FEGARY GAIETY GAYETY
TAWDRY BRAVERY GAUDERY
REGALIA BEAUETRY ELEGANCE
FINENESS FOFARRAW FOLDEROL
FOOFARAW FRIPPERY ORNAMENT
RIBANDRY

FINESPUN HAIR THIN TWITTERY

FINESSE ART CHEAT SKILL TRICK
PURITY SERENE CUNNING
ARTIFICE DELICACY SUBTLETY
THINNESS

FINFOOT SUNBIRD

FINGER TOY PAUT PLAY DIGIT
INDEX PINKY DACTYL HANDLE
MEDDLE MEDIUS PADDLE PILFER
PINKIE POLLEX ANNULAR DIGITAL
MINIMUM MINIMUS PURLOIN
DIGITIZE THRIMBLE
(— INFECTION) FELON
(FORE —) INDEX
(LITTLE —) PINKY PINKIE PIRLIE
MINIMUS AURICULAR
(RING —) ANNULAR

RINGMAN ANNULARY
(PL.) HOOKS
(PREF.) DACTYL(IO)(O) DIGITI
DIGITO
(SUFF.) DACTYLIA DACTYLOUS

FINGERFLOWER FOXGLOVE

FINGERING DOIGTE

FINGERLING PARR TROUTLET

FINGERNAIL DIGGER
(RELATING TO —) ONYCHOID
(SUFF.) ONYCHA ONYCHES
ONYCHIA ONYCHIUM ONYCHUS
ONYX

FINGERPRINT DAB ARCH LOOP
WHORL LATENT

FINGERROOT FOXGLOVE

FINGERSTALL COT

FINIAL EPI NOB TEE TOP CROP
KNOB KNOP KNOT BUNCH CREST
CROWN FINAL POPPY PRICKET
ORNAMENT PINNACLE

FINICAL NICE FUSSY CHOOSY
DAINTY DAPPER JAUNTY PRETTY
PRISSY SPRUCE CHOOSEY FINICKY
FINIKIN FOPPISH MINCING
PERJINK PICKING SMICKER
DELICATE

FINICALLY SMICKLY GINGERLY

FINICKY NICE DINKY FIKEY FIKIE
PRISSY FINICAL FINIKIN PRECISE

FINISH DO DIE END CHAR EDGE
FACE FINE MILL OVER PASS SINK
SNUG STOP BLOOM BOUND
CEASE CHARE CHEVE CLOSE
CROWN FEEZE GLACE GLAZE
LIMIT SPEED UPPER BOTTOM
BUSHEL FULFIL FULLDO PLISSE
POLISH SETTLE WINDUP ABSOLVE
ACHIEVE DEPETER EXECUTE
FLUTING FULFILL PERFECT
SURFACE COMPLETE CONCLUDE
DEPRETER DRESSING FINALIZE
FROSTING TERMINAL
(— CAREFULLY) NEATEN
(— CLOTH) BURL CONVERT
(— METAL) PLANISH
(— OF FABRIC) CIRE HOLLAND
(— OF PAPER) STIPPLE
(— OFF) DASH CRUSH ABSOLVE
ACCOMPLISH
(— STONE) COMB BOAST DROVE
(— WITH A SEAM) FELL
(— WORK) FLOOR
(CALENDERED —) CHASING
(DULL —) MAT MATTE
(GLAZED —) GLACE LACKER
LACQUER
(STUCCO —) SPATTER
(SUPERFICIAL —) BLAZONRY

FINISHED BY DID OER PAU ARCH
DONE DOWN FINE GONE OVER
PURE RIPE SHOT ENDED EXACT
KAPUT NAPOO ROUND CLOSED
NAPOOH ORNATE PERFECT
REFINED ROUNDED STOPPED
THROUGH BANKRUPT CLIMAXED
GOFFERED LUSTERED POLISHED
(— IN NATURAL COLOR) FAIR
(— WITH NAP) BRUSHED
(ABSOLUTELY —) SUNK
(HIGHLY —) SUAVE
(IMPERFECTLY —) RUDE

FINISHER EYER ENDER CORKER

GAFFER BEETLER CEMENTER
ENAMELER SOCKDOLOGER

FINISHING CRUSHING

FINITE LIMITED

FINLAND

CAPITAL: HELSINKI HELSINGFORS
COIN: PENNI MARKKA
DIVISION: IJORE VILLIPURI
GOD: TAPIO JUMALA
ISLAND: ALAND KARLO AALAND
HAILUTO VALLGRUND
ISTHMUS: KARELIA
LAKE: JUO MUO KEMI KIVI NASI
OULU PURU PYHA SIMO ENARE
HAUKI INARI KALLA LAPPA
LESTI PUULA LENTUA SAIMAA
SOUNNE SYVARI KOITERE
NILAKKA PIELINEN
LANGUAGE: AVAR LAPP UGRIC
MAGYAR OSTYAK TAVAST
SAMOYED ESTONIAN
MEASURE: KANNU TUNNA VERST
FATHOM SJOMIL OTTINGER
SKALPUND TUNNLAND
MOUNTAIN: HALTIA
NAME: SUOMI
PARLIAMENT: EDUSKUNTA
PROVINCE: HAME KYMI OULU
LAPPI VAASA KUOPIO MIKKELI
UUSIMAA
RIVER: II KALA OULU SIMO TENO
IVALO LOTTA OUNAS SIIKA
IIJOKI LAPUAN MUONIO PASVIK
TORNIO KITINEN KOKEMAKI
TOWN: ABA ABO KEM KEMI OULU
PORI VASA ENARE ESPOO
KOTKA LAHTI TURKU VAASA
IMATRA KUOPIO MIKKELI
TAMPERE HELSINKI
TRIBE: HAME VEPS VEPSE UGRIAN
KARJALAISET SUOMALAISET

FINLET PINNULE

FINN FIOUN INGER OSTIAK OSTYAK
TAVAST INGRIAN CHEREMIS
INGERMAN SWEKOMAN
(PL.) SUOMI

FINNISH
(PREF.) FENNO

FINNOCK HERLING

FINTA GIARDINIERA, LA
(CHARACTER IN —) ONESTI
ANCHISE ARMINDA BELFIORE
SANDRINA SERPETTA VIOLANTE
(COMPOSER OF —) MOZART

FIORD FJORD INLET

FIORIN KNOTGRASS

FIORITURA ORNAMENT

FIPPLE FLUTE RECORDER

FIR VER LARCH SAPIN BAUMIER
LASHORN PINABETE

FIR CLUB MOSS FOXFEET

FIRE CAN FEU LOW AGNI APOY
BALE BRIO BURN HEAT KILN
LOWE POOP SWAP SWOP ZEAL
ARDOR ARSON BLAST BLAZE
BREAK BURST EMPTY FEVER
GLEED INGLE LIGHT LOGHE
LOOSE LOUGH PLUFF SERVE
SHOOT SQUIB STOKE AROUSE
ENGHLE EXCITE FERVOR IGNITE
INCITE KINDLE SMUDGE SPIRIT

SPLEEN VULCAN ANIMATE
BONFIRE BURNING BURNOUT
CHIMNEY DISMISS EMITTER
EXPLODE FURNACE GLIMMER
INFLAME INSPIRE SMOLDER
BACKFIRE BALEFIRE CAMPFIRE
DETONATE HELLFIRE ILLUMINE
IRRITATE NEEDFIRE SMOULDER
VIVACITY PORCELAINIZE
(— A REVOLVER) FAN
(— ON) AFIRE
(— THE CHARGE) HIT
(— TWO ROUNDS) DOUBLE
(— UPON) GUN SPRAY
(CROSS —) GANTLET GAUNTLET
(DAMPENED —) SMOTHER
(FOREST —) BREAK
(LITTLE —) SPONK SPUNK
(MASSED —) ARTILLERY
(PEAT —) GREESAGH
(RUNNING-OUT —) DANDY
(SIGNAL —) BALE BEACON
BALEFIRE
(PREF.) EMPYRO IGNEO IGNI
PHLOGO PYR(ET)(ETO)(ITI)(O)
(SUFF.) PYRA

FIRE ALARM FIREBOX
FIREARM ARM GUN IRON SHOT
TUBE FIRER ORGAN PIECE RIFLE
JEZAIL MAGNUM MAUSER
MUSKET PISTOL POPPER
BOMBARD CARBINE CURRIER
DEMIHAG HANDGUN PINFIRE
SHOOTER SPANNER ARQUEBUS
BROWNING CULVERIN EXPELLER
EXPLODER PETRONEL REVOLVER
(PL.) HARDWARE ARTILLERY

FIRE ARROW MALLEOLUS
FIREBACK REREDOS MACARTNEY
FIREBALL BOLIDE
FIRE BEETLE COCUYO CUCUYO
ELATER ELATERID
FIREBOAT PALANDER
FIREBRAND BLAZE BRAND BLEERY
BOUTEFEU
FIREBRICK QUARLE
(PL.) GROG
FIREBUG BUG ARSONIST
FIRE CARRIER PORTFIRE
FIRECLAY THILL
FIRE COVER CURFEW CURPHEW
FIRECRACKER DEVIL SQUIB
BANGER PETARD SALUTE
CRACKER SNAPPER FIREWORK
WHIZBANG
FIRE-CURED DARK
FIREDAMP GAS FOULNESS
WILDFIRE
FIREDART PHALARICA
FIREDOG DOG IRON
FIRE ENGINE RIG TUB MANUAL
FIRE EXTINGUISHER SQUIRT
EXTINCTOR
FIRE FIGHTER EXEMPT HOTSHOT
FIREFLY CUCUYO FIREBUG
GLOWFLY LAMPFLY FIREWORM
GLOWWORM LAMPYRID
FIREGUARD FENDER
FIRELINE GUTTER
FIRELOCK FUSEE FUZEE SPANNER
FIREMAN VAMP FIRER FUELER
STOKER TEASER TIZEUR FIREBOY
HOSEMAN BAKEHEAD FURNACER

FIREPLACE FOCUS FOGON FORGE
FOYER GRATE INGLE TISAR
HEARTH CHIMNEY CHEMINEE
(— AND CHIMNEY) STACK
(— STONE) MANTEL
(PORTABLE —) BARBECUE
BARBEQUE
FIREPLUG PLUG HYDRANT
FIRER STOKER BLASTER
FIRESIDE SMOKE HEARTH
FIRESTAND HASTER HASTENER
FIRE THORN PYRACANTH
FIREWEED FIRETOP ROSEBAY
PILEWEED PILEWORT
FIREWOOD FIRE LENA SLAB WOOD
CHUNK FAGOT BILLET BILLOT
ELDING FIRING TALWOOD
FIREBOTE TALLWOOD TALSHIDE
FIREWORK JET SUN GERB DEVIL
GERBE PEEOY SAXON SHELL
WHEEL FIZGIG MAROON PETARD
ROCKET SALUTE SHOWER
TRACER CASCADE SERPENT
SPARKER TORPEDO FOUNTAIN
SPARKLER
(PL.) FUN FIRE
FIRE WORSHIPPER PARSI GHEBER
GHEBRE PARSEE
FIRING FIRE FUEL COUGH SALVO
BURNING DRUMFIRE
FIRKIN VESSEL
FIRM HUI PAT BUFF FAST HARD
IRON NASH SURE TAUT TRIG
TRIM CHAMP CORKY CRISP DENSE
FIRMA FIXED HARDY HOUSE
LOYAL RIGID SOLID SOUND STARK
STIFF STITH STOUT SWITH TIGHT
TOUGH HARDEN HEARTY SECURE
SETTLE SICCAR SICKER SINEWY
STABLE STANCH STEADY STEEVE
STOLID STRONG STURDY TRUSTY
ADAMANT CERTAIN COMPACT
COMPANY CONCERN CONFIRM
CONTEXT DECIDED DURABLE
STAUNCH UNMOVED CONSTANT
FAITHFUL FIDUCIAL OBDURATE
RESOLUTE SUBSTANT UNSHAKEN
(— BUT EASILY CUT) SEMISOFT
(NOT —) FUZZY
(PREF.) PAGIO
FIRMAMENT SKY DEEP POLE
CARRY CANOPY HEAVEN
EXPANSE EMPYREAN EMPYREUM
EXPANSUM
FIRMLY BUFF FAST FIRM HARD
SADLY STARK TIGHT HARDLY
SQUARE SURELY SOLIDLY
SECURELY STRONGLY
FIRMNESS BODY GRIT IRON
ETHAN PROOF FIXURE COURAGE
FIRMITY GRANITE BACKBONE
DECISION FASTNESS SECURITY
SOLIDITY STRENGTH TENACITY
FIRN NEVE
FIRST ERST FUST GULE HEAD HIGH
MAIN ALPHA CHIEF FORME NIEVE
PRIMA PRIME PRIMO MAIDEN
PRIMAL PRIMUS VIRGIN FIRSTLY
HIGHEST INITIAL LEADING
PREMIER PRIMARY EARLIEST
FOREHAND FOREMOST FORMERLY
ORIGINAL PARAVANT PREMIERE
PRINCEPS

(— PRIZE) BLUE
(— SERGEANT) TOP
(— STATE) DELAWARE
(PREF.) PRIMI PRIMO PROT(O)
(— IN TIME) ARCH
FIRSTBORN AYNE EIGNE ELDEST
FIRST-CLASS GAY TOP BOSS POSH
FLASH PRIME PUKKA BUNKUM
STUNNING
FIRST-FRUITS ANNATES
FIRSTHAND DIRECT PRIMARY
ORIGINAL
FIRST-RATE BOSS BRAG GOOD
JAKE MAIN SLAP BULLY DANDY
LUMMY PRIME SLEEK SLICK
SUPER SWELL BONSER BONZER
BOSKER CHEESY FAMOUS TIPTOP
BLIGHTY BOSHTER CAPITAL
SKOOKUM STELLAR TOPPING
CHAMPION CLINKING CLIPPING
TOPNOTCH
FIRTH ARM KYLE FRITH INLET
COPPICE ESTUARY
FISCAL BURSAL MONETARY
FISH AU ID AKU AWA AYU BIB CAT
COD DAB DAP DIB EEL FIN GAR
GIG GOO HEN IDE IHI JIG JUG
ORF RAY SAR TAI NIU BANK
BARB BASS BLAY BOCE BOGA
CARP CAST CERO CHUB CHUG
CHUM CLOD CRAB CUSK DACE
DORY DRAG DRAW DRUM ERSE
FUGU GADE GHOL GOBY GRIG
HAKE HIND HUCH HUSO JACK
JUNK LINE LING LOTE MADO
MERO MOLA OPAH PEAL PEGA
PIKE POOR POUT PRIM QUAB
RAIL RUDD RUFF SCAD SCUP
SEER SHAD SOLE SPET SPIN SPOT
TILE TORO TUNA ACARA AHOLE
AKULE ANGLE ATULE BEGTI
BETTA BINNY BLAIN BLEAK BOLTI
BOLTY BREAM BULLY BULTI
CABIO CATLA CHIRO CISCO COBIA
CONEY DANIO DORAB DRAIL
DRIFT DRIVE ELOPS ERIZO FLOAT
FLUKE FOGAS FRIAR GADID
GRUNT GUPPY HILSA HUCHO
JUREL KILLY LAKER LANCE
MANTA MIDGE MINIM MORAY
OTTER PERCH PIABA PLATY
PORGY POWAN POWER REINA
ROACH SAIDE SANGO SAURY
SHARK SKATE SMELT
SHOEK SNOOK SPRAT SQUID
SULEA SWEEP TENCH TETRA
TRABU TROLL TROUT TUNNY
UMBRA VIUVA VORAZ WAHOO
WHIFF AIMARA ALEVIN ANABAS
ANGLER BARBEL BARBER BENNET
BICHIR BISKOP BLENNY BONITO
BOWFIN BUMPER BURBOT
CALLOP CANDIL CAPLIN CARANX
CARIBE COELHO COTTID CREOLE
CUCHIA CUNNER DARTER DASSIE
DENTEX FISHET GANOID GINNEL
GULPER GUNNEL HAMLET
HAPUKU HILSAH HUSSAR INANGA
KOKOPU LAUNCE LEDGER LIGGER
LOUVAR MAIGRE MARLIN MENISE
MILTER MINNOW MOLLIE MOLOID
MULLET NONNAT PHOEBE PLAICE
POMPON PUFFER PUNECA

REDFIN REMORA ROBALO
ROUGHY RUNNER SABALO SALELE
SALEMA SALMON SAPSAP SARDEL
SAUGER SAUREL SERRAN SHINER
SIERRA SIMARA SPARID SUCKER
TAILER TAIMEN TANDAN TARPON
TAUTOG TESTAR TETARD TINOSA
TOMCOD TURBOT VENDIS
WALLER WEAVER WIRRAH
WRASSE ZINGEL ALEWIFE
ALFIONA ANCHOVY BACALAO
BARBUDO BATFISH BEARDIE
BERGYLT BERYCID BOXFISH
BRAGGLE BUFFALO BUMMALO
CABEZON CANDIRU CAPELIN
CAPLING CATFISH CAVALLA
CAVALLY CHIMERA CHROMID
CICHLID CLUPEID CONVICT
CORVINA COWFISH CRAPPIE
CROAKER CTENOID CUTLIPS
CYCLOID DRABBLE DREPANE
DRUMMER EELPOUT ESCOLAR
FATHEAD FINFISH GALJOEN
GEELBEC GEELBEK GOBIOID
GOGGLER GOLDEYE GOURAMI
GRAYSBY GROUPER GRUNION
GRUNTER GUAPENA GUAVINA
GUDGEON GULARIS GURNARD
GWYNIAD HADDOCK HAGFISH
HALIBUT HARMOOT HERRING
HINALEA HOGFISH HOUTING
ICEFISH ICHTHUS INCONNU
JAWFISH JEWFISH JUGULAR
LABROID LAGARTO LONGFIN
MACHETE MAHSEER MAYFISH
MOJARRA MOONEYE MORWONG
OARFISH OLDWIFE OQUASSA
PEGASUS PIGFOOT PINTADO
PIRANHA POISSON POLLACK
POMFRET POMPANO PUPFISH
RONQUIL SARGOAN SARDINE
SAUROID SAVELHA SAWFISH
SCALARE SCAROID SCHELLY
SCULPIN SENNETT SILURUS
SLEEPER SMUTTER SNAPPER
SOLDIER SPAWNER STERLET
SUNFISH TELEOST TOMTATE
TOPKNOT TORPEDO TUBFISH
UMBRANA UNICORN VENDACE
VIAJACA WAREHOU WAUBEEN
WHAPUKA WHAPUKU WHITING
ALBACORE ALFONSIN APOGONID
ARAPAIMA ATHERINE BAITFISH
BALISTID BIGMOUTH BILLFISH
BLENNOID BLUEBACK BLUEFISH
BOARFISH BONEFISH BRISLING
BROTULID BULLHEAD CACKEREL
CANCHITO CARANGID CARANGIN
CARDINAL CATALINA CATALUFA
CHANCITO CHIMAERA CHOANATE
CHROMIDE CORACINE CROSSOPT
CYPRINID DEALFISH DIPNEUST
DITREMID DONCELLA DRAGONET
DRUMFISH DUMBFISH ECHENEID
ELEOTRID EPISCATE FALLFISH
FILEFISH FLAGFISH FLATFISH
FLATHEAD FLOUNDER FOOLFISH
FROGFISH FUNDULUS GAMBUSIA
GEELBECK GILTHEAD GOATFISH
GOLDFISH GRAINING GRAYFISH
GRAYLING GREYSKIN HAIRFISH
HALFBEAK HANDFISH HANDLINE
HAPLOMID HARDHEAD HARDTAIL

HOMOCERC HORNFISH
HORSEMAN JACKFISH JUMPROCK
KABELJOU KARMOUTH KELPFISH
KINGFISH LADYFISH LUMPFISH
MACKEREL MENHADEN MILKFISH
MOONFISH PICKEREL PILCHARD
PIRARUCU PORKFISH QUERIMAN
ROBALITO ROCKFISH ROCKLING
ROSEFISH SAILFISH SALANGID
SANDFISH SANDGOBY SCIAENID
SCOMBRID SCOTSMAN SEERFISH
SKILFISH SKIPJACK SOAPFISH
STUDFISH STURGEON TALLYWAG
TARWHINE TERAGLIN TILEFISH
TOADFISH TREEFISH TREVALLY
WARMOUTH WEAKFISH
WHISTLER WRYMOUTH
QUILLBACK SCORPAENO
NEEDLEFISH SHEEPSHEAD
SHOVELHEAD SHOVELNOSE
SILVERSIDES MOUTHBREEDER
(— BY TROLLING) DRAIL
(— FOR EELS) GRIG SNIGGLE
(— FOR SALMON) SNIGGER
(— NETTED) LIFT
(— NOT UNDERSIZED) COUNT
KEEPER
(— TAPE) SNAKE
(— THROUGH ICE) CHUG
(— UNDERWATER) GOGGLE
(— WITH HANDS) GUMP GUDDLE
(AQUARIUM —) GUPPY RASBORA
(BLIND —) PINKFISH
(CURED —) DUNFISH
(FABLED —) MAH
(FEMALE —) RAUN SPAWNER
(FIGHTING —) PLAKAT
(HAWAIIAN —) AU
(HERALDIC —) CHABOT
(INDIAN —) ROHU
(NUMBER OF —) SCHOOL
(OLD —) MOSSBACK
(PART OF —) EYE FIN JAW ANUS
CHEEK NARIS SCALE MAXILLA
MANDIBLE OPERCULUM
PREMAXILLA
(PULPED —) POMACE
(QUANTITY OF —) MAZE
(RAW —) SASHIMI
(REFUSE —) CHUM SHACK
(SALTED —) COR
(SMOKED —) FUMADO
(SPLIT —) KLIPFISH
(STEWED —) MATELOTE
(THIN —) RACER
(YOUNG —) FRY ALEVIN
(25 LBS. OF —) STICK
(PREF.) ICHTHY(O) ISCI
(SUFF.) CHROMIS ICHTHYS
FISH BASKET POT CAUL CREEL
SLATH
FISH BOX TRUNK
FISH BRINER COBBERER
FISH CLEANER GILLER
FISH DRESSER IDLER
FISHER MART EELER PEKAN SABLE
SOBOL TAIRA TAYRA MARTEN
SEINER WEJACK MARTRIX
TRAWLER TROLLER
(SPONGE —) HOOKER
FISHERMAN (ALSO SEE ANGLER)
TOTY EELER ANGLER GIGMAN
GILLER KEDGER MAIMUL SEINER

WORMER ADMIRAL DORYMAN
DRAGMAN DRIFTER PRAWNER
RODSTER SHANKER SMELTER
STRIKER TRAWLER TROTTER
TROWMAN PETERMAN PISCATOR
SEASONER SHRIMPER
FISHERY FISHING PISCARY
SEALERY
FISHGARTH WEIR
FISHHOOK FLY GIG HOOK LARI
ANGLE DRAIL KIRBY LARIN SLEEK
ANGULE SPROAT KENDALL
ABERDEEN BARBLESS CARLISLE
LIMERICK
(PART OF —) EYE GAP BARB BEND
POINT SHANK
(PL.) PULLDEVIL
FISHING PIKING ANGLING BANKING
BASSING GRAINING SNOEKING
(— TOOL) OVERSHOT
FISHING GROUNDS HAAF
FISHING ROD GAD
FISHING TACKLE TEW LEDGER
FISHLINE GIMP TROT SNELL
TRAWL DIPSEY LIGGER BOULTER
GANGION OUTLINE SETLINE
TRIMMER HAIRLINE TROTLINE
FISH LOUSE GISLER
FISHMONGER PESSONER
FISH NEST REDD
FISHNET FLUE SEINE SETNET
FISHPOND STEW VIVER PISCINA
VIVARIUM
FISHPOUND MADRAGUE
FISH SPEAR GRANES WASTER
LEISTER
FISHTAIL UROSOME
FISHWAY PASS RACEWAY
FISHY DULL FUNNY GLASSY
VACANT
FISSION BREAKING CLEAVAGE
CLEAVING GAMOGENY SCISSION
FISSURE GAP CHAP CONE FLAW
GOOL GULL LEAK LOCH LODE
RENT RIFT RIMA RIME SEAM SLIT
TEAR VEIN VENT CHASM CHINE
CHINK CLEFT CRACK FLAKE GRIKE
PIPER PORTA SHAKE SPLIT ZYGON
CLEAVE CRANNY DIVIDE LESION
RICTUS RIMULA SPRING SULCUS
BLEMISH CREVICE FISSURA
MOFETTE OPENING SWALLET
APERTURE BLOWHOLE CLEAVAGE
COLOBOMA CREVASSE INCISURE
QUEBRADA SCISSURA TRAVERSE
(— IN BUILDING STONE) DRY
(— IN HEEL) GAUG
(— IN MAST) SPRING
(— IN PLATEAU) ABRA
(PL.) RHAGADES
(PREF.) RHAGADI
(SUFF.) SCHISIS SCHIST
FISSURED RIMATE CHAPPED
CLEFTED FISSATE
FIST JOB PUD DUKE NAVE NEIF
NIEF FOIST GRASP INDEX NIEVE
CLENCH CLUTCH DADDLE EFFORT
MAULER MAULEY PINKER STRIKE
ATTEMPT CLUBFIST FISTNOTE
PUFFBALL TIGHTWAD
FISTFIGHT TURNUP
FISTICUFF BOX NEVEL FISTIFY
FISTULA EGILOPS

(PREF.) SYRING(O)
FISTULOUS TUBULAR
FIT GO APT FAY GEE JAG PAN RIG
SET SIT ABLE AGUE BOUT FEAT
FURY GOOD HARD KINK MEET
PANG RIPE SORT SUIT TRIM TURN
WELL WHIM ADAPT ADEPT APPLY
BESIT CHINK CLICK DIGNE EXIES
FADGE FANCY FITLY FRAME FRISK
FUROR HAPPY ICTUS MATCH
PITCH QUEME QUIRK READY
RIGHT SERVE SPASM SPELL
START STOUR SWOON TALLY
ACCESS ADJUST ANSWER
ATTACK BECOME BEHOVE BESORT
DUEFUL FINISH FITTEN HABILE
HEPPEN LIABLE PROPER SEASON
SEEMLY SPLEEN SQUARE STREAK
STROKE STRONG SUITED WORTHY
ADAPTED BEHOOVE CAPABLE
CONCENT CONDIGN CONFORM
CORRECT DESPAIR FASHION
FITTING HEALTHY PREPARE
QUALIFY SEIZURE TANTRUM
WIDDRIM ADEQUATE BECOMING
DOVETAIL ELIGIBLE GLOOMING
IDONEOUS OUTBREAK PAROXYSM
PASSABLE SUITABLE SYNCOPES
(— CLOSELY) FAY CHOCK
(— CORNER TO CORNER) BUTT
(— FOR THE GALLOWS) WIDDIFOW
(— IN) GO
(— INTO SOCKET) FANG
(— LOOSELY) SLOP
(— OF ANGER) WAX FRAP FUME
HUFF RAGE TIFF FLING RAVERY
SPLEEN
(— OF DEPRESSION) HUMP
(— OF ILL HUMOR) DOD PET TIG
FUNK POUT TOUT GRUMPS
(— OF ILL TEMPER) MAD TANTRUM
(— OF ILLNESS) DROW TOUT FLING
(— OF LAUGHTER) GIRD KINK
(— OF NERVOUSNESS) TWITCHET
(— OF RESENTMENT) PIQUE SNUFF
(— OF SHIVERING) AGUE GROOSE
(— OF STUBBORNNESS) REEST
(— OF SULKS) GEE STRUM
(— OF SULLENNESS) DOD
(— OF TEMPER) WAX BAIT BIRSE
HISSY PADDY TETCH GROUCH
SPLEEN SQUALL BRAINGE
(— OF WEEPING) CRY
(— OF YAWNING) GAPE
(— ONE WITHIN ANOTHER) NEST
(— OUT) ARM BUSK BEFIT EQUIP
ASTORE CLOTHE OUTFIT APPAREL
APPOINT FURNISH HABILLE
ACCOUTER
(— RIFLE BARREL) BED
(— TIGHTLY) STUFF
(— TO BE DRUNK) SORBILE
(— TOGETHER) MESH NEST COAPT
JOINT COHERE ASSEMBLE
(— UP) RIG
(— WITH COMPACTNESS) BOX
(— WITH FETTERS) GARNISH
(RITUALLY —) KOSHER
(PL.) LUNES
(SUFF.) ABLE IBLE
FITCH LINER
FITFUL GERY CATCHY GERFUL
GLEAMY CURSORY FLIGHTY

RESTLESS UNSTABLE VARIABLE
SPASMODIC
FITLY FIT PAT DULY FEATLY
GLADLY MEETLY TIDELY APROPOS
HAPPILY PROPERLY SUITABLY
FITNESS FORM APTNESS DECENCY
DECORUM DIGNITY APTITUDE
CAPACITY IDONEITY JUSTNESS
PROPERTY CONGRUITY
FITTED APT ABLE ADAPT KEYED
SUITED ADAPTED ENGAGED
ADJUSTED ASSORTED ELIGIBLE
FITTER TUBER GASMAN
FITTING TO APT CAP DUE LUG PAT
BUTT FAIR FEAT FORK HARP
JUMP JUST KIND MEET CLEAT
HAPPY QUEME WORTH BECOME
CLENCH CLEVIS LEADER PROPER
SADDLE SEEMLY WASHER
ADAPTER CONGRUE PENDANT
SERVING SHACKLE SUCTION
TACTFUL CONDULET DECOROUS
GRACEFUL RIGHTFUL SUITABLE
RECEPTACLE
(— TIGHTLY) CLOSE
(PIPE —) CROSS ELBOW
(PL.) BRASS COVER REPAREL
FITMENTS
FIVE CINQ FUNF CINQUE EPSILON
QUINQUE
(— CENTS) JITNEY NICKEL
(— HUNDRED DOLLARS, POUNDS)
MONKEY
(— IN CRAPS) PHOEBE
(— OF TRUMPS) PEDRO
(— YEARS) LUSTRUM
(TWO —S) QUINAS
(PREF.) CINQUE LEPT(O)
PEN(T)(TA)(TH) QUINQU(E)
FIVES BALL SNACK
FIVESTONES SNOBS
FIX BOX JAM PEG PIN SET CLEW
CLUE FAST FIRM GAFF GLUE
HOLD HOLE JAMB LOCK MEND
MOOR NAIL PICK RELY SEAL SPOT
STAY AFFIX ALLOT DEFIX FOUND
GRAFT GRAVE IMBED INFIX LIMIT
PLACE PLANT POINT POSIT SEIZE
STATE STEEK STELL STICK TRYST
ADJUST ANCHOR ARREST ASSIGN
ASSIZE ATTACH CEMENT CLINCH
DEFINE ENROOT ENTAIL FASTEN
FICCHÉ FIXATE FREEZE GROUND
IMPALE REPAIR REVAMP SETTLE
SQUARE TEMPER APPOINT
ARRANGE CALCIFY CONFIRM
DELIMIT DESTINE DILEMMA
GRAPPLE IMPLANT IMPRESS
IMPRINT PREPARE STATION
PINPOINT RENOVATE TRANSFIX
(— AMOUNT) AFFEER
(— ATTENTION) NAIL
(— FIRMLY) SEAL FREEZE IMPACT
INCUBE RAMPIRE
(— PRICE) ASSIZE CHARGE SETTLE
(— UPON) CHAP AFFIX
FIXATION FETICH FETISH
(SUFF.) PAGUS PEXIA PEXIS PEXY
FIXATIVE FIXER SKATOLE
AMBRETTE EUDESMOL
HYRACEUM LABDANUM
FIXED PAT PUT SAD SET SOT FAST
FIRM FLAT HARD GIVEN SIKER

STAID UPSET FINITE FROZEN INTENT MENDED SICKER STABLE STATED STEADY STRONG CERTAIN DORMANT EMPIGHT HABITED LIMITED SETTLED SITFAST STATARY STATIVE STELLED ACCURATE ARRANGED ATTACHED CONSTANT DEFINITE EXPLICIT FASTENED IMMOBILE IRONCLAD MOVELESS RESIDENT RESOLUTE STANDING STUBBORN **(NOT —)** FLUID SHIFTY FUGITIVE **(PREF.)** APLANO

FIXEDLY SAD FAST FIRM FIXLY INTENTLY

FIXEDNESS FASTNESS

FIXER PATCH

FIXTURE ANNEX EVENT GUARD FAUCET SHIELD BRACKET CREEPER KNOCKER THIMBLE **(LIGHTING —)** SCONCE **(STORE —)** GONDOLA

FIZZING FIZZY GASSING

FIZZLE FLOP FUSS BARNEY FAILURE FLIVVER

FLABBINESS MYATONIA

FLABBY LAX FOZY LASH LIMP WEAK BAGGY FLASH FOGGY FRUSH SAPPY WOOZY CASHIE DOUGHY FEEBLE FLAGGY FLAPPY LIMBER QUAGGY WATERY FLACCID YIELDING

FLABELLUM RHIPIDION

FLACCID LIMP WOOZY FLABBY FLAGGY EMARCID FLACKED YIELDING

FLAG FAG LAG SAG SOD FAIL FANE FLAT HOOK JACK JADE LECK PINE TURF WAFT WAIF WILT CREST DROOP FAINT FLAKE SEDGE SLAKE UNION VEXIL WHEFT WHIFF BANNER BOUGEE BURGEE COLORS CORNET EMBLEM ENSIGN FANION GUIDON LEVERS PENCEL PENNON SIGNAL TABARD WIMPLE ANCIENT BEEWORT CALAMUS CATTAIL CURTAIN DECLINE DRAPEAU FANACLE LABARUM PENDANT PENNANT SCOURGE BANDEROL BRATTACH GONFALON HANDFLAG LANGUISH PAVILION STANDARD STREAMER TRICOLOR VEXILLUM WATCHMAN **(— CORNER)** UNION **(— OF DENMARK)** DANEBROG **(— OF TRANSVAAL)** VIERKLEUR **(— OF TRUCE)** KARTEL **(— OF U.S.)** GRIDIRON **(— ON LANCE)** PAVON **(BLUE — WITH WHITE SQUARE)** PETER **(CAVALRY —)** STANDARD **(KNOTTED —)** WAFT **(PIRATE —)** ROGER BLACKJACK **(SERPENT-LIKE —)** DRACO ANGUIS **(SHIP'S —)** DUSTER **(TURKISH —)** ALEM **(WATER —)** SAG **(PL.)** BUNTING

FLAG BEARER GUIDON ANCIENT

FLAGELLANT WHIPPER SCOURGER **(PL.)** ALBI

FLAGELLATE MONAS NOCTILUCA

FLAGELLUM WHIP CILIUM RUNNER KONSEAL WHIPLASH **(PREF.)** BLEPHAR(O) MASTIG(O) **(SUFF.)** KONT

FLAGEOLET PIPE ZUFOLO BASAREE LARIGOT SIBILUS ZUFFOLO MONAULOS

FLAGGING WEAK LANGUID

FLAGITIOUS WICKED CORRUPT HEINOUS CRIMINAL FLAGRANT GRIEVOUS

FLAGON GUN STOUP BOTTLE VESSEL FLACKET FLAGONET REHOBOAM

FLAGRANT BAD RED RANK GROSS ODIOUS STRONG WANTON WICKED BLATANT GLARING HATEFUL HEINOUS SCARLET VIOLENT SHAMEFUL

FLAGSHIP FLAG ADMIRAL

FLAGSTONE FLAG LECK SLAB FAVUS

FLAIL BEAT FLOG WHIP DRASH FRAIL THRAIL THRASH THRESH SWINGLE SWIPPLE STRICKLE THRESHEL

FLAIR RAY BENT NOSE ODOR SMELL GENIUS LEANING

FLAKE CHIP FILM FLAG FLAW RACK SNOW FLANK FLECK FLOCK LAMIN SCALE SLATE SPALL SPAWL STRIP APHTHA HURDLE LAMINA PALING FLAUGHT SHAVING FLOCCULE FRAGMENT **(— OF METAL)** FLITTER **(— OF SNOW)** FLAG **(PREF.)** LEPID(O) **(SUFF.)** LEPIS

FLAKY SCALY SHIVERY

FLAMBE JUBILEE

FLAMBEAU TORCH

FLAMBOYANCE BLARE PANACHE

FLAMBOYANT BAROCK FLORID GARISH ORNATE BAROQUE BUCKEYE FLAMING GORGEOUS

FLAME LOW FIRE GLOW LOWE LUNT ARDOR BLAZE FLARE FLASH GLARE GLEED INGLE LIGHT RESEPH TONGUE BURNING FLAMELET INKINDLE **(ACETYLENE —)** CALCIUM **(SMALL —)** SPUNK FLAMELET FLAMMULE **(PL.)** GLEED

FLAME SCARLET FLORENTINE

FLAME TREE KURRAJONG

FLAMING LIVE AFIRE FIERY FLAMY VIVID AFLARE ARDENT BLAZING BURNING FLARING FLAGRANT

FLAMMA, LA (CHARACTER IN —) AGNES CERVIA BASILIO DONELLO SILVANA **(COMPOSER OF —)** RESPIGHI

FLAN PLANCHET

FLANGE BEAD BOSS BEZEL COLLAR COLLET FLANCH SHROUD FEATHER DUCKBILL FOLLOWER **(— OF GIRDER)** BOOM **(WITHOUT —)** BALD

FLANGER FLAYER GOUGER

FLANK LEER LISK SIDE WING CHEEK SKIRT THIGH BORDER FLITCH

(PREF.) LAPAR(O)

FLANNEL LANA DOMETT SAXONY STAMIN WHITTLE MOLLETON SWANSKIN

FLAP FAN LUG ROB TAB TAG TAP WAP BATE BEAT BLOW CLAP FLIP FLOG FLOP GILL LOBE LOMA SLAM SLAT WAFF WELT ALARM APRON FLACK FLAFF FLICK BALLUP BANGLE LAPPET LIBBET STRIKE TONGUE WAFFLE WALLOP WINNOW AILERON BLINDER CLICKET FLACKER FLAPPET FLICKER FLOUNCE FLUTTER SWINDLE VALANCE AVENTAIL BACKFLAP COATTAIL CODPIECE TURNOVER AGITATION COMMOTION CONFUSION **(— OF BOOTEE)** FLY **(— OF GARMENT)** LAP **(— OF HAT OR CAP)** VALANCE **(— OF HINGE)** LEAF **(— ON HOLSTER)** FLOUNCE **(— ON SADDLE)** SKIRT JOCKEY **(— VIOLENTLY)** FLOG SLAT **(CARDIAC —)** CUSP **(FLESHY —)** GILL **(MUD —)** BOOT **(TROUSERS' —)** FALL

FLAPPER FLAP FLOPPER SNICKET

FLAPPING WAFF WHUTTER

FLARE BELL FLUE BLAZE FLAME FLASH FLECK FUSEE LIGHT SPIRT TORCH FLANCH SIGNAL SPREAD FLICKER TRUMPET OUTBURST **(— ON SHIPBOARD)** DUCK **(— UP)** KINDLE

FLARING BELL FLUE EVASE GAUDY AFLARE FLAMING GLARING SWAGGER BOUFFANT DAZZLING

FLASH DOT BEAT DASH LAIT LAMP LASH LEAM POOL SHOT STAB WINK BLASH BLAZE BURST FLAME FLARE FLOSH FLUFF GLADE GLAIK GLEAM GLENT GLINT LEVIN MARSH SPARK STEAM BOTTLE FILLIP GLANCE QUIVER BLUETTE FLAUGHT FOULDRE GLIMMER GLIMPSE GLISTEN GLITTER INSTANT LIGHTEN QUICKEN SHIMMER SPARKLE TWINKLE SPLINTER SUNBURST CORUSCATE SCINTILLATION **(— FORTH)** OUTRAY **(HOT —)** FLUSHING **(NEWS —)** FUDGE

FLASHBACK THROWBACK

FLASHING CURB FLASH STEEP ARDENT BRIGHT FLASHY FORWARD LAMPING SHINING CREASING METEORIC SLASHING SNAPPING

FLASHLIGHT BUG GLIM FLASH TORCH PENLITE PENLIGHT

FLASHY GAY FLAT GAUD LOUD BAVIN FIERY GAUDY NOBBY SHOWY SLEEK FLOSSY FROTHY GARISH SLANGY SPORTY STUNTY INSIPID RAFFISH TINHORN DAZZLING FLASHING SPORTING TIGERISH VEHEMENT

FLASK BOX PIG BODY HEAD HELM JACK OLPE SNAP BETTY BULGE

FRAME GIRBA GOURD BOTTLE FIASCO FLACON GUTTUS HELMET LAGENA AMPULLA BOMBOLA CANTEEN FLASKET MATRASS TICKLER WARBURG CHRISMAL CUCURBIT **(POCKET —)** TICKLER **(PREF.)** OLPIDI

FLAT DEAD DOWD DULL EVEN FADE FLUE PLAT SLOB TAME ABODE AFLAT BANAL BLAND BLUNT DUSTY HAUGH LEVEL MOLLE MUSTY PLAIN PLANE PRONE ROOMS SEBKA SLAKE VAPID WALSH AGRUFE BORING CALLOW DREARY FLASHY JEJUNE LEADEN PLANAR QUATCH SEBKHA SILENT SIMOUS DECIDED FLIPPER INSIPID INSULSE PLATOID PROSAIC SHILPIT TABULAR UNIFORM DIRECTLY LIFELESS UNBROKEN WATERISH CHAMPAIGN POINTLESS PROSTRATE **(— AND CIRCULAR)** DISCOID **(— AND SHORT)** CAMUS CAMUSE **(— IN MUSIC)** BEMOL MOLLE **(— OF SWORD)** PLAT **(MUD —)** SLOB SLAKE CORCASS **(NOT —)** BRISK **(SALT —)** SALINA **(THEATRICAL —)** JOG **(PREF.)** PLAN(I) PLAT(Y)

FLATBOAT ARK SCOW PULLBOAT

FLATCAR FLAT IDLER LORRY **(ON A —)** PIGGYBACK

FLATFISH DAB RAY BUTT DACE KITE SLIP SOLE TONG BREAM BRILL FLUKE QUIFF RHINA WHIFF ACEDIA CARTER PLAICE TURBOT HALIBUT SUNFISH TORPEDO FLOUNDER MARYSOLE

FLATHEAD SALISH

FLATIRON IRON GOOSE STEEL SADIRON

FLATLY **(PREF.)** PLANO

FLATNESS BATHOS SILENCE EVENNESS KURTOSIS **(— OF NOSE)** SIMITY

FLAT-NOSED CAMUS

FLATTEN BEAT COMB DECK EVEN PLAT CRUSH LEVEL PLUSH SPLAT BEETLE CLINCH DEJECT SMOOTH SPREAD SQUASH DEPRESS EXPLAIN PANCAKE PLANISH SUBSIDE SURBASE COMPRESS DISPIRIT

FLATTENED ECRASE OBLATE DILATED PLANATE TABULAR

FLATTER BULL CLAW COAX DAUB FAGE FUME PALP SOAP WORD CHARM FLOAT GLOZE HONEY PAINT ROOSE SLEEK SMALM BECOME BUTTER CAJOLE CRINGE FICKLE FLEECH FRAISE GLAVER KITTLE PEPPER PHRASE SAWDER SLAVER SMOOGE SOOTHE STROKE ADULATE BEGUILE BEHONEY BLARNEY FLETHER FLUTTER INCENSE PALAVER SOOTHER SWEETEN WHEEDLE BESLAVER BLANDISH BOOTLICK COLLOGUE

FLATTERER FLOIT COGGER DAUBER EARWIG GLOZER JENKINS PRONEUR SOOTHER BOOTLICK CLAWBACK COURTIER DAMOCLES INCENSER LOSENGER SLAVERER SMOOTHER
FLATTERING SOAPY SMARMY SMOOTH BUTTERY CANDIED COURTLY GLAVERING
FLATTERY BULL BUNK DAUB FLUM MUSH SOAP FRAIK GLOZE SALVE TAFFY BUTTER CARNEY FLEECH GREASE PHRASE SAWDER SLAVER BLARNEY DAUBING EYEWASH FAWNING FLETHER INCENSE PALAVER CAJOLERY ADULATION
FLATULENCE WIND VAPOR
FLATULENT GASSY WINDY TURGID POMPOUS VENTOSE FLATUOUS INFLATED
FLATWARE SILVER
FLATWORM ACOEL FLUKE PLATODE RADIATE POLYCLAD
FLAUNT BOSH SHOW WAVE BOAST SKYRE STOUT VAUNT PARADE DISPLAY FLUTTER TRAIPSE BRANDISH FLOURISH
FLAUNTING GAUDY PURPLE SKYRIN FLAGGERY
FLAVONE CHROMONE
FLAVOR GAMY GOUT MASK ODOR RASA SALT TANG ZEST AROMA ASSAI CURRY DEVIL SAPID SAPOR SAUCE SAVOR SCENT SMACK SPICE TASTE TINGE ASARUM ASSAHY INFUSE RANCIO RELISH SEASON TARAGE FLAVOUR PERFUME SUPTION HAUTGOUT PIQUANCY
(HIGH —) HOGO
(SPECIAL —) GUST
(UNPLEASANT —) TACK
FLAVORED SPICY TINCT SPICED
FLAVORFUL SAVOROUS
FLAVORING DIP ALMOND CASSIS MIREPOIS
FLAVORLESS BLAND STALE SILENT WATERISH
FLAW BUG FIB GAP LIE MAR RUB WEM BANE BLOT CHIP FLEE GALL HOLE RASE RIFT SPOT WIND BOTCH BRACK BURST CHICK CLEFT CRACK CRAZE FAULT FLAKE PLUME SPECK BLOTCH BREACH DEFECT FOIBLE LACUNA LESION BLEMISH BLISTER DEFAULT EYELAST FEATHER FISSURE NULLIFY SUNSPOT VIOLATE WHITLOW FRACTURE FRAGMENT GENDARME WINDFLAW
(— IN CASTING) BUCKLE
(— IN CLOTH) BRACK
(— IN DIAMOND) GENDARME
(— IN MARBLE) TERRACE
(— IN METAL) SNAKE
(— IN PRECIOUS STONE) FEATHER
(— IN STEEL) STAR
(— IN STONE) DRY
(— IN WICK) THIEF
(MORAL —) SMIRCH
FLAWED CRACKED
FLAWLESS CLEAN

SOUND PERFECT
FLAX LIN POB TOW CARD FLIX HARL LINE LINT ROCK GRAIN HURDS BREADS BYSSUS KORARI PEANUT PEBBLE SCUTCH LINSEED FLAXWORT HARAKEKE
(— DISEASE) PASMO
(PREF.) BYSSI BYSSO LINO
FLAXEN FLAXY BLONDE
FLAXWEED TOADFLAX
FLAY SKIN SCULP STRIP FLEECE UNCASE CENSURE PILLAGE REPROVE SCARIFY
FLEA LOP SCUD FLECH FLECK PULEX TUNGA CHEGRE CHIGOE VERMIN PULICID SANDBOY
(— INFESTED) PULICOSE
(PREF.) PULI
FLEABANE SKEVISH SCABIOUS WHITETOP
FLEA BEETLE THRIPS
FLEAM BEVEL
FLEAWORT CAMMOCK FLEASEED PSYLLIUM
FLECHE SPIRELET
FLECK FLAKE FREAK DAPPLE FLEECE POUNCE STREAK STIPPLE
FLEDERMAUS, DIE (CHARACTER IN —) ADELE FALKE FRANK ALFRED ORLOFSKY ROSALINDE EISENSTEIN
(COMPOSER OF —) STRAUSS
FLEDGED FLUSH FLIGGED
FLEDGLING SQUAB NESTER FLIGGER BIRDLING
FLEE FLY LAM RUN BOLT FLEG LOUP SCUR SHUN TURN ELOPE ELUDE SKIRR SPEED ESCAPE VANISH ABANDON ABSCOND FORSAKE SCAMPER LIBERATE SKEDADDLE
(SUFF.) FUGAL FUGE
FLEECE JIB KET TEG BUCK CAST FELL GAFF MORT PLOT ROOK SKIN TEGG TEGS FLICK PASHM PLOAT SHAVE SHEAR SHEEP SWEAT PASHIM PIGEON PUSHUM TOISON SHEARING
(— OF MEDIUM GRADE) SUPER
(POOREST PART OF —) ABB
FLEEING FUGIENT HOTFOOT RUNNING FUGITIVE
FLEER GIBE JIBE LEER FLIRE FLOUT SCOFF SNEER
FLEET BAY FAST FLIT NAVY SAIL SKIM SWIM CREEK DRAIN DRIFT EVAND FLOAT FLOTA HASTY INLET POWER QUICK RAPID SWIFT ARGOSY ARMADA FLIGHT HASTEN NIMBLE SPEEDY CARAVAN COMPANY FLOTILLA NAVARCHY WARCRAFT
FLEETING BRIEF BUBBLE CADUCE FLYING VOLAGE CURSIVE FLIGHTY PASSING POSTING SHADOWY VOLATIC CADUCOUS FUGITIVE VOLATILE
FLESH KIN BEEF BODY FELL GAME LAMB LIRE MEAT RACE WEED SLATE STOCK FAMILY MUSCLE SEASON CARNAGE KINDRED MANKIND NATURAL HUMANITY MOONLIGHT

(— ABOUT CHIN AND JAWS) GILL
(— OF CALF) SLINK
(— OF GOAT) CHEVON
(— OF KID) CABRITO
(— OF SHEEP) TRAIK
(— ON LOWER JAW) CHOLLER
(— OUT) CLOTHE
(— UNDER SKIN) FELL
(ANIMAL —) BRAWN
(DEAD —) MURRAIN
(HORSE —) JACK
(LIFELESS —) MUMMY
(PUTREFYING —) CARRION
(SUN-DRIED —) TAPA
(SUPERFLUOUS —) LUMBER
(PREF.) CARNI CRE(O) CREATO KRE(O) SARC(O)
(SUFF.) SARC
FLESHBRUSH STRIGIL
FLESH-COLORED SARCOLINE
FLESHER LINING
FLESHINESS FULLNESS CORPULENCE
FLESHLY CARNAL FLESHY SENSUAL SARKICAL
FLESHY FAT BEEFY LUSTY OBESE PLUMP PULPY STOUT ANIMAL BODILY BRAWNY CARNAL BUNTING CARNOSE SARCOUS CARNEOUS
FLETCH WING FLIGHT
FLEUR-DE-LIS LIS LYS LILY LUCY FLEUR
FLEX BEND
FLEXED PENCHE
FLEXIBILITY WHIP FLUIDITY
FLEXIBLE LIMP LUSH SOFT BUXOM LIMSY LITHE WANDY WITHY FLOPPY LIMBER LITHER PLIANT SUPPLE DUCTILE ELASTIC FINGENT FLEXILE FLEXIVE LISSOME PLIABLE SPRINGY WILLOWY WINDING WRIGGLE BENDSOME YIELDING
(PREF.) CAMPTO
FLEXURE ARCH BEND BENT CURL FOLD CURVE TWIST SIGMOID WINDING
FLICK FILM FLIP CLICK FLACK FLANK FLECK FLIRT FLISK MOVIE CINEMA
FLICKER FAIL FLIT LICK WINK BLINK FLAME FLARE FLICK FLUNK WAVER BICKER FITTER SHIVER YUCKER BLINTER FLIMMER FLITTER FLUTTER SKIMMER TREMBLE TWINKLE WHIFFLE FLICHTER HIGHHOLE
FLICKERING FLICKY FLUTTER LAMBENT FLEXUOUS UNSTEADY
FLICKERTAIL STATE NORTHDAKOTA
FLIER ACE BIRD KIWI FLYER PILOT AIRMAN AVIATOR
FLIGHT FLY GUY HOP LAM BOLT BUNK LAKE PAIR ROUT WING CHEVY FLOCK GLIDE GRICE SCRAP VOLEE CHIVVY EXODUS FUGACY HEGIRA HEJIRA JOYHOP SPIRAL BOUQUET EVASION FLAUGHT FLYOVER MIGRATE MISSION SCAMPER STEPWAY REGIFUGE STAMPEDE SWARMING

(— OF BALL) HOOK DRIVE SLICE
(— OF BIRDS) VOLARY VOLERY VOLLEY
(— OF FANCY) SALLY
(— OF GEESE) SKEIN
(— OF SNIPE) WISP
(— OF STEPS) RISE TRAP GRECE PITCH SCALE STOOP PERRON STAIRS STEPWAY STAIRWAY
(— OF WILD FOWL) SKEIN
(— OF WOODCOCK) RODING
(ABORTIVE —) ABORT
(HASTY —) TIFT
(HAWK'S —) CAREER
(HIGH —) TOWER
(IN —) ALOFT
(SUDDEN —) START STAMPEDE
(UNAUTHORIZED —) BUGOUT
(UPWARD —) SOAR
(SUFF.) FUGAL FUGE PHOBE PHOBI(A)(AC)(C) PHOBUS
FLIGHTY ANILE BARMY GIDDY LIGHT SWIFT FITFUL GARISH UNFIRM VOLAGE WHISKY FLYAWAY FOOLISH GIGGISH MOONISH ROCKETY FLEETING FREAKISH HELLICAT
(— PERSON) TRIVVET
FLIMSINESS INANITY
FLIMSY LIMP THIN VAIN WEAK FRAIL GAUDY JERRY FEEBLE PALTRY SLEAZY SLIGHT SLIMSY HAYWIRE SHALLOW TENUOUS TIFFANY GIMCRACK GOSSAMER JIMCRACK TWITTERY
FLINCH FUNK GAME JARG BLUNK BUDGE FEIGN QUAIL SHUNT START WINCE WONDE BLANCH BLENCH FALTER FLENSE RECOIL SHRINK SCRINGE SCUNNER SQUINCH
FLINCHER VELLINCH
FLINDER FLITTER SMITHERS
FLINDERSIA SILKWOOD
FLINDOSA CUDGERIE
FLING SHY BUZZ CAST DART DASH DING EMIT FLAP FLEG GIBE HURL KICK LASH PECK PICK SLAT TOSS WARP BRAID CHEAT DANCE FLIRT LANCE PITCH SHOOT SLING SNEER SWING THROW WHANG BAFFLE EFFUSE HURTLE LAUNCH PLUNGE REBUFF SPIRIT ENFORCE FLOUNCE REPULSE SARCASM SCATTER SWINDLE SHYLANCE SPANGHEW
(— MISSILES) CHUNK
(— UPWARD) HAUNCH
(HIGHLAND —) WALLOCH
FLINT CORE BLANK CHERT MISER SILEX EOLITH QUARTZ REJECT ESLABON FURISON SCRAPER GRATTOIR GUNFLINT
(PREF.) SILICEO SILICI SILICO
FLINTINESS HEART
FLINTLOCK FUSEE FUSIL FUZEE MUSKET SPANNER FIRELOCK MIQUELET SNAPHAAN
FLINTWOOD WHITETOP
FLIP SKY TAP FLAP SNAP TOSS TRIP FLANK FLICK FLIRT SLIRT SMART FILLIP FLITCH LIMBER NIMBLE PLIANT PROPEL

FLIPPANT AIRY FLIP GLIB FLUENT
LIMBER NIMBLE
FLIPPER ARM FIN PAW HAND
SWELL PADDLE FLAPPER
SPRINGER
FLIRT TOY FIKE FLIP MASH TICK
VAMP FLICK ROVER SLIRT JILLET
MASHER TRIFLE GALLANT
PICKEER TWINKLE COQUETTE
PHILANDER
FLIRTATION FIKE PASSADE
COQUETRY PHILANDER
FLIT DART FLOW SCUD FLECK
FLEET FLICK FLIRT FLOAT FLURR
HOVER QUICK SCOOT SKIFF
SWIFT NIMBLE FLICKER FLUTTER
FLITCH FLICK GAMMON
LONGWOOD MIDDLING
FLOAT BOB FLY KIT SEA BOOM
BUOY CORK DRAG FLOW FLUX
HAWK HONE HOVE LIVE PONT
RAFT RIDE SAIL SCOW SOAR
SWIM TILT WAFT WAVE BALSA
BLADE CAMEL DERBY DRIFT
DRIVE FLEET FLOOD FLUSH GRAIL
HOVER LADLE QUILL SHOAD
SWOON BILLOW BOBBER BUCKET
BUNGEY CANNEL DOBBER
PADDLE PONTON RADEAU
STREEL TOPPER CAISSON
DRINGLE FLATTER FLOTTER
FRESHEN OROPESA PAGEANT
PLANKER PLUMMET PONTOON
SLICKER LEVITATE PICKOVER
(— AIMLESSLY) DRIFT
(— DELIGHTFULLY) COWD
(— FOR HERRING NET) BOWL
(— FOR RING BUOY) LEMON
(— LOGS) DRIVE
(— OF REEDS) KELEK LIGGER
(— PAST) GLACE
(— PROPERLY) WATCH
(CANOE —) AMA
(FISHLINE —) BOB CORK BOBBER
DOBBER TRIMMER
(PLASTERER'S —) DARBY
FLOATBOARD BLADE FLOAT
LADLE
FLOATER STIFF
FLOATING FREE WAFT AWASH
LOOSE ADRIFT AFLOAT FLYING
NATANT BUOYANT FLYAWAY
PENDENT DRIFTING FLUITANT
SHIFTING UNFUNDED
FLOCCILATION TILMUS
FLOCK MOB POD BAND BANK BEVY
FOLD GAME GANG HERD MANY
PACK ROUT SAIL SORT TEAM TRIP
WISP BROOD BUNCH CHARM
COVEY CROWD DRIFT DROVE
FLAKE FLECK GROUP PLUMP
SEDGE SHOAL SWARM TRIBE
TROOP COVERT FLIGHT GAGGLE
HIRSEL MANADA MEINIE RAFTER
SCHOOL SCURRY VOLERY
COMPANY GOOSERY THICKEN
PADDLING
(— OF BIRDS) POD BANK HERD
TEAM WISP BROWN COVEY
SEDGE SIEGE TRIBE FLIGHT
VOLERY
(— OF BITTERNS) SEDGE SIEGE
(— OF DUCKS) PADDLING

(— OF FINCHES) CHARM CHIRM
(— OF GEESE) SKEIN GAGGLE
(— OF HERONS) SEDGE SIEGE
(— OF LARKS) EXALTATION
(— OF LIONS) PRIDE
(— OF MALLARDS) SORD SUTE
(— OF NIGHTINGALES) WATCH
(— OF PARTRIDGE) COVEY
(— OF PEACOCKS) MUSTER
(— OF PIGEONS) KIT LOFT
(— OF PLOVER) WING
(— OF ROOKS) ROOKERY
(— OF SANDPIPERS) FLING
(— OF SHEEP) FOLD HIRSEL
(— OF SHELDRAKE) DOPPING
(— OF SNIPE) WISP
(— OF SWANS) BANK GAME MARK
(— OF TURTLE-DOVES) DOLE
(— OF WIDGEONS) COMPANY
(— OF WILDFOWL) SCRY SKEIN
(— TOGETHER) RAFT
(SMALL —) SPRING
(PREF.) (— OF WOOL) FLOCCI
FLOCKING REPAIR
FLOE PAN
FLOG CAT TAN TAW BEAT CANE
CHOP HIDE LASH LICK LUMP
TOCO WALE WARM WELK WHIP
YANK BIRCH EXCEL FIGHT FLAIL
HORSE KNOUT LINGE QUILT
SAUCE SKEEG SWISH WHANG
BREECH COTTON LARRUP LATHER
STRIKE SWITCH THRASH WALLOP
WATTLE BALEISE BELABOR
COWHIDE SCOURGE SJAMBOK
TROUNCE CARTWHIP CHAWBUCK
SLAISTER URTICATE VAPULATE
(— WATER) SCRINGE
FLOGGER HORSING SWISHER
FLOGGING TOCO TOKO TANNING
BIRCHING WHIPPING
FLOOD SEA BORE BUOY FLOW
FLUX POUR TIDE EAGRE FLOAT
FLUSH SPATE SWAMP SWILL
WATER DELUGE EXCESS RAVINE
SLUICE SPLASH DEBACLE
FLOTTER FRESHET NIAGARA
TORRENT ALLUVION CATARACT
INUNDATE OVERFLOW
SURROUND
FLOODED AWASH AFLOAT
FLOODGATE CLOW DRAG GOLE
HATCH SLUICE STAUNCH
CATARACT PENSTOCK
FLOODING UP PROUD FLOWAGE
DILUVIAL FLOATING
FLOODLIGHT OLIVET
FLOODPLAIN BENCH DAMBO
FLOOR BECK DROP FLAT LAND
LOFT PAVE SEAT BOARD FLOAT
GRASS PIANO PIECE SOLAR
STAGE STORY BELFRY FLIGHT
GROUND SOLLAR PLANCHE
BARBECUE FLOORING HALFPACE
PAVEMENT SUBFLOOR
(— OF COAL MINE) SOLE THILL
(— OF COAL SEAM) SILL
(— OF FORGE) HEARTH
(— OF GLASS FURNACE) SIEGE
(— OF OCEAN) SEABED
(— OF SPORTS RING) CANVAS
(— OF WOOLSHED) BOARD
(FOREST —) SEEDBED

(GROUND —) TERRENO BASEMENT
(OPENWORK —S) GRATINGS
(RAISED —) LEEWAN HALFPACE
(THRESHING —) MOWSTEAD
FLOORBOARD FOOTLING
(BOAT'S —) BURDEN
FLOORING STAGE PARQUET
TERRAZZO
FLOORMAN CALLBOY
FLOP DOG BOMB SWOP WHOP
SQUAB BUMMER TURKEY
TRAGEDY
FLORA CYBELE FLORULA
(— AND FAUNA) BIOTA
FLORAL TREE LEAF
FLORENCE FLASK BETTY
FLORENCE IRIS ORRIS TREOS
FLORESTAN (WIFE OF —) LEONORA
FLORID FINE HIGH BUXOM FRESH
RUDDY ORNATE ROCOCO RUBIED
ASIATIC FLOWERY TAFFETA
BLOOMING FIGURATE RUBICUND
SANGUINE SPLENDID VIGOROUS

FLORIDIAN CRACKER
FLORIMEL (HUSBAND OF —)
MARINEL
FLORIPES (BROTHER OF —)
FIERABRAS
(HUSBAND OF —) GUY
FLOSS FLUFF SKEIN WASTE
CADDIS SLEAVE CADDICE
FLOSSER FANNER
FLOSS-SILK TREE SAMOHU
FLOTSAM JETSAM WILSAM
WAFTURE WAVESON DRIFTAGE
FLOATAGE
FLOUNCE FLAP HUFF SKIT SLAM
FLING FRILL RUCHE PEPLUM

RIPPLE ROBING ROUNCE RUFFLE
VOLANT FALBALA FALBELO
FROUNCE RUCHING FLOUNDER
FURBELOW STRUGGLE
FLOUNDER DAB GAD BUTT KEEL
POLE ROLL TOSS BREAM FLUKE
SLOSH WITCH WRELE GADOID
GROVEL MEGRIM MUDDLE PLAICE
TOLTER TURBOT WALLOP
WALLOW WARSLE BLUNDER
FLASKER FLOUNCE PLOUNCE
STUMBLE SUNFISH TOPKNOT
VAAGMAR ANACANTH FLATFISH
FOOLFISH PLUNTHER SANDLING
FLOUR AMYL ATTA DUST CONES
HOVIS BINDER CLEARS FARINA
FLOWER PATENT POLLEN SICKEN
TSAMBA WHITES BOXINGS
BRAVURA CRIBBLE CANAILLE
(— OF MALT) SMEDDUM
(COARSE —) THIRD CHISEL
BOXINGS CRIBBLE
(FINE —) CONES SUJEE
(LOW-GRADE —) TAIL
(PARTICLE OF —) CHOP
(POTATO —) FROW
(UNSORTED —) ATTA
(PREF.) ALEURO
FLOURISH TAG WAG BOOM BRAG
FUSS GROW LICK RIOT RISE
SHOW TUCK WAVE ADORN
BLOOM BOAST CHEVE GLOSS
QUIRK REIGN SHAKE SWASH
SWING SWISH TUSCH VAUNT
CATTER PARADE PARAPH
QUAVER SQUIRL THRIVE
BLOSSOM BURGEON CADENZA
DISPLAY ENLARGE FANFARE
GAMBADE GAMBADO PASSAGE
PROSPER ROULADE SUCCEED
TRIUMPH WAMPISH ARPEGGIO
BRANDISH CURLICUE INCREASE
ORNAMENT SKIRMISH
(— OF BAGPIPE) WARBLER
(— OF TRUMPET) MORT SENNET
TUCKET
FLOURISHING FAR FRIM FRUM
PERT GREEN PALMY PEART VITAL
BLOOMY FLORID GOLDEN
FLORENT HEALTHY VERNANT
THRIVING VEGETOUS
PROSPEROUS
FLOURY MEALY
FLOUT BOB GIBE JEER JERK JIBE
LOUT MOCK FLEER FLITE FRUMP
SCOFF SCOMM SCORN SCOUT
SNEER TAUNT DERIDE INSULT
BETONGUE
FLOW GO EBB ERN JET PUT RUN
SET SUE BORE COMB FLIT FLUX
FUSE GUSH HALE LAVA LAVE
MELT PASS POUR RAIL ROLL
SEND SHED SILE SLIP SOAK SWIG
TAIL TEEM TIDE WELL AVALE
DRAIN DRIFT EAGRE EXUDE
FLEAM FLEET FLOAT FLOOD
FLUSH FRESH GLIDE ISSUE QUELL
RIVER SCOOT SLIDE SPEND SPILL
SPURT SWILL TRILL ABOUND
AFFLUX COURSE CURSUS DELUGE
GUGGLE GUTTER POPPLE RECEDE
RINDLE SPRING STREAM
CURRENT DEVOLVE DISTILL

DRIBBLE EMANATE FLOWAGE
FLUTTER FLUXION ILLAPSE
INDRAFT MEANDER SPURTLE
TRINKLE TRINTLE ALLUVION
BACKWASH CURRANCE
CURRENCY DOWNFLOW EMISSION
FOUNTAIN INUNDATE
(— AGAINST) LAP LAVE BATHE
(— BACK) EBB
(— BEYOND BANKS) DEBORD
SURROUND
(— DOWN) AVALE
(— IN) INFLOW INFLOOD
(— IN RILLS) DRILL
(— IN RIVULETS) GUTTER
(— IN SPURTS) SALTATION
(— INTERMITTENTLY) HEAD
(— NOISILY) BICKER
(— OF AIR) SIDEWASH
(— OF ELECTRICITY) BOLT
OSCILLATION
(— OF METAL) CREEP
(— OF RADIO SIGNAL) BEAM
(— OF SOUNDS) CADENCE
(— OUT) EMIT ISSUE EFFUSE
SPREAD EXHAUST RESOLVE
(— OVER) BERUN
(— SLOWLY) SEEP EXUDE GLEET
(— TOGETHER) CONCUR CONFLOW
(— WITH) FLEET
(CONTINUOUS —) LAPSE
(COPIOUS —) HALE RIVER
(LAVA —) COULE COULEE
(RHYTHMICAL —) LILT
(TIDAL —) BORE AEGIR EAGER
EAGRE
(PREF.) RHEO RHYSI
(SUFF.) FLUENCE FLUENT
FLUOUS FLUX RRHAGIA RRHEA
RRHOEA
FLOWER (ALSO SEE PLANT AND
HERB) BUD GAY BEST BLOW
FLAG IRIS IXIA PINK POLE POSY
ROSE ARROW ASTER BLOOM
BLUET BREAK DAISY ELITE FANCY
FLOOR GOWAN LILAC PANSY
PHLOX TRUSS TULIP TUTTY
AZALIA CHOICE CORYMB CROCUS
CYMULE DAHLIA DATURA FLORET
MAYPOP ORCHID SCILLA SEASON
SHOWER SINGLE STEVIA UNFOLD
AMELLUS ANEMONE ARBUTUS
BLETHIA BLOSSOM BOSTRYX
CAMPANA DEVELOP ESSENCE
FLEURET FLOSCLE GAZANIA
GENTIAN GERBERA IPOMOEA
PETUNIA PICOTEE TORENIA
BELAMOUR CAMELLIA CYCLAMEN
DAFFODIL DIANTHUS GARDENIA
GERANIUM HEPATICA HIBISCUS
HYACINTH PRIMROSE SPARAXIS
(— STATE) FLORIDA
(— WITH 6 SEGMENTS) SEXFOIL
(COTTON —) SQUARE
(DEFORMED —) BULLHEAD
(DOUBLE —) BURSTER
(DRIED —S) BRAYERA
(IMAGINARY —) AMARANTH
(PART OF —) OVARY PETAL SEPAL
STALK STYLE ANTHER PISTIL
STAMEN STIGMA PEDICEL
FILAMENT PEDUNCLE PERIANTH
RECEPTACLE

(SHOWY —) ORCHIS
(STRIPED —) BIZARRE
(UNFADING —) AMARANTH
(PL.) BOUQUET
(PREF.) ANTH(O) FLORI
(SUFF.) ANTHEMA ANTHEMUM
ANTHERA ANTHEROUS ANTHERY
ANTHES ANTHOUS ANTHUS
FLORAL FLOROUS
FLOWERFLY SYRPHID
FLOWERHEAD CALATHUS
FLOWERING AFLOWER FLOWERY
ANTHESIS BLOOMING
FLOWERING GLUME LEMMA
FLOWERLESS ANANTHOUS
FLOWER-OF-AN-HOUR SHOOFLY
FLOWER-PECKER KAKAWAHIE
FLOWERPOT POT CACHEPOT
FLOWERY BLOWN BLOOMY FLORID
POSIED FLORENT PRIMROSE
FLOWING FAIR FLUX LAVE SIDE
AFLOW FLOAT FLUID FLUOR
QUICK TIDAL AFFLUX DEFLUX
FLUENT FUSILE LIVING COPIOUS
CURRENT CURSIVE EMANANT
FLUXING FLUXION FLUXIVE
RUNNING SLIDING DEFLUENT
DILUENDO FLUVIOSE
(— AT LOW SPEED) SLACK
(— BACK) EBB
(— IN) INFLUX INFLUENT
INFLUXION
(— OF GLAZE) STREAMING
(— OF TIDE) FLOOD
(— OUT) ELAPSE EFFLUENT
(— SMOOTHLY) PROFLUENT
(PREF.) **(— OUT)** EFFLUVIO
FLOWOFF RUNOFF
FLUCAN SELVAGE SELVEDGE
FLUCTUATE SWAY VARY VEER
FLEET SWING WAVER BALANCE
VIBRATE WAMPISH UNDULATE
UNSTEADY VACILLATE
FLUCTUATING WAVY HECTIC
LABILE RUBATO ERRATIC FLUXIVE
WAYWARD UNSTABLE UNSTEADY
FLUCTUATION CYCLE FADING
JIGGLE FLICKER FLUTTER
VIBRATO OSCILLATION
(— IN LAKES) SEICHE
FLUE NET BARB DOWN OPEN PIPE
THIN VENT FLARE FLUFF FLUKE
TEWEL FUNNEL TUNNEL UPTAKE
CHIMNEY OUTTAKE PASSAGE
DOWNTAKE
FLUE-CURED BRIGHT
FLUENCY SKILL
FLUENT GASH GLIB FLUID READY
FACILE LIQUID SMOOTH STREAM
COPIOUS CURRENT FLOWING
FLUIDIC RENABLE VERBOSE
VOLUBLE ELOQUENT FLIPPANT
FLUFF FUG FLUE LINT OOZE PUFF
BEARD ERROR FLOSS WHEEL
MISTAKE
FLUFFING WHEELING
FLUFFY SOFT DOWNY DRUNK
FILMY FLUEY FUZZY LIGHT
LINTEN PLUFFY FEATHERY
UNSTEADY
(NOT —) CLOSE
FLUID INK SAP MASS RASA BLOOD
FLUOR HUMOR JUICE LATEX

SERUM SPERM SWEAT WATER
FLUENT LIQUID WATERY
COOLANT FLOWING FLUIBLE
FLUXILE GASEOUS SYNOVIA
EMULSION FLOATING FLUXIBLE
FORESHOT PERSPERATION
(ANIMAL —) SERUM
(BODY —) CHYLE
(EAR —) PERILYMPH
(EGYPTIAN PRIMEVAL —) NU NUN
(ELECTRIC —) VRIL
(ETHEREAL —) ICHOR
(LIVER —) BILE
(LUBRICATING —) SYNOVIA
(MAMMARY —) MILK
(SOLDERING —) FAKE
(THICK VISCOUS —) GRUME
(WATERY —) LYE SANIES SEROSITY
(WORKING —) AIR
(PREF.) SERO
FLUIDITY LENGTH
(— UNIT) RHE
FLUKE FLUE PALM BLADE GRASP
SCALE PLAICE DISTOME PLATODE
SCRATCH FLATWORM FLOUNDER
BILHARZIA
(— OF ANCHOR) HOOK KILLICK
(— OF WHALE'S TAIL) BLADE
FLUME CHUTE DITCH SHUTE
SLUICE
FLUMMERY SOWENS WASHBREW
FLUNK BUST FAIL SKEW SPIN
FLICKER
FLUNKY SNOB TOADY COOKEE
JEAMES LACKEY FOOTMAN
SERVANT STEWARD
FLUORESCENCE BLOOM
FLUORESCENT PSYCHEDELIC
FLUORINE PHTOR PHTHOR
FLUORITE CAND FLUX FLUOR
FLURRY ADO FIT FACT FRET GUST
PIRR SPIT STIR TEAR HASTE SKIFF
SKIRL BOTHER BUSTLE SCURRY
SQUALL CONFUSE FLUSKER
FLUSTER FLUTTER FOOSTER
SWITHER WHITHER SPITTING
FLUSH JET EVEN GLOW HUSH
JUMP POOL ROSE BLOOM BLUSH
COLOR ELATE FLASH FLUSK
FRESH KNOCK LEVEL RAISE
ROUGE SCOUR START VIGOR
AFLUSH EXCITE HECTIC LAVISH
MANTLE MORASS REDDEN
RUDDLE SLUICE SPRING THRILL
ANIMATE BOBTAIL CRIMSON
SUFFUSE ABUNDANT AFFLUENT
PRODIGAL ROSINESS
(— GAME) SERVE
(— IN SKY) SUNGLOW
(NOT —) FLAT
FLUSHED RED ROSY BEAMY FIERY
FLOWN FLORID FLUSHY HECTIC
CRIMSON RUBICUND
FLUSTER PAVIE SHAKE BOTHER
FLURRY FUDDLE MUDDLE
POTHER RATTLE CONFUSE
FLUSKER FOOSTER SWITHER
BEFUDDLE FLOWSTER FLUSTRUM
FLUTE NAY FIFE FUYE PIPE AULOS
CRIMP CUENA PUNGI QUENA
STICK STYKE TIBIA TWILL CANNEL
DOUCET FLAUTO GEWGAW
GOFFER POOGYE ZUFOLO

CHAMFER DIAULOS FLAMFEW
FLUTING GAUFFER HEMIOPE
MAGADIS MATALAN PICCOLO
SIBILUS SIFFLOT TONETTE
TRANGAM WHISTLE ZUFFOLO
FLAUTINO MONAULOS RECORDER
(— OF A COLUMN) STRIGA
CHANNEL
(— STOP) VENTAGE
(CHINESE —) TCHE
(EAST INDIAN —) MATALAN
(EUNUCH —) KAZOO
(JAPANESE —) FUYE SHAKUHACHI
(LYDIAN —) MAGADIS
(MOSLEM —) NAY
(PHOENICIAN —) GINGRAS
(PL.) NEHILOTH
(PREF.) AUL(O)
FLUTED QUILLED
FLUTEMOUTH CORNETFISH
FLUTE PLAYER AULETE FLUTER
FLUTIST TIBICEN TOOTLER
AULETRIS FLAUTIST
FLUTING STRIX FULLER GADROON
STRIGIL COULISSE QUILLING
FLUTTER BAT FAN FUG BATE
BLOW BUZZ FLAP FLIT FLOW
FLUE OOZE PLAY WAFF WAVE
FLACK FLAFF FLARE FLECK FLICK
FLOSS FLURR HOVER SHAKE
WAVER BANGLE FLAUNT FLURRY
RUFFLE SWIVET WAFFLE WALLOP
WINNOW FLACKER FLAFFER
FLASKER FLATTER FLAUGHT
FLICKER FLITTER FLUSKER
SKIMMER WAGTAIL WHIFFLE
FLICHTER SQUATTER VOLITATE
(IN A —) PITAPAT
FLUTTERING AWING FLITTY
WHUTTER AFLUTTER FLICKERY
FLUTTERINGLY PITAPAT
FLUTTER-TONGUING GROWL
FLUX FLOW FUSE LASK MELT
BORAX FLOAT FLOOD ISSUE
RESIN ROSIN SMEAR SMELT
FUSION CURRENT EURIPUS
FLOWING LEAKAGE OUTFLOW
(— UNIT) WEBER MAXWELL
FLY BEE FAG FAN GAD HOP RUN
FIRK FLEA FLEE FLEG FLIT FRIT
GNAT KITE KIVU LASH LEAP MELT
RACK RAKE SAIL SCUD SMUT
SOAR SOLO WHEW WHIR WHIZ
WIND WING ZIMB AGILE ALERT
EMPID FLEET FLIER FLOAT FLURR
FLUSH FLYER GLIDE LATCH
MIDGE MUSCA OXFLY PERLA
PHORA PILOT QUICK SEDGE
SHARP SKIRL SKIRR STOUR
WHAME WHIRR ZEBUB ASILID
AVIATE BANGLE BLOWER BOTFLY
BREEZE DAYFLY ESCAPE FLIGHT
FLYBOY GADFLY GORFLY JARFLY
LEPTID MOTUCA NIMBLE PALMER
PHORID PUNKIE RANDON ROBBER
SEPSID SEROOT SPRING TIPULA
TSETSE VANISH VERMIN WINNOW
AVIGATE AVOLATE BROMMER
CANOPID CHALCID CONOPID
FORMATE GRANNOM KNOWING
LOVEBUG ORTALID PYRALIS
SCIARID TYRPHID AIRPLANE
BIBIONID BRACONID COACHMAN

DIPTERAN DROPPING EPHYDRID
EULOPHID GLOSSINA HORSEFLY
HOUSEFLY RUBYTAIL SIMULIID·
TACHINID TATUKIRA VOLITATE
(— AFTER GAME) RAKE
(— AIMLESSLY) BANGLE
(— ALOFT) SOAR TOWER
(— AWAY) CARRY
(— CLUMSILY) FLIGHTER
(— ERRATICALLY) GAD
(— INTO RAGE) FUFF RARE
(— LOW) DICE DRAG HEDGEHOP
(— NEAR THE GROUND) ACCOST
(— OUT) EXPIRE
(— RAPIDLY) SCUR SKIRR
(— TOO HIGH) SCUD
(— WIDE) MISS
(BITING —) PIUM
(FISHING —) BEE DUN OAK BUZZ
GNAT HARL HERL SMUT WASP
ZULU ABBEY ALDER BAKER FAIRY
NYMPH SEDGE BADGER BOBFLY
CADDIS CAHILL CANARY CLARET
DOCTOR HACKLE MILLER ORIOLE
WILLOW BABCOCK BUTCHER
CADDICE COLONEL DROPPER
DUBBING GRANNOM HUZZARD
SPINNER WATCHED WATCHET
BUCKTAIL CATSKILL COACHMAN
FERGUSON GOVERNOR STREAMER
WOODRUFF WRENTAIL
(MAY —) DUN DRAKE
(SHEEP —) FAG KED
(STONE —) SALLY
(PREF.) MUSCI MYI(O)
(SUFF.) MYI(A)(O)
FLYBLOWN BLOWN STRUCK
FLYBOAT FLUTE FLIGHT
FLYCATCHER TODY PEWEE PEWIT
CHEBEC COBWEB MILLER PEEWEE
PHOEBE PIPIRI RAFTER TYRANT
YETAPA ELEPAIO FANTAIL
GRIGNET GRINDER PITIRRI
TOMFOOL TYRANNI BEAMBIRD
FIREBALL FIREBIRD FLYEATER
FORKTAIL GERYGONE KINGBIRD
KISKADEE PITANGUA WALLBIRD
SCISSORTAIL
FLY, FISHING (PART OF —) EYE TAG
BODY BUTT HEAD HORN TAIL
WING CHEEK JOINT HACKLE
RIBBING TOPPING
FLYING AWING FLIGHT VOLANT
WAVING FLOTANT VOLATIC
AVIATION FLOATING
(— MANEUVER) LUFBERY
FLYING DUTCHMAN, THE
(CHARACTER IN —) ERIK SENTA
DALAND
(COMPOSER OF —) WAGNER
FLYING FISH SKIPPER VOLADOR
FLYING FOX KALONG PTEROPID
FLYING GURNARD ANGLER
BATFISH LATCHET LOPHIID
VOLADOR
FLYING LEMUR COBEGO COLUGO
KUBONG
FLYING MACHINE AVIATOR
AEROSTAT
FLYING PHALANGER CUSCUS
SQUIRREL
FLYING SQUIRREL TAGUAN
ASSAPAN

FLYMAN LOFTMAN
FLYSCH MACIGNO
FLYWHEEL FLY FLIER FLYER
WHORL WHARVE
FOAL CADE COLT FILLY PODDY
SLEEPER
FOAM FOB SUD BARM BEES BOIL
FUME HEAD KNIT REAM SCUD
SCUM SUDS WORK CREAM FROST
FROTH SPUME YEAST BUBBLE
FLOWER FLURRY FREATH IMBOST
LATHER SEETHE BLUBBER
DESPUME MELDROP
(PREF.) APHR(O) SPUMI
FOAMING AFOAM NAPPY YEASTY
SPUMOUS MANTLING
FOAMY BARMY BEADY SPUMY
SUDSY FROTHY SPUMOSE
FOB FUB SPUNG POCKET
FOCAL POINT OMPHALOS
FOCUS FIX PUT POINT PURSE
TRAIN CENTER CLIMAX DIRECT
FASTEN FIXATE HEARTH TEMPLE
NUCLEUS CONVERGE FOCALIZE
GANGLION
FODDER HAY FEED FOOD SOIL
VERT GOOMA MANGE EATAGE
FORAGE FOTHER PODDER SILAGE
STOVER FARRAGE PODWARE
PROVAND BROWSING ENSILAGE
ROUGHAGE
FODDERCAGE TUMBREL
FODDERER FOGGER
FOE ENEMY FIEND RIVAL FOEMAN
HOSTILE OPPOSER OPPONENT
WRANGLER
FOG FF DAG RAG DAMP DAZE
HAAR HAZE MIST MOKE MOSS
MURK PRIG RACK ROKE SMOG
SMUR SOUP BEDIM BRUME
CLOUD GRASS HUMOR MUDDY
SMIRR SPRAY STOUR VAPOR
MUDDLE NEBULA SALMON
STUPOR FOGGAGE OBSCURE
POGONIP SMOTHER BEWILDER
MOISTURE
(— OF THE NILE) QOBAR
(FROZEN —) BARBER
(LIGHT —) GAUZE
(SEA —) HAAR HARR
FOGBOW DOG FOGDOG SEADOG
MISTBOW FOGEATER
FOGDOG DOG STUBB FOGBOW
SEADOG FOGEATER
FOGGINESS CLOUDING
FOGGY DIM DULL HAZY MIRK
MOKY MURK ROKY DENSE DIRTY
GROSS MISKY MISTY MURKY
ROOKY ROUKY SPEWY CLOUDY
GREASY GROGGY MARSHY
MILKEN SMURRY BRUMOUS
MUDDLED OBSCURE CONFUSED
NUBILOUS VAPOROUS
FOGHORN SIREN TYFON RIPPER
MEGAFOG
FOGY FOGEY DUFFER FOGRAM
FOOZLE STODGER MOSSBACK
FOGYISH MUSTY
FOIBLE VICE FAULT FERLY FEEBLE
FAILING FRAILTY WEAKNESS
FOIL BACK BALK EPEE FILE FOIN
SOIL TAIN BLADE BLANK BLUNT
CHEAT ELUDE EVADE FALSE

STAIN STUMP SWORD TRACK
TRAIL BAFFLE BLENCH BOGGLE
CHATON DEFEAT DEFILE FLORET
OFFSET OUTWIT STIGMA STOOGE
THWART BEGUILE FAILURE
FOILING FOLIATE LAMETTA
PAILLON POLLUTE REPULSE
STONKER TRAMPLE DISGRACE
(— STRIPS) WINDOW
(FENCING —) EPEE BLUNT FLORET
FLEURET
(PART OF —) END TIP BELL GRIP
HILT BLADE FORTE GUARD POINT
BUTTON FOIBLE HANDLE
POMMEL MOUNTING
(POINTED —) TANG
(TIN —) TAIN
FOIST WISH FUDGE FATHER
SUBORN FOISTER SHOEHORN
FOLD BOW FLY LAP PEN PLY SET
WAP BEND COTE CREW CRUE
DART FAIL FALX FAUN FELD FLAP
FURL HANK HOOD LIRK LOOP
RUCK RUGA SWAG TUCK WRAP
BREAK CLASP CRIMP CRISP
CROZE DRAPE FAULD FLIPE
FLOCK FLYPE FRILL GROIN LAYER
PARMA PINCH PLAIT PLEAT PLICA
PRANK QUILL SINUS YIELD
BOUGHT BUCKLE COLLOP CREASE
CRISTA CUTTLE DEWLAP DIAPIR
DOUBLE ENFOLD FORNIX
FRENUM FURDLE GATHER
GUSSET HURDLE INFOLD LABIUM
LAPPET MANTLE PIPING PLIGHT
PUCKER RIMPLE RUMPLE WIMPLE
CAPSIZE CRINKLE CRUMPLE
EMBRACE ENVELOP FLEXION
FLEXURE PINFOLD PLACATE
PLICATE REVERSE ROLLING
ROULEAU TURNING VALVULA
CRIMPING FLECTION FLITFOLD
QUILLING SCAPULET SPLENIUM
SURROUND PLICATION REPLICATE
REFLECTION
(— CLOTH) RAG
(— DOWN) COLLAPSE
(— FOR CATTLE) BAWN
(— IN HOOD) SHOVE
(— INWARD) CRIMP
(— OF MEMBRANE) CRISTA
(— OF SKIN) APRON DEWLAP
SHEATH OMENTUM FORESKIN
MESENTERY
(— ROCKS) DEFORM
(—S OF TOGA) SINUS
(CARDIAC —) CUSP
(GEOLOGICAL —) DIAPIR CLOSURE
EXOCLINE SYNCLINE MONOCLINE
(LOOSE —) LAPPET
(RESTRAINING —) FRENUM
FRAENUM
(SHEEP —) REEVE
(PREF.) PLEXI PLICATO PLICI
PTYCH(O) SINU(ATO) VALVI VALVO
(SUFF.) FARIOUS PLEX PLICATE
PLOID
(COVERING —) STEGE STEGITE
FOLDAGE SOC SOKE
FOLDED SHUT DOUBLE FANLIKE
PLICATE PLICATED REFLEXED
WREATHED
(— AND WAVED) GYROSE

(PREF.) PLICATO
FOLDER KIT BOOK FILE FOLD
ATLAS COVER FOLIO BINDER
CLEANER HANDOUT LEAFLET
STROKER PAMPHLET
FOLDING KNOT
(— OF LEAF) PTYXIS
(— PAPER) ORIGAMI
FOLIACEOUS PHYLLOID
FOLIAGE HERB SHADE GREENS
LEAVES SHROUD BOSCAGE
GILLERY LEAFAGE LEAFERY
UMBRAGE FRONDAGE GREENERY
(CARVED —) KNOT
FOLIATED SPATHIC
FOLIATION SEXFOIL TREFOIL
CINQFOIL SEPTFOIL
FOLIC ACID PGA
FOLIO CASE ATLAS FOLIUM
FOLK DAIONE PEOPLE
(FAIRY —) SHEE SIDHE
(PL.) GENTRY
FOLKSONG SON TONADA
VOLKSLIED
FOLKSY HOMY HOMEY HOMESPUN
FOLKTALE DROLL FABULA
MARCHEN
FOLLETTO DUSIO
FOLLICLE CRYPT LACUNA OVISAC
CONCEPTACLE
FOLLOW GO PAD SUE TAG COME
COPY HUNT NEXT SEEK SHAG
TAIL TAKE TOUT ADOPT AFTER
CHASE DODGE ENSUE SNAKE
SPOOR TRACE TRACK TRAIL
TREAD ADHERE ATTEND DANGLE
FOLLER OCCUPY PURSUE RESULT
SECOND SHADOW SUIVEZ
TAGGLE HOTFOOT IMITATE
OBSERVE PROFESS REPLACE
SUCCEED VALOUWE PRACTICE
SUPPLANT
(— A POINTER'S LEAD) BACK
(— IN SUCCESSION) VARY
(— INSIDIOUSLY) DOG
(— SCENT) ROAD CARRY
(— SLOWLY) DRAGGLE
(— THROUGH) PRESS
(— TRACK) SLEUTH
(— UP) SUE ATTEND
(— UPON) WAIT
FOLLOWER FAN IST SON APER
BEAU ZANY ADEPT CHELA GILLY
BILDAR COHORT DRIVEN ENSUER
GILLIE GUDGET KNIGHT LACKEY
SEQUEL SOLTER SULTER VOTARY
ACACIAN ACOLYTE CARRIER
DEVOTEE EPIGONE FLATTER
GRIFTER POLIGAR PURSUER
RETINUE SECTARY SEQUENT
SPANIEL SUPPOST TRAILER
ADHERENT DISCIPLE FAITHFUL
FAVORITE HENCHMAN
MYRMIDON OBSERVER OFFSIDER
PARTISAN RETAINER SECTATOR
SERVITOR SATELLITE
PURSUIVANT
(— OF ART) BOHEMIAN
(— OF CELEBRITY) GROUPIE
(CAMP —) BUMMER GUDGET
LASCAR
(CRANE —) SPOTTER
(SERVILE —) SLAVE

LACKEY ANTHONY
(PL.) FOLK SECTA SEQUACES
(SUFF.) ITE
FOLLOWING LAST NEXT SECT SUIT
AFTER FIRST SUANT TRACE
TRAIN BEHIND SEQUEL ENSUANT
ENSUING SEQUENT AUDIENCE
BUSINESS SECUNDUM SEGUENDO
TRAILING VOCATION
FOLLOW-UP FOLO
FOLLY ATE SIN RAGE LAPSE MORIA
SOTIE BETISE DOTAGE LUNACY
NICETY WANWIT DAFFERY
DAFFING FOOLERY FOPPERY
IDIOTCY MADNESS MISTAKE
SOTTAGE UNSKILL FONDNESS
FOOLHEAD IDLENESS LEWDNESS
MOROLOGY NONSENSE RASHNESS
SURQUIDY UNTHRIFT UNWISDOM
WILLNESS WOODNESS SIMPLICITY
FOMALHAUT DIFDA DIPHDA
FOMENT SOW ABET BREW SPUR
ROUSE STUPE AROUSE EXCITE
INCITE AGITATE FERMENT
INSPIRE
FOND TID DAFT DEAR DOTE FAIN
FOOL FUND KIND VAIN WEAK
CRAZY SILLY STOCK STORE
ARDENT BEFOOL CARESS CHOICE
DEARLY DOTING FONDLE FONDLY
LOVING SIMPLE TENDER
AMATORY AMOROUS BEGUILE
BROWDEN FONDISH FOOLISH
INSIPID PARTIAL DESIROUS
ENAMORED SANGUINE TRIFLING
UXORIOUS
(PREF.) (— OF) PHIL(O)
(SUFF.) (— OF)
PHIL(A)(AE)(E)(OUS)(US)
FONDLE PET BABY BILL CLAP COAX
DAUT DAWT FOND NECK TICK
WALY DAUNT INGLE NURSE
WALLY CARESS COCKER CODDLE
COSSET CUDDLE CUTTER DANDLE
GENTLE KIUTLE MUZZLE PAMPER
SLAVER STROKE TANTLE TIDDLE
CHERISH FLATTER SMUGGLE
TWATTLE BLANDISH CANOODLE
FONDLING NINNY NURSLING
FONDLY DEAR FOND DEARLY
FOOLISH
FONDNESS GRA LOVE FANCY
FOLLY TASTE DOTAGE NOTION
FEELING DEARNESS WEAKNESS
(— FOR WOMEN) PHILOGYNY
(SUFF.) (— FOR) ITIS
FONS (FATHER OF —) JANUS
(MOTHER OF —) JUTURNA
FONT BILL FUND PILA BASIN
FOUNT SOURCE SPRING LAVACRE
PISCINA BENITIER DELUBRUM
FONTANEL MOLD MOULD
FENESTRA
FOOD BIT KAI PAP SAP BAIT BITE
BUNK CATE CHIH CHOP CHOW
CRAM DIET DISH EATS FARE
FARM FUEL GEAR GRUB HASH
JOCK KAIL KALE MEAT NOSH
PECK PLAT PROG SALT SOCK
STEW TACK TOKE TUCK BREAD
BROMA CHEER CHUCK FLUFF
FORAY GRILL SCAFF SCOFF
SCRAN TABLE THING TOMMY

TREAT TRIPE APPAST BUTTER
DODGER DOINGS EATING FODDER
FOSTER LIVING MAIGRE MORSEL
MUKTUK REFETE STOVER SUNKET
TACKLE TUCKER VIANDS VIVERS
WRAITH ALIMENT FAUSTER
HANDOUT INGESTA KEEPING
KITCHEN NURTURE PABULUM
PASTURE PECKAGE PROVANT
PULTURE EATABLES FLUMMERY
GRUBBERY NUTRIENT PEMMICAN
PROVIANT TRENCHER VICTUALS
PROVENDER NOURISHMENT
(— AND DRINK) BOUGE CHEER
LOWANCE
(— AND LIQUOR) GEAR
(— AND LODGING) FOUND
EASEMENT
(— BANNED DURING PASSOVER)
HAMETZ CHAMETZ
(— EATEN AS RELISH) KITCHEN
(— EATEN BETWEEN MEALS)
BAGGING
(— FOR ANIMALS) FODDER
FORAGE
(— FOR CATTLE) BROWSE TACKLE
(— FROM KELP) KOMBU
(— IN SLICES) LEACH
(— IN STOCK) LARDER
(— NOT RITUALLY CLEAN)
TEREPHAH
(— OF DUCK EGGS) BALUT
(— OF RUMINANTS) CUD
(— OF THE GODS) AMRITA
AMREETA AMBROSIA
(— OF WHALE) KRILL
(— OF WORKMEN) TOMMY
(— ON TABLE AT ONE TIME) MESS
(ASIATIC —) TEMPEH
(BEE —) CANDY
(COOKED —) CURY BAKEMEAT
(DAILY —) TUCKER
(EXTRA —) GASH
(FILLING —) STODGE
(FLAVORLESS —) HOGWASH
(GROUND —) DUST
(HAWAIIAN —) POI
(INDIGESTIBLE —) STODGE
(JAPANESE —) TERIYAKI
(LIQUID —) LAP SLOP SOUP GRUEL
LEBAN LEBEN SUPPING
(LUXURIOUS —) CATE CATES
JUNKET
(MADE OF SEVERAL —S) PANACHE
(MIRACULOUS —) MANNA
(RICH —) CHEER
(SEMILIQUID —) SWILL
(SOFT —) PAP
(STARCHY —) AMYLOID
(TAPIOCA-LIKE —) SALEP
(WATERY —) SLIPSLOP
(PREF.) SITIO SITO TROPH(O)
(SUFF.) PHAGA PHAGE PHAGIA
PHAGOUS PHAGUS PHAGY
TROPHIA TROPHIC TROPHY
(WANT OF —) ATROPHIA
FOODLESS JEJUNE VICTLESS
FOODSTUFF TRADE CEREAL
COOKABLE
FOOL APE ASS BAM BOB COD CON
DAW DOR FON FOP FOX FUN GIG
KID MUG NIT NUP POT RIG SAP
SOT TOY BULL BUTT CAKE CHUB

CLOT COLT DOLT DUPE FOND
GECK GOER GOFF GOOP GOWK
GYPE HARE HAVE HOIT JAPE JEST
JOKE JOSH MOME MUCK NIZY
POOP RACA RACH SIMP TONY
TOOT TWIT ZANY BLIND BLUFF
BUFFO CHUMP CLOWN DALLY
FUNGE GALAH GLAIK GOOSE
GREEN HORSE IDIOT KNAVE
MORON NINNY NIZEY NODDY
PATCH PATSY SAMMY SCREW
SILLY SNIPE SPOOF STICK STIFF
STIRK TOMMY TRICK BUFFLE
COUSIN CUCKOO CUDDEN
DELUDE DIMWIT DISARD DOTARD
DOTTLE FOLEYE FOOTER
GAMMON JESTER MOTLEY
MUCKER MUSARD NIDGET NIMSHI
NINCOM NUPSON SAWNEY
SHMUCK STRING TAMPER WITTOL
ASINEGO BECASSE BUFFOON
COXCOMB DAGONET DECEIVE
DIZZARD FATHEAD FOOLISH
FRIBBLE GOMERAL GOMERIL
HAVERAL JACKASS LACKWIT
MADLING MISLEAD NATURAL
OMADAWN PINHEAD PLAYBOY
SCHMUCK STOOKIE TOMFOOL
WANTWIT WITLING ABDERITE
BADINAGE DRIVELER FONDLING
HOODWINK IMBECILE MONUMENT
OMADHAUN TOMNODDY
NINCOMPOOP
(— AROUND) JIVE SKYLARK
LALLYGAG
(— AWAY) FRIBBLE
(BORN —) MOONCALF
(LEARNED —) MOROSOPH
(NATURAL —) INNOCENT
(PL.) FOOLERY
FOOLERY GAME FOLLY BARNEY
MOTLEY BAUBLERY
FOOLHARDY RASH BRASH
FOOLATUM
FOOLISH FAT SOT BETE DAFT
DUMB FOND FOOL GAGA GYPE
IDLE MADE NICE RASH SOFT VAIN
VOID WEAK ZANY BALMY BARMY
BATTY BOGGY BUGGY DILLY
DIPPY DIZZY DOILT EMPTY FONNE
GAWKY GOOFY GOOSY INANE
INEPT JERKY LOONY NODDY
POTTY SAPPY SAWNY SCREW
SEELY SILLY YAPPY ABSURD
CUDDEN DOTISH DOTTLE FONDLY
GLAKED GOTHAM GOWKIT
HARISH INSANE MOMISH MOPISH
SHANNY SIMPLE SLIGHT SOFTLY
SPOONY STOLID STULTY STUPID
TAWPIE UNWISE VACANT
ASININE DAMFOOL DOLTISH
ETOURDI FANGLED FATUOUS
FLIGHTY FOLLIAL FOPPISH
GLAIKIT GOOSISH GULLISH
IDIOTIC PEEVISH PUERILE
SOTTISH TOMFOOL UNWITTY
WANTWIT WITLESS ABDERIAN
FOOTLING FOPPERLY HEADLESS
HEEDLESS HIGHLAND IMBECILE
SENSELESS
(PREF.) STULT(I)
FOOLISHLY IDLY FONDLY SIMPLE
SIMPLY

FOOLISHNESS JAZZ PUNK FOLLY
BARNEY BUNKUM FADDLE LEVITY
LUNACY RUBBLE VANITY FATUITY
PORANGI BUNCOMBE FONDNESS
INSANITY TOMMYROT ABSURDITY
SAPPINESS
FOOT FIT PAT PAW PEG PES BASE
COOT FUSS GOER HEEL HOOF
PIED SOLE TAIL BASIS PIECE
BOTTOM CLUTCH GAMMON
PATTEN PODIUM RHYTHM
TOOTSY TRILBY WALKER FOOTING
GAMBONE MEASURE METREME
PEDICEL FOREFOOT
(— OF ANIMAL) PAD PAW HOOF
TROTTER
(— OF APE) HAND
(— OF INSECT) TARSUS
(— OF WINE GLASS) MULE
(CHINESE —) CHEK CHIH
(HALF —) SEMIPED
(LARGE AWKWARD —) CAVE
(METRIC —) IAMB BASIS DIAMB
IONIC PAEAN CHOREE DACTYL
DIIAMB IAMBUS SYZYGY ANAPEST
BACCHIC PYRRHIC SPONDEE
TROCHEE ANAPAEST BACCHIUS
CHORIAMB DOCHMIUS EPITRITE
MOLOSSUS TRIBRACH TRIMACER
(STEWED OX —) COWHEEL
(TUBE —) SUCKER
(PREF.) PED(I)(O) PEDATI
PEDICULO PEZO POD(O)
(SUFF.) PED(E)
POD(A)(AL)(E)(IA)(IUM)(OUS) PUS
FOOTAGE SETUP
FOOTBALL GRID HURLY ROUGE
FOOTER HURLING LEATHER
PIGSKIN KICKBALL
(— FORMATION) SHOTGUN
WISHBONE
(— PLAY) DELAY SWING AUDIBLE
ROLLOUT SCRAMBLE
(— PLAYER) FLANKER SLOTBACK
(KIND OF —) CAMP
FOOTBOY PAGE PEDES
FOOTBRIDGE PLANK LIGGER
FOOTLOG
FOOTED FITTIT PEDATE
(SUFF.) PEDE PODOUS
FOOTFALL PAD STEP TREAD
FOOTSTEP
FOOTGEAR PATTEN FOOTWEAR
FOOTHOLD TIP HACK STEP
FOOTING TOEHOLD
FOOTING PAR FOOT TROD BASIS
EARTH TRACK HEADING PIECING
TOEHOLD FOOTHOLD
FOOTLESS APODAL
FOOTLIGHTS FOOTS FLOATS
LIGHTS
FOOTLIKE PEDATE
FOOTMAN SKIP FLUNKY JEAMES
LACKEY VARLET DOORMAN
FOOTPAD BOTTOMER CHASSEUR
HIRCARRA WAGONMAN
FOOTPACE HALFPACE PREDELLA
FOOTPAD PAD WHYO PADDER
ROBBER FOOTMAN PADFOOT
SCOURER LANDRAKER
FOOTPATH LANE TROD JETTY
SENDA TRAIL FOOTWAY
HIGHWAY PARAPET RAMPIRE

SIDEWALK TROTTOIR
(— TO A PASTURE) DRUNG
(RAISED —) CLAPPER
FOOTPICK CASCROM
FOOTPIECE STEP
FOOTPRINT PAD PUG STEP TROD
PRICK SPOOR TRACE TRACK
TRADE TREAD FOOTING ICHNITE
PUGMARK FOOTMARK
(PREF.) ICHN(O)
FOOTREST COASTER HASSOCK
STIRRUP
FOOTROPE HORSE
FOOTS SEDIMENT
FOOTSCRAPING SAND
FOOTSORENESS SURBATE
FOOTSTALK STRIG PODIUM
PEDICEL PETIOLE PEDUNCLE
(PREF.) PEDICULO
FOOTSTEP PAD STEP TROD CLAMP
VESTIGE FOOTBEAT FORESTEP
(PREF.) ICHN(O)
FOOTSTOOL TUT LOVE MORA
STOOL BUFFET SAMBLE CRICKET
HASSOCK OTTOMAN FOOTREST
FOOT-WASHING NIPTER
FOOTWAY PATH CATWALK
FOOTPATH
(— ALONGSIDE BRIDGE)
BANQUETTE
FOOTWEAR FEET
FOP TO ADON BEAU BUCK DUDE
DUPE FOOL KNUT PRIG TOFF
DANDY FLASH PUPPY MASHER
MOPPET VANITY COXCOMB
JESSAMY GIMCRACK MACARONI
MACAROON MUSCADIN POPINJAY
SKIPJACK
FOPPISH APISH DANDY FOPPY
SAPPY SILLY DAPPER PRETTY
SPRUCE STUPID BEAUISH
BUCKISH FANGLED FINICAL
FOOLISH DANDYISH SKIPJACK
FOR P IN TO PRO TIL VER TILL
SINCE FORWHY BECAUSE
FORNENT FAVORING
(— A LONG TIME) YORE
(— CASH) SPOT
(— EXAMPLE) EG VG
(— FEAR THAT) LEST
(— INSTANCE) AS SAY
(— THE EMERGENCY) PRN
(— THE MOST PART) FECKLY
GENERALLY
(— TIME BEING) ACTUALLY
(PREF.) PRO
FORAGE ERS OAT RYE CORN GUAR
MAST PROG RAID ETAPE FORAY
BREVIT RUSSUD ZACATE
GOITCHO HAYLAGE PICKEER
BOOTHALE SCROUNGE
FORAGER OUTRIDER
FORAMEN PORE EXOSTOME
METAPORE TROCHLEA
FORAMINIFER NUMMULITE
FORAY RAID MELEE CREAGH
FURROW INROAD MARAUD
RAVAGE RAZZIA SORTIE
CHAPPOW HERSHIP PILLAGE
SPREAGH SPREATH
FORBEAR LET BEAR HELP HOLD
SHUN SIRE AVOID FORGO SPARE
WAIVE DEPORT DESIST ENDURE

PARENT RETAIN ABSTAIN
DECLINE REFRAIN RESPITE
ANCESTOR FOREBEAR
WITHDRAW
(— PROSECUTION) COMPOUND
FORBEARANCE MERCY LENITY
NONACT PARDON QUARTER
MILDNESS PATIENCE
FORBEARING CLEMENT LENIENT
PATIENT MERCIFUL TOLERANT
FORBID BAN BAR NIX DEFY DENY
FEND TABU VETO WARN DEBAR
TABOO BANISH DEFEND ENJOIN
IMPEDE OPPOSE REFUSE SHIELD
FORFEND FORWARN GAINSAY
INHIBIT WITHSAY DISALLOW
FORSPEAK PRECLUDE PROHIBIT
PROSCRIBE
FORBIDDANCE BAN VETO
FORBODE
FORBIDDEN TABU TABOO BANNED
DENIED VERBOTEN
(SOMETHING —) NONO
FORBIDDING DOUR GRIM HARD
BLACK GAUNT STERN FIERCE
GLASSY GLOOMY GRISLY ODIOUS
STRICT FORBODE GRIZZLY
REPULSIVE
FORCE GAR GUT HAP JAM LID VIM
VIS ZIP BANG BEAR BEAT BEND
BIRR BODY CLIP CRAM DINT
DOOM DRAG EDGE FECK FOSS
GRIP GUTS HEAD JAMB JINX
MAIN MAKE MANA SNAP SOCK
ABATE AGENT ARDOR BRAWL
BRING BRUSH CLAMP COACT
CRAFT CROWD CRUSH DEMON
DRAFT DRIVE EXACT EXERT
FOHAT GAVEL IMPEL KARMA
MIGHT PAINT PEISE POACH POINT
POWER PRESS PRIZE PUNCH
REPEL SHEAR SHOVE SINEW
STEAM STUFF THROW WAKAN
WREST CHARGE COERCE COMPEL
CUDGEL DURESS EFFECT EFFORT
ENERGY EXTORT HIJACK HOTBED
IMPACT IMPOSE JOSTLE OBLIGE
POWDER RAVISH SHAKTI STRAIN
STRESS WRENCH ABILITY
AFFORCE BLUSTER CASCADE
COGENCE COGENCY CONCUSS
DRAUGHT DYNAMIC IMPETUS
IMPRESS IMPULSE LASHKAR
OPPRESS REQUIRE SQUEEZE
TORMENT VIOLATE WAKANDA
ACTIVITY ADHESION AFFINITY
BULLDOZE COACTION COERCION
DYNAMISM EFFICACY HOTHOUSE
MOMENTUM PRESSURE
STRENGTH VALIDITY VIOLENCE
VIRILITY NECESSITATE
(— AIR UPON) BLOW
(— AN ENTRANCE) RANDOM
THRUST
(— APART) SUNDER DISPART
(— BACK) REPEL RAMBARRE
(— BY THREAT) SWAGGER
(— DOWN) CLEW CLUE DETRUDE
DISMOUNT
(— IN) INJECT INTRUDE
(— OPEN) BURST JIMMY SPORT
RANFORCE
(— OUT) SPEW EJECT ERUPT

EVICT EXPEL KNOCK WRING
EXTUND EXPRESS
(— PASSAGE) SQUEEZE
(— WAY) CROWD WREST WRING
(— WITH LEGAL AUTHORITY) POSSE
(ALLEGED —) OD
(ARMED —) CREW HEAD POWER
CONREY ARMAMENT BATTALIA
(CONCENTRATED —) PITH
(CONFINING —) LID
(CONSTRAINING —) STRESS
(COSMIC —) EVIL
(CREATIVE —) NATURE
(DRIVING —) STEAM SWINGE
(EVOLUTIONARY —) BATHMISM
(EXPLOSIVE —) MEGATON
(HYPOTHETICAL —) FORTUNE
(LACK OF — TO DEFEAT) UNDERKILL
(LIFE —) SHAKTI
(MAIN —) BRUNT
(MILITANT —) SWORD
(MILITARY —) FYRD LEGION
WERING BAYONET OCCUPATION
(MOVING —) SOLICITATION
(NAVAL —) FLEET
(PHYSICAL —) NERVE
(PREPONDERATING —) SWAY
(PROTECTIVE —) CONVOY
(RELIGIOUS —) SANCTITY
(SACRED —) KAMI
(SPIRITUAL —) SOUL
(UNRESTRAINED —) FURY
(UPWARD —) BUOYANCY
(PL.) ARMY WILL COLORS
(SUFF.) **(UNIT OF —)** DYNE
FORCED LABORED ENFORCED
FALSETTO SARDONIC SPURIOUS
STRAINED
FORCEFUL RUDE GREAT GUTSY
PITHY STIFF STOUT MIGHTY
PUNCHY STRONG VIRILE
DYNAMIC STHENIC VIOLENT
BRUISING ELOQUENT EMPHATIC
ENFATICO FORCIBLE VIGOROUS
TRENCHANT
FORCEFULNESS PUNCH EMPHASIS
FORCEMEAT FARCE BOUDIN
GODIVEAU QUENELLE STUFFING
FORCEPS DOG FURCA TONGS
TENAIL BULLDOG CLAMMER
PINCERS PINSONS RONGEUR
CROWBILL DENTAGRA PINCETTE
VULSELLA TENACULUM
(PREF.) FORCI LABID(O)
FORCIBLE VIVE STOUT VALID
COGENT MIGHTY POTENT
STRONG FORCIVE NERVOUS
VIOLENT WEIGHTY EMPHATIC
FORCEFUL POWERFUL PREGNANT
PUISSANT VEHEMENT VIGOROUS
FORCIBLY AMAIN SADLY HARDLY
MAINLY HEAVILY STRONGLY
FORD PASS RACK RIFT WADE
WATH DRIFT STREAM CURRENT
FORDING PASSAGE PASSING
CROSSING
(PAVED —) STEAN STEENING
FORE VAN WAY AFORE AHEAD
FRONT PRIOR FORMER FURTHER
FOREARM CUBIT CUBITAL
CUBITUS
FOREBEAR ANCESTOR
FOREBODE BODE GIVE OMEN

ABODE AUGUR CROAK BETIDE
DIVINE BETOKEN MISBODE
OMINATE PORTEND PREDICT
PRESAGE FORETELL
(— EVIL) CROAK
FOREBODING OMEN BLACK FATAL
AUGURY BODING DISMAL
GLOOMY ANXIETY BALEFUL
BANEFUL DRUTHER OMINOUS
PRESAGE BODEMENT SINISTER
ABODEMENT PROGNOSTICATION
FOREBODINGLY DIRELY
FOREBRAIN CEREBRUM
PROENCEPHALON
FORECAST BODE CAST SCHEME
CAUTION FORESEE FORESET
PREDICT FOREDEEM FOREDOOM
FORETELL PROPHESY
ADUMBRATE PREVISION
PROGNOSIS PREDICTION
PROGNOSTICATION
FORECASTLE FOCSLE ISLAND
FORECOURT VESTIBULE
FOREDOOM JINX DESTINY
FOREFACE CUSHION
FOREFATHER AYEL SIRE ELDER
PITRI PARENT ANCESTOR
FOREBEAR PROGENITOR
PRIMOGENITOR
FOREFINGER INDEX
FOREFOOT PAW PUD GRIPE
FOREFOOTING MANGANA
FOREFRONT VAN FRONT VAWARD
FOREGO FORGO WAIVE ESCHEW
ABSTAIN NEGLECT PRECEDE
REFRAIN ABNEGATE DISPENSE
RENOUNCE
FOREGOING PAST ABOVE
ANTERIOR PREVIOUS PRECEDING
FOREGROUND PROSCENIUM
FOREHEAD BROW FRONS FRONT
FRONTLET SINCIPUT
(— INDENTATION) STOP
(— MARK) KUMKUM
(HIGH —) LEPTENE
(PREF.) FRONTI FRONTO METOPO
FOREHEARTH SETTLER
FOREIGN UNCO ALIEN FREMD
WELSH ALANGE EXILED EXOTIC
FRENCH REMOTE UNKIND
DISTANT ECDEMIC EPIGENE
EXCLUDE FRAMMIT HEATHEN
OUTBORN OUTLAND OUTWARD
STRANGE BARBARIC EPIGENIC
EXTERIOR EXTERNAL FORINSEC
OVERSEAS PEREGRIN STRANGER
BARBAROUS OUTLANDISH
TRAMONTANE
(— TO) DEHORS
(PREF.) ALIENI EXOTO
FOREIGNER ALIEN HAOLE ALLTUD
GRINGO PAKEHA GREENER
OUTBORN OUTLAND PARDESI
ETRANGER OUTSIDER PEREGRIN
PORTUGEE STRANGER
MLECHCHHA OUTLANDER
(PREF.) XEN(O)
(SUFF.) XENE XENOUS XENY
FOREKNOW DIVINE FORESEE
FOREWIT
FOREKNOWLEDGE PRESAGE
FORELEG GAMB
FORELOCK TOP BANG QUIFF

COTTER TOUPET FORETOP
TOPPING FOREBUSH
FOREMAN BOSS BULL CORK JOSS
LUNA PUSH CHIEF DOGGY
BUNTER GAFFER GANGER LEADER
RAMROD SIRDAR TENTER
CAPATAZ CAPORAL CAPTAIN
FOUNDER HEADMAN MANAGER
MANDOER OVERMAN SHOOFLY
SKIDDER STEWARD FOREHAND
GANGSMAN OVERSEER
(**— OF JURY**) CHANCELLOR
FOREMOST TOP HEAD HIGH MAIN
CHIEF FIRST FORME FRONT
GRAND BANNER FORMER
LEADING RANKING SUPREME
VANMOST CHAMPION
(**— PART**) VAWARD
FOREORDAIN FATE SLATE
DESTINE FORESAY PREDOOM
FORECAST
FOREORDINATION FATE
FOREPART FRONT FOREHEAD
(**— OF FACE**) CHAP
(**— OF HORSE'S HEAD**) CHANFRIN
(**— OF SHIP**) STEM FORWARD
CUTWATER ENTRANCE
FOREPOLE LATH SPILE SPILING
FORERUN HERALD OUTRUN
PRECEDE PRELUDE ANNOUNCE
FORESHOT
FORERUNNER OMEN SIGN USHER
AUGURY HERALD ANCESTOR
FOREGOER FOURRIER OUTRIDER
PRODROME MESSENGER
PRECURSOR
FORERUNNING PRECURSE
FORESADDLE RACK
FORESEE SEE READ DIVINE
PURVEY PREVISE PROVIDE
ENVISAGE ENVISION FORECAST
FOREKNOW PROSPECT
PREFIGURE
FORESHADOW HINT FIGURE
HERALD FORERUN PATTERN
PRELUDE PRESAGE UMBRATE
FORETYPE ADUMBRATE
FORESHORE HARD SHORE
HARDWAY SEASHORE
FORESHOW BODE ABODE AUGUR
BETOKEN PORTEND SIGNIFY
FORETELL PROPHESY
FORESIGHT FEAR VISION FOREWIT
FORECAST FORELOOK PROSPECT
PRUDENCE
FORESIGHTED CAGY CAGEY
CANNY
FOREST BUSH GAPO MATA RUKH
WOLD WOOD FIRTH GLADE
GUBAT MATTA MATTO MONTE
SYLVA TAIGA WASTE WEALD
JUNGLE TIMBER BOSCAGE
CALYDON COPPICE CAATINGA
WOODLAND
(**— CITY**) PORTLAND SAVANNAH
CLEVELAND
(**— FOR DEER**) FIRTH
(**IMMENSE —**) MONTANA
(**RAIN —**) SELVA
(**SIBERIAN —**) URMAN
(**STUNTED —**) CAATINGA
KRUMMHOLZ
(**PREF.**) HYL(O) SILVI SYLVI

FORESTAGE APRON
FORESTALL BEAT HELP LURCH
STALL DEVANCE FORERUN
OBVIATE PREVENE PREVENT
FORSTEAL ANTICIPATE
FORESTALLER KIDDER GROSSER
FORESTAYSAIL JUMBO
FORESTER FOSTER WALKER
MONTERO TINEMAN TREEMAN
WOODMAN WOODSMAN
FORETASTE GUST HANSEL TEASER
EARNEST HANDSEL ANTEPAST
PROSPECT PRELIBATION
FORETELL BODE ERST READ SPAE
AUGUR INSEE WEIRD WRITE
DIVINE HALSEN HERALD BESPEAK
FORESAY PORTEND PREDICT
PRESAGE ANNOUNCE FOREBODE
FORECAST FORESHOW PROPHESY
SOOTHSAY
FORETELLING PROPHECY
FORETHOUGHT CAUTION
FORECAST PREPENSE PRUDENCE
FORETOKEN OMEN AUGUR
PORTEND PROMISE FORECAST
FORESHOW FORESIGN
FOREVER AY AKE AYE EVER ETERN
ALWAYS ETERNE ENDLESS
ETERNITY EVERMORE
FOREWARN WEIRD PREMONISH
FOREWARNING HINT PORTENT
PREMONITION
FOREWING PRIMARY
FOREWORD PROEM PREFACE
PREAMBLE
FORFEIT WED FINE LOSE TINE
WITE CHEAT CRIME DEDIT FORGO
LAPSE FOREGO SCONCE DEFAULT
ESCHEAT FORWORK PENALTY
FORFAULT
FORFEITURE FINE BLIND MULCT
TINSEL ESCHEAT FORFEIT
PENALTY
FORGE FOGE MINT TILT WELL
CLICK FALSE FEIGN SMITH STOVE
HAMMER SMITHY STEADY STITCH
STITHY SWINGE CHAFERY FALSIFY
FASHION BLOOMERY
FORGED BOGUS SPURIOUS
FORGER SMITH FALSER FALSARY
LEVERMAN
FORGERY SHAM FALSUM FICTION
BLOOMERY
FORGET LOSE OMIT WANT FLUFF
BILEVE UNKNOW UNMIND
NEGLECT OVERLOOK
FORGETFUL OBLIVIOUS
FORGETFULNESS SWIM FLUFF
LETHE AMNESIA AMNESTY
OBLIVION
(**PREF.**) LETHO
FORGET-ME-NOT MYOSOTE
FORGETTING
(**PREF.**) LETHO
FORGING HOOP CLICK JACKET
FORGIVE REMIT SPARE ASSOIL
EXCUSE PARDON ABSOLVE
CONDONE OVERLOOK
FORGIVENESS GRACE PARDON
FORGIFT
FORGIVING GRACE HUMANE
CLEMENT MERCIFUL
MAGNANIMOUS

FORGOTTEN DERELICT UNMINDED
FORINT FLORIN
FORK CROC EVIL HOOK TANG TINE
CLEFT CLOFF FURCA GLACK
GRAIN GRAIP PRONG TWIST
BISECT BRANCH CLITCH CROTCH
DIVIDE FEEDER GAFFLE HACKER
OFFSET TWISEL BIPRONG
FOURCHE FRUGGIN HAYFORK
TOASTER CROTCHET EQUULEUS
GRAINING PITCHFORK
(**— OF BODY**) SHARE
(**— OF PENNON**) FANON
(**— OF WINDPIPE**) BRONCHUS
(**MEAT —**) TORMENTOR
(**THATCHER'S —**) GROM
(**TUNING —**) DIAPASON
(**PREF.**) FURCI
FORKED BIFID FORKY FURCAL
PRONGY DIVIDED FURCATE
LITUATE BIFORKED BIRAMOUS
BRANCHED FOURCHEE SUBBIFID
FORKING STAR
FORLORN LORN LOST REFT ALONE
ABJECT FORFAIRN FORSAKEN
HELPLESS HOPELESS PITIABLE
WITLOSEN
FORM AME DIG FIG HEW HUE SET
BLEE BODY CASE CAST CAUL
DOME FLOW GARB IDEA KERN
KITE MAKE MODE MOLD PLAN
RITE SEAT THEW TURN BENCH
BLANK BLOCK BOARD BUILD
BUNCH CHART CHECK CRUSH
DUMMY EIDOS ERECT FORGE
FORMA FORME FRAME GALBE
GUISE IMAGE MATCH MEUSE
MODEL SHAPE SPELL STAMP
THROW USAGE ADJUST CHALAN
COUPON CREATE CUSTOM DEVISE
DOCKET FIGURE FILLER HANGER
INVENT MANNER REMOVE RITUAL
SCHEMA SCHOOL SPONGE STRIKE
SYSTEM TAILLE AGENDUM
ARRANGE COMPOSE CONFECT
CONTOUR DEVELOP FASHION
FEATURE FORMULA GESTALT
IMPANEL INVOICE LITURGY
MAKEDOM OUTLINE PATTERN
PORTRAY PORTURE PRODUCE
PROFILE SPECIES STATURE
BILLHEAD CEREMONY COMPOUND
CONCEIVE CONTRIVE FORMWORK
INSTRUCT LIKENESS MODALITY
ORGANIZE SEMBLANCE
(**— A HEAD**) POME
(**— A NETWORK**) PLEX
(**— A RING**) ENVIRON
(**— ASSUMED AFTER DEATH**)
KAMARUPA
(**— BRANCHES**) BREAK
(**— BY CUTTING OFF**) ABJOINT
(**— CONNECTION**) ALLY
(**— FOR BELL FOUNDING**) SWEEP
(**— FOR CONCRETE**) BOXING
(**— FOR HOLDING BARREL**) SQUAW
(**— FOR MOLD**) JACKET
(**— FOR PRESSING VENEERS**) CAUL
(**— FRUIT**) KNIT
(**— INTO A CHAIN**) CATENATE
(**— INTO BALL**) CONGLOBE
(**— INTO RINGLETS**) CRISP
(**— LEATHER**) CRIMP

(**— MOUND**) TUMP
(**— OF GOVERNMENT**) ESTATE
KINGSHIP
(**— OF PREDICATION**) CATEGORY
(**— POLITICAL SUCCESSION**) CAVE
(**— WITH PLASTER**) RUN
(**— YARN INTO THREAD**) CABLE
(**ANCESTRAL —**) BLASTAEA
STEMFORM
(**CONVENTIONAL —**) AMENITY
(**DEXTROROTATORY —**) CAMPHOR
(**DISPLAY —**) MANNEQUIN
(**IMPERFECT —**) SEMIFORM
(**IRREGULAR —**) PSEUDOMORPH
(**ISOMETRIC —**) DIPLOID
(**LINGUISTIC —**) FOSSIL GERUND
(**LITERARY —**) KNACK
(**LYRICAL —**) SESTINA
(**MUSICAL —**) RAGA SUITE
(**POETIC —**) CINQUAIN
(**POINTED —**) ANGLE
(**SCHOOL —**) SHELL
(**SHOE —**) LAST FILLER
(**SHORTENED —**) ABBREVIATION
(**SONG —**) BAR
(**SPECTRAL —**) SHADOW
(**SPEECH —**) LEXEME IDIOLECT
(**SPIRAL OR CIRCULAR —**) GYRE
(**STRUCTURE —**) MORPHOLOGY
(**TOP —**) GROOVE
(**VERB —**) FUTURE CONATIVE
DEFINITE DURATIVE
(**VERSE —**) EPODE BALLAD
PANTUM SONNET KYRIELLE
LIMERICK
(**VISIBLE —**) RUPA
(**WILD —**) AGRIOTYPE
(**WORD —**) ETYMON ANOMALY
(**PREF.**) IDO MORPH(O) PLASMATO
(**SUFF.**) FY GEN(E)(ESIA)(ESIS)
(ETIC)(IC)(IN)(OUS)(Y) IFY
MORPH(A)(AE)(IC)(ISM)(OSIS)(OTIC)
(OUS)(Y) PLASIA PLASIS
PLASM(A)(IA)(IC) PLAST(IC)(Y)
PLASY
(**HAVING — OF**) IC(AL)
(**IN THE — OF**) OID(AL)
FORMAL DRY SET BOOK PRIM
BUDGE CHILL COURT EXACT
STIFF SOCIAL SOLEMN STOCKY
ANGULAR BOOKISH LOGICAL
NOMINAL ORDERLY OUTWARD
PRECISE REGULAR SOLWARD
STARCHY STATELY STILTED
ABSTRACT ACADEMIC AFFECTED
ELEVATED FORMULAR OFFICIAL
PUNCTUAL STARCHED
FORMALDEHYDE FORMAL
MONOSE HARDENER METHANAL
FORMALISM ACADEMISM
FORMALIST PEDANT SCHOLASTIC
FORMALISTIC COURT ACADEMIC
FORMALITY FORM SASINE STARCH
BUCKRAM DECENCY WIGGERY
CEREMONY PHARISAISM
FORMALIZE STIFFEN
FORMALLY FORMLY STARCHLY
FORMAT SIZE GETUP SHAPE STYLE
FORMATION FORM RANK SPUR
BIOME FLIGHT GROWTH HARROW
MASSIF SPREAD POTENCE
BOTRYOID

(— ENCLOSING MINE WORKING) GROUND
(— ENCOUNTERED IN DRILLING) STRAY
(— OF BRAIN) FORNIX
(— OF BRANCHES) CANOPY
(— OF CRYSTAL) SHOOT
(— OF JOINT) ANKYLOSIS
(— OF PLANES) JAVELIN
(— ON TOAD) SPADE
(— RESEMBLING ICICLE) STIRIA
(BATTLE —) HERSE
(CLOUD —) NUBECULA
(DANCE —) SET
(DIAGONAL —) HARROW
(DRIPSTONE —) COLUMN
(ECOLOGICAL —) BIOME
(FLIGHT —) SQUADRON
(FOOTBALL —) SHOTGUN WISHBONE
(GEOLOGIC —) BOEL CULM CHICO STRAY MARKER MEDINA CURTAIN MANLIUS MATAWAN POTOMAC TERRAIN AQUIFUGE FERNANDO KOOTANIE KOOTENAI LOCKPORT TOPATOPA YORKTOWN
(HABIT —) FIXATION
(INDENTED —) CLEFT
(INFANTRY —) TERTIA ECHELON
(LAND —) BOOTHEEL
(MILITARY —) SNAIL FLIGHT
(NAVAL —) SCREEN
(POINTED —) BEAK
(PREF.) PLASTO
(TAIL —) CERC(O)
(SUFF.) GENESIA GENESIS OSIS POEIA POESIS POIESIS POIETIC
FORMATIVE CREANT PLASTIC DEMIURGIC
(SUFF.) POEIA POESIS POIESIS POIETIC
FORMED BUILT BOOKIT DECIDED MATURED SETTLED WROUGHT TIMBERED
(— AT BASE OF MOUNTAIN) PIEDMONT
(— INTO STEPS) GRADY
(— ON SURFACE OF EARTH) EPIGENE
(IMPERFECTLY —) ABORTIVE
(STURDILY —) BUXOM
(PREF.) APO PLASTO
FORMEE PATE PATTEE
FORMER DIE OLD ERER ERST FERN FORE LATE ONCE PAST ELDER FORME GAUGE GUIDE MAKER OTHER PRIOR BYGONE RATHER WHILOM ANCIENT ANOTHER CREATOR EARLIER FIRSTER FURTHER ONETIME PRIDIAN QUONDAM TEMPLET UMWHILE PRETERIT PREVIOUS PRISTINE SOMETIME STRICKLE UMQUHILE PRECEDING
(PREF.) PROTER(O)
FORMERLY ERE NEE OLD ERST FORE ONCE THEN YORE GRAVE WHILOM WHILST ONETIME QUONDAM SOMETIME UMQUHILE
FORMIDABLE MEAN FEARFUL ALARMING DREADFUL MENACING TERRIBLE FEROCIOUS REDOUBTABLE

(— PERSON) TARTAR
FORMING
(SUFF.) GENIC GEROUS
FORMLESS ARUPA DOUGHY ANIDIAN CHAOTIC DEFORMED INDIGEST
FORMOSA (SEE TAIWAN)
FORMULA LAW MIX DATE FIAT FORM RULE CANON CREED DHIKR GRAPH INDEX LURRY KEKULE MANTRA METHOD RECIPE THEORY RECEIPT APOLYSIS CLAUSULE DOXOLOGY EXORCISM
(— OF FAITH) KELIMA
(MAGICAL —) CARACT
(WORD —) PATERNOSTER
(PL.) RAKA RAKAH
FORMULARY SYMBOL
FORMULATE PUT CAST DRAW FRAME DEVISE CAPSULE COMPOSE FORMULE PLATFORM
FORMULATED STATED WRITTEN
FORMULATION (— OF A TRUTH) COUNT CREED DOGMA APHORISM APOTHEGM DOCTRINE
(SUFF.) (SYSTEMATIC —) ICS
FORMWORK SHUTTERING
FORNIX VAULT PSALIS
FORSAKE DENY DROP FLEE QUIT SHUN ABAND AVOID FORGO LEAVE WAIVE DEFECT DEPART DESERT FOREGO FORHOO FORLET REFUSE REJECT ABANDON DISCARD FORLESE DESOLATE FORHOOIE RENOUNCE WITHDRAW
FORSAKEN LORN FORLORN DESERTED DESOLATE LASSLORN
FORSETE (FATHER OF —) BALDER
FORSOOTH EVEN MARRY QUOTH
FORSWEAR DENY ABJURE REJECT ABANDON PERJURE ABNEGATE MANSWEAR RENOUNCE
FORSYTE SAGA (AUTHOR OF —) GALSWORTHY
(CHARACTER IN —) JON VAL JUNE MONT FLEUR HOLLY IRENE JOLLY MONTY DARTIE JOLYON PHILIP SOAMES ANNETTE FORSYTE LAMOTTE MICHAEL PROFOND PROSPER SWITHIN TIMOTHY BOSINNEY WINIFRED
FORT PA DUN LIS PAH LISS PEEL SHEE SPUR WORK COTTA REDAN SIDHE CASTLE SANGAR SCHERM SCONCE STRONG BASTION BULWARK CITADEL CLOSURE REDOUBT BASTILLE CASTILLO FASTHOLD FASTNESS FORTRESS MARTELLO PRESIDIO
(FAIRY —) LIS LIOS LISS SHEE SIDHE
(HILL —) RATH
(RUINS OF —) ZIMBABWE
(SMALL —) GURRY FORTIN BASTIDE FORTLET FORCELET
FORTE FORT STARK METIER STRONG EMINENCY STRENGTH
FORTESCUE COBBLER SCORPION
FORTH OUT AWAY FURTH
(PREF.) E OUT
FORTHCOMING PROXIMATE
FORTHRIGHT BALD BURLY

GUTTY CANDID
FORTHRIGHTLY FRANKLY
FORTHRIGHTNESS PLUMPNESS
FORTHWITH EFT NOW ANON AWAY BEDENE DIRECT BETIMES FORTHON DIRECTLY
FORTIFICATION BAWN BOMA FORT MOAT WALL REDAN TOWER ABATIS CASHEL CASTLE GLACIS LAAGER BASTION BULWARK CITADEL DEFENCE DEFENSE PARAPET PILLBOX RAMPART RAVELIN REDOUBT FORTRESS MUNITION RONDELLE STRENGTH
(LINE OF —S) TROCHA
(PART OF —) BERM MOAT ANGLE DITCH FLANK GORGE SCARP SLOPE COVERT ESCARP GLACIS PARADE BASTION CURTAIN PARAPET RAMPART SALIENT BANQUETTE TERREPLEIN COUNTERSCARP
FORTIFIED ARMED CONFIRMED
FORTIFY ARM MAN BANK FORT LINE WALL WARD FENCE SPIKE STANK BATTLE IMMURE MUNIFY MUNITE BULWARK COMFORT DEFENSE GARNISH RAMPIRE BASTILLE EMBATTLE FORTRESS RAMFORCE STOCKADE
FORTITUDE GRIT GUTS SAND FIBER FIBRE NERVE PLUCK METTLE BRAVERY COURAGE HEROISM STAMINA BACKBONE PATIENCE STRENGTH
(AUTHOR OF —) WALPOLE
(CHARACTER IN —) TAN HANZ NORA BOBBY BRANT CLARE JERRY PETER ZANTI EMILIO LAUNCE GALLEON JERRARD MONOGUE STEPHEN ZACHARY BROCKETT ROSSITER WESTCOTT CARDILLAC GOTTFRIED AITCHINSON
FORTNIGHTLY BIWEEKLY
FORTRESS (ALSO SEE FORT) BURG KEEP KASBA PIECE PLACE ROCCA CASBAH CASTLE ALCAZAR BARRIER BOROUGH CASTRUM CHATEAU CITADEL KREMLIN ZWINGER ALCAZAVA BASTILLE FASTNESS STRENGTH
(AUTHOR OF —) WALPOLE
(CHARACTER IN —) ADAM JOHN KRAFT PARIS ROGUE BENJIE CAESAR JUDITH REUBEN TEMPLE UHLAND WALTER HERRIES SUNWOOD JENNIFER MARGARET ELIZABETH GOLIGHTLY CHRISTABEL
FORTUITOUS CASUAL CHANCE RANDOM FORTUIT FORTUNEL
FORTUITY LUCK CHANCE
FORTUNATE EDI FAT HAP SRI GOOD SHRI WELL CANNY FAUST HAPPY LUCKY RIGHT WHITE DEXTER EUROUS BLESSED FAVORED WEIRDLY GRACIOUS
FORTUNATELY FAIR HAPPILY
FORTUNE DIE HAP LOT URE BAHI DOOM FALL FARE FATE HAIL LUCK PILE SEEL STAR EVENT GRACE ISSUE LINES SONSE SPEED

WEIRD WHATE CHANCE ESTATE MISHAP RICHES WEALTH DESTINY SUCCESS THEEDOM VENTURE ACCIDENT CASUALTY FELICITY STOCKING
(GOOD —) SELE SONSE SPEED THRIFT FURTHER GOODHAP BONCHIEF FELICITY
(ILL —) DOOM THRAW
(PREF.) TYCH(O)
FORTUNES OF RICHARD MAHONY (AUTHOR OF —) RICHARDSON
(CHARACTER IN —) TOM JOHN LUCY MARY ZARA CUFFY OCOCK POLLY SARAH LALLIE MAHONY RICHARD TURNHAM CUTHBERT
FORTUNE-TELLER SEER SIBYL SYBIL SPAEMAN SORTIARY SPAEWIFE
(PL.) CHALDAEI
FORTY DAYS OF MUSA DAGH (AUTHOR OF —) WERFEL
(CHARACTER IN —) TER HAIK MARIS SARKIS BEREKET GABRIEL STEPHAN GONZAGUE HAIGASUN HULIETTE KILIKIAN BAGRADIAN NOKHUDIAN
FORUM COURT PLATFORM TRIBUNAL
FORWARD ON TO AID BOG BUG GAY ABET BAIN BOLD FORE FREE HELP PERT SEND SHIP STEP AHEAD ALONG AVANT BARDY BRASH CAGER EAGER FAVOR FORTH FRACK FRECK FRONT HASTY PAWKY PUSHY RANDY READY RELAY REMIT SAUCY SERVE SPACK ULTRA AFFORD ARDENT AVAUNT BEFORE BRIGHT COMING DEVANT FORRIT FORTHY HASTEN NUZZLE ONWARD PROMPT ROUDAS SECOND TOWARD ADVANCE BETIMES EARNEST EXTREME FURTHER PROMOTE PUSHING RADICAL SOLICIT ADELANTE ARROGANT FROMWARD IMMODEST IMPUDENT MALAPERT ONCOMING PERVERSE PETULANT TELLSOME TOWARDLY TRANSMIT OBTRUSIVE
(MOST —) HEADMOST
(PREF.) ANTE
(LEANING —) PRONO
FORWARDNESS IMMODESTY
FOR WHOM THE BELL TOLLS (AUTHOR OF —) HEMINGWAY
(CHARACTER IN —) MARIA PABLO PILAR JORDAN ROBERT ANSELMO
FORZA DEL DESTINO, LA (CHARACTER IN —) CARLO ALVARO LEONORA CALATRAVA
(COMPOSER OF —) VERDI
FOSSA FOSS FOVEA GALET TRENCH VALLIS FOSSULA FOSSETTE
FOSSE DITCH GRAFF
FOSSIL CYCAD CYSTID DOLITE EOZOON FUCOID ICHITE PINITE AMBRITE BLASTID CHAMITE CRINITE ICHNITE JUNCITE LITUITE NEREITE OVULITE REMANIE

TYLOPOD ZOOLITE ZOOLITH
AISTOPOD AMMONITE
ANCODONT ASTROITE BACULITE
BALANITE BIOCHRON BLASTOID
BUFONITE CALAMITE CERATITE
CONCHITE CONODONT ECHINITE
EOHIPPUS FAVOSITE FILICITE
FUSULINA GEDANITE GYROLITH
MIMOSITE PEUCITES POLYPITE
SALIGRAM SCAPHITE SERAPHIM
SPONGOID SYNAPSID TARSIOID
CARPOLITE OSTRACODERM
(PREF.) NECR(O) ORYCT(O)
(SUFF.) LITE LITH(IC) LITIC
FOSTER REAR NURSE COCKER
HARBOR NUZZLE SUCKLE
CHERISH DEPOSIT EMBOSOM
GRATIFY INDULGE NOURISH
NOURSLE NURTURE BEFRIEND
CULTIVATE
FOSTERAGE NURSERY
FOSTERER NORRY
FOUL BAD BASE EVIL HORY RANK
ROIL VILE BAWDY BLACK DIRTY
DITCH FUNKY GRIMY GURRY
HORRY KETTY LOUSY MUDDY
MUSTY NASTY RUSTY SULLY
WEEDY CLARTY DEFAME DIRTEN
DREGGY FILTHY GREASY IMPURE
MALIGN ODIOUS PUTRID ROTTEN
SOILED SORDID UNFAIR VIROSE
ABUSIVE BEASTLY DEFACED
FULSOME HATEFUL ILLEGAL
IMBROIN NOISOME OBSCENE
PROFANE SLOTTER SMEARED
SQUALID TETROUS UNCLEAN
VICIOUS AMURCOUS ENTANGLE
FECULENT INDECENT MEPHITIC
SLOTTERY STAGNANT STINKING
TRAUCHLE WRETCHED
(— UP) BOTCH
FOULMOUTHED RIBALD ROUDAS
ABUSIVE OBSCENE PROFANE
FOULNESS FEDITY PRAVITY
(— OF MOUTH) SABURRA
FOUL-SMELLING FUNKY
FOUND FIX TRY YET BASE CAST
REST STAY BEGIN BOARD BUILD
ENDOW ERECT PLANT START
ATTACH BOTTOM DEPART
GROUND INVENT EQUIPPED
PRACTICE PROVIDED SUPPLIED
FOUNDATION BED BASE BODY
FIRM FOND FUND GIST ROOT SILL
SOLE BASIS FOUND STOCK STOOL
ANLAGE BOTTOM CRADLE
GROUND LEGACY MATRIX
PODIUM RIPRAP BEDDING
BEDROCK CHANTRY COLLEGE
MORTISE PINNING RADICAL
ROADBED SUBBASE WARRANT
BACKBONE DONATION MATTRESS
MIREPOIX PEDESTAL PLATFORM
STANDARD UNDERLAY
(— FOR WIG) CAUL
(— OF BASKET) SLATH SLARTH
(FLOATING —) CRIB
(LACE —) RESEAU
(PRECARIOUS —) STILT
FOUNDATIONER GOWNBOY
COLLEGER
FOUNDED FUSILE
FOUNDER FAIL IMAM AUTHOR

CASTER DYNAST EPONYM HELLEN
YETTER AFOUNDE STUMBLE
BELLETER MISCARRY LAMINITIS
PATRIARCH
(— OF COLONY) OECIST
FOUNT FONS FONT SOURCE
FOUNTAIN URN AQUA FOND HEAD
KELD PANT PILA SYKE WELL
DIRCE FOUNT GURGE QUELL
SURGE ORIGIN PHIALE PIRENE
SOURCE SPRING BUBBLER
CONDUIT SPRUDEL AGANIPPE
SALMACIS UPSPRING WELLHEAD
(INK —) DUCT
(SODA —) SPA
(PREF.) PEGO
(SUFF.) CRENE
FOUNTAINHEAD ORIGIN SOURCE
FOUNTAIN PEN STICK STYLO
FOUR MESS CATER DELTA DALETH
FEOWER TETRAD QUARTET
QUATRAL MURNIVAL QUADRATE
(— OF ANYTHING) GUNDA
(— OF TRUMPS) TIDDY
(— TIMES A DAY) QD QID
(— YEAR PERIOD) PYTHIAD
(GROUP OF —) TETRAD
(PREF.) QUADR(I)(U) QUADRATO
QUATER TESSARA TETR(A)
(— ATOMS OF HYDROGEN)
TETRAZ(O)
(— TIMES) QUATER TETRAKIS
(HAVING — PARTS) TETR(A)
FOURCHETTE FORGET SIDEWALL
WISHBONE
FOURFOLD FOURBLE QUATERN
**FOUR HORSEMEN OF
APOCALYPSE (AUTHOR OF —)**
IBANEZ
(CHARACTER IN —) JULIO CHICHI
MARCELO DESNOYER HARTROTT
FOURIERISM SOCIALISM
FOUR-O'CLOCK FRIARBIRD
FOURPENNY BIT JOE FLAG JOEY
GROAT
FOURTEENER SEPTENAR
FOURTH DELTA QUART FARDEL
FORPIT FERLING QUARTER
QUADRANT
(— HOUR) SEXT
(— OF BAHMANI EMPIRE) TARAF
(— OF CAKE) FARL FARLE
(— OF YEAR) RAITH
(AUGMENTED —) TRITONE
(PREF.) QUART(I) TETART(O)
FOUSSA CIVET GALET
FOVEOLA VARIOLE
FOWL HEN RED COCK GAME GRIG
JAVA ROCK SLIP BIDDY CHUCK
CLUCK COPPY DUMPY MALAY
MANOC MARAN SILKY ANCONA
ASHURA BANTAM BRAHMA
CAMBAR COCHIN HOUDAN
LAMONA LEGBAR POLISH REDCAP
SULTAN SUSSEX BUFFBAR
CAMPINE CHICKEN CORNISH
DORKING FRIZZLE HAMBURG
LEGHORN MINORCA OKLABAR
POULTRY ROOSTER SPANISH
SUMATRA COCKEREL CUBALAYA
DELAWARE DUCKWING DUNGHILL
GAMECOCK LANGSHAN
SHANGHAI SHOWBIRD VOLAILLE

(AGGREGATION OF —) RAFT
(CASTRATED —) CAPETTE
(CRESTED —) TOPKNOT
(GUINEA —) KEET COMEBACK
(MALE —) STAG
(STUFFED —) FARCI
(TAILLESS —) RUMKIN
(5-TOED —) SILKY SILKIE
FOWLER BIRDMAN
FOX DOG KIT PUG TOD ASSE FOOL
STAG WILD ADIVE BRANT CAAMA
SWIFT TRICK VIXEN ZORRO
ARCTIC BAGMAN CANDUC
COLFOX CORSAC FENNEC LOWRIE
OUTWIT RENARD RUSSEL
BEGUILE CHARLEY CHARLIE
KARAGAN REYNARD STUPEFY
VULPINE CUSTOMER MUSKWAKI
OUTAGAMI PLATINUM
FOX-AND-GEESE MERELS
FOXGLOVE POPPY POPDOCK
THIMBLE FLAPDOCK POPGLOVE
FOX GRAPE ISABELLA LABRUSCA
FOXHOUND WALKER
FOX HUNTER PINK
FOXTAIL CAUDA CHAPE COUGH
KNEED TWITCH SETARIA
GAMELOTE
FOXY SLY WILY COONY SHREWD
CUNNING VULPINE DEXTROUS
FOYER HALL LOBBY ANTEROOM
FRACAS BOUT BRAWL MELEE
MUSIC BICKER RUMPUS SHINDY
UPROAR QUARREL SHINDIG
FRACTION INCIDENT
FRACTION BIT CUT PYO FLUX
PART BREAK PIECE SCRAP
BREACH LITTLE MOIETY DECIMAL
GLUTOSE WETNESS
(— OF RADIATION) ALBEDO
(NAPHTHA —) LIGROIN
(PREF.) MER(I)(O)
(SUFF.) MER(E)(IC)(OUS)(Y)
FRACTIONAL ALIQUOT FRACTED
PARTIAL
FRACTIOUS MEAN UGLY CROSS
UNRULY CRABBED PEEVISH
WASPISH PERVERSE SNAPPISH
FRACTURE BUST FLAW REND
BILGE BREAK CLEFT CRACK FAULT
JOINT BREACH DEFORM HACKLE
DIACOPE FISSURE RUPTURE
DIACLASE FRACTION
(PREF.) RHEGMA RHEGNO
(SUFF.) CLASE RHEXIS RRHEXIS
FRACTURED SPLIT BROKEN
FRACTURING SLIP STRAIN
FAILURE
FRA DIAVOLO (CHARACTER IN —)
PAMELA DIAVOLO LORENZO
ZERLINA COCKBURN
(COMPOSER OF —) AUBER
FRAGILE FINE FROW WEAK FRAIL
FROWY LIGHT SWACK FEEBLE
FROUGH INFIRM SLIGHT TENDER
BRICKLE BRITTLE FROUGHY
SLENDER TIFFANY DELICATE
EGGSHELL ETHEREAL FRACTILE
SLATTERY BREAKABLE
FRAGILITY DELICACY
FRAGMENT BIT ORT ATOM BLAD
CHIP DRIB FLAW GROT MOIT
MOTE PART RUMP SHED SNIP

WISP ANGLE BLAUD BRACK
BREAK BROKE CATCH CHUNK
CLOUT CRUMB FRUST GIGOT
PIECE RELIC SCRAP SHARD SHERD
SHIVE SHRED SPALL SPELL SPLIT
CANTLE FARDEL FILING GOBBET
MORSEL REMAIN SCREED SHIVER
SIPPET SLIVER CANTLET EXCERPT
FLINDER FLITTER FRITTER
FRUSTUM MACERAL MAMMOCK
REMANIE REMNANT SEGMENT
SHATTER SHAVING SNIPPET
AVULSION CHIPPING DETRITUS
FRACTION OARTICLE POTSHERD
SCANTLET SKERRICK SPLINTER
(— CUT OFF) CANTLE
(— OF BONE) SEQUESTER
SEQUESTRUM
(— OF BRICK) BRICKBAT
(— OF DIAMOND) CLEAVAGE
(— OF ICE) CALF
(— OF LAVA) FAVILLA LAPILLUS
(— OF MELODY) LAY
(— OF ROCK) CRAG AUTOLITH
LAPILLUS
(— OF SAIL) HULLOCK
(— OF SOD) TAB
(— OF STONE) SCABBLING
(— OF UNFINISHED WORK) TORSO
(— OF VEIN MATERIAL) SHOAD
SHODE
(—S OF CLOUD) SCUD
(-S OF DIAMOND) BORT
(—S OF SAND) FINES
(CAST IRON —) POTLEG
(ICE —S) BRASH
(JAGGED —) BROCK
(LITERARY —) ANALECTA
(MASS OF —S) BRASH
(PLANT —) SHIVE
(SHELL —S) SHRAPNEL
(WOODY —S FOUND IN FOOD) CHAD
(PL.) BRASH FRUSH SCRAPS
CINDERS FITTERS GUBBINS
SMATTER FLINDERS LEFTOVER
SMITHERS SMITHEREENS
FRAGMENTAL CLASTIC
FRAGMENTARY HASHY SNIPPY
SCRAPPY DIVIDUAL
FRAGRANCE BALM ODOR AROMA
SCENT SMELL SWEET BREATH
FLAVOR FRAGOR BOUQUET
INCENSE PERFUME SUAVITY
FRAGRANT NOSY RICH BALMY
OLENT SPICY SWEET SAVORY
SPICED ODORANT ODOROUS
PERFUMY SCENTED AROMATIC
FLAGRANT NECTARED ODORIFIC
REDOLENT
FRAIL FINE POOR PUNY WEAK
CRAZY REEDY SEELY SILLY
BASKET BROTEL CROCKY FLIMSY
INFIRM SICKLY SINGLE SLIGHT
SLIMSY SQUEAL TICKLE TOPNET
BRITTLE BRUCKLE FRAGILE
SLENDER SLIMPSY UNHARDY
DELICATE PINDLING
FRAILTY FAULT FOIBLE INVENT
FAILING DELICACY WEAKNESS
(HUMAN —) ADAM
FRAMBESIA PIAN YAWS BUBAS
MORULA
FRAME BED BIN BOW BOX FLY

GYM MAT SET BAIL BEAM BIER
BUCK BULK BUNK CANT CASE
CAUM CELL CLAM CRIB CURB
DESK DRAG FORM FROG GATE
GILL HACK HARP HECK JACK
MOLD PORT RACK SASH SLEY
SOLE STEP AIRER ANGLE BANJO
BLADE BLIND BLOCK BUILD
CADRE CHASE CLEAT CRATE
CROOK DRAFT EASEL FLAKE
FLASK FLEAK FLOAT GRATE
HERSE HORSE MOUNT OXBOW
PERCH PRESS SCRAY SHAPE
STAND STATE STEAD STOCK
STOOL TRAIL BARROW BATTEN
BINDER BUCCAN BUCKET CASING
CHEVAL COFFIN CRADLE CRATCH
CRUTCH DECKLE DREDGE FABRIC
FENDER GANTRY GRILLE HANGER
HARROW HOTBED HURDLE
PERSON PILLAR QUADRA REDACT
REEDER SCREEN SETTLE SLEDGE
SPIDER SQUARE STAPLE TANGLE
TENTER TESTER ARMRACK
BREAKER CABINET CARRIER
CASEBOX CHASSIS COAMING
COASTER CRAMPON CRIMPER
DRAUGHT DROSSER FASHION
FRAMING FRISKET GALLOWS
GARLAND GATEWAY GIGTREE
GRATING HAYRACK HOUSING
ICEBOAT MACHINE MONTURE
OXBRAKE PORTRAY SETTING
STADDLE TRANSOM TRESTLE
TRIBBLE BARBECUE BOWGRACE
CARRIAGE CASEMENT CONCEIVE
CONTRIVE DOORCASE GRAFFAGE
GRIDIRON GRILLAGE HALBERDS
HOGFRAME PLOWHEAD
RAILROAD RECEIVER RETAINER
SKELETON THRIPPLE TRIANGLE
TURNPIKE BRANDRITH
OUTRIGGER
(— FOR ARCH) COOM COOMB
(— FOR BEEHIVE) SECTION
(— FOR CANDLES) HEARSE
(— FOR CARRYING STRAW) KNAPE
(— FOR CASK) GANTRY STALDER
(— FOR CATCHING FISH) HATCH
(— FOR CLOTHES DRYING) AIRER
(— FOR CONFINING HORSE) TRAVE
TRAVAIL
(— FOR COW'S HEAD) BAIL
(— FOR DRYING FISH) HACK HAIK
(— FOR DRYING SKINS) HERSE
(— FOR FISHING LINE) CADAR
CADER
(— FOR GLAZING LEATHER) BUCK
(— FOR HAWKS) CADGE
(— FOR KILLING PIGS) CREEL
(— FOR LENS) BOW
(— FOR ROLLER BEARINGS) CAGE
(— FOR SMOKING MEAT) BOUCAN
BUCCAN
(— FOR STACK) HAYRACK STADDLE
(— FOR WASHING ORE) BUDDLE
(— OF A VESSEL) HULL
(— OF MIND) HAZE SPITE SPIRIT
TEMPER FEELING POSTURE
(— OF PIER) JETTY
(— OF SAW) HUSK
(— OF SPINNING MULE) SQUARE
(— OF STRAW) SIME

(— OF TINWORK) MARQUITO
(— ON STAGE) CEILING
(— TO CATCH STARFISH) TANGLE
(— TO CLEAN SHIP'S BOTTOM) HOG
(— TO DRY CLOTHES) AIRER
(BELL —) SWEEP
(BOBBIN —) BANK
(CARRIAGE —) BRAKE BREAK
(COUNTING —) ABACUS
(DIVING —) LUNET LUNETTE
(EMBROIDERY —) TENT TABORET
TAMBOUR
(FISHING —) DREDGE
(GLAZIER'S —) FRAIL
(HARNESS —) HEALD
(LOOM —) SLAY SLEY LATHE
BATTEN SLEIGH
(MINING —) APRON
(PHOTOGRAPHY —) BUTTERFLY
(PORTABLE —) BIER CACAXTE
(PRINTING —) CHASE PRESS
(SHIP'S —) CANT
(SLUBBING —) BILLY
(STRETCHING —) TENT SLEDGE
TENTER
(TANNING —) BEAM
(WINDOW —) CHESS
(2-WHEELED —) GILL
(PL.) PROFILE
FRAMED NATE NATED ENGAGED
FRAMEWORK BED BENT BIER
BONE BUCK BULK CAGE CRIB
DURN GRID RACK SASH BONES
CADRE CHUTE COPSE CREEL
FLAKE SHELL STOCK BELFRY
BRIDGE BUSTLE CABANE CRADLE
DESIGN FABRIC GOCART GUARDS
HARROW HEARSE REBATO SHIELD
STROMA WATTLE CABINET
CARCASS CLIMBER COMMODE
DERRICK FRAMING FULCRUM
JACKBOX LATTICE PANNIER
REBATER RETABLE STADDLE
TRESTLE BARBECUE BEDSTEAD
BULKHEAD CARRIAGE CRADLING
CRIBWORK GRIDIRON GRILLAGE
OSSATURE SCAFFOLD SHELVING
SHOWCASE SKELETON
(— AROUND HATCHWAY) FIDDLEY
(— FOR CORNSTACK) HOVEL
(— FOR PEAL OF BELLS) CAGE
(— OF REFERENCE) SCHEMA
(— TO EXPAND SKIRTS) BUSTLE
PANNIER
(EMPTY —) HUSK
(SCULPTOR'S —) ARMATURE
FRAMING CURB LEAD BELFRY
ARMATURE BEDPLATE
**FRAMLEY PARSONAGE (AUTHOR
OF —)** TROLLOPE
(CHARACTER IN —) LUCY MARK
FANNY SMITH LUFTON THORNE
CRAWLEY ROBARTS SOWERBY
DUNSTABLE
FRANCE
(PREF.) GALLO

FRANCE
BAY: BISCAY ARACHON
CAPE: HAGUE
CAPITAL: PARIS
CHEESE: BLEU BRIE BONBEL
BOURSIN MUNSTER

CAMEMBERT MARCILLAT
ROQUEFORT
COIN: ECU SOL SOU GROS AGNEL
BLANC BLANK FRANC LIARD
LIVRE LOUIS OBOLE SAIGA
SCUTE BLANCA BLANCO DENIER
DIZAIN TESTON AGNEAUX
CENTIME TESTOON CAVALIER
NAPOLEON
DANCE: GAVOT BRANLE CANARY
CANCAN BOUTADE GAVOTTE
DEPARTMENT: AIN LOT VAR AUBE
AUDE CHER EURE GARD GERS
JURA NORD OISE ORNE TARN
AISNE INDRE ISERE LOIRE
RHONE YONNE ARIEGE CANTAL
CREUSE LOZERE NIEVRE
CORREZE GIRONDE MOSELLE
DIVISION, ANCIENT: ARLES PERCHE
NEUSTRIA AQUITAINE
AQUITANIA
DYNASTY: CAPET VALOIS
BOURBON ORLEANS CAPETIAN
MEROVINGIAN
FOOD: PATE CREPE CANAPE
MOUSSE QUICHE BRIOCHE
SOUFFLE ESCARGOT PIPERADE
POTAUFEU TOURNEDO
ISLAND: RE YEU CITE CORSE
GROIX HYERE OLERON USHANT
CORSICA
KING: ODO EUDES PEPIN CLOVIS
LOTHAIR
LAKE: ANNECY CAZAUX
MEASURE: POT SAC AUNE LINE
MINE MUID PIED VELT ARPEN
CARAT LIEUE LIGNE MINOT
PERCH PINTE POINT POUCE
TOISE VELTE ARPENT HEMINE
LEAGUE QUARTE SETIER
CHOPINE HEMINEE POISSON
SEPTIER BOISSEAU QUARTAUT
ROQUILLE QUARTERON
MILITARY ACADEMY: STCYR
SAINTCYR
MOUNTAIN: PUY DORE BLANC
CINTO FOREZ PELAT COTEDOR
MOUNIER VENTOUX
VIGNEMALE CHAMBEYRON
MOUNTAIN RANGE: ALPS ECRINS
VOSGES CEVENNES PYRENEES
MARITIMES
NAME: GAUL GAULE GALLIA
NATIONAL ANTHEM: MARSEILLAISE
NATIVE: CELT GAUL FRANK
BASQUE BRETON GASCON
NORMAN PICARD CATALAN
GALLOIS LORRAIN FRANCIEN
LIGURIAN PROVENCAL
BURGUNDIAN
PORT: CAEN BREST CALAIS
TOULON LEHAVRE BORDEAUX
CHERBOURG DUNKERQUE
MARSEILLE
PROTESTANT: HUGUENOT
PROVINCE: FOIX ANJOU AUNIS
BEARN ALSACE ARTOIS
COMTAT POITOU AUVERGNE
BRETAGNE BRITTANY LIMOUSIN
LORRAINE PROVENCE
TOURAINE
RACE TRACK: AUTEUIL
LONGCHAMPS

REPUBLIC CALENDAR: NIVOSE
FLOREAL VENTOSE BRUMAIRE
FERVIDOR FRIMAIRE GERMINAL
MESSIDOR PLUVIOSE PRAIRIAL
FRUCTIDOR THERMIDOR
VENDEMIAIRE
RESORT: PAU NICE CANNES
MENTON RIVIERA
RIVER: AIN LOT LUY LYS VAR AIRE
AUBE AUDE CHER DRAC EURE
GARD GERS LOIR OISE ORNE
TARN VIRE ADOUR AISNE
AULNE DROME INDRE ISERE
LOIRE MARNE MEUSE RHONE
RISLE SAONE SEINE SOMME
VIAUR YONNE ALLIER ARIEGE
ESCAUT SAMBRE SCARPE
VEZERE VIENNE DURANCE
GARONNE GIRONDE MAYENNE
MOSELLE CHARENTE
DORDOGNE
STOCK EXCHANGE: BOURSE
STRAIT: BONIFACIO
TOWN: AY EU AIX DAX GEX PAU
AGDE AGEN ALBI AUBY AUCH
BRON CAEN LAON LOOS METZ
NICE OPPY ORLY RIOM SENS
SETE STLO TOUL UZES VAUX
VIMY VIRE ARLES ARRAS BLOIS
BREST DIJON DINAN DOUAI
ERNEE LAVAL LILLE LISLE
LYONS NANCY NERAC NESLE
NIMES ORNES PARIS REIMS
ROUEN SEDAN TOURS TULLE
VICHY AMIENS ANGERS CALAIS
LEMANS LONGWY NANTES
PANTIN RENNES RHEIMS
SARLAT SENLIS SEVRES TARARE
TARBES TOULON TROYES
TULLUM VALOIS VERDUN
BAREGES CASTRES LIMOGES
ORLEANS ROUBAIX VALENCE
BORDEAUX CLERMONT
GRENOBLE MULHOUSE
ROCHELLE TOULOUSE
MARSEILLE STRASBOURG
TRIBE: REMI AEDUI ARVERNI
SALUVII ALLOBROGES
VERSE FORM: LAI ALBA AUBADE
RONDEL BALLADE DESCORT
RONDEAU VIRELAI VIRELAY
WATERFALL: GAVARNIE
WEIGHT: GROS MARC ONCE
CARAT LIVRE POUND TONNE
TONNEAU ESTERLIN
WIND: MISTRAL
WINE: MACON MEDOC GRAVES
CHABLIS POMEROL BORDEAUX
BURGUNDY MUSCADET
SAUTERNE CHAMPAGNE
WINE DISTRICT: MEDOC ALSACE
BORDEAUX BURGUNDY
CHAMPAGNE

FRANCESCA DA RIMINI
(CHARACTER IN —) PAOLO
FRANCESCA GIANCIOTTO
MALATESTINO
(COMPOSER OF —) ZANDONAI
FRANCHISE SOC SOKE VOTE
CHASE FERRY HONOR INFANG
CHARTER FREEDOM LIBERTY
CONTRACT FREELAGE

SUFFRAGE TENEMENT
FRANCISCAN MINOR MINORITE
FRANCOLIN COQUI TETUR TITAR
REDWING PHEASANT
FRANCOPHILE GALLOMAN
FRANGIBLE BRITTLE
FRANGIPANI SHAKEWOOD
FRANK FREE OPEN RANK BLUFF
BLUNT BURLY LUSTY NAIVE
PLAIN BRAZEN CANDID DIRECT
FORTHY HONEST SALIAN ARTLESS
GENUINE LIBERAL PROFUSE
SINCERE CAREFREE CAVALIER
GENEROUS STRAIGHT VIGOROUS
OUTSPOKEN OPENHEARTED
PLAINSPOKEN
FRANKENSTEIN (AUTHOR OF —)
SHELLEY
(CHARACTER IN —) HENRY ROBERT
VICTOR WALTON CLERVAL
JUSTINE WILLIAM ELIZABETH
FRANKENSTEIN
FRANKINCENSE THUS OLIBAN
OLIBANUM

FRANKLY FREELY OPENLY PLAINLY
CANDIDLY
FRANKNESS CANDOR FREEDOM
OPENNESS
FRANKPLEDGE BORROW FRIBORG
FRANSERIA RAGWEED
FRANTIC MAD WOOD RABID
INSANE MANIAC FURIOUS
LUNATIC VIOLENT DERANGED
FEVERISH FRENETIC FRENZIED
MANIACAL
FRAPPE ICE GRANITE
FRATERCULA MORMON
FRATERNAL BROTHERLY
DIZYGOTIC NONIDENTICAL
FRATERNITY FRAT FRARY HOUSE
ORDER FRATRY QUALITY SOCIETY
SODALITY
FRATERNIZE FRAT COTTON
FRAUD GYP DOLE FAKE GAFF
GAUD GULL JAPE JUNT LURK
RUSE SHAM SKIN WILE CHEAT
COVIN CRAFT DOLUS FAKER
FAVEL GLAIK GUILE HOCUS
LURCH SHARK SHIFT SHUCK
SWICK SWIKE TRICK BROGUE
DECEIT FIDDLE FULLAM HUMBUG
INTAKE STUMER WRENCH
FLIVVER KNAVERY ROGUERY
STUMOUR SWINDLE BOODLING
COZENAGE IMPOSTER OPERATOR
SUBTLETY TRUMPERY
FRAUDULENT SKIN WILY CRONK
COGGED CRAFTY QUACKY
ABUSIVE CROOKED CUNNING
KNAVISH CHEATING COVINOUS
FRAUDFUL GUILEFUL QUACKISH
SINISTER SPURIOUS
FRAXINELLA DITTANY RUEWORT
FRAY FRET BROIL BROOM FEAZE
MELEE RAVEL AFFRAY BUSTLE
CHAUVE FRIDGE TIFFLE CONTEST
FRAZZLE
FRAYED WORN FLAGGY RAVELED
FRAZER FINNER
FREAK FIRK FLAM WHIM FANCY
HUMOR LUSUS MOODS SCAPE

SPORT MEGRIM SPLEEN WHIMSY
CAPRICE CROTCHET ESCAPADE
FLIMFLAM WHIMWHAM
MONSTROSITY
(CRAZY —S) LUNES
FREAKISH FREAKY BIZARRE
FLIGHTY MAGGOTY WHIMSIC
CRANKISH
FRECKLE CHIT EPHELIS FRECKEN
LENTIGO SUNSPOT HEATSPOT
FRECKLED FRECKLY FLECKLED
FREE LAX LET MOD RID BOLD EASE
LISS OPEN PERT REDD SHED
SHUT CLEAN CLEAR FLUID FRANK
LARGE LISSE LOOSE READY
SCOUR SLAKE SPARE ACQUIT
DEGAGE DEVOID EXEMPT FACILE
FLUENT FREELY GRATIS IMMUNE
LOOSEN SOLUTE UNSLIP VACANT
VAGILE CLEANSE DELIVER
GRIVOIS INEXACT LASKING
LIBERAL MANUMIT RELEASE
SCIOLTO UNBOUND UNSLAVE
UNTWIST WILLING ABSOLUTE
AUTARKIC BUCKSHEE EASINESS
EXPEDITE FACILITY FREEHAND
GRIVOISE INDIGENT LAXATIVE
LIBERATE UNBRIDLE
(— AND EASY) GLIB CAVALIER
FAMILIAR
(— BROOK OF WEEDS) RODE
(— FROM) EX REDD DEVOID
DISPATCH
(— FROM AMBIGUITY) HOMELY
DECIDED
(— FROM ACCUSATION) SACKLESS
(— FROM ACIDITY) DULCIFY
(— FROM ANXIETY) CONTENT
(— FROM ARTIFICIAL) ARTLESS
(— FROM BIAS) CANDID
(— FROM CARE) EASY CARELESS
(— FROM CHARGE) FDD PURGE
FRANCO
(— FROM CONSTRAINT) CASUAL
(— FROM DEDUCTIONS) NET
(— FROM DEFECT) HAIL HALE
SOUND
(— FROM DIRT) BRIGHT
(— FROM DOUBT) RESOLVE
(— FROM ELECTRICAL CHARGE)
DEAD
(— FROM ERROR) LEAL SOUND
CORRECT ACCURATE
(— FROM EVIL) RESCUE
(— FROM EXTREMES) EQUABLE
(— FROM FLAWS) GOOD
(— FROM FROST) FRESH
(— FROM IMPURITIES) FINE DRESS
DEFECATE DEPURATE
(— FROM KNOTS) ENODE ENODATE
(— FROM MARKS) BLANK
(— FROM MICROORGANISMS)
ASEPTIC STERILE
(— FROM OBLIGATION) ACQUIT
EXCUSE
(— FROM PENALTY) ABSOLVE
(— FROM RESTRAINT) ABANDONED
(— FROM STONES) CHESSOM
(— OF DIFFICULTIES) AFLOAT
(— OF FAT) ENSEAM
(— OF OVERTONES) PURE
(— OF TAR) WRECK
(— ONE'S SELF) SOLVE

(— PLUNGER) ARM
(— THROW AREA) KEYHOLE
(PREF.) ELEUTHER(O) IMMUNO
LIBRO
(— FROM) DE
FREEBOARD QUICKSIDE
FREEBOOTER TORY RIDER ROVER
THIEF PIRATE BRIGAND CATERAN
CORSAIR PINDARI PILLAGER
RAPPAREE SNAPHANCE
FREEBORN INGENUOUS
FREEDMAN LEYSING TITYRUS
(PL.) LAET
FREEDOM RUN EASE FRITH LARGE
UHURU ACCESS STREET APATHIA
BREADTH LEISURE LIBERTY
LICENCE LICENSE RELEASE
AUTONOMY FREELAGE FREENESS
IMMUNITY IMPUNITY LARGESSE
WITHGATE
(— FROM BIAS) CANDOR
(— FROM CONSTRAINT) ABANDON
(— FROM DANGER) SECURITY
(— FROM ERROR) ACCURACY
(— FROM GUILT) SHRIVE
(— OF ACCESS) ENTREE
(— OF ACTION) SWINGE LATITUDE
(— OF SPEECH) PARISIA
(— TO PROCEED) HEAD
(CARELESS —) ABANDON
(PREF.) ELEUTHER(O)
FREEHOLD BARONY
FREEHOLDER SWAIN BONDER
YEOMAN FRANKLIN
FREEING LIVERY ACQUITAL
FREE LANCE ROUTIER
FREELY FREE LIEF LARGE LARGELY
READILY HEARTILY
FREEMAN BUR AIRE BARON CEORL
HAULD BONDER CITIZEN
FRANKLIN ROTURIER
(POOR —) THETE
FREEMASON FRATER MORGAN
NOACHITE
(ONE NOT A —) COWAN
FREESTONE HAZEL
(— STATE) CONNECTICUT
FREETHINKER INFIDEL SKEPTIC
AGNOSTIC
FREEZE ICE RIME CATCH CHILL
FROST CURDLE FRAPPE HARDEN
STARVE STEEVE CONGEAL
GLACIATE
FREEZING COLD FREEZY FRIGID
FROSTY GLACIAL CRYONICS
GELATION
(PREF.) CRY(O) KRY(O)
FREIGHT LOAD CARGO GOODS
ASTRAY BURDEN LADING
FRAUGHT HOTSHOT PLUNDER
PORTAGE TRUCKAGE
(— CAR) TRUCK
**FREISCHUTZ, DER (CHARACTER IN
—)** MAX CUNO AGATHE HERMIT
KASPAR SAMIEL AENNCHEN
(COMPOSER OF —) WEBER
FREMD FRAIM FRAMMIT
FRENCH CREOLE FRANCO
GALLIC GALLIAN
GALLICAN
(— MIXED WITH ENGLISH)
FRANGLAIS
(PREF.) FRANCO GALLO

FRENCH GUIANA (CAPE OF —)
ORANGE
(CAPITAL OF —) CAYENNE
(RIVER OF —) MARONI
(TOWN OF —) MANA KOUROU
FRENCH HONEYSUCKLE SULLA
FRENCH LAVENDER STECHADOS
FRENCHMAN GAUL PICARD
FRENCHY MONSIEUR PARLEYVOO
FRENCH MULBERRY SOURBUSH
FRENCH NUDE ALESAN
FRENCH REPUBLIC MARIANNA
MARIANNE
FRENCH SUDAN (SEE MALI)
FRENULUM TENDON
FRENUM BRIDLE FRAENUM
FRENULUM VINCULUM
FRENZIED MAD MUST RABID
RAMAGE BERSERK FANATIC
FRANTIC MADDING FRENETIC
FURIBUND POSSESSED
FRENZY AMOK FURY GERE MOON
MUST RAGE AMUCK FUROR
MANIA MUSTH FURORE RAVING
MADNESS OESTRUS SWIVVET
DELIRIUM INSANITY
FREQUENCY HERTZ PITCH
CREBRITY
FREQUENT USE BANG KEEP
HAUNT HOWFF OFTEN THICK
AFFECT COMMON HOURLY
INFEST RESORT ENHAUNT
OFTTIME CREBROUS FAMILIAR
PRACTICE ACCUSTOMED
(PREF.) SYCHNO
FREQUENTLY OFT OFTEN HOURLY
UNSELDOM
FRESH GAY HOT NEW WET FLIP
GOOD RACY SMUG WARM BRISK
CRISP GREEN MOIST QUICK
RUDDY SASSY SMART SOUND
SWEET VIVID CALLER CALVER
FLORID LIVELY MAIDEN STRONG
UNUSED VERNAL VIRENT VIRGIN
ANOTHER NOUVEAU UNFADED
VERDANT NOUVELLE ORIGINAL
SPANKING YOUTHFUL
(PREF.) CENO
(SUFF.) CENE
FRESHEN BRACE FRESH RENEW
BREEZE CALLER REVIVE CHOUNCE
PEARTEN REFRESH SWEETEN
FRENCHEN
FRESHENER BRACER
FRESHET TIDE FLOOD FRESH
SPATE TORNADO
FRESHMAN FOX BEJAN FROSH
BEJANT GREENY PENNAL
FRESHER
FRESHNESS DEW VERD NOVELTY
VERDURE VIRIDITY ORIGINALITY
FRET DIK NAG ORP RUB RUX VEX
CARK FASH FRAY FUSS GALL
GNAW RAGE STEW YIRM CHAFE
CRAKE CRISP FLISK GRATE PIQUE
WORRY WREAK ABRADE CORSIE
CRYSAL HARASS MUCKLE NETTLE
PLAGUE REPINE RIPPLE RUFFLE
CHRYSAL GRECQUE GRIZZLE
MEANDER SCRUPLE SQUINNY
ALIGREEK IRRITATE
FRETFUL CROSS GIRNY ORPIT
TEATY TEENY TESTY FRETTY

PENCEY SULLEN TATCHY TWISTY
FRECKET PEEVISH PETTISH
SPLEENY CAPTIOUS CRANKOUS
FRETSOME FROPPISH PETULANT
PINDLING QUERULOUS
FRETTED FRETTY MAGGED
FRETTING FRET EATING
FREY FREYR YNGVI
(FATHER OF —) NJORD
(SISTER OF —) FREYA
FREYA (BROTHER OF —) FREY
(FATHER OF —) NJORD
(HUSBAND OF —) ODIN
FRIABLE CRIMP CRISP CRUMP
FLAKY FRUSH MEALY SHORT
CRUMBY CRUMMY FLUFFY
PUTRID CHESSOM CRUMBLY
MOLDERY POWDERY RESOLUTE
ROTTENLY SHATTERY
(NOT —) SAD
FRIAR FRATE FREER MINIM MINOR
BHIKKU FRATER GELONG GOSAIN
LISTER BHIKSHU JACOBIN
LIMITER SERVITE BREVIGER
CAPUCHIN JACOBITE MINORIST
MINORITE PREACHER AUGUSTINE
CARMELITE CORDELIER
MENDICANT BENEDICTINE
FRIARBIRD COLDONG PIMLICO
MONKBIRD
FRIAR SKATE DOCTOR
FRICANDEAU GRENADINE
FRICASSEE POTPIE
FRICATIVE BUZZ HISS OPEN YOGH
DURATIVE
FRICTION BUZZ DRAG HISS CHAFE
WINDAGE
(PREF.) TRIBO
(SUFF.) TRIPSIS
FRICTIONLESS SMOOTH
FRIED FRIT SAUTE
FRIEDCAKE WONDER CRULLER
FATCAKE DOUGHNUT
FRIEND AME AMI AMY BOR CAD
EME PAX BHAI CHUM NABS OPPO
PARD WINE AMIGO BRICK BUDDY
INGLE NETOP TROUT AIKANE
BELAMY COBBER COUSIN
CUMMER GOSSIP INWARD
KIMMER PRINCE QUAKER
ACHATES COMRADE SOCIETY
COCKMATE COMPADRE
DEMOPHIL FEDERATE HICKSITE
INTIMADO INTIMATE TILLICUM
(— OF BRIDEGROOM) PARANYMPH
(—S NOT SPEAKING) CUTS
(CLOSE —) PRIVY COBBER
COMPADRE
(DIVINE —) SOCIUS
(FAMILIAR —) CRONY GREMIAL
SPECIAL
(GIRL —) DOXY DRAG DONEY
DOXIE STEADY
(INTIMATE FEMALE —) CUMMER
(PRIVATE —) PRIVADO
(WOMAN —) GIMMER
(PL.) FOLK KITH SOCE FOLKS
SOCIETY
FRIENDLESS FORLORN
FRIENDLINESS AMITY AFFINITY
BONHOMIE GOODWILL
FRIENDLY COSH GOOD HOLD
HOMY KIND TOSH CADGY CHIEF

COUTH GREAT HOMEY MATEY
THICK AMICAL CHATTY CHUMMY
FOLKSY FORTHY HOMELY KINDLY
SMOOTH AFFABLE AMIABLE
AMICOUS COUTHIE AMICABLE
HOMELIKE INTIMATE SOCIABLE
NEIGHBORLY
FRIENDSHIP PAX AMITY AMOUR
FRIEZE KELT FRISE CUSHION
FALDING FRISADO FRIEZING
FRIGATE ZABRA
FRIGATE BIRD IOA IWA ALCATRAS
FRIGATE MACKEREL BONITO
TASSARD
FRIGG FREA FRIJA
FRIGGA (HUSBAND OF —) ODIN
(SON OF —) BALDER
FRIGHT COW BOOF FEAR FLEG
FRAY ALARM GHAST GLIFF GLOFF
PANIC SCARE AFFRAY GASTER
GLIFFY SCHRIK TERROR STARTLE
SWITHER FRIGHTEN GASTNESS
GLIFFING
FRIGHTEN AWE COW FLY SHY SOB
BAZE BREE DARE DOSS FEAR
FLEG FLEY FRAY FUNK HARE
HAZE SHOO AFEAR AFLEY ALARM
APPAL BLUFF GALLY GHOST GLIFF
HAZEN SCARE SHORE SPOOK
AFFRAY ALARUM APPALL BOGGLE
BOOGER COWARD FLAITE FLIGHT
FRIGHT GALLEY GALLOW
AFFREUX FRECKEN SCARIFY
STARTLE TERRIFY AFFRIGHT
MISTRYST
(— BIRDS) KEEP
(PREF.) TERRI TERRORI
FRIGHTENED RAD EERY FRIT GAST
EERIE GHAST WINDY AFRAID
AGHAST SCARED SCAREY
STURTIN GHASTFUL
(EASILY —) TIMID SKITTISH
FRIGHTENING EERY DREAD EERIE
GOURY HAIRY FRIGHTY GHASTLY
SHIVERY DREADFUL FLEYSOME
FRIGHTFUL WAN GRIM UGLY
AWFUL FERLY HORRID UGSOME
AFFREUX DIREFUL FEARFUL
GASHFUL GHASTLY HIDEOUS
ALARMING DREADFUL ELDRITCH
FEARSOME GHASTFUL HORRIBLE
HORRIFIC TERRIBLE TERRIFIC
FRIGID DRY ICY COLD BLEAK FISHY
ARCTIC FROSTY FROZEN WINTRY
GLACIAL FREEZING SIBERIAN
FRIGIDITY GLARE
FRILL DIDO PURL JABOT RUCHE
RUFFLE ARMILLA FLOUNCE
SPINACH SPINAGE CHITLING
CRIMPING FRILLERY FURBELOW
(— OF HAIR) APRON
(PL.) PUFFERY FOOFARAW
FRILLERY
FRILLINESS CHICHI
FRILLING RUCHE ROUCHE
SWEEPER
FRILLY CHICHI
FRINGE WLO EDGE GILL LOMA
RUFF WELT BEARD THRUM
BORDER EDGING MARGIN PELMET
TASSEL BULLION CREPINE
EYELASH FEATHER FIMBRIA
MACRAME SELVAGE TRAILER

VALANCE WHISKER CILIELLA
FRISETTE INDUSIUM PENUMBRA
SELVEDGE TRIMMING
(— OF TEETH) PERISTOME
(SOFT —S) THRUM
(PL.) ZIZITH
(PREF.) CROSS(O) FIMBRI(O)
LACINI THYSAN(O)
FRINGED JUBATE CILIATE
LACINIATE
FRINGEFOOT UMA
FRINGEPOD LACEPOD
FRINGETAIL VEILTAIL
FRINGE TREE SHAVINGS
FRIPPERY FLIPPERY TRINKUMS
(PL.) GAUDERY
FRISK COLT FISK PLAY ROLL SKIP
WHID BOUND CAPER SKICE
CAREER CAVORT CURVET FRISCO
FROLIC TITTUP WANTON FRISCAL
FRISKLE
FRISKY GAY PERT FRISK CROUSE
FEISTY KIPPER LIVELY WANTON
BUCKISH COLTISH JIGGISH
PLAYFUL SKITTISH SPORTIVE
FRISON KNUB
FRIT FRETT CALCINE
FRITTER FOOL FRIT TEAR BOLLO
DRILL BANGLE DRIVEL LOUNGE
BEIGNET DRIBBLE FLITTER
SLATTERN
FRIVOLITY LEVITY FRIBBLE
INANITY ITEMING FUTILITY
NONSENSE NUGACITY
FRIVOLOUS GAY DAFT VAIN GIDDY
INANE LIGHT PETTY SILLY WASHY
FLIMSY FRILLY FRIVOL FROTHY
FUTILE TOYISH YEASTY FATUOUS
FRIBBLE LIGHTLY NIDGETY
SHALLOW TRIVIAL GIMCRACK
JIMCRACK SKITTISH TRIFLING
FRIVOLOUSNESS FUTILITY
FRIZZ FRIZ CREPE FRIZE FRIZZLE
FROUNCE
FRIZZED CRISPY
FRIZZLE CRAPE CREPE
FRIZZLY FUZZY CRIMPY FRIZZY
FRIZZY FUZZY CRIMPY FRIZZLY
FROCK DUD JAM GOWN JUMP
SLIP SLOP WRAP LAMMY SMOCK
TRUSS TUNIC CLERIC JERSEY
LAMMIE MANTLE ROCHET
SUKKENYE
FROCK COAT CRISPIN
FROG PAD POD KICK FROSH FROSK
FROUD PADDO PADDY RANID
RONCO ANURAN PEEPER TOGGLE
CHARLIE CRAWLER CREEPER
CROAKER CUSHION FRESHER
FROGLET PADDOCK PODDOCK
QUILKIN BULLFROG FERREIRO
FROGGING PLATANNA REPLACER
(— IN LOOM) HEATER
(— OF HORSE'S HOOF) FRUSH
CUSHION
(TREE —) NOTOTREMA
(PREF.) BATRACH(O) RANI
FROG CRAB RANININ
FROGFISH ANGLER SLIMER
TOADFISH
FROGGER CHASER TRAILER
ZOOGLER
FROGGY RANARIAN

FROGHOPPER HOPPER CERCOPID
FROGMOUTH MOPOKE MOREPORK
PODARGUE
FROGS (AUTHOR OF —)
ARISTOPHANES
(CHARACTER IN —) AEACUS
CHARON BACCHUS DIONYSUS
HERCULES XANTHIAS AESCHYLUS
EURIPIDES
(SUFF.) BATRACH(O)(US)
FROLIC BUM GAY RIG BLOW COLT
GAME GELL HAZE JINK LAKE LARK
ORGY PLAY PLOY RANT REEK
ROMP TEAR CAPER FREAK FRISK
MERRY PRANK RANDY ROUSE
SALLY SPORT SPREE BUSTER
CAVORT CURVET FRATCH
GAMBOL PLISKY POWWOW
PRANCE ROLLIX SHINDY SPLORE
VAGARY WANTON DISPORT
GAMMOCK MARLOCK PLISKIE
ROLLICK SCAMPER SKYLARK
SPANIEL STASHIE WASSAIL
CAROUSAL JAMBOREE
FROLICSOME GAY DAFT ROID
ANTIC BUXOM CADGY FRISK
GILPY LARKY FRISKY LIVELY
WANTON ANTICAL JOCULAR
LARKING LARKISH PLAYFUL
WAGGISH ESPIEGLE FRISKFUL
FROLICKY GAMESOME LARKSOME
PRANKISH SPORTFUL SPORTIVE
FROLICSOMENESS HEYDAY
FROM A AB DE EX OF FAE FRA FRO
VAN VON THROM AGAINST
(— A DISTANCE) ALOOF
(— BEGINNING TO END) THROUGH
(— ELSEWHERE) ALIUNDE
(— OFF) AFFA
(— SIDE TO SIDE) OVER CROSS
ATHWART
(— THIS PLACE) HENCE
(PREF.) AP APH APO
FROND FERN TRESS CROSIER
FRONDLET
FRONT BOW VAN BROW FACE
FORE HEAD PROW THIN AFORE
VAUNT BEFORE DEVANT FACADE
FACING FORMER OPPOSE SECTOR
VAWARD ADVANCE FORWARD
FRONTAL FURTHER OBVERSE
PALATAL PREFACE RESPECT
SLENDER FOREHEAD FOREMOST
FOREPART FORESIDE FRONTAGE
(— OF ASTROLABE) WOMBSIDE
(— OF BARN) FOREBAY
(— OF BIRD'S NECK) GUTTUR
(— OF BODY) GROUF
(— OF HEAD) VISAGE FORETOP
(— OF HELMET) VENTAIL
(— OF SHIRT) BOSOM
(— OF WATERWHEEL BUCKET)
START
(— UPON) AFFRONT
(PREF.) ANTER(O) PRO
(IN —) FORE PRO(S)(SO)
(IN — OF) ANTE ANTER(O) PRAE
PRE
FRONTAL PALL FRONT SINDON
TABULA FRONTON METOPIC
FRONTLET SUFFRONT
FRONTIER BOUND COAST FRONT
MARCH BORDER BARRIER

FRONTURE OUTLYING
(FORTIFIED —) LIMES
FRONTING OBVIOUS
FRONTISPIECE FRONT UNWAN
FRONTIS
FRONTLET TIARA FRONTAL
CHAMFRON
FRONT PAGE (AUTHOR OF —)
HECHT MACARTHUR
(CHARACTER IN —) EARL BURNS
GRANT HILDY PEGGY WALTER
HARTMAN JOHNSON WILLIAMS
FRONTPIECE GORE
FROST ICE COLD HOAR RIME RIND
(PREF.) CRYMO PAGO RHIGO
(HOAR —) PACHNO
FROSTED PRUINOSE
FROSTING ICING DIVINITY
FROSTWEED ROCKROSE
FROSTY ICY COLD RIMY CHILL
CRISP FRORE GELID GLARY
HUNCH BOREAL FRIGID FROREN
CHILLING INIMICAL PRUINOUS
(NOT —) OPEN
FROTH FOB BARM FOAM HEAD
REAM SCUM SUDS WORK CREAM
SPUME YEAST FLOWER FREATH
LATHER SPURGE
FROTHER CREOSOTE
FROTHING HUMMING MANTLING
FROTHY BARMY FOAMY REAMY
SPEWY SPUMY SUDSY FLASHY
YEASTY SPUMOSE SPUMOUS
WHIPPED
FROWARD RANK CROSS
AWKWARD PEEVISH WAYWARD
CONTRARY FROPPISH PERVERSE
PETULANT PROTERVE SHREWISH
UNTOWARD
FROWN GLUM LOUR GLOOM
GLOUT GLUMP LOWER SCOWL
GLOWER GLUNCH FROUNCE
FRONTLET
FROWNING GLUM GLUNCH
FROWZY BLOUSY BLOWSY
BLOWZY RAFFISH FROWZLED
SCABROUS SLOVENLY
FROZEN FAST FIXED FRORE FRORY
GELID GLARY FRAPPE FROREN
FRUCTIFICATION CONK AECIDIUM
BASIDIUM APOTHECIUM
FRUCTOSE ACROSE
FRUGAL EASY MILD CANNY CHARY
ROMAN SCANT SPARE SAVING
SCARCE SCOTCH CAREFUL
PRUDENT SLENDER SPARING
THRIFTY PROVIDENT
PARSIMONIOUS
FRUGALITY SPARE THRIFT
ECONOMY PARCITY MANAGERY
FRUGALLY HARD CHARILY
SAVINGLY
FRUIT BEL FIG HAW UVA AKEE
ATTA BAEL BITO COYO DATE
DIKA DROP GEAN JACK LIME
NOOP PEAR PLUM POME SEED
SLOE SNAP SORB AKENE ANISE
APPLE BERRY CLING COUMA
DRUPE GENIP GOURD GRAPE
GUAVA HAZEL ILAMA LEMON
LIMON MANGO MELON OLIVE
PAPAW PEACH RIPER SORVA
TRYMA ACHENE ACINUS ALMOND

BANANA BUTTON CEDRON
CEREZA CHERRY CITRON CITRUS
COBNUT COCHAL COCONA
DAMSON DURIAN EMBLIC
EMBOLO GUARRI JUJUBE KEEPER
LEGUME LONGAN LOQUAT
MAMMEE MARANG MAYPOP
MUYUSA NARRAS ORANGE
PAPAYA PAWPAW PELLAS
POMATO RESULT SAPOTA
SQUASH UVALHA WAMPEE
WESTME ZAPOTE APRICOT
ATEMOYA AVOCADO AZAROLE
BILIMBI BLOATER CARAWAY
CHAYOTE CHECKER CIRUELA
COCONUT CURRANT DESSERT
GEEBUNG GENIPAP GHERKIN
KUMQUAT MURCOTT PIGFACE
PRODUCT RIPENER SERVICE
SHALLON SOROSIS SOURSOP
TANGELO ACHENIUM BAYBERRY
BELLERIC BILBERRY CALABASH
CANISTEL CAPSICUM CARDAMUM
CITRANGE COCOPLUM
CUCUMBER DEWBERRY
DOGBERRY EGGFRUIT FOLLICLE
FRUITAGE FRUITERY FRUITLET
GOLKAKRA INKBERRY LIMEQUAT
OSOBERRY PIEPRINT PODOCARP
RAMBUTAN SEBESTEN SEEDBALL
SHADDOCK SWEETSOP
SYCONIUM CARYOPSIS
NECTARINE PINEAPPLE
SAPODILLA CHERIMOYER
MANGOSTEEN
(— OF CACTUS) SABRA
(— OF CAPER) CAPOT
(— OF CITRON) ETROG ETHROG
(— OF HEMLOCK) CONIUM
(— OF OAK) ACORN
(— OF PALM) SALAK PUPUNHA
(— OF ROSE) HEP HIP BUTTON
(— ON TREES) HANG
(—S COOKED IN SYRUP) COMPOTE
(AGGREGATE —) ETAERIO
DRUPETUM HETAERIO
(ASTRINGENT —) GAB GAUB
CHEBULE
(AVOCADO-LIKE —) ANAY
(CANDIED —) CONSERVE
(CARMINATIVE —) BADIAN
(COILED —) STROMBUS
(COLLECTIVE —) SYNCARP
(DRIED —) PASA CUBEB MUMMY
SABAL OREJON CAPSULE
EMBELIA
(EARLY —) PRIMEUR HASTINGS
(FALLEN —) SHEDDER WINDFALL
(FIRST —S) ANNATES BIKKURIM
PRIMICES
(FLESHY —) SYCONIUM
SARCOCARP
(GOURD —) PEPO
(GRAPEFRUIT-LIKE —) SUHA
(GRAPELIKE —) WAMPEE
(HAWTHORN —) PEGGLE
(IMPERFECT —) SPECH NUBBIN
(MASHED —) FOOL
(MEDICINAL —) AIWAIN AJOWAN
EMBELIA
(ONE-SEEDED —) AKENE ACHENE
(PALMYRA —) PUNATOO
(PLUMLIKE —) CARISSA CIRUELA

(PRESERVED —) SUCCADE
CONFITURE
(PRICKLY —) HEDGEHOG
(SELF-FERTILIZED —) AUTOCARP
(SLICED DRIED —) SNITS SNITZ
SCHNITZ
(SPURGE —) TAMPOE
(SUPERIOR —) TOPPER
(UNRIPE OAK —) CAMATA
(WINGED —) SAMARA
(WOODY —) XYLOCARP
(PREF.) CARP(O) FRUCTI FRUGI
(BEAK-LIKE —) RYNCO
(SUFF.) CARP(OUS)(US)(Y)
FRUIT BAT KALONG
FRUIT-BEARING FERTILE
FRUIT DOVE KUKU
FRUITFUL FAT FOODY BATTEL
FECUND FRUITY GRAVID FERTILE
TEEMFUL UBEROUS ABUNDANT
CHILDING FRUITIVE PREGNANT
PROLIFIC PLENTEOUS
FRUITFULNESS UBERTY FATNESS
FRUITGROWER FRUITIST
FRUITLESS DRY GELD VAIN ADDLE
BARREN FUTILE STERILE USELESS
ABORTIVE BOOTLESS
FRUIT PIGEON KUKU LUPE
KUKUPA MANUMA MANUTAGI
FRUIT STONE COB PYRENE
PUTAMEN
(PREF.) PYREN(O)
FRUMP JUDY
FRUSTRATE BALK BEAT BILK CRAB
DASH DISH FOIL LAME BAULK
BLANK BLOCK CHECK CROSS
ELUDE SMEAR THRAW WRECK
BAFFLE BLIGHT BUGGER DEFEAT
DELUDE KIBOSH OUTWIT SCOTCH
THWART ANIENTE DECEIVE
FALSIFY PREVENT CONFOUND
INFRINGE STULTIFY
FRUSTRATED DISHED MANQUE
FRUSTRATER MARPLOT
FRUSTRATING BOOTLESS
FRUSTRATION FOIL SUCK DEFEAT
FIASCO
FRUSTULE TESTULE HYPOTHECA
FRY SILE BROOD FRIZZ KRILL
SAUTE FRIZZLE GREYFISH
FRYER FRIER FRIZZER SPRINGER
FRYING PAN FRYPAN SPIDER
CREEPER SKILLET
FUCHSIA CORREA KONINI FUCHSIN
EARDROPS
FUCHSIN ROSEINE SOLFERINO
FUCHSINE RUBIN RUBINE
MAGENTA ROSANILINE
FUDDLE FUZZLE FLUSTER
FUDDLED FAP REE DOPY BOSKY
DOPEY SWASH TIPSY MAUDLIN
TOSTICATED
FUDGE HUNCH SNUDGE PENUCHE
DIVINITY
FUEL GAS OIL POB COAL COKE FIRE
PEAT UPLA ARGOL ACETOL
BUNKER ELDING FIRING SHRUFF
TIMBER COALITE PABULUM
SYNTHOL FIREBOOT FIREBOTE
GASOGENE GAZOGENE TRIPTANE
(JELLED —) NAPALM
(ROCKET —) HYDYNE
FUGITIVE HOT FLEME FLYER FUGIE

SCAMP OUTLAW FLEEING
LAMSTER REFUGEE RUNAWAY
FLEETING RUNAGATE UNSTABLE
(PL.) MANZAS
FUGUE FUGA RICERCAR
(— THEME) DUX
(PART OF —) STRETTA
FULA PEUL PEUHL FELLANI
FELLATA
FULANI PEUL PEUHL
FULCRUM BAIT GLUT
FULFILL FILL FULL KEEP MEET
HONOR ANSWER COMPLY FULFIL
REDEEM ACHIEVE PERFORM
SATISFY COMPLETE COMPLISH
ACCOMPLISH
(— A TERM) EXPIRE
FULFILLMENT PASS EFFECT
FUNCTION PERFORMANCE
(— OF GOD'S WILL) KINGDOM
(IMAGINARY —) FANTASY
FULGURATION BLICK
FULL BAD BIG FAT FOW COOL
DEEP FAIR GOOD JUST PANG
RANK TRIG TUCK AMPLE AWASH
BROAD CLEAR FLUSH LARGE
LUCKY PIENO PLAIN PLENY
ROUND SATED SOLID TIGHT
TOTAL WHOLE ENTIRE GOGGLE
HONEST STRONG BAPTIZE
BRIMFUL COPIOUS DESTROY
DIFFUSE FULFILL FULSOME
LIBERAL OROTUND PERFORM
PLENARY REPLETE TEEMING
TRAMPLE WEALTHY ABSOLUTE
ADEQUATE BOUFFANT BRIMMING
CHOCKFUL COMPLETE EXTENDED
FREQUENT PREGNANT RESONANT
THOROUGH
(— CLOTH OR YARN) WALK
(— OF AIR) LIGHT
(— OF BLANKS) LACUNOSE
(— OF CHINKS) RIMOSE
(— OF DELAY) MOROSE
(— OF DEVILTRY) HEMPY HEMPIE
(— OF DIRT) FOUL
(— OF EGGS) GRAVID
(— OF ENERGY) STOUT SWANK
(— OF FLAWS) CRAZY
(— OF FUN) FROLIC
(— OF HAPPINESS) SUNSHINY
(— OF INTEREST) AGOG
(— OF IRON) SIDEROSE
(— OF LIFE) SPUNKY ANIMATE
(— OF LOOPS) KINKY
(— OF MATTER FOR THOUGHT)
MEATY
(— OF RUSHES) SPRITTY
(— OF SAND) ARENOSE
(— OF SLEEP) SOPOROSE
(— OF SMALL OPENINGS) POROUS
(— OF SPIRIT) GENEROUS
(— OF VIGOR) FLUSH GREEN LUSTY
ANIMATED SPIRITED
(— OF ZEST) RACY
(PREF.) PLENI PLERO
(SUFF.) **(— OF)** IOUS OSE OUS
FULL-BLOODED PLETHORIC
FULL-BLOWN JUICY
FULLBODIED FAT LOFTY HEARTY
ROBUST
FULL-BOSOMED BUXOM
FULLER GAG HARDY HARDIE

ROLLER TUCKER WALKER
BLOCKER CREASER
THICKER CLOTHIER
FULL-FACED AFFRONTE AFFRONTY
FULL-FLAVORED BOLD RACY
FULL-FLEDGED SUMMED
FULL-GROWN RIPE GROWN
MATURE SEEDED
FULLNESS BODY FLAIR FLARE
FULTH PLENUM FULNESS
PLEROMA SATIETY
FULLY ALL DOWN EVEN INLY WELL
AMPLY LARGE ENOUGH FAIRLY
THRICE WHOLLY CLEARLY
LARGELY UTTERLY CLEVERLY
ENTIRELY INWARDLY MATURELY
FULMAR HAG NELLY NODDY
HAGDON NELLIE MALDUCK
MALMOCK STINKER MALLEMUCK
FULMINATE BLOW FULMINE
FULSOME FAT SUAVE FOULSOME
FUMARIC BOLETIC LICHENIC
FUMAROLE HORNITO
FUMBLE BOOT MUFF MULL PIRL
BOBBLE BOGGLE FAFFLE MUMBLE
PRODDLE MISFIELD THRUMBLE
FUMBLER STUMER BUNGLER
STUMOUR
FUMBLING HALTING
FUME FUFF RAGE REEK EWDER
SMOKE STIFE STORM SNUFFLE
FUMIGATE
FUMID SMOKY SMOKEY
FUMIGATE SMEEK SMOKE PASTIL
CYANIDE PASTILLE
FUMIGATION GASSING
FUMIGATOR AERATOR
FUMITORY FUMARIA FUMEROOT
FUMEWORT
FUN GIG GAME GELL JEST JOKE
LAKE PLAY BORAK BOURD
HUMOR KICKS MIRTH MUSIC
SPORT FROLIC GAIETY GAYETY
DAFFERY DAFFING GAMMOCK
WHOOPEE
(MAKE — OF) JAPE RIDE
(UNRESTRAINED —) HELL
FUNCTION ACT JOB RUN USE
DUTY FORM ROLE WORK POWER
ACTION AGENCY MATRIX MISTER
OFFICE SQUASH CONCEPT
FACULTY ISOLATE PERFORM
SERVICE WORKING ACTIVITY
BUSINESS MINISTRY PROVINCE
(— EFFECTIVELY) AVAIL
(—S OF JUDGES) ERMINE
(APPARENT —) STUDY
(CHEMICAL —) PARACHOR
(ECCLESIASTICAL —) DIET
(ESSENTIAL —) DHARMA
(MATHEMATICAL —) DEL FORM
METRIC INVERSE QUARTIC
(SPECIAL —) CEREMONY
(SUFF.) CY URE
FUNCTIONAL DYNAMIC
FUNCTIONARY BEADLE FLUNKY
CAPTAIN FLUNKEY CHAPRASI
FUNCTIONING AFLOAT
FUNCTIONLESS OTIOSE
FUND BOX BANK FOND MASS
CHEST KITTY MOUNT SLUSH
STOCK STORE ESCROW CHALUKA
JACKPOT RESERVE

HALUKKAH PECULIUM
(COMMON —) POT POOL
(POLITICAL —S) BARREL
(PL.) CAJA PURSE COFFER
FUNDAMENT NOCK TAIL BOTTOM
FUNDUS
FUNDAMENTAL NET BASE BASAL
BASIC KLANG PRIME VITAL
BOTTOM PRIMAL SIMPLE BASILAR
BEDROCK ORGANIC PRIMARY
RADICAL ABSOLUTE CARDINAL
ORIGINAL RUDIMENT SUBSTRAT
ULTIMATE PRIMORDIAL
RUDIMENTARY
FUNDAMENTALLY AUFOND
FUNDUS FORNIX
FUNERAL TANGI BURIAL EXEQUY
BURYING CORTEGE FUNEBRE
FUNERARY MORTUARY
FUNERAL DIRECTOR BLACKMAN
FUNEREAL BLACK FERAL DISMAL
SOLEMN FUNEBRE FUNERAL
DIRGEFUL EXEQUIAL MOURNFUL
SEPULCHRAL
FUNGI MYCOFLORA
FUNGICIDE MANEB NABAM ZINEB
FERBAM CALOMEL BORDEAUX
DICHLONE
FUNGOID MYCOID FUNGOUS
FUNGOSO (FATHER OF —) SORDIDO
FUNGUS BUNT MOLD SMUT BLACK
BRAND ERGOT FUNGE HYPHO
MOREL MOULD PHOMA SPUNK
SWARD TRUFF VALSA VERPI
AGARIC BOLETE FUNGAL MILDEW
OIDIUM AMANITA BOLETUS
CHYTRID FUNGOID GEASTER
LEPIOTA TRUFFLE AECIDIUM
CLATHRUS CORNBELL EUMYCETE
FUSARIUM HELVELLA MUCEDINE
MUSHROOM OOMYCETE
OTOMYCES PHALLOID POLYPORE
PUFFBALL RHIZOPUS SAPROGEN
SPOROGEN TREMELLA TUCKAHOE
NEUROSPORA PENICILLIUM
(UNICELLULAR —) BEES EAST
YEAST
(PREF.) AGARICI BASIDIO HYDNO
MYC(ET)(ETO)(O)
(SUFF.) MYCES MYCET(O)
MYCETE(S) MYCOSIS
(— DISEASE) OSIS
FUNK FUNG NESH
FUNNEL CAST STACK TEWEL
TRUNK FILLER FUMMEL HOPPER
SIPHON SYPHON TUNNEL
TUNNER TRUMPET TUNDISH
HYPONOME WINDSAIL
(PREF.) CHOAN(O)
(SUFF.) CHOANITE CHOANITIC
FUNNY ODD GOOD COMIC DROLL
MERRY QUEER COMICAL JOCULAR
RISIBLE STRANGE HUMOROUS
(VERY —) SPLITTING
SIDESPLITTING
FUR FOX BEAR CALF COON FLIX
FLUE FOIN GRAY GREY GRIS MINK
PEAN PELF PELL PILE SEAL VAIR
BUDGE COYPU CROSS FITCH
FLICK GENET GRISE OTTER PAHMI
SABLE SCARF SHUBA BADGER
BEAVER COUGAR DESMAN
ERMINE FISHER GALYAC JACKET

MARTIN NUTRIA PELAGE POTENT
RABBIT SPRING SUSLIK CALABER
CARACAL FITCHET FITCHEW
FURRURE MINIVER TOPCOAT
CACOMIXL ERMINOIS KOLINSKI
(— OF LAMBSKIN AND WOOL)
BUDGE
(— RESEMBLING PERSIAN LAMB)
KRIMMER
(BEAVER —) WOOM CASTOR
(GRAY —) GRAY GREY GRIS GRISE
CRIMMER LETTICE
(LAMB —) CARACUL KARAKUL
(NUMBER OF — SKINS) TIMBER
TIMMER
(RABBIT —) CONY SCUT CONEY
FLICK LAPIN HATTER SEALINE
ERMILINE
(SQUIRREL —) CALABAR
(SQUIRREL OR MARTIN —) AMICE
POPEL
(STONE MARTEN'S —) FOIN
(PL.) PELTRY FURRIERY
(PREF.) DORA
FURBEARER PLATINUM
FURBELOW DIDO FRILL FALBALA
FURBISH DO FIG RUB FAKE FINE
VAMP CLEAN SCOUR FINIFY
POLISH BURNISH VARNISH
RENOVATE
FURCATE FORKY BRANCH FURCAL
FURCULA SPRING FURCULUM
FURCULUM WISHBONE
FURFOOZ GRENELLE
FURIES ALECTO ERINYS ERINYES
MEGAERA ERINNYES TISIPHONE
FURIOUS MAD GRIM WOOD YOND
ANGRY BRAIN GIDDY IRATE LIVID
RABID SHARP FIERCE FURIAL
FURIED INSANE RENISH STORMY
ACHARNE FRANTIC HOPPING
MADDING MANKIND PELTING
RAGEOUS REDWOOD RUSHING
TEARING VIOLENT FRENZIED
MAENADIC TOWERING VEHEMENT
VESUVIAN WRATHFUL
FURIOUSLY CRAZY ANGERLY
TEARING
FURL FOLD HAND ROLL STOW
WRAP FRESE TRUSS FARDEL
FURDLE
FURLED IN
FURLONG SHOT STADE
FURLOUGH LEAVE BLIGHTY
FURNACE ARC KILN OVEN TANK
BENCH CUPEL DRIER DRYER
FORGE MOUTH TISAR BURNER
CALCAR COCKLE CUPOLA HEATER
ATHANOR CHAFERY CRESSET
FIREPOT PUDDLER ROASTER
BESSEMER BLOOMERY CALCINER
CHAUFFER FIREWORK IRONCLAD
LIMEKILN PRODUCER REFINERY
TRYWORKS
(— DOOR) TWEEL
(ALMOND —) ALMAN
(ARC —) HEROULT
(GLASS-HEATING —) TISAR
(PORTABLE —) DANDY CRESSET
FURNACEMAN BUSTLER DROSSER
SMELTER IMPROVER REHEATER
FURNISH ARM SOW DECK FEAT
FEED FILL FRET FRUB GIVE LEND

TRIM VEST ARRAY BESEE ENDOW
EQUIP FRAME INDUE PITCH
POINT SERVE SPEED STOCK
STORE STUFF AFFORD GRAITH
INSURE INVEST OUTFIT RENDER
SUPPLY ADVANCE APPAREL
APPOINT BRACKET GARNISH
INSTORE PERFORM PLENISH
PRESENT PRODUCE PROVIDE
SUFFICE ACCOUTER DECORATE
FRUBBISH MINISTER
ACCOMMODATE
(— ABUNDANTLY) FREQUENT
(— ANALYSIS) ACCOUNT
(— FULLY) CHARGE
(— REFRESHMENT) EASE
(— WITH) BESEE
(— WITH DRINK) BIRL BYRL
(— WITH MEALS) BOARD
(— WITH NEW PARTS) RETROFIT
(— WITH STEEP SLOPE) ESCARP
(— WITH STRENGTH) MAN
(— WITH WINGS) IMP
FURNISHED ARMED BODEN GARNI
(COMFORTABLY —) BEIN
FURNISHING ADVANCE FITMENT
(PL.) STUFF BAGGAGE PENATES
FURNITURE ADAM BUHL TIRE
SAMAN STOOL STUFF GRAITH
FITMENT INSIGHT MEUBLES
MOVABLE EQUIPAGE ORNAMENT
SUPELLEX TACKLING
(CHEAP —) BORAX
(SHIP'S —) HARNESS
(STORED —) LUMBER
FURORE FUROR BROUHAHA
FURRED PURED LOADED
FURRING PACKING
FURROW FUR GAP GAW RIB RUT
FURR GRIP HINT LINE PLOW RAIN
RILL ROUT RUCK SEAM SULK
CHASE DRAIN DRILL EARTH FIELD
RIGOL SCORE SEUGH STRIA
GROOVE GUTTER INDENT SULCUS
SUTURE TRENCH BREAKER
CHAMFER CHANNEL CRUMPLE
FEERING PLOWING QUILLET
SCRATCH WINDROW WRINKLE
CARRIAGE NOTAULIX THOROUGH
VALLECULA
(PREF.) AULAC(O) HOLC(O) LIRELLI
SULCI SULCO
FURROWED SEAMED EXARATE
FURROWY SULCATE TRENCHED
FURROWING KNOT DRESS
FURRY SHAGGY
FUR SEAL URSAL
FURTHER MO AID YET ALSO HELP
YOND ADDED AGAIN FRESH
SPEED SUPRA BEYOND EXTEND
SECOND ADVANCE DEVELOP
FARTHER FORWARD PROMOTE
MOREOVER REMANENT ULTERIOR
FURTHERMORE BESIDES FURTHER
OVERMORE
FURTIVE SLY PRIVY CLAMMY
SECRET SHIFTY SNEAKY
HANGDOG MEACHING MYSTICAL
SNEAKING STEALTHY THIEVISH
CLANDESTINE
FURTIVELY SLILY SLYLY SIDELINS
FURTIVENESS STEALTH
FURUNCLE BOIL

FURY HAG IRE MAD WAX BURN
RAGE ANGER BRETH DREAD
FUROR IRISH RIGOR WRATH
ALECTO BELDAM CHOLER FRENZY
FURORE MADNESS MEGAERA
WIDDRIM DELIRIUM FEROCITY
VIOLENCE WOODNESS TISIPHONE

FURZE FUN FUZZ LING ULEX WHIN
GORSE WHINCOW

FUSE RUN CAKE FLOW FLUX FRIT
FUZE MELT BLEND FOUND FUSEE
FUZEE QUILL SMELT SQUIB
SWAGE TRAIN UNITE MINGLE
SPITTER COALESCE CONCRETE
CONFLATE COPULATE PORTFIRE
SAUCISSE COLLIQUATE

FUSED CONNATE

FUSEE FUZEE SPINDLE VESUVIAN
VESUVIUS

FUSELAGE BODY
(— MEMBER) LONGERON

FUSIFORM FUSATE SPINDLE

FUSIL (DIVIDED INTO —S) PLUMETE

FUSION ZYG FLUX FUSURE
CHIASMA FLUXION CYTOGAMY
MITAPSIS PLASMOGAMY
(PREF.) ZYG(O)(OTO)
(SUFF.) APSIS

FUSS DO ADO ROW TEW COIL FAFF
FIKE FIRK FIZZ FRET ROUT SONG
STIR TIME TOUSE TOWSE TRADE
WHAUP BOTHER CADDLE
DIRDUM FANTAD FETTLE FISSLE
FISTLE FIZZLE FRAISE FUFFLE
FUSTLE HOORAY HURRAH
PHRASE POTHER RACKET SETOUT
STROTH TURNUP FOOSTER
FRIGGLE FUSSIFY NAUNTLE

POOTHER SPUFFLE SPUTTER
TAMASHA BUSINESS FOOFARAW
SCRONACH

FUSSBUDGETY SPOFFISH

FUSSINESS DAINTY FADDLE
FIKERY FOOSTER

FUSSING BOTHER

FUSSY BUSY FIKY FIXY FUDGY
PICKY CHICHI FIDFAD PROSSY
SPOFFY SPRUCE STICKY FIDGETY
NIGGLING NOTIONAL SPOFFISH
SQUEAMISH PERSNICKETY

FUSTET ZANTE FUSTIC

FUSTIAN HOLMES PILLOW
BOMBAST TWADDLE CORDUROY
MOLESKIN

FUSTIC LIME MORA FUSTET
DYEWOOD AMARILLO

FUSTINESS FOIST FROWST

FUSTY FOIST MOLDY MUSTY
FOISTY RANCID
FROWSTY MALODOROUS

FUTILE IDLE TOOM VAIN OTIOSE
USELESS BOOTLESS FECKLESS
FOOTLESS FUTILOUS HELPLESS
NUGATORY

FUTILITY VANITY NUGACITY
VAINESSE

FUTTAH WHATA

FUTURE LATER SKULD AVENIR
COMING ONWARD OPTION
TOCOME TOWARD LAVENIR
FUTURITY ONCOMING
(— TIME) MANANA

FUZZ LINTERS

FUZZY LOUSY MUZZY WOOLY
WOOLLY

FYTTE PASSUS

G

G GEE GOLF GEORGE
GA AKRA ACCRA INKRA
GAAL (FATHER OF —) EBED
GAB GOB YAP BLAB CHIN
  CHINFEST
GABBLE WAB CANK CHAT CONK
  JAVER BABBLE GAGGLE HABBLE
  PATTER RABBLE TATTER YABBLE
  CLATTER JAUNDER TWADDLE
  TWITTER SLIPSLOP SLUMMOCK
GABBRO BOJITE NORITE EUCRITE
GABION KISH KEESH BASKET
  WALING CORBEIL
GABLE GAVEL GOFOL DETAIL
  DORMER GABLET KENNEL
  MEMBER PINION AILERON
  PEDIMENT
GABON (CAPITAL OF —) LIBREVILLE
  (LAKE OF —) ANENGUE AZINGUO
  (MOUNTAIN OF —) MPELE
  IBOUNDJI
  (NATIVE OF —) FANG ADOUMA
  ECHIRA OKANDE
  (RIVER OF —) ABANGA IVINDA
  OGOOUE NGOUNIE
  (TOWN OF —) OYEM BONGO
  KANGO MITZIC OMVANE
  MAKOKOU
GABOON OKOUME
GABRIELINO TOBIKHAR
GAD GAR RUN FISK GAUD JAZZ
  RAKE JINKET GADLING TRAIPSE
  VIRETOT
  (— ABOUT) HAIK ROLL STRAM
  GALLANT TROLLOP
  (BROTHER OF —) ASHER
  (FATHER OF —) JACOB
  (MOTHER OF —) ZILPAH
GADABOUT GAD GADDER TRAIPSE
GADDI (FATHER OF —) SUSI
GADFLY GAD CLEG GLEG BRIZE
  CLEGG STOUT WHAME BOTFLY
  BREEZE GADBEE OESTRID
  TABANID HORSEFLY
  (PREF.) ESTRA ESTRI ESTRO
  OESTR(I)
GADGET DODAD GISMO GIZMO
  HICKY DINGUS DOODAD GILGUY
  HICKEY JIGGER JIMJAM WIDGET
  CONCERN DOFUNNY GIMMICK
  BUSINESS GIMCRACK JIMCRACK
  CONTRAPTION
  (PL.) GIBBLES GUBBINS
  GADGETRY
GADI (SON OF —) MENAHEM
GADUS MORRHUA
GADWALL RODGE VOLANT
  GADWELL REDWING SHUTTLE
GAEL CELT KELT SCOT GOIDEL
  GAEDHEAL
GAELIC ERSE IRISH
GAFF CLIP SPAR SPUR YARD
  GAFFLE GABLOCK GAFFLET

SLASHER GAVELOCK
  (— MACKEREL) GAMBEER
GAFFER STAGEHAND
GAG BOFF GEGG JOKE PONG SCOB
  HEAVE KEVEL SCOBE AGUAJI
  MUZZLE WHEEZE
GAGE (ALSO SEE GAUGE) LAY
  PAWN WAGE GAUGE JEDGE
  NORMA WAGER FEELER PLEDGE
  SPIDER SCANTLE STANDARD
  UDOMETER
GAHAM (FATHER OF —) NAHOR
  (MOTHER OF —) REUMAH
GAHERIS (MOTHER OF —)
  MORGANSE
GAIETY JOY GALA JEST RANT
  CHEER MIRTH BAWDRY FROLIC
  GAYETY LEVITY BAUDERY
  BEGONIA DAFFERY DAFFING
  GAYNESS JOLLITY JOYANCE
  ROLLICK BUOYANCY FESTIVAL
  HILARITY VIVACITY
GAILY GAY GAYLY BRAVELY
  LIGHTLY
GAIN BAG DAP GET NET POT WIN
  BEAR BOOT DRAW GROW HAVE
  LAND MAKE PELF SACK TILL
  ADDLE BOOTY CATCH LATCH
  LUCRE REACH SCORE ARRIVE
  ATTAIN CHIEVE DERIVE GATHER
  INCOME OBTAIN PROFIT STRAIN
  CAPTURE CONQUER EMBRACE
  GAYMENT GETTING HARVEST
  POSSESS PROCURE REALIZE
  VANTAGE WINNING CLEANING
  CONQUEST PURCHASE
  PERQUISITE
  (— ADMISSION) ENTER
  (— ADVANTAGE) GLEEK
  (— ASCENDANCY) PREVAIL
  (— BY EXTORTION) SQUEEZE
  (— BY FORTUNE) DRAW HAZARD
  (— COMMAND OF) MASTER
  (— IN FAVOR) PROPITIATE
  (— KNOWLEDGE) EDIFY LEARN
  (— OVER) ENGAGE
  (— UNDERSTANDING) SMOKE
  (— WITHOUT DEDUCTION) CLEAR
  (DISHONEST —) MEED
  (ESTIMATED —) ESTEEM
  (ILL-GOTTEN —) PELF BOODLE
  (ILLICIT —) SPLOSH
  (MATERIAL —) PUDDING
  (UNEXPECTED —) BUNCE
  (PL.) PICKING PLUNDER
  GANANCIAS
GAINFUL LUCROUS GAINSOME
GAINSAY DENY FORBID IMPUGN
  OPPOSE REFUTE RESIST DISPUTE
  RECLAIM WITHSAY AGAINSAY
GAIT BAT JOG GANG LOPE PACE
  RACK SKIP STEP TROT VOLT
  WALK AMBLE AUBIN GOING

STALK TRAIN ALLURE CANTER
  GALLOP LOUNGE SLOUCH
  SWINGE TODDLE WADDLE
  WALLOW WAMBLE WOBBLE
  DOGTROT HICKORY PIAFFER
  SAUNTER SCUTTLE SHAMBLE
  SHUFFLE WALKING WAUCHLE
  (— OF ILL-BROKEN HORSE) CHACK
  (DEFECTIVE —) WINDING
  (LIMPING —) HIRPLE
  (UNSTEADY —) STAGGER
  (4-BEAT —) AMBLE
GAITER SPAT VAMP STRAD
  BONNET BRAGAS COCKER GASKIN
  GUETRE HOGGER HUGGER
  LEGGIN PUTTEE GAMBADE
  GAMBADO LEGGING STARTUP
  BOOTIKIN CUTTIKIN
  (PL.) UPPERS GASKINS
  GAMASHES GRAMOCHES
GAIZE MALMSTONE
GAJO GORGIO
GALACTITE MILKSTONE
GALACTOSIDE IDEIN IDAEIN
GALAGO LEMUR LEMUROID
GALAL (FATHER OF —) ASAPH
  JEDUTHUN
GALANAS GAINES
GALAOR (BROTHER OF —) AMADIS
GALATEA (DAUGHTER OF —)
  LEUCIPPUS
  (FATHER OF —) NEREUS
  (HUSBAND OF —) PYGMALION
  (LOVER OF —) ACIS
  (MOTHER OF —) DORIS
  (SON OF —) PAPHUS METHARME
GALAX COLTSFOOT
GALAXY NEBULA SPIRAL
  (KIND OF —) SEYFERT
  (PREF.) GALACT(O)
GALBANUM FERULA GALBAN
  ALBETAD
GALCHA PAMIR
GALE BLOW GELL HELM WIND
  GAGEL PERRY STOUR BUSTER
  EASTER BAYBUSH BURSTER
  GALEAGE TEMPEST FLEAWOOD
  GALEWORT NORWESTER
GALEA MITRA HELMET
GALGA INGUSH
GALIBI CARIBI KALINA
GALINGALE CYPRESS WANHORN
  CHINAROOT
GALIPOT BARRAS GALLIPOT
  TACAMAHAC
GALJOEN BLACKFISH
GALL GA GAW BAIT FELL FRET
  NERVE WRING ANBURY COCKLE
  HARASS HUTZPA ANBERRY
  BEDEGAR CHUTZPA GALLNUT
  HUTZPAH KNOPPER NUTGALL
  BEDEGUAR CECIDIUM CHUTZPAH
  FLEASEED IRRITATE OAKBERRY

SEEDGALL SPURGALL TACAHOUT
  (SAND —) SALT NATRON
  SANDIVER
  (PL.) PURPLES
  (PREF.) CHOL(E)(O)
  (SUFF.) CHOLIA CHOLY
GALLANT GAY BEAU PROW BLADE
  BRAVE BULLY CIVIL JOLLY LOVER
  NOBLE PREUX SHOWY SPARK
  SWAIN DONZEL ESCORT HEROIC
  POLITE RUTTER SPARKY SQUIRE
  SUITOR AMATORY AMORIST
  AMOROSO AMOROUS CONDUCT
  GALANTE GREGORY SPARKER
  STATELY TOPPING YOUNKER
  BELAMOUR CAVALIER CICISBEO
  FEMALIST GALLIARD HANDSOME
  POLISHED
GALLANTRY GAME DRURY
  DRUERY BRAVERY COURAGE
  PROWESS CHIVALRY PARAMOUR
GALLBERRY INKBERRY
GALLED RAW
GALLEON CARAC CARRACK
  GALLOON
GALLERY POY SAP COOP GODS
  JUBE LOFT PAWN ALURE BOYAU
  ORIEL PRADO ARCADE BURROW
  DEDANS NARROW PIAZZA
  SCHOOL SOLLAR SUBWAY
  TUNNEL BALCONY GALERIE
  HEADWAY MIRADOR TERRACE
  VERANDA BARTISAN BRATTICE
  CANTORIA CORRIDOR HOARDING
  PARADISE PERAMBLE SCAFFOLD
  TRAVERSE VERANDAH
  BLINDSTORY
  (— IN BAZAAR) PAWN
  (— IN HOUSE OF COMMONS)
  VENTILATOR
  (— MADE BY INSECT) MINE
  (— OF FORT) CASEMATE
  (CHURCH —) JUBE LAFT LOFT
  (MINE —) BORD BROW SLOVAN
  (MINSTREL'S —) ORIEL
  (OPEN —) LOGGIA
  (UNDERGROUND —) HYPOGEE
  HYPOGEUM
GALLEY FUST CUDDY DRAKE FOIST
  STICK BIREME GALIOT HEARTH
  ZYGITE BASTARD CABOOSE
  DROMOND GALLIOT HEXERIS
  LYMPHAD TRIREME UNIREME
  CAMBOOSE COOKROOM
  CROMSTER GALLEASS RAMBERGE
  (— BOTTOM) SLICE
  (CHIEFTAIN'S —) BIRLING BIRLINN
  (PHILIPPINE —) CALAN
  (VIKING —) AESC DRAKE
GALLEY SLAVE FORSADO
  SFORZATO
GALLFLY CYNIPID
GALLIMAUFRY HASH

GALLINACEOUS RASORIAL
GALLINAE RASORES
GALLINAZO VIRU VULTURE
GALLING BITTER
GALLINULE COOT KORA MOHO
RAIL GORHEN PUKEKO SKITTY
MOORHEN STANKIE SULTANA
DABCHICK HYACINTH
MANUALII RAILBIRD
RICEBIRD SWAMPHEN
GALLIVANT KITE ROAM ROVE
GALLANT
GALLNUT
(PREF.) CECIDIO CEDIDO
GALLON GAWN CONGIUS
(— OF ORE) DISH
(EIGHTH —) OCTARIUS
(HALF —) POTTLE
(128 —S) LEAGUER
GALLOON ORRIS
GALLOP FOG RUN AUBIN PRICK
CANTER CAREER COURSE TITTUP
WALLOP TANTIVY
GALLOWS NUB CRAP DROP FORK
TREE BOUGH CHEAT FURCA
WIDDY GIBBET WOODIE DERRICK
FORCHES JUSTICE POTENCE
STIFLER WARYTREE
GALLOWS BIRD HEMPY WIDDY
HEMPIE HEMPSEED WIDDIFOW
CRACKROPE
GALOSH ARCTIC ZIPPER EXCLUDER
OVERSHOE
GALUTH GOLUS GOLAHI
GALVANIC VOLTAIC
GALVANIZE ZINCIFY SHERADISE
GALVANOMETER DETECTOR
REOMETER
GAMBESON WAMBAIS
GAMBIA (CAPITAL OF —) BANJUL
(COIN OF —) BUTUT DALASI
(LANGUAGE OF —) JOLA WOLOF
FULANI MALINKE
(MONEY OF —) DALASI
(NATIVE OF —) JOLA PEUL WOLOF
DIOLAS FULANI MANDINGO
SERAHULI
(TOWN OF —) KAUUR MANSA
FATOTO BINTANG BRIKAMA
KUNTAUR
GAMBIA POD BABLOH
GAMBIER CATECHU
GAMBIT MANEUVER
GAMBLE BET DICE GAFF GAME
NICK PLAY PUNT RISK SPORT
STAKE WAGER CHANCE
GAMMON HAZARD PLUNGE
FLUTTER
(— AGAINST) BUCK
GAMBLER PIKER SPORT CARROW
DEALER PLAYER PUNTER
HUSTLER PLAYMAN PLUNGER
SLICKER THROWER BLACKLEG
GAMESTER HAZARDER
GAMBLER, THE (CHARACTER IN —)
ALEXEY BLANCHE PAULINE
(COMPOSER OF —) PROKOFIEV
GAMBLING GAMING HAZARDRY
(— DEVICE) PACHINKO
GAMBLING HOUSE HELL TRIPOT
GAMBO GOOSE SPURWING
GAMBOL HOP PLAY CAPER FRISK
KEVEL PRANK CAREER CAVORT

FROLIC PRANCE GAMBADO
CAPRIOLE
GAMBREL CAMMOCK SPREADER
GAME COB FUN JEU JIG GAMY
LAKE MAIL PLAY DANCE GAMEY
PARTY SPIEL SPORT WATHE
BATTUE MORRIS QUARRY
RAMSCH VENERY JENKINS
KNICKER BREATHER FIGHTING
FOREGAME
(— FOR FISHERMEN) SKISH
(— LIKE HANDBALL) FIVES
(— LIKE HOCKEY) DODDART
(— NARROWLY WON) SQUEAKER
(— OF CAT) BILLET
(— OF FOOTBALL) BOWL CAMP
(— OF FORFEITS) KEN
(— OF HOCKEY) BANDY SHINNY
(— OF INSULTS) DOZENS
(— OF MARBLES) TAW BOWL
BONCE GULLY KEEPS KNUCKS
MIGGLES
(— OF MENTAL SKILL) GO CHESS
CHECKERS
(— OF NINEPINS) KAILS KAYLES
(— OF PRISONER'S BASE) CHEVY
CHIVVY
(— WITH BOOMERANG) BRIST
(— WITH COUNTERS) DUMPS
GOOSE
(— WITH SHUTTLECOCK) TAHYING
(BACKGAMMON —) HIT IRISH
(BALL —) CAT TUT SNOB CATCH
RUGBY SOCCER SQUASH TENNIS
CRICKET KNAPPAN BASEBALL
FOOTBALL HANDBALL SLUGFEST
SOFTBALL
(CARD —) AS HOC LOO MAW NAP
PAM PIT PUT SET BRAG CENT
FARO FISH FROG GRAB JASS
LANT PINK POOL POPE POST
RUFF SANT SKAT SLAM SNAP
SOLO STUD VINT BEAST BUNCO
BUNKO CARDS CARIE CHICO
CINCH COMET CRIMP DECOY
GILET GLEEK GRAND LEAST
MONTE NODDY OMBER OMBRE
PEDRO PITCH POKER PRIME
RUMMY SCOPA SLAMM STOPS
STUSS TRUMP WHIST BANKER
BASSET BIRKIE BOODLE BOSTON
BRIDGE CASINO CHEMMY
COMMIT ECARTE EIGHTS EUCHRE
FARMER FLINCH HEARTS HOWELL
LOADUM PANFIL PIQUET QUINZE
RAMSCH ROUNCE SLOUGH
SMUDGE SPIDER TOURNE
AUCTION AUTHORS BELOTTE
BEZIQUE CANASTA CASSINO
CAYENNE CHICAGO COONCAN
GARBAGE HUNDRED JACKPOT
PLAFOND PONTOON PRIMERO
REVERSI SCOPONE SETBACK
TRIUMPH VINGTUN VITESSE
BACCARAT BASEBALL BRISCOLA
COMMERCE CONQUIAN
CONTRACT CRIBBAGE FREAKPOT
HANDICAP IMPERIAL NAPOLEON
PATIENCE PENCHANT PENNEECH
PINOCHLE SHOWDOWN SKINBALL
SKINNING SLAPJACK TREDILLE
TRESILLO VERQUERE VIDERUFF
(CARNIVAL —) HOOPLA

(CHILDREN'S —) TAG DIBS JACKS
KICKBALL PEEKABOO
(CONFIDENCE —) RAMP BIGMITT
(COURT —) PELOTA SQUASH
TENNIS HANDBALL
(DICE —) FARE TRAY BINGO CRAPS
NOVUM RAPHE HAZARD BARBUDI
ADDITION BARBOTTE CAMEROON
HOOLIGAN
(DRAWN —) SPOIL REFAIT
(DRINKING —) HIJINKS
(EGYPTIAN —) SENT SENIT
(GAMBLING —) EO TAN FARO
HAND PICO BOULE CRAPS MACAO
MONTE POKER PROPS RONDO
STUSS BRELAN HAZARD
RONDEAU ROULETTE
(GENERAL —) HEI HIM HIT HOB
TAG TIG BALL BASE BULL BUNT
BUZZ CENT DIBS DUCK FARE
GOLF HOLE JOWL KENO MALL
POLO POOL SLAM SNOB TICK
BANDY BINGO BONCE BOULE
CHESS CHUBA CHUNK CLOSH
DARTS DOLOS, FIVES GOOSE
HALMA HOUSE IRISH JACKS
LOTTO LURCH NOVUM NULLO
PITCH PUSSY RUGBY SALTA
SALVO SCRUB TROCO WHOOP
BEAVER BEETLE CAROMS CHIVVY
CHUNKY CLUMPS COBNUT
COCKAL COOTIE CRAMBO FEEDER
GOBANG GRACES HAZARD
HOOPLA HUBBUB JEREED KAYLES
MERELE PELOTA PLUMPS
RAGMAN RINGER SEESAW
SHINNY SIPPIO SKILLO STICKS
TENNIS TIGTAG TIPCAT TIVOLI
TRIGON TRUCKS BALLOON
BEANBAG BEEBALL BOWLING
COBBLER CONKERS CROQUET
CURLING DIABOLO DODDART
DOUBLES DREIDEL ENDBALL
GOGGANS HANGMAN HURLBAT
LOGGATS MAHJONG MATADOR
MUGGINS NETBALL PALLONE
PASSAGE PEEVERS PUSHPIN
QUINTET RINGTAW SARDINE
SQUAILS STATUES TENPINS
TOMBOLA ANAGRAMS BALKLINE
BASEBALL CHARADES CHECKERS
CHOUETTE DOMINOES DOUBLETS
DRAUGHTS DUCKPINS FIVEPINS
FOOTBALL FORFEITS GIVEAWAY
HARDHEAD KICKBALL KORFBALL
LEAPFROG PARCHESI PEEKABOO
PETANQUE PURPOSES PUSHBALL
PYRAMIDS RINGTOSS ROULETTE
ROUNDERS SCRABBLE SKITTLES
STOBBALL STOWBALL
TRAPBALL VERQUERE
PARCHEESI PHILOPENA
SHUFFLEBOARD
(GUESSING —) LOVE MORA
CANUTE
(INDIAN —) CHUNKY HUBBUB
(INFERIOR —) CHECK
(JAPANESE —) GO
(MEXICAN —) FRONTENIS
(NUMBERS —) BUG
(OUTDOOR —) GOLF POLO HURLY
ROQUE RUGBY SOCCER CROQUET
HURLING BASEBALL

FOOTBALL LACROSSE
(PROGRESSIVE —) DRIVE
(PUZZLE —) GLAIK
(REHEATED —) SALMI SALMIS
(SWISS —) JASS
(THREE BOWLING —S) SERIES
(TRAPSHOOTING —) SCOOT
(WAR —) BARRIERS
(WORD —) GHOST ANAGRAMS
(PL.) LUDI
(PREF.) LUDI
GAMECOCK STAG STAIG
GAMEKEEPER GAMIE KEEPER
WALKER WARNER VENERER
WARRENER
GAMESTER DICER PLAYER
GAMBLER PLAYMAN SHARPER
HAZARDER TABLEMAN
GAMETE SPERM OOCYTE ZYGOTE
GAMETOID OOGAMETE OOSPHERE
GAMETOCYTE GAMONT
CRESCENT GONOCYTE
GAMETOPHYTE GERMLING
GAMIN TAD ARAB URCHIN
GAVROCHE
GAMMA AGMA
GAMMON BAM
GAMUT GAMME RANGE SCALE
SERIES COMPASS DIAGRAM
GANDAREWA (SLAYER OF —)
KERESASPA
GANDER STEG STAIG GANNER
(— AND GEESE) SET
GANDHARI (HUSBAND OF —)
DHRITARASHTRA
GANESA GUNPUT GANAPATI
GANG MOB SET BAND BUND CORE
CREW GING PACK PAIR PUSH
TEAM BATCH BUNCH GROUP
HORDE SPELL SQUAD CHIURM
COFFLE GAGGLE LAYOUT
MOHOCK SCHOOL COMPANY
(— MEMBER) WHYO
(— OF FISHHOOKS) PULLDEVIL
(— OF MINERS) CORE
(— OF WITCHES) COVEN
(ROWDY —) TRIBULATION
GANGLING GAWKY GANGLY
GANGLION TUMOR CEREBRUM
GANGPLANK BROW GANGWAY
GANGRENE NOMA CANKER
GANGER SPHACEL NECROSIS
MORTIFICATION
(PREF.) NECR(O) SPHACELO
GANGSTER HOOD PUNK WHYO
APACHE BANDIT COWBOY
CHOPPER
GANGUE MATRIX LODESTUFF
VEINSTONE
GANGWAY BROW ROAD SLIP
LOGWAY TUNNEL CATWALK
COULOIR GATEWAY
GANJA GUNJAH CANNABIS
GANNET BOOBY GAUNT SOLAN
PIQUERO SEAFOWL ALCATRAS
GANTRYMAN DROPMAN
GANYMEDE (BROTHER OF —) ILUS
ASSARACUS
(FATHER OF —) TROS
(MOTHER OF —) CALLIRRHOE
GAOLER (ALSO SEE JAILER) ADAM
ALCAIDE
GAP SAG FLAW GAPE GOWL GULF

MUSE NICK SLAP SLOP WANT BREAK BRECK CHASM CHAUM CHAWN CLOVE FRITH MEUSE MUSET NOTCH SHARD SHERD VUIDE BREACH GULLET HIATUS LACUNA SPREAD THROAT VACUUM CLOSING OPENING VACANCY VACUITY APERTURE DIASTEMA ENTREFER INTERVAL MULTIGAP QUEBRADA
(— IN BANK OF STREAM) GAT
(— IN FOOTBALL LINE) SLOT
(— IN MEMORY) AMNESIA
(— SERVING AS PASS) COL
(PREF.) CHASMO

GAPE GAN GAP GANT GAUP GAWK GAWP GAZE GOVE GRIN YAWN CHAUN GERNE HIATE STARE RICTUS DEHISCE INHIATE
(PREF.) CHAEN(O)

GAPER COMBER

GAPING GALP AGAPE HIANT CHAPPY CHASMA GAWISH MOUTHED RINGENT ADENOIDAL

GAR HOUND SNOOK AGUJON CHERNA GARFISH GARPIKE BILLFISH GOREFISH GURDFISH HORNBEAK HORNFISH HORNKECK LONGJAWS LONGNOSE

GARAGE HANGAR LOCKUP SIDING GARRIDGE
(ROW OF —S) MEWS

GARAVANCE CARAUNA GARBANZO

GARB (ALSO SEE APPAREL AND DRESS) COWL GEAR TOGA VEST DRESS GUISE HABIT APPAREL CLOTHES COSTUME RAIMENT
(UNIVERSITY —) ACADEMICALS

GARBAGE GASH SLOP OFFAL TRASH WASTE GIBLET REFUSE SCRAPS
(— IN, — OUT) GIGO

GARBAGEMAN DUSTMAN

GARBLE GELD JUMBLE MANGLE DISTORT GARBLING MUTILATE MISREPRESENT

GARDANT AFFRONTE

GARDEN HAW EDEN KNOT YARD ARBOR GARTH CIRCLE POMACY POMARY QUINTA ROSARY SHAMBA VERGER VIHARA ACADEMY HERBARY OLITORY ORCHARD ROCKERY TOPIARY CHINAMPA FLORETUM HORTYARD KALEYARD LEIGHTON PARADISE PARTERRE POTAGERE ROSARIUM
(— CITY) CHICAGO
(— STATE) NEWJERSEY
(BEER —) BRASSERIE
(SECLUDED —) PLEASANCE
(PREF.) HORT(I) TOPI
(SUFF.) ETUM

GARDENER MALI PONICA CROPPER PLANNER BOSTANGI

GARDEN HELIOTROPE VALERIAN

GARDENIA TIARA

GARDENING TOPIARY

GARDEN ROCKET EVEWEED

GARDEN WARBLER JACK HAYBIRD BECAFICO FAUVETTE FIGEATER

GARFISH (SEE GAR)

GARGAMELLE (SON OF —) GARGANTUA

GARGANEY TEAL CRICK

GARGANTUA AND PANTAGRUEL
(AUTHOR OF —) RABELAIS
(CHARACTER IN —) JOHN BRIDE BACBUC TRIPPE BADEBEC PANURGE ANARCHUS JOBERLIN GARGANTUA TRIBOULET GARGAMELLE GRANGOSIER HOLOFERNES PANTAGRUEL PICROCHOLE PONOCRATES ENTOMMEURES TROUILLOGAN RAMINAGROBIS

GARGANTUAN HUGE VAST GIANT HOMERIC TITANIC ENORMOUS GIGANTIC HOMERIAN

GARGET MASTITIS

GARGLE GURGLE COLLUTORY

GARGOYLE BOSS

GARIBALDI GOLDFISH

GARISH GAUDY GIDDY SHOWY CRIANT GLARING

GARISHNESS GLARE

GARLAND BAY LEI CROWN TORAN VITTA ANADEM CORONA CRANTS ROSARY WREATH CHAPLET CORANCE CORONAL FESTOON
(PREF.) STEMMATI STEPHAN(O)

GARLIC AJO MOLY RAMP CHIVE PORET ALLIUM PORRET RAMSON

GARMENT DUD TOG BACK BRAT COAT GOWN PELL PELT RAIL ROBE SARK SHAG SILK SLIP SLOP SULU VEST WEED ABAYA BUREL BURKA CENTO CLOAK CLOTH COTTE CYMAR DRESS FROCK HABIT HAORI JOSEY JUPON KHAKI MANGA NABOB SHAWL SHIFT SHIRT SIMAR SKIRT STOLE WRIEL ALPACA ATTIRE BARROW BLOUSE BURKHA CAFTAN CAMLET CAPOTE CHAMMA COTTON CYCLAS ERMINE EXOMIS FECKET HUIPIL JACKET JERSEY JUMPER KERSEY KIRTLE MOHAIR MOTLEY SARONG SHORTY SHROUD STROUD TAMEIN ZIZITH AMICTUS BROIGNE BUNTING CAMBLET CASSOCK CHIRIPA CRAWLER CUCULLA CULOTTE DOUBLET FALDING FLOCKET GROGRAM PALETOT PELISSE RAIMENT SHORTIE SURCOAT SWEATER VESTURE WRAPPER BATHROBE CAMELINE CAPUCHIN CHAUSSES COLOBIUM CORSELET COVERALL DEERSKIN EPIBLEMA GAMBESON GUERNSEY HIMATION INDUMENT PADUASOY PULLOVER SCAPULAR SEALSKIN SLIPOVER SNOWSUIT VESTMENT WEARABLE PETTICOAT REDINGOTE STROUDING
(— OF DERVISH) KHIRKAH
(— OF HERALD) TABARD
(— OF HIGH PRIEST) EPHOD
(— OF PATCHES) CENTO
(ARABIAN —) ABA
(BABY'S —) BARROW CRAWLER CREEPER
(BADLY-MADE —) DRECK
(BLUE —) MAZARINE

(BURIAL —) SHROUD
(COARSE —) BRAT STROUD
(DEFENSIVE —) JACK BROIGNE GAMBESON
(ECCLESIASTICAL —) STOLE RHASON ROCHET CASSOCK
(ETHIOPIAN —) CHAMMA
(HINDU —) SARI SAREE
(INFANT'S —) BARRY BARROW DIAPER BUNTING SLEEPER PANTYWAIST
(JAPANESE —) HAORI
(LEATHER —) BUFF
(LINEN —) LINE
(LONG —) JIBBA KANZU STOLE JIBBEH MANDYAS PELISSE HIMATION
(MEDIEVAL —) ROCHET CHAUSSES DALMATIC GAMBESON
(MONK'S —) SCAPULAR
(MOURNING —) SABLE
(ONE-PIECE —) BODYSUIT
(ONE-PIECE WOMAN'S —) CATSUIT
(OUTER —) BRAT COAT GOWN HAIK HYKE SLOP WRAP FROCK HAORI NABOB PALLA PILCH SMOCK DOLMAN ROCHET CHEMISE GALABIA PALETOT SURCOAT SWEATER HIMATION OVERSLOP
(PADDED —) TRUSS
(PENITENTIAL —) CILICE
(PULLOVER —) DASHIKI
(SLEEVELESS —) ABA CAPE COWL VEST MANTLE CUCULLA GANDURAH
(SQUARE —) KAROSS
(SYRIAN —) ABAYA
(THIN —) GOSSAMER
(TIGHT-FITTING —) HOSE COTTE TRICOT LEOTARD
(WOMAN'S —) IZAR BURKA CYMAR NABOB SIMAR BURKHA CHITON JOSEPH PEPLOS PEPLUM VISITE BLOUSON BURNOUS
(PL.) GEAR COSTUME GARNISH FLANNELS
(PREF.) RHACO

GARNER REAP STORE GATHER IMBARN COLLECT

GARNET GRENAT PYROPE ANTHRAX GRANATE OLIVINE VERMEIL ESSONITE MELANITE ROSOLITE YANOLITE CARBUNCLE RHODOLITE UVAROVITE
(YTTRIUM IRON —) YIG

GARNISH LARD TRIM ADORN DRESS EQUIP MENSE STICK FURNISH PARSLEY TOPPING CHUMMAGE DECORATE DUXELLES ORNAMENT

GARNISHED GARNI

GARNISHEE CHECK FACTOR GARNISH

GARRET ATTIC SOLAR SOLLAR MANSARD COCKLOFT

GARRISON WARD STUFF PRESIDY WARNISON

GARROTE STRANGLE

GARRULITY POLYLOGY

GARRULOUS GABBY TALKY WORDY BABBLY TONGUY VOLUBLE

GARTER GARTEN LEGLET ELASTIC STRAPPLE

GARTH CORTILE OUTGARTH

GARUM LIQUAMEN

GAS DAMP XENON FLATUS GENAPP LEAVEN OXYGEN PETROL EXHAUST KRYPTON YPERITE AFTERGAS ETHERION FIREDAMP HYDROGEN STANNANE VESICANT
(— CONSTANT) R
(COLORLESS —) OXAN OXANE KETENE GERMANE STIBINE
(EXPLOSIVE —) METHYLAMINE
(NERVE —) SARIN
(NONCOMBUSTIBLE —) INERT
(POISONOUS —) ARSINE ADAMSITE AQUINITE CYANOGEN PHOSGENE BRETONITE PHOSPHINE
(TEAR —) ACROLEIN
(VOLCANIC —) MOFETTE
(PREF.) MANO PNEUM(O)(ON)(ONO) PNEUMA PNEUMAT(O)
(CONTAINING —) PYOPNEUMO
(PRESENCE OF —) PHYS(O)
(SUFF.) **(INERT —)** ON

GASCONADE BRAG CROW BOAST BLUSTER

GASEOUS AERIFORM GASIFORM VOLATILE

GASH CUT CHOP LASH BLASH CRIMP GANCH GRIDE SCORE SLASH SLISH SCOTCH SLUICE TRENCH INCISION INCISURE
(— A FISH) RIM

GASKET LUTE CASKET GASKIN GROMMET SCISSIL

GASKIN BRAGAS

GASOLINE AVGAS JUICE PETROL BENZINE NATURAL

GASP FOB BLOW GAPE KINK PANK PANT CHINK CROAK FETCH THRATCH

GASPING CHINK

GASTRONOME EPICURE

GASTROPOD SLUG DRILL HARPA OLIVA SNAIL BUCKIE NERITE ABALONE MOLLUSK TOXIFER UNIVALVE VELUTINA PULMONATE PROSOBRANCH

GATAM (FATHER OF —) ELIPHAZ

GATE BAB BAR JET HEAD LIFT PORT SASH SLAP YATE YETT ENTRY HATCH JANUA SALLY SPRAY STICK TORAN ENAJIM ESCAPE FENDER FUNNEL HARROW INGATE LIGGAT PADDLE PORTAL RUNNER TIMBER TORANA WICKET ZAGUAN BARRIER CLICKET FIVEBAR GATEWAY LIDGATE POSTERN SHUTTER ABOIDEAU ANTEPORT DECUMANA ENTRANCE FOREGATE GURDWARA PENSTOCK TOLLGATE TOWNGATE TRIMTRAM TURNPIKE
(— OF CASTLE) BAR
(— OF DRYDOCK) CAISSON
(BACK —) POSTERN
(CUSTOMS —) BARRIER
(IRRIGATION —) CHECK TAPON TAPPOON
(LICH —) SCALLAGE TRIMTRAM

(RUNNING —) FUNNEL
(SAW —) FRAME
(SAWMILL —) SASH
(SLALOM —S) HAIRPIN
(SLUICE —) HATCH VALVE
(TEMPLE —) VIMANA
(TIDE —) ABOIDEAU ABOITEAU
(WATER —) SLUICE
(PREF.) PYL(E)
(SUFF.) PYL(E)
GATEADO DIOMATE
GATEHOUSE BAR LODGE
GATEKEEPER WARDEN CERBERUS
GATEWARD PORTITOR STILEMAN
GATEMAN GUARD
GATEPOST DURN HARR HEEL PIER
POST SHAFT POSTEL
GATEWAY DAR DOOR GATE LOKE
PORT TORU PYLON TORAN TORII
BARWAY GOPURA TORANA
PROPYLON
(COMPUTER —) PORT
GATHER GET LEK POD WIN BAND
BREW CLAN CLOT CROP CULL
FURL HERD HIVE HOST PICK REAP
RELY TUCK AMASS BANGE
BROOM BUNCH FLOCK GLEAN
GUESS INFER LEASE PLUCK RAISE
SWEEP ACCRUE COMPEL CORRAL
DECERP DERIVE GARNER HUDDLE
HUSTLE IMBARN MUSTER
RAMASS SCRAPE CLUSTER
COLLATE COLLECT COMPILE
CONGEST CONVENE CONVOKE
HARVEST RAMMASS RECRUIT
ASSEMBLE CUMULATE SHEPHERD
(— AS ARMY) HOST
(— BY SCRAPING) SCRATCH
(— GRASS SEED) STRIP
(— HEADWAY) SET
(— HERBS) SIMPLE
(— IN A HEAP) HATTER
(— IN RAGS) TAT
(— SEWING) GAGE GAUGE
(— UP) KILT
(SUFF.) LEGE
GATHERED KILTED CUMULATE
GATHERER GEDDER TUCKER
RUFFLER CHICLERO PLICATOR
PUCKERER
GATHERING HUI LED LEK SUM
FAIR FEST KNOT SING SIVA LEVEE
SHINE TRYST AFFLUX INDABA
MUDDLE PLISSE POWWOW
RUELLE SMOKER COLLECT
COMMERS COMPANY FUNFEST
HARVEST HOSTING HUSKING
JOLLITY KLATSCH MEETING
MOOTING NYMPHAL ROCKING
TURNOUT ASSEMBLY CONCLAVE
FUNCTION JAMBOREE PANIONIA
POTATION RECOURSE SINGSONG
SOCIABLE STAMPEDE
(— OF ANIMALS) DRIVE
(— OF ARMED MEN) HOSTING
(— OF CLOTH) SHIRR SHIRRING
(— OF FILM) CISSING
(— OF SCOUTS) CAMPOREE
JAMBOREE
(— PLACE) LESCHE
(BASUTO —) PITSO
(FORMAL —) HALL
(RELIGIOUS —) SHOUT

(SOCIAL —) BEE FRY BAKE BALL
CLUB DRUM STAG WINE BAILE
BINGE BINGO DANCE MIXER
SHIVOO SMOKER CANTICO
KLATSCH SHINDIG SQUEEZE
BARBECUE CAMPFIRE CLAMBAKE
TALKFEST RECEPTION
SYMPOSIUM
(STUDENTS' —) KOMMERS
(SUFF.) **(FESTIVE —)** FEST
GAU BANT
GAUCHE CLUMSY AWKWARD
GAUD GAY GAUDY FANGLE VANITY
TRINKET
GAUDINESS GLARE GLITTER
GAUDY GAY LOUD CHEAP FLARY
SHOWY VAUDY BRAZEN FLASHY
FLIMSY FLORID GARISH GAWISH
SKYRIN TAWDRY TINSEL BRANKIE
CHINTZY FLARING GAUDISH
GLARING MERETRICIOUS
GAUGE (ALSO SEE GAGE) BORE
GAGE MOOT PLUG SIZE TRAM
GADGE NORMA RANGE DENTIN
FEELER FORMER GABARI
DEPTHEN TEMPLET TRAMMEL
ESTIMATE INDICANT MEASURER
STANDARD SURFACER TEMPLATE
MANOMETER
(— FOR SLATES) SCANTLE
(RAIN —) UDOMETER
GAUGER SURVEYOR
GAUL GALLIA
(PL.) PICTONES
GAULISH
(PREF.) GALLO
GAUNT BONY GRIM LANK LEAN
SLIM THIN PINED SPARE THIRL
BARREN HAGGED HOLLOW
MEAGER MEAGRE SHELLY
HAGGARD SLENDER DESOLATE
RAWBONED CADAVEROUS
GAUNTLET TOP CUFF GLOVE
GANTLET GAINPAIN GANTLOPE
GAUR BISON SELADANG
GAUZE LISSE MARLI MARLY UMPLE
CYPRUS CYPRESS TIFFANY
CARBASUS
GAUZY FILMY
GAVE GIN GUV YAF YAFE
GAVEL HAMMER GAVELAGE
GAVIAL NAKOO LIZARD GHARIAL
LORICATE
GAVOTTE MUSETTE
GAWK GAWKY GAWNEY LUMPKIN
RAMMACK
GAWKY GOWKIT ANGULAR
AWKWARD GAWKISH
GAY MAD AIRY BOON DAFT GLAD
GLEG HIGH RORY TRIM WILD
BONNY BUXOM GAUDY JOLLY
LIGHT MERRY NITID RIANT RORTY
SUNNY VAUDY WLONK ALEGER
BLITHE CHEERY FLASHY FRISKY
FROLIC GARISH JOCUND JOVIAL
JOYFUL JOYOUS KIPPER LIVELY
SOCIAL SPORTY WANTON
BOBBISH CHIPPER FESTIVE
GALLANT GIOJOSO GLEEFUL
LARKING RACKETY SMICKER
SMILING TITTUPY WINSOME
CAVALIER DEBONAIR FROHLICH
GAMESOME PLEASANT PRIMROSE

SPARKISH SPLENDID SPORTIVE
GAY-FEATHER LIATRIS
GAYUMART **(SLAYER OF —)**
ANGROMAINYUS
(SON OF —) SIYAMAK
GAYWINGS MAYWINGS
GAZE EYE PRY CAPE GAPE GOUK
GOWK LEER LOOK MOON OGLE
PEER PORE SCAN TOOT GLAIK
GLARE GLOAT GLORE SIGHT
STARE TWIRE VISIE WLITE
ASPECT GLOWER REGARD
AFTEREYE
GAZELLE AHU GOA ADMI AOUL
CORA DAMA MOHR ADDRA ARIEL
KORIN MHORR DZEREN GROUSE
ALGAZEL CHIKARA CORINNE
DIBATAG TABITHA CHINKARA
GAZELLE HOUND SALUKI
GAZETTE COURANT JOURNAL
(— OF CRIMES) HUE
GAZEZ **(FATHER OF —)** CALEB
HARAN
(MOTHER OF —) EPHAH
GE TAPUYAN
GEAN MERRY MURIE MURRY
GUIGNE GASKINS
GEAR KIT SPUR TACK TRIM IDLER
TOOTH FOURTH GRAITH HYPOID
PINION TACKLE CLOBBER
GEARING HARNESS REVERSE
RIGGING SEGMENT TRILOBE
BACKPACK HEADGEAR
OVERDRIVE
(— OF DIVER) ARMOR
(CHAFING —) SCOTCHMAN
(DEFENSIVE —) ARMORY
(RUNNING —) CARRIAGE
(TRANSMISSION —) HIGH FIRST
SPEED FOURTH SECOND REVERSE
GEARED GIRT
GEARWHEEL UNILOBE WABBLER
WOBBLER
GEB KEB SEB
GEBER **(FATHER OF —)** URI
GECKO FANFOOT TARENTE
GEKKONID LACERTID
GEDALIAH **(FATHER OF —)** AHIKAM
(SLAYER OF —) ISHMAEL
GEELBEC SALMON TERAGLIN
GEEPOUND SLUG
GEESE SET
GEIGER TREE ALOEWOOD
SEBESTEN
GEL JELL JELLY LIVER GELATE
ALCOGEL
GELATIN AGAR GLUE COLLIN
GLUTIN GLUTOID HAITSAI
NORGINE ISINGLASS
GELATINOUS COLLOID MUCULENT
JELLYLIKE
GELD LIB GELT ALTER CASTRATE
GELDING HORSE SPADE SPADO
GEM GIM JADE ONYX OPAL RUBY
AGATE BERYL BIJOU CAMEO
JAZEL JEWEL PEARL SPARK
STONE TOPAZ ZIMME AMULET
BAGUET CRUSTA GARNET IOLITE
JASPER PEBBLE PYROPE RONDEL
ZIRCON CITRINE DIAMOND
DOUBLET EMERALD JACINTH
KUNZITE ONEGITE PERIDOT
SPARKLE ACHROITE AMATRICE

AMETHYST BAGUETTE HYACINTH
INTAGLIO MARQUISE ORIENTAL
RONDELLE SAPPHIRE SARDONYX
HIDDENITE MOONSTONE
RUBICELLE
(— CARVED IN RELIEF) CAMEO
INTAGLIO
(— ENGRAVED WITH CHARM)
ABRAXAS
(— OF IMPERFECT BRILLIANCY)
LOUPE
(— REFLECTING LIGHT IN 6 RAYS)
ASTERIA
(— STATE) IDAHO
(IMITATION —) PASTE
(UNCUT —) ROUGH CABOCHON
GEMALLI **(SON OF —)** AMMIEL
GEMARIAH **(FATHER OF —)** HILKIAH
SHAPHAN
(SON OF —) MICHAIAH
GEMMA BUD GEMMULE SOREDIUM
GEMMULE SPORE BROODSAC
GEMMY EMERALD
GEMSBOK ORYX KOKAMA
GEMSBUCK
GEMSTONE JADE STAR CHEVEE
PYROPE SPINEL EMERALD
FISHEYE CROSSCUT HYALITHE
MORGANITE
(PART OF —) BEZEL CROWN CULET
FACET TABLE GIRDLE PAVILION
GENA CHEEK
GENDER SEX KIND CLASS
FEMININE
GENE GEN ALLEL AMORPH FACTOR
LETHAL PRIMER CYTOGENE
MODIFIER POLYGENE RECESSIVE
GENERAL (ALSO SEE SOLDIER)
MAIN MOST BROAD GROSS
ATAMAN COMMON HETMAN
PUBLIC VULGAR CURRENT
GENERIC MARSHAL SUMMARY
AUFIDIUS CANIDIUS CATHOLIC
ECUMENIC ENCYCLIC OVERHEAD
PANDEMIC PUFIDIUS STRATEGE
BRIGADIER
(PL.) DIADOCHI
(PREF.) CAEN(O) CEN(O) COEN(O)
PAN
GENERALITY CREDO GENERALE
GENERALIZATION LAW AXIOM
BROMIDE
GENERALIZE WIDEN EXTEND
SPREAD BROADEN
GENERALIZED GROSS GLOBAL
GENERALLY BROADLY LARGELY
OVERALL ROUNDLY MOSTWHAT
GENERATE MAKE SIRE TEEM
BEGET BREED IMPEL SPAWN
STEAM CREATE FATHER GENDER
IMPOSE KITTLE DEVELOP INBREED
PRODUCE ENGENDER
(— PUS) DIGEST
GENERATION AGE KIND TIME
WORLD STRAIN STRIND DESCENT
DIPLOID GETTING KINDRED
GAMOBIUM GENITURE SAECULUM
THEOGONY TRIPLOID UPSPRING
OFFSPRING
(FUTURE —S) POSTERITY
(SPONTANEOUS —) ABIOGENESIS
(SUFF.)
GON(E)(IDIUM)(IMO)(IUM)(Y)

GENERATIVE GENIAL GAMETIC GENESIC GENETIC SEEDFUL SEMINAL PROLIFIC

GENERATOR KIPP BUZZER DYNAMO RULING ELEMENT DIPHASER GENERANT OSCILLATOR

GENEROSITY GRACE LARGE BOUNTY GENTRY BREADTH FREEDOM HONESTY COURTESY GOODNESS KINDNESS LARGESSE

GENEROUS BIG FREE OPEN SOFT FRANK HEFTY LARGE NOBLE LIBERAL GRACIOUS HANDSOME INSORDID LARGEOUS MAGNIFIC OPENHANDED

GENEROUSLY LUCKY MANLY KINDLY FRANKLY

GENESIS BIRTH ORIGIN BERESHIT GENETICS

GENET BERBE CIVET DAPPLE VIVERRINE

GENIAL BEIN BIEN WARM DOUCE SONSY DOULCE FORTHY FURTHY HEARTY KINDLY MELLOW MENTAL CHEERFUL GRACIOUS PLEASANT

GENIALITY BONHOMIE

GENICULATE KNEED ELBOWED

GENIE GENIUS HATHOR SANDMAN

GENII XIN JANN

GENIN BUFAGIN

GENIP GINEP JAGUA IRONWOOD

GENIPAP LANA GENIP JAGUA GUENEPE

GENISTA FURZE RETAMA

GENITAL SECRET (PL.) HARNESS PRIVITY GENITURE

GENITALS (PREF.) EDE(O)

GENIUS KA FIRE GIFT HAPI KALI TURN ANGEL BRAIN DEMON GENIO NUMEN DAEMON INGENY INGINE TALENT WIZARD DUSTMAN DUAMUTEF EINSTEIN FRAVASHI SILVANUS (— OF LANGUAGE) IDIOM

GENOA GEANE

GENOTYPE BIOTYPE LOGOTYPE

GENOUILLERE KNEELET

GENRE EPIC KIND SORT TYPE CLASS STYLE FABLIAU SPECIES CATEGORY

GENS HOUSE

GENSERIC (BROTHER OF —) GONDERIC GONTHARIS (FATHER OF —) GODIGISDUS

GENTEEL NICE GENTY GENTIL JAUNTY POLITE STYLISH GRACEFUL

GENTIAN BIT FELWORT AGUEWEED GALLWEED BALDMONEY PENNYWORT

GENTILE GOI GOY ARIAN ARYAN GOYISH HEATHEN

GENTILITY POLISH CIVILITY GENTRICE NICENESS

GENTLE MOY CALM DEFT DEWY FAIR FOND KIND MEEK MILD MURE NESH SLOW SOFT SOOT TAME BLAND CANNY LIGHT LITHE MILKY QUIET SMALL SOBER SWEET BENIGN BONAIR CADISH

DOCILE FACILE LYDIAN MODEST PLACID REMISS SILKEN SILVER SOFTLY TENDER AFFABLE AMABILE CLEMENT GRADUAL SOAKING SUBDUED DEBONAIR DELICATE DOVELIKE EGGSHELL LAMBLIKE LENITIVE MAIDENLY MANSUETE MODERATE PEACEFUL SARCENET TOWARDLY TRANQUIL (— AS OF THE WIND) LOOM

GENTLEFOLK GENTRY GENTILITY

GENTLEMAN NIB SIR BABU GENT TOFF BABOO CURIO DORAY SAHIB SENOR GEMMAN MILORD SENHOR SIGNOR YONKER BRAVERY GALLANT GENTMAN MYNHEER CAVALIER MIRABELL SEIGNEUR SEIGNIOR SQUIREEN (— COMMONER) HAT (— TRAINING FOR KNIGHTHOOD) DONZEL (COUNTRY —) SQUIRE (GIPSY —) RYE (MILITARY —) CADET (POOR —) BUCKEEN (WOULD-BE —) SHONEEN (PL.) HERREN CHIVALRY

GENTLEMAN-AT-ARMS PENSIONER

GENTLEMANLY JAUNTY

GENTLENESS FLESH LENITY AMENITY DOUCEUR CLEMENCY KINDNESS MANSUETUDE

GENTLY SOFT CANNY SOAVE EASILY FAIRLY LIGHTLY EASYLIKE PRETTILY TENDERLY

GENTRY COUNTY GENTRICE SQUIRAGE SZLACHTA

GENUBATH (FATHER OF —) HADAD

GENUFLECTION VENIE KNEELING

GENUINE ECHT GOOD LEAL PURE REAL TRUE VRAI PLAIN PUKKA SOLID ACTUAL ARRANT DINKUM DIRECT HONEST KOSHER PISTIC CURRENT GERMANE GRADELY SINCERE VERIDIC GRAITHLY STERLING (NOT —) TIN SHAM BOGUS PLASTIC PRETENDED (SEEMINGLY —) COLORABLE (SUFF.) (NOT —) ASTER

GENUINENESS VERIDITY

GENUS KIND CLASS ANALOG GENDER GENERAL (— OF ALGAE) DASYA FUCUS BANGIA CHORDA CODIUM HYPNEA NOSTOC PADINA DIATOMA LEMANEA LIAGORA PTILOTA VALONIA ZYGNEMA ANABAENA BRYOPSIS CAULERPA CERAMIUM CHONDRUS CONFERVA CUTLERIA DICTYOTA DUMONTIA GELIDIUM GOMONTIA HALIMEDA LERAMIUM LESSONIA NEMALION OOCYSTIS PALMELLA PORPHYRA STRIARIA TAONURUS ULOTHRIX (— OF AMOEBA) CHAOS (— OF AMPHIBIAN) HYLA RANA SIREN PROTEUS AMPHIUMA NECTURUS (— OF ANT) ATTA ECITON LASIUS

PONERA TERMES FORMICA PHEIDOLE TAPINOMA (— OF ANTELOPE) ORYX KOBUS BUBALIS GAZELLA MADOQUA REDUNCA ANTILOPE EGOCERUS (— OF APE) PAN PONGO SIMIA (— OF APHID) ADELGES CHERMES (— OF ARACHNID) ACARUS GALEODES (— OF ARMADILLO) DASYPUS XENURUS (— OF ASCIDIAN) CIONA MOLGULA BOLTENIA PYROSOMA (— OF ASCLEPIAD) STAPELIA (— OF AUK) ALCA ALLE (— OF BABOON) PAPIO (— OF BACTERIA) VIBRIO EIMERIA ERWINIA GAFFKYA PROTEUS SARCINA BACILLUS BRUCELLA SERRATIA SHIGELLA (— OF BADGER) MELES ARCTONYX HELICTIS (— OF BARNACLE) LEPAS BALANUS ELMINIUS (— OF BASIDIOMYCETE) BOVISTA (— OF BAT) EUDERMA PETALIA DESMODUS DIPHYLLA MOLOSSUS MORMOOPS NOCTILIO NYCTERIS PLECOTUS PTEROPUS VAMPYRUM (— OF BEAN) ABRUS (— OF BEAR) URSUS EUARCTOS MELURSUS (— OF BEAVER) CASTOR (— OF BEE) APIA APIS BOMBUS ANDRENA TRIGONA COLLETES HALICTUS MELIPONA (— OF BEETLE) AMARA FIDIA HISPA LAMIA LARIA LYTTA MELOE SAGRA ALTICA ASILUS CLERUS ELATER LYCTUS PTINUS SILPHA ACILIUS ADELOPS AGRILUS ANOBIUM ANOMALA BRUCHUS CARABUS CASSIDA EPITRIX PRIONUS SAPERDA SITARIS ADORETUS AGRIOTES APHODIUS CALOSOMA CATORAMA CYBISTER DYNASTES DYTISCUS EPICAUTA EUMOLPUS HARPALUS LAMPYRIS MEGASOMA PASSALUS POPILLIA SCOLYTUS SPHINDUS TENEBRIO DERMESTES (— OF BIRD) ARA ALCA APUS CRAX CREX GYPS JYNX MIRO MITU MOHO OTIS PICA RHEA SULA TYTO XEMA AJAJA ANOUS ANSER ARDEA ARGUS ASTUR BUCCO FALCO GAVIA GOURA GUARA GYGIS IRENA JUNCO LARUS LERWA LOXIA MIMUS MITUA MUNIA PIPRA PITTA SITTA TODUS UPUPA VIDUA VIREO ALAUDA ALCEDO ANHIMA ANTHUS AQUILA BONASA BRANTA CAPITO CIRCUS COLIUS CORVUS DACELO ELANUS FULICA GALLUS JACANA LANIUS LEIPOA LIMOSA MARECA MENURA MEROPS MILVUS MONASA NESTOR NUMIDA PASSER PASTOR PERDIX PERNIS PROGNE QUELEA RALLUS SAPPHO SCOPUS SIALIA SPINUS STERNA SYLVIA TETRAO TRERON TRINGA TROGON TURDUS TURNIX

VULTUR ANHINGA APTERYX ARTAMUS BUCEROS CACICUS CAPELLA CARIAMA CERTHIA CHIONIS CICONIA CINCLUS COLINUS COLUMBA COTINGA CUCULUS ELAENIA GALBULA GARRUPA HALCYON HIRUNDO IBYCTER ICTERUS KAKATOE LAGOPUS LOPHURA LYRURUS MALURUS MANACUS MESITES MILVAGO MOMOTUS ORIOLUS PANDION PAROTIA PIRANGA PITYLUS PLAUTUS PLOCEUS PORZANA REGULUS SEIURUS SERINUS STURNUS TANAGRA TIMALIA TOTANUS XENICUS ZENAIDA ACCENTOR ACCIPTER ACREDULA AFROPAVO AGELAIUS AMIZILIA BOTAURUS BUCORVUS BURHINUS CHAETURA COLYMBUS CORACIAS COTURNIX DELICHON DIATRYMA DINORNIS DIOMEDEA DREPANIS EMBERIZA EUPHONIA EURYPYGA FULMARUS GARRULUS GEOSPIZA GERYGONE GLAREOLA GRALLINA GYPAETUS IONORNIS LUSCINIA MACHETES MYCTERIA NEOPHRON NOTORNIS NUMENIUS OREORTYX PENELOPE PHAETHON PITANGUS PLATALEA PLEGADIS PODARGUS PRIONOPS PRUNELLA PUFFINUS RUPICOLA SALTATOR SAXICOLA SCOLOPAX SPEOTYTO SPIZELLA STRUTHIO TRAGOPAN TYRANNUS (— OF BIVALVES) MYA PINNA ANOMIA MACTRA NUCULA ETHERIA MYTILUS PANDORA COLYMBUS HINNITES PISIDIUM SAXICAVA TRIDACNA XYLOTRYA SPHAERIUM (— OF BOWFIN) AMIA (— OF BRACHIOPOD) ATRYPA CRANIA ATHYRIS DISCINA SPIRIFER (— OF BRYOZOAN) BUGULA ESCHARA FLUSTRA RETEPORA (— OF BUG) ANASA CIMEX EMESA CORIXA TINGIS (— OF BUTTERFLY) CALIGO COLIAS DANAUS MORPHO PIERIS THECLA EURYMUS JUNONIA KALLIMA LYCAENA PAPILIO STRYMON VANESSA ARGYNNIS HESPERIA LEMONIAS MELITAEA SPEYERIA (— OF CABBAGE) COS (— OF CACTUS) CEREUS NOPALEA OPUNTIA HARRISIA (— OF CANTELOUPE) CUCUMIS (— OF CAT) FELIS ACINONYX HEMIGALE (— OF CATTLE) BOS NEAT TAURUS (— OF CEPHALOPOD) SEPIA SPIRULA (— OF CETACEAN) INIA (— OF CHINK) LACUNA (— OF CHIPMUNK) EUTAMIAS (— OF CILIATE) COLPODA CHILODON EUPLOTES (— OF CIVET) FOSSA PAGUMA (— OF CLAM) ENSIS GEMMA SOLEN SPISULA (— OF COCKLE) CHIONE

(— OF COCKROACH) BLATTA
(— OF CODFISH) GADUS
(— OF CORAL) ASTREA FUNGIA
MAENDRA OCULINA PORITES
ACROPORA TUBIPORA
(— OF CRAB) UCA MAIA BIRGUS
CANCER GRAPSUS OCYPODE
PAGURUS LITHODES PORTUNUS
(— OF CRANE) GRUS
(— OF CRAYFISH) CAMBARUS
(— OF CRICKET) ACHETA GRYLLUS
(— OF CRUSTACEAN) APUS HIPPA
JASUS LIGIA MYSIS CYPRIS
LIGYDA SELLUS TRIOPS ARGULUS
ARTEMIA ASTACUS BOPYRUS
CALAPPA CHELURA DAPHNIA
EMERITA HOMARUS IDOTHEA
LERNAEA NEBALIA SQUILLA
CAPRELLA ESTHERIA GAMMARUS
LEUCIFER LIMNETIS LIMNORIA
NEPHROPS PHRONIMA
(— OF CTENOPHORE) BEROE
CESTUM
(— OF CUCUMBER) CUCUMIS
(— OF CURASSOW) CRAX
(— OF DEER) AXIS DAMA PUDU
RUSA CERVUS MAZAMA
MOSCHUS RUCERVUS
(— OF DIATOM) DIATOMA
SYNEDRA MERIDION NAVICULA
(— OF DODO) DIDUS
(— OF DOG) CUON CANIS LYCAON
(— OF DORMOUSE) GLIS
(— OF DRAGONFLY) AESCHNA
(— OF DUCK) AIX ANAS AYTHYA
MERGUS NYROCA NETTION
SPATULA CLANGULA FULIGULA
(— OF EAGLE) AQUILA
(— OF ECHINODERM) ASTERIAS
(— OF EDENTATE) MANIS
(— OF EEL) CONGER ECHIDNA
MURAENA ANGUILLA GYMNOTUS
MORINGUA
(— OF FERN) FILIX TODEA ANEMIA
AZOLLA DOODIA CYATHEA
ISOETES ONOCLEA OSMUNDA
PELLAEA WOODSIA ADIANTUM
ASPIDIUM ATHYRIUM BLECHNUM
CETERACH CIBOTIUM CLEMATIS
DAVALLIA LYGODIUM MARATTIA
SALVINIA SCHIZAEA VITTARIA
(— OF FIREFLY) LAMPYRIS
(— OF FISH) AMIA ESOX HURO
LOTA MOLA RAJA ZEUS ALOSA
BADIS BERYX BETTA DORAS
ELOPS GADUS GOBIO HUCHO
LATES MANTA MUGIL PERCA
SALMO SARDA SOLEA UMBRA
ALBULA ANABAS APOGON BAIGRE
BARBUS BELONE CARANX CLUPEA
COTTUS DIODON GERRES GOBIUS
HIODON KUHLIA LABRUS LATRIS
MOBULA MYXINE NOMEUS
PAGRUS PSETTA REMORA
SCARUS SPARUS TRIGLA TRUTTA
TURSIO WEEVER ABRAMIS
ALOPHAS ALOPIAS ARACANA
ASPREDO BROTULA CARAPUS
CLARIAS DREPANE ECHIDNA
GARRUPA GIRELLA GYMNORA
LEPOMIS LIMANDA LUCANIA
LYCODES OSMERUS PEGASUS
PRISTIS SCIAENA SCOMBER

SEPIOLA SERIOLA SIGANUS
SILLAGO SILURUS SPHYRNA
SQUALUS SYNODUS THUNNUS
TORPEDO TOXOTES TRIODON
XIPHIAS ZOARCES AMEIURUS
ANABLEPS ANGUILLA ARAPAIMA
ASTYANAX ATHERINA BALISTES
BODIANUS CARANGUS CHIMAERA
CLADODUS CTENODUS CYPRINUS
DAPEDIUS DIPLODUS DIPTERUS
DOROSOMA ECHENEIS ETRUMEUS
FUNDULUS GADOPSIS GALAXIAS
GAMBUSIA GOBIESOX HAEMULON
ICOSTEUS KYPHOSUS LEBISTES
LUTIANUS MEGALOPS MORMYRUS
MUSTELUS NOTROPIS OPHIDION
PALOMETA PANTODON
PHOCAENA POLYODON PYGIDIUM
SERRANUS SQUATINA
COREGONUS MYCTOPHUM
(— OF FLAGELLATE) COCOS
GONIUM OPHION SYNURA
VOLVOX ATTALEA CARYOTA
EUGLENA GIARDIA BORASSUS
CERATIUM EUDORINA HEXAMITA
HYDRURUS
(— OF FLEA) PULEX BOSMINA
(— OF FLY) DACUS MUSCA MYMAR
PERLA PHORA ASILUS CEPHUS
FANNIA PIMPLA RHYSSA SCIARA
TIPULA CALIROA CHALCIS DIOPSIS
EPHYDRA HYLEMYA MIASTOR
ORTALIS OSCINIS PANORPA
TACHINA THEREVA ACROCERA
AGROMYZA ANOMALON APHIDIUS
BORBORUS CHELONUS CHRYSOPA
CHRYSOPS GLOSSINA PSYCHODA
SCHEDIUS SIMULIUM STOMOXYS
(— OF FLYING SQUIRREL) BELOMYS
(— OF FOSSIL) AMPYX ERYON
ADAPIS ATRYPA BAIERA ERYOPS
GEIKIA HYENIA KLUKIA MAMMUT
OLENUS ORTHIS RHYNIA ANDRIAS
ANTEDON APTIANA ASAPHUS
DICERAS EXOGYRA GANODUS
HAMITES HYBODUS KNORRIA
LESKEYA LESLEYA LOXOMMA
MESONYX MOROPUS MYLODON
OTOZOUM PHACOPS PHIOMIA
PROAVIS PROETUS WALCHIA
AGLASPIS AGNOSTUS AMYNODON
APHELOPS ARCHELON BIRKENIA
BRONTOPS CALIPPUS CALYMENE
CAYTONIA CERATOPS CLYMENIA
CTENODUS DAPEDIUS DEINODON
DIATRYMA DINOHYUS DIPLODUS
DIPTERUS ENCHODUS ENCRINUS
EODISCUS EOHIPPUS EOSAURUS
EUSMILUS GORDONIA GRYPHAEA
HALLOPUS HELIGMUS ILLAENUS
LANARKIA LEBACHIA LECROSIA
LEGUATIA LESTODON LITUITES
MACLUREA MARRELLA METOPIAS
OLDHAMIA PLACODUS PORTHEUS
RUTIODON SMILODON SPIRIFER
STEGODON STEGOMUS
TAONURUS THELODUS XIPHODON
ZAMICRUS CONULARIA
(— OF FOX) ALOPEX VULPES
UROCYON
(— OF FROG) RANA ANURA
HYLODES
(— OF FUNGUS) FOMES IRPEX

PHOMA TUBER VALSA VERPA
ALBUGO BREMIA CAEOMA
EMPUSA FUMAGO HYDNUM
ISARIA OIDIUM PEZIZA TORULA
ZYTHIA ACRASIA AMANITA
BOLETUS CANDIDA CHALARA
CYATHUS ELSINOE ERYSIBE
FABRAEA GEASTER LEPIOTA
MONILIA NECTRIA OZONIUM
PACHYMA PYTHIUM RHIZINA
RUSSULA SIMBLUM STEREUM
STICTIS STILBUM TYPHULA
XYLARIA ACHORION AECIDIUM
AGARICUS BOTRYTIS CALVATIA
CLATHRUS CLAVARIA COLLYBIA
COPRINUS CORYNEUM CYPHELLA
CYTTARIA DAEDALEA DIPLODIA
ENDOTHIA ENTOLOMA ENTYLOMA
ERYSIPHE EXOASCUS FUSARIUM
GEASTRUM GNOMONIA
GRAPHIUM HELOTIUM HELVELLA
LENZITES MERULIUS MYCOGONE
PAXILLUS PHOLIOTA PUCCINIA
RHIZOPUS RHYTISMA SEPTORIA
SORDARIA SPICARIA TAPHRINA
TERFEZIA TRAMETES TREMELLA
TROCHILA USTILAGO USTULINA
VENTURIA CORDICEPS
(— OF GALLFLY) CYNIPS
(— OF GASTROPOD) FICUS HARPA
LIMAX OLIVA EBURNA PATELLA
TENEBRA SCYLLAEA STROMBUS
(— OF GEESE) CHEN ANSER
NETTAPUS
(— OF GNAT) SCIARA
(— OF GOAT) IBEX CAPRA
OREAMNOS
(— OF GRASS) POA ZEA AIRA COIX
AVENA BRIZA ORYZA STIPA
APLUDA ARUNDO BROMUS
ELYMUS HOLCUS LOLIUM
LYGEUM MELICA MILIUM NARDUS
PHLEUM SECALE UNIOLA ZOYSIA
BAMBUSA BUCHLOE CHLORIS
CYNODON FESTUCA HILARIA
HORDEUM LAGURUS LEERSIA
MELINIS MOLINIA PANICUM
SETARIA SORGHUM ZIZANIA
AEGILOPS AGROSTIS ARISTIDA
AXONOPUS BULBILIS CENCHRUS
DACTYLIS ELEUSINE GLYCERIA
GYNERIUM IMPERATA PASPALUM
PHALARIS SPARTINA SPINIFEX
TRISETUM TRITICUM
(— OF GRASSHOPPER) LOCUSTA
(— OF GUAN) CRAX
(— OF GULL) XEMA LARUS
(— OF HAWK) BUTEO CIRCUS
(— OF HERB) GYP IVA AMMI ARUM
BETA GEUM GLAX HEBE LENS
MEUM MUSA OLAX RUTA SIDA
SIUM ADOXA AJUGA APIOS
APIUM CALLA CANNA CAREX
CARUM CICER DALEA DRABA
ERUCA ERVUM FEDIA GALAX
GAURA GILIA GLAUX HOSTA
INULA LAPPA LAVIA LAYIA LEMNA
LINUM LOASA LOTUS LUFFA
MADIA MALVA NAPEA PANAX
PARIS PHACA PHLOX PILEA
RHEUM RHOEO RUBIA SEDUM
TACCA URENA VICIA VIGNA
VINCA VIOLA ZIZIA ACAENA

ACNIDA ACORUS ACTAEA ADONIS
ALISMA ALLIUM ALSINE AMOMUM
ANOGRA ARABIS ARALIA ARNICA
ASARUM ATROPA BACOPA
BAERIA BASSIA BELLIS BIDENS
BLITUM BLUMEA BORAGO CAKILE
CALTHA CASSIA CELSIA CICUTA
CISTUS CLEOME CNICUS COLEUS
CONIUM COPTIS COSMOS
CRAMBE CREPIS CRINUM CROCUS
CROTON CUNILA CYNARA DAHLIA
DATURA DAUCUS DIODIA DONDIA
ECHIUM ELODEA ELODES EMILIA
EUCLEA FILAGO GALEGA GALIUM
GIFOLA GYNURA ISATIS ISMENE
KOCHIA KRIGIA KUHNIA LAMIUM
LECHEA LUZULA MALOPE
MENTHA MIMOSA MONTIA
MUCUNA MUILLA NERINE
NERIUM NESLIA ONONIS OTHAKE
OXALIS PICRIS PISTIA PYROLA
RESEDA RESTIO RHEXIA RIVINA
RUPPIA SAGINA SALVIA SCILLA
SESBAN SESELI STEVIA SUAEDA
THALIA TULIPA VIORNA ZINNIA
ABRONIA ADLUMIA AETHUSA
ALEGRIA ALETRIS ALKANNA
ALPINIA ALTHAEA ALYSSUM
AMORPHA AMSONIA ANCHUSA
ANEMONE ANETHUM ANYCHIA
APHANES ARACHIS ARCTIUM
ARNEBIA ARUNCUS BABIANA
BARTSIA BEGONIA BOEBERA
BUTOMUS CACALIA CAJANUS
CALYPSO CARLINA CELOSIA
CHELONE CIRCAEA CIRSIUM
CLARKIA COMARUM CROOMIA
CURCUMA CUSCUTA CYTINUS
DATISCA DECODON DERINGA
DIASCIA DROSERA ELATINE
EOMECON EPISCIA ERODIUM
FELICIA FICARIA FRASERA
FREESIA FUMARIA GAZANIA
GERBERA GLECOMA GLYCINE
GUNNERA HALENIA HECHTIA
HEDEOMA HOMERIA HUGELIA
HYPOXIS IRESINE JASIONE
KICKXIA KNAUTIA KOELLIA
LACTUCA LAPPULA LAPSANA
LEWISIA LIATRIS LINARIA
LINNAEA LOGANIA LOPEZIA
LUNARIA LUPINUS LYCHNIS
LYTHRUM MARANTA MEDEOLA
MIMULUS MITELLA MOLLUGO
MONESES MUSCARI NEMESIA
NIGELLA OTHONNA PAEONIA
PAPAVER PAVONIA PEGANUM
PETUNIA PLUCHEA PRIMULA
RORIPPA ROTALIA RUELLIA
SALSOLA SAMOLUS SCANDIX
SENECIO SESAMUM SHORTIA
SILYBUM SINAPIS SOLANUM
SONCHUS STACHYS STATICE
SUCCISA SWERTIA TAGETES
TALINUM TELLIMA THAPSIA
THESIUM THLASPI THURNIA
TORENIA TORILIS TOVARIA
TRILISA URGINEA VALLOTA
VERBENA ZEBRINA ACALYPHA
ACANTHUS ACHILLEA ACONITUM
AGALINIS AGERATUM ALLIARIA
ALLIONIA ALOCASIA AMBROSIA
AMMOBIUM ANDRYALA ANGELICA

ANTHEMIS ANTICLEA APOCYNUM
ARCTOTIS ARENARIA ARGEMONE
ARISAEMA ASPERULA ATRIPLEX
BAPTISIA BARBAREA BARTONIA
BERGENIA BERTEROA BETONICA
BISTORTA BOLTONIA BORRERIA
BRASSICA BRUNONIA BUCHNERA
CALATHEA CAMASSIA CAMELINA
CANNABIS CAPSICUM CERINTHE
CLEMATIS COCHARUS COLLOMIA
COLUMNEA COMANDRA
COOPERIA CRASSULA CUBELIUM
DENTARIA DIANTHUS DICENTRA
DIPSACUS DISPORUM DYSSODIA
ECHINOPS EPIFAGUS ERANTHIS
EREMURUS ERIGENIA ERIGERON
ERYNGIUM ERYSIMUM EUCHARIS
EUTHAMIA FITTONIA FLAVERIA
FLOERKEA FRAGARIA GALACTIA
GENTIANA GERARDIA GESNERIA
GILLENIA GLAUCIUM GLECHOMA
GLORIOSA GLOXINIA GOODENIA
GRATIOLA GUZMANIA HELENIUM
HELONIAS HEPATICA HESPERIS
HEUCHERA HIBISCUS HIPPURIS
HOSACKIA HOTTONIA HUDSONIA
HYDROLES HYSSOPUS IONIDIUM
ISNARDIA JATROPHA JUSSIAEA
JUSTICIA KNEIFFIA KOHLERIA
LAPORTEA LAVATERA LEONOTIS
LEONURUS LEPIDIUM LEPTILON
LIMONIUM LOPHIOLA LYCOPSIS
MACLEAYA MANFREDA MANTISIA
MEDICAGO MEIBOMIA MYOSOTIS
MYOSURUS OBOLARIA OENANTHE
OPOPANAX ORONTIUM PAROSELA
PHACELIA PHORMIUM PHYMOSIA
PHYSALIS PHYSARIA PLANTAGO
PLUMBAGO POLYGALA POLYMNIA
POTERIUM PRUNELLA PSORALEA
RAPHANUS RHAGODIA SABBATIA
SAMBUCUS SANICULA SARCODES
SAROTHRA SATUREIA SCABIOSA
SCOLYMUS SESBANIA SESUVIUM
SEYMERIA SIDALCEA SILPHIUM
SOLIDAGO SPERGULA SPIGELIA
SPINACIA STOKESIA TAENIDIA
THASPIUM TIARELLA TRIBULUS
TRILLIUM TROLLIUS TUECRIUM
UVULARIA VACCARIA VALERIAN
VANELLUS VERATRUM VERNONIA
VERONICA VISCARIA WATSONIA
XANTHIUM RUDBECKIA
(— OF HERON) ARDEA EGRETTA
(— OF HORSE) EQUUS CALIPPUS
EOHIPPUS
(— OF HYDROZOAN) DIPHYES
PHYSALIA
(— OF HYENA) HYAENA CROCUTA
(— OF INSECT) NEPA APHIS EMESA
JAPYX SIREX BOREUS CICADA
COCCUS CORIXA EMPUSA ICERYA
KERMES MANTIS PHASMA
PODURA SIALIS THRIPS CHALCIS
FORMICA FULGORA LEPISMA
ORYSSUS RANATRA STYLOPS
VEDALIA BACILLUS CAMPODEA
EPHEMERA LABIDURA LACCIFER
LECANIUM LYONETIA MACHILIS
MANTISPA NERTHRUS REDUVIUS
(— OF ISOPOD) IDOTEA IDOTHEA
CIROLANA
(— OF JAY) GARRULUS

(— OF JELLYFISH) CYANEA
AURELIA AEQUOREA
(— OF JERBOA) DIPUS
(— OF KELP) AGARUM
(— OF LANGUR) SIMIAS
(— OF LEAFHOPPER) AGALLIA
EMPOASCA
(— OF LEECH) HIRUDO HAEMOPIS
(— OF LEMUR) INDRI GALAGO
(— OF LIANA) BAUHINIA
(— OF LICE) APHIS PSYLLA
ARGULUS ONISCUS BOVICOLA
ERIOSOMA GONIODES LIPEURUS
(— OF LICHEN) CORA USNEA
STICTA EVERNIA GRAPHIS
LECIDEA LOBARIA PHYSCIA
CETRARIA CLADONIA LECANORA
PARMELIA ROCCELLA STRIGULA
(— OF LIMPET) ACMAEA
(— OF LIZARD) UTA AGAMA
DRACO GEKKO AMEIVA ANGUIS
ANOLIS IGUANA EUMECES
LACERTA PYGOPUS SCINCUS
ACONTIAS CHIROTES COLEONYX
LYGOSOMA RHINEURA
(— OF LOCUST) TETRIX TETTIX
(— OF MACAW) ARA
(— OF MAMMAL) BOS SUS HOMO
LAMA ALCES BISON CAPRA
TAYRA DUGONG FRISON
AELURUS AILURUS BUBALUS
GALIDIA GYMNURA LINSANG
OTOCYON AUCHENIA CYCLOPES
CYNOGALE SURICATA TRAGULUS
(— OF MAPLE) ACER
(— OF MARSUPIAL) DASYURUS
MACROPUS POTOROUS TARSIPES
(— OF MARTEN) MARTES MUSTELA
(— OF MEDUSA) SARSIA GERYONIA
(— OF MICROSPORIDIAN) GLUGEA
(— OF MILDEW) ERYSIPHE
UNCINULA
(— OF MILLIPEDE) JULUS
(— OF MINT) ICIMUM NEPETA
MELISSA PERILLA PHLOMIS
ORIGANUM
(— OF MITE) ACARUS ACERIA
LEPTUS DEMODEX ACARAPIS
(— OF MOLD) MUCOR FULIGO
MELIOLA
(— OF MOLE) TALPA SCALOPS
SCALOPUS
(— OF MOLLUSK) ARCA DOTO LEDA
LIMA CHAMA DONAX EOLIS FICUS
HARPA LIMAX MUREX OLIVA
VENUS AEOLIS ANOMIA BANKIA
CASSIS CHITON LEPTON LUCINA
OSTREA PECTEN PHOLAS PYRULA
SEMELE TEREDO TETHYS
ACTAEON ASTARTE ATLANTA
CARDITA CARDIUM CYPRAEA
CYPRINA DOSINIA ETHERIA
EXOGYRA LINGULA TELLINA
BUCCINUM GRYPHAEA HALIOTIS
LIMACINA LUTRARIA MODIOLUS
NAUTILUS PINCTADA SCYLLAEA
STROMBUS
(— OF MONGOOSE) GALIDIA
(— OF MONKEY) AOTES AOTUS
CEBUS ATELES MACACA CACAJAO
COLOBUS NASALIS SAIMIRI
PITHECIA
(— OF MOOSE) ALCES

(— OF MOSQUITO) AEDES CULEX
(— OF MOSS) BRYUM CHILO
EUXOA MNIUM SAMIA SESIA
TINEA ACTIAS ALYPIA ARCTIA
BOMBYX COSSUS DATANA
HYPNUM LESKEA PLUSIA PSYCHE
SPHINX THYRIS URANIA AGROTIS
ALABAMA APATELA ARCHIPS
ATTACUS BARBULA CRAMBUS
FUNARIA GRIMMIA PHASCUM
PRONUBA PYRALIS SESAMIA
TORTRIX ZEUZERA ZYGAENA
ANDREAEA CATOCALA
DAWSONIA DIATRAEA DICRANUM
ENDROMIS EPHESTIA EUPREPIA
GALLERIA GELECHIA HEPIALUS
PLUTELLA PRODENIA PYRAUSTA
SATURNIA SPHAGNUM THUIDIUM
(— OF MOTH) CHILO ABRAXAS
(— OF MOUSE) MUS APODEMUS
(— OF MUSKMELON) CUCUMIS
(— OF MUSKRAT) FIBER ONDATRA
(— OF NARWHAL) MONODON
(— OF NEMATODE) ACUARIA
ALAIMUS ANGUINA NECATOR
(— OF NUDIBRANCH) GLAUCUS
(— OF OATS) AVENA
(— OF OPOSSUM) MARMOSA
(— OF ORCHID) DISA VANDA
BLETIA LAELIA PHAJUS ACINETA
AERIDES ANGULOA BRASSIA
CORDULA EUCOSIA IBIDIUM
ISOTRIA LIPARIS LISTERA
MALAXIS POGONIA VANILLA
ANGRECUM ARETHUSA BLETILLA
CALANTHE CATTLEYA CYTHEREA
FISSIPES GOODYERA MILTONIA
ONCIDIUM PERAMIUM SERAPIAS
SOBRALIA TRIPHORA
(— OF OTTER) LUTRA
(— OF OWL) BUBO NINOX STRIX
KETUPA NYCTEA AEGOLIUS
SPEOTYTO
(— OF OXEN) BIBOS
(— OF OYSTER) OSTREA AVICULA
(— OF PALM) NIPA ARECA ASSAI
COCOS HOWEA SABAL ARENGA
ELAEIS INODES KENTIA RAPHIA
RHAPIS ATTALEA BACTRIS
CALAMUS CARYOTA CORYPHA
ERYTHEA EUTERPE GEONOMA
LATANIA LICUALA PHOENIX
SERENOA THRINAX BORASSUS
HYPHAENE IRIARTEA LODOICEA
MAURITIA
(— OF PARASITE) STRIGA CUSCOTA
CUSCUTA HYDNORA OLPIDIUM
CASSYTHIA
(— OF PARRAKEET) ARATINGA
(— OF PARROT) NESTER AMAZONA
KAKATOE
(— OF PEACOCK) PAVO
(— OF PENGUIN) EUDYPTES
(— OF PHALANGER) DROMICIA
(— OF PIGEON) GOURA DUCULA
COLUMBA
(— OF PLANT) ALOE ARUM COLA
DION FABA IRIS IXIA PUYA SOJA
ADOXA AGAVE ASTER BATIS
CANNA CHARA DIOON DRYAS
INULA NAIAS PIPER RUMEX
TRAPA TYPHA XYRIS YUCCA ZILLA
ABROMA ACACIA AIZOON ALBUCA

ANANAS CACTUS CUPHEA
DATURA EXACUM FERULA IBERIS
JAMBOS JUNCUS LICHEN LILIUM
MAYACA MORAEA NUPHAR
PHRYMA RICCIA SILENE SMILAX
STRIGA URTICA VISCUM ALONSOA
ASTILBE BALLOTA CAMBOMA
CUCUMIS CYPERUS DIONAEA
DROSERA ENCELIA EPACRIS
EPIGAEA EURYALE FAGELIA
GLYCINE GODETIA HELXINE
HOOKERA ISOETES ISOLOMA
KARATAS LYCOPUS MANIHOT
MONARDA NELUMBO NITELLA
RAOULIA RICINUS STEMONA
SYRINGA TRIURUS TURNERA
WOLFFIA WYETHIA ZOSTERA
ABUTILON ACANTHUS ADIANTUM
ANABASIS ANTHYLIS BRASENIA
BRODIAEA BROMELIA CALADIUM
CAPSICUM CYCLAMEN FORCRAEA
FURCRAEA GALTONIA GASTERIA
GERANIUM LATHRAEA LATHYRUS
MARSILEA MONSTERA NYMPHAEA
PANDANUS PEDALIUM PELVETIA
PERESKIA SAURURUS SPARAXIS
THEVETIA TIGRIDIA TRITONIA
VELLOZIA VICTORIA ZINGIBER
(— OF POLYZOAN) LEPRALIA
LOXOSOMA
(— OF POPLAR) ALAMO
(— OF PORCUPINE) COENDOU
HYSTRIX
(— OF PORPOISE) INIA PHOCAENA
(— OF PRAWN) PALAEMON
(— OF PROTOZOAN) BODO HYDRA
MONAS ADELEA AMOEBA
ACINETA ARCELLA EIMERIA
STENTOR DIDINIUM EUGLYPHA
ISOSPORA UROGLENA
(— OF RABBIT) LEPUS
(— OF RACCOON) OLINGO
(— OF RAT) ANISOMYS
(— OF RHIZOPOD) AMOEBA
GROMIA LAGENA HATTERIA
PELOMYXA
(— OF RODENT) MUS CAVIA DIPUS
LEPUS ZAPUS GEOMYS LEMMUS
SPALAX CYNOMYS DINOMYS
ECHIMYS LEGGADA MERINES
NESOKIA ZYZOMYS ALACTAGA
ARVICOLA CAPROMYS CITELLUS
CRICETUS HAPLODON HYDROMYS
LAGIDIUM MICROTUS MYOTALPA
ORYZOMYS
(— OF ROTIFER) HYDATINA
PEDALION
(— OF RUST) UREDO HEMILEIA
UROMYCES
(— OF SALAMANDER) ANDRIAS
EURYCEA SIREDON TRITURUS
(— OF SCALE) KERMES LECANIUM
(— OF SCALLOP) HINNITES
(— OF SCORPION) BUTHUS
SCORPIO CHELIFER
(— OF SEA ANEMONE) MINYAS
ACTINIA
(— OF SEA FAN) GORGONIA
(— OF SEA OTTER) ENHYDRA
(— OF SEA SLUG) ELYSIA
(— OF SEA URCHIN) ARBACIA
CIDARIS DIADEMA ECHINUS
(— OF SEAL) PHOCA HYDRURGA

MIROUNGA ZALOPHUS
(— OF SEAWEED) ULVA ALARIA
(— OF SEDGE) FUIRENA SCIRPUS
SCLERIA SCHOENUS
(— OF SHARK) LAMNA GALEUS
ISURUS ACRODUS ALOPIAS
SPHYRNA SQUALUS CLADODUS
MENASPIS SQUATINA
(— OF SHEEP) OVIS
(— OF SHELL) PUPA LAMBIS
EXOGYRA LATIRUS MALLEUS
TROCHUS HAMINOEA MACLUREA
OLIVELLA TRIGONIA UMBRELLA
(— OF SHREW) SOREX BLARINA
(— OF SHRIMP) CRAGO CRANGON
(— OF SHRUB) IVA ACER BIXA
BRYA HOYA ILEX INGA ITEA MABA
OLEA RHUS ROSA SIDA THEA
ULEX ALNUS ANONA BIOTA
BUTEA BUXUS CATHA DALEA
DIRCA ERICA EURYA FICUS
HAKEA IXORA LEDUM MALUS
OCHNA PADUS RIBES RUBUS
SABIA SALIX TAXUS THUJA
TREMA UNONA URENA VITEX
ABELIA ACAENA ADELIA ALHAGI
AMYRIS ANNONA ARALIA ARONIA
AUCUBA AZALEA BAPHIA BAUERA
BETULA BLUMEA BYBLIS CANTUA
CASSIA CELTIS CERCIS CISTUS
CITRUS CLEOME CLUSIA COFFEA
CORDIA COREMA CORNUS
CORREA CROTON DAPHNE
DATURA DERRIS DIOSMA DONDIA
DRIMYS ECHIUM EVODIA FATSIA
FEIJOA GARRYA GNETUM GREWIA
GUAREA KALMIA KERRIA LARREA
LIPPIA LITSEA LUCUMA LYCIUM
MIMOSA MYRCIA MYRICA
MYRTUS OCOTEA OLINIA OPILIA
PENAEA PERSEA PIERIS PROTEA
PTELEA PUNICA QUIINA RAMONA
RANDIA ROCHEA ROYENA
RUSCUS SALVIA SAPIUM SCHIMA
SELAGO SESBAN SORBUS STEVIA
STYRAX SUAEDA TECOMA
AECULUS AMORPHA ARBUTUS
ARDISIA ARMERIA ASIMINA
ASSONIA BANKSIA BAROSMA
BENZOIN BORONIA BUMELIA
BURSERA CALLUNA CARISSA
CASASIA CERASUS CESTRUM
CLETHRA CNEORUM COLUTEA
CORYLUS COTINUS CUNONIA
CYRILLA CYTISUS DEUTZIA
DOMBEYA DURANTA EHRETIA
ENCELIA EPACRIS EPHEDRA
EUCHLEA EUGENIA EURSERA
FABIANA FUCHSIA GENISTA
GMELINA GYMINDA HAMELIA
HOVENIA KARATAS LAGETTA
LANTANA MAHONIA MERATIA
MONIMIA MORINDA MUTISIA
MYRRHIS NANDINA NEMESIA
OLEARIA OTHONNA PAVETTA
PAVONIA PENTZIA PIMELEA
PISONIA PURSHIA QUASSIA
QUERCUS RAPANEA REMIJIA
RHAMNUS RHODORA ROBINIA
ROMNEYA RUELLIA SALSOLA
SENECIO SKIMMIA SOLANUM
SOPHORA SPIRAEA SURIANA
SYRINGA TAMARIX TELOPEA

XIMENIA XYLOPIA XYLOSMA
ZELKOVA ACALYPHA ALANGIUM
ALSTONIA ANAGYRIS ATRIPLEX
BALOGHIA BAUHINIA BERBERIS
BORRERIA BUCKLEYA BUDDLEIA
CAMELLIA CAPPARIS CAPSICUM
CARAGANA CASSIOPE CASTANEA
CODIAEUM COLLETIA CONDALIA
CONNARUS COPROSMA CORIARIA
CRATAEVA DAVIESIA DENDRIUM
DILLENIA DODONAEA DOVYALIS
DRACAENA DUBOISIA EMPETRUM
EUONYMUS EUPTELEA EXOSTEMA
FRAXINUS GALACTIA GOODENIA
GORDONIA GUAIACUM HIBISCUS
HIRTELLA IONIDIUM JASMINUM
JATROPHA JUSTICIA KNIGHTIA
KRAMERIA LABURNUM LAVATERA
LAWSONIA LEONOTIS MAGNOLIA
MAYTENUS MICHELIA MYOPORUM
NOTELAEA PALIURUS PAROSELA
PHILESIA PHOTINIA PHYMOSIA
PLUMIERA POLYGALA POTERIUM
PROSOPIS PSORALEA RHAGODIA
ROLLINIA RORIDULA RUSSELIA
SAMBUCUS SATUREIA SAURAUIA
SESBANIA SOLANDRA SORBARIA
SPARTIUM TABEBUIA TORRUBIA
TRECULIA VARRONIA VERNONIA
VERONICA VIBURNUM VOCHYSIA
WITHANIA ZIZYPHUS MENZIESIA
(— OF SILKWORM) BOMBYX
(— OF SKUNK) MEPHITIS
(— OF SLOTH) BRADYPUS
(— OF SLUG) DOTO ARION DORIS
LIMAX ELYSIA GLAUCUS
(— OF SNAIL) HUA PILA CONUS
FUSUS GALBA HELIX MITRA
OVULA PHYSA THAIS TURBO
CERION EULIMA NATICA NERITA
RISSOA TRITON ANCYLUS
BITTIUM BULINUS BUSYCON
CYMBIUM LATIRUS LITIOPA
LYMNARA MELANIA MODULUS
PURPURA RANELLA VALVATA
VERTIGO VITRINA ZONITES
ACHATINA ALOCINMA ELLOBIUM
FOSSARIA GYRAULUS HELICINA
HELISOMA JANTHINA KATAYAMA
LITORINA NERITINA OLEACINA
SUCCINEA
(— OF SNAKE) BOA ERYX NAIA
NAJA ASPIS BITIS BOIGA ECHIS
ELAPS CAUSUS DABOIA ELAPHE
HURRIA ILYSIA LIGUUS NATRIX
PYTHON VIPERA ATHERIS
BOAEDON COLUBER ECHIDNA
MEHELYA OPHIDIA ZAMENIS
BOTHROPS BUNGARUS CERBERUS
CROTALUS DEMANSIA EUNECTES
FARANCIA LACHESIS MICRURUS
STORERIA TYPHLOPS
(— OF SPIDER) ARANEA LYCOSA
MYGALE AGALENA ARGIOPE
ATTIDAE NEPHILA PHOLCUS
LINYPHIA ULOBORUS
(— OF SPIROCHETE) BORRELIA
(— OF SPONGE) SYCON GEODIA
SCYPHA ASCETTA CHALINA
GRANTIA SPONGIA SYCETTA
LEUCETTA
(— OF SPOROZOAN) NOSEMA
(— OF SQUID) LOLIGO SEPIOLA

(— OF SQUIRREL) SCIURUS
(— OF SUBSHRUB) LECHEA
ARMERIA ASCYRUM BEGONIA
FELICIA ATRIPLEX COLUMNEA
(— OF SWAN) OLOR CYGNUS
(— OF TAKIN) BUDORCAS
(— OF TAPEWORM) BERTIA LIGULA
DAVAINEA HARRISIA
(— OF TAYRA) GALERA GALICTIS
(— OF TELEDU) MYDAUS
(— OF TERN) GYGIS STERNA
(— OF THISTLE) CNICUS CARDUUS
(— OF TICK) ARGAS ARGUS IXODES
HYALOMMA
(— OF TOAD) BUFO HYLA PIPA
ALYTES XENOPUS ASCAPHUS
(— OF TREE) ACER BIXA BRYA
COLA HURA ILEX INGA MABA
OLAX OLEA RHUS THEA ABIES
AEGLE ALNUS ANIBA BIOTA
BUTEA BUXUS CARYA CEIBA
CYCAS DURIO EURYA FAGUS
FICUS HAKEA HEVEA HOPEA
IXORA KHAYA LARIX MALUS
MELIA MESUA MORUS NYSSA
OCHNA PADUS PICEA PINUS
PYRUS SALIX TAXUS THUJA TILIA
TOONA TREMA TSUGA ULMUS
UNONA VITEX XYLIA ABROMA
ACHRAS AKANIA AMOMIS AMYRIS
ANDIRA ANNONA ARALIA
AUCUBA AZALEA BAPHIA BETULA
BOMBAX CANTUA CARAPA
CARICA CASSIA CEDRUS CELTIS
CERCIS CITRUS CLUSIA COFFEA
CORDIA CORNUS DATURA
DRIMYS EPERUA EPERVA EUCLEA
EVODIA FEIJOA GARRYA GENIPA
GINKGO GNETUM GREWIA
GUAREA IDESIA ILLIPE LAURUS
LITCHI LITSEA LUCUMA LYCIUM
MAMMEA MIMOSA MYRCIA
MYRICA OCOTEA OLNEYA OSTRYA
OWENIA PAPPEA PARITI PERSEA
PRUNUS PTELEA QUIINA RANDIA
ROYENA SAPIUM SAPOTA SCHIMA
SENCIO SESBAN SHOREA SIMABA
SORBUS STYRAX TECOMA
AGATHIS ARBUTUS ARDISIA
ASIMINA ASSONIA BANKSIA
BUMELIA BURSERA CANANGA
CANELLA CASASIA CATALPA
CEDRELA CERASUS CLETHRA
COPAIVA CORYLUS COTINUS
CUNONIA CUPANIA CYDONIA
CYRILLA DOMBEYA ECHINUS
EHRETIA EPACRIS EUGENIA
FERONIA GMELINA GUAZUMA
GYMINDA HAGENIA HALESIA
HICORIA HOVENIA HUMIRIA
JUGLANS KADELIA KOKOONA
LAGETTA LICANIA LINGOUM
MACLURA MICONIA MORINDA
MORINGA MURRAYA OCHROMA
OLEARIA PANGIUM PIMENTA
PISONIA PLANERA POPULUS
PROTIUM PSIDIUM QUASSIA
QUERCUS RAPANEA REMIJIA
RHAMNUS ROBINIA SCHINUS
SENECIO SEQUOIA SLOANEA
SOLANUM SOPHORA SURIANA
SYRINGA TAMARIX TECTONA
TELOPEA TORREYA TROPHIS

VATERIA XIMENIA XYLOPIA
XYLOSMA ZELKOVA AESCULUS
ALANGIUM ALBIZZIA ALSTONIA
ANTIARIS AVERRHOA BALANOPS
BALOGHIA BAUHINIA BRABEJUM
BROSIMUM BUDDLEIA CABRALEA
CAMELLIA CANARIUM CAPPARIS
CARAGANA CARPINUS CARYOCAR
CASEARIA CASTANEA CASTILLA
CECROPIA CINCHONA CODIAEUM
CONDALIA CYBISTAX DILLENIA
DIPTERYX DODONAEA DOVYALIS
DRACAENA DUBOISIA EUCOMMIA
EUONYMUS EUPTELEA EXOSTEMA
FITZROYA FRAXINUS FUNTUMIA
GARCINIA GARDENIA GORDONIA
GUAIACUM HIBISCUS HIRTELLA
HOMALIUM HYMENAEA ILLICIUM
JATROPHA KANDELIA KNIGHTIA
LABURNUM LAPORTEA LAVATERA
LECYTHIS LEUCAENA LYSILOMA
MAGNOLIA MALLOTUS MAYTENUS
MESPILUS MICHELIA MIMUSOPS
MYOPORUM NOTELAEA PHOTINIA
PISCIDIA PISTACIA PLATANUS
PLUMIERA PONCIRUS PROSOPIS
QUILLAJA RAVENALA ROLLINIA
SAMADERA SAMBUCUS
SANTALUM SAPINDUS SAURAUIA
SESBANIA SIMARUBA SPONDIAS
SWARTZIA TABEBUIA TAXODIUM
TORRUBIA TRECULIA VARRONIA
VERONICA VIBURNUM VIRGILIA
VOCHYSIA
(— OF TUNICATE) SALPA ASCIDIA
DOLIOLUM
(— OF TURTLE) EMYS AMYDA
CHELUS CHELYS CARETTA
CHELONE CLEMMYS TESTUDO
TRIONYX ARCHELON CHELONIA
CHELYDRA PELUSIOS
(— OF TWINER) STEMONA
(— OF UNIVALVE) DOLIUM
(— OF VINE) ROSA ABRUS ABUTA
PISUM TAMUS UNONA VIGNA
VITIS AKEBIA CISSUS COBAEA
DERRIS ENTADA HEDERA
MUCUNA PETREA POTHOS
SICANA SICYOS SOLLYA VIORNA
ARAUJIA BASELLA BOMAREA
BRYONIA ECHITES EMBELIA
EPACRIS FALCATA HUMULUS
IPOMOEA MIKANIA PISONIA
SECHIUM UNCARIA ZANONIA
ANAMIRTA ATRAGENE BIGNONIA
CLEMATIS COCCULUS DEGUELIA
DOLICHOS EUONYMUS JASMINUM
KENNEDYA PANDOREA PUERARIA
SECAMONE SERJANIA TACSONIA
WISTARIA
(— OF WALRUS) ODOBENUS
(— OF WASP) SPHEX VESPA
BEMBEX CYNIPS SCOLIA TIPHIA
CHRYSIS EUMENES MASARIS
MUTILLA ANDRICUS CHLORION
ODYNERUS POLISTES POMPILUS
SPHECIUS
(— OF WEASEL) MUSTELA
(— OF WEED) CAPSELLA
(— OF WEEVIL) APION HYPERA
SITONA CLEONUS CALANDRA
CALENDRA CURCULIO
(— OF WHALE) CETE ARETA KOGIA

BALAENA ORCINUS ZIPHIUS PHYSETER
(— OF WOLVERINE) GULO
(— OF WORM) DERO SPIO ALARIA
EUNICE KERRIA MERMIS NEREIS
SYLLIS ACHAETA ACHOLOE
ASCARIS DUGESIA EISENIA
FILARIA GLYCERA GORDIUS
HESIONE LEODICE POLYNOE
SABELLA SAGITTA SERPULA
SETARIA SPIRURA TUBIFEX
ARABELLA ASCAROPS BIPALIUM
BONELLIA COOPERIA DOCHMIUS
ECHIURUS FASCIOLA GEOPLANA
PHORONIS SPADELLA SUBULURA
SYNGAMUS SYPHACIA
(— OF ZORIL) ICTONYX
(PREF.) GEN(O)
(SUFF.) IA
GEODE DRUSE
GEOGRAPHER **AMERICAN** BAKER
DAVIS GUYOT ATWOOD BOWMAN
BRYANT SEMPLE DAVIDSON
MITCHELL HUNTINGTON
ARAB BAKRI
AUSTRIAN KORISTKA
PAULITSCHKE
CANADIAN PALLISER
DUTCH BLAEU
EGYPTIAN PTOLEMY
ENGLISH BEKE KEANE BEAZLEY
HAKLUYT MARKHAM RENNELL
GREENOUGH MACKINDER
FRESHFIELD
FRENCH JOMARD RECLUS VALLOT
ANVILLE DELISLE DEMANGEON
GERMAN BEHM KOHL BANSE
PENCK VOGEL ANDREE BEHAIM
CLUVER RATZEL RITTER APIANUS
EBELING GERLAND HETTNER
KIEPERT KRUMMEL PESCHEL
SCHONER BERGHAUS BRUCKNER
BUSCHING DRYGALSKI
PETERMANN RICHTHOFEN
GREEK SCYLAX STRABO MARINUS
PYTHEAS DIONYSIUS PAUSANIAS
ERATOSTHENES
HUNGARIAN TELEKI
ICELANDIC THORODDSEN
ITALIAN BALBI CODAZZI AMORETTI
MARSIGLI
POLISH LELEWEL
PORTUGUESE CORDEIRO
RUSSIAN SEMENOV KROPOTKIN
SHOKALSKI
SCOTTISH MILL BROWN
JOHNSTON
SPANISH COSA
SWEDISH HEDIN
GEOLOGIST **AMERICAN** DALY DANA
HALL KEMP KING REID TARR
CROSS GUYOT HAGUE HOBBS
LEITH MCGEE ORTON SCOTT
SMITH SPURR WHITE ARNOLD
ATWOOD BAYLEY DUTTON
FOSTER HAYDEN HOLMES IRVING
JAGGAR LAWSON LESLEY
MARCOU MATHER POWELL
SHALER UPJOHN WRIGHT
BARRELL BRANNER GILBERT
HOLLICK IDDINGS JOHNSON
MACLURE MERRILL PIRSSON
RANSOME RUSSELL TALMAGE

VANHISE LEVERETT MITCHELL
NEWBERRY PUMPELLY SILLIMAN
WINCHELL HITCHCOCK
JOHANNSEN SALISBURY
TWENHOFEL CHAMBERLIN
LOUDERBACK WASHINGTON
AUSTRALIAN DAVID
AUSTRIAN BECKE HAUER SUESS
HAIDINGER HOCHSTETTER
MOJSISOVICS
BELGIAN RENARD
CANADIAN BELL ADAMS LOGAN
WALLACE
DANISH KOCH
ENGLISH BELT TATE JUKES LYELL
SORBY ANSTED BONNEY CLARKE
FORBES HOLMES MAWSON
SCROPE DAWKINS GREGORY
HOLLAND MANTELL BUCKLAND
LYDEKKER PHILLIPS SEDGWICK
GREENOUGH MURCHISON
PRESTWICH STRICKLAND
FRENCH FOUQUE ARCHIAC
DAUBREE DELESSE BARRANDE
BEAUMONT BERTRAND
DOLOMIEU DUFRENOY
LAPPARENT
GERMAN BUCH ABICH COHEN
DECHEN ROEMER WERNER ZITTEL
ALBERTI BISCHOF CREDNER
GEINITZ LEONHARD QUENSTEDT
KEYSERLING ROSENBUSCH
ICELANDIC THORODDSEN
IRISH OLDHAM
ITALIAN MERCALLI
NEW ZEALAND HAAST
NORWEGIAN BROGGER KJERULF
RUSSIAN OBRUCHEV
SCOTTISH HALL CROLL GEIKIE
HUTTON MILLER RAMSAY
OGLIVIE PLAYFAIR
MACCULLOCH
SWEDISH ANTEVS TORELL
HISINGER NATHORST
NORDENSKJOLD
SWISS HEIM DELUC
GEOMETRIC CUBIST CUBISTIC
GEOMETRY EUCLID SPHERICS
GEOPHAGY PICA

GEORGIA
CAPITAL: ATLANTA
COLLEGE: SPELMAN MOREHOUSE
COUNTY: BIBB CLAY COBB COOK
HALL TIFT WARE BANKS BRYAN
BUTTS DOOLY EARLY FLOYD
GRADY PEACH RABUN TROUP
WORTH COFFEE COWETA
DEKALB ECHOLS ELBERT
FANNIN FULTON JASPER
LANIER OCONEE TWIGGS
WILKES CATOOSA LAURENS
LUMPKIN GWINNETT
MUSCOGEE
INDIAN: GUALE YUCHI CHIAHA
OCONEE YAMASEE
LAKE: LANIER MARTIN HARDING
NOTTELY BANKHEAD
HARTWELL SINCLAIR
MOUNTAIN: STONE KENNESAW
NATIVE: CRACKER
PRESIDENT: CARTER
RIVER: PEA FLINT ETOWAH

OCONEE PIGEON CONECUH
SATILLA ALTAMAHA
OCMULGEE
STATE BIRD: THRASHER
STATE NICKNAME: PEACH
STATE TREE: LIVEOAK
TOWN: JESUP MACON JASPER
OCILLA AUGUSTA CONYERS
DECATUR ELLIJAY GRIFFIN
VIDALIA MARIETTA
MOULTRIE SAVANNAH
VALDOSTA WAYCROSS
UNIVERSITY: EMORY GATECH
MERCER

GEORGIAN ADZHAR CRACKER
GEORGIA PINE LONGLEAF
GEPHYREAN STARWORM
GER STRANGER
GERAINT (WIFE OF —) ENID
GERANIUM DOVEFOOT FLUXWEED
SHAMEFACE
GERANIUM LAKE SPARK
NACARAT
GERANIUM PINK BERMUDA
GERBIL JIRD
GERIANOL ISOLATE
GERM BUG CHIT SEED SPARK
SPAWN SPERM GERMEN
GERMULE MICROBE SEMINAL
RUDIMENT SEEDLING SEMINARY
SEMINIUM
(— CELL) GONE
(PREF.) BLAST(O) SPERM(A)(ATI)
(ATIO)(ATO)(I)(IO)(O)
(SUFF.) BLAST(IC)(Y) SPERM(A)(AE)
(AL)(IA)(IC)(OUS)(UM)(Y)
GERMAN BALT HANS ALMAN
HEINE JERRY ALMAIN DUTCHY
HEINIE TEUTON TEDESCO
COTILLON GERMANIC TUDESQUE
(PREF.) TEUTO
GERMANDER POLY BETONY
FOXTAIL SOVENEZ
SCORDIUM
GERMANE GERMAN RELEVANT
PERTINENT
GERMANIC GOTHIC GOTHONIC
TEUTONIC
GERMAN SHEPHERD ALSATIAN

GERMANY
ANCIENT: ALMAIN ALMAINE
ANCIENT TRIBESMAN: JUTE
TEUTON VISIGOTH OSTROGOTH
CANAL: KIEL WESER LUDWIG
CAPITAL: BONN BERLIN
CHEESE: MUENSTER TILSITER
LIMBURGER
COAL REGION: RUHR SAAR SARRE
COIN: MARK KRONE TALER
GULDEN KRONEN THALER
PFENNIG GROSCHEN
DIALECT: KOLSCH KOELSCH
BALTISCH HESSISCH
DYNASTY: HOHENSTAUFEN
HOHENZOLLERN
FOOD: WURST KNODEL SPATZLE
STRUDEL MARZIPAN ROULADEN
HANSEATIC CITY: KOLN LUBECK
COLOGNE HAMBURG
LUEBECK
ISLAND: USEDOM WOLLIN

FEHMARN FRISIAN
LAKE: DUMMER WURMSEE
AMMERSEE BODENSEE
CHIEMSEE MURITZEE
CONSTANCE
LANGUAGE: DEUTSCH
MEASURE: AAM IMI OHM FASS
FUSS LAST RUTE SACK STAB
CARAT EIMER KANNE KETTE
LINIE MAASS METZE RUTHE
SIMRI MASSEL MORGEN
OXHOFT SEIDEL STRICH
JUCHART KLAFTER TAGWERK
SCHEFFEL SCHOPPEN
STUBCHEN VIERLING
MOUNTAIN: FELDBERG
WATZMANN
MOUNTAIN RANGE: ORE ALPS
HARZ RHON HARDT HUNSRUCK
NAME: REICH ASHKENAZ
GERMANIA DEUTSCHLAND
NATIVE: GOTH SAXON TEUTON
PORT: EMDEN BREMEN HAMBURG
ROSTOCK STETTIN
RESORT: EMS BADEN AACHEN
RIVER: ALZ EMS INN EDER EGER
ELBE ISAR LAHN LECH MAIN
NAAB NAHE ODER OKER REMS
RUHR SAAR SIEG ALLER DONAU
EIDER FULDA HAVEL HUNTE
ILLER LEINE LIPPE MOSEL
MULDE PEENE REGEN RHEIN
RHINE SAALE SAUER SPREE
UCKER VECHT WERRA WESER
DANUBE ELSTER KOCHER
NECKAR NEISSE RANDOW
TAUBER WARNOW ALTMUHL
JEETZEL PEGNITZ SALZACH
UNSTRUT
STATE: BADEN HESSE LIPPE
BAYERN BREMEN HESSEN
SAXONY BAVARIA HAMBURG
PRUSSIA SAARLAND
BRUNSWICK
TOWN: AUE EMS HOF ULM BONN
GERA GOCH HAAR HAMM JENA
KIEL KOLN LAHR AALEN AHLEN
EMDEN ESSEN FURTH GOTHA
HAGEN HALLE HERNE MAINZ
MOLLN NEUSS PIRNA TRIER
AACHEN ALTENA ALTONA
BARMEN BERLIN BREMEN
CASSEL DACHAU DESSAU
ERFURT KASSEL LINDEN
LUBECK MUNICH PLAUEN
TREVES BAMBERG BRESLAU
COBLENZ COLOGNE CREFELD
DRESDEN GORLITZ HAMBURG
HANOVER LEIPZIG MAYENCE
MUNCHEN MUNSTER POTSDAM
ROSTOCK SPANDAU ZWICKAU
AUGSBURG CHEMNITZ
DORTMUND DUISBURG
FREIBURG LIEGNITZ MANNHEIM
NURNBERG WURSELEN
WURZBURG DARMSTADT
KARLSRUHE MAGDEBURG
NUREMBERG OSNABRUCK
STUTTGART WUPPERTAL
DUSSELDORF HEIDELBERG
OBERHAUSEN
UNIVERSITY TOWN: FREIBURG
HEIDELBERG

WEIGHT: LOT GRAN LOTE LOTH UNZE LOTHE PFUND STEIN PRUNDE DRACHMA ZENTNER VIERLING
WINE: MOSELLE RIESLING

GERMICIDE KRELOS MERBROMIN
GERMINABLE PREGNANT
GERMINATE BUD HIT CHIP CHIT GERM SHOOT SPIRE SPRIT BRAIRD SPROUT STRIKE PULLULATE
GERMINATION CATCH
GERSHOM (FATHER OF —) LEVI MOSES
(MOTHER OF —) ZIPPORAH
GERYON (DOG OF —) ORTHUS
(FATHER OF —) CHRYSAOR
(MOTHER OF —) CALLIRRHOE
(SLAYER OF —) HERCULES
GESAN TAPUYAN CHAVANTE
GESHAM (FATHER OF —) JAHDAI
GESTATION GOING BREEDING PREGNANCY
GESTICULATE GESTURE
GESTURE CUT FIG BECK BERE GEST SIGN FILIP GESTE HONOR SANNA ACTION BECKON BREATH CUTOFF FILLIP MOTION SALUTE SIGNAL CURTSEY FASHION FLICKER MURGEON ACCOLADE CEREMONY
(— OF DERISION) SNOOK
(AFFECTED —) GAATCH
(HINDU —) NAMASTE
(OBSCENE —) BIRD
(OSTENTATIOUS —) POMP
(USELESS —) FUTILITY
GET COP GIT WIN EARN FALL GAIN GRAB HAVE HENT TAKE TILL AFONG ANNEX CATCH COVER FETCH LATCH DERIVE OBTAIN PUZZLE SECURE ACQUIRE COMPARE CONQUER PROCURE PRODUCE RECEIVE PERCEIVE
(— ABOARD) FLIP
(— ABOUT) BEGO NAVIGATE
(— ALONG) DO GEE FARE FEND AGREE FADGE FODGE SPEED FETTLE
(— AROUND) BYPASS COMPASS FINESSE FLUMMER OUTFLANK
(— AT) ATTAIN
(— AWAY) LAM RYNT SLIP EVADE CHEESE ESCAPE
(— BACK) REDEEM RETIRE RECOVER
(— BETTER OF) WAX BEST DING DOWN DAUNT FLING SHEND SHENT STICK STING JOCKEY OVERGO RECOVER OVERCOME SURMOUNT
(— BY ARTIFICE) WIND
(— BY ASKING) KICK
(— BY CUNNING) WHIZZLE
(— BY EXTORTION) GRATE
(— BY FLATTERY) COG
(— CLEAR OF) STRIP
(— DISHONESTLY) FIRK
(— DOWN) ALIGHT
(— ON) FARE BOARD CHEFE CHEVE FRAME SHIFT EXPLOIT
(— ON WELL) LIKE

(— OUT) LEAK SCRAM CHEESE OUTWIN VOETSAK
(— PAST) BEAT HURDLE
(— POSSESSION) CARRY
(— READY) GET BOUN PARE RANK BOWNE BRACE FRAME FETTLE ORDAIN APPAREL
(— RID) CAST DISH DUMP FREE JUNK SHAB TOSS ERASE SHAKE SHIFT SHOOT SLOUGH UNLOAD DELIVER DISCARD EXTRUDE DISPATCH DISSOLVE
(— SURREPTITIOUSLY) SNEAK
(— THE POINT) SAVVY
(— TO BOTTOM OF) FATHOM
(— UNDER CONTROL) RAIM
(— UP) ARISE HUDDUP UPRISE HAIRPIN
(PREF.) (— OFF) DE
GETA SABOT
GETHER (FATHER OF —) ARAM
GET-TOGETHER DO DRINK HOBNOB BAMBOCHE POTLATCH
GETUP SETOUT
GEWGAW DIE TOY WALY KNACK WALLY BAUBLE FANGLE FEGARY JIGGER FLAMFEW TRANGAM TRINKET FOLDEROL GIMCRACK JIMCRACK TRIMTRAM
GEYSER BORE JETTER

GHANA

CAPITAL: ACCRA
COIN: PESEWA
DAM: AKOSOMBO
LAKE: VOLTA BOSUMTWI
LANGUAGE: GA EWE TWI FANTI HAUSA DAGBANI DAGOMBA
MONEY: CEDI NEWCEDI
MOUNTAIN: AFADJATO
NATIVE: GA EWE AHAFO BRONG FANTI ASHANTI DAGOMBA MAMPRUSI
REGION: VOLTA ASHANTI BRONGAHAFO
RIVER: OTI PRA DAKA TANO AFRAM VOLTA ANKOBRA KULPAWN
TOWN: HO WA ODA AXIM FIAN KETA TALA TEMA ACCRA BAWKU ENCHI LAWRA LEGON SAMPA YAPEI DUNKWA KARAGA KPANDU KUMASI NSAWAM OBUASI SWEDRU TAMALE TARKWA WASIPE ANTUBIA DAMONGO MAMPONG PRESTEA SEKONDI SUNYANI WINNEBA AKOSOMBO KINTAMPO TAKORADI
WIND: HARMATTAN

GHARRY SHIGRAM
GHASTLY WAN GASH GRIM PALE BLATE GHAST LURID UNKET UNKID DISMAL GOUSTY GRISLY PALLID CHARNEL DEATHLY FEARFUL GASHFUL GRIZZLY GRUGOUS HIDEOUS MACABRE DREADFUL GRUESOME HORRIBLE SHOCKING TERRIBLE
GHAWAZI BARAMIKA
GHERKIN CUCUMBER
GHETTO JEWRY JUDAISM

GHIBELLINE WAIBLING
GHOST HAG KER BHUT HANT JUBA WAFF BUGAN CADDY DUFFY DUPPY FETCH GAIST GUEST HAUNT JUMBY LARVA PRETA SHADE SPOOK UMBRA CHUREL SOWLTH SPIRIT SPRITE TAISCH ANTAEUS ANTAIOS BOGGART BUGGANE GYTRASH PHANTOM SPECTER SPECTRE VAMPIRE BARGHEST GUYTRASH PHANTASM REVENANT
(PREF.) SPECTRO SPOOKO
GHOSTFISH WRYMOUTH
GHOSTLY EERY EERIE GOUSTY SHADOWY UNCANNY WEIRDLY CHTHONIC GHASTFUL SPECTRAL
GHOST MOTH SWIFT HEPIALID
GHOSTS (AUTHOR OF —) IBSEN
(CHARACTER IN —) HELEN JACOB ALVING OSWALD REGINA MANDERS ENGSTRAND
GHOST-WRITER SPOOK
GHOULISH SATANIC
GHUZ OGHUZ
GIAI NHANG
GIANNI SCHICCHI (CHARACTER IN —) BUOSO DONATI LAURETTA RINUCCIO SCHICCHI
(COMPOSER OF —) PUCCINI
GIANT ORC ETEN HUGE OGRE OTUS WATE YMER YMIR AFRIT BALOR CACUS HYMIR JOTUN MIMAS MIMER THRYM TITAN TROLL AFREET ALBION FAFNIR GIGANT GOEMOT PALLAS THJAZI THURSE TITYUS WARLOW ANTAEUS CYCLOPS GOLIATH WARLOCK ASCOPART BELLERUS COLBRAND GIGANTIC GOEMAGOT GOGMAGOG MASTODON MORGANTE ORGOGLIO TYPHOEUS PROCRUSTES
(1-EYED —) CYCLOPS
(100-HANDED —) GYGES COTTUS BRIAREUS
(1000-ARMED —) BANA
(PL.) ANAK ANAKIM COTTUS ALOADAE REPHAIM NEPHILIM ZAMZUMMIM
(PREF.) GIGANT(I)(O)
GIANTESS NORN ARGANTE
GIANT FULMAR NELLY STINKER STINKPOT
GIANT GRASS OTATE
GIANT HERON GOLIATH
GIANTISM ACROMEGALY
GIANT LILY FIGUE MAGUEY
GIANT PUFFBALL FUZZ FUZZBALL
GIANTS IN THE EARTH (AUTHOR OF —) ROLVAAG
(CHARACTER IN —) OLE PER ANNA HANS OLSA BERET HANSA PEDER
GIARDIA LAMBLIA
GIB JIB SHOE DEMUR SLIPPER
GIBBAR GIBBERT JUBARTAS
GIBBER CHAT CHATTER
GIBBERISH GREEK JABBER JARGON CHOCTAW ABRACADABRA
GIBBET STOB TREE CROOK JEBAT GALLOWS POTENCE EQUULEUS
GIBBON LAR WAWA UNGKA

WUYEN CAMPER HULOCK HOOLOCK SIAMANG HYLOBATE
GIBBOUS CONVEX HULCHY HUMPED SACCATE
GIBE (ALSO SEE JIBE) BOB RUB GIRD JAPE JEST JIBE PROG QUIB QUIP SKIT WIPE FLEER FLING FLIRT FRUMP GLEEK KNACK SCOFF SCOMM SCORN SLANT SNEER DERIDE GLANCE HECKLE BROCARD SARCASM RIDICULE
GIBING SNASH
GID DUNT GIDDY STURDY GOGGLES POTHERY VERTIGO
GIDDALTI (FATHER OF —) HEMAN
GIDDINESS LUNACY SOORAWN
GIDDY BARMY GLAKY LIGHT WESTY GIGLET GLAKED GOWKED GOWKIT SHANNY STURDY VOLAGE GLAIKET LARKING HALUCKET HELLICAT
GIDDY-HEADED HELLICAT
GIDEON (FATHER OF —) JOASH
GIDEONI (SON OF —) ABIDAN
GIFT BOX FOY QUO SOP BENT BOON DASH ENAM MEED SAND BONUS BRIBE CAULP CUDDY DONUM GRANT KNACK TOKEN BEFANA CADEAU DASHEE DONARY GENIUS GERSUM GIFTIE GIVING HANSEL LEGACY RECADO REGALO TALENT XENIUM APTNESS BEFFANA BENEFIT CHARISM CHARITY DEODATE DONATIO DOUCEUR ETRENNE FACULTY FAIRING GIFTURE HANDSEL PRESENT PROPINE REGALIO SUBSIDY TASHRIF TRIBUTE AMATORIO APTITUDE BENEFICE BESTOWAL BLESSING COURTESY DONATION DONATIVE GARRISON GIVEAWAY GRATUITY MORTUARY OBLATION OFFERING POTLATCH SPORTULA BENEFACTION REMEMBRANCE PHILANTHROPY PRESENTATION
(— FROM HUSBAND TO WIFE) ARRAS
(— OF GOD) GRACE
(— OF MONEY) POUCH BAKSHISH
(— OF NATURE) DOWER DOWRY
(— TO ROMAN PEOPLE) CONGIARY
(CHARITABLE —) ALMS ENAM PITTANCE
(COMPULSORY —) SIXENIA
(LIBERAL —) LARGESSE
(NATURAL —) TALENT
(NEW YEAR'S EVE —) ETRENNE HAGMENA HOGMANAY
(SPIRITUAL —) CHARISM CHARISMA
(PL.) OBLATA MISSILES
GIFTBOOK ANNUAL KEEPSAKE
GIG TUB MOZE BANDY BUGGY CHAIR GIGGE CHAISE CLATCH DENNET WHISKY CALESIN TILBURY STANHOPE
GIGANTIC HUGE GIANT MAMMOTH TITANIC COLOSSAL ENORMOUS GIGANTAL ATLANTEAN MONSTROUS BROBDINGNAGIAN
GIGGER TEASELER
GIGGLE TEHEE KECKLE NICKER

TEEHEE TITTER SNICKER TWITTER
GIGLET JIG
GIL BLAS
GIL BLAS (AUTHOR OF —) LESAGE
(**CHARACTER IN —**) GIL BLAS LEWIS
PEREZ AURORA MENCIA SCIPIO
ANTONIA ARSENIA ROLANDO
ALPHONSO DOROTHEA FABRICIO
MATTHIAS OLIVAREZ SANGRADO
GILD GILT BEGILD ENGILD ORFGILD
GILDED GILT AURATE INAURATE
GILDER TRACER
GILEAD (FATHER OF —) MACHIR
(**SON OF —**) JEPHTHAH
GILGAMESH IZDUBAR
GILL JILL QUAD GHYLL PLICA
GILLIE LAMELLA BRANCHIA
QUADRANT
(**—S OF BIVALVE**) BEARD
(**PL.**) GINNERS CHOLLERS
BRANCHIAE
(**SUFF.**) BRANCH(IA)(IATE)
GILLAR PITTO
GILLIE GILLY HENCHMAN
GILLS
(**PREF.**) BRANCHI(O)
GILLYFLOWER STOCK GILVER
GELOFRE GILLIVER
GILTHEAD CONNER MELANURE
GIMBAL GEMEL JEMBLE
GIMCRACK QUIP BAUBLE FIZGIG
GEWGAW JIMJAM TRIFLE
TRANGAM TRINKET JIMCRACK
WHIMWHAM
GIMLET SCREW WIMBLE PIERCEL
PIERCER
GIMMICK GAFF
GIMP TAR ORRIS GUIMPE GIMPING
GIN MAX CRAB GRIN LACE RUIN
TAPE CLEAN JACKY SNARE SNARL
DIDDLE GENEVA JAMBER
JAMMER SPRINGE TITTERY
TWANKAY EYEWATER HOLLANDS
SCHIEDAM SCHNAPPS
(**DROP OF —**) DAFFY
GINATH (SON OF —) TIBNI
GINGER PEPPER RATOON
AROMATIC ZINZIBER COLTSFOOT
GINGERBREAD SPICE PARKIN
GINGERLY GINGER WARILY
CHARILY EDGINGLY
GINGERROOT HAND RACE
(**PL.**) ASARUM
GINGHAM CHAMBRAY
GINKGO ICHO
GINSENG SANG FATIL PANAX
ARALIA IVYWORT REDBERRY
GIOCONDA, LA (CHARACTER IN —)
ENZO CIECA LAURA ALVISE
BARNABA GIOCONDA GRIMALDO
(**COMPOSER OF —**) PONCHIELLI
GIRAFFE OONT CAMEL DAPPLE
KAMEEL SERAPH CAMAILE
RUMINANT
GIRASOL OPAL
GIRD BELT BIND GIRR GIRT HASP
YERK CLOSE SCOFF ENGIRD
FASTEN GIRDLE SECURE ACCINGE
ENVIRON CINCTURE SURROUND
GIRDER BEAM GIRD GIRT GIRTH
TABLE TRUSS BINDER SUMMER
WARREN GIRDING TWISTER
BUCKSTAY STRINGER

GIRDING CINCTURE
GIRDLE OBI ZON BARK BELT CEST
GIRD HOOP SASH ZONA ZONE
CEINT GIRTH MITER PATTE SARPE
WAIST BODICE CESTUS CINGLE
CIRCLE MOOCHA TISSUE ZODIAC
ZONULA ZOSTER BALDRIC
BALTEUS CENTRUM CENTURE
COMPASS GIRDING SHINGLE
CEINTURE CINCTURE CINGULUM
SURROUND
(**— FOR HELMET**) TISSUE
(**— OF DIATOM**) HOOP
(**BRIDE'S —**) CEST CESTUS
(**LITTLE —**) ZONULE ZONELET
(**ROYAL —**) MALO
(**SACRED —**) KUSTI
(**PREF.**) ZON(I)(O) ZOSTERI
ZOSTERO
(**SUFF.**) PLEURA
GIRDLED RUNG
GIRL BIT GAL HER KIT POP SHE SIS
TIB TID TIT BABE BABY BINT BIRD
CHIT DAME DEEM DELL GILL JANE
JILL JUDY LASS MARY MOPS
MORT PERI PUSS SLUT WREN
BEAST FILLY FLUFF GUIDE KITTY
LUBRA QUEAN SISSY SKIRT TIDDY
TITTY TOOTS TRULL BURDIE
CALICO CLINER CUMMER DALAGA
DAMSEL DEEMIE FEMALE FIZGIG
GEISHA GIRLIE LASSIE LOVELY
MAGGIE NUMBER PIGEON SHEILA
SISTER SUBDEB TOMATO
CAMILLA COLLEEN CRUMPET
DAMOSEL MADCHEN MAUTHER
TENDREL BONNIBEL FARMETTE
FEMININE GRISETTE MUCHACHA
(**AGILE —**) YANKER
(**AWKWARD —**) HOIT
(**BEATIFIED —**) BEATA
(**BEAUTIFUL —**) BELLE
(**BOLD —**) HOIDEN HOYDEN
(**CAMP FIRE —**) ARTISAN
(**CHORUS —**) CHORINE CORYPHEE
(**CLUMSY —**) TAWPIE
(**COUNTRY —**) MEG JOAN
(**DANCING —**) ALMA DASI ALMAH
KISANG KISAENG BAYADERE
DEVADASI
(**DANCING —S**) GHAWAZI
(**DEAR —**) PEAT
(**DUMPY —**) CUTTY
(**FLIGHTY —**) GOOSECAP
(**FLIRTATIOUS —**) JADE JILLET
(**FLOWER —**) NYDIA
(**FORWARD —**) STRAP
(**FROLICSOME —**) GILPY
(**GIDDY —**) GIG GIGLET GIGLOT
JILLET
(**GREEK —**) HAIDEE
(**GYPSY —**) GITANA
(**HIRED —**) BIDDY BIDDIE
(**IMPUDENT —**) STRAP
(**JAPANESE —**) GEISHA
(**LITTLE —**) SIS COOKY SISSY
COOKIE LASSOCK
(**MISCHIEVOUS —**) CUTTY HUSSY
(**MODEST —**) BLUSHET
(**NAIVE —**) INGENUE
(**NON-JEWISH —**) SHIKSE SHICKSA
(**PERT —**) MINX HUSSY
(**PRETTY —**) PRIM BUNNY

CUTEY CUTIE
(**ROMPING —**) STAG TOMBOY
(**SAUCY —**) SNIP
(**SERVANT —**) SLUT
(**SHIFTLESS —**) MYSTERY
(**SILLY —**) SKIT
(**SINGING —**) ALMA ALMEH
(**SLENDER —**) SYLPH
(**SMALL —**) PINAFORE
(**SPIRITED —**) FILLY
(**UNATTRACTIVE —**) FRUMP
(**UNMARRIED —**) MOUSME TOWDIE
MUSUMEE MADEMOISELLE
(**WANTON —**) GIG FILLOCK
(**WILD —**) BLOWZE
(**WORKING —**) ORISETTE
(**WORTHLESS —**) HUSSY
(**YOUNG —**) BUD MODER TITTY
MAIDEN MOTHER BAGGAGE
COLLEEN FLAPPER GIRLEEN
ROSEBUD
(**PL.**) GIRLERY GIRLHOOD
(**PREF.**) PUPI
GIRL OF THE GOLDEN WEST
(**CHARACTER IN —**) DICK JACK
RANCE MINNIE JOHNSON
RAMERREZ
(**COMPOSER OF —**) PUCCINI
GIRT CINCT
GIRTH GIRD GIRT TAPE CINCH
GARTH GIRSE GRETH WANTY
CINGLE WARROK COMPASS
GIRDING SHINGLE WEBBING
GIST JET NET NUB SUM CHAT
CORE GITE KNOT MEAT PITH
GREAT HEART JOIST POINT SENSE
BURDEN KERNEL PURPORT
SUMMARY STRENGTH
GITH MELANTHY
GIVE ADD GIE HOB TIP BEAR DEAL
DOLE HAND METE SELL TAKE
WEVE WHIP YEVE ALLOW AWARD
COUGH GRANT REFER YIELD
ACCORD AFFORD BESTOW
CONFER DEMISE DOTATE FASTEN
IMPART IMPOSE IMPUTE RENDER
SUPPLY CONSIGN DELIVER
FORGIVE FURNISH PRESENT
PROPINE BEQUEATH DISPENSE
(**— A BOOST**) BOLSTER
(**— A PLACE TO**) SITUATE
(**— A REASON**) ACCOUNT
(**— A REMEDY**) MINISTER
(**— ADHERENCE**) ASSENT
(**— ADMITTANCE**) ACCEPT
(**— ADVICE**) READ ADVISE
(**— AN ACCOUNT**) TELL RELATE
REPORT
(**— AND TAKE**) GIFFGAFF
(**— ANYTHING NAUSEOUS TO**) DOSE
(**— APPROVAL**) CONSENT
(**— AS CONCESSION**) YETTE
(**— AS EXPLANATION**) ASSIGN
(**— ASSURANCE**) EFFRONT
(**— ATTENTION TO**) HEED
(**— AUTHORITY**) ENABLE EMPOWER
ACCREDIT
(**— AWAY**) PART
(**— BACK**) REFUND RETURN
RESTORE
(**— BIRTH**) KIT BEAR BORN DROP
FIND MAKE BEGET BREED ISSUE
WORLD FARROW KINDLE LITTER

DELIVER FRESHEN
(**— BY WILL**) DEVISE
(**— CARE**) NURSE
(**— CLAIM TO**) REMISE
(**— COUNSEL**) AREAD AREED
(**— CREDIT FOR**) FRIST
(**— CURRENCY TO**) PASS
(**— EAR**) HARK HARKEN LISTEN
HEARKEN
(**— EXPRESSION TO**) EMOTE FRAME
VOICE
(**— FORM**) CUT
(**— FORTH**) WARP YIELD AFFORD
CONCEIVE
(**— GROUND**) RETIRE
(**— HEED**) LOOK ATTEND
(**— IN**) BOW CONCEDE COLLAPSE
(**— IN EXCHANGE**) SWAP SWOP
(**— IN MARRIAGE**) BESTOW SPOUSE
(**— INFORMATION**) WARN
(**— INSTRUCTION**) LEAR
(**— NAME TO**) BAPTIZE
(**— NOTICE**) WARN HERALD
APPRISE PUBLISH ANNOUNCE
INTIMATE
(**— NOTICE TO APPEAR**) GARNISH
(**— OBLIQUE EDGE**) CANT
(**— OFF**) EMIT SEND SHED EXUDE
FLING DIVIDE EFFUSE EVOLVE
EXHALE EXPIRE EXCRETE
SEPARATE
(**— ONE'S SELF OVER TO**) ADDICT
(**— ONE'S WORD**) PROMISE
(**— OUT**) BOOM LEAK EXUDE ISSUE
PETAL EVOLVE EMANATE
OUTGIVE
(**— OVER**) LIN
(**— PAIN**) AGGRIEVE
(**— PLACE**) VAIL BACCARE
(**— PLEDGE**) GAGE
(**— PROMINENCE TO**) FEATURE
(**— RELUCTANTLY**) BEGRUDGE
(**— SATISFACTION**) ABY ABYE
ABEGGE
(**— SPARINGLY**) INCH
(**— STRENGTH TO**) NERVE
(**— SUPPORT**) ASSIST ANIMATE
(**— TEMPORARILY**) LEND
(**— TIP**) TOUT
(**— TONGUE**) CRY YEARN
(**— UP**) PUT BURY DROP PART
CHUCK DEMIT DEVOW FORGO
LEAVE RAISE REMIT SHOOT
SPARE SPEND ABJURE ADDICT
BETRAY DESERT DEVOTE FOREGO
MIZZLE REFUSE RELENT RENDER
RESIGN VACATE ABANDON
DEPOSIT DESPAIR FLUMMOX
FORBEAR FORGIVE REFRAIN
RELEASE ABDICATE RENOUNCE
(**— VENT TO**) EMIT ISSUE
DISCHARGE
(**— VOICE**) BOLT ACCENT
(**— WARNING**) ALERT
(**— WAY**) GO FAIL FOLD KEEL SINK
VAIL BREAK BUDGE BURST FAINT
SLAKE YIELD BUCKLE FALTER
RELENT SWERVE FOUNDER
RECLAIM SUCCUMB
(**— WITNESS**) DEPOSE
GIVEN APT DONEE NATHAN
PROMPT
(**— TO**) ALL AFTER

(SUFF.) (— TO) ABLE IBLE LEW
GIVER DONOR
(— OF LIFE) APHETA
(NAME —) EPONYM
GIVING DOLE BOUNTY DATION
REMISE
(— HELP) ADJUTANT
(— MILK) FRESH
(— NO MILK) YELD YELL
(— TROUBLE) CUMBROUS
GIZZARD GIGERIUM
GIZZARD SHAD SKIPJACK
GLABROUS BALD SMOOTH
GLABRATE LEVIGATE
GLACIATION MINDEL
(— STAGE) RISS WURM
GLACIER BRAE ICECAP STREAM
CALOTTE ICEBERG PIEDMONT
(PREF.) GLACIO
GLACIOLOGY CRYOLOGY
GLACIS ESPLANADE
GLAD GAY FAIN LIEF VAIN CANTY
HAPPY PROUD BLITHE FESTUS
GLADLY JOCUND JOYFUL JOYOUS
GLADFUL GLEEFUL JOCULAR
ANIMATED CHEERFUL CHEERING
FESTIVAL GLADSOME PLEASING
GLADDEN JOY GLAD BLESS BLISS
CHEER EXULT MIRTH BLITHE
COMFORT GLADIFY LIGHTEN
REJOICE
(PREF.) TERP(I)(SI)
GLADE LAWN LAUND SLADE
SHRADD SUNGLADE SUNSCALD
(PREF.) NEMO
GLADIATOR THRAX RETIARY
SAMNITE SECUTOR ANDABATA
GLADIOLUS GLAD IRID LILY
LEVERS LILIUM GLADIOLA
GLADLY GLAD LIEF FAINLY LIEFLY
LOVELY HAPPILY
GLADNESS JOY GLAD GLEE BLISS
MIRTH BLITHE FAINNESS
GLADSHIP PLEASURE
GLADSOME BLITHE
GLAGA KASA KUSA TALTHIB
GLAMOR SCRY UTIS OOMPH
PIZAZZ BRABBLE PIZZAZZ
BALLYHOO
GLAMORIZE POT GLORIFY
GLAMOROUS EXOTIC ALLURING
CHARMING
GLAMOUR PAZAZZ PIZAZZ PIZZAZZ
GLANCE EYE RAY SEE BEAM CAST
GLIM LEER PEEK SCRY SKEG VIEW
WINK BLENK BLINK BLUSH
CAROM FLASH GLEEK GLENT
GLIDE GLIFF GLINT GLISK GRAZE
PRINK SCREW SIGHT SKIME
SLANT SQUIZ TWIRE APERCU
ASPECT CARROM GANDER
REGARD SCANCE STRIKE VISION
EYEBEAM EYESHOT EYEWINK
GLIMPSE BELAMOUR GLIFFING
OEILLADE
(— OFF) GLACE
(— THROUGH) SAMPLE
(LOVE —) AMORET
(MELANCHOLY —) DOWNCAST
(SHARP —) DART
(SIDELONG —) SHEW SLENT
SKLENT
(SLY —) GLEG GLIME GLOAT

GLAND MILT NOIX SETA CLYER
CRYPT GONAD LIVER MAMMA
ACINUS BREAST KERNEL THYMUS
ADRENAL CRUMENA NECTARY
PAROTID PAROTIS TEARPIT
THYROID CONARIUM ENDOCRIN
FOLLICLE FOLLOWER GANGLION
GLANDULA GLANDULE
HOOFWORM PROSTATE SCIRRHUS
SPERMARY
(PREF.) ADEN(O) SCIRRH(O)
(SUFF.) ADEN SCIRRHUS
GLANDERS FARCY MALLEUS
GLANDULAR EARTHY INNATE
SEXUAL ADENOID PHYSICAL
ADENOIDAL
GLANS NUT GLAND
GLARE BEAT GAZE BLARE BLAZE
BLOOM FLAME GLAZE STARE
GLITTER ICEBLINK RADIANCE
GLARING HARD RANK GLARY
AGLARE GARISH BURNING
FLARING STARING FLAGRANT
GLASS CUP VER CALX FLAT FLUX
FRIT JENA MOIL PONY VITA
CHARK FACER FLINT GLAZE
STOOP STOUP VERRE VITRE
CALGON CEMENT CULLET
RUMMER SPECKS VITRUM
ALEYARD BIFOCAL BRIMMER
CHIRPER CRYSTAL PERLITE
SCHMELZ TALLBOY VITRITE
FROSTING OBSIDIAN SCHOPPEN
PERSPECTIVE
(— IN STATE OF FUSION) METAL
(— OF A MIRROR) STONE
(— OF BEER) BREW
(— OF BRANDY) SNEAKER
(— OF SPIRITS) CHASSE
(— OF WHISKY) KELTY RUBDOWN
(— OF WINE) APERITIF
(— STICKING TO PUNTY) COLLET
(BEER —) SHELL SEIDEL PILSNER
PILSENER
(BELL-SHAPED —) CUP CLOCHE
(BURNING —) SUNGLASS
(CHEVAL —) PSYCHE
(COLORED —) SMALT SMALTO
TINTER SCHMELZ
(COLORED —S) GOGGLES
(CUPPING —) VENTOSE
(CURVED —) LENS
(DESSERT —) COUPE
(DRINKING —) GOBLET RUMKIN
PILSNER PIMLICO SCUTTLE
TUMBLER SCHOONER
(EUROPEAN ORNAMENTAL —)
PELOTON
(EXAMINATION —) SLIDE
(FULL —) BUMPER
(FUSIBLE —) FLUX
(HALF —) SPLIT
(ICE CREAM —) SLIDER
(LEAD —) STRASS
(LIQUEUR —) PONY PONEY
(LIQUOR —) GUN
(MAGNIFYING —) LOUPE
(MASS OF MOLTEN —) PARISON
(METEORITIC —) MOLDAVITE
(OPALESCENT —) OPALINE
(OPAQUE —) HYALITHE
(PIECE OF HOT —) BIT
(PULVERIZED —) FROSTING

(REFUSE —) CALX CULLET
(RUBY —) SCHMELZE
(RUSSIAN —) CHARK
(SHERBET —) SUPREME
(SHERRY —) COPITA
(SMOKED —) SHADE
(STAINED —) VITRAIL
(TALL —) RUMMER
(THIN —) MOUSSELINE
(VOLCANIC —) PUMICE PERLITE
(WINDOW —) PANE
(WINE —) FLUTE
(PL.) SHELLS
(PREF.) HYAL(O) VITR(EO)(I)(O)
GLASSBLOWER MUMBLER
GLASS CRAB SPECTER SPECTRE
GLASSES (TINTED —) SHADES
GLASSHOUSE STOVE HOTHOUSE
GLASS-LIKE VITRIC
GLASS MENAGERIE (AUTHOR OF —
) WILLIAMS
(CHARACTER IN —) TOM JAMES
LAURA AMANDA OCONNOR
GLASSWARE AGATA AURENE
BURMESE FAVRILE OPALINE
STEUBEN VITRICS AMBERINA
GLASSWORK GLAZING GLAZIERY
GLASSWORKER GANGMAN
GLAZIER SNAPPER GLASSMAN
SERVITOR
GLASSWORT KALI KELPWORT
SALTWORT SAMPHIRE
GLASSY GLIB FILMY GLAZY
GLAZEN GLASSEN HYALINE
HYALOID VITREAL VITREOUS
(PREF.) HYAL(O)
GLAUCE (FATHER OF —) CREON
(HUSBAND OF —) JASON
GLAUCUS (FATHER OF —) MINOS
ANTHEDON SISYPHUS
HIPPOLOCHUS
(MOTHER OF —) MEROPE
PASIPHAE
GLAZE DIP LEAD SIZE SLIP GLASS
SLEET SMEAR ENAMEL QUARRY
CELADON COPERTA EELSKIN
GLASSEN GLAZING GLIDDER
COUVERTE TIGEREYE
(— OF ICE) GLARE
GLAZED FILMY GLACE GLASSEN
GLOSSED
GLAZED WARE GLOST
GLAZIER PUTTIER
(TOOL OF —) SPRIG LADKIN
GLEAM RAY BEAM GLOW LEAM
WAFT WINK BLENK BLINK BLUSH
FLASH GLAIK GLEEN GLENT GLINT
GLISK GLINT GLOSE SHINE SKIME
SPUNK STARE STEEM TWIRE
GLANCE SCANCE FOULDRE
GLIMMER GLITTER SHIMMER
CORUSCATE SCINTILLA
(— FAINTLY) SHIMMER
(— OF LIGHT) LEAM PINK GLAIK
SCANCE
(FAINT —) SCAD
GLEAMING FAW GLOW CLEAR
GLINT STEEP ABLAZE BRIGHT
GLEAMY ADAZZLE SHINING
GLOOMING
GLEAN CULL EARN REAP LEASE
GATHER COLLECT SCRINGE
GLEANER STIBBLER

GLEANING CROP GATHERING
(LITERARY —S) ANALECTA
ANALECTS
GLEBE SOD CLOD LAND SOIL
TERMON KIRKTOWN
GLEE GLY JOY SONG MIRTH SPORT
GAIETY DELIGHT ELATION
WASSAIL HILARITY MADRIGAL
GLEEFUL GAY MERRY JOYOUS
JOCULAR GLEESOME
GLEEMAN SONGMAN MINSTREL
GLEN DEN GILL GLYN GRIFF HEUCH
HEUGH KLOOF SLACK SLADE
TEMPE CANADA DINGLE POCKET
GLIADIN GLUTIN PROLAMIN
GLIB PAT FLIP SLICK CASUAL
GLOSSY OFFHAND RENABLE
SHALLOW VOLUBLE FLIPPANT
GLIDE GO SKI FLOW SAIL SILE SKIM
SLIP SLUR SOAR SWIM COAST
CREEP DANCE FLEET GLACE
GRAZE LAPSE MERGE PLANE
SCOOP SHIRL SKATE SKIFF SKIRR
SKITE SLADE SLEEK SLICK SLIDE
SLIPE STEAL GLANCE GLIDER
SASHAY SNOOVE ILLAPSE
SCRIEVE SCRITHE SKITTER
SLITHER AIRPLANE GLISSADE
VOLPLANE SEMIVOWEL
(— AWAY) ELAPSE
(— BY) PASS FLEET
(— OFF) EXIT
GLIDER BIPLANE SCOOTER
SAILPLANE
GLIDING LAPSE TRAIL SLIDING
(— OF THE VOICE) DRAG
(— OVER) LAMBENT
GLIMMER FIRE GLIM GLOW LEAM
STIM BLINK FLASH GLEAM GLOOM
STIME SIMPER BLINTER FLIMMER
GLIMPSE GLITTER SHIMMER
SPARKLE TWINKLE SUNBLINK
GLIMMERING GHOST AGLIMMER
GLOOMING
GLIMPSE IDEA WAFF WAFT BLINK
BLUSH FLASH GLIFF GLINT GLISK
SIGHT STIME TINGE TRACE WHIFF
GLANCE GLEDGE LUSTER SCANCE
GLIMMER INKLING
(BRIEF —) APERCU
(FLEETING —) SHIM SNATCH
GLINT PEEP FLASH GLEAM GLENT
GLANCE SPARKLE
GLIS MYOXUS
GLISSANDO GLISS SMEAR
GLISSADE
GLISTEN FLASH GLISK GLISS GLIST
SHINE GLISTER GLITTER SHIMMER
SPANGLE SPARKLE RUTILATE
GLISTENING SHINY AGLISTEN
GLITTER FLASH GLARE GLEAM
GLEIT GLINT GLORE SHEEN SHINE
SKYRE STARE BICKER LUSTER
SCANCE GLIMMER GLISTEN
GLISTER SKINKLE SPANGLE
SPARKLE TWINKLE BRANDISH
RADIANCE RUTILATE CORUSCATE
(FALSE —) GILT
GLITTERING GEMMY SHEEN SHINY
STEEP FULGID SPANGLY
AGLITTER GLITTERY RUTILANT
BRILLIANT CLINQUANT
GLOAMING EVE DUSK GLOAM

GLOOMING TWILIGHT

GLOAT GAZE GLUT TIRE EXULT
PREEN

GLOBAL PLANETARY

GLOBE ORB BALL BOWL CLEW
CLUE POME AGGER GEOID
MONDE MOUND ROUND SPHERE
COMPASS GEORAMA GLOBULE
GRENADE AQUARIUM ROUNDURE

GLOBEFISH FUGU TOBY TOADO
ATINGA BOTETE PUFFER
BLAASOP BURFISH OOPUHUE
BLOWFISH

GLOBEFLOWER BOLT GOLLAND
GOWLAND CORCHORUS

GLOBE THISTLE ECHINOPS

GLOBOSE COCCOID COCCOUS
CAPITATE GLOBULAR

GLOBULAR GLOBED ROTUND
GLOBATE GLOBOSE GLOBICAL

GLOBULE BEAD BLOB DROP GLOB
PEARL BUBBLE BUTTON REGULUS
GLOBULET SPHERULE
(— OF TAPIOCA) FISHEYE

GLOBULIN MAYSIN MYOSIN VIGNIN
ARACHIN CORYLIN EDESTIN
LEGUMIN TUBERIN VICILIN
ANTIBODY BIOLOGIC EXCELSIN
GLYCININ MUSCULIN ORYZENIN

GLOCKENSPIEL BELL LYRA
CARILLON

GLOMERULE GLOME FASCICLE

GLOOM DAMP DUSK MURK CLOUD
DREAR FROWN SOMBER DESPAIR
DIMNESS GLOOMTH SADNESS
DARKNESS MIDNIGHT

GLOOMY DUN SAD WAN BLUE
COLD DARK DOUR DREE DULL
EERY GLUM MIRK MURK ADUSK
ADUST BLACK BROWN DOWFF
DREAR DUSKY EERIE FERAL
GUMLY HEAVY LURID MOODY
MORNE MUDDY MUNGY MUSTY
MUZZY ROOKY SABLE SORRY
STERN SULKY SURLY SWART
TRIST CLOUDY DISMAL DREARY
DREICH DROOPY DRUMLY
GLUMMY MOROSE SOLEMN
SOMBER SULLEN TETRIC THRAWN
OBSCURE STYGIAN THESTER
DARKSOME DESOLATE DOLESOME
DOWNBEAT DOWNCAST
FUNEREAL GLOOMING LOWERING
OVERCAST TRISTFUL PESSIMISTIC

GLORIA GLORY AUREOLE

GLORIFICATION AVATAR

GLORIFY HERY LAUD BLESS DEIFY
EXALT EXTOL HERSE HONOR
PRIDE WURTH KUDIZE PRAISE
CLARIFY ELEVATE MAGNIFY
DIVINIZE EMBLAZON EULOGIZE
PROCLAIM STELLIFY

GLORIOLE HALO AUREOLE

GLORIOUS SRI DEAR DERE MERE
SHRI GRAND PROUD BRIGHT
EMINENT RENOWNED

GLORY JOY ORE SUN FACE FAME
GLOR HALO HORN BLAZE BOAST
EXULT HONOR KUDOS PRIDE
WULDER AUREOLA CLARITY
GARLAND GLORIFY RADIANCE
SPLENDOR WORTHING

GLORY-PEA KOWHAI

GLOSS GILL COLOR DUNCE GLASS
GLAZE GLOZE JAPAN SHEEN
SHINE BLANCH LUSTER LUSTRE
POSTIL REMARK VENEER BURNISH
EXPOUND VARNISH FLOURISH
PALLIATE POLITURE
(— OVER) FARD HUSH SALVE
SLEEK SOOTHE

GLOSSA LINGUA

GLOSSARY GLOSS CLAVIS

GLOSSIPHONIA CLEPSINE

GLOSSY GLOZE NITID SHINY SILKY
SLEEK SLICK SATINY SMOOTH

GLOVE KID CUFF GAGE MITT
COFFE BERLIN MITTEN CHEVRON
DANNOCK GANTLET GOMUKHI
GAUNTLET
(— FOR RUBBING SKIN) STRIGIL
(BISHOP'S —) GWANTUS
(BODY OF —) TRANK
(BOXING —) MUFFLE
(HEDGER'S —) DANNOCK
(HUSKING —) HUSKER
(PART OF —) THUMB TRANK
GUSSET BINDING FOURCHETTE

GLOVEMAKER DOMER GLOVER
CLASPER FINGERER

GLOVER TRANKER

GLOW ARC LOW AURA BURN FIRE
LEAM LOOM LOWE BLAZE BLOOM
BLUSH FLAME FLASH FLUSH
GLAZE GLEAM GLEED GLORY
GLOSS GLOZE SHINE STEAM
CORONA KINDLE WARMTH
FLUSTER LIGHTEN
(— OF PASSION) ESTUS AESTUS
(— WITH INTENSE HEAT) IGNITE

GLOWER GAZE GLOW GLARE
GLOOM GLORE

GLOWING HOT LIVE WARM
AGLOW FIERY LIGHT QUICK
RUDDY VIVID ABLAZE ARDENT
ORIENT BURNING CANDENT
FERVENT RADIANT SHINING
FLAGRANT RUTILANT

GLOWWORM FIREFLY FIREWORM
GLOWBIRD LAMPYRID

GLOZE FAWN PAINT SMOOTH
FLATTERY

GLUCINUM BERYLLIUM

GLUCOSE AME GLYCOSE
DEXTROSE

GLUCOSIDE GEIN APIIN RUTIN
TUTIN ADONIN BINDER CORNIN
DURRIN FRAXIN FUSTIN IRIDIN
PICEIN UZARIN ACACIIN ARBUTIN
DAPHNIN DIOSMIN ESCULIN
ESTEVIN GITALIN GITONIN
GITOXIN HEDERIN HELICIN
INDICAN LOGANIN LOTUSIN
LUPININ OUABAIN POPULIN
ROBININ SALICIN TABACIN
TEUCRIN ADONIDIN CARTHAME
ERICOLIN GENISTIN GOSSYPIN
MORINDIN NARINGIN PARIGLIN
PARILLIN PRUNASIN QUINOVIN
SAPONINE SCILLAIN SINIGRIN
SYRINGIN THEVETIN VERNONIN
VIBURNIN VICIANIN

GLUE PAD EPOXY MOUNT STICK
BEGLEW CEMENT FUNORI
FUNORIN STICKER STICKUM
TAUROCOL

(BEE —) PROPOLIS
(PREF.) COLL(A)(O)(OIDIO)(OIDO)
GLOEO
(SUFF.) COLL GLIA GLOEA

GLUE-LIKE
(PREF.) (— SUBSTANCE) GLI

GLUEY GLUISH STICKY STRINGY
VISCOUS ADHESIVE

GLUM CLUM DOUR GRUM SURLY
GLOOMY GLUMPY MOROSE
SULLEN DEJECTED

GLUMALES POALES

GLUME PILE FLIGHT
(FLOWERING —) LEMMA
(PL.) CHAFF

GLUSIDE SACCHARIN

GLUT CLOY FILL GULP QUAT SATE
CHOKE DRAFT GORGE BATTEN
ENGLUT EXCESS MARROW
PAMPER PAUNCH ENGORGE
GLUTTON SATIATE SURFEIT
SWALLOW OVERFEED SAGINATE
SATURATE

GLUTEAL NATAL

GLUTELIN AVENINE ORYZENIN

GLUTENIN AVENIN ZYMOME
ZYMOMIN

GLUTINOUS ROPY SIZY ROPEY
SLIMY TOUGH STICKY VISCID
(PREF.) GLOEO GLOIO

GLUTTED QUAT GORGED SATIATED

GLUTTER VEER

GLUTTON HOG PIG GLUT GORB
GUTS GULCH MIKER GLOTUM
HELLUO MACCUS EPICURE
GUTLING LURCHER MOOCHER
RAVENER SWILLER CARCAJOU
DRAFFMAN GOURMAND
GULLYGUT
(STUPID —) GRUB

GLUTTONIZE BIZLE BEZZLE

GLUTTONOUS GREEDY GLUTTON
HOGGISH GOURMAND

GLUTTONY GULE EDACITY
SURFEIT

GLYCERIDE BUTYRIN

GLYCINE SOJA

GLYCOL CARBOWAX

GLYCOPROTEIN MUCIN MUCOID

GLYCOSIDE APIIN CROCIN ACACIIN
CYMARIN DIGOXIN GITALIN
GITOXIN HEDERIN HYPERIN
LOGANIN LOTUSIN SAPONIN
ALDESIDE ANDROSIN ANTIARIN
HOLOSIDE KETOSIDE

GNARL NOB KNOB KNUR KNARL
KNURR SNIRL WARRE DEFORM

GNARLED GNARLY KNARRY
KNOTTY CRABBED KNOTTED
KNURLED

GNASH TUSK CHAMP CRASH
GANCH GRASH GRATE KNASH

GNAT KNAW SMUT MIDGE PUNKY
STOUT KNATTE SCIARA SCIARID
SCINIPH BLACKFLY DIPTERAN
GNATLING
(PREF.) CULIC(I)

GNATCATCHER SYLVIID

GNATHION MENTON

GNAW EAT NAB BITE FRET TIRE
CHELE GNARL MOUSE SHEAR
ARRODE BEFRET BEGNAW
CANKER CHAVEL NATTLE NIGGLE

ROUNGE CHIMBLE CHUMBLE
CORRODE

GNAWED
(PREF.) BROTO

GNAWING EATING RODENT
FRETFUL ARROSION ROSORIAL

GNOME NIS NISSE PECHT PYGMY
KOBOLD VAKSHA YAKSHI
GNOMIDE GREMLIN HODEKEN
ERDGEIST

GNOMON COCK INDEX STILE STYLE
FESCUE STYLUS

GNOSTIC CLEVER SHREWD
KNOWING PÉRATES EBIONITE
MANDAEAN SEVERIAN SIMONIAN
SIMONITE

GNU KOKOON BRINDLE

GO BE DO ACT GAE HOP ISH LAY
MM PEP TEE WAG BANG BEAR
BING BOWN BUSK DRAW FAND
FARE FOND GANG HARK HAUL
HUMP MOVE QUIT RAIK ROAM
ROLL SEEK SHOT SILE SLAP SNAP
STAB STEP TAKE TEEM TOUR
WADE WANE WEAR WEND WEVE
WIND WISE WORK YEAD YEDE
AMBLE BOUND CARRY CHEVE
DEMON DRESS FETCH FRAME
HAUNT KNOCK LEAVE MOSEY
PLUCK REACH SCRAM SHAKE
SLOPE SPEED TOUCH TRACE
TRACK TRENE TRINE TRUSS
WHIZZ YONGE BECOME BETAKE
CHIEVE CRUISE DEPART EXTEND
QUATCH QUETCH REPAIR RESORT
RESULT RETIRE SASHAY STRAKE
STRIKE TODDLE TRAVEL WEAKEN
JOURNEY SCRITHE DIMINISH
WITHDRAW
(— ABOUT) JET BEGO BIGAN
(— ABOUT DEJECTEDLY) PEAK
(— ABOUT GOSSIPING) COURANT
(— AHEAD) HOLD
(— AIMLESSLY) ERR BUMMLE
(— ALONG) PATH
(— ALONG WITH) ACCOMPANY
(— AROUND) SKIRT BYPASS
CIRCUE
(— ASHORE) LAND
(— ASTRAY) ERR MAR WRY MANG
WILL MISGO DELIRE FORVAY
MISWEND DEROGATE MISCARRY
(— AWAY) AGO HOP OFF BEAT
BUNK HIKE NASH PART SHOO
VADE CLEAR HENCE IMSHI LEAVE
SCRAM SHIFT BEGONE BUGGER
DEPART REMOVE VACATE
SKIDDOO ELONGATE
(— BACK IN TIME) MOUNT
(— BAD) SOUR
(— BEFORE) LEAD FOREGO
PRECEDE ANTECEDE PREAMBLE
(— BEYOND) SURPASS FOREPASS
(— BRISKLY) JUNE
(— BROKE) BUST
(— COURTING) WENCH
(— DOWN) SET SINK VAIL DROOP
SOUND DESCEND
(— EASILY) AMBLE
(— ERRATICALLY) KICK
(— FAST) HURRY SPLIT BARREL
BEELINE
(— FORTH) AGO DEPART FORTHGO

(— FORWARD) HUP HUPP ADVANCE AGGRESS PROCEED
(— FOWLING) AUCUPATE
(— FURTIVELY) SLINK SNEAK STEAL
(— HANG) SNICK
(— HEAVILY) LOB LAMPER
(— IN) ENTER INGRESS
(— IN A HURRY) SCUFFLE
(— IN HASTE) LEN LAMMAS
(— IN PURSUIT) SUE
(— INTO BUSINESS) EMBARK
(— LAME) FOUNDER
(— LEISURELY) BUMMEL JIGGET JIGGIT
(— LIGHTLY) TIPTOE
(— MAD) CRAZE MADDLE
(— NEAR) APPROACH
(— NOISILY) LARUM
(— OFF) MOG DISCHARGE
(— ON) DO GARN LAST PASS PERGE FURTHER PROCEED
(— ON BOARD) BOARD EMBARK ENTRAIN
(— ON FOOT) SHANK
(— ON TO SAY) ADD
(— OUT) EXIT ISSUE SLOCK EGRESS EXEUNT QUENCH SORTIE
(— OVER) KNEE REVOLT SURPASS OVERGANG
(— OVER AGAIN) RENEW REVISE RETRACE
(— PROSPEROUSLY) COTTON
(— QUICKLY) GET HIE BUZZ LAMP PIKE SCAT SPEED
(— RAPIDLY) LAMP SPLIT
(— SHARES) SNACK
(— SLOWLY) CRAWL CREEP
(— SLUGGISHLY) SHACK
(— SMOOTHLY) SLIP
(— STEALTHILY) SHIRK SLINK SNEAK GUMSHOE
(— SUDDENLY) CLAP SCOOT
(— SWIFTLY) SKISE STRIP HIGHBALL
(— THE ROUNDS) PATROL
(— THROUGH) SUFFER
(— THROUGH WATER) SQUATTER
(— THROUGHOUT) COAST
(— TO BED) KIP DOSS FLOP SNUG
(— TO EXCESS) DEBORD
(— TO HARBOR) VERT
(— TO PIECES) SNURP
(— TO SCHOOL) SCOLEY
(— TO SLEEP) HUSHABY
(— TO WAR) RISE
(— TOO FAR) OUTREACH
(— UP) CLIMB AMOUNT ASCEND
(— WEARILY) HAGGLE
(— WITH EFFORT) HIKE
(— WRONG) MISS FAULT CURDLE MISFARE BACKFIRE
GOAD EGG GAD GIG HAG BAIT BROD BROG DARE EDGE GAUD LASH MOVE PROD SPUR URGE WHIP YERK ANKUS HARRY IMPEL PIQUE PRICK PROGG PUNGE STING VALET INCITE NEEDLE OXGOAD ANKUSHA HOTFOOT INFLAME PROVOKE IRRITATE SLAPJACK STIMULUS
GOADMAN GADMAN GAUDSMAN GOADSTER
GOAL BYE DEN END BASE BUTT

DOLE DOOL HAIL HALE MARK METE PORT BOURN FINIS IDEAL SCOOP SCOPE SCORE STING DESIGN OBJECT SIGHTS DESTINY HORIZON TERMINUS OBJECTIVE
(— IN GAMES) HUNK
(FIELD —) BASKET
(REMOTE —) THULE
(UNATTAINABLE —) STAR
GO-ASHORE KOHUA
GOAT BOK TUR IBEX TAHR BEDEN BILLY BOVID EVECK SEROW ALPINE ANGORA AOUDAD CAPRID CHAMAL JEMLAH MAZAME NUBIAN PASANG SAANEN WETHER CHAMOIS AEGAGRUS CAPRIPED MARKHOOR BOUQUETIN
(DOMESTIC —) HIRCUS
(FEMALE —) NANNY DOELING
(MALE —) BUCK BUCKLING
(YOUNG —) KID KIDDY TICCHEN GOATLING
(PREF.) AEG(I)(O) CAPRI EGO
GOAT ANTELOPE GORAL SEROW GOORAL
GOATEE TUFT
GOATFISH MOANO
GOATHERD DAMON
GOAT-LIKE CAPRINE GOATISH HIRCINE
GOAT MOTH COSSID
GOATSBEARD ROSACEAN
GOATSKIN CRUST CASTOR CHEVRETTE
GOATSUCKER PUCK PEWKE POTOO EVEJAR BULLBAT DORHAWK GRINDER SPINNER DOORHAWK EVECHURR NIGHTJAR PAURAQUE
GOB CLOT GOAF SWAB SWOB WASTE GOBBET SWABBY
GOBBET BIT CHUNK MORSEL
GOBBLE MOP BOLT SLOP GOFFLE GORBLE
GOBBLEDYGOOK PEDAGESE
GO-BETWEEN BAWD FIXER MEANS BROKER DEALER PANDAR CONTACT MEDIATOR
GOBLET DINOS GLASS HANAP POKAL SKULL STOOP STOUP BUMPER HOLMOS RUMKIN CHALICE SCYPHUS SNIFTER TALLBOY JEROBOAM STANDARD STEMWARE
(PREF.) CALICI
GOBLIN (ALSO SEE HOBGOBLIN) COW HAG NIS PUG BHUT BOGY MARE PUCK BOGEY NISSE OUPHE POOKA BODACH BOGGLE BOOGER CHUREL EMPUSA FOLIOT SPRITE BOGGARD BOGGART BROWNIE BUGBEAR KNOCKER PADFOOT BARGHEST BOGEYMAN FOLLETTO
GOBY MAPO BULLY BIGHEAD CHALACO GOBIOID GUAVINA GUDGEON MUDFISH BULLHEAD PINKFISH SANDGOBY
GOCART SULKY WALKER STROLLER
GOD (ALSO SEE DEITY) AS EA EL ER RA VE BEL BES COG DAD DES

DEV DIS DOD EAR GAR GAW GEB GOG GOL GOM GUM ING KEB LAR LOK MEN MIN ODD ORO SEB SUN TEM TYR ULL UTU VAN AITU AMEN AMON ARES ASUR ATEO ATUA ATYS BAAL BEER BRAN BURE CHAC COCK DEUS DEVA DIEU ESUS FONS FREY GAWD GOSH HAPI HOLY HOTH INTI JOVE KANE KING LIFE LLEU LOKE LOKI LOVE LUGH MARS MIND NABU NEBO NUDD ODIN PTAH SHEN SHIN SOMA SOUL TANE THOR TIKI ULLR UTUG VAYU XIPE YAMA ZEUS ARAWN ASHUR ASURA ATTES ATTIS COMUS DAGDA DEITY DEOTA DUVEL DYAUS DYLAN EBISU ELOAH FREYR GHOST GOLES GOLLY GRAVE GUACA HESUS HIEMS HORUS HOTHR HUACA HYMEN INDRA JUDGE KINGU LADON LIBER LLUDD MENTU MIDER MOMUS NJORD NUMEN PALES PICUS SILEN TAMUZ THOTH TINIA TRUTH TYCHE URASH WAKEA WODIN WOTAN ZOMBI ADITYA ADONAI ADONAY ANSHAR ANUBIS APOLLO ASEITY AUTHOR CHAMOS CONSUS DEVATA DHARMA ELATHA ELOHIM FATHER FAUNUS GANESA HEAVEN HERMES HOENIR MEZTLI MILCOM MITHRA NEREUS NERGAL OSIRIS PATRON PENEUS PLUTUS PUSHAN SESHAT SOCIUS SOURCE SPIRIT SUTEKH SYLENE TAAROA TAMMUZ TARTAK TERAPH TRITON TRIVIA VARUNA VEDUIS VERITY VISHNU VULCAN WISDOM YAKSHA YAKSHI ZOMBIE ABRAXAS ADRANUS ALPHEUS ANTEROS BELENUS CHEMOSH DAIKOKU DELLING ETERNAL GODHEAD HANUMAN IAPETUS JEHOVAH JUPITER KANALOA MERCURY MITHRAS MUTINUS NEPTUNE NJORTHR PROTEUS PRYDERI REMPHAN ROBIGUS SAVITAR SERAPIS TRIGLAV VATICAN VEJOVIS ZAGREUS ALMIGHTY ASTRAEUS BISHAMON CAMAXTLI DEMIURGE DEVOTION DIVINITY GUCUMATZ INFINITE JIUROJIN KUKULKAN MIXCOATL MORPHEUS POSEIDON SABAZIOS SUMMANUS TANGAROA TERMINUS TUTELARY VEDIOVIS ZEPHYRUS OMNIPOTENT
(— OF AGRICULTURE) PICUS URASH FAUNUS AMAETHON NINGIRSU
(— OF ARTS) SIVA
(— OF ATMOSPHERE) HADAD
(— OF COMMERCE) MERCURY
(— OF CORN) CAT
(— OF DAY) HORUS
(— OF EARTH) BEL GEB KEB SEB DAGAN
(— OF EVIL) SET FOMOR FOMORIAN ZERNEBOCK
(— OF FERTILITY) SHANGO
(— OF FIRE) AGNI GIRRU NUSKU RUDRA VULCAN

(— OF FLOCKS) PAN
(— OF HAPPINESS) HOTEI JUROJIN
(— OF HEAVENS) ANU JUMALA
(— OF JUSTICE) FORSETE FORSETI
(— OF LEARNING) IMHOTEP
(— OF LOVE) AMOR ARES EROS KAMA BHAGA CUPID AENGUS
(— OF MOON) SIN ENZU NANNAR
(— OF NATURE) MARSYAS
(— OF POETRY) BRAGE BRAGI
(— OF RAIN) PARJANYA
(— OF SEA) LER VAN AEGIR DYAUS NEPTUNE PROTEUS PALAEMON POSEIDON
(— OF SKY) ANU GWYDION
(— OF SLEEP) HYPNOS HYPNUS MORPHEUS
(— OF SOUTHEAST WIND) EURUS
(— OF STORM) ZU ADAD ADDA ADDU MARUT RUDRA TESHUP
(— OF SUN) RA RE SHU SOL TEM TUM UTU AMON ATMU ATUM BAAL LLEU UTUG SAMAS SEKER SURYA APOLLO HELIOS SOKARI KHEPERA PHOEBUS SHAMASH PHAETHON TONATIUH
(— OF THUNDER) THOR DONAR PERUN PERKUN PEROUN SHANGO TLALOC HURAKAN TARANIS
(— OF UNDERWORLD) DIS BRAN GWYN YAMA HADES ORCUS PLUTO
(— OF VEGETATION) ATYS ATTIS
(— OF WAR) ER IRA ORO TIU TYR ARES COEL IRRA MARS MENT ODIN THOR MONTU NINIB MEXITL SKANDA CAMULUS MEXITLI NINURTA ENYALIUS NINGIRSU QUIRINUS
(— OF WEALTH) BHAGA KUBERA KUVERA PLUTUS
(— OF WIND) ADAD ADDA ADDU VAYU MARUT AEOLUS BOREAS EECATL
(— OF WISDOM) TAT THOTH
(— WILLING) DV
(BLIND —) HOTH HOTHR
(FALSE —) BAAL IDOL MAUMET
(FEMALE —) GODDESS
(HAWAIIAN —) AUMAKUA
(IMMORTAL —) AKAL
(INFERIOR —) PANISK
(PAGAN —) DEMON
(RAM-HEADED —) AMON KHNUM KHNEMU
(TIMELESS —) AKAL
(TUTELARY —) LAR
(UNKNOWN —) KA
(WOOD —) SILEN SILENUS
(PL.) DI DII KAMI AESIR IGIGI SUPERI PANTHEON TRIMURTI
(PREF.) DEI DEO THE(O)
GODDESS (ALSO SEE DEITY) AI NU ANA ANU ATE AYA DEA DON NUT OPS UNI VAC ANTA BADB BODB CACA DANA DANU ERIS ERUA FRIA HELA HERA JORD JUNO MAIA MEDB NIKE NINA NONA PELE SAGA SATI TARA UPIS ALLAT AMENT ANATH ANTUM ARURU BAUBO CERES CHLOE DEESS DIANA DIANE DIRGA DOLMA DOMNU EPONA FRIGG

HYBLA IAMBE ISTAR KOTYS
MAEVE NANAI NINTU PAKHT
PALES PARCA SALUS SEDNA
SKADI TANIT TYCHE USHAS
VENUS VESTA ADEONA AESTAS
ANATUM ANUKIT APHAIA
ATHENA BELILI BENDIS BOOPIS
BRIGIT CYRENE EOSTRE FRIGGA
GEFJON HELENA HESTIA HYGEIA
INNINA KISHAR LIBERA MOTHER
NINGAL PEITHO PHOBOS
POMONA PRORSA RUMINA
SEKHET SEMELE SKATHI SOTHIS
TANITH TEFNUT TRIVIA URANIA
VACUNA YDGRUN ANAHITA
ANAITIS ARTEMIS ASHERAH
DEMETER DERCETO FERONIA
FJORGYN GODHEAD KOTYTTO
LARENTA LARUNDA MAJAGGA
MAJESTA MINERVA MORNING
MORRIGU MYLITTA NEKHEBT
NEMESIS PALATUA PARBATI
PARVATI SALACIA ADRASTEA
AGLAUROS ANGERONA BELISAMA
CARMENTA CENTEOTL
COCAMAMA DESPOINA DICTYNNA
GULLVEIG MORRIGAN NEPHTHYS
PARBUTTY PRAKRITI RHIANNON
SEFEKHET THOUERIS VICTORIA
(— OF AGRICULTURE) BAU OPS
DEMETER CENTEOTL
(— OF AIR) AURA
(— OF BEAUTY) VENUS LAKSHMI
(— OF BURIAL) LIBITINA
(— OF CHILDBIRTH) LEVANA
LUCINA
(— OF DAWN) EOS USAS USHAS
AURORA MATUTA
(— OF DEW) HERSE
(— OF DISCORD) ATE ERIS
(— OF EARTH) GE LUA SEB ERDA
GAEA GAIA TARI ARURU DIONE
JORTH TERRA SEMELE TELLUS
THEMIS DAMKINA PERCHTA
(— OF FERTILITY) MA ISIS MAMA
NERTHUS
(— OF FLOWERS) FLORA CHLORIS
(— OF FORTUNE) TYCHE FORTUNA
(— OF GRAIN) CERES
(— OF HEALING) EIR GULA
(— OF HEALTH) DAMIA HYGEIA
VALETUDO
(— OF HEARTH) VESTA HESTIA
(— OF HISTORY) SAGA
(— OF HOPE) SPES
(— OF INFATUATION) ATE
(— OF JUSTICE) DIKE MAAT
THEMIS ASTRAEA NEMESIS
JUSTITIA
(— OF LEGISLATION) EUNOMIA
(— OF LOVE) ATHOR FREYA VENUS
FREYJA HATHOR
(— OF MAGIC) HECATE
(— OF MARRIAGE) HERA
(— OF MATERNITY) APET
(— OF MERCY) KWANNON
(— OF MOTHERHOOD) ISIS
(— OF NIGHT) NOX NYX
(— OF OCEAN) NINA
(— OF OVENS) FORNAX
(— OF PEACE) PAX IRENE
NERTHUS
(— OF PLEASURE) BES

(— OF RAINBOW) IRIS
(— OF SEASONS) DIKE HORA
(— OF THE DEAD) HEL HELA
(— OF THE HUNT) DIANA VACUNA
ARTEMIS
(— OF THE MOON) LUNA MOON
DIANA SELENA TANITH ARTEMIS
(— OF THE SEA) INO RAN DORIS
BRANWEN EURYNOME
(— OF TRUTH) MAAT
(— OF VEGETATION) OPS CERES
COTYS COTYTTO
(— OF VENGEANCE) ARA NEMESIS
(— OF VICTORY) NIKE
(— OF WAR) ENYO ANATH ANATU
ANUNIT BELLONA
(— OF WATER) ANAHITA
(— OF WEALTH) LAKSHMI
(— OF WISDOM) ATHENA MINERVA
(— OF YOUTH) HEBE JUVENTAS
(COW-HEADED —) ISIS
(ESKIMO —) SEDNA
(FERTILITY —) ASTARTE
(MARRIAGE —) VOR
(SUBORDINATE —) DEMIURGE
(THUNDER-SMITTEN —) SEMELE
KERAUNIA
(3-HEADED —) HECATE
(PL.) HORAE MATRIS POINAE
ASYNJUR
GO-DEVIL TRAVOIS ALLIGATOR
GODFATHER GOSSIP GODPAPA
PADRINO SPONSOR GODPHERE
GODHEAD DEITY GODHOOD
DIVINITY
GODLESS WICKED ATHEIST
IMPIOUS PROFANE UNGODLY
GODLESSNESS ATHEISM
GODLIKE DEIFIC DIVINE IMMORTAL
OLYMPIAN
GODLINESS PIETISM SANCTITY
GODLING DEVATA GENIUS GODKIN
GODLET PANISC DEMIGOD
PANISCUS
GODLY HOLY WISE PIOUS DEVOUT
GRACIOUS
GODMOTHER CUMMER GOSSIP
SPONSOR GODMAMMA MARRAINE
GODPARENT SPONSOR
GOD'S S
GODSON FILLEUL GODCHILD
GOD TREE CEIBA
GODWIT PICK PRINE BARKER
MARLIN SCAMMEL YARWHIP
RINGTAIL SHRIEKER SPOTRUMP
YARDKEEP YARWHELP
GOFFER QUILL FULLER GAUFFER
GOG (FATHER OF —) SHEMAIAH
GO-GETTER HUSTLER
GOGGLER SCAD
GOGLET COOJA SERAI MONKEY
SURAHI GURGLET SURAHEE
GOING FARE GAIT BOUND AGOING
WAYING PASSADO SLEDDING
(— ABOUT) AROUND
(— BEYOND OTHERS) ULTRA
(— IN) INEUNT INFARE INGOING
(— ON) FARE AGATE TOWARD
(— OUT) EGRESS
(— UP) ANABASIS
(SUFF.) GRESS
GOITER WEN GLANS GOITRE
STRUMA BRONCHOCELE

GOITERED ANTELOPE ZENU
GOITROUS STRUMOUS
GOLD OR ORO RED SOL DORE GILT
GULL ALTUN AURUM GUILD
METAL OCHER OCHRE RIDGE
SHINY GOLDEN OBRIZE ORMOLU
YELLOW BULLION SPANKER
(— PIECE) TALI
(GREENISH —) AENEUS AENEOUS
(IMITATION —) PINCHBECK
(PREF.) AUR(I) AUREO CHRYS(O)
ORI
GOLDBEATER (TOOL OF —) WAGON
GOLDCREST MOON TIDLEY
MUDDLER TROCHIL
GOLDEN RED DORE GOLD BLEST
DURRY GOLDY SUNNY AUREAL
BLONDE GILDEN GILTEN AUREATE
AUREOUS HALCYON AURULENT
DEAURATE
(— STATE) CALIFORNIA
GOLDEN ASS (AUTHOR OF —)
APULEIUS
(CHARACTER IN —) ISIS MILO FOTIS
LUCIUS CHARITES PAMPHILE
SOCRATES BYRRHAENA
LEPOLEMUS THRASILLUS
ARISTOMENES
GOLDEN BOWL (AUTHOR OF —)
JAMES
(CHARACTER IN —) ADAM STANT
MAGGIE VERVER AMERIGO
CHARLOTTE
GOLDEN CHAIN LABURNUM
GOLDEN CLUB TAWKEE TAWKIN
TUCKAHOE
GOLDEN EAGLE RINGTAIL
GOLDENEYE CUR GARROT
COBHEAD GOWDNIE BULLHEAD
IRONHEAD MORILLON WHIFFLER
WHISTLER
GOLDEN ORIOLE PIROL WITWALL
GOLDEN PLOVER KOLEA
FROGSKIN SQUEALER WHISTLER
GOLDEN RAGWORT LIFEROOT
GOLDENROD BONEWORT
SOLIDAGO JIMMYWEED
GOLDENSEAL EYEBALM EYEROOT
ICEROOT PUCCOON
GOLDEN SHINER CHUB DACE
WINDFISH
GOLDFINCH JACK FINCH GOLDY
GOWDY CANARY REDCAP
FLAXBIRD GRAYPATE
GOLDFINNY CONNER GOLDNEY
CORKWING
GOLDFISH FUNA MOOR COMET
CALICO FANTAIL CYPRINID
VEILTAIL
GOLD-OF-PLEASURE FLAX
MADWORT OILSEED
GOLDSMITH SONAR AURIFEX
ENGLISH HILLIARD
FRENCH MEISSONIER
GERMAN JAMNITZER
ITALIAN LEONI ROBBIA
WELSH MYDDELTON
GOLFER TEER
GOMER (FATHER OF —) JAPHETH
(HUSBAND OF —) HOSEA
GOMUTI EJOO IROK ARENG KITTUL
SAGWIRE SAGOWEER
GONAD GERMEN

GONCALO ALVES KINGWOOD
GONDOLA GON BARGE
GUNDALOW
GONE AWAY LOST NAPOO
(— BY) AGO DONE PAST AGONE
PASSE BEHIND BYGONE
(— OUT OF USE) EXTINCT
(— TO PIECES) HAYWIRE
**GONE WITH THE WIND (AUTHOR
OF —)** MITCHELL
(CHARACTER IN —) FRANK OHARA
RHETT ASHLEY BUTLER WILKES
CHARLES KENNEDY MELANIE
HAMILTON SCARLETT
GONG BELL CLOCK GANGSA
DOORBELL
(SERIES OF —S) BONANG
GONGORISM CULTISM
GONOPHORE MEDUSOID
SPOROSAC
GOOD BON GAY TOP TRY ABLE
BEAU BEIN BIEN BOON BRAW
FINE GAIN HEND NICE NOTE
PROW SAKE BONNY BONUM
BRAVE BULLY CANNY FRESH
GWEED JELLY KAPAI PAKKA
PUKKA SEELY SOUND VALID
BENIGN BRAWLY BUCKRA DIVINE
EXPERT FACTOR FORBYE HONEST
MABUTI PRETTY PROFIT PROPER
WEALTH BENEFIT COPIOUS
CORKING FAIRISH FORTHBY
GODLIKE GRADELY HELPFUL
LIBERAL SNIFTER STAVING
TRAINED UPRIGHT BUDGEREE
GRAITHLY INTEREST LAUDABLE
PLEASING SALUTARY SKILLFUL
SUITABLE
(EXCEPTIONALLY —) SLAMBANG
(EXTREMELY —) SLICK
(HOLD —) BEAR
(INFINITELY —) HOLY
(MIGHTY —) SKOOKUM
(NO —) DUFF NAPOO NAPOOH
(PRETTY —) FAIR TIDY
(RELATIVELY —) SMOOTH
(SUPERLATIVELY —) BRAG
BEAUTIFUL
(SUPREMELY —) IMMENSE
GORGEOUS
(SURPASSINGLY —) SUPERIOR
(VERY —) HOT TOP DANDY DICTY
GRAND NIFTY BONZER BOSHTA
BOSKER BOSHTER NAILING
SPLENDID SWINGING
(PREF.) AGATH(O) BENI EU
GOOD-BYE BY BYE TATA ADDIO
ADIEU ADIOS LULLABY FAREWELL
SAYONARA
**GOOD COMPANIONS (AUTHOR OF
—)** PRIESTLEY
(CHARACTER IN —) DEAN HUGH
NUNN ELSIE INIGO JERRY JIMMY
SUSIE TRANT JESIAH OAKROYD
ELIZABETH JOLLIFANT
LONGSTAFF MCFARLANE
JERNINGHAM
GOOD EARTH (AUTHOR OF —)
BUCK
(CHARACTER IN —) LIU LUNG
NUNG OLAN PEAR WANG CHING
HWANG LOTUS
GOOD-FOR-NAUGHT LOSEL

GOOD-FOR-NOTHING BUM ORRA SLIM SLINK DONNOT KEFFEL RIBALD STUMER BRETHEL FUSTIAN SCROYLE SHOTTEN SKEEZIX SKELLUM SKYBALD VAURIEN WOSBIRD VAGABOND

GOOD-HUMORED SONSY

GOOD-KING-HENRY BLITE ALLGOOD MARKERY MERCURY CHENOPOD

GOOD-LOOKING BRAW FAIR FOXY MOOI BONNY GAWSY COMELY PRETTY SEEMLY EYESOME GRADELY WINSOME GOODLIKE HANDSOME STUNNING

GOODLY BOON PROPER GOODLIKE

GOOD-NATURED SONSY CLEVER AMIABLE

GOODNESS BONTE BONUM MENSK PROOF BONITY BOUNTY SATTVA VIRTUE KINDNESS

GOODS FEE BONA GEAR KIND PELF CARGO STUFF TRADE WORLD WRACK ADVANCE CAPITAL CHATTEL EFFECTS FINANCE HAVINGS INSIGHT TRAFFIC CHAFFERY HIGGLERY PROPERTY
(**— BARTERED)** DICKER
(**— CAST OVERBOARD)** JETSAM
(**— SUNK IN SEA)** LAGAN LIGAN LAGEND
(**DRY —)** DRAPERY
(**HOUSEHOLD —)** INSIGHT
(**IMPERFECT —)** FENT
(**INFERIOR —)** BRACK
(**PIECE —)** CUTTANEE
(**SECONDHAND —)** BROKERY
(**SLOW-SELLING —)** JOBS
(**STOLEN — THROWN AWAY)** WAIF
(**SURPLUS —)** OVERAGE
(**VALUABLE —)** SWAG

GOOD-SIZED HEFTY GAWSIE

GOOD-TASTING DAINTY

GOODWILL GREE PHILANTHROPY

GOODY-GOODY PI MOLLYCODDLE

GOOEY CLARTY

GOOF BOOB GOOFER

GOOGLY BOSEY WRONGUN

GOON MUSCLEMAN

GOOSANDER JACKSAW RANTOCK

GOOSE ELK LAMA NENE ROUT BRANT BRENT EMDEN HANSA HOBBY ROMAN SOLAN WAVEY CAGMAG CANADA EMBDEN GALOOT GANDER GOSLET HISSER HONKER SOLAND AFRICAN BLACKIE BUSTARD GAGGLER GOSLING GRAYLAG GREASER GREYLAG OUTARDE WIDGEON BALDHEAD BARGOOSE BARNACLE BERNICLE SPURWING TOULOUSE
(**MYTHICAL —)** GANZA
(**PART OF —)** BOW EAR EYE TOE WEB BEAN BILL CAPE FOOT KEEL RUMP WING FLUFF SHANK BREAST COVERT DEWLAP SADDLE FEATHER NOSTRIL SHOULDER SECONDARY
(**PREF.)** CHEN(O)

GOOSEBERRY BLOB FABE FAPE POHA BRAGAS GOBLIN GOZILL GROZER DOWNING GASKINS GROZART CARBERRY CATBERRY DOGBERRY EATBERRY FEABERRY GOOSEGOG HOUGHTON INDUSTRY
(**PL.)** THAPES

GOOSE EGG DUCK

GOOSEFOOT BLITE ORACH BASSIA KOCHIA ORACHE QUINOA ALLSEED PIGWEED

GOOSEGIRL GOSSARD

GOOSE GRASS HERIF HARIFFE CLEAVERS

GOOSEHERD GOZZARD GOOSEBOY

GOOSENECK ROOSTER

GOPHER TUZA GAUFFRE GEOMYID MUNGOFA QUACHIL SALAMICH TUCOTUCO
(**— STATE)** MINNESOTA

GOPHERMAN SWAMPER

GOPHERWOOD FUSTIC

GORBODUC (**SON OF —)** FERREX PORREX

GORDIUS (**SON OF —)** MIDAS

GORE CLY CLOY GARE HIKE HIPE HOOK HORN PICK PIKE SHOT CRUOR GODET STICK GORING GUSSET

GOREVAN AUBURN

GORGE GAP JAM FILL GASH GAUM GLUT JAMB KHOR RENT BREAK CAJON CANON CHASM CHINE CLUSE DRAFT FARCE FLUME GULLY GURGE KLOOF PONGO POUCH STECH STRID STUFF TANGI CANYON DEFILE NULLAH RAVINE STODGE STRAIT THROAT COULOIR DATIATE DRAUGHT ENGORGE SATIATE SLABBER BARRANCA QUEBRADA

GORGED ACCOLLE

GORGEOUS VAIN GRAND SHOWY COSTLY DAZZLING GLORIOUS SPLENDID

GORGERIN NECK NECKING

GORGIBUS (**DAUGHTER OF —)** CELIE

GORGING STODGE

GORGON MEDUSA STHENO EURYALE

GORGOPHONE (**FATHER OF —)** PERSEUS
(**HUSBAND OF —)** OEBALUS PERIERES
(**MOTHER OF —)** ANDROMEDA
(**SON OF —)** ICARIUS APHAREUS LEUCIPPUS TYNDAREUS

GORILLA APE PIGMY PYGMY

GORING CORNUPETE

GORMANDIZE STECH STEGH GUTTLE

GORMANDIZER HELLUO GLUTTON

GORSE ULEX WHIN FURZE GORST

GORY BLOODY

GOSHAWK GOS ASTUR TERCEL

GOSLING GULL

GOSPEL SPELL DHARMA EVANGEL KERUGMA KERYGMA SYNOPTIC
(**— OF REDEMPTION)** CROSS
(**PL.)** TEXT

GOSSAMER MOUSEWEB STARDUST

GOSSIP EME GUP PIE AUNT BLAB BUZZ CANT CLAT CONK COZE DIRT NEWS TALK CAUSE CLACK CLASH CLYPE COOSE CRACK FERLY FRUMP GOSSY SIEVE YENTA BABBLE CACKLE CADDLE CALLET CAMPER CLAVER CUMMER FERLIE JANGLE KIMMER NORATE TATTLE TITTLE CLATTER COMPERE GOSTHER HASHGOB NASHGAB SCANDAL TATTLER TRATTLE CAUSERIE CHITCHAT GOSSIPRY QUIDNUNC SCHMOOZE NEWSMONGER

GOSSIPY BUZZY NEWSY CHATTY

GOTH GOTHIAN SUIOGOTH VISIGOTH

GOTHAM ABDERA

GOTHAMITE ABDERITE

GOTHIC OGIVAL

GOTTERDAMMERUNG
(**CHARACTER IN —)** HAGEN GUNTHER GUTRUNE SIEGFRIED WALTRAUTE BRUNNHILDE
(**COMPOSER OF —)** WAGNER

GOUGE DIG PUG BENT SCUFF CHISEL FLUKAN GOUGER HOLLOW SCRIBE FLOOKAN SCORPER SELVAGE SELVEDGE STICKING
(**— OUT)** BULLDOZE
(**V-TYPE —)** VEINER

GOUGER CHISELLER

GOURD MATE PEPO LUFFA ABOBRA JICARA PATOLA ANGURIA DISHRAG HECHIMA CALABASH CUCURBIT PEPONIDA PEPONIUM

GOURMAND EPICURE GLUTTON GORMAND

GOURMET PALATE EPICURE GOURMAND

GOUT GUT CLOT DROP SPLASH PODAGRA PODAGRY CHIRAGRA ARTHRITIS
(**SUFF.)** AGRA

GOUTTE DROP ICICLE

GOUTWEED AXWEED ASHWEED ACHEWEED AISEWEED BOLEWORT GOATWEED GOUTWORT

GOUTY PODAGRAL PODAGRIC

GOVERN RUN WIN CURB KING LEAD REDE REIN RULE SWAY WALD WARD WIND YEME GUIDE JUDGE REGLE STEER TREAT WIELD BRIDLE DIRECT MANAGE ORDAIN POLICE POLICY TEMPER COMMAND CONDUCT CONTROL PRESIDE REFRAIN DISPENSE DOMINATE IMPERATE MODERATE OVERRULE OVERSWAY POLICIZE REGULATE RESTRAIN

GOVERNED BENT

GOVERNESS ABBESS DUENNA FRAULEIN MISTRESS MADEMOISELLE

GOVERNING REGENT REGITIVE

GOVERNMENT GATE LAND RULE KREIS METRO POWER STATE STEER DURBAR HAVANA POLICY RULING CABINET CZARISM DIARCHY DYARCHY RECTION REGENCY REGIMEN TSARISM CIVILITY ENDARCHY GOBIERNO HEGEMONY ISOCRACY ISOCRYME KINGSHIP STEERING ABSOLUTISM
(**— BY FEW)** OLIGARCHY
(**— BY GOD)** THEONOMY
(**— BY MOB)** OCHLOCRACY
(**— BY WEALTHY)** PLUTOCRACY
(**— BY WOMEN)** GYNARCHY
(**— BY 10)** DECARCHY
(**— BY 2)** DIARCHY DUARCHY
(**— OF CEYLON)** DISSAVA
(**— OF TURKEY)** GATE PORTE
(**ARBITRARY —)** ABSOLUTISM
(**CHURCH —)** PRELACY
(**INDIAN —)** CIRCAR SIRCAR
(**MALAYSIAN —)** KOMPENI
(**MOROCCAN —)** MAGHZEN MAKHZAN
(**PREF.)** CRATO
(**WITHOUT —)** ANARCH(O)
(**SUFF.)** ARCH ARCHIC ARCHY CRACY CRAT(IC)

GOVERNMENTAL ARCHICAL

GOVERNOR BAN BEY DEY EARL KAID LORD NAIK TUTU VALI BANUS CLEON DEWAN DIWAN HAKIM NABOB NAZIM SHEIK SUBAH TUPAN AUTHOR DYNAST GRIEVE LEGATE MOODIR MYOWUN NAIGUE NAIQUE PATESI PENLOP RECTOR REGENT SACHEM SATRAP SHEIKH SHERIF TUCHUN WARDEN CATAPAN DAROGHA LEONATO PODESTA RECTRIX SERKALI SHEREEF TOPARCH TSUNGTU VICEROY WIELDER AUTOCRAT BURGRAVE ETHNARCH HOSPODAR LANDVOGT MISTRESS RESIDENT SUBAHDAR TETRARCH CASTELLAN PRESIDENT PROCONSUL
(**— OF ALGIERS)** DEY DISAWA
(**— OF BURMA)** WUN WOON
(**— OF EGYPT)** MUDIR
(**— OF FORTRESS)** ALCAIDE ALCAYDE
(**— OF SHIRE)** ALDERMAN
(**— OF TAMMANY)** SACHEM
(**BYZANTINE —)** EXARCH CATAPAN
(**CEYLON —)** DISAWA
(**GERMAN —)** LANDVOGT
(**GREEK —)** ETHNARCH
(**JAPANESE —)** SHOGUN TYCOON
(**PAPAL —)** LEGATE
(**ROMAN —)** TETRARCH
(**SELJUK —)** ATABEG ATABEK
(**SPARTAN —)** HARMOST
(**TURKISH —)** BEY WALI MUDIR KEHAYA

GOVERNOR-GENERAL VALI

GOWDIE SCULPIN

GOWK CUCKOO

GOWN GOR SAC GITE GORE HUKE JAMA RAIL SACK SILK TOGA BANIA DRESS FROCK GOUND HABIT JAMAH MANTO TABBY TOOSH BANIAN BANIYA CAFTAN CAMISE CANDYS CHITON JESUIT JOHNNY KIMONO KIRTLE KITTEL LEVITE MANTUA ARISARD CASSOCK GARMENT JOHNNIE SLAMKIN SULTANA SULTANE WRAPPER CAMISOLE GANDOURA MAZARINE PEIGNOIR
(**HAWAIIAN —)** MOLOKU MUUMUU

GOYA CURRANT
GOYIM GENTES
GRAB NAB NAP RAP GLAM GOPE GLAUM SCRAB CLUTCH COLLAR CRATCH DIPPER NIPPER NOBBLE SNATCH CRAPPLE GRABBLE GRAPNEL GRAPPLE NIPPERS
GRABEN TROUGH
GRABWEED BISHOPWEED
GRACE EST ORE BEAT ESTE GARB HELD SWAY ADORN COULE FAVOR HONOR MENSE MENSK MERCY SLIDE THANK VENUS BEAUTY BECOME BEDECK CHARIS POLISH RELISH THALIA AGGRACE CHARISM COMMEND DIGNITY FINESSE GRATIFY MELISMA MORDENT BACKFALL BEAUTIFY BLESSING DECORATE EASINESS ELEGANCE FELICITY GRATUITY LEVATION ORNAMENT
(— OF FORM) FLOW SWAY TOURNURE
GRACEFUL AIRY FEAT GENT BONNY GENTY GRATE COMELY FEATLY FELINE FLUENT GAINLY QUAINT SEEMLY SILKEN VENUST ELEGANT FITTING GENTEEL GRACILE SYLPHID WILLOWY CHARMING DELICATE GRACIOUS LEGGIERO MACEVOLE SWANLIKE SYLPHISH
(PREF.) ABRO HABRO
GRACEFULLY FAIR FEATLY HAPPILY LEGGIERO
GRACEFULNESS JOLLITY ELEGANCE
GRACELESS AWKWARD
GRACES CHARITES
GRACIOUS GOOD HEND HOLD KIND MILD CIVIL GODLY HAPPY LUCKY SUAVE WINLY BENIGN GENIAL GENTLE GOODLY KINDLY AFFABLE CORDIAL WINSOME BENEDICT DEBONAIR GENEROUS HANDSOME MERCIFUL PLEASING SOCIABLE BENIGNANT
GRACIOUSLY FAIR SWEETLY
GRACIOUSNESS GRACE MENSK FACILITY GRATUITY
GRACKLE BEO DAW JACKDAW BOATTAIL TINKLING TROOPIAL
GRADATION HUE CLINE ABLAUT CLIMAX NUANCE GEOCLINE STRENGTH
GRADE CUT BANK CHOP EVEN FORM MARK RANK SIZE STEP GLIDE LEVEL ORDER PLANE SCORE SIEGE STAGE ASCENT DEGREE RATING STAPLE TRIAGE FAILURE INCLINE INSPECT DEMISANG GRADIENT GRADUATE MERIDIAN STANDARD
(— DOWN) FAULT
(— LUMBER) SURVEY
(— OF BEEF) GOOD CUTTER
(— OF LUMBER) CULL
(— OF OAK) WAINSCOT
(— OF OFFICER) CORNET
(— ROAD) IMPROVE
(ABLAUT —) GUNA
(DESIGNED FOR USE IN —S 1-12) ELHI

(SUPERIOR —) SUPER
(THIRD —) FAIR
GRADER PLANER CLASSER SCRAPER
GRADIENT GRADE LAPSE SLOPE ASCENT INCLINE DOWNHILL
(SUFF.) CLINAL CLINE
GRADIN GRADINO PREDELLA
GRADUAL EASY FLAT SLOW GRAIL GENTLE LENTOUS STEPWISE PIECEMEAL
GRADUALLY GENTLY EDGINGLY GRADATIM INCHMEAL PIECEMEAL
GRADUATE GRAD GRADE ALUMNA DIVIDE FELLOW ALUMNUS GRADATE BACHELOR
(EISTEDDFOD —) OVATE
GRADUATED SCALAR MEASURED
GRADUATION CLICK
GRAFT BUD IMP PIE CION WORK GRAFF GRAVY INEYE SCION BOODLE INARCH PAYOLA SPLICE ENGRAFT IMPLANT JOBBERY SQUEEZE TOPWORK APPROACH BOODLING GRAFTING INSITION
GRAFTED ENTE
GRAFTER BOODLER
GRAFTING GRAFTAGE INSITION
(PREF.) GREFFO
GRAIL CUP GRAAL CHALICE SANGRAAL
GRAIN JOT RUN RYE WAY CORN CURN DANA KERN PILE RICE SAND SEED WALE WOOD EMMER FIBER FIBRE FUNDI GAVEL GLEBE GRIST PANIC SCRAP SPARK STUFF TRACE WHEAT ANNONA BARLEY BRAINS CEREAL CURRAN GROATS KERNEL FRUMENT GRANULE PANICLE VICTUAL GRAINING PARTICLE STRAIGHT SWEEPAGE
(— FOR MUSH) KASHA
(— FROM MASH TUN) DRAINS
(— LEFT AFTER HARVEST) GAVEL SHACK
(— MEASURE) THRAVE
(— OF BOARD) BEAT
(— OF CORN) PICKLE
(— OF GOLD) PIPPIN
(— OF WOOD) BATE
(CHAFF OF —) BRAN
(COARSE —) THIRD
(COARSELY GROUND —) MEAL GRITS KIBBLE
(DAMAGED —) SALVAGE
(EAR OF —) SPIKE RISSOM RIZZON
(GERMINATED —) MALT
(GROUND —) GRIST
(HANDFUL OF —) REAP
(HULLED —) GRITS GROUT GROATS SHELLING
(HUSKED —) SHEALING SHILLING
(MILLET —) CUSCUS
(MIXED —) MASLIN
(MIXED —S) DREDGE
(PARCHED —) GRADDAN
(REFUSE —) SHAG DRAFF
(SACRIFICIAL —) ADOR
(SHOCK OF —) COP
(STACK OF —) HOVEL
(STORED —) MOW
(STREAKED —) ROEY
(PL.) PICKLES RAGGING

(PREF.) CHONDR(I)(IO)(O) COCC(O) GRANI GRANUL(I)(O) SITIO SITO
(SUFF.) COCCAL COCCIC
GRAIN BEETLE CADELLE
GRAINER DICER BOARDER
GRAINSMAN THROWER DRAFFMAN
GRAIN SORGHUM DURRA SHALLU
GRAM KHESARI
(MILLIONTH —) GAMMA
GRAMMAR DONAT SYNTAX GRAMARY PRISCIAN
(TYPE OF —) TAGMEMIC
GRAMMARIAN PRISCIAN
GRAMPUS ORC COWFISH DOLPHIN SPRINGER
GRANARY GOLA GUNJ SILO GOLAH GUNGE LATHE GARNER GIRNEL GRANGE HORREUM RESERVE CORNLOFT GRAINERY
GRAND OLD AIRY BRAW EPIC MAIN TALL CHIEF GREAT LOFTY NOBLE PROUD SHOWY SWELL WLONK ANDEAN AUGUST COSMIC EPICAL FAMOUS GLOBAL KINGLY LORDLY SIGHTY SUPERB SWANKY EXALTER IMMENSE STATELY SUBLIME COSMICAL FOREMOST GLORIOUS GORGEOUS IMPOSING MAJESTIC SPLENDID MAGNIFICENT
(PREF.) BEL
GRAND CANYON STATE ARIZONA
GRANDCHILD OE OY OYE
(GREAT —) IEROE
GRANDDAUGHTER NIECE
GRANDEE DON GRAND OMRAH BASHAW GRANDO MAGNATE
GRANDEUR POMP STATE ESTATE FIGURE PARADE MAJESTY ELEGANCE GRANDEZA HAUTESSE NOBILITY SPLENDOR VASTNESS
GRANDFATHER AIEL NONO BOBBY GRAMP ATAVUS GRAMPS BELSIRE GRANDAD GRANDPA GRANDFER GUIDSIRE
(GREAT —) NONO
(GREAT-GREAT-GREAT —) QUATRAYLE
GRAND HOTEL (AUTHOR OF —) BAUM
(CHARACTER IN —) ANNA OTTO FLAMM GAIGERN PREYSING ELISAVETA FLAEMMCHEN KRINGELEIN GRUSINSKAYA OTTERNSCHLAG
GRANDILOQUENT TALL HEROIC TURGID BOMBAST MAGNIFIC RHETORICAL
GRANDIOSE GRAND COSMIC TURGID SUBLIME COSMICAL IMPERIAL
GRANDISSIMUS (AUTHOR OF —) CABLE
(CHARACTER IN —) KEENE AURORA HONORE JOSEPH PALMYRE AGRICOLA CLOTILDE FUSILIER NANCANOU FROWENFIELD GRANDISSIMUS
GRANDMOTHER GRAM GRAN LUCKY NANNY GRANNY GUDAME LUCKIE BELDAME NOKOMIS BABUSHKA GRANDAME

GRANDMOTHERS (AUTHOR OF —) WESTCOTT
(CHARACTER IN —) JIM EVAN ROSE ALWYN FLORA HENRY NANCY RALPH TOWER CANNON SERENA LEANDER MARIANNE
GRANDPARENT TUTU TUPUNA
GRAND SLAM VOLE
GRANDSON NEPHEW NEPOTE
GRANITE MOYITE RUNITE GREISEN SYENITE ALASKITE RAPAKIVI PEGMATITE
(— STATE) NEWHAMPSHIRE
(DECOMPOSED —) GROWAN
(PREF.) PEGMATO SYENO
GRANITEWARE GRAYWARE
GRANNY TUTU BABUSHKA
GRANT AID FEU BOOK BOON CEDE ENAM GALE GIFT GIVE HEAR LEND LOAN MISE SEND STOW YARK ADMIT AFFORD ALLOW AWARD BONUS CHART COWLE FLOAT FUERO LEASE SEIZE SPARE TITHE YETTE YIELD ACCEDE ACCORD AFFORD ASSENT BESTOW BETAKE BETEEM BOUNTY CONFER DESIGN EXTEND FIRMAN IMPART JAGEER NOVATE OCTROI PATENT PERMIT REMISE ADJUDGE APPOINT COLLATE CONCEDE CONSENT DISPONE INDULGE LICENSE PRESENT PROMISE SUBSIDY TRIBUTE APPANAGE BESTOWAL CONTRACT DONATION EXCHANGE MONOPOLY PITTANCE TRANSFER CONCESSION ACKNOWLEDGE
(— AS PROPER) ACCORD
(— OF LAND) FEU ENAM GALE PATA SASAN CASATE
(— PERMISSION) ALLOW DISPENSE
(— RELIEF) FORGIVE
(— TIME) FRIST
(INDIAN —) ENAM COWLE SASAN JAGEER JAGHIR
(PL.) PORK
GRANTING IF ALTHO REMISE ALTHOUGH ACCORDANCE
GRANTOR LESSOR
GRANULAR CORN OPEN GRAINY
GRANULATE CORN KERN GRAIN SUGAR
GRANULATED CORN GRANULAR
GRANULATION SUGARING
GRANULE GRIT GRANUM LUCULE NODULE BIOBLAST GONIDIUM GRANULET
(ALTMANN'S —S) BIOPLAST
(ICE —S) FRAZIL
(SUFF.) PLAST
GRAPE UVA VINE BERRY GRAIN PINOT TOKAY ACINUS AGAWAM ISABEL MALAGA MONICA MUSCAT RAISIN VERDEA WORDEN CATAWBA CONCORD HAMBURG MALMSEY MISSION NIAGARA SULTANA CABERNET DELAWARE GRAPELET HANEPOOT ISABELLA LABRUSCA MALVASIA MORILLON MOUNTAIN MUSCATEL NUCULANE RIESLING SLIPSKIN SYLVANER THOMPSON VINIFERA MUSCADINE

(PL.) RAPE UVAE
(PREF.) ACINI UVI UVULO
GRAPEFRUIT POMELO POMOLO
POMMELO TORONJA
GRAPE HYACINTH MUSK
GRAPE JUICE MUST SAPA STUM
GRAPENUTS TERRAPIN
GRAPEROOT BERBERIS
GRAPES
(PREF.) (BUNCH OF —) BOTRY(O)
STAPHYL(O)
**GRAPES OF WRATH (AUTHOR OF
—)** STEINBECK
(CHARACTER IN —) AL JIM TOM
JOAD NOAH ROSE CASEY MULEY
CONNIE GRAVES RUTHIE
WINFIELD
GRAPESTONE
(PREF.) ACINI
GRAPEVINE
(PREF.) AMPEL(O)
GRAPH CHART CURVE OGIVE
TRACE CONTOUR DIAGRAM
PROFILE ISOPLETH
GRAPHIC PICTORIAL PICTURESQUE
GRAPHITE WAD KISH LEAD WADD
KEESH PENCIL PLUMBAGO
MODERATOR
GRAPNEL CROW DRAG GRAB
CREEP CREEPER GRABBLE
GRAPPLE SNIGGER GRABHOOK
GRAPPLE DOG CLOSE GRASP
GRIPE LATCH BUCKLE CLINCH
GRABBLE GRAPNEL GRIPPLE
SNIGGER SNIGGLE WRESTLE
(— QUARRY) BIND
GRAPPLING IRON CLIP DRAG
CLASP CRAMP CORVUS CRAMPER
CRAMPON CREEPER GRAPNEL
GRAPPLE HARPAGO
GRAPTOLITHA XYLINA
GRASP HUG NAP SEE CLAM CLAW
CLUM FAKE FANG FIST GLAM
GRAB GRIP HAND HENT HOLD
SNAP SPAN TAKE VICE CATCH
CINCH CLAMP CLASP CLAUT
CLEUK GRIPE GROPE LATCH
SAVVY SEIZE SENSE SHAKE
SPEND CLENCH CLINCH CLUTCH
COLLAR FATHOM GOUPEN
RUMBLE SNATCH CLAUGHT
COMPASS ENCLOSE GRAPPLE
GRIPPLE SMITTLE CONCEIVE
HANDFAST HOLDFAST
(— FULLY) SWALLOW
(— MENTALLY) ENVISAGE
(— OF REALITY) EPIPHANY
(PREF.) CHADA
GRASPING HARD NIPPY SNACK
GRABBY GREEDY GRIPPY HAVING
TAKING BROKING MISERLY
PUGGING COVETOUS HANDGRIP
AVARICIOUS
GRASS BON FAG FOG POA RAY
BENT COIX DISS DOOB GAMA
HERB ICHU KANS KUSA MUNJ
MUSK RAGI TARE TORE USAR
ANKEE BARIT BROME COGON
COUCH CROFT DRAWK DRINN
FLAWN FUNDI GARSE GIRSE
GLAGA GRAMA HARIF HAVER
HICHU ILLUK KOGON KUSHA
KWEEK MELIC MUHLY PANIC

QUILA REESK ROOSA SEREH SPIRE
STIPA SUDAN ZORRA BARLEY
BHABAR BHARTI DARNEL
EMOLOA FESCUE FIORIN GLUMAL
KIKUYU QUITCH RAGGEE REDTOP
RIPGUT SCUTCH TOETOE TWITCH
ZACATE AMOURET CANNACH
DOGFOOT ESPARTO EULALIA
FESTUCA FINETOP FOXTAIL
GALLETA GOLDEYE HERBAGE
HORDEUM JARAGUA MATWEED
MUSCOVY PANICLE PASTURE
PIGROOT SETARIA SORGHUM
TIMOTHY TOCUSSO TUSSOCK
VETIVER ZACATON AEGILOPS
BLUESTEM BROWNTOP CALFKILL
CAMALOTE CELERITY COCKSPUR
DOGSTAIL DRAWLING DROPSEED
EELGRASS ELEUSINE FINEBENT
GAMELOTE MANGRASS
MATGRASS PASPALUM
SANDBURR SANDSPUR SANDSTAY
SPANIARD SPARTINA SPINIFEX
SWEEPAGE TEOSINTE WHITETOP
MARIJUANA
(— AMONG GRAIN) DRAWK
(— FOR STOCK) EATAGE
(— FOR THATCHING) BANGO
(— ON BORDER OF FIELD) RAND
(— READY FOR REAPING) SWATH
SWATHE
(AROMATIC —) KHUS CUSCUS
KHUSKHUS
(BEACH —) STAR
(BERMUDA —) DOOB SCUTCH
(COARSE —) FAG RISP TATH
COGON REESK LALANG SNIDDLE
(COUCH —) CUTCH KWEEK QUITCH
SCUTCH STROIL SQUITCH
(CURED —) HAY
(DEAD —) FOG FOGGAGE
(DITCH —) ENALID
(GOOSE —) CLIVERS CLEAVERS
(MEADOW —) POA
(NUT —) COCO COCOA
(ORCHARD —) DOGFOOT
(PART OF —) AWN TIP APEX CULM
LEAF NODE ROOT STEM BLADE
BRACT GLUME SHOOT FLORET
FLOWER LIGULE SHEATH TILLER
PEDICEL RHIZOME SPIKELET
(PASTURE —) TORE GRAMMA
(POVERTY —) HEATH
(QUAKING —) SHAKER
(REED —) CARRIZO
(REEDLIKE —) BENT DISS
(SUDAN —) GARAWI
(SWEET —) SORGO
(PREF.) CHORTO GRAMIN(I)(O)
HERBI
GRASS-EATING
(PREF.) POE
GRASSERIE JAUNDICE
GRASSHOPPER GRIG CICADA
HOPPER QUAKER SAWYER TETTIX
ACRIDID CRICKET KATYDID
SKIPPER ACRIDIAN LANGOSTA
GRASSLAND HAM LEA RAKH VELD
VELDT BOTTOM MEADOW
PATANA LEYLAND PASTURE
SAVANNA
(TRACT OF —) PRAIRIE
(PL.) SCHIH

GRASS PEA LANG KHESARI
GRASSQUIT QUAT QUIT CIVITE
GRASS TREE BLACKBOY
GRASSY HERBY
GRATE JAR FRET GRIT RASP
CHARK CHIRK DANDY DEVIL
GRIDE GRIND RANGE STOVE
ABRADE CHAFER SCRAPE SCREAR
SCREEK SCROOP GRATING
MANGRATE
(FALSE —) DANDY
GRATEFUL KIND SAPID WELCOME
THANKFUL
GRATEFULNESS GRATUITY
GRATIANO (BROTHER OF —)
BRABANTIO
(WIFE OF —) NERISSA
GRATIFICATION GLUT GUST
LUXURY RELISH REWARD SATIETY
DELICACY GRATUITY PLEASURE
TICKLING SATISFACTION
GRATIFIED GLAD PROUD
CHARMED CONTENT PLEASED
GRATIFY PAY BABY FEED LUST
AMUSE FEAST FLESH GRACE
HUMOR MIRTH QUEME SAVOR
SERVE STILL WREAK ARRIDE
FOSTER OBLIGE PAMPER PLEASE
REGALE SALUTE TICKLE AGGRATE
CONTENT DELIGHT FLATTER
GLADDEN INDULGE SATISFY
PLEASURE
(— THE PALATE) SEASON
GRATIFYING GOOD COMELY
DELICATE GRATEFUL
GRATING GRID HACK HARP HECK
JACK RACK CRATE CRUDE GRILL
HARSH RANGE RASPY TRAIL
BAFFLE CRATCH GITTER GRILLE
HOARSE RUGGED WICKET
BAFFLER ECHELLE ECHELON
BABRACOT CATAPULT GRIDIRON
METALLIC SCRANNEL STRIDENT
PORTCULLIS
GRATIS FREE FREELY BUCKSHEE
GRATITUDE THANK THANKS
GRATUITY
GRATUITOUS FREE WANTON
BASELESS NEEDLESS
GRATUITY FEE TIP BOON DASH
VAIL PILON SPIFF SPILL BOUNTY
CUMSHAW DASTURI DOUCEUR
PRESENT PRIMAGE BAKSHISH
BONAMANO BUCKSHEE
COURTESY DUSTOORI GRATUITO
REAPDOLE PERQUISITE
(CHRISTMAS —) BOX
(PL.) LARGESSE
GRAVE BED DRY LOW PIT SAD
URN BALK BASS BIER CELL CIST
DEEP DELF FOSS GRIT HIGH
HOME KIST LAIR LAKE MOLD
MOOL RUDE SADE SAGE TOMB
URNA DELFT FOSSE GRAFF
GROVE HEAVY MOULD SHEOL
SOBER STAID STIFF SUANT VAULT
BURIAL DEMURE GRIEVE HEARSE
SEDATE SEVERE SOLEMN SOMBER
SOMBRE STEADY AUSTERE
EARNEST FUNERAL PITHOLE
SERIOSO SERIOUS
SOBERLY CATONIAN
DECOROUS MATRONAL

SERMONIC SATURNINE
GRAVECLOTHES LINEN
CEREMENTS
GRAVEDIGGER RATEL BEDRAL
BURIER FOSSOR PITMAN BEDERAL
GRAVEL GRIT ARENA GEEST GRAIL
CHESIL RANGLE SAMMEL SHILLA
BALLAST CALICHE CHANNEL
RATCHEL SHINGLE STANNER
BLINDING
(— AND SAND) DOBBIN
(— DEPOSIT) LEAD
(— IN KIDNEYS) ARENA
(LOOSE —) SLITHER
(SCREENED —) HOGGINS
(PREF.) CROCO
GRAVELLY HASKY CHISELLY
GLAREOUS
GRAVELY SADLY DEEPLY
GRAVE MOUND TUMULUS
GRAVER BURIN STYLE PLASTIC
SCORPER
GRAVESTONE BAUTA PLANK
STELA STELE STONE TABLE
CIPPUS JUMPER THROUGH
GRAVEYARD CEMETERY
GRAVID HEAVY WOMBED
PREGNANT
GRAVIMETER DOODLEBUG
GRAVITATIONAL UNIT SLUG
GRAVITY WEIGHT DIGNITY
EARNEST SOBRIETY
GRAVY JUS SOP BREE FOND LEAR
BLANC BUNCE JIPPER
GRAY ASH BAT FOG ASHY BEAR
BLAE BLUE DOVE DUSK GREY
GRIS GULL HOAR IRON LEAD SALT
ACIER CAMEL CRANE HOARY
LYART MOUSE STEEL WHITE
CASTOR CINDER DENVER FROSTY
FRUSTY GREIGE GRISLY ISABEL
LEADEN NICKEL NUTRIA PEWTER
QUAKER STRING BLUNKET
CRUISER GRANITE GRIZARD
GRIZZLE GRIZZLY HUELESS
MURINUS NEUTRAL PELICAN
PILGRIM SARKARA SPARROW
ALUMINUM BLONCKET CHARCOAL
CINEREAL CINEROUS EVENGLOW
FELDGRAU PLATINUM PLYMOUTH
(DARKEST —) BLACK
(GOOSE —) LAMA
(MOLE —) TAUPE
(MOTH —) SHEEPSKIN
(STREAKED WITH —) LYARD
(VIOLET —) GRIDELIN
(PREF.) GLAUC(O) POLI(O)
GRAYBACK DOWITCH GRAYCOAT
GREYBACK
GRAY CRANE COOLEN COOLUNG
GRAY DRAB ACIER
GRAYISH NEUTRAL
GRAYLING PINK OMBRE UMBER
HERRING UMBRANA BLUEFISH
SALMONID
GRAYNESS CANITIES
GRAY PARROT JAKO
GRAYSBY CONY CONEY
GRAY WHALE RIPSACK GRAYBACK
HARDHEAD
GRAZE BITE CROP FEED SCUR SKIM
AGIST BRUSH GRASS GRIDE
RANGE SCAMP SCUFF SHAVE

SKIFF SKIRR STOCK BROWSE
CREASE FODDER GLANCE RIPPLE
SCRAPE SCRAZE PASTURE
GRAZIER PASTURER SQUATTER
TREKBOER
GRAZING BIT FEED GRASS COLLOP
RASANT FOLDING PASCUAGE
GREASE COOM SAIM SEAM ADEPS
BLECK COOMB SMEAR SPICK
ARMING AXUNGE CREESH
ENSEAM LIQUOR POMATE
ALEMITE SAINDOUX
(— IN HARD CAKES) SEAK
(PIG'S —) MORT
(WOOL —) YOK DEGRAS LANOLIN
(PREF.) SEBI
GREASE-HEELS GRAPES
GREASER DOPER
GREASEWOOD CHICO CHEMIZO
GREASY FAT GLET OILY RICH
FATTY PORKY YOLKY SMEARY
TRAINY CREESHY PINGUID
TALLOWY UNCTUOUS
GREAT BIG FAR FAT FIT OLD BARO
DEEP DREE FELL FINE GONE
GURT HUGE KEEN MAIN MUCH
RIAL SOME TALL UNCO VAST VILE
AMPLE BURRA CHIEF FELON
GRAND LARGE MEKIL STOUR
SWEET SWELL TOUGH YEDER
FIERCE GAPING HEROIC MICKLE
NATION STRONG CAPITAL
EMINENT EXTREME GALLOWS
HOWLING IMMENSE INTENSE
STAVING TITANIC VIOLENT
VOLUMED ALMIGHTY CRACKING
ELEVATED ENORMOUS FAVORITE
GALACTIC GALAXIAN GIGANTIC
HORRIBLE INFINITE PRECIOUS
TERRIFIC MONSTROUS
MAGNIFICENT
(— LAND) ALASKA
(IMMEASURABLY —) ABYSMAL
(TOO —) OVERDUE
(VERY —) MAIN SORE AWFUL
STEEP ARDENT DEADLY IMMANE
INGENT MORTAL EXTREME
FRANTIC GHASTLY HOWLING
SUBLIME DREADFUL MOUNTAIN
MONUMENTAL
(PREF.) ARCH MAGN(I) MAHA
MEG(A) MEGAL(O)
(HOW —) QUANTI
(SUFF.) MEGALY
GREAT AUK PENGUIN PINWING
GAREFOWL
GREAT BRITAIN (SEE ENGLAND)
GREATCOAT GREGO JEMMY
JOSEPH POSTEEN OVERCOAT
GREATER SUPERIOR
(PREF.) MEIZO
GREATER STITCHWORT HEAD
SNAPPER HEADACHE SNAPJACK
SNAPWORT
GREATER YELLOWLEGS YELPER
GREATEST UTMOST EXTREME
MAXIMAL
(— POSSIBLE) ALL SUPREME
**GREAT EXPECTATIONS (AUTHOR
OF —)** DICKENS
(CHARACTER IN —) JOE PIP ABEL
BIDDY DOLGE SARAH ORLICK
PHILIP PIRRIP POCKET PROVIS

BENTLEY DRUMMLE ESTELLA
GARGERY HERBERT JAGGERS
MATTHEW HAVISHAM MAGWITCH
COMPEYSON PUMBLECHOOK
GREAT GATSBY (AUTHOR OF —)
FITZGERALD
(CHARACTER IN —) JAY TOM NICK
BAKER DAISY MCKEE GATSBY
GEORGE JORDAN MYRTLE
WILSON BUCHANAN CARRAWAY
CATHERINE WOLFSHIEM
GREAT-GRANDCHILD IEROE
GREAT GRANDFATHER NONO
BESAIEL GRANDSIR
GREAT LAKE ERIE HURON
ONTARIO MICHIGAN SUPERIOR
GREATLY FAR MUY FELL MUCH
AMAIN SWITH FINELY MAINLY
STRONG SWYTHE SWEETLY
WOUNDLY MIGHTILY
GREAT MOLE RAT ZEMMI ZEMNI
GREATNESS FORCE GRANDEUR
GRANDEZA MUCHNESS
GREAT RAGWEED KINGHEAD
GREAT TITMOUSE SHARPSAW
GREAVE JAMB JAMBE JAMBEAU
(PL.) CRAP HOSE GRAVES
GREBE LEAD LOON DIVER GAUNT
WITCH DIPPER DOBBER DUCKER
FINFOOT HENBILL PYGOPOD
ARSEFOOT CARGOOSE DABCHICK
DIDAPPER GRUIFORM
GRECE GRICE DEGREE GRISSEN

GREECE

ANCIENT LOCATIONS: ELIS DORIS
PYLOS ACHAEA ACTIUM ATTICA
DELPHI EPIRUS HELLAS LOCRIS
PHOCIS SPARTA THEBES TIRYNS
BOEOTIA CORINTH EPEIROS
LACONIA MACEDON MEGARIS
MYCENAE PAESTUM
ARMY UNIT: TAXIS
BAY: ELEUSIS SALAMIS PHALERON
CAPE: KRIOS MALEA SPADA
AKRITAS MATAPAN SIDEROS
DREPANON GRAMBYSA
TAINARON
CAPITAL: ATHENS ATHENAI
COIN: OBOL HECTE DIOBOL
LEPTON STATER DRACHMA
DIOBOLON
COLUMN: DORIC IONIC
CORINTHIAN
DANCE: PYRRHIC ROMAIKA
DIALECT: COAN ATTIC DORIC
ELEAN EOLIC IONIC AEOLIC
MELIAN THERAN ACHAEAN
ARCADIAN
DISTRICT: ARTA ELIS CANEA CHIOS
CORFU CRETE DRAMA EVROS
KHIOS PELLA SAMOS ZANTE
ACHAEA ACHAIA ATTICA
EPIRUS EUBOEA KILKIS KNANIA
KOZANE LARISA LESBOS
LEUKAS PHOCIS PIERIA SERRAI
THRACE XANTHE AETOLIA
ARCADIA ARGOLIS BOEOTIA
CORINTH KAVALLA LACONIA
LARISSA LASETHI MTATHOS
PREVEZA RHODOPE CYCLADES
IOANNINA KARDITSA KASTORIA
MAGNESIA MESSENIA

PHLORINA RETHYMNE
SALONIKA THESSALY TRIKKALA
MACEDONIA
GULF: VOLOS ATHENS MESARA
PATRAI PATRAS ARGOLIS
CORINTH KAVALLA KNANION
LACONIA LEPANTO MESSINI
RENDINA SARONIC STRIMON
MESSENIA SALONIKA SINGITIC
THERMAIC TORONAIC
HOME OF GODS: OLYMPUS
ISLAND: DIA IOS KEA KOS NIO
CEOS KEOS MILO SYME SYRA
CHIOS CORFU CRETE DELOS
KASOS KHIOS LEROS MELOS
MILOS NAXOS PAROS PAXOI
PAXOS PSARA RODOS SAMOS
SARIA SYROS TELOS TENOS
THERA THIRA TINOS ZANTE
ANAPHE ANDROS CANDIA
CERIGO CHALKE EUBOEA
EVVOIA GAVDOS IKARIA ITHACA
ITHAKI LEMNOS LESBOS LEUKAS
LEVKAS PATMOS RHENEA
RHODES SIFNOS SKYROS
THASOS AMORGOS CIMOLUS
CYTHERA KERKYRA KIMOLOS
KYTHERA KYTHNOS LEVITHA
MYKONOS NISYROS SALAMIS
SIPHNOS KALYMNOS MYTILENE
SANTORIN SERIPHOS
ISLANDS: IONIAN CYCLADES
SPORADES DODECANESE
STROPHADES
LAKE: KARLA VOLVE COPAIS
KOPAIS PRESPA TOPOLIA
KASTORIA TACHINOS VISTONIS
LETTER: MU NU PI XI CHI ETA PHI
PSI RHO TAU BETA IOTA ZETA
ALPHA DELTA GAMMA KAPPA
OMEGA SIGMA THETA LAMBDA
EPSILON OMICRON UPSILON
MARKET PLACE: AGORA
MEASURE: PIK BEMA PIKI POUS
BARIL CADOS CHOUS CUBIT
DIGIT MARIS PEKHE PODOS
PYGON XYLON ACAENA BACHEL
BACILE BARILE COTULA DICHAS
GRAMME HEMINA KOILON
ORGYIA PALAME PECHYS
SCHENE AMPHORA CHENICA
CHOENIX CYATHOS DIAULOS
HEKTEUS METRETA STADION
STADIUM STREMMA CONDYLOS
DAKTYLOS DEKAPODE
DOLICHOS MEDIMNOS
METRETES PALAISTE PLETHRON
PLETHRUM SPITHAME
STATHMOS
MOUNTAIN: IDA IDHI OSSA ATHOS
PAROS ELIKON PARNON PELION
PILION WITSCH HELICON
OLYMPUS VURANON
KRAGNOVO SMOLIKAS
TAYGETOS PARNASSUS
MOUNTAINS: OETA OTHRYS
PINDUS RODOPI RHODOPE
HYMETTOS TAYGETUS
NAME: ELLAS HELLAS
PENINSULA: ACTE AKTE AKTI
MOREA SITHONIA
PELOPONNESE
PORT: SYRA CORFU PYLOS SYROS

VOLOS MEGARA PATRAI
PATRAS KAVALLA KERKYRA
PIRAEUS SALONIKA
RIVER: IRI ARDA ARTA AURO
AXIOS DOONA EVROS LERNA
ALFIOS NESTOS PENEUS PINIOS
STRUMA VARDAR ALPHEUS
EUROTAS EVROTAS ILISSOS
PENEIOS ROUFIAS SARANTA
STRIMON ACHELOUS AKHELOOS
ALIAKMON KEPHISOS
RHOUPHIA
RUINS: DELOS PELLA SAMOS
CORINTH ELEUSIS ELEVSIS
ACROPOLIS
SEA: CRETE AEGEAN IONIAN
MIRTOON
STATE: PHOCIS
TOWN: IOS KEA KOS ARTA ELIS
KYME PETA SYME YDRA ADREA
AGYIA ARGOS CANEA CHIOS
CORFU DRAMA KARYA MELOS
NAXOS NEMEA PELLA POROS
PSARI PYLOS PYRGI SAMOS
SYROS TENOS VAMOS VATHY
VOLOS VYRON ZANTE ACTIUM
ATHENS CANDIA DAPHNI
DELPHI EDESSA ITHACA JANINA
KOZANE LARISA MEGARA
NIKHIA PATRAS RHODES SERRAI
SERRES SPARTA THEBES TIRYNS
XANTHE ATHENAI CORINTH
ELEUSIS KERKYRA LARISSA
MYCENAE PIRAEUS IOANNINA
KOMOTINE MARATHON
PHARSALA SALONIKA TRIKKALA
PERISTERI
VALLEY: NEMEA
VERNACULAR: DEMOTIC
WEIGHT: MNA OKA OKE MINA
OBOL LITRA LIVRE MANEH
POUND DIOBOL DRAMME
KANTAR OBOLOS OBOLUS
STATER TALENT CHALCON
CHALQUE DRACHMA DIOBOLON
TALANTON
WOMEN: THYIAD

GREED AVARICE AVIDITY HOGGERY
CUPIDITY
GREEDINESS AVARICE AVIDITY
GULOSITY
GREEDY AVID GAIR GORB YELP
EAGER GUTTY YIVER GRABBY
GUNDIE KITISH STINGY GLUTTON
GRIPPLE HOODOCK MISERLY
PIGGISH COVETOUS ESURIENT
GRASPING RAVENOUS LICKERISH
(PREF.) LICHNO
GREEK GREW ATTIC HADJI KOINE
METIC ARGIVE IONIAN KLEPHT
ACHAIAN AEOLIAN GRECIAN
GRIFFON HELLENE GRECANIC
HELLADIC HELLENIC ITALIOTE
SICELIOT
(PREF.) GRAECO GRECO HELLENO
GREEN (ALSO SEE COLOR) LEEK
VERD VERT CRUDE FRESH
CALLOW VIRENT NOUVEAU
SINOPLE UNFIRED VERDANT
BAYBERRY IMMATURE NOUVELLE
VAGABOND VIRIDIAN
WEDGWOOD WOODLAND

(— MOUNTAIN STATE) VERMONT
(COOKED —S) SALAD
(NILE —) BOA
(PALE —) ALOE ALOES
(YELLOWISH —) GLAUZY ABSINTHE
GLAUCOUS
(PREF.) CHLOR(O) PRASEO PRASO
VERD(O) VIRID(I)
GREEN AMARANTH REDROOT
GREENBACK FROGSKIN
(PL.) GREEN LETTUCE
GREEN BAY TREE (AUTHOR OF —)
BROMFIELD
(CHARACTER IN —) CYON LILY
ELLEN GIGON IRENE JULIA SHANE
HATTIE WILLIE HARRISON
KRYLENKO TOLLIVER
GREENBRIER SMILAX
SARSAPARILLA
GREEN CORMORANT SHAG
GREENFISH BLUEFISH
GREENHEART BIBIRU BEBEERU
GREEN HERON KIALEE
GREENHORN JAY MUG YAP JAKE
PUTT IKONA GREENY SUCKER
SOFTHORN
GREENHOUSE STOVE GREENERY
HOTHOUSE ORANGERY
COOLHOUSE
GREENISH BERYL SANIOUS
GREENISH-YELLOW RESEDA

GREENLAND
AIR BASE: THULE
BAY: DISKO BAFFIN MELVILLE
CAPE: JAAL GRIVEL WALKER
BISMARCK BREWSTER
FAREWELL LOWENORN
CAPITAL: GODTHAAB
DISCOVERER: ERIC
MOUNTAIN: FOREL PAYER
KHARDYU GUNNBJORN
STRAIT: DAVIS DENMARK
TOWN: ETAH NORD THULE
UMANAK GODHAVN IVIGTUT
GODTHAAB JULIANEHAB
EGEDESMINDE SUKKERTOPPEN
HOLSTEINSBORG

GREENLING TROUT BOREGAT
BODIERON LORICATE ROCKFISH
GREEN MANSIONS (AUTHOR OF —)
HUDSON
(CHARACTER IN —) ABEL RIMA
NUFLO
GREEN MONKEY GUENON
GREENNESS VERD VERT VERDURE
VERDANCY VIRIDITY
GREEN ONION RARERIPE
GREEN PIKE JACK
GREENROOM FOYER
GREENSHANK TATTLER
GREENSTONE POUNAMU
GREEN SUNFISH REDEYE
GREENWEED WOODWAX
GREEN WOODPECKER ECCLE
SPRITE YAFFLE YOCKEL YUKKEL
HEWHALL HEWHOLE SNAPPER
SPEIGHT YAFFLER POPINJAY
WOODHACK WOODWALL
GREET CRY JOY CROW HAIL HALSE
ACCOST HERALD SALAAM SALUTE
ADDRESS RECEIVE WELCOME

GREETING HOW CIAO HIYA ALOHA
GREET HELLO HOWDY KOMBO
ACCOST CHEERO SALAAM SALUTE
SHALOM ADDRESS CHEERIO
COMMEND SLAINTE WELCOME
REMEMBRANCE
GREGARIOUS GREGAL SOCIAL
GREGE NUTRIA
GRENADA (CAPITAL OF —)
STGEORGES
(ISLAND OF —) CARRIACON
GRENADE EGG TROMBE GRENADO
FIREBALL PINEAPPLE
GRENADIER RATTAIL WHIPTAIL
GRENADINE FLORENCE
GRENDEL (SLAYER OF —) BEOWULF
GRETCHEN (BELOVED OF —) FAUST
**GRETTIR THE STRONG (AUTHOR
OF —)** UNKNOWN
(CHARACTER IN —) ATLI GEST
GLAM GRIM JARL ANGLE BJORN
EINAR ASMUND ILLUGI OGMUND
OXMAIN SKEGGI STEINN THORIR
DROMUND GRETTIR MAKSSON
HALLMUND LONGHAIR REDBEARD
SNAEKOLL STEINVOR THORFINN
THORGILS SLOWCOACH
THORBJORN THORSTEINN
GREY (SEE GRAY)
GREYHOUND GREW SALUKI
BANJARA SAPLING TUMBLER
WHIPPET
GRID BOUCAN BUCCAN GRIDDLE
GRIDIRON
(CIRCULAR —) DISC DISK
GRIDDLE COMAL GRILL GIRDLE
GRILLE BRANDER
GRIDDLE CAKE AREPA LATKE
CHAPATTY CORNCAKE FLAPJACK
SLAPJACK
GRIDIRON GRID GRILL TRAIL
BRANDER BROILER GRIDDLE
GRIEF VEX WOE CARE DILL DOLE
DOOL DREE HARM HURT MOAN
MOOD PAIN RUTH SORE TEEN
TINE AGONY DOLOR GRAME
RUING TRIAL WRONG BARRAT
DESIRE MISHAP REGRET SORROW
STOUND WONDER ANGUISH
CHAGRIN EMOTION FAILURE
OFFENSE SADNESS THOUGHT
TROUBLE WAESUCK WAYMENT
DISASTER DISTRESS HARDSHIP
(— STEM) KELLY
(SECRET —) CANKER
(PREF.) DOLORI LYPO
GRIESEN ZWITTER
GRIEVANCE BEEF GRIEF PEEVE
BURDEN BYGONE GRAVAMEN
HARDSHIP
GRIEVE VEX CARE DOLE DUMP
EARN ERME HONE HURT PAIN
PINE SIGH WAIL GRAME GRIPE
MOURN SORRY WOUND YEARN
ATHINK CORSIE LAMENT REPINE
SORROW AFFLICT CHAGRIN
CONDOLE GRIZZLE TROUBLE
WAYMENT COMPLAIN DISTRESS
GRIEVED WOE GRAME SORRY
GRIEVING SORRY
GRIEVOUS SAD DEAR DEEP DERF
HARD SORE CHARY DIRTY GRIEF
HEAVY SORRY WEARY BITTER

DREARY SEVERE SHREWD
CAREFUL HEINOUS WEIGHTY
DOLOROUS ATROCIOUS
GRIEVOUSLY DERNLY FOULLY
SORELY HEAVILY
GRIFFE SPUR
GRIFFIN GRIPE GRYPHON
EPIMACUS
GRILL REJA BRACE BROIL DEVIL
TRAIL AFFLICT BROILER GRILLADE
GRILLE FACE REJA HAZARD
GRILLROOM GROOM
GRILSE PEAL SEWIN FINNAC
GRAWLS BOTCHER FORKTAIL
GRIM DOUR GASH SOUR BLEAK
CRUEL GAUNT STERN GRIMLY
GRISLY HORRID SULLEN TORVID
GHASTLY GRIZZLY HIDEOUS
MACABRE TORVOUS PITILESS
RUTHLESS
GRIMACE MOP MOW MUG POT
FACE GIRN IRPE MOUE MUMP
YIRN FLEER MOUTH SNEER
SNOOT GIMBLE SHEYLE STITCH
MURGEON SIMAGRE
GRIMALKIN CAT HAG MOLL WITCH
BELDAM HARRIDAN
GRIME DIRT SMUT COLLY SMOUCH
SMUTCH
GRIMME COQUETOON
GRIMNESS TORVITY
GRIMP CLIMB
GRIMY DINGY GRUBBY SCABROUS
GRIN DRAD GIRN MUMP FLEER
RISUS SNEER SIMPER GRIZZLE
GRIND DIG SAP BONE BRAY CHEW
FILE GRUN MILL MULL MUZZ
SMUG SWOT CRUSH FLOAT
FLOUR GRATE GRIDE GRIST
QUERN CRUNCH DRUDGE
POWDER EMERIZE GRISTLE
SWOTTER LEVIGATE
(— COARSELY) KIBBLE
(— DIAMONDS) SKIVE
(— SMALL) BRAY
(— TEETH) GNASH GRATE GRINT
GRISBET
GRINDER CRASH MULLER BRUISER
GRINDING BREAK MOLAR
ABRASION
(— OF CORN) MULTURE
(— OF MEAL) BREAK GRIST
(— OF TEETH) BRUXISM
GRINDSTONE MANO PAVER
STONE
GRIP BITE BURR CLIP FANG FIST
HOLD HOLT TAKE VICE CHOKE
CINCH CLAMP CLASP GRASP
GRIPE PINCH SALLY SEIZE BARREL
CLINCH CLUTCH CRADLE FREEZE
EMBRACE HANDBAG HOLDING
SEIZURE ADHESION FOOTLOCK
HANDFAST HANDGRIP
HANDHOLD STAGEHAND
(— OF A SWORD) FUSEAU
(— OF BELL ROPE) SALLY
(— TO A SPAR) DOG
GRIPE CRAB FRIB BITCH CREATE
GROUSE HOLLER KVETCH NATTER
SNATCH GRIZZLE COMPLAIN
GRIPER GRIZZLER
GRIPES TORMINA
GRIPING GRIPPLE PINCHING

GRIPPER KEEPER NIPPER
GRIPPING STONY STONEY
GRIQUA BASTARD BASTAARD
GRISKINISSA (HUSBAND OF —)
ARTAXAMINOUS
GRISLY GRIM GHASTLY GRIZZLY
HIDEOUS GRUESOME
GRISON HURON GALICTIS
GRIST PABULUM
GRISTLE CARTILAGE
GRIT SAND GRIND PLUCK BOTTOM
BRAVERY DECISION GRITROCK
RUBSTONE
(PL.) CUTLINGS
GRITH MUND GYRTH
GRITTY SANDY SHARP GRISTY
CHISELLY SABULINE SABULOUS
GRIVET TOTA WAAG GEUNON
NISNAS
GRIZZLED GRISLY STREAKED
GRIZZLY BEAR (— STATE)
CALIFORNIA
GROAN MOAN ROME GRANK
GRUNT STECH COMPLAIN
GROAT BIT FLAG GILL HARP
GROATS
(PREF.) ATHERO
GROCER SPICER EPICIER PEPPERER
GROCERY BODEGA PULPERIA
GROG RUMBO TEMPER CHAMOTTE
GROGGERY SHANTY GROGSHOP
GROGGY SHAKY UNSTEADY
WAVERING
GROGSHOP SHANTY DOGGERY
GROGGERY
GROIN LISK PIER SHARE CLITCH
INGUEN GRUNZIE
(PREF.) INGUIN(O)
GROMMET BECKET COLLAR
EYELET CRINGLE GARLAND
GROMWELL PUCCOON REDROOT
SALFERN GRAYMILL
GROOM LAD MAFU NEAT SYCE
CURRY DRESS MAFOO STRAP
SWIPE TIGER BARBER BATMAN
FETTLE FOGGER GUINEA MEHTAR
OSTLER HOSTLER MARSHAL
COISTREL COISTRIL GROOMLET
STRAPPER
GROOVE RUT BEAD DADO GAIN
KERF LUCE PORT RAKE SLOT
CANAL CHASE CROZE FLUTE
GLYPH GORGE GOUGE GUIDE
JOINT QUIRK REGAL RIFLE RIGOL
SCARF SCORE STRIA SWAGE
CREASE CULLIS FULLER FURROW
GUTTER KEYWAY RABBET
RAGGLE RAGLET REBATE RIFFLE
RUNNER SCROBE SULCUS
THROAT TRENCH CHAMFER
CHANNEL GARLAND KEYHOLE
PLOWING SULCATE BOTHRIUM
GROOVING PHILTRUM
CANNELURE VALLECULA
(— IN AUGER) POD
(— IN COLUMN) FLUTE
(— IN MASONRY) RAGGLE
(— IN STAVES) CROZE
(— IN STONE) JAD
(— IN TIRE) SIPE
(— ON UPPER LIP) PHILTRUM
(— ON WEEVIL) SCROBE
(— ON WHALE) SCARF

(— UNDER COPING) GORGE
(—S ON ROCK) LAPIES
(RECTANGULAR —) REGLET
GROOVED FLUTED MILLED
EXARATE SULCATE
GROOVER FLUTER
GROPE CLAM CLAW FEEL POKE
RIPE GLAUM GRAIP FUMBLE
GUDDLE GRABBLE GRAPPLE
GROPPLE GRUBBLE SCRABBLE
GROSBEAK FINCH HAWFINCH
GROSGRAIN ROYALE
GROSS FAT DULL FOUL LUMP
RANK BROAD CRASS FOGGY
GREAT GUTTY LARGE MACRO
SLUMP THICK WHOLE ANIMAL
COARSE EARTHY FILTHY GREASY
SÖRDID STRONG BLOATED
FULSOME CLODDISH FLAGRANT
INDECENT SLUTTISH
GROSSO MATAPAN
GROTESQUE ANTIC WOOZY
ROCOCO BAROQUE BIZARRE
CROTESCO FANCIFUL
GROTTO CAVE GROT ANTRE SPEOS
CAVERN LUPERCAL
GROUCH SULK CRANK GROUSE
SOURBALL SOURPUSS
GROUND SEW SOD SUE BASE
CLOD DIRT FOLD FOND GIST
LAND MOLD REST ROOT SOIL
STAY WOLD EARTH FIELD FIRTH
FOUND MOULD PLACE SCORE
SOLUM TRAIN TUTOR VENUE
CREASE MATTER REASON
SMACKED FORELAND INITIATE
(— AT TOP OF SHAFT) BANK
(— COVERED WITH RUBBLE) TITI
(— FOR COMPLAINT) BEEF
(— OF FLAG) FIELD
(— OF LACE) FOND
(— OVERLYING TIN DEPOSIT)
BURDEN
(BOGGY —) SOG CARR SNAPE
(BROKEN —) HAG
(BURYING —) CEMETERY
(CAMPING —) AUTOCAMP
(COLLEGE —S) CAMPUS
(DUMPING —) TIP TOOM
(FALLOW —) BRISE
(FEEDING —) HAUNT
(FIRM-HOLDING —) LANDFANG
(FISHING —) HAAF
(FROZEN —) TJAELE
(GRASSY —) LAWN CLOWRE
(GRAZING —) HERDWICK
(HARD —) HARDPAN
(HUNTING —) CHASE
(LOW —) INCH SWALE TALAO
(MIDDLE —) LIMBO
(MUDDY —) SLOB
(NEW ENCLOSED —) TINING
(ORIGINAL —) URGRUND
(PARADE —) MAIDAN
(PASTURE —) HIRSEL
(RECREATION —) PARK
(RISING —) HURST HYRST
(SLOPING —) CLEVE
(SOLID —) HILL
(SPONGY —) BOG
(SWAMPY —) PUXY CRIPPLE
(UNCULTIVATED —) JUNGLE
(UNUSED —) AREA

(WET WASTE —) MOOR REESK
(PL.) GROUT STOCK
(PREF.) CHAMAE CHAME GE(O)
PEDO SOLI
(ON THE —) HUMI
GROUND HEMLOCK SHINWOOD
GROUND HOG MARMOT
GROUND IVY GILL HEWE HOVE
JILL YARROW ALEHOOF CATFOOT
GAGROOT MILFOIL TUNHOOF
FOALFOOT
GROUNDLESS IDLE FALSE
BASELESS
GROUNDLINE SETLINE
GROUNDMAN GRUNT
GROUNDMASS PASTE CEMENT
MATRIX
GROUNDNUT GOBBE PEANUT
PIGNUT
GROUND PINE FOXTAIL
STAGHORN
GROUNDSEL SIMSON DOGBUSH
SENCION SENECIO BINDWEED
BIRDSEED
GROUNDSMAN CURATOR
GROUND SQUIRREL GOPHER
GRINNY SUSLIK MEERKAT
SCIURID SOUSLIK SCIURINE
GROUND THRUSH PITTA
GROUNDWORK BASE FOND FUND
BASIS BOTTOM FUNDUS
GROUP MOB SET BAND BEVY BODY
CREW DECK FOLD GANG KNOT
PAIR RING SECT SORT STEW TREF
ARRAY BATCH BREED BUNCH
CLASS CLUMP COVEY FIRCA
FLOCK GENUS GLOBE PLUMP
SABHA SKULK SQUAD STACK
TALLY WHEEN CIRCLE CLUTCH
COHORT FAMILY GRUPPO PARCEL
RUBRIC AGGROUP BATTERY
BOILING BOUROCK BRACKET
CLASSIS CLUSTER COLLEGE
COMMUNE COMPANY CONSORT
FELLOWS FLUTTER QUOTITY
SECTION SEVERAL SOCIETY
ALLIANCE CATEGORY CLASSIFY
DIVISION FAISCEAU FLOTILLA
GROUPING
(— OF ANGELS) FLIGHT
(— OF ARTIFACTS) CACHE
(— OF BADGERS) CETE
(— OF BUILDINGS) BLOCK
(— OF CASTINGS) SPRAY
(— OF CATS) CLOWDER
(— OF CELLS) GLAND ISLET LAURA
CENTER CORONA EPITHEM
SEMILUNE
(— OF COMPUTER JOBS) BATCH
(— OF DECOYS) STOOL
(— OF DEITIES) CABEIRI
(— OF DIALECTS) AEOLIC
(— OF EELS) SWARM
(— OF EIGHT) OCTAD OCTET
OCTETTE
(— OF FAMILIES) FINE
(— OF FIVE) PENTAD CINQUAIN
(— OF FOUR) MESS QUARTET
(— OF FRIENDS) BUNCH
(— OF FURNISHINGS) ENSEMBLE
(— OF HAITIANS) COMBITE
COUMBITE
(— OF HOUSES) BOROUGH

(— OF HUTS) BUSTI KRAAL BUSTEE
(— OF ILLUSTRIOUS PERSONS)
PANTHEON
(— OF INDIAN STATES) AGENCY
(— OF ISOGLOSSES) BUNDLE
(— OF KINDRED) SIOL
(— OF KINSMEN) AHL
(— OF LAYMEN) COFRADIA
(— OF LIONS) PRIDE
(— OF LISTENERS) AUDIENCE
(— OF MARTENS) RICHESSE
(— OF MILITARY VEHICLES)
DEADLINE
(— OF MOLDINGS) DANCETTE
(— OF NINE) ENNEAD NONARY
(— OF NUCLEONS) SHELL
(— OF OFFSPRING) CLUTCH
(— OF ORGANISMS) FORM STRAIN
(— OF PARACHUTISTS) STICK
(— OF PERSONS) BAG CLUB KNOT
SWAD CROWD DROVE CIRCLE
GAGGLE KENNEL
(— OF RETORTS) BENCH SETTING
(— OF RUFFIANS) PUSH
(— OF SCHOLARS) ULAMA
(— OF SCULPTURE) MORTORIO
(— OF SEVEN) HEPTAD SEPTET
HEBDOMAD
(— OF SIX) HEXAD SENARY
(— OF SLAVES) COFFLE
(— OF SOILS) LATERITE
(— OF SOLDIERS) DRAFT COHORT
(— OF STARS) ASTERISM
(— OF STRATIFIED BEDS) FACIES
(— OF STUDENTS) SEMINAR
(— OF SYLLABLES) FOOT
(— OF SYMBOLS) FORMULA
(— OF SYMPTOMS) SYNDROME
(— OF TEN) DECADE DENARY
(— OF TENTS) CAMP CANVAS
(— OF THEATERS) CIRCUIT
(— OF THREE) TRIO GLEEK TRIAD
TRINE
(— OF TRAITS) COMPLEX
(— OF TROUT) HOVER
(— OF VERSES) SYSTEM
(— OF WEAPONS) NEST
(— OF WINGS) RUFFLE
(— OF WIRES) DROP
(— OF WORDS) ACCENT GENITIVE
(— OF 10 NOTES) DECUPLET
(— OF 1000) CHILIAD
(— OF 12) DOZEN
(— OF 2 VOWELS) DIGRAM
DIGRAPH
(— OF 40 THREADS) BEER BIER
(— OF 60 PIECES) SHOCK
(ASSISTANCE —) AINI
(ATOMIC —) LIGAND
(AUTHORITATIVE —) CONCLAVE
(AVANT-GARDE —) UNDERGROUND
(CONFUSED —) SNARL
(CORE —) CADRE
(CRIME SYNDICATE —) FAMILY
(ECOLOGICAL —) GUILD
(ETHNIC —) LI ACHANG BALAHI
BATTAK ETHNOS CHINGPAW
(ETHNOLOGICAL —) ISLAND
(EXCLUSIVE —) ELECT
(FAMILY —) GWELY
(HARMONIOUS —) DOVECOTE
(INTIMATE —) COTERIE
(KINSHIP —) SUSU

(LANGUAGE —) ATALAN
(LARGE —) PASSEL
(LINKED —) NEXUS
(LIVELY —) GALA
(NON-MOSLEM —) MILLET
(PAGAN —) BATAK BATANGAN
(PHILOSOPHICAL —) CENACLE
(POLITICAL —) BLOC PARTY
FASCIO COMMONS MACHINE
(SEGREGATED —) GHETTO
(SMALL —) PLUMP
(SOCIAL —) KITH SEPT TRIBE
FAMILY INGROUP
(PREF.) (CULTURAL —) ETHNO
(SUFF.) AD ET OME SOME
GROUPED AGMINATE
GROUPER GAG HIND MERO GUASA
HAMEL SCAMP AGUAJI BONACI
CHERNA GROPER HAMLET
WARSAW BACALAO GARLOPA
GARRUPA GOURAMI JEWFISH
REDFISH LAPULAPU REDBELLY
ROCKFISH SCIRENGA SERRANID
(YOUNG —) SNAPPER
GROUPING KIND ARRAY BATTERY
KINDRED DIVISION GROUPAGE
SODALITY SYNTAGMA
(— OF POTTERY) SERIES
GROUSE CRAB BITCH GANGA
PEEVE GORHEN GROUCH HOOTER
ATTAGEN CHEEPER GAZELLE
GORCOCK PINTAIL COMPLAIN
MOORBIRD MOORFOWL
PTARMIGAN
(YOUNG —) POULT SQUEALER
GROUT GROOT LARRY SLUSH
GROUTING
GROUTER GUNITER
GROVE CAMP HEWT HOLT MOTT
SHAW TOFT TOPE WONG ALTIS
BLUFF COPSE GLADE HURST
HYRST GARDEN GREAVE GROVET
ISLAND OLIVET SCROBE SPRING
ACADEMY ARBORET BOSCAGE
COPPICE SPINNEY THICKET
WOODING SERINGAL WODELEIE
(— OF ALDERS) CARR
(— OF MANGO TREES) TOPE
(— OF OAKS) ENCINAL
(— OF OSIERS) HOLT
(— OF SUGAR MAPLES) CAMP
(SACRED —) ALTIS SARNA
(SMALL —) SHAW
(PREF.) NAEMOR
(SUFF.) ETUM
GROVEL FAWN ROLL CREEP
CRINGE TUMBLE WALLOW
WELTER GRABBLE FLOUNDER
GROVELING PRONE WORMY
ABJECT HANGDOG REPTILE
GROW AGE BUD GET HIT ICH WAX
BOLL COME CROP ECHE ITCH
MAKE RISE SEED THEE THRO
WEAR EDIFY ISSUE PLANT PROVE
RAISE SHOOT SWELL ACCRUE
BATTEN BECOME DOUBLE
EXPAND EXTEND GATHER SPRING
SPROUT THRIVE AUGMENT
BROADEN BURGEON DEVELOP
DISTEND ENLARGE IMPROVE
NOURISH ADOLESCE FLOURISH
HEIGHTEN INCREASE THRODDEN
PROLIFERATE

(— ANGRY) STIVER
(— BETTER) IMPROVE
(— DARK) GLOAM GLOOM NIGHT
DARKEN DARKLE
(— FAINT) DIE APPAL APPALL
(— FAT) FEED BATTEN
(— IN LENGTH) ELONGATE
(— IRREGULARLY) SCRAMBLE
(— LESS) ABATE SLAKE ASSUAGE
DECREASE
(— LIGHT) DAWN
(— LUXURIANTLY) THRIVE
(— MAD) WOOD
(— MILD) GIVE
(— OLD) AGE OLD SENESCE
(— OVER) INVADE
(— PLUMP) PLIM
(— RICH) FATTEN
(— SOUND) HEAL
(— SPIRITLESS) FLAG
(— STILL) HUSH
(— STRONG) FORTIFY STORKEN
(— THIN) PEAK
(— TO HEAD) CABBAGE
(— TO STALK) SPINDLE
(— TOGETHER) KNIT ACCRETE
CONCREW COOSIFY COALESCE
(— UNDER GLASS) GLASS
(— UP) STEM ACCRUE
(— WEAK) FAINT
(PREF.) **(— TOGETHER)** SYMPHY(O)
GROWING GROWY ONGOING
CRESCENT CRESCIVE
ACCRESCENT
(— ANGRY) IRASCENT
(— IN AIR) AERIAL
(— IN CLUSTERS) RACEMOSE
(— IN GRAIN FIELDS) SEGETAL
(— IN HEAPS) ACERVATE
(— IN MEADOW) PRATAL
(— IN PAIRS) BINATE
(— IN RUBBISH) RUDERAL
(— IN WATER) AQUATIC
(— ON A STEM) CAULINE
(— OUT) ENATE
(— RAPIDLY) BOOMING
(— THICKLY) HOUSY
(— VIGOROUSLY) THRIFTY
(— WILD) SAVAGE AGRARIAN
AGRESTAL
(SUFF.) PLASIA PLASIS
PLASM(A)(IA)(IC) PLAST(IC)(Y)
PLASY
(— IN OR ON) COLE COLINE
COLOUS
GROWL YAR GNAR GURL GURR
NARR RASE ROIN ROME WIRR
YARR YIRR GARRE GNARL GNARR
GROIN SNARL GOLLAR HABBLE
GRUMBLE MAUNDER
GROWLER CLARENCE
GROWLING GROIN SURLY
GROWN THRIVEN
(— COLD) DEAD
(— HIGH) LOGGY
(— TOGETHER) ADNATE ACCRETE
(FULL —) GREAT MATURE
(WELL —) THRODDY
GROWN-UP ADULT GROWN
MATURE
GROWTH FUR WAX BUSH COAT
CORN FILM GROW JUBA RISE
SPUR SUIT DUVET FLUSH GUMMA

MAQUI STAND STOCK STOOL
SWELL BUTTON CALLUS CANCER
CLAVUS EATAGE EPULIS FRINGE
FUNGUS LANUGO SCREEN
SPROUT TYLOSE UPCOME
WASTME AUXESIS BRACKEN
COPPICE ERINEUM FUNGOID
MACCHIE SARCOID STATURE
TYLOSIS BEARDING CARUNCLE
ENDOGENY INCREASE SETATION
SWELLING UPSPRING ACCRETION
(— IN EYE) FILM
(— OF BEARD) DOWN
(— OF HAIR) SUIT
(— OF HORN) BUTTON SPIDER
(— OF PLANKTON) BLOOM
(— OF TREES) MOTTE BOSQUE
BOSCAGE COPPICE SHINNERY
(— ON HORSE'S LEG) FUSEE FUZEE
(— ON VESSEL'S BOTTOM) GARR
(ABUNDANT —) FLUSH
(DENSE —) BRUSH FOREST
SHINNERY
(DOWNY —) LANUGO
(GREEN —) GREENTH
(HARD —) STONE
(LUXURIANT —) FLOURISH
(ROUGH —) STUBBLE
(RUDIMENTARY —) STUB STUMP
(SIDE —) SPRIG
(SPARSE —) SCRAGGLE
(SUPERFICIAL —) MILDEW
(TRANSPARENT —) DRUSE
(VIGOROUS —) THRIFT
(WOODY —) BURL
(2ND — OF GRASS) FOG
(PREF.) AUXANO AUXO
(SUFF.) PHYTA PHYTE(S) PHYTIC
PHYTUM PLASTY TROPHIA
TROPHIC TROPHY
(INHIBITION OF —) STASIA STASIS
GROWTH OF THE SOIL (AUTHOR
OF —) HAMSUN
(CHARACTER IN —) AXEL ISAK
BREDE INGER OLINE OLSEN
STROM BARBRO SIVERT ARONSEN
ELESEUS REBECCA GEISSLER
LEOPOLDINE
GRUB BOB DIG EATS HUHU MOIL
MOOT ROUT STUB WORM CHUCK
GROUT MATHE SCRAN SNOUT
WROTE ASSART ESSART GRUGRU
MAGGOT MUZZLE ROOTLE
NEASCUS PIGROOT FLAGWORM
GRUBWORM MUCKWORM
SKINWORM
GRUBROOT STARWORT
GRUDGE DOWN ENVY DERRY
PEEVE SCORE SPITE ANIMUS
GROUCH GRUNCH GRUTCH
MALICE MALIGN SPLEEN DESPITE
EYELAST SIMULTY
GRUDGING JEALOUSY
GRUEL SLOP BLEERY BURGOO
CAUDLE CONGEE CROWDY SKILLY
SOFKEE BROCHAN CROWDIE
LOBLOLLY WANGRACE
GRUESOME UGLY GRISLY GROOLY
HORRID SORDID FEARFUL
GHASTLY HIDEOUS MACABRE
GRUFF BLUFF ROUGH CLUMSE
SULLEN AUSTERE BEARING
BRUSQUE CLUMPST

(PL.) TAILINGS
GRUIFORMES GRALLAE
GRUMBLE CARP GIRN GREX HONE
KREX ROIN BLEAT BROCK CROAK
DRUNT GROIN GROWL GRUMP
GRUNT MUNGE GROUCH GROUSE
GRUDGE GRUNCH MUMBLE
MUNGER MURMUR MUTTER
NOLLER PEENGE REPINE RUMBLE
SQUEAL TARROW YAMMER
CHANNER CHUNNER CHUNTER
GNATTER GRIZZLE GRUNTLE
MAUNDER MURGEON QUADDLE
SWAGGER COMPLAIN
GRUMBLER GROUCH QUADDLE
GROGNARD
GRUMBLING BITCH DRUNT GRIPE
GROIN GRUDGE MURMUR
MURGEON
GRUMPY ILL CROSS GLUMPY
GLUMPISH GRUMPISH
GRUNION SMELT
GRUNT OINK BURRO GROIN
HUMPH RONCO SARGO GRUMPH
RONCHO BURRITO CROAKER
GRUNTER GRUNTLE PIGFISH
PINFISH TOMTATE KNORHAAN
KOORHAAN PORKFISH
REDMOUTH RONCADOR
GUACHARO FATBIRD OILBIRD
GUAICURU CADUVEO
GUAM (BAY OF —) AGAT YLIG CETTI
AJAYAN UMATAC
(CAPITAL OF —) AGANA
(HARBOR OF —) APRA
(ISLAND OF —) CABRAS
(MOUNTAIN OF —) TENJO LAMLAM
(PENINSULA OF —) OROTE
(TOWN OF —) UPI ARRA ASAN
TOTO YONA AGANA LUPOG
MAGUA MERIZO UMATAC
MALOLOS
GUAMA INGA PACAY
GUAN JACU ORTALIS PHEASANT
GUANA CHANE
GUANABANA SOURSOP
GUANCHE CANARIAN
GUANO OSITE
GUAPENA SERRAN SERRANA
AGUAVINA
GUARANTEE (ALSO SEE
GUARANTY) BAIL BAND SEAL
CINCH COVER AVOUCH ENGAGE
ENSURE INSURE RATIFY SECURE
SURETY CAUTION CERTIFY
HOSTAGE WARRANT AWARRANT
GUARANTY PRESTATE SECURITY
WARRANTY
GUARANTEED ASSURED
CERTIFIED FOOLPROOF
GUARANTOR ENGAGER GRANTOR
GUARAND SPONSOR GUARANTY
GUARANTY (ALSO SEE
GUARANTEE) ANDI AVAL PAWN
SEAL CAUTIO PLEDGE WARRANT
SECURITY WARRANTY
GUARD BOW LEG NIT PAD SEE
CARE CURB HERD HOLD KEEP
KNOW LOOK REDE SAVE STOP
STUB TENT TILE WAIT WEAR
WERE WITE YEME ASKAR AWARD
BLESS BLOCK CHECK COVER
FENCE FORAY HEDGE HINGE

PILOT SCREW SKIRT TUTOR
WAKEN WATCH ASKARI BANTAY
BASKET BRACER BRIDLE BUMPER
BUTTON CONVOY DEFEND
DRAGON ESCORT FENDER GHAFIR
GUNMAN JAILER KAVASS KEEPER
MIDDLE POLICE SCREEN SECURE
SENTRY SHIELD SHROUD WAITER
WARDER YEMING BULWARK
CHERISH ESGUARD FRONTAL
GHAFFIR GHATWAL GUARDER
KEEPING PANDOUR PRESIDY
PROTECT SOULACK TRABANT
WARDAGE WARRANT CHAPERON
GARRISON MUDGUARD
OUTGUARD PEDESTAL PILOTMAN
PRESERVE SECURITY SENTINEL
SHEPHERD SPLASHER
WARDSMAN WATCHMAN
(— ON FOIL) BUTTON
(— WHILE IN TRANSIT) RIDE
(AXLE —) HOUSING
(COACH —) SHOOTER
(CONSULAR —) KAVASS
(IMPERIAL —) BOSTANGI BOSTANJI
(KEYHOLE —) LAPPET
(MOUNTED —) SHOMER
(NECK —) CAMAIL
(ON —) AWARE EXCUBANT
(PRISON —) HACK SCREW CHASER
JAILER
(STIRRUP —) TAPADERA
(SWORD —) BOW TSUBA
(WRIST —) BRACER
(PL.) HEAVIES
GUARDED WARY IMMUNE
MANNED
GUARDEDLY GINGERLY
GUARDHOUSE BRIG CLINK
BULLPEN HOOSEGOW
GUARDIAN HERD ANGEL ARGUS
TUTOR YEMER CUSTOS KEEPER
MIMING PASTOR PATRON
SHOMER WARDEN CORONER
CURATOR GARDANT GARDEEN
GRIFFIN BARTHOLO BELLERUS
CERBERUS CREANCER DEFENDER
ECKEHART FRAVASHI GOVERNOR
GUARDANT PROTUTOR TUTELARY
(— OF HOME) SIF
(WORLD —) LOKAPALA MAHARAJA
(PL.) SELLI SELLOI
GUARDIANSHIP WARD TUTELA
CUSTODY KEEPING TUITION
WARDAGE WARDING CUSTODIA
GUARDAGE TUTELAGE
WARDENRY WARDSHIP
GUARDROOM WARDROOM
GUARDSMAN GUARDEE
GUASA MERO

GUATEMALA
CAPITAL: GUATEMALA
COIN: PESO CENTAVO QUETZAL
DANCE: ELSON GUARIMBA
DEPARTMENT: PETEN IZABAL
JALAPA QUICHE SOLOLA
ZACAPA JULIAPA ESCUINTLA
GULF: HONDURAS
INDIAN: MAM CHOL ITZA IXIL
MAYA XINCA CARIBE QUICHE
POKOMAM
LAKE: DULCE GUIJA PETEN

IZABAL ATITLAN
MEASURE: VARA CUARTA FANEGA
TERCIA CAJUELA MANZANA
MOUNTAIN: AGUA FUEGO PACAYA
TACANA ATITLAN TOLIMAN
TAJAMULCO
PORT: OCOS BARRIOS LIVINGSTON
RIVER: AZUL BRAVO DULCE LAPAZ
BELIZE CHIXOY NEGINO PASION
SAMALA CHIAPAS MOTAGUA
SARSTUN POLOCHIC
RUINS: TIKAL
TOWN: OCOS COBAN VIEJA
CHAHAL CHISEC CUILCO
FLORES IZTAPA JALAPA
SALAMA SOLOLA TACANA
TECPAN YALOCH ZACAPA
ANTIGUA CUILAPA JUTIAPA
SANJOSE PROGRESO
VOLCANO: AGUA FUEGO PACAYA
TACANA ATITLAN TAJUMULCO
WEIGHT: CAJA LIBRA

GUAVA ARACA MYRTAL GUAYABA
GUAYABO GOIABADA
GUAYCURU MBAYA
GUDDLE GUMP NOODLE HANDFISH
GUDGEON PIN QUAB CHALDER
TRUNNION
GUDRUN (FATHER OF —) HETEL
GUELDER-ROSE GAITER OPULUS
DOGWOOD WHITTEN DOGBERRY
SNOWBALL VIBURNUM
GUENDOLEN (HUSBAND OF —)
LOCRINE
GUENON GRIVET NISNAS VERVET
TALAPOIN TALLAPOI MOUSTACHE
GUEREZA COLOBIN COLOBUS
GUERRILLA COWBOY GORILLA
JAYHAWK SKINNER BUSHWACK
FELLAGHA KOMITAJI
GUERRILLERO KOMITAJI
GUESS AIM CALL HARP REDE SHOT
WEEN AREAD COUNT ETTLE
FANCY INFER TWANG DEVISE
DIVINE RECKON IMAGINE
SURMISE SUSPECT
(— CORRECTLY) TOUCH
GUEST COME GOER HOST DINER
INVITEE VISITOR SYMPHILE
VISITANT
(— AT RANCH) DUDE
(UNINVITED —) SHADOW
(PL.) LEVEE COMPANY
(PREF.) XEN(O)
(SUFF.) XENE XENOUS XENY
GUFA KUFA GOOFAH KUPHAR
GUFFAW GAFF ROAR HEEHAW
GUIDANCE AIM DUCT EGIS AEGIS
STEER CONDUCT GUIDAGE
HELMAGE LEADING WISSING
AUSPICES ENGINERY REGIMENT
STEERAGE
GUIDE GUY LAY PIR TIP AIRT BEAD
CURB GAGE GATE LEAD PASS
REIN RULE SWAY WISE CARRY
CHARM DRESS FRAME GAUGE
LIGHT MAHDI MOROC PILOT
STEER TEACH WEISE ADALID
BARKER BEACON BEDWAY
CONVOY DIRECT ESCORT FORMER
GILLIE GOVERN INFORM LEADER
MANAGE POPPET CONDUCE

CONDUCT COURIER GHILLIE
INSPIRE MARSHAL MERCURY
PIONEER SHIKARI STERNER
TRACKER CALENDAR CICERONE
DIRECTOR DRAGOMAN ENGINEER
FAIRLEAD LODESMAN PEDESTAL
POLESTAR PRACTICO REPEATER
SHIKAREE SIGNPOST
(MORAL —) LABARUM
(RAILWAY —) ABC BRADSHAW
(SPIRITUAL —) PIR GURU BISHOP
DIVINE
(TRAFFIC —) MUSHROOM
(SUFF.) AGOGUE AGOGY
GUIDEBOOK ABC GUIDE WAYBOOK
BAEDEKER HANDBOOK
ROADBOOK
GUIDELINE SLUG PARAMETER
GUIDEPOST GUIDE PARSON
WAYMARK WAYPOST SIGNPOST
GUIDERIUS (FATHER OF —)
CYMBELINE
GUIDEWAY SLAY SLEY SLEIGH
SLIDEWAY SWANNECK
GUIDING POLAR BEHIND HOMING
LEADING
GUIDO (WIFE OF —) ALERIA
GUILD HUI GILD HOEY HONG YELD
CRAFT HANSA HANSE GREMIO
GUIDRY SCHOLA BASOCHE
COLLEGE COMPANY MYSTERY
GUILE DOLE WILE CHEAT CRAFT
FRAUD TRAIN CAUTEL DECEIT
HUMBUG CUNNING FALLACY
ARTIFICE
GUILELESS PLAIN CANDID HONEST
ARTLESS ONEFOLD IGNORANT
INNOCENT SACKLESS UNNOOKED
GUILLEMOT AUK COOT LARY LAVY
LOOM QUET TURR URIA ARRIE
CUTTY FROWL MURRE SCOUT
TOIST TYSTE GRYLLE LUNGIE
MAGGIE MARROT SCRABE TINKER
DOVEKEY DOVEKIE SEACOOT
SKIDDAW TARROCK WILLOCK
PUFFINET ROCKBIRD SCUTTOCK
SPRATTER
GUILT SIN SAKE WITE BLAME
CULPA FAULT PIACLE PLIGHT
NOCENCE OFFENSE HAMARTIA
INIQUITY
GUILTLESS FREE PURE CLEAN
UNSAKED INNOCENT SACKLESS
GUILTY FAULTY NOCENT WICKED
CORREAL HANGDOG NOXIOUS
PECCANT BLAMEFUL CRIMINAL
CULPABLE GUILTFUL
(— OF ERROR) LAPSED
GUINEA MEG BEAN QUID QUEED
GEORGE SHINER GEORDIE
(HALF —) SMELT

GUINEA

CAPE: VERGA
CAPITAL: CONAKRY
COIN: FRANC
ISLAND: TOMBO TRISTAO
ISLAND GROUP: LOS
MEASURE: JACKTAN
MOUNTAIN: TAMGUE
MOUNTAINS: LOMA NIMBA
NATIVE: SUSU TOMA KISSI FULANI

GUERZI MALINKE KOURANKE
LANDUMAN
RIVER: NIGER BAFING FALEME
SENEGAL KONKOURE TINKISSO
TOWN: BOKE FRIA KADE LABE
BENTY BEYLA COYAH KOULE
MAMOU DABOLA DALABA
DOUAKO FABALA KANKAN
KINDIA BOFOSSO CONAKRY
DUBREKA FARANAH KONFARA
KOUMBIA OUASSOU SIGUIRI
KEROUANE
WEIGHT: AKEY PISO UZAN BENDA
SERON QUINTO AGUIRAGE

**GUINEA-BISSAU (ARCHIPELAGO OF
—)** BIJAGOS
(CAPITAL OF —) BISSAU
(RIVER OF —) GEBA CACHEU
MANSOA CORUBAL
GUINEA FOWL KEEL KEET PEARL
MEBACK GALEENY PINTADO
COMEBACK GALLINEY
(SOUND OF —) POTRACK
GUINEA GRASS PANIC PANICLE
SACATON ZACATON GAMELOTE
GUINEA PEPPER PIMENTO
GUINEA PIG CAVY
(MALE —) BOAR BUCK
GUINEA RUSH ADRUE
GUISE HUE FORM GARB COLOR
COVER SHAPE MANNER PERSON
APPAREL CLOTHES GUISARD
LIKENESS
GUISER MUMMER
GUITAR AX AXE BOX KIT PIPA
DOBRO JAMON KITAR SITAR
TIPLE GIMBRI KITTAR SANCHO
SATTAR CITHERN CITTERN
MACHETE UKULELE CHARANGO
CHITARRA
(PART OF —) KEY NUT PEG BASE
BODY BONE FRET HEAD HEEL
HOLE NECK BRACE GUARD WAIST
BRIDGE SADDLE STRING ROSETTE
FINGERBOARD
GUITARFISH RAY BATOID
PURAQUE
GUITGUIT PITPIT
GULANCHA GILO GILOE
GULCH COULE GULLY SLUIT
CANYON COULEE RAVINE
GULDEN FLORIN GUILDER
(100,000 —) TUN
GULES MARS RUBY TORTEAU
GULF SINE CHAOS GULPH VORAGE
VORAGO
(BOTTOMLESS —) ABYSM ABYSS
GULFWEED SARGASSO
GULL COB COX MEW COBB CONY
COOT CULL DUPE FOOL GOLL
LARI MALL PINT PIRR SELL SKUA
XEME ALLAN ALLEN ANNET
BOSUN CHEAT CHUMP COBBE
COKES CROCK CULLY HOODY
JAGER LARID LARUS PEWIT
SCULL SMELT YAGER BONXIE
BUBBLE CHOUSE COUSIN JOCKEY
PEEWIT PIGEON SIMPLE TEASER
TULIAC VICTIM WAGGEL WHILLY
CROCKER DECEIVE MEDRICK
PICKMAW POPELER SCAURIE
SEABIRD SEAFOWL SWARBIE

TARROCK TRUMPIE BLACKCAP
DIRTBIRD DOTTEREL DUNGBIRD
SEEDBIRD
(LIKE A —) LAROID
GULLET MAW GULE LANE GORGE
GARGLE PECHAN THROAT
KEACORN STOMACH SWALLOW
WEASAND GURGULIO
(PREF.) ESOPHAG(O) LAEMO
LEMO RUMENO
GULLIBLE GOOFY GREEN SIMPLE
CULLIBLE
GULLIVER GRILDRIG
GULLY BOX GEO GUT DRAW GULL
RAIK RAKE SICK SIKE DONGA
DRAFT GOYLE GULCH SLAKE
SLUIT ZANJA ARROYO GULLET
GULLEY GUTTER NULLAH RAVINE
SHEUCH SHEUGH CHIMNEY
COULOIR DRAUGHT BARRANCA
GULP BOLT GAUP GLUT GULL
POOP SOPE SWIG GULCH QUILT
SLOSH SWIPE ENGLUT GLUTCH
GOBBLE GOLLOP PAUNCH
SLABBER SWALLOW SWATTLE
SLUMMOCK
(— NOISILY) SLORP
GUM ASA AMRA BLOB FILL GOOM
LOAD TUNO ALGIN AMAPA BABUL
CUMAY DHAVA ACAJOU ANGICO
BARRAS CHICLE KARAYA TOUART
TUPELO CARANNA CARAUNA
GINGIVA GUMWOOD PERRIER
BORRACHA CARABEEN DEXTRINE
DRESSING FEVERGUM
CALENDULIN
(ACACIA —) GEDDA
(AROMATIC —) MYRRH
(ASTRINGENT —) KINO
(CHEWING —) WAX
(FRAGRANT —) BUMBO
(RED —) JARRAH
(UNGRADED —) SORTS
(WOOD —) XYLAN
(PL.) ULA
(PREF.) COMMI GUMMI GUTTI
GUM ARABIC KIKAR ACACIA
ACACIN
GUMBO OKRA
GUMBOIL PARULIS
GUMBO-LIMBO JOBO BIRCH
GOMART MASTIC NEGRITO
ALMACIGO ARCHIPIN
GUMDROP GUM JUJUBE
GUMMER BIDDY BIDDIE SCRAPER
SCUFFER SCUFFLER SCUPPLER
GUMMY GLUEY CLAGGY MASTIC
GUMMOUS
GUMPTION NOUS SENSE SPRAWL
GUMS
(PREF.) GINGIV(O) ULEMO ULO
GUM SUCCORY HOGBITE
GUM TREE KARI KARRI TOOART
TOUART TUPELO EUCALYPT
GUMWEED GRINDELIA
SUNFLOWER
GUN GAT POP BREN HAKE PIAT
ROER STEN TUBE BARIL FIFTY
FIRER FUSEE FUZEE RAKER
REWET RIFLE ARCHIE BERTHA
CANNON CHASER CULVER
DUCKER INCHER JEZAIL MINNIE
QUAKER RANDOM SPIGOT SWIVEL

TUPARA CALIVER FIREARM
HACKBUT HANDGUN JINGALL
LANTACA MUZZLER AMUSETTE
ARQUEBUS CHAUCHAT CULVERIN
FIRELOCK GALLOPER OERLIKON
PEDERERO SHAGBUSH
TROMBONE
(BOAT —) BASE
(LOWER-DECK —) BARKER
(MACHINE —) CHOPPER GATLING
(SPRING —) STEL
(TOY —) SPARKLER
(PL.) FLAK CHASE ARTILLERY
GUNA RAJAS TAMAS SATTVA
GUNBOAT SKIP BARCA GONDOLA
TINCLAD
GUN CARRIAGE PANEL MADRIER
GALLOPER
GUNCREWMAN PLUGMAN
GUNDOBAD (BROTHER OF —)
GODOMAR CHILPERIC GODEGISEL
(FATHER OF —) GUNDIOCH
GUNDOG POINTER
GUNFLINT STONE
GUNI (FATHER OF —) NAPHTALI
GUNITE SHOTCRETE
GUNLOCK ROWET FIRELOCK
GUNMAN HOOD GUNSEL
GUNSMAN TORPEDO ENFORCER
GANGSTER
GUNNEL BLENNY SWORDICK
GUNNER GUN POPPER FIREMAN
SHOOTER ENGINEER
GUNNY TAT BURLAP BAGGING
SACKING
GUNNYSACK CORNSACK
GUNPOWDER SULFUR SULPHUR
GUNSIGHT VISIE HAUSSE
GUNSTOCK BLANK TIPSTOCK
GUNSTONE OGRESS PELLET
GUNTHER (SISTER OF —) KRIEMHILD
(WIFE OF —) BRUNEHILDE
GUNTRAM (BROTHER OF —)
SIGEBERT CHARIBERT CHILPERIC
(CHARACTER IN —) ROBERT
GUNTRAM FREIHILD FRIEHOLD

(COMPOSER OF —) STRAUSS
(FATHER OF —) CLOTAIRE
GUNWALE GUNNEL PORTOISE
GUNZ SCANIAN
GUPPY MILLIONS BELLYFISH
GUR GOOR KHAUR JAGGERY
VOLTAIC
GURGLE GLOX BRAWL CLUNK
QUARK SLOSH BICKER BUBBLE
BULLER BURBLE GOLLER GUGGLE
RUCKLE
GURGLINGLY TRILLIL
GURJUN YANG
GURNARD CUR TUB PIPER ELLECK
ROCHET BATFISH CAPTAIN
GRUNTER LATCHET SOLDIER
TRIGLID TUBFISH VOLADOR
HARDHEAD KNORHAAN LORICATE
GURO KWENI
GUSH JET BOIL FLOW FOAM HUSH
RAIL SLOP WALM BELCH SLUSH
SMALM SMARM SPIRT SPURT
STOUR SWOSH BURBLE PHRASE
SWOOSH WALLOW WHOOSH
SLOBBER
(SENTIMENTAL —) SLOSH
GUSHING SLOPPY SMARMY
EFFUSIVE
GUSSET GORE MITER MITRE QUIRK
PIECETTE
GUST BUB FLAN GALE GUSH WAFF
WAFT WIND BLAST FRESH SLANT
FLURRY HUFFLE SQUALL
FLAUGHT WILLIWAW WINDFLAW
(— OF RAIN) SKIT
(— OF WIND) FLAM FLAN FUFF
GALE GUSH PIRR SCUD TIFT
BERRY BLAST BLORE FLAFF
THODE SQUALL WINDFLAW
GUSTATION TASTE
GUSTO GUST ZEST VERVE RELISH
UNCTION
GUSTY DIRTY PUFFY BLASHY
BLASTY FRETFUL GUSTFUL
SQUALLY
GUT GIB BOWEL CECUM CLEAN

CAECUM CATGUT HOLLOW
STRING ELISION GRALLOCH
(FISH —) GIP GILL
(TWISTED —) THARM THERM
(PL.) MOXIE BOWELS COJONES
PUDDING ENTRAILS
GUTSY BALLSY
GUTTA SOH DROP PUAN SIAK
SUSU DUJAN GERIP SANGE
SUNDIK CAMPANA JANGKAR
SEMARUM TRENAIL TRUNNEL
HANGKANG KETAPANG
GUTTER GRIP REAN SIKE GRIPE
GULLY RIGOL SIVER SPOUT
SWEAL BOTTOM CANNEL CULLIS
GROOVE GUZZLE KENNEL RIGGOT
RUNNEL STRAND TROUGH
VENNEL CHANNEL CHENEAU
GRIZZLE
(— OF STREET) KENNEL
(MINING —) BOTTOM HASSING
(ROOF —) RONE
(PL.) LIMBERS
GUTTERMAN SWAMPER
GUTTURAL GRUM BURRY HARSH
THICK
GUY BOD CAT EGG JOE NUT BIRD
BOZO DUDE GENT GINK HUSK
JACK JOHN BLOKE COOKY JOKER
SCOUT SPOOF BUFFER COOKIE
GAZABO GAZEBO GAZOOK GILGUY
HOMBRE JASPER JIGGER MALKIN
MAUMET MAWKIN KNOCKER
BLIGHTER
GUYANA (CAPITAL OF —)
GEORGETOWN
(RIVER OF —) CUYUNI BERBICE
DEMERARA MAZARUNI
ESSEQUIBO
(TOWN OF —) ITUNI BILOKU
ISSANO MACKENZIE
(WATERFALL IN —) MARINA
KAIETEUR
GUY MANNERING (AUTHOR OF —)
SCOTT
(CHARACTER IN —) GUY MEG LUCY

BROWN DANDY HARRY JULIA
BERTRAM DINMONT GLOSSIN
SAMPSON MANNERING MERRILIES
ELLANGOWAN HATTERAICK
GUY ROPE STAY VANG
GUZ GAZ GEZ ZAR ZER GUDGE
GUZERAT KANKREJ
GUZZLE BUM GUM SOT TUN BEND
GULL SLOSH SWILL GOOZLE
GUDDLE SWATTLE SWIZZLE
GUZZLER BENDER
GWYNIAD SCHELLY
GYASCUTUS PROCK
GYLE BEER GAIL BREWING
GYMKHANA AUTOCROSS
GYMNASIUM GYM PALESTRA
TURNHALL PALAESTRA
GYMNAST SOKOL BENDER
TURNER ACROBAT TUMBLER
GYMNASTIC (— SOCIETY) SOKOL
GYNOECIUM BRUSH APOCARP
GYNOPHORE PODOGYN
GYPSUM GYP GYPS YESO GESSO
LUDIAN PARGET GYPSITE
SATINITE SELENITE ALABASTER
GYPSY FAW CALO APTAL CAIRD
GIPSY ROMNI BOSHAS GITANO
ROMANY TINKER AZUCENA
CZIGANY MOONMAN TINKLER
TZIGANE ZINCALO ZINGARO
BOHEMIAN EGYPTIAN FLAMENCO
ZIGEUNER
(NON —) GORGIO
(SEA —) BAJAU
(PL.) ROMANESE
GYRATE GYRE SPIN TURN TWIRL
WHIRL CURVET INGYRE ROTATE
REVOLVE SQUIRREL
GYRATION PRECESSION
GYRATORY GIDDY GYRAL
GYRFALCON JERKIN
GYRON GIRON ESQUIRE
GYROSE SINUATE

H

H HOW AITCH HOTEL ASPIRATE
HABERDASHER OUTFITTER
HABERDASHERY TOGGERY
HABERGEON HAUBERK
HABILIMENT GARB HABIT
   APPAREL RAIMENT CLOTHING
   (PL.) CLOTHES EQUIPAGE
HABILITATE ENABLE
HABIT LAW PAD SET USE WON
   COAT GARB GATE SUIT THEW
   WONT FROCK HAUNT TACHE
   TRADE TRICK USAGE CUSTOM
   GROOVE MANNER PRAXIS TALENT
   CLOTHES FOLKWAY HABITUS
   WONTING CROTCHET HABITUDE
   PHYSIQUE PRACTICE PRACTISE
   ASSUETUDE CONSUETUDE
   (— OF GRINDING TEETH) BRUXISM
   (BAD —) HANK VICE MISTETCH
   CACOETHES
   (DEPRAVED —) CACHEXY
   (SPEECH —S) ACCENT
   (PL.) DAPS
   (PREF.) HEXICO
HABITABLE BIGLY LIVABLE
HABITAT ECE HOME RANGE
   PATRIA STATION LOCALITY
   (PREF.) EC(O) OEC(O) OIKO
HABITATION HOLD TELD TENT
   ABODE BIELD HABIT HOUSE
   BIDING WONING DOMICILE
   DWELLING PANTHEON TENEMENT
   RESIDENCE
   (— SITE) YACATA
   (QUIET —) SHADE
   (UNDERGROUND —) HOLE
HABITUAL USUAL COMMON
   HECTIC CHRONIC REGULAR
   FREQUENT ORDINARY
HABITUATE USE HOWF ENURE
   FLESH HABIT INURE ADDICT
   SEASON HACKNEY ACCUSTOM
   ACQUAINT OCCASION
HABITUATED WONT SEASONED
   ACCUSTOMED
HABITUDE HABIT SCHESIS
HABITUE DENIZEN COURTIER
HABRONEMIASIS BURSATI
   BURSATTE
HACEK WEDGE
HACHALIAH (SON OF —) NEHEMIAH
HACK HAG HEW BOLO CHIP HAKE
   DEVIL HATCH DRUDGE FIACRE
   HACKLE HAGGLE HODMAN
   JOBBER MANGLE SCOTCH
   HACKNEY MATTOCK VETTURA
   MUTILATE
   (LITERARY —) GRUB DEVIL
HACKBERRY EGGBERRY HACKTREE
   HAGBERRY ONEBERRY
HACKBUT HAGBUT DEMIHAG
   HACKBUSH
HACK GHARRI SHIGRAM

HACKLE COMB RUFF HECKLE
   NAPPER RUFFER HATCHEL
   ROUGHER
HACKNEY HACK MIDGE NODDY
HACKNEY CARRIAGE MIDGE
   FIACRE JARVEY VETTURA
HACKNEYED HACK WORN BANAL
   HOARY TRITE CANNED CLICHE
   COMMON FOREWORN
HAD D HED HEDDE
   (— NOT) HADNA HADNT
HADAD (FATHER OF —) ISHMAEL
HADADEZER (FATHER OF —) REHOB
HADDOCK GADE GADID SCROD
   DICKEY HADDIE
   (DRIED —) CRAIL RIZZAR SPELDING
   SPELDRIN
HADE UNDERLIE
HADES PIT ADES HELL AIDES
   ORCUS PLUTO SHEOL SHADES
   TARTAR ACHERON AIDONEUS
   TARTARUS
   (FATHER OF —) SATURN
   (WIFE OF —) PROSERPINA
HADORAM (FATHER OF —) TOU
   JOKTAN
HAECCEITY THISNESS
HAEMON (FATHER OF —) CREON
   PELASGUS
   (SON OF —) THESSALUS
HAEMUS (FATHER OF —) BOREAS
   (MOTHER OF —) ORITHYIA
   (SON OF —) HEBRUS
   (WIFE OF —) RHODOPE
HAFF LAGOON
HAFNIUM CELTIUM
HAFT HEFT HOVE HELVE DUDGEON
HAFTER HANDLER
HAG ATE MARE REBEC RUDAS
   SIBYL VECKE WITCH BELDAM
   HECATE ROUDAS BELDAME
   HAGGARD HELLCAT HARRIDAN
HAGAR (MISTRESS OF —) SARAH
   (SON OF —) ISHMAEL
HAGBOAT HOGGET HOGGIE
HAGFISH HAG BORER VECKE
   MYZONT SUCKER PLACOID
   MYXINOID
HAGGARD PALE THIN GAUNT
   WISHT HAGGED
HAGGI (FATHER OF —) GAD
HAGGITH (HUSBAND OF —) DAVID
   (SON OF —) ADONIJAH
HAGGLE CHOP PRIG DODGE
   BADGER BANTER BOGGLE DICKER
   HACKER HIGGLE HUCKLE NAGGLE
   NIFFER PALTER SCOTCH THREEP
   BARGAIN CHAFFER HUCKSTER
HAGGLER DODGER
HAGGLING BARGAIN CHAFFER
HAGIOGRAPHA KETUBIM
HAGIOSCOPE SQUINT SQUINCH
HAIDA SKITTAGET

HAIL AVE HOY HALE GREET SALVE
   SPEAK STORM ACCOST BAYETE
   HAGGLE HALLOO HERALD SALUTE
   ACCLAIM
   (SOFT —) GRESIL GRAUPEL
   (PREF.) CHALAZI CHALAZO
HAILSTONE STONE
HAINAI IONI
HAIR FAX JAG RIB WIG BARB CROP
   FLUE GLIB HEAD KEMP PELF PILE
   SETA WIRE BEARD CRIMP CRINE
   FRIZZ FRONT PILUS QUIFF
   ANGORA BRILLS BRUTUS CRINET
   FIBRIL FROWZE MERKIN SETULA
   THATCH TRAGUS CULOTTE
   ELFLOCK GLOCHIS TOPKNOT
   WHISKER CAPILLUS COLLETER
   PALPOCIL TENTACLE TRICHODE
   TRICHOME VIBRISSA
   (— BROWN) ARGALI
   (— OF ANIMALS) FUR PELF
   (— OF HORSES OR COWS) CERDA
   (— OF TERRIER) FALL
   (— ON HORSE'S HOOF) CRONET
   (— ON LEAF) GLAND
   (— ON TEMPLES) HAFFET HAFFIT
   (— ON THIGHS) CULOTTE
   (— OVER EYES) BROW GLIB
   EYELASH
   (BARBED —) GLOCHIS
   (BRAID OF —) QUEUE PIGTAIL
   (BUNDLE OF —) LEECH
   (CAMEL'S —) DEER
   (COARSE —) KEMP BRISTLE
   (CURLED —) FRIZZ
   (CUTDOWN —) STUMPS
   (FALSE —) WIG JANE FRONT
   PERUKE
   (FRIZZED —) FROWZE
   (GRAY —) GRIZZLE
   (LOCK OF —) TUZ FEAK TATE
   FLOCK TRESS
   (LONG HEAVY —) MANE
   (LOOSE —) COMBINGS
   (MATTED —) SHAG ELFLOCK
   (MOP OF —) TOUSLE
   (NOSE —) VIBRISSA
   (PLANT —) COLLETER
   (ROOT —) FIBRIL
   (SNARL OF —) TANGLE
   (SOFT —) DOWN LANUGO
   (STINGING —) STING STIMULUS
   (STINGING —S) COWHAGE
   (STRAY LOCK OF —) TAG
   (STYLE —) CORNROW
   (TUFT OF —) PLUME KROBYLOS
   (WAVING LOCK OF —) WIMPLER
   (WHITE —) SNOW SNOWS
   (PL.) SETAE COWAGE COWHAGE
   HACKLES
   (PREF.) CAPILLI CHAET(I)(O)
   CHETO COME COMI CRINI
   HIRSUTO LACHN(O) PIL(I)(O)

   TRICH(O) TRICHINO VILLI
   (SUFF.) CHAETA CHAETES
   CHAETUS COMA THRICHOUS
   THRIX TRICHA TRICHI(A) TRICHY
HAIRBREADTH HERMELE WHISKER
HAIR BROWN QUAIL
HAIRBRUSH TOILETRY
HAIRCLOTH HAIR CILICE
HAIRCUT BOB CUT CROP BUTCH
   SHINGLE DUCKTAIL
HAIRDO AFRO FRISURE
HAIRDRESSER WAVER FRISEUR
   COIFFEUR
HAIRDRESSING FRISURE
   BANDOLINE
HAIR FRAME PALISADE
HAIRINESS PILOSISM PILOSITY
HAIRLESS BALD PELON CALLOW
   ATRICHIC DEPILOUS GLABROUS
HAIRLIKE TRICHOID
HAIRLINE WHISKER
HAIRPIN ACUS BODKIN SKEWER
HAIRSPLITTING FINE PILPUL
HAIRSTYLE AFRO BINGLE
HAIRWORM GORDIID GORDIOID
HAIRY FAXED MOSEY PILAR
   ROUGH COMATE COMOUS PILARY
   PILINE CRINITE CRINOSE HIRSUTE
   PILEOUS VILLOUS UNSHAVEN
   (PREF.) DASI DASY HEBE

HAITI

CAPE: FOUX
CAPITAL: PORTAUPRINCE
CHANNEL: SUD STMARC
COIN: GOURDE
DEITY: LOA
GULF: GONAVE
INDIAN: TAINO
ISLAND: VACHE GONAVE TORTUE
   NAVASSA TORTUGA
ISLAND GROUP: CAYMITES
LAKE: SAUMATRE
MAGIC: OBI OBEAH
MOUNTAIN: NORD CAHOS NOIRES
   LAHOTTE LASELLE TROUDEAU
PLAIN: NORD CAYES JACMEL
   LEOGANE ARCAHAIE CULDESAC
   GONAIVES
PRIEST: BOCOR HOUNGAN
RIVER: GUAYAMOUC ARTIBONITE
SPIRIT: LOA BAKA BOKO
TOWN: AQUIN CAYES FURCY
   LIMBE HINCHE JACMEL JEREMIE
   LEOGANE SALTROU GONAIVES
   KENSCOFF

HAKAM CACAM HAHAM CHOCHEM
   KHAKHAM
HAKE GADE HAIK LING GADOID
   CODLING HADDOCK WHITING
   ANACANTH QUODLING
HAKENKREUZLER SWASTIKA

HALBERD BILL PIKE GLAIVE
GLEAVE POLEARM PARTISAN
(PART OF —) BEAK BUTT BLADE
SPIKE
HALBERDIER DRABANT
HALCYON CALM ALCYON GOLDEN
HALE YELL FRACK FRECK TRAIL
ROBUST STRONG HEALTHY
VIGOROUS
HALER HELLER
HALF M ARF ELF DEMI HAUF HOVE
SEMI SIDE MEDIO HALFEN HALFLY
MOIETY MEDIETY
(— GALLON) POTTLE
(— OF DRAW) BRACKET
(— OF EM) EN
(— OF INNING) BOTTOM
(— OF MOLD) VALVE
(FRUIT —S) SLABS
(PREF.) DEMI HEMI SAM SEMI
(ONE AND A —) SESQUI
HALFBACK (OFFENSIVE —)
SLOTBACK
HALFBEAK GAR IHI BALAO PIPER
BALLYHOO
HALF-BLOOD DEMISANG
HALF BOOT BUSKIN BOTTINE
HALF-BREED BREED METIF METIS
SAMBO MUSTEE RAMONA
CABOCLO MESTIZO METISSE
DEMISANG HARRATIN MIXBLOOD
HALF-CASTE TOPAZ TOPASS
HALF-CRAZY FIFISH
HALF CROWN GEORGE ALDERMAN
HALF-DEAD ALAMORT
HALF DENIER MAILE MAILLE
HALF DOBRA PECA
HALF-EATEN SEMESE
HALF-FARTHING CUE MITE
MINUTE
HALF-GABLE AILERON
HALF GAINER ISANDER
HALF-GROWN HALFLIN
HALF-GUINEA SMELT
HALF HITCH ROLLING
HALF MASK LOUP DOMINO
HALF-MOON LUNETTE DEMILUNE
HALF NOTE MINIM
HALFPENCE GROCERY
HALFPENNY OB MAG MEG DUMP
GRAY GREY MAIK MAIL MAKE
MEKE OBOL SOUSE STAMP
BAUBEE BAWBEE MAILLE
HAPENNY PATRICK STUIVER
(COUNTERFEIT —) RAP GRAY
(THICK —) DUMP
HALF-PIKE SPONTON DEMIPIKE
SPONTOON
HALF-PINT CUP JACK CUPFUL
HALF REST SOSPIRO
HALF SOLE TAP
HALF STEP CHROMA
HALFTONE DROPOUT
HALF TURN DEMIVOLT
HALF-WIT DOLT DUNCE HAVEREL
TOMFOOL STAUMREL UNDERWIT
HALF-WITTED SOFT DOTTY SIMPLE
HALUCKET IMBECILE STAUMREL
HALIBUT BUT BUTT FLITCH
TURBOT FLATFISH
HALIFAX BALLYHACK
HALIOTIS ABALONE

HALIRRHOTHIUS (FATHER OF —)
NEPTUNE
(MOTHER OF —) EURYTE
(SLAYER OF —) MARS
HALL HA AULA HELL IWAN SALA
AIWAN ATRIO BALAI BURSA
CURIA DIVAN ENTRY FOYER
HOUSE OECUS SALLE SALON
ATRIUM CAMERA DURBAR
EXEDRA GARDEN LESCHE SALOON
SCHOOL SENATE TOLSEY TRANCE
APADANA CHAMBER DANCERY
GALLERY HALLWAY KURHAUS
KURSAAL MEGARON PASSAGE
VINGOLF ANTEROOM ARCHEION
ASSEMBLY BASILICA CHOULTRY
COLISEUM CORRIDOR FOREHALL
HASTROND HOSPITAL RAADZAAL
TOLBOOTH VALHALLA
(— FOR PERFORMANCES) ODEON
ODEUM
(— OF JUSTICE) COURT
(— WITH STATUES) VALHALLA
(DINING —) COMMON REFECTORY
(LECTURE —) SCHOLA
(MISSION —) CITADEL
(MUSIC —) GAFF
(TOWN —) CABILDO RATHAUS
TRIBUNAL
(UNIVERSITY —) BURSA
HALLMARK CROWN SHOPMARK
HALL OF FAME (AVIATION —) ELY
SIX BYRD LAHM LEAR LINK LUKE
MOSS POST RYAN WADE EAKER
GLENN LEMAY PIPER REEVE
ARNOLD BOEING CESSNA FOKKER
HUGHES LEVIER MARTIN ROGERS
SPAATZ SPERRY TOWERS TRIPPE
TURNER WALDEN WRIGHT
YAEGER CHANUTE EARHART
GRUMMAN LANGLEY LOENING
SHEPARD TWINING MITCHELL
NORTHROP SIKORSKY
ARMSTRONG LINDBERGH
MCDONNELL RICKENBACKER
(BASEBALL —) OTT COBB DEAN
FORD FOXX HOYT KELL KLEM
MACK MAYS MIZE RUTH WYNN
AARON BANKS BERRA COMBS
EVERS FRICK GOMEZ GROVE
HAFEY KINER LEMON LOPEZ
LYONS PAIGE PLANK RUSIE
SPAHN TERRY VANCE WALSH
WANER WHEAT YOUNG ALSTON
CHANCE CRONIN CUYLER FELLER
FRISCH GEHRIG GOSLIN KALINE
KOUFAX LAJOIE LANDIS MANTLE
MANUSH MCGRAW MUSIAL
RICKEY SISLER TINKER WAGNER
WILSON WRIGHT YAWKEY
APPLING AVERILL BURKETT
HORNSBY HUBBARD HUGGINS
JOHNSON PENNOCK RUFFING
SIMMONS SPEAKER STENGEL
TRAYNOR BOUDREAU COMISKEY
DIMAGGIO GRIFFITH MACPHAIL
MARICHAL MCCARTHY ROBINSON
WILLIAMS COVELESKI
BRICKHOUSE MARANVILLE
(BASKETBALL —) GALE GOLA PAGE
REED WEST COUSY FULKS GREER
HAGAN HYATT LUCAS MIKAN
ARIZIN BARLOW BAYLOR COOPER

FOSTER HANSON HOLMAN
KRAUSE MURPHY PETTIT PHILIP
RAMSEY ROOSMA SEDRAN
TWYMAN WOODEN BECKMAN
BRADLEY BRENNAN DEHNERT
GRUENIG KURLAND POLLARD
SCHAYES SCHMIDT SHARMAN
WACHTER BORGMANN
ENDACOTT LAPCHICK LUISETTI
MACAULEY SCHOMMER
MCCRACKEN STEINMETZ
VANDIVIER DEBERNARDI
DEBUSSCHERE
(BUSINESS —) FORD HAAS LUCE
OCHS VAIL GARST HEINZ ROUSE
SLOAN BATTEN DISNEY DORIOT
DUPONT HILTON KAISER LASKER
MELLON MORGAN OGILVY
PENNEY SCHIFF SCHWAB
EASTMAN SARNOFF WHITNEY
CARNEGIE FRANKLIN MCCORMICK
VANDERBILT ROCKEFELLER
WESTINGHOUSE WEYERHAEUSER
(FOOTBALL —) MIX RAY BELL HEIN
HUFF LARY MARA OTTO FEARS
GROZA GUYON HALAS HAYES
LAYNE LILLY LYMAN MUSSO
NEALE RINGO ROYAL BADGRO
BLANDA BUTKUS GRANGE HINKLE
KINARD MATSON MCAFEE
ROONEY THORPE TITTLE TRIPPI
UNITAS ALWORTH GILLMAN
LUCKMAN MILLNER LOMBARDI
MITCHELL WARFIELD JURGENSEN
PARSEGHIAN
(GOLF —) BERG FORD HOPE
BOROS BURKE DUTRA EVANS
HAGEN HOGAN JONES SHUTE
SMITH SNEAD ARMOUR COOPER
DIEGEL GHEZZI LITTLE NELSON
OUIMET PALMER PICARD RUNYAN
TRAVIS DEMARET GULDAHL
HARBERT MANGRUM REVOLTA
SARAZEN ZAHARIAS DEVICENZO
(THEATER —) DREW KERR BROOK
HECHT KELLY SIMON PRINCE
DUNNOCK CHAMPION KINGSLEY
LANSBURY MCARTHUR MEREDITH
SONDHEIM STRASBERG
YOUNGMANS BLOOMGARDEN
HALLOO HO HOO LOO ALEW BAWL
LURE WHOOP ACCOST TALLYHO
HALLOW BLESS HALWE DEDICATE
SANCTIFY
HALLOWED HOLY SACRED
BLESSED
HALLUCINATION DWALE
ACOASMA ACOUASM ACOUSMA
FANTASY PHONEME DELUSION
ILLUSION PHANTASY ZOOSCOPY
HALLUCINOGEN ACID
HALLUX TALON
HALLWAY ENTRY FOYER TRANCE
HALMA HOPPITY
HALMALILLE PETWOOD
HALO DOG BURR GLOR NIMB
GLORY SHINE AREOLA CIRCLE
CORONA GLORIA NIMBUS
SUNDOG AREOLET AUREOLE
BOROUGH CINCTURE
HALOHESH (SON OF —) SHALLUM
HALT HO HOP ALTO BAIT BALK
HOLD LIMP SKID STAY STOP TRIP

WAIT BAULK BLOCK BREAK CEASE
CHECK HILCH HITCH STAND STICK
ARREST BARLEY SCOTCH STANCE
CONTAIN CRIPPLE STATION
STOPPAGE
(— GAME) CALL
(— TO DOGS) TOHO
HALTER EVIL SOLE BRANK TRASH
WANTY WIDDY WITHE POISER
CAUSSON CAVESON JAQUIMA
POINTEL BALANCER NECKLACE
HALTING BODE LAME ZOPPA
CRIPPLE LIMPING
HALVE DIMIDIATE
(PL.) HALVERS
HALVING HAPLOSIS
HAM PIG GAMMON JAMBON
JARRET PESTLE GAMBONE
PROSCIUTTO
(BROTHER OF —) SHEM JAPHET
(FATHER OF —) NOAH
(PICNIC —) CALA CALI
(SON OF —) CUSH PHUT CANAAN
MIZRAIM
HAMATUM UNCIFORM
HAMESUCKEN HAMFARE
HAMITE BORAN BORANA DANAKIL
DANKALI
HAMLET KOM DORP TOON TOWN
TREF VILL ALDEA CASAL HAMEL
SITIO STEAD THORP VICUS
ALDEIA BUSTEE THORPE
CLACHAN KAMPONG KIRKTON
KIRKTOWN
(AUTHOR OF —) SHAKESPEARE
(CHARACTER IN —) OSRIC HAMLET
HORATIO LAERTES OPHELIA
BERNARDO CLAUDIUS GERTRUDE
POLONIUS REYNALDO CORNELIUS
FRANCISCO MARCELLUS
VOLTIMAND FORTINBRAS
ROSENCRANTZ GUILDENSTERN
HAMMEDATHA (SON OF —)
HAMAN
HAMMER AX AXE BIT DOG PEG
SET CALL COCK DROP HORN
MALL MASH MAUL MELL SETT
TILT CAVIL KEVEL KNOCK MADGE
POUND SMITE THUMP BEETLE
BUCKER CLOYER DRIVER FALLER
FULLER MALLET MARTEL NOPPER
OLIVER PLEXOR SCUTCH SLEDGE
TACKER TILTER KNAPPER
KNOCKER MALLEUS PLESSOR
STRIKER CRANDALL MALLEATE
MJOLLNIR SCUTCHER TREMBLER
(— FOR DRESSING STONE) KEVEL
(— OF GUNLOCK) DOG COCK
DOGHEAD
(— OUT) ANVIL
(BRICKLAYER'S —) SCOTCH
SCUTCH SCUTCHER
(LEADEN —) MADGE
(MINER'S —) BULLY
(PART OF —) BELL CLAW FACE
GRIP HEAD NECK PEEN POLL
CHEEK HANDLE
(PAVING —) REEL
(PNEUMATIC —) GUN BUSTER
(SLATE-CUTTER'S —) SAX
(STEAM —) IMPACTER IMPACTOR
(TUNING —) KEY
HAMMERED BEATEN WROUGHT

HAMMERHEAD CORNUDA
HAMMERKOP UMBER UMBRETTE
HAMMERLOCK BAR ARMLOCK
HAMMERMAN STRIKER
HAMMOCK SACK HUMMOCK
  (— CARRIED BY BEARERS) DANDY
  (— SLUNG ON POLE) MACHILA
  (WOODEN —) KATEL KARTEL
HAMMOLEKETH (BROTHER OF —)
  GILEAD
  (FATHER OF —) MACHIR
HAMPER BIN COT MAR PED TUB
  BFAT BIND CLOG CURB FLAT
  HURT LOAD SLOW TUCK BLOCK
  CABIN CRAMP CRATE MAUND
  RUSKY SERON BASKET BURDEN
  FETTER HALTER HINDER HOBBLE
  HOPPLE IMPEDE TANGLE
  BUFFALO CONFINE HANAPER
  MANACLE PANNIER PERPLEX
  SHACKLE TRAMMEL ENCUMBER
  ENTANGLE OBSTRUCT RESTRAIN
  RESTRICT STRAITEN
HAMPERING STIFLING DIFFICULT
HAMSTER CRICETID
HAMSTRING HOX HOCK LAME
  HOUGH ENERVATE
HAMUL (FATHER OF —) PHAREZ
HAMUTAL (FATHER OF —)
  JEREMIAH
  (HUSBAND OF —) JOSIAH
  (SON OF —) JEHOAHAZ ZEDEKIAH
HANAMEEL (COUSIN OF —)
  JEREMIAH
  (FATHER OF —) SHALLUM
HANAN (FATHER OF —) AZEL
  ZACCUR MAACHAH IGDALIAH
HANANI (FATHER OF —) HEMAN
  (SON OF —) JEHU
HANANIAH (FATHER OF —) AZUR
  BEBAI HEMAN ZERUBBABEL
  (GRANDSON OF —) IRIJAH
  (SON OF —) ZEDEKIAH
HANAPER HAMPER
HAND M CAT DAB FAM FIN HAN
  PAW PUD CLAW DEAL DUKE GIVE
  GOLL HALF JACK LOOF MAIN
  MANO MITT PART PASS SPAN
  CAMAY CLAUT CLEUK FLUSH
  GLAUM GRASP GRIPE INDEX
  MANUS NIEVE POWER SHARE
  STIFF STOCK BRIDGE CLUNCH
  CLUTCH DADDLE DOUBLE
  FAMBLE GOWPEN HANDLE
  MAULEY MINNIE STAGER
  WORKER CLAWKER FAMELEN
  FLAPPER FLIPPER POINTER
  WORKMAN GRAPPLER MORTMAIN
  (— COUNTING ZERO) BACCARA
  BACCARAT
  (— DOWN) DEVOLVE TRADUCE
  BEQUEATH TRANSMIT
  (— GESTURES) MUDRA
  (— IN POKER) FULL SKIP BLAZE
  FLUSH SKEET TIGER BICYCLE
  JACKPOT SKIPPER IMMORTAL
  STRAIGHT
  (— IN WHIST) MORT TENACE
  (— ON) BUCK SPREAD
  (— ON HIP) AKIMBO
  (— OVER) GIVE REACH BETEACH
  BITECHE DELIVER
  (— UP STRAW) SERVE

(— WITH 5 HIGHEST TRUMPS)
JAMBOREE
(BABY'S —) SPUD
(BIG AND UNGAINLY —) MAIG
(BRIDGE —) BID DUMMY DOUBLE
  CHICANE LAYDOWN
(CLENCHED —) FIST
(COLD —S) SHOWDOWN
(CURSIVE —) CIVILITE
(DECK —) HAWSEMAN
(DUMMY —) BOARD
(ELDEST —) EDGE SENIOR
(EUCHRE —) JAMBONE
(EXTRA — IN LOO) MISS
(FRENCH —) COULEE
(GRASPING —) CLAUT
(GREEN —) FARMER JACKEROO
(LEFT —) SINISTRA
(LONE —) JAMBONE
(PART OF —) PAD BALL HEEL PALM
  DIGIT INDEX THUMB WRIST
  CARPUS CREASE FINGER PINKIE
  THENAR MINIMUS BRACELET
  LIFELINE FINGERTIP FOREFINGER
  HYPOTHENAR TRANSVERSE
(PERSIAN —) SHIKASTA
(POKER —S) BOARD
(RANCH —) COWBOY
(REEL —) SPINDLER
(RIGHT —) DEXTER
(ROUND —) RONDE
(SECTION —) SNIPE
(SKILLFUL —) DAB
(SPARE — IN CARDS) CAT
  JAMBOREE
(UNSKILLED —) DABSTER
(UPPER —) BULGE EMINENCE
(WEAK CARD —) BUST
(PREF.) CHEIR(O) CHIR(O) MANI
  MANU PALMATI PALMI
  (SUFF.) CHEIRIA CHIRIA
HANDBAG BAG CABA NEIF CABAS
  PURSE SATCHEL ENVELOPE
  GRIPSACK POCHETTE RETICULE
  POCKETBOOK
HANDBALL PALM
HANDBARROW BIER HANDY
  TRUCK BARROW
HANDBELL SKELLAT TANTONY
HANDBILL BILL FLIER FLYER LIBEL
  DODGER
HANDBOOK VADY GRADUS
  MANUAL BAEDEKER
HANDBOW STONEBOW
HANDCAR DRAG
HANDCART PRAM DANDY HURLY
  TRUCK GOCART TROLLY TROLLEY
HANDCUFF CUFF STAY LINKER
  NIPPER STAYER MANACLE
  TRAMMEL WRISTER BRACELET
  HANDBOLT HANDLOCK LIGAMENT
  SNITCHER WRISTLET
  (PL.) IRONS SNAPS DARBIES
  NIPPERS
HANDEDNESS
  (SUFF.) CHEIRIA CHIRIA
HANDER-IN INGIVER
HANDFUL M MAN GRIP LOCK WISP
  YELM CLAUT GRIPE LITCH
  GOUPIN GOWPEN HANTLE
  YAFFLE FISTFUL MANIPLE
  (— OF GRAIN) RIP REAP SINGLE
  SONGLE

(— OF LEAVES) PATRIN
(DOUBLE —) GOWPEN
(LAST — OF HARVEST) KIRN
(SMALL —) PUGIL
HANDFUL OF DUST (AUTHOR OF —
) WAUGH
  (CHARACTER IN —) JOCK JOHN
  LAST TODD TONY BEAVER
  BRENDA MENZIES MESSINGER
HANDGRIP TUFFING
HANDGUN HAKE CALIVER
  HANDARM
HANDICAP START BURDEN DENIAL
  HAMPER HINDER IMPEDE STRIKE
  PENALTY ENCUMBER PENALIZE
HANDICAPPED CRIMP CRIMPED
HANDICRAFT MYSTERY ARTIFICE
  MECHANIC HANDCRAFT
HANDICRAFTSMAN ARTISAN
HANDILY HANDY GAINLY
HANDINESS YARAGE
HANDIWORK MACHINE
HANDKERCHIEF WIPE CLOUT
  FOGLE HANKY ROMAL STOOK
  WIPER HANKIE MADRAS NAPKIN
  SUDARY TIGNON BANDANA
  BELCHER FOULARD KERCHER
  MANIPLE ORARIUM SNEEZER
  BANDANNA KERCHIEF MOCKETER
  MONTEITH MOUCHOIR SUDARIUM
  VERNACLE VERONICA
HANDLE BOW EAR FAN LUG NIB
  NOB PAD PIN PLY USE ANSA BAIL
  BALE BOOL BUTT CROP FEEL FIST
  GAUM GRIP HAFT HALE HAND
  HANK HILT KILP KNOB LIFT RAPE
  RUNG STOP GRASP GRIPE GROPE
  HELVE MOUNT SHAFT SPOKE
  STAIL STALE START STEAL STELE
  STOCK SWING TREAT WIELD
  BECKET FETTLE FINGER FUSEAU
  HANGER LIFTER MANAGE
  MANURE POMMEL ROUNCE
  TILLER CONDUCT DUDGEON
  WOOLDER BEERPULL BELLPULL
  BITSTAIN BITSTOCK DISPENSE
  HANDGRIP HANDHOLD HANDLING
  MOPSTICK STAGHORN
  PENHOLDER MANIPULATE
  (— AWKWARDLY) FUMBLE
  THUMBLE
  (— BADLY) ILLGUIDE
  (— CLUMSILY) PAW FUMBLE
  (— IMPROPERLY) GAUM
  (— MODISHLY) GALLANT
  (— OF AXE) HELVE
  (— OF BENCH PLANE) TOAT TOTE
  (— OF CANNON) MANIGLION
  (— OF DAGGER) DUDGEON
  (— OF KETTLE) BAIL
  (— OF LADLE) SHANK
  (— OF OAR) GRASP
  (— OF PLOW) HALE STAFF START
  STILT PLOWTAIL
  (— OF PRINTING PRESS) ROUNCE
  (— OF RAKE) STALE
  (— OF SCYTHE) TACK SNATH
  SNEAD THOLE SNATHE SNEATH
  (— OF SWORD) HAFT HILT
  (— OF WHIP) CROP
  (— RECKLESSLY) FOOL
  (— ROUGHLY) MALL MAUL TOWSE
  MUZZLE GRABBLE MANHANDLE

(— VIOLENTLY) BOUNCE
(CRANK —) WINK
(CROSSBOW —) TILLER
(CURVED —) BOOL BOUL
(DETACHABLE —) KILP
(LIFTING — OF GUN) DOLPHIN
(PUMP —) BRAKE SWIPE
(ROPE —) SHACKLE
(WOODEN —) TREE
(PL.) HALES
HANDLED (EASILY —) BANTAM
HANDLER DOCKHAND
  (AIRPLANE —) AIREDALE
  (SUFF.) STER STRESS
HANDLEY CROSS (AUTHOR OF —)
  SURTEES
  (CHARACTER IN —) JOHN PIGG
  HARDY MELLO BELINDA BRAMBER
  DOLEFUL MICHAEL SWIZZLE
  JORROCKS FLEECEALL
  BARNINGTON
HANDLING USE CONTROL
  (SKILLFUL —) CONDUCT
  (UNSKILLFUL —) BUNGLING
HANDMAID ANCILLA
HANDOUT DOWN
HANDRAIL BAR RAIL MANROPE
  BANISTER EASEMENT MOPSTICK
  TOADBACK
HANDSHAKE SHAKE SHRUG
HAND-SHAPED PALMATE
HANDSOME BRAW FAIR FINE
  MOOI NICE PERT TALL BONNY
  FETIS FITTY FUSOM LUSTY
  ADONIC BRAWLY CLEVER COMELY
  FARAND GOODLY HEPPEN LIKELY
  PROPER SEEMLY ADONIAN
  AVENANT ELEGANT FEATISH
  FEATOUS FEWSOME GALLANT
  LIBERAL SMICKER GOODLIKE
  STUNNING VENEREAN WEELFARD
HANDSOMELY FAIRLY HANDSOME
HANDSTONE MANO
HAND STRAP TOGGEL TOGGLE
HANDSTROKE TALLY
HANDWORK TOOLING
HANDWRITING PAW FIST HAND
  WRITE DUCTUS NESHKI NIGGLE
  SCRIPT SCRIVE BATARDE
  WRITING BACKHAND HANDWRIT
HANDY DAB DEFT GAIN NEAT
  WEME JEMMY LUSTY QUEME
  READY TIGHT ADROIT CLEVER
  HEPPEN KNACKY DEXTROUS
  EXPEDITE HANDSOME SKILLFUL
HANDYMAN MOZO JUMPER
  GREASER SWAMPER
HANG NUB TOP CRAP DRAG FALL
  HANK KILT PEND TREE TUCK
  DRAPE DROOP HOVER KETCH
  NOOSE SCRAG STRAP SWING
  TRINE TRUSS TWIST ANHANG
  APPEND DEPEND GIBBET HALTER
  IMPEND SLOUCH STRING TALTER
  DOGGONE HANGING LANTERN
  STRETCH SUSPEND
  (— ABOUT) DRING HOVER
  (— AROUND) KNOCK HANKER
  SLINGE
  (— BACK) LAG BOGGLE
  (— BEHIND) PLOD
  (— CRIMINAL) STRAP TOTTER
  (— DOWN) DIP LOP LAVE DROOP

DEPEND FESTOON PROPEND
(— HEAVILY) SWAG
(— LOOSELY) BAG SAG FLAG FLOW
LOLL BANGLE DANGLE PAGGLE
(— ONE'S HEAD) SLINK
(— OUT) LILL
(— OVER) WAUVE IMPEND
WHAUVE
(— PICTURE NEAR CEILING) SKY
(— SOGGILY) TROLLOP
(— WITH TAPESTRY) TAPIS
(PREF.) CREMO
HANGAR DOCK GARAGE AIRDOCK
HANGER PASSIVE SHABBLE
BASELARD WHINYARD
(— FOR CARCASSES) STANG
(COAT —) SHOULDER
(CRANK —) BRACKET
(LACE-MAKING —) WORKER
(SWORD —) CARRIAGE
HANGER-ON BUR CAD BURR SPIV
LEECH TOADY CLIENT HANGBY
HEELER LACKEY SPONGE
LACQUEY PENDING PARASITE
(— OF CELEBRITY) GROUPIE
HANGING FLAG HEMP TURN
ARRAS BAGGY DRAPE SWING
CELURE DORSEL DOSSER DERRICK
DRAPERY PENDENT PENSILE
ANTEPORT HANGMENT
PARAMENT
(— LOOSE) LOPPY BAGGED
(— LOW) SIDE
(— THREATENINGLY) IMMINENT
(LIMPLY —) FLAGGY SLIMPSY
(WALL —) CEILING TENTURE
KAKEMONO
(PL.) TAPIT TAPPET DRAPERY
PARAMENT
HANGMAN KETCH HANGER
HANGIE TOPMAN DERRICK
GREGORY TOPSMAN VERDUGO
CARNIFEX SCRAGGER
(HALTER OF —) TOW
HANGMAN'S DAY FRIDAY
HANGNAIL AGNAIL
HANGOUT NEST JOINT SCATTER
HANGOVER HOLDOVER RESIDUUM
HANG-UP BAG
HANIEL (FATHER OF —) ULLA
HANK HASP SKEIN BOBBIN
SELVAGEE
(— OF FLAX) HEAD
(— OF TWINE) RAN
(— OF YARN) SLIP
HANKER HANK LONG LINGER
HANKERING ITCH HANKER
HANKUL ENMUN ONMUN
HANNAH (HUSBAND OF —)
ELKANAH
(SON OF —) SAMUEL
HANNIEL (FATHER OF —) EPHOD
HANOCH (FATHER OF —) REUBEN
HANS BRINKER (AUTHOR OF —)
DODGE
(CHARACTER IN —) HANS RAFF
GLECK HILDA GRETEL BOEKMAN
BRINKER MEVROUW
HANSOM CAB SHOFUL SHOWFUL
HANUMAN ENTELLUS
HANUN (FATHER OF —) NAHASH
ZALAPH
HAP REDE CHANCE

FORTUNE HAPPING
HAPHAZARD CASUAL CHANCE
CHANCY RANDOM BUCKEYE
SCRATCH CARELESS SCRAMBLY
SLAPDASH TUMULTUARY
HAPHAZARDLY ANYHOW
HAPLESS POOR UNLUCKY
HAPLY HAPS HAPPILY
HAPPEN BE DO GO HAP COME
COOK FALL FARE GIVE LUCK PASS
RISE TIDE TIME BREAK EVENE
EVENT LIGHT OCCUR SHAPE
ARRIVE BECOME BEFALL BETIDE
CHANCE TUMBLE FORTUNE
STUMBLE SUCCEED BECHANCE
OVERCOME
(— TOGETHER) CONCUR
HAPPENING HAP FACT EVENT
THING CHANCE TIDING TIMING
INCIDENT OCCASION
OCCURRENCE
(ACTUAL —) FACT
(UNEXPECTED —) ACCIDENT
HAPPILY FAIN FITLY GLADLY
JOYOUSLY
HAPPINESS JOY WIN GLEE SELE
SONS WEAL BLISS GLORY MIRTH
SOOTH FELICE WEALTH DELIGHT
ECSTASY FELICIA RAPTURE
UTILITY FELICITY GLADNESS
HILARITY
HAPPY FIT COSH FAIN GLAD GLEG
SELI WELY BONNY FAUST FELIX
LIGHT LUCKY MERRY PROUD
SEELY SONSY SUNNY WHITE
BLITHE BONNIE BRIGHT JOYFUL
COMICAL GLEEFUL HALCYON
JOCULAR PERFECT SEELFUL
WEALFUL WEIRDLY BLISSFUL
CAREFREE DISPOSED FROHLICH
GRACIOUS SUNSHINE
(PREF.) FELICI
HARA-KIRI SEPPUKU
HARAN (BROTHER OF —) ABRAHAM
(DAUGHTER OF —) ISCAH MILCAH
(FATHER OF —) CALEB TERAH
(MOTHER OF —) EPHAH
(SON OF —) LOT
HARANGUE ORATE CONCIO
PATTER SERMON SPEECH TIRADE
ADDRESS DECLAIM EARBASH
DIATRIBE PERORATE
HARASS FAG GIG HAG HOX MAG
NAG RAG TAW VEX BAIT CARK
FRAB FRET GALL GNAW HAKE
HALE HARE HAZE HOCK JADE
PAIL PUSH RIDE SEEK TIRE TOIL
TOSS WORK ANNOY BESET BULLY
CHAFE CHASE CHEVY CHIVY
CURSE FLISK GRIND GRIPE HARRY
HURRY PRESS TARGE TEASE
TRASH WEARY WORRY BADGER
BOTHER CHIVVY CHOUSE
CUMBER FERRET HASSLE HATTER
HECKLE HECTOR HESPEL HOORAY
HURRAH INFEST MOLEST
MURDER OBSESS PESTER PINGLE
PLAGUE POTHER PURSUE
AFFLICT AGITATE BEDEVIL
DRAGOON HAGRIDE HARRAGE
OPPRESS PERPLEX PROVOKE
TERRIFY TORMENT TRAVAIL
TROUBLE TURMOIL BULLYRAG

DISTRACT DISTRESS EXERCISE
FORHAILE IRRITATE SPURGALL
SUPPRESS PERSECUTE
(— MENTALLY) GRUDGE
HARASSED BESTEAD HARRIED
HAUNTED
(— BY) BEFORE
HARASSING WARM
HARBINGER ANGEL USHER
HERALD FORAGER FORAYER
FURRIER OUTRIDER PRODROME
(— OF SUMMER) SWALLOW
HARBOR REE BEAR DOCK HOLD
PIER PORT BASIN BAYOU CHUCK
CREEK HAVEN HITHE SLADE
BREACH BUNDER COTHON
FOSTER REFUGE OUTPORT
PORTLET SEAPORT SHELTER
CARENAGE ENHARBOR SHIPRADE
(— A CRIMINAL) RESET
(SUBMARINE —) PEN
HARBOR SEAL DOTANT DOTARD
RANGER SEALCH TANGFISH
HARD DRY FIT ILL COLD DEAR
DOUR DURE FAST FIRM IRON
MEAN NASH OPEN CHAMP CLOSE
CORKY HARSH HORNY ROCKY
SMART SNELL SOLID SOUND
STEEL STERN STIFF STONY STOOR
STOUT TIGHT BOARDY BRAWNY
COARSE FLINTY GLASSY KITTLE
KNOBBY KNOTTY ROBUST
RUGGED SEVERE STARKY STINGY
STRICT STRONG STURDY UNEATH
UNNETH WOODEN ADAMANT
ARDUOUS AUSTERE CALLOUS
HARDWAY HORNISH ONEROUS
SUBDURE CORNEOUS DILIGENT
HARDBACK HARDENED
IRONHARD OBDURATE PETROSAL
RIGOROUS SCLEROID SCLEROSE
TOILSOME
(— BY) FORBY FORTHBY
(— TO BEAR) FIERCE
(— TO MANAGE) SALTY
(— TO PLEASE) FINICKY CONCEITY
(— TO REACH) CUMBROUS
(— TO READ) BLIND
(— TO SATISFY) EXIGENT
EXIGEANT
(— TO SELL) STICKY
(— TO UNDERSTAND) DIFFUSE
(PREF.) DURO SCLER(O) STERE(O)
HARD-BILL SEEDEATER
HARD-BITTEN GNARLED
HARDEN SET TAW BAKE BEEK
CAKE FIRM HARN KERN SEAR
BRAZE ENURE FLESH INURE
STEEL STONE BRONZE ENDURE
FREEZE OBDURE OSSIFY POTASH
SEASON TEMPER CALCIFY
EMBRAWN PETRIFY STIFFEN
THICKEN CONCRETE ENHARDEN
INDURATE SOLIDIFY
(— QUILL) DUTCH
(CASE —) STEEL
HARDENED DRAW HARD LOST
SALTED CALLOUS COCTILE
CRUSTED FIBROUS INDURATE
OBDURATE
HARDENING SET POROMA
SCLEROMA OSSIFICATION
HARDHACK SPIREA

IRONBUSH WHITECAP
HARDHEAD LION BOCHE
HARDHEARTED STERN STONY
OBDURATE
HARDICANUTE (FATHER OF —)
CANUTE
(HALF-BROTHER OF —) HAROLD
(MOTHER OF —) EMMA
HARDIHOOD PLUCK COURAGE
AUDACITY
HARDLY ILL SCANT BARELY
RARELY SCARCE UNEATH
SCARCELY
HARDNESS SEG GRAIN PROOF
RIGOR STEEL DURESS DURITY
ADAMANT HARDSHIP SEVERITY
SOLIDITY
(— OF CHARACTER) HEART
HARD-OF-HEARING DULL DUNCH
DEAFISH
HARDPAN PAN CLAYPAN
MOORPAN MOORBAND ORTSTEIN
HARDSHIP HARD GRIEF PINCH
RIGOR STOUR THRONG UNWEAL
SQUEEZE ASPERITY HARDNESS
(PL.) EXTREMES
HARDTACK PANTILE
(— AND MOLASSES) BURGOO
HARD TIMES (AUTHOR OF —)
DICKENS
(CHARACTER IN —) JUPE JAMES
SISSY JOSIAH LOUISA SLEARY
THOMAS SPARSIT STEPHEN
GRAGRIND BLACKPOOL
BOUNDERBY HARTHOUSE
MCCHOAKUMCHILD
HARDWARE TRIM IRONWARE
(COMPUTER —) MONITOR
HARDWOOD HARD BREAKAX
LEAFWOOD
HARDWORKING EIDENT
HARDY DOUR HARD WIRY LUSTY
MANLY STOUR STOUT TOUGH
GARDEN HUGMED RUGGED
STURDY SPARTAN STUBBED
GAILLARD GALLIARD STUBBORN
HARE PUG WAT BAWD CONY PUSS
SCUT BAWTY CUTTY LEPUS
PUSSY MALKIN MAUKIN BELGIAN
LEPORID POUSSIE VENISON
BAUDRONS KLIPHAAS LEPORINE
(— IN FIRST YEAR) LEVERET
(— TRACK) PRICK
(FEMALE —) DOE
(GREAT —) MANABOZHO
(LITTLE CHIEF —) CONY PIKA
(MALE —) BUCK
(PATAGONIAN —) MARA
(SIBERIAN —) TOLAI
(PL.) FLICK
(PREF.) LAG(O) LEPORI
HAREBELL BLAWORT THIMBLE
BLAEWORT BLUEBELL
HAREBRAINED GIDDY WINDY
HARELIP LAGOSTOMA
HAREM SERAI ZENANA ANDERUN
HAREMLIK SERAGLIO
HAREPH (FATHER OF —) CALEB
(SON OF —) BETHGADER
HARE'S-EAR MODESTY BUPLEVER
HARHAIAH (SON OF —) UZZIEL
HARIJAN PANCHAMA
HARL WHIRL

HARLEQUIN DUCK SQUEALER
(FEMALE —) LADY
(MALE —) LORD
HARLOT PUG DRAB LOON SLUT
HIREN PAGAN QUEAN RAHAB
STRAP TWEAK WHORE RIBALD
TOMBOY DELILAH MERMAID
WAGTAIL MERETRIX MISWOMAN
STRUMPET
(PREF.) PORN(O)
HARLOTRY PUTAGE BITCHERY
HARM NEY NOY NYE WEM ARME
BALE BANE DERE HURT SCAT
SORE TEEN WERD ANNOY GRAME
HERME LOATH QUALM SHEND
SPOIL TOUCH WATHE WEMMY
WOUGH WOUND WRAKE WREAK
WRONG DAMAGE DAMNUM
DANGER GRIEVE INJURE INJURY
SCATHE SORROW WONDER
DESPITE DISEASE FORFEIT
IMPEACH TROUBLE UNQUERT
BUSINESS DISAVAIL DISSERVE
ENDAMAGE MISCHIEF NOCUMENT
NUISANCE
(— REPUTATION) DEFAME
(DO —) ENVY
(PREF.) NOCI
HARMFUL BAD EVIL HARM NASTY
NOXAL NOCENT NOCIVE NOYFUL
UNSELY BANEFUL HURTFUL
NOISOME NOXIOUS DAMAGING
INIMICAL SINISTER PERNICIOUS
HARMFULNESS VICE MALICE
HARMINE BANISTERINE
HARMLESS SAFE SELI TAME
CANNY SEELY SILLY WHITE
DOVISH FEARLESS HURTLESS
INNOCENT SACKLESS UNHARMED
HARMONIA (DAUGHTER OF —) INO
AGAVE SEMELE AUTONOE
(FATHER OF —) MARS
(HUSBAND OF —) CADMUS
(MOTHER OF —) VENUS
(SON OF —) POLYDORUS
HARMONIC OVERTONE
HARMONICA HARP EUPHON
SYRINX AEOLINE PANPIPE
ARMONICA ZAMPOGNA
HARMONIOUS HAPPY SWEET
COSMIC SILKEN UNITED MUSICAL
SPHERAL TUNEFUL BALANCED
CHARMING HARMONIC PEACEFUL
ACCORDING CONCINNOUS
CONCORDANT
(PREF.) SYMPHO
HARMONITE RAPPIST RAPPITE
HARMONIUM ORGAN VOCALION
HARMONIZE GO FIT GEE KEY JIBE
SORT TUNE AGREE ATONE BLEND
CHORD GROUP HITCH RHYME
ACCORD ASSORT COTTON
COMPORT CONCENT CONCORD
CONSORT ORDINATE
ACCOMMODATE
HARMONIZING HENOTIC
HARMONY SUIT TUNE CHIME
CHORD UNITY ACCORD ATTUNE
COSMOS HEAVEN MELODY
UNISON BALANCE CONCENT
CONCERT CONCORD CONSENT
CONSORT KEEPING RAPPORT
DIAPASON FABURDEN SYMPATHY

SYMPHONY CONGRUITY
HARNEPHER (FATHER OF —)
ZOPHAH
HARNESS TUG GEAR HAME LEAF
REIN BRACE CROWN DRAFT
FRONT GEARS SLING TRACE
COLLAR FETTLE GULLET INSPAN
TACKLE DRAUGHT GEARING
GIGTREE LORMERY SIMBLOT
TOGGERY DRAWGEAR ENCLOSER
HEADGEAR TACKLING TURNBACK
(— FOR LOOM) LEAF HEALD
MOUNTING
(— FOR PULLING GUNS) BRICOLE
(DECORATIVE —) CAPARISON
(PART OF —) BIT REIN GIRTH
TRACE COLLAR BLINDER
CRUPPER BELLYBAND BREECHING
CHECKREIN
(WEAVING —) HEADLE HEDDLE
HARNESSED ANTELOPE GUIB
GUIBA BOSCHBOK BUSHBUCK
HARNESS MAKER KNACKER
WHITTAW
HAROLD I HAREFOOT
HARP ARPA FORK LYRE VINA
NABLA NANGA HARPER SABECA
CHROTTA DECHORD SAMBUKE
AUTOHARP CLARSACH
(CELTIC —) TELYN CLARSACH
(FINNISH —) KANTELA KANTELE
(ICELANDIC —) LANGSPIL
(JAPANESE —) KOTO
(JEW'S —) TRUMP
(PART OF —) BASE BODY FOOT
NECK BOARD PEDAL PILLAR
STRING
(PERSIAN —) SANG
(TRIANGULAR —) TRIGON
TRIGONON
HARPOON IRON FIZGIG GRAINS
FISHGIG HARPAGO STRIKER
HARPAGON
HARPOONED FAST
HARPOONER STRIKER
HARP SEAL HARP BEATER
SADDLER
HARPSICHORD SPINET CEMBALO
CLAVIER CLAVECIN HASPICOL
HARPY HAG AELLO CELAENO
OCYPETE PODARGE
HARQUEBUS HAGBUT CALIVER
HACKBUT ARQUEBUS
HARQUEBUSIER CARABIN
HARRIER HAWK KAHU BEAGLE
FALLER MILLER PUTTOCK
HARROWER
HARROW COG CHIP DISC DISK
DRAG HARO TINE BRAKE BREAK
HERSE DREDGE DRUDGE FALLOW
LADDER SPADER CUTAWAY
LACERATE OXHARROW
HARROWED HAGGARD
HARROWING TINE TINING
TEARING
(— OF HELL) ANASTASIS
HARRY HAG BRACE CHIVEY
CHIVVY FERRET HARASS CRUCIFY
HARSH ILL ACID BULL DOUR FOUL
HARD HASH HASK IRON RUDE
SOUR ACERB ACRID ASPER BRUTE
CRONK CRUDE GRILL GRUFF
HEAVY HUSKY RASPY ROUGH

ROUND RUVID SHARP SNELL
STARK STERN STIFF STOUR
STOUT BRUTAL COARSE FLINTY
GRAVEL GRISLY HOARSE RAGGED
RASPED RUGGED SEVERE
SHREWD STURDY SULLEN TETRIC
UNKIND UNRIDE AUSTERE
CRABBED RASPING RAUCOUS
SQUAWKY VIOLENT ABRASIVE
ACERBATE ASPERATE ASPEROUS
CATONIAN CLASHING DRACONIC
GRAVELLY GRINDING GUTTURAL
JANGLING OBDURATE RIGOROUS
SCABROUS SCRANNEL STRIDENT
STROUNGE STUBBORN TETRICAL
UNGENTLE UNKINDLY
(— OF VOICE) STEER
HARSHLY HARD HARSH SHORTLY
HARSHNESS WOLF RIGOR DURESS
CATOISM CRUDITY CRUELTY
DUREZZA RAUCITY ACERBITY
ACRIMONY ASPERITY FELLNESS
HARDNESS HASKNESS
MORDANCY SEVERITY
HART SPADE VENISON
HARTEBEEST ASSE TORA TORI
BUBAL CAAMA KAAMA KONZE
LECAMA BUBALIS CONGONI
KONGONI SASSABY
HART'S-TONGUE LONGLEAF
HARUM (SON OF —) AHARHEL
HARUMAPH (SON OF —) JEDAIAH
HARUSPEX ARUSPEX ARUSPICE
EXTISPEX
HARUZ (DAUGHTER OF —)
MESHULLEMETH
HARVEST IN WIN CROP HEAP RABI
REAP SLED SNAP FOISON GATHER
HAIRST RUBBEE COMBINE
GRABBLE INGATHER SHEARING
HARVESTER COMBINE
HARVEST FISH WHITING
MOONFISH STARFISH
HARVEST HOME KIRN MELL
HOCKEY HORKEY
HARVESTING SLEDDING
HARVESTMAN CARTER CARTARE
HARY JANOS (COMPOSER OF —)
KODALY
HAS S AS HATH
(— NOT) NAS AINT
HASADIAH (FATHER OF —)
ZERUBBABEL
HAS-BEEN WUZZER
HASH RAPE MINCE HACHIS
MUDDLE RAGOUT
HASHABIAH (COMPANION OF —)
EZRA
(FATHER OF —) BUNNI KEMUEL
JEDUTHUN MATTANIAH
HASHABNIAH (SON OF —)
HATTUSH
HASHISH HEMP ASSIS
HASHUBAH (FATHER OF —)
ZERUBBABEL
HASID ASSIDEAN
HASKALAH (FOLLOWER OF —)
MASKIL
HASP COP HAPS COPSE SPRENT
HASSAR DORAD
HASSOCK TUT BOSS PESS POUF
TOIT TRUSH BUFFET TUFFET
HASTE HIE POST RACE RAGE RAPE

CHASE FEVER HASTY HURRY
SPEED BUSTLE FLURRY SWIVET
DISPATCH RAPIDITY STROTHER
PRECIPITATION
(HEADLONG —) SPURN
(IN —) HOTFOOT
(IN GREAT —) AMAIN
HASTEN HIE RAP RUN BUSK DUST
FIRK PELL PLAT POST RACE RAPE
RUSH SPUR URGE CATCH CHASE
DRIVE FLEET HASTE HURRY
PRESS PREST SLATE SPEED STEER
EXPEDE SCURRY STREAK SWITHE
ADVANCE FORWARD HACKNEY
HOTFOOT PREVENT QUICKEN
SLITHER SWIFTEN WITHHIE
DISPATCH EXPEDITE ACCELERATE
(— AWAY) FLEE SHERRY SQUIRR
HASTILY HOTLY RAPELY RASHLY
FOOTHOT HOTFOOT HYINGLY
HEADLONG
HASTY FAST RAPE RASH BRASH
FLEET QUICK FLYING RAPELY
CURSORY HOTHEAD HURRIED
PEPPERY TEARING HASTEFUL
HEADLONG SUBITANE
(TACTLESSLY —) BRASH
HAT DIP FEZ LID NAB ATTE BAKU
COIF DISC DISK FELT FLAT HIVE
HOOD KNAB MOAB SLOP TILE
TOPI BEANY BENJY BENNY BERET
BOXER CADDI CORDY DERBY
DICER GIBUS JERRY KELLY MILAN
MITER MITRE SHELL TARAI TERAI
TOPEE TOQUE TRUSH ABACOT
BEANIE BEAVER BOATER BOWLER
BRETON BUMPER CADDIE
CASQUE CLAQUE CLOCHE
COCKUP COIFFE FEDORA HELMET
PANAMA PILEUS RAFFIA SAILOR
SHOVEL SLOUCH TOPPER
TURBAN VIGONE BANDEAU
BANGKOK BLOOMER BRIMMER
BYCOKET CATSKIN CAUBEEN
CHAPEAU FANTAIL HATTING
HATTOCK HOMBURG LEGHORN
PETASOS PILLBOX PLATEAU
PLATTER SALACOT SCRAPER
SHALLOW SKIMMER SMASHER
STETSON BONGRACE CAPELINE
GOSSAMER HEADGEAR JIPIJAPA
MONTABYN MUSHROOM
NABCHEAT RAMILIES REHOBOAM
ROUNDLET SOMBRERO
(— BLOCKER) ROPER
(— OF MERCURY) PETASUS
(BEAVER —) CASTOR
(CLERGYMAN'S —) SHOVEL
(COCKED —) BICORNE RAMILIE
SCRAPER
(COWBOY —) STETSON
(FABRIC —) TOQUE
(FELT —) DERBY JERRY TARAI
TERAI ALPINE BOWLER TRILBY
BILLYCOCK
(HIGH —) KYL PLUG TILE TOPPER
(IRON —) GOSSAN GOZZAN
(MILITARY —) BUSBY BEARSKIN
(OILSKIN —) SQUAM
(OPERA —) GIBUS CLAQUE
(PART OF —) BOW BRIM CROWN
PINCH LINING BINDING HATBAND
SWEATBAND

(PITH —) TOPI TOPEE
(SILK —) KYL BEAVER SHINER CATSKIN
(STIFF —) TILE DERBY KELLY BOATER BOWLER SAILOR
(STOVEPIPE —) CAROLINE
(STRAW —) BAKU FLAT HOOD KADY KATY TOYO BENJY BENNY CADDY STRAW BASHER BOATER PANAMA LEGHORN
(TOP —) PLUG TOPPER
(UNBLOCKED —) CONE
(WATERPROOF —) TARPAULIN
(WIDE-BRIMMED —) FLAT BENJY TARAI SMASHER SUNDOWN
(3-CORNERED —) TRICORN
HATBAND BAND WEED WEEPER
HAT BRIM LEAF TARFE TURNUP
HATCH HECK BREED BROOD CLECK CLOCK COVEY GUICHET UNSHELL DISCLOSE INCUBATE
HATCHERY CHICKERY
HATCHET MOGO HACHE GWEEON THIXLE FRANCISC TOMAHAWK **(PREF.)** SECURI
HATCHING CLETCH BREEDING ECLISION
HATCHWAY HATCH SCUTTLE
HATE FIRE TEEN ABHOR SPITE DETEST HATRED LOATHE UNLOVE DESPITE
HATEFUL FOUL LOTH BLACK CURST DIRTY HATEL LOATH CURSED ODIOUS HEINOUS HIDEOUS ACCURSED FLAGRANT ABOMINABLE
HATER ULYSSES
HATH MOOLUM
HATHATH (FATHER OF —) OTHNIEL
HATING (PREF.) MIS(O)
HAT MONEY TAMPANG
HATRED DOSA ENVY HATE HELL ONDE HAINE ODIUM SPITE ENMITY RANCOR AVERSION ABHORRENCE
(— OF CHILDREN) MISOPEDIA
(— OF MARRIAGE) MISOGAMY
(— OF MEN) MISANDRY MISANTHROPY
(— OF NEW IDEAS) MISCAINEA
(— OF REASONING) MISOLOGY
(— OF WOMEN) MISOGYNY **(PREF.)** MIS(O)
HATTER GADGER HURRER
HATTUSH (FATHER OF —) HASHABNIAH
HAUBERK BYRNIE
HAUGHTILY BIGLY
HAUGHTINESS AIR PRIDE HEIGHT MORGUE ORGUIL DISDAIN HAUTEUR STOMACH HAUTESSE
HAUGHTY DAIN HIGH RANK STAY DIGNE DORTY HUFFY LOFTY LUSTY POTTY PROUD STOUT SURLY TAUNT FEISTY FIERCE HAUGHT QUAINT DISTANT HAUTAIN HONTISH PAUGHTY STATELY SUBLIME ARROGANT CAVALIER DEIGNOUS FASTUOUS GLORIOUS IMPERIAL INSOLENT ORGULOUS PRIDEFUL SCORNFUL SNIFFISH SUPERIOR

TOPLOFTY PEREMPTORY
HAUL KEP LUG RUG TEW TOW TUG DRAG DRAW DRAY HALE HURL JUNK PULL SKID TAKE TOTE TRAM BOUSE DRAVE HEAVE LIGHT ROUSE SNAKE TRACT TRICE TRAVOY DRAUGHT SCHLEPP CORDELLE HANDBANK
(— AFT) TALLY
(— DOWN) STRIKE
(— IN) GATHER
(— LOGS) TODE SLOOP SWAMP SIWASH HANDBANK
(— OF FISH) TACK DRAVE
(— OF NET) LIFT
(— SAIL) BUNT CLEW CLUE
(— SHIP) SPRING
(— TO DECK) BOARD
(— UP AND FASTEN) TRICE
(— WITH TACKLE) BOUSE
HAULAGE DOOK
HAULAGEWAY GANGWAY
HAULING HALE CARTAGE
HAUNCH HIP HOOK HUCK HANCE HUCKLE **(PL.)** GRUG HUNKERS
HAUNT DEN HANT HOME HOWF KEEP NEST WALK GHOST HOWFF SPOOK STALK INFEST KENNEL OBSESS OUTLAY PURSUE REPAIR PURLIEU FREQUENT PRACTICE
(— OF ANIMALS) LIE HOME
(FAMILIAR —) SLAIT
HAUNTED SPOOKY
HAUNTING BESETTING
HAUSTELLATE GLOSSATE
HAUSTORIUM SINK SINKER SUCKER
HAUTBOY OBOE WAIT
HAUTEUR PRIDE HEIGHT MORGUE
HAVE A AN OF OWN HOLD BOAST ENJOY OUGHT WIELD POSSESS
HAVEN ARK HOPE PIER PORT HITHE HARBOR HAVENET
HAVILAH (FATHER OF —) CUSH JOKTAN
HAVING (SUFF.) IOUS OSE OUS
HAVOC HOB HELL WASTE RAVAGE
HAW HOI HECK SLOE WIND WYND BOOTS PEGGLE ALISIER

HAWAII

BAY: POHUE HALAWA KIHOLO MAMALA KAMOHIO KANEOHE WAIAGUA KAWAIHAE MAUNALUA
BEACH: WAIKIKI
CAPITAL: HONOLULU
CHANNEL: AUA KAIWI KALOHI PAILOLO
COUNTY: MAUI KAUAI HAWAII HONOLULU
CRATER: KILAUEA
DESERT: KAU
DISTRICT: KONA PUNA
FISH: ULUA AKULE MOANO
FORMER NAME: SANDWICH
HARBOR: PEARL
HEAD: DIAMOND
ISLAND: MAUI OAHU KAUAI KAULA LANAI NIIHAU MOLOKAI
MOUNTAIN: KAALA KOHALA

KAMAKOU MAUNAKEA LANAIHALE
MOUNTAIN RANGE: KOHALA KOOLAU WAIANAE
NATIVE: KANAKA
STATE BIRD: GOOSE
STATE FLOWER: HIBISCUS
STATE NICKNAME: ALOHA
STATE TREE: CANDLENUT
TOWN: EWA AIEA HANA HILO LAIE PAIA KAPAA KEAAU LIHUE MAILI KAILUA KEKAHA PAHALA HONOKAA KAHULUI KANEOHE WAHIAWA WAIANAE WAILUKU HONOLULU PAPAIKOU
TREE: KOA NAIO WILIWILI
VALLEY: MANOA
VOLCANO: KILAUEA HUALALAI MAUNAKEA MAUNALOA

HAWAIIAN KANAKA KAMAAINA
HAWFINCH KATE GROSBEAK
HAWK IO EYAS KITE ALLAN BATER BUTEO CADGE EYESS HOICK HOUGH REACH RIVER STOOP BAWREL FALCON FOOTER HIGGLE KEELIE MERLIN MUSKET OSPREY PALLET PEDDLE RAMAGE RAPTOR RIFLER SHIKRA VERMIN BUZZARD GOSHAWK HAGGARD HARRIER HERONER KESTREL LENTNER STANIEL SWOOPER BRANCHER CARACARA HARROWER LENTINER PASSAGER ROUGHLEG SPARHAWK TALENTER TARTARET MORTARBOARD
(— FIGHT) CRAB
(CAGE FOR —S) MEW
(CROP OF —) GORGE
(FEMALE —) FORMAL FORMEL
(MALE —) JACK TASSEL TERCEL
(YOUNG —) EYAS NIAS BOWET BOWESS BRANCHER **(PREF.)** HIERACO
HAWKER CRIER CRYER BADGER CADGER COSTER DUFFER JOWTER PEDDER PETHER CAMELOT CHAPMAN HIGGLER MERCURY PEDDLER CRATEMAN GLASSMAN HUCKSTER
HAWKEYE STATE IOWA
HAWKING FALCONRY
HAWK PARROT HIA
HAWKWEED DINDLE BUGLOSS FIREWEED OXTONGUE
HAWSE BAG JACKASS
HAWSER FAST WARP HEADLINE
HAWTHORN HAW MAY QUICK THORN AIGLET MAYBUSH COCKSPUR MAYBLOOM MAYTHORN QUICKSET
(FRUIT OF —) HAZEL PEGGLE
HAY HEI RIP MATH RAKH RISP FETTLE STOVER WINDLIN SWEEPAGE
(— CUT FINE) CHAFF
(— PUT IN BARN) END
(BUNDLE OF —) TRUSS
(PILE OF —) TUMBLE
(ROW OF —) WINDROW
(SECOND-GROWTH —) EDDISH
(SMALL LOAD OF —) HURRY
(SMALL PIECE OF —) TATE

HAYCOCK MOW COIL HOVEL QUILE SHOCK DOODLE HIPPLE LAPCOCK HAYSHOCK
HAYFIELD PARK RAKH MOWING
HAYFORK PIKE PICKEL
HAYLOFT LOFT TALLET SCAFFOLD
HAYMAKER PICKMAN
HAYMOW GOAF HAYLOFT OVERDEN OVERHEAD
HAYRACK HECK HAYRIG THRIPPLE
HAYSTACK COB PIKE RICK HOVEL HAYRICK STACKAGE
HAYSUCK EYSOGE
HAY SWEEP BUCK
HAYWARD MEADSMAN
HAZAN CANTOR CHAZZAN
HAZARD DIE LAY LOT JUMP PAWN RISK WAGE JENNY LOSER PERIL CHANCE DANGER NIFFER BALANCE IMPERIL VENTURE ENDANGER JEOPARDY
HAZARDOUS NICE NASTY RISKY CHANCY QUEASY RISQUE UNSAFE UNSURE PARLOUS PERILOUS
HAZARDOUSLY CHANCILY
HAZE FOG URE FILM GLIN MIST REEK SMOG TRUB DEVIL GAUZE HAZLE SMEETH
(— AND SMOKE) SMAZE
HAZEL AGLET AIGLET COBNUT MUFFIN FILBERT HAZELNUT NOISETTE
(— FOR THATCHING) SPRAYS
HAZEL HOE PULASKI
HAZELNUT NIT HAZEL FILBERT
HAZEL TREE AVELLANO
HAZILY DIMLY
HAZINESS HAZE GRAYOUT
HAZO (FATHER OF —) NAHOR
(MOTHER OF —) MILCAH
HAZY DIM FOGGY MISTY MUZZY SMOKY THICK VAGUE CLOUDY DREAMY OBSCURE SMUISTY NEBULOUS
HE A E HI HO HEH HEY HIM HYE SHE ILLE THON CESTUI
(— DIED) OB
(— GAVE AND DEDICATED) DDD
(— MADE) F FEC
(— PAINTED IT) PNXT
(— READS) LEG
(— WAS NOT FOUND) NEI
HEAD BIT BUT COP DON FAT MIR NAB NOB PEN POW TOP BEAN BOSS CAPE COCO CONK COSP CROP DATU DEAN DOME HELM JOLE JOWL KAID KNOB LEAD MAKE MASK NOLL PASH PATE POLL RAIS TURN YEAD ALDER ATTIC BLADE BLOCK BONCE CHIEF CHUMP CROWN DATTO MAZER ONION RISER SCALP SHODE SKULL START TIBBY TROPE BELFRY BLANCH CABEZA CENTER CHAULE COBBRA COCKER DAROGA EXARCH GARRET GATHER HEADER KAISER MAHANT MAZARD NAPPER NODDLE PALLET RUBRIC SCONCE CAPITAL CAPTAIN COCONUT COSTARD COSTREL COXCOMB CRUMPET CUPHEAD GENARCH HEADING HEGUMEN NUCLEUS

PRELATE TOPKNOT CALABASH
CEPHALON DECURION DIRECTOR
DUFFADAR FOUNTAIN HEADLINE
INITIATE PHYLARCH POINTING
TOPPIECE CAPERNOITIE
(— IN PARTICULAR DIRECTION)
STEM
(— OF ABBEY) ABBOT
(— OF ALEMBIC) MITER MITRE
(— OF BEAR, WOLF OR BOAR) HURE
(— OF CABBAGE) LOAF
(— OF CEREAL) EAR
(— OF CHAIR) MAKER
(— OF CLOVER) COB SUCKER
(— OF COLUMN) CHAPITER
(— OF COMET) COMA
(— OF CONVENT) ABBESS
SUPERIOR
(— OF CRIME SYNDICATE) CAPO
(— OF DANDELION) BLOWBALL
(— OF DRILL BRACE) CUSHION
(— OF FAMILY) ALDER COARB
COMARB GOODMAN
(— OF FISH) JOWL
(— OF GANG) TINDAL
(— OF GOVERNMENT) MUKHTAR
(— OF GRAIN) ICKER
(— OF GUILD) ALDERMAN
(— OF HAIR) SUIT CRINE FLEECE
CHEVELURE
(— OF HARPOON) BOMB
(— OF HERRING) COB
(— OF JEWISH ACADEMY) GAON
(— OF LANCE) MORNE MOURNE
(— OF LOOM) JACQUARD
(— OF MONASTERY) HEGUMEN
(— OF MUSHROOM) BUTTON
(— OF MUSICAL INSTRUMENT)
SCROLL
(— OF NUNNERY) DAME
(— OF ORDER) MURSHID
(— OF PROJECTILE) OGIVE
(— OF RING) CHATON
(— OF RIVET) BULLHEAD
FLATHEAD SNAPHEAD
(— OF SEPT) COARB COMARB
(— OF STATE) CAUDILLO PRINCEPS
(— OF TAPEWORM) SCOLEX
(— OF TREE) COMA
(— OF 10 MONKS) DEAN
(— ON) SQUARE
(— PREMATURELY) BUTTON
(— USED AS TARGET) SARACEN
(BAKED SHEEP'S —) JAMES JEMMY
(BALD —) PILGARLIC
(BARBED —) FLUKE
(DRAGON'S —) RAHU
(FLOWER —) DAISY ARNICA
BUTTON PINBALL
(FLOWER —S) CURD ANTHEMIS
(FROM — TO FOOT) CANAPE
(LATHE —) POPPET
(NAIL —) ROSEHEAD
(POPPY —) POST
(PRINTED —) BOXHEAD
(SEED — OF FLAX) HOPPE
(SHRUNKEN —) TSANTSA
(PL.) GEONIM
(PREF.) CEPHAL(O) CORY(PH)(PHO)
CRANIO
(SUFF.) CEPHALIC CEPHALOUS
CEPHALUS CEPHALY PATE
HEADACHE HEAD SODA

BUSTHEAD HEADWARK MIGRAINE
CEPHALALGY
HEADBAND MITER MITRE VITTA
CARCAN DIADEM TAENIA CIRCLET
GARLAND CARCANET FOOTBAND
STEPHANE
HEADBOROUGH VERGES
HEADCAP SETHEAD CAPELINE
HEADDRESS FLY TOP TOY APEX
COIF FRET HEAD HORN KELL
PARE POUF TETE TIRE TOUR
AEGIS AMPYX CROWN GABLE
LAUTU PASTE POLOS PSHEM
SHAKO TIARA TOWER VITTA
ALMUCE ATTIRE ATTOUR BONNET
CASQUE CORNET FAILLE HENNIN
KENNEL KULLAH MOBCAP PINNER
TIRING TUINGA BANDORE
COMMODE FLANDAN MORTIER
PSCHENT STEEPLE TABLITA
THERESE TRESSON TUTULUS
BILIMENT BINNOGUE BYCOCKET
CAPRIOLE COIFFURE HEADGEAR
HEADTIRE KAFFIYEH MASKETTE
STEPHANE TRESSURE
(— OF DOGES) TOQUE
(— OF GODS) MODIUS
(— OF POPE) REGNUM
(— WITH LONG LAPPET) PINNER
(HIGH —) TOWER STEEPLE
FONTANGE
(WIDOW'S —) BANDORE
HEADED KNOTTED
(— OUT) RIZZOMED
(SUFF.) PATED
HEADER BINDER BONDER NOBBER
SADDLE KNOBBER HEADSMAN
STRETMAN
HEADFAST HEADROPE
HEADFIRST HEADLONG
HEADFOREMOST TOPSAIL
HEADFRAME POPPET GALLOWS
HEADGEAR (ALSO SEE
HEADDRESS) HIVE PASTE
BONNET BRIDLE HEADWEAR
HEADHUNTER LAKHER TAIYAL
ATAIYAL QUIANGAN
HEADING END HEAD STOW
LEMMA PILOT TROPE WICKET
CAPTION DIPHEAD HEADILY
STENTON WITCHET FOREHAND
STENTING
HEADLAND KOP PEN RAS BILL
CAPE HEAD MULL NASE NAZE
NESS NOOK NOUP PEAK SCAW
THRUM FORELAND PROMONTORY
HEADLESS ACEPHALOUS
(PREF.) ACEPHALO
HEADLINE HEAD LABEL BANNER
CAPTION DROPLINE SCREAMER
STREAMER SCAREMONGER
HEADLONG FULL RANK AHEAD
HASTY PRONE STEEP SUDDEN
RAMSTAM TANTIVY GADARENE
HEADLING RECKLESS
PRECIPITATE
HEADMAN BAAS JARL CHIEF
DATTO MALIK PATEL POMBO
VIDAN ATAMAN CABEZA HETMAN
INDUNA LOWDAH LULUAI POTAIL
TOPMAN KOMARCH ALDERMAN
CABOCEER CAPITANO HEADSMAN
KONOHIKI MALGUZAR

MOKADDAM PENGHULU
PRINCEPS STAROSTA TENIENTE
HEADMASTER HEAD RECTOR
REGENT PRECEPTOR
HEADMOST FOREMOST
HEADNOTE SYLLABUS
HEADPIECE CAP POT BASKET
CASQUE HELMET PALLET TESTER
TREMOR BASINET BRASSET
CASQUET CHAMFRON TESTIERE
HEADPIN KINGPIN
HEADQUARTERS BASE DEPOT
YAMEN AGENCY FONDACO
EXCHANGE BATTALION
HEADROPE BALK BAULK HEADLINE
HEADSET PHONES
HEADSHIP CHIEFTY
(SPIRITUAL —) KHALIFAT
HEADSPACE OUTAGE
HEADSTALL HALTER BRADOON
BRIDOON JAQUIMA
HEADSTOCK POPPET
HEADSTRONG RASH COBBY
RACKLE STOCKY UNRULY
HOTSPUR RAMSTAM VIOLENT
WAYWARD PERVERSE STUBBORN
HEADWAITER CAPTAIN
HEADWAY WAY DENT SEAWAY
WAYGATE HEADROOM
HEADWORD ENTRY
HEADY BOLD NAPPY HUFFCAP
HEAL CURE HALE MEND SAIN
AMEND COVER LEECH SALVE
SOUND WHOLE PHYSIC RECURE
SUPPLE TEMPER WARISH
CLEANSE GUARISH RECOVER
REDRESS RESTORE MEDICATE
(— OVER) INCARN
HEALD CAMB DUPE HAVEL
HEALER CURER ALTHEA SHAMAN
POWWOWER PRACTITIONER
(SUFF.) IATRIST
HEALING IATRIC POWWOW
BALSAMIC CURATION IATRICAL
SANATION
(PREF.) IATR(O)
(SUFF.) IATRIA IATRIC(S) IATRIST
IATRY
HEALTH SAP HAIL HEAL SONS
QUART SALEW LIKING PLEDGE
SALUTE SANITY EUCRASY
SLAINTE EUCRASIA TONICITY
VALETUDE VALIDITY
(GOOD —) PLIGHT VERDURE
(ILL —) SICKNESS
(NORMAL —) USUAL
(PREF.) HYGE(I) HYGI SALUTI
HEALTHFUL HEALTHY HYGIENIC
SALUTARY SANATORY SANITARY
HEALTHY FIT FIER FIRM HALE
IRON SAFE SANE TIDY WELL
BONNY HODDY QUART SOUND
STOUT VALID ENTIRE HEARTY
ROBUST BOUNCING LAUDABLE
SALUTARY SANITARY VEGETOUS
VIGOROUS
(PREF.) SANI
HEAP COP CUB HOT MOW PIE SOW
TON BALE BING BULK DECK DESS
HILL HOTT LEET PILE POKE POOK
RAFF REEK RUCK SESS TASS
TUMP AMASS CLAMP CLUMP
COUCH CROWD SHOCK SORUS

STACK WOPSE BURROW HIPPLE
HOTTER ISLAND JALOPY MEILER
OODLES QUARRY RICKLE RUCKLE
SCRAPE SORITE TOORIE BOUROCK
CUMULUS ENDORSE HAYCOCK
HAYRICK HURROCK TOOROCK
TUMMELS WINDROW BASURALE
CONGERIES ACCUMULATE
ACCUMULATION
(— HAY) UNCOCK
(— OF DEAD BODIES) CARNAGE
(— OF GAME) QUARRY
(— OF GRAIN) BING
(— OF MORTAR) BINK
(— OF ORE) PANEL MONTON
(— OF PRODUCE) BURY CLAMP
(— OF REFUSE) BURROW BASURAL
(— OF RUBBISH) GAGING
(— OF SILVER ORE) TORTA
(— OF SLAIN) CARNAGE
(— OF STONES) AHU MAN CAIRN
SCRAE SCREE HURROCK
MONTJOY
(— OF VEGETABLES) HOG
(— REPROACHES) KICK
(— TOGETHER) AGGEST HOWDER
LUMBER CUMULATE
(— UP) HILL SACK AGGEST
ACERVATE AGGERATE OVERHEAP
(COMBUSTIBLE —) PYRE
(MANURE —) HOTT MIXEN
(PROMISCUOUS —) RAFF
(PREF.) CUMULI CUMULO SOREDI
SORI SORO THOMO
HEAPED COCKED ACERVATE
CUMULATE
HEAR EAR LIST OYES OYEZ LEARN
LITHE HARKEN LISTEN HEARKEN
(— DIRECTLY) IMPINGE
(PREF.) ACOU(O) AUDIO
HEARD AUDIBLE
(EASILY —) CLEAR
HEARER AUDIENT AUDITOR
HEARING EAR LIST OYER AUDIT
SOUND ASSIZE AUDIENCE
AUDITION
(PREF.) ACOU(O)
(SUFF.) ACOUSIA ACOUSIS
ACUSIA ACUSIS
HEARKEN HARK HEAR HEED LIST
TEND LITHE ATTEND HARKEN
INTEND
HEARSAY REPORT ACCOUNT
HEARSE HACK CATAFALCO
HEART AB COR CORE GIST HATI
PUMP RAAN SOUL YOLK BOSOM
BOWEL CHEER JARTA QUICK
BREAST CENTER CENTRE DEPTHS
HASLET MIDDLE NATURE TICKER
VISCUS COURAGE EMOTION
ESSENCE FEELING
(— OF DIXIE) ALABAMA
(— OF ROTTEN TREE) DADDOCK
(DEAR —) DILIS
(PREF.) CARDI(A)(O) CORDI
PHREN(O)
(AROUND THE —) PERICARDI(O)
(SUFF.) CARDIA CARDIUM
HEARTACHE SORROW
HEARTBEAT STROKE
(SUFF.) CROTIC
HEARTBREAK HOUSE (AUTHOR OF
—) SHAW

(CHARACTER IN —) DUNN ELLIE
MANGAN HESIONE MAZZINI
HUSHABYE SHOTOVER
UTTERWORD
HEARTBURN PYROSIS
HEART CHERRY GASKINS
HEARTEN BIELD CHEER HEART
SPIRIT EMBOLDEN INSPIRIT
HEARTFELT DEAR DEEP REAL
TRUE INFELT INWARD CORDIAL
GENUINE SINCERE
HEARTH EARD SOLE TEST ASTRE
CUPEL EARTH FOCUS FOGON
FOYER SMOKE CHIMNEY
(— GODDESS) VESTA
HEARTILY INLY AGOOD DEARLY
FREELY WARMLY SHEERLY
DINGDONG INWARDLY STRONGLY
HEARTINESS GOODWILL
HEARTLESS SARDONIC
HEARTLESSNESS CYNICISM
**HEART OF MIDLOTHIAN (AUTHOR
OF —)** SCOTT
(CHARACTER IN —) MEG JOHN
DAVID DEANS EFFIE MADGE
BUTLER GEORGE JEANIE REUBEN
GEORDIE PORTEUS STAUNTON
ROBERTSON MURDOCKSON
HEARTSEASE PANSY
HEARTTHROB DUNT
HEARTWOOD ALOES HEART
SAPAN SPINE GUAYAB BUBINGA
DURAMEN TRUEWOOD
HEARTY REAL WARM BUXOM
COBBY FRECK HEAVY STOUT
DEVOUT ENTIRE ROBUST STANCH
BOBBISH CORDIAL EARNEST
HEALTHY RAFFING SINCERE
HEARTFUL VIGOROUS
BOISTEROUS
HEAT HET HOT RUT SUN TAP BOIL
FIRE GLOW SALT WARM ARDOR
BEATH BROIL CALOR CAUMA
CHAFE FEVER PRIDE PROUD
STECH TEPOR TRIAL ACHAFE
ANNEAL DEGREE DIGEST FERVOR
HEATEN IGNITE SCORCH SEASON
SIZZLE SPARGE WARMTH
CALCINE CALORIC ENCHAFE
FERMENT FLUSTER INCENSE
INFERNO PASSION SWELTER
UPERIZE CALIDITY
(— GENTLY) SOAK
(— OF BATTLE) PRESS
(— SCRAP IRON) BUSHEL
(— SWEETEN, AND SPICE) MULL
(— TOBACCO) SAP
(ROWING —) REPECHAGE
(SCORCHING —) EWDER
(PREF.) CALORI PYR(O)
THERM(ATO)(O)
(BURNING —) KAUMO
(MODIFIED BY —) COCTO
(SUFF.) THERM(Y)
HEATED WARM FIERCE STEAMY
HEATER GAT GUN FIRE COCKLE
PISTOL SMOKER CHAFFER
CHOFFER LATROBE
HEATH BENT YETH BESOM BRIAR
BRIER ERICA ERICAD COMMONS
HEATHER RHODORA CRAKEBERRY
(PREF.) ERICO
HEATHEN AKKUM PAGAN ETHNIC

PAYNIM GENTILE PROFANE
SARACEN GENTILIC
HEATHENISM ODINISM OTHINISM
PAGANISM
HEATHER BENT GRIG LING BROOM
ERICA HEATH HADDER
HEATHERY LINGY
HEATH PEA CARMELE
HEATING BAKEOUT BURNING
HEATLESS ATHERMIC
HEAVE GAG BUNG HEFT HOVE
KECK LIFE QUAP FETCH HOIST
SCEND SURGE BUCKLE KECKLE
POPPLE ESTUATE
HEAVEN SKY HIGH ABOVE BLISS
DYAUS ETHER GLORY ASGARD
CANAAN HIMMEL SVARGA
SWARGA URANUS WELKIN
KINGDOM OLYMPUS DEVALOKA
EMPYREAL EMPYREAN PARADISE
SVARLOKA
(12TH PART OF —) HOUSE
(PL.) ARCH LIFT LANGI HEIGHT
REGION SPHERE ELEMENT
TENGERE EMPYREAN KAMALOKA
(PREF.) URAN(I)(O) URANOSO
HEAVENLY ABOVE DIVINE ANGELIC
BLESSED URANIAN ETHEREAL
OLYMPIAN AMBROSIAL
**HEAVEN'S MY DESTINATION
(AUTHOR OF —)** WILDER
(CHARACTER IN —) BAT HERB
BRUSH COREY EFRIM LOUIE
MCCOY BURKIN CROFUT GEORGE
JESSIE MARGIE MORRIE DOREMUS
QUEENIE ROBERTA BLODGETT
ELIZABETH
HEAVENWARD ZIONWARD
HEAVER COALY DANNER HEFTER
HEAVILY SOSS CLOIT CLYTE HEAVY
PLUMP SADLY SOUSE SWACK
HEAVINESS DOLE HEFT GLOOM
POISE WEIGHT GRAVITY
HEAVY FAT HOT SAD CLIT DEEP
DOWF DULL HARD BEEFY BURLY
DENSE DOWFF DUNCH GRAVE
GREAT GROSS HEFTY HOGGY
STIFF THARF THERF THICK
WROTH CHARGE CLUMPY
CLUMSY DOUGHY DRAGGY
HEARTY LEADEN LIVERY LOGGER
SODDEN STODGY STRONG STUPID
WOODEN INSIPID LABORED
LIVERED LUMPING MASSIVE
ONEROUS OUTSIZE PESANTE
WEIGHTY CUMBROUS GRIEVOUS
PERSANTE PREGNANT
THUMPING PONDEROUS
SATURNINE
(PREF.) BARY GRAVI HADR(O)
HEAVY-FOOTED SOGGY LEADEN
INFICETE
HEBDOMADARY WEEKLY
HEBE (FATHER OF —) JUPITER
(HUSBAND OF —) HERCULES
(MOTHER OF —) JUNO
HEBER (GRANDFATHER OF —) ASHER
(SON OF —) SOCHO
(WIFE OF —) JAEL
HEBREW RABBINIC
**HEBRIDES
(ISLAND OF—)** IONA
HEBRON (FATHER OF —) KOHATH

HECATE TRIVIA
(FATHER OF —) PERSES
(MOTHER OF —) ASTERIA
HECKLE BAIT GIBE HACK BADGER
HARASS HECTOR HATCHEL
HECTIC ETIK SEPTIC HECTIVE
FEVERISH FRENETIC FRENZIED
HECTOLITER VAT
(5.82 —S) LEAGUER
HECTOR BAIT HUFF BULLY HARRY
TEASE WORRY HARASS HECKLE
BLUSTER BRAVADO BROWBEAT
(FATHER OF —) PRIAM
(MOTHER OF —) HECUBA
(SLAYER OF —) ACHILLES
(WIFE OF —) ANDROMACHE
HECUBA (DAUGHTER OF —)
POLYXENA
(FATHER OF —) DYMAS CISSEUS
(HUSBAND OF —) PRIAM
(SON OF —) PARIS HECTOR
HELENUS POLYDORUS
HEDDA GABLER (AUTHOR OF —)
IBSEN
(CHARACTER IN —) THEA BRACK
DIANA HEDDA EILERT GABLER
GEORGE TESMAN ELVSTED
JULIANA LOVBERG
HEDDLE CAMB DOUP HAVEL
HEALD
(PL.) CAAM
HEDGE BAR HAW HAY HYE OXER
SAVE BEARD EDDER FENCE FRITH
FUDGE HOVER MOUND QUICK
COPPER FRIGHT RADDLE
ENCLOSE QUICKSET RUFFMANS
SEPIMENT SURROUND THICKSET
(PREF.) SEPI SEPTATO
(SUFF.) SEPTATE
HEDGE BINDWEED CREEPER
HELLWEED WOODBINE
HEDGEHOG ORCHEN URCHIN
ECHINUS ERICIUS YLESPIL
HEDGEPIG HERISSON
HEDGE LAUREL TARATA
HEDGE MUSTARD BANKWEED
FLUXWEED
HEDGE NETTLE STACHYS
HEDGE PARSLEY HOGWEED
HEDGE-PRIEST PATRICO
HEDGE SPARROW DICKY DONEY
DICKEY EYSOGE PHILIP CHANTER
DUNNOCK HAYSUCK PINNOCK
TITLING ACCENTOR
HEDGEWOOD LAYER
HEED CARK COME CURE GAUM
HEAR KEEP LOOK MIND NOTE
RECK TEND TENT VISE WARE
YEME AWAIT TASTE VALUE
ATTEND INTENT NOTICE REGARD
REMARK REWARD CAUTION
OBSERVE RESPECT SUSPECT
THOUGHT OBSERVATION
HEEDFUL WARE ATTENT DILIGENT
VIGILANT REGARDFUL
HEEDLESS RASH BLIND DIZZY
GIDDY BLITHE REMISS UNWARY
LANGUID UNHEEDY CARELESS
LISTLESS MINDLESS
RECKLESS WISTLESS
NEGLECTFUL
HEEDLESSLY BLIND HEADLONG
HEEL TIP BUTT CALX FROG HIELD

SPIKE TALON DOTTLE INCLINE
BOOTHEEL
(— IN) SHOUGH
(— OF GATE) HARR
(— OF HORSESHOE) SPONGE
(— OF SWORD BLADE) TALON
RICASSO
(— OVER) SEEL TILT CAREEN
(PREF.) CALCANEO TAL(I)(O)
HEEL BEVEL RAND
HEEL PLATE SHOD CLEAT
HEFT WEIGHT
HEFTY HEAVY
HE-GOAT
(PREF.) HIRCO
HEIFER IO QUI QUEE QUEY QUOY
BULLER STOCKER
(— IN 2ND YEAR) STIRK
(YEARLING —) BURLING
HEIGH-HO HECH
HEIGHT SUM ACME ALTO APEX
FELL HIGH LOFT MOTE PINK TUNE
CREST HICHT STATE ALTURE
INCHES SUMMIT CEILING
COMMAND HEIGHTH STATURE
SUPREME ALTITUDE EMINENCE
HAUTESSE SIDENESS VERTICAL
ACROPOLIS
(— OF FASHION) GO
(— OF PROSPERITY) GLORY
(— OF ROOM) STUD STUDDING
(— OF SAIL) HOIST
(GREATEST —) NOON SUMMIT
ZENITH
(ROCKY —) KNOT
(PREF.) ACR(O) BATHO BATHY
BATO HYPS(I)(O)
HEIGHTEN ENDOW EXALT FORCE
RAISE ACCENT BOLSTER
ENHANCE SUBLIME
(— FLAVOR) PETUNE
HEINOUS SWART CRYING WICKED
SCARLET FLAGRANT GRIEVOUS
HEIR SCION SPRIG COHEIR HERITOR
APPARENT PARCENER
(— APPARENT) ATHELING
ETHELING
(CELTIC —) TANIST
(FEMALE —) DISTAFF
(PREF.) HEREDI HEREDO
HEIRESS BEGUM PORTIA FORTUNE
HERITRIX
HEIRLOOM
(PL.) CIMELIA
HEL (FATHER OF —) LOKI
(MOTHER OF —) ANGURBODA
HELAH (HUSBAND OF —) ASHUR
(SON OF —) TEKOA
HELEB (FATHER OF —) BAANAH
HELEK (FATHER OF —) GILEAD
HELENUS (FATHER OF —) PRIAM
(MOTHER OF —) HECUBA
(SON OF —) CESTRINUS
(WIFE OF —) ANDROMACHE
HELEZ (FATHER OF —) AZARIAH
HELI (SON OF —) JOSEPH
HELIANTHEMUM SUNROSE
HELICAL SPIRAL
HELICAON (FATHER OF —)
ANTENOR
(MOTHER OF —) THEANO
(WIFE OF —) LAODICE
HELICOPTER HOVER COPTER

CHOPPER WINDMILL
(— TO REMOVE CASUALTIES)
DUSTOFF
(ARMED —) GUNSHIP
HELIOPOLIS ON
HELIOS HYPERION PHAETHON
(DAUGHTER OF —) CIRCE PASIPHAE
(FATHER OF —) HYPERION
(MOTHER OF —) THEIA
(SISTER OF —) EOS SELENE
(SON OF —) AEETES PHAETHON
HELIOSIS SUNBURN
HELIOTROPE HELIO BENNET
SETWALL GIRASOLE TURNSOLE
VALERIAN
HELIPORT SKYPORT
HELIX COIL SPIRAL
HELIXIN HEDERIN
HELL PIT POT HECK PAIN ABYSS
AVICI BLAZE DEUCE HADES
SHEOL BLAZES NARAKA TARTAR
TOPHET TUNKET ABADDON
GEHENNA HELLBOX INFERNO
TORMENT TARTARUS
BARATHRUM PERDITION
PANDEMONIUM
(PREF.) TARTARO
HELLBENDER TWEEG MENOPOME
HELLE (BROTHER OF —) PHRIXUS
(FATHER OF —) ATHAMAS
(MOTHER OF —) NEPHELE
HELLEBORE POKE BUGBANE
ITCHWEED LINGWORT
LUNGWORT NOSEWORT
POKEROOT VERATRUM
EARTHGALL
HELLEN (FATHER OF —) DEUCALION
(MOTHER OF —) PYRRHA
(SON OF —) DORUS AEOLUS
XUTHUS
(WIFE OF —) ORSEIS
HELLER HALER HALERZ
HELLERI SWORDTAIL
HELL-FIRE BRIMSTONE
HELLGRAMMITE DOBSON SIALID
CLIPPER CRAWLER SPRAWLER
HELLISH HELLY SATANIC STYGIAN
DEVILISH INFERNAL TOPHETIC
HELLO HALLO HILLO HULLO HILLOA
HELM KEY STEER STERN TIMON
HELMET TIMBER STEERAGE
HELMET CAP POT CASK HELM
HOOD ARMET CREST GALEA
MAZER MOUND BARBEL BEAVER
CASQUE CASTLE GALERA
HEAUME MORION PALLET SALADE
SALLET TESTER BASINET
CASQUET GALERUM GALERUS
AVENTAIL BURGANET BURGONET
HEADGEAR KNAPSCAP SCHAPSKA
SKULLCAP TARNHELM TESTIERE
(— PART) VENTAIL
(PITH —) TOPI TOPEE
(PREF.) GALEI
HELMET-SHAPED GALEATE
HELMSMAN PILOT STEER
GLAUCUS TIMONEER
HELON (SON OF —) ELIAB
HELP AID BOT ABET BACK BOOT
CAST LIFT STOP AVAIL BOOST
FAVOR FRITH HEEZE RESET
SPEED START STEAD YELDE
ASSIST HELPER RELIEF REMEDY

SECOND SUCCOR UPTAKE
BENEFIT BESPEED BESTEAD
CHEVISE COMFORT FORWARD
FURTHER HELPING IMPROVE
PRESIDY PROMOTE REDRESS
RELIEVE SUPPORT SUSTAIN
ADJUMENT BEFRIEND SUFFRAGE
(— FORWARD) FRANK FURTHER
(— ON) ADVANCE
(— ONWARD) FORWARD
(— OUT) FIRK
(HIRED —) LABOR
HELPER AID CAD FOAL HELP MATE
PAGE ANSAR AIDANT BARBOY
COOKEE DIENER FLUNKY JUMPER
NIPPER TENTER WAITER ADJOINT
ADJUNCT ADJUTOR ANCILLA
CASHBOY GALOPIN SUMPMAN
SWAMPER HELPMATE OFFSIDER
SCULLION TROUNCER
(— IN GLASSWORKS) SNAPPER
(BLACKSMITH'S —) STRIKER
(CHIMNEY SWEEP'S —) CHUMMY
(COOK'S —) SLUSHY
(COOPER'S —) TUBBIE
(HORSESHOER'S —) FLOORMAN
(PICKPOCKET'S —) BULKER
(YOUNG —) FOAL
HELPFUL GOOD AIDANT AIDFUL
HELPLY SECOND SPEEDY USEFUL
ADJUVANT HELPSOME OBLIGING
SINGULAR SERVICEABLE
HELPING HELP AIDANT PORTION
SERVING ADJUTORY ADJUVANT
HELPLESS NUMB SILLY ABJECT
UNABLE AIDLESS FORLORN
FECKLESS HAVELESS REDELESS
HELPLESSNESS ADYNAMIA
HELTER-SKELTER TAGRAG
PELLMELL
HELVE HELM SHAFT
HELVE HAMMER OLIVER
HEM HUM WLO FELL SLIP WELT
HEDGE SPLAY PURFLE TURNUP
HEMMING TURNING SURROUND
(— AND HAW) HAVER
(— GLOVE) WRIST
(— IN) BOX LAP BEBAY BESET
IMPALE BESIEGE COMPASS
ENCLOSE ENVIRON STRAITEN
SURROUND
(— IN FISH) EBB
(— OF SAIL) TABLING
(— OF TROUSERS) CUFF
(PREF.) LIMBI
HEMAM (BROTHER OF —) HORI
(FATHER OF —) LOTAN
HEMAN (FATHER OF —) JOEL ZERAH
(GRANDFATHER OF —) SAMUEL
HEMATITE ORE OLIGIST SANGUINE
HEMDAN (FATHER OF —) DISHON
HEMICRANIA MIGRAINE
HEMIEPES ENOPLION
HEMIMORPHITE CALAMINE
HEMIOLIC SESCUPLE
HEMISTICH SECTION
HEMITHEA (BROTHER OF —) TENES
(FATHER OF —) CYCNUS
(MOTHER OF —) PROCLEA
HEMLOCK BUNK CASH KELK
BENNET CICUTA COWBANE
DEATHIN SHINWOOD
HEMOPHILIAC BLEEDER

HEMORRHAGE STAXIS APOPLEXY
BLEEDING HEMOPTOE PETECHIA
HEMOSTATIC RHATANY ERIGERON
HEMP IFE KEF KIF TOW BANG CARL
POOA RINE SANA SUNN ABACA
BHANG DACHA DAGGA FIQUE
GANJA HURDS MURVA RAMIE
SABZI SISAL AMBARY CABUYA
FIMBLE LIAMBA NALITA SINAWA
AMYROOT CABULLA GAGROOT
NIYANDA PANGANE PITEIRA
SOSQUIL BIRDSEED CANNABIS
CHUCKING LOCOWEED
NECKWEED NEPENTHE
MARIJUANA
(PREF.) CANNABI
HEMP AGRIMONY EUPATORY
HEMPWEED
HEMPEN NOGGEN
HEMP NETTLE IRONWORT
HEMPWEED BONESET DUCKBLIND
HEN FOWL BIDDY CHUCK LAYER
BROODY MABYER PULLET
CLOCKER HOVERER PARTLET
LANGSHAN
(— THAT HAS NOT LAID) TOWDIE
(— WITH CHICKENS) CLUCK
(— WITH SHORT LEGS) GRIG
(BROODY —) SITTER
(FATHER OF —) ZEPHANIAH
(FATTENED —) POULARD
(1-YEAR-OLD —) YEAROCK
HENBANE HEBENON CHENILLE
HENCE AWAY ERGO HYNE THUS
AVAUNT HETHEN HEREOUT
HENCEFORTH YET HENCE
HENCHMAN FELLOW SATRAP
SERVANT FOLLOWER RETAINER
UNDERLING
HEN COOP CAVY CAVIE
HENGEST (BROTHER OF —) HORSA
(KINGDOM FOUNDED BY —) KENT
(SON OF —) AESC
HEN HARRIER FALLER KATABELLA
(IMMATURE —) RINGTAIL
(MALE —) MILLER
HENNA MENDY ALCANNA
ALHENNA CAMPHIRE
HENNIN STEEPLE
HENPECK NAG
HENRY QUAD HAWKIN SECOHM
HEINRICH QUADRANT
HENRY ESMOND (AUTHOR OF —)
THACKERAY
(CHARACTER IN —) HOLT FRANK
HENRY JAMES MOHUN ESMOND
RACHEL STUART BEATRIX
FRANCIS
HENRY IV-PART I (AUTHOR OF —)
SHAKESPEARE
(CHARACTER IN —) JOHN OWEN
PETO BLUNT HENRY PERCY POINS
EDMUND SCROOP THOMAS
VERNON WALTER DOUGLAS
HOTSPUR MICHAEL QUICKLY
RICHARD BARDOLPH FALSTAFF
GADSHILL MORTIMER ARCHIBALD
GLENDOWER LANCASTER
WESTMORELAND
HENRY IV-PART II (AUTHOR OF —)
SHAKESPEARE
(CHARACTER IN —) DAVY DOLL
FANG JOHN PETO WART BLUNT

GOWER HENRY POINS RUMOR
SNARE FEEBLE MORTON MOULDY
PISTOL SCROOP SHADOW SURREY
THOMAS MOWBRAY QUICKLY
SHALLOW SILENCE TRAVERS
WARWICK BARDOLPH BULLCALF
CLARENCE FALSTAFF HARCOURT
HASTINGS HUMPHREY COLEVILLE
LANCASTER TEARSHEET
WESTMORELAND
NORTHUMBERLAND
HENRY V (AUTHOR OF —)
SHAKESPEARE
(CHARACTER IN —) NYM GREY
JAMY YORK ALICE BATES COURT
GOWER HENRY LEWIS EXETER
ISABEL PISTOL SCROOP THOMAS
BEDFORD BOURBON CHARLES
MONTJOY ORLEANS WARWICK
BARDOLPH BURGUNDY FLUELLEN
GRANDPRE RAMBURES WILLIAMS
ERPINGHAM KATHARINE
MACMORRIS SALISBURY
GLOUCESTER WESTMORELAND
HENRY VIII (AUTHOR OF —)
SHAKESPEARE
(CHARACTER IN —) ANNE VAUX
BUTTS DENNY HENRY SANDS
BULLEN LOVELL SURREY THOMAS
WOLSEY ANTHONY BRANDON
CRANMER NORFOLK SUFFOLK
CAMPEIUS CAPUCIUS CROMWELL
GARDINER GRIFFITH NICHOLAS
PATIENCE GUILDFORD
KATHARINE BUCKINGHAM
ABERGAVENNY
HENRY VI-PART I (AUTHOR OF —)
SHAKESPEARE
(CHARACTER IN —) JOAN JOHN
LUCY HENRY BASSET EDMUND
TALBOT THOMAS VERNON
ALENCON BEDFORD CHARLES
RICHARD SUFFOLK WARWICK
WILLIAM BEAUFORT BURGUNDY
FASTOLFE GARGRAVE MARGARET
MORTIMER REIGNIER GLANSDALE
LAPUCELLE SALISBURY
WOODVILLE GLOUCESTER
PLANTAGENET
HENRY VI-PART II (AUTHOR OF —)
SHAKESPEARE
(CHARACTER IN —) SAY CADE DICK
HUME IDEN JACK JOHN VAUX
BEVIS GOFFE HENRY PETER
SMITH EDWARD GEORGE HORNER
SCALES ELEANOR HOLLAND
MATTHEW MICHAEL RICHARD
SIMPCOX STANLEY SUFFOLK
WARWICK BEAUFORT CLIFFORD
HUMPHREY JOURDAIN
MARGARET SOMERSET STAFFORD
ALEXANDER SALISBURY
SOUTHWELL BUCKINGHAM
BOLINGBROKE PLANTAGENET
HENRY VI-PART III (AUTHOR OF —)
SHAKESPEARE
(CHARACTER IN —) BONA HUGH
JOHN HENRY LEWIS MARCH
EDMUND EDWARD EXETER
GEORGE OXFORD RIVERS
BOURBON NORFOLK RICHARD
RUTLAND STANLEY WARWICK
CLIFFORD HASTINGS MARGARET

MONTAGUE MORTIMER
PEMBROKE SOMERSET STAFFORD
MONTGOMERY PLANTAGENET
WESTMORELAND
NORTHUMBERLAND
HEP (NOT —) ICKY
HEPATICA AI TRINITY
HEPATITIS FAVISM JAUNDICE
HEPHAESTUS LEMNIAN
(FATHER OF —) ZEUS
(MOTHER OF —) HERA
(WIFE OF —) CHARIS
HEPHZIBAH (HUSBAND OF —)
HEZEKIAH
(SON OF —) MANASSEH
HER A ARE SHE HARE HERS HURE
HERA JUNO
(FATHER OF —) KRONOS
(HUSBAND OF —) ZEUS
HERALD BODE LYON USHER
BEADLE DECLARE FORERUN
PREFACE STENTOR BLAZONER
PRECURSE PROCLAIM ROTHESAY
MESSENGER
HERALDIC FECIAL FETIAL
HERALDRY ARMORY
HERB ANU APE PIA RUE UDO WAD
ALOE ANET ANYU ARUM COUS
DILL HEMP IRID LEEK MINT MOLY
POLY RAPE SAGE SOLA WOAD
WORT YAMP YARB AWIWI BLITE
BRUSH CHIVE CREAT CROUT
DAGGA DAISY DRABA GALAX
GAURA GILIA GRASS HOSTA
LOASA LUFFA MEDIC MUNGO
NANCY SEDGE SOLAH STOCK
SULLA THYME ZIZIA ALLIUM
ARALIA ARNICA AXSEED BAGPOD
BAMBAN BANANA BLINKS
BORAGE CANCER CATGUT CATNIP
CENIZO CICELY CISTUS CLOVER
COCASH COLEUS CONIUM
COWISH COWPEA ELODEA
ENDIVE ERYNGO FENNEL GALAXY
GINGER HARMEL HYSSOP KOCHIA
KRIGIA KRIGLA LOOFAH LOVAGE
RAMTIL RATTLE ROBERT SESAME
SESELI SHEVRI WASABI ABRONIA
ALPINIA ALTHAEA ALYSSUM
AMORPHA AMSONIA ANCHUSA
ANEMONE ANGELON ARACHIS
BABIANA BABROOT BARTSIA
BIRDEYE BLINKER BONESET
BUGSEED BUGWEED CHICORY
CUDWEED CULVERS DEWDROP
DYEWEED EPISCIA ERODIUM
FREESIA FROGBIT FUMMORY
GERBERA GINSENG GOITCHO
GOSMORE GOUAREE GUAYULE
GUNNERA HARMALA HEDEOMA
HENBANE HERBLET IRESINE
ISOLOMA JONQUIL LABIATE
LEWISIA LINNAEA MARANTA
MIMULUS MUDWEED MUDWORT
MULLEIN MUSTARD NAILROD
NEMESIA NIEVETA PAVONIA
PETUNIA PINESAP PINWEED
PUCHERA ROSELLE SAFFLOR
SALSIFY SEEDBOX SKIRRET
SOWBANE SPIGNEL STACHYS
ABELMOSK ABELMUSK ACANTHUS
ACONITUM AGERATUM ALOCASIA
ALUMROOT AMBROSIA

AMMOBIUM ANGELICA
ARGEMONE ASPHODEL
BEDSTRAW CALATHEA
CAPEWEED CARELESS CENTAURY
CHENILLE COLLOMIA COSTMARY
COWWHEAT CRASSULA
CROMWELL DANEWEED
DEERWEED DROPWORT
ECHINOPS EGGPLANT EREMURUS
ERIGERON EUCHARIS FEVERFEW
FLEABANE FOWLFOOT GAYWINGS
GERARDIA GESNERAD GESNERIA
GHETCHOO GLOXINIA GOATROOT
GUZMANIA HAREBELL HEPATICA
HEUCHERA HIBISCUS HOLEWORT
HONEWORT HOROKAKA
HUDSONIA IRONWEED LICORICE
LOCOWEED MANDRAKE
MANFREDA MANYROOT
MARDOWRT MARJORAM
MARTYNIA MURRNONG PHACELIA
PINKROOT PLUMBAGO
POKEWEED SACALINE SAINFOIN
SALICORN SAMPHIRE SANDBURR
SCABIOUS SHINLEAF SMALLAGE
SNOWDROP SOAPROOT
SOAPWORT STAPELIA SUNDROPS
TETRIFOL TOCALOTE WOODRUFF
MONEYWORT PUSSYTOES
RUDBECKIA SAXIFRAGE
NASTURTIUM PENNYCRESS
PERIWINKLE SARRACENIA
(— COUNTERACTING POISON)
CANCER
(— OTHER THAN GRASS) FORB
(AROMATIC —) MINT ANISE CLARY
CATNIP CAAPEBA CHERVIL
DITTANY
(BIENNIAL —) LEEK PARSLEY
ANGELICA
(BULBOUS —) LILY CANNA ALLIUM
CRINUM GARLIC NERINE SQUILL
BABIANA SHALLOT DOGTOOTH
SLANGKOP
(FABULOUS —) MOLY PANAX
PANACE
(FLOATING —) FROGBIT
(FORAGE —) FITCHES GOITCHO
(MEDITERRANEAN —) CRAMBE
(POISONOUS —) CONIUM HEMLOCK
MONKSHOOD
(PL.) POTAGERIE
HERBAGE HAY BITE GRASS GRAZE
PICHI ADONIS SACATE ZACATE
GRAZING
HERB EVE IVA IVY
HERB GRACE RUE
HERBICIDE IPE DIURON SILVEX
DALAPON MONURON PARAQUAT
PICLORAM PROPANIL SIMAZINE
HERB IMPIOUS DOWNWEED
HOARWORT
HERB PARIS TRUE ONEBERRY
TRUELOVE
HERB ROBERT JENNY ROBIN
ROBERT
HERCULEAN HUGE
HERCULES ERCLES ALCIDES
HERSHEF OETAEUS OVILLUS
HERAKLES
(BROTHER OF —) IPHICLES
(CAPTIVE OF —) IOLE
(FATHER OF —) JUPITER

(MOTHER OF —) ALCMENA
(WIFE OF —) HEBE MEGARA
DEIANIRA
HERCULES ALLHEAL OPOPANAX
HERCULES-CLUB ARALIA IVYWORT
RUEWORT SHOTBUSH
HERD BOW GAM MOB BAND CREW
GAME GANG HEAD RACE ROUT
RUCK TAIL TEAM TRIP DROVE
FLOCK HEARD TROOP CAVIYA
CHOUSE HIRSEL HUDDLE
MANADA MEINIE REMUDA
SPREAD THRAVE CREAGHT
RANGALE SHEPHERD
(— CATTLE) TAIL WRANGLE
(— OF CATTLE) FLOTE
(— OF COLTS) RAG
(— OF HORSES) RACE HARAS
HARRAS
(— OF SEALS) PATCH
(— OF WHALES) GAM
(— OF WILD SWINE) SOUNDER
HERDBOY BOUCHAL
HERDER DROVER FEEDER
HERDBOY
HERDSMAN AMOS SENN GAUCHO
HERDER LOOKER PASTOR
HERDBOY LLANERO THYRSIS
VAQUERO BEASTMAN DAMOETAS
GARTHMAN NEATHERD
PASTORAL PASTURER RANCHERO
SWANHERD WRANGLER
HERE ADSUM READY WHERE
HEREAT HITHER PRESENT
(— AND THERE) ABOUT ABROAD
AROUND PASSIM SPARSIM
HEREAFTER BEYOND
HEREDITAMENT LAND
HEREDITARY INBORN INNATE
KINDLY LINEAL PATERNAL
HEREIN WITHIN
HERESY DOCETISM KETZEREI
MISBELIEF
HERETIC BUGGER KETZER ZINDIQ
LOLLARD PATARIN PROFANE
SECTARY JUDAIZER MISCREANT
SABELLIUS MISBELIEVER
(PL.) ACEPHALI
HERETICAL HERETIC HETERODOX
MISCREANT
HERETO HITHER
HERETOFORE ERST BEFORE
ERENOW EREWHILE FORMERLY
**HEREWARD THE WAKE (AUTHOR
OF —)** KINGSLEY
(CHARACTER IN —) BRAND GODIVA
MARTIN WILLIAM ALFTRUDA
HEREWARD TORFRIDA
LIGHTFOOT
HERITAGE HEIRDOM HEIRSHIP
PATRIMONY
HERMA MERCURY
HERMAPHRODITE MOPH SCRAT
ANDROGYNOUS
HERMAPHRODITIC BISEXED
BISEXUAL MONOECIOUS
HERMAPHRODITISM GYNANDRY
HERMAPHRODITUS (FATHER OF —)
MERCURY
(MOTHER OF —) VENUS
HERMENEGILD (FATHER OF —)
LEOVIGILD
HERMES MERCURY

AGORAIOS CYLLENIUS
(FATHER OF —) ZEUS
(MOTHER OF —) MAIA
HERMIA (BELOVED OF —) LYSANDER
(FATHER OF —) EGEUS
HERMIONE (FATHER OF —)
MENELAUS
(HUSBAND OF —) PYRRHUS
(MOTHER OF —) HELEN
HERMIT ARME MUNI HANIF MINIM
ANCHOR SANTON SULLEN
ASCETIC EREMITE RECLUSE
TAPASVI ANCHORET MARABOUT
SOLITARY
HERMITAGE ASHRAM ASHRAMA
RECLUSE
HERNIA BURST RAMEX BREACH
RUPTURE MEROCELE
(SUFF.) CELE COELE COELUS
HERO CID KIM RAB AJAX EGIL IDAS
KAMI MAUI NALA NATA OFFA
RINK YIMA ADAPA BERNE DEBON
ETANA FAUST GHAZI HODER
HOTHR IRAYA KIPPS MARKO
ORSON TASSO TIMON VOTAN
EGMONT FIGARO GIDEON GOLIAS
HEROIC IASION IOLAUS MAUGIS
MINYAS OSSIAN PELHAM PENROD
RIENZI ROLAND RUSTAM SIGURD
TARZAN USHEEN VATHEK
ALCESTE BOGATYR DEMIGOD
FAUSTUS GLUSKAP INGOMAR
JAMSHID MACBETH MANRICO
MARMION MAZEPPA ORLANDO
OTHELLO PALADIN RAFFLES
TANCRED THALABA THESEUS
TROILUS ULYSSES VOLPONE
WERTHER WIDSITH WIELAND
ACADEMUS ARGONAUT
CHAMPION FANSHAWE
FERUMBAS FRITHJOF GAEDHEAL
GILGAMES LAMMIKIN MALAGIGI
MORGANTE OROONOKO
PALMERIN PARSIFAL PERICLES
RASSELAS RODOMONT
SUPERMAN TRISTRAM WAVERLEY
(LOVER OF —) LEANDER
(TRIBAL —) JUDGE
HERODIAS (BROTHER OF —)
AGRIPPA
(FATHER OF —) ARISTOBULUS
(HUSBAND OF —) HEROD
HEROIC EPIC FELL GREAT NOBLE
EPICAL FEATLY EXTREME
GALLANT VALIANT FEARLESS
HEROICAL HOMERIAN INTREPID
SPLENDID
HEROIN JUNK SCAG SKAG SNOW
HORSE SMACK
HEROINE AIDA EMMA MIMI RUTH
JULIE MEDEA NORMA SEDNA
THAIS ESTHER FEDORA GUDRUN
HELENA JUDITH JULIET MARTHA
MIGNON PAMELA PHEDRE
RAMONA ROMOLA SALOME SILVIA
TRILBY UNDINE ERMINIA EVELINA
GALATEA GINEVRA GRAINNE
HEROESS MONIMIA SHIRLEY
ZENOBIA ZULEIKA ATALANTA
ISABELLA MARGARET PATIENCE
POMPILIA ROSMUNDA SOFRONIA
HEROISM VALOR BRAVERY
COURAGE PROWESS

HERON QUA POKE SOCO CRAIG CRANE EGRET FRANK HERNE PADDY QUAWK YABOA AIGRET GAULIN KIALEE KOTUKU QUAKER SQUAWK BITTERN CRABIER GOLIATH HANDSAW QUABIRD SQUACCO BOATBILL GAULDING HERONSEW UMBRETTE
(— FLOCK) SIEGE
HERON'S-BILL ERODIUM
HERPES DARTRE TETTER
HERPES ZOSTER ZONA SHINGLES
HERRING ALEC BRIT CHUB SILD BLOAT CAPON CISCO DORAB HILSA MARAY MATIE SPRAT KIPPER POLLAN TAILOR BLOATER CLUPEID NAILROD ROLLMOP SHADINE BLUEBACK BRISLING BUCKLING CROPSHIN GRAYBACK QUODDIES SCUDDAWN STRADINE
(— SEASON) DRAVE
(— UNIT) LAST MAZE
(FEMALE —) RAUN
(LAKE —) KIYI CISCO
(RED —) CAPON SOLDIER
(SMOKED —) BLOATER
(YOUNG —) COB BRIT SILD SILE SILL SOIL WILE BRITT COBBE MATIE SPRAT SARDINE SPERLING
(2, 3 OR 4 —S) WARP
HERS HERN SHISN
HERSE (FATHER OF —) CECROPS
(SISTER OF —) AGRAULOS
(SON OF —) CEPHALUS
HERSELF HI HER SELF ITSELF
HERSHEF ARSAPHES
HESHVAN BUL CHESHVAN
HESIONE (FATHER OF —) LAOMEDON
(HUSBAND OF —) TELAMON
(RESCUER OF —) HERCULES
HESITANCY HANG
(— IN SPEECH) BALBUTIES
HESITANT SHY CAGY CHARY GROPING HALTING SUSPENSE
(NOT —) FACILE
HESITATE COY HEM STAY STOP CHECK CRANE DEMUR DOUBT FORCE PAUSE STAND STICK SUSSY WAVER BOGGLE FALTER HANKER LINGER MAMMER RELUCT SCOTCH TARROW TARTLE BALANCE PROFFER SCRUPLE STAGGER STAMMER SWITHER THRIMBLE
(— IN SPEAKING) HACKER
HESITATING JUBUS HALTING BACKWARD DOUBTFUL JUBEROUS TIMOROSO
HESITATION HANG HINK WAND PAUSE STAND STICK SUSSY SWITHER
HESPERUS VESPER
HESRON (FATHER OF —) REUBEN
HESSIAN BURLAP
HESTIA (FATHER OF —) KRONOS
(MOTHER OF —) RHEA
HETAERA LAIS THAIS PHRYNE MISTRESS
HETER-
(PREF.) XEN(O)
HETERODOX HERETIC SINISTRAL
HETERODOXY HERESY CACODOXY

HETEROGENEOUS MIXED MOTLEY UNLIKE DIVERSE PIEBALD ASSORTED
HETEROMYS SACCOMYS
HETEROSEXUAL STRAIGHT
HETEROTROPHIC HOLOZOIC
HETEROXENOUS INDIRECT
HETEROZYGOUS CROSS SPLIT IMPURE
HETMAN ATAMAN
HEW CUT HAG CHIP SNAG STUB SHRED SLICE
(— OUT) CARVE
(— STONE) CHAR
HEWER JOEY GETTER GIDEON FACEMAN
HE WHO GETS SLAPPED (AUTHOR OF —) ANDREYEV
(CHARACTER IN —) ALFRED ZINIDA BENZANO BRIQUET JACKSON MANCINI REGNARD CONSUELO
HEX WITCH VOODOO WHAMMY
HEXAGON SEXANGLE
HEXAGONAL HEX DIMETRIC
HEXAGRAM PENTACLE
HEXAMETER MIURUS RHOPALIC
(DACTYLIC —) EPOS HEROIC
HEXOBARBITAL EVIPAL
HEXOSAN MANNAN GLUCOSAN MANNOSAN
HEYDAY MAY HIGHDAY
HEZEKIAH (FATHER OF —) AHAZ NEARIAH
(MOTHER OF —) ABI
HEZION (SON OF —) TABRIMON
HEZRON (FATHER OF —) PHAREZ REUBEN
HIATUS GAP BREAK CHASM BREACH HIATAL LACUNA
HIBERNATE SHACK WINTER SLUMBER
HIBERNATING LATITANT
HIBERNIA EIRE ERIN IRELAND JUVERNA
HIBERNIAN IRISHMAN IVERNIAN
HIBISCUS ROSELLE
HICCUP YEX YOX HICK HOCKET HOQUET SINGULTUS
HICK BOOR HIND JAKE BACON BUSHMAN CORNBALL
HICKORY NOGAL PIGNUT BULLNUT SHAGBARK
HICKORY NUT TRYMA PIGNUT BULLNUT KISKITOM
HICKWALL ECCLE HECKLE HICKWAY
HIDDEN HID SHY DEEP DERN LOST TECT BLIND CLOSE DOGGO DUSKY PERDU PRIVY ARCANE BURIED COVERT INNATE LATENT MASKED MYSTIC OCCULT SECRET VEILED BOSOMED CLOUDED COVERED CRYPTIC OBSCURE RECLUSE SUBTILE ABDITIVE ABSTRUSE CRYPTOUS HIDEAWAY PALLIATE SCREENED SECLUDED SNEAKING CRYPTICAL RECONDITE
(PREF.) CRYPT(O) KRYPT(O)
HIDE HOD WRY BUFF BURY CASE CROP DARK DERN FELL FELT HILL HOOD JOUK LEAN MASK PELL PELT SCAB SKIN SKUG SNUG STOW VEIL WELL BELIE BELLY

BLIND CACHE CLOAK CLOUD COUCH COVER DITCH EARTH FLANK GLOSS LAYNE LOSHE MANSE PLANT SHADE SPOIL STASH STEER TAPIS BURROW BUSHEL CASATE EMBOSS ENCAVE ENWOMB FOREST HUDDLE IMBOSK MANENT PELAGE SCREEN SHADOW SHIELD SHROUD ABSCOND CONCEAL COWHIDE EMBOWEL FLAUGHT OBCLUDE OVERLAY SECLUDE SECRETE SPREADY TAPPICE CARUCATE DISGUISE ENSCONCE HIDELAND HOODWINK PALLIATE PLOWLAND SQUIRREL SUPPRESS CLANDESTINE
(— AS AN EEL) MUD
(— IN WOODS) WOOD BUSHWACK
(— UNDER) BUSHEL
(CALF'S —) DEACON
(DRESSED —S) LEATHER
(HALF OF —) BEND
(HAVING SOFT —) MELLOW
(SHEEP'S —) SLAT
(TANNED —) CROP
(THICKEST —S) BACKS
(UNDRESSED —) KIP
(PL.) JUFTI JUFTS
(PREF.) DERM(AT)(ATO)(O) DORA
(SUFF.) DERM(A)(ATOUS)(IA)(IS)(Y)
HIDE-AND-GO-SEEK BOGLE WHOOP BOGGLE
HIDEAWAY MEW LAIR
HIDEBOUND BORNE NARROW BIGOTED
HIDEOUS FELL GASH GRIM UGLY AWFUL TOADY DEFORM GRIMLY GRISLY HORRID ODIOUS OGRISH GHASTLY DEFORMED DREADFUL FIENDISH GRUESOME HORRIBLE SHOCKING TERRIBLE MONSTROUS
HIDEOUSLY FOULLY
HIDING DERN MICHING SECRECY ABDITIVE HIDEAWAY
HIEMAL WINTRY
HIERACIUM DINALE HAWKWEED
HIERARCHY SATRAPY
HIEROGLYPH CIPHER
(PL.) SIGNARY
HIGGLE HUCK HAGGLE
HIGH UP ALT AIRY DEAR HAUT MAIN MUCH RANK TALL ACUTE ALOFT BRENT CHIEF CLOSE FIRST GREAT LOFTY MERRY NOBLE SHARP STEEP BOMBED COSTLY SHRILL ZONKED EMINENT EXALTED HAUGHTY STICKLE SUBLIME TOPPING VIOLENT ELEVATED FOREMOST PIERCING TOWERING
(— AND MIGHTY) HOGEN
(— IN CHROMA) STRONG
(— IN PITCH) ALT ACUTE
(— IN RANK) MUCH
(— PITCH) ORTHIAN
(MOST —) SERENE
(PRETTY —) STIFFISH
(VERY —) TAUNT RAREFIED RARIFIED
(PREF.) ALTI HYPS(I)(O)
(ON —) HYPS(I)(O)
HIGHBORN NOBLE GENEROUS

HIGHBOY TALLBOY
HIGHBRED SOFT REFINED
HIGHBROW EGGHEAD
HIGH-CLASS CLASSY UPSTAGE
HIGH-CLIMBER TOPPER
HIGH-COLORED BLOWSY BLOWZY
HIGH-CROWNED COPATAIN
HIGHER OVER ABOVE SENIOR SUPERIOR
(PREF.) SUPER(O) SUPRA
HIGHEST ACE TOP HEXT FIRST EXTREME MAXIMAL SUPREME BUNEMOST HIGHMOST OVERMOST
(— IN DEGREE) LAST
HIGHFALUTIN PAUGHTY
HIGH-FED BEANY
HIGH-FLAVORED GAMY
HIGH-FLOWN TALL TUMID
HIGH-HANDED CAVALIER
HIGHLAND RAND CERRO
HIGHLANDER GAEL TARTAN NAINSEL PLAIDMAN REDSHANK TREWSMAN UPLANDER
(PL.) TREWS TARTAN
HIGHLIGHT ADORN HEIGHTEN PINPOINT SALIENCE
HIGHLY THRICE
HIGH-MINDED HAUGHT
HIGHNESS ALTESSE ALTEZZA ALTITUDE
(— OF PRICE) DEARTH
HIGH-PITCHED ACUTE PROUD PIPING TREBLE ORTHIAN SHRIEKY
HIGH-POWERED MAGNUM
HIGH-PRICED DEAR
HIGH-RIGGER TOPPER
HIGH-SOUNDING BIG BOMBAST MAGNIFIC SONORANT SONOROUS SOUNDING
HIGH-SPIRITED CRANK FIERY FIERCE LIVELY GALLANT GINGERY RAMPANT CAVALIER VASCULAR
HIGH-SPIRITEDNESS SPLEEN
HIGH-STRUNG TENSE NERVOUS
HIGH-TONED TONY DICTY DICKTY
HIGHWAY VIA WAY BELT ITER PATH PIKE ROAD TOBY BOLOS ARTERY CAUSEY COURSE RUMPAD SKYWAY STREET BELTWAY CALZADA FREEWAY RAMPIRE THRUWAY ARTERIAL AUTOBAHN BROADWAY CAUSEWAY CHAUSSEE HIGHROAD MOTORWAY SPEEDWAY
(— ROBBERY) TOBY
(LOCATED OFF THE —) DEVIOUS
(PART OF —) EXIT GORE LANE LOOP RAMP ACCESS BRIDGE ISLAND MEDIAN DIVIDER ROADWAY JUNCTION OVERPASS SHOULDER UNDERPASS INTERSECTION
HIGHWAYMAN PAD RIDER SCAMP BANDIT CUTTER PADDER RODMAN BRIGAND FOOTPAD LADRONE PRANCER RODSMAN TOBYMAN BIDSTAND DAMASTES HIGHTOBY HIJACKER LANÇEMAN OUTRIDER BANDOLERO
HIGH-WROUGHT INTENSE
HIKE MUSH MARCH TRAMP RAMBLE

HILARIOUS MAD RORTY JOVIAL JOCULAR RAUGHTY CHIRPING GLORIOUS

HILARITY GIG JOY GLEE LAUGH MIRTH GAIETY GAYETY DEVILRY JOLLITY WHOOPEE MERRIMENT

HILKIAH (FATHER OF —) AMZI HOSAH

(SON OF —) ELIAKIM GEMARIAH JEREMIAH

HILL BEN DEN DUN HOE HOW KOP LOW PUY VAN ALTO BANK BERG BRAE BULT BUMP COTE DAGH DENE DOWN DRUM FELL HIGH HONE KNAP LOMA LUMP MESA MOOR MOTE NOUP PAHA TOFT ZION BARGH BUTTE CERRO CLIFF COAST HEUGH KNOCK KNOLL KOPJE MORRO MOUND MOUNT STILL SWELL TELLE WATCH ASCENT BARROW BEACON COBBLE COLLIS COPPLE CUESTA HEIGHT HEUVEL LOMITA SPRUNT STRONE CAELIAN CAPITOL COLLINE DRUMLIN HILLOCK NUNATAK PICACHO SOWBACK VIMINAL AREOPAGY CATOCTIN DRUMLOID FOOTHILL MONTICLE QUIRINAL MONADNOCK

(— OF SAND) DENE DUNE

(— OF STRATIFIED DRIFT) KAME

(— UP) MOLD

(BROAD-TOPPED —) LOMA

(CONICAL —) LAW PAP PINGO

(CRAGGY —) TOR

(FORTIFIED —) RATH

(HIGH —) BEN

(ISOLATED —) HUM TOFT BARGH BUTTE

(LAST —) STRONE

(LOW —) HOW BAND WOLD KOPPIE SOWBACK

(NIPPLELIKE —) PAP

(NORTH AFRICAN —) JEBEL DJEBEL

(RESIDUAL —) CATOCTIN

(ROUNDED —) DODD HONE MAMELON

(SHARP-POINTED —) KIP KIPP PIKE

(SMALL —) KNAP KNOLL KOPJE KOPPIE HILLOCK MOLEHILL

(STEEP —) BREW BROW STILL

(STONY —) ROACH

(SUGAR-LOAF —) SPITZKOP

(WOODED —) HOLT HURST

(PREF.) BUNO

HILLOCK HOW LOW NOB BOSS BULT DOWN KAME KNAP KNOB TERP TOFT TUMP BERRY HEAVE HURST KNOCK KNOLL KOPJE MOUND TOMAN BARROW BURROW COPPET HILLET HUMMOCK MAMELON TUMMOCK TUMULUS MOLEHILL

HILLSIDE BENT BRAE COTE EDGE CLEVE FALDA SLADE FELLSIDE SIDEHILL

HILLTOP DOD NAB PIKE RISE KNOLL

HILLY KNOBBY

HILT HAFT BASKET POIGNET HANDGRIP

(— OF DAGGER) DUDGEON

(PART OF —) BOW CUT GRIP RING

GUARD BUTTON POMMEL CAPSTAN LANGUET QUILLON RICASSO CROSSPIECE COUNTERGUARD

HILUM EYE SCAR HILUS PORTA NUCLEUS CICATRIX

HIM A EN HE HEM HIN MUN

HIMATION PALLION PALLIUM

HIMERUS (FATHER OF —) LACEDAEMON

(MOTHER OF —) TAYGETE

(SISTER OF —) CLEODICE

HIMSELF HIM IPSE SELF HISSEL ITSELF HERSELF HISSELF

HIND ROE CONY HINE HINT CONEY HEARST HINDER VENISON CABRILLA

HIND-BODY ABDOMEN

HINDBRAIN RHOMBENCEPHALON

HINDER BAR DAM KEP LET MAR ROB CLOG HELP SLOW SLUG STAY STOP TENT WARN AFTER BLOCK CHEAT CHECK CHOKE CRAMP DEBAR DELAY DETER EMBAR ESTOP HEDGE SLOTH THROW TRASH ARREST CUMBER DETAIN FORBID FORLET HAMPER HARASS HINNER IMPEDE IMPEND INJURE RETARD RETRAL SCOTCH TAIGLE UNHELP ABSTAIN DEPRIVE FORELAY IMPEACH INHIBIT OCCLUDE PREVENT TRACHLE ENCUMBER HANDICAP IMPEDITE OBSTRUCT PRECLUDE PROHIBIT POSTICOUS

(PREF.) POSTERO

HINDERED FOUL

HINDERER LETTER

HINDERMOST LAG ACHTER

HINDQUARTER HIND HAUNCH

(HALF —) LEG

(PL.) FOUCH CRUPPER HAUNCHES

HINDRANCE BAR LET RUB BALK CURB REIN SLUG STAY STOP BLOCK CHECK DELAY HITCH TRASH ARREST CUMBER DENIAL HINDER OBJECT UNHELP SHACKLE UNSPEED DISCOUNT DRAWBACK HOLDBACK OBSTACLE PULLBACK

HINDU BABU BABOO SUDRA BABHAN BANIAN BANYAN GENTOO JAJMAN KALWAR KHATRI NAYADI SHUDRA THAKUR VAISYA MUSAHAR VAIRAGI

(— ASCETIC) SADHU

(— ASSOCIATION) SANGH

(— CASTE) TELI VARNA

(— CUSTOM) SATI SUTTEE

(— ENERGY) SAKTI SHAKTI

(— IDOL) SWAMI

(— INTERJECTION) OM AUM

(— PHILOSOPHY) VEDANTA

(— PRACTICE) PURDAH

(— RITE) PUJA POOJA

(— SAGE) RSI RISHI

(— SCRIPTURE) VEDA

(— VARNA MEMBER) SUDRA

(— WORSHIPER) SAKTA

(— WRITING) VEDA

(— WRITINGS) SMRTI TANTRA

(TWICE-BÓRN —) KSATRIYA

HINDUSTANI URDU HINDI OORDOO DAKHINI

HINDWING BALANCER

HINGE RUN BAND BUTT FLAP HARR TRIM TURN CARDO CROOK GEMEL JOINT MOUNT NODUS SKELL SKEWL TWIST DEPEND GARNET GEMMEL GIMMER HANGLE JIMMER SNIBEL CHARNEL COXCOMB FULCRUM HOLDBACK

(— OF BIVALVE SHELL) CARDO

(— OF HELMET) CHARNEL

(— TOGETHER) SCISSOR

(HALF OF —) FLAP

(PHILATELIC —) STICKER

(PREF.) GINGLYMO

HINGED SWING

(SUFF.) POMATOUS

HINNY BURDON FUNNEL JENNET

HINT CUE ASTE ITEM MINT TANG WIND WINK CHEEP IMPLY INFER POINT SPELL STEER TOUCH TRACE WHIFF ALLUDE GLANCE OFFICE SMATCH TIPOFF WHEEZE INKLING LEADING MEMENTO POINTER SUGGEST UMBRAGE WHISPER WRINKLE ALLUSION INDICATE INNUENDO INTIMATE TELLTALE

HINTERLAND BLED BACKLAND

HIP HEP COXA HUCK PITCH SHOOP HAUNCH HUCKLE HIPBERRY

(— JOINT) THURL

(— OF ROSE) BERRY CHOOP SHOOP

(— OF TARGET) SPOT

(PREF.) COX(O) ISCHI(O) OSPHY(O)

HIPBONE FINBONE PINBONE EDGEBONE SIDEBONE

HIPPARCHUS (BROTHER OF —) HIPPIAS

(FATHER OF —) PISISTRATUS

HIPPARETE (BROTHER OF —) CALLIAS

(FATHER OF —) HIPPONICUS

(HUSBAND OF —) ALCINIADES

HIPPEUS KNIGHT

HIPPIE FREAK

HIPPOCAMPUS ERGOT HIPPO

HIPPOCOON (BROTHER OF —) TYNDAREUS

(FATHER OF —) OEBALUS

(MOTHER OF —) GORGOPHONE

(SLAYER OF —) HERCULES

HIPPODAMIA (FATHER OF —) ADRASTUS OENOMAUS

(HUSBAND OF —) PELOPS PEIRITHOUS

(SON OF —) ATREUS TROEZEN PITTHEUS THYESTES

HIPPOLYTUS (FATHER OF —) THESEUS

(MOTHER OF —) HIPPOLYTE

(STEPMOTHER OF —) PHAEDRA

HIPPOMENES (FATHER OF —) MEGAREUS

(MOTHER OF —) MEROPE

(WIFE OF —) ATALANTA

HIPPONACTEAN SCAZON

HIPPOPOTAMUS HIPPO ZEEKOE BEHEMOTH BUNODONT

HIPPOTHOE (FATHER OF —) MESTOR

(MOTHER OF —) LYSIDICE

(SON OF —) TAPHIUS

HIPPOTRAGUS OZANNA EGOCERUS

HIRAH (COMPANION OF —) JUDAH

HIRE FEE JOB HAVE MEED RENT SIGN WAGE PREST WAGES EMPLOY ENGAGE RETAIN SALARY BESPEAK CHARTER CONDUCE CONDUCT FREIGHT STIPEND

(— CATTLE) TACK

HIRED PAID TEEKA TICCA WAGED

HIRELING HACK VENAL HACKNEY MYRMIDON WAGELING MERCENARY PENSIONER PENSIONARY

HIRSUTE HAIRY SHAGGY

HIS S AS ES IS HISN

HISPID STRIGOSE STRIGOUS

HISS BLOW FUFF HISH HIZZ QUIZ SISS SIZZ GOOSE WHISS FISSLE FIZZLE SIFFLE WHOOSH WHISTLE SIBILATE

(— OF SWORD) SOUGH

HISSING BIRD AFFLATUS SIBILANT

HISTONE GLOBIN

HISTORIAN MORONI STORIER ANNALIST

AMERICAN FAY FOX BEER DODD FISH HART SHEA ADAMS BEARD BEMIS ELSON FORCE GIBBS GROSS HAZEN MAHAN MOORE MUNRO MYERS SMITH STONE USHER ABBOTT BARBER BARZUN BECKER BEESLY BOURNE BOWERS FISHER GREENE HANSEN LATANE LOWELL MALONE MOTLEY MUZZEY NEVINS PAXSON REEVES RHODES SLOANE SPARKS STILES TURNER WINSOR ANDREWS BASSETT CHAPMAN CHEYNEY CLELAND DUNNING GAYARRE HEADLEY HULBERT JAMESON LEARNED MCELROY MORISON PALFREY PARKMAN RIDPATH SCHMITT SHANNON VANTYNE BANCROFT BOTSFORD BRODHEAD COMMAGER COOLIDGE HILDRETH JOHNSTON MCMASTER PENNIMAN PHILLIPS PRESCOTT ROBINSON STEPHENS THWAITES TRUMBULL BEVERIDGE GROSVENOR MACDONALD PRIESTLEY STEVENSON MCLAUGHLIN WESTERMANN OBERHOLTZER ROSTOVTZEFF SCHLESINGER

ARGENTINIAN FUNES LOPEZ MITRE CARBIA

AUSTRIAN BIBI SRBIK ARNETH LORENZ HORMAYR LOSERTH MENGHIN PRIBRAM ASCHBACH HELLWALD WURZBACH

BELGIAN JUSTE HYMANS GACHARD HASSELT LAURENT PIRENNE

CANADIAN BEGG BRYCE WRONG GARNEAU BOURINOT CASGRAIN

CHINESE PANKU

COLOMBIAN ACOSTA RESTREPO

CZECH GOLL PALACKY

DANISH HOLM ALLEN BARFOD
AAGESEN AAGESON BRANDES
MOLBECH WORSAAE PEDERSEN
HAMMERICH NEERGAARD
DUTCH BOR BLOK GEYL FRUIN
HOOFT JAPIKSE BARLEAUS
HUIZINGA
ENGLISH COXE DYER HALL HYDE
MUIR OMAN PAUL ROSE STOW
TOUT WARD ACTON BIRCH
BROWN CARTE DAVIS DIXON
DORAN DOYLE EDMER FIRTH
FYFFE GOOCH GREEN GUEST
HELPS INNES PARIS SMITH TERRY
TOOKE WELLS BARKER BUCKLE
BURNET CAMDEN COLOMB
CREASY FINLAY FISHER FROUDE
GIBBON GILDAS HALLAM MILMAN
POWELL ROSCOE SEELEY STRYPE
STUBBS TURNER WARNER
WILSON BEAZLEY BOULGER
COULTON DOUGLAS FORSTER
FREEMAN HASSALL HAYWARD
KNOLLES LANGTON LINGARD
MITFORD POLLARD RALEIGH
SYMONDS ADOLPHUS GAIRDNER
GARDINER KINGLAKE MACAULAY
MAITLAND MARRIOTT OLDMIXON
PALGRAVE PHILLIPS PROTHERO
ARMSTRONG KINGSFORD
ROBERTSON TEMPERLEY
TREVELYAN HAVERFIELD
FINNISH FORSMAN
FRENCH FAY SEE DROZ FAIN
DURUY FILON FLACH GIDEL
GLOTZ GOYAU MABLY MONOD
NAUDE RENAN SOREL AULARD
BALUZE BEMONT BONNET DANIEL
DAUDET GERARD GUIZOT
HAUSER MARTIN MASSON
MATTER MIGNET OZANAM
ROMIER THIERS VANDAL VERTOT
ZELLER BARANTE BLONDEL
CHENIER CHERUEL FAGNIEZ
FAURIEL JULLIAN LAGORCE
LANFREY LAVISSE LERMINA
MADELIN MEZERAY PFISTER
RAMBAUD THIERRY DEBIDOUR
DUCHESNE GODEFROY
HANOTAUX LUCHAIRE MICHELET
PARFAICT RULHIERE BEAUCOURT
BONNEMERE BOURGEOIS
HERICAULT SEIGNOBOS
SIEGFRIED TILLEMONT
DESJARDINS GUIGNEBERT
ROHRBACHER CHANTELAUZE
GERMAN DAHN HEHN KAPP KOCH
LENZ NIEM ALZOG FALKE JAFFE
KLOPP KOSER LUDEN MEYER
MOSER PERTZ RANKE RIEHL
SYBEL VEHSE VOGEL VOIGT
WAITZ WEBER ZEUSS ABELIN
BELOCH BOHMER HEEREN
KUGLER MENZEL ONCKEN PREUSS
QUIDDE RITTER SICKEL WUTTKE
ANDREAS DROYSEN DUMMLER
ECKHART FISCHER FORSTER
HAEBLER HELMOLT HETTNER
KEUTGEN LEHMANN LINDNER
ROTTECK RUVILLE SCHAFER
SCHMIDT SCHULTE BRESSLAU
DELBRUCK DONNIGES FLEMMING
GALLETTI GERVINUS HOETZSCH

HOFFMANN KAUFMANN
KROMAYER LEDEBOUR SCHLOZER
FREIDRICH LAMPRECHT
SCHIEMANN SCHMOLLER
SLEIDANUS ARCHENHOLZ
BAUMGARTEN BIEDERMANN
HIRSCHFELD LAPPENBERG
MARHEINEKE POSCHINGER
TREITSCHKE ZIMMERMANN
BRANDENBURG FALLMERAYER
GARDTHAUSEN GREGOROVIUS
SECKENDORFF
GREEK DURIS GREEN ARRIAN
BIKELAS EPHORUS LAMBROS
SOZOMEN TIMEAUS DEXIPPUS
HERODIAN POLYBIUS XENOPHON
CRATIPPUS HERODOTUS
HESYCHIUS PHILISTUS
TIMAGENES ANAXIMENES
CLITARCHUS HELLANICUS
HIERONYMUS PHYLARCHUS
THEOPOMPUS THUCYDIDES
ARISTOBULUS MEGASTHENES
OLYMPIODORUS AGATHARCHIDES
HUNGARIAN FEJER TOLDY PAULER
TELEKI FESSLER FRAKNOI
MAILATH MARCZALI SZILAGYI
IRISH BURY LECKY GILBERT
WADDING
ITALIAN AMARI CANTU VOLPE
CANALE CIAMPI DENINA EMILIO
FEDELE GIOVIO NOVATI VASARI
ACCOLTI FERRERO VILLANI
VILLARI AMMIRATO CIBRARIO
GIANNONE MOLMENTI MURATORI
BERTOLINI LIUTPRAND SALVEMINI
MEXICAN ALAMAN PEREYRA
CLAVIJERO BUSTAMANTE
NORWEGIAN KOHT LANGE MUNCH
DIETRICHSON
PERUVIAN ULLOA
POLISH KUBALA BIELSKI CHODZKO
DIUGOSZ LELEWEL SZUJSKI
ASKENAZY BOBRZYNSKI
KUCHARZEWSKI
PORTUGUESE GOES MELO LOPES
BARROS CASTANHEDA
ROMAN LIVY CORDUS FLORUS
TROGUS SALLUST TACITUS
APPIANUS VALERIUS EUTROPIUS
SUETONIUS FENESTELLA
RUMANIAN IORGA KOGALNICEANU
RUSSIAN KAVELIN POGODIN
BRUCKNER KARAMZIN MILYUKOV
TURGENEV VENGEROV
POKROVSKI HRUSHEVSKY
KOSTOMAROV
SCOTTISH MILL BOECE BROWN
LAING BURTON TYTLER CARLYLE
GILLIES NEILSON SPALDING
MACKINTOSH
SPANISH AVILA XEREZ PINELO
PULGAR TORENO DESCLOT
GOMARRA HERRERA MARIANA
MONCADA FERRERAS LAFUENTE
SEPULVEDA MONTESINOS
SWEDISH DALIN BESKOW GEIJER
CARLSON FRYXELL FORSSELL
MESSENIUS
SWISS KOPP BLUMER GELZER
MULLER STUMPF TSCHUDI
SISMONDI GAGLIARDI
BURCKHARDT

HISTORICAL GENETIC
HISTORIOGRAPHER SCALD SKALD
HISTORY STORY ANNALS LEGEND
RECORD SURVEY ACCOUNT
ANCESTRY PROPHECY RELATION
(— OF EXPERIENCES) MEMOIRS
(— OF JAPAN) KOJIKI
(LIFE —) COURSE
(TRIBAL —) PHYLOGENY
HISTRIONIC ACTORY ACTORISH
ACTRESSY
HIT BAT BOP BOX DOT GET HAT
JOB PEG PIP WOW BASH BEAN
BEAT BELT BIFF BLOW BOFF BUST
CHOP CONK DONG FOUR GOLD
NAIL PINK POKE PUCK PUNT
RUFF SLAM SOCK SWAT SWIP
TAKE TANK TUNK WART WIPE
ANGLE CHECK CLOUT CLUNK
CROWN FIVER FLICK GOUFF
KNOCK POTCH PRANG PUNTA
PUNTO SCORE SLASH SLOSH
SMASH SMITE SNICK SWIPE
TAINT TOUCH VENUE ATTAIN
DOUBLE FOURER HURTLE SCLAFF
STRIKE VOLLEY ATTAINT
BOFFOLA CONNECT MUZZLER
SANDBAG WHERRET BLUDGEON
BOUNDARY LENGTHER STRICKEN
(— A KEY) STRIKE
(— BALL) CUR FLY DINK DRIVE
SHOOL SKITE SNICK
(— BUNT) DRAG
(— GAME) STOP
(— GENTLY) BABY
(— GOLF BALL) CAN BLAST
EXPLODE
(— HARD) DUMP SLOG SLUG
PASTE SKELP SOUSE DEVVEL
STOUSH STONKER
(— IN BOXING) LEADOFF
(— IN FIELD HOCKEY) CORNER
(— IN TILTING) TAINT
(— IT OFF) CLICK
(— LIGHTLY) KISS
(— ON BULL'S-EYE) GOLD
(— POORLY) DUB
(— SHARPLY) CLIP
(— SUDDENLY) ZAP
(— TOGETHER) CLASH
(— UPON) FIND
(— WITH FOOT) KICK SPURN
(BASE —) BINGLE DOUBLE SAFETY
SINGLE TRIPLE SCRATCH
SMOTHER
(CRICKET —) SLOG BOUNDARY
(EASILY —) SITTING
(FENCING —) HAI HAY VENUE
(SHARP —) LICK
(SMASH —) SOCKEROO
HITCH JET TUG HALT HIKE ITCH
KNOT PULL CATCH HOTCH SPELL
TRACE HIRSLE INSPAN MAGNUS
CONTRETEMPS
(NOSE —) BOZAL
HITCHHIKE HOP THUMB
HITCHHIKER PICKUP
HITCHING KNOT SHRUG
HITHER HERE
HITHERTO YET BEFORE
HIT-OR-MISS CASUAL CHANCE
HOBNOB CARELESS
HITTER SWATTER

HITTING BATTING SLOGGING
HITTITE HATTI KHATTI TABALIAN
HIVE GUM BIKE SKEP PYCHE
STAND STATE STOCK SWARM
APIARY ALVEARY BEEHIVE
SWARMER
(— PLACED OVER ANOTHER) SUPER
HIVES CROUP UREDO
HLORRITHI THOR THORR
HOAGIE TORPEDO
HOAR GRAY RIME HOARY
HOARD HEAM POSE SAVE AMASS
HUTCH MISER STOCK COFFER
MAGPIE MUCKER STOUTH
GENIZAH HUSBAND SQUIRREL
TREASURE
HOARDER MUCKER STORER
HUSBAND
HOARFROST RAG HOAR RIME
RIND
HOARINESS HOAR ROOP MUCOR
HOARSE RAW FOGGY GRUFF
HEAZY HUSKY RAWKY ROKEY
ROUGH ROUPY STOUR CROAKY
CROUPY RASPED ROUPIT
GRATING RAUCOUS
HOARSENESS FROG ROUP QUACK
RAUCITY HASKNESS BARYPHONIA
HOARY AGED GRAY GREY HOAR
WHITE FROSTY ANCIENT
HOARISH INCANOUS
HOATZIN ANNA HANA HOACTZIN
HOAX BAM COD FUN GAG HUM
KID RAG RIG BILK DUPE FAKE
GAFF GEGG GUNK JOSH QUIZ
RAMP RUSE SELL SHAM SKIT
CHEAT FRAUD GREEN SHAVE
SPOOF TRICK WINDY CANARD
DIDDLE HUMBUG STRING
BLAFLUM DECEIVE FLIVVER
ARTIFICE
HOB HUB PUNCH MATRIX
HOBAB (BROTHER-IN-LAW OF —)
MOSES
HOBBER LEANER
HOBBLE GIMP LOCK SPAN BUNCH
HILCH HITCH STILT STUMP
HABBLE HIRPLE HOPPLE LANGLE
LANKET TOLTER CRAMBLE
CRAMMEL CRIPPLE SHACKLE
SHAFFLE SPANCEL STAGGER
TRAMMEL SIDELINE
HOBBLEBUSH DOGWOOD
HOBBY BUG FAD HOBBLER
AVOCATION
HOBBYHORSE HOBBY PLAYMARE
HOBBYIST BUG
HOBGOBLIN (ALSO SEE GOBLIN)
COW HAG HOB PUG BOGY PUCK
BOGEY BUCCA BUGAN POKER
SCRAT SPOOK BOODIE BOWSIE
EMPUSA SPOORN BUGABOO
RAWHEAD BOGGLEBO COLTPIXY
POPLEMAN PUCKEREL
WORRICOW
HOBNAIL HOB HUB PUNCH
TACKET
HOBNAILED TACKETY
HOBO BO BOE BUM STIFF
HOCK HAM HOX HEEL HOUGH
HUXEN SINEW SKINK JARRET
CAMBREL GAMBREL HOCKSHIN
SUFFRAGO

HOCKEY HURLY HORKEY HURLEY SHINNY CAMMOCK HURLBAT
(— STAR) ORR
HOCKEY STICK HOOKY HURLY STICK BULGER SHINNY CAMBUCA CAMMOCK DODDART HURLBAT
HOCUS-POCUS FAKERY HUMBUG FLIMFLAM QUACKERY
HOD TRAY
(FATHER OF —) ZOPHAH
HODAVIAH (FATHER OF —) HASSENUAH
HOD CARRIER PADDY
HODESH (HUSBAND OF —) SHAHARAIM
HODGEPODGE CHOW HASH MESS OLIO RAFF SALAD BOLLIX JUSSEL MAGPIE MEDLEY MELANGE CHIVAREE CHOWCHOW HOTCHPOT KEDGEREE MISHMASH PASTICHE PORRIDGE SCRAMPUM PATCHWORK
HODOMETER VIAMETER
HOE BROD CHIP CLAT HACK HOWE SHIM CLAUT LARRY THIRD CHONTA HACKER PAIDLE PECKER SARCLE GRUBBER PULASKI SCRAPER SCUFFLE GRIFFAUN
(— HANDLE) STAIL
(HORSE —) NIDGET NIGGET
(PART OF —) BLADE SHANK HANDLE FERRULE
HOECAKE CORNCAKE
HOG BEN SOW BOAR GALT GILT PORK DUROC GRUNT SHOAT BARROW HOGGET HOGGIE PORKER PORKET YORKER BACONER BUTCHER GRUNTER HOGLING MONTANA BABIRUSA BUNODONT HEREFORD LANDRACE VICTORIA RAZORBACK
(PREF.) SUI
HOGAN LODGE TEPEE DWELLING
HOGBACK FLATIRON HOGFRAME
HOGCHOKER SOLE
HOGFISH CAPITAN LADYFISH LORICATE SCORPION
HOGGER HUGGER HOGHEAD
HOGGISHNESS GRILL GRYLL
HOGLAH (FATHER OF —) ZELOPHEHAD
HOGNOSE SNAKE ADDER FLATHEAD
HOG PLUM AMRA JOBO
HOGSHEAD CASK CARDEL
HOG'S-MEAT TOSTON HOGWEED
HOG-TIE HAMPER
HOGWASH DRAFF SWASH SWILL PIGWASH
HOIST FID HEFT KILT LIFT SWAY SWIG WHIM WHIP CRANE ERECT HEAVE HEEZE HEIST HOICK HOOSH HORSE RAISE WEIGH JAMMER LAUNCH LIFTER TUGGER WHIMSY DERRICK
(— A LOG) CANNON
(— ANCHOR) CAT
(— FISH) BRAIL
(— FLUKES) FISH FANCHER
HOISTED (— TIGHT) ATRIP
HOISTMAN CAGEMAN
HOKUM BLAA BLAH HOKE JUNK
HOLD HOD OWN BULK DEEM FEEL

FILL GAUM GIVE GRIT HANK HAVE HELD HEND HILT HOLE HOLT HOOK KEEP LOCK NAIL RELY SOFT STOW AFONG AHOLD AHOLT BELAY CARRY CINCH CLAMP CLING GRASP GRIPE LATCH LEASE PAUSE POISE ROCCA STORE WOULD ADHERE ADSORB ARREST CLUTCH DETAIN HANDLE INTERN MANURE OCCUPY REGARD REPUTE RETAIN ADJUDGE CAPTURE CLAUGHT CONFINE CONTAIN ENCLOSE FERMATA GRAPPLE HOLDING RECEIVE SEIZURE SUBSIST SUSPEND COMPRISE FOOTHOLD FOREHOLD HANDFAST HANDHOLD HEADLOCK HOLDFAST PURCHASE THURROCK
(— A BELIEF) SUPPOSE
(— AS PRECIOUS) TREASURE
(— AS TRUE) ACCEPT
(— AT BAY) DOMPT
(— BACK) STOP WELL BELAY LAYNE BOGGLE DETAIN FLINCH HINDER RETIRE SHRINK CONTAIN DETRACT FORBEAR INHIBIT RECLAIM REFRAIN SLACKEN HESITATE SUPPRESS WITHDRAW
(— BACK ON LEASH) TRASH
(— CLOSELY) CRADLE CUDDLE
(— CONSULTATION) ADVISE
(— CORONER'S INQUEST) CROWN
(— DEAR) CHERISH
(— DOWN) PINION CONTAIN
(— FAST) FIX BAIL BITE CLING SNARL CLENCH CLINCH SECURE STABLE
(— FIRMLY) CLIP INSIST

(— FORTH) SPIEL
(— FROM) ABSTAIN
(— GOOD) APPLY SERVE
(— IN CHECK) REIN GOVERN REPRESS COMPESCE
(— IN CONTEMPT) SMILE DISPRIZE
(— IN PLACE) ANCHOR
(— OF PLASTER) KEY
(— ON COURSE) STEM FETCH STAND
(— ON FINAL NOTE) TENOR
(— ON SHORE) LANDFAST
(— OUT) DREE LAST STAY OFFER EXTEND PROTEND STRETCH SUSTAIN
(— PROTECTIVELY) LAP
(— TIGHTLY) CLIP STICK
(— TOGETHER) BOND COHERE CONSIST
(— UP) BEAR HALT STAY ERECT HEIST IMPEDE UPHOLD RUMPADE SUPPORT SUSTAIN TRADUCE
(— UP BY LEADING STRINGS) DADE
(— UP TO CONTEMPT) FLEER
(— UP TO PUBLIC NOTICE) GIBBET
(SHIP'S —) HOLE HOLL FISHHOLD
(WRESTLING —) CROTCH KEYLOCK CHANCERY HEADLOCK SCISSORS SIDEHOLD
(PREF.) CHADA
HOLDBACK DAM
HOLDER WYE HAVER STOCK DIPPER SOCKET CRACKER

CASSETTE JAGIRDAR
(— FOR CARRYING GLASS) FRAIL
(— FOR COIL) SPOOL
(— FOR CUP) ZARF
(— FOR FLOWERS) FROG
(— FOR FOOD) COZY COSEY
(— FOR TOOLS) TURRET
(— FOR WHIP) BUCKET
(— OF GRANT) ENAMDAR
(ALLOTMENT —) CLERUCH
(CANDLE —) SPIDER GIRANDOLE
(LAMP —) BODY
(PL.) GRIPPERS
(PREF.) PORTE
HOLDFAST CLINCH HAPTERON
HOLDIKEN HADDIN
HOLDING HAL COPY COTE HOLD TAKE GRASP HONOR HADDIN POFFLE TENANT TENURE TENANCY COMMENDA
(— DIFFERENT OPINIONS) APART
(— FAST) IRON
(— OF OFFICE) OCCUPATION
(— OF SECURITIES) CARRY
(PL.) FLOCKS PROPERTY
HOLDUP HEIST STICKUP
HOLE CAN CUP EYE GAP PIT TAP BORE BURY LEAK MAIL MUSE PECK PINK POCK PUKA WANT CHINK DITCH FLOSS FOSSE MEUSE SINUS SLACK SPRUE SQUAT TEWEL THIRL THURL BURROW CAVITY CENTER CENTRE CRANNY CRATER EYELET HOLLOW LACUNA OBTAIN OILLET PIERCE POCKET POUNCE WEEPER BLOWOUT BOGHOLE BOTHROS DIBHOLE EYEHOLE KEYHOLE MORTICE MORTISE OILHOLE OPENING PINHOLE POTHOLE SCUTTLE SWALLET VENTAGE ACCEPTER APERTURE BLOWHOLE BOREHOLE COALHOLE CRABHOLE FUMAROLE HANDHOLE KNOCKOUT KNOTHOLE OVERTURE PEEPHOLE POSTHOLE PUNCTURE WELLHOLE WINDHOLE PERTUSION PERFORATION
(— CAUSED BY LEAK) GIME
(— FOR WIRE) HUB HUBB
(— IN BANK OF STREAM) GAT
(— IN GARMENT) FRACK
(— IN GUILLOTINE) LUNET LUNETTE
(— IN HEDGE) SMEUSE
(— IN HIDE) BOTHOLE
(— IN KEEL) LIMBER RUFFLE
(— IN KIVA) SIPAPU
(— IN ONE STROKE) ACE
(— IN STREAM BED) DUMP
(— IN WIND INSTRUMENT) LILL
(— INTO MOLD) GEAT SPRUE
(— THREE BELOW PAR) ALBATROSS
(AIR —) SPIRACLE
(BREATHING —) SUSPIRAL
(DEEP —) POT GOURD
(FOX —) KENNEL
(GOLF —) CUP DOGLEG
(MELON —) GILGAI
(RABBIT —) CLAPPER
(SAND —) BUNKER
(SINK —) SOAKAWAY
(SPY —) JUDAS
(TO —) GOBBLE HAZARD
(VOLCANIC —) FUMAROLE

(WATER —) DUB CHARCO
(WELL-LIKE —) CASCAN
(PREF.) TREMATO TROGLO
HOLIDAY HOL PLAY TIDE WAKE FERIE FESTA MERRY FIESTA JOVIAL FESTIVE HALEDAY PLAYDAY YEARDAY PASSOVER SHABUOTH WAYGOOSE
(HALF —) REMEDY
(PL.) FERIA
HOLINESS PIETY HALIDOM SANCTITY SANCTIMONY
HOLLA SOLA
HOLLAND (ALSO SEE NETHERLANDS) FROGLAND
HOLLANDAISE GULASH GOULASH
HOLLAND BLUE ORION
HOLLANDER DUTCHMAN
HOLLANDS GIN GENEVA
HOLLER HALLO HOLLO HALLOO KYOODLE
HOLLO SOLA
HOLLOW DEN DIP KEX BOSS BOWL CAVE COMB COOM COVE DALK DELL DENT DINT DISH DOCK DOKE FOLD GORE HOLE HOLL HOWE KEXY KHUD SINK SLOT THIN VOID WAME BASIN BIGHT CAVUM CHASE CLEFT CUPPY DELVE DOWFF EMPTY GAUNT GOYLE GULCH GULLY HEUCH LAIGH NOTCH SCOOP SINUS SLOCK SWAMP WOMBY ARMPIT BULLAN CAVITY CORRIE DIMPLE HOLLER INDENT KETTLE MATRIX POCKET RECESS SOCKET SUNKEN VACANT WALLOW BOXLIKE CONCAVE UNSOUND VACUITY CAVITARY CHELIDON CORELESS CRUCIBLE FISTULAR FOSSETTE NOTCHING SPECIOUS
(— AMONG HILLS) SWAG SLOCK
(— IN COIL OF CABLE) TIER
(— IN HILL) COOM CLASH COMBE COOMB CORRIE
(— IN TILE) KEY
(— OF ARM) LEAD ARMPIT
(— OF EAR) ALVEARY
(— OF HANDS) GOUPEN GOWPEN
(— OF HORSE'S TOOTH) MARK
(— OF KNEE) HAM
(— OF ROOF) VALLEY
(— OUT) CUT DIG BORE HOWK KERF CAVERN EXCISE
(LONG —) GROOVE
(NOT —) SOLID FARCTATE
(PASSING —) CRESCENT
(ROUND —) CIRQUE
(SECLUDED —) GLEN
(SPRINGY —) GAW
(WOODED —) GULLY
(PREF.) CAEL(I)(O) CAVI CAVO CEL(O) COEL(I)(O)
(SUFF.) COELOUS COELUS
HOLLOWED HOWKIT CONCAVE SPOUTED
HOLLOW-EYED HAGGARD
HOLLOWNESS VANITY INANITY VACUITY CONCAVITY
HOLLY HOLM HULL ILEX MATE DAHOON HOLLIN HULVER TOLLON YAUPON CATBERRY INKBERRY MILKMAID

HOLLYHOCK HOCK ALTHEA
MALLOW
HOLM ISLET ISLAND BOTTOMS
HOLOFERNES (SLAYER OF —)
JUDITH
HOLOTHURIAN TREPANG
HOLY SRI SHRI HUACA SAINT
SANTO DEVOUT DIVINE SACRAL
SACRED BLESSED PERFECT
SAINTLY SINLESS BLISSFUL
INNOCENT REVEREND SPIRITUAL
SANCTIMONIOUS
(— MAN) SADHU
(— OF HOLIES) ADYT ADYTUM
(ALL —) PANAGIA
(PREF.) HAGI(O) HIER(O)
HIERATICO HOSIO SANCTI
SANCTO SEMNO
(SUFF.) HIERIC
HOLY BASIL TULCE TOOLSY
HOLY SPIRIT PARACLETE
HOLY STONE BEAR BIBLE
HOLY WOOD LIGNUM
HOMAGE FEE COURT HONOR
YMAGE FEALTY MANRED INCENSE
LOYALTY MANRENT MANSHIP
OVATION SERVICE TREWAGE
EMINENCE OBEISANCE
(SUPREME —) LATRIA
HOME BYE DEN HAM BASE HAME
HUNK WIKE ABODE ASTRE BEING
DOMUS FOYER HAUNT SMOKE
HEARTH BLIGHTY SHELTER
DOMICILE FIRESIDE ROOFTREE
(— FOR THE POOR) HOSPICE
(— OF THE BLESSED) GIMLE
(FUNERAL —) CHAPEL
(HARVEST —) KERN KIRN MELL
HOCKEY
(REST —) FARM HOSTEL
(PREF.) (RETURN —) NOST(O)
HOMELAND HAVAIKI
HOMELESS ROOFLESS VAGABOND
HOMELIKE HOMEY HAMEIL HAMILT
HOMISH HOMESOME
HOMELINESS YEOMANRY
HOMELY FOUL UGLY PLAIN
DUDGEN RUGGED PLAINLY
EVERYDAY FAMILIAR HOMELIKE
HOME PLATE RUBBER
HOMER KOR CHOMER
HOME RUN SWAT SWOT BLAST
HOMESICKNESS HEIMWEH
NOSTALGIA
HOMESPUN KERSEY RUSSET
RAPLOCH
HOMESTEAD TOFT TREF ONSET
PLACE WORTH TYDDYN FARMERY
ONSTEAD STEADING
HOMESTEADER NESTER
HOMETHRUST HAI HAY
HOMEWORK PREP
HOMICIDE DEATH MORTH KILLING
HOMILETIC KERYSTIC
HOMILY PRONE OMELIE POSTIL
SERMON
HOMINY SAMP NASAUMP
HOMOEOMERY GERM SEED
(PL.) SPERMATA
HOMOGENEITY SAMENESS
HOMOGENEOUS LIKE SOLID
GLOBAL SIMPLE COMPACT
MASSIVE SIMILAR

(PREF.) HOL(O) IS(O)
HOMOGENOUS ENTIRE
HOMOLOGUE CYANINE HOMOTYPE
(PREF.) NOR
HOMOPHONY MONODY
HOMORGANIC COGNATE
HOMOSEXUAL (FEMALE —) DIKE
DYKE
HOMOZYGOUS PURE ISOGENIC

HONDURAS

CAPITAL: TEGUCIGALPA
COIN: PESO CENTAVO LEMPIRA
DEPARTMENT: YORO COLON
COPAN VALLE OLANCHO
GULF: FONSECA
INDIAN: MAYA PAYA SUMO ULVA
CARIB LENCA PIPIL TAUIRA
JICAQUE MISKITO MOSQUITO
ISLAND: ROATAN
ISLANDS: BAY BAHIA
LAKE: CRIBA YOJOA BREWER
MEASURE: VARA MILLA MECATE
TERCIA CAJUELA MANZANA
MOUNTAINS: PIJA AGALTA
CELAQUE
PORT: LACEIBA TRUJILLO
RIVER: COCO SICO ULUA AGUAN
LEMPA NEGRO TINTO WANKS
PATUCA SULACO GUAYAPE
OLANCHO SEGOVIA SANTIAGO
RUINS: TENAMPUA
TOWN: TELA YORO COPAN LAPAZ
ROATAN GRACIAS LACEIBA
TRUJILLO YUSCARAN
JUTICALPA
WEIGHT: CAJA LIBRA

HONE HO STROP STROKE STRICKLE
HONEST FAIR GOOD JAKE TRUE
AFALD FRANK ROUND SOUND
WHITE CANDID DEXTER DINKUM
ENTIRE PROPER RUSTIC SINGLE
SQUARE SINCERE UPRIGHT
RIGHTFUL STRAIGHT
HONESTLY TRULY DINKUM
HONEST INDEED SINGLY SQUARE
SQUARELY
HONESTY FAITH HONOR SATIN
EQUITY LUNARY REALTY VERITY
JUSTICE LUNARIA PROBITY
BOLBONAC FAIRNESS FIDELITY
MOONWORT SATINPOD
YEOMANRY
HONEY MEL MELL HINNY
HONEYBUN
(— BEVERAGE) MULSE
(ROSE-FLAVORED —) RODOMEL
(PREF.) MELI(TTO) MELL(I)
HONEYBEE (ALSO SEE BEE) BEE
GYNE KING DRANE DRONE QUEEN
DINGAR DRONER EGATES
CYPRIAN DEBORAH DESERET
KOOTCHA MELISSA STINGER
ACULEATE ANGELITO
HONEY BUZZARD PERN
HONEYCOMB COMB FRAME
WAXCOMB
(PREF.) CERIO FAVI
HONEYCREEPER IIWI MAMO
PALILA DREPANID GUITGUIT
HONEYDEW MANNA MILDEW
HONEY EATER OO IAO TUI MOHO

MINER TENUI MANUAO MAOMAO
ROSTER BELLBIRD WURRALUH
HONEYED SWEET HYBLAN SUGARY
SUGARED HYBLAEAN LUSCIOUS
HONEY GUIDE MOROC
HONEY MESQUITE ALGAROBA
HONEYPOD
HONEY PLANT HOYA HUAJILLO
HONEYSUCKLE VINE SUCKLE
WEIGELA BINDWEED SUCKLING
WOODBINE

HONG KONG

BAY: SHEKO REPULSE
CAPITAL: VICTORIA
COIN: CENT DOLLAR
DISTRICT: WANCHAI
GARDENS: TIGERBALM
ISLAND: LANTAO
MOUNTAIN: CASTLE VICTORIA
PENINSULA: KOWLOON
TOWN: KOWLOON

HONK KONK YANG CRONK
HONOR BAY ORE FAME FETE HORN
KUDO ADORE CROWN GLORY
GRACE HERRY IZZAT MENSE
MENSK SPEAK TREAT CREDIT
DECORE ENHALO ESTEEM
HOMAGE HONOUR LAUREL
PRAISE REVERE SALUTE WORTHY
DIGNITY EMBLAZE GLORIFY
HONESTY MANSHIP RESPECT
WORSHIP ACCOLADE DECORATE
GRANDEZA TASHREEF
(PL.) ACES
(PREF.) TIMO
HONORABLE DEAR FREE GOOD
DIGNE NOBLE OPIME WHITE
GENTLE HONEST HONORA
LORDLY SQUARE UPRIGHT
GENEROUS HANDSOME
HONORARY
HONORABLENESS HONESTY
HONORABLY GENTLY
HONORARIUM SALARY DOUCEUR
ALTARAGE HONORARY
HONORED GOOD FAMOUS LAUREL
LAURELED PRESTIGIOUS
HONORIFIC MAGNIFIC
HOOD HOW COIF COWL HEAD
HUDE JACK AMICE ALMUCE
BIGGIN BONNET BURLET CALASH
CAMAIL CANOPY CAPOTE CUTOFF
DOMINO FUNNEL MANTLE RAFFIA
BANGKOK BASHLYK CALOTTE
CAPUCHE BLINDAGE CALYPTRA
CAPUCCIO CAPUTIUM CHAPERON
CUCULLUS FOOLSCAP LIRIPIPE
LIRIPOOP MAZARINE TROTCOZY
NITHSDALE
(— AND CAPE COMBINED)
FALDETTA
(— FOR EVENING WEAR) CAPELINE
(— OF BOILER) VOMIT
(— OF CARRIAGE) HEAD
(— OF MAIL) COIF CAMAIL COIFFE
(— OF VEHICLE) TOP CAPOTE
(— ON CUPBOARD) TREMOR
(— ON HORSES) BLINKER
(— OVER DOOR) MARQUISE
(LENS —) SUNSHADE
(MONK'S —) COWL

(STIRRUP —) TAPADERO
(STRAW —) JAVA
(WOMAN'S —) SURTOUT VOLUPER
HOODED COWLED GALEATE
CUCULLATE
HOODED CROW HOODIE
GRAYBACK GREYBACK
HOODED MERGANSER SMEW
SNOWL SPIKE TADPOLE
TOWHEAD MOSSHEAD
HOODED SEAL WIG HOOD
HOODCAP
HOODLUM HOOD PUNK BADDY
BADDIE SKOLLY LURCHER
HOOLIGAN LARRIKIN
HOODOO JINX
HOODWINK MOP DUPE FOOL SEEL
BLEAR BLIND BLUFF CHEAT
BAFFLE CLOYNE DELUDE
GAMMON WIMPLE AVEUGLE
BEGUILE BLINKER DECEIVE
MISLEAD INVEIGLE
HOOEY BUSHWAH
HOOF CLOOF CLOOT COFFIN
UNGUIS UNGULA CLOOTIE
HOOFLET FOREHOOF
(PREF.) UNGULI
HOOK DOG GAB JIG PEW TUG CLIP
DRAG FLAG GAFF HAKE HUCK
KILP MEAK NOCK PEVY PRIN
PUGH SETT SKID STAY TACK
CATCH CHAPE CLEEK CLICK
CRAMP CROME CROOK DRAIL
HAMUS ONCIN PEAVY PREEN
SARPE SPOON TACHE UNCUS
BECKET DETENT HANGLE HINGLE
PINTLE TENTER AGRAFFE
GAMBREL GRUNTER HAMULUS
HITCHER HOOKLET KNUCKLE
NUTHOOK PELICAN PENNANT
PINHOOK POTHOOK RAMHEAD
SNIGGLE SPERKET UNCINUS
BOATHOOK CROTCHET
GRABHOOK PORTHOOK PULLBACK
VULSELLA WEEDHOOK
(— FISH) FOUL HANG SNAG DRAIL
HITCH STRIKE SNIGGLE FISHHOOK
(— FOR BACON) COMB
(— FOR KETTLE) KILP HANGLE
TRAMMEL
(— FOR POT) DRACKEN POTHOOK
SLOWRIE
(— FOR TWISTING HEMP) WHIRL
WHIRLER
(BENCH —) JACK
(BOAT —) HITCHER
(BOXING —) CROSS
(COUPLING —) JIGGER
(LONG-HANDLED —) HOCK MEAK
(MUSICAL —) FLAG PENNANT
(PRUNING —) SARPE CALABOZO
(REAPING —) HINK TWIBILL
(SAFETY —) CLEVIS
(SKIDDING —S) GRAB
(2 —S FASTENED AT SHANKS)
DOUBLES
HOOKAH KALIAN CHILLUM
HOOKED ADUNC UNCATE UNCOUS
ADUNCAL FALCATE HAMATED
HAMULAR ADUNCATE ADUNCOUS
AQUILINE HAMIFORM UNCINATE
HOOKEDNESS ADUNCITY
HOOKER-OUT STICKMAN

HOOK-SHAPED ANKYROID
HOOKUP CIRCUIT
HOOKWORM STRONGYL
HOOLIGAN ROUGH ROWDY TOUGH
  APACHE GOONDA LARRIKIN
  (PL.) AMALAITA
HOOP RIB BAIL BAND BOND BOOL
  CLIP GIRD GIRR PASS RING TIRE
  GARTH GIRTH FRETTE HOOPLE
  LAGGIN WICKET CIRCLET
  GARLAND TROCHUS TRUNDLE
  (— FOR A SPAR) BANGLE
  (— FOR BARREL) BAND GIRD GIRTH
  (— FOR LAMPSHADE) HARP
  (— FOR ORE BUCKET) CLEVIS
  (— FOR WINNOWING GRAIN)
  WEIGHT
  (— NET) TRUNK
  (— OF WHEEL) STRAKE
  (— TO STRENGTHEN GUN) FRETTE
  (HALF —) BAIL BALE
HOOPED RUNG
HOOPOE HOOP UPUPA WHOOP
  IRRISOR DUNGBIRD PICARIAN
HOOPSKIRT TUBTAIL
HOOP SNAKE WAMPUM
HOOSE HUSK
HOOSIER SCHOOLMASTER
  (AUTHOR OF —) EGGLESTON
  (CHARACTER IN —) BUD PETE
  JONES MEANS RALPH SMALL
  WHITE HANNAH MARTHA
  SANDER SHOCKY WALTER
  HAWKINS JOHNSON MATILDA
  PEARSON THOMSON
HOOSIER STATE INDIANA
HOOT CURR WHOO WHOOP
  WHOOT EXPLODE ULULATE
HOOVE BLOAT
HOP HIP NIP FLIP JUMP LEAP
  BOUND HITCH SWINE FLIERS
  GAMBOL SPRING TITTUP
  CROWHOP HOPBIND HOPVINE
  LUPULUS SKIPPER
HOPBUSH AKE AKEAKE
HOP CLOVER SHAMROCK
  SUCKLING
HOPE WON DEEM SPES TROW
  COMBE THINK TRUST DESIRE
  EXPECT PERDUE ESPEIRE
  THOUGHT SPERANZA VELLEITY
  (VAIN —) PIPE WANHOPE
HOPEFUL FOND BUOYANT
  SANGUINE WENLICHE
HOPELESS DULL ABJECT FORLORN
  DOWNCAST
HOPELESSNESS ANOMIE DESPAIR
HOPHNI (BROTHER OF —) PHINEHAS
  (FATHER OF —) ELI
HOP HORNBEAM DEERWOOD
  HARDHACK IRONWOOD
HOPI MOKI MOQUI
HOP-LIKE LUPULINE
HOPPER CURB JACK BUNKER
  CLOSET HAPPER MACARONI
HOPPLE HOBBLE PASTERN
  SIDELANG
HOPS SHATTER
  (— BETWEEN 2 AND 4 YEARS) OLDS
HOPSCOTCH POTSY HOPPERS
  PALLALL PEEVERS
HOP TREE RUEWORT WINGSEED
HORDE ARMY CAMP CLAN PACK

CROWD GROUP SWARM LEGION
  THRONG
  (INNER —) BUKEYEF
HOREHOUND HENBIT MARVEL
  WONDER MARRUBE
HORI (FATHER OF —) LOTAN
  (SON OF —) SHAPHAT
HORIZON LAYER VERGE COMPASS
  FINITOR ORTERDE SKYLINE
HORIZONTAL LEVEL LINEAR
  NAIANT ACLINAL STRAIGHT
HORIZONTALLY FLATLY BARWAYS
  BARWISE ENDLONG FESSWAYS
  FESSWISE
HORMIGO QUIRA
HORMONE CORTIN LUTEIN
  EQUILIN ESTRIOL ESTRONE
  GASTRIN INSULIN RELAXIN
  STEROID THEELIN THEELOL
  ANDROGEN ENDOCRIN ESTROGEN
  FLORIGEN GALACTIN LACTOGEN
  OESTRIOL SECRETIN CORTISONE
HORN BEAK BATON BUGLE CONCH
  CORNO CORNU SHOOT ANTLER
  CLAXON KLAXON OXHORN
  TOOTER ALPHORN ALTHORN
  ANTENNA BUFFALO CLARONE
  FOGHORN HELICON HUTCHET
  OUTHORN PRICKET SHOPHAR
  UNICORN BEAKIRON BUCKHORN
  CLAVICOR CORNICLE OLIPHANT
  SLUGHORN STAGHORN
  WALDHORN NOISEMAKER
  (— NOTE) MORT
  (— OF COW) SCUR
  (— OF CRESCENT MOON) CUSP
  (— OF DILEMMA) PIKE
  (— OF DRINK) SLOSH
  (— OF YOUNG STAG) BUNCH
  (BUDDING —) SHOOT
  (DRINKING —) RHYTON
  (ENGLISH —) CA
  (FRENCH —) CORNO
  (GREY —) COLUMN
  (HUNTER'S —) HUTCHET
  WALDHORN
  (INSECT'S —) ANTENNA
  (IVORY —) OLIFANT
  (RAM'S —) SHOPHAR
  (RUDIMENTARY —) SLUG
  (STUNTED —) SCUR
  (PREF.) CORNEO CORNI CORNU
  (SUFF.) CERA(S) CEROS CEROUS
  CERUS CORN
HORNBEAM HARDBEAM
  HARDHACK HORNWOOD
  IRONWOOD
HORNBILL TOCK CALAO TOUCAN
  BUCEROS HOMURAI BROMVOEL
  PICARIAN YEARBIRD
HORNBLENDE SIDERITE
HORNED FORKED CORNUTE
  (PREF.) CERA CERVI CORNEO
  CORNI CORNU
HORNED DACE CHUB
HORNED POUT CATFISH
HORNED SCREAMER ANHIMA
  KAMACHI KAMICHI UNICORN
HORNED VIPER WAMPUM
  CERASTES
HORNET VESPA VESPID STINGER
HORNGELD CORNAGE
HORNLESS NAT NOT MOIL POLL

DODDY MULEY POLEY DODDED
  HUMBLE HUMMEL MAILIE MULLEY
  POLLED ACEROUS
HORNPIPE MATELOTE
HORN POPPY SQUATMORE
HORNSTONE CHERT KERALITE
HORNTAIL SIREX ORYSSID
  UROCERID WOODWORM
HORNWORT COONTAIL
  HORNWEED
HORNY WAUKIT CALLOUS
  CERATOID CORNEOUS KERASINE
  KERATOID
HORNYHEAD CHUB
HOROSCOPE SCOPE THEME
  FIGURE GENESIS NATIVITY
HORRIBLE DIRE GRIM UGLY
  AWFUL BLACK GREAT GRISLY
  HORRID GEARFUL GHASTLY
  HIDEOUS HORRENT UNSLOGH
  DREADFUL GRUESOME HORRIFIC
  SHOCKING TERRIBLE MONSTROUS
HORRID GRIM UGLY AWFUL
  ROUGH RUGGED SNUFFY
  UGSOME WICKED HIDEOUS
  DREADFUL GRUESOME HORRIBLE
  SHOCKING
HORRIFIC FEARFUL
HORRIFIED AGHAST GHASTLY
  HORRENT
HORRIFY APPAL AGRISE DISMAY
  ENHORROR
HORROR FEAR DREAD TERROR
  CONSTERNATION
  (PL.) JIMJAMS
HORSA (BROTHER OF —) HENGIST
HORS D'OEUVRE CANAPE RELISH
  OUTWORK ZAKUSKA
  (PL.) ASSIETTE
HORSE BAY CUT DUN GEE GRI NAG
  PAD POT RIP TIT ARAB AVER
  BARB DOON GOER GROG HACK
  HAND HOSS JADE MARE MOKE
  PRAD PROD QUAD RACK RIDE
  ROAN ROIL SKIN STUD TEAM
  TURK WEED YAWD ZAIN AIVER
  ARION ARVAK BEAST BIDET
  BLACK BROCK CAPLE CAPUL
  CHUNK CREAM CROCK DUMMY
  EQUID FAVEL GLYDE GRANI
  HAIRY HOBBY MILER MOREL
  PACER PINTO PIPER POLER
  PUNCH RACER ROGUE RUNSY
  SCREW SHIER SHIRE SKATE
  SOMER STEED STIFF TACKY
  WALER WIDGE ALEZAN AMBLER
  BANKER BOLTER BRONCO
  BRUMBY BUCKER BUSSER CABBER
  CALICO CASTER CHASER CHEVAL
  COLLOP CURTAL CUSSER DAPPLE
  DOBBIN DRIVER ENTIRE EQUINE
  FENCER FILLER GANGER GARRON
  GLEYDE GRULLA HUNTER
  JUMPER KEFFEL LEADER MAIDEN
  MORGAN NUBIAN ORLOFF
  OUTLAW PELTER PLATER POSTER
  PULLER RACKER ROARER ROUNCY
  RUNNER SAVAGE SORREL STAGER
  TARPAN TRACER TURKEY
  VANNER WARPER WEAVER
  ALSVINN ALSVITH ARABIAN
  BARBARY BELGIAN BOARDER
  CABALLO CHARGER CLICKER

CLIPPER COACHER COCOTTE
  COURSER CRIBBER CRIOLLA
  CRITTER DRAFTER FLEMISH
  GALATHE GELDING GIGSTER
  GRUNTER HACKNEY KNACKER
  LEEFANG MONTURE MUSTANG
  NEIGHER PACOLET PALFREY
  PIEBALD PRANCER PRANKER
  RATTLER REESTER REFUSER
  REMOUNT RUNAWAY SADDLER
  SLEDDER SLEEPER SPANKER
  STAGGIE STEPPER SUFFOLK
  SUMPTER TRAPPER TRESTLE
  TROOPER TROTTER WHEELER
  ARDENNES BATHORSE BUCKSKIN
  CHESTNUT CHEVALET COCKTAIL
  COLICKER CREATURE CYLLAROS
  DEMISANG DESTRIER EOHIPPUS
  FOOTROPE FRIPPERY GALLOPER
  GALLOWAY HRIMFAXI KADISCHI
  MACHINER OUTSIDER PALOMINO
  RIDGLING ROADSTER SKEWBALD
  STIBBLER TRIPPLER WHISTLER
  YARRAMAN
  (— ACT) MANAGE
  (— CERTAIN NOT TO WIN) STIFF
  (— ESTABLISHMENT) HARAS
  (— LOSING FIXED RACE) STUMER
  STUMOUR
  (— OF UNIFORM DARK COLOR) ZAIN
  (— RACE) WALKOVER
  (— THAT WON'T START) STICK
  (—S RUNNING BEHIND) RUCK
  (ARABIAN —) ARAB KOHL ARABIAN
  (BALKY —) JIB JIBBER
  (BROKEN-DOWN —) JADE CROCK
  SCREW DURGAN GARRAN
  (CALICO —) PINTO
  (CASTRATED —) GELDING
  (CLUMSY —) STAMMEL
  (DECREPIT —) SKATE GLEYDE
  (DRAFT —) HAIRY PUNCH SHIRE
  BEETEWK BELGIAN SUFFOLK
  PERCHERON
  (DROVE OF —S) ATAJO
  (EASY-PACED —) PAD
  (FALLOW —) FAVEL
  (FAMILY —) DOBBIN
  (FAST —) GANGER
  (FEMALE —) MARE FILLY
  (FLEMISH —) ROIL
  (GRAY —) SCHIMMEL
  (HIGH-SPIRITED —) STEPPER
  (IMAGINARY —) AULLAY
  (IMMUNIZED —) BLEEDER
  (INFERIOR —) PLUG CAYUSE
  PLATER
  (JUMPING —) LEPPER
  (MALE —) STALLION
  (NEAR —) HAND
  (OLD —) JADE PROD YAUD AIVER
  CROCK
  (PACK —) BIDET SUMPTER
  (PART OF —) EAR EYE JAW RIB
  FACE HOCK HOOF KNEE LOIN
  MANE NECK NOSE POLL TAIL
  BELLY CHEEK CROUP ELBOW
  FLANK MOUTH THIGH BREAST
  CANNON GASKIN HAUNCH STIFLE
  BUTTOCK CORONET FETLOCK
  FOREARM NOSTRIL PASTERN
  WITHERS FOREHEAD FORELOCK
  SHOULDER THROATLATCH

(RANGE —) FANTAIL
(ROAN —) SCHIMMEL
(SADDLE —) MOUNT
(SHAFT —) SHAFTER THILLER
(SHAGGY —) ALTAI
(SLUGGISH —) HOG
(SMALL —) NAG TIT BIDET GENET
HOBBY CANUCK JENNET
GALLOWAY
(STOCKY —) COB
(TEAM OF —S) CARTWARE
(TEAM OF 3 —S WITH LEADER)
UNICORN
(TRICK —) SIMON
(UNBROKEN —) BRONCO
(VICIOUS —) LADINO
(WILD —) FUZZY BRUMBY
KUMRAH OUTLAW TARPAN
JUGHEAD BANGTAIL FUZZTAIL
WARRIGAL
(WINGED —) PEGASUS
(WORN-OUT —) HACK GARRAN
KNACKER CROWBAIT
(WORTHLESS —) JADE SHACK
KEFFEL
(YOUNG —) TIT COLT FOAL STAG
STOT STAGGIE
(2-YEAR OLD —) TWINTER
(3 —S ABREAST) TROIKA
(3 —S ONE BEHIND ANOTHER)
RANDEM
(4 —S ABREAST) QUADRIGA
(PL.) MANADA STABLE UNICORN
(PREF.) HIPP(O)
(SUFF.) HIPPUS
HORSE BALM KNOBWEED
KNOTROOT RICHWEED
HORSE BLANKET RUG MANTA
HORSE BOY TRACER
HORSE CHESTNUT CONKER
HORSECLOTH HOUSE HOUSING
HORSE DEALER COPER CHANTER
COURSER
HORSE-EYE JACK XUREL
HORSE FENNEL SESELI
HORSEFLESH JACK
HORSEFLY BOT GAD CLEG CLEGG
STOUT BOTFLY BREEZE GADBEE
GADFLY BULLDOG DEERFLY
TABANID
HORSEHAIR SETON
HORSELAUGH GUFFAW
HORSELEECH ALUKAH
HORSELOAD SEAM
HORSE MACKEREL TUNNY
SAUREL
HORSEMAN RIDER CHARRO
COWBOY HUSSAR KNIGHT
RUTTER COURIER PICADOR
PRICKER CAVALIER GALLOPER
(PL.) HORSE CAVALRY
HORSEMANSHIP CAVALRY
HORSEMINT RIGNUM
HORSE MUSHROOM WHITECAP
HORSE NETTLE SOLANUM
HORSEPLAY HIJINKS
(PANTOMIME —) RALLY
HORSEPOWER SOUP
HORSEPOX GREASE
HORSE-RADISH MAROR MOROR
REDCOLL
HORSE-RADISH TREE BEN BEHN
BEHEN

HORSESHOE TIP SHOE PLATE
HOBBER LUNETTE
HORSETAIL TAIL PRELE TOADPIPE
HORSETAIL LICHEN TREEHAIR
HORSETAIL TREE AGOHO AGOJO
HORSEWEED COCASH COWTAIL
HOGWEED FIREWEED
SCABIOUS
HORTATORY EMOTIVE
HORTICULTURIST (ALSO SEE
BOTANIST)
HORUS SEPT SOPT SEPTI
HORMAKHU
(FATHER OF —) OSIRIS
(MOTHER OF —) ISIS
HOSACKIA ACMISPON
HOSE LINE VAMP HOSEN GASKIN
BROGUES BULLION HOSIERY
CHAUSSES HANDLINE HOSEPIPE
HOSEA (FATHER OF —) BEERI
HOSHAIAH (SON OF —) AZARIAH
JEZANIAH
HOSHEA (FATHER OF —) NUN
AZAZIAH
HOSIERY HOSE KNITWEAR
(— WORKER) LOOPER
HOSPICE IMARET DIACONIA
HOSPITAL
HOSPITABLE DOUCE CLEVER
DOULCE SOCIAL CORDIAL
FRIENDLY
HOSPITAL BEDLAM CRECHE
SPITAL COLLEGE LAZARET
PESTHOUSE POLYCLINIC
HOSPITALITY SALT MENSE
XENODOCHY
HOSPODAR VOIVOD GOSPODAR
HOST SUM ARMY FYRD WARE
CROWD JASON MAKER POWER
SWARM WERED LEGION LODGER
NATION THRONG BALEBOS
COMPANY FYRDUNG SACRING
VIANDER LANDLORD PARTICLE
MULTITUDE
(— OF INVADERS) HERE
(EUCHARISTIC —) LAMB SACRING
(PL.) SABAOTH
(SUFF.) XENOUS XENY
HOSTA NIOBE FUNKIA
HOSTAGE BORROW PLEDGE
SURETY RANSOMER
HOSTEL INN ENTRY HOSTAGE
KINGDOM HOSPITAL
HOSTELRY AUBERGE
HOSTESS TAUPO LANDLADY
CHATELAINE
HOSTILE FOE HARD ALIEN BLACK
ENEMY FREMT HATEL STOUT
DEADLY FRIGID INFEST ADVERSE
ASOCIAL FIENDLY OPPOSED
UNQUERT WARLIKE CONTRARY
INIMICAL OPPOSITE
HOSTILITY WAR FEID FEUD HATE
ANIMUS ENMITY HATRED
RANCOR SCHISM DAGGERS
RUPTURE
(PL.) WAR ARMS ARMOR
WARFARE
HOSTLER NAGMAN OSTLER
HORSEBOY
HOT WARM ADUST CALID EAGER
FIERY ARDENT ESTIVE FERVID
IGNITE SULTRY TORRID ANIMOSE

ANIMOUS BOILING BURNING
CANDENT FERVENT PEPPERY
THERMAL CAYENNED FEVERISH
SEETHING SIZZLING
(— WATER) SOUP
HOTBED BED NEST HOTHOUSE
HOT-BLOODED VASCULAR
HOTBOX SMOKER STINKER
HOTEL INN SPA FLOP FONDA
HOUSE HYDRO HOSTEL HOTTLE
POSADA FLEABAG FONDACO
FUNDUCK GASTHOF HOSTELRY
(— NEAR AIRPORT) AIRTEL
(WATERSIDE —) BOATEL
HOTELKEEPER HOTELIER
HOTHAM (FATHER OF —) HEBER
HOTHAN (SON OF —) SHAMA
JEHIEL
HOT-HEADED BRAINISH MADBRAIN
HOTHIR (FATHER OF —) HEMAN
HOTHOUSE STEW STOVE PINERY
FRUITERY
HOT ROD DRAGSTER
HOT-TEMPERED PEPPERY
CHOLERIC SPITFIRE
HOTTENTOT NAMA TOTTY
HOTNOT KOKANA WITBOOI
QUAEQUAE
(PL.) BALAO BALAWU
HOUND DOG PIE BAIT HARL HUNT
MUTE BRACE BRACH ENTRY
HARRY LEASH LIMER SLATE
AFGHAN BASSET BEAGLE HUNTER
JOWLER LEAMER LUCERN SLEUTH
TUFTER CURTISE ENTRADA
GELLERT REDBONE SKIRTER
BARUKHZY BLUETICK BRATCHET
COURSING FOXHOUND
(BITCH —) BRACH
(CRY OF —) MUSIC
(EXTINCT —) TALBOT
(RELAY OF —S) VANLAY
(SLEUTH —) TALBOT
(SPECTRAL —) SHUCK
(PL.) RACHES
HOUND'S-TONGUE TORYWEED
HOUR URE TIDE TIME CURFEW
GHURRY
(CANONICAL —) NONE SEXT PRIME
MATINS TIERCE ORTHROS
VESPERS COMPLINE EVENSONG
(HALF —) BELL
(KILOWATT —) KELVIN
(LAST —S) DEATHBED
(STUDY —) PREP
(6 —S) QUADRANT
(PREF.) HORO
HOURGLASS (PART OF —) BULB
SAND FRAME WAIST
HOURLY HORAL HORARY
HOUSE BOX KEN CASA CRIB DOME
DUMP FIRM FLET HALL HELL
HOLE HOME RACE ROOF STOW
ABODE ADOBE AERIE BAHAY
BANDA COVER DACHA DOMUS
HOOCH HOOSE JACAL LODGE
MEESE PLACE STAGE WHARE
BESTOW BIGGIN BOTTLE CAMARA
CASITA CASTLE CHEMIS CLOTHE
DUPLEX FAMILY HEARTH HOOTCH
MAISON PALACE PARISH SINGLE
STABLE WIGWAM BASTIDE
BIGGING CABOOSE CASSINE

EUDEMON FAZENDA HOGGERY
HOUSING MESUAGE QUARTER
SHELTER AEDICULA BARADARI
BUNGALOW DOMICILE DOVECOTE
DWELLING MEDSTEAD MESSUAGE
TENEMENT NOVITIATE
(— AND LAND) DEMESNE
(— AND 5 ACRES) COTE
(— FOR DOGS) KENNEL
(— FOR WOMEN) HAREM
(— IN BOROUGH) HAW
(— OF A MARABOUT) KOUBA
(— OF CORRECTION) BRIDEWELL
(— OF KNIGHTS TEMPLARS)
PRECEPTORY
(— OF LEGISLATURE) SEANAD
CHAMBER ASSEMBLY
(— OF PARLIAMENT) COMMONS
LAGTING
(— OF PROSTITUTION) CRIB BAGNIO
BORDEL
(— OF REFUGE) MAGDALEN
MAGDALENE
(— OF THIEVES) KEN
(— OF WORSHIP) BETHEL CHURCH
(— WITH TRIANGULAR FRONT)
AFRAME
(APARTMENT —) INSULA
(ASTROLOGICAL —) ANGLE
(AUSTRALIAN —) HUMPY
(CHANGE —) DRY
(CHAPTER —) CABILDO
(CLAY —) ADOBE TEMBE
(COACH —) REMISE
(COMMUNAL —) MORONG
(COUNTRY —) PEN DACHA CASINO
GRANGE QUINTA BASTIDE
CHATEAU
(COW —) VACCARY
(DAIRY —) WICK
(EATING —) COOKSHOP
(ESKIMO —) IGLU IGLOO TOPEK
KASHGA KASHIMA
(FIJI —) BURE
(FORTIFIED —) GARRISON
(GAMBLING —) BANK HELL
RIDOTTO
(GOVERNMENT —) KONAK
(GRINDING —) HULL
(GROUP OF —S) CLUSTER
(HAWAIIAN —) HALE
(LODGING —) INN KIP HOST ENTRY
HOTEL HOSTEL
(LOG —) TILT
(MANOR —) HAM HALL COURT
PLACE SCHLOSS SEIGNEURY
(PLANETARY —) TOWER
(POULTRY —) ARK HENNERY
(PUBLIC —) INN HOSTEL SHANTY
CANTEEN SNUGGERY
(RANCH —) HUT
(RELIGIOUS —) CELL CONVENT
KELLION MONASTERY
PRESBYTERY
(RENTED —) LET
(REST —) DAK KHAN SERAI
(RETREAT —) CENACLE
(ROOMING —) DOSS FLOP
FLEABAG
(ROYAL —) AERIE
(SENATE —) CURIA
(SMALL —) COT HUT BACH CELL
CABIN HOVEL SHACK CASITA

COTTAGE MAISONETTE
(SOD —) SODDY
(STILT —) CHIKEE CHICKEE
(SUMMER —) TRELLIS
(TENEMENT —) LAND CHAWL
(THATCHED —) BANDA
(TOY —) COBHOUSE
(TURKISH —) KONAK
(PREF.) DOMI ECO OECO OIKO
STEG(O)
(SUFF.) OECA OECIA STEGE
STEGITE
HOUSEBOAT BARGE HOUSER
WANGAN WANIGAN DAHABEAH
HOUSEBREAKER MILL JACOB
MILLKEN
HOUSEBREAKING CRACK
HOUSECARL THINGMAN
HOUSECOAT DUSTER
HOUSEFINCH BURION LINNET
REDHEAD
HOUSEHOLD HIRED HOUSE
FAMILY HOUSAL MEINIE MENAGE
FIRESIDE MAINPAST
(PREF.) EC(O) OEC(O) OIKO
HOUSEHOLDER ASTRER
GOODMAN GUIDMAN NAUKRAR
FRANKLIN
HOUSEKEEPER HUSSY MATRON
HOUSELEEK JUBARB AYEGREEN
HOMEWORT SENGREEN SILGREEN
HOUSEMATE DOMESTIC
HOUSE OF MIRTH (AUTHOR OF —)
WHARTON
(CHARACTER IN —) GUS BART
JUDY LILY GRYCE PERCY SIMON
BERTHA DORSET GEORGE SELDEN
TRENOR LAURENCE PENISTON
ROSEDALE
HOUSE OF SEVEN GABLES
(AUTHOR OF —) HAWTHORNE
(CHARACTER IN —) MAULE PHOEBE
VENNER JAFFREY CLIFFORD
HEPZIBAH HOLGRAVE PYNCHEON
HOUSEWARMING INFARE
HOUSEWIFE DAME FRAU FROW
WIFE HUSSY VROUW BUSHWIFE
HAUSFRAU
(MEAN —) NIP
HOUSEY-HOUSEY BINGO
HOUSING BOX BASE CASE DRUM
TRAP BANJO BLIMP GLOBE
HOUSE KIOSK BARREL RADOME
SHIELD HOUSAGE SHELTER
DOGHOUSE PADCLOTH PECTORAL
PEDESTAL SHABRACK
(HORSE'S —) BASE
(RADAR —) BLISTER
(PL.) HOLSTERS
HOVA IMERINA
HOVEL HUT COSH CREW CRIB
CRUE HELM HULK HULL BOTHY
CHOZA HUTCH LODGE BOTHIE
BURROW CRUIVE PONDOK
HOVELER HOBBLER HUFFLER
HOVEN BLOATING
HOVER BAIT FLIT HANG HOVE
BROOD POISE FLUTTER HOVERER
HOW AS FOO HOO HOWE HOWEER
HOWEVER QUOMODO WHEREBY
HOWDAH TOWER AMBARI
AMBAREE
HOWEVER BUT THO YET ONLY

HOWSO STILL THOUGH
HOW GREEN WAS MY VALLEY
(AUTHOR OF —) LLEWELLYN
(CHARACTER IN —) HUW BETA
DAVY IVOR OWEN EVANS IANTO
GWILYM IESTYN MARGED
MORGAN BRONWEN ANGHARAD
GRUFFYDD
HOWITZER HOWITZ LICORN
UNICORN
HOWITZER SHELL OBUS
HOWL WAP WOW BAWL GOWL
GURL HURL RAVE WAUL WAWL
YAWL YOLL YOUT YOWL TIGER
WHEWL WRAWL BEHOWL
STEVEN ULULATE
(— VOCIFEROUSLY) TONGUE
HOWLER BONER ERROR
ARAGUATO
HOWLER MONKEY MONO ARABA
HOWLER GUARIBA GUEREBA
STENTOR ALOUATTE
HOWLING ULULANT
HOY TJALK BILANDER CRUMSTER
HOYDEN MEG BLOWZE RIGSBY
TOMBOY
HREIDMAR (SON OF —) REGIN
FAFNER FAFNIR
H-SHAPED ZYGAL
HUAMUCHIL INGA
HUAVE WABI HUABI
HUB HOB BOSS NAVE STOCK
CENTER CENTRE FAUCET HUBBLE
SOCKET SPIDER OMPHALOS
(— AND SPOKES) SPEECH
HUBBLE-BUBBLE CALEAN KALIAN
CALAHAN
HUBBUB DIN COIL STIR CLAMOR
FRAISE HUBBLE RABBLE RACKET
TUMULT BOBBERY CLUTTER
BROUHAHA HUBBABOO
ROWDYDOW SPLATTER
HUCHEN HUSO
HUCHNOM TATU
HUCKLEBERRY HURT ERICAD
CRACKERS
HUCKLEBERRY FINN (AUTHOR OF
—) TWAIN CLEMENS
(CHARACTER IN —) JIM TOM DUKE
FINN HUCK JANE KING POLLY
SALLY SUSAN WILKS JOANNA
PHELPS SAWYER WATSON
DOUGLAS GRANGERFORD
SHEPHERDSON
HUCKSTER BADGER CADGER
KIDDER HAGGLER KIDDIER
TRUCKER OUTCRIER
HUDDLE RUCK HUNCH CRINGE
CROUCH FUMBLE HOWDER
HURTLE SCRUMP SHRIMP SHRINK
CROODLE SCRINCH SCROOCH
SCRUNCH SHUFFLE
HUDIBRAS (AUTHOR OF —) BUTLER
(CHARACTER IN —) RALPHO
CROWDERO HUDIBRAS
SIDROPHEL
HUE RUD BLEE BLUE COND CYAN
CHLOR COLOR GREEN LEMON
SHOUT TAINT TINCT CHROMA
(DULL —) DRAB
(SOMBER —) DARK
HUELESS GRAY GREY
HUFF DOD BLOW RUFF TIFF

DRUNT SNUFF OFFENSE
HUFFY FUFFY SHIRTY
HUG CLIP COLL COUL MOLD CREEM
CRUSH HALSE PRESS CUDDLE
HUDDLE HUGGLE STRAIN
CHERISH EMBRACE SQUEEZE
HUGE BIG FELL MAIN VAST ENORM
GIANT GREAT JUMBO LARGE
STOUR HEROIC IMMANE BANGING
BUMPING DECUMAN HIDEOUS
IMMENSE MASSIVE MONSTER
TITANIC COLOSSAL ENORMOUS
GALACTIC GIGANTIC MOUNTAIN
PYTHONIC SLASHING SWAPPING
THUMPING THWACKING
MOUNTAINOUS
HUGENESS ENORMITY
HUGUENOT CAMISARD
HUGUENOTS, LES (COMPOSER OF
—) MEYERBEER
HUISACHE WABI AROMO CASSIE
POPINAC OPOPANAX
HUL (FATHER OF —) ARAM
(GRANDFATHER OF —) SHEM
HULDAH (HUSBAND OF —)
SHALLUM
HULK CHOP HULL CORSE
HULL HUD POD BODY BULK HULK
HUSK PILL BURSE CASCO SWELL
(— OF COTTON BOLL) BUR BURR
(— OF SHIP) BODY HULK BOTTOM
(PART OF —) BEAM DECK KEEL
RAIL BATTEN RABBET CEILING
FUTTOCK KEELSON GARBOARD
PLANKING STRINGER WATERWAY
STANCHION SHELFPIECE
SPIRKETING
HULLABALOO DIN FLAP CLAMOR
HUBBUB RACKET BROUHAHA
HUM BUM BLUR BRUM BUZZ HUSS
TUNE CHIRM CROON DRONE
FEIGN SOUGH SOWFF
HUMBLE TEEDLE FREDDON
TRUMPET
HUMAN BEING MANLY FINITE
FLESHY HUMANE MORTAL
MANNISH HOMININE HUMANIST
(PREF.) HOMIN(I)
HUMAN BEING MAN WIGHT
MORTAL PERSON ADAMITE
CREATURE RATIONAL
(PREF.) ANTHROP(O)
HUMAN COMEDY (AUTHOR OF —)
SAROYAN
(CHARACTER IN —) BESS MARY
ARENA HOMER KATEY TOBEY
ACKLEY GEORGE GROGAN
HUBERT LIONEL MARCUS
THOMAS BYFIELD ULYSSES
MACAULEY SPANGLER
HUMANE CIVIL KINDLY TENDER
MERCIFUL
HUMANELY MANLY
HUMANITARIAN (ALSO SEE
PHILANTHROPIST) PUBLIC
PHILANTHROPIC
HUMANITY FLESH MENSK WORLD
MANHEAD MANHOOD MANSHIP
SPECIES ADAMHOOD HUMANISM
KINDNESS LENITUDE
HUMBLE LOW BASE HOWE MEAN
MEEK MILD MURE POOR TAME
VAIL ABASE ABATE BUXOM DEMIT

DIMIT LOWER LOWLY PLAIN SILLY
SMALL SOBER WORMY ATTERR
DEJECT DEMEAN DEMISS EMBASE
HONEST MASTER MODEST
REDUCE SIMPLE SLIGHT UNPUFF
AFFLICT DEGRADE DEPRESS
FOOLISH IGNOBLE MORTIFY
OBSCURE CONTRITE DISGRACE
(— ONESELF) STOOP GROVEL
HUMBLED SMALL ABASED
DEJECTED
HUMBLENESS HUMILITY
HUMBLER INFERIOR
HUMBLING SETDOWN ABJECTION
HUMBLY SIMPLE
HUMBUG GAS GUM HUM KID
BUNK FLAM GAFF GAME GUFF
JAZZ SHAM CHEAT FRAUD FUDGE
GUILE JOLLY SPOOF SPOOK TRICK
BARNEY BLAGUE GAMMON
BLARNEY FLUMMER VERNEUK
FLIMFLAM FLUMMERY
HUCKMUCK IMPOSTER NONSENSE
HUMDINGER LULU ONER DOOZY
DINGER HUMMER SNORTER
RIPSNORTER
HUMDRUM IRKSOME PROSAIC
BOURGEOIS
HUMERUS ARM
HUMID WET DAMP DANK MOIST
SOGGY STICKY SULTRY WETTISH
HUMOROUS
HUMIDITY
(PREF.) HYGR(O)
HUMILIATE ABASE ABASH SCALP
SHAME NIDDER NITHER DEGRADE
MORTIFY UNPLUME DISGRACE
HUMILIATED SMALL ASHAMED
HUMILIATION DUST COMEDOWN
DISGRACE
HUMILITY MODESTY MEEKNESS
MILDNESS
HUMIN MELANIN
HUMMEL FALTER
HUMMING AHUM BROOL SINGING
HUMMINGBIRD RUBY STAR
MANGO SYLPH TENUI TOPAZ
AMAZON COQUET HERMIT
HUMMER ROSTER SAPPHO
COLIBRI EMERALD HUMBIRD
JACOBIN RAINBOW SNOWCAP
TROCHIL WARRIOR CALLIOPE
COQUETTE FIRETAIL FROUFROU
MIMOTYPE PICARIAN SAPPHIRE
WHITETIP
HUMMOCK HUMP CHENIER
HAMMOCK TUSSOCK
HUMOR CUE PIN TID WIT BABY
BILE CANT COAX MOOD TIFF VEIN
WHIM FRAME IRONY TUTOR
MEGRIM PAMPER PHLEGM SANIES
SOOTHE SPLEEN SPRITE TEMPER
FOOLING GRATIFY INDULGE
VITREUM VITRINA ARCHNESS
DISHUMOR DROLLERY EYEWATER
FUMOSITY SANGUINE VITREOUS
(BAD —) BATS THROW
(ILL —) BILE DUDGEON
(QUIET —) DRYNESS
(SLIMY —) HIPPOMANES
HUMORIST JOKER FUNSTER
FUNMAKER FUNNYMAN
AMERICAN NYE LEAF SHAW WARD

LEWIS SHUTE SMITH LELAND
LOOMIS MASSON ROGERS
MARQUIS THOMSON PERELMAN
STREETER SULLIVAN SHILLABER
AUSTRIAN SAPHIR
CANADIAN LEACOCK
ENGLISH PAIN WARD SEAMAN
FRENCH RABELAIS
GERMAN RICHTER
IRISH MAHONY
HUMOROUS DROLL FUNNY
PAWKY QUEER JOCOSE COMICAL
GIOCOSO PLAYFUL WAGGISH
PLEASANT SARDONIC
HUMP BOSS HUNK BULGE BUNCH
CROUP CRUMP HULCH HUNCH
GIBBER GIBBUS HUMMIE GIBBOUS
(PREF.) HYB(O)
HUMPBACK LORD CRUMP PUNCH
KYPHOSIS
HUMPBACKED HUMPED HUMPTY
GIBBOSE GIBBOUS
(PREF.) CYPH(O) HYB(O)
HUMPBACKED SALMON HADDO
HOLIA
HUMPED HULCH HUMPY HUTCH
HUMPTY HUNCHY BUNCHED
HUMPHRY CLINKER (AUTHOR OF —
) SMOLLETT
(CHARACTER IN —) JERRY LYDIA
GEORGE WILSON BRAMBLE
CLINKER HUMPHRY JENKINS
MATTHEW MELFORD OBADIAH
TABITHA DENNISON WINIFRED
LISMAHAGO
HUMUS MOR MOLD MULL HUMIN
MOULD
HUNCH HUMP HUNK HULCH
HUNCHET SCRUNCH
HUNCHBACK URCHIN HUMPBACK
HUNCHBACK OF NOTRE DAME
(AUTHOR OF —) HUGO
(CHARACTER IN —) CLAUDE
FROLLO PHOEBUS ESMERALDA
GRINGOIRE QUASIMODO
CHATEAUPERS
HUNDRED RHO CENT CENTUM
HUNDER HUNNER CANTRED
CANTREF CENTARY
(— THOUSAND) LAC LAKH
(NINE —) SAN SAMPI
(5 —) D
(PREF.) CENT(I) HECATO
HECATOM HECATON HECT(O)
HUNDREDFOLD CENTUPLE
HUNDRED-HANDED BRIAREAN
HUNDREDTH CENTESIMAL
(— OF INCH) POINT
(— OF RIGHT ANGLE) GRAD GRADE
HUNDREDWEIGHT CENT CENTAL
CENTENA CENTNER HUNDRED
QUINTAL
HUNGARIAN HUN KUMAN
MAGYAR
(PREF.) UGRO

HUNGARY

CANAL: SIO SARVIZ
CAPITAL: BUDAPEST
COIN: GARA BALAS LENGO FILLER
FORINT KORONA
COUNTY: VAS PEST ZALA BEKES
FEJER HEVES TOLNA NOGRAD

SOMOGY BARANYA
DANCE: CZARDAS
DYNASTY: ARPAD ANGEVIN
FOREST: BAKONY
GYPSY: SZIGANE TZIGANE
KING: BELA GEZA IMRE ARPAD
ISTVAN KALMAN MATTHIAS
LAKE: FERTO BALATON VELENCE
BLATENSEE
MEASURE: AKO HOLD JOCH YOKE
ANTAL ITCZE MAROK METZE
HUVELYK MERFOLD
MOUNTAIN: KEKES BAKONY
MECSEK BORZSONY KORISHEGY
MOUNTAIN RANGE: BUKK MATRA
MECSEK CARPATHIAN
MUSICAL INSTRUMENT: TAROGATO
NATIVE: HUN SERB CROAT GYPSY
MAGYAR SLOVAK UGRIAN
PLAIN: PUSZTA
REGIME: KADAR
RIVER: DUNA MURA RAAB RABA
SAJO ZALA BODVA DRAVA
DRAVE IPOLY KAPOS KOROS
MAROS RABCA TARNA TISZA
DANUBE HENRAD POPRAD
SZAMOS THEISS ZAGYVA
VISTULA BERRETYO
TOWN: ABA ACS OZD VAC BUDA
EGER GYOR MAKO PAPA PECS
PEST TATA ZIRC KOMLO
CEGLED MOHACS SOPRON
SZEGED DBRECEN MISKOLC
SZENTES DEBRECEN SZEGEDIN
WEIGHT: VAMFONT VAMMAZSA
WINE: EGER TOKAJ TOKAY
SZEKSZARD

HUNGER BELL CLEM WANT ACORIA
DESIRE FAMINE CRAVING
HUNGRY YAP HOWE KEEN LEER
YAUP EMPTY THIRL HOLLOW
JEJUNE PECKISH YAPPISH
ANHUNGRY ESURIENT
HUNK DAD DAUD JUNK MOUNTAIN
(— OF BREAD) TOMMY
HUNT DOG GUN JAG MOB RUN
GREW JACK LARK PUMP SEAL
SEEK SHOP CHASE CHEVY DRIVE
HOUND REVAY TRACK TRAIL
BATTUE BEAGLE BREVIT CHEVVY
COURSE FALCON FERRET SEARCH
SHIKAR VANLAY ENCHASE
AUCUPATE PIGSTICK SCROUNGE
VENATION
(— BIG GAME) GHOOM
(— DEER) FLOAT
(— DOWN) QUARRY
(— DUCKS) TOLL
(— FOX) CUB
(— WITH HAWK) FLY
(— WITH SPEAR) STICK
HUNTER GUN HUNT PINK JAGER
BIRDER CHASER GUNNER JAEGER
NIMROD THERON ACTAEON
BUSHMAN CATCHER COURSER
MONTERO SHIKARI SHOOTER
SKIRTER STALKER TRAILER
VENERER CEPHALUS CHASSEUR
FIELDMAN HUNTSMAN TRAILMAN
(— ON SNOW) CRUSTER
(BUFFALO —) CIBOLERO
(MYTHOLOGICAL —) GWYN ORION

(RING OF —S) TINCHEL TINCHILL
HUNTING DRAG HANK AHUNT
WATHE SHIKAR VENERY CUBBING
GUNNING BEAGLING PURCHASE
SHOOTING SURROUND VENATION
(— SIGNAL) SEEK
HUNTSMAN WHIP HUNTER
JAEGER ACTAEON CATCHER
COURSER MONTERO SCARLET
VENATOR VENERER CHASSEUR
HUPHAM (FATHER OF —) BENJAMIN
HUR (GRANDSON OF —) BEZALEEL
(SON OF —) REPHAIAH
HURAM (FATHER OF —) BELA
HURDLE TRAY FLAKE FRITH PANEL
STALE STICK DOUBLE RADDLE
SLEDGE WATTLE
HURDS TOW
HURDY-GURDY LIRA ROTA
LANTUM VIELLE SAMBUKE
HUMSTRUM SYMPHONY
HURI (SON OF —) ABIHAIL
HURL BUM BUN CAST CLOD DASH
DUST FIRE PASH PELT PICK SLAT
SOAK SOCK DRIVE FLING HEAVE
LANCE PITCH SLING SMITE SPANG
SWING THIRL THROW WHIRL
THRILL HURLBAT SWITHER
WHITHER JACULATE PRECIPITATE
HURLY-BURLY HURL RACKET
UPROAR
HURRAH HAIL HUZZA HOORAY
HURRAY BRAVISSIMO
HURRICANE BAGUIO PRESTER
FURACANA FURICANE WILDWIND
HURRIED HASTY RAPID THRONG
HASTEFUL SNATCHED
HURRY ADO FOG NIP RAP RUB
RUN BUSK DUST HUMP PELL
PLAT POST RAPE RESE RUSH STIR
TIFT TROT URGE WHIR CHASE
CROWD HASTE HYPER LURRY
MOSEY PRESS SESSA SKIRT SPEED
STAVE STOUR WHIRL BUCKET
BUNDLE BUSTLE HASTEN HUSTLE
POWDER STROTH TATTER
WHORRY HOTFOOT QUICKEN
SCUDDLE SKELTER SLITHER
WHITHER DISPATCH EXPEDITE
SPLUTTER ACCELERATE
(— A HORSE) SPUR
(— ABOUT) SCOUR
(— AWAY) FLEE BUNCH SCREW
SKIRT
(— CLUMSILY) TAVE TEAVE
(— NOISILY) SPLUTTER
(— OFF) DUST
(— UP) BUSK
HURT CUT HOT NOY DERE FIKE
GALL HARM PAIN SCAT ABUSE
BLAME GRIEF GRIPE PINCH SORRY
SPITE THORN WATHE WOUND
BRUISE DAMAGE GRIEVE IMPAIR
INJURE INJURY LESION MIFFED
MITTLE PAINED PUNISH SCATHE
STRAIN STROKE WINGED AFFLICT
HURTING OFFENCE OFFENSE
SCADDLE MISCHIEF NUISANCE
(— EASILY) FROISSE
(— FEELINGS) CUT TOUCH
(— REPUTATION) LIBEL
(— SEVERELY) KILL
(EASILY —) GINGER

(PREF.) NOCI
HURTFUL BAD ILL EVIL MALIGN
NOCENT NOCIVE NOUGHT
SHREWD TAKING BALEFUL
BANEFUL HARMFUL MALEFIC
NOCUOUS NOXIOUS SCADDLE
UNQUERT GRIEVOUS HURTSOME
SCATHFUL
HURTLE HURL FLING THIRL
HUSBAND EKE MAN WER BOND
CHAP FERE KEEP LORD MAKE
MATE SAVE SIRE BARON CHURL
HOARD HUBBY MATCH STORE
MANAGE MASTER MISTER
SPOUSE CONSORT GOODMAN
GUIDMAN HENPECK PARTNER
CONSERVE
(— OF ADULTRESS) CUCKOLD
(AFFIANCED —) FUTURE
(SUPPLEMENTARY —) PIRRAURU
(PL.) PUNALUA
(PREF.) MARITI
HUSBANDMAN BOND BOOR CARL
CLOWN COLON RUSTIC TILLER
ACREMAN HUSBAND PLOWMAN
TILLMAN AGRICOLE
HUSBANDRY GAINER GAINOR
THRIFT ECONOMY MANAGERY
HUSH SH HSH MUM PAX HESH
HOOT LULL BURKE SHUSH STILL
WHISH WHIST WHUSH HUDDLE
BESTILL HUSHABY SILENCE
HUSHED QUIET STILL GENTLE
WHISHT
HUSHIM (HUSBAND OF —)
SHAHARAIM
HUSK BUR COD HUD KEX SID ARIL
BARK BURR COAT COSH HOSE
HUCK HULK PILL SEED SHIV SKIN
HOOSE SCALE SHACK SHALE
SHAUP SHELL SHILL SHOOD
SHUCK SHUDE COLDER DEHUSK
FLIGHT SLOUGH BOLSTER
CARCASS CASCARA
(— OF NUT) SHACK BOLSTER
(— OF OATS) SHUD SHOOD FLIGHT
(CORN —) HOJA
(PL.) BHUSA CHAFF BHOOSA
HULKAGE SHELLING
(PREF.) LEMMO LEPO LOPO
SILIQUI
(SUFF.) LEMMA
HUSKY HUSK CODDY FOGGY THICK
FURRED BUIRDLY HULKING
BOUNCING SIBERIAN
HUSSITE TABORITE
HUSSY MINX SLUT BESOM CUTTY
GIPSY GYPSY MADAM STRAP
HIZZIE LIMMER DROSSEL
HUSTINGS BEMA
HUSTLE FAN PEG HUMP JUMP
BLITZ SKELP BUCKET BUNDLE
BUSTLE JOSTLE RABBLE RUSTLE
SCUFTER
HUSTLECAP PINCH
HUSTLER HUSTLE PEELER BUSTLER
FIREBALL
HUT COE COT BARI BUTT COSH
COTE CREW CRIB HALE HULK
HULL ISBA IZBA SHED SKEO TENT
TILT BASHA BENAB BOHIO BOOTH
BOTHY CABIN CHAWL CHOZA
HOVEL HUMPY HUTCH JACAL

KRAAL LODGE SCALE SETER
SHACK SHIEL TOLDO TOPEK
WHARE WURLY BOHAWN
BOTHAN CANABA CHALET
GUNYAH GUNYEH MIAMIA
PONDOK RANCHO REFUGE
SAETER SCONCE SHANTY SHELTY
WIGWAM WIKIUP BALAGAN
BARRACK BOUROCK CAMALIG
COTTAGE GOONDIE HUDDOCK
HUTMENT SHEBANG YAKUTAT
BARABARA CHANTIER RONDAWEL
SHIELING THOLTHAN TUGURIUM
(— FOR TEMPORARY USE) CORF
(— IN VIETNAM) HOOCH HOOTCH
(— OVER MINING SHAFT) COE
(ABORIGINAL —) MIMI WURLY
GUNYAH MIAMIA WURLEY
GOONDIE
(FISHERMAN'S —) SKEO SKIO
(HEATED —) HOTHOUSE
(HERMIT'S —) CELL
(NAVAJO —) HOGAN
(POULTRY —) IGLOO
(SAMOYED —) CHUM
(SENTRY —) BOX
(SIBERIAN —) JURT
(SOUTH AFRICAN —) STRUIS
(PREF.) CALIO
HUTCH ARK BUDDLE RABBITRY
HUTIA UTIA JUTIA PILORI
HUZ (FATHER OF —) NAHOR
HYACINTH LILY MUSK LILIUM
CROWTOE FLOATER GREGGLE
JACINTH BLUEBELL CROWFOOT
HAREBELL JACOUNCE
HYACINTH BEAN LABLAB
BONAVIST BONNYVIS DOLICHOS
HYACINTHUS (FATHER OF —)
AMYCLAS
(MOTHER OF —) DIOMEDE
HYALOGEN NEOSSIN
HYBRID DZO ZHO MULE ZOBO
CROSS GRADE HINNY LIGER
COYDOG GALYAK MOSAIC MULISH
SPLAKE TURKEN BASTARD
BIGENER CATTALO JERSIAN
MONGREL PLUMCOT ZEBRASS
ZEBRULA ZEBURRO CARIDEER
CITRANGE KAFERITA LIMEQUAT
ZEBRINNY
(PREF.) NOTH(O)
HYBRIDIZE CROSS
HYDRANT CHUCK FIREPLUG
(PART OF —) NUT CHAIN BARREL
BONNET STANDPIPE
CONNECTION
HYDRANTH SIPHON SYPHON
HYDRATE SLAKE
HYDRAULIC

(PREF.) HYDR(I)(O)
HYDRAZINE DIAMIDE
HYDRAZOATE AZIDE
HYDRIA KALPIS
HYDROCARBON ARENE CUMOL
FREON GUTTA IDRYL INDAN
IRENE TOLAN XYLOL ALKANE
ALKYNE ALLENE BUTANE BUTYNE
CARANE CETANE CETENE
CYMENE DECANE ETHANE
ETHENE HEXINE INDANE INDENE
MELENE NONENE OCTANE
OCTENE OCTINE PICENE PINENE
PYRENE RETENE TOLANE TOLUOL
XYLENE AMYLENE AZULENE
BENZENE CHOLANE CYCLENE
DECALIN ETHERIN FULVENE
HEPTANE HEPTENE HEPTYNE
LYCOPIN MUCKITE MYRCENE
OLEFINE PENTINE PENTYNE
PHYTANE PROPANE STYRENE
TETROLE TOLUENE BIPHENYL
CADALENE CADINENE CAMPHANE
CARBURAN CEROTENE CETYLENE
CHRYSENE CORONENE
CUMULENE DECYLENE DIOLEFIN
DIPHENYL DOCOSANE DYSODILE
EICOSANE ETHYLENE EUDALENE
FLUORENE HEXYLENE ILLIPENE
ISOPRENE LYCOPENE MENTHENE
NONYLENE OCTYLENE PARAFFIN
PRISTANE PYRACENE RUTYLENE
SABINENE SQUALENE STILBENE
(SUFF.) YLENE
HYDROCHLORIC ACID
(SUFF.) CHLORHYDRIA
HYDROCYANIC PRUSSIC
HYDRODAMALIS RHYTINA
HYDROEXTRACTOR BUZZER
WHIZZER
HYDROFLUORIC PHTHORIC
HYDROGEN HYDRO PROTIUM
HYDROGRAPHER AMERICAN
MAURY MITCHELL
ENGLISH SMYTH MURRAY
GERMAN NEUMAYER
NORWEGIAN SVERDRUP
HYDROHEMATITE TURGITE
HYDROID POLYP OBELIA ACALEPH
ZOOPHYTE
HYDROLEA NAMA
HYDROMEL ALOJA
HYDROMETER SPINDLE
HYDROPERITONEUM ASCITES
HYDROPHOBIA LYSSA RABIES
HYDROPHOBIC LYSSIC
HYDROPHYLLIUM BRACT
HYDROXIDE ALKALI HYDRATE
HYDRIDE
HYDROXYL

(SUFF.) (CONTAINING —) OLIC
HYDROZINCITE CALAMINE
HYENA HINE DABUH SIMIR
HYAENID
HYGIENIC SANITARY
HYGRODEIK PAGOSCOPE
HYLAS (FATHER OF —) THIODAMAS
(LOVER OF —) DRYOPE
(MOTHER OF —) MENODICE
HYLLUS (FATHER OF —) HERCULES
(MOTHER OF —) DEIANIRA
(SLAYER OF —) ECHEMUS
(WIFE OF —) IOLE
HYLOZOIST PHYSICIST
HYMEN CHERRY BRIDEGOD
MAIDENHEAD
HYMENIUM THECIUM
HYMENOCALLIS ISMENE
HYMN ODE FUGE LAUD SING
DIRGE GATHA PAEAN PSALM
YASHT YMPNE ANTHEM CARVAL
CHORAL HIMENE HIRMOS
MANTRA ORPHIC THEODY VESPER
CHORALE EXULTET HEIRMOS
INTROIT CANTICLE CATHISMA
DOXOLOGY ENCOMIUM
PSALMODY SEQUENCE TRISAGION
TROPARION
(— COLLECTION) MENAION
(MEXICAN —) ALABADO
(PL.) HYMNODY
HYMNAL HYMNARY HYMNBOOK
HYPATIA (AUTHOR OF —) KINGSLEY
(CHARACTER IN —) AMAL MIRIAM
AUFUGUS HYPATIA ORESTES
PELAGIA RAPHAEL VICTORIA
HERACLIAN PHILAMMON
HYPERBOLE AUXESIS
HYPERCORACOID RADIAL
SCAPULA
HYPERCRITICAL NICE CAPTIOUS
CRITICAL
HYPERDULIA ADORATION
HYPEREMIA RUBOR
HYPEREMIC CONGESTED
HYPERENOR (BROTHER OF —)
EUPHORBUS POLYDAMAS
(FATHER OF —) PANTHOUS
(MOTHER OF —) PHRONTIS
(SLAYER OF —) MENELAUS
HYPERICUM TUTSAN
HYPERION (DAUGHTER OF —)
AURORA
(FATHER OF —) URANUS
(MOTHER OF —) GAEA
(WIFE OF —) THEA
HYPERON BARYON
HYPEROPIC FARSIGHTED
HYPERSENSITIVITY ATOPY
ALLERGY

HYPHA STOLON
HYPHEN BAND
(PL.) LEADERS
HYPNOTIC AMYTAL BROMAL
CHLORAL SECONAL BARBITAL
NARCEINE SOPORIFIC
HYPNOTISM DEVIL BRAIDISM
HYPNOSIS MESMERISM
HYPNOTIST OPERATOR SVENGALI
HYPOBLAST ENDODERM
HYPODERM
HYPOCHONDRIA HIP HYP HYPO
MEGRIM
HYPOCHONDRIAC ARGAN HIPPY
HIPPIST ATRABILIAR
HYPOCOTYL RADICLE TIGELLA
TIGELLUS
HYPOCRISY SHAM POPEHOLY
PHARISAISM
HYPOCRITE CANT BIGOT CHEAT
FACER FRAUD BLIFIL CAFARD
HUMBUG MUCKER MAWWORM
SIMULAR CHADBAND DECEIVER
TARTUFFE
HYPOCRITICAL FALSE SLAPE
DOUBLE CANTING PLASTER
POPEHOLY SPECIOUS
HYPOCYCLOID ASTROID
HYPODERMIS SKIN
HYPOPHARYNX LINGUA LABIELLA
HYPOSTASIS PERSON
HYPOSTATIZE ENTIFY
HYPOSTOME MANUBRIUM
HYPOTENUSE SUBTENSE
HYPOTHESIS SYSTEM THEORY
PREMISE WEGENER SUPPOSAL
POSTULATE
HYPOTHETICAL IDEAL
HYPOTRACHELIUM GORGERIN
HYPSEUS (DAUGHTER OF —)
CYRENE
(FATHER OF —) PENEUS
(MOTHER OF —) CREUSA
(WIFE OF —) CHLIDANOPE
HYPTIS OREGANO
HYRAX DAS CONY CONEY DAMAN
WABUR DASSIE WABBER
ASHKOKO KLIPDAS HYRACOID
HYRMINA (FATHER OF —) EPEUS
(HUSBAND OF —) PHORBAS
(SON OF —) ACTOR
HYRNETHO (BROTHER OF —)
AGELAUS CALLIAS EURYPYLUS
(FATHER OF —) TEMENUS
(HUSBAND OF —) DEIPHONTES
HYSTERIA MOTHER NERVES
PIBLOKTO TARASSIS
(PRONE TO —) VAPORISH
(RELIGIOUS —) LATA
HYSTERICAL NERVOUS SHRIEKY

I

I A Y HI HY CHE ICH ISS SHE ITEM UTCH INDIA UTCHY
(— AM) ISE CHAM ICHAM
(— HAD) CHAD
(— WILL) CHILL ICHÜLLE
(— WOULD) CHUD
IALEMUS (FATHER OF —) APOLLO
(MOTHER OF —) CALLIOPE
IALMENUS (BROTHER OF —) ASCALAPHUS
(FATHER OF —) ARES APOLLO
(MOTHER OF —) ASTYOCHE CALLIOPE
IAMB IAMBIC IAMBUS
(DOUBLE —) DIIAMB
IAMUS (FATHER OF —) APOLLO
(MOTHER OF —) EVADNE
IAPETUS (FATHER OF —) URANUS
(MOTHER OF —) GAEA
(SON OF —) ATLAS MENOETIUS
(WIFE OF —) ASIA CLYMENE
IAPYGIANS MESSAPII
IAPYX (BROTHER OF —) DAUNIUS PEUCETIUS
(FATHER OF —) LYCAON DAEDALUS
IASION (BROTHER OF —) DARDANUS
(FATHER OF —) ZEUS JUPITER
(LOVER OF —) CERES DEMETER
(MOTHER OF —) ELECTRA
(SON OF —) PLUTUS
IATROCHEMICAL SPAGYRIC
IATROCHEMISTRY SPAGYRIC
IBANAG CAGAYAN
IBEX KYL TEK TUR ZAC KAIL BEDEN EVECK IZARD JAELA EVICKE SAKEEN
IBHAR (FATHER OF —) DAVID
IBIS GUARA GANNET HADADA JABIRU TURKEY CICONIID IRONHEAD
IBNEIAH (FATHER OF —) JEROHAM
ICARIUS (BROTHER OF —) TYNDAREUS
(DAUGHTER OF —) ERIGONE PENELOPE
(FAITHFUL DOG OF —) MOERA
(FATHER OF —) OEBALUS
(MOTHER OF —) GORGOPHONE
ICARUS (FATHER OF —) DAEDALUS
(MOTHER OF —) NAUCRATE
ICE YS GEAL FROST GLACE CRYSTAL VERGLAS
(— IN ROUGH BLOCKS) RUBBLE
(ANCHOR —) FRAZIL
(DRIFTING FRAGMENT OF —) PAN CALF
(PATCH OF —) RONE
(PINNACLE OF —) SERAC
(RIDGE OF —) HAMMOCK HUMMOCK
(SEA —) GLACON SLUDGE
(SHORE —) FAST

(SLUSHY —) SISH
(SOFT —) SLOB LOLLY
(THIN NEW —) DISH PANCAKE
(THIN OR FLOATING —) FLOE GRUE BRASH
(WATER —) SHERBET
(PREF.) CRYSTALL(I)(O) GLACI(O)
(SUFF.) CRYST
ICEBERG BERG GROWLER FLOEBERG
ICEBOAT SKEETER
ICE CREAM BISK CREAM GLACE AUFAIT BISQUE NOUGAT TASTER SPUMONI TORTONI
ICE CREAM CONE CORNET
ICED COLD GLACE FRAPPE
ICEFISH SALANGID
ICEHOUSE (— WORKER) AIRMAN

ICELAND

BALLAD: RIMUR
BAY: FAXA HUNA
CAPITAL: REIKJAVIK REYKJAVIK
COIN: AURAR EYRIR KRONA
DISH: SKYR SVIO BLOOMOR HAROFISK
EPIC: EDDA SAGA
FIRST SETTLER: ARNARSON
FJORD: BREIDHA
GEYSER: GRYLA
GIANT: ATLI
GLACIER: HOFSJOKULL LANGJOKULL VATNAJOKULL
HERO: BELE ERIC LEIF SIGUROSSON
LAKE: MYVATN THORISVATN
MEASURE: SET ALIN LINA ALMUD TURMA ALMENN ALMUDE FERFET POTTUR FATHMUR FERALIN FERMILA OLTUNNA SJOMILA
MOUNTAIN: JOKUL
PARLIAMENT: ALTHING
REPUBLIC: LYOVELDIO
RIVER: HVITA JOKULSA THJORSA
TOWN: AKRANES AKUREYRI KEFLAVIK KOPAVOGUR
VOLCANIC ISLAND: SURTSEY
VOLCANO: LAKI ASKJA HEKLA ELDFELL
WATERFALL: GULL DETTI GULLFOSS DETTIFOSS
WEIGHT: PUND POUND

ICHABOD (FATHER OF —) PHINEHAS
(GRANDFATHER OF —) ELI
ICHNEUMON URVA NYMSS MEERKAT VANSIRE
ICHOROUS GLEETY
ICHU HICHU STIPA
ICICLE ICARY ICKLE YOKEL TANGLE SHOGGLE SHOOGLE COCKBELL

ICINESS GLARE
ICING ICE PIPING ALCORZA FROSTING MERINGUE
ICON IKON EIKON IMAGE DEESIS
ICONOCLAST DEBUNKER
ICONOSTASIS DIASTYLE
ICTEROHEMATURIA CARCEAG
ICTONYX ZORILLA
ICTUS ACCENT DOWNBEAT
ICY GELID BOREAL FRIGID WINTRY GLACIAL
ID ES ORF GARDON SYPHILID

IDAHO

CAPITAL: BOISE
COUNTY: ADA GEM BUTTE CAMAS LATAH LEMHI POWER TETON BLAINE BONNER CARNAS CASSIA JEROME OWYHEE BENEWAH KOOTENAI
DAM: OXBOW BROWNLEE
INDIAN: BANNOCK KALISPEL NEZPERCE SHOSHONI
LAKE: BEAR GRAYS PRIEST
MOUNTAIN: RYAN BORAH RHODES TAYLOR BIGBALDY BLUENOSE
MOUNTAIN RANGE: CABINET SELKIRK
NICKNAME: GEM
RIVER: SNAKE LOCHSA SALMON PAYETTE
SPRINGS: SODA HOOPER LAVAHOT
STATE BIRD: BLUEBIRD
STATE FLOWER: SYRINGA
TOWN: BUHL MALAD NAMPA BURLEY DRIGGS DUBOIS MOSCOW WEISER CASCADE CHALLIS ORIFINO REXBURG POCATELLO

IDAS (BROTHER OF —) LYNCEUS
(FATHER OF —) APHAREUS
(MOTHER OF —) ARENE
(WIFE OF —) MARPESSA
IDDO (FATHER OF —) ZECHARIAH
(SON OF —) AHINADAB
IDE ORFE
IDEA EGG GIG KINK EIDOS IMAGE THING ANONYM DHARMA ECTYPE FIGURE INTENT NOTICE NOTION RECEPT THREAP THROPE BEGRIFF CONCEIT CONCEPT GIMMICK GLIMPSE MAROTTE OPINION PROJECT SPECIES SURMISE THOUGHT GIMCRACK NOTIONAL PRECONCEPTION
(—S OF LITTLE VALUE) STUFF
(CENTRAL —) ARGUMENT
(COMMONPLACE —) SHIBBOLETH
(CONSERVATIVE —S) FOGYISM
(DOMINANT —) CLOU
(DULL STUPID —S) STODGE
(FAINT —) GLIMMER

(FALSE —) FALLACY
(FANTASTIC —) VAPOR MAGGOT
(FAVORITE —) HORSE
(FIXED —) TICK
(FUNDAMENTAL —) KEYNOTE
(IRRATIONAL —) FOLLY
(MAIN —) POINT
(MUSICAL —) SENTENCE
(ODD —) FREAK
(OVERWORKED —) CLICHE
(PLATONIC —) ESSENCE
(RECURRING —) BURDEN
(STALE —S) BILGE
(SUPERSTITIOUS —) FREIT
(TRANSCENDENT —) FORM
(PL.) EIDE THOUGHT
(PREF.) IDEO
IDEAL ISM IDEA DREAM AERIAL BEAUTY DOMNEI DREAMY MENTAL UNREAL PATTERN PERFECT UTOPIAN ABSTRACT FANCIFUL IDEALITY NOTIONAL QUADRATE ORIFLAMME
(— OF BEAUTY) KALON
IDEALISM IDEOLOGY
IDEALIST IDEIST UTOPIAN FICHTEAN UTOPIAST
IDEALIZE PLATONIZE
IDEALIZED POETICAL
IDENTICAL LIKE SAME SELF VERY ALIKE EQUAL EVENLY PROPER CORRECT IDENTIC NUMERIC SELFSAME
IDENTIFICATION IDENT DOCUMENT EQUATION RECOGNITION
IDENTIFIED SIGNATE
IDENTIFIER BIRDER
IDENTIFY PEG TAB MARK NAME RANK SPOT IDENT PLACE TALLY FINGER DISCERN DIAGNOSE PINPOINT
(— WITH) ENTER
IDENTITY SEITY UNITY IPSEITY ONENESS EQUALITY SAMENESS
IDEOGRAPH CHARACTER
(PL.) KANJI
IDEOGRAPHIC REAL
IDEOLOGICAL MENTAL
IDIOBLAST SPHERE IDIOSOME
IDIOCY ANOIA ANOESIA FATUITY IDIOTRY MOROSIS IDIOTISM
IDIOM CANT ARGOT JUANG DORISM IFUGAO JARGON MEDISM SPEECH AEOLISM ANOMALY GRECISM PEHLEVI TURKISM DANICISM DORICISM IDIOTISM IONICISM LANGUAGE LOCALISM PARLANCE RURALISM
IDIOMORPHIC EUHEDRAL
IDIOPHONE RATTLE
IDIOSOME SPHERE

IDIOSYNCRASY WAY IDIASM RUMNESS

IDIOT FON OAF SOT DAFF DOLT FOOL AMENT BOOBY DUNCE FONNE CRETIN HOBBIL NIDGET NIDIOT DULLARD NATURAL OMADAWN PINHEAD IMBECILE INNOCENT SLAVERER
(AUTHOR OF —) DOSTOEVSKI
(CHARACTER IN —) LEF GANYA AGLAYA PARFEN MYSHKIN NATASYA EPANCHIN ROGOZHIN FILIPOVNA ARDALIONOVITCH

IDIOTIC DAFT ZANY IDIOT FATUOUS FOOLISH WANTWIT IMBECILE

IDLE COLD DEAD HACK HAKE HANG HULL JAUK LAKE LAZE LAZY LUSK MUZZ SOFT SORN TICK VAIN VOID DALLY EMPTY SHOOL SLIVE THOKE WASTE COOTER DAIDLE DANDER DREAMY FOOTER GAMMER LOUNGY OTIANT OTIOSE SLIMSY TEETER TIDDIE TIFFLE TRIFLE TRUANT UNUSED VACANT DRONISH IDLEFUL IDLESET LOAFING SAUNTER SHACKLE SLUMBER SLUTHER UNLUSTY VACUOUS WHIFFLE BASELESS BOOTLESS FAINEANT INACTIVE INDOLENT SHAMMOCK SLAISTER SLOTHFUL TRIFLING WORKLESS
(TO BE —) SLOTH

IDLENESS LAZE RUST SLOTH IDLETY IDLESET IDLESSE IGNAVIA VACANCY VACUITY FLANERIE IDLEHOOD INACTION
(— PERSONIFED) LAURENCE LAWRENCE
(LIVE IN —) MAROON

IDLER BUM GAUM HAKE JAUK KERN LOON DRONE BADAUD BUMBLE DONNOT IDLEBY LUBBER PLAYER QUISBY RODNEY STALKO TRUANT BLELLUM BUCKEEN DAWDLER FAITOUR FRANION IDLESBY LOLLARD LOUNGER LOUTHER LURDANE SLOUNGE TRIFLER DOLITTLE FAINEANT IDLESHIP LAYABOUT LAZARONE UNWORKER WHIFFLER

IDLE WHEEL IDLER RUNNER

IDLY TOOMLY VAGUELY

IDMON (DAUGHTER OF —) ARACHNE
(FATHER OF —) APOLLO
(MOTHER OF —) CYRENE ASTERIA

IDOCRASE EGERAN CYPRINE VESUVIAN

IDOL GOD BAAL ICON JOSS TIKI WOOD ZEMI ANITO BESAN EIKON GUACA HOBAL HUACA IMAGE STOCK SWAMI IDOLET IDOLUM MAMMET MAUMET MINION PAGODA POPPET PUPPET TERAPH EIDOLON MAHOMET BAPHOMET MAUMETRY PANTHEUM
(HEATHEN —) DEVIL
(PREF.) EIDOLO IDOLO

IDOLATER AKKUM PAGAN HEATHEN IDOLIST

IDOLATROUS PAGAN IDOLISH

IDOLATRY BAALISM IMAGERY ADULTERY MAUMETRY

IDOLIZE GOD IDOL ADORE ADMIRE WORSHIP

IDUMAEAN EDOMITE

IDUN (HUSBAND OF —) BRAGI

IDYIA (DAUGHTER OF —) MEDEA
(FATHER OF —) OCEANUS
(HUSBAND OF —) AEETES
(MOTHER OF —) TETHYS
(SON OF —) APSYRTUS

IDYL IDYLL BUCOLIC ECLOGUE

IDYLLIC HALCYON PASTORAL THEOCRITEAN

IDYLLS OF THE KING (AUTHOR OF —) TENNYSON
(CHARACTER IN —) BORS ENID BALAN BALIN ISOLT ARTHUR ELAINE GARETH GAWAIN MERLIN MODRED VIVIEN ETTARRE GALAHAD GERAINT LYNETTE PELLEAS BEDIVERE LANCELOT TRISTRAM GUINEVERE PERCIVALE

IF AN AND GIF GIN THO GEVE IFFEN SOBEIT THOUGH PROVIDED
(— EVER) ONCE
(— NOT) BUT ELSE NISI
(PREF.) QUASI

IF WINTER COMES (AUTHOR OF —) HUTCHINSON
(CHARACTER IN —) MARK NONA EFFIE MABEL PERCH SABRE TYBAR BRIGHT FARGUS HAROLD FORTUNE TWYNING

IGAL (FATHER OF —) JOSEPH NATHAN

IGDALIAH (SON OF —) HANAN

IGEAL (FATHER OF —) SHEMAIAH

IGERNA (HUSBAND OF —) UTHER GORLOIS
(SON OF —) ARTHUR

IGNEOUS PLUTONIC
(PREF.) PLUTONO

IGNIS FATUUS WISP SPUNKIE WILDFIRE

IGNITE TIND FLASH LIGHT SHOOT ILLUME KINDLE CALCINE LIGHTEN

IGNITED LIVING BURNING

IGNITER SPARKER

IGNITION FIRE LIGHTING

IGNOBLE LOW BASE MEAN VILE ABJECT GRUBBY SORDID CURRISH SERVILE UNNOBLE BASEBORN SHAMEFUL

IGNOBLY BASELY

IGNOMINIOUS BASE VILE INFAMOUS SHAMEFUL

IGNOMINY SHAME REBUKE SCANDAL DISGRACE DISHONOR

IGNORAMUS IDIOT IGNARO SIMPLE AMHAAREZ

IGNORANCE IRONY TAMAS AGNOSY AVIDYA AVIJJA BETISE NICETY RUDITY UNSKILL DARKNESS IDIOTISM NESCIENCE
(BOLD —) BAYARD
(FEIGNED —) IRONY
(PREF.) AGNOIO

IGNORANT LAY DARK NICE RUDE VAIN GREEN GROSS SILLY INGRAM SIMPLE ARTLESS SECULAR UNAWARE UNCOUTH UNKNOWN IMPERITE INNOCENT INSCIENT INSCIOUS NESCIENT UNTAUGHT BENIGHTED

IGNORANTLY SIMPLY

IGNORE BALK BLOW SINK SNUB VAIN BAULK BLINK ELIDE BYPASS MISKEN SLIGHT DESPISE MISKNOW NEGLECT CONFOUND OVERJUMP OVERLEAP OVERLOOK OVERPASS

IGOROT BONTOK NABALOI KANKANAI

IGUANA GUANA GUANO LEGUAN

IGUVINE UMBRIAN

IJO DJO BONI BONNY

IKKESH (SON OF —) IRA

ILAIRA (FATHER OF —) LEUCIPPUS
(HUSBAND OF —) CASTOR
(MOTHER OF —) PHILODICE
(SISTER OF —) PHOEBE

ILEUM
(PREF.) ILEO

ILEUS MISERERE

ILIA RHEA
(FATHER OF —) NUMITOR
(SON OF —) REMUS ROMULUS

ILIAD (AUTHOR OF —) HOMER
(CHARACTER IN —) AIAS HELEN PARIS PRIAM ATHENA HECTOR NESTOR ACHILLES DIOMEDES MENELAUS ODYSSEUS PANDARUS AGAMEMNON APHRODITE PATROCLUS ANDROMACHE

ILIONE (BROTHER OF —) POLYDORUS
(FATHER OF —) PRIAM
(HUSBAND OF —) POLYMNESTOR
(MOTHER OF —) HECUBA
(SON OF —) DEIPYLUS

ILK KIN

ILL BAD EVIL ILLY SICK AEGER CRONK CROOK DONCY FUNNY WISHT GROGGY INJURY POORLY SICKLY UNWELL SICKISH VICIOUS MISCHIEF PHYSICAL
(— AT EASE) ASHAMED AWKWARD FAROUCHE
(PREF.) MAL(E) MIS

ILL-ADVISED FOOLISH

ILL-BEHAVED UNTHEWED

ILL-BEING ILLTH

ILL-BODING DIRE DISMAL

ILL-BRED HOYDEN CADDISH CHURLISH PLEBEIAN MISLEARED

ILL-CHOSEN UNSORTED

ILL-CONSIDERED HASTY

ILL-DEFINED BLIND VAGUE MONGREL

ILLEGAL BLACK LAWLESS UNLAWFUL WRONGOUS ADULTERINE
(NOT —) COLD

ILLEGALITY UNLAW

ILLEGIBLE BLIND

ILLEGITIMACY BASTARDY

ILLEGITIMATE BASE BASTARD BOOTLEG NATURAL NOTHOUS MISBEGOT NAMELESS UNLAWFUL WRONGFUL MISBEGOTTEN
(PREF.) NOTH(O)

ILL-FATED UNHAPPY UNSONCY UNCHANCY

ILL-FAVORED UGLY UNSONCY

ILL-FORMED SCRAWLY INFORMED

ILL HUMOR TID BILE DRUNT

GRUMP THRAW FANTEE SPLEEN DUDGEON FANTIGUE

ILL-HUMORED FOUL GLUM CROOK DUDDY GRUMPY MOROSE STUFFY SULLEN CROOKED FRETFUL PEEVISH

ILLIBERAL LITTLE NARROW INSULAR BANAUSIC GRUDGING

ILLICIT SLY BLACK ILLEGAL UNLAWFUL

ILLIMITABLE INFINITE

ILLINOIS	
CAPITAL: SPRINGFIELD	
COLLEGE: AURORA EUREKA OLIVET QUINCY SHIMER	
COUNTY: BOND CASS COOK KANE OGLE COLES MACON BUREAU DUPAGE GRUNDY HARDIN MASSAC PEORIA IROQUOIS MACOUPIN SANGAMON	
FRENCH SETTLEMENT: CAHOKIA	
HILLS: SHAWNEE	
INDIAN: FOX SAUK	
LAKE: MICHIGAN	
NICKNAME: SUCKER PRAIRIE	
PRESIDENT: REAGAN	
RIVER: OHIO ROCK WABASH ELKHORN MACKINAW SANGAMON	
STATE BIRD: CARDINAL	
STATE FLOWER: VIOLET	
STATE TREE: OAK	
TOWN: PANA ALEDO ALTON CAIRO CARMI DIXON FLORA LACON OLNEY PARIS PEKIN ALBION CANTON EUREKA GALENA HARDIN HAVANA HERRIN JOLIET OTTAWA PEORIA QUINCY SKOKIE URBANA VIENNA CHICAGO DECATUR GENESEO MENDOTA NOKOMIS TAMPICO ROCKFORD	

ILLINOISIAN SUCKER

ILLIPE BASSIA VIDORICUM

ILLITERATE UNREAD IGNORANT MUSELESS UNTAUGHT

ILL-MADE AWKWARD

ILL-NATURED ACID UGLY NASTY SURLY CRABBY SNARLY SULLEN THWART CANKERY PEEVISH

ILLNESS DROW TOUT BRASH CHILL TRAIK MORBUS PLUNGE DISEASE SICKNESS
(MENTAL —) MONOMANIA
(MINOR —) HURRY
(MOMENTARY —) DROW
(SUDDEN —) WEED SWEAM

ILL-NOURISHED SHELLY

ILLOGICAL MAD SPURIOUS

ILL-OMENED DISMAL UNLUCKY

ILL-SHAPED WEEDY

ILL-SMELLING FUSTY STINKING

ILL-TEMPERED ILL FESS MEAN PUXY ACRID CHUFF NURLY RATTY CAMMED CHUFFY CURSED GIRNIE SHRILL SNAGGY RAMPANT ROPABLE VICIOUS CAMSHACH LUNGEOUS SHREWISH VIXENISH MALODOROUS

ILL-TREAT FOB HOIN MISDO AFFRONT

ILLUMINATE FIRE LIMN CLEAR
LIGHT ENLIMN ILLUME KINDLE
BESHINE CLARIFY EMBLAZE
LIGHTEN MINIATE RADIATE
EMBRIGHT FLOURISH ILLUMINE
LUMINATE
(— FAINTLY) TWILIGHT
ILLUMINATION E GLIM GLORY
LIGHT SHINE LIGHTING LUMINARY
(— INCREASE) WOMP
(— UNIT) PHOT
ILLUMINE SUN FIRE LAMP CLEAR
LUMINE ENLIGHT
ILL-USAGE ABUSE
ILLUSION MAYA DEATH ERROR
FAIRY FANCY FLESH TRICK
MATTER CHIMERA ELUSION
FALLACY FICTION MOCKERY
PHANTOM RAINBOW ZOLLNER
DELUSION PHANTASM PRESTIGE
ILLUSIVE PHANTOM
ILLUSORY FALSE EVANID
FATUOUS PHANTOM TRICKSY
APPARENT ILLUSIVE SPECTRAL
ILLUSTRATE INSTANCE
ILLUSTRATION CUT GAY ICON
IKON SHOW SPOT INSET FIGURE
COMPARE DISIMILE EXEMPLUM
INSTANCE VIGNETTE
ILLUSTRATIVE CLASSIC
ILLUSTRIOUS GRAND NOBLE
NOTED SHEEN BRIGHT CANDID
HEROIC EMINENT EXALTED
GLORIED SHINING GLORIOUS
HEROICAL LUCULENT MAGNIFIC
PRECLARE RENOWNED SPLENDID
STARLIKE BRILLIANT
REDOUBTABLE
(MOST —) ILMO ILLMO
ILL WILL SPITE ENMITY GRUDGE
MALICE MAUGER MAUGRE
RANCOR DESPITE AMBITION
ILL-WISHER FOE
ILUS (FATHER OF —) TROS
(MOTHER OF —) CALLIRRHOE
(SON OF —) LAOMEDON
ILVAITE YENITE LIEVRITE
ILYSIA TORTRIX
IMAGE DAP GOD MAP FORM ICON
IDOL IKON JOSS MAKE SEAL SIGN
SPIT TIKI AGNUS DITTO EPHOD
FANCY HERMA IMAGO MEDAL
MORAL PAINT PRINT SAMMY
SANTO SHAPE SIGIL SWAMI
SWAMY TOTEM AGALMA ALRAUN
EFFIGY EMBLEM FIGURE MAUMET
MODULE POPPET RECEPT REFLEX
SHRINE SPHINX STATUE SVAMIN
TERAPH VISAGE WEEPER
EIDOLON EXPRESS FANTASY
GODLING IMAGERY KATCINA
PICTURE PROPOSE CONCEIVE
DAIBUTSU OPTOGRAM PORTRAIT
SURPRINT ZOOMORPH
SEMBLANCE SIMILITUDE
SIMULACRUM RESEMBLANCE
(— IN CHINESE COSTUME)
MANDARIN
(— OF CHRIST) SUDARIUM
(— OF DEITY) SWAMI GODKIN
SVAMIN GODLING
(— OF SAINT) BULTO SAINT SANTO
GEORGE SANTON

(— OF WOOD) XOANON
(— RECALLED BY MEMORY) IDEA
(CULT —) JOSS
(FALSE —) GHOST
(GOOD-LUCK —) ALRAUN ALRUNA
(HEAVENLY —) FRAVASHI
(LINGERING —) SHADE
(MENTAL —) FANCY IMAGO
RECEPT CONCEPT FANTASY
SPECIES PHANTASM
(RADAR —) BLIP
(REFLECTED —) SHADOW SPECIES
(SEQUENCE OF —S) REVERIE
(VAGUE —S) FRINGE
(PL.) IMAGERY TERAPHIM
(PREF.) EID(O)(OLO) EIKON(O)
ICON(O) IDOLO IKON(O) TYP(I)(O)
IMAGERY ICONISM
IMAGINARY IDEAL AERIAL
FEIGNED FICTIVE SHADOWY
CHIMERAL CHIMERIC FANCIFUL
FICTIOUS MYTHICAL NOTIONAL
QUIXOTIC ROMANTIC SCENICAL
VISIONAL BARMECIDE
IMAGINATION CHIC BRAIN FANCY
FLAME NOTION FANTASY
PROJECT THOUGHT
(DROLL —) HUMOR
IMAGINATIVE FORMFUL CREATIVE
FANCIFUL POETICAL
IMAGINE SEE WIS REDE WEEN
DREAM FANCY FEIGN FRAME
GUESS IMAGE THINK DEVISE
FIGURE IDEATE INVENT RECKON
COMPASS CONCEIT CONJURE
FANCIFY FANTASY FEATURE
PICTURE PORTRAY PROJECT
PROPOSE SUPPOSE SURMISE
SUSPECT CONCEIVE DAYDREAM
JEALOUSE
IMAGINED FANCIED SUPPOSED
IMAGINER FANCIER
IMAGINING FICTION PHANTOM
IMAM IMAUM MAHDI
IMBALANCE DRIVE DYSCRASIA
IMBECILE MAD DOTE FOOL AMENT
ANILE DAFFY IDIOT CRANKY
DOTARD DOTING DOTISH
CONGEON FATUOUS
IMBECILITY AMENTIA FATUITY
IMBIBE DRINK SMACK ABSORB
SPONGE INHAUST SWALLOW
IRRIGATE
IMBIBING SUCTION
IMBIBITORY SPONGY
IMBRIUS (FATHER OF —) MENTOR
(SLAYER OF —) AJAX
(WIFE OF —) MEDESICASTE
IMBRUE EMBREW INSTEEP
IMBUE SOAK STEW COLOR CROWN
EMBUE INDUE SCENT STEEP
TINCT ENSOUL IMBIBE INFUSE
LEAVEN SEASON ANIMATE
INGRAIN INSENSE INSTILL
SATURATE TINCTURE
IMBUED INSTINCT REDOLENT
IMHOTEP (FATHER OF —) PTAH
(MOTHER OF —) SEKHMET
IMIDE LACTIM SACCHARIN
IMITATE APE COPY ECHO MIME
MOCK ZANY ENSUE FORGE IMAGE
MIMIC AFFECT ANSWER FOLLOW
SEMBLE COPYCAT EMULATE

PAGEANT PATTERN PASTICHE
RESEMBLE SIMULATE
(PREF.) MIMO
IMITATION COPY FAKE SHAM
DUMMY IMAGE MIMIC ALPACA
ANSWER BUMPER ECTYPE
SHADOW CAMBLET FOULARD
IMITANT MIMESIS MOCKAGE
MOCKERY CHENILLE PARROTRY
PASTICHE POSTIQUE
(— OF COIN) COUNTER
(BURLESQUE —) TRAVESTY
(COTTON —) CAMBRIC
(EXAGGERATED —) BURLESQUE
(UNSUBSTANTIAL —) GHOST
(PREF.) NE
(SUFF.) EEN ETTE
IMITATIVE ARTY MIMIC ARTFUL
ECHOIC SHODDY MIMETIC
SIMULAR SLAVISH APATETIC
EPIGONAL
IMITATOR APE MIME ZANY MIMIC
COPIER COPYIST EPIGONE
EMULATOR EPIGONUS HOMERIST
(SUFF.) MIMUS
IMMACULATE CLEAN CANDID
CHASTE BLOTLESS SPOTLESS
UNSOILED
IMMANENCE INBEING
IMMATERIAL MENTAL SLIGHT
ETHEREAL FORMLESS SEPARATE
TRIFLING
IMMATURE RAW CRUDE GREEN
SAPPY SMALL VEALY YOUNG
BOYISH CALLOW JEJUNE LARVAL
NEANIC TENDER GIRLISH HALFLIN
IMPUBIC LADDISH NOUVEAU
PUERILE UNBAKED JUVENILE
NEPIONIC UNWEANED SHIRTTAIL
IMMATURITY NONAGE
IMMEASURABLE UNTOLD
ABYSMAL INFINITE
IMMEDIACY HERE
IMMEDIATE DIRECT MODERN
PARATE SUDDEN INSTANT
PRESENT PROXIMAL SYNECTIC
POSTHASTE
IMMEDIATELY PDQ TIT ANON
AWAY FAST JUST ONCE SOON
PLUMB RIGHT ASTITE DIRECT
PRESTO PRONTO SUBITO
DIRECTLY HEREUPON OUTRIGHT
STRAIGHT
IMMEDIATENESS INSTANCY
IMMEMORIAL DATELESS
IMMENSE HUGE VAST GRAND
GREAT LARGE UNMEET UNRIDE
TITANIC ENORMOUS GIGANTIC
INFINITE SLASHING WHOOPING
PLANETARY
IMMENSELY EVER
IMMENSITY VAST IMMANE
IMMENSE ENORMITY GRANDEUR
HUGENESS
IMMERSE DIP SINK SOAK COVER
DOUSE MERGE MERSE SOUSE
STEEP DRENCH PLUNGE BAPTIZE
BOWSSEN DEMERGE EMBATHE
ENSTEEP IMMERGE DISSOLVE
IMMERSED DEEP INNATE
IMMERSION DIP DUNKING
MERSION
IMMERSIONIST DIPPER

IMMIGRANT LAG BALT ISSEI
JIMMY METIC POMMY GUINEA
HALUTZ CHALUTZ INCOMER
PILGRIM COMELING
IMMINENCE INSTANCY
IMMINENT TOWARD PENDING
PROXIMATE
IMMOBILE FIXED STILL FROZEN
DORMANT GLACIAL TRANCED
MOVELESS
(PREF.) ANKYL(O)
IMMOBILIZATION FUSION
FIXATION
IMMOBILIZE FREEZE SPLINT
STIFFEN
IMMOBILIZED STIFF
IMMODERATE FREE DIZZY UNDUE
LAVISH UNMETH EXTREME
OVERWEENING
IMMODERATENESS EXCESS
IMMODEST FREE BRAZEN
OBSCENE INDECENT PETULANT
UNCHASTE
IMMORAL BAD ILL EVIL IDLE
LOOSE WRONG WANTON
CORRUPT VICIOUS CULPABLE
DEPRAVED INDECENT SLIPPERY
IMMORTAL DIVINE ENDLESS
ETERNAL GODLIKE UNDYING
ENDURING UNDEADLY
IMMORTALITY AMRITA ATHANASY
ETERNITY
IMMOVABLE PAT SET FAST FIRM
FIXED RIGID ADAMANT SITFAST
CONSTANT IMMOBILE IMMOTIVE
OBDURATE
IMMUNE FREE SALTED
REFRACTORY
IMMUNITY SOC CHARTER
FREEDOM LIBERTY WOODGELD
PROTECTION
IMMURE MURE WALL CONFINE
CLOISTER IMPRISON
IMMUTABILITY ONENESS
IMMUTABLE ETERNAL
IMNAH (FATHER OF —) ASHER
IMOGEN (FATHER OF —) CYMBELINE
(HUSBAND OF —) POSTHUMUS
IMP PUG LIMB DEMON DEVILET
DEVILING DEVILKIN FOLLETTO
IMPACT HIT JAR BEAT BITE BLOW
BUMP DASH DUSH JOLT SLAM
BRUNT CLASH FEEZE PEISE POISE
PULSE SHOCK SKITE GLANCE
STROKE CONTACT IMPULSE
COLLISION
(HAVING STRONG —) GUT
IMPAIR MAR BLOT HARM HURT
MAIM MANK SOUR WEAR ALLOY
CLOUD CRACK CRAZE DECAY
ERODE QUAIL SPOIL TAINT
ACRAZE DAMAGE DEADEN
DEFACE HINDER INJURE LABEFY
LESSEN REDUCE SICKEN WEAKEN
WORSEN BLEMISH CRIPPLE
DISABLE IMPEACH REFRACT
SHATTER STRETCH VITIATE
DECREASE ENFEEBLE IMBECILE
IMPERISH INFRINGE LABEFACT
(— BY INACTIVITY) RUST
(— ESSENTIALLY) RUIN
IMPAIRED HURT STALE CROCKY
FLYBLOWN

(— BY AGE) FUSTY
(— IN TONE) BREATHY
(PREF.) DYS
IMPAIRMENT ALLAY FAULT SPOIL
DOTAGE IMPAIR INJURY LESION
BEATING DEFICIT DISEASE
EROSION WEARING AKINESIA
PAIRMENT
(— OF CONSCIOUSNESS) ABSENCE
IMPALA PALLA PALLAH REDBUCK
ROOIBOK ROODEBOK ROOYEBOK
IMPALE BAIT SPIT GANCH GANSH
SPEAR SPIKE STAKE STICK STING
SKIVER TRANSFIX
IMPALPABLE ELUSIVE
IMPART GIVE SHED TELL BREAK
DRILL SHARE YIELD BESTOW
COMMON CONFER CONVEY
DIRECT IMPUTE INSTIL PARTEN
REVEAL DELIVER DIVULGE
PURPORT DISCOVER INSTRUCT
INTIMATE
(— TONE) TONE
(— ZEST) ANIMATE
IMPARTIAL EVEN FAIR JUST
EQUAL LEVEL CANDID NEUTER
UNBIASED
IMPARTIALITY CANDOR EQUITY
EQUACITY EVENNESS
IMPARTIALLY FAIRLY EQUALLY
IMPASSABLE WICKED INVIOUS
PASSLESS ROADLESS TRACKLESS
IMPASSE LOGJAM DEADLOCK
IMPASSION COMMOVE
IMPASSIONED ARDENT FERVID
FERVENT FEVERISH PERFERVID
IMPASSIVE FROZEN STOLID
PASSIVE STOICAL PHLEGMATIC
IMPASSIVENESS APATHY
MORGUE STOICISM
IMPATIENT HOT ANTSY EAGER
HASTY SHARP TESTY FRETFUL
PEEVISH RESTIVE TIDIOSE
CHOLERIC PETULANT
IMPATIENTLY HASTILY
IMPEACH CALL ACCUSE CHARGE
INDICT ARRAIGN CENSURE
IMPLEAD TRAVERSE
IMPEACHMENT APPEAL
IMPECCABLE SINLESS
IMPECUNIOUS POOR
IMPEDE BOG DAM GUM JAM LET
MAR CLOG GRAB JAMB KILL SLUG
SNAG ANNOY BLOCK CHECK
CHOKE DELAY EMBAR ESTOP
HITCH SLOTH SPOKE BAFFLE
FETTER FORBID FORSET HAMPER
HARASS HINDER HOBBLE PESTER
RETARD STYMIE IMPEACH
PREVENT SHACKLE ENCUMBER
HANDICAP OBSTRUCT PRECLUDE
IMPEDIMENT BAR RUB CLOG
SNAG STOP BLEAR BLOCK HITCH
SPOKE STICK BURDEN RUBBER
SCOTCH BLINDER EMBARGO
OBSTACLE OBSTANCY
(— IN SPEECH) HAAR HALT
IMPEDIMENTA STUFF
IMPEDING CATCH HEAVY FOULING
IMPEL PAT PUT BEAR CALL
CAST GOAD HURL MOVE SEND
URGE WHIP CARRY DRIVE FEEZE
FORCE KNOCK PRESS PRICK

PULSE COMPEL EXCITE INCITE
INDUCE PROPEL ACTUATE
DESTINE INSPIRE INSTINCT
MOTIVATE
(— TO GREATER SPEED) GATHER
IMPELLER RUNNER
IMPEND BREW HANG DEPEND
OVERHANG
IMPENDING TOWARD PENDENT
PENDING IMMINENT MENACING
IMPENETRABLE HARD DENSE
MURKY PROOF THICK AIRTIGHT
HARDENED
IMPENITENT OBDURATE
IMPERATIVE VITAL PRESSING
MASTERFUL
IMPERCEPTIBLE OCCULT SUBTLE
IMPERFECT ILL HALF POOR AMISS
BLIND FUZZY ROUGH BOTCHY
FAULTY PLATIC ATELENE STICKIT
UNWHOLE VICIOUS INPARFIT
MUTILOUS
(PREF.) ATEL(O)
IMPERFECTED INCHOATE
IMPERFECTION BUG RUB WEN
FLAW KINK MOLE SLUR VICE
ERROR FAULT BLOTCH DEFECT
FOIBLE BLEMISH CRUDITY
DEFAULT DEMERIT FAILING
FRAILTY WEAKNESS
(— IN BOTTLE) HEELTAP
(— IN GLASS) STRIA STREAK
(— IN LEATHER) FRIEZE
(— IN SILK) CORKSCREW
(— IN WICK) THIEF WASTER
IMPERFECTIVE ATELIC
IMPERFECTLY ILL HALF AMISS
ROUGHLY
IMPERFORATION ATRESIA
IMPERIAL TUFT ROYAL KINGLY
PURPLE MAJESTIC
IMPERIALIST CAESAR
IMPERIL RISK EXPONE EMPERIL
ENDANGER JEOPARDY
IMPERIOUS SURLY LORDLY
HAUGHTY DESPOTIC IMPERIAL
MASTERLY PRESSING MASTERFUL
IMPERISHABLE ETERNAL
UNDYING ENDURING IMMORTAL
IMPERMANENCE ANICCA
IMPERMANENT FLEETING
IMPERSONAL COLD DEADPAN
INHUMAN ABSTRACT
IMPERSONATE POSE TYPIFY
PERSONIFY
IMPERSONATION GENIUS
IMPERSONATOR ACTOR CACHINA
KACHINA KATCINA
IMPERTINENCE PAWK SNASH
AUDACITY
IMPERTINENT GAY FREE PERT
RUDE FRESH SASSY SAUCY
PUSHING IMPERENT IMPUDENT
OBTRUSIVE OFFICIOUS
MEDDLESOME
IMPERTURBABILITY ATARAXY
ATARAXIA SANGFROID
IMPERTURBABLE COOL PLACID
GLACIAL TRANQUIL
UNFLAPPABLE
IMPERVIOUS DEAD GASTIGHT
HARDENED HERMETIC
MOTHPROOF

(SUFF.) PROOF
IMPETUOSITY BIRR FURY HASTE
WRATH FOUGUE POWDER
RANDOM SPLEEN
IMPETUOUS HOT RAMP RUDE
BRASH EAGER FIERY FRECK
HASTY HEADY SHARP ARDENT
BROTHE FIERCE FLASHY LAVISH
RACKLE STRONG BUCKISH
FURIOUS HOTHEAD HOTSPUR
RAMSTAM VIOLENT BRAINISH
EMPRESSE HEADLONG SLAPDASH
VEHEMENT PRECIPITATE
IMPETUS BIRR FARD SEND DRIFT
GRACE SWING YMPET BENSEL
IMPACT POWDER RAVINE SWINGE
SWOUGH IMPULSE MOMENTUM
IMPINGE FALL IMPACT ASSAULT
CROSSCUT
IMPINGEMENT IMPACT
IMPIOUS UNHOLY ATHEIST
ATHEOUS GODLESS UNGODLY
DOWNWEED HOARWORT
NEFANDOUS NEFARIOUS
IMPISH IMPY ELFISH PUCKISH
WARLOCK
IMPLACABLE STOUT DEADLY
MORTAL
IMPLACABLY FATALLY
IMPLANT FIX IMP SOW HAFT ROOT
GRAFT INFIX INLAY ENRACE
ENROOT FASTEN INFUSE INSTIL
ENFORCE ENGRAFT IMPRESS
INSPIRE ENTRENCH INSTINCT
IMPLANTED INBORN INSITE
IMPLEMENT (ALSO SEE TOOL) AX
AXE BAT CARD DISC DISK FORK
GRAB HACK HONE HOOK LOOM
PLOW SPUD SPUR TOOL CROOK
DRILL FLINT LANCE SCRUB SHEAR
SLICK SPADE SPOON STEEL STICK
TRIER AMGARN BEAMER BLADER
BROACH COLLAR COOLER DIBBLE
DREDGE DRIVER DUSTER EOLITH
FLAKER FLUTER HACKER
HARROW INVOKE LADDER LIPPER
LUNATE MARKER MEALER
PACKER PADDLE PALLET PESTLE
PLOUGH RIMMER SCREEN SCYTHE
SEATER SEEDER SERVER SHEARS
SHOVEL SICKLE SLICER SMOOTH
BREAKER CHOPPER CLEANER
CLEAVER ENFORCE FLESHER
FLYFLAP GAROTTE GRUBBER
HARPOON HUSTLER KNAPPER
MATTOCK NUTPICK SKIMMER
SLABBER SLASHER SLEEKER
SLICKER SPATTLE SPATULA
SPITTLE SPURTLE STAMPER
STICKER SWATHER UTENSIL
AGITATOR BUSHWACK MEASURER
SCUTCHER SEARCHER SHREDDER
SKETCHER SPLITTER SPREADER
STRIPPER TERRACER THWACKER
TOLLIKER TRANCHET TWEEZERS
WARKLOOM WORKLOOM
NUTCRACKER
(— FOR CUTTING CHEESE) HARP
(— FOR HANGING POT) HALE
(— TO PREVENT MALT FROM
OVERFLOWING) STROM
(—S OF HUSBANDRY) WAINAGE
(ANCIENT —) POINT SLICE

AMGARN EOLITH NEOLITH
RACLOIR PALEOLITH
(BAKER'S —) PEEL
(CLIMBING —) CREEPER
(ESKIMO —) ULU
(GARDENING —) HOE RAKE SEEDER
SICKLE
(HEDGING —) TRAMP
(IRRIGATION —) CROWDER
(LOGGING —) TODE
(POTTER'S —) PALLET SPATTLE
(PREHISTORIC —) CELT FLAKER
(SHOVEL-LIKE —) SCOOP
(SOLDERING —) DOCTOR
(TORTURE —) ENGINE
(UPROOTING —) MAKE
(WINNOWING —) FAN
(PL.) GEAR CUTLERY GAINAGE
FLAUGHTS
(SUFF.) LABE
IMPLEMENTATION PERFORMANCE
IMPLICATE DIP ENWRAP CONCERN
EMBROIL INCLUDE INVOLVE
IMPLICATION CLAIM IMPLIAL
INNUENDO
IMPLICIT COVERT
IMPLIED TACIT IMPLICIT
IMPLORATION PETITION
IMPLORE ASK BEG CRY PRAY
CHARM CRAVE PLEAD INVOKE
OBTEST BESEECH CONJURE
ENTREAT SOLICIT PETITION
IMPLY HINT ARGUE CARRY COUCH
INFER EMPLOY ENTAIL IMPORT
INDUCE CONNOTE CONTAIN
INCLUDE INVOLVE PRESUME
SIGNIFY SUGGEST SUPPOSE
PREDICATE
IMPOLITE RUDE UNCIVIL
IMPOLITENESS CRUDITY
IMPONDERABLE FRIGORIC
IMPORT SAY WIT BEAR BODY
TOUR DRIFT FORCE IMPLY MORAL
SCOPE SENSE SOUND SPELL
VALOR AMOUNT CHARGE
DENOTE INGATE INTENT MATTER
SPIRIT BETOKEN MEANING
PRETEND SIGNIFY CARRIAGE
INDICATE
(PL.) INWARDS
IMPORTANCE BORE MARK PITH
FORCE POISE WORTH CHARGE
IMPORT MATTER MOMENT
REMARK STRESS STROKE WEIGHT
ACCOUNT ESSENCE GRAVITY
VALENCY EMPHASIS MAGNITUDE
SIGNIFICANCE
**IMPORTANCE OF BEING
EARNEST** (AUTHOR OF —) WILDE
(CHARACTER IN —) JACK ALGIE
PRISM CECILY EARNEST
ALGERNON WORTHING
BRACKNELL GWENDOLEN
MONCRIEFF
IMPORTANT BIG DEAR DREE HIGH
MAIN REAL GRAVE GREAT
GAPING NEEDLE STRONG URGENT
VALOUR CAPITAL CENTRAL
CRUCIAL EMINENT MATTERY
PIVOTAL SERIOUS EVENTFUL
MATERIAL PRESSING
MOMENTOUS OVERBEARING
SIGNIFICANT

(MOST — ONE OF GROUP) FLAGSHIP
IMPORTER MILLINER
IMPORTUNATE URGENT INSTANT
DEVILING EXIGEANT PRESSING
IMPORTUNE BEG WOO BEAT BONE
PRIG TOUT PRESS TEASE
BESEECH BESIEGE INSTANT
SOLICIT TERRIFY INSTANCE
IMPORTUNITY BRASS URGENCY
IMPOSE LAY SET TOP CLAP GIVE
LEVY MUMP POLE SORN ABUSE
APPLY CLAMP INPUT STAMP
TRUMP BURDEN CHARGE ENJOIN
ENTAIL FASTEN FATHER IMPONE
IMPUTE BLAFLUM DICTATE
INFLICT IRROGATE
(— UPON) FOB GAG HUM LAY
DUPE SELL CULLY TRAIL BLUDGE
DELUDE EXCISE HUMBUG NUZZLE
CULLION DECEIVE HOODWINK
IMPOSED BOUNDEN
IMPOSING BIG EPIC BUDGE BURLY
GRAND HEFTY NOBLE PROUD
AUGUST EPICAL FEUDAL PORTLY
HAUGHTY POMPOUS STATELY
HANDSOME MAGNIFIC SONORANT
SONOROUS
(— UPON) PRACTICE PRACTISE
IMPOSITION BAM COD HUM LEVY
SELL TAIL GOUGE IMPOT CHOUSE
GAMMON INTAKE TAILLE
IMPOSAL ARTIFICE IMPOSURE
(MILITARY —) CESS
(SCHOOL —) PENSUM
IMPOSSIBLE OUT HOPELESS
IMPOST LAY TAX CAST LEVY TAIL
TASK TOLL ABWAB ANNALE
AVANIA EXCISE GABELLE
POUNAMU TALLAGE TONNAGE
TRIBUTE CHAPTREL SPRINGER
(PL.) CUSTOMS
IMPOSTOR FOB FAKE GULL IDOL
CHEAT FAKER FRAUD GOUGE
QUACK BUNYIP FOURBE HUMBUG
MUMPER EMPIRIC FAITOUR
PROCTOR SHAMMER PHANTASM
IMPOSTURE BAM GAG FAKE HOAX
SHAM CHEAT FRAUD TRICK
DECEIT HUMBUG JUGGLE
ARTIFICE DELUSION JUGGLERY
IMPOTENCE ACRATIA UNMIGHT
WEAKNESS
IMPOTENCY UNWELTH
IMPOTENT WEAK FRIGID PAULIE
UNABLE STERILE UNMIGHTY
IMPOUND FIND POIND POUND
INTERN PINFOLD
IMPOVERISH PILL CLOUD BEGGAR
IMPOOR SICKEN DEPLETE
DEPRESS EMPOVER BANKRUPT
POVERISH
IMPOVERISHED POOR OBOLARY
BANKRUPT INDIGENT
IMPRACTICAL CRAZY FECKLESS
IMPRECATE WISH
IMPRECATION DASH OATH PIZE
WISH BLAME CURSE DAMME
DAMMIT CONSARN ANATHEMA
IMPREGNABILITY STRENGTH
IMPREGNABLE FAST PROOF
IMPREGNATE BIG HOP DOPE FILL
LIME MILT BREED IMBUE STOCK
STUFF TINCT AERATE CHARGE

INFORM INFUSE LEAVEN SEASON
SETTLE ASPHALT ENVENOM
IMPREGN CHROMATE CONCEIVE
CREOSOTE FRICTION FRUCTIFY
GRAPHITE MEDICATE PERMEATE
SATURATE SILICATE TINCTURE
(SUFF.) (— WITH) URET(UM)
IMPREGNATED BRED COATED
IMPRESS FIX BITE COIN DING DINT
ETCH MARK AFFIX BRAND CLAMP
CRIMP DRIVE GRAVE GRILL INFIX
PRESS PRINT REACH SEIZE STAMP
STEAD WRITE AFFECT ENSEAL
FASTEN INCUSE INDENT SALUTE
STRIKE ANTIQUE ENGRAVE
ENSTAMP IMPLANT IMPREST
IMPRINT INSENSE AUTOTYPE
INSCRIBE NEGATIVE
(— DEEPLY) DELVE ENGRAVE
(— SUDDENLY) SMITE
(— WITH FEAR) AFFRIGHT
(FAIL TO —) UNDERWHELM
IMPRESSED BLIND ANTIQUE
INDENTED
IMPRESSIBLE WAXY
IMPRESSION CUT HIT AURA CAST
CHOP DENT DINT IDEA MARK
MOLD SEAL STEP STIR FANCY
GOUGE IMAGE MOULD PRINT
STAMP STATE ECTYPE EFFECT
ENGRAM FIGURE INCUSE OFFSET
SIGNET STRIKE EOPHYTE
ETCHING FANTASY IMPRESS
MOULAGE OPINION SEALING
SQUEEZE STENCIL TOOLING
BLANKING ENGRAMMA NEGATIVE
PRESSION PRESSURE STAMPAGE
TOOLMARK PHOTOGENE
(— OF DIE) CLICHE
(— ON COIN) CROSS
(— WITHOUT INK) ALBINO
(AUDITORY —) SOUND
(DOUBLE —) MACKLE MACULE
(IMMEDIATE —) APERCU
(LUMINOUS —) PHOSPHENE
(MAKE AN — ON) GRAB
(MENTAL —) GRAVING
(STRONG —) HUNCH
(TRANSITORY —) SNAPSHOT
(VIVID —) SPLASH
(PREF.) TYP(I)(O)
(SUFF.) TYPAL TYPE TYPIC TYPY
IMPRESSIONABLE SOFT WAXY
WAXEN TENDER PLASTIC
PASSIBLE
IMPRESSIONIST LUMINIST
IMPRESSIVE BIG FAT EPIC AWFUL
GRAND NOBLE PROUD EPICAL
SOLEMN PESANTE STATELY
TEARING TELLING WEIGHTY
FORCIBLE IMPOSING SMASHING
SONORANT SONOROUS
STUNNING MAGNIFICENT
IMPRINT DINT ETCH SIGN STEP
PRESS STAMP CUTOFF FASTEN
STRIKE ENGRAVE ENSTAMP
IMPRESS APREYNTE COLOPHON
EPIGRAPH PRESSION PRESSURE
STAMPAGE
(— ON CHEEK) FASTEN
IMPRISON JUG LAG NUN BOND
GAOL HULK JAIL QUOD SEAL
SHOP WARD CROWD EMBAR

GRATE COMMIT IMMURE JIGGER
PRISON SLOUGH CONFINE
INTOWER BASTILLE
IMPRISONED FAST
IMPRISONMENT BAND BOND
ARREST CHAINS DURESS PRISON
CUSTODY DURANCE
IMPROBABLE FISHY UNLIKE
UNLIKELY
IMPROMPTU GLIB MAGGOT
SUDDEN OFFHAND
IMPROPER BAD PAH PAW AMISS
LARGE SPICY UNDUE UNFELE
UNJUST ILLICIT INDECENT
PERVERSE TORTIOUS UNSEEMLY
WRONGOUS MALODOROUS
IMPROPERLY AMISS
IMPROPRIETY SOLECISM
IMPROVE FIX BEET GAIN GOOD
GROW HELP MEND AMEND EDIFY
EMEND GRADE MOISE SMART
TOUCH BETTER ENRICH PROFIT
ADVANCE BENEFIT CORRECT
CULTURE ELEVATE PERFECT
PROMOTE RECTIFY UPSWING
(— APPEARANCE OF HORSE)
BISHOP
(— APPEARANCE OF TEA) FACE
(— CONDUCTIVITY) AGE
IMPROVED BETTER
IMPROVEMENT AMENDS PICKUP
POLICY PROFIT REFORM REDRESS
UPSWING
IMPROVIDENT PRODIGAL
WASTEFUL
(— PERSON) MICAWBER
IMPROVISATION THEME CALYPSO
IMPROVISE JAM COOK FAKE PONG
VAMP ADLIB FANTASY
(— MUSICALLY) JAM FAKE
NOODLE
IMPRUDENCE FOLLY
IMPRUDENT FESS RASH FALSE
UNWARY FOOLISH RECKLESS
IMPUDENCE GALL BRASS CHEEK
MOUTH NERVE SLACK BRONZE
PUPPYISM
IMPUDENT BOLD COXY FACY RUDE
BANTY BARDY BRASH FRESH
GALLY LIPPY SASSY SAUCY
BRASSY BRAZEN CHEEKY STOCKY
BIGGETY CHUNKED FORWARD
GALLOWS PERKING INSOLENT
MALAPERT AUDACIOUS
BAREFACED
IMPUDENTLY COOLY COOLLY
FRESHLY
IMPUGN DENY FALSE DISPUTE
IMPEACH
IMPULSE FIT BIAS RESE SEND
URGE DRIVE NISUS SPEND START
DESIRE MOTIVE SIGNAL SPLEEN
YETZER CALLING CONATUS
IMPETUS INSTINCT MOVEMENT
STIRRING
(BLIND —) ATE
(ELECTRICAL —) KICK
(SPONTANEOUS —) ACCORD
(SUDDEN —) SPLEEN
(SUPERNATURAL —) AFFLATUS
(PREF.) OSMO
IMPULSION SWING IMPULSE
IMPULSIVE QUICK

FITFUL HEADLONG
IMPURE DRY FOUL LEWD GROSS
HORRY MUDDY FILTHY TURBID
UNPURE MONGREL SCABBED
UNCLEAN VICIOUS INDECENT
MACULATE PRURIENT
MACULATED
IMPURITY CRUD DONOR DROSS
FEDITY ACCEPTER ACCEPTOR
FOULNESS
(— IN LINT) SHALE
(— IN MINERAL) GANG GANGUE
(PL.) SCUM GARBLE SLUMMAGE
IMPUTABLE OWING
IMPUTATION SCANDAL
IMPUTE LAY PUT RET ARET EVEN
WITE COUNT REFER ARRECT
CHARGE FASTEN IMPOSE OBJECT
RECKON REPUTE ASCRIBE
ENTITLE IMPEACH
IN A I N Y AT TO BAJO INBY INTO
UPON ALONG INTIL
(— A FAINT) AWAY
(— A SERIES) SERIATIM
(— A STATE OF ACTION) ENERGIC
(— ACCORDANCE) AFTER
(— ADDITION) EKE TOO ALSO
ABOVE AGAIN ALONG FORBY
STILL BEYOND BESIDES FARTHER
FURTHER MOREOVER OVERPLUS
THERETIL
(— ADVANCE) AHEAD FORTH
BEFORE
(— ANY CASE) EVER HOWEVER
(— BEHALF OF) PRO
(— CASE THAT) AUNTERS
(— CIRCULATION) ABROAD
(— CONNECTION WITH) FORNENT
FERNINST
(— EARNEST) AGOOD
(— EXCESS OF) OVER
(— FACT) SOOTH TRULY INDEED
ITSELF MERELY VERILY ACTUALLY
VERAMENT
(— FAITH) IVADS EFECKS YFACKS
(— FRONT) FORE AFACE FORNE
AGAINST PARAVANT
(— FULL) ALONG
(— GOOD SEASON) BETIMES
(— GOOD SPIRITS) BOBBISH
(— GRACEFUL MANNER) ADAGIO
(— JEST) AGAME
(— NO MANNER) NOWISE
NAEGATES
(— ONE DIRECTION) ANON
(— ORDER) FOR ATAUNT
ATAUNTO
(— PLACE OF) FOR WITH INSTEAD
(— POSSESSION) WITHIN
(— PROGRESS) AFOOT TOWARD
(— PROPER MANNER) DULY
(— RESPECT TO) ANENT
(— RETURN FOR) AGAINST
(— ROTATION) ABOUT
(— SO FAR AS) AS QUA
(— SOLE CONTROL) ABSOLUTE
(— SOOTH) PARFEY PERFAY
(— SPITE OF) FOR ALTHO MALGRE
AGAINST DESPITE MALGRADO
(— SUSPENSE) PENDING
(— THE DOING OF) WITH
(— THE FIELD) ABROAD
(— THE FIRST PLACE) IMP IMPRIMIS

(— THE FUTURE) HENCE
(— THE MORNING) MANE
(— THE REAR) AREAR ASTERN
(— THE REGIONS OF UNBELIEVERS) IPI
(— THE SAME PLACE) IBID IBIDEM
(— THE SAME WAY) AS
(— TOWARD) INOWER
(— TRUTH) MARRY SOOTH CERTES INDEED VERILY SOOTHLY FORSOOTH
(— VAIN) WASTELY
(— VIEW OF THE FACT THAT) SEEING
(— WHAT MANNER) HOW QUOMODO
(NOT —) OUT
(PREF.) A IL IM IN INTRO IR
INABILITY (— TO FEED) APHAGIA
(— TO MASTICATE) AMASESIS
(— TO SPEAK) ALOGIA ANEPIA DUMBNESS
(— TO WALK) ABASIA
INACCESSIBILITY FASTNESS
INACCESSIBLE COY REMOTE UNGAIN WICKED SHADOWY
INACCURATE SOUR FALSE LOOSE FAULTY UNJUST INEXACT IMPROPER SLIPSHOD
INACHUS (DAUGHTER OF —) IO
(FATHER OF —) OCEANUS
(MOTHER OF —) TETHYS
(SON OF —) PHORONEUS
INACTION RUST
INACTIVATE MOTHBALL
INACTIVE LAX DEAD DRUG FLAT IDLE LAZY MESO SLOW HEAVY INERT NOBLE SLACK SULKY ASLEEP SEDENT STATIC SUPINE TORPID CESSANT DORMANT PASSIVE RESTIVE COMATOSE COMATOUS DEEDLESS DILATORY FAINEANT SLOTHFUL SLUGGISH THEWLESS THOWLESS QUIESCENT
INACTIVITY SLOTH ANERGY TORPOR ANERGIA ABEYANCE IDLENESS CESSATION SEGNITUDE
INADEQUACY DEFECT FRAILTY SCARCITY
INADEQUATE BAD BARE POOR THIN INEPT SCANT SHORT SLACK FEEBLE STRAIT FOOLISH INVALID SLENDER HIGHLAND INFERIOR MISERABLE
(PREF.) MAL
INADEQUATELY BADLY SLACK SLACKLY
INADVERTENCE LAPSUS
INADVERTENT CARELESS
INAJA JAGUA
INALIENABLE INHERENT
INAMORATA AMORADO AMORETTO
INANE DIZZY EMPTY JERKY SILLY VAPID JEJUNE VACANT FATUOUS FOOLISH INSIPID VACUOUS IMBECILE SLIPSLOP TRIFLING
INANGA MINNOW
INANIMATE DEAD DULL BRUTE INERT DEADLY STOLID STUPID LIFELESS
INANIMITY CONSENSUS

INANITY FATUITY VACUITY
INAPPLICABLE SPURIOUS
INAPPROPRIATE INEPT UNAPT UNDUE FOREIGN UNHAPPY
(SOMETHING —) CAMP
INAPT BACKWARD FOOTLESS
INARTICULATA LYOPOMA
INARTICULATE DUMB LAME THICK
INARTISTIC CRUDE ARTLESS
INATTENTION ABSENCE NEGLECT APROSEXIA
INATTENTIVE DEAF SLACK ABSENT REMISS SUPINE DREAMSY UNTENTY CARELESS DISTRAIT HEEDLESS MINDLESS
INAUDIBLE SECRET
INAUDIBLY INWARDLY SECRETLY
INAUGURATE AUGUR BEGIN HANDSEL INITIATE
INAUGURATION HANDSEL
INAUSPICIOUS BAD ILL EVIL FOUL ADVERSE OBSCENE OMINOUS UNHAPPY UNLUCKY SINISTER
INAUTHENTIC SPURIOUS
INBORN GENIAL INBRED INNATE NATIVE CONNATE NATURAL HABITUAL INHERENT
INBRED INBORN INNATE
INBREED SELF
INBREEDING ENDOGAMY
INCA INGUA OREJON
INCALCULABLE UNTOLD SUMLESS UNKNOWN
INCA MAGIC FLOWER CANTUT CANTUTA
INCANDESCENCE GLOW
INCANDESCENT BRIGHT
INCANTATION CHARM DAWUT SPELL CARMEN FETISH MANTRA CANTION CHANTRY GREEGREE
INCAPABLE DEAD NUMB UNABLE HANDLESS
INCAPACITATE NAPOO UNFIT NOBBLE UNABLE DISABLE
INCAPACITATED FLAT DISABLED STRICKEN
INCARCERATE IMMURE CONFINE IMPRISON
INCARNATE BODIED EMBODY CARNATE ENFLESH HUMANIFY PERSONIFY
INCARNATION RAMA IMAGE ADVENT AVATAR GENIUS MNEVIS TERTON HUTUKTU EPIPHANY PERSONIFICATION
INCAUTIOUS RASH UNWARY UNCHARY UNTENTY CAREFREE RECKLESS
INCENDIARY FIREBUG ARSONIST BOUTEFEU
INCENSE CENSE INFLAME KETURAH PROVOKE IRRITATE THYMIAMA
(— INGREDIENT) ONYCHA
(— VESSEL) SHIP
(PREF.) THURI
INCENSED RAW IRATE WROTH WRATHFUL
INCENTIVE BROD GOAD SPUR PRICK MOTIVE IMPETUS IMPULSE INCITIVE STIMULUS MOTIVATION
INCEPTION ORIGIN ANCESTRY
INCESSANT STEADY

ENDLESS CONSTANT
INCESSANTLY FOREVER
INCH UNCH PRIME UNCIA
(ABOUT 7 —S) FISTMELE
(100TH OF —) POINT
(4 —S) HANDFUL
(48TH OF —) IRON
(9 —S) SPAN
INCHOATE FORMLESS
INCIDENT GO EVENT LIABLE CAUTION EPISODE PASSAGE SUBJECT ACCIDENT CASUALTY OCCASION OCCURRENCE
(AMUSING —) BAR BREAK
(LITERARY —) BIT
INCIDENTAL BY BYE SIDE STRAY CASUAL EPISODIC GLANCING INCIDENT OCCURRENT
INCIDENTALLY BYHAND OBITER APROPOS
INCINERATE COMBUST CREMATE
INCINERATOR BURNER SALAMANDER
INCIPIENCE BUD
INCIPIENT INITIAL GERMINAL INCHOATE
INCISE CHOP RASE LANCE INCIDE CHANNEL ENGRAVE
INCISION CUT GASH SLIT SNIP ISSUE SCORE BROACH SCOTCH STREAK CUTDOWN DIACOPE APLOTOMY CECOTOMY COLOTOMY
(SUFF.) TOMY
INCISIVE ACID KEEN CRISP SHARP BITING BRUTAL CUTTING ACULEATE PIERCING TRENCHANT
INCISIVENESS MORDANCY
INCISOR CUTTER NIPPER GATHERER
INCITE EGG HIE HOY PUT SIC TAR ABET BEET BUZZ EDGE FIRE GOAD LASH MOVE PROD SICK SNIP SPUR STIR URGE WHET AWAKE CHIRK IMPEL PRICK PROKE SPARK SPURN STING TEMPT AROUSE BESTIR ENTICE EXCITE EXHORT FILLIP FOMENT HALLOO INDUCE KINDLE NETTLE PROMPT UPSTIR ACTUATE ANIMATE COMMOVE INCENSE INSPIRE PROMOVE PROVOKE QUICKEN SOLICIT INCITATE MOTIVATE
(— SECRETLY) SUBORN
(— TO ATTACK) SET HIRR SOOL
INCITEMENT GOAD PROD SPUR STING MOTIVE EGGMENT STIRRING
(— OF LITIGATION) BARRATRY
INCITER FEEDER MONITOR INCENSOR INCENTOR
INCLEMENCY RIGOR CRUELTY TYRANNY ASPERITY HARDNESS SEVERITY
INCLEMENT RAW HARD RUDE SOUR GURLY STARK COARSE RUGGED SEVERE UNFINE UNKINDLY
(NOT —) OPEN CIVIL
INCLINATION DIP GEE MAW PLY SET BENT BIAS BROO CANT CARE DRAG DRAW EDGE FALL GUST

HANG LEAN LIKE LIST LOVE LUST MIND SLEW TURN VEIN WILL BEVEL BOSOM DRAFT DRIFT FANCY GRAIN HABIT HIELD HUMOR KNACK LURCH PITCH POISE SLANT SLOPE STUDY SWING TASTE THEAT TREND AFFECT ANIMUS ANLAGE ASCENT DESIRE DEVICE GATHER GENIUS INTENT LIKING MOTION NOTION PONDUS RELISH SQUINT TALENT YETZER APTNESS CONATUS COURAGE CURRENT DESCENT DRAUGHT FANTASY INKLING LEANING STOMACH VERSANT WILLING APPETITE APTITUDE CLINAMEN DEVOTION GRADIENT PENCHANT TENDENCY VELLEITY VERGENCY WOULDING PROCLIVITY PROPENSITY
(— DOWNWARD) DIP DESCENT HANGING
(— OF OARSMAN'S BODY) LAYBACK
(INWARD —) BATTER
(PREDOMINATE —) STRENGTH
INCLINE APT BOW DIP KIP TIP WRY BEAR BEND BIAS BREW CANT CAST DOCK DOOK DOOR DROP GIVE HANG HEEL HELD HILL LEAN LIKE LIST PECK PEND RAKE SEEL STAY SWAY TILT TURN BEVEL CLIMB CLINE DROOP FLECT HIELD JINNY OFFER PITCH SHAPE SLANT SLOPE SOUND VERGE AFFECT GLACIS INTEND SHELVE STEEVE UPBROW DECLINE DESCEND GANGWAY PROPEND PROCLINE PROCLIVE
(— SKI) EDGE
(PREF.) CLIN(O)
INCLINED APT SIB BENT CANT FAIN LIEF RIFE VAIN ARAKE GIVEN PRONE READY COUCHE MINDED PROMPT SLOPED SUPINE FORWARD HANGING OBLIQUE PRONATE STUDIED AFFECTED DISPOSED ENCLITIC PREGNANT PROPENSE SIDELING TALENTED
(— TO DRINK) BIBULOUS
INCLINING HILLY SHELVY SLOPING CERNUOUS PROPENSE SIDELING
(SUFF.) CLINIC CLINOUS
INCLUDE ADD LAP HAVE TAKE ANNEX COUCH COVER IMPLY EMPLOY ENSEAM RECKON BELOUKE COLLECT CONNOTE CONTAIN EMBRACE IMMERSE INVOLVE RECOUNT SUBSUME COMPRISE CONCLUDE
(— IN LIST) ENGROSS
INCLUDING TO CUM
INCLUSIVE GRAND CAPABLE CATHOLIC
INCLUSIVELY BROADLY
INCLUSUS RECLUSE
INCOHERENT FUZZY BROKEN RAVING INCHOATE
INCOHERENTLY IDLY
INCOMBUSTIBLE APYROUS ASBESTIC
INCOME GAIN PORT RENT LIVING PEWAGE PEWING PROFIT SALARY FACULTY INTRADO INTRATE

PRODUCE REVENUE STIPEND
INTEREST PROCEEDS
POCKETBOOK
(— OF BENEFICE) ANNAT
(ANNUAL —) RENTE
(UNFORESEEN —) GRAVY
INCOMMENSURATE UNEQUAL
INCOMMODE VEX ANNOY MOLEST
PLAGUE TROUBLE DISQUIET
INCOMPARABLE ALONE
INCOMPATIBILITY SOLECISM
ANTIPATHY
INCOMPATIBLE ALIEN
REPUGNANT
INCOMPETENT INEPT UNFIT
SLOUCH UNABLE UNMEET
FECKLESS HANDLESS HELPLESS
SPLITTER
INCOMPLETE WANE BLIND ROUGH
BROKEN UNDONE DIVIDED
LACKING PARTIAL IMMATURE
INCHOATE SEGMENTAL
(PREF.) ATEL(O) DEMI SEMI
INCOMPLETELY BADLY HALVES
INCOMPOSITE PRIME
INCOMPREHENSIBILITY
ACATALEPSY
INCOMPREHENSIBLE PARTIAL
COCKEYED
INCONCLUSIVE FUZZY
INCONGRUITY JAR ANOMALY
SOLECISM
INCONGRUOUS ALIEN ABSURD
ANOMALOUS
INCONNU CONY NELMA CONNIE
SHEEFISH
INCONSEQUENTIAL NUGATORY
INCONSIDERABLE WEAK LIGHT
PETTY LITTLE
INCONSIDERATE RASH UNKIND
ASOCIAL RECKLESS
INCONSISTENCY HOLE
INCONSISTENT ALIEN
REPUGNANT
INCONSPICUOUS OBSCURE
INCONSTANCY CHANGE LEVITY
INCONSTANT FICKLE BRUCKLE
FLUXILE MOONISH MUTABLE
SLIDING VARIOUS FLUXIBLE
MOVEABLE STRUMPET VARIABLE
CHAMELEON MERCURIAL
VERSATILE
INCONTESTABLE SURE CLEAN
CERTAIN POSITIVE
INCONTINENCE ENURESIS
INCONTINENT LOOSE LAXATIVE
INCONTROVERTIBLE GRAND
INCONVENIENCE FASH BOTHER
CUMBER STRESS SQUEEZE
DISQUIET
INCONVENIENT UNKED CLUMSY
UNBANE UNGAIN AWKWARD
UNHANDY ANNOYING UNCHANCY
UNTOWARD
INCOORDINATION ASTASIA
INCORPORATE MIX FOLD FUSE
JOIN ANNEX KNEAD MERGE
UNITE ABSORB EMBODY ENGRAIN
ENTRAIN INWEAVE INCORPSE
(— IN WALL) ENGAGE
INCORPOREAL AERY BODILESS
ASOMATOUS
INCORRECT BAD ILL OFF FALSE

WRONG PECCANT UNRIGHT
UNSOUND VICIOUS PERVERSE
(PREF.) CAC(O)
INCORRIGIBLE HARD
INCORRUPTIBLE IMMORTAL
INCREASE UP ADD EIK EKE IMP
WAX BUMP ECHE GAIN GROW
HELP HIKE ITCH JACK JUMP
MEND MORE MUCH PLUS PUSH
RISE SOAR THEE THRO BOOST
BUILD BULGE CLIMB CROWD
FLUSH FRESH HEAVE LARGE
RAISE SPURT SWELL ACCENT
ACCESS ACCRUE BETTER BIGGEN
CHANGE CREASE DEEPEN
DOUBLE EXPAND EXTEND
EXTENT GATHER GROWTH
SPREAD SPRING ADVANCE
AMPLIFY AUCTION AUGMENT
AUXESIS BALLOON DISTEND
ELEVATE ENGROSS ENHANCE
ENLARGE GREATEN IMPROVE
INFLATE MAGNIFY STEEPEN
SURCRUE ACCRESCE ADDITION
COMPOUND FLOURISH HEIGHTEN
LENGTHEN MAJORATE MAXIMATE
MAXIMIZE MULTIPLY THRODDEN
PROPAGATE PROLIFERATE
(— AT USURY) OCKER
(— GREATLY) ACCUMULATE
(— HEAT OF KILN) RUSTLE GLISTER
(— IN BUSINESS) UPBEAT
(— IN PAY) FOGY FOGIE
(— IN STRENGTH) FRESHEN
(— KNOWLEDGE) ENRICH
(— POWER) SOUP
(— PRICE BY BIDDING) CANT
(— SPEED) JAZZ ACCELERATE
(— STITCHES) FASHION
(— SUDDENLY) LEAP
(PRICE —) RIST
(SHORT-TERM —) BOOMLET
(PREF.) AUXO
(SUFF.) AUXE OSIS
INCREASING GROWING CRESCENT
CRESCIVE DILATANT SWELLING
(— RAPIDLY) BOOMING
INCREDIBLE TALL STEEP DAMNED
FABULOUS
INCREDULITY UNBELIEF
INCREDULOUS INFIDEL
INCREMENT DOSE DELTA
INCREASE
INCRIMINATE ACCUSE
INCRUST FOUL
INCRUSTATION CRUD MOSS
CRUST SCALE TARTAR FOULING
FURRING
INCUBATE SIT BROOD CLOCK
COVER HATCH
INCUBATION PASSAGE
INCUBATOR FURNACE HATCHER
COUVEUSE ISOLETTE
INCUBUS DUSE MARE DUSIO
NIGHTMARE
INCULCATE BREED INFIX INCULK
INFUSE IMPLANT IMPRESS
INSTILL
INCULCATED BRED
INCUMBENT COARB BEARER
INCUR RUN BEAR GAIN WAGE
CONTRACT
INCURABLE BOOTLESS HOPELESS

INCURRENT INHALANT
INCURSION RAID ROAD FORAY
INFALL INROAD RAZZIA DESCENT
HOSTING INBREAK INCURSE
ANABASIS INVASION
INCUS AMBOS ANVIL
INDEBTED DEBTFUL BEHOLDEN
INDEBTEDNESS DEBT SCORE
INDECENCY IMPURITY PRIAPISM
RIBALDRY
INDECENT PAW BLUE FOUL LEWD
RANK BAWDY GROSS NASTY
SAUCY GREASY IMPURE PAWPAW
SMUTTY CURIOUS GRIVOIS
IMMORAL OBSCENE IMMODEST
IMPROPER SHAMEFUL UNCOMELY
INDECISION DEMUR DOUBT
MAYBE POISE SWITHER
INDECISIVE DRAWN HALTING
INDECISIVENESS SUSPENSE
INDECOROUS RUDE COARSE
FORWARD UNCIVIL IMMODEST
IMPOLITE IMPROPER INDECENT
UNSEEMLY UNTOWARD
INDEED SO ARU NAY TOO WIS YEA
AWAT DEED EVEN IWIS JUST
SURE MARRY QUOTH TIENS
ATWEEL ITSELF PARDIE SURELY
FAITHLY FRANKLY FORSOOTH
VERAMENT
INDEFATIGABLE TIRELESS
INDEFENSIBLE INVALID
INDEFINABLE NAMELESS
INDEFINITE HAZY FUZZY GROSS
LOOSE VAGUE DIVERS INEXACT
AORISTIC
INDEFINITELY IN
INDELIBLE FAST FIXED
INDELICATE RAW FREE WARM
BROAD GROSS ROUGH COARSE
GREASY IMPOLITE IMPROPER
UNSEEMLY
INDEMNIFICATION RELIEF
INDEMNIFY PAY RECOUP SATISFY
WARRANT
INDENT JAG BRIT DENT GIMP
MUSH NICK CHASE DELVE NOTCH
STAMP TOOTH WHEEL BRUISE
CRENEL ENGRAIL GAUFFER
INDENTATION CHOP DENT DINT
DOKE FOIL KINK SCAR BOSOM
BULGE CLEFT CRENA DINGE
NOTCH SINUS DIMPLE FURROW
GROOVE INDENT RECESS IMPRESS
CRENELLE TOOTHING
(— IN BOTTLE) KICK
(— IN DOG'S FACE) STOP
(— IN SHELL) EYE
INDENTED WAVED CRENATE
NOTCHED SINUATE
INDENTURE BIND INDENT
ESCALLOP SYNGRAPH
INDEPENDENCE AUTARKY
FREEDOM AUTARCHY
(— OF GOD) ASEITY ASEITAS
(POLITICAL —) SWARAJ
INDEPENDENT FREE PROUD
SEEKER BIGGITY DIVIDED
MUGWUMP SECTARY ABSOLUTE
PECULIAR POSITIVE SEPARATE
(STATISTICALLY —) ORTHOGONAL
(PREF.) SELF
INDEPENDENTLY APART

INDESCRIBABLE TERMLESS
INEFFABLE
INDETERMINATE AORISTIC
FORMLESS INFINITE
INDEX PIE FIST HAND ARNETH
ELENCH PIGNET TONGUE
POINTER ALPHABET EXPONENT
REGISTER
(COMPUTER —) KWIC KWOC
INDIA BHARAT

INDIA	
CAPE:	COMORIN
CAPITAL:	NEWDELHI
CASTE:	JAT MAL AHIR GOLA JATI
	MALI DHOBI SANSI SUDRA
	VARNA DACOIT DHANUK
	LOHANA VAISYA AGARWAL
	BRAHMAN DHANGAR
COAST:	MALABAR
COIN:	LAC PIE ANNA FELS LAKH
	PICE TARA ABIDI CRORE PAISA
	RUPEE
COLLEGE:	TOL
DESERT:	THAR
DISTRICT:	SIBI NASIK PATNA
	SIMLA ZILLAH MALABAR
	NELLORE MOFUSSIL
GULF:	KUTCH CAMBAY MANNAR
ISLAND:	CHILKA
LAKE:	WULAR CHILKA COLAIR
	DHEBAR SAMBAHR
LANGUAGE:	URDU HINDI TAMIL
	TELUGU SANSKRIT
MEASURE:	ADY DHA GAZ GUZ
	JOW KOS LAN SER BYEE COSS
	DAIN DHAN HATH JAOB KUNK
	MOOT PARA RAIK RATI SEIT
	TAUN TENG TOLA AMUNA
	BIGHA CAHAR COVID CROSA
	DANDA DRONA GARCE GIREH
	HASTA PALLY PARAH RATTI
	SALAY YOJAN ADHAKA ANGULA
	COVIDO CUDAVA CUMBHA
	GEERAH LAMANY MOOLUM
	MUSHTI PALGAT PARRAH
	ROPANI TIPREE UNGLEE
	YOJANA ADOULIE DHANUSH
	GAVYUTI KHAHOON NIRANGA
	PRASTHA VITASTI OKTHABAH
MOUNTAIN:	MERU GHATS KAMET
	MASTUJ TANKSE KALAHOI
	SIWALIK VINDHYA SULEIMAN
MOUNTAIN RANGE:	SATPURA
	VINDHYA ARAVALLI HIMALAYA
NATIVE:	TODA HINDU TAMIL
PROVINCE:	HAR ASSAM BIHAR
	ANDHRA BENGAL KERALA
	MADRAS MYSORE ORISSA
	PUNJAB GUJARAT HARYANA
	KASHMIR MANIPUR
REGION:	MALABAR
RIVER:	AI DOR SON TEL KOSI KUSI
	NIRA REHR SIND BETWA BHIMA
	DAMOH GOGRA INDUS JAWAI
	RAPTI SANKH SONAR TAPTI
	TUNGA CHENAB GANGES
	KISTNA PENNER SUTLEJ
	WARDHA CAUVERY CHAMBAL
	IRAWADI KRISHNA NARMADA
	NARMEDA HEMAVATI
	HYDASPES MAHANADI
	NERBUDDA VINDHYAS

SEAPORT: DAMAN BOMBAY COCHIN MADRAS CALCUTTA
STATE: ASSAM BIHAR KERALA MYSORE ORISSA PUNJAB GUJARAT MANIPUR
STRAIT: PALK
TERRITORY: DIU GOA DAMAN MINICOY AMINDIVI
TOWN: DIU AGRA DAMA GAYA PUNA REWA ADONI AKOLA ALWAR ARCOT BHERA DACCA DATIA DELHI GIROT KALPI PATAN PATNA POONA SALEM SIMLA SURAT TEHRI AJMERE AMBALA BARELI BARODA BHOPAL BOMBAY CHAMBA COCHIN DUMDUM HOWRAH INDORE JAIPUR KANPUR LAHORE MADIRA MADRAS MADURA MEERUT MULTAN MUTTRA MYSORE NAGPUR RAMPUR UJJAIN ALIGARH BENARES BIKANER CALICUT CAWNPUR DINAPUR GWALIOR JODHPUR KARACHI KURNOOL LASWARI LUCKNOW RANGOON RANGPUR AMRITSAR BHATINDA BHATPARA CALCUTTA DINAPORE JABALPUR KOLHAPUR MANDALAY MIRZAPUR PESHAWAR SHOLAPUR SRINAGAR VARANASI
TRIBE: AO GOR BHIL BADAGA SHERANI
WATERFALL: JOG GOKAK CAUVERY
WEIGHT: MOD PAI SER VIS DHAN DRUM KONA MYAT PALA PANK PICE RAIK RATI RUAY SEER TANK TOLA YAVA ADPAD BAHAR CANDY CATTY HUBBA MASHA MAUND PALLY POUAH RATTI RETTI RUTEE TICAL TICUL TIKAL ABUCCO DHURRA KARSHA CHITTAK PEIKTHA

INDIAN LO RED ROJO INJUN TAWNY ABNAKI INDISH BHARATI HOSTILE NAIKPOD REDSKIN LONGHAIR MUSKOGEE PENOBSCOT SHAHAPTIAN NARRAGANSET
(AMERICAN —) AIS AUK FOX HOH KAW OTO REE SAC SIA UTE WEA ZIA ADAI COOS CREE CROW DOEG ERIE EYAK HANO HOPI HUPA IOWA KATO KOSO MOKI MONO OTOE OTTO PIMA PIRO SAUK TANO TAOS TEWA TIOU TOAG UTAH WACO YUMA ZUNI ACOMA ALSEA BANAK BIDAI CADDO CHAUI COMOX CONOY COREE CREEK HANIS HOOPA HUECO HURON JEMEZ KANIA KANSA KAROK KERES KIOWA KOROA KUSAN LENCA LIPAN MAKAH MANSO MIAMI MINGO MODOC MOQUI NAMBE OMAHA OSAGE OSTIC OZARK PECOS PINAL PIUTE PONCA SAMBO SARSI SEWEE SIOUX SITKA SKIDI SLAVE SNAKE SOOKE TETON TEXAS TIGUA TONTO TWANA TYIGH UINTA

UNAMI WAPPO WASCO WASHO WIYOT YAMEL YAZOO YUCHI YUROK AGAWAM AHTENA APACHE ATSINA ATUAMI AVOYEL BILOXI CALUSA CAYUGA CAYUSE CHATOT CHERAW CHETCO COOSUC CUPENO DAKOTA DIGGER EYEISH FARAON GILENO HAINAI HAISLA ISLETA KAIBAB KAINAH KANSAS KICHAI KOSIMO KUITSH LAGUNA LENAPE MANDAN MAUMEE MAYEYE METOAC MICMAC MIKMAK MOHAVE MOHAWK MUNSEE NASHUA NATICK NAUSET NAVAHO NAVAJO NEUTER NOOTKA OGLALA ONEIDA OREJON OTTAWA PAIUTE PAPAJO PATWIN PAWNEE PEORIA PEQUOD PEQUOT PIEGAN PODUNK PUEBLO QUAPAW QUERES RIKARI SALISH SAMISH SANTEE SAPONI SATSOP SENECA SHASTA SILETZ SIOUAN SIWASH SKAGIT SOKOKI SUMASS SUMDUM SUTAIO SYLVID TAPOSA TENINO TOHOME TOLOWA TONGAS TUNICA TUTELO UMPQUA WALAPI WAPATO WATALA WAXHAW WEANOC WIKENO WINTUN YAKIMA YAMASI ZUNIAN ABENAKI ALABAMA ALIBAMU AMERIND ANDARKO ANDASTE ARIKARA ATAKAPA AYAHUCA BANNOCK CAHOKIA CALOOSA CATAWBA CHILCAT CHILULA CHINOOK CHOCTAW CHUMASH CHUMAWI CIBECUE CLALLAM CLATSOP COCHITI COLCINE COWLITZ DEADOSE DHEGIHA DWAMISH ESSELEN GOSHUTE HELLELT HIDATSA HUCHNOM HUICHOL INGALIK JUANENO KANAWHA KLAMATH KOASATI KOHUANA KOPRINO KUNESTE KUTCHIN KUTENAI LUISENO MASHPEE MASKOKI MOHEGAN MOHICAN MONACAN MONSONI MONTAUK MOUSONI NANAIMO NASCAPI NATCHEZ NIANTIC NIMKISH NIPMUCK OJIBWAY PACIFID PADUCAH PAMLICO PICURUS QUAITSO SALINAN SANETCH SANPOIL SERRANO SHAPTAN SHAWANO SHAWNEE SIKSIKA SIUSLAW SONGISH SPOKANE SQUAXON STIKINE TAMAROA TESUQUE TIMUCUA TLINGIT TONKAWA TUALATI TULALIP TUTUTNI UGARONO WAILAKI WALPAPI WAMESIT WANAPUM WASHAKI WEWENOC WHILKUT WICHITA WISHOSK WITUMKI WYANDOT YANKTON YAQUINA YAVAPAI YOJUANE YONKALA ABSAROKA ACHOMAWI ACHUMAWI ALGONKIN AMERICAN AMOSKEAG APALACHI ARIVAIPA ARKANSAS ASTAKIWI ATFALATI ATSUGEWI CAHINNIO CAHUILLA CANARSIE CHAWASHA CHEHALIS CHEMAKUM CHEROKEE

CHEYENNE CHIMAKUM CHOPTANK CHOWANOC CLACKAMA COLUMBIA COLVILLE COMANCHE COQUILLE COYOTERO DELAWARE DIEGUENO ETCHIMIN FLATHEAD HITCHITI HUNKPAPA ILLINOIS IROQUOIS KALISPEL KAWAIISU KICKAPOO KIKATSIK KLASKINO KLIKITAT KONOMIHU LAMANITE MALECITE MASCOTIN MENOMINI MIKASUKI MINITARI MISSOURI MOGOLLON MUSCOGEE MUSKWAKI NEHANTIC NESPELIM NOTTOWAY OKINAGAN ONONDAGA PAMUNKEY PANAMINT PATUXENT PAVIOTSO PENACOOK PISHQUOW POWHATAN PUYALLUP QUATSINO QUERECHO QUILEUTE QUINAULT ROCKAWAY SAHAPTIN SAULTEUR SAVANNAH SEMINOLE SHIVWITS SHOSHONE SIHASAPA SINGSING SINKIUSE SINKYONE SINTSINK SISSETON SOUHEGAN SQUAMISH SQUEDUNK TLAKLUIT TOBIKHAR TOPINISH TSIHALIS TUSHEPAW TUSKEGEE UMATILLA WABANAKI WACHUSET WAHPETON WETUMPKA YAHUSKIN YAMACRAW DOUSTIONI SQUAWTITS
(BRAZILIAN —) BUGRE
(CANADIAN —) DENE COMOX HAIDA SLAVE TINNE DOGRIB HAISLA LASSIK MICMAC SARSEE BEOTHUK GOASILA KHOTANA KOYUKON CHISEDEC COWICHAN HEILTSUK KIMSQUIT KWAKIUTL LILLOOET SALTEAUX SHUSHWAP
(FEMALE —) SQUAW KLOOCH
(MALE —) BUCK SANNUP SIWASH
(MEXICAN —) MAM OVA CHOL CORA JOVA MAYA MAYO ROTO SERI TECA TECO XOVA AZTEC CHIZO CHORA HUABI HUAVE KAMIA NAHUA OPATA OTOMI YAQUI ZOQUE CAHITA CHOCHO CONCHO EUDEVE KILIWI NEVOME OTONIA PAKAWA TARASC TOLTEC ZOTZIL ACOLHUA AKWAALA AMISHGO CHATINO CHINCHA CHINIPA CHONTAL COTONAM COUHIMI GUASAVE HUASTEC HUAXTEC MAZATEC MISTECA MIXTECA NAYARIT SINALOA TEGUIMA TEHUECO TEPANEC TEPEHUA TZENTAL TZOTZIL ZACATEC ZAPOTEC CHANABAL CHAPANEC CHUCHONA COLOTLAN COMANITO CONICARI GUASAPAR HUASTECO IRRITILA JACALTEC JANAMBRE LACANDON LAGUNERO TARUMARI TECPANEC TEXCOCAN TEZCUCAN TOTONACO TZAPOTEC YUCATECO
(OTHER —) GE ITE ONA URO URU YAO AGAZ ANDE ANTA ANTI AUCA BABU CAME CANA CARA CHUJ COTO CUNA DENE DIAU DUIT INCA ITEN ITZA IXIL MOJO MOXO MURA MUSO MUZO PEBA PIRO RAMA TAMA TAPE TATU

TOBA TRIO TUPI TUPY ULUA ULVA ACROA ARARA ARAUA ARUAC AUETO BAURE BETOI BRAVO BUGRE CAITE CAMPA CANCA CARIB CHANE CHIMU CHITA CHOCO CHOKO CHOLA CHOLO CHONO COCTO COLAN CUEVA DIRIA GUANA GUATO HUARI JAVAH KASKA LENCA MOCOA MOZCA OPATA OYANA PALTA PAMPA PASSE PETEN PINTO PIOJE PIOXE PIPIL POKAN POKOM QUITU SENCI SIUSI SMOOS TAINO UAUPE UMAUA VEJOZ WAURA XINCA YAGUA YAMEO YUNCA YUNGA AGUANO AIMARA AKAVAI AKAWAI AMORUA ANDOKE ANTISI APANTO APARAI APIACA ARAWAK AROACO ATORAI AYMARA BABINE BANIVA BETOYA BORORO BRIBRI BRUNKA CAHETE CAIGUA CANCHI CANELO CARAHO CARAJA CARAYA CARIRI CAUQUI CAVINA CAYAPA CHAIMA CHARCA CHAYMA CHICHA CHISCA CHOCOI CHORTI COCAMA COCOMA COCORA COFANE COLIMA COTOXO CUCAMA CULINO CUMANA DOGRIB DORASK GALIBI GOYANA GUAIMI GUAQUE GUAYMI HUARPE HUBABO IGNERI INCERI IXIAMA JIVARO JUCUNA JUMANA JURUNA KARAYA KEKCHI KUCHIN LENGUA LUCAYO MACUSI MAKUSI MANGUE MANIVA MIRANA MUYSCA NAHANE NASCAN OMAGUA OTOMAC PAPAGO PKOMAM PURUHA QUICHE SABUJA SACCHA SALIBA SALIVA SAMUCU SEKANE SETIBO SIPIBO SUERRE TACANA TAGISH TAHAMI TAMOYO TAPAJO TAPUYA TARUMA TAUNA TICUNA TIMOTE TOTORO TUCANO TUNEBO UIRINA UITOTO VILELA WAIWAI WITOTO WOOLWA YAHGAN YAHUNA YARURO YURUNA ZAPARA ACHAGUA ACKAWOI AKAMNIK ANDAQUI ANGAITE APALAII APINAGE ARECUNA ARHUACO BEOTHUK BILQULA CACHIBO CAINGUA CALIANA CAMACAN CARANGA CARIBAN CARIBEE CARRIER CASHIBO CHARRUA CHIBCHA CHIMANE CHIMILA CHIRINO CHONCHO CHOROTE CHUMULU CHUNCHO CHURAPA CHUROYA CIBONEY CJACOGO COROADO FRENTON FUEGIAN GITKSAN GOAHIVO GOAJIRA GUAHIVO GUARANI GUARAYO GUARANY GUARRAU GUARUAN GUATUSO GUETARE HUANUCO HUATUSO ITONAMA JACUNDA JICAQUE KALIANA KOPRINO KULIANA LUCAYAN MAIPURE MISKITO MONGOYO MORCOTE NICARAO PAMPERO PAYAGUA PEDRAZA PIARROA POKOMAM PUELCHE PUQUINA QUECHUA QUEKCHI

RANQUEL SARIGUE SATIENO
SHUSWAP SINSIGA SIRIONE
TAHLTAN TALUCHE TALUHET
TAMANAC TARIANA TARRABA
TAYRONA TELEMBI TIMBIRA
TIRRIBI TSONECA UARAYCU
UCAYALE VOYAVAI WOYAWAY
YUSTAGA ZUTUHIL AGUARUNA
AHOUSAHT AKIYENIK ALACALUF
AMAHUACA APOLISTA ARAQUAJU
AWISHIRA BOTOCUDO CAINGANG
CALINAGO CANAMARY CANOEIRO
CAQUETIO CARIBISI CARIJONA
CARIPUNA CAYUBABA CHAMBOIA
CHANDALA CHAVANTE CHIQUITO
CHIRIANA COLORADO COMIAKIN
CONCHUCU CORABECA
CUSTENAU GUAYAQUI
GUAYCURU JAVITERO KANHOBAL
KLASKINO LOROKOTO MACARANI
MAYORUNA MISSKITO MOSQUITO
NIQUIRAN OCHOZOMA OROTINAN
PACAVARA PALENQUE
PARUKUTU PINALENO POIGUARA
POKONCHI POPOLOCO POTYUARA
PUPULUCA QUATSINO QUERENDY
QUIMBAYA SHIRIANA SNONOWAS
SUBTIABA TADOUSAC TAPACURA
TENAKTAK TOCOBAGA
TOROMONA TSATTINE
TUMUPASA UAREKENA
URUKUENA USPANTEC
YURUCARE
(SPANISH-AMERICAN —) CHOLO

INDIANA
CAPITAL: INDIANAPOLIS
COLLEGE: BALL BETHEL DEPAUW
GOSHEN MARIAN PURDUE
WABASH
COUNTY: JAY CASS CLAY KNOX
OWEN PIKE RUSH VIGO BOONE
FLOYD WELLS JASPER TIPTON
DAVIESS PULASKI
INDIAN: MIAMI HAWNEE
LAKE: MONROE MANITOU
WAWASEE MICHIGAN
NATIVE: HOOSIER
RIVER: OHIO WHITE WABASH
STATE BIRD: CARDINAL
STATE FLOWER: PEONY
STATE TREE: TULIP
TOWN: GARY PERU PAOLI VEVAY
ALBION ANGOLA BRAZIL
GOSHEN JASPER KOKOMO
MUNCIE SHOALS WABASH

INDIAN BEECH KURUNJ
INDIAN BREAD TUCKAHOE
INDIAN CORN KANGA MAIZE
CHOLUM JAGONG MEALIES
INDIAN FIG SABRA
INDIAN FISH FLATFISH
INDIAN GOOSEBERRY EMBLIC
INDIAN HEMP KEF KIF SANA
DAGGA SABZI AMYROOT
DOGBANE
INDIANIAN HOOSIER
INDIAN JALAP TURPETH
INDIAN LICORICE JEQUIRITY
INDIAN MADDER MUNJEET
INDIAN MALLOW SIDA DAGGA
PIEPRINT

INDIAN MILLET JONDLA
INDIAN MULBERRY AL AAL ACH
ALROOT
INDIAN PIPE FITROOT EYEBRIGHT
WAXFLOWER
INDIAN POKE ITCHWEED
INDIAN RED BOLE
INDIAN SHOT ALIIPOE
INDIAN TOBACCO GAGROOT
LOBELIA PUKEWEED SOURBUSH
INDIAN YELLOW PIOURY PURREE
INDIC (— LANGUAGE) URDU VEDIC
INDICATE RUN SAY BODY CITE
HINT LOOK MAKE MARK READ
SHOW ARGUE INDEX INFER POINT
PROVE SPEAK ALLUDE ATTEST
BETRAY DENOTE DESIGN EVINCE
FINGER IMPORT NOTIFY REVEAL
BESPEAK BETOKEN CONNOTE
DECLARE DISPLAY PORTEND
SIGNIFY SPECIFY ADMONISH
ANNOUNCE DECIPHER DISCLOSE
EVIDENCE MANIFEST OUTPOINT
REGISTER SIGNALIZE
(— BY SOUNDING) STRIKE
(— WILLINGNESS) AGREE
INDICATION BECK CLEW CLUE
HINT LEAD MARK NOTE SHOW
SIGN CURVE INDEX PROOF SCENT
TOKEN AUGURY BEACON INDICE
REMARK SAMPLE SIGNAL
AUSPICE MENTION PROFFER
SYMPTOM ALLUSION ARGUMENT
EVIDENCE MONITION MONUMENT
NOTATION SIGNANCE TELLTALE
(— OF APPROVAL) CACHET
(— OF CONTROL) COLLAR
(— OF LIGHT) AUREOLE
(— OF OFFICE) SEAL
(OBSCURE —) SHADOW
(VAGUE —) GLIMMER
(PL.) INDICIA
INDICATOR PIN HAND SIGN FLOAT
INDEX LITMUS SHOWER STYLUS
TARGET LACMOID POINTER
DETECTOR TELLTALE
(— OF BALANCE) COCK
(— OF HOUR) GNOMON
(ECONOMIC —) LAGGER LEADER
INDICIA POSTAGE
INDICT DITE CRIME PANEL ACCUSE
ATTACH CHARGE INDITE
ARRAIGN ARTICLE IMPEACH
TROUNCE WARRANT
INDICTMENT CHARGE DITTAY
INDIFFERENCE APATHY PHLEGM
ATARAXY DISDAIN ATARAXIA
COLDNESS EASINESS FROIDEUR
INDIFFERENT COLD COOL DEAD
DRAM EASY SOSO ALOOF BLASE
EQUAL SOBER CASUAL DEGAGE
FRIGID SUPINE CALLOUS
LANGUID NEUTRAL DETACHED
LISTLESS LUKEWARM MEDIOCRE
RECKLESS SUPERIOR UPSITTEN
APATHETIC
INDIFFERENTIST POLITIC
INDIFFERENTLY DRYLY HUMDRUM
INDIGENCE NEED WANT PENURY
BEGGARY POVERTY TENUITY
INDIGENE ENDEMIC
INDIGENOUS DESI
NATIVE DOMESTIC

HOMEBORN ABORIGINAL
INDIGENT POOR BEGGARLY
INDIGESTIBLE STUDGY
INDIGESTION APEPSY APEPSIA
DYSPEPSY
INDIGNANT ANGRY WROTH
ANNOYED UPTIGHT INCENSED
INDIGNATION IRE ANGER WRATH
DESPITE DISDAIN DUDGEON
JEALOUSY
INDIGNITY CUT SLUR SCORN
INSULT SLIGHT AFFRONT
OFFENCE CONTUMELY
INDIGO ANIL NILL SHOOFLY
(PREF.) INDI(CO)
INDIRECT SLY SIDE DEVIOUS
OBLIQUE CIRCULAR GLANCING
OVERHEAD OVERWART SIDELONG
SIDEWAYS SIDEWISE
ROUNDABOUT
(— WAY) AMBAGE
INDIRECTION CIRCUITY
INDIRECTLY SECONDHAND
INDIRECTNESS OBLIQUITY
INDISCREET RASH HASTY SILLY
WITLESS CARELESS HEEDLESS
INDISCRETION FOLLY FREDAINE
INDISCRIMINATE MIXED MINGLED
SWEEPING PROMISCUOUS
INDISCRIMINATELY PELLMELL
INDISPENSABLE NEEDFUL
CRITICAL
INDISPOSED ILL MEAN SICK ILLISH
UNWELL
INDISPOSITION AIL BRASH
MALADY AILMENT SICKNESS
(— TO MOTION) INERTIA
INDISPUTABLE SURE CERTAIN
EVIDENT MANIFEST POSITIVE
APODICTIC
INDISTINCT DIM DARK DULL HAZY
FAINT FUZZY INNER LIGHT MISTY
MUDDY SHADY THICK VAGUE
BLEARY CLOUDY DREAMY
INWARD SLURRY WOOLLY
BLEARED BLURRED OBSCURE
SHADOWY UNCLEAR NEBULOUS
(— IN UTTERANCE) CHOKING
INDISTINCTNESS BLUR
CONFUSION
INDITE PEN DITE DRAW
INDIVIDUAL GEE MAN ONE HEAD
SORT UNIT BEING MONAD THING
PROPER SINGLE SPIRIT VERSAL
APOMICT ATAVISM AZYGOTE
BIONTIC DIPLOID EIDETIC ISOLATE
MONADIC NUMERIC SEVERAL
SPECIAL EVERYONE IDENTITY
SEPARATE SINGULAR SOLITARY
SPECIMEN PERSONAGE
(COLOR-BLIND —) MONOCHROMAT
(COUNTRIFIED —) HOBNAIL
(DESPICABLE —) HEEL
(DULL —) BOEOTIAN
(FOOLISH —) SOP
(HAUGHTY —) POT
(IDENTICAL —) CLONE
(IMMATURE —) ADULTOID
(IMPUDENT —) BOLDFACE
(INDEPENDENT —) MAVERICK
(IRRITABLE —) SNAPPER
(LEADING —) KEY
(MOSAIC —) GYNANDER

(MUTANT —) SALTANT
(PHYSIOLOGICAL —) BION
(PROSAIC —) PHILISTINE
(ROUGH-LOOKING —) BOHUNK
(SKILLED —) ADEPT
(SLOVENLY —) GROBIAN
(STUPID —) HOBBIL
(TRICKY —) BILK
(UNDERSIZED —) KIT KITT
(WINGED —) ALATE
(YOUNG —) KID
(PL.) FRY
INDIVIDUALITY KA SEITY QUALITY
SELFDOM HECCEITY IDENTITY
SELFHOOD
INDIVIDUALIZE ATOMIZE
INDIVIDUALLY APART APIECE
SINGLY PROPERLY
INDIVIDUATION AHANKARA
INDIVISIBLE PUNCTUAL
INDO-CHINESE SERIFORM
INDOCTRINATE BRIEF INSTRUCT
INDO-EUROPEAN ARIAN ARYAN
JAPHETIC
INDOLE KETOLE
INDOLENCE SLOTH LANGUOR
IDLESHIP MUSARDRY SLUGGING
(— PERSONIFIED) LAURENCE
LAWRENCE
INDOLENT IDLE LAZY FAINT INERT
SWEER DROWSY OTIOSE SUPINE
DRONISH LANGUID WILSOME
FAINEANT INACTIVE LISTLESS
LOUNGING SLOTHFUL SLUGGISH
PICKTOOTH
INDO-MALAYAN (— TREE) SUPA

INDONESIA
CAPITAL: DJAKARTA
COIN: RUPIAH
GULF: BONE TOLO TOMINI
ISLAND: ALOR BALI BURU JAVA
CERAM IRIAN SUMBA WETAR
BAWEAN BORNEO BUTUNG
FLORES KOMODO LOMBOK
MADURA PELENG CELEBES
SALAJAR SUMATRA SUMBAWA
SULAWESI
ISLAND GROUP: EWAB SUNDA
BANJAK NATUNA ANAMBAS
MOLUCCA TABELAN SABALANA
LAKE: RANAU TOWUTI
LANGUAGE: BAHASA MALAYAN
MOUNTAIN: BULU NIUT RAJA
DEMPO MURJO NIAPA LEUSER
SLAMET MENJAPA OGOAMAS
SAMOSIR KATOPASA KERINTJI
MAHAMERU RINDJANI
TALAKMAU
MOUNTAINS: MULLER BARISAN
QUARLES SCHWANER
NATIVE: BUGI
PROVINCE: RIAU ATJEH DJAMBI
MALUKU LAMPUNG BENGKULU
RIVER: HARI MUSI DIGUL KAJAN
PAWAN BARITO KAMPAR
KAPUAS MAHAKAM
SEA: JAVA BANDA CERAM TIMOR
FLORES ARAFURA CELEBES
STRAIT: SUNDA LOMBOK
MAKASSAR
TOWN: PALU MEDAN MALANG
MANADO BANDUNG KENDARI

MAKASAR SEMARANG SURABAJA PALEMBANG SURAKARTA
VOLCANO: GEDE AGUNG DEMPO RAUNG MARAPI MERAPI SINILA SLAMET SUNDORO TAMBORA KERINTJE RINDJANI
WEIGHT: CATTY OUNCE THAIL

INDONESIAN NESIOT SADANG
INDOORS WITHIN
INDRA SAKKA SAKRA
INDUBITABLE SURE EVIDENT APPARENT MANIFEST UNIVOCAL
INDUCE GET DRAW LEAD MOVE URGE WORK ARGUE BRIBE BRING CAUSE IMPEL INFER TEMPT WEIGH ADDICT ADJURE ALLURE ENGAGE ENTICE IMPORT INCITE INVITE OBTAIN REDUCE SEDUCE SUBORN ACTUATE PREVAIL PROCURE PROVOKE SOLICIT MOTIVATE PERSUADE WIREDRAW
(— BY BRIBERY) FIX
INDUCEMENT MOTIVE REASON FEATURE PERSUASION
INDUCT STALL INSTAL INITIATE
INDUCTANCE HENRY
INDUCTION EPAGOGE
INDULGE PET BABY CADE CANT FEED GLUT ALLOW HUMOR JOLLY SPOIL TUTOR WALLY WREAK COCKER FOSTER PAMPER PETTLE DEBAUCH GRATIFY
(— IN PRIDE) PRIDE
(— TO EXCESS) PAMPER DEBAUCH SURFEIT
INDULGED CADE
INDULGENCE LAW BINGE FAVOR FOLLY MERCY SPREE EXCESS INDULT PARDON PATENT JUBILEE QUIENAL SURFEIT COURTESY DELICACY EASINESS GLUTTONY POCULARY
(SEXUAL —) LECHERY
INDULGENT FOND GOOD MEEK MILD SPOONY LENIENT TOLERANT
INDURATE HARDEN INDURE
INDURATED SCLEROID SCLEROUS
INDURATION SCLEROMA
INDUSTRIOUS BUSY DEEDY EIDENT STEADY OPEROSE PAINFUL DILIGENT SEDULOUS VIRTUOUS WORKSOME
INDUSTRY TOIL LABOR SCREEN VIRTUE CERAMICS SEDULITY
INDWELLING IMMANENT INHERENT
INE (WIFE OF —) AETHELBURH
INEBRIATE SOUSE EBRIATED
INEBRIATED DRUNK DRINKY
INEFFACEABLE INBURNT INDELIBLE
INEFFECTIVE DUD WEAK CLUMSY DREEPY FLABBY FUTILE FLACCID HALTING STERILE BUMBLING
INEFFECTIVELY ILL BADLY FEEBLY
INEFFECTUAL WAN DEAD IDLE TAME VAIN VOID JERKY FUTILE SPINDLY USELESS BOOTLESS FAINEANT FIDDLING NUGATORY
INEFFICIENT ILL LAME POOR

CLUMSY DOLESS ROTTEN UNABLE SLOUCHY USELESS FECKLESS HANDLESS
INELEGANT RUDE HOYDEN AWKWARD
INELOQUENT WANMOL
INEPT INAPT ABSURD AWKWARD FOOTLESS MALADROIT
INEPTITUDE PIFFLE
INEQUAL ROUGH
INEQUALITY ODDS CAHOT ANOMALY EVECTION IMPARITY NUTATION
INEQUITABLE HARD
INERADICABLE LASTING INDELIBLE PERMANENT
INERT DEAD DULL LAZY SLOW HEAVY NOBLE SULKY LEADEN SODDEN STUPID SUPINE TORPID PASSIVE INACTIVE INDOLENT LIFELESS SLOTHFUL SLUGGISH STAGNANT THEWLESS THOWLESS
INERTIA TAMAS
INESCAPABLE DEAD NECESSARY
INESTIMABLE SUMLESS PRICELESS
INEVITABILITY FINALITY
INEVITABLE DUE SURE DIRECT CERTAIN FATEFUL
INEXACT FREE ROUGH CLOUDY
INEXHAUSTIBLE INFINITE
INEXORABLE STERN STONY STRICT RIGOROUS
INEXPEDIENCY IMPOLICY
INEXPEDIENT UNWISE
INEXPENSIVE LOW CHEAP REASONABLE
INEXPERIENCED RAW PUNY CRUDE FRESH YOUNG UNSEEN KITLING STRANGE INEXPERT INSOLENT PRENTICE UNTRADED
INEXPERT ILL RUDE CRUDE GREEN SIMPLE
INEXPLICABLE FELL
INFAMOUS BASE RUDDY BLOODY NOTOUR ODIOUS BLEEDING FLAGRANT NIDERING SHAMEFUL NEFARIOUS OPPROBRIOUS
INFAMY STAIN BAFFLE DEFAME SHONDE DISHONOR IGNOMINY OPPROBRIUM
INFANCY CRADLE BABYHOOD
INFANT BABE BABY TINY WEAN CHILD MINOR PREMIE CHRISOM MILKSOP PREEMIE BALDLING BANTLING
(NAKED —) SCUDDY
(NEWLY-BORN —) NEONATUS
(VORACIOUS -) KILLCROP
INFANTILE BABYISH
INFANTRY FOOT FANTERIE FOOTFOLK
INFANTRYMAN ASKAR ZOUAVE DOGFACE DRAGOON DOUGHBOY PIOUPIOU SOREFOOT VOETGANGER
INFATUATE FOOL ASSOT BESOT
INFATUATED MAD FOND GONE ASSOT CRAZY DOTTY ENTETE ENGOUEE FOOLISH BESOTTED
INFATUATION ATE PASH RAVE CRUSH FOLLY BEGUIN
(TRANSIENT —) CRAZE
(SUFF.) (— FOR) MANE MANIA(C)

(— WITH) ITIS
INFECT SMIT TAINT CANKER DEFILE EMPEST ENTACH INFEST POISON CORRUPT DISEASE POLLUTE SMITTLE CONTAMINATE
INFECTED FUNGUSED
(NOT —) BLAND
INFECTION COLD DOSE SMIT FELON TAINT FUNGUS
INFECTIOUS TAKING SMITTLE CATCHING SMITABLE SMITTING VIRULENT
INFEFTMENT SASINE
INFER DRAW PICK TAKE GUESS JUDGE DECIDE DEDUCE DEDUCT DERIVE DIVINE GATHER INDUCE REASON COLLECT INCLUDE PRESUME SURMISE CONCLUDE CONSTRUE
INFERENCE EDUCT SEQUEL ANALOGY SEQUELA ILLATION SEQUENCE SEQUITUR OBSERVATION PRESUMPTION
INFERIOR BAD BUM DOG ILL JAY LOW OFF SAD EVIL LESS MEAN POOR PUNK SLIM SOUR WAFF BASER BAUCH BELOW CHEAP DOGGY GROSS LOUSY LOWER PETTY PLAIN SCALY SCRUB WORRY BEHIND CAGMAG COARSE COMMON CRAPPY FEEBLE FEMALE IMPURE LESSER MEASLY PALTRY PEDARY PUISNE PUISNY ROTTEN SECOND SHABBY SHODDY WOODEN BADDISH CRIPPLE HUMBLER NAGGISH POPULAR SCRUBBY SUBJECT ABNORMAL ANTERIOR DEROGATE ORDINARY PARAVAIL TERRIBLE
(PREF.) DEMI INFRA SUB
(SUFF.) ASTER EEN
(— ONE) LING
INFERIORITY LESSNESS MEANNESS
INFERNAL BLACK AVERNAL BLASTED ETERNAL HELLISH SATANIC SHEOLIC STYGIAN CHTHONIC DAMNABLE DEVILISH PLUTONIC PLUTONIAN
INFERTILE DEAD DEAF DOUR LEAN POOR THIN CLEAR STERILE
INFEST COE VEX BESET INFECT PESTER PLAGUE OVERRUN TORMENT
INFESTATION SCALE PLAGUE STRIKE MYIASIS LOAIASIS PEDICULOSIS
INFESTED MITY BLOWN BROOD BUGGY FLUKY FLUKED GRUBBY HAUNTED FLYBLOWN
INFIDEL DEIST KAFIR GIAOUR PAYNIM ATHEIST SARACEN SKEPTIC AGNOSTIC MISCREANT MISBELIEVER
INFIDELITY PERFIDY ADULTERY TRAHISON
INFIELD INTOWN DIAMOND
INFILTRATE FILTER CRETIFY COLONIZE
INFILTRATION SEEPAGE ADIPOSIS SATURATION
INFINITE CHAOS COSMIC ENDLESS ETERNAL IMMENSE
INFINITENESS ETERNITY

INFINITESIMAL PUNCTUAL
INFINITIVE SUPINE VERBID
(FRENCH —) ETRE
INFINITY OLAM ANANTA ETERNITY
INFIRM LAME WEAK ANILE CRAZY CRONK SHAKY CRANKY FEEBLE SICKLY UNFIRM UNSURE CASALTY CRAICHY DOWLESS DWAIBLE FRAGILE INVALID SAPLESS UNFEARY DODDERED FIRMLESS INSECURE RESOLUTE UNSTRONG
INFIRMITY WOE CRAZE DOTAGE FOIBLE UNHEAL DISEASE FAILING FRAILTY UNMIGHT DEBILITY SICKNESS WEAKNESS
INFIX INLAY INSET ENGRAVE IMPLANT INGRAIN
INFIXED INHERENT
INFLAME BURN FIRE GOAD HEAT STIR ANGER BLAIN FLAME SCALD SHAME AROUSE ENAMOR EXCITE FESTER IGNITE INCEND KINDLE MADDEN RANKLE EMBRASE FLUSTER INCENSE ESCHAUFE
INFLAMED RED ANGRY FIERY ABLAZE FRETTY TORRID FLAGRANT
INFLAMMABLE FIERY ARDENT TOUCHY PICEOUS TINDERY
INFLAMMATION ACNE FIRE ANGER FELON GLEET SCALD SEBEL AGNAIL ANCOME BLIGHT CANKER DEFLUX GREASE IRITIS CATARRH CECITIS CHAFING COLITIS COXITIS FISTULA GONITIS ILEITIS QUITTOR SUNBURN ADENITIS ANGIITIS AORTITIS BURSITIS CHILITIS CYCLITIS CYSTITIS SHINGLES
(SUFF.) ITIS
INFLATE HOVE HUFF KITE PLIM PUFF BLOAT BOLNE HEAVE SWELL DILATE EMBOSS EXPAND HUFFLE INBLOW TUMEFY BLADDER BOMBAST DISTEND FORBLOW OUTSWELL SUFFLATE
INFLATED TRIG BLOWN FLOWN GASSY PUFFY TUMID TURGID BOMBAST BULLATE FUSTIAN OROTUND STILTED SWOLLEN TURGENT BLADDERY OUTBLOWN TOPLOFTY TUMOROUS VANITOUS BOMBASTIC OVERBLOWN PLETHORIC
INFLATION FLATUS CADENCE TYMPANY
INFLECT COMPARE DECLINE
INFLECTION SIGN TONE ARSIS ACCENT FLEXION LATINISM MODULATION
INFLECTIONAL FORMAL
INFLEXIBILITY ACAMPSIA
INFLEXIBLE ACID DOUR FIRM HARD IRON EAGER SOLID STERN STIFF STONY STOUR SEVERE STRICT STUFFY ADAMANT RESTIVE GRANITIC IRONCLAD OBDURATE PREFRACT RESOLUTE RIGOROUS STIFFISH STUBBORN ADAMANTINE
INFLICT DO ADD PUT SET GIVE SEND INFER YIELD IMPOSE RAMROD STRIKE

(— CHASTISEMENT) WREAK
(— HURT) BRUISE
(— INJURY) AGGRIEVE
(— PAIN) LAY CHASTISE
INFLORESCENCE CHAT CYME
AMENT ARROW BRUSH SPIKE
UMBEL CORYMB FLOWER RACEME
SPADIX TASSEL BOSTRYX
PANICLE THYRSIS CYATHIUM
FASCICLE NUCAMENT
INFLOW INSET AFFLUX INCOME
INFLUX INCOURSE
INFLOWING AFFLUENT
INFLUENCE IN WIN BEND BIAS
COAX DRAG DRAW HAND HANK
HEFT LEAD MOVE PULL PUSH
RULE SUCK SWAY BRIBE CHARM
CLOUT COLOR ENACT FORCE
GRACE IMPEL MOYEN POWER
REACH SPELL VAPOR VOGUE
WEIGH AFFECT ALLURE CREDIT
EFFECT GOVERN IMPORT INDUCE
INFLOW INFLUX MOTIVE OBSESS
PONDUS SALUTE SHADOW
STROKE WEIGHT ACTUATE
ATTINGE ATTRACT BEARING
BEWITCH BLARNEY BOSSDOM
CAPTURE CONCUSS CONTROL
DISPUTE ENCHANT GRAVITY
IMPRINT INCLINE INSPIRE
MASTERY SUASION TENDRIL
DOMINION HEGEMONY INTEREST
LEVERAGE MEDICINE PRESTIGE
SANCTION STRENGTH CAPTIVATE
(— BY GIFTS) GREASE
(— CORRUPTLY) BRIBE
(— OF GODS) MANA
(— OF THE STARS) BLAS
(— UNREASONABLY) OBSESS
(ATTEMPT TO —) JAWBONE
(BENIGN —) UNCTION
(CONTROLLING —) SWAY
(CORRUPTING —) SMOUCH
SMUTCH
(DEPRESSING —) CHILL
(DIABOLICAL —) DEVILDOM
(DISRUPTIVE —) GREMLIN
(DOMINANT —) GENIUS STREAM
(DULLING —) DAMPER
(ELEVATING —) LIFT
(HARMFUL —) UPAS GRUDGE
(INJURIOUS —) RUST
(MALEVOLENT —) DISASTER
(MALIGN —) TAKING
(PERNICIOUS —) BALE BLAST
(SINISTER —) MALICE
(SOOTHING —) SALVE
(SURROUNDING —) AIR AMBIENCE
(UNDER — OF ALCOHOL OR DRUGS)
ZONKED
INFLUENCING INFUSIVE
INFLUENTIAL BIG GRAVE
POWERFUL
INFLUENZA FLU LEUMA GRIPPE
PINKEYE
INFLUX STORM INCOME INFLOW
INRUSH ILLAPSE
(— IN A MINE) COURSE
(— OF TIDE) INSET
INFOLD WRAP IMPLY TWINE
EMPLOY INWRAP ENVELOP
INVOLVE CONVOLVE
INFORM KEN BEEF BLOW FINK

NOSE POST SHOP SHOW TELL
WARN WISE LEARN PEACH
ADVISE ASSURE DELATE DETECT
NOTIFY PREACH SNITCH WITTER
APPRISE EDUCATE IMPEACH
INSENSE PARTAKE POSSESS
RESOLVE SIGNIFY SUGGEST
ACQUAINT DENOUNCE INFORMED
INSTRUCT SPARSILE
INFORMAL BREEZY CASUAL
CHATTY COMMON FOLKSY
TWEEDY INTIMATE SLIPSHOD
SOCIABLE NEGLIGENT OFFICIOUS
INFORMANT AUTHOR INFORMER
SYCOPHANT
INFORMATION AIR GEN OIL WIT
CLEW CLUE DOPE INFO LORE
NEWS NOTE TALE WIRE WORD
DATUM GRIFF SCOOP SKILL
ADVICE INSIDE LIGHTS NOTICE
APPRISE PEMICAN READOUT
TIDINGS WITTING BRIEFING
NOTITION PEMMICAN
(— ON VIDEO SCREEN) DISPLAY
(BODY OF —) DIGEST
(INCIDENTAL —) SIDELIGHT
(SECRET —) ARCANUM
(SUFF.) ANA IANA
INFORMED UP HEP WISE AWARE
WITTY KNOWING LEARNED
INFORMER FINK NARK NOSE PIMP
SPIV STAG RUSTY SNEAK SPLIT
BEAGLE CANARY FINGER SETTER
SNITCH TELLER DELATOR
STOOLIE TANQUAM APPROVER
PROMOTER SQUAWKER
SQUEAKER SQUEALER TELLTALE
INFORTUNE MARS SATURN
INFRACTION BREACH OFFENCE
TRESPASS
INFRARED ULTRARED
INFREQUENCY SELDOMCY
INFREQUENT RARE SELDOM
FUGITIVE UNCOMMON
INFRINGE IMPOSE INVADE TRENCH
IMPINGE INFRACT INTRUDE
ENCROACH REFRINGE TRESPASS
INFRINGEMENT FOUL BREACH
TRESPASS VIOLENCE
INFRINGER PIRATE
INFULA FANON LABEL LAPPET
HEADBAND
INFUNDIBULUM FUNNEL PAVILION
INFURIATE ENRAGE ENFELON
INFUSE DRAW MASK IMBUE IMMIT
SPOIL STEEP AERATE AERIFY
IMMISS INFLOW INFORM INFUND
INVEST LEAVEN BREATHE DISTILL
ENGRAIN IMPLANT INFOUND
INSPIRE INSTILL SUFFUSE
SATURATE
(— TEA) TRACK
(— WITH HATRED) TURN
INFUSED SHOT
INFUSION SHADE CARDIN INCOME
TISANE HORDEATE
(— OF MALT) WORT GROUT
(BITTER —) RUE
INFUSORIAN LEPOCYTE
INGA GUAVA
INGATE GATE LEDGE TEDGE
INGATHERING HARVEST
INGENIOUS SLY CUTE FAST FEAT

FINE ACUTE SHARP SMART WITTY
ADROIT BRAINY CLEVER CRAFTY
DAEDAL GIFTED KNACKY PRETTY
QUAINT SUBTLE CUNNING
POLITIC SKILLFUL
INGENUITY ART WIT ENGINE
ADDRESS COMPASS ARTIFICE
CONTOISE INDUSTRY QUENTISE
INGENUOUS FREE FRANK NAIVE
PLAIN CANDID HONEST SUBTLE
ARTLESS NATURAL SINCERE
INNOCENT
INGENUOUSNESS NAIVETE
INGEST EAT INCEPT ENGLOBE
SWALLOW
INGESTION SLURP
INGOT GAD SOW WEDGE LINGOT
NIGGOT CROPHEAD
(— OF BRASS) STRIP
(— OF SILVER) SHOE TING SCHUYT
(SILVER —S) SYCEE
(SOAKING —S) HEAT
INGRAIN GRAIN INFUSE ENFLESH
INGRAINED INWORN
INGRATE SNAKE
INGRATIATE FLATTER
INGRATIATING BLAND SILKY
SLEEK SLICK SOAPY SILKEN
SMOOTH
INGRATITUDE UNTHANK
INGREDIENT FACTOR AMALGAM
BINDING ELEMENT ADJUVANT
(ACTIVE —) ANIMA
(FUNDAMENTAL —) BASIS
(FUSIBLE —) BOND
(MAIN —) BASE
INGRESS ENTRY ENTRANCE
INGROWTH APODEMA
INGUEN GROIN
INHABIT BIG WIN WON COVER
DWELL HABIT OCCUPY BEDWELL
INDWELL POSSESS POPULATE
INHABITANT INMATE BURGHER
CITIZEN DENIZEN DWELLER
PEOPLER BORDERER CONFINER
DEMESMAN HABITANT INCOLANT
INHOLDER
(— OF ALASKA) SOURDOUGH
(— OF BORDER REGION) MARCHER
(— OF CITY) CIT CITIZEN
(— OF INDIA) BHARATA
(— OF JUNGLE) JUNGLI
(— OF SWISS ALPS) GRISON
(— OF TORRID ZONE) ASCIAN
(— OF VIRGINIA) COOHEE
(— OF WISCONSIN) BADGER
(EARTH —) TERRAN
(PL.) SIDE WARE
(SUFF.) COLA ITE OT OTE
INHABITING
(SUFF.) COLE COLINE COLOUS
INHALATION SNUFF BREATH
(PREF.) ANEM(O)
INHALE DRAW TAKE SMOKE SNIFF
SNUFF ATTRACT BREATHE
INHAUST INSPIRE RESPIRE
ASPIRATE
(— A DRUG) SNORT
(PREF.) INSPIRO
INHALER SNIFTER
INHARMONIOUS ABSURD RUGGED
ABSONANT
INHERE CONSIST INEXIST

INHERENCE INBEING
INHERENT KIND INBORN INNATE
INWARD NATIVE PROPER INGENIT
HABITUAL IMMANENT INTEGRAL
INTERNAL RESIDENT
INHERIT HEIR SUCCEED
INHERITANCE KIND ENTAIL
HEIRDOM HEIRSHIP HEREDITY
HERITAGE LANDFALL VACANTIA
(— OF CATTLE) ERF
(PARTICULATE —) MENDELISM
INHERITED INBORN INNATE
CONGENITAL
(SUFF.) CLINOUS CLINY
INHIBIT COOP CURB SNUB CRIMP
DETER FORBID STIFLE SUPPRESS
INHIBITED COLD
INHIBITION AKINESIS
INHIBITOR PARGYLINE
PHENELZINE
INHIBITORY COLYTIC
INHOSPITABLE STERN DESERT
INHUMAN FELL CRUEL BRUTAL
FIERCE IMMANE SAVAGE BESTIAL
MANLESS DEVILISH KINDLESS
INHUMANE WANTON
INHUMANITY CRUELTY
INHUME BURY INTER ENTOMB
INIMICAL BAD FROSTY HOSTILE
INIQUITOUS ILL DARK WRONG
SINFUL WICKED NEFARIOUS
INIQUITY SIN EVIL VICE CRIME
GUILT DARKNESS MISCHIEF
INITIAL LETTER VIRGIN ASPIREE
PRINCIPAL
(INTERWOVEN —S) CIPHER
(PL.) PERFINS
INITIATE HEAD MYST OPEN ADEPT
ADMIT BEGIN BREAK ENTER
EPOPT FOUND START GROUND
INDUCE INDUCT INVENT LAUNCH
MYSTES ORPHIC BAPTIZE INSTALL
INSTATE OPERATE ORPHEAN
SYMMIST YTIGGER COMMENCE
ESOTERIC INCHOATE ORIGINATE
INITIATION DIKSHA OPENING
ENTRANCE
(— OF GROWTH) BUDBREAK
INITIATIVE PEP LEAD GETUP
ACTION AMBITION GUMPTION
OVERTURE
INJECT DRIVE IMMIT
(— DRUGS) MAINLINE
INJECTION JAG HYPO SHOT
BOOSTER CLYSTER INSERTION
INJUDICIOUS UNWISE
INJUDICIOUSNESS ACRISY
INJUNCTION HEST BEHEST
CHARGE IMPOSE RUBRIC BIDDING
DICTATE EXPRESS MANDATE
PRECEPT
INJURE DO GAS ILL MAR BURN
CHEW DERE ENVY GALL HARM
HURT MAUL TEAR TEEN WERD
ABUSE BLAST CRAZE DIRTY
MISDO RIFLE SCALD SHEND
SMITE SPOIL STEER WOUND
WRONG BRUISE DAMAGE DEFACE
DEFECT DEPAIR GRIEVE HINDER
IMPAIR INJURY MANGLE NOBBLE
PUNISH RANKLE SCATHE SCOTCH
STRAIN AFFLICT AFFRONT
CONTUSE DAMNIFY DESPITE

FORWORK MISBEDE TERRIFY
AGGRIEVE DISASTER DISSERVE
FORSLACK IMPERISH INTERESS
MISCHIEF MISGUIDE MUTILATE
PREJUDGE SPURGALL
(— BY ASPERSION) SPATTER
(— BY FALSE REPORT) SLANDER
(— BY GLANCE OF BASILISK) STRIKE
(— BY TREADING UPON) FITTER
(— SCENT) STAIN
(— SERIOUSLY) DO KILL SPOIL
(— SLIGHTLY) ANNOY
(— THE BACK) CHINK
(— WITH GRENADE) FRAG
(SEVERELY —) WASTE
INJURED HURT LESED BLASTED
INJURIOUS BAD ILL EVIL NOCENT
NOYANT NOYFUL SHREWD
ABUSIVE HARMFUL HURTFUL
NOXIOUS SCADDLE DAMAGING
GRIEVOUS SINISTER TORTIOUS
TORTUOUS WRACKFUL
WRONGFUL PERNICIOUS
INJURIOUSLY HEAVILY
INJURY ILL JAM MAR BALE BANE
BURN EVIL HARM HURT JEEL
LOSS RUIN SCAT TEEN TORT
WITE ABUSE BLAME CHAFE
CRUSH GRIEF SCALD SCORE SPITE
SPOIL TOUCH WATHE WRACK
WRONG BREACH BRUISE DAMAGE
DANGER IMPAIR LESION SCATHE
STRAIN STROKE TRAUMA
BEATING DESPITE EXPENSE
OFFENSE OUTRAGE PAYMENT
SCADDLE SCRATCH SORANCE
BUSINESS CASUALTY CREPANCE
INTEREST MISCHIEF NUISANCE
(— OF HORSES) TREAD CREPANCE
(— OF PLANTS) SUNSCALD
(CHIEF —) FOCUS
(SERIOUS —) MAYHEM
INJUSTICE WRONG INJURY
INJURIA UNRIGHT HARDSHIP
INEQUITY
(GROSS —) INIQUITY
INK BEAT COLOR ARNEMENT
ATRAMENT
(PRINTER'S —) CYAN
INK-BALL DABBER PUMPET
INKER SLOSHER
INKING PAD TOMPION
INKLE SPINEL
INKLING HINT ITEM SCENT
GLIMMER GLIMPSE UMBRAGE
INKSTAND STANDISH
INKWELL FOUNT INKSTAND
INKY BLACK ATRAMENTOUS
INLAID PIQUE CONTISE
(— WORK) KOFTGARI
INLAND MAUKA INMORE INWARD
MIDLAND INTERIOR
INLAY PICK PIKE COUCH HATCH
INLET PIQUE SPELL CRUSTA
ENAMEL IMPAVE INDENT NIELLO
TARSIA ENCHASE ENCRUST
INCRUST COMMESSO
INLAYING TARKASHI
INLET ARM BAY CUT GEO RIA VOE
COVE DOCK HOPE MERE SLEW
WICK BAYOU BRACE CHUCK
CREEK FIORD FJORD FLEET
HAVEN LOGAN LOUGH STOMA

ESTERO HARBOR INFALL SLOUGH
TONGUE DOGHOLE INDRAFT
SUCTION CALANQUE SEAPOOSE
(— OF THE SEA) EA
(MUDDY —) SUMP
(TIDAL —) GAP
INLIER WINDOW
INLYING INNERLY
INMATE FISH LODGER TENANT
BEADSMAN DOMESTIC PRISONER
INMOST SECRET RETIRED
INN PUB KHAN STOP VENT ANGEL
FONDA HOTEL MESON TAMBO
VENTA CABACK HARBOR HOSTEL
HOSTRY IMARET POSADA PUBLIC
SHANTY ALBERGE AUBERGE
BOLICHE CAFENEH CAFENET
FONDACO FONDOUK HOSTAGE
LOCANDA OSTERIA SOJOURN
SURAHEE CHOULTRY GASTHAUS
HOSTELRY ORDINARY SERAGLIO
WAYHOUSE ROADHOUSE
INNARDS GIZZARD INWARDS
STUFFING
INNATE BORN KIND INBORN
INBRED CONNATE INGRAIN
NATURAL INSTINCT
(— QUALITY) LARGESS
INNER BEN ENTAL INSIDE INWARD
INWITH MENTAL INTERIOR
INTERNAL PECTORAL
(— LIGHT) SEED
(PREF.) ENT(O) ESO
(— PARTS OF BODY) BATHY
INNER MONGOLIA (CAPITAL OF —)
HOHHOT HUHEHOT
INNERMOST UPPER INMOST
MIDMOST INTIMATE
INNINA ISHTAR
INNING END HAND HEAD FRAME
(PL.) KNOCK WICKET
INNKEEPER HOST DUENA TAPPER
VENTER GOODMAN HOSTESS
HOSTLER PADRONE BONIFACE
(PL.) CAUPONES
INNOCENCE BLUET WHITE
CANDOR PURITY SIMPLICITY
INNOCENT SOT FREE NAIF PURE
CANNY CLEAR NAIVE SEELY SILLY
WHITE CHASTE DOVISH HONEST
SIMPLE CHRISOM LAMBKIN
UPRIGHT ARCADIAN HARMLESS
IGNORANT PASTORAL PRIMROSE
SACKLESS UNGUILTY ZACCHEUS
INNOCUOUS HARMLESS INNOCENT
INNOVATE NOVELIZE
INNOVATION NOVEL NOVELTY
INNOVATOR HERETIC
INNUENDO HINT SLUR SLIPE
INNUMERABLE MYRIAD
NUMBERLESS
INO (BROTHER OF —) POLYDORUS
(FATHER OF —) CADMUS
(HUSBAND OF —) ATHAMAS
(MOTHER OF —) HARMONIA
(SISTER OF —) AGAVE SEMELE
AUTONOE
(SON OF —) LEARCHUS PALAEMON
MELICERTES
INOCULATE SEED PLANT INFUSE
ENGRAFT EQUINATE
INOCULATION JAG
INOCULUM STAB STREAK

INOFFENSIVE HARMLESS
INOPERATIVE OFF DEAD
NUGATORY
INOPPORTUNE UNTIMELY
INORDINATE WILD UNDUE
ENORMOUS
INORGANIC MINERAL
INOSITOL DAMBOSE
INPOURING INFLUX
INQUEST CROWN QUEST ASSIZE
OFFICE INQUIRY
INQUIET UNEASY
INQUILINE GUEST
INQUIRE ASK AXE SEEK QUERY
SPERE DEMAND FRAYNE SEARCH
EXAMINE HEARKEN QUESTION
INQUIRER ASKER QUERENT
INQUIRY PROBE QUERY THANK
TRIAL DEMAND EXAMEN TRACER
DOCIMASY QUESTION RESEARCH
SCRUTINY SPEERING
INQUISITION CUSTOM INQUIRY
QUAESTIO
INQUISITIVE NOSY PEERY PRYING
CURIOUS MEDDLING QUIZZICAL
INROAD RAID BREACH INBREAK
INVASION
INSALUBRIOUS NOXIOUS
INSANE MAD WUD DAFT WOOD
BALMY BATTY BUGGY CRAZY
DIPPY QUEER WRONG CRANKY
LOCOED SCREWY FLIGHTY
FRANTIC FURIOUS LUNATIC
WITLESS BUGHOUSE DEMENTED
DERANGED DISTRACT
INSANITY RAGE CRACK CRAZE
FOLIE MANIA FRENZY LUNACY
MADNESS VESANIA DELIRIUM
DEMENTIA WOODNESS
ACROMANIA PSYCHOSIS
INSATIABLE GREEDY
INSCRIBE DELVE ENTER WRITE
BLAZON DOCKET ENDOSS INDITE
LEGEND LETTER SCRIBE SCRIVE
SCROLL ASCRIBE ENDORSE
ENGROSS DEDICATE DESCRIBE
EMBLAZON ENSCROLL INTITULE
INSCRIBED INWRIT WRITTEN
DESCRIPT
INSCRIPTION HEAD ELOGY
CACHET LEGEND LETTER
ELOGIUM EPIGRAM EPITAPH
MENTION TITULUS WRITING
COLOPHON EPIGRAPH GRAFFITO
INSCRIPT SCRIBING
(— ON ROCK) PETROGLYPH
(— ON TOMBSTONE) ELOGE
ELOGIUM
(3-LETTER —) TRIGRAM
INSCRUTABLE EQUIVOCAL
MYSTERIOUS
INSECT ANT BEE BUG DOR DUN
ELF FLY NIT ANER FLEA GNAT
GOGO GYNE MOTH PELA PEST
PUPA SPIT WASP WETA ZIMB
APHID APHIS BICHO BORER FLYER
GOGGA GUEST IMAGO LOUSE
MINER ROACH SCALE BEETLE
BLIGHT CALLOW CICADA CIXIID
EARWIG EMBIID HAWKER HOPPER
INSTAR MANTIS NITTER PODURA
PSOCID SAPPER SAWFLY THRIPS
VERMIN WALKER WEEVIL

ATTACUS BLATTID BOATMAN
BRUMMER BUZZARD CRAWLER
CREEPER CRICKET CYNIPID
DEALATE DRUMMER EARWORM
FIREBUG FIREFLY GALLFLY
GIRDLER GRAYFLY HEXAPOD
JAPYGID KATYDID PHASMID
SANDBOY SCINIPH SKIPPER
SPECTRE STAINER STYLOPS
TERMITE VAGRANT WEBWORM
ALDERFLY ALKERMES BLACKFLY
BRACONID DIPTERAN FIREBRAT
FULGORID GLOWWORM
HOMOPTER HORNTAIL LACEWING
LECANIUM MEALYBUG
PRONYMPH SEMIPUPA SEXUPARA
SPHECOID STINKBUG STYLOPID
SYMPHILE
(PART OF —) EYE CLAW COXA
WING FEMUR TIBIA CERCUS
LABRUM PALPUS TARSUS
THORAX ABDOMEN ANTENNA
OCELLUS MANDIBLE SPIRACLE
OVIPOSTOR PROTHORAX
TYMPANIUM MESOTHORAX
METATHORAX OVIPOSITER
TROCHANTER
(PREF.) ENTOM(O)
(SUFF.) CORIS
INSECTICIDE DDD DDT DIP CUBE
FLIT MIREX NALED TIMBO ALDRIN
DERRIS ENDRIN RONNEL
CALOMEL ISODRIN LINDANE
MENAZON OVICIDE PHORATE
CHLORDAN CULICIDE DIELDRIN
FENTHION NICOTINE ROTENONE
SCHRADAN ANTRYCIDE
MALATHION PARATHION
PYRETHRUM
INSECTIVORE AGOUTA DESMAN
MOONRAT ALAMIQUI
INSECURE DICKY EEMIS LOOSE
SHAKY INFIRM TICKLE UNFAST
UNSAFE UNSURE CASALTY
INSEMINATE BREED
INSENSATE SURD FATUOUS
INSENSIBILITY DAMP APATHY
STUPOR TORPOR
INSENSIBLE DEAD DULL LOST
NUMB BRUTE DENSE MARBLE
SEARED WOODEN DATELESS
APATHETIC
INSENSITIVE DEAD BLUNT STONY
OBTUSE STUPID BOORISH
INSEPARABLE WRAPPED
INSERT SLIP SPUD STOP BOTCH
DICKY ENROL ENTER FUDGE
IMMIT INFER INFIX INLET INSET
STUFF COLLET GUSSET INWORK
INWEAVE GATEFOLD INTROMIT
SANDWICH SLASHING SUBTRUDE
THROWOUT
(— IN SHOE) CUSHION
(SKIRT —) GORE
(— SURREPTITIOUSLY) FOIST
INSERTION FLOWER BEADING
INSET GODET INSERT
(DRESS —) MOTIF
INSHEATHE EMBOSS
INSIDE IN BEN ATHIN INBYE INNER
INWITH KEYHOLE INTERIOR
(— OF ANGLE BAR) BOSOM
(— OF OUTER EAR) BUR BURR

(PREF.) END(O)
INSIDIOUS SLY SNARY COVERT SUBTLE GUILEFUL
INSIGHT KEN SIGHT APERCU THEORY NOSTRIL
INSIGNIA TYPE ORDER SIGNS COLLAR GEORGE CADUCEUS COMMENDA HERALDRY OPINICUS PONTIFICALS
INSIGNIFICANCE NOTHINGNESS
INSIGNIFICANT NULL POOR PUNY DINKY FOOTY PETIT PETTY POTTY SCRUB SMALL HUMBLE NAUGHT PALTRY PUISNE SIMPLE SLIGHT FOOLISH NAUGHTY NIFLING NOMINAL PELTING PIMPING SCRUBBY TENUOUS TRIVIAL BAUBLING INFERIOR PEDDLING PITIABLE SNIPPING TRIFLING TRIPENNY
INSINCERE FALSE DOUBLE FEIGNED ARTIFICIAL
INSINCERITY ARTIFICE DISGUISE
INSINUATE HINT MINT WIND CRAWL SCREW TWIST ALLUDE GLANCE INFUSE INSTIL WRITHE IMPLANT INNUATE
INSINUATING SNIDE SILKEN SMARMY
INSINUATION HINT INKLING
INSIPID DRY WAW DEAD FADE FLAT FOND FOZY LASH TAME BANAL BAUCH BLAND FLASH INANE PROSY STALE VAPID WALSH WAUGH FLASHY FRIGID JEJUNE SWASHY THREEP WAIRSH WALLOW EXOLETE FATUOUS INSULSE MAWKISH PROSAIC SAPLESS SHILPIT WEARISH WEERISH LIFELESS UNSAVORY WATERISH
INSIST AVER PRESS THREAP CONSIST
(— PEEVISHLY) CRAIK
(— UPON) SOLICIT
INSISTENCE URGENCY INSTANCY
INSISTENT LOUD ADAMANT INSTANT EMPHATIC FRENZIED IMPOSING
INSOLE CUSHION SLIPSOLE
INSOLENCE GUM CHEEK PRIDE SNASH HUBRIS DISDAIN AUDACITY SURQUIDY CONTUMELY PETULANCE
INSOLENT FACY PERT RUDE WISE BARDY BRASH LUSTY PROUD CHEEKY LORDLY WANTON ABUSIVE DEFIANT PAUGHTY ARROGANT IMPUDENT PETULANT SCORNFUL AUDACIOUS
INSOLUBLE HOPELESS
INSOMNIA AHYPNIA AGRYPNIA
INSOUCIANT CAVALIER
INSPECT SEE VET CASE ESPY LOOK BRACK CHECK SIGHT VISIT INLOOK PERUSE SURVEY EXAMINE OVERSEE CONSIDER OVERLOOK OVERVIEW
(— CASUALLY) BROWSE
(— COINS) SHROFF
(— MERCHANDISE IN BALTIC) BRACK
INSPECTION EYE PRY VIEW CHECK

SIGHT REVIEW SURVEY BEDIKAH CHECKUP INSIGHT INSPECT PERUSAL VIDIMUS OVERHAUL OVERVIEW SCRUTINY
(— OF CLOTH) ALNAGE
INSPECTOR SAYER SNOOP BISHOP CENSOR CONNER JUMPER LOOKER VIEWER GRAINER MOOCHER PERCHER SAMPLER SNOOPER VEADORE EXAMINER SEARCHER
(— OF COAL) KEEKER
(— OF COTTON LOOMS) TACKLER
(— OF ELECTRIC LAMPS) AGER
(ECCLESIASTICAL —) EXARCH
INSPIRATION FIRE SIGH POESY ANIMUS SPIRIT SPRITE IMPULSE MADNESS PEGASUS AFFLATUS AGANIPPE INFLATUS
(— IN ORATORY) HWYL
INSPIRE FIRE MOVE CHEER ELATE EXALT SPARK BEACON INBLOW INCUSS INDUCE INFORM INFUSE KINDLE PROMPT ACTUATE ANIMATE EMBRAVE ENFORCE ENLIVEN HEARTEN IMPLANT PREMOVE QUICKEN SUGGEST CATALYZE ENTALENT INSPIRIT MOTIVATE SUFFLATE
INSPIRED VATIC AFFLATED DAEMONIC ENTHEATE VISIONED
INSPIRER SOUL
INSPIRING INFUSIVE SPLENDID STIRRING
INSPIRIT CHEER HEART ROUSE SPIRIT ANIMATE CHERISH COMFORT ENLIVEN HEARTEN INSPIRE QUICKEN ALACRIFY
INSPISSATE STIFFEN THICKEN
INSPISSATED STIFF THICK
INSTABILITY SLIDDER FLUIDITY
INSTALL SEAT CHAIR STALL INDUCT INVEST ENSTOOL POSSESS ENTHRONE INITIATE
INSTALLATION INDUCTION
(— OF MINISTER) INFARE
(MILITARY —) GARRISON
INSTALLMENT KIST SERIAL EARNEST CONTRACT
(— OF SERIAL) HEFT
(— OF WAGES) COMPO
(— SELLER) TALLYMAN
(FIRST —) HANDSEL
(NEXT —) SEQUEL
INSTANCE CASE PINK SAMPLE EXAMPLE PURPOSE ENSAMPLE EXEMPLAR
(EXTREME —) CAPSHEAF
INSTANT POP HINT WHIP WINK BLICK CLINK CRACK FLASH GLENT GLIFF GLISK JIFFY POINT SHAKE SOUND START TRICE WHIFF WIGHT BREATH FLIFFY MINUTE MOMENT SECOND PRESENT CLIFFING
(PRECISE —) TIME
INSTANTANEOUS PRESTO DIRECTLY
INSTANTANEOUSLY OUTRIGHT
INSTANTLY SLAP SWITH PRONTO SWITHE DIRECTLY MOMENTLY
INSTAR STAGE
INSTEAD EITHER

(PREF.) ANTI PRO
INSTEP WRIST TARSUS
(PREF.) PEDI(O)
INSTIGATE EGG ABET GOAD MOVE SPUR URGE IMPEL ATTICE ENTICE EXCITE FOMENT INCITE INDUCE INVOKE PROMPT SPIRIT SUBORN ACTUATE INCENSE INSTINCT
INSTIGATION MOTION MOTIVE EGGMENT INSTANCE INSTINCT
INSTIGATOR AUTHOR MOTIVE SOURCE MONITOR
INSTILL GRAFT INFIX IMPART INFUSE INSTIL BREATHE IMPLANT
INSTINCT KIND FILLED NATURE CHARGED IMPULSE CAPACITY TENDENCY
INSTINCTIVE INNATE NATURAL INHERENT ORIGINAL
INSTITUTE BEGIN BRING ERECT FOUND RAISE STUDY FOMENT INVENT KINDLE ORDAIN ACTIVATE
(— MEMBER) PIARIST
INSTITUTION BANK CAMP FOLD CLINIC FRIARY SCHOOL ACADEMY CHARITY COLLEGE GALLERY JUBILEE LIBRARY SHELTER STATION VERITAS SEMINARY ORPHANAGE OBSERVATORY PENITENTIARY
(— FOR HOMELESS CHILDREN) PROTECTORY
(— FOR INSANE) ASYLUM
(CHARITABLE —) SPITTLE DEACONRY HOSPITAL
(DRUIDICAL —) GORSEDD
INSTRUCT KEN REAR SHOW WISE BREED COACH DRILL EDIFY ENDUE GUIDE TEACH TRAIN CHARGE DIRECT GROUND INDUCE INFORM LESSON PREACH REFORM SCHOOL COMMAND EDUCATE INSENSE POSSESS ADMONISH DOCUMENT
(— BEFOREHAND) PRIME
INSTRUCTED SCIENCED
INSTRUCTION LORE ADVICE ASSIZE CHARGE LESSON COUNSEL PRECEPT TUITION WISSING COACHING DOCTRINE DOCUMENT MONITION PEDAGOGY PROPHECY TEACHING TUTELAGE
(COMPUTER —) MACRO
(DIVINE —) LAW
(SACRED —) TORAH
(SERIES OF COMPUTER —S) LOOP
(PL.) BRIEF BRIEFING
INSTRUCTIVE DOCENT DIDACTIC
INSTRUCTOR DON SOAK SCREW TUTOR MENTOR REGENT ACHARYA CRAMMER MONITOR TEACHER BEACHBOY CHAIRMAN ELDERMAN
INSTRUMENT (ALSO SEE MUSICAL INSTRUMENT) DEED TOOL WRIT AGENT SLANG THEME FACTUM UTENSIL SYNGRAPH
(— FOR ACQUIRING KNOWLEDGE) ORGANON
(— NOT UNDER SEAL) PAROL
(— OF DESTRUCTION) SWORD
(— OF DIVINATION) EPHOD

(— OF TORTURE) BOOT RACK BRAKE BRANK FURCA GADGE WHEEL TUMBREL BARNACLE SQUEEZER SCARPINES PILLIWINKS
(—S OF WAR) ENGINERY
(CALCULATING —) ABACUS
(FINANCIAL —) ITEM
(LEGAL —) DEED GRANT FACTUM SASINE SCRIPT CHARTER CODICIL DUPLICATE
(METEOROLOGICAL —) LIDAR
(NEGOTIABLE —) HUNDI HOONDEE
(OFFICIAL —) SLANG
(PREHISTORIC —) CELT
(SCIENTIFIC OR OTHER —) AWL FAN HOE KEY MET RAX SAX BROG CLAM COMB DIAL DRAG FILE FORK GAGE HOOK PALM PLOW RACK RING SPAR ARMIL BEVEL BLADE BRACE BRAKE CHAIN CLAMP CORER DATER DOLLY DRILL FLAIL FLOAT FLUKE GAUGE GLASS INDEX KNIFE LADLE LEVER METER MISER PILOT RAZOR SCALE SCOPE SLATE SLICE SLING SPADE SPEAR SPRAY STAMP STEEL SWIFT THROW TONGS TUNER WHISK ABACUS BEATER BEETLE BODKIN BRIDGE CHOWRY CIRCLE DOUCHE ENGINE ERASER FERULE FOLDER GRATER LEAPER MORTAR NEEDLE PALLET PESTLE PICKER PLOUGH PULLER PUMPER RAMMER RASPER RATTLE RUBBER SCALER SCORER SCRIBE SCUTCH SCYTHE SHEARS SQUARE SQUIRT STADIA STRAIK STROBE STYLET STYLUS TACKLE TICKER WIMBLE ALIDADE BELLOWS BREAKER CADRANS CLEAVER COMPASS DIOPTER DOLABRA DOUBLER FISTUCA GRAFTER GRAINER GRAPPLE HATCHEL LAYOVER MASSEUR MEASURE OOMETER OOSCOPE PAVIOUR PELORUS PIERCER PINCERS PRICKER PRINTER PYROPEN QUADRAT SCRAPER SEXTANT SHOCKER SHUTTLE SLITTER SOUNDER SPLAYER SPRAYER STRIGIL SUNDIAL SWINGLE TRAMMEL TRIMMER WHISTLE ANALEMMA ATOMIZER BARNACLE BIRDCALL BLOWPIPE BUTTERIS CALLIPER COALRAKE DECAPPER DETECTOR DIAGRAPH DIPMETER DIVIDERS EQUULEUS ERGMETER EXPLORER FATHOMER GEOPHONE HOROLOGE IMPLUM IRISCOPE ISOGRAPH ISOSCOPE JOVILABE MESOLABE MHOMETER ODOMETER OHMMETER PHOTOMER QUADRANT RECORDER RINGHEAD RUMMAGER SCISSORS SEARCHER SQUEEGEE STILETTO STRICKLE TJANTING TRIANGLE VELLINCH VIAGRAPH YAWMETER
(SURGICAL OR MEDICAL —) GAG HOOK SPUD FLEAM PROBE SCALA SCOOP SNARE SOUND STAFF STYLE BILABE BOUGIE BROACH GORGET LANCET SEEKER TREPAN

TROCAR UNGULA VECTIS XYSTER
AGRAFFE AIRDENT DILATER
FORCEPS HARPOON LEVATOR
LIGATOR MYOTOME PELICAN
PLUGGER RONGEUR SCALPEL
SOUNDER SYRINGE TRACTOR
TRILABE TURNKEY ANOSCOPE
AURILAVE AXOMETER BISTOURY
DIRECTOR DIVULSOR ECRASEUR
ELEVATOR EXSECTOR HEMOSTAT
KERATOME MYOGRAPH
SPECULUM TREPHINE
(VOID —) NULLITY
(PREF.) (POINTED —) SCOLO
(WIND —) AEOLO
(SUFF.) LABE METER
METR(E)(O)(Y) STAT(IC)
(MUSICAL —) INA
(SURGICAL REMOVAL —) ECTOME
INSTRUMENTAL MEDIATE
ORGANIC SERVILE SERVIENT
MINISTERIAL
INSTRUMENTALIST KLEZMER
SIDEMAN
INSTRUMENTALITY HAND MEANS
AGENCY MEDIUM CHANNEL
COUNCIL MINISTRY
**(— FOR ACQUISITION OF
KNOWLEDGE)** ORGANON
(NAVAL —S) BEACH
INSUBORDINATE FACTIOUS
MUTINOUS UNWIELDY
INSUBORDINATION MUTINY
INSUBSTANTIAL AIRY INANE
FROTHY SLENDER SPECTRAL
INSUBSTANTIALITY FRAILTY
INSUFFICIENCY PAUCITY
(PREF.) OLIG(O)
INSUFFICIENT POOR WANE SHORT
SCANTY
INSUFFICIENTLY BARELY FEEBLY
THINLY
INSULATE ISLE ISLAND ISOLATE
INSULATION LAGGING ISOLATION
INSULATOR NOB KNOB CLEAT
TAPLET VITRITE MEGOHMIT
STANDOFF
(PL.) STRING
INSULT CAG FIG JOEY RUMP SLAP
SLUR ABUSE CHECK FLOUT
FRUMP SLANG INJURE INJURY
OFFEND OUTRAY RUFFLE SCRAPE
ABUSION AFFRONT OFFENCE
OUTRAGE BRICKBAT DISHONOR
CONTUMELY
INSULTING RUDE ABUSIVE
ARROGANT INSOLENT
INSULTINGLY FOULLY
INSURANCE LINE CHOMAGE
COVERAGE INDEMNITY
(— AGENT) TWISTER
(UNEMPLOYMENT —) DOLE POGEY
INSURE COVER ASSURE ENSURE
FURNISH
INSURER ABANDONEE
INSURGENT REBEL RISER CHOUAN
OAKBOY TAIPING BARRABAS
CAMISARD STEELBOY
INSURRECTION RIST MUTINY
REVOLT UPROAR OUTBREAK
SEDITION UPRISING REBELLION
INSURRECTO GUGU
INTACT SOUND WHOLE

ENTIRE MAIDEN
(PREF.) INTEGRI
INTAGLIO ENTAIL DIAGLYPH
(PART OF —) INCAVO
INTANGIBLE VAGUE SUBTLE
AERIFORM SLIPPERY
INTEGER SUM NORM TOTITIVE
INTEGRAL FLUX NEEDFUL
INTEGRANT ELEMENT
INTEGRATE FUSE PIECE COMBINE
FULFILL ORGANIZE
INTEGRATED FUSED INTEGRAL
INTEGRATION BALANCE
HARMONY
INTEGRITY HONOR TRUTH
HONESTY JUSTICE PROBITY
CHASTITY STRENGTH SINCERITY
INTEGUMENT KEX ARIL PILL SKIN
TESTA TUNIC SWATHE CUTICLE
ENVELOP EPIDERM EXODERM
PRIMINE TUNICLE VELAMEN
EPISPERM PERISARC SCABBARD
SECUNDINE
(PREF.) SCYT(O)
(SUFF.) DERM(A)(ATOUS)(IA)(IS)(Y)
INTELLECT MIND NOUS HEART
INWIT MAHAT SKILL BRAINS
NOTICE REASON SPIRITS
THINKING
(HIGHEST —) NOUS
INTELLECTUAL BLUE GAON IDEAL
BOOKSY BRAINY NOETIC SOPHIC
BRAHMIN EGGHEAD GNOSTIC
CEREBRAL LONGHAIR SOPHICAL
DIANOETIC SPIRITUAL
INTELLIGENCE AIR CIT SAT CHIT
KNOW MIND NEWS NOTE NOUS
WORD AGIEL SAVVY SENSE
ADVICE BRAINS ESPRIT INGENY
NOTICE PSYCHE WITTING
MENTALITY
(— IN EGYPTIAN LORE) CHU
(— OF PLANET JUPITER) JOPHIEL
(LACKING —) VACUOUS
(LIVELY —) WIT
INTELLIGENT APT GASH PERT
ACUTE ALERT SMART SPACK
AKAMAI BRAINY BRIGHT CLEVER
MENTAL SHREWD SPRACK
WITFUL KNOWING INFORMED
LUMINOUS RATIONAL SKILLFUL
INTELLIGENTSIA CLERISY
INTELLIGIBLE CLEAR PLAIN
LUMINOUS PELLUCID PERVIOUS
REVELANT PERCEIVABLE
INTELLIGIBLY SIMPLY
INTEMPERANCE ACRASY EXCESS
ACRASIA OUTRAGE
INTEMPERATE SHRILL SURFEIT
(NOT —) SWEET
INTEND GO AIM FIX CAST MEAN
MIND MINT PLAN PLOT TEND
ALLOT ALLOW ETTLE TIGHT
ATTEND DESIGN RECKON
BEHIGHT DESTINE FORELAY
PRETEND PROPOSE PURPORT
PURPOSE FOREMIND MEDITATE
PRETENSE
INTENDED ON SUPPOSED
INTENSE HOT ACID COLD DEEP
HARD HIGH KEEN BLANK DENSE
GREAT HEAVY QUICK SHARP
TENSE VIVID ARDENT BRAZEN

FIERCE INTENT PITCHY SEVERE
STRONG BURNING CHARGED
CHRONIC CUTTING EXTREME
FERVENT FRANTIC FURIOUS
VICIOUS VIOLENT EGYPTIAN
GRIEVOUS POWERFUL PROFOUND
SEETHING TERRIFIC VEHEMENT
INTENSELY STIFF HIGHLY ACUTELY
CURSEDLY FERVIDLY MORTALLY
SHREWDLY
INTENSIFICATION
(PREF.) DE
INTENSIFIED ACUTE
INTENSIFY RISE URGE EXALT
RAISE ACCENT DEEPEN BOLSTER
ENFORCE ENHANCE IMPROVE
INFLAME MAGNIFY SHARPEN
THICKEN CONDENSE HEIGHTEN
INCREASE REDOUBLE
INTENSION INTENT MEANING
INTENSITY EDGE HEAT ARDOR
DEPTH DRIVE FEVER FIELD VIGOR
ACCENT DEGREE DOSAGE FERVOR
FRENZY STRESS CURRENT
FEROCITY STRENGTH VIOLENCE
(— OF DISEASE) ACUITY
(— OF EMOTION) ARDENCY
INTENSIVE HARD HIGH EXTENDED
INTENSIVELY HARD SOLIDLY
INTENT SET DEEP DOLE FELL HENT
MIND RAPT TENT BEADY CAUSE
DRIFT ETTLE FIXED HEART PRICK
SCOPE TENOR TENSE EFFECT
SPIRIT COUNSEL INTENSE
PRESENT PURPOSE STUDIED
WISTFUL
(CRIMINAL —) DOLE
(EVIL —) DOLUS
INTENTION AIM END GOAL HENT
MIND VIEW WILL HEART SCOPE
ANIMUS ATTENT DESIGN DEVICE
EFFECT INTENT OBJECT REGARD
COUNSEL COURAGE EARNEST
FORESET MEANING PROPOSE
PURPORT PURPOSE SUPPOSE
THOUGHT PRETENSE OBJECTIVE
(CRIMINAL —) DOLE
INTENTIONAL SET WILLFUL
WILLING WITTING INTENDED
INTENTLY BUSILY WISHLY
EAGERLY FIXEDLY
INTER BURY EARTH ENTER GRAVE
PLANT ENTOMB INHUME
INEARTH
INTERACTION COUPLING
INTERAGENT MEDIUM MIDDLER
INTERBREED CROSS
INTERBREEDING APOGAMY
MIXTURE PANMIXY CROSSING
INTERCALATE INSERT
INTERCALATION EMBOLISM
INTERCEPT KEP HEAD KEEP STOP
CATCH NORMAL ABSCISS
TRAMMEL GAINCOPE INTERPEL
RETRENCH
INTERCEPTION CUTOFF
INTERCESSION MOYEN DIPTYCH
PLEADING
INTERCESSOR MEANS PLEADER
ADVOCATE MEDIATOR
INTERCHANGE CHANGE ANAGRAM
COMMUTE PASSAGE PERMUTE
COMMERCE EXCHANGE

(— OF OPINION) COUNSEL
(— OF WORDS) SPEECH
(PREF.) TRANS
INTERCHANGEABLE FUNGIBLE
INTERCHANGED CROSS
INTERCOLUMNIATION EUSTYLE
SYSTYLE DIASTYLE
INTERCOMMUNICATION LIAISON
INTERCONNECTED SYNDETIC
INTERCONNECTION BONDING
INTERCOURSE GAM DEAL MANG
MONG TRADE TRUCK TURGY
BAWDRY HOBNOB NEGOCE
COITION DEALING MIXTURE
QUARTER SOCIETY TRAFFIC
BUSINESS COMMERCE CONVERSE
RECOURSE RELATIONS
INTERDICT BAN TABU TABOO
FORBID UTRUBI INHIBIT PROHIBIT
SUPPRESS
INTERDICTION VETO
INTEREST BUG DIP FAD USE BENT
GOOD HAND HOLD PART CLOSE
COLOR DRIVE FAVOR FETCH
GAVEL HOBBY RENTE RIGHT
STAKE STUDY USAGE USURA
USURY BEHALF ENGAGE EQUITY
ESTATE FAENUS FERVOR FINGER
INCOME USANCE ATTRACT
CONCERN RESPECT USAUNCE
CONTANGO INCREASE VIGORISH
(— OF HUSBAND) CURTESY
(— ON LAND) CLOSE
(ACTIVE —) SYMPATHY
(EXORBITANT —) JUICE
(LEGAL —) EASEMENT
(POLITICAL —) FENCE
(SECURITY —) LIEN
(SPECIAL —) MEAT ANGLE
INTERESTED HIPPED ENGAGED
SERIOUS CONCERNED
(— IN) INTO
INTERESTING FRUITY CURIOUS
PIQUANT STORIED ABSORBING
INTERFERE CUT MAKE ANNOY
BLOCK CHECK HITCH POACH
BAFFLE HAMPER HINDER HOBBLE
IMPEDE MEDDLE STRIKE TAMPER
INTRUDE INTROMIT
(— SLIGHTLY) BRUSH
(— WITH) AIL JOLT MESS CROSS
HECKLE BLANKET DISTURB
INTERFERENCE BALK CHOKE
THUMP HINDER JOSTLE MEDDLE
CONFLICT FREINAGE
INTERFERING CUT
INTERFEROMETER ETALON
INTERFLUVE DOAB
INTERGROWTH PERTHITE
INTERIM BREAK VACANCY
INTERIOR BEN BELLY BOSOM
INNER ENTIRE INLAND INWARD
INWITH MIDDLE GIZZARD
ENTRAILS INTERNAL
(— OF CUPOLA) CALOTTE
(— OF TEMPLE) CELLA
(— OF VESSEL) HOLD
(— PART) MANTLE
INTERJECT POKE ENTER SQUIB
INJECT THRUST
INTERJECTION (ALSO SEE OATH)
AW ER HA LO BAH COO FIE GEE
GIP GUP HAH HEH HEY OOH

AHEM AHOY ALAS ANAN CHUT
EGAD FORE GOSH HECH HOLA
JOVE ODSO OOPS OUCH PISH
ADIOS ALACK ARRAH FAUGH
GOODY HEIGH MAFEY MARRY
MUSHA OHONE PROST PSHAW
SUGAR TENEZ ATWEEL BARLEY
CRIKEY CRIPES EUREKA HARROW
OUTCRY PHOOEY PROSIT
CARAMBA CRIMINE LACKADAY

INTERLACE LACE WARP BRAID
WEAVE ENLACE PLEACH ENTRAIL
INWEAVE WREATHE
INTERLACED BRACED FRETTED
PLEACHED
INTERLACEMENT KNOT
INTERLACING RETE TWINY
INTERLINING DOUBLER
INTERLOCK KNIT LOCK MESH
PITCH ENGAGE FINGER TANGLE
DOVETAIL
INTERLOPE INTRUDE
INTERLUDE JIG JEST LETUP
COMEDY VERSET TEMACHA
TRIUMPH ANTIMASK ENTRACTE
ENTREMES RITORNEL VERSETTE
PARENTHESIS
(OPERATIC —) RITORNELLO
(ROMANTIC —) IDYL IDYLL
INTERMEDDLER STRANGER
INTERMEDDLING GESTION
INTERMEDIARY MEAN AGENT
MOYENER MEDIATOR TRAMPLER
MIDDLEMAN
INTERMEDIATE MEAN MESNE
FILLER ISATIN MEDIAL MEDIUM
MIDDLE NEUTRAL MIDDLING
(PREF.) MEDI MES(O)
INTERMEDIATOR BROKER
INTERMENT BURIAL BURYING
DEPOSIT HUMATION
INTERMINABLE ETERNAL INFINITE
TIMELESS UNENDING
INTERMINGLE MIX BRAID
COALESCE IMMINGLE INTERMIT
INTERMIX
INTERMINGLED AMONG AMONGST
INTERMINGLING
(SUFF.) MIXIS
INTERMISSION REST WAIT BREAK
DWELL PAUSE DEVALL RECESS
NOONING RELACHE RESPITE
INTERVAL SURCEASE VACATION
(— OF FEVER) APYREXIA
(— OF PAIN) SABBATH
INTERMISSIVE CESSANT
INTERMIT CEASE DEFER DEVAUL
SUSPEND
INTERMITTENT BROKEN FITFUL
PERIODIC
INTERMIX BLEND MEDLEY MINGLE
INTERMIXTURE CROSS INTIMACY
INTERNAL INLY INNER ENTIRE
INLAND INNATE INSIDE INWARD
DOMESTIC
(PREF.) INTRA
INTERNALLY INLY INSIDE INWARD
INWARDLY
INTERNODE ROSETTE
INTERPELLATION FLOWER
INTERPENETRATED SHOT
INTERPLAY AUSPICE
INTERPOLATE FARCE FARSE FOIST

FUDGE INSERT THRUST
INTERPOLATION GAG FARSE
INTERPOSE BAR CHOP POKE
DEMUR OBJECT THRUST THWART
MEDIATE
INTERPRET MAKE OPEN READ
SCAN TAKE AREAD AREED FANCY
GLOSS GLOZE RECHE DEFINE
DIVINE INTEND CLARIFY
COMMENT DECLARE ENGLISH
EXPLAIN EXPOUND CONSTRUE
DECIPHER SIMPLIFY
INTERPRETATION REDE GLOSS
SENSE GOSPEL STRAIN ANAGOGE
BARAITA COMMENT DOBHASH
EPIKEIA MEANING CABALISM
EXEGESIS INNUENDO MOONSHEE
SOLARISM SOLUTION
INTERPRETER BROKER DUBASH
UNDOER EXEGETE LATINER
MUNCHEE CABALIST DRAGOMAN
EXPONENT LINKSTER TRUCHMAN
(— OF SCRIPTURE) TROPIST
(PL.) HAHAM SELLI SELLOI
CHOCHEM HAKAMIM
INTERRELATED INTIMATE
INTERRELATIONSHIP ACCORD
LIAISON COMMERCE
INTERROGATE ASK TARGE
DEBRIEF EXAMINE INQUIRE
INTERROGATION EROTESIS
QUESTION
INTERROGATORY EROTETIC
INTERRUPT CUT MAR NIP CHOP
STOP TAKE BREAK CHECK CRACK
EMBAR ARREST DERAIL DERANGE
DISRUPT FORBREAK INTERMIT
INTERPEL OBSTRUCT
INTERRUPTED BROKEN CHOPPY
SNATCHY
INTERRUPTER BUZZER
INTERRUPTION CESS JUMP STOP
BLOCK BREAK CHECK DWELL
LAPSE PAUSE BREACH HIATUS
HOCKET HOQUET ISLAND
OUTAGE CAESURA CUTBACK
DIASTEM BLOCKING BREAKAGE
SOLUTION STOPOVER
(WITHOUT —) FLUSH
INTERRUPTOR TIKKER BREAKER
CHOPPER RHEOTOME
INTERSECT CUT CROSS BISECT
INCISE CROSSCUT
INTERSECTING CRUCIAL
COMPITAL
INTERSECTION LEET CHINE CROSS
CURVE CHIASMA CROSSING
CROSSWAY JUNCTION
INTERSEXUAL EPICENE
INTERSEXUALITY GYNANDRY
INTERSPACE SPACE POCKET
INTERSPERSE DOT SALT SHED
MEDDLE THREAD CHECKER
INTERSOW SPRINKLE
INTERSTICE PORE SEAM CHINK
GRATE SPACE AREOLA AREOLE
RIFFLE CELLULE VACUITY
(PL.) CANCELLI
INTERSTRATIFY INTERBED
INTERTWINE KNIT LACE WARP
TWINE FELTER TANGLE WAMPLE
WARPLE WRITHE ENSNARL
COMPLECT IMPLEACH INTERTEX

INTERTWINED INWOUND
INTERTWIST RADDLE
INTERVAL GAP LAG CENT GULF
REST SAND SEXT SPOT STEP
BLANK BREAK COMMA CYCLE
FIFTH LAPSE PRIME QUINT SIXTH
SPACE SWING TENTH THIRD
BREACH DECIMA DEGREE DIESIS
DITONE FOURTH MERLON
SECOND SLATCH SYSTEM
ADVANCE DIASTEM DISCORD
HEADWAY HEMIOLA INTERIM
PASTIME RESPITE SCHISMA
SETTIMO STADIUM TRITONE
DIAPASON DIAPENTE DISTANCE
ELEVENTH ENTRACTE FONTANEL
INTERACT MICROTONE
PARENTHESIS
(— BETWEEN FINGERS) SUBVOLA
(— BETWEEN ROPE STRANDS)
CONTLINE
(— OF BRIGHTNESS) FLICKER
(— OF FAIR WEATHER) SLATCH
(— OF HARSH WEATHER) SNAP
(— OF SEMITONE) APOTOME
(— OF TIME) WINDOW
(REST —) SOB
(SHORT —) STREAK
(TIME —) HEADWAY
INTERVALE BOTTOM
INTERVENE CHOP STEP STRIKE
MEDIATE OBVIATE STICKLE
INTERCUR
INTERVENING MESNE MIDDLE
MEDIANT
(PREF.) INTER
INTERVIEW BUZZ CONTACT
AUDIENCE CONGRESS
INTERWEAVE MAT PLAT CRISP
PLAIT PLASH PLEACH RADDLE
TANGLE WATTLE ENTWINE
TEXTURE TRELLIS COMPLECT
ENTANGLE IMPLEACH INTERTEX
INTERWEAVING BREDE CROWN
INTIMATE
(— OF INITIALS) CIPHER
INTERWOVEN INWOVEN IMPLICIT
INTIMATE
INTESTINAL INNER ENTERAL
ENTERIC SPLANCHNIC
INTESTINE GUT ROPE BOWEL
INNER THARM INWARD MIDDLE
THAIRM
(PORTION OF —) JEJUNUM
(PL.) VISCUS INGANGS CHITLINS
(PREF.) COL(O) ENTER(O)
INTHROW RIDGE
INTIMACY LIAISON PRIVACY
AFFINITY CHUMMERY GOSSIPRY
INTRIGUE MUTUALITY
(UNDUE —) LIBERTY
INTIMATE SIB BOON GRIT HINT
HOME HOMY KIND NEAR NEXT
PACK TOSH BOSOM CHIEF CLOSE
GREAT HOMEY PALLY PRIVY
THICK ALLUDE ENTIRE FRIEND
HOMELY INTIME INWARD NOTICE
SECRET STRAIT STRICT THRANG
THRONG CHAMBER CLOSEUP
GREMIAL INNERLY INNUATE
KEYHOLE PRIVADO PRIVATE
SIGNIFY SPECIAL SUGGEST
COCKMATE ESPECIAL FAMILIAR

FREQUENT FRIENDLY INDICATE
INTIMADO
(MOST —) MIDMOST
(PL.) FOLKS
INTIMATELY INLY NEAR TOSH
WELL COZILY CLOSELY INWARDLY
INTIMATION CUE HINT ITEM
WARN WIND SCENT NOTICE
OFFICE GLIMMER INKLING
CIRCULAR INNUENDO MONITION
INTIMIDATE COW HAZE ABASH
BULLY COWER DAUNT DETER
PSYCH HECTOR PSYCHE TERRIFY
BROWBEAT BULLDOZE BULLYRAG
FRIGHTEN
INTO IN INTIL WITHIN
(PREF.) IL IM IN INTRO IR
INTOLERABLY PLAGUY
INTOLERANCE BIGOTRY
INTOLERANT CLOSED BIGOTED
INTONATION FALL ITALICS
INTONE CANT SING TONE CHANT
CHAUNT ENTUNE MODULATE
CANTILLATE
INTOXICANT BOZA
INTOXICATE FOX TIP TOX CORN
FLAW GOOF SOAK TODDY
FUDDLE MUDDLE SOZZLE SPRING
TIPSIFY DISGUISE OVERTAKE
SPRINKLE
INTOXICATED CUT FAP LIT WET
HIGH LUSH RIPE SHOT SOSH TOFT
TOSY BOSKY BUFFY DRUNK
FRESH FRIED FUNNY HEADY
LACED NAPPY PIPED TIGHT
BLOTTO BOILED GROGGY LOADED
LOOPED MELLOW PIPPED QUAINT
SCREWY SKEWED SLEWED
SLOPPY SODDEN SOSHED SOZZLE
STEWED TANKED UPPISH UPPITY
ZONKED EBRIATE EXALTED
FLECKED JINGLED POTSHOT
SCREWED SLOPPED SMASHED
SPIFFED SQUIFFY UNSOBER
BESOTTED COCKEYED DELEERIT
ELEVATED OVERSEEN OVERSHOT
PLEASANT SQUIFFED TEMULENT
TOXICATE
INTOXICATING HARD HEADY
STARK HUFFCAP
INTOXICATION WINE FUDDLE
IVRESSE LOCOISM DISGUISE
EBRIOSITY TEMULENCE
(— OF ANIMALS) DUNZIEKTE
INTRACTABLE BAD HARD SALTY
STACK SURLY FIERCE KITTLE
SULLEN THWART UNRULY
CRABBED HAGGARD RESTIVE
ROPABLE WAYWARD CHURLISH
INDOCILE MUTINOUS OBDURATE
PERVERSE SHREWISH
INTRADOS SOFFIT
INTRANSITIVE NEUTER
INTREPID BOLD BRAVE HARDY
HEROIC PRETTY SAVAGE
DOUGHTY VALIANT RESOLUTE
INTREPIDITY GAME COURAGE
INTRICACY KNOT INTRIGUE
INTRICATE HARD MAZY BLIND
DAEDAL IMPLEX KNOBBY KNOTTY
SUBTLE TANGLY TRICKY
COMPLEX CRABBED CURIOUS
GORDIAN PERPLEX PUZZLED

SINUOUS INVOLUTE INVOLVED ANFRACTUOUS

INTRIGUE PLOT ANGLE CABAL CLOAK STORY AFFAIR AMOUNT BRIGUE DECEIT SCHEME CONNIVE FACTION FINAGLE JOBBERY TRINKET TRINKLE ARTIFICE CHEATING COLLOGUE PRACTICE PRACTISE STRATEGY TRIPOTER

INTRIGUER JESUIT SCHEMER DESIGNER TRINKETER

INTRIGUING EXCITING SCHEMING

INTRINSIC REAL TRUE INBORN INBRED INNATE INWARD NATIVE GENUINE NATURAL ABSOLUTE IMMANENT INHERENT INTERNAL INTIMATE

INTRINSICALLY PERSE PROPERLY

INTRODUCE READ DEBUT ENTER FRONT IMMIT INFER PLANT START USHER BROACH HERALD INDUCE INDUCT INFUSE INJECT INSERT INVECT INVOKE LAUNCH PREFER FORERUN IMPLANT INSTILL INVEIGH PRECEDE PREFACE PRELUDE PRESENT SHUFFLE SPONSOR ACQUAINT INNOVATE INTROMIT WIREDRAW (— **AIR INTO**) AERATE (— **AS FIRST ACT**) INITIATE (— **FROM WITHOUT**) IMPORT (— **SURREPTITIOUSLY**) FOIST

INTRODUCTION LASSU PROEM PRONE INTRADA INTROIT ISAGOGE MENTION PREFACE ENTRANCE EXORDIUM PREAMBLE PROLOGUE PRELUSION (— **INTO STOMACH**) GAVAGE (— **OF DRAMA**) PROTASIS (— **OF NOVELTY**) CHANGE (**MUSICAL** —) INTRO INTRADA OVERTURE (SUFF.) PHORESIS

INTRODUCTORY EXORDIAL ISAGOGIC LIMINARY PROTATIC SYSTATIC PRELUSIVE PRELIMINARY

INTROIT REQUIEM

INTRORSE ANTICAL

INTROSPECTION INLOOK REFLEX

INTRUDE JET ABATE BARGE CRASH POACH BOTHER CHISEL INGYRE INJECT INVADE IRRUPT THRUST AGGRESS OBTRUDE ENCROACH INFRINGE TRESPASS

INTRUDER INTRUS INCOMER INVADER STRANGER

INTRUSION INVASION

INTRUSIVE NOSY FRESH NOSEY SPURIOUS (PREF.) XEN(O)

INTUITION HUNCH PRESAGE INSTINCT

INTUITIONIST EIDETIC

INULIN ALANTIN

INUNDATE FLOW DROWN FLOOD INUND SWAMP DELUGE OVERFLOW SUBMERGE SURROUND

INUNDATION FLOW FLOOD WATER DELUGE ALLUVIO FRESHET ALLUVION FLOODAGE OVERFLOW

INURE URE BREAK ENURE STEEL HARDEN SCHOOL SEASON ACCUSTOM INDURATE ACCLIMATIZE

INVADE ASSAIL INTRUDE ENCROACH INTRENCH TRESPASS

INVADER HUN PICT

INVADING INGRUENT

INVAGINATION GULLET

INVALID BAD BUM NULL CHRONIC NUGATORY

INVALIDATE UNDO AVOID BREAK CANCEL INFIRM IMPROVE INVALID VITIATE

INVALUABLE COSTLY PRECIOUS PRICELESS

INVARIABLE STEADY UNIFORM CONSTANT

INVARIABLENESS ONENESS

INVARIABLY EVER ALWAYS

INVASION RAID INROAD DESCENT INBREAK INJURIA

INVECTIVE ABUSE HOKER SATIRE RAILING DIATRIBE REPROACH

INVEIGH RANT INVECT DECLAIM DENOUNCE

INVEIGLE COAX ROPE WILE CHARM DECOY SNARE ALLURE ENTICE SEDUCE

INVENT COIN FIND FORM MINT VAMP FEIGN FRAME FRUMP CREATE DESIGN DEVISE IDEATE CONCOCT CONJURE CONTRIVE DISCOVER

INVENTED MADE

INVENTION FANCY DEVICE FINDAL NOTION FANTASY FICTION FIGMENT FORGERY WITCRAFT (**DRAMATIC** —) IBSENISM

INVENTIVE ADROIT FERTILE CREATIVE MECHANIC ORIGINAL PREGNANT

INVENTIVENESS WIT ARTIFICE

INVENTOR TALOS COINER FINDER FRAMER MINTER CREATOR MINTMAN ENGINEER ARTIFICER **AMERICAN** LEE BELL COLT FELT GRAY HALL HOWE HUNT IVES LAND LOWE OTIS READ WOOD ADAMS ALLEN BLAKE BROWN DAVIS EARLE EVANS FIELD FITCH GIBBS HYATT LOCKE MCKAY MOODY MOREY MORSE NOYES PRATT TESLA WHITE BENDIX BORDEN BORTON BOYDEN CAHILL CHURCH CLYMER CURTIS DURYEA EDISON FOLMER FRENCH FULTON GARAND GAYLEY GORDON GORRIE HAMLIN HAYNES HORGAN HUGHES HUSSEY JANNEY JUDSON PORTER SAXTON SHOLES SINGER SPERRY WESSON WILCOX WILSON ACHESON APPLEBY BABBITT BETHELL BIGELOW BRADLEY CORLISS EASTMAN GODFREY HAMMOND HOLLAND JENKINS KNOWLES LANSTON PERKINS PULLMAN SELLERS STEVENS TAINTER WHITNEY BACHRACH BERLINER BIRDSEYE BOGARDUS BUSHNELL DEFOREST ELLSBERG ERICSSON GILLETTE GOODYEAR

WATERMAN BURROUGHS BUTTERICK DRAWBAUGH HOTCHKISS MCCORMICK HERRESHOFF WESTINGHOUSE **AUSTRIAN** KEMPELEN **BELGIAN** BAEKELAND **DUTCH** DREBBEL **ENGLISH** KAY MOON WATT MILLS SMITH AYRTON BRUNEL DONKIN GURNEY HOLDEN LISTER BESEMER BURGESS GAUDENS MORLAND MURDOCK STARLEY CROMPTON STURGEON ACKERMANN APPLEGATH ARKWRIGHT ARMSTRONG HEATHCOAT WHITWORTH CARTWRIGHT HARGREAVES STEPHENSON **FRENCH** FOUCHE GIRARD LENOIR MONIER PROGIN DAGUERRE DELSARTE JACQUARD CHASSEPOT MONTGOLFIER **GERMAN** DREYSE MAUSER FLETTNER **GREEK** CTESIBIUS ARCHIMEDES **IRISH** BRENNAN **ITALIAN** MARCONI **NORWEGIAN** KRAG **SCOTTISH** BARR WATT BAIRD DUNLOP MILLER GREGORY NEILSON TWADDELL SYMINGTON **SWEDISH** DALEN POLHEM **SWISS** VETTERLI

INVENTORY BILL LIST STOCK ACCOUNT INVOICE TERRIER ANAGRAPH DATABASE REGISTER SCHEDULE

INVERSE (PREF.) OB

INVERSION WALDEN CHIASMUS ENTROPION (— **OF STITCHES**) PURL

INVERT CANT TURN REVERT REVERSE

INVERTASE SUCRASE

INVERTED AWKWARD

INVEST DON DUB PUT BELT FUND GARB GIFT GIRD GIRT GOWN LOCK SINK VEST WRAP BELAY BLOCK ENDOW ENDUE FEOFF INDUE CLOTHE EMBODY ENROBE FORSET OCCUPY ORDAIN BESIEGE COMPASS ENFEOFF ENVELOP INSTATE OBSERVE BENEFICE BLOCKADE SURROUND (— **ONESELF**) COVER ASSUME (— **WITH**) INFEFT (— **WITH AUTHORITY**) SCEPTER ACCREDIT (— **WITH ENERGY**) CATHECT (— **WITH SOVEREIGN DIGNITY**) ENTHRONE (SUFF.) (— **WITH ATTRIBUTES OF**) FY IFY

INVESTED GARTERED

INVESTIGATE SPY SIFT CHECK PROBE SOUND STUDY EXCUSS FATHOM SEARCH DISCUSS EXAMINE EXPLORE INQUIRE INDAGATE SCRUTATE (— **QUICKLY**) SKIP

INVESTIGATION CHECK PROBE TRIAL EXAMEN PILPUL SEARCH

DELVING INQUEST INQUIRY LEGWORK ZETETIC ANALYSIS QUESTION RESEARCH SCRUTINY SOUNDING

INVESTIGATOR SNOOP TRIER SLEUTH GUMSHOE SPOTTER FIELDMAN

INVESTING AMBIENT

INVESTITURE VESTURE INDUMENT

INVESTMENT DOG FLIER CUTICLE CATHEXIS PANNICLE

INVETERATE BLACK SWORN ROOTED CHRONIC HARDENED

INVIDIOUS ENVIOUS HATEFUL

INVIGORATE PEP BRACE CHEER RAISE RENEW VIGOR VIVIFY COMFORT ENFORCE ENLIVEN FORTIFY INNERVE INSINEW REFRESH INSPIRIT

INVIGORATING BRISK CRISP FRESH TONIC VITAL HEARTY LIVELY BRACING CORDIAL VEGETANT

INVIOLABILITY SANCTITY

INVIOLABLE SACRED SECURE STYGIAN

INVIOLATE SACRED

INVISIBLE HID BLIND SECRET UNSEEN VIEWLESS SIGHTLESS (PREF.) APHAN(O) CRYPT(O) KRYPT(O)

INVITATION BID CALL CARD INVITE BIDDING CALLING (— **TO CONTEND**) DARE

INVITE ASK BID WOO BEAR CALL LURE PRAY TOLL CLEPE COURT LATHE TEMPT TRYST ALLURE DESIRE ENTICE INDITE ATTRACT CONVITE PROVOKE REQUEST SOLICIT

INVITING ADORABLE HOMELIKE

INVOCATION WISH DAWUT NANDI BISMILLAH

INVOICE BILL BRIEF CHALAN FACTURE MANIFEST BORDEREAU

INVOKE WISH CLEPE EVOKE APPEAL ATTEST OBTEST CONJURE ENTREAT PROVOKE SOLICIT INVOCATE

INVOLUCRE HULL HUSK CUPULE CALYCLE CALYCULE EPICALYX

INVOLUNTARY FORCED REFLEX HELPLESS

INVOLUTE INVOLVED

INVOLUTED SCREWY

INVOLUTION ATRESIA

INVOLVE DIP LAP MIX MIRE WRAP BROIL CARRY COUCH IMPLY RAVEL DIRECT EMPLOY ENGAGE ENTAIL HANKLE INWRAP TANGLE COMPORT CONCERN CONNOTE EMBRACE EMBROIL ENSNARE ENTWINE ENVIRON IMMERSE INCLUDE ENCUMBER ENTANGLE INTEREST (— **IN DIFFICULTY**) STEAD

INVOLVED IN DEEP GONE INTO BLIND KNOTTY COMPLEX ENGAGED PLAITED IMPLICIT INVOLUTE CONCERNED ANFRACTUOUS

INWARD ENTAD INNER INWITH BENWARD INNERLY HOMEFELT

(PREF.) IL IM IN INTRO IR OB
INWICK INRING
IO (BROTHER OF —) PHORONEUS
(FATHER OF —) INACHUS
(SON OF —) EPAPHUS
IODINE
(PREF.) (REMOVAL OF —) DESIODO
IOLAUS (COMPANION OF —)
HERCULES
(FATHER OF —) IPHICLES
(MOTHER OF —) AUTOMEDUSA
(WIFE OF —) MEGARA
IOLE (FATHER OF —) EURYTUS
(HUSBAND OF —) HYLLUS
IOLITE IBERITE PELIOMA
ION ACID ADION ANION CATION
ISOMER KATION LIGAND
AMPHION HYDRION OXONIUM
SPECIES ZWITTERION
(— DURATION) LIFETIME
(FATHER OF —) XUTHUS
(MOTHER OF —) CREUSA
(SON OF —) GELEON ARGADES
HOPLETES AEGICORES
(PREF.) IONTO
(SUFF.) (CHARGED —) ONIUM
IONIA (GULF OF —) ARTA
IONIZATION BURST
IOPHON (FATHER OF —) SOCRATES
(MOTHER OF —) NICOSTRATE
IOTA JOT WHIT GHOST TITTLE
SCRUPLE
IOU MARKER

IOWA

CAPITAL: DESMOINES
COLLEGE: COE DORDT LORAS
CORNELL PARSONS GRINNELL
WARTBURG
COUNTY: IDA LEE SAC CASS LINN
PAGE POLK TAMA ADAIR
BOONE CEDAR EMMET FLOYD
LUCAS SIOUX BREMER KEOKUK
OBRIEN DUBUQUE KOSSUTH
MAHASKA OSCEOLA
LAKE: CLEAR STORM SPIRIT
NICKNAME: HAWKEYE
PRESIDENT: HOOVER
RIVER: CEDAR SKUNK BIGSIOUX
MISSOURI
STATE BIRD: GOLDFINCH
STATE FLOWER: WILDROSE
STATE TREE: OAK
TOWN: ADEL AMES LEON ALBIA
MASON ONAWA OSAGE PERRY
SIOUX ALGONA ELDORA
KEOKUK LEMARS MARION
SIBLEY VINTON ANAMOSA
OTTUMWA WATERLOO
DAVENPORT

IOWAN HAWKEYE
IPECAC ITOUBOU
IPHIANASSA (FATHER OF —)
PROETIUS
(HUSBAND OF —) BIAS
(MOTHER OF —) ANTIA
IPHICLUS (BROTHER OF —)
HERCULES
(FATHER OF —) PHYLACUS
AMPHITRYON
(MOTHER OF —) ALCMENA

(SON OF —) PODARCES
PROTESILAUS
(WIFE OF —) CLYMENE
IPHIDAMAS (FATHER OF —)
ANTENOR
(MOTHER OF —) THEANO
(SLAYER OF —) AGAMEMNON
IPHIGENIA (BROTHER OF —)
ORESTES
(FATHER OF —) AGAMEMNON
(MOTHER OF —) CLYTEMNESTRA
(SISTER OF —) ELECTRA
IPHIMEDIA (HUSBAND OF —)
ALOEUS
(SON OF —) OTUS EPHIALTES
IPHINOE (FATHER OF —) PROETUS
(MOTHER OF —) ANTIA
(SISTER OF —) LYSIPPE
IPHIANASSA
IPHIS (FATHER OF —) LIGDUS
(MOTHER OF —) TELETHUSA
(WIFE OF —) IANTHE
IPHITUS (BROTHER OF —) CLYTIUS
(FATHER OF —) EURYTUS
(SISTER OF —) IOLE
(SLAYER OF —) HERCULES
IPIL VESI
IPOMOEA NIL NILL BATATAS
MANROOT TURBITH TURPETH
SCAMMONY
IPSEITY SELFHOOD
IRA (FATHER OF —) IKKESH
IRACUND IREFUL
IRAD (FATHER OF —) ENOCH
(GRANDFATHER OF —) CAIN
(SON OF —) MEHUJAEL

IRAN

CAPE: HALILEH
CAPITAL: TEHRAN TEHERAN
COIN: PUL ASAR CRAN LARI RIAL
BISTI DARIC DINAR LARIN
SHAHI TOMAN STATER ASHRAFI
KASBEKE PAHLAVI
DESERT: KERMAN
FORMER NAME: PERSIA
GOVERNORSHIP: ILAM YAZD
SEMNAN ZANJAN HAMADAN
LORESTAN
LAKE: NIRIS NIRIZ TASHT TUZLU
URMIA SAHWEH SISTAN
MAHARLU NEMEKSER
URUMIYEH
LANGUAGE: ZEND PAHLAVI
MEASURE: GAZ GUZ MOV ZAR ZER
CANE FOOT GAREH JERIB KAFIZ
MAKUK QASAB ARTABA
CHARAC CHEBEL GARIBA
GHALVA OUROUB CAPICHA
CHENICA FARSAKH FARSANG
MANSION MISHARA PAIMANEH
PARASANG SABBITHA
STATHMOS
MOUNTAIN: CUSH KUSH HINDU
KHOSF ARARAT HAMUNT
BINALUD KHORMUJ SABALAN
DEMAVEND
MOUNTAIN RANGE: ELBURZ
SIAHAN ZAGROS JAGATAL
PEOPLE: LUR KURD MEDE SART
KAJAR MUKRI PERSE TAJIK
HADJEMI PERSIAN
PORT: JASK BUSHIRE PAHLEVI

PROVINCE: FARS GILAN KERMAN
TEHRAN ESFAHAN KHORASAN
KORDESTAN
RIVER: MAND MUND SHUR ARAKS
JAGIN KARUN RABCH SEFID
BAMPUR GORGAN HALIRI
TIGRIS KARKHEH MASHKEL
SAFIDRUD ZAYENDEH
EUPHRATES
STRAIT: HORMUZ
TOWN: FAO KOM AMOL SARI YAZD
AHVAZ KHVOY NIRIZ RASHT
RESHT ABADAN DEZFUL
GORGAN KASVIN KERMAN
MASHAD MESHED SHIRAZ
TABRIZ TAURIS HAMADAN
ISFAHAN SANANDAJ
WEIGHT: SER DRAM DUNG ROTL
SANG SEER ABBAS ARTEL
MAUND PINAR RATEL BATMAN
DIRHEM GANDUM KARWAR
MISCAL NAKHOD NIMMAN
ABBASSI TCHEIREK

IRANIAN TAT SART GALCHA
SHUGNI BACTRIAN BARTANGI
(— SOVEREIGN) SHAH

IRAQ

CAPITAL: BAGDAD BAGHDAD
COIN: DINAR DIRHAM
DISTRICT: BASRA KURDISTAN
FORMER NAME: MESOPOTAMIA
MOUNTAINS: ZARGOS KURDISTAN
OASIS: MANIYA
PEOPLE: ARAB KURD
PORT: FAO BASRA
RIVER: ZAB TIGRIS EUPHRATES
TOWN: ANA HIT AFAQ AMARA
BAIJI BASRA ERBIL HILLA
MOSUL NAJAF HILLAH KIRKUK
TIKRIT KARBALA

IRASCIBILITY BILE CHOLER
IRASCIBLE WARM ANGRY CROSS
FIERY GASSY HASTY IRATE SHARP
TECHY TESTY CRANKY IREFUL
SPUNKY TETCHY TOUCHY
ANGULAR BILIOUS FRETFUL
IRACUND PEEVISH TINDERY
TOUSTIE WASPISH CAPTIOUS
CHOLERIC PETULANT SNAPPISH
STOMACHY
IRATE ANGRY HEATED CHOLERIC
WRATHFUL
IRE FURY ANGER WRATH
IREFUL ANGRY JEALOUS

IRELAND

BAY: MAL CLEW SLIGO BANTRY
DINGLE GALWAY TRALEE
DONEGAL DUNDALK KILLALA
BLACKSOD DROGHEDA
CAPE: CLEAR
CAPITAL: TARA DUBLIN BELFAST
COIN: RAP REAL
COUNTY: CORK DOWN LEIX MAYO
CAVAN CLARE KERRY LOUTH
MEATH SLIGO ANTRIM ARMAGH
CARLOW GALWAY OFFALY
TYRONE ULSTER DONEGAL
KILDARE LEITRIM WEXFORD
WICKLOW KILKENNY LIMERICK

MONAGHAN FERMANAGH
LONDONDERRY
ISLAND: ARAN TORY SALTEE
RATHLIN
LAKE: DOO KEY REE TAY CONN
DERG ERNE MASK CARRA
GOWNA LEANE RAMOR BODERG
COOTER ENNELL DROMORE
OUGHTER SHEELIN
MEASURE: MILE BANDLE
MOUNTAIN: OX CAHA ANTRIM
GALTEE KEEPER MOURNE
MULREA DONEGAL ERRIGAL
KENNEDY KIPPURE WICKLOW
LEINSTER
MOUNTAIN RANGE: GALTY STACKS
COMERAGH
OTHER NAME: EIRE ERIN BANBA
IERNE IRENA ULSTER BOGLAND
HIBERNIA INISFAIL
PEOPLE: CELT ERSE GAEL CELTIC
HIBERNIAN
PERTAINING TO: CELTIC GAELIC
POINT: CAHORE CARNSORE
PORT: COBH
PROVINCE: ULSTER MUNSTER
LEINSTER CONNAUGHT
RIVER: LEE BANN DEEL ERNE
NORE SUIR BOYNE CLARE
FEALE FLESK FOYLE LAUNE
BANDON BARROW LIFFEY
KENMARE MUNSTER SHANNON
TOWN: CORK NAAS TRIM ADARE
CAVAN ENNIS OMAGH SLIGO
ARMAGH CARLOW DUBLIN
GALWAY LURGAN TRALEE
LIMERICK TIPPERARY

IRENE (FATHER OF —) JUPITER
(MOTHER OF —) THEMIS
IRENIC CALM HENOTIC PEACEFUL
IRENICA AITESIS
IRI (FATHER OF —) BELA
IRIDESCENCE LUSTER LUSTRE
REFLET
IRIDESCENT SHOT IRISED IRIDINE
IRISATE OPALINE PAVONINE
IRIS EYE SET FLAG LILY LUCE LUCY
SEGG AZURE IREOS ORRIS SEDGE
FLAGON LEVERS LILIAL LILIUM
SHADOW SUNBOW ALCAZAR
BABIANA FLAGGER GLADDON
FLAGLEAF
(FATHER OF —) THAUMAS
(MOTHER OF —) ELECTRA
(PREF.) IRID(O) IRIDICO IRIDIO
IRISH ERSE EIRANN IRISHRY
MILESIAN
(— KING) RIG
(ILLITERATE —) KEELMAN
(PREF.) HIBERNO
IRISHMAN MAC PAT CELT GAEL
KELT SCOT GREEK IRISH PADDY
YREIS TEAGUE GRECIAN IRISHER
MILESIAN ORANGEMAN
(LEARNED —) OLLAMH
IRISH MOSS SLOKE CHONDRUS
IRISHWOMAN HARP
IRK BORE ITCH ANNOY WEARY
BOTHER
IRKSOME DULL WARM WEARY
HUMDRUM OPEROSE PAINFUL
TEDIOUS ANNOYING TIRESOME

IROKO ODUM ODOOM MUVULE KAMBALA

IRON BIT DOG IRE AIRN MARS WIRE ANGLE ANVIL BASIL BRAND DRAIL DRIFT FLOSS HORSE NEGRO PRESS SPIKE STEEL WAVER ANCONY BEATER CALKER CAUTER FERRUM GAGGER GOFFER JAGGER OSMUND CAUTERY COBIRON CRAMPER FERRITE FURISON GAMBREL GAUFFER PRICKER SADIRON FLATIRON TRICOUNI
(— FOR CLOSING STAVES) HORSE
(— OF MILLSTONE) RIND RYND
(— ORE) LIMNITE
(— PIECES) POTLEG
(— PLATE) TRAMP
(— SUPPORTING SPIT) COBIRON
(— TO SUPPORT BEAM) TORSEL
(ANGLE —) LATH STIFFENER
(BASKETWORK —) BEATER
(BOOM —) WITHE WYTHE
(BRANDING —) BURN
(CAST —) METAL YETLIN SPIEGEL YETLING PROMETAL SEMISTEEL
(CLIMBING —) GAFF SPUR CREEPER
(CRUDE CASTING OF —) PIG
(DRIVING —) CLEEK
(GLASSBLOWING —) BAIT
(GOLF —) JIGGER
(GRAPPLING —) CRAMPON CRAMPOON
(HATTER'S —) SLUG
(MASS OF WROUGHT —) BLOOM
(METEORIC —) SIDERITE
(PASTY —) SPONGE
(PIG —) SPIEGEL KENTLEDGE
(PRIMING —) DRIFT
(PUDDLING —) RABBLE
(RUSSIAN —) SABLE
(SHEET —) TERNE
(SOLDERING —) COPPER
(SPECULAR —) HEMATITE
(TAILOR'S —) GOOSE
(TAMPING —) DRIVER
(8 PIGS OF CAST —) FODDER
(PL.) GARTERS
(PREF.) FERRI FERRO SIDER(O)
(SUFF.) SIDERITE

IRONBARK MUGGA

IRON BROWN NEGRO

IRONCLAD ARMORED IRONSIDE

IRON, GOLF (PART OF —) TOE FACE GRIP HEAD HEEL NECK NOSE SOLE HOSEL SHAFT

IRON GRAY BAT

IRON HAT GOSSAN

IRONIC ACERB ACERBIC SATIRIC SARCASTIC

IRONICAL BLAND CRUEL PAWKY

IRON-LIKE MARTIAL

IRON MAN TALUS

IRONMONGERY HARDWARE

IRON-OXIDE RED TARRAGONA

IRONSMITH FERRER

IRONSTONE DOGGER SIDERITE

IRONWEED FLATTOP VERNONIA WINGSTEM

IRONWOOD TITI COLIMA MOPANE MOPANI PURIRI WAMARA CYRILLA JOEWOOD AXMASTER

BURNWOOD FIREWOOD

IRONWORKER LOHAR MOSCHI

IRONWORT SIDERITE

IRONY SATIRE ASTEISM SARCASM RIDICULE

IROQUOIS HURON MINGO CAYUGA MENGWE

IRRADIATE XRAY EMBEAM

IRRATIONAL MAD REE SURD WILD BRUTE SILLY ABSURD RAVING STUPID BESTIAL FOOLISH

IRRECONCILABLE HOSTILE FRONDEUR

IRREDUCIBLE BASIC

IRREGULAR ODD DUMB WILD BUMPY EROSE FANCY MIXED WOPSY ATYPIC CATCHY FITFUL PATCHY RAGGED RUGGED SPOTTY UNEVEN UNLIKE WEEWAW ANAXIAL ATACTIC BAROQUE CATERAN CRABBED CROOKED CURSORY DEVIOUS DIFFORM ERRATIC FRECKET MUTABLE SCRAWLY SNATCHY UNEQUAL WAYWARD ABNORMAL ATYPICAL DOGGEREL INFORMAL PINDARIC SCRAGGLY SCRAMBLY UNLAWFUL UNSTABLE UNSTEADY VARIABLE AMORPHOUS PROMISCUOUS
(— IN SHAPE) BAROQUE
(PREF.) AMETR(O) ANOM ANOMAL(O)

IRREGULARITY SNAG DEFECT RUFFLE ANOMALY ACCIDENT
(— IN YARN) SNICK

IRREGULARLY UNDULY

IRRELIGIOUS PAGAN WICKED HEATHEN IMPIOUS PROFANE SENSUAL

IRREMEDIABLE HELPLESS HOPELESS

IRREPROACHABLE SPOTLESS

IRRESISTIBLE MESMERIC OPPOSELESS

IRRESISTIBLY FATALLY

IRRESOLUTE FICKLE INFIRM UNSURE WANKLE DOUBTFUL UNSTABLE

IRRESPONSIBLE WILDCAT CAREFREE FECKLESS SKITTISH

IRRESPONSIVE LEADEN

IRRETRIEVABLE HOPELESS

IRREVERENCE IMPIETY

IRREVERENT ATHEIST AWELESS IMPIOUS PROFANE

IRREVOCABLE DEAD

IRREVOCABLY FATALLY FINALLY

IRRIGATE FLOAT WATER SYRINGE

IRRIGATION KAREZ

IRRIGATOR FLOATER

IRRITABILITY BATE NERVES SPLEEN ERETHISM SORENESS VAGOTONY SENSITIVITY

IRRITABLE BAD EDGY BIRSY CROOK FIERY FUSSY HASTY HUFFY JUMPY MUSTY NAGGY RASPY TETTY TILTY TOITY CRANKY GROWLY NETTLY PATCHY SNUFFY SPUNKY STOCKY TEETHY TETCHY TOUCHY CRABBED FRATCHY FRETFUL HORNETY HUFFISH KICKISH

PECKISH PEEVISH SPLEENY TEDIOUS TWITCHY WASPISH LIVERISH PETULANT SNAPPING SNAPPISH STOMACHY SPLENETIC

IRRITANT PHOSGENE

IRRITATE BUG EAT GET IRE IRK NAG RUB TAR TEW TRY VEX BURN CRAB FIRE FRET GALL GOAD GRIG GRIT ITCH NARK RILE ROIL SOUR TEEN ANGER ANNOY CHAFE EAGER FRUMP GRATE GRILL GRIPE PEEVE PIQUE STING TARRY ABRADE BOTHER FRIDGE GRAVEL HARASS HECTOR NETTLE RUFFLE AFFRONT INCENSE INFLAME NERVOUS PROVOKE STOMACH ACERBATE

IRRITATED RILY SORE HUFFY RAGGY MUFFED SHIRTY EMPORTE FRATCHED SOREHEAD
(EASILY —) TESTY

IRRITATING ACRID HARSH CORSIE ELVISH GRAVEL FRETFUL GALLING IRKSOME PUNGENT RASPING ANNOYING FRETSOME GRAVELLY NETTLING SCRATCHY SPITEFUL STINGING TIRESOME MADDENING NETTLESOME

IRRITATION FRET TEEN BIRSE PIQUE STEAM NEEDLE RUFFLE TEMPER WARMTH ANTPRICK FLEABITE PINPRICK VEXATION

IRRUPTION BREAK INROAD INBREAK INBURST ERUPTION INVASION

IRU (FATHER OF —) CALEB

IS S YS BEES
(— NOT) NIS AINT ISNT

ISAAC (FATHER OF —) ABRAHAM
(MOTHER OF —) SARAH
(SON OF —) ESAU JACOB
(WIFE OF —) REBEKAH

ISABELLA (BROTHER OF —) CLAUDIO
(HUSBAND OF —) BIRON VILLEROY VINCENTIO
(LOVER OF —) ZERBINO
(SLAYER OF —) RODOMONT

ISABELLE (GUARDIAN OF —) SGANARELLE
(HUSBAND OF —) VALERE

ISAIAH ESAY ESAIAS
(FATHER OF —) AMOZ

ISANDER (BROTHER OF —) HIPPOLOCHUS
(FATHER OF —) BELLEROPHON
(SISTER OF —) LAODAMIA

ISCAH (BROTHER OF —) LOT
(FATHER OF —) HARAN
(SISTER OF —) MILCAH

ISCHEMIA ANEMIA

ISCHIAL SCIATIC

ISEULT (FATHER OF —) HOEL ANGUISH
(HUSBAND OF —) MARK
(LOVER OF —) TRISTAN

ISFENDIYAR (BROTHER OF —) BISHUTAN
(FATHER OF —) GUSHTASP
(SLAYER OF —) RUSTAM
(SON OF —) BAHMAN

ISHBAK (FATHER OF —) ABRAHAM
(MOTHER OF —) KETURAH

ISHBOSHETH (FATHER OF —) SAUL

ISHI (SON OF —) ZOHETH

ISHIAH (FATHER OF —) IZRAHIAH

ISHMAEL (FATHER OF —) AZEL ABRAHAM JEHOHANAN NETHANIAH
(MOTHER OF —) HAGAR
(SON OF —) ZEBADIAH

ISHMAIAH (FATHER OF —) OBADIAH

ISHPINGO CINNAMON

ISHSHAKKU PATESI

ISHTAR NINNI

ISHUAH (FATHER OF —) ASHER

ISHUI (FATHER OF —) SAUL
(MOTHER OF —) AHINOAM

ISINGLASS AGAR LEAF MICA PIPE KANTEN CARLOCK

ISIS (BROTHER OF —) OSIRIS
(FATHER OF —) SATURN
(MOTHER OF —) RHEA

ISLAM ABBASID

ISLAMIC (— CUSTOM) SUNNA

ISLAND CALF CAYO HOLM INCH ISLE JAVA POLO ENNIS MALTA MAYDA AVALON ITHACA OGYGIA REFUGE RIALTO CIPANGO JAMAICA MADEIRA TOWHEAD BLEFUSCU CALAURIA DOMINICA GUERNSEY LILLIPUT LUGGNAGG
(— IN EVERGLADES) HAMMOCK
(— OF REIL) INSULA
(ARTIFICIAL —) CRANNOG
(CORAL —) ATOLL
(FABLED —) MERU UTOPIA
(FLOATING —) HOVER
(FLYING —) LAPUTA
(FORTIFIED —) CRANNOG
(LEGENDARY —) BRAZIL OBRAZIL
(LITTLE —) AIT KAY KEY ISLET
(LOW —) KEY
(ROCKY —) SKERRY
(SANDY —) BEACH BARRIER
(SMALL —) CAY ISLE ISLET NUBBLE SANDKEY
(PREF.) NESO

ISLANDER KANAKA ISLEMAN INSULARY

ISLE IZLE ISLET SKERRY

ISLET OE AIT CAY KEY EYOT HAFT HOLM ILOT MOTU ROCK ISLOT STACK NUBBLE

ISMENE (FATHER OF —) OEDIPUS
(MOTHER OF —) JOCASTA
(SISTER OF —) ANTIGONE

ISOBAR MEIOBAR MESOBAR PLEIOBAR

ISOGRAM ISOPLETH

ISOLATE SPORE ENISLE ISLAND DISSECT SECLUDE COLONIZE INSULATE PRESCIND SEPARATE SEQUESTER

ISOLATED LONE POCKET UNIQUE OUTLYING SOLITARY STRANDED SECESSIVE

ISOLATION HERMITRY LONENESS SOLITUDE SEQUESTER

ISOMER PYRAN TOSYL XYLENE CUMIDINE DECOSANE DODECANE

ISOMERIC ISO ALLO

ISOMETRIC ALLO CUBIC REGULAR TESSULAR

ISOPLETH GEOTHERM

ISOPOD SLATER ASELLUS BOPYRID

GRIBBLE EPICARID
ISOTOPE IONIUM THORON
ACTINON CARRIER PROTIUM
TRITIUM
ISOTYPE COTYPE SYNTYPE
ISPAGHUL SPOGEL
ISPAHAN HERAT HERATI

ISRAEL
CAPITAL: JERUSALEM
COIN: AGORA POUND SHEKEL
COLLECTIVE FARM: KIBBUTZ
DESERT: NEGEV
FORMER NAME: CANAAN
PALESTINE
GULF: AQABA
LAKE: HULEH TIBERIAS
MEASURE: CAB HIN KOR LOG
BATH EPHA EZBA OMER REED
SEAH CUBIT EPHAH HOMER
KANEH QANEH
MOUNTAIN: NAFH SAGI HARIF
MERON RAMON ATZMON
CARMEL
PLAIN: ESDRAELON
RIVER: FARIA MALIK SOREQ
JORDAN QISHON SARIDA
YARKON LAKHISH
SEA: DEAD GALILEE
SEAPORT: EILAT ELATH ASHDOD
TELAVIV
TOWN: ACRE RAMA HAIFA HOLON
JAFFA JENIN JOPPA RAMLE
SAFAD BATYAM HEBRON
NABLUS JERICHO NATANYA
TELAVIV TULKARM NAZARETH

ISRAELI SABRA
(— STUDY CENTER) ULPAN
ISRAELITE JEW SAINT HEBREW
JACOBITE
(PL.) ZION
ISSUE END ISH COME EMIT FALL
FLOW GIVE GUSH HEAD MISE
REEK TERM VENT ARISE COUNT
EVENT FRUIT LOOSE OUTGO
SETON SOURD UTTER EFFECT
EFFUSE EGRESS EMERGE ESCAPE
EXITUS MUTTON RESULT SEQUEL
SETTER SPRING UPPING BALLOON
DEBOUCH DESCENT DRIZZLE
EMANATE ESSENCE EXSURGE
OUTCOME PROCEED PROGENY
REDOUND REFLAIR SUCCESS
EXPEDITE FONTANEL INCREASE
ISSUANCE KINDLING OUTGOING
(— AND ORDER) BID
(— SLOWLY) EXUDE
(— SPASMODICALLY) BELCH
(— SUDDENLY) SALLY
(— WITH FORCE) SPOUT
(BOND —) CONSOL
(FAVORABLE —) SPEED FORTUNE
(FINAL —) FATE UPSHOT UTMOST
(NUMEROUS —) SPAWN
(REAL —) CRUX
ISSUED OUT
ISSUING EMANANT JESSANT
MANATION
ISTHMUS BALK STRAIT TARBET
ISTLE PITA IXTLE JUAMAVE
GUAPILLA
IT HE HIT MUN TAGGER

(— FOLLOWS) SEQ SEQU
(— HAS BEEN SWORN) JURAT
ITALIAN ITALIC AUSONIAN
MACARONI
ITALIANA IN ALGIERI, L'
(CHARACTER IN —) ELVIRA
TADDEO LINDPRO ISABELLA
MUSTAPHA
(COMPOSER OF —) ROSSINI
ITALITE VESBITE
ITALY AUSONIA HESPERIA
SATURNIA

ITALY
CAPE: TESTA CIRCEO LICOSA
LINARO COLONNE FALCONE
PASSERO RIZZUTO SANVITO
TEULADA VATICANO
CAPITAL: ROMA ROME
CHEESE: ROMANO FONTINA
RICOTTA BELPAESE PARMESAN
TALEGGIO
COIN: LIRA LIRE TARI GRANO
PAOLI PAOLO SCUDO SOLDO
DANARO DENARO DUCATO
SEQUIN TESTONE ZECCHINO
FAMILY: ASTI ESTE AMATI CENCE
DORIA BORGIA MEDICI SFORZA
FOOD: PASTA PIZZA SCAMPI
GNOCCHI LASAGNE POLENTA
RAVIOLI RISOTTO SPUMONI
TORTONI CAPONATA LINGUINE
MACARONI PEPERONI
GULF: GAETA GENOA OROSEI
SALERNO TARANTO CAGLIARI
ORISTANO
ISLAND: ELBA LERO CAPRI LEROS
PONZA GIGLIO ISCHIA LINOSA
SALINA SICILY USTICA ALICUDI
ASINARA CAPRAIA GORGONA
LEVANZO PANAREA PIANOSA
SICILIA VULCANO FILICUDI
SARDINIA
ISLANDS: EGADI LIPARI TUSCAN
PELAGIE PONTINE TREMITI
LAKE: COMO ISEO NEMI GARDA
ALBANO LESINA LUGANO
VARANO BOLSENA PERUGIA
MAGGIORE BRACCIANO
MEASURE: PIE ORNA CANNA
PALMA PALMO PIEDE PUNTO
SALMA STAIO STERO BARILE
MIGLIE MIGLIO MOGGIO RUBBIO
TAVOLA TOMOLO BOCCALE
BRACCIO SECCHIO GIORNATA
POLONICK QUADRATO
MOUNTAIN: ETNA ROSA VISO
AMARO BLANC CORNO SOMMA
CIMONE BERNINA VESUVIUS
MOUNTAIN RANGE: ALPS ORTLES
APENNINES MARITIMES
NATIVE: ITALO LATIN OSCAN
ROMAN SABINE TIRANO
TUSCAN LOMBARD SIENESE
LIGURIAN VENETIAN
PASS: FREJUS BERNINA BRENNER
SPLUGEN
PORT: BARI POLA ZARA GENOA
TRANI ZADAR RIMINI SALERNO
TRIESTE
PROVINCE: ASTI COMO ENNA PISA
AOSTA CUNEO FORLI LECCE
NUORO PARMA PAVIA RIETI

SIENA UDINE FOGGIA MATERA
MODENA PADOVA RAGUSA
TRENTO VERONA BRESCIA
PISTOIA SASSARI VITERBO
REGION: CARSO APULIA LATIUM
MARCHE MOLISE PUGLIA SICILY
UMBRIA ABRUZZI LIGURIA
TUSCANY VENETIA CALABRIA
CAMPANIA LOMBARDY
PIEMONTE SARDINIA
RESORT: LIDO SANREMO
TAORMINA
RIVER: PO ADDA AGRI ANIO ARNO
LIRI NERA RENO SELE TARO
ADIGE CRATI MANNU OGLIO
PARMA PIAVE SALSO STURA
TIBER TIRSO ANIENE BELICE
MINCIO OFANTO PANARO
RAPIDO SANGRO SIMETO
TANARO TEVERE TICINO
BIFERNO BRADANO CHIENTI
METAURO MONTONE OMBRONE
PESCARA RUBICON SECCHIA
TREBBIA VOLTURNO
SEA: IONIAN ADRIATIC LIGURIAN
STRAIT: MESSINA OTRANTO
BONIFACIO
TOWN: BRA RHO ACRI ALBA ASTI
BARI COMO DEGO ELEA ENNA
ESTE FANO GELA IESI LODI
NARO NOLA PISA POLA ROMA
ROME ACQUI ANZIO AOSTA
ASOLA AVOLA CAPUA CUNEO
EBOLI FIUME FORLI GENOA
IMOLA LECCE LUCCA MASSA
MILAN MONZA OSTIA PADUA
PARMA PAVIA SIENA TEANO
TRENT TURIN UDINE VELIA
ALCAMO AMALFI ANCONA
ANDRIA AREZZO CEFALU
FAENZA FOGGIA GENOVA
MANTUA MESTRE MILANO
MODENA NAPLES NAPOLI
NOVARA RIVOLI SPEZIA TRENTO
VARESE VENICE VERONA
BERGAMO BOLOGNA BOLZANO
BRESCIA CARRARA CASERTA
CATANIA COSENZA CREMONA
FERRARA FIRENZE GORIZIA
IMPERIA LEGHORN LIVORNO
MARSALA MESSINA PALERMO
PERUGIA PISTOIA POMPEII
RAVENNA TARANTO TRIESTE
BRINDISI CAGLIARI FLORENCE
PIACENZA SORRENTO
SYRACUSE
VOLCANO: ETNA SOMMA
VULCANO VESUVIUS
STROMBOLI
WATERFALL: FRUA TOCE
WEIGHT: CARAT LIBRA ONCIA
POUND CARATO DENARO
LIBBRA OTTAVA
WINE: SOAVE CHIANTI MARSALA
ORVIETO

ITCH EWK EACH REEF RIFF YEUK
YEWK YUKE PSORA TICKLE
ITCHING SCABIES PRURITUS
CACOETHES VANILLISM
(PREF.) ACARI ACARO PSOR(O)
ITCHING ITCHY YEUKY PRURIENT
PRURITUS URTICANT

ITEM ANA JOB TOT ENTRY POINT
THING DETAIL PARCEL ARTICLE
SEVERAL PARTICULAR
(— IN SERIES) COURSE
(— OF PROPERTY) CHATTEL
(— OF VALUE) ASSET
(APPENDED —) ADDENDUM
(COLLECTOR'S —) SPOIL
(DECORATIVE —) CONCEIT
(LUXURY —) BOUTIQUE
(NEWS —) DISPATCH
(UNPUBLISHED —S) ANECDOTE
(VALUELESS —) BEAN
(PL.) CHECKAGE
ITEMIZE DETAIL
ITERATION PLEONASM
ITHIEL (FATHER OF —) JESAIAH
ITHRA (SON OF —) AMASA
(WIFE OF —) ABIGAIL
ITHRAN (FATHER OF —) DISHON
ITHREAM (FATHER OF —) DAVID
(MOTHER OF —) EGLAH
ITHURIEL'S-SPEAR GRASSNUT
ITINERANT ERRANT AMBULANT
STROLLING PERIPATETIC
ITINERARY DIET JOURNAL
WAYBILL
(— OF ROYAL PROGRESS) GEST
ITINERATION EYRE
ITS HIS
ITSELF IT HERSELF
ITTAI (FATHER OF —) RIBAI
ITYS (FATHER OF —) TEREUS
(MOTHER OF —) PROCNE
ITZA PETEN
IULUS ASCANIUS
IVANHOE (AUTHOR OF —) SCOTT
(CHARACTER IN —) JOHN BRIAN
GIRTH ISAAC LUCAS ROBIN
WAMBA CEDRIC ROWENA ULRICA
MAURICE REBECCA RICHARD
WILFRED REGINALD BEAUMANOIR
IVATAN BATAN
IVORY EBURE DENTINE ELEPHANT
(DUST OF —) EBURINE
(WALRUS —) RIBZUBA RIBAZUBA
IVORY BLACK ABAISER

IVORY COAST
CAPE: PALMAS
CAPITAL: ABIDJAN
DAM: BANDAMA
LANGUAGE: DIOULA
MOUNTAIN: NIMBA
PEOPLE: ABE AKAN ATLE KOUA
KROU MANDE ABOURE LAGOON
MALINKE VOLTAIC
RIVER: KOMOE BANDAMA
CAVALLY SASSANDRA
TOWN: MAN DALOA TABOU
BOUAKE GAGNOA KORHOGO
SASSANDRA

IVORY GULL SNOWBIRD
IVORY NUT ANTA TAGUA JARINA
COROZO
IVORY PALM TAGUA COROJO
COROZO
IVORY TREE PALAY
IVY TOD GILL HOVE IVIN JILL PICRY
ARALIA HEDERA HIBBIN ALEHOOF
ARALIAD IVYWORT BINDWEED
FOALFOOT
(PREF.) HEDERI

IWW WOBBLY

IXION (FATHER OF —) PHLEGYAS

(SISTER OF —) CORONIS

(WIFE OF —) DIA

IYNX (FATHER OF —) PAN

(MOTHER OF —) ECHO

IZHAR (FATHER OF —) KOHATH

IZMIR SMYRNA

J

J JAY JIG JULIETT

JAALAM (FATHER OF —) ESAU

JAAL GOAT BEDEN JAELA

JAASIEL (FATHER OF —) ABNER

JAAZANIAH (FATHER OF —) AZUR
SHAPHAN JEREMIAH

JAB GAG GIG JAG JOB POKE STAB
STICK

JABAL (BROTHER OF —) JUBAL
(FATHER OF —) LAMECH
(MOTHER OF —) ADAH

JABBER CHAT JAVER BURBLE
GABBER GABBLE JOBBER YABBER
YATTER CHATTER

JABESH (SON OF —) SHALLUM

JABIRU STORK CICONIID

JABOT RUFFLE

JACANA PARRA

JACARANDA BROWN DATE
TALLYHO

JACARE CAIMAN CAYMAN

JACHIN (FATHER OF —) SIMEON

JACINTH LIGURE

JACK DIB FLAG JACA CRICK DICKY
KNAVE NANCA COLORS KATHAL
SCALET SETTER WENZEL
MATADOR BLOCKING JACKFISH
POLIGNAL SOURJACK TURNSPIT
UPLIFTER
(— IN BOWLS) BABY MARK KITTY
MASTER MISTRESS
(— IN CARDS) PAM PUR TOM
BOWER CNAFE KITTY KNAPE
KNAVE MAKER KNIGHT VARLET
WENZEL VARLETTO
(— OF CLUBS) NODDY BRAGGER
MATADOR
(— OF SAME SUIT) NOB
(— OF TRUMPS) TOM JASS JASZ
BOWER HONOR PLAYBOY
(PIANO —) HOPPER STICKER
SAUTEREAU
(SPINNING —) BEAT

JACKAL DIEB JACK KOLA THOS
CANID CANINE DRAGON SILVER
THOOID SIACALLE

JACKAROO RINGNECK

JACKASS JACK

JACKASS FISH MORWONG
TERAKIHI

JACK BEAN OVERLOOK

JACK CREVALLE TORO

JACKDAW DAW KAE JACK SHELL
CADDOW CARDER CHOUGH
KADDER CADESSE DAWCOCK
DAWPATE GRACKLE

JACKER SLIPMAN TORCHER

JACKET SAC COAT ETON JACK
JUMP JUPE SACK VEST ACTON
COVER DICKY JUPON PARKA
POLKA SHRUG WAMUS BANIAN
BASQUE BIETLE BLAZER BOLERO
CARACO CORSET DOLMAN
FECKET GANSEY JERKIN JERSEY
JUMPER RAILLY REEFER SACQUE
SADDLE SLEEVE SLIVER SONTAG
TABARD TEMIAK WAMPUS
WARMUS ZOUAVE BEDGOWN
CANEZOU LOUNGER NORFOLK
PALETOT PALTOCK PEACOAT
RISTORI SPENCER SURCOAT
SWEATER CAMISOLE CARDIGAN
CHAQUETA HANSELIN JIRKINET
MACKINAW OVERSLOP PENELOPE
SEALSKIN CARMAGNOLE
ROUNDABOUT
(— FOR TURKEY) APRON
(— LINED WITH STEEL) PLACCATE
(— OF INDIA) BANIAN BANIYA
(— UNDER ARMOR) ACTON TRUSS
HAQUETON
(CROCHETED —) SONTAG
(HOODED —) GREGO ANORAK
GRIEKO
(HUSSAR'S —) PELISSE
(KIND OF —) MAO NEHRU
(LADY'S —) BRUNSWICK
(LOOSE —) VAREUSE
(MALAY —) BAJU BADJU KABAYA
(PART OF —) FOB HEM DART FLAP
SEAM VENT GORGE LAPEL
BUTTON COLLAR INSEAM PIPING
POCKET REVERS SLEEVE
ARMHOLE OUTSEAM
BUTTONHOLE
(PEASANT'S —) SAYON
(UNDRESS MILITARY —) SHELL
(WORK —) BAWNEEN

JACKFRUIT JACA KATHAL
SOURJACK

JACKHAMMER SINKER PLUGGER

JACKKNIFE JACK PIKE BARLOW

JACKMAN SHELLMAN

JACK-OF-ALL-TRADES DOCTOR
TINKER GIMCRACK

JACKSCREW CRICK

JACKSMELT PEIXEREY

JACKSNIPE GID JED JACK PEERT
SCAPE SNIPE SNIGHT CHOROOK
CREAKER JUDCOCK SQUATTER

JACKSTAY JACK HORSE PARREL
JACKROD RAILWAY

JACKSTRAW SPILIKIN

JACK TREE NANGKA

JACOB ISRAEL
(BROTHER OF —) ESAU
(DAUGHTER OF —) RACHEL
DEBORAH
(FATHER OF —) ISAAC
(MOTHER OF —) REBEKAH
(SON OF —) JOSEPH

JACOB'S LADDER POLEMONIUM

JACQUARD FACONNE

JADA (BROTHER OF —) SHAMMAI
(FATHER OF —) ONAM

JADE YU DUN TIT HACK JAUD
MINX PLUG SLUT TIRE HUSSY
QUEAN TRASH BEJADE HARASS
RANNEL AXSTONE HILDING
POUNAMU
(DIRTY —) SLAISTER

JADED FORGONE SHOPWORN
DISJASKIT

JADEITE YU

JAEGER LARI SKUA ALLAN BOSUN
LARID SHOOL BONXIE TEASER
TULIAC TRUMPIE DIRTBIRD
DUNGBIRD

JAEL (HUSBAND OF —) HEBER
(VICTIM OF —) SISERA

JAFFIER (WIFE OF —) BELVIDERA

JAG BUN JOG BARB GIMP JAUG
LOAD SOSH TOOT SKATE TOOTH
INDENT

JAGELLO (WIFE OF —) HEDWIG

JAGGED JAGGY HACKLY RAGGED
RUGGED SCRAGGY SHAGGED
SNAGGED INDENTED SCRAGGLY
TATTERED

JAGGERY GUR GOOR GOUR
KHAUR KHAJUR KITTUL

JAGUAR CAT OUNCE TIGER
PANTHER UTURUNCU

JAHANGIR (FATHER OF —) AKBAR

JAHATH (FATHER OF —) LIBNI
SHIMEI SHELOMOTH

JAHAZIAH (FATHER OF —) TIKVAH

JAHAZIEL (FATHER OF —) HEBRON
ZECHARIAH

JAHDO (FATHER OF —) BUZ
(SON OF —) JESHISHAI

JAHLEEL (FATHER OF —) ZEBULUN

JAHZEEL (FATHER OF —) NAPHTALI

JAI ALAI PELOTA
(— COURT) FRONTON

JAIL CAN GIB JUG BOOB CAGE
COOP CRIB DUMP GAOL HELL
HOLD HOLE KEEP LAKE LOCK
NICK STIR WARD CHOKY CLINK
GRATE KITTY LIMBO LODGE
POKEY TENCH TRONK BUCKET
CARCEL COOLER ENJAIL JIGGER
LIMBUS LOCKUP TOLZEY FREEZER
FURNACE GEHENNA KIDCOTE
PINFOLD SLAMMER TOLLERY
BASTILLE CALABOZO HOOSEGOW
IMPRISON MILLDOLL TOLLHALL
BRIDEWELL CALABOOSE
(— TERM) JOLT

JAILBIRD LAG

JAILER ADAM GAOLER KEEPER
WARDEN ALCAIDE TURNKEY
INCLUDER

JAIR (FATHER OF —) KISH
(SON OF —) ELHANAN MORDECAI

JAKAN (FATHER OF —) EZER

JAKE FINE HICK FELLOW

JAKES AJAX GONG

JALAP MECHOACAN

JALON (FATHER OF —) EZRA

JALOPY HEAP CLUNKER

JAM DIP CRAM JAMB BLOCK
CHOKE CROWD STICK KONFYT
THRONG JACKPOT

JAMAICA (CAPITAL OF —)
KINGSTON
(RIVER OF —) BLACK COBRE
MINHO
(TOWN OF —) MAYPEN
PORTANTONIO SPANISHTOWN

JAMAICA COBNUT OUABE
PIGNUT

JAMAICA DOGWOOD BABASCO
BARBASCO FISHWOOD

JAMAICAN RAINBIRD TOMFOOL

JAMAICA VERVAIN GERVAO

JAMAICIN BERBERINE

JAMB DURN ALETTE HAUNCH
REVEAL DOORPOST
(PL.) COVING

JAMES JEM JIM JIMMY SEAMAS
SHAMUS
(BROTHER OF —) JOHN JESUS
JOSES
(COUSIN OF —) JESUS
(FATHER OF —) CLOPAS
(MOTHER OF —) MARY SALOME

JAMIN (FATHER OF —) RAM SIMEON

JANAKA (DAUGHTER OF —) SITA

JANAMEJAYA (FATHER OF —)
PARIKSHIT

JANE EYRE (AUTHOR OF —)
BRONTE
(CHARACTER IN —) EYRE JANE
JOHN MARY REED ADELE DIANA
ELIZA GRACE POOLE BERTHA
BESSIE EDWARD ELLIOT INGRAM
LEAVEN RIVERS TEMPLE VARENS
BLANCHE FAIRFAX GEORGIANA
ROCHESTER

JANGLE CLAM SQUABBLE

JANGLING HARSH JANGLY
AJANGLE

JANISSARY CREOLE RABIRUBIA

JANITOR DURWAN PORTER
SERVITOR

JANIZARY SOLAK SOLACH

JANNA (FATHER OF —) JOSEPH
(SON OF —) MELCHI

JANSENIST RIGORIST

JANUARY (— IN SPANISH) ENERO

JANUS IANUS BIFRONT

JAOB JOW

JAPAN NIPPON YAMATO CIPANGO

JAPAN

BAY: ISE MUTSU OTARU ARIAKE
ATSUMI SENDAI SURUGA
TOYAMA WAKASA UCHIURA
CAPE: TOI ESAN MINO NOMA SHIO
SOYA SUZU ERIMO KYOGA
RURUI MUROTO NOJIMA

TODOGA SHIRIYA ASHIZURI SHAKOTAN

CAPITAL: TOKIO TOKYO

COIN: BU RIN SEN YEN OBAN KOBAN OBANG TEMPO ICHEBU ITZEBU KOBANG

ISLAND: IKI SADO AWAJI BONIN HONDO KURIL REBUN HONSHU KIUSHU KURILE KYUSHU RYUKYU CIPANGO LOOCHOO RISHIRI SKIKOKU HOKKAIDO IKISHIMA OKIGUNTO OKUSHIRI TSUSHIMA YAKUJIMA

ISLAND GROUP: OKI GOTO BONIN VOLCANO

LAKE: BIWA TOYA TOWADA CHUZENJI KUTCHAWA SHIKOTSU INAWASHIRO

MEASURE: BU JO SE BOO CHO KEN TAN HIRO SHAKU TSUBO

MOUNTAIN: ZAO FUJI ASAHI ASAMA YESSO ASOSAN ENASAN HIUCHI KIUSIU YARIGA FUJISAN HAKUSAN KUJUSAN TOKACHI FUJIYAMA

PORT: OTARU YAHATA YAWATA

PREFECTURE: MIE GIFU NARA OITA SAGA AICHI AKITA CHIBA EHIME FUKUI GUMMA HYOGO IWATE KOCHI KYOTO SHIGA AOMORI KAGAWA MIYAGI NAGANO TOYAMA NIIGATA OKINAWA SAITAMA TOTTORI NAGASAKI WAKAYAMA YAMAGATA TOKUSHIMA

SEA: SUO AMAKUSA

STRAIT: KII BUNGO OSUMI NEMURO TANEGA TOKARA TSUGARU TSUSHIMA

STREET: GINZA

TOWN: OME TSU GIFU KOBE KURA MITO NAHA NARA OITA OTSU SAGA UEDA AKITA ATAMI CHIBA FUKUI KIOTO KOCHI NIKKO OSAKA OTARU SAKAI UJINA URAWA CHOSHI MATSUE NAGOYA SASEBO SENDAI TAKADA TOYAMA FUKUOKA NIIGATA OKAYAMA OKAZAKI SAPPORO HAKODATE KAMAKURA KANAZAWA KAWASAKI KUMAMOTO NAGASAKI YOKOHAMA YOKOSUKA HIROSHIMA

VOLCANO: ASO USU FUJI ASAMA ASOSAN HAKUSAN FUJIYAMA

WATERFALL: KEGON

WEIGHT: MO FUN KIN KON RIN SHI KATI KWAN NIYO CARAT CATTY MOMME PICUL KWAMME HIYAKKIN

JAPAN CEDAR SUGI
JAPANESE JAP JAPONIC
JAPANESE APRICOT UME
JAPANESE CHERRY SAKURA
JAPANESE DEER SIKA
JAPANESE GELATIN AGAR
JAPANESE IRIS SHADOW
JAPANESE PERSIMMON KAKI
JAPANESE PLUM KELSEY
JAPANESE PORGIE TAI
JAPANESE QUINCE JAPONICA

JAPANESE VELVET BIRODO
JAPE GAUD JOKE BEGUNK
JAPHETH (BROTHER OF —) HAM SHEM
  (FATHER OF —) NOAH
  (SON OF —) JAVAN
JAPHIA (FATHER OF —) DAVID
JAPONICA ASTILBE
JAQUENETTA (LOVER OF —) ARMADO
JAR TUN CELL JANG JARG JOLT JURR OLLA BANGA BOCAL CADUS CRUSE KADOS SHOCK DOLIUM HUSTLE HYDRIA IMPACT JUDDER KALPIS PANKIN PINATA PITHOS TINAJA CANOPUS CONCUSS POTICHE PSYKTER STAMNOS TERRINE MARTABAN STINKPOT
  (BELL —) CLOCHE
  (BULGING —) OLLA
  (EARTHENWARE —) CAN NAN CROCK GAMLA PIPKIN PITHOS TERRINE
  (POROUS —) GURGLET
  (SQUAT —) KORO
  (STONE —) STEEN STONE CROPPA
  (WATER —) KANG BANGA CHATTI CHATTY GUMLAH HYDRIA
  (2-HANDLED —) AMPHORA
  (PREF.) DOLIO URCEI
JARASANDHA (FATHER OF —) BRIHADRATHA
  (SLAYER OF —) BHIMA
JARED (SON OF —) ENOCH
JARGON CANT JIVE RANE SLUM ARGOT LINGO SLANG LINGUA LINSEY PATOIS PATTER PIDGIN SHELTA SIWASH CHINOOK CHOCTAW DIALECT JARGOON PALAVER BARRIKIN KEDGEREE PARLANCE POLYGLOT SCHMOOZE SHOPTALK
  (THIEVES' —) FLASH
  (TINKER'S —) KENNICK
  (UNINTELLIGIBLE —) BARAGOUIN
JARHA (MASTER OF —) SHESHAN
JARIB (FATHER OF —) SIMEON
JARRING JARG RUDE SOUR HARSH ROUGH DARING STRIDENT
JASHUB (FATHER OF —) BANI ISSACHAR
JASMINE BELA MALATI PIKAKE JESSAMY WOODBINE
JASPER JASPIS MORLOP DIASPER BASANITE CREOLITE
JATAYU (FATHER OF —) GARUDA
  (SLAYER OF —) RAVANA
JAUNDICE AURIGO GULSACH ICTERUS JANDERS YELLOWS JAUNDERS GRASSERIE
  (PREF.) ICTER(O)
JAUNDICED ICTERODE
JAUNT TRIP SALLY JAUNCE VAGARY JOURNEY
JAUNTILY AIRILY BOUNCILY
JAUNTING CAR SIDECAR OUTSIDER
JAUNTY PERK PERT TRIM COCKY PERKY SASSY DAPPER JANTEE SHANTY FINICAL PERKING DEBONAIR

JAVA

INDONESIAN NAME: DJAWA
ISLAND: BALI LOMBOK MADURA
MEASURE: PAAL
MOUNTAIN: GEDE MURJO RAOENG SEMERU SLAMET SEMEROE SOEMBING
PORT: BATAVIA SURABAJA TJILATJAP
RIVER: SOLO LIWUNG BRANTAS
TOWN: BOGOR DESSA KEDIRI MALANG BANDUNG BATAVIA· JAKARTA SEMARANG SURABAJA
WEIGHT: POND TALI

JAVA ALMOND PILI CANARI KANARI TALISAY
JAVA COTTON KAPOK
JAVA HEAD (AUTHOR OF —) HERGESHEIMER
  (CHARACTER IN —) TAOU YUEN RHODA EDWARD GERRIT JEREMY NETTIE VOLLAR AMMIDON DUNSACK WILLIAM
JAVAN (FATHER OF —) JAPHETH
JAVANESE KRAMA KROMO
JAVANESE SKUNK TELEDU
JAVA PLUM DUHAT JAMBUL LOMBOY JAMBOOL
JAVA SPARROW MUNIA PADDY RICEBIRD
JAVELIN COLP DART PILE ACLYS PILUM JAREED LANCET ASSAGAI HARPOON HURLBAT JAVELOT ACONTIUM GAVELOCK
JAW JIB BEAK CHAP CHAW CHOP JOWL WANG ANVIL CHAFT CHEEK CHOKE SCOLD CHAWLE FEELER JAWBONE MAXILLA MANDIBLE
  (— OF FORCEPS) BEAK
  (— OF SPIDER) FANG
  (— OF VISE) CHAP
  (—S OF BIRD) BILL
  (FALSE —) CLAMP
  (RECEDING NOSE AND UNDERSHOT —) LAYBACK
  (PL.) MAW BITS THROAT
  (PREF.) (UNDER —) GENYO
  (SUFF.) GNATHA(E) GNATHI(A)(C)(SM) GNATHOUS GNATHUS
JAWBONE JOWL WANG MAXILLA CHAWBONE
  (PREF.) MAXILLI MAXILLO
JAWBREAKING CRACKJAW
JAY JAYPIET SIRGANG BLUECOAT MEATBIRD
JAYHAWKER KANSAN
JAZERANT GESSERON
JAZZ BOP JIVE HOTCHA
JEALOUS YELLOW EMULOUS ENVIOUS
JEALOUSY ENVY YELLOWS EMULATION ZELOTYPIA
JEAN FROCKING
JEAN-CHRISTOPHE (AUTHOR OF —) ROLLAND
  (CHARACTER IN —) ADA JEAN GRAZIA KRAFFT LOUISA MICHEL COLETTE LORCHEN OLIVIER STEVENS MELCHIOR GRUNEBAUM

JEANPAULIA BAIERA
JEATERAI (FATHER OF —) ZERAH
JECHOLIAH (HUSBAND OF —) AMAZIAH
  (SON OF —) UZZIAH AZARIAH
JEDAIAH (FATHER OF —) HARUMAPH
JEDIAEL (FATHER OF —) SHIMRI MESHELEMIAH
JEDIDAH (HUSBAND OF —) AMON
  (SON OF —) JOSIAH
JEER BOB BOO MOB GECK GIBE GIRD JAPE JEST JIBE MOCK SKIT WIPE FLIRT FLOUT FLUTE FLYTE FRUMP GLAIK LAUGH SCOFF SCOMM SNEER TAUNT CHIACK DERIDE BARRACK RIDICULE
JEERING BIRD FLOUT DERISIVE
JEHALELEL (SON OF —) AZARIAH
JEHIEL (BROTHER OF —) JEHORAM
  (FATHER OF —) HOTHAN HACHMONI JEHOSHAPHAT
  (SON OF —) GIBEON OBADIAH SHECHANIAH
JEHIZKIAH (FATHER OF —) SHALLUM
JEHOADDAN (HUSBAND OF —) JOASH
  (SON OF —) AMAZIAH
JEHOAHAZ (FATHER OF —) JEHU JOSIAH JEHORAM
  (SON OF —) JEHOASH
JEHOASH (FATHER OF —) AHAZIAH JEHOAHAZ
JEHOHANAN (SON OF —) ISHMAEL
JEHOIACHIN (FATHER OF —) JEHOIAKIM
JEHOIADA (FATHER OF —) PASEACH
  (SON OF —) BENAIAH
  (WIFE OF —) JEHOSHEBA
JEHOIAKIM (FATHER OF —) JOSIAH
  (SON OF —) JEHOIACHIN
JEHONADAB (FATHER OF —) RECHAB
JEHONATHAN (FATHER OF —) UZZIAH
JEHORAM (BROTHER OF —) AHAZIAH
  (FATHER OF —) AHAB JEHOSHAPHAT
  (SLAYER OF —) JEHU
  (WIFE OF —) ATHALIAH
JEHOSHAPHAT (FATHER OF —) ASA AHILUD NIMSHI PARUAH
  (SON OF —) JEHU JEHORAM
JEHOSHEBA (FATHER OF —) JORAM
  (HUSBAND OF —) JEHOIADA
  (SON OF —) JOASH
JEHOVAH JAH LORD JAHVE YAHWEH
  (— WITNESS) PIONEER
JEHOZABAD (FATHER OF —) OBEDEDOM
  (MOTHER OF —) SHOMER SHIMRITH
JEHOZADAK (FATHER OF —) SERAIAH
  (SON OF —) JESHUA
JEHU (FATHER OF —) HANANI JOSIBIAH JEHOSHAPHAT
  (SON OF —) JEHOAHAZ
  (VICTIM OF —) JEHORAM

JEHUDI (FATHER OF —) NETHANIAH
JEHUSH (FATHER OF —) ESHEK
JEJUNE DRY ARID MEAGER INSIPID
JEKAMIAH (FATHER OF —)
SHALLUM
JELL COME FIRM
JELLY GEAL JEEL JELL GELEE
CULLIS JUJUBE ALCOGEL
FISNOGA GELATIN JELLIFY
FLUMMERY HYDROGEL QUIDDANY
MARMALADE
(AGAR-AGAR —) KANTEN
(CALF'S-FOOT —) SULZE
(FRUIT —) ROB
(MEAT —) ASPIC
(PREF.) GELATI
JELLYFISH JELLY QUARL CARVEL
MEDUSA ACALEPH AURELIA
BLUBBER MEDUSAN SLOBBER
SUNFISH SCYPHULA SEACROSS
STROBILA
(PART OF —) ARM BELL MOUTH
MARGIN STOMACH TENTACLE
UMBRELLA MANUBRIUM
(PREF.) MEDUSI
JELLYLIKE SLABBY
JEMIMA (FATHER OF —) JOB
JEMMY BETTY
JEMUEL (FATHER OF —) SIMEON
JENNY MULE BETTY JINNY
JEOPARDIZE STAKE EXPOSE
HAZARD IMPERIL ENDANGER
JEOPARDY RISK PERIL DANGER
HAZARD
JEPHTHAH (FATHER OF —) GILEAD
JEPHUNNEH (SON OF —) CALEB
JEQUIRITY BEAN EYEN RUTTEE
JERAH (FATHER OF —) JOKTAN
JERAHMEEL (FATHER OF —) MAHLI
HEZRON HAMMELECH
JERBOA GERBIL JUMPER
JERED (FATHER OF —) MAHALALEEL
(SON OF —) ENOCH
JEREED TZIRID
JEREMIAD TRAGEDY
JEREMIAH (DAUGHTER OF —)
HAMUTAL
(FATHER OF —) HILKIAH
(SON OF —) JAZANIAH
JEREMOTH (SON OF —) ELAM
HEMAN MUSHI ZATTU
JERIMOTH (DAUGHTER OF —)
MAHALATH
(FATHER OF —) BELA DAVID
HEMAN MUSHI AZRIEL BECHER
JERIOTH (HUSBAND OF —) CALEB
JERK BOB GAG JET NUD TIT BOUT
CANT FIRK GIRD HIKE JERT JIRT
JOLT JOUK KICK PECK SNAP SNIG
YANK YERK BRAID CHUCK FLIRT
HITCH HOICK SCHMO SLIRT
SNAKE SPANG SURGE TWEAK
TWICK FILLIP JIGGER SWITCH
TWITCH WRENCH FLOUNCE
SACCADE SCHMUCK SPANGHEW
JERKED MEAT TASAJO
JERKILY HITCHILY
JERKIN SAYON JACKET
JERKY NERVY SHARP CHOPPY
ELBOIC FLICKY FLINGY HITCHY
JIGGETY CHOPPING PALMODIC
RATCHETY SACCADIC
JEROBOAM REHOBOAM

(FATHER OF —) JOASH NEBAT
(WIFE OF —) ANO
JEROHAM (FATHER OF —) PASHUR
(SON OF —) ADAIAH AZAREEL
AZARIAH ELKANAH IBNEIAH
JERSEY FROCK SHIRT GANSEY
TRICOT ZEPHYR MAILLOT SINGLET
CAMISOLE GUERNSEY
JERUSALEM ZION ARIEL SOLYMA
AHOLIBAH
JERUSALEM ARTICHOKE TUBER
CANADA GIRASOL
JERUSALEM CHERRY SOLANUM
JERUSALEM DELIVERED (AUTHOR
OF —) TASSO
(CHARACTER IN —) HUGH OTHO
SWENO ARMIDA OLINDO ALADINE
ERMINIA GODFREY RINALDO
TANCRED ARGANTES BOUILLON
CLORINDA SOLIMANO SOPHRONIA
JERUSALEM OAK AMBROSIA
JERUSALEM SAGE PHLOMIS
SAGELEAF
JERUSALEM THORN CASCOL
RETAMA
JERUSHA (FATHER OF —) ZADOK
(HUSBAND OF —) UZZIAH
JESAIAH (BROTHER OF —) PELATIAH
(FATHER OF —) HANANIAH
JESHAIAH (FATHER OF —)
JEDUTHUN REHABIAH
(MOTHER OF —) ATHALIAH
JESHARELAH (FATHER OF —)
ASAPH
JESHER (FATHER OF —) CALEB
(MOTHER OF —) AZUBAH
JESIAH (FATHER OF —) UZZIEL
JESSAMINE JASMINE WOODBINE
JESSE (FATHER OF —) OBED
(SON OF —) DAVID
JESSICA (FATHER OF —) SHYLOCK
(HUSBAND OF —) LORENZO
JEST BAR BOG COD COG FUN GAB
JOE TAX BULL GAME GAUD GIRD
JAPE JOKE JOSH PLAY QUIP QUIZ
RAIL SKIT BOURD BREAK CHAFF
CLOWN DROLL FLIRT GESTE
GLEEK SPORT THING BANTER
GLANCE JAPERY RAILLY TRIFLE
DICTERY GAMMOCK JOLLITY
WAGGERY DROLLERY RAILLERY
(— SPITEFULLY) SLENT
JESTER FOOL MIME BUFFO CLOWN
DROLL IDIOT JAPER JOKER PATCH
WAMBA DISOUR MOTLEY YORICK
BADCHAN BOURDER BUFFOON
DIZZARD DROLLER JOCULAR
JUGGLER PICADOR SCOFFER
SCOGGIN TOMTRAM MERRYMAN
OWLGLASS PLEASANT RAILLEUR
TRINCULO
JESTING DROLL JAPERY SCOPTIC
WAGGISH
(RUDELY —) INFICETE
JESUI (FATHER OF —) ASHER
JESUIT PAULIST TERTIAN
IGNATIAN LOYOLITE
JESUS GEE GIS IHC IHS JHS YHS
JESU WISDOM
(SAYINGS OF —) AGRAPHA
JET BOLT TAIL TANG BREAK
DUMBY DUMMY JETTO SALLY
SCOOT SPOUT SPRAY SPURT

CANDLE DELUGE DOUCHE
GAGATE SQUIRT FANTAIL
JETTEAU SPATTER SPURTER
FOUNTAIN SOFFIONE UPSPRING
(— OF FLAME) TONGUE
(— OF METAL) BREAK
(— OF VOLCANIC STEAM) STUFA
(SMALL —) SQUIB
(SUBSONIC —) AIRBUS
JET-BLACK BUGLE
JETHER (FATHER OF —) EZRA JADA
GIDEON
(SON OF —) AMASA
(SON-IN-LAW OF —) MOSES
JETHRO (DAUGHTER OF —)
ZIPPORAH
(SON-IN-LAW OF —) MOSES
JETTING SALIENT
JETTISON DUMP JETSAM
JETTY JET PEN DIKE GROIN JUTTY
BRIDGE OVERHANG
JEUSH (FATHER OF —) ESAU BILHAN
REHOBOAM
(MOTHER OF —) AHOLIBAMAH
JEW SAINT ESSENE JUDEAN
LITVAK SEMITE SMOUCH SMOUSE
TOBIAD BARABAS GRECIAN
KARAITE MARRANO APIKOROS
CONVERSO GALICIAN JUDAHITE
LANDSMAN SEPHARDI
(—S OUT OF ISRAEL) DIASPORA
(BALKAN —) LADINO
JEWEL GEM JOY DROP OUCH
BIJOU REGAL STONE BROOCH
GEORGE TRIFLE CRAPAUD
GARLAND POUNDER
(PL.) BULSE PERRIE
JEWELER GEMMARY LAPIDARY
JEWELRY ICE JUNK OUCH PARURE
COLLARET LAPIDARY
(MOCK —) LOGIE
(PIECE OF —) GAUD
JEWELS OF THE MADONNA
(CHARACTER IN —) GENNARO
MALIELLA RAFFAELE
(COMPOSER OF —) WOLFFERRARI
JEWELWEED CEROLINE EARJEWEL
SNAPWEED
JEWFISH MERO GUASA WARSAW
PERCOID JUNEFISH MULLOWAY
SERRANID
JEWISH JUDAIC SEMITIC
(— BODY) VAAD
(— COMMUNITY) KEHILLAH
(— QUARTER) MELLAH
(— SCHOOL) ALJAMA
(PREF.) JUDAEO JUDEO
JEW OF MALTA (AUTHOR OF —)
MARLOWE
(CHARACTER IN —) JACOMO
MARTIN ABIGAIL BARABAS
MATHIAS CALYMATH ITHAMORE
LODOWICK BELLAMIRA
BERNARDINE
JEWRY GHETTO JUDAISM
JEW'S-HARP HARP TROMP TRUMP
GEWGAW FLAMFEW TRANGAM
GUIMBARD
JEW'S MALLOW DESI
JEZANIAH (FATHER OF —)
HOSHAIAH
JEZEBEL GILLIVER
(FATHER OF —) ETHBAAL

(HUSBAND OF —) AHAB
(SLAYER OF —) JEHU
JEZER (FATHER OF —) NAPHTALI
JEZOAR (FATHER OF —) ASHER
(MOTHER OF —) HELAH
JEZREEL (FATHER OF —) HOSEA
JIB GIB BALK BAULK DEMUR GIGUE
STICK GIBBET SPITFIRE
JIBE (ALSO SEE GIBE) GEE KAY
GAFF GIBE JAPE JERK MOCK SKIT
AGREE FLIRD MARCH SNACK
THRUST
JIBSAM (FATHER OF —) TOLA
JIDLAPH (FATHER OF —) NAHOR
JIFFY JIFF BRAID FLISK WHIFF
GLIFFY GLIFFING
JIG BUCK FRISK GIGUE SQUID
GARLIC JIGGER JIGGET JITTER
LOCATOR
(— FOR WASHING ORE) HUTCH
(FISHING —) PILK
JIGGER SHOT DANDY PIQUE
DOODAD GADGET JIGMAN
VATMAN CHIGGER
JIGGLE DIDDLE JUGGLE TEETER
JILT GUNK KICK SACK BEGOWK
BEGUNK MITTEN
JIMMY BETTY JAMES JEMMY
JIMNA (FATHER OF —) ASHER
JIMSONWEED DATURA DEWTRY
JIMSON FIREWEED STRAMONY
JINGLE TUNE CHIME CHINK CLINK
DINGLE RICKLE TINKLE CHINKLE
CLERIHEW DINGDONG JINGLING
(MEANINGLESS —) SPORT
JINGLING SMIT JANGLE RIGADIG
TINKLING
JINGO WARRIOR WARMONGER
JINGOISM CHAUVINISM
JINKER WHIM
JINN DJIN DJINN JANN AFRIT EBLIS GENIE
AFREET DJINNI SHAITAN
(PL.) JINNI
JINNI MARID AFREET ALUKAH
GENIUS YAKSHA YAKSHI JINNIYEH
JINRIKIMAN KURUMAYA
JINRIKISHA GOCART KURUMA
RICKSHAW
JINX HEX JONAH HOODOO
JIPIJAPA CHIDRA PANAMA
PALMILLA TOQUILLA
JITTERBUG TRUCKING
JITTERY EDGY JUMPY TENSE
SPOOKY AJITTER
JIVARO JIBARO SHUARA XIBARO
JOAB (BROTHER OF —) ASAHEL
ABISHAI
(MOTHER OF —) ZERUIAH
(SLAYER OF —) BENAIAH
(UNCLE OF —) DAVID
(VICTIM OF —) ABNER
JOAH (FATHER OF —) ASAPH
JOAHAZ ZIMMAH OBEDEDOM
(SON OF —) EDEN
JOAHAZ (SON OF —) JOAH
JOAN JUG JONE
(— OF ARC) PUCELLE
JOANNA (FATHER OF —) RHESA
(HUSBAND OF —) CHUZA
JOASH (FATHER OF —) AHAB
BECHER AHAZIAH SHEMAAH
JEHOAHAZ
(SON OF —) GIDEON

(VICTIM OF —) ZECHARIAH
JOB LAY TUT CHAR CRIB FIST
SHOP TURN BERTH CHORE FIRST
PLACE BILLET HOBJOB HUSTLE
JOBSITE SWEATER BUSINESS
POSITION
(EASY —) BLUDGE
(FATHER OF —) ISSACHAR
(SMALL —) CHORE JOBBLE
JOBAB (FATHER OF —) JOKTAN
JOBBER BRAGER DEALER FLUNKY
BROGGER COURSER
JOB'S TEARS COIX ADLAI ADLAY
JOCHEBED (HUSBAND OF —)
AMRAM
(SON OF —) AARON MOSES
JOCKEY JOCK ROPER WASTER
CHANTER EQUISON TURFITE
SKIPJACK
(— FOR POSITION) DICE
(DISC —) DEEJAY
JOCOSE JOCO LEPID JOCULAR
JOCOTE MOMBIN
JOCOTE DE MICO BARBAS
JOCULAR GAY AIRY GLAD JOKY
DROLL FUNNY HAPPY JOLLY
MERRY WITTY BLITHE ELATED
JAPISH JOCOSE JOCUND JOKISH
JOVIAL JOYFUL JOYOUS LIVELY
BUOYANT COMICAL FESTIVE
GLEEFUL PLAYFUL WAGGISH
ANIMATED CHEERFUL DEBONAIR
GLADSOME HUMOROUS
JOCATORY JOKESOME
LAUGHING MIRTHFUL
BURLESQUE
JOCULARITY FUN WAGGERY
JOCUND BUDGE MERRY JOCANT
JOCULAR
JOE JO
(HALF —) JOANNES JOHANNES
JOED (FATHER OF —) PEDAIAH
JOEL (BROTHER OF —) NATHAN
(FATHER OF —) NEBO SAMUEL
ZICHRI PEDAIAH PETHUEL
IZRAHIAH
(SON OF —) HEMAN
JOELAH (FATHER OF —) JEROHAM
JOE-PYE WEED EUPATORY
JOEWOOD JOEBUSH BARBASCO
IRONWOOD
JOG BOB HOD JAG JIG JOT MOG
KICK POKE SHOG SPUD STIR TROT
WHIG DUNCH HOTCH MOSEY
NUDGE TWEAK DIDDLE JITTER
JOGGLE JUNDIE
(— ALONG) FADGE FODGE
(— AWKWARDLY) DODGE
(— WITH ELBOW) DUNCH
JOGGER LAYBOY
JOGGLE HOTCH JUGGLE SHOGGLE
SHOOGLE
JOGLI (SON OF —) BUKKI
JOHA (FATHER OF —) BERIAH
JOHANAN (FATHER OF —) JOSIAH
KAREAH TOBIAH AZARIAH
ELIOENAI HAKKATAN
(SON OF —) AZARIAH
JOHANNES JOE PECA
JOHN IAN JEAN JOCK JONE JUAN
SEAN JOHANN SEAGHAN
GIOVANNI
(BROTHER OF —) JAMES

(FATHER OF —) ZEBEDEE
ZACHARIAS
(MOTHER OF —) SALOME
ELISABETH
**JOHN BROWN'S BODY (AUTHOR
OF —)** BENET
(CHARACTER IN —) CLAY JACK
LUCY LUKE DUPRE SALLY SOPHY
SPADE VILAS ELLYAT MELORA
SHIPPY WINGATE WEATHERBY
BRECKINRIDGE
JOHNNYCAKE CORNCAKE
JOIADA (FATHER OF —) ELIASHIB
JOIAKIM (FATHER OF —) JESHUA
JOIN ADD COP FAY MIX OUP PAN
TAG TIE UNY ALLY COPE FAIR
FUSE GAIN GLUE KNIT LINK MEET
MELL SEAM SOUD TAIL TEAM
YOKE ANNEX BLEND ENTER
FRANK GRAFT JOINT MERGE
TENON UNITE WRING ACCEDE
ADJECT ADJOIN ASSIST ATTACH
CEMENT COCKET COMMIT
CONCUR ENGAGE INDENT
JOGGLE MARROW MINGLE PIECEN
RELATE RELIDE SPLICE STITCH
STRIKE COMBINE CONJOIN
CONNECT CONTACT INJOINT
JOINING SHACKLE ACCOUPLE
COALESCE COMPOUND COPULATE
DOVETAIL JUNCTION
ACCOMPANY
(— BATTLE) JOUST ENGAGE
(— BY SEWING) STITCH SUTURE
(— CLOSELY) FAY AFFY WELD
GRAFT
(— IN COMBAT) BUCKLE
(— IN MARRIAGE) WED TACK
HITCH COUPLE
(— THE PARTS OF) PIECE
(— TOGETHER) CLOSE COAPT
FRANK HITCH COUPLE ENGLUE
ENJOIN ASSEMBLE COAGMENT
COALESCE
(— UP) ACCEDE
(PREF.) ARTIO
JOINED JOINT ALLIED DIRECT
SEAMED ACCOLLE ADJUNCT
APPINED EMBOITE ADJUGATE
COMBINED CONJUNCT COPULATE
INTEGRAL
(PREF.) GAM(ETO)(O) ZEUCTO
ZEUGLO
JOINER SNUG WRIGHT JOINTER
JOINING BAR JOIN SEAM BRIDE
CLOSE SPLICE BETWEEN JOINDER
ADDITION JUNCTION JUNCTIVE
JUNCTURE SYNECTIC
JOINT BED HAR HIP BUTT COXA
FISH HEAD HELL HOCK JOIN KNEE
LITH LOCK SEAL SEAM TUCK
ANKLE BRAZE BUILD CARDO
CHASE ELBOW MITER MITRE
PLACE SCAPE SCARF SPALD
UNION UNITE WRIST BOXING
COMMON HAUNCH MUTUAL
SCARPH SPLICE STIFLE SUTURE
TOGGLE UNITER ARTHRON
ARTICLE COGGING DIGITAL
FETLOCK FLEXURE ISCHIUM
JOINING KNUCKLE SCATTER
SHIPLAP SIAMESE CONJOINT
CONJUNCT COUPLING DIACLASE

DOVETAIL FLASHING JOINTURE
JUNCTURE SUBJOINT SUFFRAGO
TROCHOID VARIATOR
(— ABOVE HOCK) STIFLE
(— OF BIRD'S WING) FLEXURE
(— OF FLAIL) CAPEL
(— OF MEAT) BARON SADDLE
(— OF SHIP) CHASE
(— OF STEM) NODE
(ANKLE —) COOT
(ELBOW —) NOOP
(FLEXIBLE —) HINGE
(GROOVED —) RABBET
(HIP —) COXA THURL
(MASONRY —) JOGGLE
(MINING —) CLEAT SLINE
(QUARRYING —) CUTTER
(SCARF —) BOXING
(UNIVERSAL —) CARDAN
(VERTICAL —) BUILD
(WHEEL-LIKE —) TROCHITE
(PREF.) ARTHR(O) ARTI CO
CONDYL(O) HARMO HOM(O)
JOINTED ARTHROUS
JOINTED CHARLOCK KRAUT
RUNCH
JOINTER JOINER SKIMMER
JOINT FIR EPHEDRA
JOINT GRASS PASPALUM
JOINTLY
(PREF.) CO COL COM CON COR
JOIST GEEST LEDGE BRIDGE
RAGLIN DORMANT SLEEPER
CARRIAGE
(PL.) PIGGIN JOISTING
JOJOBA PIGNUT SHEEPNUT
JOKE BAR DOR FUN GAB GAG GIG
JOE KID ROT WIT FOOL GAFF
GAME GAUD GEGG JAPE JEST
JOSH LICE NOTE QUIP QUIZ TYPE
BREAK CRACK FLIRT GLEEK GRIND
LAUGH PRANK RALLY SPORT
TRICK BANTER JAPERY PLISKY
WHEEZE JOKELET WAGGERY
CHESTNUT
(PRACTICAL —) BAR FUN GAG RIG
HOAX REAK SHAVIE HOTFOOT
(STALE —) CHESTNUT
(PL.) JAPERY
JOKER BUG DOR WAG CARD
CLOWN GRIND SLAVE FARCER
FOOLER GAGGER JOKIST
FARCEUR GIMMICK FUNNYMAN
HUMORIST JOKESTER
JOKESTER WAG WIT
JOKIM (FATHER OF —) SHELAH
JOKING JOSH BANTER JOCOSE
(PRACTICAL —) GAME
JOKSHAN (FATHER OF —)
ABRAHAM
(MOTHER OF —) KETURAH
(SON OF —) DEDAN SHEBA
JOKTAN (FATHER OF —) EBER
JOLLIFICATION RAG RANT BEANO
JOLLY SINDIG
JOLLITY MIRTH GAIETY HILARITY
JOLLITRY
JOLLY GAY KID BOON BUXOM
GAWSY MERRY RORTY SONSY
WALLY BLITHE CROUSE JOVIAL
STRING JOCULAR RAUGHTY
DISPOSED
JOLLY BOAT YAWL DANDY

JOLT JET JIG JOG JOT JUT BELT
BUMP DIRD DIRL HIKE JOWL
JUMP KICK SHOG JAUNT HOTTER
IMPACT JOGGLE JOSTLE JOUNCE
JUMBLE
JOLTING JERKY BUMPITY HOTTERY
JONA (SON OF —) PETER
JONADAB (COUSIN OF —) AMNON
(FATHER OF —) SHIMEAH
(UNCLE OF —) DAVID
JONAH JINX JONAS HOODOO
(FATHER OF —) AMITTAI
JONAN (FATHER OF —) ELIAKIM
JONATHAN (BROTHER OF —)
JOHANAN
(COMPANION OF —) DAVID
(FATHER OF —) SAUL ASAHEL
JOIADA KAREAH ABIATHAR
(SON OF —) MEPHIBOSHETH
JONQUIL JONK LILY DAFFODIL
JORAM (FATHER OF —) TOI AHAB
JEHOSHAPHAT

JORDAN

CAPITAL: AMMAN
COIN: DINAR
GULF: AQABA
MOUNTAIN: BUKKA DABAB ATAIBA
MUBRAK
REGION: PEREA BASHAN PERAEA
RIVER: JORDAN YARMUK
TOWN: AQABA ARIHA IRBID
KARAK ZARQA ZERKE NABLUS
JERICHO

JORIM (FATHER OF —) MATTHAT
JOSE (FATHER OF —) ELIEZER
JOSEPH JOSEY GIUSEPPE
(FATHER OF —) HELI JACOB JUDAH
MATTHIAS
(MOTHER OF —) RACHEL
(SON OF —) IGAL JESUS
(WIFE OF —) MARY ASENATH
**JOSEPH ANDREWS (AUTHOR OF —
)** FIELDING
(CHARACTER IN —) ADAMS BOOBY
FANNY PETER JOSEPH PAMELA
POUNCE THOMAS WILSON
ANDREWS GOODWILL SLIPSLOP
JOSEPHINE BLUSH PHENY
JOSEPH VANCE (AUTHOR OF —)
DEMORGAN
(CHARACTER IN —) JOE BONY
JANEY NOLLY SIBYL VANCE
JOSEPH LOSSIE THORPE VIOLET
BEPPINO DESPREZ PHEENER
RANDALL SPENCER PERCEVAL
CHRISTOPHER MACALLISTER
JOSES (BROTHER OF —) JESUS
(FATHER OF —) ELIEZER
JOSH GUY KID RIB JOKE CHAFF
STRING
JOSHAVIAH (FATHER OF —)
ELNAAM
JOSHBEKASHAH (FATHER OF —)
HEMAN
JOSHI JOTI JOTISARU
JOSHUA JESUS
(FATHER OF —) NUN JOZADAK
JOSIAH (FATHER OF —) AMON
ZEPHANIAH
(MOTHER OF —) JEDIDAH
JOSIBIAH (SON OF —) JEHU

JOSTLE JOG JOLT JOSS PUSH
SHOG CROWD ELBOW HUNCH
JUNDY SHOVE HURTLE HUSTLE
JOGGLE JUNDIE JUSTLE
SHOULDER
JOSTLING SCRAMBLE
JOT ACE DOT ATOM IOTA MARK
MITE TARE WHIT GRAIN MINIM
POINT TWINT WIGHT TITTLE
SCRUPLE SYLLABLE
(— DOWN) NICK
JOTHAM (FATHER OF —) GIDEON
UZZIAH
(MOTHER OF —) JERUSHAH
JOTTING TOT
JOTUNN GEIRROTH
JOUNCE HIKE JOLT JAUNT
JOURNAL TOE BOOK DIARY PAPER
BLAZER SERIAL DAYBOOK
DIURNAL GAZETTE GUDGEON
JOURNEY CASHBOOK NOCTUARY
TRUNNION
(SEA —) LOGBOOK
JOURNAL BEARING RHODING
JOURNALISM NEWSWRITING
JOURNALIST SCRIBE WRITER
BYLINER DIARIAN
AMERICAN NEW BAUM CAIN COBB
CROW DALY EDGE HOWE HUNT
KENT MOTT OTIS OWEN PAGE
PECK PRAY REED REID ROSS
SNOW WEBB WEED ADAMS
BACHE BAKER BEACH BEALS
BEEBE BRANN BROUN CREEL
DUANE EARLY ELSER FISKE
FLYNN GREEN GUILD HARTE
HOUSE IRWIN JAMES KROCK
LEWIS LOCKE MCCOY MOLEY
MOORE MORSE NOYES OGDEN
OHARA PAINE PIATT POORE
PRIME RALPH REEDY SAXON
STONE STOWE SWING SWOPE
TOWLE UPTON WALSH WHITE
YOUNG ZEVIN ASBURY BAILEY
BIERCE BISHOP BLIVEN BONSAL
BOWERS BURMAN CHILDS
CROUSE FOWLER GILDER GILMER
GODWIN GRAHAM GRAVES
GREENE HARVEY HASKIN HATTON
HERSEY HOWARD HOWELL
KEIRAN KENNAN LAFFAN
LAWSON LELAND MANTLE
MARDEN MEDILL MILLER MILLIS
MORRIS MORTON MOWRER
NELSON NEWELL PEGLER
REDMAN RESTON RIDDER
RUNYON SAVAGE SEAMAN
SEATON SELDES SHIRER STREIT
TAYLOR TILTON TUCKER TURNER
WALKER WALTER WARMAN
WILCOX WILSON ANTHONY
BARRETT BIGELOW BRENNAN
BULLARD CARROLL DANIELS
EASTMAN EDWARDS FARRELL
FEARING FISCHER FREEMAN
GALLICO GARRETT GIBBONS
GREELEY GUNTHER HALLOCK
HASSARD KENDALL LOSSING
MANNING MARQUIS MELONEY
OCONNOR OURSLER OVERTON
POLLARD PRINGLE RANDALL
RAYMOND REDPATH RITCHIE
RUSSELL SANBORN SERVISS

SMALLEY STANTON VANLOON
VEILLER VILLARD WELLMAN
WHEELER WOLFERT BROWNELL
CREELMAN JOHNSTON
LAWRENCE LIPPMANN MCINTYRE
MCKELWAY MEREDITH PULITZER
ROBINSON STARRETT STEFFENS
STILLMAN STODDARD SULLIVAN
THOMPSON TOWNSEND
WESTCOTT WHITLOCK WILLIAMS
BENEFIELD BERNSTEIN
MACDONALD MARCOSSON
MCCORMICK MOREHOUSE
PATTERSON WATTERSON
WOOLLCOTT CHAMBERLIN
WEITZENKORN
ARGENTINIAN AVELLANEDA
AUSTRALIAN DONALD FAWKNER
PATERSON
AUSTRIAN BAHR SEIDL HEVESI
SAPHIR CASTELLI
CANADIAN LAUT BROWN DAFOE
PAASSEN DECELLES FRECHETTE
CZECH CAPEK NERUDA HAVLICEK
DANISH JORGENSEN
GOLDSCHMIDT
DUTCH SCHIMMEL
ENGLISH LOW MEE BELL FYFE
GORE LANE LUCY MAIS SIMS
BANKS BLAKE COTES CROWE
DICEY DORAN GIBBS LEWIS MIALL
MOULT SCOTT SHIEL STEAD
STEED WERTH ARKELL ARNOLD
BAINES BARKER BEGBIE BENHAM
BOADEN BROOKS BUCKLE
CANTON CASTLE CHIROL DILLON
FORBES GARVIN GIBBON HANNAY
MACKAY MANNIN MAYHEW
MURRAY NORMAN REEVES
SQUIRE TRAILL WATSON BOLITHO
BYWATER CHORLEY COBBETT
ENNEVER HAMMOND HERBERT
HORABIN LEHMANN MEYNELL
ROBERTS SHORTER SPENDER
WALLACE BAERLEIN CARSWELL
CHISHOLM COURTNEY FLETCHER
HOBHOUSE LAWRENCE
LOCKHART MONTAGUE
MORRISON ROBINSON SLOCOMBE
STEEVENS STRACHEY TOWNSEND
WOODFALL BLANCHARD
COLQUHOUN GREENWOOD
LESTRANGE MACDONELL
MONYPENNY THORNBURY
BALLANTYNE BRAILSFORD
CHATTERTON CHESTERTON
FONBLANQUE HUDDLESTON
MASSINGHAM THURSFIELD
HOLLINGSHEAD
FRENCH BLUM KARR MACE PUJO
BULOZ CAPUS CLAIR DUPUY
GOSSE GRIMM HAMEL HAVES
HERVE MEYER MILLE SOREL
STEEG VERON BERTIN CARNOT
CARREL DAUDET DELORD
DUCAMP FONTAN FRERON
GOZLAN HEBERT LEROUX
MAZADE NISMAN PICHON ROMIER
SARCEY UZANNE BRISSOT
CARRERE CHARMES GENOUDE
HAUREAU LARBAUD LINGUET
MICHAUD MIRBEAU NALECHE
RECOULY REINACH REYBAUD

SCHERER SIMONDS TABOUIS
TILLIER VIARDOT CALMETTE
CLARETIE DUJARDIN GIRARDIN
GUEROULT JOUVENEL MAZELINE
NEFFTZER PELLETAN PERTINAX
PROUDHON QUILLARD
RENAUDOT RIVAROLI VEUILLOT
BAINVILLE CAILLAVET CAVAIGNAC
DESCHAMPS MIRECOURT
ROCHEFORT SAUERWEIN
VACQUERIE BARTHELEMY
DESMOULINS LACRETELLE
MONTLOSIER TASCHEREAU
TAILLANDIER MONTALEMBERT
GERMAN LONS BUSCH THOMA
BECKER DREYER EISNER GORRES
GROSSE GUBITZ HARDEN
BARTELS FRANZOS GUTZKOW
HAMMANN KALISCH MARTENS
BERNHARD ROHRBACH
LIEBNECHT SCHUCKING
STREICHER BEUMELBURG
POSCHINGER
HUNGARIAN BAJZA BALAZS
HUSZAR MORICZ RAKOSI
IRISH BELL LYND LESLIE OBRIEN
OKELLY PIGOTT DESMOND
OCONNOR ROLLESTON
ITALIAN ANCONA MONETA
BATTISTI ALBERTINI FEDERZONI
JAPANESE INUKAI FUKUZAWA
KAWAKAMI
NEW ZEALAND BALLANCE
NORWEGIAN FINNE VINJE
PARAGUAYAN BENITEZ
PERUVIAN CANDAMO
RUSSIAN KATKOV CHERNOV
NOVIKOV DOBROLYUBOV
SCOTTISH BELL REID BLACK
MUNRO CHALMERS CARRUTHERS
SWEDISH THORILD STRANDBERG
SWISS DROZ FAZY MEYER MURET
DUCOMMUN
WELSH EVANS
JOURNEY BE GO JOG RUN WAY
DIET EYRE FARE FORE GAIT GANG
GATE HIKE JUMP RACE RAIK RIDE
ROAD STEP TOUR TREK TRIP
TURN WENT BROAD COVER
DRIVE JAUNT REISE SITHE TRAIK
TRAIL TURUS WEENT COMINO
ERRAND FLIGHT HEGIRA JUNKET
TRAVEL VAGARY EMBASSY
ENTRADA EXCURSE JORNADA
JOURNAL MEANDER PASSAGE
STRETCH TRAVAIL TROUNCE
WALKING WAYFARE GODSPEED
PROGRESS PILGRIMAGE
(— BY SEA) VOYAGE
(— DOWNSTREAM) DESCEND
(DAY'S —) DIET
(DESERT —) JORNADA
(FATIGUING —) TRAIK
(LONG —) TREK
(TEDIOUS —) TRANCE
(PL.) PERIPATETICS
JOURNEYING CRUISE
JOURNEYMAN YEOMAN
JOUST PLAY TILT JOSTLE JUSTLE
TOURNEY
JOUSTER TILTER
JOVIAL GAY BOON JOVY BULLY
JOLLY MERRY GENIAL HEARTY

MELLOW WANTON BACCHIC
HOLIDAY JOCULAR CONVIVIAL
RANTIPOLE
JOVIALITY JOLLITY ROLLICK
HILARITY
JOWL CHOW CHAULE
(PL.) CHOPS
JOY JO WIN GLEE LIST PLAY BLISS
CHEER DREAM EXULT MIRTH
REVEL GAIETY HEYDAY DELIGHT
ECSTASY ELATION JOYANCE
RAPTURE REVELRY FELICITY
GLADNESS HILARITY PLEASURE
JOYFUL GAY GLAD BEAMY JOLLY
BLITHE FESTUS JOCUND JOVIAL
JOYANT JOYOUS GAUDFUL
GLADFUL GLEEFUL JOCULAR
GLADSOME
JOYFULLY FAIN FAINLY GLADLY
JOYOUSLY
JOYLESS DESOLATE LUSTLESS
UNBLITHE
JOYOUS GAY GLAD JOLLY MERRY
YOUSE BLITHE JOVIAL FESTIVE
GIOJOSO GLEEFUL JOCULAR
SMILING FRABJOUS FROHLICH
SUNSHINY
JOYOUSNESS HILARITY
JOZABAD (FATHER OF —) JESHUA
JOZACHAR (VICTIM OF —) JOASH
JUBAL (FATHER OF —) LAMECH
(MOTHER OF —) ADAH
JUBILANT ELATED JOYFUL
EXULTANT
JUBILATION JOY JOYANCE
JUBILEE
JUDA (FATHER OF —) JOSEPH
HANANIAH
(MOTHER OF —) JOANNA
JUDAH (FATHER OF —) JACOB
(MOTHER OF —) LEAH
JUDAHITE JEW
JUDAISM JEWISM HEBRAISM
JUDAS TREE CERCIS
JUDEA JEWRY
JUDEO-SPANISH LADINO
**JUDE THE OBSCURE (AUTHOR OF
—)** HARDY
(CHARACTER IN —) SUE DONN
JUDE FAWLEY RICHARD
ARABELLA DRUSILLA BRIDEHEAD
PHILLOTSON
JUDGE (ALSO SEE JURIST) DAN
JUS SEE WIG CADI CAID CAZY
DEEM DOOM HOLD IMAM JUEZ
JURY KAZI QADI RATE RULE SCAN
AWARD COUNT COURT DAYAN
GAUGE HAKIM INFER JUDEX
MINOS OPINE PUNEE TRIER
WEIGH BREHON CENSOR CRITIC
DANIEL DECERN DEEMER DICAST
DOOMER INTEND JUDGER JURIST
OPINER PUISNE SAMSON SAMUEL
SETTLE SQUIRE ACCOUNT
ADJUDGE ALCALDE ARBITER
BENCHER BRIDOYE CENSURE
DISCERN FLAGMAN FOUJDAR
HELIAST JURYMAN JUSTICE
MUNSIFF PODESTA REFEREE
SCABINE SHAMGAR SUPPOSE
APPRAISE CENTENAR CONCLUDE
CONSIDER DEEMSTER DEMPSTER
DIRECTOR DOOMSMAN

DOOMSTER ESTIMATE FOREDEEM
JEPHTHAH JUDGMENT JUDICATE
LINESMAN MINISTER MITTIMUS
ORDINARY QUAESTOR RECORDER
REGICIDE SCABINUS STRADICO
(— OF UNDERWORLD) AEACUS
(PREF.) KRIT(O)
JUDGMENT ACT EYE BOOK DEEM
DOME DOOM REDE VIEW ARRET
AWARD FANCY JUISE SENSE
SIGHT SKILL TASTE ADVICE
ASSIZE DECREE ESTEEM JUWISE
OUSTER STEVEN ACCOUNT
CENSURE CONCEIT HOLDING
OPINION THOUGHT VERDICT
WITTING DECISION ESTIMATE
JUDICIAL JUDICIUM SAGACITY
SAPIENCE SENTENCE THINKING
PREJUDICE OBSERVATION
(PREF.) GNOMO
JUDICATORY SYNOD
JUDICIOUS SAGE WISE POLITIC
PRUDENT CRITICAL JUDICIAL
MODERATE SENSEFUL SENSIBLE
WISELIKE
JUDITH (FATHER OF —) BEERI
(HUSBAND OF —) ESAU
JUDITH PARIS (AUTHOR OF —)
WALPOLE
(CHARACTER IN —) ADAM EMMA
JOHN CARDS DAVID PARIS STANE
JUDITH REUBEN WALTER
WARREN DOROTHY FRANCIS
GAUNTRY GEORGES HERRIES
SUNWOOD WILLIAM FORESTER
JENNIFER CHRISTABEL
FERNYHIRST
JUDO (— EXERCISES) KATA
(— PRACTICE) RANDORI
(— SCHOOL) DOJO
(EXPERT LEVEL IN —) DAN
JUG CAN EWER JACK JUST ASCUS
ASKOS BUIRE GAMLA GOTCH
JORUM JUBBE STEAN BOGGLE
CROUKE GOGLET GOMLAH
HYDRIA CREAMER PITCHER
CRUISKEN LECYTHUS LEKYTHOS
OENOCHOE PROCHOOS
(— WITH SPOUT) BUIRE DOLLIN
(ALE —) TOBY
(BEER —) BOCK
(BULGING —) GOTCH
(LEATHER —) JACK BOMBARD
(ONE-HANDLED —) URCEUS
(SPOUTLESS —) OLPE
JUGATED BAJOIRE
JUGGLE TRICK BAFFLE FUMBLE
CONJURE SHUFFLE
JUGGLER HARLOT CONJURER
JONGLEUR TREGETOUR
JUGLONE NUCIN
JUGULARES DERIPIA
JUGUM FIBULA JUGULUM
JUICE JUS SEW BREE BROO FOND
OOZE SUCK ANIMA BLOND BLOOD
GRAVY HUMOR LASER MOBBY
PERRY CASIRI CREMOR JIPPER
SUCCUS CAMBIUM AGUAMIEL
HYPOCIST VERJUICE
(— OF COCONUT) MILK
(— OF TREE) SAP LYCIUM
JELUTONG
(— OF UNRIPE FRUIT) OMPHACY

(APPLE —) CIDER
(CANE —) SLING
(CASSAVA —) CASSAREEP
CASSARIPE
(CONCENTRATED —) SIRUP SYRUP
(DRIED —) ALOE KINO
(FERMENTED —) SURA GRAPE
(FRUIT —) ROB ROHOB
(GRAPE —) MUST SAPA STUM
(INSPISSATED —) HYPOCIST
(INTOXICATING —) SOMA
(LETTUCE —) THRIDACE
(MEAT —) BLOND
(POPPY —) CHICK MECONIUM
(TOBACCO —) AMBEER AMBIER
(PL.) ESSENCE HUMIDITY
(PREF.) CHYL(I)(O) MYRO OPO
(SUFF.) CIDAL CIDE
JUICY FAT FRIM FRUM NAISH
SAPPY FRUITY SUCCOSE
WATERISH
JUJUBE BER ELB TSAO LOTUS
LOTEBUSH LOTEWOOD ZIZYPHUS
JUKEBOX PICCOLO NICKELODEON
JULIUS CAESAR (AUTHOR OF —)
SHAKESPEARE
(CHARACTER IN —) CATO CASCA
CINNA CLITO PORTA VARRO
BRUTUS CAESAR CICERO CIMBER
DECIUS JULIUS LUCIUS MARCUS
STRATO CASSIUS FLAVIUS
LEPIDUS MESSALA PUBLIUS
ANTONIUS CLAUDIUS LIGARIUS
LUCILIUS MARULLUS METELLUS
OCTAVIUS PINDARUS POPILIUS
TITINIUS CALPURNIA DARDANIUS
TREBONIUS VOLUMNIUS
ARTEMIDORUS
JUMBLE PI PIE ROG HASH MESS
MUSS RAFF BOTCH BOLLIX
BUMBLE FUDDLE GARBLE
HUDDLE JABBLE JUMPER JUNGLE
MEDLEY MOMBLE MUDDLE
PALTER RAFFLE WELTER WUZZLE
CLUTTER CONFUSE EMBROIL
GOULASH SHUFFLE DISORDER
MISHMASH PASTICHE RHAPSODY
SMACHRIE
(— OF SOUNDS) LURRY
JUMBLED CRAZY HASHY JUMBLY
MEDLEY HUDDLING MACARONIC
JUMP HOP LEP NIP DART JETE
LEAP LUTZ SKIP SKIT STEN STOT
TUMB BOUND CAPER FENCE
HALMA SALTO SAULT SPANG
SPEND START STOIT VAULT
DOUBLE FOOTER HURDLE INSULT
LAUNCH SPRING SPRUNT STARRE
WALLOP CISEAUX CROWHOP
SALTATE SKYLARK BALLONNE
(— ABOUT) SKIT CAPER
(— FROM AIRCRAFT) BAIL BALE
(— IN FENCING) BALESTRA
(— ON HORSEBACK) LARK
(— ON SKATES) AXEL SALCHOW
(— TO CONCLUSION) SALTUS
(PL.) ALLEGRO
JUMPER LAMMY SWAGE BARKER
LEPPER HANDYMAN
JUMPING SALIENT SALTANT
JUMPING JACK PANTINE
JUMPY ITCHY NERVOUS
JUNCO SNOWBIRD

JUNCTION HIP FROG JOIN CLOSE
CROWN RAPHE UNION FILLET
INFALL CONTACT JOINING
MEETING UNITION ABUTMENT
JUNCTURE CONSERTION
(— OF EARTH AND SKY) HORIZON
(— OF STREAMS) GRAINS
(— OF THREADS) FELL STOP
(— ON TOOTH) CERVIX
JUNCTURE PASS PINCH CRISIS
STRAIT ARTICLE BRACKET
JOINING OPHRYON EXIGENCY
JOINTAGE JOINTURE OCCASION
QUANDARY
JUNEBERRY SHADBLOW
SHADBUSH SERVICEBERRY
JUNE BUG BUZZARD DUMCLOCK
JUNGLE BUSH RUKH SHOLA
BOONDOCK
(AUTHOR OF —) SINCLAIR
(CHARACTER IN —) ONA JACK
DUANE JONAS CONNOR JURGIS
MARIJA RUDKUS ANTANAS
ELZBIETA STANISLOVAS
JUNGLE BENDY WEENONG
JUNGLE BOOK (AUTHOR OF —)
KIPLING
(CHARACTER IN —) KAA KHAN
AKELA BALOO HATHI SHERE
BULDEO MESSUA MOWGLI
TABAQUI BAGHEERA BANDARLOG
JUNIOR PUNY CADET YOUNG
PUISNE YOUNGER
JUNIPER CADE EZEL GORSE GORST
RETEM SAVIN SABINE
JUNK CRAM GEAR GOOK TOPE
DRECK REFUSE SCULCH DISCARD
PLUNDER TONGKANG
(WORTHLESS —) SLUM
JUNKET TRIP KNACK JINKET
SAFARI
JUNKMAN TATTER SCRAPMAN
SCAVENGER
JUNO MONETA PRONUBA
JUNO AND THE PAYCOCK
(AUTHOR OF —) OCASEY
(CHARACTER IN —) JACK JUNO
MARY BOYLE JERRY JOXER
DEVINE JOHNNY BENTHAM
CHARLIE TANCRED
JUPITER JOVE STATOR FORTUNE
MUSHTARI TERMINUS
(PREF.) JOVI ZENO
JUPITER'S BEARD JOUBARB
SENGREEN
JUR LWO LUOH
JUREL RUNNER CREVALLE
HARDTAIL
JURGEN (AUTHOR OF —) CABELL
(CHARACTER IN —) LISA HELEN
JURGEN MERLIN SEREDA ANAITIS
CHLORIS DESIREE DOLORES
DOROTHY KOSHCHEI GUENEVERE
JURISDICTION SOC BAIL SOKE
FUERO HONOR REALM VERGE
ABBACY BANDON BEYLIK DANGER
DIWANI RIDING SPHERE DEANERY
DEWANEE DROSTDY EMIRATE
FOUDRIE KHANATE BAILIERY
CHAPELRY FOUJDARY LIGEANCE
PASHALIC PROVINCE
(— OF BISHOP) SEE
(COERCIVE —) SWORD

(MORMON —) KEYS
(SUFF.) DOM
JURISPRUDENCE LAW BYRLAW
REPORTS
JURIST JUDGE MUFTI BREHON
LAWYER DOTTORE
AMERICAN DAY JAY LEE BOND
DANA DANE DYER GOFF GRAY
HALL HUNT KENT NOTT POPE
REED RUSK SHAW TAFT TAIT
WARE ZANE BETTS BLACK BLAIR
BROWN CASEY CHASE DAVIS
DAWES DUANE EATON FIELD
FREAR GRIER LAMAR LOGAN
MOODY MOORE PAINE RANDA
SMITH STONE STORY TANEY
TYLER WAITE WAYNE WEARE
WHITE WYTHE YATES BAYLOR
BREWER BURGER BURTON
BUTLER BYRNES CATRON CLARKE
COOLEY CURTIS DANIEL DARROW
DULLES FOLGER FORTAS FULLER
GASTON GIBSON HARLAN
HOLMES HUDSON HUGHES
JEROME KENYON LANDIS LOWELL
LURTON MARTIN MILLER MINTON
MORRIS MURPHY NELSON
PARKER PECORA PETERS PITNEY
POWELL SEWALL STRONG
SUMNER SWAYNE UPSHUR
VINSON WARREN WILBUR
BALDWIN BRADLEY CARDOZO
CLAYTON CUSHING DOUGLAS
DRAYTON GRIFFIN JACKSON
JOHNSON LINDSEY MCKENNA
PARSONS ROBERTS SANBORN
SANFORD SHERMAN STEVENS
STOWELL TRIMBLE WHARTON
WHEATON ANDERSON
BLACKMUN BRANDEIS CLIFFORD
GOLDBERG GRISWOLD GROSSCUP
KIRCHWAY LAWRENCE
MACVEAGH MARSHALL
MATTHEWS MCKINLEY MITCHELL
PENFIELD ROSENMAN RUTLEDGE
SEDGWICK STAFFORD
WALWORTH WOODBURY
ELLSWORTH GREENLEAF
GROESBECK HOPKINSON
PENDLETON SHARSWOOD
UNDERWOOD WHITTAKER
BLATCHFORD MCREYNOLDS
POINDEXTER TROWBRIDGE
WASHINGTON FRANKFURTER
VANDEVANTER
ARGENTINIAN CALVO DRAGO
ALBERDI QUESADA CASTILLO
AUSTRIAN GROSS UNGER GLASER
ZELLER REDLICH LAMMASCH
RINTELEN SCHMERLING
BELGIAN NYS PICARD LAURENT
DESCAMPS GERLACHE
BOLIVIAN SILES SAAVEDRA
BRAZILIAN PESSOA BARBOSA
BARROSO PECANHA
CANADIAN CARON JETTE ARMOUR
DAVIES MULOCK STUART
DOHERTY LACOSTE FOURNIER
HAULTAIN NEWCOMBE RICHARDS
ROBINSON HALIBURTON
FITZPATRICK
CHILEAN EGANA DONOSO
COSTA RICAN CARRILLO

CZECH HACHA
DUTCH GEER ASSER LODER GROTIUS OPZOOMER BYNKERSHOEK
ENGLISH MAY AMOS CAVE COKE HALE HOLT KING REID ANSON BOWEN BRYCE GROVE HURST IMPEY JAMES MAINE PRATT SCOTT TWISS VINER ABBOTT ATKYNS AUSTIN BARNES CARSON DAVIES FINLAY GATLEY HENLEY HEWART HUGHES MERSEY NORTON PALMER SANKEY SELDEN AMULREE DARLING GODFREY HOLLAND JENKINS MOULTON PLOWDEN CAMPBELL CHALMERS HAILSHAM JEFFREYS CALDECOTE FORTESCUE HERSCHELL LITTLETON OPPENHEIM BLACKSTONE FITZHERBERT
FRENCH ADAM GIDE MOLE DOMAT FLACH WEISS COCHIN DEMETZ DONEAU DUGUIT GOHIER HOTMAN MERLIN PITHOU DECAZES HENAULT LECONTE NOGARET RENAULT CUJACIUS DUMOULIN GODEFROY PASQUIER PORTALIS AGUESSEAU BEAUMANOIR EPREMESNIL LAFERRIERE
GERMAN UZ BAR FALK GANS HUGO KAHL POST WACH ZORN CROME FRANK HANEL KRAUS MOSER SPAHN TEMME WITTE AEGIDI AHRENS FICKER GERBER GNEIST HITZIG KELSEN LABAND

MEZGER PREUSS BOCKING COCCEJI GOLDAST GOSCHEL HEFFTER KOSTLIN RICHTER THIBAUT WICHERT ANCILLON DERNBURG EICHRODT FISCHART GEFFCKEN HABERLIN HEDEMANN HUFELAND ALTHUSIUS EBERMAYER FEUERBACH HINSCHIUS KIRCHMANN PUFENDORF HEINECCIUS KOHLRAUSCH GOLDSCHMIDT KANTOROWICZ MITTERMAIER HOLTZENDORFF
GREEK POLITES
INDIAN SAPRU
IRISH BALL MORRIS OHAGAN MACNEILL FITZGIBBON
ITALIAN AZO FIORE ROCCO ACCORSO ALCIATI CARRARA GRAVINA MANCINI TANUCCI BARTOLUS BULGARUS GAROFALO IRNERIUS ANZILOTTI ROMAGNOSI FILANGIERI PIERANTONI
JAPANESE ADACHI
MEXICAN IGLESIAS
NEW ZEALAND STOUT BULLER MANING
NORWEGIAN FALSEN HAGERUP
PANAMANIAN PORRAS
PARAGUAYAN BAEZ
PERUVIAN CORNEJO
ROMAN GAIUS LABEO CELSUS FRONTO PAULUS ULPIAN SABINUS SALVIUS PAPINIAN PROCULUS SCAEVOLA SULPICIUS TRIBONIAN MODESTINUS GREGORIANUS

RUSSIAN KAVELIN MARTENS MUROMTSEV MEYENDORFF VINOGRADOFF POBEDONOSTSEV
SCOTTISH HOME CRAIG FORBES ERSKINE GIFFORD JEFFREY LORIMER BROUGHAM
SPANISH GALVEZ PINELO AGUSTIN
SWEDISH UNDEN
SWISS DUBS MUSY HILTY HUBER LARDY MEILI BLUMER DELOLME
URUGUAYAN BRUM
JUROR JURAT ASSIZER JURYMAN CENTUMVIR
JURY ARRAY PANEL QUEST ASSIZE JURATA COUNTRY EMPANEL INQUEST
(— COUNTY) VISNE
JURYMAN DICAST JURIST ASSIZER
JURY-RIGGED HAYWIRE
JUST ALL DUE EVEN FAIR FLOP LEAL ONLY TRUE EQUAL FIRST LEVEL NOBUT ROUND VALID ZADOC CANDID GIUSTO HONEST JUSTIN JUSTUS MERELY SQUARE EQUABLE LEESOME UPRIGHT ACCURATE LIEFSOME RATIONAL RIGHTFUL SKILLFUL UNBIASED
(— AS) AFTER
(— HOVE CLEAR) ATRIP
(— IN TIME) SONICA
(ONLY —) HARDLY SCARCELY
JUSTAUCORPS JUSTICO
JUSTICE LAW DOOM RIGHT SKILL DHARMA EQUITY REASON HONESTY SHALLOW SILENCE DEEMSTER JUDGMENT JUSTITIA JUSTNESS RECORDER

(— OF PEACE) BEAK SQUIRE
(AUTHOR OF —) GALSWORTHY
(CHARACTER IN —) HOW RUTH DAVIS FROME JAMES FALDER WALTER CLEAVER COKESON WILLIAM HONEYWILL
(PREF.) DICAEO
JUSTIFIABLY FAIRLY
JUSTIFICATION CALL COLOR EXCUSE APOLOGY DEFENCE WARRANT APOLOGIA
JUSTIFIED FAIR JUST
JUSTIFY AVOW CLEAR PROVE SALVE DEFEND EXCUSE HONEST EXPLAIN RECTIFY SUPPORT WARRANT DARRAIGN MAINTAIN SANCTION UNDERPIN VINDICATE
JUSTLY WELL TRULY EVENLY FAIRLY EQUALLY HANDILY SQUARELY
JUSTNESS SQUARE FITNESS JUSTICE ACCURACY
JUSTUS JESUS
JUT HANG BULGE JETTY JUTTY BEETLE EXTEND IMPEND EXTRUDE
JUTE PAT DESI PAUT DAISEE ARAMINA CHINGMA
JUTTING HANGING
JUVENILE TEEN YOUNG JEJUNE PUERILE YOUTHFUL
JUXTAPOSED ADJACENT
JUXTAPOSITION BALANCE CONTACT CONTRAST NEARNESS

K

K KA KAY KILO KING
KAABA CAABA ALCAABA
KABAYA BADJU CABIE
KABELJOU KOB
KABISTAN KUBA
KABOB KEBOB SHASLIK
KABUKALLI CUPIUBA
KACHA (FATHER OF —) BRIHASPATI
KACHARI BODO
KACHIN SINGFO SINGPO
CHINGPAW
KADAGA COORG
KADAMBARI (FATHER OF —)
CHITRARATHA
(MOTHER OF —) MADIRA
KAFFIR KATI XOSA FINGO TEMBU
CAFFRE INFIDEL TAMBUKI
WAIGULI
(— BOY) UMFAAN
KAGU GRUIFORM
KAHODA (SON OF —) ASHTAVAKRA
KAIKAWAKA CEDAR
KAIKAWUS (FATHER OF —)
KAIQUBAD
(WIFE OF —) SAUDABAH
KAIKEYI (HUSBAND OF —)
DASHARATHA
(SON OF —) BHARATA
KAIKHUSRAU (FATHER OF —)
SYAWAUSH
(MOTHER OF —) FARANGIS
KAINGIN SWIDDEN
KAKI TRIUMPH
KAKU (GRANDFATHER OF —) ZOHAK
(SLAYER OF —) MINUCHIHR
KALAPOOIAN LAKMIUT
KALE COLE KAIL COLLARD
SPROUTS BORECOLE
KALEVALA (AUTHOR OF —)
UNKNOWN
(CHARACTER IN —) KULLERVO
ILMARINEN VAINAMOINEN
LEMMINKAINEN
KALI (HUSBAND OF —) SIVA SHIVA
KALMASHAPADA (FATHER OF —)
SUDASA
KALMUCK ELEUT UIRAD KHOSHOT
KALPA EON AEON
KALUMPIT ANAGEP
KAMA (DAUGHTER OF —) TRISHA
(FATHER OF —) DHARMA
(MOTHER OF —) LAKSHMI
SHRADDHA
(SON OF —) ANIRUDDHA
(WIFE OF —) RATI PRITI
KAMAHI BIRCH TOWAI
KAMALA WURRUS ROTTLERA
KAME AS
KAMICHI SCREAMER
KAMPUCHEA (SEE CAMBODIA)
KANA IROFA IROHA
KANGAROO ROO EURO BILBI FLIER
FLYER TUNGO BOOMER FOSTER
WOILIE DIDELPH POTOROO
WALLABY BETTONGA BOONGARY
FILANDER FORESTER WALLAROO
(FEMALE —) DOE GIN
(YOUNG —) JOEY
KANGAROO APPLE GUNYANG
POROPORO
KANGAROO RAT JERBOA
BETTONG POTOROO
KANHOBAL CONOB
KANKANAI IGOROT
KANS KUSA GLAGA KUSHA
GLAGAH
KANSA (FATHER OF —) UGRASENA
(SLAYER OF —) KRISHNA
KANSAN JAYHAWK

KANSAS
CAPITAL: TOPEKA
COLLEGE: BAKER TABOR BETHANY
STERLING WASHBURN
COUNTY: ELK GOVE LINN LYON
NESS RENO GEARY PRATT
ROOKS TREGO BARTON COFFEY
NEMAHA NEOSHO BOURBON
LABETTE ATCHISON
FORT: RILEY SCOTT
INDIAN: KANSA KIOWA PAWNEE
WICHITA COMANCHE
LAKE: CHENEY KIRWIN NEOSHO
MILFORD
MOUNTAIN: SUNFLOWER
NATIVE: JAYHAWK
NICKNAME: JAYHAWKER
SUNFLOWER
PRESIDENT: EISENHOWER
RIVER: SALINE SOLOMON
ARKANSAS MISSOURI
STATE BIRD: MEADOWLARK
STATE FLOWER: SUNFLOWER
STATE TREE: COTTONWOOD
TOWN: ALMA GOVE HAYS IOLA
COLBY DODGE HOXIE LAKIN
LEOTI SEDAN LARNED SALINA
ABILENE CHANUTE LIBERAL
ULYSSES WICHITA

KAOLIANG SORGHUM
KAPOK CEIBO FLOSS
KARAISM ANANISM
KARAKA KOPI
KARA KIRGHIZ BURUT BOUROUT
KARATAS PITA
KARATE (— SCHOOL) DOJO
(EXPERT LEVEL IN —) DAN
KAREN SGAU SGAW
KARENNI PADAUNG
KARMA FATE
(BAD —) DEMERIT
KARNA (FATHER OF —) SURYA
(MOTHER OF —) KUNTI PRITHA
(SLAYER OF —) ARJUNA
KARTTIKEYA (FATHER OF —)
RUDRA SHIVA
KASKA NAHANE
KAT KHAT QUAT CAFTA
KATE KAI
KATHERINE (HUSBAND OF —)
PETRUCHIO
KAUNAS KOVNO
KAURI COWRIE BERAIROU
KAUSHALYA (HUSBAND OF —)
DASHARATHA
(SON OF —) RAMA
KAVA AVA AWA YAQONA
KAVAKAVA YANGGONA
KAW AKHA
KAYANUSH (BROTHER OF —)
FARIDUN PURMAYAH
KAZOO BAZOO GAZOO ZARAH
HEWGAG MIRLITON
KEEL FIN BACK SEEL BARGE
CARINA CRISTA RADDLE SERRULA
(— OF BIRD'S MANDIBLE) GONYS
(AFTERPART OF —) SKAG SKEG
(PREF.) CARINI
KEEN DRY FLY GAY SHY YAP ACID
DEAR FINE GAIR GLEG HIGH
HOWL NUTS PERT TART TEEN
WAIL WARM WILD ACUTE BREME
BRIEF BRISK EAGER QUICK SHARP
SMART SNELL SPICY VIVID
ARGUTE ASTUTE BITTER CAOINE
GREEDY LIVELY SEVERE SHREWD
SHRILL CUNNING HAWKING
MORDANT PARLISH PARLOUS
PUNGENT SERIOUS THIRSTY
OBSERVANT SAGACIOUS
TRENCHANT PERSPICACIOUS
(PREF.) OXY
KEENER HOWLER
KEENLY KEEN FELLY DEARLY
ACUTELY
KEENNESS EDGE ACUITY ACUMEN
PUNGENCY
(— OF SIGHT) ACIES
KEEN-SCENTED NASUTE
NOSEWISE
KEEN-SIGHTED EAGLE
KEEP HUG HAVE HOLD SALT SAVE
WAIT WITE BLESS ROCCA WITIE
COFFER DETAIN REDUIT CONFINE
CONTAIN DEFORCE HUSBAND
KEEPING OBSERVE RESERVE
CONSERVE MAINTAIN PRESERVE
RESTRAIN WITHHOLD
(— A COURSE) CAPE
(— A SCHOOL) DOJO
(— A SMALL SHOP) CRAME
(— A WOUND OPEN) TENT
(— ABREAST) FOLLOW
(— AFLOAT) BUOY
(— AN EYE ON) STAG
(— APART) DOTTLE ISOLATE
SEPARATE
(— AT A DISTANCE) ESTRANGE
(— AWAY) ABSENT
(— AWAY FROM) ABHOR AVOID
(— BACK) DAM HAP ROB STAY
ARREAR DETAIN RETARD
RESERVE
(— COMPANY WITH) GANG MOOP
CONSORT
(— FREE) ESCHEW
(— FROM BOILING OVER) KEEL
(— FROM BURNING) REDD
(— HIDDEN) HOARD SECRETE
(— IN) CAGE
(— IN CIRCULATION) WIND
(— IN EXCITEMENT) ALARM
ALARUM
(— IN MIND) RETAIN
(— IN ORDER) TARGE
(— IN STOCK) CARRY
(— IN THE TRACK) GATHER
(— OFF) FEND WEAR EXPEL
SHIELD
(— OUT) BAR EXPEL
(— POSSESSION) HARBOR
(— SCORELESS) BLANK
(— SECRET) HUSH WHIST
(— STRAIGHT) DIRECT
(— TABS ON) FINGER
(— TIME) GO
(— TO ONESELF) BOSOM
(— UNTIL YEAR OLD) HOG
(— UP) SUBSIST SUSTAIN
CONTINUE
(— WAITING) DELAY
(— WARM) STIVE STOVE FOSTER
(— WATCH) BARK TOUT WAIT
BEWAKE
(PREF.) SOZ(O)
(— OFF) ALEXI
KEEPER NAB KEEP SCREW TUTOR
YEMER CUSTOS GAOLER JAILER
LIFTER LOOKER PARKER PASTOR
RAHDAR RANGER WARDEN
BAILIFF CURATOR GEARMAN
PIKEMAN PROVOST BEARWARD
DEERHERD DOLLYMAN
ELDERMAN FEWTERER
GUARDANT GUARDIAN
HOUNDMAN TRAITEUR
WARRENER
(— OF CATTLE) HAYWARD
(— OF DOGS) FEWTERER
(— OF ELEPHANT) MAHOUT
(— OF PRISON) GAOLER JAILER
WARDEN ALCAIDE PROVOST
(DOOR —) DURWAN
KEEPING CARE WARD TRUST
CHARGE CUSTODY DETAINER
KEEPSAKE DRURY TOKEN
GIFTBOOK SOUVENIR
KEEVE TUB KIEVE
KEG CAG PIN TUB CADE CASK
KNAG WOOD ANKER BARRICO
COSTREL
KELP KILP LEAG VAREC WRACK

305

GIRDLE SEAWEED BELLWARE
KELPIE NIX BARB
KELT SLAT LIGGER
KENAF DA GOMBO MESTA AMBARI
KANAFF PAPOULA STOKROOS
KENILWORTH (AUTHOR OF —)
SCOTT
(CHARACTER IN —) AMY HUGH
TONY GILES JANET SMITH
ALASCO DICKIE DUDLEY EDMUND
FOSTER SLUDGE SUSSEX VARNEY
WALTER GOSLING MICHAEL
RALEIGH RICHARD ROBSART
WAYLAND DOBOOBIE ELIZABETH
LAMBOURNE LEICESTER
TRESSILIAN FLIBBERTIGIBBET
KENNEL STALL VENERY VENISON
DOGHOUSE
KENO HOUSE
KENTISH (— UNIT) YOKE

KENTUCKY
CAPITAL: FRANKFORT
COLLEGE: BEREA ASBURY CENTRE
BRESCIA URSULINE
COUNTY: BATH BELL BOYD HART
TODD ADAIR BOYLE TRIGG
WOLFE ESTILL MENIFEE
MAGOFFIN
INDIAN: SHAWNEE CHEROKEE
IROQUOIS
LAKE: CUMBERLAND
RIVER: DIX OHIO SALT BARREN
STATE BIRD: CARDINAL
STATE FLOWER: GOLDENROD
STATE NICKNAME: BLUEGRASS
STATE TREE: TULIP
TOWN: INEZ BEREA CADIZ DIXON
HYDEN MCKEE PARIS CORBIN
HARLAN HAZARD GLASGOW
GREENUP PADUCAH DANVILLE
COVINGTON LEXINGTON
OWENSBORO

KENYA
BAY: FORMOSA
CAPITAL: NAIROBI
COIN: SHILLING
LAKE: MAGADI RUDOLF NAIVASHA
VICTORIA
LANGUAGE: LUO KIKUYU SWAHILI
MEASURE: WARI
MOUNTAIN: ELGON KENYA KULAL
NYIRU MATIAN LOGONOT
PEOPLE: LUO MERU BANTU
KAMBA KISII LUHYA MASAI
NANDI KIKUYU OGADEN
BALUHYA HAMITIC HILOTIC
TURKANA KIPSIGIS
RIVER: LAK ATHI TANA KEIRO
TURKWELL
TOWN: MERU KITUI NAROK KIPINI
KISUMU MOYALE NAKURU
NAYUKI ELDORET MALINDI
MOMBASA

KERCHIEF CURCH ROMAL RUMAL
ANALAV CYPRUS MADRAS
NAPKIN PEPLUM CYPRESS
KERCHER PANUELO THERESE
BABUSHKA BANDANNA HEADRAIL
KAFFIYEH KINGSMAN

KERESAPA (BROTHER OF —)
URVAKHSHAYA
(FATHER OF —) THRITA
KERF CARF SKAFF GROOVE
UNDERCUT
KERI QRI KERE
KERMANSHAH COCONUT
KERMES GRAIN
KERNEL NUT BUNT CORE KERN
MEAT PITH BERRY GOODY GROAT
ACINUS ALMOND CARNEL PICKLE
NUCLEUS PICHURIM
(CORN —S) HOMINY
(UNHUSKED —S) CAPES
(PL.) NIXTAMAL
(PREF.) CARY(O) KARY(O)
KEROGEN SAPROPEL
KEROSINE PARAFFIN
KERSENNEH ERS ERVIL
KERSEY WASHER ORDINARY
KESTREL FANNER KEELIE STANIEL
STANNEL STANCHEL WINDHOVER
KETA CHUM
KETCH SAIC
KETONE IRONE ACETOL ARMONE
CARONE CARVOL COTOIN
HEXONE IONONE QUINOL
ACETOIN ACETONE ACYLOIN
BENZOIN CAMPHOR CARVONE
DYPNONE FLAVONE JASMONE
MUSCONE PHORONE SHOGAOL
THUJONE ACRIDONE ANTHRONE
BAECKEOL BUTANONE BUTYRONE
CHALCONE CHALKONE
CHROMONE DEGUELIN EXALIONE
FENCHONE MENTHONE PROPIONE
PULEGONE ROTENONE STEARONE
TAGETONE THIENONE VALERONE
XANTHONE
KETTLE LEAD STEW DIXIE BOILER
CANNER FESSEL MARMIT MASLIN
TRIPOD VESSEL CALDRON SKILLET
STEWPOT CALABASH FLAMBEAU
KETTLEDRUM NAKER ATABAL
KETTLE TIMBAL TYMBAL TIMBALE
TYMPANY
KEVEL CAVEL KNAPPER
KEX KECKSY
KEY CAY KAY CLEW CLUE CRIB
FLAT JACK KING NOTE PLUG
PONY DITAL SCREW TASTO
WREST BUTTON CHIAVE CIPHER
CLAVIS COTTER SAMARA SPLINE
WINDER DIGITAL LANGUET
PASSKEY SPEAKER LATCHKEY
TONALITY
(— FOR TUNING HARP) WREST
(— OF KEYBOARD INSTRUMENT)
CHIP MANUAL
(— OF LIFE) ANKH
(— OF ORGAN) TASTO DIGITAL
(— OF PIANO) IVORY NATURAL
(— OF SPINET) CHIP
(— ON WOODWIND INSTRUMENT)
LANGUET SPEAKER
(— UP) STRING
(—S OF CARILLON) CLAVECIN
(ARITHMETICAL —) ADDITIVE
(ASH —) PIGEON
(FALSE —) GLUT
(FEATHER —) FIN STOP SPLINE
FEATHER
(PART OF —) BOW BLADE

WARDING SHOULDER SERRATION
(SKELETON —) GILT TWIRLER
(TELEGRAPH —) BUG TAPPER
(WHITE —) NATURAL
(PREF.) CLAVI CLEID(O) CLEIST(O)
(SUFF.) CLEISIS CLISIS
KEYBOARD CLAVIER PEDALIER
(PREF.) CLAVI
KEYHOLE KEY LOCKHOLE
KEYNOTE A B D E KEY MESE TONIC
FINALIS
KEYSTONE KEY QUOIN VERTEX
SAGITTA VOUSSOIR
(— STATE) PENNSYLVANIA
KEYWAY SPLINE KEYSLOT
KEZIA (FATHER OF —) JOB
KHA KA KHMU KACHE LAMET
KHALAT SEERPAW
KHAN CAN CHAM HAWN SERAI
TACON CHAGAN KHAKAN
KHAS-KURA NEPALI PAHARI
PARBATI GORKHALI
KHATTISH HATTIC
KHEDIVE QUITEVE
KHELLIN VISAMMIN
KHOTANA KOYUKON
KHUSKHUS CUSCUS VETIVER
KIANG ONAGER CHIGETAI
HEMIONUS
KIBBLE GIG KETTLE
KIBBLER CRACKER
KICK BOOT FICK FLEG FLIG FOOT
FUNK HEEL HOOF LASH PORR
POTE PUNT SHIN TURF YERK
ANGLE BUNCH FLING KEVEL
PAUSE PUNCH SKELP SPANG
SPURN CHARGE CORNER FITTER
KICKER KICKUP OBJECT SPIRAL
VOLLEY DROPOUT FOUETTE
KICKOFF DROPKICK PLACEKICK
(— ABOUT) SPARTLE
(— AS A HORSE) FLING WINCE
(— HEELS UP) SPURN
(— ON SHINS) HACK SHINNER
(BALLET —) BRUSH
(SOCCER —) CORNER
(SWIMMING —) THRASH
KICKER TEDDER WINCER
KID COD FUN POD TUB FAWN
FOOL JIVE JOKE CHILD FAGOT
HORSE JOLLY KIDDY SPOOF
KIDLET SQUIRT DECEIVE EANLING
FATLING TICCHEN YOUNGER
CHEVEREL YEANLING
KIDDING JOKE SPOOFERY
KIDNAP STEAL ABDUCT PANYAR
SPIRIT
KIDNAPER PLAGIARY SNATCHER
SPIRITER
KIDNAPING SNATCH PLAGIUM
PLAGIARY
KIDNAPPED (AUTHOR OF —)
STEVENSON
(CHARACTER IN —) ALAN BRECK
COLIN DAVID RIACH SHUAN
BALFOUR RANSOME CAMPBELL
EBENEZER HOSEASON
RANKEILLOR
KIDNEY NEAR NEER REIN TYPE
NEPHRON
(PL.) REINS ROGNONS
(PREF.) NEPHR(O) RENI RENO
(SUFF.) NEPHRITIS NEPHROSIS

KIDNEY BEAN FRIJOLE
(PL.) FASELS
KIER KEEVE PUFFER
KIESELGUHR DOPE GUHR
KILL DO BAG END GET MOW OFF
OUT PIP ZAP BANE BOLO COOK
COOL DOWN FELL MORT NECK
SLAY TAME WING BLAST BRAIN
CROAK CULLE FETCH FORDO
GANCH MISDO NAPOO QUELL
SABER SCRAG SHOOT SMITE
SNUFF SPEED SPEND SPILL SPOIL
STALL STICK SWELT SWORD
WASTE CORPSE DEADEN DIDDLE
FAMISH FINISH HANDLE IMPALE
MARTYR MURDER POISON
STARVE UNLIVE ACHIEVE
BUTCHER DESTROY EXECUTE
FLATTEN HATCHET KILLING
MORTIFY SMOTHER STONKER
SUICIDE DEATHIFY DISPATCH
DISSOLVE IMMOLATE JUGULATE
STILETTO
(— ANIMALS) CONTROL
(— BY STONING) LAPIDATE
(— BY SUBMERSION) STIFLE
(— CALF AFTER BIRTH) DEACON
(— CATTLE) PITH
(— EVERY TENTH) DECIMATE
(— GAME) SATCHEL
(— OFF) ENECATE
(— SMALL GAME) BARK
(— TIME) GOOF
(— WITH GRENADE) FRAG
KILLDEER KILLDEE DEERKILL
KILLED KILT WINGED SKITTLED
(FRESHLY —) GREEN
KILLER GUN BRAVO GUNMAN
SLAYER TORPEDO MURDERER
THRESHER
(SUFF.) CIDAL CIDE
KILLER WHALE ORCA DOLPHIN
GRAMPUS
KILLIFISH KELLY KILLY MINNOW
COBBLER GUDGEON MAYFISH
MUDFISH PANCHAX FUNDULUS
ROCKFISH SACALAIT STUDFISH
SWAMPINE MUMMICHOG
KILLING FELL KILL MORT QUELL
TUANT MURDER CLEANUP
HANGING CLEANING DISPATCH
FELICIDE HOMICIDE
MANSLAUGHTER
(MERCY —) EUTHANASIA
KILLJOY NARK GLOOM LEMON
SOURPUSS
KILN BING KEEL LEHR OAST CULLE
DRIER GLAZE STOVE TILER
COCKLE CUPOLA TILERY
FURNACE CALCINER LIMEKILN
KILOGRAM (— OF MARIJUANA OR
HEROIN) KEY
(— OF NARCOTIC) KEY
KILOMETER LI
KILORAD KRAD
KILT QUELT PIUPIU FILIBEG
PHILIBEG PETTICOAT
KILTER SKEET
KIM (AUTHOR OF —) KIPLING
(CHARACTER IN —) ALI KIM OHARA
ARTHUR HURREE LURGAN
MAHBUB BENNETT KIMBALL
CREIGHTON MOOKERJEE

KIN SIB KATI KITH CATTY CUNNE
FLESH FAMILY AFFINITY
RELATION

KIND ILK KIN LOT BOON CAST FAIR
FORM GOOD HAIR HEND LIKE
MAKE MEEK MILD MODE MOLD
NICE RATE SELY SOFT SORT SUIT
TRIM TYPE WING BREED BROOD
CLASS GENRE GENUS GESTE
ORDER SPICE STAMP BENIGN
BLITHE FACILE GENDER GENTLE
GOODLY HUMANE KIDNEY KINDLY
MANNER MISTER NATURE SPEECE
STRAIN STRIPE TENDER CLEMENT
EDITION FASHION FEATHER
FLESHLY LENIENT QUALITY
REGIMEN SPECIAL SPECIES
SPECKLE FRIENDLY GENEROUS
MANSUETE OBLIGING BENIGNANT
INDULGENT OFFICIOUS
PERSUASION
(— OF) A
(— OF PEOPLE) FOLK
(DIFFERENT IN —) DIVERS
(DISTINCTIVE —) BRAND
(OF EVERY —) ALKIN
(PREF.) GEN(O)

KINDLE BEET BLOW FIRE LUNT
MOVE TAKE TEND TIND FLAME
LIGHT QUICK SPUNK ACCEND
ALIGHT DECOCT ENFIRE EXCITE
IGNITE ILLUME EMBLAZE ESPRISE
INCENSE INFLAME SOLICIT
KINDLING

KINDLINESS CANDOR

KINDLING FIRE BAVIN FAGOT
TINDER IGNITION

KINDLY FAIR GAIN KIND NESH
AGREE COUTH HENDE NAISH
BENIGN BLITHE COUTHY GENIAL
HOMELY AMIABLE BENEFIC
INNERLY FAVOROUS GENEROUS
GRACIOUS QUEMEFUL TOWARDLY

KINDNESS LOVE ALOHA FAVOR
BOUNTY CANDOR LENITY
BENEFIT SERVICE CLEMENCY
EASINESS GOODNESS HUMANITY
LENITUDE MILDNESS

KIND OF
(SUFF.) EE

KINDRED KIN SIB KIND KITH
BLOOD FLESH HOUSE FAMILY
KOBONG NATION STRIND
COGNATE KINFOLK KINSMEN
RELATED SIBSHIP AFFINITY
COGNATION CONGENIAL
CONGENEROUS

KINE KYE COWS

KINETIC ACTUAL
(— POTENTIAL) L

KING RI SO BAN DAM LOT LUD PUL
REX REY RIG ROY AGAG AMON
ATLI BALI BELI BIJA BORS BRAN
BRES CRAL CZAR JEHU KRAL LEIR
MARK NUDD NUMA OMRI OTTO
PHUL RAJA RIAL TSAR TZAR
WANG YIMA ARDRI BALOR BELUS
CONOR CREON DAGDA DAHAK
EGLON ETZEL GYGES HIRAM
HOGNI HOSEA IPHIS IXION JOASH
LAIUS LLUDD LYCUS MESHA
MIDAS MINOS NADAB NEGUS
NORSE NUADA PEKAH PRIAM
RAJAH SAMMY SWAMI ZIMRI
ZOHAK AEOLUS AGENOR AILILL
ALBOIN ALONSO ALOROS ARIOCH
BLADUD CODRUS DIOMED
DUNCAN ELATHA FINGAL FRODHI
FROTHI GOEMOT INKOSI KABAKA
LEMUEL LYCAON MEMNON
MINYAS NESTOR NODONS
OENEUS OGYGES PELEUS PELIAS
SAUGHT SHESHA SVAMIN TEUCER
URIENS UZZIAH VASUKI ADMETUS
AHAZIAH AMAIMON AMYCLAS
ANGEVIN ARDRIGH ARTEGAL
ATHAMAS BAGINDA BELINUS
BUSIRIS CACIQUE CEPHEUS
CROESUS ELIDURE EPAPHUS
EPOPEUS ETHBAAL EURYTUS
GUNTHER HYGELAC INACHUS
JAMSHID JEHOASH JEHORAM
KINGLET LAERTES LATINUS
LEONTES MENAHEM MONARCH
PANDION PHINEUS POLYBUS
REGULUS ROMULUS ROYALET
SMERDIS SOLOMON VOLSUNG
ACRISIUS ADRASTUS AEGYPTUS
ALBERICH AMRAPHEL ASNAPPER
BAHMANID BRENNIUS CLAUDIUS
COPHETUA ELDORADO ETEOCLES
GILGAMES GOEMAGOT
GOGMAGOG GORBODUC
HEZEKIAH HROTHGAR JEHOAHAZ
JEROBOAM KINGLING LAOMEDON
LISUARTE MANASSEH MELIADUS
MENELAUS ODYSSEUS
ORCHAMUS OSNAPPAR OVERKING
PADISHAH PEKAHIAH PENTHEUS
RAMESSID REHOBOAM RODERICK
RODOMONT ROITELET SARPEDON
SHEPHERD SISYPHUS TANTALUS
(— AND QUEEN OF TRUMPS) BELLA
(— CHANGED TO WOLF) LYCAON
(— OF ARMS) GARTER NORROY
(— OF BEASTS) LION
(— OF DWARFS) ALBERICH
(— OF FAIRIES) OBERON
(— OF TRUMPS) HONOR
(IRISH —) RI RIG ARDRI ARDRIGH
(POLYNESIAN —) ALII ARII ARIKI
(PREF.) REGI

KINGBIRD PIPIRI PETCHARY

KINGBOLT KING KINGPIN MAINPIN

KING CRAB LIMULID LIMULUS
PANFISH

KINGDOM WEI REALM REIGN
WORLD ESTATE MONERA
MORVEN REGION SAXONY
MITANNI

KINGFISH BARB CERO HAKE HAKU
MINK OPAH TOMCOD CHENFISH
SCIAENID TOMMYCOD

KINGFISHER HALCYON PODITTI
TOROTORO

KING JOHN (AUTHOR OF —)
SHAKESPEARE
(CHARACTER IN —) JOHN BIGOT
ESSEX HENRY JAMES LEWIS
MELUN PETER ARTHUR BLANCH
ELINOR GURNEY HUBERT PHILIP
ROBERT DEBURGH LYMOGES
BRETAGNE PANDULPH
PEMBROKE CHATILLON
CONSTANCE SALISBURY
FAULCONBRIDGE

KING LEAR (AUTHOR OF —)
SHAKESPEARE
(CHARACTER IN —) KENT LEAR
CURAN EDGAR REGAN ALBANY
EDMUND OSWALD GONERIL
BURGUNDY CORDELIA CORNWALL
GLOUCESTER

KINGLET REGULI

KINGLY REGAL ROYAL REGNAL
BASILIC IMPERIAL MAJESTIC
PRINCELY

KING PARAKEET WELLAT

KING'S HENCHMAN, THE
(CHARACTER IN —) EADGAR
AELFRIDA AETHELWOLD
(COMPOSER OF —) TAYLOR

KINGSHIP STOOL THRONE
KINGDOM ROYALTY DEVARAJA
KINGHOOD

KING SOLOMON'S MINES
(AUTHOR OF —) HAGGARD
(CHARACTER IN —) GOOD JOHN
JOSE ALLAN HENRY KHIVA
TWALA CURTIS GAGOOL GEORGE
IGNOSI UMBOPA FOULATA
SCRAGGA INFADOOS SILVESTRE
VENTVOGEL QUATERMAIN

KING'S PEACE GRITH

KING'S ROW (AUTHOR OF —)
BELLAMANN
(CHARACTER IN —) DRAKE ELISE
JAMIE NOLAN RANDY RENEE
TOWER CASSIE GORDON LOUISE
MCHUGH PARRIS SANDOR
PERDOFF MONAGHAN
CASSANDRA WAKEFIELD

KING'S SCHOLAR TUG

KING VULTURE PAP PAPA

KININ KALLIDIN

KINK NIB SNICK BUCKLE DOGLEG
KINKLE
(— IN ROPE) GRIND

KINKAJOU POTTO HEYRAT
APOROSO

KINKING FLUTING

KINKY NAPPY ENCOMIC KINKLED

KINO BIJA BIJASAL

KINSHIP SIB BLOOD NASAB STOOL
ENATION KINDRED SIBNESS
SIBSHIP AFFINITY AGNATION
RELATION PROPINQUITY

KINSMAN KIN SIB ALLY BLOOD
AFFINE AGNATE COUSIN FRIEND
BROTHER GOTRAJA KINDRED
WINEMAY BANDHAVA RELATION
RELATIVE COLLATERAL

KINSWOMAN SISTER KINDRED
RELATIVE

KIP SKIP GRASSER KIPSKIN
UPSTART

KIRGHIZ QYRGHYZ

KIRGIZ (MOUNTAIN RANGE IN —)
ALAI

KIRIBATI (CAPITAL OF —) TARAWA
BAIRIKI
(FORMER NAME OF —)
GILBERTISLANDS
(ISLAND OF —) BERU MAKIN
ABAIANG ABEMAMA NONOUTI
TABITEUEA

KIRN MELL

KISH (FATHER OF —) JEHIEL
(SON OF —) SAUL

KISS BA LIP NEB BASS BUSS PECK
PREE MOUTH POGUE SLAKE
SMACK BEKISS CARESS SALUTE
SLAVER SMOOCH SMOUCH
OSCULATE
(— OF PEACE) PAX
(— WETLY) SLOBBER
(STOLEN —) SMOORICH

KISSING LIPWORK

KIT CHIT DUFFEL KITTEN OUTFIT
POCHETTE
(LUMBERMAN'S —) TURKEY
(MESS —) CANTEEN

KITCHEN BUT GALLEY CABOOSE
CUISINE KITCHIE COOKROOM

KITE LAP CHIL CYTE HAWK GLEDE
CHILLA DRACHE DRAGON ELANET
FALCON PREYER SENTRY MILVINE
PUDDOCK PUTTOCK FORKTAIL
HELLKITE

KITTEN KIT KITTY KITTLE CATLING
KITLING

KITTIWAKE GULL WAEG ANNET
KITTY PICKUP HACKLET TARROCK
TIRRLIE

KITTY CAT POT BADRANS
BAUDRONS

KIVA ESTUFA

KIWI APTERYX
(BROWN —) ROA

KLAMATH WEED AMBER
GOATWEED

KLANG PHONE

KLIPSPRINGER KAINSI KLIPBOK

KLONDIKE CANFIELD SOLITAIRE

KNACK ART FEAT FEEL GATE GIFT
HANG CATCH QUIRK SKILL TRICK
SLEIGHT WRINKLE INSTINCT

KNACKER CLAPPER
(PL.) BONES

KNAPSACK WALLET MOCHILA
MUSETTE SNAPBAG SNAPSACK

KNAPWEED SWEEP BLUETOP
FLATTOP BALLWEED BELLWEED
BOLEWEED BULLWEED
BUNDWEED CENTAURY
CLUBWEED CROPWEED
HARDHEAD IRONHEAD IRONWEED
KNOTWEED MATFELON

KNAVE BOY ELF LAD NOB PAM
PUR TOM JACK BOWER CHEAT
DROLE MAKER NODDY ROGUE
TIGER COQUIN FRIPON HARLOT
KNIGHT PICARO RASCAL VARLET
WENZEL CAMOOCH CUSTREL
PEASANT VILLAIN BEZONIAN
COISTREL SWINDLER VARLETTO

KNAVERY ROPERY CATZERIE
PATCHERY RASCALITY

KNAVISH ROGUISH SCAMPISH

KNAWEL KNOTWEED KNOTWORT

KNEAD ELT TEW MOLD POST
BRAKE STOCK PETRIE MASSAGE
(— HIDES) STOCK

KNEADING (— MACHINE) BRAKE

KNEE GENU HOCK CROOK
KNAPPER SLEEPER SUFFRAGO
(— HOLLOW) HAM
(— OF COMPOSING STICK) SLIDE
(PREF.) GENU GONY

KNEECAP CAP ROTULA PATELLA
(PL.) MARROWBONES

KNEEL SIT KNEE COUCH

SHIKO KOWTOW
KNEELER SPRINGER
KNEELING SHIKO BENDED
KNEEPAN ROTULA PATELLA
KNELL BELL RING TOLL KNOLL
STROKE
KNICKKNACK TOY KNACK TRICK
GEWGAW NOTION PRETTY
BIBELOT GIMCRACK
KNIFE DAH DIE PIN SAX ULU BOLO
BUCK MOON SAEX SHIM SHIV
SPUD TANG BOWIE BURIN CHIVE
CUTTO FACON GULLY KNIVE
KUKRI PANGA SHANK SHAVE
SKEAN SLICE BARLOW BARONG
CAMPIT CARVER SLICER COUTEL
CUTTLE CUTTOE DAGGER
DOCTOR JIGGER PANADE
PARANG PAVADE PORKER PULLER
RIMMER SICKLE SLICER TREVET
TRIVAT WORKER BREAKER
CATLING CHOPPER COUTEAU
FIPENNY KIOTOME MACHETE
PALETTE SCALPEL SEVERER
SKINNER SLASHER SNICKER
STICKER SUNDANG TICKLER
WHITTLE BELDUQUE BILLHOOK
CALABOZO JOCTELEG SERPETTE
THWITTLE YATAGHAN
SNICKERSNEE
(— FOR BREAKING FLAX) BEATER
(— FOR LEATHER) PIN
(— FOR RUBBER DOUGH) DOCTOR
(BLACKSMITH'S —) BUTTERIS
(BURMESE —) DAH DAO DOW
(CURRIER'S —) CLEANER
(ENGRAVER'S —) CRADLE
(ESKIMO —) ULU
(MORO —) BARONG
(PART OF —) NEB TIP WEB BACK
EDGE HEEL HILT BLADE CHOIL
GUARD POINT RIVET FULLER
HANDLE POMMEL BOLSTER
QUILLON ROCASSO
(SHOEMAKER'S —) BUTT
(SURGICAL —) CATLING SCALPEL
BISTOURY EXSECTOR
(TANNER'S —) GRAINER
KNIFE-PLEATED KILTED
KNIGHT N ELF SIR ADUB GANO
TULK EQUES EQUIS HORSE LANCE
RIDER THANE TOLKE CABALL
ERRANT KEMPER PENCEL RITTER
ROGERO GENILON PALADIN
YOUNKER ALMANZOR BACHELOR
BANNERET CAVALIER COLVILLE
GANELONE IRONCLAD ISENBRAS
PALMERIN RUGGIERO
(— IN CHESS) HORSE
(— OF ROUND TABLE) GAN BORS
OWEN GARETH GAWAIN MODRED
CARADOC CRADOCK GALAHAD
GANELON EGLAMORE LANCELOT
PALMERIN PERCIVAL TRISTRAM
(CARPET —) DAMMARET
KNIGHTHOOD CAVALRY
KNIGHTS (AUTHOR OF —)
ARISTOPHANES
(CHARACTER IN —) CLEON DEMUS
NICIAS AGORACRITUS
DEMOSTHENES
KNIPHOFIA TRITOMA
KNIT SET BIND KNOT PLAIT PURSE

UNITE WEAVE COMPACT
CONNECT WRINKLE CONTRACT
(— STOCKINGS) SHANK
KNITTED FLAT WOVEN
KNITTING (— OF BONES) POROSIS
KNITTING LOOP STEEK
KNITTING NEEDLE WIRE
KNOB BOB BUR NOB NUB BEAD
BOLL BOSS BURR CLUB DENT
HEAD HEEL KNOP KNOT KNUB
LIFT NODE NOOP PULL SNUG
STUD TORE BERRY BULLA BUNCH
FORTE GEMMA KNURL NATCH
ONION PLOOK PLUKE BUTTON
CROCHE EMBOSS NOBBLE
NUBBLE PIMPLE PISTON POMMEL
FERRULE HORNTIP KNOBBLE
BELLPULL DOORKNOB DRAWSTOP
OMPHALOS
(— OF HAIR) TOORIE
(— OF ROCK) BUHR BURR
KNUCKLE
(— ON BILL OF SWAN) BERRY
(— ON BUTT OF CANNON) GRAPE
(— ON CHAIR) POMMEL
(— ON DEER'S ANTLER) OFFER
CROCHE
(— ON ROPE) MOUSE
(PREF.) CONDYL(O) TYL(O)
KNOBBED NODOSE TOROSE
BULLATE TUBEROUS TYLOTATE
KNOBBY GOUTY KNOTTY TOROSE
WHELKY GOUTISH KNOBBLY
SCRAGGED
KNOCK CON DAD HIT JOW JUT
POP PUN RAP WAP BANG BASH
BEAT BUMP CALL CHAP CHOP
DASH DAUD DING DUMP DUNT
HACK JOLT JOWL KNAP NOCK
NOIT PINK PLUG POLT POSS
PUSH ROUT SLAM SLAY SNOP
TANK TIRL WHAP WHOP CLOUR
CLUMP KNOIT POUND SMITE
SNOCK STAVE STRAM THUMP
BOUNCE DUNTLE KNATCH
KNETCH STOTER CANVASS
PINKING
(— ABOUT) RUMBLE
(— DOWN) MOW DROP DUMP FELL
FLOOR GRASS LEVEL SMITE
SOUSE HURTLE RAFFLE UNPILE
(— OFF) SECURE
(— ON HEAD) MAZER MAZARD
(— OUT) OUT SAP CONK COOL
KAYO FLATTEN STIFFEN
(— UNCONSCIOUS) COLDCOCK
(— WITH THE HORNS) DISH
(IGNITION —) PING
KNOCKER CROW RISP HAMMER
WHACKER
(DOOR —) CROW HAMMER
RAPPER
KNOCK-KNEED VARUS VALGUS
KNOCKOUT KO KAYO CRUSHER
NOBBLER
(PRETENDED —) DIVE
KNOLL NOB HIGH KNAP KNOB
KNOW TOFT HEAVE HURST
HYRST MOUND SHOAL COPPLE
BOUROCK HUMMOCK
KNOP NOB KNOB KNOSP KNAPPE
KNOT BOB BOW BUN FAG NIB NOB
NUB PIN TIE BEND BURR CHOU

CLOD CLOT CLUB HARL KILL
KNAG KNAR KNOB NODE NOIL
NURL SLUG SNUB TRUE WAFT
WALL BUNCH CROWN DUNNE
GNARL GNARR HALCH HALSH
HATCH HITCH KNURL MOUSE
NODUS NOEUD SNARL SNICK
SWIRL TWIST WARRE BOUGHT
BUTTON CLINCH CROCHE FINIAL
GRANNY MASCLE SORTIE TANGLE
BOWKNOT BOWLINE CHIGNON
COCKADE GORDIAN MAYBIRD
CICISBEO DRAWKNOT GRAYBACK
KNITTING SLIPKNOT TRUELOVE
SHEEPSHANK
(— IN CLOTH) FAG NEP BURL
(— IN COTTON FIBERS) NEP
(— IN SIGNAL FLAG) WAFT WEFT
WHEFT
(— IN WOOD) PIN BURL BURR
KNAG KNAR SNUB GNARL KNAUR
KNURL
(— IN YARN) SLUG SNICK
(— OF HAIR) BOB BUN COB PUG
CLUB KNURL CHIGNON
(— OF RIBBONS) FAVOR
(EMBROIDERY —) PICOT
(LOVE —) AMORET
(ORNAMENTAL —) BOW
(SHOULDER —) WING
(WALL —) WALE
(PREF.) NODI
KNOTGRASS LIGNUM HOGWEED
PIGWEED BINDWEED BIRDWEED
DOORWEED KNOTWEED
KNOTWORT PINKWEED
POLYGONY WIREWEED
KNOTTED KNIT NOUE TIED NOWED
NODOSE SWIRLY CRABBED
NODATED SCRAGGY
KNOTTY HARD CRAMP GOUTY
NODAL COMMON CRAGGY
GNARLY KNAGGY KNOBBY
KNURRY NODOSE NODOUS
COMPLEX GNARLED GOUTISH
JOINTED KNARRED KNOTTED
SCABROUS
KNOTWEED LIGNUM ALLSEED
HOGWEED JUMPSEED POLYGONY
POLYGONUM
KNOW CAN CON KEN WIS WIT
WOT CITE HAVE SABE WEET WIST
WOTH SAVVY SKILL COGNIZE
(— NOT) NOOT
(—S NOT) NOTE
(DID NOT —) KENDNA
(DO NOT —) KENNA
KNOWABLE SENSABLE
KNOW-HOW SAVVY SKILL
KNOWING FLY HEP HIP SLY FOXY
GASH SPRY WISE AWARE CANNY
DOWNY JERRY LEERY SPACK
WITTY EXPERT SCIENT SCIOUS
SHREWD WITFUL WITTER
GNOSTIC SAPIENT
(— SUPERFICIALLY) SCIOLOUS
(SUFF.) GNOSIA GNOSIS GNOSTIC
GNOSY
KNOWINGLY CANNILY SCIENTER
SHREWDLY WITTERLY
KNOWLEDGE CAN WIT BOOK KITH
KNOW LAIR LEAR LORE NOTE
INWIT JNANA SKILL VIDYA

ADVICE AVIDYA CLERGY GNOSIS
NOESIS NOTICE WISDOM
CUNNING DIANOIA HEARING
KNOWING MEANING SCIENCE
WITTING DAYLIGHT DOCTRINE
EPISTEME LEARNING LETTRURE
NOTITION PRUDENCE SAPIENCE
SCIENTIA COGNIZANCE
(— OF SPIRITUAL TRUTH) GNOSIS
(FAMILIAR —) HANG
(LATER —) AFTERWIT
(MYSTERIOUS —) ARCANUM
(PIECEMEAL —) SMATTER
(PRIVATE —) PRIVITY
(PUBLIC —) LIGHT
(SLICK —) ANGLE
(SLIGHT —) INKLING SMATTER
(SUPERFICIAL —) SCIOLISM
(SUPERIOR —) MASTERY
(SUPREME —) PRAJNA
(SYSTEMATIZED —) SCIENCE
(UNIVERSAL —) PANSOPHY
(PREF.) EPISTEMO GNOSIO
(SUFF.) GNOSIA GNOSIS GNOSTIC
GNOSY ICS SOPH(ER)(IC)(IST)(Y)
KNOWLEDGEABLE KNOWING
SKILLED STUDIED
KNOWN EVER COUTH COMMON
(ACTUALLY —) SPECIOUS
(LITTLE —) FAMELESS
(NOT —) DARK SILENT
(OTHERWISE — AS) ALIAS
(PUBLICLY —) EXOTERIC
(UNMISTAKABLY —) STATED
(WIDELY —) COMMON
KNOW-NOTHING SAM
KNUCKLE KNUCK JARRET
(PREF.) CONDYL(O)
KNUCKLEBONE DIB DOLOS TALUS
COCKAL SHACKLE
KNURL MILL NULL DWARF SNARL
KNURLING NULLING REEDING
KNULLING
KOALA BEAR BAALU BALOO SLOTH
KOOLAH WOMBAT CARBORA
PHALANGER
KOANGA (CHARACTER IN —) JOSE
PEREZ SIMON KOANGA PALMYRA
MARTINEZ
(COMPOSER OF —) DELIUS
KOBOLD NIS GNOME NISSE
HODEKEN HUTCHEN
KOEL KOIL KOKIL RAINBIRD
KOHATH (FATHER OF —) LEVI
(SISTER OF —) JOCHEBED
KOHL COHOL ALCOHOL
KOHLRABI BROMATIUM
KOKAN LAMPATIA
KOKO LEBBEK
KOKUM GARCINIA
KOKUMIN BAN
KOLA COLA BICHY GOORANUT
KOLAIAH (SON OF —) AHAB
KOMBU KOBU KAMBOU CHAKOBU
KOMMETJE WALLOW COMITJE
KONAK YALI
KOOKABURRA KOOKA JACKASS
KOPECK KAPEIKA
KORAH (FATHER OF —) ESAU IZHAR
ELIPHAZ
(MOTHER OF —) AHOLIBAMAH
KORAKAN RAGI RAGGI RAGGY
KORAN KITAB QURAN ALCORAN

(SECTION OF —) SURA SURAH
KORE DESPOINA
  (FATHER OF —) IMNAH
KOREA (SEE NORTH KOREA OR
  SOUTH KOREA)
KOREC MIRA
KORINA LIMBA
KOS COAN
KOSHER (NOT —) TREF
KOSIN KOUSSIN TAENNIN
  BRAYERIN
KOSO PANAMINT
KOULAN GOUR
KOVANSHCHINA (CHARACTER IN —
) ENNA IVAN MARFA ANDREY
  DOSIFEY GOLITSYN KHOVANSKY
  (COMPOSER OF —) MUSSORGSKY
KOWHAI GOAI PELU LOCUST
  SOPHORA
KOWTOW KNEEL SHIKO
KOYUKON TENA KHOTANA
KRAAL CRAW MANYATTA
  ZIMBABWE
KRAIT ADDER KORAIT BUNGARUM

KRATER KELEBE
KRAUNHIA WISTARIA
KREIS CIRCLE
KREUTZER SONATA (AUTHOR OF —
) TOLSTOY
  (CHARACTER IN —) LIZA VASYLA
  POZDNISHEF TRUKHASHEVSKY
KRIEMHILD (BROTHER OF —)
  GERNOT GUNTHER GISELHER
  (FATHER OF —) GIBICH
  (HUSBAND OF —) ATTILA
  SIEGFRIED
KRIS CREASE CREESE DAGGER
KRISHNA VASUDEVA
  (BROTHER OF —) BALARAMA
  (FATHER OF —) VASUDEVA
  (FOSTER FATHER OF —) NANDA
  (FOSTER MOTHER OF —) YASHODA
  (MOTHER OF —) DEVAKI
  (UNCLE OF —) KANSA
KRISTIN LAVRANSDATTER
  (AUTHOR OF —) UNDSET
  (CHARACTER IN —) ULF IVAR
  GAUTE MUNAN SIMON SKULE

ERLEND JOFRID NAAKVE AASHILD
HALVARD KRISTIN LAVRANS
RAMBORG ULVHILD BJORGULF
JARDTRUD NIKULAUS
RAGNFRID ANDRESSON
BJORGULFSON IVARSDATTER
LAVRANSDATTER
KRONE CROWN CORONA
KRU KROOBOY KROOMAN
KRUMMHORN CREMONA
  CROMORNE
KSHATRIYA THAKUR
KUA MAKUA MAKWA
KUBA BUSHONGO KABISTAN
KUDZU VINE KOHEMP
KUI KHONDI
KU KLUXER KLUXER KLUCKER
  KLANSMAN
KUKURUKU IKPERE
KULANAPAN POMO
KUMAN POLOVTZY
KUMBUK ARJAN ARJUN
KUMMEL ALLASCH
KUMQUAT NAGAMI

KUNTI
  (FATHER OF —) PANDU SHURA
  (SON OF —) BHIMA KARNA
  ARJUNA YUDHISHTHIRA
KURRAJONG CALOOL LACEBARK
KURUKH ORAON
KUSA DARBHA
KUSHAIAH (SON OF —) ETHAN
KUSIMANSEL MANGUE
KUTCHIN LOUCHEUX
KUWAIT (CAPITAL OF —) ALKUWAIT
  (OIL FIELD OF —) WAFRA BAHRAH
  BURGAN SABRIYA MINAGISH
  RAUDHATAIN
  (OTHER NAME OF —) KOWEIT
  KUWEIT
  (TOWN OF —) MAGWA AHMADI
  HAWALLI ABDULLAH FAHAHEEL
KVASS BEER QUASH
KWENI GURO
KYANITE DISTHENE
KYPHOSIS HUMPBACK
KYURINISH LESGHIN LEZGHIAN

L

L EL LIMA FIFTY

LAADAH (FATHER OF —) SHELAH
  (GRANDFATHER OF —) JUDAH
LAADAN (FATHER OF —) GERSHOM
LAAGER LEEGTE LEAGUER
LABAN (DAUGHTER OF —) LEAH
  RACHEL
  (FATHER OF —) BETHUEL
  (SISTER OF —) REBEKAH
LABDACUS (FATHER OF —)
  POLYDORUS
  (MOTHER OF —) NYCTEIS
  (SON OF —) LAIUS
LABDANUM MYRRH
LABEL TAG BILL FILE MARK FICHE
  STAMP TALLY TITLE DIRECT
  DOCKET TICKET ENDSEAL
  LAMBEAU STICKER
  (— ON SUIT OF CLOTHES) ETIQUET
LABELLUM LIP LABEL
  (PART OF —) HYPOCHIL
LABIAL ROUND
LABIATE HOREHOUND
LABIUM LIP LABRUM
LABOR ADO FAG TUG WIN CARK
  MOIL TASK TAVE TILL TOIL WORK
  BEGAR DELVE GRAFT GRIND
  HEAVE PAINS SWEAT SWINK
  TEAVE TREAD WHILE YAKKA
  CORVEE DRUDGE EFFORT
  HAMMER STRIVE BULLOCK
  FATIGUE MANUARY OPIFICE
  PROCURE SERVICE SLAVERY
  TRAVAIL TROUBLE TURMOIL
  BUSINESS DRUDGERY EXERTION
  GROANING INDUSTRY LABORAGE
  STRUGGLE
  (— ARDUOUSLY) BILDER
  (— HARD) THRASH THRIPPLE
  (— UNDER) SUFFER
  (DAY'S —) DARG JOURNEY
  (DIFFICULT —) DYSTOCIA
  (EXCESSIVE —) STRAIN
  (FORCED —) BEGAR CORVEE
  (HARD —) HARD BULLWORK
  (HIRED —) TOGT
  (IMPOSED —) TASKAGE
  (MENTAL —) HEADWORK
  (SEVERE —) AGON
  (UNPAID —) CORVEE
LABORATORY LAB SHOP KITCHEN
  OFFICINA WORKSHOP
LABORED HEAVY FORCED SWEATY
  STRAINED
LABORER (ALSO SEE WORKER AND
  WORKMAN) BOY BHAR ESNE
  HIND JACK JOEY MOZO PEON
  TOTY BAGDI CHURL GUASO
  HUNKY NAVVY PALLI PINER STIFF
  BALAHI BEGARI BOHUNK COALER
  COOLIE DAYMAN DILKER DOCKER
  FELLAH FLUNKY FOGGER HEAVER
  HODMAN HOLEYA JIBARO

LUMPER RAFTER TASKER
WAYMAN WORKER BRACERO
BYWONER CREWMAN DAYSMAN
DIGGORY DIRGLER DRAINER
DVORNIK GRECIAN HOBBLER
MANUARY MAZDOOR PICKMAN
PIONEER PIPEMAN PLOWMAN
SANDHOG SCOURER SHIPPER
SMASHER SOUGHER SPALLER
STOCKER SWINKER TOTYMAN
WORKMAN BIJWONER CHAINMAN
COTTAGER DOLLYMAN
FARMHAND FLOORMAN
GANGSMAN HODMAN
SPADEMAN SPALPEEN STRAPPER
TIDESMAN ROUSTABOUT
(INEXPERIENCED —) GREENER
LABORIOUS HARD HEAVY STIFF
  TOUGH SWEATY UPHILL
  ARDUOUS OPEROSE SLAVISH
  TOILFUL DILIGENT LABOROUS
  TOILSOME
LABRADOR TEA LEDUM
  GOWIDDIE
LABURNUM AWBER
LABYRINTH MAZE CIRCUIT
  MEANDER
LABYRINTHINE TORTUOUS
LAC LACCA LACQUER
LACE VAL BEAT BEST FOND GOTA
  LASH PEAK FILET LACIS LIVEN
  ORRIS POINT SCREW SPRIG
  WEAVE BLONDE CADDIS CORDON
  DEFEAT EDGING GRILLE LACING
  LASHER THRASH TUCKER VENISE
  ALENCON ALLOVER BULLION
  CURRAGH CUTWORK FOOTING
  GALLOON GUIPURE HONITON
  LATCHET MACRAME MALINES
  MECHLIN MELANGE NANDUTI
  TAMBOUR TATTING TORCHON
  TROLLEY ARGENTAN BOBBINET
  BONEWORK BOOTLACE BRUSSELS
  DENTELLE ILLUSION LACEWORK
  LIMERICK PEARLING STAYLACE
  COLBERTINE NEEDLEPOINT
  (— EDGING) PUNTILLA
  (— IN PLACE OF COLLAR) RUCHE
  (— MAKER) TWISTHAND
  (— PATTERN) TOILE
  (KIND OF —) CLUNY
  (KNOTTED —) TATTING
LACEBARK LAGETTO DAGUILLA
  LACEWOOD
LACE BUG TINGITID
LACEDAEMON (DAUGHTER OF —)
  CLEODICE
  (FATHER OF —) ZEUS JUPITER
  (MOTHER OF —) TAYGETE
  (SON OF —) HIMERUS
  (WIFE OF —) SPARTA
LACERATE REND TEAR GANCH
  ENGORE HARROW MANGLE

SCARIFY FRACTURE
LACERATION RIP TEAR WOUND
LACEWING NEUROPTERAN
LACEWOOD SYCAMORE
LACEWORK DENTELLE
LACHRYMOSE SAD TEARY WEEPY
  MAUDLIN
LACINARIA LIATRIS
LACING LACET LINGEL ECHELLE
  LANGUET
  (RAWHIDE —S) BABICHE
LACINIATION DAG
LACK FAIL LANK LIKE LOSS MAIM
  MISS NEED VOID WANE WANT
  FAULT MINUS DEARTH DEFECT
  INLAIK ABSENCE BLEMISH
  DEFAULT FAILURE PAUCITY
  VACANCY SCARCITY SOLITUDE
  WANTROKE
  (— CONFIDENCE) DOUBT
  (— FAITH) DIFFIDE
  (— HARMONY) DISAGREE
  (— OF APPETITE) ANOREXIA
  (— OF CLARITY) DARKNESS
  (— OF CONFIDENCE) MISTRUST
  (— OF COORDINATION) ASYNERGY
  DYSERGIA
  (— OF DEVELOPMENT) AGENESIS
  (— OF EARNESTNESS) ITEMING
  (— OF EFFUSIVENESS) RESERVE
  (— OF EMOTION) APATHY
  (— OF ENERGY) ATONY ANERGY
  ATONIA
  (— OF FLAVOR) SILENCE
  (— OF FORESIGHT) MYOPIA
  (— OF HARMONY) DISCORD
  DISUNITY
  (— OF INTENTION) ACCIDENT
  (— OF INVOLVEMENT) DISTANCE
  (— OF ORDER) ATAXY ATAXIA
  DISARRAY
  (— OF PATRIOTISM) INCIVISM
  (— OF REFINEMENT) CRUDITY
  (— OF SENSE) FOLLY
  (— OF SENSE OF SMELL) ANOSMIA
  (— OF STEADINESS) LEVITY
  (— OF SYMPATHY) DYSPATHY
  (— OF VIGOR) LANGUOR
  (— OF VITALITY) ANEMIA
  ADYNAMIA
  (— OF WIND) CALM
  (— OF WORTH) IMMERIT
  (— STRENGTH) DROOP
LACKADAISICAL LANGUID
  LISTLESS
LACKEY SKIP SLAVE LACQUEY
  STAFFIER
LACKING BUT SHY BARE FREE
  SANS WANT ALACK GNEDE
  MINUS SHORT ABSENT BARREN
  DEVOID WITHIN WANTING
  DESOLATE INDIGENT
  (PREF.) LONCH(O)

LACKLUSTER DULL FISHY CLOUDY
  GLASSY
LACONIC CURT SHORT CONCISE
  POINTED SPARTAN SUCCINCT
LA CORUNA GROIN
LACQUER LAC DOPE DUCO JAPAN
  CHATON LACKER URUSHI
  VARNISH
LACRIMAL
  (PREF.) DACRY(O)
LACTATION (— PERIOD) NOTE
LACTONE CUMARIN LIMONIN
  MECONIN DIKETENE
LACTOSCOPE PIOSCOPE
LACUNA GAP BREAK
LACUSTRINE LAKISH
LAD BOY BUB MAN BOYO CARL
  CHAP DICK HIND JOCK LOON
  SNAP BILLY BUCKO CADDY CHIEL
  GROOM YOUTH BURSCH CADDIE
  CALLAN FELLOW LADDIE LADKIN
  MANNIE NIPPER SHAVER
  CALLANT MUCHACHO SPRINGER
  STRIPLING
  (AWKWARD —) GROMET
  GRUMMET
  (MISCHIEVOUS —) GAMIN
  (MY —) AVICK
  (SERVING —) GILLIE GOSSOON
LADDER STY STEE JACOB SCALE
  AERIAL BANGOR ESCAPE PULEYN
  GANGWAY POLEYNE POMPIER
  (FIREMAN'S —) STICK
  (FISH —) FISHWAY
  (JACOB'S —) CHARITY
  (REVOLVING —) POTENCE
  (ROPE —) ETRIER
LADDIE JOCKEY LATHIE LADDOCK
  LADDIKIE
LADE BAIL LAVE LADEN TRUSS
  BURDEN FRAUGHT
  (— INTO COOLER) STRIKE
LADEN HEAVY BELAST LOADED
  FRAUGHT FREIGHT GESTANT
LADING LOAD CARGO BURDEN
  FREIGHT
LADINO SPANIOL
LADLE DIP JET GAWN SKEP CLATH
  CYATH KEACH STOOP DIPPER
  LADING CUVETTE CYATHUS
  KYATHOS POTSTICK
  (— OUT SOUP) SLEECH
  (— WITH HANDLES) CYATH SHANK
  CYATHUS KYATHOS SKIPPET
  (BRINE —) LOOT
  (LARGE —) SCOOP
  (PREF.) ARYTENO
LADRONE TULISAN LATHERIN
LADY BIBI BURD DAME RANI
  DONNA HANUM BEEBEE DOMINO
  FEMALE KADINE KHANUM
  RAWNIE SAHIBA SENORA
  LADYKIN MADONNA SENHORA

BELAMOUR SINEBADA
(— OF HIGH RANK) BEGUM
(— OF HOUSE) GOODWIFE
(BEAUTIFUL —) CLEAR
(LEADING —) PREMIERE
(TURKISH —) KHANUM
(PL.) LADYHOOD
LADYBUG VEDALIA
LADYFISH WRASSE PUDIANO
BONEFISH BONYFISH DONCELLA
LADYLIKE FEMALE
LADYLOVE LADY DELIA MINION
MISTRESS
LADY'S-COMB NEEDLES
LADY'S-MANTLE DEWCUP
PADELION
LADY'S-SLIPPER DUCK YELLOW
NERVINE YELLOWS UMBILROOT
(PREF.) CYPRI CYPRO
LADY WINDERMERE'S FAN
(AUTHOR OF —) WILDE
(CHARACTER IN —) LORTON
ERLYNNE AUGUSTUS MARGARET
DARLINGTON WINDERMERE
LAEL (SON OF —) ELIASAPH
LAERTES (FATHER OF —) ARCESIUS
(MOTHER OF —) CHALCOMEDUSA
(SON OF —) ULYSSES
(WIFE OF —) ANTICLEA
LAG DRAG DRAW SLOG DELAY
TRAIL HOCKER LAGGER LINGER
LOITER STRING DRIDDLE LAGGING
(— IN PRODUCTION) SLIPPAGE
LAGGARD SLOW TARDY LAGGER
TORTOISE
LAGGING TARDY JACKET DEADING
LAGGARD CLEADING DRAWLING
FOREPOLE
LAGNIAPPE TIP GIFT BONUS
PILON PRESENT
LAGOMORPH PIKA RABBIT
LAGOON HAFF POOL BAYOU
LIMAN LAGUNA SALINA
LAHAD (FATHER OF —) JAHATH
LAHMI (BROTHER OF —) GOLIATH
LAID (— ACROSS WALL) INBOND
(— DOWN) THETIC THETICAL
(— WASTE) BARE
LAIR DEN LAY FORM HOLD SHED
COUCH EARTH HAUNT LODGE
MEUSE SQUAT HARBOR KENNEL
SPELUNK
(— OF FOX) KENNEL
(— OF OTTER) HOLT HOVER
(— OF WILD BOAR) SOUNDER
LAISH (SON OF —) PHALTIEL
LAISSE TIRADE
LAITY FOLK LAYMEN PEOPLE
LAIUS (FATHER OF —) LABDACUS
(SON OF —) OEDIPUS
(WIFE OF —) JOCASTA
LAKE LAY SEA VLY BAHR JAIL JHIL
LAGO LLYN LOCH MERE MOAT
SHOR TANK TARN VLEI VLEY
BAYOU CHOTT JHEEL LERNA
LIMAN LOUGH SPARK TUBIG
LAGOON NYANZA STROND
ANCYLUS CARMINE LAKELET
TURLOUGH
(CASHEW —) AUBURN
(DRY —) PLAYA
(FENNY —) BROAD
(MOUNTAIN —) TARN

(RELATING TO —S) LIMNAL
(SALT —) SHOT CHOTT SHOTT
SALINA SALINE
(SMALL —) GURGES MARIGOT
(TEMPORARY —) PINAG
(YELLOW —) PINK
(PREF.) LIMN(I)(O)
(SUFF.) LIMNION
LAKE CARP DRUM LAKER
LAKE HERRING KIYI CISCO
GRAYBACK
LAKE TROUT POGY TOGUE
LAKE WHITEFISH POLLAN
LAKME (CHARACTER IN —) LAKME
GERALD NILAKANTHA
(COMPOSER OF —) DELIBES
LAKSHMANA (FATHER OF —)
DURYODHANA
(SLAYER OF —) ABHIMANYU
LAKSHMI SRI SHREE
(HUSBAND OF —) VISHNU
LAMA ELK AUCHENIA
LAMB BUM PET PUR CADE DEAR
DUPE LOME SOCK YEAN AGNUS
PESAH PODDY AGNEAU COSSET
HIEDER LAMBIE LAMKIN PESACH
SUCKER WASTER WEANER
CHILVER EANLING FATLING
HOGLING PASCHAL PERSIAN
RUFFIAN TWAGGER BAAHLING
LAMBLING PASSOVER YEANLING
(— AND WHEAT) KIBBE
(SCYTHIAN —) BAROMETZ
(SHOULDER OF —) BANJO
(SIDE OF —) CONCERTINA
LAMBASTE CREAM SQUABASH
LAMBENT BRIGHT RADIANT
LAMBREQUIN MANTLING
LAMBSKIN LAMB BAGDAD
BAGHDAD SALZFELLE
LAMB'S QUARTERS MUCKWEED
LAMB'S WOOL WASSAIL
LAME BUM GAME HALT LAHN
GAMMY GIMPY GRAVEL TINSEL
CRIPPLE CRIPPLY HALTING
HIPHALT GORGERIN SPAVINED
(— A HORSE) STUB NOBBLE
(— WITH HORSESHOE NAIL) ACCLOY
LAMECH (DAUGHTER OF —)
NAAMAH
(SON OF —) NOAH JABAL JUBAL
TUBALCAIN
(WIFE OF —) ADAH ZILLAH
LAMELLA PLICA FOLIUM FORNIX
LAMELLIBRANCH PELECYPOD
LAMENESS HALT
LAMENT CRY WEY CARE DOLE
HONE HOWL KEEN MEAN MOAN
PINE SIGH TEAR WAIL WALY
WEEP CROON DUMKA GREET
KINAH MOURN PLAIN QINAH
BEHOWL BEMOAN BEWAIL
BEWEEP COMMOS KOMMOS
PLAINT REGRET REPINE SORROW
SQUAWK THREAP YAMMER
BEMOURN CONDOLE DEPLORE
EJULATE ELEGIZE GRIZZLE
REGRATE THRENOS WAYMENT
COMPLAIN CORONACH
MOURNING THRENODY
ULLAGONE WELLAWAY
LAMENTABLE YEMER FUNEST
RUEFUL DOLEFUL PITIFUL

PITIABLE PLAINFUL YAMMERLY
LAMENTATION KEEN MOAN WAIL
DOLOR LINOS RUING TANGI
LAMENT PLAINT REGRET
SORROW THRENE PLANGOR
TRAGEDY WAYMENT WILLAWA
CORONACH MOURNING PATHETIC
WAILMENT WELLAWAY
LAMENTING
LAMINA FILM LAME LAMP LEAF
OBEX BLADE FLAKE LAMIN PLATE
SCALE SHELL TABLE FOLIUM
CAPSULE
LAMINATE LEAFY FLAGGY
LAMINATED BUILT FOLIATE
TABULAR
LAMINATION SLABBING
LAMINITIS FOUNDER
LAMMAS DAY GULE TERM
LAMMERGEIER AREND OSSIFRAGE
LAMP ARC EYE SEE DAVY GLIM
INKY JACK SLUT ALDIS ARGAND
ASTRAL BULLET HELION LAMPAD
TARGET ILLUMER LAMPION
LAMPLET LANTERN LUCERNE
LUCIGEN SUNLAMP SUNSPOT
AEOLIGHT CIRCLINE GASLIGHT
SIDELAMP TORCHERE
PHOTOFLASH PHOTOFLOOD
(— FOR FIREPLACE) KYLE
(CHIMNEYLESS —) TORCH
(DARKROOM —) SAFELIGHT
(IRON —) CRUSIE
(MAKESHIFT —) BITCH
(NIGHT —) VEILLEUSE
(PART OF —) CAP CORD HARP
SHELL FINIAL NIPPLE SOCKET
SWITCH WASHER NECKWING
(SAFETY —) DAVY GEORDIE
(STAGE —S) BATTEN
(4-CORNERED —) CHILL
(PL.) CLUSTER
(PREF.) LYCHNO
LAMPBLACK LINK SOOT
LAMPETIA (FATHER OF —) APOLLO
HELIOS
(MOTHER OF —) NEAERA
(SISTER OF —) PHAETHUSA
LAMP HOLDER HUSK
LAMPLIGHTER LEERIE
LAMPOON PIPE SKIT GESTE LIBEL
SQUIB IAMBIC SATIRE BERHYME
PASQUIN COCKALAN RIDICULE
SATIRIZE PASQUINADE
LAMPOONER PASQUIL PASQUIN
LAMPREY PRIDE LAMPER MYZONT
RAMPER SAYNAY SUCKER
LAMPERN
LAMP RING CRIC
LAMPSHADE GLOBE
(PART OF —) RIB RING SHADE
SPIDER
LAMPSTAND TORCHERE
LAMPWICK MATCH
LANATE WOOLY LANOSE WOOLLY
LANCE PIC CANE DART SHAFT
SPEAR STAFF BROACH ELANCE
GLAIVE GLEAVE LANCET ROCKET
LANCELET SPICULUM
(KING ARTHUR'S —) RON
LANCE GUARD VAMPLATE
LANCE HEAD MORNE SOCKET
LANCELET AMPHIOXUS

LANCER LANCE SOWAR UHLAN
LANCE REST QUEUE FEWTER
LANCET FLEAM FLEEM LANCELET
LANCEWOOD YAYA CIGUA
CANELA YARIYARI
LAND ERD ERF NOD RIB AGER DIRT
FOLD GALE GISH GORE JODO
MARK SITE SOIL EARTH EJIDO
ETHEL FIELD GLEBE JUGER PLANT
SHORE SOLUM ALIGHT ASSART
FUNDUS GROUND COMMONS
COUNTRY DEMESNE ELLASAR
HOLDING LANDING LIBRATE
QUILLET TERRENE ALLODIAL
BOOKLAND COMMONTY
FARMLAND FLEYLAND FOLKLAND
POMERIUM PRAEDIUM
(— A PLANE) GREASE
(— BETWEEN FURROWS) SELION
(— BETWEEN RIVERS) DOAB
(— CLEARING) KAINGIN
(— CONVERTED TO TILLAGE)
TWAITE THWAITE
(— HAVING VALUE OF POUND PER
YEAR) LIBRATE
(— IN CONACRE) MOCK
(— IN GRASS) LAYER
(— LEFT FALLOW) ARDER
(— MEASURE) RIG
(— OF BLISS) GOKURAKU
(— OF GIANTS) UTGARTHAR
(— OF MANSION) DEMESNE
(— OF OPPORTUNITY) ARKANSAS
(— OF PLENTY) GOSHEN
(— OF REGION) MOLD MOULD
(— PLOWED IN A DAY) JORNADA
(— RECOVERED FROM SEA) INTAKE
INNINGS
(— REGULARLY FLOODED) SALTING
(— SURROUNDED BY WASTE) HOPE
(— UNIT) URE KIPUKA MECATE
MORGEN MANZANA VIRGATE
(ALLUVIAL —) BATTURE
(ANCESTRAL —) ETHEL
(ARABLE —) LEA LEY LAINE
(ARID —) DESERT STEPPE
(BOTTOM —) SLASH CALLOW
STRATH
(CHURCH —) GLEBE TERMON
(CHURCH —S) CROSS
(CLEARED —) ASSART
(COMMON —) EJIDO EXIDO STRAY
(CONTINENTAL —) MAIN
(CULTIVATED —) FARM ARADA
TILTH CULTURE FEERING
WAINAGE LABORAGE METAIRIE
(ENCLOSED —) CLOSE INTAKE
(FREEHOLD —) MULK
(GRAVELLY —) GEEST GRAVES
(GRAZING —) GRASS HIRSEL
HIRSLE FEEDING
(HEATHY —) ROSLAND
(HERITABLE —) ODAL UDAL
(IMAGINARY —) FAERIE COCKAYNE
LILLIPUT
(LEASED —) TACK
(LONG STRIP OF —) SLANG SPONG
(LOW —) BOG FEN GALL INKS
CARSE BOTTOM
(LOW RICH —) CARSE
(NATIVE —) SOD KITH BLIGHTY
BIRTHDOM HOMELAND
(OBDURATE —) TILL

(PARCEL OF —) FEU LOT MOCK
(PASTURE —) HA ALP FEED HOGA
WALK GRASS VELDT LEASON
SCATHOLD SCATLAND
(PLATEAU —) HIGHVELD
(PLOWED —) ARADA FALLOW
FURROW BREAKING
(PRIVATE —) SEVERAL
(PROMISED —) CANAAN
(PURE —) JODO SUKHAVATI
(RECLAIMED —) POLDER
(RESOWN —) HOOKLAND
(ROUGH —) BRAKE
(SAVANNAH —S) LALANG
(SCRUBBY —) SCROG SCROGS
(SMALL PARCEL OF —) SUERTE
(SWAMPY —) WOODSERE
(TIMBER —S) STICKS
(WASTE —) HEATH
(WESTERN —) HESPERIA
(WET —) SOAK SWAMP SWANG
(WOODED —S) STICKS
(PL.) ACRES SUCKEN LAENDER
NOVALIA
(PREF.) CHERSO CHOR(O)
(SUFF.) GAEA GEA
LANDBOOK TERRIER
LANDED PRAEDIAL
LANDFORM CUSP CUESTA
LANDHOLDER LAIRD COSCET
TALUKDAR
LANDHOLDING BARONY
LANDING BANK YARD STAITH
LANDAGE ARRIVAGE FOOTPACE
HALFPACE LANDFALL
(ABRUPT —) PANCAKE
(CRASH —) PRANG
(SMOOTH —) GREASER
LANDING PLACE GHAT HARD
SCALE PALACE ARRIVAGE
LANDING STAGE MEAR STAGE
STAIR STAITH STELLING
LANDLADY WIFE DUENA
PADRONA GOODWIFE
LANDLOCK EMBAY
LANDLORD HOST LESSOR
GOODMAN PADRONE ZAMINDAR
LANDMARK COPA DOLE DOOL
MARK MERE BAKEN BOUND
CAIRN MARCH MEITH SENAL
CIPPUS SEAMARK
LANDMASS BULGE
LANDOWNER THANE BONDER
SQUIRE CACIQUE EFFENDI
FREEMAN BHUMIDAR FRANKLIN
ZAMINDAR
(PL.) GAMORI GEOMOROI
LANDSCAPE VIEW BOCAGE
PAYSAGE SCENERY LANDSKIP
LANDSLIDE SLUMP LANDFALL
LANDSLIP
LANDSMAL MAL NYNORSK
LAND SPRING LAVANT
LANDVOGT BAILIFF
LANE GUT WAY GANG LOAN LOKE
PASS RACE VEIN WIND WYND
ALLEY CHASE DRANG DRONG
ENTRY BOREEN VENNEL
LANEWAY LOANING TWITTEN
DRIFTWAY
(AIR TRAFFIC —) CORRIDOR
(NARROW —) CHAR CHARE TEWER
BOREEN RUELLE

(OCEAN —) SEAWAY
LANGUAGE (ALSO SEE DIALECT)
BAT LIP CHIB CODE LEED RUNE
TALE TESO LEDEN LINGO SLANG
LANGUS LINGUA SPEECH TONGUE
YABBER ACCENTS CABLESE
DIALECT IDIOLECT LEGALESE
PARLANCE PILIPINO
(— THAT CONDEMNS) ABUSE
(ARTIFICIAL —) RO IDO NEO ARULO
NOVIAL VOLAPUK ESPERANTO
(BANTU —) KIRUNDI
(COMPUTER —) BAL ALGOL BASIC
COBOL SNOBOL FORTRAN
(FIGURATIVE —) IMAGERY
(FLORID —) SILLABUB
(FOOLISH —) STUFF FLUMMERY
(FOUL —) SMUT ORDURE
(GYPSY —) CALO
(IMPUDENT —) SNASH
(INCOMPREHENSIBLE —) CHOCTAW
(INTERNATIONAL —) ANGLIC
(LATIN —) GRAMMAR HUMANITY
(NONSENSICAL —) BANTER
(OBSCENE —) BAWDY BAWDRY
(ORDINARY —) PROSE
(OVERPRETENTIOUS —) BOMBAST
(PERT —) SAUCE
(PIDGIN —) SABIR CAVITENO
FANAKALO
(PLAIN —) CLEAR
(PROPAGANDISTIC —) NEWSPEAK
(SECRET —) ARGOT
(SHOWY —) FLUBDUB
(SPECIFIC —) GA GE HO MO VU AIS
AKA ATA EDO EFE EPE EVE EWE
FAN FON FOX FUL GEG HET ICA
IJO ILA KAI KAU KOL KOT KRU
KUI LAB LAI LAZ MON MRU SIA
TWI UDI YAO ZIA AFAR AGAO
AGAU AGNI AHOM AINU AKAN
AKIM ALUR AMBO ANDI ANTA
ARUA AVAR BARI BEJA BIAK
BODO BONI BORA BUBE BUGI
BULU CARA CHAM CHIN CHOL
CHUJ COOS CORA COTO CREE
CROW CUNA DENE DOBU DYAK
EFIK EKOI ERIE EYAK FANG FIJI
FULA FUNG GARO GEEZ GHEG
GOLA GOLD HARE HEHE HOPI
HOVA HULA HUPA IBAN IDJO
IJAW IXIL KADU KAFA KAMI KAVI
KAWI KELE KOCH KOMI KONO
KOTA KUKI KURI LAHU LAKH
LAPP LASI LATI LAZI LESU LETT
LUBA MANX MAYA MOLE MORO
NAGA NAMA NIAS NIUE NUBA
NUPE OGOR PALA PALI PEGU
PEUL PUME RAMA SAHO SERB
SERI SGAW SHAN SIUS SORB
SULU SUMO SUMU SUSU TAAL
TIAM TIBU TINO TODA TSHI TUPI
TUPY VEPS VOTE XOSA ZULU
ALEUT ALSEA ARAUA AUETO
AZTEC BAJAU BALTI BANTU
BASSA BATAK BATTA BAURE
BEMBA BHILI BICOL BILIN BONNY
CAMPA CARIB CAYUA CHANE
CHIMU CHOCO CHOPE COFAN
COIBA COMAN CUEVA CUMAN
CUNZA CZECH DAFLA DAYAK
DIERI DINKA DUALA DUTCH
DYULA EMPEO FANTI FINGO

FUNJI GAFAT GALLA GANDA
GETAN GETIC GOLDI GONDI
GREBO GREEK GUAMO GUATO
GURMA GYPSY HABAB HAIDA
HAIKH HATSA HAUSA HINDI
HUABI HUARI HURON HUSKY
HYLAM IGALA ILOKO IRAYA IRISH
JAKUN JATKI JUANG JUTIC
KABYL KAMBA KAMIA KANDH
KAREN KAROK KHASI KHMER
KHOND KHUZI KIOWA KISSI KIWAI
KOINE KOLIS KONDE KONGO
KORKU KORWA KOTAR KUMUK
KUMYK KUSAN KWOMA LAMBA
LAMUT LANGO LATIN LENCA
LENDU LHOKE LHOTA LIMBA
LIMBU LUIAN LUNDA MAGHI
MAHRA MAHRI MALAY MALTO
MAORI MAZUR MBUBA MEDIC
MENDI MIKIR MODOC MOSSI
MUONG MURMI MURUT NAHUA
NOGAI NORSE NYORO ORAON
ORIYA OROMO OSAGE OSCAN
PALAU PAMIR PELEW PEUHL
PLATT PUNIC RONGA SAKAI
SAMAL SANTO SAXON SCOTS
SERER SHILH SHINA SHONA SICEL
SIKEL SLAVE SOTHO SOYOT
SUOMI SWAZI TAINO TAMIL TELEI
TONGA TURKI UDISH UIGUR
URIYA UZBEK VOGUL WAYAO
WELSH WOLOF YAKUT YUNCA
ZERMA ABIPON ABKHAS ACAWAI
ACHOLI ADIGHE ADZHAR AFGHAN
AHTENA ALTAIC ANDAKI ANDHRA
ANDOKE ANGAMI APACHE
APANTO APIACA ARABIC ARANDA
ARAONA ARAWAK ARUNTA
ATAROI AVANTI AYMARA
BAGOBO BAHASA BAITSI BAKELE
BANIVA BASQUE BASUTO BEAVER
BHOTIA BHUMIJ BIHARI BILAAN
BILOXI BOHUNK BONTOC BORORO
BRAHUI BRETON BRIBRI BUKAUA
BULGAR BURIAT CAGABA CANITA
CARAJA CARIAN CARIRI CAUQUI
CAVINA CAYAPA CAYUGA CAYUSE
CEBUAN CHAGGA CHAIMA
CHANGO CHOCHO CHOKWE
COCAMA CONIBO COPTIC CREOLE
DAKOTA DANISH DOGRIB
DYERMA ESKIMO EUDEVE
FRENCH FULANI FULNIO FUTUNA
GADDAN GALCHA GALIBI GATHIC
GENTOO GERMAN GILAKI GILIAK
GILYAK GOTHIC GUAIMI GUETAR
GUINAU GULLAH GURIAN HAINAN
HANTIK HARARI HATTIC HEBREW
HERERO HIBITO IBANAG IBIBIO
IFUGAO IGNERI IGOROT INDIAN
INDOIS INUSI INUPIK ISINAI
ISLETA IVATAN KABARD KACHIN
KAFFIR KAIBAL KALMUK KAMASS
KANAKA KANURI KATIRI KEKCHI
KHALKA KHAMTI KHARIA
KHOWAR KIKUYU KILIWA
KODAGA KODAGU KOIARI KOIBAL
KOLAMI KOREAN KORYAK KOTIAK
KPELLE KUNAMA KURNAI
KURUKH KYURIN LADINO LAGUNA
LAHNDA LAHULI LENAPE LEPCHA
LIBYAN LIUKIU LIVIAN LUSHAI
LUVIAN LUWIAN LYCIAN LYDIAN

MAGAHI MAGYAR MANCHU
MANOBO MBONDO MBUNDA
MEDIAN MEGREL MICMAC
MINOAN MISHMI MISIMA
MOHAWK MONTES MUYSCA
MYSIAN NEPALI NEWARI NINGPO
NOOTKA NUBIAN NYANJA
OJIBWA ONEIDA OORIVA OSTIAK
OTOMAC OVAMPO PAHARI
PAIUTE PALAIC PAPAGO PAPUAN
PASHTO PAZAND POLISH PUSHTO
PUSHTU RASHTI REJANG
ROMANY SAFINE SAKIAN SALISH
SAMOAN SANGIL SANGIR SARCEE
SASSAK SAVARA SEDANG SEKANI
SELKUP SELUNG SEMANG SENECA
SENUFO SESUTO SHARRA SHASTA
SILETZ SINDHI SLOVAK SOMALI
SONRAI SUBIYA SURHAI SUSIAN
TARTAR TAVGHI TELEGU TELEUT
TETTUM THONGA TIPURA
TUNGUS VANNIC VOTYAK
YANKEE YARURA YORUBA
ZAREMA ABENAKI ACHAGUA
AEQUIAN AKWAALA AKWAPIM
ALABAMA ALTAIAN AMANAYE
AMHARIC AMORITE AMUESHA
APINAYE ARAMAIC ARAPAHO
ARAUCAN ARECUNA ARGOBBA
ARICARA ARMORIC ASHANTI
ASURINI ATACAMA ATAKAPA
AUSTRAL AVESTAN AXUMITE
BAGHELI BAGIRMI BAINING
BAKONGO BALANTE BALUCHI
BAMBARA BANGALA BANNACK
BASHKIR BENGALI BEOTHUK
BERBERI BHOTIYA BHUTANI
BOSNIAN BRITISH BULANDA
BUNDELI BUNYORO BURMESE
BUSHMAN CALIANA CALINGA
CARRIER CASHIBO CATALAN
CATAWBA CAWAHIB CHACOBO
CHARRUA CHATINO CHEBERO
CHECHEN CHIBCHA CHIMILA
CHINOOK CHIRINO CHIWERE
CHONTAL CHOROTI CHUKCHI
CHUMASH CHUROYA CHUVASH
CIBONEY CIMBRIC CLALLAM
COCHIMI CORNISH COTONAM
COWLITZ CYMRAEG DAGBANE
DAGOMBA DANAKIL DANKALI
DARGHIN DEUTSCH DHEGIHA
DRAVIDA ENGLISH ESCUARA
ESSELEN EUSKERA FINNISH
FLEMISH FOOCHOW FRIESIC
FRISIAN GAULISH GOAJIRO
GUAHIBO GUARANI GUAYAKI
GURUNSI GYARUNG HAITIAN
HANUNOC HIDATSA HITTITE
HUASTEC HUCHNOM HUICHOL
HURRIAN IBERIAN ILOKANO
ILONGOT INGALIK IPURINA
ITALIAN ITELMES ITONAMA
JACUNDA JAGATAI KAKHYEN
KALINGA KALMUCK KANAMARI
KANAUJI KANNADA KASHUBE
KASSITE KIKONGO KIPCHAK
KIRANTI KIRGHIZ KIRUNDI
KLAMATH KOASATI KONKANI
KOYUKON KUBACHI KULAMAN
KURDISH KUTCHIN KUTENAI
LAMPONG LATVIAN LESGHIN
LINGALA LOATUKO LUGANDA

MAGADHI MAHICAN MALINKE
MALTESE MAPUCHE MARATHI
MASKOKI MERCIAN MEXICAN
MINAEAN MINGREL MISKITO
MITANNI MOABITE MOCHICA
MONUMBO MORATTY MORISCO
NAHUATL NICOBAR OJIBWAY
OSMANLI OSSETIC PAHLAVI
PALAUNG PANJABI PARBATE
PERMIAK PERMIAN PERSIAN
PICTISH PRAKRIT PUNJABI
PUQUINA QUECHUA QUERCHI
SABAEAN SALINAN SAMBALI
SAMNANI SAMNITE SAMOYED
SANDAWE SANTALI SANTANA
SEMITIC SERBIAN SHAWANO
SHAWNEE SHILLUH SHIPIBO
SHUSWAP SIAMESE SIRIONO
SIUSLAW SOGDIAN SONGHAI
SONGISH SORBIAN SPANIOL
SPANISH STIKINE SUBANUN
SVANISH SWAHILI SWEDISH
TAGALOG TIBETAN TUAMOTU
TURKISH UMBRIAN UMBUNDU
VISAYAN WALLOON WENDISH
YENISEI YIDDISH ZABERMA
ZONGORA ABANEEME ACHINESE
ACHUMAWI AKKADIAN AKSUMITE
ALACALUF ALBANIAN ALFURESE
AMAHUACA AMERICAN
AMMONITE ANGOLESE
ANNAMESE ANZANIAN APALACHI
ARMENIAN ASSAMESE ASSYRIAN
ATJINESE AWISHIRA BACTRIAN
BALINESE BARBACOA BECHUANA
BHOJPURI BISCAYAN BOSNISCH
BOTOCUDO CAHUILLA CAINGANG
CANARESE CANOEIRO CAQUETIO
CARELIAN CARIJONA CAYUBABA
CHALDEAN CHAMORRO CHEHALIS
CHEMAKUM CHEYENNE
CHINGPAW CHIQUITO CHITRALI
COCONUCA COLUMBIA
COMANCHE CORAVECA
CROATIAN CUSTENAU DELAWARE
DIEGUENO EGYPTIAN ELAMITIC
ETHIOPIC ETRUSCAN FALISBAN
FORMOSAN FRANKISH FULFULDE
GALICIAN GALLEGAN GEORGIAN
GERMANIC GORKHALI GUAICURU
GUJARATI HADENDOA HAWAIIAN
HITCHITI ILLINOIS ILLYRIAN
IROQUOIS JAPANESE JAVANESE
KANARESE KANAWARI KANKANAI
KASHMIRI KASUBIAN KERMANJI
KIMBUNDU KOLARIAN LANDSMAL
LANUVIAN LIGURIAN LIHYANIC
LILLOOET LIVONIAN LUSATIAN
MADURESE MAHRATTI MAKASSAR
MALAGASY MANDINGO
MARSHALL MASOVIAN
MAYATHAN MAZOVIAN
MONGOLIC MUSKOGEE NUMIDIAN
NYAMWEZI ONONDAGA OSSETIAN
PAMPANGO PHRYGIAN PILIPINO
POLABIAN PORTUGAL PRUSSIAN
RABBINIC ROMANIAN SABELLIC
SANSKRIT SAWAIORI SCOTTISH
SCYTHIAN SEBUNDOY SEECHELT
SHAMBALA SHIRIANA SHOSHONE
SICILIAN SKIPETAR SLAVONIC
SOUTHRON SQUAMISH SUBARIAN
SUBTIABA SUMATRAN SUMERIAN

TAHITIAN TALMUDIC TAMASHEK
THRACIAN TURCOMAN VENETIAN
VOLSCIAN WOGULIAN YUGOSLAV
YUKAGHIR CANAANITE
MONGOLIAN
(SWAHILI —) KISWAHILI
(UNCLEAN —) SEWERAGE
(UNIVERSAL —) PASILALY
(WELSH —) CYMRAEG
(PL.) BALTIC FINNIC MAHORI
SEMITIC SUDANIC ILLYRIAN
(PREF.) GLOSS(O) GLOTT(I)(O) KI
(SUFF.) ESE GLOT
LANGUE D'OC LEMOSI LIMOSI
LANGUET LANGUID LANGUAGE
LANGUID WAN LANK DOWIE FAINT
DREAMY FEEBLE SICKLY SUPINE
TORPID CARELESS FLAGGING
HEEDLESS INDOLENT LISTLESS
SLUGGISH
LANGUISH DIE FADE FALL FLAG
PINE WILT DROOP DWINE FAINT
QUAIL SWOON SICKEN WITHER
DECLINE
LANGUISHING FADE SICK
LANGUID
LANGUOR KEF KIF ENNUI DEBILITY
LASSITUDE
LANGUR DOUC MAHA LOTONG
LUTONG SIMPAI WANDEROO
LANK LEAN THIN GAUNT LANKY
SLANK MEAGER MEAGRE
SCRANKY SLUNKEN
LANKY LEAN RENKY SLINK GANGLY
GANGLING
LANOLIN LANUM DEGRAS
LANSEH DUKU LANSA LANZON
LANTANA OREGANO
LANTERN (ALSO SEE LAMP) BUAT
BOUET BOWET CROWN DARKY
LIGHT CUPOLA LOUVER PHAROS
SCONCE THOLUS CIMBORIO
LANTHORN
(— ON ROOF) FEMEREIL
(DARK —) DARKY ABSCONCE
ABSCONSA
(ELEVATED —) PHAROS
(OPTICAL —) EPISCOPE
LANTERN FISH INIOME
LANTERN FLOUNDER MEGRIM
LANTERN FLY FULGORID
LANTERN PINION RUNDLE
TRUNDLE
LANYARD CORD WAPP
GILGUY LANIARD
BACKROPE
LAODAMIA (BROTHER OF —)
ISANDER HIPPOLOCHUS
(FATHER OF —) ACASTUS
BELLEROPHON
(HUSBAND OF —) PROTESILAUS
(MOTHER OF —) HIPPOLYTE
(SLAYER OF —) ARTEMIS
(SON OF —) SARPEDON
LAODICE (FATHER OF —) PRIAM
(HUSBAND OF —) HELICAON
(MOTHER OF —) HECUBA
LAOIGHIS LEIX
LAOMEDON (DAUGHTER OF —)
HESIONE
(FATHER OF —) ILUS
(MOTHER OF —) EURYDICE
(SON OF —) PRIAM CLYTIUS

LAOS
CAPITAL: VIENTIANE
COIN: KIP
MEASURE: BAK
MOUNTAIN: BIA LAI LOI SAN COPI
KHAT ATWAT KHOUNG TIUBIA
PEOPLE: LU KHA LAO MEO YAO
THAI
RIVER: NOI DONE KHONG MEKONG
NAMHOU SEBANG
TOWN: NAPE PAKSE XIENG
PAKLAY THAKHEK
SAVANNAKHET
LUANGPRABANG
WATERFALL: MEKONG

LAP LEP LIP BARM FOLD GORE LICK
SLAP SLOD SOSS SUCK WASH
WELT SKIVE LAPPER LAPPET
SHOVEL INTERLAP
(— IN STEEL) SPILL
(— OF STRAKES) LAND
LAPACHOL TECOMIN
LAPBOARD PANEL
LAPDOG MESSAN MESSET SHOUGH
LAPEL LAPPET REVERE REVERS
LAPIDARY STONER GEMMARY
LAPIDIST
LAPIDOTH (WIFE OF —) DEBORAH
LAPILLUS RAPILLO
(PL.) CINDER
LAPIS LAZULI AZURE
LAP-JOINTED CLINCH
LAPP LAPPISH LAPPONIC
LAPPED FOLIATED
LAPPET LAP PAN BARBE FANON
LABEL CORNET INFULA PINNER
(PREF.) LACINI
LAPSE DROP FADE FALL HALT SLIP
ERROR FAULT FOLLY SPACE
TRACT EFFLUX HIATUS LAPSUS
DELAPSE ESCHEAT FAILURE
PASSAGE PROCESS RELAPSE
RESOLVE SLIDING ABEYANCE
CADUCITY
(— OF MEMORY) BLACKOUT
(MENTAL —) ABERRATION
(PL.) LACHES
LAPSED CADUCOUS
LAPSING CADUCOUS
LAPSTRAKE CLINCH
LAPWING WEEP WYPE PEWIT
PEEWEE PEEWIT PLOVER TIRWIT
HORNPIE PEEWEEP PIEWIPE
TEUCHIT FLOPWING PEESWEEP
TEEWHAAP TERUTERU
LARBOARD PORT BABURD
LARCENY THEFT FELONY ROBBERY
BURGLARY STEALAGE
LARCH ALERCE LARICK JUNIPER
EPINETTE TAMARACK
LARD MORT SAIM ADEPS DAUBE
ENARM FLARE FLECK FLICK
AXUNGE ENLARD INLARD
NEUTRAL SAINDOUX
LARDED PIQUE CADUCE
CADUCOUS
LARDER CAVE PANTRY SPENCE
BUTTERY LARDINER
LARGE BIG BULL FEAT GOOD LONG
MAIN ROOM TALL AMPLE BULKY
BURLY GRAND GREAT GROSS

HUSKY JOLLY LARGY MACRO
MAXIM RENKY ROUND SMART
SPACY WALLY GAWSIE GOODLY
HEROIC MAXIMA STRONG TRABAL
BOWERLY CAPITAL COPIOUS
FAIRISH FEARFUL HEALTHY
HULKING LASKING LIBERAL
MASSIVE OUTSIZE SIZABLE
BOUNCING CHOPPING OUTSIZED
PLUMPING SENSIBLE SWACKING
(— AND HOLLOW) CAVAL
(— AND ROUND) SIDE
(— IN DIAMETER) STOUT
(APPALLINGLY —) HIDEOUS
(EXTRA —) MAXI
(EXTREMELY —) GIANT DECUMAN
GIGANTIC
(FAIRLY —) SMART
(INDEFINITELY —) NTH INFINITE
(MODERATELY —) FAIR TIDY
PRETTY
(UNUSUALLY —) HEAVY SKELPIN
SKELPING
(VERY —) HUGE JUMBO ROYAL
BOXCAR BUMPER INGENT NATION
GOLIATH INTENSE BEHEMOTH
SLAPPING SPANKING SWINGING
WHACKING
(PREF.) MACR(O) MEGA MEGAL(O)
(HOW —) QUANTI
LARGE-FOOTED MEGAPOD
LARGE-FRAMED ROOMY
LARGE-LETTERED UNCIAL
LARGELY BIG HARD BIGLY
LARGENESS BULK MICKLE
BREADTH FREEDOM GIANTISM
LARGEOUR
LARGEST BEST MAXIMUS
LARIA BRUCHUS
LARIAT ROPE LASSO RIATA
CABESTRO
LARK GAME ROMP FROLIC PEEWEE
SCHEME GAMMOCK LAVROCK
LAYROCK SKYLARK CALANDER
LAVEROCK
LARKA KOLS HO
LARKSPUR LOCOWEED
LARNITE BELITE
LARRIGAN PAC
LARRIKIN NUT ROWDY HOODLUM
LARVA BOT BLOW BOTT CRAB
GRUB HUHU SLUG TURK WOLF
WORM ALIMA ASCON BARDY
BRUKE ERUCA LEECH OTTER
REDIA SYCON CORBIE COSSID
DRAGON EPHYRA GRUGRU
HOPPER LEPTUS LEUCON LOOPER
MAGGOT MEASLE NIGGER
PEDLAR TORCEL WABBLE
WORMIL WOUBIT ATROCHA
BUDWORM CADELLE CREEPER
DIPORPA FIGWORM FLYBLOW
GORDIAN HYDATID HYPOPUS
PEDDLER PLANULA PLUTEUS
PREPUPA VELIGER WIGGLER
ACTINULA ANTIZOEA ARMYWORM
BOLLWORM BOMBYCID
BOOKWORM CASEWORM
CERCARIA COENURUS CYRTOPIA
DEUTOVUM DROPWORM
EPHYRULA FIREWORM FURCILIA
GEOMETER GILTTAIL GLOWWORM
GNATWORM LEAFTIER

LEAFWORM MEALWORM MUCKWORM NAUPLIUS PILIDIUM ROOTWORM SCYPHULA SEMIPUPA SILKWORM SKINWORM SPANWORM SPRAWLER STAGWORM SUBIMAGO TORNARIA VERMICLE WASPLING WIREWORM WOODGRUB WOODWORM

LARVACEA ATREMATA COPELATA
LARVAL NEPIONIC
LARYNGITIS CROUP
LARYNX
  (PREF.) LARYNG(O)
LASCIVIOUS LEWD NICE SALT HORNY LUBRIC WANTON BLISSOM FLESHLY GOATISH PAPHIAN PRURIENT SALACIOUS
LASCIVIOUSNESS LECHERY ASELGEIA LUXURITY LUBRICITY
LASERWORT SILPHIUM
LASH CUT BEAT FIRK FLOG JERK LACE WELT WHIP WIRE YERK LEASE LEASH SCORE SKEEG SLASH THONG TRICE WHALE CANVAS CILIUM LAINER LAUNCH STRIPE SWINGE SWITCH FLYFLAP KURBASH SCOURGE
  (— BOWSPRIT) GAMMON
  (— TOGETHER) RACK
LASHER THONGMAN
LASHING YARK YERK GAMMON LISTING MOUSING SEIZING SLATING FRAPPING
  (PL.) OODLES OODLINS SLITHERS
LASS TIB GILL PRIM TRULL DAMSEL KUMMER LASSIE DAMOZEL LASSIKY TENDREL MUCHACHA
LASSITUDE COPOS LANGUOR LETHARGY
LASSO LASH LAZO ROPE RIATA LARIAT CABESTRO
LAST ABY LAG DURE HOLD KEEP RIDE SAVE ABIDE FINAL SERVE ABEGGE ENDURE LATEST LATTER REMAIN ULTIMA UTMOST DARREIN DERNIER EXTREME PERDURE SUPREME CONTINUE EVENTUAL HINDMOST LATEMOST REARMOST TERMINAL ULTIMATE AFTERMOST
  (— BUT ONE) PENULT
  (— OUT) SPIN STAY
  (AT —) FINALLY
  (THE —) OMEGA
  (PREF.) ESCHATO POSTREMO ULTIMO
LAST DAYS OF POMPEII (AUTHOR OF —) BULWER LYTTON
  (CHARACTER IN —) IONE BURBO JULIA NYDIA DIOMED ARBACES CLODIUS GLAUCUS SALLUST APAECIDES
LASTING FIXED LASTY DURANT DURING STABLE ABIDING DURABLE DUREFUL CONSTANT ENDURING LIVELONG REMANENT STANDING
  (— FOR LONG PERIOD) AEONIC AEONIAL
  (— FOR ONE DAY) DIARY DIURNAL
LASTINGNESS STAY DURATION
LAST OF THE MOHICANS

(AUTHOR OF —) COOPER
(CHARACTER IN —) CORA WEBB ALICE DAVID GAMUT MAGUA MUNRO NATTY UNCAS BUMPPO DUNCAN HAWKEYE HEYWARD MONTCALM CHINGACHGOOK
LAST PURITAN (AUTHOR OF —) SANTAYANA
  (CHARACTER IN —) JIM IRMA ROSE ALDEN BOBBY EDITH MARIO PETER WEYER BOWLER OLIVER DARNLEY HARRIET SCHLOTE BUMSTEAD
LAST SUPPER CENA COENA MAUNDY
LAT STAMBHA
LATCH FLY PIN HASP RISP CATCH CHAIR CLICK CLINK SNECK SNICK KEEPER CLICKET
LATCHET DAG TAB SANDAL LANGUET
LATCHING LASKET
LATCHKEY CLICKET PASSKEY
LATE LAG NEW DEEP RIPE SLOW TARDY TARDIVE UMWHILE ADVANCED LATEWARD SOMETIME UMQUHILE
  (— IN DEVELOPING) SEROTINOUS
LATE GEORGE APLEY (AUTHOR OF —) MARQUAND
  (CHARACTER IN —) JOHN MARY APLEY AMELIA GEORGE ELEANOR HORATIO MONAHAN OREILLY WILLIAM WILLING BOSWORTH PRENTISS CATHARINE
LATELY LATE ALATE NEWLY
LA TENE MARNEAN
LATENT HIDDEN MASKED ABEYANT DORMANT PASSIVE LATITANT QUIESCENT
  (PREF.) CRYPT(O) KRYPT(O)
LATER POI SIN ANON POST SYNE AFTER ELDER BEHIND FUTURE LATTER PUISNE ANOTHER INFERIOR UMQUHILE
  (PREF.) HYSTERO INFRA META POST
LATERAL SIDE
  (PREF.) PLEUR(O)
LATERALLY SIDELONG
LATERITE CABOOK KUNKUR
LATEST LAST LATTER FARTHEST FURTHEST
LATEX GUTTA SORVA ANTIAR SENAMBY
LATH BAT LAG SLAT SPAIL SPALE SPELL SWALE REEPER SPLENT SPLINT STOOTH LATHING FOREPOLE LATHWORK
LATHE LAY SLEY TURN LAITH THROW BEATER WISKET
  (— FOR CYLINDERS) BROAD
  (— OF LOOM) LAY
  (TURNING —) THROW
  (WATCHMAKER'S —) TURN TURNS MANDREL
LATHER FOAM SUDS FROTH FREATH SAPPLES
LATHERED SOAPY
LATIN ROMAN HISPERIC LATINITY SCATTERMOUCH
  (— COMPOSITION) VULGUS
LATIN-AMERICAN LATIN LADINO

LATINO HISPANIC
LATINUS (DAUGHTER OF —) LAVINIA
  (FATHER OF —) FAUNUS
  (SON-IN-LAW OF —) AENEAS
  (WIFE OF —) AMATA
LATITUDE SCOPE WIDTH EXTENT HEIGHT
  (HELIOCENTRIC —) LIMIT
LATONA (DAUGHTER OF —) DIANA
  (FATHER OF —) COEUS
  (MOTHER OF —) PHOEBE
  (SON OF —) APOLLO
LATRIA ADORATION
LATRINE BOG REAR PRIVY TOILET BOGGARD
LATTER LAST FINAL RECENT SECOND PRESENT
  (— PORTION) AUTUMN
LATTICE GRATE HERSE TWINE PINJRA UMBREL GRATING CANCELLI
  (— OF POINTS) SATIN
  (MOVING —) APRON
  (PREF.) CLATHR
LATTICED CLATHRATE
LATTICE PLANT LACELEAF
LATTICEWORK ARBOR GRATE GRATING ESPALIER TUKUTUKU

LATVIA

CAPITAL: RIGA
COIN: LAT RUBLIS KAPEIKA SANTIMS
MEASURE: STOF KANNE STOFF STOOF VERST ARSHIN KULMET SAGENE VERCHOC KROUCHKA POURVETE
NAME: LATVIJA LETTLAND LETTONIE
PEOPLE: LETT
RIVER: AA OGRE DVINA GAUJA VENTA SALACA LIELUPE
TOWN: CESIS LIBAU DVINSK LIBAVA TUKUMS JELGAVA LIEPAJA REZEKNE DUNABURG VALMIERA DAUGAVPILS
WEIGHT: LIESPFUND

LAUAN KALUNTI
LAUD EXTOL PRAISE ADVANCE APPLAUD COMMEND GLORIFY MAGNIFY EMBLAZON EULOGIZE MACARIZE
LAUDATION PUFF EULOGY PRAISE PANEGYRIC
LAUDATORY SNEER EPENETIC PRAISING
LAUGH GAFF CHUCK FLEER LEUGH RISUS ARRIDE NICKER TITTER CHORTLE GRIZZLE SNICKER SNIGGER SNIRTLE TWITTER LAUGHTER
  (— CONTEMPTUOUSLY) SNORT DERIDE
  (— GLEEFULLY) CHECKLE
  (— HYSTERICALLY) CHECKLE
  (— IN AFFECTED MANNER) GIGGLE
  (— IN COARSE MANNER) FLEER GUFFAW
  (— LIKE HEN) CACKLE
  (— LOUDLY) GAFF GUFFAW
  (— QUIETLY) GULE SMUDGE CHUCKLE SNIRTLE

(BELLY —) BOFF BOFFOLA
(LOUD —) GAUSTER
LAUGHABLE ODD RICH COMIC DROLL FUNNY MERRY QUEER WITTY AMUSING COMICAL RISIBLE STRANGE WAGGISH FARCICAL HUMOROUS LAUGHING PLEASANT SPORTIVE RIDICULOUS
LAUGHING RIANT RIDENT IRRISION
  (— MATTER) MOWS
LAUGHING GULL PEWIT
LAUGHING OWL WEKAU WHEKAU
LAUGHINGSTOCK GUY BUTT JEST JOKE SONG SPORT DERISION RIDICULE
LAUGHTER JOKE MIRTH RISUS SNIRT CACKLE LAWTER SPLEEN HILARITY RISIBILITY
  (HYSTERICAL —) CACHINNATION
  (PREF.) GELOTO
LAUNCE LANT LANCE SMELT AMMODYTE SANDLING
LAUNCH PUT BURST DRIVE LANCE ELANCE STRIKE BAPTIZE PINNACE PROMOTE STEAMER VIBRATE CATAPULT
  (— HOSTILELY) DIRECT
LAUNCHER (ROCKET —) BAZOOKA
LAUNDER TYE WASH TRUNK SLUICE STRAKE LAUNDRY
LAUNDRESS TRILBY LAVENDER
LAUNDRY WASH LAVATORY
LAUREL BAY IVY LAURY UNITE WICKY DAPHNE KALMIA MALLET MYRTLE CAJEPUT IVYWOOD WOEVINE BREWSTER CALFKILL
  (GROUND —) ARBUTUS
LAUREL OAK ACAJOU
LAURIC PICHURIC
LAURUSTINE VIBURNUM
LAUSUS (FATHER OF —) NUMITOR MEZENTIUS
  (SISTER OF —) ILIA
  (SLAYER OF —) AMULIUS
LAUTVERSCHIEBUNG SHIFT
LAVA AA ASHES SPINE COULEE LATITE SCORIA VERITE FAVILLA LAPILLO MALPAIS ASPERITE ORENDITE PAHOEHOE
  (MUD —) MOYA LAHAR
  (SCORIACEOUS —) AA SLAG
  (SLAGGY —) SCORIA
LAVABO LAVATORY
LAVAGE LAVATION LAVEMENT
LAVALAVA SULU
LAVAN KALUNTI
LAVATORY BASIN CHALET CLOSET LAVETTE WASHROOM CLOAKROOM
LAVE LIP WASH BATHE SPLASH
LAVENDER BEHN ASPIC BEHEN SPICK SPIKE INKROOT LAVANDIN STICHADO
LAVENGRO (AUTHOR OF —) BORROW
  (CHARACTER IN —) JOHN MOLL ARDRY HERNE PETER ISOPEL JASPER BERNERS FRANCIS LEONORA TAGGART LAVENGRO SAPENGRO SLINGSBY WILLIAMS WINIFRED PETULENGRO

LAVER SION SLAKE SLOKE LOUTER PHIALE AMANORI CISTERN CANTHARUS

LAVINIA (FATHER OF —) LATINUS **(HUSBAND OF —)** AENEAS **(MOTHER OF —)** AMATA

LAVISH FREE LASH LUSH FLUSH LARGE SPEND SPORT WASTE COSTLY WANTON COPIOUS OPULENT PROFUSE GENEROUS LUCULLAN PRODIGAL SQUANDER WASTEFUL REDUNDANT MUNIFICENT

LAVISHNESS WASTE FINERY LAVISH

LAW ACT FAS IUS JUS LAY LEX ADAT DOOM JURE RULE CANON DROIT NOMOS TORAH BYELAW BYRLAW DECREE DHARMA EQUITY BROCARD DANELAW DERECHO HALACHA HALAKAH JUSTICE PRECEPT SETNESS STATUTE JUDGMENT JUDICIAL ROGATION STATEWAY TANISTRY ORDINANCE **(—S OF MANU)** SUTRA SUTTA **(BEDOUIN —)** THAR **(DIETARY —S)** KASHRUTH **(ISLAMIC —)** ADA BAI ADAT SHERI SHARIA SHERIAT. **(MARRIAGE —)** LEVIRATE **(OPPOSING —)** ANTINOMY **(PROPOSED —)** BILL **(UNIVERSAL —)** HEAVEN **(PL.)** LORS **(PREF.)** JURIS LEGI LEGO NOM(O) THESMO **(SUFF.)** LEGE NOMY

LAW-ABIDING LAWFUL

LAWBREAKER FELON HOUGHER

LAWFUL DUE LEAL TRUE VERY LEGAL LICIT LOYAL VALID KINDLY LEEFUL ENNOMIC LEESOME INNOCENT LIEFSOME RIGHTFUL

LAWGIVER MINOS MOSES SOLON LAWYER LAWMAKER

LAWLESS LEWD UNRULY ILLEGAL MOBBISH ANARCHIC

LAWLESSNESS ANOMY ANOMIE ANARCHY

LAWMAKER LEGIFER

LAWN ARBOR GRASS LINON SWARD UMPLE CYPRUS BATISTE QUINTIN TIFFANY

LAWSUIT LIS CASE SAKE SECTA ACTION BRABBLE

LAWYER (ALSO SEE JURIST) JET PEAT AVOUE PATCH SHARK BREHON JURIST LAWMAN LEGIST SQUIRE WRITER COUNSEL MUKHTAR TEMPLAR DEFENDER LEGISTER TRAMPLER BARRISTER MOUTHPIECE PETTIFOGGER

LAX DULL FREE LASH LAZY LINK SLOW SWAG WIDE LARGE LOOSE RELAX SLACK TARDY REMISS BACKWARD INACTIVE DISSOLUTE NEGLIGENT

LAXATIVE LAX LASK CASCARA APERIENT HYDROMEL LAPACTIC RELAXANT SOLUTIVE TARAXACUM

LAXITY LASCHETY LATITUDE

LAY LIE SET CLAP LAIC LEWD SLEY SONG WAGE BIGHT CIVIL COUCH DITTY LATHE LEDGE QUIET STAKE STILL COMMON HAZARD IMPOSE IMPUTE APPEASE ASCRIBE LAYDOWN POPULAR SECULAR SIRVENTE TEMPORAL **(— ASIDE)** DOFF DOWN DUMP SHUCK DEPOSE DIVEST DEPOSIT PIGEONHOLE **(— AWAY)** STORE **(— BARE)** BARE NAKE TIRL TIRVE DENUDE DETECT OPPOSE UNCOVER DENUDATE **(— CLAIM)** ASSERT BESPEAK ARROGATE **(— CROSSWISE)** COB **(— DOWN)** ABDICATE PRESCRIBE **(— EGGS)** BLOW WARP LEDGE OVIPOSIT **(— FLAT)** SQUAT ADPRESS **(— HOLD OF)** FANG GRIP HENT TAKE GRIPE LATCH ATHOLD ATTACH COLLAR COMPRISE **(— IN BIGHTS)** JAG **(— IN COIL)** FLEMISH **(— IN PLEATS)** FOLD **(— LOW)** STREW STRIKE **(— OF LOOM)** BEATER **(— ON)** APPLY INFLICT **(— OPEN)** BREAK CHINE EXPOSE UNMASK **(— OUT)** FRAY PLAT RANGE SPELD SPEND BEWARE DESIGN EXTEND SPREAD STREAK STREEK CHECKER DEVELOP STRETCH CONTRIVE **(— PRONE)** LEVEL **(— RUBBLEWORK)** SNECK **(— SIEGE)** INVEST **(— SMOOTH)** EVEN **(— SNARE FOR RABBITS)** HAY **(— STONE)** PAVE **(— STRAIGHT)** COMB **(— TYPE)** CASE **(— UP)** HEAP HIVE ADDLE HOARD HUTCH STOCK TREASURE **(— WASTE)** PEEL WEST HARRY HAVOC HARASS RAVAGE DESTROY DESOLATE FORWASTE

LAYBOY JOGGER

LAYDOWN LAYOUT SPREAD

LAYER BED LAY BARK CAKE COAT DASS FACE FILM FLAP FOLD LAIR LOFT RIND SEAM SKIN WEFT ZONA CHESS COUCH COVER CRUST CUTIS FLAKE FLASH LEDGE SCALE CARPET COURSE FASCIA FILLER FOLIUM INTINE LAMINA LISSOM STREAK BLANKET COATING CUTICLE EPICARP FEATHER FLAVEDO GANGMAN INLAYER LAMELLA PACKING PHELLEM PROPAGO PROVINE STRATUM SUBCOAT SUPPORT ECTOCYST ECTOSARC ENDOCYST ENDODERM EPIBLAST EPIBLEMA EPISPORE EPITHECA INTERBED MOLLISOL PERIOPLE PERISARC SUBCRUST PERIPLAST PHELLODERM **(— IN FUNGI)** HYMENIUM

(— OF ATMOSPHERE) MESOSPHERE OZONOSPHERE **(— OF BLOOD VESSEL)** EXTIMA EXTERNA **(— OF CELLS)** EXINE CORTEX EXTINE CAMBIUM PHELLEM TAPETUM PERICYCLE **(— OF CLAY)** GLEY VARVE SELVAGE SELVEDGE **(— OF EARTH)** SPIT **(— OF FAT)** LEAF FINISH **(— OF FELT)** BAT BATT **(— OF FIBER)** LAP **(— OF FINE MATERIAL)** CUSHION **(— OF FOREST GROWTH)** SUBSTORY OVERSTORY **(— OF FUEL)** FIREBED **(— OF GLASS)** CASING **(— OF IRIS)** UVEA **(— OF MEAT)** SPINE **(— OF MORTAR)** SCREED **(— OF NERVE FIBERS)** ALVEUS **(— OF ORGANIC MATTER)** FLOOR **(— OF PLASMA)** BUFFCOAT **(— OF ROCK)** CAP SHELF SHELL SLATE FOLIUM SEPTUM BLISTER SKULLCAP **(— OF ROOTS)** SOLE **(— OF SEDIMENT)** WARP **(— OF SHALE)** BONE **(— OF SHEEPSKIN)** FLESHER **(— OF SHOE HEEL)** LIFT **(— OF SILT)** VARVE **(— OF SKIN)** DERM DERMA EPIDERM **(— OF SOIL)** SOLUM CALLOW CASING HARDPAN HORIZON **(— OF STONES)** DASS DESS **(— OF TANBARK)** HAT **(— OF TISSUE)** BED DARTOS FASCIA SEROSA ELASTICA EPIBLEMA PERIDERM **(— OF TOBACCO LEAVES)** HANGER **(— OF TURF)** FLAW KERF **(— OF WHITE MATTER)** CAPSULE **(— OF WOOD)** CORE **(BONY —)** LAMELLA CEMENTUM **(BOTTOM —)** BEDDING **(FLAT —)** BED FLAP FLAKE **(FROZEN —)** PERMAFROST **(GERM —)** MESODERM **(IMPERVIOUS —)** LINING **(OUTER —)** HUSK **(PREF.)** LAMELLI LAMIN(I) PTYCH(O) STRATI **(SUFF.)** CLINAL CLINE LAMIN **(— OF SKIN)** DERMIS **(GERM —)** BLAST(IC)(Y)

LAYERING LAP GOOTEE STOOLING

LAYMAN LAIC CLERK IDIOT DEACON SECULAR DEFENSOR EXHORTER EXOTERIC FAMILIAR STRANGER WORLDMAN

LAYOFF FURLOUGH

LAYOUT MISE DUMMY SETOUT **(— OF CARDS)** TABLEAU

LAZARETTO SPITAL SPITTLE

LAZARUS (SISTER OF —) MARY MARTHA

LAZINESS LAZE SLOTH SLOUCH OISIVITY

LAZULITE SIDERITE

LAZY ARGH IDLE LASS DOXIE

DRONY FAINT INERT LINGY LUSKY RESTY SLOAN SLOTH CLUMSY LIMPSY LURDAN LUTHER ORNERY SWEERT TRAILY CLUMPST DRONISH LUSKISH PEAKISH SLIVING DROGHLIN FAINEANT FECKLESS INDOLENT LITHERLY OSCITANT SLOTHFUL SLUGGARD THOWLESS TRIFLING SHIFTLESS

LEA LAY GRASS LAYER LAYLAND LEALAND

LEACH TAP LETCH SOFTEN

LEAD GO TEE VAN WIN BEAR DADE GIVE GROW HAVE HEAD HERD LEED SLIP TAKE TEEM WORK BLAZE BOUND BRING CARRY GREBE GUIDE MAYNE PILOT PRESA SOUND START TRAIN TREAT CONVEY DEDUCE DIRECT ESCORT INDUCE INDUCT LEADER SATURN BEGUILE CAPTAIN CONDUCE CONDUCT LEADING MARSHAL PIGTAIL PIONEER PLUMBUM PLUMMET LEADSMAN MANUDUCE MANUDUCT SQUIRREL **(— A BAND)** BATON **(— AND SUPPORT)** DADE **(— ASIDE)** CHAR SINGLE **(— ASTRAY)** ERR MANG TURN WARP BEFOOL BETRAY ENTICE WANDER WILDER DEBAUCH MISLEAD MISWEND PERVERT SOLICIT TRADUCE BEWILDER INVEIGLE MISGUIDE **(— AWAY)** CHAR ABDUCT DIVERGE **(— BACK)** REDUCT **(— FORCIBLY)** ESCORT **(— IN CARD GAME)** SNEAK WHITECHAPEL **(— IN RACE)** LAP **(— IN SINGING)** PRECENT **(— INTO ERROR)** ABUSE DELUDE **(— MONOXIDE)** MASSICOT **(— ON)** TRAIL **(— PASSIVE EXISTENCE)** VEGETATE **(— POISONING)** PLUMBISM **(BLACK —)** WAD WADD GRAPHITE **(COLOR —)** PLOMB **(DEEP-SEA —)** DIPSY DIPSEY **(MOCK —)** BLENDE **(OVERLAPPING —)** DRIP **(PLUMBING —)** BLUEY **(SYMBOL FOR —)** PB **(WHITE —)** KREMS CERUSE **(PREF.)** GALENO MOLYBD(O) PLUMB(I)(O) **(SUFF.)** AGOGUE AGOGY

LEAD-COLORED WAN BLAE

LEADEN HEAVY PLUMBEAN

LEADER BO BOH COB DUX HOB MIR CAST COCK DUCE DUKE HEAD HOBB JEFE NAIG NAIK OMDA SOUL TYEE CHIEF DOYEN ELDER FIRST MAHDI MOSES OMDEH PILOT SEYID TRACE ARCHON CALIPH DESPOT HEADER HONCHO RECTOR SAYYID TYCOON ACREMAN ADVISER CAPTAIN CONDUCT DEMAGOG DRUNGAR FOREMAN FUEHRER INDUCER PRIMATE ACCENTOR CAUDILLO DIRECTOR FUGLEMAN

HEADSMAN HERETOGA
LODESMAN PANDARUS STRATEGE
PENDRAGON PROTAGONIST
(— OF ARMY) VAIVODE VOIVODE
(— OF DACOITS) BOH
(— OF GUISERS) SKUDLER
(— OF MINING GANG) CORPORAL
(— OF MUTINEERS) ELECTO
(— OF REVOLT) ANARCH
(BAND —) BATONEER
(CHOIR —) CANTOR PRECENTOR
(CHORUS —) CHORAGUS
(COSSACK —) HETMAN
(FASCIST —) RAS
(INTELLECTUAL —) BRAIN
(MOB —) MOBOCRAT
(POLITICAL —) SACHEM
(PRAYER —) IMAM
(RELIGIOUS —) AGA AGHA SHEIKH
(SCOUT —) AKELA SIXER
(SPIRITUAL —) GURU SADDIK
GUARDIAN
(SUFF.) ARCH ARCHIC ARCHY
LEADERSHIP LEAD AEGIS MANRED
CONDUCT IMAMATE LEADING
MANRENT CHIEFDOM GUIDANCE
HEADSHIP HEGEMONY
(— BY TALENTED) MERITOCRACY
LEADING BIG BEST COCK DUCT
HEAD LEAD MAIN CHIEF FIRST
BANNER PREMIER STELLAR
GUIDANCE PROMINENT
(— OUTWARD) EMISSARY
(— TO NOTHING) IDLE
LEADSMAN SOUNDER
LEADWORK PLUMBAGE PLUMBING
LEADWORT CROWTOE PLUMBAGO
LEAF PAD BACK BARB BUYO FLAG
FLAP FOIL FOLD GEAR PAGE
PALM STUB BLADE BLANK FLIER
FLYER FOLIO FROND GRASS
GUARD LEAVE SCALE SEPAL
SIGHT SPILL TEPAL BONNET
CADJAN CARPEL COUPON
FOLIUM FRAISE FULZIE NEEDLE
PEPPER DAMIANA FOLDOUT
HARNESS LEAFLET TREFOIL
WITNESS PHYLLADE PHYLLOME
MICROPHYLL
(— FAT) FLICK
(— FROM AXIL) BRACT
(— OF BOOK) PAGE FOLIO INSET
PLATE FLYLEAF
(— OF CALYX) BARB
(— OF CORN) HUSK
(— OF COROLLA) PETAL
(— OF DOOR) VALVE
(— OF HEDDLES) GEAR
(— OF PALM) FAN OLA PAN CHIP
OLLA FROND LATANIER
(— OF SPRING) BACK
(BETEL —) PAN SIRIH
(BIBLE —) COSTMARY
(DEAD —) FLAG
(HOLLOW —) PHYLLODE
(PART OF —) RIB TIP APEX BASE
LOBE STEM VEIN BLADE SINUS
LAMINA MARGIN MIDRIB PETIOLE
LEAFSTALK
(RUDIMENTARY —) CATAPHYLL
(SPRING —) WRAPPER
(STRAWBERRY —) FRAISE
(THIN —) LAMELLA

(TOBACCO —) LUGS STRIP CUTTER
WRAPPER
(WASTE GOLD —) SKEWING
(PREF.) FOLI(O) PETAL(I)(O)
PHYLL(I)(O)
(SUFF.) FOLIATE FOLIOUS
PETALOUS PHYLL(A)(OUS)(UM)(Y)
LEAFAGE FOLIAGE
LEAFHOPPER HOPPER JASSID
THRIPS HOMOPTER
LEAFLET PINNA TRACT MAILER
FOLIOLE STUFFER
(-S DROPPED FROM AIR) BUMF
(PAIR OF —S) JUGUM
(PL.) SENNA CAROBA
LEAFLIKE PHYLLINE
LEAFMOLD KOLINSKY
LEAFY GREEN LEAVY FOLIATE
FOLIOSE FRONDOSE
LEAGUE BOND BUND BANDY
BOARD GUEUX HANSA PARTY
UNION WHEEL CIRCUIT COMPACT
ALLIANCE SYSTASIS COALITION
(— OF NATIONS) GENEVA
(BUSH —S) STICKS
LEAGUED FEDERATE
LEAH (DAUGHTER OF —) DINAH
(FATHER OF —) LABAN
(HUSBAND OF —) JACOB
(SISTER OF —) RACHEL
(SON OF —) LEVI JUDAH REUBEN
SIMEON ZEBULUN ISSACHAR
LEAK BLOW SEEP WEEP GEYZE
SPUNK INLEAK SIGGER SPRING
ZIGGER LEAKAGE MELTERS
SCREEVE
(— IN ELECTRIC CIRCUIT) FAULT
LEAKAGE ESCAPE SEEPAGE
(— OF ELECTRICITY) CREEPAGE
(— OF GAS) SLIP
(— OF WIND) RUNNING
LEAKING ALEAK DRIBBLE NAILSICK
LEAKY LEAK UNTIGHT GIZZENED
LEAL FAITHFUL
LEAN BEAR BEND BONY HANG
HEEL LANK PEND POOR PRIN
RACY RELY REST SEEL STAY
SWAY THIN TOOM EMPTY GAUNT
HIELD LANKY LEANY SLANK
SOUND SPARE STOOP HOLLOW
MEAGER RECUMB SKINNY SPRING
UPLEAN ANGULAR FATLESS
HAGGARD INCLINE SCRAGGY
SCRAWNY SLUNKEN STRINGY
MACILENT SCRAGGED SCRANNEL
(— FOR SUPPORT) ABUT
(— FORWARD) PROCLINE
(— OVER) WHAUVE
(PREF.) CLIN(O)
LEANDER (LOVE OF —) HERO
LEANDRE (FATHER OF —) GERONTE
(LOVER OF —) LUCINDE
LEANER HOBBER
LEANING DRIFT FLAIR PENCHE
HANGING ACCLINAL ENCLITIC
FROMWARD PROPENSE
PROCLIVITY PROPENSITY
(— BACKWARD) SUPINE
(STRONG —) GENIUS PENCHANT
LEANNESS LANK POVERTY
SPARENESS
LEAN-TO SHED LINTER OUTSHOT
SKILLION

LEAP FLY HOP POP BEND DART
DIVE FALL GIVE JUMP LOPE LOUP
RAMP RISE SKIT WIND BOUND
BREAK CAPER DANCE EXULT
FLIER FLYER FRISK LUNGE PRIME
SALTO SAULT SCOPE SCOUP
SPANG STEND VAULT BOUNCE
BREACH CURVET INSULT LAUNCH
SPRENT SPRING SPRUNT WALLOP
REBOUND SALTARY SALTATE
SUBSULT BUCKJUMP LEAPFROG
SPANGHEW UPSPRING
(— BACK) RESULT SPRUNT
(— FOR JOY) EXULT
(— IN DANCING) STOT
(— LIGHTLY) SKIP
(— OF HORSE) CURVET BALOTADE
CAPRIOLE CROUPADE
(— OF WHALE) BREACH
(— OUT) SALLY
(— OVER) FREE OVER SKIP CLEAR
HURDLE
(— UPON) ASSAIL
(BALLET —) JETE ASSEMBLE
CABRIOLE
(FROLICSOME —) CAPER
(SUICIDAL —) BRODIE
(PL.) ALLEGRO
(PREF.) SCIRTO
LEAPING GAMBOL SPRING
RAMPANT SALIENT SALTANT
LEARCHUS (BROTHER OF —)
MELICERTA
(FATHER OF —) ATHAMAS
(MOTHER OF —) INO
LEARN DO CON GET SEE WIT ARAL
FIND HAVE HEAR LEAR LERE
EDIFY GLEAN STUDY RECORD
REALIZE RECEIVE DISCOVER
ASCERTAIN
(— FROM EXPERIENCE) ASSAY
LEARNED BLUE SEEN LERED
LORED DUCTUS BOOKISH
CLERKLY CUNNING ERUDITE
STUDIED TUITIVE ACADEMIC
CLERGIAL LETTERED OVERSEEN
POLYMATH PROFOUND SCIENCED
(— MAN) OLLAV
(AFFECTEDLY —) INKHORN
(SOMETHING TO BE —) LIRIPIPE
LEARNEDLY CLERKLY
LEARNER PUPIL NOVICE SCHOLAR
TRAINEE PRENTICE ABECEDARIAN
(LATE —) OPSIMATH
LEARNING ART WIT BOOK LEIR
LERE LORE CLERGY WISDOM
APPRISE CUNNING GRAMMAR
INSIGHT LETTERS WISTING
BOOKLEAR BOOKLORE DOCTRINE
HUMANISM LETTRURE MATHESIS
PEDANTRY
(SUFF.) MATHY
LEASE FEU FEW LET SET FARM
HIRE RENT TACK COWLE DIMIT
FIRMA LISSE DEMISE POTTAH
RENTAL ASSEDAT CHARTER
SETTING BACKTACK SUBLEASE
LEASEHOLDER LIVIER
LEASH LEAD LYME SLIP LEASE
TRASH COUPLE STRING SWINGE
(— OF HOUNDS) HARL
(DOG —) SLIP TRASH TIRRET
(HAWK'S —) LOYN LUNE

TIRRET CREANCE
LEASING LOCATIO
LEAST LEST MINIMAL MINIMUM
MINIMUS
(AT —) HURE
LEAST FLYCATCHER CHEBEC
LEAST SANDPIPER PEEP OXEYE
STINT
LEATHER ELK KID BEND BOCK
BUFF CALF CAPE HIDE NAPA
SEAL ADUST ALUTA BALAT FLANK
NIGER RETAN SUEDE BULGAR
CASTOR CHROME LIZARD ORIOLE
OXHIDE PEBBLE RUSSET SKIVER
TURKEY BELTING BUFFING
CANEPIN CHAMOIS COWHIDE
COWSKIN DEGRAIN DOGSKIN
DONGOLA HEADCAP HOGSKIN
KIDSKIN MURRAIN PANCAKE
PECCARY PERSIAN SAFFIAN
ANTELOPE BUCKSKIN BULLNECK
CABRETTA CALFSKIN CAPESKIN
CHEVEREL COLTSKIN CORDOBAN
CORDWAIN DEERSKIN GOATSKIN
KANGAROO LAMBSKIN SHAGREEN
SHEEPSKIN
(— FOR DRESSING FLAX) RIBSKIN
(— FROM SHEEPSKIN) ROAN
(— SHREDS) MOSLINGS
(— STRIP) RAND
(ARABIAN —) MOCHA
(ARTIFICIAL —) KERATOL
PEGAMOID
(BOARDED —) BOX
(CORDOVAN —) CORDOBAN
CORDWAIN
(GRAINED —) ROAN
(MOROCCO —) LEVANT MAROQUIN
(PATCH OF —) CLOUT
(PRUSSIAN —) SPRUCE
(RUSSIAN —) YUFT BULGAR
RUSSIA JUCHTEN
(SHEEPSKIN —) BOCK BUCK
MOCHA
(SOFT —) OOZE ALUTA
(SUPERIOR —) BUFF
(THICK —) BUTT
(WASH —) LOSH LOSHE
(PREF.) SCYT(O)
LEATHERBACK LUTH
LEATHERFISH LIJA FOOLFISH
LEATHERJACKET FILEFISH
ZAPATERO
LEATHERLEAF CASSANDRA
LEATHERWOOD DIRCA WICOPY
BURNWOOD FIREWOOD
IRONWOOD LEADWOOD
ROPEBARK
LEATHERWORKER TAWER
BEDDER CHAMAR MADIGA
FLUFFER CHUCKLER
LEAVE GO GET LET BUNK DROP
FADE FLEE HOOK LEAF PART
QUIT VADE VOID WALK AVOID
CONGE FAVOR FORGO GRACE
SHOVE WAIVE BUGGER BUGOFF
DEPART DESERT DEVOID FORLET
PERMIT RETIRE SECEDE STRAND
VACATE FORLEIT FORLESE
FORSAKE LARGESS LIBERTY
LICENSE FAREWELL PATIENCE
UNTENANT PERMISSION
SABBATICAL

(— ALONE) FORBEAR DESOLATE
(— BEHIND) LET PLANT DISTANCE
OUTSTRIP
(— BRIGHT TRAIL) STREAM
(— BY WILL) BEQUEATH
(— COVER) BREAK
(— HASTILY) SCUR SKIRR
(— HURRIEDLY) CUT BLOW FLEE
JUMP SCAT SKIP
(— IN ISOLATION) MAROON
(— IN SAFEKEEPING) CHECK
(— NOTHING TO BE DESIRED)
SATISFY
(— OF ABSENCE) ABSIT EXEAT
LIBERTY FURLOUGH
(— OFF) CEASE DEVAL PETER
BILEVE CHEESE DESIST SURCEASE
(— OUT) BATE OMIT SKIP SLIP
ELIDE
(— PORT) CLEAR
(— QUICKLY) SCREW
(— SECRETLY) STEAL
(— SUDDENLY) KITE
(— UNDONE) PRETERMIT
LEAVED
(SUFF.) PHYLLOUS
LEAVEN ZYM ZYMO RAISE YEAST
INFUSE RAISING SOURING
(PREF.) ZYM(O)
LEAVENING EMPTINGS
LEAVES PATRIN FOLIAGE LEAFAGE
LEAFERY
(— OF BAOBAB TREE) LALO
(— OF ORCHID) FAHAM
(— OF TOBACCO) LEAF FLYINGS
SECONDS
(— ON STEM AFTER WITHERING)
INDUVIAE
(— USED AS STYPTIC) MATICO
(BOILED — OF POTHERB) CHARD
(DRIED —) LAUHALA
(FALLEN —) DUFF
(MEDICINAL —) COCA FILE BUCCO
BUCKU FARFARA FUMARIA
(PALM —) ATAP ATTAP CADJAN
CAJANG
(TEA —) SOUCHONG
(WITHERED —) PININGS
(SUFF.) **(HAVING —)** CLEMA
PHYLLOUS
(NUMBER OF —) MO
LEAVE-TAKING VALE ADIEU
CONGEE PARTING WAYGANG
FAREWELL WAYGOING
LEAVING BIT ORT TAG
(PL.) RAFF SNUFF REFUSE
RESIDUE RESIDUUM
(PREF.) LIPO

LEBANON
CAPITAL: BEIRUT BEYROUTH
COIN: LIVRE PIASTRE
MOUNTAIN: ARUBA HERMON
SANNINE KENISSEH
PLAIN: ELBIKA
RIVER: JOZ LYCOS DAMOUR
LITANI HASBANI LEONTES
ORONTES KASEMIEH
SEAPORT: TYRE SAIDA SIDON
BEIRUT
TOWN: SUR TYRE ALEIH HALBA
SAIDA SIDON ZAHLE
JUNIYE ZAHLAH QARTABA

TRIPOLI MERJUYUN
VALLEY: BEQAA

LEBBEK KOKO KOKKO SIRIS
LEBKUCHEN LEKACH
LECHER GOAT LUXUR PALLIARD
LECHEROUS LEWD SALT PRIME
RANDY WANTON BOARISH
CODDING GOATISH LUSTFUL
LIKEROUS SCABROUS SPORTIVE
STUPROUS SALACIOUS
(PREF.) LUBRI
LECHERY LUXURY
LECTERN DESK EAGLE LUTRIN
LATERAN LATTERIN
LECTION GOSPEL EPISTLE READING
PERICOPE PROPHECY
LECTIONARY LEGEND
LECTOR LISTER READER
LECTURE JOBE CREED FORUM
HOMILY LECTOR LESSON SERMON
ADDRESS EARBASH HEARING
PRELECT READING JOBATION
ORDINARY
LECTURER DOCENT LECTOR
READER DRYASDUST
LEDA (DAUGHTER OF —) HELEN
CLYTEMNESTRA
(FATHER OF —) THESTIUS
(HUSBAND OF —) TYNDAREUS
(SON OF —) CASTOR POLLUX
LEDGE BEAD BERM DESS LINE STEP
ALTAR BENCH CLINT LINCH SHELF
SNOUT BEARER OFFSET SETTLE
STANCE CHANNEL LEDGING
RETABLE
LEDGEMAN BREAKER
LEDGER BOOK SLAB LIEGER
JOURNAL OVERLIER
LEDGER BOARD RIBBON
LEE LEW LEEWARD
LEECH GILL HARPY LEACH APODAN
SANGSUE BDELLOID HELMINTH
(PREF.) BDELL(A) HIRUDINI
(SUFF.) BDELLA
LEEK FOUAT ALLIUM PORRET
SCALLION SENGREEN ROCAMBOLE
(— COLORED) PRASINE
(PREF.) PRASEO PRASO
LEEK GREEN RESEDA
LEER LEAR LOOK OGLE FLEER
LEERY SKIME SMIRK TWIRE
LEERFISH GARRICK
LEES LAGS ADDLE DRAFF DREGS
DROSS GROUT AMURCA BOTTOM
DUNDER MOTHER ULLAGE
GROUNDS EMPTINGS SEDIMENT
WINEDRAF
LEEWAN SOFA DIVAN
LEEWARD DOWNWIND
LEEWAY DRIFT
LEFT G CAR KAY GAWK NEAR PORT
OTHER TOWARD DESERTED
(— EYE) OL OS
(PREF.) LAEV(O) LEV(O) SINISTR(O)
LEFT HAND MG MS SM SIN
GAUCHE
(— PAGE) VERSO
LEFTHANDED CAR GAUCHE
AWKWARD DUBIOUS OBLIQUE
KITHOGUE SOUTHPAW
LEFT-HANDER SOUTHPAW
LEFTOVER END ORT REMNANT

SURPLUS REMAINDER
(TOBACCO —) TOPPER
(PL.) SCRAN ANALECTS
LEG ARM GAM PEG PIN CRUS
GAMB JAMB LIMB TRAM BOUGH
GAMBE JAMBE REACH SHANK
STICK STUMP BENDER GAMBON
GAMMON LEGLET MOGGAN
OVIGER PESTLE PLANTA PROLEG
WALKER FORELEG TRESTLE
FORELIMB
(— OF CRUSTACEAN) PODITE
(— OF HAWK) ARM
(— OF LAMB) GIGOT WABBLER
WOBBLER
(— OF TABLE) BALUSTER
(— OF WHEELBARROW) STILT
(— USED FOR FOOD) PESTLE
(—S OF ARTIFICIAL FLY) HACKLE
(ARTIFICIAL —) PYLON
(FURNITURE —) CABRIOLE
(MILK —) WEED
(TROUSER —) SLOP
(WIRE —S) SLING
(WOODEN —) PEG STUMP TIMBER
(PL.) PROPS TONGS STAMPS
STICKS
(PREF.) SCEL(O)
(SUFF.) SCELES
(LOWER —) CNEMA CNEMIA
CNEMIC CNEMUS
LEGACY ENTAIL LEGATE BEQUEST
HERITAGE WINDFALL
LEGAL LEAL LICIT SOUND VALID
LAWFUL SQUARE JURIDIC
RIGHTFUL
LEGALISM NOMISM SCRIBISM
LEGALISTIC COURT
LEGATE ENVOY DEPUTY EXARCH
LEGATUS CONSULAR LEGATARY
PANDULPH
LEGATION MISSION
LEGATO SMOOTH
LEGEND EDDA MYTH POSY SAGA
TALE FABLE STORY TITLE THREAP
CAPTION CUTLINE HAGGADA
(MAP —) KEY
(PREF.) MYTHO
LEGENDARY FABLED FICTIOUS
LEGERDEMAIN PRESTIDIGITATION
LEGERDEMAINIST JUGGLER
LEGGING SPAT COCKER BOTTINE
GAMBADO JAMBEAU BALATONG
BOOTIKIN CHIVARRA
(LEATHER —) STRAD
(PL.) CHAPS SHANKS BROGUES
COGGERS GAMASHES LEATHERS
OVERALLS
LEGIBLE FAIR READABLE
LEGION HOST TERZO TERZIO
LEGIONARY ANT DRIVER
FORAGER
LEGISLATION DYSNOMY
LAWMAKING
LEGISLATOR SOLON LAWGIVER
LAWMAKER
LEGISLATURE DIET COURT THING
LAGTING RIKSDAG LANDRATH
RIGSRAAD
LEGITIMATE JUST TRUE VERY
LEGAL LEGIT LOYAL HONEST
KINDLY KOSHER LAWFUL REABLE
SQUARE NATURAL LEGITIME

LEGITIMATELY FAIRLY MULIERLY
LEGPIECE JAMBEAU
LEGUME POD GUAR PULSE
LOMENT PODDER COCHLEA
LEGUMEN PODWARE SOYBEAN
STROMBUS
LEHUA OHIA
LEIPOA LOWAN MEGAPOD
PHEASANT
LEISHMANIASIS UTA ESPUNDIA
LEISTER SPEAR WASTER
LEISURE TIME TOOM VOID OTIUM
RESPITE VACANCY VACATION
LEISURELY SLOW SOODLY TIMELY
TOOMLY GRADUAL PICKTOOTH
LELEX (FATHER OF —) NEPTUNE
POSEIDON
(MOTHER OF —) LIBYA
(SON OF —) MYLES
LEMAN UNDERPUT
LEMMING CRICETID
LEMMUS MYODES
LEMNISCUS FILET FILLET
LAQUEUS
LEMON DOG DUD CEDRA CHLOR
LEMONY CEDRATE FAILURE
KUMQUAT
LEMONADE COOLER
LEMON GRASS TANGLAD
LEMON SOLE MARYSOLE
LEMON VERBENA ALOYSIA
LEMUR MAKI VARI AVAHI INDRI
KOKAM LORIS POTTO SIFAC
ADAPID COBEGO COLUGO
GALAGO KUBONG MACACO
MAHOLI MONKEY SIFAKA
APOSORO MEERKAT NATTOCK
PRIMATE SEMIAPE TARSIER
AMPONGUE BABAKOTO
MONGOOSE PRIMATAL TARSIOID
LEND OCKER PREST SECOND
ADVANCE IMPREST
(— AT INTEREST) GAVEL
(— ITSELF) ALLOY
LENDING (— AGENCY) MOUNT
LENGTH LUG DREE TOWT PITCH
SCOPE SIDTH COURSE EXTENT
TOWGHT FOOTAGE DISTANCE
LEGITUDE SIDENESS
(— ATHWARTSHIP) ABURTON
(— OF BRIDGE) BAY
(— OF CABLE) SCOPE SHACKLE
(— OF CHAIN) SHOT
(— OF CLOTH) CUT
(— OF FIBER) STAPLE
(— OF FISHING LINE) CAST
(— OF GEAR TOOTH) FACE
(— OF HAIR) KNOT
(— OF HAIR IN FISHING LINE) IMP
(— OF LINE) LOYN
(— OF METAL) SHAPE
(— OF MOUTH) GAPE
(— OF NET) LEAD
(— OF PISTON STROKE) TRAVEL
(— OF ROPE) DRIFT SPOKE BRIDLE
COURSE STOPPER
(— OF SERVICE) STANDING
(— OF SHOEMAKER'S THREAD) END
(— OF THREAD) STITCH
(— OF TILE) GAUGE
(— OF TIMBER) BALK FLITCH
(— OF TRIP) GATE
(— OF WINDMILL ARM) WHIP

(— OF YARN) KNOT TAPE CHASE
SKEIN
(— UNIT) FERMI
(AT FULL —) ALONG
(CONTINUOUS —) STRETCH
(FOCAL —) FOCUS
(UNIT OF —) PIC PIK ROD FOOT
INCH KILO PIKE REED VARA
WRAP YARD METER SHAKU
POLLEX FURLONG PLETHRON
(UTMOST —) EXTREME
(PREF.) MEC(O)
LENGTHEN EKE LONG DILATE
EXPAND EXTEND LENGTH
AMPLIFY DISTEND PRODUCE
PROLONG STRETCH ELONGATE
INCREASE PROTRACT
(— BY INTERPOLATION) FARSE
LENGTHENING HOLD ECTASIS
DIASTOLE
LENGTHWISE ALONG ALENGTH
ENDLONG ENDWAYS ENDWISE
VERTICAL
LENGTHY LONG LARGE PROLIX
LONGFUL EXTENDED
LENIENCY FAVOR MERCY LENITY
CHARITY CLEMENCY LENIENCE
LENIENT LAX EASY KIND MILD
SOFT FACILE GENTLE HUMANE
LENITIVE
LENITIVE MILD MITIGANT
SEDATIVE
LENITY MERCY HUMANITY
KINDNESS LENITUDE
LENO GAUZE
LENS EYE CROWN GLASS OPTIC
FLASER PEBBLE READER
APLANAT BIFOCAL CONCAVE
CONTACT DOUBLET ACHROMAT
EYEGLASS EYEPIECE HYPERGON
LENTICLE LUNETTES MENISCUS
MAGNIFIER
(WITHOUT —) APHAKIA
(PREF.) PHAC(O)
LENT CAREME IMPREST
LENTICULAR PHACOID
LENTIGO FRECKLE
LENTIL LENS LINT TILL LENTILE
LENTICLE
(PREF.) PHAC(O)
LEOFRIC (FATHER OF —) LEOFWINE
(WIFE OF —) GODIVA
LEONORE (GUARDIAN OF —) ARISTE
(SISTER OF —) ISABELLE
LEONTOCEBUS MIDAS
LEOPARD PARD TIGER PARDAL
WAGATI LIBBARD PAINTER
PANTHER PARDALE CATAMOUNT
(SNOW —) IRBIS OUNCE
LEOVIGILD (SON OF —)
ERMENEGILD
(WIFE OF —) GOISWINTHA
LEPCHA RONG RONGPA
LEPER LAZAR MESEL LAZARUS
LEPIDOMELANE ANNITE
LEPIDOPTERA GLOSSATA
LEPIDOPTERIST AURELIAN
LEPIDOSIS SCALING
LEPRECHAUN ELF SPRITE
LURACAN
LEPROSY LEPRA MESEL SCALL
ALPHOS LAZARY MESELRY
LEPROUS MESELY MESELED

LEPTON MITE MUON
LEPTOSPIROSIS JAUNDICE
LERP LAAP
LESBIAN EROTIC SAPPHIC TRIBADE
SAPPHIST
LESION PIT GALL HIVE SORE
CRATER ESCHAR LEPRID
ANTHRAX CHANCRE FISSURE
LEPROMA BEESTING ERUPTION
LEUKEMID TERTIARY

LESOTHO

CAPITAL: MASERU
COIN: RAND
FORMER NAME: BASUTOLAND
LANGUAGE: SOTHO SESOTHO
MOUNTAINS: MALUTI
PEOPLE: BASOTHO
RIVER: ORANGE CALEDON
TOWN: LERIBE MASHAI MORIJA
  PITSENG QUTHING SEKAKES
  MAFETENG
WATERFALL: MALETSUNYANE

LESPEDEZA SERICEA
LESS FEW MIN MENO FEWER
MINOR LESSER SMALLER
WANTING
(— BY A COMMA) MINOR
(PREF.) HYPO MEIO MIMIO MIO
(— THAN NORMAL) HYPO
LESSEE FARMER TERMOR
HUURDER TACKSMAN
LESSEN CUT EBB BATE DOCK EASE
FAIK FRET KILL LESS SINK WANE
ABATE BREAK LOWER MINCE
SMALL TAPER BUFFER DEADEN
DEJECT IMPAIR INLESS MINIFY
MINISH NARROW REBATE
REDUCE WEAKEN AMENUSE
ASSUAGE CURTAIL DEPLETE
DEPRESS ELEVATE LIGHTEN
RELIEVE SHORTEN CONTRACT
DECREASE DEROGATE DIMINISH
DISCOUNT EMBEZZLE MITIGATE
MODERATE PALLIATE
(— FORCE) GELD
(— IN VALUE) SHRINK CHEAPEN
(— SENSITIVITY) DULL
(— STRENGTH) WEAR
(— TENSION) RELAX
(— VELOCITY) DEADEN
LESSENING LETUP PERDITION
LESSER PETIT MINUTE SMALLER
INFERIOR
(PREF.) MI(O) MINI
(SUFF.) (— ONE) ET ETTE
LESSER CELANDINE PILEWORT
LESSON TAX LEAR TASK STUDY
EXAMPLE LECTURE PRECEPT
READING DOCUMENT LIRIPOOP
(DIFFICULT —) SOAK
(TORAH —) PARASHAH
LESSOR SETTER
LEST UNLESS ANANTER
ANAUNTERS
LET LAT SET HIRE ALLOW LEASE
LEAVE LETTEN PERMIT SUFFER
TENANT
(— BAIT BOB) DIB
(— BECOME KNOWN) SPILL
(— BURN) BISHOP
(— CONTINUE) DRILL

(— DOWN) VAIL DEMIT DIMIT
LOWER STOOP STRIKE SUBMIT
(— DOWN ROCK FACE) ABSEIL
(— FALL) DROP VAIL AVALE
AWALE DEPOSE
(— FLY) PEG BOLT FIRE WING
(— GO) DROP FAIK QUIT DEMIT
BILEVE DEMISE DISMIT UNHAND
DISCARD UNSEIZE
(— HIM TAKE) SUM
(— IN) IMMIT INLET IMMISS
ADHIBIT
(— IT BE REPEATED) REPET
(— IT STAND) STET
(— KNOW) ACQUAINT
(— LAND) GAVEL
(— LOOSE) FREE SLIP LIBERATE
(— OUT) BLAB TEAM WAGE BREAK
SPILL ARRENT BROACH
(— SLIP) BALK BAULK CHECK
FOREGO
LETDOWN HANGOVER
LETHAL FATAL DEADLY MORTAL
LETHARGIC INERT DROWSY
SLEEPY TORPID DORMANT
PASSIVE COMATOSE COMATOUS
SLUGGISH SLUMBROUS
LETHARGY COMA SLOTH STUPOR
TORPOR SLUMBER HEBETUDE
INACTION SOPITION
LETO LATONA
LETT BALT
LETTER EF EL EM EN EX HE PE AIN
AYN BEE CEE CHI DAK DEE EDH
ESS ETA ETH GEE HET JAY KAY
LIL MEM NUN PEE SIN TAV TAW
TEE VEE WAW YOD YAK YOK ZED ZEE
ALEF ALIF AYIN BETA BETH BILL
BULL CHIT DEAD HETH IOTA
KAPH RESH SHIN SORT TETH
YODH YOGH AITCH ALEPH BLIND
BREVE CAPON DELTA DEMIT
FAVOR GAMMA GIMEL GRAPH
KAPPA KNOWN KOPPA SADHE
SIGMA STAVE STIFF ZAYIN
ACCENT ADVICE ANSWER BILLET
CADJAN CARTEL CHARTA
COCKUP DALETH FAVVER ITALIC
LAMBDA LAMEDH MEDIAL
SAMEKH SCRIPT SIGLUM SUNNUD
SYMBOL VERSAL CODICIL COLLINS
CONTROL DIGAMMA DIPLOMA
EPISTLE EPSILON KAREETA
MISSIVE SPECIAL AEROGRAM
ASCENDER ENCYCLIC MONITORY
NUNDINAL PASTORAL
(— OF DEFIANCE) CARTEL
(— OF PERMISSION) EXEAT
(—S DIMISSORY) APOSTOLI
(—S OF MARQUE) MART
(ANGLO-SAXON —) EDH ETH
THORN
(AUTHORIZING —) BREVE
(BEGGING —) SCREEVE
(BLACK —) GOTHIC
(BREAD AND BUTTER —) COLLINS
(CAPITAL —) CAP UNCIAL CAPITAL
FACTOTUM MAJUSCULE
(FRIENDLY —) SCREED
(INITIAL —) BLOOMER
(LOVE —) POULET
(LOWERCASE —) MINISCULE
(OBSOLETE —) EPISEMON

(OFFICIAL —) BRIEF
(PAPAL —) BULL TOME BREVE
ENCYCLIC
(PRIVATE —) BOOK
(SHORT —) CHIT LINE NOTE BILLET
LETTERET
(SILENT —) MUTE
(SMUGGLED —) KITE
(SUBSCRIPT —) SUBFIX
(WORD —) LOGOGRAM
(PL.) MAIL APOSTOLI
(PREF.) EPISTOLO
LETTER BOX APARTADO
LETTER CARRIER CORREO
MAILMAN POSTMAN
LETTERER SKETCHER
LETTERING FAC WRITE INCUSE
LETTERPRESS TEXT CAPTION
LETTING FIRMA LOCATIO
LETTING-OUT DROPPING
LETTUCE COS BIBB GRASS SALAD
KARPAS SALLET ICEBERG
ROMAINE FIREWEED MILKWEED
LETUSHIM (FATHER OF —) DEDAN
LEUCIPPE (BROTHER OF —)
CALCHAS
(FATHER OF —) MINYAS THESTOR
(SISTER OF —) THEONOE
(SON OF —) TEUTHRAS
LEUCIPPUS (BROTHER OF —)
APHAREUS
(DAUGHTER OF —) PHOEBE
HILAIRA
(FATHER OF —) OENOMAUS
PERIERES
(MOTHER OF —) GORGOPHONE
(WIFE OF —) PHILODICE
LEUCITE LENAD
LEUCITITE ITALITE SPERONE
ALBANITE CECILITE
LEUCOCYTE POLY NEOCYTE
HEMAMEBA MONOCYTE OXYPHILE
LEUCOMA ALBUGO WALLEYE
LEUCORRHEA WHITES
LEUCOTHEA (FATHER OF —)
ORCHAMUS
(MOTHER OF —) EURYNOME
LEUKEMIA CHLOROMA LEUKOSIS
LEVANT EASTERN WORMSEED
LEVANTINE SCATTERMOUCH
LEVEE DIKE DYKE WALL WEIR
DURBAR STOPBANK
LEVEL BONE EVEN FAIR FLAT GLAD
LUTE PLAT RAZE SHIM VIAL
COUCH EQUAL FLUSH GRADE
PLAIN PLANE POINT SLICK SOLID
CHARGE DOUBLE EVENLY FIELDY
NIVEAU SLIGHT SMOOTH STRIKE
TUNNEL FLATTEN GALLERY
GANGWAY REGULAR DEMOLISH
LEVELLER SUBGRADE
(— A RAFTER) EDGE
(— AFTER PLOWING) BUSH
(— AND SCATTER) GELD
(— OF SOCIETY) STRATUM
(— OF STAGE) STUDY
(— OFF) HAMMER BULLDOZE
(— PLACE) PLANILLA
(COMMON —) PAR
(ENERGY —) SINGLET
(EYE —) EYELINE
(HIGHER —S) BRASS
(HIGHEST —) SUMMIT

(LOWEST —) FLOOR BOTTOM
HARDPAN
(MINING —) KIP HEAD GALLERY
GANGWAY
(STRATIGRAPHIC —) HORIZON
(TOP —) HIGH CEILING
(PREF.) PLAN(I)
LEVELED BENT
LEVELER DIGGER
(PL.) ACEPHALI
LEVELING EGALITE EGALITY
LEVER KEY PRY BEAM GAUL HOOK
HORN JACK SWAY TREE BRAKE
FLAIL FLIRT HELVE PEDAL PINCH
PLUTO PRIZE SPOON STANG
STANK SWIPE THROW BINDER
CLUTCH COUPER DETENT FEELER
GAFFLE HAMMER HEAVER
HOPPER LOWDER PORTER
ROCKER TAPPET TILLER BALANCE
BOOTLEG POINTER RAMHEAD
SHIPPER SWINGLE TREADLE
TRIGGER TUMBLER BACKFALL
GAVELOCK SELECTOR THROTTLE
(— ARM) NIGGER
(— FOR CROSSBOW) GAFFLE
GARROT
(— FOR TURNING RUDDER) HELM
TILLER
(— IN KNITTING MACHINE) JACK
(— IN TIMEPIECE) PALLET
(— LIKE CANTHOOK) PEAVY PEAVIE
(— OF GIN) START
(GEARSHIFT —) STICK
(ORGAN —) BACKFALL
(SPINNING —) BOOTLEG
(SPOKELIKE —) SWINGLE
(THROTTLE —) GUN
(WEAVING —) LAM LAMM SWELL
BINDER TIPPLER
LEVERAGE PRY PRIZE
LEVI (FATHER OF —) JACOB
ALPHAEUS
(MOTHER OF —) LEAH
(SON OF —) KOHATH MERARI
GERSHON
LEVIGATE DUST
LEVITY FOLLY HUMOR GAIETY
WHIFFLERY
LEVOROTATORY LAEVO
LEVOGYRE NEGATIVE
LEVY CUT TAX CESS MISE REAR
LEVEL RAISE ASSESS EXTEND
EXTENT IMPOSE IMPOST UPTAKE
IMPRESS TRIBUTE DISTRAIN
DISTRESS SHIPPAGE
(— A TAX) GELD GELT TAIL STENT
(— DISTRESS) DRIVE
(IRISH —) MART
LEVYING EXACTION
LEWD NICE BAWDY FOLLY PRIME
RANDY HARLOT IMPURE LACHES
LUBRIC RAKISH WANTON HIRCINE
LEERING LUSTFUL OBSCENE
RAMMISH RIGGISH SCARLET
SENSUAL WHORISH PRURIENT
SLUTTISH UNCHASTE SALACIOUS
LEWDNESS FOLLY RAKERY
LECHERY HARLOTRY PUTANISM
LUBRICITY SCULDUDDERY
LEXICOGRAPHER AMERICAN GOVE
ALLEN CARHART WEBSTER
WHEELER WORCESTER

BRAZILIAN MORAES
ENGLISH WYLD COLES DYCHE
SCOTT SMITH BAILEY BLOUNT
CRAGIE FARMER FLORIO FOWLER
MURRAY ONIONS WALKER
BRADLEY CAWDREY JOHNSON
MINSHEU WITHALS BULLOKAR
COCKERAM COTGRAVE
AINSWORTH COCKERELL
PARTRIDGE STORMONTH
RICHARDSON
FRENCH LITTRE BEAUJAN
GODEFROY LAROUSSE FURETIERE
GERMAN ERMAN MURET SACHS
FLUGEL SCHNEIDER
GREEK POLLUX SUIDAS
PAMPHILUS
ICELANDIC BLONDAL
ITALIAN CESARI CALENUS
FANFANI FACCIOLATI FORCELLINI
POLISH LINDE
SCOTTISH GRANT OGILVY
LEXICON CALEPIN WORDBOOK
LIABILITY DEBT DEBIT CHARGE
TRIBUTE OBLIGATION
LIABLE APT ABLE OPEN GUILTY
EXPOSED OBVIOUS ONEROUS
SUBJECT AMENABLE INCIDENT
(SUFF.) ABLE IBLE
LIAISON BOND AFFAIR AFFAIRE
LINKING INTIMACY INTRIGUE
LIANA CIPO BEJUCO GUARANA
BUSHROPE
LIANG TAEL
LIAR LEAR ANANIAS BOUNCER
CRACKER CRAMMER PROCTOR
WARLOCK WERNARD FABULIST
LIBATION AMBROSIA
LIBEL DEFAME MALIGN VILIFY
SLANDER
LIBELOUS FAMOUS SCANDALOUS
LIBER PHLOEM
LIBERAL FAIR FREE GOOD OPEN
WHIG BROAD FRANK LARGE
NOBLE SOLUTE JANNOCK
PROFUSE ADVANCED CATHOLIC
GENEROUS HANDSOME
LARGEOUS PRODIGAL SEPARATE
MUNIFICENT
(CANADIAN —) GRIT
(NOT —) CHARY SPARE
LIBERAL ARTS MUSES
LIBERALITY LARGE BOUNTY
BREADTH CHARITY FREEDOM
HONESTY LARGESS
LIBERALLY LARGE BROADLY
LIBERATE FREE QUIT FRITH REMIT
UNGYVE UNWRAP DELIVER
MANUMIT RELEASE UNSLAVE
UNFETTER UNTHRALL
LIBERATION FREEDOM RELEASE
DELIVERY KAIVALYA DISCHARGE
(— OF SPORE) ABSCISSION

LIBERIA
CAPITAL: MONROVIA
CUSTOM: SANDE
HILLS: BOMI
MEASURE: KUBA
MOUNTAIN: UNI NIETE NIMBA
WUTIVI
MOUNTAINS: BONG SATRO
PEOPLE: GI KRU KWA VAI VEI

GOLA KROO KROU TOMA BASSA
GIBBI GISSI GREBO KPELLE
KROOBY KRUMAN KROOBOY
MANDINGO
RIVER: CESS LOFA MANO LOFFA
MANNA MORRO CESTOS
DOUOBE STJOHN STPAUL
CAVALLY SANPEDRO
TOWN: GANTA GRIBO REBBO
HARPER ZORZOR NANAKRU
TAPPITA BUCHANAN
MARSHALL SASSTOWN

LIBERTINE ROUE PUNKER
PANURGE STRIKER LOTHARIO
LOVELACE STRINGER
LIBERTY MAY SOC EASE LARGE
LEAVE SCOPE ACCESS SCOUTH
STREET FREEDOM LARGESS
LICENSE WITHGANG
(— OF ACTION) PLAY SWING
(— OF ENTRANCE) INGRESS
(— OF GOING OUT) ISH
(— OF TURNING PIGS INTO FIELDS)
SHACK
(— TO BUY AND SELL) TOLL
(— TO HUNT) CHASE
(PARTIAL — OF HAWK) HACK
(SEXUAL —) INTIMACY
(UNDUE —) HEAD
LIBERTY CAP PILLEUS
LIBIDINIZATION EGOISM
LIBIDINOUS FLESHY FLESHLY
LIBNI (FATHER OF —) MAHLI
GERSHON
LIBRA AS PONDUS
LIBRARIAN AMERICAN COLE DANA
HILL HUNT KOCH LANE DEWEY
EAMES GREEN MUDGE POOLE
SMITH CUTTER FOLSOM HUMMEL
JEWETT PUTNAM WINSOR
EDMANDS SONNECK VANNAME
WELLMAN BARTLETT BOSTWICK
COGSWELL MACLEISH SAUNDERS
SPOFFORD YARMOLINSKY
ENGLISH BOND COXE PANIZZI
THOMPSON
FRENCH DUPUY OMONT
BONNECHOSE TASCHEREAU
GERMAN EBERT BURGER
PERUVIAN ULLOA
SPANISH MACHADO
LIBRARY AMBRY BIBLE MUSEUM
BHANDAR BOOKERY ATHENEUM
LIBRETTO BOOK WORD TESTO
TEXTBOOK

LIBYA
ALPHABET: TIFINAGH
CAPITAL: BENGASI BENGAZI
TRIPOLI
COIN: DIRHAM
DESERT: FEZZAN MURZUK
MURZUQ
GULF: SIDRA SIRTE
MEASURE: SAA BOZZE DONUM
JABIA TEMAN BARILE MISURA
MATTARO
MOUNTAIN: BETTE
OASIS: JALO KUFRA SEBHA
FEZZAN GIOFRA TAZERBO
GIARABUB
SEAPORT: HOMS DERNA SIDRI

TOBRUK BENGAZI
TOWN: BRAK DERJ HOMS BARKA
DERNA SEBHA SIDRI UBARI
ZAWIA ELMARJ GARIAN
MURZUQ REMADA TOBRUK
MISURATA
WEIGHT: KELE UCKIA GORRAF
TERMINO KHAROUBA

LICE CREEPERS
(FISH —) EPIZOA
LICENSE CHOP GALE HEAD EXEAT
LEAVE SLANG SWING BANDON
CAROON FIRMAN INDULT PATENT
PERMIT READER TICKET
CAROOME CERTIFY CROTTLE
FACULTY FREEDOM INDULTO
LIBERTY LICENCE PLACARD
WARRANT ESCAMBIO IMMUNITY
MORTMAIN PASSPORT TEZKIRAH
(— FOR CART) CAROOME
(— PLATE) NUMBER
(PEDDLER'S —) SLANG
LICENTIOUS GAY LAX FREE LEWD
WILD FRANK LARGE LOOSE
FILTHY RIBALD UNRULY WANTON
CYPRIAN FLESHLY IMMORAL
LAWLESS LIBERAL UNYOKED
LICENTIOUSNESS DIRT LICENSE
LICHEN RAG MOSS MANNA USNEA
ARCHIL CORKIR KORKIR ORCHIL
CROTTAL CROTTLE CUDBEAR
EVERNIA OAKMOSS PARELLA
ARCHILLA CAPEWEED LECANORA
LUNGWORT PARMELIA ROCKHAIR
TREEHAIR WARTWORT
LICIT LEGAL LAWFUL LEEFUL
LICK LAP LIKE SUCK MOUTH SLAKE
CONQUER
LICKER-IN TUMBLE
LICKING LAMBENT GRUELING
LICKSPITTLE LACKEY
LICORICE POMFRET SWEETROOT
LICORICE PILL CACHOU
LICYMNIUS (FATHER OF —)
ELECTRYON
(MOTHER OF —) MIDEA
(SISTER OF —) ALCMENA
(SLAYER OF —) TLEPOLEMUS
(WIFE OF —) PERIMEDE
LID DIP BRED DECK TYMP COVER
BRIDLE EYELID POTLID CLAPPER
CLICKET CLOSURE SCUTTLE
SHUTTER COVERCLE OPERCULUM
(SUFF.) POMATOUS
LIE FIB GAB KIP LAY LIG LIN SIT
YED CRAM FALL FLAW LIGG REST
RIDE WHID DEVIL DWELL FABLE
FEIGN LEASE STAND STORY
BOUNCE FITTEN PALTER RAPPER
RESIDE SPRAWL VANITY YANKER
BOUNCER CONSIST CRACKER
CRAMMER CRUMPER FALSITY
GRABBLE LEASING PLUMPER
TWISTER UNTRUTH WHACKER
WHISKER WHOPPER MENDACITY
TARADIDDLE PREVARICATE
(— ALONGSIDE) ACCOST
(— AROUND) COMPASS
(— AT ANCHOR) HOVE
(— AT FULL LENGTH) STRETCH
(— CONCEALED) DARKLE
(— CONTIGUOUS) CONFINE

(— DETECTOR) POLYGRAPH
(— DORMANT) SLEEP
(— DOWN) LEAN COUCH CHARGE
(— FLAT ON BELLY) GROVEL
(— HEAD TO WIND) TRY
(— HIDDEN) LURK MICHE TAPPISH
(— IN AMBUSH) HUGGER
(— IN BED) KIP THOKE
(— IN WAIT) AWAIT LOWER
AMBUSH FORELAY
(— IN WATER) DOUSE DROWN
(— LOW) TAPPICE
(— NEXT TO) ADJOIN
(— OPPOSITE TO) SUBTEND
(— OVER) COVER
(— PRONE) GROVEL GRABBLE
(— PROSTRATE) STREEK
(— QUIET) SNUDGE
(— SNUG) CUDDLE
(— UNEVENLY) SAG
(— WITH SAILS FURLED) HULL
(BIG —) CAULKER
(IMPUDENT —) BOUNCE
(MONSTROUS —) STRAMMER
(PREF.) (— HID) LANTHAN(O)
LANTHO

LIECHTENSTEIN
CAPITAL: VADUZ
CASTLE: GUTEMBURG
MOUNTAIN: RHATIKON
RIVER: RHINE SAMINA
ROMAN NAME: RHAETIA
TOWN: HAAG BALZER SCHAAN
NENDELN
TRIBE: ALAMANN

LIED BALLAD
LIEF DEAR LEAVE LEEVE LIEVE
FREELY GLADLY BELOVED
LIEUTENANT LUFF ZANY LOUEY
JAYGEE KEHAYA CAIMAKAM
QAIMAQAM TENIENTE WOODVILE
LIFE IT VIE ZOE HIDE JIVA PUFF
SNAP TUCK VALE ANIMA BEING
BLOOD DEMON HEART LIFER
QUICK SWEAT BIOSIS BREATH
CANDLE COURSE ENERGY SPIRIT
SPRITE LIFELET LIFEWAY VITALITY
VIVACITY
(— AFTER DEATH) FUTURITY
(— IN HEAVEN) GLORY
(— IN SOCIETY) SAMSARA
SANSARA
(— OF FURNACE LINING) CAMPAIGN
(— OF THE SEA) HALIBIOS
(ACADEMIC —) ACADEMIA
(ANIMAL —) FLESH
(ANIMAL AND PLANT —) BIOS
BIOTA BIOLOGY EDAPHON
(CLOISTERED —) VEIL
(INTELLECTUAL —) JIVATMA
(MONASTIC —) CLOISTER
(MORAL —) DAENA
(MOSS —) BRYOLOGY
(PLANT —) FLORA BOTANY
(ROBUST —) JUICE
(SINGLE —) CELIBACY
(TERRESTRIAL —) GEOBIOS
(WAY OF —) BAG SCENE
(WITHOUT —) AZOIC
(PREF.) BI(O) EMBIO PSYCH(O)
VIT(A)(O)

(NOT —) ABIO
(SUFF.) BIA BIONT BIOSIS BIOTIC
BIOUS BIUM BIUS BY PSYCHE
LIFE BELT SAFETY
LIFEBLOOD BLOOD SWEAT
LIFE-FORCE KUNDALINI
LIFE FOR THE TSAR, A
(CHARACTER IN —) SOBININ
SUSANIN ANTONIDA
(COMPOSER OF —) GLINKA
LIFELESS ARID DEAD DULL FLAT
AMORT HEAVY INERT VAPID
ANEMIC TORPID SAPLESS
DESOLATE GRIPLESS INACTIVE
(PREF.) ABIO
LIFELESSLY DEADLY INERTLY
LIFELESSNESS ANEMIA
LIFELIKE VIVE QUICK EIDETIC
NATURAL ANIMATED SPEAKING
LIFE PRESERVER FLOAT NEDDY
LIFETIME AGE DAY WORLD LIVING
LIFEDAY DURATION LIFELONG
LIFE WITH FATHER (AUTHOR OF —)
DAY
(CHARACTER IN —) DELIA GULICK
CLARENCE MARGARET
LIFT WIN BOOM BUOY CAST COCK
HEFT JACK REAR TOSS WEVE
ARSIS BOOST BREAK ELATE
HEAVE HITCH HOICK HOIST
HOOSH MOUNT PRESS RAISE
SPOUT STEAL WEIGH BUCKET
CLEECH SNATCH ELEVATE
ENHANCE HEELTAP NAUNTLE
BOOKLIFT CHAIRWAY ELEVATOR
LEVITATE
(— HAT) DOFF
(— IN VEHICLE) SETDOWN
(— OF WAVE) SCEND
(— ONESELF) SOAR
(— QUICKLY) PERK
(— UP) HOVE CRANE ERECT EXALT
EXTOL HORSE WEIGH ADVANCE
ELEVATE NAUNTLE
(— WITH BLOCK AND TACKLE)
BOUSE
LIFTED ARRECT SUBLIME
LIFTER GAGGER SERVER HOISTER
HOISTMAN
LIFTING HIKE UPTAKE
LIFT VALVE POPPET
LIGAMENT BAND BOND ARTERY
FRENUM PAXWAX STRING
ZONULE ARMILLA LIGATURE
(PREF.) DESM(A)(IDI)(IDIO)(O)
SYNDESM(O)
LIGAMENTOUS DESMOID
LIGATE BAR
LIGATURE CLAM PLICA DIGRAM
PNEUMA STIGMA DIGRAPH
FUNICLE LIGAMENT LIGATION
(— OE) ASH
LIGGER TRIMMER
LIGHT BUG DAY GAY HAP LAW SHY
SUN AIRY EASY FAIR FALL FINE
FIRE FLIT FLUX GLIM LAMP LEET
LUNT MILD SLUT SOFT BAVIN
BLAZE CORKY FANAL FILMY
FLAME FLEET FUFFY LEGER
LOUGH MERRY PITCH QUICK
SHEER SPILL WHITE BEACON
BRIGHT CHAFFY FLOATY FLOSSY
FLUFFY FROTHY GENTLE HAPPEN

ILLUME KINDLE LANCET LUSTER
LUSTRE MARKER PASTEL PHAROS
SIGNAL SLUSHY STINGY STRIKE
SUTTLE VOLAGE BENGOLA
BUOYANT CRESSET FRAGILE
GLITTER LAMBENT SFOGATO
SMITHER SUMMERY TORTAYS
TRIVIAL UNGRAVE BACKFIRE
DAYLIGHT DELICATE DIAPHANE
ELECTRIC EXPEDITE FEATHERY
GASLIGHT GOSSAMER LEGGIERO
LUMINARY PALOUSER SUNLIGHT
SUNSHINE
(— AND BRILLIANT) LAMBENT
(— AND FIRE ON HORSE'S MANE)
HAG
(— AND FREE) FLYAWAY
(— AND QUICK) VOLANT
(— CANDLES) TOLLY
(— FROM NIGHT SKY) AIRGLOW
(— IN WINDOW) LANCET
(— OF MORNING) AURORA
(— ON TV SCREEN) SNOW
(— UP) FLASH GLOZE ILLUME
RELUME GLORIFY
(— UPON) STRIKE
(BRIGHT —) GLARE GLEAM
(BURST OF —) FLASH
(CIRCLE OF —) HALO NIMBUS
(EMIT COHERENT —) LASE
(FAINT —) GLIMMER SCARROW
(FEEBLE —) TAPER GLIMMER
(FITFUL —) SHIMMER
(HARBOR —) BUG
(INDICATOR —) BEZEL
(INNER —) SEED
(NEBULOUS —) CHEVELURE
(NEW —) SEPARATE
(NIGHT —) MORTAR
(PARKING —S) DIMMERS
(PATCH OF —) CURSOR
(PERSIAN GOD OF —) MITHRAS
(REFLECTED —) SKYME
(SHIP'S —) FANAL
(SMALL —) TAPER
(TRAFFIC —) BLINKER
(WAVERING —) FLICKER
(PL.) BUFF
(PREF.) LUCI LUMIN(I)(O) PHOS
PHOT(O)
LIGHT-COLORED BLONDE
LIGHTEN ALAY CLEAR LEVIN LIGHT
RAISE ALLEGE BLEACH ENCLEAR
FOULDRE MOLLIFY SWEETEN
THUNDER LEVIGATE
LIGHTENING BREAK
(— OF HAIR) FROSTING
LIGHTER KEEL SCOW ACCON
BARGE CASCO PRAAM WHERRY
DROGHER GABBARD GONDOLA
PONTOON CHOPBOAT
LIGHTERMAN KEELER KEELMAN
LIGHT-GREEN
(PREF.) CHLOR(O)
LIGHT-HEADED IDLE BARMY LIGHT
LIVELY CARRIED GLAIKET
SKITTISH
LIGHT-HEARTED GAY GLAD GIDDY
BUOYANT WINSOME CAREFREE
DEBONAIR VOLATILE
LIGHTHEARTEDNESS BUOYANCY
LIGHTHOUSE FANAL LIGHT MINAR
BEACON PHAROS LANTERN

(PREF.) PHARO
LIGHT IN AUGUST (AUTHOR OF —)
FAULKNER
(CHARACTER IN —) DOC JOE GAIL
LENA ALLEN BROWN BURCH
BYRON GROVE HINES LUCAS
BOBBIE BURDEN JOANNA
EUPHEUS CHRISTMAS
HIGHTOWER
LIGHTLESS APHOTIC
(PREF.) APHOTO
LIGHTLY LIGHT AIRILY FAIRLY
HOVERLY LEGGIERO SLIGHTLY
LIGHT-MINDED BLITHE ETOURDI
LIGHTNESS CHEER VALUE GAIETY
LEVITY AIRINESS BUOYANCY
LEGERETE LEGERITY
(— OF MOVEMENT) BALLON
LIGHTNING BOLT FIRE LAIT LEVIN
FULMEN METEOR FOULDRE
SULPHUR THUNDER FIREBALL
FIREBOLT WILDFIRE
LIGHT-O'-LOVE COCOTTE LEVERET
LIGHT-TEXTURED FOZY
LIGHTWOOD FATWOOD
LIGIA LIGYDA
LIGNEOUS WOODY XYLOID
LIGNIN LIGNOSE XYLOGEN
LIGNITE JET
LIGNUM VITAE GUAYACAN
POCKWOOD
LIGROIN BENZINE CANADOL
LIGULA LANGUET
LIGULE STRAP LIGULA
LIKE AS DIG DOTE LIST LOVE ALIKE
ENJOY EQUAL FANCY SAVOR
TASTE ADMIRE AFFECT BELIKE
LIKELY MATTER PLEASE SEMBLE
SIMILE CONCEIT SIMILAR
SEMBLANT SUITABLE SEMBLABLE
(— A GLAND) ADEMOSE ADENOUS
(— BETTER) PREFER
(— HAIR) CRINITE
(VERY —) SIAMESE
(PREF.) HOME(O) HOMOE HOMOI
SYM
(SUFF.) AR EOUS IC(AL) INE IS ISH
ISTIC LY ODE OID(AL) SOME
LIKELIHOOD APTNESS
LIKELY APT FAIR LIKE READY
LIABLE PROOFY SEEMLY GRADELY
SMITTLE APPARENT FEASIBLE
POSSIBLE PROBABLE
PROSPECTIVE
(MOST —) BELIKE
LIKEN EVEN LIKE REMENE SEMBLE
COMPARE ASSEMBLE CREDIBLE
RESEMBLE SIMILIZE
LIKENESS DAP BLEE ICON IDOL
MAKE SECT BLUSH DUMMY GLIFF
IMAGE MORAL SHAPE EFFIGY
FIGURE STATUE ANALOGY
KINSHIP PATTERN PICTURE
RETRAIT EQUALITY HOMOLOGY
PARALLEL PORTRAIT SEMBLANCE
SIMILARITY
(PERFECT —) SPIT
LIKEWISE EKE TOO ALSO ITEM
EITHER EQUALLY LIKEWAYS
(— NOT) NOR
LIKHI (FATHER OF —) SHEMIDAH
LIKING GOO GRA PAY GOUT GUST
LIKE LIST LUST FANCY FLAIR

GUSTO HEART SHINE SKILL SMACK TASTE THEAT SWALLOW AFFINITY APPETITE FONDNESS PENCHANT
(ECCENTRIC —) FOIBLE
(SUFF.) (— FOR) PHIL(A)(AE)(E)(IA)(ISM)(IST)(OUS)(US)(Y)

LIKUTA
(PL.) MAKUTA

LILAC LILAS MAUVE LAYLOCK

LILACIN SYRINGIN

LILIOM (AUTHOR OF —) MOLNAR
(CHARACTER IN —) WOLF JULIE MARIE FICSUR LILIOM LOUISE MUSKAT LINZMAN HOLLUNDER

LILY ALOE IXIA KELP SEGO AZTEC CALLA CLOTE AUGUST LILIUM VALLEY COCUISA MONOCOT ASPHODEL LILYWORT MARTAGON NENUPHAR
(AFRICAN —) AGAPANTHUS
(CLIMBING —) GLORIOSA
(PALM —) TI
(SEA —) CRINOID
(WATER —) CANDOCK CAMALOTE
(PREF.) LIRIO
(SUFF.) CRINUS

LILY OF THE VALLEY LILIUM MUGGET MUGUET MUGWET LILYWORT SHINLEAF

LIMA BEAN HABA LIMA

LIMB ARM LEG CLAW FOOT KNOT LITH TRAM WING ARTUS BOUGH SPALD SPAUL SWAMP BRANCH MEMBER PODITE FEATURE FLIPPER FORCEPS PLEOPOD NECTOPOD
(PREF.) MEL
(SUFF.) **(CONDITION OF —)** MELIA

LIMBA AFARA FRAKE

LIMBER BAIN FLIP LIMP LUSH LINGY LITHE LISSOM SEMMIT SUPPLE SWANKY BRUSHER BRUTTER KNOTTER LIMMOCK PLIABLE FLEXIBLE FLIPPANT

LIME CALX LIMA CEDRA CEDRAT CHUNAM CITRON FUSTIC
(— IN BRICK) BOND
(WILD —) COLIMA
(PREF.) CAL(AREO)(I)(IO)(O)

LIMEN THRESHOLD

LIMESTONE CAM HUM CALP CAUK CAUM LIAS LYAS MALM POROS ROACH CLUNCH KUNKUR OOLITE CIPOLIN SCAGLIA PISOLITE TRAVERTINE
(— REGION) KARST
(DECOMPOSED —) ROTTENSTONE

LIME TREE LIME TEIL LINDEN

LIMIT END FIX BIND BUTT FINE HOLD LINE LIST MARK MERE PALE TAIL BLOCK BOUND COAST GAUGE HEDGE SCANT STENT STINT VERGE BORDER BOURNE DEFINE EFFLUX EXTENT FINISH FINITE HAMPER LENGTH MODIFY NARROW PALING SCRIMP TROPIC UPSHOT ASTRICT CLOSURE COMPASS CONFINE CONTENT HORIZON MAXIMUM MEASURE OUTSIDE BOUNDARY CONTRACT DEADLINE IMPRISON LIMITARY LIMITATE OUTGOING OUTREACH

RESTRAIN RESTRICT SOLSTICE TERMINUS PARAMETER
(— EFFECT) ALLAY
(— IN A FOREST) BAIL
(— MOTION) HOLD
(— OF STATUTE) PURVIEW
(— OF VISION AT SEA) KENNING
(EXTREME —) HEIGHT
(LOWER —) FLOOR
(UPPER —) CEILING
(UTTER —) EXTREME
(PL.) AMBIT CANCELS ENVIRONS PERIMETER
(PREF.) ORI

LIMITATION TAIL FRAME STINT DENIAL CLOTURE RESERVE
(PL.) SWADDLE

LIMITED MILD TAIL BORNE BRIEF SHORT SMALL FINITE NARROW STINTY STRAIT BOUNDED SPECIAL CONFINED DEFINITE LIMITARY PAROCHIAL SECTARIAN MEASURABLE PROVINCIAL RESTRICTED
(— IN APPEAL) CHICHI
(— IN SCOPE) MODERATE

LIMITING DEFINITE ADJECTIVE EXCLUSIVE

LIMITS (NEAR OUTER — OF PLAY) DEEP

LIMMA DIESIS

LIMMU EPONYM

LIMON (BROTHER OF —) SCEPHRUS
(FATHER OF —) TEGEATES
(MOTHER OF —) MAERA

LIMONENE CINENE CARVENE CITRENE

LIMONIUM STATICE

LIMOUSINE BERLIN SALOON SUBURBAN

LIMP HIP HOP CLOP GIMP HALT HIMP HOIT SOFT THIN HENCH HILCH HITCH LINGY LOOSE LOPPY SLAMP STILT FLABBY FLIMSY HAMBLE HIMPLE HIRPLE HOBBLE LENNOW LIMBER LIMPSY FLACCID LIMMOCK SHAFFLE UNSMART DRAGGLED DROOPING CLAUDICATION

LIMPET CHINK OPIHI SHELL ACMAEA LIMPIN FLIDDER

LIMPID PURE CLEAR LUCID BRIGHT CRYSTAL PELLUCID

LIMPING LAME GIMPY LIMPY ZOPPA HALTING

LIMPLY LANKLY

LINAGE SPACE

LINALOOL LICAREOL

LINCHPIN FORELOCK

LINCTUS LOOCH LOHOCH LOHOCK

LINDEN LIN LIME LYNE TEIL TILIA TILLET LINWOOD BASSWOOD DADDYNUT WOODLIND

LINE BAR BOX FIX RAY ROW TAW BOFF CASE CEIL COLA CRIB DASH FACE FILE GAME GAPE LACE LARD LATH LEAD LING MAIN MARK RACE RANK RULE STOP TAUM WHIP AGONE FAINT FEINT FLEET HATCH LIGNE LINEA METER RANGE SCORE STRIA TOUCH TRACE TRAIL TRAIN TWIST BINDER CABURN CEVIAN

CREASE DEGREE DOUBLE EARING GASKET ISOBAR ISOHEL ISOPAG ISOTAC METIER NETTLE SECANT SECOND SPRING STRING STRIPE AZIMUTH BABBITT CATLINE CONTOUR CREANCE ENVELOP GUNLINE HIPLINE ISOCHOR ISOGRAM ISOHYET ISONEPH ISORITH ISOSTER ISOTOME KNITTLE MARLINE NACARAT SCRATCH WINDROW BALKLINE BISECTOR BOUNDARY BUSINESS CHAMPAIN DATELINE DEADLINE DIAGONAL DIAMETER DRAGLINE DRUMLINE FISHBACK GANTLINE GEODESIC GIRTLINE HAIRLINE HANDLINE HEXAPODY ISOGLOSS ISOGONIC ISOPHANE ISOPHENE ISOPLERE ISOTHERE ISOTHERM LANDWIRE LIFELINE MARTINET SLIPBAND STRINGER SUBCLONE SUBSTILE SUBSTYLE UPSTROKE PERPENDICULAR
(— AROUND STAMP) FRAME
(— AS CENTER FOR REVOLVING) AXIS
(— HEARTH) FIX FETTLE
(— IN GLASS) STRING
(— IN HAT) HEADLINE
(— MINESHAFT) TUB
(— OF ACTION) LAY
(— OF BATTLE) FRONT
(— OF BUSINESS) WAY
(— OF CELLS) ANNULUS
(— OF CLIFFS) SCARP BREAKS
(— OF COLOR) SLASH STREAK
(— OF DANCERS) CHAIN
(— OF DESCENT) SIDE STEM STIRP STOCK PHYLUM STRAIN ANCESTRY BREEDING
(— OF DETERMINANT) COLUMN
(— OF DEVELOPMENT) STREET
(— OF DEVOLUTION) ENTAIL
(— OF FIBERS) CHRYSAL
(— OF FIRE HOSE) LEAD
(— OF FLOTATION) BEARINGS
(— OF FORTIFICATION) LIMES ENCEINTE
(— OF HAY) WAKE WALLOW
(— OF HEALTH) HEPATICA
(— OF HIGH TIDE) LANDWASH
(— OF HOUSES) BLOCK
(— OF INTERSECTION) GROIN BUTTOCK
(— OF JUNCTION) MEET SEAM
(— OF MERCHANDISE) NAMEPLATE
(— OF MERCURY) HEPATICA
(— OF PERSONS) QUEUE CORDON STICKLE
(— OF PORES) HATCHING
(— OF SOLDIERS) RAY FILE RANK WAVE CORDON
(— OF STITCHING) BASTING
(— OF TIMBERS) BOOM STOCKADE
(— OF TREES) SCREEN
(— OF TYPE) SLUG KICKER
(— OF UNION) SUTURE
(— ON A LETTER) SERIF
(— ON BOOK COVER) BAND
(— ON COAT) GORGE
(— ON DOLPHIN) STOP
(— ON HIGHWAY) BARRIER
(— THAT CUTS ANOTHER) SECANT

(— TO BIND CABLES) CABURN
(— TO FASTEN SAIL) EARING GASKET
(— TO RAISE FLAG) LANIARD LANYARD
(— TO START RACE) TRIG
(— TOUCHING ARC) TANGENT
(— UP) LAY
(— WITH BRICKS) GINGE
(— WITH PANELLING) WAINSCOT
(— WITH STONES) STEEN STEYN
(— WITH TIMBER) CRIB
(ANCHOR —) RODING
(BEARING —) CUT
(BOUNDARY —) MERE FENCE BORDER ISOGLOSS
(BOUNDING —) SIDE BOUNDARY PERIMETER
(BRIEF —) ITEM
(COASTAL —) SEAMARK
(CONNECTING —) LIGATURE
(CONTINUOUS —) STRETCH
(CURVED —) ARC SLUR SWEEP
(DEMARCATION —) BOMBLINE
(DIAGONAL —) BIAS
(DIVIDING —) EDGE MIDRIB DIVISION FRONTIER
(ELECTRIC —) HIGHLINE
(FACIAL —) TRAIT
(FINISHING —) TAPE WIRE
(FISHING —) TOME TROT FLEET SNELL SNOOD LEADER LEDGER NORSEL BACKING BOULTER OUTLINE SPILLER SPILLET TRIMMER BLOWLINE CORKLINE FISHLINE SNAGLINE TROTLINE
(HORIZONTAL —) LEVEL
(IMAGINARY —) AGONE HINGE GROOVE ISOBAR ISOGAM ISOHEL ISOPAG HORIZON ISOBASE ISOBATH ISOGRIV ISOHYET ISOLINE ISOTACH ISOBRONT ISOCHASM ISOCHEIM ISOCHLOR ISOCHORE ISOCRYME ISOGLOSS ISOPHOTE ISOPLETH ISOSTERE ISOTHERM
(INCLINED —) CANT
(LONGITUDINAL —) MERIDIAN
(MEDIAN —) RAPHE
(METRICAL —) EIGHT STAFF STICH DIMETER SAPPHIC STICHOS MONOMETER OCTAMETER PENTAMETER
(MINESHAFT —) BRATTICE
(MUSICAL —) ACCOLADE
(NAUTICAL —) EARING LACING GESWARP MARLINE PAINTER RATLINE DOWNHAUL MESSENGER
(ONE-TENTH OF —) GRY
(PERPENDICULAR —) CATHETUS
(PLOTTED —) ADIABAT
(RADIATING —) BEAM
(RAILROAD —) STEM STUB
(RAISED —) RIDGE
(SPECTRUM —) GHOST DOUBLET SINGLET TRIPLET MULTIPLET
(STARTING —) SCRATCH
(STRAIGHT —) CHORD BEELINE STRAIGHT
(SUPPLY —) AIRLIFT UMBILICAL
(SURVEYING —) WAD BASE CHAIN
(THEATRICAL —S) FAT
(TOW —) CORDELLE

(TRANSPORTATION —) FEEDER CARRIER
(WAVY —) SQUIGGLE
(ZIGZAG —) DANCETTE
(42 —S) LENGTH
(PREF.) LINEO STICHO
(SUFF.) STICH(OUS)
(STRAIGHT —) TRIX
LINEAGE GET KIN KIND RACE TEAM BIRTH BLOOD SPACE STIRP STOCK FAMILY HAVAGE NATION PARAGE SOURCE SPRING STRAIN DESCENT KINDRED PROGENY SUCCESS ANCESTRY PEDIGREE PARENTAGE
LINEAL DIRECT
LINEAMENT LINE TRACT TRAIT FEATURE
LINEAR RUNNING
LINECUT ZINCO
LINED MASONED
LINEMAN FORWARD WIREMAN CHAINMAN
LINEN LIN BUCK LAWN CRASH IRISH TOILE BARRAS DAMASK DIAPER RAINES SENDAL BATISTE DORNICK HOLLAND LOCKRAM TABLING BARANDOS OSNABURG PLATILLA
(— CLOSET) LOCKER
(— FOR SHIRTS) SARKING
(— TO COVER CHALICE) PALL
(CHINESE —) KOMPOW
(COARSE —) HARN BARRAS
(FINE —) LAKE LAWN BYSSUS DAMASK DIAPER RAINES
(HOUSEHOLD —) NAPERY TABLING
(SCRAPED —) LINT
(SPANISH —) CREA
(PREF.) BYSSI BYSSO LINO
LINER SHIP BASKET SCRIBER STEAMER
LINES
(PREF.) **(TWO CROSSED —)** CHIASMO CHIASTO
LINET (BROTHER OF —) LIONES
(HUSBAND OF —) GARETH
LINEUP SHOWUP
LING BURBOT DRIZZLE STOKVIS
LINGA DILDO
LINGCOD CULTUS
LINGER LAG HANG HOVE LING STAY CLING DALLY DELAY DEMUR DWELL HAUNT HOVER PAUSE TARRY DRETCH HANKER LOITER TAIGLE TARROW DRINGLE
LINGERER LUNGIS LAGGARD
LINGERIE FRILLIES PRETTIES
LINGERING SLOW DELAY MOROSE TARDANT DRAGGING
LINGO BAT CANT JARGON LINGUA PATTER DIALECT
LINGUA GLOSSA TONGUE
LINGUAL GLOSSAL
LINGUIST (ALSO SEE PHILOLOGIST)
LINGUISTIC GLOTTIC
LINGUISTICS GRAMMAR PHILOLOGY
LINIMENT EIK EMBROCHE OPODELDOC
LININ PLASTIN
LINING FUR BACK COAT BAIZE BRASS FACING PANNEL BABBITT

BUSHING CEILING FURRING FURRURE THIMBLE TINNING TUBBING CLEADING DOUBLING DOUBLURE FIREBACK SHEETING UNDERLAY WAINSCOT PERCALINE
(— FOR WELL) STEENING STEYNING
(— OF BEARING) JEWEL
(— OF CYLINDER) BUSH
(— OF FURNACE) BASQUE FIREBACK
(— OF HAT) TIP
(— OF SMELTING LADLE) SCULL
(MINESHAFT —) CRIB
(WOODEN —) LAG BRATTICE
(SUFF.) PLEURA
LINK JAR TIE TOW JOIN KNIT LUNT SHUT YOKE CLEEK COMMA NEXUS COPULA COUPLE FASTEN FETTER TOUGHT CODETTA CONNECT COUPLER ENCHAIN INVOLVE LIAISON SHACKLE CATENATE IDENTIFY VINCULUM COLLIGATE
(— ARMS) CLEEK
(— IN NETWORK) LEG
(COMPOUND —) SWIVEL
(WOODEN —) LAG
LINKAGE BOND CELL COUPLING LINKWORK
LINKED CONNEX CATENATE INTEGRAL
LINKING HOOKUP ANNECTANT
(— DEVICE) LINCHPIN
LINKMAN LINKBOY LIGHTMAN
LINKS MACHAIR
LINNET FINCH TWITE LENARD LINTIE REDPOLL REDFINCH
LINSANG CIVET ZINSANG
LINSEED LINGET
LINSEY-WOOLSEY WINCEY
LINT FLY FLUE FLICK CADDIS CADDICE CHARPIE CARBASUS
(SCRAPED —) XYSTUS
LINTEL CAP CLAVY HANCE CLAVEL DARNER SUMMER SQUINCH TRANSOM BRESSUMMER
LINUS (BROTHER OF —) ORPHEUS
(FATHER OF —) APOLLO OEAGRUS ISMENIUS
(MOTHER OF —) CALLIOPE PSAMATHE
LION CAT LLEW MORNE SHEDU SIMBA LIONEL LIONET LEOPARD
(MOUNTAIN —) PUMA COUGAR
(PREF.) LEON LEONT(O)
LION MONKEY LEONCITO
LION-TAILED MONKEY MACACO MACAQUE WANDEROO
LIP BLOB EDGE MASK PUSS APRON CHOPS GROIN MOUTH SPOUT TUTEL LABIUM LABRUM ROUTER CHILOMA LABELLUM UNDERLIP
(— DISEASE) PERLECHE
(— OF BELL) SKIRT
(— OF COROLLA) GALEA
(— OF FLOWER) HELM
(— OF ORCHID) SLIPPER
(— OF PITCHER) BEAK
(—S OF MOOSE) MUFFLE
(FLAT —) APRON
(LOWER —) JIB FIPPLE
(PL.) LABRAS CUSHION

(PREF.) CHEIL(O) CHIL(O)
(SUFF.) CHIL(IA)(O)(US)
LIPARITE RHYOLITE
LIPASE PIALYN
LIPIDE CERIDE ADIPOID STERIDE TETHELIN
LIPOCHROME LUTEIN
LIPOID FAT
LIPOMA STEATOMA
LIPPED LABIATE
(SUFF.) LABIATE
LIPPIA WRIGHT ALOYSIA
LIP PLUG LABRET TEMETA
LIPPY STIMPART
LIPS
(PREF.) LABIO
LIQUEFIED FUSILE POTATE REMISS RESOLVED
LIQUEFY RUN FUSE MELT RELENT LIQUATE DISSOLVE ELIQUATE
LIQUEUR EAU OUZO RAKI AURUM CREME NOYAU CHASSE GENEPI KUMMEL PASTIS PERNOD RACKEE STREGA ANESONE CORDIAL CURACAO PERSICO RATAFIA RATIFIA ABSINTHE ADVOCAAT ALKERMES ANGELICA ANISETTE CALVADOS MANDARIN PRUNELLE VESPETRO MARASCHINO BENEDICTINE
(PL.) EAUX
LIQUID AQUA BREE BLASH DRINK FLUID LEACH MOIST ACETAL FLUENT FURANE AEROSOL BUCKING CINEOLE EYEWASH FLOWAGE VINASSE BLACKING EFFLUENT EFFUSION EXCITANT FURFURAN LEACHATE LIBATION SOLUTION
(— AFTER SALT CRYSTALLIZATION) BITTERN
(— IN CELL) EXCITANT
(— UNIT) TUN CHENG SHENG SHING POTTLE MUTCHKIN PUNCHEON
(ACID-RESISTANT —) GROUND
(COLORING —) HENNA
(COOKING —) BREE BROO BROTH STOCK
(DISABLING —) MACE
(DISTILLED —) SPIRIT
(FILTHY —) ADDLE
(INSULATING —) ASKAREL
(OILY —) ANILINE CHLORAL PICAMAR CARDANOL CREOSOTE
(PERFUMED —) COLLEN COLOGNE
(REFUSE —) SCOURAGE
(REFUSE —S) SEWAGE
(SIZING —) GLAIK
(STERILIZED —) JOHNIN
(STINKING —) CACODYL
(SYRUPY —) HONEY
(TANNING —) LIME
(THICK —) DOPE SIRUP SYRUP
(THICK, STICKY —) GLOP
(VISCOUS —) TAR SCHRADAN
(VOLATILE —) ETHER ALCOHOL DILUENT LIGROIN
(WEAK —) BLASH SLIPSLOP
(PREF.) LATICI
LIQUIDATE SINK SETTLE
LIQUIDATION CLEANUP
LIQUOR ALE BUB DEW GAS LAP

OKE PAD POT RUM SUP TAP WET BEER BREE FIRE FIZZ GEAR GROG LUSH PURL SUCK SWIG TAPE TIFF BOGUS BUDGE CEBUR DRINK GLASS HOOCH JUICE KEFIR MOBBY NAPPY PERRY PISCO SAUCE SHRAB SHRUB SICER SKINK STICK BOTTLE CASSIS CHICHA DIDDLE DOCTOR FOGRAM FUDDLE GATTER GENEVA GUZZLE HYDROL KIRSCH MASTIC MESCAL POTTLE ROTGUT SAMSHU STRUNT TIPPLE WHISKY BITTERN BRACKET BRAGGET GROCERY PHLEGMA SPUNKIE SUCTION TAPLASH TEQUILA WAIPIRO WHISKEY ABSINTHE BRAGWORT EYEWATER HYDROMEL MEDICINE OKOLEHAO POTATION RUMBOOZE FIREWATER
(— CABINET) TANTALUS
(— CASE) GARDEVIN
(— FROM MUST) ARROPE
(— FROM PEARS) PERRY PERRIE
(— FROM WOOL-SCOURING) SUD SUDS
(— MIXED WITH WINE) DOCTOR
(— SALE) ABKARI
(— TAKEN IN SODA WATER) CINDER
(ACID —) VERJUICE
(ALCOHOLIC —) GIN ARAK HOOCH ARRACK BRANDY SAMSHU AQUAVIT BITTERS SNOOTFUL
(ALCOHOLIC —S) ARDENT
(BITTER —) TIRE
(CHEAP —) SMOKE
(COLORLESS —) GLYCID GLYCOL GLYCIDOL GUAIACOL
(CRAB APPLE —) WHERRY
(DISTILLED —) DEW SOTOL GRAPPA PHLEGM SCHNAPPS
(DRUGGED —) HOCUS
(HARD —) BOOZE
(INTOXICATING —) GROG LOAD LUSH TAPE BUDGE GUZZLE KUMISS HASHISH MOONSHINE
(MALT —) ALE BUB BEER STOUT ENTIRE PORTER STINGO
(MOTHER —) HYDROL BITTERN
(POT —) BREWIS
(RICE —) SAMSHU
(SPIRITUOUS —) DEW GROG MOBBY STRUNT WAIPIRO KAOLIANG
(STRAIGHT —) SHORT
(STRONG —) RUG TUBA VINO HOGAN RUMBO STINGO
(TAN —) OOZE
(TANNING —) LAYAWAY TAILING
(WATERED —) BLASH
(WEAK —) BULL SLIPSLOP
LIRA LIRE ZWANZIGER
(ONE-TWENTIETH —) SOLDO
LIRIPIPE TIPPET
LISSOME LITHE LIMBER NIMBLE SUPPLE SVELTE FLEXIBLE
LIST TIP BILL FILE HEEL LEET NOTE POLL ROLL ROON ROTA SWAG BRIEF CANON GISTS INDEX PANEL SCORE SCRIP SCROW SLATE AGENDA CENSUS COLUMN DETAIL DOCKET ERRATA HUDDLE LEGEND PURREL RAGGER

RAGMAN RECORD ROSTER
SCREED SCROLL SERIES CATALOG
CITATOR COMPILE DIPTYCH
ITEMIZE LISTING NOTITIA
WAYBILL CALENDAR CINCTURE
HANDLIST PLATBAND REGISTER
SCHEDULE SYNONYMY TITULARY
(— OF BOOKS) CANON
(— OF CANDIDATES) LEET SLATE
TERNA
(— OF CONTESTANTS) DRAW
SEEDING
(— OF DISEASES) NOSOLOGY
(— OF JURORS) TALES
(— OF MAP SYMBOLS) LEGEND
(— OF PASSERS WITHOUT HONORS)
GULF
(— OF RATES) TARIFF
(— OF THEATRICAL PARTS) CAST
(GENEALOGICAL —) BEGATS
(IMPRESSIVE —) ARRAY
(LEGAL —) TABLEAU
(PRAYER —) BEADROLL
(WINE —) CARD
(PL.) CAREER BARRACE
LISTEL QUADRA
LISTEN HARK HEAR LIST TEND
TENEZ ATTEND HARKEN INTEND
WHISPER
(— TO) DIG EAR HARK HEAR
CATCH ATTEND
LISTENER AUDITOR OTACUST
LISTENING PRICK AUDIENT
HEARING
(PREF.) ACOU
LISTER SULKY RIDGER
LISTERA OPHRYS
LISTING ITEM FRAME PARADE
LASHING
(— OF JURORS) ARRAY
LISTLESS DOPY DULL WOFF
DOWFF FAINT DONSIE SUPINE
LANGUID UNLISTY UNLUSTY
CARELESS INDOLENT THOWLESS
TONELESS UNHEARTY
LISTLESSLY DAVIELY
LISTLESSNESS ACEDIA APATHY
UNLUST VACUITY
LISUARTE (DAUGHTER OF —)
ORIANA
(FATHER OF —) ESPLANDIAN
LITANY AITESIS ROGATION
LITERAL VERBAL TEXTUAL
LITERALLY SIMPLY
LITERARY BLUE BOOKISH
LITERATE
(— MATERIAL) KITSCH
(SUFF.) (— STYLE) ESE
LITERATE LETTERED
LITERATI CLERISY
LITERATURE FICTION LETTERS
CLAPTRAP
(— CLANDESTINELY DISTRIBUTED)
SAMIZDAT
(SACRED —) VEDA SRUTI
(WISDOM —) CHOKMAH HOKHMAH
LITHE BAIN SWACK CLEVER LIMBER
SILKEN SUPPLE SVELTE WANDLE
LISSOME FLEXIBLE

LITHUANIA
CAPITAL: VILNA WILNA VILNIUS
COIN: LIT LITAS MARKA CENTAS

FENNIG OSTMARK AUKSINAS
SKATIKAS
FORMER CAPITAL: KOVNO KAUNAS
NAME: LITVA LIETUVA
PEOPLE: BALT LETT ZHMUD
LITVAK YATVYAG
RIVER: NEMAN NERIS RUSNE
VENTA DUBYSA LIELUPE
NEMUNAS PREGOLYA
TOWN: MEMEL VILNA JELGAVA
VILNIUS KAPSUKAS KLAIPEDA
SIAULIAI

LITHUANIAN BALT ZHMUD
LITIGANT SUITOR
LITIGATE LAW PLEAD CONTEST
LITIGATION LAW LIS MOOT SUIT
LAWING PLEADING PLEASHIP
LITMUS LAKMUS TURNSOLE
LITOTES MEIOSIS
LITTER DIG PIG BIER RAFF REDD
BREED CABIN CLECK DOOLY
DRECK HAULM MULCH SEDAN
DOOLIE FARROW GOCART KINDLE
KITTEN MAHMAL REFUSE
CLUTTER LETTIGA LOUSTER
MAMMOCK NORIMON RUBBISH
RUMMAGE SCAMBLE BRANCARD
CARRIAGE KINDLING MUNCHEEL
PAVILION STRETCHER
(— FOR LIVESTOCK) BEDDING
(— OF PIGS) FAR FARE FARROW
(— ON PACK ANIMAL) CACOLET
(CAMEL —) KAJAWAH
(FOREST —) DUFF
LITTERED FOUL
LITTLE FEW LIL WEE CURN LITE
TINY VEEN CHOTA CRUMB SMALL
TASTE WHONE BITTIE DAPPER
LEETLE MINUTE PETITE PICKLE
PUSILL KENNING MODICUM
THOUGHT FRACTION SNIPPING
(— BY LITTLE) EDGINGLY
INCHMEAL
(— LESS THAN) ABOUT
(— MUSICALLY) POCO
(— ONE) BUTCHA POPPET
(A —) SOMEWHAT
(INDEFINITELY —) NTH
(PREF.) OLIG(O) PARVI PAUCI
PUSILL(I) STEN(O)
(SUFF.) ISK KIN STENOSIS
(— ONE) CLE ELLA ETTE IE ILLA
LITTLE DEMON (AUTHOR OF —)
SOLOGUB
(CHARACTER IN —) SASHA
LIUDMILA PYLNIKOV PEREDONOV
RUSTILOVA NEDOTYKOMKA
LITTLE DORRIT (AUTHOR OF —)
DICKENS
(CHARACTER IN —) AMY JOHN
CASBY FANNY FLORA ARTHUR
DORRIT EDWARD PANCKS
CHIVERY CLENNAM MEAGLES
WILLIAM BLANDOIS PLORNISH
BARNACLES
LITTLE MINISTER (AUTHOR OF —)
BARRIE
(CHARACTER IN —) DOW ROB
ADAM GAVIN MICAH NANNY
BABBIE OGILVY DISHART
MCQUEEN RINTOUL WEBSTER
MARGARET

LITTLENESS ATOMITY
LITTLE WOMEN (AUTHOR OF —)
ALCOTT
(CHARACTER IN —) JO AMY MEG
BETH DEMI JOHN BHAER DAISY
FRITZ KIRKE MARCH BROOKE
CARROL LAURIE MARMEE
LAURENCE THEODORE
LITTORAL COAST
LITURGY FORM RITE ABODAH
MAARIB MINHAG NEILAH
MINCHAH MYSTERY HIERURGY
SHAHARIT
LIVE BE USE WIN KEEP LEAD STAY
ALERT ALIVE DWELL EXIST GREEN
HABIT LEEVE QUICK SHACK VITAL
HARBOR LIVELY LIVING REMAIN
RESIDE BREATHE INHABIT
SUBSIST CONTINUE CONVERSE
VIGOROUS
(— AT ANOTHER'S EXPENSE)
COSHER
(— BY BEGGING) CADGE SKELDER
(— BY STRATAGEMS) SHARK
(— FROM DAY TO DAY) EKE
(— IN CONTINENCE) CONTAIN
(— IN LUXURY) STATE
(— IN PEACE) COEXIST
(— IN SAME PLACE) STALL
(— ON) SURVIVE
(— RIOTOUSLY) JET
(— TEMPORARILY) CAMP
(— THROUGH) PASS TIDE
(— TOGETHER) AGREE COHABIT
(— WELL) BATTEN
LIVE-BOX CAR
LIVE-FOREVER LULANG ORPINE
LIVELIHOOD BEING BREAD LIVING
LIFEHOOD
LIVELINESS PEP BRIO FIRE FIZZ
LIFE PUNCH SPUNK BOUNCE
ESPRIT GAIETY SPIRIT ENTRAIN
SPARKLE ACTIVITY VITALITY
VIVACITY
LIVELONG LEELANG ENDURING
LIVELY GAY TID AIRY BRAG CANT
FAST FESS GLEG KECK LIVE PERT
RACY TAIT TRIG VITE VIVE WARM
YARE AGILE ALERT ALIVE BONNY
BRISK BUXOM CANTY CHIRK
COBBY CORKY CRISP DESTO
FRESH FRISK JAZZY KEDGE KINKY
MERRY PAWKY PEART PEPPY
POKEY RUDDY SASSY SMART
VIVID WHICK ACTIVE BLITHE
BOUNCY BRIGHT CHEERY CHIRPY
COCKET CROOSE CROUSE DAPPER
FIERCE FRISCH GINGER JOCUND
KIPPER LIVING NIMBLE QUIVER
SEMMIT SPARKY SPRACK TROTTY
VEGETE WHISKY WIMBLE
ALLEGRO ANIMATE ANIMOSE
BOBBISH BUCKISH BUOYANT
GIGGISH GIOCOSO JOCULAR
KINETIC LEBHAFT POINTED
ROUSING SPIRITY SPRINGY
TITTUMY TITTUPY WINCING
ANIMATED BOUNCING CHIRRUPY
FRISKFUL FRISKING GALLIARD
SANGUINE SKITTISH SMACKING
SPANKING SPIRITED SPORTIVE
STEERING STIRRING TRIPSOME
VEGETOUS VOLATILE SPARKLING

(— PERSON) SWINGER
(TO BE —) SWING
LIVEN LACE CHEER ANIMATE
LIVE OAK ENCINA
LIVER MAW FOIE HEPAR VISCUS
PUDDING
(— ATROPHY) LUPINOSIS
(— OF LOBSTER) TOMALLEY
(PREF.) HEPAT(O) HEPATICO
LIVERPOOL (NATIVE OF —)
SCOUSER
LIVERWORT HEPATICA
MOSSWORT
LIVERY SUIT CLOTH LIVRE
UNIFORM CLOTHING
LIVESTOCK FEE WARE STOCK
STORE STUFF CHATTEL BESTIALS
FATSTOCK
LIVE WIRE HUSTLER
LIVID HAW WAN BLAE BLUE
LIVING KEEP ALIVE BEING BREAD
GOING QUICK VITAL WHICK
AROUND LIVELY VIABLE ZOETIC
ANIMATE SUPPORT ANIMATED
BENEFICE
(— IN THE WORLD) SECULAR
(— IN WAVES) LOTIC
(— NEAR THE GROUND) EPIGEAN
(— ON BANKS OF STREAMS) RIPAL
RIPARIAN
(— THING) QUICK
(BARE —) CRUST
(ECCLESIASTICAL —) BENEFICE
(PREF.) ONT(O) VIVI
(— ORGANISMS) BIO
(SUFF.) (— IN OR ON) COLE COLINE
COLOUS
LIVRE FRANC
LIXIVIATE LEACH
LIXIVIUM LYE
LIZARD DAB EFT GOH UMA UTA
DABB GILA IBIT SEPS TEGU TEJU
URAN AGAMA ANOLE BLUEY
DRACO GECKO GUANO SKINK
SNAKE SWIFT TEIID TOKAY
TWEEG VARAN AMEIVA ANGUID
ARBALO DRAGON GOANNA
HARDIM IGUANA LACERT LEGUAN
MOLOCH TEIOID WORRAL
ZONURE BUMMAJO CAUDATE
CHEECHA DIAPSID MONITOR
REPTILE SAURIAN SCINCID
SCINCUS TUATARA TUCKTOO
BASILISK KAKARIKI MOKAMOKA
SCINCOID SCORPION SLOWWORM
TEGUEXIN WHIPTAIL ZONUROID
CHAMELEON PLEURODONT
(PREF.) LACERTI SAUR(O)
(SUFF.) SAUR(A)(IA)(IAN)(US)
LIZARD FISH ULAE INIOME
SOAPFISH SPEARING
LLAMA ALPACA VICUNA GUANACO
LLUDD NUDD
LO SEE ECCE
LOACH DOJO BEARDIE MUDFISH
LOAD JAG LUG TON BUCK CARK
CRAM DECK DRAW FILL HAUL
LADE LAST LUMP PACK RAKE
SEAM STEM STOW TOTE TURN
BARTH CARGO DRAFT PITCH
PRIME STACK TRUSS TURSE
BURDEN CHARGE COMBLE
DEMAND FODDER FOTHER

HAMPER LADING LOADEN
THRACK WEIGHT BALLAST
CARLOAD DERRICK DRAUGHT
ENDORSE FRAUGHT FREIGHT
ONERATE OPPRESS BACKPACK
CARRIAGE ENCUMBER HEADLOAD
SHIPLOAD PLANELOAD
(— A DIE FOR CHEATING) COG
(— FABRICS) WEIGHT
(— OF COAL) KEEL
(— OF HAY OR CORN) HURRY
(— OF LAMBS) DECK
(— OF LOGS) PEAKER BUNKLOAD
(— OF WOOL) TOD
(— ON BACK) ENDORSE INDORSE
(— SHIP) STEM
(— TO CAPACITY) SATURATE
(— TO EXCESS) ENCUMBER
(ELECTRIC —) DEMAND
(HORSE —) SEAM SUMAGE
(LAST — OF GRAIN) WINTER
(SMALL —) JAG JAGG JOBBLE
(PL.) BUSHEL
LOADER CHARGER
LOADING LADING MARGIN
ARRASTRE
LOADSTONE MAGNET SIDERITE
LODESTONE
LOAF BAP BUM COB AZYM HACK
HAKE HULL LAKE MIKE SLIM
SORN BANGE BREAD BRICK
DRING MOUCH SHOOL SLIVE
SLOSH BLUDGE BROGUE CADDLE
DIDDLE GEORGE HALLAH RODNEY
SLINGE WASTEL HOOSIER
MANCHET SHACKLE SLOUNGE
SOLDIER OBLATION PANHAGIA
QUARTERN SHAMMOCK
(— AROUND) HULL HOWFF SLOSH
RODNEY
(— OF BREAD) COB BATON FADGE
MICHE TOMMY HALLAH TAMMIE
(BROWN —) GEORGE
(ROUND —) BUN COBURG
(SMALL —) BAP COB NACKET
(SUGAR —) TITLER
LOAFER BUM CAD YOB BEAT GRUB
STIFF BUMBLE BUMMER CADGER
KEELIE SLOUCH SLOVEN BLUDGER
COASTER FAITOUR HOODLUM
SLINKER SOLDIER COBERGER
HOOLIGAN LARRIKIN LAYABOUT
SEASONER
LOAFING IDLE MIKE
LOAM RAB LAME MALM MARL SLIP
LOESS REGUR CLEDGE
LOAMY MELLOW
LOAN DHAN LEND LENT PREST
CREDIT DONATE MUTUUM
ADVANCE FIXTURE IMPREST
LOANBLEND HYBRID
LOATH LOTH LAITH LEATH SWEER
DAINTY BACKWARD
LOATHE UG HATE SHUN ABHOR
LAITH WLATE AGRISE DETEST
DESPISE SCUNDER SCUNNER
NAUSEATE
LOATHING NAUSEA REVOLT
DISGUST SCUNNER
LOATHLY LAIDLY
LOATHSOME FOUL UGLY VILE
POCKY LAIDLY UNLIEF HATEFUL
LOATHLY MAWKISH OBSCENE

TETROUS WLATFUL DEFORMED
NAUSEOUS WLATSOME
NEFANDOUS ABOMINABLE
LOBBY HALL FOYER NARTHEX
PASSAGE TAMBOUR ANTEROOM
COULISSE
LOBBYIST PROMOTER
LOBE ALA FIN LAP AXIS LIST MALA
ALULA EXITE FIBER FIBRE FLUKE
GALEA LOBUS THECA TOOTH
UVULA EARLAP FILLET FOLIUM
GLOSSA INSULA LAPPET LIGULE
LOBING MANTLE VANNUS VERMIS
AROLIUM AURICLE HEMAPOD
LACINIA LOBULUS AMYGDALA
EPICHILE GLABELLA LABELLUM
PALPIFER PHYLLOID SQUAMULE
(PREF.) **(— OF BRAIN)** LEUC(O)
LOBED CUT LOMATINE
(SUFF.) FID FIDATE
LOBSTER CRAY HOMARD DECAPOD
SHEDDER CRAWFISH CRAYFISH
LANGOSTA MACRURAN
(— ENCLOSURE) CRAWL
(— LESS THAN 10 INCHES LONG)
JOE
(FEMALE —) HEN
(NORWAY —) SCAMPO
(SMALL —) PAWK NANCY
(UNDERSIZED —) SHORT
LOBSTER POT COY CRAIL CREEL
TRUNK FISHPOT
LOBULARIA KONIGA
LOCAL HOME NATIVE LIMITED
TOPICAL VICINAL REGIONAL
EPICHORIC
(NOT —) AZONIC
(PREF.) TOP(O)
LOCALE SITE LOCAL PLACE SCENE
LOCALITY SPA HAND PLAT SPOT
LOCUS PLACE POINT SITIO SITUS
STEAD HABITAT LATITUDE
POSITURE SITUATION
(BARREN —) GALL
(BEAUTIFUL —) XANADU
(GUARDED —) POST
LOCALIZE SITUATE POSITION
LOCATE SITE SPOT PITCH PLACE
BESTOW BILLET SETTLE SITUATE
PINPOINT
(— AT INTERVALS) SPOT
(— WATER) DIVINE
LOCATED SET FIXED SEATED
SITUATED
(— OFF THE HIGHWAY) DEVIOUS
LOCATING SYSTEM SOFAR
LOCATION FALL HOME PLOT SEAT
PLACE SITUS WHERE UBIETY
AMENITY STATION HOMESITE
STANDING
(ESSENTIAL —) EYE
(FOREST —) CHANCE
(GEOGRAPHIC —) SEAT
(MINING —) MYNPACHT
(NATURAL —) HABITAT
(SUFF.) TOPE TOPY
LOCH LOUGH LOCHAN
LOCK COT KEY FEAK FRIB HOLD
TRIM YALE CHUBB CLASP SASSE
DUBBEH ENLOCK LUCKEN
DAGLOCK EARLOCK KEYLOCK
PINLOCK SPANNER DEADLOCK
FORELOCK

(— IMPROPERLY) BIND
(— IN RIVER) SASSE
(— OF HAIR) COT TAG TUZ COTT
CURL FEAK TATE FLAKE FLOCK
FLUKE QUIFF TRESS TANGLE
COWLICK EARLOCK FRIZZLE
SERPENT WIMPLER FORELOCK
SIDELOCK
(— OF WOOL) TAG COTT FRIB
FLOCK STAPLE HASLOCK
(— UP) JAIL STOW CABINET
(CANAL —) COFFER CHAMBER
(DIRTY —) FRIB
(MATTED —) COT COTT DAGLOCK
(MUSKET —) ROWET
(PART OF —) REWET STRIKE
(WHEEL —) REWET
LOCKED FAST LUCKEN
LOCKER HUTCH ASCHAM
LOCKERMAN NIBBLER SCOTCHER
SNIBBLER
LOCKET BRELOQUE
LOCKJAW TETANUS TRISMUS
LOCKNUT JAMNUT KEEPER
LOCKOUT SHUTOUT
LOCKSMITH LOCKYER
LOCKUP JUG GAOL JAIL LOCK
LOGS CHOKY CLINK TRONK
COOLER HOOSEGOW
ROUNDHOUSE
LOCOMOTION FLYING LATION
LOCOMOTIVE HOG PIG PUG BOGY
GOAT HOGG MULE SHAG TANK
BOGIE DINKY DUMMY MOGUL
PILOT DIESEL DOCTOR DOLLIE
DONKEY ENGINE LOADER PUSHER
SMOKER YARDER BOBTAIL
BOOSTER SHUNTER STEAMER
CALLIOPE CHOOCHOO
COMPOUND DOLLBEER
(— WITHOUT CARS) WILDCAT
(EXTRA —) HELPER
(PART OF —) CAB ROD BELL DOME
HOSE LAMP STEP BRACE HINGE
PILOT TRUCK BOILER JACKET
TENDER COUPLER SANDBOX
WHISTLE CYLINDER HANDRAIL
INJECTOR SANDPIPE HEADLIGHT
RESERVOIR DRIVEWHEEL
SMOKESTACK
LOCOMOTOR ATAXIA TABES
LOCOWEED LOCO LEGUME
PEAVINE
LOCRINE (DAUGHTER OF —)
SABRINA
(FATHER OF —) BRUTE BRUTUS
LOCULUS THECA
LOCUS PLACE EVOLUTE SURFACE
SYNAPSE CONCHOID ENVELOPE
HOROPTER
LOCUST WETA BRUKE CICAD
HONEY ACACIA CICADA QUAKER
SKIPPER TETRIGID VOETGANGER
LOCUST TREE CAROB ACACIA
LOCUST ROBINIA ALGAROBA
LODE LEAD REEF VEIN LEDGE
COURSE FEEDER QUARRY
SCOVAN COUNTER
LODESTONE MAGNET SIDERITE
TERRELLA
LODGE DIG HUT INN LIE BEAT
CAMP HOST KEEP ROOM STAY
STOW TENT BOWER CABIN

COUCH COURT GROVE GUEST
HOGAN HOTEL HOUSE HOWFF
LAYER LOGIS STICK TARRY
ALIGHT BESTOW BILLET BURROW
COSHER GESTEN GRANGE HOSTEL
RESIDE SETTLE BARRACK
LODGING QUARTER SOJOURN
EMBOLIZE HARBINGE
(— AND EAT) COSHER
(— FOR SAFEKEEPING) DEPOSIT
(— IN COURT) BOX
(LOCAL —) COURT
(SPORTSMAN'S —) SHEAL
LODGEPOLE PINE TAMARACK
LODGER INMATE ROOMER TENANT
LODGING BED CRIB FERM GIST
HAFT HOST NEST GEAST LOGIS
HARBOR HOSTEL LIVERY HOSPICE
HOUSING COUCHANT GUESTING
(— FOR SOLDIERS) CASERN
(— OF MARABOUT) KOUBA
(VILE —) KENNEL
(PL.) PAD DIGS DIGGINGS
LODGINGHOUSE INN KIP GITE
STOP HOTEL LOGIA LOCANDA
PENSION HOSTELRY
LODICULE SQUAMULA SQUAMULE
LODOLETTA (CHARACTER IN —)
ANTONIO FLAMMEN LODOLETTA
(COMPOSER OF —) MASCAGNI
LOESS LIMON
LOFT BALK FLAT GOLF JUBE LAFT
ATTIC SOLAR GARRET SOLLAR
HAYLOFT COCKLOFT SCAFFOLD
TRAVERSE
(HAY —) TALLET TALLIT
LOFTIEST SUPREME
LOFTINESS PRIDE HEIGHT DIGNITY
MAJESTY EMINENCE GRANDEUR
HIGHNESS CELSITUDE
(— OF SPIRIT) MAGNANIMITY
LOFTSMAN LINESMAN
LOFTY AIRY HIGH LOFT TALL
BRENT ELATE GRAND GREAT
NOBLE PROUD SKYEY STEEP
WINGY AERIAL ANDEAN HAUGHT
TOPFUL TOWERY UPWARD
WINGED ANDESIC ARDUOUS
EMINENT EXCELSE HAUGHTY
SUBLIME ARROGANT ELEVATED
GENEROUS MAJESTIC OLYMPIAN
TOWERING
LOG NOG BUNK CLOG DRAG SKID
CHOCK CHUCK CHUNK PIECE
STICK STOCK BATTEN BILLET
PEAKER PEELER SADDLE SAWLOG
BACKLOG DAYBOOK DEADMAN
DEGRADE JOURNAL LOGBOOK
DEADHEAD
(— AS ANCHOR) DEADMAN
(— AS RAFTER) VIGA
(— BINDING A RAFT) SWIFTER
(— CAR) BUNK
(— FASTENED TO TRAP) DRAG
(— SUPPORTING MINE ROOF) NOG
(— WITH SPIKES IN END)
DEADENER
(— WITHOUT BARK) BUCKSKIN
(ENCLOSED —S) BOOM
(FLOATING —) DRIVE
(LOAD OF —S) PEAKER
(PILE OF —S) DECK ROLLWAY
(SAWED —) BOULE

(SLABBED —) CANT
(SMALL —) LOGGET
(SPLIT —) PUNCHEON
(STRIPPED —) BATTEN
(SUNKEN —) DEADHEAD
LOGANIN MELIATIN
LOGARITHM DENSITY
(— SYMBOL) PF PH PK RH
(NEGATIVE —) PH
LOGBOOK LOG JOURNAL
LOGE BOX BOOTH LODGE STALL
LOGGER RIDER BOWMAN DECKER
FALLER GOPHER HOOKER LIMBER
MARKER SCORER CHOPPER
FROGGER GRABBER SPOTTER
CATTYMAN
LOGGIA LODGE BALCONY
MIRADOR
LOGIC NYAYA LOGICS CANONIC
WITCRAFT
(— OF DISCOVERY) HEURETIC
LOGICAL SANE RAISONNE
RATIONAL
LOGISTILLA (SISTER OF —) ALCINA
MORGANA
LOGMAN CHASER CHOPPER
LOGO EMBLEM
LOGOGRAM IDEOGRAM
LOGOS WORD
LOGOTYPE SIG
LOG PERCH DARTER HOGFISH
ROCKFISH
LOGROLLING BIRLING
(— TOURNAMENT) ROLEO
LOGWOOD BRAZIL ADMIRAL
DYEWOOD BLUEWOOD HYPERNIC
CAMPEACHY
LOGY DROWSY GROGGY
LOHAN RAKAN
LOHENGRIN (CHARACTER IN —)
ELSA HENRY ORTRUD FREDERICK
GOTTFRIED LOHENGRIN
TELRAMUND
(COMPOSER OF —) WAGNER
(FATHER OF —) PARSIFAL
(WIFE OF —) ELSA
LOIN LEER LISK ALOYAU LUNYIE
(PORK —) GRISKIN
(2 UNCUT —S) BARON
(PL.) REINS FILLET SADDLE
(PREF.) LUMB(O) OSPHY(O)
LOINCLOTH IZAR MALO MARO
DHOTI LUNGI PAGNE PAREU
MOOCHA PANUNG DHOOTIE
LOIS (DAUGHTER OF —) EUNICE
(GRANDSON OF —) TIMOTHY
LOITER LAG CLUG FOOL HAKE
HANG HAWM HAZE HOVE LOUT
MIKE MUCK SLUG COOSE DELAY
DRAWL KNOCK MOUCH SHOOL
SIDLE TARRY COOTER DAWDLE
LAGGER LINGER MUCKER STRAKE
TAIGLE PROJECT SHAFFLE
LALLYGAG LOLLYGAG SCOWBANK
SLAMMOCK SLUMMOCK
LOITERER DRONE IDLER LAGGER
LAGGARD LURCHER
LOITERING SLIMSY LAGGARD
LOKAPALA MAHARAJA
LOKI (DAUGHTER OF —) HEL
(FATHER OF —) FARBAUTI
(MOTHER OF —) NAL LAUFEY
ANGRBODHA

(SLAYER OF —) HEIMDALL
(WIFE OF —) SIGYN ANGURBODA
LOLL FUG LOUT FROWST LOLLUP
LOUNGE SOZZLE SPRAWL
RECLINE SCAMBLE SCOWBANK
LOLLAPALOOZA LULU ONER
LOLLIPOP LOLLY SUCKER
SUCKABOB
LOLO NOSU
LONDON SMOKE COCKAGNE
(BRIDGE IN —) TOWER ALBERT
PUTNEY CHELSEA WATERLOO
(DISTRICT OF —) SOHO ACTON
ADELPHI ALSATIA BRIXTON
CHELSEA MAYFAIR
(MONUMENT IN —) GOG MAGOG
NELSON CENOTAPH VICTORIA
(RIVER OF —) THAMES
(STREET OF —) BOND FLEET
CANNON SAVILE DOWNING
WARDOUR HAYMARKET
(SUBURB OF —) KEW FINCHLEY
LONDONER FLATCAP
LONE LANE SOLE ALONE APART
SINGLE SOLITARY
(— STAR STATE) TEXAS
LONELINESS ONENESS VACANCY
SOLITUDE
LONELY LORN ONLY SOLE VAST
ALONE UNKET UNKID WISHT
ALANGE DEAFLY SULLEN
DEAVELY FORLORN LONEFUL
SOLEYNE DESOLATE SECLUDED
SOLITARY
(PREF.) EREM(O)
LONESOME ALONE DOLEY LONELY
LANESOME SOLITARY
LONG HO DIE FAR FIT YEN ACHE
DREE HANK HONE ITCH LANG
SIDE TALL WILN WISH YAWN
CRAVE DREAM GREEN LATHY
LONGA MOURN STARK WEARY
YEARN ARIGUE ASPIRE DESIRE
DREICH HANKER HUNGER LINGER
LONGUS PROLIX STOUND THIRST
LENGTHY TEDIOUS WEILANG
GEMINATE INFINITE
(— AGO) FERN LANGSYNE
(— AND SLENDER) REEDY SQUINNY
(— AND UNIFORM IN WIDTH)
LINEAR
(— FOR) CARE HONE COVET
CRAVE TASTE ASPIRE DESIRE
SUSPIRE
(— RESTLESSLY) ITCH
(— SINCE) YORE
(EXTRA —) MAXI
(TEDIOUSLY —) MORTAL
(PREF.) DOLICH(O) LONGI LONGO
MACR(O) MEC(O)
LONG-BILLED CURLEW SMOKER
LONGBOAT SLOOP
LONG-BODIED RACY RANGY
LONGERON SPAR
LONGEVITY VIVACITY
(— CHARACTER) SHOU
LONGING YEN ENVY ITCH LUST
PINE WISH BRAME YEARN DESIRE
HANKER TALENT THIRST ATHIRST
CRAVING THIRSTY WILLING
WISHFUL WISTFUL APPETENT
APPETITE CUPIDITY HOMESICK
PRURIENT

LONGINGLY WISTLY
LONGITUDINALLY ENDLONG
LONG-LASTING CHRONIC
LONGLEGS STILT
LONGLINE BULTOW
LONG-LIVED LONGEVE MACROBIAN
LONGSHOREMAN DOCKER
HOBBLER WHARFIE DOCKHAND
ROUSTABOUT
LONG-STANDING OLD
LONG-SUFFERING MEEK PATIENT
ENDURING PATIENCE
LONG-TAILED WHIDAH REDBILL
LONG TOM SKIPPER
LONG-WINDED PROLIX PROSAIC
LOOK LA LO AIR EYE KEN SEE SPY
CAST GAWK GAZE GIVE GLOM
HEED KEEK LATE LUCK MARK
MIEN POKE SEEM SWAP VIEW
WAIT ACIES BLUSH DEKKO FAVOR
FLASH GLEAM GLEER GLIFF GLINT
SCREW SIGHT SQUIZ VIZZY WLITE
APPEAR ASPECT EYEFUL GANDER
GLANCE REGARD REWARD VISION
EYESHOT EYEWINK INSIGHT
SEEMING DISCOVER LANGUISH
OEILLADE
(— ABOUT) BELOOK SPECTATE
(— AFTER) TENT ATTEND FATHER
FETTLE PROCURE
(— ASKANCE) GLIM LEER SKEW
BAGGE GLENT GLEDGE SKLENT
(— AT) DIG SEE GLOM LAMP VIEW
VISE GLISK ADVISE BEHOLD
REGARD REWARD CONSIDER
SPECTATE
(— CLOSELY) PRY ESPY SCAN
(— CROSS-EYED) SHEYLE
(— DOWN UPON) SNOB DESPISE
(— DULLY) BLEAR
(— FIXEDLY) GAZE KYKE GLORE
STARE
(— FOR) SPY FOND SEEK GROPE
EXPECT PROPOSE RESPECT
(— FORWARD) EXPECT FORESEE
ENVISAGE ENVISION
(— GLANCINGLY) BLINK
(— IN SNEAKING MANNER) SNOOP
(— INTENTLY) GLOSE VISIE
GLOWER EYEBALL
(— INTO) SOUND SEARCH
(— OBLIQUELY) GLIME GOGGLE
SQUINT
(— OF DERISION) FLEER
(— OF PLANETS) ASPECTS
(— OUT) FEND MIND CHEESE
JIGGERS OUTLOOK
(— OVER) SCAN TOISE BROWSE
SURVEY EXAMINE
(— SEARCHINGLY) PEER PORE
TOOT
(— SLYLY) PEEP GLINK
(— SOUR) GLUNCH
(— STEADFASTLY) GLOAT
(— SULKY) LUMP
(— SULLEN) LOUR LOWER
(— UPON AS) ACCOUNT
(— WILDLY) GLOP WAUL WHAWL
(— WITH FAVOR) SMILE
(AMOROUS —) SMICKER
(ANGRY —) SCOWL
(BRIEF —) GLIM GLINT GLIMPSE
(LOVING —) BELGARD

(QUICK —) SCRY GLENT
(SEARCHING —) SCRUTINY
(SEVERE —) FROWN
(SIDELONG —) GLEE GLIME
(SLY —) GLEG GLIME TWIRE
(SULLEN —) GLOOM GLOUT
GLUNCH
(TENDER —) LANGUISH
(WANTON —) LEER
(PL.) DAPS
(PREF.) **(— THROUGH)** PERSPECTO
LOOKER BEAUTY HERDSMAN
SEARCHER
LOOKER-ON BEHOLDER
LOOK HOMEWARD ANGEL
(AUTHOR OF —) WOLFE
(CHARACTER IN —) BEN GANT
LUKE DAISY ELIZA HELEN JAMES
LAURA EUGENE GROVER OLIVER
LEONARD MARGARET
LOOKING BACKWARD (AUTHOR
OF —) BELLAMY
(CHARACTER IN —) WEST EDITH
LEETE JULIAN BARTLETT
PILLSBURY
LOOKOUT HUER TOUT SCOUT
WATCH BANTAY CONNER
TOOTER FUNERAL OUTLOOK
ATALAYAN BANTAYAN BARTIZAN
COCKATOO PROSPECT
TOWERMAN WATCHOUT
OBSERVATORY
LOOM BEAM BULK HULK LEEM
DOBBY FRAME GLOOM BEETLE
DOBBIE DRAWLOOM HANDLOOM
JACQUARD OVERPICK
(— ATTACHMENT) LAPPET
(PREF.) HIST(O)
LOOM AXLE ROCKTREE
LOOM BAR EASER DAGGER
LOOMFIXER TACKLER
LOOM HARNESS LEAF HEADLE
SIMBLOT MOUNTING
LOON DIVER IMBER WABBY
COBBLE DUCKER GUNNER
WHABBY PYGOPOD
LOOP BOW EYE LUG NOB TAB TAG
ANSA BEND COIL FAKE HANK
KINK KNOB KNOP LEAF LINK
LOUP PURL BIGHT BRIDE CHAPE
COQUE GUIDE KINCH LACET
LATCH NOOSE PEARL PICOT
SHANK STRAP TERRY WITHY
BECKET BILLET BUCKLE FOLIUM
HANGER HOLDER KEEPER KINKLE
PARRAL SPIRAL STAPLE STITCH
TWITCH COCKEYE COUPURE
CRINGLE CRUPPER GROMMET
KNUCKLE LATCHET SEGMENT
ANTINODE COURONNE
(— AND THIMBLES) CLEW CLUE
(— BY ICESKATER) SPOON
(— IN KNITTING) STEEK
(— IN MINER'S ROPE) SLUG
(— IN NEEDLEWORK) BRIDE
(— OF INTESTINES) KNUCKLE
(— OF IRON) OOLLY
(— OF ROPE) FAKE BIGHT FLAKE
KINCH NOOSE ANCHOR BECKET
PARRAL SNORTER SNOTTER
(— OF SCABBARD) FROG
(— OF TUBING) SCROLL
(— ON ARMOR) VERVELLE

(**— ON SAIL**) LASKET
(**— ON SPINNING FRAME**) BAND
(**— ON SWORD BELT**) HANGER
(**HANGING —**) FESTOON
(**HEDDLE —**) DOUP
(**ORNAMENTAL —**) PICOT
(**SHOULDER —**) EPAULET
(**SURGICAL —**) CURET CURETTE
(**TIGHT —**) KINK KINKLE
(**PREF.**) FUNDI
LOOPER INCHWORM SPANWORM
LOOPHOLE LOOP CHINK MEUSE
EYELET OILLET WICKET BARBICAN
PORTHOLE
LOOSE GAY LAX EMIT FREE GLAD
LASH LIMP OPEN SOFT UNDO
WIDE WILD BAGGY CRANK FRANK
LARGE LIGHT RELAX SLACK
VAGUE WASHY ADRIFT FLUFFY
LIMBER SLOPPY SOLUTE SPORTY
SUBURB UNBIND UNGIRT UNLASH
WOBBLY ABSOLVE CHESSOM
FLYAWAY IMMORAL MOVABLE
RELAXED SHOGGLY STRINGY
UNBOUND UNHITCH UNTIGHT
DIFFUSED DISCINCT FLOATING
INSECURE LAXATIVE SHATTERY
UNSTABLE
(**— ARROW**) BOLT
(**MORALLY —**) FRANK
(**PREF.**) LAXI
LOOSE-JOINTED LANKY SHACKLY
LOOSELY SLACK LARGELY SLACKLY
LOOSEN LAX BREAK SLACK UNTIE
LAXATE LIMBER UNBEND
RESOLVE SLACKEN UNGRIPE
UNLOOSE UNSCREW DISHEVEL
UNSTRING
(**— ANCHOR**) TRIP
(**— ROCK**) GAD
LOOSENESS SLACK LAXITY
LATITUDE
(**PREF.**) LYO
LOOSENING START SOLUTIVE
SOLUTORY
(**PREF.**) LYS(I)
LOOSESTRIFE KILLWEED
PEATWEED PEATWOOD
PRIMWORT
LOOSING
(**SUFF.**) LYSE LYSIS LYST LYTE
LYTIC LYZE
LOOT SACK SWAG BOOTY HARRY
SPOIL STEAL THEFT BOODLE
MARAUD HERSHIP PILLAGE
PLUNDER SNAFFLE
LOOTING SACK
LOP DOD LAP CLIP DODD OCHE
SNED SNIG TRIM SHRAG SHRED
SHRUB STUMP TRASH TWINE
SHROUD SNATHE TRASHIFY
TRUNCATE
(**— OFF**) COW DOD CROP DODD
HEAD SNAG SNED PRUNE SHRED
TRUNK DEFALK AMPUTATE
LOPE SHAG
LOPPED
(**PREF.**) (**— OFF**) TRUNCATO
LOPPER CLABBER
LOPPINGS SHROUD
LOQUACIOUS GABBY FUTILE
LOQUACITY PRATE PRATTLE
FUTILITY

LOQUAT BIWA NISPERO
LORAL FRENAL
LORD BEL DAM DEN DON GOD HER
LOR MAR SID SIR DION DOMN
EROS HERR LAUK LOSH NAIK SIRE
TUAN ANGUS ARAWN BARON
LAFEU LIEGE LUDDY NIGEL
OMRAH RABBI SAHIB SWAMI
DOMINE DUMAIN KYRIOS PRABHU
SAYYID SIGNOR TANIST THAKUR
CAMILLO CERIMON JACQUES
JEHOVAH MARCHER OGTIERN
VAVASOR BHAGAVAT DESPOTES
DRIGHTEN GRANDPRE LORDLING
MARGRAVE OVERLORD PALATINE
SEIGNEUR SEIGNIOR SUPERIOR
SUZERAIN THALIARD
(**— OF DARKNESS**) HYLE
(**— OF WORLD**) LOKINDRA
(**FEUDAL —**) DAUPHIN VAVASOR
SUZERAIN
(**JAPANESE —**) KAMI
LORD CHANCELLOR WOOLPACK
LORD JIM (**AUTHOR OF —**) CONRAD
(**CHARACTER IN —**) JIM DAIN
BROWN STEIN WARIS MARLOW
DORAMIN
LORDLINESS PRIDE
LORDLY PROUD SUPERB
ARROGANT DESPOTIC
LORDOSIS SWAYBACK
LORDSHIP NAVY DYNASTY
ERECTION SEIGNORY SIGNORIA
LORE LEAR LORUM MASTAX
LEARNING
LORGNETTE STARER
LORICA LORIC SHEATH SHIELD
LORIKEET PARROT WARRIN
CORELLA WEROOLE
LORIS KOKAM LEMUR SLOTH
LEMUROID
LORN ALONE
LORNA DOONE (**AUTHOR OF —**)
BLACKMORE
(**CHARACTER IN —**) FRY TOM ALAN
JOHN RIDD ANNIE DOONE DUGAL
ENSOR LORNA CARVER FAGGUS
JEREMY REUBEN BRANDIR
STICKLES HUCKABACK
LORRY DRAG RULLY CAMION
ROLLEY
LORY LOORY CORELLA LORIKEET
LOSE LET TIN AMIT DROP TINE
WANT FORGO LAPSE LEASE TRAIL
GAMBLE MISLAY FORBEAR
FORFEIT FORLESE SLATTER
(**— AT CARDS**) BUST
(**— BET**) WRONG
(**— BRILLIANCE**) FAINT
(**— BY DEATH**) BURY
(**— BY GAMING**) GAME
(**— BY STUPIDITY**) BLUNDER
(**— CONTROL**) BLOW CRACK
(**— COURAGE**) DREEP TAINT
(**— FLAVOR**) FOZE APPAL APPALL
(**— FORCE**) COLLAPSE
(**— FRESHNESS**) FADE WILT
WITHER
(**— HEART**) JADE FAINT QUAIL
COLLAPSE
(**— HOPE**) DESPAIR DESPOND
(**— LUSTER**) TARNISH
(**— MOISTURE**) GUTTATE

(**— NERVE**) CHICKEN
(**— OFFICE**) FALL
(**— ONE'S BREATH**) CHINK
(**— ONE'S WAY**) STRAY
(**— POWER**) FAIL DISSOLVE
(**— SELF-POSSESSION**) ABASH
(**— SPIRIT**) JADE
(**— STRENGTH**) GO FADE FAIL PALL
WEAKEN LANGUISH
(**— VISION**) DAZZLE
(**— WARMTH**) COOL CONGEAL
(**— WEIGHT**) ENSEAM
LOSS ACE COST HARM LEAK LOST
MISS LAPSE QUALM WASTE
BURIAL DAMAGE DAMNUM
DEFEAT INJURY TINSEL AVERAGE
DEBACLE DEFICIT EXPENSE
JACTURE LEAKAGE LEESING
MISTURE REPRISE AMISSION
BREAKAGE CLEANING MISSMENT
PERDITION SACRIFICE
(**— BY EVAPORATION**) ULLAGE
(**— BY SIFTING**) ULLAGE
(**— IN WORKING**) SLIPPAGE
(**— OF ABILITIES**) COLLAPSE
(**— OF ACTIVITY**) AKINESIA
(**— OF APPETITE**) ASITIA ANOREXIA
(**— OF CONSCIOUSNESS**) SWOON
ABSENCE APOPLEXY BLACKOUT
FAINTING
(**— OF ELASTICITY**) SET
(**— OF ELECTRICITY**) EFFLUVE
(**— OF EXPRESSION**) AMIMIA
(**— OF HAIR**) DEFLUX ALOPECIA
PTILOSIS
(**— OF HONOR**) ATIMY
(**— OF HOPE**) DESPAIR
(**— OF MEMORY**) AMNESIA
BLACKOUT
(**— OF PRESTIGE**) DISHONOR
(**— OF SCENT**) CHECK
(**— OF SENSE OF SMELL**) ANOSMIA
(**— OF SIGHT**) ANOPSY ANOPSIA
(**— OF SIZE**) WANE
(**— OF SOUND**) APOCOPE SYNCOPE
APHERESIS
(**— OF SPEECH**) ALALIA APHASIA
APHONIA
(**— OF VOICE**) ANAUDIA APHONIA
(**— OF VOWEL**) APHESIS
(**— OF WILL POWER**) ABULIA
(**CONTRACT —**) LESION
(**SUFF.**) ZEMIA
LOST ASEA GONE LORN TINT
STRAY WASTE ASTRAY BUSHED
HIDDEN NAUGHT FORFEIT
FORLORN MISSING CONFUSED
OBSCURED BENIGHTED
(**— IN THOUGHT**) PREOCCUPIED
LOST HORIZON (**AUTHOR OF —**)
HILTON
(**CHARACTER IN —**) HUGH BRIAC
CHANG HENRY CONWAY LOTSEN
BARNARD CHARLES ROBERTA
BRINKLOW MALLISON PERRAULT
RUTHERFORD
LOST LADY (**AUTHOR OF —**)
CATHER
(**CHARACTER IN —**) IVY BLUM NIEL
FRANK OGDEN PETERS HERBERT
ELLINGER POMMEROY
CONSTANCE FORRESTER
LOT CUT HAP PEW CHOP CROP

DEAL DOLE DOOM DRAW FALL
FATE HEAP PACK PART PILE REDE
SKIT SLEW SLUE SORS SORT
BATCH BLOCK BREAK BUNCH
CAVEL FIELD GRACE GRIST GROSS
LINES SHARE SHOOT SIGHT SITHE
STAND TEEMS TROOP WEIRD
AMOUNT BARREL BOODLE
BUNDLE CHANCE DICKER FARDEL
OODLES PARCEL TICHEL BOILING
DESTINY FEEDLOT FORTUNE
OODLINS PORTION SANDLOT
BACKYARD CABOODLE JINGBANG
MOUTHFUL RIMPTION
WOODLAND
(**— OF PERSONS**) BOODLE
(**— OF TEA**) BREAK
(**— OF 60 PIECES**) SHOCK
(**BUILDING —**) ERF
(**BURIAL —**) LAIR
(**FATHER OF —**) HARAN
(**GREAT —**) SWAG
(**MISCELLANEOUS —**) RAFT
(**SISTER OF —**) ISCAH MILCAH
(**UNCLE OF —**) ABRAHAM
(**VACANT —**) COMMON COMMONS
(**PREF.**) CLERO SORTI
LOTAN (**FATHER OF —**) SEIR
LOTION WASH EYEWASH
EYEWATER LAVATORY
LOTS HEAPS TEEMS BUSHEL
HODFUL
LOTTERY AMBO LOTTO TERNO
RAFFLE TOMBOLA
LOTTO KENO BINGO TOMBOLA
(**— GAME**) HOUSE
LOTUS LOTE LOTOS PADMA
NELUMBO WANKAPIN
LOTUS TREE SADR ZIZYPHUS
LOUCHEUX KUTCHIN
LOUD HARD HIGH MAIN CRUDE
FORTE GAUDY GREAT HEAVY
SHOWY STARK STOUR WIGHT
BRASSY BRAZEN COARSE CRIANT
FLASHY GARISH HOARSE VULGAR
BLATANT CLAMANT HAUTAIN
VIOLENT BIGMOUTH FRENZIED
PIERCING SLAMBANG STREPENT
STRIDENT VEHEMENT
STREPITANT
LOUDLY BOST ALOUD FORTE
STARK
LOUDNESS STRESS SONORITY
MAGNITUDE
(**— UNIT**) PHON SONE
LOUDSPEAKER WOOFER SPEAKER
TWEETER BULLHORN SQUAWKER
LOUD-SPOKEN RANDY
LOUIS LUIGI LODOWIC

LOUISIANA
CAPITAL: BATONROUGE
COLLEGE: LSU TULANE DILLARD
GRAMBLING
COUNTY: CADDO ACADIA PARISH
TENSAS LAFOURCHE
CULTURE: TCHEFUNCTE
DIALECT: CREOLE
FESTIVAL: MARDIGRAS
INDIAN: ADAI WASHA ATAKAPA
LAKE: IATT CLEAR LARTO BORGNE
SALINE DARBONNE MAUREPAS
MOUNTAIN: DRISKILL

NATIVE: CAJUN CREOLE ACADIAN
NICKNAME: CREOLE PELICAN
PARISH: WINN CADDO ACADIA
IBERIA SABINE TENSAS
ORLEANS RAPIDES OUACHITA
CALCASIEU
RIVER: RED AMITE BOEUF SABINE
TENSAS OUACHITA
STATE BIRD: PELICAN
STATE FLOWER: MAGNOLIA
STATE TREE: CYPRESS
STREAM: BAYOU
TOWN: JENA MANY HOMER
HOUMA EDGARD GRETNA
MINDEN MONROE RUSTON
BASTROP VIDALIA BOGALUSA
TALLULAH NEWORLEANS

LOUISIANIAN CAJUN ACADIAN
LOUNGE HAWM LOAF LOLL SORN
SOSS BANGE TRAIK DACKER
FROUST FROWST GLIDER LOLLUP
LOPPET RIZZLE SLINGE SOZZLE
LAMMOCK SAUNTER SLOUNGE
LOUNGER IDLER SLOUNGER
LOUSE BOB BUG SOW CRAB
CRUMB BOOGER BRAULA COOTIE
GISLER PALMER SISTEN VERMIN
MORPION PUCERON GRAYBACK
(FISH —) GISLER ARGULUS
(PLANT —) APHID APHIS
(WOOD —) SOW SLATER
(YOUNG —) NIT
(PREF.) ONISCI PEDICUL(I)(O)
LOUSEWORT RATTLE SNAFFLES
LOUSINESS PEDICULOSIS
LOUSY SEEDY CRAPPY CRUMMY
PEDICULOUS
LOUT HOB LOB LUG YOB BOOR
CHUB COOF GAUM GAWK JAKE
LOON NOWT SWAB SWAD BOOBY
CHUMP CUDDY GNOFF LOOBY
LOURD ROBIN THRUM WHAUP
YAHOO BOHUNK CLUNCH GOBBIN
HOBLOB LOURDY LUBBER LUNGIS
SLOUCH TRIPAL BUMPKIN
GROBIAN HALLION HAWBUCK
LOBCOCK PALOOKA
LOBLOLLY
(COUNTRY —) KERN BUMPKIN
LOUTISH SWAB HULKY SLOOMY
BOORISH HULKING VILLAIN
BOEOTIAN CLOWNISH
LOUVER SLAT LOUVRE LUFFER
DIFFUSER FEMERELL
(PL.) SHUTTER
LOVABLE AMABEL CUDDLY
AMIABLE ADORABLE DOVELIKE
LOVESOME
LOVABLENESS DEARNESS
LOVAGE SMELLAGE
LOVE GRA LOO AMOR EROS KAMA
LIKE ALOHA AMOUR CUPID
DRURY FANCY HEART MINNE
AFFECT TENDRE CHARITY
EMBRACE FEELING PASSION
DEVOTION KINDNESS LOVEHOOD
PARAMOUR
(— IN RETURN) REDAME
(— OF COUNTRY) PATRIOTISM
(— OF MARVELOUS) TERATISM
(— TO EXCESS) IDOLIZE
(— TOWARD DEITY) BHAKTI

(CHRISTIAN —) CHARITY
(INTENSE —) FIRE
(NATURAL —) STORGE
(SELF-GIVING —) AGAPE
(UNLAWFUL —) LEMANRY
(PREF.) ERO(TO)
(SUFF.) PHIL(A)(AE)(E)(IA)
(ISM)(IST)(OUS)(US)(Y)
LOVED DEAR BELOVED
(MUCH —) SWEET
LOVE FEAST AGAPE
LOVE KNOT AMORET
LOVELINESS BEAUTY
LOVELOCK EARLOCK
LOVELY DREAMY LOVING TENDER
AMIABLE AMOROUS ADORABLE
LOVESOME
LOVEMAKING AMOUR
LOVER GRA LAD MAN BEAU CHAP
AMANT AMOUR DRURY LEMAN
ROMEO SPARK SWAIN AMADIS
AMANTE MARROW MINION
SQUIRE ADMIRER AMORIST
AMOROSO CELADON GALLANT
PATRIOT SPARKER SPECIAL
SPRUNNY AMORETTO BELAMOUR
CASANOVA CICISBEO PARAMOUR
STREPHON
(MODEL —) LEILAH
(SILLY —) SPOON
LOVE SEAT CAUSEUSE
LOVE'S LABOR'S LOST (AUTHOR
OF —) SHAKESPEARE
(CHARACTER IN —) DULL MOTH
BOYET MARIA ARMADO DUMAIN
ADRIANO BEROWNE COSTARD
MERCADE ROSALINE FERDINAND
KATHERINE NATHANIEL
HOLOFERNES JAQUENETTA
LONGAVILLE
LOVING DEAR FOND TENDER
AMATORY AMOROUS
(PREF.) PHIL(O)
(SUFF.) PHIL(A)(AE)(E)(OUS)(US)
LOW BAS BOO LAW MOO BASE
BASS KEEN MEAN NEAP OPEN
ORRA ROUT SLOW VILE WEAK
BLORE DIRTY GROSS HEDGE
LAICH PUTID SHORT SMALL
SNIDE THIRD CALLOW EARTHY
FILTHY GENTLE GRUBBY HARLOT
HUMBLE LIMMER MENIAL ORNERY
RASCAL RIBALD SECRET SHABBY
SILKEN TURPID VULGAR BESTIAL
IGNOBLE RAFFISH REPTILE
SLAVISH SUBMISS SOUTERLY
(— AS OF A VOWEL) OPEN
(— DOWN) SIDE
(— IN LIGHTNESS) DULL
(— IN PERCEPTION) CRUDE
(— IN PITCH) GRAVE
(— IN PRICE) MODERATE
(— IN QUALITY) HEDGE
(— IN SATURATION) GRAYISH
(— IN SPIRITS) BLUE DOWN
GLOOMY DOWNCAST
(— IN TONE) SOFT SUBMISS
(— IN WATER) RACE
(— NUMBERS) MANQUE
(— POINT) TROUGH
(IMMEASURABLY —) ABYSMAL
(PREF.) CHAMAE CHAME TAPIN(O)
LOWBORN WAFF

LOWBRED BASTARD PLEBEIAN
LOW-DOWN BUCKASS
LOWER CUT DIP LOW BASE BATE
DOWN DROP DUCK FELL SINK
VAIL ABASE ABATE ALLOY AVALE
BELOW BLAME COUCH COWER
DECRY DEMIT DOUSE FROWN
GLOOM LEVEL SCOWL STOOP
BEMEAN DEBASE DEJECT
DEMEAN EMBASE GLOWER
HUMBLE JUNIOR LESSEN MODIFY
NETHER REDUCE SETTLE STRIKE
SUBDUE SUBMIT BENEATH
DECLASS DEGRADE DEPRESS
SHORTEN DIMINISH DOWNWARD
INFERIOR MODERATE
(— BANNER) VAIL
(— BY HALF STEP) FLAT
(— IN ESTEEM) CHEAPEN
DEROGATE
(— IN PITCH) FLAT SHADE
(— ONESELF) SINK BEMEAN
DESCEND
(— PRICES) BEAR
(— SAIL) AMAIN
(— THE HEAD) STOOP
(PREF.) BATH(O)(Y) CATO INFERO
INFRA NERTERO
(— IN STATUS) INFRA
(MAKE —) DE
LOWERING DIP DUCK DOWLY
HEAVY LAPSE BEETLE SULLEN
PEJORATION
(— OF BODY) FONDU
(— OF LAND) ABLATION
LOWEST LAST LEAST EXTREME
LOWMOST PRIMARY PARAVAIL
NETHERMOST
(— CLASS) LAG
(— POSSIBLE) KNOWDOWN
LOWING MUGIENT
LOWLAND LAICH POLDER
LALLAND DOWNLAND
(— BESIDE RIVER) INKS
(BARREN —) LANDES
LOWLANDER SAXON ZHMUD
SASSENACH
LOWLIER LESS
LOWLY LOW BASE SILLY HUMBLE
BASEBORN
LOW-LYING CALLOW LALLAN
INFERIAL SUBJECTED
LOW-MINDED BASE MEAN
LOWNESS LOWTH
(— OF PITCH) GRAVITY
(— OF SPIRITS) GLOOM SPLEEN
MEGRIMS
LOW-PITCHED GRUFF
LOW-SPIRITED HIPPED DEJECTED
LOW SUNDAY QUASIMODO
LOY SLICK
LOYAL FAST FEAL FIRM HOLD LEAL
REAL TRUE LIEGE PIOUS SOUND
ARDENT HEARTY LAWFUL SECRET
STANCH CONSTANT FAITHFUL
STALWART YEOMANLY
LOYALIST TORY
LOYALLY SURELY
LOYALTY ARDOR FAITH FEALTY
HOMAGE LEALTY REALTY SPIRIT
REALITY DEVOTION FIDELITY
CONSTANCY NATIONALISM
LOZENGE TAB JUBE COIGN QUOIN

CACHOU JUJUBE MASCLE PASTIL
QUARRY ROTULA RUSTRE TABLET
TABULE TROCHE CREMULE
DIAMOND TABELLA PASTILLE
ROSEDROP
(— OF CEMENT) WAFER
LOZI ROZI BAROTSE
LSD ACID
LUBBER LOUT SWAB LOOBY
SLOUCH LOBCOCK LILBURNE
LUBBERLY AWKWARD
LUBRICANT DOPE GREASE
AQUADAG UNGUENT
LUBRICATE OIL DOPE GLIB GREASE
LUBRIFY
LUBRICATOR OILER OILCAN
LUCARNE LUCOMBE
LUCE GED
LUCENT BRIGHT LUCIBLE
LUCERNE LEGUME ALFALFA
LUCIA DI LAMMERMOOR
(CHARACTER IN —) LUCY EDGAR
HENRY ARTHUR ASHTON
BUCKLOW RAVENSWOOD
(COMPOSER OF —) DONIZETTI
LUCIANA (SISTER OF —) ADRIANA
LUCID SANE CLEAR AERIAL BRIGHT
LIMPID CRYSTAL DILUCID
LITERATE LUCULENT LUMINOUS
LUCIDITY SANITY CLARITY
LUCIFER DEVIL PHOSPHOR
LUCK HAP CESS EURE SONS SPIN
GRACE ISSUE CHANCE THRIFT
FORTUNE HANDSEL SUCCESS
VENTURE HAMINGJA
(BAD —) ACE DOLE DEUCE
HOODOO UNLUCK AMBSACE
MISCHANCE
(BAD — TO YOU) YLAHAYLL
(GOOD —) HAP FORTUNE
THEEDOM
(ILL —) UNHAP DIRDUM DISGRACE
MISHANTER
(RELATING TO —) ALEATORY
(UNEXPECTED —) BUNCE
LUCKILY HAPPILY
LUCKY HOT CANNY HAPPY JAMMY
SEELY SONSY CHANCY LUCKLY
LUCKFUL GRACIOUS
PROVIDENTIAL
LUCRATIVE FAT GOOD GAINFUL
LUCRE SWAG DROSS
LUCREZIA BORGIA (CHARACTER IN
—) ALFONSO GENNARO LUCREZIA
(COMPOSER OF —) DONIZETTI
LUD (FATHER OF —) SHEM
LUDICROUS AWFUL COMIC DROLL
ABSURD COMICAL FOOLISH
HIDEOUS RISIBLE FARCICAL
BURLESQUE
LUDO UCKERS
LUFF DERRICK
LUFFA LOOFAH SPONGE
LUG EAR HUG TUG WAG SNUG
SPUD TOTE ZULU PATCH WALTZ
LUGGAGE SWAG TRAPS HATBOX
BAGGAGE TRUSSERY
(AIRPLANE —) CARRYON
LUGGAGE CASE IMPERIAL
LUGGAR JAGGAR JUGGER LAGGAR
LUGGER CAT TOUP ZULU FIFIE
LUGUBRIOUS BLACK TEARY
BALEFUL DOLEFUL DOLOROUS

LUGWORM LOB LUG LOBWORM SANDWORM
LUIGINO TEMIN
LUISA MILLER (CHARACTER IN —) WURM LUISA MILLER WALTER RODOLFO FREDERICA
(COMPOSER OF —) VERDI
LUKEWARM LEW LUKE TEPID WLACH
LULL CALM DRUG FODE HUSH ROCK CROON HUSHO LETUP SLACK STILL SOPITE HUSHABY HUSHEEN
LULLABY LULL BALOO BALOW LULLAY HUSHABY HUSHEEN ROCKABY
LULLING DROWSY CIRCEAN
LULU DOOZY DOOZER SNORTER HUMDINGER
LUMBER BURR DEAL RAFF NANMU STOCK STRIP CUMBER FINISH FLITCH RAFFLE REFUSE SAMCHU SHORTS TIMBER DEGRADE DUNNAGE GUMWOOD RUMMAGE TRUNDLE STEPPING
(INFERIOR —) SAPS SCOOT
LUMBERING AWKWARD LUMBERLY LUMBROUS
LUMBERJACK JACK LOGGER TOPPER TIMBERER
LUMBERMAN PINER DOGGER SCORER CHOPPER GIRDLER TIMBERER
LUMINANCE HELIOS
LUMINARY LIGHT CANDLE PLANET
LUMINESCENCE FLAME
LUMINOSITY FIRE GLOW LIGHT VALUE
LUMINOUS LIGHT LUCID SHINY BRIGHT LUMINANT
LUMMOX LOBSTER PALOOKA
LUMP BAT BOB COB CUB DAB DAD FID GOB JOB LOB NIB NOB NUB WAD BLOB BURL CLAG CLAM CLOT COOL COWL DUNT JUNK KNOB KNOT NIRL PONE SWAD TOKE BLOOM BUNCH CHUCK CHUNK CLAUT CLUMP CLUNK GLEBE HUNCH KNOLL KNURL MOUSE SLUMP STONE WEDGE WODGE CLUNCH DOLLOP GOBBET HUBBLE HUDDLE LUMPET NUBBLE NUGGET CLUMPER CLUNTER PUMPKNOT
(— IN CLOTH) BURL
(— IN GLASS) YOLK
(— OF BLACK LEAD) SOP
(— OF BLOOD) CLOD
(— OF CLAY) BAT
(— OF COAL) NUBBLING
(— OF DOUGH) DIP
(— OF FAT) KEECH
(— OF GLASS) BLOOM
(— OF IRON) OOLLY
(— OF LAVA) BOMB
(— OF LINT) SLUG
(— OF MEAT) OLIVE
(— OF METAL) MASS SLUG
(— OF ORE) ROCK HARDHEAD
(— OF RUBBER) THIMBLE
(— OF SALT) SALTCAT
(— OF WOOD) CHUMP
(— OF YEAST) BEE

(— ON HORSE'S BACK) SITFAST
(— ON SKIN) MILIUM
(LARGE —) BLAD DOLL HUNK
(LITTLE —) NODULE KNOBBLE
(ROUNDED —) CLOT
(PREF.) THROMB(O)
LUMPFISH GROSS PADDLE SUCKER
LUMPISH STODGY CHUCKLE
LUMPSUCKER PADDLE
LUMPY GOBBY CHUNKY CLOGGY CLUNCH COBBLY STODGY BUNCHED
LUNACY MOON FOLLY MADNESS DELIRIUM INSANITY
LUNARIA SATINPOD
LUNARY VOLVELLE
LUNATIC GELT LOONY BEDLAM MADMAN MANIAC FANATIC FRANTIC CRACKPOT MOONLING MOONSICK
LUNCH CUT BAIT CRIB TIFF BEVER PIECE SNACK BRUNCH NACKET TIFFIN UNDERN BAGGING ELEVENS DEJEUNER DRINKING ELEVENER LUNCHEON NUNCHEON COLLATION
(DAIRY —) CREMERIE
(MINER'S —) SNAP
LUNCHEON CRIB LUNCH STULL TIFFIN DEJEUNE DINETTE NOONMEAT
LUNCHROOM EATERY
LUNETTE OUTWORK
LUNG PULMO DRAGON LONGUE
(PREF.) PNEO PNEUM(A)(ATO)(O)(ON)(ONO) PULMO PULMON(I)
LUNGE FOIN PASS SPAR POINT VENUE CHARGE ALLONGE
LUNGFISH CYCLOID DIPNOAN MUDFISH SIRENOID
LUNGS LIGHTS VISCUS BELLOWS
(PERTAINING TO —) PULMONIC
LUNKHEAD DOLT JUGHEAD
LUNULE ALBEDO
LUO DHOLUO
LUPINE SUNDIAL
LURCH JOLL STOT SWAG PITCH STOIT CAREEN STOITER STUMBLE SWAGGER
LURCHING DRUNKEN ROLLING
LURE CON JAY BAIT HOOK ROPE TOLL WISE DECOY DRILL FEINT SLOCK SNARE SNOOK SPOON SQUID STALE TEMPT TROLL ALLURE CAPPER CLARET ENTICE ENTRAP RABATE SEDUCE TREPAN VELURE GUDGEON INVEIGH PHANTOM PITFALL WOBBLER BUCKTAIL INVEIGLE LUREMENT
(— INTO GAMBLING) HUSTLE
(— OF CARRION) TRAIN
(— WILDFOWL) STOOL
LURI ALUR
LURID RED PURPLE SULTRY CRIMSON GHASTLY
LURK DARE LOUT COUCH LOWER SKULK SLINK SNEAK AMBUSH DARKLE
LURKING LURKY GRASSANT LATITANT
LUSCIOUS FOND RICH SWEET CREAMY DULCET DELICATE

LUSH RICH GREEN LUSTY MOIST SAVORY FERTILE OPULENT PROFUSE THRIVING
LUST HELL KAMA BLOOD PRIDE DESIRE LIBIDO LIKING LUXURY NICETY PASSION COVETISE CUPIDITY CARNALITY
(SUFF.) LAGNIA
LUSTER NAIF GLASS GLINT GLOSS SHEEN SHINE WATER LUSTRE POLISH REFLET BURNISH GLIMPSE GLISTER LUSTRUM NITENCY FULGENCE LUSTRATE RADIANCY SPLENDOR
(— OF FIBER) BLOOM
(BRONZE-LIKE —) SCHILLER
LUSTERLESS WAN DEAD DULL FISHY STARY
LUSTFUL HOT GAMY GOLE LEWD RANK SALT CADGY LUSTY PRIME RANDY RUTTY WANTON BEASTLY CODDING FLESHLY FULSOME GOATISH JEALOUS RAMMISH RUTTISH LIKEROUS SALACIOUS
LUSTFULNESS SATYRISM
LUSTILY CRANK HOTLY
LUSTING ITCHY
LUSTRATION ABHISEKA
LUSTROUS CLEAR DOGGY NITID BRIGHT GLOSSY ORIENT SHEENY SILKEN SILVER SHINING SPLENDID
LUSTY BRAG CANT BURLY CRANK FLUSH FRACK FRANK FRECK GUTSY HARDY JUICY RANDY STIFF STOUT GAWSIE ROBUST STURDY LUSTFUL LUSTICK BOUNCING PHYSICAL SKELPING SPORTIVE VIGOROUS
LUTE TAR BIWA LAUD DOMRA NABIA NABLE REBAB REBEC SAROD CITOLE ENLUTE LORICA LUTING SCREED VIELLE ANGELOT BANDORE DICHORD DYPHONE MANDOLA MANDORE MINIKIN PANDORE THEORBO VIHUELA ANGELICA ARCHLUTE PENORCON TAMBOURA TEMPLATE TRICHORD
LUTER DAUBER PASTER
LUTJANID JEWFISH

LUXURIANT GOLE LUSH RANK RICH FRANK PROUD LAVISH WANTON OPULENT PROFUSE RAMPANT TEEMING PAMPERED PRODIGAL
LUXURIANTLY FATLY
LUXURIATE BASK REVEL FROWST WALLOW WANTON
LUXURIOUS HIGH LUSH NICE

POSH RANK SOFT GAUDY PLUSH SWANK CAPUAN DELUXE GILDED PALACE SILKEN SWANKY WANTON APICIAN ELEGANT DELICATE LUCULLAN PRODIGAL REGALADO SENSUOUS TRYPHENA TRYPHOSA
LUXURIOUSLY HIGH DELUXE
LUXURY FRILL FINERY OUTRAGE DELICACY ELEGANCE PLEASURE RICHNESS PRINCELINESS
LUXURY-LOVING DELICATE
LYCANTHROPE WEREWOLF
LYCAON (DAUGHTER OF —) CALLISTO
(FATHER OF —) PELASGUS
LYCEUM PLATFORM
LYCHNIS FIREBALL NONESUCH
LYCIUM RUSOT
LYCOPODIUM MOSS FOXTAIL CROWFOOT STAGHORN
LYCURGUS (BROTHER OF —) POLYDECTES
(FATHER OF —) DRYAS EUNOMUS
(SON OF —) OPHELTES
LYCUS (BROTHER OF —) AEGEUS PALLAS IPHINOE
(FATHER OF —) PANDION
(MOTHER OF —) PYLIA
(WIFE OF —) DIRCE
LYDIA MAEONIA
LYE LEY BOUK BUCK STRAKE LESSIVE LIXIVIUM SOAPLEES
LYING FLAT FALSE LEASE CRETISM LEASING MENTERY ACCUBATION MENDACIOUS
(— APART) DISSITE
(— AT BASE OF MOUNTAINS) PIEDMONT
(— CLOSE) QUAT
(— DOWN) DOWN LODGED CUMBENT DORMANT COUCHANT
(— HID) LATITANT
(— IDLE) INACTIVE
(— ON BACK) SUPINE
(— ON FACE) PRONE PROCUMBENT
(— OVER) JACENT
(— UNDER GRASS) LEA
LYING-IN INLYING CHILDBED GROANING
LYMPH CHYLE VIRUS
(PREF.) CHYL(O)
(SUFF.) CHYLIA
LYMPHAD GALLEY
LYMPHANGITIS WEED FILLING
LYMPHATIC LACTEAL
LYMPHOGRANULOMA BUBO
LYMPHOMATOSIS FISHEYE
LYNCEUS (BROTHER OF —) IDAS
(FATHER OF —) AEGYPTUS APHAREUS
(WIFE OF —) HYPERMNESTRA
LYNCH HANG DEWITT
LYNX LOSSE OUNCE PISHU BOBCAT GORKUN LUCERN CARACAL LUCIVEE WILDCAT CARCAJOU
LYRE ASOR HARP LYRA SHELL CHELYS KINNOR KISSAR TRIGON CITHARA TESTUDO BARBITON PHORMINX TRICHORD TRIGONON
LYREBIRD LYRETAIL PHEASANT
LYRIC LAY LIED HOKKU LAEAN MELIC GHAZEL TENSON CANCION

CHANSON DESCORT MADRIGAL
(HAVING — AND DRAMATIC QUALITIES) SPINTO

(LOVE —) ALBA
(PL.) SONG
LYSIPPE (FATHER OF —) PROETUS

(HUSBAND OF —) MELAMPUS
(MOTHER OF —) ANTIA
(SISTER OF —) IPHINOE IPHINASSA

LYTTA WORM

M

M EM EMMA MIKE METRO
  (WRONG USE OF —) MYTACISM
M-1 GARAND
MAACAH (HUSBAND OF —) DAVID
  (SON OF —) ABSALOM
MAACHAH (FATHER OF —) NAHOR
  URIEL TALMAI
  (HUSBAND OF —) JEHIEL MACHIR
  REHOBOAM
  (MOTHER OF —) REUMAH
  (SON OF —) HANAN ABIJAH
  ACHISH ABSALOM SHEPHATIAH
MAADAI (FATHER OF —) BANI
MA'AM MARM MISTRESS
MAARIB ARBIT ARBITH
MAASEIAH (FATHER OF —) ADAIAH
  BARUCH SHALLUM
  (SON OF —) AZARIAH ZEDEKIAH
  ZEPHANIAH
MAATH (FATHER OF —)
  MATTATHIAS
MAAZ (FATHER OF —) RAM
MACA ENIMAGA
MACABRE SICK HORRIBLE
MACACA PITHECUS
MACADAMIZE METAL
MACAO (CHINESE NAME OF —)
  AOMEN
  (ISLAND OF —) TAIPA COLOANE
MACAQUE KRA BROH BRUH
  MACAC TOQUE MACHIN RHESUS
  RILAWA WANDEROO
MACARIA (FATHER OF —)
  HERCULES
  (MOTHER OF —) DEIANIRA
MACARIZE LAUD
MACARONI DITALI
MACARONIC SKEW
MACAW ARA ARARA PARROT
  MARACAN ARACANGA COCKATOO
MACBETH (AUTHOR OF —)
  SHAKESPEARE
  (CHARACTER IN —) ROSS ANGUS
  BANQUO DUNCAN HECATE
  LENNOX SEYTON SIWARD
  FLEANCE MACBETH MACDUFF
  MALCOLM MENTEITH CAITHNESS
  DONALBAIN
MACE CROC MALL MAUL POKER
  VERGE MALLET SPARTH CATTAIL
  (PART OF —) HEAD HILT SPIKE
  FLANGE HANDLE
  (REED —) DOD DODD
  (ROYAL —) SCEPTER SCEPTRE
MACE-BEARER BEADLE VERGER
  MACEMAN
MACERATE RET SOUR STEEP
MACHAON (BROTHER OF —)
  PODALIRIUS
  (FATHER OF —) AESCULAPIUS
  (MOTHER OF —) CORONIS
MACHETE GULOC PARANG
  CURTAXE CUTLASH CUTLASS

MACHI (COMPANION OF —) CALEB
  JOSHUA
  (SON OF —) GEUEL
MACHIAVELLIAN CRAFTY
  CUNNING GUILEFUL
MACHINATION ARTIFICE INTRIGUE
  SCHEMERY
MACHINE (ALSO SEE DEVICE AND
  ENGINE) GIN HOG JIG SAW AGER
  BABY COMB GEAR JACK LIFT
  MULE PUMP RASP TRAY WHIM
  WINK ADDER AWNER BALER
  BENCH BILLY BOARD BRAKE
  BREAK COPER CRANE DEVIL
  EDGER ERNIE FRAME FUDGE
  FUGAL JENNY JERRY JOLLY
  LATHE LAYER METER MIXER
  MOWER NAVVY RAKER RESAW
  ROVER SCREW SETUP SHEEN
  SIZER STAMP SULKY TRONE
  VINER WILLY BARKER BEADER
  BEAMER BEATER BEETLE BENDER
  BILLER BINDER BOLTER BUCKLE
  BUMPER BUTTER CANTER
  CAPPER CARDER CONCHE
  COOLER CREWER DECKER
  DOFFER DONKEY DRAPER
  DREDGE DUSTER ENGINE FLAKER
  FOLDER FOOTER FORMER
  GADDER GAPPER GLAZER
  GRADER GRATER GUMMER
  HEADER HEMMER HOBBER
  HOGGER HOOPER HULLER
  HUSKER IRONER JIGGER JORDAN
  KICKER LEGGER LIFTER LINTER
  LOGGER MAILER MANGLE MILLER
  MITRER NAPPER NETTER NIBBER
  NIPPER PACKER PEGGER PINNER
  PLATER PUMPER RIPPER ROSSER
  ROTARY ROUTER SANDER
  SCUTCH SEALER SEAMER SHAKER
  SHAPER SHAVER SINGER SKIVER
  SLICER SORTER SPACER STOCKS
  STOKER TEDDER TENTER TWINER
  VANNER WASHER WELDER
  WILLOW ABRADER AUTOMAT
  AVIATOR BACKHOE BATCHER
  BELLOWS BLENDER BLUNGER
  BOTTLER BRANNER BREAKER
  CANDROY CAPSTAN CHIPPER
  COMBINE CRUSHER DIBBLER
  DRESSER EMULSOR ENCODER
  ENROBER ERECTOR EXOSTRA
  FLANGER FLOSSER FREEZER
  GARNETT GLASSER GRAINER
  GRINDER GROOVER GROUTER
  HUMIDOR IRONMAN JOINTER
  KNITTER KNOTTER MACHINA
  MANGLER MATCHER MITERER
  PERRIER PLODDER PLUCKER
  POTCHER PRINTER QUILLER
  REPRESS RIVETER ROASTER
  SAMMIER SCALPER SHEARER

  SHEETER SIROCCO SLABBER
  SLASHER SLITTER SLOTTER
  SLUBBER SLUGGER SMASHER
  SPALLER SPEEDER SPINNER
  SPONGER SPOOLER SPRAYER
  STACKER STAMPER STAPLER
  STEAMER STEMMER STICKER
  TENONER TEREBRA TOOTHER
  TRAMPER TREATER TRIMMER
  TRUSSER TWILLER TWISTER
  TYPOBAR WHIPPER WHIZZER
  AERIFIER AIRCRAFT BROACHER
  CALENDER CANCELER CARTONER
  CLINCHER COLLATOR COMPRESS
  DUNGBECK ELEPHANT EXPLODER
  EXTRUDER FILATORY FINISHER
  FLYWINCH FORKLIFT GATHERER
  HARDENER HAYMAKER HERCULES
  HUMMELER IMPACTER KILLIFER
  MORTISER MOULINET ODOGRAPH
  OROGRAPH PROFILER PULSATOR
  SCHIFFLI SCUTCHER SHREDDER
  SOFTENER SPLITTER SPREADER
  SPRIGGER SQUEEZER STITCHER
  STRANDER STRIPPER SURFACER
  TEMPERER THREADER THRESHER
  THROSTLE TRAVELER TRISPAST
  TUNNELER UPSETTER WINNOWER
  ADDRESSER
MACHINE GUN STINGER
  CHAUCHAT
MACHINERY MINT TOPCAP
  SUCCULA APPARATUS
MACHINE SHOP TURNERY
MACHINIST FRILLER THINNER
  MACHINER
MACHIR (FATHER OF —) AMMIEL
  MANASSEH
MACHISMO MACHO
MACHNADEBAI (FATHER OF —)
  BANI
MACKEREL CHAD PETO SCAD TINK
  BLINK OPELU SNOEK TUNNY
  BONITO SAUREL TINKER BLINKER
  BLOATER SCOMBER TASSARD
  ALBACORE HARDHEAD SCOMBRID
  SEERFISH
  (— ABOUT 8 OR 9 INCHES) TINK
  TINKER
  (PICKLED —) SCALPEEN
  (POOR BONY —) SLINK SLINKER
  (YOUNG —) SPIKE
  (PREF.) SCOMBRI
MACKLE SLUR SHAKE MACULA
MACROGAMETE OVUM
MACROSCOPIC GROSS
MACROSPECIES LINNEON
MAD FEY AWAY GITE GYTE HYTE
  WOOD YOND ANGRY BATTY
  BRAIN CRAZY DIPPY FOLLE RABID
  BEDLAM FRENZY INSANE MANIAC
  WOODEN BERSERK BONKERS
  FANATIC FRANTIC FURIOUS

  LUNATIC MADDING MADDOCK
  MANKIND REDWOOD WITLESS
  DELIRANT DEMENTED DISTRACT
  INFORMAL MANIACAL MINDLESS
  RAVENING POSSESSED

MADAGASCAR
CAPITAL: ANTANANARIVO
FORMER NAME:
MALAGASYREPUBLIC
ISLAND GROUP: ALDABRA
LAKE: ITASY ALAOTRA
MEASURE: GANTANG
NATIVE: HOVA SAKALAVA
PEOPLE: HOVA COTIER MARINA
RIVER: IKOPA MANIA SOFIA
MANGOKY MANGORO ONYLAHY
TOWN: IHOSY MANJA TULEAR
MAJANGA NOSSIBE TSIVORY
TAMATAVE ANTISIRABE

MADAI (FATHER OF —) JAPHET
MADAM MEM MUM BAWD MAAM
  PANI DONNA MADAME SENORA
  SENHORA SIGNORA GOODWIFE
  MISTRESS SINEBADA
MADAMA BUTTERFLY
  (CHARACTER IN —) SUZUKI
  CIOCIOSAN PINKERTON
  SHARPLESS
  (COMPOSER OF —) PUCCINI
MADAME BOVARY (AUTHOR OF —)
  FLAUBERT
  (CHARACTER IN —) EMMA LEON
  BOVARY DUPUIS HOMAIS
  CHARLES HELOISE ROUAULT
  LHEUREUX RODOLPHE
  BOULANGER
MADAR YERCUM
MADDEN ENRAGE INCENSE
  INFLAME DISTRACT
MADDENED ENRAGED FRENZIED
MADDER GAMENE LIZARY ALIZARI
  GARANCE MUNJEET TANAGRA
  GARANCIN SPURWORT
  WOODRUFF
MAD-DOG SKULLCAP MADWEED
  HOODWORT
MADE SET BUILT COMPACT
  PREPARED TIMBERED
  (— FLUID BY HEAT) FUSILE
  (— OF DISSIMILAR PARTS) MIXED
  (— OF FLAX) LINEN
  (— OF GRAIN) OATEN CEREAL
  (— OF IVORY) EBURNEAN
  (— OF SILVER) ARGENT
  (— OF STONE) STONEN
  (— OF TWIGS) VIRGAL
  (— SHORT) CURTAL
  (— TART) EUCHRED
  (— TO ORDER) BESPOKEN
  (— TRANSLUCENT) AJOURE
  (— UP) ACCRETE

(— WITH CEDAR) CEDARN
(PREF.) (— OF) DIA
(SUFF.) (— OF) INE
MADE-BEAVER SKIN CASTOR
MADEIRA ISLANDS (ISLAND OF —)
GRANDE DEZERTE
(TOWN OF —) FUNCHAL
(WINE OF —) BUAL TINTA
MALMSEY SERCIAL VERDELHO
MADELON POLIXENE
MADHOUSE ASYLUM BEDLAM
MADHUCA BASSIA ILLIPE
MADLY WOOD CRAZY
MADMAN GELT BEDLAM MANIAC
FURIOSO LUNATIC WOODMAN
MADNESS MAD FURY MOON
WOOD FOLIE FOLLY FUROR
MANIA BEDLAM FRENZY LUNACY
DEWANEE ECSTASY MOONERY
WIDDRIM DELIRIUM DEMENTIA
PIBLOKTO WILLNESS WOODNESS
WOODSHIP
(PREF.) LYSSO MANIC
(SUFF.) MANE MANIA(C)
MADONNA LADY VIRGIN
MADREPORE FUNGID
MADRIGAL ENSALADA
MADRONA LAUREL MANZANITA
MADTOM TADPOLE
MADWORT ALYSSUM BUGLOSS
MAENAD FROW BASSARID
BACCHANTE
(PL.) BACCHAE
MAFIC FEMIC
MAFURA ROKA ELCAJA
MAGANI BAGANI
MAGAZINE BOOK DRUM FLAT
IGLOO SLICK STORE RETORT
ALMACEN JOURNAL CASSETTE
(BLACKWOOD'S —) MAGA
MAGDALEN MAUDLIN
MAGGOT MAD GRUB MAWK
WORM METHE GENTLE WARBLE
WORMIL MADDOCK SKIPPER
MUCKWORM
MAGIC JUJU MAYA RUNE CRAFT
FAIRY GOETY SPELL TURGY
GOETIC TREGET VOODOO
ALCHEMY CANTRIP CONJURY
DEVILRY GLAMOUR GRAMARY
MAGICAL SORCERY BRUJERIA
HECATEAN WIZARDRY
NECROMANCY
(BLACK —) GOETY GOETIC
MALEFICE
(WHITE —) TURGY
MAGICAL WIZARD WONDER
HERMETIC NUMINOUS THEURGIC
**MAGIC FLUTE, THE (CHARACTER
IN —)** PAMINA TAMINO
PAPAGENA PAPAGENO SARASTRO
MONOSTATOS
(COMPOSER OF —) MOZART
MAGICIAN MAGE BOKOR MAGUS
UTHER CUNJAH GOETIC GOOFER
GUFFER MAGIAN MERLIN
WABENO WIZARD CHARMER
GWYDION KOSCHEI WARLOCK
WIELARE WISEMAN CONJURER
FETISHER SORCERER THEURGIC
TROLLMAN ARCHIMAGE
MAGIC MOUNTAIN (AUTHOR OF —)
MANN

(CHARACTER IN —) HANS NAPHTA
BEHRENS CASTORP CAUCHAT
CLAVDIA JOACHIM ZIEMSSEN
KROKOWSKI PEEPERKORN
SETTEMBRINI
MAGISTERIAL LOFTY PROUD
AUGUST CURULE LORDLY
HAUGHTY STATELY ARROGANT
DOGMATIC
MAGISTERY MASTERY
MAGISTRACY AMT PRYTANY
MAGISTRATE BEAK FOUD EPHOR
JUDGE JURAT MAYOR PRIOR
REEVE AMTMAN ARCHON
AVOYER BAILIE BAILLI CENSOR
CONSUL FISCAL KOTWAL SYNDIC
ALCALDE BAILIFF BURGESS
DUUMVIR ECHEVIN EPHORUS
JUSTICE NOMARCH PODESTA
PRAETOR PREFECT PROVOST
STEWARD SUFFETE TRIBUNE
ALABARCH ALDERMAN CAPITOUL
DEFENSOR DEMIURGE DICTATOR
GOVERNOR MITTIMUS PHYLARCH
PRYTANIS RECORDER STRADICO
STRATEGE HUNDREDER
CORREGIDOR
(— IN CHANNEL ISLANDS) JURAT
(— OF ANCIENT ROME) EDILE
(— OF VENICE AND GENOA) DOGE
(MOHAMMEDAN —) CADI CADY
SHERIF
(SCOTCH —) PROVOST STEWARD
MAGMA ICHOR
MAGMATIC JUVENILE
MAGNANIMITY HEIGHT FREEDOM
MAGNANIMOUS BIG FREE GREAT
LARGE LOFTY NOBLE HEROIC
EXALTED GENEROUS
MAGNATE BARON MOGUL
BASHAW TYCOON
MAGNESIA PULVIL
MAGNET FIELD ADAMAS MAGNES
ADAMANT SOLENOID TERRELLA
MAGNETISM IT DEVIL OOMPH
MAGNETITE LOADSTONE
LODESTONE
MAGNETIZE TOUCH SATURATE
MAGNETOMETER DOODLEBUG
MAGNIFICATION POWER
MAGNIFICENCE GITE POMP FLARE
GLORY STATE PARADE JOLLITY
ROYALTY GRANDEUR SPLENDOR
MAGNIFICENT RIAL GRAND NOBLE
PROUD ROYAL AUGUST LAVISH
IMMENSE POMPOUS STATELY
SUBLIME GLORIOUS GORGEOUS
MAGNIFIC PALATIAL PRINCELY
SPLENDID
MAGNIFICENT OBSESSION
(AUTHOR OF —) DOUGLAS
(CHARACTER IN —) BRENT HELEN
JOYCE NANCY WAYNE DAWSON
HUDSON ROBERT ASHFORD
MERRICK
MAGNIFY LAUD BLESS ERECT
EXALT PRAISE ADVANCE DISTEND
ENLARGE GLORIFY GREATEN
INCREASE MAXIMIZE MULTIPLY
MAGNIFYING
(PREF.) MICR(O)
MAGNIFYING GLASS LOUPE
READER

MAGNILOQUENT TURGID
BOMBAST
MAGNITUDE BULK MASS SIZE
DATUM LEVEL SOLID EXTENT
FIGURE PERIOD EXTREME
CONSTANT FUNCTION INFINITE
MAGNOLIA YULAN BIGBLOOM
CUCUMBER MAURICIO
(— STATE) MISSISSIPPI
MAGOG (FATHER OF —) JAPHETH
MAGPIE MAG PIE PIET PYAT CISSA
KOTRI MADGE NINUT MARGET
NANPIE PIANET PIEMAG SIRGANG
HAGISTER MARGARET PHEASANT
PIENANNY
MAGPIE LARK PEEWEE GRALLINA
MAGPIE ROBIN DAYAL DHYAL
MAGUEY AGAVE MESCAL
CANTALA
MAGYAR SZEKEL SZEKLER
MAHALAH (MOTHER OF —)
HAMMOLEKETH
(UNCLE OF —) GILEAD
MAHALATH (FATHER OF —)
ISHMAEL JERIMOTH
(HUSBAND OF —) ESAU REHOBOAM
MAHALI (FATHER OF —) MERARI
MAHATMA SAGE ARHAT
MAHAZIOTH (FATHER OF —)
HEMAN
MAH-JONGG WOO
MAHLAH (FATHER OF —)
ZELOPHEHAD
MAHLI (FATHER OF —) MUSHI
MERARI
MAHLON (DAUGHTER OF —) NAOMI
(SON OF —) ELIMELECH
(WIFE OF —) RUTH
MAHOE EMAJAGUA
MAHOGANY SIPO ALMON CAOBA
CEDAR ROHAN ACAJOU AGUANO
SAPELE THITKA ALBARCO
AVODIRE BAYWOOD GUNNUNG
MADEIRA RATTEEN TABASCO
BANGALAY HARDTACK TANGUILE
(INDIAN —) TOON
(PHILIPPINE —) BAGTIKAN
MAHONIA ASHBERRY ODOSTEMON
MAHOUND MACON
MAHUA FULWA MOWHA MOWRA
MADHUCA PHULWARA
MAHUANG EPHEDRA
MAIA (FATHER OF —) ATLAS
(MOTHER OF —) PLEIONE
(SON OF —) MERCURY
MAID MAY AYAH GIRL LASS MEDE
SLUT CHINA WENCH WOMAN
MAIDEN SLAVEY TWEENY VIRGIN
ANCILLA GENERAL MAIDKIN
PHYLLIS PUCELLE WENCHEL
BONIBELL BRANGANE HANDMAID
SUIVANTE TIREMAID
(— IN WAITING) DAMSEL DAMOZEL
(— OF HONOR) MARIE
(— OF-ALL-WORK) SLAVEY
GENERAL
(KITCHEN —) SCOGIE
(LADY'S —) AYAH ABIGAIL
TIREMAID
(NURSE —) BONNE
(OLD —) TABBY SPINSTER
(WAITING —) ABIGAIL SUIVANTE
MAIDEN MAY BIRD BURD DAME

GIRL MAID DALAGA DAMSEL
FROKIN MEISJE COLLEEN CYDIPPE
DAMOZEL MADCHEN
DAUGHTER
(— WITH BASKET ON HEAD)
CANEPHOR
(PREF.) PARTHENO
MAIDENHAIR GINGKO ADIANTUM
MAIDENLY VIRGIN GIRLISH
VIRGINAL
MAIDEN PINK SPINK DIANTHUS
MAIDSERVANT LASS BIDDY
BONNE SKIVVY ANCILLA LISETTE
MAIEUTIC HEBAMIC
MAIGRE BAR SCIAENID WEAKFISH
MAIL BAG DAK HOOD POST
MATTER AIRMAIL JACKPOT
MAILBAG ORDINAR POSTAGE
POSTBAG SEAPOST TAPPALL
ORDINARY
(IMPROPERLY ADDRESSED —) NIX
NIXY
MAILBAG BAG POUCH POSTBAG
MAILBOX POST PILLAR POSTBOX
MAILLECHORT ARGENTON
MAILLOT SWIMSUIT
MAILMAN POSTMAN BREVIGER
MAIM LAME BREAK TRUNK
HAMBLE MANGLE MAYHEM
SCOTCH CRIPPLE MUTILATE
TRUNCATE
(— AN ANIMAL) LAW MANK
MAIMED GAMMY SPAVINED
(PREF.) PERO
MAIN HIGH LINE MOST CHIEF
GRAND GREAT PRIME SHEER
MIGHTY CAPITAL LEADING
CARDINAL FOREMOST

MAINE
CAPITAL: AUGUSTA
COLLEGE: BATES COLBY BOWDOIN
COUNTY: KNOX WALDO KENNEBEC
AROOSTOOK PENOBSCOT
SAGADAHOC PISCATAQUIS
INDIAN: ABNAKI
LAKE: GRAND SEBEC SEBAGO
RANGELEY SCHOODIC
MOOSEHEAD CHESUNCOOK
MOUNTAIN: BIGELOW CADILLAC
KATAHDIN
NATIVE: MANIAC
RIVER: SACO KENNEBEC
AROOSTOOK KENNEBAGO
PENOBSCOT
STATE BIRD: CHICKADEE
STATE FLOWER: PINECONE
STATE NICKNAME: LUMBER
PINETREE
STATE TREE: PINE
TOWN: BATH ORONO AUBURN
BANGOR BELFAST HOULTON
KITTERY MACHIAS BOOTHBAY
LEWISTON OGUNQUIT
PORTLAND SKOWHEGAN

MAINLAND
(PREF.) EPEIRO
MAINLY BROADLY CHIEFLY
LARGELY
MAINSTAY KEY ATLAS SINEW
STOOP PILLAR BACKBONE
RELIANCE

MAIN STREET (AUTHOR OF —) LEWIS
(CHARACTER IN —) ERIK HUGH WILL CAROL MILFORD VALBORG KENNICOTT
MAINTAIN AVOW BEAR FEND FIND HOLD KEEP LAST SAVE ADOPT ARGUE CARRY CLAIM ESCOT SALVE ADHERE ALLEGE ASSERT AVOUCH DEFEND INTEND RETAIN THREAP UPHOLD UPKEEP CONFIRM CONTEND DECLARE DISPUTE JUSTIFY NOURISH SUBSIST SUPPORT SUSTAIN CONTINUE PRESERVE
(— AS TRUE) AVOUCH SOOTHE
(— POSITION) STALL
(— WITHOUT REASON) ARROGATE
MAINTAINER FOUNDER RETAINER
MAINTENANCE KEEP LIVING UPKEEP ALIMONY CUSTODY FINDING KEEPING PREBEND SERVICE
(— OF POPULATION) BALANCE
MAITHILI TIRHUTIA
MAIZE CORN GRAIN CEREAL INDIAN JAGONG STAPLE MEALIES DJAGOONG
(— CRUSHED WITH PESTLE) STAMP
MAJAGUA HAU BARU BOLA MAHO MOJO BURAO GUANA MAHOE PURAU BALIBAGO CORKWOOD EMAJAGUA
MAJESTIC HIGH AWFUL GRAND LOFTY REGAL ROYAL AUGUST KINGLY SUPERB STATELY SUBLIME ELEVATED IMPERIAL MAESTOSO SPLENDID
MAJESTY DIGNITY AUGUSTUS GRANDEUR KINGSHIP
MAJOON BANG BHANG
MAJOR BEY DUR DURUM SHARP CAPITAL GREATER MAGGIORE
MAJOR BARBARA (AUTHOR OF —) SHAW
(CHARACTER IN —) LOMAX SARAH CUSINS BARBARA CHARLES STEPHEN ADOLPHUS BRITOMART UNDERSHAFT
MAJORITY BODY BULK FECK CORPSE SUBSTANCE
(ABSOLUTE —) QUORUM
MAKARAKA IDDIO
MAKARI KOTOKO
MAKE DO CUT GAR LET MAY FORM GIVE LEVY BRAND BUILD CAUSE COVER FETCH FORGE FRAME SEIZE SHAPE STAMP AUTHOR COBBLE CREATE GRAITH INDUCE RENDER CONFECT FASHION IMAGERY IWURCHE PERFORM PRODUCE CONTRIVE GENERATE
(— A DIFFERENCE) SKILL
(— A MESS OF) PIE
(— A RUG) HOOK
(— A VISIT) COSHER
(— ACKNOWLEDGMENT) CONFESS
(— ACTIVE) ENERGIZE
(— AMENDS) ABYE ATONE ABEGGE ANSWER REDEEM EXPIATE REDRESS
(— ANGRY) GRAMY WRATH
(— ATTRACTIVE) GILD

(— AWAY WITH) ABOLISH EMBEZZLE
(— BARE) STRIP DENUDE
(— BELIEVE) LET PRETEND
(— BETTER) AMEND HEIGHTEN
(— BLUE) HIP
(— BRIGHT) ENGILD ILLUME CLARIFY
(— BRISK) PERK
(— BROWN) TAN
(— BY STAMPING) MINT
(— CANDLE) DIP DRAW
(— CERTAIN) ASSURE ENSURE
(— CHANNEL IN) THROAT
(— CHEERFUL) SOLACE
(— CHOICE) OPT CHOOSE SELECT
(— CLAMMY) ENGLEIM
(— CLEAR) DECLARE DEVELOP DISCUSS EXHIBIT EXPOUND LIGHTEN DESCRIBE
(— COLD) REFREID
(— COMPLETE) SPHERE
(— CONSPICUOUS) ENNOBLE
(— CONTENT) SATISFY
(— CULTIVABLE) EMPOLDER
(— CUT PRIOR TO LAYERING) TONGUE
(— DESTITUTE) BEREAVE
(— DIFFERENT) ALTER CHANGE
(— DIRTY) MOIL GRIME
(— DISPLAY OF) AFFECT DISCOVER
(— DRUNK) FOX SOUSE FUDDLE SOZZLE
(— DRY) HAZLE HAZZLE
(— EARLIER) ADVANCE
(— EFFERVESCENT) AERATE
(— EFFIGY) GUY
(— END OF) SNIB FETCH
(— ENDURING) ANNEAL
(— EQUAL) WEIGH EQUATE
(— EVEN) GLAZE LEVEL WEIGH SQUARE
(— FACES) GIMBLE MURGEON
(— FALSE PRETENSES) SHAM
(— FAST) FIX BAIL FAST GIRD KNIT MAKE STOP BELAY HITCH BUCKLE FASTEN SECURE
(— FAT) BATTEN
(— FIRM) FIX BRACE FASTEN
(— FIT) APTATE STRIKE
(— FOOL OF) DOR BORE DOLT DORRE BEGOWK DOODLE
(— FOOLISH) DAFF GREEN NUGIFY STULTIFY
(— FOOTSORE) SURBATE
(— FROTHY) MILL
(— FULL) FARCE FULFILL
(— FUN OF) GUY KID GAFF JAPE JEST JOSH RIDE DROLL GLAIK SCOUT SMOKE
(— FUSS OVER NOTHING) FAFF
(— GLAD) FAIN
(— GLASS) FOUND
(— GLOSSY) SLEEK
(— GLOW) FURNACE
(— GOLDEN) ENDORE
(— GOOD) ABET
(— GRINDING NOISE) GRINCH
(— GURGLING SOUND) CROOL
(— HAPPY) BLESS ENJOY REFORM BEATIFY SATISFY FELICIFY
(— HARD) TAW STEEL ENDURE HORNIFY

(— HARDY) FASTEN
(— HEADWAY) STEM WALK ENFORCE
(— HELPLESS) STAGGER
(— HOLY) BLESS SACRE HALLOW SANCTIFY
(— HORSE SEEM YOUNGER) BISHOP
(— ILL) MORBIFY
(— IMMOBILE) FREEZE
(— IMPACT) ASSAIL
(— INCURSION) HARRY
(— INSIGNIFICANT) MICRIFY
(— INTO BUNDLE) FARDEL
(— INTO LAW) ENACT
(— INVALID) DAMASK
(— JOINT) SYPHER
(— KNOWN) BID OUT GIVE WISE AREAD BEKEN BREAK KITHE SOUND SPEAK BEWRAY BROACH COUTHE DENOTE DESCRY EXPOSE INFORM REVEAL SPREAD CONFESS DECLARE DELIVER DIVULGE PUBLISH SIGNIFY UNCOVER ANNOUNCE DECIPHER DISCLOSE DISCOVER INDICATE PROCLAIM PROMULGE
(— LESS DENSE) THIN RAREFY
(— LESS SEVERE) MITIGATE
(— LIABLE) DANGER
(— LOVE) WOO COURT SPOON GALLANT
(— LUKEWARM) WLECCHE
(— LUSTERLESS) FLATTEN
(— MANIFEST) EVINCE EXPLAIN
(— MELANCHOLY) HYP
(— MELODIOUS) ATTUNE
(— MELODY) DREAM
(— MENTION) SPEAK
(— MERRY) JET GAUD CHEER SPORT FROLIC SHROVE DISPORT REHAYTE
(— METALLIC SOUND) CHINK
(— MISTAKE) ERR BOOB GOOF
(— MONOTONOUS NOISE) DRONE
(— MORAL) ETHICIZE
(— MUCH OF) DAWT DANDLE
(— MURMURING NOISE) BUM
(— NEAT) FEAT SMUG TIDY GROOM
(— NEST) TIMBER
(— NONMAGNETIC) DEGAUSS
(— NUMB) DAZE ETHERIZE
(— OFF) BAG BOLT HOOK ANNEX HEIST MOSEY SLOPE SPIRIT SCARPER
(— ONE) UNE
(— ONE'S WAY) AIRT BORE TRADE
(— OPEN) AIR PATEFY
(— OUT) FARE FILL GLEAN SKILL DISCERN DECIPHER
(— OVER) TURN ALIEN CHANGE RECOCT DELIVER REFORGE
(— PALE) CHALK
(— PLEASANT) SWEETEN
(— POIGNANT) SAUCE
(— PREGNANT) ENWOMB
(— PROGRESS) GAIN STEM GATHER
(— PROUD) WLENCH
(— PUBLIC) BLOW BLAZE BREAK BLAZON DELATE DIVULGE FANFARE PUBLISH BULLETIN
(— QUIET) ALLAY QUIET APPEASE

(— RATTLING NOISE) TIRL
(— READY) DO BUN GET BOUN BOWN BUSK YARK BELAY BOWNE DRESS PREST PRIME FETTLE GRAITH ADDRESS APPAREL DISPOSE PREPARE
(— RECORD OF) REFER
(— REFERENCE) MENTION
(— RESISTANCE) REBEL
(— RESOLUTE) STEEL
(— RETURN FOR) REQUITE
(— RICH) FREIGHT IMBURSE
(— ROSY) FLUSH
(— RUSTLING SOUND) FISSLE FISTLE
(— RUTTING CRY) FREAM
(— SCANTY LIVING) EKE
(— SERIES OF NOTES) TINKLE
(— SHIFT) SCAMBLE
(— SIGN OF CROSS) BLESS
(— SMALL) MICRIFY BELITTLE
(— SMALLER) MINIFY COMPRESS
(— SMOOTH) SLAB GLAZE SLEEK GENTLE HAMMER SCRAPE LEVIGATE
(— SOFT) NESH GENTLE
(— SOGGY) SOP
(— SOUR) FOX WIND
(— SPIRITLESS) MOPE
(— SPORT OF) LARK
(— SPRUCE) PERK SMARTEN
(— STRAIGHT) ADDRESS
(— STRONG) STEEL FASTEN FORTIFY
(— STUPID) MOIDER STULTIFY
(— SUITABLE) ADAPT
(— SURE) SEE INSURE
(— TIPSY) FLUSTER
(— TRANSITION TO) MODULATE
(— UP) UP COOK FORM SPELL INDITE SETTLE ANALYZE COMPACT COMPOSE COMPUTE CONCOCT CONFECT FASHION COMPOUND COMPRISE DISPENSE
(— UP ACCOUNTS) BREVE
(— USE OF) FEE BUSK APPLY AVAIL BROOK SERVE SPEND EMPLOY EXECUTE IMPROVE UTILIZE
(— VIBRANT SOUND) CHIRR
(— VOID) ABATE ANNUL
(— WAR) WARRAY
(— WET) DRAGGLE
(— WHISTLING NOISE) WHEW
(— WHITE) BLANCH BLEACH CANDIFY
(— WORSE) IMPAIR PEJORATE
(PREF.) POETICO POETO
(SUFF.) EN FECT FEIT FIC(AL)(ATE)(ATION)(ATIVE)(ATOR) (ATORY)(E)(ENCE)(ENT)(IAL)(IARY) (IENT) FIER FIQUE FY IFY POEIA POESIS POIESIS POIETIC
MAKE-BELIEVE BORAK DUMMY ASSUMED PRETENCE
MAKER DOER JACK KNAVE SMITH FACTOR FORGER FORMER WORKER WRIGHT CREATOR DECLARER OPERATOR
(— OF ARROWS) FLETCHER
(— OF BARRELS) COOPER
(— OF POTS) POTTER
(— OF SADDLETREES) FUSTER
(— OF SONGS) BULBUL

(— OF TALLOW) CHANDLER
(DRIP-COFFEE —) MACCHINETTA
(SUFF.) STER STRESS
MAKESHIFT JURY RUDE JERRY
TOUSY BEWITH CUTCHA KUTCHA
APOLOGY JACKLEG STOPGAP
RESOURCE TIMENOGUY
MAKEUP FACE BUILD GETUP
HABIT PAINT ROUGE SETUP
SHAPE FACIES FORMAT ANATOMY
CONSIST FEATURE EYELINER
PHYSIQUE TRAVESTY
MAQUILLAGE
MAKING FACT
(SUFF.) FACIENT
FACT(ION)(IVE)(ORY)
MALABAR BAY
MALABAR ALMOND KAMANI
ALMENDRO
MALACEAE POMACEAE PYRACEAE
MALADJUSTMENT SCAR
MALADROIT ILL INEPT AWKWARD
UNHANDY BUNGLING
MALADY AMOK EVIL MORB CAUSE
GRIEF ONCOME AILMENT DISEASE
ILLNESS DISORDER MISCHIEF
SICKNESS
(SUFF.) (— ARISING FROM) ITIS
MALAGASY LEMURIAN
MALAGASY REPUBLIC (SEE
MADAGASCAR)
MALAGIGI (COUSIN OF —) RINALDO
MALAPROPISM SLIPSLOP
MALAR JUGAL
MALARIA AGUE MIASMA SHAKES
QUARTAN PALUDISM
(— PARASITE) VIVAX
MALARIAL PALUDAL PALUDOSE
PALUDOUS

MALAWI
CAPITAL: LILONGWE
COIN: KWACHA TAMBALA
FORMER CAPITAL: ZOMBA
FORMER NAME: NYASALAND
HIGHLANDS: SHIRE
LAKE: NYASA
LANGUAGE: YAO CEWA BANTU
  NGONI TONGA NYANJA
  TUMBUKA
MOUNTAIN: MLANJE
PEOPLE: YAO BANTU CHEWA
  NGURU NYANJA
RIVER: SHIRE
TOWN: DOWA CHOLO MZUZU
  NCHEU ZOMBA KARONGA
  BLANTYRE LILONGWE
VALLEY: RIFT

MALAY AMOK ASIL AMUCK BAJAU
ILOCO JAKUN MANOBO ILOKANO
MALAYAN (— TREE) TERAP
MALAY APPLE OHIA JAMBO
KAVIKA

MALAYSIA
CAPITAL: KUALALUMPUR
COIN: TRA TRAH
ISLAND: ARU GOA KAI OBI OMA
  ALOR BALI GAGA JAVA MUNA
  MURU SULU AMBON BANDA
  BOHOL BUTON CERAM LUZON
  MISOL PANAY SANGI SUMBA

TIMOR WETAR BANGKA
  BOEFON BOEROE BORNEO
  BUTUNG FLORES LOMBOK
  MADURA PELENG SANGIR
  TALAUR WAIGEU AMBOINA
  CELEBES JAMDENA MINDORO
  MOROTAI PALAWAN SALAJAR
  SALWATI SUMATRA SUMBAWA
  BELITONG DJAILOLO TANIMBAR
ISTHMUS: KRA
LANGUAGE: TAGALOG
MOUNTAIN: BULU NIUT RAJA
  MURJO NIAPA LEUSER SLAMET
  BINAIJA RINDJANI
PEOPLE: ATA BAJAU SEMANG
  BISAYAN TAGALOG VISAYAN
RIVER: KUTAI PERAK BARITO
  PAHANG
STATE: KEDAH PERAK SABAH
  JOHORE PAHANG PENANG
  PERLIS MALACCA SARAWAK
TOWN: IPOH DAVAO ILOILO
  KANGAR KUPANG MANADO
  KUANTAN KUCHING MALACCA
  SANDAKAN SEREMBAN
WEIGHT: TAEL WANG TAMPANG

MALCHAM (FATHER OF —)
SHAHARAHIM
(MOTHER OF —) HODESH
MALCHIAH (FATHER OF —) HARIM
PAROSH RECHAB
MALCHIEL (FATHER OF —) BERIAH
MALCHIRAM (FATHER OF —)
JEHOIACHIN
MALCHISHUA (FATHER OF —) SAUL
MALCONTENT FRONDEUR
MALDIVES (CAPITAL OF —) MALE
MALE HE DOG HIM MAN BUCK
BULL COCK JACK ADULT MANLY
SPEAR JOHNNY MANFUL MASCLE
VIRILE LALAQUI MANKIND
MANLIKE MANNISH PURUSHA
(— OF ANIMALS) TOM BUCK BULL
JACK STUD STALLION
(EFFEMINATE —) NANCE
(GELDED —) GALT
(YOUNG —) GROOM
(PREF.) ANDR(O)
(SUFF.) ANDRIA ANDROUS
ANDRY
MALECITE ETCHEMIN
MALEDICTION BAN WISH CURSE
MALISON ANATHEMA
MALEFACTOR BADDY FELON
BADDIE CULPRIT CRIMINAL
EVILDOER
MALEFIC TAKING
MALEFICENT BALEFUL
MALELEEL (FATHER OF —) CAINAN
MALEO MEGAPOD
MALE ORCHIS CUCKOO CROWTOE
CULLION PURPLES RAGWORT
CROWFOOT
MALEVOLENCE SPITE ENMITY
GRUDGE HATRED MALICE
RANCOR SPLEEN MALIGNITY
MALEVOLENT ILL EVIL FELL
MALIGN HATEFUL HOSTILE
SPITEFUL RANCOROUS
MALFEASANCE MISCONDUCT
MALPRACTICE
MALFORMATION CURL ERROR

HEMITERY MONSTROSITY
(— OF CARNATION) TWITTER
(— OF FRUIT) CATFACE
MALFORMED SHAMBLE
MALFUNCTION GLITCH

MALI
ANCIENT CITY: TIMBUKTU
CAPITAL: BAMAKO
FORMER NAME: FRENCHSUDAN
LAKE: DO DEBO GAROU KORAROU
LANGUAGE: DOGON DYULA
  MANDE MARKA PEULH
  BAMBARA MALINKE SENOUFO
  SONGHAI
MOUNTAIN: MINA MANDING
PEOPLE: MOOR PEUL TUAREG
  BAMBARA MALINKE SONGHAI
  SENOULFO
RIVER: BANI BAGOE BAKOY NIGER
  BAOULE AZAOUAK SENEGAL
TOWN: GAO SAN KATI KITA NARA
  BAMBA KAYES MOPTI NIONO
  NIORO SEGOU SIKASSO

MALICE DOLE ENVY HAIN PIQUE
SPITE VENOM VIRUS ENMITY
GRUDGE RANCOR SPLEEN
DESPITE AMBITION MALIGNITY
MALEVOLENCE
MALICIOUS SHREW TEENY BITTER
DOGGED MALIGN WANTON
HATEFUL HEINOUS LEERING
SPITOUS VICIOUS CANKERED
NARQUOIS SINISTER SPITEFUL
VENOMOUS VIPEROUS
MALIGN ILL FOUL ABUSE LIBEL
WRONG BEWRAY DEFAME REVILE
VILIFY ASPERSE DEPRAVE
HURTFUL SLANDER BLASPHEME
MALIGNANCY FEROCITY
MALIGNANT EVIL ATTRY BLACK
FELON FERAL SWART ATTERY
MALIGN BALEFUL ENVIOUS
HATEFUL HELLISH PEEVISH
REPTILE VICIOUS WARLOCK
CANKERED SHREWISH SPITEFUL
VENOMOUS VIPEROUS VIRULENT
WRATHFUL RANCOROUS
MALIGNITY GALL LIVER VENOM
VIRUS HATRED MALICE RANCOR
DESPITE
MALINGER MIKE DODGE SKULK
MALINGERER SCONCER
MALL WALK ALLEE
MALLARD TWISTER
(FLOCK OF —S) SORD SUTE
PADDLING
MALLEABLE MILD SOFT DUCTILE
PLASTIC BATTABLE
MALLEIN MORVIN
MALLEMUCK MOLLIE MALMARSH
MALLET MALL MAUL MELL GAVEL
BEATER BEETLE DRIVER HAMMER
DRESSER FLOGGER STRIKER
PLOWMELL
(— FOR BREAKING CLODS) BILDER
(CURRIER'S —) MACE
(HATTER'S —) BEATER
(PAVER'S —) TUP
(PREF.) MALLEI MALLEO SPHYRA
MALLEUS HAMMER OSSICLE
PLECTRUM

MALLOTHI (FATHER OF —) HEMAN
MALLOW MAW DOCK HOCK ALTEA
KOKIO MALVA MAUVE TAUPE
CHEESE ESCOBA GEMAUVE
ABUTILON PIEPRINT
MALLUCH (FATHER OF —) BANI
MALMSEY MALVASIA MALVOISIE
MALNUTRITION CACHEXY
CACHEXIA CACOTROPHY
MALODOROUS GAMY HIGH NOSY
RANK FETID SMELLY VIROSE
VIROUS NOISOME
MALT WORT
(GROUND —) GRIST
(REMAINS OF —) DRAFF
MALTA (ANCIENT NAME OF —)
MELITA
(CAPITAL OF —) VALLETTA
(ISLAND OF —) GOZO COMINO
(TOWN OF —) QORMI RABAT
HAMRUN SLIEMA XAGHRA
ZABBAR BIRKIRKARA
MALTASE GLUCASE
MALTHA BREA
MALTHOUSE MALTING
MALTOSE AMYLON
MALTREAT MAUL ABUSE DIGHT
DEFOUL DEMEAN HESPIL HUSPEL
MISUSE THREAT BEDEVIL
MISGUIDE MANHANDLE
MALTREATMENT ABUSE
MALVA DOCK MALLOW
MAMAMU MU
MAMBA COBRA ELAPOID
MAMMA MA MOM MAMA WIFE
MOMMA WOMAN MOTHER
MAMMAL OX ASS BAT CAT COW
DOG FOX PIG YAK BEAR BOAR
COON DEER GOAT HARE LION
LYNX MINK MOLE PUMA SEAL
ZEBU BEAST BISON CAMEL COATI
COYPU GENET HORSE HYENA
LEMUR LLAMA MOOSE OKAPI
OTTER PANDA RATEL SABLE
SHEEP SHREW SKUNK SLOTH
SWINE TAPIR TIGER WHALE ZORIL
ALPACA ANIMAL BADGER
COUGAR CULPEO DESMAN
DUGONG FISHER FOUSSA
GOPHER GRISON JAGUAR
MARTEN MONKEY OCELOT
TENREC VICUNA WALRUS
WOMBAT BUFFALO CARIBOU
DOLPHIN ECHIDNA GIRAFFE
GLUTTON GUANACO HIPPOID
HUANACO MANATEE OPOSSUM
PECCARY POLECAT PRIMATE
RACCOON SUCKLER SURICAT
TARSIER TYLOPOD WILDCAT
AARDVARK AARDWOLF
ANTELOPE BANXRING CACOMIXL
CREODONT ELEPHANT FALANAKA
HEDGEHOG KINKAJOU MAMMIFER
PANGOLIN PINNIPED REINDEER
SQUIRREL PRONGHORN
RHINOCEROS
MAMMALIA MASTOZOA
MAMMEE ABRICO ABRICOT
MAMMILLA PAP TEAT NIPPLE
MAMMOTH HUGE LARGE GIGANTIC
MAMRE (BROTHER OF —) ANER
ESHCOL
MAN BO HE BOY GEE GUY HIM LAD

TAO WAT WER BUCK CHAL CHAP COVE DICK EARL GENT GOME HOMO JACK JONG MALE RINK TULK BERNE BIMBO BIPED BLOKE CHURL COVEY CULLY FORCE FREKE GROOM GUEST HEART HOMME HORSE JOKER SEGGE SWAIN WIGHT BIMANE CHIELD CUFFIN FELLOW HOMBRE MANTZU WEPMAN BIMANUS HOMONID KINSMAN MANKIND

(— AFFECTING FOREIGN WAYS) MACARONI

(— DRESSED AS WOMAN) BESSY MALINCHE

(— IN DEBT) DYVOUR

(— IN PRIVATE STATION) IDIOT

(— IN TUG-OF-WAR) ANCHOR

(— LEADING 12TH NIGHT) BEAN

(— OF ALL WORK) MOZO

(— OF AUTHORITY) AGHA SEIGNIOR

(— OF BEAUTY) APOLLO

(— OF BRASS) TALOS

(— OF GREAT WEALTH) NABOB

(— OF HIGH RANK) CHAM KHAN THAKUR GRANDEE

(— OF SUBSTANCE) IDLEMAN

(— OF THE COMMON PEOPLE) JACK

(— OF VIGOR) WYE

(— OF VIOLENCE) RABIATOR

(— OF WAR) ANDREW CARAVEL CRUISER

(— TO MAN) SINGLE

(ARTIFICIAL —) GOLEM

(BACKGAMMON —) BLOT BUILDER

(BALD —) PILGARLIC

(BEST —) BRIDEMAN PARANYMPH

(BIG —) COB BRUISER MUGWUMP

(BRISK —) SPARK

(CASTRATED —) SPADO EUNUCH

(CHIEF —) FOREMAN OPTIMATE

(CHURLISH —) NABAL BODACH

(CLEANING —) BUSBOY

(COMMON —) CARL STREET YEOMAN

(COVETOUS —) HUNKS

(CRAFTY —) FOX

(CRUEL —) OGRE BRUTE

(DISAGREEABLE —) GLEYDE

(DISLIKED —) CUT

(DISSOLUTE —) RAKE

(ECCENTRIC —) GEEZER

(EDUCATED —) EFFENDI

(EFFEMINATE —) DILDO FAIRY NANCE PUNCE SISSY JESSIE COCKNEY MEACOCK MIDWIFE MILKSOP ANDROGYN MOLLYCODDLE

(END —) BONES BRAKE

(ENLISTED —) GI SNIPE AIDMAN AIRMAN KEEPER STORES ARMORER STRIKER SONARMAN

(ENTIRE —) EGO

(EXTINCT —) TEPEXPAN

(FAITHFUL —) TRUEMAN

(FANCY —) PONCE

(FASHIONABLE —) TOUPET ELEGANT FOPLING GALLANT

(FIRST —) ASK ADAM ASKR TIKI FOREMAN

(FLASHILY-DRESSED —) LAIR

(FOPPISH —) BLOOD

(FREE —) LIBER

(GRAY-HAIRED —) GRIZZLE

(GREAT —) VAVASOR

(HARDHEARTED —) KNARK

(HAUGHTY —) BASHAW

(HOLDUP —) FOOTPAD

(HOLY —) SADHU SAINT SANNYASI

(HONORS —) WRANGLER

(IDEAL —) SUPERMAN

(IMMORAL —) REP

(INEFFECTUAL —) DUFFER

(INSANE —) FURIOSO

(LADY'S —) FOPLING DAMMARET

(LAME —) BACACH

(LEARNED —) ULEMA LAMDAN OLLAMH PUNDIT SAVANT SOPHIST

(LECHEROUS —) SATYR

(LEWD —) BROTHEL

(LIAISON —) COURIER

(LITERARY —) GIGADIBS

(LITTLE —) MANNET SHRIMP MANNIKIN

(LUSTFUL —) GOAT

(MAINTENANCE —) CAMPMAN

(MARRIED —) HUSBAND BENEDICT

(MEDICINE —) PEAI DOCTOR SHAMAN ANGAKOK

(MEEK —) MOSES

(MIGHTY —) SAMSON

(ODD-JOB —) JOEY

(OLD —) HAG OLD BOOL CUFF GAFF CRONE DOBBY UNCLE BODACH DUFFER FATHER GAFFER NESTOR GERONTE STARETS ECKEHART VELYARDE PATRIARCH

(OLD-CLOTHES —) POCO

(ONE-ARMED —) WINGY

(ONE-EYED —) ARIMASP

(OVERFASTIDIOUS —) DUDE

(PARTY —) SIDESMAN

(PRIMITIVE —) URMENSCH

(PRINCIPAL —) HERO TOPARCH

(RASH —) HOTSPUR

(RICH —) DIVES CROESUS

(RIGHTEOUS —) SADDIK

(RIGHT-HAND —) HENCHMAN

(SERVING —) GARCON

(SOUND-EFFECTS —) CRAWK

(STERN —) GRIMSIRE

(STRAIGHT —) STOOGE

(STRONG —) KWASIND

(STRONG-ARM —) HOOD GORILLA

(STUPID —) SUBMAN

(THICKSET —) GRUB KNAR SPUD

(TOUGH —) KNAR

(UNEMPLOYED —) BATLAN

(UTILITY —) JUMPER

(VICIOUS —) YAHOO

(WHITE —) BOSTON BUCKRA PAKEHA CACHILA

(WHITE — LIVING WITH ABORIGINE) COMBO

(WILD —) WOODMAN WOODWOSE

(WISE —) NAB HAKAM SABIO SOLON SOPHY NESTOR WIZARD SOLOMON TOHUNGA

(WIZENED —) GNOME

(WOMANISH —) JENNY

(WRETCHED —) CAITIFF

(YOUNG —) BOY LAD JONG PUNK YOUTH BOCHUR DAMSEL EPHEBE KNIGHT BOUCHAL BUCKEEN YOUNKER COCKEREL SPRINGAL

(PREF.) ANDR(O) ANTHROP(O) HOMI(NI)

(SUFF.) ANDRIA ANDROUS ANDRY ENGRO VIR(ATE)

MAN-ABOUT-TOWN FLANEUR

MANABOZHO MICHABOU WINABOJO

MANACLE BAND BOND DARBY HAMPER TIRRET SHACKLE HANDCUFF HANDLOCK

(PL.) IRONS CHAINS

MANAGE DO GET MAN RUN BEAR BOSS CURB FEND HACK HOLD KEEP LEAD MAKE RULE TEND TOOL WIND WORK BROOK CARRY DIGHT FORTH FRAME GUIDE MAYNE ORDER SHIFT SPEND STEER SWING WIELD CONVEY DEMEAN DEVISE DIRECT FETTLE GOVERN HANDLE INTEND MANURE TEMPER AGITATE CONDUCT DISPOSE EXECUTE FINAGLE HUSBAND MINSTER OFFICER OPERATE SOLICIT STEWARD CONTRIVE ENGINEER NEGOTIATE

(— AWKWARDLY) FOOZLE

(— CLUMSILY) KEVEL

(— SKILLFULLY) MANIPULATE

(— TO BEAR) AFFORD

MANAGEABLE EASY YARE BANTAM DOCILE WIELDY DUCTILE FLEXIBLE YIELDING

MANAGEMENT CARE HEEL WORK CHARGE CONDUCT CONTROL ECONOMY GESTION RUNNING CARRIAGE DEMEANOR ENGINERY MANAGERY MANEUVER REGIMENT STEERAGE STEERING

(DOMESTIC —) MENAGE HUSBANDRY

(GOOD —) EUTAXY

(SKILLFUL —) PRACTICE PRACTISE

MANAGER BOSS DOER AGENT DAROGA DEPUTY PURSER SYNDIC AMILDAR CURATOR ERENACH HUSBAND STEWARD WIELDER AUMILDAR DIRECTOR DISPOSER ENGINEER HERENACH INSTITOR

(— OF ENTERTAINERS) ROADIE

(— OF FARM) HIND GRIEVE

(ASSISTANT —) CAPORAL

(MINE —) CAPTAIN

(POLITICAL —) FUGLEMAN

(SUFF.) EER

MANAHATH (FATHER OF —) SHOBAL

MANAKIN PIPRA

MAN-AT-ARMS KNIGHT

MANATEE COWFISH HOGFISH MERMAID LAMANTIN MUTILATE SIRENIAN

MANBARKLAK JARANA KAKARAL

MANCALA WARI

MANCHU SHERRY

MANCHURIA (CHINESE NAME FOR —) MANCHOW

(PENINSULA OF —) LIAOTUNG

(PROVINCE OF —) JILIN LIAONING HEILONGJIANG

(RIVER OF —) AMUR LIAO YALU ARGUN USSURI SUNGARI

MANDAEAN SABAEAN

MANDANE (FATHER OF —) ASTYAGES

(HUSBAND OF —) CAMBYSES

(SON OF —) CYRUS

MANDARIN TOWKAY CHINESE

MANDARIN ORANGE SATSUMA

MANDATE BREVE ORDER BEHEST CHARGE DECREE FIRMAN BIDDING COMMAND PRECEPT PROCESS MANDAMUS MANDATUM WARRANTY

(— OF GOD) JUDGMENT

MANDATORY OBLIGATORY

MANDIBLE BEAK JOWL SETA RAMUS JAWBONE GNATHITE

(— PART) MALA

MANDINGO MANDE MALINKE WANGARA

MANDOLIN OUD MANDORA

MANDRAKE ALRAUN DUDAIM

MANDREL BALL STUD SLEEVE CHEMISE SPINDLE TRIBLET

MANDRICARDO (BELOVED OF —) ANGELICA

(FATHER OF —) AGRICAN

(SLAYER OF —) ORLANDO

MANDRILL MAIMON MORMON

MANE JUBA MONE CREST PITRI ENCOLURE

MAN-EATER REQUIN REQUIEM

MANEGE TRAIN

MANEUVER PLAY TURN WISE GAMBIT JOCKEY MANURE PESADE VRILLE FINAGLE FINESSE ARTIFICE DEMARCHE ENGINEER EXERCISE STRATEGY WINDLASS

(— IN AUTO RACING) SLINGSHOT

(— IN SPACE) DOCK

(— IN SURFING) CUTBACK

(— OF MOTORCYCLE OR BICYCLE) WHEELIE

(- GENTLY) EASE

(AERIAL —) BUNT LOOP SPIN FISHTAIL WINGOVER

(BULLFIGHTING —) VERONICA

(ILLEGAL —) GAME

(ROCK-CLIMBING —) LAYBACK

(SKIING —) SNOWPLOW

(WRESTLING —) ESCAPE BUTTOCK

MANEUVERABLE YARE

MANEUVERING FINESSE FLANKING

MANGE ITCH REEF SCAB CANKER DARTARS SCABIES

MANGER BIN BUNK CRIB HECK STALL CRATCH

MANGLE MAR HACK MOUTH BRUISE GARBLE HACKLE IRONER MAGGLE MURDER MAMMOCK LACERATE MUTILATE

MANGO DIKA AMHAR AMINI BAUNO AMCHOOR CARABAO PAHUTAN

(POINT OF —) NAK

MANGOSTEEN SANTOL GARCINIA

MANGROVE BACAO GORAN MANGLE MYRTAL BACAUAN CERIOPS COURIDA HANGALAI LANGARAI

MANGUE CHOLUTECA CHOROTEGA

MANGY SCABBY ROINISH SCABETIC

MANHANDLE MESS ROUGH SCRAG

MANHATTAN TRANSFER (AUTHOR OF —) DOSPASSOS
(CHARACTER IN —) BUD GUS JOE HERF JOHN RUTH STAN CONGO ELLEN EMERY EMILE HARRY JIMMY SUSIE GEORGE MCNIEL NELLIE OKEEFE PRYNNE BALDWIN HARLAND MERIVALE PEARLINE THATCHER GOLDWEISER OGLETHORPE
MANHOOD ADAMHOOD
MANIA RAGE CRAZE FUROR FRENZY DELIRIUM HYSTERIA INSANITY CACOETHES
MANIAC KILLER MADMAN FANATIC LUNATIC
MANIFEST HAVE NUDE OPEN RIFE SENE SHOW APERT CLEAR FRANK GROSS KITHE NAKED OVERT PLAIN PROVE SPEAK SUTEL ARRANT ATTEST COUTHE EVINCE EXTANT GRAITH LIQUID OSTEND PATENT PHANIC APPROVE BETOKEN CONFESS DECLARE EVIDENT EXHIBIT EXPRESS OBVIOUS SIGNIFY VISIBLE APPARENT DISCLOSE DISCOVER INDICATE PALPABLE PROCLAIM
(NOT —) LATENT
(PREF.) PHANER(O) PHANTA(SMO) PHANTO
MANIFESTATION ACT SON BEAM COMA SIGN GLINT AVATAR COMING EFFECT OSTENT ADVANCE DISPLAY EXPRESS OUTSIDE SHOWING EPIPHANY MANIFEST
(BARELY PERCEPTIBLE —) SCINTIL
(BRIEF —) GLEAM
(DIVINE —) SPIRIT SHEKINAH
(HORRIBLE —) CHIMAERA
(MORAL —) SOUL
(VAGUE —) GLIMMER
(SUFF.) PHANE PHANOUS PHANT PHANY
MANIFESTLY WITTERLY
MANIFESTO PLACARD
MANIFOLD MANY TURRET VARIOUS FELEFOLD MANYFOLD MULTIPLE MULTIPLEX REPLICATE
(SUFF.) PLOID
MANIKIN ECORCHE PANTINE PHANTOM HOMUNCIO HOMUNCLE MANNIKIN
MANILA HEMP ABACA
MANIOC CASSAVA CATELLA MANDIOCA
MANIPLE FANON ORALE FANNEL COMPANY HANDFUL SUDARIUM
MANIPULATE COG COAX COOK DIAL FAKE HAND STIR TOOL CROOK HUMOR KNEAD SHAPE TREAT WIELD CHIVVY GOVERN HANDLE JOCKEY MANAGE WANGLE SHUFFLE
(— BY DECEPTIVE MEANS) RIG
MANIPULATION PASS JUGGLERY MANAGERY
MANITO ORENDA POKUNT MANITOU TAMANOAS
MANITOBA (CAPITAL OF —) WINNIPEG
(RIVER OF —) RED SEAL SWAN NELSON ROSEAU SOURIS PEMBINA CHURCHILL SASKACHEWAN
(TOWN OF —) CARMAN BRANDON DAUPHIN KILLARNEY SWANRIVER
MANKIND MAN FLESH SHEEP WORLD BIMANA SPECIES HUMANITY UNIVERSE MORTALITY
MANLIKE MALE MANLY MANNISH HOMINOID
MANLINESS ARETE VIRTUS MANSHIP
MANLY BOLD MALE HARDY MANNY DARING VIRILE MANLIKE
MAN-MADE CULTURAL SYNTHETIC
MANNA TREHALA WINDFALL
MANNER AIR BAT JET LAT WAY FORM GAET GARB GATE KIND MAKE MIEN MODE RATE SORT THEW TOUR WISE WONE GUISE LATES SHAPE STYLE TENUE TRICK COURSE CUSTOM METHOD MISTER STRAIN ADDRESS AMENITY FASHION QUALITY QUOMODO CARAPACE DEMEANOR LANGUAGE
(— OF APPROACH) ABORD
(— OF DOING) ACTION
(— OF HANDLING) HAND
(— OF MAKING ANYTHING) FACTURE
(— OF SITTING) ASANA
(— OF SPEAKING) SLUR SOUGH ACCENT GRAMMAR PARLANCE
(— OF WALKING) STEP
(AFFECTED —) AIR
(AMUSING —) DROLLERY
(ARROGANT —) BRAG HAUTEUR
(FORBIDDING —) SHELL
(FORMAL —) STARCH
(HABITUAL —) SONG
(OUTWARD —) TOUR FRONT
(SMOOTH —) JAPAN
(SWAGGERING —) SIDE PANACHE
(UNUSUAL —) SINGULARITY
(USUAL —) HABIT
(PL.) ADDRESS CORNERS HAVINGS BREEDING
(SUFF.) WISE
(AFTER THE — OF) FASHION
(IN A —) LY
(IN THE — OF) IC(AL)
MANNERED CUTE MORATE THEWED
MANNERISM POSE TRICK IDIASM
(PL.) DAPS
MANNERLY CIVIL POLITE
MANNERS MORES HAVANCE HAVINGS BEAUETRY BREEDING
MANNITOL MANNITE PUNICIN
MANOAH (SON OF —) SAMSON
MAN-OF-WAR CARAVEL
MAN-OF-WAR FISH PASTOR
MANON (CHARACTER IN —) MANON GRIEUX LESCAUT BRETIGNY
(COMPOSER OF —) MASSENET
MANON LESCAUT (CHARACTER IN —) MANON GRIEUX GERONTE
(COMPOSER OF —) PUCCINI
MANOR HAM HOF BURY HALL

TOWN VILL BARONY COMMOTE MANSION LORDSHIP TOWNSHIP
MANPOWER BRAWN LABOR
MANROOT IPOMOEA
MANROPE LIMMER
MANSERVANT (ALSO SEE SERVANT) LAD MOZO GROOM VALET ANDREW BUTLER TEABOY
MANSFIELD PARK (AUTHOR OF —) AUSTEN
(CHARACTER IN —) TOM MARY WARD FANNY HENRY JULIA MARIA PRICE YATES EDMUND NORRIS THOMAS BERTRAM CRAWFORD RUSHWORTH
MANSION DOME SEAT HOTEL HOUSE MANSE SIEGE TOWER CASTLE HARBOR HOSTEL CHATEAU
(— OF THE MOON) ALNATH
MANSLAUGHTER BLOOD FELONY HOMICIDE
MANTEL CLAVY CLAVEL
MANTELET MANTA MANTLE MANTLET GALAPAGO
MANTELPIECE BRACE PAREL CLAVEL MANTEL MANTLING
MANTICORE MONTEGRE
MANTIS CAGN RACER REARER MANTOID PROPHET
MANTIS CRAB SQUILLA
MANTLE CAPA HOSE PALL REAM ROBE CLOAK CREAM FROCK JABUL LAMBA PALLA TUNIC CAMAIL CAPOTE KHIRKA KIRTLE ROCHET SLAVIN SOLMAN TABARD CHLAMYS CHRISOM CHUDDAR FERIDJI MANTEAU PAENULA PALLIUM SLEEVES WHITTLE WRAPPER BARRACAN CHRYSOME MANTELET REGOLITH RICINIUM STOCKING
(PREF.) CHLAMYD(O) PHARO
MANTLEROCK REGOLITH
MANTO (DAUGHTER OF —) TISIPHONE
(FATHER OF —) HERCULES TIRESIAS
(HUSBAND OF —) RHACIUS
(SON OF —) OCNUS MOPSUS AMPHILOCHUS
MANTRA OM DHARANI GAYATRI MANTRAM SAVITRI
MANTUA MANTY SEMAR
MANTZU MIAOTZE
MANUAL VADY COACH GREAT TUTOR PORTAS CAMBIST CEMBALO DIDACHE MANUARY BOMBARDE HANDBOOK KEYBOARD ORDINARY PORTHORS SYNOPSIS
(MAGICIAN'S —) GRIMOIRE
(NAVIGATION —) BOWDITCH
MANUAO IAO
MANUBRIUM HYPOSTOME
MANUFACTURE COIN FAKE MAKE FORGE PERFORM PRODUCE WORKING BOOKWORK
(— OF LIQUOR OR DRUGS) ABKARI
(ILLEGAL —) COINING
MANUFACTURED STORE
MANUFACTURER BRAND MAKER WRIGHT DISKERY

SPINNER SUPPLIER
MANUMIT FREE LIBERATE
MANURE HOT MIG DUNG LIME MUCK SAUR SOIL TATH FECES GUANO MIXEN FULZIE SEASON SLEECH COMPOST FOLDING GOODING POUDRET DRESSING WORTHING
MANURED BONED
MANUS HAND
MANUSCRIPT CODEX FLIMSY MATTER SCRIPT UNCIAL CURSIVE PANDECT PAPYRUS PINTURA WITNESS EXEMPLAR PARCHMENT
MANX CAT RUMPY
MANX SHEARWATER CREW PUFFIN SCRABE SCRABER
MANY TEN FELE MUCH SERE FORTY GREAT MAINT MOULT OODLES TWENTY ENDLESS JILLION SEVERAL VARIOUS MANIFOLD COUNTLESS
(BEING —) NUMEROUS
(GOOD —) HANTLE
(GREAT —) MORT RAFF SWITH
(PREF.) MULT(I) PLURI POLY
(HOW —) POSO QUOT
MANYATTA KRAAL
MANY-COLORED BONT
MANY-HANDED BRIAREAN
MANYPLIES FARDEL OMASUM
MANYROOT RUELLIA
MANY-SIDED VARIOUS
MAO NEHRU
MAOCH (SON OF —) ACHISH
MAORI (— IMAGE) TIKI
(— LAW) UTU
(— VILLAGE) PA PAH KAINGA
(NOT —) PAKEMA
MAP KEY CARD DICE PLAT PLOT CARTE CENTO CHART DRAFT INSET QUART STILL DRAUGHT GRAPHIC CARTGRAM GATEFOLD PLATFORM
(PREF.) CARTO CHARTO
MAPAU MAPLE MATIPO TARATA PIRIPIRI
MAPLE MAZER DOGWOOD SYCAMORE WINGSEED
(FLOWERING —) ABUTILON
(GROVE OF —) SAPBUSH
MAR BLOT SCAR SMIT SNIP BLOOM BOTCH SHEND SPILL SPOIL BLOTCH DEFACE DEFEAT DEFORM EFFACE IMPAIR INJURE MANGLE BLEMISH DISGRACE
MARABOU STORK ARGALA MORABIT ADJUTANT
MARANAO LANAO
MARASMUS MARCOR ATHREPSIA
MARAUD RAID DACOIT PICKEER PILLAGE
MARAUDER TORY BANDIT BUMMER LOOTIE PIRATE CATERAN LADRONE
(PL.) BLACKS
MARAUDING BANDITRY OUTRIDING
MARBLE MIB MIG PEA POT TAW ALLY BOOL BOWL DUCK DUMP MARL AGATE AGGIE ALLEY BONCE COMMY IMMIE IVORY LINER PUREY RANCE DOGGLE

MARMOR MARVEL MIGGLE PARIAN PEEWEE STEELY CARRARA CIPOLIN GLASSIE GRIOTTE KNICKER PARAGON PITCHER SHOOTER BROCATEL DOLOMITE KNUCKLER
(BLACK —) JET
(IMITATION —) SCAGLIOLA
(SIENA —) BROCATELLO
(PL.) TAW BOWLS PLUMPS HUNDRED
MARBLED MIRLY
MARCH FILE HIKE LIDE MARK MUSH SLOG ROUTE TRACE TRINE TROOP WALTZ DEFILE DOUBLE PARADE REVIEW DEBOUCH STRETCH FOOTSLOG PROGRESS
(— BEHIND) COVER
(— IN FRONT OF) LEAD
(— OBLIQUELY) INCLINE
(DAY'S —) ETAPE
(PL.) FRONTIER
MARCHING (— UP) ANABASIS
MARCHIONESS MARCHESA MARQUISE
MARCOT GOOTE
MARCOTTAGE GOOTEE
MARE SEA YAD YADE YAUD GILLIE GILLOT GRASNI HUNTRESS
MARE'S-TAIL HIPPURID
MARGARET MEG META MARGET MARGOT GRETCHEN
MARGATE PORGY
MARGAY TIGER
MARGIN HEM RIM VAT BANK BRIM BROW CURB EDGE FOLD HAIR INCH LIMB LIST RAND BRINK EAVES MARGE VERGE BORDER FRINGE LABRUM LACING CUSHION DRAUGHT MARGENT SELVAGE HAIRLINE
(— OF CARAPACE) DOUBLURE
(— OF CIRCLE) LIMB
(— OF LIP) PROLABIUM
(— OF PAGE) BACK
(— OF SAFETY) LEEWAY
(— OF SHELL) LABRUM LIMBUS
(— OF SUPERIORITY) LEAD
(— OF WING) TERMEN
(—S OF HERD) SWING
(NARROW —) ACE NECK
(SEA —) COAST
MARGOSA NIM NEEM NEEMBA
MARGRAVE RUDIGER MARKGRAF
MARIA (FATHER OF —) OCTAVIO PETROBIUS
(HUSBAND OF —) PETRUCHIO
MARIANA SILYBUM
MARIGOLD GOLD GULL SAMH AZTEC BOOTS GOLDE GOOLS HELIO BACLIN BUDDLE GOLDCUP GOLDING GOLLAND KINGCUP MARYBUD TAGETES
MARIJUANA BOO POT WEED DAGGA GRASS MOOCAH LOCOWEED MARYJANE
(ONE OUNCE OF —) LID
(ONE WHO TAKES —) POTHEAD
(OUNCE OF —) CAN
(PUFF ON — CIGARETTE) TOKE
MARINE JOLLY GALOOT GULPIN GYRENE TOPMAN MARINAL HALIMOUS MARITIME NAUTICAL AEQUOREAL THALASSIC
(PREF.) ENALI(O) THALASS(O) THALASSI(O) THALATTO
MARINER MARINE SAILOR SEALER SEAMAN BUSCARLE SEAFARER WARRENER
(PL.) SEAFOLK
MARINHEIRO ACAJOU
MARIONETTE PUPPY POPPET PUPPET
MARITAL INTIMATE HUSBANDLY
MARITIME MARINE HALIMOUS NAUTICAL
MARJORAM AMARACUS
MARK AIM END HOB HUB MOT POP BELT BLOT BUOY BUTT CHOP CLIP DELE DINT FAZE FIST GOAL KEEL LINE MIND NOTE RIST SCAR SEAR SIGN SMOT SMUT SPOT TEND TEXT TICK VIRE WAND WIND BADGE BOTTU BRAND BREVE CHANT CHECK CLOUD DATUM DITTO DRAFT FLECK FRANK GHOST GRADE HILUM KNIFE LABEL MARCH MARCO MEITH NOKTA POINT PRINT PROOF ROVER SCART SCOPE SCORE SCUFF SPOOR STAMP SWIRL TOKEN TOUCH TRACE TRACK TRACT WATCH WHITE ACCENT ALPIEU BEACON BESPOT BLOTCH BUTTON CARACT DAGGER DAPPLE DENOTE DIRECT INDICE LETTER MARKER NOTICE OBJECT SMUTCH STREAK STRIKE STROKE SUCKER SYMBOL TARGET UPSHOT WICKER WITTER BETOKEN CHARBON COCKSHY DEMERIT DIAMOND DRAUGHT EROTEME EXCUDIT FINMARK IMPRESS IMPRINT INSIGNE KENMARK SCARIFY SERRATE SIGNARY SPECKLE STRIATE SYMPTOM VESTIGE WAYMARK BRACELET CROWFOOT DATEMARK DIASTOLE DISPUNCT EVIDENCE FOOTMARK FOOTSTEP IDENTIFY IDEOGRAM MONUMENT NOTATION
(— A BIRD) BAND
(— AFTER ASSAY) TOUCH
(— AS SPURIOUS) ATHETIZE
(— BY BURNING) CHAR
(— BY CUTTING) SCRIBE
(— BY PLOWING) STRIKE
(— CROSSWISE) CRANK
(— DENOTING CORRUPT PASSAGE) OBELUS
(— DIRECTIONS) ADDRESS
(— IN ARCHERY) CLOUT HOYLE ROVER WHITE
(— IN BOOK) PRESSMARK
(— IN CANON) LEAD
(— IN CURLING) TEE COCK
(— IN QUOITS) MOT
(— INDICATING CONTRACTION) CORONIS
(— INDICATING DIRECTION) ARROW
(— OF ACKNOWLEDGEMENT) ACCOLADE
(— OF DISGRACE) STAIN STIGMA
(— OF DISHONOR) ABATEMENT
(— OF DISTINCTION) BELT
(— OF ESTEEM) LAUREL GARLAND
(— OF OFFICE) SEAL
(— OF OWNERSHIP) SWANMARK
(— OF PURITY) HALLMARK
(— OF REFERENCE) OBELISK
(— OF SIGNATURE) CROSS
(— OF SUPERIORITY) BELL
(— OF WEAVER) KEEL
(— OFF) SUBTEND
(— OFF LAND) FEER PHEER
(— ON ANIMAL'S FACE) BLAZE STRIPE
(— ON CHART) VIGIA
(— ON EXAM) PASS
(— ON FEATHER) BAR SPANGLE
(— ON FOREHEAD) KUMKUM
(— ON PENNSYLVANIA BARNS) HEXAFOOS
(— ON SHEEP) SMIT BUIST
(— ON SHIP) SURMARK
(— ON SKIN) PLOT CREASE
(— ON STAMP) CONTROL
(— OUT) RUN CANCEL DELINE AIRMARK APPOINT COMPART DESCRIBE
(— OVER GERMAN VOWEL) UMLAUT
(— OVER LETTER N) TILDE
(— OVER LONG VOWELS) MACRON
(— RIGS) FEER
(— SHEEP OR CATTLE) BASTE BUIST DEWLAP
(— TIME) BEAT COUNT
(— TO BE ATTAINED) BOGEY BOGIE
(— TO GUIDE VESSELS) MYTH
(— TO SCARE DEER) SHEWEL
(— TRANSVERSELY) LADDER
(— UNDER LETTER C) CEDILLA
(— WITH LINES) HATCH CAMLET
(— WITH POINTED ROLLER) GRILL
(— WITH RIDGES) RIB
(— WITH STRIPES) WALE STREAM
(— WITH TAR) BASTE
(ACCENT —) VERGE
(ANGULAR —) HOOK
(BALLOT —) SCRATCH
(BOUNDARY —) DOOL MEAR MERE TERM WIKE MEITH STAKE LANDMARK
(CADENCY —) BRISURE
(CANCELLATION —) BUMPER KILLER
(DIACRITICAL —) TIL TILDE TITTLE
(DIRTY —) SMIRCH
(DISTINCTIVE —) BADGE INDICIA
(DISTINGUISHING —) ITEM COCARDE EARMARK INSIGNE
(DOUBLE-DAGGER —) DIESIS
(EASY —) YAP SMELT PIGEON
(EIGHTH —) URE
(EXACT —) NICK
(EXCLAMATION —) SCREAMER
(IDENTIFICATION —) MOLE CREST SPLIT SIGNET WATTLE EARMARK KENMARK LUGMARK COLOPHON
(LOW-WATER —) DATUM
(MAGICAL —) SIGIL
(MERIDIAN —) MIRE
(MUSICAL —) PRESA CORONA
(PARAGRAPH —) PILCROW
(PROOFREADER'S —) STET CARET
(PUNCTUATION —) DASH STOP BRACE BREVE COLON COMMA HYPHEN PERIOD BRACKET DIERESIS ELLIPSIS DIACRITIC SEMICOLON PARENTHESIS
(RED —) HICKEY
(SECTARIAN —) BOTTU TILAKA
(SKATE —) CUSP
(SMALL ROUND —) DOT
(TRAMP'S —) MONICA MONNIKER
(WHITE —) RACHE
(PL.) POINTING
(PREF.) STIGONO
MARKED FAR GREAT SCORED SEVERE SPOTTY COLORED EMINENT MARCATO POINTED SCARRED SPECKED SPOTTED
(— BY COLORED RINGS) AREOLATE
(— BY FURROWS) RIVOSE
(— BY INTELLIGENCE) ABLE
(— BY PROSTRATION) ALGID
(— BY REFINEMENT) ELEGANT
(— BY RIDGES) SERRIED
(— BY SHREWDNESS) ADROIT
(— BY SIMILARITY) AKIN
(— BY SIMPLICITY) ATTIC
(— BY WAVY LINES) GYROSE
(— OUT) DISTINCT
(— SPOTS OR LINES) MACULATE
(— UP) FOUL
(— WITH BANDS) ZONATE
(— WITH SMALLPOX) FRETTEN
(— WITH SPOTS OR LINES) NOTATE
(— WITH WHITE) BAUSOND
(EXTREMELY —) INTENSE
MARKEDLY BYOUS
MARKER HOB HUB IOU DOLE FLAG MARK SPAD STUMP TYPER BUTTON GUIDON HOBBLE HUBBLE TABBER DAYMARK SCRIBER
MARKET CURB GUNJ MART PORT SALE SOOK VEND VENT CHEAP CROSS GUNGE HALLE PASAR PRICE TRONE TRYST BAZAAR BOURSE MERCAT OUTLET PARIAN RIALTO STAPLE POULTRY CHEAPING DEBOUCHE EMPORIUM EXCHANGE MACELLUM
(CATTLE —) TRISTE
(MEAT —) SHAMBLES
MARKETABLE SUK SUQ SOUK STAPLE SALABLE VENDIBLE
MARKETING (SYSTEM OF —) ADMASS
MARKETPLACE SUK SUQ SOUK TRON AGORA CHAWK CHOWK HALLE PLAZA BAZAAR RIALTO EMPORIUM
MARKING EYE HOOD COLLAR CLOUDING SCARRING SCRIBING
(— OF WOOD) CURL GRAIN
(— ON FEATHER) SPANGLE
(— ON MARS) CANAL
(—S ON STEEL) DAMASK
(ANIMAL —) SADDLE SHIELD
(CATTLE —) JINGLEBOB
(CRESCENT-SHAPED —) LUNULA LUNULE
(DROP-SHAPED —) GUTTA
(POSTAL —) INDICIA OVERPRINT
(RINGLIKE —) ANNULUS
(STRIPED —) STRAKE
MARKKA FINMARK

MARKSMAN SHOT MARKER PLUFFER SHOOTER SHOTMAN SHOOTIST
MARL MALM MARLITE
MARLI MARIE
MARLIN AU AGUJA
MARLINESPIKE FID JAEGER PRICKER STABBER
MARMALADE CHEESE SQUISH CODINIAC
MARMALADE TREE CHICO MAMEY MAMMIE SAPOTE ZAPOTE
MARMOSET MICO TITI SAGOIN JACCHUS OUITITI QUIRCAL SAIMIRI TAMARIN WISTITI ORABASSU
MARMOT BOBAC PAHMI GOPHER SUSLIK SCIURID SIFFLEUR WHISTLER
MARMOTA ARCTOMYS
MAROON AZTEC PICNIC CIMARRON
MARQUEE CANOPY MARQUISE
MARQUISE NAVETTE
MARQUISETTE LENO
MARRANOS ANUSIM
MARRED CUPPY SCABBY SLURRED SPECKED
MARRIAGE MUTA DAIVA HYMEN KARAO BEENAH BRIDAL BUCKLE SPLICE SPOUSE EXOGAMY NUPTIAL PUNALUA SPOUSAL WEDDING WEDLOCK CONUBIUM LEVIRATE OPSIGAMY
(— AFTER DEATH OF FIRST SPOUSE) DIGAMY
(— AT ADVANCED AGE) OPSIGAMY
(— BELOW POSITION) HYPOGAMY
(— CONTRACT) KETUBAH
(— OUTSIDE FAMILY) EXOGAMY
(— PORTION) TOCHER
(— WITH AN INFERIOR) MESALLIANCE
(— WITHIN GROUP) ENDOGAMY
(PREF.) GAMO
(SUFF.) GAM(AE)(IST)(OUS)(Y) GAMETE
MARRIAGEABLE NUBILE
MARRIED COVERT WEDDED ESPOUSED
(NOT —) SOLE
MARROW KEEST MARIE MERCH MERGH MEDULLA
(PREF.) MEDULLI MYEL(O) MYELINO
(SUFF.) MYELIA MYELITIS
MARRY TIE WED FAST WIFE WIVE CLEEK MATCH BUCKLE CROTCH ENSURE MARROW SPLICE HUSBAND NUPTIAL WEDLOCK DESPOUSE
(— OFF) BESTOW
(PREF.) GAMETO GAMO
(SUFF.) GAM(AE)(IST)(OUS)(Y) GAMETE
MARS ARES MAMERS MARMAR MAVORS MASPITER TEUTATES
(FATHER OF —) JUPITER
(MOTHER OF —) JUNO
(SON OF —) REMUS ROMULUS
(PREF.) AREO
MARSH BOG FEN HAG CARR DANK FELL FLAM FLAT HOPE JHIL MASH

MIRE OOZE QUAG ROSS SOIL SUDS TARN VLEI VLEY WASH WHAM FLASH GLADE JHEEL LIMAN SLACK SLASH SLUMP SWAMP MORASS PALUDE PUDDLE CIENAGA CORCASS POCOSIN PONTINE QUAGMIRE STROTHER TURLOUGH
(SALT —) SALT SEBKA SALINA SALINE
(PREF.) ELO HELO LIMN(I)(O) PALUDI
MARSHAL ARRAY ORDER MUSTER PARADE JERONIMO MARECHAL MOBILIZE
(— FACTS) HASH
MARSHBUCK SITUTUNGA
MARSH ELDER JACKO
MARSH FEVER HELODES
MARSH GAS METHANE
MARSH HARRIER PUDDOCK PUTTOCK
MARSHLAND MAREMMA
MARSHMALLOW MALLOW WYMOTE
MARSH MARIGOLD BOOTS CAPER CRAZY GOOLS DRAGON GAMOND GOWLAN COWSLIP ELKSLIP GOLDCUP KINGCOB KINGCUP MARYBUD DRUNKARD
MARSH PENNYWORT PENNYROT WATERCUP
MARSH PINK SABBATIA
MARSH TEA LEDUM
MARSH TREFOIL BUCKBEAN
MARSH WREN LONGBILL
MARSHY BOGGY FOGGY MOORY MOSSY PONDY SNAPY SPEWY CALLOW MARISH PLASHY QUAGGY QUASHY SLUMPY HELODES MOORISH PALUDAL QUEACHY PALUDINE WATERISH
MARSILEA NARDOO
MARSUPIAL KOALA QUOLL CUSCUS POSSUM WOMBAT BETTONG DASYURE OPOSSUM KANGAROO BANDICOOT PETAURIST
MART STAPLE EMPORIUM
MARTEN FOIN PEKAN SABLE SOBOL FISHER MARTRIX MUSTELID MUSTELIN
(GROUP OF —S) RICHESSE
(SUFF.) ICTIS
MARTENSITE SORBITE
MARTHA (CHARACTER IN —) JULIA NANCY LIONEL MARTHA HARRIET PLONKETT
(COMPOSER OF —) FLOTOW
MARTIAL BELLIC WARLIKE WARRIOR BELLICAL MILITARY
MARTIN MARTLET SWALLOW MARTINET
MARTIN CHUZZLEWIT (AUTHOR OF —) DICKENS
(CHARACTER IN —) GAMP MARK MARY SETH JONAS MERCY SARAH GRAHAM MARTIN TAPLEY ANTHONY CHARITY PECKSNIFF CHUZZLEWIT
MARTINMAS TERM
MARTYR STEPHEN WITNESS SUFFERER

MARTYRDOM MARTYRY PASSION
MARVEL MARL MUSE FERLY SELLY ADMIRE WONDER MAGNALE MIRACLE MONSTER PORTENT PRODIGY SELCOUTH ADMIRATION
MARVELOUS FAB EPATANT MIRIFIC STRANGE FABULOUS WONDROUS MIRACULOUS
MARY MOLL POLL MAMIE MAURA MOLLY MIRIAM MARILLA

> **MARYLAND**
> **BATTLESITE:** ANTIETAM
> **CAPITAL:** ANNAPOLIS
> **COLLEGE:** HOOD GOUCHER STJOHNS
> **COUNTY:** KENT CECIL TALBOT CALVERT HARFORD ALLEGANY SOMERSET
> **INDIAN:** CONOY NANTICOKE
> **LAKE:** PRETTYBOY
> **MOUNTAIN:** BACKBONE
> **NATIVE:** WESORT TERRAPIN
> **NICKNAME:** COCKADE OLDLINE
> **RIVER:** CHESTER POTOMAC CHOPTANK PATUXENT
> **STATE BIRD:** ORIOLE
> **STATE TREE:** OAK
> **TOWN:** BELAIR DENTON EASTON ELKTON TOWSON LAPLATA ABERDEEN BETHESDA POCOMOKE BALTIMORE

MARYSOLE CARTER LEADER CARTARE
MARZIPAN MARCHPANE
MASAI WAKWAFI WAKWAVI
MASCEZEL (BROTHER OF —) GILDO
MASCOT BILLIKEN
MASCULINE MALE BUTCH DOGGY MACHO RUDAS VIRILE LALAQUI MANLIKE
(EXAGGERATEDLY —) MACHO
(PREF.) ANDR(O) MASCULO
(SUFF.) ANDRIA ANDROUS ANDRY
MASCULINITY (EXAGGERATED AWARENESS OF —) MACHISMO
MASH PAP BEER CHAP MASA MASK MESH SLOP CHAMP CREEM SMASH SMUSH MUDDLE STILLAGE
(FATHER OF —) ARAM
MASHED CHAPPED DAUPHINE
MASHER FLIRT BEETLE
MASJID MOSQUE
MASK FACE HIDE JEST LOUP SLUR VEIL BLOCK BLOOP CLOAK COVER GRILL GUISE LARVE POINT VIZOR DOMINO GRILLE MUZZLE SCREEN VEILER VIZARD BECLOUD CONCEAL CURTAIN MASKOID ANTEMASK DEFILADE DISGUISE MASCARON PRETENSE
(— OUT) CROP
(GAS —) CANARY
(HALF —) LOO LOUP DOMINO
(PL.) AREITO
MASKED LARVATED VIZARDED
MASKED BALL (CHARACTER IN —) HORN ANGRI AMELIA RENATO TOMASI ULRICA ARMANDO RIBBING SAMUELE ARVIDSON

GUSTAVUS RICCARDO ANCKERSTROEM
(COMPOSER OF —) VERDI
MASKER GUISARD MASQUER
MASKING MUMMERY MUMMING COLORING
MASKLIKE PERSONATE
MASLIN MESTLEN MASHLOCH MUNGCORN MASSELGEM
MASNADIERI, I (CHARACTER IN —) CARLO AMALIA FRANCESCO MASSIMILIAN
(COMPOSER OF —) VERDI
MASON LAYER BUILDER MASONER COMACINE KNOBBLER LAMMIKIN SCUTCHER
MASONRY ASHLAR MANTLE BACKING BLOCAGE MOELLON NOGGING ISODOMUM QUOINING ROCKWORK RUBBLEWORK
MASQUE MASK COMUS DEVICE ANTIMASK DISGUISE
MASQUER REX
MASQUERADE MASK GUISE DOMINO MASQUE PARADE MASKERY DISGUISE
MASQUERADER RAGSHAG
MASQUERADING CARNIVAL
MASS BAT BED GOB SOP WAD BODY BULK CLOD GOUT HEAP HEFT KNOT LEAD LUMP MOLE OBIT STOW SWAD AMASS BATCH BLOOM CLAMP CLASH CLUMP CROWD CRUST DIRGE GLOBE GORGE GROSS MATTE MISSA PRESS SLUMP SOLID SPIRE STORE WODGE COMMON GOBBET NUGGET PROPER VOLUME WEIGHT BOUROCK CONGEST DENSITY MASKINS MESKINS MYSTERY REQUIEM SALOMON CALAPITE CONGERIE ENDOSOME FLOCCULE MOUNTAIN MYCETOMA SOULMASS ACCUMULATION
(— IN THE WHITE NILE) SUDD
(— OF BACTERIA) SLIME BAREGINE SYMPLASM
(— OF BLOSSOMS) BLOW
(— OF BLUBBER) MELON
(— OF BRANCHES) SPRAY
(— OF BUBBLES) FOAM
(— OF BUSHES) SHAG
(— OF CARPELS) SOREMA
(— OF CELLS) COMB CANCER MORULA CUMULUS STALACE PULVINUS
(— OF CLOUDS) BANK
(— OF COAL) JUD
(— OF COLORS) BLOB
(— OF COTTON) FUSSOCK
(— OF CURED RUBBER) LOAF
(— OF DEBRIS) SLIDE
(— OF DOUGH) DUMPLING
(— OF FIBERS) KAPOK
(— OF FILAMENTS) FLOCCUS MYCELIUM
(— OF FILTH) GORE
(— OF FRAGMENTS) BRASH
(— OF GAS) PROMINENCE
(— OF GOLD) BONANZA
(— OF HAIR) GLIB TOUPET
(— OF HYPHAE) MEDULLA

(— OF ICE) BERG CALF FLOE FLAKE PATCH ICICLE STURIS GROWLER ICEBERG FLOEBERG
(— OF INSECTS) CACHE
(— OF IRON) BALL BLOB CORE BLOOM INDUCTOR
(— OF LAVA) BOMB SPINE
(— OF LEAVES) FOLIAGE
(— OF LIMESTONE) HUM
(— OF LOOSE BOULDERS) CLATTER
(— OF METAL) SOW INGOT BUTTON
(— OF MOLTEN GLASS) GOB BLOOM GATHER PARISON
(— OF MUD) CLASH
(— OF ORE) BACK SLUG BUNNY SQUAT REGULUS
(— OF PEOPLE) CROWD HORDE
(— OF POMACE) CHEESE
(— OF ROCK) DOME NECK HORSE LEDGE NAPPE SCALP SNOUT INLIER SARSEN BOULDER FOOTWALL
(— OF SAND) PAAR
(— OF SOAP) CURD
(— OF SPORES) SORUS
(— OF SUGAR) FONDANT
(— OF SUGAR CRYSTALS) STRIKE
(— OF TISSUE) COLLAR GANGLION NUCELLUS
(— OF WATER) HEAD
(— OF YARN) COP BALLOON
(— OF YOLK) LATEBRA
(— OVERHANGING) CORNICE
(— TOGETHER) HUDDLE
(—S OF DRIFTWOOD) EMBARRAS
(ALPINE —) FLYSCH
(AMORPHOUS —) JUMBLE SYMPLASM
(BILLOWY —) CLOUD
(BUSHY —) SHOCK
(COMPACT —) BRIQUET
(CONCENTRATION OF MOON —) MASCON
(CONFUSED —) COT JUMBLE JUNGLE PILEUP CLUTTER RUMMAGE SHUFFLE
(DISORDERLY —) SCRAMBLE
(EGG —) BUNION CULTCH SPONGE
(FATTY —) BEAN HEADSKIN
(FECAL —) SCYBALUM
(FLATTISH —) DAB
(FLUFFY —) PUFF
(FLUID —) FLUOR
(GLASSY —) SLAG
(GLOBULAR —) MOORBALL
(INDISTINCT —) SMUDGE
(IRREGULAR —) CUB
(LIVING —) BLASTEMA
(MOIST —) PULP
(MOUNTAIN —) OROGEN
(NUCLEAR —) SHIELD
(OVERSPREADING —) PALL
(PART OF —) INTROIT
(PEAR-SHAPED —) BOULE
(POROUS —) FILTER
(PROJECTING —) BOSS
(PULPY —) SQUELCH
(RECTANGULAR —) BRICK
(ROOT —) SOLE
(ROUNDED —) COB NOB KNOB BOLUS KUGEL BULLET RONDLE
(SEDIMENTARY —) GOBI

(SHAPED —) PAT LOAF
(SHAPELESS —) JELLY
(SLIPPERY —) SIND SLUD SLUDDER
(SLUSHY —) POSH
(SOFT —) MASH MOXA MUMMY
(STICKY —) CLAG
(SWOLLEN —) CERE
(TANGLED — OF HAIR) MOP KNURL
(UNCTUOUS —) LANOLIN
(UNIT OF —) DALTON
(UPRIGHT —) COLUMN
(PL.) MEINY MEINIE TRENTAL POPULACE
(PREF.) ONCO
(SUFF.) IUM OME
MASSA (FATHER OF —) ISHMAEL

MASSACHUSETTS
CAPE: ANN COD
CAPITAL: BOSTON
COLLEGE: SMITH AMHERST SIMMONS WHEATON WILLIAMS RADCLIFFE WELLESLEY
COUNTY: DUKES ESSEX BRISTOL NORFOLK SUFFOLK BERKSHIRE NANTUCKET BARNSTABLE
INDIAN: NAUSET POCOMTUC
ISLAND: DUKES NANTUCKET
LAKE: ONOTA QUABBIN ROHUNTA WEBSTER
MOUNTAIN: BRODIE POTTER ALANDER EVERETT GREYLOCK
MOUNTAIN RANGE: BERKSHIRE
POND: WALDEN
PRESIDENT: KENNEDY
RIVER: NASHUA CHARLES CONCORD QUABOAG TAUNTON CHICOPEE DEERFIELD MERRIMACK
STATE BIRD: CHICKADEE
STATE FLOWER: MAYFLOWER
STATE NICKNAME: BAY OLDBAY OLDCOLONY
STATE TREE: ELM
TOWN: AYER LYNN OTIS ATHOL BARRE LENOX AGAWAM DEDHAM GROTON LOWELL NAHANT NATICK REVERE SAUGUS WOBURN HOLYOKE IPSWICH PEABODY TAUNTON BROCKTON CHICOPEE COHASSET SCITUATE UXBRIDGE YARMOUTH CAMBRIDGE NANTUCKET WORCESTER PITTSFIELD SPRINGFIELD
UNIVERSITY: CLARK TUFTS HARVARD BRANDEIS

MASSACRE SLAY POGROM CARNAGE SCUPPER BUTCHERY SLAUGHTER
MASSAGE WISP KNEAD FACIAL PETRIE SHAMPOO TRIPSIS LOMILOMI ANATRIPSIS
MASSAGER MASSEUR VIBRATOR
MASSECUITE GUR FILLMASS
MASSED DENSE
MASSENA QUAIL COPPY
MASSIVE BIG BEAMY BULKY GROSS HEAVY LUSTY MASSY SOUND STERN STRONG HEALTHY HULKING VOLUMED TIMBERED MONUMENTAL

MAST BUCK MAIN POLE SPAR OVEST STICK STING DRIVER JIGGER MIZZEN ARTEMON ASHERAH MASTAGE PANNAGE SPANKER FOREMAST JURYMAST MAINMAST SHIPMAST MIZZENMAST
(FALLEN —) SHACK
(SIXTH —) DRIVER
MASTAX TROPHI
MASTER DON HER JOE MAS RAB SAB SIR ARCH BAAS BEAK BOSS COCK FACE HERR JOSS KING LORD MIAN SIRE TUAN BWANA MARSE MASSA RABBI SAHIB SWAMI SWAMY SWELL BRIDLE BUCKRA CASTER DEACON DOMINE HUMBLE MAITRE PATRON RECTOR RHETOR SIRCAR WAFTER CAPTAIN CONQUER DOMINIE DOMINUS EFFENDI MAESTRO NAKHODA OGTIERN PADRONE RABBONI AMAISTER BARGEMAN BEMASTER KINGFISH LANDLORD MAGISTER OVERCOME SLOOPMAN SURMOUNT VANQUISH
(— OF CEREMONIES) EMCEE VERGER COMPERE CHAIRMAN
(— OF CRAFT) KAHUNA
(— OF HOUSEHOLD) BALABOS GOODMAN
(— OF REVELS) ALYTARCH
(— OF WHALER) SPOUTER
(FENCING —) LANISTA
(INFERIOR —) KNIFER
(PREF.) ARCH
MASTER-AT-ARMS JAUNTY JAUNTIE
MASTER BUILDER (AUTHOR OF —) IBSEN
(CHARACTER IN —) ALINE HILDA BROVIK RAGNAR SOLNESS
MASTERFUL BOSSY LORDLY VIRILE HAUGHTY ARROGANT MAGERFUL PEREMPTORY
MASTER OF BALLANTRAE (AUTHOR OF —) STEVENSON
(CHARACTER IN —) CHEW DASS BALLY BURKE HENRY JAMES TEACH ALISON DURRIE GRAEME FRANCIS SECUNDRA MACKELLAR DURRISDEER
MASTERPIECE TOPPIECE
MASTERY GREE GRIP GRIPE COMMAND MAISTRY OVERHAND
MASTHEAD FLAG HIGTOP
MASTICATE GUM CHAW CHEW
MASTICATORY PAN BUYO
MASTIC BULLY JOCUM JOCUMA
MASTIC TREE ACOMA AUSUBO COCUYO COCULLO LENTISK
MASTIFF ALAN MASTY BANDOG TIEDOG
MASTIGONEME FLIMMER
MASTITIS CLAP WEED GARGET
MAST TREE ASAK
MASTURBATE ABUSE
MASTURBATION ONANISM FROTTAGE
MASTWOOD POON KAMANI
MAT COT RUG TOD BASS FLAT FLET FOOT HAIR MOSS NIPA

PACE RAFT SHAG TAUT DOILY KILIM TATTY COTTER FELTER FOOTER PAUNCH PETATE TARGET COASTER CUSHION DOORMAT KAITAKA MATTING FOOTPACE FROSTING MATTRESS SPANDREL
(— BORDER) TANIKO
(BOWLING —) FOOTER
(FIBER —) IE BASS
(PALM-LEAF —) YAPA
(PICTURE-FRAME —) FLAT
(POLYNESIAN —) LAUHALA
(SCOURING —) BEAR
(TABLECLOTH —) GARDNAP
(PL.) DUNNAGE
MATACHIN BOUFFON
MATACO CORONADO
MATADOR MAT ESPADA CAPEADOR
(— MOVEMENT) PASE
MATCH GO CAP VIE BOUT COPE EVEN FERE LUNT MAKE MATE MEET MILL MOTE PAIR PEEL PEER SIDE SUIT AMATE EQUAL FIRER FUSEE FUZEE MOUSE PARTY RIVAL SPUNK TALLY VENUE VESTA ASSORT BESORT CANCEL COMMIT FELLOW KIPPIN MARROW QUADER RUBBER SAMPLE SWATCH COMPEER EXAMPLE IGNITER ILLUMER KINDLER KIPPEEN LIGHTER LUCIFER PARAGON PAREGAL PATTERN PENDANT SINGLES APPROACH BONSPIEL BREATHER CONGREVE EUPYRION FOURSOME INFLAMER LOCOFOCO PARALLEL PORTFIRE REANSWER VESUVIAN VESUVIUS SEMIFINAL PREMINIARY QUARTERFINAL
(— AT DICE) MAIN
(BOXING —) SPAR FIGHT PRELIM SLUGFEST
(CURLING —) SPIEL BONSPIEL
(DANCING —) KANTIKEY
(DISHONEST —) CROSS
(GOLF —) NASSAU FOURSOME
(SCOLDING —) FLYTE
(SHOOTING —) TIR SHOOT
(SLOW —) LUNT SMIFT SQUIB
(TILTING —) CAROUSEL
(PL.) LIGHTS
MATCHED ASSORTED
MATCHING MARROW SUITABLE
MATCHLESS ALONE UNIQUE NONESUCH PEERLESS
MATCHMAKER SHADCHAN
MATE CAWK FERE METE PAIR PEER BILLY BREED BUDDY BULLY CHINA CLASP CULLY DICKY MATCH PARTY TALLY YERBA BUNKIE COBBER FELLOW FUTURE MARROW PAREIL BROTHER COMPEER COMRADE CONSORT HUSBAND PARAGON NEIGHBOR PIRRAURA
(BOATSWAIN'S —) BUFFER
(GUNNER'S —) LADY
(SECOND —) DICKY
MATERIAL FINE MOLD GAUZE GOUGE HYLIC METAL MOULD PASTE PLASS STUFF THING TRADE BORROW CARNAL CYANUS

FABRIC GRAITH HOGGIN MATTER
PAPREG PUBLIC THINGY APPAREL
FOOTING SUBJECT TEXTILE
UNIDEAL WEIGHTY ADDITIVE
CORPORAL ECONOMIC EQUIPAGE
RELEVANT SENSIBLE SNOODING
TANGIBLE THINGISH OBJECTIVE
PHENOMENAL
(— ELIMINATED) CULLAGE
(— FOR FERMENTING) GUILE
(— FOR OYSTER BEDS) CULCH
CULTCH
(— IN GRAIN) DOCKAGE
(— IN MAKING CEMENT) ADDITION
(— IN NEEDLEWORK) INKLE
(— OF CORDED SILK) CRYSTAL
(— OF SCREENINGS) HOGGIN
HOGGING
(— REMOVED BY SAW CUT) KERF
(— USED IN WAXING) BALL
(— WEIGHED) DRAFT DRAUGHT
(—S FOR MAKING GLASS) FRIT
(ABSORBENT —) DOPE
(ALLUVIAL —) SHINGLE
(ANCIENT —) MURRA MURRHA
(ARTISTIC —) KITSCH
(BAGGING —) HOPSACK
(BITUMINOUS —) KEROGEN
(BONY —) COSMINE
(BUILDING —) LATH ADOBE BRICK
STAFF SWISH TABBY TAPIA
SILLAR CONCRETE
(BUILDING —S) TIGNUM
(CLAY —) TAPIA
(CLAYEY —) GOUGE
(COLORING —) TINCTION
(COMBUSTIBLE —) KINDLING
(CONSTRUCTION —) BREEZE
(CORE —) NIFE
(CUSHIONING —) AIRFOAM
(DEPOSITED —) FOOTS
(DIAMOND —) BORT
(DOWNY —) FLUE
(DRESS —) FOULE VOILE PEELING
COTILLON EOLIENNE
(DYEING —) SUMAC SUMACH
(EMBOSSED —) CLOQUE
(EMROIDERY —) ARRASENE
(EXCAVATED —) SPOIL
(FACING —) ENAMEL
(FISSIONABLE —) STUFF
(FOUNDATION —) UNDERLAY
(GLUTINOUS —) GELATIN
(GRANULAR —) BASIS
(HARD —) CARBIDE
(HEAT-RESISTANT —) ALSIFILM
(ILLUSTRATIVE —) ART
(INSECTICIDAL —) SCABRIN
(INSULATING —) KERITE PECITE
BLANKET LAGGING OKONITE
MEGOTALC
(LEFTOVER —S) ARISINGS
(LOOSE —) SAND GRAVEL
DETRITUS
(MINING REFUSE —) ATTLE
(MINUTE —) SESTON
(NUTRITIVE —) FUEL
(ORGANIC —) EXINITE
(PAPER-THIN —) FOIL
(PATCHING —) BOTCH
(PETRIFIED —) GEMSTONE
(POLISHING —) RABAT
(POWDERED —) FINES

(PRIMORDIAL —) BLASTEMA
(RAW —) STOCK STAPLE
(REFRACTORY —) GROG BULLDOG
CASTABLE
(RESIDUAL —) CEMENT
(RESOURCE —) SWIPE
(REVERSIBLE —) DAMASK
(SEDIMENTARY —) SILT
(SILK —) HONAN PEKIN FOULARD
SARCENET
(SLIMY —) GLIT SWARF
(SMOKING —) KEF KIF
(STIFF —) CANVAS
(STIFFENING —) BOXING
(TANNING —) BADAN SYNTAN
(THIN SLICE OF —) WAFER
(TILE-STRENGTHENING —) WEB
(TRASHY —) SLUSH
(TWEEDY —) HOMESPUN
(TYPE-HIGH —) BEARER
(UNPUBLISHED —) INEDITA
(UPHOLSTERY —) LAMPAS
(VOLCANIC —) EJECTA
(WATERPROOF —) KERATOL
(WORTHLESS —) GARBLE
(WOVEN —) LAPPET
(PL.) STOCK STUFF
(PREF.) HYL(O)
(SUFF.) **(PLASTIC —)** PLASM(A)
MATERIALISM HYLISM SOMATISM
(DIALECTICAL —) DIAMAT
MATERIALISTIC SENSATE
SENSUAL BANAUSIC
MATERIALIZE REIFY DESCEND
MATER LECTIONIS GRAPHY
MATERNITY WARD NATUARY
MATGRASS NARD MATWEED
MATH MUTH MONASTERY
MATHEMATICIAN ALGORIST
GEOMETER
AMERICAN SEE FINE WEST WEYL
BROWN FISKE HARDY MASON
MOORE SMITH YOUNG CAJORI
KASNER KEYSER LEHMER LOOMIS
MILLER NEWTON OSGOOD PEIRCE
RUNKLE VEBLEN DICKSON
GODFREY METZLER NEUMANN
SAFFORD BANNEKER BIRKHOFF
BOWDITCH COOLIDGE FRANKLIN
MURNAGHAN HUNTINGTON
WILCZYNSKI
AUSTRIAN HAGEN DOPPLER
PURBACH
BELGIAN LEMAITRE
BRAZILIAN GUSMAO
DUTCH BLAEU VLACQ CEULEN
STEVIN HUYGENS SNELLIUS
GRAVESANDE MUSSCHENBROEK
EGYPTIAN PTOLEMY
ENGLISH DEE LAMB MUIR PELL
ALLEN BOOLE COTES ELLIS
HARDY MURIS ROUTH SHARP
SMITH WALES ATWOOD BARLOW
BARNES BARROW BRIGGS CAYLEY
COCKLE DARWIN DIGGES GUNTER
HADLEY HUTTON KELVIN LARMOR
NEWTON ROBINS STOKES TAYLOR
WALLIS WEDDLE BABBAGE
DODGSON HARRIOT LUBBOCK
MAKEHAM MASERES PEACOCK
RECORDE RUSSELL WHEWELL
WHISTON CLIFFORD GLAISHER
GOMPERTZ LEYBOURN

MACMAHON OUGHTRED
RAYLEIGH DUNSTABLE GREENHILL
NICHOLSON TODHUNTER
WHITEHEAD WHITTAKER
WOODHOUSE CODDINGTON
GELLIBRAND SACROBOSCO
SAUNDERSON
FRENCH BIOT FINE LAME LEVY
BORDA BOREL CHEZY COMTE
LEROY MONGE PRONY RAMUS
STURM VIETE BEAUNE BEZOUT
BOSSUT CAUCHY FERMAT FERNEL
GALOIS JORDAN MOIGNO PICARD
BOUGUER BROCARD CHASLES
CHUQUET COURNOT DARBOUX
GERMAIN GOURSAT HERMITE
KOENIGS LACROIX LAPLACE
POINSOT POISSON PUISEUX
VERNIER ALEMBERT BERTRAND
CLAIRAUT CORIOLIS DEMOIVRE
GERGONNE HACHETTE
HADAMARD LAGUERRE LEBESGUE
LEGENDRE MERSENNE MONTUCIA
PAINLEVE POINCARE PONCELET
ROBERVAL BRIANCHON
CONDORCET DESARGUES
DESCARTES LIOUVILLE
BURCKHARDT DEPARCIEUX
MAUPERTUIS
GERMAN GAUSS HESSE KLEIN
MAYER MISES PASCH PFAFF
RUNGE WOLFF BALMER CANTOR
JACOBI KUMMER MOBIUS
MULLER STIFEL APIANUS
CLEBSCH FRIESEN HILBERT
KASTNER LAMBERT PLUCKER
RIEMANN WIDMANN ARONHOLD
BLASCHKE DEDEKIND DROBISCH
LEIBNITZ MERCATOR RHATICUS
SCHOTTKY SCHUBERT DIRICHLET
GRASSMANN KRONECKER
LINDEMANN BIEBERBACH
EISENSTEIN HINDENBURG
PRINGSHEIM TSCHIRNHAUS
WEIERSTRASS KONIGSBERGER
GREEK CONON PAPPUS DIOCLES
ANTIPHON AUTOLYCUS
OENOPIDES SOSIGENES
ARCHIMEDES DIOPHANTUS
PYTHAGORAS DINOSTRATUS
HUNGARIAN BOLYAI
INDIAN ARYABHATA RAMANUJAN
IRISH BALL SALMON HAMILTON
BROUNCKER
ITALIAN CEVA BALDI FRISI PEANO
AGNESI GRANDI CARDANO
CREMONA PACIOLI RICCATI
BRIOSCHI CAMPANUS MALFATTI
BOSCOVICH CAVALIERI FIBONACCI
TARTAGLIA BELLAVITIS
MASCHERONI TORRICELLI
JAPANESE SEKI
NORWEGIAN LIE ABEL STORMER
GULDBERG
POLISH BARTEL CIOLEK WRONSKI
PORTUGUESE NUNES
RUSSIAN KRYLOV LIAPUNOV
CHEBYSHEV KOVALEVSKI
LOBACHEVSKI
SCOTTISH TAIT IVORY KEILL
LESLIE NAPIER BURGESS FORSYTH
GREGORY PLAYFAIR STIRLING
SWISS EULER AMSLER CRAMER

GULDIN BYRGIUS STEINER
BERNOULLI CHRISTOFFEL
MATHEMATICS MATHESIS
MATING NICK COUPLE DIALLEL
BREEDING HOMOGAMY PANMIXIA
(RANDOM —) PANGAMY
MATRASS BOLTHEAD CUCURBIT
MATRED (DAUGHTER OF —)
MEHETABEL
(FATHER OF —) MEZAHAB
MATRIMONIAL MARITAL NUPTIAL
SPOUSAL CONJUGAL
MATRIMONIO SEGRETO, IL
(CHARACTER IN —) FIDALMA
PAOLINO CAROLINA ELISETTA
GERONIMO ROBINSON
(COMPOSER OF —) CIMAROSA
MATRIMONY WEDLOCK
MARRIAGE
MATRIMONY VINE JASMINE
JESSAMY BOXTHORN
MATRIX PI BED MAT SORT PLASM
SHELL SLIDE DYADIC MASTER
MOTHER STRIKE STROMA
CALYMMA FORMULA MATRICE
PATTERN PROPLASM
MATRON DAME
MATTAN (SON OF —) SHEPHATIAH
MATTANIAH (FATHER OF —) BANI
ELAM HEMAN ZATTU
(SON OF —) ZACCUR
MATTE SLURRY REGULUS
MATTED COTTY FELTY PINNY
FELTED TAGGED TAUTED WAUKIT
STRINGY FELTLIKE CESPITOSE
MATTENAI (FATHER OF —) JOIARIB
MATTER RES BONE CASE GEAR
HYLE ITEM RECK WHAT AMPER
FORCE PARTY SKILL STUFF
THEME TOPIC AFFAIR ARGUFY
BEHALF DITTAY IMPORT ARTICLE
CONCERN MATERIA SHEBANG
SIGNIFY SUBJECT BUSINESS
COMETHER MATERIAL
(— ADDED TO BOOK) APPENDIX
(— AROUND THE TEETH) TOPHUS
(— CONSTITUTING PERFUME)
ESSENCE
(— IN DISPUTE) ISSUE
(— OF BUSINESS) SHAURI
(— OF CONCERN) FUNERAL
(— OF INTEREST) GRIST
(— TO) CONCERN
(ALLUVIAL —) GEEST
(BRAIN —) ALBA
(CARTILAGINOUS —) GRISTLE
(COLORING —) DYE COLOR CROCK
EOSIN MORIN PIURI ALNEIN
BUTEIN FUSTIC INDIGO ORCEIN
PIOURY CARMINE CASTORY
CUDBEAR LIGULIN OENOLIN
PIGMENT PUNICIN XANTHIN
ALGOCYAN ALIZARIN BRAZILIN
FUSTERIC LAPACHOL SCOPARIN
TINCTION
(CORRUPT —) PUS ATTER
(DECAYED ORGANIC —) DUFF
(ESSENTIAL —) POINT
(EXPLANATORY —) HAGGADA
(FATTY —) SEBUM
(FECAL —) SIEGE
(FILTHY —) GUNK
(FOREIGN —) SOIL DROSS

(FOUL —) FILTH SORDES
(FRONT —) FOREWORD
(GELATINOUS —) BREAK SPAWN
(GRAY —) GLIOSA CINEREA
(HYPOTHETICAL —) PROTYLE
(INANIMATE —) AJIVA
(INFECTIOUS —) MIASMA
(MINERAL —) FLOAT FLOATS
(NERVE —) CINEREA
(POTENTIAL —) PRAKRITI
(PRIMARY —) PRADHANA
(PRINTED —) BOX DISPLAY
(PULVERIZED —) ATTRITUS
(READING —) BODY
(SLIMY —) GLAIR
(SMALL —) MINUTIA
(SOFT —) PASH
(SUBJECT —) SCOPE CONTENT
(SUPPURATIVE —) PUS
(TRIVIAL —) JOKE
(TYPESET —) CHASE
(WASTE —) DIRT DRAFF DROSS
RAMMEL SEWAGE EXCRETA
(WORTHLESS —) SLAG CHAFF
GARBAGE
(WRITTEN —) SCRIVE
(PL.) HARNESS SQUARES
(PREF.) HYL(O)
(SUFF.) (COLORING —) PHYLL
MATTER-OF-FACT DRY PROSE
LITERAL PROSAIC
MATTER-OF-FACTNESS PROSE
MATTHAN (GRANDSON OF —)
JOSEPH
MATTHEW (FATHER OF —)
ALPHAEUS
MATTING MAT TAT BAST BEAR
BUMP SIRKI TATTY SAWALI
TATAMI COCOMAT RABANNA
MATTOCK MAT BILL HACK MATAX
PICKAX TUBBAL TWIBIL GRUBBER
MATTRESS BED MAT TICK DIVAN
QUILT RESAI REZAI PALLET
BISCUIT MATRACE PALLIASSE
MATURATE MATTER
MATURE AGE OLD BOLD FULL
GRAY RIPE ADULT MANLY RIPEN
SHOOT ACCRUE AUTUMN
DECOCT DIGEST MELLOW SEASON
SEEDED CONCOCT DEVELOP
FURNISH PERFECT PROVECT
MATURATE
(PREF.) TEL(E)(O)
MATURED ADULT GROWN
FORMED HEADED MELLOW
SEEDED HOMOGAMY
(SEXUALLY —) HIGH
MATURING (— EARLY) RATHRIPE
MATURITY AGE RIPENESS
MATWEED NARDUS
MATZOTH MATZOS AFIKOMEN
MAUDLIN BEERY MOIST FUDDLED
MAUDLINISM BATHOS
MAUL FAN PAW TUG MALL MELL
GAVEL GLAUM BEATER BEETLE
BEMAUL MUZZLE SCAMBLE
MAUND MAO MEIN MAHAN
MAUNDER HAVER
MAUNDY NIPTER MANDATE
MAURITANIA (CAPITAL OF —)
NOUAKCHOTT
(MONEY OF —) OUGUIYA
(RIVER OF —) SENEGAL

(TOWN OF —) ATAR NEMA AGMAR
KAEDI OUJAF
MAURITIUS (CAPITAL OF —)
PORTLOUIS
(CHANNEL OF —) QUOIN
(ISLAND OF —) AGALEGA GABRIEL
RODRIGUEZ
(RIVER OF —) GRAND POSTE
REMPART
(TOWN OF —) VACOAS TRIOLET
CUREPIPE SOUILLAC
MAUSOLEUM MOLE TOMB SHRINE
TURBEH BARADARI
MAUVE MALLOW PURPLE
MAUVINE
MAVEN EXPERT
MAW MAA CROP GORGE CROPPY
THROAT
MAWKISH CUTE SAPPY SOPPY
SOUPY WALSH DRIPPY SICKLY
VANILLA
MAXILLA SETA GNATHITE
CULTELLUS
MAXILLIPED JAWFOOT GNATHITE
MAXIM SAW SAY DICT ITEM NORM
RULE TEXT WORD ADAGE AXIOM
GNOME LARGE MOTTO DICTUM
SAYING SYMBOL BROCARD
DICTATE IMPRESA PRECEPT
PROVERB APHORISM APOTHEGM
DOCTRINE MORALISM PROTASIS
SENTENCE
(PL.) LOGIA
MAXIMUM FULL MOST PEAK
CREST EXTREME OUTSIDE
SUMMARY ULTIMATE
MAXIXE CARIOCA
MAXWELL LINE WEBER
MAY CAN MUN MOTE MOWE MUST
PRIME SHALL HEYDAY
HAWTHORN SYCAMORE
(3D OF —) RUDMASDAY
MAYA PRAKRITI
MAYAN COCOM
(— CALENDAR PERIOD) UAYEB
UINAL
(— GOD) CHAC CHAAC
MAYAPPLE MANDRAKE
MAYBE MEBBE HAPPEN PERHAPS
POSSIBLY
MAY DAY BELTANE
MAYFISH ROCKFISH
MAYFLOWER ARBUTUS
MAYFLY DUN DOON DRAKE NAIAD
DAYFLY SPINNER EPHEMERA
MAYHEM FELONY
MAYONNAISE MAYO GOULASH
DRESSING
(GARLIC —) AIOLI
MAYOR MAIRE BAILIFF DEMARCH
PODESTA PROVOST PALATINE
(BULGARIAN —) KMET
(SPANISH —) ALCALDE
MAYOR OF CASTERBRIDGE
(AUTHOR OF —) HARDY
(CHARACTER IN —) JOPP SUSAN
DONALD NEWSON FARFRAE
LESUEUR LUCETTA MICHAEL
RICHARD HENCHARD ELIZABETH
TEMPLEMAN
MAYORSHIP CHAIR
MAYPOLE SHAFT
MAYPOP MAYCOCK MARACOCK

MAYWEED BALDER COTULA
MATHER HOGWEED COMPOSIT
DILLWEED
MAZE JUNGLE WARREN CONFUSE
BEWILDER LABYRINTH
MAZEPPA (CHARACTER IN —)
MARIA ANDREY MAZEPPA
KOCHUBEY
(COMPOSER OF —) TCHAIKOVSKY
MAZUMA (ALSO SEE MONEY)
LUCRE
MCCOY QUILL
ME I MA US
MEAD MEATHE BRAGGET
HYDROMEL METHEGLIN
MEADOW LEA ABEL MEAD VEGA
WISH WONG FIELD GRASS LEASE
MARSH SWALE WARTH CALLOW
PARAMO SAETER SMOOTH
POTRERO THWAITE CHINAMPA
(ARTIFICIAL —) CHINAMPA
(IRISH —) BAAN
(LOW —) ING INCH INGE HAUGH
CALLOW
(PREF.) PRATI
(SUFF.) ING
MEADOW CROWFOOT
FROGWORT
MEADOW GRASS POA
MEADOWLAND ALP MOWING
MOWLAND
MEADOWLARK ACORN MEDLAR
MEADOW MOUSE VOLE
MEADOW PEA COWPEA
MEADOW PIPIT WEKEEN CHEEPER
TIETICK TITLING LINGBIRD
TWITLARK
MEADOW SAFFRON UPSTART
COLCHICUM
MEADOW SAXIFRAGE SESELI
MEADOWSWEET SPIREA
MEADWORT
MEAGER BALD BARE LANK LEAN
NICE POOR THIN GAUNT NAKED
SCANT SILLY SKIMP SOBER SPARE
JEJUNE LEEPIT LENTEN MEAGRE
NARROW PILLED SCANTY SLIGHT
SPARSE STINGY SCRAGGY
SCRANNY SCRIMPY SCRUBBY
SLENDER SPARING STARVED
STERILE MARGINAL SCRANNEL
SCRATCHY MISERABLE
MEAGERLY BARELY SPARELY
SPARINGLY
MEAGERNESS ECONOMY EXILITY
TENUITY SPARENESS
MEAL AMYL ATTA BAKE CENA
CHOW FARM FEED HASH KAIL
MEAT MONG NOSH TUCK COENA
FLOUR MANGE SCOFF BUFFET
COMIDA DINNER FARINA MANGER
POLLEN REPAST SPREAD SQUARE
SUPPER UNDERN BLOWOUT
COOKOUT CRIBBLE MELTITH
NAGMAAL NOONING SETDOWN
ALMUERZO CORNMEAL
EVENMETE MEALTIDE ORDINARY
TRENCHER
(— AND WATER) DRAMMOCK
(— FROM CASSAVA ROOT) FARINE
FARINHA
(— GROUND BY HAND) GRADDAN
(— OF FELLOWSHIP) AGAPE

(— STIRRED WITH MILK) STUROCH
(ACORN —) RACAHOUT
(COARSE —) GRIT GROUT KIBBLE
CRIBBLE GURGEONS
(COLLEGE —) HALL
(CORN —) MASA ATOLE NOCAKE
(ELABORATE —) FEAST BANQUET
(FIRST —) ALMUERZO
(FULL —) GORGE
(HASTY —) SNAP CHACK
(HEARTY —) AIT
(IMPROMPTU —) BITE CHECK
(LIGHT —) BAIT BEVER CHACK
CHECK FOURS NUNCHEON
(MIDDAY —) NOON
(MORNING —) BRUNCH
(PERTAINING TO —) PRANDIAL
(PURIM —) SEUDAH
(SCANTY —) PICK
(SMALL —) SNAP MORSEL
(SOLITARY —) SULLEN
(UNSORTED —) ATTA
(PL.) TUCKER
(PREF.) ATHERO
MEALTIDE MELTITH
MEALTIME CHOW MELTETH
MEALY FLOURY FARINOSE
PERONATE
MEALYBUG COCCID
MEAN LOW BASE CLAM HARD
LEAN MIDS NICE POKY POOR SLIM
VILE AGENT ARGUE DINGY DIRTY
DUSTY FOOTY GRIMY KETTY
LOUSY MANGY MESNE MEZZO
MIDST MINGY MOYEN MUCKY
NASTY PETIT PETTY RATTY
RUNTY SCALD SCALL SCALY
SCRUB SEEDY SILLY SMALL SNIDE
SNIVY SORRY SOUND SPELL
ABJECT BEMEAN COMMON
DENOTE DESIGN DIRTEN FEEBLE
FROWZY FRUGAL GRUBBY
HUMBLE HUNGRY IMPORT INSECT
INTEND LEADEN LITTLE MEASLY
MEDIAL MEDIUM MENIAL MIDDLE
NARROW ORNERY PALTRY
PEANUT PILLED POKING RASCAL
SCABBY SCREWY SCUMMY
SCURVY SHABBY SLIGHT SNIFTY
SNIPPY SORDID SQUALL STRAIT
TEMPER YELLOW AVERAGE
CAITIFF CHANNEL CHETIVE
COMICAL CONNOTE HACKNEY
HILDING IGNOBLE MESQUIN
MISERLY MOTETUS OBSCURE
PEAKING PELTING PIGGISH
PIMPING PITIFUL PORTEND
REPTILE ROINISH SCABBED
SHABBED SIGNIFY VICIOUS
BEGGARLY CHURLISH DOGGEREL
MEDIOCRE MIDDLING NIGGLING
PICAYUNE PITIABLE RASCALLY
RIFFRAFF SHAMEFUL SNEAKING
TWOPENNY WRETCHED
MEANDER WIND STRAY TWINE
CIRCLE WIMPLE WINDLE SERPENT
WINDING STRAGGLE
MEANING WIT HANG DRIFT SENSE
SOUND IMPORT INTENT SEMEME
PURPORT PURPOSE CARRIAGE
INNUENDO SENTENCE STRENGTH
REFERENCE SIGNIFICANCE
(BASIC —) EFFECT

(DOUBLE —) WHIM EQUIVOKE
(ESSENTIAL —) CORE CONTENT
(IMPLIED —) EMPHASIS
(MANIFEST —) FACE
(REAL —) SPIRIT
(SECONDARY —) OVERTONE
(SECRET —) HEART
(SENSE THE — OF) READ
MEANINGFUL RICH PREGNANT
MEANINGFULNESS BODY
MEANINGLESS BANAL ABSURD
FECKLESS SENSELESS
(— LETTER OR CODE) NULL
MEANNESS BEGGARY
MEANS MIDS AGENT DRIVE MESNE
MOYEN PURSE THEME AGENCY
AVENUE ENGINE MATTER MIDDES
POCKET STRING WRENCH
BALANCE BENEFIT DEMESNE
FACULTY FASHION QUOMODO
COURTESY
(— OF COMMUNICATION) CANAL
COMMERCE
(— OF DEFENSE) HORN HEDGE
SHIELD BULWARK
(— OF ESCAPE) CHINK SCAPE
FLIGHT
(— OF LIVING) ALIMONY
(— OF OFFENSE) ARM
(— OF PROTECTION) SAFETY
(— OF SUPPORT) HOLD ALIMENT
SUPPORT
MEANSPIRITED POOR SUPINE
CURRISH BANAUSIC RECREANT
MEANTIME MEAN WHILE WHILES
INTERIM
MEANTONE TERTIAN
MEANWHILE WHILST INTERIM
MEANTIME
MEASLES RUBEOLA MORBILLI
(BLACK —) ESCA APOPLEXY
MEASURE (ALSO SEE UNIT AND
WEIGHT) AR BU EM EN HO KO LI
MO RI SE TU AAM ARE AUM BAG
CAB CHO DRA ELL FAT FEN FIT
FOU FUN GAD GAZ GUZ HIN HOB
IMI KAB KAN KIP KOR KOS LEA
LOG LUG MAU MIL MOY PIK RIG
RIN ROD SAA SHO TON TUN VAT
VOG WEY ACRE ALMA AUNE
BARN BATH BEKA BOLL BOUW
BUTT CADE CENT CHIH COOM
COSS DEPA DOSE DRAA DRAM
DYNE EPHA EPHI FALL FANG
FOOT FULL GAGE GERA GILL GIRT
GOAD GRAM GREX HAND HATT
HIDE HOOP HOUR IMMI INCH
KNOT KOKU LAST MEAL METE
MILE MUID NAIL NOOK OMER
PACE PINT PIPE POLL REAM RIME
ROOD ROPE ROTL SAAH SACK
SALM SEAH SEAM SIZE SKEP
SPAN STEP TAKT TAPE TIME
TRAM TRUG TSUN VARA WIST
YARD ALMUD AMBER ANKER
ARDAB ARDEB ARURA BEKAH
BIGHA BLANK BODGE BRASS
CABAN CABLE CABOT CANDY
CARAT CARGA CATTY CAVAN
CHAIN CHANG CHING CLOVE
COOMB CRANS CUBIT CUMAL
CUNIT DENUM DEPOH DIGIT
DRAFT DUNAM DUNUM EPHAH

GAUGE GERAH GIRTH HOMER
HUTCH JUGER LABOR LAGEN
LIANG LIBRA LIGNE LIPPY LITER
LITRE MEITH METER METRE
MINIM MODEL OUNCE PEISE
PERCH PLANK POUND QUIRE
RASER RHYME SALMA SCALE
SCORE SHAKU SHENG SHING
SIEVE SLEEP STACK STERE STONE
STOOP STOUP THERM TOISE
TOVET TRACE VERST YOJAN
APATAN ARCHIN ARPENT ARSHIN
ASSIZE BARREL BATMAN BEMETE
BOVATE BUNDLE BUSHEL
CANADA CANTAR CHOMER
CHOPIN COLLOP COUDEE COVIDO
CUERDA DAVACH DAVOCH
DECARE DEGREE DENIER DIPODY
DIRHAM DRACHM ENGLER
EXTENT FANEGA FATHOM
FEDDAN FINGER FIRKIN FIRLOT
FLAGON FODDER FORPET FOTHER
GALLON GRAMME HALEBI HIDAGE
KISHEN LEAGUE MICRON MODIUS
MODULE MOGGIO MORGEN
NUMBER OITAVA OUROUB
OXHIDE QANTAR REASON
SAZHEN SETIER SQUARE STERAD
STRIKE SULUNG TERMIN THRAVE
WINDLE YOJANA ADOULIE
AMPHORA ANAPEST ARSHINE
BATTUTA BRACCIO BREADTH
CADENCE CALIPER CALORIE
CENTARE CENTNER CENTRAD
CHITTAK COMPASS CONGIUS
CONTAIN DECIARE DIOPTER
DRACHMA DRAUGHT ENTROPY
FARSAKH FARSANG FRUNDEL
FURLONG HECTARE HEMINEE
KILIARE NOCKTAT QUARTAN
QUARTER SCHEPEL SCRUPLE
SECCHIO SKEPFUL SKIPPLE
SPANGLE SPINDLE STADION
STADIUM TERTIAN VIRGATE
ALQUEIRE CAPACITY CARUCATE
CENTIARE CHETVERT CRANNOCK
DACTYLIC DECAGRAM DECIGRAM
DESIATIN DIAPASON HOGSHEAD
INNOCENT LANDYARD
METEWAND MUTCHKIN
PARASANG PLOWGANG
PLOWGATE SCHOONER
SCHOPPEN STANDARD
PRECAUTION
(— DEPTH) SOUND
(— FOR DRINKS) JIGGER
(— FOR FISH) COT VOG CRAN LAST
DRAFT HAMPER DRAUGHT
(— FOR SHELLFISH) WASH
(— OF BEER) HANDLE
(— OF BUTTER) SPAN
(— OF CHAFF) FAN
(— OF COAL) TEN CORF KEEL
CHALDER CHALDRON
(— OF DEVELOPMENT) AGE
(— OF DIAMONDS) BULSE
(— OF DISCREPANCY) LEEWAY
(— OF EELS) BIND STICK
(— OF EFFICIENCY) DUTY
(— OF FURS) MANTLE
(— OF GRAIN) MOY COOP
(— OF HERRINGS) MEASE
(— OF LIQUOR) FIFTH

(— OF MERCURY) FLASK
(— OF MINING CLAIMS) MERE
(— OF PEAS) COP
(— OF RAISINS) FRAIL
(— OF ROTATION) ANGLE
(— OF SILK) DRAMMAGE
(— OF STRAW) KEMPLE
(— OF SUPERIORITY) LEAD
(— OF TIMBER) TON STANDARD
(— OF WAR) BLOCKADE
(— OF WATCHES) LIGNE
(— OF WATERCRESS) HAND
(— OF WEIGHT FOR ARROWS)
SHILLING
(— OF WHISKY) CRUISKEN
CRUISKEEN
(— OF WOOD) CORD STACK
(— OF WOOL FINENESS) BLOOD
(— OF WORK) POOL
(— OF YARN) LEA RAP CLEW HEER
THREAD SPANGLE SPINDLE
(— OUT) BATCH
(ANGULAR —) ARC
(COERCIVE —) SANCTION
(COUNTERFEIT —) SLANG
(DANCE —) TRACE
(DUE —) MANNER
(FULL —) SATIETY
(QUANTITATIVE —) MAGNITUDE
(ROAD —) SCHENE
(RUSSIAN —) VERST SAGENE
(SANCTIONED —) STANDARD
(PREF.) METR(O)
(SUFF.) METER METR(E)(O)(Y)
(BY A SPECIFIED —) MEAL
MEASURED NUMEROUS
MEASURE FOR MEASURE
(AUTHOR OF —) SHAKESPEARE
(CHARACTER IN —) ELBOW FROTH
LUCIO PETER ANGELO JULIET
POMPEY THOMAS CLAUDIO
ESCALUS MARIANA VARRIUS
ABHORSON ISABELLA OVERDONE
FRANCISCA VINCENTIO
BARNARDINE
MEASURELESS ENDLESS INFINITE
MEASUREMENT GAGE DEPTH
GAUGE LEVEL MEITH METAGE
DIALING MEASURE SOUNDING
(— FOR TAXATION) HIDE HIDAGE
(— OF CLOTH) ALNAGE
(— OF FINENESS) SET SETT
(LUMBER —) LAST
MEASURER METER
MEASURING
(SUFF.) METRY
MEAT BEEF FISH FOOD LAMB LEAN
LIFT PORK FLESH STEAK VIFDA
VIVDA BUCCAN CAGMAG FLEECE
MATTER NUTTON TARGET
PECKAGE
(— AND FISH) LAULAU
(— COOKED WITH SKEWERS)
SASSATIE
(— DRIED IN SUN) JERKY CHARQUI
PEMMICAN
(— OF CONCH) SCUNGILI
(— OF KID) CAPRETTO
(— WITH VEGETABLES) STEW
MULLIGAN
(BOILED —) SOD SODDEN BOUILLI
(BROILED —) GRISKIN GRILLADE
(BUFFALO —) FLEECE

(CANNED —) SPAM
(CHOPPED —) BURGER
(COCONUT —) COPRA
(CURED —) HAM
(CUT OF —) ARM
(DRIED —) MUMMY
(FAT —) SPECK
(FROZEN —) FRIGO
(INFERIOR —) CAGMAG STICKING
(JERKED —) BILTONG CHARQUI
(LEAN —) MUSCLE
(MINCED —) CHUET JIGOTE
RISSOLE SANDERS
(POTTED —) RILLETT
(RABBIT —) LAPAN
(RAGOUT OF —) HARICOT
(ROAST —) BREDE CABOB
(ROLLED —) BIRD
(SALTED —) JUNK MART
(SIDE —) SOWBELLY
(SMOKED —) BUCCAN
MEAT CURER BATHMAN
MEAT HOOK GAMBREL
MEAT JELLY ASPIC
MEATLESS PARVE LENTEN PAREVE
MEAT PIE PASTY
MEATUS BUR BURR ALVEARY
MEATY PITHY
MECATE MCCARTY
MECHANIC JOINER WRIGHT
ARTISAN FELTMAN SHOPMAN
WORKMAN BANAUSIC OPERATIVE
MECHANICAL FROZEN INHUMAN
METALLIC AUTOMATIC
(NOT —) HORMIC
MECHANICALLY BLINDLY
MECHANISM FAN BOND FEED
GEAR KITE LIFT MOTE APRON
CATCH CROWD FORCE ORGAN
SHAKE SLIDE SPARK STEER
ACTION BOTTOM CUTOFF INFEED
MOTION SICKLE STRIKE AUTOVAC
BUILDER CHANNEL CONTROL
EJECTOR GIGBACK GRIPPER
GUNLOCK HOLDOUT SETTING
TRIPPER ACTUATOR ELEVATOR
KINETICS RACKWORK SELECTOR
SETWORKS SIGNALER STEERING
STOPWORK THROWOUT
(— OF HEREDITY) PANGENESIS
MECHANIZE DESKILL AUTOMATE
MECHLIN MALINES
MECONIN OPIANYL
MEDAL STAR AWARD STAMP
PLAQUE MEDALET OSCELLA
VERNICLE MEDALLION
MEDALLION CAMEO TONDO
PADUAN PATERA PANHAGIA
MEDAN (FATHER OF —) ABRAHAM
(MOTHER OF —) KETURAH
MEDDLE TIG FOOL MELL MESS
MIRD POKE TOUCH DABBLE
FIDDLE FINGER HECKLE POTTER
PUTTER TAMPER TANGLE TINKER
MEDDLER SNOOP SNOOPER
BUSYBODY KIBITZER STICKLER
STIFFLER BUTTINSKY
MEDDLESOME FRESH NEBBY
MEDDLING BUSY
MEDEA (BROTHER OF —) ABSYRTUS
APSYRTUS
(FATHER OF —) AEETES
(HUSBAND OF —) JASON AEGEUS

(MOTHER OF —) IDYIA
(SISTER OF —) CHALCOPE
CHALCIOPE
MEDIA ELASTICA
MEDIAL MEDIAN MEDIUM MIDDLE
AVERGAGE
MEDIAN MEDIAL MESIAL AVERAGE
(— STRIP) MALL TERRACE
MEDIANT THIRD
MEDIATE MEAN REFEREE
MEDIATING MIDDLE MIDWAY
MEDIATOR MEANS MEDIUM
DAYSMAN MIDDLER PLACATER
STICKLER MODERATOR
MEDIC HOP NONESUCH
SHAMROCK
MEDICAL IATRIC PHYSIC IATRICAL
PAEONIAN
(— WORK) ALMONING
(PREF.) (— TREATMENT) IATR(O)
MEDICAMENT SMEGMA FRONTAL
EPULOTIC
MEDICINAL IATRIC PHYSIC
MEDICAL THERIAL PHYSICAL
SALUTARY THERICAL OFFICINAL
MEDICINE DRUG MUTI PEAI DROPS
GRUEL STEEL STUFF TONIC
TRADE AMULET ECLEGM ELIXIR
MAGUAL PHYSIC POWDER
REMEDY SIMPLE ALOETIC
ANODYNE ANTACID CORDIAL
HEPATIC LUCHDOM MIXTURE
OPORICE PLACEBO POROTIC
PYROTIC SPLENIC AROMATIC
DIAPENTE DIGESTER DRUGGERY
EARDROPS ECCRITIC EMULGENT
LAXATIVE LEECHDOM LENITIVE
LOBLOLLY PECTORAL PHARMACY
PULMONIC RELAXANT SPECIFIC
STOMATIC PRESCRIPTION
(CHINESE —) SENSO
(QUACK —) NOSTRUM
(SYSTEM OF —) AYURVEDA
(UNIVERSAL —) PANACEA
(PL.) GALIANES
(PREF.) IAMATO IATRO
PHARMACO
MEDICINE MAN PEAI DOCTOR
KAHUNA PIACHE POWWOW
SHAMAN SINGER ANGEKOK
TOHUNGA CONTRARY
POWWOWER
MEDIEVAL OLD GOTHIC
MEDIOCRE HACK MEAN SUCH
MEDIUM AVERAGE INFERIOR
MIDDLING MODERATE PASSABLE
MEDITATE CAST CHEW MUSE
BROOD GLOAT STUDY THINK
WEIGH PONDER RECORD BETHINK
COMMENT IMAGINE PREPEND
REFLECT REVOLVE COGITATE
CONSIDER PURPENSE RUMINATE
MEDITATION MOYEN STUDY
THINK DHYANA MUSING REVERIE
THOUGHT HIGGAION
MEDITATIVE MUSING MUSEFUL
PENSIVE RUMINANT
MEDITERRANEAN MIDLAND
MEDIUM BATH EVEN LENS MEAN
ETHER JUICE MIDST MOYEN
ORGAN BALIAN BISTER BISTRE
DIGEST MIDDLE MIDWAY ORACLE
SLUDGE TEMPER PSYCHIC

VEHICLE MEDIOCRE SHOWCASE
CONTINUUM
(— OF EXCHANGE) CURRENCY
(— OF TRANSMISSION) AIR
AIRWAVE
(CULTURE —) AGAR STAB BROTH
HYRAX SLANT CULTURE
BOUILLON
(ENVELOPING —) SWATH
(REFINING —) ALEMBIC
MEDIUM, THE (CHARACTER IN —)
FLORA MONICA
(COMPOSER OF —) MENOTTI
MEDLAR MESPIL LAZAROLE
MEDLEY OLIO BABEL REVUE
JUMBLE CHIVARI CLANGOR
FARRAGO GOULASH MELANGE
MIXTURE BROUHAHA KEDGEREE
MACARONI MISHMASH RHAPSODY
SLAMPAMP VARIORUM
CHARIVARI MACEDOINE
MEDOC WINE LAFITTE
MEDREGAL BONITO
MEDULLA PITH MARROW
MEDULLA OBLONGATA BULB
MEDUSA JELLY QUARL GORGON
BLUBBER GERYONID
(FATHER OF —) PHORCYS
(MOTHER OF —) CETO
(SLAYER OF —) PERSEUS
(PL.) BRACT
MEEK LOW DAFT MURE LOWLY
GENTLE HUMBLE PACIFIC
LAMBLIKE YIELDING
MEEKNESS MANSUETUDE
MEERSCHAUM PIPE GRAVEL
KIEFEKIL SEPIOLITE
MEET FIT KEP SEE COPE FACE FILL
HENT NOSE ABIDE CLOSE CROSS
FRONT GREET INCUR OCCUR
PIECE TOUCH ANSWER BATTLE
BEMEET COMBAT CONCUR FULFIL
INVENT SEMBLE CONTACT
CONVENE CONVENT COUNCIL
FULFILL SATISFY ASSEMBLE
CONFRONT CONVERGE GAINCOPE
(— A BET) SEE
(— A NEED) SUFFICE
(— AT END) BUTT
(— FACE TO FACE) AFFRONT
(— SQUARELY) ENVISAGE
(— VIOLENTLY) CHECK HURTLE
(— WITH) GET SEE BUMP FIND
STRIKE
(ATHLETIC —) GALA GYMKHANA
MEETING MOD FEIS MOOT CLOSE
FORUM SABHA SHINE STOUR
SYNOD TRYST ACCESS AUMAGA
CAUCUS CHAPEL CLINIC HUDDLE
POWWOW SEANCE CABINET
CHAPTER COLLEGE CONTACT
CONVENT COUNCIL JOLLITY
MOOTING OCCURSE REVIVAL
SEMINAR SITTING SYNAXIS
ASSEMBLY CONGRESS CONSULTA
DELEGACY ECCLESIA EXERCISE
JUNCTION OSCULANT TERTULIA
WARDMOTE CONCOURSE
COLLOQUIUM
(— OF BARDS) GORSEDD
(— OF NEIGHBORS) HUSKING
(— OF SCHOLARS) LEVY
(— OF WITCHES) ESBAT

(— OF WORSHIPERS) SERVICE
(ANGLO-SAXON —) GEMOTE
(GENERAL —) PRIME
(NOT —) PARALLEL
(POLITICAL —) CAUCUS
(PRIVATE —) CONCLAVE
(SECRET —) CABAL CONSULT
CONCLAVE
(SOCIAL —) CLUB JOLLY HOBNOB
(TOWN —) TUNMOOT
MEETINGHOUSE MORADA
MEETING PLACE AMBALAM
CENACLE TINWALD
MEGAPHONE VAMPHORN
MEGAPODE MALEO LEIPOA
MEGARA (FATHER OF —) CREON
(HUSBAND OF —) HERCULES
MEGAREUS (FATHER OF —)
HIPPOMENES
(MOTHER OF —) OENOPE
(SON OF —) EUIPPUS
(WIFE OF —) IPHINOE
MEGILP GUMPTION
MEHETABEL (HUSBAND OF —)
HADAD
(MOTHER OF —) MATRED
MEHIR (FATHER OF —) CHELUB
MEHTAR BUNGY BHUNGI
MEHUJAEL (FATHER OF —) IRAD
MEIOSIS LITOTES REDUCTION
**MEISTERSINGER VON
NURNBERG, DI (CHARACTER IN —
)** EVA HANS VEIT DAVID FRITZ
SACHS POGNER KOTHNER
WALTHER STOLZING MAGDALENE
BECKMESSER
(COMPOSER OF —) WAGNER
MELAMPUS (BROTHER OF —) BIAS
(FATHER OF —) AMYTHAON
(MOTHER OF —) IDOMENE
(SON OF —) MANTIUS ANTIPHATES
(WIFE OF —) LYSIPPE
MELANCHOLIA ATHYMY ATHYMIA
SADNESS
MELANCHOLIC HYPPISH
MELANCHOLY WO LOW SAD WOE
BLUE DRAM DULL DUMP MARE
ADUST BLUES DEARN DOWIE
DREAR DUSKY GLOOM SORRY
WISHT GLOOMY SOMBER SOMBRE
SORROW SPLEEN SULLEN
YELLOW CHAGRIN DOLEFUL
DUMPISH ELEGIAC SADNESS
SPLEENY THOUGHT ATRABILE
LIVERISH TRISTFUL
MELANESIAN DOBUAN KANAGA
KANAKA EFATESE
MELANGE GOMBO GUMBO
SMORGASBORD
MELANIPPUS (FATHER OF —)
THESEUS HICETAON
(LOVER OF —) COMAETHO
(MOTHER OF —) PERIGUNE
(SON OF —) IOXUS
MELANISM PHAEISM
MELANTERITE INKSTONE
MELANTIUS (SISTER OF —) EVADNE
MELATOPE EYE
MELCHI (FATHER OF —) ADDI
JANNA
MELCHIAH (SON OF —) PASHUR
MELD SET SAMBA SPREAD BOLIVIA
DECLARE

MELEA (FATHER OF —) MENAN
MELEAGER (FATHER OF —) OENEUS
(MOTHER OF —) ALTHAEA
MELECH (FATHER OF —) MICAH
MELEE BRAWL MEDLEY DOGFIGHT
PELLMELL WINGDING
MELIA (FATHER OF —) OCEANUS
(SON OF —) ISMENUS TENERUS
AEGIALEUS PHORONEUS
MELIBOEA (FATHER OF —)
AMPHION
(HUSBAND OF —) NELEUS
(MOTHER OF —) NIOBE
MELIORATE MITIGATE
MELISMA JUBILUS
MELL KIRN
MELLIFLUOUS SUGARED
HYBLAEAN
MELLOW AGE OMY HAZE LUSH
MALM PLUM RICH RIPE SOFT
FRUSH RIPEN FLUTED GOLDEN
MATURE
MELLOWED BEERY
MELODIOUS SOFT SOOT TUNY
SWEET TUNED ARIOSO DULCET
MELODIC MUSICAL SIRENIC
SONGFUL TUNABLE TUNEFUL
CANOROUS CHARMING
NUMEROUS SOUNDFUL
(EXCESSIVELY —) SIRUPY SYRUPY
MELODRAMA HAM TANK
MELODY AIR HUM LAY ARIA NOTE
TUNE CANTO CHANT CHARM
DREAD MELOS MIRTH NIGUN
CANTUS CHORAL GHAZEL
MONODY NIGGUN STROKE
CANZONA CANZONE CHORALE
DESCANT HARMONY MEASURE
MELISMA PLANXTY ROSALIA
CARILLON CAVATINA DIAPASON
VOCALISE
(— COMPASS) AMBITUS
(MOURNFUL —) DUMP
(SYNAGOGAL —S) CHAZANUT
HAZANUTH
MELON PEPO GOURD MANGO
CASABA CITRON DUDAIM
MAYCOCK CUCURBIT HONEYDEW
PEPONIDA PEPONIUM
MELT FLY RIN RUN BLOW FADE
FLOW FLUX FUSE THAW FOUND
LEACH SMELT SWEAL SWELT
TOUCH GUTTER RELENT SOFTEN
DISTILL FORMELT RESOLVE
DISCANDY DISSOLVE ELIQUATE
COLLIQUATE
(— AWAY) SWEAL
(— DOWN) RENDER
(— IRREGULARLY) DROZE
MELTED RUN FONDU FUSED
FUSILE
MELTING SOFT FUSILE FUSION
MELTWATER OUTWASH
MEMBER LIMB LITH PART BRANCH
FELLOW FILLET GIRDER SOCIUS
AMANIST COMPART ERANIST
FAIRING ALBRIGHT AULARIAN
BRIDLING
(— OF ANSAR) HELPER
(— OF BALLET) FIGURANT
(— OF BAND) SIDEMAN
(— OF BODYGUARD) HUSCARL

(— OF BROTHERHOOD) ESSENE SENUSSI
(— OF CLAN) CHILD CALEBITE
(— OF CLERGY) DEFENSOR
(— OF COAST GUARD) SPAR
(— OF COUNCIL) CONSUL HEEMRAAD
(— OF COURT) DICAST EPHETE
(— OF CREW) HAND IDLER LAYER DRIVER STROKE BOWSMAN FORETOP BRAKEMAN SHAREMAN
(— OF CULT) ANGEL AMIDIST
(— OF FACULTY) COUNSEL LECTURER
(— OF FAMILY) FETII
(— OF FRATERNAL ORDER) ELK SHRINER FORESTER KIWANIAN
(— OF FRATERNITY) GREEK
(— OF FRENCH ACADEMY) IMMORTAL
(— OF GANG) HENCHMAN
(— OF GENTRY) SEIGNEUR
(— OF GIRL SCOUTS) BROWNIE
(— OF GREEK ARMY) EVZONE
(— OF GUILD) COMACINE HOASTMAN
(— OF HOUSEHOLD) FAMILIAR
(— OF HUNTING PARTY) STANDER
(— OF INN OF COURT) ANCIENT BENCHER
(— OF ITALIAN ARMY) ALPINO
(— OF KNOW-NOTHING PARTY) SAM
(— OF LEGISLATURE) SOLON DEPUTY DELEGATE
(— OF LITERARY GROUP) FELIBRE
(— OF MIDDLE CLASS) BURGHER
(— OF PARLIAMENT) CONTENT THINGMAN
(— OF PRIMROSE LEAGUE) KNIGHT
(— OF RELIGIOUS ORDER) DAME FRIAR EUDIST FRAILE FRATER HERMIT JESUIT SISTER ALEXIAN BEGUINE BRINSER DERVISH HUSSITE SEPARTE SERVANT SERVITE CENOBITE EXORCIST HUMANIST SALESIAN
(— OF RETINUE) SEQUEL SEQUENT
(— OF RUSSIAN ARISTOCRACY) BOIAR BOYAR BOYARD
(— OF SAME GENUS) CONGENER
(— OF SECRET ORGANIZATION) DEMOLAY
(— OF SECRET SOCIETY) BOXER DANITE
(— OF SECT) BABI BABEE DRUSE HASID KHOJA AUDIAN BEREAN BRAHMO CATHAR DIPPER DOPPER IBADHI JUMPER KHLYST SMARTA AISSAWA AJIVIKA AUDAEAN CAINITE CHASSID DREAMER EMPIRIC EUCHITE IBADITE ISAWIYA ISMAILI RAPPIST SENUSSI SEVENER AQUARIAN CALIXTIN DARBYITE DUKHOBOR EBIONITE FAMILIST GLASSITE LABADIST MANDAEAN SADDUCEE SEVERIAN SHAFIITE SIMONIAN
(— OF STAFF) ATTACHE
(— OF STATE) CITIZEN
(— OF STOCK EXCHANGE) BOARDMAN

(— OF TEAM) SPARE BOBBER KICKER
(— OF TRIBE) LEVITE JUDAHITE LAMANITE
(— OF UPPER CLASS) EFFENDI
(— OF VARNA) SUDRA SHUDRA
(— OF WHITE RACE) HAOLE
(— OF WINDOW) APRON
(—S OF CLASS) FRY
(—S OF PROFESSION) FACULTY
(—S OF SECT) SKOPTSY
(—S OF TRIBUNAL) ACUERDO
(ARCHITECTURAL —) FAN ARCH FLAT SILL SPAN GABLE SOCLE STILE STILT CORBEL FASCIA CONSOLE CORNICE
(CHURCH —) GREEK LATIN DANITE DUNKER KIRKER TUNKER AZYMITE BAPTIST BEGHARD BROTHER DUNKARD KIRKMAN SECEDER ARMENIAN BRYANITE CATHOLIC DISCIPLE DOWIEITE JACOBITE
(CHURCH —S) FAITHFUL
(EVERY —) ALL
(FEEBLEST —) WRIG
(FULL —) GREMIAL
(OLDEST —) FATHER
(OVERHANGING —) BRACKET
(POLITICAL —) CADET ENDEK SHIRT GUELPH HUNKER LEADER APRISTA LEFTIST LIBERAL ABHORRER BUCKTAIL DEMOCRAT HERODIAN LABORITE
(PROJECTING —) TENON
(SECRET —) CRYPTO
(SENIOR —) DOYEN
(TENSION —) HANGER
(TERMINAL —) TOE
(SUFF.) AD CRAT
(— OF A CLASS) ANDER
MER(E)(IC)(IS)(OUS)(Y)
MEMBERS
(SUFF.) **(— OF THE FAMILY)** IDAE
(— OF THE SUBFAMILY OF) INAE
MEMBERSHIP SEAT GARTER GUILDRY
MEMBRANE RIM WEB CAUL COAT DURA FELL HEAD TELA GALEA HYMEN VELUM AMNION AMNIOS EXTINE INTINE MENINX MOTHER MUCOSA PLEURA RETINA SEPTUM SEROSA TIMBAL TUNICA TYMPAN BLANKET CAPSULE CHORION CHOROID CUTICLE DECIDUA EPICYTE HYALOID OOLEMMA PUTAMEN STRATUM VELAMEN ECTODERM ENDOCYST ENVELOPE EPENDYMA EPISPORE EXOLEMMA INDUSIUM INTEXINE LABELLUM PATAGIUM PELLICLE STRIFFEN ALLANTOIS PERIPLAST PERITONEUM
(— OF ORANGE) ZEST
(NICTITATING —) HAW
(TYMPANIC —) TYMPAN MYRINGA DRUMHEAD DRUMSKIN
(PL.) ADNEXA ANNEXA MENINGES
(PREF.) CHORI(O) HYMEN(O) MENING(O) MYRINGO VEL(I)
(SUFF.) YMENITIS
MEMBRANOUS HUSKY SKINNY

HYMENOID SCARIOSE SCARIOUS
MEMENTO RELIC TOKEN MEMORY TROPHY KEEPSAKE REMINDER SOUVENIR
MEMINNA PEESOREH
MEMNON (FATHER OF —) TITHONUS
(MOTHER OF —) AURORA
(SLAYER OF —) ACHILLES
MEMOIR ELOGE RECORD HISTORY MEMORIAL
MEMORABLE GRAND SIGNAL CLASSIC NOTABLE MEMORIAL NAMEABLE NOTEWORTHY
MEMORANDA (SET OF —) TICKLER
MEMORANDUM BILL CHIT NOTE SLIP BRIEF JURAT CAHIER CIPHER DOCKET MEMOIR MINUTE TICKET JOTTING MEMORIAL NOTANDUM PROTOCOL BORDEREAU
MEMORIAL AHU AGALMA CAHIER FACTUM MEMOIR MEMORY RECORD TROPHY DENKMAL MEMENTO MENTION EBENEZER MONUMENT REMEMBRANCE
MEMORIZE LEARN MANDATE REMEMBER
MEMORY MIND HEART IMAGE STORE RECALL RECORD MEMENTO STORAGE MEMORIAL SOUVENIR
(— ON COMPUTER CHIP) RAM ROM
(— SUBDIVISION) PAGE
(COMPUTER —) STACK
(OF POOR —) FLUFFY
(PAINFUL —) SCAR
(SMALL COMPUTER —) SCRATCHPAD
(PREF.) MNEM(I)(O)
(SUFF.) MNESIA(C) MNESIS MNETIC
MEN THEY ORANG INNUIT MANHEAD MANHOOD MANKIND MENFOLK HUMANITY
MENACE BOAST IMPEND THREAT BOGEYMAN MINATORY THREATEN
MENACING STOUT SURLY FIERCE TOWARD MINATORY MINACIOUS
MENAHEM (FATHER OF —) GADI
(VICTIM OF —) SHALLUM
MEN-AT-ARMS CHIVALRY
MEND DO FIX BEET DARN HEAL HELP STOP TINK AMEND CLOUT EMEND GRAFT MOISE PATCH COBBLE DOCTOR FETTLE RANTER REFORM REPAIR SOLDER SPETCH TINKLE IMPROVE INWEAVE REDRESS RIGHTLE
(— BY ADDING FEATHERS) IMP
(— CLUMSILY) BOTCH
(— MEN'S CLOTHES) BUSHEL
MENDACIOUS FALSE DISHONEST
MENDACITY LYING DECEIT FALSITY UNTRUTH
MENDER TINKER KETTLER BEATSTER
MENDICANCY BEGGARY
MENDICANT NAGA DANDI FAKIR FRIAR UDASI BEGGAR BHIKKU FAKEER FRATER GOSAIN AJIVIKA BAIRAGI EUCHITE VAIRAGI PANDARAM SANNYASI PASSIONIST

MENDING COBBLE
MENEL NELL
MENELAUS (BROTHER OF —) AGAMEMNON
(FATHER OF —) ATREUS PLISTHENES
(MOTHER OF —) AEROPE
(SISTER OF —) ANAXIBIA
(WIFE OF —) HELEN
MENHADEN POGY PORGY BUNKER CHEBOG SHINER ALEWIFE BUGFISH BUGHEAD CLUPEID ELLFISH FATBACK OLDWIFE SAVELHA SHADINE WHITING BONYFISH HARDHEAD
MENHIR BOUTA GORSEDD PEULVAN CATSTONE HAGIOLITH
MENIAL FAG BASE LOON PAGE KNAVE DRIVEL HARLOT POTBOY VARLET SERVILE SLAVISH BANAUSIC SCULLION SERVITOR
MENISCOID CRESCENT
MENNONITE HOOKER AMISHMAN AMMANITE HUTERITE
MENOETIUS (BROTHER OF —) ATLAS PROMETHEUS
(FATHER OF —) ACTOR
(MOTHER OF —) AEGINA
(SON OF —) PATROCLUS
MENOPAUSE CLIMAX
MENSTRUATE FLOW
MENSTRUATING SICK
MENSTRUATION FLOW CURSE FLUOR CRAMPS PERIOD COURSES
(FIRST —) MENARCHE
(PREF.) MENO
(SUFF.) **(— CONDITION)** MENIA
MENSTRUUM SOLVENT
MENTAL IDEAL GENIAL INWARD MINDLY PHRENIC PSYCHIC CEREBRAL
MENTALITY MIND SENSE ACUMEN REASON SPIRIT PSYCHISM
MENTHA LABIATE
MENTHANE TERPANE
MENTHOL CAMPHOR
MENTION CALL CITE HINT MIND MING MINT NAME CHEEP CLEPE SPEAK TOUCH MEMBER NOTICE SPEECH MEANING SPECIFY SUGGEST CITATION INSTANCE MEMORATE REHEARSE REMEMBER REFERENCE REPETITION
(— BY NAME) NEMN NEMME NEMPNE
(— CASUALLY) DROP
(HONORABLE —) ACCESSIT
MENTOR TEACHER CICERONE
MENTUM PERULA
MENU CARD CARTE
(COMPUTER —) DISPLAY
MEONOTHAI (FATHER OF —) OTHNIEL
MEPACRINE ATABRIN ATABRINE
MEPERIDINE DEMEROL
MEPHIBOSHETH (BROTHER OF —) ARMONI
(FATHER OF —) SAUL JONATHAN
(MOTHER OF —) RIZPAH
(SON OF —) MICHA
MEPHISTOPHELIAN SATANIC

MEPROBAMATE MILTOWN
MERAB (FATHER OF —) SAUL
  (HUSBAND OF —) ADRIEL
MERARI (FATHER OF —) LEVI
MERCAPTAN THIOL
MERCEDARIAN NOLASCAN
  RANSOMER
MERCENARY HACK VENAL JACKAL
  HESSIAN PINDARI HIRELING
  WAGELING
MERCER SILKMAN
MERCERIZE SCHREINER
MERCHANDISE CARGO CHEAP
  GOODS STUFF WARES ARTWARE
  CHAFFER SHIPPER TRAFFIC
  CHAFFERY SALEWARE
  (CHEAP SHODDY —) BORAX
  (RETURNED —) COMEBACK
MERCHANT ARAB SETH SETT TELI
  WALLA BADGER FACTOR KITELY
  NEPMAN RETAIL TAIPAN TRADER
  ANTONIO CHAPMAN GOLADAR
  HANSARD HOWADJI CHANDLER
  HUCKSTER MARCHAND
  POVINDAH SOUDAGUR
  (GRAIN —) LAMBADI
  (GREAT —) TAIPAN
  (HINDU —) BUNIA BUNNIA
  (WINE —) VINTNER
MERCHANT OF VENICE (AUTHOR
  OF —) SHAKESPEARE
  (CHARACTER IN —) GOBBO TUBAL
  PORTIA ANTONIO JESSICA
  LORENZO NERISSA SALANIO
  SALERIO SHYLOCK BASSANIO
  GRATIANO LEONARDO SALARINO
  STEPHANO BALTHASAR
  LAUNCELOT
MERCIFUL KIND MILD HUMANE
  RUEFUL TENDER CLEMENT
  LENIENT MILDFUL PITIFUL
  SPARING GRACIOUS QUEMEFUL
MERCILESS GRIM CRUEL SHARP
  BLOODY FIERCE SAVAGE
  WANTON PITILESS
MERCURY HG AZOCH AZOTH
  DRAGON HERMES SPIRIT CHIBRIT
  MARKERY TEUTATES
  QUICKSILVER
  (FATHER OF —) JUPITER
  (MOTHER OF —) MAIA
MERCY LAW ORE HORE PITY RUTH
  GRACE GRITH BLITHE LENITY
  CHARITY CLEMENCY LENIENCY
  COMPASSION
  (PREF.) MISERI
MERE BARE NUDE ONLY PURE
  PUTE SOLE VERY NAKED SHEER
  SINGLE
  (PREF.) PSIL(O)
MEREL PIN
MERELY BUT JUST ONLY BARELY
  PURELY SIMPLY SINGLY SOLELY
  ALONELY UTTERLY ENTIRELY
  SCARCELY
MEREMOTH (FATHER OF —) BANI
  URIAH
MERETRICIOUS CHEAP GAUDY
  GILDED TAWDRY PUNKISH
MERGANSER SMEE SMEW HARLE
  SNOWL SPIKE HERALD SAWNEB
  WEASER BRACKET GARBILL
  JACKSAW RANTOCK SAWBILL

TADPOLE TOWHEAD TWEEZER
  WHEEZER EARLDUCK MOSSHEAD
  SHELDRAKE
MERGE FUSE JOIN MELD BLEND
  ENTER GLIDE UNIFY VERGE
  MINGLE COALESCE COMMERGE
  CONFLATE LIQUESCE
MERGING BLEND FUSION
MERICARP COCCUS
MERIDIAN (THOSE LIVING UNDER
  SAME —) ANTOECI
MERINGUE KISS
MERINO DELAINE
MERISTEM PERIBLEM
MERIT DUE EARN MEED PUNY
  BROOK FOUND THANK WORTH
  DESERT PRAISE VIRTUE WRIHTE
  DEMERIT DESERVE PUDDING
  (— CONSIDERATION) COUNT
  (POSSESSING —) WORTHY
MERITED JUST
  (NOT —) INDIGN
MERITORIOUS CAPITAL MERITORY
  THANKFUL VALOROUS
MERL BLACKIE
MERLIN (MISTRESS OF —) VIVIEN
MERLON COP
MERMAID NIXIE SIREN MERROW
  MERWOMAN
MERMAN SEAMAN MANFISH
MERODACH (FATHER OF —) EA
  (WIFE OF —) ZARPAINT
MEROPE **(BROTHER OF —)**
  PHAETHON
  (FATHER OF —) ATLAS OENOPION
  PANDAREUS CRESPHONTES
  (HUSBAND OF —) POLYBUS
  SISYPHUS POLYPHONTES
  (MOTHER OF —) PLEIONE
  CYPSELUS HARMOTHOE
  (SISTER OF —) AEDON CLEOTHERA
  (SON OF —) AEPYTUS
MEROPODITE FEMUR MEROS
MEROZOITE AGAMETE
MERRILY GAILY GAMELY LIGHTLY
  LUSTICK JOYOUSLY
MERRIMENT FUN JOY GALE GLEE
  JEST UTAS DERAY MIRTH FROLIC
  SPLEEN DAFFERY DAFFING
  FESTIVE JOLLITY WAGGERY
  HILARITY
MERRY GAY BOON CANT GLAD
  GOLE BONNY BUXOM CADGY
  CRANK DROLL JOLLY LIGHT
  LUSTY MURRY SUNNY VOGIE
  VOKIE BLITHE COCKET FROLIC
  JOCANT JOCOSE JOCUND JOVIAL
  JOYOUS LIVELY FEASTLY GLEEFUL
  HOLIDAY JOCULAR LUSTICK
  RAFFING WINSOME CHIRPING
  DISPOSED FESTIVAL GAMESOME
  GLEESOME LAUGHING PLEASANT
  SPANKING SPORTFUL SPORTIVE
  CONVIVIAL
  (UNREASONABLY —) DAFT
MERRY-ANDREW AIRY ZANY
  ANTIC DROLL JESTER BUFFOON
MERRY-GO-ROUND CAROUSEL
  TURNABOUT ROUNDABOUT
MERRYMAKING ALE MAY RAG
  KIRN PLOY REVEL GAIETY JUNKET
  RACKET SPLORE CARNIVAL
MERRYTHOUGHT WISHBONE

MERRY WIDOW (CHARACTER IN —)
  ZETA HANNA MIRKO DANILO
  GLAWARI
  (COMPOSER OF —) LEHAR
MERRY WIVES OF WINDSOR
  (AUTHOR OF —) SHAKESPEARE
  (CHARACTER IN —) NYM ANNE
  FORD HUGH JOHN PAGE CAIUS
  EVANS ROBIN RUGBY FENTON
  PISTOL SIMPLE QUICKLY
  SHALLOW SLENDER WILLIAM
  BARDOLPH FALSTAFF
MERUS PALM
MESA HILL LOMA BENCH MESILLA
  PLATEAU TERRACE CARTOUCH
MESADENIA CACALIA
MESCAL PEYOTE PEYOTL WOKOWI
  MEXICAL CHALLOTE
MESCALERO FARAON
MESECH (FATHER OF —) JAPHET
MESENTERY CROW RUFFLE
MESH MASK MOKE CHAIN PITCH
  SHALE ACCRUE ENGAGE MASCLE
  SCREEN INTERLOCK SCREENING
  (— IMPROPERLY) BUTT
  (IN —) DIRECT
MESHA (FATHER OF —) CALEB
  SHAHARAIM
  (MOTHER OF —) HODESH
MESHED ENGAGED
MESHEZABEEL (FATHER OF —)
  ZERAH
  (SON OF —) PETHAHIAH
MESHILLEMOTH (FATHER OF —)
  IMMER
MESHULLAM (FATHER OF —)
  BERECHIAH BESODEIAH
  ZERUBBABEL
  (SON OF —) SALLU
MESHULLEMETH (FATHER OF —)
  HARUZ
  (HUSBAND OF —) MANASSEH
  (SON OF —) AMON
MESOCARP FLESH
MESOMORPHIC SOMAL SOMATIC
  ATHLETIC
MESON RHO KAON PION
  BARYTRON MESOTRON
MESOPODIUM PETIOLE
MESOPOTAMIA (TREE OF —) HOMA
MESOTONIC TERTIAN MEANTONE
MESQUITE HONEY KEAWE PACAY
  CASHAW ALGAROBA HONEYPOD
  IRONWOOD MOSQUITO
MESS JAG JAM MIX MUX PIE SOP
  CLAT FIST HASH JAMB MUCK
  MULL MUSS SLUB SOSS STEW
  SUSS BOTCH CAUCH JAKES
  STREW SWILL BOLLIX BUNGLE
  CADDLE CLATCH JUMBLE
  MUCKER PICKLE PUDDLE SOZZLE
  TUMBLE MAMMOCK MULLOCK
  SCAMBLE SLOTTER COUSCOUS
  DISORDER LOBLOLLY SHAMBLES
  SLAISTER
  (— AROUND) JUKE
  (— OF FOOD) SAND
  (GREASY —) GAUM
  (SLOPPY —) SLOBBER SLAISTER
MESSAGE CHIT MODE SAND SEND
  WIRE WORD RUMOR BREVET
  CIPHER ERRAND GOSPEL LETTER
  SCROLL BLINKER BODWORD

DEPECHE EMBASSY MISSION
  SENDING TIDINGS AEROGRAM
  CREDENCE DISPATCH
  (— BY FLAGS) HOIST
  (— FROM GOD) ANGEL
  (CHRISTIAN —) EVANGEL
  (CIPHER —) SCYTALE
  (COMPLIMENTARY —) RECADO
  (SEQUENCE OF —S) QUEUE
MESSALIAN EUCHITE
MESSENE (FATHER OF —) TRIOPAS
  (HUSBAND OF —) POLYCAON
MESSENGER BODE PEON POST
  SAND SEND TOTY VAUX ANGEL
  ENVOY MUMMU VISOR BEADLE
  BROKER BUNENE CHIAUS HERALD
  LEGATE NUNCIO PIGEON RUNNER
  APOSTLE CARRIER CASHBOY
  CONTACT COURANT COURIER
  EXPRESS FORAGER FORAYER
  MALACHI MERCURY MESSAGE
  MISSIVE NAMTARU PATAMAR
  TOTYMAN TROTTER TRUMPET
  EMISSARY FOREGOER HIRCARRA
  LOBBYGOW NUNCIATE ORDINARY
  PORTATOR APPARITOR
  (— OF APSU AND TIAMAT) MUMMU
  (— OF GOD) ANGEL
  (— OF SHAMASH) BUNENE
  (— OF THE GODS) HERMES
  MERCURY
  (MOUNTED —) COSSID ESTAFET
  (RELIGIOUS —) APOSTLE
  (UNDERWORLD —) NAMTARU
MESSIAH CHRIST WOVOKA
  (MUSLIM —) MAHDI
MESSMATE YUBA
MESSUAGE HAW TOFT MEESE
  MIDSTEAD
MESSY GOOEY SLOPPY SOZZLY
  STICKY
MESTIZO CHOLO LADINO
  CURIBOCA MAMELUCO
MESTOR (DAUGHTER OF —)
  HIPPOTHOE
  (FATHER OF —) PERSEUS
  (MOTHER OF —) ANDROMEDA
  (WIFE OF —) LYSIDICE
METAL ORE TIN BODY DIET GOLD
  IRON LEAD ZINC BARIUM CESIUM
  CHROME COBALT COPPER INDIUM
  LATTIN NICKEL ORMOLU OSMIUM
  RADIUM SILVER SODIUM
  BISMUTH CADMIUM CALCIUM
  HAFNIUM IRIDIUM LITHIUM
  MERCURY RHENIUM RHODIUM
  THORIUM TUTANIA URANIUM
  YTTRIUM ALUMINUM ANTIMONY
  CHROMIUM DEADHEAD
  PLATINUM RUBIDIUM SCANDIUM
  TANTALUM TINCTURE TITANIUM
  TUNGSTEN VANADIUM
  (— IN MASS) BULLION
  (— IN SHEETS) LEAF PLATE
  (BABBITT —) LINING
  (BASE —) BILLON
  (DECORATED —) TOLE
  (GROUND —) BRONZING
  (HEAVIEST —) OSMIUM
  (IMPURE MASS OF —) REGULUS
  (LIGHTEST —) LITHIUM
  (LIQUID —) MERCURY
  (MASS OF —) INGOT

(MOLTEN —) TAP SQUIRT
(OLD POT —) POTIN
(PERFORATED —) STENCIL
(PIECE OF CRUDE —) SLUG
(POINTED —) NAIL
(POROUS —) SPONGE
(SEMIFINISHED —) SEMIS
(SHEET —) LATTEN DOUBLES
KALAMEIN
(WASTE —) GATE
METALLIC HARD THIN TINNY
METALLOPHONE SARON
(BALINESE —) GANGSA
METALLURGIST AMERICAN HUNT
HOLLEY PETERS SHIMER
ENGLISH PERCY MUSHET THOMAS
HADFIELD
FRENCH HEROULT
METALWARE TOLE LORMERY
GRAYWARE PONTYPOOL
METALWORK ZOGAN
METALWORKER BARMAN FOONER
FORKMAN FOUNDER SUDSMAN
METAMERE SOMITE SEGMENT
MEROSOME
METAMERIC SEGMENTAL
METAMORPHIC
(PREF.) BLAST(O)
METAMORPHOSE TURN SHAPE
INDENIZE TRANSMEW
METAMORPHOSIS METABOLE
PETALODY PHYLLODY SEPALODY
(SUFF.) ODY
METANIRA (HUSBAND OF —)
CELEUS
(SON OF —) DEMOPHON
TRIPTOLEMUS
METAPHOR IMAGE TROPE FIGURE
KENNING
METAPHORICAL FIGURAL
FIGURATE TROPICAL
METASTOMA LABIUM
METATE QUERL
METE DEAL DOLE GIVE ALLOT
AWARD MATCH SERVE MEASURE
APPORTION
METEMPSYCHOSIS SAMSARA
METEOR STAR ARGID CETID COMID
DRAKE LUPID LYRID URSID
ANTLID AUGUST BOLIDE BOOTID
CORVID CYGNID DRAGON HYDRID
LIBRID LYNCID LYRAID PHASMA
PISCID TAURID AQUARID AQUILID
ARIETID AURIGID CAMELID
CANCRID CEPHEID CORONID
GEMINID MEATURE ORIONID
PEGASID PERSEID POLARID
PRODIGY COLUMBID CRATERID
DRACONID ERIDANID FIREBALL
FORNAXID HERCULID LACERTID
SAGITTID SCORPIID SHOTSTAR
TOUCANID VIRGINID
(SUFF.) ID
METEORITE BAETYL BOLIDE
ANDRITE ATAXITE EUCRITE
AEROLITE AEROLITH BAETULUS
BAETYLUS IREOLITE SIDERITE
SKYSTONE
METEOROLOGIST AMERICAN EDDY
ESPY WARD ROTCH FERREL
MARVIN CLAYTON REDFIELD
CARPENTER
AUSTRIAN FALB HANN PERNTER

ENGLISH REID SHAW DINES
GALTON GLAISHER
FRENCH MOREUX PELTIER
GERMAN DOVE FICKER WEGENER
BRUCKNER NEUMAYER
NORWEGIAN MOHN SVERDRUP
RUSSIAN TILLO
SCOTTISH MILL BUCHAN
SWEDISH MALMGREN
SWISS WILD DELUC
METEOROLOGY AEROLOGY
METER IONIC METRE SEVEN
ALCAIC RHYTHM CADENCE
GAYATRI MEASURE SUBMETER
VIAMETER YAWMETER
(CUBIC —) STERE
(MILLIONTH OF —) MICRON
(NETHERLANDS —) ELL
(SQUARE —) CENTIARE
(VEDIC —) GAYATRI
(10 CUBIC —S) DEKASTERE
(10,000 —S) GREX
METHADONE AMIDONE
METHANE FORMENE
METHANOL WOODINE CARBINOL
METHEGLIN MEAD
METHOD ART WAY DART FORM
GARB GATE KINK LINE MIDS
MODE REDE RULE SORT ORDER
STYLE TRACK USAGE COURSE
ENGINE MANNER STEREO SYSTEM
FASHION PROCESS TACTICS
WRINKLE ADJUVANT STANDARD
(— OF ANGLING) HARLING
(— OF APPEALING) DHARNA
DHURNA
(— OF COLORING TEA) FACING
(— OF CONSTRUCTION) JACAL
(— OF CULTIVATION) JUM JOOM
STUMPING
(— OF DIETING) BANTING
(— OF DISTILLATION) DESCENT
(— OF ELECTION) SCRUTINY
(— OF FATTENING POULTRY)
GAVAGE
(— OF INDUCTION) CANON
(— OF MILKING) NIEVLING
(— OF MURAL DECORATION) KHASI
(— OF PROCEDURE) GAME
(— OF SELECTING POPE) SCRUTINY
(— OF TRACKING) DOVAP
(— OF TREATMENT) SCOPE
(CLEVER —) KINK KINKLE
(FIXED —) FORMULA
(MEDICAL —) CUSHION
(OUTMODED —) ARCHAISM
(PAINTING —) GOUACHE
(PRINTING —) AQUATONE
(SCIENTIFIC —) BACONISM
(SURVEYING —) STADIA
(USUAL —) COURSE PRACTICE
METHODICAL TRIG EXACT
FORMAL SEVERE ORDERLY
REGULAR ORDINARY ORDINATE
METHODIST JUMPER WESLEYAN
SWADDLING
METHODIZE ORDER REGULATE
METHUSAEL (FATHER OF —)
MEHUJAEL
(SON OF —) LAMECH
METHUSELAH (FATHER OF —)
ENOCH
METHYLAL FORMAL

METICULOUS FUSSY NARROW
STICKY CAREFUL FINICAL FINICKY
PARTICULAR
METION (BROTHER OF —) CECROPS
(FATHER OF —) ERECHTHEUS
(MOTHER OF —) PRAXITHEA
METONYM SYNONYM
METRICAL MEASURED
(— QUANTITY) MATRA
METRICS PROSODY
METRONOME (PART OF —) BOX
KEY CASE PIVOT SCALE SHAFT
WEIGHT PENDULUM
METROPOLIS CITY SEAT CAPITAL
METROPOLITAN EPARCH EXARCH
METTLE PITH SAUL PRIDE SPUNK
GINGER SPIRIT COURAGE
SMEDDUM
METTLESOME FIERY PROUD
SKEIGH SPUNKY STUFFY FLIGHTY
GINGERY SPIRITED
MEUSE
(PREF.) (RIVER —) MOSA
MEW PEN WOW CAGE CAST COOP
GULL MEWL MOLT SHED MEUTE
MIAOU MIAOW HIDEAWAY
INTERMEW SEEDBIRD
CONFINEMENT
MEWER WRAWLER
MEWL WRAWL
MEWS ALLEY COURT STREET
STABLES
MEXICAN CHOLO LEPERO
WETBACK
(AMERICAN OF — DESCENT)
CHICANO
MEXICAN-AMERICAN PACHUCO
MEXICAN ELM MEZCAL
MEXICAN ONYX TECALI
MEXICAN PERSIMMON CHAPOTE
MEXICAN POPPY ARGEMONE
MEXICAN TEA BASOTE APASOTE
FISHWEED WORMSEED

MEXICO
CAPITAL: MEXICOCITY
COIN: PESO TLAC ADOBE CLACO
TLACO AZTECA CENTAVO
PIASTER
LAKE: CHAPALA
MEASURE: PIE VARA ALMUD BARIL
JARRA LABOR LEGUA LINEA
SITIO FANEGA PULGADA
MOUNTAIN: BUFA BLANCO
CUPULA PEROTE ORIZABA
PENINSULA: BAJA YUCATAN
PEOPLE: MAM CHOL CORA MAYA
MIXE PIMA SERI TECO XOVA
AZTEC NAHUA OPATA OTOMI
ZOQUE EUDEVE MIXTEC TOLTEC
NAYARIT TEPANEC TOTONAC
ZACATEC ZAPOTEC TEZCUCAN
TOTONACO ZACATECO
RIVER: BRAVO LERMA BALSAS
GRANDE PANUCO TABASCO
GRIJALVA SANTIAGO
STATE: LEON NUEVO COLIMA
OAXACA SONORA CHIAPAS
DURANGO HIDALGO NAYARIT
SINALOA TABASCO YUCATAN
CAMPECHE QUINTANA
VERACRUZ
TOWN: LEON LAPAZ TEPIC ARIZPE

COLIMA JALAPA JUAREZ
MERIDA OAXACA PARRAL
POTOSI PUEBLA CANANEA
DURANGO GUAYMAS MORELIA
ORIZABA PACHUCA TAMPICO
TORREON CULIACAN
MAZATLAN MONCLOVA
SALTILLO TLAXCALA VERACRUZ
VOLCANO: COLIMA TOLUCA
JORULLO PARICUTIN
POPOCATEPETL
WEIGHT: BAG ONZA CARGA LIBRA
MARCO ADARME ARROBA
OCHAVA TERCIO QUINTAL

MEZAHAB (DAUGHTER OF —)
MATRED
MEZZANINE ENTRESOL
MIAROLITIC DRUSY
MIASMA REEK MALARIA
MAREMMA
MIB MIGGLE
MIBSAM (FATHER OF —) SIMEON
ISHMAEL
MICA DAZE TALC GLIST SLUDE
BIOTITE GLIMMER ALURGITE
FUCHSITE PHENGITE PHLOGOPITE
MICAH (FATHER OF —) UZZIEL
MERIBBAAL
(SON OF —) ABDON
MICAH CLARKE (AUTHOR OF —)
DOYLE
(CHARACTER IN —) JACOB MICAH
SAXON CLANCY CLARKE GERVAS
JOSEPH REUBEN DECIMUS
STEPHEN LOCKARBY MONMOUTH
TIMEWELL
MICAIAH (FATHER OF —) IMLAH
MICE (BREEDING PLACE FOR —)
MURARIUM
MICHA (FATHER OF —)
MEPHIBOSHETH
(SON OF —) MATTANIAH
MICHAEL MIKE MICKY MICHEL
MIGUEL
(FATHER OF —) IZRAHIAH
JEHOSHAPHAT
(SLAYER OF —) JEHORAM
(SON OF —) OMRI SETHUR
MICHAH (FATHER OF —) UZZIEL
MICHAIAH (FATHER OF —) URIEL
GEMARIAH
(HUSBAND OF —) REHOBOAM
(SON OF —) ABIJAH
MICHAL (FATHER OF —) SAUL
(HUSBAND OF —) DAVID PHALTI

MICHIGAN
BAY: SAGINAW THUNDER
KEWEENAW STURGEON
CAPITAL: LANSING
COLLEGE: ALMA WAYNE ADRIAN
ALBION CALVIN OLIVET
OWOSSO OAKLAND
COUNTY: BAY CASS IRON LUCE
CLARE DELTA IONIA IOSCO
ALCONA OCEANA OGEMAW
OSCODA OTSEGO GOGEBIC
OSCEOLA TUSCOLA KALKASKA
INDIAN: OTTAWA
LAKE: BURT TORCH HOUGHTON
MOUNTAIN: CURWOOD
NATIVE: WOLVERINE

MICHIGAN
NICKNAME: LAKE WOLVERINE
RIVER: CASS BRULE HURON
  DETROIT SAGINAW STCLAIR
  ESCANABA MONTREAL
  MENOMINEE
STATE BIRD: ROBIN
STATE FLOWER: APPLEBLOSSOM
STRAIT: MACKINAC
TOWN: MIO ALMA CARO HART
  FLINT IONIA LANSE ADRIAN
  ALPENA BADAXE OWOSSO
  PAWPAW WARREN DETROIT
  LANSING LIVONIA PONTIAC
  SAGINAW ANNARBOR CADILLAC
  ESCANABA KALKASKA
  MANISTEE MUNISING
  MUSKEGON CHEBOYGAN
  KALAMAZOO

MICIPSA (FATHER OF —) MASINISSA
MICONIA TAMONEA
MICROBAR BARYE
MICROBE GERM
MICROBIOLOGIST AMERICAN
  NATHAN
  FRENCH LWOFF
  SWISS ARBER
MICROCEPHALIC PINHEAD
MICROFILM (SHEET OF —) FICHE
MICROMETER MU BIFILAR
  (— CALIPER) MIKE
MICRON MU
MICRONESIAN KANAGA NAURUAN
  (— ISLAND) NUI GUAM ROTA TRUK
  MAKIN NAURU WOTHO MAJURO
MICROORGANISM BUG GERM
  AZOFIER BUTYRIC MICROBE
  BACILLUS MYCOPLASMA
MICROPHONE BUG MIKE
  PARABOLA
  (REMOVE CONCEALED —) DEBUG
MICROPYLE FORAMEN
MICROSCOPE GLASS SCOPE
  (PART OF —) ARM BASE CLIP KNOB
  LENS LIMB TUBE STAGE FILTER
  HOLDER APERTURE EYEPIECE
  CONDENSER DIAPHRAGM
  NOSEPIECE OBJECTIVE
  ADJUSTMENT
MICROSCOPIC SMALL MINUTE
MICROSECOND (HUNDREDTH OF —)
  SHAKE
MICROSPECIES JORDANON
MICROSPOROPHYLL STAMEN
MICROTONE SRUTI SHRUTI
MICROTUS ARVICOLA
MIDBRAIN MESENCEPHALON
MIDDAY NOON UNDERN MIDNOON
  NOONDAY MERIDIAN NOONTIME
MIDDEN BASURAL SAMBAQUI
MIDDLE MEDIO MESNE NAVEL
  CENTER MEDIAL MEDIAN
  CENTRAL MEDIATE MEDILLE
  (— OF SAIL) BUNT
  (— OF SHIP) WAIST
  (— OF WINTER) HOLL HOWE
  (PREF.) MEDI(O) MES(O) MESIO
  MEZZO
MIDDLE-AGED MIDDLING
MIDDLE EAST (— NATIVE) WOG
MIDDLEMAN BUTTY BROKER
  DEALER FOGGER JOBBER LUMPER
  BUMAREE BUMMAREE BUTTYMAN

  HUCKSTER REGRATER
MIDDLEMARCH (AUTHOR OF —)
  ELIOT
  (CHARACTER IN —) FRED TYKE
  WILL CALEB CELIA GARTH JAMES
  RIGGS VINCY BROOKE EDWARD
  JOSHUA CHETTAM LYDGATE
  RAFFLES TERTIUS CASAUBON
  DOROTHEA LADISLAW NICHOLAS
  ROSAMOND BULSTRODE
  FEATHERSTONE
MIDDLER PLATEMAN
MIDDLETONE HALFTONE
MIDDLING FAIR MEAN SOSO
  NEUTRAL MEDIOCRE MEETERLY
  (PL.) DUNST FARINA SHARPS
  SIZINGS SEMOLINA WEATINGS
MIDGE GNAT SMUT PUNKY
  MIDGET MINGIE PUNKIE WEEVIL
MIDIAN (FATHER OF —) ABRAHAM
  (MOTHER OF —) KETURAH
MIDMOST
  (PREF.) MESATI
MIDNIGHT NOON NOONTIDE
MIDPOINT BASION PORION
  STOMION GNATHION
MIDRIB COSTA SHAFT MIDVEIN
  (— OF LEAF) PEN
MIDRIFF APRON SKIRT
  (PREF.) PHREN(O)
MIDSHIPMAN WART MIDDY PLEBE
  REEFER SNOTTY OLDSTER
MIDST DEPTH CENTER MIDDLE
  MIDWARD
  (PREF.) **(IN THE —)** INTER
MIDSUMMER DAY JOHNSMAS
MIDSUMMER NIGHT'S DREAM
  (AUTHOR OF —) SHAKESPEARE
  (CHARACTER IN —) MOTH PUCK
  SNUG EGEUS FLUTE SNOUT
  BOTTOM COBWEB HELENA
  HERMIA OBERON QUINCE
  THESEUS TITANIA LYSANDER
  DEMETRIUS HIPPOLYTA
  STARVELING MUSTARDSEED
  PHILOSTRATE PEASEBLOSSOM
MIDWAY MEDIO GAYWAY
  HALFWAY
MIDWIFE BABA DHAI GAMP
  HOWDY LUCKY COMMER
  CUMMER GRANNY HOWDIE
  KIMMER LUCINA LUCKIE GRANNIE
  HEBAMME
MIEN AIR BROW PORT VULT
  ALLURE ASPECT DEMEAN
  MANNER OSTENT BEARING
  DEMEANOR PORTANCE
MIG MIB DUCK
MIGHT ARM BULK MOTE FORCE
  MOUND POWER SHOULD
  STRENGTH
  (PREF.) CRATO
MIGHTILY HEFTILY
MIGHTINESS (HIGH —) HOGEN
MIGHTY FELL HIGH KEEN MAIN
  MUCH RANK RICH VAST FELON
  GREAT HEFTY STERN STOOR
  POTENT STRONG VIOLENT
  ENORMOUS FORCEFUL
  POWERFUL PUISSANT SAMSONIC
  (PREF.) DEIN(O) DIN(O)
  MEG(A)(AL)(ALO)
MIGNON (CHARACTER IN —)

  MIGNON MEISTER SPERATA
  WILHELM LOTHARIO
  (COMPOSER OF —) THOMAS
MIGNONETTE WELD WOLD
  RESEDA LUTEOLA
MIGRAINE MEGRIM
MIGRANT MOVER
MIGRATE RUN FLIT TREK DRIFT
  FLIGHT COLONIZE
MIGRATION TREK EXODUS FLIGHT
  EELFARE EMOTION PASSAGE
  DIASPORA
MIGRATORY PEREGRINE
MIKADO DAIRI
MIKIR ARLENG
MIKLOTH (FATHER OF —) JEHIEL
  (MOTHER OF —) MAACHAH
MILCAH (FATHER OF —) HARAN
  ZELOPHEHAD
  (HUSBAND OF —) NAHOR
MILD LEW MOY CALM COLD EASY
  FAIR LENT MEEK NESH PLUM
  SOFT TAME WARM BALMY BLAND
  BUXOM GREEN LIGHT LITHE
  MELCH MELSH MILKY NAISH
  QUIET BENIGN FACILE GENIAL
  GENTLE HUMBLE KINDLY REMISS
  SMOOTH AFFABLE AMIABLE
  CLEMENT LENIENT VELVETY
  BENEDICT DOVELIKE FAVONIAN
  LENITIVE MERCIFUL SARSENET
  SOOTHING TRANQUIL
  (PREF.) LENI
MILDEW OIDIUM
MILDLY FEEBLY GENTLY
MILDNESS MILD LENITY SUAVITY
  CLEMENCY HUMILITY KINDNESS
MILE (NAUTICAL —) KNOT KAIRI
  (ONE-EIGHTH —) FURLONG
  (SEA —) NAUT
  (SIXTY —S) DEGREE
  (3 —S) HOUR LEAGUE
MILESTONE MILLIARY
MILETUS (FATHER OF —) APOLLO
  (MOTHER OF —) ARIA DEIONE
  (SON OF —) BYBLIS CAUNUS
  (WIFE OF —) CYANEE
MILFOIL AHARTALAV
MILIEU CLIMATE TERRAIN
  AMBIENCE
MILITANT WARRISH FIGHTING
  (ONE WITH — ATTITUDE) HAWK
MILITARISTIC PRUSSIAN
MILITARY MARTIAL WARLIKE
  MILITANT SOLDIERY
  (— POST) THANA
  (— SCIENCE) LOGISTICS
MILITIA FYRD ARRAY MILICE
MILITIAMAN CHOCO UHLAN
  LUMPER TRAINER FENCIBLE
  SHIRTMAN
  (TURKISH —) TIMARIOT
MILK COW LAC FUZZ LAIT PAIL
  SKIM BLEED JUICE MILCH MULCT
  BOTTLE ELICIT RAMMEL STROKE
  SUCKLE EXPLOIT
  (— CLOSELY) JIB
  (— DRY) STRIP
  (— OUT) EMULGE
  (— PAN) LEAD
  (— PRODUCT) KHOA
  (— SICKNESS) TIRES
  (BREAST —) SUCK DIDDY

  (COW'S —) MESS
  (CURDLED —) SKYR TYRE TAYER
  LOPPER CLABBER TATMJOLK
  (FERMENTED —) KUMISS MATZOON
  (NEW —) RAMMEL
  (PINT OF —) PINTA
  (SOUR —) SKYR WHIG BONNY
  BLEEZE BLINKY CLABBER
  JOCOQUE
  (WATERY —) BLASH
  (PREF.) GALACT(O) LACT(I)(O)
  (SUFF.) GALACTIA
MILK CART KIT PRAM BUNGEY
MILKFISH AWA BANGOS SABALO
  SAVOLA BANDENG SABALOTE
MILKING (— PARLOR) BAIL
  (— TIME) MEAL
MILKLESS PARVE PAREVE
MILKMAN KITTER CHALKER
MILK PAIL TRUG LEGLEN
MILK SHAKE FRAPPE
MILK SNAKE ADDER
MILKSOP SOP MOLLY COCKNEY
  MEACOCK
MILKWOOD MELKHOUT
MILKWORT SENECA CENTAURY
  GAYWINGS POLYGALA
MILKY MILCHY LACTARY LACTEAL
  OPALOID LACTEOUS
MILKY WAY
  (PREF.) GALACT(O)
MILL FULL MILN STAR BREAK
  FLOUR KNURL QUERN CHERRY
  FANNER STAMPS BLOOMER
  MOLINET PUGMILL SMUTTER
  ARRASTRA ARRASTRE BUHRMILL
  SPINNERY TRAPICHE WALKMILL
  (CHOCOLATE —) MOLINET
  (FULLING —) STOCKS
  (SHINGLING —) FORGE
  (SUGAR —) CENTRAL TRAPICHE
  (PREF.) MOLARI MYL(O)
MILLBOARD TARBOARD
MILLDAM WEIR WARREN
  WARRANT
MILLED GRAINED
MILLENARIAN CHILIAST
MILLENIUM CHILIAD
MILLER MILLMAN STOCKER
  MULTURER NILLWARD
MILLER'S-THUMB BLOB CULL
  CABOT CHABOT COTTOID
  MUDDLER BULLHEAD
MILLET BUDA KODA KOUS MOHA
  ARZUN BAJRA CHENA CUMBU
  DUKHN DURRA GRAIN HIRSE
  KODRA MILLY PANIC PROSO
  TENAI WHISK BAJREE DHURRA
  HUREEK JONDLA JOWARI MILIUM
  RAGGEE DAGASSA PANICLE
  ZABURRO BIRDSEED KADIKANE
  (PREF.) MILIO
MILLHAND CROPMAN
MILLILITER MIL
MILLIMETER LI
  (THOUSANDTH OF —) MICRON
MILLINER ARTISTE MODISTE
MILLING GRAINING
MILLION CONTO QUENT
  (10 —) CRORE
  (1000 —) MILLIARD
  (PL.) GUPPY
  (PREF.) MEGA

MILLIONTH
(PREF.) **(ONE —)** MICR(O)
MILLIPEDE JULID POLYPOD
DIPLOPOD PILLWORM RINGWORM
WIREWORM
MILLISECOND SIGMA
MILL ON THE FLOSS (AUTHOR OF
—) ELIOT
(CHARACTER IN —) BOB TOM KENN
LUCY DEANE GLEGG GUEST JAKIN
WAKEM MAGGIE PHILIP PULLET
STEPHEN STELLING TULLIVER
MILLPOND DAM MILLDAM
BINNACLE MILLPOOL
MILLRACE LADE LEAD LEAT
FOREBAY TAILRACE MILLSTREAM
MILLRYND INK
MILLSTONE RYND STONE BEDDER
LEDGER LIGGER RUNNER
(LOWER —) METATE
(UPPER —) MANO
(PL.) RUN
MILLSTREAM DAM LADE FLEAM
MILLWORKER DOGGER
MILO SORGHUM
MILPA LADANG
MILQUETOAST CASPAR
MILT MILK SEED SPLEEN
MILTONIST DIVORCER
MIMAS (FATHER OF —) THEANO
(MOTHER OF —) AMYCUS
(SLAYER OF —) MEZENTIUS
MIME ACTOR MIMER MIMIC
(PL.) MIMIAMBI
MIMEOGRAPH RONEO
MIMIC APE HIT COPY MIME MINT
MOCK MOCKER MONKEY
BUFFOON COPYCAT IMITATE
PAGEANT
(PREF.) MIM(EO)(O)
MIMICRY APERY MIMESIS
MOCKAGE MOCKERY
MIMOSA AROMA CASSIE ALBIZZIA
HUISACHE TURMERIC
MINCE CHOP SHEAR FINICK
MINCED HACHE
MINCEMEAT GIGOT MINCE
MINCING NIMINY FINICAL MINIKIN
MIGNIARD SKIPJACK
MINCINGLY FINE GINGERLY
MIND CIT CHIT HEAD HEED MOOD
NOTE NOUS RECK SOUL BESEE
BRAIN PHREN SENSE SKULL
WATCH ANIMUS MATTER NOTICE
PSYCHE REGARD COURAGE
SENSORY SUBJECT THINKER
THOUGHT
(CONSCIOUS —) SENTIENT
(INFINITE —) GOD
(RIGHT FRAME OF —) TUNE
(STATE OF —) BAG
(YEAR'S —) MINNING
(PREF.) MENTI NOO PHREN(O)
PSYCH(O)
(SUFF.) **(CONDITION OF —)** THYMIA
MINDFUL HEEDY MINDLY HEEDFUL
OBSERVANT
MIND READER MENTALIST
MINE BAL DIG PIT DELF HOLE HUEL
MEUM BARGH DELFT DELPH
METAL STOPE WHEAL COYOTE
GOPHER GROOVE RESCUE
BONANZA BORASCA COALPIT

MINERAL OPENCUT TORPEDO
GOLCONDA MYNPACHT
PROSPECT
(— BY BLASTING) SHOOT
(— IRREGULARLY) GOPHER
(— PASSAGE) SLUM
(COAL —) ROB COALPIT COLLIERY
(MILITARY —) FOUGADE
FOUGASSE CAMOUFLET
(OLD —) GWAG
(RICH —) GOLCONDA
(TIN —) STANNARY
(UNPRODUCTIVE —) DUFFER
SHICER BORASCA
MINER PECK PICK PYKE BARER
DOGGY ARTIST BUCKER CUTTER
DAMMER DELVER DIGGER
GANGER GETTER HAGGER
JUMPER MATTER PELTER REEFER
SNIPER STOPER TINNER TOPMAN
VANNER COLLIER CRUTTER
DIRGLER FEIGHER GEORDIE
GROOVER HITCHER HUTCHER
LEADMAN PICKMAN PIKEMAN
PIONEER PLUGMAN ROCKMAN
SNUBBER ENTRYMAN HEADSMAN
STRIPPER WINZEMAN
(— WHO WORKS ALONE) HATTER
MINERAL JET GEET HOST MINE
SPAR BERYL BLOOM EARTH
FLUOR GLEBE GUEST LENAD
SQUAT TRONA ACMITE ALAITE
AUGITE BARITE BARYTE BLENDE
CASTOR CERITE COCKLE CURITE
DAVYNE EGERAN EHLITE ERRITE
GALENA GARNET GLANCE
GYPSUM HALITE HAUYNE HELVIN
HUMITE ILLITE IOLITE LABITE
MIXITE NATRON NOSEAN NOSITE
PINITE RUTILE SALITE SILICA
SPHENE SPINEL ADAMINE
ADAMITE ADELITE ALTAITE
ALUMITE ALUNITE AMOSITE
ANATASE APATITE ATOPITE
AXINITE AZORITE AZULITE
AZURITE BAUXITE BAZZITE
BELLITE BIOTITE BISMITE BITYITE
BOHMITE BOLEITE BORNITE
BRUCITE CALCITE CELSIAN
CYANITE DIAMOND DICKITE
DUFTITE EDENITE EPIDOTE
ERIKITE ERINITE EUCLASE
FLOKITE GAGEITE GAHNITE
GEDRITE GLADITE GOTHITE
GUMMITE HELVITE HESSITE
HOPEITE HOWLITE HULSITE
IHLEITE ILVAITE INESITE INYOITE
ISERITE JADEITE JARLITE JOSEITE
KEMPITE KERNITE KOPPITE
KOTOITE KYANITE LANGITE
LARNITE LAURITE LAUTITE
LEHIITE LEIFITE LEONITE LEPTITE
LEUCITE LOWEITE MARTITE
MELLITE MULLITE OKENITE
OLIVINE PALAITE PENNINE
PETZITE PYRITES RATHITE
REALGAR RETZIAN RHAGITE
RINKITE ROMEITE ROSSITE
SENAITE SODDITE SVABITE
SYLVITE THORITE TURGITE
ULEXITE UTAHITE UVANITE
VAUXITE VOGLITE VRBAITE
WARBITE WIIKITE ZEOLITE

ZINCITE ZOISITE ZORGITE
ZUNYITE AIKINITE ALLANITE
ALLUVIAL ALUNOGEN AMBONITE
ANAUXITE ANCYLITE ANDORITE
ANKERITE ARIEGITE ARMENITE
ARTINITE ASBOLITE AUGELITE
AUTUNITE AWARUITE BADENITE
BAKERITE BARARITE BARYLITE
BAVENITE BETAFITE BEYERITE
BILINITE BIXBYITE BLAKEITE
BLOEDITE BOOTHITE BORACITE
BOWENITE BRAGGITE BRAUNITE
BRAVOITE BROMLITE BRONZITE
BROOKITE BRUSHITE CALCSPAR
CARBOCER CEROLITE CHIOLITE
CHLORITE CHROMITE CIMOLITE
CINNABAR CLEVEITE COHENITE
COLUSITE COOKEITE COSALITE
CREEDITE CROCOITE CRYOLITE
DANALITE DAPHNITE DATOLITE
DELTAITE DENDRITE DIALLAGE
DIASPORE DIGENITE DIOPSIDE
DIOPTASE DIXENITE DOLOMITE
DYSODILE EGUEIITE ELIASITE
ELPIDITE EMBOLITE ENARGITE
EPSOMITE ERIONITE EUCOLITE
EULYTINE EULYTITE EUXENITE
EVANSITE FASSAITE FAYALITE
FELDSPAR FERSMITE FIBROITE
FLINKITE FLUORITE FOOTEITE
FUCHSITE FUSINITE GEMSTONE
GENTHITE GIBBSITE GINORITE
GOETHITE GOYAZITE GRIPHITE
GROTHINE GROUTITE GYROLITE
HANKSITE HANUSITE HARTTITE
HATCHITE HAUERITE HAUYNITE
HEMATITE HOMILITE HUGELITE
IDOCRASE INDERITE IODYRITE
JALPAITE JAROSITE JEZEKITE
KALINITE KAMACITE KASOLITE
KEHOEITE KLEINITE KOKTAITE
KOLSKITE KRAUSITE LAGONITE
LAVENITE LAZULITE LAZURITE
LEVYNITE LEWISITE LIMONITE
LINARITE LOMONITE LOWIGITE
MARSHITE MEIONITE MELILITE
MELONITE MESITITE MESOLITE
MIERSITE MIMETITE MISENITE
MOLYSITE MONAZITE MONETITE
MORAVITE MOSESITE NADORITE
NASONITE NEPOUITE NOCERITE
NOSELITE OXAMMITE PEGANITE
PETALITE PIMELITE PINNOITE
PISANITE PODOLITE PORODINE
PRICEITE PRIORITE RINNEITE
ROSELITE SAGENITE SALEEITE
SALESITE SAPONITE SASSOLIN
SCAWTITE SHANDITE SHARPITE
SHORTITE SIDERITE SMALTITE
SMITHITE SODALITE SPADAITE
SPURRITE STANNITE STIBNITE
STILBITE STOLZITE STRUVITE
STURTITE SZMIKITE TAGILITE
TANGEITE TEALLITE TENORITE
TILASITE TITANITE TRIPLITE
TROILITE TYROLITE TYSONITE
URANOTIL VEGASITE VOLTAITE
VOLTZITE WEHRLITE WEISSITE
WELLSITE WILKEITE WURTZITE
XENOLITE XENOTIME YENTNITE
ZARATITE MILLERITE MUSCOVITE
NEPHELINE NICCOLITE
PHENACITE WILLEMITE

(BLACK —) JET GEET CERINE
YENITE KNOPITE NIOBITE
ALLANITE GRAPHITE HIELMITE
ILMENITE ONOFRITE MAGNETITE
SAMARSKITE
(BLUE —) MOLYBDENITE
(BRIGHT —) BLENDE
(BROWN —) CERINE EGERAN
GUILDITE JAROSITE
(FIBROUS —) ASBESTOS
(GRAY-WHITE —) TRONA HOPEITE
(GREEN —) AMESITE GAHNITE
ILESITE PRASINE PREHNITE
SMECTITE
(MOTTLED —) SERPENTINE
(ORANGE —) SANDIX
(RADIATED —) ASTROITE
(RADIOACTIVE —) CURITE
(RARE —) CYMRITE EUCLASE
TYCHITE BARYLITE
(RED —) GARNET RHODOCHROSITE
(SOFT —) TALC KERMES
(TRANSPARENT —) MICA POLLUX
ABRAZITE SODALITE
(WHITE —) BARITE HOWLITE
STILBITE
(YELLOW —) TOPAZ PYRITES
PENTLANDITE
(YELLOWISH-GREEN —) EPIDOTE
ECDEMITE
(PREF.) ORYCT(O)
(SUFF.) CLASE INE ITE LITE
LITH(IC) LITIC XENE
MINERALOGIST **AMERICAN** HUNT
KUNZ BRUSH KRAUS EGLESTON
WHITLOCK CLEAVELAND
AUSTRIAN BORN BECKE WULFEN
HAIDINGER TSCHERMAK
ENGLISH BROOKE CLARKE GREGOR
MILLER PHILLIPS
FRENCH HAUY ROME DAUBREE
FRIEDEL LACROIX LAUMONT
DOLOMIEU DUFRENOY
BRONGNIART
GERMAN MOHS COHEN RASPE
DECHEN KOBELL WERNER ZIRKEL
KARSTEN NEUMANN LEONHARD
QUENSTEDT
ITALIAN SELLA BRUGNATELLI
RUSSIAN FERSMAN
SWEDISH GAHN HISINGER
SEFSTROM CRONSTEDT
BLOMSTRAND
MINERAL TAR MALTHA
MINERAL WATER SELTZER
MINERVA MENFRA
MINESWEEPER ALGERINE
MINGLE MIX FUSE JOIN MELL
MOLD MONG MOOL ADMIX BLEND
MERGE TWINE COMMIX FELTER
HUDDLE JUMBLE MEDDLE
MEDLEY COMBINE COALESCE
CONFOUND
(PREF.) MISCE
MINGLED FUSED MEDLEY
CONFUSED
(PREF.) MYXTI
MINGLING
(PREF.) MIXO
(SUFF.) MIXIS
MINIATURE BABY SMALL LITTLE
POCKET MINIKIN
MINIMAL BASAL LIMINAL

MARGINAL

MINIMIZE DECRY MINCE LESSEN MINIFY SMOOTH SCISSOR BELITTLE DISCOUNT

MINIMUM BARE BEDROCK

MINING WORK MINERY SPATTER GROOVING

MINION PEAT SATAN MIGNON DARLING MINIKIN CREATURE SATELLITE

MINIONETTE EMERALD

MINISTER PRIG CLERK DEWAN ELDER ENVOY HAMAN PADRE VIZIR ATABEG DEACON DIVINE GALLAH HELPER PANDER PARSON PASTOR PESHWA PRIEST VIZIER BROTHER DOMINIE OFFICER PESHKAR PREFECT PALATINE PREACHER
(— OF FINANCE) DEWAN
(— TO) TEND SERVE INTEND
(— WITHOUT SETTLEMENT) STIBBLER
(PRIME —) PADRONE

MINISTRANT
(PL.) SELLI SELLOI

MINISTRATION SERVICE TENDANCE

MINISTRY SERVICE

MINIUM SANDIX

MINIVER LASSET

MINK FAG HURON NORSE VISON JACKASH KOLINSKY MUSTELIN PLATINUM

MINNESOTA
CAPITAL: STPAUL
COLLEGE: BETHEL STOLAF WINONA BEMIDJI HAMLINE AUGSBURG CARLETON
COUNTY: LYON PINE TODD ANOKA MOWER AITKIN DAKOTA ISANTI ITASCA MCLEOD NOBLES ROSEAU WASECA WILKIN CHISAGO WABASHA CROWWING HENNEPIN OTTERTAIL
INDIAN: SIOUX OJIBWA CHIPPEWA
LAKE: LEECH ITASCA BEMIDJI SUPERIOR
MOUNTAIN: EAGLE MISQUAH
MOUNTAIN RANGE: CUYUNA MESABI MISQUAH
NICKNAME: NORTHSTAR
RIVER: RAINY STCROIX
STATE BIRD: LOON
STATE TREE: REDPINE
TOWN: ADA ELY MORA ANOKA EDINA FOLEY AUSTIN CHASKA DULUTH MILACA NEWULM WADENA WASECA WINONA BEMIDJI FOSSTON HIBBING IVANHOE MANKATO BRAINERD PIPESTONE

MINNESOTAN GOPHER

MINNOW PINK BANNY GUPPY HITCH MINIM MINNY BAGGIE MENNON DOGFISH FATHEAD GULARIS PHANTOM PINHEAD PINKEEN BONYTAIL CYPRINID FLATHEAD GAMBUSIA MOONFISH SATINFIN

(PL.) MENISE

MINOR FLAT LESS MOLL WARD PETIT PETTY INFANT LESSER SLIGHT

MINORESS CLARE CLARISSE

MINORITY FEW NONAGE INFANCY

MINOS (DAUGHTER OF —) ARIADNE PHAEDRA
(FATHER OF —) JUPITER LYCASTUS
(MOTHER OF —) EUROPA
(SLAYER OF —) COCALUS
(SON OF —) ANDROGEOS DEUCALION
(WIFE OF —) PASIPHAE

MINSTER CHADBAND

MINSTREL BARD LUTER BADHAN HARPER JOCKEY BADCHAN GLEEMAN JOCULAR PARDHAN PIERROT SONGMAN JONGLEUR

MINSTRELSY GLEE DREAM

MINT COIN NANA SAGE AJUGA BASIL ORGAN THYME HYSSOP SAVORY STRIKE ALLHEAL BALLOTA CAPMINT LABIATE MONARDA OLITORY OREGANO PERILLA PHLOMIS POTHERB STACHYS BERGAMOT CALAMINT IRONWORT LAMPWICK LAVENDER MARJORAM SAGELEAF SELFHEAL SKULLCAP PATCHOULI PATCHOULY PENNYROYAL PEPPERMINT

MINTER MONEYER

MINUCHIHR (DAUGHTER OF —) NAUDAR
(FATHER OF —) IRAJ

MINUET MINAWAY

MINUS LESS WANTING

MINUTE FINE NICE TINY CLOSE MINIM PRIME SMALL ATOMIC MOMENT NARROW INSTANT SCRUPLE DETAILED
(24 —S) GHURRY
(PL.) ACTA

MINX JADE PEAT SLUT SNIP HUSSY HUZZY LIMMER SNICKET

MIRACLE SIGN ANOMY MARVEL WONDER PRODIGY THEURGY
(PREF.) THAUMA(TO)

MIRACLE PLAY GUARY

MIRACULOUS MARVELOUS

MIRAGE SERAB CHIMERA FLYAWAY LOOMING ILLUSION TOWERING

MIRANDA (FATHER OF —) PROSPERO
(LOVER OF —) FERDINAND

MIRE BOG DUB CLAY GLAR LAIR MOIL SLOB SLUB SLUE SLUR ADDLE CLART EMBOG FANGO GLAUR LATCH SEUGH SLAKE SLOSH SLUSH SQUAD STALL SLOUGH SLUDGE SLUTCH CLABBER GUTTERS SLUBBER LOBLOLLY WORTHING

MIREILLE (CHARACTER IN —) RAMON OURRIAS VINCENT MIREILLE
(COMPOSER OF —) GOUNOD

MIRIAM (BROTHER OF —) MOSES

MIRITI PALM ITA BURITI MORICHE

MIRLITON KAZOO

MIRO TOMTIT

MIRROR FLAT BERYL GLASS IMAGE STEEL STONE PEEPER PSYCHE REFLEX SHINER SHOWER CONCAVE HORIZON REFLECT DIAGONAL SPECULUM
(PREF.) CATOPTRO

MIRTH GLEE CHEER DREAM SPORT GAIETY BAUDERY DISPORT JOLLITY HILARITY
(CONTEMPTUOUS —) SPORT
(VIOLENT —) SPLEEN

MIRTHFUL CADGY MERRY RIANT FESTIVE GLEEFUL JOCULAR DISPOSED LAUGHFUL CONVIVIAL

MIRY OOZY PUXY LAIRY MUCKY SLAKY CLAGGY CLASHY LUTOSE MIRISH POACHY SLABBY GUTTERY SLOUGHY

MISADVENTURE GRIEF ACCIDENT CALAMITY CASUALTY DISASTER MISHANTER

MISANTHROPE CYNIC TIMON
(AUTHOR OF —) MOLIERE
(CHARACTER IN —) ORONTE ALCESTE ARSINOE ELIANTE CELIMENE PHILINTE

MISANTHROPIC CYNICAL

MISANTHROPY CYNICISM TIMONISM

MISAPPLIED ABUSIVE

MISAPPLY ABUSE CROOK WREST DISUSE MISUSE

MISAPPREHEND MISTAKE

MISAPPREHENSION ILLUSION

MISBECOME MISSIT MISSEEM

MISBEHAVE MISUSE MISBEAR MISFARE MISHAVE MISLEAD MISGUIDE

MISBEHAVIOR MALVERSATION

MISBELIEF MISCREED

MISCALCULATE DUTCH MISCAST MISCOUNT

MISCALL BECALL MISNAME

MISCARRIAGE FAIL MISHAP FAILURE ABORTION
(PREF.) ECTRO

MISCARRY FAIL WARP ABORT MISGO FOUNDER MISFARE MISGIVE BACKFIRE

MISCARRYING ABORTIVE

MISCELLANEOUS CHOW ORRA SUNDRY ASSORTED CHOWCHOW

MISCELLANY VARIA MEDLEY WHATNOT CHOWCHOW GIFTBOOK

MISCHANCE CALAMITY CASUALTY DISASTER

MISCHIEF HOB ILL BALE BANE EVIL HARM HURT JEEL WRACK INJURY MURCHY SORROW WONDER DEVILRY KNAVERY MALICHO SCADDLE DEVILTRY MALLECHO

MISCHIEF-MAKING URCHIN

MISCHIEVOUS BAD SLY ARCH IDLE PIXY ROYT ELFIN HEMPY PIXIE ROYET ELFISH ELVISH GALLUS HEMPIE IMPISH NOCENT NOYANT SHREWD SULLEN WICKED GALLOWS HARMFUL KNAVISH LARKISH MOCKING NAUGHTY PARLISH PLISKIE PUCKISH ROGUISH SCADDLE UNHAPPY UNLUCKY WAGGISH

LITHERLY LUNGEOUS SPORTIVE SPRITISH VENOMOUS WANSONSY

MISCHIEVOUSNESS ROGUERY

MISCONCEPTION DELUSION ILLUSION

MISCONDUCT CULPA DOLUS OFFENCE OFFENSE DISORDER MALFEASANCE

MISCONSTRUCTION STRAIN

MISCONSTRUE MISJUDGE

MISCREANT KNAVE

MISDEED ILL MISS SLIP AMISS UNWRONG DEFAULT FORFEIT OFFENCE OFFENSE DISORDER

MISDEMEANOR SIN CRIME FAULT DELICT OFFENCE OFFENSE DISORDER

MISDIRECT PERVERT MISGUIDE

MISER CUFF SKIN CHUFF CHURL FLINT GRIPE HAYNE HUNKS NABAL SCRAT SCRIB CODGER HUDDLE NIPPER PELTER SCRIMP SNUDGE WRETCH DRYFIST GOBSECK NIGGARD SCRAPER CHINCHER GATHERER HAPTERON HARPAGON HOLDFAST MUCKERER MUCKWORM PINCHGUT CURMUDGEON

MISERABLE WOE EVIL GRAY PUNK SOUR DAWNY DEENY DUSTY MISER WOFUL YEMER ABJECT CHETIF CRUMBY CRUMMY ELENGE FEEBLE PRETTY UNSELY WOEFUL BALEFUL FORLORN PITIFUL SCRUFFY UNHAPPY WANSOME FORSAKEN PITIABLE SCRANNEL UNTHENDE WRETCHED

MISERABLES, LES (AUTHOR OF —) HUGO
(CHARACTER IN —) JEAN JAVERT MARIUS COSETTE EPONINE FANTINE VALJEAN JONDRETTE MADELEINE PONTMERCY THENARDIER FAUCHELEVANT

MISERERE SUBSELLA

MISERLINESS AVARICE MISERISM SNUDGERY TENACITY

MISERLY WOE GARE MEAN NEAR GRIPPY KNIVEY STINGY CHINCHE PELTING WANSITH SCRAPING SNUDGERY

MISERY WO WOE BALE RUTH GNEDE GRAME WREAK THREAT ANGUISH MISEASE TRAGEDY CALAMITY DISTRESS WANDRETH WOWENING

MISFIRE SKIP SNAP

MISFORTUNE ILL BLOW DOLE DREE EVIL HARM RUTH TEEN CROSS CURSE HYDRA SCATH TRAIK DAMAGE DIRDUM MISERY MISHAP RUBBER SCATHE SORROW UNHEAL UNLUCK WANHAP WROATH AMBSACE MALHEUR MISCARE MISFALL MISFATE MISLUCK REVERSE TRAGEDY TROUBLE UNSELTH UNSPEED CALAMITY DISASTER DISGRACE DISTRESS MISCHIEF ADVERSITY MISCHANCE

MISGIVING DOUBT QUALM

MISGOVERN MISRULE

MISGUIDED WET
MISHAEL (BROTHER OF —)
ELIZAPHAN
(FATHER OF —) UZZIEL
MISHAM (FATHER OF —) ELPAAL
MISHANDLE BUNGLE
MISHAP SLIP GRIEF SHUNT SITHE
UNHAP WANHAP FORTUNE
MISTIDE ACCIDENT CASUALTY
MISCHIEF PRATFALL
(MINOR —) GLITCH
MISHEARING OTOSIS
MISHIT DUFF
MISHMA (BROTHER OF —) MIBSAM
(FATHER OF —) ISHMAEL
MISHMASH BOTCH GOULASH
MISINFORM MIZZLE
MISINTERPRET WARP WREST
WRITHE MISREAD PERVERT
MISCOUNT
MISJUDGE MISDEEM MISWERN
MISLAY LOSE DISPLACE MISPLACE
MISLEAD COG ERR BUNK DUPE
GULL HOAX HYPE JIVE BLUFF
CHEAT FALSE SHUCK BETRAY
DELUDE SEDUCE WILDER
CONFUSE DEBAUCH DECEIVE
MISLEAR INVEIGLE MISGUIDE
BAMBOOZLE
MISLEADING JIVE BLIND FALSE
CIRCEAN TORTIOUS
MISMANAGE MULL BLUNK
BLUNDER MISLEAD MISRULE
ILLGUIDE MISGUIDE
MISOGYNIC CYNICAL
MISPLACE MISLAY MISPUT MISSET
DISPLACE
MISPLACED MALPOSED
MISPLAY BLOW DUFF ERROR
FLUFF FUMBLE
MISPRINT LITERAL
MISPRONOUNCE MISCALL
STUMBLE
MISQUOTE GIVE
MISREPRESENT SKEW ABUSE
BELIE COLOR MISUSE DISTORT
FALSIFY SLANDER MISCOLOR
MISREPRESENTATION FRAUD
CALUMNY DAUBERY GARBLING
MISS ERR HIP FAIL LACK LOSE SKIP
SLIP SNAB FORGO HANUM MISSY
PANNA SKIRT DESIRE KUMARI
FRAULEIN MISTRESS OVERLOOK
OVERSLIP SENORITA
(CLOSE —) SHAVE
MISSEL BIRD MAVIS SHIRL DRAINE
JAYPIE MISTLE SHRITE SYCOCK
CHERCOCK
MISSHAPE DEFORM
MISSHAPEN UGLY BLOWN
DEFORM THRAWN DEFORMED
UNSHAPED MALFORMED
(PREF.) DYSMORPHO
MISSILE ABM GUN BALL BIRD
BOLT DART NIKE SHOT PLUMB
SHAFT STONE BULLET SEEKER
BOMBARD GRENADE MISSIVE
OUTCAST PROJECT AERODART
BRICKBAT PROJECTILE
(DEFECTIVE —) DUD
(PL.) MITRAILLE
(PREF.) TELI
MISSING LACK WANT

ABSENT WANTING
(— OF CUE) FLUFF
(PREF.) E
MISSION SAND TASK CHARGE
ERRAND SORTIE VISITA MESSAGE
BUSINESS DEVOTION LEGATION
NUNCIATURE
MISSIONARY APOSTLE COLPORTER

MISSISSIPPI
CAPITAL: JACKSON
COLLEGE: RUST ALCORN
BELHAVEN MILLSAPS
TOUGALOO
COUNTY: TATE HINDS JONES
LAMAR LEAKE PERRY YAZOO
ALCORN ATTALA COPIAH
JASPER PANOLA TIPPAH
TUNICA CHOCTAW NESHOBA
NOXUBEE ITAWAMBA
YALOBUSHA
INDIAN: TIOU BILOXI TUNICA
CHOCTAW NATCHEZ
CHICKASAW
LAKE: ENID SARDIS BARNETT
GRENADA OKATIBBEE
MOUNTAIN: WOODALL
NATIVE: MUDCAT TADPOLE
NICKNAME: BAYOU MAGNOLIA
RIVER: LEAF PEARL YAZOO
BIGBLACK
STATE BIRD: MOCKINGBIRD
STATE FLOWER: MAGNOLIA
STATE TREE: MAGNOLIA
TOWN: IUKA MARKS BILOXI
HELENA LAUREL PURVIS
TUNICA TUPELO WINONA
BELZONI CORINTH GRENADA
NATCHEZ WIGGINS BOGALUSA
GULFPORT MERIDIAN
KOSCIUSKO

MISSIVE NOTE BILLET LETTER
EPISTLE MESSAGE MISSILE

MISSOURI
CAPITAL: JEFFERSONCITY
COLLEGE: AVILA DRURY TARKIO
LINCOLN WEBSTER STEPHENS
COUNTY: RAY COLE DENT IRON
LINN ADAIR BARRY HENRY
MACON RALLS TANEY GRUNDY
PETTIS PLATTE DAVIESS
NODAWAY
INDIAN: OSAGE
LAKE: OZARKS TABLEROCK
MOUNTAIN: TAUMSAUK
NATIVE: PUKE PIKER
NICKNAME: SHOWME BULLION
PLATEAU: OZARK
PRESIDENT: TRUMAN
RIVER: OSAGE
STATE BIRD: BLUEBIRD
STATE FLOWER: HAWTHORN
STATE TREE: DOGWOOD
TOWN: AVA EDINA ELDON HAYTI
LAMAR MACON MILAN ROLLA
BUTLER GALENA KAHOKA
NEOSHO POTOSI BETHANY
BOLIVAR CAMERON LEBANON
MOBERLY PALMYRA SEDALIA
STLOUIS HANNIBAL SIKESTON

MISSTATEMENT ERRATUM
MISSTEP TRIP
MIST DAG FOG MUG URE DAMP
DRIP DROW FILM HAAR HAZE
MOKE RACK ROKE SCUD SMUR
BRUME CLOUD DRISK GAUZE
STEAM MIZZLE NEBULE SEREIN
SERENE SMEETH
(COLD —) DROW BERBER
(DRIZZLING —) SMUR DRISK SMIRR
SMURR
(SMOKY —) SMOG
(WHITE —) HAG
(PL.) SMOKES
(PREF.) NEBULI NIMBI
MISTAKE ERR BALK GAFF GOOF
MISS SLIP TRIP ERROR FAULT
FLUFF GAFFE LAPSE BARNEY
BOBBLE ESCAPE MISCUE SLIPUP
STUMER BLOOMER BLUNDER
CONFUSE DEFAULT JEOFAIL
STUMOUR WRONGER CONFOUND
MISPRINT MISPRISE
(STUPID —) BUBU BONER
CLANGER
(PL.) ERRATA
MISTAKEN WRONG ASTRAY
OVERSEEN OVERSHOT TORTIOUS
MISTER DON REB HERR SENOR
SENHOR SIGNOR GOODMAN
SIGNIOR GOVERNOR
MISTFLOWER EUPATORY
MISTILY FOGGILY
MISTINESS FILM
MISTLETOE MISSEL ALLHEAL
GADBUSH
MISTREAT BANG VIOLATE
MISTRESS MRS PUG TOY AMIE
BIBI DAME DOLL DOXY LADY MISS
PURE AMIGA AMOUR DOLLY
DONNA DUENA FANCY LEMAN
LUCKY MADAM NANCY WOMAN
BEEBEE MINION MISSIS MISSUS
NEAERA PARNEL SAHIBA SENORA
TACKLE WAHINE BEDMATE
DELILAH HERSELF HETAERA
KITTOCK LEVERET METREZA
PADRONA SENHORA SIGNORA
SULTANA CAMPASPE DESPOINA
DULCINEA FARMWIFE GOODWIFE
GUDEWIFE HAUSFRAU LADYLOVE
LANDLADY MIGNIARD PARAMOUR
PECULIAR SINEBADA TIMANDRA
COURTESAN
(— OF CEREMONIES) FEMCEE
MISTRUST MISTROW SURMISE
DISTRUST JEALOUSE JEALOUSY
MISDOUBT
MISTY HAZY MOKY BLEAR DAGGY
FILMY FOGGY MISKY MOCHY
MOOTH MURKY RAWKY ROKEY
ROUKY BLURRY CLOUDY GREASY
MIZZLY SMURRY STEAMY
BRUMOUS OBSCURE NEBULOUS
NUBILOUS VAPOROUS
MISUNDERSTAND MISKNOW
MISTAKE
MISUNDERSTANDING
MALENTENDU
MISUSE ABUSE ABUSION PERVERT
MALTREAT
MITE BIT ATOM CENT DITE DRAM
ATOMY BICHO SPECK ACARID

ACARUS CHIGOE LEPTUS MINUTE
SMIDGE ACARIAN BDELLID
CHIGGER DEMODEX SMIDGEN
ARACHNID DIBRANCH FARTHING
HANDWORM ORIBATID SANDMITE
(PREF.) ACAR(I)(O)
MITER MITRE TIMBER TIMBRE
MITERWORT COOLWORT
MITICIDE ACARICIDE
PHOSPHAMIDON
MITIGATE BALM COOL EASE HELP
ABATE ALLAY DELAY MEASE
RELAX REMIT SLAKE ASLAKE
LENIFY LESSEN MODIFY PACIFY
SOFTEN SOOTHE SUCCOR
TEMPER ASSUAGE COMMUTE
CUSHION ELEVATE MOLLIFY
QUALIFY RELEASE RELIEVE
SWEETEN PALLIATE ALLEVIATE
(— PAIN) PLASTER
MITIGATING LENITIVE
MITOCHONDRION SARCOSOME
MITTEN BOOT CUFF MITT MUFF
LOOFIE MUFFLE NIPPER MUFFLER
MIX BOX BEAT CARD DASH FUSE
JOIN KNIT MELL MENG MESS STIR
ADMIX ALLOY BLEND BRAID
IMMIX KNEAD MISCE TWINE
BLUNGE CAUDLE COMMIX
CRUTCH GARBLE JUMBLE
MEDDLE MEDLEY MINGLE
MUDDLE PERMIX STODGE
TEMPER WUZZLE BLUNDER
SHUFFLE SWIZZLE
CONFOUND LEVIGATE
SCRAMBLE
(— AND STIR WHEN WET) PUG
(— CONFUSEDLY) BROIL
(— FLOCKS) BOX
(— LIQUORS) BREW
(— PLASTER) GAGE GAUGE
(— TEA) BULK
(— WINE) PART
(— WITH YEAST) BARM
(— WOOL OF DIFFERENT COLORS)
TUM
(CONCRETE —) SOUP
MIXABLE MISCIBLE
MIXED CHOW IMPURE MEDLEY
MOTLEY PIEBALD STREAKY
CHOWCHOW
(— BLOOD) MESTIZO
(— CHALICE) KRASIS
(— UP) HAYWIRE
(NOT —) SINCERE
(PREF.) MIXO
MIXER HOG BANBURY MUDDLER
PICKLER
(CEMENT —) BOXMAN
(CONCRETE —) PAVER
MIXTURE AIR MIX BODY BREW
DASH FEED HASH MANG MONG
MULL OLIO PUER SOUP STEW
ALGIN ALLOY BLEND BLENT
BROMO DOUGH GUMBO SALAD
STUFF FOURRE GARBLE GUNITE
LIGNIN MASLIN MEDLEY MELLAY
MINGLE MOTLEY TEMPER
AMALGAM COMPOST CUSTARD
FARRAGO FILICIN FORMULA
GOULASH HEADING KOGASIN
MELANGE MISTION MISTURA
MIXTION MONGREL OLLAPOD

RECEIPT TIMBALE ALKYLATE
BLENDURE DRAMMOCK
EMULSION POSSODIE POWSOWDY.
SOLUTION MACEDOINE
MENAGERIE MISCELLANY
SALMAGUNDI SMORGASBORD
(— ADDED TO WINE) DOSAGE
(— ATTRACTIVE TO PIGEONS)
SALTCAT
(— FOR CAKE) BATTER
(— FOR DRESSING LEATHER)
DUBBIN DUBBING
(— OF ALE AND OATMEAL) STOORY
(— OF ALKALOIDS) ADONIDIN
JABORINE
(— OF BARKS) TONGA
(— OF CEMENT AND STONE)
BUMICKY
(— OF CLAY AND CHALK) MALM
(— OF CLAY AND ROCK) BODY
(— OF CLAY AND SAND) LOAM
(— OF DRUGS) SPECIES
(— OF ELEMENTS) DIDYMIUM
(— OF FEEDS) MASH
(— OF IMPURE ARSENIDES) SPEISS
(— OF OATS AND BARLEY) DREDGE
(— OF PRINCIPLES) EUONYMIN
(— OF PROTEINS) CROTIN
(— OF SALTS) SOYATE
(— OF SAND AND STONES) CHAD
(— OF SAWDUST AND GLUE)
BADIGEON
(— OF SHALE AND SANDSTONE)
HAZLE
(— OF SLAG AND ORE) BROWSE
(— OF VINEGAR AND HONEY)
OXYMEL
(— OF VITAMINS) BIOS
(— OF WHITE AND BLACK) GRIZZLE
(— OF WINE, HONEY AND SPICES)
CLARY
(— TO ADULTERATE LIQUORS)
FLASH
(— TO DOCTOR WINE) GEROPIGA
(— TO WHITEN BREAD) HARDS
(— USED AS A FERMENT) BUB
(— USED AT SEDER) HAROSET
CHAROSES
(ACUTE —) ACUTA
(AERIFORM —) GAS
(CARVER'S —) COMPO
(CAULKING —) BLARE
(CLAY —) COB SLIP
(COATING —) COLOR
(CONFUSED —) MESS CHAOS
FUDDLE SOZZLE
(CRUMBLY —) STREUSEL
(EXPLOSIVE —) DUALIN FIREDAMP
(FOOD —) FILLING
(FREEZING —) CRYOGEN
(GILDING —) ASSIETTE
(HYDROCARBON —) ABIETENE
(ITALIAN CONDIMENT —) TAMARA
(JUMBLED —) BOTCH PASTICHE
(MECHANICS' —) PUTTY
(PLASTIC CEMENT —) CLOY
(PRESERVATIVE —) STUFF
(SEASONED —) STUFFING
(SMOKING —) CHARAS CHURRUS
(TANNING —) PURE
(THICKENING —) ROUX
(UNPALATABLE —) DRAMMOCK
(WATERY —) SLURRY

(WELDING —) THERMIT
(SUFF.) CRASE CRASIS CRASY
MIZZAH (FATHER OF —) REUEL
(GRANDFATHER OF —) ESAU
MIZZEN DANDY
MIZZONITE DIPYRE
MKS UNIT JOULE
MNEMONIC MEMORIAL
MOAN HONE MOON REEM WAIL
CROON GROAN MOURN MUNGE
QUIRK SOUGH MUNGER
MOANING SOUGH DIRGEFUL
MOAT FOSS DITCH FOSSE GRAFF
RUNDEL
MOB CREW HERD RAFF ROUT
COHUE CROWD HURRY PLEBE
PLEBS MOBILE RABBLE TUMULT
VOULGE DOGGERY CANAILLE
RIFFRAFF VARLETRY CLAMJAFRY
(PREF.) OCHLO
MOBCAP MOB
MOBILE THIN FLUID ROVING
MOVEABLE
MOBSTER HOODLUM
MOBY DICK (AUTHOR OF —)
MELVILLE
(CHARACTER IN —) AHAB STUBB
ISHMAEL FEDALLAH QUEEQUEG
STARBUCK
MOCCASIN PAC CONGO TEGUA
SHOEPACK
(— WITH LEGS) LARRIGAN
(PL.) SHANKS
MOCCASIN FLOWER NERVINE
MOCHA BARK
MOCHICA YUNCA
MOCHILA MACHEER KNAPSACK
MOCK BOB DOR GAB MOW COPY
DEFY GECK GIBE GIRD JAPE JEER
JEST JIBE PLAY QUIZ BOURD
DORRE ELUDE FLEER FLIRT FLOUT
FRUMP HOKER KNACK MIMIC
RALLY SCOFF SCORN SCOUT
SLEER SPORT TAUNT BEMOCK
DELUDE DERIDE ILLUDE NIGGLE
IMITATE MURGEON RIDICULE
MOCKER MOWER GIRDER
BOURDER FLOUTER SCORNER
RAILLEUR
MOCKERNUT BULLNUT
MOCKERY DOR GAB MOW GLEE
JEER BOURD DORRE FARCE
FLOUT GLAIK SCOFF SPORT
BISMER HETHING LUDIBRY
MOCKADO MOCKAGE DERISION
ILLUSION RIDICULE SCOFFERY
MOCKING GAB ACID SPORT
SCOPTIC IRRISORY NARQUOIS
SARDONIC TRUMPERY
MOCKINGBIRD MIMUS MOWER
MOCKER
MOCK ORANGE SYRINGA
PHILADELPHUS
MOCOA COCHE
MODE CUT JET TON WAY FORM
GATE MOOD RAGA TONE TWIG
WISE FERIO FINAL GENUS MODUS
STATE STYLE ACTING BAROCO
CESARE COURSE DATISI FAKOFO
FANGLE FESAPO MANNER
METHOD BAMALIP CALEMES
CAMENES DABITIS DARAPTI
DIBATIS DIMARIS DIMATIS

DISAMIS FAPESMO FASHION
FERISON FESTINO CELARENT
DOKMAROK FELAPTON FRESISON
TONALITY
(— OF BEHAVIOR) THEW HABITUDE
(— OF BEING) CATEGORY
(— OF CONDUCT) LAW
(— OF DRESS) HABIT TENUE
(— OF DRESSING HAIR) MADONNA
(— OF EXPRESSION) IRONY
(— OF MORAL ACTION) CONDUCT
(— OF PARTITIONING) CANT
(— OF PROCEDURE) ORDER SYSTEM
(— OF RULE) REGIME
(— OF SPEECH) ACCENT LATINISM
PARLANCE
(— OF STANDING) STANCE
(— OF STRUCTURE) BUILD
(PREVAILING —) GARB
(TEMPORARY —) VOGUE
MODEL WAX COPY FORM MOLD
NORM CANON DUMMY IDEAL
LIGHT MOULD NORMA SHAPE
DESIGN FUGLER GABARI MODULE
PRAXIS SOURCE BOZZETO
DIORAMA EXAMPLE GABARIT
MODULET PARAGON PATTERN
PICTURE SAMPLER CALENDAR
ENSAMPLE EXEMPLAR EXEMPLUM
FORMULAR FUGLEMAN
MAQUETTE MODELLER MODULIZE
PARADIGM PROPLASM SPECIMEN
TYPORAMA MANNEQUIN
PLANETARIUM
(— OF HUMAN BODY) FORM
MANIKIN
(— OF STATUE) ESQUISSE
(INFERIOR —) JALOPPY
(MATHEMATICAL —) SPACE
(PRELIMINARY —) MAQUETTE
PROPLASM
(PREF.) TYP(I)(O)
MODERATE BATE COOL CURB
EASE EASY EVEN MEEK SOFT
ABATE ALLAY ALLOY LIGHT
LOWER MEZZO MODER REMIT
SLACK SLAKE SOBER SWEET
ARREST BRIDLE DECENT GENTLE
LESSEN MEANLY MIDWAY
MODEST MODIFY REMISS SEASON
SOFTEN SUBMIT TEMPER
CENTRAL CHASTEN CONTROL
SLACKEN ATTEMPER CENTRIST
MEETERLY MIDDLING MITIGATE
MODERATO ORDINATE PALLIATE
PASSABLE CONTINENT
ABSTEMIOUS MEASURABLE
REASONABLE
(— IN BURNING) SOFT
(— OF THE WIND) LOOM
MODERATELY GEY FAIR MEAN
MEANLY MEETLY PRETTY
MIDWISE MEETERLY MIDDLING
MODERATENESS CLEMENCY
MODICITY
MODERATION MEAN STAY MINCE
SPARE MANNER MEDIUM REASON
COMPASS MEDIETY MODESTY
SOBRIETY ABATEMENT
IMMODESTY
MODERATO MASSIG
MODERATOR ANCHORMAN
MODERN NEW LATE

RECENT NEOTERIC
MODEST COY SHY DEFT MURE
NICE PURE SNUG BLATE DOUCE
LOWLY QUIET SMALL CHASTE
DEMURE HUMBLE PUDENT
SIMPLE VIRGIN CLERKLY PUDICAL
DISCREET MAIDENLY PUDIBUND
RESERVED RETIRING SHAMEFUL
VERECUND VIRTUOUS
MODESTY AIDOS PUDOR NICETY
DECENCY PUDENCY SHYNESS
CHASTITY FOREHEAD HUMILITY
PUDICITY
MODICUM DROP BREAK SPICE
PENNORTH SCANTLING
SEMBLANCE PENNYWORTH
MODIFICATION BOB ECAD FORM
SALT CHANGE ENGRAM FACIES
SANDHI SINGLE UMLAUT
ENGRAMMA
(— OF A REMEDY) TINCTION
(GLOTTAL —) STOP
MODIFIED VARIANT
MODIFY EDIT VARY ALTER AMEND
HEDGE TOUCH BUFFER CHANGE
DOCTOR MASTER TEMPER
ARABIZE COMPARE FASHION
QUALIFY ATTEMPER DENATURE
GRADUATE MODERATE
FAUCALIZE
(— ARTICULATION) COLOR
(— COLOR) TONE
MODILLION ANCON MODEL TRUSS
CARTOUCH
MODISH CHIC MODY SOIGNE
TIMISH TONISH STYLISH
MODISHNESS CHIC
MODRED (FATHER OF —) ARTHUR
(MOTHER OF —) MARGAWSE
MODULATE SINK INFLECT QUALIFY
MODULATION ACCENT CHANGE
CADENCE BUNCHING PASSAGIO
MODULE LEM
MOGUL PADISHAH
MOHAIR MOIRE
MOHAMMED MAHOMET
MAHOUND MUDEJAR PROPHET
(UNCLE OF —) ABBAS
MOHAMMEDAN MOSLEM PAYNIM
MAHOMET
MOHAMMEDANISM TURBAN
TURKERY MAUMETRY
MOHAWK NICKER
MOHR MHORR GAZELLE
MOHUR MOOR AHMEDI
MOIETY MEDIETY
MOIST WET DAMP DANK DEWY
NESH UVID DABBY GIVEY GREEN
HUMID JUICY MADID MOCHY
SAMMY SAPPY SLACK SOAKY
SOCKY SPEWY SWACK WASHY
WEEPY CLAMMY MOISTY STICKY
WETTISH HUMOROUS MUCULENT
(PREF.) HUMI(DI) HYGR(O) UDO
MOISTEN DIP WET DAMP MOIL
BASTE BATHE BEDEW JUICE
LATCH LEACH STEEP WOKIE
DABBLE DAMPEN HUMECT
HUMIFY IMBRUE MADEFY SPARGE
TEMPER HUMIDIFY IRRIGATE
IRRORATE
(— LEATHER) SAM SAMMY
MOISTURE DEW WET BREE DAMP

DANK ROKE HUMOR MOIST WATER PHLEGM AQUOSITY HUMIDITY
(— DEFICIENT) XERIC
(— IN STONE) SAP
(— ON BEARD) BARBER
(CONDENSED —) BREATH
(REMOVE CONDENSED —) DEFOG
(PREF.) HUMI(DI) HYGR(O) UDO
MOJARRA SHAD PATAO
MOKI MOGUEY MOKIHI
MOKSHA MUKTI
MOLAR WANG FORMAL MOLARY GRINDER
(PREF.) MYL(O)
MOLASSES DIP LICK CLAGGUM THERIAC TREACLE LONGLICK
(PREF.) MELASSI
MOLD DIE FEN PIG PLY SOW CALM CAST CURB FORM MULL MUST SOIL TRAP BLOCK CHAPE CHILL FRAME INGOT MODEL MOULD MUCOR PLASM PRINT SHAPE SHARE STENT STINT VALVE COFFIN GABARI INFORM LINGET MATRIX SQUARE BASTARD FASHION FESTOON MATRICE RILLETT SANDBOX SKILLET TEMPLET COQUILLE FUMAGINE HOODMOLD PROPLASM TEMPLATE WHISKERS PENICILLIUM
(— FOR METAL) SOW SKILLET
(— OF ASPIC) DARIOLE
(— OF SHIP) SWEEP
(— THAT ATTACKS HOPS) FEN
(CHEESE —) CHESSEL
(SLIME —) MYCETOZOAN MYXOMYCETE
(PREF.) PLASM(ATO)(O)
(SUFF.) PLASIA PLASIS PLASM(A)(IA)(IC) PLAST(IC)(Y) PLASY
MOLDAVITE TEKTITE
MOLDBOARD REEST
(— SURFACE) WREST
MOLDED FICTILE
MOLDER MURL CAPPER MANGLE MOSKER FIGURER PLASTER PLASTIC
MOLDINESS MUST FINEW MUCOR VINEW
MOLDING BEAD COVE CYMA DADO GULA KEEL LIST OGEE OVAL CABLE FILET GORGE LABEL LEDGE ROVER STAFF BANDLE BASTON BILLET CASING COLLAR CONGEE COVING FILLET LISTEL MULLER REGLET SQUARE ZIGZAG ANNULET BEADING CABLING CHAPLET CORNICE DOUCINE ECHINUS EYEBROW FINGENT HIPMOLD LOZENGE MOULAGE NECKING SURBASE TONDINO TRINGLE ASTRAGAL BAGUETTE BANDELET CASEMATE CASEMENT CINCTURE CYMATION CYMATIUM DANCETTE DOGTOOTH FUSAROLE HOODMOLD KNURLING MOULDING NAILHEAD NECKMOLD ARCHIVOLT BOLECTION
(CONCAVE —) GORGE CONGEE SCOTIA CAVETTO
(CONVEX —) REED CABLE OVOLO THUMB TORUS BASTON REEDING ASTRAGAL FUSAROLE
(OGEE —) TALON
(OUTSIDE —) BACKBAND
(PL.) TORI LEDGMENT
MOLDY FUSTY HOARY MUCID MUGGY MUSTY VINNY FOISTY MOULDY FOUGHTY
MOLE COB UNT COBB MAIL OONT PIER PILE TAPE WANT JUTTY MOODY NEVUS TALPA TAUPE ANICUT MOUDIE HYDATID TALPOID MOLDWARP MOONCALF SORICOID STARNOSE UROPSILE ZANDMOLE
(PREF.) TALPI
MOLE CRICKET CHANGA
MOLECULE ACID ATOM BASE AMMINE DIPOLE HYDROL LIGAND PRIMER HYDRONE SPECIES TEMPLATE OCTAPEPTIDE
MOLEHILL TUMP HOYLE WANTHILL
MOLE RAT SEMNI ZEMMI ZOKOR SLEPEZ SPALACID ZANDMOLE
MOLEST GALL HAUNT TEASE BOTHER HARASS HECKLE INFEST PESTER MISLEST TROUBLE
MOLID (FATHER OF —) ABISHUR
(MOTHER OF —) ABIHAIL
MOLL FLANDERS (AUTHOR OF —) DEFOE
(CHARACTER IN —) MOLL JEMMY ROBIN FLANDERS
MOLLIFY HUSH RELAX ADULCE GENTLE PACIFY RELENT SOFTEN SOOTHE TEMPER ASSUAGE DULCIFY SWEETEN ATTEMPER MITIGATE UNRUFFLE
MOLLIFYING MILD SUPPLING
MOLLUSK ARK CLAM CONE PIPI SPAT BORER CHAMA CHANK CHINK CLAMP CONCH COWRY DORIS DRILL MUREX PINNA SNAIL VENUS AEOLID BAILER BUBBLE CERION CHITON COCKLE COURIE DOLIUM JINGLE LEPTON LIMPET MUSSEL NERITA OYSTER PECTEN PHOLAD PURPLE SEMELE STROMB ABALONE ADMIRAL ASTARTE BIVALVE CARDITA DECAPOD JUNONIA MOLLUSC PIDDOCK SALPIAN SCALLOP TOHEROA TREPANG TROPHON DUCKFOOT FIGSHELL HALIOTIS NAUTILUS PTEROPOD SAXICAVA STROMBUS UNIVALVE VERMETUS SHELLFISH NUDIBRANCH PERIWINKLE
(— TRIBE) NAIADES
(LARVAL —) VELIGER
(YOUNG —) SPAT
MOLLYCODDLE MOLLY WANTON INDULGE MILKSOP
MOLOSSUS (FATHER OF —) PYRRHUS
(MOTHER OF —) ANDROMACHE
MOLT MEW CAST MUTE SHED MOULT DISCARD EXUVIATE INTERMEW
MOLTEN FUSED
MOLTING BROKEN ECDYSIS
MOLUCCAS (ISLAND OF —) ARU KAI OBI BURU LETI SULA AMBON BABAR BANDA CERAM WETAR BATJAN TIDORE MOROTAI TERNATE TANIMBAR HALMAHERA
MOLUS (BROTHER OF —) EVENUS
(DAUGHTER OF —) MOLIONE
(FATHER OF —) ARES MARS
(MOTHER OF —) DEMONICE
MOLYBDENUM (EXCESS OF —) TEART
MOMBIN JOCOTE
MOMENT MO GIRD HINT SAND TICK AVAIL BLINK BRAID CLINK CRACK GLIFF GLISK JIFFY SHAKE SNIFT SPURT STOUN TRICE VALUE FILLIP GLIFFY MINUTE PERIOD SECOND STOUND WEIGHT YAWING ARTICLE INSTANT INSTANCE MOMENTUM TWINKLING
(— FOR LEGERDEMAIN ACTION) TEMPS
(— OF STRESS) CRISE
(APPROPRIATE —) PLACE
(CRITICAL —) BIT INCH CORNER
(DECISIVE —) CRISIS
(EXACT —) BIT POINT
(OPPORTUNE —) KAIROS
(SCHEDULED —) TIME
MOMENTARY MOMENTAL TRANSIENT
MOMENTOUS FELL GRAVE EPOCHAL FATEFUL WEIGHTY EVENTFUL PREGNANT
MOMENTOUSNESS GRAVITY
MOMENTUM WAY FORCE SPEED IMPETUS
MON PEGUAN TALAING

MONACO
ANCIENT NAME: MONOECUS
CAPITAL: MONACO MONACOVILLE
DYNASTY: GRIMALDI
LANGUAGE: FRENCH
PEOPLE: MONEGASQUES
PRINCE: LOUIS ALBERT HONORE ANTOINE CHARLES RAINIER FLORESTAN
RIVER: VESUBIE
SECTION: MONTECARLO LACONDAMINE MONACOVILLE

MONAD ATOM JIVA HENAD MONAS
MONADIC UNARY
MONADNOCK BARABOO
MONARCH KING QUEEN DANAID DIADEM PRINCE DANAINE EMPEROR AUTOCRAT
MONARCHIAN PRAXEAN
MONARCHICAL KINGLY
MONARCHY KINGDOM
MONASTERY WAT ABBEY BADIA LAURA RIBAT TEKKE TEKYA FRIARY MANDRA VIHARA BONZERY CERTOSA CONVENT KHANKAH MINSTER MONKERY CLOISTER LAMASERY
(ALGERIAN —) RIBAT
(BUDDHIST —) TERA KYAUNG BONZERY LAMASERY
(CARTHUSIAN —) CERTOSA
(HINDU —) MATH
(MOSLEM —) TEKKE

TEKYA KHANKAH
(PREF.) MANDRI
(SUFF.) MINSTER
MONASTIC MONKLY MONKISH ABBATIAL CENOBIAN MONACHAL
MONASTICISM MONKERY MONKISM
MONETARY EXPLICIT PECUNIARY NUMISMATIC
MONEY (ALSO SEE COIN) AES BOX DIB FAT FEE FEI GET OOF ORO SAP TIN WAD CASH COAT COIN COLE CRAP CUSH DUBS DUST FUND GATE GELT GILT GOLD HOOT JACK JAKE KALE LOOT LOUR MALI MINT MOSS MUCK PELF ROLL SALT SAND SHAG SOAP SWAG BEANS BLUNT BRASH BRASS BREAD BUNCE BUNTS CHINK CHIPS CLINK DARBY DIMES DOUGH DUMPS FUNDS GREEN GRIGS IMPUT LOLLY LUCRE MEANS MOOLA MOPUS OCHER PURSE RHINO ROCKS ROWDY SCADS SHINY SMASH SPUDS STIFF STUFF SUGAR ARGENT BARATO BARREL BOODLE CHANGE CUNYIE DANARO DINERO FARLEU FARLEY FEUAGE FLIMSY FUMAGE GRAITH HANSEL KELTER MAZUMA POCKET SHEKEL SILLER SILVER SPENSE SPLOSH STAMPS STEVEN STUMPY TALENT WISSEL ADVANCE CHATTEL CHINKER COUNTER CRACKER CRUSADE DEPOSIT FALDAGE GUNNAGE OOFTISH SCRATCH SPANKER SPECIES STOCKER CRIMPAGE CURRENCY DEMIMARK INCOMING INTEREST SPENDING STERLING STOCKING XERAPHIN
(— BET) COMEBACK
(— DUE) DEVOIRS
(— FOR LIQUOR) WHIP
(— LENT) LUMBER
(— OF ACCOUNT) ORA
(— PAID TO BIND BARGAIN) ARLES
(— TAKEN IN) DRAWING
(ADDITIONAL —) BONUS
(AVAILABLE —) CAPITAL
(BAR —) BONK TANG
(BASE —) SHICE
(BRIBE —) SOAP BOODLE
(COUNTERFEIT —) BOGUS QUEER BOODLE DUFFER SHOWFUL SLITHER
(EARNEST —) ARLES ARRHA DEPOSIT HANDSEL HANDGELD HANDSALE
(EXPENSE —) DIET
(EXTORTED —) PROTECTION
(FERRY —) NAULUM
(HARD —) SPECIE
(HAT —) TAMPANG
(HAVING NO —) FLYBLOWN
(INVESTED —) STOCK
(PAPER —) GREEN CABBAGE CURRENCY FROGSKIN
(PASSAGE —) SHIPHIRE
(PRIZE —) PEWTER
(PROTECTION —) ICE
(PUSH —) SPIFF

(READY —) CASH DARBY PREST READY STUFF STUMPY
(REFUNDED —) DRAWBACK
(SHELL —) PEAG HAWOK WAKIKI WAMPUM
(SILVER —) SYCEE
(SMALL SUM OF —) SPILL
(STANDARD BANK —) BANCO
(SUBSISTENCE —) BATTA
(TRAVELLING —) VIATICUM
(WIRE —) LARI LARIN LARREE
MONEYBAG FOLLIS
MONEY BELT ZONE
MONEY BOX TILL CHEST PIRLIE
MONEY-CHANGER SARAF SHROFF CAMBIST ARGENTER
MONEY-CHANGING AGIO
MONEY DRAWER TILL SHUTTLE
MONEYED RICH WEALTHY
MONEYLENDER BANYA CHETTY USURER LOMBARD MAHAJAN MARWARI SHYLOCK BUMMAREE
MONEYMAKING BANAUSIC
MONEYWORT MANG MYRTLE PRIMWORT
MONGOL HUN KALKA BALKAR BURIAT DAGHUR SHARRA BERBERI KALMUCK KHALKHA SILINGAL
(PL.) HU
MONGOLIA (CAPITAL OF —) ULAANBAATAR
(DESERT IN —) GOBI
(MONEY OF —) TUGHRIK
(RIVER OF —) ORHON DZAVHAN KERULEN SELENGE
(TOWN OF —) ONON MUREN DARHAN BULAGAN CHOIREN TAMTSAK ULANBATOR CHOYBALSAN
MONGOOSE MUNG URVA CIVET MUNGO MONGOE MEERKAT VANSIRE
MONGREL CUR DOG FICE FIST MUTT CROSS FEIST LIMER POOCH SCRUB HYBRID PYEDOG BASTARD CURRISH PIEBALD DOGGEREL
MONILIALES HYPHO
MONIMIA (GUARDIAN OF —) ACASTO
(HUSBAND OF —) CASTALIO
(LOVER OF —) POLYDORE
MONISM HENISM ONEISM
MONITION TUITION
MONITOR CRT MARKER MENTOR LANTERN PREFECT
MONITOR LIZARD IBID IBIT URAN VARAN WARAL GOANNA WORRAL MONITOR KABARAGOYA
MONK BO FRA COWL LAMA MARO ARHAT BONZE CLERK FRATE FRIAR PADRE YAHAN ARAHAT BHIKKU CULDEE GALLAH GETSUL GOSAIN MONACH SANTON VOTARY CALOYER CLUNIAC GALLACH JACOBIN STARETS STUDITE ATHONITE BACHELOR BASILIAN MARABOUT MONASTIC OLIVETAN SANNYASI TALAPOIN TRAPPIST BALDICOOT CELESTINE THELEMITE BERNARDINE CISTERCIAN
(PL.) AGAPETI ACOEMETI

MONKEY APE CAY ORA PUG SAI TUP BEGA BROH BRUH DOUC KAHA MONA MONK MONO SAKI SIME TITI TOTA WAAG ZATI ARABA CEBID DIANA JACKO JOCKO KAHAU MUNGA OATAS PATAS PONGO PUGGY SAJOU TOQUE UNGKA BANDAR COAITA COUXIA GRISON GRIVET GUENON HOWLER LANGUR MACACO MARTEN MIRIKI MONACH NISNAS OUBARI PINCHE RILAWA SAMIRI SIMIAN SIMPAI TEETEE VERVET WARINE WEEPER WISTIT BHUNDER COLOBIN GUARIBA GUEREZA HANUMAN KALASIE LUNGOOR MACAQUE MEERKAT MOUSTOC OUAKARI PRIMATE ROLOWAY SAIMIRI SAPAJOU STENTOR TAMARIN ARAGUATO CAIARARA CAPUCHIN DURUKULI ENTELLUS LEONCITO MANGABEY MARMOSET MARTINET MUSTACHE ORABASSU PRIMATAL TALAPOIN TCHINCOU WANDEROO BRACHYURA MALBROUCK
(LIKE A —) PUGGISH
(PREF.) PITHEC(O)
MONKEY BREAD BAOBAB ADANSONIA
MONKEY FLOWER MIMULUS
MONKEYPOT LECYTH KAKARALI LECYTHIS SAPUCAIA
MONKEY PUZZLE BUNYA PINON PINION
MONKEYSHINE DIDO SINGERIE
(PL.) HORSE
MONKFISH MONK RHINA SQUATINA
MONKISH CENOBIAN MONASTIC
MONK PARROT LORO
MONKSHOOD ATIS ACONITE ACONITUM NAPELLUS MOUSEBANE
MONO MONACHI
MONOACETATE ACETIN
MONOCARPELLARY SIMPLE
MONOCHORD MAGAS MAGADIS UNICHORD
MONOCHROME CAMAIEU MONOTINT
MONOCLE QUIZ LORGNON EYEGLASS
MONOCLINOUS PERFECT
MONOECISM SYNOECY SYNOEKY
MONOGRAM IHS JHS YHS CIPHER HERALD CHRISMON
MONOGRAPH STUDY MEMOIR BULLETIN DISCOURSE
MONOLITH MENHIR PILLAR
(CIRCLE OF —S) CROMLECH
MONOLITHIC GLOBAL
MONOLOGIST DISEUSE
MONOLOGUE MONOLOGY SOLILOQUY
MONOPHTHONGAL PURE
MONOPHTHONGIZE SMOOTH
MONOPHYSITE AGNOETE AGNOITE JACOBITE
(PL.) ACEPHALI
MONOPLANE TAUBE PARASOL
MONOPODE SKIAPOD
MONOPOLIZE LURCH ABSORB

CONSUME ENGROSS
MONOPOLY REGIE TRUST CARTEL APPALTO
MONOSACCHARIDE OSE DIOSE HEXOSE KETOSE MONOSE GLYCOSE HEPTOSE PENTOSE PYRANOSE
MONOTONOUS ARID DEAD DULL FLAT WASTE DREARY SAMELY SODDEN ADENOID HUMDRUM INSIPID IRKSOME TEDIOUS BORESOME DRUDGING SAMESOME SINGSONG UNVARIED VEGETABLE
MONOTONY DRAB DRYNESS HUMDRUM DULLNESS SAMENESS
MONOXENOUS DIRECT
MONSIEUR BEAUCAIRE (AUTHOR OF —) TARKINGTON
(CHARACTER IN —) BEAU MARY NASH VALOIS CARLISLE MIREPOIX PHILLIPE MOLYNEAUX WINTERSET CHATEAURIEN
MONSOON VARSHA
MONSTER OGRE BILCH LARVA MORMO RAHAB TERAS UNMAN ELLOPS GERYON MAKARA SHRIMP TYPHON BICORNE CHIMERA CYCLOPS DIDYMUS DIPYGUS ECHIDNA GRENDEL GRIFFIN GRIFFON PRODIGY SLAPPER UNBEAST WARLOCK JANICEPS LINDWORM MOONCALF TARASQUE TYPHOEUS UROMELUS LEVIATHAN
(— WITH 100 EYES) ARGUS
(— WITH 100 HANDS) BRIAREUS
(FABULOUS —) KRAKEN TANIWHA
(FEMALE —) HARPY LAMIA SCYLLA
(HALF-BULL HALF-MAN —) MINOTAUR
(INVISIBLE —) BUNYIP
(MAN-DEVOURING —) OGRE LAMIA
(MYTHICAL —) HARPY SCYLLA SPHINX CHIMERA WARLOCK MINOTAUR
(SEA —) BELUE PHOCA KRAKEN PISTRIX ZIFFIUS WASSERMAN
(SUPERNATURAL —) LARVA
(TWO-BODIED —) DISOMUS
(WATER —) NICKER
(9-HEADED —) HYDRA
(PREF.) TERAT(O)
(SUFF.) PAGUS
MONSTRANCE SUN
MONSTROSITY FREAK DIPYGUS MONSTER ABORTION IMMANITY MOONCALF TERATISM
(SUFF.) DYMUS
MONSTROUS VAST ENORM GIANT FIENDLY FLAMING HIDEOUS TITANIC BEHEMOTH COLOSSAL DEFORMED ENORMOUS FLAGRANT GIGANTIC PYTHONIC SLAPPING NEFARIOUS PRODIGIOUS
MONTAGNARD SEKANI

MONTANA
CAPITAL: HELENA
COLLEGE: CARROLL
COUNTY: HILL TETON TOOLE CARBON CUSTER FERGUS MCCONE WIBAUX BIGHORN PONDERA RAVALLI CHOUTEAU FLATHEAD MISSOULA
INDIAN: CROW ATSINA SALISH ARAPAHO KUTENAI SIKSIKA SHOSHONE
LAKE: HEBGEN FLATHEAD FORTPECK MEDICINE
MOUNTAIN: AJAX BALDY COWAN SPHINX TORREY GRANITE HILGARD TRAPPER GALLATIN PENTAGON SNOWSHOE
MOUNTAIN RANGE: CRAZY LEWIS POCKY BIGBELT
NICKNAME: BIGSKY MOUNTAIN TREASURE
RIVER: MILK TONGUE KOOTENAI MISSOURI
STATE BIRD: MEADOWLARK
STATE FLOWER: BITTERROOT
TOWN: BUTTE HAVRE MALTA TERRY CIRCLE CONRAD HARDIN HELENA HYSHAM SCOBEY BOZEMAN CHINOOK CHOTEAU EKALAKA FORSYTH GLASGOW ROUNDUP BILLINGS MISSOULA

MONTANIST PHRYGIAN

MONTENEGRO
CAPITAL: CETINJE
COIN: PARA FLORIN PERPERA
LAKE: SCUTARI SHKODER
MOUNTAIN: DURMITOR
NAME: ZETA ILLYRIA CRNAGORA TSERNAGORA
PORT: BAR ULCINJ ANTIVARI DULCIGNO
RIVER: IBAR ZETA DRINA MORACA
TOWN: NIKSIC CETINJE TITOGRAD PODGORICA

MONTH AB AV BUL MAY PUS SOL ZIF ZIW ABIB ADAR AHET APAP ASIN ELUL IYAR JETH JULY JUNE KUAR MAGH MOON TYBI AGHAN APRIL ASARH CHAIT IYYAR MAIUS MARCH NISAN PAYNI RABIA RAJAB SAFAR SAWAN SEBAT SHVAT SIVAN SIWAN TEBET THOTH TIZRI UINAL AUGUST BHADON CHOIAK JUMADA JUNIUS KARTIK KISLEV KISLEW KISLEY MECHIR MESORE NISSAN NIVOSE PAOPHI PHAGUN SAPHAR SHABAN SHABAT TAMMUZ TEBETH TISHRI VEADAR ABAGHAN APRILIS BAISAKH BYSACKI CHAITRA CHISLEV ETHANIM FLOREAL HESHVAN JANUARY MARTIUS OCTOBER PACHONS PHALGUN RAMADAN SARAWAN SHAABAN SHAWWAL THAMMUZ VENTOSE BRUMAIRE DECEMBER DULKAADA FEBRUARY FERVIDOR FRIMAIRE GAMELION GERMINAL MESSIDOR MUHARRAM NOVEMBER PLUVIOSE POSEIDON PRAIRIAL SEXTILIS ZULKADAH SEPTEMBER
(IN NEXT —) PROXIMO
(IN PRECEDING —) ULTIMO
(PRESENT —) INSTANT

(SIX —S) SEMESTER
(PREF.) MENO
(SUFF.) MESTER
MONTHLY MENSAL
MONUMENT VAT WAT LECH TOMB
CROSS STONE TABUT TITLE
BILITH DOLMEN HEARSE HEROON
MEMORY RECORD TROPHY
ARCHIVE CHAITYA CHHATRI
CHORTEN DENKMAL FUNERAL
TRILITH BILITHON CENOTAPH
MEMORIAL MONOLITH TROPAION
(— IN CHURCH) SACELLUM
(— OF BALEARIC ISLES) TALAYOT
(— OF HEAPED STONES) CAIRN
(PILLARLIKE —) SHAFT STELA
STELE
MOO LOW
MOOCH BUM CADGE SPONGE
MOOCHER MIKER CADGER
GRAFTER SKELDER
MOOD CUE FIT TID MIND TIFF TIFT
TONE TUNE VEIN WHIM DEVIL
FRAME FREAK HEART HUMOR
SPITE PLIGHT SPIRIT SPLEEN
SPRITE STRAIN TALENT TEMPER
CAPRICE FANTASY FEATHER
JUSSIVE ATTITUDE OPTATIVE
(— IN LOGIC) BARBARA
(— OF BAD TEMPER) MAD DORTS
(— OF DEPRESSION) LETDOWN
(CROSS —) FRUMPS
(FRIVOLOUS —) JEST
(GROUCHY —) DODS
(IRRITABLE —) GRIZZLE
(PENSIVE —) MELANCHOLY
(SULKY —) PET
(SULLEN —) STRUNT SULLENS
MOODY SAD GLUM SULKY BROODY
GLOOMY MOROSE SULLEN
MOODISH PENSIVE
MOON BUAT LAMP LUNA MAHI
DIANA LUNET LUCINA PHOEBE
CHANDRA CYNTHIA LEWANNA
LUNETTE MOONLET FOGEATER
MENISCUS SATELLES
(AREA ON —) TERRA
(FULL —) PLENILUNE
(NEW —) PRIME
(PART OF COURSE OF —) MANSION
(WANING —) WANIAND
(PREF.) LUNI MENI SELEN(I)(O)
MOON AND SIXPENCE (AUTHOR OF —) MAUGHAM
(CHARACTER IN —) AMY ATA DIRK
TIARE BLANCHE CHARLES
COUTRAS STROEVE STRICKLAND
MOONBLIND LUNATIC
MOONEYE HIODONT
MOONEYE CISCO BLOATER
MOON-EYED LUNATIC
MOONFISH OPAH SUNFISH
JOROBADO
MOONFLOWER ACHETE
MOONLIGHT FLESH MOONGLOW
MOONRAT GYMNURE
MOONSET MOONDOWN
MOONFALL
MOONSHINE MOON SHINE SHINNY
BOOTLEG BLOCKADE
MOONSTONE (AUTHOR OF —)
COLLINS
(CHARACTER IN —) CUFF EZRA

JOHN BLAKE BRUFF CANDY
LUKER RACHEL GABRIEL GODFREY
ROSANNA FRANKLIN JENNINGS
SPEARMAN VERINDER
ABLEWHITE BETTEREDGE
HERNCASTLE MURTHWAITE
MOONSTRUCK LUNATIC
MOONWORT LUNARY HONESTY
MOOR FEN BENT FELL MOSS POST
BEACH BERTH HOVEL TURCO
COMONTE MARRANO MOGRABI
MOORMAN MORESCO MORISCO
COMMONTY
(INFERTILE —) LANDE
MOOR COCK GORCOCK MUIRCOCK
MOORING DOCK MOORAGE
MOORLAND ROSLAND OUTFIELD
MOOSE BELL ELAND CERVID
ORIGNAL
(YOUNG —) CALF
MOOSEWOOD DIRCA
MOOT MUTE STIR PORTMOOT
MOP BOB SOP SWAB MALKIN
MERKIN MOPPET SCOVEL
(— FOR CLEANING CANNON)
MERKIN
(— OF HAIR) TOUSLE
(BAKER'S —) MALKIN MAWKIN
MOPANE IRONWOOD
MOPE MUMP PEAK POUT SULK
BOODY BROOD GLOOM
MOPING FUSTY DUMPISH
MOPSUS (FATHER OF —) AMPYCUS
RHACIUS
(MOTHER OF —) MANTO CHLORIS
MORA LOVE TIME LIMMA SEMEION
MORAL TAG PURE CIVIL ETHIC
EPIMYTH ETHICAL UPRIGHT
HONORARY
(PL.) THEW
MORALISTIC DIDACTIC
MORALITY MORALS VIRTUE
MORALIZING PI
MORASS BOG FLOW MOSS ROSS
SUMP FLUSH MARSH SLACK
POLDER SLOUGH QUAGMIRE
MORAY PUSI ELGIN HAMLET
MURAENA
MORBID SICK MORBOSE PECCANT
MORDANT HANDLE SPIRIT
CAUSTIC STRIKER SCATHING
MORDECAI (FATHER OF —) JAIR
(WARD OF —) ESTHER
MORE MO MAE PIU OTHER HELDER
(— OR LESS) HALFWAY
(— THAN) BUT OVER ABOVE
RISING PLUSQUAM
(— THAN ADEQUATE) AMPLE
(— THAN ENOUGH) TOO
(— THAN HALF) BETTER
(— THAN ONE) SEVERAL
(— THAN ONE OR TWO) SUNDRY
(— THAN SUFFICIENT) ABUNDANT
(— THAN THIS) YEA
(LITTLE —) ADVANTAGE
(PREF.) MALLO PLEIO PLEO PLIO
(— THAN) PLU SUPER
MOREEN TABBY
MOREL HELVELLA MORIGLIO
MORELLO MOREL GRIOTTE
MULBERRY
MOREOVER EFT EKE TOO ALSO
MORE AGAIN EITHER BESIDES

FARTHER FURTHER THERETO
LIKEWISE OVERMORE
MOREPORK PEHO RURU MOPOKE
MOPEHAWK
MORGUE LIBRARY MORTUARY
MORION CABASSET
MORMON COHAB SAINT DANITE
PATRIARCH
(— STATE) UTAH
MORNING GAY MORN MATIN
MORROW UNDERN COCKCROW
MORNTIME
(IN THE —) MANE
MORNING GLORY NIL KOALI
TWINER GAYBINE IPOMOEA
MANROOT PILIKAI BINDWEED
SCAMMONY MOONFLOWER
(— GROWING AMONG GRAIN) BEAR
MORNING STAR VENUS DAYSTAR
LUCIFER MERCURY BARTONIA
MORO LUTAO SAMAL YAKAN
ILLANO JOLOANO MARANAO
MOROCCO MAROQUIN

MOROCCO

CAPE: NUN NOUN
CAPITAL: RABAT
COIN: OKIA RIAL OKIEH DIRHAM
MOUZOUNA
DISTRICT: ERRIF
FRENCH NAME: MAROC
MEASURE: KALA SAAH FANEGA
IZENBI TOMINI
MOUNTAIN: TOUBKAL
MOUNTAIN RANGE: RIF ATLAS
PEOPLE: MOOR BERBER KABYLE
MOSLEM MUSLIM
PORT: SAFI CEUTA RABAT SAFFI
AGADIR TETUAN LARACHE
MAZAGAN MELILLA MOGADOR
TANGIER
PROVINCE: CEUTA MELILLA
RIVER: DRA SOUS WADI SEBOU
TENSIFT MOULOUYA
TOWN: FES FEZ SAFI OUJDA
RABAT AGADIR MEKNES
KENITRA TANGIER TETOUAN
MARRAKECH CASABLANCA
WEIGHT: ROTL ARTAL ARTEL
GERBE RATEL KINTAR QUINTAL

MORON FOOL AMENT IMBECILE
MORONITY MOROSIS
MOROSE ACID GLUM GRUM SOUR
MOODY RUSTY SURLY CRUSTY
GLOOMY SEVERE STINGY SULLEN
CRABBED CROOKED PEEVISH
STROUNGE SATURNINE
SPLENETIC
MOROSELY CRUSTILY
MOROSENESS ASPERITY
MORPHEME BASE ETYMON
COGNATE
MORPHOLOGICAL FORMAL
MORRIS MILL MERELS
MORSEL BIT NIG ORT TIT BITE
GNAP SNAP SCRAN BUCKONE
MORCEAU NOISETTE PARTICLE
SKERRICK
(— OF CHEESE) TRIP
(— OF CHOCOLATE) BUD
(— OF SEASONED MEAT) GOBBET
(CHOICE —) TIDBIT TITBIT

(PREF.) PSOMO
MORTAL BEING DYING FATAL
HUMAN VITAL DEADLY FINITE
LETHAL BRITTLE DEATHLY
DEATHFUL
(FIRST —) YAMA
MORTALITY FLESH MURRAIN
MORTALLY DEADLY FATALLY
MORTAR DAB COMPO DAGGA
GROUT LARRY ROYAL SORKI
SWISH CANNON CEMENT
HOLMOS MINNIE POTGUN
BEDDING COEHORN DAUBING
PERRIER POUNDER PUGGING
SOORKEE
(— AND PESTLE) DOLLY DOLLIE
(— EXTRUDED BETWEEN LATHS)
KEY
(— FOR ROCKETS) TROMBE
(— FOR SALUTES) CHAMBER
(— MADE WITH STRAW) BAUGE
(INFERIOR —) SLIME
(SMALL —) HOBIT ROYAL TINKER
(THIN —) LARRY
MORTARBOARD CATERCAP
TRENCHER
MORTAR BOAT PALANDER
MORTGAGE DIP LAY BOND LIEN
ENGAGE MONKEY OBLIGE
WADSET WEDDEED THIRLAGE
MORTGAGOR REVERSER
MORTIFICATION ENVY SHAME
SPITE CHAGRIN GANGRENE
NECROSIS VEXATION
MORTIFIED ASHAMED
MORTIFY ABASE ABASH SHAME
SPITE HUMBLE CHAGRIN CRUCIFY
MACERATE
MORTISE GAIN COCKET
(SIDE OF —) CHEEK
MORTUARY MORGUE FUNERARY
SAWLSHOT SEPULCHRAL
MORWONG TARAKIHI
MOSAIC AUCUBA EMBLEM MUSIVE
SCREEN FRISOLEE INTARSIA
TERRAZZO
(POTATO —) CRINKLE
MOSLEM MOOR HADJI HAFIZ
HANIF ISLAM MALAY SALAR
PAYNIM SHIITE TURBAN ISLAMIC
MOORMAN SANGGIL SARACEN
ISLAMITE SANGUILE
(— SCHOLAR) ULAMA
MOSQUE JAMI MOSCH DURGAH
MASJID MESKED
MOSQUITO GNAT AEDES CULICID
GAMBIAE SKEETER ANOPHELE
DIPTERAN
(PREF.) CULIC(I) EMPID(O)
MOSS FOG MNIUM USNEA
HYPNUM MUSKEG AEROGEN
FOXFEET GULAMAN HAIRCAP
PILIGAN TORTULA CROWFOOT
MOSSWORT SPHAGNUM
STAGHORN
(— HANGING FROM TREE) WEEPER
(PL.) MUSCI
(PREF.) BRY(O) MUSC(I)(O)
SPHAGNI SPHAGNO
MOSSBUNKER MENHADEN
MOSSHORN STEER
MOSSI MOLE MORE
MOSSI-GURUNSI GUR

MOSS PINK PHLOX
MOSSTROOPER RIDER
MOSSY FOGGY HOARY MUSCOSE
MOST BEST MOSTLY FARTHEST
(PREF.) PLEISTO
MOSTLY MOST FECKLY CHIEFLY
MOSTDEAL
MOT JEST
MOTE ATOM ATOMY FESCUE
MOATHILL
MOTEL COURT
MOTH GEM NUN PUG DART HAWK
MOTE PAGE ACREA APPLE ATLAS
EGGAR EGGER FLAME GAMMA
IMAGO MORMO PISKY PLUME
SAMIA SWIFT THORN USHER
WITCH ANTLER BAGONG BUGONG
BURNET COSSID DAGGER
DATANA HERALD HUMMER
JUGATE LACKEY LAPPET MILLER
MOODER MUSLIN PLUSIA PRALID
QUAKER RUSTIC SPHINX THISBE
TINEID TISSUE TUSSUR VENEER
ARCTIAN ARCTIID BAGWORM
BUDWORM CRAMBID CRININE
DELTOID DRINKER EMERALD
EMPEROR EUCLEID FESTOON
FIGWORM FOOTMAN FRENATE
HOOKTIP NOCTUID PEGASUS
PSYCHID PYRALIS SLICKER
STINGER SYLINID TINEOLA
TORTRIX TUSSOCK URANIID
VAPORER ZYGENID AEGERIID
ARMYWORM BOMBYCID
CATOCALA CECROPIA CINNABAR
COCHYLIS FISHTAIL FORESTER
GEOMETER GOLDTAIL GRISETTE
HAWKMOTH HEPIALID
KNOTHORN MOTHWORM
PHYCITID PLUTELLA SPHINGID
SPRAWLER WAINSCOT SATURNIID
PALMERWORM
(— BREEDER) AURELIAN
(VERY SMALL —) MICRO
(PREF.) PHALAENO SETO
MOTH BALL REPELLER
MOTHER INA MOM DAME MAMA
MADRE MAMMA MAMMY MATER
MINNY MODUR MITHER MULIER
VENTER GENETRIX
(— OF THE GODS) RHEA
(DIVINE —) MATRIGAN
(GREAT —) AGDISTIS
(NOURISHING — OF MAN) CYBELE
(SEVEN —S) MATRIS
(SIDE OF —) ENATE
(PREF.) MADRE MATR(I)(O) METRO
MOTHERLAND COUNTRY
MOTHERLY MATERNAL MATRONAL
MOTHER-OF-PEARL NACRE PEARL
MOTIF SPRIG DESIGN DEVICE
MOTIVE SCALLOP APPLIQUE
MORESQUE
MOTILE ZO ZOO
MOTION WAY FARD FEED GIRD
MOVE SIGN WHID HURRY PAVIE
APPORT MOMENT MOTIVE
TRAVEL UNREST IMPULSE
ACTIVITY MOVEMENT OVERTURE
(— OF AIR) AIRFLOW
(— OF CONTEMPT) FICO
(— OF HORSE) AIR
(— TO) ALLATIVE

(ABRUPT —) CHOP
(CAM —) COULIER
(CIRCULAR —) GYRE COMPASS
(CONFUSED —) GURGE
(DANCE —) CAPER
(DIZZY —) SWIMBEL
(EXPRESSIVE —) GESTURE
(FORWARD —) HEADWAY
(GLIDING —) SWIM SKITTER
(HEAVING —) ESTUS AESTUS
(HURRIED —) HUSTLE
(ILLEGAL —) BALK BAULK
(IRREGULAR —) SWAG
(JERKING —) BOB LIPE JIGGLE
(LATERAL —) DRIFT
(QUIVERING —) TREMOR
(RAPID —) SCOUR BRATTLE
(REARING —) PESADE
(RECIPROCATING —) SEESAW
(ROTARY —) SWAY BACKSPIN
SIDESPIN
(SHOWY —) FANFARE
(SIDEWAYS —) CRAB
(SLOW —) CRAWL
(SPINNING —) ENGLISH
(SUNWISE —) DEASIL
(SWIMMING —) FLUTTER
(UPWARD —) HEAVE
(VIGOROUS —) SKELP
(VIOLENT —) JERK RAPT BENSEL
(WAVERING —) SHAKE
(WAVING —) WAFF
(WHIRLING —) SWIRL
(PREF.)
CIN(E)(EMATO)(EMO)(ET)(ETO)
KIN(E)(EMATO)(EMO)(ET)(ETO)
KINESI MOTI MOTO PHORO
(SUFF.) CINESIA KINESIA KINESIS
KINETIC
MOTIONLESS DEAD ASLEEP
STATIC IMMOBILE STAGNANT
STIRLESS
MOTION PICTURE PIC CINE FILM
FLICK MOVIE BIOPIC CINEMA
TALKIE CHEAPIE SMELLIE
FLICKERS PHOTODRAMA
(PL.) SILENTS
(PREF.) CINE(MATO)(MO)(T)(TO)
MOTIVATE PROPEL ACTUATE
ANIMATE INSPIRE
MOTIVATED COVERT
MOTIVE GOAD SAKE SPUR CAUSE
MOTIF SCORE ACTUAL DESIRE
OBJECT REASON REGARD SPRING
ATTACCO IMPULSE PATTERN
RESPECT RINCEAU SUBJECT
INSTANCE STIMULUS
(ALLEGED —) PRETEXT
(CHIEF —) MAINSPRING
MOTLEY MIXED MEDLEY RAGTAG
MOTTLED PIEBALD
(PREF.) PARTI PARTY
MOTMOT HOUTOU SAWBILL
PICARIAN
MOTOR AUTO TOOT TOUR MOVER
ENGINE BOOSTER ROTATOR
TURBINE EFFERENT OUTBOARD
MOTORBIKE MOPED
MOTORBOAT KICKER LAUNCH
AUTOBOAT RUNABOUT
HYDROFOIL
MOTORCAR MOTOR DOODLEBUG
(MINIATURE — FOR RACING) KART

MOTORCYCLE BIKE CYCLE MOTOR
STEED TRICAR CHOPPER
AUTOETTE MINIBIKE TRICYCLE
(PART OF —) HORN SEAT TANK
TIRE BRAKE GUARD LEVER LIGHT
VALVE WHEEL CLUTCH FENDER
SADDLE SIGNAL CALIPER
EXHAUST MUFFLER TOOLBOX
HANDGRIP THROTTLE GEARSHIFT
TAILLIGHT TENSIONER
CARBURETOR TACHOMETER
SPEEDOMETER
(SMALL —) MINIBIKE
MOTORIST AUTOIST
MOTORMAN CARMAN WATTMAN
TROLLYMAN
MOTORTRUCK DRAY LORRY
CAMION BOBTAIL FLATBED
MOTTLE CHECK TABBY SPONGE
MOTTLED JAZZ PIED CHINE PINTO
TABBY MARLED MOTLEY
RUMINATE SPLASHED
MOTTO MOT WORD AXIOM POESY
CACHET DEVICE EUREKA LEGEND
REASON IMPRESA EPIGRAPH
(— IN A RING) POSY
(— OF CALIFORNIA) EUREKA
(— OF MAINE) DIRIGO
MOUE FACE
MOUFLON MUSIMON
MOULDER CRUMBLE
MOULIN CHIMNEY
MOUND AHU COP HOW LAW LOW
BALK BANK BOSS BUND BUTT
GOAL HILL HUMP KNOW MOLE
POME TELL TEPE TERP TUFT
TUMP AGGER BERRY DHERI
ESKAR ESKER KNOLL MONDE
MOTTE MOUNT PINGO RAISE
STUPA TOMAN BARROW CAUSEY
MEILER RIDEAU ANTHILL
BOUROCK HILLOCK MAMELON
BACKSTOP BARBETTE SNOWBANK
TEOCALLI
(— ABOUT A PLANT) TUMP
(— FOR MEMORIAL) CAIRN
(— IN BUILDING MATERIAL) DIMPLE
(— OF DETRITUS) WASH
(— OF ICE) DOME
(— OF WOOD TO BE CHARRED)
MEILER
(BURIAL —) LAW LOW TOR TOLA
BERRY GUACA HUACA BARROW
KURGAN TUMULUS
(FORTIFIED —) DUN
(GLACIAL —) KAME
(MILITARY —) BARBETTE
(PALISADED —) MOTTE
(VOLCANIC —) HORNITO
(PREF.) BUNO
MOUND BIRD MEGAPODE
MOUNT BEN STY BACK HEAD RIDE
RISE SCAN ARISE BIPOD BOARD
CLIMB HEAVE HINGE SPEEL SPIRE
SWARM ASCEND ASPIRE BREAST
MORIAH CHARGER COLLINE
HAIRPIN HARNESS BESTRIDE
MOUNTAIN MOUNTING
MOUNTURE SURMOUNT
(— A HORSE) FORK LIGHT WORTH
(— BY STEPS) SCAN
(— ON PIN) STICK
(— ON WINGS) SOAR

(STEREOTYPE —) CORE
MOUNTAIN BEN KOP BERG CIMA
DAGH FELL KLIP KNOB MONS
MONT NEBO PICO PIKE JEBEL
MOUNT RANGE BARROW
BUNDOC GILEAD GUNONG
HEIGHT PISGAH HELICON
MONTURE NUNATAK
MONADNOCK
(— INHABITED BY SPIRIT) GUACA
HUACA
(— MASS) OROGEN
(— PASS) GHAT GHAUT
(— STATE) MONTANA
(— TRACT) DUAR
(AT BASE OF —) PIEDMONT
(FABLED —) KAF MERU
(GREEK —) OSSA PELION HELICON
OLYMPUS MAENALUS
(HIGH —) ALP
(ROUND —) REEK
(SMALL —) NOB KNOB BUTTE
(SNOW —) JOKUL
(SUBMARINE —) GUYOT
SEAMOUNT
(PREF.) MONTI ORE(O) ORI ORO
MOUNTAIN ASH SORB SORBUS
DOGBERRY MOZEMIZE ROUNTREE
WINETREE
MOUNTAIN BEAVER SEWELLEL
MOUNTAIN BINDWEED
SOLDANEL
MOUNTAIN CAP SCALP
MOUNTAIN CLIMBER CRAGSMAN
MOUNTAIN CRANBERRY
FOXBERRY
MOUNTAINEER WASIR WAZIR
HEIDUC HAYDUCK HILLMAN
ORESTES MONTESCO TIERSMAN
(PL.) GUTI GUTIANS
MOUNTAIN GOAT IBEX MAZAME
MOUNTAIN LAUREL IVY HEATH
ERICAD KALMIS LAUREL
IVYWOOD CALFKILL
(THICKET OF —) SLICK
MOUNTAIN LINNET TWITE
MOUNTAIN LION PUMA COUGAR
MOUNTAIN MAHOE EMAJAGUA
MOUNTAIN MISERY TARWEED
MOUNTAINOUS RANGY VICIOUS
MOUNTAIN PARSLEY FLUELLEN
MOUNTAIN RANGE KAF QAF TIER
SIERRA SAWBACK DINDYMUS
MOUNTAIN SICKNESS VETA
MOUNTAINSIDE FELLSIDE
MOUNTAINTOP MAN DOME
MOUNTAIN WOOD ROCKWOOD
MOUNTEBANK ANTIC BALADIN
BALADINE IMPOSTOR OPERATOR
MOUNTED CARDED SADDLE
EASELED EQUITANT
MOUNT ETNA MONGIBEL
MOUNTING MOUNT SCAPE
ASCENT FLIGHT MONTANT
SOAKING ASPIRANT INCABLOC
MOUNTURE
(— OF GEM) CHASE
(STYLE OF —) SETTING
MOURN DOLE KEEN SIGH WAIL
PLAIN GRIEVE LAMENT SORROW
GRIZZLE
MOURNER WAILER WEEPER
(HIRED —) SALLIE SAULIE

(PROFESSIONAL —) MUTE BLACK KEENER
MOURNFUL SAD BLACK MINOR SORRY WEEPY RUEFUL DERNFUL FUNEBRE SIGHFUL WAILFUL DEJECTED DIRGEFUL ELEGIOUS FUNEREAL MAESTIVE MESTFULL PLANTFUL YEARNFUL PLAINTIVE
MOURNING DOLOR SHIVA DISMAL SORROW WIDOWED
(— CLOTH) RADZIMIR
MOURNING BECOMES ELECTRA
(AUTHOR OF —) ONEILL
(CHARACTER IN —) ADAM EZRA ORIN BRANT DAVID HAZEL NILES PETER MANNON LAVINIA CHRISTINE
MOUSE MURINE MYGALE RODENT VERMIN ARVICOLE CRICETID MYOMORPH
(LIKE A —) MURIFORM
(MEADOW —) VOLE
(STRIPED —) KUSU
(PREF.) MURI MY(O) SMINTHO
(SUFF.) MYS
MOUSEBIRD COLY
MOUSE DEER PLANDOK
MOUSE GRAY SAKKARA SPARROW
MOUSETRAP TIPE
MOUSING KEEPER
MOUTH OS GAB GAM GOB JIB MUG MUN NEB ORF ROW YAP BEAK BEAL BOCA HEAD MUSS PUSS SHOP TRAP YAWN BAZOO BOCCA BRACE CHOPS CODON STOMA TUTEL GEBBIE KISSER MUZZLE RABBLE RICTUS SUCKER THROAT CLAPPER FLUMMER ORIFICE OSTIOLE STOMACH LORRIKER PAVILLON
(— AND THROAT) COPPER WHISTLE
(— OF CANYON) ABRA
(— OF GLASS FURNACE) BOCCA
(— OF HARBOR) BOCA
(— OF PERITHECIUM) OSTIOLE
(— OF RIVER) BEAL BOCA LADE ENTRY FIRTH INFLUX OSTIUM ESTUARY OSTIARY OUTFALL
(— OF SHAFT) BRACE
(— OF TRUMPET) BELL CODON PAVILLON
(— PARTS OF ARTHROPOD) TROPHI
(KILN —) KILNEYE KILNHOLE
(SORE — OF SHEEP) ECTHYMA
(WRY —) MURGEON
(PL.) ORA
(PREF.) BUCCO ORI ORO OSCULI STOM(A)(AT)(ATO)(O)
(SUFF.) STOMA(TA)(TE)(TOUS) STOME STOMI(A) STOMOUS STOMUM STOMY
MOUTHFUL GAG GOB SUP GNAP GOLEE GOBBET
MOUTHPART BILL
MOUTHPIECE BAR BEAK BOCAL MOUTH FIPPLE SYRINX PROPHET
(— OF BAGPIPE) MUSE
(— OF PIPE) STEM
MOUTHWASH GARGLE COLLUTORIUM
MOUTH-WATERING SALIVANT
MOVABLE FREE LOOSE MOBILE PORTABLE REMUABLE

(PL.) MEUBLES
MOVE GO ACT FIG GEE GET WAG BOOM BORE BUCK BUMP CALL DRAW FIRK FLIT GOAD HEAT KNEE MAKE PIRL ROLL SILE SPUR STEP STIR SWAY WORK ANKLE BLITZ BUDGE CARRY CAUSE CROWD DRAFT HEAVE IMPEL LIGHT MARCH MUDGE QUECH REMUE ROUSE SHAKE SHIFT TOUCH GAMBIT HANDLE HUSTLE INCITE INDUCE KINDLE MOTION PROMPT QUITCH REMBLE SASHAY STRAKE ACTUATE AGITATE ANIMATE DISTURB DRAUGHT FLUTTER INSPIRE MIGRATE PROVOKE AMBULATE BULLDOZE CATAPULT DEMARCHE DISLODGE DISPLACE MOTIVATE
(— A RESOLUTION) FIRST
(— ABOUT) ROLL WEND DISPACE SHUFFLE CONVERSE LOCOMOTE
(— ACROSS) THWART
(— ACTIVELY) YANK
(— AIMLESSLY) POKE BOGUE
(— ALONG) SHOG
(— APART) ABDUCT SPREAD
(— AS IN STUPOR) DAVER
(— ASIDE) SKEW
(— ASUNDER) SINGLE
(— AT TOP SPEED) LICK
(— AWAY) CUT MOG DECAMP RECEDE
(— AWKWARDLY) HODGE HIRSEL LARRUP SHAMBLE SLUMMOCK
(— BACK) FADE ARSLE RECUR RECEDE RETIRE RETREAT
(— BACKWARD AND FORWARD) GIG SWAY DARTLE DIDDLE SHUFFLE SHUTTLE
(— BOOM OR SAIL) JIB
(— BRISKLY) FAN HALE STIR FRICK FRIKE FRISK KNOCK SQUIRT TRANCE TRAVEL WHIPPET
(— BY FITS AND STARTS) JIFFLE
(— BY JERKS) HITCH JIGGET JIGGLE JINKLE
(— BY SMALL SHOCKS) JOG
(— BY WHEELS) ROLL TRUNDLE
(— CHESS PIECE) DEVELOP
(— CLUMSILY) HOIT JOLL PAUT BARGE KEVEL HIRSEL LUMBER TOLTER GALUMPH STUMBLE
(— COMPUTER VIDEO DISPLAY) SCROLL
(— DIAGONALLY) CATER
(— DOWN) SILE STOOP DECLINE DESCEND
(— FORCIBLY) SHOVE
(— FORWARD) BREAK ADVANCE PROGREDE
(— FURTIVELY) LEER GLIDE SLINK SLIVE SNEAK STEAL
(— GRADUALLY) EDGE
(— HAPHAZARDLY) BUCKET
(— HASTILY) SCUR SKIRR
(— HAUGHTILY) SWOOP
(— HEAVILY) LUG LUMP FLUMP LUMBER
(— IN AGITATION) SEETHE
(— IN AWKWARD MANNER) GANGLE
(— IN CIRCLES) MILL PURL

(— IN MARBLES) FULK
(— IN RIPPLES) CURL
(— IN SHUFFLING MANNER) MOSEY
(— IN SMALL DEGREES) INCH
(— IN WATER) SQUELCH
(— IN WAVES) LAP CRINKLE
(— INWARDLY) ENMOVE
(— JERKILY) JAG BUCK FLIP KICK FLIRT BUCKET TWITCH
(— LANGUIDLY) MAUNDER
(— LAZILY) HULK
(— LEISURELY) AMBLE
(— LIGHTLY) BRUSH FLUFF
(— LOOSELY) SLOP
(— NERVOUSLY) DITHER
(— NIMBLY) KILT LINK WHIP DANCE
(— OFF) FIRK RYNT MOSEY MORRIS
(— ON) MOG VAMP AVAUNT SUCCEED WHIGFARE
(— OUT) BLOW
(— OUT OF SIGHT) SINK
(— QUICKLY) BOB FIG CLIP DUCK FIRK FLAX FLIT GIRD JINK KITE SCUR WHAP WHEW WHID WHOP YANK FLASH GLENT SKEET SKIRR SKITE SPANK SQUIB STAVE STOUR THROW NIDDLE STRIKE WALLOP SKIMMER
(— QUIETLY) SLIP
(— RAPIDLY) BANG BOLT BUZZ HEEL HURL SKIR THUD CHASE GLINT SCOUR CAREER GIGGIT HURTLE WHIRRY AGITATE CLATTER HIGHTAIL
(— RESTLESSLY) FIG GAD FIKE ITCH CHURN SQUIB JIFFLE KELTER
(— SHAKILY) HOTTER
(— SIDEWISE) CRAB EDGE SIDLE SLENT
(— SLOWLY) LAG MOG INCH PANT PAUT SLUG BOGUE CRAWL CREEP DRAWL FUDGE SHLEP SLOOM SNAIL HAGGLE LINGER SCHLEP SCHLEPP TRINTLE
(— SMOOTHLY) SLIP DRIFT FLOAT GLIDE SLEEK GLISSADE
(— SPIRALLY) GYRATE
(— STEADILY) FORGE
(— STEALTHILY) GLIDE SLINK SMOOT SNAKE
(— STIFFLY) CRAMBLE CRAMMEL
(— SUDDENLY) BOLT LASH YERK GLENT START FLOUNCE STARTLE
(— SWIFTLY) CUT FLY BOOM HARE LEAP RAKE SCUD SPIN BREEZE COURSE WUTHER SWIFTEN
(— THROUGH AIR) FLY
(— TO AND FRO) FAN FLOP DODGE SHAKE WIGWAG AGITATE
(— TO ANOTHER PLACE) ADJOURN
(— TO LEEWARD) DRIVE
(— TREMULOUSLY) WAPPER
(— UNEASILY) FIDGET
(— UNSTEADILY) BICKER BUMBLE FALTER HOBBLE WABBLE WAMBLE WELTER WOBBLE BLUNDER STAGGER STUMBLE
(— UP AND DOWN) BOB HOWD SEESAW TEETER
(— UPWARD) ARISE

ASCEND GRADUATE
(— VESSEL) KEDGE
(— VIGOROUSLY) FLOG STRAY
(— VIOLENTLY) DASH FLOG HURL LASH LEAP SWASH AGITATE COMMOVE
(— WAVERINGLY) FLEET
(— WEAKLY) FLAG
(— WITH BEATING MOTION) FLAP
(— WITH EFFORT) ACHE
(— WITH LEAPS) SKIP SPRING
(— WITH NOISY ACTIVITY) BUSTLE
(— WITH SHORT TURNS) ZIGZAG
(CHESS —) KEY COOK NECK PLOY GAMBIT KEYMOVE
(SUCCESSFUL —) SCORE
(SUDDEN —) GAMBADE
MOVED MOSSO ANIMATE FRANTIC INSTINCT
(— BY LOVE) AMOROUS
(EASILY —) FLESHLY SKINLESS
MOVEMENT EDDY MOTO PLAY STIR CARRY CAUSE FLICK FLISK FLOAT FRONT GESTE MUDGE TREND UKIYO ACTION CURSUS ENTREE MOMENT MOTION PIAFFE SPRAWL STROKE CURRENT FURIANT GAMBADO GESTURE KINESIS PIAFFER UKIYOYE BUSINESS CHARTISM FEMINISM FUTURISM HASKALAH STIRRING PERIPATETICS
(— BY ORGANISMS) TAXIS
(— FOR POLITICAL UNION) ENOSIS
(— FROM POINT TO POINT) PASSAGE
(— IN BULLFIGHT) SUERTE
(— OF AIR) SPIRIT
(— OF CHORUS) STROPHE
(— OF CLOUDS) CARRY
(— OF COMPUTER BITS) SHIFT
(— OF HORSE) LEVADE PIAFFE
(— OF LOOM) MOUSING
(— OF PLANTS) NUTATION
(— OF PROTOPLASM) CYCLOSIS
(— OF ROPE) SURGE
(— OF SHIP) STERNWAY
(— OF TIDE) LAKIE
(— OF TROOPS) LIFT
(— OF WATER) BOBBLE
(— TOWARD GOAL) STRIDE
(AGITATED —) WORKING
(ART —) CUBISM
(AVANT-GARDE —) UNDERGROUND
(BACKWARD —) BACKUP BACKLASH BACKWASH
(BALLET —) PLIE FRAPPE FOUETTE FLICFLAC
(BOBBING —) BOBBLE
(BODILY —) ACTION
(BOWEL —) LAXATION
(BOXING —) SPAR
(BRISK —) SNAP
(BROWNIAN —) PEDESIS
(CAVALRY —) CARACOLE
(CIRCULAR —) CYCLING
(CLEVER —) PAW
(DANCE —) FRIS BRISE CLOSE GIGUE GLIDE LASSU SPIRAL BATTERIE
(DARTING —) FLIRT
(DOWNWARD —) DECLINE
(DROLL —) GAMBADE GAMBADO

(ENLIGHTENMENT —) HASKALAH
(EXPANSION —) BOOM
(FENCING —) VOLT
(FLAPPING —) FLAFF
(FORWARD —) SWEEP ADVANCE PROGRESS INCESSION PROCESSION
(FROLICKING —) FRISK GAMBOL
(GRADUAL —) CREEPISM
(GYMNASTIC —) KIP SWING DISMOUNT
(HUMOROUS —) BURLA
(INDEPENDENCE —) SWADESHI
(INVOLUNTARY —) REFLEX
(JAPANESE ART —) YAMATO YAMATOE
(JERKING —S) BALLISM
(JERKY —) SNATCH
(JERKY EYE —) SACCADE
(LATERAL —) LEEWAY
(MASS —) STAMPEDE
(MASSAGE —) SCIAGE
(MILITARY —) BOUND MANEUVRE
(MUSICAL —) AIR DUET BURLA DUMKA LARGO ADAGIO ENTREE FINALE PRESTO SARABAND SYMPHONY
(OSCILLATING —) HUNT
(PAINTING —) FAUVISM TACHISM VORTICISM
(POETRY —) IMAGISM
(POLITICAL —) LEFTISM GAULLISM
(QUADRILLE —) POULE
(QUICK —) PAW DART WHID WHIP YERK GLENT SHAKE GLANCE
(RATIONALISTIC —) DEISM
(REELING —) STAGGER
(RELIGIOUS —) JOCISM BABIISM PIETISM STUNDISM
(RETROGRADE —) SLIP CREEP
(RETURN —) BACKHAUL
(RHYTHMIC —) DANCE
(ROCKING —) HOWD
(ROWING —) HOICK
(SKATING —) MOHAWK CHOCTAW
(SKILLED —) SUERTE
(SPASMODIC —) JUMP HICCUP SPRUNT HICCOUGH
(SPRINGY —) LILT
(STEALTHY —) SLINK
(SUDDEN —) HITCH SPANG START FLICKER
(SWAYING —) SWAG
(SWEEPING —) SWINGE
(SWIFT —) SWOOSH
(THEOLOGICAL —) ARIANISM
(TUMULTUOUS —) HORROR EMOTION
(TURNING —) CARACOLE
(UP AND DOWN —) SEESAW
(UPWARD —) BULGE SCEND
(UPWARD — OF VESSEL) SCEND
(WALKING —) AMBLE
(WATCH —) EBAUCHE BAGUETTE
(ZIGZAG —) TACK MEANDER
(PREF.) KIN(O) KINESI KINETO
(SUFF.) CINESIA KINESIA KINESIS KINETIC
MOVEMENTS
(SUFF.) (PERFORMANCE OF —) PRACTIC PRAXIA PRAXIS
MOVER MOTIVE CLIPPER
MOVIE (ALSO SEE MOTION

PICTURE) FLICK FLICKS SLEEPER MELODRAMA
(PL.) PICTURES
MOVIES (DEVOTEE OF —) CINEPHILE
MOVING WAY HIGH ASTIR GOING QUICK AFLOAT MOVENT ANIMATE CURRENT AMBULANT FLITTING PATHETIC POIGNANT TOUCHING AFFECTING
(— ABOUT) AROUND AMBULANT
(— AIMLESSLY) ERRANT
(— BACKWARDS) CRAB
(— DOWN LINE) ACTIVE
(— FORWARD) ADVANCE
(— HAPHAZARDLY) AFLOAT
(— IN MANY DIRECTIONS) DIFFUSE
(— RAPIDLY) STICKLE SKELPING
(— SLOWLY) SOFT GLACIAL TEDIOUS
(— TO AND FRO) AGITATED
(NOT —) STICKY STABILE
MOVINGLY PATETICO
MOW CUT BARB GOAF SKIM TASS CRADLE SCYTHE SICKLE DESECATE
(— BEANS) THROAT
(— FOR STORING GRAIN) TOSS
(— OF CORN) CANSH
(HAY —) TASS
MOWER MEADER
(FOREMOST —) LORD
MOWING MATH MOWTH SHEAR
MOZA (FATHER OF —) CALEB ZIMRI
MOZAMBIQUE (CAPE OF —) DELGADO
(CAPITAL OF —) MAPUTO
(LAKE OF —) CHUALI NHAVARRE
(MONEY OF —) METICAL
(RIVER OF —) SAVE MSALU RUVUMA LIMPOPO LUGENDA ZAMBEZI
(TOWN OF —) MAUA TETE BEIRA MAPAI ZUMBO CHEMBA MANICA NAMAPA PAFURI CHIMOIO NAMPULA
MOZZETTA CAMAIL
MR HERR SIGNOR SIGNIOR SIGNORE
MR MIDSHIPMAN EASY (AUTHOR OF —) MARRYAT
(CHARACTER IN —) EASY JACK AGNES MESTY WILSON REBIERA GASCOIGNE MIDDLETON
MRS FRAU MISS PANI HANOUM SENORA SENHORA SIGNORA GOODWIFE
MRS DALLOWAY (AUTHOR OF —) WOOLF
(CHARACTER IN —) PETER SALLY SETON SMITH WALSH HOLMES KALMAN WILLIAM BRADSHAW CLARISSA DALLOWAY SEPTIMUS
MRS WARREN'S PROFESSION
(AUTHOR OF —) SHAW
(CHARACTER IN —) FRANK PRAED VIVIE CROFTS GEORGE SAMUEL WARREN GARDNER
MUCH FAR FELE MICH REAL WELL GREAT HEAPS MOLTO MOULT SIZES MICKLE MUCHLY ABUNDANT MUCHWHAT
(— CALLED FOR) LEEFTAIL
(PRETTY —) GAILY GAYLY

(SO —) ALL SUCH TANTO INSOMUCH
(TOO —) TROP TROPPO
(VERY —) ALL BADLY GREAT HEAPS LOADS SWITHE SWYTHE APLENTY GEYLIES GREATLY
(PREF.) ERI MULT(I) POLY SYCHNO
(HOW —) POSO QUANTI
MUCH ADO ABOUT NOTHING
(AUTHOR OF —) SHAKESPEARE
(CHARACTER IN —) HERO JOHN PEDRO URSULA VERGES ANTONIO CLAUDIO CONRADE FRANCIS LEONATO BEATRICE BENEDICK BORACHIO DOGBERRY MARGARET BALTHASAR
MUCILAGE GUM MUCUS MUCAGO
MUCILAGINOUS MALACOID
MUCK CACK SOIL
MUCOID BLENNOID
MUCUS SNOT MUCOR BUBBLE MUCAGO PHLEGM SNIVEL PITUITE
(PREF.) BLENN(I)(O) MUC(I)(O)(OSO) MYX(O)
(SUFF.) MYXA
MUD DAB FEN CLAY DIRT DUBS FANC GLAR LAIR MIRE MOIL SAUR SIND SLAB SLEW SLOB SLOP SLUB SLUD SLUE SLUR SUMP CLART FANGO GLAUR GUMBO SLAKE SLIME SLOSH SLUSH SPOSH SQUAD WAISE PELOID SLOUGH SLUDGE CLABBER GUTTERS MURGEON SLOBBER SLODDER SLUDDER SLUTHER SULLAGE
(LACUSTRINE —) GYTTJA
(OF DRIED —) CUTCHA
(PREF.) LIMI LIMO PEL(O) TELMAT(O)
MUDAR AK AKUND ASHUR MADOR YERCUM AKMUDDAR
MUDCAP ADOBE
MUD CAT FLATHEAD
MUDCAT STATE MISSISSIPPI
MUDDLE MIX BALL DOZE HASH MASH MESS MULL MUZZ SOSS ADDLE SNAFU BEMUSE BURBLE FANKLE FOITER FUDDLE HUDDLE JUMBLE MAFFLE MIZZLE MOFFLE MUCKER POTHER PUDDLE TANGLE BECLOUD BEDEVIL BLUNDER CONFUSE EMBROIL FLUSTER POOTHER STUPEFY BEFUDDLE BEWILDER CONFOUND DISORDER FLIUNDER
MUDDLED ADDLE BEERY FOGGY FUZZY MUSED MUZZY DRUMLY GROGGY BESOTTED CONFUSED
MUDDY DEEP FOUL GLET OOZY ROIL SICK DIRTY DROVY DUBBY GUMLY ROILY SLAKY CLAGGY CLARTY CLASHY DREGGY DROUMY DRUMLY GROUTY LIMOUS PUDDLY SALLOW SLABBY SLOBBY SLOPPY SLUBBY SLUDGY TURBID CLATCHY GUTTERY MUDDIFY MUDDISH SLOUGHY CLABBERY LUTULENT SLOBBERY
(— BY STIRRING) STUDDLE
MUDFISH BOWFIN KOMTOK
MUDFLOW LAHAR MUDSPATE
MUDGUARD WING CUTTOO SPLASHER

MUDHOLE PULK SLOUGH LOBLOLLY
MUD MINNOW DOGFISH MUDFISH
MUD PUPPY DOGFISH
MUERMO ULMO
MUFF BLOW BOBBLE MUFFLE SNUFFKIN
MUFFIN COB GEM SINK COBBE HAZEL SINKER MANCHET PIKELET POPOVER
MUFFLE MOB MOP PAD DAMP DULL MUTE NOSE WRAP BUMBLE DEADEN MUZZLE SHROUD STIFLE ENVELOP
(— A BELL) CLAM
(— THE HEAD) MOBLE
MUFFLED DEAD DEAF DULL CLOSE THICK HOLLOW INWARD MOBBED WRAPPED
MUFFLER SCARF MUFFLE SILENCER
MUFTI JURIST CIVVIES
MUG TOT BOCK CANN FACE STEIN NOGGIN PEWTER SCONCE SEIDEL CANETTE GODDARD BLACKPOT PANNIKIN SCHOPPEN
(ALE —) TOBY
(LIQUOR —) CAN GUN
MUGGER GOA HAM
MUGGING YOKING
MUGGINS SNIFF
MUGGY FOZY MUNGY PUGGY STICKY MUGGISH PUTHERY
MUGWORT BULWAND MUGWEED
MUISCA CHIBCHA
MUISHOND ZORIL ZORILLE
MULATTO PARDO GRIFFE GRIQUA GRIFFIN TERCERON
MULBERRY AL AAL ACH AUTE KOZO MORE WAUKE ALROOT MURREY MORELLO SOURBUSH SYCAMINE
(PREF.) MOR(I)
MULBERRY FIG SYCAMORE
MULCT FINE CHECK AMERCE SCONCE FORFEIT PENALTY
MULE BUCKER HYBRID ACEMILA IRONMAN JARHEAD JUGHEAD RATTAIL SUMPTER CENCERRO HARDTAIL QUADROON QUATERON
(DROVE OF —S) ATAJO MULADA
(MOHAMMED'S —) ALBORAK
MULE ARMADILLO MULITA
MULE DRIVER SKINNER
MULE SHOE PLANCHE
MULETEER ASSMAN ARRIERO
MULISH BALKY STUPID STUBBORN OBSTINATE
MULL CHAW BOSOM FETTLE MULMUL STEATIN
MULLEIN TORCH AGLEAF ICELEAF DOVEWEED FELTWORT FOXGLOVE HAGTAPER LUNGWORT VERBASCO
MULLER DAMPENER
MULLET BOBO LISA LIZA BOURI GARAU KANAE MOLET HARDER MULLOID GOATFISH MUGILOID SPRINGER
(UNPIERCED —) STAR
MULLIGRUBS COLIC
MULLION MONIAL

MULLOWAY JEWFISH KINGFISH SCIAENID
MULTICOLORED CALICO
MULTIFARIOUS MANIFOLD
MULTIFARIOUSNESS VARIETY
MULTIFORM DIVERSE
MULTILINGUAL POLYGLOT
MULTIPLE DECUPLE PARALLEL SEPTUPLE MULTIPLEX
MULTIPLICAND FACIEND
MULTIPLICATION INCREASE DUPLATION
MULTIPLICITY MULTEITY
MULTIPLIER FACIENT COFACTOR
MULTIPLY VIE BREED LAYER DOUBLE INVOLVE ENGENDER INCREASE MANIFOLD PROPAGATE PROLIFERATE
MULTIPLYING (PREF.) POLY
MULTITUDE ARMY CRAM HEAP HIVE HOST ROUT RUCK CLOUD CROWD FLOTE MEINY POWER SHOAL SWARM HIRSEL HOTTER LEGION MAMPUS MEINIE NATION THRONG SMOTHER PLURALITY (PL.) FLOCKS
MULTITUDINOUS LEGION MYRIAD MANIFOLD NUMEROUS
MULTIVALENT POLYAD
MULTURE THIRL THIRLAGE
MUM CLUM DARK MUMMER
MUMBLE CHEW MOUP MUMP BROCK CHELE MOUTH CHAVEL FAFFLE FUMBLE HOTTER HUMMER MAFFLE MOFFLE PALTER DRUMBLE FLUMMER GRUMBLE
MUMBLER MAFFLER
MUMBLETY-PEG KNIFE
MUMMER ACTOR GUISER GUISARD
MUMMERY MORRIS HODENING PUPPETRY
MUMMICHOG MUDFISH
MUMMY CONGO MUMMIA SKELET (PREF.) MOMIO
MUMMY BROWN BAY SNUFF TAMARACK
MUMMY CASE SLEDGE
MUMPS BRANKS PAROTITIS
MUNCH CHEW NOSH CHUMP MANGE MUNGE
MUND GRITH
MUNDA KOLARIAN
MUNDANE WORLD EARTHLY FLESHLY SECULAR TERRENE SUBSOLAR
MUNG BEAN MUG GRAM MONGOE BALATONG
MUNIA MAYA PADDA
MUNICIPAL TOWN CIVIL
MUNICIPALITY CITY TOWN CABILDO
MUNIFICENCE BOUNTY ROYALTY
MUNIFICENT ROYAL LIBERAL MUNIFIC PROFUSE MAGNIFIC PRINCELY OPENHANDED
MUNJ MOONJA MANJEET (CULMS OF —) SIRKI SIRKY
MUNTIACUS CERVULUS
MUNTJAC KAKAR RATWA KIDANG
MURAL TOPIA FRESCO
MURCIA (RIVER OF —) SEGURA

(TOWN OF —) MULA LORCA TOTANA
MURDER OFF BANE KILL SLAY BLOOD BURKE DEATH SCRAG FELONY KILLING MURDRUM MURTHER THUGGEE HOMICIDE MASSACRE THUGGERY THUGGISM PATRICIDE
(PREMEDITATED —) HIT
MURDERER BANE CAIN KILLER ASSASSIN
MURDER IN THE CATHEDRAL
(COMPOSER OF —) PIZZETTI
MURDEROUS FELL GORY CRUEL FELON BLOODY CARNAL SAVAGE DEATHFUL SANGUINARY
MURKINESS GLOOM
MURKY DARK BLACK DIRTY MIRKY MUDDY CLOUDY PUDDLY
MURMUR HUM BRUM BURR CLUM HUZZ MUSE BRAWL BROOL GRANK INKLE MOURN RUMOR SOUCH SOUGH BABBLE BURBLE GRUDGE GRUTCH HUMMER MUTTER PIPPLE REPINE RUMBLE CROODLE MURGEON WHIMPER WHISPER WHITTER COMPLAIN
(— AGREEABLY) CHIRM
(— OF STREAM) PURL
(CONFUSED —) BABBLE
(DEEP —) BROOL
MURMURING BUZZ BRABBLE MURGEON RUMOROUS
MURRAH SURTI
MURRAL DALAG
MURRE TINK ARRIE LUNGIE STRANY TINKER ROCKBIRD
MURREY SANGUINE
MUSA SABA
MUSANG POWCAT POLECAT
MUSCA FLY
MUSCADINE BULLACE SCUPPERNONG
MUSCAT (SEE OMAN)
MUSCLE EYE BOWR LIRE THEW FLESH MOUSE PSOAS SINEW BENDER BICEPS CORACO FLEXOR LACERT PENNON RECTUS SOLEUS TENSOR AGONIST AMBIENS CANINUS DELTOID DILATOR ERECTOR EVERTOR FLECTOR MUSCULE NASALIS OBLIQUE ROTATOR SCALENE SCALLOP TRICEPS VAGINAL ABDUCTOR ADDUCTOR ADJUSTER ANCONEUS ARRECTOR ATOLLENT BIVENTER DIDUCTOR EXTENSOR GEMELLUS GRACILIS INVERTOR MASSETER MENTALIS OBLIQUUS OMOHYOID OPPONENS PALMARIS PATHETIC PECTORAL PERONEUS PROCERUS PRONATOR RETENTOR SCALENUS SERRATUS SPINALIS SPLENIUS TEMPORAL TIBIALIS OBTURATOR SARTORIUS
(HAVING LUMPY —S) LOADED
(THIGH —) HAMSTRING
(PL.) BRAWN THEWS
(PREF.) INO MUSCUL(O) NERVI NERVO
(SUFF.) EUS MYA MYARIA
MUSCLE SUGAR INOSITE INOSITOL

MUSCOVY DUCK PATO SCOVY
MUSCULAR ROPY HEFTY HUSKY THEWY BRAWNY ROBUST SINEWY STRONG TOROSE NERVOUS ATHLETIC
MUSCULATURE DETRUSOR
(SUFF.) (HAVING —) MYA MYARIA
MUSE CLIO DUMP MESE MULL NETE REVE AMUSE AOIDE DREAM ERATO MNEME STUDY THINK HYPATE MELETE PONDER THALIA URANIA EUTERPE REFLECT CALLIOPE COGITATE CONSIDER MEDITATE POLYMNIA RUMINATE MELPOMENE POLYHYMNIA TERPSICHORE
(— OF ASTRONOMY) URANIA
(— OF COMEDY) THALIA
(— OF EPIC POETRY AND ELOQUENCE) CALLIOPE
(— OF HISTORY) CLIO
(— OF LOVE POETRY) ERATO
(— OF MIMIC ART) POLYHYMNIA
(— OF POETRY AND DANCE) TERPSICHORE
(— OF THE FLUTE) EUTERPE
(— OF TRAGEDY) MELPOMENE
(PL.) PIERIDES
MUSEUM MUSEE
(PREF.) MUSEO
MUSH KASHA SLUSH MUSHER SEPAWN SOFKEE POLENTA SAGAMITE SCRAPPLE
MUSHI (FATHER OF —) MERARI
MUSHROOM FAT CEPE FLAT DEATH MITRA MOREL AGARIC BEAVER BUTTON FUNGUS BLEWITS BOLETUS BROILER LEPIOTA MUSHRUMP WHITECAP CHAMPIGNON SHAGGYMANE CHANTERELLE
(PART OF —) CAP GILL RING STEM STALK STIPE VOLVA PILEUS ANNULUS MYCELIUM
(PREF.) MYC(O) MYCET(O)
MUSHY SOFT SOPPY
MUSIC RAG DRAG GLEE JAZZ NOME BEBOP CANOR CHIME DREAM GIMEL GYMEL MURKY NOISE SWING DREHER MUSICA DESCANT FORLANA LANCERS LANDLER MUSICAL MUSICRY FALSETTO FANDANGO GUARACHA
(— OF WEST INDIES) REGGAE
(CALYPSO —) GOOMBAY
(CONCERTED —) ENSEMBLE
(COUNTRY —) BLUEGRASS
(EVENING —) DREAM SERENA
(IDENTIFYING —) SIG
(JAPANESE COURT —) GAGAKU
(JAZZ OR FOLK —) SKIFFLE
(LIVELY —) GALOP FURLANA
(MORNING —) AUBADE
(PATTERN OF HINDU —) TALA
(RECORDED BACKGROUND —) MUZAK
(RESOUNDING —) HIGGAION
(ROCK —) BIGBEAT BUBBLEGUM
(SAD —) MESTO
(SENTIMENTAL —) SCHMALZ SCHMALTZ

(STACCATO —) SECCO
(UNSOPHISTICATED —) FUNK

(ZULU —) KWELA
MUSICAL LYRIC SWEET LIQUID LYRICAL TUNABLE TUNEFUL CANOROUS HARMONIC NUMEROUS
(— DIRECTION) BIS PIU ARCO BRIO FINE MENO POCO ANIME ASSAI DOLCE GRAVE GUSTO LARGO LENTO MEZZO MOLTO MOSSO OSSIA PRIMO SECCO SEGUE SOPRA TACET TEMPO TUTTI ADAGIO ARIOSO DOPPIO FREDDO MARCIA PRESTO RUBATO SEMPRE SIMILE SUBITO TENUTO TROPPO VELOCE VIVACE AGITATO ALLEGRO AMABILE ANIMATO ATTACCA FURIOSO GIOCOSO MARCATO MORENDO PIETOSO SORDINO TREMOLO DOLOROSO MAESTOSO MODERATO SALTANDO SEMPLICE SPICCATO CRESCENDO GLISSANDO OBBLIGATO SOSTENUTO SPIRITOSO
(SUFF.) (— DEVICE) INA INE
(— INSTRUMENT) INA
MUSICAL INSTRUMENT AX AXE GLY GUE KIN OUD QIN TAR UKE ZEL ALTO ASOR BELL CRUT DRUM GLEE GLEW GORA HARP HORN KOTO LIRA LUTE LYRE OBOE ROTE SANG SAWM TAAR TUBA VINA VIOL ANVIL AULOS BANJO BLOCK BUGLE CELLO CHENG CRWTH CUICA DOMRA FLUTE GORAH GOURA GUDOK GUIRO GUSLA GUSLE KAZOO MBIRA NABLA ORGAN RAMKI REBAB REBEC ROCTA RUANA SAROD SHAWM SHELL SHENG TARAU TELYN TRUMP VIOLA ZANZE ZINKE BALAFO BONANG CABASA CITOLE CORNET CROUTH CYMBAL DOUCET FIDDLE GENDER GLARIN GUITAR GUSLEE JARANA RAPPEL REBECK RIBIBE SABECA SANCHO SANTIR SPINET TABRET TREBLE TYMPAN URHEEN VIOLET VIOLIN ZITHER ALTHORN ANGELOT ANKLONG ARGHOOL BAGPIPE BANDORE BANDURA BASSOON BAZOOKA CELESTA CHEKKER CHIKARA CITHARA CLARINA CLAVIER CLAVIOL DICHORD DOLCIAN DOLCINO DULCIAN FISTULA FLUTINA GAMELIN GITTERN HELICON KANTELE MAGADIS MARIMBA OCARINA PANDURA PIBCORN RACKETT SAMISEN SARANGI SARINDA SAXHORN SERPENT SISTRUM SORDONO THEORBO TRUMPET UKULELE URANION ADIAPHON AKALIMBA AUTOHARP AUTOPHON BARBITON BOUSOUKI BOUZOUKI CALLIOPE CASTANET CLARINET CORNPIPE CRESCENT DULCIMER DYOPHONE EUPHONON FIDICULA FLAUTINO

HORNPIPE HUMSTRUM
KRUMHORN LAPIDEON
MARTENOT MELODION NEGINOTH
NEHILOTH PENORCON PHONIKON
PSALTERY SCHWEGEL SERINGHI
SOURDINE SYMPHONY
TAMBOURA TAROGATO TRIANGLE
TRICHORD TROMBONE VIRGINAL
ZAMBOMBA ACCORDION
BOMBARDON SAXOPHONE
MELLOPHONE
(AFRICAN —) KORA MBIRA
(BALINESE —) GANGSA
(STRINGED — OF INDIA) SARANGI
(PL.) BRASS FAMILY STRINGS
PERCUSSION
MUSICALITY HARMONY
MUSIC HALL GAFF MELODEON
MUSICIAN BARD WAIT ASAPH
LINOS VIOLA BOPPER BUSKER
MUSICO PLAYER VIOLER VIOLIN
BANDMAN BOPSTER CELLIST
GAMBIST ORPHEUS TWANGER
VIOLIST KORAHITE MARIACHI
MINSTREL MUSICKER THRUMMER
TWANGLER CITYBILLY
MINNESINGER
(PL.) ENSEMBLE WAITSMEN
MUSING PENSIVE MUSARDRY
MUSK MOOST CATTAIL MIMULUS
AMBRETTE FIXATIVE
(PREF.) MOSCHI
MUSK DEER CERVID KASTURA
MUSKELLUNGE LONGE MUSKIE
MUSKET FUSIL FUZIL MATCH
DRAGON JINGAL BUNDOOK
CALIVER ENFIELD GINGALL
BANDHOOK BISCAYAN BISCAYEN
CULVERIN ESCOPETA SNAPHAAN
TOPHAIKE
MUSKET BALL GOLI
MUSKETEER FUSILEER STRELITZ
MUSKET FORK GAFFLE
MUSK MALLOW ABELMOSK
MUSKMELON MANGO ATAMON
WUNGEE SPANSPEK
CANTALOUPE
MUSKOGEE CREEK SEMINOLE
MUSK OX OVIBOS
(WOOL OF UNDERCOAT OF —)
QIVIUT
MUSKRAT SQUASH ONDATRA
MUSQUASH
MUSK SHREW SONDELI
MUSK TURTLE STINKER STINKPOT
MUSKWOOD CAOBA
MUSKY MOSCHATE
MUSLIM LAZ ALIM SIDI SWAT
TURK ARAIN HAFIZ IBADHI
KAZAKH TURBAN ABBADID
AYYUBID BAGIRMI BASHKIR
IBADITE KHAKSAR MUDEJAR
SUNNITE ALAOUITE ISLAMIST

ISLAMITE QADARITE SIFATITE
(— BEADS) TASBIH
(— BROTHERHOOD) TARIQA
(— CHIEF) RAIS REIS
(— DOCTRINE) TAWHID
(— FOUNDATION) WAKF WAQF
(— JUDGE) CAID QAID
(— MYSTIC) SUFI
(— PLAY) TAZIA
(— PRACTICE) PURDAH
(— PRINCIPLE) TAQIYA
(— SCHOLARS) ULAMA ULEMA
(— SECT) WAHHABI MURJIITE
(— TOMB) TABUT
(— TREE) TUBA
(PL.) SHIA SHIAH SUNNI
MUSLIN BAN MULL DORIA SWISS
GURRAH MULMUL SHALEE SHILLA
TANJIB BETEELA FACTORY
JAMDANI ORGANDY STENTER
COTELINE SEERHAND TARLATAN
(PL.) COSSAS
MUSQUASH ONDATRA
MUSS FUFFLE RUMPLE GLOMMOX
UNDRESS
MUSSEL CLAM UNIO NAIAD
ANODON JINGLE LACERT MUCKET
PALOUR BIVALVE GLOCHID
MYTILID UNIONID BULLHEAD
DEERHORN
(PREF.) CONCH(O) MYTILI MYTILO
MUSSELCRACKER BISKOP
MUST BIT BUD BUT MAN MAY
MUN BOOD MAUN MOTE SAPA
STUM DULCE SHALL
(— BE TAKEN) SUM
(— NOT) MAUNNA
MUSTACHE WALRUS VALANCE
WHISKER
MUSTACHE MONKEY MOUSTOC
MUSTANG PONY BRONCO SPHINX
MUSTARD CRESS SENVY SINEWY
AWLWORT CADLOCK KEDLOCK
SINAPIS CHADLOCK CHARLOCK
FLIXWEED AUBRIETIA
(PREF.) SIN
MUSTARD GAS YPERITE
MUSTARD PLASTER SINAPISM
MUSTELUS GALEUS
MUSTER LEVY ENROL RAISE
SPUNK GATHER HOSTING
MARSHAL RECRUIT
MUSTINESS FUST MUST
MUSTY HOAR FUNKY FUSTY
HOARY MOLDY MUCID RAFTY
VINNY FOISTY FROWZY RANCID
FOUGHTY FROWSTY COBWEBBY
MUTABLE FICKLE MUTATORY
VARIABLE
MUTATE SPORT
MUTATION SHIFT SPORT CHANGE
MUANCE SILKIE ANAGRAM
VARIANT SALTATION

(VOWEL —) UMLAUT
MUTE PAD DUMB ECHO LENE
SURD BLACK MEDIA WHIST
DAMPER MUFFLE SILENT STIFLE
TENUIS SORDINE SOURDINE
(— AT FUNERAL) SALLIE
(— FOR TRUMPET) DERBY
MUTED DULL SORDO STILL
DISCREET SOURDINE
MUTENESS SILENCE DUMBNESS
MUTILATE MAR HACK MAIM
BREAK GARBLE HAMBLE INJURE
MANGLE MARTYR MITTLE
CONCISE CASTRATE EMBEZZLE
(— AN ANIMAL) LAW
MUTILATION STRIP CONCISION
MUTINEER PANDY MUTINADO
MUTINOUS UNRULY
MUTINY REVOLT STRIFE
REBELLION
MUTINY ON THE BOUNTY
(AUTHOR OF —) HALL NORDHOFF
(CHARACTER IN —) BYAM BLIGH
PEGGY ROGER GEORGE ROBERT
TEHANI BURKITT ELLISON
MAIMITI STEWART TINKLER
WILLIAM FLETCHER MILLWARD
MORRISON MUSPRATT CHRISTIAN
MUTISM ALALIA
MUTTER CROOL MOTRE HOTTER
HUMMER MUMBLE MURMUR
PATTER THROAT CHANNER
CHUNNER CHUNTER GRUMBLE
MAUNDER TOOTMOOT
MUSSITATE
MUTTERING GROWL
MUTTON BRAXY VIFDA VIVDA
MOUTON BRAXIES
(LEG OF —) CABOB WABBLER
WOBBLER
MUTTONBIRD OII
MUTTONFISH SAMA ABALONE
EELPOUT MOJARRA
MUTUAL COMMON RECIPROCAL
(PREF.) CO INTER
MUZZLE NOSE MOUTH SNOUT
FOREFACE
(— FOR FERRET) COPE
(— OF CANNON) CHOPS
MUZZLE-LOADER CAPLOCK
MUZZLER
MYALGIA COURBATURE
MYALL YARRAN WARRIGAL
MY ANTONIA (AUTHOR OF —)
CATHER
(CHARACTER IN —) JIM JAKE LENA
OTTO WICK ANTON CUZAK
FUCHS LARRY BURDEN CUTTER
ANTONIA DONOVAN HARLING
LINGARD MARPOLE AMBROSCH
SHIMERDA
MYCELIUM SPAWN MYCELE
TAPESIUM

MYCTERIA TANTALUS
MY DEAR MACHREE
MYDRIATIC PHENYLEPHRINE
MYIASIS STRIKE
MYNA MINA MYNAH GRACKLE
MYNES (BROTHER OF —)
EPISTROPHUS
(FATHER OF —) EVENUS
(WIFE OF —) BRISEIS
MYOCOMMA FLAKE
MYRIAD HOST TOMAN COUNTLESS
MYRIAPOD JULID POLYPOD
PAUROPOD MILLIPEDE
MYRRH STACTE
MYRRHA (SON OF —) ADONIS
MYRTLE MYRT LILAC BALTIC
JAROOL ARRAYAN JAPONICA
RAMARAMA
MYSELF SELF MYSEN HERSELF
MYSID SHRIMP
MYSOST PRIMOST
MYSTERIES OF PARIS (AUTHOR OF
—) SUE
(CHARACTER IN —) FLEUR SARAH
CICELY MURPHY WALTER
FERRAND GEORGES JACQUES
RODOLPH CHOUETTE CLEMENCE
HARVILLE POLIDORI MACGREGOR
RIGOLETTE
MYSTERIES OF UDOLPHO
(AUTHOR OF —) RADCLIFFE
(CHARACTER IN —) EMILY DUPONT
MORANO MONTONI LUDOVICO
STAUBERT VILLEFORT
LAURENTINI VALANCOURT
MYSTERIOUS DIM DARK DEEP
EERY SELI EERIE SABLE WAKON
ARCANE EXOTIC MYSTIC OCCULT
SECRET CRYPTIC PUCKISH
UNCANNY UNCOUTH ABSTRUSE
ESOTERIC NUMINOUS SIBYLLIC
CRYPTICAL
MYSTERIOUSLY DARKLY EERILY
HEIMLICH
MYSTERY MIST RUNE CABALA
ENIGMA SECRET ARCANUM
PROBLEM SECRECY
(PREF.) MYST(ERI)(ERIO)(ICO)
MYSTIC SUFI OCCULT ORPHIC
SECRET EPOPTIC ESOTERIC
MYSTICAL MISTY MYSTIC
ANAGOGIC TELESTIC
MYSTICALLY GHOSTLY
MYSTICISM SUFIISM
MYSTIFY BEAT BEFOG BOTHER
MUDDLE PUZZLE BECLOUD
CONFUSE BEWILDER
MYTH SAGA FABLE LEGEND
MYTHOS ALLEGORY
MYTHICAL FABLED FABULOUS
FICTIOUS

N

N EN NU nan NOVEMBER

NAAM (FATHER OF —) CALEB

NAAMAH (BROTHER OF —)
TUBALCAIN
(FATHER OF —) LAMECH
(MOTHER OF —) ZILLAH
(SON OF —) REHOBOAM

NAARAH (HUSBAND OF —) ASHUR

NAASSENE OPHITE

NAB HAT NIB GRAB HEAD KNAB
NAIL CATCH SEIZE ARREST
CLUTCH COLLAR NIBBLE NOBBLE
SNATCH CAPTURE APPREHEND

NABAL (WIFE OF —) ABIGAIL

NABALOI IBALOI IGOROT

NABK NUBK NABAK NEBUK
NABBUK NEBACK NEBBUK
NEBBUCK

NABOB DIVES NAWAB NOBOB
DEPUTY VICEROY GOVERNOR
PLUTOCRAT
(— DEPUTY) NAWAB
(PL.) NABOBRY

NACELLE CAR BOAT BASKET
CHASSIS COCKPIT SHELTER

NACHSCHLAG SPRINGER
AFTERNOTE

NACKET BOY CAKE LUNCH
NOCKET

NACRE PEARL SHELLFISH

NADAB (FATHER OF —) AARON
SHAMMAI
(MOTHER OF —) ELISHEBA

NADIR BATHOS BEDROCK
(OPPOSED TO —) ZENITH

NAG CUT RAG TIT BAIT FRAB FRET
FUSS GNAW JADE MOKE PLUG
PONY PROD SNAG TWIT YAFF
ANNOY COBRA HOBBY HORSE
SCOLD SKATE SNAKE STEED
TEASE BADGER BERATE BOTHER
DOBBIN GARRAN GLEYDE HAGGLE
HARASS HECKLE HECTOR KEFFEL
PADNAG PESTER PLAGUE
ROUNCY WANTON HACKNEY
HENPECK TORMENT DINGDONG
HARANGUE IRRITATE PARAMOUR
(AMBLING —) HOBBY

NAGA SEMA COBRA KABUI LHOTA
SNAKE

NAGGING NIGGLING

NAGKASSAR SURIGA

NAGOR TOHI ANTELOPE
REEDBUCK

NAHANE KASKA

NAHATH (FATHER OF —) ZOPHAI

NAHBI (FATHER OF —) VOPHSI

NAHOOR SHA SNA SHEEP URIAL
BHARAL OORIAL

NAHOR (BROTHER OF —) HARAN
ABRAHAM
(FATHER OF —) SERUG
(SON OF —) TERAH

(WIFE OF —) MILCAH

NAHSON (FATHER OF —)
AMMINADAB
(SISTER OF —) ELISHEBA
(SON OF —) SALMON

NAHUATL AZTEC CAZCAN MEXICA

NAHUM ELKOSHITE

NAIAD NAIS NYMPH MUSSEL
HYDRIAD

NAIL CUT FIX HOB NAB PIN TEN
BOSS BRAD BRAG BROD CLAW
CLOY DUMP HOOF PILE SLUG
SPAD STUB STUD TACK TRAP
AFFIX CATCH CLOUT DRIVE
GROPE PLATE SCALE SEIZE SPEED
SPICK SPIKE SPRIG TALON
BULLEN CLENCH CLINCH COOLER
CORKER DETAIN FASTEN GARRON
HAMMER SECURE SINKER TACKET
TENTER TINGLE UNGUIS UNGULA
CAPTURE CLINKER FASTENER
HOLDFAST ROSEHEAD SPARABLE
SPIKELET TENPENNY TRICOUNI
(— BITING) ONYCHOPHAGIA
(— GROWTH) ONYCHAUXIS
(HEADLESS —) SPRIG
(HOOKED —) TENTER TENTERHOOK
(INGROWN —) ONYXIS ACRONYX
(MARKING —) SPAD SPEED
(OLD HORSESHOE —) STUB
(SHOEMAKER'S —) CLOUT
SPARABLE
(TOED —) TOSHNAIL
(PREF.) GOMPHO HELO ONYCH(O)
UNGUI
(SUFF.) ONYCHA ONYCHES
ONYCHIA ONYCHIUM ONYCHUS
ONYX

NAILROD STICKWEED

NAIVE OPEN RACY FRANK GREEN
CANDID JEJUNE SIMPLE ARTLESS
NATURAL CHILDISH INNOCENT
UNTAUGHT CHILDLIKE GUILELESS
INGENUOUS PRIMITIVE
UNTUTORED UNWORLDLY
(— GIRL) INGENUE

NAIVETE GREENNESS SIMPLICITY

NAKED BALD BARE MERE NUDE
OPEN CLEAR EXACT PLAIN STARK
ADAMIC BARREN CUERPO
SCUDDY SIMPLE EXPOSED
LITERAL OBVIOUS MANIFEST
STARKERS STRIPPED SMOCKLESS
UNADORNED UNCLOTHED
UNCOVERED
(PREF.) GYMN(O) NUDI

NAKED OAT PILLAS PILCORN
PILKINS

NAKEDWOOD MABI SNAKEWOOD

NAKHI MOSO MOSSO

NAKONG SITUTUNGA

NAMAYCUSH CREE FISH LAKER
LONGE LUNGE TOGUE TROUT

LONGUE SISCOWET

NAMBY-PAMBY INANE SILLY
VAPID CODDLE INSIPID KEEPSAKE

NAME DUB FIX NOM SET CALL CITE
FAME NAIL NOMB NOUN TERM
ALIAS CLAIM CLEPE COUNT ETHIC
NEVEN NOMEN POINT QUOTE
STYLE TITLE ADDUCE APPEAL
GOSSIP MONICA REPUTE SELECT
ALLONYM APPOINT BEHIGHT
DECLARE ENTITLE EPITHET
MENTION MONIKER SPECIFY
VOCABLE CATEGORY CHRISTEN
COGNOMEN IDENTIFY IDENTITY
INDICATE ENUMERATE
PATRONYMIC
(— TABLET) FACIA
(— WRITTEN BACKWARDS)
ANANYM
(ADDED —) AGNAME AGNOMEN
(ALTERNATIVE —) BUNCH
(ANCESTOR'S —) EPONYM
(ANOTHER —) ALIAS
(ASSUMED —) PEN ALIAS
ONOMASTIC PSEUDONYM
SOBRIQUET
(BAD —) CACONYM
(DAY —) AHAU
(DERIVATION OF —) EPONYMY
(FIRST —) FORENAME PRAENOMEN
(GOOD —) HONOR CREDIT
(PEN —) PSEUDONYM
(REGISTERED —) AFFIX
(TECHNICAL —) ONYM
(WELL-SUITED —) EUONYM
(PREF.) NOMEN ONOMATO
(SUFF.) NOMEN NYM ONYM

NAMED DIT CITED HIGHT NEMPT
DUBBED YCLEPT ONYMOUS
YCLEPED

NAMELESS BAS

NAMELY FOR VIZ SCIL NOTED
TOWIT FAMOUS SCILICET

NAMEPLATE MASTHEAD
(AUTOMOBILE —) MARQUE

NAMESAKE EPONYM JUNIOR
HOMONYM

NAMIBIA (BAY OF —) WALVIS
(CAPITAL OF —) WINDHOEK
(DESERT OF —) KALAHARI
(PEOPLE OF —) NAMAS BANTUS
BUSHMEN OVAMBOS

NANA (AUTHOR OF —) ZOLA
(CHARACTER IN —) NANA ROSE
HUGON LOUIS SATIN FONTAN
GEORGE HECTOR MIGNON
MUFFAT SABINE XAVIER ESTELLE
STEINER BEUVILLE DAGUENET
FAUCHERY PHILIPPE DECHOUARD

NANDI BANANDE MUNANDI
KIPSIKIS

NANDU RHEA

NANISM DWARFISM

NANNAR SIN

NANNY GOAT NURSE

NANTICOKE TOAG

NAOMI MARA
(DAUGHTER-IN-LAW OF —) RUTH

NAOS CELLA SHRINE TEMPLE

NAP GIG KIP NOD RAS CALK CAMP
DOWN DOZE FUZZ LINT OOZE
PILE RUFF SHAG WINK COVER
DOVER FLUFF GRASP SEIZE SLEEK
SLEEP STEAL CATNAP DROWSE
SIESTA SNOOZE EMERIZE
SLUMBER
(TO RAISE —) TEASE

NAPE NOD CUFF NECK NUKE POLL
NUCHA NUQUE SCRAG SCUFT
SCURF TURNIP NODDLE SCRUFF
NIDDICK
(PREF.) NUCH(I)

NAPERY LINEN DAMASK DOILIES
NAPKINS

NAPHTALITE ENAN AHIRA

NAPHTHA NEFTE PETROLEUM

NAPKIN CLOTH DOILY TOWEL
DIAPER NAPERY KERCHIEF
SUDATORY HANDCLOTH
SERVIETTE

NAPLES BISCUIT LADYFINGER

NAPLESS BARE HARD

NAPOLEON (— III) LOUIS
BOUSTRAPA
(BATTLE OF —) ULM ACRE JENA
WATERLOO
(BIRTHPLACE OF —) CORSICA
(BROTHER-IN-LAW OF —) MURAT
(GAME LIKE —) PAM
(ISLAND OF —) ELBA HELENA
CORSICA
(MARSHALL OF —) NEY
(MOTHER OF —) HORTENSE
(PLACE OF VICTORY FOR —) LODI
LIGNY

NAPPE DECKE

NAPPY ALE DISH DOWNY HEADY
WOOLY LIQUOR SHAGGY STRONG
WOOLLY COTTONY FOAMING
VILLOUS

NARCISSUS LILY PLANT CRINUM
EGOIST FLOWER LILIUM JONQUIL
POLYANTHUS
(FATHER OF —) CEPHISSUS
(LOVED BY —) ECHO
(MOTHER OF —) LIRIOPE
(TRUMPET —) DAFFODIL

NARCOTIC (ALSO SEE DRUG) KAT
KEF BANG DOPE DRUG HEMP
JUNK BHANG DAGGA ETHER
OPIUM HEROIN OPIATE ANODYNE
COCAINE CODEINE HASHISH
METOPON NARCEIN HYPNOTIC
MORPHINE TAKROURI DIACODION
MARIJUANA SOPORIFIC
CHLORODYNE

(— AGENT) GAZER
(— DOSE) LOCUS
(— PLANT) DUTRA MANDRAKE
(SMALL AMOUNT OF —) SNIFTER
(PL.) JUNK STUFF
NARCOTINE OPIANE
NARD SPICE ANOINT RHIZOME
MUSKROOT SPIKENARD
NARDOO ARDOO NARDU CLOVER
NARGIL COCONUT
NARGILEH PIPE HOOKA HOOKAH
NARGHILE
NARK SPY VEX NOTE ANNOY
TEASE OBSERVE INFORMER
IRRITATE
NARRA NAGA ASANA APALIT
NARRATE SPIN TELL BRUIT STATE
STORY DEPICT DETAIL DEVISE
RECITE RELATE REPORT DISCUSS
RECOUNT STORIFY DESCRIBE
REHEARSE
NARRATION TALE FABLE STORY
DETAIL ACCOUNT HAGGADA
RECITAL SYNAXAR ALLEGORY
DELIVERY DIEGESIS HAGGADAH
NARRATIVE EPIC JOKE MYTH
SAGA TALE CONTE DRAMA FABLE
PROSE STORY COMEDY JATAKA
LEGEND ACCOUNT EPISODE
HISTORY MEMOIRS MIDRASH
NOVELLA PARABLE RECITAL
ALLEGORY ANECDOTE APOLOGUE
ARETALOGY HAGIOLOGY
(— OF VOYAGE) PERIPLUS
(— POEM) EPIC EPOS SAGA
(BRIEF —) ANECDOTE
(PL.) ACTA EXEMPLA
NARRATOR TESTO TELLER
RELATOR SAGAMAN TALESMAN
RACONTEUR
NARROW JERK LEAN MEAN NEAR
POKY SLIT TRUE BORNE CLOSE
CRAMP PINCH RIGID SCANT
SHARP SMALL SOUND TAPER
ANGUST BIASED LINEAR LITTLE
MEAGER STRAIT STRICT TWITCH
BIGOTED ERICOID LIMITED
PRIMARY SLENDER THRIFTY
CONDENSE CONTRACT
PAROCHIAL PROVINCIAL
(— DOWN) CONFINE
(— DOWN STAVES) BUCK
(— INLET) RIA
(NOT —) CATHOLIC
(VERY —) HAIRBREADTH
(PREF.) AUGUSTI DOLICH(O)
STEN(O)
(SUFF.) STENOSIS
NARROWED LISTED INSWEPT
CONTRACT ANGUSTATE
NARROWING CAP CHOKE INTAKE
STENOSIS
NARROWLY WIDE STRAITLY
NARROW-MINDED BORNE PETTY
NARROWNESS BIAS BIGOTRY
LOCALISM PAROCHIALISM
NARSINGA TRUMPET
NARTHECIUM ABAMA
NARTHEX HALL STOA ENTRY
FOYER LOBBY PORCH PORTICO
PRONAOS VESTIBULE
NARWHAL MONODON
NASAB NUSUB KINSHIP

NASAL NOSY NARINE RHINAL
TWANGY ADENOID STRINGY
(PREF.) NASIO RHIN(O)
NASCENCY BIRTH ORIGIN GENESIS
BEGINNING
NASEBERRY SAPODILLA
NASHGAB OAF GOSSIP
NASI OFFICER PATRIARCH
NASICORN RHINOCEROS
NASTIKA ATHEIST
NASTURTIUM CAPUCINE
NOSEWORT RADICULA
STURSHUM STURTION
NASTY BAD PAH FOUL MEAN UGLY
DIRTY SNIDE FILTHY HORRID
ODIOUS RIBALD BAGGAGE
BEASTLY DEFILED HARMFUL
OBSCENE SQUALID UNCLEAN
INDECENT NAUSEOUS
DANGEROUS MALICIOUS
OFFENSIVE
NAT NOT DEMON SPIRIT
NATA (WIFE OF —) NANA
NATAL INBORN INNATE NATIVE
GLUTEAL CONGENIAL
NATAL BROWN MAHAL
NATAL PLUM AMATUNGULA
NATANT AFLOAT FLOATING
SWIMMING
NATATORIUM BATH POOL
NATCHEZ STINKER STINKARD
NATION BENI FOLK GEAT HOST
LAND LEDE RACE VOLK AEDUI
CASTE CLASS FANTE FANTI
REALM STATE TRIBE FANTEE
GEATAS PEOPLE WAGOGO
ARVERNI COUNTRY SOCIETY
LANGUAGE COMMUNITY
MANDATORY MINISTATE
MULTITUDE
(— SYMBOL) FLAG CREST
(HEBREW —) JACOB
(LARGE —) COLOSSUS
(PREF.) ETHN(O)
NATIONAL CITIZEN FEDERAL
GENTILE GENTILIC
(— DEMOCRACY) ENDEX
NATIONALISM JINGOISM
PHYLETISM
NATIONALIST CHINA (SEE
TAIWAN)
NATIONALITY FLAG
NATIVE (ALSO SEE PEOPLE AND
TRIBE) ABO ITE RAW SON TAO
BORN FREE GOOK HOME KIND
LIVE NEIF WILD INNER NATAL
PUNTI EPIROT GENIAL INBORN
INNATE KINDLY MOTHER NORMAL
SIMPLE VIRGIN CITIZEN DENIZEN
DZUNGAR ENDEMIC GENUINE
NATURAL PAISANO POLISTA
DOMESTIC GRASSCUT HABITUAL
HOMEBORN HOMEMADE
INHERENT LANDSMAN ORIGINAL
PRIMEVAL PRISTINE RESIDENT
YAMMADJI ABORIGINE
CONGENIAL INGRAINED
INHERITED INTRINSIC ORIGINARY
TAWNYMOOR ABORIGINAL
(— BEAR) KOALA
(— BEECH) FLINDOSA
(— MINERAL) LIVE
(— OF ALBANIA) SKIPETAR

(— OF BENGAL) KOL
(— OF CHINA) CELESTIAL
(— OF FENS) SLODGER
(— OF FLORIDA KEYS) CONK
CONCH
(— OF ILLINOIS) SUCKER
(— OF IRELAND) BOGTROTTER
(— OF LONDON) COCKNEY
(— OF LOW CLASS) TAO
(— OF MADAGASCAR) HOVA
(— OF MALAYA) INFIEL
(— OF MANCHESTER) MANCUNIAN
(— OF MARITIME PROVINCES)
BLUENOSE
(— OF N. CAROLINA) TARHEEL
(— OF NEW GUINEA) BOONG
(— OF NEW SOUTH WALES)
CORNSTALK
(— OF PHILIPPINES) GUGU
(— OF SCOTLAND) GEORDIE
(— OF SOUTHERN ILLINOIS)
EGYPTIAN
(— OF W. AUSTRALIA) GROPER
(— PLANT) INDIGINE
(— WHO TEACHES) CATECHIST
(BORN AND BRED AS A —) CREOLE
(FREE —) TIMAWA
(UNCIVILIZED —) MYALL
(SUFF.) ESE ITE OT OTE
(— OF) ER IER YER
NATIVE SON (AUTHOR OF —)
WRIGHT
(CHARACTER IN —) JAN MAX MARY
BORIS MEARS BESSIE BIGGER
DALTON ERLONE THOMAS
BRITTEN BUCKLEY
NATIVITY BIRTH JATAKA GENESIS
GENITURE HOROSCOPE
NATTERJACK NEWT TOAD
NATTY CHIC NEAT POSH TIDY TRIG
TRIM NIFTY SMART SPICY
DAPPER JAUNTY SPRUCE
FOPPISH VARMINT
NATURAL RAW BORN EASY FOOL
HOME KIND OPEN RACY REAL
WILD NAIVE USUAL CANCEL
CASUAL COMMON CONJON
CRETIN DIRECT HOMELY INBORN
INBRED INNATE KINDLY MOTHER
NATIVE NORMAL PHYSIC ARTLESS
GENUINE QUADRUM REGULAR
INHERENT LIFELIKE ORDINARY
PHYSICAL UNCOINED PRIMITIVE
REALISTIC UNASSUMED
UNFEIGNED
(— LOGARITHM) LN
(— TALENT) DOWER FLAIR
(NOT —) AFFECTED
(PREF.) PHYSI(O) PHYSICO
NATURALIST AMERICAN LEA COPE
DALL MUIR SNOW WARD FLAGG
HYATT LEIDY LUCAS MASON
ORTON ABBOTT AKELEY BARTON
GODMAN HOLDER MORTON
NELSON SAVAGE STORER
ANDREWS BACHMAN BUCKLEY
DITMARS FUERTES MERRIAM
SCUDDER COOLIDGE HALDEMAN
HOLBROOK JENNINGS
BURROUGHS INGERSOLL
RAFINESQUE
AUSTRALIAN BANFIELD
DANISH BERGSOE WINSLOW

DUTCH CAMPER HOEVEN
HOMBERG SWAMMERDAM
LEEUWENHOEK
ENGLISH RAY BELL BAKER BANKS
BATES BRADY GOSSE LEACH
NORTH DARWIN SLOANE
BORLASE CATESBY DUGMORE
EDWARDS NEEDHAM PENNANT
WALLACE BRODERIP BURCHELL
LYDEKKER STEBBING SWAINSON
BOWERBANK JEFFERIES
CARRUTHERS TEGETMEIER
WILLIAMSON
FRENCH BELON CHENU BUFFON
CUVIER BAILLON DAUBENY
DUMERIL GERVAIS LAMARCK
LESUEUR ORBIGNY POUCHET
POUPART REAUMUR ADDANSON
AUDEBERT BONPLAND DESHAYES
LACEPEDE RONDELET CASTELNAU
DAUBENTON BROUSSONETT
GERMAN OKEN WIED JAGER
LIBAU SEITZ MULLER PALLAS
MARTIUS NEUWIED SCHWANN
SIEBOLD STELLER CHAMISSO
ERXLEBEN HUMBOLDT
JUNGHUHN SCHUBERT
EHRENBERG KIELMEYER
BURMEISTER KEYSERLING
TREVIRANUS ESCHSCHOLTZ
SOEMMERING SCHLAGINTWEIT
ITALIAN REDI RISSO BONELLI
BROCCHI FABRONI FONTANA
SCOPOLI AMORETTI MARSIGLI
ALDROVANDI SPALLANZANI
VALLISNIERI
NORWEGIAN ASBJORNSEN
RUSSIAN EICHWALD FEDCHENKO
CHIKHACHEV
SCOTTISH BROWN BAIKIE FORBES
HERDMAN JARDINE THOMSON
RICHARDSON MACGILLIVRAY
SPANISH COBO AZARA MUTIS
SWEDISH ARTEDI FORSKAL
ZETTERSTEDT
SWISS HEER HUBER BONNET
GESNER AGASSIZ TSCHUDI
SAUSSURE TREMBLEY CLAPAREDE
POURTALES RUTIMEYER
NATURALIZE ADAPT ADOPT
ACCUSTOM ACCLIMATE
ENDENIZEN HABITUATE
NATURALLY SN KINDLY GENIALLY
NATURALNESS EASE NAIVETE
NATURE ILK BENT BIOS CAST CLAY
FORM HAIR KIND MAKE MOOD
RACE SORT TRIM TYPE COLOR
OUSIA SHAPE STATE TENOR
ANIMAL DHARMA FIGURE
HEAVEN KIDNEY PHYSIS STRIPE
ESSENCE FEATHER INBEING
QUALITY SPECIES PRAKRITI
UNIVERSE CHARACTER
QUALIFICATION
(— DIVINITY) NYMPH
(— GOD) PAN
(— GODDESS) CYBELE ARTEMIS
(— OF GOD) DIVINITY
(— PRINT) PHYTOGRAPH
(— SPIRIT) NAT
(— WORSHIP) PHYSIOLATRY
(APPARENT —) STUDY
(CONCEALED —) LATENCY

(DIVINE —) DEITY
(EMOTIONAL —) HEART
(ESSENTIAL —) ESSE FORM GENIUS
(GOOD —) BONHOMIE
(HUMAN —) FLESH MANHEAD
MANKIND
(INHERENT —) GENIUS
(INTRINSIC —) BOTTOM
(MORAL —) ETHNOS
(OF THE SAME —) HOMOGENEOUS
(ORGANIC —) BIOS
(PERT. TO —) COSMO
(ROUGH —) SPINOSITY
(SPECIAL —) IDIOM
(SPIRITUAL —) INTERNAL
(TRUE —) PROPRIETY
(ULTIMATE —) ESSENCE
(UNREGENERATE —) ADAM
(PREF.) PHYSI(O)
(SUFF.) (HAVING — OF) IC ICAL
(OF — OF) EOUS
NAUGHT NIL EVIL ZERO AUGHT
NAGHT OUGHT CIPHER NOUGHT
WICKED NOTHING USELESS
WORTHLESS
NAUGHTY BAD PAW SAD EVIL
WRONG PAWPAW SHREWD
WICKED OBSCENE WAYWARD
IMPROPER
NAUPATHIA SEASICKNESS
NAURU (CAPITAL OF —) YAREN
(DISTRICT OF —) BOE EWA AIWO
IJUW BAITI BUADA NIBOK UABOE
YAREN ANABAR ANETAN
MENENG ANIBARE
(FORMER NAME OF —)
PLEASANTISLAND
(TOWN OF —) ANNA ORRO
ANABAR RONAWI YANGOR
NAUSEA PALL QUALM DISGUST
NAUSITY LOATHING SICKNESS
ANTIPATHY DIZZINESS
NAUSEATE TURN TWIST WLATE
REVOLT SICKEN DISGUST
SCUNNER STOMACH DISTASTE
SCOMFISH
NAUSEATED ILL SICKISH
QUALMISH SQUEAMISH
NAUSEATING NASTY WAUGH
QUEASY BILIOUS FULSOME
BRACKISH STAWSOME
LOATHSOME REVOLTING
SICKENING
NAUSEOUS OFFENSIVE
NAUSICAA (FATHER OF —)
ALCINOUS
(MOTHER OF —) ARETE
NAUSITHOUS (FATHER OF —)
NEPTUNE POSEIDON
(MOTHER OF —) PERIBOEA
(SON OF —) ALCINOUS
NAUTICAL (ALSO SEE NAVIGATION)
NAVAL MARINE NAUTIC MARINAL
OCEANIC TARRISH MARITIME
NAVIGABLE
(— FLAG) CORNET PENNON
NAUTILUS MOLLUSK ARGONAUT
ARGONAUTA
(— COMMANDER) NEMO
NAVAHO DINE NAVAJO LONGHAIR
(— GROUP) OUTFIT
(— RITE) WAY
NAVAL SEA MARINE

NAUTICAL NAVIGABLE
(— DEPOT) BASE
(— FORCE) NAVY FLEET ARMADA
SQUADRON
(— JAIL) BRIG
NAVAL OFFICER AMERICAN ROE
CONE DALE DYER HART HULL
HUSE KING LAND LEVY LUCE
MAYO SIMS ALLEN AMMEN
BARRY BEALE CAPPS CLARK
DAVIS DEWEY EVANS FISKE
FOOTE GRANT JONES LEAHY
LEARY MAHAN PERRY PRATT
ROWAN STARK WALKE BARNEY
BENSON BIDDLE BREESE CONNER
EBERLE GREENE NEALS HEWITT
HOWELL KEARNY KIMMEL KNIGHT
MCCAIN MORRIS NIMITZ PALMER
PORTER RODMAN SCHLEY
SEMMES TALBOT TOWERS
TUCKER WILKES BRISTOL
BULLOCH CHESTER CUSHING
DALGREN DECATUR ELLIOTT
GLEAVES GRIDLEY HOLLINS
HOPKINS KIMBALL KINKAID
MOFFETT NIBLACK SCHENCK
SIGSBEE STEWART TRUXTUN
WHIPPLE WILLSON WINSLOW
BUCHANAN CAPERTON
CHADWICK CHAUNCEY
FARRAGUT GHORMLEY
INGRAHAM LAWRENCE PAULDING
PERCIVAL RICKOVER ROBINSON
ROUSSEAU SHUBRICK SPRUANCE
STANDLEY STIRLING THATCHER
GLASSFORD PILLSBURY
SCHROEDER SELFRIDGE
BAINBRIDGE GREENSLADE
MACDONOUGH WAINWRIGHT
GOLDSBOROUGH
BELGIAN GERLACHE
BRAZILIAN MELLO
DANISH HOLM JUEL AMDRUP
ADELAER
DUTCH TROMP RUYTER ALMONDE
DEWINTER HELFRICH
ENGLISH BALL BYNG HOOD HOPE
HOWE LUCE MEUX ALLIN ANSON
BAYLY BLAKE BLIGH BOYLE
BROKE FOLEY HARDY HAWKE
LEAKE LYONS NOBLE TRYON
AYLMER AYSCUE BEATTY
BENBOW BOWERS BURNEY
CARDEN COFFIN COLOMB FENNER
GORDON HALSEY HERVEY
HORNBY JERRAM LAWSON
LAYTON LITTLE MADDEN
MONSON NELSON OSBORN
PARKER RODNEY SYFRET VERNON
WILSON ADDISON BARCLAY
BEDFORD BELCHER CRADOCK
DOUGLAS GAMBIER HARWOOD
HAWKINS JACKSON MCCLURE
MORESBY NASMITH SEYMOUR
ANDERSON BEAUFORT
BOSCAWEN BROTHERS
COCHRANE JELLICOE TRELAWNY
TYRWHITT BACKHOUSE
BERESFORD CALLAGHAN
CHATFIELD COLLINSON
FREMANTLE GRENVILLE
NARBROUGH NICHOLSON
CODRINGTON CUNNINGHAM

SOMERVILLE TROUBRIDGE
FITZMAURICE
FRENCH BELLOT DARLAN FORBIN
GRASSE COURBET DUPERRE
ESTAING FARRERE GUICHEN
MOUCHEZ CORBIERE FLEURIAS
FLEURIEU MUSELIER NOAILLES
CASABIANCA
GERMAN KONIG HIPPER MULLER
RAEDER BEHNCKE CAPELLE
DOENITZ TIRPITZ JACHMANN
GREEK KANARES MIAOULES
HUNGARIAN HORTHY
ITALIAN LAURIA JACCHINO
RICCARDI
JAPANESE ITO KATO TOGO URIU
KONDO OKADA SAITO YONAI
NAGANO NOMURA SHIMADA
YOSHIDA KAMIMURA SUETSUGU
NORWEGIAN TORDENSKJOLD
PERUVIAN GRAU
PORTUGUESE CASTRO
RUSSIAN GREIG KOLCHAK
MAKAROV ALEKSEEV APRAKSIN
KUZNETSOV
SCOTTISH BARTON
SPANISH ULLOA GRAVINA
SWEDISH LINDMAN EHRENSVARD
**NAVARRAISE, LA (CHARACTER IN
—)** ANITA ARAQUIL GARRIDO
ZUCCARAGA
(COMPOSER OF —) MASSENET
NAVE HOB HUB NEF APSE BODY
FIST PACE AISLE NATHE NIEVE
CENTER
NAVEL NOMBRIL OMPHALOS
UMBILICUS
(PREF.) OMPHAL(O) UMBILI(CI)
(SUFF.) OMPHALUS
NAVIGABLE BOATABLE PORTABLE
NAVIGATE KEEL SAIL DRIVE GUIDE
SKIFF STEER AVIATE COURSE
CRUISE DIRECT MANAGE TRAVEL
CONDUCT CONTROL JOURNEY
OPERATE TRAVERSE ASTROGATE
NAVIGATION HOMING VOYAGE
NAUTICS PASSAGE SAILING
TRAFFIC CABOTAGE SHIPPING
(— MEASURE) TON KNOT SEAM
FATHOM
(— SYSTEM) LORAN TACAN
(SYSTEM OF —) DECCA
NAVIGATOR FLYER NAVVY PILOT
AIRMAN AVIATOR COPILOT
LABORER AERONAUT SEAFARER
SPACEMAN NEPTUNIAN
NEPTUNIST
DANISH BERING
DUTCH HARTOG BARENTS
HOUTMAN LEMAIRE HEEMSKERK
ENGLISH FOX BYRON DIXON
DRAKE BARLOW BUTTON CLERKE
HUDSON SOMERS BARLOWE
GILBERT GOSNOLD RALEIGH
WEDDELL CAVENDISH
LANCASTER VANCOUVER
CHANCELLOR WILLOUGHBY
FRENCH BETHENCOURT
BOUGAINVILLE
GERMAN BEHAIM KOTZEBUE
GREEK EUDOXUS PYTHEAS
ITALIAN ZENO VESPUCCI
PORTUGUESE CAM DIAS DIAZ

GAMA CUNHA ZARCO CABRAL
GARCIA QUEIROS GILIANES
MAGELLAN FERNANDES
RUSSIAN LUTKE GOLOVNIN
KRUSENSTERN
SPANISH CANO GALI NINO SOLIS
PINZON TORRES FERNANDEZ
NAVITE BASALT
NAVVY HAND WORKER LABORER
NAVIGATOR
NAVY FLEET SHIPFERD
(— BOARD) ADMIRALTY
(— OFFICER) CPO AIDE MATE
BOSUN CHIEF ENSIGN ADMIRAL
ARMORER CAPTAIN COMMANDER
COMMODORE
(— RADIO OPERATOR) SPARKS
(— VESSEL) PT SUB CARRIER
CRUISER FLATTOP DESTROYER
SUBMARINE TRANSPORT
NAWOB NABOB NUWAB RULER
VICEROY
NAY NO NAI NEI NOT DENY EVEN
NYET FLUTE NEVER DENIAL
REFUSE REFUSAL NEGATIVE
NAZARD STOP NASAT
NAZE NASE HEADLAND
NAZI BROWN HITLERITE
(— SYMBOL) FYLFOT SWASTIKA
NAZIM VICEROY GOVERNOR
NEAERA (DAUGHTER OF —) AUGE
EVADNE LAMPETIS PHAETHUSA
(FATHER OF —) PEREUS
(HUSBAND OF —) ALEUS STRYMON
(SON OF —) CEPHEUS LYCURGUS
AMPHIDAMAS
NEANDERTHAL CAVEMAN
NEANIC IMMATURE YOUTHFUL
NEAR AD AT BY IN GIN KIN NAR
AKIN BAIN DEAR FAST GAIN
HARD HEND INBY NEXT NIGH
ABOUT ANEAR ANENT ASIDE
CLOSE EWEST FORBY HANDY
HENDE JUXTA MATCH NUDGE
ROUND SHORT TOUCH ALMOST
AROUND BESIDE CLIMAX HEREBY
NARROW STINGY TOWARD
WITHIN ADVANCE AGAINST
FORTHBY SIMILAR THRIFTY
VICINAL ADJACENT APPROACH
IMMINENT INTIMATE
CONTIGUOUS
(— AKIN) GERMANE
(— POINT) PP
(— THE BEGINNING) EARLY FORMER
(— THE EQUATOR) LOW
(— THE MOUTH) ADORAL
(— THE SURFACE) EBB FLEET
(— THE WIND) HIGH AHOLD
(CONVENIENTLY —) HANDSOME
(PREF.) AC AD AF AG AL AP AS
AT BY ENGY EPH EPI JUXTA PERI
PLESI(O) PROS
NEARBY AROUND GAINLY LOCALLY
ADJACENT
NEARER HITHER
(— FRANCE) CISALPINE
(— ROME) CISALPINE
(— THE REAR) AFTER
(PREF.) (— IN TIME) CIS CITRA
NEAREST NEXT EWEST CLOSEST
NEARMOST PROCHAIN PROXIMAL
IMMEDIATE PROXIMATE

(— THE STERN) AFTERMOST
(PREF.) PROXIMO
NEARIAH (FATHER OF —) ISHI
SHEMAIAH
NEARLY GAIN JUST LIKE MOST
MUCH ABOUT CLOSE ALMOST
FECKLY PRACTICALLY
NEARNESS AFFINITY VICINITY
PROPINQUITY
NEARSIGHTED MYOPIC PURBLIND
NEAT GIM NET COSH COWS DEFT
DINK FEAT FEEL FEIL GENT JIMP
MACK NICE OXEN PRIM PURE
SMUG SNOD SNUG TIDY TOSH
TRIG TRIM BULLS CLEAN CLEAR
COMPT CRISP DINKY DONCY
DONSY DOUCE EXACT FEATY
FETIS GENTY JEMMY NATTY
NIFTY PREST QUEME SMART
SMIRK SPICK TERSE TIGHT
ADROIT BOVINE CATTLE CLEVER
DAINTY DAPPER DIMBER DONSIE
HEPPEN MINION POLITE QUAINT
SPANDY SPRUCE BANDBOX
CONCISE FEATOUS ORDERLY
PERJINK PRECISE REFINED
SHAPELY TRICKSY UNMIXED
MENSEFUL SKILLFUL STRAIGHT
TASTEFUL DEXTEROUS
SHIPSHAPE UNDILUTED
WHOLESOME
NEATLY SNUG DEFTLY FAIRLY
FEATLY SMARTLY SPRUCELY
NEATNESS MENSE DEFTNESS
ELEGANCE SPRUCERY
NEB EAR NIB TIP BEAK BILL NOSE
POINT SNOUT
NEBAIOTH (FATHER OF —) ISHMAEL
NEBAT (SON OF —) JEROBOAM
NEBO (FATHER OF —) MARDUK
MERODACH
(WIFE OF —) TASHMET

NEBRASKA
CAPITAL: LINCOLN
COLLEGE: DANA DOANE
DUCHESNE HASTINGS
COUNTY: GAGE LOUP OTOE DEUEL
DUNDY KEITH SARPY CHERRY
COLFAX FURNAS HOOKER
NEMAHA VALLEY BUFFALO
ANTELOPE BOXBUTTE
KEYAPAHA
INDIAN: OTO OMAHA PONCA
PAWNEE
PRESIDENT: FORD
RIVER: LOGAN DISMAL PLATTE
ELKHORN NIOBRARA
STATE BIRD: MEADOWLARK
STATE FLOWER: GOLDENROD
STATE NICKNAME: BLACKWATER
CORNHUSKER TREEPLANTERS
STATE TREE: ELM
TOWN: ORD ALMA COZAD OMAHA
PONCA TRYON WAHOO GERING
MULLEN NELIGH PENDER
TEKAMAH OGALLALA
REDCLOUD THEDFORD
UNIVERSITY: CREIGHTON

NEBRIS FAWNSKIN
NEBULA SKY CRAB SPOT
VAPOR BALAXY GALAXY

SPIRAL PLANETARY
NEBULIZE ATOMIZE
NEBULOUS DIM DARK HAZY
FOGGY MISTY MUDDY VAGUE
CLOUDY MYSTIC TURBID
CLOUDED EVASIVE SHADOWY
UNCLEAR DREAMLIKE
NECESSARILY NEEDS NEEDLY
PERFORCE
NECESSARY NEEDY PRIVY VITAL
FRIEND TOILET KINSMAN
NEEDFUL FORCIBLE INTEGRAL
OBLIGATE BEHOVEFUL ESSENTIAL
INTRINSIC
(PL.) ALIMENT MISTERS
NECESSITATE FORCE IMPEL
COMPEL DEMAND ENTAIL OBLIGE
REQUIRE CONSTRAIN
NECESSITY USE CALL DUTY FATE
FOOD LACK MUST NEED TASK
WANT DRINK ANANKE BEHOOF
BESOIN MISTER MUSCLE NEEDBE
URGENCY PERFORCE
REQUIREMENT
(— OF MOVING) ZUGZWANG
(BY —) PRESENTLY
(PL.) BREAD
(PREF.) DEONTO
NECK COL NUB PET CAPE CRAG
CROP HALS KISS WAKE BEARD
CHOKE CRAIG HALSE SCRAG
SPOON SWIRE TRAIL BEHEAD
CARESS CERVIX COLLET COLLUM
FONDLE STRAIT CHANNEL
EMBRACE ISTHMUS SQUEEZE
TUBULUS LALLYGAG
(— ARTERY) CAROTID
(— MUSCLE) SCALENUS
(— OF BOTTLE) THROTTLE
(— OF LAMB) TARGET
(— OF VOLCANO) CORE
(BACK OF —) NOD NAPE NUCH
NUQUE SCRUFF NIDDICK
(BOW —) HAWSE
(PERT. TO —) JUGULAR CERVICAL
(RED —) ROOINEK
(PREF.) CERVIC(I)(O) COLLI DER(O)
TRACHEL(O)
(SUFF.) DERUS
NECK AND NECK TIE EVEN CLOSE
NECKBAND BAND COLLAR COLLET
SHIRTBAND
NECKCLOTH BOA TIE RUFF AMICE
CHOKE SCARF STOLE CHOKER
CRAVAT BURDASH NECKTIE
PANUELO STARCHER BARCELONA
SOLITAIRE STEINKIRK
NECKERCHIEF GIMP RAIL FOGLE
BELCHER FOULARD NECKLET
KERCHIEF NECKATEE NECKCLOTH
NECKENGER
NECKING COLLAR GORGERIN
NECKLACE BEE LEI TORC BEADS
CHAIN NOOSE CARCAN CHOKER
COLLAR GORGET SANKHA
TAWDRY TORQUE BALDRIC
CHAPLET RIVIERE SAUTOIR
LAVALIER NEGLIGEE ESCLAVAGE
(PREF.) MONILI
NECKLINE COWL SCOOP
NECK RUFF FRAISE QUELLIO
NECKTIE BOW TIE ASCOT
SCARF CHOKER CRAVAT

GRAVAT OVERLAY
(— PARTY) HANGING LYNCHING
(PART OF —) EDGE SEAM TACK
APRON SHELL FACING MARGIN
POCKET HEMMING TIPPING
NECKBAND INTERLINING
NECROMANCER GOETIC
MAGICIAN
NECROMANCY GOETY MAGIC
GRAMARY SORCERY WIZARDRY
EGROMANCY
NECROPOLIS CEMETERY
NECROPSY AUTOPSY
NECROSIS MORTIFICATION
NECTAR HONEY AMRITA
AMBROSIA
NECTAR BIRD EATER HONEY
SUNBIRD
NECTARINE BRUNION NECTRON
NECTARIN
NECTARY SPUR GLAND
NECTARIUM
NEDABIAH (FATHER OF —)
JECONIAH
NEDDER ADDER
NEDDY HORSE DONKEY
NEE BORN
NEED ASK NUD LACK TAKE THAR
WANT CRAVE DRIVE THARF
BEHOOF BEHOVE BESOIN
DEMAND DESIRE EGENCE MISTER
STRAIT BEHOOVE NEEDHAM
POVERTY REQUIRE URGENCY
DISTRESS EXIGENCY MISCHIEF
EMERGENCE EXTREMITY
NECESSITY
NEEDED NECESSARY
NEEDFIRE WILDFIRE
NEEDFUL VITAL INTEGRAL
ESSENTIAL NECESSARY REQUISITE
NEEDLE SEW VEX YEN ACUS DARN
GOAD TIER WIRE ANNOY BLUNT
POINT SHARP SPIKE STRAW
STYLE BODKIN DARNER STYLUS
OBELISK PRICKER PROVOKE
SPICULE TUMBLER
(— HOLE) EYE
(— SORTER) HANDER
(COMB. FORM) ACU
(PART OF —) EYE HOLE CROWN
POINT SHANK
(PINE —) SPILL
(PINE —S) PININGS
(PL.) TWINKLES
(PREF.) ACU RAPHI RAPHIDI
NEEDLE BUG NEPID RANATRA
NEEDLEBUSH URY PINBUSH
NEEDLEFISH GAR SNOOK AGUJON
BELONID LONGJAW
NEEDLE GUN RIFLE DREYSE
NEEDLELIKE ACUATE ACERATE
ACEROSE ACEROUS ACIFORM
ACICULAR BELONOID SPLINTERY
NEEDLEMAN TAILOR
NEEDLE-POINTED ACEROSE
NEEDLESHAPED ACIFORM
ACETIOUS
NEEDLESS AMOK
NEEDLESTONE NATROLITE
NEEDLEWORK SEWING SAMPLER
SEAMING TATTING KNITTING
WOOLWORK HEMSTITCH
INSERTION

NEEDY BARE POOR INDIGENT
NEEDSOME HUNGARIAN
PENNILESS PENURIOUS
NECESSITOUS
NEEP NEPE TURNIP
NE'ER-DO-WELL BUM PELF LOSEL
SKELLUM SCHLEMIEL SHIFTLESS
WORTHLESS RAPSCALLION
NEFANDOUS IMPIOUS EXECRABLE
NEFARIOUS WICKED HEINOUS
IMPIOUS FLAGRANT HORRIBLE
INFAMOUS ATROCIOUS
NEFERT (HUSBAND OF —)
AMENEMHAT
NEGATE DENY SUBLATE
NEGATION NAY NOT EMPTY
DENIAL REFUSAL ANNULMENT
NONENTITY
(PREF.) DIS
NEGATIVE NA NE NO CON NAE
NAY NIT NIX NON NOR NOT NUL
DENY FILM VETO MINUS NEVER
NAYWARD STAMPER APOPHATIC
PRIVATIVE
(— PREFIX) IL IM IN IR UN DIS NON
(— PRINCIPLE) YIN
(PHOTOGRAPHIC —) CLICHE
(PREF.) INEQUI
NEGLECT DEBT FAIL HANG OMIT
SHUN SLIP FAULT FORGO SHIRK
SLOTH WAIVE BYPASS CESSER
FOREGO FORGET IGNORE LACHES
LOITER PERMIT SLIGHT DEFAULT
DISOBEY FAILURE OVERSEE
RESPECT FORSLACK OMISSION
OVERLOOK OVERSLIP RECKLESS
DISREGARD MISLIPPEN
OVERSIGHT PRETERMIT
MISPRISION
(— OF DUTY) INCIVISM
NEGLECTED TACKY SHABBY
UNDONE DORMANT OBSOLETE
NEGLECTFUL LAX REMISS
CARELESS DERELICT HEEDLESS
RECKLESS DISSOLUTE NEGLIGENT
NEGLIGEE ROBE MANTEAU
MATINEE UNDRESS PEIGNOIR
NIGHTGOWN DISHABILLE
NEGLIGENCE CULPA LACHES
DEFAULT LASCHETY DISREGARD
OVERSIGHT
NEGLIGENT LAX LASH SOFT SLACK
CASUAL OVERLY REMISS
CARELESS DERELICT DISCINCT
RECKLESS SLOVENLY YEMELESS
DISSOLUTE NEGLECTFUL
NEGLIGIBLE FAT
NEGOTIATE DEAL SELL BROKE
FLOAT TREAT TROKE TRUCK
TRYST ADVISE ASSIGN CONFER
DICKER DIRECT MANAGE PARLEY
SETTLE ARRANGE BARGAIN
CHAFFER CONDUCT CONSULT
DISCUSS ENTREAT CONCLUDE
ENTREATY TRANSACT TRANSFER
TEMPORIZE
NEGOTIATION DEAL DICKER
PARLEY TREATY PASSAGE
ENTREATY PRACTICE
NEGRITO ATA ATI ITA AETA AKKA
BATWA BLACK KARON SEMANG
TAPIRO ABENLEN BAMBUTE
NEGRITUDE SOUL

NEGRO FON JUR LUO LWO SUK
AKIM ALUR BENI BINI BONI EGBA
FONG IRON MADI MOKE NUBA
NUPE SIDI BENIN BLACK BONGO
CUFFY DINKA DJUKA FULUP
FUZZY HATSA MUNGO SEPIA
SEREC SMOKE TEMNE GULLAH
HUBSHI AKWAPIM DAHOMAN
GEECHEE QUASHIE SANDAWE
SHELLUH SHILLUK BECHUANA
ETHIOPIAN MANGBATTU
(— BLOOD) TARBRUSH
(GOLD COAST —) GA FANTI
(LIBERIAN —) KRU VAI VEI GREBO
ICROO KRUMAN KROOBOY
(MALE —) BUCK
(OLD —) UNCLE
NEHEMIAH (FATHER OF —) AZBUK
HACHALIAH
NEHUSHTA (FATHER OF —)
ELNATHAN
(HUSBAND OF —) JEHOIAKIM
(SON OF —) JEHOIACHIN
NEIGH NIE NVE WHI HINNY NICKER
WHINNY WIGHER WHICKER
NEIGHBOR BOR ADJOIN BORDER
FELLOW NEIPER ACCOLENT
BORDERER CONFINER UCALEGON
(PL.) KITH CONFINES
(SUFF.) GETON
NEIGHBORHOOD WAY AREA
HAND VENUE BARRIO LOCALE
REGION PURLIEU SECTION
DISTRICT ENVIRONS PRESENCE
PROCINCT VICINAGE VICINITY
BAILIWICK COMMUNITY
PROXIMITY TERRITORY
VOISINAGE
NEIGHBORING NIGH NEARBY
CONFINE VICINAL ACCOLENT
ADJACENT
NEIGHBORLY FOLKSY FOLKSEY
AMICABLE
NEITHER NOT NATHER NITHER
NOWDER
(— RIGHT NOR WRONG)
ADIAPHOROUS
NELEUS (BROTHER OF —) PELIAS
(DAUGHTER OF —) PERO
(FATHER OF —) NEPTUNE
(MOTHER OF —) TYRO
(SON OF —) NESTOR
(WIFE OF —) CHLORIS
NELLORE ONGOLE
NEMA EELWORM FILAMENT
NEMATODE ROUNDWORM
NEMATOCYST CNIDA
DESMONEME PENETRANT
NEMATODE ROUNDWORM
NEMESIS BANE FATE UPIS AGENT
AVENGER PENALTY
NEMUEL (BROTHER OF —) ABIRAM
DATHAN
(FATHER OF —) ELIAB SIMEON
NENTSI SAMOYED SAMOYEDE
NEOPHYTE TYRO EPOPT NOVICE
AMATEUR CONVERT BEGINNER
PROSELYTE YOUNGLING
NEOPLASM TUMOR GROWTH
TUMOUR SARCOMA NEWGROWTH
NEOTERIC NEW LATE FRESH
NOVEL MODERN RECENT
NEP KNOT CATNIP

CATMINT CLUSTER

NEPENTHE DRUG PLANT POTION
ANODYNE
NEPHEG (FATHER OF —) DAVID
IZHAR
NEPHELE (DAUGHTER OF —) HELLE
(HUSBAND OF —) ATHAMAS
(SON OF —) LEUCON PHRIXUS
NEPHELINE LENAD MINERAL
SOMMITE ELEOLITE
NEPHEW OY OYE NEVE VASU
NEFFY NEVOY NIECE NEPOTE
BENVOLIO
NEPHRITE YU JADE AXSTONE
POUNAMU TREMOLITE
NEPTUNE LER PAN SEA GREEN
OCEAN PLATE SEAGOD
(BROTHER OF —) PLUTO JUPITER
(CONSORT OF —) SALACIA
(DISCOVERER OF —) GALLE
(EMBLEM OF —) TRIDENT
(FATHER OF —) SATURN
(MOTHER OF —) RHEA
(SISTER OF —) JUNO
NER (SON OF —) ABNER
NEREID NYMPH NEREIS THALIA
THETIS CYMODOCE
NEREIDES (FATHER OF —) NEREUS
(MOTHER OF —) DORIS
NERGAL (BROTHER OF —) NINAZU
(FATHER OF —) ENLIL
(MOTHER OF —) NINLIL
NERI (FATHER OF —) MELCHI
(SON OF —) SALATHIEL
NERIAH (FATHER OF —) MAASEIAH
(SON OF —) BARUCH SERAIAH
NERISSA (HUSBAND OF —)
GRATIANO
NERO TYRANT FIDDLER
(MOTHER OF —) AGRIPPINA
(SUCCESSOR TO —) GALBA
(VICTIM OF —) LUCAN SENECA
(WIFE OF —) OCTAVIA
NERONE (CHARACTER IN —) MAGO
NERO SIMON FANUEL RUBRIA
ASTERIA
(COMPOSER OF —) BOITO
NERVE RIB BEND CORD GALL GRIT
GUTS LINE SAND VEIN CHEEK
CHORD CRUST PLUCK PUDIC
SINEW SPUNK STEEL TENON
VAGUS VIGOR APLOMB COSTAL
DARING DENTAL ENERGY FACIAL
HUTZPA LUMBAR RADIAL SACRAL
STRING AXILLAR CHUTZPA

COELIAC COURAGE HUTZPAH
SAPHENA SCIATIC SPINDLE
ABDUCENS AUDACITY BOLDNESS
CERVICAL CHUTZPAH COOLNESS
EFFERENT EMBOLDEN STRENGTH
TEMERITY AUTONOMIC
ENCOURAGE EYESTRING
ACCELERATOR
(— CELL) ANAXON NEURON
DIAXONE DENDRAXON
(— CENTER) BRAIN CORTEX
PLEXUS
(— FIBERS) PONS
(— NETWORK) RETIA PLEXUS
(— SLEEP) NEURO HYPNOTISM
(PL.) HORRORS JITTERS
(PREF.) NEUR(I)(O)
(SUFF.) NEURA(L) NEURE NEURIA
NEURIC
NERVELESS DEAD WEAK BRAVE
INERT UNNERVED FOOLHARDY
POWERLESS
NERVOUS EDGY TOEY FUSSY
GOOSY JUMPY TENSE TIMID
WINDY FIDGET SINEWY SPOOKY
TOUCHY UNEASY FEARFUL
FRETFUL JITTERY RESTIVE
SCADDLE NEUROTIC TIMOROUS
EXCITABLE SENSITIVE
TREMULOUS TWITTERLY
(— MALADY) APHASIA NEURITIS
(— SEIZURE) TIC ANEURIA
NERVURE RIB COSTA NERVE
NEURON CUBITAL
NERVY BOLD RASH JERKY PUSHY
BRAZEN SINEWY STRONG
FORWARD JITTERY IMPUDENT
INTREPID VIGOROUS EXCITABLE
NESS RAS CAPE SKAW SUFFIX
HEADLAND
NEST BED DEN EST JUG WEB AERY
BIKE BINK DRAY DREY EYRY
HOME LAIR NIDE REDD SHED
TRAP ABODE AERIE BROOD EYRIE
HAUNT HOUSE NIDUS SWARM
CLUTCH COLONY CUDDLE
HOTBED RESORT WURLEY
CABINET LODGING RETREAT
VESPIARY WITHYPOT LARVARIUM
PENDULINE RESIDENCE
TERMITARY
(— OF ANIMALS) BED
(— OF ANT) FORMICARY
(— OF BOXES) INRO
(— OF EGGS) CLUTCH
(SQUIRREL'S —) CAGE
(PREF.) CALIO NIDI OECO
(SUFF.) OECA OECIA
NESTER FLEDGLING
NESTLE JUG LAP LIE PET NEST
SNUG NICHE SPOON BURROW
CUDDLE FIDGET NUZZLE PETTLE
SETTLE SNUDGE CHERISH
SHELTER SNUGGLE SNUZZLE
NESTLING BABY BIRD EYAS NEST
POULT SQUAB CUDDLE RETREAT
BIRDLING NIDULATE FLEDGLING
**NEST OF GENTLEFOLK (AUTHOR
OF —)** TURGENEV
(CHARACTER IN —) LIZA FYODOR
PANSHIN VARVARA KALITINE
PAVLOVNA LAVRETSKY
NESTOR SAGE SOLON LEADER

ADVISER ADVISOR COUNSELOR
PATRIARCH
(FATHER OF —) NELEUS
(MOTHER OF —) CHLORIS
(SON OF —) ANTILOCHUS
(WIFE OF —) ANAXIBIA EURYDICE
NESTORIAN WISE
NET BAG GIN HAY LAM POT WEB
CAUL FIKE FLAN FLEW FLUE FYKE
GAIN HAAF KELL LACE LAUN
LAWN LEAD LEAP MESH MOKE
NEAT PURE RETE SALE SEAN TOIL
TRAP TRIM WEIR BRAIL CATCH
CLEAN CLEAR DRIFT GAUZE LACIS
PITCH POUND SCOOP SEIZE
SNARE SNOOD TRAWL TRINK
TULLE YIELD BAGNET BASKET
BRIGHT COBWEB ENTRAP FABRIC
GROUND LEADER MALINE MASILE
PANTER PROFIT RAFFLE SAGENE
SAPIAO TOWNET TUNNEL
DRAGNET ENSNARE FLYTAIL
LAMPARA MALINES NETWORK
PROTECT RETICLE RINSING
SCRINGE SHELTER SPILLER
STALKER TRAINEL TRAMMEL
MESHWORK SALAMBAO
BUCKSTALL RETICULUM
(PREF.) DICTY(O) DIKTYO(N) RETI
RETINO
NETHANEEL (BROTHER OF —)
DAVID
(FATHER OF —) ZUAR JESSE
OBEDEDOM
(SON OF —) SHEMAIAH
NETHANIAH (FATHER OF —) ASAPH
ELISHAMA
(SON OF —) JEHUDI ISHMAEL
NETHER DOWN BELOW LOWER
UNDER NEDDER DOWNWARD
INFERIOR INFERNAL

ZWOLLE HAARLEM TILBURG UTRECHT AALSMEER ENSCHEDE NIJMEGEN AMSTERDAM EINDHOVEN GRONINGEN ROTTERDAM
WEIGHT: ONS LAST LOOD POND BAHAR GREIN KORREL WICHTJE ESTERLIN

NETHERWORLD HADES SHADES
NETLIKE MESHY NETTY RETIARY RETICULAR
NETTING BAR CAUL LING MESH SCREEN DEEPING FISHNET FOOTING BOBBINET WIREWORK
NETTLE VEX FRET LINE ANNOY CNIDA ETTLE PEEVE PIQUE STING HENBIT ORTIGA RUFFLE SPLICE URTICA AFFRONT BLUBBER BLUETOP KNITTLE PROVOKE STINGER IRRITATE CLOWNHEAL GLIDEWORT PELLITORY SMARTWEED
(— RASH) HIVES UREDO URTICARIA
(— TREE) LOTUS GYMPIE
(WHITE DEAD —) ARCHANGEL
(PREF.) CNID(O)
NETWORK WEB CAUL FRET GRID KELL MAZE MESH MOKE RETE CHAIN LACIS BRIDGE COBWEB CRADLE PLEXUS RESEAU SAGENE SYSTEM DRAGNET DIPLEXER GRIDIRON KNITTING WATTLING RETICULUM
(— OF BLOOD VESSELS) TOMENTUM
(— OF CRACKS) CRACKLE
(— ON MAP) GRATICULE
(NUCLEAR —) SKEIN
(PL.) RETIA
NEUME PES VIRGA CLIVIS PNEUMA PODATUS PUNCTUM VIRGULA CLIMACUS QUILISMA SEQUENCE TORCULUS SCANDICUS
NEURAL DORSAL NERVAL NEURIC
NEURALGIA SCIATICA COSTALGIA
NEURILEMMA
(PREF.) LEMMO
NEURITE AXON AXONE
NEUROGLIAL
(PREF.) GLI(O)
NEUROLOGIST AMERICAN BEARD DERCUM PRINCE COLLINS CORNING
AUSTRIAN FREUD
ENGLISH ASH GOWERS
FRENCH RAYMOND DEJERINE
GERMAN NISSL GUDDEN MOBIUS
PORTUGUESE MONIZ
NEUROTIC DRUG NERVOUS
(— CONDITION) LATAH
NEUTRAL GRAY INERT SWEET AMORAL MIDDLING NEGATIVE UNBIASED COLORLESS IMPARTIAL
(— IN COLOR) SOBER
(OPTICALLY —) INACTIVE
NEUTRALIZE KILL ANNUL BLUNT ERASE CANCEL ABOLISH BALANCE CORRECT DESTROY NULLIFY VITIATE NEGATIVE OVERRIDE SATURATE FRUSTRATE
NEUTRINO LEPTON

NEVADA
CAPITAL: CARSONCITY
COUNTY: NYE ELKO LANDER STOREY WASHOE MINERAL PERSHING
INDIAN: WASHO PAIUTE
LAKE: MUD MEAD RUBY TAHOE WALKER PYRAMID WINNEMUCCA
PEAK: BOUNDARY
RIVER: REESE TRUCKEE HUMBOLDT
STATE BIRD: BLUEBIRD
STATE FLOWER: SAGEBRUSH
STATE NICKNAME: SILVER SAGEBRUSH
STATE TREE: ASPEN
TOWN: ELY ELKO RENO EUREKA FALLON NELLIS PIOCHE SPARKS TONOPAH LASVEGAS LOVELOCK

NEVE ICE FIRN SNOW NEPHEW GLACIER
NEVER NAY NIE NOT NARY NARRA NIVER NOWHEN
NEVER-NEVER DREAMLAND
NEVERTHELESS BUT YET STILL ALWISE THOUGH ALGATES HOWBEIT HOWEVER WHETHER NATHELESS NONETHELESS
NEVUS MOLE SPOT TUMOR NAEVUS SPIDER SPILUS FRECKLE LENTIGO SPILOMA BIRTHMARK
NEW NEO NEU RAW LATE NOVA FRESH GREEN MOIST NOVEL YOUNG MODERN RECENT UNUSED VIRGIN ANOTHER FOREIGN STRANGE UNTRIED UPSTART INITIATE NEOTERIC ORIGINAL YOUTHFUL BEGINNING
(— BUT YET OLD) NOVANTIQUE
(BRAND —) SPICK
(COMB. FORM) NEO
(PREF.) CAEN(O) CEN(O) NE(O) NOV(I)(O)
(SUFF.) CENE
NEWBORN YEANLING
NEW BRUNSWICK (CAPITAL OF —) FREDERICTON
(COUNTY OF —) KINGS QUEENS SUNBURY MADAWASKA
(MOUNTAIN OF —) CARLETON
(TOWN OF —) BURTON MONCTON BATHURST GAGETOWN
NEW CALEDONIA (— BIRD) KAGU
(CAPITAL OF —) NOUMEA
(ISLAND OF —) HUON BELEP DEPINS LOYALTY WALPOLE
(SEAPORT OF —) NOUMEA
NEWCASTLE GOTHAM
NEWCOMER CADET SETTLER COMELING FRESHMAN JACKEROO MALIHINI RINGNECK GREENHORN IMMIGRANT KIMBERLIN
NEWCOMES (AUTHOR OF —) THACKERAY
(CHARACTER IN —) ANN KEW JOHN BRIAN CLARA CLIVE ETHEL JAMES ROSEY ALFRED BARNES BINNIE HOBSON RIDLEY THOMAS NEWCOME PULLEYN FARINTOSH MACKENZIE

NEW DEAL (— AGENCY) CCC NRA NYA TVA
NEWEL POST VICE SPINDLE
NEW ENGLAND (— INHABITANT) YANK YANKEE JONATHAN
(— SETTLER) PILGRIM PURITAN
NEWFOUNDLAND (— CAPE) RAY RACE BAULD
(— HOUSE) TILT
(— INHABITANT) OUTPORTER
(CAPITAL OF —) STJOHNS
(ISLAND OF —) BELL FOGO GROAIS MIQUELON
(RIVER OF —) GANDER HUMBER EXPLOITS
(TOWN OF —) GANDER HOWLEY WABANA CORNERBROOK

NEW GUINEA
BAY: ORO MILNE HOLNICOTE GOODENOUGH COLLINGWOOD
CAPITAL: PORTMORESBY
GULF: HUON PAPUA
ISLAND: BUKA MANUS MUSSAU
ISLAND GROUP: CRETIN NINIGO SAINSON SOLOMON
MOUNTAIN: ALBERT VICTORIA
NATIVE: ARAU BOONG KARON PAPUAN
PORT: LAE DARU WEWAK MADANG
RIVER: FLY HAMU SEPIK KIKORI PURARI AMBERNO
TOWN: LAE WAU DARU SORON AITAPE KIKORI RABAUL SAMARAI

NEW HAMPSHIRE
CAPITAL: CONCORD
COLLEGE: DARTMOUTH
COUNTY: COOS BELKNAP GRAFTON MERRIMACK
LAKE: SQUAM OSSIPEE SUNAPEE UMBAGOG WINNIPESAUKEE
MOUNTAIN: MORIAH PAUGUS WAUMBEK CHOCORUA MONADNOCK
MOUNTAIN RANGE: WHITE
NOTCH: CRAWFORD FRANCONIA
PRESIDENT: PIERCE
RIVER: SACO ISRAEL BELLAMY SOUHEGAN MERRIMACK PISCATAQUA
STATE NICKNAME: GRANITE
TOWN: DOVER KEENE EXETER NASHUA HANOVER LACONIA OSSIPEE

NEW HEBRIDES (CAPITAL OF —) VILA
(ISLAND OF —) EPI TANA EFATE MAEWO MABRIM MALEKULA

NEW JERSEY
CAPITAL: TRENTON
COLLEGE: UPSALA
COUNTY: ESSEX OCEAN SALEM UNION BERGEN CAMDEN MERCER MORRIS SUSSEX WARREN PASSAIC MONMOUTH
INDIAN: DELAWARE
PRESIDENT: CLEVELAND

RIVER: DENNIS HAYNES MANTUA RAMAPO MULLICA PASSAIC RARITAN COHANSEY TUCKAHOE
STATE BIRD: GOLDFINCH
STATE FLOWER: VIOLET
STATE NICKNAME: GARDEN
STATE TREE: REDOAK
TOWN: LODI SALEM CAMDEN NEWARK NEWTON NUTLEY RAHWAY TOTOWA BAYONNE CLIFTON HOBOKEN HOHOKUS MATAWAN NETCONG ORADELL PARAMUS PASSAIC TEANECK TENAFLY TRENTON WYCKOFF CARTERET FREEHOLD METUCHEN PATERSON SECAUCUS WATCHUNG HACKENSACK
UNIVERSITY: RUTGERS PRINCETON

NEWLY ANEW AGAIN AFRESH LATELY FRESHLY NEWLINS RECENTLY
NEWMARKET MICHIGAN SARATOGA GRABOUCHE

NEW MEXICO
CAPITAL: SANTAFE
COUNTY: LEA EDDY LUNA MORA QUAY TAOS OTERO CATRON CHAVES DEBACA HIDALGO SOCORRO VALENCIA
CULTURE: MIMBRES
INDIAN: SIA TANO TEWA TIWA ZUNI JEMEZ PECOS APACHE NAVAHO NAVAJO PUEBLO
MOUNTAIN: WHEELER
RIVER: UTE GILA PECOS SANJOSE
STATE BIRD: ROADRUNNER
STATE FLOWER: YUCCA
STATE NICKNAME: SUNSHINE LANDOFENCHANTMENT
STATE TREE: PINON PINYON
TOWN: JAL MORA AZTEC BELEN RATON CLOVIS DEMING GALLUP GRANTS ARTESIA SANTAFE SOCORRO CARLSBAD LASVEGAS TUCUMCARI ALAMOGORDO

NEWNESS NOVITY
NEWS BUZZ DOPE UNCA UNKO WORD CLASH FERLY ADVICE BUDGET CRACKS FERLIE GOSPEL NOTICE REPORT EVANGEL KHUBBER TIDINGS WITTING NOUVELLE KNOWLEDGE SPEERINGS
(— AGENCY) AP UP DNB INS UPI TASS ANETA DOMEI REUTERS
(— BEAT) SCOOP
NEWSBOY NEWSY CAMELOT CARRIER PAPERBOY
NEWSCASTER ANCHORMAN
NEWSMONGER GOSSIP TATTLER NOVELANT NOVELIST QUIDNUNC REPORTER
NEWSPAPER RAG NEWS DAILY ORGAN PAPER PRESS SHEET TIMES ARRIBA HERALD SERIAL SUNDAY COURANT DIURNAL GAZETTE JOURNAL MERCURY TABLOID TRIBUNE NEWSPRINT

(— USED BY PICKPOCKET) STIFF
(PL.) PRESS
NEWSPAPERMAN PRESSMAN
NEWSSTAND BOOTH KIOSK STALL
STAND BOOKSTALL
NEWSWORTHY NEWSY
NEWT ASK EFT ESK EVET EBBET
EFFET LIZARD TRITON AXOLOTL
CRAWLER CREEPER REPTILE
MANKEEPER
NEW YEAR'S DAY NAURUZ
NOROOSE NOWROZE
NEW YEAR'S EVE HAGMENA
HOGMANAY

NEW YORK
AVENUE: PARK FIFTH MADISON
FLATBUSH
BAY: JAMAICA PECONIC
MORICHES
BOROUGH: BRONX KINGS QUEENS
BROOKLYN MANHATTAN
BUILDING: RCA PANAM CHRYSLER
FLATIRON
CANAL: ERIE GOWANUS
CAPITAL: ALBANY
COLLEGE: BARD CCNY IONA PACE
FINCH UNION HUNTER VASSAR
WAGNER ADELPHI BARNARD
CANISIUS HAMILTON SKIDMORE
COUNTY: ERIE BRONX ESSEX
KINGS TIOGA WAYNE YATES
BROOME CAYUGA NASSAU
ONEIDA OSWEGO OTSEGO
PUTNAM QUEENS SENECA
ULSTER CHEMUNG GENESEE
NIAGARA STEUBEN SUFFOLK
CHENANGO DUTCHESS
HERKIMER ONONDAGA
RICHMOND ROCKLAND
SARATOGA SCHUYLER
INDIAN: CAYUGA MOHAWK
ONEIDA SENECA MOHICAN
MONTAUK IROQUOIS
ONONDAGA
ISLAND: FIRE LONG ELLIS STATEN
FISHERS LIBERTY SHELTER
GOVERNORS MANHATTAN
LAKE: ERIE CAYUGA GEORGE
ONEIDA OTISCO OTSEGO
OWASCO PLACID SENECA
CONESUS HONEOYE ONTARIO
SARANAC SCHROON SUCCESS
SARATOGA
MOUNTAIN: BEAR MARCY
MOUNTAINS: TACONIC CATSKILL
ADIRONDACK
NICKNAME: EMPIRE GOTHAM
PRESIDENT: FILLMORE VANBUREN
ROOSEVELT
PRISON: TOMBS ATTICA SINGSING
RIVER: TIOGA HARLEM HOOSIC
HUDSON MOHAWK OSWEGO
GENESEE NIAGARA
SQUARE: TIMES UNION HERALD
MADISON
STATE BIRD: BLUEBIRD
STATE FLOWER: ROSE
STATE NICKNAME: EMPIRE
EXCELSIOR
STATE TREE: SUGARMAPLE
STREET: WALL BOWERY
BROADWAY

SUBWAY: BMT IND IRT LEX
TOWN: RYE OVID ROME DELHI
ILION ISLIP NYACK OLEAN
OWEGO UTICA ATTICA AUBURN
CARMEL COHOES ELMIRA
GOSHEN ITHACA MALONE
ONEIDA OSWEGO TAPPAN
WARSAW ARDSLEY BABYLON
BATAVIA BUFFALO CONGERS
ENDWELL GENESEO HEWLETT
MAHOPAC MASSENA MERRICK
MINEOLA MONTAUK ONEONTA
PENNYAN POTSDAM SUFFERN
SYOSSET WANTAGH YAPHANK
YONKERS BETHPAGE CATSKILL
HERKIMER KINGSTON OSSINING
SYRACUSE TUCKAHOE
ROCHESTER
UNIVERSITY: LIU NYU ADELPHI
COLGATE CORNELL FORDHAM
HOFSTRA YESHIVA COLUMBIA
WATERFALL: NIAGARA

NEW YORK CITY (BOROUGH OF —)
BRONX QUEENS BROOKLYN
MANHATTAN STATENISLAND
(COUNTY OF —) BRONX KINGS
QUEENS RICHMOND
(ISLAND OF —) WARD ELLIS
RANDALL WELFARE
(PARK OF —) GRANT BRYANT
BATTERY CENTRAL
(SUBWAY OF —) BMT IND IRT

NEW ZEALAND
BAY: OHUA HAWKE LYALL
AWARUA CLOUDY GOLDEN
FITZROY PEGASUS POVERTY
RANGAUNU
CAPE: EGMONT FAREWELL
PALLISER
CAPITAL: WELLINGTON
GULF: HAURAKI
ISLAND: OTEA STEWART
PUKETUTU
LAKE: OHAU HAWEA TAUPO
PUKAKI PUPUKE TEANAU
TEKAPO WANAKA BRUNNER
ROTORUA WAKATIPU
MOUNTAIN: COOK FLAT OWEN
CHOPE LYALL MITRE OTARI
EGMONT STOKES AORANGI
PIHANGA TUTAMOE TYNDALL
ASPIRING EARNSLAW
NATIVE: ATI ARAWA MAORI
RINGATU
PENINSULA: MAHIA OTAGO
RIVER: MOKAU ORETI WAIPA
CLUTHA TAIERI TAMAKI
WAIHOU WAIROA MATAURA
WAIKATO WAITAKI CLARENCE
MANAWATU WANGANUI
RANGITIKEI
STRAIT: COOK FOVEAUX
TOWN: LEUIN ORETI OTAKI TAUPO
CLUTHA FOXTON NAPIER
NELSON OAMARU PICTON
TIMARU DUNEDIN MANUKAU
RAETIHI ROTORUA AUCKLAND
HAMILTON KAWAKAWA
CHRISTCHURCH
VOLCANO: RUAPEHU NGAURUHOE
TONGARIRO

WATERFALL: BOWEN HELENA
STIRLING SUTHERLAND

NEXT POI NEAR SYNE THEN UNTO
WISE AFTER EWEST FIRST LATER
NEIST RIGHT BESIDE COMING
SECOND TIDDER TOTHER
CLOSEST NEAREST DIRECTLY
PROCHAIN PROCHEIN ADJOINING
IMMEDIATE
(— AFTER) THEN FOLLOWING
(— IN ORDER) EKA
(— MONTH) PROXIMO
(— OF KIN) GOEL
(— TO LAST) PENULT
(PREF.) (— IN ORDER) EKA
NEXUS TIE BOND LINK CHAIN
NGAIO KIO KAIO NAIO TREE
NHANG GIAI
NIAM-NIAM ZANDE AZANDE
AZANDI ZANDEH AZANDEH
BABUNGERA
NIB NEB PEN BEAK BILL KINK TEAT
POINT PRONG SCORER
NIBBLE EAT NAB NIB NIP BITE
GNAW KNAB KNAP MOOP MOUP
NOSH PECK PICK CHAMP GNARL
MOUSE PIECE SHEAR ARRODE
BROWSE CHAVEL NATTLE PICKLE
PILFER CHIMBLE GNABBLE
GNATTER KNABBLE SNAGGLE
NIBELUNGENLIED (AUTHOR OF —)
UNKNOWN
(CHARACTER IN —) UTA ETZEL
HAGEN IRING GERNOT HUNOLD
LUDGER BLOEDEL GUNTHER
ORTLIEB BRUNHILD DANKWART
DIETRICH GISELHER KRIEMHILD
SIEGFRIED HILDEBRAND
NIBLICK BLASTER
NICANOR (WIFE OF —) CLEOPATRA

NICARAGUA
CAPITAL: MANAGUA
COIN: PESO CENTAVO CORDOBA
DEPARTMENT: LEON BOACO RIVAS
CARAZO ESTELI MADRIZ
MASAYA ZELAYA MANAGUA
ISLAND: OMETEPE
LAKE: MANAGUA
MEASURE: VARA CAHIZ MILLA
SUERTE TERCIA CAJUELA
ESTADAL MANZANA
MOUNTAIN: MADERA MOGOTON
PORT: CORINTO
RIVER: COCO TUMA WANKS
GRANDE ESCONDIDO
TOWN: LEON BOACO RIVAS
MASAYA OCOTAL SOMOTO
GRANADA MANAGUA JINOTEGA
MATAGALPA CHINANDEGA
WEIGHT: BAG CAJA TONELADA

NICCOLITE ARITE KUPFERNICKEL
NICE APT FIT FEAT FINE GOOD
JUMP KIND NEAT NYCE PURE
TRIM CANNY EXACT FUSSY NIECE
SWEET BONITA BONITO DAINTY
GENTIL MINUTE PEACHY QUAINT
QUEASY SPICED STRICT SUBTLE
TICKLE CORRECT ELEGANT
FINICAL GENTEEL MINCING
PERJINK PICKING PRECISE

PRUDISH REFINED DECOROUS
DELICATE EXACTING PLEASANT
PLEASING TICKLISH PARTICULAR
SCRUMPTIOUS
(TOO —) SUPERFINE
(PREF.) (PERTAINING TO —)
NICENO
NICELY JUMP
NICETY HAIR DELICACY JUSTNESS
CRITICISM CURIOSITY PRECISION
(PL.) PERJINKITIES
NICHE BAY WRO APSE CANT COVE
NOOK SLOT AMBRY HERNE HOVEL
NIECE NITCH PLACE ALCOVE
ANCONA BOXING COVERT
CRANNY EXEDRA GROOVE
MIHRAB RECESS RINCON EDICULE
HOUSING RETREAT ROUNDEL
AEDICULA CREDENCE TOKONOMA
HABITACLE TABERNACLE
NICHOLAS NICKLEBY (AUTHOR OF
—) DICKENS
(CHARACTER IN —) BRAY HAWK
KATE FRANK GRIDE NOGGS
RALPH SMIKE NEWMAN SQUEERS
VINCENT CRUMMLES MADELINE
MULBERRY NICHOLAS NICKLEBY
WACKFORD CHEERYBLE
MANTALINI
NICIPPE (FATHER OF —) PELOPS
(HUSBAND OF —) STHENELUS
(MOTHER OF —) HIPPODAMIA
(SON OF —) EURYSTHEUS
NICK CUT JAG MAR NAG NOB CHIP
DENT DINT HACK NACK SLAP SLIT
CHEAT CHICK GOUGE NITCH
NOTCH PRICK SCORE SLACK
SNICK TALLY TRICK ARREST
RECORD DEFRAUD
(— OF TIME) GODSPEED
NICKEL JIT COIN JITNEY NIMBUS
(ALLOY OF —) INVAR KONEL
MONEL
(CONTAINING —) NICCOLIC
(SYMBOL OF —) NI
NICKELODEON JUKEBOX
NICKER NEIGHER
NICKNAME DUB DOEG NICK ALIAS
AGNAME BYWORD HANDLE
MONICA TONAME CRACKER
EKENAME MISNAME MONIKER
NICKERY COGNOMEN MONARCHO
MONICKER TARTUFFE SOBRIQUET
NICKNAMING PROSONOMASIA
NICOMEDE (HALF-BROTHER OF —)
ATTALE
(STEPMOTHER OF —) ARSINOE
NICOSTRATA (FATHER OF —)
LADON
(HUSBAND OF —) ECHENUS
(SON OF —) EVANDER
NICOSTRATUS (BROTHER OF —)
MEGAPENTHES
(FATHER OF —) MENELAUS
(MOTHER OF —) HELEN
NICOTINIC ACID NIACIN
NICTATE WINK BLINK CLOSE
TWINK TWINKLE NICTITATE
NIDDICK NAPE
NIDE NID NEST BROOD LITTER
NIDGE NIG SHAKE QUIVER
NIDGET HOE FOOL IDIOT
NIDOR ODOR AROMA SAVOR

SCENT SMELL
NIECE OY OYE NEPHEW
NIELLO TULA
NIEPA NIOTA KARINGHOTA
NIEVE FIST HAND NEIF SERF NATIVE
NIFTY FINE GOOD KEEN SMART STYLISH
NIGER JOLIBA KWORRA RAMTIL
(CAPITAL OF —) NIAMEY
(MOUTH OF —) NUN
(NATIVE OF —) PEUL HAUSA DJERMA FULANI SONGHA TOUBOU TUAREG
(OASIS IN —) KAOUAR
(REGION OF —) AIR
(RIVER OF —) DILLIA
(TOWN OF —) SAY GAYA TERA BAGAM FACHI GOURE MADAMA MARADI TAHOUA ZINDER

NIGERIA
CAPITAL: LAGOS
COIN: KOBO NAIRA
NATIVE: ARO EBO EDO IBO IJO VAI BENI EBOE EFIK EJAM EKOI NUPE BENIN HAUSA FULANI YORUBA
PLATEAU: JOS
PORT: LAGOS CALABAR
PROVINCE: ISA OYO KANO NUPE ONDO IJEBU OGOJA WARRI OWERRI ADAMAWA
RIVER: OLI GANA YOBE BENUE NIGER KADUNA SOKOTO GONGOLA HADEJIA KOMADUGU
STATE: IMO OYO KANO OGUN ONDO BENUE BORNO KWARA LAGOS BAUCHI SOKOTO ANAMBRA GONGOLA
TOWN: ABA ADO EDE ISA IWO JOS BIDI BUEA KANO OFFA YOLA AKURE ENUGU IKEJA LAGOS MINNA ZARIA BAUCHI IBADAN ILESHA ILORIN KADUNA MUSHIN OWERRI TAKOBA CALABAR ONITSHA OSHOGBO ABEOKUTA
TREE: AFARA

NIGGARD CARL CHURL CLOSE MISER NIGON PIKER SCART TIGHT NIGGER SCRIMP SCRUNT STINGY CHINCHE DRYFIST NITHING PUCKFIST SCRIMPER EARTHWORM PINCHBECK PINCHFIST PUCKFOIST SKINFLINT
NIGGARDLY MEAN CLOSE STINT NARROW NIGHLY SCANTY SCREWY SKIMPY SORDID STINGY STRAIT CHINCHE MISERLY PARSIMONIOUS
NIGGERFISH CONY HIND CONEY GROUPER GUATIVERE
NIGGLING PETTY PICAYUNE
NIGH AT NEAR ANEAR ANIGH CLOSE ALMOST NEARLY ADJACENT
NIGHT PM EVE DARK NUIT DARKY DEATH NACHT NOCHE SLEEP DARKMANS DARKNESS
(— AND DAY) NYCHTHEMERON
(CHILDREN OF —) ERINYS

FURIES ERINNYES
(COMB. FORM) NYCTI
(DEPTH OF —) HOLL
(GODDESS OF —) NOX NYX
(LAST —) YESTREEN
(NORSE —) NATT NOTT
(PERT. TO —) NOCTURNAL
(STAY OUT ALL —) PERNOCTATE
(PREF.) NOCT(I)(O) NYCT(I)(O)
NIGHT APE DURUKULI
NIGHT BELL (CHARACTER IN —) ENRICO SERAFINA PISTACCHIO
(COMPOSER OF —) DONIZETTI
NIGHT BLINDNESS NYCTALOPIA
NIGHTCAP HOW COWL DOWD HOUVE PIRNY BIGGIN PIRNIE DORMEUSE SUNDOWNER
NIGHTCLUB CAFE CLUB SPOT AGOGO BOITE BISTRO NITERY CABARET DANCERY NIGHTERY
NIGHTDRESS SLOP WILYCOAT WYLIECOAT
NIGHTFALL EEN EVE DARK DUSK EVEN SHUTTING TWILIGHT
(OCCURRING AT —) ACRONICAL
NIGHTGOWN SLOP TOOSH NIGHTY BEDGOWN NIGHTIE WYLIECOAT
NIGHTHAWK PISK CUIEJO BULLBAT
NIGHTINGALE JUG BULBUL FLORENCE PHILOMEL ROSSIGNOL
(— SOUND) JUG
(SWEDISH —) LIND JENNY
(PL.) WATCH
NIGHTJAR PUCK POTOO EVEJAR DERHAWK SPINNER WHEELER MOREPORK POORWILL NIGHTHAWK
NIGHT LAMP VEILLEUSE
NIGHTMARE ALP HAG MARA MESS DREAM FANCY FIEND VISION INCUBUS CACODEMON CAUCHEMAR EPHIALTES
(— CAUSER) MARE
NIGHTMARE ABBEY (AUTHOR OF —) PEACOCK
(CHARACTER IN —) EMILY FATOUT FLOSKY GLOWRY STELLA TOOBAD CELINDA CYPRESS ASTERIAS LISTLESS SCYTHROP GIROUETTE MARIONETTA CHRISTOPHER
NIGHTSHADE HERB DWALE MOREL HENBANE MORELLE PETUNIA SANDBUR SOLANUM TROMPILLO
NIGHT'S LODGING (AUTHOR OF —) GORKY
(CHARACTER IN —) LUKA BARON PEPEL SAHTIN BUBNOFF NATASHA ALYOSCHKA KVASCHNYA KOSTILIOFF WASSILISSA
NIHIL NIL NICHIL NOTHING
NIHILIST ANARCHIST SOCIALIST
NIKE (BROTHER OF —) BIA ZELUS CRATOS
(FATHER OF —) PALLAS
(MOTHER OF —) STYX
NIL ZERO NILGAI IPOMOEA NOTHING

NILE
ARABIC NAME: ALBAHR

AS GOD: HAPI
BIRD: IBIS WRYNECK
BOAT: BARIS CANGIA NUGGAR DAHABEAH
CAPTAIN: RAIS REIS
DAM: ASWAN
FALLS: RIPON
FISH: BAGRE SAIDE BICHIB DOCMAC MORMYRID MORMYROID
ISLAND: RODA PHILAE
LATIN NAME: NILUS
NATIVE: MADI NILOT
NEGRO: JUR LUO LWO SUK
PLANT: SUDD LOTUS
REGION: NUBIA
SOURCE: TSANA
TOWN: QUS ABRI ARGO IDFU ISNA QINA ASYUT CAIRO REJAF SAITE ROSETTA
TRIBUTARY: ATBARA KAGERA
VALLEY DEPRESSION: KORE

NILE GREEN BOA
NILGAI NIL NYLGAU ANTELOPE NEELGHAU
NIMBLE FLY DEFT FLIP FLIT GLEG LISH SPRY SWAK YALD YARE AGILE BRISK FLEET LIGHT NIPPY QUICK SWACK TRICK WIGHT YAULD ACTIVE ADROIT CLEVER FEIRIE LIMBER LISSOM LIVELY PROMPT QUIVER SPRACK SUPPLE VOLANT WANDLE DELIVER LISSOME SWIPPER FLIPPANT TRIPPING CITIGRADE SENSITIVE SPRIGHTLY
(PREF.) PRESTI
NIMBLENESS HASTE AGILITY SLEIGHT LEGERITY DEXTERITY LIGHTNESS
NIMBLE-WITTED VOLABLE
NIMBUS AURA HALO NIMB CLOUD GLORY SHINE VAPOR GLORIA AUREOLA AUREOLE
NIMIETY EXCESS
NINAZU (BROTHER OF —) NERGAL
(FATHER OF —) ENLIL
(MOTHER OF —) NINLIL
NINCOMPOOP ASS DOLT FOOL POOP NINNY NINCOM WITLING BLOCKHEAD SIMPLETON
NINE IX NIE NYE TEAM COMET POTHOOK
(— A.M.) UNDERN MIDMORN
(— ANGLED FIGURE) NONAGON
(— DAYS DEVOTION) NOVENA
(— FOLD) NONUPLE
(— HEADED MONSTER) HYDRA
(— HUNDRED) SAN
(— INCHES) SPAN
(— OF CLUBS OR DIAMONDS) COMET
(— OF DIAMONDS) BRAGGER
(— OF TRUMPS) DIX MENEL SANCHO
(— YEAR CYCLE) JUGLAR
(GROUP OF —) ENNEAD
(MUSIC FOR —) NONET
(PREF.) ENNE(A) NON(A) NOVEM NOVEN
NINEBARK ROSACEAN SEVENBARK
NINEHOLES BUMBLEPUPPY

NINEPIN KAIL SQUAIL SKITTLE SKITTLES
(PL.) BOWLS KEELS KAYLES NINEPEGS
NINETEENTH LARIGOT
NINETIETH NONAGESIMAL
NINETY KOPPA
NINEVEH (FOUNDER OF —) NINUS
NINE WORLDS HEL ASGARD ALFHEIM MIDGARD NIFLHEIM VANAHEIM JOTUNNHEIM MUSPELLSHEIM SVARTALFAHEIM
NINLIL (HUSBAND OF —) ENLIL
(SON OF —) NERGAL NINAZU
NINNI ISHTAR
NINNY DOLT FOOL LOUT DUNCE IDIOT NONNY PATCH SAMMY SPOON FONDLE NOODLE SAPHEAD FONDLING BLOCKHEAD NIDDICOCK PEAKGOOSE SIMPLETON
NINON SHEER
NINSUN (SON OF —) GILGAMESH
NINTH (EVERY —) NONAN ENNEATIC
(PREF.) NON(A)
(SUFF.) NON(A)
NINTU (DAUGHTER OF —) UTTU
(HUSBAND OF —) ENKI
(SON OF —) NINSAR
NINURTA (FATHER OF —) ENLIL
NINUS (FATHER OF —) BELUS
(SON OF —) NINYAS
(WIFE OF —) SEMIRAMIS
NIOBATE TODDITE SIPYLITE COLUMBATE
NIOBE HERB HOSTA FUNKIA
(BROTHER OF —) PELOPS
(FATHER OF —) TANTALUS
(HUSBAND OF —) AMPHION
(SISTER-IN-LAW OF —) AEDON
NIOBIC COLUMBIC
NIOBIUM COLUMBIUM
NIP CUT SIP VEX BITE BUMP CLIP DRAM GIVE KNIP NIPE PECK SNUB TANG TAUT TUCK BLAST CHEAT CHECK CHILL CLAMP DRAFT FROST PINCH SEIZE SEVER SNAPE SNEAP THIEF BENUMB BLIGHT CATNIP TIPPLE TWITCH WITHER SARCASM SQUEEZE WETTING COMPRESS FROSTBITE VELLICATE
NIPA PALM ATAP ATTAP DRINK
NIPPER BOY LAD CLAW CRAB GRAB HAND BITER CHELA MISER THIEF CUNNER URCHIN GRIPPER INCISOR BRAKEMAN
NIPPERS DOG NIP BITS NIPS TONGS GRATER PLIERS TURKIS FORCEPS PINCERS OSTEOTOME
NIPPLE BUD DUG PAP TIT BEAN TEAT DIDDY DUMMY SPEAN NIBBLE PILLAR MAMILLA PAPILLA THELIUM
(— POINT) THELION
(PREF.) EPITHELI(O) MAMM(I)(ILLI) MAST(O) PAPILLI PAPILLO THEL(O)
NIPPLEWORT BALLOGAN WARTWEED WARTWORT
NIPPY BOLD SHARP
NIREUS (FATHER OF —) CHAROPUS
(MOTHER OF —) AGLAIA

(SLAYER OF —) EURYPYLUS
NIRVANA EMPTINESS
NIS NIX NISSE GOBLIN KOBOLD
  BROWNIE
NISAN ABIB
NISUS POWER EFFORT IMPULSE
  ENDEAVOR
  (DAUGHTER OF —) SCYLLA
  (FATHER OF —) PANDION
  HYRTACUS
  (MOTHER OF —) IDA
NITER NITRE PETER PETRE POTASH
  SALTPETER
NITHER BLAST DEBASE SHIVER
  TREMBLE
NITID GAY BRIGHT GLOSSY SPRUCE
  SHINING LUSTROUS NITIDOUS
NITO AGSAM
NITON RADON
NITRATE SALT ESTER COTTON
  AZOTATE
  (PREF.) NITR(O)
NITRIC AZOTIC
NITRIDE BORAZON
NITRITE AZOTITE
NITROGEN GAS AZOTE ALKALIGEN
  (PREF.) AZ(O)
NITROGLYCERIN TNT SOUP NITRO
  SIRUP SYRUP GLONOIN GLONOINE
NITWIT DAW NIT DOLT DOPE
  DRONGO DIZZARD SIMPLETON
NIX NO HARD NECK NICKER
  NOBODY SPIRIT SPRITE UNDINE
  NOTHING
NJAVE ADJAB DIAVE
NJORD (DAUGHTER OF —) FREYA
  (SON OF —) FREY
  (WIFE OF —) SKADHI
NO NA NE NAE NAH NAW NAY NIT
  NIX NUL BAAL BALE NONE
  NYET NAPOO AIKONA NAPOOH
  NOGAKU
  (— ONE) NIX NEMO
  (— POINTS IN TENNIS) LOVE
  (PREF.) NULLI
NOADIAH (FATHER OF —) BINNUI
NOAH NOE
  (DOVE OF —) COLUMBA
  (FATHER OF —) LAMECH
  ZELOPHEHAD
  (GRANDFATHER OF —)
  METHUSALEH
  (GRANDSON OF —) ARAM
  (GREAT-GRANDSON OF —) HUL
  (MEXICAN —) COXCOX
  (RAVEN OF —) CORVUS
  (SON OF —) HAM SEM SHEM
  JAPHETH
  (WINE CUP OF —) CRATER
NOB NAB BLOW HEAD NAVE
  KNAVE SWELL HANDLE
  TIPTOPPER
NOBEL PRIZE (— IN CHEMISTRY)
  BERG HAHN HOFF KUHN TODD
  UREY ALDER ASTON BOSCH
  CURIE DEBYE DIELS EIGEN FLORY
  FUKUI HABER LIBBY NATTA
  PREGL SODDY SYNGE TAUBE
  CALVIN HARDEN HASSEL KARRER
  LELOIR NERNST PERUTZ PRELOG
  RAMSAY SANGER SUMNER
  WERNER WITTIG BERGIUS
  BUCHNER GIAUQUE GILBERT

KENDREW MOISSAN NORRISH
ONSAGER OSTWALD RUZICKA
SEABORG SEMENOV WALLACH
WIELAND WINDAUS LANGMUIR
MULLIKEN TISELIUS
(— IN ECONOMICS) ARROW KLEIN
OHLIN SIMON TOBIN DEBREU
FRISCH MYRDAL KUZNETS
SCHULTZ STIGLER FRIEDMAN
LEONTIEF
(— IN LITERATURE) BOLL BUCK
GIDE MANN SHAW AGNON BUNIN
CAMUS ELIOT HESSE HEYSE
LEWIS PERSE SACHS YEATS
ANDRIC BELLOW ELYTIS EUCKEN
FRANCE MILOSZ NERUDA ONEILL
SARTRE SINGER TAGORE BECKETT
CENETTI GOLDING KIPLING
LAXNESS MAURIAC MISTRAL
MONTALE ROLLAND RUSSELL
BJORNSON CARDUCCI FAULKNER
LAGERLOF CHURCHILL
HEMINGWAY PASTERNAK
STEINBECK LAGERKVIST
MAETERLINCK
(— IN MEDICINE) DAM CORI DALE
HESS KATZ KOCH ROSS ROUS
WALD ARBER BLOCH BOVET
BUMET CHAIN CRICK CURIE DOISY
EULER GOLGI HENCH HUBEL
KREBS KROGH LOEWI LURIA
LYNEN MINOT MONIZ MONOD
OCHOA SNELL TATUM YALOW
BARANY BEADLE BEKESY BORDET
CARREL CLAUDE DOMAGK ECCLES
ENDERS FLOREY GASSER GRANIT
HOLLEY HUXLEY KOCHER KOSSEL
LORENZ PALADE PAVLOV RICHET
SPERRY WIESEL AXELROD
BEHRING FIBIGER HERSHEY
HODGKIN KHORANA LAVERAN
NATHANS NICOLLE SCHALLY
THELLER DELBRUCK MCCLINTOCK
(— IN PEACE) ORR THO HULL KING
MOTT PIRE ROOT SATO ASSER
BAJER BALCH BEGIN DAWES
FRIED GOBAT LANGE PASSY
SADAT ADDAMS ANGELL BRANDT
BRIAND BUNCHE BUTLER CASSIN
CREMER DUNANT MONETA
NANSEN QUIDDE WALESA
WILSON BORLAUG BUISSON
JOUHAUX KELLOGG LUTHULI
PAULING RENAULT THERESA
BRANTING CORRIGAN ESQUIVEL
SAKHAROV KISSINGER
ROOSEVELT SODERBLOM
SCHWEITZER HAMMARSKJOLD
(— IN PHYSICS) LEE BOHR BORN
HESS LAMB LAUE MOTT NEEL
RABI RYLE TAMM TING WIEN
YANG BASOV BETHE BLOCH
BOTHE BRAGG BRAUN CURIE
DALEN DIRAC ESAKI FERMI
GABOR HERTZ KUSCH PAULI
SEGRE ALFVEN BARKLA CRONIN
FOWLER GLASER HEWISH
LANDAU PERRIN PLANCK STRUTT
TOWNES WIGNER YUKAWA
BARDEEN GLAEVER GLASHOW
KAPITSA LORENTZ MARCONI
RICHTER EINSTEIN ROENTGEN
CHANDRASEKHAR

NOBILITY RANK ELITE GRACE
  GENTRY STATUS DIGNITY
  KWAZOKU PEERAGE QUALITY
  STATION BARONAGE SZLACHTA
  ELEVATION
  (MEMBER OF TATAR —) MURZA
  (ROMAN —) RAMNES
NOBLE DON ALII DOGE DUKE EARL
  EDEL EPIC FAME FREE GENT
  GOOD GRAF HIGH JARL JUST
  KAMI KUGE LORD PEER PURE
  RIAL ARIKI ATHEL BARON BROAD
  BURLY COUNT DUCAL ERECT
  ETHEL FURST GRAND GREAT
  HIRAM KHASS LOFTY MANLY
  MORAL MURZA PROUD ROYAL
  STATE AUGUST COUSIN DAIMIO
  EPICAL FLAITH GENTLE GESITH
  HAUGHT HEROIC JUNKER KINGLY
  LORDLY LUCUMO MANFUL
  SIRDAR SUPERB THAKUR
  WORTHY YONKER ACERBAS
  CACIQUE GALLANT GLAUCUS
  GLORIED GRANDEE HIDALGO
  LIBERAL MAGNATE MARQUIS
  PATRICK STAROST STATELY
  STEWARD SUBLIME TOISECH
  VOLPONE PANGLIMA PRINCELY
  (MINOR —) VIDAME
NOBLEMAN DUKE EARL EMIR
  LORD PEER SOUL BARON COUNT
  ORLOV PARIS THANE COUSIN
  MILORD ORLOFF THAKUR YONKER
  GRANDEE HIDALGO MAGNATE
  MARQUIS STAROST VOLPONE
  YOUNKER ADELIGER ALDERMAN
  ALMAVIVA BELARIUS MARCHESE
  MARQUESS LANDGRAVE
  MAGNIFICO
NOBLENESS HONOR DIGNITY
  (— OF BIRTH) EUGENY
NOBLEWOMAN LADY MILADY
  DUCHESS PEERESS BARONESS
  COUNTESS
NOBODY NIX NEMO NONE NADIE
  NOMAN SCRUB SCARAB NOTHING
  JACKSTRAW
NOCENT GUILTY HARMFUL
  HURTFUL NOXIOUS CRIMINAL
NOCTURNAL NIGHT NOXIAL
  NIGHTLY NIGHTISH MOONSHINE
  (— ANIMAL) COON POSSUM
  OPOSSUM
  (— BIRD) OWL
  (— CARNIVORE) RATEL
  (— MAMMAL) BAT LEMUR
  (— SIGNS) ZODIAC
NOCTURNE LULLABY UHTSONG
  PAINTING SERENADE
NOD BOB BOW ERR NAP NID NIP
  BECK BEND DOZE NAPE SIGN SLIP
  SWAY WINK DROOP LAPSE
  ASSENT BECKON DODDLE
  DROWSE NODDLE NUTATE
  SALUTE SIGNIFY
NODDING DROWSY NUTANT
  ANNUENT CERNUOUS DROOPING
  NUTATION
NODDLE HEAD PATE BRAIN
NODDY AUK FOOL JACK NOIO
  TERN KNAVE NINNY DROWSY
  FULMAR NOODLE SLEEPY
  HACKNEY TOMNODDY SIMPLETON

NODE BOW BUMP KNOB KNOT
  LUMP PLOT JOINT NODUS POINT
  TUMOR BULBIL NODULE DILEMMA
  GRANULE KNUCKLE FOLLICLE
  PHYTOMER SWELLING TUBERCLE
  (— OF GRASS) KNOT
  (— OF POEM) PLOT
  (— OF STEM) JOINT
NODULE BOB AUGE BUMP KNOT
  LUMP MASS NODE YOLK FLINT
  GEODE PHYMA MILIUM BLISTER
  CATHEAD GRANULE LEPROMA
  NABLOCK SARCOID AMYGDALE
  AMYGDULE COALBALL TUBERCLE
  WHITEHEAD
  (— OF FLINT) CORE
  (CHALCEDONY —) ENHYDROS
  (PL.) BEADING
NOEL XMAS CAROL NOWEL
  NATALIS CHRISTMAS
NOGAH (FATHER OF —) DAVID
NOGGIN ALE CUP MUG NOG PEG
  PIN GILL HEAD PAIL PATE DRINK
  GOGGAN NAGGIN NOODLE
NOHAH (FATHER OF —) BENJAMIN
NOIL FIBER PINION
NOISE (ALSO SEE SOUND) ADO AIR
  BUM DIN GIG HUM POP ROW
  BANG BOOM BRAY BUMP BURR
  CLAM COIL HOOT KLOP MUSH
  PEAL RALE RASH REEL RERD
  ROTE ROUT SLAM ZING ALARM
  BABEL BLARE BLAST BLOOP
  BRAWL BRUIT BURLE CHANG
  CHIRM CLICK DREAM GRASS
  JERRY KNOCK LARRY LARUM
  LEDEN PLASH QUONK REERE
  RERDE RUMOR SLURP SNORE
  SOUND STEER SWISH WHANG
  BICKER CACKLE CLAMOR DUNDER
  GOBBLE GOSSIP HUBBUB NORATE
  OUTCRY PUDDER RACKET
  RANTAN RATTLE REPORT SPLASH
  SQUAWK STEVEN STRIFE TUMULT
  UPROAR BLUSTER BRATTLE
  CLITTER CLUTTER CRACKLE
  ORATION SCANDAL SPATTER
  STREPOR STRIDOR FLICFLAC
  QUONKING TINTAMAR
  CONFUSION
  (EARTHQUAKE —) BRONTIDES
  (ELECTRIC —) GRASS
  (PREF.) **(— OF FALLING OBJECT)**
  KER
NOISELESS QUIET STILL SWEET
  TACIT SILENT APHONIC CATLIKE
NOISEMAKER BELL HORN GRAGER
  RATTLE CLAPPER SQUEAKER
NOISETTE HAZEL HAZELNUT
NOISOME FOUL RANK FETID
  NASTY PUTRID RANCID HARMFUL
  HURTFUL NOXIOUS NUISOME
  STINKING OFFENSIVE
  MALODOROUS
NOISY LOUD CLASHY CREAKY
  BLATANT DINSOME FRANTIC
  MOILING RACKETY RIOTOUS
  ROUTOUS BRAWLING CLATTERY
  SONOROUS STREPENT HILARIOUS
  RATTLEBAG SCAMBLING
  BOISTEROUS
NOLL HEAD NODDLE NOODLE
NOMA CANKER

NOMAD ARAB BEJA LURI MOOR
SAKA SHUA ALANI GYPSY IGDYR
JAREG ROVER SHUWA NOMADE
ROAMER ROVING SEMITE SLUBBI
TUAREG BAZIGAR BEDOUIN
SARACEN SCENITE SHORTZY
SHUKRIA SOLUBBI TOUAREG
KABABISH SCYTHIAN SHINWARI
AMALEKITE MIGRATORY
(— PEOPLE) ALANI
(PL.) AKHLAME
NOMADIC ERRATIC VAGRANT
VAGABOND FOOTLOOSE
ITINERANT
NOMBRIL NAVEL
NOM DE PLUME PENNAME
TELONISM PSEUDONYM
NOME ELIS NOMOS MELODY
NOMARCHY PROVINCE
NOMENCLATURE LIST NAME
TERM ONYMY NAMING GLOSSARY
REGISTER CATALOGUE
NOMINAL PAR BASIC PAPER
FORMAL SLIGHT UNREAL TITULAR
TRIVIAL PLATONIC TRIFLING
(— RECOGNIZANCE) DOE
NOMINATE CALL LEET NAME
ELECT NEVEN SLATE SELECT
APPOINT ENTITLE PRESENT
PROPOSE SPECIFY DESIGNATE
POSTULATE
NOMINY SPEECH RIGMAROLE
NONAGE NEANT INFANCY
MINORITY PUPILAGE
NONAGREEMENT DISSENT
NON-ALCOHOLIC SMALL
NO NAME (AUTHOR OF —) COLLINS
(CHARACTER IN —) NOEL CLARE
FRANK GARTH KIRKE NORAH
ANDREW GEORGE WRAGGE
BARTRAM BYGRAVE LECOUNT
MAGDALEN VANSTONE
NON-ARAB SHANGALLA
NONASPIRATE LENE
NONBELIEVER PAGAN ATHEIST
AGNOSTIC
NONCE NANES NONES NOANCE
PRESENT PURPOSE OCCASION
NONCHALANT COOL GLIB ALOOF
CASUAL JAUNTY CARELESS
DEBONAIR NEGLIGENT
NON-CHRISTIAN PAYNIM INFIDEL
NONCITIZEN TENSOR PEREGRINUS
NONCLERICAL LAY LAIC
NONCOMBUSTIBLE APYROUS
NONCOMMITTAL NEUTRAL
NONCONFORMIST REBEL
NONCON BEATNIK DEVIANT
FANATIC HERETIC SECTARY
BOHEMIAN RECUSANT DISSENTER
(— IN ART) FAUVE
NONCONFORMITY HERESY
ADHARMA DISSENT NEGLECT
REFUSAL RECUSANCE
RECUSANCY
NONCONTINUOUS DISCRETE
NON-CONVERGENCE ABERRATION
NONDISCLOSURE FRAUD
NONDO LOVAGE ANGELICO
NONDUALISM ADVAITA
NONE NO UN NAE NIN NANE NARY
NEEN NONES
(PREF.) NULLI

NONEGO NOTSELF
NONELASTIC BROAD
NONENTITY ZERO AUGHT CIPHER
NOBODY NOUGHT NOTHING
NULLITY NEGATION
NONESSENTIAL CASUAL FRILLY
UNNEEDED EXTRINSIC
(— IN RELIGION) ADIAPHORON
NONESUCH APPLE MODEL
PARAGON PATTERN PARADIGM
MATCHLESS NONPAREIL
UNRIVALED
NON-EXISTENCE ABSENCE
NOTHING
NONEXISTENT NULL NAPOOH
NOUGHT NONBEING BARMECIDE
(PRACTICALLY —) FAT
(PREF.) NULLI
NONFEASANCE BREACH
NON GRATA UNWELCOME
NONGYPSY GAJO
NONINJURY AHIMSA
NON-JEW GOI GOY
NONJUROR USAGER
NON-LATIN SAXON
NONLEGATO DETACHE DETACHED
NON-MOSLEM GENTILE
NONMOTILE
(PREF.) APLANO
NONNASAL ORAL
NONPAREIL BEST POPE TYPE
PARAGON PERFECT SUPREME
UNEQUAL NONESUCH PEERLESS
UNRIVALED
NONPAYMENT DISHONOR
NONPLUS SET FAZE POSE STOP
BLANK FLOOR POSER STICK
STUMP TRUMP BAFFLE GRAVEL
PUZZLE RATTLE CONFUSE
MYSTIFY PERPLEX STAGGER
QUANDARY DULCARNON
EMBARRASS
NONPLUSSED BLANK FOOLISH
NONPOISONOUS EDIBLE
NONPROFESSIONAL BUM LAY
LAIC AMATEUR
NONSENSE BAH GAS GUP PAH
ROT BILK BLAA BLAH BOSH BUFF
BULL BUNK COCK CRAP FLAM
FLUM GAFF GOOK GUFF JIVE
JUNK PISH POOH PUNK TOSH
BALLS BILGE BLASH DROOL FOLLY
FUDGE HAVER HOOEY NERTS
SPOOF STITE STUFF TRASH TRIPE
WAHOO BABBLE BETISE BLAGUE
BUNKUM DRIVEL FADDLE FOLDER
FOOTLE KIBOSH LINSEY NAVERS
PIFFLE RUBBLE SQUISH TRIVIA
BLARNEY BLATHER EYEWASH
FARRAGO INANITY LOCKRAM
RHUBARB RUBBISH TOSHERY
TRIFLES TWADDLE BUNCOMBE
CLAPTRAP COBBLERS DISHWASH
FALDEROL FLIMFLAM FLUMMERY
GALBANUM MACARONI
MOROLOGY PISHPOSH PISHTOSH
SKITTLES SPLUTTER TOMMYROT
TRUMPERY ABSURDITY FRIVOLITY
MOONSHINE POPPYCOCK
SILLINESS BALDERDASH
CODSWALLOP
(— CREATURE) GOOP SHOO SNARK
SHIMOO

NONSENSICAL ABSURD
NONSURFER HODAD
NON-VIOLENCE AHIMSA
NOODLE BEAN FOOL HEAD NIZY
NOLL PATE MOONY NINNY NIZEY
NODDY PASTA PASTE SAMMY
BOODLE GUDDLE NODDLE
NOGGIN DAWCOCK LOKSHEN
NOGHEAD NOUILLE BLOCKHEAD
SIMPLETON CAPERNOITIE
(— DISH) PANSIT RAVIOLI
KREPLACH
(PL.) MEIN FARFEL FERFEL
LASAGNA LASAGNE LOKSHEN
FETTUCINI
NOOK IN BAY OUT WRO CANT
COVE GLEN HERN HOLE NALK
NUCK NUIK ANGLE HALKE HERNE
NEUCK NICHE ALCOVE CANTLE
CORNER CRANNY RECESS
CREVICE NOOKERY RETREAT
NOON M APEX DINE NOWN SEXT
DINNER MIDDAY UNDERN
MIDNOON MERIDIAN
NOONDAY (— REST) NAP SIESTA
MERIDIAN
NOOSE TIE TOW BOND DULL FANK
GIRN HEMP LACE LOOP ROPE
TRAP BIGHT CATCH GRANE HITCH
HONDA KINCH LASSO LATCH
LEASH SNARE SNARL WIDDY
CAUDLE CHOKER CLINCH ENTRAP
HALTER LARIAT SPRING TETHER
TIPPET TWITCH CHOCKER
ENSNARE EXECUTE LANIARD
LANYARD SPRINGE NECKLACE
SQUEEZER TWITCHEL
(— FOR HAULING LOG) CHOKER
CHOCKER
(— FOR SNARING FISH) DULL
(— IN A CORD) KINCH
(HANGMAN'S —) SQUEEZER
NOOTKA AHT AHOUSAHT
MOATCAHT MOOACHAHT
NORATE NOISE RUMOR GOSSIP
NORAX (FATHER OF —) HERMES
MERCURY
(MOTHER OF —) ERYTHEA
NORDIC ARIAN ARYAN
NORI AMANORI
NORITE GABBRO OLIGOSITE
NORM PAR MODE RULE TYPE
CANON GAUGE MODEL NORMA
DHARMA MEDIAN AVERAGE
MODULUS PATTERN STANDARD
TEMPLATE
NORMA MOLD RULE GAUGE
MODEL SQUARE PATTERN
TEMPLET STANDARD TEMPLATE
(CHARACTER IN —) NORMA
ADALGISA POLLIONE
(COMPOSER OF —) BELLINI
NORMAL PAR FULL HOME JUST
MEAN SANE WISE CLEAR ERECT
USUAL FORMAL NATIVE SCHOOL
AVERAGE NATURAL NEUTRAL
REGULAR TYPICAL ORDINARY
STANDARD CUSTOMARY
NORMANDY (BEACH IN —) OMAHA
(CAPITAL OF —) ROUEN
(RIVER IN —) EURE ORNE SEINE
NORN FATE URTH WURD WYRD

NORNA SKULD URDHR URTHR
VERDHANDI VERTHANDI
NORSEL BAND LINE ORSEL FILLET
NOSSEL ORSELLER
NORTH SEPTENTRION
(PREF.) ARCT(O)

NORTH AMERICA
(ALSO SEE SPECIFIC COUNTRIES)
ISLAND: LONG BANKS PARRY
BAFFIN BERMUDA VICTORIA
ANTICOSTI ELLESMERE
NEWFOUNDLAND
LAKE: ERIE HURON NIPIGON
ONTARIO MANITOBA MICHIGAN
REINDEER SUPERIOR WINNIPEG
ATHABASCA NETTILING
MOUNTAIN: WOOD LOGAN WALSH
ROBSON STEELE TOLUCA
LUCANIA PARICUTIN
TAJUMULCO POPOCATEPETL
NATION: CANADA MEXICO
UNITEDSTATES
RIVER: GILA MILK JAMES LIARD
OSAGE PEACE PEARL PECOS
SNAKE YUKON BALSAS BRAZOS
FRASER HUDSON MOBILE
NEOSHO PANUCO PLATTE
POWDER SABINE TANANA
KLAMATH KOYUKUK POTOMAC
SUSITNA CIMARRON COLUMBIA
DELAWARE MISSOURI
NIOBRARA PENOBSCOT
PORCUPINE RIOGRANDE
STLAWRENCE MISSISSIPPI

NORTH CAROLINA
CAPE: FEAR LOOKOUT HATTERAS
CAPITAL: RALEIGH
COLLEGE: ELON CATAWBA
DAVIDSON
COUNTY: ASHE DARE HOKE HYDE
NASH PITT WAKE AVERY DAVIE
GATES ROWAN SURRY BERTIE
BLADEN CRAVEN ONSLOW
YADKIN YANCEY CATAWBA
PAMLICO CURRITUCK
INDIAN: ENO COREE CHERAW
MORATOK PAMLICO
CHOWANOC HATTERAS
MOUNTAIN: HARRIS MITCHELL
PRESIDENT: POLK JOHNSON
RIVER: HAW TAR NEUSE CHOWAN
LUMBER PEEDEE YADKIN
ROANOKE
SOUND: BOGUE CROATAN
PAMLICO
STATE BIRD: CARDINAL
STATE FLOWER: DOGWOOD
STATE NICKNAME: TARHEEL
OLDNORTH TURPENTINE
STATE TREE: PINE
TOWN: BOONE SYLVA BURGAW
DOBSON DURHAM LENOIR
SHELBY SPARTA EDENTON
HICKORY ROXBORO TARBORO
GASTONIA CHARLOTTE
UNIVERSITY: DUKE

NORTH DAKOTA
CAPITAL: BISMARCK

COLLEGE: JAMESTOWN
COUNTY: DUNN EDDY SLOPE STARK WELLS DICKEY DIVIDE GRIGGS KIDDER OLIVER TRAILL PEMBINA ROLETTE
INDIAN: MANDAN ARIKARA HIDATSA
MOUNTAIN: WHITEBUTTE
RIVER: RUSH CEDAR HEART JAMES SOURIS DESLACS SHEYENNE WILDRICE
STATE BIRD: MEADOWLARK
STATE FLOWER: ROSE PRAIRIE
STATE NICKNAME: SIOUX FLICKERTAIL
STATE TREE: ELM
TOWN: MOTT CANDO FARGO MINOT ROLLA AMIDON LAKOTA LINTON MOHALL BOWBELLS NAPOLEON

NORTHERN PIKE ARCTIC BOREAL NORLAND NORTHEN
(— BEAR) POLAR RUSSIA
(— CONSTELLATION) URSA ANDROMEDA

NORTH KOREA
CAPITAL: PYONGYANG
COIN: JUN WON HWAN
PROVINCE: CHAGANG KANGWON TANGGANG
RIVER: NAM YALU IMJIN TUMEN TAEDONG
TOWN: HAEJU HEIJO KEIJO ANDONG ANTUNG HYESAN JUSHIN POCHON SAINNI WONSAN HAMHUNG HUICHON HUNGNAM KAESONG KANGGYE SARIWON SINUIJU CHONGJIN

NORTH STAR STATE MINNESOTA

NORTH VIETNAM
CAPITAL: HANOI
COIN: XU DONG
COMMUNIST PARTY: VIETCONG
GULF: TONKIN TONKING
MOUNTAIN: FANSIPAN
NATIVE: HOA MAN MEO TAY KINH NUNG THAI MUONG
NEWSPAPER: NHANDAN
PORT: BENTHUY HONGGAI HAIPHONG
REGION: ANNAM TONKIN
RIVER: BO CA DA LO MA CHU GAM KOI CHAY NHIHA
TOWN: VINH BACNINH CAOBANG DONGHOI NAMDINH VIETTRI HAIPHONG THANHHOA

NORTHWEST TERRITORY
(CAPITAL OF —) YELLOWKNIFE
(DISTRICT OF —) FRANKLIN KEEWATIN MACKENZIE
(RIVER OF —) BACK KAZAN DUBAWNT COPPERMINE
(TOWN OF —) RAE INUVIK DISCOVERY SNOWDRIFT

NORWAY
CAPE: NORDKYN NORDKAPP
CAPITAL: OSLO

COIN: ORE KRONE
COUNTY: AMT OSLO FYLKE TROMS BERGEN TROMSO FINMARK HEDMARK OPPLAND OSTFOLD NORDLAND ROGALAND TELEMARK VESTFOLD
DANCE: GANGAR HALLING SPRINGAR SPRINGLEIK
FJORD: OSLO SOGNE HARDANGER TRONDHEIM
INLET: IS KOB RAN ALST ANDS BOKN NORD OFOT SALT SUNN TYRI VEST FIORD FJORD FOLDA LAKSE SOGNE BJORNA HADSEL HORTENS TRONDHEIM
ISLAND: VEGA BOMLO DONNA FROYA HITRA HOPEN SENJA SMOLA ALSTEN AVEROY BOUVET HINNOY KARMOY KVALOY SOLUND SOROYA VANNOY GURSKOY LOFOTEN MAGEROY SEILAND JANMAYEN SVALBARD RINGVASSOY
LAKE: ALTE ISTER MJOSA SNASA FEMUND ROSTAVN TUNNSJO ROSTVATN
MEASURE: FOT MAL POT ALEN MAAL KANDE FATHOM SKIEPPE
MOUNTAIN: SOGNE KJOLEN NUMEDAL BLODFJEL SNOHETTA TELEMARK USTETIND
PARLIAMENT: LAGTING STORTING ODELSTING
PLATEAU: DOURE FJELD HARDANGER
RIVER: OI ENA ALTA OTRA RANA TANA BARDU BEGNA GLAMA LAGEN ORKLA OTTER RAUMA REISA GLOMMA LOUGEN NAMSEN PASVIK DRAMSELVA
TOWN: GOL NES BODO MOSS ODDA OSLO VOSS BJORT FLORO HAMAR MOLDE SKIEN SKJAK BERGEN HORTEN LARVIK NARVIK ALESUND ARENDAL DRAMMEN SANDNES STAVANGER
WATERFALL: VETTI SKYKJE VORING
WEIGHT: LOD MARK PUND SKAALPUND BISMERPUND

NORWEGIAN (FORM OF —) BOKMAL
(LITERARY FORM OF —) NYNORSK
NOSE CAP NEB NIZ PRY PUG SPY BEAK BOKO CONK NASE GROIN LORUM NASUS SCENT SMELL SNIFF SNOOP SNOUT TRUNK BEEZER CYRANO DETECT GNOMON MUFFLE MUZZLE NOZZLE PECKER ROOKIE SEARCH SNITCH SOCKET ADVANCE PERFUME SMELLER DISCOVER INFORMER OLFACTOR PERCEIVE PROBOSCIS SCHNOZZLE
(— A LOG) SNIPE
(— BAG) MORRAL
(— CARTILAGE) SEPTUM
(— DISEASE) OZENA OZOENA
(— DIVE) VRILLE
(— FLUTE) PUNGI POOGYE
(— INFLAMMATION) CORYZA RHINITIS

(— MEDICINE) ERRHINE
(— OF ANIMAL) GROIN
(— OPENING) NARE
(— PARTITION) VOMER
(— PIECE) NASAL
(— RING) PIRN
(BLUNT —) SNUB
(FLAT —) PUG SNUB
(PREF.) NAS(I)(O) NASUTI RHIN(O)
(SUFF.) RHINA RHINE RHINIA RHINOUS RHINUS RRHINE RRHINIA
NOSEBAND BOSAL MUSROL CAVESSON
NOSEBLEED EPISTAXIS RHINORRHAGIA
NOSEGAY BOB ODOR POSY POESY SCENT TUTTY BOUQUET CORSAGE PERFUME
NOSINESS CURIOSITY
NOSING CURB
NOSTALGIA LONGING YEARNING
NOSTALGIC ELEGIAC ELEGIACAL
NOSTOLOGY GERIATRICS
NOSTRADAMUS SEER PROPHET PHYSICIAN
NOSTRIL ALA NARE NARIS THIRL THRILL BLOWHOLE
(PERT. TO —) NARIAL NARINE
(PL.) NARES NARIS SNUFFERS
(PREF.) NARI
NOSU LOLO
NOSY BEAKY PRYING CURIOUS FRAGRANT INTRUSIVE
NOT NA NE NAE NAY NOR PAS BAAL BAIL BALE NICHT SHORN SORRA NOUGHT POLLED SHAVEN NEITHER HORNLESS NEGATIVE
(— ANY) NO NUL NANE NARY NONE NAIRY NOKIN STEAD
(— AT ALL) NEVER LITTLE NOWAYS NOWHIT NOWISE
(— FINAL) NISI
(— THE SAME) OTHER ANOTHER DIFFERENT
(— TO BE REPEATED) NR
(— WANTED) DETROP SUPERFLUOUS
(ALMOST —) SCARCELY
(COULD —) NOTE
(PREFIX MEANING —) IL IM IN IR UN NON
(PREF.) A ANTI DIS E IL IM IN IR NON UM UN
NOTABLE VIP FINE FABLED FAMOUS GIFTED NOTARY SIGNAL UNIQUE EMINENT STORIED SUBLIME DISTINCT ESPECIAL EVENTFUL HISTORIC MEMORABLE NOTORIOUS NOTEWORTHY
NOTARY NOTAR GRAFFER GREFFIER NOTEBOOK OBSERVER OFFICIAL SCRIVENER
NOTARY PUBLIC TABELLION
NOTATION HOLD MEMO NOTE ENTRY SYSTEM MARKING
(PHONETIC —) ROMIC
NOTATOR NOTER RECORDER
NOTCH CUT DAG DAP GAP HAG JAG JOG PEG COPE DENT DINT GAIN GIMP KERF MUSH NICK NOCK SLAP SLOT SNIP STEP WARD CRENA GABEL GRADE

HILUM SCORE SHARD SHERD SWICK TALLY CRENEL CROTCH DEFILE DEGREE HOLLOW INDENT JOGGLE RAFFLE RECORD SCOTCH CRENATE GUDGEON SERRATE INCISION UNDERCUT
(— BETWEEN HILLS) SLAP
(— ON VERTEBRAE) HYPANTRUM
(— TO FELL TREE) UNDERCUT
NOTCHED EROSE JAGGY RAGULE RAGULY SERRATE CRENATED
NOTE BON DOG IOU JOT KEY SEE TEN UNE BILL CARD CENT CHIT ESPY FAME FLAT GOOD HEED MARK MEMO NAME NOIT SIGN SOLE SONG TENT TONE TUNE VIEW CHECK FIVER GLOZE LABEL PRICK SHORT SIXTH SOUND STIFF TENTH TOKEN TRAIT TWANG ATTEND BILLET DEGREE EXCUSE FIGURA FLIMSY LETTER MELODY MINUTE NOTICE POLICY RECORD REGARD REMARK RENOWN REPORT SECOND STRAIN TENNER BETOKEN COMMENT DISCORD MESSAGE MISSIVE NATURAL OBSERVE PUNCTUS REDBACK ANNOTATE BLUEBACK BRADBURY BREVIATE DISPATCH EMINENCE MARGINAL PERCEIVE POSTFACE TREASURY GREENBACK POSTSCRIPT
(— FROM TRAIN) BUTTERFLY
(— OF ASSAULT) WARISON
(— OF HUMOR) TRAIT
(— OF SCALE) DO FA LA MI RE SI SO TI UT ARE SOL
(— OF SNIPE) SCAPE
(— OF WARNING) WATCHWORD
(— ON SHOPHAR) TEKIAH
(— TO RECALL DOG) FORLOIN
(—S ON HUNTING HORN) SEEK
(ALTERED —) ACCIDENTAL
(BANK —S) CABBAGE
(BASS —) DRONE
(BIRD'S —) JUG CHIRP
(BUGLE —) MOT
(EIGHTH —) UNCA QUAVER
(EMBELLISHING —) ORNAMENT
(ESCAPE —) ECHAPPEE
(EXPLANATORY —) ANAGRAPH SCHOLIUM ANNOTATION
(FUNDAMENTAL —) ROOT
(GRACE —) NACHSCHLAG
(HALF —) MINIM
(HARSH —) BLOB
(HIGHEST —) ELA
(HIGH-PITCHED —) BEEP
(LEADING —) SUBTONIC
(LONG —) LARGE
(LOVE —) POULET
(LOWEST —) KEY GAMUT
(MARGINAL —) TOT QUOTE POSTIL APOSTIL
(MUSICAL —) ALT RAY MESE MIND BREVE GAMUT SHARP ALAMIRE MEDIANT PUNCTUS LICHANOS PARAMESE PIZZICATO
(NONHARMONIC —) CAMBIATA
(POUND —) BRADBURY
(PROMISSORY —) DOG GOOD HUNDI CEDULA ASSIGNAT

(QUARTER —) CROTCHET SEMIMINIM
(SIXTEENTH —) DEMIQUAVER SEMIQUAVER
(SIXTY-FOURTH —) HEMIDEMISEMIQUAVER
(THIRTY-SECOND —) SUBSEMIFUSA DEMISEMIQUAVER
(TWO —S) DUPLET
(WARBLING —) CHIRL
(WHOLE —) SEMIBREVE
(100-POUND —) CENTURY
(PL.) ANA GAMUT STRAIN NUMBERS TIRALEE MARGINALIA
NOTEBOOK LOG DIARY NOTARY RECORD STREET JOURNAL
NOTECASE WALLET POCKETBOOK
NOTED COUTH FAMED GREAT NAMELY EMINENT INSIGNE RENOWNED DISTINGUE
NOTEPAPER BOUDOIR
NOTEWORTHY BIG SOLEMN EMINENT NOTABLE SALIENT SPECIAL BODACIOUS MEMORABLE OBSERVABLE
NOTHING NIL NIX FREE LUKE NILL WIND ZERO AUGHT BLANK NIHIL ZILCH CIPHER NAUGHT NOBODY NOUGHT TRIFLE NULLITY SCRATCH USELESS BAGATELLE
(— BUT) ALL
(— DOING) NAPOO NAPOOH
(— MORE THAN) MERE
(— OTHER THAN) ONLY
NOTHINGNESS NOT NADA ZERO NOUGHT VACUITY NIHILITY
NOTICE AD BAN SEE SPY CALL ESPY GAUM GOME HEED IDEA KEEP MARK MIND NEWS NOTE PIPE RIDE SIGN SPOT TWIG ALARM AWAIT COUNT EDICT FLOAT NOTAM ORDER QUOTE ADVICE ALLUDE BILLET ESPIAL NOTION PERMIT READER REGARD REMARK REWARD AFFICHE ARTICLE DISCERN MENTION OBSERVE PLACARD PROGRAM WARNING BULLETIN MONITION PERCEIVE WITTERING
(— UNEXPECTEDLY) CATCH
(ADVANCE —) HERALDRY PREMONITION
(COMMENDATORY —) PUFF BLURB
(DEATH —) OBIT OBITUARY
(FAVORABLE —) RAVE
(LEGAL —) CAVEAT
(MARRIAGE —) BANS BANNS
(OFFICIAL —) EDICT SUMMONS BULLETIN CITATION
(PUBLIC —) BAN EDICT BULLETIN SPOTLIGHT
NOTICEABLE CRUDE GROSS FLASHY MARKED SIGNAL EVIDENT NOTABLE POINTED SALIENT HANDSOME PALPABLE STRIKING OBTRUSIVE PROMINENT CONSPICUOUS OUTSTANDING
(UNDESIRABLY —) CONSPICUOUS
NOTIFICATION DRUM NOTE AVISO NOTICE SUMMONS
(PUBLIC —) SIGN
NOTIFY ALL BID CRY JOG CITE PAGE TELL WARN ADVISE

INFORM NOTICE SIGNAL APPRISE DECLARE FRUTIFY PUBLISH ACQUAINT INTIMATE
NOTION BEE GEE BUZZ IDEA IDEE KINK MAZE OMEN VIEW WHIM FANCY FREIT IMAGE SENSE THING WARES BELIEF CEMENT DESIRE DONNEE GADGET MAGGOT NOTICE THEORY VAGARY BROMIDE CONCEIT CONCEPT FANTASY INKLING MAROTTE OPINION THOUGHT WRINKLE CATEGORY FOLKLORE PHANTASY SUPPOSAL WHIMWHAM INTENTION SENTIMENT WHIRLIGIG
(FALSE —) IDOL
(FIXED —) TICK
(FOOLISH —) VAPOR VAPOUR
(PUERILE —) BOYISM
(SUPERSTITIOUS —) FREET FREIT
(VISIONARY —) ABSTRACTION
(PL.) SMALLS SMALLWARE
NOTORIETY FAME ECLAT GLORY HONOR RUMOR RENOWN REPUTE PUBLICITY
NOTORIOUS BIG KNOWN ARRANT COMMON CRYING FAMOUS NOTARY STRONG EVIDENT NOTABLE NOTOIRE APPARENT FLAGRANT INFAMOUS MANIFEST EGREGIOUS
NOTORNIS TAKAHE
NOTUS (BROTHER OF —) EURUS BOREAS ZEPHYRUS
(FATHER OF —) AEOLUS ASTRAEUS
(MOTHER OF —) EOS
NOTWITHSTANDING BUT FOR THO YET EVEN WITH ALGATE MAUGER MAUGRE AGAINST ALGATES DESPITE HOWBEIT HOWEVER ALTHOUGH NATHLESS WHATRECK
NOUGAT NUT CANDY NUTSHELL
NOUGHT BAD NIL NOT NOWT ZERO NOCHT WRONG NOTHING USELESS WORTHLESS
NOUMENAL ONTAL ONTIC
NOUN MANE WORD THING SUPINE NOMINAL CONSTRUCT INCREASER
(INDECLINABLE —) APTOTE
(KIND OF —) COMMON PROPER DIPTOTE REGULAR TRIPTOTE MONOPTOTE
(QUOTATION —) HYPOSTASIS
(VERBAL —) GERUND
NOURISH AID FEED FOOD GROW BREED NORSH NURSE TRAIN BATTLE BREAST FOISON FOSTER NORICE REFETE SUCCOR SUCKLE SUPPLY CHERISH DEVELOP EDUCATE NURTURE NUTRIFY PROVIDE SUPPORT SUSTAIN MAINTAIN CULTIVATE REPLENISH STIMULATE
(PREF.) NUTRI
NOURISHING ALMA RICH ALIBLE BATTLE HEARTY STRONG NUTRIENT ALIMENTAL HEALTHFUL NUTRITIVE WHOLESOME NUTRITIOUS
NOURISHMENT DIET FARE FETE FOOD KEEP MEAT MANNA

FOISON FOSTER ALIMENT PABULUM PASTURE NUTRIMENT REFECTION
(PREF.) THREPSO
NOURONIHAR (FATHER OF —) FAKREDDIN
(LOVER OF —) VATHEK
NOUS MIND REASON ALERTNESS INTELLECT
NOUVEAU RICHE PARVENU UPSTART
NOVA SCOTIA (CAPITAL OF —) HALIFAX
(COUNTY OF —) DIGBY HANTS PICTOU
(STRAIT OF —) CANSO
(TOWN OF —) TRURO PICTOU SYDNEY ARICHAT BADDECK DARTMOUTH
NOVA SCOTIAN ACADIAN BLUENOSE
NOVEL HOT NEW BOOK EPIC RARE FRESH PROSE RECIT ROMAN STORY DARING RECENT SERIAL THRILL FICTION ROMANCE STRANGE UNUSUAL NEOTERIC ORIGINAL THRILLER UNCOMMON NARRATIVE PAPERBACK
(BRIEF —) CONTE
(PREF.) CAEN(O) CEN(O)
NOVELIST (ALSO SEE AUTHOR)
NOVELTY FAD NEWEL RENEW CHANGE NEWNESS PRIMEUR WRINKLE CURIOSITY FRESHNESS
NOVEMBER 1 SAMUIN SAMHAIN
NOVEMBER 11 MARTINMAS
NOVICE DUB HAM BOOT COLT PUNK PUNY TIRO TYRO CHELA GOYIN PUPIL ROOKY YOUTH DRONGO RABBIT ROOKIE TYRONE ACOLYTE AMATEUR CONVERT GRIFFIN LEARNER STARTER STUDENT YOUNKER BACHELOR BEGINNER FRESHMAN INEXPERT NEOPHYTE ARCHARIOS GREENHORN NOVITIATE ABECEDARIAN
NOVITIATE FUCHS NOVICERY PROBATION
NOW NOO YET ARAH HERE ARRAH NONCE SINCE TODAY EVENOO EXTANT ANYMORE CURRENT INSTANT PRESENT FORTHWITH PRESENTLY
(— AND THEN) SOMETIMES STOUNDMEAL
(BUT —) ERSTWHILE
(JUST —) ENOW FRESH
NOWADAYS ANYMORE
NOWEL DRAG
NOX NYX
(BROTHER OF —) EREBUS
(FATHER OF —) CHAOS
NOXIOUS BAD ILL EVIL FETID DEADLY NOCENT NOYOUS PUTRID BALEFUL BANEFUL DAMPISH HARMFUL HURTFUL NOCUOUS NOISOME SCADDLE TEDIOUS VICIOUS INFAMOUS VIRULENT INJURIOUS MIASMATIC OFFENSIVE PESTILENT POISONOUS PERNICIOUS
(— AIR) MALARIA

(MORALLY —) UNWHOLESOME
NOZZE DI FIGARO, LE (CHARACTER IN —) FIGARO BARTOLO BASILIO SUSANNA BARBARINA CHERUBINO MARCELLINA
(COMPOSER OF —) MOZART
NOZZLE BIB JET TIP BEAK BIBB NOSE ROSE VENT GIANT SNOUT SPOUT TWEER GROVEL OUTLET MONITOR NIAGARA ORIFICE SHUTOFF ADJUTAGE ROSEHEAD VERMOREL NOSEPIECE
(BLAST FURNACE —) TUYERE
(MINING —) GIANT
NUANCE SHADE NICETY FINESSE GRADATION VARIATION
NUB EAR HUB JAG KEY NOB CORE CRUX GIST HANG KNOB KNOT KNUB LUMP NECK PITH SNAG HEART NUDGE POINT KERNEL NUBBIN EXECUTE
NUBBIN EAR STUB STUMP
NUBIA WRAP CLOUD SCARF
NUBIAN NUBA BARABRA HADENDOA
(— MUSICAL INST.) SISTRUM
NUBILOUS FOGGY MISTY VAGUE CLOUDY OBSCURE
NUCHA NAPE NECK NUKE NUCHE
NUCLEAR ELEMENTARY
NUCLEATE SEED
NUCLEOLUS
(PREF.) PYREN(O)
NUCLEON MESON BARYON MESOTRON
NUCLEOSIDE VICINE INOSINE CYTIDINE ADENOSINE
NUCLEUS HUB CELL CORE GERM KERN PITH ROOT SEED CADRE FOCUS HEART MIDST SPERM UMBRA CENTER COLONY DEUTON KARYON KERNEL MIDDLE ISOTOPE NIDULUS HABENULA MEROCYTE MESOPLAST
(— OF CELL) KARYON
(— OF STARCH GRAIN) HILUM
(— OF SUNSPOT) UMBRA
(ATOMIC —) SPECIES
(CELL —) SYNCARYON HEMIKARYON
(PREF.) (— OF CELL) CARY(O) KARY(O)
NUCLIDE ISOTONE
NUDE BARE LOOSE MODEL NAKED SEASAN STATUE UNCLAD DENUDED EXPOSED PICTURE PAINTING STARKERS STRIPPED UNDRESSED
(FRENCH —) ALESAN
(NOT —) DECENT
(RUN —) STREAK
NUDGE JOG NOG NUB WAG GOAD JOLT KNUB LUMP POKE POTE PROD PUSH BLOCK CHUCK DUNCH ELBOW
NUDISM NATURISM GYMNOSOPHY
NUDIST ADAMITE NUDIFIER GYMNOSOPH
NUGATORY IDLE NULL VAIN EMPTY PETTY FUTILE HOLLOW INVALID TRIVIAL USELESS TRIFLING FRUSTRATE WORTHLESS

NUGGET EYE LOB GOLD HUNK LUMP MASS SLUG PRILL YELLOW

NUISANCE BANE BORE EVIL HARM HURT PAIN PEST STING INJURY PLAGUE TERROR VEXATION ANNOYANCE

NULL NIL VOID EMPTY INEPT IRRITE INVALID NULLIFY USELESS VACUOUS NUGATORY FRUSTRATE

NULLAH GORGE GULLY NULLA NALLAH RAVINE

NULLIFY BEAT FLAW LAME NULL UNDO VETO VOID ABATE ANNUL ELIDE ERASE LAPSE CANCEL DEFEAT NEGATE OFFSET REPEAL REVOKE ABOLISH COUNTER DESTROY ABROGATE EVACUATE STULTIFY FRUSTRATE

NULLIFYING DIRIMENT

NULLITY NIHILITY

NUMB DEAD DRUG DULL DAZED FUNNY STONY ASLEEP BENUMB CLUMSY DEADEN STUPID TORPID STUPEFY ENFEEBLE HEBETATE HELPLESS RIGESCENT TABETLESS

NUMBER SUM BAND BODY COPY CURN DRAW FECK HERD HOST LOTS MAIN MANY MESS MORT SLEW SURD TALE TELL COUNT DATUM DIGIT FOLIE GRIST GROUP INDEX ISSUE SCADS SCORE STAND TOTAL WHOLE ADDEND AMOUNT BUNDLE CIPHER ENCORE FACTOR FIGURE FILLER HIRSEL MYRIAD POLICY RECKON SCALAR TICHEL CHIFFER COMPUTE DECIMAL DIVISOR FOLIATE NUMERIC SEVERAL CARDINAL FRACTION NUMERATE QUANTITY CALCULATE · MAGNITUDE MULTITUDE MULTIPLIER MULTIPLICAND
(— BETWEEN 4 AND 10) MAIN
(— OF ARROWS) END
(— OF ATOMS) CHAIN
(— OF BEASTS) HERD
(— OF BOMBS) STICK
(— OF BRICKS) CLAMP
(— OF CATTLE) SOUM
(— OF FUR SKINS) TIMBER
(— OF HANKS OF YARN TO POUND) COUNT
(— OF HAWKS) CAST
(— OF HONEYBEES) CLUSTER
(— OF NEEDLES) GAGE GAUGE
(— OF POEMS) EPOS
(— OF SHEARERS) BOARD
(— OF TEA CHESTS) BREAK
(— OF THREADS PER INCH) PITCH
(— OF TRICKS) BOOK
(— OF WORDS) FOLIO
(— THROWN IN CRAPS) POINT
(—S GAME) BUG
(BALLET —) ENTREE
(CARDINAL —) ONE TWO ALEF ALEPH THREE
(COMPLEX —) IMAGINARY
(CONSIDERABLE —) WHEEN HATFUL FISTFUL
(DESCRIBABLE —) SCALAR
(EXCESS —) ADVANTAGE
(EXCESSIVE —) SPATE
(EXTRA —) ENCORE

(GOLDEN —) PRIME
(GOOD —) THRAVE
(GREAT —) LAC HEAP HOST LAKH MORT BREAK HIRST MEINY POWER SHOAL SIGHT SWARM LEGION MYRIAD INFINITE INFINITY THOUSAND MULTITUDE MULTIPLICITY
(GREAT —S) FLOCKS
(GREATER —) MO
(INDEFINITE —) LAC STEEN SUNDRY THRAVE JILLION SEVERAL THREAVE UMPTEEN
(IRRATIONAL —) SURD
(LARGE —) ARMY FECK HERD HOST LUMP PECK SLEW ARRAY CROWD FORCE POWER SCADS SHEAF SPATE STACK STORE WORLD GALLON GOOGOL HIRSEL HIRSLE LEGION MELDER BILLION JILLION PLURALITY
(LARGE —S) STRENGTH
(LEAF —) FOLIO
(LEAST WHOLE —) UNIT
(ODD —S) IMPAIR
(OPPOSITE —) COUSIN
(ORDINAL —) FIRST THIRD SECOND
(PUT ON SERIAL —) FOLIO
(SMALL —) FEW CURN CURRAN HANDFUL PAUCITY SPATTER
(TOTAL —) AMOUNT
(VAST —) HORDE
(WHOLE —) ALL DIGIT INTEGER
(PREF.) ARITHM(O) ARITHMETICO LOGARITHMO NUMERO
(SUFF.) ARITHM PLY
(— TERMINATION) TEEN
(— THAT FILLS) FUL FULL
(ORDINAL —) ETH

NUMBERED MENE

NUMBERING TALE COUNT FOLIATION

NUMBERS
(PREF.) **(ODD —)** PERISSO

NUMBFISH TORPEDO

NUMBING WARELESS

NUMBLES UMBLES INNARDS NOMBLES VISCERA ENTRAILS

NUMBNESS STUPOR TORPOR STUPIDITY
(PREF.) NARC(O)

NUMEN DEITY GENIUS SPIRIT VESTAL DIVINITY

NUMERAL (ALSO SEE NUMBER) SUM WORD DIGIT CIPHER FIGURE LETTER CHAPTER NUMERIC
(— STYLE) ROMAN ARABIC
(CLOCK —) CHAPTER

NUMERATIVE PEN SEGREGATIVE

NUMEROUS BIG LOTS MAIN MANY RANK RIFE GREAT LARGE STOUR DIVERS GALORE LEGION MYRIAD SUNDRY UNRIDE COPIOUS CROWDED ENDLESS FEARFUL FERTILE PROFUSE SEVERAL TEEMING UMPTEEN ABUNDANT FREQUENT MANIFOLD MULTIPLE POPULOUS THRONGED EXTENSIVE MULTIFOLD NUMBERFUL PLENTIFUL
(— AND POWERFUL) MAIN
(MODERATELY —) FAIR

(VERY —) EXCESSIVE
(PREF.) MYRI

NUMIDIA (BIRD OF —) DEMOISELLE
(CITY OF —) HIPPO
(KING OF —) JUGURTHA

NUMITOR (GRANDSON OF —) REMUS ROMULUS

NUMSKULL NUM DAFF DOLT FLAT BOOBY DUNCE LACKWIT BONEHEAD BLOCKHEAD LAMEBRAIN

NUN BIRD SMEW CLARE CLERK MONIAL PIGEON SISTER TERESA VESTAL VOWESS CLUNIAC CONFINE DEANESS DEVOTEE EXTERNE MINCHEN MONKESS RECLUSE TEATINE THEATIN BASILIAN CHAPLAIN CLARISSE PRIORESS TITMOUSE URBANIST URSULINE VISITANT VOTARESS ANGELICAL CARMELITE LORETTINE PRIESTESS RELIGEUSE
(— BIRD) MONASE TITMOUSE
(— HEADDRESS) WIMPLE
(— HOOD) FAILLE
(— MOTH) TUSSOCK
(— ORDER) MARIST TRAPPIST DOMINICAN LORETTINE
(CHIEF —) ABBA ABBESS MOTHER
(LATIN —) VESTA
(SON OF —) JOSHUA

NUNCIATE NUNCIO ANNOUNCER MESSENGER

NUNCIO ENVOY NUNCE LEGATE NUNTIUS DELEGATE MESSENGER

NUNCUPATE DECLARE DEDICATE INSCRIBE PROCLAIM DESIGNATE PRONOUNCE

NUNCUPATIVE ORAL SPOKEN UNWRITTEN

NUNNERY ABBEY NUNRY CONVENT CLOISTER MINCHERY
(HEAD OF —) ABBESS

NUPSON FOOL SIMPLETON

NUPTIAL BRIDAL GENIAL THORAL MARITAL WEDDING ESPOUSAL HYMENEAL MARRIAGE
(PL.) SPOUSAL ESPOUSAL HYMENEALS WIFETHING

NUQUE NAPE NECK

NURSE AMAH AYAH BABA CARE DHAI FEED NANA NUSS REAR SUCK TEND BONNE MAMMY NANNY NORSH ATTEND BAYMAN CRADLE FOMENT FOSTER GRANNY KEEPER NANNIE NORICE NUZZLE SISTER SITTER SUCKLE UMFAAN CHERISH FURTHER NOURISH NURTURE PROMOTE CULTIVATE ENCOURAGE NURSEMAID
(— A GRIEVANCE) SULK
(— OF HIAWATHA) NOKOMIS
(— OF ULYSSES) EURYCLEA
(— OF ZEUS) AMALTHEA CYNOSURA
(— SHARK) GATA
(GULLIVER'S —) GLUMDALCLITCH
(WET —) DHAI DHOLL

NURSERY RACE CRECHE BROODER FOSTERAGE

NURSLING BABY NORRY NURRY

FOSTER FOUNDLING
(PREF.) THREMMATO

NURTURE CARE DIET FEED FOOD REAR TEND BREED NURSE TRAIN COCKER CRADLE FOSTER NUZZLE CHERISH EDUCATE SUPPORT BREEDING NORTELRY TRAINING EDUCATION ESTABLISH NUTRIMENT
(PREF.) TROPH(O)

NUSAIRI ANSARIE

NUT ACA BEN BUR COB GUY JOU NIT TAP ANTA BURR COLA CORE DOLT FOOL FROG HEAD KOLA LORE MAST NITE PILI PITH SEED TASK ACORN BETEL BONGA BUNGA CRANK FLAKE FRUIT GLANS HAZEL HICAN JUVIA PECAN TRYMA ALMOND BONDUC BRAZIL CASHEW FELLOW HICCAN ILLIPE KERNEL PEANUT PIGNON PINION PYRENE CASTANA FILBERT HICKORY PROBLEM APPLENUT BEECHNUT BREADNUT CHESTNUT GOORANUT LARRIKIN CAPOTASTO CHINKAPIN ECCENTRIC MACADAMIA PHILOPENA
(— COAL) ANTHRACITE
(— GRASS) SEDGE
(— OF VIOLIN BOW) FROG
(— PINE) PIGNON PINOON PIGNOLIA
(CASHEW —) SEDGE ANACARD
(CONSORT OF —) GEB KEB SET
(DAUGHTER OF —) ISIS NEPHTHYS
(FALLEN —S) SHACK
(PALM —) BETEL LICHI BABASSU COCOANUT COQUILLA
(PERT. TO —) NUCAL
(RIPE —) LEAMER
(RUSH —) CHUFA
(SON OF —) RA OSIRIS
(PL.) MASTAGE
(PREF.) CARY(O) KARY(O) NUCI

NUT-BEARING NUCIFEROUS

NUTCRACKER XENOPS CRACKER PILLORY MEATBIRD NUTCRACK NUTHATCH NUCIFRAGA NUTPECKER

NUTHATCH SITTA TOMTIT XENOPS JARBIRD SITTINE TITMOUSE NUTJOBBER

NUTHOOK BEADLE CONSTABLE

NUTLET NUCULE PYRENA PYRENE GYROLITH

NUTMEG SEED TREE SPICE BEAVER CALABASH NOTEMIGGE NOTEMUGGE
(— COVERING) MACE
(— STATE) CONNECTICUT
(PREF.) MYRISTICI

NUTRIA FUR COYPU GREGE NEUTRIA RAGONDIN

NUTRIENT STARTER
(PLANT —S) SIDEDRESS
(PL.) FOOD HEMOTROPHE

NUTRIMENT DIET FOOD KEEP VIANDS ALIMENT PABULUM SUPPORT NOURISHMENT

NUTRITION EUTROPHY TROPHISM
(IMPERFECT —) DYSTROPHY DYSTROPHIA

(PREF.) TROPH(O)
(SUFF.) TROPHIA TROPHIC TROPHY
NUTRITIOUS BATTLE BAITTLE TROPHIC
NUTRITIVE ALIBLE
NUT-SHAPED NUCIFORM
NUTSHELL SHELL INCLUDER
NUTTY GAGA LOCO NUTS RACY ZANY BUGGY CRAZY QUEER SPICY FRUITY LOVING SPRUCE AMOROUS FOOLISH PIQUANT ZESTFUL DEMENTED PLEASANT ECCENTRIC FLAVORFUL
NUX VOMICA SNAKEWOOD
NUZZLE DIG PET ROOT NURSE SNUFF BURROW CARESS FONDLE FOSTER NESTLE NUDDLE

NURTURE SNOOZLE SNUGGLE SNUZZLE
NYCTEUS (BROTHER OF —) LYCUS
(DAUGHTER OF —) ANTIOPE
(FATHER OF —) HYRIEUS
(MOTHER OF —) CLONIA
NYE EYAS NEST NIDE BROOD FLOCK
NYMPH FLY GIRL MAIA MITE MUSE PINK PIXY PUPA TICK AEGLE DRYAD HOURI LARVA NAIAD NIXIE OREAD SIREN SYLPH BYBLIS CYRENE DAMSEL DAPHNE HELICE HESTIA KELPIE MAIDEN NEREID SPRITE SYRINX UNDINE CORYCIA ERYTHEA HESPERA LIRIOPE OCEANID CALLISTO CYNOSURA EURYDICE MARPESSA PROSOPON

BUTTERFLY HAMADRYAD
(— BELOVED BY PAN) SYRINX
(— BELOVED OF NARCISSUS) ECHO
(— OF FOUNTAIN) EGERIA SALMACIS
(— OF HILLS) OREAD
(— OF MEADOWS) LIMONIAD
(— OF MESSINA STRAIT) SCYLLA
(— OF MT. IDA) OENONE
(CITY —) POLIAD
(LAKE —) NAIAD LIMNIAD
(OCEAN —) SIREN GALATEA
(QUEEN OF —S) MAB
(RIVER —) NAIS NAIAD
(SEA —) MERROW NEREID CALYPSO GALATEA MERMAID
(WATER —) NAIS EGERIA LURLEI

UNDINE APSARAS HYDRIAD JUTURNA RUSALKA EPHYDRIAD
(WOOD —) DRYAD NAPEA ARETHUSA
(PL.) HYADS THRIAI CAMENAE
(PREF.) NYMPHO
NYMPHAEA CASTALY CASTALIA
NYMPHOMANIAC (BOVINE —) BULLER
NYROCA AYTHYA
NYSSA TUPELO
NYSTAGMUS TIC WINK
NYX NOX NIGHT
(— PERSONIFIED) NIGHT
(BROTHER OF —) EREBUS
(DAUGHTER OF —) DAY ERIS LIGHT
(HUSBAND OF —) CHAOS
(SON OF —) CHARON

O

O HO OH OCH ZERO CIPHER OMICRON

OAF AUF BOOR DOLT FOOL LOUT CLOWN DUNCE IDIOT OUPHE YOKEL MUCKER NASHGAB PALOOKA POMPION BLOCKHEAD FOUNDLING SCHLEMIEL SIMPLETON

OAHU (— BIRD) JIBI

OAK CLUB CORK HOLM ILEX BRAVE BRIAR EMORY HOLLY ROBLE ROBUR ACAJOU BAREEN CERRIS ENCINA KERMES STRONG TOUMEY VALOMA AMBROSE BELLOTA BELLOTE DURMAST EGILOPS KELLOGG PALAYAN TURTOSA BEEFWOOD BLUEJACK CHAMPION CHAPARRO FLITTERN WAINSCOT BLACKJACK CHINKAPIN QUERCITRON
(— BARK) CRUT
(— FRUIT) MAST ACORN CAMATA BELLOTE
(JERUSALEM —) AMBROSE
(WHITE —) ROBLE
(YOUNG —) FLITTERN
(PREF.) DRY(O) QUERCI

OAKUM OCCAM

OAKWOOD MESA

OAR AIR BOW PLY ROW PALM PEEL POLE ALOOF BLADE ROWER SCULL SPOON SWAPE SWEEP YULOH PADDLE PALLET PROPEL OARSMAN PROPELLER
(— BLADE) PALM PEEL WASH
(— FULCRUM) LOCK THOLE OARLOCK ROWLOCK
(BOW —) GOUGER
(HANDLE OF —) GRASP
(INBOARD PORTION OF —) LOOM
(PART OF —) GRIP LOOM BLADE SHAFT
(STERN —) SCULL SKULL
(PREF.) COPE(O) REMI

OARLOCK LOCK THOLE ROWLOCK

OARSMAN OAR REMEX ROWER BOWMAN STROKE BENCHER SCULLER WATERMAN

OASIS BAR OJO SPA MERV SIWA WADI WADY SPRING

OAST HOST KILN OVEN COCKLE OASTHOUSE

OAT AIT WOT FEED FOOD PIPE POEM SKEG SONG AUCHT CHEAT GRAIN HAVER PEARL ANGORA EGILOPS
(— HUSK) SHOOD FLIGHT
(— RENT) AVENAGE
(EDIBLE PORTION OF —) GROATS
(FALSE WILD —S) FATUOID
(HUSKED —) SHEALING
(NAKED —) PILLAS PILCORN
(UNTHRASHED —) OATHAY

(WILD —S) HAVERGRASS
(PL.) CORN GRAIN HAVER GROUTS PROVENDER WHITECORN

OATCAKE CAPER HAVERCAKE SOURBREAD

OATEN AITEN

OATH OD ADS BAN DAD DOD GAD GAR GOL GOR GUM ODD SAM VOW BOND CRUM CUSS DARN DRAT ECOD EGAD GEEZ GOSH HECK JEEZ JING NIGS OONS SANG SLID SLUD WORD BEDAD BEGAD BEGOB BLIMY CURSE DAMME DEUCE GOLLY HOKEY MORDU PARDY SACRE SFOOT SLIFE SNIGS SWEAR YERRA ADSBUD APPEAL CRACKY CRIKEY CRIPES CRUMBS FEALTY JABERS JERNIE NEAKES PARDIE PLEDGE RAPPER SBLOOD SLIGHT STRUTH ZOUNDS BEGORRA BEGORRY BEJESUS BYRLADY CORBLEU GADSLID GEEWHIZ GEEWIZZ JEEPERS JIMMINY MORBLEU ODSFISH ODZOOKS PROMISE THUNDER ANATHEMA BEJABERS BODYKINS CRICKETY GADZOOKS JURAMENT PITIKINS SANCTION SEREMENT SNIGGERS SPLUTTER AFFIDAVIT BEJABBERS BLASPHEMY DODGASTED EXPLETIVE PROFANITY SACRAMENT SLIDIKINS SWEARWORD

OATMEAL OATS STODGE YELLOW POTTAGE DRAMMOCK PORRIDGE
(— BREAD) ANACK JANNACK
(— CAKE) PONE SCONE

OATS (MIXED ROLLED —) GRANOLA
(PREF.) AVENO

OBADIAH ABDIAS
(FATHER OF —) AZEL JEHIEL SHEMAIAH
(SON OF —) ISHMAIAH

OBAL (FATHER OF —) JOKTAN

OBCLUDE HIDE OCCLUDE

OBDURATE FIRM HARD BALKY HARSH INERT ROCKY ROUGH STARK STONY DOGGED INURED MULISH RUGGED SEVERE STURDY SULLEN ADAMANT CALLOUS HARDENED PERVERSE STUBBORN IMPASSIVE UNBENDING

OBEAH OBI OBIA CHARM FETISH VOODOO

OBECHE ARERE AYOUS SAMBA

OBED (FATHER OF —) BOAZ JARHA SHEMAIAH
(MOTHER OF —) RUTH
(SON OF —) JESSE AZARIAH

OBEDEDOM (FATHER OF —) JEDUTHUN

OBEDIENCE ORDER FEALTY CONTROL SERVICE

DOCILITY OBEISANCE

OBEDIENT BENT RULY TALL TAME BUXOM DOCILE PLIANT DEVOTED DUTEOUS DUTIFUL HEEDFUL MINDFUL ORDERLY SUBJECT AMENABLE BIDDABLE YIELDING ATTENTIVE OBSERVING SERVIABLE TRACTABLE
(— TO THE HELM) HANDY

OBEDIENTIARY PRIOR

OBEDIENT PLANT DRAGONHEAD

OBEISANCE BOW LEG JOUK BINGE CONGE HONOR SALAM CONGEE CRINGE CURTSY FEALTY HOMAGE SALAAM CURTSEY DEFERENCE HUMBLESSO REFERENCE

OBELISK MARK PYLON SHAFT DAGGER GUGLIA GUGLIO NEEDLE OBELUS PILLAR AGUGLIA MONUMENT HAGIOLITH

OBERON KING POEM FAIRY OPERA SATELLITE
(CHARACTER IN —) HUON PUCK FATIMA OBERON TITANIA SHERASMIN
(COMPOSER OF —) WEBER
(WIFE OF —) TITANIA

OBESE FAT FOZY PLUMP PUDGY PUFFY PURSY STOUT FLESHY PORTLY PYKNIC ROTUND TURGID ADIPOSE PORCINE PURSIVE BLUBBERY LIPAROUS CORPULENT

OBESITY FAT FATNESS LIPOSIS ADIPOSIS FOZINESS ADIPOSITY

OBEY EAR HEAR HEED MIND DEFER YIELD COMPLY FOLLOW OBEISH SUBMIT CONFORM EXECUTE OBSERVE OBTEMPER
(— HELM) STEER

OBFUSCATE DIM CLOUD DARKEN MUDDLE OBFUSK CONFUSE MYSTIFY OBSCURE PERPLEX STUPEFY BEWILDER

OBI OBE SASH CHARM OBEAH FETICH FETISH GIRDLE

OBIT MASS REST DEATH NOTICE OBITAL DECEASE RELEASE SERVICE OBITUARY NECROLOGY OBSEQUIES

OBITUARY NECROLOGY

OBJECT AIM END TAP BALK BEEF CARE CARP FINE GOAL IDEA ITEM KICK MAIN MIND PASS SAKE WHAT ARGUE CAVIL DEMUR GRIPE PINCH POINT SCOPE SIGHT TELOS THING AFFAIR DESIGN EMBLEM ENTITY FIGURE GADGET INTENT MATTER MOTIVE OPPOSE TARGET ARTICLE DINGBAT DISLIKE DISSENT MEANING PROTEST PURPOSE QUARREL REALITY RECLAIM NOUMENON TENDENCY CHALLENGE

INTENTION SPECTACLE
(— HAVING FLAWS) SPOIL
(— OF AMBITION) MAIN
(— OF ART) VASE CURIO VIRTU ANTIQUE BIBELOT FIGURINE
(— OF CRITICISM) BUTT
(— OF DEVOTION) IDOL TOTEM FETISH
(— OF DISGUST) UG
(— OF DREAD) BOGY BOGEY BOGIE BOGGIE BUGBEAR
(— OF KNOWLEDGE) SCIBILE
(— OF PILGRIMAGE) CAABA KAABAH
(— OF PURSUIT) SHADOW
(— OF RELIANCE) STAY
(— OF RIDICULE) FUN GAME
(— OF SCORN) GECK SCOFF BYWORD HISSING DERISION
(— OF TERROR) BUG
(— OF THOUGHT) CONSTRUCT
(— OF WONDER) ADMIRATION
(— TO BE TILTED AT) QUINTAIN
(BELOVED —) MINION DARLING MISTRESS
(BULKY —) WODGE
(CONICAL —) ACORN
(CONSPICUOUS —) LANDMARK
(CONTAMINATED —S) FOMITES
(CURVED —) BELLY
(CYLINDRICAL —) BOLE
(DECORATIVE —) BIBELOT
(DESIRABLE —) GRAIL
(FACTORY-MADE —S) ARTWORK
(MINUTE —) ATOM MITE
(ROUND —) COB RONDEL TRINDLE TRUNDLE
(SACRED —) URIM ZOGO GUACA HUACA SHRINE CHURINGA
(SILLY —) INANITY
(SMALL —) PIRLIE
(TRANSCENDENTAL —) ENTITY
(ULTIMATE —) TELOS
(UNIDENTIFIED FLYING —) BOGEY
(VILE —S) SCUM
(WORTHLESS —) SPLINTER
(PREF.) **(FILTHY OR DIRTY —)** RHYPARO RHYPO

OBJECTION OB BAR BUT BEEF CRAB FUSS KICK CAVIL DEMUR DOUBT BOGGLE CHESON QUARREL QUIBBLE SCRUPLE QUESTION CHALLENGE CRITICISM EXCEPTION

OBJECTIONABLE VILE AWFUL HORRID GHASTLY UNLUSTY UNLIKELY FRIGHTFUL OBNOXIOUS OFFENSIVE

OBJECTIVE AIM END FAIR GAME GOAL HOME REAL SAKE OUTER ACTUAL AMORAL ANIMUS DESIGN MOTIVE TARGET PURPOSE DETACHED TANGIBLE UNBIASED

DIRECTION INTENTION POSITIVAL QUAESITUM ULTIMATUM

OBJECTOR (CONSCIENTIOUS —) CONCHY

OBJURGATE BAN JAW DAMN ABUSE CHIDE CURSE DECRY BERATE REBUKE REPROVE UPBRAID VITUPER EXECRATE CASTIGATE

OBLATE MONK OFFER DEDICATE MONASTIC

OBLATION CORBAN OFLETE SACRED CHARITY ANAPHORA DEVOTION OFFERING SACRIFICE

OBLIGATE COMMIT STRICT

OBLIGATED BOUND LIABLE BEHOLDEN

OBLIGATION DUE IOU TIE VOW BAIL BAND BOND CALL DEBT DUTY KNOT LOAD LOAN MUST NOTE OATH ONUS SEAL CHECK OUGHT SCORE ARREAR BURDEN CHARGE CONSOL CORVEE CUSTOM FEALTY PLEDGE ANNUITY BONDAGE PROMISE TRIBUTE CONTRACT HYPOTHEC SECURITY WARRANTY AGREEMENT LIABILITY
(— NOT TO MARRY) CELIBACY
(— TO RENDER RENT) CUSTOM
(MORAL —) BOND DUTY
(PL.) STRINGS

OBLIGATORY BINDING BOUNDEN FORCIBLE IMPOSING LIGATORY INCUMBENT MANDATORY

OBLIGE PUT HOLD PAWN DRIVE FAVOR FORCE COMPEL ENGAGE PLEASE GRATIFY REQUIRE CONCLUDE MORTGAGE OBLIGATE CONSTRAIN ACCOMMODATE

OBLIGED FAIN BOUND DEBTED BOUNDEN DEBTFUL FAVORED PLEASED PLEDGED BEHOLDEN GRATEFUL OBSTRICT BEHOLDING OBLIGATED

OBLIGING KIND BUXOM CIVIL CLEVER TOWARD AMIABLE FAVOROUS AGREEABLE COURTEOUS FAVORABLE OFFICIOUS

OBLIQUE AWRY BIAS SIDE SKEW ASKEW BEVEL CROSS SLANT ASLANT ASWASH LOUCHE SQUINT THWART ASKANCE AWKWARD CROOKED EMBELIF EVASIVE SCALENE SIDLING SLOPING DIAGONAL INCLINED INDIRECT SIDELONG SIDEWAYS SIDEWISE SLANTING TORTUOUS INDICULAR UNDERHAND
(— IN MINING) CLINIC
(— STROKE) SLASH SOLIDUS
(— WORK) SWASHWORK
(PREF.) LECHRI(O) LOX(O) PLAGI(O)

OBLIQUELY AGEE AWRY BIAS AGLEE ASIDE ASKEW AWASH SLANT SLOPE ASLANT ASWASH ASKANCE ASQUINT EMBELIF BIASWISE SIDELONG SIDEWAYS SIDEWISE

OBLIQUITY BIAS DIRT SWEEP DIRTINESS

OBLITERATE INK BLOT DELE RASE

RAZE WIPE ANNUL BLACK COVER ERASE SMEAR CANCEL DELETE EFFACE SPONGE ABOLISH DESTROY EXPUNGE OUTRAZE SCRATCH OVERSCORE

OBLITERATION BLOT RASURE ERASURE NEGATION SYNIZESIS

OBLIVION LETHE LIMBO PARDON AMNESTY NIRVANA SILENCE OUBLIANCE

OBLIVIOUS AMORT BLISSFUL HEEDLESS OBLIVIAL FORGETFUL

OBLONG CHITON EVELONG AVELONGE EVENLONG ELONGATED
(ROUNDED —) ELLIPSE

OBLOQUY ABUSE BLAME ODIUM INFAMY CALUMNY CENSURE REPROOF CONTEMPT DISGRACE DISHONOR OBLICQUE

OBNOXIOUS FOUL PERT VILE CURST CURSED FAULTY HORRID LIABLE ODIOUS RANCID SEPTIC HATEFUL INVIDIOUS OFFENSIVE REPUGNANT VERMINOUS

OBOE PIPE REED WAIT AULOS SHAWM SURNAI SURNAY HAUTBOY MUSETTE PIFFERO CHIRIMIA HAUTBOIS SCHALMEY SZOPELKA CHALUMEAU
(— DI CACCIA) TENOROON FAGOTTINO
(BASS —) RACKETT
(PREF.) AUL(O)

OBOLE MAIL MAILLE

OBSCENE PAW FOUL LEWD NAST BAWDY GROSS NASTY ROCKY COARSE FILTHY IMPURE RIBALD SMUTTY VULGAR KNAVISH PROFANE IMMODEST INDECENT LOATHSOME OFFENSIVE REPULSIVE SALACIOUS
(— CULT) AISCHROLATREIA

OBSCENITY DIRT RIBALDRY SCULDUDDERY
(PREF.) COPR(O)

OBSCURATION COVER ECLIPSE

OBSCURE DIM FOG BLUR BLOT DARK DEEP HARD HART HAZY HIDE PALE SLUR BEDIM BEFOG BLACK BLANK BLEND BLIND CLOUD COVER DUSKY FAINT FOGGY GLOOM INNER LOWLY MIRKY MISTY MUDDY MURKY SHADE SMEAR STAIN VAGUE BEMIST CLOUDY DARKEN DARKLE DEADEN DELUDE GLOOMY HUMBLE MYSTIC OCCULT OPAQUE REMOTE SHADOW SOMBER SUBTLE BECLOUD BENIGHT CLOUDED CONCEAL CONFUSE CRABBED CRYPTIC ECLIPSE ENCRUST ENVELOP OBLIQUE OVERLAY OVERTOP SHADOWY SLUBBER TARNISH UNCLEAR UNKNOWN UNNOTED ABSTRUSE DARKLING DISGUISE DOUBTFUL FAMELESS MYSTICAL NAMELESS NUBILOUS OBSTRUSE ORACULAR OVERSILE CALIGINOUS
(MAKE —) BECLOUD
(PREF.) APHAN(O)

OBSCURED HAZY HIDDEN

BLINDED CLOUDED DUSKISH DARKSOME DISGUISED INFUSCATE

OBSCURITY FOG MIST CLOUD GLOOM SHADE CALIGO SHADOW DIMNESS OPACITY PRIVACY SILENCE DARKNESS TENEBRES BLINDNESS SECLUSION
(DELIBERATE —) OBLIQUITY
(PL.) MURLEMEWES

OBSECRATE BEG PRAY BESEECH ENTREAT PETITION

OBSEQUIES MASS OBIT PYRE WAKE RITES SERVICE FUNERALS

OBSEQUIOUS SLICK MENIAL SUPPLE COURTLY DEVOTED DUTEOUS DUTIFUL FAWNING SERVILE SLAVISH VERNILE CRINGING OBEDIENT OBEISANT TOADYING ASSIDUOUS ATTENTIVE COMPLIANT
(— PERSON) LIMBERHAM

OBSEQUY RITE EXEQUY RITUAL FUNERAL CEREMONY

OBSERVANCE ACT FORM RITE RULE FREET HONOR CUSTOM REGARD KEEPING CEREMONY PRACTICE ADHERENCE ATTENTION DEFERENCE INDICTION SOLEMNITY
(— OF PROPRIETIES) DECORUM BREEDING ETIQUETTE
(RELIGIOUS —) NOVENA SACRAMENT
(REVERENTIAL —) PUJA
(SUPERSTITIOUS —) FREET FREIT
(PL.) FUNERAL CEREMONY

OBSERVANT ALERT EYEFUL CAREFUL HEEDFUL MINDFUL DILIGENT VIGILANT WATCHFUL REGARDFUL PERCEPTIVE

OBSERVATION EYE SPY HEED IDEA NOTE RAOB VIEW SIGHT WATCH ESPIAL LOGION NOTICE REGARD REMARK AUSPICE AUTOPSY COMMENT CONTACT DESCANT OPINION EYESIGHT GAZEMENT SCHOLION SCHOLIUM ASSERTION ATTENTION ESPIONAGE COGNIZANCE PERCEPTION
(— BY BALLOON) PIBAL
(ECOLOGICAL —S) ANNUATION
(PRELIMINARY —) PROEM

OBSERVATIONISM SCHAULUST

OBSERVATORY LICK TOWER LOOKOUT PALOMAR

OBSERVE LO EYE SEE SPY ESPY HEED HOLD KEEP LOOK MAKE MARK MIND NARK NOTA NOTE OBEY SPOT TENT TOUT TWIG WAIT YEME ABIDE QUOTE SMOKE STUDY UTTER WATCH ADHERE ADVERT ATHOLD BEHOLD DETECT DEVISE FOLLOW NOTICE NOTIFY REGARD REMARK SURVEY COMMENT DISCERN EXPRESS MENTION PERCEIVE PRESERVE WITNESS PROFESS RESPECT SPECTATE ADVERTISE CELEBRATE SOLEMNIZE
(— CLOSELY) SMOKE
(— DULLY) BLEAR

(— OPPOSING POSITION) KEY

OBSERVER O BIRDER CORNER WATCHER AUDIENCE INFORMER ONLOOKER BYSTANDER SCRUTATOR SPECTATOR

OBSESS RIDE BESET HAUNT HARASS INVEST OBSEDE BESIEGE HAGRIDE POSSESS PREOCCUPY

OBSESSED CRAZY DOTTY HAPPY HIPPED BESOTTED

OBSESSION TIC CRAZE MANIA SIEGE MAGGOT ECSTASY FIXATION
(SUFF.) **(— WITH)** ITIS

OBSIDIAN CORE LAVA IZTLE IZTLI LAPIS

OBSOLETE OLD DEAD PAST DATED PASSE BYGONE EFFETE ABOLETE ANCIENT ARCHAIC CLASSIC DISUSED EFFACED EXTINCT OUTWORN OUTDATED OUTMODED OVERWORN DISCARDED

OBSTACLE BAR DAM LET BOYG BUMP DRAG JUMP OBEX SNAG STAY STOP BLOCK CHECK CLAMP CRIMP FENCE HITCH HYDRA SPOKE STICK STILE ABATIS BUNKER FRAISE HOCKET HURDLE LOGJAM OBJECT RETARD ANSTOSS BARRIER CHICANE FIVEBAR STOPPER BLOCKADE MOLEHILL BARRICADE CONDITION HINDRANCE ROADBLOCK TURNAGAIN
(— TO VIRTUE) SLANDER
(GOLF —) HAZARD
(INSURMOUNTABLE —) IMPASSE

OBSTETRICIAN ACCOUCHEUR

OBSTETRICS TOCOLOGY MAIEUTICS MIDWIFERY

OBSTINACY BRASS CONTUMACY

OBSTINATE SET SOT DOUR FIRM SULY BALKY FIXED ROWDY RUSTY STIFF STOUT TOUGH ASSISH CUSSED DOGGED KNOBBY MULISH STEEVE STUFFY STUPID STURDY SULLEN THRAWN UNRULY ASININE BULLISH CRABBED FROWARD PEEVISH RESTIVE WILLFUL CROTCHED OBDURATE PERVERSE PREFRACT RECUSANT RENITENT STOMACHY STUBBORN FORERIGHT PIGHEADED STONEWALL TENACIOUS
(NOT —) SUPPLE

OBSTREPEROUS LOUD WILD NOISY RORTY UNRULY RAUGHTY CLAMOROUS

OBSTRUCT BAR DAM DIT GAG JAM CLOG COOP CRAB DITT FILL FOUL JAMB STOP TRIG TRIP BESET BLANK BLOCK CHAIN CHECK CHOKE CROSS DELAY HEDGE THROW ARREST CUMBER FORBAR HAMPER HOBBLE IMPEDE OPPOSE PESTER RETARD STIFLE THWART WAYLAY WINDER BARRIER FORELAY OCCLUDE BLOCKADE EMBOLIZE ENCUMBER FLOUNDER OBTURATE OPPILATE BARRICADE

EMBARRASS INCOMMODE

OBSTRUCTION BAR DAM GAG LET
RUB BOOM BUMP CLOG SLUG
SNAG STAY STOP BLOCK CHOKE
GORCE HITCH SPOKE HAMPER
TAPPEN THWART BARRACE
BARRAGE BARRIER BLINDER
CHOKAGE EMBOLISM OBSTACLE
STOPPAGE EMPHRAXIS
OCCLUSION
(— IN OILWELL) BRIDGE
(— IN RIVER) GORGE
(— IN TEAT) SPIDER
(— IN VALVE) GAG
(— OF BLOOD VESSEL) EMBOLISM
(— OF PINE LEAVES) TAPPEN
(INNER —) LOAD

OBTAIN BEG BUM BUY EKE GET
PAN WIN EARN FANG FIND GAIN
HENT REAP ANNEX CADGE
CATCH ETTLE REACH AREACH
ARECHE ARRIVE ATTAIN BORROW
DERIVE EXPEDE SECURE SPONGE
ACHIEVE ACQUIRE CAPTURE
CHEVISE COMPASS DEMERIT
EXTRACT POSSESS PREVAIL
PROCURE RECEIVE SUCCEED
PURCHASE SCROUNGE
(— BY CHANCE) DRAW
(— BY HEAT) EXCOCT
(— BY REQUEST) IMPETRATE
(— BY THREAT) EXTORT
(— CONTROL) ENGROSS
(— DISHONESTLY) CROOK SHARP
FLEECE NOBBLE SKELDER
(— MONEY FROM) BLEED
(— PERMISSION) CLEAR

OBTAINABLE GOING GETTABLE
AVAILABLE DERIVABLE
SECURABLE

OBTAINED (— AT SCENE OF CRIME)
LATENT

OBTRUDE DIN JET SORN EJECT
EXPEL GLARE FLAUNT IMPOSE
MEDDLE THRUST INTRUDE
INTERFERE

OBTRUSIVE FRESH PUSHY GARISH
BLATANT FORWARD PUSHING
BUMPTIOUS INTRUSIVE

OBTUND DULL BLUNT QUELL
DEADEN

OBTURATOR MUSHROOM

OBTUSE DIM DULL BLINK BLUNT
CRASS DENSE THICK BOVINE
OPAQUE STUPID STUBBED
BOEOTIAN HEBETATE PURBLIND
(NOT —) ACUTE

OBVERSE FACE FRONT CONVERSE
(— OF COIN) MAN HEAD

OBVIATE PREVENT PRECLUDE
FORESTALL

OBVIOUS LOUD OPEN BROAD
CLEAR CRUDE FRANK GROSS
NAKED OVERT PLAIN SLICK
STARK LIABLE PATENT BLATANT
EVIDENT EXPOSED GLARING
SHALLOW SUBJECT VISIBLE
APPARENT DISTINCT MANIFEST
PALPABLE BAREFACED
PROMINENT
(NOT —) DEEP INNER ARCANE
HIDDEN MASKED OCCULT SECRET
SUBTLE DELICATE DOUBTFUL

PROFOUND INEVIDENT

OBVOLUTE CONTORTED
OVERLAPPING

OCA OKA TUBER OXALIS SORREL
SOURSOP

OCARINA CAMOTE

OCCASION SEL BOUT CALL GIVE
HINT NEED SELE SITH TIDE TIME
TURN BREAK BREED CASUS
CAUSE CHARE EVENT INFER
NONCE RAISE SITHE SLANT
STOUR WHILE YIELD AFFAIR
AUTHOR CHANCE COURSE
EXCUSE PERIOD REASON STOUND
CHESOUN INSPIRE OPENING
PRETEXT QUARREL CEREMONY
ENGENDER EXIGENCY FUNCTION
INCIDENT INSTANCE CONDITION
ENCHEASON HAPPENING
(— GRIEF) GRIEVE
(— OF EXCITEMENT) ALARM
ALARUM
(DEFINITE —) TIDE
(EXCITING —) BLAST
(FAVORABLE —) ADVANTAGE
(FESTIVE —) UTAS BEANO
HOLIDAY SHINDIG BEANFEAST
MERRYMAKING
(HAPPY —) SIMHAH SIMCHAH
(SOCIAL —) COFFEE
(SPECIAL —) CEREMONY

OCCASIONAL ODD ORRA STRAY
ANTRIN CASUAL DAIMEN SCARCE
POPPING EPISODIC FUGITIVE
SPORADIC IRREGULAR

OCCASIONALLY EVERY BETIMES
SOMETIME SOMETIMES

OCCASIVE SETTING WESTWARD

OCCIDENTAL WEST PONENT
WESTERN HESPERIAN
WESTERNER

OCCLUDE SHUT SORB CLOSE
ABSORB OBSTRUCT

OCCLUSAL MORSAL

OCCLUSION CORONARY
ARTICULATION
(SUFF.) CLEISIS CLISIS

OCCULT MAGIC ARCANE HIDDEN
LATENT MYSTIC SECRET VOODOO
ALCHEMY CRYPTIC ECLIPSE
UNKNOWN ESOTERIC MYSTICAL
SIBYLLIC CONCEALED RECONDITE
SIBYLLINE
(— SCIENCE) ESOTERICS
(PREF.) CRYPT(O) KRYPT(O)

OCCULTATION ECLIPSE

OCCULTISM MAGIC CABALA
MYSTERY

OCCUPANCY POSSESSION

OCCUPANT HOLDER INMATE
RENTER TENANT CITIZEN
DWELLER RESIDENT INCUMBENT
(— OF THEATER GALLERY) GOD
(SUFF.) ITE

OCCUPATION ART JOB LAY USE
CALL GAME LINE NOTE PLOY TOIL
WORK BERTH CRAFT GRAFT
TRADE BILLET CAREER EMPLOY
METIER RACKET SPHERE TENURE
THRIFT CALLING CONCERN
CONTROL MYSTERY PURSUIT
QUALITY SERVICE ACTIVITY
BUSINESS FUNCTION INDUSTRY

INVASION PLUMBING VOCATION
(— OF MIND) ABSORPTION
(SUBORDINATE —) HOBBY
AVOCATION

OCCUPIED BUSY FULL HELD KEPT
RAPT TOOK ACTIVE INTENT
ENGAGED ABSORBED CAPTURED
(FULLY —) ENGROSSED

OCCUPY LIE SIT USE BUSY FILL
HAVE HOLD KEEP TAKE WARM
AMUSE BELAY BESET DWELL
ABSORB BETAKE EMPLOY ENGAGE
EXPEND FULFIL OBTAIN TENANT
COHABIT CONCERN CONTAIN
ENGROSS ENTREAT IMPROVE
INHABIT INVOLVE OVERSIT
PERVADE POSSESS SWALLOW
DISSOLVE GARRISON INTEREST
POPULATE POURPRISE
(— ILLEGALLY) JUMP
(— QUARTERS) CAMP

OCCUR BE GO COME COOK FALL
GIVE MAKE MEET PASS RISE SORT
ARISE BREAK CLASH EXIST INCUR
LIGHT APPEAR ARRIVE BEFALL
BETIDE CHANCE HAPPEN
PROCEED TRANSPIRE
(— AGAIN) RECUR REPEAT
(— BY CHANCE) LIGHT
(— TO) CROSS ENTER STRIKE

OCCURRENCE GO HAP CASE FACT
ITEM NOTE REDE EVENT WEIRD
EPISODE PASSAGE INCIDENT
JUNCTURE OCCASION
ENCOUNTER FREQUENCE
HAPPENING
(CHANCE —) ADVENTURE
CONTINGENT
(COMMON —) USE FREQUENCY
(FREQUENT —) COMMUNITY
(SIMULTANEOUS —) COINCIDENCE
(SUDDEN —) ZAP
(SUPERNATURAL —) MIRACLE
(UNEXPECTED —) SUDDEN
BLIZZARD BOMBSHELL
(UNFORTUNATE —) CASUALTY
(UNUSUAL —) ODDITY

OCCURRING (— AT NIGHTFALL)
ACRONICAL
(— AT REGULAR INTERVALS) HORAL
(— AT TWILIGHT) CREPUSCULAR
(— BY TURN) ALTERNATE
(— EVERY EIGHT DAYS) OCTAN
(— EVERY FOURTH YEAR)
PENTETERIC
(— FREQUENTLY) COMMON
(— IN USUAL PLACE) ENTOPIC

OCEAN SEA BLUE BRIM DEEP MAIN
POND BRINE DRINK ARCTIC
INDIAN EXPANSE NEPTUNE
PACIFIC ATLANTIC ANTARCTIC
(— FLOATING MATTER) ALGAE
LAGAN FLOTSAM
(— ROUTE) LANE
(— SPRAY) IRONWOOD
CREAMCUPS
(— SWELL) SEA
(ON THE —) ASEA
**(RELATING TO — BELOW 6000
METERS)** HADAL

OCEANIA MALAYA AUSTRALIA
MELANESIA POLYNESIA
(SACRED OBJECT OF —) ZOGO

OCEANIC NAVAL MARINE PELAGIC
NAUTICAL AEQUOREAL

OCEANOGRAPHER (ALSO SEE
HYDROGRAPHER)

OCEANUS TITAN
(DAUGHTER OF —) DORIS OCEANID
EURYNOME
(FATHER OF —) URANUS OURANOS
(MOTHER OF —) GAEA GAIA
(SISTER OF —) TETHYS
(SON OF —) NEREUS
(WIFE OF —) TETHYS

OCELLUS EYE EYELET STEMMA
EYESPOT

OCELOT CAT TOGER LEOPARD
WILDCAT

OCHER RUD SIL KEEL OAKER
OCHRE TIVER ABRAUM RADDLE
ALMAGRA TANGIER
(BLACK —) WAD WADD
(RED —) RUD KEEL TIVER ABRAUM
REDDLE RUBRIC RUDDLE
KOKOWAI
(YELLOW —) SIL SPRUCE

OCOTILLO COACHWHIP
CANDLEWOOD

OCRAN (SON OF —) PAGIEL

OCREA OCHREA SHEATH

OCTAHEDROID HYPERCUBE
TESSERACT

OCTAVE UTAS UTIS EIGHT EIGHTH
OTTAVA HUITAIN DIAPASON
SHEMINITH
(— FLUTE) FLAUTINO
(— OF THE SEVENTH) FOURTEENTH
(— SINGING) MAGADIZE
(DIMINISHED —) SEMIDIAPASON
(FATHER OF —) ARGANTE
(TRIPLE —) TRIDIAPASON

OCTAVIA (BROTHER OF —)
AUGUSTUS
(HUSBAND OF —) ANTONY

OCTAVO EIGHTS

OCTET OCTAVE OCTUOR HUITAIN
OTTETTO

OCTOPUS HEE POLYP POULP
PREKE SQUID CUTTLE CATFISH
POLYPOD POLYPUS SCUTTLE
DIBRANCH OCTOPEAN DEVILFISH
(— ARM) TENTACLE
(AUTHOR OF —) NORRIS
(CHARACTER IN —) DYKE TREE
HILMA LYMAN HOOVEN MAGNUS
SARRIA BEHRMAN CARAHER
DELANEY DERRICK PRESLEY
RUGGLES VANAMEE ANNIXTER
SHELGRIM CEDARQUIST
GENSLINGER
(SECRETION OF —) INK

OCTOROON METIS MESTEE
MUSTEE MESTIZO METISSE
OCTAROON

OCTROI TAX GRANT PRIVILEGE

OCTUPLE EIGHTFOLD

OCUBY RUM

OCULAR OPTIC VISUAL OCULARY
OPTICAL ORBITAL EYEPIECE

OCULUS MUNDI OPAL

OCYRRHOE (FATHER OF —) CHIRON
(MOTHER OF —) CHARICLO

ODD AUK AWK OUT RUM FELL
LEFT LONE ORRA RARE ANTIC
CRAZY DIPPY DROLL EXTRA

FLAKY FUNKY FUNNY IMPAR
KINKY OUTRE QUEER UNKET
UNKID WEIRD FLAKEY IMPAIR
QUAINT SINGLE UNEVEN UNIQUE
AZYGOUS BAROQUE BIZARRE
COMICAL CURIOUS ERRATIC
STRANGE UNEQUAL UNUSUAL
FANCIFUL FREAKISH PECULIAR
SINGULAR UNPAIRED BURLESQUE
ECCENTRIC FANTASTIC
GROTESQUE LAUGHABLE
SQUIRRELY UNMATCHED
WHIMSICAL
(— JOBMAN) JOEY
(PREF.) AZYGO IMPARI
ODDBALL SPOOK
ODDITY GIG QUIP JIMJAM
RUMNESS QUIZZITY PECULIARITY
(PL.) PURLICUES
ODDMAN UMPIRE ARBITER
FLOATER REFEREE
ODDS BISK EDGE CHALK PRICE
BISQUE DISCORD DISPUTE
QUARREL HANDICAP VARIANCE
ADVANTAGE DISPARITY
(— AND ENDS) ORTS BROTT
REFUSE SCRAPS GIBLETS
SECONDS FEWTRILS REMNANTS
SHAKINGS ETCETERAS
FRAGMENTS
(AT —) ACROSS
(EXTRAVAGANT —) POUNDAGE
(FAVORABLE —) PERCENTAGE
ODE HYMN POEM SONG LYRIC
PAEAN PSALM MONODY ODELET
CANZONA CANZONE EPICEDE
CANTICLE PALINODE PINDARIC
SERENATA STASIMON EPICEDIUM
EPINICION PARABASIS
ODED (SON OF —) AZARIAH
ODENATHUS (WIFE OF —) ZENOBIA
ODEON HALL ODEUM GALLERY
THEATER
ODIN OTHIN WODAN WODEN
WOTAN
(BROTHER OF —) VE VILI
(CREATED BY —) ASK EMBLA
(DAUGHTER-IN-LAW OF —) NANNA
(DESCENDANT OF —) SCYLD
(FATHER OF —) BOR BORR
(HALL OF —) VALHALLA
(HORSE OF —) SLEIPNER SLEIPNIR
(MANSION OF —) GLADSHEIM
(MOTHER OF —) BESTLA
(PALACE OF —) SYN
(RAVEN OF —) HUGIN MUNIN
(RING OF —) DRAUPNIR
(SHIP OF —) NAGLFAR
SKIDBLADNIR
(SON OF —) TYR THOR VALI BALDR
BALDER
(SPEAR OF —) GUNGNIR
(SWORD OF —) GRAM
(THRONE OF —) HLIDSKJALF
(WIFE OF —) FRIA RIND FRIGG
RINDR FRIGGA
(WOLF OF —) GERI FREKI
ODIOUS FOUL LOTH UGLY VILE
LOATH INFAND ODIBLE HATABLE
HATEFUL HEINOUS HIDEOUS
DAMNABLE FLAGRANT
INFAMOUS ABHORRENT
INVIDIOUS OBNOXIOUS
OFFENSIVE REPUGNANT
ODIUM HATRED STIGMA DISLIKE
AVERSION DISFAVOR DISGRACE
DISHONOR ANTIPATHY
(PUBLIC —) ENVY
ODOACER (FATHER OF —) EDECON
ODOMETER ODOGRAPH VIAMETER
WAYWISER HODOMETER
PEDOMETER
ODONTALGIA TOOTHACHE
ODOR AIR FUME FUNK NOSE OLID
TANG WAFF WAFT AROMA
EWDER FETOR FLAIR FUMET
NIDOR SCENT SMACK SMELL
SNUFF SPICE STINK BREATH
FLAVOR FOETOR HODURE
REPUTE STENCH BOUQUET
ESSENCE FUMETTE NOSEGAY
PERFUME VERDURE PUNGENCE
EFFLUVIUM EMPYREUMA
FRAGRANCE REDOLENCE
(— FROM FLOWERS) FUME
(— OF GAME) FUMET
(— OF HAY) NOSE
(BAD —) EWDER FROWST STENCH
(DISGUSTING —) STINK
(FOUL —) FIST MEPHITIS
(FRESH —) YMUR
(PUNGENT —) SPICE
(SPICY —) BALM
(STUDY OF —S) OSMICS
(PREF.) OSM(O)
(SUFF.) OSMA OSPHRESIA
ODORIFEROUS BALMY OLENT
ODOROUS FRAGRANT
ODOROUS FOUL BALMY OLENT
SMELLY ODORANT AROMATIC
FRAGRANT NIDOROSE NIDOROUS
PERFUMED REDOLENT SCENTFUL
SMELLFUL
ODYSSEUS ULYSSES
(DOG OF —) ARGOS
(FATHER OF —) LAERTES SISYPHUS
(FRIEND OF —) MENTOR
(ISLAND OF —) ITHACA
(SON OF —) TELEGONUS
TELEMACHUS
(WIFE OF —) PENELOPE
ODYSSEY (AUTHOR OF —) HOMER
(CHARACTER IN —) ARETE CIRCE
HELEN AEOLUS NESTOR
EUMAEUS ALCINOUS MENELAUS
NAUSICAA ODYSSEUS PENELOPE
DEMODOCUS EURYCLEIA
TEIRESIAS POLYPHEMUS
TELEMACHUS
OEAX (BROTHER OF —) PALAMEDES
(FATHER OF —) NAUPLIUS
(MOTHER OF —) CLYMENE
OEBALUS (FATHER OF —) TELON
(SON OF —) ICARIUS HIPPOCOON
TYNDAREUS
(WIFE OF —) GORGOPHONE
OECIST OEKIST COLONIZER
OEDIPUS OEDIPAL
(BROTHER-IN-LAW OF —) CREON
(DAUGHTER OF —) ISMENE
ANTIGONE
(FATHER OF —) LAIUS
(FOSTER MOTHER OF —) PERIBOEA
(MOTHER OF —) JOCASTA
(SON OF —) ETEOCLES POLYNICES
(WIFE OF —) JOCASTA

OEIL-DE-BOEUF OCULUS
OEILLADE OGLE ELIAD EYLIAD
GLANCE ILLIAD
OENEUS (DAUGHTER OF —) GORGE
DEIANIRA
(FATHER OF —) PORTHEUS
(SON OF —) TOXEUS TYDEUS
MELEAGER
(WIFE OF —) ALTHAEA
OENOCHOE OLPE PROCHOOS
OENOMAUS (DAUGHTER OF —)
HIPPODAMIA
(FATHER OF —) ARES MARS
(MOTHER OF —) STEROPE
(SON OF —) LEUCIPPUS
DYSPONTEUS HIPPODAMUS
OENOMETER VINOMETER
OENONE (FATHER OF —) CEBREN
(LOVER OF —) PARIS
(SON OF —) CORYTHUS
OENOPION (DAUGHTER OF —)
MEROPE
(FATHER OF —) DIONYSUS
(WIFE OF —) HELICE
OESTRID FLY
(— LARVA) BOT
OESTRUS RUT FURY HEAT STING
DESIRE ESTRUS FRENZY IMPULSE
STIMULUS
OEUVRE OPUS WORK
OF A O BY DE OFF VAN VON FROM
HAVE TILL WITH ABOUT
(— AGE) AE
(— ALL) AVA ALDER ALLER
(— COURSE) NATCH
(— DEATH) M
(— EACH) ANA PER SING
(— THIS DAY) HODIERNAL
(— THIS MONTH) HM
(SUFF.) AL AR ILE INE ISH ISTIC
ITIC ITIOUS ORIOUS ORY
OFF BY AFF FAR ODD WET AFAR
AGEE AWAY DOFF DOWN GONE
ALONG ASIDE RIGHT WONKY
WRONG ABSENT CUCKOO
DEPART REMOTE DISTANT
FURTHER REMOVED SEAWARD
TAINTED ABNORMAL OPPOSITE
(— GUARD) TARDY
(— THE PATH) ASTRAY
(— THE SUBJECT) AFIELD
(— THE WIND) ROOM ROOMWARD
(FAR —) DISTANT
(PREF.) AP APH APO DE
OFFAL GURRY WASTE REFUSE
CARRION DOGMEAT GARBAGE
LEAVING RUBBISH GRALLOCH
(— OF FISH) GURRY STOSH
(MILLING —S) GRIT
OFF-BEAT KOOKY
OFFBREAK GOOGLY
OFF-CENTER ECCENTRIC
EXCENTRIC
OFF-COLOR BLUE RISQUE
SUGGESTIVE
OFFEND CAG ERR PET SIN VEX
GALL HARM HUFF HURT MIFF
RASP RASS ABUSE ANGER ANNOY
GRATE GRILL PIQUE SHOCK SPITE
TOUCH WRONG AGUILT ATTACK
GRIEVE INJURE INSULT NETTLE
REVOLT AFFRONT DEFAULT
DISDAIN MORTIFY OUTRAGE

PROVOKE REGRATE STOMACH
UMBRAGE VIOLATE CONFRONT
DISTASTE IRRITATE TRESPASS
DISOBLIGE DISPLEASE
OFFENDED HUFF MIFF SORE
AVERTED FROISSE INJURED
INSULTED
OFFENDER SINNER CULPRIT
MISDOER PECCANT HABITUAL
OFFENDANT
(FIRST —) STAR
OFFENSE PET SIN HUFF LACK SLIP
WITE ABUSE CRIME ERROR FAULT
GRIEF GUILT MALUM PIQUE
SNUFF ATTACK BIGAMY DELICT
FELONY PIACLE PRITCH REATUS
STRUNT AFFRONT DEFAULT
DEMERIT DUDGEON LARCENY
MISDEED OUTRAGE SCANDAL
UMBRAGE PECCANCY TRESPASS
EXTORTION INDECORUM
INDIGNITY THEFTBOTE
(— AGAINST LAW) MALUM DELICT
DELICTUM
(— AGAINST MORALITY) EVIL
CRIME
(SLIGHT —) PECCADILLO
OFFENSIVE BAD ACID EVIL FOUL
HARD UGLY BILGY CRUDE DIRTY
FETID GROSS NASTY SLIMY
COARSE FROWZY GARISH HORRID
RANCID RIBALD ROTTEN ABUSIVE
BEASTLY FULSOME HATEFUL
HIDEOUS NOISOME PECCANT
RASPING SCARLET DREADFUL
INVADING MEPHITIC SHOCKING
STINKING UNSAVORY
LOATHSOME OBNOXIOUS
REPUGNANT REVOLTING
SCANDALOUS
OFFER GO BID PUT BODE GIVE
HAND LEND PLEA SHOW TAKE
TEND DEFER HEAVE PARTY
SHORE START ADDUCE AFFORD
ALLEGE DELATE INJECT OBLATE
OPPOSE PREFER SUBMIT SUPPLY
TENDER ADVANCE BIDDING
COMMEND EXHIBIT PRESENT
PROFFER PROPINE PROPOSE
SUGGEST OVERTURE PROPOSAL
VOLUNTEER
(— EXCUSE) ALIBI
(— FOR SALE) HAWK EXPOSE
(— IN SACRIFICE) IMMOLATE
(— PROOF) APPROVE
(— PUBLICLY) JACTITATE
(— TO VERIFY) AVER
(— UP) APPEAL
(LAST —) ULTIMATUM
(SOLEMN —) PLEDGE
(UNACCEPTED —) POLLICITATION
OFFERING BID ALMS BALI DALI
DEAL GIFT HOST SOMA DOLLY
ENTRY CORBAN NUZZER OFLETE
PIACLE PRESENT RETABLO
TRIBUTE ANATHEMA DEVOTION
DONATION LIBATION OBLATION
PESHKASH PIACULUM SACRIFICE
(— TO GOD) CORBAN DEODATE
(— TO HOUSEHOLD DEITIES) BALI
(EUCHARISTIC —) ANAPHORA
(PEACE —S) PACIFICS
(RELIGIOUS —) OBLATION

(SACRIFICIAL —) HOLOCAUST
(THEATRICAL —) FLUFF
(PL.) HIERA ALTARAGE INFERIAE
OFF-GLIDE EXIT VOCULE DETENTE
OFFHAND AIRY CURT GLIB SOON
ADLIB BLUSH HASTY ABRUPT
BREEZY CASUAL BRUSQUE
READILY CARELESS CAVALIER
GLANCING INFORMAL
EXTEMPORE IMPROMPTU
UNSTUDIED
OFFICE HAT JOB SEE BOMA DUTY
NONE PART POST ROLE ROOM
SHOP TASK TOGA WIKE WORK
PLACE STINT TRUST WIKEN
YAMEN ABBACY AGENCY BUREAU
CHARGE DAFTAR DIWANI DUFTER
METIER MISTER BULLPEN
CAMARIN CENTRAL DEWANEE
DROSTDY EDILITY MYSTERY
SERVICE STATION SURGERY
AEDILITY CAPACITY CUTCHERY
ENSIGNCY FUNCTION KINGSHIP
MINISTRY POSITION PROVINCE
WOOLPACK BAILIWICK
BANKSHALL SITUATION
(— BOY) CHOKRA
(— CHIEF) BOSS MANAGER
(— OF BISHOP) LAWN
(— OF JUDGE) BENCH ERMINE
(— OF PROFESSOR) CHAIR
(— OF ROMAN CURIA) DATARY
DATARIA
(— OF RULER) REGENCY
(— OF THE DEAD) DIRGE
(— WORKER) CLERK STENO TYPIST
SECRETARY
(BRANCH —) WING
(CASHIER'S —) CAISSE
(CLERICAL —) CASSOCK
(DIVINE —) AKOLUTHIA
(ECCLESIASTICAL —) FROCK
BENEFICE EXORCIST
(HIGH —) DIGNITY
(LITURGICAL —) SEXT SERVICE
(MAGISTRATE'S —) KACHAHRI
(MORNING —) ORTHRON ORTHROS
(NAVAL —S) BEACH
(PAY —) WANIGAN
(POLICE —) NICK
(PRIESTLY —) SACERDOCY
(PRINTING —) CHAPEL IMPRIMERY
(RECORD —) CHANCERY
(RESIGN AN —) DEMIT
(TIMEKEEPER'S —) PENNYHOLE
(SUFF.) ATE CY DOM SHIP URE
OFFICEHOLDER IN WINNER
OFFICIAL PLACEMAN
OFFICER (ALSO SEE OFFICIAL) COP
TAB AIDE EXEC EXON FLAG HOLD
NASI SWAB VOGT AGENT CHIEF
CRIER DEWAN DIWAN GRAND
GRAVE GROOM JURAT SEWER
TAXOR USHER ALCADE BEADLE
BEAGLE BEDRAL BUTLER CENSOR
DEPUTY DIRECT ENSIGN GAILLI
GEREFA HERALD KOTWAL
LAWMAN LICTOR MANAGE
ORATOR PARNAS REDTAB SYNDIC
TINDAL ADJOINT AGISTOR
ALNAGER ASSIZER BAILIFF
COMMAND CONDUCT CORONER
DUUMVIR EPAULET FEDERAL

FEODARY GAVELER GENERAL
JEMADAR KLEAGLE LOBSTER
MUSTANG NAPERER PANTLER
PATROON REGIDOR SANCTUM
SCHEPEN SHERIFF SPEAKER
STEWARD WHIPPER WOODMAN
ADJUTANT ALDERMAN ALGUACIL
ANDREEVE BANNERET
CHAFFWAX COFFERER CURSITOR
DOORWARD FORESTER
GOVERNOR GRASSMAN
MERESMAN MINISTER PALATINE
QUESTEUR DEMPSTER TIPSTAFF
VISCOUNT WOODWARD
CONSTABLE DIKEGRAVE
FINANCIER INTENDANT
MODERATOR PAYMASTER
SCHOOLMAN TAHSILDAR
(— OF CHURCH) ABBOT ELDER
DEACON SEXTON ANTISTES
DEFENSOR LAMPADARY
SACRISTAN
(— OF COURT) MACER MASTER
BAILIFF FEODARY FILACER
CURSITOR DEMPSTER EXAMINER
SERGEANT ASSOCIATE
BYRLAWMAN SURROGATE
(— OF FORESTS) AGISTER AGISTOR
(— OF KING'S STABLES) AVENER
(BARDIC —) DRUID
(CAVALRY —) CORNET
(CHIEF —) NASI DEWAN DAROGA
PARNAS PRESIDENT
(CUSTOMS —) GAGER SHARK
GAUGER JERQUER DOUANIER
SEARCHER SURVEYOR TIDESMAN
(GREEK —) STRATEGOS
STRATEGUS
(JAPANESE —) SHIKKEN
(MASONIC —) EAST KING DEACON
STEWARD
(MILITARY —) NAIG NAIK COMES
MAJOR SUBAH ENSIGN NAIQUE
RANKER SARDAR SIRDAR
CAPTAIN COLONEL GENERAL
JEMADAR MARSHAL SUBADAR
WARRANT COMMANDER
RABSHAKEH SHAVETAIL
(MINOR —) CHINOVNIK
(MONASTERY —) CELLARER
(MUNICIPAL —) SCHOUT
(NAVAL —) CPO EXON MATE SWAB
BOSUN ENSIGN PURSER YEOMAN
ADMIRAL CAPTAIN MUSTANG
SPOTTER YOUNKER SUNDOWNER
(PAPAL —) DATARY
(POLICE —) PIG PEON RURAL
EXEMPT JAVERT KOTWAL
RUNNER SBIRRO ALYTARCH
SEARCHER THANADAR DETECTIVE
ROUNDSMAN
(PRESIDING —) CHAIRONE
CHAIRPERSON
(PUBLIC —) JUDGE FISCAL NOTARY
PODESTA
(ROMAN —) LICTOR
(SHERIFF'S —) FANG BEAGLE
BAILIFF BULLDOG HUISSIER
(SHIP'S —) MATE FANTOD
(STAFF —) TAB AIDE REDTAB
ADJUTANT
(TURKISH —) AGA AGHA MUTE
VIZIR VIZIER BIMBASHI BINBASHI

(UNIVERSITY —) DEAN PROVOST
(WARRANT —) MACHINIST
(PL.) BRAID BRASS STAFF
OFFICIAL (ALSO SEE OFFICER) AGA
BEG DEY VIP AMIN BOSS KUAN
KWAN TRUE AGENT AHONG
AMALA AMBAN AMEEN AMLAH
CLERK EDILE EPHOR GYANI HAJIB
HOMER JURAT LIMMU LINER
MAYOR NAZIR REEVE SAHIB
AEDILE ARCHON ATABEG
BASHAW CENSOR CONSUL
EPARCH EPONYM FISCAL FORMAL
GABBAI GRIEVE HAZZAN HERALD
LAWMAN MASTER NOTARY
PANDIT PREVOT RABMAG SATRAP
SCRIBE SEALER SINGER TAOTAI
TAOYIN TRONER VERGER
WARDEN WEDANA ALMONER
APOSTLE ASIARCH BURGESS
CERTAIN JEMADAR LANDRAT
MARSHAL MOORMAN PRISTAW
REFEREE STALLAR STARTER
SUBASHI ALDERMAN APPROVED
CARDINAL CELLARER CUSTOMER
DOGBERRY GOVERNOR LINESMAN
MANDARIN PRYTANIS VESTIARY
WHIFFLER EXECUTIVE
MAJORDOMO OMBUDSMAN
SELECTMAN MAGISTRATE
(— APPROVAL) VISA VISE
(— DECREE) WRIT UKASE
(BLUNDERING —) DOGBERRY
(EISTEDDFOD —) DRUID
(PALACE —) PALADIN
(POMPOUS —) BUMBLE
(PRETENTIOUS —) PANJANDRUM
(PL.) KEYS PHAR OMLAH
OFFICIATE ACT FILL SERVE SUPPLY
PERFORM CELEBRATE
OFFICIATOR DEICIDE
OFFICIOUS BUSY COOL PERT
SAUCY FORMAL FORTHY PUSHING
ARROGANT IMPUDENT INFORMAL
MEDDLING OFFICIAL INBEARING
PRAGMATIC
OFFING OFF FUTURE PICTURE
OFFISH CLAMMY UPSTAGE
OFFSCOURINGS MUD SCURF
OFF-SEASON LAYOFF
OFFSET SLAB STEP ALTAR CRIMP
ERASE POISE CANCEL CONTRA
JOGGLE REDEEM SETOFF
BALANCE COUNTER LATERAL
RETREAT SETBACK PROPAGULE
(— ON BULB) SPLIT
OFFSHOOT GET PUP ROD SON
LIMB SPUR BOUGH ISSUE SCION
SHOOT SPRIG BRANCH FILIAL
GROWTH MEMBER OFFSET
SPROUT ADJUNCT APOPHYSIS
FILIATION OUTGROWTH
RAMIFICATION
(— OF LAKE) BAYOU
OFFSHORE DEEPWATER
OFFSPRING BOY FRY IMP KID KIN
SON BRAT BURD CHIT HEIR SEED
SLIP BIRTH BREED BROOD CHILD
FRUIT ISSUE SCION SPAWN
BEGATS DUSTEE EMBRYO FOSTER
GRIQUA JUMART PROLES RESULT
STRAIN STRIND MORISCO
NISHADA OUTCOME PRODUCE

PRODUCT PROGENY YOUNGER
CHILDREN DAUGHTER DEMISANG
GENITURE INCREASE KINDLING
BAIRNTEAM MUSTAFINA
(— OF FAIRIES) CHANGELING
(— OF NEGRO AND MULATTO)
GRIFFE
(— OF WITCH) HAGSEED HOLDIKEN
(MYTHICAL —) JUMART
(PREMATURE —) CASTLING
(PREF.) GEN(O) GON(O) PAEDO
PEDO PROLI
(SUFF.) ITE TOKOUS
OF HUMAN BONDAGE (AUTHOR
OF —) MAUGHAM
(CHARACTER IN —) CAREY EMILY
ERLIN FANNY NORAH PRICE
SALLY WEEKS LAWSON LOUISA
NESBIT PHILIP ROGERS THORPE
ATHELNY CLUTTON HAYWARD
MILDRED WILLIAM CRONSHAW
WILKINSON
OFICINA WORKS OFFICE FACTORY
OFLETE WAFER OBLATION
OFFERING
OF, MICE AND MEN (AUTHOR OF —)
STEINBECK
(CHARACTER IN —) SLIM CANDY
SMALL CROOKS CURLEY GEORGE
LENNIE MILTON
OFTEN OFT AFTEN OFTLY
COMMON EFTSOONS FREQUENT
REPEATED
(VERY —) CONTINUALLY
OF TIME AND THE RIVER
(AUTHOR OF —) WOLFE
(CHARACTER IN —) ANN GANT
JOEL WANG BASCOM ELINOR
EUGENE PIERCE ROBERT WEAVER
COULSON FRANCIS HATCHER
MORNAYE PENTLAND
OGDOAD EIGHT OCTOAD OGDOAS
OCTONARY
OGEE (ALSO SEE MOLDING) CYMA
GULA TALON MOLDING
OGIVAL HEATER
OGLE EYE GAZE LEER LOOK MASH
STARE GLANCE EXAMINE
MARLOCK SMICKER OEILLADE
OGRE ORC BOYG BRUTE DEMON
GHOUL GIANT HUGON TYRANT
YAKSHA BUGABOO BUGBEAR
MONSTER WINDIGO
OGRESS PELLET GUNSTONE
OGTIERN LORD MASTER
OGYGIAN ANCIENT PRIMEVAL
OH OU OW ACH OUCH

OHIO	
CAPITAL: COLUMBUS	
COLLEGE: KENT HIRAM KENYON XAVIER ANTIOCH OBERLIN DEFIANCE	
COUNTY: ERIE PIKE ROSS DARKE MIAMI STARK GALLIA HARDIN SUMMIT LICKING CUYAHOGA HAMILTON	
INDIAN TRIBE: ERIE WYANDOT	
NATIVE: BUCKEYE	
NICKNAME: BUCKEYE	
PRESIDENT: TAFT GRANT HAYES HARDING GARFIELD HARRISON MCKINLEY	

RIVER: MIAMI MAUMEE SCIOTO CUYAHOGA MUSKINGUM
STATE BIRD: CARDINAL
STATE FLOWER: CARNATION
STATE TREE: BUCKEYE
TOWN: ADA LIMA TROY ADENA AKRON BEREA CADIZ NILES XENIA CANTON DAYTON LORAIN MENTOR TOLEDO CHARDON COLUMBUS SANDUSKY CLEVELAND

OIL BEN FAT ILE ULE BALM CHIA DIKA FUEL ZEST BRIBE CRUDE JUICE OLEUM SMEAR STOCK TRAIN ULYIE ULZIE ACEITE ANOINT BINDER BUTTER CARDOL CHRISM CREESH EUPION GREASE LIQUOR SAFROL SMOOTH ZACHUN CEDRIUM ESSENCE LANOLIN MYRRHOL PHLOROL RETINOL VETIVER BERGAMOT COUMARAN ERIGERON GINGEROL PHTHALAN SDRAVETS TETRALIN CARVACROL LUBRICATE PETROLEUM
(— BEETLE) MELOE MELOID
(— CAKE) SEEDCAKE
(— CAN) OILER
(— CASK) RIER
(— FROM ORANGE FLOWERS) NEROLI
(— LAMP) LUCIGEN
(— OF TURPENTINE) CAMPHENE CAMPHINE
(— PALM) OILBERRY
(— PAN) SUMP
(— PLANT) SESAME
(— ROCK) SHALE LIMESTONE
(— TREE) EBOE POON TUNG MAHWA
(— VESSEL) DRUM OLPE CRUET CRUSE TANKER CRESSET
(— WELL) DUSTER GASSER GUSHER WILDCAT
(BUTTER —) GHEE
(COAL —) PHOTOGEN
(CONSECRATED —) CHRISM
(FISH —) GURRY
(FIXED —) COCUM KOKAM KOKUM
(FLOWER —) ABSOLUTE
(FRAGRANT —) ATAR OTTO ATTAR OTTAR CAFFEOL BERGAMOT CAFFEONE GERANIOL
(INFERIOR —) MIDDLING
(LINSEED —) CARRON LINOLEUM
(MINERAL —) NAPHTHA KEROSENE
(PINE —) FROTHER
(PUNGENT —) CAJUPUT
(SESAME —) GINGILI SIRITCH
(SOLID —) KIKUEL
(VEGETABLE —) MACASSAR
(VULCANIZED —) FACTICE
(WHALE —) SPERM TRAIN
(PREF.) ELAEO ELAIO ELEO OLEI OLEO
OILBIRD FATBIRD GUACHARO
OILFISH ESCOLAR
OILSEED TIL TEEL SESAME LINSEED RAPESEED
OILSKIN OIL OILER SQUAM OILCASE OILCOAT SLICKER
OILSTONE HONE

SHALE WHETSTONE
OILY FAT GLIB BLAND FATTY LOEIC OLEIC SLEEK SOAPY SUAVE GREASY OILISH OLEOSE OLEOUS SMARMY SMOOTH SUPPLE PINGUID SERVILE SLIPPERY UNCTUOUS COMPLIANT PLAUSIBLE
(PREF.) LIPAR(O)
OINTMENT UNG BALM MULL NARD PASTE SALVE SMEAR BALSAM CERATE CEROMA CHARGE CHRISM GREASE POMADE REMEDY UNGUENT EYESALVE POPULEON REMOLADE SPIKENARD WHITFIELD
(— OF GODS) AMBROSIA
OJIBWAY CHIPPEWA SAULTEUR CHIPPEWAY
OKA OCHA OQUE OQUI OCQUE
OKAPI GIRAFFINE
OKAY OK YES HUNK OKEH HUNKY APPROVE CORRECT SANCTION AUTHORIZE
OKIA OKET OUNCE
OKINAWA (CAPITAL OF —) NAHA

OKLAHOMA

CAPITAL: OKLAHOMACITY
COLLEGE: CAMERON LANGSTON PHILLIPS
COUNTY: KAY COAL LOVE ADAIR ATOKA CADDO GREER OSAGE ALFALFA OKFUSKEE OKMULGEE
INDIAN TRIBE: WACO WICHITA TAWAKONI
LAKE: EUFAULA OOLOGAH
MOUNTAINS: OUACHITA
NATIVE: OKIE SOONER
NICKNAME: SOONER
RIVER: RED GRAND WASHITA ARKANSAS CANADIAN CIMARRON
STATE FLOWER: MISTLETOE
STATE TREE: REDBUD
TOWN: ADA JAY ALVA ENID HUGO ALTUS MIAMI PONCA TULSA ELRENO GUYMON IDABEL LAWTON MADILL TALOGA VINITA ANTLERS SAPULPA SHAWNEE ANADARKO FORTSILL MUSKOGEE

OKRA GOBO OKRO BAMIA BENDY GOBBO GOMBO GUBBO GUMBO OCHRA BENDEE MALLOW BANDAKA BANDICOY BANDIKAI
OLD AGY ELD AGED AULD COLD WOLD YALD ANILE HOARY STALE WOULD FORMER FOROLD INFIRM MATURE SENILE SHABBY VETUST AGEABLE ANCIENT ANTIQUE ARCHAIC ELDERLY FORWORN OGYGIAN UMWHILE DECREPIT MEDIEVAL OBSOLETE DODDERING HACKNEYED SENESCENT VENERABLE
(— AND MELLOW) CRUSTY
(— BAILEY) GAOL JAIL PRISON
(— CLOTHESMAN) POCO
(— FAITHFUL) GEYSER
(— HAND) LONGTIMER
(— MAID) SPINSTER THORNBACK

(— MAN) ANTIQUITY WHITEBEARD
(— SOD) EIRE ERIN IRELAND
(— SQUAW) DIVER HOUND MOMMY CALLOO CALLOW COWEEN DUCKER QUANDY OLDWIFE SCOLDER COCKAWEE LONGTAIL SHARPTAIL SOUTHERLY
(— WOMAN) HAG CRONE GAMMER
(BEING LESS THAN 13 YEARS —) PRETEEN
(GROWING —) SENESCENT
(OF —) WHILOM ERSTWHILE
(PREF.) PALAE(O) PALAI(O) PALE(O) SENI
(— AGE) GER(I)(O) GERATO GERONT(O) PRESBY(O)
(— MAN) GER(I)(O) GERONT(O) PRESBY(O)
OLD AND THE YOUNG (AUTHOR OF —) PIRANDELLO
(CHARACTER IN —) COSTA MAURO SALVO SELMI AURITI GIULIO AURELIO CORRADO MORTARA ROBERTO CAPOLINO DIANELLA FLAMINIO GERLANDO IPPOLITO NICOLETTA LAURENTANO
OLD BAY STATE MASSACHUSETTS
OLD CURIOSITY SHOP (AUTHOR OF —) DICKENS
(CHARACTER IN —) KIT DICK FRED NELL BRASS QUILP SARAH CODLIN JARLEY MARTON THOMAS BARBARA NUBBLES SAMPSON SWIVELLER CHRISTOPHER
OLD DOMINION STATE VIRGINIA
OLDER MORE ALDER ELDER SENIOR ANCESTOR
OLDEST
(PREF.) EO
OLD-FASHIONED CORNY DOWDY FUSTY PASSE FOGRAM FOGRUM QUAINT STODGY ANCIENT ANTIQUE ARCHAIC ARRIERE ELDERLY VINTAGE FRUMPISH OBSOLETE CRINOLINE PRIMITIVE RINKYDINK OLDFANGLED
OLD FRANKLIN STATE TENNESSEE
OLD LINE STATE MARYLAND
OLD MAID (AUTHOR OF —) WHARTON
(CHARACTER IN —) JOE TINA DELIA JAMES LOVELL CLEMENT RALSTON SPENDER CHARLOTTE
OLD MORTALITY (AUTHOR OF —) SCOTT
(CHARACTER IN —) JOHN BASIL EDITH HENRY JENNY MAUSE CUDDIE MORTON BALFOUR FRANCIS GRAHAME OLIFANT BOTHWELL DENNISON EVANDALE HEADRIGG MARGARET BELLENDEN CLAVERHOUSE
OLD-TIMER SOURDOUGH
OLD WIVES' TALE (AUTHOR OF —) BENNETT
(CHARACTER IN —) JOHN CYRIL POVEY BAINES CHIRAC GERALD SAMUEL SCALES SOPHIA HARRIET FAUCAULT CONSTANCE CRITCHLOW
OLD-WOMANISH ANILE

OLEANDER LAUREL NERIUM DOGBANE ROSEBAY
OLEFIN ALKENE
OLEIC RAPIC RAPINIC
OLEORESIN GUM ANIME APIOL ELEMI TOLUS BALSAM GURJUN IRIDIN COPAIBA GALIPOT LABDANUM TACAMAHAC
OLFACTION NOSE SMELL OSMESIS SMELLING ESPHRESIS
OLIGARCHIC FEUDAL
OLIGARCHY KREMLIN
OLIGOCLASE SUNSTONE
OLIMPIA (HUSBAND OF —) BIRENO OBERTO
OLINDO (HUSBAND OF —) SOFRONIA
(SAVIOR OF —) CLORINDA
OLIO STEW MEDLEY MELANGE MIXTURE MISHMASH MACEDOINE PASTICCIO POTPOURRI
OLIPHANT HORN ELEPHANT
OLIPRANCE ROMP SHOW FROLIC JOLLITY
OLIVE OLEA MORON BRUNET LIERRE OLIVER OXHORN PIMOLA RESEDA BAROUNI CITRINE MISSION MORILLON OLEASTER
(— FLY) DACUS
(AMERICAN —) DEVILWOOD
(OVERRIPE —) DRUPE
(PREF.) DRUPI
(—OIL) ELAEO ELAIO ELEO
OLIVER NOLL HAMMER HOLLIPER
(BROTHER OF —) ORLANDO
(WIFE OF —) CELIA
OLIVER TWIST (AUTHOR OF —) DICKENS
(CHARACTER IN —) BILL JACK NOAH ROSE TOBY BATES FAGIN HARRY MONKS NANCY SALLY SIKES TWIST BEDWIN BUMBLE CORNEY EDWARD MAYLIE OLIVER CHARLEY CRACKIT DAWKINS GRIMWIG LEEFORD BROWNLOW CLAYPOLE LOSBERNE SOWERBERRY
OLIVET PEARL
OLIVIA (HUSBAND OF —) SEBASTIAN
OLIVINE PERIDOT
OLLA JAR JUG OLE POT OLAY PUCHERA PUCHERO
OLLA PODRIDA HASH OLIO MEDLEY POTPOURRI
OLM PROTEUS SALAMANDER
OLOGY ISM SCIENCE
OLYMPIAN CELESTIAL
OLYMPIAS (FATHER OF —) NEOPTOLEMUS
(HUSBAND OF —) PHILIP
(SLAYER OF —) CASSANDER
(SON OF —) ALEXANDER
OLYNTHUS ASCULA
OMAGUA CAMBEVA
OMAH SASQUATCH
OMAN (CAPITAL OF —) MASQAT MUSCAT
(LANGUAGE OF —) ARABIC BALUCHI
(MOUNTAIN OF —) SHAM HAFIT HARIM NAKHL TAYIN AKHDAR
(NATIVE OF —) ADNAN QAHTAN BALUCHI
(TOWN IN —) SUR NIGWA MASQAT

MATRAH SALALAH
OMAR (FATHER OF —) ELIPHAZ
OMASUM BOOK BOUK BIBLE
FARDEL MANYPLIES
OMBER SOLO UMBRE HOMBRE
MEDIATOR QUADRILLE
OMEGA END LAST
OMELET AMLET AMELET FOOYUNG
FOOYOUNG FRITTATA
OMEN BODE LUCK SIGN ABODE
AUGUR BODER FREET FREIT
GUEST TOKEN WEIRD WHATE
AUGURY HANDEL HANSEL
AUSPICE PORTENT PRESAGE
PRODIGY WARNING CEREMONY
FOREBODE SOOTHSAY
HARBINGER
OMENTUM WEB CAUL ZIRBUS
EPIPLOON
OMINOUS DIRE DOUR GRIM BLACK
FATAL BODING DISMAL SHREWD
AUGURAL BALEFUL BANEFUL
BODEFUL DIREFUL DOOMFUL
FATEFUL MENACING SINISTER
THUNDERY PROPHETIC
PORTENTOUS
OMISSION OUT BALK BAULK
CHASM SALTUS DEFAULT
FAILURE MISPICK NEGLECT
SILENCE PASSOVER OVERSIGHT
(— OF A LETTER) APOCOPE
(— OF SYLLABLES) SYNCOPE
(TACIT —) SILENCE
OMIT CUT LET BALK BATE DROP
EDIT KILL MISS PASS SKIP SLIP
ABATE ELIDE OBMIT SPARE
BELEVE CANCEL DELETE EXCEPT
FORGET IGNORE DISCARD
EXPUNGE NEGLECT DISCOUNT
OVERLEAP OVERLOOK OVERSKIP
OVERSLIP DISREGARD PRETERMIT
OMITTED VIDE
OMMATIDIUM FACET FACETTE
OMNIBUS BUS BUSS BARGE
HERDIC JOGGER PIRATE
AUTOBUS MOTORBUS KITTEREEN
OMNIPOTENT GOD ABLE DEITY
GREAT ARRANT MIGHTY
ALMIGHTY POWERFUL
UNEQUALED UNLIMITED
OMNIPRESENCE UBIQUITY
OMNISCIENT WISE LEARNED
POWERFUL PANSOPHIC
OMOPLATE SCAPULA
OMPHALE (FATHER OF —)
IARDANUS
(HUSBAND OF —) TMOLUS
(SON OF —) TANTALUS
OMPHALOS HUB BOSS KNOB
NAVEL CENTER UMBILICUS
OMRI (FATHER OF —) BECHER
MICHAEL
(SON OF —) AHAB
ON O AN IN TO ONE SUR ATOP
AWAY OVER UPON ABOUT ABOVE
AHEAD ALONG ANENT WITHIN
FORWARD
(— A HATCH) ABROOD
(— ACCOUNT OF) IN FOR
(— ALL SIDES) ABOUT AROUND
(— AND ON) EVER FOREVER
TEDIOUS
(— EARTH) BELOW

(— END) TOGETHER
(— FOOT) UP AFOOT TOWARD
FOOTBACK
(— HAND) ALONG
(— HIGH) ALOFT
(— THE CONTRARY) BUT RATHER
(— THE MOVE) AFOOT
(— THE OTHER HAND) BUT AGAIN
HOWEVER ALTHOUGH
(— THE OTHER SIDE) OVER ACROSS
(— THE WAY) AWAY AGATE
(— TIME) PROMPT
(— TOP OF) ATOP ABOVE ALOFT
(— WHAT ACCOUNT) WHY
(FATHER OF —) PELETH
(PREF.) IL IM IN IR SUPER
ONAGER ASS GOUR KULAN
KOULAN ONAGRA ALACRAN
CATAPULT SCORPION
ONAM (FATHER OF —) SHOBAL
JERAHMEEL
(MOTHER OF —) ATARAH
ONAN (FATHER OF —) JUDAH
ONCE ANE EEN ERST AINCE ONCET
WHILE YANCE FORMER WHILOM
QUONDAM UMWHILE FORMERLY
SOMETIME UMQUHILE WHENEVER
ERSTWHILE
(— MORE) YET AGAIN ENCORE
ITERUM
(AT —) PRESTO
ONDATRA FIBER
ONE J AE AN HE UN ACE AIN ANE
ANY EIN MAN OON TAE UNA UNE
WON YAE YAN YEN YIN YOU
SAME SOLE SOME TANE TEAN
THIS TONE TOON UNAL UNIT
WHON WONE ALONE ALPHA
UNITY WOONE ABOARD FELLOW
PERSON SINGLE UNIQUE UNITED
CERTAIN NUMERAL PRONOUN
SIMPLUM UNBROKEN SINGLETON
UNDIVIDED UNMARRIED
(— AFTER ANOTHER) ABOUT
TANDEM SERIALLY SERIATIM
(— BORN A SERF) NEIF NEIFE
(— BY ONE) APIECE SINGLY
OVERHEAD
(— CONDEMNED WRONGFULLY)
CALAS
(— CURIOUS TO KNOW ALL)
QUIDNUNC
(— DETESTED) WARLING
(— DEVOTED TO PARTICULAR ART)
IST
(— EASILY TRICKED) CULLY
(— ENGAGED IN MARAUDING)
LOOTIE
(— ENROLLED IN ARMY) DRAFTEE
(— GIVEN TO DEVILTRY) HELLION
(— INSTRUCTED IN SECRET SYSTEM)
EPOPT
(— LATE) SERO
(— NOT A REGULAR MASON)
COWAN
(— OF PAIR) FELLOW DOUBLET
(— OF TRIPLETS) TRILLING
(— OVERZEALOUS) HYPER
(— SENT FORTH) APOSTLE
(— TENTH) TITHE
(— THAT UNDERGOES CHANGE)
MUTANT
(— THOUSAND) MIL

(— TWENTY-FOURTH) CARAT
(— UNKNOWN) QUIDAM
(— VERSED IN LITERATURE) SAVANT
(— WHO BRINGS MEAT TO TABLE)
DAPIFER
**(— WHO DISPLAYS
FASTIDIOUSNESS)** EPICURE
(— WHO DOCTORS SOMETHING)
COOK
(— WHO EXCELS) ACE
(— WHO FABRICATES) SMITH
(— WHO FOLLOWS ARMY) SUTLER
(— WHO FORSAKES FAITH)
APOSTATE
(— WHO FRUSTRATES PLAN)
MARPLOT
**(— WHO HAS ATTAINED
PERFECTION)** SIDDHA
(— WHO IS AWAY) ABSENTEE
**(— WHO IS STRANGE OR
ECCENTRIC)** WEIRDO
(— WHO LOADS SHIP) BUNKER
**(— WHO MAKES LIVING BY
TRICKERY)** CADGER
(— WHO MANAGES) GERENT
(— WHO REGULATES GUN) TRAINER
(— WHO REMOVES NUISANCE)
ABATOR
(— WHO REPRESENTS NEWEST) NEO
(— WHO TESTS) CONNER
**(— WHOSE MIND IS IMPAIRED BY
AGE)** DOTARD
**(— WITH FIRST-HAND
INFORMATION)** INSIDER
(BLESSED —) BHAGAVAT
(EVIL —) WOND SHAITAN SHEITAN
(EXTRAORDINARY —) DOOZY
DOOZER
(LITTLE —) BUTCHA PICKANINNY
(LOVED —) MINION
(NOT —) NARY
(SWEET —) HONEYCOMB
(TIMELESS —) AKAL
(PREF.) HENO MON(O) UNI
(— AND A HALF TIMES) SESQUI
(— AND THE SAME) HOM(O)
(— ANOTHER) ALLELO
(— BILLIONTH) NANO
(— MILLIONTH) MICR(O)
(— TRILLIONTH) PICO
(SAME —) AUT(O) AUTH(I)
(SUFF.) (— BELONGING) AN EAN
IAN
(— BELONGING TO) IE ING
(— BELONGING TO A GROUP) ID
(— BELONGING TO A LINE) IE
(— HAVING) ANDER
(— HAVING TO DO WITH) IE
(— OF A KIND) ING
(— OF A QUALITY) IE
(— SKILLED) AN EAN IAN
(— THAT ADVOCATES A DOCTRINE)
IST
(— THAT DABBLES)
(— THAT DOES) ER IER YER
(— THAT HAS) ER IER YER
(— THAT MAKES) IST
(— THAT OPERATES)
(— THAT PERFORMS) ER IER IST
YER
(— THAT PRACTICES) IST
(— THAT PRODUCES) ER IER IST
YER

(— THAT SPECIALIZES) IST
(— THAT STUDIES)
(— THAT YIELDS) ER IER YER
**(— OCCUPATIONALLY CONNECTED
WITH)** ER IER YER
(LESSER —) IDIUM
(LITTLE —) IE
(SMALL —) IDIUM IUM
ONEGITE AMETHYST GEMSTONE
ONENESS UNION UNITY CONCORD
ONEHOOD UNICITY UNITUDE
IDENTITY SAMENESS AGREEMENT
ONE-NIGHT STAND GIG
ONEROUS HARD HEAVY ARDUOUS
ONEROSE WEIGHTY EXACTING
GRIEVOUS LABORIOUS
ONESELF
(PREF.) SUI
(BY, FOR, PERT. TO —) AUT(O)
AUTH(I)
ONE-SIDED ECCENTRIC
UNILATERAL
ONETIME FORMER FORMERLY
ERSTWHILE
ONFALL ONSET ATTACK ASSAULT
ON-GLIDE TENSION ENTRANCE
ONION BOLL CEPA LEEK LILY SYBO
CIBOL INGAN PEARL ALLIUM
LILIUM PORRET BERMUDA
CEBOLLA HOLLEKE PICKLER
SHALLOT AYEGREEN RARERIPE
SCALLION VALENCIA
(ROPE OF —S) REEVE
(SEASONED WITH —S) LYONNAISE
(STRING OF —S) TRACE
ONKOS TOPKNOT
ONLOOKER BOOK GAZER WITNESS
AUDIENCE BEHOLDER OVERSEER
BYSTANDER SPECTATOR
ONLY ALL BUT JUST LONE MERE
ONCE SAVE SOLE AFALD ALONE
ARRAH FIRST MERED NOBUT
OLEPY ANERLY BARELY MERELY
NOBBUT SIMPLE SINGLE SINGLY
SOLELY ALLENARLY EXCEPTING
(— THIS) MERE
(BEING —) SIMPLE
ONMUN HANGUL HANKUL
ONOMATOPOEIA
(PREF.) KE(R)
ONOMATOPOEIC ECHOIC IMSONIC
MIMETIC IMITATIVE
ONRUSH BIRR SHAKE ATTACK
TIDEWAY
ONSET DASH DINT FALL FARD
RESE RUSH BRAID BREAK BRUNT
FAIRD FRUSH START STORM
STOUR VENUE ACCESS AFFRET
ATTACK CHARGE COURGE
IMPACT INSULT ONDING ONFALL
POWDER THRUST ASSAULT
BRATTLE BEGINNING ENCOUNTER
ONSLAUGHT
ONSETTER CAGER HITCHER
ONSLAUGHT LASH BLAST ONSET
ATTACK ASSAULT DESCENT
SISERARA SALIAUNCE
ONSTEAD ONSET FARMHOUSE
HOMESTEAD
ONTARIO (CANAL IN —) TRENT
RIDEAU
(CAPITAL OF —) TORONTO
(LAKE IN —) SIMCOE

(TOWN IN —) EMO GALT LONDON OTTAWA WINDSOR HAMILTON KINGSTON KITCHENER
ONTO ATOP ABOARD
ONTOGENY DEVELOPMENT
ONTOLOGY METAPHYSICS
ONUS DUTY LOAD BLAME BURDEN CHARGE WEIGHT INCUBUS
ONWARD AWAY AHEAD ALONG FORTH UPWARD FORTHON FORWARD TOWARDS FORERIGHT
ONYX ONIX NICOLO TECALI ONYCHIN JASPONYX SARDONYX
(MEXICAN —) ALABASTER
OOCYTE PROGAMETE GAMETOCYTE
OODLES HEAP LOTS MANY RAFTS SCADS SLEWS LASHINGS SLITHERS ABUNDANCE
OOGONIUM NUCULE OOCYST OOGONE
OOLAK WOLLOCK
OOLITE PISOLITE ROESTONE
OOLONG TEA
OOMPH PEP VIGOR ENERGY
OOPAK TEA
OORALI CURARE
OORIAL SHA SHEEP URIAL
OOTHECA OVISAC
OOZE OZ BOG MUD SEW SOP DRIP EMIT LEAK MIRE SEEP SLEW SLOB SLUE WEEP EXUDE GLEET MARSH SLIME SWEAT WEEZE EXHALE SICKER SLEECH SLOUGH SLUDGE SQUASH SQUDGE STRAIN SCREEVE TEICHER PERCOLATE
(— OUT) SEW SPEW SPUE
(PREF.) STACTO
OOZING WEEPY SQUDGY SEEPAGE SPEWING WEEPING
OOZY OASY SEEPY WASHY SLEECHY ULIGINOUS
OPAH CRAVO SUNFISH KINGFISH MARIPOSA MOONFISH
OPAL GEM NOBLE RESIN FIORITE GIRASOL HYALITE ISOPYRE JASPOPAL MENILITE SEMIOPAL CACHOLONG GEYSERITE
OPALESCENT OPALED OPALINE IRISATED
OPALEYE GREENFISH
OPAQUE DIM DARK DULL DENSE MUDDY SHADY THICK VAGUE OBTUSE STUPID CLOUDED OBSCURE ABSTRUSE EYESHADE
OPEN GO DUP LAX OPE AIRY AJAR BARE FAIR FLUE FREE GIVE PERT UNDO VIDE AGAPE APERT BEGIN BLOWN BREAK BROAD BURST CHINK CLEAR CRACK FLARE FRANK FRESH LANCE LOOSE MUSHY NAKED OVERT PLAIN RELAX SPALD SPLAT SPLAY START UNBAR UNPEG UNTIE APPERT CANDID DIRECT ENTAME EXPAND EXPOSE FACIAL FORTHY GAPING HONEST LIABLE OUVERT PATENT PUBLIC SINGLE SPREAD UNBOLT UNFOLD UNFURL UNGLUE UNLOCK UNROLL UNSEAL UNSHUT UNSPAR UNSTOP UNTINE UNWINK VACANT ARTLESS BLOSSOM

DISPART FIELDEN OBVIOUS OUTLINE SINCERE THROUGH UNCLOSE UNHINGE APPARENT COMMENCE DISCLOSE EXPLICIT EXTENDED INITIATE MANIFEST PERVIOUS RESERATE UNFASTEN CHAMPAIGN OSTENSIBLE
(— A VEIN) BROACH
(— AIR) ALFRESCO
(— AND CLEANSE) WILLOW
(— CLOTH) SCUTCH
(— COUNTRY) VELDT WEALD
(— EYES OR LIPS) SEVER
(— THE WAY) INVITE PIONEER
(— TO PURSUIT) FAIR
(— UP) START DEVELOP DISPART DISCLOSE
(— VIOLENTLY) SPORT
(— WIDE) YAWN EXPAND STRETCH
(— WIDELY) GAPE
(FULLY —) WIDE AGAPE YAWNING
(HALF —) MID AJAR
(TOO —) OVERBARISH
OPENBILL OPENBEAK
OPENED APPAUME ECHAPPE
OPENER KEY KNOB LATCH SESAME APERIENT
(— IN POKER) PAIR JACKS
(FURROW —) SHOE STUBRUNNER
(OYSTER —) HUSKER
OPENHANDED FREE LIBERAL GENEROUS RECEPTIVE
OPENING OS CUT EYE GAP YAT ANUS BOLE BORE DAWN DOOR DROP FENT FLUE GATE HOLE LOOP PASS PORE PORT PYLA RIFT RIMA SLAP SLIT SLOT SPAN VENT VOID YAWN YEAT BLEED BRACK BREAK CHASM CHINK CLEFT CROSS DEBUT GRILL HILUM INLET LIGHT MOUTH SCOOT SINUS START THIRL WIDTH ADITUS AVENUE BREACH CASING CHANCE GRILLE HIATUS INTAKE LACUNA MEATUS OILLET OUTLET PORTAL SLUICE SPREAD AIRPORT CREVASS CREVICE DISPLAY FISSURE ORIFICE OUTCAST SWALLET APERIENT APERTURE BUNGHOLE CREVASSE ENTRANCE OVERTURE PLUGHOLE SCISSURE TEASEHOLE
(— BELOW PENTHOUSE) GALLERY
(— FOR ESCAPE) MUSE MEUSE
(— FROM SEA) INDRAFT
(— IN ANTHER) STOMIUM
(— IN DECK) SCUTTLE
(— IN EARTH) MOFETTE
(— IN FLOOR OR ROOF) HATCH SKYLIGHT
(— IN GARMENT) FENT ARMHOLE
(— IN LOCK TUMBLER) GATING
(— IN MINE) EYE ADIT RAISE SHAFT WINZE WINNING
(— IN MOLD) POUR
(— IN PICTURE FRAME) SIGHT
(— IN PILLAR OF COAL) JENKIN JUNKING
(— IN ROCK) GRIKE
(— IN SALMON TRAP) SLAP
(— IN SEA CAVE) GLOUP
(— IN SKIRT) PLACKET

(— IN SPONGE) APOPYLE
(— IN STAGE) DIP
(— IN TENNIS COURTS) GRILLE HAZARD GALLERY
(— IN TROUSERS) SPARE
(— IN VAULT) LUNET LUNETTE
(— IN WALL) BOLE DREAMHOLE
(— OF BALL) PROMENADE
(— OF BUD) ANTHESIS
(— OF EAR) BUR.BURR
(— OF ESOPHAGUS) CARDIA
(— OF GEYSER) CRATER
(— OF HOCKEY GAME) BULLY
(— OF PRAIRIE) BAY
(— OF SHELL) GAPE
(— THROUGH BULWARKS) GANGWAY GUNPORT SCUPPER
(— TO ASH PIT) GLUT
(— WIDE) DEHISCENT
(— WITH LID) SCUTTLE
(— WITHOUT TREES) BLANK
(— IN EARTH) GROTTO CHIMNEY SWALLOW
(ARCHED —) ALCOVE ARCADE
(CHECKERS —) ALMA DYKE FIFE CROSS CENTER SOUTER BRISTOL GLASGOW PAISLEY WHILTER DEFIANCE SWITCHER
(CHESS —) DEBUT GAMBIT DEFENCE DEFENSE
(EROSIONAL —) FENSTER
(FUNNELLIKE —) CHOANA
(GRILL —) GUICHET
(JAR —) PITHOIGIA
(MOUTHLIKE —) STOMA OSTIUM
(SMALL —) PORE SLOT CHINK STOMA CRANNY EYELET LACUNA CATHOLE CREVICE DOGHOLE FORAMEN GUICHET PINHOLE QUARREL FENESTRA
(WINDOWLIKE —) SPLITE FENESTRA
(PREF.) APERTO CHASMO TREMATO
(SUFF.) PORA PORE PYL(E) STOMA(TA)(TE)(TOUS) STOME STOMI(A) STOMOUS STOMUM STOMY TREMA(TA)
OPENLY BARELY FREELY BROADLY FRANKLY PUBLICE ROUNDLY STRAIGHT
OPEN-MINDED LIBERAL
OPENMOUTHED GAPING GREEDY RAVENOUS CLAMOROUS
OPENNESS FREEDOM PATENCY DAYLIGHT FRANKNESS ROUNDNESS
OPENWORK LATTICE TRACERY CAGEWORK FILIGREE FRETTING FRETWORK
OPEN-WORKED AJOURISE
OPERA AIDA FAUST LAKME MANON NORMA THAIS TOSCA BOHEME CARMEN DAPHNE ERNANI LOUISE MIGNON OTELLO RIENZI SALOME ELEKTRA FIDELIO BURLETTA FALSTAFF IOLANTHE LOKACOLO PARSIFAL TRAVIATA WALKYRIE LOHENGRIN PAGLIACCI RHEINGOLD RIGOLETTO SIEGFRIED TROVATORE
(— DIVISION) SCENA
(— GLASS) GLASS JUMELLE

LORGNET LORGNETTE
(— HAT) GIBUS CLAQUE
(— SONG) ARIA
(— STAR) DIVA
(COMIC —) BUFFA BURLETTA
(HORSE —) WESTERN
(SPANISH —) ZARZUELA
(TV OR RADIO —) SOAP
(16TH CENTURY —) PASTORALE
OPERANT EFFICIENT OPERATIVE
OPERATE GO ACT CUT MAN RUN PUSH TAKE WORK DRIVE MULES AFFECT EFFECT MANAGE CONDUCT PROCEED FUNCTION
(— BY HAND) MANIPULATE
(— GUNS) SERVE
(— MINE) FLUSH
(— RADIO) BLOOP
OPERATIC LYRIC
OPERATING GOING
(FULLY —) AFLOAT
OPERATION DEED PLAY BLAST ACTION AGENCY EFFECT VIRTUE PROCESS CREATION EXERCISE FUNCTION PRACTICE EXECUTION INFLUENCE PROCESSUS
(SUFF.) (— FOR OPENING) STOMY
OPERATIONS
(SUFF.) ICS
OPERATIVE EYE HAND ARTIST LIVING ARTISAN OUVRIER MECHANIC DETECTIVE EFFECTIVE
OPERATOR DEL DOER AGENT BAKER DEWER NABLA PILOT QUACK BEAMER BILLER BOLTER BUMPER BUSMAN CAPPER DEALER DEGGER DRIVER DUNGER DYADIC GAGGER JOCKEY KICKER RAGGER TRADER AVIATOR BREAKER CENTRAL CHEESER DENTIST FACIENT GLASSER JOGGLER MANAGER OPERANT SURGEON IDENTITY MOTORMAN CONDUCTOR
(INFERIOR —) PLUG
(RADIO —) HAM SPARKS SPARKER
(TRUCK —) GIPSY GYPSY
(SUFF.) STER STRESS
OPERCULUM LID FLAP ONYCHA OPERCLE APTYCHUS COVERING EYESTONE MANDIBLE
OPERETTA ZARZUELA
OPEROSE BUSY IRKSOME DILIGENT LABORIOUS
OPHELIA (BROTHER OF —) LAERTES
(FATHER OF —) POLONIUS
OPHELTES (FATHER OF —) LYCURGUS
(NURSE OF —) HYPSIPYLE
OPHIDIAN ASP EEL SNAKE CONGER REPTILE SERPENT
OPHIR (FATHER OF —) JOKTAN
OPHITE CAINIAN CAINITE
OPHIUROID ARGUS
OPHRAH (FATHER OF —) MEONOTHAI
OPIATE DOPE DRUG HEMP DWALE OPIUM DEADEN ANODINE HYPNOTIC NARCOTIC SEDATIVE DORMITARY PAREGORIC SOPORIFIC
OPIFICER OPIFEX WORKMAN ARTIFICER

OPINE DEEM JUDGE THINK PONDER BELIEVE SUPPOSE OPINIATE

OPINION CRY EYE MOT BOOK DOXY FAME IDEA MIND VIEW WEEN DOGMA FANCY FUTWA GUESS HEART SENSE SIGHT TENET THINK VARDI VARDY VOICE ADVICE ASSENT BELIEF DEVICE DICTUM ESTEEM GROUND NOTION REPUTE SCHISM CENSURE CONCEIT CONCEPT CONSENT COUNSEL DIANOIA FEELING HOLDING MEASURE SEEMING THINKSO THOUGHT TROWING VERDICT DECISION DOCTRINE JUDGMENT SUFFRAGE PREJUDICE SENTIMENT PERSUASION
(COLLECTION OF —S) SYMPOSIUM
(EXAGGERATED —) BIGHEAD
(EXPRESSION OF —) VOTE
(FAVORABLE —) BROO ESTEEM
(MOHAMMEDAN —) FUTWA
(SET OF PROFESSED —S) CREDO
(UNORTHODOX —) HERESY
(WRONG —) CACODOXY
(PREF.) DOXO
(SUFF.) DOX(Y)

OPINIONATED DOGMATIC CONCEITED OBSTINATE PRAGMATIC

OPINIONATIVE ENTETE

O PIONEERS (AUTHOR OF —) CATHER
(CHARACTER IN —) LOU CARL EMIL IVAR FRANK MARIE OSCAR AMEDEE BERGSON SHABATA TOVESKY ALEXANDRA LINDSTRUM

OPIUM HOP MUD DOPE DRUG OPIE POST CHANDU CHANDOO MECONIUM TOXICANT
(— ALKALOID) CODEIN CODEINE MORPHINE NARCOTIN NARCOTINE PAPAVERIN
(— POPPY) NEPENTHE
(OF —) THEBAIC
(TINCTURE OF —) LAUDANUM
(PREF.) MECON(O) OPIO

OPIUMISM THEBAISM

OPOSSUM QUICA YAPOK POSSUM YAPOCK MARMOSE OYAPOCK SARIGUE VULPINE MARSUPIAL PHILANDER TACUACINE
(— SHRIMP) MYSID MYSOID

OPPONENT FOE ANTI ENEMY PARTY RIVAL ALOGIAN NEMESIS OPPOSER ADVERSARY ASSAILANT
(— OF GOV CLINTON) BUCKTAIL
(— OF WAR) PEACENIK
(BOORISH —) BOEOTIAN
(IMAGINARY —) WINDMILL

OPPORTUNE FIT PAT HAPPY LUCKY READY TIMELY APROPOS FITTING TIMEFUL SUITABLE FAVORABLE

OPPORTUNELY TIMELY APROPOS HAPPILY

OPPORTUNIST CREEPER

OPPORTUNISTIC SHUFFLING

OPPORTUNITY GO MAY OPE SEL EASE HENT MEAN MINT ROOM SELE SHOT TIDE TIME SIGHT SLANT SPACE ACCESS CHANCE SEASON SQUEAK LEISURE OPENING RESPITE VANTAGE APPROACH FACILITY OCCASION ADVANTAGE
(— TO PROCEED) WAY
(FAVORABLE —) SHOW TIME

OPPOSE PIT VIE WAR BUCK COPE DEFY FACE HEAD MEET NOSE STEM WARN WEAR ARGUE BLOCK CHECK CLASH CROSS FIGHT FRONT OCCUR REBEL REBUT REPEL BATTLE BREAST COMBAT DEFEND NAYSAY OBJECT OBTEND OPPUGN REPUGN RESIST THWART WITHER CONTEST COUNTER GAINSAY OBVIATE REVERSE WITHSET CONFLICT CONFRONT CONTRARY CONTRAST FRONTIER OBSTRUCT TRAVERSE ENCOUNTER WITHSTAND ANTAGONIZE
(— BY ARGUMENT) REBUT
(— ONE IN AUTHORITY) REBEL DEFORCE

OPPOSED ANTI ALIEN AVERSE ADVERSE AGAINST COUNTER HOSTILE CONTRARY ABHORRENT ANTARCTIC REPUGNANT
(PERSISTENTLY —) RENITENT

OPPOSING RELUCTANT
(PREF.) COUNTER

OPPOSITE TO ANENT POLAR ACROSS ANENST AVERSE FACING WITHER ADVERSE COUNTER FORNENT INVERSE OBVIOUS REVERSE ANTIPODE CONTRARY CONTRAST CONVERSE ANTIPODAL REPUGNANT RECIPROCAL
(— MIDDLE OF SHIP'S SIDE) ABEAM
(— OF TRUTH) DEVIL
(— THE ALTAR) WEST
(— THE SUN) ANTISOLAR
(PREF.) ANTI ENANTIO
(DO THE —) DIS

OPPOSITION CON FLAK ATILT CLASH STOUR THWART DISCORD CLASHING CONTRAST OBSTACLE POLARITY ANIMOSITY COLLISION HOSTILITY RENITENCY
(ELECTRICAL —) IMPEDANCE
(PREF.) (IN —) CONTRA

OPPRESS SIT HOLD LADE LOAD PEIS RACK RAPE RIDE SWAY THEW CROWD CRUSH GRIND GRIPE HEAVY PEISE POISE PRESS WEIGH WRONG BETOIL BURDEN DEFOIL DEFOUL EXTORT HARASS HARROW NIDDER NITHER RAVISH SUBDUE THREAT AFFLICT DEPRESS INGRATE OVERLAY REPRESS SQUEEZE TRAMPLE CONFRONT DISTRESS ENCUMBER PRESSURE SUPPRESS OVERPOWER OVERTHROW OVERWEIGH OVERWHELM
(— WITH DREAD) HAGRIDE
(— WITH HEAT) SWELTER

OPPRESSED SERVILE

OPPRESSION ROD GRIPE PRESS BURDEN THRALL MIZRAIM DULLNESS PRESSURE EXTORTION GRIEVANCE LASSITUDE

OPPRESSIVE HOT DIRE DOWY HARD CLOSE DOWIE FAINT HARSH HEAVY BITTER LEADEN SCREWY SEVERE SMUDGY SULTRY TORRID URGENT WEIGHT ONEROUS SLAVISH GRIEVOUS GRINDING RIGOROUS

OPPRESSIVELY STRAIT

OPPRESSIVENESS LANGUOR

OPPRESSOR CSAR CZAR NERO TSAR TZAR EGLON TYRANT INCUBUS

OPPROBRIUM ENVY ABUSE ODIUM SCORN SHAME INFAMY INSULT CALUMNY DISDAIN OFFENSE SCANDAL DISGRACE DISHONOR REPROACH CONTUMELY

OPS (ASSOCIATE OF —) CONSUS
(CONSORT OF —) SATURN
(DAUGHTER OF —) CERES
(FESTIVAL OF —) OPALIA
(PERSONIFICATION OF —) FAUNA TERRA TELLUS

OPT CULL PICK WISH ELECT CHOOSE DECIDE OPTATE SELECT

OPTIC EYE OCULAR VISUAL

OPTICAL VISIBLE
(— APPARATUS) LENS GLASS ALIDAD ALIDADE OPTOMETER PERISCOPE TELESCOPE

OPTIMIST UTOPIANIST

OPTIMISTIC GLAD ROSY SUNNY JOYOUS BULLISH HOPEFUL ROSEATE EUPEPTIC SANGUINE EXPECTANT

OPTION UP CALL DOWN CHOICE SPREAD REFUSAL STRADDLE PRIVILEGE

OPTIONAL ELECTIVE VOLUNTARY PERMISSIVE

OPULENT FAT LUSH RICH WELI AMPLE FLUSH PLUSH SHOWY LAVISH MONEYED PROFUSE WEALTHY ABUNDANT AFFLUENT LUXURIANT PLENTIFUL SUMPTUOUS

OPUS WORK ETUDE STUDY
(OVERLABORED —) LUCUBRATION

OQUASSA QUASKY

OR NE ARE AUT ERE ORE GOLD OSSIA OTHER TOPAZ EITHER YELLOW

ORACHE SALTBUSH GREASEWOOD

ORACLE SEER TRIP SIBYL TRIPOD TRIPOS DIVINER AUTOPHONE

ORACULAR OTIC VATIC ORPHIC DELPHIC VATICAL DELPHIAN PYTHONIC PROPHETIC

ORAL ALOUD PAROL VOCAL BUCCAL PAROLE SONANT SPOKEN VERBAL UTTERED UNWRITTEN NONCUPATIVE

ORALE FANON

ORANGE KING MOCK CERES CHILE CHILI CHINO FLAME GENIP HEDGE JAFFA NAVEL OSAGE TENNE AURORA BODOCK BRAZIL COPPER MIKADO NAVAHO SUNTAN TEMPLE TITIAN UVALHA COWSLIP FLORIDA LEATHER MACLURA NARTJIE PAPRIKA PONCEAU PUMPKIN RANGPUR SEVILLE TANGELO TANGIER BERGAMOT BIGARADE CHINOTTI CLAYBANK FLAMINGO HONEYDEW JACINTHE MANDARIN MARATHON MOROCCAN POMANDER SUNBURST VALENCIA BUCCANEER CARNELIAN PERSIMMON TANGERINE
(— GRASS) KNITWEED PINEWEED
(— HAWKWEED) FIREWEED HIERACIUM
(— MEMBRANE) ZEST
(— MILKWORT) CANDYWEED
(— PIECE) LITH SEGMENT
(— ROCKFISH) FLIOMA
(— SEED) PIP
(— TREE) SATSUMA
(BROWNISH —) SPICE
(LARGE —) KING
(MOCK —) SERINGA
(OSAGE —) HEDGE BODOCK
(SOUR —) CURACAO BIGARADE CHINOTTO
(SWEET —) CHINA CHINO

ORANGEBIRD TANAGER

ORANGE HAWKWEED PAINTBRUSH

ORANGELEAF KARAMU

ORANGEMAN MARKSMAN

ORANGEWOOD OSAGE

ORANG LAUT BAJAU

ORANGUTAN APE MIAS ORANG PONGO SATYR SATIRE SATURY PRIMATE SALTIER SATYRUS WOODMAN WOODSMAN

ORAON KURUKH

ORATE PLEAD SPEAK SPIEL SPOUT ADDRESS DECLAIM LECTURE BLOVIATE HARANGUE DISCOURSE SPEECHIFY

ORATION EULOGY HESPED SERMON ADDRESS CONCION HARANGUE SUASORIA OLYNTHIAC PANEGYRIC PHILIPPIC
(— OF CICERO) PHILIPPIC
(FUNERAL —) ELOGE ELOGY MONODY ELOGIUM ENCOMIUM

ORATOR RHETOR DEMAGOG SPEAKER STUMPER CICERONE BOANERGES DEMAGOGUE PLAINTIFF SPOKESMAN

ORATORICAL ELOQUENT RHETORICAL

ORATORIO ELIJAH RORATORIO

ORATORY CHAPEL SACRARY ORACULUM SPEAKING ELOCUTION ELOQUENCE PROSEUCHE
(EXAGGERATED —) RHETORIC

ORB EYE SUN BALL MOON STAR EARTH GLOBE MOUND ORBIT CIRCLE PLANET SPHERE CIRCUIT ENCLOSE ENCIRCLE SURROUND FIRMAMENT

ORBED LUNAR ROUND GLOBATE

ORBIT AUGE PATH APSIS CYCLE TRACK CIRCLE SOCKET SPHERE CIRCUIT ELLIPSE EYEHOLE ECCENTRIC
(POINT IN —) APSIS APOGEE EPIGEE SYZYGY PERIGEE

ORC OGRE ORCA GIANT WHALE GRAMPUS

ORCHARD HOLT TOPE ARBOR GROVE ARBOUR GARDEN HUERTA OLIVET VERGER ARBUSTUM FRUITERY PEACHERY POMARIUM SUGARBUSH
(— **GRASS**) DOGFOOT COCKSFOOT

ORCHESTRA BAND GROUP CHAPEL CAPELLE CONSORT GAMELAN KAPELLE ENSEMBLE GAMELANG SYMPHONY SINFONIETTA PHILHARMONIC
(— **BELLS**) GLOCKENSPIEL
(— **CIRCLE**) PARQUET PARTERRE
(**SECTION OF** —) BRASS WINDS WOODS STRINGS WOODWINDS PERCUSSION

ORCHESTRATE SCORE ARRANGE COMPOSE

ORCHESTRION HARMONICON APOLLONICON

ORCHID FAAM FAHAM PETAL VANDA CYMBID DUFOIL LAELIA PURPLE AERIDES ANGULOA BOATLIP CALYPSO CULLION FLYWORT LYCASTE POGONIA VANILLA ARETHUSA CALANTHE DENDROBE GYNANDER LABELLUM ONCIDIUM RAMSHEAD SATYRION CORALROOT HABENARIA PUTTYROOT TWAYBLADE SNAKEMOUTH

ORCHIS CROWTOE CROWFOOT CRAKEFEET

ORDAIN LAW PUT DEEM DOOM LOOK MAKE SEND WILL WITE ALLOT ENACT JAPAN ORDER SHAPE WIELD WRITE DECREE PRIEST ADJUDGE APPOINT ARRANGE BEHIGHT COMMAND DESTINE DICTATE FORTUNE INSTALL PREPARE PRESCRIBE

ORDEAL FIRE GAFF TEST AGONY TRIAL CALVARY GAUNTLET
(— **TREE**) AKAZGA TANGHIN TANGUIN

ORDEAL OF RICHARD FEVEREL
(**AUTHOR OF** —) MEREDITH
(**CHARACTER IN** —) TOM LUCY BERRY CLARE MOUNT ADRIAN AUSTIN BLAIZE CAROLA HARLEY RIPTON FEVEREL RICHARD BAKEWELL THOMPSON GRANDISON DESBOROUGH MONTFALCON

ORDER BAN BID RAY SAY TAX BOON CALL CASE CHIT FIAT FORM ORDO RANK RULE SAND SECT STOP SUIT TELL TIFF TRIM WILL WORD ALIGN ARRAY CHIME CLASS DIGHT EDICT GENUS GRADE GUIDE HAVOC PRESS QUIET RANGE SHIFT STATE TAXIS WHACK ASSIGN AVAUNT BEHEST BILLET CEDULA CHARGE COSMOS CURFEW DECREE DEGREE DEMAND DIRECT ENJOIN FIRMAN FOLLOW GRAITH HOOKUM INDENT KILTER MANAGE METHOD NATURE ORDAIN POLICE POTENT SERIES SETTLE SYNTAX SYSTEM ADJUDGE ARRANGE BESPEAK

BIDDING BOOKING COMMAND COMPOSE DISPOSE EMBARGO FLOATER MANDATE PRECEPT PROCESS SOCIETY CATEGORY KODASHIM METHODIZE ORDINANCE PRESCRIBE
(— **OF ANGELS**) CHOIR QUIRE MIGHTS THRONES DOMINIONS PRINCIPALITIES
(— **OF BATTLE**) BATTALIA
(— **OF BELLS**) CHANGE
(— **OF COURT**) SIST VACATUR
(— **OF HOLY BEINGS**) HIERARCHY
(— **OF WORSHIP**) AGODUM
(— **OFF**) TURN
(— **TOBACCO LEAF**) CASE
(**CIVIL** —) EUNOMY
(**COSMIC** —) TAO RITA
(**GOOD** —) EUTAXY
(**KNIGHTHOOD** —) DANNEBROG
(**LACKING** —) AMISS MESSY MUSSY ROUGH CHAOTIC UNKEMPT CONFUSED
(**LEGAL** —) SIST STET WRIT DAYWRIT SUMMONS SENTENCE SUBPOENA
(**LOWER** — **OF MAN**) ALALUS
(**MINOR CHURCH** —) BENET
(**MONASTIC** —) SAMGHA SANGHA ACOEMETI
(**PROPER** —) TRAIN
(**TRAIN** —) FLIMSY
(**TURKISH** —) MEDJIDIE
(**UNIVERSAL** —) KIND
(**WRITTEN** —) CHECK DRAFT BILLET DRAUGHT
(**PREF.**) (**REVERSE** —) OB
(**SUFF.**) TACTIC TAXIS TAXY
(— **OF ANIMALS**) INI

ORDERED BANDBOX BESPOKE REGULAR SCRAPED COHERENT
(**WELL** —) TRIM

ORDERLINESS METHOD SYSTEM CLARITY DECORUM

ORDERLY AIDE DULY NEAT PEON RULY SNOD TIDY TRIM CRISP SOWAR SUWAR BATMAN BURSCH COSMIC FORMAL MODEST ORDENE GRADELY REGULAR SHAPELY DECOROUS GALLOPER GRAITHLY OBEDIENT PEACEABLE SHIPSHAPE

ORDINANCE LAW DOOM FIAT RITE BYLAW EDICT ASSIZE DECREE RECESS CONTROL MANDATE SETNESS STATUTE WORKING DECRETUM JUDICIAL REGIMENT TAKKANAH DIRECTION

ORDINANT DIHELY DIHELIOS DIHELIUM

ORDINARY LAY LOW SOS BEND FESS LALA MEAN PALE PALL RUCK BANAL CHIEF CROSS NOMIC PLAIN PROSE USUAL CANTON COMMON FILLET FLANCH MODERN NORMAL PAIRLE SIMPLE VULGAR AVERAGE MUNDANE NATURAL PROSAIC ROUTINE SALTIRE SAUTIER TRIVIAL VULGATE EVERYDAY FAMILIAR HABITUAL MEDIOCRE MIDDLING PLEBEIAN RUMTYTOO WORKADAY QUOTIDIAN SHAKEFORK

ORDINATE ORDER ORDAIN APPOINT ORDERLY REGULAR MODERATE TEMPERATE

ORDNANCE LAW GUNS ARMOR ORGUE FALCON MINION PETARD PEDRERO RABINET SERPENT WEAPONS BASILISK PETERERO ARTILLERY

ORDO ORDER ALMANAC DIRECTORY

ORDURE
(**PREF.**) SCAT(O) SCORI

ORE (**ALSO SEE MINERAL**) TIN CHAT DISH DRAG FELL GOLD IRON LEAD MINE POST PULP ROCK CRAZE CRUDE FAVOR GLORY GRACE HONOR MANTO MERCY METAL PRILL COPPER CUPRITE FLOATER RESPECT SEAWEED SMEDDUM CLEMENCY KNOCKING CARBONATE REVERENCE
(— **CRUSHER**) DOLLY
(— **DEPOSIT**) LODE SCRIN BONANZA
(— **LAYER**) SEAM STOPE
(— **LOADING PLATFORM**) PLAT
(— **MASS**) SQUAT
(— **NOT DRESSED**) WORK
(— **WITH STONE ADHERING**) CHAT CHATS
(**BEST** —) CROP
(**BROKEN** —) DIRT
(**COPPER** —) HORNITE ATACAMITE MALACHITE
(**CRUDE** —) HEADS
(**CRUSHED** —) SCHLICH
(**CUBE** —) SIDERITE
(**EARTHY-LOOKING** —) PACO
(**HORSEFLESH** —) BORNITE
(**IMPURE** —) SPEISS HALVANS
(**IRON** —) OCHER OCHRE MINION IRONMAN LIMNITE MINETTE OLIGIST TURGITE HEMATITE TACONITE JACUTINGA
(**LEAD** —) BOOZE GALENA ARQUIFOUX
(**LUMP OF** —) HARDHEAD
(**MERCURY** —) GRANZA CINNABAR
(**SOLID** —) RIB
(**TIN** —) ROWS CRAZE SCOVE WHITS FLORAN TINSTUFF
(**WORTHLESS** —) SLAG DROSS MATTE
(**ZINC** —) SMITHSONITE

OREAD PERI NYMPH

OREGON TRAIL (**AUTHOR OF** —) PARKMAN
(**CHARACTER IN** —) SHAW HENRY QUINCY FRANCIS PARKMAN CHATILLON DESLAURIERS

OREN (**FATHER OF** —) JERAHMEEL

ORE-PRODUCING QUICK

ORESTES (**COMPANION OF** —) PYLADES
(**FATHER OF** —) AGAMEMNON
(**FRIEND OF** —) PYLADES
(**MOTHER OF** —) CLYTEMNESTRA
(**SISTER OF** —) ELECTRA IPHIGENIA
(**WIFE OF** —) HERMIONE

ORGAN CUP GILL LIMB PART CHELA FLOAT GREAT HEART MEANS PAPER REGAL SERRA ELATER FEEDER FEELER HAPTOR MEDIUM SPLEEN SUCKER CLASPER CONSOLE JOURNAL ARMATURE EFFECTOR ISOGRAFT MAGAZINE MELODEON MELODICA MYCETOME OOGONIUM EQUIPMENT HARMONIUM NEWSPAPER PORTATIVE
(— **GALLERY**) LOFT
(— **OF HEARING**) EAR
(— **OF SCORPION**) PECTEN
(— **OF SENSE**) SENSE SENSORY
(— **OF SILKWORM**) FILATOR
(— **OF TOUCH**) TACTOR TACTUS
(— **PIPE**) REED FLUTE SCHWEGEL
(— **STOP**) ECHO HARP OBOE SEXT TUBA VIOL ACUTA DOLCE FLUTE GAMBA ORAGE QUINT TENTH VIOLA BIFARA CURTAL CYMBAL DECIMA DULCET FUGARA GEDACT NASARD OCTAVE SCHARF TIERCE TROMBA BASSOON BOMBARD BOURDON CELESTE CLARION CREMONA DOLCIAN DOUBLET DULCIAN FAGOTTO GEDECKT MELODIA PICCOLO POSAUNE SERPENT TERTIAN TRUMPET TWELFTH VIOLINA BOMBARDE CARILLON CLARINET DIAPASON DIAPHONE DULCIANA GEMSHORN REGISTER TENOROON TROMBONE WALDHORN BOMBARDON CORNOPEAN DOUBLETTE HARMONICA PRINCIPAL SAXOPHONE CLARABELLA
(— **VIBRATO**) TREMOLO
(**BRISTLELIKE** —) SETA
(**CHINESE** —) SANG CHENG

(HAND —) SERINETTE
(OLFACTORY —) NOSE
(RESPIRATORY —) LUNG
(SMALL —) REGAL
(SWIMMING —) CTENE
(VOCAL — OF BIRDS) SYRINX
(WASTE —) KIDNEY
(PREF.) (INTERNAL —) VISCER(I)(O)
ORGANIC VITAL INBORN NATURAL
INHERENT
ORGANISM WOG BODY ECAD
GERM GUEST PLANT AEROBE
ANIMAL EMBRYO SYSTEM
DIPLONT DISEASE MACHINE
PLANONT SUSCEPT HEMAMEBA
PATHOGEN PLANKTER
MESOPHILE POLYMORPH
(— CHARACTERISTIC) MIXIS
(COLD-BLOODED —) POIKILOTHERM
(COMPOUND —) STOCK
(FOSSIL —) EOZOON
(MINUTE —) AMEBA MONAD
SPORE
(MODIFIED —) ECAD
(PELAGIC —S) NEKTON
(POLITICAL —) LEVIATHAN
(SIMPLE —) MONAD
(SMALL AIRBORNE —S)
AEROPLANKTON
(PL.) BENTHON BENTHOS
HAYSEED NEUSTON PLEUSTON
(PREF.) BIO ONT(O)
(SUFF.) ACEAN ONT PHORA
(SIMPLE —) MONAS
ORGANIZATION ART BIG ITO CLUB
FIRM KLAN CADRE FIDAC FORUM
HOUSE MAFIA SETUP AUMAGA
CHURCH OUTFIT SURVEY SYSTEM
CHARITY COMPANY CONCERN
DEMOLAY ECONOMY GIDEONS
MENORAH SOCIETY CONGRESS
PATRONAGE STRUCTURE
(— OF ACTORS) COMPANY
(— OF DEALERS) AUCTION
(— OF EXPERIENCE) SCHEMA
(— WITH MANY BRANCHES)
OCTOPUS
(ARMY —) LANDSTORM
(AUXILIARY —) AID SYNODICAL
(COLLEGE —) FRAT ALUMNA
ALUMNI ALUMNUS SORORITY
(HARMONIOUS —)
ORCHESTRATION
(JEWISH —) ITO MENORAH
(MUSICAL —) BAND COMBO
CAPELLE KAPELLE ENSEMBLE
ORCHESTRA
(POLICE —) GESTAPO
(POLITICAL —) PARTY VEREIN
HETAERIA HETAIRIA APPARATUS
(SAMOAN —) AUMAGA
(SECRET —) WOW BPOE ELKS
MOOSE MASONS MIDEWIN
(SOCIAL —) POLICE
(WAR VETERANS —) AVC DAV GAR
SAR VFW FIDAC AMVETS
(WOMEN'S —) DAR WAF WRC
WCTU SORORITY
(YOUTH —) KOMSOMOL
ORGANIZE FORM EDIFY FOUND
MODEL ORDER RALLY DESIGN
EMBODY ARRANGE MODULIZE
REGIMENT UNIONIZE BLUEPRINT

INSTITUTE INTEGRATE
STRUCTURE
ORGANIZED FORMED ORGANIC
TOGETHER
(BADLY —) INCONDITE
ORGIASTIC BACCHIC
SATURNALIAN
ORGY LARK RITE ROMP BINGE
REVEL SPREE FROLIC SHINDY
REVELRY WASSAIL CAROUSAL
CEREMONY SATURNALIA
(PL.) ORGIACS DEBAUCHERIES
ORIANA (FATHER OF —) LISUARTE
(HUSBAND OF —) MIRABEL
(LOVER OF —) AMADIS
ORIBI OUREBI ANTELOPE
BLEEKBOK PALEBUCK
ORIEL BAY CHAPEL DORMER
RECESS WINDOW BALCONY
GALLERY MIRADOR PORTICO
CORRIDOR
ORIENT DAWN EAST ADAPT BUILD
PEARL PLACE SHEEN ADJUST
LEVANT LOCATE LUSTER RISING
GLOWING INCLINE RADIANT
SUNRISE LUSTROUS SPARKLING
ORIENTAL ASIAN PEARL BRIGHT
INDIAN ORTIVE RISING EASTERN
SHINING INDOGEAN LUSTROUS
PELLUCID PRECIOUS BRILLIANT
LEVANTINE
ORIENTATION ASPECT PHORIA
STRIKE COLORING LOCALITY
ORIFICE BUNG HOLE PORE PORT
VENT INLET MOUTH STOMA
TREMA BLOWER CAVITY OUTLET
RICTUS SIPHON THROAT
CHIMNEY EARHOLE FORAMEN
OPENING OSCULUM OSTIOLE
APERTURE FUMAROLE INTROITUS
(— IN VOLCANIC REGION)
FUMAROLE
(— OF INFUNDIBULUM) LURA
(BREATHING —) SPIRACLE
(VOLCANIC —) BLOWER
(PREF.) TREMATO
(— OF STOMACH) PYLOR(O)
(SUFF.) PYL(E) TREMA(TA)
ORIGANUM ORGANY MARJORAM
ORGAMENT
ORIGILLE (FATHER OF —)
MONODANTE
(LOVER OF —) GRIFONE
(SISTER OF —) BRANDIMARTE
ORIGIN NEE GERM KIND RISE ROOT
SEED BIRTH CAUSE RADIX START
STOCK FATHER GROWTH NATURE
PARENT SOURCE SPRING EDITION
GENESIS LINEAGE UPSTART
NASCENCE UPSPRING BEGINNING
INCEPTION OFFSPRING
PARENTAGE PROVENANCE
(— ON EARTH) EPIGENE
(FOREIGN —) ECDEMIC
(PREF.) (ANCIENT —) PALAE(O)
PALAI(O) PALE(O)
(SUFF.) GENY
ORIGINAL NEW HOME SEED FIRST
FRESH NOVEL PRIME STOCK
FONTAL MASTER MOTHER NATIVE
PRIMAL PRIMER SAMPLE PIONEER
PRIMARY RADICAL SEMINAL
NASCENCY PRISTINE AUTHENTIC

AUTOGRAPH BEGINNING
INVENTIVE OFFSPRING PRIMITIVE
(NOT —) DERIVED
(PREF.) ARCH(AE)(AEO)(E)(EO)(I)
ORIGINALITY INGENUITY
ORIGINATE COIN COME DATE
GROW HEAD MAKE MOVE OPEN
REAR RISE SIRE ARISE BEGIN
BIRTH BREED CAUSE ENDOW
FOUND HATCH RAISE START
AUTHOR CREATE DERIVE DESIGN
DEVISE FATHER INVENT PARENT
SPRING CAUSATE DESCEND
EMANATE PIONEER PROCEED
PRODUCE COMMENCE CONCEIVE
CONTRIVE DISCOVER GENERATE
INITIATE INSTITUTE
ORIGINATION DESCENT GENESIS
BREEDING ORIGINAL COSMOGONY
ETYMOLOGY
ORIGINATOR AUTHOR FATHER
CREATOR INVENTOR GENERATOR
PROGENITOR
ORIOLE PIROL BUNYAH LARIOT
LORIOT CACIQUE FIGBIRD
PEABIRD FIREBIRD GOLDBIRD
HANGBIRD HANGNEST TROUPIAL
ORION RIGEL ALGEBAR
(BELT OF —) ELLWAND
(FATHER OF —) HYRIEUS POSEIDON
(GUIDE OF —) CEDALION
(HOUND OF —) ARATUS
(SLAYER OF —) ARTEMIS
ORITHYIA (DAUGHTER OF —)
CHIONE CLEOPATRA
(FATHER OF —) ERECHTHEUS
(MOTHER OF —) PRAXITHEA
(SON OF —) ZETES CALAIS
ORKNEY ISLANDS (CAPITAL OF —)
KIRKWALL
(ISLAND OF —) HOY POMONA
ROUSAY SANDAY STRONSAY
ORLANDO (BELOVED OF —)
ROSALIND
ORLE ORLET BORDER FILLET
WREATH BEARING CHAPLET
TRESSURE
ORLOP DECK ARLOUP
ORMENUS (FATHER OF —)
CERCAPHUS
(SON OF —) AMYNTOR
ORMER ABALONE
ORMOLU GILT GOLD ALLOY BRASS
VARNISH
ORNAMENT BOB DUB FLY FOB
GAY JOY PIN POT TAG TEE TOY
URN BALL BOSS CURL CUSP DICE
ETCH FALL FRET FROG GAUD
GEAR HUSK KNOP LEAF NULL
OUCH RULE STAR TOOL TRIM
WALY WING ADORN BRAID BULLA
CHASE CROSS CROWN DECOR
EXORN FUSEE GRACE GUTTA
HELIX HONOR INLAY KNOSP
LUNET MENSK MENSO OVOID
PATCH POPPY PRUNT SPANG
SPRAY SPRIG STALK TRAIL TRICK
WALLY AMULET ANKLET ATTIRE
BEDAUB BEDECK BILLET BRANCH
BROOCH BUTTON CIMIER COLLAR
DIAPER DOODAD EDGING EMBOSS
ENRICH FALLAL FINERY FLORET
FLOWER GORGET INSERT LABRET

LUNULA NIELLO OFFSET PAMPRE
PARURE PATERA ROCOCO
ROSACE RUNTEE SETOFF TABLET
TAHALI TEMPLE TIRADE
AGREMEN AKROTER AMALAKA
BIBELOT BUCRANE CIRCLET
COCARDE CORBEIL CROCKET
DIGLYPH EARPLUG ECHINUS
EMBLEMA ENGRAVE ENHANCE
FRIGGER FURNISH GADROON
GARNISH NETSUKE RINCEAU
SEXFOIL STRIGIL TREFOIL
TRINKET ACCOLADE ANAGLYPH
APPLIQUE BRELOQUE DECORATE
FLOURISH GIMCRACK LAVALIER
MORESQUE PALMETTE ROCAILLE
SWASTIKA POPPYHEAD
(— FOR HEAD) MIND TARGET
(— ON SHIP) BADGE APLUSTRE
(CHILD'S —) GAY
(CLAW-LIKE —) GRIFFE
(DRESS —) FROG LACE JABOT
SEQUIN SPANGLE
(FANTASTIC —) ANTIC
(HAIR —) TETTIX
(HEAD —) TIARA TEMPLE
(HORSE COLLAR —) HOUNCE
(MUSICAL —) TURN MORDENT
BACKFALL PRALLTRILLER
(PENDANT —) BOB BULLA ANADEM
BANGLE TASSEL EARRING
LAVALIER
(ROOF —) ANTEFIX
(SHOULDER —) EPAULET
(TAWDRY —) GINGERBREAD
(PL.) FIGGERY KNAVERY
AGREMENS
ORNAMENTAL FANCY CHICHI
FRILLY LILYTURF BLUEBEARD
NASTURTIUM SEMPERVIVUM
ORNAMENTATION BOSS FOIL
ACORN DECOR ADORNO BABERY
CHICHI CILERY DICING BARBOLA
CUSPING ECHELLE LACWORK
STYLING ACANTHUS APPLIQUE
FROUFROU HEADWORK PURFLING
ROCAILLE STAFFAGE TRESSURE
(CHEAP —) TINSEL
(EXTRAVAGANT —) ROCOCO
(MUSICAL —) GRUPPO GRUPPETTO
SCHLEIFER
ORNAMENTED FIGURY FOILED
ORNATE TAWDRY ADORNED
FLOUNCY FROSTED TREFLEE
WROUGHT GOFFERED SINNOWED
ELABORATE STELLATED
ORNATE GAY FINE FANCY FUSSY
GIDDY SHOWY DRESSY FLORID
FLOSSY PURPLE SUPERB
AUREATE BAROQUE FLOWERY
TAFFETA MANDARIN OVERRIPE
SPLENDID ELABORATE
UNNATURAL
(EXTREMELY —) GIDDY
ORNERY CONTRARY
ORNITHOLOGIST AUDUBON
BIRDMAN
AMERICAN CORY OBER COUES
STONE BAILEY BREWER BUTLER
CASSIN KEELER MILLER TORREY
WILSON XANTUS AUDUBON
BRASHER CHAPMAN FORBUSH
HENSHAW NUTTALL RIDGWAY

SHUFELDT TOWNSEND
CANADIAN NASH
ENGLISH DIXON GOULD CLARKE
LATHAM SHARPE KIRKMAN
FRENCH LEVAILLANT
GERMAN NAUMANN REICHENOW
KLEINSCHMIDT
NEW ZEALAND BULLER
OROONOKO (WIFE OF —) IMOINDA
OROTUND FULL CLEAR SHOWY
MELLOW STRONG POMPOUS
RESONANT SONOROUS
BOMBASTIC
ORP FRET WEEP
ORPAH (HUSBAND OF —) CHILION
(SISTER-IN-LAW OF —) RUTH
ORPHAN PIP WARD FOUNDLING
STEPCHILD
ORPHANED ORBATE
ORPHEUS (BIRTHPLACE OF —)
PIERIA
(FATHER OF —) APOLLO OEAGRUS
(MOTHER OF —) CALLIOPE
(WIFE OF —) EURYDICE
ORPHREY BAND BORDER
ORPIMENT ORPIN HARTAL SPIRIT
ARSENIC HARTAIL ZARNICH
ORPINE SEDUM LIVELONG
BAGLEAVES EVERGREEN
ORRA ODD IDLE ORROW
WORTHLESS
ORRIS GIMP IRIS LACE BRAID
ORRICE GALLOON
ORSINO (WIFE OF —) VIOLA
ORT BIT END TAG CRUMB SCRAP
MORSEL REFUSE TRIFLE LEAVING
REMNANT FRAGMENT LEFTOVER
ORTHOCLASE ADULARIA
AMAZONITE
ORTHODOX GOOD GREEK SOUND
USUAL PROPER CANONIC
CORRECT ACCEPTED CATHOLIC
STANDARD CUSTOMARY
ORTHODOXY PIETY TRUTH
SOUNDNESS
ORTHOGRAPHY WRITING
ORTHOPTERON WALKER
ORTNIT (BROTHER OF —)
WOLFDIETRICH
ORTOLAN BIRD RAIL SORA
BUNTING BOBOLINK WHEATEAR
ORTSTEIN HARDPAN
ORYX BEISA PASANG PASENG
GAZELLE GEMSBOK ANTELOPE
LEUCORYX
OS BONE ESKAR ESKER MOUTH
OPENING ORIFICE
OSAGE ORANGE HEDGE OSAGE
BODOCK BOWWOOD
OSCILLATE LOG WAG HUNT ROCK
SWAY VARY SQUEG SWING
WAVER WEAVE SHIMMY FEATHER
VIBRATE FLUCTUATE
OSCILLATION HOWL WAVE SHOCK
SEICHE SHIMMY SQUEAL FLUTTER
LIBRATION VIBRATION
(— OF EARTH'S AXIS) NUTATION
OSCULATE BUSS KISS
OSCULATION TACNODE
OSCULATORY PAX
OSIER ROD WAND EDDER SALIX
SKEIN SPLIT WITHY BASKET
SALLOW WICKER WILLOW

DOGWOOD WILGERS REDBRUSH
(— CAGE) TUMBREL
(— WILLOW) TWIGWITHY
OSIRIS HERSHEF UNNEFER
(BROTHER OF —) SET SETH
(CROWN OF —) ATEF
(FATHER OF —) GEB KEB SEB
(MOTHER OF —) NUT
(SISTER OF —) ISIS
(SON OF —) HORUS ANUBIS
(WIFE OF —) ISIS
OSMANLI TURK TURKISH
OSPREY GLED HAWK OSSI GLEDE
PYGARG BALBUSARD OSSIFRAGE
OSSATURE SKELETON OSSEMENTS
OSSE DARE ATTEMPT PRESAGE
PROMISE VENTURE PROPHESY
RECOMMEND UTTERANCE
OSSEOUS BONE BONY SPINY
LITHIC OSTEAL
OSSIAN (FATHER OF —) FINN
OSSICLE BONE INCUS ADORAL
STAPES ALVEOLE BONELET
MALLEUS SCUTELLA
OSSIFICATION OSTOSIS
UROSTEON METOSTEON
SIDEBONES
OSSUARY URN TOMB GRAVE
VAULT OSSARIUM
OSTEND SHOW REVEAL EXHIBIT
MANIFEST
OSTENSIBLE NOMINAL SEEMING
APPARENT SPECIOUS
OSTENT AIR MIEN SIGN TOKEN
DISPLAY PORTENT
OSTENTATION DOG POMP PUFF
SHOW CLASS ECLAT FLARE PRIDE
STRUT SWANK VAUNT PARADE
VANITY DISPLAY FLUTTER
PAGEANT PORTENT PRESAGE
FLOURISH FRIPPERY PRETENCE
PRETENSE SHOWINESS
SPECTACLE
OSTENTATIOUS ARTY LOUD VAIN
GAUDY SHOWY SWANK FLASHY
SPORTY SWANKY TURGID
FLAUNTY GLARING OBVIOUS
POMPOUS SPLASHY SPLURGY
FASTUOUS ELABORATE
OSTERIA INN TAVERN
OSTIOLE PORE MOUTH STOMA
OPENING ORIFICE APERTURE
OSTRACISM PETALISM
OSTRACIZE BAN BAR CUT SNUB
EXILE BANISH PUNISH REJECT
ABOLISH BOYCOTT CENSURE
EXCLUDE BLACKBALL PROSCRIBE
OSTRACON SHELL FRAGMENT
POTSHERD
OSTRICH EMU RHEA NANDU
BREVIPEN STRUCION
(— FEATHER) BOO
(JERKED —) BILTONG
(PREF.) STRUTHI(O)(ONI)
OSTYAK KHANTY
OSWALD (FATHER OF —)
ETHELFRITH
(SLAYER OF —) PENDA
OSWEGO TEA BALM
OTAHEITE TAHITI
(— APPLE) HEVI MACUPA MACUPI
OTALGIA EARACHE
OTHELLO MOOR

(AUTHOR OF —) SHAKESPEARE
(CHARACTER IN —) IAGO BIANCA
CASSIO EMILIA MONTANO
OTHELLO GRATIANO LODOVICO
RODERICO BRABANTIO
DESDEMONA
(ENSIGN OF —) IAGO
(FRIEND OF —) IAGO
(LIEUTENANT OF —) CASSIO
(WIFE OF —) DESDEMONA
OTHER HE MO ELSE MORE ALTER
FORMER NOTHER SECOND
TIDDER TOTHER ALTERUM
FURTHER DISTINCT DIFFERENT
(— THAN) SAVE
(PL.) LAVE REST LUTRA
(PREF.) ALL(O) HETER(O)
OTHERNESS ALTERITY
OTHERWISE OR NOT ELSE ENSE
ALIAS SECUS ALITER EXCEPT
BESIDES ELSEHOW ELSEWAYS
OTHNI (BROTHER OF —) CALEB
(FATHER OF —) KENAZ SHEMAIAH
(WIFE OF —) ACHSAH
OTIC AURAL AUDITORY ORACULAR
AURICULAR
OTIONIA (FATHER OF —)
ERECHTHEUS
(MOTHER OF —) PRAXITHEA
(SISTER OF —) PANDORA
PROTOGONIA
OTIOSE IDLE LAZY VAIN ALOOF
FUTILE OTIANT REMOTE STERILE
USELESS INACTIVE INDOLENT
REPOSING
OTOLITH SAGITTA LAPILLUS
OTOSTEON
OTOLOGIST AURIST
OTTAVINO PICCOLO
OTTER DOG FUR PUP FISH NAIR
PELT BITCH HURON LOUTRE
SIMUNG TACKLE ANNATTO
PERIQUE MAMPALON MUSTELIN
PARAVANE
(— TAIL) POLE
(DEN OF — S) HOLT
(SEA —) KALAN
OTTOMAN (ALSO SEE TURKEY)
POUF SEAT TURK COUCH DIVAN
SQUAB STOOL FABRIC OTHMAN
POUFFE SULTANE FOOTSTOOL
(— COURT) PORTE
(— GOVERNOR) PASHA
(— LEADER) OSMAN
(— PROVINCE) VILAYET
(— STANDARD) ALEM
(— SUBJECT) RAIA RAYAH
OUABE HOGNUT
OUAKARI ACARI UKARI MONKEY
UAKARI
OUCH OH OW ADORN BEZEL CLASP
JEWEL NOUCH BROOCH FIBULA
NOUCHE BRACELET NECKLACE
ORNAMENT
OUGHT BIT BUD BUT MOW BOOD
BOOT MOTE MUST ZERO SHALL
BELONG CIPHER NAUGHT
NOUGHT SHOULD BEHOOVE
OUISTITI WISTITI MARMOSET
OUNCE URE OKET OKIA ONCA
ONCE ONZA OKIEH UNCIA
CHEETAH LEOPARD WILDCAT
(CHINESE —) LIANG

(EIGHT —S) CUPFUL
(HALF —) SEMUNCIA
(ONE-16TH OF —) DRAM
(ONE-20TH OF —) EASTERLING
(ONE-8TH OF —) DRAM
OUPHE ELF OOF OUF GOBLIN
OUR UR ORE URE WER WIR HORE
NOTRE UNSER
(— LORD) NS
(— SAVIOR) NSIC
(PREF.) NOSTRI
OURICURY LICURI LICURY
CABECUDO
**OUR MUTUAL FRIEND (AUTHOR OF
—)** DICKENS
(CHARACTER IN —) JOHN WEGG
WREN BELLA BETTY FANNY
HEXAM JENNY JESSE SILAS
BOFFIN EUGENE HARMON
HIDGEN JULIUS LIZZIE WILFER
BRADLEY CHARLEY CLEAVER
HANDFORD WRAYBURN
HEADSTONE HENRIETTA
NICODEMUS ROKESMITH
OURSELVES USSELF USSELS
USSELVEN
OUR TOWN (AUTHOR OF —)
WILDER
(CHARACTER IN —) JOE WEBB
EMILY GIBBS HOWIE SIMON
WALLY GEORGE CROWELL
NEWSOME REBECCA STIMSON
GORUSLOWSKI
OUSIA NATURE ESSENCE
SUBSTANCE
OUST BAR BUMP FIRE SACK CHUCK
EJECT EVICT EXPEL BANISH
DEBOUT REMOVE CASHIER
DISCARD DISMISS SUSPEND
DISSEIZE FORJUDGE ELIMINATE
OUSTING AMOTION
OUT EX AWAY DOWN HORS FORTH
ABSENT BEGONE ISSUED
OOTWITH OUTWARD EXTERNAL
PUBLISHED
(— AT ELBOWS) SCRUFFY
(— LOUD) BOST
(— OF) EX FROM DEHORS
OUTWITH
(— OF BREATH) BLOWN
(— OF COMMISSION) BUNG
(— OF DATE) OLD DOWDY PASSE
OUTWORN TIMEWORN
OVERDATED
(— OF DOORS) ABROAD FOREIGN
THEREOUT
(— OF EXISTENCE) AWAY
(— OF KILTER) ALOP AWRY CRANK
BROKEN
(— OF ONE'S MIND) FEY DAFT
DELEERIT
(— OF ORDER) AMISS KAPUT
FAULTY DEFICIENT
(— OF PLACE) AMISS INEPT
(— OF PLAY) DEAD FOUL
(— OF SIGHT) DOGGO INVISIBLE
(— OF SORTS) CROOK CROSS
HUMPY NOHOW COMICAL
PEEVISH
(— OF THE WAY) BY BYE ASIDE
BLIND CLEAR CLOSE AFIELD
GEASON REMOTE
(— OF THIS LIFE) HYNE

(— OF TUNE) FALSE SCORDATO
(FARTHER —) UTTER
(PREF.) E ECT(O) EXO PRO
(— OF) EC
OUTAGE VENT ULLAGE
HEADSPACE
OUT-AND-OUT GROSS PLUMB
SHEER SWORN UTTER ARRANT
DIRECT WHOLLY REGULAR
ABSOLUTE COMPLETE CRASHING
OUTRIGHT
OUTBREAK FIT ROW RASH RIOT
BURST SALLY EMEUTE PLAGUE
REVOLT RUCKUS TUMULT
UPROAR BOUTADE OUTCROP
RUCTION BLIZZARD ERUPTION
OUTBURST EXPLOSION
(— OF DISEASE) PANDEMIC
(— OF EMOTIONALISM) HYSTERIA
(— OF TEMPER) MOORBURN
(REVOLUTIONARY —) PUTSCH
(SUDDEN —) SPURT
OUTBUILDING BARN SHED LODGE
PRIVY BARTON GARAGE HEMMEL
OUTHOUSE SKEELING SKILLING
BACKHOUSE
OUTBURST BOUT CROW FLAW
FUME GALE GUST RAGE TEAR
TIFF AGONY BLAST BLAZE BLURT
BREAK BRUNT BURST FLARE
FLASH GEARE SALLY SPATE
START STORM ACCESS BLOWER
BLOWUP ESCAPE FANTAD
FANTOD GOLLER TIRADE TUMULT
BLOWOUT BOUTADE OUTCROP
PASSION TANTRUM TORRENT
ERUPTION EXPLOSION
(— OF ANGER) FIT GERE GEARE
TATTER
(— OF ORATORY) SQUIRT
(— OF SPEECH) STRAIN
(— OF TEMPER) FUFF TIFF
BLOWOUT
(SPACE —) SUPERNOVA
OUTCAST EXILE LEPER RONIN
SHREW ABJECT PARIAH WRETCH
AOUTLET ISHMAEL MISSILE
OUTWALE CASTAWAY CHANDALA
REJECTED VAGABOND DIALONIAN
(HOMELESS —) ARAB
(JAPANESE —) ETA RONIN
(PYRENEES —) CAGOT
OUTCOME END OUT FATE TERM
CLOSE EDUCT EVENT HATCH
ISSUE LOOSE PROOF UPSET
BROWST EFFECT EXITUS OUTLET
PERIOD RESULT SEQUEL UPSHOT
EMANATE PROGENY SUCCESS
FATALITY AFTERMATH
OUTCROP CROP REEF LEDGE
BASSET INLIER BLOSSOM
BLOWOUT OUTBREAK OUTBURST
OUTCROPPING BULT SCABROCK
OUTCRY CAW CRY HUE YIP BAWL
BRAY DITE GAFF HOWL REAM
ROAR SCRY UTAS YARM YELL
ALARM BOAST DITTY NOISE
OUTAS SHOUT STINK WHAUP
BELLOW CLAMOR HOLLER
RACKET SCREAM SHRIEK STEVEN
TUMULT CALLING EXCLAIM
PROTEST SCREECH SHILLOO
COMPLAINT PHILLILEW

(PUBLIC —) STINK
OUTDATED CRINOLINE
OUTDISTANCE DROP SKIN OUTGO
SURPASS OUTSTRIP
OUTDO CAP COB COP COW POT
TOP BANG BEAT BEST FLOG WHIP
EXCEL OUTGO REVIE TRUMP
WORSE DEFEAT EXCEED OUTACT
NONPLUS OUTPACE SURPASS
OUTMATCH OUTSHINE
OVERCOME
OUTDOORS FORTH OUTBY
OUTBYE OUTSIDE
OUTER BUT OVER ALIEN ECTAD
ECTAL UPPER UTTER FOREIGN
OUTSIDE OUTWARD EXTERIOR
EXTERNAL FORINSEC
(PREF.) EPH EPI EXO
OUTER MONGOLIA (SEE
MONGOLIA)
(COIN OF—) MONGO TUGRIK
OUTERMOST FINAL UTTER
UTMOST EVEREST EXTREME
OUTWARD FARTHEST REMOTEST
OUTFACE DEFY RESIST SUBDUE
CONFRONT OVERCOME
OUTFIELDER GARDENER
OUTSCOUT
OUTFIT KIT RIG GANG GARB REAR
REEK SUIT TEAM UNIT DRESS
EQUIP GETUP HABIT TROUP
ATTIRE CONREY DUFFEL FITOUT
LAYOUT CLOTHES FURNISH
SHEBANG EQUIPAGE FURNITURE
GRUBSTAKE
(INFANT'S —) LAYETTE
(SPARE —) CHANGE
OUTFLANK OUTWING OVERWING
OUTFLOW FLUX DRAIN ISSUE
OUTGO EFFLUX ESCAPE
OUTPOUR
OUTGO EXIT EXCEL ISSUE OUTDO
EFFLUX EGRESS EXCEED OUTLAY
OUTLET OUTRUN OUTCOME
PRODUCT SURPASS OUTSTRIP
OUTGROWTH ALA BUD JAG ARIL
FOOT HAIR LEAF MOSS SPUR
CLAMP FRUIT HILUM HYPHA
SCALE SPINE ACULEA COCKLE
CUPULE FIBRIL ENATION
FEATHER ISIDIUM APPENDIX
CARUNCLE EPIDERMA HAPTERON
INDUSIUM OFFSHOOT
CARBUNCLE EMERGENCE
OSTEOPHYTE
(PLANTS —) OVULE
OUTGUESS PSYCH PSYCHE
OUTHOUSE SHED SKEO BIFFY
LODGE PRIVY BIGGIN LINHAY
OUTHUT LATRINE SKEELING
SKILLION
(PL.) STEADING
OUTING OUT SKIP STAY TRIP
JUNKET PICNIC COOKOUT
HOLIDAY CLAMBAKE VACATION
WAYGOOSE EXCURSION
WAYZGOOSE
OUTLANDER PARDESI
OUTLANDISH ALIEN KINKY EXOTIC
REMOTE BIZARRE FOREIGN
STRANGE UNCOUTH PECULIAR
BARBAROUS FANTASTIC
GROTESQUE UNEARTHLY

OUTLAST ELAPSE SURVIVE
OVERBIDE
OUTLAW BAN BAR CACO HORN
TORY EXILE EXLEX FLEME RONIN
ARRANT BADMAN BANDIT
BANISH BRUMBY COWBOY
DACOIT UNLEDE BANDIDO
ISHMAEL FUGITATE FUGITIVE
PROHIBIT PROSCRIBE
PROSCRIPT
(IRISH —) WOODKERN
(JAPANESE —) RONIN
(PL.) MANZAS
OUTLAWED ILLEGAL ILLICIT
LAWLESS
OUTLAWRY BAN EXILE UTLAGARY
OUTLAY COST MISE OUTGO
EXPENSE PENSION
OUTLET BORE DRIP EXIT VENT
ISSUE EGRESS ESCAPE EXITUS
FUNNEL OUTAGE OPENING
FUMEDUCT OVERFLOW SINKHOLE
AVOIDANCE
(— FOR COASTAL SWAMP) BAYOU
(— FOR SMOKE) FEMERALL
(— OF CARBURETOR) BARREL
(— OF SPRING) EYE
(AIR —) GRILL GRILLE
(ELECTRIC —) POINT
OUTLIER KLIP KLIPPE
OUTLINE MAP BOSH ETCH FLOW
FORM LINE PLAN PLAT BRIEF
CHALK CHART DRAFT FRAME
MODEL SHAPE TRACE AGENDA
APERCU DESIGN DOODLE FIGURE
FILLET LAYOUT SCHEMA SCHEME
SCROLL SKETCH SURVEY
CAPSULE CONTOUR CROQUIS
DRAUGHT ELEMENT EXTRACT
FEATURE GABARIT ISOTYPE
PROFILE SUMMARY CONTORNO
DESCRIBE ESQUISSE SKELETON
SYLLABUS SYNOPSIS GUIDELINE
TREATMENT
(— HASTILY) SPLASH
(— OF A SCIENCE) GRUNDRISS
(— OF ANIMAL'S BODY) UNDERLINE
(— OF COLUMN) ENTASIS
(— OF PLAY) SCENARIO
(— SHARPLY) ITALICIZE
(CURVING —) SWING
(DOUBLE —) FRINGE
(SHADOWY —) GHOST
OUTLIVE OUTLAST OUTWEAR
SURVIVE OVERBIDE
OUTLOOK MIND VIEW FRONK
FRONT VISTA ASPECT CLIMATE
LOOKOUT PURVIEW FRONTAGE
OUTSIGHT PROSPECT MENTALITY
(BRASH —) FACE
(MEDICAL —) PROGNOSIS
(SELF-CONFIDENT —) SWAGGER
OUTMANEUVER HAVE OUTPLAY
OUTMODED COLD DATED KAPUT
PASSE RUSTY BYGONE EFFETE
ANTIQUE ELDERLY VINTAGE
OBSOLETE
OUT-OF-DATE RINKYDINK
OUTPLAY HAVE
OUTPOST STATION FOREPOST
OUTGUARD
OUTPOURING FLOW GALE GUSH
FLOOD RIVER SPATE EARFUL

LAVISH STREAM OUTFLOW
FUSILLADE
OUTPUT CUT GET CROP MAKE
EXPEL GRIST POWER YIELD
ENERGY UPCOME TURNOUT
OUTRAGE RAPE ABUSE INSULT
OFFEND RAVISH ABUSION
AFFRONT OFFENSE
VIOLATE VIOLENCE
INDIGNITY
OUTRAGEOUS ENORM DAMNED
HEINOUS OBSCENE UNGODLY
FLAGRANT INFERNAL SHAMEFUL
SHOCKING ATROCIOUS
DESPERATE MONSTROUS
OUTRANK CAMP PREFER SURPASS
OUTRE ODD BIZARRE STRANGE
ECCENTRIC
OUTREACH CHEAT EXCEED
EXTEND OUTWIT SEARCH
DECEIVE SURPASS OVERREACH
OUTRIDER HAYDUK HEIDUK
HEYDUCK
(PL.) SWING
OUTRIGGER BOOM PROA BUMKIN
RIGGER SPIDER
OUTRIGHT RUN BALD CLEAN
TOTAL WHOLE DIRECT ENTIRE
OPENLY WHOLLY ABSOLUTE
COMPLETE DIRECTLY ENTIRELY
OUTRIVAL WIN EXCEL OUTDO
DEFEAT ECLIPSE SURPASS
OUTRUN BEAT COTE NICK PASS
OUTGO EXCEED ATRENNE
FORERUN OUTFOOT PREVENT
OUTRUSH GUST
OUTSET START OFFSET SETOUT
BEGINNING THRESHOLD
OUTSHED SKIPPER
OUTSHINE BLIND EXCEL OUTDO
STAIN DAZZLE DEFACE
DISTAIN SURPASS
OVERSHINE
OUTSIDE BUT OUT BOUT FREE
RIND OUTBY UTTER AFIELD
OUTFACE SURFACE EXTERIOR
EXTERNAL
(— BOUNDS) ALOGICAL
(— OF) BESIDE
(COMB. FORM) ECTO
(PREF.) EC ECT(O) EXO EXTERO
EXTRA EXTRO
OUTSIDER ALIEN OUTMAN
BOUNDER ISHMAEL EXOTERIC
STRANGER EXTRANEAN
FOREIGNER PHILISTER
(PL.) OUSTITI
OUTSKIRTS SIDE SKIRTS PURLIEU
OUTSHIFTS
OUTSMART SLICK
OUTSPOKEN BOLD FREE LOUD
APERT BLUFF BLUNT BROAD
FRANK NAKED PLAIN ROUND
CANDID DIRECT ARTLESS
EXPRESS EXPLICIT
OUTSTANDING ACE BIG ARCH
RARE SOME AMONG FAMED
NOTED SMASH BANNER FAMOUS
GIFTED HEROIC MARKED SIGNAL
SNAZZY UNPAID EMINENT
PALMARY SALIENT STELLAR
SUBLIME SUPREME TOPPING
FABULOUS INSPIRED PREMIERE

SEASONED SKELPING SLAMBANG
SMACKING STANDOUT TOWERING
BEAUTIFUL PRINCIPAL
PROMINENT UNSETTLED
MONUMENTAL NOTICEABLE
PREEMINENT

OUTSTAY TARRY

OUTSTRETCHED STENT
EXPANDED EXTENDED

OUTSTRIP CAP TOP WIN BEST
COTE LEAD LOSE PASS EXCEL
OUTDO STRIP EXCEED OUTRUN
DEVANCE SURPASS DISTANCE
OVERCOME TRANSCEND

OUTVIE SURPASS OUTSTRIP

OUTWARD ECTAD OUTER OVERT
DERMAD EXODIC EXTERN
FORMAL EXTREME VISIBLE
APPARENT EXTERIOR EXTERNAL
OBSOLETE OUTFORTH EXTRINSIC

OUTWEIGH WEIGH OUTPOISE
OVERBEAR OVERSHADE
PREPONDERATE

OUTWIT FOX POT BALK BEST DISH
FOIL HAVE BLOCK CHECK CROSS
BAFFLE EUCHRE FICKLE JOCKEY
OVERGO THWART STONKER
OUTGUESS OUTSHARP CROSSBITE
OVERREACH CIRCUMVENT

OUTWORK BRAY JETTY FLECHE
TENAIL BULWARK BARBICAN
HORNWORK TENAILLE
HORSESHOE

OUTWORKER BONDAGER

OUTWORN WAPPENED

OUZEL PIET AMSEL COLLY OUSEL
OWZEL DIPPER THRUSH
WHISTLER

OVAL O ELLIPSE STADIUM VESICAL
VULVATE AVELONGE NUMMULAR
VULVIFORM

OVARY CORAL GONAD GERMEN
OARIUM OOPHORON
(PREF.) OOPHOR(O) OV(I) OVARI(O)
OVATO

OVATION HAND APPLAUSE

OVEN OON UMU KILN LEAR LEER
LEHR OAST BAKER BENCH GLAZE
GLOOM HANGI KOHUA TANUR
TILER CALCAR MUFFLE CABOOSE
FURNACE KITCHEN
(— FORK) FRUGGAN FRUGGIN
(— MOP) SCOVEL

OVENBIRD BAKER FURNER
HORNERO TEACHER ACCENTOR

OVER BY BYE OER TOO ALSO
ANEW ATOP BACK DEAD DONE
GONE UPON ABOVE AGAIN ALOFT
ATOUR ATURN CLEAR ENDED
EXTRA VAULT ABROAD ACROSS
AROUND BEYOND DESSUS
EXCESS UPWARD SURPLUS
THROUGH FINISHED
(— AGAINST) FORNENT
(— AND ABOVE) ATOP ATOUR
BESIDES
(ALL —) NAPOO NAPOOH
SURTOUT
(PREFIX) SUR SUPER SUPRA
(PREF.) EPH EPI HYPER OB PERI
SUPER SUR

OVERABUNDANCE WASTE
EXCESS SURPLUS PLETHORA

OVERACT HAM EMOTE OUTDO
BURLESQUE

OVERALLS SLIP CHAPS JEANS
TONGS DENIMS

OVERARCH COVE

OVERAWE COW ABASH BULLY
DAUNT BUFFALO CONCUSS
BROWBEAT

OVERBEARING HIGH PROUD
LORDLY OVERLY HAUGHTY
ARROGANT BULLYING DOGMATIC
INSOLENT PRUSSIAN SNOBBISH
IMPERIOUS MASTERFUL

OVERBLOUSE SHELL

OVERBLOWN RECHERCHE

OVERBURDEN COVER HOIST
PESTER CONGEST OVERLAY
ENCUMBER STRIPPING
SURCHARGE

OVERBUSY FUSSY PRAGMATIC

OVERCAST DIM SEW BIND DARK
DULL GLUM WHIP CLOUD HEAVY
SERGE CLOUDY DARKEN GLOOMY
LOWERY CLOUDED NUBILOUS

OVERCHARGE GYP RUSH SOAK
CROWD GOUGE STICK STING
BURDEN EXCISE OPPRESS
EXTORTION

OVERCOAT MINO BENNY GREGO
JEMMY SHUBA BANGUP CAPOTE
RAGLAN SLIPON TABARD TOPPER
ULSTER PALETOT SPENCER
SURTOUT TOPCOAT BENJAMIN
COONSKIN TAGLIONI COTHAMORE
GREATCOAT INVERNESS

OVERCOATING DUFFEL DUFFLE

OVERCOME DO AWE GET MOW
WAR WIN BEAT BEST DING LICK
LOCK MATE POOP SACK SUNK
TAME WAUR CHARM CRUCH
DAUNT DROUK DROWN FORDO
STILL STOOP THROW APPALL
BEATEN BUSHED CRAVEN DEFEAT
EXCEED EXPUGN FOREDO
HURDLE MASTER MOIDER
OUTRAY PLUNGE SUBDUE VICTOR
CONFUTE CONQUER DEPRESS
ENFORCE RECOVER SMOTHER
CONVINCE OUTSTRIP SUPERATE
SURMOUNT SURPRISE
PROSTRATE
(— DIFFICULTIES) SWIM
(— WITH FATIGUE) FORDO FOREDO
(— WITH WEARINESS) HEAVY
(BE — BY HEAT) SWELTER

OVERCONFIDENT SECURE
POSITIVE

OVERCROWD PESTER CONGEST
SURCHARGE

OVERDAINTY TAFFETA

OVERDECORATED GARISH

OVERDEVELOPED GAUDY

OVERDO EXCEED EXHAUST
FATIGUE PERCOCT OVERCOOK
OVERWORK BURLESQUE

OVERDONE FUSTIAN EXUBERANT

OVERDOSE OD SICKENER

OVERDRESS SAC SACK DIZEN
SACQUE POLONAISE

OVERDRIED SLEEPY

OVERDUE BACK LATE TARDY
UNPAID ARREARS BELATED
DELAYED EXCESSIVE

OVEREAGER FEVERISH FEVEROUS

OVEREAT GORGE SLOFF SATIATE
GOURMAND

OVERELABORATE NIGGLE
LABORED

OVEREXERT TORLE STRAIN
TORFEL OVERPLY

OVERFED RANK FULSOME

OVERFLOW REE COME FLUX REAM
SLOP SWIM TEEM VENT BRIME
FLOAT FLOOD SPATE SPILL
ABOUND DEBORD OUTLET SPILTH
OVERRUN REDOUND BOILOVER
EXUNDATE INUNDATE OUTSWELL
SUBMERGE CATACLYSM
(— FROM MOLD) SPEW SPUE

OVERFLOWING FLOW AWASH
FLOAT DELAVY DELUGE ALLUVIO
COPIOUS FRESHET PROFUSE
INUNDANT EXUBERANT
LANDFLOOD SUPERFLUX

OVERGARMENT SMOCK BLOUSE
DUSTER

OVERGROWN FOZY RANK GAWKY
BRANCHY FULSOME SPRATTY
SPRITTY

OVERHAND WHIP

OVERHANG JUT BEND EAVE RAKE
BULGE JETTY BEETLE SHELVE
TOPPLE FANTAIL OVERLAP
PROJECT SUSPEND

OVERHANGING BEETLE SHELVY
HANGING PENDENT PENSILE
BEETLING IMMINENT
OBUMBRANT PENTHOUSE
PRECIPITOUS

OVERHAUL EXAMINE OVERHAIL
RENOVATE FOREREACH

OVERHEAD COST ABOVE ALOFT
BURDEN ONCOST UPKEEP
EXPENSE OVERTOP

OVERHEAT PARBOIL SCOUTHER

OVERINDULGE PAMPER DEBAUCH

OVERLAP LAP RIDE SYPHER
SHINGLE IMBRICATE INTERSECT

OVERLAPPING JUGATE RIDING
EQUITANT OBVOLUTE IMBRICATE
(— IN FUGUE) STRETTA STRETTO

OVERLAVISH BAROQUE

OVERLAY CAP LAP CEIL COAT
WHIP APPLY COUCH COVER
GLAZE PATCH PLATE CEMENT
CRAVAT SPREAD STUCCO VENEER
ENCRUST OPPRESS OVERLIE
SMOTHER APPLIQUE TEMPLATE
(— WITH GOLD) BEAT GILD

OVERLOAD GLUT CHARGE
ENCUMBER SURCHARGE

OVERLOADED PLETHORIC
PLETHOROUS

OVERLOOK BALK MISS OMIT PASS
SKIP SLIP WINK BLINK FORGO
ACQUIT EXCUSE FOREGO FORGET
IGNORE MANAGE OVERGO
ABSOLVE COMMAND CONDONE
FORGIVE INSPECT MISKNOW
NEGLECT CONFOUND DOMINATE
DISREGARD DISSEMBLE

OVERLOOKER GAITER

OVERLOOKING (INTENTIONAL —)
AMNESTY

OVERLORD LIEGE DESPOT ISWARA
SATRAP TYRANT ISHVARA

SUZERAIN TYRANNIZE

OVERLY CAP TOO

OVERLYING JESSANT BROCHANT
INCUMBENT

OVERMAN CHIEF LEADER ARBITER
FOREMAN REFEREE OVERSEER
SUPERMAN

OVERMANTLE (— TREATMENT)
TRUMEAU

OVERMASTER GET

OVERMATCH BEST DEFEAT
EXCEED SURPASS VANQUISH

OVERMODEST PRIM PRUDISH

OVERMUCH TOO EXCESS SURPLUS
EXCESSIVE
(PREF.) HYPER

OVERNICE FEAT FUSS SAUCY
DAINTY QUAINT SPRUCE FINICKY
PRECISE DENTICAL PRECIOUS
SQUEAMISH

OVERPAINT CLOBBER

OVERPLAY HAM

OVERPOWER AWE BEAT ROUT
RUSH CRUSH DROWN QUELL
SWAMP WHELM COMPEL DEFEAT
DELUGE ENGULF MASTER
OVERGO SUBDUE WRIXLE
CONQUER CONTROL OPPRESS
REPRESS CONVINCE OUTSCOUT
SCUMFISH SURPRISE
(— WITH HEAT) SWELT
(— WITH LIGHT) DAZZLE

OVERPOWERING DIRE FIERCE
KILLING DAZZLING STUNNING
DESPERATE MONSTROUS

OVERPRAISE OVERSELL

OVERPRECISE MIM PRISSY
FINICKY CLERKISH NIGGLING
PRECIEUSE

OVERREACH DO POT DUPE GRAB
CHEAT COZEN CHOILE GREASE
NOBBLE OUTWIT OVERGO
DECEIVE

OVERREADY FORWARD

OVERREFINED QUAINT PRECIOUS

OVERRIPE FRACID SQUSHY
SQUUSHY

OVERRIPENESS SEED

OVERRULE VETO GOVERN
ABROGATE OVERCOME

OVERRULING GREAT
PREDOMINANT

OVERRUN TEEM BESET CRUSH
SWARM DELUGE EXCEED INFEST
INVADE OVERGO RAVAGE SPREAD
DESTROY

OVERSEAS OUTREMER

OVERSEE TEND WATCH DIRECT
HANDLE MANAGE SURVEY
EXAMINE INSPECT NEGLECT
DISREGARD SUPERVISE

OVERSEER BAAS BOSS CORK JOSS
EPHOR GRAVE REEVE BISHOP
CENSOR DRIVER GAFFER GRIEVE
KEEKER MIRDHA TINDAL WARDEN
BAILIFF CAPATAZ CAPORAL
CURATOR FOREMAN HEADMAN
KANGANI MANAGER MANDOER
MAYORAL OVERMAN PRISTAW
TAPSMAN BANKSMAN CHAPRASI
DECURION MARTINET SURVEYOR
VILLICUS
(— OF MACHINERY) TENTOR

(— OF MINE) CAPTAIN
(SPIRITUAL —) PASTOR PRIEST
OVERSENSITIVE TICKLISH
OVERSENTIMENTAL SOFT SLOPPY
OVERSHADOW DIM CLOUD COVER
DWARF SHADE TOWER DARKEN
EFFACE ECLIPSE OBSCURE
UMBRAGE BESCREEN DOMINATE
OVERCAST
OVERSHOE GUM BOOT GUME
ARCTIC GAITER GALOSH GOLOSH
PATTEN RUBBER SANDAL
FLAPPER EXCLUDER FOOTHOLD
PANTOFLE
OVERSIGHT EYE CARE HOLE SLIP
ERROR FAULT GAFFE LAPSE
WATCH CHARGE BLUNDER
CONTROL JEOFAIL MISTAKE
OMISSION TUTELAGE DIRECTION
(LEGAL —) JEOFAIL
OVERSKIRT PEPLUM PANNIER
OVERSOFT QUASHY
OVERSPREAD FOG CAST CLOT
DECK PALL BATHE BREDE CLOUD
COVER SMEAR STREW CLOTHE
DELUGE DOODLE INDUCE
SCATTER SUFFUSE BESPREAD
OVERSTATE MAGNIFY
EXAGGERATE
OVERSTEP PASS EXCEED SURPASS
OVERSTRAINED EPITONIC
OVERSUPPLIED RANK
OVERT OPEN PATENT PUBLIC
OBVIOUS APPARENT MANIFEST
OVERTAKE PASS ATAKE CATCH
ATTAIN BEFALL DETECT ENSNARE
OVERHIE FOREHENT OVERHAUL
(— BY DARKNESS) BENIGHT
OVERTASK DRIVE
OVERTAX HOIST EXCEED STRAIN
STRESS
OVERTHROW TIP CAST DASH
DOWN FALL FELL FOIL FOLD
HURL RAZE ROUT RUIN RUSH
WALT WEND ALLAY CRUSH
EVERT FLING LEVEL QUASH
UPSET WORST WRACK WRECK
DEFEAT DEJECT DEPOSE REPUTE
SLIGHT TOPPLE TUMBLE UNSEAT
WRITHE AFFLICT CONQUER
CONVELL DESTROY DISMISS
RUINATE SUBVERT UNDOING
UNHORSE WHEMMLE CONFOUND
DEMOLISH OVERCOME OVERTURN
REVERSAL SUPPLANT
VANQUISH CHECKMATE

CONFUSION OVERWHELM
(— BY TRIPPING) CHIP
OVERTONE PARTIAL HARMONIC
OVERTOP COW OVERREACH
OVERTURE OFFER PROEM
ADVANCE OPENING PRELUDE
APERTURE PROPOSAL SINFONIA
VORSPIEL
(INDECENT —) ASSAULT
OVERTURN TIP CAVE COUP KEEL
TILT WALT WELT TERVE THROW
UPEND UPSET WELME WHALM
WHELM SLIGHT TIPPLE TOPPLE
WELTER CAPSIZE DESTROY
PERVERT REVERSE SUBVERT
WHEMMLE
(— A WATCHMAN) BOX
OVERWEENING MISPROUD
PRESUMPTUOUS
OVERWEIGHT OUTGANG
OVERWHELM BOWL BURY SINK
SLAY AMAZE COVER CRUSH
DROOK DROUK DROWN FLOOD
SEIZE SPATE SWAMP CUMBER
DEFEAT DELUGE ENGULF OBRUTE
PLUNGE QUELME QUENCH
ASTOUND BOMBARD CONFUTE
CONQUER ENGROSS FLATTEN
IMMERSE INFLOOD OPPRESS
SMOTHER ASTONISH DISTRESS
INUNDATE OVERCOME SUBMERGE
AVALANCHE
OVERWHELMED ACCABLE
OVERWORK HOIN TIRE TOIL
SWEAT STRAIN SURMENAGE
OVINE OVIN OVILE SHEEP
SHEEPLIKE
OVIPOSITOR TEREBRA
OVOID OVATE OBOVOID
OVOLO OVAL THUMB BOLTEL
OVULE EGG NIT GERM SEED
EMBRYO OVULUM GEMMULE
SEEDLET
OVUM EGG OVAL SEED SPORE
OOSPERM OOSPHERE
OWAIA TREE BOBO
OWE DUE OWN REST AUGHT
OUGHT SHALL POSSESS
ATTRIBUTE
OWER DEBTOR
OWL ULE BUBO LULU MOMO RURU
SURN TYTO UTUM JENNY MADGE
NINOX PADGE SCOPS STRIX
TAWNY WEKAU AZIOLA HOOTER
HOWLET KETUPA MUCARO
RAPTOR STRICH VERMIN

WHEKAU BOOBOOK HARFANG
KATOGLE WAPACUT WOOLERT
BILLYWIX COQUIMBO MOREPORK
(— CALL) HOOT
(LIKE AN —) STRIGINE
(YOUNG —) UTUM OWLET
(PREF.) STRIGI
OWN AIN OWE AVOW FESS HAVE
HOLD HOWE MEET NAIN SELF
ADMIT AUGHT OUGHT MASTER
CONCEDE CONFESS POSSESS
PROSPER ACKNOWLEDGE
(PREF.) (ONE'S —) IDIO
OWNER BEL MALIK WALLA
HOLDER DOMINUS HERITOR
ODALLER PROPRIETOR
(— OF ESTATE) ALIRD
(— OF FISHING PLANT) PLANTER
(— OF SLAVES) PATRON
(— OF YACHT) AFTERGUARD
(PLANTATION —) COLON
(SHEEP —) NABAL
OWNERSHIP ODAL UDAL AUGHT
TITLE CORNER SEIZIN SEIZURE
SEVERAL TENANCY DOMINIUM
PROPERTY COMMUNITY
POSSESSION
OX YAK ANOA AVER BEEF BUFF
BULL GAUR MUSK NAWT NEAT
NEWT NOWT OWSE REEM RUNT
STOT URUS ZEBU AIVER BISON
BUGLE GAYAL SANGA STEER
TOLLY TSINE BOVINE MITHAN
ROTHER BANTENG BUFFALO
KOUPREY TWINTER SELADANG
TALLOWER
(CAMBODIAN —) KOUPREY
KOUPROH
(HORNLESS —) MOIL
(SMALL —) RUNT
(TAME —) COACH
(WILD —) URE ANOA BUFF GAUR
REEM URUS BISON BUGLE
BANTIN BANTENG BUFFALO
SELADANG
(YEARLING —) STIRK
(YOUNG —) STOT
(PREF.) BOVI BU
OXBLOOD KAZAK COPTIC KAZAKH
OXBOW INCIDENT (AUTHOR OF —)
CLARK
(CHARACTER IN —) GIL DREW ROSE
CANBY CROFT GRIER JOYCE
MAPEN TYLER CARTER DAVIES
DONALD GERALD MARTIN
OSGOOD RISLEY TETLEY

FARNLEY KINKAID
OXEN NOWT OWSEN CATTLE
OXEYE BOCE GOLD ASTER CLOUD
DAISY GOLDE DUNLIN PLOVER
TARPON
OXFORD DOWN SHOE CLOTH
OXONIAN SLIPPER
OXGANG OSKEN BOVATE OXGATE
OXLAND PLOWGANG
OXIDATION RUST
OXIDE EARTH FLOSS CADMIA
HAFNIA MOILES ZAFFER CALCINE
GUMMITE KERNITE LIMONITE
DJALMAITE
(— OF CALCIUM) LIME
(— OF IRON) RUST COLCOTHAR
MAGNETITE
OXLIP PAGLE PAIGLE PRIMULA
MILKMAID PRIMROSE PRIMWORT
OXSHOE CUE
OXYGEN GAS OZONE OXYGENIUM
(PREF.) OXO
OXYGENATE AERATE VENTILATE
OYSTER COPIS COUNT PINNA
PLANT SHELL COTUIT HUITRE
NATIVE REEFER BIVALVE
MOLLUSK PANDORE RATTLER
SHARPER BLUEPOINT GREENGILL
LYNNHAVEN
(— BED) PARK STEW LAYER SCALP
CLAIRE SCALFE OYSTERAGE
(— CATCHER) OLIVE PYNOT TIRMA
KROCKET PIANNET REDBILL
SCOLDER SHELDER PILWILLET
SKELDRAKE
(— CRAB) PINNOTERE
(— FOSSIL) OSTRACITE
(— MEASURE) WASH
(— PLANT) SALSIFY
(— SHELL) HUSK TEST SHUCK
(— SMALLER THAN QUARTER)
BLISTER
(— SOLD BY POUND) COUNT
(IRISH —) POWLDOODY
(ROCK —) CHAMA
(VEGETABLE —) SALSIFY
(YOUNG —) SET SPAT
(2,3, OR 4 —S) WARP
(PREF.) OSTRE(I)(O)
OYSTERFISH TAUTOG TOADFISH
OZARK STATE MISSOURI
OZEM (BROTHER OF —) DAVID
(FATHER OF —) JESSE
OZNI (FATHER OF —) GAD
OZOCERITE MALTHA NEFTGIL
OZONE AIR

P

P PAPA PETER
PA DAD PAW FORT PAPA DADDY FATHER VILLAGE STOCKADE
PABULUM FOOD FUEL PROG CEREAL ALIMENT SUPPORT NUTRIMENT
PAC BOOT SHOE MOCCASIN
PACA CAPA CAVY LAVA LABBA AGOUTI RODENT
PACE FIG PAD RIP WAY BEMA CLIP GAIT LOPE PASS PELT RACK RATE STEP TEAR TROT WALK AMBLE BRAWL CANTO SLINK SPACE SPEED STEEK SWING TEMPO TRACE TREAD CANTER GALLOP STRAIT STRIDE CHANNEL CHAPTER DOGTROT MEASURE PASSAGE SCUTTLE
(**FAST —**) ROMP
(**RAPID —**) CLIP CRACKER
(**SLOW —**) JOG CRAWL CREEP
(PL.) MANAGE
PACER HORSE AMBLER SPANKER TRIPPLER
PACHISI LUDO UCKERS PARCHESI
PACHYDERM HIPPO RHINO ELEPHANT
PACIFIC CALM MEEK MILD IRENE IRENIC PLACID SERENE PEACEFUL TRANQUIL PEACEABLE
(**— ISLAND PINE**) IE KOU IEIE LEHUA
PACIFIER DUMMY COMFORTER
PACIFIST BOLO
PACIFY PAY CALM EASE LULL STAY ABATE ALLAY AMESE MEASE PEASE QUELL QUIET STILL PECIFY SERENE SETTLE SOFTEN SOOTHE APPEASE ASSUAGE MOLLIFY PLACATE QUALIFY STICKLE MITIGATE ALLEVIATE RECONCILE
PACK JAM PUN WAD BALE CADE CRAM DECK FILL GANG JAMB LADE LOAD PAIR ROUT STOW SWAG TAMP TOTE TUCK COUCH CRAME CROWD DRESS FLOCK HORDE SKULK SOMER STEVE STORE STUFF TRUSS BARREL BODDLE BOODLE BUDGET BUNDLE CARTON DUFFLE EMBALE ENCASE FARDEL HAMPER IMPACT PARCEL STEEVE THWACK TURKEY WALLET PANNIER PORTAGE RUMMAGE SUMPTER KNAPSACK
(**— ANIMAL**) ASS MULE BURRO CAMEL HORSE LLAMA DONKEY PACKER
(**— BUILDER**) GOBBER
(**— JURY**) WATER
(**— LOOSELY**) HOVER
(**— OF BEARS**) SLOTH
(**— OF CARDS**) STOCK
(**— OF DOGS**) CRY KENNEL
(**— OF FOXES**) GROUP SKULK
(**— OF HOUNDS**) CRY HUNT MUTE
(**— OFF**) WAG SHANK TURSE
(**— ROAD**) PACKWAY
(**— TIGHTLY**) STIVE
PACKAGE PAD BALE BOLT PAIR DUMMY TRUSS BINDLE BUNDLE PACKET PARCEL SAMPLE SEROON DORLACH
(**— OF CIGARETTES**) DECK
(**— OF GOLDBEATER'S SKINS**) SHODER
(**— OF LEAF**) BOOK
(**— OF PEPPERS**) ROBBIN
(**— OF STAMPS**) KILOWARE
(**— OF VELLUM**) KUTCH
(**— OF VENEER**) FLITCH
(**— OF WOOL**) BAG PAD BUTT FADGE
(**YARN —**) CONE CHEESE
PACKER BALER LINER ROPER CANNER
PACKET BOAT BOOK DECK ROLL SCREW BUNDLE PARCEL SACHET
(**— OF A DRUG**) BAG
(**— OF VELLUM**) CUTCH KUTCH
PACKHORSE SOMER JAGGER PACKER SUMPTER
PACKING CUP RAGS GAUZE PAPER STRAW WASTE GASKET GROMMET STOWAGE STOPPING
(**— MATERIAL**) BALINE GASKET
(**CLAY —**) LUTE
PACKINGHOUSE MEATWORKS
PACKMAN HAWKER
PACKSACK KYACK
PACKSADDLE BAT BARDEL APAREJO
PACT MISE ACCORD CARTEL PACTUM TREATY BARGAIN COMPACT LOCARNO ALLIANCE CONTRACT COVENANT AGREEMENT CONCORDAT
PAD MAT WAD WAY BLAD BOSS FROG LURE MUTE PATH PUFF ROAD ROLL SHOE WALK WASE BLOCK INKER PERCH PILCH QUILT STENT STINT STUFF TABBY TRAMP BASKET BUFFER BUSTLE DAUBER HOLDER JOCKEY NUMNAH PADDLE PADNAG PANNEL PILLOW SPONGE TABLET TRUDGE VELURE WREATH BOLSTER BOMBAST CUSHION FOOTPAD PILLION SASHOON
(**— IN CRIB**) BUMPER
(**— OF ROPE**) PUDDING PUDDENING
(**— OF STRAW**) SUNK WASE
(**— ON HORSE'S FOOT**) FROG
(**ETCHER'S —**) DABBER
(**FENCING —**) PLASTRON
(**HAIR —**) RAT MOUSE TOQUE
(**INKING —**) INKER TOMPION
(**MEDICAL —**) PLEDGET
(**PERFUMED —**) SACHET
(**SADDLE —**) PANEL PILLOW PILLION
(**PREF.**) TYL(O)
PADAUK CORAIL
PADDER MANGLE
PADDING TABBY CADDIS BOLSTER BOMBAST BUSHING CADDICE FILLING PACKING ROBBERY WADDING MAHOITRE STUFFING
PADDLE OAR ROW SPUD WADE ALOOF CANOE SLICE SPANK BUCKET DABBLE PETTLE PUNISH STRIKE TODDLE SPANKER SPURTLE LUMPFISH
(**— BOX**) WHEELHOUSE
(**— FOR FLOUR**) SLICK
(**TAILOR'S —**) BEATER
PADDLEFISH GANOID DUCKBILL STURGEON POLYODONT SPADEFISH SPOONBILL
PADDOCK LOT FROG PARK CLOSE FIELD SLEDGE GARSTON LOANING BIRDCAGE
PADDYMELON QUOKKA PADMELON
PADISHAH SULTAN PADASHA POTSHAW
PADLOCK LOCK FASTEN SECURE CLOSING FASTENER HORSELOCK
(**— LINK**) SHACKLE
PADRE MONK CLERIC FATHER PRIEST CHAPLAIN
PADRONA LANDLADY MISTRESS
PADRONE BOSS CHIEF MASTER PATRON LANDLORD INNKEEPER
PAEAN ODE HYMN SONG PRAISE OUTBURST TRIUMPHAL
PAGAN ATA BUID BATAK BUKID APAYAO BAGOBO BANGON BILAAN BONTOC ETHNIC PAYNIM SABIAN ALANGAN DUMAGAT GENTILE HEATHEN INFIDEL SARACEN SUBANUN UNGODLY IDOLATOR
PAGANDOM PAYNIM
PAGE BOY CALL LEAF MOTH SIDE CHILD FACER FOLIO GROOM SHEET DONZEL ERRATA SUMMON VARLET BUTTONS CALLBOY FUNNIES PAVISER SERVANT CHASSEUR HENCHMAN ICHOGLAN
(**— BOTTOM**) TAIL
(**BLANK —S**) CANCEL
(**FACING —S**) SPREAD
(**LADY'S —**) ESCUDERO
(**LAST FEW —S**) BACK
(**LEFTHAND —**) VERSO
(**RIGHTHAND —**) RECTO OUTPAGE
(**TITLE —**) TITLE UNWAN RUBRIC
(PL.) ODDMENTS
PAGEANT JEST POMP SHOW ANTIC PARADE RIDING TABLEAU TAMASHA TRIUMPH AQUACADE CAVALCADE SPECTACLE WATERWORK
PAGEANTRY POMP PARADE HERALDRY SPLENDOR
PAGIEL (FATHER OF —) OCRAN
PAGLIACCI (CHARACTER IN —) BEPPE CANIO NEDDA TONIO SILVIO
(**COMPOSER OF —**) LEONCAVALLO
PAGODA PON TAA HOON WATT TEMPLE VARELLA
(**PART OF —**) TEE ROOF TOPE STUPA FINIAL BALCONY
PAHOUIN FAN FANG
PAHUTAN PAHO
PAID EVEN RESOLUTE
(**— IN COIN**) DRY
(**— IN FULL**) SATISFIED
PAIL CAN COG PAN SOA SOE BEAT BOWK GAWN MEAL STOP TRUG BOWIE COGUE CRUCK DANDY ESHIN SKEEL STOOP BLICKY BUCKET COGGIE HARASS KETTLE LEGLEN NOGGIN PIGGIN SITULA THRASH COLLOCK
(**MILK —**) KIT SOE TRUG ESHIN LEGLEN
(**ON WHEELS**) DANDY
(**PART OF —**) EAR RIM BODY CURL HANDLE
(**POTTERY —**) SEAU
(**SMALL —**) KIT BLICKY BLICKIE
(**WOODEN —**) COG COGUE LUGGIE PIGGIN
PAIN GYP ACHE AGRA BALE CARE CARK DOLE FRET GRUE HARM HURT PANG SITE SORE TEEN TINE WARK AGONY BEANS CRAMP DOLOR GRIEF GRIPE PINCH PINSE SCALD SMART STING STOUN THRAW THROE WOUND WRING BARRAT GRIEVE MISERY SHOWER STITCH TWINGE AFFLICT ALGESIS ANGUISH EARACHE HURTING MYALGIA OFFENCE PENALTY TORTURE TRAVAIL TROUBLE AGGRIEVE DISTRESS FLEABITE
(**— IN BACK**) NOTALGIA SCIATICA
(**— IN HAND**) CHIRAGRA
(**— IN SIDE**) STEEK
(**— OF MIND**) AGONY
(**— RELIEVER**) OPIATE ANODYNE ASPIRIN
(**FILL WITH —**) YEARN
(**SHARP —**) WRING
(**STOMACH —**) GRIPES GNAWING
(**WRENCHING —**) TORSION
(PL.) FASH LABOR WHILE

EFFORT TROUBLE
(PREF.) ALG(IO)(O) DOLORI NOCI
PENO
(SUFF.) AGRA ALGIA ALGIC
ODYNE ODYNIA
PAINFUL BAD ILL DIRE EVIL FELL
SORE SOUR TART ANGRY CRUEL
SHARP SORRY BITTER STICKY
TENDER THORNY BALEFUL
GRIPING HURTFUL IRKSOME
LABORED PENIBLE PUNGENT
EXACTING TERRIBLE TORTUOUS
DIFFICULT HARROWING
(PREF.) MOGI
PAINSTAKING BUSY LOVING
NARROW CAREFUL PENIBLE
DILIGENT EXACTING STUDIOUS
ASSIDUOUS ELABORATE
PAINT BICE BLOT COAT DAUB
DRAW FARD GAUD LIMN PENT
PICT SOIL COLOR FEIGN FUCUS
GRAIN ROUGE STAIN BEDAUB
DAZZLE DEPICT ENAMEL FRESCO
OPAQUE SHADOW SKETCH
BESMEAR PORTRAY PRETEND
SCUMBLE AIRBRUSH DECORATE
DEPEINCT DESCRIBE DISGUISE
URFIRNIS CALCIMINE
(— A PIPE) SOIL
(— FACE OR BODY) FUCUS PARGET
(— HASTILY) SQUIGGLE
(— SKETCHILY) SPLASH
(— THROUGH PATTERN) STENCIL
(— WITH COSMETICS) POP POT
FARD
(PREF.) PICTO
PAINTBRUSH WICKAWEE
NOSEBLEED
(PART OF —) HAIR CRIMP HANDLE
BRISTLE FERRULE
PAINTED PINTO FUCATE PASTOSE
PINTADO FUCOIDAL GOFFERED
(— BEAUTY) VANESSA
(— BUNTING) POP NONPAREIL
(— CUP) WICKAWEE PAINTBRUSH
(— WAKE-ROBIN) SARA
PAINTER BRUSH FAUVE ARTIST
DAUBER PICTOR PANTHER
SIGNIST SIGNMAN WORKMAN
BRUSHMAN LUMINIST MURALIST
NAZARENE STIPPLER DECORATOR
TACTILIST
(PL.) ECLECTICS
AMERICAN AHL COX GAG LOW
RAY RIX AMES BAER BEAL COLE
DABO DANA GRAY HART HAYS
HOWE HURD KOST LOEB LUKS
NEAL PAGE POOR REID UFER
WEIR WEST WOOD ABBEY AGATE
AIKEN ALDIS BACON BAKER
BARSE BEARD BEAUX BETTS
BOGGS BROOK BROWN BRUSH
BUNCE CHASE CHILD CRANE
CURRY DAVIS DEWEY EATON
ENNIS FIENE FLAGG FOOTE GILES
GRANT GROLL HEALY HENRI
HOMER INMAN IPSEN JONES
LAHEY LUCAS MARSH MINOR
MOORE MORAN MYERS OGDEN
PEALE PERRY POORE RYDER
SHINN SLOAN SMITH TRYON
UPTON WALDO WAUGH WEBER
WEEKS WHITE WOOLF WYANT

WYETH YOUNG BENSON BENTON
BOGERT BOUCHE BROWNE
CADMUS CHAPIN CHURCH
COLMAN COOPER COPLEY
COTTON CRANCH CURRAN
DANIEL DANNAT DAVIES DEARTH
DECAMP DEMUTH DEWING
DUNLAP DURAND EAKINS FERRIS
FORBES FOSTER FOWLER GUERIN
HAGGIN HARVEY HASSAM
HAYDEN HEATON HERTER
HOPPER INGHAM INNESS JOUETT
KINNEY KNIGHT LAWSON LEVINE
LOOMIS MARTIN MEIERE MILLER
MOSLER MURPHY NEAGLE
NOURSE OAKLEY PARTON PEARCE
POWELL QUIDOR SAMPLE
SAVAGE SINGER STELLA STUART
SYMONS TANNER TAUBES
TURNER VEDDER WRIGHT
ZORACH ADDISON ALLSTON
AUDUBON BANVARD BELLOWS
BINGHAM BRINLEY CAMERON
CARLSON CARROLL CHAPMAN
CHRISTY CORBINO COUDERT
CROPSEY DOUGHTY EDWARDS
ELLIOTT FASSETT FREEMAN
GARNSEY GIFFORD GRIFFIN
GROPPER HARDING HARNETT
HIBBARD HIGGINS HUBBARD
HUBBELL JOHNSON KENDALL
KENSETT LAFARGE LATHROP
MACEWEN MATHEWS MCENTEE
METCALF MUNSELL NAEGELE
OKEEFFE PARRISH PEIXOTO
PROCTOR SCUDDER SIMMONS
SMIBERT SPENCER STIMSON
WATROUS WIGGINS ATCHISON
BARTLETT BECKWITH BICKNELL
BILLINGS BOUGHTON BRACKMAN
BRADFORD BREVOORT BRIDGMAN
CORNWELL COSTIGAN DUVENECK
FAULKNER HAMILTON HARRISON
HOVENDEN HUTCHINS
JOHANSEN KRONBERG
LOCKWOOD MATTESON
MELCHERS PHILLIPS REINHART
RICHARDS ROCKWELL ROSSITER
SHATTUCK SPEICHER TRUMBULL
WHISTLER WILMARTH
WOODBURY ALEXANDER
ARMSTRONG BEMELMANS
BERDANIER BERNSTEIN
BIERSTADT BITTINGER
BLAKELOCK DAUGHERTY
DEKOONING HALLOWELL
HAWTHORNE REMINGTON
ROTHERMEL SCHREIBER
TWACHTMAN VANDERLYN
WENTWORTH BLASHFIELD
BURCHFIELD CLINEDINST
EILSHEMIUS FARNSWORTH
HUNTINGTON MACCAMERON
WHITTREDGE BERNINGHAUS
DELLENBAUGH PRENDERGAST
BLUMENSCHEIN BRECKENRIDGE
DAINGERFIELD CROWNINSHIELD
ARGENTINIAN CENTURION
AUSTRIAN ALT FUHRICH
AMERLING HAUSMANN
DANHAUSER DEFREGGER
KOKOSCHKA FRIEDLANDER
PETTENKOFEN

BELGIAN CLAYS ENSOR NAVEZ
VIGNE BEIFVE KEYSER WIERTZ
GALLAIT GUFFENS LALAING
PAUWELS STEVENS WAPPERS
WAUTERS WILLEMS BAERTSON
LAERMANS BROUCKERE
EVENEPOEL TONGERLOO
BRAEKELEER CHAMPAIGNE
VERBOECKHOVEN
CANADIAN COTE KANE FORBES
OBRIEN WALKER WATSON
CHINESE SHUBUN
CZECH KUPKA MANES MUCHA
BROZIK
DANISH JUEL BLOCH CARLSEN
DAISGAARD MARSTRAND
WILLUMSEN ZAHRTMANN
ABILDGAARD ECKERSBERG
DUTCH BOL DOU BECK BEGA
CORT CUYP GOES GOGH HAAS
HALS HEDA HEEM LAAR LELY
LOOY MAES MEER NEER AELST
BAUER BOSCH BOUTS BRUYN
CODDE DAVID GOYEN HELST
KETEL MARIS METSU NEEFS
OVENS VELDE VROOM WITTE
BACKER DECKER EGMONT FLINCK
GELDER HEYDEN KESSEL MANDER
MESDAG MIERIS MULIER OSTADE
POTTER RUYSCH TOOROP
WEENIX AERTSEN AERTZEN
ASSELYN BERCHEM BEYEREN
CRABETH DOUFFET HOBBEMA
ISRAELS KONINCK LASTMAN
LIEVENS LOMBARD PATINIR
POURBUS VERMEER WYNANTS
AGRICOLA DOESBURG DUJARDIN
EECKHOUT GOLTZIUS HUYSMANS
JONGKIND KOEKKOEK LAIRESSE
MOREELSE RUYSDAEL TERBORCH
BLOEMAERT CORNELISZ
FABRITIUS HOEFNAGEL
HONTHORST HOUBRAKEN
MIEREVELT MONDRIAAN
MOUCHERON REMBRANDT
STEENWILK WOUWERMAN
BACKHUYSEN BERCKHEYDE
CAMPHUYSEN EVERDINGEN
GESELSCHAP LINGELBACH
BREKELENKAM HONDECOETER
POELENBURGH HOOGSTRAETEN
ENGLISH COX EGG BIRD BONE
COLE COPE EAST ETTY EVES GILL
HAAG HOOK HUNT JOHN LEAR
NASH OPIE SWAN WARD WEIR
BLAKE BROCK BROWN CRANE
CROME DAVIS DOYLE FURSE
LEWIS LUCAS MOORE ORPEN
STARK STEER STONE TONKS
UWINS WATTS WELLS ABBOTT
ASHTON BARKER BOXALL BROOKS
BROWNE CARTER CHALON
COATES COOPER COSWAY
COTMAN COWPER COZENS
CROFTS DEWINT DOBSON FILDES
GIRTIN GLOVER HACKER HAYDON
HOLMES KNIGHT LAVERY
LAWSON LEADER MARTIN
MCEVOY MULLER NEWTON
OLIVER OULESS SEVERN SMIRKE
STUART STUBBS TURNER VARLEY
WALKER ANSDELL BAYLISS
BEECHEY CAMERON CLAUSEN

COLLIER DANIELL DICKSEE
GILBERT GUEVARA HERBERT
HODGSON HOGARTH HOLIDAY
HOLROYD LINNELL MILLAIS
MORLAND POYNTER RIVIERE
RUSSELL SOLOMON ZOFFANY
ARMITAGE ATKINSON AUMONIER
BEAUMONT BRANGWYN
CALDERON CALLCOTT CORBOULD
CRESWICK EASTLAKE FIELDING
HILLIARD LANDSEER LEIGHTON
MUNNINGS REDGRAVE REYNOLDS
RICHMOND RICKETTS ROSSETTI
STOTHARD WATERLOW
WHISTLER AMSHEWITZ
BEARDSLEY BONINGTON
BOURGEOIS COLLINSON
CONSTABLE GREENAWAY
NORTHCOTE STANFIELD
THORNHILL BROCKHURST
KENNINGTON WATERHOUSE
WOOLDRIDGE ROTHENSTEIN
GAINSBOROUGH
FINNISH EDELFELT
FLEMISH BLES BRIL EYCK BALEN
CLAUS CLEVE COXIE COQUES
CRAYER BLOEMEN BROUWER
CANDIDO BRUEGHEL CHRISTUS
CRAESBEECK
FRENCH ZO ARP BIDA CAIN DORE
DUFY ETEX HEIM HUET LAMI
TROY BIARD CAZIN CHERY CORNU
COROT DAVID DEGAS DOYEN
DUPRE FRERE JONAS LEGER
LHOTE MANET MONET MOROT
PATER VEBER VOUET BAUDRY
BERARD BERAUD BOILLY BONNAT
BONVIN BOUDIN BOUTON
BRAQUE BRETON CALLOT CARREY
CHABAS CHERET CHERON
CORMON COTTET COUDER
COUSIN COYPEL DAUBAN DERAIN
DOUCET DUBUFE FAVORY FORAIN
FORBIN FRIESZ GERARD GEROME
GERVEX GIGOUX GRANET GREUZE
GUERIN HEBERT HENNER INGRES
LAHIRE LATOUR LEBLON LEBRUN
LELEUX LEPINE MARTIN MERSON
MILLET MIRBEL MOREAU MULLER
RENOIR SIGNAC STELLA TISSOT
TROYON VANLOO VERNET VIBERT
WEERTS BARRIAS BESNARD
BONHEUR BONNARD BOUCHER
BOUCHOR BOURDON CABANEL
CEZANNE CHARDIN CHARLOT
COGNIET COURBET COUTURE
DAMERON DORIGNY DROUAIS
FERRIER FLANDIN FOUQUET
GARNIER GAUGUIN GENDRON
HEDOUIN HERSENT JEANRON
LAFOSSE LANSYER LAURENS
LEBOURG LEGRAND LEHMANN
LEMOYNE LESUEUR LORRAIN
MAIGNAN MARQUET MATISSE
MIGNARD MORISOT NATTIER
PICABIA POUSSIN PRUDHON
RESTOUT ROUAULT UTRILLO
WATTEAU BELLANGE BERCHERE
CARRIERE CHARTRAN CONSTANT
DAGUERRE DALAUNAY DAUBIGNY
DESCAMPS DETAILLE DROLLING
ESPAGNAT FLANDRIN GALIMARD
JOUVENET KLINGSOR LANDELLE

LATOUCHE LEFEBVRE LENEPVEU
LEPRINCE OZENFANT PARROCEL
PISSARRO ROUSSEAU SCHEFFER
STEINLEN VUILLARD WILLETTE
BOULANGER CHATILLON
CHENAVARD COUBERTIN
DEBUCOURT DEHODENCQ
DELABORDE DELACROIX
DELAROCHE DESPORTES
FALGUIERE FRAGONARD
GERICAULT GLEISPACH
GUILLEMET HENNIQUIN
LAURENCIN METZINGER
SCHUSSELE BARTHOLOME
BOUGUEREAU BOULLONGNE
BRASCASSAT CHASSERIAU
DESBROSSES GUILLAUMET
GUILLAUMIN HARPIGNIES
JACQUEMART MEISSONIER
BRACQUEMOND CARMONTELLE
LARGILLIERE DESVALLIERES
LOUTHERBOURG
GERMAN DIX MAX ADAM DIEZ
HESS JANK LENZ MARC MARR
SOHN UHDE VEIT BEGAS BEHAM .
BINCK BRUYN DURER EBERS
EMELE ERNST FOLTZ FRIES FUGER
GRAFF GROSZ HOFER KNAUS
KUEHL LEIBL MACKE MEYER
MUCKE NEHER OESER PECHT
PENCZ STUCK THOMA VOGEL
BECKER BRACHT BRAITH BUHLER
BURGER EBERLE ECHTER FITGER
FRIESE GEBLER GUSSOW HECKEL
HENSEL HERLIN HERTEL HEYDEN
HUBNER KELLER KOBELL KRAFFT
KRUGER LANGER LOFFTZ MAREES
MENZEL MULLER RETHEL
WERNER BALDUNG BARTELS
BLECHEN CORINTH CRANACH
FLICKEL GENELLI HOFMANN
HOLBEIN KLINGER KOPSICH
KRELING LENBACH LESSING
LOCHNER PRELLER RICHTER
SCHWIND STEUBEN AGRICOLA
AMBERGER CARSTENS
DETTMANN FIORILLO GEBHARDT
GRUTZNER HABERLIN HENDRICH
KAULBACH KIRCHNER KOLLWITZ
KUGELGEN KULMBACH
ROTTMANN SCHIRMER SCHREYER
ZEITBLOM ACHENBACH
AINMILLER ALTDORFER
BENDEMANN BLEIBTREU
BURGKMAIR CORNELIUS
ELSHEIMER ENGELHARD
FRIEDRICH GRUNEWALD
HABERMANN KNACKFUSS
MEYERHEIM MODERSOHN
PASSAVANT TISCHBEIN
ALDEGREVER CAMPHAUSEN
HECKENDORF HILDEBRAND
SCHROEDTER WOHLGEMUTH
ZIMMERMANN CHODOWIECKI
HASENCLEVER HILDEBRANDT
HUCHTENBERG MORGENSTERN
SCHRAUDOLPH LINDENSCHMIT
ROTTENHAMMER WINTERHALTER
GREEK GYSIS AETION NICIAS
ZEUXIS APELLES PAUSIAS
EUPOMPUS ARISTIDES
EUPHRANOR MELANTHUS
PAMPHILUS TIMANTHES

AGATHARCUS PARRHASIUS
POLYGNOTUS PROTOGENES
GUATEMALAN MERIDA
HUNGARIAN LOTZ ZICHY VADASZ
WAGNER SZINYEI MUNKACSY
IRISH BARRY DANBY BURTON
FORBES PETRIE MACLISE
COSTELLO MULREADY
ITALIAN MOLA RENI ROSA TURA
VAGA BACCI CAFFI CAMPI CARPI
COSSA COSTA DANTI FERRI FETTI
FOPPA GATTI GENGA IORIS LUINI
MELZI PALMA PENNI PRETI RICCI
SANTI SPADA VANNI VINCI
ABBATE ALBANI ALLORI AVANZO
BATONI CALCAR CESARI CIARDI
CRESPI FRANCO GIOTTO MORONI
NITTIS PASINI PREDIS RICCIO
ROMANO SACCHI SODOMA
SOLARI SUARDI TITIAN VASARI
VERRIO AMIGONI APPIANI
BARBARI BAROCCI BARTOLI
BASSANO BELLINI BERNINI
BOLDINI CENNINI CHIRICO
CIGNANI CORTONA FALCONE
FRANCIA MARATTI MARTINI
MORELLI MUZIANO OGGIONO
PALIZZI PERUZZI RAPHAEL
STROZZI TIBALDI TIEPOLO
UCCELLO VECELLI ZUCCARO
BACICCIO BAGLIONI BARBIERE
BOCCIONI BONFIGLI CAGLIARI
CARDUCCI CARRIERA CASANOVA
CASTELLO CIPRIANI COGHETTI
CORENZIO GRIMALDI MAGNASCO
MAINARDI MANTEGNA MICHETTI
MONTAGNA POCCETTI
PONTORMO SALVIATI SEVERINI
UBERTINI VAROTARI VERONESE
VIVARINI ASPERTINI BECCAFUMI
CAMUCCINI CANTARINI
CAVALLINI CORREGGIO
FRANCESCA GHISLANDI
MAZZOLINO PIAZZETTA
SCHIAVONE SEGANTINI
BELTRAFFIO BOCCACCINO
BORGOGNONE BOTTICELLI
CAMPAGNOLA CARAVAGGIO
LORENZETTI MODIGLIANI
PROCACCINI SIGNORELLI
SQUAREIONE TINTORETTO
VERROCCHIO ZUCCARELLI
ANGUISCIOLA CASTIGLIONE
GENTILESCHI PRIMATICCIO
ALBERTINELLI BALDOVINETTI
FRANCESCHINI MICHELANGELO
PARMIGIANINO PINTURICCHIO
JAPANESE KANO OKYO BUSON
IWASA SOSEN TORII GOSHUN
KOETSU KYOSAI JAKUCHU
JOSETSU SOTATSU HARUNOBU
KIYOMASU KIYONAGA KIYONOBU
MORONOBU TOYOKUNI
HIROSHIGE KIYOMITSU
TSUNETAKA
LITHUANIAN SOUTINE
MEXICAN CANTU OROZCO RIVERA
TAMAYO SIQUEIROS
CASTELLANOS
NORWEGIAN DAHL GUDE
KROHG MUNCH LERCHE
MUNTHE SINDING
FEARNLEY WERENSKIOLD

POLISH BENDA GERSON MATEJKO
GROTTGER CHELMINSKI
MARCOUSSIS WYSPIANSKI
PORTUGUESE FONSECA
RUSSIAN BAKST BENOIS BERMAN
GRABAR BURLIUK CHAGALL
ROERICH LARIONOV LEVITSKI
MALEVICH CHELISHEV KANDINSKI
LISSITZKY RODCHENKO
AIVAZOVSKI BOGOLYUBOV
BASHKIRTSEV VERESHCHAGIN
SCOTTISH BONE FAED HILL ALLAN
GRANT PATON SCOTT AIKMAN
ARCHER BARKER BROUGH
DUNCAN GEDDES GORDON
GRAHAM HARVEY LAUDER LEITCH
MANSON MURRAY PETTIE WILKIE
DOUGLAS GUTHRIE LORIMER
MACBETH NASMYTH RAEBURN
THOMSON CHALMERS
MACWHIRTER ORCHARDSON
SPANISH ARCO CANO DALI GOYA
GRIS MAZO MIRO MOYA GRECO
MACIP CEREZO COELLO PAREJA
RIBERA RINCON VARGAS
ALVAREZ HERRERA IRIARTE
MADRAZO MORALES MURILLO
ORRENTE PACHECO PICASSO
RIBALTA ZULOAGA CESPEDES
PRADILLA ZAMACOIS ZURBARAN
VELASQUEZ ZUBIAURRE
BERRUGUETE
SWEDISH DAHL ZORN BERGH
ROSLIN LARSSON FAGERLIN
LUNDGREN HELLQUIST
JOSEPHSON LILJEFORS
SWISS KLEE LIPS MIND ASPER
DIDAY ITTEN MEYER CALAME
GLEYRE MANUEL BOCKLIN
BUCHSER DISTELI LIOTARD
PETITOT VAUTIER KAUFFMANN
PAINTING ART OIL PAT DAUB
PATA DRAFT MURAL PIECE TABLE
WATER CANVAS CROUTE FRESCO
MINERY TITIAN BODEGON
CAMAIEU CARTOON COMBINE
DAUBING GRADINO GRAPHIC
HISTORY PAYSAGE FROTTAGE
PREDELLA SEAPIECE SYMPHONY
AQUARELLE MINIATURE
(— EQUIPMENT) OIL BRUSH EASEL
PAINT CANVAS PALLET
(— IN COLLOIDAL MEDIUM)
TEMPERA
(— OF EVERYDAY LIFE) GENRE
(— OF FOLIAGE) BOSCAGE
(— ON PLASTER) SECCO FRESCO
(— WITH OPAQUE COLORS)
GOUACHE
(ACTION —) TACHISM
(CIRCULAR —) TONDO
(PREHISTORIC —) PICTOGRAM
PICTOGRAPH
(RELIGIOUS —) PIETA TANKA
(SCENIC —) SCAPE
(SMALL —) TABLET
(TEMPERA —) SECCO
(THREE PANEL —) TRIPTYCH
(PL.) GENRE
(SUFF.) CHROMY
PAIR DUO TWO ZYG CASE DIAD
DUAD DUAL DYAD MATE SIDE
SPAN TEAM TWIN YOKE BRACE

MARRY MATCH TWAIN UNITE
COUPLE GEMINI COUPLET
DOUBLET JUMELLE TWOSOME
(— OF FILMS) BIPACK
(— OF MILLSTONES) RUN
(— OF SHOTS) BRACKET
(— OF TONGS) GRAMPUS GRAPPLE
(— OF WINGS) SHEARS
(— ROYAL) PARIAL
(ONE OF —) IMPAIR NEIGHBOR
(PL.) GEMELS
(PREF.) GEMINI ZYG(O)(OTO)
(SUFF.) ZYGOUS
PAIRED GEMEL JUGATE ZYGOUS
JUMELLE
PAISLEY PRINT SHAWL DESIGN
FABRIC
PAIUTE DIGGER
PAJAMAS SHALWAR SLEEPER
PAKHT (HUSBAND OF —) PTAH

PAKISTAN

BAY: SOYMIANI
CANAL: NARA ROHRI
CAPE: FASTA JADDI JIWANI
CAPITAL: ISLAMABAD
COIN: ANNA RUPEE
DAM: TARBELA
LANGUAGE: URDU PUSHTU SINDHI
  BALUCHI BENGALI PUNJABI
MOUNTAIN: TIRICHMIR
MOUNTAIN RANGE: MAKRAN
  KIRTHAR HIMALAYA SULAIMAN
NATIVE: BENGAL PATHAN SINDHI
  BALUCHI PUNJABI
PORT: CHALNA KARACHI
PROVINCE: SIND PUNJAB
RIVER: NAL BADO RAVI ZHOB
  DASHT INDUS CHENAB GANGES
  JAMUNA JHELUM KUNDAR
  PORALI
STATE: DIR SWAT KALAT KHARAN
  CHITRAL KHAIRPUR
TOWN: DACCA CHALNA KHULNA
  LAHORE MULTAN QUETTA
  KARACHI SIALKOT LYALLPUR
  PESHAWAR SARGODHA
WEIGHT: SEER TOLA MAUND

PAKTONG TUTENAG
PAL BO ALLY CHUM JACK PARD
BILLY BUDDY BUTTY CHINA
CRONY LOUKE COBBER COPAIN
DIGGER FRIEND COMRADE
PARTNER COMPANION
PALACE SALE CHIGI COURT SERAI
STEAD CASTLE ELYSEE LOUVRE
PALAIS ALCAZAR EDIFICE
LATERAN MANSION PALAZZO
TRIANON VATICAN ZWINGER
BASILICA SERAGLIO WHITEHALL
(— OF SATAN) PANDEMONIUM
(FAIRY —) SHEE SIDHE
PALADIN HERO PEER ANSEIS
ASTOLF KNIGHT CHAMPION
DOUZEPER
PALAL (FATHER OF —) UZAI
PALAMEDES (BROTHER OF —) OEAX
SFORZA ACHILLES
(FATHER OF —) NAUPLIUS
(MOTHER OF —) CLYMENE
(SLAYER OF —) CORINDA
PALAMON (RIVAL OF —) ARCITE

(WIFE OF —) EMELYE
PALANQUIN JAUN JUAN KAGE
KAGO DANDI DOOLI DOOLY PALKI
SEDAN DOOLIE LITTER PALKEE
TONJON NORIMON
PALATABLE SAPID SPICY TASTY
DAINTY SAVORY MOREISH
DELICATE LUSCIOUS PLEASING
SAPOROUS AGREEABLE
DELICIOUS TOOTHSOME
PALATAL SOFT FRONT VELAR
GUTTURAL
PALATALIZED MOUILLE
PALATE TASTE VELUM RELISH
GOURMET URANISCUS
(SOFT —) UVULA
(PREF.) URAN(O)(OSO)
PALATIAL LARGE ORNATE
STATELY SPLENDID
PALATINE CAPE OFFICER PALADIN
PALATIAL
PALAVER GASH SLUM TALK
CAJOLE DEBATE GLAVER JARGON
PARLEY CHATTER FLATTER
WHEEDLE CAJOLERY FLATTERY
PALE DIM WAN ASHY BLOC FADE
GREY GULL LILY PALL SICK THIN
WHEY ASHEN BLAKE BLATE
BLEAK CLOSE FAINT FENCE
GREEN LIGHT LINEN LIVID LURID
MEALY STAKE STICK VERGE
WHITE ANEMIC BLANCH CHALKY
CHANGE DOUGHY FALLOW
FEEBLE PALLID PASTEL PICKET
REGION REMISS SICKLY SILVER
WATERY WHITEN DEFENSE
GHASTLY HAGGARD INSIPID
OBSCURE SHILPIT DELICATE
WATERISH
(IN —) HAURIENT
(PREF.) LIRO PALLIDI POLI(O)
PALEA PALET SQUAMELLA
PALENESS WAN PALLOR
ACHROMA
PALEONTOLOGIST AMERICAN
GABB HALL LULL MEEK BERRY
MARSH CLARKE FOSTER GRABAU
OSBORN BEECHER GREGORY
MERRIAM WALCOTT KNOWLTON
SPRINGER WILLIAMS SCHUCHERT
WACHSMUTH WILLISTON
AUSTRIAN SUESS HOERNES
MOJSISOVICS ETTINGSHAUSEN
ENGLISH TATE CAUTLEY MANTELL
DAVIDSON WOODWARD
BOWERBANK PARKINSON
FRENCH BOULE GAUDRY
BARRANDE
GERMAN ZITTEL BEYRICH
QUENSTEDT
SOUTH AFRICAN BROOM
SCOTTISH FALCONER
PALESTINE (SEE ISRAEL)
PALETOT COAT JACKET OVERCOAT
GREATCOAT
PALFREY HORSE PALFRY
PALIMPSEST TABLET PARCHMENT
PALING PALE FENCE FLAKE LIMIT
PALIS STAKE PICKET FENCING
BLENCHING
PALISADE HAY BOMA PALE PEEL
CLIFF FENCE RIMER STAKE FRAISE
HURDIS PICKET BARRIER

ENCLOSE FORTIFY HURDIES
STACKET TAMBOUR ESPALIER
(MILITARY —) CIPPUS
(PL.) BAIL BARRIER
PALL FOG BORE CLOY PALE SATE
CLOAK CLOTH FAINT QUALM
STALE WEARY MANTLE NAUSEA
SHROUD DISGUST SATIATE
ANIMETTA MORTCLOTH
PALLET BED COT PAD COUCH
QUILT PADDLE BLANKET
MATTRESS PLANCHER
PALLIARD BEGGAR LECHER
RASCAL VAGABOND
PALLIATE EASE HIDE MASK VEIL
ABATE CLOAK COLOR COVER
GLOSS GLOZE LITHE BLANCH
LESSEN REDUCE SMOOTH SOFTEN
SOOTHE CONCEAL CUSHION
SHELTER DISGUISE MITIGATE
PALLID WAN ASHY PALE PALY
BLEAK MEALY WASHY WAXEN
WHITE SALLOW GHASTLY
BLOODLESS COLORLESS
INNOCUOUS
PALL-MALL MAIL
PALLOR ASH WAN PALE ASHES
PALENESS
PALLU (FATHER OF —) REUBEN
(SON OF —) ELIAB
PALM ADY DOM ITA ATAP BRAB
BURI BUSU COCO DATE DOUM
FLAT HIDE JARA KOKO LOOF
NIOG NIPA PAWN SAGO SLIP
TARA ARCHA ARECA ARENG
ASSAI BONGA BUNGA CARRY
COCOA COYOL CURUA DATIL
FOIST HOWEA INAJA JAGUA
LOULU MACAW MERUS NIKAU
RATAN SABAL SALAK TECUM
TUCUM UNAMO YAGUA YARAY
ANAHAO ASSAHY BACABA BURITI
CHONTA COHUNE COROJO
COROZO GEBANG GOMUTI
GRUGRU JAMBEE JUPATI KENTIA
KITTUL LAWYER LONTAR NIBONG
PACAYA RAFFIA ROTANG THENAR
TOOROO TROPHY APRICOT
BABASSU BACTRIS CARANDA
CONCEAL COQUITO ERYTHEA
GEONOMA MORICHE PALMYRA
PUPUNHA SAGWIRE TALIPOT
TROOLIE URUCURI JACITARA
LATANIER MACAHUBA PIASSAVA
(— FERN) PONJA
(— FOOD) NUT COCO DATE NIPA
SAGO SURA ASSAI TAREE TODDY
COCONUT
(— JUICE) SURA
(— LEAF) OLA OLLA CAJAN FROND
(— LILY) TI
(— OF HAND) FLAT LOOF VOLA
TABLE THENAR
(— OFF) COG FOB TOP SHAB FOIST
TRUMP
(— OUT) APPAUME
(BETEL —) ARECA BONGA PUGUA
PINANG
(CLIMBING —) RATTAN
(FEATHER —) HOWEA GOMUTI
URUCURI
(SPINY —) PEACH GRIGRI GRUGRU
(PREF.) CYCAD(I)(O) PALMATO

PALMI PALPI PALPO
PALMARY CHIEF PALMAR
SUPERIOR
PALMATE FLAT BROAD LOBED
WEBBED
PALMER LOUSE FERULE STROLL
TRAVEL VOTARY WANDER
FOISTER PILGRIM
PALMETTO CABBAGE PALMITO
BIGTHATCH
(— STATE) SOUTHCAROLINA
PALMISTRY CHIROMANCY
PALMODIC JERKY
PALMYRA BRAB TALA LONTAR
RONIER TADMOR BASSINE
(QUEEN OF —) ZENOBIA
PALP FEEL TOUCH CAJOLE FEELER
HANDLE PALPUS FLATTER
TENTACLE
PALPABLE BALD RANK PLAIN
PATENT AUDIBLE EVIDENT
OBVIOUS TACTILE APPARENT
DISTINCT MANIFEST TANGIBLE
CORPOREAL
PALPATION THROB TOUCH
WALLOP DIPPING PITAPAT
PALPEBRA EYELID
PALPITATE PANT QUAP THROB
FLACKER FLICKER FLUTTER
PULSATE
PALPITATION BEAT DUNT PANT
FLICKER FLUTTER PULSATION
SALTATION THROBBING
(— OF HEART) THUMB
PALSIED SHAKY SHAKING
PARALYZED TOTTERING
TREMBLING TREMULOUS
PALSY PARLESIE PARALYSIS
PALTER FIB LIE BABBLE HAGGLE
MUMBLE PARLEY TRIFLE BARGAIN
CHAFFER CHATTER QUIBBLE
SHAFFLE
PALTIEL (FATHER OF —) AZZAN
PALTRY BALD BARE BASE MEAN
ORRA PUNY SCAB VILE WAFF
CHEAP FOOTY MINOR PETTY
SCALD SCALL SCRUB SILLY TRASH
CHETIF FLIMSY JITNEY SHABBY
SLIGHT TRASHY WOEFUL HILDING
PELTING PIMPING PITEOUS
PITIFUL ROYNISH RUBBISH
SCABBED SCRUBBY TRIVIAL
PICAYUNE PICKLING PIDDLING
TRIFLING
PALUDAL MARSHY
PAMELA (AUTHOR OF —)
RICHARDSON
(BROTHER OF —) PHILOCLEA
(CHARACTER IN —) JACOB DAVERS
JERVIS JEWKES PAMELA
ANDREWS SWYNFORD
(FATHER OF —) BASILIUS
PAMPA PLAIN PRAIRIE
PAMPAS (— CAT) KODKOD PAJERO
(— DEER) MAZAME
PAMPER PET BABY CRAM DELT
GLUT POMP HUMOR SPOIL TUTOR
WALLY CARESS COCKER CODDLE
COSHER COSSET CUDDLE CUITER
DANDLE FONDLE MAUNGE
POSSET TIDDLE CHERISH
COCKNEY FORWEAN GRATIFY
INDULGE SATIATE

SMOODGE SAGINATE
PAMPHLET JACK LEAD QUIRE
SHEET TRACT FOLDER BOOKLET
CATALOG LEAFLET NOVELET
BROCHURE CHAPBOOK
WORKBOOK CATALOGUE
NEWSLETTER
PAN FIT TAB VLY MELL PART PRIG
VLEI WASH AGREE BASIN BATEA
COVER GRAND SHEET UNITE
CENSER FRACHE LAPPET PANKIN
PATINA SPIDER VESSEL CRANIUM
CREAMER HARDPAN PORTION
ROASTER SKILLET SUBSOIL
PANNIKIN RIDICULE
(— FOR COALS) BRAZIER
(— OF BALANCE) BOWL BASIN
SCALEPAN
(— WITH 3 FEET) POSNET
(EARTHENWARE —) PANCHEON
(EVAPORATING —) ROOM COVER
TACHE SALTPAN
(GOD —) FAUNUS
(IRON —) YET FRACHE
(LONG-HANDLED —) PINGLE
(MILK —) LEAD
(OIL —) SUMP
(PREF.) PATELLI PATELLO
PANACEA CURE BEZOAR ELIXIR
REMEDY SOLACE CUREALL
GINSENG HEALALL NEPENTHE
CATHOLICON
PANACHE STYLE

PANAMA
CAPITAL: PANAMA
COIN: BALBOA
COUNTY: DARIEN HERRERA
CROP: ABACA CACAO
GULF: DARIEN SANBLAS CHIRIQUI
MOSQUITO
ISLAND: COIBA
LAKE: GATUN
MEASURE: CELEMIN
MOUNTAIN: CHICO GANDI
COLUMAN SANTIAGO
MOUNTAIN RANGE: VERAGUA
PENINSULA: AZUERO
PORT: CRISTOBAL
PROVINCE: COCLE COLON
CHIRIQUI VERAGUAS
RIVER: CHEPO SAMBU TUIRA
BAYANO PANUGO CHAGRES
TOWN: COLON DAVID AZUERO
BALBOA PANAMA PENONOME
SANTIAGO
TREE: YAYA MARIA QUIRA ALFAJE
CATIVO

PANAMA HAT JIPIJAPA
PANAMINT KOSO
PANCAKE BLIN FLAM AREPA
CREPE FADGE FLAWN KISRA
LEFSE TOURT BLINTZ FRAISE
FROISE CRUMPET FLAPPER
FLIPPER FRITTER HOTCAKE
PIKELET CORNCAKE FLAPJACK
FLIPJACK
(PL.) LEFSEN
PANCREAS BUR NUT
PAND PAWN DRAPERY
PANDA WA WAH BEARCAT
PANDAREUS (DAUGHTER OF —)

AEDON MEROPE CLEOTHERA
(FATHER OF —) MEROPS
(WIFE OF —) HARMOTHOE
PANDARUS (BROTHER OF —) BITIAS
(FATHER OF —) LYCAON ALCANOR
PANDAVA BHIMA
PANDECT COMPENDIUM
PANDEMONIUM DIN HELL CHAOS
NOISE TUMULT UPROAR
DISORDER CONFUSION
PANDER BAWD PIMP BULLY CATER
BROKER MICHER PURVEY
RUFFIAN WHISKIN PROCURER
BAWDSTROT
PANDION (BROTHER OF —)
PLEXIPPUS
(DAUGHTER OF —) PROCNE
PHILOMELA
(FATHER OF —) CECROPS PHINEUS
ERICHTHONIUS
(MOTHER OF —) CLEOPATRA
(SON OF —) BUTES LYCUS NISUS
AEGEUS PALLAS ERECHTHEUS
(WIFE OF —) PYLIA
PANDORA BANDORE
(BROTHER OF —) PROMETHEUS
(HUSBAND OF —) EPIMETHEUS
PANDOWDY PIE DESSERT
PANDU (BROTHER OF —)
DURYODHANA
(FATHER OF —) DHRITARASHTRA
PANE GLASS GLAZE LOZEN PANEL
QUIRK SHEET SHOCK SLASH
QUARRY QUARREL SECTION
PORTLIGHT
PANEGYRIC ELOGE ELOGY EULOGY
PRAISE ORATION TRIBUTE
ENCOMIUM LAUDATION
PANEL FIN PAN JURY SKIN BOARD
GROUP LABEL TABLE ABACUS
ASSIZE COFFER HURDLE MIRROR
PADDLE PILLOW ROSACE TABLET
TYMPAN CAISSON CONSOLE
FLIPPER LACUNAR DECORATE
MANDORLA MEDALLION
(— IN FENCE) LOOP
(— IN GARMENT) LAP STEAK
(CIRCULAR —) ROUNDEL
(GAUZE —) SCRIM
(GLAZED —) LAYLIGHT
(LEGAL —) ARRAY
(RECESSED —) ORB COFFER
LACUNAR
(SUNKEN —) CAISSON CASSOON
(3-PART —) TRIPTYCH
PANFISH SCUP
PANG ACHE CRAM FILL GIRD PAIN
STAB TANG AGONY PINCH PRONG
SPASM STANG STOUN STUFF
THROE SHOWER STOUND TWINGE
ANGUISH TRAVAIL
(PL.) GNAWINGS
PANGLOSS (PUPIL OF —) CANDIDE
PANGOLIN MANID MANIS
ANTEATER EDENTATE TANGILIN
PANGWE FAN FANG
PANHANDLE BEG CADGE SKELB
SKILDER
(— STATE) WV WVA
PANIC FEAR FRAY FUNK WILD
ALARM AMAZE CHAOS SCARE
FRIGHT SCHRIK TERROR SWITHER
CONSTERNATION

PANICKY FUNKY
PANICLE JUBA WHISK ANTHELA
PANNIER BAG PED SERON BASKET
CAJAVA CURAGH DORSEL
DORSER DOSSAL DOSSER PANTRY
CORBEIL CURRACK KAJAWAH
KEDJAVE
PANOPE (FATHER OF —) NEREUS
(MOTHER OF —) DORIS
PANOPEUS (BROTHER OF —) CRISUS
(COMPANION OF —) AMPHITRYON
(DAUGHTER OF —) AEGLE
(FATHER OF —) PHOCUS
(MOTHER OF —) ASTERIA
PANOPLY POMP ARMOR UNIFORM
PANORAMA VIEW RANGE SCENE
SWEEP VISTA NEORAMA PICTURE
SCENERY CYCLORAMA
POLYORAMA
PANPIPE SICU SIKU QUILL ANTARA
SYRINX ZAMPOGNA
PANSY FANCY PENSE VIOLA
KISSES PENSEE VIOLET TRINITY
FANTASQUE HEARTEASE
(PREF.) VIOL
PANT FAB ACHE BEAT BLOW FUFF
GAPE GASP HECH LONG PANK
PECH PEGH PINE PIPE PUFF TIFT
FLAFF HEAVE QUIRK STECH
SUGGE THROB YEARN ANHELE
ASPIRE FRIESE PANTLE PULSATE
PANTAGRUEL (COMPANION OF —)
PANURGE
(FATHER OF —) GARGANTUA
(MOTHER OF —) BADEBEC
PANTALOONS PANTS TROUSERS
PANTHEA (HUSBAND OF —)
ABRADATUS
PANTHEIST AMALRICIAN
PANTHEON TEMPLE ROTUNDA
VALHALL VALHALLA
PANTHER CAT PARD PUMA
COUGAR JAGUAR LEOPARD
PAINTER PANTILE
PANTIES SCANTIES
PANTILE TILE IMBREX BISCUIT
HARDTACK
PANTING ANHELOSE ANHELOUS
PANTOGRAPH EIDOGRAPH
POLYGRAPH
PANTOMIME PLAY PANTO
PANTRY CAVE STUE AMBRY
COVEY CUDDY CLOSET LARDER
SPENCE BUTLERY BUTTERY
PANNIER PANTLER SERVERY
SPICERY CUPBOARD
PANTS JEANS LEVIS BRIEFS
SLACKS DRAWERS JODHPUR
BREECHES BRITCHES KICKSIES
KNICKERS SNUGGIES TROUSERS
(— WITH WIDE BOTTOMS) BELLS
(LEATHER —) CHAPS LEDERHOSEN
(WIDE-LEGGED —) PALAZZO
PANUELO COLLAR RUFFLE
KERCHIEF NECKCLOTH
PANURGE (COMPANION OF —)
PANTAGRUEL
PANZER TANK
PAOLO (LOVER OF —) FRANCESCA
PAP DUG TIT POBS TEAT NIPPLE
EMULSION FLUMMERY
PAPA PA DAD PAP PAW POP SIN
BABA EVIL DADDY LOVER PAPPY

BABOON FATHER POTATO PRIEST
HUSBAND VULTURE
PAPAL (ALSO SEE POPE) POPAL
PAPANE POPELY APOSTOLIC
PAPAW PAPA ASIMEN PAPAIO
ASIMINA CORAZON JASMINE
PAPAYA PAPAW LECHOSA
PAPER LIL WEB BILL BOND BLANK
BROKE ESSAY STUDY THEME
ASTHMA BINDLE CARTEL PAPIER
REPORT RETREE VESSEL CHEVIOT
EXHIBIT JOURNAL WRITING
YOSHINO DOCUMENT
MONOGRAPH NEWSPRINT
ONIONSKIN PARCHMENT
VALENTINE
(— FOLDER) STROKER
(— MAKER) WASHERMAN
(— NAUTILUS) ARGONAUT
(— PULP) WATERLEAF
(— QUANTITY) PAGE REAM QUIRE
SHEET BUNDLE
(ABSORBENT —) BLOTTER
TOWELLING
(ALBUMINIZED —) SAXE
(BUILDING —) FELT
(BUNDLE OF —S) DUFTER DOSSIER
(CHINESE —) INDIA
(COMMERCIAL —) PORTFOLIO
(DAMAGED —) BROKE CASSE
SALLE RETREE
(DEFECTIVE —) BROKES
(DRAWING —) TORCHON
(FOLDED —) SADDLE AIRPLANE
(GLOSS —) GILL
(HARD —) PELURE
(HEAVY —) FELT
(LAVATORY —) BUMF
(LINING —S) SKIPS
(NEGOTIABLE —) STIFF
(OFFICIAL —) TARGE HOOKUM
DOCUMENT
(PARCHMENT —) VELLUM
PERGAMYN
(PHOTOGRAPHIC —) SEPIA
(SIZE OF —) CAP COPY DEMI NOTE
POST POTT TOWN ATLAS CROWN
FOLIO JESUS LARGE LEGAL ROYAL
SIXMO ALBERT BILLET CASING
LETTER MEDIUM THIRDS
BASTARD CABINET EMPEROR
THEOREM ELEPHANT FOOLSCAP
IMPERIAL
(STRIP OF —) TAPE
(THIN —) FLIMSY PELURE TISSUE
ONIONSKIN
(TOILET —) BUMF
(UNCUT —) BOLT
(WALL —) TENTURE
(WATERMARKED —) BATONNE
(WRAPPING —) SKIP KRAFT
SEALING SCREENING
(WRITING —) FLAT LINEN
WEDDING
(PREF.) PAPYRO
PAPERBARK CAJEPUT MILKWOOD
PAPERBOARD BENDER VENEER
CARDBOARD CHIPBOARD
PULPBOARD
PAPILLA CERAS DEIRID NIPPLE
PAPULA MAMMULA THELIUM
(PL.) CERATA
PAPILLOMA ANGLEBERRY

PAPIO MORMON
PAPIST TORY PAPANE CATHOLIC
POPELING
PAPPUS DOWN AIGRETTE
THISTLEDOWN
PAPPY PA DAD PAW PAPA SOFT
MUSHY PULPY FATHER
SUCCULENT
PAPRIKA PIMENTO PIMIENTO
PAPUA (BAY OF —) DYKE MILNE
ACLAND HOLNICOTE
(CAPITAL OF —) PORTMORESBY
(MONEY OF —) KINA
(RIVER OF —) FLY KIKORI PURARI
(TOWN OF —) LAE BUNA DARU
WEWAK GOROKA KIKORI
MADANG SAMARAI
PAPUAN ARAU BIAK HULA KATE
BUANG EKARI KIWAI KWOMA
SIVAI SULKA BAITSI BANARO
IATMUL KEREWA KOIARI
ARAPESH BAINING
PAPULE WHELK PIMPLE
PAPYRUS REED PAPER SEDGE
BIBLOS GLUMAL SCROLL
BULRUSH
(— STRIP) ORIHON
PAR BY NORM EQUAL NORMAL
AVERAGE EQUALITY
(ONE OVER —) BOGIE
(ONE UNDER —) BIRDIE
(TWO UNDER —) EAGLE
PARA FODDA PERAU PARRAH
PARABLE MYTH TALE FABLE
STORY APOLOG BYWORD MASHAL
SAMPLE BYSPELL PROVERB
ALLEGORY APOLOGUE FORBYSEN
LIKENESS SIMILITUDE
PARABOLA ARC CURVE ANTENNA
PARACETAMOL PANADOL
PARACHUTE SILK CHUTE BROLLY
DROGUE PATAGIUM STREAMER
(SMALL —) BALLUTE
PARACHUTIST PATHFINDER
(PL.) STICK
PARACLETE AIDER HELPER
PLEADER ADVOCATE CONSOLER
COMFORTER
PARADE JET TOP POMP SHOW
WALK MARCH STRUT FLAUNT
MUSTER REVIEW STROLL
CORTEGE DISPLAY EXHIBIT
MARSHAL CEREMONY EXERCISE
FLOURISH GRANDEUR SPLENDOR
PAGEANTRY
(— GROUND) MAIDAN
(— OF BULLFIGHTERS) PASEO
(UNSUBSTANTIAL —) PAGEANT
PARADED AFFICHE
PARADISE EDEN JODO BLISS
JENNA AIDENN GOLOKA HEAVEN
PARVIS ELYSIUM NIRVANA
(— OF INDRA) SVARGA SWARGA
(— TREE) ACEITUNA STAVEWOOD
PARADOX KOAN ANTINOMY
PARADOXURE MUSANG
PARAFFIN ALKANE
PARAGON GEM HERO PINK TYPE
IDEAL MODEL PEARL APERSEE
PATTERN PEROPUS PHOENIX
NONESUCH NONPAREIL
(— OF KNIGHTHOOD) PALADIN
PARAGRAPH ITEM SIGN CAPUT

PAUSE CLAUSE NOTICE RUBRIC ARTICLE INITIAL PILCROW SECTION CAUSERIE MATERIAL PEELCROW PERSONAL SUBLEADER
(— MARK) PILCROW
(UNIMPORTANT —S) BALAAM

PARAGUAY

CAPITAL: ASUNCION
COIN: GUARANI
DEPARTMENT: GUAIRA ITAPUA OLIMPO CAAZAPA BOQUERON
LAKE: VERA YPOA YPACARAI
LANGUAGE: GUARANI
MEASURE: PIE LINE LINO VARA LEGUA LINEA CORDEL CUADRA CUARTA FANEGA
PLAIN: CHACO
RIVER: YPANE ACARAY PARANA CONFUSO
TOWN: LUQUE PILAR CAACUPE CAAZAPA TRINIDAD CONCEPCION VILLARRICA
WEIGHT: QUINTAL

PARAKEET CONURE PARROT WELLAT ROSELLA ARATINGA KAKARIKI POPINJAY ROSEHILL GREENLEEK
PARALLEL EVEN LIKE ALONG EQUAL MATCH SECOND EXAMPLE FRONTAL PARAGON PENDANT ANALOGUE LIKENESS MULTIPLE QUANTITY
(PREF.) ORTH(O) PAR(A)
PARALLELEPIPED CUBOID
PARALLELISM PARITY ANALOGY
PARALLELOGRAM RHOMB OBLONG SQUARE RHOMBUS RHOMBOID RECTANGLE
PARALYSIS CRAMP PALSY POLIO SHOCK PARESIS DIPLEGIA PARAPLEGIA POLIOMYELITIS
(SUFF.) LYSE LYSIS LYST LYTE LYTIC LYZE
PARALYZE DARE DAZE STUN PALSY SCRAM ASTONY BENUMB CONGEAL IMPALSY PETRIFY TORPEDO TORPEFY
PARALYZED NUMB PALSIED CRIPPLED
PARAMORPHINE THEBAINE
PARAMOUNT ABOVE CHIEF RULER SOVRAN CAPITAL SUPREME DOMINANT SUPERIOR SUZERAIN SOVEREIGN
PARAMOUR DOLL PRIM PURE LEMAN LOVER WOMAN WOOER AMORET FRIEND MASTER MINION FRANION GALLANT HETAERA RUFFIAN SERVANT SPECIAL SULTANA STALLION BOYFRIEND
PARAPET BUTT WALL BAHUT REDAN BARBET BONNET FLECHE PARPEN TRENCH BULWARK PLUTEUS RAILING RAMPART BARTIZAN ENVELOPE TRAVERSE
PARAPH RUBRIC
PARAPHERNALIA GEAR EQUIPAGE APPARATUS EQUIPMENT TRAPPINGS
PARAPHRASE FARSE REWORD

TARGET TARGUM PREFACE THARGUM VERSION TRANSLATE
PARASITE BUG BUR FLY BURR MOSS SPIV TRYP CHARK DRONE LEECH SHARK TOADY VIRUS FEEDER FUNGUS GNATHO SHADOW SPONGE SUCKER BLEEDER BYWONER SPONGER TAGTAIL DICYEMID ENTOZOON EPIPHYTE HANGERON SLAVERER INFESTANT POTHUNTER SACCULINA SPARGANUM SYCOPHANT TOADEATER TUBHUNTER
(— ON TROUT) SUG
(PL.) ECTOZOA ENTOZOA DRIFTWOOD
(PREF.) **(VEGETABLE —)** PHYT(I)(O)
PARASITIC CYTOZOIC TRENCHER BIOPHILOUS
(— JAEGER) SHOOI DIRTBIRD
PARASOL SHADE AOGIRI SHADOW ROUNDEL TIRESOL KITTYSOL SUNSHADE UMBRELLA
(— MUSHROOM) LEPIOTA
(PREF.) UMBELL(I)
PARAVANE OTTER
PARBOIL CODDLE
PARBOILED LEEPIT
PARCEL DAK LOT DAWK DEAD DEAL DOLE METE PACK PART WISP BULSE BUNCH GROUP PIECE BUNDLE DIVIDE FARDEL PACKET PASSEL CONACRE PACKAGE PORTION COMMODITY
(— OF DIAMONDS) SERIES
(— OF GROUND) LOT PICK CLOSE SOLUM SUERTE CONACRE PENDICLE
(— OF HEMP FIBER) PIG
(— OF JEWELS) BULSE
(— OUT) ALLOT
PARCH DRY FRY BURN COOK SEAR ROAST TOAST PEARCH RIZZER SCORCH BRISTLE BRUSTLE GRADDAN SHRIVEL TORREFY TORRIFY
(PREF.) TORRE XER(O)
PARCHED ARID HUSK SERE ADUST FIERY GIZZEN TORRID THIRSTY SCORCHED
PARCHING URENT
PARCHMENT LARK FOREL CHARTA MEZUZAH PAPYRIN SCYTALE DRUMHEAD SHEEPSKIN PALIMPSEST
(— PAPER) DOCKET PERGAMYN
(FINE —) VEL VELLUM
(PIECE OF —) MEMBRANE
(ROLL OF —) PELL SCROLL
PARD PAL CHUM TIGER FRIEND LEOPARD PANTHER PARTNER COMPANION
PARDON FREE CLEAR COVER GRACE MERCY REMIT SPARE ACQUIT ASSOIL EXCUSE SHRIVE ABSOLVE AMNESTY CONDONE FORGIVE OVERLOOK REPRIEVE TOLERATE EXCULPATE
PARDONABLE VENIAL VENIABLE EXCUSABLE
PARDONER QUESTOR QUAESTOR
PARE CUP CHIP COPE FLAY PEEL

SKIN FRIZZ SHAVE SKELP SKIVE SLIPE SPADE CHISEL REDUCE REMOVE RESECT CURTAIL FLAUGHT WHITTLE
(— LEATHER) SKIVE
(— SOD) BURNBEAT
(— STAVES) BUCK
(— STONE) BOAST
PAREGORIC ANODYNE MITIGATING
PAREL PARELL APPAREL CLOTHING ORNAMENT
PARENCHYMA AMYLOM MESOPHYL
PARENT DAD DAM MAMA PAPA SIRE DADDY ELDER MATER PATER AUTHOR FATHER MOTHER ORIGIN FORBEAR GENITOR ANCESTOR BEGETTER FILICIDE GUARDIAN
PARENTAGE KIND BIRTH BROOD FAMILY ORIGIN PROGENY ENGENDURE
PARENTHESIS HOOK ASIDE PAREN BRACKET TOENAIL INNUENDO INTERVAL INTERLUDE
(PL.) HOOKS CURVES
PAREVE NEUTRAL
PARGET COAT GYPSUM PARIET PLASTER DECORATE WHITEWASH
PARGO MUTTONFISH
PARHELION DOG SUN SUNDOG
PARIAH PAREA ISHMAEL OUTCAST
PARIAN CHINA MARBLE PORCELAIN
PARIETAL SOMAL SOMATIC
PARI-MUTUEL TOTE TOTALIZER
PARING CHIP FOIL SHRED SPECK GUBBIN PARURE PEELING
(FISH —S) GUBBINS
(PL.) BOXING
PARIS ALEXANDER
(— AIRPORT) ORLY
(FATHER OF —) PRIAM
(MOTHER OF —) HECUBA
(PALACE IN —) ELYSEE LOUVRE TUILERIES
(RIVER OF —) SEINE
(STOCK EXCHANGE IN —) BOURSE
(SUBWAY IN —) METRO
(WIFE OF —) OENONE
PARISH CURE HOUSE TITLE CHARGE SOCIETY PECULIAR OUTPARISH
(— HEAD) PASTOR PRIEST MINISTER
(— MEETING) VESTRY
PARISIAN LUTETIAN
PARISINA (BELOVED OF —) HUGO
(HUSBAND OF —) AZO
PARISON BLOW GATHERING
PARITY ANALOGY EQUALITY LIKENESS GRAVIDITY
PARK HAY PEN HOLE STOP WAIT GREEN LEAVE CIRCLE DAPHNE GARDEN PRATER COMMONS DIAMOND PADDOCK TERRACE PARADISE TETRAGON
PARKA PARCA ANORAK JACKET PULLOVER
PARKLEAVES TUTSAN
PARLANCE TALK IDIOM SPEECH DICTION DISCOURSE
PARLAY DOUBLE

PARLEY DODGE PARLE SPEAK TREAT UTTER CONFER INDABA PALTER PAROLI DISCUSS PALAVER PARLING PARLANCE DISCOURSE TEMPORIZE NEGOTIATION
PARLIAMENT DIET RUMP TING COURT SENAT CORTES FANTAN MAJLIS SAEIMA COUNCIL ESTATES KNESSET LAGTING RIKSDAG TYNWALD CONGRESS CONVERSE STORTING VOLKSRAAD
(GREEK —) BOULE
(SCAND. —) THING
PARLIAMENTARIAN APRONEER
PARLOR BEN BOOR HALL FOREROOM LOCUTORY SNUGGERY SOLARIUM
(COUNTRY —) SPENCE
(MILKING —) BAIL
PARLORMAID MATRON
PARLOUS KEEN RISKY CLEVER SHREWD CUNNING CRITICAL PERILOUS DANGEROUS HAZARDOUS
PARMASHTA (FATHER OF —) HAMAN
PARMESAN GRANA
PARNACH (SON OF —) ELIZAPHAN
PAROCHIAL PETTY NARROW PAROCHIAN SECTARIAN
PARODIST SPOOFER
PARODY RIB SKIT SPOOF SATIRE TRAVESTY BURLESQUE IMITATION
PAROLE FAITH PLEDGE LICENSE PROMISE
PARONOMASIA PUN AGNOMINATION
PARONYCHIA FELON PANARIS WHITLOW NAILWORT
PAROTITIS MUMPS
PAROXYSM FIT KINK PANG AGONY COLIC QUIRK SPASM STORM STOUR THROE ACCESS ATTACK FRENZY ORGASM RAPTUS SHOWER RAPTURE EPITASIS AGITATION
PARR PAR SAMLET SCEGGER SKEGGER BRANDLIN BRANDLING
PARROT ARA HIA KEA COPY ECHO JAKO KAKA LORO LORY POLL VAZA ARARA CAGIT MACAW MIMIC POLLY AMAZON CAIQUE CONURE KAKAPO REPEAT TIRIBA CORELLA GRASSIE ITERATE LORILET COCKATOO LORIKEET LOVEBIRD PARAKEET PICARIAN POPINJAY BROADTAIL COCKATEEL
(PREF.) PSITTAC(I)
PARROT FISH LORO SCAR LANIA LAUIA SCAUR VIEJA COTORO SCARUS LABROID MUDFISH OLDWIFE BLUEFISH
PARRY FEND STOP WARD AVOID BLOCK DODGE EVADE FENCE PRIME QUART SIXTE OCTAVE PARADE QUINTE SECOND THWART TIERCE COUNTER DEFLECT EVASION
PARSE PACE PEARCE ANALYZE DIAGRAM DISSECT CONSTRUE ANATOMIZE

PARSEGHIAN ARA
PARSHANDATHA (FATHER OF —)
HAMAN
PARSI ZOROASTRIAN
(— **HOLY BOOK**) AVESTA
(— **PRIEST**) MOBED DASTUR
PARSIFAL (CHARACTER IN —)
KUNDRY TITUREL AMFORTAS
KLINGSOR PARSIFAL GURNEMANZ
(**COMPOSER OF —**) WAGNER
PARSIMONIOUS GARE MEAN
NEAR NIGH CLOSE MINGY NIPPY
SCANT SPARE TIGHT FRUGAL
NARROW SCARCE SCOTCH
SKIMPY SORDID STINGY STRAIT
MISERLY SCRIMPY SPARING
COVETOUS GRASPING GRUDGING
SCREWING WRETCHED
MERCENARY NIGGARDLY
PENURIOUS RETENTIVE
ABERDONIAN
PARSLEY ACHE CUMIN UMBEL
CICELY CONIUM ELTROT KARPAS
CHERVIL HOGWEED FLUELLIN
PARSLEY CAMPHOR APIOL
APIOLE
PARSNIP TANK WYPE UMBEL
CONIUM MADNEP CADWEED
HOGWEED SKIRRET BUNDWEED
QUEENWEED
(**WATER —**) SIUM
PARSON RECTOR CROAKER
PATRICO PERSONA MINISTER
PREACHER GUIDEPOST
(**COUNTRY —**) RUM
(PL.) PARSONRY
PARSONAGE GLEBE MANSE
RECTORY PASTORATE
PASTORIUM
PARSON BIRD POE TUI KOKO
TUWI POEBIRD POYBIRD
PART DEL END LOT PAN DEAL
DOLE FECK GRIN HAET HALF
HAND NECK PANE ROLE ROVE
SECT SHED SIDE SOME TEAR
TWIN AUGHT PARTY PIECE
QUOTA SEVER SHARE SHODE
SNACK SPLIT TWAIN BEHALF
CANTON CLEAVE DEPART DETAIL
DIVIDE FEEDER FINGER MEMBER
MINUTE MOIETY PARCEL PORTIO
QUORUM SECTOR SINGLE
SUNDER UNYOKE DISJOIN
ELEMENT FEATURE FRUSTUM
PORTION SECTION SEGMENT
SEVERAL ALIENATE DISSEVER
DIVISION ELIQUATE FRACTION
LIRIPIPE
(— **HAIR**) SHADE
(— **OF ANIMAL'S TAIL**) DOCK
(— **OF BEEF**) CHUCK SKINK
(— **OF BLAST FURNACE**) BOSH
BELLY
(— **OF BOW**) PEAK
(— **OF CAM WHEEL**) LOBE
(— **OF CANNON**) CHASE
(— **OF COMPASS**) FLY
(— **OF CONCERTO**) CEMBALO
(— **OF CONFIRMATION SERVICE**)
ALAPA
(— **OF CROSSBOW**) LATH
(— **OF DIAMOND**) BEZEL
(— **OF FLEECE**) LEECH

(— **OF FOWL'S COMB**) BLADE
(— **OF GUN SHIELD**) APRON
(— **OF HARBOR**) FAIRWAY
(— **OF HAWK'S BEAK**) CLAP
(— **OF HIDE**) RANGE
(— **OF HOOKAH**) CHILLUM
(— **OF MASS**) INTROIT
(— **OF POETIC FOOT**) ARSIS
(— **OF PORK LOIN**) GRISKIN
(— **OF RIVER**) FRESH
(— **OF SADDLE TREE**) FORK
(— **OF STAIR TREAD**) NOSING
(— **OF STAMEN**) ANTHER
(— **OF SWORD**) FORTE
(— **OF SWORD BLADE**) FOIBLE
(— **OF TEMPLE**) CELLA
(— **OF TONGUE**) DORSUM
(— **OF TURTLE**) CALIPEE
(— **OF VIOLIN BOW**) BAGUET
(— **OF WHEEL**) SPEECH
(— **THAT REVOLVES**) ROTOR
(— **WITH**) GIVE LOSE SELL LEAVE
DONATE ABANDON
(— **OF CHAIR**) SPLAT
(**ACCOMPANYING —**) BURDEN
OBBLIGATO
(**ASSUMED —**) FIGURE
(**BAGLIKE —**) SAC
(**BEST —**) FAT YOLK CREAM
FLOWER MARROW
(**BRISTLELIKE —**) SETA
(**BROADEST — OF PLANK**) TOUCH
(**CENTRAL —**) HUB BODY CORE
HEART KERNEL
(**CHOICE —**) ELITE
(**CLEAR — OF LIQUID**) SWIM
(**CLOSING —**) HEEL
(**COARSE — OF FLAX**) HURDS
(**CONICAL —**) BULLET
(**CURVED —**) START
(**DEPRESSED —**) HOLLOW
(**DISTANT —S**) FARNESS
(**DUPLICATE —**) SPARE
(**EDIBLE — OF CLAM**) CHEEK
(**ESSENTIAL —**) PITH
(**ESSENTIAL —S**) STAMINA
(**FIFTH —**) QUINTUS
(**FINAL —**) LAST SHANK EPILOG
(**FIRST —**) FRONT PRIME VAUNT
INITIAL BEGINNING
(**FOURTH —**) FARDEL FORPIT
FERLING
(**FRONT —**) VAUNT BREAST
FORESIDE
(**GREATER —**) HEFT SUBSTANCE
(**HARDEST —**) BRUNT
(**HIGHEST —**) CROPCROWNHEIGHT
(**HUNDREDTH —**) CENTESM
(**IMPAIRING —**) ALLOY
(**IN —**) HALVES
(**INDETERMINATE —**) PERCENTAGE
(**INNERMOST —**) FUND
(**INNERMOST —S**) PENETRALIA
(**INSTRUMENTAL —**) HAND
CONTINUO
(**INTERLACED —**) TWINE
(**INTRODUCTORY —**) PROTASIS
(**LARGE —**) FORCE
(**LATERAL — OF HEAD**) CHEEK
(**LATTER —**) HEEL SHANK
(**LEAST —**) STITCH
(**LOWER —**) SECONDO
(**LOWER — OF ROBE**) BASES

(**LOWEST —**) FOOT BOTTOM
GROUND DESCENT
(**MAIN —**) BODY BULK SUBSTANCE
(**MATERIAL —**) GIST
(**MIDDLE —**) DEEP CENTER
(**MIDDLE — OF NIGHT**) HOWE
(**MINOR —**) BIT COG
(**MINUTE —**) PRICK TITTLE
(**MISSING —**) LACUNA
(**MOST IMPORTANT —**) EYE
FOREHAND
(**MOST SERIOUS —**) DICKENS
(**OF HORSE'S THIGH**) GASKIN
(**OVERDUE —**) ARREAR
(**PRINCIPAL —**) BODY MAIN GROSS
(**PRIVATE —**) THING MEMBER
(**PROJECTING —**) ARM JAG JET JOG
APSE LOBE SPURN
(**PROTUBERANT —**) BOSS BULGE
(**REJECTED —S**) CHANKINGS
(**REMAINING —**) BUTT DREG HEEL
(**REMOTEST —**) EXTREMITY
(**RINGLIKE —**) ANNULUS
(**ROOTLIKE —**) RADICLE
(**ROUNDED —**) BULB
(**SAWLIKE —**) SERRA
(**SECRET —**) RECESS
(**SLENDER —**) NECK
(**SMALL —**) BIT ATOM FLOW TITHE
DETAIL MINUTE SNIPPET
(**SMALLEST —**) ATOM WHIT MINIM
(**SOFT — OF BREAD**) CRUMB
(**SOFT — OF VEIN**) LEATH
(**SOLO —**) CALL
(**STAMEN —**) ANTHER
(**STILL — OF WATER**) KELD
(**SWINGING —**) FLAIL
(**TELLING —**) POINT
(**TENTH —**) TITHE
(**THIN — OF WALL**) ALLEGE
(**THIRD —**) THIRDENDEAL
(**TOP —**) HEADPIECE
(**TWELFTH —**) INCIA POINT UNCIAL
(**UPPER —**) CHIEF RIDGE
OVERPARTY
(**UPPERMOST —**) TOP PEAK CHIEF
UPSIDE TOPSIDE
(**VAUDEVILLE —**) OLIO
(**VITAL —**) HEART
(**WINGLIKE —**) ALA
(**WORST —**) DEPTH
(**WORTHLESS —**) DREGS
(**24TH —**) CARAT
(**360TH —**) DEGREE
(PREF.) MER(I)(O) PARTI
(SUFF.) MER(E)(IC)(IS)(OUS)(Y)
TOMA TOME TOMIC TOMOUS
TOMY
PARTAKE BITE PART SHARE
DIVIDE PARTEN PARTICIPATE
(— **OF**) USE HAVE SHARE TASTE
TOUCH IMPART
PARTAN CRAB
PARTED PARTITE
PARTHAON (FATHER OF —)
AGENOR
(**MOTHER OF —**) EPICASTE
(**SON OF —**) OENEUS
(**WIFE OF —**) EURYTE
PARTHENIA (HUSBAND OF —)
ARGALUS
PARTHENIUS (BROTHER OF —)
PANDION

(**FATHER OF —**) PHINEUS
(**MOTHER OF —**) CLEOPATRA
PARTHENOGENETIC AGAMIC
AGAMOUS
PARTIAL HALF PART SEMI BIASED
UNFAIR COLORED HALFWAY
UNEQUAL HARMONIC INCLINED
PARTISAN PROPENSE SKELETON
FAVORABLE SEGMENTAL
PARTICULAR RESPECTIVE
(PREF.) DEMI MER(I)(O) MES(O)
SEMI
PARTIALITY FAVOR RESPECT
AFFECTION SPECIALTY
PARTIALLY HALF HALFWAY
HALFWISE
PARTICIPANT BOOK ACTOR PARTY
MEMBER PARTNER DUETTIST
PARTABLE PARTISAN
(**SUBORDINATE —**) STOOGE
(PL.) FIELD
PARTICIPATE JOIN SIDE ENTER
SHARE ENGAGE ENLIST IMPART
COMPETE PARTAKE
(— **IN**) GO HAVE JOIN STAY STAND
TASTE COMMON STICKLE
PARTICIPATION HAND PLOT
SOCIETY INTEREST
(**COMMON —**) COMMUNITY
PARTICIPATOR
(SUFF.) STER STRESS
PARTICIPLE VERBID
PARTICLE ACE BIT DOT FIG GRU
JOT RAY ATOM BETA CORN CROT
CURN DUST GRUE HAET IOTA
KNIT MITE MOTE SNIP SPOT STIM
WHIT ALPHA BOSON FLAKE FLECK
GHOST GRAIN MESON OMEGA
POINT QUARK SHRED SIGMA
SPECK STARN STIME THRUM
TWINT FILING GEIGER LEPTON
MOMENT PANGEN PARTON
RIZZOM SMIDGE SMITCH TITTLE
VIRION AMICRON FERMION
GEMMULE GRANULE NUCLEUS
PSYCHON SINGLET SMIDGIN
TACHYON ACCEPTER NEUTRINO
SMIDGEON SYLLABLE MICROSOME
POSITRINO SCINTILLA
(— **IN BLOOD**) EMBOLUS
(— **IN INTERNAL EAR**) OTOCONIUM
(— **OF FIRE**) SPARK
(— **OF GOLD**) COLOR
(— **OF SOOT**) ISEL IZLE SMUT AIZLE
(— **S IN BEER**) FLOATERS
(— **S OF GRAIN**) CHOP
(**ATOMIC —**) ION BARYON HADRON
LEPTON ELECTRON
(**COLLECTION OF CHARGED —S**)
PLASMA
(**COMBINING —**) ACCEPTOR
(**ELECTRIFIED —**) ION ANION
PROTON POSITRON
THERMION
(**ELEMENTARY —**) MUON NEUTRON
NEUTRINO
(**FINE ICY —S**) SLEET
(**GROUP OF —S**) MESON
(**HYPOTHETICAL —**) QUARK
(**JAGGED —**) SPLINTER
(**LEAST POSSIBLE —**) MINIM
(**LINGUISTIC —**) SERVILE
(**MINUTE —**) JOT ORT RAY ATOM

GRAIN SPECK RAMENT GRANULE
MOLECULE RAMENTUM
CORPUSCLE
(NEGATIVE —) NOR NOT
(NUCLEAR —S) FALLOUT
(POSITIVELY-CHARGED —) CATION
KATION
(SMALL —) NIP BLEB CORN MOTE
CRUMB GRAIN SPECK AMICRON
GRANULE SPRINKLE SUBMICRON
(TINY —) ATOMY
(ULTIMATE —) PSYCHON
(UNCHARGED —) LAMBDA
(PL.) DUST FINES SWARF SIZINGS
CUTTINGS FURFURES
(SUFF.) PLAST
(— OF A KIND) ID
PARTI-COLORED PIED FANCY
MOTLEY PARTED PIEBALD
BUTTERFLY HARLEQUIN
PARTICULAR AND ATOM FIXY
ITEM NICE SELF SOME FUSSY
PARTY POINT THING CHOOSY
DAINTY DETAIL MINUTE MOROSE
REGARD SINGLE STICKY ARTICLE
CAREFUL CERTAIN CORRECT
FINICKY PRECISE PRIVATE
RESPECT SEVERAL SPECIAL
UNUSUAL CLERKISH CONCRETE
ESPECIAL PECULIAR PICKSOME
PRECIOUS SINGULAR SUBALTERN
RESPECTIVE
(NOT —) INCURIOUS
PARTICULARLY ONLY EXTRA
SINGLY SPECIAL EXPRESSLY
SPECIALLY
PARTING DEATH GOODBYE
FAREWELL
(— AS OF HAIR) SHED
PARTISAN PIKE SIDER STAFF
BIASED FACTOR FAUTOR MARIAN
ZEALOT CALOTIN DEVOTEE
GUISARD PARTNER ADHERENT
CRISTINO ESPOUSER FAVORITE
FENNOMAN FOLLOWER
HENCHMAN JACOBITE MOSSBACK
SIDESMAN STALWART URBANIST
HIGHFLIER MAZZINIST
OCHLOCRAT OLIVERIAN
SECTARIAN TERRORIST
(NOT —) CATHOLIC
(PL.) FOLLOWING
(SUFF.) CRAT
PARTITION BAR CUT DAM FIN
FLAG SEPT WALL SHOJI SPEER
STAGE WITHE BAFFLE DIVIDE
PARPAL PARPEN SCONCE SCREEN
SEPTUM BARRIER CLOISON
ENCLOSE GRATING PINFOLD
PORTION SCANTLE BRATTICE
BULKHEAD CLEAVAGE DIVISION
STOPPING TRAVERSE
DASHBOARD DAYABHAGA
ICONOSTAS MESENTERY
STOOTHING
(— BETWEEN STALLS) TRAVIS
TREVIS TRAVISS
(— IN CHIMNEY) WITH WITHE
(— IN CORAL) TABULA
(— IN COTTAGE) SPEER HALLAN
(— IN FRUIT) REPLUM
(— IN LOUDSPEAKER) BAFFLE
(— IN WATERWHEEL) WREST

(— OF ESTATE) BOEDELSCHEIDING
(— OF LATH AND PLASTER)
STOOTHING
(HORIZONTAL —) STAGE
(MINING —) SOLLAR BRATTICE
STOPPING
(PL.) CANCELLI
PARTLET HEN WOMAN PERTELOT
PARTLY WHAT PARCEL PARTIM
HALFLINGS
(PREF.) SEMI
PARTNER BOY PAL ALLY HALF
MATE PARD WIFE BUDDY BUTTY
PARTY FELLOW MARROW SHARER
COMRADE CONSORT HUSBAND
CAMARADA COPEMATE SIDEKICK
YOKEMATE
(— OF DUMMY) VIVANT
(DANCING —) GIGOLO CAVALIER
(PREF.) CO
PARTNERSHIP HUI AXIS FIRM
HOUSE FUSION CAHOOTS
COMPANY CONSORT SOCIETY
SOCIETEIT
PARTRIDGE HUN BIRD KYAH YUTU
LERWA RUDGE TITAR CHUKAR
REDLEG SEESEE CHEEPER
PATRICK SHRIMPI TINAMOU
BOBWHITE FRANCOLIN
FRENCHMAN TETRAONID
(— NOISE) JUCK
(SAND —) TEHOO
(YOUNG —) CHEEPER SQUEALER
PARTRIDGEBERRY BOXBERRY
COWBERRY EYEBERRY ONEBERRY
SNOWBERRY TWINBERRY
PARTS
(PREF.) **(SIDE —)** ALI
PART-SONG MADRIGAL
PART-TIME PARCEL
PARTURITION EUTOCIA TRAVAIL
CHILDBED DELIVERY DYSTOCIA
(SUFF.) TOKY
PARTY DO BAL BEE CRY TEA CAMP
CLAN DRUM GALA SECT SIDE
BINGE BLAST BRAWL BUNCH
CABAL COVEY CRUSH GROUP
LEVEE COMITE FIESTA FROLIC
FRONDE GERMAN INFARE JUNKET
PERSON SETOUT SHINDY
SHOWER BLOWOUT CANTICO
COMPANY FACTION GREGORY
PATARIA SHINDIG CLAMBAKE
DRINKING FENNOMAN POTLATCH
POUNDING SOCIABLE SQUANTUM
TERTULIA CONCISION INCLINING
MERRIMENT
(— GIVEN AT HOME) HUDDLE
(AFTERNOON —) TEA RECEPTION
(BEACH —) CLAMBAKE
(BOISTEROUS —) JAMBOREE
(BRIDAL —) SEND SHOWER
(DANCING —) HOP GERMAN
CANTICO HOEDOWN RIDOTTO
FANDANGO
(DRINKING —) KNEIPE MOLLIE
POTATION SYMPOSIUM
(DRUNKEN —) BLIND
(EVENING —) BALL SOIREE
GREGORY ROCKING TERTULIA
(FISHING —) HUKILAU
(HUNTING —) FAID
(INFORMAL —) SOCIABLE TERTULIA

(IRISH —) HOOLEY
(LARGE —) ROUT
(MASQUERADE —) GUISE
(MEN'S —) STAG SMOKER
(POLITICAL —) SAM SIDE WAFD
HOOKS LABOR CAUCUS FRONDE
SWARAJ ZENTRUM MINSEITO
KENSEIKAI SQUADRONE
OPPOSITION
(POPULAR —) HOOKS
(ROWDY —) BLOWOUT
(SCOUTING —) ESPIAL
(SUPPLY —) BRIGADE
(TEA —) DRUM TEMPEST
(THIRD —) STRANGER
PARUAH (SON OF —)
JEHOSHAPHAT
PARULIS GUMBOIL
PARVENU SNOB ARRIVE UPSTART
ARRIVIST MUSHROOM ARRIVISTE
PARVIS PARADISE
PARZIFAL (FATHER OF —) GAMURET
(MOTHER OF —) HERZELOIDE
PASACH (FATHER OF —) JAPHLET
PASCH PACE PAQUE EASTER
PASSOVER
PASCHAL LAMB CANDLE SUPPER
PASSOVER
PAS DE DEUX DUET
PASE FAROL NATURAL VERONICA
PASEAH (FATHER OF —) ESHTON
PASEAR WALK AIRING EXCURSION
PROMENADE
PASHA DEY EMIR BASHAW
PASAHAW
PASHTO AFGHAN
PASIPHAE (BROTHER OF —) AEETES
(CHILD OF —) ARIADNE PHAEDRA
(DAUGHTER OF —) ARIADNE
PHAEDRA
(FATHER OF —) HELIUS
(HUSBAND OF —) MINOS
(MOTHER OF —) PERSA
(SISTER OF —) CIRCE
PASQUEFLOWER BADGER
GOSLING APRILFOOL
PASQUINADE PIPE SQUIB SATIRE
LAMPOON PASQUIL
PASS BY GO COL DIE END FIG GAP
SAG USE ABRA BEAL CEDE CHIT
COMP COVE DREE DROP FALL
FARE FLIT FOIN GATE GHAT GULF
HALS HAND HAVE JARK LANE
LEAD PACE RIDE ROLL SEEK SILE
SLAP SLIP STEP WADE WALK
WEAR WEND WIND ALLOW
CANTO DREIE ENACT FLEET
GHAUT GORGE HALSE HURRY
KOTAL LAPSE LITHE LUNGE
NOTCH OCCUR ORDER PAPER
PUNTA REACH RELAY SHAKE
SHOOT SMITE SPEND STRIP
TRADE UTTER WASTE WHELM
YODEL BILLET CHALAN CONVEY
COUPON DEFILE DEMISE ELAPSE
EXCEED HAPPEN PASSUS PERMIT
RAVINE SPIRAL TICKET TRAVEL
TWOFER ABSOLVE ALLONGE
APPROVE BREATHE DESCEND
DEVOLVE DIFFUSE ENTREAT
LATERAL OVERGET PASSAGE
UNDERGO JUNCTURE REBOLERA
PURWANNAH SAFEGUARD

(— A BALL) FEED HEEL
(— ABRUPTLY) LEAP
(— ALONG) BANDY DERIVE
(— AWAY) DIE SET FLEE VADE
WING DEPART EXPIRE PERISH
FORFARE FORTHGO OVERDRIVE
(— BACK AND FORTH) FIG
CRISSCROSS
(— BAD COIN) SMASH
(— BETWEEN HILLS) BEAL SLAP
SLACK
(— BY) COTE OMIT SKIP VADE
WEND APASS CLEAR FORGO
FOREGO IGNORE OVERGO
INTERMIT OVERHEAVE
(— GRADUALLY) FADE
(— IN BULLFIGHT) SUERTE
(— IN POKER) BREATHE
(— INTO USE) ENURE INURE
(— JUDGMENT ON) DEEM DECERN
SENTENCE
(— LIGHTLY) BRUSH SKATE
SKITTER
(— OFF) SHAM FOIST
(— ON) LEAK PACE DELATE
(— ONE'S LIFE) TRADE
(— OUT) CONK DEBOUCH
EXHAUST
(— OVER) DO HIP BALK FREE SKIM
SKIP SLIP COVER CROSS ELIDE
FLEET SCOUR SWEEP TRANCE
OVERHIP INTERMIT OVERLOOK
OVERPOST PROGRESS TRAVERSE
(— OVER LIGHTLY) SKIM SWEEP
OVERSKIP
(— OVER QUICKLY) SCUD FLEET
(— QUICKLY) FLIT SPIN SPEED
STRIKE
(— THROUGH) CROSS REEVE
TRACE DIVIDE OVERGO PIERCE
SUFFER EXCURSE PERVADE
OVERPASS OVERRIDE PERMEATE
PROGRESS PENETRATE
(— THROUGH A BLOCK) REEVE
(— THROUGH NARROW WAY) THRID
THREAD
(— TIME) DRIVE SPEND TRADE
(— UNHAPPILY) DREE
(— UP) REJECT DECLINE
DISREGARD
(— WITH DIFFICULTY) WADE
(— WITH VIOLENCE) RAKE
(CUSTOMS —) CARNET
(FENCING —) FOIN BOTTE LUNGE
PUNTA
(FOOTBALL —) FLY FLARE
FORWARD LATERAL PITCHOUT
(FORWARD —) AERIAL
(HOCKEY —) CENTER
(LONG — IN FOOTBALL) BOMB
(MOUNTAIN —) COL GAP NEK SAG
GATE GHAT SLIP CLOVE GHAUT
KLOOF KLOOT KOTAL POORT
SWIRE SWIRL BEALACH
(NARROW —) ABRA GULF CLOSE
SLYPE DEFILE
(SUDDEN —) LUNGE
PASSABLE FIT FAIR SOSO TOLLOL
GENUINE ADEQUATE MEDIOCRE
MODERATE POSSIBLE TRAVELED
PERMEABLE TOLERABLE
(PREF.) BATO
PASSABLENESS INDIFFERENCE

PASSABLY SEEMLY
PASSAGE CUT GAT GUT ROW VIA WAY WRO ADIT BELT BORD DOOR EXIT FARE FLUE FORD GANG GATE HALL ITER LANE PACE PASS PAWN RACE RAMP SLIP SLUM VENT WELL AISLE ALLEY ALURE BAYOU BEARD BOGUE CANAL CHOPS CHUTE CLOSE CREEK CRUSH DRAFT DRIFT DRIVE ENTRY FLYBY FORTE GLADE GOING GORGE INLET JETTY MEUSE PATCH PORCH SHUNT SLYPE SOUND ACCESS ADITUS APORIA ARCADE ATRIUM AVENUE BRIDGE BURROW BYPASS CAREER COURSE DEFILE DROMOS EGRESS ELAPSE FAUCES HIATUS MEATUS PARODE RELIEF SCREEN SLUICE STRAIT TRAJET TRANCE TRAVEL TUNNEL VOYAGE ARCHWAY BALTEUS CHANNEL CHAPTER CHIMNEY CONDUIT COULOIR COUPURE DIAZOMA DOGTROT DRAUGHT ESTUARY EXCERPT FISTULA FRAUGHT GALLERY GANGWAY GATEWAY ISTHMUS JOURNEY MANHOLE OFFTAKE OUTTAKE PARADOS PROCESS TRANSIT APPROACH AQUEDUCT CITATION CLOISTER COMMERCE DEBOUCHE DELETION PARADIGM PERICOPE SENTENCE SHIPPING SINUSOID SPILLWAY
(— IN BOOK) WHERE EXCERPT
(— IN JEWISH SCRIPTURE) PARASHAH
(— OF THREAD) FLOAT
(— TO STOMACH) SWALLOW
(— TO TOMB) DROMOS SYRINX
(—S OF LITERATURE) BEAUTIES
(AIR —) FLUE THIRL WINDWAY THIRLING VENTIDUCT
(ANATOMICAL —) ITER
(CENSORED —) CAVIAR
(CONTINUOUS —) LAPSE
(COVERED —) OPE PAWN PEND
(DIFFICULT —) APORIA
(LITERARY —) TEXT QUOTE EXCERPT SNIPPET QUOTATION
(MINE —) RUN ADIT HEAD ROOF SLUM DRIVE LEVEL SHAFT THIRL AIRWAY STENTON UNDERCAST
(MUSICAL —) CUE CODA LINK BREAK FORTE STAVE ARIOSO FUGATO LEGATO PRESTO REPEAT CADENZA CODETTA FANFARE STRETTO FLOURISH SPICCATO STACCATO SYMPHONY VOCALISE PIZZICATO RITARDANDO
(NARROW —) GUT HASS ALLEY CREEP GORGE JETTY NOTCH SLYPE SMOOT DEFILE GULLET NARROW STRAIT
(SECRET —) BOLTHOLE
(SECURE OF) CARRY
(SUBTERRANEAN —) POSTERN
(SWIFT —) FLIGHT
(VAULTED —) PEND
(WATER —) TICKLE TICKLER
(PREF.) MEATO
(SUFF.) PLANIA PORA PORE

PASSAGE HAWK TARTARET PASSENGER
PASSAGE TO INDIA (AUTHOR OF —) FORSTER
(CHARACTER IN —) AZIZ ADELA CECIL MOORE RONALD STELLA GODBOLE HEASLOP QUESTED FIELDING
PASSAGEWAY (ALSO SEE PASSAGE) BORD FLUE GANG HALL LANE PACE PASS PEND PORT RACE SHED SLIP WENT YAWN AISLE ALLEY ALURE CHUTE DRIFT DRONG ENTRY GOING LUMEN RAISE SHOOT SMOOT STULM ACCESS AIRWAY AVENUE COURSE DINGLE FUNNEL GUTTER INTAKE MANWAY RUNWAY TRANCE ZAGUAN DOORWAY GALLERY SLIPWAY TWITTEN WALKWAY WAYGATE CALLEJON CORRIDOR HATCHWAY
(CLEARED — IN CROWD) HALL
(COVERED —) ARCADE CLOISTER
(MINE —) BORD BOARD DRIFT SLANT STULM WINZE
(NARROW —) SLIP AISLE SMOOT
(SLOPING —) RAMP
PASSANT PAST CURRENT CURSORY PASSING EPHEMERAL
PASSE AGED PAST WORN FADED BELATED OBSOLETE OUTMODED
PASSENGER FARE INSIDE FERRYMAN TRAVELER WAYFARER
(— WHO AVOIDS PAYING FARE) NIP STOWAWAY
(— WITHOUT TICKET) HARE
(AIRPLANE —) BIRDMAN
(UNBOOKED —) CAD
(PL.) WAYBILL
PASSEPARTOUT SPANDREL
PASSERBY PASSER PASSANT BYPASSER SAUNTERER
PASSERINE OSCINE PERCHER
PASSIFLORA TACSO
PASSING DEATH DYING ELAPSE CURSORY DIADROM PASSADO RUNNING SLIDING ELAPSING FLEETING ENACTMENT EPHEMERAL WAYFARING
(— BETWEEN) INTERCURRENT
(— BY) COTE
(— INTO EACH OTHER) FONDU
(— OF HOURS) TIME
(— OF TIME) EFFLUX
(SLOWLY —) LAG
PASSION IRE WAX BATE FIRE FURY HEAT LOVE LUST PASH RAGA RAGE TEAR TIDE WILL ZEAL ANGER ARDOR BLOOD BRAME CHAFE DEVIL ERROR FLAME LETCH MANIA RAJAS SPUNK WRATH AFFECT CHOLER DESIRE FERVOR MOTHER PELTER SATTVA SPLEEN TALENT WARMTH EARNEST EMOTION EROTISM FEELING OUTRAGE VULTURE APPETITE DISTRESS VIOLENCE PADDYWACK
(— FOR DOING GREAT THINGS) MEGALOMANIA
(— FOR MUSIC) MELOMANIA
(ANGRY —) FUNK

(ANIMAL —) KAMA
(PREF.) PASSI PATH(O)
(SUFF.) (— FOR) MANE MANIA(C)
PASSIONATE HOT FOND WARM WILD FIERY GUTSY QUICK WHITE ARDENT FERVID FIERCE FUMOUS IREFUL STORMY SULTRY TORRID AMOROUS FLAMING PEPPERY THERMAL VIOLENT CHOLERIC FRENETIC VASCULAR VEHEMENT WRATHFUL DIONYSIAN IRASCIBLE
PASSIONATELY HASTILY FERVIDLY
PASSIONFLOWER MAYPOP BULLHOOF
PASSIONLESS COLD FREDDO APATHETIC
PASSIVE INERT STOIC PATHIC STOLID PATIENT FEMININE INACTIVE SIGNLESS YIELDING APATHETIC
PASSIVENESS QUIETISM
PASSOVER PESAH PHASE PASQUE PESACH
(— FESTIVAL) SEDER
(JEWISH —) EASTER
PASSPORT CHOP PASS CONGE CONGEE DUSTUK DUSTUCK FURLOUGH TESCARIA TEZKIRAH SAFEGUARD
PASSUS PACE PART PASS STEP CANTO DIVISION
PASSWORD SIGN WORD TOKEN DUSTUK TESSERA WATCHWORD
PAST BY AGO WAS GONE YOND YORE AFTER AGONE APAST ASIDE ENDED SINCE BEHIND BYGONE FOREBY PRETER ANOTHER FOREGONE PRETERIT COMPLETED
(LONG —) HIGH
(RECENTLY —) OTHER
(TIME NOT LONG —) YESTERDAY
(PREF.) PRETER RETRO
PASTA ORZO LASAGNA LINGUINE LINGUINI MACARONI MANICOTTI SPAGHETTI
PASTE HIT PAP BEAT BLOW DIKA DUFF GLUE MISO PACK PATE CREAM DOUGH FALSE GESSO HENNA PUNCH STICK ATTACH BATTER CERATE FASTEN GROUND PANADA RASTIK STRASS BUCKETY CLOBBER COLOGNE DRAWOUT FILLING GORACCO GUARANA STICKUM BADIGEON BARBOTINE
(— FOR CAULKING) BLARE
(— FOR LINING HEARTHS) BRASQUE
(— FOR SHOES, BOOTS) CLOBBER BLACKING
(— OF CLAY) BATTER
(— TO FILL HOLES IN WOOD AND STONE) BADIGEON
(ALIMENTARY —) FEDELINI SCUNGILLI SPAGHETTI
(AROMATIC —) PASTILE
(COLORING —) HENNA
(DRIED —) GUARANA
(EARTHY —) ENGOBE
(FISH —) BAGOONG
(MEDICATED —) ELECTUARY
(PORCELAIN —) PATE
(POTTER'S —) BARBOTINE

(TOBACCO —) GORACCO
(WEAVER'S —) SOWENS BUCKETY
PASTEBOARD CARD SHAM CARTON FLIMSY TICKET MATBOARD
PASTEDOWN LINING
PASTEL WOAD LIGHT CRAYON PICTURE DELICATE
PASTEL BLUE OADE WOAD
PASTEN HOBBLE TETHER PASTOUR SHACKLE
PASTILLE CACHOU CANDLE LOZENGE
PASTIME GAY TOY GAME PLOY HOBBY SPORT GOSSIP OLEARY SAILING PASTANCE AMUSEMENT DIVERSION ABRIDGMENT
PASTOR HERD ANGEL RABBI CURATE KEEPER PRIEST RECTOR DOMINIE VICAIRE GUARDIAN MINISTER SHEPHERD
PASTORAL POEM DRAMA RURAL RUSTIC BUCOLIC CROSIER IDYLLIC NOMADIC ROMANCE ARCADIAN THEOCRITEAN
PASTORALIST SQUATTER
PASTRY PIE FLAN HUFF PUFF SOCK TART TUCK CORNET DANISH ECLAIR ABAISSE BRIOCHE CARCAKE STRUDEL BAKEMEAT NAPOLEON TALMOUSE TURNOVER APPLEJACK
(— COOK) PASTLER
(— SHELL) BOUCHEE DARIOLE TIMBALE TALMOUSE
(— STRIPS) LATTICE
(— WHEEL) JAGGER
(SWEET —) DOUCET
PASTURAGE FEED GANG GATE STRAY COLLOP EATAGE FORAGE HERBAGE SHEEPGATE
PASTURE ALP FOG HAG HAM ING LEA PEN TYE BENT FEED GAET GANG GATE GISE GIST HAFT HALF HEAF HOGA INGE KEEP PARK RAIK AGIST DRIFT EJIDO GRASS GRAZE LAYER LEASE RANGE VELDT INTAKE MEADOW OUTRUN SAETER COWGATE FOGGAGE GRAZING HERBAGE LEALAND POTRERO VACCARY VICTUAL HERDWICK OUTFIELD SHEEPWALK
(— GRASS) TORE GRAMA
(— IN STUBBLE) SHACK
(— LAND) RAKE TACK LEASOW
(HILL —) HOGA
(MOUNTAIN —) SETER SAETER SHIELING
(SHEEP —) HEAF EWELEASE
(SHETLAND I. —) SETER
(SUMMER —) AGOSTADERO
(WET —) SLINK
PASTURELAND BENT SOUM
PASTURING RELIEF PANNAGE
PASTY PIE PATE SLAB PATTY DOUGHY FRACID SAMBOUSE
PAT APT DAB DIB TAP TIG BLOW CLAP GLIB JUMP PALP TICK CHUCK FITLY FIXED IMPEL THROW CARESS DABBLE PRETTY SMOOGE SOOTHE STRIKE STROKE TIMELY APROPOS CHERISH

FITTING PATAPAT READILY SUITABLE PERTINENT SEASONABLE
PATAGIUM TEGULA TIPPET SCAPULA PARACHUTE PTERYGODE
PATAGONIA (DEITY OF —) SETEBOS **(RODENT OF —)** CAVY MARA **(TREE OF —)** MANIU ALERCE ALERSE
PATAMAR COURIER PATTAMAR MESSENGER
PATAYAN YUMAN
PATCH BIT EKE FLY BOUT LAND MEND SKIP SPOT SWAB SWOB VAMP BLAZE BODGE CLOUT CLUMP COVER FRIAR FUDGE PIECE SAVER SCRAP SPECK SPLAT BLOTCH COBBLE COOPER DOLLOP GORGET MOUCHE PARCEL REVAMP SOLDER SPETCH SWATCH TINKLE CLAMPER CLOBBER INWEAVE PELIOMA REMNANT
(— AS ORNAMENT) MOUCHE
(— CLUMSILY) BOTCH CLOUT CLAMPER
(— OF COLOR) CLOUP DAPPLE SPLASH SPECULUM
(— OF DARK HAIR) SMUT
(— OF DIRT) MIRE
(— OF FEATHERS) BIB CAP PTERYLA
(— OF ICE) RONE
(— OF LAND) RODHAM
(— OF LEATHER) SPECK
(— OF LIGHT) GLADE
(— OF PRINT) FUDGE
(— OF RUFFLED WATER) ACKER
(— OF SALIVA) SIXPENCE
(— OF TIRE) BOOT
(— ON BOAT) TINGLE
(— ON PRINTED PAGE) FRIAR
(— ON THROAT) GORGET
(— TOGETHER) CONSARCINATE
(— UP) HEAL MEND
(BALD —) AREA
(LIVID —) PELIOMA
(OOZY —) SPEW SPUE
(OPEN — IN FOREST) CAMPO
(SHOULDER —) FLASH
PATCHOULI PACCIOLI PATCHLEAF
PATCHWORD WASTEWORD
PATCHWORK BOTCH CENTO CENTON JUMBLE SCRAPS PATCHERY FRAGMENTS PASTICCIO
PATE PIE TOP HEAD BROWN PASTE PASTY PATTY BADGER NODDLE NOGGIN COSTARD COXCOMB
PATELLA CAP PAN DISH VASE ROTULA KNEECAP KNEEPAN WHIRLBONE
PATEN ARCA DISC DISH DISK PLATE PATINA PLATEN VESSEL
PATENT ARCA BALD OPEN BERAT BROAD OVERT PLAIN SUNNUD CHARTER EVIDENT LICENSE OBVIOUS APPARENT ARCHIVES MANIFEST PALPABLE PRIVILEGE
PATENTED BREVETE
PATER FATHER PRIEST
PATERFAMILIAS MASTER

PATERNAL FATHERLY
PATERNITY FATHER ORIGIN
PATESI ISHSHAKKU
PATH ARC PAD RIG RUN RUT TAN WAY BERM FARE GATE LANE LEAD LINE LODE RACE RACK ROAD TRIG TROD WALK ALLEY BYWAY GOING JETTY PISTE ROUTE SPACE TRACK TRACT TRADE TRAIL BOSTAL BYPASS CAMINO CASAUN CIRCLE COMINO COURSE GROOVE SLEUTH SPHERE SWATHE TRENCH CHANNEL ERGODIC FAIRWAY FOOTWAY HIGHWAY LANDWAY MEANDER PASSAGE RODDING SIDEWAY TARIQAT TOWPATH TRAFFIC TRUNDLE WAYGATE BORSTALL CENTRODE CROSSCUT DRIFTWAY TRAILWAY TWITCHEL CROSSWALK
(— BETWEEN HEDGES) TWITCHEL
(— CUT IN MOWING) SWATH SWATHE
(— FOLLOWED BY ENERGY) ERGODIC
(— MADE BY ANIMAL) PIST PISTE
(— OF CELESTIAL BODY) ORBIT
(— OF CLOUDS) RACK
(— OF MOVING POINT) CURVE LOCUS
(— OF RACE) STRIP
(— UP STEEP HILL) BOSTAL BORSTAL BORSTALL
(BRIDLE —) SPURWAY
(CLOSED —) CIRCUIT
(FORTIFICATION —) RELAIS
(GARDEN —) ALLEE
(NARROW —) BERM RACK TRIG RODDIN TROCHA RODDING
(PHILIPPINE FOOT —) SENDA
(STONE-PAVED —) STEEN
(SUFI —) TARIQAT
(WINDING —S) AMBAGES
(PREF.) HODO ODO
(SUFF.) ODE OID
PATHAN TURI AFRIDI SIVATI BAJOURI BANGASH PAYTHAN DANGARIK
PATHETIC SAD SILLY TEARY TENDER FORLORN PITIFUL DOLOROSO PATETICO PITIABLE POIGNANT STIRRING TOUCHING AFFECTING
PATHFINDER (AUTHOR OF —) COOPER
(CHARACTER IN —) CAP DAVY MUIR MABEL NATTY BUMPPO DUNHAM JASPER MACNAB CHARLES WESTERN SANGLIER ARROWHEAD CHINGACHGOOK
PATHIC MORBID VICTIM PASSIVE CATAMITE DISEASED SUFFERER SUFFERING
PATHOGEN VIRUS
PATHOLOGICAL
(SUFF.) (— CONDITION) IA
PATHOLOGIST AMERICAN OPIE ROUS SLYE EWING MOORE SMITH WELCH MOHLER FLEXNER HEKTOEN PRUDDEN WARTHIN WHIPPLE RICKETTS
CANADIAN WESBROOK

DANISH FIBIGER
ENGLISH ADAMI BOYCE PAGET ANNETT FLOREY WRIGHT
GERMAN HENLE KLEBS TRAUBE ZENKER VIRCHOW COHNHEIM RECKLINGHAUSEN
IRISH STOKES
ITALIAN GUARNIERI
PATHOS BATHOS SNIVEL POIGNANCY
PATHWAY (ALSO SEE PATH) RUN LANE PATH RACK SLADE COURSE RAMBLA RAMBLE RODDIN BORSTAL RODDING
(RAISED —) CAUSEY CAUSEWAY
PATIENCE CALM THILD BEARANCE STOICISM COMPOSURE ENDURANCE FORTITUDE
PATIENT CASE CURE MEEK SOBER BOVINE PASSIVE ENDURING THOLEMOD SUFFERANT
(— OF ASYLUM) BEDLAM
(BE —) BEAR
(HYDROPATHIC —) WATERER
(MEDICAL —) CURE
PATIO COURT COURTYARD
PATOIS CANT GOMBO GUMBO CREOLE JARGON PATTER DIALECT GUERNSEY
(FRENCH —) JOUAL
PATRIARCH JOB ABBA ENOS LEVI NASI NOAH PAPA POPE ALDER ELDER JACOB PITRI DESPOT JOSEPH NESTOR ABRAHAM ANCIENT VETERAN VENERABLE
(ETHIOPIAN —) ABUNA
PATRICIAN NOBLE EMPEROR PATRICK NOBLEMAN GENTLEMAN
PATRIMONY PORTION ANCESTRY HERITAGE LONGACRE
PATRIOT LOVER AMATEUR
PATRIOTIC PUBLIC ENVELOPE NATIONAL
PATRIPASSIAN NOETIAN
PATROCLUS (FATHER OF —) MENOETIUS
(MOTHER OF —) PERIAPIS POLYMELE STHENELE
(SLAYER OF —) HECTOR
PATROL GUARD SCOUT WATCH STOOGE PATROLE PROTECT
PATROLMAN COP GUARD FLATFOOT INSPECTOR
PATRON BUYER GUEST STOOP AVOWRY CLIENT FATHER FAUTOR JAJMAN ACCOUNT PADRONE PATROON PROCTOR SPONSOR ADVOCATE CHAMPION CUSTOMER DEFENDER GUARDIAN MAECENAS
(PL.) FOLLOWING
PATRONAGE AEGIS FAVOR AVOWRY CUSTOM FAVOUR ACCOUNT AUSPICE FOMENTO HEARING AUSPICES BUSINESS PADROADO
(— AND CARE) AUSPICE
(POLITICAL —) PAP
PATRONAL TITULAR
PATRONIZE USE DEIGN FAVOR DEFEND FATHER PROMOTE PROTECT EMPATRON FREQUENT
PATROON TRACT

CAPTAIN SUPPORTER
PATTEE FORMY FORMEE
PATTEN BASE CLOG FOOT SHOE SKATE STAND STILT CHOPIN GALOSH RACKET SANDAL CREEPER RACQUET SUPPORT CIOPPINO SNOWSHOE
PATTER CANT TALK TIRL LINGO HAPPER JARGON BLATHER BLATTER CHATTER DIALECT
PATTERING PITAPAT
PATTERN CUT FUR SET BASE CAST COMB COPY FORM GIMP IDEA LAUE MOLD NORM PLAN SEME STAR WAVE BISON BYSEN CHECK DECOR DISME DRAFT EPURE GUIDE IDEAL INLAY MODEL MOIRE MOULD NOTAN PLAID SEMEE SHAPE WATER BASKET BURELE CANVAS CHECKS DESIGN DIAPER ENTAIL ETOILE FABRIC FIGURE FLORAL FORMAT FORMER LACERY MAGPIE MATRIX MIRROR MODULE MUSTER ONDULE PATRON POUNCE RANDOM RECIPE SAMPLE SQUARE STRIPE SYSTEM ALLOVER CHEVRON EXAMPLE FACONNE FILLING FOLKWAY GESTALT GRIZZLE HOBNAIL MEANDER MEANING MULLION PARAGON PROJECT SAMPLER SLEIGHT STENCIL TEMPLET CALENDAR DENTELLE DYNAMICS FILIGREE HATCHING ILLUSION OVERSHOT PARADIGM PLATFORM STRICKLE PROTOTYPE
(— IN BRAIN) GYRATION
(— OF BEHAVIOR) HABIT DISPLAY
(— OF CADENCE) CURSUS
(— OF HINDU MUSIC) TALA
(— OF LARGE SQUARES) DAMIER
(— OF SCARS) KELOID
(— OF SEPARATE OBJECTS) SEME
(— OF STRESS) SUPERFIX
(— OF TARTAN) SET SEET SETT SETTE
(— ON PAPER) BURELAGE
(— ON STAMP) GRILL GRILLE
(— USED BY SILVERSMITHS) WORK BOROON
(-S ON SILK) ARMURE
(CHARACTERISTIC BEHAVIOR —) BIT
(CROSS-BARRED —) PLAID
(FACIAL —) BLAZE
(FRET —) KEY
(GARMENT —) SLOPER
(HAT —) BLOCK
(KNITTING —) ARGYLE
(MASONRY —) SPICATUM
(MELODIC —) RAGA
(PORCELAIN —) FITZHUGH
(RUG —) AINALEH
(SHOE —) FORME
(SKATING —) EDGE
(SOCIAL —) FAMILISM
(SPEECH —) IDIOLECT
(STRIPED —) BARRE
(SYMBOLIC —) MANDALA
(TAILOR'S —) PROTRACTOR
(TATTOO —) MOKO
(TREE —) HOM HOMA
(WEAVING —) DRAW
PATTERNED GOFFERED

PATTY TABLET BOUCHEE PRALINE PATTYPAN VOLAUVENT
(— **SHELL**) DARIOLE TALMOUSE CROUSTADE
PATULOUS OPEN SPREAD DISTENDED
PAUCITY LACK DEARTH FEWNESS EXIGUITY SCARCITY
PAUL PAOLO
(**ASSOCIATE OF** —) DEMAS SILAS TITUS ARTEMAS BARNABAS
PAULDRON POLLET EPAULET PALERON POLDRON POLLETTE
PAULINA (**HUSBAND OF** —) CAMILLO ANTIGONUS
PAULLU (**BROTHER OF** —) MANCO HUASCAR
PAULOPOST DEUTERIC
PAULOWNIA KIRI
PAUNCH TUN KITE KYTE BELLY PENCH RUMEN ABDOMEN STOMACH GUNDYGUT POTBELLY
PAUNCHY BLOATED
PAUPER BEGGAR INDIGENT ROUNDSMAN
PAUPERISM BEGGARY
PAUSANIAS (**FATHER OF** —) CLEOMBROTUS
PAUSE HO HEM HALT HANG HOLD LULL REST RUFE STAY STOP WAIT ABIDE BREAK CEASE CHECK COMMA DELAY DEMUR DEVAL DWELL HOVER LETUP LIMMA POISE SELAH TARRY TENOR BREACH BREATH CORONA CUTOFF FALTER HANKER HIATUS PERIOD STANCE CAESURA FERMATA RESPITE VIRGULE BREATHER INTERVAL
(— **BEFORE HURDLE**) DWELL
(**SUDDEN** —) CHECK
(**PL.**) LIMMATA CAESURAE
PAUT PAW POKE POWT STAMP FINGER
PAVANE DANCE PADUAN
PAVE LAY TAR PATH STUD TILE COVER FLOOR CAUSEY COBBLE QUARRY SMOOTH OVERLAY PREPARE RUDERATE
(— **WITH STONES**) STEEN CAUSEY
PAVED COBBLED
PAVEMENT SARN SLAB HEARTH PAEPAE TELFORD ASAROTUM FLAGGING FLOORING PATHMENT PEDIMENT PITCHING SIDEWALK TROTTOIR WASHBOARD
PAVER CUBER PAVIOR
PAVID TIMID AFRAID FEARFUL
PAVILION BASE FLAG TELD TENT FOLLY KIOSK PINNA ROYAL CANOPY ENSIGN HOWDAH LITTER PANDAL PALLION COVERING GLORIETTE
PAVILLON CHINOIS CRESCENT
PAVING FLAG SETT BLOCK BRICK DALLE PAVER STEAN STEEN STONE COBBLE TARMAC ASPHALT TELFORD PITCHING FLAGSTONE
(**SQUARE** —) MITCHEL
PAVIS COVER PAVADE PAVOIS SHIELD PROTECT
PAW PAT PUD TOE CLAW FOOT GAUM GRAB HAND MAUL PATY

PAUT PORT FLAIL PATTE TRICK CLUTCH FUMBLE HANDLE PATTEE CRUBEEN FLIPPER FORELEG FOREFOOT
PAWKY SLY ARCH BOLD CANNY SAUCY CRAFTY LIVELY SHREWD CUNNING FORWARD SQUEAMISH
PAWL COG DOG BOLT HAND SEAR STOP TENT TRIP CATCH CLICK DETENT FINGER PALLET TONGUE CLAWKER RATCHET
PAWN DIP POP WED FINE GAGE HOCK SOAK VAMP WAGE SPOUT SWEAT ENGAGE LUMBER OBLIGE PIGNUS PLEDGE WADSET COUNTER HOSTAGE PEACOCK CHESSMAN MOSKENEER TRIBULATION
(**PL.**) PHALANX
PAWNBROKER MOUNT UNCLE BROKER LUMBERER MONEYLENDER
PAWNEE PANEE SKIDI WATER ALMOND BISCUIT PLEDGEE
PAWNIE PAWN PEACOCK
PAWNSHOP PAWN SPOUT LUMBER LOMBARD POPSHOP
PAX BOARD PEACE TRUCE FRIEND TABLET
PAXWAX WHITELEATHER
PAY DO BUY FEE TIP ANTE FOOT FORK GIVE MEET RENT SOLD WAGE BATTA CLEAR COUGH DOUSE PLANK SCREW SHEPE SOUND WAGES YIELD ANSWER BETALL DEFRAY IMPEND REWARD SALARY SETTLE COMMUTE DEADRAY HALVANS IMBURSE REQUITE SATISFY SOULDIE STIPEND TRIBUTE RECOMPENSE
(— **ATTENTION**) DIG SEE COME GAUM HARK HEED TENT ADVERT REGARD
(— **COURT TO**) NUT SUE GALLANT
(— **DOWN**) DOUSE
(— **FLIRTATIOUS ADVANCES**) QUEEN
(— **FOR**) ABY BUY BYE COUP ABIDE COVER ESCOT STAND ABEGGE
(— **FOR LIQUOR**) BIRL
(— **HEAVY PENALTY**) SMART EXPIATE
(— **HOMAGE**) CHEFE CHEVE CHIVE SALAAM ADULATE
(— **IN ADVANCE**) IMPRESS
(— **MONEY**) PINGLE
(— **OF SOLDIER**) SAWDEE
(— **OFF**) LIFT SINK ACQUIT
(— **OUT**) VEER BLEED SPEND STUMP EXPEND DISBURSE
(— **PENALTY**) ABY ABYE
(— **TAXES**) GILD
(— **UP**) ANTE QUIT SETTLE LIQUIDATE
(— **WITH IOU**) VOWEL
(**ADVANCE** —) IMPREST
(**DAILY** —) DIET
(**EXTRA** —) BATTA BONUS KICKBACK
(**SMALL** —) SCREW
PAYABLE DUE C4RTAL
PAYEE HOLDER ENDORSER

PAYMASTER BAKSHI BUKSHI PURSER BUKSHEE PAGADOR
PAYMENT CRO DUE FEE TAX BILL CENS DOES DOLE DUTY ERIC FEAL FINE GALE GILD HIRE LEVY MAIL MISE TACK TOLL BONUS CANON CLAIM GAVEL MAILL MENSE MODUS PREST PRICE YIELD ANGILD BOUNTY CHARGE LINAGE LOBOLA OUTLAY PAYOLA PLEDGE REBATE RETURN REWARD TARIFF ADVANCE ALIMONY ANNUITY BENEFIT CUSTOMS DEPOSIT FOOTAGE GARNISH PANNAGE PENSION PRIMAGE SOLUTIO STIPEND SUBSIDY SUBSIST TREWAGE TUITION CASUALTY FOREGIFT GRATUITY KICKBACK MALIKANA MARITAGE MONEYAGE TREASURY WOODGELD HEADPENNY MALGUZARI
(— **FOR INJURY**) UTU
(— **FOR LABOR**) MEED
(— **FOR OFFENSE**) ENACH
(— **FOR RELEASE**) LOOSING
(— **FOR RERUN**) RESIDUAL
(— **OF FEE**) FEAL
(— **OF MINERS**) FOOTAGE YARDAGE
(— **ON DELIVERY**) COD
(— **TO SECURE FAVOR**) PAYOLA
(**ADVANCE** —) ANTE
(**DEMAND** —) DUN BILL
(**EVADE** —) BILK DEFAULT
(**HOMICIDE'S** —) KELCHIN
(**PERIODICAL** —) GALE GAVEL
PAYNIM PAGAN PANIME HEATHEN INFIDEL PAGANDOM
PAYOFF FIX BRIBE CLIMAX PROFIT REWARD DECISIVE RECKONING
PEA DAL TUR DHAL GRAM LANG SEED ARHAR CHICK CICER GANDUL LEGUME PIGEON PODDER CARMELE CATJANG KHESARI PODWARE TANGIER GARVANRO MARROWFAT
(— **DOVE**) ZENAIDA
(— **HARVESTER**) VINER
(— **PETAL**) KEEL
(**EARLY** —**S**) HASTINGS
(**PARCHED** —**S**) CARLS CARLINS
(**PL.**) POIS GRAIN
(**PREF.**) PISI
PEABIRD ORIOLE WRYNECK
PEACE PAX CALM EASE FINE LIOS LISS REST AMITY FRITH GRITH LISSE QUIET TRUCE REPOSE SAUGHT SHALOM CONCORD HARMONY REQUIEM
(— **OF MIND**) ATARAXIA
(**GODDESS OF** —) IRENE
(**SYMBOL OF** —) DOVE TOGA OLIVE
(**PREF.**) PACI
PEACEABLE FAIR SOME CIVIL DOUCE QUIET STILL GENTLE SILVER ORDERLY PACIFIC SOLOMON AMICABLE SACKLESS
PEACEFUL CALM SOME SOBER STILL IRENIC PLACID SILVER HALCYON ORDERLY PACIFIC
PEACE PIPE CALUMET
PEACH BLAB PAVY CLING PAVIE SNEAK SPLIT TRUMP ACCUSE

BETRAY CARMAN CROSBY FOSTER INDICT INFORM OREJON PEENTO SALWEY BRUNION ELBERTA PERSIAN PIENTAO WHITTLE CRAWFORD ISABELLA RARERIPE ROSEWORT NECTARINE VICTORINE
(— **STATE**) GEORGIA
(— **STONE**) PUTAMEN
PEACHBLOW FAKIR
PEACHY FINE DANDY
PEACOCK MAO PAON PAVO PAWN POSE PEKOK STRUT PAJOCK PAVONE POWNIE PEAFOWL PHASIANID
(— **TAIL**) TRAIN
(**CONGO** —) AFROPAVO
PEACOCK BITTERN SUN
PEACOCK BUTTERFLY IO
PEACOCK FISH WRASSE
PEACOCK FLOWER FLAMBEAU POINCIANA
PEA CRAB PINNOTERE
PEAG TAX TOLL BEADS PAAGE PEACK PEAGE PEDAGE WAMPUM
PEAI PIAY PIACHE
PEA JACKET PEACOAT
PEAK BEN NAB NOB PAP PIC TOP TOR ACME APEX BEAK CIMA CUSP DENT DOLT DOME KNOB KNOT PICO PIKE TOLT BLOOM CREST CROWN PIQUE PITCH PITON POINT SLINK SNEAK SPIRE STEAL STUMP CLIMAX CUPULA SHASTA SHRINK SUMMIT ZENITH EPITOME MAXIMUM PICACHO CENTROID
(— **OF ANCHOR**) PEE
(— **OF CAP**) SCOOP
(— **OF ENERGY**) NUCLEUS
(**ICE** —) SERAC
(**ISOLATED** —) TOLT
(**SHARP** —) HORN AIGUILLE
(**SNOW-CAPPED** —) DOME CALOTTE
(**PREF.**) ACR(O)
PEAKED WAN PALE THIN DRAWN PIKED SHARP COPPED SICKLY SLIMSY POINTED SLIMPSY
PEAKEDNESS KURTOSIS
PEAL CLAP RING TOLL CHIME CRACK GRILSE SHOVEL MINNING RESOUND SUMMONS THUNDER CARILLON
(— **OF THUNDER**) CLAP REEL
PEANUT BUR FLAX MANI MEAN PETTY PINDA GOOBER PINDAL ARACHIS BEENNUT ARACHIDE EARTHPEA GRASSNUT KATCHUNG VALENCIA MONKEYNUT
(— **DISEASE**) TIKKA
PEA POD COB PYSE QUASH PESCOD
(**POORLY FILLED** —) POP
(**UNRIPE** —) SQUASH
PEAR BOSC BURY DIEGO MELON NELIS SABRA BEURRE BURREL COLMAR PANINI SECKEL WARDEN WINTER KIEFFER PEPERIN PRICKLY AMBRETTE BERGAMOT BLANQUET MUSCATEL TASAJILLO
(**PRICKLY** —) TUNA NOPAL OPUNTIA
(**PREF.**) PIRI PIRO PYRI

PEAR HAW THORN
PEARL GEM MABE TERN GRAIN
NACRE ONION PICOT UNION
BOUTON OLIVET ORIENT
BAROQUE BDELLIUM BLISTER
PARAGON CATARACT MOONBEAM
MARGARITE
(— WEIGHT) TANK
(IMITATION —) OLIVET
(IRREGULAR —) SLUG
(PIERCED —) WIDOW
(SEED —) ALIOFAR
(SMOKED —) MITRAILLE
(PREF.) PERLI
PEARL BLUE METAL
PEARL BLUSH ROSETAN
**PEARL FISHERS, THE (CHARACTER
IN —)** LEILA NADIR ZURGA
NOURABAD
(COMPOSER OF —) BIZET
PEARL MILLET KOUS BAJRA
CUMBU DUCHN DUKHN KOUSE
JONDLA DAGASSA
PEARLSIDES ARGENTIN
PEARLWEED SAGINA POVERTY
SEALWORT
PEARLY NACRY NACROUS
MARGARIC PRECIOUS
PEARLY EVERLASTING LIVELONG
MOONSHINE
PEAR-SHAPED FULL MELLOW
ROUNDED PYRIFORM
PEASANT TAO BOND BOOR HERA
HIND KERN KONO KOPI PEON
RAYA RYOT SERF BAIRU BOWER
CHURL KNAVE KULAK RAYAH
SWAIN CARLOT COTMAN COTTAR
FARMER FELLAH RASCAL RUSTIC
BONDMAN LABORER PAISANO
VILLAIN CHOPSTICK CONTADINO
(— CLASS) JACQUERIE
(— OF INDIA) RYOT KISAN RAIYAT
(ARABIC —) FELLAH
(IRISH —) KERN KERNE
(RUSSIAN —) KULAK MUZHIK
MUZJIK
PEASANTS (AUTHOR OF —)
REYMONT
(CHARACTER IN —) KUBA ROCH
ANTEK HANKA SIMON YAGNA
YANEK BORYNA NASTKA TERESA
MATTHEW MATTHIAS
DOMINIKOVA
PEASE CROW TERN
PEASHOOTER TRUNK BLOWER
PISTOL BLOWGUN
PEAT GOR PET SOD VAG COOM
FUEL MIST MOOR MUCK MULL
TURF COOMB YARFA LAWYER
MINION YARPHA DARLING
FAVORITE
(— BOG) CESS YARPHA
(— CUTTER) PINER
(— SPADE) SLADE TUSKAR
TWISCAR
(DRIED — FOR FUEL) VAG
(LAYER OF —) FLAW
PEA TREE KATURAI
PEATY KETTY
PEBA PEVA ARMADILLO
PEBBLE DIB FLAX JACK PLUM
CHUCK SCREE STONE BANTAM
COGGLE GIBBER GRAVEL QUARTZ

SHILLA SYCITE CHUCKIE CRYSTAL
SHINGLE STANNER JACKSTONE
(PL.) BEACH DREIKANTER
(PREF.) CALCULI CHALICO
PSEPH(O) THRIO
PEBBLY BEACHY
PECAN NOGAL PACANE
PECCADILLO FAULT OFFENSE
MISCHIEF
PECCANT FAULTY MORBID
CORRUPT SINNING DISEASED
PECCARY JAVALI WARREE
TAGASSU TAYASSU JAVELINA
TAYASSUID
PECK DAB DOT JOB NIP BEAK BILL
CARP FOOD GRUB HOLE JERK
KISS PYKE PITCH PRICK STOCK
THROW HATFUL NIBBLE PEGGLE
PICKLE PIERCE STROKE CHIMBLE
(1-4TH OF —) LIPPY FORPET
FORPIT LIPPIE
PECKER BILL NOSE COURAGE
SPIRITS
PECTEN COMB MARSUPIUM
PECTORAL SANDPIPER JACK
PERT PEERT BROWNY BROWNIE
CHOROOK CREAKER FATBIRD
HAYBIRD KRIEKER SQUATTER
TRIDDLER JACKSNIPE
PECULATE STEAL MISUSE
EMBEZZLE
PECULIAR ODD VERY QUEER
WEIRD PROPER QUAINT UNIQUE
CURIOUS PRIVATE SEVERAL
SPECIAL STRANGE UNUSUAL
SEPARATE SINGULAR SPECIFIC
PECULIARITY KINK IDIOM QUIRK
TRAIT TRICK TWIST IDIASM
ODDITY AEOLISM FEATURE
IRISHRY CROTCHET HEADMARK
MANNERISM PROPRIETY
SINGULARITY
(— IN BOWL) BIAS
(— OF SPEECH) IDIOLOGISM
(CROTCHETY —) FIKE
PECUNIARY POCKET MONETARY
FINANCIAL
PED BASKET HAMPER PANIER
PEDAGOGUE TUTOR PEDANT
DOMINIE SQUEERS TEACHER
THWACKUM
PEDAGOGY SCHOOL DIDACTICS
EDUCATION
PEDAHEL (FATHER OF —) AMMIHUD
PEDAHZUR (SON OF —) GAMALIEL
PEDAIAH (BROTHER OF —)
SALATHIEL
(DAUGHTER OF —) ZEBUDAH
(FATHER OF —) PAROSH
(SON OF —) JOEL
PEDAL LEVER SWELL TREADLE
FOOTFEED PEDALIAN THROTTLE
(— COUPLER) TIRASSE
(PIANO —) CELESTE
PEDANT PRIG DUNCE TUTOR
DORBEL PURIST TASSEL
ACADEME PEDAGOG GAMALIEL
DRYASDUST OLOFERNES
PEDANTIC BLUE STODGY BOOKISH
DONNISH ERUDITE INKHORN
TEACHING SCHOLASTIC
PEDDLE HAWK SELL CADGE SHOVE
TRANT TRUCK HIGGLE MEDDLE

PIDDLE RETAIL COLPORT
PEDDLER ARAB SMOUS BADGER
BODGER CRAMER JAGGER
JOWTER MUGGER STROLL
WALKER YAGGER NIGGLER
PACKMAN ROADMAN SANDBOY
SWADDER TROGGER TRUCKER
HUCKSTER BOXWALLAH
DUSTYFOOT
(— OF DOPE) FIXER
(— OF DRESS PIECES) DUDDER
(— OF FISH) RIPIER RIPPIER
(— OF SHAM JEWELRY) DUFFER
(BOOK —) COLPORTEUR
(ITINERANT —) SMOUS SMOUSE
SMOUSER STROLLER
(MOHAM. —) BORA
(STREET —) CAMELOT
(WARES OF —) TROGGIN
PEDESTAL ANTA BASE BASIS
BLOCK SOCLE STAND PILLAR
PODIUM ROCKER AKROTER
SUPPORT PADMASANA
ACROTERIUM
PEDESTRIAN PED DULL FOOT
SLOW HIKER FOOTER HOOFER
WALKER FOOTMAN PROSAIC
PLODDING WINGLESS
PONDEROUS VOETGANGER
PERIPATETIC
PEDICEL RAY STEM SCAPE STALK
PEDUNCLE FOOTSTALK
PEDIGREE STEMMA DESCENT
LINEAGE ANCESTRY PETEGREU
PUREBRED
PEDIMENT FRONTAL FRONTON
FASTIGIUM
PEDIPALP
(PL.) LABIUM
PEDOMETER ODOGRAPH
WAYWISER
PEDRERO PERRIER PETRARY
PEDUNCLE STEM SCAPE STALK
STIPES PEDICEL EYESTALK
HYPOCARP
(PL.) CRURA
PEEK PEEP PIKE GLANCE GLIMPSE
PEEKABOO PEEP BOPEEP PEEPEYE
PEEL BARK HARL HULL HUSK PARE
RIND SKIN FLAKE FLIPE SCALE
SLIPE STAKE STRIP CORTEX
SHOVEL SPITTLE UNDRESS
BARKPEEL ORANGEADO
(— OFF) HARL CRAZE FLAKE
SHUCK
(BAKER'S —) PALE SPITTLE
(ORANGE OR LEMON —) ZEST
ORANGEAT
PEELER CRAB BOBBY CORER
HUSTLER SHEDDER SPUDDER
PILLAGER
PEELING RIND SKIN PARING
PARURE
PEEN PIN PYNE RIVET
PEEP PIP PRY SPY COOK JEEP KEEK
KOOK PEEK PEER PINK PULE SKEG
STEP TOOT TOTE TOUT CHEEP
CHIRP DEKKO GLINT PIPIT SNOOP
TWEET DEGREE GLANCE SQUEAK
SQUINNY PEEKABOO
(— SHOW) RAREE
PEEPER EYE TOM FROG KEEK
VOYEUR

PEEPHOLE PEEP JUDAS EYELET
CREVICE
PEEPING NOSY PRYING
PEER PRY DUKE EARL FEAR GAZE
LOOK LORD MATE PEEP PINK
TOOT TOUT BARON EQUAL GLINT
GLOZE MATCH NOBLE RIVAL
STARE STIME THANE TWIRE
APPEAR FELLOW OLIVER PINKER
COMPERE
PEERAGE RANK DEBRETT DIGNITY
BARONAGE NOBILITY TENEMENT
PEER GYNT (AUTHOR OF —) IBSEN
(CHARACTER IN —) ASE BOYG
GYNT PEER ANITRA HEGSTAD
SOLVEIG
PEERING SQUINNY
PEERLESS SUPREME MATCHLESS
NONPAREIL UNRIVALED
PEESWEEP FINCH PEWIT LAPWING
PEEWEEP
PEEVE IRK ANNOY GRUDGE NETTLE
IRRITATE
PEEVISH SOUR CROSS DORTY
PENSY SNACK TECHY TEENY
TESTY TETTY THRAW TIFFY
WEMOD CRUSTY FRANZY GIRNIE
HIPPED PATCHY SNARLY SNUFFY
SULLEN TATTER TOUCHY TWARLY
TWAZZY TWITTY UPPISH UPPITY
VAPORY CRABBED FRATCHY
FRECKET FRETFUL FROWARD
GROUCHY PETTISH SPLEENY
TEDIOUS TIFFISH WASPISH
CAPTIOUS PERVERSE PHRAMPEL
PINDLING SANSHACH TWANKING
FRAMPOLD,PETULANT
PEEVISHLY CRUSTILY
PEEVISHNESS PET PETULANCE
PEEWEE BOOT RUNT TINY PEWEE
MARBLE LAPWING
PEG FIX HOB HUB NOB NOG PIN
HOBB KING KNAG PLUG SCOB
SHAG SKEG STEP CLEAT DOWEL
DRINK NOTCH PERCH PITON
PRONG SPELL SPILE SPILL STAKE
THOLE THROW TOOTH WADDY
DEGREE DOWELL FAUCET
MARKER NORMAN PICKET
REASON SPIGOT TAPOUN TIPCAT
PINNING PRETEXT SCOLLOP
SPERKET SUPPORT TRENAIL
(— FOR PLAYING GAME) CAT
SPILIKIN
(— FOR SADDLES) SPERKET
(— OF STRINGED INSTRUMENT)
CHEVILLE
(— OUT) DIE FAIL
(BELAYING —) KEVEL
(IRON —) PITON
(THATCH —) SCOB
PEGA REMORA
PEGALL BASKET PACKALL
PEGASUS QUAVIVER HYPOSTOME
PEG TOP PIRY PEERY PEERIE
PEG WOFFINGTON (AUTHOR OF —)
READE
(CHARACTER IN —) PEG RICH VANE
HARRY MABEL CIBBER COLLEY
CHARLES TRIPLET POMANDER
WOFFINGTON BRACEGIRDLE
PEIGNOIR GOWN DRESS KIMONO
NEGLIGEE

PEISE BLOW FORCE PASSE POISE POIZE IMPACT WEIGHT BALANCE POISURE

PEKAH (FATHER OF —) REMALIAH
(SLAYER OF —) HOSHEA

PEKAHIAH (FATHER OF —) MENAHEM
(SLAYER OF —) PEKAH

PEKAN WEJACK

PEKING MAN SINANTHROPUS

PELAGE FUR COAT HAIR PILAGE

PELAGIC MARINE AQUATIC OCEANIC PELAGIAN

PELAIAH (FATHER OF —) ELIOENAI

PELALIAH (FATHER OF —) AMZI

PELATIAH (FATHER OF —) BENAIAH HANANIAH

PELEG (BROTHER OF —) JOKTAN
(FATHER OF —) EBER

PELET (FATHER OF —) JAHDAI AZMAVETH

PELETH (FATHER OF —) JONATHAN
(SON OF —) ON

PELEUS (BROTHER OF —) TELAMON
(FATHER OF —) AEACUS
(HALF-BROTHER OF —) PHOCUS
(MOTHER OF —) ENDEIS
(SON OF —) PELIDES ACHILLES
(WIFE OF —) THETIS ANTIGONE

PELF GAIN BOOTY LUCRE MONEY SPOIL TRASH PILFER PILFRE REFUSE RICHES WEALTH COMPOST

PELIAS (BROTHER OF —) NELEUS
(DAUGHTER OF —) ALCESTIS
(FATHER OF —) POSEIDON
(MOTHER OF —) TYRO
(SON OF —) ACASTUS
(WIFE OF —) ANAXIBIA PHYLOMACHE

PELICAN DOVE ALCATRAS ONOCROTAL
(— STATE) LOUISIANA

PELISSE POSTIN POSTEEN

PELL BEAT PELE PELT HURRY PEELE HASTEN

PELLAGRA MAIDISM PELAGRA

PELLEAS (BELOVED OF —) MELISANDE
(BROTHER OF —) GOLAUD

PELLEAS ET MELISANDE
(CHARACTER IN —) ARKEL GOLAUD YNIOLD PELLEAS ALLEMONDE GENEVIEVE MELISANDE
(COMPOSER OF —) DEBUSSY

PELLES (DAUGHTER OF —) ELAINE

PELLET BB WAD BALL CAST PILL SHOT BOLUS PRILL STONE BEEBEE BULLET FECULA OGRESS PILULE CASTING GRANULE PALLION TRATTLE BUCKSHOT GUNSTONE HAILSTONE
(SNOW —S) GRAUPEL
(PL.) SHOT

PELLICLE FILM SCUM SKIN CRUST CUTICLE EPISTASIS

PELLINORE (SLAYER OF —) GAWAIN
(SON OF —) TORRE DORNAR LAMEROK PERCIVAL AGGLOVALE

PELLITORY BERTRAM BERTRUM WALLWORT

PELL-MELL RUSH MELPELL DISORDER HEADLONG

PELLOCK PALACH PORPOISE

PELLUCID CLEAR BRIGHT LIMPID ORIENT CRYSTAL

PELMA TRACK

PELMET CORNICE VALANCE PALMETTE

PELOPONNESUS (CITY OF —) SPARTA
(PEOPLE OF —) MOREOTE
(RIVER GOD OF —) ALPHEUS

PELOPS (FATHER OF —) TANTALUS
(SON OF —) ATREUS TROEZEN PITTHEUS THYESTES
(WIFE OF —) HIPPODAMIA

PELORIA EPANODY

PELT FUR KIT BEAR BEAT BLOW CAPE CAST CLOD COON DASH FELL HIDE HURL KITT PELL PUSH RACK SKIN BESET CHUNK FITCH HURRY SABLE SLASH SPEED STONE WHACK BADGER BEAVER FISHER PELTER PEPPER SERVAL SPRING BETHUMP COONSKIN
(— OF SEAL, WITH BLUBBER) SCULP
(— WITH MISSILES) BUM SQUAIL
(— WITH STONES) LAPIDATE
(BEAVER —) BLANKET

PELTAST SOLDIER TARGETEER

PELTATE SCUTATE

PELTER SKEET

PELTING SLASHING

PELTRY FURS SKINS

PELUDO POYOU ARMADILLO

PELVIS
(PREF.) PELVI(O) PELYCO PYEL(O)
(SUFF.) PELLIC

PEN COT CUB GET HOK MEW PAR PIN STY BOLT CAGE COOP CROO CROW FAUD FOLD JAIL STUB WALK YARD BUGHT CRAWL CREEP CUBBY HUTCH KRAAL POINT QUILL STYLE WRITE BOUGHT CORRAL CRUIVE FASTEN FLIGHT HURDLE INDITE RECORD STYLUS ZAREBA CONFINE WARKLOOM
(— CATTLE) STANCE
(— FOR CATTLE) CUB LOT CREW CRUE LAIR REEVE
(— FOR ELEPHANTS) KRAAL
(— FOR HOGS OR SLAVES) CRAWL
(— OF CUTTLEFISH) GLADIUS
(— POINT) NEB NIB STUB
(— UP) FRANK STIVE
(AUTHOR'S —) STYLE STYLUS
(FOUNTAIN —) STICK
(MUSIC —) RASTRUM
(REED —) CALAMUS

PENALIZE CHECK

PENALTY BETE CAIN DOOM FINE LOSS PAIN BEAST JUISE MULCT AMENDE AMERCE SOLACE FORFEIT NEMESIS SURSIZE BLOODWIT HARDSHIP SCAFFOLD
(DRINKING —) KELTIE

PENANCE TAP SORE SHRIFT SORROW REMORSE SUFFERING

PEN CASE PENNER POPPET

PENCEL FLAG PENNON STREAMER PENNONCEL

PENCHANT BENT TASTE FOIBLE GENIUS LIKING LEANING FONDNESS

PENCIL PEN RED WAD BLUE LEAD WADD LINER SHEAF SKETCH STYLUS POINTEL CHARCOAL KEELIVINE
(PART OF —) CASE LEAD POINT ERASER FERRULE SHOULDER
(SLATE —) CAM CALM SKAILLIE
(PL.) STATIONERY
(PREF.) PENCILLI PENICILLI

PENCILWOOD MORDORE

PENDANT BOB JAG DROP FLAG JAGG PEND TAIL AGLET BULLA GUTTA POINT AIGLET LUSTER PALAOA PLAYER TABARD TARGET TASSEL EARDROP LANGUET SUPPORT LAVALIER

PENDENNIS (AUTHOR OF —) THACKERAY
(CHARACTER IN —) BELL AMORY EMILY FANNY FOKER HELEN HENRY LAURA ARTHUR BOLTON GEORGE JEMIMA BLANCHE FRANCIS ALTAMONT COSTIGAN CLAVERING PENDENNIS WARRINGTON THISTLEWOOD

PENDENT LOP BAGGED ICICLE HANGING PROMISS

PENDICLE POFFLE

PENDULOUS LOP SLOUCH HANGING NODDING PENSILE CERNUOUS DROOPING

PENDULUM SWING PENDLE SWINGEL SWINGLE VIBRATILE
(INVERTED —) NODDY

PENELOPE (FATHER OF —) ICARIUS
(FATHER-IN-LAW OF —) LAERTES
(HUSBAND OF —) ULYSSES ODYSSEUS
(MOTHER OF —) PERIBOEA
(SON OF —) TELEMACHUS
(SUITOR OF —) AGELAUS

PENEPLAIN STRATH ENDRUMPF

PENETRABLE PERVIOUS

PENETRATE CUT DIG DIP SEE BITE BORE DIVE GORE PASS PINK SINK STAB WADE BREAK DRILL DRIVE ENTER IMBUE PROBE SEIZE THIRL CLEAVE FATHOM FICCHE GIMLET INVADE PIERCE RIDDLE SEARCH STRIKE THRILL WIMBLE DISCERN PERVADE PERCOLATE PERFORATE
(— MENTALLY) ENTER
(— ONE'S MIND) SOAK

PENETRATED (EASILY —) MELLOW

PENETRATING ACID KEEN ACUTE LEVEL NASAL SHARP ASTUTE DEADLY SHREWD SHRILL SUBTLE GIMLETY INGOING INTRANT KNOWING PUNGENT PERCEANT PIERCING REACHING TRENCHANT

PENETRATION DEPTH ACUMEN FATHOM INROAD INGOING INSIGHT SEEPAGE INCISION INVASION SAGACITY

PENEUS (DAUGHTER OF —) DAPHNE
(FATHER OF —) OCEANUS
(MOTHER OF —) TETHYS
(SON OF —) HYPSEUS

PENGUIN AUK DIVER GENTU ARCTIC DIPPER GENTOO JOHNNY PINWING BREVIPED MACARONI
(PL.) IMPENNES
(PREF.) SPHENISCI SPHENISCO

PENGUIN ISLAND (AUTHOR OF —) FRANCE
(CHARACTER IN —) MAEL CLENA CRRES DRACO OLIVE PYROT TALPA AGARIC KRAKEN TRINCO VISIRE EVELINE BOSCENOS CLARENCE GREATANK JOHANNES OBEROSIA CHATILLON MARBODIUS

PENINNAH (HUSBAND OF —) ELKANAH
(SON OF —) SAMUEL

PENINSULA CAPE MULL NECK INDIA BILAND BYLAND ISLAND PENILE CHERSONESE

PENIS
(PREF.) BALAN(I)(O) PHALL(O) POSTH(E)(IO)(O)

PENITENCE RUE REGRET SORROW PENANCE PENANCY REMORSE

PENITENT RUER SORRY HUMBLE WEEPER MOURNER STANDER CONTRITE
(— OF 3RD STAGE) KNEELER

PENITENTIARY JUG PEN JAIL STIR TENCH PRISON PENITENT

PENMAN CLERK AUTHOR SCRIBE WRITER

PENMANSHIP HAND SCRIPT PENSHIP WRITING

PENNANT FANE FLAG WHIP COLOR ROGER BANNER CORNET ENSIGN PENCIL PENNON PENSIL PINION PINNET MEATBALL REPEATER STREAMER

PENNILESS POOR BROKE NEEDY BANKRUPT INDIGENT STRAPPED PLACKLESS

PENNON FLAG VANE WING ANVIL BANNER PENCIL PENOUN PINION FEATHER GONFANON

PENNON SPAR PEGGYMAST

PENNSYLVANIA
CAPITAL: HARRISBURG
COLLEGE: JUNIATA URSINUS LYCOMING
COUNTY: ELK ERIE PIKE YORK BERKS BUCKS PERRY TIOGA LEHIGH CAMBRIA JUNIATA LUZERNE VENANGO WYOMING LYCOMING
MOUNTAIN RANGE: POCONO ALLEGHENY
NATIVE: AMISH DUTCH
PRESIDENT: BUCHANAN
RIVER: LEHIGH CLARION JUNIATA LICKING TOWANDA CALDWELL DELAWARE SCHRADER ALLEGHENY SCHUYLKILL MONONGAHELA SUSQUEHANNA
STATE BIRD: GROUSE
STATE FLOWER: LAUREL
STATE NICKNAME: KEYSTONE
STATE TREE: HEMLOCK
TOWN: ERIE ETNA PLUM YORK AVOCA MEDIA EASTON EMMAUS SHARON ALTOONA EPHRATA HERSHEY READING TOWANDA BRYNMAWR SCRANTON SHAMOKIN BETHLEHEM CHARLEROI GETTYSBURG PITTSBURGH

UNIVERSITY: PITT DREXEL LEHIGH TEMPLE BUCKNELL DUQUESNE VILLANOVA

PENNY DY AES MEG RED SOU WIN GILL WING WINN BROON BROWN OULAP PENCE COPPER FOLLIS SALTEE STIVER BROWNIE STERLING
   (— DREADFUL) HORRIBLE
   (DUTCH —) STIVER
   (HALF —) HALFLIN
   (OLD SCOTCH —) TURNER
   (PL.) PENCE FOLLES
PENNYCRESS FANWEED STINKWEED
PENNY-PINCHING STINGY
PENNYROYAL PULIOL HEDEOMA HILLWORT TICKWEED SQUAWWEED
PENNYWEIGHT DWT PENNY WEIGHT STERLING
PENNYWORT ROTGRASS
PENROD (AUTHOR OF —) TARKINGTON
   (CHARACTER IN —) CRIM JONES SARAH PENROD MARJORIE SCHOFIELD
PENSION WAGE PAYMENT STIPEND SUBSIDY TRIBUTE GRATUITY MALIKANA
PENSIONER COD
PENSIVE MESTO MOODY PENSY SOBER DREAMY MUSING PENCEY WISTFUL THOUGHTY MELANCHOLY
PENT CAGED PENNED CONFINED ENCLOSED RESERVOIR
PENTACLE STAR HEXAGRAM PENTAGRAM
PENTAD QUINTAD
PENTASTICH POEM UNIT STANZA STROPHE
PENTATEUCH TORAH
PENTECOST SHABUOTH WHITSUNDAY
PENTHESILEA (SLAYER OF —) ACHILLES
PENTHEUS (FATHER OF —) ECHION
   (GRANDFATHER OF —) CADMUS
   (MOTHER OF —) AGAVE
PENTHOUSE CAT PENT ROOF SHED AERIE ANNEX HANGAR LOOKUM SHADOW PLUTEUS BULKHEAD SKEELING SKILLION APPENTICE
PENTOSAN ARABAN
PENTOSE APIOSE RIBOSE
PENTYL AMYL
PENURIOUS MEAN POOR BARREN SCANTY STINGY MISERLY WANTING INDIGENT HIDEBOUND NIGGARDLY
PENURY WANT BEGGARY BORASCO POVERTY SCARCITY INDIGENCE PRIVATION
PEON HAND PAWN SERF SLAVE PELADO THRALL FOOTMAN LABORER PEASANT SOLDIER CONSTABLE
PEONY PINY MOUTAN
PEOPLE (ALSO SEE NATIVE AND TRIBE) ARO FUL LOG MEN PUL TAT VAI YAO AKRA ASHA BENI BUGI CHIN CHUD EMIM FOLK FULA GARO GENS HERD HIMA HUMA IRON LAND LEDE LUBA LURI PHUD PHUL PHUT RACE RAIS REMI SAFI SARA SEBA SERE TEMA THEY TODA TOMA TULU USUN VITI VOLK WARE AFIFI AVARS BENIN BONGO CATTI CHAGA COURS DEMOS DUALA EDONI ELYMI FOLKS FULAH GENTE GOMER HAUSA JACKS KAREN LAITY LANAO LENDU LUREM MARSI MASAI NOGAI ORANG PUNAN QUADI RAMBO ROTSE SACAE SALAR SAURA SHAKA STOCK TAURI VOLTA WARUA WORLD ABABUA ACHUAS AFSHAR AISSOR ANGAMI ANGLES ARUNTA AVIKOM BAHIMA BAKELE BAKUBA BALUBA BELTIR BOSHAS BULLOM CIMBRI COMMON DAOINE GENTRY GILAKI GILEKI HAUSSA HERERO HERULI KANWAR KPUESI KRUMAN MANTZU MINYAE MOSCHI NATION OVAMPO PAMIRI PUBLIC RAMUSI RUTULI SAFINI SAMBAL SATRAE SEMANG SHARRA TADJIK TAGAUR TELUGU TUNGUZ TURSHA VENETI VOLCAE WACAGO WAHIMA YNDOYS YUECHI ZAMBAL ACHANGO ASTOMOI BAGANDA BAGARRA BAKALAI BANGALA BANGASH BAROTSE BUNYORO DARDANI DENIZEN DURZADA FALISCI GAETULI GENERAL GEPIDAE GOAJIRO GUHAYNA INHABIT IRISHRY ISSEDOI ITALICI KINDRED KURANKO MAKONDE MESHECH MITANNI NABALOI PICENES PICTAVI PUKHTUN ROHILLA SAMBURU SENONES SILURES SUKKIIM TIRURAI VESTINI WABUNGA WACHAGA WAKAMBA WANGONI POPULATE
   (— HAVING DISTINCT LANGUAGE) TONGUE
   (— OF FASHION) FLOSS
   (— OF GOOD BREEDING) GENTRY GENTILITY
   (ABORIGINAL —) JAKUN KHMER KODAGU SEKHWAN
   (ANCIENT —) CARA CHAM JUNG ELYMI GETAE HURRI ICENI SACAE SERES SICULI DARDANI FALISCI FIRBOLG KIPCHAK SEQUANI SILURES
   (BIBLICAL —) ALUR IBAD IBAN MAGOG IBANAG SOMALI GADDANG
   (CAVE-DWELLING —) HORITE
   (COMMON —) DEMOS PLEBE VULGAR VULGUS TILIKUM SNOBBERY
   (EXTINCT —) KOT CHONO COFAN COREE CHANGO CHATOT GUINAU HIBITO SAPONI SHIRINO
   (FOREST —) SAKAI SAORA SAURA
   (HONORABLE —) HONESTY
   (LOWEST CLASS OF —) CANAILLE
   (MARITIME —) LAMUT
   (MOUNTAIN —) HUZUL HUTZUL
   (NOMADIC —) SHUA HORDE IGDYR IHLAT SHUWA HABIRU SHAGIA SARACEN SHAMMAR SHORTZY SHUKRIA
   (OLD —) ANCIENTRY
   (ORDINARY —) LAYFOLK
   (PAGAN —) IRAYA HANUNOO SUBANUN
   (POWERFUL GROUP OF —) MAFIA
   (PRIMITIVE —) DAFLA IRULA KADIR KURUKH CHENCHU
   (WHITE —) ALBICULI
   (PL.) MAKHZAN
   (PREF.) DEM(O) ETHN(O) PLEBI POPULI
PEOPLED ABAD SETTLED POPULATE
PEORIA MASCOUTEN
PEP GO VIM DASH MOXIE VERVE VIGOR ENERGY GINGER ANIMATE QUICKEN ACTIVITY
PEPLUM GOWN SKIRT TUNIC PEPLOS OVERSKIRT
PEPO GOURD MELON SQUASH PUMPKIN PEPONIDA PEPONIUM
PEPPER CAVA IKMO ITMO KAVA SIRI BETEL CHILI MANGO PIPER SIRIH MATICO TOPEPO CAYENNE PAPRIKA PIMENTA RELIENO JALAPENO KAVAKAVA
   (JAVA —) CUBEB
   (RED —) LADYFINGER
   (PREF.) PIPERI PIPERO
PEPPER-AND-SALT JASPER
PEPPERGRASS CRESS CANARY ANOUNOU COCKWEED
PEPPERMINT MENTHE LABIATE
PEPPER TREE MOLLE HOROPITO PIMIENTO
PEPPERWORT DITTANDER
PEPPERY HOT FIERY SAUCY SPICY TOUCHY PIQUANT PUNGENT SPIRITED STINGING
PEPPY GINGERY
PEPTIDE KININ
PEPTONE ASCARON
PER BY THE EACH THROUGH
PERADVENTURE HAP DOUBT MAYBE CHANCE MAPPEN MAYHAP HAPPILY PERHAPS POSSIBLY
PERAMBULATE WALK RAMBLE STROLL PERAMBLE TRAVERSE
PERAMBULATION WEND
PERAMBULATOR BUGGY WAGON BASSINET VIAMETER WAYWISER PEDOMETER
PERATE OPHITE
PERCEIVE SEE ESPY FEEL FIND GAUM HEAR KNOW LOOK MIND NOTE SCAN TWIG SCENT SENSE SMELL TASTE TOUCH BEHOLD COTTON DESCRY DIVINE FIGURE NOTICE REMARK SURVEY COGNIZE DISCERN OBSERVE REALIZE SENSATE COMPRISE DESCRIBE UNDERNIM RECOGNIZE
PERCENTAGE CUT AGIO PART SHARE PROFIT PORTION SCALAGE CONTANGO DEFLATOR PROPORTION
   (MINING —) LEY

PERCEPT IDEA
PERCEPTIBLE PUBLIC NOTABLE TACTILE VISIBLE APPARENT PALPABLE SENSIBLE TANGIBLE TRACTABLE PERCEIVABLE
   (FAINTLY —) SHADOWY
   (HARDLY —) FAINT
   (PREF.) ESTHETO
PERCEPTION RAY BUMP GAUM TACT SAVOR SCENT SENSE SIGHT ACUMEN VISION CLOSURE FEELING GLIMMER NOSTRIL BEARINGS DELICACY OUTSIGHT COGNITION SENSATION SENTIMENT
   (DIM —) GLIMMER
   (MENTAL —) TACT TOUCH SENSATION
   (SPIRITUAL —) WISDOM
PERCEPTIVE ACUTE QUICK SHARP SUBTLE KNOWING PIERCING SENSITIVE
PERCH BAR BAS LUG PEG ROD SIT BASS JOUK MADO OKOW PERK PIKE POLE POPE RUFF SEAT BARSE BEGTI BEKTI BLOCK LIGHT REACH ROOST RUFFE STAFF STANG ALIGHT BUGARA CALLOP COMBER PERCID SANDER SAUGER SETTLE ZANDER ZINGEL ALFIONE HOGFISH STATION ROCKFISH MARTENIKO TRUMPETER MADEMOISELLE
   (2-YEAR OLD —) EGLING
   (PREF.) PERCI
PERCHANCE HAPLY MAYBE AUNTERS FORTUNE PERHAPS POSSIBLY
PERCHER STAKER
PERCHTA BERTHA
PERCOLATE MELT OOZE PERK SEEP SIFT SILT SIPE SOAK WEEP DRILL EXUDE LEACH EXHALE FILTER STRAIN
PERCOLATION SIPING SEEPAGE LEACHING
PERCOLATOR SIPER BIGGIN CAFETIERE DISPLACER
PERCUSSION BLOW IMPACT STROKE PNEUMATIC
   (— IN MASSAGE) TAPOTEMENT
PERDITA (FATHER OF —) LEONTES
   (MOTHER OF —) HERMIONE
PERDITION HELL LOSS RUIN BOWWOWS BALLYWACK DAMNATION
PEREGRINATE TOUR WALK TRAVEL WANDER JOURNEY SOJOURN TRAVERSE
PEREGRINE ALIEN EXOTIC ROVING PILGRIM STRANGE IMPORTED
PEREGRINE FALCON SAKER GENTLE TASSEL TERCEL
PEREGRINE PICKLE (AUTHOR OF —) SMOLLETT
   (CHARACTER IN —) TOM VANE PIPES SALLY EMILIA HAWSER PICKLE APPLEBY GRIZZLE GAMALIEL GAUNTLET HATCHWAY HORNBECK TRUNNION PEREGRINE CADWALLADER
PEREMPT QUASH DEFEAT DESTROY

PEREMPTORY FLAT FINAL UTTER EXPRESS HAUGHTY ABSOLUTE DECISIVE DOGMATIC POSITIVE ESSENTIAL MASTERFUL

PERENNIAL HERB CAREX LIANA PEONY SEDUM BANANA CENTRO BLUEWEED CONSTANT ENDURING KNAPWEED TOADFLAX CONTINUAL EVERGREEN PENNYWORT PERPETUAL RECURRENT

PERESH (FATHER OF —) MACHIR (MOTHER OF —) MAACHAH

PERFECT ALL AOK BACK BORN CURE FILL FINE FULL HOLY PURE SURE EXACT FINAL FULLY IDEAL PLAIN RIGHT RIPEN SHEER SOUND TOTAL UTTER WHOLE ENTIRE EXPERT FINISH MATURE POLISH REFINE SPHERE CERTAIN CONCOCT CONTENT CORRECT CROWNED DEVELOP GEMLIKE IMPROVE PLENARY PRECISE SINLESS SPHERAL TYPICAL COMPLETE COPYBOOK FLAWLESS INFINITE INTEGRAL REPLENISH (— IN RIGHTEOUSNESS) HOLY (— SCORE) MAX (PREF.) TEL(E)(EO)

PERFECTA EXACTA

PERFECTED EXACT SUMMED FINISHED PERQUEIR

PERFECTION ACME BEST PINK BLOOM IDEAL BEAUTY FINISH PLENTY FULLNESS PARAGON FINALITY FINENESS MATURITY RIPENESS ERUDITION (STATE OF —) SIDDHI (TYPE OF —) PARAGON

PERFECTIVE TELIC

PERFECTLY SPAN QUITE IDEALLY PERQUEIR

PERFIDIOUS FALSE SNAKY DISLEAL SNAKISH DISLOYAL SPITEFUL FAITHLESS

PERFIDY DECEIT TREASON FALSEHOOD FALSENESS TREACHERY

PERFORATE EAT DOCK HOLE DRILL PRICK PUNCH SIEVE THIRL PIERCE POUNCE RIDDLE THRILL PINHOLE PUNCTURE PENETRATE TEREBRATE (— A STAMP) CENTER

PERFORATED OPEN CRIBROSE

PERFORATION BORE HOLE THIRL TORET BROACH EYELET STIGMA TRESIS FORAMEN PINHOLE SEPTULA STENCIL FENESTRA DIABROSIS PERTUSION (SUFF.) TRESIA

PERFORM DO ACT CUT KIP CHAR FILL FULL HAVE KEEP LAST MAKE PLAY SHOW STEP CHARE DIGHT ENACT EXERT FETCH ACQUIT COMMIT EFFECT FULFIL RENDER ACHIEVE EXECUTE EXHIBIT EXPLOIT FUNGIFY FURNISH IWURCHE OPERATE PRESENT PRESTATE PROSECUTE (— AWKWARDLY) BOGGLE (— BADLY) BOLLIX (— BRILLIANTLY) STAR SPARKLE

(— CLUMSILY) THUMB BUNGLE (— FULLY) END (— HASTILY) SKIMP SCAMP, (— HURRIEDLY) SLUR (— IN DANCING) FIGURE (FAIL TO — EFFECTIVELY) CHOKE

PERFORMANCE ACT JOB DEED FEAT HAND SHOW TEST WORK CAPER SLANG SPORT STUNT ACTING ACTION BALLET EFFECT HORARY MASQUE ACCOUNT ACROAMA BENEFIT BOOKING CONCERT EXPLOIT MATINEE MUMMERY RELEASE SHOWING FAREWELL FUNCTION PRACTICE STERACLE OPERATION (— FOR ONE) SOLO (— OF DUTY) FEASANCE (— OF OBLIGATION) SOLUTIO (— VARIATIONS) COUNTER (— WITH SENTIMENTALITY) DROOL (ARAB —) FANTASIA (BRILLIANT —) BRAVURA (CHRISTMAS EVE —) GOMBAY (CLUMSY —) BUNGLE (DRAMATIC —) TOPENG PANTOMIME (FIRST —) OPENING PREMIERE (INEPT —) BOMB (NO —) RELACHE (PAST —) FORM (TRIAL —) AUDITION (VULGAR —) BLOWOFF (WRONG —) MISPRISION (SUFF.) LOG(ER)(IA)(IAN)(IC)(ICAL) (IST)(UE)(Y)

PERFORMER ACT DOER GEEK MOKE STAR ACTOR SHINE ARTIST DANCER KINKER LEADER PLAYER WORKER ACROAMA ACROBAT ARTISTE GAMBIST HORNIST HOTSHOT SOLOIST EXECUTOR SPARKLER HAMFATTER HEADLINER (— ON SEVERAL INSTRUMENTS) MOKE (— WITH NEGRO DIALECT) HAMBONE (BURLESQUE —) GRINDER (CIRCUS —) LEAPER (INFERIOR —) HAM SHINE (SUFF.) ANT ENT

PERFUME ATAR BALM FUME MUSK NOSE OTTO AROMA ATTAR CENSE CIVET MYRRH SCENT SMELL SPICE CARVOL CHYPRE EMBALM FLAVOR IONONE BOUQUET CARVONE DIAPASM ESSENCE INCENSE JASMINE NOSEGAY ODORIZE SWEETEN BERGAMOT MARECHAL ORANGERY PATCHOULI (— BASE) MUSK CIVET NEROL NEROLI (POWDERY —) PULVIL

PERFUNCTORY CURSORY CARELESS SLIPSHOD SLOVENLY APATHETIC

PERGOLA ARBOR BOWER RAMADA BALCONY TRELLIS

PERHAPS HAPS MAYBE ABLINS BELIKE HAPPEN MAPPEN MAYHAP ABLINGS AIBLINS

LIGHTLY PERCASE YIBBLES POSSIBLY PERCHANCE

PERI ELF FAIRY SPRITE

PERIAPT CHARM AMULET

PERICARP BUR BOLL BURR BLADDER

PERICHOLE, LA (CHARACTER IN —) ABDRES PIQUILLO PERICHOLE (COMPOSER OF —) OFFENBACH

PERICLES (AUTHOR OF —) SHAKESPEARE (CHARACTER IN —) BOULT CLEON DIANA GOWER MARINA THAISA CERIMON DIONYZA ESCANES LEONINE PERICLES PHILEMON THALIARD ANTIOCHUS HELICANUS LYCHORIDA SIMONIDES LYSIMACHUS (FATHER OF —) XANTHIPPUS (MISTRESS OF —) ASPASIA (MOTHER OF —) AGARISTE (SON OF —) PARALUS XANTHIPPUS (TEACHER OF —) ZENO DAMON

PERICLYMENUS (BROTHER OF —) NESTOR (FATHER OF —) NELEUS POSEIDON (MOTHER OF —) CHLORIS MELIBOEA

PERICRANIUM HEAD BRAIN

PERIDOTITE PICRITE EULYSITE JOSEFITE SAXONITE WEHRLITE

PERIERES (FATHER OF —) AEOLUS (MOTHER OF —) ENARETE (SON OF —) APHAREUS LEUCIPPUS (WIFE OF —) GORGOPHONE

PERIGEE EPIGEUM

PERIGYNIUM UTRICLE

PERIL RISK WERE WATHE CRISIS DANGER HAZARD MENACE SCYLLA THREAT THRONG TRANCE DISTRESS JEOPARDY CHARYBDIS

PERILOUS KITTLE DOUBTFUL DREADFUL INFAMOUS DANGEROUS HAZARDOUS

PERIMETER RIM CIRCUIT OUTLINE BOUNDARY PERIPHERY

PERIOD GO AGE DOT END EON ERA AEON DATE LIFE RACE SPAN STOP TERM TIDE TIME YEAR AVAIL CLOSE CYCLE EPACT EPOCH LABOR LAPSE PATCH POINT SPACE SPELL STAGE CUTOFF GHURRY HEMERA MOMENT PARODY PICTUN SEASON STOUND ACCOUNT DICOLON FLORUIT PASTIME SESSION STADIUM STRETCH DURATION INDUCIAE INSTANCE LIFETIME SENTENCE (— ENDING FROST) FRESH (— FOR WHICH ENJOYED) TENURE (— IN DEVELOPMENT) STAGE (— OF ACTION) GO BOUT (— OF DECLINE) SUNSET EVENING (— OF DRYNESS) DROUTH DROUGHT (— OF FAIR WEATHER) SLATCH (— OF FESTIVITY) WAKES (— OF GLOOM) DEAD (— OF GRACE) DAY (— OF HAPPINESS) MILLENNIUM (— OF HEAT) CALLING (— OF HUMID WEATHER) SIZZARD

(— OF IMMATURITY) SWADDLE (— OF INSTRUCTION) LESSON (— OF LIFE) AGE ELD SPAN (— OF MILITARY SERVICE) HITCH (— OF MOTILITY) SWARMING (— OF MOURNING) SHIVA SHIBAH (— OF PERFORMING) STANZA (— OF PLAY) HALF CHUKKER QUARTER (— OF RECREATION) HOLIDAY VACATION (— OF REMISSION) JUBILEE (— OF REST) SMOKO BREATHER (— OF REVOLUTION OF HEAVENLY BODY) ORB (— OF TIME) DAY HOUR WEEK YEAR MONTH DECADE MINUTE SECOND (— OF WORK) SHIFT SPELL STINT (— OF 10 YEARS) DECADE (— OF 100 YEARS) AGE CENTURY (— OF 1000 YEARS) CHILIAD MILLIAD (— OF 14 MINUTES, 24 SECONDS) CENTIDAY (— OF 2 MONTHS) DIMESTER (— OF 2 YEARS) BIENNIUM (— OF 20 TUNS) KATUN (— OF 20 YEARS) KATUN (— OF 260 DAYS) TONALMATL (— OF 4 YEARS) QUADRENNIUM (— OF 5 DAYS) PENTAD (— OF 5 YEARS) LUSTRE LUSTRUM (— OF 50 YEARS) JUBILE JUBILEE (— OF 7 DAYS) HEBDOMAD (— OF 7 YEARS) SEPTENARY (— PRECEDING IMPORTANT EVENT) EVE (CLASS —) HOUR (CULTURAL —) HORIZON (DEFINITE —) MOMENT (DISTINCTIVE —) EPOCH (DULL —) SLACK (EVOLUTIONAL —) HEMERA (GEOLOGICAL —) JURA KAROO EOCENE ALGOMAN HORIZON NEOCENE CAMBRIAN DEVONIAN JURASSIC SILURIAN TERTIARY TRANSVAAL (HAPPY —) MILLENIUM (HYPOTHETICAL —) ACME (JAPANESE CULTURAL —) JOMON (LONG —) EON AEON CYCLE (MEETING —) SESSION (MENSTRUAL —) TERMS (OCCASIONAL —) SNATCH (OF JAPANESE CULTURAL —) YAYOI (PENITENTIAL —) LENT (RECURRING —) EMBER (SHORT —) BIT FIT BLINK SHAKE SPELL SPURT SNATCH (WAITING —) MORATORIUM (WET —) PLUVIAL (SUFF.) (OF A —) CHRONOUS

PERIODIC ERAL ANNUAL CYCLIC ETESIAN REGULAR FREQUENT SEASONAL (NOT —) LOOSE ACYCLIC

PERIODICAL DAILY ORGAN PAPER SHEET ANNUAL DIGEST REVIEW ETESIAN FANZINE JOURNAL REGULAR TABLOID DREADFUL EXCHANGE MAGAZINE

EPHEMERIS PICTORIAL
PERIODICALLY TERMLY
PERION (SON OF —) AMADIS
PERIPATETIC ROVING RAMBLING
ITINERANT
PERIPHERAL DEEP OUTER DISTAL
DISTANT EXTERNAL MARGINAL
PERIPHERY LIP RIM BRIM DOME
EDGE AMBIT LIMIT SKIRT AREOLA
BORDER BOUNDS FRINGE
AMBITUS CONTOUR SUBURBS
SURFACE CONFINES PERIMETER
PERIPHRASTIC AMBAGIOUS
PERISCOPE ALTISCOPE
HYPOSCOPE OMNISCOPE
PERISH DIE FADE FALL RUIN TINE
TYNE QUAIL SPILL SWELT WASTE
DEPART EXPIRE STARVE DESTROY
FORFARE MISCARRY
(— GRADUALLY) FADE
PERISHABLE SOFT DYING CADUKE
BRITTLE FUGITIVE
PERISHED MUSHY

PERISTOME FRINGE
PERITE SKILLED
PERITHECIUM ALVEOLA
PERITONEUM RIM SIPHAC
PERIWIG FLASH GALERA PERUKE
TOUPEE GALERUM PERWICK
CHEVELURE
PERIWINKLE PERY PIRE WINK
PERRY SNAIL MYRTLE WINKLE
DOGBANE PINPATCH SENGREEN
BLUEBUTTON
PERJINK NEAT TRIM PRECISE
PERJURE FORSWEAR
PERJURED MANSWORN
PERK BRISK PERCH PREEN PRINK
FRESHEN SMARTEN
PERKY AIRY PERT COCKY JAUNTY
CHIPPER
PERMANENCE STAY STABILITY
PERMANENT FIXED STABLE
ABIDING DURABLE LASTING
STATIVE CONSTANT ENDURING
REMANENT STANDING INDELIBLE
PERMANENTLY KEEPS
PERMEABLE POROUS PERVIOUS
PERMEATE FILL SEEP SOAK BATHE
IMBUE DRENCH INFORM INVADE
ANIMATE PERVADE DOMINATE
SATURATE PENETRATE
PERMEATED SHOT
PERMEATION SATURATION
PERMIAN DYAS DYASSIC
PERMISSIBLE FREE VENIAL
POSSIBLE CONGEABLE
(NOT —) NEFAS
PERMISSION MAY FIAT LIEF PASS
CONGE DARST FAVOR GRACE
GRANT LEAVE ACCESS ACCORD
PERMIT CONSENT LIBERTY
LICENSE SANCTION
(— TO BE ABSENT) ABSIT
(LETTER OF —) EXEAT
PERMISSIVE TOLERANT
CONCESSORY
PERMIT LET CHIT CHOP GIVE LEVE
PASS ADMIT ALLOW CONGE
EXEAT FAVOR GRACE GRANT
LEAVE SERVE ACCORD BETEEM

CEDULA DUSTUK ENDURE
ENTREE SUFFER CONCEDE
CONSENT DUSTUCK FACULTY
LICENSE PLACARD POMPANO
WARRANT DISPENSE
(— NEGATIVELY) TOLERATE
(— TO TAKE) SOAK
(CUSTOMS —) CARNET
PERMITTED FREE LOOT LICIT
ALLOWED INNOCENT SUPPOSED
(— BY LAW) LEGAL
PERMUTATION BARTER CHANGE
EXCHANGE
PERNICIOUS BAD ILL EVIL FATAL
QUICK SWIFT DEADLY MALIGN
WICKED BALEFUL BANEFUL
HARMFUL HURTFUL NOISOME
NOXIOUS RUINOUS
PERNIO CHILBLAIN
PERO (BROTHER OF —) NESTOR
(FATHER OF —) NELEUS
(HUSBAND OF —) BIAS
(MOTHER OF —) CHLORIS
(SON OF —) ASOPUS
PEROPUS PARAGON
PERORATION EPILOG PERIOD
CLOSING PURLICUE
PEROXISOME MICROBODY
PERPEND JUMPER PARPEN
PONDER REFLECT THROUGH
PERPENDICULAR SINE ERECT
PLUMB SHEER ABRUPT NORMAL
APOTHEM UPRIGHT BINORMAL
CATHETUS EVENDOWN VERTICAL
(MUTUALLY —) ORTHOGONAL
PERPENDICULARITY APLOMB
PERPENDICULARLY BOLT SHEER
SHEERLY
PERPETRATE DO PULL COMMIT
EFFECT PERFORM
PERPETUAL ETERN ENDLESS
ETERNAL CONSTANT INFINITO
UNENDING CONTINUAL
PERENNIAL
PERPETUALLY EVER ALWAYS
FOREVER
PERPETUATE CONTINUE ETERNIZE
MAINTAIN
PERPLEX CAP MAR SET VEX BEAT
CLOG DOIT DOZE FIKE MAZE
STUN AMAZE BESET BLAIK STUMP
TWIST BAFFLE BOGGLE BOTHER
BUNKER CUMBER DARKEN
FEAGUE FICKLE GRAVEL HAMPER
HARASS HOBBLE KITTLE MAMMER
MITHER MOIDER MUDDLE
PLAGUE POTHER POTTER PUTTER
PUZZLE RAFFLE RIDDLE TWITCH
WILDER WRIXLE BEDEVIL
BUMBAZE CONFUSE DIFFUSE
EMBROIL FLUMMOX MYSTIFY
NONPLUS PLUNDER STAGGER
STUMBLE TORMENT BEWILDER
CONFOUND SURPRISE WINDLASS
BAMBOOZLE
PERPLEXED MAZY ANXIOUS
NONPLUS PUZZLED CONFUSED
TROUBLED INTRICATE
TOSTICATED
PERPLEXING HARD MAZY SPINY
CRABBY KNOBBY KNOTTY
CARKING COMPLEX CRABBED
QUISCOS BAFFLING

PERPLEXITY FOG KNOT WERE
BRAKE FOITER HOBBLE PUCKER
PUZZLE TAKING TANGLE ANXIETY
NONPLUS STICKLE TROUBLE
POSEMENT SURPRISE CONFUSION
LABYRINTH PUZZLEMENT
(MENTAL —) STUDY
(RELIEVE OF —) CLEAR
PERQUISITE FEE TIP LOCK PERK
VAIL GOUPIN GOWPEN INCOME
ADJUNCT APANAGE VANTAGE
CONQUEST GRATUITY
(PL.) PICKING
PERRIER PEDRERO
PERRINIST LIBERTINE
PERSE BLUE
(DAUGHTER OF —) CIRCE PASIPHAE
(FATHER OF —) OCEANUS
(HUSBAND OF —) HELIOS
(SON OF —) AEETES PERSES
PERSECUTE VEX BAIT ANNOY
CHASE HARRY HOUND WRACK
WRONG HARASS PESTER PURSUE
AFFLICT CRUCIFY DRAGOON
OPPRESS TORMENT TORTURE
PERSECUTED JOB REFUGEE
PERSECUTOR TORQUEMADA
PERSEPHONE KORE DESPOINA
PRAXIDIKE
(DAUGHTER OF —) CORA KORE
(FATHER OF —) ZEUS JUPITER
(HUSBAND OF —) HADES PLUTO
(MOTHER OF —) CERES DEMETER
PERSES (BROTHER OF —) AEETES
(DAUGHTER OF —) HECATE
(FATHER OF —) CRIUS HELIOS
(MOTHER OF —) PERSE EYRYBIA
(SISTER OF —) CIRCE PASIPHAE
PERSEUS RESCUER CHAMPION
(FATHER OF —) ZEUS JUPITER
(GRANDFATHER OF —) ACRISIUS
(MOTHER OF —) DANAE
(STAR OF —) ATIK ALGOL
(VICTIM OF —) MEDUSA
(WIFE OF —) ANDROMEDA
PERSEVERANCE GRIT MOXIE
STAMINA INDUSTRY PATIENCE
TENACITY CONSTANCY
PERSISTENCE
PERSEVERE PEG CANK KEEP PLUG
TORE ABIDE STICK INSIST REMAIN
PERSIST CONTINUE
PERSEVERING BUSY HARD STILL
PATIENT RESOLUTE SEDULOUS
ASSIDUOUS INSISTENT
PERSIA (SEE IRAN)
PERSIAN PERSE GILAKI HAJEMI
IRANIC DURZADA HADJEMI
IRANIAN MEMNONIAN
(— RED DEER) MARAL
PERSICARY REDLEG REDLEGS
REDSHANK HEARTEASE
HEARTSEED PEACHWORT
PERSIFLAGE BANTER RAILLERY
PERSIMMON KAKI SIMON SIMMON
ZAPOTE CHAPOTE HYAKUME
TRIUMPH
(— TREE) GAB GAUB LOTUS
PERSIST HOLD KEEP LAST URGE
ADHERE ENDURE INSIST REMAIN
PREVAIL SUBSIST CONTINUE
PERSEVERE
PERSISTENCE GUTS
(SUFF.) STASIA STASIS

PERSISTENCY TENACITY
PERSISTENT SET DREE FIRM HARD
GREAT STOUT TOUGH DOGGED
DREECH GRITTY HECTIC SLEUTH
DURABLE RESTANT RESTIVE
CONSTANT ENDURING HOLDFAST
OBDURATE RESOLUTE SEDULOUS
STUBBORN ASSIDUOUS
OBSTINATE PERENNIAL PRIMITIVE
RELENTLESS
PERSISTING
(PREF.) MENO
PERSON BOD CAT EGG EGO GUY
MAN ONE BABY BODY CHAL CHAP
COVE DUCK FISH FOOD FORM
GINK HOOK LEDE LIFE NABS PRIG
SELF SOUL BEING BOSOM CHILD
COOKY GHOST HEART HUMAN
PARTI PARTY PIECE STICK THING
WATCH WIGHT ANIMAL BUGGER
ENTITY FELLOW GALOOT GAZABO
JOHNNY KIPPER NUMBER SINNER
SISTER SPIRIT SPRITE ARTICLE
BLISTER WAGTAIL SPECIMEN
TILLICUM
(— ACTING FOR ANOTHER) PROXY
(— ASSOCIATED WITH WORK)
WALLAH
(— BEARING HEAVY BURDEN)
CAMEL
(— BEHIND THE TIMES) FOGY
FOGEY
(— BRINGING GOOD LUCK) MASCOT
**(— FROM WHOM FAMILY IS
DESCENDED)** STIRPS
(— NAMED) NOMINEE
(— NOT IN THE KNOW) LAME
(— NOT OF NOBLE BIRTH)
ROTURIER
(— OF AGE) COOT FALDWORTH
(— OF CONSEQUENCE) BIGGIE
BIGWIG TALLBOY
(— OF COURAGE) SPARTAN
(— OF INFLUENCE) CAPTAIN
HEAVYWEIGHT
(— OF MEAN BIRTH) GUTTERBLOOD
(— OF RANK) STATE MAGNATE
EMINENCE MAGNIFICO
PERSONAGE
(— RESEMBLING ANOTHER) SOSIA
(— TO SERVE WRIT) ELISOR
(— TOO STRONG FOR ASSAILANT)
TARTAR
(— WHO IS UP-TO-DATE) SWINGER
(— WHO PERFORMS MENIAL TASKS)
DOGSBODY
(— WHO TAKES AMPHETAMINES)
PILLHEAD
(— WITH MENTAL TWIST) CRANK
(— WITH NERVOUS DISORDERS)
NEUROTIC
(— WITH QUEER IDEAS) ROZUM
(— WITHOUT STAMINA) JELLYFISH
(—S IN AMBASSADOR'S SUITE)
COMES
(ABJECT —) SLAVE CRAWLER
(ABSENT-MINDED —) MUSARD
(ADMIRABLE —) PIPPIN
(AFFECTED —) POSEUR MINNICK
GIMCRACK
(AGGRESSIVE —) SHOVER
HOTSHOT
(AMUSING —) COMIC

(ANNOYING —) FIEND NUDNICK
(ARABIZED —) MOZARAB
(ARROGANT —) HUFF TENGU
(ATTRACTIVE —) CUTEY CUTIE KILLER KNOCKOUT
(AVARICIOUS —) YISSER
(AWKWARD —) PUT GAWP HICK MUFF RUBE SLAM STAG STEG KLUTZ STIFF GUFFIN TUMFIE HOOSIER LOBSTER SCHLEPP KITHOGUE SHLEPPER SLOMMACK SPELDRIN
(BAD —) UNSEL
(BALD —) BALLARD BALDHEAD SKINHEAD BALDICOOT
(BANISHED —) WRETCH
(BAPTIZED —) MEMBER ILLUMINATO
(BASE —) CUT RASCAL CAITIFF HILDING PUTTOCK
(BELOVED —) FLAME HEARTROOT
(BIG-BELLIED —) GORBELLY
(BLACK —) BLECK
(BOASTFUL —) BLOWER GASCON
(BOORISH —) GOOP
(CALLOW —) GORLIN SMARTY GOSLING
(CANONIZED —) SAINT
(CARELESS —) HASH TASSEL
(CHICKENHEARTED —) HEN
(CHILDISH —) BAUBLE WHIMLING
(CHUNKY —) JUNT
(CHURLISH —) TIKE TYKE
(CIRCLE OF —S) COTERIE
(CLEVER —) BIRD WHIZ WHIZZ MERCURY
(CLOWNISH —) BUFFOON HOBNAIL VILLAIN
(CLUMSY —) DUB LOB BOOB GAWK SLOB TIKE TYKE JUMBO STAUP STIFF DUFFER KEFFEL LUMMOX HODMADOD
(COARSE —) COW STIRK BABOON MUCKER
(COMBATIVE —) DRAGON GAMECOCK
(COMMONPLACE —) MUT MUTT BROMIDE
(CONCEITED —) IT HUFF COXCOMB PRAGMATIC
(CONFUSED —) FOOSTERER
(CONSERVATIVE —) HUNKER MOSSBACK
(CONTEMPTIBLE —) YAP HEEL PUKE SCAB SKIN SWAB CATSO SHRUB SKITE SKUNK SNIPE TWERP INSECT SHICER STINKER BLIGHTER WHIFFLER PETTITOES
(COWARDLY —) FUGIE SISSY SLINK SQUIB
(CRAFTY —) TOD FILE SHARK JESUIT
(CRAZED —) PSYCHOPATH
(CRINGING —) SNAKE SNOOL FLUNKY SPANIEL
(CRUEL —) LAMB FIEND MALISON
(CUNNING —) PIE
(DAINTY —) MIMMOCK
(DEAD —) DEFUNCT DECEASED DECEDENT
(DECREPIT —) CROCK WITHERLING
(DEFORMED —) CRILE CALIBAN HODMADOD

(DENSE —) DUFFER
(DEPRAVED —) SKATE
(DESPICABLE —) SCAB HOUND SLAVE CAITIFF
(DESTITUTE —) PAUPER
(DIMINUTIVE —) BANTY MIDGE BANTAM MIDGET NIFFNAFF
(DIRTY —) SWEEP DRIVEL HOWLET
(DISABLED —) DUCK CRIPPLE INVALID
(DISAGREEABLE —) GOOP PILL QUAT SKITE RATBAG
(DISGRUNTLED —) SOREHEAD
(DISHONEST —) ROGUE ROTTER BEZONIAN
(DISLIKED —) WARLING
(DISREPUTABLE —) RIP
(DISSOLUTE —) RIBALD ROUNDER STRIKER
(DOLTISH —) BLOCK SWINE
(DRUNKEN —) LUSH TUMBREL TUMBRIL
(DULL —) LOB BORE DODO GOON GOOP GRUB LUMP MOME MOPE SLOB CLUNK DROUD PRUNE SCHMO STICK STOCK LURDAM LACKWIT LOBCOCK NUDNICK OPACITY
(DULL-WITTED —) DOPE GUMP DUNCE
(DWARFISH —) AGATE CROWL SHURF
(DYING —) MORIBUND
(ECCENTRIC —) COON GINK KOOK TIKE TYKE GAZABO GAZEBO FANTAST ODDBALL
(EFFEMINATE —) SOFTY SQUAW CODDLE SOFTIE WANTON BADLING SOFTLING SMOCKFACE
(ELDERLY —) SENIOR SOAKER GRAYHEAD
(EMACIATED —) FRAME WASTREL SKELETON
(EMPTY-HEADED —) NITWIT
(ENROLLED —) MEMBER
(ENTERTAINING —) COMEDIAN
(EVIL —) QUED SCUM QUEDE SHREW
(EXPERIENCED —) EXPERT SOAKER STAGER
(EXPERT —) ACE DAB
(EXTORTIONATE —) SCREW
(EXTRAORDINARY —) ONER BUSTER
(FADED —) SHARGAR SHARGER
(FAMOUS —) DON NOTORIETY
(FANTASTIC —) KICKSHAW
(FARSIGHTED —) PRESBYOPE
(FASHIONABLE —) GIMCRACK
(FASTIDIOUS —) MIMMOCK DELICATE
(FAT —) GURK BLIMP FATSO QUILT SQUAB STOUT
(FATUOUS —) GOOP
(FAWNING —) COGGER SPANIEL
(FEEBLEMINDED —) FEEB IDIOT MORON IMBECILE
(FEROCIOUS —) LAMB
(FICKLE —) ROVER MOONCALF
(FINE —) WHIPPA
(FLABBY —) HUDDERON
(FLASHY —) KID FLASHER
(FOOLISH —) FOP COOT GUMP

HOIT JERK BOOBY SOFTY BAUBLE DOODLE DOTARD DRIVEL HOWLET GOSLING GUBBINS HAVEREL
(FOUL —) DREVILL
(FRANK —) TELLTRUTH
(FUSSY —) FAD FADDLE GRANNY SPOFFY GRANNIE
(GAY —) GRIG HUZZA
(GIDDY —) SCATTERBRAIN
(GOOD-FOR-NOTHING —) KET PELF TASSEL WASTER WANHOPE WASTREL
(GOSSIPING —) SHULER SHUILER
(GOSSIPY —) BIGMOUTH QUIDNUNC NEWSMONGER
(GOSSIPY, TALKATIVE —) YENTA
(GRAVE —) SOBERSIDES
(GREEDY —) GORB GANNET GRASPER PUTTOCK
(GROTESQUE —) GUY GOLLIWOGG PUNCHINELLO
(GRUMPY —) SOURBELLY
(GULLIBLE —) JAY BOOB GULPIN LOBSTER FLATHEAD SHLEMIEL WOODCOCK
(GYPSY —) CHI CHAI
(HANDLESS —) SAMMY
(HARD —) MALISON
(HATEFUL —) TOAD
(HEAVY —) STODGER
(HEAVY-SET —) LUMP
(HOT-TEMPERED —) SPARK
(HUMPBACKED —) LORD
(HUNGRY —) HUNGARIAN
(IDLE —) BUMMLE RAGABASH SLUGGARD
(IGNORANT —) BABE BOOB PORK IDIOT IGNARO
(ILL-BRED —) BOOR CHURL CLOWN
(ILL-MANNERED —) GRUB SKUNK
(ILL-NATURED —) CRAB HUNKS PATCH
(ILL-TEMPERED —) CRAB ETTERCAP TAISTREL
(IMMATURE —) BUD SQUAB GORLIN
(IMMORAL —) REP PERDU IMPURITAN
(IMPASSIVE —) BLOCK
(IMPERTINENT —) PAUK PAWK SNIP
(IMPORTANT —) HONOR MOGUL MUGWUMP
(IMPOTENT —) SPADO
(IMPUDENT —) SAUCE SQUIRT SAUCEBOX
(INANE —) SHAUP
(INEXPERIENCED —) BABE INGENUE BEGINNER
(INFERIOR —) BATA SHRUB SHABBLE
(INSIGNIFICANT —) DAB MUT MUTT QUAT BILSH CREEP JOKER SHURF SPRAT SQUIB ABLACH PEANUT NEBBISH PINKEEN WHIFFET GNATLING GRILDRIG PIGWIGEON
(INSINUATING —) WHILLY
(INTRACTABLE —) BUCKIE TARTAR HAGGARD HARDCASE
(IRASCIBLE —) TOUCHWOOD
(IRRITATING —) BOT

(LAME —) VULCAN
(LANK —) TANGLE GANGEREL WINDLESTRAW
(LARGE —) CHUNK WHIPPA SKELPER STODGER STRAPPER
(LASCIVIOUS —) SUCCUBUS
(LAST — IN CONTEST) MELL
(LAZY —) BUM DAW HOIT POKE IDLER TRAIL LORDAN LURDAN BLELLUM LAZYLEGS SLUGABED SLUGGARD
(LEAN —) RIBE TANGLE SHARGER THINGUT
(LEARNED —) CLERK ERUDIT ACHARYA SCHOLAR LITERATO WISEACRE LITERATUS
(LIGHTHEADED —) BEEHEAD
(LITERATE —) SCHOLAR
(LITTLE —) SMOLT SMOUT
(LIVELY —) GRIG BIRKIE HEMPIE WHISKER
(LOUD-VOICED —) STENTOR
(LOW —) PACK SCUM RASCAL BEASTMAN
(LOW SOCIETY —) MUDSILL
(LUBBERLY —) OAF
(LUMBERING —) PUMPKIN TUMBREL TUMBRIL
(LUMPISH —) DROUD
(LUSTY —) BILCH BILSH
(MAD —) MADLING
(MARRIED —) WIFE SPOUSE HUSBAND MATRIMONY
(MEAN —) RIP SCAB CHURL HOUND MISER SKATE SNEAK SHICER BASTARD DOGBOLT BEZONIAN HUCKSTER STINKARD EARTHWORM
(MEDDLESOME —) BREVIT HESSIAN
(MENTALLY UNBALANCED —) MATTOID
(MISCHIEVOUS —) IMP LIMB PEST TOOL HEMPIE HELLION WHIPSTER
(MISERABLE —) SNAKE SWELP WRETCH
(MISERLY —) SKATE SCROOGE PINCHGUT PINCHBACK
(MONSTROUS —) WAMPUS
(NAIVE —) JERK CLUCK GUNSEL INGENUE INNOCENT
(NASTY —) BLEEDER
(NEGLECTED —) TACKY TACKEY
(NIMBLE —) MERCURY
(NOISY —) YAP HOWLET
(OBJECTIONABLE —) CUR COYOTE FOUTER
(OBSTINATE —) DONKEY STIFFNECK
(ODD —) GIG CURE QUIZZY RATBAG CAUTION
(OFFENSIVE —) TICK SKITE STINKER
(OLD-FASHIONED —) FRUMP
(PALTRY —) PELTER
(PASSIONATE —) FUME
(PECULIAR —) BIRD CASE
(PEEVISH —) GRIZZLER SPLENETIC
(PERNICKETY —) FIKE
(PERT —) PIE FLIRT
(POLISHED —) SMOOTHY SMOOTHIE
(POMPOUS —) PUFFIN POMPIST
(POT-BELLIED —) GORREL
(PRIVATE —) JUDEX

(PROSAIC —) PHILISTINE
(PRYING —) POKER PEEPER
SMELLER
(PUGNOSED —) CAMUS CAMUSE
(PUNY —) SCART SHILP SHRIMP
TITMAN
(PURITANICAL —) WOWSER
(QUEER-LOOKING —) JIGGER
(QUERULOUS —) GRUMP JACKDAW
(QUICK-TEMPERED —) SPUNKIE
WILDCAT SPITFIRE
(RAGGED —) ROTO SHAGRAG
TATTERWAG
(RAPACIOUS —) SHARK CATERER
(RECKLESS —) MADCAP RAMSTAM
(RED-HAIRED —) BRIQUE
(REFRACTORY —) BUCKIE
(RESTLESS —) RAMPLER RAMPLOR
RANTIPOLE
(RETICENT —) CLAM
(RICH —) MONEYBAGS
(RIDICULOUS —) GOOF HARE
MONIMENT MONUMENT
(RIOTOUS —) ROARER
(ROUGH —) TOWSER
(ROUGH-LOOKING —) RULLION
(RUDE —) HICK PORK RULE CHURL
CLOWN GROBIAN
(RUSTIC —) COON KERN KERNE
HAYSEED HOMESPUN
(SAINTLY —) SADDIK
(SAUCY —) PIET
(SCRAWNY —) SCART SCRAG
(SELF-CENTERED —) HEEL DEVIL
FLANEUR
(SELF-RIGHTEOUS —) PHARISEE
(SENSUAL —) SWING CARNALIST
(SHAMEFUL —) BISMER
(SHORT —) CRILE FADGE KNURL
STUMP
(SHOWY —) FLASH FLASHER
HOTSHOT
(SHREWD —) FILE YEPE
HARDHEAD SNOLLYGOSTER
(SICK —) SICK MALADE PATIENT
AEGROTANT
(SILENT —) MUM MUMCHANCE
(SILLY —) FOP CAKE GUMP SOFT
DOBBY GOOSE SOFTY SPOON
CUCKOO NIMSHI SOFTIE
GOOSECAP LIRIPIPE LIRIPOOP
SOFTHEAD
(SILLY OR CRAZY —) DINGBAT
(SIMPLE —) DRIP LAMB IDIOT
PIGWIGEON
(SKINNY —) SCRAE SCARECROW
(SLATTERNLY —) SLATE
(SLIM —) SWABBLE
(SLOTHFUL —) SLOWBELLY
(SLOVENLY —) HASH SLOB SLORP
TRAIL STREEL SLOMMACK
STREELER
(SLUGGISH —) LUMP DOLDRUM
DRUMBLE LOBCOCK
(SLY —) COON SLYBOOTS
SNECKDRAW SNICKDRAW
(SMALL —) GRIG AGATE DWARF
SPRAT INSECT MORSEL POPPET
SACKET GNATLING
(SOPHISTICATED —) WELTKIND
(SPIRITLESS —) MOPE STICK
(SPITEFUL —) HELLCAT ETTERCAP
(SPRUCE —) SPRUSADO

(STINGY —) CHURL HAYNE STINGY
(STOCKY —) STUMP
(STOLID —) CLAM THICKSKIN
(STRANGE —) WAMPUS
(STRANGE OR ECCENTRIC —)
WEIRDO
(STRAY —) WAIF
(STUBBORN —) BUCKY STOUT
BUCKIE
(STUNTED —) URF SCRUNT
SHARGAR
(STUPID —) ASS DUB JAY MUT
BETE BOOB DODO DOLT DOPE
DRIP GAUM GAWP GOOF GUMP
HASH HOIT JERK MOKE MUTT
BLOCK BUCCA CLUCK CLUNK
CUDDY DUNCE HOBBY JUKES
LOACH MORON SHEEP STIFF
STIRK STOCK STUPE SUMPH
SWINE THICK WAMUS ZOMBI
BOODLE DAWKIN DIMWIT
DODUNK DONKEY DUFFER
GANDER GILLIE GRANNY GUNSEL
LUMMOX LURDAN NITWIT
NOODLE SACKET SHMUCK
STUPEX TUMFIE TUMPHY ZOMBIE
BLUNTIE DULLARD FATHEAD
FUSSOCK HOWFING JACKASS
JUGHEAD MUDHEAD PINHEAD
SAPHEAD SCHMUCK SCHNOOK
BONEHEAD BULLHEAD DOTTEREL
DUMBBELL FLATHEAD GAMPHREL
IRONHEAD MEATHEAD
MOLDWARP MUMPHEAD
STUNPOLL THICKWIT
HODMANDOD MUMCHANCE
THICKHEAD
(STUPID, FOOLISH —) YOYO
(STURDY —) LUMP CHUNK
STALWART
(SULKY —) GLUMP GRUMP SUMPH
GROUCH
(SURLY —) CRUST HUNKS
(TACITURN —) OYSTER
(TALKATIVE —) GASSER BLELLUM
BIGMOUTH
(TALL, AWKWARD —)
GAMMERSTANG
(TENDER —) LAMBKIN
(THICKSET —) NUGGET
(THIN —) BEANPOLE
(THIRD —) GOOSEBERRY
(THOUGHTLESS —) AIRLING
SKIPPER BIRDBRAIN
(TIMID —) NEBBISH MILQUETOAST
(TIMID OR MEEK —) NEBBISH
(TINY —) KEEROGUE
(TIRESOME —) BORE PILL BROMIDE
(TREACHEROUS —) JUDAS SNAKE
VIPER GUNSEL SERPENT
(TRICKY —) SLYBOOTS
(TROUBLESOME —) COW PEST
HELLION HESSIAN
(TRUSTWORTHY —) TRAIST
STANDBY
(UNATTRACTIVE —) GOON GRUB
SCUG CREEP
(UNBENDING —) STIFF
(UNCHASTE —) SHORTHEELS
(UNCIVILIZED —) VISIGOTH
(UNCOUTH —) APE PUT STIFF
YAHOO BABOON SLOMMACK
ROUGHNECK

(UNDERSIZED —) DURGAN
SPARROW
(UNFAITHFUL —) INFIDEL
(UNGAINLY —) CLATCH
(UNHANDY —) FOUTER
(UNHAPPY —) UNSEL
(UNIQUE —) ONER
(UNKNOWN —) INCONNU
STRANGER
(UNMARRIED —) MAIDEN SINGLE
AGAMIST BACHELOR CELIBATE
SPINSTER
(UNPRACTICAL —) MUFF
(UNREASONABLE —) DUFFER
(UNSCRUPULOUS —) CATSO KNAVE
(UNSOPHISTICATED —) JAY HICK
NYAS HAYSEED CORNBALL
INNOCENT
(UNTHANKFUL —) INGRATE
(UNTIDY —) SLOVEN STREEL
SLAISTER
(UNWIELDY —) FUSTILUGS
(USELESS —) POOP SWAB UNSEL
BAUCHLE
(VALOROUS —) HERO
(VENOMOUS —) SPITPOISON
(VIGOROUS —) SNEEZER
(VIOLENT —) DRAGON BANGSTER
SPITFIRE
(VORACIOUS —) HUNGARIAN
(VULGAR —) MUCKER
(WANTON —) RIG FLIRT WHIPSTER
(WASTEFUL —) SCATTERGOOD
(WEAK —) SCART SHILP SOFTY
WHIMLING
(WEAK OR INEFFECTUAL —) WIMP
(WEAK-MINDED —) SAPHEAD
TOTTYHEAD
(WEALTHY —) MONEYBAGS
(WELL-BORN —) FREE
(WHITE —) FAY OFAY GRIFFIN
EUROPEAN PALEFACE
(WICKED —) DEVIL SATAN SHREW
UNLEAD UNLEDE SATANIST
(WILD —) HELLCAT RANTIPOLE
(WILY —) PIE
(WITHERED —) RUNT
(WITLESS —) WITHAM WITTOME
SLABBERER
(WITTY —) WITSHIP SPARKLER
(WORNOUT —) HUSHEL
(WORTHLESS —) YAP FILE GEAR
HOIT JADE LOON SCUM TOOT
CRUMB LOREL LOSEL SCOUT
SHAND BAUBLE BUGGER FELLOW
FOUTRA SHICER BUDMASH
GULLION BLIGHTER VAGABOND
PHARMAKOS
(WRETCHED —) MISER MISERY
(YOUNG —) CUB KID COLT LAMB
CHILD HEMPY SMOLT SMOUT
SPRIG YONKE GUNSEL HEMPIE
JUNIOR CHICKEN CHOOKIE
GRISTLE LAMBKIN JUVENILE
STRIPLING
(PL.) FRY PERSONNEL
(PREF.) PROSOP(O)
(SUFF.) (FEMALE —) INE
PERSONABLE COMELY SHAPELY
HANDSOME
PERSONAGE DON DUSE NIBS
BLOKE FIGURE SHOGUN TYCOON
(GREAT —) MOGUL SOPHI

SOPHY SUFFEE
PERSONAL SELF PRIVY DIRECT
PRIVATE CHATTELS CORPORAL
INTIMATE
(— EFFECTS) DUNNAGE
(PREF.) IDIO
PERSONALITY EGO AURA DRAW
SELF SOUL BEING ETHOS HEART
EGOITY FIGURE CONTROL
FACULTY DEMIURGE PRESENCE
SELFHOOD SELFNESS
PERSONATE ACT FEIGN MIMIC
MASKED PERSON TYPIFY
PRESENT
PERSONATION (SHAM —) IDOL
PERSONIFICATION SOUL GENIUS
(— OF DIVINE VIRTUE) EON
(— OF JUSTICE) THEMIS
PERSONIFY EMBODY INCARNATE
PERSONIZE
PERSONNEL BLOOD STAFF
KITCHEN PHYSIQUE
PERSPECTIVE OPTICS DISTANCE
TELESCOPE
PERSPICACIOUS KEEN ACUTE
ASTUTE SHREWD
(MAKE —) CLEAR
PERSPICACITY WIT ACUMEN
PERSPICUOUS CLEAR LUCID
PLAIN PRECISE VISIBLE MANIFEST
LIGHTSOME
PERSPIRATION DEW SUDOR
SUINT SWEAT HIDROSIS
OLIGIDRIA SUDORESIS
PERSPIRE PUG MELT BREAN
SWEAT SWELTER TRANSPIRE
PERSUADE CON GET WIN COAX
GAIN MOVE RULE SNOW TICE
URGE WISE ARGUE BRING EDUCE
SUADE SWADE WEISE ADVISE
ARGUFY ASSURE CAJOLE ENGAGE
ENTICE INDUCE REMOVE SUBORN
CONVERT DISPUTE ENTREAT
IMPRESS PREVAIL SATISFY
CANOODLE INFLUENCE
PERSUADED PLIABLE GULLIBLE
RESOLVED SENSIBLE
PERSUASION KIND SORT BELIEF
OPINION SUASION JUDGMENT
(AUTHOR OF —) AUSTEN
(CHARACTER IN —) ANNE CLAY
MARY CROFT ELLIOT LOUISA
WALTER BENWICK CHARLES
RUSSELL WILLIAM HARVILLE
MUSGROVE ELIZABETH
FREDERICK HENRIETTA
WENTWORTH
PERSUASIVE COGENT WINNING
INDUCTIVE PLAUSIBLE PROTEPTIC
(PREF.) PITHANO
PERT BOLD CHIC FESS FLIP KECK
SPRY TRIM ALERT ALIVE BARDY
BRISK COCKY DONSY KISKY
PEART PERKY PIERT QUICK SASSY
SAUCY SMART TAUNT CHEEKY
CLEVER COCKET COMELY DAPPER
FRISKY SWASHY THWART
BOBBISH PAUGHTY INSOLENT
PETULANT
(— TALK) CHELP
PERTAIN BE LIE BEAR COME LONG
BELIE TOUCH AFFEIR BEFALL
BELIMP BELONG RELATE

RETAIN CONCERN
(— TO) RINE
PERTAINING (— TO ABDOMEN)
ALVINE
(— TO AIR) AURAL PNEUMATIC
(— TO ALL NATURE) PAMPHYSIC
(— TO ANIMALS) ZOIC
(— TO ANKLE) TARSAL
(— TO APOLLO) PYTHIAN
PAEONIAN
(— TO APOSTLE) PETRINE
(— TO APPETITES) ORECTIC
(— TO ARMPIT) AXILLAR
(— TO ARMY) MARTIAL STRATONIC
(— TO ARROW) SAGITTAL
(— TO ATHENA) PALLADIAN
(— TO BACK) DORSAL TERGAL
(— TO BATH) BALNEAL
(— TO BEAM) TRAGAL
(— TO BEARD) BARBAL
(— TO BED) THORAL
(— TO BEES) APIAN APIARIAN
(— TO BELLY) ALVIN ALVINE
VENTRAL VENTRIC
(— TO BIBLICAL LAW) LEVITIC
(— TO BIRDS) AVIAN AVINE
ORNITHIC VOLUCRINE
(— TO BIRTH) NATAL
(— TO BISHOP) LAWN
(— TO BITTER TASTE) PICRIC
(— TO BLACK SEA) PONTIC
(— TO BODIES AT REST) STATIC
(— TO BODY) SOMAL SOMATIC
(— TO BONE) OSSAL OSTEAL
(— TO BOSOM) GREMIAL
(— TO BRACELET) ARMILLARY
(— TO BRANCHES) RAMOUS
(— TO BREADMAKING) PANARY
(— TO BREAKFAST) ENTACULAR
(— TO BREAST) PECTORAL
(— TO BREASTBONE) STERNAL
(— TO BRISTLES) SETAL
(— TO BROTHEL) STEWISH
(— TO BUNCH) COMAL
(— TO CALF) VITULINE
(— TO CALF OF LEG) SURAL
(— TO CART) PLAUSTRAL
(— TO CARTHAGINIANS) PUNIC
(— TO CARVING) GLYPHIC
(— TO CAVE) SPELEAN SPELUNCAR
(— TO CHAIN) CATENARY
(— TO CHAMBER) CAMERAL
(— TO CHARIOTEER) AURIGAL
(— TO CHEEK) MALAR
(— TO CHESS) SCACCHIC
(— TO CHINA) SINIAN SINISIAN
(— TO CITY) CIVIC URBAN
(— TO CLAN) SEPTAL
(— TO CLAY) BOLAR
(— TO CLOTHES) VESTIARY
VESTURAL
(— TO COINS) NUMMARY
NUMISMATIC
(— TO COLOR) CHROMATIC
(— TO COMB) PECTINAL
(— TO CONSTRUCTION) TECTONIC
(— TO CONTESTS) AGONISTIC
(— TO CORK) SUBERIC SUBEROUS
(— TO COUGH) TUSSAL TUSSIVE
(— TO COURT) AULIC JUDICIAL
JUDICIARY
(— TO CROCKERY) PIG
(— TO CROWN) CORONAL

(— TO DANCING) SALTATORY
TRIPUDIAL
(— TO DAUGHTER OR SON) FILIAL
(— TO DAWN) EOAN
(— TO DEFENSE) PHYLACTIC
(— TO DESERTS) EREMIC
(— TO DIAPHRAGM) PHRENIC
(— TO DINNER) CENATORY
PRANDIAL
(— TO DOVE) COLUMBINE
(— TO DREAMS) ONEIRIC ONIROTIC
(— TO DRINKING) BIBITORY
(— TO DUNG) STERCORAL
(— TO EARTH) GEAL TELLURIC
TERRANEAN
(— TO EARTHQUAKE) SEISMAL
SEISMIC
(— TO EAST) EOAN
(— TO ESSENCE) BASIC
(— TO EUNUCH) SPADONIC
(— TO EVENING) VESPER
(— TO EYELIDS) BLEPHARAL
(— TO FACE) PROSOPIC
(— TO FAIR) NUNDINAL
(— TO FAITH) PISTIC
(— TO FEET) PEDAL PEDARY
(— TO FERMENTATION) ZYMIC
ZYMOTIC
(— TO FIELDS) AGRARIAN
(— TO FINGERS) DIGITAL
(— TO FISHING) HALIEUTIC
(— TO FLEAS) PULICENE PULICOSE
(— TO FLESH) SARCOUS
(— TO FLOCK) GREGAL
(— TO FLOOD) DILUVIAL DILUVIAN
(— TO FLOWERS) FLORAL ANTHINE
(— TO FOREARM) CUBITAL
(— TO FOREHEAD) METOPIC
(— TO FORM) MORPHIC
(— TO FOX) VULPINE
(— TO FRESH WATER) LIMNETIC
(— TO FROGS) ANURAN RANINE
(— TO FRUIT) POMONAL POMONIC
(— TO FUNERALS) EXEQUIAL
(— TO FUNGUS) MYCETOID
(— TO FURNACE) FORNACIC
(— TO GALLOWS) PATIBULARY
(— TO GARDEN) HORTULAN
(— TO GARRISON) PRESIDIAL
(— TO GENTILES) ETHNIC
(— TO GLASS) VITREOUS
(— TO GOATS) CAPRIC
(— TO GOVERNMENT) ARCHICAL
POLITICAL
(— TO GRANDPARENTS) AVAL
(— TO GRINDING) MOLINARY
(— TO GROUND) SOLARY
(— TO GROVE) NEMORAL
(— TO GULLS) LARINE
(— TO GUMS) ULETIC GINGIVAL
(— TO HAIR) PILAR CRINAL PILARY
(— TO HAND) CHIRAL MANUAL
(— TO HAWKS) ACCIPITRINE
(— TO HEAD) CEPHALIC
(— TO HEAP) ACERVAL
(— TO HEART) CARDIAC
(— TO HEAT) CALORIC THERMAL
THERMIC
(— TO HIPS) SCIATIC
(— TO HOLIDAY) FERIAL
(— TO HORIZON) MUNDANE
(— TO HORSE) EQUINE HIPPIC
CABALLINE

(— TO HOSPITALITY) XENIAL
XENIAN
(— TO HOUSE) DOMAL
(— TO HUNGER) FAMELIC
(— TO HUNTING) VENATIC
VENERIAL CYNEGETIC
(— TO INTELLECT) NOETIC
(— TO INTESTINES) ALVIN ALVINE
(— TO JAW) MALAR GNATHAL
GNATHIC
(— TO JOURNEY) VIATIC
(— TO KIDNEY) RENAL NEPHRIC
(— TO KNOWLEDGE) GNOSTIC
(— TO LAKES) LACUSTRINE
(— TO LAP) GREMIAL
(— TO LAUGHING) GELASTIC
(— TO LAUGHTER) RISORIAL
(— TO LEARNING) PALLADIAN
(— TO LEG) CRURAL
(— TO LICE) PEDICULAR
(— TO LIFE) VITAL ZOETIC
(— TO LINE) FILAR
(— TO LIPS) LABIAL
(— TO LIVER) HEPATIC JECORAL
(— TO LOINS) LUMBAR
(— TO LOVE) EROTIC AMATORY
(— TO LUCK) ALEATORY
(— TO LUNGS) PULMONIC
PNEUMONIC PULMONARY
(— TO MANKIND) COMMON
ANTHROPIC
(— TO MARBLE) MARMORIC
(— TO MARKET) NUNDINAL
(— TO MARRIAGE) MARITAL
HYMENEAL
(— TO MARS) AREAN MAMERTINE
MAVORTIAL
(— TO MASS) MOLAR
(— TO MASTER) HERILE
(— TO MEADOWS) PRATAL
(— TO MEAL) PRANDIAL
(— TO MECCA) MECCAWEE
(— TO MEMORY) MNESTIC
MNEMONIC
(— TO MIDDAY) MERIDIAN
(— TO MILK) LACTARY LACTEAL
(— TO MILL) MOLINARY
(— TO MIND) PHRENIC
(— TO MIRROR) SPECULAR
(— TO MOISTURE) HYGRIC
(— TO MOON) LUNAR SELENIC
SELENIAN
(— TO MORNING) MATIN MATINAL
MATUTINAL
(— TO MOTION) GESTIC KINETIC
(— TO MOUNTAINS) MONTANE
(— TO MOUTH) ORAL OSCULAR
STOMATIC
(— TO MUSCLE) SARCOUS
(— TO MUSIC) HARMONIC
(— TO MYSTERIES) TELESTIC
(— TO NAMES) ONOMASTIC
(— TO NAVEL) OMPHALIC
(— TO NECK) JUGULAR
(— TO NEPHEW) NEPOTAL
(— TO NIGHT) NOCTURNAL
(— TO NOSE) NASAL RHINAL
(— TO NUT) NUCAL
(— TO NUTRITION) TROPHIC
(— TO OAK) QUERCINE
ROBOREOUS
(— TO OCEAN) PELAGIC
OCEANOUS THALASSIC

(— TO OLD AGE) SENILE GERATIC
GERONTIC
(— TO OPEN SKY) SUBDIAL
(— TO PARLOR) BEN BOOR
(— TO PASTURES) PASCUAL
(— TO PAWNBROKER) AVUNCULAR
(— TO PEACOCK) PAVONINE
(— TO PEARL) MARGARIC
(— TO PERSPIRATION) SUDORIC
(— TO PICTURE) ICONIC
(— TO PIGS) PORCINE
(— TO PINE) WARRYN
(— TO PLAGUE) LOIMIC
(— TO PLEASURE) HEDONIC
(— TO POETRY) MUSAL IAMBIC
(— TO POISON) TOXIC
(— TO POTTERY) CERAMIC
(— TO PRIESTS) SACERDOTAL
(— TO PRISON) CARCERAL
(— TO PULSE) SPHYGMIC
(— TO PUNISHMENT) PENAL
PUNITIVE
(— TO PURIFICATION) LUSTRAL
(— TO QUEEN) REGINAL
(— TO RAIN) HYETAL PLUVIAL
(— TO RAINBOW) IRIDAL
(— TO REMOTE PLACE) FORANE
(— TO RESONANCE) SYNTONIC
(— TO RING) ARMILLARY
(— TO RISING) ORTIVE
(— TO RIVER) AMNIC POTAMIC
RIVERINE FLUMINOSE
(— TO RIVER BANK) RIPARIAN
(— TO ROAD) VIATIC
(— TO ROCK) PETREAN SAXATILE
(— TO ROD) BACULINE
(— TO RUBBISH) RUDERARY
(— TO SABLES) ZIBELINE
(— TO SAIL) VELIC
(— TO SALVATION) SOTERIAL
(— TO SANDARAC) THYINE
(— TO SATURDAY) SABBATINE
(— TO SEAL) PHOCINE SIGILLARY
SPHRAGISTIC
(— TO SEAM) SUTURAL
(— TO SEASHORE) LITTORAL
(— TO SEAWEED) ALGOUS
(— TO SENSE OF TASTE) GUSTATIVE
(— TO SHEEP) VERVECINE
(— TO SHEPHERDS) PASTORAL
(— TO SHERIFF) VICONTIEL
(— TO SHIN) CNEMIAL
(— TO SHIP) NAVICULAR
(— TO SHOPMAN) APOTHECAL
(— TO SHOULDER) ALAR SCAPULAR
(— TO SIGNS) SEMIC SEMANTIC
(— TO SILVER) LUNAR ARGENTAL
(— TO SISTER) SORORAL
(— TO SKIN) DERIC DERMAL
CUTICULAR
(— TO SLEEP) SOMNIAL
MORPHETIC
(— TO SNAKE) ANGUINE
(— TO SNOW) NIVAL
(— TO SOFT PALATE) VELAR
(— TO SOIL) DAPHIC
(— TO SONG) MELIC
(— TO SPECTACLE) THEORIC
(— TO SPEECH) PHEMIC
(— TO SPINAL CORD) MYELIC
(— TO SPRING) VERNAL
(— TO STARS) ASTRAL STELLAR
SIDEREAL

(— TO STATE AFFAIRS) PRAGMATIC
(— TO STEPMOTHER) NOVERCAL
(— TO STOMACH) GASTRIC
(— TO STORKS) PELARGIC
(— TO SULPHUR) THIONIC
(— TO SUMMER) ESTIVAL AESTIVAL
(— TO SUN) SOLAR HELIAC
(— TO SUNDAY) DOMINICAL
(— TO SUNDIAL) SCIATHERIC
(— TO SUPPER) CENATORY
(— TO SURFACE OF ANYTHING) FACIAL
(— TO SWALLOWS) HIRUNDINE
(— TO SWEAT) SUDORIC
(— TO SWIMMING) NATATORY
(— TO SWINEHERD) SYBOTIC
(— TO TAIL) CAUDAL
(— TO TAILOR) SARTORIAL
(— TO TANNING) SC
(— TO TEARS) LACRIMAL LACHRYMAL
(— TO TEMPO) AGOGIC
(— TO THE BEAUTIFUL) ESTHETIC AESTHETIC
(— TO THIEVING) KLEPTISTIC
(— TO THIGH) CRURAL
(— TO THREAD) FILAR
(— TO THROAT) GULAR JUGULAR
(— TO TILE) TEGULAR
(— TO TIN) STANNIC
(— TO TITHES) DECIMAL
(— TO TITMICE) PARINE
(— TO TOMB) TOMBAL
(— TO TONGUE) GLOSSAL LINGUAL
(— TO TORTOISES) CHELONIAN
(— TO TOUCH) TACTILE
(— TO TOWER) TURRICAL
(— TO TREES) DENDRAL ARBOREAL
(— TO TWENTY) VICENARY
(— TO UNCLE) AVUNCULAR
(— TO UNDERGROUND WATER) VADOSE PHREATIC
(— TO VESSEL) VASAL
(— TO VIRGIN) PARTHENIAN
(— TO VOW) VOTAL
(— TO WAGON) PLAUSTRAL
(— TO WALLS) MURAL PARIETAL
(— TO WAR) POLEMICAL
(— TO WASPS) VESPAL VESPINE
(— TO WAX) CERAL
(— TO WEAVING) TEXTORIAL
(— TO WEIGHT) BARIC PONDERAL PONDERARY
(— TO WELL) PHREATIC
(— TO WHALES) CETIC
(— TO WHEAT) VULGARE
(— TO WHEELS) ROTAL
(— TO WHETSTONES) COTICULAR
(— TO WIFE) UXORIAL
(— TO WIND) EOLIAN PNEUMATIC
(— TO WINE) VINIC VINOUS
(— TO WINE-MAKING) OENOPOETIC
(— TO WINGS) ALAR PTERIC EXRUPEAL PTEROTIC
(— TO WINTER) HIEMAL
(— TO WISDOM) PALLADIAN
(— TO WOMANKIND) MULIEBRAL
(— TO WOODPECKERS) PICINE
(— TO WOODS) SYLVAN NEMORAL
(— TO WORMS) VERMICULAR
(— TO WOUNDS) VULNERAL
(— TO WRIST) CARPAL
(— TO YESTERDAY) PRIDIAN

(— TO YEW) TAXINE
(SUFF.) (—TO) AL AR ORIOUS ORY
PERTINACIOUS FIRM STIFF DOGGED ADHERING STUBBORN OBSTINATE
PERTINENCE RELEVANCE
PERTINENCY FORCE
PERTINENT APT FIT PAT HAPPY COGENT PROPER TIMELY ADAPTED APROPOS GERMANE POINTED TELLING INCIDENT MATERIAL RELATIVE RELEVANT
PERTLY CROUSE
PERTURB BITE GRATE UPSET WORRY DISMAY AGITATE CONFUSE CONTURB DERANGE DISTURB TROUBLE
PERTURBATION DISMAY FLIGHT POTHER POOTHER STICKLE TROUBLE TURMOIL EVECTION AGITATION
PERTURBED UNEASY
PERTUSSIS COUGH CHINCOF CHINCOUGH

PERU

CAPITAL: LIMA
COIN: SOL LIBRA DINERO CENTAVO
DEPARTMENT: ICA LIMA PUNO CUSCO CUZCO JUNIN PIURA TACNA ANCASH LORETO TUMBES
DESERT: SECHURA
ISLAND: CHINCHA
LAKE: TITICACA
LANGUAGE: AYMARA QUECHUA
MEASURE: TOPO VARA GALON CELEMIN FANEGADA
MOUNTAIN: HUAMINA COROPUNA HUASCARAN
PERIOD: RECUAY
RIVER: NAPU RIMAC SANTA TIGRE MORONA YAGUAS YAVARI CURARAY MARANON PASTAZA UCAYALI AMAZONAS APURIMAC HUALLAGA URUBAMBA
TOWN: ICA LIMA PUNO CUZCO PAITA PISCO PIURA TACNA CALLAO TUMBES IQUITOS AREQUIPA CHICLAYO TRUJILLO
VOLCANO: MISTI YUCAMANI
WEIGHT: LIBRA QUINTAL

PERUKE WIG FLASH GALERA TOUPEE GALERUM PERIWIG WIGGERY
PERUSAL SIGHT LECTURE SCRUTINY
PERUSE CON READ SCAN STUDY HANDLE SEARCH SURVEY EXAMINE INSPECT
PERUVIAN BARK CALISAYA CINCHONA
PERVADE FILL BATHE IMBUE DRENCH INSTIL OCCUPY THREAD INSTILL PERMEATE TRAVERSE
PERVADED STIFF
PERVASIVE POIGNANT
PERVERSE AUK AWK CAM CAR AWRY WOGH WRAW CROSS DONSY GAMMY THRAW WROTH CUSSED DIVERS LOUCHE

THRAWN THWART WICKED WILFUL WRAIST AWKWARD CRABBED CROOKED DIVERSE FORWARD FROWARD OBLIQUE PEEVISH WAYWARD CAMSHACH CRANKISH STUBBORN
PERVERSELY AUK AWK AWRY ATHWART OVERWART
PERVERSION WREST ABUSION
(— OF TASTE) MALACIA
PERVERT WRY DRAW RACK RUIN SKEW TURN WARP ABUSE CROOK GLOSS TWIST UPSET WREST DEBASE DETORT DIVERT GARBLE INVERT MISUSE POISON VOYEUR WRENCH WRITHE CONTORT CORRUPT DEGRADE DEPRAVE DEVIATE DISTORT MISTURN SUBVERT TRADUCE VITIATE MISWREST
PERVERTED BAD WICKED ABUSIVE AWKWARD CORRUPT TWISTED VICIOUS
PERVERTER WRESTER
PERVIOUS LEACHY PERVIAL PERVADING
PES NEUME TENOR PODATUS
PESKY VERY PLAGUY ANNOYING DEVILING EXTREMELY
PESO DURO CONANT DOLLAR CAROLUS PATACAO
PESSIMISM WELTSCHMERZ MISERABILISM
PESSIMIST ALARMIST JEREMIAH WORRYWART
PESSIMISTIC GLOOMY ALARMED BEARISH CYNICAL DOWNBEAT
PEST BOT BANE TICK WEED MOUSE MYZUS TRAIK INSECT MENACE PLAGUE SCHELM SORROW VERMIN NUDNICK SCOURGE MEALYBUG SANDMITE BUTTINSKY
PESTER DUN HOX NAG RIB TIG HAKE ANNOY DEVIL TEASE WORRY BADGER BOTHER HARASS INFEST MOLEST BEDEVIL TORMENT TROUBLE OBSTRUCT PERSECUTE
PESTHOUSE LAZARET LAZARETTO
PESTICIDE BIOCIDE FUMIGANT
PESTILENCE LUES PEST DEATH QUALM PLAGUE MURRAIN EPIDEMIC MORTALITY
PESTILENT FATAL DEADLY VEXING NOXIOUS
PESTLE MIX BRAY GRIND PESTL PILUM STAMP BEETLE BRAYER MULLER PISTIL CHAPPER POUNDER STAMPER
PET TOY CADE COAX DAUT DEAR DUCK HUFF LAMB NECK PEAT SOCK SULK TIFF DRUNT DUCKY HUMOR QUIET SPOIL SPOON TETCH CARESS CODDLE COSHER COSSET CUDDLE DANDLE DAUTIE DAWTIE FADDLE FANTAD FANTOD FONDLE GENTLE PAMPER PETKIN SMOOCH SQUALL STROKE WANTON CHERISH DARLING INDULGE PINKENY TANTRUM TIDLING UMBRAGE WHITHER CANOODLE FAVORITE

TIDDLING PADDYWACK
PETAL ALA HELM HOOD LEAF WING BANNER
(— IN PEA FLOWER) VEXILLUM
(— OF IRIS) STANDARD
(UPPER —) HOOD BANNER
(PL.) COROLLA
PETALIA NYCTERIS
PETARD PITTARD FIREWORK
PETATE BANIG
PETECHIA STIGMA
PETER P FADE FAIL PEAK SAFE WANE CEASE PEDRO PIERS PIERRE SIGNAL DWINDLE
(— OUT) FIZZLE
(BROTHER OF —) ANDREW
(FATHER OF —) JONAS
PETER GRIMES (CHARACTER IN —) ELLEN PETER GRIMES ORFORD BALSTRODE
(COMPOSER OF —) BRITTEN
PETER IBBETSON (AUTHOR OF —) DUMAURIER
(CHARACTER IN —) DEANE MADGE MIMSY PETER LINTOT GREGORY PLUNKET IBBETSON PASQUIER
PETER PAN (AUTHOR OF —) BARRIE
(CHARACTER IN —) PAN HOOK JOHN NIBS SMEE PETER WENDY TINKER DARLING MICHAEL TOOTLES MARGARET SLIGHTLY
PETHAHIAH (FATHER OF —) MESHEZABEEL
PETHEUL (SON OF —) JOEL
PETIOLE STEM SPINE STALK STIPE PODEON PEDUNCLE PHYLLODE LEAFSTALK
PETITE SMALL LITTLE MIGNON MIGNONNE
PETITION ASK BEG SUE BILL BOON PLEA PRAY SUIT VOTE WISH APPLY ORATE PLEAD APPEAL DESIRE INVOKE MOTION PLACIT PRAYER STEVEN ADDRESS BESEECH ENTREAT IMPLORE ORATION SOLICIT ROGATION SUFFRAGE
(MAKE —) SUE
(PL.) PRECES
PETITIONER BEGGAR ORATOR SUITOR BEADSMAN APPLICANT ENTREATER PLAINTIFF
PETO WAHOO
PETREL BILL TITI CAHOW MITTY NELLY PRION WITCH SPENCY TEETEE ASSILAG GLUTTON KAEDING PINTADO SEABIRD SEAFOWL STINKER ALLAMOTH FORKTAIL STINKPOT ALLAMOTTI MALLEMUCK NIGHTHAWK
PETRIFY DAZE DEADEN STONIFY STUPEFY LAPIDIFY FOSSILIZE GORGONIZE
PETRIFYING STONY GORGON
PETROL GAS GASOLINE
PETROLATUM VASELINE
PETROLEUM OIL CRUDE PETROL NAPHTHA
(— INDUSTRY) OILDOM
(CRUDE —) MAZOUT
PETRUCHIO (WIFE OF —) KATHERINE
PE-TSAI PECHAY

PETTED CADE DANDILY
PETTICOAT BAJO GORE KILT SLIP
SOUS DICKY GREEN JUPON
PAGNE SOUSE KIRTLE LUHINGA
PLACKET WHITTLE BALMORAL
BASQUINE WILYCOAT
(— OF TARGET) GREEN
PETTIFOG FOG CAVIL BICKER
PETTIFOGGER FOGGER SHYSTER
LEGULEIAN
PETTINESS NAGGLE PARVINIMITY
PETTING COLLING
PETTISH DORTY HUFFY FRETFUL
PEEVISH PLAINTIVE
PETTY TIN BASE JERK MEAN ORRA
PUNY VAIN BANAL GRIMY MINOR
PETIT PUNEE SMALL MEASLY
MINUTE PALTRY PEANUT POKING
PUISNE PUSILL SNIFTY KITLING
PIMPING TRIVIAL TWATTLE
CHILDISH FIDDLING INFERIOR
NIGGLING NUGATORY PEDDLING
PICAYUNE PIFFLING SNIPPETY
TRIFLING PAROCHIAL
(PREF.) MICR(O)
(SUFF.) (— ONE) EEN
PETULANCE PROCACITY
PETULANT PERT CROSS SAUCY
SHORT TESTY TIFFY FEISTY
SULLEN WANTON WILFUL
CRABBED FRETFUL FROWARD
HUFFISH PEEVISH WASPISH
PERVERSE SNAPPISH
PEULTHAI (FATHER OF —)
OBEDEDOM
PEUMUS BOLDU
PEW BOX PUE BOUT DESK PFUI
PUGH SEAT SLIP BENCH BUGHT
STALL BOUGHT
PEWEE PEWIT PEEWEE PEEWIT
PEWIT PEESWEEP
PEWTER CUP BIDRI BIDRY MONEY
PUDER BIDERY TRIFLE PEAUDER
SADWARE TUTENAG
(— MARK) TOUCHMARK
PEYOTE HIKULI
PFENNIG PENNING
PHAEDRA (AUTHOR OF —) RACINE
(CHARACTER IN —) ARICIA OENONE
PHAEDRA THESEUS HIPPOLYTUS
THERAMENES
(FATHER OF —) MINOS
(HUSBAND OF —) THESEUS
(MOTHER OF —) PASIPHAE
(SISTER OF —) ADRIADNE
(SON OF —) ACAMAS DEMOPHON
PHAETON DUKE FAETON SPIDER
STANHOPE
PHAETON BUTTERFLY
BALTIMORE
PHALANGER TAIT ARIEL TAPOA
CUSCUS TAGUAN OPOSSUM
PENTAIL SQUIRREL
PHALAROPE LOBIPED COOTFOOT
LOBEFOOT WHALEBIRD
PHALERA BEAD BOSS DISK STUD
CAMEO
PHALTI (FATHER OF —) LAISH
PHANTASM DREAM FANCY GHOST
VAPOR FIGURE SHADOW SPIRIT
FANTASY PHANTOM SPECIES
SPECTER SPECTRE
PHANTASMAL UNREAL SPECTRAL

PHANTASUS (BROTHER OF —)
ICELUS MORPHEUS PHOBETOR
THANATOS
(FATHER OF —) HYPNOS SOMNUS
(MOTHER OF —) NYX
PHANTASY FANCY FANTASY
PHANTASIA
PHANTOM IDOL BOGEY BOGLE
DUMMY GHOST IMAGE PHASM
SHADE SHAPE UMBRA BOGGLE
DOUBLE FANTOM IDOLON
IDOLUM SHADOW SPIRIT
BUGBEAR EIDOLON ELUSIVE
FANTASY FEATURE SPECIES
SPECTER ILLUSORY ADAMASTOR
SIMULACRUM
PHANUEL (DAUGHTER OF —) ANNA
PHARAOH ALE FARO PHARO
TYRANT BUSIRIS
PHARAOH'S HEN VULTURE
PHAREZ (BROTHER OF —) ZARAH
(FATHER OF —) JUDAH
(MOTHER OF —) TAMAR
PHARISEE MUGWUMP NICODEMUS
PHARMACEUTICAL MERCURIAL
(SUFF.) (— PRODUCT) EIN EINE IN
INE
PHARMACIST DRUGGIST
DISPENSER
PHARMACY FERMACY
DRUGSTORE
PHAROS CLOAK LIGHT TORCH
BEACON LANTERN
PHARYNGEAL FAUCAL
PHARYNX MASTAX PROBOSCIS
(PREF.) LAEMO LEM(O)
PHASE EFT END LEG FAZE SIDE
ANGLE FACET GRADE STAGE
ASPECT AVATAR BACKLASH
PASSOVER DICHOTOMY
(INITIAL —) BUD
(LOWEST —) BATHOS
(TRANSITORY —) STREAK
PHASM FANTOM METEOR PHASMA
PHANTOM
PHEASANT CHIR GUAN ARGUS
CHEER KALIJ MINAL MONAL
GROUSE LEIPOA MAGPIE MONAUL
MOONAL PUKRAS KALLEGE
FIREBACK ITHAGINE RINGNECK
TRAGOPAN MACARTNEY
(BREEDING PLACE FOR —S) STEW
(BROOD OF —S) NID NYE NIDE
(YOUNG —) POULT
PHEASANT CUCKOO COUCAL
PHEASANT DUCK PINTAIL
MERGANSER
PHEASANT FINCH WAXBILL
PHEASANT'S-EYE ROSAIRBY
PHEBE (HUSBAND OF —) SILVIUS
PHELLEM CORK SUBER
PHENOBARBITOL LUMINAL
PHENOCRYST INSET
PHENOL LACCOL THYMOL ALOESOL
CREOSOL DURENOL EUGENOL
ORCINOL CHAVICOL RESORCIN
PHENOMENA
(SUFF.) ICS
PHENOMENON FIRE ANOMY
COLOR EVENT IMAGE ARTHUS
EFFECT METEOR MIRAGE
SHADOW ISOTOPY MIRACLE
PARADOX PROCESS SYMPTOM

ASTERISM PRAKRITI SIDERISM
SUNQUAKE LANDSPOUT
PHENYLSALICYLATE SALOL
PHERES (BROTHER OF —) AESON
AMYTHAON
(DAUGHTER OF —) IDOMENE
PERIAPIS
(FATHER OF —) CRETHEUS
(MOTHER OF —) TYRO
(NEPHEW OF —) JASON
(SON OF —) ADMETUS LYCURGUS
PHIAL CUP FIAL VIAL CRUET
BOTTLE VESSEL
PHILABEG KILT FILIBEG
PHILANDER FOOL WOLF DALLY
FLIRT SMOCK
PHILANTHROPIC HUMANE
PHILANTHROPIST ALTRUIST
HUMANITARIAN
AMERICAN DIX CASE HOLT LICK
RICE SAGE VAUX EVANS GERRY
LENOX MILLS ODGEN PRATT
SMITH TRASK COOPER CRERAR
GEORGE GIRARD GURLEY HAYDEN
LOWELL MILLER MURPHY PEPPER
PHIPPS PUTNAM ROBERT TAPPAN
COCHRAN CORNELL DOREMUS
FARNHAM GILBERT GRELLET
LAZARUS MILBANK PARRISH
PEABODY RUTGERS RYERSON
SHEPARD STEWART CARNEGIE
CORCORAN HARKNESS LEWISOHN
PHILLIPS ROBINSON STERLING
ROSENWALD SHEFFIELD
CRITTENTON SULZBERGER
AUSTRIAN FRANKL
ENGLISH FRY GUY COBBE CORAM
CORRY KYRLE SHARP WAUGH
GURNEY KENYON COWDRAY
HIBBERT MONTAGU KINNAIRD
MACAULAY SOMERSET FAITHFULL
MONTEFIORE OGLETHORPE
SHAFTESBURY WHITTINGTON
WILBERFORCE
FRENCH MANCE MARBEAU
MONTYON MICHELIN MIRAMION
GERMAN FALK HIRSCH MULLER
FLIEDNER
INDIAN JEEJEEBHOY
IRISH RICE GONNE MADDEN
RUSSIAN NOVIKOV
SCOTTISH DALE HERIOT FINDLAY
GUTHRIE
SWEDISH NOBEL
SWISS DUNANT
PHILANTHROPY CHARITY
ALMSGIVING
PHILIP PIP PHILP SPARROW
PHILIPPIC SATIRE SCREED TIRADE
ABUSIVE DIATRIBE

PHILIPPINES
ARCHIPELAGO: SULU
CAPITAL: BAGUIO MANILA
COIN: PESO PESETA CENTAVO
SENTIMO
FIBER: ERUC ABACA BUNTAL
ISLAND: CEBU BATAN BOHOL
LEYTE LUZON PANAY SAMAR
NEGROS MASBATE MINDORO
PALAWAN ROMBLON
MINDANAO
LAKE: TAAL LANAO

LANGUAGE: MORO BICOL IBANAG
ILOCANO TAGALOG VISAYAN
MEASURE: LOAN BRAZA CABAN
CAUAN CHUPA GANTA APATAN
BALITA QUINON
MOUNTAIN: APO IBA MAYON
PULOG BANAHAO
NATIVE: ATA ATI ITA TAO AETA
ATTA ETAS MORO SULU BICOL
TAGAL VICOL IGOROT TIMAUA
BISAYAN TAGALOG FILIPINO
PROVINCE: ABRA CEBU SULU
ALBAY CAPIZ DAVAO LANAO
RIZAL BATAAN CAVITE IFUGAO
ILOILO TARLAC SURIGAO
RIVER: ABRA AGNO MAGAT PASIG
AGUSAN LAOANG CAGAYAN
MINDANAO PAMPANGA
TOWN: IBA AGOA BOAC CEBU
JOLO MATI ALBAY DAVAO
DIGOS LAOAG PASAY VIGAN
APARRI BAGUIO CAVITE ILAGAN
ILOILO MANILA BACOLOD
BASILAN DAGUPAN CALOOCAN
TREE: DAO IBA TUA TUI ACLE
ANAM ATES BOGO DITA IPIL
GUIJO LAUAN LIGAS ALUPAG
ANAHAU ARANGA ANONANG
APITONG TINDALO ALMACIGA
AMPALAYA
VOLCANO: APO TAAL MAYON
BULOSAN CANLAON
WEIGHT: CATTY FARDO PICUL
PUNTO LACHSA QUILATE
CHINANTA

PHILISTINE BOOB GIGMAN
MUCKER BABBITT GITTITE
BOEOTIAN BARBARIAN
BOURGEOIS HYPOCRITE
(PL.) PULESATI PURASATI
CAPHTORIM
PHILOLOGIST LAVENGRO
LINGUIST
AMERICAN BUCK COOK HART
TODD WOOD ADLER BROWN
CHILD CURME GIBBS HEMPL
MARCH MARSH BENDER BRIGHT
MARDEN PRINCE REEVES
EMERSON GEROULD GUDEMAN
HOPKINS KENNEDY LEARNED
SHELDON HARRISON TRUMBULL
GREENOUGH BLOOMFIELD
STURTEVANT
AUSTRIAN MINOR MULLER
KARAJAN REINISCH SCHONBACH
COLOMBIAN CUERVO MARROQUIN
CZECH HANKA GEBAUER
JUNGMANN DOBROVSKY
DANISH RAFN RASK VERNER
HEIBERG MOLBECH THOMSEN
JESPERSEN WESTERGAARD
DUTCH KATE KERN BRINK VRIES
VREESE WINKEL HEINSIUS
HEREMANS UHLENBECK
HUYDECOPER VALCKENAER
HEMSTERHUIS
ENGLISH WYLD ASTON EARLE
ELLIS NARES SAYCE SKEAT TOOKE
CONWAY CRAGIE MORRIS
MURRAY ONIONS THORPE
WERNER WRIGHT GARNETT
GOMPERZ SKINNER WEEKLEY

BOSWORTH CHADWICK
STEPHENS WEYMOUTH
COLERIDGE DONALDSON
FURNIVALL
FINNISH SETALA CASTREN
FRENCH ADAM BREAL DOLET
EGGER HENRY LEBAS MEYER
RENAN BRUNOT LAMBIN WAILLY
BRACHET BURNOUF MEILLET
LEFEBVRE VAUGELAS
CHABANEAU QUICHERAT
HOVELACQUE DARMESTETER
GERMAN AST ABEL BIRT BOPP
DIEZ FICK HIRT JULG KERN MOGK
PAUL POTT WOLF BERGK BLANC
BLASS BOCKH EBERT GREIN
GRIMM HAASE HAGEN HAUPT
HEYNE HEYSE JUSTI KLOTZ
KRAPF KRAUS KROLL LEHRS
MEYER NIESE PAULY ZEUSS
BECKER BEKKER BENFEY CHRIST
FREUND FRISCH HENZEN JACOBI
JACOBS KELLER KOCHLY MARTIN
MULLER PASSOW REISKE VAHLEN
VIETOR ADELUNG BARTSCH
BERNAYS BRANDIS BURSIAN
CORSSEN CREUZER CURTIUS
DINDORF DUNTZER GERLAND
KIEPERT KORTING LEPSIUS
LESKIEN MATZNER OSTHOFF
RIBBECK RITSCHL RUHNKEN
SANDERS SCHERER SIEVERS
WEIGAND WELCKER WISSOWA
ZARNCKE ZUPITZA AUFRECHT
BEHAGHEL BISCHOFF BOTTIGER
BRUGMANN FOERSTER GRAEVIUS
HOFFMANN HUMBOLDT
MASSMANN SCHRADER THIERSCH
WEINHOLD WESTPHAL XYLANDER
ACIDALIUS BAUMSTARK
BERNHARDY BUSCHMANN
ETTMULLER FRISCHLIN
GABELENTZ HOLTZMANN
KIRCHHOFF KOSCHWITZ
STEINTHAL TRAUTMANN
HOLTHAUSEN STREITBERG THURNEYSEN
VOLLMOLLER BARTHOLOMAE
HUNGARIAN REVAI HUNFALVY
DOBRENTEJ ENDLICHER
ICELANDIC JONSSON EGILSSON
MAGNUSSON VIGFUSSON
ITALIAN ASCOLI MONACI NOVATI
OVIDIO COMPARETTI
CASTELVETRO CASTIGLIONE
NORWEGIAN AASEN BUGGE
KONOW MUNCH
POLISH ZAMENHOF
ROZWADOWSKI
PORTUGUESE COELHO
RUMANIAN HASDEU
RUSSIAN GROT VOSTOKOV
SCHIEFNER
SCOTTISH GRANT BAIKIE MURRAY
SWEDISH IHRE LUNDELL
AHLQUIST SODERWALL
ZACHRISSON
SWISS MAHLY ISELIN
PHILOLOGY SEMITICS
PHILOMACHUS MACHETES
PHILOMELA STOP FILOMEL
(FATHER OF —) PANDION
(RAVISHER OF —) TEREUS

(SISTER OF —) PROCNE
(SLAIN BY —) ITYS
(VICTIM OF —) ITYS
PHILOSOPHER WIT SAGE CYNIC
STOIC ARTIST IONIAN LEGIST
DOTTORE ELEATIC ERISTIC
SCHOLAR SOPHIST SUMMIST
THINKER ZETETIC ACADEMIC
EPOCHIST MAGICIAN VIRTUOSO
ACADEMIST ALCHEMIST
DIALECTIC PHYSICIAN
SCHOOLMAN
AMERICAN HUME LADD MEAD
ADLER ALBEE BOWEN BOWNE
DEWEY EDMAN FISKE JAMES
LEWIS MOORE PERRY QUINE
ROYCE UPHAM HARRIS HICKOK
HYSLOP LANGER SNIDER CALKINS
HOCKING HOWISON NEWBOLD
WILLIAMS ALEXANDER
SANTAYANA
ARAB AVICENNA
AUSTRIAN BUBER EXNER DEUBLER
MEINONG STEINER ZIMMERMANN
RATZENHOFER
BELGIAN MERCIER DELBOEUF
BRAZILIAN MAGALHAES
CANADIAN MURRAY STEWART
CHINESE MOTI MENCIUS
CZECH MASARYK SMETANA
DANISH SIBBERN HOFFDING
KIERKEGAARD
DUTCH BOLLAND HEYMANS
SPINOZA OPZOOMER
ENGLISH CASE JOAD MILL MORE
WARD BACON BROAD COTES
GREEN HOOKE JONES LAIRD
LEWES LOCKE MOORE PALEY
STOUT SULLY BAYNES FOWLER
GODWIN GURNEY HOBBES
LATHAM MCCABE NEWTON
NORRIS OCKHAM TAYLOR AINSLIE
BALFOUR BENTHAM COLLIER
HALDANE HARTLEY HERBERT
HODGSON INGELBY JACKSON
RUSSELL SPENCER STEPHEN
STEWART WHEWELL CORNFORD
COURTNEY CUDWORTH GLANVILL
HOBHOUSE MUIRHEAD SCHILLER
SIDGWICK BOSANQUET
MACKENZIE WHITEHEAD
CUMBERLAND HUTCHINSON
FINNISH WESTERMARCK
FRENCH DROZ BAYLE COMTE
GUYAU HELLO JANET LEROY
LIARD MABLY RAMUS SIMON
TAINE BERARD BONALD COUSIN
GILSON GOBLOT LEROUX PASCAL
QUESNE RAYNAL SARTRE VALERY
ABAUZIT ABELARD BARTHEZ
BERGSON BURIDAN CABANIS
DAMIRON DIDEROT GERANDO
HOLBACH MAISTRE MILHAUD
REYNAUD ALEMBERT BOURDEAU
BOUTROUX CHARTIER FOUILLEE
GASSENDI GILLOUIN JOUFFROY
LAFFITTE MARITAIN MEYERSON
ROUSSEAU VACHEROT
BALLANCHE CONDILLAC
CONDORCET DESCARTES
HELVITIUS LACHELIER
SCHWEITZER MONTESQUIEU
LAROMIGUIERE

GERMAN BIEL HAYM KANT KRUG
MARX OKEN PREL BAUER CARUS
COHEN DREWS ENGEL FRIES
GROOS HEGEL LIPPS LOTZE
MARBE MEYER RIEHL STEIN UTITZ
WAITZ WOLFF BENEKE CAROVE
EUCKEN FICHTE GABLER GEIGER
GEYSER GRUPPE HEINZE HERDER
JACOBI KRAUSE KRONER LASSON
MAIMON MESSER MULLER
PRANTL RITTER STUMPF ULRICI
ZELLER ZIEHEN BRUCKER
BRUNNER CRUSIUS DEUSSEN
DILTHEY DRIESCH DUHRING
ERDMANN HAECKEL HENNING
HERBART JUNGIUS KNUTZEN
LASAULX LAZARUS PAULSEN
STIRNER STRAUSS VOLKELT
CARRIERE CASSIRER DROBISCH
EBERHARD FORTLAGE
HARTMANN HERTLING LASSWITZ
LEIBNITZ MICHELET MICHELIS
PANNWITZ REINHOLD AVENARIUS
BILFINGER CORNELIUS DIETERICI
EHRENFELS FEUERBACH
GOCLENIUS LEISEGANG
NIETZSCHE SCHELLING
THOMASIUS TIEDEMANN
VAIHINGER VORLANDER
BAUMGARTEN HILLEBRAND
ROSENKRANZ FRAUENSTADT
MENDELSSOHN SCHOPENHAUER
SCHLEIERMACHER
TRENDELENBURG
GREEK BION ZENO CEBES DAMON
LYCON PLATO CRATES EUCLID
PHAEDO PYRRHO STRATO THALES
CRANTOR DEMONAX EUDEMUS
PROCLUS TIMAEUS ALCMAEON
APULEIUS CRATYLUS DIODORUS
DIOGENES EPICURUS MELISSUS
MENIPPUS NUMENIUS PHAEDRUS
PORPHYRY SOCRATES
ARCHELAUS ARISTOTLE
CARNEADES CHARMIDES
CLEANTHES CRITOLAUS
DAMASCIUS EPICTETUS
EUBULIDES FAVORINUS
HIEROCLES LEUCIPPUS
MENEDEMUS PANAETIUS
PANTAENUS PHILOLAUS
ANAXAGORAS ANAXARCHUS
ANAXIMENES ARCESILAUS
ARISTIPPUS CHRYSIPPUS
DEMOCRITUS EMPEDOCLES
HERACLITUS IAMBLICHUS
METRODORUS PARMENIDES
PHERECYDES POSIDONIUS
PROTAGORAS PYTHAGORAS
SIMPLICIUS SPEUSIPPUS
XENOCRATES XENOPHANES
ANAXIMANDER ANTISTHENES
ARISTOXENUS CLITOMACHUS
DICAEARCHUS CALLISTHENES
PHILOSTRATUS THEOPHRASTUS
HUNGARIAN ERDELYI
INDIAN GHOSE
IRISH BERNARD BERKELEY
MOLYNEUX
ITALIAN NIFO VERA VICO ABANO
BRUNO CONTI CROCE FERRI
ARDIGO FICINO PAPINI VANINI
AQUINAS CANTONI FERRARI

FRANCHI GENTILE MAMIANI
TELESIO UBERWEG GIOBERTI
ALGAROTTI CESALPINO
CAMPANELLA FIORENTINO
POMPONAZZI BONAVENTURA
PICCOLOMINI
NORWEGIAN MONRAD
POLISH LIBELT WRONSKI
LUTOSLAWSKI
PORTUGUESE ACOSTA
ROMAN BOETHIUS CORNUTUS
PLOTINUS
RUSSIAN BERDYAEV CHICHERIN
SCOTTISH HOME HUME MILL REID
SETH CAIRD FLINT FRASER
VEITCH FERRIER STEWART
WALLACE FERGUSON HAMILTON
STIRLING HUTCHESON
CALDERWOOD MACKINTOSH
SPANISH VIVES BALMES SUAREZ
SWEDISH BOSTROM ATTERBOM
SWEDENBORG
SWISS WYSS AMIEL HILTY
PREVOST HABERLIN
PHILOSOPHER'S STONE ADROP
MICROCOSM
PHILOSOPHIC SAGE
PHILOSOPHY ETHICS GOSPEL
MAGISM SYSTEM TAOISM
APRISMO COSMISM DUALISM
INQUIRY MIMAMSA SANKHYA
SCEPSIS ACTIVISM HINDUISM
HUMANISM IDENTISM IDEOLOGY
LEGALISM OCCAMISM STOICISM
ABSURDISM NOUMENISM
SOCRATISM VEDANTISM
(— OF LIFE) LIGHTS
PHILTER DRUG CHARM WANGA
FILTER POTION AMATORY
PHINEHAS (FATHER OF —) ELI
ELEAZAR
(GRANDFATHER OF —) AARON
PHINEUS (BROTHER OF —) CADMUS
CEPHEUS
(FATHER OF —) BELUS AGENOR
(MOTHER OF —) ANCHINOE
TELEPHASSA
(SISTER OF —) EUROPA
(WIFE OF —) IDAEA CLEOPATRA
PHLEBOTOMIZE BLEED VENESECT
PHLEBOTOMUS TATUKIRA
PHLEGM FLEM GLEET MUCUS
WATER FLEUME PITUITE
MOUSEWEB
PHLEGMATIC CALM COOL DULL
SLOW INERT MUCOID SLEEPY
WATERY VISCOUS COMPOSED
SLUGGISH APATHETIC
IMPASSIVE
PHLEGYAS (DAUGHTER OF —)
CORONIS
(FATHER OF —) ARES MARS
(MOTHER OF —) CHRYSE
(SLAYER OF —) APOLLO
(SON OF —) IXION
PHLOEM BAST LIBER LEPTOME
PHLOGISTIC FIERY HEATED
BURNING FLAMING
PHLOMIS SAGELEAF
PHLOX CYME FLOX ALBION
BEACON COBAEA
PHOCUS (FATHER OF —) AEACUS
ORNYTION

(HALF-BROTHER OF —) PELEUS
TELAMON
(MOTHER OF —) PSAMATHE
(SON OF —) CRISIUS PANOPEUS
(WIFE OF —) ANTIOPE
PHOEBE FEBE FIVE MOON DIANA
PEWEE ARTEMIS
(BROTHER OF —) CASTOR POLLUX
POLYDEUCES
(DAUGHTER OF —) LETO
(FATHER OF —) URANUS
LEUCIPPUS TYNDAREUS
(MOTHER OF —) GAEA LEDA
(SISTER OF —) HELEN
CLYTEMNESTRA
PHOEBUS SUN APOLLO PHOIBUS
PHOENICIA (COLONY OF —)
CARTHAGE
(GODDESS OF —) TANIT BALTIS
TANITH ASTARTE
(KING OF —) AGENOR
(TOWN OF —) ACRE TYRE SIDON
SAREPTA
PHOENIX (BROTHER OF —) CILIX
CADMUS THASUS PHINEUS
(FATHER OF —) AGENOR AMYNTOR
(MOTHER OF —) CLEOBULE
TELEPHASSA
(PUPIL OF —) ACHILLES
(SISTER OF —) EUROPA
PHOLAS PIDDOCK
PHONEME MORPH TONEME
LARYNGAL
PHONEMIC BROAD
PHONOGRAM LOGOGRAM
SINOGRAM
PHONOGRAPH VIC PHONO
VICTROLA
(— RECORD) DISK PLATTER
PHONY FAKE JIVE SHAM BOGUS
FAKER FALSE BRUMMY BUNYIP
PHONEY PLASTIC IMPOSTOR
SPURIOUS
PHORONEUS (DAUGHTER OF —)
NIOBE
(FATHER OF —) INACHUS
(MOTHER OF —) MELIA
(SISTER OF —) IO
(SON OF —) APIS IASUS AGENOR
PELASGUS
(WIFE OF —) CERDO LAODICE
PHOSPHATE EHLITE FLOATS
APATITE CABOCLE CACOXENE
GRIPHITE MONAZITE
PHOSPHORESCENCE BRIMING
MARFIRE
PHOSPHORESCENT PHOSPHOR
NOCTILUCOUS
PHOTISM SYNOPSY
PHOTOENGRAVER
ZINCOGRAPHER
PHOTOENGRAVING HALFTONE
HELIOGRAPH
PHOTOGENE AFTERIMAGE
PHOTOGRAPH MUG PIC FILM
LENS SNAP CARTE IMAGE PANEL
PHOTO PINUP SHOOT STILL
CANDID GLOSSY MOSAIC RETAKE
SCENIC STEREO AIRVIEW PICTURE
TINTYPE LIKENESS PORTRAIT
POSITIVE SNAPSHOT TABLETOP
CYCLOGRAM MAMMOGRAM
(— SIZE) PANEL

(X-RAY —) SKIAGRAM
PHOTOGRAPHER PHOTOG
LENSMAN CAMERIST
CAMERAMAN PAPARAZZO
SHUTTERBUG
PHOTOGRAPHY STEREO
CALOTYPE PHOTOGENY
PHOTOMETER LUCIMETER
PHOTOMONTAGE COLLAGE
PHOTON BOSON TROLAND
PHRASE CRY HIT MOT SET CRIB
FUSS HAVE IDEA TERM WORD
COMMA COUCH IDIOM LABEL
LEMMA POINT STATE STYLE
TOPIC TROPE BYWORD CLAUSE
CLICHE DITTON DORISM GRUPPO
HOBNOB NOTION PNEUMA
PRAISE SAVING SLOGAN
ATTACCO DICTION EPITHET
PASSAGE CONCEIVE DIVISION
DORICISM FLATTERY IDEOGRAM
IRISHISM LATINISM LEITMOTIV
(— DIFFERENTLY) TURN
(— UNCTUOUSLY) DROOL
(MUSICAL —) RIFF POINT ATTACCO
SUBJECT
(PET —) SHIBBOLETH
(REDUNDANT —) CHEVILLE
(STOCK —) CANT
(TRITE —) CLICHE
(WELL-TURNED —) STROKE
PHRASEOLOGY CANT STYLE
DIALECT DICTION WORDING
LOCUTION PARLANCE
PHRATRY CLAN
PHRENETIC PYTHIAN FRENETIC
PHRENIC MENTAL
(PL.) PSYCHOLOGY
PHRIXOS (FATHER OF —) ATHAMAS
(MOTHER OF —) NEPHELE
(SISTER OF —) HELLE
PHRONTIS (BROTHER OF —) ARGUS
MELAS CYTISSORUS
(FATHER OF —) PHRIXUS
(HUSBAND OF —) PANTHOUS
(MOTHER OF —) CHALCIOPE
(SON OF —) EUPHORBUS
HYPERENOR POLYDAMAS
PHRYGIA (GOD OF —) ATYS ATTIS
SABAZIOS
(KING OF —) MIDAS
PHRYNIN BUFIDIN
PHTHISIS DECAY
PHUVAH (FATHER OF —) ISSACHAR
PHYLACTERY FILACTERY
(PL.) TEFILLIN TEPHILLIN
PHYLE TRIBE
PHYLOMACHE (DAUGHTER OF —)
ALCESTIS
(FATHER OF —) AMPHION
(HUSBAND OF —) PELIAS
(SON OF —) ACASTUS
PHYLUM HOKA CLASS HOKAN
NADENE BRYOZOA ANNELATA
ANNELIDA CHORDATA DIVISION
LIGNOSAE PORIFERA
PHYMA TUMOR
PHYSALIS POP POPPER
TOMATILLO
PHYSETER CATODON
PHYSIC CURE HEAL FISIC PURGE
TRADE REMEDY MEDICAL
NATURAL RELIEVE DRUGGERY

PHYSICAL ILL LUSTY SOMAL
BODILY CARNAL DISTAL NATURAL
SOMATIC CORPORAL CURATIVE
EXTERNAL MATERIAL CORPOREAL
(PURELY —) BRUTE
PHYSICIAN ASA DOC PILL CURER
GALEN HAKIM LEECH MEDIC
QUACK ARTIST BAIDYA DOCTOR
FELLOW HEALER INTERN MEDICO
DOTTORE EMPIRIC SURGEON
ALIENIST RESIDENT SAWBONES
SUNDOWNER
(— OF THE GODS) PAEAN
(PREF.) IATRO JATEO JATO
(SUFF.) IATRIST
AMERICAN RAY BARD COIT DICK
DREW FITZ HARE HOLT KING
LUST PARK SALK BIGGS BRILL
BRUSH CABOT COHEN DRAKE
FLINT GOLER KNOPF LOGAN
MINOT SMITH SPOCK TONER
TULLY TYSON WHITE BARKER
BATTEY BENNET BROOKS CARTER
CLARKE FISHER FOSTER HEISER
HOOKER HORNER HOSACK JOSLIN
KEELEY KNIGHT LAZEAR MILLER
MORGAN MORROW MURPHY
ODWYER PARRAN STILES STILLE
STORER STRONG TILTON WALKER
WATSON ALVAREZ CAMMANN
CHAPMAN DARLING DICKSON
FRANCIS GERHARD GILBERT
HAGGARD HEPBURN HOPKINS
JACKSON JANEWAY ROBBINS
TROLAND TRUDEAU BARTLETT
BILLINGS BOYLSTON FISHBEIN
GUERNSEY GWATHMEY
HAMILTON KIRTLAND KNOWLTON
MITCHELL PETERSON RICHARDS
ROCKWELL SHATTUCK SPALDING
TOWNSEND WOODWARD
BLACKWELL STERNBERG
CLENDENING GOLDBERGER
STEPHENSON WATERHOUSE
ZAKRZEWSKA CASTIGLIONI
ARAB AVICENNA ABDALLATIF
ARGENTINIAN BUNGE
AUSTRIAN BARANY BREUER
MESMER OPPOLZER ENNEMOSER
ROKITANSKY
BELGIAN WIER
BRAZILIAN CHAGAS KUBITSCHEK
CANADIAN CRAIK DAFOE FISET
GRANT OSLER REEVE ASHTON
MCCRAE BANTING RODDICK
MACPHAIL
CZECH VANCURRA
DANISH GRAM WORM LANGE
FINSEN BARTHOLIN
DUTCH GRAAF BOERHAAVE
INGENHOUSZ
ENGLISH BUDD GOOD HAKE HALL
HUME MEAD PAVY SNOW BARRY
BRUCE CAIUS DOVER DRAKE
FLUDD JAMES JONES JURIN
LOWER PAGET ACLAND BRIGHT
BROWNE CLARKE DOBELL
GARROD HARVEY HAVERS
HUNTER JENNER MANSON
PARKES RINGER SLOANE TREVES
WILLIS ADDISON ALLBUTT
BENNETT CHAPMAN CONOLLY
COPLAND DEARDEN GLISSON

HODGKIN NABARRO PRINGLE
SKINNER STANTON WHARTON
ANDERSON ANDREWES
BARNARDO BASHFORD BIRKBECK
BUCHANAN GRENFELL HEBERDEN
PRICHARD SYDENHAM
BLACKMORE BROADBENT
LANKESTER RADCLIFFE
FOTHERGILL
FRENCH CLOT DENIS DUPRE
HAYEM PINEL WIDAL ANDRAL
ASTRUC AUZOUX BERARD FERNEL
LEPINE LITTRE MARTIN PLANTE
VAQUEZ BAILLON BECHAMP
DAVAINE DUMERIL GRASSET
LAENNEC LAVERAN LECLUSE
MANTOUX MENIERE NICOLLE
PECQUET QUESNAY VINCENT
BOUCHARD DUCHENNE
LANDOUZY LEVADITI BOUILLAUD
BROUSSALS LAMETTRIE
BAILLARGER BRETONNEAU
CASSEGRAIN LANCEREAUX
POISEUILLE SCHWEITZER
BROUSSONETT
GERMAN ERB BINZ EBEL GALL
KOCH MUCH REIL ZINN BLOCH
CARUS FAUST FRANK LINGG
OSANN REMAK BRUCKE CORDUS
DOBLIN KERNER KORTUM LEYDEN
MEIBOM NORDAU OERTEL
OLBERS PEUCER AGRIPPA
BASEDOW BERENDT KAMPFER
NEISSER BRUNFELS ERXLEBEN
FLEMMING HOFFMANN
HUFELAND ZIEMSSEN DOLLINGER
FORSSMANN HAHNEMANN
NICOLAIER NOTHNAGEL
SCHONLEIN DETTWEILER
FRIEDREICH LANGERHANS
GREEK GALEN RUFUS AETIOS
CTESIAS SORANUS ALCMAEON
DEMOCEDES ORIBASIUS
PRAXAGORAS ASCLEPIADES
HIPPOCRATES ERASISTRATUS
IRISH JOYCE STOKES GOGARTY
SIGERSON
ITALIAN BOTTA GOLGI ASELLI
FARINI MAZZEI BAGLIVI BELLINI
CARDANO GALVANI BACCELLI
LOMBROSO SCALIGER
BLANDRATA CESALPINO
FRACASTORO MONTESSORI
TOSCANELLI VALLISNIERI
NORWEGIAN HANSEN
PARAGUAYAN BARBERO
RUMANIAN BABES
RUSSIAN DAHL VERESAEY
VORONOFF
SALVADORAN MOLINA
SCOTTISH LIND MOIR BLANE
BROWN ARNOTT BRIDIE BUCHAN
CHEYNE CULLEN FERGUS FORBES
BRUNTON CANTLIE JAMESON
SIMPSON GRAINGER ARBUTHNOT
ARMSTRONG PITCAIRN
CHRISTISON MACALISTER
RUTHERFORD ABERCROMBIE
SPANISH CHANCA SERVETUS
SWEDISH MUNTHE ZANDER
ACHARIUS
SWISS GOLL AMMAN PEYER
ROLLIER ZWINGER PARACELSUS

VENEZUELAN VARGAS
PHYSICIST HYLOZOIST
  AMERICAN AMES CREW GUNN
  HALL HULL LAMB LAND LANE
  MORE PAGE RABI ROOD ROSA
  TING WOOD YANG ZINN ALTER
  BACHE BARUS BAUER BETHE
  BLOCH COHEN DUANE EWELL
  HENRY KUSCH LEMON LYMAN
  MAYER PUPIN SEGRE STERN
  SWANN YALOW BEDELL BRIGGS
  CONDON COOPER FRANCK
  GERMER GLASER LOOMIS MORLEY
  NIPHER PIERCE SLOANE TELLER
  TOLMAN TOWNES VARIAN
  WIGNER WRIGHT ALLISON
  BABCOCK BARDEEN BURGESS
  CARHART COMPTON FEYNMAN
  GODDARD GODLOVE LECONTE
  NICHOLS PURCELL RANDALL
  RENWIEK RICHTER ROWLAND
  SZILARD WHEELER ANDERSON
  BLODGETT BRATTAIN BRIDGMAN
  DAVISSON HASTINGS LAWRENCE
  MILLIKAN SHOCKLEY STRATTON
  THOMPSON VANALLEN VANVLECK
  WINTHROP BITTINGER
  GOODSPEED HUMPHREYS
  INGERSOLL LAURITSEN
  MICHELSON RAINWATER
  SCHWINGER HOFSTADTER
  MENDENHALL RENTSCHLER
  RUTHERFURD SCHRIEFFER
  TROWBRIDGE CHAMBERLAIN
  OPPENHEIMER
  ARGENTINIAN CERNUSCHI
  AUSTRIAN HESS MACH DOPPLER
  PRECHTL BOLTZMANN
  SCHRODINGER
  BELGIAN PLATEAU
  CANADIAN TORY HERZBERG
  DANISH BOHR OERSTED
  MOTTELSON
  DUTCH WAALS ZEEMAN HUYGENS
  LORENTZ ZERNIKE HARTSOEKER
  KAMERLINGH MUSSCHENBROEK
  ENGLISH EVE LAMB LEES MOTT
  ASTON BOYLE BRAGG DIRAC
  GROVE JEANS JOULE LODGE
  NICOL AITKEN BARKLA CANTON
  DALTON DARWIN FRISCH KELVIN
  STOKES ANDRADE BARRETT
  CROOKES DANIELL FARADAY
  GILBERT GUTHRIE HARTREE
  MICHELL MOSELEY THOMSON
  TYNDALL APPLETON BLACKETT
  CHADWICK HAUKSBEE POYNTING
  RAYLEIGH SCHUSTER CALLENDAR
  COCKCROFT HEAVISIDE
  JOSEPHSON GLAZEBROOK
  RICHARDSON RUTHERFORD
  WHEATSTONE
  FRENCH BIOT HIRN NEEL CORNU
  FABRY JAMIN MALUS PAPIN
  PETIT WEISS BRANLY CARNOT
  CLAUDE COTTON DULONG FIZEAU
  FORTIN NIEPCE NOLLET PERRIN
  RAOULT SAVART VIOLLE BABINET
  BEUDANT BLONDEL COULOMB
  FOURIER FRESNEL JOUBERT
  KASTLER MASCART PELTIER
  REAUMUR SAUVEUR AMONTONS
  ARSONVAL DESPRETZ FOUCAULT

  LANGEVIN LIPPMANN MARIOTTE
  POUILLET REGNAULT BECQUEREL
  BRILLOUIN CAILLETET
  GUILLAUME LISSAJOUS
  CHARDONNET
  GERMAN MIE OHM BORN DOVE
  KORN LAUE LENZ REIS WIEN
  BOTHE BRAUN BUDDE DEBYE
  ERMAN HERTZ HOLTZ JOLLY
  KUNDT MAYER STARK VOIGT
  WEBER BALMER ELSTER HANKEL
  KOENIG LAMONT LENARD
  LUMMER MAGNUS NERNST
  PLANCK RIECKE RITTER ZEUNER
  AEPINUS BRODHUN CHLADNI
  FECHNER GEHRCKE HITTORF
  LAMBERT NEUMANN PLUCKER
  PRANDTL QUINCKE REGENER
  RUDOLPH SCAEFER SEEBECK
  TOEPLER WULLNER CLAUSIUS
  EINSTEIN GUERICKE ROENTGEN
  SCHUMANN FEDDERSEN
  GOLDSTEIN HALLWACHS
  KIRCHHOFF MOSSBAUER
  SCHEIBLER STEINHEIL
  WIEDEMANN BARKHAUSEN
  FAHRENHEIT KOHLRAUSCH
  PRINGSHEIM SCHWEIGGER
  SIEDENTOPF SOMMERFELD
  LICHTENBERG
  GREEK CTESIBIUS
  INDIAN BOSE SAHA RAMAN
  IRISH JOLLY STONEY WALTON
  ANDREWS TOWNSEND
  FITZGERALD
  ITALIAN RIIS FERMI PORTA RIGHI
  VOLTA ALDINI NOBILI BORELLI
  CAVALLO GALILEI GALVANI
  MELLONI VENTURI AVOGADRO
  BECCARIA BELTRAMI BLASERNA
  FERRARIS GRIMALDI PALMIERI
  BOSCOVICH PACINOTTI
  TORRICELLI
  JAPANESE ESAKI YUKAWA
  TOMONAGA
  NORWEGIAN GIAEVER BJERKNES
  HANSTEEN
  POLISH WROBLEWSKI
  RUSSIAN TAMM BASOV FRANK
  LANDAU KAPITZA LEBEDEV
  SAKHAROV CHERENKOV
  PROKHOROV
  SCOTTISH KERR TAIT WATT
  DEWAR EWING NOBLE WILSON
  MAXWELL RANKINE STEWART
  BREWSTER
  SWEDISH EDLEN ALFVEN EDLUND
  NILSON ANGSTROM SIEGBAHN
  ARRHENIUS BENEDICKS
  SWISS WILD EULER ARGAND
  LARIVE PICTET PICCARD PREVOST
  ALLAMAND
PHYSIC NUT TUBA CURCAS
  PIGNON TARTAGO
PHYSIOCRAT ECONOMIST
PHYSIOGNOMY MUG FACE PHIZ
  VIZNOMY PORTRAIT VISENOMY
PHYSIOLOGIST **AMERICAN** IVY
  LUSK HOUGH CANNON DALTON
  GASSER HARVEY HOWELL
  CARLSON SCHALLY COURNAND
  ERLANGER HARTLINE GUILLEMIN
  HENDERSON OSTERHOUT

  ARGENTINIAN HOUSSAY
  AUSTRALIAN ECCLES
  AUSTRIAN STEINACH
  BELGIAN HEYMANS
  CANADIAN BEST
  CZECH PURKINJE
  DANISH KROGH
  DUTCH DONDERS EINTHOVEN
  ENGLISH DALE HILL KATZ BEALE
  HALES LOWER ADRIAN DARWIN
  FOSTER HUXLEY RIVERS WALLER
  BAYLISS HERRING HODGKIN
  BARCROFT MARSHALL STARLING
  ELLIOTSON SHERRINGTON
  FRENCH BERT MAREY RICHET
  BEAUNIS BERNARD FLOURENS
  MAGENDIE DUTROCHET
  POISEUILLE
  GERMAN FICK VOIT BUDGE GOLTZ
  KUHNE REMAK WUNDT HENSEN
  HERING LUDWIG MULLER PREYER
  WAGNER BURDACH PFLUGER
  VERWORN WARBURG MEISSNER
  MEYERHOF VALENTIN
  HEIDENHAIN
  ITALIAN BOVET MOSSO
  MANTEGAZZA
  RUSSIAN CYON PAVLOV
  SCOTTISH MACLEOD
  SWEDISH EULER GRANIT
  HOLMGREN
  SWISS HESS
PHYSIOLOGY BIONOMY ZOONOMY
PHYSIOTHERAPY PATTERNING
PHYSIQUE BODY BUILD
  COOST HABIT FIGURE
  STRENGTH
PHYSOCARPUS NEILLIA
  OPULASTER
PHYSOSTIGMINE ESERE ESERINE
PHYTOMER PHYTON PODIUM
PI JUMBLE CONFUSE PREACHY
  CONFUSION
PIA PI GABI GABGAB MARMOT
PIACLE SIN CRIME GUILT OFFENSE
PIAN YAWS FRAMBESIA
PIANETTE PYNOT PIANINO
PIANIST CEMBALIST CLAVIERIST
PIANO SOFT FLOOR GRAND GRANT
  STORY FLUGEL GENTLY SOFTLY
  SPINET SQUARE CLAVIAL
  CLAVIER GIRAFFE PIANOLA
  QUIETLY UPRIGHT
  MELOTROPE
  (AFRICAN —) KALIMBA
  (PART OF —) ARM KEY LEG LID
  DESK FALL HEEL LYRE PROP
  CHEEK PEDAL STRING KEYSLIP
  KEYBOARD
PIASSAVA IYO JARA BAHIA
  PIACABA
PIASTER KURUS
PIATTI CYMBALS
PIAZZA PORCH SQUARE BALCONY
  GALLERY PORTICO VERANDA
  PIAZZETTA
PIC PEAK LANCE PIQUE PICADOR
PICA M EM LINE
PICARD PYKAR
PICARO KNAVE ROGUE TRAMP
  BOHEMIAN VAGABOND
PICAROON ROGUE PICARO PIRATE
  CORSAIR WRECKER

PICAYUNE PIC PETTY MEASLY
  PALTRY TRIVIAL
  PISTAREEN
PICCADILL RABATA REBATE
  REBATO
PICCOLO BUSBOY JUKEBOX
  FLAUTINO OTTAVINO
PICHICIAGO ARMADILLO
  CHLAMYPHORE
PICK NIB OPT BILL CULL GAFF
  HACK LIFT PIKE PILK SHOT WALE
  ADORN BEELE BREAK CAVIL
  ELECT FLANG LEASE PILCH PLUCK
  PRIDE PRIME CHOICE CHOOSE
  GATHER PICKAX PUDDLE TWITCH
  BARGAIN CASCROM DIAMOND
  DRESSER MANDREL
  (— APART) TOW
  (— KNOTS FROM) BURL
  (— OUT) CULL SPOT TAKE
  WELE CRONE GLEAN
  GARBLE SELECT
  (— POCKETS) FIG FILE FOIST
  TOUCH
  (— TOBACCO) STRIP
  (FILLING —) ABB
PICKAX PIX BEDE BILL PIKE
  GURLET TUBBER TWIBIL TWIBILL
PICKED PICK TRIM PIKED CHOSEN
  DAINTY PEAKED SELECT
  ADORNED POINTED
  (PREF.) LECTO
PICKER COD HOPPER
  (BERRY —) HURTER
  (PEA —) VINER
PICKEREL JACK SNAKE DUNLIN
  SAUGER SLINKER
  WALLEYE
PICKERELWEED TULE WAMPEE
PICKER-UP FINDER
PICKET PEG PALE POST TERN
  FENCE STAKE FASTEN PALING
  TETHER ENCLOSE FORTIFY
  OUTPOST PICQUET PALISADE
  OUTPICKET
PICKLE BOX ALEC DILL MESS PECK
  ACHAR BRINE GRAIN MANGO
  SAUCE SOUSE ATSARA CAPERS
  DAWDLE HIGDON KERNEL KIMCHI
  MUDDLE NIBBLE PIDDLE PILFER
  PLIGHT TRIFLE CONDITE CONFECT
  GHERKIN TROUBLE VITRIOL
  MARINADE
  (FISH —) ALEC
PICKLED DRUNK MURIATED
  POWDERED MARINATED
PICKLOCK LOCK PICKER
PICK-ME-UP SCREW PICKUP
PICKPOCKET DIP FIG GUN NIP
  BUNG FILE WIRE DIVER FILER
  FOIST BULKER BUZZER CANNON
  DIPPER FIGBOY HOOKER NIPPER
  RATERO FOISTER MOBSMAN
  CLYFAKER CUTPURSE KNUCKLER
  BUZZGLOAK
  (HELPER OF —) STALL BULKER
PICKUP BRUSH TRUCK ARREST
  BRACER ANACRUSIS
PICKWICK PAPERS (AUTHOR
  OF —) DICKENS
  (CHARACTER IN —) BOB SAM MARY
  ALLEN EMILY TRACY ALFRED
  HUNTER JINGLE PERKER SAWYER

TUPMAN WARDLE WELLER
WINKLE BARDELL RACHAEL
SLAMMER ARABELLA AUGUSTUS
CLUPPINS ISABELLA PICKWICK
NATHANIEL SMORLTORK
SNODGRASS
PICNIC FRY BALL GIPSY GYPSY
BURGOO FROLIC JUNKET
MAROON OUTING SHOULDER
SQUANTUM SUMMERING
WAYZGOOSE
PICOT LOOP PEARL PERLE
PICOTAH SWEEP PACOTA
PICTOGRAPH GLYPH PICTOGRAM
PICTORIAL GRAPHIC
PICTURE GAY MAP OIL COPY DAUB
ICON IKON LIMN SIGN VIEW
DECAL FRAME IMAGE LINER
PAINT PHOTO PIECE PINAX PRINT
SCENE SHAPE STAMP STORY
TABLE CACHET CANVAS CHROMO
CUTOUT DEPICT EMBLEM MARINE
PASTEL SEMBLE SHADOW STEREO
TABLET CUTAWAY DIORAMA
DIPTYCH EMBLEMA ETCHING
EXHIBIT FASHION FEATURE
GOUACHE GRAPHIC HISTORY
MIZRACH PAYSAGE PORTRAY
PORTURE RETRAIT SCENERY
TABLEAU VANDYKE AIRSCAPE
AUTOTYPE DESCRIBE DROLLERY
ENVISION IDEOGRAM KAKEMONO
LANDSKIP LIKENESS MAKIMONO
MONOTINT OVERDOOR PAINTING
PANORAMA PORTRAIT PROSPECT
RITRATTO SEASCAPE SINGERIE
SKYSCAPE TRIPTYCH VIGNETTE
ENCAUSTIC
(— IN BOOK) GAY
(— IN 3 COMPARTMENTS)
TRIPTYCH
(— MAT) SPANDREL
(— OF MONKEYS) SINGERIE
(— ON ROLLER) KAKEMONO
MAKIMONO
(— PUZZLE) REBUS JIGSAW
(—S IN BOOKS) BABY
(COMIC —) DROLLERY
(RELIGIOUS —) TANKA
(STEREOSCOPIC —) ANAGLYPH
(THREE-DIMENSIONAL —)
HOLOGRAM
(PREF.) PINAC(O)
PICTURE OF DORIAN GRAY
(AUTHOR OF —) WILDE
(CHARACTER IN —) ALAN GRAY
VANE BASIL HENRY JAMES SIBYL
DORIAN WOTTON CAMPBELL
HALLWARD
PICTURESQUE VIVID EXOTIC
QUAINT SCENIC GRAPHIC IDYLLIC
ROMANTIC PICTORIAL
PICUL TAN PICO PIKOL
PIDDLE PICK PLAY DAWDLE PICKLE
PUTTER TRIFLE
PIDDLING JERK PALTRY TRIVIAL
USELESS FOOTLING TRIFLING
JERKWATER
PIDDOCK DACTYL PHOLAD
PHOLAS
PIDGIN LANGUAGE SABIR
PIE PAI FLAM FLAN HEAP MESS
PATE PILE TART DOWDY FLAWN

PASTY PATTY TORTA TOURT
AFFAIR BRIDLE CHEWET MAGPIE
PASTRY TOURTE COBBLER
SMASHER STRUDEL BAKEMEAT
CRUSTADE FLAPJACK PANDOWDY
SURPRISE TURNOVER
SMASHOVER
PIEBALD PIE PIED PIET MIXED
PIETY PINTO CALICO MOTLEY
SKEWBALD
PIECE BAT BIT COB CUT DAM FIG
JOB LAB LOG MAN TUT GIRL
MIND PART PISE PLAY BLYPE
DAGON DRAMA DWANG FLOOR
PEZZO SCRAP SHARD SHERD
SHRED SLICE SNODE STEEK
STUCK THROW COLLOP FARDEL
FUGATO GOBBET PARCEL STITCH
CANTLET EXAMPLE FLINDER
FLITTER MORCEAU OPINION
PICTURE PORTION SEGMENT
DUOLOGUE EMBOLIUM
FANDANGO PAINTING
(— AT END) HEELPIECE
(— FOR TWO) DUET DUOLOGUE
(— IN CHECKERS) DAM
(— IN ORGAN) THUMPER
(— OF ARMOR) JAMB JAMBE
(— OF BAD LUCK) DIRDUM
(— OF BLANKET) DAGON
(— OF BLUBBER) BIBLE
(— OF DECEPTION) BEGUNK
(— OF DECORATED METAL) NIELLO
(— OF FALSE HAIR) JANE
(— OF FIBER) NOIL
(— OF FIRED CLAY) TILE
(— OF GROUND SURROUNDED BY
WASTE) HOPE
(— OF HARD WOOD) MOOT
(— OF LAND) ERF HAM LOT BUTT
GORE LEASE SPONG SQUAT
HUERTA RINCON SECTION
CLEARAGE SOLIDATE
(— OF LIGHT ORDNANCE) ASPIC
(— OF LINEN) AMIT AMICE
(— OF LOG) SLAB
(— OF MAST) TONGUE
(— OF MATZOTH) AFIKOMEN
(— OF MEAT) EYE HEEL RAND
COLLOP EPIGRAM
(— OF METAL) JAG COIN JAGG
SPRAG
(— OF MONEY) COG SOU SHINER
(— OF NEEDLEWORK) SAMPLER
(— OF NONSENSE) FUDGE
TRIMTRAM
(— OF ORE) CHAT
(— OF PROPERTY) CHOSE
(— OF SAIL) HULLOCK
(— OF SEPARATED LAND) BUTT
(— OF SKIN) BLYPE
(— OF SKIN FOR GLOVE) TRANK
(— OF SLATE) SLAT
(— OF SOAP) BALL
(— OF SOMETHING EDIBLE) STULL
(— OF TIMBER) FISH COULISSE
FOREHOOK
(— OF TOAST) SLINGER
(— OF TOBACCO) FIG
(— OF TRACK) LEAD RUNBY
(— OF TRICKERY) CROOK CANTRIP
(— OF TURF) FLAG DIVOT SCRAW
SHIRREL

(— OF WOOD) KIP LATH APRON
BOARD CHUMP CHUNK PLANK
SPOON WADDY BILLET COMMON
STOWER TIMBER LIPPING
(— OF WORK) JOB CHAR TURN
(— OF WRITING) SCREED SCREEVE
(— OUT) EKE
(— SPLIT OFF) SPLINT
(— TO PREVENT SLIPPING) CLEAT
(—S OF MACARONI) DITALI
DITALINI
(ARTILLERY —) DRAKE SAKER
LANTACA
(BACKGAMMON —) BLOT STONE
(BROAD —) SHEET
(BROKEN —) BRACK MAMMOCK
FRACTION
(BUTTING —) HURTER
(CHESS —) PIN KING PAWN ROOK
QUEEN BISHOP CASTLE KNIGHT
OFFICER
(DREAMY —) REVERIE
(END — OF BUCKET) CANT
(FLAT —) FLAP FLAKE
(FUR —) PALATINE
(GOLD —) SLUG TALI
(IN —S) LIMBMEAL
(IRREGULAR —) SNAG
(LARDED — OF MEAT) DAUB
(LARGE —) HUNK MOLE STULL
DOLLOP
(LITERARY —) CAMEO
(LITTLE —) STNEKI SCANTLING
(LONG —) STRIP
(MOVABLE — IN VIOLIN BOW) NUT
(MUSICAL —) ITEM CHORO DANCE
ETUDE CHASER LESSON ALLEGRO
ANDANTE BLUETTE CONCERTO
DUOLOGUE ENTRACTE OVERTURE
INVENTION
(NARROW —) LABEL STAVE STRIP
(ODD — OF CARPENTRY)
DUTCHMAN
(ROTATING —) CAM ROTOR
SPINDLE
(SAMPLE —) SWATCH
(SHAPELESS —) DUMP MAMMOCK
(SIDE —) RIB JAMB JAMBE
(SINGLE —) LENGTH
(SLENDER —) SPILL SLIVER
(SMALL —) BIT BOB NOB PEA CHIP
SNIP TATE CRUMB PATCH PRILL
SCRAP SPECK MORSEL SIPPET
DRIBLET FLITTER PALLION
SPLINTER
(SMALL — OF FLESH) GIGOT
(SMALL — OF WOOD) KIP
(SMALL —S) MATCHWOOD
(STRENGTHENING —) DWANG
HURTER
(TAPERING —) GORE GUSSET
(THICK —) JUNK HUNCH
(THIN —) SHIM FLAKE SHIVE SLICE
(WEDGESHAPED — OF WOOD) GLUT
SHIM
(100-REAL GOLD —) ISABELLA
(25-CENT —) CUTER
(4-DOLLAR GOLD —) STELLA
(PL.) MATERIAL NOBLEMEN
PIECEWORK SETWORK TUTWORK
TASKWORK
PIECEWORKER JOBBER
PIECRUST BREAD COFFIN ABAISSE

PIED PINTO SHELD MAGPIED
PIEBALD
PIED ANTELOPE BONTEBOK
PIEDFORT PATAGON
PIED WAGTAIL COB COBB PEER
PILE PILLAR WAGGIE WASHER
WATERIE SEEDBIRD WASHDISH
WASHTAIL
PIEPLANT RHUBARB RHAPONTIC
PIER COB ANTA BELT COBB DOCK
MOLE PILE QUAY TILT GROIN
JETTY JOWEL JUTTY LEVEE STILT
WHARF BRIDGE BUNDER
MULLION STAGION PIEDROIT
STELLING
(— SUMMER) SUMMER
(HALF —) RESPONSE
PIERCE CUT DAB DAG DEG DIG
JAB JAG RIT BARB BEAR BITE
BORE BROB BROD CLOY DART
DIRL GORE HOLE HOOK LACE
LACK PASS PINK POKE PROB
PROG RIVE ROVE STAB STOB
TAME TANG WHIP BREAK DRIFT
DRILL ENTER GOUGE GRIDE
LANCE PERCH PITCH POACH
PREEN PROBE PRONG SHEAR
SNICK SPEAR SPIKE STEEK STICK
STING THIRL ATTAME BROACH
CLEAVE DAGGER EMPALE FICCHE
GIMLET IMPALE LAUNCH PRITCH
RIDDLE SEARCH SKEWER STITCH
STRIKE THRILL THRING THRUST
WIMBLE ASSAGAI JAVELIN
ENTHRILL LACERATE PUNCTURE
PENETRATE
(PREF.) FORAMINI
PIERCED AJOURE CRIBRAL
PERTUSE CRIBROSE PERFORATE
PIERCING SHY FELL HIGH KEEN
LOUD TART ACUTE CLEAR EAGLE
SHARP SNELL ARROWY BITTER
BORING SHREWD SHRILL SNITHE
SNITHY CUTTING GIMLETY
POINTED PUNGENT DRILLING
INCISIVE PERCEANT POIGNANT
POUNCING STABBING STICKING
PENETRATIVE
PIERHEAD MOLEHEAD
PIET PYOT DIPPER MAGPIE
PIETIST LABADIST
PIETISTIC DEVOUT
PIETY HONOR LOYALTY PIETISM
DEVOTION SANCTION GODLINESS
PIFFLE BUFF FOLDEROL
PIG (ALSO SEE HOG, SWINE) COW
FAR HAM HOG SLIP BACON
BONAV BROCK CHEAT CHUCK
GRICE INGOT PIGGY SHOAT
APEREA BONHAM COCHON
FARROW GUSSIE HOGGIE PORKET
PORKIN SUCKER TITMAN WEANER
BONNIVE GLUTTON GRUMPHY
HOGLING PIGLING ROOKLER
GRUNTLING
(BROOD OF —S) TEAM
(CASTRATED —) BARROW
(EIGHT —S) FODDER
(PART OF —) EAR EYE HAM BUTT
HOCK JOWL LOIN POLL TAIL TEAT
FLANK SNOUT PICNIC FATBACK
FOREFOOT SHOULDER SPARERIB
TENDERLOIN

(SMALLEST — OF LITTER) DOLL TITMAN ANTHONY DILLING TANTANY TANTONY
(SUCKLING —) ROASTER
(UNDERSIZED —) RUNT TITMAN TEATMAN
(YOUNG —) ELT FAR SLIP GRICE GURRY BONEEN BONHAM SQUEAKER
(PREF.) HYO
(SUFF.) CHOERUS
PIG DEER BABIRUSA
PIGEON DOO NUN OWL TOY BARB CLAY DOVE JACK KING KITE LUPE RUFF RUNT SPOT BALDY DOWVE FRILL HOMER KOKLA PIPER SQUAB WONGA CULTER CULVER CUSHAT DODLET DRAGON FEEDER HELMET JEWING MAGPIE MANUMA MAUMET MODENA POUTER PRIEST ROCKER SHAKER TRERON TURBIT TURNER WATTLE ANTWERP CARNEAU CARRIER CROPPER FANTAIL FINIKIN JACINTH JACOBIN MALTESE PINTADO SWALLOW TIPPLER TUMBLER BALDHEAD CAPUCHIN FINIKING HORSEMAN MANUTAGI RINGDOVE SASSOROL SQUABBER SQUEAKER SQUEALER FRILLBACK TOOTHBILL
(CLAY —) BIRD GYROPIGEON
(STOOL —) PIG NARK
PIGEON BLOOD GARNET
PIGEON HAWK MERLIN
PIGEONHOLE BOX SLOT LABEL SHELVE ANALYZE CELLULE CLASSIFY CUBBYHOLE
(PL.) STOCK
PIGEON HOUSE COT DOOKET DOVECOT COLUMBARY
PIGEON PEA DAL TUR TARE ARHAR DAHIL GANDUL TURNER TURNOR CATJANG
PIGEON WOODPECKER FLICKER
PIGGERY PIGS PIGSTY HOGGERY POTTERY SWINERY CROCKERY
PIGGIN HANDY PIPKIN
PIGHEADED WILLFUL PERVERSE STUBBORN OBSTINATE
PIGHTLE PIKLE PICKLE PIDDLE PIGTAIL
PIG IRON GRUNDY
PIGLET PORKLING
PIGLIKE SUIFORM SUILINE SWINISH
PIGMENT (ALSO SEE DYE, COLOR) BLUE HEME BROWN COLOR EARTH GREEN HUMIN MORIN MUMMY PAINT STAIN TONER BRONZE CEROID CERUSE IDAEIN LITHOL MALVIN ORANGE PURPLE SIENNA VIOLET BEZETTA GOUACHE PAINTRY PUCCOON STAINER TURACIN ALTHAEIN COLORANT EXTENDER GOSSYPOL MELANOID PAINTURE TINCTURE UROPHEIN VERDITER
(— FOR WOODWORK) KOKOWAI
(— IN BUTTERFLY WING) PTERIN
(BLACK —) ABAISER MELANIN
(BLUE —) BICE SMALT CYANIN ALTHEIN CERULEUM MARENNIN
(BLUE-GREEN —) LEUCOCYAN

(BROWN —) MUMMY SEPIA UMBER BISTER FUSCIN ASTERIN SINOPIA
(BROWNISH-YELLOW —) SIENNA
(GRAPE —) ENIN OENIN
(GREEN —) VERDITER
(MADDER-ROOT —) RUBIATE
(ORANGE-RED —) REALGAR
(PLANT —) CYANIN
(RED —) HAEM LAKE ARUMIN PATISE SANDYX AMATITO KOKOWAI PUCCOON SCARLET SINOPIA CAPSUMIN URORUBIN URRHODIN VERMILION
(RED-VIOLET —) TURACIN
(WHITE —) CERUSE ANATASE LITHOPONE
(YELLOW —) FLAVIN PURREE ETIOLIN FISETIN GAMBOGE PUCCOON CAROTENE DIATOMIN GALANGIN GENTISIN MASSICOT ORPIMENT UROBILIN
(PREF.) CHROM(AT)(ATO)(I)(IDIO)(O)
PIGMENTATION COLOR LENTIL ARGYRIA LENTIGO JAUNDICE NIGRITIES
(SUFF.) CHROMIA
PIGNUS PAWN PLEDGE
PIGNUT ARNOT ARNUT HOGNUT
PIGS' FEET CRUBEEN PETTITOES
PIGSKIN SADDLE FOOTBALL
PIGSNEY EYE DARLING
PIGSTY FRANK CRUIVE HOGCOTE HOGGERY PIGGERY SWINESTY
PIGTAIL PLAIT QUEUE COLETA
PIGWASH SWILL
PIGWEED QUINOA BEETROOT CARELESS GOOSEFOOT
PIK DRA PICKI PICKL ENDAZE ENDASEH
PIKA CONY HAIR HARE LEPORID LAGOMORPH
PIKE GED DORE DORY GADE GEDD JACK LUCE TANG TOUG TUCK HAKED LUCET SNAKE SNOOK STING VOUGE SALMON SAUGER JAVELIN WALLEYE BLOWFISH GLASSEYE JACKFISH NORTHERN PARTISAN PICKEREL POULAINE TURNPIKE MUSKELLUNGE
PIKELET CRUMPET
PIKEMAN PIKE WATTLEBOY
PIKE PERCH FOGASH PERCID SANDER SAUGER ZANDER
PIKER TRAMP VAGRANT TELLTALE TIGHTWAD VAGABOND
PILASTER ANTA PIER RIDGE ALETTE ALLETTE RESPOND TELAMON
PILCHARD FUMADO ALEWIFE SARDINE MENHADEN
PILDASH (FATHER OF —) NAHOR
(MOTHER OF —) MILCAH
PILE COP FUR LOT NAP PIE TIP BALE BANK BING BULK BUNG BURR COCK DASS DECK DESS DOWN HACK HAIR HEAP LEET LOAD PEEL PIER POLE POOK PYRE REEK RUCK SESS SHAG SPUD AMASS CANCH CLAMP CROWD FAGOT POINT SPILE SPIRE STACK STILT TOWER CASTLE FAGGOT FENDER FILLER GALGAL PILLAR

RICKLE RUCKLE FORTUNE JAVELIN PYRAMID REACTOR SPINDLE CROWBILL INCREASE SANDPILE
(— CROSSWISE) COB
(— CURD) CHEDDAR
(— OF BRICKS) HACK CLAMP
(— OF CLOTH) LAY
(— OF HAY) RICK SHOCK DOODLE HAYCOCK HAYRICK
(— OF ICE) HUMMOCK
(— OF LOGS) DECK
(— OF PLATES) BUNG
(— OF REFUSE) DUSTHEAP
(— OF SALT FISH) BULK
(— OF SEALSKINS) PAN
(— OF SHEAVES) SESS
(— OF SHEETS) LIFT
(— OF STONES) ISLAND STONAGE WARLOCK
(— OF TOBACCO) BULK
(— OF WOOD) STRAND
(— TO BE BURNT) PYRE
(— UP) BIG BULK CORD RICK COMPILE ACCUMULATE
(— WHEAT SHOCKS) STITCH
(IRON —) SPINDLE
(LITTLE —) HOT HOTT
(LOOSE —) RICKLE
(ROCK —) HOODOO
(SMALL —) COCK CANCH
(PL.) FIG DRIFT
PILEA ADICEA
PILEATED WOODPECKER LOGCOCK WOODCOCK
PILE DRIVER TUP FISTUCA HERCULES IMPACTER
(— DOLLY) FOLLOWER
(— WEIGHT) RAM TUP MONKEY
PILEUS CAP MITRA PILEOLUS
PILEWORT CRAIN CRANE FICARY FIGWORT CELANDINE
PILFER NIM NIP ROB CRIB HOOK PELF PICK PILK PRIG SMUG SNIG FILCH MICHE MOOCH PILCH PROWL SHARP SLOCK STEAL SWIPE FINGER MAGPIE MOOTCH NIBBLE PICKLE SMOUCH SNITCH CABBAGE MANAVEL PLUNDER PURLOIN SNAFFLE UNHITCH PETTIFOG SCROUNGE
PILFERER PRIG PIKER TAKER SLOCKER FINGERER SLOCKSTER
PILFERING CRIB MICHING PICKING THIEVISH
PILGRIM HAJI HADJI HAJJI PALMER PELERIN PEREGRIN WAYFARER
PILGRIMAGE TRIP TURUS VOYAGE JOURNEY
(— TO MECCA) HADJ
(BRETON —) PARDON
PILGRIM BROWN FRIAR
PILGRIM'S PROGRESS (AUTHOR OF —) BUNYAN
(CHARACTER IN —) POPE PAGAN PIETY SLOTH PLIANT SIMPLE CHARITY DESPAIR HOPEFUL SINCERE APOLLYON FAITHFUL GOODWILL PRUDENCE WATCHFUL CHRISTIAN FORMALISM HYPOCRISY IGNORANCE KNOWLEDGE

OBSTINATE DISCRETION EVANGELIST EXPERIENCE PRESUMPTION
PILING SPILING STOCKADE
(PL.) STARLING
PILL PIL ROB BALL BARK GOLI PEEL POOL CREEK CACHOU EXTORT UNHAIR DESPOIL DIURNAL GLOBULE GRANULE PARVULE PILLULE PREFORM BASEBALL GOOFBALL BLACKBALL CIGARETTE
(AROMATIC —) CACHOU
(LARGE —) BALL BOLUS
(LITTLE —) PILULA PILULE
PILLAGE LOOT PEEL PILL PREY SACK BOOTY FORAY HARRY REAVE RIFLE SPOIL HARROW MARAUD PICORY RAPINE RAVAGE DESPOIL PICKEER PLUNDER RANSACK ROBBERY BOOTHALE EXPILATE PURCHASE SPOLIATE DEVASTATE
PILLAGER PEELER PILLER ROBBER SACKER SPOILER SNAPHANCE
PILLAGING EXECUTION PREDATORY
PILLAR COG HERM JAMB PACK PIER PILE POST PROP STUD TERM JAMBE NEWEL SHAFT STELA STELE STOCK STONE STOOP STUMP CIPPUS COLUMN HERMES PILLER STAPLE BEDPOST DEADMAN TRESTLE TRUMEAU BOUNDARY MASSEBAH PEDESTAL RESPONSE STANCHION
(— CAPPED WITH SLAB) BILITH
(— IN LARGE DOORWAY) TRUMEAU
(— IN MINE) STOOK STUMP
(— OF COAL) SPURN STOOK STOOP
(— SUPPORTING ARCH) RESPONSE
(— SURMOUNTED BY HEAD) HERMES
(—S OF HERCULES) ABILA CALPE
(BUDDHIST —) LAT
(CHANGED TO —) OLENUS
(EARTH —) HOODOO
(SACRED —) ASHERAH
(SEMITE —) MASSEBAH
(STONE —) CIPPUS
(TEMPORARY —) DEADMAN
(4-SIDED —) OBELISK
(PL.) CRURA
(PREF.) CION(O) STELO STYL(I)(O)
(SUFF.) STELE STYLAR STYLE STYLI(C) STYLOUS
PILLARIST STYLITE
PILLAS PILCORN PILKINS
PILLBOX SCATULA
PILLBUG ISOPOD KEESLIP MILLEPED PILLWORM CHEESELIP
PILLED BALD SHAVEN TONSURED
PILLION PAD PILLOW SADDLE CUSHION
PILLORY CANG THEW JOUGS TRONE CANGUE CRUCIFY HALSFANG
PILLOW COD BOTT DAWN PEEL PILE REST FLOAT WANGER BOLSTER CUSHION FUSTIAN HEADING OREILLE PULVINAR
(PREF.) PULVILLI PULVIN(I)
PILLOWCASE COD BEAR PILL SHAM PILLIVER

PILLOWY PULVINAR
PILM DUST
PILON BONUS LAGNIAPPE
PILOSE HAIRY PILEOUS
PILOT ACE SPY KIWI COACH
GUARD GUIDE STEER AIRMAN
ESCORT MANAGE THAMUS
AVIATOR CAPTAIN CONDUCT
HOBBLER LODEMAN SHIPMAN
WINGMAN AIREDALE GOVERNOR
HELMSMAN PALINURUS
WHEELSMAN COWCATCHER
(AUTHOR OF —) COOPER
(AUTOMATIC —) GEORGE
(CHARACTER IN —) TOM GRAY
ALICE JONES MERRY COFFIN
DILLON EDWARD HOWARD
MANUAL MUNSON CECILIA
PLOWDEN RICHARD GRIFFITH
DUNSCOMBE KATHERINE
BARNSTABLE CHRISTOPHER
BORROUGHCLIFFE
(DUD —) PRUNE
PILOT BIRD PLOVER
PILOT FISH ROMERO JACKFISH
AMBERFISH
PILOTHOUSE TEXAS CHARTHOUSE
PILUM PESTLE JAVELIN
PIMENTA MYRTAL
PIMENTO PIMENTA ALLSPICE
PIMIENTO
PIMP MACK BULLY CADET FAGOT
PONCE SNEAK MACRIO PANDER
RUFFIAN INFORMER PROCURER
PURVEYOR SCOUNDREL
SOUTENEUR
PIMPERNEL BURNET WAYWORT
EYEBRIGHT MARGELINE
WINCOPIPE
PIMPLE GUM NOB PAP BURL KNOB
PUSH QUAT SPOT BLAIN BOTCH
HICKY PLOOK PLOUK PLUKE
WHELK BLOTCH BOUTON BUTTON
PAPULA PAPULE TETTER
BUBUKLE PUSTULE PIMGENET
WHEYWORM
(PREF.) CHALAZI CHALAZO
PAPULI PAPULO
PIN FID FIX HOB HUB LAG LEG NOG
PEG PEN ACUS APEX AXLE BANK
BOLT MOOD PEEN POST PRIN
PROP PYNE RUNG STUD DRIFT
HUMOR KAYLE POINT PREEN
SPILL THOLE BOBBIN BODKIN
BROACH BROOCH CALIGO COTTER
CURLER FASTEN HATPIN JOGGLE
NORMAN PINNET SKEWER SPIGOT
TEMPER TENPIN TOGGEL TONGUE
TRIFLE BAYONET CONFINE
ENCLOSE GUDGEON HAIRPIN
IMPOUND LOCKPIN PUSHPIN
SPINDLE TAMPION TANGENT
TUMBLER WOOLDER FORELOCK
PINNACLE
(— FOR FITTING PLANKS) SETBOLT
(— IN AXLETREE) LINCHPIN
(— IN RIFLE) TIGE
(— OF DIAL) STYLE GNOMON
(— OF LANTERN PINION) RUNDLE
(— OF WATCH) DART
(— ON CLAVICHORD KEY) TANGENT
(— TO HOLD BEDCLOTHES)
BEDSTAFF

(— USED AS TARGET) HOB
(BELAYING —) CAVIL
(BOWLING —) DUCKPIN HEADPIN
KINGPIN SLEEPER
(BOWLING —S) DEADWOOD
(CARPENTRY —) DOWEL
(COUPLING —) DRAWBOLT
(ENGAGING —) BAYONET
(HAIR —) BARRETTE
(HEADED —) RIVET
(JEWELED —) PROP
(OAR —) THOLE
(ORNAMENTAL —) AGLET AIGLET
(PIVOT —) PINTLE
(SMALL —) LILL MINIKIN MICROPIN
(SPLIT —) COTTER FORELOCK
(SURVEYOR'S —) ARROW
(TAPERED —) DRIFT
(TIRLING —) RISP
(WOODEN —) SPILE TRENAIL
(PL.) LEGS KAILS DEADWOOD
(PREF.) PERONEO PERONO
PINACOID BASE HEMIDOME
PINAFORE BRAT SLIP TIDE TIDY
TIER TYER DAIDLY PINNER
SAVEALL SLIPPER GABERDINE
PINBALL BAGATELLE
PINBALL MACHINE PACHINKO
PINCASE POPPET
PINCE-NEZ NIPPER LORGNON
NOSEPINCH
PINCERS TEU TEW CLAM CHELA
TUARN PLIERS TURKIS WYNRIS
FORCEPS MULLETS NIPPERS
PINCHER PINSONS TWEEZERS
PINCH NIP TOP VEX WRY BITE
CLAM HURT POOK PUSH STOP
TAIT TATE TUCK CHACK CRIMP
GRIPE HINCH PUGIL SNUFF
SQUAT STEAL STINT TAPER
THEFT TWEAK WRING ARREST
CLUTCH EXTORT HARASS
NARROW SNITCH STRAIT STRESS
TWITCH SCRINCH SQUEEZE
JUNCTURE PRESSURE SHORTAGE
STRAITEN VELLICATE
(— OF SNUFF) SNEESH SNEESHIN
(— WITH COLD) NIRL
(— WITH HUNGER) CLAM CLEM
PINCHBECK SHAM CHEAP
SPURIOUS PRETENDED
PINCHED CHITTY WASTED
HAGGARD PUNGLED SQUINCH
PINCHING CHACK
PINCHPENNY CARL MISER
NIGGARD NIGGARDLY
PINDARIC ODE WILD
PINE IE ARA LIM CHIL CHIR FADE
FLAG HALA HONE IEIE KAIL WANT
AGGAG DROOP DWAIN GRIEF
KAURI MATAI MATSU MOURN
OCOTE PINON WANZE WEARY
WRIST YEARN APACHE AROLLA
DUSTER FAMINE GRIEVE HUNGER
LAMENT PANDAN SHRINK
SORROW STARVE TOATOA
TORFEL WITHER CYPRESS
DAISING DWINDLE FORPINE
FOXTAIL JEFFREY LAUHALA
TARWOOD TORMENT TORTURE
AKAMATSU AUSTRIAN GALAGALA
LANGUISH LOBLOLLY LONGLEAF
PINASTER STAGHORN

TANEKAHA VANQUISH
(— AWAY) PEAK DROOP DWINE
SNURP WANZE WINDER FORPINE
MACERATE
(AUSTRALIAN —) BEEFWOOD
(GROUND —) FOXTAIL
(PITCH —) THYME
(PREF.) PINI PITYO
PINEAPPLE BOMB NANA PINA
PINO PITA ANANA ANANAS
ABACAXI GRENADE
PINE FINCH SISKIN
PINE MARTEN SABLE
PINE NEEDLE SHAT SPILL PINING
ALFILARIA
(PL.) TWINKLES
PINE TREE STATE MAINE
PINFEATHER PEN STUMP STIPULE
PINFISH CHUB SPOT JIMMY PORGY
SARGO
PINFOLD POUND
PING KNOCK
PINGRASS ALFILERIA
PINGUIN MAYA ANANAS AGUAMAS
PINUELA HUIPILLA
PINGUITUDE FATNESS OBESITY
OILINESS
PINION NOIL WING PINON QUILL
PENNON SARCEL SECURE
LANTERN PINACLE SHACKLE
TRUNDLE FLIGHTER WALLOWER
PINION WHEEL MOBILE
PINITOL SENNITE MATEZITE
PINK JAG PIP CYME DAWN DECK
FADE MICE PING STAB WINK
ADORN BLINK CORAL ELITE
MOVED SWELL WOUND AURORE
BISQUE CHERUB FIESTA HEIGHT
MINNOW POUNCE SHRIMP SILENE
TATTOO ZEPHYR ANNATTO
ARBUTUS BEGONIA BERMUDA
BLOSSOM CAMPION EXTREME
PARAGON REVEREE SANDUST
TUSSORE CONFETTI COQUETTE
DECORATE DIANTHUS GILLIVER
LIMEWORT RADIANCE RECAMIER
PINKED JAGGED
PINKIE PIRLIE
PINKROOT REDROOT WORMWEED
STARBLOOM
PINNA EARFLAP PINNULE
APHLEBIA AURICULA PAVILION
PINNACE BARK CROWN WOMAN
BARQUE PINNAGE MISTRESS
PINNACLE IT PIN TOP ACME APEX
CREST CROWN SERAC SPIRE
THUMB FINIAL HEIGHT SUMMIT
GENDARME
(ICE —) SERAC
(ROCKY —) TOR HOODOO
AIGUILLE GENDARME
PINNATE WINGED
PINNER PINDER FLANDAN STICKER
PINNIPED SEAL
PINOCHLE BINOCLE GOULASH
AIRPLANE
(— SCORE) MELD
PINPILLOW PIMPLO
PINPOINT ISOLATE
(— OF LIGHT) GLEAM
PINT O GULL PINNET SWIGGER
OCTARIUS
(FOURTH —) GILL JACK

(HALF —) CUP NIP GILL JACK
CUPFUL NIPPERKIN
(9-10THS —) MUTCHKIN
PINTADO CERO PIED SIER SEARER
SIERRA SPOTTED KINGFISH
PINTAIL DUCK SMEE SPIKE SPRIG
GROUSE SMETHE CRACKER
LADYBIRD LONGNECK PIKETAIL
PINTANO PILOT COCKEYE
CHIRIVITA
PINTID EMPEINE
PINTO BEAN ROSILLO
PINWEED
(PL.) LECHEA
PINWHEEL WINDMILL
PINWORM NEMA OXYURID
PIN WRENCH SPANULE
PIONEER BLAZE GUIDE MINER
GROPER HALUTZ SETTLE
CHALUTZ EXPLORE EARLIEST
EMIGRANT ORIGINAL RAWHIDER
VOORTREKKER
PIONEERS (AUTHOR OF —) COOPER
(CHARACTER IN —) JOHN GRANT
HIRAM JONES NATTY BUMPPO
LOUISA OLIVER TEMPLE
EDWARDS RICHARD DOOLITTLE
EFFINGHAM ELIZABETH
CHINGACHGOOK
PIOUS PI HOLY WISE FROOM
GODLY MORAL SEELY DEVOUT
DIVINE INWARD PIETIC CANTING
DUTIFUL GODDARD PITEOUS
SAINTED SAINTLY FAITHFUL
RELIGIOUS
PIP DIE CHIP ECHO KILL PAIP PEEP
SPOT SPECK ACINUS DEFEAT
PIPPIN BLACKBALL
PIPAL BO FIG
PIPE TD BIN GUN HUB TAP TEE
BUTT CALL CANE DALE DRIP
DUCT FLUE HOSE LINE MAIN
MUTE PULE REED TILE TUBE
WEEP WORM BLAST BRAIL BRIAR
CANAL CANEL CINCH CRANE
CROSS CUTTY HOOKA PROBE
PUNGI QUILL RIDER RISER SPOUT
STAND STRAW TEWEL TRUMP
TRUNK VOICE BRANCH BURROW
CALEAN CASING DUCTUS FAUCET
FILLER GEWGAW HEWGAG
HOGGER KINURA NIPPLE NOTICE
NOZZLE OFFLET OFFSET POOGYE
RANKET SLEEVE SLOUCH SLUICE
SUCKER TROWEL TUBULE
TUNNEL UPTAKE WEEPER
CHANNEL CHANTER CHIBOUK
CONDUIT DUCTURE FISTULA
HYDRANT SERVICE SPARGER
SPINDLE SUCTION TALLBOY
TWEEDLE WHISTLE CALIDUCT
DOWNTAKE GALOUBET
LAMPHOLE MIRLITON NARGHILE
NARGILEH PENSTOCK SEMIDOLE
SUSPIRAL TELLTALE THRIBBLE
(— AS NAVIGATION AID) SPINDLE
(— BENDER) HICKEY
(— BOWL) STUMMEL
(— FOR CONDUCTING WATER)
LEADER
(— JOINT) TURNOUT
(— OF ORE) BUNNY
(— OF PAN) SYRINX

(— OF QUEEN BEE) TEET
(— ON BAGPIPE) DRONE CHANTER
(— SUPPORT) CRADLE
(— TAB) TACK
(— TO MUFFLE TRUMPET) SORDINE
(— USED IN WELL) STRING
(— WITH SOCKET ENDS) HUB
(BOWL AND STEM OF —) STUMMEL
(CEREMONIAL —) CALUMET
(CLAMMING —) BRAIL
(CONNECTING —) HOGGER
(FLUE —) LABIAL
(HEATING —) CALIDUCT
(MUSICAL —) BODY GEWGAW
FISTULA SORDINE HORNPIPE
SCHWEGEL
(OATEN —) OAT
(ORGAN —) FLUE KINURA LABIAL
ERZAHLER SCHWEGEL
TREMOLANT
(ORGAN —S) MONTRE
(PART OF —) BIT BOWL STEM
SHANK SHAPE SADDLE
MOUTHPIECE
(PEACE —) CALUMET
(PROJECTING —) BRACKET
(SEWER —) SLANT
(SHEPHERD'S —) REED LARIGOT
CHALUMEAU
(SNAKE-CHARMER'S —) PUNGI
(TOBACCO —) GUN CLAY BRIAR
BRIER CUTTY HOOKA STRAW
CALEAN DUDEEN HOOKAH
BULLDOG CHIBOUK CHILLUM
CORNCOB BILLIARD CALABASH
MEERSCHAUM
(TOY —) HEWGAG
(VERTICAL —) STACK LAMPHOLE
(WATER — FOR ENGINE) SLOUCH
(4 LENGTHS OF —) FOURBLE
(PREF.) AUL(O) SIPHON(O)
SOLEN(O) SYRING(O) TUBI TUBO
TUBULI TUBULO
PIPECLAY CAM CAUM
PIPED DRUNK JETTED
PIPEFISH EARL LONGJAW
NEEDLEFISH
PIPELAYER YARNER
PIPESTEM STOPPEL STOPPLE
PIPETTE PIPET TASTER
PIPEWORT HATPIN WOOLWEED
PIPING HOSE SOFT VERY CRYING
ROULEAU WAILING WEEPING
TRANQUIL
PIPING CROW CASSICAN
FLUTEBIRD
PIPIRI PITIRRI
PIPISTRELLE BAT NOCTULE
PIPIT PEEP TEETAN WEKEEN
CHEEPER SKYLARK TIETICK
TITLARK TITLING WAGTAIL
LINGBIRD TWITLARK
PIPPIN PIP APPLE PEPPIN RIBSTON
PIPSISSEWA EVERGREEN
WINTERGREEN
PIQUANCY SALT ZEST JUICE
FLAVOR GINGER TARTNESS
PIQUANT BOLD RACY JUICY
NUTTY SALTY SHARP SPICY
TASTY ZESTY LIVELY SEVERE
CUTTING PEPPERY PUNGENT
POIGNANT STINGING
PIQUE FRET GOAD PEAK PICK PIKE

PYKE TICK ANNOY PRISE SNUFF
SPITE STING HARASS MALICE
NETTLE PRITCH STRUNT CHIGGER
OFFENSE PROVOKE UMBRAGE
IRRITATE MARCELLA
PIRACY CAPTURE PIRATISM
PIRAGUA CANOE DUGOUT
PIROGUE PETTIAGUA
PIRANHA PIRAI CARIBE PIRAYA
PIRARUCU PAICHE ARAPAIMA
PIRATE CAPER ROVER ROBBER
VIKING CATERAN CORSAIR
PICKEER SCUMMER ALGERINE
MAROONER PICAROON
BUCCANEER SALLEEMAN
(— FLAG) ROGER BLACKJACK
PIRENE (FATHER OF —) ASOPUS
ACHELOUS
(MOTHER OF —) METOPE
(SON OF —) CENCHRIAS
PIRIPIRI BIRK BIRCH MAPAN
PIRL SPIN TWINE TWIST REVOLVE
PIRN QUILL BOBBIN PIRNIE
SPINDLE
PIROGUE CANOE PERIOQUE
PIROPLASM BABESIA
PIROSHKI PIROGEN
PISCINA POOL TANK BASIN
SACRARY LAVATORY SACRARIUM
PISE CAJON PISAY
PISHOGUE CHARM SPELL SORCERY
WITCHERY
PISMIRE ANT EMMET
PISOLITE PEASTONE
PISTACHIO FISTIC PISTICK
PISTIL CHIVE CARPEL UMBONE
POINTEL
(PL.) GYNECIUM
(PREF.) GYN(AE)(AEO)(E)(EO)(O)
GYNAECO GYNANDRO GYNECO
(SUFF.) GYN
PISTILLATE FEMALE
PISTOL DAG GAT GUN POP ROD
BULL COLT DAGG IRON TACK
FLUTE RIFLE STICK BARKER
BUFFER BULDER BULLER CANNON
DRAGON HEATER POTGUN RIFFLE
ROSCOE BULLDOG DUNGEON
SHOOTER TICKLER DERINGER
PETRONEL REPORTER REVOLVER
PEPPERBOX
(TOY —) SPARKLER
PISTON BUCKET FORCER PALLET
SUCKER EMBOLUS PLUNGER
(— HUB) SPIDER
PIT PET POT PUT BURY CIST DELF
DELL DISC DISK FOSS HELL HOLE
KHUD KIST LAKE MINE PLAY PUTT
SILO SINK SUMP SWAG TURN
WEEM WELL ABYSM ABYSS
CRYPT DELFT DITCH FOSSA
FOVEA FROST GRAVE LEACH
MATCH PITCH PORUS SLACK
SLUIG TREAD AREOLE BORROW
BUNKER KERNEL OPPOSE RADDLE
WALLOW ABADDON ALVEOLA
AMPULLA BOTHROS CHARPIT
FOSSULA FOXHOLE HANDLER
LATRINE MEGARON PINHOLE
VARIOLE WINNING CESSPOOL
CYPHELLA DOWNFALL FAVEOLUS
FENESTRA POCKMARK PUNCTULE
WELLHOLE

(— FOR BAKING) IMU UMU
(— FOR OFFERINGS) BOTHROS
(— OF STOMACH) MARK WIND
ANTICARDIUM
(— OF THEATER) GROUND
PARTERRE
(— ON COCKROACH HEAD)
FENESTRA
(— ON LICHENS) LACUNA
CYPHELLA
(— SACRED TO DEMETER)
MEGARON
(AUTHOR OF —) NORRIS
(BITTER —) STIPPEN
(BOTTOMLESS —) ABYSS ABADDON
BARATHRUM
(CHARACTER IN —) PAGE WESS
LAURA CURTIS GRETRY JADWIN
SHELDON CORTHELL CRESSLER
DEARBORN
(COAL —) HEUCH HEUGH
WINNING
(FODDER —) SILO
(MAORI —) RUA
(MIRY —) SLUIG
(RIFLE —) SANGAR
(ROOFED —) CIST KIST
(SALT —) VAT PEZOGRAPH
(SAND —) BUNKER
(SMALL —) AREOLE LACUNA
STAPLE
(TANNING —) LIME LAYER LEACH
HANDLER LAYAWAY SUSPENDER
(PREF.) BOTHR(I)(IO)(O) FOVEI
PITA PITO YUCCA ARGHAN
PITCH DIP FIT KEY LAB MEL PIC
BUCK CANT CHAT CODE COOK
DING FALL FORK HURL PECK PICK
PLUG RAKE TELL TONE TOSS
ABODE BOOST BUNCH CHUCK
FLING LABOR LURCH PLANT
SLENT SLOPE SPIEL THROW
TWIRL BINDER DIRECT ENCAMP
FILLER LENGTH MALTHA MANJAK
PLUNGE SQUARE TOTTER
TUMBLE VOLLEY WICKET
CURRENT NARRATE ALKITRAN
OVERHANG
(— AT A MARK) LAG
(— FROM FIR TREES) ALKITRAN
(— OF HELIX) JAW
(— TENT) TELD
(ABOVE —) SHARP
(AUCTION —) SETBACK
(BASEBALL —) CURVE STRIKE
CRIPPLE SPITTER FADEAWAY
KNUCKLER SPITBALL BRUSHBACK
(BELOW —) FLAT
(COBBLER'S —) CODE
(FULL —) VOLLEY
(GLANCE —) MANJAK MANJACK
(HIGH —) BLOOPER
(HIGHEST —) PRIDE
(IDENTITY IN —) UNISON
(MINERAL —) BITUMEN
(PREF.) MISERI
PITCH APPLE COPEI CUPAY
PITCHBLENDE CLEVEITE
PITCHED SET
(PREF.) (— BELOW BASS) CONTRA
PITCHER JUG JACK OLLA PILL PRIG
BUIRE CROCK CRUET GALON
GORGE GOTCH AFTABA CROUKE

GALLON HURLER POURIE STRAIN
URCEUS CANETTE CHUCKER
FLINGER GROWLER STARTER
STOPPER TWIRLER URCEOLE
AIGUIERE ASCIDIUM OENOCHOE
SOUTHPAW MOUNDSMAN
(— AND CATCHER) BATTERY
(— FOR BEER) GROWLER
(— OF ORCHID) BUCKET
(— SHAPED LIKE MAN) TOBY
(— WITH ONE HANDLE) URCEUS
(BULGING —) GOTCH
(EARTHEN —) GEORG GORGE
(RELIEF —) FIREMAN
(RELIEF —S) BULLPEN
(REMOVE — FROM BASEBALL GAME)
DERRICK
(WIDEMOUTHED —) EWER
PITCHER PLANT BISCUIT FLYTRAP
FEVERCUP FOXGLOVE WATERCUP
NEPENTHES SKUNKWEED
PITCHFORK EVIL PICK PIKE PICKEL
SHEPPECK PITCHPIKE
(THATCHER'S —) GROOM
(PL.) HARD
PITCHHOLE CAHOT
PITCHMAN VENDER SALESMAN
PITCH PINE THYME
PITCH PIPE TUNER EPITONION
PITCHSTONE RETINITE
PITCHY BLACK
PITEOUS MEAN PALTRY PITIFUL
MERCIFUL MOURNFUL PIERCING
PITFALL PIT FALL TRAP SNARE
DANGER TRAPFALL
PITH JET PUT SAP CORE GIST
MEAT PULP PUTT SOLA HEART
VIGOR ENERGY KERNEL MARROW
ESSENCE EXTRACT MEDULLA
NUCLEUS PAPYRUS STRENGTH
(PREF.) MEDULLI METR(O) PULPE
PULPI PULPO
PITH HELMET TOPI TOPEE
PITHINESS BREVITY
PITHON (FATHER OF —) MICAH
PITH TREE AMBATCH
PITHY CRISP MEATY SAPPY TERSE
STRONG CONCISE LACONIC
MARROWY
PITIABLE SAD POOR SEELY WOFUL
RUEFUL WOEFUL FORLORN
PITIFUL
PITIFUL MEAN MEEK RUTH SILLY
SORRY PALTRY RUEFUL TENDER
HANGDOG RUESOME RUTHFUL
MERCIFUL PATHETIC
PITILESS GRIM CRUEL STERN
STONY BRASSY SAVAGE
RUTHLESS UNPITIED MERCILESS
PITMAN GEORDIE
PITTANCE BIT ALMS DOLE GIFT
MITE SONG TRIFLE BEQUEST
PITTED FOVEATE OPPOSED
PUNCTATE ALVEOLATE
PITTER STONER
PITTHEUS (DAUGHTER OF —)
AETHRA
(FATHER OF —) PELOPS
(PUPIL OF —) THESEUS
PITURI BEDGERY PITCHERY
PITY RUE MEAN MOAN PETE PITE
RUTH MERCY PIETY REIVE SCATH
BEMOAN PATHOS MERCIFY

REMORSE WAESUCK CLEMENCY
SYMPATHY COMPASSION

PIVOT TOE CRUX SLEW SLUE TURN
HEART CENTER SLOUGH WORDLE
GUDGEON TRAVERSE TRUNNION

PIVOTAL POLAR CENTRAL
TROCHOID

(— POINT) KNUCKLE

PIVOTING DISHRAG

PIVOT STAND PEDESTAL

PIXILATED DAFFY DOTTY DRUNK
PIXIE BEMUSED PUCKISH
TOUCHED CONFUSED

PIXY ELF FAIRY PYGMY ROGUE
IMPISH RASCAL SPRITE PUCKISH
ROGUISH

PIZE OATH PISE CURSE

PLACABLE WEAK QUIET PACABLE
PEACEFUL YIELDING FORGIVING

PLACARD BILL POST TITLE POSTER
TICKET AFFICHE REDLINE
STOMACHER

PLACATE CALM GENTLE PACIFY
PLEASE SOOTHE APPEASE
FORGIVE

PLACE L DO BIT FIX PUT SET AREA
HOLE LIEU PLAT PLOT POSE POST
RANK ROOM SEAT SITE SITU
SPOT STEL STEP STOW TEXT VICE
YARK BEING ESTER ESTRE HOUSE
JOINT LOCUS PLAZA POINT POSIT
SCENE SITUS STALL STATE STEAD
STELL STOUR WHERE BESTOW
CHARGE GROUND IMPOSE INVEST
LAYOUT LOCALE LOCATE OFFICE
POSSIE ROOMTH ALLODGE
ARRANGE DEPOSIT KITCHEN
STATION ABDITORY ALLOCATE
DIGGINGS EMPORIUM LOCATION
POSITION

(— ALONE) ISOLATE

(— ALTERNATELY) STAGGER

(— APART) ENISLE

(— BEFORE) APPOSE PREFIX

(— BY FORCE) PILT

(— CROSSWISE) THWART

(— FISH IN SALTING BIN) KENCH

(— FOR CATTLE) CAMP

(— FOR DUMPING RUBBISH) SHOOT

(— FOR HAWKING) RIVER

(— FOR MILKING COWS) LOAN

(— FOR MORTAR AND BRICK) FROG

(— FOR PHEASANTS) STEW

(— FOR PRAYERS) IDGAH

(— FOR RABBITS) WARREN

(— FOR RECEPTION) RECEIPT

(— FOR RUBBISH DEPOSITS)
LAYSTALL

(— FOR SEETHING) STEW

(— FOR SLEEPING) BED BUNK DOSS
FLOP LAIR LIBKIN

(— FOR STROLLING) PROMENADE

(— FOR TORTURE) CATASTA

(— FOR TRAINING HORSES) LONGE

(— FROM WHICH JURY IS TAKEN)
VENUE

(— IN) INNEST

(— IN COMPACT MASS) STOW

(— IN ORDER) ARRAY ENRANK

(— IN WATERFALL) LEAP

(— OF AMUSEMENT) GAFF

(— OF ASSEMBLY) AGORA CURIA
KGOTLA SYNAGOG

(— OF BLOODSHED) ACELDAMA

(— OF BURIAL) AHU KIL KILL LAIR
GRAVE LAYSTOW CATACOMB
CEMETERY GOLGOTHA LAYSTALL

(— OF BUSINESS) BANK AGENCY
KNACKERY

(— OF CONCEALMENT) DEN BOMA
BLIND STALE HIDING HIDEOUT
HIDEAWAY

(— OF CONFINEMENT) BRIG CAGE
COOP LIMBO PRISON BULLPEN

(— OF CONFUSION) BABEL
TROYTOWN

(— OF CREMATION) GHAT

(— OF CRUCIFIXION) GOLGOTHA

(— OF DESTRUCTION) ABADDON

(— OF DETENTION) BAGNIO

(— OF DWELLING) WANE

(— OF ENTERTAINMENT) INN JOINT
DANCERY HANGOUT HOSTELRY

(— OF EXERTION) ARENA

(— OF EXILE) PATMOS

(— OF IDYLLIC BEAUTY) XANADU

(— OF MISERY) HELL

(— OF NETHER DARKNESS) EREBUS

(— OF NOISE) BABEL

(— OF PROTECTION) PORT SCUG

(— OF REFUGE) ARK BAST HOLD
ASYLUM ADULLAM HIDEOUT

(— OF RESIDENCE) SOIL DOMICILE

(— OF RESORT) PURLIEU

(— OF RESTRAINT) LIMBO PINFOLD

(— OF SACRIFICE) ALTAR

(— OF SAFETY) GRITH HAVEN
WARRANT

(— OF SECURITY) GRITH ASYLUM
CORRAL HARBOR GARRISON

(— OF SHELTER) LEW HOLD JOUK
COVER

(— OF SUBMISSION) CANOSSA

(— OF TORMENT) GOLGOTHA

(— OF WORSHIP) HEIAU BETHEL
CHAPEL CHURCH DESERT SHRINE
TEMPLE GURDWARA SYNAGOGUE

(— SIDE BY SIDE) APPOSE

(— STRUCK BY LIGHTNING)
BIDENTAL

(— WHERE FOOD IS KEPT) LARDER

(— WHERE MEAT IS SMOKED)
BUCAN BUCCAN

(— WHERE OUTCASTS GATHER)
HELL

(— WHERE ROADS CROSS) LEET

(— WHERE STREAM IS RAPID)
SHARP

**(— WHERE TROOPS HALT
OVERNIGHT)** ETAPE

(— WHERE 4 OR MORE WAYS MEET)
CARFAX

(BOGGY —) SLACK SLUMP

(BREEDING —) NIDUS LOOMERY
SEMINARY PELICANRY

(CHIEF —) HEADSHIP

(CIRCULAR —) ORBELL

(CONFINED —) CRIB

(CONSECRATED —) HIERON

(DRINKING —) BOOZER
MUMHOUSE

(DRY —) SEARING

(DWELLING —) BY BYE DEN SEE
BAWN HAFT HIVE HOME ABODE
BEING HOUSE HOWFF SOJOURN
HABITACLE

(EATING —) CAFE GRUBBERY

(EMPTY —) BLANK SPACE

(ENCLOSED —) BIN HAY WORTH
SEVERAL CLOISTER

(ESSENTIAL —) EYE

(FAMILIAR —) KITH

(FAULTY — IN THREAD) TRAP

(FILTHY —) STY

(FIRST —) BLUE LEAD STRAIGHT

(FORTIFIED —) LIS LISS CASTLE
FASTNESS

(GARRISONED —) PRESIDIO

(GATHERING —) SHOP AGORA
FOYER JOINT LESCHE

(GRASSY —) LAUND

(HALTING —) MARAH

(HIDING —) MEW CACHE HIDEL
HOARD STASH COVERT HIDDELS
RETREAT STOWAWAY

(HIGH —) EMINENCE

(HOLLOW —) GULF HOLE HOLL
SCOOP CAVITY ALBERCA
SINKHOLE

(INHABITED —) ABADI

(LANDING —) GHAT HARD HITHE
LEVEE SCALE BUNDER PALACE
HELIPORT

(LEVEL —) PLANILLA

(LODGING —) CAMP LOGIS BIDING
BILLET LIBKEN

(LOOKOUT —) TOOT

(LURKING —) HOLD HOLE HOARD
HULSTER

(MARKET —) AGORA TRONE
MARKET RIALTO

(MARSHY —) SLEW SLOO SLUE
SLUMP SLOUGH

(MEETING —) CLUB PNYX COURT
FORUM GUILD TRYST TOLSEL
TOLZEY AMBALAM KLAVERN
TINWALD

(MUDDY —) SOIL

(NESTING —) JUG NIDARY

(OPEN —) ENAJIM

(OTHERWORLDLY —) EMPYREAN

(POLLING —) BOOTH

(RAVELED —) FRAY

(REMOTE —) JERICHO

(RESTING —) LAY CAMP FORM
GIST LAIR PARAO CRADLE

(ROCKY —) ROCHER

(SACRED —) HAREM HIERON
CHAITYA SANCTUM

(SALTING —) SALADERO

(SECRET —) LAIR ADYTUM CORNER
CRANNY

(SECURE —) REDOUBT

(SHADY —) GLOOM SWALE
FRESCADE UMBRACLE

(SHELTERED —) NOOK SCUG
SUCCOR

(SPAWNING —) REDD

(STEEP —) PITCH

(STOPPING —) HALT MANZIL

(STORAGE —) DEPOT HOARD
LODGE SPICERY STORAGE
STOWAGE DOCKYARD

(SWAMPY —) FLUSH SOUGH

(THIRD —) SHOW

(TIGHT —) JAM JAMB

(WATCH —) TOOTHILL

(WATERING —) ABREUVOIR

(WEAK —) BLOT

(WET —) DANK

(WORN —) ABRASION

(WRETCHED —) DEN MISERY

(PL.) LOCI

(PREF.) CHOR(O) LOCO TOP(O)

(DRY —) XER(O)

(TAKES — OF) PRO VICE

(SUFF.) ESE THESIS THESTE
THETIC TOPE TOPY

(— FOR) ARIUM ORIUM ORY

(— OF) ARY

(— OF DOING) ERY

(— OF GROWING, BREEDING) ERY

(— OF KEEPING) ERY

(— OF SELLING) ERY

PLACEBO SOP TOADY VESPERS
PARASITE

PLACED FIXED BESTEAD

(— ON ITS SIDE) LAZY

PLACEHOLDER VARIABLE

PLACE-NAME TOPONYM

PLACENTA MAZA REPLUM

(PREF.) MAZ(O)

PLACENTAL MAZIC

PLACID CALM COOL EVEN MEEK
MILD SOFT DOWNY QUIET SUANT
SUENT GENTLE SEDATE SERENE
SMOOTH PACIFIC TRANQUIL
THROBLESS

PLACKET FENT SPARE WOMAN
CLOSING PETTICOAT

PLAGAL MODE
(PREF.) HYPO

PLAGIARISM CRIB PLAGIUM

PLAGIARIST TAKER COPYIST

PLAGIARIZE CRIB LIFT STEAL

PLAGUE DUN IMP POX VEX FRAB
FRET GNAW PEST TWIT BESET
CURSE DEATH DEUCE HARRY
QUALM TEASE TRAIK WEARY
WORRY WOUND BOTHER BURDEN
HAMPER HARASS INFEST PESTER
PESTIS SORROW WANION
DESTROY MURRAIN PERPLEX
SCOURGE TORMENT TORTURE
TROUBLE BEPESTER HANDICAP
OUTBREAK PESTILENCE

(PREF.) LEMO LOIMO PESTI
PESTO

PLAGUY VERY PESKY VEXING
MURRAIN PESTFUL INFERNAL

PLAICE FLUKE FLATFISH
FLOUNDER

PLAID CALM FAKE MAUD PLOD
TARTAN BRACKEN BRECHAN

PLAIN DRY LOW BALD BARE CHOL
EASY EVEN FLAT OPEN PLAT RIFE
VEGA WALD WOLD BLAIR BLUNT
BROAD CAMPO CORAH FIELD
FRANK GREEN GROSS LAUND
LEVEL LLANO MOURN NAKED
PAMPA PROSE ROUND SEBKA
SECCO SILLY SMALL SOBER
TALAO UNORN BEMOAN BEWAIL
CHASTE CUESTA GRAITH HOMELY
HONEST HUMBLE LENTEN
MACHAR MAIDAN PARAMO
PUSZTA RUSTIC SABANA SEVERE
SIMPLE SINGLE SMOOTH ARTLESS
EVIDENT GENUINE IDAVOLL
LEGIBLE OBVIOUS POPULAR
SAVANNA TERRACE UNARTED
APPARENT CAMPAIGN DISTINCT

EVERYDAY EXPLICIT FAMILIAR HOMEMADE HOMESPUN ITHAVOLL PALPABLE PIEDMONT SEMPLICE STRAIGHT
(— AMONG TREES) LAUND
(— OF ARGENTINA) PAMPA
(— OF RUSSIA) STEPPE
(ALKALI —S) USAR
(ALLUVIAL —) APRON CARSE HAUGH
(ARCTIC —) TUNDRA
(DESOLATE —) CHOL
(HEATHY —) LANDE
(LOW-LYING —) MACHAR MACHAIR
(MARSHY —) BLAIR
(NOT —) MEALYMOUTHED
(SALINE —) SEBKA SEBKHA
(SALT —) SALADA
(SLOPING —) HOPE CUESTA CONOPLAIN
(SMALL GRASSY —) CAMAS CAMASS QUAMASH
(TREELESS —) BLED TUNDRA SAVANNA SAVANNAH
(UNOCCUPIED —) DESERT
(PL.) VIZCACHA
(PREF.) LITI PEDI(O) PLAN(I)
PLAIN CHANT CF
PLAINCLOTHESMAN SPLIT
PLAINLY FAIR BARELY FAIRLY FLATLY SIMPLY BROADLY FRANKLY DIRECTLY
PLAINNESS PROSE INNOCENCE
PLAINSMAN LLANERO
PLAINSONG GROUND
PLAINT WAIL PLANT LAMENT COMPLAINT
PLAINTEXT CLEAR
PLAINTIFF SUER ACTOR ORATOR PURSUER QUERENT
PLAINTIVE SAD CROSS PINING DOLENTE ELEGIAC FRETFUL MOANFUL PEEVISH PETTISH DOLOROSO MANGENDO PETULANT WAILSOME SORROWFUL
PLAIT CUE PLY KNIT PAIR PLAT RUFF TURN WALE WAND BRAID BREAD CRIMP FETCH FITCH PEDAL PINCH QUEUE QUILL QUIRK TRACE TRESS WEAVE BORDER DOUBLE GATHER GOFFER PLEACH PLIGHT RUMPLE TUSCAN WIMPLE WRITHE CRIMPLE FROUNCE PIGTAIL SCALLOM COMPLECT
(— FOR HAT) DUNSTABLE
(— OF STRAW) MILAN TRACE
(SERIES OF —S) KILTING
PLAITED PLISSE DEVIOUS PLICATE
PLAITING PLISSE LEGHORN NATTIER
PLAN AIM ART LAY WAY CARD CAST COUP DART FOOT GAME HANG IDEA MIND MOOD PLAT PLOT REDE WENT ALLOW BRIEF CHART DARTY DRAFT DRIFT ETTLE FRAME HOBBY MODEL REACH SHAPE TRACE ADVICE AGENDA BEREDE BUDGET CIPHER DECOCT DESIGN DEVISE ENGINE FIGURE INTEND LAYOUT METHOD MODULE ORDAIN PROJET

SCHEMA SCHEME SURVEY THEORY ARRANGE CONCERT CONCOCT COUNSEL DRAWING FORELAY NOSTRUM OUTLINE PATTERN PROJECT PURPOSE THOUGHT COGITATE CONSPIRE CONTRIVE ENGINEER FORECAST FOREGAME LANDSKIP MEDITATE PLATFORM PRACTICE SCHEDULE SKELETON STRATEGY CALCULATE
(— AHEAD) FORECAST
(— OF FUTURE PROCEDURE) PROGRAM
(— ON A FLOOR) EPURE
(— TOGETHER) CONCERT
(CUNNING —) WHEEZE
(GROUND —) TRACE GRUNDRISS
(INSURANCE —) TONTINE
(5-YEAR —) PIATILETKA
PLANARIAN PLATODE TRICLAD FLATWORM PLATYHELMINTH
PLANE BEAD DADO FACE FLAT HOLL MILL AXIAL CHUTE CROZE FACET GLIDE HOULE HOWEL LEVEL MESON SHOOT STICK TABLE WHISK AEQUOR BEADER HOLLOW REEDER ROUTER SMOKER SNIBEL COURIER INSHAVE JOINTER NONSKED SURFACE WITCHET BULLNOSE DECLINER LEEBOARD MERIDIAN RECLINER SYCAMORE TRAVERSE

(— CURVE) ROSE
(— HANDLE) TOAT TOTE
(— OF CLEAVAGE) BACK
(— OF EARTH'S ORBIT) ECLIPTIC
(— OF ROCK) BED
(—S OF GUNNERY FIRE) SHEAF
(ENEMY —) BANDIT
(INCLINED —) RAMP SLIP
(MOLDING —) HOLL HOULE HOLLOW
(PERSPECTIVE —) TABLE
(RABBET —) PLOW RABAT PLOUGH REBATE FILLETER
(SLOPING —) CUESTA
PLANER JOINTER SURFACER
PLANER TREE HORNBEAM SYCAMORE
PLANET SUN BODY IRIS JOVE MARS MOON STAR EARTH GLOBE HYLEG PLUTO SHREW VENUS WORLD SATURN SPHERE URANUS VULCAN ALMUTEN ANARETA BENEFIC FORTUNE JUPITER MERCURY NEPTUNE PRIMARY CHASUBLE LUMINARY RECEPTOR TERRELLA WANDERER
(— IN A NATIVITY) ALMUTEN
(BENEVOLENT —) FORTUNE
(CONTROLLING —) LORD
(HYPOTHETICAL —) VULCAN
(MALEFICENT —) SHREW
(RULING —) DOMINATOR
(SMALL —) IRIS ASTEROID TERRELLA
PLANETARIUM ORRERY
PLANETOID UNDINE ASTEROID
PLANE TREE CHINAR PLATAN COTONIER PLANTAIN SYCAMORE
PLANET-STRICKEN SIDERATED

PLANISPHERE ASTROLABE METEOROSCOPE
PLANK CLAM HOOD PATA PLAT RAIL SOLE WAIR BOARD CLAMP PATTA SHIDE SWALE THEAL DAGGER FLITCH PLANCH ROOFER STRAKE CLAPPER CROSSER DEPOSIT MADRIER RIBBAND STEALER FOREPOLE GARBOARD STRINGER
(— AS PROTECTION) SHOLE
(— OVER BROOK) CLAM
(— 6 FT. X 1 FT.) WARE
(—S IN BRIDGE) CHESS
(—S LESS THAN 6 FT.) DEAL
(CURVED —) SNYING
(ROUGHHEWN —) SLAB
PLANK DRAG RUBBER
PLANK END STUB
PLANKING GORE RACK HATCH SWALE CEILING LAGGING BERTHING BRATTICE GARBOARD WATERWAY
PLANKSHEER WATERWAY
PLANKTON KRILL SESTON
PLANNED PREPENSE
PLANNING (TECHNIQUE FOR —) PERT
PLANOMILLER SLABBER
PLANT AJI BED SET SOW ACHE ALGA ARUM BURY CROP FAST HERB HIDE MORE RAPE SALT SEED SLIP TREE WORT ABACA AGAVE AJWAN ARGEL CAROA CHIVE CLOTE CLOVE EARLY FANCY GRAFT HEATH INTER INULA JALAP KEIKI ORACH PITCH SEDUM SHRUB YERBA ACACIA AJOWAN AKELEY ALASAS ANNUAL BEDDER CACOON CALALU CARROT COKERY COTTON DERRIS DIBBLE ESCAPE FICOID FORCER GALAXY GROWTH KARREE LENTIL LIGGER MANUKA MEDICK MESCAL ORPINE PEPINO SETTLE SPRING ULLUCU YARROW ABANDON ALKANET ALYSSUM BREWERY CARDOON CONCEAL CUTTING DAGGERS ENCELIA HAEMONY IMPLANT JIKUNGU LETTUCE PALMIET PICKERY RAMBONG SAWMILL ABUTILON AGERATUM AGRIMONY ANGLEPOD BIENNIAL BLUEBELL CONSOUND DRAWLING DYEHOUSE EMERGENT ENGINERY FUMEROOT GASWORKS GROMWELL HAWKWEED HONEWORT KNAPWEED LARKSPUR PHILODENDRON
(— BY SPADING) SPIT
(— DEEPLY) HEEL
(— DISEASE) NECROSIS
(— FIRMLY) BRACE
(— GROWING IN WATER) BILDERS HYDROPHYTE
(— IN ROWS) DRILL
(— OF MEADOWS) POOPHYTE
(— OF THE DEAD) ASPHODEL
(— OUTGROWTH) OVULE
(— ROOTED IN GROUND) LIANA LIANE

(— SUPPORTING PARASITES) SUSCEPT
(— TREE) MOTCH
(— WITH NO DISTINCT MEMBERS) THALLUS
(— WITH THREE PISTILS) TRIGYN
(— WITH THREE STAMENS) TRIANDER
(— 2ND CROP) ETCH
(AIR —) FLOPPERS
(ANCIENT —) CYCAD
(AQUATIC —) ALISMA NUPHAR SUGAMO TAWKEE AMBULIA AWLWORT FROGBIT DUCKWEED PONDWEED PICKERELWEED
(AROMATIC —) MINT NARD BASIL CUMIN TANSY THYME AMOMUM CUMMIN CARAWAY DITTANY ALBAHACA CALAMINT LAVENDER SPIKENARD
(AUSTRALIAN —) LILAC STYLO LIGNUM LANCEPOD
(BULBOUS —) GALTONIA
(CENTURY —) PITA
(CLIMBING —) VETCH LAWYER ULLUCE ULLUCU CORALITA
(COMPOSITE —) SUCCORY HAWKWEED SNEEZEWEED
(CONSECRATED —) HAOMA
(CREATED —) BARAMIN
(CREEPING —) IPECAC KAREAO KAREAU PENNYWORT
(CROSSBRED —) HYBRID
(CRUSHING —) BREAKER
(DWARF —) CUMIN STUNT
(DYE —) WAD ANIL WOAD WOLD WOALD MADDER
(E. INDIAN —) JATI
(ETIOLATED —) ALBINO
(FIBER —) ALOE FLAX HEMP PITA CAJUN RAMIE SISAL
(FLOWERING —) HOP ROSE DAISY HOLLY POPPY ORCHID VIOLET HAWTHORN LARKSPUR POLYGALA PRIMROSE SNOWDROP
(FORAGE —) RAPE ALFALFA DAINCHA
(FOSSIL —) CALAMITE
(GERMINATING —) SPIRE
(GRAIN —) TEFF
(HEDGE —) ESPINO
(HEMP —) FIMBLE
(IMMATURE —) KEIKI
(LEAFLESS —) ULEX DODDER RESTIAD TRIURID
(MALE —) MAS MACRANDER
(MARSH —) FERN CALLA JUNCUS CATTAIL BUCKBEAN
(MEDICINAL —) ALOE HERB ERICA ARNICA CATNEP CATNIP IPECAC SIMPLE ACONITE BONESET GENTIAN LOBELIA CAMOMILE
(NON-FLOWERING —) FERN
(NURSERY —) SEEDLING
(PEPPER —) ARA
(PHILIPPINE —) ABACA
(PISTILLATE —) FEMALE
(POISONOUS —) COWBANE DEATHIN SAMNITIS
(POTTED —) BONSAI LANTANA
(POWER —) HYDRO
(PRICKLY —) BRIAR BRIER CACTUS CARDON NETTLE TEASEL

TEAZEL PRICKFOOT
(PUNGENT —) PEPPER
(RAPIDLY-GROWING —) FILLER
(REEDY —) SPRIT
(RENDERING —) KNACKERY
(SENSITIVE —) MIMOSA
(SIBERIAN —) BADAN
(SPINOUS —) KANTIARA
(STAMINATE —) HUSBAND
(SUBMERGED —) ENALID
(SUCCULENT —) ALOE HERB
GASTERIA HAWORTHIA
HOUSELEEK
(SWORD-LEAVED —) LEVERS
(THALLOPHYTIC —) LICHEN
(TRAILING —) ARBUTUS
(TUFTED —) DRYAS
(TWINING —) SMILAX WINDER
CLIMBER BINDWEED SCAMMONY
(UNIDENTIFIED —) HORDOCK
(WATER —) LIMU LOTUS AQUATILE
STARFRUIT
(WEEDY —) DOCK KNAWEL
(YOUNG —) SET SPRINGER
(PL.) FLORA
(PREF.) BOTAN(O) PHYT(I)(O)
(SUFF.) AD CHORE COCCUS
OECIA PHYTA PHYTE(S) PHYTIA
PHYTIC PHYTUM
PLANTAGENET ANGEVIN
PLANTAIN COCK PALA ABACA
ALISMA FINGER PISANG WABRON
BENTING NETLEAF RIBWORT
SITFAST BALISIER BUCKHORN
FIREWEED FLEAWORT ISPAGHUL
PLANTANO RATSBANE RIBGRASS
ROADWEED WAYBREAD
PLANTAIN EATER TOURACO
SPLITBEAK
PLANTAIN LILY FUNKIA
PLANTATION PEN HOLT WALK
FINCA GROVE BOSKET BOWERY
COLONY ESTATE SHAMBA SPRING
YERBAL CAFETAL FAZENDA
NOPALRY PINETUM THICKET
ARBUSTUM HACIENDA TRAPICHE
VINEYARD
(HEMP —) LATE
(WILLOW —) SALICETUM
PLANTED LISTED
PLANTER SNAG COLON SOWER
FARMER SETTLER PLANTATOR
PLANTING GROVE SATION
PLANTING STICK DIBBLE
PLANT LOUSE APHID PSYLLID
PUCERON HOMOPTER
PLANTS
(SUFF.) ACEAE ALES INEAE
PLAQUE CHIP PINAX PLATE
PLATEAU SARCOID NAMEPLATE
STOMACHER
PLASH LIP DASH BLASH PLOSH
PLOUT PLEACH PUDDLE SPLASH
SPATTER SPECKLE
PLASMA LATEX PLASM
PLASTER CAST DAUB HARL LEEP
LOCK TEER CLEAM GATCH PARGE
SLICK SMALM STAFF TOPIC TREAT
CHARGE CHUNAM CLATCH
GAGING MORTAR PARGET
SPARGE STOOTH STUCCO BLISTER
MALAGMA DIACULUM DIAPALMA
SINAPISM VESICANT CATAPLASM

(— BETWEEN LATHS) CAT
(— OF PARIS) GESSO GYPSUM
(— WITH COW DUNG) LEEP
(COARSE —) GROUT
(MEDICAL —) SALVE TOPIC TREAT
CHARGE SPARADRAP
(MUSTARD —) SINAPISM
(2 COATS OF —) RENDERSET
PLASTERBOARD GYPSUM
PLASTERED DRUNK SOUSED
SWACKED
PLASTERER DAUBER DAUBSTER
PARGETER SPREADER
PLASTERING KEY SETWORK
ROUGHCAST
PLASTIC FOAM RICH SIRUP LABILE
PLIANT ACETATE CATALIN
CRYSTAL DUCTILE FICTILE
ORGANIC CREATIVE FLEXIBLE
LAMINATE MELAMINE PHENOLIC
TECTONIC UNCTUOUS
FORMATIVE
PLASTICIZER CAMPHOR
PLASTRON DICKEY CALIPEE
PLAT BED FLAT FOOD PLAN PLOT
SLAP BRAID LEVEL PLACE PLAIN
PLAIT BUFFET WATTLE ARRANGE
FLATTEN PLATEAU QUADRAT
PLATANIST SUSU
PLATANUS PLANE COTONIER
SYCAMORE
PLATBAND IMPOST LINTEL
EPISTYLE
PLATE BAT CAP CUT DIP DOD EAR
FIN GIB WEB ANAL BACK BRIN
CASE CAST CURB DIAL DISK DROP
FISH GILL GONG GULA HOME
HOOF LAME LEAF MOLD NAIL
ORAL RETE ROSE SHOE SHUT
SLAB SOLE STUD TACE TRAY
AMPYX ANODE BASAL BELLY
BLADE CHAIR CLAMP CLEAT
CLOUT FACIA FENCE FLOOR
FLUKE FORCE GLAND GUARD
GULAR LAMEL PATEN PYGAL
SCALE SCUTE SHEET SHOLE SLICE
STAMP STAVE STRAP TABLE
TASSE TERNE TRAMP UNCUS
WATER ADORAL BAFFLE BRIDGE
BUCKLE CASTER CIRCLE CLICHE
COLLAR COPPER COSTAL CRUSTA
DAMPER DASHER EPIGNE FASCIA
FILLER FOLIUM FRIZEL GENIAL
GNOMON GORGET GUSSET
LABIAL LAMINA LOREAL MASCLE
MATRIX MENTAL MENTUM
MOTHER PALLET PATTEN PLATEN
RADIAL SCREEN SCUTUM SEPTUM
SERVER SHEATH SHROUD SPLINT
STAPLE TARSUS TEGMEN TURTLE
TYMPAN VESSEL BESAGNE
BOLSTER BRACKET BRACTEA
BUCCULA BUCKLER CHARGER
CLYPEUS COASTER CORNULE
CORONET CRYSTAL DOUBLER
ETCHING FRIZZLE FRONTAL
GRAVURE HUMERAL INKBLOT
MORDANT MYOTOME NEPTUNE
PETALON PRIMARY ROSTRAL
ROUNDEL SPANGLE STEALER
STEELER TERGITE TESSERA
VENTRAL ASSIETTE BEDPLATE
BIQUARTZ BRACHIAL CELLOCUT

DIASCOPE DRAWBACK ELECTRUM
EPIGYNUM EPIPROCT EPISTOME
FIREBACK FLOUNDER SKEWBACK
STAPLING STRINGER SUBPLATE
SURPRINT
(— COVERING KEYHOLE) DROP
(— COVERING MIDDLE EAR)
TEGMEN
(— IN AIRPLANE WING) SPOILER
(— IN BATTERY) GRID
(— IN ORGAN PIPE) LANGUET
(— IN STEAM BOILER) SPUT
DASHER
(— OF BALEEN) BLADE
(— OF BLAST FURNACE) TYMP
(— OF CTENOPHORE) COMB
(— OF GELATIN) BAT
(— OF GLASS) SLIDE
(— OF JAW) AURICLE
(— OF PRECIOUS METAL) BRACTEA
(— OF SOAP FRAME) SESS
(— OF SUNDIAL) GNOMON
(— ON FIREPLACE) BLOWER
(— ON LANCE SHAFT) VAMPLATE
(— ON PLOW) MOLDBOARD
(— ON SADDLE) SIDEBAR
(— ON SATCHEL STRAP) OLIVE
(— ON THROAT OF FISH) GULAR
(— ON WATERWHEEL) SHROUD
(—S OF CARDING MACHINE) ARCH
(—S OF GUN CARRIAGE) FLASK
(ARMOR —) SPLINT AILETTE
PALLETTE
(COLLECTION —) BROD
(COMMUNION —) PATEN
(DEEP —) MAZARINE
(DORSAL —) ELYTRUM ALINOTUM
(EARTHEN —) MUFFIN
(FASHION —) SWELL
(FIREPLACE —) IRONBACK
(FLAT —) APRON
(GOLD — ON FOREHEAD) PATA
PATTA
(GROOVED TRAM —) GULLY
GULLEY
(GUARD —) SHELL
(HINGED —) SHUT
(HOME —) DISH
(HOT —) GRILL GRILLE
(IRON —) CLOUT STAVE LATTEN
MARVER LAPSTONE SKEWBACK
MOLDBOARD TURNPLATE
TURNSHEET
(LARGE —) DOUBLER
(LOCK —) SELVEDGE
(NAME —) FACIA
(PERFORATED —) DOD GRID
WORTLE PINNULE
(PITCHER'S —) SLAB MOUND
(RIMLESS —) COUPE
(SIEVE —) LATTICE
(SIFTING —) TROMMEL
(THIN —) LAME LAMP LAMINA
LAMELLA
(THIN TIN —) TAIN LATTEN
TAGGERS
(WALL —) PAN RASEN TORSEL
(WOODEN —) TRENCHER
(PREF.) ELASM(O) LAMELLI
LAMIN(I) PLAC(O)
(SUFF.) (COVERING —) STEGE
STEGITE
PLATEAU PLAT PUNA FJELD

KAROO KARST TABLE CAUSSE
HAMADA MESETA NIVEAU
PARAMO SABANA UPLAND
ANASAZI PLATFORM
(PL.) BARRENS
PLATEHOLDER CASSETTE
PLATEN ROLL
PLATER VATMAN CLAIMER
COLLARMAN
PLATFORM TOP BANK BEMA DAIS
DECK DRIP DROP DUCK FLAT
GHAT KITE PACE PLAT STEP
WING APRON BENCH BLIND
BLOCK CHAIN DUKAN FLAKE
FLOAT HEIAU SOLEA STAGE
STAND STOEP STOOL STOOP
STULL STUMP TOLDO ARBOUR
AZOTEA BRIDGE DESIGN GANTRY
HURDLE ISLAND MACHAN
PAEPAE PALLET PERRON PILLAR
PODIUM PULPIT RUNWAY SETTLE
SLEDGE ALMEMAR BALCONY
BATTERY CATWALK ESTRADE
FORETOP GALLERY LANDING
LOGEION PADDOCK PATTERN
ROLLWAY ROSTRUM SKIDWAY
SOAPBOX TRIBUNE BARBETTE
FOOTPACE HUSTINGS SCAFFOLD
STALLAGE MORTARBOARD
(— FOR ACTORS) LOGEION
THEOLOGIUM
(— FOR ALTAR) PREDELLA
(— FOR DRYING FISH) FLAKE
(— FOR PUBLIC SPEAKING) BEMA
PODIUM TRIBUNE
(— FOR STORING FOOD) WHATA
(— IN CHURCH) SOLEA
(— IN SYNAGOGUE) ALMEMAR
(— IN TEMPLE) DUKAN
(— IN TREE) MACHAN
(— OF GALLOWS) DROP
(— ON RUNNERS) SLEDGE
(— ON STEAMER) SPONSON
(— ON TOP OF HOUSE) AZOTEA
(— ON WHEELS) SKID DOLLY FLOAT
(— TO SUPPORT MINERS) STULL
(BOARDING —) RAMBADE
(GUN —) BARBET SPONSON
BARBETTE
(LEADSMAN'S —) CHAIN
(MINE —) STULL SOLLAR SOLLER
(MOHAMMEDAN STONE —)
MASTABA
(MOUNTED —) SKID
(NAUTICAL —) FORETOP MAINTOP
ROUNDTOP
(ORE —) BUDDLE
(RAILROAD —) DOCK DOCKEN
TRAINWAY
(RAISED —) DAIS PYAL STAND
STOEP STOOL STOOP EXEDRA
LISSOM PANTALAN
(ROCK —) STANCE
(SLEEPING —) KANG
(STAIRCASE —) HALFPACE
HATHPACE
(WOOD —) PLANCHER
PLATING ARMOR SKIRT
PLATINUM COSTLY PLATINA
PLATITUDE TRUISM BROMIDE
DULLNESS STALENESS TRITENESS
PLATONIST IDEIST
PLATOON SQUAD VOLLEY

PELOTON PLOTTON
PLATTER DISH DISK LANX ASHET
GRAIL PLATE RECORD CHARGER
TRENCHER
PLATY MOON MOONFISH
PLATYPUS DUCKBILL DUCKMOLE
MALLANGONG
PLAUDIT APPLAUD APPROVAL
ENCOMIUM
(PL.) PRAISE APPLAUSE
PLAUSIBILITY COLOR
PLAUSIBLE FAIR OILY SNOD SLEEK
GLOSSY SMOOTH AFFABLE
POPULAR CREDIBLE PROBABLE
PROVABLE SPECIOUS SUITABLE
OSTENSIBLE
PLAY FUN JEU JIG RUN RUX TOY
AUTO BEAR COME DAFF DEAL
DICE DRAW FAIR GAME JEST
LAKE MOVE MUCK PLEE PUNT
ROMP SPIN TUNE WAKE CARRY
CHARM DALLY DRAMA ENACT
FLIRT FROST HORSE SHOOT SOTIE
SOUND SPIEL SPORT STUCK
WREAK YEDDE ACTION COMEDY
COQUET DANDLE DIVIDE FILLER
FROLIC GAMBLE GAMBOL GAMING
GHOSTS MUSERY NUMBER
PIDDLE ROLLIX TRIFLE CONSORT
CUTBACK DISPORT EXECUTE
EXPLOIT GUIGNOL HISTORY
HOLIDAY MIRACLE PAGEANT
PASSION PERFORM PRELUDE
STAGERY VENTURE BURLETTA
MORALITY SKITTLES MELODRAMA
(— A DOMINO) SET POSE
(— A PART) DO ACT ENTER
GAMMON GUIZARD
(— A PIPE) CHARM
(— ABOUT) SPANIEL
(— AGAINST) BUCK
(— AN INSTRUMENT) BOW BLOW
SWAY FINGER TWEEDLE
(— AT COURTSHIP) FLIRT
(— BAGPIPE) SKIRL DOODLE
DOUDLE
(— BY STROKES) STRIKE
(— FANFARE) FLOURISH
(— FAST AND LOOSE) PALTER
(— FIRST CARD) LEAD
(— FLORIDLY) DIVIDE
(— FOR TIME) STALL
(— GOLF BALL) DRIVE
(— IMPOSTER) MUMP
(— IN MUD) MUDLARK
(— IN POOL) BURST
(— IN STREAKS) FORK
(— IN TRIGGER) CREEP
(— JAZZ) BLOW
(— LEGATO) SUSTAIN
(— LOOSELY) WAVE
(— LOUT) SWAB SLUBBER
(— MEAN TRICKS) SHAB
(— NERVOUSLY) FIDGET
(— OF COLORS) IRIS
(— OF FOAM) HOOD
(— OF LIGHT) GLORY
(— ON WORDS) PUN CLENCH
CLINCH PARAGRAM CALEMBOUR
PARONOMASIA
(— THE BUFFOON) DROLL
(— THE BULLY) BLUSTER
(— THE FOOL) HOIT

(— THE HYPOCRITE) FACE
(— THE TOADY) SUPE
(— TRICKS) COD JAPE JINK
(— TRUANT) KIP WAG JOUK MICHE
MOOCH MOUCH PLUNK TRONE
MOOTCH
(— UNSKILLFULLY) STRUM FOOZLE
(— WITH) DANDLE
(AMOROUS —) GAME
(BOISTEROUS —) ROMP
(BRIDGE —) COUP ECHO SIGNAL
SQUEEZE
(END —) SHAKE
(FARCICAL —) SOTIE
(FOOTBALL —) DOWN KEEP SWING
KEEPER SAFETY AUDIBLE
COUNTER CUTBACK ROLLOUT
SPINNER
(IN —) ALIVE
(MASKED —) GUISE
(MIRACLE —) AUTO GUARY
MIRACLE
(RAPID CHESS —) SKITTLES
(USED IN —) LUSORY
(PL.) THEATER VANGELI
PLAYA BEACH SEBKA SALINA
SEBKHA
**PLAYBOY OF THE WESTERN
WORLD** (AUTHOR OF —) SYNGE
(CHARACTER IN —) QUIN KEOGH
MAHON SHAWN PEGEEN CHRISTY
FLAHERTY MARGARET
CHRISTOPHER
PLAY-BY-PLAY DETAILED
PLAYER IT CAP END BACK DUCK
SIDE ACTOR BLACK COLOR
GUARD BANKER BUSKER FEEDER
STAGER STROLL TENTER ALTOIST
FIELDER FORWARD GAMBLER
STRIKER TRIFLER TURQUET
BUDGETER GAMESTER
HORNSMAN STROLLER
(— IN CHESS) BLACK WHITE
(— IN CHOUETTE) CAPTAIN
(— OF JAZZ) CAT
(— WHO CUTS CARDS) PONE
(— WHO IS IT) HE
(— WHO SCORES ZERO) DUCK
(— WITH LOWEST SCORE) BOOBY
(BACKGAMMON —) TABLER
(BASEBALL —) SHORT SACKER
CATCHER FIELDER LEADOFF
PITCHER BACKSTOP
(BASKETBALL —) CAGEMAN
HOOPMAN HOOPSTER
(BOWLING —) LEAD
(CARD —) EAST HAND PONE WEST
BLIND DUMMY NORTH OMBRE
SOUTH JUNIOR SENIOR BRAGGER
DECLARER
(CRICKET —) LEG BOWLER INNING
(CROQUET —) MALLET
(DICE —) SHOOTER
(FLUTE —) AULETE
(FOOTBALL —) END GUARD SLANT
BUCKER CENTER TACKLE
BLOCKER FLANKER GRIDDER
SNAPPER FULLBACK HALFBACK
SCATBACK SLOTBACK
(KEY —) PIVOT
(LACROSSE —) HOME COVER
POINT ATTACK STICKMAN
(LEAPFROG —) BACK

(POKER —) AGE
(RUGBY —) SCRUM HOOKER
(SOCCER —) CAP INNER BOOTER
(STUPID —) HAM
(TENNIS —) SMASHER
(TWO OR MORE —S) PLATOON
(UNSKILLFULLY —) DUB
(VOLLEYBALL —) SPIKER
(WEAK —) RABBIT
PLAYFUL SLY ELFIN MERRY FRISKY
GAMBOL JOCOSE LUSORY TOYISH
WANTON COLTISH GIOCOSO
JIGGISH JOCULAR TOYSOME
GAMESOME HUMOROUS
LARKSOME SPORTFUL SPORTIVE
KITTENISH
(IRRESPONSIBLY —) MISCHIEVOUS
PLAYFULLY SCHERZANDO
PLAYFULNESS FUN BANTER
GAMMICK GAMMOCK
PLAYGROUND OVAL CLOSE
TOTLOT PLAYSTOW PLAYSTEAD
PLAYHOUSE HOUSE MOVIE
CINEMA THEATER
PLAYING FROLIC LAKING
(— CARD) ACE JACK KING TREY
DEUCE QUEEN TAROT
(— CARDS) DECK
(— LIGHTLY) LAMBENT
PLAYTHING DIE TOY HOOP KNACK
PLAIK SPORT BAUBLE LAKING
SUCKER TRIFLE PLAYOCK
PLAYWRIGHT AUTHOR
DRAMATIST PLAYMAKER
AMERICAN ADE BAUM DALY
HART HOYT RICE SHAW
BARRY COHAN DAVIS DOBIE FITCH
GREEN LEWIS ODETS RIVES
SMITH WILDE YOUNG BARAKA
BARKER BARRAS BEAHAN BOLTON
BOOTHE BROOKS FLAVIN
GOLDEN HOWARD HUGHES
LAWSON LERNER MEGRUE
MILLER NUGENT ONEILL
THOMAS TOTTEN WALKER
WALTER WEXLEY WILDER
ANDREWS BEHRMAN BELASCO
BLOSSOM CARROLL COLLIER
HELLMAN HOPWOOD HURLBUT
KAUFMAN LINDSAY MOELLER
PEABODY RICHMAN RYSKIND
SAROYAN SHELDON SHIPMAN
SPEWACK VEILLER ANDERSON
CARLETON COLLISON CONNELLY
KINGSLEY KIRKLAND MITCHELL
SHERWOOD WILLIAMS
BALDERSON MACARTHUR
MIDDLETON MOREHOUSE
NICHOLSON STALLINGS
BOUCICAULT WEITZENKORN
AUSTRALIAN CHAMBERS
AUSTRIAN BLEI COLLIN MULLER
NISSEL WERFEL NEUMANN
ZEDLITZ CASTELLI WILDGANS
SCHONTHAN SCHNITZLER
HOFMANNSTHAL
BELGIAN MAETERLINCK
CANADIAN ROSE
CZECH JERABEK JIRASEK
DANISH EWALD TANDRUP
BERGSTROM BUCHHOLTZ
OEHLENSCHLAGER
DUTCH FEITH HOOFT COSTER

EMANTS VONDEL BREDERO
ENGLISH FRY GAY KYD LEE BEHN
BELL FORD HILL LEVY LONG NASH
ROWE SHAW SIMS TATE TUKE
BARRY BROME BYRON DUKES
FIELD HOOLE JONES LEMON
LEWIS LILLO LODGE MILNE
MOORE MUNRO ORCZY PEELE
SMITH WOODS ALBERY BOADEN
CANNAN CASTLE CIBBER
COWARD COWLEY CROWNE
DAVIES DEKKER DENNIS DIBDIN
GRAHAM GREENE HOWARD
JONSON KENNEY LYTTON
MANLEY MORTON MONDAY
NABBES PINERO PINTER PORTER
ROWLEY SETTLE STEELE TAYLOR
WILSON ACKLAND BARNETT
BARRETT BENNETT BURNAND
CHAPMAN CHETTLE EDWARDS
FLECKER GILBERT HARWOOD
HEYWOOD JERROLD JOHNSON
MARLOWE MARMION MARSTON
MERRICK MITFORD MOTTEUX
NICHOLS OSBORNE PLANCHE
PRESTON SHIRLEY SIMPSON
SITWELL SOWERBY WEBSTER
BEAUMONT CLIFFORD CONGREVE
DAVENANT ETHEREGE FIELDING
FITZBALL FLETCHER HAMILTON
HOLCROFT HOUGHTON
JOHNSTON KNOBLOCK LONSDALE
MORRISON PHILLIPS ROBINSON
SHADWELL THEOBALD THURSTON
TOURNEUR VANBRUGH WILLIAMS
ZANGWILL BOTTOMLEY
BRIGHOUSE GOLDSMITH
GREENWOOD ISHERWOOD
KILLIGREW MASSINGER
MIDDLETON MONCRIEFF
MONKHOUSE SIEVEKING
SOUTHERNE VANDRUTEN
WYCHERLEY BROADHURST
CARTWRIGHT DRINKWATER
GALSWORTHY PHILLPOTTS
SHAKESPEARE
ESTONIAN TAMMSAARE
FINNISH KIVI TAVASTSTJERNA
FRENCH BLUM KOCK PYAT VADE
BELOT BLOCH CAMUS CAPUS
CARRE CEARD COLLE CUREL
DUCIS FABRE FEVAL FLERS GENET
PIRON WOLFF AUGIER BAYARD
BECQUE BELLOY BRIEUX COLLIN
COOLUS DONNAY DOUCET
FAVART LESAGE MAIRET MONVEL
MOREAU PAGNOL PARODI
PICARD RAYNAL ROTROU
SARDOU SCRIBE SOUMET
ANCELOT ANOUILH BARBIER
BERNARD BORNIER BOUILLY
BOUVIER CLAUDEL COCTEAU
DENNERY FERRIER GRESSET
HERVIEU IONESCO LABICHE
LAPLACE LARIVEY LAVEDAN
LEGOUVE MEILHAC MEURICE
MOLIERE MORTIER NUITTER
PONSARD ROSTAND SANDEAU
SARMENT SEDAINE VILDRAC
ANDRIEUX BARRIERE BATAILLE
BEAUVOIR BENJAMIN CROISSET
DANCOURT DUMANOIR FAUCHOIS
MARIVAUX MONTEPIN QUINAULT

VOLTAIRE BENSERADE BERNSTEIN
BOURSAULT CORNEILLE
DELAVIGNE DUVEYRIER
LEMERCIER VACQUERIE
CAMPISTRON CLAIRVILLE
DESTOUCHES BEAUMARCHAIS
GERMAN BAB BABO BEER KIND
LENZ BLOEM ERNST HALBE JOHST
LAUBE SORGE UNRUH ZWEIG
ANGELY BRECHT DREYER KAISER
KLEIST KORNER REUTER WEISSE
BARLACH BENEDIX BRONNEN
GUTZKOW KLINGER LESSING
RAUPACH REDWITZ VULPIUS
BRENTANO GRYPHIUS KOTZEBUE
LISSAUER SCHILLER WOLZOGEN
BEYERLEIN GANGHOFER
IMMERMANN SUDERMANN
UECHTRITZ WILBRANDT
AUFFENBERG BLUMENTHAL
FEUCHTWANGER
GREEK ALEXIS SOPHRON
CRATINUS PHILEMON RHINTHON
AESCHYLUS EURIPEDES
SOPHOCLES ANTIPHANES
PHRYNICHUS PHERECRATES
ARISTOPHANES
HUNGARIAN TOTH DOCZI JOKAI
VAJDA MOLNAR ZILAHY
BESSENYEI KISFALUDY SZIGLIGETI
ICELANDIC KAMBAN
SIGURJONSSON
IRISH BEHAN COLUM KELLY
SYNGE WILDE WILLS YEATS
ERVINE MARTYN OCASEY
BECKETT DUNSANY GREGORY
GRIFFIN MATURIN OKEEFFE
SHEILDS ORIORDAN SHERIDAN
BICKERSTAFFE
ITALIAN CECCHI GIRAUD ALFIERI
BENELLI CARRERA GIACOSA
GOLDONI MARENCO TORELLI
RUCELLAI SABATINI CHIARELLI
NICCOLINI PIRANDELLO
JAPANESE CHIKAMATSU
MEXICAN GAMBOA
NORWEGIAN BOJER IBSEN
HEIBERG BJORNSON KIELLAND
POLISH ASNYK FREDRO SZUJSKI
ZAPOLSKA ZEROMSKI ZULAWSKI
NALKOWSKA WYSPIANSKI
BELCIKOWSKI BOGUSLAWSKI
KORZENIOWSKI
PORTUGUESE SILVA BIESTER
ROMAN NAEVIUS PLAUTUS
TERENCE PACUVIUS
RUMANIAN BLAGA
RUSSIAN KRYLOV CHEKHOV
KAPNIST KIRSHON TOLSTOI
BULGAKOV CHIRIKOV FONVIZIN
POTEKHIN SUMBATOV
ABLESIMOV BOBORYKIN
YUSHKEVICH KHMELNITSKI
LAZHECHNIKOV
SCOTTISH BEITH BARRIE
DAVIDSON ROBERTSON
SPANISH CRUZ LARRA RUEDA
CANETE ENCINA ZAMORA
MORATIN DIAMANTE FERNANDEZ
SWEDISH BESKOW EDGREN
BLANCHE HEDBERG MESSENIUS
LAGERKVIST STREINDBERG
SWISS ILG FAESI

WELSH EVANS
PLAZA PLACE PLEIN SQUARE
ZOCALO
(— DE TOROS) BULLRING
PLEA BAR BID PLY MOOT NOLO
SUIT ALIBI CLAIM PLEAD ABATER
APPEAL EXCUSE REFUGE
APOLOGY CONTEND DEFENCE
LAWSUIT PRETEXT QUARREL
DILATORY ENTREATY PLACITUM
PRETENSE
PLEACH PLAIT PLASH INTERLACE
PLEAD BEG SUE MOOT PLEA PRAY
PRIG SHOW URGE COUNT ORATE
ALLEGE APPEAL ASSERT PLAYTE
PURSUE ENTREAT IMPLORE
SOLICIT WRANGLE ADVOCATE
LITIGATE
(— FOR) SOLICIT PETITION
PLEADER ACTOR VAKIL PATRON
SUITOR VAKEEL COUNTOR
ADVOCATE
PLEADING PLEA PAROL ANSWER
PAROLE ADVOCACY COGNOVIT
DEMURRER INTENDIT MEMORIAL
PLEASANT FUN GAY BEEN BIEN
BRAW FAIR FINE GLAD GOOD
HEND JOLI NEAT TRIM WEME
AMENE BIGLY BONNY CANNY
COUTH CUSHY DOUCE DRUNK
DUCKY GREEN HAPPY HENDE
HODDY JOLLY LEPID LISTY LUSTY
MERRY NUTTY QUEME SMIRK
SUAVE SWEET TIPSY WALLY
WETHE COMELY DAINTY DULCET
GENIAL KINDLY PRETTY SAVORY
SMOOTH AFFABLE ELEGANT
FARRAND JANNOCK LEESOME
WINSOME DELICATE GLORIOUS
GRATEFUL HEAVENLY LIEFSOME
LIKESOME LOVESOME THANKFUL
TOWARDLY GEMUTLICH
(PREF.) HEDY
PLEASANTLY FAIR WINLY FAIRLY
AFFABLY SWEETLY GENIALLY
LIKINGLY
PLEASANTNESS GAIETY NAAMAN
AMENITY SUAVITY JOCUNDITY
PLEASANTRY WIT JEST JOKE
SPORT BANTER JESTING JOLLITY
WAGGERY
PLEASE PAY GAME LIKE LIST LUST
SUIT WANT WISH AGREE AMUSE
BITTE CHARM ELATE FANCY
HUMOR QUEME SAVOR TASTE
ARRIDE KITTLE OBLIGE REGALE
SOOTHE TICKLE AGGRATE
APPLESE CONTENT DELIGHT
GLADDEN GRATIFY PLACATE
REJOICE SATISFY
(— FORWARD) FS
PLEASED FAIN FOND GLAD APAID
HAPPY PROUD BUCKED CONTENT
GLADSOME
(BE —) GAME
PLEASING AMEN COOL GLAD
GOOD LIEF NICE SOFT AMENE
DICTY NIFTY SOOTH SWEET
CLEVER COMELY DREAMY FACILE
FLASHY GAINLY LIKING LUSTLY
MELLOW PRETTY AMIABLE
BLESSED CORKING DARLING
LIKABLE LIKEFUL TUNABLE

WELCOME CHARMING DELICATE
FAVOROUS FETCHING GRACEFUL
GRACIOUS GRATEFUL HEAVENLY
INVITING LIKESOME PLACABLE
PLAUSIVE SPECIOUS PLAUSIBLE
PERSONABLE
(— TO EAR) HARMONIC
(— TO EYE) EESOME
(— TO HEAR) FAIR
(VERY —) SNAZZY
PLEASURABLE GOOD JOLLY
ANIMAL MIRTHFUL
PLEASURE JO EST FUN JOY BANG
BOOT EASE ESTE GREE KAMA LIST
LUST PLAY WILL BLISS KICKS
MIRTH SAVOR SOOTH TASTE
DAINTY DEDUIT GAIETY GAYETY
LIKING LUXURY NICETY VOLUPT
COMFORT DELIGHT GRATIFY
JOLLITY JOYANCE VOLUPTY
DELICACY FRUITION GLADNESS
HILARITY VOLUPTAS
(SELFISH —) LECHERY
(STOLEN —) STOUTH STOWTH
(PL.) DELICIAE
PLEASURE SEEKER FRANION
PLEAT SET FOLD KILT POKE RUCK
FLUTE FRILL PINCH PLAIT PRANK
GUSSET SUNRAY
PLEATED PLICATE SUNBURST
PLEBE PLEBS FRESHMAN
PLEBEIAN LOW BASE PLEB SNOB
COMMON HOMELY VULGAR
IGNOBLE LOWBORN POPULAR
BASEBORN EVERYDAY HOMESPUN
INFERIOR MECHANIC ORDINARY
ROTURIER RUPTUARY
PLEBISCITE VOTE DECREE
PLECTRUM PICK SPUR QUILL
UVULA MALLEUS POINTEL
PLECTRON
(— OF HARP) FESCUE
PLEDGE LAY VAS VOW WAD WED
AFFY BAND CLAP EARL GAGE
HAND HEST HOCK PASS PAWN
WAGE WOID WORD FAITH SIKER
SPOUT STAKE SWEAR SWEAT
TOKEN TROTH TRUTH WAGER
ARREST BORROW COMMIT
ENGAGE IMPAWN IMPONE
LUMBER PAROLE PIGNUS PLEVIN
PLIGHT SICCAR SICKER VADIUM
WADSET BARGAIN BETROTH
CAUTION CREANCE EARNEST
HOSTAGE PROMISE BOTTOMRY
MORTGAGE SECURITY SPONSION
VADIMONY
(— IN DRINKING) PROPINE
PLEDGED HIGHT SWORN ASSURED
ENGAGED PIGNORATE
(— TO MARRY) SURE
PLEDGET DOSSIL PENICIL
PLEIADES MAIA MEROPE ALCYONE
CELAENO ELECTRA STEROPE
TAYGETA
PLEIN-AIRIST LUMINIST
PLEISTHENES (FATHER OF —)
ATREUS
(MOTHER OF —) AEROPE
(SON OF —) MENELAUS
AGAMEMNON
PLENARY FULL ENTIRE PLENAL
PERFECT ABSOLUTE COMPLETE

PLENITUDE PLENITY PLEROMA
FULLNESS PLETHORA
ABUNDANCE
PLENTEOUS RICH COPIOUS
FERTILE AFFLUENT FRUITFUL
GENEROUS ABOUNDING
EXUBERANT
PLENTIFUL OLD FULL RANK RICH
RIFE AMPLE HEFTY LARGE ROUTH
SONSY STORE ENOUGH FOISON
GALORE LAVISH SONSIE COPIOUS
FERTILE LIBERAL OPULENT
PROFUSE UBEROUS ABUNDANT
FRUITFUL NUMEROUS
EXUBERANT
PLENTIFULLY RIFE FREELY GALORE
APLENTY
PLENTY WON BAIT COPY MANY
RAFF SONS AMPLE CHEAP COPIA
FOUTH PRICE ROUTH SONSE
TEEMS FOISON SCOUTH UBERTY
LASHINGS
(GREAT —) ABUNDANCE
PLEON TELSON ABDOMEN
PLEONASM ITERATION
MACROLOGY TAUTOLOGY
PLETHORA RASH EXCESS PLENUM
PLURISY FULLNESS PLEURISY
POLYEMIA PROFUSION REPLETION
PLETHORIC TUMID TURGID
SWOLLEN INFLATED
PLEURISY EMPYEMA
PLEURON SCAPULA
PLEXUS RETE GLOMUS NETWORK
PROPLEX GENIPLEX
PLIABLE WAXY WEAK LITHY
WAXEN DOCILE LIMBER PLIANT
SEMMIT SUPPLE BOWABLE
FICTILE FINGENT FLEXILE PLASTIC
WINDING CUSHIONY FLEXIBLE
COMPLIANT
PLIANCY FLEXURE FACILITY
PLIANT APT FLIP SWAK AGILE
BUXOM LITHE SWACK YOUNG
DOCILE LIMBER SUPPLE WANDLE
DUCTILE FLEXILE PLASTIC
PLIABLE SLIPPER WILLOWY
APPLIANT FLEXIBLE SUITABLE
WORKABLE SEQUACIOUS
PLICA FOLD TRICHOMA
PLICATE FOLD PLEAT FOLDED
FANLIKE PLAITED
PLIERS BENDER FLEXOR GRATER
FLECTOR PINCERS
PLIGHT PLY FOLD ARRAY BRAID
DRESS PLAIT POINT STATE
WOVEN ATTIRE ENGAGE PICKLE
PLEDGE PLISKY STRAIT TAKING
BETROTH MISCHIEF QUANDARY
PLIGHTED ASSURATE
PLIM PLUM STOUT SWELL INFLATE
PLIABLE
PLINTH ORLE ORLO BLOCK SOCLE
ABACUS PATAND QUADRA
SUBBASE FOOTSTALL SCAMILLUS
PLISTHENES (FATHER OF —)
ATREUS
(MOTHER OF —) CLEOLA
(SON OF —) MENELAUS
AGAMEMNON
(WIFE OF —) AEROPE ERIPHYLE
PLOD JOG GRUB PLOT SLOG STOG
TORE TROG VAMP POACH TRAMP

TRASH DRUDGE SLOUCH
TRUDGE PLUNTHER
(— **ALONG**) PEG TORE
(— **THROUGH MUD**) SLOUGH
PLODDER GRUB DIGGER SLOGGER
PLOIARIA EMESA
PLONK WINE
PLOP FLUMP PLUMP HEAVILY
PLOT BREW CAST MARK PACK
PLAN PLAT CABAL DRIFT CONTOUR
GLEBE GRAPH GREEN HATCH
MODEL PLECK SCALD STORY
STUDY WATCH ACTION BRIGUE
CLIQUE DESIGN DEVISE GARDEN
MALIGN MYTHOS SCHEME
SHAMBA TAMPER AGITATE
COLLUDE COMPACT COMPASS
CONJECT CONNIVE CONTOUR
DRAUGHT FEEDLOT LAZYBED
MACHINE PRETEND QUADRAT
QUARTER SWIDDEN ARGUMENT
COGITATE CONSPIRE CONTRIVE
INTRIGUE PRACTICE PROTRACT
SEMINARY MACHINATE
(— **OF GRASS**) SONK
(— **OF LAND**) ERF LOT PLAT SHOT
FORTY MILPA PATCH PLECK
SPLAT COMMON SCHERM
SHAMBA HAGGARD LAZYBED
SEVERAL
(— **OF 1-2 ACRE**) ERF
(— **SECRETLY**) WHISPER
(**GARDEN —**) BED ERF QUINTA
QUARTER
(**UNPRODUCTIVE —**) HIRST
PLOTTER PACKER HATCHER
JACOBIN SCHEMER DESIGNER
ENGINEER
PLOUK KNOB PIMPLE
PLOVER DROME KOLEA OXEYE
PILOT SANDY STILT KILDEE
QUAILY TURNIX COLLIER
COURSER DOTTREL LAPWING
MAYCOCK OWLHEAD PAPABOT
WRYBILL BULLHEAD DOTTEREL
DULWILLY HILLBIRD KILLDEER
RINGNECK SPURWING SQUEALER
TOADHEAD WHISTLER WIREBIRD
SANDERLING
PLOW EAR ERE BOUT DISK FOIL
HINT MOLE PLOD RIVE ROVE
SLUG STIR SULK SULL TILL BREAK
FLUNK SPLIT SULKY THROW
ARAIRE BUSTER DIGGER FALLOW
FURROW GOPHER JUMPER LISTER
PLOUGH RAFTER ROOTER RUTTER
SULLOW BACKSET BREAKER
HUSBAND SCOOTER SULCATE
TWISTER FIREPLOW FURROWER
GANGPLOW SNOWPLOW
TURNPLOW
(— **CROSSWISE**) THORTER
(— **HANDLE**) STILT
(— **LIGHTLY**) SKIM RIFFLE
(— **PART**) PINHEAD
(**PL.**) OUTSIGHT
PLOWBOY YOKEL
PLOWING ARDER EARTH ARDURE
ARATION CARUAGE STIRRING
PLOWLAND CARUE CARVE TILTH
CARUCATE TEAMLAND
PLOWMAN PLOWER TILLER
ACREMAN

PLOWSHARE LAY SLIP SOCK
LAVER REEST SHARE JUMPER
(— **BONE**) VOMER PYGOSTYLE
(**PREF.**) VOMERO
PLOY BENT BOWED SPORT
RAMBLE TACTIC PURSUIT
ACTIVITY ESCAPADE
PLUCK GO PUG ROB TUG BOUT
CROP CULL DRAG GAME GRAB
GRIT PELT PICK PILL POOK PULL
RACE RASE RASH SAND TUCK
ARBER ARBOR BREAK DRAFT
HANGE MOXIE NERVE PILCH
PLOAT PLUME RANCH SMITE
SPUNK STEAL STRIP AVULSE
DECERP EVULSE FLEECE GATHER
PIGEON PLITCH PLOUGH QUARRY
SNATCH SPIRIT TWINGE TWITCH
COURAGE DEPLUME PLUNDER
BOLDNESS DECISION DEMOLISH
GAMENESS VELLICATE
PURTENANCE
(— **AS A STRING**) TIRL PINCH
(— **FEATHERS**) STUB
(— **LEAVES**) BLADE
(— **OF SHEEP OR CALF**) RACE
GATHER
(— **UP COURAGE**) CHEER
(— **WOOL BY HAND**) ROO
PLUCKED PLUMED PIZZICATO
PLUCKY GAMY SANDY BANTAM
GRITTY SPUNKY FIGHTING
PLUG BUG FID PEG PIN TAP TOP
WAD BLOW BONE BOTT BUNG
FILL JADE ROOT SHOT SLOG STOP
SWAT SWOT BOOST DOWEL
DUMMY PILOT PUNCH SHACK
SKATE SPILE STUFF SWEAT
BOUCHE BOXING BULLET
COMEDO DOSSIL DOTTLE FIDDLE
SPIGOT BOUCHON BUSHING
CHAMBER CHUGGER FERRULE
STOPPER STOPPLE DRIVECAP
FUSEPLUG PELELITH STOPCOCK
(— **FOR CANNON**) TAMPION
(— **IN GRENADE**) BOUCHON
(— **IN ORGAN PIPE**) STOPPLE
TAMPION
(— **OF CLAY**) BOTT
(— **OF OAKUM**) FID
(— **OF VOLCANO**) CORE
(— **TO HOLD NAIL**) DOOK
(— **UP**) CLAM STOP ESTOP
RAMFORCE
(**FISHING —**) BUG
(**LIP —**) LABRET
(**NOSE —**) TEMBETA TEMBETARA
(**WASTE —**) WASHER
(**WATER —**) HYDRANT
PLUG-IN JACK
PLUG-UGLY THUG ROWDY TOUGH
RUFFIAN ROUGHNECK
PLUM GAGE JOBO RISE ISLAY
JAMAN PRUNE SWELL BEAUTY
CHENEY DAMSEL DAMSON
KELSEY MUSSEL SAPOTE APRICOT
BULLACE BURBANK FORTUNE
ORLEANS QUETSCH PRUNELLO
ROSACEAN ROSEWORT VICTORIA
WINDFALL
(**COCO —**) ICACO
(**JAVA —**) DUHAT JAMBUL
JAMBOOL JAMBOLAN

(**WILD —**) SKEG SLOE ISLAY
(**PREF.**) PRUNI
PLUMAGE ROBE RUFF FLUFF
HACKLE SHROUD FEATHER
FLOCCUS JUVENAL PENNAGE
FEATHERS PARADISE PTILOSIS
PLUMB BUNG SHEER BOTTOM
BULLET SINKER EXACTLY
PLUMMET UTTERLY ABSOLUTE
COMPLETE DIRECTLY ENTIRELY
VERTICAL
PLUMBAGO LUSTER LUSTRE
GRAPHITE LEADWORT
PLUMB BOB PLUMMET
PLUMBISM SATURNISM
PLUMB LINE MERKHET
PLUM CURCULIO TURK WEEVIL
PLUME PEN TIP TUFT CREST
EGRET PRIDE PRUNE DEPRIVE
DESPOIL FEATHER PANACHE
AIGRETTE
(— **ON HELMET**) CREST PANACHE
(— **ON HORSE**) PLUMADE
(— **ON TURBAN**) CULGEE
(**EGRET —**) OSPREY
(**MILITARY —**) PANACHE
PLUME NUTMEG SASSAFRAS
PLUMMET LEAD FLOAT PLUMB
WEIGHT
PLUMMING BRONZING
PLUMP FAT BOLD FAIR FLOP FULL
PLOP SLAP SOSS TIDY BLUNT
BONNY BUXOM CLUMP FLUMP
FUBBY FUBSY GROUP JOLLY
PLUNK SAPPY SLEEK SMACK
SONSY SQUAB STOUT THICK
BONNIE CHUBBY CRUMBY
CRUMMY DIRECT FATTEN FLATLY
FLESHY FODGEL GAWSIE PLUNGE
PUBBLE ROTUND BLUNTLY
BUNTING CLUSTER DISTEND
FULSOME RIBLESS THRODDY
CHOPPING FLESHFUL
(— **AND ROSY**) BUXOM
(— **AND ROUND**) CHUBBY
(**NOT —**) ANGULAR
(**PLEASINGLY —**) ZAFTIG ZOFTIG
PLUM POCKET FOOL
PLUMULE BLASTUS FEATHER
GEMMULA GEMMULE GEOBLAST
ACROSPIRE
PLUNDER GUT ROB BOOT FANG
JUNK LOOT PILL POLL PREY RAPE
REIF RIPE RUMP SACK SWAG
BEROB BOOTY CHEAT GAINS
HARRY PLUCK PREDE RAVEN
REAVE RENNE RIFLE SCOFF
SHAVE SPOIL STRIP BEZZLE
BOODLE CREACH DACOIT FLEECE
FORAGE HARROW MANAUD
PANYAR PROFIT RAPINE RAVAGE
DESPOIL ESCHEAT FREIGHT
PILFERY PILLAGE RANSACK
SACKAGE SPREAGH SPULZIE
BOOTHALE FREEBOOT
PLUNDERER THIEF BANDIT
BUMMER PEELER POLLER RAPTOR
ROBBER VANDAL ROUTIER
SPOILER MARAUDER RAPPAREE
PLUNDERING PREY SACK MARAUD
RAPINE ESCHEAT HERSHIP
PURCHASE SPECHERY SPOILFUL
SPOILING PREDATORY

PLUNGE BET DIG DIP CAVE DIVE
DOOK DUCK DUMP JUMP PURL
PUSH RAKE RISK SINK SOSS
BURST DOUSE FLING PITCH
PLUMP SOUSE SWOOP FOOTER
GAMBLE LABOR LAUNCH
SPLASH THRUST WALLOP
BRAINGE DEMERGE IMMERSE
PLOUNCE SUBMERGE
(— **INTO**) CLAP ENGULF IMMERGE
(— **INTO WATER**) ENEW
(**GAMBLING —**) RAKER
PLUNGER RAM SWAB FORCE
DUCKER POMMEL BLUNGER
STRIKER
PLUNGING FLING
PLUNK DIVE PLONK PLUCK PLUMP
DOLLAR SUPPORT SUDDENLY
PLUNTHER PLOD FLOUNDER
PLURAL
(**SUFF.**) IM
PLURALIST TOTQUOT
PLURALITY MAJORITY MORENESS
TRIALITY
(**PREF.**) POLY
PLUS AND GAIN WITH EXTRA
SURPLUS ADDITION INCREASE
POSITIVE
PLUSH EASY BEAVER VELOUR
SUPERIOR
PLUSHY SWANK SWANKY
PLUTEUS WAGON PARAPET
PLUTO DIS HADES ORCUS
(**BROTHER OF —**) JUPITER
NEPTUNE
(**FATHER OF —**) SATURN
(**WIFE OF —**) PROSERPINE
PLUTOCRAT NABOB RICHARD
PLUTONIC HYPOGENE INTRUSIVE
VULCANIAN
PLUTUS (ASSOCIATE OF —) TYCHE
EIRENE
(**FATHER OF —**) IASION
(**MOTHER OF —**) CERES DEMETER
PLY RUN BEAT BEND BIAS CORD
CORE DRAM FOLD MOLD SAIL
URGE ADAPT APPLY EXERT LAYER
STEER TWIST WIELD YIELD
COMPLY DOUBLE HANDLE
TRAVEL EXERCISE
(— **WITH DRINK**) BIRL ROSIN
(— **WITH DRUGS**) HOCUS
(**OF ONE —**) SINGLE
PNEUMA NEUM SOUL NEUME
BREATH SPIRIT
PNEUMATIC HAMMER GUN
PNEUMATOCYST FLOAT
PNEUMONIA PULMONITIS
POACH PUG ROB COOK DROP
POKE PUSH SINK BLACK DRIVE
FORCE POTCH STEAL BLEACH
PLUNGE INTRUDE
POACHED EGGS MOONSHINE
POACHER BLACK POGGE SPOACH
LURCHER STALKER WIDGEON
BALDPATE BULLHEAD
(**SALMON —**) REBECCA REBEKAH
(**PL.**) BLACKS
POALES GLUMALES
POCHARD DUCK SMEE DIVER
POKER SCAUP DUNAIR DUNKER
DUNBIRD REDHEAD WHINGER
GOLDHEAD WHINYARD

POCHETTE KIT VIOLIN HANDBAG
POCKET BOX CLY FOB PIT CLAY
KICK POKE PRAT BASIN BURSE
MEANS POUCH PURSE STEAL
ACCEPT BECKET CASING CANTINA
PLACKET SWALLOW TROUSER
ENVELOPE ISOLATED MONETARY
PROFONDE SUPPRESS
CONDENSED MINIATURE
(— A WRONG) PURSE
(— IN BOOK BINDER) STATION
(— OF NET) BOWL
(BILLIARD —) POT HOLE HAZARD
(MAGICIAN'S —) PROFONDE
(NOODLE —S) KREPLACH
(ORE —) CHURN BONANZA
(SMALL —) FOB
(TROUSER —) PRAT BECKET
(WATER —) TINAJA ALBERCA
(PL.) KREPLACH
(PREF.) PERO
POCKETBOOK BAG KICK SKIN
PURSE INCOME READER WALLET
HANDBAG LEATHER BILLFOLD
NOTECASE
POCKET GOPHER TUZA QUACHIL
POCKETING COUP
POCKETKNIFE BARLOW PENKNIFE
PIGSTICKER
POCKMARK PITHOLE
POD BAG COD GAM KID POP SAC
BALL BEAN BOLL HUSK POKE
SWAD BURSE CAROB FLOCK
POUCH QUASH SHAUP SHELL
SHUCK SNAIL WHAUP CHILLI
LEGUME PESCOD SCHOOL
HARICOT PEASCOD SILIQUA
PEASECOD PODOCARP POTBELLY
SEEDCASE TAMARIND
(— FORMING) KID
(— OF LEGUME) KID
(— OF MESQUITE) HONEYPOD
(EXPLOSIVE —) SANDBOX
(SUBTERRANEAN —) EARTHNUT
(UNRIPE —) SQUASH
(PL.) PIPI SUNT BABUL GARAD
BABLAH GARRAT COWHAGE
GONAKIE ALGAROBA DIVIDIVI
(PREF.) SILIQUI
PODALIRIUS (BROTHER OF —)
MACHAON
(FATHER OF —) ASCLEPIUS
PODARCES (BROTHER OF —)
PROTESILAUS
(FATHER OF —) IPHICLUS
PODDED BOLLED
PODIUM DAIS FOOT WALL
LECTERN
PODOCARP YACCA
PODWARE PODDER
PODZOL SPODOSOL
POEM GEM LAI LAY ODE DUAN
EPIC JOSE MELE POSY RUNE
SONG CENTO DIRGE DITTY HAIKU
IWEIN METER STAFF VERSE
AMHRAN AUBADE BALLAD
CACCIA CARMEN CYCLIC DIXAIN
EPOPEE EROTIC ESTRIF HEROID
MELODY MONODY NOSTOS
PIYYUT SESTET SONNET TENSON
TERCET BUCOLIC CANTARE
CANTATA CANZONE DESCORT
DIZAINE ECLOGUE ELEGIAC

FLITING GEORGIC SOTADIC
TRIOLET VIRELAI VIRELAY
VOLUSPA ACROSTIC AMOEBEUM
BRINDISI CANTICLE DINGDONG
DOGGEREL INVICTUS LIMERICK
MADRIGAL TELESTIC THEOGONY
TRISTICH TROCHAIC VERSICLE
MONORHYME ROUNDELAY
(— ABOUT DEBATE) ESTRIF
(— ABOUT SHEPHERDS) ECLOGUE
(— GREETING DAWN) AUBADE
(— OF LAMENTATION) ELEGY
(— OF RETRACTION) PALINODE
(— OF 10 LINES) DIZAINE
(— OF 14 LINES) SONNET
(AMATORY —) EROTIC SONNET
(EPIC —) EPOS EPOPEE LUSIAD
THEBAID
(HOMELY —) DIT
(IRISH —) AMHRAN
(JAPANESE —) HAIKU TANKA
(LITURGICAL —) VIDDUI VIDDUY
SELIHOTH
(LOVE —) AMORETTO
(LYRIC —) LAI LAY ODE ALBA
EPODE GHAZEL RONDEL
CANZONA PARTIMEN
(PART OF —) PASSUS
(PASTORAL —) IDYL IDYLL
BUCOLIC
(PERSIAN —) GHAZAL
(RELIGIOUS —) HYMN
(RURAL —) GEORGIC
(SACRED —) PSALM YIGDAL
(SATIRICAL —) IAMBIC KASIDA
(SHORT —) DIT DITTY EPILOG
SONNET CANZONE EPIGRAM
EPILOGUE EPYLLION
(TONE —) BALLADE
(WELSH —) CYWYDD
(PL.) AZAHROT MAKINGS
(SUFF.) STICH
POET OG RSI BARD FILE FILI FIRI
LARK MUSE SCOP SWAN ARION
LAKER LINOS LINUS LYRIC MAKAR
MAKER ODIST RISHI SAYER SCALD
SKALD FINDER GNOMIC IBYCUS
LAKIST LYRIST SHAPER SINGER
DICHTER ELEGIAC EPICIST IDYLIST
IMAGIST MUSAEUS ORPHEUS
PROPHET CONCRETE FERAMORZ
GEORGIAN LAUREATE LUTANIST
MINSTREL SONGSTER TROUVERE
MINNESINGER
(IRISH —) FILI
(MEDIOCRE —) RIMER RHYMER
(MINOR —) BARDIE
ALBANIAN FISHTA
AMERICAN LOW POE AGAR BURR
CARY CONE DALY HEAD NASH
READ REED SAXE SILL SNOW
TATE TOWN VERY WARE ADAMS
AIKEN AKINS ALLEN AUDEN
BACON BEERS BOGAN BROWN
CLAPP CLARK COLES CRANE
DAMON DRAKE ENGLE FICKE
FIELD FINCH FROST GUEST
HAYNE HOVEY JOLAS MOODY
PIATT POUND PRIME RIDGE RILEY
STORY TOWNE WELBY WILDE
WYLIE ARNOLD BARLOW BRALEY
BRANCH BROOKS BRYANT
BURTON CARMER CAWEIN CIARDI

CLARKE COATES COFFIN CRANCH
CULLEN CUTTER DARGAN
DUNBAR FISHER GILDER GUINEY
HOLMES HOOPER KEELER KILMER
LANIER LEDOUX LOWELL MILLER
MONROE MORGAN MORTON
NORTON OSGOOD SAVAGE
SEEGER THOMAS TIMROD
WRIGHT AINSLIE BABCOCK
CHIVERS CROWELL EMERSON
FEARING FRENEAU HALLECK
HILLYER JEFFERS KNOWLES
LAFARGE LAZARUS LINDSAY
MARKHAM MIFFLIN MOULTON
PARSONS PATCHEN PEABODY
PROCTOR ROBERTS RUSSELL
SHAPIRO SHERMAN STEDMAN
TAGGARD THAXTER WATTLES
WHITMAN BRAINARD CARLETON
CONKLING CUMMINGS DINSMOOR
FISHBACK FLETCHER GINSBURG
HAGEDORN MACLEISH NEIHARDT
PETERSON PHILLIPS PROKOSCH
ROBINSON SANDBURG SCOLLARD
SPOFFORD STERLING STODDARD
TEASDALE THOMPSON TRUMBULL
WHITTIER AUSLANDER
COOLBRITH DICKINSON
GUITERMAN HENDERSON
KREYMBORG OPPENHEIM
TUCKERMAN WURDEMANN
COATSWORTH LONGFELLOW
BRAITHWAITE RITTENHOUSE
ARAB TARAFA
ARGENTINIAN ASCASUBI
ECHEVERRIA
AUSTRALIAN GORDON TURNER
AUSTRIAN VOGL KAFKA BACHER
FRANKL GRAZIE WERFEL
NEUMANN ZEDLITZ CASTELLI
WILDGANS WURZBACH ZINGERLE
HAMERLING HOFMANNSTHAL
BELGIAN GILKIN GIRAUD EEKHOUD
ELSKAMP HASSELT CAMMAERTS
RODENBACH VERHAEREN
BRAZILIAN GAMA COSTA AZEVEDO
GUIMARAES MAGALHAES
BULGARIAN VAZOV BOTYOV
CANADIAN FISET PRATT SCOTT
CARMAN MACKAY FERLAND
JOHNSON LAMPMAN SERVICE
CAMPBELL CRAWFORD
DRUMMOND MACDONALD
CHILEAN NERUDA MISTRAL
CHINESE LIPO TUFU POCHUI
MEISHENG
COLOMBIAN ARBOLEDA
CUBAN VALDES
CZECH CECH GOLL ERBEN FRIDA
HALEK HANKA JEBAVY KVAPIL
MACHAR NERUDA
DANISH BOYE RODE EWALD
HAUCH KINGO PLOUG ARREBO
JENSEN RAHBEK BLICHER
CLAUSEN HOSTRUP KAALUND
WINTHER BAGGESEN BODTCHER
INGEMANN JACOBSEN
AARESTRUP GRUNDTVIG
JORGENSEN GERSTENBERG
DUTCH CATS GOES KATE POOT
BEETS BERGH EEDEN FEITH
HAREN HOOFT DECKER EMANTS
LENNEP LOGHEM VERWEY

VONDEL BELLAMY BREDERO
HELMERS TOLLENS BARLEAUS
SECUNDUS BILDERDIJK
HEEMSKERCK HUYDECOPER
BROEKHUIZEN
ECUADORIAN OLMEDO
ENGLISH GAY MAY MEW PYE BELL
BIGG COOK CORY DYER GALE
GRAY HAKE HALL HILL HOOD
HUNT LEAR NOEL OWEN POPE
TATE VAUX ADAMS BASSE BLAKE
BLUNT BROWN BRYAN BYROM
BYRON CAREW CAREY CLARE
COOKE DIXON DONNE DOYLE
GOOGE GOULD GOWER GREEN
JONES KEATS KEOWN LEWIS
MASON MERRY MILNE MINOT
MONRO MOORE MYERS NADEN
NOYES PAYNE PERCY PRAED
PRIOR SMART SMITH SWAIN
WATTS WAUGH WELLS WHITE
WOLFE WOODS WYATT YOUNG
ABBOTT ANSTEY ARNOLD AUSTIN
BAILEY BARLOW BARNES BARTON
BINYON BOWLES BRETON
BROOKE BROWNE BUTLER
CANTON CAPERN CARTER
CLOUGH CORBET COTTON
COWLEY COWPER CRABBE
DANIEL DAVIES DENHAM DOBELL
DOBSON DOMETT DOWSON
DRYDEN EUSDEN FENTON
GIBSON GLOVER GODLEY GRAVES
GREENE HARVEY HAWKER
HAYLEY HEMANS HOWARD
JONSON KENYON LANDON
LANDOR MACKAY MARTIN
MASSEY MCLEOD MILMAN
MILNES MILTON MORRIS MUNDAY
NESBIT ROGERS SAVAGE SCOGAN
SEWARD STRODE SYMONS
TAYLOR THOMAS TREECE
TRENCH WALLER WARNER
WARREN WATSON WITHER
WOLCOT WOTTON AINSLIE
BAMFORD BLUNDEN BRIDGES
CAEDMON CAMPION CHAPMAN
CHAUCER COKAYNE COLLINS
COPPARD CRASHAW DOUGHTY
DRAYTON ELLIOTT FAUSSET
FLATMAN FLECKER FRAUNCE
FREEMAN GIBBONS GIFFORD
HERRICK HEWLETT HOPKINS
HOUSMAN INGELOW KENNEDY
KIPLING LAYAMON LYDGATE
MANNYNG MARVELL MONTAGU
NEWBOLT NICHOLS PATMORE
PEACOCK PHILIPS POMFRET
PROCTER QUARLES SASSOON
SEYMOUR SHELLEY SITWELL
SKELTON SKIPSEY SOUTHEY
SPENSER SYMONDS TICKELL
TREVENA VAUGHAN WEBSTER
WOOLNER AKENSIDE BEAUMONT
BETJEMAN BLAGMIRE BRANFORD
BRERELEY BROWNING BUCHANAN
CAMPBELL CHALONER DAVENANT
FALCONER GREVILLE HAMILTON
HOCCLEVE LANGLAND LOVELACE
MACNEICE MOULTRIE OVERBURY
ROSSETTI SHADWELL STERLING
SUCKLING TENNYSON THOMPSON
TRAHERNE WHISTLER ALDINGTON

ARMSTRONG BARNFIELD
BLANCHARD BOTTOMLEY
CALVERLEY CAMBRIDGE
CHALKHILL CHURCHILL
CLEVELAND COLERIDGE
CONSTABLE GASCOIGNE
GOLDSMITH HABINGTON
LANGHORNE MASEFIELD
MONKHOUSE ROSCOMMON
SACKVILLE SHENSTONE
SOUTHWELL SWINBURNE
SYLVESTER UNDERHILL
WHITEHEAD BLOOMFIELD
BOURDILLON BRATHWAITE
CHATTERTON DRINKWATER
FITZGERALD MONTGOMERY
SOMERVILLE WORDSWORTH
ABERCROMBIE SHAKESPEARE
TURBERVILLE CHAMBERLAYNE
OSHAUGHNESSY
FINNISH MANNINEN RUNEBERG
ARWIDSSON TAVASTSTJERNA
FRENCH NAU AIDE BAIF FORT
GHIL GRAS KAHN LABE VIAU
ARENE CARCO DIERX DORAT
GACON GREGH GUYAU HARDY
MAROT MURET PIRON RETTE
SCEVE SULLY TASTU AICARD
ARAGON AUGIER AUTRAN
BARTAS BELLAY BERTIN BRETON
BRUNET DANIEL DEREME
DUPONT ELUARD FRANCE
GUERIN HUGUES JAMMES
LEBRUN MORICE MUSSET PARODI
PRADON RACINE REBOUL RICARD
RICTUS SAMAIN THIARD VALERY
VILLON ANCELOT AUBANEL
BARBIER BOCCAGE BONNARD
BORNIER BOUCHOR BOURGET
BRIZEUX CARRERE CAZALIS
CLAUDEL COCTEAU DELTEIL
FEYDEAU GILBERT GRESSET
HENRIOT HEREDIA JODELLE
LAPRADE MAYNARD MISTRAL
MOLINET PONSARD REGNIER
RIMBAUD RONSARD ROSTAND
SCARRON SEGRAIS VICAIRE
VILDRAC AJALBERT ANDRIEUX
BEAUVOIR BERANGER BERGERAT
BERTRAND BOUILHET CHAULIEU
COLLERYE GRECOURT GRINGORE
MALHERBE MALLARME
PEROCHON QUILLARD QUINAULT
RABELAIS ROUSSEAU VERLAINE
BELMONTET BOUFFLERS
CHAPELAIN CREBILLON
DELAVIGNE DESCHAMPS
LAMARTINE LEMERCIER
MONTREUIL ARLINCOURT
BARTHELEMY BAUDELAIRE
BOISROBERT CHENEDOLLE
DESPORTES MALFILATRE
CHANTAVOINE GRANDMOUGIN
DESHOULIERES
GERMAN UZ BAUM BOIE DACH
KLAJ LENZ RIST VOSS AYRER
BOHME BRANT BUSCH FRANK
GLEIM HARDT HEBEL HEINE
HERTZ HOLTY LANGE LOGAU
OPITZ RAABE RILKE SORGE STEIN
UNRUH WEBER BECKER BRECHT
BROGER BURGER FOLLEN GEORGE
GOETHE GOTTER GRABBE

HAMMER HEBBEL HESSUS
JORDAN KARSCH KERNER KLEIST
KNEBEL KOBELL KORNER LEFORT
MORIKE MULLER TIEDGE TOLLER
UHLAND ULRICH WALDIS WEISSE
WERNER ALLMERS BARLACH
BARTHEL BOTTGER BROCKES
BUCHNER FONTANE FORSTER
GELLERT HARRIES HENRICI
KALBECK KOPSICH MALTITZ
NEUMARK REDWITZ RUCKERT
VISCHER WALTHER WIELAND
BAUMBACH BIERBAUM
BRENTANO ECKSTEIN FLEMMING
FREIDANK GRYPHIUS HAGEDORN
HOFFMANN JUNGHANS
KAUFMANN LISSAUER
MAHLMANN OVERBECK SCHEFFEL
SCHILLER SCHUBART STOLBERG
WERNICKE ACIDALIUS BECHSTEIN
BULTHAUPT HOLDERLIN
IMMERMANN KIRCHBACH
KLOPSTOCK MOSENTHAL
NIETZSCHE RODENBERG
WILBRANDT BODENSTEDT
CREIZENACH FASTENRATH
HARDENBERG KOSEGARTEN
MATTHISSON WECKHERLIN
FREILIGRATH KOLBENHEYER
SCHNECKENBURGER
GREEK ION BION AGIAS ARION
HOMER ERINNA HESIOD IBYCUS
NONNUS PALLES PIGRES PINDAR
SAPPHO AGATHON ALCAEUS
ARCHIAS BIKELAS CORINNA
HERODAS ISYLLUS LESCHES
MOSCHUS MUSAEUS PALAMAS
RHIANUS SOLOMOS THESPIS
ANACREON COLUTHUS DIAGORAS
HIPPONAX NICANDER PANYASIS
PHILETAS PISANDER STASINUS
THEOGNIS TYRTAEUS EUPHORION
LYCOPHRON SIMONIDES
TERPANDER TIMOTHEUS
PARTHENIUS PHOCYLIDES
SEFERIADES THEOCRITUS
ASCLEPIADES BACCHYLIDES
HERMESIANAX STESICHORUS
CHRISTOPOULOS
HINDU BHARTRIHARI
HUNGARIAN ADY TOTH AMADE
ARANY GARAY REVAI SZASZ
MADACH PETOFI BALASSA
CZUCZOR KOLCSEY MAILATH
BACSANYI GYONGYOSI KISFALUDY
VOROSMARTY
ICELANDIC EGILSSON
GUNNARSSON JOCHUMSSON
THORODDSEN HALLGRIMSSON
SIGURJONSSON
INDIAN BILHANA
IRISH BANIM COLUM DAVIS
MOORE TIGHE TYNAN WILDE
WILLS WOLFE YEATS ANSTER
BROOKE CLARKE DARLEY DEVERE
FIGGIS GRAVES MAGINN MANGAN
SKRINE BARRETT DRENNAN
DUNSANY HIGGINS MACGILL
STARKEY CAMPBELL FERGUSON
FLECKNOE LEDWIDGE MCCARTHY
STEPHENS ALLINGHAM
LARMINNIE MACDONAGH
ITALIAN REDI VIDA ZENO BELLI

BERNI BONDI BOSSI CASTI DANTE
GUIDI MOLZA MONTI PORTA
PRAGA PRATI PULCI TASSO
CIAMPI GIUSTI GROSSI MAMELI
MARINI PARINI POERIO REVERE
ALEARDI ARIOSTO BERCHET
BOIARDO FOLENGO FRUGONI
GUARINI MARRADI MAZZONI
MONTALE PASCOLI ZANELLA
ALAMANNI BACCELLI BIBBIENA
CARDUCCI CHIARINI COSTANZO
FILICAIA GUERRINI LEOPARDI
MARTELLI NENCIONI PETRARCH
RUCELLAI TANSILLO ARNABOLDI
BARBERINI BROFFERIO CALZABIGI
CESAROTTI CHIABRERA
MARINETTI RAPISARDI
ANGIOLIERI CANNIZZARO
FIRENZUOLA METASTASIO
PINDEMONTE BRACCIOLINI
CRESCIMBENI FORTEGUERRI
JAPANESE BASHO AKAHITO
NOGUCHI
LITHUANIAN MAIRONIS
NEW ZEALAND DUGGAN
NICARAGUAN DARIO
NORWEGIAN MOE KRAG IBSEN
AANRUD HANSEN GARBORG
WELHAVEN
PERSIAN HAFIZ SAADI ANVARI
DAKIKI HATIFI NIZAMI FIRDAUSI
PERUVIAN CHOCANO
POLISH POL ASNYK LANGE
POTOCKI SZUJSKI UJEJSKI
WITTLIN ZALESKI KLONOWIC
KRASICKI ZEROMSKI ZULAWSKI
GASZYNSKI KARPINSKI KRASINSKI
BRODZINSKI DANILOWSKI
KONOPNICKA LOBODOWSKI
MALCZEWSKI MICKIEWICZ
SARBIEWSKI WIERZYNSKI
WYSPIANSKI KOCHANOWSKI
LENARTOWICZ SZYMONOWICZ
PORTUGUESE MELO QUITA
BOCAGE CAMOES CASTRO
GONZAGA QUENTAL RESENDE
RIBEIRO CASTILHO FERREIRA
JUNQUEIRO PALMEIRIM
NASCIMENTO
ROMAN CATO OVID CINNA LUCAN
VARRO ACCIUS BAVIUS ENNIUS
HORACE VERGIL AVIENUS
NAEVIUS STATIUS AFRANIUS
SEDULIUS TIBULLUS VALERIUS
LUCRETIUS PROPERTIUS
RUMANIAN BLAGA EMINESCU
ALEXANDRI ALECSANDRI
RUSSIAN FET MEI BLOK BUNIN
BUGAEV ESENIN IVANOV MAIKOV
RYLEEV BALMONT BRYUSOV
GNEDICH KAPNIST KOLTSOV
NIKITIN PUSHKIN NEKRASOV
POLONSKI TYUTCHEV BESTUZHEV
DERZHAVIN KHERASKOV
KHOMYAKOV LERMONTOV
PASTERNAK ZHUKOVSKI
BARATYNSKI BATYUSHKOV
MAYAKOVSKI PLESHCHEEV
BOGDANOVICH VOZNESENSKY
YEVTUSHENKO
SCOTTISH ADAM AIRD GRAY
HOGG LANG MURE THOM AYTON
BRUCE BURNS JACOB LOGAN

SCOTT SHARP SMITH YOUNG
AYTOUN DUNBAR GRAHAM
HERVEY LEYDEN MALLET MICKLE
MILLER MURRAY NICOLL POLLOK
RAMSAY WILSON BAILLIE
BARBOUR BARCLAY BEATTIE
CLELAND DOUGLAS GRAHAME
KENNEDY LINDSAY PRINGLE
TENNANT THOMSON ANDERSON
COCKBURN DAVIDSON
DRUMMOND HAMILTON
HENRYSON MACNEILL MAITLAND
ALEXANDER BELLENDEN
BLACKLOCK FERGUSSON
GILFILLAN STEVENSON
BALLANTINE CUNNINGHAM
MACDIARMID MOTHERWELL
MONTGOMERIE
SOUTH AFRICAN LANGENHOVEN
SPANISH CRUZ MENA RUIZ VEGA
DURAN RIOJA CANETE CETINA
VIRUES ALCAZAR BECQUER
GALLEGO HERRERA IRIARTE
JIMENEZ MORATIN SALINAS
AGUILERA BALBUENA CORONADO
FIGUEROA MANRIQUE VILLEGAS
ALEIXANDRE CASTILLEJO
CIENFUEGOS ESPRONCEDA
SANTILLANA VILLAMEDIANA
SWEDISH DALIN BESKOW CREUTZ
LIDNER TEGNER WALLIN
DALGREN EKELUND LEOPOLD
RYDBERG ATTERBOM BELLMANN
BORJESON BOTTIGER BRINKMAN
KELLGREN LAGERLOF LENNGREN
LEVERTIN NICANDER ADLERBETH
KARLFELDT MARTINSON
MESSENIUS FAHLCRANTZ
LAGERKVIST STAGNELIUS
STRANDBERG WENNERBERG
OXENSTIERNA
SWISS ILG AMIEL FAESI MEYER
GESSNER LAVATER FROHLICH
LEUTHOLD
SYRIAN GIBRAN
TURKISH FUZULI
URUGUAYAN FIGUEROA
WELSH DAVID HUGHES WILLIAMS
POETASTER BARDET BAVIAN
BAVIUS POETITO BARDLING
VERSEMAN
POETIC ODIC LYRIC STILTED
PEGASEAN POEMATIC
POETRY SONG BLANK MELIC
POEMS VERSE EPOPEE POESIS
SONIOU DOGGREL KALEVALA
(FINNISH —) RUNES
(GOD OF —) BRAGI
(HEROIC —) EPOS
(KIND OF —) CONCRETE
(MUSE OF —) ERATO THALIA
EUTERPE CALLIOPE
POGGE BULLHEAD
POGROM RIOT PILLAGE MASSACRE
POGY POGIE MENHADEN
POIGNANT APT HOME KEEN
ACUTE SHARP SMART BITING
BITTER MOVING SEVERE URGENT
CUTTING POINTED PUNGENT
SATIRIC INCISIVE PIERCING
PRESSING STINGING STRIKING
TOUCHING AMAREVOLE
POINCIANA DELONIX FLAMBEAU

GULMOHAR FLAMBOYER
POINSETTIA BANNER FIREFLOWER
POINT AIM DOT JOT NAK NEB NIB
NUB PEG PIN RES WAY APEX
BACK BOKE CHAT CUSP FORK
GAFF GAME GOOD HEAD HOLD
ITEM KNOT LACE LOOK NAIL
PEAK PICK PILE PINT SPOT STOP
WHET BEARD CHALK DIGIT
FOCUS INDEX LEVEL MUCRO
PITCH PRICK PUNCH PUNCT
PUNTA PUNTO REFER STAND
TEACH THING TOOTH ALLUDE
BROACH CRAYON CUSPIS CUTOFF
DEGREE DIRECT FLECHE JUGALE
MATTER NOSING PERIOD THESIS
TITTLE VERTEX ZYGION APICULA
ARTICLE BENEFIT CACUMEN
CRUNODE ESSENCE GATEWAY
PUNCTUM PUSHPIN SHARPEN
TANJONG TRAGION ANNOUNCE
PUNCTULE STRIPPER PARTICULAR
(— AT ISSUE) BEEF CRUX
(— AT WHICH LEAF SPRINGS) AXIL
(— BEHIND EAR) ASTERION
(— FOR PHONOGRAPH RECORD)
STYLE
(— IN CAPSTAN) STRIPPER
(— IN CONSONANT) DAGHESH
(— IN DEBATE) ISSUE
(— IN ORBIT OF PLANET) AUGE
APSIS APOGEE SYZYGY APOJOVE
PERIGEE APASTRON APHELION
(— IN QUESTION) ISSUE
(— IN SEVEN-UP) GIFT
(— IN SOME GAMES) PUNT
(— NEAREST EARTH) PERIGEE
(— OF A BORDER) VANDYKE
(— OF ANCHOR) BILL
(— OF ANTLER) PRONG
(— OF ANVIL) HORN
(— OF CELESTIAL SPHERE)
ANTAPEX
(— OF CHIN) BUTTON
(— OF CONTACT) EPHAPSE
(— OF CRESCENT MOON) CUSP
(— OF DECLINE) EBB
(— OF DIVERGENCE) AXIL
(— OF ECLIPTIC) LAGNA SOLSTICE
(— OF EPIGRAM) STING
(— OF FAITH) ARTICLE
(— OF HONOR) PUNDONOR
(— OF INTEREST) CLOU
(— OF INTERSECTION) FOOT
STAURION
(— OF JAVELIN) SAGAIE
(— OF JUNCTION) MEET BREGMA
LAMBDA
(— OF LABEL) LAMBEAU
(— OF LAND) ODD CAPE SPIT
MORRO HEADLAND
(— OF LEAF) MUCRO
(— OF LIFE) HYLEG
(— OF LIGHT) GLINT SPANGLE
(— OF LIGHTNING ROD) AIGRETTE
(— OF LIPS) CHEILION
(— OF MANGO) NAK
(— OF ONSET) BRINK
(— OF ORIGIN) HIVE SOURCE
FOUNTAIN
(— OF PEN) NEB NIB
(— OF PETAL) LACINULA
(— OF REFERENCE) STYLION

(— OF ROCK) NUNATAK
(— OF STAG'S HORN) START
(— OF STORY) KNOT
(— OF STYLUS) CUTTER
(— OF SUPPORT) BEARING
(— OF TEMPERATURE) SOLIDUS
(— OF TIME) DATE INSTANT
JUNCTURE
(— OF TOOTH) CUSP
(— OF UMBRELLA) FERRULE
(— OF VIEW) EYE ANGLE FRONT
SLANT COLORS CORNER GROUND
RESPECT FUTURISM
(— OF VIOLIN BOW) HEAD
(— OF WEAPON) ORD BARB
(— ON AUGER OR BIT) SPUR
(— ON BACKGAMMON BOARD)
FLECHE
(— ON CURVE) TACNODE
(— ON JAW) GONION
(— ON STAG'S HORN) BROACH
(— ON SUNDIAL) NODE
(— OUT) SHOW DIGIT INFER
ASSIGN DIRECT ENSIGN FINGER
MUSTER NOTIFY REMARK
PRESAGE INDICATE
(APPROPRIATE —) PLACE
(ASTROLOGICAL —) INGRESS
(BARBED —) FORK
(BLUNT —) MORNETTE
(CARBON —) CRAYON
(CARDINAL —) EAST WEST HINGE
NORTH SOUTH
(CARDINAL —S) CARDINES
(CENTRAL —) OMPHALOS
(CHRONOLOGICAL —) ERA EPOCH
(COMPASS —) E N S W NE NW SE
SW ENE ESE NNE NNW SSE SSW
WNW WSW AIRT AIRTH RHUMB
COURSE
(CRITICAL —) JUMP
(CROWNING —) CAPSHEAF
CAPSTONE
(CRUCIAL —) CRUX
(CULMINATING —) HEAD COMBLE
(DOUBLE — OF CURVE) ACNODE
CRUNODE
(ESSENTIAL —) MAIN
(EXACT —) TEE
(EXCESS —S) LAP
(EXCLAMATION —) BANG
SCREAMER
(EXTREME —) END
(FARTHEST —) APOGEE SOLSTICE
(FINAL —) UPCOME
(FIXED —) ABUTMENT
(GLAZIER'S —) SPRIG
(HALFWAY — IN CRIBBAGE) CORNER
(HIGHEST —) TIP ACME APEX
AUGE NOON PEAK CREST FLOOD
APOGEE CLIMAX CULMEN HEIGHT
PERIOD SUMMIT VERTEX ZENITH
EVEREST MAXIMUM MERIDIAN
SOLSTICE
(KNOTTY —) CRUX NODUS
(LAST —) END
(LATERAL —) ALARE
(LOWEST —) NADIR BOTTOM
BEDROCK
(LOWEST — OF HULL) BILGE
(MAIN —) JET SUM GIST
(MEDIAN —) HORMION
(NO —S) LOVE

(ONE'S STRONG —) FORTE
(PEDAL —) DRONE
(PIVOTAL —) KNUCKLE
(PRECISE —) NICK
(PROJECTING —) CRAG PEAK
BEARD
(SHARP —) JAG PRICK PRICKLE
(SIGNIFICANT —) MILESTONE
(SINGLE —) ACE
(SKULL —) TYLION
(SORE —) NERVE
(STARTING —) BASE
(STATIONARY —) SPINODE
(STRIKING —) SALIENCE
(STRONG —) FORTE
(TAPERING —) ACUMEN
(TENNIS —) LET CHASE BISQUE
(TENTH OF —) MOMENT
(TERMINAL —) GOAL BOURN
BREAK AIRPORT
(TO THE —) COGENT
(TOP —) TUFT
(TURNING —) CARDO EPOCH CRISIS
(UNIPLANAR —) UNODE
(UTMOST —) EXTREME SUBLIME
(VANTAGE —) TOWER
(VOWEL —) SERE SEGOL SEGHOL
(WEAK —) BLOT
(PREF.) KENTRO MUCRONI PUNC-
TATO PUNCTI PUNCTO STIGMATI
STIGMEO STIGMO
POINT-BLANK BLUNT PLAIN POINT
DIRECT WHOLLY EXPRESS
DIRECTLY
**POINT COUNTER POINT (AUTHOR
OF —)** HUXLEY
(CHARACTER IN —) JOHN LUCY
MARK BURLAP ELINOR GILRAY
PHILIP RACHEL SIDNEY WALTER
WEBLEY BIDLAKE CARLING
EVERARD QUARLES RAMPION
BEATRICE MARJORIE SPRANDRELL
TANTAMOUNT
POINTED SET ERDE HOME ACUTE
EXACT FIXED PEAKY PIKED
TANGY TERSE FITCHE LIVELY
OXEOTE PEAKED PECKED PICKED
SPIRED ANGULAR FITCHEE
LACONIC PRECISE SPICATE
ZESTFUL ACICULAR ACULEATE
COPATAIN CULTRATE DIACTINE
PUNCTUAL STELLATE ACUMINATE
(PREF.) OXY
POINTEDNESS BARB
POINTER TIP YAD COCK HAND
WAND DUBHE INDEX POINT
FESCUE FINGER GUNDOG INDICE
SILKER STYLUS FLUSHER
INDICANT SIGNITOR
(— IN GREAT BEAR) DUBHE
DUBBHE
(— ON ASTROLABE) ALMURY
(— ON GAUGE) ARM
(BUILDER'S —) RAKER
(TEACHER'S —) FESCUE
(PL.) MEN GUARDS YADAYIM
POINTLESS DRY ILL DULL FLAT
INANE SILLY VAPID FRIGID
STUPID INSIPID WITLESS
MUTICOUS
POINTSMAN TRAPPER LATCHMAN
SWITCHMAN
POISE PEE PEA CALM HEAD REST SWAY

TACT BRACE PEIZE APLOMB
OFFSET PONDER BALANCE
BEARING DIGNITY OPPRESS
POISURE DELIVERY EASINESS
SERENITY
(— RECIPROCAL) RHE
POISED SET FACILE HOVERING
NERVELESS
(BE —) LIBRATE
POISER HALTER
POISON FIG GAS BANE BIKH DRAB
DRUG GALL TUBA VERY ATTER
TAINT TOXIN VENOM VIRUS
ANTIAR DERRIS INFECT RANKLE
TOXIFY TOXOID ACONITE
BABASCO CORRUPT ENVENOM
FLYBANE MINERAL PERVERT
PHALLIN TANGHIN VITIATE
ACQUETTA DELETERY RATSBANE
VENENATE SAXITOXIN
(— IN DEATH CUP) PHALLIN
(ARROW —) HAYA INEE URALI
URARE URARI ANTIAR ANTJAR
CURARE CURARI DERRIS OURARI
OUABAIN
(FISH —) AKIA CUBE TIMBO
DERRIS HAIARI BABASCO
BARBASCO
(RAT —) ANTU
(VIRULENT —) BIKH TANGHIN
(PREF.) PHARMACO VENENI
VENENO VIRU
POISONED BUCKEYED TOXICATE
VENENATE VENOMOUS
POISONER SEPSIN CANIDIA
VENEFIC VENOMER
POISON HEMLOCK BUNK CICUTA
POISONING PYEMIA UREMIA
ARGYRIA GASSING JIMMIES
BOTULISM MYCETISM PLUMBISM
ICHTHYISM LATHYRISM
SATURNISM SELENOSIS
POISON IVY CLIMATH MARKERY
MERCURY MARKWEED
POISON OAK YEARA
POISONOUS ATTRY TOXIC ATTERY
VENENE VIROSE VIROUS BANEFUL
NOISOME NOXIOUS DELETERY
MEPHITIC TOXICANT VENENATE
VENOMOUS VIRULENT
MALIGNANT
(PREF.) TOX(I)(IC)(ICO)(O)
POISON SUMAC BURTREE
DOGWOOD
POISON TOBACCO HENBANE
POISONWOOD BUMWOOD
POITREL ARMOR PECTRON
POKE BAG DAB DIG DUB HIT JAB
JOG PUG PUR TIG WAD BROD
PAUT PORR PROD PROG RAUK
RUCK SACK SOCK STAB STIR
NIDGE POACH PROKE PROTE
PUNCH ROUSE STEER STOKE
COWBOY DAWDLE INCITE PIERCE
POCKET POUNCE POUTER
PUGGLE PUTTER WALLET
PRODDLE
(— ABOUT) ROKE ROUT RUMMAGE
(— AROUND) ROOT SCROUNGE
(— FUN) COD
(— LIGHTLY) POTTER PUTTER
(— WITH FOOT) SCUFF
(— WITH NOSE) SNUZZLE

POKE-IN STRANDER
POKELOKEN BOGAN LOGAN
POKER DART DRAW FLIP POIT
PORR POTE STUD BLUFF BOGIE
CURATE GOBLIN STOKER
ACEPOTS FRUGGAN LOWBALL
PASSOUT POCHARD SHOTGUN
BASEBALL COALRAKE JACKPOTS
MISTIGRI SHOWDOWN
(**— CHIP**) JETON JETTON
(**— HAND**) RUNT FLUSH SKEET
KILTER PELTER STRAIGHT
(**FORM OF —**) DRAW STUD
(**HOT —**) SALAMANDER
POKEWEED POKE POCAN SCOKE
COAKUM GARGET FOXGLOVE
INKBERRY REDBERRY
POKY DEAD DULL JAIL SLOW
DOWDY POKEY POKING SHABBY
STODGY STUFFY STUPID
CRAMPED TEDIOUS
POLAK BALSA POLLACK

POLAND
CAPITAL: WARSAW
COIN: DUCAT GROSZ MARKA
ZLOTY FENNIG HALERZ KORONA
DANCE: POLKA MAZURKA
KRAKOWIAK POLONAISE
GENTRY: SZLACHTA
LAKE: GOPLO MAMRY SNIARDWY
MEASURE: CAL MILA MORG PRET
LINJA SAZEN STOPA VLOKA
WLOKA CWIERK KORZEC
KWARTA LOKIEC GARNIEC
MOUNTAIN: RYSY TATRA SUDETEN
NAME: POLONIA SARMATIA
NATIVE: SLAV MARUR SILESIAN
PARLIAMENT: SEJM SEYM SENAT
PROVINCE: OPOLE KIELCE
RIVER: BUG SAN ALLE BRDA
GWDA LYNA NYSA ODER STYR
BIALA BZURA DRANA DWINA
NOTEC SERET WARTA WISTA
NEISSE NIEMEN PILICA PRIPET
PROSNA STRYPA WIEPRZ
VISTULA WISTOKA DNIESTER
TITLE OF ADDRESS: PAN PANI
PANIE
TOWN: LWO KOLO LIDA LODZ
LVOV OELS BREST BYTOM
CHELM POSEN RADOM SRODA
TORUN VILNA GDANSK GDYNIA
GRODNO KRACOW KRAKOW
LUBLIN POZNAN TARNOW
WARSAW ZABRZE BEUTHEN
BRESLAU CHORZOW GAROCIN
GLIWICE LEMBERG LITOUSK
WROCLAW GLEIWITZ
KATOWICE SZCZECIN
TARNOPOL
WEIGHT: LUT FUNT UNCYA
KAMIAN CENTNER SKRUPUL

POLAR ARCTIC EMANANT PIVOTAL
DIRECTRIX
POLARIS ALRUCABA
POLE BAR LAT LEG LUG POL POY
ROD SKY XAT BEAM BIND BROG
COPE FALL HOOK KENT MAST
NEAP PALO PERK PIKE PROP SKID
SPAR TREE UFER CABER FOCUS
MASUR MAZUR PERCH QUANT
REACH SHAFT SPEAR SPOKE
STAFF STANG STILT STING STODE
SWAPE SWIPE BEACON BORITY
CROTCH FLOWER IMPOSE JUFFER
KILLIG RICKER RISSLE RYPECK
SPONGE STOWER TONGUE
BARLING HEAVENS TOWMAST
ALESTAKE FLAGPOLE FOOTPICK
POLANDER STANDARD
(**— AS EMBLEM OF SOVEREIGNTY**)
KAHILI
(**— AS HOLDFAST FOR BOATS**)
RYPECK
(**— FOR BEARING COFFIN**) SPOKE
(**— FOR PROPELLING BOAT**) POY
(**— FOR TOSSING**) CABER KEBAR
(**— HOLDING SAIL**) BOOM MAST
SPRIT
(**— MARKING SAND DUNE**) BALIZE
(**— OF TIMBER WAGON**) NIB
JANKER
(**— OF VEHICLE**) NEAP
(**— ON TWO WHEELS**) JANKER
(**— SEPARATING HORSES**) BAIL
(**— USED AS SIGN**) ALEPOLE
ALESTAKE
(**— WITH BIRD DECOY**) STOOL
(**BOAT —**) SPRIT
(**CARRIAGE —**) NIB BEAM
(**COUPLING —**) REACH
(**FIR —**) UFER UPHER JUFFER
(**FISHING —**) WAND
(**FORKED —**) CROTCH
(**LOGGING —**) JANKER KILHIG
KILLIG
(**LONG —**) PEW
(**MANGROVE —**) BORITY
(**MINE —S**) LAGGING
(**NEGATIVE —**) CATHODE
(**PUNT —**) QUANT STOWER
(**RANGE —**) FLAG
(**SACRED —**) ASHERAH
(**SHEPHERD'S —**) KENT
(**SPRINGY —**) BINDER
(**STABLE —**) BAIL
(**STOUT —**) KILHIG RICKER
(**WATER-RAISING —**) SWEEP
(**SUFF.**) KONT
POLEAX STAFF POLEARM
POLECAT FITCH SKUNK ZORIL
FERRET FICHAT WEASEL
FOUMART FOULMART PERWITSKY
SARMATIER
(**— PELT**) FITCH
POLE FLOUNDER SOLE
POLEHEAD TADPOLE
POLESTAR STAR GUIDE POLARIS
LODESTAR
POLICE MAN HEAT GUARD WATCH
GOVERN CONTROL JEMADAR
OCHRANA POLIZEI PROTECT
TOXOTAE OPRICHNIK
(**SECRET —**) CHEKA
POLICEMAN COP JOE KID NAB PIG
BOGY BULL FLIC FUZZ GRAB JACK
JOHN PEON SLOP TRAP ZARP
BOBBY BOGEY BULKY BURLY
GAZER PEACE RURAL SCREW
SEPOY ASKARI BADGER BOBBIE
COPPER FISCAL FLATTY HARMAN
JOHNNY PEELER REDCAP ROZZER
RUNNER SHAMUS CRUSHER
FOOTMAN GHAFFIR GUMSHOE
JEMADAR OFFICER SHOOFLY
TROOPER ZAPTIAH ZAPTIEH
BARGELLO BLUECOAT DOGBERRY
FLATFOOT GENDARME MINISTER
PATROLMAN
(**CLUB OF —**) BILLY STAFF
SPONTOON TRUNCHEON
(**PL.**) FINEST
POLICE STATION THANA
BARGELLO KOTWALEE
POLICY WIT DEAL FRONT ORDER
GOVERN NUMBER TICKET
WISDOM AUTARKY COUNSEL
CUNNING FLOATER LEFTISM
LOTTERY TONTINE VOUCHER
ACTIVISM ARTIFICE SAGACITY
STATEWAY PLURALISM
(**CHOSEN —**) COURSE
(**PL.**) APRISMO
POLISH BOB LAP MOP RUB RUD
BUFF DUCO FILE POLE CLEAN
FRUSH GLAZE GLOSS GRACE
RABAT ROUND SHINE SLICK
STONE AFFILE BARREL LUSTER
PUNISH REFINE RUMBLE SHAMMY
SLIGHT SMOOTH STREAK
BEESWAX BURNISH CHAMOIS
FURBISH LACQUER PERFECT
PLANISH VARNISH ELEGANCE
LEVIGATE SIMONIZE URBANIZE
SARMATIAN
POLISHED FINE COMPT ROUND
SHINY SLICK TERSE BUFFED
FACETE GLOSSY INLAND POLITE
SMOOTH ELEGANT GALLANT
GENTEEL POLITIC REFINED
CULTURED
(**NOT —**) BLIND
POLISHER BUFFER GLAZER
WAGWAG WIGWAG DOLLIER
GLOSSER LAPIDARY SMOOTHER
POLISHING SANDING FROTTAGE
LIMATION
(**— MATERIAL**) RABAT
POLITE NEAT TIDY TRIM BLAND
CIVIL SUAVE GENTLE SMOOTH
URBANE COURTLY GALLANT
GENTEEL DELICATE DISCREET
LUSTROUS ATTENTIVE
COURTEOUS
POLITENESS FINISH TASHRIF
CIVILITY COURTESY ELEGANCE
URBANITY
POLITES (**FATHER OF —**) PRIAM
(**MOTHER OF —**) HECUBA
POLITIC WARY WISE SUAVE
ARTFUL CRAFTY CUNNING
TACTFUL DISCREET PROVIDENT
POLITICAL (**— ASSN.**) VEREIN
(**— PARTY**) GOP TORY WHIG
LABOR
POLITICIAN BOSS STATIST
WARWICK PIPELAYER
STATESMAN
POLITY SERFISM
POL INES (**SON OF —**) FLORIZEL
POLL COW DOD NOT POW ROB
CHUB COLL DODD HEAD NAPE
NOTT PASH CROWN SKULL STRIP
CENSUS FLEECE PARROT
CANVASS DESPOIL PILLAGE
PLUNDER POLLARD
POLLACK LOB GADE LAIT GADID
LYTHE BILLET LAITHE SAITHE
BADDOCK SILLOCK WALLEYE
BLUEFISH COALFISH GRAYFISH
LORICATE MOULRUSH
POLLARD CHU COW DOD BRAN
POLL STAG SHEEP CHEVAN
DODDLE DOTARD BOLLING
LOPPARD WOODSERE
POLLARD TREE DOTARD RUNNEL
POLLED NOT NOTT POLEY
HORNLESS
POLLEN DUST MEAL FLOUR
FARINA POWDER BEEBREAD
(**— BRUSH**) SCOPA
(**— TUBE**) SPERMARY
POLLER VOTER BARBER POLLSTER
POLLEX THUMB
POLLINATE SELF FECUNDATE
FECUNDIZE FERTILIZE
POLLINATING SIBBING
POLLIWOG TADPOLE
POLLOCK PODLER
POLLUTE FOIL FOUL SOIL BLEND
DIRTY SMEAR TAINT BEFOUL
DEFILE INFECT MUDDLE RAVISH
ADULTER DEBAUCH PROFANE
SLOTTER VIOLATE
POLLUTED FOUL DRUNK TURBID
CORRUPT
POLLUTING FILTHY
POLLUTION STAIN SULLAGE
FOULNESS IMPURITY
POLLUX POL HERCULES
(**BROTHER OF —**) CASTOR
(**MOTHER OF —**) LEDA
POLO (**PERIOD IN —**) CHUKKER
POLONAISE POLACCA
FACKELTANZ
POLONIUS CORAMBIS
(**DAUGHTER OF —**) OPHELIA
(**SON OF —**) LAERTES
POLT BLOW THUMP STROKE
POLTERGEIST GHOST SPIRIT
POLTROON IDLER COWARD
CRAVEN WRETCH DASTARD
COWARDLY SLUGGARD
POLYANDRIUM CEMETERY
POLYBUS (**FATHER OF —**) ANTENOR
(**MOTHER OF —**) THEANO
(**WIFE OF —**) MEROPE PERIBOEA
POLYDAMAS (**BROTHER OF —**)
EUPHORBUS HYPERENOR
(**COMPANION OF —**) HECTOR
(**FATHER OF —**) PANTHOUS
(**MOTHER OF —**) PHRONTIS
POLYDORE (**BROTHER OF —**)
CASTALIO
POLYDORUS (**FATHER OF —**) PRIAM
CADMUS HIPPOMEDON
(**MOTHER OF —**) HECUBA
HARMONIA
(**SLAYER OF —**) POLYMNESTOR
(**SON OF —**) LABDACUS
(**WIFE OF —**) NYCTEIS
POLYGALA GAYWINGS
POLYGON DECAGON HEXAGON
NONAGON HEPTAGON PENTAGON
CHILIAGON MULTANGLE
POLYGRAPH KEELER
POLYHEDRON BEAD PRISM
PRISMATOID
POLYMER DIMER HYDROL
MANNAN MUREIN

HEXAMER OLIGOMER
(— UNIT) MER

POLYNESIA
CHESTNUT: RATA
IMAGE: TIKI
ISLAND: COOK LINE SAMOA
TONGA EASTER ELLICE
PHOENIX
ISLE: MOTU
KING: ALII ARII ARIKI
LANGUAGE: UVEA TAGALOG
MOUND: AHU
NATIVE: ATI MAORI KANAKA
NIVEAN TONGAN NESOGAEAN
PRINCIPLE: TIKI
WOMAN: WAHINE

POLYNESIAN MAORI KANAKA
TONGAN FUTUNAN
POLYNICES (BROTHER OF —)
ETEOCLES
(FATHER OF —) OEDIPUS
(MOTHER OF —) JOCASTA
(WIFE OF —) ARGIA
POLYNOMIAL CUBIC
POLYP CORAL HYDRA TUMOR
ZOOID ISOPOD HYDRULA
OCTOPOD
POLYPARY ZOARIUM
POLYPHONY ORGANUM
FABURDEN COUNTERPOINT
POLYPIDOM CORMUS
POLYSACCHARIDE LEVAN
GELOSE GLYCAN INULIN IRISIN
MANNAN AMYLOSE DEXTRAN
FUCOSAN HEXOSAN POLYOSE
GALACTAN GLYCOGEN LICHENIN
SECALOSE SINISTRIN
POLYXENA (FATHER OF —) PRIAM
(MOTHER OF —) HECUBA
POLYZOAN POLYP CESTODE
RADIATE
POMACE MUST RAPE POMMY
STOCK STOSH CHEESE
POMADE CIDER POMATUM
LIPSTICK OINTMENT
POMANDER CASE POUNCET
POMATO TOPATO
POME BALL APPLE GLOBE
JUNEBERRY
POMEGRANATE GRENAT
GRENADE BALAUSTA
POMELO SHADDOCK GRAPEFRUIT
POMERANIA (CAPITAL OF —)
STETTIN
(CITY IN —) THORN TORUN
ANKLAM
(ISLAND IN —) RUGEN USEDOM
(PROVINCE IN —) POMORZE
POMFRET BULLY HENFISH
POMME DE TERRE POTATO
POMMEL BOB FIB NOB BEAT HORN
KNOB PAIK PAKE TORE NEVEL
BRUISE BUFFET CRUTCH FINIAL
PLUMMET
POMP BRAG FARE WEAL BOAST
PRIDE STATE ESTATE PAMPER
PARADE RIALTY SCHEME SPRUNK
BOBANCE DISPLAY PAGEANT
PANOPLY SPLURGE CEREMONY
EQUIPAGE GRANDEUR SEMBLANT
SPLENDOR

POMPANO DART JUREL ALLICE
CARANX PERMIT ALEWIFE
COBBLER OLDWIFE CARANGID
MACKEREL
(— CLAM) COQUINA
POMPOSITY TUMOR TUMOUR
BIGHEAD BIGNESS BOMBAST
POMPOUS BIG BUG BUDGE JELLY
LARGE SHOWY TUMID WIGGY
ASTRUT AUGUST TURGID
BLOATED BOMBAST FUSTIAN
OROTUND STILTED SWOLLEN
TURGENT BEWIGGED INFLATED
MAGNIFIC SWELLING TOPLOFTY
IMPORTANT PONTIFICAL
PORTENTOUS
PONCEAU GRANAT
PONCHO MANGA RUANA
POND (ALSO SEE POOL) LAY LUM
DELF DIKE MOAT PULK SLEW
STEW TANK VLEI VLEY CANAL
DECOY DELFT LACHE LETCH
STANK WAYER CLAIRE LAGOON
LOCHAN PUDDLE SALINA SLOUGH
SPLASH STAGNE MULLETRY
(— FOR OYSTERS) CLAIRE
(— MAN) JACKER
(ARTIFICIAL —) AQUARIUM
(DIRTY —) SOAL
(FISH —) VIVER GURGES PISCINA
(FISH STORING —) STEW
(SMALL —) KHAL
(STAGNANT —) DUB
(PREF.) LACO LIMN(I)(O)
PONDER CON CAST CHAW MUSE
PORE ROLL TURN BROOD STUDY
VOLVE WEIGH ADVISE EXPEND
REASON RECORD REMORD
BALANCE COMPASS EXAMINE
IMAGINE PERPEND REFLECT
REVERIE REVOLVE APPRAISE
COGITATE CONSIDER MEDITATE
PONDERABILITY WEIGHT GRAVITY
PONDEROUS DULL SLOW BULKY
GRAVE HEAVY SOGGY AWKWARD
WEIGHTY UNWIELDY IMPORTANT
PONDEROUSNESS HEFT
POND HEN COOT
PONDMAN JACKER
PONDOKKIE HUT HOVEL
PONE CAKE LUMP WRIT PAUNE
PUDDING SWELLING
PONGEE PAUNCHE SHANTUNG
PONIARD STAB BODKIN DAGGER
STYLET POINADO
PONOCRATES (PUPIL OF —)
GARGANTUA
PONT FERRY FLOAT BRIDGE
FERRYBOAT
PONTIANAC JELUTONG
PONTIC DUMMY
PONTICELLO BREAK MAGAS
PONTIFF POPE BISHOP PRIEST
PONTIFEX
PONTIFICAL AARONIC
PONTIL PUNTY
PONTOON FLOAT RHINO BRIDGE
PONY CAB RAW TAT CAVY TROT
YABU BIDET DALES GRIFF PAINT
PINTO POWNY TACKY TRICK
WELCH WELSH BASUTO BHUTIA
BRONCO CAYUSE EXMOOR
GARRAN SHELTY TANGUN

TATTOO ENGLISH HACKNEY
MANIPUR MUSTANG SHELTIE
FORESTER GALLOWAY SHETLAND
(STUDENT'S —) CRIB TROT BICYCLE
(PL.) DALES
POODLE SHOCK BARBET
POOH POWWAW
POOK HEAP PICK PULL PLUCK
STACK
POOKA PUCK GOBLIN SPECTER
POOL (ALSO SEE POND) CAR DIB
DUB LAY LUM PIT POL POT POW
BANK BOOK CARR DIKE DUMP
FARM FLOW JHIL LAKE LIDO LINN
LLYN LUMB MERE PANT PEEL
PLUD POLK POND PULE PULK
RING SINK SLEW SOIL SWAG
TANK TARN WEEL BAYOU BOWLY
DECOY FLASH FLUSH FRESH
JHEEL KITTY LETCH LOUGH
MEARE PLASH PLUMB SLACK
STANK STELL STILL THERM
TRUNK CARTEL CHARCO FLODGE
LAGOON LASHER PLUNGE
PUDDLE SILOAM SPLASH STABLE
CARLINE CATHOLE CUSHION
JACKPOT PLASHET SNOOKER
STAGNUM INTERLOT QUINIELA
(— AT JERUSALEM) BETHESDA
(— BELOW WATERFALL) LIN LINN
LLYN
(— IN BOG) HAG
(— WITH SALMON NETS) STELL
(— WITHOUT OUTLET) STAGNUM
(ARTIFICIAL —) CUSHION
(AUCTION —) CALCUTTA
(BETTING —) EXACTA PERFECTA
TRIFECTA
(DIRTY —) SUMP
(FISH —) TRUNK STEWPOND
(MOUNTAIN —) TARN
(MUDDY —) LETCH
(SWIMMING —) BATH LIDO
PISCINA NATATORY NATATORIUM
(PREF.) LIMN(I)(O) STAGNI
POON DILO PEON PUNA DOMBA
KEENA TAMANU SIRPOON
MASTWOOD
POONGHIE RAHAN PRIEST PUNGYI
PHONGHI TALAPOIN
POOP DOCK FIRE GULP TOOT
CHEAT COZEN STERN BEFOOL
ISLAND DECEIVE EXHAUST
HINDDECK OVERCOME
POOR BAD OFF SAD BASE EVIL
FOUL LEAN LEWD PUNK SICK
SOUR THIN DINKY EXILE FOOTY
GROSS JERRY KETTY SCALY SEELY
SILLY SOBER SORRY UNORN
FEEBLE HUMBLE HUNGRY
LEADEN MEAGER MEAGRE
MEASLY PILLED PORAIL PRETTY
SCANTY SHABBY STREET CODFISH
HAPLESS NAUGHTY SCRAWNY
SCRUBBY SQUALID TRIVIAL
UNLUCKY INDIGENT ORDINARY
PRECIOUS SCRANNEL SNEAKING
TERRIBLE UNTHENDE PENNILESS
PENURIOUS
(— BOY) HERO
(PREF.) MAL(E) PTOCHO
POORHOUSE MEASONDUE
POORLY ILL BADLY SADLY BARELY

FEEBLY SIMPLY SLIGHT SHABBILY
(PREF.) DYS
POOR SOLDIER FRIARBIRD
POORTITH POVERTY
POOR WHITE (AUTHOR OF —)
ANDERSON
(CHARACTER IN —) JIM JOE TOM
HUGH CLARA MCVEY SARAH
STEVE HUNTER SHEPARD
WAINSWORTH BUTTERWORTH
POP GO DOT GUN HIT TRY BLOW
DART HOCK JUMP PAWN SODA
BREAK CLOOP CRACK KNOCK
SHOOT ATTACK EFFORT FATHER
POPPER STROKE THRUSH
ASSAULT ATTEMPT CONCERT
EXPLODE INSTANT REDWING
BACKFIRE SUDDENLY
POPDOCK FOXGLOVE
POPE PAPA PAPE RUFF BISHOP
PUFFIN SHRIKE PONTIFEX
FISHERMAN
(PREF.) PAPI PAPO POPO
POPERY POPEISM PAPISTRY
POPE'S-EYE NUT NOIX
POPGUN SCOOT PENGUN POTGUN
PLUFFER
POPINJAY PARROT PAPINGO
POPLAR ABBEY ABELE ALAMO
ASPEN BAHAN LIARD BALSAM
POPPLE BAUMIER ABELTREE
WHITEBARK
POPLIN TABINET
POPOLOCA CHOCHO
POPPY HEAD BLAVER CANKER
COPROSE EARACHE PONCEAU
REDWEED ARGEMONE BALEWORT
BOCCONIA HEADACHE
DANNEBROG SQUATMORE
COQUELICOT
(CORN —S) SOLDIERS
(PREF.) MECON(O)
POPPYCOCK BOSH FOLLY STUFF
HAVERS
POPPYFISH POMPANO
POPPY SEED MAW MOHNSEED
POPULACE MOB MASS CROWD
DEMOS PLEBS MASSES MOBILE
PEOPLE PUBLIC COUNTRY
MULTITUDE
(PREF.) DEM(O) OCHLO
POPULAR LAY POP COMMON
GOLDEN PUBLIC SIMPLE VULGAR
CROWDED DEMOTIC VULGATE
APPROVED FAVORITE PEOPLISH
PLEBEIAN
POPULARITY VOGUE CLAPTRAP
POPULATE MAN BREED PLANT
WORLD PEOPLE INHABIT
POPULATION DEME COLONY
FLOTSAM KINDRED TOPODEME
UNIVERSE
(PREF.) DEM(O)
POPULUS SALIX
PORATHA (FATHER OF —) HAMAN
PORBEAGLE LAMNA SHARK
LAMNID LAMNOID
PORCELAIN JU KO CHINA MURRA
SPODE BISQUE MURRHA NANKIN
BISCUIT CELADON DRESDEN
NANKEEN NANKING MANDARIN
STEATITE
(JAPANESE —) KUTANI

(VARIETY OF —) CAEN KUAN ARITA HIZEN IMARI KYOTO AMSTEL PARIAN SEVRES BUDWEIS DRESDEN LIMOGES MEISSEN SWANSEA COALPORT HAVILAND KAKIEMON CHANTILLY

PORCH HOOD STOA LANAI STOEP STOOP INGANG PARVIS PIAZZA PORTAL RAMADA BALCONY GALERIE GALILEE NARTHEX PASSAGE POIKILE PORTICO PRONAOS VERANDA ANTENAVE SOLARIUM TRANSEPT VESTIBULE
(FRONT —) ANTICUM

PORCUPINE QUILL URSON CAWQUAW COENDOU ERECTER ERICIUS PORKPEN HEDGEHOG HEDGEPIG
(PREF.) HYSTRICO

PORCUPINE ANTEATER ECHIDNA

PORCUPINE FISH ERIZO ATINGA BURFISH DIODONT

PORCUPINE GRASS SPINIFEX

PORE GAZE GLOSE GLOZE STARE STOMA STUDY TRYPA BROWSE PONDER ALVEOLA CINCLIS OSTIOLE TUBULUS BAJONADO JOLTHEAD LENTICEL POROSITY

PORGY TAI SCUP PARGO PLUMA POGGY BESUGO BRAISE MAMAMU PAGRUS SPARID MARGATE PINFISH MENHADEN SPADEFISH

PORK HAM HOG PIG LARD BACON BRAWN MONEY SWINE BALDRIB LARDOON MIDDLING
(— AND SALMON) LAULAU
(— CHOP) BALDRIB GRISKEN
(— SHOULDER) HAND
(FRIED CUBE OF —) CUCHIFRITO
(SALT —) BACON SPECK SOWBELLY

PORKFISH SISI CATALINETA

PORKY FAT GREASY

PORNOGRAPHIC LEWD CURIOUS OBSCENE

PORNOGRAPHY CURIOSA ESOTERICA

POROUS OPEN LIGHT LEACHY CELLULAR

PORPHYRY ELVAN EURITE ELVANITE GRORUDITE

PORPOISE WHALE PALACH PUFFER COWFISH DOLPHIN HOGFISH PELLOCK PULLOCK SNUFFER CETACEAN GAIRFISH

PORRECT EXTEND TENDER PRESENT

PORRET LEEK ONION PORETT SCALLION

PORRIDGE KHIR POBS SAMP ATOLE BROSE GROUT GRUEL BURGOO CROWDY SEPAWN SKILLY SOWENS TARTAN BROCHAN BURGOUT OATMEAL POBBIES POLENTA POTTAGE FLUMMERY SAGAMITE
(PREF.) POLTO

PORRINGER TASTER TRINKET

PORT GATE GOAL LEFT MIEN WICK WINE CARRY CREEK HAVEN HITHE SALLY SCALE STATE APPORT HARBOR INPORT REFUGE AIRPORT BEARING DIGNITY

LIBERTY OUTPORT ANTEPORT DEMEANOR LARBOARD MALTOLTE PORTHOLE PRESENCE

PORTABLE MOBILE MOVABLE BEARABLE

PORTAGE PACK CARGO CARRY TARBET FREIGHT TONNAGE HAULOVER

PORTAL DOOR GATE ENTRY PORCH DOORWAY ENTRANCE

PORTAMENTO DRAG GLIDE SCOOP SLIDE PORTATO GLISSADE

PORTCULLIS BAR SHUT HERSE ORGUE SARASIN CATARACT SARRASIN

PORTE GATE

PORTE-MONNAIE PURSE

PORTEND BODE AUGUR DIVINE EXTEND BESPEAK BETOKEN PREDICT PRESAGE DENOUNCE FOREBODE FORECAST FORETELL

PORTENT AYAH LUCK SIGN SOUND TOKEN AUGURY MARVEL OSTENT WONDER AUSPICE PREDICT PRESAGE PRODIGY CEREMONY DISASTER SOOTHSAY PROGNOSTIC

PORTENTOUS AWFUL GRAVID BODEFUL DOOMFUL FATEFUL OMINOUS POMPOUS DOOMLIKE DREADFUL INFLATED SINISTER

PORTER ALE BEER MOZO CADDY HAMAL STOUT TAMEN BADGER BEARER CADDIE COOLIE DARWAN DURWAN ENTIRE KHAMAL REDCAP SUISSE DROGHER DVORNIK HUMMAUL JANITOR PITCHER REMOVER BADGEMAN BUMMAREE CARGADOR CHAPRASI LODGEMAN PORTITOR RECEIVER
(— AND STOUT) COOPER
(JAPANESE —) AKABO
(MEAT —) PITCHER
(MEXICAN —) TAMEN

PORTFOLIO BLAD

PORTIA (HUSBAND OF —) BRUTUS
(LOVER OF —) BASSANIO
(MAID OF —) NERISSA

PORTIA TREE MAHO BENDY MAHOE

PORTICO STOA WALK XYST ORIEL PORCH XYSTA ZAYAT EXEDRA PARVIS PIAZZA SCHOOL XYSTUS BALCONY DISTYLE GALLERY NARTHEX PARVISE PRONAOS TERRACE VERANDA PORTICUS POSTICUM VERANDAH

PORTION BIT CUP CUT DAB JAG LAB LOT PAN BLAD DALE DEAL DOLE DOSE FATE FECK JAGG PART SIZE WHAT DOWER PIECE RATIO SHARE SLICE SNACK WHACK CANTLE CANTON COLLOP DETAIL GOBBET MATTER PARCEL RASHER EXCERPT PARTAGE SECTION SEGMENT TODDICK TRANCHE FRACTION FRAGMENT PITTANCE QUANTITY SCANTLET FODDERING
(— DRUNK) DRAFT DRAUGHT
(— OF ACTOR'S PART) LENGTH
(— OF ARROW) BREAST

(— OF BIRD SONG) TOUR
(— OF BREAD OR BEER) CUE
(— OF CITRUS RIND) ALBEDO
(— OF ESTATE) LEGITIM
(— OF FARMLAND) BEREWICK
(— OF FLOODPLAIN) BANCO
(— OF FODDER) JAG
(— OF FOOD) HELP GOBBET HELPING
(— OF HIDE) HEAD
(— OF LAND) BLOCK PATTI INTAKE DIVISION DONATION
(— OF LIQUOR) STICK DIVIDEND
(— OF LITURGY) ANAPHORA
(— OF MAST) HOUSING HOUNDING
(— OF PASTURE) BREAK
(— OF POEM) STRAIN
(— OF RUG) GRIN
(— OF SERPENT'S BODY) TRAIN
(— OF STEM) BOON
(— OF STORY) SNATCH
(— OF STREAM) LAVADERO
(— OF TEA) DRAWING
(— OF TIME) SPAN DISTANCE
(— OF TOBACCO) CUD
(— OF TONGUE) BLADE
(ADDITIONAL —) RASHER
(ALLOTTED —) MOIRA SCANTLING
(BRIDE'S —) DOWRY
(CLOTTED — OF BLOOD) CRUOR
(COARSER —) BOLTINGS
(EARLY —) SPRING
(INHABITED — OF EARTH) ECUMENE
(LARGE —) SKELP
(LATTER —) AUTUMN EVENING
(MAIN —) CORPSE
(MARRIAGE —) DOT DOTE TOCHER
(MINUTE —) GRAIN
(MOST VALUABLE —) CHIEF
(PERCEPTIBLE —) KENNING
(REPRESENTATIVE —) SAMPLE
(SIGNIFICANT —) CHAPTER
(SIZABLE —) DUNT
(SMALL —) BIT DAB DOT DRAM DROP SOSH TAIT TATE CHACK SPICE SPUNK SHADOW KENNING MODICUM REMNANT SCANTLE SMIDGEN SOUPCON SCANTLET
(SMALL — OF LIQUOR) DOLLOP HEELTAP
(TRIFLING —) SMACK
(SUFF.) (BY A SPECIFIC —) MEAL

PORTLY FAT FULL AMPLE STOUT GAUCIE GOODLY STATELY SWELLING OVERBLOWN

PORTMANTEAU BAG HOOK VALISE POCKMANKY

PORTRAIT BUST ICON IKON IMAGE IMAGO MODEL PIECE KITKAT STATUE VISAGE PORTRAY RETRAIT LIKENESS RITRATTO VERONICA MINIATURE
(— ON COIN) EFFIGY

PORTRAIT OF A LADY (AUTHOR OF —) JAMES
(CHARACTER IN —) MERLE PANSY RALPH ARCHER CASPAR EDWARD GEMINI ISABEL OSMOND ROSIER GILBERT BANTLING GOODWOOD TOUCHETT HENRIETTA STACKPOLE WARBURTON

PORTRAY GIVE LIMN LINE BLAZE ENACT IMAGE PAINT CIPHER

CLOTHE DEPICT FIGURE SHADOW FEATURE IMITATE PICTURE DECIPHER DESCRIBE RESEMBLE

PORTUGAL

BAY: SETUBAL
CAPE: ROCA MONDEGO ESPICHEL
CAPITAL: LISBON
COIN: JOE REI PECA REAL CONTO COROA DOBRA INDIO ESCUDO MACUTA PATACA TESTAO VINTEM CENTAVO CRUSADO MOIDORE EQUIPAGA
COLONY: MACAO TIMOR ANGOLA GUINEA PRINCIPE
DISTRICT: BEJA FARO BRAGA EVORA HORTA PORTO VISEU LEIRIA LISBOA
ISLAND: TIMOR
ISLANDS: MADEIRA
MEASURE: PE ALMA BOTA MEIO MOIO PIPA VARA ALMUD BRACA FANGA GEIRA LEGOA LINHA MILHA PALMO ALMUDE CANADA COVADO QUARTO ALQUIER ESTADIO FERRADO SELAMIN ALQUEIRE TONELADA
MOUNTAIN: ACOR GEREZ MARAO MOUSA PENEDA ESTRELA MONCHIQUE
RIVER: SOR TUA LIMA MINO MIRA SADO SEDA TAGO TEJO DOURO MINHO SABAR TAGUS VOUGA ZATAS CAVADO CHANCA TAMEGA ZEZERE MONDEGO GUADIANA
TOWN: BEJA FARO OVAR BRAGA EVORA HORTA PORTO VISEU GUARDA OPORTO COIMBRA FUNCHAL SETUBAL BRAGANCA
UNIVERSITY: COIMBRA
WEIGHT: GRAO ONCA LIBRA MARCO ARROBA OITAVA ARRATEL QUINTAL
WINE: PORT

PORTUGUESE
(PREF.) LUSO

PORTULACA MOSS PURSLANE

PORWIGLE TADPOLE

POSAUNE TROMBONE

POSE SET SIT HOARD MODEL OFFER PLANT STICK BAFFLE NONPLUS PEACOCK POSTURE PRESENT PROPOSE POSITION PRETENSE PROPOUND QUESTION MANNERISM

POSEIDON NEPTUNE EARTHSHAKER
(BROTHER OF —) ZEUS
(FATHER OF —) KRONOS
(MOTHER OF —) RHEA
(WIFE OF —) AMPHITRITE

POSER FACER POSEUR PUZZLE STAYER STICKER STUMPER TWISTER EXAMINER STICKLER BANDARLOG

POSH RITZY SWAGGER

POSING OPPOSAL
(— TECHNIQUE) PLASTIQUE

POSIT FIX PUT SET PLACE AFFIRM ASSUME

POSITING PONENT

POSITION LAY LIE HANG LINE POSE RANK SITE CENSE COIGN PLANT POINT POSTE SIEGE SITUS STAND STATE STEAD ASSIZE FIGURE HEIGHT OCTAVE OFFICE STANCE UBIETY VALGUS POSTURE STATION ATTITUDE CAPACITY DOCTRINE VOCATION PLACEMENT
(— OF AFFAIRS) STATUS
(— OF FEAR) GAZE
(— OF HEAVENLY BODY) HARBOR
(— OF VESSEL) GAUGE HEIGHT
(— WITH NO ESCAPE) IMPASSE
(— WITH NO RESPONSIBILITY) SINECURE
(BALLET —) POINTE
(CHESS —) ZUGZWANG
(COMMANDING —) PRESTIGE
(DEFENSIVE —) OUTWORK
(DISTINGUISHED —) HONOR
(EMBARRASSING —) FIX HOLE LURCH CORNER
(FENCING —) CARTE SIXTE SIXTH QUARTE TIERCE SACCOON SECONDE SEPTIME
(FOREMOST —) HEAD LEAD STEM
(INITIAL —) ANLAUT
(MEDIAL —) INLAUT
(RELATIVE —) RANK PLACE TERMS BEARING FOOTING STANDING
(SOCIAL —) CASTE STATE VALOUR
(SYMBOLIC —) HASTA
(SUFF.) TOPE TOPY
POSITIONAL SITUAL
POSITIVE POS POZ COOL DOWN FLAT PLUS SURE BASIC SHEER UTTER ACTIVE DIRECT THETIC GENUINE HEALTHY ABSOLUTE CONCRETE DECISIVE DEFINITE DOGMATIC EXPLICIT INHERENT RESOLUTE SIGNLESS THETICAL
(THREE —S) KROMOGRAM
POSITIVELY BUT POS FLAT PLUS QUITE FAIRLY INDEED STRICTLY
POSITIVISM COMTISM CERTAINTY DOGMATISM
POSITRON LEPTON
POSSESS GET OWE OWN HAVE HOLD WALD BOAST BROOK OUGHT REACH WIELD MASTER OBTAIN OCCUPY BEDEVIL ENVELOP FURNISH INHABIT INHERIT INSTALL INSTATE SMITTLE ACQUAINT DOMINATE INSTRUCT
POSSESSED MAD CALM COOL OUGH CRAZED JERUSHA ENTHEATE
(— BY EVIL SPIRIT) DEMONIAC
(AUTHOR OF —) DOSTOEVSKI
(CHARACTER IN —) BLUM DASHA FEDKA MARIE MARYA PYOTR YULIA SHATOV DROZDOV LIPUTIN NIKOLAI STEPHAN VARVARA KIRILLOV LIZAVETA LYAMSHIN PETROVNA SHIGALOV LEBYADKIN STAVROGIN VIRGINSKY KARMAZINOV TIMOFYEVNA VERHOVENSKY
POSSESSION AVER HAND HOLD YHTE AUGHT GRASP STATE CLUTCH CORNER HAVIOR SASINE

SEISIN SEIZIN WEALTH CONTROL COUNTER DEMESNE DEWANEE FINGERS KEEPING MASTERY SEIZURE CONQUEST DEFIANCE PROPERTY
(— OF COMMON FEATURES) AFFINITY
(— OF KNOWLEDGE) SCIENCE
(— WITH QUIET ENJOYMENT) SEISIN SEIZIN
(BURDENSOME —) ELEPHANT
(LOST — OF BALL) TURNOVER
(RELIGIOUS —) POWER
(TEMPORAL —S) WORLD
(TEMPORARY —) LEND
(PL.) ALLS STORE STUFF WRACK DOMAIN ESTATE GRAITH PROPER CAPITAL FORTUNE HAVINGS LIVINGS
POSSET CURDLE PAMPER POWSOWDY BALDUCTUM MERRYBUSH
POSSIBILITY MAY MAYBE POSSE CHANCE PROSPECT QUESTION
POSSIBLE ABLE RIFE MAYBE LIKELY EARTHLY ELIGIBLE FEASIBLE PROBABLE PROBABLY POTENTIAL CONTINGENT PRACTICABLE
(BARELY —) OUTSIDE
POSSIBLY MAPPEN LIGHTLY PERHAPS PERCHANCE PERADVENTURE
POSSUM TAIT FEIGN PRETEND
POST DAK SET TIE BITT BOMA CAMP CRIB DAWK DOLE FAST FORT MAIL META POLE ROOM SPOT SPUD STOB STUD TREE BERTH CHEEK CLOSH CRANE NEWEL PLACE SPILE SPRAG STAKE STAND STILT STING STOCK STODE STOOP STULP STUMP BILLET CIPPUS COLUMN CROTCH FENDER GIBBET INFORM OFFICE PICKET PILLAR SAMSON SCREEN STAPLE STOOTH STOWER TRUNCH ASHERAH BOLLARD COURIER GARETTA PLACARD POSTAGE POSTBOX QUARTER STATION STUDDLE UPRIGHT BANISTER DEADHEAD LEGPIECE MAKEFAST PRESIDIO PUNCHEON QUINTAIN STRADDLE STANCHION
(— AS RACE MARKER) META
(— ON PIER) FAST BOLLARD DEADHEAD
(BOUNDARY —) TERM STOOP TERMINUS
(CHIMNEY —) SPEER
(CUSTOMS —) CHOKEY
(DECK —) BITT
(DOOR OR GATE —) DURN
(ECCLESIASTIC —) BENEFICE
(FENCE —) DROPPER
(HANGING —) GIBBET
(INDIAN MILITARY —) TANA TANNA THANA
(MILITARY —) FORT GARRISON
(MOORING —) BITT DOLPHIN
(OBSERVATORY —) CUPOLA
(SACRED —) ASHERAH
(SIGN —) PARSON
(PREF.) STELO

POSTAGE POST INDICIA STAMPAGE
POSTAGE-FREE FRANCO
POSTAGE STAMP DUE HEAD STICKER
POSTBOY YAMSHIK YEMSCHIK POSTILION
POSTCARD (— COLLECTOR) DELTIOLOGIST
POST CHAISE JACK POCHAY POSCHAY
POSTER BILL CLAP SNIPE CLAPPE AFFICHE PLACARD SHOWING STICKER STREAMER
POSTERIOR BACK REAR CAUDAL DORSAL POSTIC RETRAL ADAXIAL BUTTOCKS
(PL.) WHEERIKINS
(PREF.) OPISTH(O) UR(O)
POSTERIORLY RETRAD
POSTERITY SEQUEL KINDRED FUTURITY
POSTERN SIDE CLOCKET KLICKET PRIVATE POSTICUM
POSTHOUSE YAM MUTATION
POSTICHE WIG SHAM SWITCH TOUPEE PRETENSE SPURIOUS
POSTIL HOMILY COMMENT
POSTILION COURIER POSTBOY YAMSHIK
POSTLUDE SORTIE SORTITA EPILOGUE
POSTMAN MAIL CORREO MAILBAG MAILMAN
POST OFFICE BOMA CORREO POSTHOUSE
POSTPONE OFF STAY WAIT DEFER DELAY FRIST REFER REMIT WAIVE FUTURE LINGER RELONG RETARD ADJOURN DEGRADE OVERSET PROLONG RESPECT SUSPEND CONTINUE PROROGUE REPRIEVE WITHHOLD
POSTPONED DEFERRED
POSTPONEMENT MORA STAY DELAY RESPECT RESPITE
POSTRIDE COURIER POSTILION
POSTSCRIPT EKE ENVOY
POST SUPPORT CROWFOOT
POSTULANT NOVICE
POSTULATE AXIOM CLAIM POSIT ASSERT ASSUME DEMAND THESIS PERHAPS PREMISE PETITION PRINCIPLE
POSTURE SET POSE SEAT SITE ASANA FRONT HEART PLACE SHAPE SQUAT STATE LOUNGE SLOUCH STANCE BEARING CROWHOP STATION STATURE ATTITUDE CARRIAGE POSITION
(— OF DEFENSE) GUARD
(DANCE —) HOLD
(KNEELING —) SHIKO
POSY POESY TUTTY FLOWER BOUQUET NOSEGAY ANTHOLOGY
POT BAG CAN COOP FOOL JUST LEAD OLLA PINT POOL RUIN CREWE CROCK CRUSE DIXIE KITTY SHANT SHOOT ALUDEL CHATTY CHYTRA JORDAN JORDEN KETTLE MARMIT MASLIN MONKEY OUTWIT PINGLE PIPKIN POCKET POSNET BRAISER CHAMBER

CUVETTE DECEIVE POTSHOT SEETHER SKILLET YETLING FAVORITE JACKSHEA PRESERVE MARIJUANA
(— FOR CATCHING FISH) COOP
(— OF BRASS) LOTA MASLIN
(— OF DRINK) SHANT
(— WITH 3 FEET) POSNET
(BULGING —) OLLA
(BUSHMAN'S —) JACKSHAY JACKSHEA
(CHAMBER —) JERRY JORDAN JORDEN COMMODE JEROBOAM
(CHIMNEY —) CAN TUN
(EARTHEN —) OLLA CROCK CHATTY PIPKIN
(LEATHER —) GISPIN
(LOBSTER —) COY TRUNK
(LONG-HANDLED —) PINGLE
(MELTING —) CREVET CRUCIBLE
(PART OF —) EAR LIP RIM BASE BODY FOOT NECK SPOUT HANDLE
(PEAR-SHAPED —) ALUDEL
(SMALL ROUND —) LOTA LOTAH
(TEA —) TRACK
(12-GALLON —) DIXY DIXIE
POTABLE DRINK BEVERAGE POTATORY
POTAGE SOUP BROTH
POTAMOGETON PONDWEED PONDGRASS
POTASH KALI SALINE PEARLASH POLVERINE
(— FACTORY) ASHERY
POTASSIUM K KALIUM POTASS
(— DICHROMATE) CHROME
POTASSIUM NITRATE GROUGH
POTATION POT DRAM DRAFT DRINK LIBATION
POTATO PAP YAM CHAT PAPA SPUD YAMP FLUKE IDAHO RURAL TATER TUBER BATATA CAMOTE KUMARA LUMPER MURPHY PRATEY SKERRY BURBANK EPICURE SOLANUM BLUENOSE
(— BALL) NOISETTE
(— MASHER) RICER CHAPPER
(— SLICES) LATTICE
(— STATE) IDAHO MAINE
(—S AND CABBAGE) COLCANNON
(FRENCH FRIED —) CHIP
(FRENCH FRIED —S) GAUFRETTES
(JAPANESE —) IMO
(STEWED —S) STOVIES
(WITH —S) PARMENTIER
(PL.) WARE CHUNO
POT BEARER POTIFER
POTBELLIED KEDGE PODDY STOMACHY ABDOMINOUS
POTBELLY PAUNCH TUNBELLY
POTBOY GANYMEDE
POTE KICK MOPE POIT POKE PUSH NUDGE PLATE POKER SHOVE THRUST
POTEEN POTHEEN WHISKEY POTWHISKY
POTENCE STUD CROSS GIBBET
POTENCY FORCE POWER VIGOR ORENDA VIRTUE EFFICACY STRENGTH VITALITY OPERATION
POTENT ABLE MAIN RICH STAY STIFF CAUSAL COGENT CRUTCH MIGHTY STRONG DYNAMIC

SUPPORT WARRANT FORCIBLE
POWERFUL PUISSANT VIGOROUS
VIRTUOUS VIRULENT
POTENTATE KING RULER HUZOOR
POTENT PRINCE DICTATOR
DOMINION SOVEREIGN
POTENTIAL EH LATENT VIRTUAL
IMPLICIT INCHOATE POSSIBLE
PREGNANT
(— **ENERGY**) ERGAL
(**EXCESS** —) OVERVOLTAGE
POTENTIALITY POSSE POWER
DUNAMIS DYNAMIS POTENCY
CAPACITY PREGNANCY
POTGUN PISTOL POPGUN
BRAGGART
POTHER ADO VEX FUSS STEW STIR
WORRY BOTHER BUSTLE HARASS
POTTER PUTTER PUZZLE PERPLEX
TURMOIL
POTHERB WORT CLARY WERTE
GREENS CHERVIL OLITORY
POTWORT QUELITE SPINACH
TAMPALA
POTHOLE POT RUT KETTLE TINAJA
POTHOOK HAIK HAKE CROOK
HANGLE RACKAN SLOWRIE
TRAMMEL COTTEREL
POTHOUSE TAVERN ALEHOUSE
MUGHOUSE
POTION DOSE DRUG DRAFT DRINK
DWALE STUFF DRENCH POISON
AMATORY MIXTURE PHILTER
PHILTRE NEPENTHE
POTIPHERAH (DAUGHTER OF —)
ASENATH
POTLATCH GIFT FEAST PARTY
POTLACH FESTIVAL
POT MARIGOLD GOLD GOLDE
SUNFLOWER
POTPOURRI HASH OLIO STEW
MASLIN MEDLEY POTPIE RAGOUT
FANTASIA PASTICHE JAMBALAYA
SALMAGUNDI
POTRO COLT
POTSHERD BIT PIG TEST CROCK
SHARD SHERD FRAGMENT
OSTRACON PANSHARD
POTTAGE SEW SOUP SOWL STEW
BERRY BROTH BRUET BREWIS
BROWET POTAGE OATMEAL
PULMENT
POTTED DRUNK CANNED
(— **MEAT**) RILLETT
POTTER FAD FUSS MUCK POKE
ANNOY DAKER TRUCK BOTHER
DABBLE DACKER DAIDLE DIDDLE
DISHER DODDER FIDDLE FOOTLE
FOTTER JOTTER KUMHAR
MUDDLE NANTLE NIGGLE PETTLE
POUTER TIDDLE TIFFIE TIFFLE
TRIFLE CLOAMER CROCKER
DISTURB FIGURER FOSSICK
HANDLER NAUNTLE PERPLEX
PLOWTER PRODDLE THROWER
TROUBLE CERAMIST TERRAPIN
(— **OFFICIOUSLY**) TEW
(**MACHINE OF** —) JOLLY
POTTERER TWIRLER
POTTERY POT BANK CHUN DELF
GROG WARE BIZEN CROCK DELFT
GLOST ROUEN SPODE BASALT
FICTIL KASHAN MIMPEI ASTBURY

BELLEEK BOCCARO BRISTOL
DIPWARE FIGMENT JETWARE
KAMARES POTBANK POTWARE
POTWORK REDWARE SATSUMA
TICKNEY TZUCHOU BUCCHERO
CERAMICS FIGULINE GRAYWARE
SANTORIN SLIPWARE
BROWNWARE
(— **CIVILIZATION**) MINYAN
(— **CULTURE**) PUCARA
(— **DECOR**) MISHIMA
(— **DECORATED WITH SCRATCHING**)
GRAFFITO
(**ANCIENT** —) KAMARES
GRAYWARE
(**BLACK** —) BASALT BUCCHERO
(**CHINESE** —) KUAN YIHSING
(**CRUSHED** —) GROG
(**HINDU** —) UDA
(**RICHLY COLORED** —) MAJOLICA
(**UNGLAZED** —) BISCUIT
POTTERY TREE CARAIPE
POTTINGER COOK POTYCARY
POTTO LEMUR APOSORO
KINKAJOU
POTTY CRAZY FOOLISH TRIVIAL
SNOBBISH
POUCH BAG COD JAG POD SAC
BELL CYST POCK POKE BULGE
BURSA POKKE PURSE BUDGET
CAECUM CRUMEN GIPSER
PACKET POCKET PURSET SACHET
ALFARGA ALFORJA CANTINA
CRUMENA GIPSIRE MAILBAG
MOCHILA OVICYST SCROTUM
SPORRAN SWALLOW BURSICLE
PROTRUDE SPEUCHAN
MARSUPIUM
(— **OF FLY**) AEROSTAT
(— **ON DEER'S NECK**) BELL
(**PILGRIM'S** —) SCRIP
(**TOBACCO** —) DOSS
(PREF.) PERO PHASCO
PHASCO(O) THYLAC(O)
POUCH OF DOUGLAS
(PREF.) CULDO
POUF PUFF OTTOMAN
POULAINE PIKE CRAKOW
POULPE POULP CUTTLE OCTOPUS
POULTICE QUILT STUPA STUPE
MALAGMA EPITHEME SINAPISM
CATAPLASM
POULTRY FOWL HENS DUCKS
GEESE PULLEN PEAFOWL
PIGEONS PULLERY TURKEYS
CHICKENS PULLAILE VOLAILLE
POUNAMU JADE PUNAMU
NEPHRITE
POUNCE NAB CHOP CLAP JUMP
POKE SWAP SWOP FLECK PRICK
PUNCH SOUSE SWOOP TALON
EMBOSS PIERCE TATTOO
BOBCOAT DESCEND SPRINKLE
(— **UPON**) TIRE STOOP
POUND L LB BUM DAD LIB PIN
PUN SOV BEAT CHAP DRUB FRAM
PELT PIND POON POSS PUND
QUID SKIT THUD TRAP TUND
CRUSH FRAME KNOCK LABOR
LIVRE NEVEL STAMP THUMP
TRAMP WEIGH BATTER BRUISE
HAMMER LUMBER NICKER
POUNCE PRISON THRASH

CONTUND CONTUSE PINFOLD
THUNDER LAMBASTE RESTRAIN
(— **FINE**) BRAY
(**FISH** —) KEEP MADRAGUE
(**ISRAELI** —**S**) LIROTH
(**100** —**S**) CENTAL CENTURY
(**12** —**S OF BUTTER**) GAUN
(**1-8TH OF** —) HANDFUL
(**25** —**S**) PONY PONEY
(**32, 56, OR 75** —**S OF RAISINS**) FRAIL
(**500** —**S**) MONKEY
POUNDMASTER PINDER PINNER
PONDER
POUR JAW RUN TUN YET BIRL
BREW DROP EMIT FILL FLOW
GOSH GUSH HELD LASH LAVE
RAIN TEEM TOOM VENT FLOOD
FLUSH HEELD HIELD POWER
SLIDE SOUSE SPILL SPOUT
SWARM TRILL AFFUSE DECANT
SLUICE STREAM CASCADE
CHANNEL DIFFUSE SUFFUSE
(— **AWAY**) STAVE
(— **BACK**) REFUND
(— **BEER OR WINE**) BIRL
(— **CLUMSILY**) SLOSH
(— **COPIOUSLY**) HALE
(— **DOWN**) RASH SILE SHOWER
DESCEND DISPUNGE
(— **FORTH**) SHED TIDE VENT WELL
DISTILL OVERFLOW
(— **FREELY**) SWILL
(— **FROM ONE VESSEL TO ANOTHER**)
DECANT JIRBLE TRANSFUSE
(— **IN**) INFUSE INFOUND INHELDE
(— **IN DROP BY DROP**) INSTIL
INSTILL
(— **LIKE RAIN OR TEARS**) LASH
(— **MELTED WAX**) BASTE
(— **MOLTEN LEAD**) YOTE
(— **OFF**) SLUICE
(— **OIL UPON**) ANOINT
(— **OUT**) FILL SEND SHED SKINK
STOUR UTTER EFFUSE LIBATE
DIFFUND DIFFUSE
(— **UPON**) AFFUSE
(PREF.) CHYMI
(SUFF.) CHYME
POURBOIRE TIP GRATUITY
TRINKGELD
POURER TEEMER INFUSER
POURING AFFUSION
(SUFF.) ENCHYSIS
POURPOINT GIPON JUPON QUILT
DOUBLET
POUT BIB MOP MAID MOUE PUSS
SULK BLAIN BOODY GROIN
BRASSY BRASSIE CATFISH
EELPOUT BULLHEAD PROTRUDE
POUTERIA LUCUMA
POUTING BOUDERIE
POVERTY LACK NEED WANE
WANT DEARTH PENURY BEGGARY
DEFAULT MISEASE TENUITY
DISTRESS POORTITH PUIRTITH
SCARCITY WANDRETH NECESSITY
(SUFF.) PENIA
POVERTY PLANT HEATH HEATHER
LINGWORT
POVERTY-STRICKEN POOR NAKED
NEEDY SQUALID SHIRTLESS
POWDER BRAY DUST KISH MILL
MULL SAND CHALK CURRY ERBIA

FLOUR GRIND HEMOL KOSIN
PICRA STOUR CEMENT CHARGE
CHINOL DECAMP DERMOL
EMPASM ESCAPE FARINA FILITE
GERATE KAMALA KERMES
KUMKUM MELLON PEYTON
PINOLE POUNCE RACHEL SMEETH
YTTRIA ALCOHOL BESTREW
BROCADE LUPULIN SCATTER
SMEDDUM SPACKLE SPODIUM
ALGAROTH CATAPASM DYNAMITE
FLUMERIN PALEGOLD
(— **A SHIELD**) GERATE
(— **FOR BRONZING**) BROCADE
(— **OBTAINED BY SUBLIMATION**)
FLOWERS
(— **TO MASK SWEAT ODOR**)
EMPASM EMPASMA
(— **USED IN CHOCOLATE**) PINOLE
(**ABRASIVE** —) EMERY
(**ANTHELMINTIC** —) KOSIN
(**ANTIMONY** —) KOHL
(**ASTRINGENT** —) BORAL
(**BLEACHING** —) CHEMIC CHLORIDE
(**BROWNISH** —) LIGNIN
(**CATHARTIC** —) KAMALA
(**COLORING** —) HENNA
(**FINE** —) DUST POUNCE ALCOHOL
(**FLUORESCENT** —) FLUMERIN
(**GOA** —) ARAROBA
(**GOLD** —) VENTURINE
(**GRAPHITIC** —) KISH
(**GRAY** —) ANTU
(**HAIR** —) MUST
(**MALT** —) SMEDDUM
(**PERFUMED** —) ABIR PULVIL
SACHET
(**PINK** —) CALAMINE
(**POISONOUS** —) ROBIN
(**PURPLE** —) CUDBEAR
(**REDDISH** —) ABIR KUMKUM
SIMMON
(**ROSE-COLORED** —) ERBIA
(**SACHET** —) PULVIL
(**SILICEOUS** —**S**) SILEX
(**SMOKELESS** —) FILITE PEYTON
CORDITE AMBERITE INDURITE
SOLENITE
(**WHITE** —) CHINOL YTTRIA
HYPORIT SCANDIA HALAZONE
LANTHANA PARAFORM
(**YELLOW** —) KOSIN DERMOL
MELLON LUPULIN MALARIN
SAMARIA TANNIGEN
(PREF.) PUMICI
POWDERED SEME SPICED PICKLED
SEASONED
POWDER PUFF PLUFF
POWDERY MEALY PRUINOSE
POWER ARM ART JUS ROD SAY
SUN VIS BEEF BULK DINT GIFT
GRIP HAND HANK HEAP HORN
IRON KAMI MAIN MANA MAYA
SOUP SWAY WALD WILL AGENT
CROWN DEMON DEVIL FORCE
GRACE HUACA HYDRO INPUT
LURCH MIGHT SINEW SKILL
STEAM VALUE VIGOR WAKON
WIELD YARAK AGENCY APPEAL
BREATH CLUTCH CREDIT DANGER
DEGREE DOUGHT EFFORT
ENERGY FOISON IMPACT MOLOCH
SHAKTI STROIL STROKE SWINGE

TALENT VIRTUE WEIGHT ABILITY
BALANCE BOSSDOM COMMAND
CONTROL DEMESNE DESTINY
DUNAMIS DYNAMIS ENTHEOS
FACULTY POTENCY VALENCY
VOLTAGE WAKONDA ACTIVITY
AUTONOMY CAPACITY CLUTCHES
COERCION DELEGACY DEMIURGE
DISPOSAL DOMINION INTEREST
LEVERAGE LORDSHIP SEIGNORY
STRENGTH PUISSANCE
PREROGATIVE
(— FROM SUPREME BEING) EON
AEON
(— OF ACID) BASICITY
(— OF ATTORNEY) PROXY
(— OF ATTRACTION) ALLURE
(— OF CHOICE) LIBERTY
(— OF DIVORCE) TAFWIZ
(— OF ENTRY) INGRESS
(— OF GIVING) PROPINE
(— OF HEARING) AUDITION
(— OF KNOWING) JNANASHAKTI
(— OF MANIFESTATION) MAYA
(— OF MOVING AT SEA) YARAGE
(— OF PERFORMING) ART
(— OF RESISTANCE) STAMINA
(— OF TRANSMUTATION) ALCHEMY
(— OF VISION) KEN
(— OF WINE) SEVE
(— TO ATTRACT) DUENDE
(— TO CONVINCE) FORCE
(—S OF EVIL) HELL
(AUTHOR OF —) FEUCHTWANGER
(CHARACTER IN —) REB KARL
ISAAC JOSEF MARIE NAEMI
ANSELF GABRIEL SIBYLLE
LANDAUER MAGDALEN
ALEXANDER SELIGMANN
WEISSENSEE OPPENHEIMER
(CIVIL —) CAESAR
(COERCIVE —) SWORD
(DIVINE —) MOIRA
(ELEVATING —) LIFT
(EMOTIONAL —) STOMACH
(EXTRAPHYSICAL —) MANA
(FIFTH —) SURSOLID
(FOCAL —) DIOPTRY
(GROWTH —) BATHMISM
(HYPOTHETICAL —) FORTUNE
(IMPERSONAL —) WAKAN WAKON
WAKANDA
(INTELLECTUAL —) WIT
(LEGAL —) JUS
(MAGIC —) ORENDA
(MAGNETIC —) MAGNES
(MENTAL —) HABITUS
(MORMON —) KEYS
(NATURAL —) OD
(OCCULT —) MAGIC
(PERSUASIVE —) RHETORIC
(PERUVIAN —) HUACA
(POLITICAL —) DOMINIUM
(RATIONAL —) EYE
(REFLECTIVE —) ALBEDO
(ROYAL —) RIAL
(SACRED —) KAMI
(SECOND —) SQUARE
(SOVEREIGN —) SWAY THRONE
(SPIRITUAL —) NGAI
(STAYING —) BOTTOM STAMINA
(SUPERNATURAL —) CHARISMA
(SUPREME —) EMPIRE

HEAVEN IMPERIUM
(THIRD —) CUBE
(VITAL —) SPIRITS
(PREF.) CRATO DYN(A)(AMI)(AMO)
(SUFF.) OD ODIC
(RULING —) CRACY CRAT(IC)
POWERBOAT SEDAN SKIFF GLIDER
CRUISER STINKPOT GASOLINER
POWERFUL BIG FAT ABLE DEEP
HIGH MAIN RANK RICH VERY
FORTE HEFTY HUSKY LUSTY
STARK STOUT VALID VIVID
WIGHT WILDE COGENT HEROIC
MIGHTY POTENT SEVERE STRONG
CAPABLE FECKFUL INTENSE
POLLENT RICHARD SKOOKUM
STAVING VALIANT FORCIBLE
PUISSANT VIGOROUS
(PREF.) MEGA
POWERLESS WEAK FEEBLE
UNABLE HELPLESS IMPOTENT
POWWOW PAWAW CONFAB
FROLIC COUNCIL MEETING
SESSION CONJURER
POX ROUP CANKER PLAGUE
VARIOLA
(FOWL —) SOREHEAD
(SHEEP —) OVINIA
POYOU PELUDO ARMADILLO
PRABHU LORD CHIEF WRITER

PRACTICABLE AGIBLE DOABLE
USABLE VIABLE FEASIBLE
OPERABLE POSSIBLE
PRACTICAL HARD UTILE ACTIVE
ACTUAL THINGY USEFUL
OPERARY VIRTUAL WORKING
BANAUSIC HOMESPUN PRACTIVE
THINGISH
(— JOKE) WAGGERY
(NOT —) PROFESSORY
PRACTICALLY ALMOST NEARLY
REALLY VIRTUALLY
PRACTICE ACT ISM LAW SUE TRY
URE USE KEEP LIVE PLAN PLOT
ADOPT APPLY ASSAY DRILL
FOUND GUISE HABIT HAUNT
TRADE TRAIN TREAD USAGE
CUSTOM EMPLOY FOLLOW
GROOVE OCCUPY PRAXIS RECORD
BRUSHUP ENHAUNT KNOCKUP
OPERATE PROCEED PROFESS
RANDORI USANCE ACTIVISM
ALARMISM EXERCISE FREQUENT
GALENISM OBSERVANCE
(— CHEATING) FOIST
(— DECEPTION) DEACON
(— DILIGENTLY) PLY
(— FRAUD) SHARK
(— HYPOCRISY) CANT
(— OF AN ART) PRAXIS
(— OF MEDICINE) GALENISM
(— ROWING) TUB
(— WITCHCRAFT) HEX
(BINDING —) LAW
(CEREMONIAL —) RITE
(COMMUNAL —) SUNNA SCHEME
SUNNAH INTRIGUE
(CORRUPT —) ABUSE WHORE
(DIPLOMATIC —) ALTERNAT
(DISHONEST —S) CROSS
(HORTICULTURAL —) CUTTAGE
(MEDICAL —) ALLERGY

(RELIGIOUS —) CULT CULTUS
(SUPERSTITIOUS —) FREET
(UNDERHAND —) JUGGLING
(VICIOUS —) MOLOCH
(SUFF.) CY ERY ICS ISM
PRACTICED EXPERT VERSED
PRACTIC SKILLED VETERAN
HACKNEYED
PRACTICING EXERCENT
PRACTITIONER DOCTOR HEALER
LAWYER NOVICE LEARNER
EXERCENT FELDSHER HUMANIST
HERBALIST HOMEOPATH
NATUROPATH
(SUFF.) ICIAN PATH(IA)(IC)(Y)
PRAD HORSE
PRAENOMEN AULUS CAIUS GAIUS
TITUS GNAEUS LUCIUS MANIUS
MARCUS SEXTUS SERVIUS
SPURIUS MAMERCUS NUMERIUS
TIBERIUS
PRAESEPE CRIB CRATCH MANGER
BEEHIVE
PRAGMATIC BUSY BUSYBODY
DOGMATIC MEDDLING OFFICIOUS
PRACTICAL
PRAIRIE BAY BLED CAMAS PAMPA
PLAIN CAMASS MEADOW
PLATEAU QUAMASH
(— STATE) ILLINOIS
(AUTHOR OF —) COOPER
(CHARACTER IN —) ASA BUSH INEZ
PAUL WADE ELLEN HOVER NATTY
WHITE ABIRAM BUMPPO ESTHER
BATTIUS ISHMAEL HARDHEART
MIDDLETON
PRAIRIE BERRY TROMPILLO
PRAIRIE CHICKEN GROUSE
PRAIRIE DOG GOPHER MARMOT
PRAIRIE WOLF COYOTE
PRAISE CRY LOF FUME HERY LAUD
LOSE LOVE PRES ADORE ALLOW
ALOSE BLESS CAROL CHANT
CRACK DEIFY EXTOL GLORY
HERSE HONOR KUDOS PLAUD
PRIZE ROOSE SALVE VALUE
WURTH ANTHEM BELAUD
EULOGY FRAISE HILLEL KUDIZE
LOANGE LOVING ORCHID SALUTE
TONGUE ACCLAIM ADULATE
APPLAUD COMMEND FLATTER
GLORIFY MAGNIFY NOSEGAY
PLAUDIT PUFFING TRIBUTE
WORSHIP ACCOLADE APPLAUSE
BLESSING DOXOLOGY ENCOMIUM
EULOGIZE PROCLAIM PANEGYRIC
(— BE TO GOD) LD
(— IN THANKSGIVING) JOY
(— INORDINATELY) FUME
(— OF ANOTHER'S FELICITY)
MACARISM
(— TO GOD ALWAYS) LDS
(EFFUSIVE —) FUSS
(EXAGGERATED —) PUFFERY
(EXCESSIVE —) FLATTERY
ADULATION PANEGYRIC
(EXTRAVAGANTLY —) PUFF
(INSINCERE —) CLART DAUBING
(PUBLIC —) PRECONY
(SING FALSE —S) CHANT
PRAISED JUDAH JUDITH
LAURELED
(UNDULY —) BEPUFFED

PRAISEWORTHY WORTHY
AMIABLE GLORIOUS LAUDABLE
SPLENDID EXEMPLARY
PRAJAPATI KA PITRI
PRAKRIT PALI MAGADHI
PRAM CARRIAGE HANDCART
PUSHCART STROLLER
PRANCE STIR BRANK CAPER
DANCE JAUNT PRANK CANARY
CAREER CAVORT CURVET
GAMBOL JAUNCE TITTUP TRANCE
PRANKLE SWAGGER CAKEWALK
PRANCER HORSE DANCER
CAPERER
PRANK JIG RAG RIG DECK DIDO
FOLD GAME GAUD JEST LARK
PLOY PRAT REAK ADORN ANTIC
CAPER FREAK SHINE SKITE TRICK
VAGUE BROGUE CURVET FEGARY
FIGARY FROLIC GAMBOL SHAVIE
VAGARY MARLOCK SPANGLE
ESCAPADE FREDAINE PRANCOME
RIGWIDDIE MONKEYSHINE
(PL.) REX GAMES JINKS
PRANKISH TRICKSY
PRASINE LEEK
PRAT PUSH NUDGE TRICK
PRATE GAB BUCK BUKH BUKK
CARO CHAT CLAP CLAT TALK
BLATE BOAST CLASH SCOLD
BABBLE CACKLE CLAVER JANGLE
SQUIRT TONGUE BLATHER
BLATTER BLETHER CHATTER
CLATTER PALAVER PRATTLE
TWATTLE
PRATING GAFF CHATTER
PRATIQUE CUSTOM PRODUCT
PRATTLE GUP CHAT CLACK
BABBLE BURBLE CACKLE JANNER
JAUNER YATTER BLATTER
CHATTER CLATTER GABNASH
JAUNDER NASHGAB PRITTLE
TRATTLE TWADDLE CHITCHAT
BAVARDAGE
PRATTLING CHAVISH
PRAWN CARID NIPPER PENEID
SHRIMP SQUILLA CARIDEAN
CARIDOID CREVETTE MACRURAN
(SUFF.) CARIS
PRAWN KILLER SQUILLA
PRAXIS HABIT ACTION CUSTOM
PRACTICE
PRAY ASK BEG BID BLESS CRAVE
DAVEN SOUGH VOUCH INVITE
BESEECH ENTREAT IMPLORE
REQUEST WRESTLE INVOCATE
(— FOR) BOON
PRAYA BUND BEACH STRAND
PRAYER ACT AHA AVE CRY VOW
BEAD BENE BOON PLEA SUIT
VOTE AGNUS ALENU NAMAZ
SALAT SHEMA ABODAH APPEAL
ECTENE ERRAND LITANY MANTRA
MATINS ORISON STEVEN VESPER
YIZKOR BIDDING COMPLIN
FATIHAH GAYATRI GEULLAH
KADDISH MEMENTO ORATION
PRECULE PREFACE TAHANUN
ANAPHORA APOLYSIS CATHISMA
DEVOTION KEDUSHAH MISERERE
PETITION SUFFRAGE TEHINNAH
REQUIESCAT
(— BEADS) ROSARY

(**— BOOK**) MAHZOR MISSAL SERVICE
(**— LEADER**) IMAM
(**— OF DISMISSAL**) APOLYSIS
(**— RUG**) NAMAZLIK
(**— SHAWL**) TALLITH
(**— STICK**) BAHO PAHO
(**— TOWER**) MINARET
(**CANONICAL —S**) BREVIARY
(**CHIEF MOHAMMEDAN —**) NAMAZ
(**HINDU —**) GAYATRI
(**INWARD —**) ACT
(**JEWISH —**) ALENU ABODAH GEULLAH HOSHANA KADDISH
(**LAST — OF DAY**) COMPLIN
(**LONG —**) CATHISMA
(**LORD'S —**) PATERNOSTER
(**MUSLIM —**) SALAH SALAT KHUTBAH
(**OPENING —**) COLLECT
(**SHORT —**) GRACE COLLECT
(**SILENT —**) SECRET
(**PL.**) HOURS NORITO TIKKUN CHAPLET
(**PREF.**) EUCHO
PRAYING ORISON IMPRECANT
PREACH EDIFY SOUGH TEACH EXHORT GOSPEL SERMON DELIVER HOMILIZE PREDICATE
PREACHER KHATIB MAGGID PARSON TUBMAN DARSHAN LOLLARD MARTEXT PROPHET ROUNDER TEACHER TUBBIST TUBSTER EXHORTER KOHELETH MINISTER PARDONER PULPITER QOHELETH SERMONER SPINTEXT SWADDLER VARTABED BOANERGES
(**PL.**) PULPIT
PREACHING SPELL PULPIT SERMON HEARING KERUGMA KERYGMA PROPHECY PULPITRY SPELLING
PREACHY DIDACTIC
PREAMBLE PREFACE WHEREAS
PREARRANGED SET
PREBEND CANONRY
PREBENDARY PROVEND
PRE-CAMBRIAN MOINE EOZOIC ARCHEAN PRIMARY HURONIAN TORRIDONIAN
PRECARIOUS NEAR DICKY RISKY SHAKY CASUAL INFIRM NARROW UNSURE DUBIOUS TRICKLE CATCHING DELICATE INSECURE PERILOUS UNSTABLE DANGEROUS UNCERTAIN
PRECAUTION CARE GUARD CAUTEL SAFEGUARD
PRECEDE LEAD FOREGO HERALD FORERUN PREFACE PREVENT ANTECEDE PREAMBLE
PRECEDENCE PAS LEAD PRIMACY HERALDRY PRIORITY
(**RIGHT OF —**) PAS
(**SOCIAL —**) LEVEL
PRECEDENT LEAD SIGN MODEL TOKEN USAGE INSTANCE ORIGINAL SPECIMEN STANDARD AUTHORITY
PRECEDING OLD FORE WEST BEFORE FORMER LEADING ADJACENT PREVIOUS

(**— ALL OTHERS**) FIRST
(**PREF.**) ANTE
PRECENTOR CANTOR PSALMIST LETTERGAE
PRECEPT LAW HEST LINE RULE TORA WRIT ADAGE AXIOM BREVE MAXIM ORDER SUTRA SUTTA TORAH BEHEST DICTATE MANDATE WARRANT DOCTRINE DOCUMENT LANDMARK
PRECEPTIVE DIDACTIC MANDATORY
PRECEPTOR TUTOR MASTER
PRECINCT BEAT AMBIT BOUND CLOSE VERGE DOMAIN HIERON VIHARA COLLEGE LENAEUM SOCIETY TEMENOS BANLIEUE DISTRICT ENVIRONS
(**PL.**) AMBIT
PRECIOUS CUTE DEAR FINE LIEF RARE VERY CHARY CHERE GREAT HONEY CHICHI CHOICE COSTLY DAINTY GOLDEN PEARLY POSING SILVER TENDER PRECISE AFFECTED ORIENTAL OVERNICE VALUABLE WORTHFUL PRICELESS
PRECIOUSNESS PRICE
PRECIPICE LIN KHUD LINN LLYN PALI CLIFF KRANS SCREE SHEER STEEP KRANTZ CLOGWYN DOWNFALL HEADWALL
PRECIPITATE GEL CURD HURL RASH HASTY HURRY SHOOT SPEED STEEP ABRUPT COAGEL HASTEN SLUDGE SUDDEN TUMBLE UNWARY DISTILL LYCOPIN SUBSIDE TRIGGER CATALYZE HEADLONG PROCLIVE SEDIMENT SETTLING
(**— DYE**) STRIKE
PRECIPITATELY HEADLING HEADLONG SLAPDASH
PRECIPITATION HAIL MIST RAIN SNOW HASTE SLEET VIRGA
PRECIPITOUS FULL RASH BRANT BRENT HASTY STEEP ABRUPT CHICHI STEEPY SUDDEN PRERUPT HEADLONG
PRECIS JUNONIA SUMMARY ABSTRACT
PRECISE DRY SET FLAT HARD JUMP JUST NEAT NICE TIDY TRIG TRIM TRUE VERY CLEAN CLOSE EXACT PRESS RIGID SOUND FORMAL NARROW RIGORE STARCH STRICT BUCKRAM CAREFUL CERTAIN CLERKLY CORRECT EXPRESS PERFECT PERJINK STARCHY ABSOLUTE ACCURATE DEFINITE EXPLICIT HAIRLINE PINPOINT PUNCTUAL RIGOROUS
PRECISELY BUT EVEN JUST CLEAN SHARP FINELY JUSTLY STRAIT EXACTLY
PRECISENESS RIGOR RIGOUR PRIMNESS
PRECISIAN PRIG PURITAN
PRECISION NICETY CLARITY ACCURACY DELICACY ELEGANCE JUSTNESS
PRECISIONIST PEDANT
PRECLUDE BAR DENY STOP CLOSE

CROSS DEBAR ESTOP FORBID HINDER IMPEDE OBVIATE PREVENT SILENCE CONCLUDE INTERPEL PROHIBIT ANTICIPATE
PRECOCIOUS PRECOX UNRIPE FORWARD PREMATURE RATHERIPE
PRECONCEIVE IDEATE
PRECONCEPTION PRENOTION
PRECONDITION PRIUS
PRECURSOR USHER HERALD INITIAL ANCESTOR PRODROME WAYMAKER HARBINGER HEMIAUXIN PROGENITOR
PREDACITY RAVEN RAVIN
PREDATOR COACTOR
PREDATORY HUNGRY HARMFUL RAVENOUS
PREDECESSOR ANCESTOR FOREGOER
(**PL.**) OLDERS
PREDELLA FOOTPACE
PREDESTINATION FATE DESTINY ELECTION
PREDESTINE DOOM SLATE FOREDOOM FOREPOINT
PREDETERMINE DESTINE FORECAST
PREDICAMENT BOX FIX JAM NODE SOUP SPOT CLASS LURCH STATE STEAD PICKLE PLIGHT SCRAPE DILEMMA IMPASSE CATEGORY JUNCTURE QUANDARY
PREDICANT FRIAR PREACHER DOMINICAN
PREDICATE BASE FOUND AFFIRM ASSERT PRAISE PREACH COMMEND DECLARE EXTREME PREDICT PROCLAIM
PREDICT LAY BODE CALL DOPE READ REDE SPAE AUGUR WEIRD HALSEN FORESAY PRESAGE FOREBODE FORECAST FORETELL PROPHESY SOOTHSAY AUSPICATE PROGNOSTICATE
(**— EVIL**) CROAK
PREDICTION DOPE WEIRD AUGURY BODING BODWORD PORTENT PRESAGE BODEWORD FORECAST PROPHECY VATICINE
PREDILECTION BIAS HANG FANCY FAVOR LIKING RELISH FONDNESS
PREDISPOSE BEND INCLINE SUBJECT
PREDISPOSED PRONE PARTIAL TENDING INCLINED
PREDISPOSITION ITCH DIATHESIS
PREDOMINANCE MAJORITY REGNANCY ASCENDANCY
PREDOMINANT GREAT RULING CAPITAL REIGNING SUPERIOR CULMINANT HEGEMONIC
PREDOMINATE RULE DOMINE EXCEED GOVERN PREVAIL
PREE KISS PRIE TEST TASTE TRIAL PRYING SAMPLE PROVING TASTING
PREEMINENT BIG TOP ARCH HIGH STAR FIRST GRAND GREAT PALMARY PASSING STELLAR SUPREME FOREMOST PRECLARE SPLENDID SUPERIOR

PARAMOUNT PREPOTENT
(**PREF.**) ARCH
PREEMPT COLLAR
PREEN PIN PERK PICK TRIM WHET DRESS GLOAT PLUME PRINK PRUNE SWELL TRICK BROOCH GODWIT SMOOTH REPLUME
(**— WINGS**) WHET
PREFACE FRONT PROEM USHER HERALD PRESAY EPISTLE PRECEDE PREPOSE EXORDIUM FORETALK FOREWORD PREAMBLE PROLOGUE
PREFATORY PROEMIAL PRELIMINARY
PREFECT WALI EPARC GRAVE EPARCH MONITOR PROVOST GOVERNOR PRESIDENT
PREFECTURE EPARCHY
(**CHINESE —**) FU
(**JAPANESE —**) KEN
(**TIBETAN —**) JONG
PREFER LAY LIKE LOVE BRING ELECT EXALT FAVOR OFFER CHOOSE PROFER SELECT OUTRANK PREFECT PRESENT PROMOTE PROPOSE SURPASS
PREFERABLE LIEF RIGHT RATHER ELIGIBLE
PREFERENCE GOO LIKE FAVOR CHOICE DESIRE LIKING RATHER DRUTHERS FAVORITE PRIVILEGE PROMOTION PRECEDENCE
PREFERMENT DIGNITY
PREFIGURE TYPE IDEATE SHADOW TYPIFY FORERUN FORESEE PREDICT FORESHOW PROPHESY ADUMBRATE
PREFIX DUN DOON PREPOSE
PREGNANCY CYESIS TROUBLE ACCYESIS FETATION OOCYESIS GESTATION
PREGNANT BIG GONE OPEN GREAT HEAVY QUICK READY BAGGED CAUGHT COGENT GRAVID PAROUS ENCEINT FERTILE GESTANT TEEMING WEIGHTY CHILDING FORCIBLE GERMINAL PRESSING
PREHALLUX CALCAR
PREHEND SEIZE
PREHISTORIC OGYGIAN IMMEMORIAL
PREINDICATE PRESAGE FORESHOW
PREJUDICE BIAS DOWN HARM HURT KINK TURN DERRY AGEISM DAMAGE IMPAIR INJURY SEXISM SCUNDER SCUNNER JAUNDICE PREJUDGE
PREJUDICED BIGOTED INSULAR PARTIAL
PREJUDICIAL BIASED HURTFUL CONTRARY DAMAGING INIMICAL SINISTER
PRELATE CHIEF LEADER PRIEST HIERARCH ORDINARY SUPERIOR MONSIGNOR
PRELIMINARY PRIOR PRELIM PREFACE PRELUDE LIMINARY PREAMBLE PREVIOUS PREFATORY
PRELUDE PROEM VERSET DESCANT FORERUN INTRADA

PREFACE ANTELUDE BORSPIEL OVERTURE RITORNEL VERSETTE VORSPIEL

PREMATURE RATH UNRIPE IMMATURE PREVIOUS TIMELESS UNTIMELY

PREMEDITATE FORNCAST PURPENSE

PREMEDITATED SET STUDIED PREPENSE

PREMIER CHIEF FIRST OLDEST LEADING EARLIEST

PREMISE LEMMA MAJOR ASSUME GROUND REASON SUMPTION

PREMIUM USE AGIO BACK AWARD BONUS FANCY PRIZE SHAVE USURY BOUNTY DEPORT REWARD GRASSUM CONTANGO DONATIVE FOREGIFT GIVEAWAY
(UNDERCOVER — FOR SEATS) ICE

PREMIXED INSTANT

PREMONITION OMEN HUNCH NOTICE BODWORD PRESAGE WARNING BODEWORD FORESCENT

PREMUNE SALTED

PREOCCUPATION HEART INSIGHT FIXATION

PREOCCUPIED DEEP LOST RAPT CRAZY ABSENT FILLED INTENT CRACKED ABSORBED ENGROSSED

PREPARATION DIA FIG BALM DIBS DOPE PREP CREAM FLASH GLAZE JELLY READY ACETUM BLEACH BLUING DERRIS FACIAL LOTION MEGILP NEBULA PEPSIN SIMPLE ADDRESS APPREST CLEANER DIPPING EMANIUM ESSENCE ETHIOPS EXTRACT FITNESS FONDANT LINCTUS MELLITE PLACEBO TRYPSIN VARNISH ABSTRACT CONSERVE COSMETIC FIXATURE GELOSINE INHALANT LAUDANUM MEDICINE RACAHOUT TRAINING MAKEREADY PROVISION
(— CONTAINING HONEY) MELLITE
(— FOR COLORING LIQUORS) FLASH
(— OF GRAPEJUICE) DIBS
(AROMATIC —) ELIXIR
(CHEESE —) FONDU
(CHEESELIKE —) YOGURT CROWDIE YOGHURT
(COSMETIC —) HENNA
(ENZYME —) KOJI
(EYELID —) KOHL
(IMPURE RADIOACTIVE —) EMANIUM
(INTOXICATING —) BOZA GANJA
(MEDICAL —) STUFF
(OPIUM —) LAUDANUM
(SALINE —) LICK
(SLOPPY —) SLIBBERSAUCE
(SWEET —) DULCE
(UNCTUOUS —) CERATE

PREPARATORY PRIMAL PIONEER PRELIMINARY

PREPARE DO FIT FIX GET LAY ABLE BOUN BUSK COOK GIRD MAKE PARE PLOT PREP TILL YARK ATTLE BLEND BOWNE BRACE DIGHT DRAFT DRESS EQUIP FRAME ORDER PREDY READY TRAIN ADJUST DESIGN GRAITH ORDAIN ADDRESS AFFAITE APPAREL APPOINT CONCOCT CONFECT DISPOSE EDUCATE PRODUCE PROVIDE QUALIFY INSTRUCT
(— BANQUET) COVER
(— BY BOILING) BREW DECOCT
(— BY HEAT) FRIT
(— CAPON) SAUCE
(— FISH) CALVER
(— FOOD) DO COOK
(— FOR BUILDING) FRAME
(— FOR BURIAL) EMBALM
(— FOR DISPLAY) DRESS
(— FOR PUBLICATION) EDIT
(— HASTILY) RASH
(— HEMP) TAW
(— LAND) CURE
(— ONESELF) ADDRESS
(— TEASEL HEADS) CARP

PREPARED UP APT BUN FIT SET BAAN BOON BOUN BOWN GIRT RIPE YARE ALERT BOUND PREST READY GRAITH CURRIED EQUIPPED TOGETHER
(QUICKLY —) RUNNING

PREPAREDNESS PROCINCT

PREPENSE DESIGN FORETHOUGHT

PREPONDERANCE MAJORITY DOMINANCE

PREPONDERATE EXCEED INCLINE SURPASS DOMINATE OUTWEIGH PERSUADE

PREPOSSESS BIAS PREVENT

PREPOSSESSING WINNING

PREPOSSESSION BENT BIAS FETICH FANTASY PREJUDICE

PREPOSTEROUS RICH INEPT ABSURD FOOLISH LAPUTAN GROTESQUE RIDICULOUS

PREPUCE
(PREF.) POSTH(E)(IO)(O)

PREROGATIVE GRACE HONOR RIGHT ESNECY REGALE FACULTY PECULIAR PRIVILEGE

PRESA LEAD

PRESAGE BODE HINT OMEN OSSE SIGN ABODE AUGUR TOKEN AUGURY BETIDE BETOKEN FORESEE OMINATE PORTEND PREDICT FOREBODE FORECAST FOREDOOM FORETELL INDICATE PREAMBLE PROPHESY

PRESBYTER ELDER PRIEST PRESTER ANTISTES MINISTER

PRESBYTERIAN WHIG CLASSIC

PRESBYTERY CLASSIS SENIORY EXERCISE PARSONAGE CONSISTORY

PRESCIENCE PRESAGE FORESIGHT PREVISION

PRESCIND SEVER DETACH

PRESCRIBE SET TAX ALLOT GUIDE LIMIT ORDER ASSIGN DEFINE DIRECT ENJOIN INDITE ORDAIN APPOINT CONFINE CONTROL DICTATE RESTRAIN

PRESCRIBED SET BASIC THETIC POSITIVE THETICAL FORMULARY

PRESCRIPT LAW COMMAND MANDATE PRECEPT

PRESCRIPTION RX BILL FORM CIPHER RECIPE DICTATE FORMULA RECEIPT

PRESENCE EYE FACE SELF BEING ASPECT BEARING COMPANY ASSEMBLY INSTANCE
(DIRECT —) IMMEDIACY

PRESENT AIM BOX NOW BILL BOON GIFT GIVE HAND HERE MEED NEAR NIGH SAND SHOW BEING CUDDY DOLLY ENTER FEOFF GRANT NONCE OFFER PLACE RAISE READY STAGE THERE ACCUSE ACTUAL ADDUCE ALLEGE AROUND BESTOW BOUNTY BROACH CADEAU CLOTHE CUMSHA DONATE DURANT HANSEL KHILAT LATTER MODERN NEARBY PREFER REGALE REGALO RENDER XENIUM COMMEND CUMSHAW DISPLAY DOUCEUR ETRENNE EXHIBIT EXPOUND FAIRING FURNISH HANDSEL INSTANT LARGESS PERFORM PORRECT PRETEND PROPINE RELEASE RESIANT TASHRIF BLESSING CONGIARY DONATION GRATUITY INSTANCE LAGNIAPPE OFFERING PESHKASH RESIDENT SOULCAKE SPORTULA
(— AS GIFT) DASH
(— FOR ACCEPTANCE) TENDER
(— FROM PUPIL TO TEACHER) MINERVAL
(— IN DETAIL) DISCUSS
(— IN MIND) DEAR
(— ONESELF) APPEAR
(— TO SOLDIERS) CONGIARY
(— TO STRANGER) XENIUM
(— TO VIEW) YIELD
(— WITHOUT WARRANT) OBTRUDE
(ALWAYS —) CHRONIC
(BRIDEGROOM'S —) HANDSEL
(CEREMONIAL —) KHILAT
(NOT —) ABSENT

PRESENTATION BILL GALA GIFT SHOW DROLL IMAGE DHARMA MUSTER SCHEMA BILLING DISPLAY EPITOME HOOKUPU MUSICAL PRESENT SPECIES ANALYSIS BESTOWAL DELIVERY DONATION EXPOSURE CANDLEMAS PERFORMANCE

PRESENTIMENT FEELING PRESAGE BODEMENT FOREFEEL PRENOTION PREMONITION

PRESENTLY NOW ANON ENOW SOON SHORTLY DIRECTLY

PRESERVATION FILING SAVING KEEPING SERVATION

PRESERVATIVE SALT BORAX SPICE SUGAR CONSERVE TREATMENT

PRESERVE CAN JAR CORN HAIN HOLD KEEP SALT SAVE BLESS GUARD SERVE SPARE SWEET WITIE ATHOLD BOTTLE COMFIT DEFEND EMBALM FREEZE GOGGLE POWDER RETAIN SECURE SHIELD UPHOLD CONDITE FORFEND KYANIZE PROTECT RAISINE RESERVE SUCCADE SUSTAIN CHOWCHOW CONSERVE ENSHRINE MAINTAIN MOTHBALL PARADISE WITHSAVE
(— BY BOILING WITH SUGAR) CANDY
(— BY SALTING) CORN CURE SALT
(— OF GRAPES) RAISINE
(— WOOD) KYANIZE PAYNISE
(GAME —) MOOR SHIKARGAH
(HUNTING —) WALK
(PL.) KONFYT

PRESERVED WET CONFECT BRANDIED POWDERED

PRESIDE RULE GUIDE DIRECT MODERATE
(— OVER) KEEP

PRESIDENCY MADRAS PRYTANY

PRESIDENT MIR FOUD PREX PREXY PROXY REEVE DEACON RECTOR PRAESES PREFECT
(— OF GUILD) DEAN
(— OF SUPREME COURT) LAWMAN
(— OF TRADE) DEACON

PRESIGNIFY PRESAGE FORETOKEN

PRESS FLY HUG JAM SIT BEAR BEND CRAM DOME DROP DRUK HORN HUSH IRON JAMB KISS PLOT SERR THEW TUCK URGE VICE YERK ARGUE BESET BRIZZ CHAFE CHIRT CRIMP CROWD CRUSH DRIVE EXACT FORCE KNEAD MIDST PRIZE SCREW SHREW SMASH STAMP STUFF TWIST WEIGH WRING ASSAIL CHISEL CLOSET COARCT CRUNCH GOFFER HARASS JOBBER KVETCH MANGLE NUDDLE PREACE SQUASH STRAIN STRESS THRAST THREAP THREAT THREEP THRIMP THRING THRONG THRUST AFFLICT ARMOIRE ATTEMPT BESEECH BESIEGE CONCISE CRUMPLE EMBRACE ENVIRON FLATBED IMPRESS MACHINE OPPRESS SCROOGE SCRUNGE SQUEEZE THRUTCH AGGRIEVE CALENDER COMPRESS PRESSURE SCROUNGE SQUEEGEE SURROUND
(— AGAINST) CONTACT
(— CLOSE) NUDDLE
(— CLOSELY AND PAINFULLY) MASH
(— DOWN) QUAT
(— FOR WINE) TORCULAR
(— FORWARD) DRIVE BREAST
(— HARSHLY) GRIND
(— IN CHEESE VAT) CHISEL CHIZZEL
(— INTO) THRIMBLE THRUMBLE
(— ON ANVIL) HORN
(— ONWARD) STRETCH
(— OUT) EXTRUDE
(— PAINFULLY) PINCH
(— PAPER) COUCH
(— TOGETHER) SERRY
(— UPON) ELBOW DOWNBEAR
(— WITH HEAD OR HORNS) BOX
(— WITH VIOLENCE) DRIVE
(PREF.) PIEZO PRESSI
(SUFF.) (— TOGETHER) ARCTIA

PRESS AGENT FLACK

PRESSED SERRIED
(— WITH BUSINESS) THRONG
(— WITH LEFTHAND FOREFINGER) BARRED

PRESSES
(SUFF.) (— CLOSE) NASTIC

PRESSING RASH ACUTE CRYING URGENT CLAMANT EARNEST EXIGENT INSTANT SQUEEZE CRITICAL PREGNANT NECESSITOUS

PRESSMAN PIG MINDER PROVER PRINTER

PRESSURE JAM HEAD HEAT PEND PUSH SWAY DRIVE FORCE IMAGE PINCH STAMP BURDEN DURESS STRESS THRONG WEIGHT BEARING MERCURY PUSHING SQUEEZE TENSION URGENCY EXACTION EXIGENCY FUGACITY PRESSION
(— GROUP) LOBBY
(— OF CIRCUMSTANCE) NECESSITY
(— OF 1 DYNE) BARAD
(— ON INSTRUMENT STRING) STOP
(— UNIT) TORR MICRON
(LIQUID —) HEAD
(MANUAL —) TAXIS
(UNIT OF —) TORR OSMOL PASCAL
(VAPOR —) FUGACITY
(PREF.) PIEZO TONO

PRESSURE COOKER STEAMER AUTOCLAVE

PRESSWORK BACKUP

PRESTIDIGITATOR PALMER JUGGLER PYTHONIC

PRESTIGE FACE MANA CASTE IKBAL IZZAT KUDOS PLACE CACHET STATUS STATURE ILLUSION INFLUENCE

PRESTO QUICKLY SPEEDILY

PRESUME BEAR DARE GROW IMPLY INFER ASSUME EXPECT DARESAY SUPPOSE ARROGATE

PRESUMING ARROGANT FAMILIAR

PRESUMPTION GALL JOLLITY OUTRAGE PRESUME AUDACITY SUCCUDRY SURQUIDY

PRESUMPTUOUS BOLD PERT FRESH PROUD WICKED WILFUL FORWARD HAUGHTY ARROGANT ASSUMING FAMILIAR INSOLENT FOOLHARDY

PRESUPPOSE IMPLY POSIT ASSUME EXPECT PREMISE FORETAKE

PRESUPPOSITION PREMISE

PRETA PETA

PRETEND ACT LET FAKE MAKE MOCK SHAM CLAIM FEIGN AFFECT ASPIRE ASSERT ASSUME GAMMON INTEND OBTEND POSSUM RECKON SEMBLE ATTEMPT PORTEND PRESUME PROFESS SUPPOSE VENTURE SIMULATE
(— IGNORANCE) CONNIVE
(— TO) FA

PRETENDED FAKE SHAM BOGUS FALSE IRONIC PSEUDO UNREAL ALLEGED ASSUMED COLORED FEIGNED SEEMING SIMULAR AFFECTED IRONICAL SIMULATE

PRETENDER FOP FAKE IDOL CHEAT COWAN FAKER FRAUD QUACK PSEUDO SEEMER AEOLIST CLAIMANT IMPOSTOR INTENDER TARTUFFE MOUNTEBANK
(— TO LEARNING) SCIOLIST

PRETENDING FICTION

PRETENSE ACT AIR FACE GRIM MASK MIEN PLEA RUSE SCUG SHAM SHOW SIGN WILE CLOAK COLOR COVER FEINT GLOSS GLOZE STUDY EXCUSE HUMBUG CHARADE DAUBERY FAITERY FASHION FICTION GRIMACE PRETEXT PURPOSE UMBRAGE ARTIFICE DISGUISE POSTICHE POSTIQUE SEMBLANT

PRETENSION PARADE VANITY PRETEXT

PRETENTIOUS BIG BRAG HIGH SIDY BRANK FLASH GAUDY PUFFY SHOWY BRAGGY CHICHI GEWGAW GLOSSY PUFFED ROCOCO SHODDY TINSEL BOMBAST POMPOUS STILTED TINHORN TOPPING BRAGGART OVERBLOWN RECHERCHE

PRETENTIOUSNESS SIDE SWANK

PRETERMIT OMIT NEGLACT SUSPEND INTERRUPT

PRETERNATURAL GOUSTY GOUSTIE STRANGE ABNORMAL UNCOMMON UNEARTHLY
(— BEING) MARE

PRETEXT PEG FLAM MASK PLEA VEIL CLOAK COLOR COVER GLOSS SALVO STALL EXCUSE REFUGE SCONCE APOLOGY UMBRAGE OCCASION PRETENCE PRETENSE

PRETTIFY EYEWASH

PRETTY APT GEY PAT ABLE BRAW CUTE DEFT FAIR FEAT FINE GAIN GENT GOOD JOLI MILD MOOI POOR TRIM BONNY DINKY DINK POOTY PURTY QUITE SWEET BONITA DIMBER FINELY INCONY MINION PRATTY RATHER TRETIS CLEMENT CUNNING DOLLISH GENTEEL BUDGEREE PRECIOUS
(— WELL) GAILY GAYLY

PRETTY-PRETTY KEEPSAKE

PREVAIL WIN BEAR BEAT REIGN WIELD INDUCE OBTAIN CONQUER PERSIST SUCCEED TRIUMPH DOMINATE
(— BECAUSE BEYOND CONTROL) RAGE
(— OVER) OVERRIDE OVERRULE SURMOUNT
(— UPON) GET FOLD LEAD ARGUFY ENTICE INDUCE OBTAIN ENTREAT OVERSWAY

PREVAILING RIFE GOING USUAL CURRENT DOMINANT

PREVALENCE RUN

PREVALENT UP RIFE BRIEF COMMON POTENT VULGAR CURRENT GENERAL POPULAR RAMPANT REGNANT CATHOLIC EPIDEMIC POWERFUL

PREVARICATE LIE EVADE STRAY SKLENT WANDER QUIBBLE SHUFFLE WHIFFLE

PREVARICATOR LIAR JESUIT

PREVENT BAR LET HELP KEEP NILL SHUN STAY STOP TENT WARN AVERT CHECK DEBAR DETER ESTOP ARREST DEFEND FORBID FORLET HINDER OUTRUN RETAIN

REVOKE SECURE FORFEND FORLEIT IMPEACH INHIBIT OBVIATE OCCLUDE PRECEDE RETRACT ANTEVERT INTERPEL PARALYZE PRECLUDE PROHIBIT WITHHOLD
(— OPPONENT FROM SCORING) CHICAGO

PREVENTION PREFACE ESTOPPEL OBSTACLE PREJUDICE

PREVIEW SNEAK FUTURAMA

PREVIOUS HASTY PRIOR BEFORE FORMER RATHER EARLIER LEADING FOREGONE PRECEDING

PREVIOUSLY ERE YET ERST FORE SUPRA BEFORE ALREADY HASTILY PRIORLY FORMERLY HITHERTO

PREVISION FORESEE FORECAST FORESIGHT

PREY ROB FEED GAME SOYL TIRE BOOTY PREDE RAVEN RAVIN SPOIL QUARRY RAVAGE RAVINE VICTIM CAPTURE PILLAGE PLUNDER ROBBERY SPREATH VULTURE
(— UPON) DEVOUR PICAROON DEPREDATE
(HAWK'S —) PELT

PREYER KITE

PRIAM (DAUGHTER OF —) CREUSA POLYXENA CASSANDRA
(GRANDFATHER OF —) ILUS
(SLAYER OF —) PYRRHUS
(SON OF —) PARIS HECTOR TROILUS
(WIFE OF —) HECUBA

PRIAPISM TENTIGO

PRICE LAY ANTE COST FARE FEER FIAR FIER FOOT ODDS PRYS RATE BRIBE CHEAP CLOSE VALUE WORTH CHARGE FIGURE HANSEL TARIFF AVERAGE CATALOG CRANAGE EXPENSE FURNACE HANDSEL PRETIUM STORAGE CARRIAGE FERRIAGE INTEREST
(— FOR KEEPING GOODS) STORAGE
(HIGH —) DEARTH
(LOW —) WANWORTH
(PROPER —) VALUE
(REDUCED —) SALE BARGAIN
(RISING —S) BOOM INFLATION

PRICELESS RARE COSTLY UNIQUE UNSALABLE

PRICK DOT JAG BROD BROG DROB FOIN GOAD JAGG PECK PING PROG SPUR STAB TANG URGE DRESS ERECT POINT PREEN PUNCH STEEK BROACH GALLOP INTENT LAUNCH POUNCE PRITCH SKEWER STITCH TARGET THRUST TWINGE ACANTHA POINTED BULLSEYE
(— OUT) SPOT
(— PAINFULLY) STING
(— WITH NAIL) CLY CLOY ACCLOY
(PREF.) STIGMATI STIGMEO STIGMO

PRICKED PIQUE

PRICKER PROD NEEDLE STABBER

PRICKET DAG SNUFFER SPITTER

PRICKING SMART PUNGENT RETRACT POIGNANT POINTURE PUNCTION

(SUFF.) NYXIS

PRICKLE PIKE SETA BRIAR SPEAR SPINE THORN BASKET BRIER ACANTHA ACULEUS PRINKLE SPICULA STICKLE STIMULUS

PRICKLY BURRY JAGGY SHARP SPINY URCHIN BEARDED SPINOSE SPINOUS STICKLY THISTLY ACULEATE ECHINATE MURICATE SCABROUS SCRATCHY SPICULAR STICKERY STINGING VEXATIOUS
(PREF.) ICHIN(O)

PRICKLY ASH RUEWORT

PRICKLY HEAT MILIARIA

PRICKLY PEAR TUN TUNA NOPAL SABRA OPUNTIA PINPILLOW

PRICKLY-POINTED PUNGENT

PRICKLY POPPY ARGEMONE COCKSCOMB

PRIDE HEAT HORN LUST POMP RUFF ADORN CREST GLORY ORGUL PLUME PREEN PRIME WLANK EXCESS HUBRIS METTLE NOSISM VANITY COMPANY CONCEIT DISDAIN EGOTISM GLORIFY HAUTEUR STOMACH SURQUIDY WLONKHEDE
(— ONESELF) PIQUE
(EXCESSIVE —) SWELLING ARROGANCE
(MASCULINE —) MACHISMO

PRIDE AND PREJUDICE (AUTHOR OF —) AUSTEN
(CHARACTER IN —) JANE MARY DARCY KITTY LUCAS LYDIA BENNET GEORGE BINGLEY COLLINS WICKHAM CAROLINE DEBOURGH GARDINER CATHERINE CHARLOTTE ELIZABETH FITZWILLIAM

PRIDEFUL FASTUOUS

PRIEST EN ABBE CURA CURE DEAN EZRA IMAM MAGA CLERK COHEN EPULO IMAUM ISIAC MOBED PADRE PATER SABIO SARIP VICAR ZADOK ABACES AMAUTA BHIKKU BISHOP DASTUR DIVINE FALMEN FATHER FLAMEN GALLAH GALLUS GELONG GETSUL GOSAIN JETHRO KAHUNA LEVITE POWWOW SHAMAN ANANIAS ARBACES CALCHAS CASSOCK CHANTER DESTOUR DUSTOOR GALLACH LAOCOON PANDITA PAPALOI PATENER PATRICO PHINEAS POONGEE PRESTER STOLIST TEACHER TOHUNGA BABAYLAN BEROSSOS CHRYSEIS HANANIAH KASHYAPA MINISTER PANDARAM PENANCER PONTIFEX POONGHIE SACERDOS SEMINARY SOGGARTH SYRIARCH TALISMAN VARDAPET ZADOKITE OFFICIANT SHAVELING
(— OF APOLLO) CALCHAS CHRYSEIS
(— OF CYBELE) CORYBANT
(— OF RAMA) KASHYAPA
(— OF RHEA) CURETE
(BABYLONIAN —) BEROSSOS
(BUDDHIST —) LAMA BHIKKU GELONG POONGEE POONGHIE TALAPOIN
(CHIEF —) SYRIARCH

(CHIEF — OF SHRINE) EN
(EGYPTIAN —) ARBACES
CHOACHYTE
(ETRUSCAN —) LUCUMO
(EUNUCH —) GALLUS
(FRENCH —) PERE SULPICIAN
(GYPSY —) PATRICO
(HIGH —) ELI SARIP DASTUR
KAHUNA DESTOUR PHINEAS
PONTIFF PRELATE CAIAPHAS
HIERARCH JEHOIADA PONTIFEX
(HINDU —) PANDARAM
(INCA —) AMAUTA
(LAMAIST —) GETSUL
(MAORI —) TOHUNGA
(MORO —) SARIP PANDITA
(MOSLEM —) ALFAQUI TALISMAN
(PAGAN —) BABAYLAN
(PARISH —) CURA CURE PAPA
POPE PARSON PERSON SECULAR
(ROMAN —) EPULO FLAMEN
(TIBETAN —) LAMA
(VAISHNAVA —) GOSAIN
(VOODOO —) BOCOR BOKOR
(PL.) LUPERCI
PRIEST-DOCTOR SHAMAN
WABENO
PRIESTESS NUN ENTUM HORSE
MAMBO MAMBU BACBUC PYTHIA
DIOTIMA MAMALOI PHOIBAD
PHITONES PYTHONESS
(— OF APOLLO) PYTHIA PHOEBAD
(— OF THE BOTTLE) BACBUC
(BABYLONIAN —) ENTUM
(VOODOO —) HORSE
PRIESTFISH CHERNA ROCKFISH
PRIESTHOOD SALII SACERDOCY
PRIEST-KING PATESI
PRIESTLY LEVITIC SACERDOTAL
PRIG BEG FOP BRAD BUCK NAIL
SMUG DANDY FILCH PLEAD
STEAL THIEF FELLOW HAGGLE
PERSON PILFER TINKER ENTREAT
PURITAN QUIBBLE
PRIGGER THIEF
PRIGGISH PRUDISH
PRIM MIM NEAT TRIG TRIM MIMZY
DEMURE FORMAL MIMSEY PRISSY
PRIVET PROPER STUFFY MISSISH
PERJINK PRECISE PRIMSIE
STARCHY
PRIMACY CHIEFTY PRIMITY
HEADSHIP
PRIMA DONNA DIVA STAR
PRIMARY CYAN BASIC CHIEF FIRST
PRIME CAUCUS DIRECT FONTAL
MANUAL MAGENTA RADICAL
ARCHICAL CARDINAL HYPOGENE
ORIGINAL PRIMEVAL PRINCIPAL
(PREF.) ARCHI PROT(E)(EO)
PRIMATE BISHOP GALAGO LEADER
PREMAN PRINCIPAL PREHOMINID
PRIME MAY FANG FILL LOAD MAIN
CHIEF COACH FIRST PRIDE TONIC
YOUTH CHOICE FLOWER SPRING
CENTRAL LEADING LUSTFUL
PREPARE DOMINEER ORIGINAL
YOUTHFUL PRINCIPAL
PRIME MINISTER ATABEG
PREMIER
PRIMER ABC CAP DONAT WAFER
READER CORDERY HORNBOOK
PRIMEVAL OLD NATIVE ANCIENT

OGYGIAN PRIMARY PRISTINE
PRIMITIVE
PRIMING MORSING TWOPENNY
CLEARCOLE
PRIMING IRON DRIFT
PRIMING WIRE PICKER
PRIMITIVE DARK CRUDE EARLY
FIRST GROSS NAIVE PLAIN PRIME
FANTEE GOTHIC PRIMAL SAVAGE
SIMPLE ANCIENT ARCHAIC
PRIMARY PRISCAN BACKVELD
BARBARIC EARLIEST IGNORANT
ORIGINAL PRISTINE ABORIGINAL
PRIMORDIAL
(PREF.) ARCH(AE)(AEO)(E)(EO)(I)
PALAE(O) PALE(O)
PRIMNESS STARCH PRUDERY
PRIMORDIAL CRUDE FIRST
PRIMARY ARCHICAL EARLIEST
PRIMEVAL
PRIMORDIUM BUD ANLAGE
BLASTEMA
PRIMP PRIM ADORN PREEN PRINK
PRIMROSE GAY OXLIP SPINK
FLOWER SUNCUP COWSLIP
FLOWERY PRIMULA SCABISH
AURICULA PLUMROCK SCURVISH
AFTERGLOW PIMPERNEL
POLYANTHUS
PRIMULA OXLIP COWSLIP
PRIMWORT
PRINCE MIN RAS DUKE EARL EMIR
IMAM KHAN KING KNEZ LORD
NASI RAJA RANA RIAL SAID
WANG ALDER EBLIS EMEER
FURST GEBIR MIRZA PWYLL
RAJAH SAYID ARJUNA DESPOT
DYNAST SHERIF SOLDAN
BHARATA ELECTOR GLAUCUS
HELENUS MONARCH TANCRED
TOPARCH ZERBINO ARCHDUKE
ATHELING CARDINAL FLORIZEL
HOSPODAR MAMILIUS OROONOKO
RASSELAS SARPEDON
PENDRAGON
(— OF ABYSSINIA) RAS RASSELAS
(— OF APOSTATE ANGELS) DEVIL
EBLIS
(— OF ARGO) DIOMED DIOMEDES
(— OF BOHEMIA) FLORIZEL
(— OF DARKNESS) DEVIL SATAN
(— OF DEMONS) BEELZEBUB
(— OF DYFED) PWYLL
(— OF SALERNO) TANCRED
(— OF SCOTLAND) ZERBINO
(— SOLD INTO SLAVERY)
OROONOKO
(— WITH CHARLEMAGNE) ASTOLF
ASTOLFO
(ANGLO-SAXON —) ADELING
ATHELING
(ARAB —) SHERIF
(CHINESE —) WANG
(ETRUSCAN —) LUCUMO
(GERMAN —) FURST ELECTOR
(INDIAN —) RAJA RANA RAJAH
BHARATA AHLUWALIA
(LYCIAN —) GLAUCUS SARPEDON
(MOHAMMEDAN —) SOLDAN
(MOSLEM —) IMAM SAID SAYID
SAYYID SHEIKH SOLDAN
(PETTY —) SATRAP VERGOBRET
(SERVIAN —) CRAL

(SLAVIC —) KNEZ
(TROJAN —) HELENUS
PRINCE EDWARD ISLAND (BAY
OF —) ROLLA EGMONT ORWELL
MALPEQUE
(CAPITAL OF —) CHARLOTTETOWN
(TOWN OF —) ABNEY SOURIS
TIGNISH MONTAGUE
GEORGETOWN SUMMERSIDE
PRINCELY NOBLE ROYAL KINGLY
STATELY SOVEREIGN
PRINCE'S FEATHER LILAC
PILEWORT
PRINCESS AIDA ELSA RANI DANAE
PALLA RANEE SARAH CREUSA
GLAUKE ILDICO MADAME PSYCHE
ANTIOPE CORONIS PHYLLIS
DRAUPADI MAHARANI
(— CHANGED INTO CROW) CORONIS
(— MOTHER OF ZEUS) ANTIOPA
ANTIOPE
(— OF ARGOS) DANAE
(— OF CORINTH) CREUSA GLAUKE
(— WHO SLEW ATTILA) ILDICO
(MOHAMMEDAN —) BEGUM
(THRACIAN —) PHYLLIS
(TYRIAN —) DIDO
PRINCEWOOD CYP BARIA CYPRE
CERILLO CANALETE SALMWOOD
PRINCIPAL ARCH BOSS HEAD HIGH
MAIN STAR CHIEF FIRST GRAND
GREAT PRIME STOCK AUCTOR
CORPUS MASTER STAPLE
CAPITAL CAPTAIN CENTRAL
CHATTEL DECUMAN DOMINUS
PREMIER PRIMARY SALIENT
STELLAR CARDINAL ESPECIAL
FOREMOST OFFICIAL PRESTANT
PRINCELY
(— OF SCHOOL) PRECEPTOR
HEADMASTER
(POLITICAL —) PLANK
(PREF.) ARCH PROT(O)
PRINCIPALITY ZUPA ARZAVA
ARZAWA ORANGE SATRAPY
APPANAGE DESPOTAT
PRINCEDOM
PRINCIPLE JUS LAW RTA TAO
BASE FATE RITA RULE SEED YANG
AGENT AXIOM BASIS CANON
CAUSE DATUM PRANA SPARK
STUFF TENET ANIMUS ARABIN
CNICIN COGITO CORTIN ELIXIR
EMBRYO FAGINE GOSPEL
ARCHEUS BROCARD BUFAGIN
CLYSSUS ELEMENT FORMULA
GENERAL PRECEPT QUASSIN
RADICAL THEOREM URGRUND
DOCTRINE GOSSYPOL INTIMISM
LANDMARK NICOTINE SANCTION
SPECIFIC TINCTURE
(— ACCEPTED AS TRUE) CANON
(— FROM TOAD) BUFAGIN
(— IN BEECHNUTS) FAGINE
(— OF BLESSED THISTLE) CNICIN
(— OF COTTONSEED) GOSSYPOL
(— OF EXISTENCE) TATTVA
(— OF INDIVIDUATION) AHANKARA
(— OF KEY IN MUSIC) TONALITY
(— OF REST) ADHARMA
(COSMIC —) HEAVEN URGRUND
PRAJAPATI
(DOGMATIC —) DICTUM

(ELEMENTARY —) BROCARD
(FEMALE —) YIN SAKTI
(FIRST —) ABC SEED ARCHE
(FUNDAMENTAL —) GROUNDSEL
(GERMINAL —) STAMEN
(GOVERNING —) HINGE
(GUIDING —) SQUARE
(LIFE —) SOUL GHOST PRANA
(MALE —) YANG PURUSHA
(MOHAMMEDAN THEOLOGICAL —)
IJMA
(MORAL —) SCRUPLE
(NARCOTIC —) FAGINE
(ONTOLOGICAL —) DHARMA
(PRIMAL —) APEIRON
(PROMINENT —) KEY
(RHYTHMICAL —) ACCENT
(SPIRITUAL —) SOUL
(SUMMARY OF —S) CREED
(VITAL —) JIVA SPIRIT STAMEN
ARCHAEUS
PRINK PERK PRIG WINK ADORN
PRICK PRIMP PRUNE BEDECK
SMUDGE
PRINT CUT GAY GUM RUN DRUK
MARK TYPE FUDGE PORTY PRESS
SEPIA STAMP BANNER BORDER
CARBON CARBRO ENFACE LETTER
STRIKE BROMOIL DROPOUT
DUOTYPE ENGRAVE GRAPHIC
GRAVURE IMPRESS PUBLISH
TRACING VANDYKE VESTIGE
WOODCUT AQUATONE CALOTYPE
CHLORIDE DRYPOINT HALFTONE
INSCRIBE LEIMTYPE MONOTYPE
POSITIVE URUSHIYE
PHOTOENGRAVING
(— OF WILD MAMMAL) PUG
(— OTHER SIDE) BACK
(— TO RIGHT) ADSCRIPT
PRINTED FONTED
PRINTER TYPO TWICER PRESSMAN
IMPRIMENT
(AID TO —) DEVIL
(PL.) TYPOTHETAE
AMERICAN DAY GOUDY GREEN
RUDGE AITKEN DRAPER DUNLAP
ROGERS THOMAS UPDIKE WILSON
ZENGER GARNETT BRADFORD
WOODWORTH
AUSTRIAN WELSBACH
DUTCH BOMBERG ELZEVIR
ENSCHEDE
ENGLISH CAVE JONES WORDE
BLOUNT BOWYER BULMER
BUTTER CAXTON OGILBY
AWDELAY COPLAND CROWLEY
GRAFTON HANSARD NICHOLS
BRADSHAW ROYCROFT
WOODFALL WHITTINGHAM
FRENCH DIDOT DOLET MOREL
COLINES PLANTIN ESTIENNE
GERMAN FUST ZELL KONIG LUFFT
FROBEN MENTEL ZAINER PFISTER
RATDOLT AMERBACH GRYPHIUS
SCHOFFER BREITKOPF
TAUCHNITZ
ITALIAN BODONI GIUNTA
CASTALDI MANUTIUS
JAPANESE HARUNOBU
SCOTTISH SMELLIE BALLANTYNE
SWISS GERING
PRINTER'S DEVIL FLY

PRINTING TIRAGE EDITION VIGOREUX CHARACTER IMPRIMERY
(LAST —) THIRTY
PRION PETREL
PRIONID BEETLE
PRIONODON LINSANG
PRIOR ERE OLD FORE PAST EIGNE ELDER FORMER RATHER ALREADY EARLIER FARTHER ANTERIOR FOREHAND HITHERTO PREVIOUS PRECEDING
(PREF.) ANTE EPH EPI
(— TO) ANTE PRAE PRE SUPRA
PRIORITY PRIVILEGE PRECEDENCE PREFERMENT
(PREF.) PRAE PRE
PRIORY ABBEY NUNNERY CLOISTER PRIORATE
PRISCA (HUSBAND OF —) AQUILA
PRISM BLOCK NICOL CYLINDER SPECTRUM WERNICKE REFRACTOR
PRISMATIC SHOWY BRILLIANT
PRISON GIB JUG BRIG COOP GAOL HELL HOCK HOLD HOLE JAIL KEEP LAKE NICK QUAD QUOD SHOP STIR WARD BAGNE CHOKY CLINK FLEET GRATE KITTY LIMBO LODGE POUND RATEL TENCH TRONK VAULT BAGNIO BAILEY BUCKET CARCEL CARCER COOLER JIGGER LUMBER RATTLE BASTILE BOCARDO BULLPEN COLLEGE COMPTER CONFINE COUNTER DUNGEON FREEZER GEHENNA KIDCOTE LUDGATE NEWGATE SLAMMER DARTMOOR HOOSEGOW TOLBOOTH TRIBUNAL CALABOOSE PENITENTIARY
(— CAMP) OFLAG
(— IN ROME) TULLIANUM
(AUSTRALIAN —) TENCH
(UNIVERSITY —) CARCER
PRISONER CON POW MUTE LIFER DETENU INMATE REMAND CAITIFF CAPTIVE CONVICT GAOLBIRD JAILBIRD LONGTIMER
PRISONER OF ZENDA (AUTHOR OF —) HOPE
(CHARACTER IN —) ROSE SAPT FRITZ FLAVIA RUDOLF MICHAEL DEMAUBAN BURLESDON ANTOINETTE RASSENDYLL TARLENHEIM
PRISONER'S BASE CHEVY CHIVY
PRISSY PRIM FUSSY DAINTY FINICKY PRUDISH PRIGGISH SISSIFIED
PRISTINE NEW PURE FIRST FRESH ANCIENT PRIMARY ORIGINAL PRIMEVAL PRIMITIVE UNSPOILED
PRIVACY RECESS SECRET PRIVITY RETREAT SECRECY DARKNESS INTIMACY INTIMITY SOLITUDE SECLUSION
(IN —) ASIDE
(PL.) VERENDA
PRIVATE SNUG ALONE CLOSE GUIDE KHASS PRIVY SHARE CLOSET COVERT INWARD POCKET SECRET STANCH POSTERN SECRECY SEVERAL SOLDIER

CIVILIAN DOMESTIC ESOTERIC HOMEFELT INTERNAL INTIMATE PERSONAL SINGULAR UMBRATILE
(PREF.) CRYPT(O) KRYPT(O) PRIVI
PRIVATEER CAPER MARQUE PIRATE ALABAMA CORSAIR CRUISER DUNKIRK PICKEER
PRIVATELY ASIDE INWARDLY SECRETLY
PRIVATION LOSS WANT PINCH PENURY PERISH ABSENCE POVERTY HARDSHIP
PRIVET PRIM HEDGE SKEDGE IBOLIUM PRIMWORT PRIMPRINT
PRIVILEGE UP PUT SOC BOTE DOWN HAND STAR TEAM CLAIM ENTRY FAVOR FRANK GRACE HONOR REGAL RIGHT THEAM EXCUSE INDULT MUNITY OCTROI OPTION PATENT WARREN CHARTER FALDAGE FREEDOM LIBERTY MITZVAH PASSAGE GRANDEZA STANDAGE PERQUISITE PREROGATIVE
(— TO USE THINGS) BOTE
(ACQUIRED —) EASEMENT
(POKER —) EDGE
(POOL —) STAR
PRIVILEGED CURULE EXEMPT LICENSED CHARTERED
(— PLACE) WARREN
PRIVY WC AJAX GONG REAR BIFFY DRAFT ISSUE JAKES PETTY QUIET SIEGE CLOACA CLOSET OFFICE SECRET DRAUGHT FOREIGN LATRINE PRIVATE DONICKER FAMILIAR INTIMATE OUTHOUSE PERSONAL STEALTHY WARDROBE
PRIZE CUP FEE GEM PRY BELL BEND GAME GREE PALM PREY PRIX RATE RISK AWARD BACON BOOTY LEVER PLATE PLUME PRICE PURSE STAKE VALUE WAGER ESTEEM GLAIVE PRAISE PREMIO TROPHY BENEFIT CAPTURE GARLAND PREMIUM ESTIMATE LEVERAGE PURCHASE REPRISAL TREASURE
(— FOR LAST) MELL
(FIRST —) BLUE
(LOTTERY —) LOT TERN
(THEATER —) OBIE
PRIZE CUP PEWTER
PRIZED DEAR CHARY
PRIZEFIGHT GO BOUT MILL MATCH SCRAP BARNEY
PRIZEFIGHTER BOXER BLEEDER FIGHTER SLUGGER PUGILIST
PRIZE MONEY GUNNAGE
PRO TO FOR FAVORING
PROA PARO PRAU PROW PAROO PRAHU CARACOA
PROBABILITY ODDS SHOW CHANCE PERCENTAGE
PROBABLE MAYBE LIKELY PROBAL TOPICAL APPARENT FEASIBLE POSSIBLE
PROBABLY BELIKE LIKELY
PROBATION TEST PROOF TRIAL PAROLE EVIDENCE
PROBATIONER STIBBLER
PROBE PICK SEEK SIFT STOG TENT ENTER GROPE SOUND FATHOM

SEARCH SEEKER STYLET THRUST TRACER ACCOUNT EXAMINE INQUIRY SOUNDER GYROMELE
PROBITY HONESTY INTEGRITY RECTITUDE
PROBLEM NUT SUM WHY BOYG CRUX DUAL ISSE KNOT BLAIK HYDRA POSER APORIA ENIGMA BUGBEAR DILEMMA FUNERAL GORDIAN GRUELER TICKLER EXERCISE HEADACHE JEOPARDY QUESTION STICKLER SITUATION
(CHESS —) DUAL MOVER SUIMATE MINIATURE
PROBLEMATICAL DUBIOUS DOUBTFUL PUZZLING UNCERTAIN UNDECIDED
PROBOSCIS NOSE SNOUT TRUMP TRUNK ANTLIA LINGUA SIPHON SYPHON TONGUE ROSTRUM
PROBOSCIS MONKEY KAHA KAHAU
PROCAINE NOVOCAINE
PROCAVIA HYRAX
PROCEDURE BIAS FORM HAVE VEIN DRAFT ORDER TENOR TRACK AFFAIR COURSE METHOD POLITY SYSTEM DRAUGHT PROCESS PRODUCT ACTIVITY PROTOCOL OPERATION
(PRESCRIBED —S) CEREMONY
(ROUNDABOUT —) CIRCUITY
(SECRET —) STEALTH
(STANDARDIZED —) BIT
(UNWISE —) FOLLY
PROCEED DO GO BANG BEAR FAND FARE FLOW FOND HAVE MAKE MARK MOVE PASS ROAM ROLL SEEK STEP TAKE TOOL TOUR WEAR WEND WIND YEAD YEDE YEED AMBLE ARISE DRESS FOUND FRAME ISSUE MARCH REACH TRACE BREEZE INTEND PURSUE RESULT SPRING STRAKE STRIKE TRAVEL ADVANCE AGGRESS DEVOLVE EMANATE FORTHGO PRETEND STRETCH CONTINUE PROGRESS
(— AIMLESSLY) CIRCLE
(— ALONE) SINGLE
(— AWKWARDLY) SHLEP SCHLEP SCHLEPP
(— CLUMSILY) FLOUNDER
(— OBLIQUELY) CUT
(— RAGGEDLY) HALT
(— RAPIDLY) RAKE STRETCH
(— UNSTEADILY) DRIDDLE
(— WITH DIFFICULTY) STRUGGLE
(PL.) TAKE VAIL AVAILS INCOME PROFITS PROVENT RETURNS PREVENUE
PROCEEDING ACT DEED FARE PLOY STEP AFFAIR AMPARO COURSE DOMENT ISSUANT MEASURE ONGOING PASSANT QUIETUS TEMANET WARRANT CONCURSO INSTANCE PLACITUM PRACTICE
(— BY THREES) TERNARY
(— FROM GOD) DIVINE
(— FROM THE EARTH) TELLURIC
(COURT —S) TRIAL ACTION
(INDIRECT —S) AMBAGES

(PARLIAMENTARY —S) HUSTINGS
(RECORDED —S) ACTA
PROCERITY HEIGHT TALLNESS
PROCESS RUN FANG FOOT TINA WRIT CREST FURCA HAMUS MUCRO SPINA CALCAR CAPIAS CILIUM COURSE FEELER HABEAS INTEND METHOD REPORT ACCOUNT BARBULE FURCULA GOBBING HAMULUS ISOLATE LAMELLA MANDATE SPATULA SUMMONS ACROMION ACTIVITY APPENDIX AUTOTYPE FILAMENT FRENULUM GRAINING INSTANCE MANUBRIUM OPERATION
(— OF BONE) HORN
(— OF CHANGE) ACTION
(— OF CREATING VACUUM) EXHAUST
(— OF DYEING) BATIK HANKING
(— OF METALPLATING) ACIERAGE
(— OF PACKING) GOBBING
(— OF REASONING) ALGEBRA
(— OF SUPPLYING WANTAGE) ULLING
(— ON FISH'S HEAD) LACINIA
(— PAPER) CONVERT
(— TO RECOVER LAND) DADENHUDD
(— TO REGAIN USE) RECYCLE
(ABRUPT —) MUCRO
(ALCHEMICAL —) CIBATION DIPLOSIS
(ARTISTIC —) FROTTAGE
(CALENDERING —) SWISSING
(CARBON —) AUTOTYPE
(CERAMIC —) FIRING
(COATING —) BLOOMING
(CURVED —) HAMUS
(DEVELOPMENTAL —) ANCESTRY
(EARLIKE —) AURICLE
(FALCONRY —) IMPING
(FINISHING —) BRUSHING CRABBING
(FORKED —) FURCA FURCULA
(HELMETLIKE —) CASQUE
(HOOKLIKE —) HAMULUS
(HORNSHAPED —) CORNICLE
(INTELLECTUAL —S) COGITO
(KNOBLIKE —) BOSS
(LEGAL —) BAIL SUIT CAUSE ATTAINT INSTANCE
(MATHEMATICAL —) ADDITION DIVISION
(MENTAL —) COMPOUND
(MINING —) STOPING
(MOVIE-MAKING —) SLATING
(NERVE-CELL —) DENDRON
(NERVELIKE —) AXON AXONE
(PHOTOGRAPHIC —) CARBRO
(POINTED —) AWN SPINE STYLUS LANGUET
(PRINTING —) OFFSET GRAVURE STENCIL INTAGLIO
(REORGANIZATION —) HEMIXIS
(SMALL POINTED —) AWN
(SPINNING —) JACKING
(SPINOUS —) ACANTHA
(TEXTILE —) DECATING
(WEAVING —) HATCHING
(WINGLIKE —) ALA FIN
(PREF.) TYP(I)(O)
(DRY —) XER(O)

(SUFF.) AL ANCE ANT ENCE ESIS
IAL ING ISATION ISM IZATION
OSIS SIS TH TYPAL TYPE TYPIC
TYPY
(— OF BECOMING) ESCENCE

PROCESSED DOWN FINISHED

PROCESSION POMP WALK CORSO
DRIVE TRACE TRAIN BRIDAL
EXEQUY LITANY PARADE STREAM
CORTEGE FUNERAL THIASOS
TRIONFO TRIUMPH ENTRANCE
MOHARRAM PROGRESS
MOTORCADE
(BOISTEROUS —) SKIMMITY
(IRISH CIVIC —) FRINGES
(SUFF.) CADE

PROCLAIM BID CRY BAWL DEEM
HORN OYES OYEZ SCRY SING
TOOT TOUT BLARE BLAZE BOAST
CLAIM GREDE KNELL SOUND
SPEAK BLAZON BOUNCE DEFAME
HERALD INDICT OUTCRY CLARION
DECLARE DIVULGE PROTEST
PUBLISH TRUMPET ANNOUNCE
DENOUNCE RENOUNCE
PROMULGATE
(— ALOUD) ROAR
(— PUBLICLY) PRECONIZE
(— WITH BIG TALK) BOUNCE

PROCLAMATION CRY HUE BANS
FIAT OYEZ RERD SCRY BANDO
BANNS BLAZE EDICT UKASE
PLACARD PROGRAM

PROCLIVITY BENT ANLAGE
APETITE APTNESS LEANING
TENDENCY

PROCNE (FATHER OF —) PANDION
(HUSBAND OF —) TEREUS
(SISTER OF —) PHILOMELA
(SON OF —) ITYS

PROCONSUL GALLIO PROVOST

PROCRASTINATE LAG TIME
DEFER DELAY LINGER ADJOURN
POSTPONE PROROGUE
TEMPORIZE

PROCRASTINATION DELAY
CUNCTATION

PROCREANT FRUITFUL

PROCREATE WIN SIRE BEGET
ENGENDER GENERATE OCCASION

PROCREATION INCREASE

PROCREATOR AUTHOR

PROCRIS (FATHER OF —)
ERECHTHEUS
(HOUND OF —) LAELAPS
(HUSBAND OF —) CEPHALUS

PROCTOR LIAR PROG ACTOR
AGENT PROXY BEGGAR RECTOR
MONITOR PROCUTOR

PROCUMBENT HUMIFUSE
PROSTRATE

PROCURABLE PARABLE

PROCURATOR PROXY PILATE
PROCTOR

PROCURE GET WIN FANG FIND
GAIN GIVE HALE BRING INFER
TOUCH EFFECT INDUCE OBTAIN
ACHIEVE ACQUIRE COMPARE
CONQUER CONTRIVE PURCHASE

PROCURER PIMP PROXENET
PURVEYOR

PROCURESS AUNT BAWD
HACK LENA PANDER

COMMODE PINNACE

PROD DAB EGG GIG JAB JOB JOG
BROD BROG GOAD HEEL POKE
PROG GOOSE HURRY NUDGE
PROBE INCITE JOSTLE THRUST
IRRITATE

PRODIGAL PROD FLUSH LARGE
COSTLY LAVISH WANTON
WASTER PROFUSE SPENDER
WASTRIE WASTRIFE PROFLIGATE

PRODIGALITY WASTE WASTRY
WASTRIFE PROFUSION

PRODIGIOUS HUGE VAST GIANT
AMAZING IMMENSE STRANGE
ABNORMAL ENORMOUS GIGANTIC
MONSTROUS PORTENTOUS

PRODIGY OMEN SIGN MARVEL
OSTENT WIZARD WONDER
MIRACLE MONSTER PORTENT
CEREMONY

PRODITION TREASON BETRAYAL

PRODUCE DO GO ANTE BEAR
FORM GIVE GROW MAKE REAR
SHOW TEEM WAGE BEGET BIRTH
BREED BRING BROOD BUILD
CARRY CAUSE DRIVE FORGE
FRAME HATCH ISSUE RAISE
SPAWN THROW TRADE YIELD
APPORT CREATE EFFECT
GROWTH INCOME INVENT
INWORK PARENT SECURE
ADVANCE ANIMATE COMPOSE
DEPROME GIGNATE INSPIRE
OUTWORK PRODUCT PROLONG
PROVENT CONCEIVE CONFLATE
ENGENDER GENERATE INCREASE
LENGTHEN OFFSPRING
(— A COPY OF) TYPE
(— AN EFFECT) ACT AFFECT
(— AUDIBLE EFFECT) SOUND
(— CROPS) CARRY
(— DULL APPEARANCE) CHILL
(— FREELY) PULLULATE
(— FRUIT) TEEM
(— HEAT) ENRAGE
(— IN SPECIFIED FORM) FORMAT
(— PAID FOR RENT) CAIN
(— SHARP NOISE) CRINK
(AGRICULTURAL —) PODWARE
(FARM —) HUSBANDRY
(MINING —) LEY
(SUFF.) FER(ENCE)(ENT)(OUS)
FIC(AL)(ATE)(ATION)(ATIVE)(ATOR)
(ATORY)(E)(ENCE)(ENT)(IAL)(IARY)
(IENT) FIQUE GEN(E)(ESIA)(ESIS)
(ETIC)(IC)(IN)(OUS)(Y)

PRODUCED
(SUFF.) GENETIC

PRODUCER GASMAN BEARING
SHOWMAN DIRECTOR GAZOGENE
OUTPUTTER
(SUFF.) ARIAN EER

PRODUCING IN PROCREANT
(PREF.) EXO
(SUFF.) GENIC GEROUS
GON(E)(IDIUM)(IMO)(Y) IGEROUS
PARA PAROUS

PRODUCT HEIR ITEM BRAND
CHILD FRUIT GROSS OUTGO
SPAWN ALCLAD EFFORT FABRIC
GROWTH RESULT UPCOME
FALLOUT OUTTURN PRODUCE
PROGENY TURNOUT

OUTBIRTH OFFSPRING
(— OF ROCK DECAY) LATERITE
(—S OF LAND) ESPLEES
(—S OF ORCHARD) BIKKURIM
(ADDITION —) ADDUCT
(CHEESE AND MILK —S) GERVAIS
(CHOICE —) CAVIAR
(COMPLETED —) TURNOFF
(LEGISLATIVE —) ACT
(MATHEMATICAL —) SQUARE
(MINERAL —) HUTCH
(OXIDATION —) SUBSCALE
(RESIDUAL —) LATERITE
(SECONDARY —) CONGENER
(SURPLUS —S) ARISINGS
(TRANSFORMATION —) BAINITE
(WASTE —) RESIDUENT
(WORTHLESS —) CHAFF
(SUFF.) ADE
(COMMERCIAL —) INE
(MANUFACTURED —) ITE

PRODUCTION WORK FORGE FRUIT
GROSS PIECE YIELD GROWTH
OUTPUT EDITION GUIGNOL
PRODUCE ARTIFICE INDUCTION
OPERATION
(— OF MEDIUM) APPORT
(— OF YOUNG) INCREASE
(BEST —S) FAT
(SUCCESSFUL —) HIT
(SUFF.) GENY POEIA POESIS
POIESIS POIETIC

PRODUCTIVE FAT RICH LOOSE
QUICK ACTIVE BATTLE PAROUS
STRONG CAUSING FERTILE
GAINFUL HEALTHY TEEMFUL
TEEMING CHILDING CREATIVE
FRUITFUL GERMINAL PLENTEOUS
(SUFF.) POEIA POESIS POIESIS
POIETIC

PROEM PREFACE PRELUDE
PROHEIM FOREWORD OVERTURE
PREAMBLE

PROETUS (BROTHER OF —)
ACRISIUS
(DAUGHTER OF —) IPHINOE
LYSIPPE IPHIANASSA
(FATHER OF —) ABAS
(MOTHER OF —) OCALEA
(WIFE OF —) ANTEA

PROFANATION VIOLENCE
SACRILEGE

PROFANE LAY NOA BLUE FOUL
ABUSE COARSE DEBASE DEFILE
DEFOIL DEFOUL UNHOLY VULGAR
WICKED GODLESS IMPIOUS
POLLUTE SECULAR UNGODLY
VIOLATE WORLDLY TEMPORAL
UNHALLOW

PROFANITY OATH CURSE CURSING
LANGUAGE BLASPHEMY

PROFESS OWN AVOW ADMIT
CLAIM AFFECT AFFIRM ALLEGE
ASSERT ASSUME FOLLOW
PRESUME PRETEND PURPORT
PRACTICE

PROFESSION ART BAR LAW COAT
FEAT GAME WALK CRAFT FAITH
FORTE TRADE CAREER CHURCH
EMPLOY METIER MISTER CALLING
FACULTY QUALITY SERVICE
ADVOCACY BUSINESS COACHING
FUNCTION PEDAGOGY

SOLDIERY VOCATION
(SUFF.) SHIP

PROFESSIONAL PRO COLT PAID
HIRED EXPERT SKILLED TRAINED
FINISHED

PROFESSOR DON PROF HANIF
KHOJA LAWYER REGENT ADJOINT
ACADEMIC CIVILIAN EMERITUS

PROFESSORSHIP CHAIR FAUTEUIL

PROFFER BID CAP GIVE TEND
TENT DEFER DODGE ESSAY OFFER
EXTEND OPPOSE PREFER PROFRE
TENDER ATTEMPT PRESENT
HESITATE

PROFICIENCY SIGHT SKILL ABILITY
APTNESS MAITRISE

PROFICIENT ADEPT EXPERT
MASTER SALTED VERSED
PERFECT SKILLED SKILLFUL

PROFILE FORM FLANK PURFLE
SKETCH CONTOUR OUTLINE
SECTION PSYCHOGRAPH
(— OF RIVERBED) THALWEG

PROFIT AID GET NET WIN BOOT
GAIN MEND NOTE SKIN VAIL
AVAIL EDIFY FRAME GRIST LUCRE
SCALP SPEED BEHOOF INCOME
MAKING PAYOFF RETURN
ACCOUNT ADVANCE BENEFIT
CLEANUP FURTHER GETTING
IMPROVE MILEAGE PLUNDER
REVENUE VANTAGE WINNING
CLEANING INCREASE INTEREST
PERCENTAGE PERQUISITE
(— BY) BROOK
(INORDINATE —) BUNCE
(UNDERCOVER —) SQUEEZE
(PL.) GRAVY ISSUE AVAILS
JALKAR ESPLEES

PROFITABLE FAT GOOD UTILE
GOLDEN PLUMMY GAINFUL
HELPFUL PAYABLE BEHOVELY
ECONOMIC PROVABLE REPAYING
VAILABLE REWARDING

PROFITLESS BOOTLESS

PROFLIGATE ROUE DEFEAT
CORRUPT IMMORAL RIOTOUS
SPENDER VICIOUS WASTREL
DEPRAVED FLAGRANT OVERCOME
RAKEHELL WASTEFUL
ABANDONED

PROFOUND DEEP HARD WISE
ABYSS DEPTH HEAVY OCEAN
SOUND THICK PITCHY STRONG
ABYSMAL INTENSE ABSTRUSE
COMPLETE PREGNANT REACHING
THOROUGH

PROFUNDITY ABYSS DEPTH
FATHOM DEEPNESS

PROFUSE FREE LUSH SLAB FRANK
GALORE LAVISH COPIOUS LIBERAL
OPULENT ABUNDANT GENEROUS
PRODIGAL SQUANDER WASTEFUL
REDUNDANT

PROFUSELY HEARTILY

PROFUSION WASTE EXCESS
LAVISH FLUENCY OPULENCE
REDUNDANCY

PROG FOOD GOAD POKE PROD
PROWL TRAMP BEGGAR FORAGE
PROCTOR

PROGENITOR BURI MANU ROOT
SIRE PITRI STOCK

PARENT ANCESTOR
PROGENY BED GET IMP KIN BURD
CLAN KIND SEED TEAM BROOD
CHILD FRUIT ISSUE STRAIN
STRIND INCROSS KINDRED
LINEAGE OUTCOME PRODUCT
CHILDREN FRUITAGE INCREASE
OUTBIRTH OUTCROSS OFFSPRING
(— OF WATER-BUFFALO AND YAK)
DZO
(— OF WITCH AND DEMON) HOLD
(INSECT —) SOCIETY
PROGNOSIS FORECAST
PROPHASIS
PROGNOSTIC OMEN SIGN TOKEN
AUSPICE OMINOUS PRESAGE
PROPHECY
PROGNOSTICATE BODE AUGUR
SPELL BETOKEN CONJECT
PREDICT PRENOTE FOREBODE
FORESHOW FORETELL PROPHESY
PROGNOSTICATION RACE
PRESAGE FOREBODE FORECAST
PROGRESS PROPHECY
PROGNOSTICATOR SEER DOOMER
PROPHET HARUSPEX
PROGRAM CARD SHOW FORUM
AGENDA DESIGN SCHEME
AGENDUM PREFACE CLAMBAKE
FESTIVAL GIVEAWAY GUIDANCE
JAMBOREE PLAYBILL SCHEDULE
SEQUENCE SYLLABUS
(COMPUTER —) DOS FIRMWARE
(COMPUTER —S) SOFTWARE
(HEALTH —) MEDICAID MEDICARE
(PART OF COMPUTER —) BRANCH
PROGRAMMA EDICT DECREE
PREFACE PROGRAM
PROGRESS WAY BIRL DENT FARE
GAIN GROW MOVE RACE RISE
STEM STEP TOUR WEAR WEND
WENT BUILD DRIFT FORGE GOING
MARCH SWING WEENT ASCENT
BUFFET COURSE GROWTH
STREEK ADVANCE DEVELOP
FOOTING HEADWAY IMPROVE
JOURNEY ONGOING PASSAGE
PROCESS PROFICIENCY
(— CLUMSILY) SCRAMBLE
(— ERRATICALLY) FLAIL
(— FEEBLY) DODDER
(— INTELLIGENTLY PLANNED)
TELESIA TELESIS
(— NOISILY) CHORTLE
(— SLOWLY) CRAWL
(SINGLE —) THROUGH
PROGRESSED FAR
PROGRESSION WAY SWING
COURSE GALLOP ADVANCE
PASSAGE PROGRESS SEQUENCE
(— OF CHORDS) SWIPE
(MUSICAL —) SKIP
(SMOOTH —) SLIDE
PROGRESSIVE ACTIVE ONWARD
FORWARD GRADUAL LIBERAL
PROGRESSIVELY STILL
PROHIBIT BAN BAR STOP VETO
BLOCK DEBAR ESTOP DEFEND
ENJOIN FORBID HINDER OUTLAW
FORFEND FORWARN INHIBIT
PREVENT DISALLOW PRECLUDE
SUPPRESS PROSCRIBE
PROHIBITED HOT TABU TABOO

ILLEGAL ILLICIT UNLAWFUL
VERBOTEN
PROHIBITING VETITIVE
PROHIBITION BAN NAY NON VETO
ORDER BARRIER DEFENCE
DEFENSE EMBARGO FORBODE
ESTOPPEL
PROHIBITIONIST DRY PUSSYFOOT
PROJECT GAB GAG JET JUT LAP
TUT BEAM CAST GAME IDEA
PLAN POKE PUSH SAIL SWIM
BULGE CHART DRAFT DRIVE
IMAGE JETTY JUTTY SETUP
SHOOT STICK THROW BEETLE
DESIGN DEVICE ESTATE EXTEND
FILLIP OUTJUT PROPEL SCHEME
SCREEN SHELVE EXTRUDE
GOSPLAN IMAGINE KNUCKLE
OUTCROP PATTERN BUSINESS
CONTRIVE OUTREACH OUTSHOOT
OVERHANG PROPOSAL PROTRUDE
SPANGHEW
(UNETHICAL —) SCHEME
(VISIONARY —) BABEL
PROJECTILE BALL BOLT CASE
SHOT SHAFT TRACER OUTCAST
POUNDER FIREBALL SHRAPNEL
(— DESIGNED TO SET FIRE TO
HOUSES) CARCASS
(EXPLOSIVE —) BOMB SHELL
(SUBMARINE —) TORPEDO
(PL.) LEAD SHOT SALVO STUFF
PROJECTING BEETLE SHELVY
EMINENT JUTTING OUTSHOT
PENDENT SALIENT SNAGGLED
PROMINENT OUTSTANDING
(PREF.) PRO
PROJECTION ARM CAM COG DOG
EAR FIN GIB JET JOG JUT NAB
NAG NUT TOE BEAK BOSS BROW
BUHR COAK COCK CROC CUSP
HEEL HORN KEEL KICK KINK KNAG
KNOB KNOP LOBE RIDE SAIL
SNUG SPUD SPUR TEAT WING
BULGE CLEAT EJECT ELBOW
FENCE FURCA JUTTY SALLY
SCRAG SHANK SHOOT SPIKE
TOOTH BRANCH CALCAR CORBEL
CROSET FUSULA HEARTH ICICLE
MENTUM NOSING PALATE RELISH
TAPPET BREAKER CONSOLE
DRAWING EPAULET EYEBROW
ORILLON PRICKER PRICKLE
RESSAUT AJUTMENT CASCABEL
DENTICLE EMINENCE FOOTLOCK
OVERHANG SALIENCE SHOULDER
SPROCKET STERIGMA APOPHYSIS
OUTTHRUST PROMINENCE
(— CONNECTING TIMBER) COAK
(— EXTENDING BACKWARD) BARB
(— FROM CASTING) SPRUE
(— FROM SHIP'S KEEL) SPONSON
(— IN CLOCK) SQUARE
(— IN ORCHIDS) MENTUM
(— OF FOREHEAD) ANTINION
(— OF JAW) GNATHISM
(— OF PEAT) HAG
(— OF RAFTER) SALLY
(— OF TERRITORY) PANHANDLE
(— ON CANNON) CASCABEL
(— ON CHURCH SEAT) MISERICORD
(— ON GUN) CROC LUMP

(— ON HARNESS) HAME
(— ON HORSE'S LEG) FETLOCK
(— ON HORSESHOE) STICKER
(— ON LOCK) FENCE STUMP
(— ON MAST) STOP
(— ON OVARY) STIGMA
(— ON POCKETKNIFE) KICK
(— ON SALMON JAW) GIB
(— ON WHEEL) GUB GROUSER
GROUTER
(— OVER AIR PORT) EYEBROW
(FIREPLACE —) HOB
(JAGGED —) SNUG
(SHARP —) BARB FANG
(SUBMERGED —) KNOLL
(PL.) GRAIN BARLEY
PROJECTOR KINO LANTERN
PLANNER SCHEMER BIOSCOPE
EPISCOPE VITASCOPE
PROLAMIN ZEIN SEINE GLIADIN
HORDEIN KAFIRIN SECALIN
PROLAPSE PTOSIS BLOWOUT
FALLING
PROLETARIAN POPULAR
PROLETARIAT MASSES
PROLIFIC BIRTHY BREEDY BROODY
FECUND FERTILE PROFUSE
TEEMING ABUNDANT FRUITFUL
SPAWNING
(BE —) INCREASE
PROLIX LARGE WORDY DIFFUSE
LENGTHY PROSAIC TEDIOUS
VERBOSE TIRESOME WEARISOME
PROLIXITY REDUNDANCY
PROLOGUE BANS BANNS INDEX
PREFACE
PROLONG DREE LENG LONG SPIN
DEFER DELAY DRIVE ELONG
TWINE DILATE EXTEND LINGER
SPREAD DISPACE PRODUCE
RESPITE SUSTAIN CONTINUE
ETERNIZE LENGTHEN POSTPONE
PROROGUE PROTRACT
PROLONGATION BEAK AORTA
CONUS STIPE STYLE FERMATA
ACROSOME GYNOBASE LABELLUM
PROLONGED GREAT PROLIX
DELAYED EXTENDED SOSTENUTO
PROMENADE BUND MAIL MALL
PIER PROM WALK CORSO FRONT
PASEO PRADO MARINA PARADE
PASEAR ALAMEDA GALLERY
FRESCADE BOULEVARD
(CARRIAGE —) TOUR
PROMETHEUS (BROTHER OF —)
ATLAS MENOETIUS EPIMETHEUS
(FATHER OF —) IAPETUS
(MOTHER OF —) CLYMENE
PROMETHEUS UNBOUND
(AUTHOR OF —) SHELLEY
(CHARACTER IN —) ASIA IONE
EARTH JUPITER MERCURY
PANTHEA HERCULES
DEMOGORGON PROMETHEUS
PROMINENCE BUR NOB BOSS
BURR CUSP KNOB NOOP UMBO
AGGER BULLA CREST GRAIN
OLIVA SWELL TUBER TYLUS
ACCENT CALCAR NODULE
TRAGUS BILLING BUTTOCK
CONDYLE FASHION HAMULUS
KNUCKLE LINGULA AMYGDALA
EMINENCY EMPHASIS GLABELLA

PULVINAR SALIENCE TUBERCLE
MONTICULE PROMONTORY
(PREF.) TUBERCULI TUBERCULO
TUBERI
PROMINENT BIG BOLD BEADY
BRENT GREAT STEEP BEETLE
MARKED SIGNAL BLATANT
BOLTING CAPITAL EMINENT
JUTTING LEADING NOTABLE
OBVIOUS SALIENT AQUILINE
BEETLING MANIFEST STRIKING
NOTICEABLE CONSPICUOUS
(SOCIALLY —) SWELL
PROMISCUOUS LIGHT CASUAL
RANDOM CARELESS
PROMISCUOUSLY TAGRAG
PROMISE VOW AVOW BAND HEST
HETE HOPE HOTE OSSE PASS
PLEA SURE WORD FAITH GRANT
HIGHT TRUTH ASSURE BEHEST
ENGAGE FIANCE HALSEN INSURE
PAROLE PLEDGE PLIGHT PROMIT
BEHIGHT BETROTH WARRANT
CONTRACT COVENANT
GUARANTY BETROTHAL
OBLIGATION
(— IN MARRIAGE) BETROTH
ESPOUSE AFFIANCE
(— TO PAY) NOTE ACCEPT
(— TO TAKE IN MARRIAGE) AFFY
PROMISED VOTARY
(— IN MARRIAGE) SURE HIGHT
ENGAGED
PROMISING APT FAIR BRIGHT
LIKELY PROOFY TOWARD
GRADELY TOWARDLY
PROMISSORY NOTE IOU HUNDI
HOONDI TICKET
PROMONTORY HOE NAB BEAK
BILL HEAD MULL NAZE NESS
NOOK NOUP PEAK SCAW SKAW
TOOT ELBOW MORRO POINT
REACH SNOUT SALIENT
FORELAND HEADLAND
PROMOTE AID HELP LOFT PUSH
AVAIL BOOST EXALT NURSE RAISE
SERVE SPEED ASSIST EXCITE
FOMENT FOSTER LAUNCH PREFER
ADVANCE DIGNIFY ELEVATE
FORWARD FURTHER IMPROVE
PREFECT PRODUCE PROMOVE
SUCCEED SUPPORT INCREASE
SUBSERVE
PROMOTER AGENT FRIEND
ABETTOR BOOSTER BUBBLER
BROACHER HUMANIST
PROJECTOR
(SUFF.) ANT
PROMOTION LIFT REMOVE
ADVANCE PROMOVAL
PROMPT APT CUE MOVE URGE
YARE ALERT FRACK PREST QUICK
READY SERVE SWIFT WILLY
YEDER EXCITE INDITE MATURE
NIMBLE SPEEDY SUDDEN
ANIMATE FORWARD PROVOKE
SUGGEST PUNCTUAL REMINDER
(— TO EVIL) SUGGEST
PROMPTER CUER CALLER
MEMORIST ORDINARY SOUFFLEUR
PROMPTING CALL BEHEST BEHIND
MOTIVE
(SPIRITUAL —) LEADING

PROMPTITUDE ALACRITY

PROMPTLY UP PAT TID TIT SOON
TITE PRONTO YARELY PRESTLY
QUICKLY DIRECTLY SPEEDILY

PROMPTNESS ALACRITY CELERITY
DISPATCH

PROMULGATE SPREAD DECLARE
PUBLISH PROCLAIM

PRONAOS ANTICUM

PRONE APT BENT EASY FLAT FREE
GRUF BUXOM GIVEN GROOF
JACENT LIABLE SUPINE BEASTLY
BESTIAL DORMANT SUBJECT
ADDICTED COUCHANT DISPOSED
DOWNWARD PROPENSE
(— TO TAKE UP FADS) ISMY
(NATURALLY —) PROLIVE

PRONENESS
(SUFF.) **(— TO)** ITIS

PRONG NEB NIB PEG PEW BILL
FANG FORK HOOK PUGH SPUR
TANG TENG TINE TING GRAIN
SPADE SPEAN SPRONG FOURCHE
TICKLER GRAINING
(— FOR EXTRACTING BUNG)
TICKLER
(— FOR FISH) PEW PUGH
(— OF ANTLER) KNAG TIND TINE
POINT
(— OF FORK) SPEAN

PRONGHORN CABREE CABRIT
MAZAME BERENDO BERRENDO

PRONOUN HE IT ME MY WE YE
ANY HER HIM HIS ONE OUR SHE
THY WHO YOU OURS THAT THEM
THEY THOU WHAT WHOM YOUR
THINE WHICH WHOSE ITSELF
MYSELF HERSELF HIMSELF
OURSELF WHOEVER YOURSELF
OURSELVES
(GENDERLESS —) THON

PRONOUNCE SAY PASS ACUTE
SPEAK UTTER PREACH RECITE
TONGUE ADJUDGE BEHIGHT
CENSURE MOUILLE ASPIRATE
(— FREE) ABSOLVE
(— GUILTY) CONDEMN
(— HOLY) BLESS

PRONOUNCED HIGH MARKED
DECIDED HOWLING INTENSE
MOVABLE
(— AS FRICATIVE) GRASSEYE
(— PALATALLY) MOUILLE
(NOT —) SOFT

PRONOUNCEMENT FIAT CURSE
DICTUM DICTAMEN

PRONTO QUICK QUICKLY
PROMPTLY

PRONUNCIATION BROGUE
DICTION ETACISM LIAISON
DELIVERY ENCLISIS ORTHOEPY
(BAD —) CACOEPY CACOLOGY
LABDACISM
(BROAD —) PLATEASM
(CORRECT —) ORTHOEPY
(ROUGH —) BUR BURR

PROOF SAY MARK PULL SLIP TEST
ESSAY PREWE TOKEN TOUCH
TRIAL CLENCH GALLEY ORDEAL
REASON RESULT REVISE ATTEMPT
OUTCOME PROBATE SHOWING
UTTERLY VOUCHER WARRANT
ANALYSIS CACOLOGY DOCUMENT
EVICTION EVIDENCE GOODNESS
MONUMENT
(— OF WRONGDOING) GOODS
(— SPIRIT OF WINE) SVT
(ABSOLUTE —) APODIXIS
(INDIRECT —) APAGOGE
(PL.) STRING WARRANTY

PROOFREADER MARK CAP DELE
STET CARET

PROP LEG BROB BUNT POST REST
SPUR STAY STUD TRIG APPUI
BRACE PERCH PUNCH RANCE
SCOTE SHORE SHOVE SOUSE
SPRAG SPURN STAFF STELL
STOOP STULL COLUMN CROTCH
CRUTCH PILLAR SCOTCH SHORER
STAYER UPHOLD BOLSTER
FULCRUM PINNING STUDDLE
SUPPORT SUSTAIN BUTTRESS
CROTCHET DUTCHMAN
UNDERLAY UNDERSET
(— AS TRAP) TEEL
(— FOR CART) NEAP
(— FOR ROOF OF MINE) GIB
(— UP) CUSHION SCAFFOLD
(PREF.) FULCI

PROPAGANDA BOLOISM
AGITPROP BALLYHOO

PROPAGATE BREED HATCH LAYER
EXTEND SPREAD STRIKE DIFFUSE
GEMMATE PRODUCE PUBLISH
ENGENDER GENERATE INCREASE
MULTIPLY POPULATE TRANSMIT
PROCREATE

PROPAGATION BREED BREEDING
DIVISION INCREASE LAYERAGE
OFFSPRING
(SUFF.) GAM(AE)(IST)(OUS)(Y)
GAMETE

PROPEL ROW CALL CAST FIRE FLIP
KENT POLE PUSH SEND URGE
DRIVE FLICK IMPEL KNOCK PRICK
RANGE SPANK THROW HURTLE
LAUNCH PROJECT
(— BALL) STROKE
(— BOAT) OAR ROW SET KENT
POLE SCULL BUSHWACK
(— BOAT WITH FEET) LEG
(— ONESELF) HAUL
(— PUCK) CARRY
(— SUDDENLY) ZAP

PROPELLER FAN HELIX SCREW
AIRSCREW WINDMILL

PROPENSITY YEN BENT ITCH
LURCH APTNESS IMPULSE
LEANING PRONITY APPETITE
FONDNESS INTEREST TENDENCY

PROPER FIT OWN GOOD JUST
MEET TRUE WELL PREST RIGHT
UTTER COMELY DECENT HONEST
LAWFUL MODEST SEEMLY
CAPITAL CORRECT FITTING
GRADELY SEEMING SKILFUL
THRIFTY ABSOLUTE BECOMING
CONGREVE DECOROUS
FORMULAR IDONEOUS PECULIAR
RIGHTFUL SORTABLE SUITABLE
VIRTUOUS
(APPARENTLY —) SPECIOUS
(BE — TO) BESEEM
(PREF.) CURIO ORTH(O)

PROPERLY DULY WELL FITLY
TRULY ARIGHT FAIRLY FEATLY
GLADLY MEETLY RIGHTLY

PROPERTY AVER BONA DHAN
TOOL WAIF ASSET AUGHT GOODS
GRANT MOYEN STATE STOCK
THING WORTH APPEAL DEVISE
ESTATE HAVIOR KELTER LIVING
MUSHAA REALTY TALENT USINGS
WEALTH ACQUEST APANAGE
CHATTEL DEMESNE ESCHEAT
ESSENCE FACULTY FITNESS
HARNESS HAVINGS QUALITY
WARISON ALLODIAL CATALLUM
HOLDINGS PECULIUM
POSSESSION PARAPHERNALIA
(— BELONGING TO WOMAN)
STRIDHAN
(— FROM WIFE TO HUSBAND) DOS
(— GIVEN BY WILL) DEVISE
(— OF MATTER AT REST) INERTIA
(— SECURED DISHONESTLY) HARL
(— SEIZED BY FORCE) SPOIL
(ABSOLUTE —) ALODIUM
(ENEMY —) HEREM
(LANDED —) DOMAIN ESTATE
DEMESNE PRAEDIUM
(MOVABLE —) GEAR CHATTEL
EFFECTS CATALLUM
(PERSONAL —) FEE BONA GOODS
STUFF INSIGHT PLUNDER
(PRIVATE —) SEVERAL
(RURAL —) FINCA
(STOLEN —) PELF MAINOR
STEALTH
(THEATRICAL —S) PROPS
(WITHOUT —) LACKLAND
(SUFF.) ISM

PROPHECY SPAE WEIRD EXHORT
PREACH PREDICT BODEMENT
FORECAST FORESHOW SOOTHSAY
VATICINE SIBYLLISM PROGNOSTIC

PROPHESY OSSE SPAE AREAD
AUGUR DIVINE EXHORT PREACH
OMINATE PORTEND PREDICT
ARIOLATE FORETELL

PROPHET GAD AMOS JOEL SEER
ANGEL AUGUR DRUID ELIAS
HOSEA JONAH MICAH MOSES
NAHUM SILAS SYRUS ARIOLE
BALAAM DANIEL ELIJAH HAGGAI
ISAIAH MERLIN MORONI NATHAN
PYTHON SAMUEL EZEKIEL
MALACHI SPAEMAN HABAKKUK
JEREMIAH
(PL.) VATES NEBIIM
(PREF.) VATI

PROPHETE, LA (CHARACTER IN —)
JOHN FIDES BERTHA OBERTHAL
(COMPOSER OF —) MEYERBEER

PROPHETESS ANNA ANNE HULDA
SIBYL PYTHIA DEBORAH PHOIBAD
SEERESS VOLUSPA DRUIDESS
SPAEWIFE CASSANDRA
PYTHONESS

PROPHETIC FATAL VATIC MANTIC
FATEFUL FATIDIC MANTIAN
DELPHIAN ORACULAR SIBYLLIC
VATICINAL
(SUFF.) MANTIC

PROPINE TIP GIFT EXPOSE PLEDGE
PROFFER

PROPINQUITY KINSHIP AFFINITY
NEARNESS VICINITY PROXIMITY

PROPITIATE MILD ATONE PACIFY
APPEASE RECONCILE

PROPITIATORY HILASMIC

PROPITIOUS FAIR KIND HAPPY
LUCKY BENIGN DEXTER KINDLY
HELPFUL PRESENT FRIENDLY
GRACIOUS MERCIFUL TOWARDLY
FAVORABLE PROMISING
AUSPICIOUS

PROPONENT BACKER ADVOCATE
SUPPORTER

PROPORTION END LOT DOSE SIZE
CHIME FRAME QUOTA RATIO
SCALE SHARE ACCORD DEGREE
EXTENT FORMAT QUOTUM
ANALOGY BALANCE COMPASS
CONTENT MEASURE EURYTHMY
QUANTITY SYMMETRY
PERCENTAGE
(— OF CATTLE TO GIVEN AREA)
SOUM
(— OF MALT IN BREWING) STRAIK
(— OF REFLECTED LIGHT) ALBEDO
(ALLOTTED —) STENT STINT
(EXACT —) SQUARE
(SMALL —) TITHE

PROPORTIONATENESS CONTOUR

PROPOSAL BID KITE MOVE PLAN
PLEA VOEU GRACE OFFER PARTY
DEMAND FEELER MOTION MOTIVE
PROJECT PROPOSE PURPOSE
OVERTURE SCHEDULE SENTENCE
PROPOSITION
(TENTATIVE —) SNIFF

PROPOSE FACE MOVE PLAN POSE
SHOW WISH OFFER ALLEGE
DESIGN INJECT INTEND MOTION
ADVANCE EXHIBIT IMAGINE
PROPINE PURPOSE SUPPOSE
CONFRONT CONVERSE
PROPOUND
(— FOR DISCUSSION) MOOT
(— RESOLUTION) FIRST
(— TENTATIVELY) SUGGEST

PROPOSITION R FACT AXIOM
MODAL OFFER THEME AFFAIR
CONNEX MEMBER PORISM
GENERAL INVERSE PREMISS
PROBLEM PURPOSE THEOREM
TYCHISM BUSINESS CONTRARY
EMPIREMA IDENTITY IRENICON
JUDGMENT NEGATION OVERTURE
PROPOSAL PROTASIS SENTENCE
SINGULAR SUPPOSAL
(— IN LOGIC) TERMAL OBVERSE
(— LEADING TO CONCLUSION)
PREMISE
(PARTICULAR NEGATIVE —) O
(PRELIMINARY —) LEMMA
(UNIVERSAL NEGATIVE —) E

PROPOUND POSE OFFER POSIT
START STATE INVOKE PROPOSE
PURPOSE

PROPOUNDER HYLICIST

PROPRIETOR LORD LAIRD MALIK
OWNER MASTER PATRON TANIST
YEOMAN ESQUIRE PATROON
ABSENTEE BONIFACE SQUARSON
TALUKDAR YEOWOMAN

PROPRIETY GRACE IDIOM MENSE
ESTATE NATURE REASON
DECENCY DECORUM ESSENCE
FITNESS HOLDING MODESTY
CIVILITY PROPERTY ETIQUETTE

PROPROCTOR RECTOR

PROPULSION DRIFT EJECTION

PROPULSIVE ELASTIC

PRORATE ALLOT ASSESS DIVIDE
APPORTION

PROROGUE DEFER ADJOURN
PROLONG POSTPONE PROTRACT

PROSAIC DRAB DULL FLAT FOOT
PROSE PROSY PROLIX STODGY
STOLID STUPID FACTUAL
HUMDRUM INSIPID LITERAL
TEDIOUS SOULLESS TIRESOME
WORKADAY

PROSCENIUM FRAME STAGE

PROSCRIBE BAN TABU EXILE
TABOO FORBID OUTLAW REJECT
PROHIBIT

PROSCRIPTION EXILE OUTLAWRY

PROSE CHAT PROSY GOSSIP
PROSAIC TEDIOUS SEQUENCE
ELOQUENCE

PROSECUTE LAW SUE HOLD URGE
CARRY ENSUE ACCUSE CHARGE
DEDUCE FOLLOW INDICT INTEND
PURSUE IMPLEAD PROCESS

PROSECUTION PURSUANCE

PROSECUTOR DA FISCAL
PURSUER SAKEBER PROMOTER
QUAESTOR
(PUBLIC —) ACTOR

PROSELYTE CONVERT NICOLAS
NEOPHYTE PURSUANT
(JEWISH —) GER

PROSER HAVERER GRATIANO

PROSODY METER METRICS

PROSPECT HOPE VIEW SCENE
SPECK VISTA CHANCE CHIEVE
FUTURE REGARD SEARCH SURVEY
COMMAND EXPLORE FOSSICK
HORIZON LOOKOUT OUTLOOK
PROJECT RESPECT LANDSKIP
OFFSCAPE
(— FOR GOLD) SPECK
(— WITHOUT SYSTEM) GOPHER
(FORBIDDING —) DESERT

PROSPECTING LOAMING

PROSPECTIVE VIEW WATCH
LOOKOUT EXPECTED

PROSPECTOR SNIPER FOSSICKER
SOURDOUGH
(LONE —) HATTER

PROSPECTUS PROGRAM

PROSPER DO DOW FAY HIE LIKE
RISE THEE CHEVE CHIVE EDIFY
FRAME LIGHT SPEED BATTEN
THRIVE BLOSSOM SUCCEED
WELFARE FLOURISH

PROSPERITY HAP GLEE GOOD
SEEL SONS WEAL IKBAL SONSE
HEALTH THRIFT FORTUNE
SUCCESS THEEDOM WELFARE
FLOURISH
(GOD OF —) FREY
(INCREASE IN —) UPTICK

PROSPERO (DAUGHTER OF —)
MIRANDA
(SERVANT OF —) ARIEL
(SLAVE OF —) CALIBAN

PROSPEROUS UP FAT BEEN BEIN
BIEN BOON GOOD FELIX FLUSH
HAPPY LUCKY PALMY SONSY
EUROUS GILDED SONSIE WELSOM
HALCYON HEALTHY THRIFTY

THRIVEN WEIRDLY SUNSHINE
THRIVING WEALSOME

PROSTITUTE BAG BAT CAT COW
DOG MOB AUNT BAWD DOXY
DRAB HACK MAUX MISS MUFF
PUNK SLUT STEW TART TRUG
BROAD CRACK MAWKS PAGAN
POULE STALE WHORE BULKER
CALLET CHIPPY DEBASE GIRLIE
HARLOT HOOKER LIMMER
MUTTON RANNEL TOMATO
TRADER VIZARD BAGGAGE
BROTHEL CRUISER CYPRIAN
HACKNEY HETAERA HUSTLER
PAPHIAN PINNACE POLECAT
PUCELLE SELLARY BERDACHE
COMMONER CUSTOMER
HACKSTER MAGDALEN MERETRIX
OCCUPANT RUMBELOW
SLATTERN STRUMPET VENTURER
COURTESAN
(PREF.) PORN(O)

PROSTITUTION BORDEL SACKING
BORDELLO HARLOTRY PUTANISM

PROSTRATE LOW FELL FLAT GRUF
RASE RAZE FLING GROOF PRONE
STOOP THROW ATTERR CUMBER
FALLEN REPENT WEAKEN
FLATTEN DEJECTED HELPLESS
OVERCOME PROSTERN
DEPRESSED
(— ONESELF) HURKLE
(BECOME —) FALL

PROSTRATION SHOCK KOWTOW
COLLAPSE
(BURMESE —) SHIKO

PROSY DRY DULL JEJUNE
HUMDRUM INSIPID PROSAIC
PROSISH TEDIOUS TIRESOME

PROTAGONIST HERO ACTOR
LEADER PALADIN ADVOCATE
ANTIHERO CHAMPION

PROTAMINE SALMINE STURINE
CLUPEINE

PROTEAN EDESTAN VARIABLE

PROTECT CAP BANK BIEL BIND
DIKE FEND FORT HILL KEEP REDE
SAVE WARD WEAR BLESS CHAIN
CLOUT COURE COVER FENCE
GANGE GRATE GUARD HEDGE
PAVIS SHADE SHEND UMBER
ASSERT BORROW SHIELD DEFEND
SCREEN SHADOW WARISH
BULWARK CHERISH CUSHION
FASCINE FORFEND SECLUDE
SHELTER SUPPORT WARRANT
BESTRIDE CHAMPION DEFILADE
PRESERVE SAFEGUARD
(— AGAINST RAIN) FLASH
(— BY COVERING) HILL
(— BY WINDING WITH WIRE) GANGE
(— FROM INTRUSION) TILE TYLE
(— IRON OR STEEL) BARFF

PROTECTED SAFE SHADY IMMUNE
CLOUTED GUARDED SHEATHED
SHIELDED
(PREF.) IMMUNO

PROTECTING TUTELAR TUTELARY
SECUREFUL

PROTECTION LEE EGIS HOLD
WARD WING AEGIS ARMOR BIELD
COVER GRITH GUARD SHADE
TARGE TOWER AMULET ASYLUM

AVOWRY CONVOY ESCORT
FENDER REFUGE SAFETY SCONCE
SCREEN SHADOW SHROUD
AUSPICE CUSTODY DEFENCE
HOUSING MANTLET SHELTER
TUITION UMBRAGE WARRANT
BLINDAGE COVERAGE DEFILADE
PASSPORT SECURITY TUTAMENT
TUTELAGE WARDSHIP
SAFEGUARD
(— FOR SAILOR) HORSE
(— FROM LOSS) INDEMNITY
(— FROM RAIN) OMBRIFUGE
(— FROM SUN) HAVELOCK
(— FROM WEATHER) LEWTH
(— RIGHT) MUND
(VALUABLE —) EDMUND
(WISE —) RAYMOND

PROTECTIVE (— SURFACE)
LAGGING

PROTECTOR BIB GUARD BRACER
FAUTOR KEEPER PATRON REGENT
WARRANT DEFENDER GUARDIAN
PECTORAL PRESIDENT
(— OF PROSTITUTE) BULLY
(— OF VINEYARDS) PRIAPUS

PROTEGE WARD PUPIL SMIKE

PROTEIN ZEIN ABRIN ACTIN OPSIN
RICIN SOZIN AVIDIN CASEIN
FIBRIN GLOBIN MYOGEN ALBUMIN
AMANDIN ELASTIN GELATIN
GLIADIN HISTONE HORDEIN
KERATIN LIVETIN MUCEDIN
PROTEID SERICIN ALEURONE
COLLAGEN COLLOGEN FERRITIN
GLOBULIN GLUTELIN GORGONIN
IPOMOEIN PROLAMIN PROPERDIN
PROTAMINE
(RICH IN —S) NARROW

PROTEINASE PAPAIN PEPSIN

PROTEOSE ALBUMOSE ELASTOSE
GELATOSE

PROTESILAUS (BROTHER OF —)
PODARCES
(FATHER OF —) IPHICLUS
(MOTHER OF —) ASTYOCHE
(SLAYER OF —) HECTOR
EUPHORBUS
(WIFE OF —) LAODAMIA
POLYDORA

PROTEST AVER BEEF FUSS HOWL
KICK BROCK CROAK DEMUR
AFFIRM ASSERT BOWWOW
EXCEPT HOLLER OBJECT OBTEST
PLAINT SQUAWK SQUEAL
CONTEST INSPIRE PUBLISH
RECLAIM RHUBARB SCRUPLE
TESTIFY HARRUMPH PROCLAIM
(— AGAINST) ABHOR
(— AGAINST INJUSTICE) HARO

PROTESTANT ALASCAN GENEVAN
GOSPELER HELVETIC HUGUENOT
MORAVIAN SWADDLER

PROTEUS OLM AMOEBA

PROTHESIS CREDENCE PARABEMA

PROTHORAX COLLAR CORSELET
MANITRUNK

PROTOCOL PROCEDURE

PROTOPINE FUMARINE

PROTOPLASM PLASMA PLASSON
SARCODE OVOPLASM PERIPLAST
SOLEPLATE

PROTOPLAST CELL ENERGID

PROTOTYPE IDEAL MODEL
FATHER EXAMPLE PATTERN
ANTITYPE EXEMPLAR

PROTOZOAN AMEBA FORAM
MONAD MONER AGAMETE
ARCELLA BABESIA BODONID
CILIATE PROTIST RADIATE
STENTOR DIDINIUM HYPOZOAN
PARAMECIUM
(PL.) MICROZOA

PROTRACT DRAG DRAW DREE
PLOT SPIN DEFER DELAY DRIVE
TRACT TRAIL TRAIN DILATE
EXTEND LINGER SPREAD
DETRACT PROLONG CONTINUE
LENGTHEN PROROGUE

PROTRACTED DREE LONG DREICH
PROLIX LENGTHY DRAGGING
EXTENDED

PROTRUDE BUG JUT LILL LOLL
PEER POKE POUT BLEAR BULGE
BUNCH POUCH SHOOT START
STICK STRUT SWELL EXSERT
EXTEND EXTRUDE KNUCKLE
PROJECT PROTEND HERNIATE
OUTPOINT OUTREACH OUTSHOOT

PROTRUDING STEEP ASTRUT
BUNCHY GOGGLE BLABBER
EMINENT JUTTING OBTRUSIVE

PROTRUDINGLY ASTRUT

PROTRUSION JAG LAP NOB BURR
KNOB POUT HERNIA SALIENCE
SHOULDER TYLOSOID
PROJECTION

PROTUBERANCE BUD HUB JAG
NOB NUB WEN BEAN BOLL BOSS
BULB BUMP HEEL HUMP JAGG
KNAP KNOB KNOP KNOT LUMP
NODE PUFF SCAB SNAG STUB
UMBO WART BULGE BUNCH
CAPUT GLAND GNARL HUNCH
KNURL SWELL TORUS TUBER
TUMOR BREAST CALLUS HUBBLE
PIMPLE POMMEL CRANKLE
EXTANCY PAPILLA EMINENCE
FLANKARD MAMELEON NODOSITY
SWELLING APOPHYSIS
PROJECTION
(— AT BASE OF BIRD'S BILL) CERE
SNOOD
(— BEARING SPINE) UMBO
(— FROM SWELLING) PUFF
(— IN SIDE OF DEER) FLANKARD
(— ON A CASTING) SCAB
(— ON BONE) CONDYLE EMINENCE
(— ON HORSE'S HOOF) BUTTRESS
(— ON MANDIBLE OF GEESE) BEAN
(— ON SADDLEBOW) POMMEL
(— ON SALAMANDER) BALANCER
(— ON TONGUE) PAPILLA
(KNOBLIKE —) CAPUT
(OCCIPITAL —) INION
(RAGGED —) JAG JAGG
(ROUGH —) HUB
(SKIN —) WEN MOLE WART
PIMPLE
(PREF.) TORO

PROTUBERANT BULGY BUMPY
PROUD STRUT TUMID BUCKED
EXTANT GOGGLE BOTTLED
BULGING BUNCHED EMINENT
GIBBOUS SALIENT SWOLLEN
PROMINENT PROTRUSIVE

(REGULARLY —) CONVEX

PROUD FESS GLAD HIGH IKEY LOFT
PERK RANK SIDE VAIN BRANT
CHUFF GELLY GREAT JELLY LOFTY
NOBLE ORGUL PRIDY SAUCY
STEEP STIFF STOUT VOGIE WINDY
WLONK COPPED ELATED FIERCE
LORDLY ORGUIL PENCEY QUAINT
SKEICH SKEIGH UPPISH UPPITY
VAUNTY HAUGHTY SUBLIME
SWOLLEN TOPPING ARROGANT
EXULTANT GLORIOUS IMPOSING
INSOLENT ORGULOUS SPLENDID
STOMACHY TOPLOFTY
OVERBEARING

PROUDLY HIGH

PROVE TRY FAND FOND PREE
SHOW TEST ARGUE ASSAY EVICT
TAINT TASTE TEMPT ARGUFY
EVINCE SUFFER VERIFY BALANCE
CONFESS CONFIRM CONVICT
DERAIGN IMPROVE JUSTIFY
CONCLUDE CONVINCE EVIDENCE
INDICATE INSTRUCT MANIFEST
(— FALSE) BELIE BETRAY FALSIFY
(— GUILTY) ATTAINT
(— ONESELF) ACQUIT
(— OUT) SERVE
(— TITLE) DEDUCE
(— VALID) DEFEND

PROVED TRIED EXPERT PROBATE

PROVENCAL LANGUEDOC
ROMANESQUE

PROVENDER HAY CORN FEED
FOOD OATS STRAW PABULUM
PROVAND PROVIANT

PROVERB SAW SAY REDE WORD
ADAGE AXIOM CREED GNOME
SOOTH BALLAD BYWORD DITTON
DIVERB MASHAL SAYING SPEECH
SYMBOL WHEEZE BYSPELL
IMPRESA NAYWORD PARABLE
APHORISM FORBYSEN PAROEMIA
SCHOLION SCHOLIUM SENTENCE
SOOTHSAY
(PREF.) PARAMIO PAROEMIO

PROVIDE DO FIT SEE FEND FILL
FIND GIRD LEND LOOK BLOCK
CATER ENDOW ENDUE EQUIP
SPEED STOCK STORE AFFORD
FOISON PURVEY SUBORN SUPPLY
COMPARE EXHIBIT FORESEE
FURNISH INSTORE PREPARE
ACCOUTER APPANAGE DISPENSE
PURCHASE
(— AHEAD OF TIME) ADVANCE
(— AMUSEMENT) DISTRACT
(— FOOD) GRUB CATER SCAFF
(— FOR) FEND SERVE CHEVEYS
CHEVISE PROVANT
(— STINGILY) SKINCH
(— SUPPORT) ESCOT
(— WITH) BESEE
(— WITH DOWRY) DOT
(— WITH HIP-ROOF) COOT
(— WITH LOAN) ACCOMMODATE

PROVIDED IF BODEN FIXED READY
SOBEIT PROVISO INSTRUCT
PREPARED

PROVIDENCE THRIFT ECONOMY
PRUDENCE

PROVIDENT WARY WISE FRUGAL
SAVING CAREFUL

PRUDENT THRIFTY

PROVINCE LAN AREA NOME WALK
AIMAK BANAT FIELD MOUTH
NATAL NOMOS REALM SHENG
SHIRE SUBAH BANNAT EMPIRE
EYALET MALAGA MONTON
OBLAST REGION SIRCAR SPHERE
SYSSEL YAMATO DEMESNE
DONGOLA EPARCHY MUDIRIA
PURVIEW RECTORY VILAYET
APPANAGE DISTRICT FUNCTION
MUDIRIEH NOMARCHY TERRITORY
(SUBDIVISION OF EGYPTIAN —)
KISM
(PL.) OUTLAND

PROVINCIAL HICK BORNE CRUDE
NARROW RUSTIC STUFFY
INSULAR MOFUSSIL SUBURBAN
PAROCHIAL PRESIDIAL

PROVINCIALISM LOCALISM

PROVISION BOARD CHECK GRIST
FODDER MATTER PURVEY
STOVER UNLESS WRAITH
APPREST CAUTION CODICIL
DOWNSET KEEPING SLEEPER
VICTUAL WARNISH WARNISON
(—S FOR JOURNEY) VIATICUM
(BOUGHT —S) ACATES ACATERY
(SUBORDINATE —) ITEM
(PL.) CHOW FOOD JOCK KEEP
LOAN PROG BOUGE CATES
CHUCK SCRAN STORE TERMS
TOMMY ANNONA VIANDS VIVRES
COMMONS WARNAGE WAYFARE
VICTUALS

PROVISO SALVO CAVEAT CLAUSE
CAUTION CONDITION

PROVOCATION TEEN APPEAL
INCENTIVE

PROVOCATIVE GUTTY SALTY
AGACANT PIQUANT IRRITANT
APPEALING

PROVOKE BOG EGG GIG IRE TAR
VEX BEAR DARE HUFF MOVE PICK
STIR TARR TEEN URGE WORK
ANGER ANGRY ANNOY EAGER
EVOKE FRUMP PIQUE TAUNT
TEMPT APPEAL ELICIT EVINCE
EXCITE GRIEVE HARASS INCITE
KINDLE NETTLE PROMPT
SUMMON TICKLE AFFRONT ILLICIT
INCENSE INFLAME INSPIRE
VROTHER CATALYZE IRRITATE

PROVOKING AGACANT

PROVOST JUDGE PRIOR REEVE
KEEPER WARDEN STEWARD

PROW BOW BEAK SPUR STEM
PRORE SNOUT SPERON STEVEN
DIVIDER GALLANT VALIANT
(— OF GONDOLA) FERRO

PROWESS FEAT PROW VALOR
NOBLEY BRAVERY COURAGE

PROWL OWL PROG ROAM LURCH
MOOCH MOUSE RAVEN BREVIT
RAMBLE

PROWLER WALKER SLASHER
TENEBRION

PROWLIKE PROREAN

PROWLING GRASSANT

PROXIMATE NEXT CLOSE DIRECT
CLOSEST NEAREST PROXIME
IMMINENT PROXIMAL

PROXIMITY SHADOW NEARNESS

PRESENCE VICINITY PROPINQUITY
NEIGHBORHOOD

PROXY VICE AGENT VICAR BALLOT
MANDAT PROCTOR
(PL.) ELECTION

PRUDE PRIG COMSTOCK

PRUDENCE CARE METIS ADVICE
CAUTEL WISDOM CAUTION
COUNSEL SLEIGHT FORECAST
FORELOOK

PRUDENT FIT SAFE SAGE WARE
WARY WISE CANNY DOOSE
DOUCE SOLID SYKER VERTY
FRUGAL QUAINT SEKERE SICCAR
POLITIC THRIVEN CAUTIOUS
DISCREET PROVIDENT

PRUDISH NICE PRIM MIMZY
MIMSEY PRIGGISH PUDIBUND
VICTORIA

PRUDISHNESS NICETY PUDENCY

PRUNE COW LOP TOP CLIP COLL
COUL GELD PLUM SNED SPUR
TAME TRIM CLEAN DRESS KNIFE
PLUMB PREEN PRIME PURGE
SHEAR SHRAG SHRED SHRUB
TRASH TWIST DEHORN REFORM
SHRIDE SNATHE SWITCH
AMPUTATE CASTRATE RETRENCH
(— SEVERELY) DEHORN
(IMPERFECTLY RIPENED —) FROG

PRUNING HOOK SARPE CALABOZO

PRUNING KNIFE SERPETTE

PRUNING SHEARS SECATEUR

PRURIENT ITCHY

PRURITIS ITCH

PRUSSIAN PRUTENIC

PRY GAG KEEK NOSE NOTE PEEK
PEEP PEER TEET TOOT JIMMY
LEVER PRIZE SNOOP BREVIT
FERRET PIGGLE POTTER PUTTER
CROWBAR GUMSHOE LEVERAGE
(— ABOUT) OWL MOUSE SNOOK
SCROUNGE
(— INTO) BREVIT
(— INTO AND REPEAT) RAVE

PRYING NOSY NOSEY PEERY
CURIOUS PEEPING

PSALM ODE HYMN SONG DIRGE
GATHA TRACT ANTHEM CANTATE
CHORALE INTROIT MISERERE
(100TH —) JUBILATE
(95TH —) VENITE
(98TH —) CANTATE

PSALMS HALLEL
(BOOK OF —) PSALTER

PSALTERIUM BOOK LYRA
OMASUM PSALTER PSALTERY

PSALTERY GUSLA CITOLE
SAUTREE SAUTERIE

PSEUDO FAKE MOCK SHAM BOGUS
FALSE FEIGNED SPURIOUS
(PREF.) NE

PSEUDOCARP HIP

PSEUDOLOGIST LIAR

PSEUDONYM ALIAS ANONYM
JUNIUS

PSHAW SHA POOH SUGAR SHUCKS

PSITTACOSIS ORNITHOSIS

PSORIASIS ALPHOS

PSYCHE MIND SELF SOUL

PSYCHIATRIST SHRINK ALIENIST
AMERICAN BRILL MEYER OLIVER
SALMON SPITZKA MENNINGER

AUSTRIAN ADLER
GERMAN ZIEHEN JASPERS
SWISS JUNG BLEULER

PSYCHOANALYST FREUDIAN

PSYCHOLOGIST AMERICAN HALL
HOLT LADD DODGE LAIRD RHINE
URBAN WELLS ANGELL BORING
GESELL HAINES HUNTER KOFFKA
PRINCE STRONG TERMAN
WATSON ALLPORT BALDWIN
GODDARD NEWBOLD TROLAND
LANGFELD MARSHALL SEASHORE
PILLSBURY SCRIPTURE
WOODWORTH CARRINGTON
HOLLINGWORTH
ARGENTINIAN INGENIEROS
AUSTRIAN ADLER
DANISH LANGE
ENGLISH WARD BUCKE ELLIS
MYERS OGDEN STOUT SULLY
GURNEY MORGAN AVELING
BARTLETT MAUDSLEY
FRENCH BINET JANET SIMON
BEAUNIS
GERMAN KROH GEISE MARBE
STERN WUNDT KOHLER MULLER
PREYER RUBNER ZIEHEN
JAENSCH MEUMANN
SCOTTISH BAIN
SWISS JUNG

PSYCHOLOGY HORMISM
HEDONICS ANIMASTIC
FORMALISM

PSYCHOPATH MATTOID

PSYCHOSIS INSANITY PARANOIA
SENILITY MELANCHOLIA

PSYCHOTIC MAD CRAZY INSANE

PSYLLA DIMERAN

PSYLLIUM FLEAWORT

PTAH (— EMBODIED) APIS
(ASSOCIATED WITH —) SEKHET

PTARMIGAN RYPE GROUSE
LAGOPODE

PTEROCARPUS LINGOUM

PTEROSAUR DIAPSID

PTERYGIUM WEBEYE

PTERYGOID EXTERNUM

PTERYLA TRACT

PTISAN TEA TISANE

PTOLEMY SOTER
(WIFE OF —) CLEOPATRA

PTOMAINE NEURIN SEPSIN
SAPRINE GADININE PUTRESCINE

PTOUS (FATHER OF —) ATHAMAS
(MOTHER OF —) THEMISTO

PUAH (FATHER OF —) ISSACHAR
(SON OF —) TOLA

PUB BAR INN BISTRO BOOZER
LOUNGE SHANTY TAVERN

PUBBLE FAT FULL PLUMP

PUB-CRAWL BARHOP

PUBERTY
(PREF.) HEBE

PUBES
(PREF.) EPISIO PUBI(O) PUBO

PUBESCENCE DOWN SCURF
YOUTH TOMENT TOMENTUM

PUBESCENT HIRSUTE VILLOUS
(PREF.) HEBE

PUBLIC KUNG OPEN TOWN APERT
CIVIC OVERT WORLD COMMON
SOCIAL VULGAR GENERAL
OMNIBUS POPULAR EXTERNAL

MATERIAL NATIONAL MULTITUDE
(GENERAL —) GALLERY
PUBLICAN BUNG FARMER KEEPER
TAVERNER ZACCHEUS
CATCHPOLL
PUBLICATION BOOK ORDO BIBLE
FOLIO ISSUE SHEET ANNUAL
BLAZON DIGLOT SERIAL WEEKLY
ALMANAC BOOKLET ELZEVIR
JOURNAL MONTHLY WRITING
BIWEEKLY BULLETIN DOCUMENT
EMISSION EXCHANGE PRODROME
EPHEMERIS PERIODICAL
(KIND OF —) MIMEO NUDIE
PUBLIC HOUSE BAR INN PUB
BOOZER PUBLIC SALOON
HOSTELRY POTHOUSE
PUBLICIST AGENT SOLON WRITER
PUBLICITY AIR BLAZE ECLAT
BUILDUP PUFFERY RECLAME
BALLYHOO BROUHAHA DAYLIGHT
HERALDRY PROMOTION
PUBLICIZE CRY PLUG BLURB
BREAK BRUIT HERALD BALLYHOO
HEADLINE PROPAGATE
PUBLIC SQUARE PLAZA PLEIN
ZOCALO
PUBLISH AIR ASH BLOW CALL EDIT
EMIT VEND VENT CARRY ISSUE
PRINT SPEAK UTTER BLAZON
BROACH DEFAME DELATE
EVULGE EXPOSE SPREAD
CENSURE DECLARE DIFFUSE
DIVULGE GAZETTE PROTEST
RELEASE DENOUNCE DISCLOSE
EVULGATE PROCLAIM PROMULGE
(— BANNS OF MARRIAGE) CRY
SPUR OUTASK
(— IN CHURCH) ASK
(— WITHOUT AUTHORIZATION)
PIRATE
PUBLISHER CRIER EDITOR
PRINTER STATIONER
AMERICAN COX LEA BONI DODD
FUNK GINN HOLT KNOX LUCE
NAST OCHS BOBBS BROWN
CAREY GODEY JONES KNOPF
MCRAE SIMON SMITH STERN
CHILDS CURTIS DUTTON FARRAR
FIELDS HARPER HARRIS HEARST
LITTLE MOSHER MUNSEY PAYSON
PUTNAM STOKES THOMAS
UPDIKE VICTOR WALKER WILSON
ZENGER BINGHAM COLLIER
CONNERS LOTHROP MIFFLIN
POULSON SADLIER SCRIPPS
SHUSTER TICKNOR BANCROFT
BARTLETT HOUGHTON RINEHART
SCHUSTER SCRIBNER WAGNALLS
DOUBLEDAY LIVERIGHT
MCCORMICK LIPPINCOTT
AUSTRALIAN THEODORE
DUTCH ELZEVIR
ENGLISH BELL BOHN LANE PAUL
LUCAS MOXON MUDIE UNWIN
WARNE FROWDE KNIGHT LINTOT
MILLAR NEWNES TONSON TOTTEL
BEMROSE BENTLEY BRACKEN
CASSELL CHAPMAN DEBRETT
JENKINS METHUEN NEWBERRY
RICHARDS WHITAKER
HEINEMANN PICKERING
RIVINGTON ROUTLEDGE

VIZETELLY WHITCHURCH
BEAVERBROOK
FRENCH DIDOT HETZEL LEMERRE
PLANTIN HACHETTE GALIGNANI
GERMAN COTTA MEYER FROBEN
PERTHES TEUBNER BAEDEKER
BROCKHAUS TAUCHNITZ
ITALIAN RICORDI
SCOTTISH BLACK SMITH CADELL
CREECH NELSON CHAMBERS
BLACKWOOD CONSTABLE
MACMILLAN
PUCCOON GROMYL ALKANET
GROMWELL BLOODROOT
PUCE FLEA
PUCK ELF LOB PUG BLOW BUTT
DISK POKE POOK DEMON DEVIL
FAIRY PEWKE SPORT RUBBER
SPRITE STRIKE PUCKREL
HOBGOBLIN
PUCKER DRAW FULL RUCK PURSE
REEVE RIVEL TIZZY COCKLE
COTTER FURROW LUCKEN
RUCKLE WRINKLE CONTRACT
AGITATION CONSTRICT
PUCKERED PURSY BULLATE
COCKLED ROUCHED WRINKLED
BULLIFORM
PUCKFIST BRAGGART PUFFBALL
PUCKISH PUXY ELFIN IMPISH
WHIMSICAL
PUDDING DICK DUFF LINK SAGO
BOMBE DOWDY KUGEL MERIT
BURGOO FENDER HACKIN HAGGIS
HAUPIA JAUDIE SPONGE TANSEY
TARTAN DESSERT ADEQUACY
BLOODING HEDGEHOG LIVERING
PANDOWDY WHITEPOT
CHARLOTTE
(— CONTAINING KALE) TARTAN
(— OF FLOUR) DUFF
(BOILED —) HOY
(FRUIT —) HEDGEHOG
(HASTY —) MUSH SEPON SUPAWN
(HAWAIIAN —) HAUPIA
(MEAT —) ISING CHEWET HACKIN
HACKING
(SUET —) KUGEL
PUDDINGWIFE PUDIANO
DONCELLA GLUEFISH
PUDDLE DUB PANT PLUD POOL
PULK ROIL SLAB SLOP SOSS SUMP
FLUSH PLANT PLASH PUDGE
CHARCO FLODGE KENNEL
MUDDLE PUDDER SPLASH
TAMPER CONFUSE PLASHET
SLODDER SPUDDLE BEFUDDLE
(MUD —) DUB SLOP LOBLOLLY
PUDDLEBALL LOOP
PUDDLER'S RABBLE STRIKE
PUDENCY MODESTY DELICACY
PUDGY MIRY BULKY MUDDY
SQUAT CHUBBY SPUDDY
PUDU VENADA
PUEBLO ANASAZI
PUELCHE PAMPA TEHUELET
PUERILE WEAK SILLY BOYISH
JEJUNE TRIVIAL CHILDISH
IMMATURE YOUTHFUL

CAPITAL: SANJUAN
ISLAND: MONA CULEBRA VIEQUES
LAKE: LOIZA CARITE CAONILLAS
MEASURE: CUERDA CABALLERIA
RIVER: CAMUY CANAS YAUCO
ANASCO TANAMA FAJARDO
TOWN: CAYEY COAMO PONCE
ANASCO DORADO MANATI
ARECIBO BAYAMON FAJARDO
GUAYAMA HUMACAO
MAYAGUEZ

PUFF GUF POP BLOW BRAG DRAG
FLAM FLAN GUFF GUST HUFF
PANT PECH SHOW WAFF WAFT
BLURB BLURT ELATE ERUPT
EXTOL FLUFF QUIFF SKIFF STECH
SWELL WHIFF CAPFUL EXPAND
FLATUS BLUSTER EXPLODE
GRATIFY INFLATE WHIFFET
BRAGGART OVERRATE WINDGALL
BOUILLON
(— FROM SHELL BLAST) BURST
(— OF WIND) FLAM TIFT SCART
SLANT FLATUS HUFFLE
(— ON MARIJUANA CIGARETTE)
TOKE
(— OUT) BELL BLUB VENT BLOUSE
BLUBBER EFFLATE INFLATE
(— OUT SMOKE) EFFUME
(— UP) BLOW HUFF RISE BLOAT
HEAVE BLADDER
(— VIOLENTLY) BLAST
(CREAM —) DUCHESSE
(SUDDEN —) FLAN FLAW GUST
PUFFBALL FIST FUZZ PUFF SMOKE
FUNGUS PUFFIN BULLFICE
BULLFIST PUCKFIST SNUFFBOX
PUFFBIRD BARBET MONASE
NUNLET DREAMER NUNBIRD
BARBACOU
PUFFED BLUB BOLLEN BLOATED
SOUFFLE SWOLLEN ARROGANT
INFLATED
(— OUT) BAGGY BOUFFANT
(— UP) RANK POBBY ASTRUT
BLOATED SWOLLEN TURGENT
VENTOSE
(BE — UP) BELL
PUFFER ATINGA BALLER BLOWER
SLIMER TAMBOR BURFISH
EGGFISH BLOWFISH TOADFISH
PUFFIN LOOM PAPE POPE MARROT
MULLET MARROCK WILLOCK
COCKANDY PARAKEET
TOMNODDY TOMNORRY
(HAWAIIAN —) AO
PUFFY SOFT BAGGY BLOAT FAFFY
GUMMY GUSTY PURSY CHUBBY
FLUFFY PURFLY PURSIVE
SWOLLEN BLADDERY BOUFFANT
DROPSICAL
PUG FOX IMP PET BOXER CHAFF
GOUGE SPOOR TRACK TRAIL
CAMOIS CAMUSE GOBLIN
MONKEY MISTRESS PUGILIST
FOOTPRINT
PUGILIST PUG MILLER BRUISER
SLOGGER
PUGNACIOUS BELLICOSE
PUG-NOSED CAMUS CAMUSE
PUISNE PUNY LATER PETTY
JUNIOR YOUNGER INFERIOR

PUISSANCE ARMY FORCE POWER
CONTROL POTENCY PROWESS
DOMINION STRENGTH
PUJUNAN MAIDU
PUKKA GOOD REAL GENUINE
LASTING COMPLETE SUPERIOR
AUTHENTIC
PUKRAS PHEASANT KOKLAS
PULCHRITUDE GRACE BEAUTY
PULE CRY PEEP CHIRP COWRY
WHINE SNIVEL WHIMPER
PULING PULY SPINDLY WHINING
PULITZER PRIZE **(— IN LETTERS)**
BOK LEE NYE AGAR AGEE BATE
BUCK CARO COLT EDEL FEIS GALE
GRAU HART INGE LASH LEVY
MACK MOTT RICE WOUK AIKEN
AKINS ALBEE AUDEN BAKER
BEMIS BENET BRUCE BULEY
CHASE CLAPP CURTI DAVIS
DRURY DUGAN FROST HECHT
ISAAC JAMES KRAMM KUMIN
LEECH MABEE MAMET MOSEL
OPPEN PLATH PUPIN PUSEY
SAGAN TEALE UNGER WELTY
ABBOTT BAILYN BECKER BELLOW
BUTLER CATHER CATTON CREMIN
CROUSE DEGLER DURANT FERBER
FRINGS HANDIN HERSEY HORGAN
KAMMEN KENNAN KIDDER
KINNEL LARKIN LOWELL MAILER
MASSIE MILLAY NORMAN ONEILL
SHAARA TOLAND UPDIKE
WALKER WARNER WILDER
WILSON ZINDEL ASHBERY
BURROWS CHEEVER DILLARD
ERIKSON JUSTICE KAUFMAN
KENNEDY LAFARGE LINDSAY
LITWACK LOESSER MCFEELY
NEMEROV RODGERS SAROYAN
SHEEHAN TUCHMAN VIERECK
BOORSTIN FAULKNER KINGSLEY
MACLEISH MARQUAND MICHENER
SANDBURG SCHORSKE SCHUYLER
SHERWOOD SINCLAIR VANDOREN
HEMINGWAY STEINBECK
HOFSTADTER
(— IN MUSIC) HUSA IVES TOCH
WARD CRUMB KUBIK MOORE
RANDS ROREM BARBER CARTER
HANSON PISTON PORTER
ARGENTO BASSETT COPLAND
MARTINO MENOTTI SCHUMAN
SOWERBY THOMSON WERNICK
ZWILICH COLGRASS DRUCKMAN
KIRCHNER SESSIONS WUORINEN
DELLOJOIO DAVIDOVSKY
DELTREDICI SCHWANTNER
PULL IN PU EAR LUG POO POU
ROG RUG TIT TOW CHUG CLAW
DRAG DRAW DUCT HALE HARL
HAUL HOOK RUGG SWIG TIRE
TREK TUSH TWIG YANK BOUSE
BREAK BUNCH CLOUT DRAFT
HEAVE HITCH IMPEL PLUCK
POLLE PROOF TRICE TWEAK
ASSUME COMMIT GATHER
OBTAIN PLITCH RUGGLE SCHLEP
SECURE TWITCH UPROOT
WRENCH ATTRACT EXTRACT
(— A BELL) SET
(— ABOUT) TEW SOOL TOSE TOZE
MOUSLE

(— APART) RAVE REND TEAR DIVULSE
(— AWAY) AVEL AVELL WREST REVULSE
(— BY EARS) SOLE SOWL
(— DOWN) UNPILE DESTROY DEMOLISH
(— HERE AND THERE) TOOZLE TOUSLE
(— NOSE) SNITE
(— OF DRUM) EAR
(— OFF) CROP DRAW STRIP AVULSE
(— ON FISHING ROD) STRIKE
(— ON ROPE) BOWSE
(— OUT) RAX EXTRACT OUTBRAID
(— QUICKLY) YANK
(— ROUGHLY) WAP TOWSE WOUSE
(— SUDDENLY) TRICE
(— THE LEG) STRING
(— TOGETHER) KNOT ATTRACT
(— TRIGGER) SQUEEZE
(— UP) LOUK
(— UP BY THE ROOTS) ARACE
(— WITH JERK) HOICK SWITCH
(ZIPPER —) SLIDER
PULLDEVIL SCROUGER SCRODGILL
PULLER KNOCKER
PULLER-IN CLICKER
PULLET HEN EAROCK EEROCK EIRACK MABYER POULARD POULAINE
PULLEY RIM CONE DRUM BLOCK FUSEE FUZEE IDLER TRICE WHEEL DRIVEN IDLEBY JOCKEY POLYVE RIGGER SHEAVE SHIVER WHARVE CAPSTAN FERRULE TIGHTER TRUCKLE WHARROW PULLISEE PURCHASE TROCHLEA
(PL.) TRISPAST JACKANAPES
PULLOVER JERSEY SWEATER
PULLULATE BUD TEEM SWARM MULTIPLY
PULMONATE LUNGED
PULMONIC PNEUMONIC
PULP PAP PUG CHUM MUSH BROKE JELLY NERVE SLUSH STOCK STUFF MARROW SQUEEZE SQUELCH
(FOOD —) CHYME
PULPIT PEW TUB AMBO BEMA DESK WOOD CHAIR PREACH ROSTRUM TRIBUNE
(— BOARD) TYPE
(— FOR CHOIR BOOKS) ANALOGION
(MOSLEM —) MIMBAR MINBAR
(OPEN-AIR —) TENT
PULPY SOFT SPEWY FLABBY FLESHY SIDDER SIDDOW BACCATE SQUELCHY
PULSATE BEAT BRIM FLAP PANT PUMP THROB COURSE STRIKE PALPITATE
PULSATION BEAT BEATING HEARTBEAT LIFEBLOOD VIBRATION
(— OF ARTERY) ICTUS
PULSE DAL BEAT DOHL TAKT URAD WAVE POUCE STUFF THROB BATTUTA IMPULSE PULSIDGE SPHYGMUS VITALITY
(PREF.) PALMO SPHYGMO
(SUFF.) CROTIC

PULSING VIBRANT
PULVERIZATION TRIPSIS
PULVERIZE BRAY BUCK DRAG FINE MEAL MULL STUB BRAKE CRUSH FLOUR GRIND POUND BRUISE POWDER ATOMIZE DEMOLISH VANQUISH COMMINUTE MICRONIZE
PULVERIZED FINE POWDERED
PULVERIZER MULLER
PULVERULENT DUSTY CRUMBLY POWDERY
PULVILLUS PAD
PUMA COUGAR PAINTER PANTHER
PUME YARURA
PUMICE PUMEX PUMIE
PUMMEL FIB BEAT DRUB PAIK SLAT POUND SLATE THUMP POUNCE
PUMP GIN GUN FORK JACK COURT FORCE HEART PLUMB SLUSH DOCTOR DORSAY FORCER SINKER VOLUTE BOOSTER DOWNTON EJECTOR EVACTOR PITWORK SLUDGER SYRINGE TOEPLER BEERPULL ELEVATOR INFLATER INJECTOR PULSATOR PULSOMETER
(— ON SHIPS) DOWNTON
(GAS —) BOWSER
(HAND —) GUN
(MINE —) SET
(SET OF —S) LIFT
PUMP DOCTOR GRATHER
PUMPER RACKER
PUMPERNICKEL BOMBERNICKEL
PUMPKIN PEPO CHUMP GOURD PEPON QUASH CASHAW CITRUL CUCURB CUSHAW SQUASH QUASHEY CUCURBIT PEPONIDA
PUMPKINSEED RUFF SUNNY FLATFISH FLOUNDER REDBELLY
PUN NICK WHIM ALLUDE CLINCH QUIBBLE EQUIVOKE PARAGRAM CALEMBOUR PARANOMASIA ANNOMINATION
PUNCH DAB DIG FIB HUB JAB SET BASH BELT BLOW BOFF BUST DING PLUG POKE SETT SOAK SOCK TIFF BUMBO DOUSE DRIFT FORCE GLOGG PASTE PENCH SHORT SLOSH CANCEL INCUSE PATRIX PAUNCH SHAPER STINGO STRIKE TRACER MATTOIR PERLOIR SANGRIA STARTER EMBOSSER GROUNDER PRITCHEL PUNCTURE SWATCHEL THICKSET
(CHASING —) TRACER
(DOG OF —) TOBY
(ETCHER'S —) MATTOIR
(HORSESHOE —) PRITCHEL
(OVAL —) PLAISHER
(WIFE OF —) JUDY
PUNCHBOARD PUSHCARD
PUNCH BOWL SNEAKER
PUNCHCARD (GROUP OF —S) DECK
PUNCHED PERTUSE
PUNCHEON CASK PULE SNAP PUNCH
PUNCHER COWBOY SOCKER
PUNCHINELLO CLOWN BUFFOON PUGENELLO
PUNCH PRESS BEAR DROP

PUNCHY POUNCY FORCEFUL
PUNCTILIOUS NICE EXACT STIFF FORMAL CAREFUL POINTED PRECISE PUNCTUAL
PUNCTUAL DUE EXACT PROMPT CAREFUL PRECISE ACCURATE DEFINITE DETAILED EXPLICIT
PUNCTUATE MARK STOP POINT EMPHASIZE
PUNCTUATION MARK DOT DASH STOP BRACE COLON COMMA PRICK SLASH HYPHEN PERIOD STIGME BRACKET VIRGULE ELLIPSIS SEMICOLON
PUNCTURE HOLE PICK PINK PROD STAB DRILL POINT PRICK PUNCH STICK NEEDLE PIERCE PIQURE DEFLATE DESTROY PUNCTUM CENTESIS PINPRICK
(SUFF.) NYXIS STIXIS
PUNCTURED CRIBLE
PUNDIT SAGE SVAMI SWAMI CRITIC PANDIT TEACHER
PUNGENCY NIP HEAT SALT SNAP ACRIMONY KEENNESS PIQUANCY SALTNESS
PUNGENT HOT TEZ BOLD FELL KEEN RACY RICH SALT TART ACRID ACUTE BRISK NIPPY QUICK SHARP SMART SNELL SPICY TANGY BITING BITTER SHRILL SNAPPY CAUSTIC MORDANT PEPPERY PIQUANT POINTED TELLING CAYENNED PIERCING POIGNANT STABBING STINGING
PUNGI BIN
PUNIC PUNICAL FAITHLESS
PUNISH FIT FIX PAY BUCK CANE COLT COOK CUCK FINE FLOG GATE SORT WIPE ABUSE BIRCH CURSE ORDER SCOUR SHEND SLATE SPILL STOCK STRAP TWINK WREAK AMERCE AVENGE CAMPUS FERULE FOLLOW IMMURE LESSON REFORM SCHOOL STRAFE STRIKE CHASTEN CONSUME CORRECT CORRIGE DEPLETE PENANCE REQUITE SCOURGE CARTWHIP CHASTISE DISTRAIN CASTIGATE
(— BY BLOW ON PALM) PANDY
(— BY COMPENSATION) FINE AMERCE
(— BY CONFINEMENT) GATE
(— BY FINE) MULCT
(— BY LASHING WRISTS) BUCK
PUNISHING HARD GRUELING
PUNISHMENT GIG FINE LASH PAIN PINE RACK SACK WITE YARD BEANS GRUEL LIBEL PANDY PEINE SMART WRACK WREAK DESERT DIRDUM FERULE LESSON PICKET EXAMPLE GALLOWS GANTLET JANKERS PAYMENT PENALTY PENANCE PENANCY REVENGE SCOURGE HERISSON JUDGMENT PUNITION STOCKING SUPPLICE EXECUTION
(CAPITAL —) SCAFFOLD
(MILITARY —) JANKERS
PUNITIVE PENAL PUNITORY
PUNK BAD BOY MUG FUNK JERK MONK POOR PUNG CONCH

SPONK SPUNK AMADOU BUNKUM NOVICE HOODLUM RUFFIAN BEGINNER GANGSTER INFERIOR NONSENSE STRUMPET TERRIBLE TOUCHWOOD
PUNKIE MIDGE MIDGET
PUNNING ALLUSIVE BIVERBAL
PUNSCH ARRACK
PUNSTER WAG SPEED
PUNT BET HIT POY KENT KICK QUANT GAMBLE GARVEY SKERRY
PUNTER BIDDER GAMBLER SCALPER SERVITOR
PUNY WEAK DAWNY DEENY DWARF FRAIL PETTY SCRAM WEARY JUNIOR MAUGER NOVICE PUISNE RECENT SICKLY SPROTY MANIKIN PIMPING QUEECHY SHILPIT YOUNGER DROGHLIN INFERIOR PINDLING RECKLING
(— PERSON) TITMAN
PUP PUPPY WHELP
PUPA EGG NYMPH PUPPET TUMBLER WIGGLER FLAXSEED WRIGGLER CHRYSALIS
PUPIL BOY GYTE TYRO WARD BLACK CADET CHILD ELEVE NORRY NURRY RAPIN TUTEE ALUMNA GRADER INFANT JUNIOR SENIOR LEARNER PAULINE SCHOLAR SOJOURN STUDENT ABSENTEE BLUECOAT DISCIPLE RUGBEIAN SCHOOLER
(— AT HEAD OF CLASS) DUX
(— IN STUDIO) RAPIN
(— OF EYE) BLACK PEARL SIGHT
(ANGLO-INDIAN —) CHELA
(BOARDED —) SOJOURN
(GERMAN —) ABITURIENT
(PREF.) COR(E)(O)
(SUFF.) CORIA
PUPILAGE (WARDSHIP PEDANTISM
PUPPET BABY DOLL DUPE IDOL MOTE BABBY DROLL DUMMY MAUMET MOTION POPPIN STOOGE WAJANG WAYANG GUIGNOL DROLLERY MARIONET MARIONETTE
(— PLAY) WAJANG
(— SHOW) VERTEP
(PREF.) PUPI
PUPPIS STERN
PUPPY FOP PUP DOLL DOUGH WHELP PUPPET
(FEMALE —) GYP
(GREYHOUND —) SAPLING
PURBLIND BISME BISSON
PURCHASABLE VENAL CORRUPT
PURCHASE BUY WIN EARN FISH GAIN KOOP WHIP BOOTY HEDGE PRIZE DUPLEX EFFECT EMPTIO TACKLE ACQUIRE BARGAIN EMPTION PILLAGE PROCURE BARRATRY
(— AND FATTEN CATTLE) HIGGLE
PURCHASER BUYER EMPTOR VENDEE CHAPMAN POULTER SHOPPER CUSTOMER
PURE NET CAST EVEN FAIR FINE FREE FULL GOOD HOLY MERE NEAT PUTE TRUE CLEAN CLEAR FRESH MORAL NAKED SHEER STARK SYCEE UTTER WHITE

WHOLE CANDID CHASTE ENTIRE IMMIXT LIMPID PISTIC SIMPLE VESTAL VIRGIN ANGELIC CATHARI GENUINE PERFECT SINCERE ABSOLUTE ABSTRACT COMPLETE DOVELIKE INNOCENT PRISTINE SERAPHIC SPOTLESS VIRGINAL VIRTUOUS SPIRITUAL
(PREF.) KATHARO

PUREE DAL SOUP CREAM

PURGATIVE PURGE SENNA CALOMEL DIASENE DRASTIC TURPETH ALOEDARY APERIENT CLEANSER ELATERIN EVACUANT CATHARTIC ABSTERSIVE

PURGATORY PAIN SWAMP

PURGE LAX RID FIRE FLUX SOIL CLEAR RHEUM SCOUR DRENCH PHYSIC REMOVE SEETHE SHRIVE SPURGE CHISTKA CLEANSE DETERGE ABSTERGE

PURIFICATION BAPTISM ELUTION LUSTRUM VASTATION

PURIFY TRY BOLT FINE PURE WASH CLEAN PURGE SNUFF BLEACH DISTIL FILTER REFINE SETTLE SPURGE WINNOW BAPTIZE CHASTEN CLEANSE EPURATE EXPIATE LAUNDER MUNDIFY SUBLIME SWEETEN DEPURATE EXORCISE FILTRATE LUSTRATE SANCTIFY SCAVENGE SPRINKLE
(— ORE) DILVE
(— SUGAR) CLAY

PURIFYING SMECTIC DEPURANT

PURIRI TEAK BULREEDY IRONWOOD

PURITAN PRIG SAINT CANTER CROPPY BLUENOSE CATHARAN GOSPELER PRECISIAN ROUNDHEAD

PURITANICAL BLUE STRICT GENTEEL PRECISE

PURITANI, I (CHARACTER IN —) ARTHUR ELVIRA TALBOT WALTON HENRIETTA
(COMPOSER OF —) BELLINI

PURITY PURE ASSAY HONOR WHITE CANDOR SATTVA VIRTUE FINESSE CHASTITY FINENESS PURENESS
(— OF BREED) PEDIGREE

PURL RIB EDDY KNIT PEARL UPSET RIPPLE TOTTLE CAPSIZE OVERTURN

PURLIEU HAUNT
(PL.) BOUNDS CONFINES ENVIRONS

PURLIN RIB

PURLOIN CAB CRIB WEED ANNEX BRIBE FILCH STEAL SWIPE FINGER PILFER PIRATE CABBAGE SNAFFLE SURREPT ABSTRACT SCROUNGE

PURPLE GAY VIOL REGAL SHOWY ARGYLE BLATTA BLOODY CROCUS EVEQUE MIGNON ARDOISE FUCHSIA FUCHSIN HEATHEN LOGWOOD PETUNIA PONTIFF PURPURE AMARANTH BURGUNDY CAMERIER CYCLAMEN EGGPLANT EMINENCE IMPERIAL MAUVETTE MULBERRY WISTARIA

(DELICATE —) MAUVE
(VISIBLE —) RHODOPSIN
(PREF.) PORPHYR(O) PURPUREO PURPURI PURPURO

PURPLE FISH MUREX

PURPLE GALLINULE SULTAN SULTANA HYACINTH

PURPLE LAND (AUTHOR OF —) HUDSON
(CHARACTER IN —) JOHN LAMB ANITA MARCO COLOMA LUCERO MARCOS MONICA SANTOS ANSELMO BARBUDO CALIXTO GANDARA HILARIO ISIDORA PAQUITA PERALTA RICHARD DEMETRIA MARGARITA CARRICKFERGUS

PURPLE LOOSESTRIFE KILLWEED
PURPLE MEDIC ALFALFA
PURPLE RAGWORT JACOBY
PURPLE SANDPIPER REDLEG REDLEGS ROCKBIRD

PURPORT FECK GIST PORT DRIFT SENSE TENOR DESIGN EFFECT IMPART IMPORT INTEND INTENT BEARING MEANING PROFESS PURPOSE COVERING DISGUISE STRENGTH

PURPOSE GO AIM END GOAL IDEA MAIN MEAN MIND MINT PLAN SAKE TALK TEND VIEW WEEN WILL ARTHA CAUSE ETTLE HEART LEVEL POINT SCOPE STUDY THINK DESIGN DEVICE EFFECT INTEND INTENT OBTENT PREFIX REASON SCHEME COMPASS COUNSEL DESTINE EARNEST IMAGINE MEANING PROPOSE THOUGHT DEVOTION FUNCTION PLEASURE PROPOUND DISCOURSE
(ALLEGED —) PRETEXT
(FIXED —) HEART
(INSIDIOUS —) CAUTEL
(MORAL —) ETHOS

PURPOSEFUL AIMFUL POINTED
PURPOSELESS WASTE AIMLESS FECKLESS
PURPOSIVE TELIC HORMIC
PURPURA MUREX PURPLES PELIOSIS
PURPURE GOLP GOLPE PURPLE MERCURY
PURR MURR THRUM WHURL DUNLIN

PURSE BAG CLY JAN BUNG CLAY CLOY FISC KNIT POKE PUSS SKIN BULSE BURSE DUMMY FUNDS MEANS POUCH SPUNG COMMON FOLLIS GIPSER POCKET PUCKER READER SHAMMY ALMONER GIPSIRE LEATHER SPORRAN BUCKSKIN BURSICLE CRUMENAL AUMONIERE POCKETBOOK
(PREF.) BURSI

PURSE CRAB PAGURID
PURSER CLERK BURSAR BOUCHER PINCHGUT NIPCHEESE

PURSING MIMP
(— OF MOUTH) PRIM

PURSLANE PURPIE PUSSLY PIGWEED PUSSLEY PORTULACA
PURSLANE TREE SPEKBOOM

PURSUANCE SUING SEQUENCE

PURSUE BAY RUN SUE HUNT SEEK CHASE CHEVY CHIVY ENSUE HOUND QUEST SLATE STALK TRADE COURSE FOLLOW GALLOP TRAVEL BEDEVIL HOTFOOT CONTINUE PRACTICE
(— ZIGZAG COURSE) TACK

PURSUER FOLLOWER PLAINTIFF QUESTRIST

PURSUIT FAD HUNT SUIT CAPER CAUSE CHASE CHEVY CRAFT HOBBY COURSE SEARCH ASSAULT ACTIVITY ENTREATY PROSECUTION
(— OF WISDOM) PHILOSOPHY
(FAVORITE —) MEAT

PURSUIVANT BUTE MARCH FALCON ORMOND ATHLONE CARRICK ANTELOPE DINGWALL FOLLOWER

PURSY FAT OBESE PUFFY ASTHMATIC

PURULENT PYIC ATTRY ATTERY

PURVEY PANDER SUPPLY FORESEE PROVIDE

PURVEYOR CATER TAKER ACHUAS PROWER CATERER ACHATOUR MANCIPLE

PUS WARE AMPER FESTER MATTER WORSUM QUITTER
(PREF.) PURI PURO PY(O)
(CONTAINING — AND GAS) PYOPNEUMO

PUSH CA DUB JAM JOG JUR PUT BANG BIRR BOIL BOOM BORE BUNT DING DUSH FLOG KENT PICK PILT PING PORR POSS POTE SHOG STOP BLITZ BOOST BRUSH BUNCH CROWD CRUSH DRIVE DUNCH ELBOW GOOSE HUNCH NUDGE PINCH POACH POUSE SCAUT SHOVE SKELP STICK STOVE EXTEND HURTLE HUSTLE JOGGLE JOSTLE POTTER PROPEL THRING THRONG THRUST ASSAULT IMPETUS IMPULSE OPERATE PERPLEX SHUFFLE THRUTCH CONTRUDE INCREASE SHOULDER STRAITEN DISMISSAL
(— ALONG) TUSH
(— APART) SPREAD
(— ASIDE) SHOG
(— BY STICK) KENT POLE
(— FORWARD) BUCKET ADVANCE
(— GENTLY) NUDGE
(— INTO) INVADE
(— MONEY) SPIFF
(— ON) BEAR YERK
(— OUT) DEBOUT LAUNCH
(— RUDELY) BARGE HORSE HUSTLE
(— TO FULL STRIDE) EXTEND
(— TOGETHER) CONTRUDE
(— UP) BOOST
(— WITH ELBOW) ELBOW HUNCH
(— WITH FEET) DIG SCAUT
(— WITH HEAD) BUNT BUTT
(STRONG —) BEVEL

PUSH BUTTON PUSH PRESSEL
PUSHCART BARROW TROLLEY
PUSHER PLUNGER TRAILER TRAMMER WHEELER
PUSHING OBTRUSIVE PROTRUSIVE

PUSHY FORWARD AGGRESSIVE
PUSILLANIMOUS WEAK TIMID FEEBLE COWARDLY TIMOROUS
PUSS CAT FACE HARE CHEET CHILD MOUTH RABBIT BAUDRONS
PUSTULE NOB BEAL BURL KNOB POCK PUSH QUAT WART ACHOR AMPER BLAIN WHEAL WHELK BLOTCH FESTER PIMPLE TETTER ANTHRAX BLISTER ERUPTION WHEYWORM

PUT DO BET LAY PIT SET BANG BUTT FILL GIVE GROW PILT REST URGE ADAPT APPLY DIGHT DRIVE FOCUS PLACE STALL STATE STEAD STEEK STELL WAGER ASSIGN BESTOW DECAMP IMPOSE INVEST PHRASE REPOSE SPROUT THRUST DEPOSIT EMPLACE EXPRESS INFLICT SUBJECT
(— AN END TO) DATE SNIB ABATE NAPOO SNUFF SPIKE STASH STILL STINT SOPITE STANCH ABOLISH ASSUAGE EXPIATE SATISFY ABROGATE DEMOLISH SURCEASE
(— ANOTHER IN PLACE OF) RELIEVE
(— APART) DISPART
(— ASIDE) BLOW HAIN SAVE SHUNT REJECT SHUFFLE
(— AT REST) HUSH
(— AWAY) STOW COVER ELONG HUTCH SHIFT RECOND DIVORCE
(— BACK) REMIT REMISE
(— BACK INTO USE) RESTORE
(— BEFORE) PROFER ANTEPONE
(— DOWN) LAY DEMIT QUASH QUELL DEPOSE SQUASH DEPRESS OPPRESS REPRESS SILENCE DIMINISH SUPPRESS
(— EDGE ON) TED
(— FLAX UPON A DISTAFF) DIZEN
(— FORTH) GEM BLOW CAST GIVE PUSH EXERT LANCE PROFER STRETCH
(— FORTH BLOSSOMS) GEM
(— GRAIN IN BARN) END
(— IN) ENTER INSERT INTROMIT
(— IN AGONY) THROE
(— IN CHARGE) COMMIT
(— IN CLAIM) PRETEND
(— IN COMPETITION) PIT
(— IN DANGER) SCUPPER
(— IN DREAD) ADRAD
(— IN MOTION) AROUSE
(— IN OPERATION) LAUNCH
(— IN ORDER) DO SET REDD SIDE SORT TRIM DIGHT MENSE SHIFT TRICK ADJUST DAIKER GRAITH ORDAIN SETTLE ARRANGE CLARIFY DISPOSE REDRESS INSTRUCT
(— IN PLACE) POSE
(— IN POSSESSION) SEISE
(— IN PRISON) WARD
(— INFORMATION INTO) ADDRESS
(— INTO BARN) END
(— INTO CASE) SHEATHE
(— INTO CIRCULATION) EMIT SPRING
(— INTO ECSTASY) ENTRANCE
(— INTO EFFECT) EXECUTE SANCTION
(— INTO IRONS) BOLT

(— INTO RHYTHM) METER METRE
(— LIQUOR INTO CASK) TUN
(— OFF) DAFF DOFF HAFT DEFER
DELAY DEMUR FOIST PARRY
REMIT REPRY SHIFT TARRY
THROW LINGER RETARD SHELVE
ADJOURN FORSLOW PROLONG
RESPITE POSTPONE PROROGUE
PROCRASTINATE
(— ON) DON HYPE APPLY CRACK
DRAPE ENDUE MOUNT STAGE
ASSUME INVEST ADDRESS
(— ON AIRS) PROSS FINICK REVEST
(— ON ALERT) ALARM
(— ON COVER) HACKLE
(— ON GUARD) ALERT CAUTION
(— ON HAT) COVER
(— ON PRETENSE) AFFECT
(— ON SALE) SHOP
(— ON SHORT ALLOWANCE) SCRIMP
(— ON STRING) ENFILE
(— OUT) GET OUT DOUT OUST
DOWSE EVICT EXERT OUTED
SLAKE SLOCK RETIRE DISMISS
EXCLUDE EXTINCT FORJUDGE
(— OUT BATSMAN) SKITTLE
(— OUT OF ACTION) HAMPER
(— RIGHT) AMEND
(— ROAD METAL ON) STEEN
(— SUDDENLY) CLAP
(— THROUGH A STRAINER) TAMMY
(— TO FLIGHT) AFLEY FEAZE FLEME
GALLY
(— TO RIGHTS) SORT DIGHT
(— TO SHAME) DASH ABASH
SHEND UPBRAID
(— TO SLEEP) OPIATE SOPITE
SOPORATE
(— TO USE) STOW APPLY BESTOW
(— TO WORK) HARNESS
(— TOGETHER) ADD JOIN BUILD
COMPILE COMPOSE CONCOCT
CONFECT PREPARE ASSEMBLE
COMPOUND
(— UP) ANTE ERECT FLUSH
DISPENSE

(— UP HAY) BOTTLE
(— UP WITH) GO BEAR BIDE HACK
ABIDE BROOK ENDURE SUFFER
COMPORT STOMACH SWALLOW
TOLERATE
(— UPON) GAMMON
(— WITH ANOTHER) APPOSE
(SUFF.) STOLE
PUTAMEN PYRENE
PUTCHER PUTLOG PUTCHEN
PUTLOCK
PUTREFACTION ROT DECAY
SEPSIS
(SUFF.) SEPSIS SEPTIC
PUTREFACTIVE SEPTIC
(PREF.) SEPTICO
PUTREFY ROT ADDLE DECAY
SWEAT FESTER POLLUTE
PUTRESCE
PUTRESCENT PUTRID ROTTEN
PUTRID FOUL RANK SOUR VILE
LOUSY ADDLED RANCID ROTTEN
CORRUPT DECAYED FRIABLE
VICIOUS DEPRAVED
MALODOROUS
(PREF.) SAPR(O) SEPTI SEPTO
(SUFF.) SEPSIS SEPTIC
PUTT CLOWN BORROW GOBBLE
PUTTEE PAT PATA GAITER
BANDAGE LEGGING
PUTTER FUSS MESS MUCK POKE
TRUCK CADDLE DAWDLE MUCKER
MUCKLE PIDDLE TINKER FRIGGLE
PUTTY BEDDING
PUTTYROOT CRAWFOOT
PUTZ CRECHE
PUXY SWAMPY QUAGMIRE
PUZZLE CAP GET SET BEAT CRUX
DEAD LICK POSE BEFOG GRIPH
POSER QUEER REBUS STICK
BAFFLE BOTHER ENIGMA FICKLE
FOITER GLAIKS JIGSAW KITTLE
RIDDLE CONFUSE MYSTERY
MYSTIFY NONPLUS PERPLEX
STICKER TAISSLE TANGRAM
TRANGAM ACROSTIC BEFUDDLE

BEWILDER CONFOUND DISTRACT
DUMFOUND ENTANGLE INTRIGUE
REMBLERE CROSSWORD
PUZZLED ASEA PERPLEXED
PUZZLING KNOTTY CURIOUS
KNOTTED RIDDLING DIFFICULT
PROBLEMATIC
PYCNANTHEMUM KOELLIA
PYCNOGONID SPIDER
PYGARG ADDAX OSPREY
PYGIDIUM PODEX
PYGMALION (AUTHOR OF —) SHAW
(BELOVED OF —) GALATEA
(CHARACTER IN —) HILL LIZA
CLARA HENRY ALFRED FREDDY
HIGGINS EYNSFORD DOOLITTLE
PICKERING
(FATHER OF —) BELUS MUTGO
AGENOR
(MURDERED BY —) SICHAEUS
(SISTER OF —) DIDO
(STATUE FASHIONED BY —)
GALATEA
PYGMY ELF AKKA AMBA DOKO
ACHUA AFIFI ATOMY BATWA
DWARF GNOME PIXIE PIGMEW
WOCHUA ACHANGO ASHANGO
MANIKIN DWARFISH NEGRILLO
VAALPENS DANDIPRAT
PYGMY GOOSE GOSLET
PYGMY RATTLESNAKE
MASSASAUGA
PYGOSTYLE VOMER
PYKNIC SQUAT STOCKY STHENIC
MUSCULAR
PYLADES (COMPANION OF —)
ORESTES
(FATHER OF —) STROPHIUS
(MOTHER OF —) ANAXIBIA
(SON OF —) MEDON STROPHIUS
(WIFE OF —) ELECTRA
PYRAMID BENBEN HOPPER
TEOCALLI
(— OF CRAYFISH) BUISSON
(DOUBLE —) TWIN ZIRCONOID
(INVERTED —) HOPPER

PYRAMIDAL HUGE ENORMOUS
IMPOSING
PYRAMIDICAL TAPER
PYRAMUS (LOVER OF —) THISBE
PYRAZINE ALDINE PIAZIN DIAZINE
PYRE BALE PILE TOPHET BONFIRE
BALEFIRE
PYRIDOXIN ADERMIN
PYRITE BALE MUNDIC
(PL.) BRAZIL STANNITE
FIRESTONE MAGISTRAL
MARCASITE
PYROCLES (BROTHER OF —)
CYMOCLES
(FATHER OF —) ACRATES
PYROLA LIMONIUM SHINLEAF
PYROMANIAC FIREBUG ARSONIST
PYRONE CUMALIN
PYROPHYLLITE PENCIL
PYROTECHNICS FIREWORKS
PYROXENE ACMITE AUGITE SALITE
SAHLITE AEGIRITE DIALLAGE
DIOPSIDE WOLLASTONITE
PYROXENITE ARIEGITE MARCHITE
OSTRAITE NIKLESITE
PYRRHIC DIBRACH
PYRRHULOXIA GROSBEAK
BULLFINCH
PYRRHUS (FATHER OF —) AEACIDES
(MOTHER OF —) PHTHIA
(SON OF —) PTOLEMY SOPATER
(WIFE OF —) ANTIGONE
PYRROLE AZOLE
PYTHON ADJIGER PEROPOD
ANACONDA
PYTHONESS WITCH PHITONES
PYTHONIC HUGE INSPIRED
ORACULAR MONSTROUS
PROPHETIC
PYX BOX CAPSA CASKET CHRISM
VESSEL BINNACLE CHRISMAL
CIBORIUM
PYXIDIUM CAPSULE

Q

Q KU CUE KUE QUEEN QUEUE QUEBEC

QATAR (CAPITAL OF —) DOHA
(TOWN OF —) RUWAIS UMMSAID

QUA HERON QUABIRD

QUACK PUFF WHACK CROCUS SALVER SUBTLE EMPIRIC IMPOSTOR OPERATOR SANGRADO CHARLATAN
(PREF.) PSEUD(O)

QUACKERY HUMBUG

QUADRAGESIMA LENT

QUADRANGLE QUAD CLOSE COURT TETRAGON

QUADRANT BOW RADIAL SQUARE QUARTER TETRANT ALTIMETER

QUADRATE SUIT AGREE IDEAL QUADER SQUARE PERFECT BALANCED

QUADRIC CONICOID

QUADRILATERAL TRAPEZIA TETRAGRAM
(PL.) TESSARA

QUADRILLE CONTREDANSE
(PL.) LANCERS

QUADRILLION
(PREF.) ASTRA PETA QUEGA

QUADRILLIONTH
(PREF.) FEMTO

QUADROON QUATERON TERCERON

QUADRUPED BABIRUSA

QUADRUPLE FOURBLE FOURFOLD

QUADRUPLED
(PREF.) TETRAKIS

QUADRUPLET FOURLING QUARTOLE

QUAFF QUAX TOOT DRINK QUASS WAUCHT CAROUSE TRILLIL

QUAG BOG MARSH SHAKE QUIVER

QUAGMIRE BOG FEN GOG HAG QUA SOG LAIR PUXY QUAW MARSH MIZZY SWAMP MORASS PUDDLE SLOUGH BOGMIRE PUCKSEY WAGMOIRE

QUAHOG CLAM COHOG VENUS BULLNOSE

QUAIL COW LOWA WEET COLIN COWER DAUNT ORTYX QUAKE SPOIL WASTE BLENCH CURDLE FLINCH SHRINK TURNIX WITHER DECLINE HEMIPOD TREMBLE BOBWHITE
(YOUNG —) SQUEALER

QUAINT DRY ODD NAIVE BIZARRE STRANGE FANCIFUL HANDSOME PICTURESQUE
(— IN APPEARANCE) FUNKY

QUAKE JAR QUOG RESE CHILL QUAIL SHAKE DITHER QUIVER SHIVER WAMBLE FLUTTER SHUDDER TREMBLE
(PREF.) PALLO

QUAKER ASPEN HERON FRIEND OBADIAH WHACKER HICKSITE TREMBLER BEACONITE BROADBRIM SHADBELLY
(— STATE) PENNA PENNSYLVANIA

QUAKER GRAY ACIER

QUAKING ASPEN QUAKY TREPID SHAKING TREMBLING

QUAKING GRASS BRIZA COWQUAKE WAGWANTS

QUALIFICATION NATURE RESERVE SHADING CAPACITY

QUALIFIED FIT ABLE MEET FITTED FITTEN LIKELY CAPABLE ELIGIBLE SUITABLE AUTHENTIC
(NOT —) INAPT INHABILE

QUALIFIER MODIFIER

QUALIFY FIT DASH ADAPT ALLAY ALLOY EQUIP HEDGE ENABLE MODIFY SOFTEN TEMPER ABSOLVE CERTIFY ENTITLE LICENSE PREPARE GRADUATE MODERATE RESTRAIN RESTRICT

QUALITIES
(SUFF.) ERY ICS

QUALITY Y BRAN BUMP CHOP COST FEEL GUNA LEAD SORT COLOR GRACE STATE TRAIT ASSIZE BARREL FABRIC STRAIN THREAD TIMBER TIMBRE ADJUNCT CALIBER KINSHIP STATURE ACCIDENT MOVEMENT PROPERTY TONEBRAND
(— OF MIND) CALIBER CALIBRE
(— OF PERSONAL EMOTIONS) PATHOS
(— OF PHOTOGRAPH) CONTRAST
(— OF TONE) TIMBRE
(— OF VOWELS) LENGTH
(— PECULIAR TO ONESELF) SEITY
(AESTHETIC —) TASTE
(ARTISTIC —) VIRTU
(ATTRACTIVE —) TAKE
(BASIC —) GRAIN
(BASIC —S) STUFF
(COLOR —) TONE
(ESSENTIAL —) ALLOY SPECIES SUCHNESS
(GOOD —) THEW
(HEREDITARY —) STRAIN
(IMPECCABLE —) FINISH
(INCISIVE —) BITE
(INNATE —) LARGESS
(INTELLECTUAL —) BROW
(NATURAL —) TARAGE
(OBJECTIONABLE —) ANILITY
(OF HIGH —) FRANK
(OF LOW —) SHLOCK SCHLOCK
(PERVASIVE —) AROMA
(PHYSICAL —S) BOTTOM
(PRIMAL —) GUNA
(PUNGENT —) SNAP
(RELATIVE —) RATE

(SECONDARY —) OVERTONE
(SPATIAL —) MAGNITUDE
(SPRINGY —) SPINE
(STRUCTURAL —) TEXTURE
(SUBDUED —) SHADE
(SUBTLE —) BOUQUET
(SUPERIOR —) SUPER FINENESS
(TRIED —) TOUCH
(UNESSENTIAL —) ACCIDENT
(UNUSUAL —) SURD
(WAVY — OF HAIR) FLIX
(SUFF.) ACITY ANCE ANCY CY ENCE ENCY HEAD HOOD ICE ICITY ILITY ITY MENT NESS SHIP TY
(— THAT FILLS) FUL FULL
(CHARACTERIZED BY —) SOME

QUALITY STREET (AUTHOR OF —) BARRIE
(CHARACTER IN —) BROWN LIVVY PATTY SUSAN BLADES PHOEBE THROSSEL VALENTINE

QUALM CALM DROW PALL NAUSEA SQUEAM SCRUPLE

QUALMISH TEWLY SICKISH SQUEAMISH

QUAMOCLIT MOONFLOWER

QUANDARY FIX PUXY PUZZLE TANGLE DILEMMA NONPLUS SWITHER DOLDRUMS JUNCTURE

QUANDONG PEACH

QUANT RYPECK

QUANTIC NONIC OCTIC SEPTIC SEXTIC QUADRIC QUINTIC

QUANTIFIER PREFIX

QUANTITATIVE METRIC

QUANTITY BAG JAG SUM SUP BODY DEAL DISH DOSE FECK JAGG LIFT MASK SOME SOUD WARE BATCH BREAK CLASH GRIST KITTY SIEGE TROOP WHEEN ACTION ADDEND AMOUNT BAGFUL BOTTLE BUDGET DICKER EFFECT FOTHER HANTLE NUMBER PARCEL SPINOR THRAVE CONTENT FOOTAGE PORTION QUANTUM GLASSFUL KNIFEFUL LADLEFUL PARAMETER
(— OF ARROWS) SHEAF
(— OF BUTTER) CHURNING
(— OF CLOTHES) BUCKING
(— OF COTTONSEED) CRUSH
(— OF CUT TREES) FALL
(— OF DRINK) HOOP DRAFT DRAUGHT
(— OF ELECTRICITY) FARADAY
(— OF EXPLOSIVE) CHARGE
(— OF FISH OR GAME) TAKE CATCH DRAFT DRAUGHT
(— OF GRAIN) GAVEL
(— OF HAY) LOCK TRUSS
(— OF IRRIGATION WATER) DUTY
(— OF LIQUID) DROP JAUP SLASH GOBBET JABBLE

(— OF LIQUOR) HEELTAP
(— OF LUMBER) RUN
(— OF MEAL) MELDER
(— OF METAL) BLOW
(— OF MUD) CLASH
(— OF NARCOTICS) BINDLE
(— OF PAPER) TOKEN
(— OF PRODUCE) BURY
(— OF RAISINS) FRAIL
(— OF THREAD) LEASE
(— OF WOOD) HAG FATHOM
(ESTIMATED —) WEY
(EXCESSIVE —) GLUT SPATE
(FIXED —) CONSTANT
(GREAT —) HOST MORT MUCH HIRST SHOAL SIGHT STORE BARREL FOREST SLATHER TUMMELS
(LARGE —) ACRE BOLT DEAL FECK HEAP MASS PECK SCAD SLEW FLOOD FORCE GRIST JORUM POWER SCADS SHEAF STACK STORE BUCKET BUSHEL DICKER DOLLOP GALLON MATTER MELDER CLUTHER SKINFUL HECATOMB MOUNTAIN PLURALITY
(LEAST —) BEDROCK
(MINUTE —) DRAM DROP SHADE SCRUPLE PARTICLE
(NOTEWORTHY —) CHUNK
(RELATIVE —) DEGREE
(SETTLED —) SIZE
(SIZABLE —) SCUMP
(SMALL —) ACE BIT SUP CURN DASH DUST HAET HAIR HARL IOTA PEAK SOSH SPOT CANCH PRILL SMACK SPICE SQUIB TOUCH JOBBLE MORSEL PICKLE SAMPLE SONGLE STIVER CAPSULE CURTSEY DRIBBLE DRIBLET EPSILON HANDFUL MODICUM SMICKET SPATTER TODDICK FARTHING MOUTHFUL PENNORTH SCANTLET PENNYWORTH
(UNDIRECTED —) SCALAR
(VARYING —) SKID
(SUFF.) **(— THAT FILLS)** FUL FULL

QUANTUM MAGNON PHONON PHOTON ISOSPIN

QUAPAW KWAPA ARKANSAS

QUARANTINE DETAIN ISOLATE SANCTION

QUARENTENE ROOD FURLONG

QUARREL JAR WAP YED BEEF CHIP DEAL FEUD FRAY FUSS JARL JOWL MIFF NIFF ODDS PICK PLEA SPAT TIFF WHID BRACK BRAWL BRIGE BROIL FLITE FLUSK GRUFF HURRY JOWER NOISE PIQUE SCOLD SCRAP SHINE STOUR UPSET WRALL AFFRAY BARNEY BLOWUP BREACH BREEZE BRIGUE

DEBATE DIFFER DUSTUP FRACAS
FRATCH GARROT JANGLE
MATTER QUARRY RIPPET SQUARE
SQUEAL STRIFE THREAP THREEP
THWART BRABBLE BRATTLE
DISGUST DISPUTE FACTION
OUTCAST PRABBLE RUCTION
SIMULTY STASHIE SWAGGER
TUILZIE WRANGLE DISAGREE
MOORBURN SCRAFFLE SPLUTTER
SQUABBLE TRAVERSE
(— IN WORDS) JANGLE
(NOISY —) ROW FRACAS KICKUP
(PETTY —) MIFF SPAT TIFF
QUARRELING BICKER CONTEK
CHIDING CONTECK
QUARRELSOME RIXY UGLY
ROWTY FEISTY CURRISH SCRAPPY
DRAWLING FRAMPOLD FRATCHED
PETULANT PHRAMPEL BELLICOSE
BUMPTIOUS FRACTIOUS
LITIGIOUS CONTENTIOUS
(NOT —) AMICABLE
QUARRELSOMENESS SQUARING
WARIANCE
QUARRIED (NOT —) LIVE
(PREF.) ORYCTO
QUARRIER FACEMAN QUARION
QUARRY DELF GAME LODE MEAT
CHASE DELFT DELPH PLUCK
LATOMY REWARD LATOMIA
LOZENGE
(HAWK'S —) MARK
QUARRYMAN SCABBLER
SCAPPLER
QUART SHANT WHART
(METRIC —) LITER
(ONE-HALF —) PINT
(TWO —S) MAGNUM
(1-8TH —) GILL
(2 —S) FLAGON
(4 —S) GALLON
QUARTE FOURTH
QUARTER AIRT PART STUD EAVER
GRITH TRACT BARRIO BEHALF
BESTOW CANTON COLONY
FARDEL HARBOR SECTOR
CONTRADA FAUBOURG FIERDING
STANDARD POBLACION
(— IN BATTLE) GRITH
(— OF A POUND) TRIPPET
(— OF BEEF OR MUTTON) BOUT
(— OF CITY) BLOCK GHETTO
(— OF COMPASS) PLAGE
(— OF FLAG) CANTON
(— OF HOUR) POINT
(— OF HUNDRED) FIERDING
(— OF YEAR) RAITH
(— ONESELF) SORN
(— UPON) LAY
(JEWISH —) ALJAMA
QUARTERING LASKING
CHUMMAGE
QUARTER NOTE CROTCHET
QUARTER REST SOSPIRO
QUARTERS BOTHY BILLET BOTHIE
LIVERY MENAGE FARDELS
CHUMMERY DIGGINGS
LODGMENT
(— FOR IMMIGRANTS) HOSTEL
(— OF SALVATION ARMY)
BARRACKS
(HIGH —) AERY EYRY AERIE EYRIE

(JUNIOR OFFICERS' —) GUNROOM
(MEN'S —) SELAMLIK
(MONASTERY —) FRATRY
QUARTET FOURSOME
QUARTILE SQUARE TETRAGON
QUARTO FOURS
QUARTZ IRIS ONYX SARD AGATE
CHERT FLINT PRASE TARSO
TOPAZ JASPER MORION PEBBLE
PLASMA SILICA ALENCON CITRINE
CRYSTAL RUBASSE SINOPLE
AMETHYST BASANITE SARDONYX
SIDERITE YENTNITE BUHRSTONE
BURRSTONE
QUARTZITE GANISTER SILCRETE
QUASH CASS CRUSH QUELL SPIKE
SQUAT SOPITE CASSARE
PEREMPT SUPPRESS
QUASI
(PREF.) SEMI
QUAT FOUR GLUT SQUASH
SATIATE UPSTART
QUATERNION TETRAD QUADRATE
QUATREFOIL TRESSURE
(DOUBLE —) EIGHTFOIL
QUAVER QUAP CROMA SHAKE
TRILL WAVER CHROMA FALTER
QUIVER WABBLE WOBBLE WRIBLE
FREDDON VIBRATE
QUAVERY WARBLY UNSTEADY
QUAY KEY POW QUAI LEVEE
BUNDER STRAND
QUEACH BOG FEN MARSH
THICKET
QUEASINESS KECK SICKNESS
QUEASY NICE SICK SQUEEZY
DELICATE NAUSEATED
SQUEAMISH
QUEBEC (LAKE OF —) MINTO
BIENVILLE MISTASSINI
(TOWN OF —) AMOS HULL AMQUI
LAVAL MAGOG PERCE BASSIN
VERDUN JOLIETTE MONTREAL
LAPRAIRIE
QUEBRACHO BREAKAX AXMASTER
IRONWOOD AXBREAKER
QUEBRADA BROOK GULLY RAVINE
FISSURE
QUECHUA INCAN KICHUA
QUEEN REG DAME FERS LADY
MEDB RANI AEDON BEGUM FIERS
RANEE ATOSSA REGINA ROXANA
TAILTE TAMARA ARGANTE
ATHALIA CANDACE JOCASTE
OMPHALE PHEARSE STATIRA
TITANIA BRUNHILD GERTRUDE
GLORIANA GUINEVER MAHARANI
(— AND KING OF TRUMPS) BELLA
(— CITY) CINCINNATI
(— IN CHESS) FERS LADY FIERS
(— OF CLUBS) SPADILLA
(— OF DENMARK) GERTRUDE
(— OF ETHIOPIA) CANDACE
(— OF FAIRY LAND) MEDB
GLORIANA
(— OF GEORGIA) TAMARA
(— OF GOTHS) TAMORA
(— OF HEARTS) ELIZABETH
(— OF HEAVEN) HERA
(— OF JUDAH) ATHALIA
(— OF LYDIA) OMPHALE
(— OF SHEBA) BALKIS BILKIS
(— OF SPADES) BASTA LIZZY

(— OF THE ADRIATIC) VENICE
(— OF THE ANTILLES) CUBA
(— OF THE EAST) ZENOBIA
(— OF THEBES) JOCASTA
(— OF TRUMPS) HONOR
(FAIRY —) MAB ARGANTE TITANIA
(INDIAN —) RANI SUNK MAHARANI
(MOHAMMEDAN —) BEGUM
QUEEN ANNE'S LACE UMBEL
QUEEN BEE KING
QUEEN ELIZABETH DIANA ORIANA
CYNTHIA
QUEENFISH WAHOO CROAKER
DRUMFISH
QUEENLY HAUGHTY REGINAL
MAJESTIC
QUEENROOT YAWSHRUB
QUEEN'S-DELIGHT YAWSHRUB
QUEENSLAND HEMP SIDA
JELLYLEAF
QUEER HEX ODD RUM HARM
DICKY DIPPY DROLL FAINT FUNNY
GIDDY NUTTY RUMMY COCKLE
FIFISH HIPPED QUEASY QUISBY
UNIQUE AMUSING COMICAL
CURIOUS DISRUPT ERRATIC
STRANGE TOUCHED WHIMSIC
FANCIFUL OBSESSED PECULIAR
(— THING) QUOZ
QUEERNESS ODDITY
QUEEST RINGDOVE
QUELL DIE CALM FLOW HUSH KILL
QUAY SLAY ABATE ALLAY CRUSH
QUASH QUIET YIELD PACIFY
PERISH REDUCE SOOTHE SPRING
STANCH STIFLE KILLING REPRESS
SQUELCH SUPPRESS
QUEME QUIM HANDY WHEAM
COMELY PLEASE GRATIFY
PLEASANT
QUENCH COOL DAMP SIND ALLAY
CHECK CRUSH SLAKE SLOCK STILL
STANCH STIFLE ASSUAGE
SLOCKEN AUSTEMPER
QUENCHED EXTINCT
QUENCHER STANCH
QUENCHING FRITTING
**QUENTIN DURWARD (AUTHOR OF
—)** SCOTT
(CHARACTER IN —) CARL CROYE
LOUIS LESLEY PHILIP PIERRE
TOISON BALAFRE CHARLES
DURWARD EBERSON HERMITE
LAMARCK LUDOVIC QUENTIN
TRISTAN WILLIAM CRAWFORD
HAMELINE ISABELLE HAYRADDIN
JAQUELINE MAUGRABIN
CREVECOEUR
QUERCINE OAKEN
QUERECHO VAQUERO
QUERELA AUDITA
QUERENT INQUIRER PLAINTIFF
QUERN KERN MILL METATE
MILLSTONE
QUERULOUS WHINY FRETFUL
PEEVISH NATTERED PETULANT
IRRITABLE
QUERY ASK DOUBT DEMAND
INQUIRE INQUIRY QUESTION
QUEST ASK BAY GAPE SEEK
DEMAND EXAMINE PURSUIT
SEEKING VENTURE
QUESTING OUTREACH

QUESTION ASK HOW SPY POSE
QUIZ TALK ARGUE DOUBT DREAD
QUERY ACCUSE CHANCE CHARGE
DEMAND LEADER MATTER
PONDER REASON SHRIVE
EXAMINE INQUIRE INQUIRY
PROBLEM PURPOSE SCRUPLE
OVERTURE RELEVANT RESEARCH
STICKLER CATECHISE
(— AMBIGUOUSLY WORDED)
RIDDLE
(— FRETFULLY) RAME
(BAFFLING —) POSER
(PERPLEXING —) STUMPER
(RHETORICAL —) EROTEMA
(UNSOLVED —) CRUX
(ZEN —) KOAN
QUESTIONABLE FISHY QUEER
SHAKY UNSAFE BATABLE
CLOUDED DUBIOUS DOUBTFUL
PROBLEMATIC
(NOT —) DECENT
QUESTIONER APPOSER INQUIRER
QUESTIONING DUBIOUS
QUIZZICAL
QUESTION MARK QUERY QUAERE
EROTEME
QUESTIONNAIRE POLL
INVENTORY
QUETCH STIR TWITCH
QUETZAL QUESAL TROGON
QUEUE CUE COLA LINE BRAID
PIGTAIL CROCODILE
QUEY KOY WHY WHEY HEIFER
QUIBBLE COG PUN BALK CARP
QUIB QUIP CAVIL DODGE EVADE
QUIRK SALVO AMBAGE BAFFLE
BICKER HAFFLE PALTER BRABBLE
CAPTION CHICANE QUIBLET
QUIDDIT QUILLET SHUFFLE
PETTIFOG QUILLITY SCRAFFLE
CONUNDRUM
QUIBBLING CHICANERY
QUICA OPOSSUM SARIGUE
QUICK APT RAD YAP FAST FLIT
GLEG KECK KEEN LISH LIST PERT
RATH RIFE SNAP SOON WHAT
WHIT WICK YARE AGILE ALIVE
APACE BRISK CHEAP FLEET
HASTY MERRY NIFTY NIPPY
PREST RAPID READY SHARP
SHORT SNACK SNELL SWIFT
SWITH TOSTO TRICK VISTO
YARRY ACTIVE CLEVER FACILE
KITTLE NIMBLE PROMPT PRONTO
SNAPPY SPEEDY SUDDEN
DARTING SCHNELL SHUTTLE
DEXTROUS TRIPPING CITIGRADE
(— AND NEAT) DEFT
(— AS A FLASH) WHIP
(— IN PERCEPTION) ACID
(— IN RESPONSE) GNIB
(— TO DETECT) SMOKY
(— TO FLARE UP) GASSY
(— TO LEARN) APT
(— TO MOVE) YARE
(LIGHT AND —) VOLANT
(PREF.) OXY TACHEO TACHISTO
TACHO TACHY
QUICKEN PEP MEND STIR WHET
HURRY SPEED ACUATE AROUSE
HASTEN INCITE KINDLE REVIVE
VIVIFY ANIMATE ENLIVEN

PROVOKE REFRESH SHARPEN
EXPEDITE INSPIRIT ACCELERATE
QUICKENING FLICKER REVIVAL
STIRRING
QUICKLY TID TIT CITO FAST RIFE
SOON TIVY WHIP YARE NEWLY
RADLY RATHE SHARP SKELP
SNACK SNELL SWITH TIGHT
WIGHT YEPLY ASTITE BELIVE
HOURLY PRESTO PRONTO RASHLY
EFTSOON PRESTLY READILY
SPEEDILY WIKIWIKI
(— AND WITH FORCE) SWAP
(MORE —) TIDDER TITTER
STRETTO
QUICKNESS HASTE SPEED
ACUMEN AGILITY SMEDDUM
ACTIVITY CELERITY DISPATCH
KEENNESS SAGACITY
(MENTAL —) NOUS SLEIGHT
LEGERITY
QUICKSAND FLOW SYRT SYRTIS
SWALLOW
QUICK-SELLING LEEFTAIL
QUICKSILVER OREMIX MERCURY
TIERRAS HEAUTARIT
QUICK-SPEAKING PROMPT
QUICK-TEMPERED DONCY DONSY
PEPPERY IRASCIBLE
QUICK-WITTED APT SHARP
SMART NIMBLE KNOWING
QUID FID CHEW SOVEREIGN
(— OF TOBACCO) CUD FID
QUIDDANY JELLY SYRUP
CODINIAC
QUIDDITY QUIBBLE WHATNESS
QUIDNUNC GOSSIP BUSYBODY
QUIESCENCE KAIF STASIS
DORMANCY
QUIESCENT QUIET LATENT STATIC
RESTING INACTIVE
QUIET QT ST COY LAY CALM COSH
DEAD DUMB EASE EASY HUSH
LOUN LOWN LULL REST ROCK
SNUG SOFT WEME ACCOY CANNY
CIVIL DOWNY LEVEL PEACE
PEASE QUATE QUELL QUEME
RESTY SALVE SHADY SILKY SLEEP
SOBER SQUAT STILL SUANT
WHIST DREAMY GENTLE PACIFY
PLACID RETIRE SAUGHT SEDATE
SERENE SETTLE SILENT SMOOTH

SOFTLY SOOTHE SOPITE STEADY
STILLY HUSHFUL ORDERLY
REQUIEM RESTFUL SILENCE
COMPOSED DECOROUS PEACEFUL
TRANQUIL UNRUFFLE
(— DOWN) DILL
(MAKE —) ALLAY
(STEALTHILY —) SLINKY
QUIETEN SOPITE
QUIETISM MOLINISM
QUIETLY LOW FAIR CANNY STILL
WINLY EVENLY GENTLY SOFTLY
TIPTOE
QUIETNESS REST REPOSE
SERENITY
QUIETUDE CALM INERTION
QUIETUS REST DEATH RELEASE
QUILL COP PEN RIB PIRN FLOAT
STALK BOBBIN FESCUE PINION
SLEEVE BRISTLE CALAMUS
PRIMARY TRUNDLE
(— FOR WINDING THREAD) COP
(— OF FEATHER) BARREL
(PORCUPINE —) PEN
QUILLBACK SAILFISH SKIMBACK
QUILLWORT ISOETES FERNWORT
QUILT BEAT GULP WALT WELT
WHIP DUVET REZAI CADDOW
CHALON PALLET THRASH
SWALLOW MATTRESS POULTICE
COMFORTER
QUILTING MARCELLA
QUIMPER NICE
QUINCE SKEG COYNE ANGERS
SQUINCH JAPONICA
(BENGAL —) BEL BAEL BALE BHEL
QUINCE SEED CYDONIUM
QUININE KINA SPECIFIC
(PREF.) CHIN(O)
QUINK BRANT
QUINONE EMBELIN
QUINSY ANGINA PRUNELLA
QUINTAIN FAN
QUINTE FIFTH
QUINTESSENCE CREAM ELIXIR
CLYSSUS OSMAZOME
QUINTILLION
(PREF.) EXA NEBU
QUINTILLIONTH
(PREF.) ATTO
QUINTUPLE QUINARY FIVEFOLD
QUINIBLE

QUIP GIBE JAPE JEST JOKE CRACK
QUIRK SALLY SCOFF TAUNT
CONCEIT QUIBBLE
QUIRA CAOBA ROBLE HORMIGO
VENCOLA MACAWOOD
QUIRE CHOR SEXTERN
(20 —S) REAM
(PL.) INSIDES
QUIRK BEND KINK QUIP TURN
CLOCK CROOK TWIST CONCEIT
QUIBBLE FLOURISH PAROXYSM
MANNERISM PECULIARITY
QUIRQUINCHO PICHI PELUDO
QUIRT WHIP ROMAL
QUIS WOODCOCK
QUISLING APOSTATE
QUIT GO DROP NASH PART QUAT
AVOID BELAY CEASE DOUSE
LEAVE SHIFT SHOOT STASH
WHITE BEHAVE CIVITE DESERT
DESIST FOREGO RESIGN SECEDE
VACATE ABANDON FORSAKE
RELEASE UNTENANT
QUITCH COUCH QUICK SCUTCH
TWITCH
QUITCLAIM DEED ACQUIT
RELEASE DISCHARGE
QUITE SO ALL BUT GEY BRAW
EVEN FAIR FREE FULL JUST PLAT
WELL CLEAR CLOSE FULLY SHEER
STARK CLEVER DAMNED ENOUGH
JUSTLY MERELY TOTALLY
PERFECTLY
(NOT —) HARDLY
(PREF.) DE
QUITERIA (HUSBAND OF —)
CAMACHO
QUITRENT CANON
QUITS EVEN EVENS UPSIDES
QUITTER PUS SLAG PIKER
COWARD JUMPER SHIRKER
TURNBACK
QUIVER DIRL QUAG QUOG BEVER
NIDGE QUAKE SHAKE TRILL
WAVER WIVER BICKER COCKER
DIDDER DINDLE SHEATH SHIMMY
SHIVER TREMOR WAMBLE
DORLACH FLUTTER FRISSON
SHUDDER TREMBLE TWIDDLE
TWINKLE TWITTER VIBRATE
FLICHTER WERSLETE
(PREF.) PALLO

QUIVERING ASPEN AGUISH
DIDDER DITHER QUAGGLE
QUAKING AGITATED ATREMBLE
QUIVER TREE KOKERBOOM
QUIXOTIC ERRANT IMAGINARY
VISIONARY
QUIZ ASK GUY HOAX MOCK CHAFF
QUEER EXAMINE QUESTION
RIDICULE
QUIZZICAL ODD QUEER QUIZZY
CURIOUS WHIMSICAL
QUO KA
QUOD JAIL QUAD PRISON
QUOIN COIN ANGLE GOIGN
CORNER LOZENGE KEYSTONE
VOUSSOIR
QUOIT CIST DISC DISH DISK LINER
DISCUS HOBBER CROMLECH
QUOMODO HOW WAY MEANS
MANNER
QUONDAM OLD ONCE WHILE
FORMER ONETIME SOMETIME
QUORATEAN KAROK
QUORUM CORAM HOUSE MINYAN
MAJORITY
QUOTA PART BOGEY SHARE
QUOTIENT PROPORTION
QUOTATION TAG PRICE QUOTE
EXTRACT SNIPPET EPIGRAPH
(— DEVELOPED INTO ESSAY) CHRIA
QUOTATION MARK GUILLEMET
QUOTE CITE COAT COTE MARK
NAME NOTE ADDUCE ALLEGE
RECITE REPEAT EXCERPT
EXTRACT OBSERVE REHEARSE
(— SARCASTICALLY) FLOUT
QUOTH CO KO CUTH QUAD QUOD
SAID SPOKE UTTERED
QUOTIDIAN DAILY TRIVIAL
ORDINARY
QUOTIENT QUOTE FRACTION
MILLESIMAL
QUO VADIS (AUTHOR OF —)
SIENKIEWICZ
(CHARACTER IN —) ACTE NERO
PAUL CHILO LYGIA PETER URSUS
CROTON EUNICE GLAUCUS
VINICIUS PETRONIUS TIGELLINUS
QUTB POLE

R

R AR ROGER ROMEO
  (UVULAR —) BURR
RA RE RAE SHU TEM ATMU BACIS
  HORUS MENTU KHEPERA SOKARIS
RAAMAH (FATHER OF —) CUSH
  (SON OF —) DEDAN SHEBA
RABBAN MASTER TEACHER
RABBET CHECK GROOVE
  BACKJOINT FILLISTER
RABBI TANA AMORA CACAM
  HAKAM TANNA MASTER SABORA
  KHAKHAM TEACHER GAMALIEL
  SABORAIM
  (PL.) AMORAIM TANNAIM
RABBIT BUN REX TAN BUNT CONY
  JACK POLE RACK BUNNY CAPON
  CREAM CUNNY DUTCH FRIER
  LAPIN ANGORA ASTREX CONEEN
  HAVANA OARLOP PARKER POLISH
  SILVER TAPETI WOOLER BEVEREN
  CONYNGE FLEMISH LEPORID
  SNOWSHOE WARRENER
  (— BURROW) CLAPPER
  (— FUR) CONY SCUT CONEY FLICK
  LAPIN FLITCH
  (— MEAT) LAPAN
  (— SKIN) RACK
  (— TAIL) SCUT
  (— WARREN) CONYGER
  (CASTRATED —) CAPON
  (FEMALE —) DOE
  (MALE —) BUCK
  (YOUNG —) KITTEN
  (PL.) FLICK WARREN
RABBITFISH SPINY
RABBLE MOB TAG GING HERD
  RAFF ROUT SCUM FRAPE SCAFF
  SCUFF TRASH MEINIE RADDLE
  RAFFLE RAGTAG RASCAL TAGRAG
  DOGGERY PUDDLER RABBLER
  RANGALE TRAFFIC BRAGGERY
  CANAILLE RAGABASH RIFFRAFF
  VARLETRY RASCALITY
  CLAMJAMFRY
  (DISORDERLY —) HERD
RABBLE-ROUSER DEMAGOG
RABID MAD RAGING FRANTIC
  FURIOUS RABIOUS RABITIC
  FRENZIED RAVENING VIRULENT
RABIES LYSSA MADNESS PIBLOKTO
  RAVENING
  (PREF.) LYSSO RABI
RACCOON COON COATI GUARA
  TEJON AGUARA MAPACH
  WASHER AGOUARA ARCTOID
  RATTOON RINGTAIL CRABEATER
RACE CAP CUP LOG ROD RUN
  BENT CONE DASH DRAG GEST
  HUMP KIND LINE NAME RAIS
  RAZE RING RINK TEAM TRAM
  BLOOD BREED BROOD BRUSH
  CASTE CHEVY CORSO DERBY
  FLESH HOUSE ISSUE PLATE

PURSE RATCH REACH ROUTE
SPEED STAKE STAMM STIRP
STOCK BROOSE CHEVVY COURSE
FAMILY NATION PEOPLE PHYLON
RUNOFF SPRING STIRPS STRAIN
STRIND BIOTYPE CENTURY
CLAIMER CLASSIC HACKNEY
HUNDRED KINDRED LINEAGE
MATINEE NURSERY PROGENY
PROSAPY RACEWAY REGATTA
STADIUM FUTURITY HANDICAP
MARATHON WALKOVER
OFFSPRING ORIENTEERING
(— A HORSE) CAMPAIGN
(— AT WEDDING) BROOSE BROUZE
(— FOR BALL-BEARINGS) CONE
(— OF BARLEY) BENT
(— OF GODS) VANIR
(— OF PEOPLE) VANS AMALS
  VANIR HAZARA SAKAIS YADAVA
  BAMBUTE FIRBOLG GIANTRY
  NISHADA RASENNA REPHAIM
  AMALINGS
(— OF UNDERGROUND ELVES)
  DROW
(— OF WINDMILL) CURB
(HORSE —) AGON DERBY PLATE
  SPRINT MATINEE FUTURITY
  WALKOVER
(HUMAN —) MAN MANKIND
  SPECIES MORTALITY
(IMPROMPTU —) BRUSH
(JUMPING —) SCURRY
(LENTEN —S) TORPIDS
(LONG —) ENDURO
(MILL —) LADE
(MOTORCYCLE —) SCRAMBLE
  MOTOCROSS
(PRELIMINARY —) HEAT
(ROWING —) SCULLS REGATTA
(RUNNING —) MILE RELAY SPRINT
  HUNDRED HURDLES
(SHORT —) BICKER
(SHORT-DISTANCE —) DASH
  SCURRY SPRINT
(SKI —) SLALOM DAUERLAUF
(TIDAL —) ROOST
  (PL.) FOURS
  (PREF.) ETHN(O) GEN(O) PHYL(O)
RACECOURSE LIST OVAL PIST
  RING TURF EPSOM CAREER
  CIRCUS CURSUS DROMOS STADIE
  STRETCH GYMKHANA SPEEDWAY
  (PREF.) DROM(O)
  (SUFF.) DROME
RACEHORSE DOG PONY PACER
  RACER CHASER SLEEPER
  TROTTER BANGTAIL
  (— THAT HAS NEVER WON) MAIDEN
  (INFERIOR —) PLATER HAYBURNER
  (2-YEAR OLD —) JUVENILE
  (PL.) RUCK
RACEME STRIG PANICLE

RACEMOSE BOTRYOSE
RACER CRACK SNAKE RUNNER
  BICYCLIST CINDERMAN
RACETRACK OVAL DROMOS
  FURLONG AUTODROME
RACEWAY CANAL TRACK GROOVE
  CHANNEL FISHWAY
RACHEL POWDER
  (FATHER OF —) LABAN
  (HUSBAND OF —) JACOB
  (SISTER OF —) LEAH
  (SON OF —) JOSEPH BENJAMIN
RACHIS SPINE SPINDLE
  (— OF HOP STROBILE) STRIG
RACHITIS RICKETS
RACIAL GENTILE GENTILIC
  PHYLETIC
RACIST COLOR
RACK GIN RAK RAT TUB BINK
  BUCK CASE HACK HECK SHOG
  TACK AMBLE BRAKE DRIER DRYER
  FLAKE FRAME POKER THROW
  TOUSE TRAIN WRACK WRECK
  WRING CIRCLE CRATCH CUDGEL
  ENGINE NIPPER PULLEY TREBLE
  WRENCH AFFLICT AGONIZE
  PENRACK POTTARO TORMENT
  TORTURE BARBECUE EQUULEUS
  PINEBANK SAWHORSE
  (— ATTACHED TO WAGON)
  SHELVING OUTRIGGER
  (— FOR BARRELS) JIB
  (— FOR CHINAWARE) FIDDLE
  (— FOR DISHES) BINK
  (— FOR FEEDING) HACK HAYRACK
  (— FOR FODDER) HECK CRATCH
  (— FOR PLATES) CREEL
  (— FOR STORAGE) FLAKE
  (— IN THRESHER) SHAKER
  (DRYING —) CRIB TREBLE
  (WOODEN —) BUCAN
RACKED WRUNG TORTURED
RACKET BAT DIN GAME RORT
  BANDY MUSIC RAZOO CLAMOR
  CROSSE DRIVER HUBBUB HUSTLE
  RAQUET RATTLE BUSINESS
  REVELING STRAMASH
  (PART OF —) CAP BUTT CORD GRIP
  HEAD HEEL TAPE YOKE CROWN
  FLAKE SHAFT HANDLE PALLET
  STRING THROAT BINDING
  SHOULDER THROATPIECE
  (TENNIS —) SCUFE
RACKETEER HOOD HUSTLER
  GANGSTER
RACKETT CERVALET CERVELAT
RACKING FIERCE
RACKMAN TOPMAN
RACON BEACON
RACONTEUR STORYTELLER
RACQUET CROSSE GAZELLE
RACY GAMY LEAN SEXY JUICY
  SALTY SMART SPICY LIVELY

RISQUE PIQUANT PUNGENT
ZESTFUL SPIRITED MERACIOUS
RAD EAGER QUICK READY AFRAID
  ELATED
RADAR (— NAVIGATION SYSTEM)
  LANAC
  (— SYSTEM) OBOE
RADARSCOPE PPI HSCOPE
RADDAI (BROTHER OF —) DAVID
  (FATHER OF —) JESSE
RADDLE PIT BEAT SCAR RAVEL
  RUDDLE THRASH SEPARATOR
RADHA (FOSTER SON OF —) KARNA
  (HUSBAND OF —) ADHIRATHA
RADIAL RAY QUADRANT
  (PREF.) RADIO
RADIANCE RAY GLOW LEAM
  GLARE GLEAM GLINT GLORY
  LIGHT SHINE LUSTER AUREOLA
  GLITTER SPLENDOR
RADIANT BEAMY SHEEN SHINY
  ABLAZE BRIGHT GOLDEN LUCENT
  SHEENY AURORAL BEAMFUL
  BEAMING FULGENT LAMBENT
  GLORIOUS LUSTROUS RELUCENT
  SPLENDID BRILLIANT
  (— INTENSITY) J
  (PREF.) STILPNO
RADIATE RAY BEAM POUR SHED
  SHINE EFFUSE SPREAD EFFULGE
  EMANATE ACTINOID
RADIATED PENCILED STELLATE
RADIATION AURA LIGHT
  INFRARED
  (— DOSAGE) REM REP
  (— UNIT) LANGLEY
  (UNIT OF —) REM
RADIATOR HEATER EMANATOR
  (SET OF —S) STACK
RADICAL KEY SURD BASAL GROUP
  RADIX ROUGE ULTRA CAPRYL
  HEROIC CAPITAL CAPROYL
  DRASTIC EXTREME FORWARD
  HERETIC JACOBIN LEFTIST
  LEVELER LIBERAL PRIMARY
  CARDINAL LOCOFOCO
  (CHEMICAL —) ACYL AMYL CARYL
  CETYL GROUP ACETYL ADENYL
  CAPRYL PHENYL PHYTYL
  HALOGEN LINALYL CARBAMYL
  QINNAMAL
  (SUFF.) **(ACID —)** OYL
  (BIVALENT —) YLENE
RADICALISM EXTREMISM
  JACOBINISM
RADICEL ROOTLET
RADICLE (— THAT DEVELOPS IN
  GRAIN) COME
RADIENT ORIENT
RADIO AIR SET WIRELESS
  (— OPERATOR) HAM SPARKS
  (— SYSTEM) TBS
RADIOGRAM FLIMSY

RADIOGRAPH EXOGRAPH SKIAGRAM

RADIOISOTOPE TRACER

RADISH RUNCH DAEKON DAIKON RIFART CADLOCK CRADLOCK CRUCIFER CROSSWEED

RADIUS RAYON SPOKE SWEEP THROW ADRADIUS

RADIX BASE ROOT ETYMON RADICLE

RADON NITON THORON ACTINON EXRADIO

RADULA RIBBON TONGUE

RAFF LOW IDLE SCUM SWEEP TRASH COMMON JUMBLE LUMBER RABBLE RAFFLE RAGTAG SNATCH RUBBISH

RAFFISH RAKISH TAWDRY UNKEMPT

RAFFLE MOVE RAFF JUMBLE RABBLE REFUSE RUBBISH

RAFT COW CRIB MOKI BALSA BATCH FLOAT TABLE DINGEY DINGHY JANGAR MOKIHI PIPERY RADEAU JANGADA ZATTARE CATAMARAN
(— OF INVERTED POTS) GHARNAO
(— OF LOGS) BOOM CRIB
(— WITH CABIN) COW
(BAMBOO —) RAKIT
(FIRE —) CATAMARAN
(LUMBER —) BATCH

RAFT DOG RAKER

RAFTER HIP BALK BLAD FIRM SILE SOIL SPAR SPUR VIGA BAULK BLADE CABER RIDGE BOUGAR BULKER COUPLE CARLINE CHEVRON RAFFMAN SLEEPER
(— OF TURKEYS) FLOCK

RAFTY RAW DAMP FUSTY MUSTY RANCID

RAG JAG LAP TAT HAZE HOAX JAGG SAIL ANNOY CLOUT PRANK SCOLD SCRAP SHRED WIPER GIBBOL LIBBET RAGGLE TAGRAG TATTER FLITTER REMNANT TORMENT RAGSTONE STRAGGLE NEWSPAPER
(— GATHERER) TATTER
(CURLING —) CRACKER
(FLAPPING —) WALLOP
(TARRED —) HARDS
(PL.) DUDS CADDIS FITTERS RAGGERY FLITTERS

RAGAMUFFIN MUFFLIN BEGGARLY SHABROON TITMOUSE

RAGAU (FATHER OF —) PHALEC

RAGE GO AWE FAD RAG WAX BAIT BATE BEEF FARE FOAM FRET FUFF FUME FUNK FUNX FURY GLOW GRIM HEAT PELT RAMP RASE RESE TAVE TEAR WOOD ANGER BRETH CHAFE CRAZE FUROR PADDY STORM TEAVE TEVEL VOGUE WRATH FRENZY FURORE PELTER TYAUVE BLUSTER FASHION MADNESS PASSION RUFFIAN TEMPEST INSANITY WOODNESS PADDYWACK
(BE IN A —) RANT

RAGFISH ICOSTEID

RAGGED DUDDY HARSH FRAYED JAGGED SCOURY UNEVEN SHAGRAG SHREDDY TATTERY SCRAGGLY SCRATCHY TATTERED

RAGGED ROBIN ROBIN CUCKOO

RAGGEE MAND RAGI MARUA MANDUA KORAKAN ELEUSINE

RAGGLE-TAGGLE MOTLEY

RAGING HOT GRIM WILD YOND RABID FIERCE FURIAL FERVENT MADDING PELTING VIOLENT FLAGRANT FURIBUND WRATHFUL

RAGOUT SALMI GOULASH HARICOT TERRINE SALPICON CHIPOLATA PULPATONE
(— OF GAME) SALMI SALMIS

RAGPICKER BUNTER RAGMAN TATTER

RAGWEED HAYWEED HOGWEED AMBROSIA IRONWEED KINGHEAD KINGWEED RICHWEED FRANSERIA

RAGWORT CUSHAG JACOBY BENWEED CAMMOCK SEGGROM LIFEROOT

RAHAM (FATHER OF —) SHEMA
(SON OF —) JORKOAM

RAID RADE ROAD TALA FORAY HARRY PINCH REISE REIVE BODRAG CREACH FORAGE HARASS INROAD MOLEST PANYAR RAZZIA BODRAGE BORDRAG CHAPPOW DESCENT JAYHAWK OUTFALL OUTRAKE OUTRIDE OUTROAD SPREATH COMMANDO SPOILING
(— ORCHARDS) SCRUMP
(AIR —) BLITZ
(BOMBING —) PRANG
(CATTLE —) SPREAGH SPREATH
(MAKE A — ON) BUST
(WARLIKE —) HERSHIP

RAIDER REDLEG BUSHWACK

RAIL BAN BAR BULL COOT GIRD JEST KOKO LIST MOHO RANT RAVE SKID SORA TRAM WEKA WING CRAKE EASER FENCE GUARD PLATE RAVEL REILE SCOFF SCOLD SLENT STANG STANK STEEL SWEAR BANTER BEDWAY CALLET FENDER RUNNER SKITTY TIKLIN BIDCOCK BILCOCK COURLAN INVEIGH OARCOCK RACKWAY TOPRAIL BULLHEAD CANCELLI CORNBIRD PORTLAST TOADBACK VIGNOLES BRANDRETH BRANDRITH
(— AT) JEST CURSE SCOFF RATTLE REVILE BETONGUE
(— OF BED) STOCK
(— OF RAILWAY SWITCH) TONGUE
(— ON GUN PLATFORM) TRINGLE
(— ON HAY VEHICLE) THRIPPLE
(— ON SHIP) FIFE
(ALTAR —) SEPTUM
(ARCHED —) HOOPSTICK
(CHAIR —) LEDGE
(FENCE —) RIDER
(PART OF —) BED TIE FROG JOINT SPIKE BALLAST SLEEPER CROSSTIE BASEPLATE FISHPLATE
(PL.) RAILING CANCELLI RAILROAD
(PREF.) RALLI

RAIL CHAIR CARRIAGE

RAILING BAR SEPT GRATE RAVEL FENDER FIDDLE GITTER VEDIKA BARRIER GALLERY PARAPET CANCELLI ESPALIER HANDRAIL PARCLOSE TRAVERSE

RAILLERY GAFF HASH JEST JOKE RAGE CHAFF RALLY SPORT BANTER BLAGUE HOORAY HURRAH SATIRE TRIFLE MOCKERY BADINAGE DICACITY RABULOUS RIDICULE PERSIFLAGE

RAILROAD EL ROAD YARD STEEL COALER FEEDER GRANGER TRAMWAY CEINTURE ELEVATED
(— CAR) IDLER

RAILROAD CHAIR SADDLE

RAILSPLITTER MAULER

RAILWAY ROAD TUBE COGWAY SUBWAY COGROAD INCLINE TRANVIA WIREWAY ASCENSOR PLATEWAY TRAMROAD FUNICULAR CREMAILLERE

RAIMENT RAY GARB CLOTH APPAREL CLOTHES VESTURE CLOTHING DRESSING WARDROBE
(SPLENDID —) SHEEN
(SUFF.) ESTHES

RAIN WET ISLE MIST SMUR ULAN WEET BLASH STORM DELUGE MIZZLE SERENE SHOWER SOAKER DRIZZLE DOWNPOUR SPRINKLE
(— AND SNOW) SLEET
(— HEAVILY) TEEM
(— LIGHTLY) SMUR SPIT SPRINKLE
(— OF SPARKS) SHOWER
(DRIZZLING —) DAG
(FINE —) MIST SEREIN SERENE
(GOD OF —) PARJANYA
(HEAVY —) PASH SPOUT
(LIGHT —) SEREIN WEATHER HEATDROPS
(SHORT —) SHOWER
(SUDDEN —) SKEW
(WHIRLING —) SKIRL
(WIND-DRIVEN —) SCAT
(PL.) VARSHA
(PREF.) HYET(O) OMBRI OMBRO PLUVI(O)

RAINBIRD KOEL TOMFOOL STORMBIRD
(— OF JAMAICA) HUNTER

RAINBOW ARC BOW ARCH IRIS GAMUT METEOR SUNBOW ILLUSION
(AUTHOR OF —) LAWRENCE
(BROKEN —) WINDDOG WINDGALL
(CHARACTER IN —) TOM ANNA WILL ANTON LYDIA LENSKY URSULA BRANGWEN SKREBENSKY
(PREF.) IRID(O)

RAINBOW FISH GUPPY MAORI

RAINBOW RUNNER SKIPJACK SHOEMAKER

RAINBRINGER KACHINA

RAINCOAT MAC MACK MINO PONCHO BURSATI OILSKIN SLICKER GOSSAMER MACINTOSH MACKINTOSH

RAINFALL PLOUT SKIFF SKIFT ONDING STEMPLOW

RAIN GAGE UDOMETER

RAINSPOUT RONE

RAINSTORM WET SPATE SCOWTHER

RAIN TREE SAMAN ZAMAN GUANGO ZAMANG ALGAROBA GENISARO MONKEYPOD

RAINY WET KICK FRESH JUICY RAYNE SAPPY WEETY BLASHY DRIPPY HYETAL PLUNGY SPONGY PLUVIAL PLUVINE SHOWERY WEEPING CLUTTERY PLUVIOUS SLATTERY
(— SEASON) VARSHA

RAISE END SET WIN BUMP BUOY GROW HAIN HEFT HIGH HIKE HOVE JACK KICK LEVY LIFT MAKE OVER REAR ROOF STIR TELD TOSS AREAR BLOCK BOOST BREED BUILD CAIRN CHOCK CRANE DIGHT ELATE ENSKY ERECT EXALT FORCE GREET HANCE HEAVE HEEZE HEVEN HOISE HOIST HORSE LEAVE MOUND MOUNT PRICK RISER ROUSE VOICE ARRECT ASSIST BETTER CREATE DOUBLE EMBOSS EXHALE GATHER LEAVEN MUSTER NANTLE PREFER REMOVE RISING UPHOLD UPLIFT ADDRESS ADVANCE COLLECT ELEVATE ENHANCE LIGHTEN NOURISH PRESENT PROMOTE RECRUIT UPSHOOT ANGELIZE HEIGHTEN INSPIRIT RELEVATE
(— A BUMP) CLOUR
(— A NAP) MOZE TEASE TEASEL TEAZLE
(— ALOFT) SPHERE
(— ANCHOR) CAT
(— BY ASSESSMENT) LEVY
(— BY HAND) NOB
(— CLAMOR) BRAWL
(— IN PITCH) SHARP
(— OBJECTIONS) CAVIL BOGGLE
(— ONESELF) CHIN
(— TO HIGH DEGREE) STRAIN
(— TO 3RD POWER) CUBE
(— UP) BUOY AREAR ELATE EXALT EXTOL ELEVATE CIVILIZE

RAISED HIGH UPSET ARRECT HOGGED BULLATE EXALTED ELEVATED MOUNTANT UPLIFTED UPRAUGHT

RAISIN FIG PASA PLUM LEXIA ZIBEB REYSON CURRANT SULTANA MUSCATEL
(PL.) SPICE

RAISING ATOLLENT

RAJ RULE REIGN

RAJA KING CHIEF RULER PRINCE PANGLIMA

RAJMAHAL CREEPER JITI CHITI JETEE JEETEE

RAJPUT SAMMA SUMRA GAHRWAL RAZBOOCH

RAKE GO HOE RIP WAY COMB PATH RACK RAFF RAVE REAP ROAM ROUE ROVE RUCK BLOOD CLAUT PITCH SCOOP SCOUR SULKY TIGER PLUNGE RABBLE ROLLER SEARCH RANSACK SCRATCH LOTHARIO SCRAPPLE
(— GRAIN) GAVEL
(— UP IN ROWS) HACK
(— WITH GUNFIRE) SCOUR

STRAFE ENFILADE
(— WITHOUT TEETH) LUTE
(BUCK —) SWEEP
(CRANBERRY —) SCOOP
(HORSE-DRAWN —) GLEANER
(OYSTER —) GLEANER
(PART OF —) BOW TANG TINE
TOOTH HANDLE FERRULE
RAKEHELL RASCAL IMMORAL
LIBERTINE
RAKER GUMMER ROOKER
RAKISH SLANG JAUNTY SPORTY
WANTON DASHING CARELESS
DEVILISH RANTEPOLE RANTIPOLE
RALE RATTLE SIFFLE SIBILUS
RHONCHUS
RALLENTANDO DRAG RITARD
RALLY KID DRAG JOKE MOCK RELY
STIR BULLY JOLLY QUEER BANTER
DERIDE REVIVE COLLECT
CAMPOREE CLAMBAKE RIDICULE
SPEAKING
RAM PUN TIP TUP BUCK CRAM
PACK RAME STEM TEAP TOOP
ARIES CHOKE CRASH POACH
ROGER SLIDE BEETLE CHASER
RANCID ROSTRUM BULLDOZER
WETHERHOG WETHERTEG
(— OF WAR VESSEL) SPUR
(CASTRATED —) WETHER
(FATHER OF —) HEZRON
JERAHMEEL
(SON OF —) AMMINADAB
(PREF.) CRIO
RAMA MELCHORA
(FATHER OF —) DASHARATHA
(MOTHER OF —) KAUSHALYA
(WIFE OF —) SITA
RAMADA ARBOR PORCH
RAMAGE WILD RAMMISH
UNTAMED
RAMAGE HAWK BRANCHER
RAMBLE RAKE ROAM ROVE SKIR
WALK JAUNT PROWL RANGE
TRACE TROLL DODDER RUMBLE
STROLL VAGARY WAMBLE
WANDER ENRANGE EXCURSE
SAUNTER SPROGUE TROUNCE
FLAGARIE SCRAMBLE SPATIATE
(— AIMLESSLY) HAZE
RAMBLING GAD VAGARY CURSORY
DEVIOUS WINDING DESULTORY
SCATTERED
RAMBUNCTIOUS RUDE WILD
ROUGH UNRULY UNTAMED
VIOLENT
RAMBUTAN SOAPWORT
RAMENTUM PALEA PALET SCALE
SHAVING
RAMIE HEMP RHEA ORTIGA
RAMIFICATION ARM RAMUS
BRANCH OFFSHOOT OUTGROWTH
RAMIFY BRANCH SPRANGLE
RAMMAN ADAD ADDA ADDU
RAMMED EARTH PISE
RAMMEL TRASH RUMMLE RUBBISH
RAMMER TUP HEAD BOSER
PUNNER WORMER
RAMONA (HUSBAND OF —)
ALESSANDRO
RAMOSE CLADOSE BRANCHED
RAMOTH (FATHER OF —) BANI
RAMP ROB RUN BANK EXIT HOAX

RAGE RANK SLIP CREEP STORM
EASING FROLIC GARLIC FOOTPAD
SLIPWAY SWINDLE GRADIENT
RAMPAGE RAGE ROMP BINGE
SPRAY SPREE STORM RANDAN
RAMPAGEOUS UNRULY GLARING
RAMPANT VIOLENT
RAMPANT RANK PROFUSE
SALIANT SALIENT SEGREANT
RAMPART BRAY LINE WALL
AGGER ARGIN ABATIS VALLUM
ABATTIS BULWARK DEFENSE
PARAPET RAMPIER BARBICAN
MUNITION BARRICADE
RAMPER LAMPREY
RAMPIKE SNAG RAUNPICK
ROUNSPIK
RAMROD FORMAL GUNSTICK
RAMSHACKLE RUDE UNRULY
RICKETY SHACKLY UNSTEADY
RAMSON RAMP GARLIC BUCKRAM
(PL.) RAMS
RAMSTAM RASH HEADLONG
RECKLESS
RAN ARN
(HUSBAND OF —) AESIR
RANCEL SEARCH RANSACK
RANCH RUN FARM TEAR FINCA
CHACRA OUTFIT SPREAD
WRENCH STATION ESTANCIA
HACIENDA
RANCHE NATURAL
RANCHER COWMAN GRAZIER
SHEEPMAN CATTLEMAN
RANCID RAM RANK SOUR FROWY
RAFTY RASTY REEST RESTY
FROWZY ODIOUS ROTTEN
MALODOROUS
RANCOR GALL HATE SPITE ENMITY
GRUDGE HATRED MALICE
ACRIMONY
RANCOROUS ACRID VENOMOUS
MALIGNANT ACRIMONIOUS
(NOT —) GOOD
RAND EDGE ROON RUND BORDER
HIGHLAND
RANDAN SPREE RANTAN UPROAR
RAMPAGE
RANDOM BANK FORCE LOOSE
STRAY CASUAL CHANCE CHANCY
AIMLESS RANDALL RENDOUN
SHOTGUN UNAIMED VAGRANT
ALEATORIC
(AT —) HOBNOB
(SOMEWHAT —) LONG
RANDY LEWD RUDE RUDAS SPREE
BEGGAR VIRAGO LUSTFUL
RIOTOUS CAROUSAL
RANGE KEN ROW ALLY AREA BEAT
GATE GAUT GHAT LINE RAIK
RAKE RANK ROAM ROVE SCUM
SHOT TOUR WALK ALIGN BLANK
CARRY FIELD GAMUT HILLS ORBIT
REACH SCOPE SCOUR SHOOT
SPACE STAND START SWEEP
SWING VERGE COURSE DANGER
EXTEND EXTENT LENGTH RADIUS
RAMBLE SCOUTH SPHERE STROLL
WANDER BOWSHOT COMPASS
DEMESNE EARSHOT GUNSHOT
HABITAT HORIZON PURVIEW
CLASSIFY DIAPASON EARREACH
EYEREACH LATITUDE PANORAMA

(— FOR FOOD) FORAGE
(— OF ARROW) FLIGHT
(— OF BRICK) COURSE
(— OF FOOD) FARE
(— OF FREQUENCIES) SPECTRUM
(— OF GOVERNANCE) DOMAIN
(— OF GUN) CARRY RANDOM
GUNSHOT
(— OF HILLS) GAUT GHAT HUMP
TIER CHAIN GHAUT RIDGE SIERRA
SAWBACK BACKBONE
(— OF ORGANISM) BIOZONE
(— OF PASTURE) GANG
(— OF PLANKS) STRING
(— OF PRINTING TYPES) SERIES
(— OF SIGHT) KEN SCAN EYESHOT
KENNING
(— OF TONES) KEY SCALE
GRADATION
(— OF VISION) EYE SIGHT KENNING
(— OF WAVELENGTH) BAND
(— OVER) SWEEP
(— TOP) COOKTOP
(ARCHERY —) BUTTS GREEN
(COOKING —) KITCHENER
(PART OF —) CAP DOOR FLUE
HEAD KNOB OVEN RACK TRIM
VENT GRATE GUARD GUIDE
HINGE PANEL BURNER GASKET
HANDLE WINDOW BROILER
CONTROL GRIDDLE DRIPPLATE
BACKSPLASH
(SHOOTING —) MES GALLERY
(TEMPERATURE —) CONE
RANGE FINDER STADIA
MEKOMETER
RANGE POLE PICKET
RANGER ROVER ROBBER
MONTERO FIREWARD
RANGOON SHERRY
RANGY OPEN ROOMY SPACIOUS
RANK RAY ROW SEE DANK FOOT
FORM FOXY GOLE GREE LINE
RAMP RATE ROOM SEED SOUR
STEP TIER CENSE CHOIR CLASS
FETID FRANK FUSTY GRADE
GROSS HONOR LEVEL MARCH
ORDER PLACE QUIRE RANGE
ROWTY SIEGE SPACE STALL
STAND STATE TCHIN TRAIN
AFFAIR AGREGE DEGREE ERMINE
ESTEEM FIGURE LAVISH PARAGE
RATING SPHERE STATUS STRONG
CALIBER CALLING DIGNITY
DUKEDOM EARLDOM FOOTING
GLARING RAMMISH RAMPANT
STATION WORSHIP ABSOLUTE
EARLSHIP ENSIGNCY EQUIPAGE
FLAGRANT GENTRICE LADYSHIP
PALPABLE STINKING
MALODOROUS
(— AND FILE) RUCK RANGALE
(— OF GENTLEMEN) GENTRY
GENTILITY
(— OF SERGEANT-AT-LAW) COIF
COIFFE
(ACADEMIC —) AGREGE
(BOTTOMMOST —) CELLAR
(HIGH —) PURPLE DIGNITY
EMINENCE
(LOWEST —) SCOURING
(MILITARY —) GRADE AIRMAN
CORNET CHAOUSH

(NOBLE —) ADELAIDE
(ONE HIGHEST IN —) SUPREMO
(SAME —) KIND
(SOCIAL —) CLASS ESTATE
HERALDRY POSITION
(SUFF.) CY HEAD HOOD
RANKLE FRET CHAFE FESTER
INJURE RANCOR DESTROY
INFLAME
RANSACK RIG DRAG RAKE RIPE
SACK SEEK RIFLE DACKER
RANCEL SEARCH PLUNDER
RUMMAGE
RANSOM FINE RAME REDEEM
RESCUE RESGAT EXPIATE
RANSTEAD TOADFLAX
RANT CAVE HUFF RAIL RAND
MOUTH REVEL ROUSE SCOLD
SPOUT STEVEN BOMBAST
CAROUSE DECLAIM FROTHING
RODOMONTADE
(— AND RAVE) FAUNCH
RANTING RANTISM TEARCAT
RANTIPOLE WILD CARROT RAKISH
SEESAW ROMPING
RANULA CYST FROGTONGUE
(PREF.) BATRACH(O)
RANUNCULUS MOSS GOLLAND
CROWFOOT HEDGEHOG
BUTTERCUP
RAOULIA HAASTIA
RAP BOB CON BLOW CHAP GRAB
KNAP TIRL TUNK WRAP CLICK
CLINK FLIRT KNOCK STEAL
TOUCH BARTER HANDLE YANKER
RAPACIOUS CRUEL GREEDY
TAKING RAVENING RAVENOUS
RAPACITY RAVEN RAVIN CUPIDITY
EXTORTION VULTURISM
RAPE COLE ABUSE COLZA FORCE
NAVET NAVEW TOUCH ATTACK
FELONY RAPEYE TURNIP ASSAULT
DESPOIL NAVETTE OPPRESS
OUTRAGE PLUNDER RAPTURE
STUPRUM VIOLATE COLESEED
COLEWORT DISHONOR STUPRATE
SUPPRESS
RAPE OF THE LOCK (AUTHOR OF —
) POPE
(CHARACTER IN —) ARIEL BETTY
PETRE PLUME SPLEEN BELINDA
UMBRIEL CLARISSA THALESTRIS
RAPESEED COLZA RAVISON
RAPHA (FATHER OF —) BINEA
RAPHU (SON OF —) PALTI
RAPHUS DIDUS
RAPID GAY FAST CHUTE HASTY
MOSSO QUICK ROUND SAULT
SHARP SHOOT SHUTE TOSTO
WINGY RIFFLE SPEEDY WINGED
CURSIVE SCHNELL SKELPIN
STICKLE TANTIVY SLAPPING
SPEEDFUL OVERNIGHT
(—S IN RIVER) SAULT DALLES
RIFFLE STICKLE CATARACT
(MORE —) STRETTO
RAPIDITY HASTE SPEED RADEUR
CELERITY VELOCITY
RAPIDLY APACE CHEAP FLEETLY
HASTILY SPEEDILY QUICKFOOT
RAPIER TUCK TUKE BILBO ESTOC
SHARP STOCK VERDUN TOASTER
RAPINE FORCE RAVIN PILLAGE

PLUNDER VIOLENCE
RAPPACCINI (DAUGHTER OF —)
BEATRICE
RAPPAREE ROBBER CREAGHT
VAGABOND
RAPPORT ACCORD HARMONY
RELATION AGREEMENT
RAPSCALLION ROGUE RASCAL
VILLAIN HOSEBIRD VAGABOND
RAPT LOST WRAP TENSE INTENT
RAVISH TRANCE CARRIED
ENGAGED RAPTURE ABDUCTED
ABSORBED ECSTATIC
RAPTORES RAPACES
RAPTURE JOY BLISS DELIGHT
ECSTASY PAROXYSM RHAPSODY
RAPTUROUS RHAPSODIC
RARA AVIS PHENIX RARITY
WONDER PHOENIX
RARE FINE REAL SELD THIN ALONE
EARLY GREAT ANTRIN CHOICE
GEASON INCONY SCARCE SEENIL
SELDOM SINDLE SPARSE SUBTLE
SULLEN UNIQUE ANTERIN
CURIOUS TENUOUS UNUSUAL
CRITICAL SELDSEEN SINGULAR
UNCOMMON RECHERCHE
(PREF.) AREO MANO SPAN(I)(O)
RAREFACTION POROSIS
RAREFIED HIGH THIN SUBTILE
ABSTRUSE AETHERED ESOTERIC
RAREFY THIN DILUTE EXTENUATE
RARELY SELDEN SELDOM
RARENESS RARITY TENUITY
SCARCITY
RARITY SWAN CURIO RELIC
RARIETY TENUITY RARENESS
(PL.) CURIOSA
RASCAL BOY CAD DOG IMP LOW
RAP BASE DUCK FILE KITE LOON
MEAN SHAG SMAK CATSO FILTH
GANEF GIPSY KNAVE ROGUE
SCAMP SHELM SLAVE SMAIK
THIEF ABLACH BEGGAR BRIBER
BUDZAT BUGGER COQUIN
HARLOT LIMMER RABBLE RAGGIL
RIBALD SCHELM SORROW TINKER
BLEEDER CAMOOCH CULLION
GLUTTON HALLION HESSIAN
NEBULON PEASANT RAPTRIL
SHELLUM SKEEZIX SKELLUM
VILLAIN BEZONIAN BLIGHTER
HOSEBIRD LIDDERON PALLIARD
PICAROON RAKEHELL RUBIATOR
SCALAWAG SPALPEEN TAISTREL
VAGABOND WIDDIFOW
RAPSCALLION
RASCALITY FOIST RABBLE
KNAVERY ROGUING RASCALRY
RASCALLY BASE MEAN ROOKY
ARRANT GALLUS LIMMER
GALLOWS KNAVISH RAGGILY
SHAGRAG WIDDIFOW
RASE PULL RAIS RAZE ERASE
PLUCK INCISE SNATCH
RASH ID CUT BRASH HARDY
HASTY HEADY SLASH SLICE
DARING SUDDEN UNWARY
URGENT BULRUSH HOTSPUR
RABBISH RAMSTAM ROSEOLA
BLIZZARD CARELESS ERUPTION
EXANTHEM HEADLONG HEEDLESS
MADBRAIN OVERSEEN PRESSING

RECKLESS TEMEROUS
(SUFF.) ANTHEMA
(SKIN —) ID IDE
RASHER SLICE COLLOP TRIFLE
COLOPPE
RASHLY HEADILY HEADLONG
RASHNESS RAGE RESE HASTE
ACRISY TEMERITY HEADINESS
RASKOLNIK POPOVETS
RASP RUB FILE RAPE ERUCT
GRATE TOOTH RAPEYE RUBBER
RUGINE RIFFLER DENTICLE
(SHOEMAKER'S —) FLOAT
RASPBERRY AKPEK BAZOO MOLKA
AVARIN RASPIS PLUMBOG
ARNBERRY BLACKCAP BOGBERRY
CUTHBERT MULBERRY RESPASSE
ROSACEAN SALMONBERRY
RASPING HARSH ROUGH STOOR
STOUR HOARSE RASION RAZZLY
GRATING RAUCOUS GUTTERAL
(PL.) SCOBS
RASPY HARSH GRATING SCREAKY
SCRABBLY
RASSE CIVET WEASEL
RASSELAS (AUTHOR OF —)
JOHNSON
(CHARACTER IN —) IMLAC PEKUAH
NEKAYAH RASSELAS
(MENTOR OF —) IMLAC
(SISTER OF —) NEKAYAH
RAT BUCK DAMN DRAT HEEL NOKI
ROTN SCAB VOLE KIORE LOUSE
METAD RATON SELVA ZEMMI
ZEMNI CRABER MURINE RODENT
ROTTAN SLEPEZ VERMIN YUNGAS
CUSHION CONFOUND INFORMER
MYOMORPH
(INDIAN —) KOK
RATAPLAN RATTAN RATTLE
RATCH RASH REND ROCH SPOT
NOTCH STREAK RATCHET
STRETCH
RATCHET DOG PAWL CLICK
DETENT ROCHET
RAT CHINCHILLA ABROCOME
RATE LAY RAG SET CESS CHOP
DEEM GAIT GIVE HAND KIND
RANK RATA ABUSE CULET CURVE
PRIZE RATIO REBUT SCOLD STENT
STYLE VALUE ZAKAT ASSIZE
GALLOP ACCOUNT BESHREW
CARTAGE DESERVE FASHION
MILLAGE REPROVE CLASSIFY
ESTIMATE QUANTIFY
(— HIGHLY) PRICE
(— OF ASCENT) GRADE
(— OF DRAINAGE) FREENESS
(— OF EXCHANGE) BATTA
(— OF INTEREST) COUPON
DISCOUNT
(— OF MOTION) BAT SPEED
(— OF MOVEMENT) PACE TEMPO
(— OF RECKONING) FOOT
(— OF SPEED) BAT AGOGE
(— OF TAX) CENSE
(— OF TRANSFER) FLUX
(— OF TUITION) CULET
(— SCHEDULE) TARIFF
(AT ANY —) HURE
(BIRTH —) NATALITY
RATE BOOK STREET
RATEL BADGER BURIER

RATH CAR HILL REUT RUTH EARLY
MOUND QUICK REUTE SWIFT
BETIMES CHARIOT YOUTHFUL
RATHER Y BUT GEY LIKE SOON
LOURD QUITE ASTITE BEFORE
FAIRLY HELDER KINDLY PRETTY
RUTHER SEEMLY TIDDER TITTER
EARLIER INSTEAD MIDDLING
SOMEWHAT
(— THAN) ERE BEFORE
RATIFICATION AMEN RATE
SANCTION
RATIFY AMEN PASS SEAL SIGN
VISA ENSEAL FASTEN OBSIGN
APPROVE CONFIRM SCEPTER
CANONIZE ROBORATE SANCTION
VALIDATE
RATING RANK CENSE CLASS
GRADE WRITER STANDING
RATIO Q PI GAIN RATE SINE SLIP
INDEX RESON SETUP SHEAR
ASPECT CAMBER DECADE
QUOTUM REASON REYSON
SECANT AVERAGE PORTION
CONTRAST SOLIDITY MULTIPLIER
PROPORTION
RATIOCINATION LOGIC THOUGHT
REASONING
RATION DOLE RATIO ALLOCATE
(— OF BREAD) TOMMY
(ANIMAL —) CHOW
(EXTRA —S) BUCKSHEE
(HOG —) SWILL
(PL.) FOOD BOUCH ETAPE
COMMON
RATIONAL SANE LUCID SOBER
LOGICAL REASONAL SENSIBLE
THINKING
RATIONALIZE THOB EXPLAIN
RATITE EMU MOA EMEU KIWI
RHEA OSTRICH STRUTHIAN
RAT KANGAROO TUNGO
POTOROO SQUEAKER
RATOON SHOOT SPROUT SUCKER
RATTAIL MULE ARREST
GRENADIER
RATTAN CANE SEGA ROTAN
BEJUCO ROTANG SWITCH
RATTOON
RATTLE DIN BIRL BURL REEL RICK
TIRL CHINK CLACK CROTAL
GRAGER HENPEN HURTLE
MARACA RACKLE RICKLE RIFFLE
ROTTLE RUCKLE RUTTLE
CHACKLE CLACKER CLAPPER
CLATTER CLICKET CREAKER
GNATTER GROGGER SHATTER
SISTRUM SKELLAT CAIXINHA
CHOCALHO COWWHEAT
NOISEMAKER
(CRIER'S —) CLAPPER
(IRON —) SKELLAT SKILLET
(PREF.) CROTALI
(SUFF.) CROTIC
RATTLEBRAINED MADCAP
RATTLER LIE ROMBLE RUMBLER
RATTLESNAKE BELLTAIL
CASCABEL CASCAVEL CROTALID
MASSASAUGA SIDEWINDER
(— PLANTAIN) NETLEAF RATSBANE
RATTLESNAKE ROOT BUGBANE
JOYLEAF
RATTLETRAP GEWGAW

TRIFLE RICKETY
RATTLING REEL BRISK HUSKY
SLAPPING SPLENDID CREPITANT
RATTY NASTY SHABBY UNKEMPT
WORTHLESS
RATWA MUNTJAC
RAUCOUS LOUD HARSH COARSE
HOARSE SQUAWKY STRIDENT
RAUN ROE ROWN SPAWN
RAUPO CATTAIL
RAVAGE EAT PREY RIOT RUIN
SACK FORAY HARRY HAVOC
SPOIL WASTE FORAGE DESPOIL
DESTROY OVERRUN PILLAGE
PLUNDER DEFLOWER DESOLATE
POPULATE SPOLIATE
RAVANA (SISTER OF —)
SHURPANAKHA
RAVE MAD RAGE RAND WOOD
AWEDE BLURB CRUSH RATHE
ROUSE STORM TAVER DELIRE
TAIVER WANDER
RAVEL FAG RUN FRAY FRET REYLE
SNARL EVENER LADDER RADDLE
RUNNER SLOUGH TANGLE
CONFUSE INVOLVE PERPLEX
RAILING UNWEAVE
RAVELIN RABLIN OUTWORK
DEMILUNE
RAVEN CRAKE RALPH CORBEL
CORBIE CORBIN FORAGE RAVINE
WAYBIRD
(BRIGHT —) BERTRAM
(SUFF.) CORAX
RAVENING CRUEL RABIES
RAVENOUS GREEDY LUPINE
TOOTHY WOLFISH RAPACIOUS
VORACIOUS
RAVINE DEN GAP GUT LIN DELL
DRAW GILL GULL KHOR KHUD
LINN LLYN SIKE WADI BREAK
BUNNY CHASM CHINE CLOVE
COULE DONGA FLUME GHYLL
GLACK GORGE GOYAL GOYLE
GRIFF GRIKE GULCH GULLY
HEUCH KLOOF SLADE SLAKE
STRID ARROYO CLEUCH CLOUGH
COULEE DIMBLE DINGLE DUMBLE
GULLET GULLEY HOLLOW NULLAH
RAMBLA SHEUGH STRAIT
BARRANCA QUEBRADA
RAVING RAVERY DELIRANT
FRENZIED DELIRIOUS
RAVISH ROB RAPE ABUSE CHARM
FORCE HARRY SPOIL ABDUCT
ATTACK DEFILE AFFORCE
CORRUPT DELIGHT ENFORCE
OPPRESS OUTRAGE OVERJOY
PLUNDER POLLUTE VIOLATE
VITIATE DEFLOWER ENTRANCE
STUPRATE SUPPRESS UNMAIDEN
RAVISHER RAPTER RAVENER
RAVISHMENT ECSTASY RAPTURE
TRANSPORT
RAW RA ROW BRUT LASH REAR
RUDE BLEAK CHILL CRUDE FRESH
GREEN HARSH NAKED RAFTY
SHARP WERSH BITTER CALLOW
COARSE CUTCHA KUTCHA UNRIPE
VULGAR WAIRSH NATURAL
NOUVEAU UNBOUND VERDANT
WEARISH WEERISH IMMATURE
RAWBONED UNCOOKED

UNEDITED VISCERAL
(— AND COLD) CRIMPY
(PREF.) OMO
RAWBONED RAW BONY LEAN
GAUNT LANKY SCRAG SCRAWNY
RAWHIDE WHIP WHANG COWHIDE
COWSKIN GREENHIDE PARFLECHE
RAWNESS CRUDITY
RAY BEAM BETA DORN SOIL WIRE
ALPHA BRAND DRESS EQUIP
FLAIR FLAKE FLATH GLEAM
GLEED ORDER RAYON ROKER
SKATE BATOID CHUCHO OBISPO
RADIAL RADIUS RAIOID SEPHEN
STREAM TRYGON VISUAL BATFISH
COWFISH DEWBEAM DRILVIS
FIDDLER HOMELYN PLACOID
RAIMENT TORPEDO WAIREPO
BRACHIUM MOONBEAM
NUMBFISH PLOWFISH PYLSTERT
STINGRAY
(— OF LIGHT) GLINT SPEAR
GLANCE SUNRAY SUNBEAM
(— OF STARFISH) ARM
(FEMALE —) MAID
(FIN —) SPINE
(WITHOUT —S) ABACTINAL
(PREF.) BATO
(ELECTRIC —) NARC(O)
RAYED
(PREF.) ACTIN(IO)(O)
(SUFF.) ACT(INE)
(— WITH IMPAIRMENT) LEXIA
RAYON BEAM RADIUS DUCHESS
RAZE CUT FLAT RUIN ARASE
ERASE LEVEL STREW ARRACE
EFFACE SCRAPE SLIGHT UNPILE
DESTROY SCRATCH SUBVERT
UNBUILD DEMOLISH
RAZOR SHIV TUSK MUSSEL RASOIR
SHAVER RATTLER SLASHER
CUTTHROAT
(PREF.) XYR(O)
RAZORBACK STATE ARKANSAS
RAZOR-BILLED AUK FALK TINK
MURRE NODDY SCOOT SCOUT
SKOOT TINKER SKIMMER WILLOCK
ROCKBIRD
RAZOR CLAM PIROT RASOR
SOLEN SPOUT RASOIR
RAZZ PAN CHIACK RIDICULE
RASPBERRY
RAZZIA RAID FORAY INCURSION
RAZZING RAZOO
RE RAY ANENT ACTION MATTER
REGARDING
REACH GO GET HIT RAX RUN WIN
BEAT COME FIND GAIN HAWK
HENT MAKE PUSH REEK REIK
RYKE SHOT SORT SPAN SPIT
TEND BRACE CROSS FETCH
GRASP PERCH RANGE RETCH
TOUCH ADVENE ARRIVE ATTAIN
DANGER EXTEND FATHOM
LENGTH OBTAIN SNATCH STREEK
STRIKE ACHIEVE COMPASS
CONTACT GUNSHOT OVERGET
POSSESS RECOVER STRETCH
(— ACROSS) SPAN OVERSTRIDE
(— AN END) STAY
(— BY EFFORT) ATTAIN
(— BY FIGURING) STRIKE
(— FORTH) EXTEND

(— GOAL) HAIL
(— OF WATER) LODE
(— OUT) UTTER SPREAD STRETCH
(— TO) LINE
(— TOTAL) AMOUNT
(— UNDERSTANDING) AGREE
(— WITH END) ABUT
(EXTREME —) PITCH STRETCH
(TRY TO —) ASPIRE
(ULTIMATE —) PITCH
REACHER INGIVER
REACT ACT BUCK BEHAVE
RETROACT
REACTION BELT BUZZ KAHN WOHL
START WIDAL FAVISM RECOIL
BLOWOFF EMOTION FEELING
SETBACK BACKLASH BACKWASH
EXCHANGE GUARDING KICKBACK
RECEPTION
(— TIME) LATENCY
(ADVERSE —) BACKLASH
(ANGRY —) RISE
(VIOLENT —) SONG
REACTIONARY WHITE BOURBON
BACKWARD
REACTIVATED AWAKE ACTIVE
REACTIVATOR ACTIFIER
REACTOR PILE CHOKER FURNACE
INDUCTOR
READ GO CON KRI QRI SEE CALL
KERE QERI TURN CHOKE JUDGE
SOLVE WRITE PERUSE RELATE
FORESEE LEARNED LECTION
PREDICT ABOMASUM DECIPHER
FORETELL INDICATE OVERLOOK
(— ALOUD) LINE DEACON
(— HERE AND THERE) BROWSE
(— MECHANICALLY) RETINIZE
(— OF) SEE
(— OFF) DICTATE
(— PROOF) HORSE
(— RAPIDLY) DIP SKIM GOBBLE
(— SLOWLY) SPELL
(— SYSTEMATICALLY) FREQUENT
(— WITH PROFOUND ATTENTION)
PORE STUDY
READER PURSE DIPPER LECTOR
LISTER MAFTIR GRANTHI PISTLER
DEVOURER
(CHILD'S —) TENPENNY
(CHURCH —) LECTOR ANAGNOST
(PL.) FOLLOWING
READILY PAT LIEF YERN APTLY
PREST YERNE EASILY GAINLY
PROBABLY SPEEDILY
READINESS ART EASE GIFT PRESS
SKILL BELIEF GRAITH ADDRESS
FLUENCY FREEDOM ALACRITY
FACILITY GOODWILL
(IN —) APOISE AGAINST
READING KRI QRE QRI KERE KERI
QERI KTHIB KETHIB LESSON
LECTION LECTURE PERUSAL
SETTING
(PL.) PROCINCT
READING DESK AMBO LECTERN
READJUST MEND ADVANCE
(— TYPE) OVERRUN
READY UP APT BUN FIT RAD YAP
BAAN BAIN BOON BOUN BOWN
FREE GIRT GLIB GNIB RIFE RIPE
TALL YARE APERT EAGER FRACK
HANDY HAPPY PREDY PREST

PRIME QUICK SWIFT THERE TIGHT
ADROIT APPERT FACILE GRAITH
HEARTY PROMPT PREPARE
PRESENT RENABLE WILLING
CHEERFUL DEXTROUS HANDSOME
PREGNANT PREPARED PROVIDED
SKILLFUL
(— A COMPUTER) BOOT
(— FOR ACTION) ARM EXPEDITE
(— WITH WORDS) FLUENT
(NOT —) SET BOUND GROOM
FORWARD DISPOSED IMPROMPT
INCLINED
READY-MADE SALE STORE
BOUGHT
REAGENT ETCHANT REACTOR
TITRANT ALTERANT REACTIVE
NINHYDRIN
REAIA (FATHER OF —) MICAH
REAL BODY FAIR GOOD LEAL LEVY
PURE RIAL TRUE VERY VRAI
PAKKA PUCKA PUKKA RIGHT
ROYAL SOLID SOOTH ACTUAL
DINKUM ENTIRE HONEST THINGY
CORDIAL GENUINE GRADELY
SINCERE THINGAL CONCRETE
DEFINITE EXISTENT GRAITHLY
POSITIVE THINGISH
(EXTERNALLY —) TANGIBLE
(HALF —) PICAYUNE
(1-8TH —) TLAC TLACO
REALGAR ARSENIC ROSAKER
ZARNICH SANDARAC
REALISM REALITY LITERALISM
NATURALISM
REALISTIC HARD SOBER VIVID
EARTHLY LIFELIKE PROBABLE
REALITY FEAT TRUE BEING SOOTH
THING TRUTH ACTUAL DASEIN
EFFECT VERITY EARNEST
SUBJECT IDENTITY OVERSOUL
POSITIVE REALNESS TRUENESS
(LIMITED —) SOMEWHAT
(ULTIMATE —) GOD SOURCE
DIVINITY SUBSTANCE
(PL.) REALIA
REALIZATION PASS SENSE
CRUSHER FRUITION AWAKENING
REALIZE GAIN KNOW FETCH
LEARN SENSE EFFECT FULFIL
ACQUIRE CONCEIVE RECOGNIZE
REALIZED BODILY
(FULLY —) COMPLETE
REALLY ARU WIS ARAH HALF JUST
ARRAH TRULY WISHA FINELY
INDEED SIMPLY SURELY VERILY
ACTUALLY
(NOT —) ILL ALMOST
REALM LAND SOIL BOURN CLIME
RANGE REIGN REWME RICHE
BOURNE CIRCLE DEMAIN EMPIRE
HEAVEN REALTY REGION SPHERE
DEMESNE GAELDOM KINGDOM
NOTALIA ROYALME TERRENE
CLUBLAND DEVILDOM DOMINION
ELDORADO GHOSTDOM
GIPSYDOM NOTOGAEA
(— OF DARKNESS) PO
(— OF FABULOUS RICHNESS)
ELDORADO
(— OF THOR) THRUTHHEIM
THRUTHVANG
(MARINE —) NOTALIA TROPICALIA

(VISIONARY —) CLOUDLAND
(SUFF.) DOM
(— OF ANIMAL LIFE) ALIA
REALTY FEALTY REAUTE ROYALTY
REAM FOAM RIME SEED SKIM
CHEAT CREAM FROTH FRAISE
RHYMER STRETCH
(PL.) INSIDES OUTSIDES
REAMER BUR BURR SPUD DRIFT
RIMER BROACH CHERRY FRAISE
RANCER RHYMER RIMMER
WIDENER
REANIMATE WAKE RENEW REVIVE
RECREATE
REANIMATED AWAKE
REAP BAG CUT REP CROP RIPE
GLEAN SHEAR GARNER GATHER
SICKLE HARVEST
REAPER LORD COCKER TASKER
WINNER CRADLER SHEARER
SICKLER
(GRIM —) DEATH
REAPING HOOK SICKLE TWIBIL
CROTCHET
REAPPEARANCE RENTREE
EMERSION
REAR AFT BACK BUNT HIND HINT
JUMP LIFT STEN TOSS BREED
BUILD CARVE ERECT JUNCH
STEND ACHTER AROUSE CRADLE
FOSTER NURSLE SUCKLE
APPREAR ARRIERE EDUCATE
ELEVATE NOURISH NURTURE
UPBRING BUTTOCKS HINDMOST
REARWARD
(— CAREFULLY) TIDDLE
(NEARER THE —) AFTER
(TO THE —) BACK BEHIND
(TO THE — OF) ABAFT
REARED (— BY HAND) CADE
(DELICATELY —) SOYLED
REARHORSE MANTIS
REARING CABRE FRESNE PESADE
FORCENE RAMPANT
(— UP) STEND
REARRANGE DO ADJUST JIGGER
REORDER READJUST
REARRANGEMENT WAGNER
DIAGENESIS
REARWARD AFT BACKWARD
REASON PEG WAY HOTI NOUS
REDE SAKE TALK ARGUE CAUSE
COLOR COUNT LOGOS PROOF
RATIO SCORE SENSE SKILL THING
THINK TOPIC EXCUSE GROUND
MANNER MATTER MOTION
NOESIS ACCOUNT PREMISE
QUARREL SUBJECT TUITION
ARGUMENT ENCHESON LOGICIZE
VERNUNFT
(— FOR PRIDE) BOAST
(LACKING —) INEPT
(PREF.) RATI
REASONABLE FAIR JUST SANE
SOBER NATURAL SKILFUL
FEASIBLE MODERATE RATIONAL
SENSIBLE
REASONABLENESS EPIKY EPIKIKA
FITNESS FAIRNESS SOBRIETY
REASONABLY SOON
REASONER (FALLACIOUS —)
SOPHIST
REASONING LOGIC THOUGHT

ERGOTISM RATIONAL
(CLUMSY —) ARGAL
(FALLACIOUS —) CIRCLE
SOPHISTRY PARALOGISM
REASSEMBLE RELY
REASSEMBLY RALLY
REASSUME REVOKE REPRISE
REAVE ROB REFE SEIZE SPLIT
REMOVE DESPOIL PILLAGE
PLUNDER UNRAVEL
REB RABBI REBEL MISTER
REBAB GUSLE
REBATE BLUNT CHECK LESSEN
RIBBET DIMINISH DISCOUNT
DRAWBACK KICKBACK
REBEC LYRE SAROD RIBIBE
RUBIBLE
REBECCA (AUTHOR OF —)
DUMAURIER
(CHARACTER IN —) JACK BAKER
FRANK GILES MAXIM FAVELL
JULYAN CRAWLEY DANVERS
BEATRICE DEWINTER
(FATHER OF —) ISAAC
REBEKAH (BROTHER OF —) LABAN
(FATHER OF —) BETHUEL
(HUSBAND OF —) ISAAC
(SON OF —) ESAU JACOB
REBEL REB KICK RISE TURN BRAND
FAUVE ANARCH CROPPY MUTINE
REVOLT FRONDEUR MALCONTENT
(— IN ART) FAUVE
(PL.) REBELDOM
REBELLION MUTINY PUTSCH
REVOLT MISRULE UPRISING
REBELLIOUS RUSTY ANARCHIC
MUTINOUS AUDACIOUS
INSURGENT
REBIRTH REVIVAL
REBORN REDIVIVUS
REBOUND DAP HOP HANG KISS
STOT CANON CAROM STITE
BOUNCE CANNON CARROM
RECOIL RESILE RESULT BRICOLE
REDOUND RICOCHET SNAPBACK
(— ERRATICALLY) KICK
REBOUND CLIP RETAINER
REBUFF SLAP SNIB SNUB CHECK
FLING NOSER REPEL DEFEAT
DENIAL REBUKE REBUTE REFUTE
REPULSE
REBUILD MEND
REBUKE NIP WIG BAWL RATE
REDD SNEB SNIB SNUB TRIM
BARGE BLAME CHECK CHIDE
DRESS SAUCE SCOLD SNAPE
SNEAP TOUCH DIRDUM GANSEL
LESSON RATING RATTLE REHETE
REMORD THREAP CENSURE
CHIDING CORRECT HOTFOOT
LECTURE REPROOF REPROVE
SARCASM BLESSING BUSINESS
CHASTISE KEELHAUL REPROACH
SCORCHER THREAPEN UNDERNIM
CASTIGATE
REBUS BADGE ENIGMA PUZZLE
RIDDLE
REBUT REPEL RECOIL REFUTE
REPULSE RETREAT DISPROVE
RECALCITRANT UNRULY
RENITENT OBSTINATE RESISTANT
RECALL CITE BRING UNSAY
REMAND REMIND RETURN

REVOKE UNLOOK BETHINK
RECLAIM RETRACE RETRACT
REVIVAL UNSHOUT REMEMBER
WITHCALL WITHDRAW
REPRODUCE
(— FONDLY) CHERISH
RECANT UNSAY ABJURE REVOKE
UNSING DISAVOW RETRACT
SWALLOW PALINODE RENOUNCE
RECANTATION PALINODE
RECAPITULATE SUM UNITE
RECITE REPEAT RECOUNT
REHEARSE REITERATE
SUMMARIZE
RECAPITULATION EPANODOS
RECAPTURE RETAKE RECOVER
RECEDE DIE EBB BACK FADE STEP
VARY RECUR DEPART DIFFER
RETIRE SHRINK DECLINE DIGRESS
RETREAT CONTRACT DIMINISH
ELONGATE WITHDRAW
RECEIPT CHIT RECU RESET
APOCHA BINDER RECIPE
WARRANT
(PL.) GATE TAKE SALES INCOME
ENTRADA
RECEIVE GET BEAR FALL GAIN
HAVE HOLD TAKE ADMIT AFONG
CATCH GREET GUEST LATCH
RESET ACCEPT ASSUME BORROW
DERIVE GATHER HARBOR RECULE
BELIEVE CONTAIN EMBRACE
INHERIT SUSTAIN UNDERFO
PERCEIVE
(— A CRIMINAL) RESET
(— AS GUEST) FANG HOST VANG
GREET
(— AS MEMBER) INCEPT
(— AS REWARD) REAP
(— FROM LOTTERY) DRAW
(— SHEETS) FLY
(— WITH PLEASURE) GRATIFY
(PREF.) RECIPIO
RECEIVER FENCE PHONE PERNOR
SINDICO CYMAPHEN DONATARY
REHEATER
(— IN BANKRUPTCY) SINDICO
(— OF INCOME) PERNOR
(— OF STOLEN GOODS) LOCK
FENCE
(TELEGRAPH —) INKER INKWRITER
(TELEPHONE —) PHONE CYMAPHEN
RECEIVING PERNANCY
RECENSION REVIEW SURVEY
CENSURE CRITIQUE
RECENT HOT NEW LATE PUNY
ENDER FRESH GREEN HOURLY
LATELY LATTER MODERN
CURRENT HOLOCENE NEOTERIC
(MOST —) LAST
(PREF.) CAEN(O) CEN(O) NE(O)
(SUFF.) CENE
RECENTLY ANEW JUST LATE
NEWLY LASTLY LATELY FRESHLY
LATTERLY
RECENTNESS YOUTH
RECEPTACLE ARK BIN BOX CAN
CUP DIP FAT PAN TIN TUB URN
VAT BATH BOAT BOWL CASE
CELL CIST DOVE DROP FACK
FONT HELL HOLD INRO LOOM
RACK RECU SAFE SINK TIDY TOUR
ARBOR CARRY CREEL KIOSK KITTY

RESET SCOOP STEAN STEEN
TABLE TORUS BASKET BUCKET
BUTLER CARTON CUPULE DIPPER
DRAWER HAMPER HOPPER
MORTAR PITCHI POCKET SHRINE
TABLET TROUGH ASHTRAY
CAPSULE CARRIER CORBULA
DUSTBIN ENVELOP HEADBOX
LATRINE OMNIBUS OSSUARY
PARISON RECEIPT SANDBOX
SETTLER SOAPBOX STOWAGE
TRAVOIS BURSICLE CANISTER
CESSPOOL FOREBOOT GYNOBASE
HONEYPOT LOCKFAST OSSARIUM
OVERFLOW PERFUMER SPITTOON
STOCKPOT SEPULCHER
(— FOR ABANDONED INFANTS)
TOUR
(— FOR BONES) OSSUARY
OSSARIUM
(— FOR BROKEN TYPE) HELL
(— FOR BUTTER) RUSKIN
(— FOR COAL) BUNKER
(— FOR CONVEYING) APRON
(— FOR DRY ARTICLES) FAT
(— FOR FOUL THINGS) SINK
(— FOR GLASS BATCH) ARBOR
(— FOR HOLY WATER) FONT
(— FOR ORE-CRUSHING) MORTAR
(— FOR POKER CHIPS) KITTY
(— FOR SACRED RELICS) TABLE
SHRINE TABLET SEPULCHRE
(— FOR SAVINGS) SOCK
(— FOR SEWING MATERIALS) TIDY
(— FOR TREASURE) HANAPER
(— FOR TYPE CASES) RACK
(— FOR VOTES) SITULA
(— IN BOTTLE-MAKING MACHINE)
PARISON
(— OF CLAY OR STONE) STEAN
STEEN
(— OF FLOWER) THALAMUS
(— ON WEIGHING SCALES) PAN
(— OVER ALTAR) DOVE
(CLAY —) BOOT
(DILATED —) GYNOBASE
(ELECTRICAL —) BASEPLUG
(INCENSE —) ACERRA
(OPEN —) TRAY
(PURSELIKE —) BURSICLE
(TAILOR'S —) HELL
(WOODEN —) SEBILLA
(SUFF.) CLINE CLINIC CLINIUM
RECEPTION TEA ROUT COURT
CRUSH DIFFA LEVEE SALON
TREAT ACCOIL DURBAR RUELLE
SOIREE SQUASH ACCUEIL
COUCHEE MATINEE OVATION
PASSAGE RECEIPT RECUEIL
TEMPEST WELCOME ASSEMBLY
FUNCTION GREETING PERNANCY
REACTION SOCIABLE
ACCEPTANCE
(— AT BEDTIME) COUCHEE
(— OF NATIVE PRINCES) DURBAR
(— OF SOUND) AUDIO
(ARABIC —) DIFFA
(CORDIAL —) WELCOME
(CROWDED —) SQUASH
(FASHIONABLE —) LEVEE SALON
(WEDDING —) INFARE
RECEPTIVE OPEN SENSORY
OPENHANDED

RECEPTOR STOCK RECEIVER
DOMINATOR
RECERCELEE SARCELLY
RECESS ALA ARK BAY BOX COD
CUP PAN BOLE BUNK COVE DEEP
HOLE NOOK TRAP AMBRY BOSOM
BOWER CANAL CAVUM CLEFT
CREEK HAVEN HITCH INLET
NICHE ORIEL PRESS SINUS
ALCOVE ANCONA CAVERN
CENTER CHAPEL CIRQUE CLOSET
COFFER CRANNY EXEDRA
GROTTO INDENT LOCULE RABBET
REBATE BEDSITE CONCAVE
CREVICE LOCULUS MANHOLE
RETREAT SINKING INTERVAL
LOCKHOLE OVERTURE TABLINUM
TOKONOMA TRAVERSE VACATION
PIGEONHOLE
(— BETWEEN CAPES) BAY
(— FOR FAMILY RECORDS)
TABLINUM
(— FOR HINGE LEAF) PAN
(— FOR PIECE OF SCULPTURE)
ANCONA
(— IN CHURCH WALL) AMBRY
(— IN COLON) HAUSTRUM
(— IN JAPANESE HOUSE)
TOKONOMA
(— IN MOUNTAIN) CIRQUE
(— IN ROCK) HITCH
(— IN SIDE OF HILL) CORRIE
(— IN SIDE OF ROOM) ALA
(— IN WALL) BOLE NICHE ALCOVE
(— ON STAGE) CANOPY
(INMOST —) BOSOM
(PL.) FLASH
RECESSED SUNK SUNKEN
RECESSION BUST RETREAT
RECESSIVE BACKWARD RECEDING
RETIRING WITHDRAWN
RECHAB (SON OF —) MALCHIAH
JEHONADAB
RECHERCHE RARE CHOICE EXOTIC
CURIOUS PRECIOUS UNCOMMON
EXQUISITE
RECIDIVIST REPEATER
RECIPE RX FORM RULE FORMULA
RECEIPT
RECIPIENT HEIR DONEE ALMSMAN
DONATEE DONATORY LAUREATE
(SUFF.) EE
RECIPROCAL CROSS COMMON
MUTUAL SECANT SEESAW
(— OF A POISE) RHE
(— OF VISCOSITY) FLUIDITY
(PREF.) COUNTER INTER
RECIPROCATE REPAY RETURN
REQUITE RETROACT
RECIPROCITY SHU ISOPOLITY
MUTUALITY
RECITAL TALE ASHRE CITAL RECIT
STORY EXPOSE LITANY PARADE
REPEAT TIKKUN READING
RELATION REPETITION
(— OF PRAYER) GEULAH HAMOTZI
KEDUSHAH
(UNTRUE —) TALE
(SUFF.) LOG(ER)(IA)(IAN)(IC)(ICAL)
(IST)(UE)(Y)
RECITATION DHIKR READING
RECITAL RHAPSODY
RECITATIVE SCENA

CHANSON PARLANDO

RECITE SAY CARP TELL STATE
INTONE RECKON RELATE RENDER
REPEAT DECLAIM DECLINE
DICTATE NARRATE RECOUNT
REHEARSE
(— AS ELOCUTION EXERCISE)
DECLAIM
(— IN MONOTONE) INTONE
(— METRICALLY) SCAN
(— MONOTONOUSLY) CHANT
CHAUNT
(— NUMBERS) COUNT
(— PRAYERS) BENSH DAVEN
(— TIRESOMELY) THRUM
(— WITH GREAT EASE) RUSH
RECITER SCALD SKALD ANTERI
DISEUR CONTEUR DISEUSE
HOMERIST ILIADIST RHAPSODE
RECITING CHARM
RECK RAK CARE DEEM PASS
MATTER REGARD CONCERN
CONSIDER ESTIMATE
RECKLESS RASH WILD BLIND
FOLLE PERDU MADCAP RACKLE
SAVAGE GALLOWS RAMSTAM
CARELESS HEADLONG HEEDLESS
BLINDFOLD
RECKLESSLY FAST BLIND
RAMSTAM HEADLONG HEADFIRST
RECKLESSNESS BAYARD
RECKON RET ARET CAST DATE
ITEM RATE RECK RELY TALE TELL
TOTE ALLOT AUDIT CLAIM CLASS
COUNT JUDGE PLACE RETTE
SCORE TALLY THINK ASSIGN
FIGURE IMPUTE NUMBER REPUTE
TOTTLE ACCOUNT ASCRIBE
COMPUTE INCLUDE PRETEND
RECOUNT SUPPOSE SUPPUTE
CONSIDER ESTIMATE
(— IN) INCLUDE
RECKONING TAB BILL NICK POST
SHOT TAIL TALE COUNT SCORE
TALLY COMPOT LAWING REASON
TAILYE TOTTLE ACCOUNT
DAYTALE TAILZEE COMPUTUS
(TAVERN —) LAWING
RECLAIM IN TAME ASSART OBJECT
RECALL REDEEM REFORM RESCUE
SUBDUE PROTEST RECOVER
RESTORE
(— FROM SAVAGE STATE) CIVILIZE
RECLAIMANT GOEL
RECLINE LIE LIG LEAN LOLL REST
COUCH ACCUMB RECUMB
UPLEAN DISCUMB
(— LANGUIDLY) GAULSH
RECLINING CUMBENT ACCUMBENT
ACCUBATION
RECLUSE NUN MONK CULDEE
HERMIT REMOTE ASCETIC
EREMITE INCLUSA INCLUSE
ANCHORET INCLUSUS SECLUDED
SOLITARY SCIOPHYTE SOLITAIRE
(PL.) SECLUSE
RECOGNITION FAME SPUR HONOR
SENSE CREDIT STATUS FEELING
KENNING KNOWING AGNITION
SANCTION ANAGNOSIS
(— OF ACHIEVEMENT) LAUREL
CITATION
(SUFF.) GNOSIA GNOSIS

GNOSTIC GNOSY

RECOGNIZE KEN SEE WIT ESPY
FACE KNOW SPOT TELL ADMIT
ALLOW BLINK CROWN HONOR
KEETH KITHE KYTHE ACCEPT
ACKNOW AGNIZE BEKNOW
COUTHE REVISE CORRECT
DISCERN REALIZE ACCREDIT
(— IN ANY CAPACITY) AGNIZE
RECOGNIZED GOOD CLEAR
KNOWN CLASSIC FAMILIAR
RECOIL SHY BALK KICK TURN
REBUT SHRUG SHUCK START
STRAM BLENCH BOUNCE FLINCH
RECULE RESILE RESULT RETORT
SHRINK REBOUND REDOUND
REVERSE BACKLASH REJOUNCE
(WITHOUT —) DEADBEAT
RECOLLECT RECALL RECORD
RETAIN BETHINK COMPOSE
RECOVER RECOLETO REMEMBER
RECOLLECTION MIND MEMORY
RECALL RECORD MINDING
THOUGHT MEMORIAL SOUVENIR
ANAMNESIS
RECOMMENCE RENEW REOPEN
RESUME REPRISE
RECOMMEND MOVE OSSE PLUG
TOUT WISH ADVISE COMMIT
PRAISE PREFER COMMEND
CONSIGN COUNSEL ENTRUST
ADVOCATE RECOMMIT
RECOMMENDATION CHIT VOEU
ADVISE COUNSEL TESTIMONY
(PARTY —) COUPON
(SERVANT'S —) CHIT
RECOMPENSE PAY MEED MEND
MENSE QUITS REPAY YIELD
AMENDS BOUNTY HADBOT
RECOUP REWARD SALARY
GUERDON IMBURSE PAYMENT
PREMIUM REQUITE RESTORE
SATISFY SERVICE
RECONCILE GREE WEAN ADAPT
AGREE ATONE ACCORD ADJUST
SETTLE SHRIVE REUNITE
HARMONIZE
RECONCILED FAIN VAIN SAUGHT
RECONCILIATION ATONE ACCORD
SAUGHT REUNION IRENICON
RECONDITE DARK DEEP HIGH
HIDDEN MYSTIC OCCULT SECRET
CRYPTIC CURIOUS OBSCURE
RETIRED ABSTRACT ABSTRUSE
ESOTERIC
RECONNAISSANCE RECCE RECCO
RECCY SURVEY
RECONNOITER SCOUT RECALL
SURVEY EXAMINE PICKEER
DISCOVER REMEMBER
RECONSIDER REVIEW FORTHINK
RECONSTRUCT RECAST REPAIR
REEVOKE REMODEL RESTORE
RECORD CAN CUT BOOK CARD
DATE DISC ITER MARK NICK PAGE
ROLL SING SLIP WICK ALBUM
CHART DIARY ENACT ENTER
ENTRY FASTI GRAPH JUMBO
PRICK QUIPO QUIPU SIJIL SLATE
STYLE TITLE ANNALS CHARGE
DOCKET LEGEND MEMOIR SCROLL
SPREAD WARBLE ACCOUNT
CALENDS CITATOR DUBBING

KALENDS LEXICON MENTION
MYOGRAM SHOWING TICKLER
TRACING ANAGRAPH ARCHIVES
CYLINDER ENTRANCE ERGOGRAM
HERDBOOK INSCROLL JUDGMENT
KYMOGRAM LAUEGRAM
MARIGRAM MELOGRAM
MEMORIAL MONUMENT
ONDOGRAM PANCHART PRESSING
REGISTER REMEMBER SCHEDULE
STUDBOOK OBSERVATION
OSCILLOGRAM
(— BY NOTCHES) SCORE
(— OF CAR MOVEMENTS) JUMBO
(— OF DOCUMENT) PROTOCOL
(— OF EVENTS) FASTI
(— OF FOOTPRINTS) STIBOGRAM
(— OF HUMANITY'S FATE) SIJIL
SIJILL
(— OF JOURNEY) JOURNAL
ITINERARY
(— OF LOAN) CHARGE
(— OF MUHAMMAD'S SAYINGS)
HADIT
(— OF MUSCULAR WORK)
ERGOGRAM
(— OF PROCEEDINGS) ACTA ITER
JOURNAL MINUTES
(COMPUTER —) PRINTOUT
(COURT —) EYRE
(DAILY —) DIARY
(DEMONSTRATION —) DEMO
(FORMAL —) ACT
(HISTORICAL —) STORY
(MAGNETIC —) DISK FLOPPY
(PHONOGRAPH —) DISC DISK
MONO SINGLE BISCUIT SHELLAC
(SHIP'S —) LOG
(PL.) LIBER ANNALS ARCHIVE
MEMORABILIA
(PREF.) DISC(I)(O)
(SUFF.) GRAM GRAPH(ER)(IA)(IC)(Y)
RECORDER FLUTE BOOKER
FLAUTO NOTATOR GREFFIER
REGISTER
RECORDING ALBUM ALIVE LABEL
CUTTING
(— AWARD) GRAMMY
RECOUNT MING TELL COUNT
DEVISE RECITE REGARD RELATE
REPEAT SPREAD EXPRESS
HISTORY NARRATE CONSIDER
DESCRIBE REHEARSE
RECOUP DEDUCT REGAIN
RECOVER INDEMNIFY
RECOUPLING HOOKUP
RECOURSE SUIT ACCESS APPEAL
REFUGE RESORT STRING REGRESS
RESTAUR RISORSE
(HAVE —) RECUR
RECOVER DOW COUR COWR CURE
FIRM HEAL KERE COVER RALLY
REACH UPSET BOUNCE RECURE
REGAIN RESCUE RESUME RETAKE
RETIRE REVERT REVOKE WARISH
DELIVER OVERGET OVERPUT
OVERSET READEPT RECLAIM
RECRUIT REPAREL REPRISE
RESTORE RETRIEVE
RECOVERER DIGESTER
RECOVERY CURE RECOUR
RECURE REMEDY RETURN
SALVAGE COMEBACK

SNAPBACK RECLAMATION
RECREANT FALSE CRAVEN
YELLOW APOSTATE COWARDLY
DESERTER RECRAYED
RECREATE AMUSE EVOKE REVIVE
RECREATION PLAY SPORT SOLACE
RENEWAL ACTIVITY DIVERSION
PALINGENY
(PERIOD OF —) HOLIDAY VACATION
RECREATIVE PLAYING
RECREMENT SLAG DROSS SCORIA
RECRUIT BLEU BOOT FRESH RAISE
SPROG GATHER INTAKE MUSTER
RECREW REPAIR REVIVE RECOVER
REFRESH RESTORE ASSEMBLE
BEZONIAN CONSCRIPT
(RAW —) ROOKY ROOKIE
RECTAL
(PREF.) ARCHO
RECTANGLE BOX SQUARE
CHECKER
(COTTON —) HUIPIL
(CURVILINEAR —) TESSERA
(WOVEN —) SINKER
RECTANGULAR SQUARE BOXLIKE
EMERALD
RECTIFICATION REFORM
LIMATION
RECTIFIER DIODE VALVE COLUMN
DETECTOR EXCITRON
RECTIFY AMEND EMEND RIGHT
ADJUST BETTER DETECT REFORM
REMEDY CORRECT IMPROVE
REDRESS EMENDATE REGULATE
RECTITUDE DOOM EQUITY
JUSTICE PROBITY
RECTOR RULER LEADER PARSON
PERSONA INCUMBENT
RECTUM SIEGE TEWEL
(PREF.) ARCHO PROCT(O) RECTO
RECUMBENT IDLE PRONE JACENT
CUMBENT LEANING RESTING
INACTIVE REPOSING
RECUPERATE MEND RALLY
REFETE REGAIN RECOVER
RECRUIT RETRIEVE
RECUR CYCLE REFER REPEAT
RESORT RETURN REOCCUR
REVOLVE REAPPEAR
(— CONSTANTLY) HAUNT
RECURRENCE RESORT RETURN
ATAVISM REPRISE ITERANCE
ITERANCY RECOURSE
(— OF SOUND) CADENCE
(SUFF.) LY
RECURRENT CYCLIC FREQUENT
PERENNIAL
RECURRING ROLLING CONTINUAL
(— ANNUALLY) ETESIAN
(— EVERY THIRD DAY) TERTIAN
(— EVERY 72 HOURS) QUARTAN
(— ON NINTH DAY) NONAN
NONANE
(— ON SEVENTH DAY) SEPTAN
(CONSTANTLY —) ETERNAL
(CONTINUALLY —) CONSTANT
(SUFF.) ENNIAL
RECURVED REFLEX ERICOID
RECUTTING FRESHING
RED (ALSO SEE COLOR) GOYA
GULY PINK PUCE ROJO ROSY
RUBY ANGRY CANNA CORAL
FIERY JUDAS ROUGE RUDDY

RUFUS ARCHIL AZALEA BLOODY CERISE FLORID FULGID GARNET HECTIC NECTAR ORCHIL ORIENT RAISIN RUBRIC TITIAN TRYPAN VERMIL WANTON CARMINE GLOWING NACARAT PIMENTO RADICAL RUBELLE RUBIOUS STAMMEL VERMILY ARMENIAN AUBUSSON BORDEAUX CARDINAL CHOLERIC COLORADO FLAGRANT MANDARIN MOROCAIN RUBICUND SANGUINE ARTILLERY COQUELICOT

(— AND INFLAMED) BLOODSHOT

(— PLANET) MARS

(ANTIQUE —) CANNA

(BRIGHT —) TULY CHERRY PUNICIAL VERMILION

(DARK —) CLARET

(EUREKA —) PUCE

(FIERY —) MINIUM

(GRAYISH —) AZALEA

(HERALDIC —) GULES

(IRON OXIDE —) AGATE TARRAGONA

(PURPLISH —) LAKE MURREY MAGENTA

(WAX —) COPPER

(YELLOWISH —) MAROON

(PREF.) ERYTHR(O) PHENIC(O) PHOENIC(O) PYRRH(O) PYRRO RHOD(O) RUBE RUBI RUBO RUBRI RUBRO RUFI RUFO

RED ADMIRAL VANESSA

RED AND THE BLACK (AUTHOR OF —) STENDHAL

(CHARACTER IN —) SOREL FOUQUE JULIEN PIRARD DERENAL VALENOD MATHILDE

RED-BACKED SHRIKE POPE

RED BADGE OF COURAGE

(AUTHOR OF —) CRANE

(CHARACTER IN —) JIM HENRY WILSON CONKLIN FLEMING

RED BANEBERRY REDBERRY TOADROOT

RED BAY PERSEA

RED-BELLIED (— TERRAPIN) SLIDER SKILPOT

(— WOODPECKER) CHAB

RED-BREASTED BREAM FLATFISH FLOUNDER

RED-BREASTED KNOT GRAYBACK GREYBACK

REDBUD CERCIS JUNEBUD

RED CAMPION ROBIN SOLDIER

RED CEDAR SAVIN SABINA JUNIPER

RED CLOVER SAPLING TREFOIL TRIFOLY

RED CURRANT GOYA RIZZLE TIZZAR

REDD RID COMB OPEN LITTER NEATEN REFUSE RESCUE SETTLE ARRANGE DELIVER SMARTEN UNBLOCK UNRAVEL

RED DEER OLEN SPAY STAG

(FEMALE —) HIND

(MALE —) HART STAG

REDDEN RUD FIRE RUBY BLUSH FLUSH LIGHT ROUGE RUDDY BLOODY RUBIFY RUBRIC RUDDLE EMPURPLE

REDDISH REDDY RUDDY RUFUS FLUSHY GINGER RUFOUS COLORADO PYRRHOUS RUBICUND

RED DRUM SPOT REDFISH

REDEAR SHELLCRACKER

REDEEM BUY WIN SAVE ALESE CLEAR LOUSE REPRY BORROW OFFSET RANSOM DELIVER FULFILL JUSTIFY RECLAIM WITHBEG AGAINBUY LIBERATE

REDEEMER GOEL SAVIOR

REDEMPTION RANSOM REFORM SAFETY SALVATION

REDEYE BASS RUDD VIREO SUNFISH

RED-EYE CATSUP CICADA WHISKY

RED-EYED VIREO REDEYE GRASSET PREACHER

RED-FACED FLUSHED SCARLET

REDFIN DACE SHINER REDHORSE YELLOWFIN

REDFISH SALMON FATHEAD ROSEFISH

RED GOOSEFOOT PIGWEED SOWBANE

RED GROUPER MERO NEGRE REDBELLY

RED GROUSE GORHEN GORCOCK LAGOPODE MOORBIRD MUIRFOWL

RED GUM JARRAH EUCALYPT

RED GURNARD CUR ELLECK ROCHET SOLDIER

RED-HAIRED RUFUS CARROTY

REDHEAD DIVER FINCH POCHARD KIZILBASH

RED HIND GRAYSBY GROUPER CABRILLA

REDHORSE REDFIN SUCKER

REDIA SPOROSAC

REDIRECT DISPLACE READDRESS

REDISTILL COHOBATE

REDISTRIBUTE FRESHEN REASSIGN

RED LAVER SLOKE

REDNESS RED RUD GLOW HEAT RUDD RUBOR ERYTHEMA RUBEDITY

(— OF SKY) AURORA

REDO REDACT RESTYLE

(— UNSKILLFULLY) BOTCH

RED OCHER TIVER ABRAUM RUDDLE

REDOLENCE BALM AROMA SCENT

REDOLENT RICH ODOROUS SCENTED AROMATIC FRAGRANT SMELLING

RED OSIER WILLOW REDBRUSH

REDOUBLE REECHO INTENSIFY

REDOUBT FEAR MASK DREAD SCHANZ SCONCE BULWARK

REDOUND TURN ACCRUE BILLOW CONDUCE REFLECT OVERFLOW

RED RASPBERRY CUTHBERT

REDRESS HEAL DRESS REDUB AVENGE OFFSET REFORM RELIEF REMEDE REMEDY REPAIR ADDRESS CORRECT RECTIFY REFOUND RELIEVE

RED ROCKFISH TAMBOR

REDROOT PIGWEED

RED ROVER (AUTHOR OF —) COOPER

(CHARACTER IN —) ARK FID DICK HENRY AFRICA DELACY SCIPIO WILDER WYLLYS BIGNALL GRAYSON GERTRUDE RODERICK

RED SAGE LANTANA

RED SANDALWOOD CHANDAM

REDSHANK CLEE TEUK SHAKE GAMBET REDLEG YELPER PELLILE TATTLER

REDSKIN RED ROJO TAWNY INDIAN

REDSTART YELPER BRANTAIL FIRETAIL WHITECAP FIREFLIRT

RED STOPPER EUGENIA IRONWOOD

RED-TAILED (— HAWK) REDTAIL

(— TROPIC BIRD) KOAE

RED-TAPISM BEADLEDOM

RED-THROATED LOON WABBY

REDTOP COUCH FIORIN FINETOP FINEBENT FURZETOP BLUEJOINT

REDUCE CUT BATE CLIP DOCK DROP EASE PARE PULL THIN ABASE ABATE ALLAY APPAL BREAK DRAFT ELIDE LOWER QUELL SCANT SHAVE SLAKE SLASH SMELT ATTRIT DEDUCE DEFALK DEJECT DELETE DEPOSE DILUTE HUMBLE LESSEN REBATE REDUCT SHRINK SUBACT SUBDUE WEAKEN ABANDON ABRIDGE ASSUAGE ATOMIZE CHANCER CONQUER CURTAIL DEFLATE DEGRADE DEPLETE DWINDLE ECLIPSE FRITTER INHIBIT RESOLVE RETREAT SCISSOR SHORTEN SUBJECT ABSTRACT ATTEMPER CONDENSE DECREASE DIMINISH MINIMIZE

(— ACCORDING TO FIXED RATIO) SCALE

(— ANGLE) CHAMFER

(— BULK) BLEND

(— LUMBER) SIZE

(— PROFITS) SQUEEZE

(— PURITY) ALLOY

(— STONE BLOCKS) SPALL SPAWL

(— THE VALUE) DECRY BEGGAR DEPRAVE

(— TO A MEAN) AVERAGE

(— TO ASHES) CREMATE

(— TO CARBON) CHAR

(— TO FINE PARTICLES) ATOMIZE MICRONIZE

(— TO FLAT SURFACE) LEVEL

(— TO INSIGNIFICANCE) DROWN

(— TO LOWER GRADE) BREAK DEMOTE DEGRADE

(— TO NIL) CLOSE

(— TO NOTHING) ANNUL

(— TO PASSIVITY) CHINAFY PROSTRATE

(— TO POWDER) GRIND PULVERIZE

(PREF.) DE

REDUCED SUNK TAIL BROKEN CURTATE DWARFED DEGRADED WEAKENED VESTIGIAL

REDUCTION BUST LETUP SLASH CUTBACK CUTDOWN DOCKAGE SHAVING ANALYSIS DILUTION DISCOUNT ABATEMENT SHRINKAGE

(— IN FORCE) RIF

(— IN PITCH) DROP

(— IN PRICE) SAVING CONCESSION

(SUFF.) LYSE LYSIS LYST LYTE LYTIC LYZE

REDUNDANCY EXCESS NIMIETY SURPLUS PLEONASM PLETHORA VERBIAGE MACROLOGY TAUTOLOGY

REDUNDANT WORDY LAVISH PROFUSE SURPLUS VERBOSE SWELLING EXCESSIVE

REDWING POP THRUSH WINDLE GADWALL WINNARD

REDWOOD MAD AMBOYNA BARWOOD FURIOUS SEQUOIA MAHOGANY

RE-ECHO REWORD REBOUND RESOUND REDOUBLE

REED NAL RIE RIX SAG BENT JUNK PIPE PIRN RODE SLEY TULE ARROW DONAX SPEAR TWILL BENNEL RADDLE SAGGON CALAMUS FISTULA WHISTLE WINDING ABOMASUM

(— FOR WARPING) WRAITHE

(— FOR WINDING THREAD) PIRN SPOOL

(— IN ORGAN) VIBRATOR

(— OF LOOM) COMB

(FOXTAIL —) DOD

(GIANT —) DONAX

(MUSICAL —) OAT

(WEAVER'S —) SLAY SLEY RADDLE SLEIGH

(PL.) SPEAR

(PREF.) ARUNDI CALAM(I)(O)

REED BENT CARRIZO

REEDBIRD BOBOLINK

REEDBUCK BOHOR NAGOR REITBOK

REED BUNTING RINGBIRD

REED CANARY GRASS SPIRE DAGGERS

REED END TONGUE

REEDING GADROON MILLING STRIGIL GRAINING

REED MACE RAUPO CATTAIL MATREED

REED ORGAN MELODEON HARMONIUM

REED PIPE MIRLITON

REED WARBLER PITBIRD

REEDY THIN WEAK FRAIL TWILLED

REEF CAY KAY KEY CAYO LODE RYFT SCAR VEIN ATOLL LEDGE SHELF STICK BOILER REEFER SADDLE SKERRY BAGREEF BALANCE BIOHERM MAKATEA TOMBOLO

REEFER CAR COAT STICK JACKET MUGGLES

REEK FOG FUG EMIT FUME HEAP MIST PILE RICK RISE VENT EQUIP EXUDE ISSUE NIDOR SMEEK SMOKE STEAM VAPOR EXHALE OUTFIT EMANATE

(— WITH CORRUPTION) FESTER

REEL PIRN RANT ROCK SPIN STOT SWAB SWIM TURN GIDDY SPOOL SWIFT TRULL WAVER WHEEL WHIRL WINCE WINCH BOBBIN RECOIL SWERVE TOTTER TUMULT WAGGLE WALTER WELTER

WINDER WINDLE WINNLE WINTLE
BALLOON STAGGER SWABBLE
TITUBATE
(— FOR DRAWING SILK) FILATURE
(— FOR WARP DRYING) BALLOON
(— FOR WINDING YARN) PIRN
SWIFT
(— OFF A STORY) SCRIEVE
(— USED FOR YARN) CRIB
(DYEING —) WINCE
(FISHING —) TROW TROLL TRULL
WINCH
(PL.) REVELS
REELER TWINER
REELING TURN AREEL LURCH
FILATURE STAGGERY WAMBLING
REEM MOAN URUS UNICORN
REEVE REE REFE THREAD BAILIFF
PROVOST STEWARD OVERSEER
REFECTION MEAL RELIEF REPAST
HOGMANAY
REFECTORY FRATER FRATRY
REFER DEFER LEAVE POINT
ADVERT ALLUDE APPEAL ASSIGN
CHARGE COMMIT DELATE DIRECT
IMPUTE PREFER RELATE SUBMIT
ASCRIBE REJOURN RELEGATE
(— TO) SEE CITE INTEND
CONCERN CONSULT MENTION
INTIMATE
(— TO SOMETHING REPEATEDLY)
HARP
REFEREE BREHON UMPIRE ARBITER
AUDITOR
REFERENCE TAB FOLIO REMIT
SIGIL APPEAL REGARD RENVOI
BEARING MEANING RESPECT
ALLUSION HANDBOOK INNUENDO
RELATION
(— WORK) ATLAS INDEX ALMANAC
LEXICON CATALOGUE GAZETTEER
(SATIRICAL —) GLANCE
REFERENDUM POLL MANDATE
REFINE RUN TRY BOLT EDIT FILE
FINE PURE CUPEL EXALT PLAIN
SLICK SMELT AFFINE DECOCT
EXCOCT FILTER GARBLE SMOOTH
CONCOCT ELEVATE PERFECT
SUBLIME SWEETEN CIVILIZE
HUMANIZE URBANIZE
(— AS GOLD) TEST CARAT
(— PULP) JORDAN
(— SUGAR) CLAY
(— WINE) FORCE
REFINED FINE GENT NEAT NICE
TRIE ATTIC EXACT PURED TERSE
CHASTE EXCOCT INLAND NIMINY
POLITE QUAINT SUBTLE CLEANLY
COURTLY ELEGANT GENTEEL
PRECISE SCRAPED AUGUSTAN
DELICATE ELEVATED HIGHBRED
PRECIEUS PRECIOUS SERAPHIC
RECHERCHE
(NOT —) CRUDE
(TOO —) FINESPUN
REFINEMENT GRACE NICETY
POLISH CULTURE FINESSE
DELICACY ELEGANCE POLITURE
SUBTLETY URBANITY PRECIOSITY
REFINER TRIER JORDAN PURIFIER
REFINING HUMAN FINING
CULTURE AFFINAGE
REFINISH ANTIQUE

REFLECT COW CHEW MUSE PORE
SHOW BLAZE FLASH GLASS GLINT
IMAGE SHINE STUDY THINK
ADVISE DAZZLE DEBATE MIRROR
PONDER RECORD REFLEX RELUCE
RETORT RETURN REVISE STEVEN
EXPRESS PERPEND REDOUND
REFRACT SHIMMER COGITATE
CONSIDER MEDITATE REDOUBLE
RUMINATE
(— IRREGULARLY) SCATTER
(— UPON) SPECULATE
REFLECTED DERIVED MIRRORED
SPECULAR
REFLECTING
(SUFF.) ESCENT
REFLECTION ECHO FOLD IDEA
SKIT BLAME GHOST GLARE
GNOME DEBATE MUSING PONDER
REFLEX RETURN SHADOW
CENSURE COUNSEL SPECIES
THOUGHT EYESHINE MOONPATH
THINKING
(— OF SELF IN ANOTHER'S EYES)
BABY
REFLECTIVE PENSIVE
THOUGHTFUL
(— POWER) ALBEDO
REFLECTOR DISH FLAT CRITIC
HASTER SHINER TAMPER
HORIZON DIFFUSER HASTENER
SPECULUM
REFLEX COPY IMAGE TROPISM
ALLUSION
(NOT —) IDEOMOTOR
REFLUX EBB EBBING REFLOW
REFOREST REBOISE
REFORM MEND AMEND EMEND
PRUNE BETTER REBUKE REPAIR
CENSURE CORRECT DISBAND
RECLAIM RECTIFY REDRESS
REFORMATORY COLLEGE
MAGDALEN
REFORMER APOSTLE UTOPIAN
UTOPIAST JANSENIST
REFRACT DIVIDE REFLECT
REFRINGE
REFRACTION REBATE REBOUND
DIACLASIS
REFRACTOR PRISM
REFRACTORY TOUGH SULLEN
UNRULY WANTON ALUNDUM
FROWARD MULLITE RESTIVE
VICIOUS WAYWARD MUTINOUS
PERVERSE STUBBORN
CAMSTEERY REBELLIOUS
REFRAIN BOB TAG CURB DOWN
KEEP SHUN AVOID FORGO SPARE
WONDE BURDEN CHORUS DESIST
FOREGO LUDDEN RETAIN THRAIN
ABSTAIN FORBEAR LULLABY
REFREIT REPRISE TORNADA
FABURDEN FALDERAL OVERCOME
OVERWORD REPETEND RESTRAIN
WITHDRAW
(— FROM) CAN HELP AVOID SPARE
WAIVE FOREGO RESIGN ABSTAIN
(— FROM INDULGENCE) ABSTAIN
(— FROM TELLING) LAYNE
(— FROM USING) BOYCOTT
(— OF SONG) BOB TAG DOWN
FOOT WHEEL BURDEN CHORUS
FALDEROL

(MEANINGLESS —) DERRY
DUCDAME
REFRESH FAN COOL REST CHEER
FRESH SLAKE CAUDLE REFECT
REFETE REGALE REHETE REPOSE
REVIVE UNTIRE COMFORT
FORTIFY FRESHEN QUICKEN
RECRUIT IRRIGATE RECREATE
REFRESHING DEWY BALMY FRESH
TONIC CALLER LIVING BRACING
COOLING
REFRESHMENT BAIT LUNCH
CHARITY NUNCHEON REFRESCO
COLLATION
(PL.) FOURS
REFRIGERANT ICE FREON COOLER
AMMONIA COOLING CRYOGEN
REFRIGERATE CHILL
REFRIGERATION CRYOGENY
REFRIGERATOR FRIG FRIDGE
ICEBOX FREEZER CONDENSER
(— CAR) REEFER
REFUGE ARK DIVE HOLT HOME
PORT ROCK SOIL BIELD GRITH
HAVEN OASIS RESET ASYLUM
BILBIE COVERT HARBOR REFUTE
RESORT SPITAL SUCCOR ALSATIA
CRANNOG RESERVE RETREAT
SHELTER UMBRAGE WARRANT
BOLTHOLE CRANNOGE FORTRESS
HIDEAWAY MAGDALEN
RESOURCE SAFEHOLD
REFUGEE REFFO COWBOY FUIDHIR
FUGITIVE
REFULGENT BRIGHT SHINING
RELUCENT BRILLIANT
REFUND REPAY UPSET REFOUND
RESTORE DRAWBACK KICKBACK
REFURBISH DUST RENEW REVAMP
FRESHEN BRIGHTEN RENOVATE
REFUSAL NAY VEE WARN WONT
DENIAL MITTEN NAYSAY REPULSE
ACCISMUS DECLINAL NEGATION
NEGATIVE
(— TO SPEAK) APHRASIA
REFUSE ASH NAY NIL ORT SUD
BALK COOM DENY DUST JUNK
KEMP NAIT NILL NITE PELF PELT
REDD SCUM SKIM SOIL SUDS
WARN BAVIN COOMB CRAWN
DEADS DRAST DROSS EXPEL
FLOCK NITTE OFFAL RENAY
REPEL SCRAN STENT STUFF
SWASH SWILL TRADE TRASH
WAIVE WASTE COLDER DANDER
DEBRIS FORBID LITTER LUMBER
MIDDEN NAYSAY PALTRY PELTRY
RAFFLE RAMMEL RECUSE REFUGE
REJECT SCRUFF SCULCH SHORTS
SHRUFF SORDES SORDOR SPILTH
BACKING BAGGAGE BROCKLE
DECLINE DETRACT DETRECT
DISAVOW DISOBEY FORSAKE
GARBAGE GUBBINS MULLOCK
OFFSCUM OUTCAST PRUNING
RUBBISH SOILAGE SULLAGE
WITHNAY WITHSAY CRASSIER
DENEGATE DISALLOW DISCLAIM
GARBLING LEAVINGS RIFFRAFF
SWEEPAGE WITHHOLD
OFFSCOURING
(— ADMISSION) CLOSE
(— FROM CHARCOAL

(OR COKE) BREEZE
(— FROM COFFEE BERRIES)
TAILINGS
(— FROM CUTTING UP WHALE)
GURRY
(— FROM MELTING METALS) SLAG
DROSS SCORIA
(— FROM SIFTING COFFEE-BEANS)
TRIAGE
(— FROM THRESHING) HUSK
COLDER
(— GREASE) COOM COOMB
(— OF MINE) DEAD
(— OF CROP) STOVER
(— OF FLAX) PAB POB HARDS
HURDS
(— OF FRUITS) MUST
(— OF GRAIN) PUG BRAN
(— OF GRAPES) MARC
(— OF INSECT) FRASS
(— OF MALT) DRAFF
(— OF MINE) BING
(— OF OIL MILLS) SHODE
(— OF PLANTS) ROSS
(— OF SILK) STRASS
(— OF SPICES) GARBLE
(— OF WHALE) FENKS GURRY
TWITTER
(— OF WOOL) BACKINGS
(— TO APPROVE) VETO
(— TO COMPLY) STONEWALL
(— TO GO) JIB BALK
(— TO RECOGNIZE) CUT
(— TO SUPPORT) BOLT
(— TO TALK) DUMMY
(BREWERY —) DRAFF
(FISH —) CHUM GUBBINS
(FOOD —) SWILL
(LEATHER —) SPETCHES
(PLANT —) SCROFF
(STREET —) FULLAGE SCAVAGE
REFUTATION DISPROOF ELENCHUS
HYPOBOLE REBUTTER
REFUTE DENY AVOID REBUT REFEL
ASSOIL CONFUTE CONVELL
CONVICT REPROVE REVINCE
CONFOUND DISPROVE INFRINGE
REDARGUE
REGAIN READEPT RECOVER
RETRIEVE
(— SOMETHING LOST) RECOUP
REGAL REAL ROYAL KINGLY
PURPLE RIGGAL RIGOLE STATELY
IMPERIAL MAJESTIC PRINCELY
REGALIAN SPLENDID
REGALE FETE FEAST TREAT
PLEASE DELIGHT REFRESH
REGALIA KIT ROYALTY
REGALO GIFT BONUS TREAT
REGAN (FATHER OF —) LEAR
(HUSBAND OF —) CORNWALL
(SISTER OF —) GONERIL CORDELIA
REGARD CON CARE DEEM FIND
GAUM GAZE GIVE HEED HOLD
LIKE LOOK MARK MIND RATE
RECK SAKE TELL YEME ADORE
COUNT FAVOR HONOR TREAT
WEIGH ADDEEM ADMIRE ASPECT
BEHOLD ESTEEM FIGURE GLANCE
HOMAGE IMPUTE INTEND LIKING
MOTIVE NOTICE RECKON REMARK
REWARD SURVEY ACCOUNT
ADJUDGE CONCERN OBSERVE

RESPECT RESPITE CONSIDER
ENVISAGE ESTIMATE
(— AS) SEE
(— AS HOPELESS) DEPLORE
(— AS OBJECT OF GREAT INTEREST)
LIONIZE
(— AS PROPER) ACCEPT
(— HIGHLY) ADMIRE CONSIDER
(— WITH PROFOUND RESPECT)
REVERE VENERATE
(— WITH REPUGNANCE) ABHOR
(ATTENTIVE —) EYE
(MENTAL —) EYE
(PL.) COMPLIMENTS
(SUFF.) SCOPE SCOPIC SCOPUS
SCOPY
REGARDED (— WITH AFFECTION)
DEAR AFFECTED
REGARDING ABOUT ANENT
APROPOS
REGARDLESS DEAF CARELESS
HEEDLESS RECKLESS
(— OF THAT) BUT
REGATTA HENLEY LIBERTY
REGEM (FATHER OF —) JAHDAI
REGENCY RULE DOMINION
REGENERATE RENEW REFORM
REVIVE RECLAIM GRACIOUS
RENOVATE
(NOT —) CIVIL
REGENERATION REBIRTH
NEOGENESIS
REGENT RULER RULING WARDEN
SHIKKEN GOVERNOR PANGERANG
PROTECTOR
(— DIAMOND) PITT
(— OF NORTH) KUBERA KUVERA
REGIME FASCISM CAFETERIA
REGIMEN CURE DIET KEEP RULE
REGIMENT
REGIMENT BUFF RULE COLOR
TERCIO GUIDANCE INFANTRY
SLASHERS
(BRITISH —) GRAYS GREYS
(COSSACK —) PULK
(FRAMEWORK OF —) CADRE
(INDIA —) PULTON PULTUN
(SPANISH —) TERCIO
(TURKISH —) ALAI
(28TH —) SLASHERS
REGION DO END ERD EYE GAU
WON AREA BELT KITH KNOT
NECK PART SOIL WONE WOON
ZONE CLIME COAST EARTH
EXURB INDIA MARCH PAGUS
PLACE PLAGE REALM SHIRE
TRACT TROAD ALKALI BORDER
CENTER DESERT DOMAIN EXTENT
GILEAD GROUND GUIANA TATARY
CLIMATE CONFINE COUNTRY
DEMESNE ENCLAVE IMAMATE
KINGDOM MALABAR STATION
TARTARY CHIEFDOM CLUBLAND
DEMERARA DISTRICT ENVIRONS
EPISTOME FLATLAND FORTRESS
FRONTIER KRATOGEN LAKELAND
LATITUDE NAPHTALI PROVINCE
REGIMENT SERICANA STANNARY
TERRITORY
(— ABOVE MOUTH) EPISTOMA
EPISTOME
(— ADJACENT TO BOUNDARY)
MARCH

(— BEYOND ATMOSPHERE) SPACE
(— BEYOND DEATH) CANAAN
(— BORDERING ON HELL) LIMBO
(— FAR AWAY) STRAND
(— IN FIBER) MICELLE
(— NEAR EQUATOR) DOLDRUMS
(— NOTED FOR MANY CONFLICTS)
COCKPIT
(— OF AMPLITUDE) ANTINODE
(— OF CHROMOSOME) PUFF
(— OF COLD AND DARKNESS)
NIFLHEL NIFLHEIM
(— OF DEAD) AMENTI UTGARTHAR
(— OF JAPAN) DO
(— OF MARS) LIBYA
(— OF OCEAN) COUNTRY
(— OF ORIGIN) CRADLE
(— OF PHOTOSPHERE) FACULA
(— OF SHIFTING SAND) ERG
(— OF SIMPLE PLEASURE) ARCADY
ARCADIA
(— OF SOURCE OF GOLD) OPHIR
(— OF TISSUE) FIELD
(— WITHOUT LAW) ALSATIA
(— WITHOUT WOODS) WOLD
WEALD
(CELESTIAL —S) LANGI
(COASTAL —) LITTORAL
(CULTIVATED —) GARDEN
(DARKISH —S ON MARS) MARE
(DESERT —) ERG HAMADA
(DESERTED —) WASTE
(DESOLATE —) PUNA
(DISTANT —) THULE
(E. INDIAN —) DESH
(ELEVATED —) ALTITUDE
(FOREST —) TAIGA
(FORESTED —) MONTANA
(GEOGRAPHICAL —) BOWL SIDE
(HEAVENLY —) SPHERE
(IDEAL —) JINNESTAN
(INFERNAL —S) ABYSS TARTAR
TARTARUS
(LARGE —) COMPAGE
(LIMESTONE —) KARST
(MOUNTAINOUS —) SIERRA
(OPEN —) SAVANNAH
(ORIENTAL —) INDOGAEA
(STAGNANT —) EDDY
(SUPERIOR —) HIGH
(TREELESS —) HIGHMOOR
(UPPER —) HIGH LOFT
(UPPER —S) ETHER
(WOODED —) FOREST
(PL.) DIGGINGS
(PREF.) NESO
(SUFF.) DOM NESE NESIA(N)
NESUS
REGIONAL LOCAL SECTIONAL
REGISTER PIE BEAR BOOK FREE
LIST MARK PILE POLL READ ROLL
STOP ALBUM DIARY ENROL
ENTER FASTI GRILL SIJIL SLATE
ANNALS BEHAVE ENROLL LEDGER
MUSTER RECORD REGEST
ALMANAC ASCRIBE CALENDS
CATALOG COUCHER DIPTYCH
INDORSE KALENDS NOTITIA
ROTULET ANAGRAPH ARCHIVES
CADASTER CALENDAR GREFFIER
INDICATE INSCRIBE MENOLOGY
PEDIGREE POLLBOOK TOLLBOOK
STROHBASS

(— OF JUDGMENTS) DOCKET
(LOWEST —) CHALUMEAU
(MIDDLE —) CLARINO
(OFFICIAL —) TABLEAU CADASTER
REGISTRAR GUARD BURSAR
ACTUARY PATWARI PUTWARI
GREFFIER RESIDENT
REGISTRY FLAG STUDBOOK
REGLET FILET BATTEN FILLET
RIGLET
REGRATER HUCKSTER
REGRESS EGRESS RETURN
ANALYSIS RECOURSE
REGRET REW RUE RUTH GRIEF
DESIRE RELENT REPENT SORROW
DEPLORE REGRATE REMORSE
FORTHINK REPINING
REGRETFUL BAD SORRY REPINING
REGRETTABLE DIRTY DOLOROUS
REGULAR DUE SET EVEN FULL
JUST WEAK SOBER SUANT SUENT
USUAL FORMAL GIUSTO NORMAL
SQUARE STATED STEADY
CANONIC CERTAIN CORRECT
NATURAL ORDERED ORDERLY
ORDINAL PERFECT TYPICAL
UNIFORM COMPLETE CONSTANT
DECOROUS FORMULAR HABITUAL
ORDINARY ORDINATE TESSERAL
(PREF.) SYM
REGULARITY METHOD SQUARE
SYSTEM EVENNESS SYNAPHEA
(— OF NATURE) LAW
REGULARLY DULY EVEN ORDERLY
PROPERLY STATEDLY
REGULATE SET RATE RULE WIND
BOOST FRAME GUIDE ORDER
RIGHT SHAPE ADJUST ASSIZE
BEHAVE DIRECT GOVERN MASTER
RADDLE SETTLE SQUARE TEMPER
ARRANGE CONTROL DISPOSE
MEASURE QUALIFY RECTIFY
ATTEMPER MODERATE MODULIZE
(— FOOD) DIET
(— PITCH) KEY STOP
REGULATED ORDENE ORDERED
ORDERLY
REGULATING BEHIND
REGULATION LAW RULE BYLAW
ORDER REGLE USUAL CURFEW
ZABETA CONTROL PRECEPT
STATUTE VOICING DISPOSAL
STEERAGE
(— OF PRICE) ASSIZE
(DORMITORY —S) PARIETALS
REGULATOR GUIDE DISPOSER
GOVERNOR
REGULUS MATTE SLURRY KINGLET
REHABIAH (FATHER OF —) ELIEZER
(GRANDFATHER OF —) MOSES
REHABILITATE REABLE REPONE
RESTORE REINSTATE
REHASH RECHAUFFE
REHEARSAL CALL HEARSAL
HERSALL PREVIEW CLAMBAKE
NARRATION
REHEARSE TELL TRAIN DETAIL
RECITE RELATE DECLINE
NARRATE RECOUNT DESCRIBE
PRACTICE
REHEAT FLASH
REHOB (SON OF —) HADADEZER
REHOBOAM ROBOAM

(FATHER OF —) SOLOMON
(MOTHER OF —) NAAMAH
REICHSTAG DIET
REIF PLUNDER ROBBERY
REIGN RING RULE REALM RICHE
EMPIRE GOVERN KINGDOM
PREVAIL REGIMENT REGNANCY
(— IN INDIA) RAJ
REIMBURSE PAY REPAY DEFRAY
RECOUP REFUND REBURSE
INDEMNIFY
REIN CURB STOP CHECK SWING
THONG GOVERN BABICHE
LEATHER PLOWLINE RESTRAIN
(PL.) LINES RIBBONS
REINCARNATION REBIRTH
REINDEER REIN CERVID TARAND
CARIBOU CERVINE CERVOID
RANGIFER
REINDEER MOSS SWARD
REINFORCE BAR GUY BACK FACE
STAY BRACE FORCE INLAY STUFF
SUPER CRADLE DOUBLE GUSSET
HARDEN MUSCLE SUPPLY
AFFORCE BOLSTER BULWARK
ENFORCE GROMMET NERVATE
STIFFEN SUPPORT
(— ROAD) SKID
REINFORCED KEYED SPLICED
REINFORCEMENT CREW FUEL
STAY BRACE HURTER CUNETTE
SPLICING STRAINER
(PL.) SUCCOR SUPPLY
REINVIGORATE QUICK REVIVE
RECRUIT RENERVE
REITERATE BACK DING REITER
REPEAT RESUME ITERATE
REHEARSE
REIVER CATERAN
REJECT BEG ORT CAST DEFY DICE
FAIL JILT KICK NILL SPIN ABHOR
BANDY BELIE BRUSH CHECK
EJECT REFEL REPEL SCOUT
SPURN WAIVE ABJECT ABJURE
DELETE DESERT IGNORE RECUSE
REFUSE REFUTE RESPUE RETORT
ABANDON CASHIER CONTEMN
DECLINE DISCARD DISMISS
FORSAKE PROJECT REPROVE
REPULSE ABNEGATE ATHETIZE
DISALLOW DISCLAIM FORSWEAR
NEGATIVE RENOUNCE
THROWOUT
(— A STUDENT) PLUCK PLOUGH
(— COPY) SPIKE
REJECTED OFFCAST OUTCAST
CASTAWAY
REJECTION SACK BRUSH SPURN
DENIAL MITTEN REBUFF REFUSAL
REPULSE DEFIANCE TURNDOWN
(— OF DOCTRINE) HERESY
REJOICE JOY FAIN GAME CHEER
ENJOY EXULT GLORY BLITHE
PLEASE DELIGHT GLADDEN
MAFFICK JUBILATE
REJOICING GLEE MIRTH OVATION
FESTIVITY
REJOIN TAUNT ANSWER REUNITE
REJOINDER REPLY ANSWER
COUNTER RESPONSE
REJUVENATE UNOLD
REKEM (FATHER OF —) HEBRON
REKINDLE RELUME REVIVE

RELAPSE SINK WEED LAPSE
RECIDE RETURN BACKSET
SUBSIDE BACKCAST WITHDRAW
RECIDIVISM
RELATE SAY ALLY BEAR JOIN READ
TELL PITCH REFER SPELL STATE
TOUCH ALLUDE ASSERT DELATE
DETAIL DEVISE RECITE REPORT
REPUTE COGNATE CONCERN
DECLARE INVOLVE NARRATE
PERTAIN RECOUNT CALABASH
DESCRIBE REHEARSE APPERTAIN
(— TO) TOUCH
RELATED KIN SIB AKIN ALLIED
AFFINED
(— BY FATHER'S SIDE) AGNATE
(— INVERSELY) RECIPROCAL
(— ON MOTHER'S SIDE) ENATE
ENATIC COGNATE
(PREF.) **(— BY REMARRIAGE)** STEP
RELATING (ALSO SEE PERTAINING)
(— TO) AGAINST
(— TO A RECENT PAST) ERST
(SUFF.) **(— TO)** AL ATIVE IAL IC(AL)
ILE INE ISH ISTIC ITIC ITIOUS
RELATION KIN SIB TALE BLOOD
FETII AFFINE DATIVE REGARD
ACCOUNT BEARING HISTORY
KINSHIP KINSMAN RAPPORT
RESPECT SCHESIS TELLING
AFFINITY HABITUDE RELATIVE
TENDENCY REFERENCE
REHEARSAL RISHTADAR
PROPORTION
(— BETWEEN SPECIES) AFFINITY
(— OF LIKENESS) ANALOGY
(BLOOD —) KIN SIB
(FIXED —) RATIO
(FRIENDLY —S) AMITY
(SYNTACTIC —) FUNCTION
(WORKING —) GEAR
RELATIONSHIP KIN BLOOD
ACTION AGENCY AMENITY
AMITATE ANALOGY ANGULUS
BEARING CONTACT KINDRED
KINSHIP LIAISON RESPECT
SIBNESS SIBREDE SOCIETY
AFFINITY AGNATION CONTRAST
GOSSIPRY RELATIVE SYMPATHY
COGNATION FILIATION
(BUSINESS —) ACCOUNT
(CLOSE —) BOSOM AFFIANCE
INTIMACY BELONGING
(INHARMONIOUS —) OUTS
(MARITAL —) BED
(MATHEMATICAL —) PARITY
(MUTUAL —) TERMS SYMMETRY
(SEXUAL —) AFFAIR
(SOCIAL —) FOOTING
RELATIVE KIN ALLY BLOOD AFFINE
AGNATE ALLIED COUSIN GERMAN
KINDRED KINSMAN APPOSITE
COGNATUS RELATION RELEVANT
PERTINENT
(PL.) KIN SIB FOLK KINDRED
KINFOLK KINNERY KINSFOLK
RELAX LAX GIVE REST ABATE
BREAK LOOSE REMIT SLACK
DIVERT LAXATE SOFTEN UNBEND
UNGIVE UNKNIT DEBLOCK
RELEASE RESOLVE SLACKEN
UNPURSE MITIGATE UNBUCKLE
UNCLENCH

RELAXATION EASE LAZE REST
ATONY CREEP LETUP RELAX
SOLACE DETENTE LETDOWN
RELACHE BREATHER DIVERSION
RELAXED LAX LASH LOOSE SLACK
SONSY REMISS SONSIE INFORMAL
RESOLVED UNBENDED UNBRACED
RELAXING ANIMAL ANODYNE
DETENTE
(— POINT) SEAR
RELAY SPELL RELIEF REMUDA
AVANTLAY REPEATER
(— OF DOGS) VAUNTLAY
(— OF PALANQUIN BEARERS) DAK
RELEASE LES LET BAIL DROP EMIT
FREE LESE LIOS LISS SHED SLIP
TRIP UNDO ERUPT EXEEM LEISS
LOOSE MUKTI REMIT SLAKE
ACQUIT ASSOIL DEMISE EXCUSE
EXEMPT LAUNCH MOKSHA
REMISE SPRING UNBEND UNTACK
UNWORK ABSOLVE APATHIA
DELIVER DETENTE DISBAND
FREEDOM QUIETUS SOLUTIO
UNSTICK DESTROY DISPENSE
DISSOLVE LIBERATE DISCHARGE
RELINQUISH
(— AS DOGS) UNLEASH
(— DANCING PARTNER) BREAK
(— EMOTION) ABREAST
(— FROM CONFINEMENT) UNMEW
UNPEN SPRING STREET
(— FROM DEBT) FREITH
(— FROM MILITARY) INVALID
(— FROM SLAVERY) MANUMIT
(— ON ONE'S WORD) PAROLE
(PRESS —) HANDOUT
RELEASED OFF FREE EXEMPT
RELEGATE DOOM EXILE BANISH
COMMIT DEMOTE REJECT
DEGRADE
(— TO OBSCURITY) DOWN
RELENT COME MELT ABATE YIELD
REGRET REPENT LIQUEFY
MOLLIFY SLACKEN
RELENTLESS GRIM HARD HARSH
STERN STONY BITTER SAVAGE
STRICT AUSTERE PITILESS
RIGOROUS
RELEVANCE PRECISION
PERTINENCE
RELEVANT APT VALID GERMAN
APROPOS GERMANE APPOSITE
MATERIAL PERTINENT
RELIABILITY STEEL CREDENCE
RELIABLE GOOD HARD SAFE SURE
TRUE PUKKA SOLID SOUND
THERE TRIED TRUST WHITE
DINKUM STEADY TRUSTY
CERTAIN FAITHFUL SOOTHFUL
STRAIGHT
RELIANCE HOPE TRUST CREDIT
AFFIANCE MAINSTAY
(— ON FAITH) FIDEISM
RELIC HUACO REMAIN ANTIQUE
HALIDOM LEAVING MEMENTO
RELIQUE VESTIGE SOUVENIR
SURVIVAL
(PL.) CORPSE HALIDOM REMAINS
(PREF.) LIPSANO
RELICT WIDOW REMANIE
RESIDUAL SURVIVOR EPIBIOTIC
RELIEF AID LAX SOB BOOT BOTE

EASE HELP RELAY SCRUB SPELL
SWING ESCAPE REMEDY SUCCOR
COMFORT FEEDING REDRESS
RILIEVO EASEMENT REPOUSSE
(TEMPORARY —) HITCH
(SUFF.) LYSE LYSIS LYST LYTE
LYTIC LYZE
RELIEVE ROB BEET EASE FREE
HELP LIOS LISS ALLAY LIGHT
LISSE LITHE RIGHT SLAKE SPARE
SPELL ASSIST LESSEN PHYSIC
REMEDY REMOVE RESCUE
SOOTHE SUCCOR UNMAZE
ASSUAGE COMFORT DELIVER
DEPRIVE FRESHEN LIGHTEN
REDRESS REFRESH SUCCEED
SUPPORT SUSTAIN SWEETEN
ALIGHTEN DIMINISH MITIGATE
RELEVATE
(— A SAIL) SPILL
(— OF OFFICE) AX AXE
(— OF SIN) CONFESS
RELIGIEUSE NUN CLERGESS
RELIGION BON DIN LAW SECT
BONBO CREED DAENA FAITH
OBEAH PIETY SOPHY DHARMA
SHINTO SYSTEM TAOISM ELOHISM
JAINISM JUDAISM ORPHISM
PERSISM RELIGIO SIKHISM
SYNAGOG BUDDHISM CAODAISM
HINDUISM MAZDAISM PEYOTISM
SHAMANISM
(— OF ABRAHAM) HANIFIYA
(— OF TIBET) BON
(CHRISTIAN —) WAY
(UNORTHODOX —) CULT
RELIGIOSE PIETISTIC
RELIGIOUS PI HOLY EXACT GODLY
PIOUS RIGID DEVOUT DIVINE
SACRED FERVENT GHOSTLY
ZEALOUS SPIRITUAL
(— HOUSE) KELLION
RELINQUISH LAY LET CEDE DROP
QUIT DEMIT FORGO GRANT
LEAVE WAIVE YIELD CANCEL
DESERT RESIGN ABANDON
FORSAKE RELEASE ABDICATE
ABNEGATE LINQUISH RENOUNCE
RELIQUARY ARCA CHEF CASKET
CHASSE COFFER MEMORY SHRINE
STEEPA TABLET CHORTEN
HALIDOM MEMORIA FERETORY
RELISH CHOW DASH EDGE GOUT
GUST LIKE SOUL SOWL TANG
ZEST ACHAR ENJOY GUSTO RELES
SAVOR SOWLE SPICE TASTE
TRACE ATSARA DEGUST FLAVOR
LIKING PALATE SAVOUR
BOTARGO OUTWORK STOMACH
APPETITE FONDNESS PICCALILLI
(— FOR FOOD) CHAW
(INTELLECTUAL —) TASTE
(MENTAL —) PALATE
(ROMAN —) GARUM
(SALT OR ACID —) ACHAR
RELUCENT RADIANT SHINING
GLEAMING
RELUCT TARROW
RELUCTANCE GRUDGE AVERSION
ANTIPATHY RENITENCE
(— UNIT) REL
RELUCTANT SET SHY CAGY LOTH
NICE CHARY LOATH SWEER

THRAW AFRAID AVERSE DAINTY
FORCED SWEERT UNFAIN
ASHAMED HALTING BACKWARD
GRUDGING LOATHFUL RENITENT
THRAWART
RELY AFFY BANK BASE LEAN LITE
REST STAY COUNT RALLY TRUST
DEPEND GROUND RECKON
REPOSE CONFIDE
(— ON) LIPPEN VENTURE
REMAIN LIE SIT BIDE REST STAY
STOP ABIDE CLING DWELL LEAVE
STAND TARRY THOLE BELIVE
ENDURE MANENT RESIDE
SUBSIST SURVIVE CONTINUE
(— AWAKE) VIGILATE
(— IN DEADLOCK) HANG
(— MOTIONLESS) STAGNATE
(— UNDER HEAT TREATMENT) SOAK
**(— UNDISTURBED AFTER HEAT
TREATMENT)** AGE
(— UNUSED) LIE
(— UPRIGHT) STAND
(—S IN MASH TUN) GRAINS
(—S IN PIPEBOWL) TOPPER
(—S OF CANE) BEGASS BAGASSE
(—S OF FIRE) EMBER EMBERS
(—S ON STAGE) MANET
(ANIMAL —S) SPOILS
(FOSSIL —) EXUVIAE
(FOUL —S) SCURF
(PL.) CHAR DUST ASHES DECAY
DRAFF GHOST SHARD SHERD
BURIAL DEBRIS FOSSIL RELIEF
CARCASS REMNANT RESIDUE
RELIQUIAE
(PREF.) MENO
REMAINDER NET HEEL LAVE REST
PLUGS ARREAR EXCESS RELIEF
BALANCE REMNANT RESIDUE
SURPLUS LEAVINGS LEFTOVER
RESIDUAL RESIDUUM
(— OF ATOM) CORE
(PL.) GARBLINGS LEFTMENTS
REMAINING OVER BIDING
REMNANT LEFTOVER REMANENT
RESIDUAL
(PREF.) MENO
REMALIAH (SON OF —) PEKAH
REMARK DIG SAY SEE GIRD HEED
NOTE WORD GLOSS STATE TOKEN
EARFUL GAMBIT NOTICE REGARD
COMMENT DESCANT DISCANT
OBSERVE PERCEIVE OBSERVATION
(— BRIEFLY) GLANCE
(AMIABLE —) DOUCEUR
(AMUSING —) GAG
(BANAL —) PLATITUDE
(BITING —) BARB
(CLEVER —) NIFTY
(CONCLUDING —S) ENVOI
(CUTTING —) DIG SPINOSITY
(DULL —) BROMIDE
(EMBARRASSING —) BREAK
(EXPLANATORY —) SCHOLION
SCHOLIUM
(FOOLISH —) INANITY
(ILL-TIMED —) CLANGER
(INSULTING —) SLUR
(JEERING —) JEST SKIT
(LAUGH-PROVOKING —) GAG
(SARCASTIC —) HIT GIRD SLANT
(SATIRICAL —) JEST SKIT SGAFT

(SHARP —) GANSEL STINGER
(SILLY —) FADAISE
(STALE —S) BILGE
(UNCOMPLIMENTARY —) BRICKBAT
(WITTY —) JEST CRACK ZINGER
REMARKABLE SOME FORBY
GREAT SIGNAL STRONG NOTABLE
STRANGE UNUSUAL FABULOUS
MARKABLE SINGULAR SPANKING
STRIKING UNCOMMON
BODACIOUS NOTICEABLE
PHENOMENAL
(NOT —) INCURIOUS
REMARKABLY UNCO UNKO JOLLY
UNCOW DEUCED UNCOLY
SIGNALLY
REMEDIAL RELEVANT SALUTARY
REMEDILESS BOOTLESS
REMEDY AID BOT BOOT BOTE
CURE GAIN HALE HEAL HELP
REDE AZOTH MANDS REDUB
SHERE TOPIC PHYSIC RECOUR
RECURE RELIEF REPAIR RESIDY
URETIC ANTACID CORRECT
DRASTIC ICTERIC OTALGIC
PLASTER RECTIFY REDRESS
RELIEVE ANTIDOTE MEDICINE
PHARMACY RECOVERY REMEDIAL
SPECIFIC
(— COUNTERACTING POISON)
TREACLE ANTIDOTE
(— FOR ALL DISEASES) PANACEA
CATHOLICON
(— FOR DIZZINESS) DINIC
(— FOR JAUNDICE) ICTERIC
(— TO REDUCE FEVER) FEBRIFUGE
(CHINESE —) SENSO
(EXTERNAL —) TOPIC
(FAVORITE —) NOSTRUM
(SECRET —) ARCANUM
(TAPEWORM —) EMBELIA
(TOOTHACHE —) TONGA
(UNIVERSAL —) AZOTH
CATHOLICON
(WITHOUT —) BOOTLESS
REMEMBER MEM MIN MEAN MIND
MINE MING IDEATE MEMBER
RECALL RECORD REMIND RETAIN
REWARD BETHINK MENTION
RECOLLECT
(— REMORSEFULLY) REMORD
REMEMBRANCE MIN MIND
MEMORY RECORD MEANING
MINDING MINNING MEMORIAL
REMINDER SOUVENIR
**REMEMBRANCE OF THINGS
PAST** (AUTHOR OF —) PROUST
(CHARACTER IN —) MOREL SWANN
MARCEL ODETTE RACHEL ROBERT
VEDURIN GILBERTE VINTEUIL
ALBERTINE DECHARLUS
GUERMANTES
REMIND JOG MIN MIND MINE
MING IMMIND PROMPT
REMEMBER
REMINDER MEMO PROD TWIT
TOUCH PROMPT MINDING
MONITOR SOUVENIR REFRESHER
REMINISCENCE MEMORY RECALL
ANAMNESIS
REMISE RETURN RELEASE REPLACE
CARRIAGE
REMISS LAX LAZY MILD PALE

FAINT SLACK TARDY BEHIND
DILUTED LANGUID CARELESS
DERELICT DILATORY HEEDLESS
NEGLIGENT
REMISSION CURE LIOS LISS
PARDON REMISE LOOSING
REMITTAL
REMISSNESS LACHES LASHNESS
REMIT SEND COVER LOOSE RELAX
CANCEL EXCUSE PARDON
REMAND REMISS RESIGN
ABSOLVE FORGIVE RELEASE
SUSPEND ABROGATE MITIGATE
MODERATE
REMNANT END TAG BUTT DREG
FENT REST RUMP RUND RELIC
STUMP TRACE REMAIN LEAVING
REMAINS SURVIVOR
(— OF CLOTH) FENT
(— OF FOOD) CRUST
(— OF ROCK MASS) KLIP KLIPPE
(— OF VEIL) ANNULUS
(—S OF FILLETS) SCISSEL
(—S OF VEIL) CORTINA
(VESTIGIAL —) SHADOW
(PL.) EPIPLASM
REMODEL MEND RECAST CONVERT
REMONSTRANCE PROOF ADVICE
COUNSEL PROTEST REPROOF
EVIDENCE
REMONSTRANT ARMINIAN
REMONSTRATE ARGUE OBJECT
PROTEST REPROVE COMPLAIN
REMORA CLOG DRAG PEGA
SUCKER GUAICAN PEGADOR
ECHENEID LOOTSMAN STAYSHIP
STOPSHIP SUCKFISH
REMORSE HELL PITY RUTH PRICK
REGRET REMORD AYENBITE
PENITENCE
(— OF CONSCIENCE) GRUDGE
REMORSEFUL BAD PITIFUL
CONTRITE GUILTSICK
REMOTE FAR OFF BACK DEEP
FERN HIGH LONG ALOOF HOARY
UTTER ALENGE DISTAL ELENGE
EXEMPT OTIOSE SECRET DEVIOUS
DISSITE DISTANT EXTREME
FAILING FARAWAY FOREIGN
OBSCURE OUTSIDE ABDITIVE
ABSTRUSE ARMCHAIR BACKVELD
INTERIOR OUTLYING OUTWORLD
SECLUDED SOLITARY
OUTLANDISH
(— FROM LIFE) SCHOOLISH
(MOST —) ULTIMA EXTREME
HINDMOST ULTIMATE
(PREF.) DIST(O) PALAE(O) PALE(O)
REMOTELY CLEAN DISTANTLY
REMOTENESS AWAYNESS
DISTANCE
REMOTER FARTHER ULTERIOR
REMOVABLE DATIVE REMOTIVE
REMOVAL AX AXE EXILE AMOTION
CLEANUP ERASION ABLATION
EXCISION EXERESIS OFFGOING
REMOTION
(— OF COAL) GETTING
(— OF ICE FROM GLACIER)
ATTRITION
(— OF LAND) AVULSION
(SUFF.) CENOSIS
(SURGICAL —) ECTOMY

REMOVE GET PUT RID BATE COMB
DELE DRAW FILE FLIT FREE LIFT
MOVE PARE PEEL PULL QUIT
RAZE VOID WEED APART AUFER
AVOID BLAST BRUSH CLEAR
EMITY ERASE EVOID HEAVE HOIST
LIGHT PLANE RAISE REPEL SHIFT
SHUCK SLASH SLIPE STRIP SWEEP
WAIVE BANISH CANCEL CHANGE
CONVEY DEDUCT DEGREE
DEPART DEPOSE EFFACE ELOIGN
EXEMPT EXPORT MINISH RELEVE
REMBLE SPIRIT AMOLISH DEPRIVE
DESCENT DISMISS DISPOST
DIVORCE EXCERPT RESCIND
RETRACT REVERSE STRANGE
SUBDUCT SUBLATE ABSTRACT
ASPIRATE DISPLACE DISPLANT
ESTRANGE EVACUATE RETRENCH
SUPPLANT TRANSFER WITHDRAW
OBLITERATE
(— A STITCH) DECREASE
(— BARK FROM LOG) ROSS
(— BIT BY BIT) SCAMBLE
(— BY CUTTING) ABLATE
(— BY DEATH) SNATCH
(— CLOTHING) DOFF STRIP
(— COLOR) BLEACH
(— COVER) UNCAP
(— DEFECTS) SCARF
(— DIRT) BLADE GARBLE
(— EXCESS METAL) CUT
(— FROM CHECKER BOARD) HUFF
(— FROM OFFICE) DEPOSE RECALL
DISMISS
(— FROM REMEMBRANCE) COVER
(— GILLS) BEARD
(— HAIR) DEPILATE
(— HUSKS AND CHAFF) GELD
(— INSIDES OF FISH) GIB GIP
(— JUDGE) ADDRESS
(— LOWER BRANCHES) BRASH
(— MAST) UNSTEP
(— ORE) EXTRACT
(— PARTICLES OF GOLD LEAF) SKEW
(— PITCHER FROM BASEBALL GAME)
DERRICK
(— POTATOES) GRABBLE
(— QUEEN BEE) DEMAREE
(— QUIETLY) ABSTRACT
(— ROOTS) GRUB
(— SEED FROM FLAX) RIBBLE
(— SEEDS) STONE
(— SKIN) HULL HUSK
(— SOUND FROM TAPE) BLIP
(— SPROUTS FROM) CHIT
(— STALK FROM) STRIG
(— STAMENS) CASTRATE
(— TABLECLOTH) DRAW
(— THE TOP OF) COP
(— TO AVOID TAX) SKIM
(— TROUSERS) DEBAG
(— WASTE TO FIBER) GARNETT
(— WOOL) BELLY
(— WORKS OF STOLEN WATCH)
CHURCH
(PREF.) DE
REMOVED UP OFF AWAY ALIEN
ALOOF APART REMOTE DISTANT
SEMOTED ABSTRACT
REMOVER MOVER CROPMAN
KNOTTER
REMUDA CAVY

CAVAYARD CAVYYARD
REMUNERATE PAY REPAY
REWARD GRATIFY SATISFY
CONSIDER REIMBURSE
REMUNERATION PAY REWARD
SALARY PAYMENT
REMUNERATIVE GAINFUL
REWARDING
REMUS (BROTHER OF —) ROMULUS
RENAISSANCE NARA REBIRTH
REVIVAL
RENAL NEPHRIC NEPHRITIC
RENCOUNTER CLASH FIGHT
DEBATE CONTEST CONFLICT
REND PULL RENT RIVE TEAR TOIL
BREAK BURST DIVEL RATCH
ROWEL SEVER SPLIT WREST
CLEAVE SCREED WRENCH
ABSCIND DIVULSE RUPTURE
WREATHE DISPIECE DISTRAIN
FRACTURE LACERATE SPLINTER
(— AND DEVOUR) TIRE
RENDER DO PAY PUT TRY BEAR
DRAW ECHO EMIT MAKE RENT
RIND DEFER PRICK REPAY YIELD
RECITE REPEAT RETURN DELIVER
PRECARY REFLECT REQUITE
RESTORE SERVICE TALLAGE
TRANSMIT
(— ACID) PRICK
(— AGREEABLE) DULCIFY
(— AS LARD) TRY
(— ASSISTANCE TO SHIP) FOY
(— CAPABLE) ACTIVATE
(— CLEAR) OPEN
(— FIT) ADAPT
(— GODLIKE) DEIFY
(— HEAVY WITH FOOD) STODGE
(— HOMAGE) ATTORN
(— IMMUNE) FRANK VASTATE
(— INEFFECTIVE) VITIATE
(— KNOTTY) GNARL
(— OBLIQUE) SPLAY
(— OBSCURE) DARKLE
(— OF BOON WORK) PRECARY
(— QUIET) ACCOY
(— SENSELESS) STUN ASTONISH
(— TURBID) ROIL
(— UNFIT) DENATURE
(— UNSTABLE) UNHINGE
(— VERDICT) PASS
(— VOID) CASS DEFEAT
(SUFF.) EN
RENDERED RENDU TRIED
RENDERING RENDU ENGLISH
VERSION RENDITION
(— OF SCENE) STUDY
RENDEZVOUS DATE HAUNT TRYST
REFUGE HANGOUT MEETING
RETREAT
(— FOR SHIPS) DOWN
RENDITION ACCOUNT CONDUCT
DELIVERY
RENEGADE DORAX PERVERT
TRAITOR APOSTATE RECREANT
RENEGADO RUNAGADO
RUNAGATE TURNCOAT
RENEGE BEG NIG DENY RENIG
DESERT REVOKE RETRACT
FAINAIGUE
RENEW NEW REST FRESH RECALL
REFORM RENOVE REPEAT
RESUME REVIVE INSTORE

REBUILD REFRESH REPLACE RESTORE OVERHAUL REJUVENATE
(— **MORTAR**) REPOINT
(— **WINE**) STUM

RENEWAL RENEW REVIVAL NOVATION

RENNET LAB RUEN VELL STEEP RENNIN RUNNET EARNING ABOMASUM YEARNING CHEESELIP

RENOUNCE PUT CEDE DEFY DENY QUIT DEVOW FORGO RENAY WAIVE ABJURE DISOWN FORLET FORSAY RECANT REFUSE REJECT RENEGE RESIGN REVOKE ABANDON DECLARE FORLEIT FORSAKE RETRACT WITHSAY ABDICATE ABNEGATE DISCLAIM FORSPEAK FORSWEAR MANSWEAR PROCLAIM RELINQUISH

RENOVATE DUST RENEW REVIVE FURBISH REFRESH RESTORE OVERHAUL RENOVIZE
(— **HAT**) MOLOKER MOLOCKER

RENOWN BAY BRAG FAME ECLAT GLORY KUDOS PRICE RUMOR ESTEEM LUSTER RENONE REPORT EMPRISE SWAGGER WORSHIP PRESTIGE NOTORIETY

RENOWNED FAMED NOBLE NOTED FAMOUS EMINENT RENOMME GLORIOUS MAGNIFIC RENOMMEE

RENT LET SET TAX FARM GALE GAPE HIRE MAIL RACK RIME RIVE SLIT TEAR TOLL WAGE BREAK CANON CENSO CUDDY ENDOW GANCH GAVEL SPLIT BLANCH BREACH BROKEN CENSUS CHASMA CRANNY CUSTOM GAUNCH INCOME SCHISM SCREED STRENT CHARTER CHIEFRY CORNAGE CRACKED CREVICE FISSURE MAILING MOLLAND ONSTAND RENTAGE REVENUE RUPTURE TRIBUTE CHAMPART CHIEFERY HEADRENT STALLAGE VECTIGAL WAYLEAVE LANDGAFOL
(— **BY BOAR'S TUSK**) GANCH GAUNCH
(— **IN LIEU OF SUPPER**) CUDDY
(— **OF LAND PAID IN KIND**) CAIN
(**ANNUAL** —) CANON
(**EARTHQUAKE** —) SCARLET
(**GROUND** —) CENSO CENSUS
(**OATS IN LIEU OF** —) AVENAGE

RENTAL KAIN PORT TONNAGE TRIBUTE TUNNAGE

RENTED LETTEN

RENTER FARMER RANTER CHIPPER BOXHOLDER

RENUNCIATION DENIAL APOSTASY DEFIANCE DISAVOWAL REJECTION SACRIFICE

REP CANNELE DROGUET POPELINE

REPAIR DO EIK EKE FIX IMP HEAL HELP MEND TINE AMEND BOTCH DIGHT EMEND HAUNT RALLY REDUB RENEW STORE TRADE UPSET ASTORE BUSHEL COBBLE COGGLE COOPER DOCTOR FETTLE

RECURE REFORM REMEDY REPASS RESORT RETURN UPKEEP CORRECT INFAINT REDRESS REPAREL RESTORE SERVICE FLOCKING OVERHAUL RETRIEVE REVIVIFY
(— **BOAT**) CAREEN
(— **CLUMSILY**) BOTCH
(— **FENCE**) MOUND
(— **ROAD**) SKID
(— **SHOE**) FOX TAP

REPAIRED VAMPED

REPAIRER DOCTOR BOTCHER COBBLER WOFFLER CEMENTER
(**SHOE** —) JACKMAN BENCHMAN
(**TEXTILE** —) SMASHER

REPAIRMAN FETTLER

REPARATION BOTE AMENDS REMEDY REWARD DAMAGES REDRESS REPAIRS REQUITAL

REPARTEE WIT KNACK REPLY BANTER RETORT RIPOST RIPOSTE BACKCHAT BADINAGE COMEBACK GIFFGAFF

REPAST BAIT FEED FOOD MEAL BEVER FEAST TREAT DRINKING COLLATION
(— **BETWEEN MEALS**) BEVER BRUNCH BANQUET
(**HASTY** —) SNACK
(**LIGHT** —) BAIT VOID VOIDEE COLLATION

REPAY MEED QUIT APPAY TALLY YIELD ACQUIT ANSWER REFUND RETORT RETURN REWARD IMBURSE REQUITE RESTORE REIMBURSE

REPEAL ANNUL CANCEL RECALL REVOKE ABANDON ABOLISH RESCIND REVERSE ABROGATE DEROGATE DISENACT RENOUNCE

REPEAT SAY ECHO GAIT RAME RANE SHOW TELL DITTO QUOTE RECUR RENEW RESAY REVIE THRUM ANSWER RENDER RESUME RETAIL SECOND DECLINE DIVULGE ITERATE PRESENT REPLICA REPRISE DINGDONG REDOUBLE REHEARSE REPLICATE
(— **BY ROTE**) PARROT
(— **GLIBLY**) SCREED
(— **MONOTONOUSLY**) CUCKOO DINGDONG
(— **OF PATTERN**) GAIT
(— **TIRESOMELY**) DIN

REPEATED OFTEN CONSTANT FREQUENT PERENNIAL

REPEATEDLY OFT EVERY THRICE

REPEATER GUN RIFLE WATCH PISTOL FLOATER HOLDOVER

REPEL FEND TURN WARD FENCE REBUT DEFEND REBEAT REBUFF REFUSE REFUTE REJECT REPUGN RESIST REVOLT DISGUST PELLATE REPULSE PROPULSE

REPELLANT REPUGNANT

REPELLENT DOPE GRIM HARSH CAMPHOR HATEFUL SQUALID
(**INSECT** —) DEET

REPELLING HARD SICKLY

REPENT REW RUE MOURN GRIEVE REGRET REPTANT CREEPING FORTHINK

REPENTANCE REW RUE PITY RUTH RUING REGRET SORROW PENANCE REMORSE

REPENTANT ATTRITE PENITENT

REPERCUSSION ECHO TENOR RECOIL REPULSE BACKWASH

REPERTORY REP BOOK LIST INDEX ARSENAL CATALOG

REPETITION BIS REP COPY ECHO PLOCE REVIE TROLL DILOGY REPEAT MENTION RECITAL REPLICA REPRISE IDENTITY ITERANCE ITERANCY NEMBUTSU PALILOGY PARROTRY RECOVERY REDOUBLE REHEARSAL
(— **IN REVERSE ORDER**) EPANODOS
(— **OF HOMOLOGOUS PARTS**) MERISM
(— **OF SPEECH FORMS**) ROTE
(— **OF WORD**) ANAPHORA BATTOLOGY
(**NEEDLESS** —) REDUNDANCY
(**UNINSPIRED** —) STENCIL
(**PREF.**) (**PATHOLOGICAL** —) PALI

REPHAEL (**FATHER OF** —) SHEMAIAH

REPHAH (**FATHER OF** —) EPHRAIM

REPHAIAH (**FATHER OF** —) HUR TOLA BINEA

REPHAIM EMIM

REPINE FRET PINE WEAKEN COMPLAIN

REPINING MURMUR REGRET PLAINTIVE

REPLACE SWAP SWOP RENEW REPAY SHIFT STEAD CHANGE FOLLOW REFUND REMISE REPONE SUPPLY FRESHEN PREEMPT RESTORE SUCCEED DISPLACE SUPPLANT REPLENISH

REPLACEMENT CUT ERSATZ
(— **FOR HAND**) HOOK
(— **OF CONSONANT**) LENITION

REPLENISH CHUNK REFIT RENEW SUPPLY NOURISH PERFECT PLENISH REPLETE RESTORE SUFFICE

REPLETE FAT FULL RIFE SATED STOUT STUFF FILLED GORGED IMPLETE COMPLETE HONEYPOT

REPLETION FULTH FULNESS SURFEIT FULLNESS PLETHORA SATURITY

REPLICA BIS PUP COPY IDEA CHARM IMAGE REVIE FACSIMILE

REPLICATION ECHO REPLY ANSWER REJOINDER

REPLY CAP JAWAB KNACK RESAY ANSWER REJOIN RETORT RETURN REPLIAL RESOUND RESPOND REPARTEE REPLIQUE RESPONSE SIMILITER

REPORT CRY POP SAY FAME ITEM NOTE TELL VENT VOTE WORD AUDIT BRUIT COVER CRACK NOISE REFER ROUND RUMOR SCALE SOUND STATE STORY VOICE BREEZE CAHIER CREDIT DELATE DETAIL FINGER GOSSIP RAPORT RECITE RELATE RENOWN REPUTE RETURN RUMBLE SPEECH STEVEN SURVEY THREAP ACCOUNT HANSARD HEARING HEARSAY INKLING KHUBBER

NARRATE OPINION PROCESS RECITAL ADVISORY DECISION DESCRIBE HEMOGRAM VERBATIM GRAPEVINE
(— **NEWS**) COVER
(— **OF GUN**) CLAP
(— **OF INFRACTION**) GIG
(— **OF PROCEEDINGS**) CAHIER
(— **OF TIMBER SURVEYOR**) CRUISE
(**ABSURD** —) CANARD
(**BELIEVED** —) CREDIT
(**CASUAL** —) FABLE
(**COMMON** —) CRY FAME SPEECH
(**FALSE** —) SHAVE CANARD FURPHY SLANDER
(**FLYING** —) SOUGH
(**HONORABLE** —) TONGUE
(**LAW** —) CASE
(**MILITARY** —) STATE SITREP
(**NEWS** —) FLASH SCOOP
(**NOISY** —) RUMBLE
(**OFFICIAL** —) HANSARD
(**POPULAR** —) RUMOR RUMOUR
(**PUBLIC** —) FAME
(**UNFAVORABLE** —) SKIN
(**UNVERIFIED** —) VOICE GRAPEVINE
(**VAGUE** —) BREEZE

REPORTER LEGMAN PISTOL CREEPER NEWSMAN NEWSHAWK PRESSMAN STRINGER PAPARAZZO
(**SOCIETY** —) JENKINS
(**YOUNG** —) CUB

REPORTING BEAT COVERAGE

REPOSE RO BED LIE PUT AFFY CALM EASE RELY REST PEACE PLACE POISE QUIET SLEEP REPAST RECLINE EASINESS QUIETUDE SERENITY
(— **LAZILY**) FROWST
(**DREAMY** —) KEF

REPOSITORY ARK AMBRY CAPSA DEPOT HOARD VAULT ARMORY CASKET MUSEUM VESTRY ARCHIVE CABINET CAPSULE GENIZAH GRANARY HANAPER SPICERY ARCHIVES MAGAZINE TREASURY SEPULCHER

REPOSOIR REPOSE

REPOSSESS PULL RECOVER

REPREHEND NIP WARN BLAME CHIDE REBUKE CENSURE REPRISE REPROVE CRITICIZE

REPREHENSIBLE ILL AMISS BLAMABLE CRIMINAL CULPABLE SCABROUS

REPREHENSION BLAME REBUKE CENSURE OBLOQUY REPROOF

REPRESENT GIVE LIKE LIMN SHOW TYPE SHADE DEPICT SEMBLE TYPIFY DISPLAY EXHIBIT FASHION PICTURE PORTRAY PROTEST TRADUCE DEFIGURE DESCRIBE RESEMBLE PERSONATE
(— **CONCRETELY**) THING
(— **IN LANGUAGE**) ACT BODY DRAW ENACT IMAGE SPEAK BLAZON CLOTHE EMBODY FIGURE SAMPLE BETOKEN EXPRESS DECIPHER
(— **ON STAGE**) ACT

REPRESENTATION SUN BUST FORM ICON IDEA IDOL IKON SHOW SWAG ANGLE DRAFT

FANCY IMAGE INSET LABEL
MEDAL TABUT AVOWAL BUDDHA
EFFIGY FIGURE FLEECE MODULE
OBJECT SCHEMA SCHEME SKETCH
SUNRAY WAYANG ANATOMY
DIORAMA DRAUGHT DRAWING
EPITOME EXPRESS EXTRACT
FOLIAGE MAJESTY SCENERY
TABLEAU BESTIARY BLAZONRY
CREATION EPIPHANY EXTERIOR
IDIOGRAM LIKENESS TYPORAMA
SIMULACRUM RESEMBLANCE
(— OF SERPENT) BASIL DRAGON
BASILISK
(— OF SHRINE OF HUSAIN) TABUT
(— OF VISION) AISLING
(DIPLOMATIC —) DEMARCHE
(FACSIMILE —) TYPORAMA
(FAINT —) SHADOW
(FUNERAL —) CADAVER
(GRAPHIC —) CHART BISECT
(HERALDIC —) LEOPARD LIONCEL
(MENTAL —) FANCY IMAGE
(MINIATURE —) MODEL
(SYMBOLIC —) ALLEGORY
REPRESENTATIVE REP FAIR TYPE
AGENT ENVOY VAKIL ASSIGN
COMMON DEPUTY EMBLEM
LEDGER SAMPLE VAKEEL
BURGESS GRIEVER TRIBUNE
TYPICAL DECURION DELEGATE
EMISSARY EXPONENT FIELDMAN
GASTALDO INTIMATE OBSERVER
SALESMAN SPECIMEN
(— OF ATMOSPHERE) AERIAL
(MANUFACTURER'S —) BLOCKMAN
(PL.) COMMONS
REPRESS CURB HUSH BLUNT
BRIDE CHAIN CHECK CHOKE
CRUSH DAUNT DROWN QUELL
SQUAT BRIDLE COERCE DEADEN
REBUKE STIFLE SUBDUE CONTROL
DEPRESS INHIBIT REPRIME
SILENCE SWALLOW COMPRESS
OVERBEAR RESTRAIN RESTRICT
RETRENCH REVOCATE STRANGLE
SUPPRESS WITHHOLD
REPRESSED SULLEN STIFLED
REPRIEVE DELAY GRACE ESCAPE
REPRISE RESPITE SUSPEND
POSTPONE
REPRIMAND WIG BAWL CALL
CHEW JACK SKIN SLAP SLON
SNEB SNIB TASK CHECK CREED
SLATE SLOAN SPANK TARGE
BOUNCE CARPET EARFUL REBUKE
ROCKET STRAFE CENSURE
CHAPTER LECTURE REPROOF
REPROVE DRESSING WRAGGING
REPRINT COPY DEPRINT OFFPRINT
REIMPOSE TAUCHNITZ
REPRISAL PRIZE MARQUE REPRISE
REQUITAL RECAPTION
REPROACH ILL TAX BLOT GIBE
JIBE LACK NOSE NOTE RAIL SLUR
SPOT TEEN TWIT WITE ABUSE
BLAME BRAID BRAND CHIDE
SCOLD SHEND TAUNT WHITE
AYWORD BISMER INFAMY REBUKE
REVILE UPCAST VILIFY BLEMISH
CENSURE CONDEMN REPROOF
REPROVE SLANDER UMBRAID
UPBRAID WITHNIM BETONGUE

DISHONOR REDARGUE REVILING
CONTUMELY OPPROBRIUM
REFLECTION
REPROACHFUL BITTER ABUSIVE
SHAMEFUL
REPROBATE HARD LOST SCAMP
DISOWN RASCAL REJECT SINNER
ABANDON CENSURE CORRUPT
EXCLUDE REPROVE DEPRAVED
DISALLOW HARDENED
SCALAWAG SKALAWAG
REPRODUCE BUD HIT COPY BREED
SPORE RECITE REPEAT PORTRAY
AUTOTYPE MULTIPLY REFIGURE
REMEMBER PROCREATE
REPRODUCTION CAST COPY REVI
IMAGE PRINT ECTYPE RECALL
STEREO EDITION ELECTRO
EXOGAMY FISSION REPLICA
REVIVAL APOMIXIS BLOCKOUT
GAMOGAMY HOMOGAMY
LIKENESS
(— OF SOUND) AUDIO
(SUFF.) GAM(AE)(IST)(OUS)(Y)
GAMETE
GON(E)(IDIUM)(IMO)(IUM)(Y)
REPROOF PROD RATE BLAME
CHECK LESSON REBUKE CHIDING
LECTURE SETDOWN JOBATION
REPROACH REPROVAL SCOLDING
TAXATION JAWBATION
(GENTLE —) ADMONITION
REPROVE RAG TAP BAWL FLAY
FRIE JOBE RATE SNIB TRIM
BLAME CHECK CHIDE CRAWL
SCOLD SHEND SHENT SNEAP
BERATE CHASTE REBUKE REFORM
SCHOOL THREAT CENSURE
CONDEMN CORRECT IMPROVE
LECTURE UPBRAID WITHNIM
ADMONISH CHASTISE KEELHAUL
REDARGUE REPROACH
UNDERNIM WITHTAKE
REPTILE LOW MEAN WORM
GUANA SNAKE VIPER GAVIAL
LIZARD MOLOCH TURTLE
CRAWLER CREEPER DIAPSID
GHARIAL PROTEUS SAURIAN
SERPENT TUATARA BASILISK
CREEPING CYNODONT DINOSAUR
GALESAUR MESOSAUR
MOSASAUR PLIOSAUR STEGOMUS
SYNAPSID TORTOISE ALLIGATOR
CROCODILE PELYCOSAUR
PLESIOSAUR
(PART OF —) EYE JAW PIT BODY
FANG SCALE TOOTH BUTTON
RATTLE SHEATH TONGUE
SEGMENT
(PREF.) HERPET(I)(O)
REPTILIAN HERPETIC
REPUBLIC STATE SOVIET
POBLACHT
(FRENCH —) MARIANNE
(IDEAL —) ICARIA
(IMAGINARY —) OCEANA
REPUBLICAN RED QUID
STALWART SANSCULOT
REPUDIATE DEFY ABJURE DISOWN
RECANT REFUTE REJECT DECLINE
DISAVOW DISCARD DIVORCE
RETRACT DISCLAIM DISVOUCH
RENOUNCE

(— DEBTS) NOTCHEL
REPUDIATING NAKIR
REPUGNANCE ENMITY HATRED
HORROR DISGUST DISLIKE
DISTASTE LOATHING
REPUGNANT ALIEN DIRTY NASTY
ADVERSE HATEFUL OPPOSED
INIMICAL OPPOSITE ABHORRENT
OBNOXIOUS REPULSIVE
REPULSE FOIL ROUT RUSH CHECK
FLING REBUT REFEL REPEL
SMEAR DEFEAT DENIAL REBUFF
REBUTE REFUSE REJECT
REPULSION UG DISLIKE AVERSION
REPULSIVE COLD DAIN EVIL LOTH
UGLY VILE LOATH GREASY LAIDLY
FULSOME HATEFUL LOATHLY
SQUALID SCABROUS UNHONEST
REPUTABLE GOOD HONEST
WORTHY CREDIBLE ESTIMABLE
REPUTATION REP FAME LOSE
NAME NOTE ODOR PASS GLORY
HONOR IZZAT NOISE RUMOR
SAVOR VOICE CREDIT ESTEEM
RECORD RENOWN SHADOW
LAURELS OPINION RESPECT
WORSHIP STANDING
(EVIL —) INFAMY
(GOOD —) STANDING
REPUTE FAME ODOR RANK WORD
NOISE SAVOR THINK RECKON
REGARD STATUS OPINION
RESPECT WORSHIP ESTIMATE
JUDGMENT POSITION
(ILL —) SLANDER
REPUTED DIT PUTATIVE
REQUEST ASK BEG BOON CALL
PLEA PRAY SEEK SUIT TELL WISH
CLAIM LIBEL QUEST YEARN
APPEAL BEHEST DEMAND DESIRE
DIRECT ENCORE INVITE MOTION
BESPEAK COMMAND ENTREAT
INQUIRY REQUIRE SOLICIT
ENTREATY INSTANCE PETITION
ROGATION
(— FOR HELP) SOS
(STRONG —) DUN DEMAND
REQUIEM HYMN MASS REST DIRGE
PEACE QUIET REPOSE REQUIN
REQUIN SHARK TOMMY
REQUIRE ASK HAVE LACK NEED
TAKE WANT CLAIM CRAVE EXACT
FORCE GAVEL COMPEL DEMAND
DEPEND DESIRE ENJOIN ENTAIL
EXPECT GOVERN MISTER OBLIGE
BEHOOVE DICTATE INVOLVE
SOLICIT
REQUIRED DUE SET SUPPOSED
NECESSARY OBLIGATORY
REQUIREMENT CALL NEED LEGAL
ORDER BEHEST DEMAND
NECESSITY
(PL.) EXIGENCE EXIGENCY
REQUIRING
(PREF.) END(O)
REQUISITE DUE NEED NEEDY
VITAL NEEDFUL ESSENTIAL
NECESSARY
REQUISITION ORDER DEMAND
INDENT EMBARGO REQUEST
REQUITAL WAR APPAY MERIT
REPAY SERVE TALLY YIELD
ACQUIT DEFRAY REWARD

GRATIFY PAYMENT REVENGE
CONSIDER FORYIELD REPRISAL
REQUITE SERVE RECOMPENSE
RECIPROCATE
RERAILER DIAMOND
REREAD DOUBLE
RERECORD DUB
REREDOS SCREEN BRAZIER
DRAPERY RETABLO FIREBACK
REARDOSS
REREMOUSE BAT
RERUN (PAYMENT FOR —) RESIDUAL
RES POINT THING MATTER
SUBJECT
RESCIND LIFT ANNUL CANCEL
REMOVE REPEAL REVOKE
ABOLISH RETRACT RETREAT
ABROGATE
RESCRIPT EDICT ORDER DECREE
LETTER EPISTLE
RESCUE RID FREE HELP REDD
SAVE BORROW RANSOM REDEEM
RESKEW SUCCOR WARISH
DELIVER RECLAIM RECOVER
RELEASE SALVAGE DELIVERY
LIBERATE RECOURSE
RESEARCH ARBEIT SEARCH
ENQUIRY INQUIRY
RESECT EXCISE
RESEDA LEEK MENNUET
MORILLON
RESEMBLANCE SWAP PARITY
SIMILE ANALOGY AFFINITY
LIKENESS PARALLEL VICINITY
SIMILARITY
(DIM HAZY —) BLY
(SLIGHT —) BLUSH
RESEMBLE AGREE BRAID FAVOR
IMAGE LIKEN APPEAR DEPICT
FIGURE RECALL SEMBLE
COMPARE IMITATE PORTRAY
ASSEMBLE SIMULATE
(SUFF.) ODE OID OPSIS
RESEMBLING LIKE SAME SEMBLE
SIMILAR SEMBLANT
(— AN EGG) OVULARIAN
(— COMB) PECTINAL
(— GOOSE) ANSERINE
(— HORSE) EQUOID
(— IVORY) EBURNEAN EBURNEOID
EBURNEOUS
(— LADDER) SCALARIFORM
(— SALT) HALOID
(— STAR) STELLATE
(— WALL) MURAL
(SUFF.) AR ARY FUL EOUS FORM
ITIC IFORM OIDAL ACEOUS
RESENT HATE MEAN INDIGN
MALIGN STOMACH SUGGEST
RESENTFUL HARD HURT BITTER
SULLEN ENVIOUS JEALOUS
STOMACHY
RESENTMENT HURT DEPIT PIQUE
SNUFF SPITE CHOLER ENMITY
GRUDGE HATRED MALICE
RANCOR DISDAIN DUDGEON
OFFENCE OFFENSE STOMACH
UMBRAGE JEALOUSY HEARTBURN
RESERVATION DIBS SALVO SPACE
SAVING UNLESS BOOKING
CAUTION KEEPING PROVISO
RESERVE FORPRISE RESERVAL
(MENTAL —) SALVO SCRUPLE

RESERVE BOOK CAVE FUND HOJU HOLD KEEP SALT SAVE SPARE BACKUP NICETY SEPONE SEPOSE TRIARY BACKLOG CAUTION CONTROL DIGNITY SEPOSIT SHYNESS TENENUE COLDNESS DISTANCE FALLBACK FORPRISE IMMODEST WITHHOLD STOCKPILE
(HOME —S) LANDSTURM
(MILITARY —) HOJU YOBI TRIARY TRIARII LANDWEHR
(MONETARY —) CUSHION
(PL.) FAT KOKUMIN STRENGTH

RESERVED COY DRY SHY COLD UNCO ALOOF CHARY SAVED BOOKED CLOSED DEMURE MODEST SILENT STANCH COSTIVE DISTANT RETIRED STRANGE RETICENT RETIRING STANDOFF TACITURN WITHHELD
(— FOR ROYAL USE) KHASS
(NOT —) COMMON

RESERVOIR DAM BOSS FONT KEEP LAKE PENT SUMP TANK BASIN FOUNT STANK STORE CENOTE SIPHON SOURCE SYPHON CISTERN CLEARER FAVISSA FOREBAY IMPOUND PISCINA RECEIPT AFTERBAY DEPOSITO FOUNTAIN MAGAZINE STANDAGE
(— OF WEATHERGLASS) STAGNUM

RESET HELP ABODE ALTER RECEPT RESORT SUCCOR RECEIPT REPLANT SHARPEN WELCOME

RESHEPH (FATHER OF —) EPHRAIM

RESIDE BIG WIN BIDE BIGG HOME LIVE STAY TELD WONT ABIDE DWELL LODGE REMAIN CONSIST SOJOURN HABITATE
(— TEMPORARILY) LIE STOP

RESIDENCE DUN WON DOON HALL HOME SEAT SEMI STAY WENE WONE ABODE COURT DAIRI DEMUR HOUSE MAHAL MANSE YAMUN BIDING DUKERY ELYSEE HOSTEL MANOIR TENSER DEANERY DROSTDY EMBASSY SOJOURN CURATAGE DOMICILE DWELLING LEGATION RESIANCE RESIANCY RESIDUUM SEDIMENT SETTLING PREFECTURE
(— FOR STUDENTS) INN
(— OF ARCHBISHOP) PALACE
(— OF CHIEF OF VILLAGE) TATA
(— OF ECCLESIASTIC) MANSE DEANERY CURATAGE
(— OF FRENCH PRESIDENTS) ELYSEE
(— OF MANDARIN) YAMEN YAMUN
(— OF MIKADO) DAIRI
(— OF PRIEST) CONVENTO
(— OF SOVEREIGN) PALACE
(— OF SULTAN) SERAGLIO
(FORTIFIED —) DUN
(HILL —) RATH
(OFFICIAL TURKISH —) KONAK
(RURAL —) SEAT FARMSTEAD
(SUMMER —) MAHAL
(TEMPORARY —) STAY

RESIDENT GER FIXED LEGER LIVER INMATE LEDGER STABLE CITIZEN DENIZEN DWELLER PRESENT RESIANT RESIDER RESTING HABITANT INHERENT KAMAAINA MINISTER OCCUPANT
(— AT A UNIVERSITY) GREMIALE
(— OF HAWAII) KAMAAINA
(— OF NEWFOUNDLAND) LIVYER
(— OF WEST. AUSTRALIA) GROPER
(ALIEN —) GER METIC
(CHINESE — OF TIBET) AMBAN
(FOREIGN-BORN —) ALIEN
(OLD —) STANDARD
(SUFF.) ESE ITE
(— OF) ER IER YER

RESIDUAL RELICT REMANIE REMANENT

RESIDUE ASH DREG FOOT GUNK HEEL LAFE LAVE LEES REST SILT SLAG UNIT MAZUT SHARD SHERD BEGASS BORING BOTTOM GRUFFS RELICS BAGASSE CINDERS REMAINS HARDHEAD LEAVINGS LEFTOVER REMANENT RESIDUUM SEMICOKE TAILINGS
(— FROM FAT) CRAP
(— FROM OLIVES) SANZA
(— FROM REFINING TIN) HARDHEAD
(— IN STILL) BOTTOM BOTTOMS
(— OF COAL) COKE SEMICOKE
(— OF COKE) BREEZE
(— OF COMBUSTION) ASH
(— OF HONEYCOMB) SLUMGUM
(— OF PETROLEUM) MAZUT ASTATKI
(— OF SHINGLES) SPALT
(FRIABLE —) CALX
(INSOLUBLE —) MARC
(PL.) TANKAGE

RESIDUUM TAIL BOTTOM DEPOSIT RESIDUE SEDIMENT

RESIGN QUIT DEMIT FORGO REMIT YIELD PERMIT SUBMIT ABANDON COMMEND DELIVER FORGIVE ABDICATE RENOUNCE RELINQUISH

RESIGNATION PATIENCE DEMISSION SURRENDER

RESILIENCE GIVE LIFE BOUNCE RECOIL SPRING REBOUND BUOYANCY

RESILIENT TOUGH BOUNCY LIVELY SUPPLE WHIPPY ELASTIC SPRINGY FLEXIBLE

RESIN ALK LAC BALM BATU BREA HASH TOLU ALKYD AMBER ANIME COPAL CUMAR ELEMI EPOXY GUGAL GUGUL KAURI PITCH ROSEL ROSET SIRUP SYRUP ANTIAR BINDER CHARAS CONIMA DAMMAR GOOGUL GUACIN HARTIN MASTIC STORAX TAMANU ACOUCHI ACRYLIC AMBRITE BENZOIN BISABOL DERRIDE FLUAVIL GAMBOGE IONOMER LADANUM PERSPEX SAGAPEN SHELLAC ALKITRAN ALMACIGA BAKELITE BDELLIUM CACHIBOU CANNABIN COLOPHAN EUOSMITE FORMVAIL GALAGALA GALLIPOT GEDANITE GUAIACUM MALAPAHO MELAMINE OPOPANAX PHENOLIC SANDARAC SCAMMONY
(— DRAWN FROM TREES) CHIP
(— FROM HEMP) CHARAS
(— FROM NORWAY SPRUCE) THUS

(— OF FIR TREE) BLOB
(FOSSIL —) AMBER AMBRITE HARTITE GEDANITE GLESSITE RETINITE
(GRADE OF —) SORTS
(GUM —) GUGUL LASER MYRRH ANTIAR BISABOL GAMBOGE BDELLIUM SAGAPENUM
(NARCOTIC —) CHARAS CHURUS
(TURPENTINE —) ALK GALIPOT COLOPHONY
(PREF.) RETIN(O)
(SUFF.) RETIN

RESINOID ALNUIN HELONIN LOBELIN ASCLEPIN CERASEIN CHELONIN TRILLIIN

RESINOUS ROSETY ROSETTY

RESIST BUCK DEFY FACE STAY REPEL STAND DEFEND IMPUGN OPPOSE REPUGN WITHER CONTEST DISPUTE GAINSAY KNUCKLE RESERVE WITHSET OUTBRAVE OUTSTAND
(— AUTHORITY) REBEL DEFORCE
(— SEPARATION) ATTRACT

RESISTANCE DRAG LOAD OHMAGE REBUFF WITHER BALLAST ANTITYPY BLOCKAGE FASTNESS FRICTION HARDNESS OBSTACLE SEDITION
(— OF COTTON FIBERS) DRAG
(— OF KEYS) ACTION
(— THAT EXPLOSIVE MUST OVERCOME) BURDEN BURTHEN
(— TO ATTACK) DEFENCE DEFENSE
(— TO CHANGE) INERTIA
(— TO COLOR CHANGE) FASTNESS
(— TO DISEASE) PREMUNITION
(— TO SLIPPING) BOND
(UNIT OF —) OHM

RESISTANT HARD STOUT STABILE STUBBORN
(— TO CHANGE) FAST STICKY

RESISTING OBSTANT RELUCTANT

RESISTOR BLEEDER DIVERTOR RHEOSTAT

RESOLUTE BOLD FIRM GRIM BRAVE FIXED HARDY MANLY STERN STIFF STOUT GRITTY MANFUL PLUCKY STABLE STANCH STEADY STUFFY STURDY ANIMOSE ANIMOUS DECIDED CONSTANT FAITHFUL INTREPID POSITIVE STALWART STUBBORN UNSHAKEN

RESOLUTELY TALLY FIRMLY STOUTLY

RESOLUTION VOW SAND THEW NERVE PARTY PLUCK POINT STARCH ACUERDO BESLUIT CENSURE COURAGE MANHEAD MANHOOD PURPOSE RESOLVE THOUGHT ANALYSIS DECISION DIERESIS ENACTURE STRENGTH CONSTANCY

RESOLVE ACT BEND MELT REDE SOIL UNDO LAPSE RELAX SALVE SOLVE SOYLE UNTIE VOUCH ADJUST ADVICE ASSOIL DECIDE DECREE FACTOR INCIDE REDUCE SETTLE STEVEN ABSOLVE ANALYZE APPOINT BETHINK CONSULT PURPOSE CONCLUDE

DISSOLVE UNRIDDLE UNTANGLE RECONCILE
(— GRAMMATICALLY) PARSE
(— INTO ELEMENTS) ANALYSE ANALYZE

RESOLVED BENT BOUND INTENT CERTAIN INTENSE RESOLUTE
(HALF —) GOOD

RESONANCE BODY EMPATHY RAPPORT RESOUND SYNTONY TYMPANY SONORITY VIBRANCY MESOMERISM

RESONANT BIG BRASS RINGY OROTUND RINGING SILVERY VIBRANT CANOROUS PLANGENT SONORANT SONOROUS SOUNDFUL SOUNDING

RESORT GO RUN SPA BEAT DOME HOWF LIDO SEEK TEEM TOUR TURN CAUSE FRAME HAUNT HOWFF JOINT RECUR RESET VISIT ESCORT FINISH REPAIR RETURN REVERT THRONG COMPANY PIMLICO RECOURSE RESOURCE TEETOTUM
(— TO) SEEK
(— TO DEVIOUS METHODS) FINAGLE
(BATHING —) PLAGE
(DISREPUTABLE —) KEN DIVE
(DRINKING —) DOGGERY
(EVIL —) ROOKERY
(LOW —) KEN DIVE STEW SPITAL
(MEANS OF —) REFUGE
(WORKINGMEN'S —) TEETOTUM

RESOUND DIN DUN ECHO PEAL RING SOUND REECHO EXPLODE REBOUND RESPEAK VIBRATE REDOUBLE

RESOUNDING BRASS REVERB REBOANT EMPHATIC FORCEFUL PLANGENT RESONANT RUMOROUS
(— WITH TALK) ABUZZ

RESOURCE WON BOOT FUND WONE MEANS SHIFT REFUGE RESORT STOPGAP PURCHASE
(PL.) EASE FOND GAIN FUNDS MEANS PURSE SINEW BOTTOM FACULTY FOISONS PURCHASE STRENGTH POCKETBOOK

RESOURCEFUL APT FENDY SHARP SMART ADROIT CLEVER FACILE SHIFTY PLANFUL

RESOURCEFULNESS SENSE SHIFT AGILITY

RESPECT ORE WAY DUTY FACE HEED HORE LOOK MARK DEFER DULIA FRONT HONOR IZZAT PARTY VALUE ASPECT BEHALF DETAIL ESTEEM HALLOW HOMAGE NOTICE REGARD CONCERN OBSERVE RESPITE SUSPECT TASHRIF WORSHIP CONSIDER HABITUDE RELATION VENERATE
(PL.) DEVOIR

RESPECTABLE GOOD NICE SMUG DOUCE DECENT PROPER FRUSANT CULOTTIC

RESPECTFUL AWFUL CIVIL CAREFUL DUTEOUS DUTIFUL HEEDFUL REVERENT

RESPECTIVE SEVERAL

RESPIRATION SIGH EUPNEA
ANAPNEA DYSPNEA EUPNOEA
ROARING GRUNTING
(PREF.) PNEO
PNEUM(A)(O)(ON)(ONO)
PNEUMATO SPIRO
RESPIRATOR MUZZLE CUIRASS
INHALER
RESPIRE BLOW LIVE REST EXHALE
REVIVE BREATHE SNUFFLE
SUSPIRE
RESPITE SOB REST STAY TRUE
DELAY FRIST LETUP PAUSE
BARLEY BREATH LAYOFF REGARD
REMISE LEISURE RESPECT
INTERVAL REPRIEVE SURCEASE
RESPLENDENCE GLORY SHEEN
FULGENCE FULGENCY SPLENDOR
RESPLENDENT LUCID SHEEN
. BRIGHT GILDED ORIENT SILVER
AUREATE SHINING GLORIOUS
GORGEOUS LUSTROUS SPLENDID
SUNSHINY
RESPOND REACT REPLY ANSWER
RETURN TRISAGION
(— TO LURE) STOOL
(— WARMLY) RISE
RESPONDENT ANSWERER
APPELLEE
RESPONSE AMEN ECHO CHORD
REPLY SNAFF ANSWER EARFUL
VOLLEY INTROIT RESPOND
ANTIPHON BEHAVIOR INSTINCT
REACTION REANSWER RECEPTION
(— OF KEYS) ACTION
(— OF SHIP) STEERING
(— TO GRAVITY) GEOTAXIS
RESPONSIBILITY BABY BALL CARE
DUTY ONUS WITE BLAME GUILT
TRUST CHARGE RACKET
RESPONSIBLE GOOD SOLID
DIRECT LIABLE AMENABLE
RESPONSION REPLY ANSWER
(PL.) SMALLS
RESPONSIVE OPEN SOFT WARM
GUILTY MUTUAL NIMBLE SUPPLE
TENDER MEETING AMENABLE
SENSIBLE
(— TO BEAUTY) ESTHETIC
(NOT —) IMMUNE
RESPONSIVENESS TOUCH
FEELING
RESPONSORY ANTHEM LIBERA
GRADUAL RESPOND
REST BED LAY LIE PUT SET SIT SOB
BASE BLOW CALM CAMP EASE
HANG HEEL LAIR LAVE LEAN LIOS
LISS PROP RELY RIDE RUST STAY
STOP COUCH FOUND LEATH
PAUSE PEACE POISE QUIET
RENEW ROOST SLEEP SPELL
STAND TRUST WREST ANCHOR
BOTTOM FAUCRE FEWTER
GROUND INSIST REMAIN REPOSE
SETTLE SIESTA STEADY UNTIRE
ADHARMA BALANCE BREATHE
CAESURA CLARION COMFORT
GALLOWS NOONING RECLINE
REFRESH RELACHE REMNANT
REQUIEM RESIDUE RESPITE
SILENCE SLUMBER SOJOURN
SUFFLUE SUPPORT SURPLUS
AKINESIS INTERVAL QUIETUDE

STANDOFF VACATION
(— FOR SPEAR OR LANCE) QUEUE
FAUCRE FEWTER
(— FOR SUPPORT) ABUT
(— FOR TYMPAN) GALLOWS
(— HORSE) WIND
(— IDLY) SLUG
(— LAZILY) FROWST
(— ON PLANER) SIDEHEAD
(— ON SUPPORT) BOTTOM
(— UPRIGHT) STAND
(HALF —) MINIM SOSPIRO
(LATHE —) STEADY
(LEG — ON SADDLE) CRUTCH
(MUSKET —) GAFFLE
(NOONDAY —) NAP SIESTA
(QUARTER —) SOSPIRO
(PREF.) PAULO
RESTATE REHASH
RESTATEMENT SUMMARY
RESTAURANT CAFE DINER GRILL
HOUSE PLACE BISTRO BUFFET
EATERY AUTOMAT BEANERY
CABARET CANTEEN OSTERIA
TEAROOM HIDEAWAY BRASSERIE
CHOPHOUSE TRATTORIA
(— KEEPER) BISTRO TRAITEUR
(SMALL —) CAFF
RESTFUL COOL SOFT QUIET
PLACID EASEFUL RELAXED
SOOTHFUL TRANQUIL
RESTHARROW WHIN CAMMOCK
SITFAST LANDWHIN
RESTHOUSE KHAN SERAI
AMBALAM CHHATRI KHANKAH
RESTING DORMANT
(PREF.) STATO
RESTING PLACE (ALSO SEE
RESTHOUSE) FORM GIST GITE
STAGE CHHATRI DHARMSALA
RESTITUTION AMENDS RETURN
RECOVERY
RESTIVE BALKY FUDGY ITCHY
RESTY RUSTY FIDGETY UNRESTY
UNWAYED CONTRARY INACTIVE
RESTLESS SKITTISH SLUGGISH
STUBBORN UNWIELDY
RESTLESS ANTSY FIKIE FUDGY
ITCHY FITFUL HAUNTY HECTIC
ROVING UNEASY AGITATO
ERETHIC FIDGETY FLIGHTY
FRETFUL INQUIET RAMPLER
RAMPLOR RESTIVE TEWSOME
TOSSING UNQUIET UNRESTY
VARIANT WAKEFUL FEVERISH
FEVEROUS STEERING
(— FLYCATCHER) GRINDER
RESTLESSNESS FIKE STIR FIDGET
UNREST DISQUIET JACTATION
RESTORATION REPAIR RETURN
RENEWAL RESTORE REVIVAL
EXCHANGE RECOVERY REMITTER
RESTORAL RECLAMATION
RESTORATIVE ACOPON BALSAMIC
SALUTARY SANATIVE ANALEPTIC
RESTORE FIX CURE HEAL AMEND
BLOCK COVER REDUB REFER
RENEW REPAY STORE YIELD
ASTORE DOCTOR RECALL REDEEM
REFORM REFUND RELATE
RENDER REPONE REVERT REVIVE
CONVERT ENSTORE INPAINT
REBUILD RECLAIM RECOVER

RECRUIT REFOUND REFRESH
REPLACE REVOLVE DECOHERE
REANSWER RECREATE RESTITUE
RETRIEVE
(— CONFIDENCE) REASSURE
(— TO CIVIL RIGHTS) INLAW
(— TO HEALTH) CURE HEAL MEND
(— TO ORDER) STILL
RESTRAIN BIT DAM BATE BIND
BOLT BUCK COOP CRIB CURB
DAMP GRAB GYVE HEAD HEFT
KEEP REIN SHUT SINK SNEB SNIB
SNUB STAY STEM STOP STOW
BRANK CHAIN CHECK COART
CRAMP DETER GUARD LEASH
MINCE POUND REPEL SHUNT
SOBER STILL STINT TRASH
ARREST BOTTLE BRIDLE CHASTE
COERCE DETAIN ENJOIN FETTER
FORBID GOVERN HALTER HAMPER
HINDER KENNEL OBLIGE REBUKE
RETAIN RETIRE REVOKE STIFLE
STRAIN TEMPER ABRIDGE
ABSTAIN CHASTEN COHIBIT
CONFINE CONTAIN CONTROL
ENCHAIN EXCLUDE INHIBIT
INJUNCT QUALIFY RECLAIM
REFRAIN REPRESS RETRACT
SHACKLE SNAFFLE SWADDLE
BULLDOZE COMPESCE COMPRESS
HANDCUFF IMPRISON RESTRICT
SIDELINE WITHDRAW WITHHOLD
(— BY FEAR) OVERAWE
(— HAWK'S WING) BRAIL
(— MOTION) SNUB
(PREF.) ISCH(O)
RESTRAINED SOBER CHASTE
MODEST SEVERE ASHAMED
DISCREET RESERVED RITENUTO
RESTRAINT BIT BEND CLOG CURB
HEFT STAY STOP CHECK CRAMP
FORCE LEASH SPARE STENT
STINT TRASH ARREST BRIDLE
DURESS FETTER STAYER
AWEBAND BONDAGE CONTROL
DURANCE EMBARGO MANACLE
RESERVE SNAFFLE TRAMMEL
HEADREST SOBRIETY
(— OF GOODS) HOCK
(BEYOND —) APE
RESTRICT PEG TIE CURB HOLD
BOUND CHAIN COART FENCE
HEDGE STINT THIRL COARCT
COERCE CORRAL CORSET ENTAIL
HAMPER NARROW ASTRICT
COHIBIT COMBINE QUALIFY
REPRESS SCANTLE SWADDLE
CONTRACT DEROGATE DIMINISH
RESTRAIN STRAITEN
(— MEANING) MODIFY
RESTRICTED CLOSE CRAMP LOCAL
CLOSED FINITE NARROW STRAIT
STRICT OBLIGATE PAROCHIAL
RESTRICTION STENT STINT
BURDEN DENIAL BARRIER
CONFINE RESERVE BLACKOUT
CABOTAGE
(PL.) BARS SWADDLE
RESTRICTIVE SEVERE BINDING
STYPTIC COACTIVE LIMITARY
LIMITING CONFINING
RESTY LAZY RESTIVE INACTIVE
INDOLENT SLUGGISH

RESULT GO END OUT ECHO FALL
FATE FAVE GROW RISE TAKE
BACON BRING CHILD ENSUE
EVENT FRUIT FUDGE ISSUE
PROOF EFFECT EFFORT ENDING
EVOLVE FINISH FOLLOW GROWTH
RECOIL REVERT SEQUEL SPRING
UPCOME UPSHOT ENTRAIN
FALLOUT FINDING OUTCOME
PROCEED PURPOSE REBOUND
REDOUND SUCCEED SUCCESS
FRUITAGE SEQUENCE OFFSPRING
(— FAVORABLY) SUCCEED
(— FROM) SUE
(ALGEBRAIC —) DUAL EXPANSION
(AS A —) AGAIN
(INCONCLUSIVE —) DOGFALL
(INEVITABLE —) NEMESIS
(PATHOLOGICAL —S) ALCOHOLISM
(REWARDING —) HAY
(SECONDARY —) SEQUELA
(PL.) AFTERINGS
(SUFF.) ISATION IZATION
RESULTANT CONCEPT OUTCOME
PROGENY
RESUME RENEW REOPEN RECOVER
SUMMARY CONTINUE PURLICUE
REASSUME RENOVATE REOCCUPY
(PL.) EXCERPTA
RESURRECTION RISE RIST UPRIST
REBIRTH REVIVAL
RESURRECTION PLANT
FERNWORT
RESUSCITATE REVIVE QUICKEN
SUSCITE REVIVIFY
RESUSCITATION KATSU RENEWAL
REVIVAL
RET RAIT RATE SOAK DEWROT
RETABLE PREDELLA
RETAIL REGRATE HUCKSTER
(— STORE) WAREHOUSE
RETAILER DEALER CLOTHIER
HUCKSTER
RETAIN HAVE HEFT HOLD KEEP
SAVE CATCH ATHOLD CONTAIN
RESERVE CONTINUE MAINTAIN
PRESERVE
(— MOMENTUM) DRIFT
RETAINER FOOL HEWE LACKEY
MENIAL RIBALD SEQUEL YEOMAN
HOBBLER HUSCARL JACKMAN
LACQUEY PANDOUR SERVANT
TRAVERS EMPLOYEE FOLLOWER
HENCHMAN MYRMIDON
BURKUNDAZ PENSIONER
(JAPANESE —) SAMURAI
(PL.) FOLK
RETALIATE REPAY AVENGE
RETORT REQUITE RECIPROCATE
RETALIATION QUITS MARQUE
TALION REPRISAL REQUITAL
(MAKE —) TURN
(VINDICTIVE —) REVENGE
RETALIATORY COUNTER
(PREF.) COUNTER
RETARD LAG CHOP DAMP DRAG
SLOW STEM BRAKE DEFER DELAY
ELONG TARDY TARRY THROW
TRASH BACKEN BELATE DEADEN
DETAIN HINDER INHIBIT SLACKEN
ENCUMBER OBSTRUCT PROTRACT
RESTRAIN
RETARDANT (FIRE —) BORAX

RETARDATION LAG DRAG DELAY ARREST
RETARDED DARK BEHIND LAGGED SIMPLE OVERAGE
RETARDING LENTANDO
RETCH GAG BOKE KECK HEAVE REACH VOMIT KECKLE RECCHE STRAIN
RETCHING HEFT
RETEM JUNIPER
RETENTION MEMORY RETAIN HOLDING KEEPING RETINUE (SUFF.) STASIA STASIS
RETIARIUS RETIARY GLADIATOR
RETICENCE RESERVE SECRECY RESTRAINT
RETICENT DARK SNUG CLOSE SECRET SILENT MIMMOUD SPARING BOUTONNE
RETICENTLY HEIMLICH
RETICULATE MESHED NETTED
RETICULE BAG CABAS SACHET WORKBAG CARRYALL RIDICULE
RETICULUM NET MITOME NETWORK MATTULLA
RETINOL CODOL
RETINOPHORE VITRELLA
RETINUE CREW GING PORT ROUT SUIT TAIL COURT MEINY SUITE TIRED TRAIN FAMILY REPAIR RETAIN COMPANY CORTEGE SOWARRY EQUIPAGE TENDANCE BODYGUARD
(— OF CAVALRY) SOWARRY
(VILLAINOUS —) BLACKGUARD
RETIRE GO GET DRAW GIVE AVOID LEAVE MICHE REBUT DEPART LOCATE RECALL RECEDE RECESS RECOIL SHRINK SURVEY PENSION REGRADE RETRACT RETREAT WITHDRAW
(— IGNOMINIOUSLY) SLINK
(— IN CRICKET) BOWL
RETIRED QUIET SECRET DEVIOUS OBSCURE OUTGONE PRIVATE RETRAIT SECLUSE SHADOWY ABSTRUSE EMERITUS SECLUDED SOLITARY
(— FROM PLAY) DOWN
RETIREMENT SHADE RECESS RETOUR SECESS PRIVACY PRIVATE RETREAT FIRESIDE SOLITUDE
RETIRING SHY NESH TIMID DEMURE MODEST FUGIENT RESERVED UMBRATIC RECESSIVE
(— ROOM) RECAMERA
RETORT MOT QUIP RISE SNAP VENY QUIRK REPAY REPLY ANSWER REGEST RETURN RIPOST BOMBOLA CORNUTE CRUSHER PELICAN REFLECT SQUELCH BACKWORD BLIZZARD COMEBACK MAGAZINE RECEIVER REPARTEE
(CURT —) SNAPHANCE
(GROUP OF —S) SETTING
(PUNNING —) CLINCH
(WITTY —) KNACK ZINGER
RETRACE RECALL FLYBACK RETREAT UNTREAD BACKTRACK
RETRACT BACK UNSAY ABJURE DISOWN RECALL RECANT RECEDE REVOKE SHRINK UNLOOK

RESCIND RETREAT SWALLOW PALINODE RENOUNCE WITHDRAW
RETRACTED INNER
RETRACTION PALINODE PALINODY
RETREAT DEN DOME DROP FADE GIVE LAIR NEST ROUT ARBOR AVOID BOWER LODGE NICHE QUAIL QUIET SHADE START ASHRAM ASYLUM BACKUP CASTLE RECEDE RECESS REFUGE RESILE RETIRE REVOLT CABINET DESCEND PRIVACY RETIRAL RETRACT SHELTER ANABASIS CRAWFISH DISMARCH FALLBACK FASTNESS NESTLING RECOURSE RECULADE SOLITUDE STAMPEDE WITHDRAW CREEPHOLE KATABASIS
(— FOR FISH) HOD
(FORTIFIED —) REDUIT
(RELIGIOUS —) ASRAM ASHRAM
(SECURE —) STRENGTH
(SHADY —) ALCOVE
RETRENCH OMIT EXCISE LESSEN REDUCE ABRIDGE CURTAIL SHORTEN
RETRENCHMENT CUT RAMPART EXCISION RETIRADE LESSENING
RETRIBUTION PAY PAYOFF RETURN REWARD WISSEL MANNAIA PENALTY REVENGE REQUITAL
RETRIEVE SHACK RECALL RECURE REGAIN REPAIR RESCUE REVIVE CORRECT RECOVER RESTORE SALVAGE
RETRIEVER FINDER GUNDOG LABRADOR WATERRUG
RETROFLEX DEMAL CORONAL CEREBRAL INVERTED REFLEXED
RETROGRADE RECEDE RETRAL DECLINE INVERSE OPPOSED REGREDE RETREAT BACKWARD DECADENT REARWARD WITHDRAW
RETROGRESS SINK REGRESS BACKSLIDE
RETROGRESSION SINK REGRESS RETREAT FALLBACK
RETUND DULL TURN BLUNT REFUTE
RETURN EBB GET COME TURN VAIL RECUR REFER REPAY REPLY VISIT YIELD AIRWAY ANSWER HOMING REMISE RENDER REPAIR REPASS REPORT RESORT RETIRE RETORT RETOUR REVERT CLEANUP PAYMENT REBOUND REDOUND REFLECT REPRISE REQUITE RESTORE REVENUE ATTOURNE DIVIDEND ELECTION EPANODOS FEEDBACK PICKINGS REACCESS REANSWER RECOURSE RECOVERY REDITION REFLECTION RECIPROCATE
(— FROM DEATH) ARISE
(— OF MERCHANDISE) COMEBACK
(— TENNIS BALL) RALLY
(— TO ORIGINAL CONDITION) RECYCLE
(— TO ZERO) FLYBACK
(GROUNDED —) BOND

(TENNIS —) GET BOAST
RETURNING REDIENT REMEANT REDITION
RETURN OF THE NATIVE (AUTHOR OF —) HARDY
(CHARACTER IN —) VYE CLYM VENN DAMON CANTLE JOHNNY DIGGORY NUNSUCH WILDEVE EUSTACIA THOMASIN CHRISTIAN YEOBRIGHT
REUBEN (FATHER OF —) JACOB
(MOTHER OF —) LEAH
REUEL (FATHER OF —) ESAU
(MOTHER OF —) BASHEMATH
(SON OF —) ELIASAPH
REUNION COLLEGE ADHESION HERENIGING
(— WITH BRAHMA) NIRVANA
REUNITE RALLY REUNE REJOIN RECONCILE
REVEAL BID BARE BLAB HINT JAMB KNOW OPEN SHOW TELL WRAY BREAK EXERT SPEAK SPLIT UNRIP UNTOP UTTER YIELD ACCUSE APPEAR BETRAY BEWRAY DESCRY DETECT EVINCE IMPART OSTEND PATEFY SPRING UNHELE UNLOCK UNMASK UNVEIL UNWRAP BESPEAK CLARIFY CONFESS DEVELOP DISPLAY DIVULGE UNCLOAK UNCOVER UNSHALE UNTRUSS DECIPHER DISCLOSE DISCOVER INDICATE MANIFEST UNBURDEN UNSHADOW UNSHROUD
(— BY SIGNS) EXHIBIT
(— SECRETS) BABBLE
(— UNINTENTIONALLY) BETRAY
REVEILLE DIAN DIANA LEVET ROUSE SIGNAL TRAVALLY
REVIVER (DISTILLING —) BOLTHOLE
REVEL JOY MASK RANT RIOT BIZLE COMUS FEAST GLOAT GLORY WATCH BEZZLE FROLIC GAVALL SPLORE TRESCA WALLOW WANTON CAROUSE DELIGHT ROISTER TRESCHE CAROUSAL DOMINEER FESTIVAL WITHDRAW
(NOISY —) JAMBOREE
(PL.) REVELRY
REVELATION TORA TORAH EXPOSE ORACLE REVEAL BATHKOL BATHQOL SHOWING GIVEAWAY OVERTURE APOCALYPSE
(— OF GOD'S WILL) LAW
(SUDDEN —) KICK
REVELER GREEK RANTER RIOTER FRANION PIERROT ROISTER BACCHANT CAROUSER MERRYMAKER
REVELRY JOY ORGY RIOT RIOTISE WASSAIL CARNIVAL CAROUSAL FESTIVAL
REVENANT GHOST WRAITH SPECTER
REVENGE HELL WREAK WROIK AVENGE ULTION REQUITE REQUITAL REVANCHE
REVENGED EVEN
REVENUE RENT JAGIR MANSE YIELD INCOME ENTRADA FINANCE

PROFITS HACIENDA INCOMING
(— FROM WATER RIGHTS) JALKAR
(— REVENUE PAID TO POPE) ANNAT
(GOVERNMENT —) JAGHIR
(STATE —) HACIENDA
REVERBERATE DIRL ECHO RING REPEL RETORT REVERB REBOUND REDOUND REFLECT RESOUND
REVERBERATING REBOANT RESONANT SOUNDING
REVERBERATION ECHO REDOUND REBOATION
REVERE ADORE HONOR ADMIRE ESTEEM HALLOW RESPECT WORSHIP VENERATE
REVERED (PREF.) SEMNO
REVERENCE AWE ORE CULT FEAR DREAD HONOR MENSK PIETY WURTH HOMAGE REGARD WORSHIP DEVOTION VENERANT VENERATE WORTHING
(— FOR ANIMALS) ZOISM
(IRRATIONAL —) FETICH FETISH
REVEREND SRI SHRI SHREE SVAMI SWAMI POTENT STRONG (PREF.) SEBASTO
REVERENT DEVOUT STRONG AWESOME DUTIFUL
REVERENTIAL PIOUS SOLEMN
REVERIE DUMP DWAM MUSE DREAM DWALM STUDY PONDER MEMENTO MOONING DAYDREAM TRAUMEREI
REVERSAL KNOCK CHANGE DOUBLE SWITCH BACKCAST BACKFLIP OVERTURN THROWBACK TURNABOUT (PREF.) ALL(O)
REVERSE BACK DOWN FACE FLOP JOLT ANNUL CHECK UPSET VERSO CHANGE DEFEAT INVERT REPEAL RETURN REVERT REVOKE BACKSET COUNTER INVERSE PUTBACK RETREAT REVERSO SETBACK SNIFTER SUBVERT BACKCAST CONTRARY CONVERSE OPPOSITE OVERRULE OVERTURN RAMVERSE TRAVERSE WATERLOO
(— OARS) SHEAVE
(— OF COIN) PILE TAIL WOMAN
(— OF NOTE) BACK
(— PAGE OF BOOK) VERSO REVERSO (PREF.) DE DIS DYS
(— ORDER) OB
REVERSED BACK INVERSE REVERTED ROVESCIO
(NOT —) DIRECT
REVERSI QUINOLAS
REVERSION SCRAPS ATAVISM ESCHEAT REMNANT FEEDBACK REVERTAL REVERTER THROWBACK
REVERT ANNUL ADVERT RESORT RESULT RETOUR RETURN REVOKE ESCHEAT RESTORE RECOURSE BACKSLIDE
(— TO A SUPERIOR) FALL
REVETMENT SODWORK
REVIEW HASH VIEW REVIE NOTICE REVISE SURVEY BRUSHUP RECENSE REJUDGE CRITIQUE

REVIEWAL REVISION

REVILE CALL RAIL ABUSE BLEIR BRAWL REBUT SCOLD SHEND SHENT SLANG MISSAY MISUSE VILIFY INVEIGH MISCALL MISNAME BACKBITE DISGRACE EXECRATE REPROACH

REVILING ABUSE ABUSION BLASPHEMY

REVISE EDIT ALTER REDACT REFORM REVIEW CORRECT RECENSE REFLECT REVISIT OVERHAUL

REVISER REDACTOR REFORMER REVIEWER

REVISION REVIEW SURVEY REVISAL REVIEWAL EPANAGOGE

REVITALIZER BRACER

REVIVAL IMAGE PICKUP REBIRTH REPRISE WAKENING

REVIVE DAW EBB WAKE FETCH QUICK RALLY RENEW ROUSE EXHUME GINGER RECALL RELIVE REVERT REVOKE EKPHORE ENLIVEN FRESHEN FURBISH QUICKEN REFRESH RESPIRE RESTORE RECREATE REDIVIVE REKINDLE RENOVATE RETRIEVE (**— FIRE**) CHUNK

REVOCATION REPEAL REVERSAL ADEMPTION

REVOICE ECHO

REVOKE LIFT ADEEM ANNUL RENIG CANCEL RECALL RECANT RENEGE REPEAL REVERT ABOLISH COMMUTE FINAGLE RECLAIM RESCIND RETREAT REVERSE ABROGATE REVOCATE (**— A LEGACY**) ADEEM

REVOLT ARISE REBEL REPEL START MUTINY OFFEND RELUCT UPROAR MUTATION OUTBREAK SEDITION UPRISING JACQUERIE REBELLION

REVOLTING GARISH HORRID BILIOUS FEARFUL HATEFUL HIDEOUS DREADFUL

REVOLT OF THE ANGELS (AUTHOR OF —) FRANCE (**CHARACTER IN —**) MAX ZITA ISTAR ARCADE AUBELS JULIEN SOPHAR MAURICE GILBERTE SARIETTE ESPARVIEU THEOPHILE EVERDINGEN

REVOLUTION GYRE RIOT TOUR TURN CYCLE WHEEL CHANGE ANARCHY CIRCUIT REVOLVE GYRATION MUTATION NOVATION ROTATION SEDITION REBELLION

REVOLUTIONARY RED RADICAL MUSCADIN ROTATING BOLSHEVIK

REVOLUTIONIST JACOBIN REDSHIRT

REVOLVE BIRL GYRE PIRL ROLL SPIN TIRL TURN WELT ORBIT PIVOT THROW TREND TROLL TWINE VERSE WHEEL WHIRL CENTER CIRCLE GYRATE PONDER ROTATE SPHERE SWINGE WAMBLE AGITATE VERSATE CONSIDER OVERTURN REVOLUTE (**CAUSE TO —**) TRUNDLE

REVOLVER GAT GUN ROD RIFLE

STICK CANNON CUTTER HOGLEG PISTOL RIFFLE BULLDOG DUNGEON (**PART OF —**) ROD BORE BUTT GATE GRIP SPUR BLADE FRAME GUARD LATCH SIGHT SLIDE STRAP BARREL HAMMER HANDLE MUZZLE CHAMBER TRIGGER CYLINDER BACKSTRAP

REVOLVING ORBY VOLUBLE GYRATORY VOLUTION (**PREF.**) (**—AROUND**) CIRCUM.

REVUE SHOW REVIEW FOLLIES

REVULSION FEAR REACTION

REWARD FEE PAY UTU GREE MEED RENT SPUR WAGE AMEED BOOTY BRIBE CROWN LOWER MERIT PLUME SHEPE YIELD BOUNTY DESERT GERSUM PAYOFF SALARY TROPHY WEDFEE AUREOLE GUERDON PREMIUM RENTAGE SOSTRUM STIPEND WARISON CONSIDER DIVIDEND EXACTION REMEMBER REQUITAL ACKNOWLEDGE (**— FOR INFORMATION ON CATTLE THIEVES**) TASCAL (**— OF VICTORY**) CROWN (**— TO HOUNDS**) HALLOW (**ILLUSORY —**) CARROT (**UNEXPECTED —**) JACKPOT (**PREF.**) LUCRI

REWARDED APAID BOUNTIED

REWARDING FAT PREMIANT (**FINANCIALLY —**) JUICY

REWRITTEN PALIMPSEST

REZAI ROSEI COVERLET MATTRESS

REZON (FATHER OF —) ELIADAH

RHABDUS SCOPULA

RHADAMANTHUS (FATHER OF —) JUPITER (**MOTHER OF —**) EUROPA

RHAPSODIC CONFUSED EFFUSIVE RAPTUROUS

RHAPSODY JUMBLE MEDLEY BOMBAST ECSTASY RAPTURE REVERIE (**— SECTION**) LASSU

RHATANY LEGUME

RHEA EMU EMEU NANDU NANDOW RATITE OSTRICH AGDISTIS AVESTRUZ (**DAUGHTER OF —**) JUNO CERES VESTA (**FATHER OF —**) URANUS (**HUSBAND OF —**) SATURN (**MOTHER OF —**) GAEA (**SON OF —**) PLUTO NEPTUNE

RHEBOK PEELE REHBOC

RHEINGOLD, DAS (CHARACTER IN —) ERDA LOGE FREIA WOTAN FAFNER FASOLT FRICKA HUNDING ALBERICH SIEGMUND SIEGLINDE (**COMPOSER OF —**) WAGNER

RHENIUM BOHEMIUM

RHEOMETER STROMUHR

RHEOSTAT DIMMER

RHESA (FATHER OF —) ZOROBABEL

RHESUS BANDAR BUNDER MONKEY BHUNDER MACAQUE (**FATHER OF —**) EIONEUS STRYMON (**MOTHER OF —**) CALLIOPE

RHETORIC SPEECH BOMBAST PROSAIC ELOQUENCE

RHETORICAL FLORID PURPLE AUREATE FORENSIC SWELLING

RHETORICIAN ORATOR RHETOR

RHEUM GORE TEARS CHOLER SPLEEN

RHINARIUM MUFFLE

RHINE REAN DITCH RUNNEL

RHINESTONE DEWDROP (**PL.**) GLITTER

RHINO CASH MONEY PONTOON

RHINOCEROS FOW ABADA BADAK RHINO BORELE KEITLOA UNICORN UPEYGAN NASICORN

RHINOCEROS BEETLE UANG SCARABAEID

RHINOCEROS HORNBILL TOPAU

RHIPIDION FLABELLUM

RHIZOID RHIZINA ROOTLET

RHIZOME KAVA NARD ARUKE CAAPI STOCK ARALIA ARNICA ASARUM GINGER IPECAC STOLON BERBERY CALAMUS CULVERS GENTIAN SCOPOLA ZEDOARY ASPIDIUM BARBERRY BERBERIS HELONIAS KAVAKAVA TRILLIUM TRITICUM VERATRUM (**PL.**) INULA GERANIUM

RHODE (FATHER OF —) POSEIDON (**MOTHER OF —**) HALIA (**SON OF —**) PHAETHON

RHODE ISLAND

CAPITAL: PROVIDENCE
COLLEGE: BROWN BRYANT
COUNTY: KENT BRISTOL NEWPORT
INDIAN: NIANTIC
MOTTO: HOPE
NATIVE: GUNFLINT
NICKNAME: LITTLEHODY
RIVER: PAWTUXET PAWCATUCK BLACKSTONE
STATE FLOWER: VIOLET
STATE TREE: MAPLE
TOWN: BRISTOL NEWPORT WARWICK CRANSTON KINGSTON PAWTUCKET

RHODE ISLAND BENT FURZETOP

RHODE ISLANDER GUNFLINT

RHODESIA (SEE ZIMBABWE)

RHODODENDRON ROSEBAY SPOONHUTCH (**THICKET OF —**) SLICK

RHOMB LOZEN WHEEL CIRCLE LOZENGE

RHOMBUS DIAMOND LOZENGE

RHONCHUS RALE SNORE SNORT WHEEZE

RHUBARB ROW FLAP RHEUM HASSEL CITRINE DISPUTE YAWWEED ARGUMENT PIEPLANT

RHYME CHIME CLINK VERSE CRAMBO POETRY RHYTHM TINKLE MEASURE (**— ROYAL**) TROILUS (**PL.**) RIMUR

RHYOLITE LIPARITE

RHYTHM BEAT STOT TIME CHIME METER PULSE SWING CADENCE RAGTIME BACKBEAT MOVEMENT SEQUENCE

RHYTHMICAL CADENCED MEASURED NUMEROUS ACCENTUAL (**NOT —**) RAGGED

RIA CREEK INLET

RIAL COIN RYEL ROYAL KINGLY SPLENDID

RIALTO MART BRIDGE EXCHANGE

RIANT GAY RIDENT LAUGHING MIRTHFUL

RIATA LASSO LARIAT

RIB FIN KID BULB CORD DIKE JOKE PURL SLAT WALE WIFE CORSE COSTA GROIN NERVE OGIVE PEARL RIDGE VARIX VITTA WHELP BRANCH LIERNE NEEDLE PARODY RIPPLE SCROLL TIMBER TONGUE BRISTLE FEATHER NERVURE PLEURAL STRATUM FORMERET SIDEBONE (**— IN GROINED ROOF**) SPRINGER (**— OF INSECT WING**) VEIN (**— OF SHIP**) WRONG (**— OF VIOLIN**) BOUT (**—S OF UMBRELLA**) FRAME (**SHORT —S**) CROP (**STRENGTHENING —**) FEATHER (**PL.**) SLATS (**PREF.**) COST(I)(O) PLEUR(I)(O) (**SUFF.**) COSTAL COSTATE PLEURA PLEUROUS

RIBALD LEWD ROGUE COARSE RASCAL VULGAR

RIBALDRY HASH HARLOTRY

RIBAND RIBBON SCROLL

RIBBED RIBBY CORDED COSTATE

RIBBING SPOOFERY

RIBBON BAR BOW FOB PAN BEND COST PADS BRAID CORSE FILET LABEL PADOU PIECE RUBAN SHRED TASTE BENDEL CADDIS CORDON FERRET FILLET LISERE RADULA RECORD RIBAND SHOWER STRING TAENIA TAWDRY TISSUE TONGUE BANDING SAUTOIR TORSADE BANDEROL BOOKMARK FRAGMENT TRESSURE PETERSHAM (**— AS BADGE OF HONOR**) CORDON (**— AS HEADDRESS**) TRESSOUR TRESSURE (**— FOR BORDER**) LISERE (**— HANGING FROM CROWN**) JESS (**— USED FOR GARTERS**) CADDIS CADDICE (**COLORED —S**) DIVISA (**END OF —S**) FATTRELS (**FLOATING —**) PAN (**KNOT OF —S**) SORTIE (**LINGUAL —**) TONGUE (**SILK —**) CORSE PADOU TASTE (**WATERED —**) PADS (**PL.**) REINS (**PREF.**) TAENI(A)(O) (**SUFF.**) TENE

RIBBON FERN PTERIS

RIBBONFISH GARFISH GUAPENA AGUAVINA BANDFISH DEALFISH

RIBBONLIKE TAENIATE TAENIOID TAENIFORM

RIBBON TREE AKAROA HOIHERE HOUHERE LACEBARK

RIBGRASS WINDLES BUCKHORN HARDHEAD PLANTAIN

RIBWORT KLOPS HEADMAN RATTAIL SOLDIER WINDLES HARDHEAD HEADSMAN PLANTAGO

RICCIARDETTO (SISTER OF —) BRADAMANTE

RICE AUS AMAN BORO PADI PAGA RISE SELA TWIG ARROZ BATTY BIGAS CANIN CHITS GRAIN MACAN PADDY PALAY PATNA BRANCH CEREAL CONGEE SIDDHA ANGKHAK MANOMIN RISOTTO
(— BOILED WITH MEAT) PILAF PILAU PILAW
(— COOKED WITH MEAT) RISOTTO JAMBALAYA
(— FIELD) SAWAH
(— IN HUSK) PALAY
(— OF 2ND OR 3RD GRADE) CHITS
(— POLISHINGS) DARAC
(BOILED —) CANIN KANIN
(HUSKED —) CHAL
(INFERIOR —) PAGA
(LONG-STEMMED —) AMAN
(MOUNTAIN —) SMILO
(SHORT-STEMMED —) AUS
(SPRING —) BORO
(UNCOOKED —) BIGAS
(UNMILLED —) PADI PADDY
(WILD —) MANOMIN
(PREF.) ORYZ(I) RIZI

RICEBIRD BUNTING CACIQUE SPARROW BOBOLINK

RICE FLOWER PIMELEA

RICEGRASS BARIT SACATE ZACATE

RICH FAT ABLE DEEP FAIR HIGH LUSH OOFY WARM GLEBY OPIME PLUMP RITZY ROUND TINNY VIVID BATFUL COSTLY DAEDAL FRUITY HEARTY PLUMMY PLUSHY PODDED SUPERB ULRICA AMUSING BAITTLE COPIOUS FERTILE MONEYED OPULENT PINGUID PLASTIC WEALTHY ABUNDANT AFFLUENT GENEROUS HUMOROUS LUSCIOUS
(— IN FAME) RODERICK
(— IN GIFTS) PREMIOUS
(— IN INTEREST) JUICY
(— IN MALT) HEAVY
(— IN SILICA) ACID
(— IN TIMBRE) GOLDEN
(— MAN) DIVES
(— OF SOIL) PINGUID
(NOT —) PLAIN

RICHARD DICCON

RICHARD CARVEL (AUTHOR OF —) CHURCHILL
(CHARACTER IN —) FOX JONES CARVEL DOROTHY MANNERS RICHARD WALPOLE

RICHARD II (AUTHOR OF —) SHAKESPEARE
(CHARACTER IN —) JOHN ROSS YORK BAGOT BUSHY GAUNT GREEN HENRY PERCY EDMUND PIERCE SCROOP SURREY THOMAS AUMERLE HOTSPUR LANGLEY MOWBRAY NORFOLK RICHARD STEPHEN BERKELEY HEREFORD

FITZWATER LANCASTER SALISBURY WILLOUGHBY BOLINGBROKE NORTHUMBERLAND

RICHARD III (AUTHOR OF —) SHAKESPEARE
(CHARACTER IN —) ANNE JOHN YORK DERBY HENRY JAMES LOVEL BLOUNT DORSET EDWARD GEORGE MORTON OXFORD RIVERS ROBERT SURREY THOMAS TYRREL WALTER BRANDON CATESBY HERBERT NORFOLK RICHARD STANLEY TRESSEL URSWICK VAUGHAN BERKELEY CLARENCE HASTINGS MARGARET RATCLIFF RICHMOND BOURCHIER ELIZABETH ROTHERHAM BRAKENBURY BUCKINGHAM GLOUCESTER CHRISTOPHER

RICHES GOLD PELF WEAL LUCRE WORTH MAMMON TALENT WEALTH FORTUNE OPULENCE RICHESSE TREASURE

RICHLY HIGH AMPLY FATLY FULLY DEARLY

RICHNESS BODY SUMEN LUXURY ELEGANCE FECUNDITY

RICHWEED RAGWEED COOLWEED

RICK GOAF GOFE REKE CANCH RICKLE SPRAIN WRENCH CORNRICK

RICKETS RACHITIS

RICKETY SHAKY SHACKY SHACKLY UNSOUND RACHITIC SHATTERY UNSTABLE TOTTERING RAMSHACKLE

RICKMATIC CONCERN BUSINESS

RICOCHET SKIP SKITE GLANCE REBOUND

RICTUS GRIN GRIMACE

RID FREE QUIT SHED SHUT CLEAR EGEST REDDE SCOUR SHIFT ACQUIT REMOVE DELIVER
(— OF INSECTS) BUG
(— OF LICE) CHAT
(— OF WEEDS) CLEAN
(— ONESELF OF) DOFF DEPOSIT DISPATCH

RIDDANCE SHUT RELIEF DISPATCH

RIDDER SIFT SIEVE RIDDLE

RIDDLE SIFT BLAIK GRIPH REBUS DEBASE ENIGMA FOITER PUZZLE RUDDLE SCREEN CORRUPT CRIBBLE EXPLAIN GRIDDLE GRIPHUS MYSTIFY PERPLEX PROBLEM CRATEMAN PERMEATE
(— AS GRAIN) REE
(PL.) MURLEMEWES

RIDDLER CRATEMAN

RIDE GO RIB BAIT DOSA HACK HURL LAST LIFT PRIG SAIL TOOL CROSS DRIVE TEASE BANTER CANTER DEPEND DODGEM GALLOP JUMBLE NOTICE SADDLE HAYRIDE JOYRIDE OVERLAP SURVIVE TANTIVY BESTRIDE
(— FAST) PRICK POWDER
(— HARD) POUND BUCKET
(— IN HIRED VEHICLE) JOB
(— ON A WAVE) BODYSURF
(— ON HORSE) BOOT LARK BURST JOCKEY SCHOOL

(— RECKLESSLY) BRUISE
(— TO HOUNDS) GO
(AMUSEMENT PARK —) SWING

RIDER TACK ANNEX CROSS HAZER LABEL COWBOY JOCKEY SITTER ALLONGE CODICIL NAGSMAN PRICKER CAVALIER DESULTOR HORSEMAN
(DUKEY —) BRAKEMAN
(DUMMY —) CROSS

RIDERS TO THE SEA (AUTHOR OF —) SYNGE
(CHARACTER IN —) NORA MAURYA BARTLEY MICHAEL

RIDGE AAS ARM BAR FIN RIB RIG RYG BALK BAND BANK BARB BROW BULT BURR BUTT COMB DRUM FRET FULL HACK HILL KEEL LINK LIST PAHA PUFF RAIN REAN ROLL SHIN SPUR WAVE WELT BARGH CHINE COSTA CREST EARTH EAVES GONYS GYRUS JUGUM KNURL LEDGE LINCH RINGE RUDGE SCOUT SHANK SPINE TORUS VARIX WHELP BRIDGE CARINA COLLOP CREASE CRISTA CUESTA CULMEN DIVIDE DORSUM FRENUM RAFTER RIDEAU SADDLE SELION SUMMIT ANNULET APODEMA BREAKER BUCCULA COLLINE COSTULA EYEBROW EYELINE HOGBACK HUMMOCK INTHROW PROPONS RIGGING SOWBACK WINDROW WITHERS WRINKLE YARDANG CATOCTIN CINGULUM FOREDUNE HEADLAND RESTBALK SHOULDER
(— BETWEEN FURROWS) STITCH RESTBALK
(— IN BREASTPLATE) TAPUL
(— IN COAL SEAM) HORSEBACK
(— IN HORSE'S MOUTH) EAR
(— MADE BY PLOWING) HACK SELION
(— MADE BY TOOL) BUR BARB BURR
(— OF BIRD'S BILL) CULM CULMEN
(— OF BRAIN CORAL) COLLINE
(— OF BREASTBONE) KEEL
(— OF CLAY) DOWLE
(— OF EARTH) BALK
(— OF FLESH) COLLOP
(— OF HORSE'S NECK) CREST
(— OF LAND) BULT RAIN SELION STITCH HOGBACK
(— OF SAND IN WATER) REEF SANDBAR
(— OF SCAPULA) SPINE
(— OF SCREW) THREAD
(— OF SNOW) SASTRUGA ZASTRUGA
(— OF UNPLOWED LAND) LINCH LINCHET
(— OF WAVE) CREST
(— ON BOOK) HUB
(— ON CLOTH) WALE
(— ON CROWN OF TOOTH) CINGULUM
(— ON FINGERBOARD OF GUITAR) FRET
(— ON FISH SCALE) CIRCULUS
(— ON FRUITS OF CARROT FAMILY) JUGUM

(— ON GLUMES) CARINA
(— ON MOLLUSK SHELL) COSTULA
(— ON OVULE) RAPHE
(— ON SEA FLOOR) SWELL
(— ON SEASHORE) STANNER
(— ON SHEET METAL) BEAD
(— ON SIDE OF SADDLE) PUFF
(— ON SKIN) WALE
(— ON VIOLIN) NUT
(— PROTECTING CAMP) RIDEAU
(— WITH SHARP SUMMIT) HOGBACK
(—S ON ROCK) LAPIES
(ANATOMICAL —) CARINA
(BEACH —) FULL
(CHEWING —) ENDITE
(CONNECTING —) HAUSE
(CONVOLUTED —) GYRUS
(DRAINAGE —) BREAKER
(GLACIAL —) OS KAME PAHA ESKAR ESKER ESCHAR NUNATAK
(HAIRLIKE —) LIRA
(ICE —) SERAC
(ISOLATED —) BARGH
(LONG STONY —) RAND
(MOUNTAIN —) COMB CHINE SIERRA BACKBONE
(NARROW —) DRUM RAZORBACK
(PROJECTING —) HOE SCOUT
(RESIDUAL —) CATOCTIN
(ROCK —) CLEAVER
(SAND —) DUNE ESKER WAVEMARK
(SEEDED —) DRILL
(SHARP-CRESTED —) ARETE ARRIS
(SLIGHT —) PROPONS
(SNOW —) ZASTRUGA
(UNPLOWED —) BALK BAULK
(WOODED —) CHENIER
(PL.) OSAR KNURLING

RIDGED RIDGY SHARP MILLED PORCATE CARINATE

RIDGELING RIG REGALD RIDGIL RIGGOT RIGINAL

RIDGEPOLE ROOFTREE

RIDICULE FUN GUY MOB PAN RIG TAX GAME GIBE JEER JEST JIBE JOEY MOCK PLAY QUIZ RAZZ SKIT TROT TWIT BORAK CHAFF CLOWN HORSE IRONY MIMIC MOMUS QUEER RALLY SCOFF SCOUT SMOKE SNEER TAUNT BANTER DERIDE EXPOSE RAILLY SATIRE BUFFOON LAMPOON MOCKERY SARCASM DERISION RAILLERY SATIRIZE SPOOFERY BURLESQUE

RIDICULOUS DOTTY DROLL FUNNY SILLY ABSURD INSANE COMICAL FOOLISH MOCKING DERISIVE DERISORY FARCICAL INDECENT COCKAMAMY MONSTROUS

RIDING AWHEEL LIVELY OVERLAP PRICKANT SHIVAREE TRITHING CHEVACHIE
(— ACADEMY) MANAGE MANEGE
(— CROP) ROD
(— WHIP) CROP QUIRT

RIDOTTO BALL REDOUTE

RIEM RHEIM RIMPI STRAP THONG

RIENZI (CHARACTER IN —) COLA IRENE PAOLO ORSINI RIENZI ADRIANO COLONNA STEFANO RAIMONDI

(COMPOSER OF —) WAGNER
RIFE EASY FULL RANK QUICK READY ACTIVE FILLED NIMBLE STRONG CURRENT REPLETE ABUNDANT INCLINED MANIFEST NUMEROUS
RIFFLE REEF RIFF WAVE RAPID RIPPLE SHUFFLE WATERFALL
RIFFRAFF MOB RAFF SCUM SCAFF TRASH RABBLE REFUSE RUBBISH CANAILLE POPULACE RAGABASH
RIFLE RIG ROB KRAG LOOT RIPE PIECE YAGER CARBIN JEZAIL JUZAIL RIFFLE SNIDER ARISAKA BULLPUP BUNDOCK BUNDOOK CARABIN CARBINE DESPOIL ENFIELD ESCOPET MARTINI PILLAGE PLUNDER RANSACK SPORTER BANDHOOK REPEATER SPLITTER STRICKLE TAKEDOWN CHASSEPOT
  (— BALL CASING) THIMBLE
  (— PIN) TIGE
RIFLEMAN JAGER JAEGER
  (PL.) RIFLERY
RIFT RIVE BELCH CHASM CRACK SPLIT CLEAVE DIVIDE BLEMISH FISSURE CREVASSE
  (— IN TIMBER) LAG
RIG RI FIG REG HOAX JEST JOKE REEK WIND DRESS EQUIP GETUP PRANK RIDGE SPORT STORM TRICK BANTER CLOTHE GUNTER ROTARY SADDLE SCHEME MARCONI SPUDDER SWINDLE BACKSTAY RIDICULE SEMITRAILER
  (TRUCKING —) SEMI
RIGADOON DANCE RIGODON
RIGEL REGEL ALGEBAR
RIGGED (FULLY —) ATAUNT
RIGGER CLIMBER SLINGER SCAFFOLD
RIGGING NET GEAR ROOF RIDGE TACKLE APPAREL CLOTHING JACKSTAY TACKLING
RIGHT DUE FEE FIT IUS OFF REE SAY SOC BANG DUTY FAIR FLOP GALE GOOD HAND ITER JUST LIEN REAL RECT REET SANE SLAP SOKE TEAM TRUE WELL CLAIM DRESS DROIT ENTRY EXACT FAVOR FERRY LEGAL RICHT SOUND STRAY TECHT TITLE ACTION ACTUAL ANGARY BALLOT DEMAND DEXTER EATAGE EQUITY PROPER PUTURE ANNUITY APANAGE AUBAINE BENEFIT CORRECT DERECHO DESIRED FACULTY FALDAGE FITTING FOLDAGE FREEDOM GENUINE HAYBOTE LIBERTY LICENSE PRENDER RECTIFY RELIEVE SLAPDAB UPRIGHT WARRANT BANALITY BLOODWIT FIREBOOT FORESTRY HEIRSHIP INTEREST LIFERENT SEIGNORY SLAPDASH STALLAGE STRAIGHT SUFFRAGE SUITABLE THIRLAGE PREROGATIVE
  (— AND LEFT) HAY HEY
  (— AS COMMAND TO HORSES) REE
  (— EYE) OD
  (— HAND) MD OPENBAND

  (— IN A THING) INTEREST
  (— IN WIFE'S INHERITED PROPERTY) CURTESY
  (— OF CHOICE) OPTION
  (— OF EXIT) ISH
  (— OF FREE QUARTERS) CORODY
  (— OF HOLDING COURT) TEAM
  (— OF INQUIRY) SOKEN
  (— OF OWNERSHIP) TITLE COMMONTY
  (— OF PASTURAGE) FEED STINT EATAGE COWGATE COMMONAGE HORSEGATE
  (— OF PRECEDENCE) PAS
  (— OF PRESENTATION) ADVOWSON
  (— OF PROTECTION) MUND
  (— OF USING ANOTHER'S PROPERTY) EASEMENT
  (— OF USING GRASSLAND) EATAGE
  (— SIDE) OFFSIDE
  (— TIME) TID
  (— TO COLLECT REVENUE) DIWANI DEWANEE DEWANNY
  (— TO COMMAND) IMPERIUM
  (— TO CUT WOOD) VERT GREENHEW
  (— TO DRAW WATER) HAUSTUS
  (— TO DRIVE BEAST) ACTUS
  (— TO PASS OVER LAND) ITER
  (— TO SEIZE PROPERTY) ANGARY
  (— TO SHOOT FIRST) CAST
  (— TO WORK IN MINE) BEN
  (ALL —) HUNK JAKE HUNKY
  (FEUDAL —) CUDDY THIRL THIRLAGE
  (FISHING —) PISCARY
  (INDIAN LEGAL —) HAK HAKH
  (LEGAL —) IUS JUS JURE DROIT ACCESS APPEAL COMMON FISHERY HYPOTHEC
  (LEGAL —S) JURA
  (MILLER'S —) SOKEN
  (MINING —) GALE
  (NOT —) ACUTE
  (PROPERTY —) DOMINIUM
  (WIDOW'S —) TERCE TIERCE
  (PL.) DIBS JURA
  (PREF.) DEXIO DEXTR(O) ORTH(O) RECT(I)
  (— HAND) DEXIO DEXTR(O)
RIGHT ANGLE RECTANGLE
  (HUNDREDTH OF —) GRAD GRADE
RIGHTEOUS GOOD JUST GODLY MORAL ZADOC ZADOK DEVOUT FITTING PERFECT SKILFUL UPRIGHT INNOCENT VIRTUOUS
RIGHTEOUSNESS DOOM DHARMA EQUITY JUSTICE HOLINESS JUDGMENT JUSTNESS MORALITY RECTITUDE
RIGHTFUL DUE JUST TRUE LEGAL KINDLY LAWFUL PROPER FITTING
RIGHTFULNESS JUSTICE
RIGHT-HANDED DEXTRAL SKILLED DEXTROUS CLOCKWISE
RIGHT-HANDWISE DEASIL DESSIL DEISEAL CLOCKWISE
RIGHTLY RITE FITLY ARIGHT FAIRLY JUSTLY HANDILY PERQUEER SUITABLY
RIGHT WHALE BOWHEAD BALAENID MYSTICETE NORDCAPER

RIGID SET ACID CARK FIRM HARD HIGH FIXED SOLID STARK STERN STIFF STONY STOUT TENSE TONIC TOUGH FORMAL FROZEN MARBLY SEVERE STARCH STICKY STRICT AUSTERE IRONCLAD RIGOROUS STRAIGHT INELASTIC STRINGENT
  (— IN SELF-DENIAL) ASCETIC
RIGIDITY FROST RIGOR RIGOUR BUCKRAM SETNESS HARDNESS STIFFNESS
RIGMAREE COIN TRIFLE
RIGMAROLE RANE NOMINY RABBLE RAGMAN SLAMPAMP SLAMPANT AMPHIGORY
RIGOLETTO (CHARACTER IN —) GILDA MANTUA MADDALENA RIGOLETTO SPARAFUCILE
  (COMPOSER OF —) VERDI
RIGOR TYRANNY ASPERITY HARDNESS SEVERITY
RIGOROUS FIRM HARD CLOSE CRUEL EXACT HARSH HEFTY RIGID STERN STIFF TOUGH BITTER FLINTY SEVERE STRAIT STRICT STRONG AUSTERE DRASTIC PRECISE SPARTAN DISTRICT DRACONIC EXACTING IRONCLAD STRAIGHT
  (MORALLY —) PURITANIC
  (NOT —) INEXACT
  (UNDULY —) HARSH
RILE VEX ROIL ANGER PEEVE IRRITATE
RILL PURL SIKE CLEFT DRILL PRILL GROOVE RUNLET RILLOCK RIVULET BROOKLET RIVELING TRICKLET ARROYUELO WATERSHUT
RILLSTONE VENTIFACT
RIM HEM LIP BEAD BRIM CURB EDGE SHOE BEZEL BRINK CHIME EAVES FELLY FRAME HELIX SKIRT BORDER CALKER CHOANA FILLET FLANGE MARGIN EXCIPLE
  (— HOLDING WATCH CRYSTAL) BEZEL BEZIL
  (— OF BASKET) HOOP
  (— OF COROLLA) ANNULUS
  (— OF CRATER) SOMMA
  (— OF EAR) HELIX
  (— OF GEM) GIRDLE
  (— OF HORSESHOE) WEB
  (— OF INSECT'S WING) TERMEN
  (— OF JELLYFISH) VELUM
  (— OF SANIO) CRASSULA
  (— OF TIN) LIST
  (— OF WHEEL) FELLY FELLOE STRAKE
  (— ON CASK) CHIMB CHIME CHINE
  (— ON CLOG) CALKER
  (— SURROUNDING FLAGELLUM) CHOANA
  (EXTERNAL —) FLANGE
  (PROTECTIVE —) BANK
  (RAISED —) BOSS
  (PREF.) AMBO
RIMA CHINK CLEFT RIMULA FISSURE
RIME RIM HOAR RIND RUNG CRACK CRUST FROST ROUND CRANREUCH
RIMPLE FOLD RIPPLE WRINKLE

RINALDO (BELOVED OF —) ANGELICA
  (COUSIN OF —) ORLANDO
  (FATHER OF —) AYMON
  (HORSE OF —) BAYARD
RIND BARK PEEL PILL RYND SKIN CRUST FROST SWARD CITRON SWARTH
  (— OF HAM) SKIN
  (— OF MEAT) SPINE
  (— OF POMEGRANATE) GRANATUM
  (— OF ROASTED PORK) CRACKLING
  (PREF.) LEMMO LEPO
  (SUFF.) LEMMA
RING GO BEE BOW BUR CUP DEE DIE EKE FAM JOW ORB PIT RIM AMBO BAIL BAND BELL BONG BURR CRIC CURB DING DIRL ECHO GYRE HOOP JING LOOP MAIL PASS PEAL RACE RINK RUSH SHUT SING TANG TOLL VIRL WISP AMBON ANLET ARENA BAGUE CAROL CHIME CHINK CLANG CYCLE GRAIN GROUP GUARD GUIDE JEWEL KNELL LUNET PISTE RIGOL ROUND ROWEL TORUS VERGE WAFER WITHE BANGLE BECKET BROUGH BUTTON CIRCLE CIRCUS CIRQUE CLIQUE COLLAR COLLET DINDLE EYELET FAMBLE GIMMER GIRDLE HARROW KEEPER LARIGO LEGLET RINGLE RUNDLE RUNNER SIGNET TORQUE TURRET VIROLE WASHER ANNULUS ARMILLA CIRCLET CIRCUIT CLAPPER COMPASS COUPLER CRINGLE DIAMOND FAMELEN FERRULE GALLERY GARLAND GROMMET GUDGEON MANILLA NUCLEUS PACKING RESOUND ROWLOCK SHACKLE STIRRUP THIMBLE VIBRATE BRACELET BULLRING CINCTURE CORONULE DINGDONG DRAUPNIR DUSTBAND ENCIRCLE FAIRLEAD PACIFIER SONORITY SURROUND TRAVELER
  (— A TREE) FRILL
  (— AROUND ARTICULAR CAVITY) AMBON
  (— AROUND MOON) BROCH
  (— AROUND NIPPLE) AREOLA
  (— AT EACH END OF CINCH) LARIGO
  (— ATTACHED TO JIB) HANK
  (— BELLS) FIRE
  (— FOR CARRYING SHOT) LADLE
  (— FOR SECURING BIRD) VERVEL
  (— FOR TRAINING HORSES) LONGE
  (— FORMING HANDLE OF KEY) BOW
  (— OF ANNULATED COLUMN) BAGUE
  (— OF BOILER) STRAKE
  (— OF COLOR) STOCKING
  (— OF DOTS AROUND EDGE OF COIN) GRAINING
  (— OF LIGHT) GLORY
  (— OF ODIN) DRAUPNIR
  (— OF PILES) STARLING
  (— OF RIDING SCHOOL) PISTE
  (— OF ROPE) HANK BECKET GARLAND GROMMET SNORTER SNOTTER
  (— OF SPINES) CORONULE
  (— OF STANDING STONES) CAROL

(— OF TWO HOOPS) GEMEL GEMMEL
(— OF WAGONS) CORRAL LAAGER
(— ON BATTLEAX) BUR BURR
(— ON BIRD'S TIBIA) ARMILLA
(— ON DECK) CRANCE
(— ON GUN CARRIAGE) LUNET LUNETTE
(— ON HINGE) GUDGEON
(— ON LAMP) CRIC
(— ON LANCE) BURR
(— ON UMBRELLA ROD) RUNNER
(— SUPPORTING LAMPSHADE) GALLERY
(— SURROUNDING BUGLE) VIROLE
(— SUSPENDING COMPASS) GIMBAL
(— TO ENCLOSE DEER) TINCHEL TINCHILL
(— UNDER BEEHIVE) EKE
(— USED AS MONEY) MANILLA
(— USED AS VALVE) WAFER
(— WITH GROOVED OUTER EDGE) THIMBLE
(— WITH VIBRATION) DIRL
(BLACKSMITH'S —) BOLSTER
(BRIGHT —) HALATION
(CERVICAL —) TORQUE
(CURTAIN —) EYE
(FINGER —) HOOP
(FLESHY —) ANNULUS
(HARNESS —) DEE BUTTON LARIGO TERRET TORRET TURRET
(HAWK'S —) VERVEL
(INTERLINKED METAL —S) MAIL
(JOINED —) GIMMER GIMMOR
(LITTLE —) ANNULET
(LUMINOUS —) BROUGH
(MOUNTAINEER'S —) KARABINER
(NOSE —) PIRN
(OIL —) WIPER
(PACKING —) LUTE
(PART OF —) BAND CLAW PRONG SHANK STONE COLLET SETTING HALLMARK
(PLAITED —) RUSH WISP
(SURGICAL —) CURETTE
(TAPERING SHANK —) BELCHER
(TARGET —) SOUS SOUSE
(TOOTHED IRON —) HARROW
(TOP OF —) BEZEL BEZIL
(PREF.) CRICO CYCL(O) GYRO
(HAVING OPENED —) SECO
RING AND THE BOOK (AUTHOR OF —) BROWNING
(CHARACTER IN —) PAUL GUIDO PIETRO GIUSEPPE POMPILIA VIOLANTE COMPARINI CAPONSACCHI FRANCESCHINI
RINGDOVE QUIST CUSHAT CUSHIE QUEEST TOOZOO ZOOZOO COWSHOT COWSHUT
RINGED GYRATE ZONATE ANNULAR ANNULOSE
RINGED SNAKE COLUBRID
RINGER CHEER YOUTH COWBOY CROWBAR STOCKMAN
RINGHALS COBRA
RINGING BELL BRIGHT FERVID JANGLE CLANGOR OROTUND SINGING DECISIVE RESONANT SONORANT SONOROUS TINNIENT TINNITUS
(CHANGE —) CINQUES SINGLES

RINGLET CURL LOCK TENDRIL
(— ON FOREHEAD) FAVORITE
(PREF.) CIRR(I)(O)
RING-NECKED TORQUATE
RING-NECKED DUCK DOGY SCAUP MOONBILL RINGBILL BLACKJACK
RING OUZEL AMSEL THRUSH WHISTLER
RING PLOVER SANDY COLLIER KILLDEE DULWILLY RINGNECK
RING-SHAPED ANNULAR CRICOID ANNULARY ANNULATE CIRCULAR
RINGWORM TINEA KERION TETTER SERPIGO
RINGWORM BUSH SENNA
RINK ALLEY GLACIARIUM
RINSE NET SIND WASH RANGE RENCH RENSH RINGE SCIND SCOUR SWILL BLUING DOUCHE CLEANSE
RINSING NET SIND FLUSH RESIDUE
RIOT DIN HURL BRAWL REVEL WORRY ATTACK CLAMOR EXCESS JUMBLE MEDLEY RANTAN SPLORE TUMULT ANARCHY CONFUSE DESPOIL REVELRY BLOODWIT CAROUSAL
RIOTOUS ROID ROYD WILD NOISY RANDY RANTY HEMPIE RANDIE STORMY WANTON BACCHIC PROFUSE ROARING ABUNDANT BACCHIAN
RIP RIT COOP REAT TEAR BREAK SHARK SHRED SLITE UNSEW BASKET RIPPLE UNSEAM
RIPE FIT BOLD LATE DRUNK READY MATURE MELLOW SIDDER SIDDOW DIGESTED FINISHED SEASHORE SUITABLE
(EARLY —) HASTY RARERIPE
(PREF.) HADR(O)
RIPEN AGE ADDLE AUGUST DIGEST MELLOW CONCOCT CRIMSON DEVELOP PERFECT COMPLETE MATURATE
RIPENESS MATURITY
RIPHATH (FATHER OF —) GOMER
RIPOSTE REPLY RETORT THRUST REPARTEE
RIPPER RIPSAW BOBSLED HUMDINGER
RIPPET FUSS TUMULT UPROAR DISPUTE QUARREL
RIPPING FINE GRAND SWELL CAPITAL TIPPING SPLENDID
RIPPLE CURL FRET PURL RIFF SEED WAVE ACKER CRISP TWINE COCKLE DIMPLE JABBLE LIPPER RIMPLE RUFFLE RUMBLE WIMPLE CRINKLE WAVELET WRINKLE
(— ALONG) DADE
RIPPLING BREAK BULGE JABBLE ARIPPLE
(— OF SEA) LIPPER
(— ON SURFACE) HORROR
RIPSAW RIPPER SPLITSAW
RIPSNORTER SNIFTER HUMDINGER
RISE COME DRAW FLOW GROW HEAD HIGH HIKE HOLT HOVE LIFT PLUM SOAR ARISE BEGIN CANCH CHEER CLIMB ERECT HEAVE HOIST MOUNT OCCUR PITCH

PLUFF PROVE RAISE ROUSE SCEND SOURD STAND START SURGE SWELL TOWER YEAST ASCEND ASCENT ASPIRE AURORA BILLOW EMERGE GROWTH HAPPEN HEIGHT ORIGIN RESULT RETORT SOURCE SPRING THRIVE UPDIVE UPREAR ADVANCE APPLAUD HUMMOCK REDOUND UPHEAVE UPSHOOT EMINENCE FLOURISH HEIGHTEN INCREASE LEVITATE SCENSION UPSPRING
(— ABOVE) OVERLOOK SURMOUNT
(— ABRUPTLY) SKYROCKET
(— AGAIN) RESURGE
(— AND FALL) LOOM HEAVE WELTER
(— AS PRICE) MEND
(— GRADUALLY) LOOM
(— IN BLISTERS) YAW
(— IN CLOUDS) STOOR
(— IN MINE FLOOR) HOGBACK
(— IN PRICES) BULGE
(— IN VALUE) IMPROVE
(— OF CURVE) CAMBER
(— OF HAWK AFTER PREY) MOUNTY
(— OF SHIP'S LINES) FLIGHT
(— OF WATER) FLOOD
(— PRECIPITOUSLY) SKY
(— RAPIDLY) KITE
(— SHARPLY) BREAK
(— SUDDENLY) BOOM SPRING
(— SWIFTLY) BOIL
(— TO BAIT) TAKE
(— TO GREAT HEIGHT) TOWER
(— TO PEAK) SWELL
(— UP) FUME REAR ASCEND INSURRECT
(CURVED —) HANCE
(SHARP —) HOGBACK
RISE OF SILAS LAPHAM (AUTHOR OF —) HOWELLS
(CHARACTER IN —) TOM COREY IRENE SILAS LAPHAM PERSIS ROGERS PENELOPE BROMFIELD
RISER HEAD RAISE FEEDHEAD INSURGENT
RISHI RSI POET SAGE SAINT DEVARSHI KASHYAPA MAHARSHI
RISIBLE FUNNY GELASTIC LAUGHABLE
RISING BOIL BULL RIST ARISE ARIST ORIENT PUTSCH SOURCE STRAKE UPREST UPWITH MONTANT PUSTULE SURGENT EMERGENT INCREASE MOUNTANT NAISSANT ONCOMING ASSURGENT EXCEEDING
(— ABRUPTLY) BOLD
(— AND FALLING) TIDAL
(— AS OF HAWK) SOURCE
(— BY DEGREES) GRADIENT
(— GRADUALLY) SOFT
(— HIGH) AERIAL
(— SHARPLY) ABRUPT
(— STEEPLY) BLUFF
(— TO BREATHE) HAURIENT
(POPULAR —) EMEUTE
RISK GO RUN SET GAGE JUMP LUCK PAWN PERIL RISCO STAKE STAND THROW WAGER WATHE CHANCE DANGER GAMBLE HAZARD IMPAWN PLIGHT

THREAT BALANCE IMPERIL VENTURE ENDANGER EXPOSURE
(PL.) COVERAGE
RISKY BOLD DICEY CHANCY DARING KITTLE RISQUE PARLISH PARLOUS TECHOUS TICKLISH
RISP BUSH RASP STEM TWIG STALK BRANCH SCRATCH
RISQUE BLUE RACY BROAD DARING SCABROUS
RISSOLE CROQUETTE
(PL.) CECILS
RISS-WURM NEUDECKIAN
RISURREZIONE (CHARACTER IN —) DIMITRI KATUSHA SIMONSON
(COMPOSER OF —) ALFANO
RIT CUT RIP RUT REND SLIT TEAR SCRATCH
RITE KEX ASAL BORA BRIS FORM HAKO SOMA BRITH HONOR RIGHT SRADH ABDEST AUGURY EXEQUY FETISH OFFICE PANSIL PIACLE POOJAH RITUAL BAPTISM FUNERAL KATCINA LITURGY MYSTERY OBSEQUY SRADDHA TASHLIK CEREMONY HIERURGY HUSKANAW MORTUARY PIACULUM OBSERVANCE
(PL.) CULT SACRA SERVICE
RITUAL FORM RITE SOLEMN AGENDUM HAGGADA LITURGY OBSEQUY SERVICE CEREMONY VISPARAD VISPERED
(PRAYER —) PUJA
RITZY HAUGHTY SNOBBISH
RIVAGE BANK RIVE COAST SHORE
RIVAL VIE EVEN PEER SIDE MATCH COMPETE CORRIVE EMULATE PARAGON CORRIVAL EMULATOR OPPONENT
(PREF.) ANT(I) ANTH(O)
RIVALRY VIE GAME STRIFE PARAGON JEALOUSY STRIVING EMULATION
RIVALS (AUTHOR OF —) SHERIDAN
(CHARACTER IN —) BOB JACK LUCY ACRES JULIA LYDIA LUCIUS ANTHONY ABSOLUTE BEVERLEY LANGUISH MALAPROP MELVILLE OTRIGGER FAULKLAND
RIVE RIP PLOW REND STAB TEAR CRACK REAVE SEVER SPLIT WEDGE CLEAVE SUNDER THRUST SHATTER FRACTURE
RIVELING RULLION
RIVER EA LE LEE REE RIO TJI ALPH AVON BAHR GEON ILOG KILL WADI WADY BAYOU CREEK FLOOD GANGA GIHON GJOLL GLIDE HABOR INLET KIANG TCHAI BARCOO GUTTER KHUBUR NYANZA STRAIT STREAM CHANNEL COCYTUS ESTUARY FROEMAN ILISSUS PHARPAR RUBICON SENEGAL AFFLUENT ERIDANUS PACTOLUS STAIRCASE
(— CHANNEL) ALVEUS
(— NEAR GATE OF HEL'S ABODE) GJOLL
(— OF ATTICA) ILISSUS
(— OF DAMASCUS) PHARPAR

(— OF LYDIA) PACTOLUS
(— OF PARADISE) GEON GIHON
(— OF QUEENSLAND) BARCOO
(— OF UNDERGROUND)
PHLEGETHON
(— OF UNDERWORLD) STYX LETHE
ACHERON COCYTUS FLEGETON
(AFRICAN —) NYANZA SENEGAL
(CHINESE —) HO KIANG
(EGYPTIAN —) BAHR NILE
(FULL —) BANKER
(JAVANESE —) TJI
(MINOR —) BAYOU
(SACRED —) ALPH GANGA
(SMALL —) BACHE TCHAI
(PREF.) FLUVI(O) POTAM(O)
(SUFF.) POTAMIA POTAMUS
RIVERBANK RIPA RIPE
RIVERBED LAAGTE BATTURE
(DRY —) WADI WADY
RIVERBOAT COG BARGE FOIST
PULWAR
RIVER DUCK TEAL MALLARD
WIDGEON GREENWING
RIVERINE (— FISH) HUCHO
RIVERWEED WATERWEED
RIVET STUD CLINK ROOVE
PANHEAD FLATHEAD
(— ATTENTION) GRIP
(— HEAD) CUPHEAD
RIVULET RUN BURN GILL LAKE
MOTH RILL SIKE BACHE BATCH
BAYOU BOURN BROOK GHYLL
RITHE RINDLE RUNLET RUNNEL
STREAM STRIPE STRYPE
CHANNEL RIVERET BROOKLET
RIXY TERN
RIZPAH (LOVER OF —) SAUL
(SON OF —) ARMONI
MEPHIBOSHETH
RIZZAR DRY PARCH RASOUR
RAZOUR CURRANT HADDOCK
RIZZOM BIT EAR RISOM STALK
STRAW RISSOM
ROACH HOG BUTT ROCK SPOT
BRAISE BLATTID SUNFISH
ROAD LEG PAD TAO VIA WAY BELT
BORD CASH DRAG DRUN FARE
GAET GANG GATE LINE LODE
LOKE PASS PATH PAVE PIKE
RADE RAID RIDE RODE ROTE
ROUT SLAB SPUR WENT BARGH
BLAZE BYWAY CLOSE DRIFT
DRIVE DROVE FORAY GAITE
GOING METAL PRAYA ROUTE
TRACE TRACK BYROAD CAMINO
CAREER CAUSEY CHEMIN COURSE
DUGWAY FEEDER RIDING
ROUGHT RUNWAY SLOUGH
STREET TARMAC TRAJET BEELINE
CALZADA CARTWAY ESTRADA
GANGWAY HIGHWAY LANDWAY
OUTGANG PACKWAY PASSAGE
RAILWAY RAMPIRE ROADWAY
ROLLWAY SKIDWAY TELFORD
AUTOBAHN BEALLACH BLACKTOP
BROADWAY CHAUSSEE
CORDUROY FOOTRILL HORSEWAY
OVERPASS RIDGEWAY SPEEDWAY
TRACKWAY TRAMROAD
TRAVERSE TURNPIKE
WAGONWAY ROADSTEAD
(— BORDERING SHORE) PRAYA

(— FOR LOGGING) SKIDWAY
CROSSHAUL
(— IN COAL MINE) BORD BOARD
FOOTRILL
(— ON CLIFF) CORNICHE
(— SCRAPER) HARL HARLE
(— SURFACE) TELFORD
(CEMENT OR CONCRETE —) SLAB
(COUNTRY —) BOREEN DRIFTWAY
(DESCENDING —) BAHADA BAJADA
(IMPASSABLE —) SLOUGH IMPASSE
(IMPROVISED —) CASH
(MILITARY OR PUBLIC —) AGGER
(NARROW —) DRANG DRUNG
RODDIN
(PAVED —) CALZADA CHAUSSEE
(PRINCIPAL —) ARTERY
(PRIVATE —) LOKE DRIVE
DRIVEWAY
(RAISED —) AGGER RAMPIRE
CAUSEWAY
(ROMAN —) ITER CAUSEY
(SIDE —) BRANCH SHUNPIKE
(STEEP —) BRAE PATH BARGH
SPRUNT
(TEMPORARY —) SHOOFLY
(UNIMPROVED —) DROVE
(ZIGZAG —) SWITCHBACK
(PREF.) ODO VIA
(SUFF.) ODE OID
ROADBED BALLAST BITUMEN
ROADBOOK MAP ITINERARY
ROAD DONKEY ROADER
ROADMAN PEDDLER SALESMAN
CANVASSER
ROADMASTER OVERSEER
ROAD RUNNER CUCKOO PAISANO
ROADSIDE HEDGE
ROADSTEAD RAID DOWNS
ROADSTER BUGGY TRAMP DRIVER
BICYCLE RUNABOUT RACEABOUT
SPEEDSTER
ROADWAY DECK EXIT STREET
MACADAM SLIPWAY TRUCKWAY
ROAM GO ERR RUN WAG RAKE
RAME RAVE ROIL ROLL ROVE
WALK GIPSY GYPSY KNOCK
RANGE SCAMP SPACE STRAY
TAVER VAGUE WAVER BANGLE
RAMBLE STROLL SWERVE TAIVER
VAGARY WANDER GALLANT
PROCEED SQUANDER VAGABOND
(— FURTIVELY) PROWL
ROAMING ERROR NOMADIC
ROAMAGE FUGITIVE
(PREF.) PLAN(O)
ROAN HORSE GRIZZLE
ROANOKE WAMPUM
ROAR CRY BAWL BEAL BELL BERE
BOOM BRAY CAVE HOWL HURL
RAIR RARE RERD ROIN ROME
ROOP ROUT YELL BLARE BROOL
CRACK RERDE ROUST SHOUT
SNORE BELLOW BULDER BULLER
CLAMOR GOLLAR GOLLER
RUMMES SCREAM SHRIEK STEVEN
BLUSTER RUMMISH ULULATE
(— AS BOAR) FREAM
(— LIKE WIND) HURL
(— OF SURF) ROTE
(LOW —) BROOL
ROARING RUT LOUD AROAR BRISK
ROUST BELLOW BOOMING

RIOTOUS THRIVING
ROARING BOY TWIBIL TWIBILL
ROARING GAME CURLING
ROARING MEG CANNON
ROAST RAZZ ROTI SOAK BREDE
BROWN PARCH ASSATE CODDLE
REMOVE TORREFY TORRIFY
BARBECUE RIDICULE
(— IN ASHES) BRY
(STUFFED —) FARCI
ROASTED ASADO
(NOT —) GREEN
ROASTER BURNER SCORCHER
ROASTING ASSATION
ROASTING JACK TURNSPIT
ROB COP PAD EASE FAKE FLAP
MILL NICK PEEL PELF PICK PILL
POLL PREY PULL RAMP RIPE ROLL
TOBY BENIM BRIBE FLIMP HARRY
HEAVE HEIST LURCH PINCH
PLUCK PLUME PROWL REAVE
RIFLE ROIST SHAKE SPOIL SPUNG
STEAL STRUB TOUCH HARROW
HIJACK HUSTLE PILFER RAVISH
RIPOFF STRIKE THIEVE BEREAVE
DEPRIVE DESPOIL PLUNDER
RUMPADE SNAFFLE UNPURSE
DEFLOWER SPOLIATE
(— HOUSE) MILL
(— OF CHASTITY) DEFILE
(— OF FORCE) COOL
(— OF JOY) DESOLATE
(— OF VIGOR) ETIOLATE
(— WITH VIOLENCE) RAMP
ROBALO SNOOK SNOWK
SERGEANT
ROBBED RUBATO
(NOT —) UNPILLED
ROBBER PAD FOMOR LARON THIEF
BANDIT BRIBER DACOIT FORMOR
HOLDUP LATRON RIFLER
BRIGAND CATERAN FOOTPAD
HEISTER LADRONE MOONMAN
PANDOUR PRANCER RAVENER
ROUTIER SPOILER TOBYMAN
BARABBAS FOMORIAN PILLAGER
RABIATOR BANDOLERO
(— ON HIGH SEAS) PIRATE
(— WHO USES VIOLENCE)
RABIATOR
(GRAVE —) GOUL GHOUL
(HIGHWAY —) PAD FOOTPAD
TOBYMAN
(INDIAN MURDEROUS —) DACOIT
(IRISH —) WOODKERN
(MOUNTAIN —) CHOAR
(NIGHT —) MOONMAN
(SEA —) FOMOR FORMOR
FOMORIAN
(WANDERING —) ROUTIER
(PREF.) LESTO
(SUFF.) LESTES
ROBBERY JOB JUMP REIF RIFE
HEIST SCREW STALE FELONY
HOLDUP STOWTH BRIBERY
DACOITY LARCENY PILLAGE
PLUNDER REAVERY STICKUP
THUGGEE PURCHASE SPOLIATION
(— ON HIGH SEAS) PIRACY
(HIGHWAY —) TOBY
ROBE GOWN VEST KANZU STOLA
CHIMER KIMONO KITTEL MANTLE
PEPLOS REVEST ARISAID

BUFFALO GALABIA SURCOAT
VESTURE PARAMENT WOLFSKIN
(— FOR THE DEAD) HABIT
(— OF MONARCH) PLUVIAL
(— PRESENTED BY DIGNITARY)
KHALAT KHILAT
(— REACHING TO ANKLES) TALAR
(ACTOR'S —) SYRMA
(BAPTISMAL —) CHRISOM
(BISHOP'S —) CHIMER CHIMERE
(CIRCULAR —) CYCLAS
(CORONATION —) COLOBIUM
DALMATIC
(DERVISH'S —) KHIRKA KHIRKAH
(EMPEROR'S —) PURPLE
(FUNERAL —) SABLE
(JEWISH —) KITTEL
(KING'S —) DALMATIC
(LOOSE —) MANT CAMIS CAMUS
CYMAR SIMAR SYMAR MANTUA
MANTEAU
(MASQUERADE —) VENETIAN
(MEXICAN —) MANGA
(MONK'S —) HAPLOMA
(OLD-FASHIONED —) SAMARE
(OUTER —) JAMA
(TARTAN —) ARISAID
(TURKISH —) DOLMAN
(WHITE —) CHRISOM
(PL.) ACADEMICALS
ROBERT DOB POP RAB DOBBIN
POPKIN
ROBERT OF LINCOLN BOBOLINK
ROBIN PINFISH REDDOCK
RUDDOCK TOOTLER WINGFISH
REDBREAST
ROBIN GOODFELLOW ELF PUCK
FAIRY SPRITE HOBGOBLIN
ROBINIA LOCUST
ROBIN SANDPIPER KNOT
DOWITCHER
ROBORANT TONIC
ROBOT GELEM GOLEM AUTOMAT
TELEVOX
ROB ROY (AUTHOR OF —) SCOTT
(CHARACTER IN —) ROB OWEN
DIANA FRANK ANDREW MACFIN
MORRIS VERNON TRESHAM
WILLIAM CAMPBELL FREDERICK
INGLEWOOD MACVITTIE
RASHLEIGH HILDEBRAND
FAIRSERVICE OSBALDISTONE
ROBUST ABLE FIRM HAIL HALE
HARD IRON RUDE BONNY HARDY
HUSKY LUSTY RENKY SOUND
STARK STIFF STOUR STOUT
TOUGH VALID WALLY HEARTY
RUGGED SINEWY STRONG
STURDY HEALTHY NERVOUS
STHENIC VALIANT MUSCULAR
PITHSOME STALWART SWACKING
VIGOROUS STRAPPING
(NOT —) SLENDER
ROBUSTNESS VALIDITY
ROC BIRD BOMB RUKH ROQUE
SIMURG SIMURGH
ROCHET CLOAK SMOCK CAMISIA
ROCK CAP JOW LOG PAY RAG
DAZE HOST KLIP REEL RUKH SIAL
SIMA SWAY SWIG TOSS BRACK
CLIFF FLOOR GREET GRUSS
HORSE LEDGE ROACH ROQUE
SHAKE SHOWD SKARN STONE

TRILL CRADLE FACIES GROUND OOLITE PELITE TOTTER BRECCIA COUNTRY FOLIATE GREISEN CIMINITE PHYLLITE SILTSTONE
(— AROUND DRILL HOLE) COLLAR
(— CHUNK) KNUCKLE
(— DEBRIS) SCREE
(— IN ANOTHER ROCK) XENOLITH
(— IN MINE) CAPPING
(— IN SEA) STACK
(— SURFACE) KARREN
(— VIOLENTLY) STAGGER
(ARTIFICIAL —) GRANOLITH
(BALD —) SCALP
(BANDED —) BAR
(BARE —) SCARTH
(CAP —) COVER
(COMPACT —) BASEMENT
(CONGLOMERATE —) PSEPHITE
(COUNTRY —) RIDER
(CRUSHED —) GREET
(CRYSTALLINE —) ELVAN DUNITE SCHIST DIORITE GREISEN ECLOGITE
(DECAY OF —S) GEEST LATERITE
(DECOMPOSED —) GOSSAN GOZZAN
(DENSE —) ADINOLE
(DISINTEGRATED —) SAPROLITE
(EXTRUSIVE —) DACITE SPILITE ANDESITE CIMINITE
(FELDSPATHIC —) PETUNTSE
(FISSILE —) SHALE SHAUL
(FLUID —) LAVA
(FRAGMENTAL —) PSEPHITE
(GABBROITIC —) EUCRITE
(GLASSY —) PITCHSTONE
(GRANULAR —) GABBRO OOLITE DIORITE IJOLITE KOSWITE MYLONITE PSAMMITE QUARTZITE
(GRANULATED —) GRUSS
(GREEN —) OPHITE
(HARD —) WHIN KIMGLE WHINSTONE NOVACULITE
(HIGH —) SCOUT
(IGNEOUS —) BOSS SIAL SIMA TRAP BASALT DUNITE GABBRO URTITE FELSITE GRANITE MINETTE PICRITE SYENITE DOLERITE ESSEXITE RHYOLITE TONALITE
(IMPURE —) CHERT
(INSULAR —) SKERRY
(INSULATED —) SKERRY
(INTRUSIVE —) HORTITE MINETTE MAENAITE
(IRON-BEARING —) GAL
(ISOLATED —) SCAR SCARR SCAUR
(JUTTING POINT OF —) KIP
(MANTLE —) REGOLITH
(METAMORPHIC —) SKARN GNEISS SCHIST BUCHITE GONDITE LEPTITE ECLOGITE HORNFELS LIMURITE
(MICA-BEARING —) DOMITE
(MOLTEN —) MAGMA
(MOTTLED —) SERPENTINE
(PLUTONIC —) TAWITE HOLLAITE TURJAITE
(POROUS —) TUFA TUFF ARSOITE
(PROJECTING —) CLINT
(PULVERIZED —) FLOUR
(RARE —) ALNOITE

(ROUGH —) CRAG KNAR SCARTH
(ROUNDED —) ROGNON SHEEPBACK
(SEDIMENTARY —) CRAG IRONSTONE SANDSTONE
(SHARP —) NEEDLE AIGUILLE
(SLATY —) PLATE SCHALSTEIN
(SOFT —) MALM
(SOLID —) GIBBER
(STUDY OF —S) LITHOLOGY
(SUBMERGED —) SHELF
(UNDERLYING —) FLOOR
(VOLCANIC —) TUFA TUFF BASALT DACITE DOMITE LATITE TAXITE PEPERIN ANDESITE ASHSTONE EUTAXITE RHYOLITE TEPHRITE TRACHYTE
(WASTE —) MULLOCK
(WORTHLESS —) GANG GANGUE
(PL.) ROCHER
(PREF.) FELSO PETR(I)(O) RHYO RUPI SAXI
(SUFF.) CLAST ITE LITE LITH(IC) LITIC PHYRE PHYRIC
ROCKAWAY CARRIAGE
ROCK BADGER CONY HYRAX
ROCK BASS REDEYE CABRILLA
ROCK-BREAKER
(SUFF.) FRAGE
ROCKBRUSH ROSILLA
ROCK CEDAR SABINO
ROCK CRESS ARABIS SICKLEPOD
ROCK DEBRIS TALUS
ROCK DOVE SOD
ROCK-DWELLING SAXATILE
ROCKER CRADLE SHOOFLY
ROCKET DRAKE REBUKE STREAK YELLOW CONGREVE SKYLIGHT STARSHIP FIREDRAKE
(DYER'S —) WELD WOLD WOALD WOULD
ROCKET SALAD ROQUETTE
ROCKFISH BASS JACK RENA REINA VIUVA FLIOMA GOPHER RASHER TAMBOR CORSAIR GARRUPA GROUPER BOCACCIO CHINAFISH GREENLING
ROCK HARE KLIPHAAS
ROCK HIND MERO AGAUJI
ROCK HOPPER MACARONI
ROCKLING BAUD GADE ROKER SORGHE WHISTLER
ROCK NATIVE SNAPPER
ROCK PIPIT TIETICK
ROCK RABBIT PIKA HYRAX HYRACOID
ROCKROSE CISTUS PINWEED HUDSONIA ROCKCIST SAGEROSE DAYFLOWER SUNFLOWER
ROCK SALT EMOL AMOLE HALITE
(BLOCK OF —) PIG
ROCK SANDWORT CYME
ROCKSHAFT SHAFT ROCKER WEIGHBAR
ROCK TROUT BOREGAT GREENLING
ROCKWEED TANG FUCUS FUCOID SEATANG SEAWEED
(PREF.) FUCI
ROCK WHITING KELPFISH STRANGER
ROCKWORK ROCAILLE
ROCKY DAFT HARD STONY CLINTY

OBSCENE PETREAN PETROUS UNCOUTH OBDURATE UNSTABLE DIFFICULT RUPELLARY
(PREF.) TRACHY
ROCKY MOUNTAIN (— GOAT) MAZAME
ROCOCO ORNATE QUAINT BAROCCO BAROQUE OUTMODED
ROD BAR BOW CUE GAD GUY LUG PIN TIE BOLT CALM CAME CANE CORE FALL FORK GOAD GONG LINK MACE POLE RAVE SCOB SNAP STEM STUD WAND WHIP YARD ARBOR BIRCH CATCH DOWEL LYTTA OSIER PERCH POWER PUNCH REACH ROUND SETUP SHOOT SPELK SPILL SPOKE SPRAG STAFF STANG STEEL STICK STING TEYNE TOMMY TRACE VERGE WIPER BALEYS BROACH CANARY CARBON CENTER CRUTCH ETALON FERULA FINGER GLOWER HANGER PISTOL PITMAN PODGER RADDLE RAMMER SKEWER SPRING STADIA SWITCH TOGGLE WATTLE WICKER BACULUS CROPPIE DRAWROD ELLWAND FEATHER FESTUCA PLUNGER POINTER POTHOOK PRICKER PROBANG PROLONG SCALLOM SCEPTER SPINDLE STADIUM STICKER TYRANNY VIRGULA WHISKER WINDING AXOSTYLE BACKSTAY BILBERRY BODSTICK BOWSTAVE DIPSTICK JACKSTAY KINGBOLT REVOLVER STRAINER TRAVELER WEEDHOOK
(— AS SYMBOL OF OFFICE) VERGE
(— BEARING TRAFFIC SIGNAL) STANCHION
(— FOR ALIGNING HOLES) PODGER
(— FOR CARRYING GLASS) FORK
(— FOR DISCIPLINE) YARD FERULA FERULE
(— FOR FASTENING THATCH) SPELK SPRINGLE
(— FOR FIREARM BORE) WIPER
(— FOR GLASS-MAKING) PUNTY FASCET PONTEE PONTIL CROPPIE
(— FOR HOLDING MEAT) SPIT
(— FOR TRANSMITTING MOTION) TRACE
(— IN ARC LAMP) CARBON
(— IN CRICKET) STUMP
(— IN INTERFEROMETER) ETALON
(— IN MINE PUMP) SPEAR
(— IN NERNST LAMP) GLOWER
(— IN SPINNING WHEEL) SPINDLE
(— OF CELLS) NOTOCHORD
(— OF FOUNDRY MOLD) LANCE
(— OF LOOM) SHAFT
(— OF WOOD) SCOB
(— ON LOGGING TRUCK) RAVE
(— POINTED AT BOTH ENDS) SKEWER
(— SYMBOLIZING AUTHORITY) BACULUS
(— TO BIND A CONTRACT) FESTUCA
(— TO FASTEN SAILS) JACKSTAY
(— TO IMMERSE SHEEP) CRUTCH
(— TO URGE BEAST) GOAD PROD
(— UPSET AT ONE END) SETUP

(— USED AS KEY) TOMMY
(— WITH ENDS AT RIGHT ANGLES) STRAINER
(— WITH SPONGE ON END) PROBANG
(— WITH T-HEAD) TOGGLE
(AXIAL —) VIRGULA AXOSTYLE
(BASKETRY —) OSIER SLATH
(BUNDLE OF —S) DRIVER
(CARTILAGINOUS —) LYTTA COLUMELLA
(CLAMMING —) BRAIL
(CONNECTING —) PITMAN
(CURTAIN —) TRINGLE
(DANCER'S —) CROTALUM
(DIVINING —) TWIG DOWSER
(FISHING —) GAD CALCUTTA
(FLEXIBLE —) RADDLE WATTLE
(FORKED —) CRUTCH
(GEM-CUTTING —) SETTER
(GRADUATED —) STADIA STADIUM
(IRON —) SNAP BETTY
(KNITTING —) NEEDLE
(LEAD —) CAME
(LOGGING —) CANARY
(MEASURING —) JUDGE SPILE STADIA ELLWAND METEWAND METEYARD
(PLIABLE —) WINDING
(SMALL —) LANCE
(STRENGTHENING —) RIB
(SUPPLE —) SWABBLE
(TETHERING —) STAKE
(THIN —) TEYNE SCALLOM
(TIE —) ANCHOR
(UMBRELLA —) STRETCHER
(WITHE —) BILBERRY
(PREF.) BACULI RHABD(O) RHAPIDO VERGI
RODENT RAT CONY DEGU HARE MARA MOCO MOLE PACA PIKA UTIA VOLE CONEY COYPU GUNDI HUTIA JUTIA LEROT MOUSE TUCAN ZOKOR AGOUTI BEAVER BITING CURURO GERBIL GLIRID GNAWER GOPHER JERBOA MARMOT MURINE MUROID RABBIT SOKHOR BLESMOL CHINCHA DIPODID GEOMYID GNAWING HAMSTER LEMMING LEVERET MUSKRAT ABROCOME CAPIBARA DORMOUSE LEPORIDE OCTODONT SEWELLEL SPALACID SQUIRREL TUCOTUCO VISCACHA VIZCACHA ANOMALURE PORCUPINE
RODEO ROUNDUP
RODERICK RANDOM (AUTHOR OF —) SMOLLETT
(CHARACTER IN —) TOM STRAP OAKHUM RANDOM BOWLING MELINDA SNAPPER CRAMPLEY NARCISSA RODERICK WILLIAMS QUIVERWIT
RODLIKE VIRGATE RHABDOID
RODMAN CLASHY CLASHEE CHAINMAN
RODOMONTADE BRAG RANT BOAST BLUSTER BOMBAST BRAGGART
RODOMONTE (BELOVED OF —) DORALICE
(VICTIM OF —) RUGGIERO

ROD-SHAPED RHABDOID
VIRGULATE
ROE RA DOE FRY PEA RAA RAE
HIND KELK RAUN ROUN ROWN
CORAL TRUBU CAVIAR
ROEBUCK GIRL CHEVREUIL
ROGER RAM HODGE ROGUE
ROGUE BOY GUE IMP NYM HEMP
KEMP KITE LOON ROAG CATSO
CRACK CRANK DROLE GIPSY
GREEK GYPSY HEMPY KNAVE
SCAMP SHELM BEGGAR BORGER
BUGGER CANTER CHOUSE
COQUIN CURTAL HARLOT LIMMER
PICARA PICARO RASCAL SORROW
TINKER BLEEDER ERRATIC
FOISTER HALLION LADRONE
PANURGE SHARPER SKELLUM
SWINGER VILLAIN COMROGUE
HEMPSEED PICAROON SCALAWAG
SWINDLER WHIPJACK
ROGUE HERRIES (AUTHOR OF —)
WALPOLE
(CHARACTER IN —) ALICE DAVID
PRESS SARAH STARR DEBORAH
DENBURN FRANCIS HERRIES
MARGARET MIRABELL
OSBALDISTONE
ROGUERY ROPERY KNAVERY
LOONERY WAGGERY PATCHERY
PRIGGISM TRICKERY TRUANTRY
ROGUISH SLY ARCH HEMPY
ROGUY WICKED KNAVISH
TRICKSY VAGRANT WAGGISH
ESPIEGLE SCAMPISH DISHONEST
ROGUISHNESS KNAVERY
ARCHNESS
**ROI DE LAHORE, LE (CHARACTER
IN —)** ALIM SITA SCINDIA
(COMPOSER OF —) MASSENET
ROIL VEX FOUL RILE ANNOY
BLUNDER DISTURB STUDDLE
BEWILDER DISORDER IRRITATE
ROILED TURBID
ROISTER REVEL ROIST SCOUR
CAROUSE GALRAVAGE
ROISTERER MUN GREEK HUZZA
BUSTER HECTOR RIOTER
SCOURER TWIBILL EPHESIAN
ROISTERING HOYDEN
ROKE FOG DAMP MIST REEK ROWK
STIR FOGGY SMOKE STEAM
VAPOR
ROKELAY ROCOLO
ROLAND (BETROTHED OF —) AUDE
(COMPANION OF —) OLIVER
(HORN OF —) OLIVANT
(SWORD OF —) DURANDAL
(UNCLE OF —) CHARLEMAGNE
ROLE BIT JOB LEAD PART ROTE
HEAVY FIGURE CLOTHES
BUSINESS FUNCTION LIRIPIPE
(SMALL —) CAMEO
ROLL BAP BUN ROW WEB BOLT
COIL CURL FILE FLOW FURL LIST
MILL PASS REEL ROAM ROTA
SWAG WELT WIND WRAP BAGEL
BIALY BREAD BUILD DANDY
DICKY ENROL FLUTE ROYLE SPLIT
TOMMY TRILL TROLL WHELM
BILLOW BUNDLE CIRCLE ELAPSE
ENFOLD GOGGLE GROVEL KIPFEL
LEGEND MUSTER PONDER

RECORD ROSTER ROTATE SCROLL
UPWIND VOLUME WAMBLE
WANDER WHELVE WINTLE
WREATH BISCUIT BOLILLO
BRIOCHE CROCKET ENVELOP
MANCHET NOTITIA REVOLVE
ROTULET ROTULUS ROULEAU
STRETCH TERRIER TRINDLE
TRUNDLE TWISTER BROTCHEN
CANNELON CONSIDER CRESCENT
JACKROLL LAMINATE PORTEOUS
REGISTER SEDERUNT SPREADER
VOLUTATE
(— A BALL) BOWL
(— ABOUT) WALTER SCAMBLE
(— AS A SHIP) SEEL LURCH
(— AS STONE) REEL
(— BY) WALK
(— CLOSELY) FURL
(— EYES) WALL WAUL WHAWL
GOGGLE
(— GLASS) MARVER
(— INTO A BALL) CLEW CLUE
(— OF BREAD) BAP SEMMEL
TAMMIE
(— OF CLOTH) BOLT DOSSIL
WREATH
(— OF COINS) ROULEAU
(— OF DOUGH) TWIST
(— OF DRIED BARK) QUILL
(— OF DRUM) HURRY RATTAN
(— OF DUST) KITTEN
(— OF FIBERS) ROVING
(— OF HAIR) PUFF ROACH ROWEL
CROCKET
(— OF HAY) WAKE
(— OF LINT OR LINEN) TENT DOSSIL
(— OF LUGGAGE) SWAG
(— OF MINCED MEAT) RISSOLE
(— OF OFFENDERS) PORTEOUS
(— OF PAPER) SPILL STOMP STUMP
(— OF PARCHMENT) BOOK PELL
(— OF ROULETTE WHEEL) COUP
(— OF SPUN YARN) PRICK
(— OF TOBACCO) CAROT CIGAR
PRICK SEGAR CAROTTE
(— OF WALLPAPER) BOLT
(— OF WHEAT BREAD) MANCHET
(— OF WOOL) ROVE ROVING
CARDING
(— ON CASTERS) TRUCKLE
(— ON LITTLE WHEELS) TRUNDLE
(— ONWARD) DEVOLVE
(— OVER) COMB JOLL WELTER
(— TO RUB DOWN DRAWING)
STUMP
(— TOGETHER) CONVOLVE
(— UP) FURL STOW COLLAR
(— UP SLEEVES) REEVE
(BLANKET —) BINDLE SHIRALEE
(BREAKFAST —) BIALY
(DANDY —) DANCER
(HOLLOW —) CANNELON
(LONG —) FLUTE
(PADDED —) BURLET
(PENNY —) TOMMY
(TWISTED — OF WOOL) SLUB
(WHIP —) BACKREST
(PREF.) HELI(C)(CO)
ROLLED (— IN SUGAR) SANDED
ROLLER FLY BOWL BRAY DRUM
JACK LEAD MILL PUCK RUBY
BREAK DANDY FINER GODET

INKER RIDER SHELL WAVER
WINCH BRAYER BREAST DOFFER
DUCTOR FASCIA MANGLE
ROWLET RUNNER CARRIER
CLEARER MOIETER TRUCKLE
HEDGEHOG SQUEEGEE STRIPPER
TROUPAND
(— FOR MASSAGER) ROULETTE
(— IN HORSE'S BIT) CRICKET
(— IN ORGAN) TRUNDLE
(— IN STEELWORKS) COGGER
(— TO CLEAR FABRIC) MOIETER
(CARDING —) BREAST WORKER
SQUIRREL STRIPPER
(CHINESE —) SIRGANG
(DREDGING —) HEDGEHOG
(DROP —) DUCTOR
(GRINDING —) BREAK
(INKING —) BRAYER
(PLAYER ON — DERBY TEAM)
JAMMER
(PRINTING —) DANDY SHELL
BRAYER DAMPENER
(ROUND IN — DERBY) JAM
(STONE —) MAMMY TOTER
(SURGICAL —) FASCIA
(TOOTHED —) PRICK PRICKER
ROLLER COASTER SWITCHBACK
ROLLERMAN BRAKER JACKMAN
LEVERMAN
ROLLER SKATE PEDOMOTOR
ROLLICK PLAY ROMP FROLIC
ROLLIX
ROLLICKING GAY WILD MERRY
JOVIAL LIVELY
ROLLING CURL GOGGLE WHEELY
SWAYING TRILLED LURCHING
VOLUTION
(— OF SCROLL) GELILAH
(— OF SHIP) LABOR
ROLLTOP TAMBOUR
ROLY-POLY ROTUND PUDDING
TUMBLER SALTWORT
ROM RO GYPSY ROMANY
ROMAN BRAVE LATIN NOBLE
PAPAL ANTIQUA UPRIGHT
GOWNSMAN
(— COLLAR) RABAT
ROMAN CATHOLIC ROME ROMAN
PAPIST ROMIST JEBUSITE
BABYLONIC
ROMANCE WOO GEST ANTAR
FANCY FEIGN GESTE KATHA
NOVEL STORY ANTARA UTOPIA
FANTASY FICTION ROMANZA
ROMAUNT
(— LANGUAGE) FRENCH ITALIAN
SPANISH
ROMAN-FLEUVE SAGA

ROMANIA

CANAL: BEGA
CAPITAL: BUCHAREST
COIN: BAN LEI LEU LEY
COUNTY: OLT ARAD CLUJ DOLJ
GORJ IASI ARGES BACAU BIHOR
BUZAU ILFOV MURES NEAMT
SALAJ SIBIU TIMIS
DISTRICT: ALBA BANAT BIHOR
DOBRUJA DOBROGEA
MARAMURES
LAKE: SINOE
MOUNTAIN: BIHOR NEGOI CODRUL

RODNEI CALIMAN PIETROSU
OLD NAME: DACIA
PASS: ROSUL
PROVINCE: ARDEAL MOLDAVIA
WALACHIA
RIVER: ALT OLT JIUL PRUT ALUTA
ARGES BUZDU MOROS MURES
OLTUL SCHYL SIRET TIMIS
TISZA VEDEA CRASNA DANUBE
ARGESUL MURESUL SOMESUL
BISTRITA IALOMITA
RIVER PORT: BRAILA GALATI
GALATZ
TOWN: ARAD CLUJ IASI BACAU
CERNA JASSY NEAMT SIBIU
TURNU BRAILA BRASOV GALATI
GALATZ LUPENI CRAIOVA
FOCSANI PLOESTI SEVERIN
CERNAVTI KISHENEF TEMESVAR
KOLOZSVAR

ROMANIST MISSARY
ROMANIZATION LATINXUA
ROMANSH LADIN
ROMANTIC AIRY WILD IDEAL
ARDENT DREAMY GOTHIC POETIC
UNREAL FERVENT FABULOUS
FANCIFUL
ROMANY RO ROM GIPSY GYPSY
ROMAN
ROMANY RYE (AUTHOR OF —)
BORROW
(CHARACTER IN —) DALE JACK
BELLE ISOPEL JASPER URSULA
BERNERS MURTAGH LAVENGRO
SYLVESTER PETULENGRO
ROME (CHAPEL IN —) SISTINE
(FOUNDER OF —) ROMULUS
(HILL IN —) CAELIAN VIMINAL
AVENTINE PALATINE QUIRINAL
(OLD PORT OF —) OSTIA
(RIVER IN —) TIBER
ROME HAUL (AUTHOR OF —)
EDMONDS
(CHARACTER IN —) BEN DAN JOE
RAE SOL LUCY BERRY JACOB
KLORE MOLLY WAMPY CALASH
GURGET HARROW HECTOR
JOTHAM JULIUS SAMSON TINKLE
WEAVER WILSON FORTUNE
LARKINS TURNESA WILLIAM
FRIENDLY CASHDOLLAR
BUTTERFIELD
**ROMEO AND JULIET (AUTHOR OF
—)** SHAKESPEARE
(CHARACTER IN —) JOHN PARIS
PETER ROMEO JULIET TYBALT
ABRAHAM CAPULET ESCALUS
GREGORY SAMPSON BENVOLIO
LAURENCE MERCUTIO
MONTAGUE BALTHASAR
ROMOLA (AUTHOR OF —) ELIOT
(CHARACTER IN —) DINO LUCA
TITO BARDO CALVO LILLO
MONNA PIERO TESSA MELEMA
ROMOLA BRIGIDA NICCOLO
BERNARDO BALDASARRE
ROMP REG RIG HEMP LARK PLAY
ROIL FRISK SHIRL SPORT TRAIN
FROLIC GAMBOL HOORAY
HOYDEN HURRAH RIPPET
COURANT GAMMOCK RAMMACK
RUNAWAY

ROMPERS JUMPER JUMPERS
ROMPING ROYT HEMPY ROYET
RONCADOR GRUNT CROAKER
SCIAENID
RONDO ROTA
RONE BUSH BRAKE GUTTER
THICKET
RONG LEPCHA
RONGA THONGA
RONSDORFER ZIONITE ELLERIAN
ROOD RUD REED ROPE CROSS
SPAWN STANG CRUCIFIX
ROODLES RANGDOODLES
ROOF TOP ATAP BACK DECK DOME
FLAT ATTAP COVER HOUSE RAISE
RISER SHELL THACK AZOTEA
BONNET CUPOLA SUMMIT
TECTUM CHOPPER CRICKET
GAMBREL MANSARD RIGGING
TECTURE BULKHEAD HOUSETOP
SAWTOOTH SEMIDOME
PENTHOUSE
(— MEMBER) PURLIN
(— OF CARRIAGE) IMPERIAL
(— OF CAVERN) DOME
(— OF MINING CAGE) BONNET
(— OF MOUTH) PALATE
(— OF NASOPHARYNX) VAULT
(— OF RAILWAY CAR) DECK
(— OVER DOOR) APPENTICE
(— OVER STAGE) SHADOW
(— PORTION) MONITOR
(AUTOMOBILE —) FASTBACK
(CLOTH —) CHUTT
(FALSE —) CRICKET
(FLAT —) LEADS AZOTEA TERRACE
(STEEPLY TAPERING —) SPIRE
(THATCHED —) ATAP ATTAP
CHOPPER
(VAULTED —) DOME
(PREF.) STEG(O) TECTI TECTO
(SUFF.) STEGE STEGITE
ROOFING HEALING SHINDLE
PANTILING TECTIFORM
ROOK GYP ROC CROW DUPE RUKH
CHEAT CRAKE JUDGE TOWER
BLACKY CASTLE DEFRAUD
CASTILLO SWINDLER
ROOKERY ROOST RUMPUS
BUILDING
ROOKIE COLT DRONGO NOVICE
RECRUIT BEGINNER
ROOM PAD WON AULA CAFE CRIB
FARM HALL KILN LIEU PLAY SALA
SEAT SLUM WAME WENE WONE
ATTIC BERTH CUDDY DIVAN
EWERY HOUSE LODGE OECUS
PLACE SALLE SCOPE SHACK
SOLAR SPACE STALL STOVE
STUDY BELFRY BREAST CAMERA
CASINO CHAPEL ESTUFA EXEDRA
HAMMAM LEEWAY MARGIN
PARVIS SCOUTH SINGLE SMOKER
SOLLAR STANCE STANZA STUDIO
CABINET CAMARIN CHALMER
CHAMBER EPINAOS FREEZER
GALLERY HOLDING HYPOGEE
KITCHEN LAUNDRY LIBRARY
SEMINAR SERVERY SMOKERY
SURGERY AEDICULA ASSEMBLY
BASEMENT CAPACITY DRYHOUSE
HOTHOUSE HYPOGEUM
LAVATORY NYMPHEUM

PLAYROOM SCULLERY SWEATBOX
TABLINUM THALAMUS
PRESSROOM
(— ADJOINING SYNAGOGUE)
GENIZAH
(— BEHIND FACADE) ATTIC
(— BETWEEN KITCHEN AND DINING
ROOM) SERVERY
(— CONTAINING FOUNTAIN)
NYMPHEUM
(— DUG IN CLIFF) HYPOGEE
HYPOGEUM
(— FOR ACTION) LEEWAY
(— FOR BATHING) HAMMAM
(— FOR CONVERSATION) EXEDRA
LOCUTORY
(— FOR FAMILY RECORDS)
TABLINUM
(— FOR KEEPING FOOD) LARDER
PANTRY
(— FOR PAINTINGS) GALLERY
(— FOR PRIVATE DEVOTIONS)
ORATORY
(— FOR PUBLIC AMUSEMENTS)
CASINO THEATER
(— FOR STOWAGE) LASTAGE
(— FOR TABLE LINEN) EWERY
(— IN COAL MINE) BREAST
(— IN HAREM) ODA ODAH
(— IN KEEP) DUNGEON
(— IN PREHISTORIC BUILDING) CELL
(— IN REAR OF TEMPLE) EPINAOS
(— IN SIDE OF LARGER ROOM) ALA
(— IN TOWER) BELFRY
(— OF STUDENTS' SOCIETY) HALL
(— ON SHIP) CABIN STOKEHOLD
(— OVER CHURCH PORCH) PARVIS
(— OVER STAGE) SHADOW
(— TOGETHER) CHUM
(— UNDER BUILDING) CELLAR
(CHILDREN'S —) NURSERY
(COTTAGE —) END
(DINING —) CENACLE DINETTE
REFECTORY TRICLINIUM
(DRAWING —) SALON SALOON
(DRESSING —) SHIFT BOUDOIR
CAMARIN VESTUARY WARDROBE
TIREHOUSE
(ESKIMO ASSEMBLY —) KASHGA
(EXHIBITION —) THEATER
(GRINDING —) HULL
(HEATED —) STEW
(HIGH —) AERY EYRY AERIE EYRIE
(INNER —) BEN INBY INBYE
SPENCE
(INSULATED —) FREEZER
(LECTURE —) AUDITORY
(LIVING —) HOUSE LANAI SALON
SERDAB SOLARIUM VOORHUIS
(MONASTERY —) CELL LAVABO
(NARROW —) CRIB
(OCTAGONAL —) TRIBUNA
(PRIVATE —) SNUG SCHOLA
CONCLAVE
(PUEBLO ASSEMBLY —) ESTUFA
(READING —) ATHENEUM
(RECEPTION —) DIVAN PARLOR
KURSAAL MANDARAH
(REFRIGERATED —) COOLER
(RETIRING —) RECAMARA
(ROMAN —) ATRIUM AEDICULA
FUMARIUM
(ROUND —) ROTUNDA

(SEA —) BERTH
(SECLUDED —) DEN
(SERIES OF —S) SWEEP
(SITTING —) SEAT SITTER BOUDOIR
(SLEEPING —) DORMER BEDROOM
DORMITORY
(SMALL —) ALA CELL SNUG STEW
ZETA CUBBY CUDDY LOBBY
CLOSET CUBICLE SNUGGERY
(SMOKING —) DIVAN DIWAN
TABAGIE
(SORTING —) SALLE
(STEAM —) STOVE
(STORAGE —) CAMARIN MAGAZINE
THALAMUS
(SWEATING —) SUDARIUM
SUDATORY LACONICUM
(THRONE —) AIWAN
(TOP —) GARRET IMPERIAL
(UPPER —) SOLAR
(VAULTED —) CAMERA
(PREF.) STEG(O)
(SUFF.) STEGE STEGITE
ROOMMATE CHUM ROOMY
ROOMIE
ROOMY WIDE LARGE RANGY
SPACY ROOMSOME SPACIOUS
CAPACIOUS COMMODIOUS
ROOSE RUSE EXTOL PRAISE
FLATTER BOASTING BRAGGING
ROOST EVE SIT BAUK JOUK TIDE
PERCH GARRET HARBOR LODGING
ROOKERY SHELTER
ROOSTER COCK GAME GALLO
MANOC GAMECOCK
ROOT DIG PRY ROI TAP BASE BULB
CHAY CHOY GRUB MOOR MOOT
MORE PLUG PULL RACE SPUR
TAIL CHEER FIBER FRUIT GROOT
GROUT HEART IREOS LAPPA
RADIX STOCK ALRAUN BOTTOM
CARROT CATGUT GROUND
MUZZLE ORIGIN SENEGA SETTLE
SUMBAL SUMBUL ACONITE
ALKANET AZAFRAN BIACURU
BONIATA CALUMBA CHICORY
COLUMBO CRAMPON GINSENG
IMPLANT IPOMOEA NUNNARI
PAREIRA RADICAL RUMMAGE
TURPETH DEDENDUM EARTHNUT
PNEUMATOPHORE
(— BRANCH) TAPOUN
(— CONTAINING STARCH) KOONTI
(— DEEPLY) SCREW
(— OF GINGER) RACE
(— OF ORCHID) CULLIONS
(— OF TARO) EDDO
(— OF TOOTH) FANG
(— OF TREE) TANG SPURN
(— OF WORD) THEME
(— OUT) GRUB STUB STOCK
EVULSE DISPLANT SUPPLANT
(— TUBERCLE) CLOG
(— WORD) ETYMON
(— YIELDING RED DYE) CHAY CHOY
CHAYA
(—S FOR SEWING CANOES) WATAP
WATAPEH
(—S OF ACONITE) BIKH NABEE
(CANDIED —) ERYNGO
(CUSCUS —S) VETIVER
(DRIED —) JALAP ALTHEA SENECA
BRYONIA KRAMERIA

LICORICE SCAMMONY
(DRIED —S) INULA IPECAC
KRAMERIA VERATRUM
(EDIBLE —) YAM BEET EDDO
RADISH TURNIP WASABI PARSNIP
RUTABAGA TUBERCLE
(FERN —) ROI
(FINE —) STRING
(FRAGRANT —S) VETIVER
(MASS OF FIBROUS —S) SPONGE
(MEDICINAL —) JALAP LAPPA
GINSENG
(PROJECTING —) SPUR
(ROASTED BEET —) BONKA
(STUMP AND —) MOCK
(PL.) CULVERS
(PREF.) RADICI RHIZ(O)
(SUFF.) RHIZA RHIZOUS
ROOTCAP CALYPTRA SPONGIOLE
ROOTED FIXED CHRONIC
(DEEPLY —) BESETTING
ROOTER FAN PLUGGER
ROOTLESS ARRHIZAL
ROOTLET VIVER CRAMPON
RADICEL RADICLE
(PL.) COME CULMS
ROOTSTOCK PIP ROI RACE TARO
CROWN ORRIS CASAVA DANNUM
GINGER ORIGIN PANNUM STOLON
BISCUIT MISHMEE TURMERIC
ORRISROOT
ROPE GAD GUY TIE TOW TUG CEEL
COLT CORD FALL FAST GUSS
HEMP JEFF JUNK LIFT LINE ROOD
SEAL SOAM SPAN STAY TACK
TAIL TAUM TOME VANG WARP
BRACE BRAIL CABLE CABUL
CHECK CHORD LASSO LONGE
SHANK STRAP STROP SWEEP
TRACE TWIST WANTY WIDDY
WITHE CABLET HALTER INHAUL
LARIAT LISSOM LIZARD MECATE
PINION RAPEYE RUNNER SHROUD
SLATCH STRAND STRING TETHER
WARROK AWEBAND BEDCORD
BOBSTAY CATFALL CRINGLE
ENTRAIL HALYARD HAYBAND
LASHING LEEFANG OUTHAUL
PAINTER PAZAREE PENDANT
PIGTAIL SEAMING SERPENT
SERVICE STIRRUP SWIFTER
BACKBONE BACKSTAY BUNTLINE
CABESTRO CORDELLE DOWNHAUL
DRAGLINE FOREFOOT FORETACK
HALLIARD HAULYARD INHAULER
JACKSTAY LIFELINE NECKLACE
PASSAREE PROLONGE ROUNDING
SEQUENCE THRAMMLE
BREECHING
(— A STEER) HEEL
(— COLLAR) PARRAL PARREL
(— CONNECTING NETS) BALK BAULK
(— COVERING) QUILTING
(— FOR FASTENING GATE) CRINGLE
(— FOR FISH) STRINGER
(— FOR TRAINING HORSE) LONGE
(— FOR TYING CATTLE) CEEL SEAL
AWEBAND
(— HANDLE) FETTLE SHACKLE
(— HOLDING RAFT TOGETHER)
BRAIL
(— JOINT) TUCK
(— OF HAIR) CABESTRO

(— OF ONIONS) REEVE
(— OF STRAW) GAD SIME VINE
SIMON SUGAN FETTLE SIMMON
SOOGAN
(— OF 10 OR MORE INCHES) CABLE
(— ON DERRICK) TELEGRAF
(— ON FISHING NET) PINION
SEAMING
(— ORNAMENTATION) TORSADE
(— PASSING AROUND DEADEYE)
STRAP STROP
(— STOLEN FROM DOCKYARD)
RUMBO
(— WITH HOOK AND TOGGLE)
PROLONGE
(— WITH SWIVEL AND LOOP)
TOGGEL TOGGLE
(— WOUND AROUND CABLE)
KECKLING
(—S IN RIGGING) CORDAGE
(ANCHOR —) RODE VIOL VOYAL
(BELL —) TYALL HANGER
(CIRCUS —) JEFF
(DRAFT —) SOAM
(DRAG —) GUSS
(FLAG-RAISING —) HALYARD
(FOOT —) HORSE
(GRASS —) SOGA
(GUIDE —) DRAGLINE
(HANDLE —) FETTLE
(HANGMAN'S —) HEMP TIPPET
(HARNESS —) TRACE HALTER
(HARPOON —) FOREGOER
(MOORING —) HEADFAST
(NAUTICAL —) TIE TYE COLT FANG
LIFT STAY VANG BRACE BRAIL
SHEET SLING STRAP STROP
GILGUY HAWSER INHAUL LACING
RATLIN SHROUD BOBSTAY
BOWLINE CATFALL GESWARP
LANYARD LEEFANG OUTHAUL
PAINTER PAZAREE PENDANT
PENNANT PIGTAIL RATLINE
SNORTER SNOTTER STIRRUP
STOPPER SWIFTER BACKBONE
BACKSTAY BUNTLINE DOWNHAUL
FORETACK JACKSTAY PASSAREE
ROUNDING SELVAGEE WOOLDING
TIMENOGUY
(PART OF —) SLATCH
(SHORT —) SHANK
(SHORT CART —) WANTY
(SMALL HANDMADE —) FOX
(SMUGGLER'S —) LINGTOW
(TALLOWED —) GASKET
(TETHERING —) SPANCEL
(TOW —) CORDELLE
(WIRE —) HAULBACK JACKSTAY
(WORN OR POOR —) JUNK
(PL.) CORDAGE
(PREF.) FUN(I) RESTI SPIR(O)
ROPEBAND RABAND
ROPE-DANCER ACROBAT
ROPEMAKER FOLLOWER RATLINER
ROPEWALKER FUNAMBULO
ROPEWAY TRAMWAY WIREWAY
CABLEWAY
ROPY SINEWY STRINGY VISCOUS
MUSCULAR GLUTINOUS
ROQUE CROQUET
ROQUELAURE CLOAK ROCOLO
ROCKLAY
RORIPA RADICULA

RORQUAL SEI FINBACK
ROSADER (BELOVED OF —)
ROSALYNDE
(BROTHER OF —) TORRISMOND
ROSAMUNDA (FATHER OF —)
CUNIMOND
(HUSBAND OF —) ALBOIN
ROSARY BEADS CORONA TASBIH
BEADING PSALTER BEADROLL
(— BEAD) GAUD GAUDY
(MOHAMMEDAN —) COMBOLOIO
ROSE ASH GUL KNOT MOSS ROIS
BRIAR BRIDE BUCKY FLUSH
RHODA CANKER OPULUS
POMPON BOURBON BURBANK
GLAIEUL HUGONIS LOZENGE
MANETTI MONTHLY OPHELIA
RAMBLER AGRIMONY COLUMBIA
DOGBERRY LOKELANI PEDELION
(COTTON —) CUDWEED
(DWARF —) POLYANTHA
(HYBRID —) NOISETTE
(PREF.) RHOD(O) ROSEO ROSI
ROSO
(SUFF.) RHODIN
ROSE ACACIA ROBINIA
ROSE APPLE JAMBO JAMBOS
JAMBOSA
ROSEATE SPOONBILL AJAJA
ROSE-BREASTED (— COCKATOO)
GALAH
ROSEBUSH ROSER BALWARRA
ROSE CAMPION LYCHNIS
ROSE-COLORED OPTIMISTIC
(— STARLING) PASTOR TILYER
ROSEFISH BRIM BREAM BERGYLT
REDFISH
(YOUNG —) SNAPPER
ROSE HIP CHOOP CHOUP
ROSELLE SORREL SABDARIFFA
ROSEMARY COSTMARY
MOORWORT ROSMARINE
ROSE MOSS PURSLANE
PORTULACA
ROSENKAVALIER, DER
(CHARACTER IN —) OCHS SOPHIE
FANINAL MARIANDL OCTAVIAN
MARSCHALLIN
(COMPOSER OF —) STRAUSS
ROSET BRAZIL
ROSETTE CHOU KNOT ROSACE
ROSULA COCKADE
ROSEWOOD BUBINGA MOLOMPI
JACARANDA PALISANDER
ROSH (FATHER OF —) BENJAMIN
ROSIN FLUX ROSET COLOPHONY
(— SPIRIT) PINOLIN
ROSS SCALP
ROSSER BARKER PEELER SCALPER
SLIPPER
ROSTER LIST ROTA SCROLL
REGISTER
ROSTRATE BEAKED
ROSTRUM PEW AMBE BEAK BEMA
GUARD SNOUT PULPIT ACROTER
TRIBUNE
ROSY ROSEN BLUSHY AURORAL
HEALTHY AUROREAN BLOOMING
BLUSHFUL RUBICUND
ROT COE RET DOTE DOZE DROP
FOUL JOKE LEAK POKE SOUR
WROX DECAY SPOIL TEASE
BLUING FESTER ROTTEN

CORRUPT HOOFRUT PUTREFY
NONSENSE STAGNATE
(— BY EXPOSURE) RET
(— OF GRAPES) SLIPSKIN
(APPLE —) FROGEYE
(FOOT —) FOUL
(FRUIT —) LEAK
(LIVER —) COE
(PREF.) PYTHO
ROTA LIST ROLL ROSTER ROTULA
ROTARY CIRCLE GYRATORY
ROUNDABOUT
(PREF.) ROTO
ROTATE RUN BIRL GYRE ROLL SPIN
TURN PIVOT RABAT SCREW
WHEEL GYRATE REVOLVE
TRUNDLE ROTIFORM ALTERNATE
(— CAMERA) PAN
(— HIPS) GRIND
ROTATING VOLUBLE
ROTATION SPIN TURN ROUND
TWIRL GYRATION SPINNING
WHIRLING
(— ON BALL) STUFF
(DEVICE INDICATING SPEED OF —)
TACH
(STOP —) DESPIN
ROTCHE BULL RATCH ROTGE
DOVEKEY DOVEKIE BULLBIRD
ROTE CRWTH HEART ROTTA
REPEAT
ROTIFER POLYP LIPOPOD
LORICATE PLOIMATE
ROTIFORM TROCHAL
ROTL RATTEL WEIGHT ROTTOLO
(PL.) ARTAL ARTEL
ROTOGRAVURE ROTO COLOROTO
ROTOR IMPELLER
ROTTED PECKY
ROTTEN BAD FOUL PUNK ROXY
SOUR ADDLE DAZED MOSEY
PUTID ADDLED AMPERY FRACID
MOOSEY PUTRID DECAYED
SPOILED DEPRAVED UNSTABLE
(HALF —) DOTED DOATED
(PARTIALLY —) DRUXY
(PREF.) PUTRE PUTRI SAPR(O)
ROTTENSTONE TRIPOLI
ROTTING SLEEPY CARIOUS
ROTTLERA KAMALA
ROTULA ROUND TROCHE KNEEPAN
PATELLA
ROTUND FAT PLUMP ROUND
STOUT CHUBBY SUBROUND
ROTURIER PEASANT PLEBEIAN
RUPTUARY
ROUE RAKE RAKEHELL DEBAUCHEE
ROUGE RED FARD BLUSH PAINT
FUCATE REDDEN RUDDLE
CLINKER SCRIMMAGE
(ANIMAL —) CARMINE
ROUGH RU ROW RUF BEAT FOUL
GURL HARD HASK LAMB ROID
ROYD RUDE THUG WILD ACRID
ASPER BLUFF BLUNT BRUTE
CHURL CRUDE DIRTY GOBBY
GROFF GURLY HAIRY HARSH
HEFTY JAGGY LUMPY REWCH
ROUCH ROWDY RUGGY RUVID
STARK STEER STERN STOUR
TOUGH TOUSY WIGHT BORREL
BROKEN BRUSHY BURRED
CHOPPY COARSE COBBLY CRABBY

CRAGGY ELBOIC HACKLY HISPID
HOARSE HOBBLY HORRID HUBBLY
INCULT JAGGED KEELIE KNAGGY
KNOTTY NOGGEN RAGGED
RAMAGE RASPED ROBUST RUFFLE
RUGGED RUMBLY RUSTIS SEVERE
SHAGGY SKETCH STICKY TOOSIE
TRYING UNEVEN UNFEEL UNFELE
UNFINE UNKIND UNMILD UNRIDE
ABUSIVE AUSTERE BOORISH
BRISTLY CRABBED HIRSUTE
INEQUAL INEXACT JARRING
RABBISH RAMMAGE RAPLOCH
RAUCOUS RUFFLED SCABRID
STICKLE STICKLY UNCOUTH
UNKEMPT VICIOUS ABRASIVE
ASPERATE CHURLISH DEPOLISH
IMPOLITE LARRIKIN OBDURATE
SCABROUS SCRAGGED STUBBORN
UNGENTLE UNTENDER
MANHANDLE SCABERULOUS
(— EDGES) FASH
(— IT) SIWASH
(— UP) MESS
(— UP ARROW FEATHERS)
SPRANGLE
(MAKE —) SHAG
(PREF.) ASPERI DASI DASY
TRACHY
ROUGHAGE FODDER AVERAGE
BALLAST BULKAGE CELLULOSE
ROUGH-AND-READY BURLY
TOWSY TOWZIE MAKESHIFT
ROUGHCAST HARL PARGET
SPARGE ROUGHHEW SLAPDASH
ROUGHEN FRET GAIG HACK EMERY
FEAZE FLOCK FROST TOOTH
ABRADE CRISLE STIVER CRIZZLE
ENGRAIL SCRATCH ASPERATE
UNSMOOTH
(— BRICK WALL) STAB
ROUGHER BULLDOGGER
(PONY —) STRANDER
ROUGH-HOB GASH
ROUGHING IT (AUTHOR OF —)
TWAIN CLEMENS
(CHARACTER IN —) HANK MARK
SLADE TWAIN YOUNG BRIGHAM
ERICKSON
ROUGH-MILL GASH
ROUGHNECK ROWDY TOUGH
MUCKER UNCOUTH BANGSTER
ROUGHNESS GAFF GRAIN SCUFF
TOOTH RUFFLE CRIZZLE CRUDITY
ACRIMONY ASPERITY
(— OF SEA) LIPPER
(— OF SKIN) GOOSESKIN
GOOSEFLESH
(— OF WALL) KEY
ROUGHOMETER VIAGRAPH
ROULADE VOLATA ARPEGGIO
ROULETTE FILET FILLET TROCHOID
(HIGH — NUMBERS) PASSE
(1-18 IN —) MANQUE
(13-24 IN —) MILIEU
ROUNCEVAL GIANT LARGE
MONSTER GIGANTIC
ROUND BALL BEAT BEND BOLD
BOUT FAST FULL GIRO HEAD
RICH ROON ROTA TOUR TRIM
WALK ABOUT AMPLE BEADY
BRISK CATCH DANCE GLOBE
HAMBO HARSH LARGE MOONY

ORBED PLAIN ROMAN RONDO
SPOKE TROLL TUBBY CIRCLE
COURSE ENTIRE MELLOW NEARLY
ROTUND ROUNDY RUBBER
RUNDLE SPHERY SPIRAL STOWER
STREAK ZODIAC ANNULAR
CIRCUIT SHAPELY CIRCULAR
COMPLETE CROSSBAR ENCIRCLE
GLOBULAR SONOROUS LABIALIZE
(— EDGES OF TIMBER) BEARD
(— END OF LOG) SNIPE
(— FREQUENTLY GONE OVER) BEAT
(— IN BOWLING) FRAME
(— IN CARDS) GRAND
(— IN ROLLER DERBY) JAM
(— OF ACTIVITIES) SWING
(— OF APPLAUSE) HAND JOLLY
SALVO PLAUDIT
(— OF CHAIR) BALUSTER
(— OF KNITTING) BOUT
(— OF LADDER) STAVE
(— OF PLAY) LAP
(— OFF) TOP CROWN FILLET
(— OUT) ORB BELLY INTEGRATE
(— UP) CORRAL WRANGLE
SCROUNGE
(PLUMP AND —) CHUBBY
(SWEDISH —) HAMBO
(PREF.) GLOBI GLOBO PERI
ROTUNDI ROTUNDO
TROCH(I)(LEI)(O) VENTR(I)(O)
ROUNDABOUT PLUMP DETOUR
ROTARY CURVING DEVIOUS
CAROUSEL CIRCULAR INDIRECT
TORTUOUS AMBAGIOUS
(— MOVEMENT) WINDLASS
ROUNDED FULL BOMBE BOWLY
CONVEX MELLOW ROTUND
TERETE WHELKY ARRONDI
BUNTING COMPASS CONCAVE
GIBBOUS SCUTATE SHAPELY
COMPLETE FINISHED HOOPLIKE
SONOROUS
(— OUT) PLUM
(PREF.) TERETI
ROUNDEL HEURT PLATE POMME
PELLET FOUNTAIN
(— AZURE) HURT
(— GULES) TORTEAU TORTEAUX
(— OR) BEZANT BYZANT
(— PURPURE) GOLP GOLPE
(— SABLE) GUNSTONE
(— SANGUINE) GUZE
(— VERT) POMEY
ROUNDER SOAKER WASTREL
INFORMER
ROUNDERS TUT PATBALL
TUTBALL
ROUNDHEAD SWEDE CROPPY
WEAKFISH
ROUND HERRING SHADINE
STRADINE
ROUNDHOUSE BARN POOP
LOCKUP
ROUNDNESS ROTUND SPHERICITY
(— OF RIBS) SPRING
ROUND POMPANO PERMIT
PALOMETA
ROUND ROBIN ANGLER SERIES
PANCAKE SEQUENCE
ROUNDSMAN VANMAN
SWINGMAN WATCHMAN
ROUNDUP RODEO CAMBER

GATHER MUSTER
ROUNDWORM NEMA ASCARID
EELWORM GORDIAN HELMINTH
NEMATODE STRONGYL
ROUP ROLP ROOP CROAK CLAMOR
AUCTION SHOUTING
ROUSE DAW GIG HOP JOG BAIT
BEET CALL DRAW FIRK GOAD
MOVE RANT RAVE STIR WAKE
WHET AMOVE ERECT MOUNT
RAISE START STEER UPSET
WAKEN ABRADE ABRAID AROUSE
BESTIR EXCITE FOMENT KINDLE
NETTLE RATTLE REVIVE RUFFLE
WECCHE AGITATE ANIMATE
DISTURB EKPHORE ENLIVEN
HEARTEN INFLAME STARTLE
INSPIRIT IRRITATE
(— TO ACTION) HIE ALARM
ALARUM BESTIR ALACRIFY
ROUSING LIVELY
ROUSTABOUT FLOORMAN
RAZORBACK
ROUT MOB MOW DRUM FUSS
HERD BRANT CHASE COHUE
CROWD EJECT FLOCK LURCH
SMEAR SMITE SNORE CLAMOR
DEFEAT FLIGHT NUMBER RABBLE
SOIREE THRONG UPROAR
CONFUSE CONQUER DEBACLE
SCATTER SPARPLE TEMPEST
ASSEMBLY CONFOUND DISTRESS
VANQUISH
(BACCHIC —) THIASUS
ROUTE WAY BELT GATE GEST LINE
PASS PATH SEND TRACE TRACK
AIRWAY CAREER COURSE CUTOFF
SKYWAY TRAJET CHANNEL
CIRCUIT LANDWAY PASSAGE
SHUTTLE CORRIDOR DISTANCE
LIFELINE SHORTCUT TRAVERSE
(— MARKED OUT) ITER
(— TO DEFEAT) SKIDS
(CIRCUITOUS —) DETOUR
(MIGRATION —) FLYWAY
(OCEAN —) LANE
(PREF.) ODO
ROUTH PLENTY ABUNDANT
ROUTINE RUT ROTA DRILL GRIND
ROUTE TROLL GROOVE HARNESS
EVERYDAY ORDINARY
(COMPUTER —) BOOTSTRAP
(DOMESTIC —) HOMELIFE
(ENTERTAINMENT —) SHTICK
(THEATRICAL —) SCHTICK
(WEARISOME —) TREADMILL
ROVE RUN RAKE ROVE ROAM
GUESS KNOCK RANGE ROWAN
SCOUR SPACE STRAY FORAGE
MARAUD RAMBLE STROLL
WANDER SPATIATE STRAGGLE
TRANSCUR
(— ON THE WING) FLIT
ROVER FLIRT HOYLE STAKE STRAY
MASHER RANGER VIKING
GANGREL SCUMMER MARAUDER
SLIVERER TRAVELER WANDERER
COLORADAN
ROVING END SLUB NOMAD VAGUE
ARRANT ERRANT DEVIOUS
NOMADIC RAMPLER VAGRANT
GADABOUT RAMBLING RESTLESS
SLUBBING VAGABOND

MIGRATORY RANTIPOLE
**(— IN SEARCH OF KNIGHTLY
ADVENTURE)** ERRANTRY
ROW LAY OAR RIG SET DUST FILE
LINE MUSS PULL RANK RULE TIER
ALLEY BRAWL CHESS FIGHT
MOUTH NOISE ORDER RAMMY
RANGE RINGE SCOLD SCRAP
SWATH TRAIN BARNEY BERATE
COURSE DUSTUP GARRAY KICKUP
LISSOM PADDLE POTHER RACKET
RUCKUS RUMPUS SHINDY STREET
STROKE BOBBERY BRULYIE
QUARREL RUCTION SHINDIG
CATEGORY OUTBURST REMIGATE
SQUABBLE
(— BACKWARD) STERN
(— OF BENCHES) STACK
(— OF CASKS) LONGER
(— OF CORN, BARLEY, ETC.) RIG
(— OF DRY HAY) STADDLE
(— OF GRAIN) SWATH SWATHE
(— OF GRASS) HACK SWATH
(— OF GUNS) TIRE
(— OF HOUSES) CRESCENT
(— OF LAMPS) BATTEN
(— OF SEATS) BARRERA
(— OF SEED) DRILL
(— OF STAKES) ORGUE
(— OF STONES) CORDON
(— OF TREES) ESPALIER
(— OF VEGETABLES) RINGE
(-S OF BALCONY) MEZZANINE
(DISORDERLY —) RAG
(PL.) EPEIRA
(PREF.) STICHO
(SUFF.) STICH(OUS)
ROWAN RAN RODDIN
ROWAN TREE CARE SORB WICKY
WITCH RODDEN RODDIN WICKEN
WIGGEN QUICKEN RANTREE
WHITTEN WITCHEN ROUNTREE
ROWBOAT GIG OAR BARK OARS
PLAT BARIS COBLE DINGY FUNNY
KOBIL SCULL SKIFF BARQUE
CAIQUE DINGHY LURKER WHERRY
SCULLER
(— SEAT) TAFT
(CLINKER-BUILT —) FUNNY
(FLAT-BOTTOMED —) DORY
(PART OF —) RING SEAT STEM
SOCKET THWART GUNWALE
OARLOCK PAINTER ROWLOCK
TRANSOM
(SMALL —) COG
ROWDY TOU BHOY CASH MONEY
RORTY ROUGH TOUGH TOMBOY
UNRULY VULGAR HOODLUM
RAFFISH BARRATER LARRIKIN
STUBBORN ROUGHNECK
ROWDYISM YAHOOISM
ROWEN EDGROW RAWING
AFTERMATH ROUGHINGS
ROWENA (FATHER OF —) HENGIST
(GUARDIAN OF —) CEDRIC
(HUSBAND OF —) IVANHOE
VORTIGERN
ROWER URGER GALIOT STROKE
OARSMAN STERNMAN CAIQUEJEE
(— ON UPPER SEATS) THRANITE
(OUTERMOST —) THALAMITE
(SECOND LEVEL —) ZYGITE
ROWING CREW

ROWLOCK LOCK CRUTCH
OARLOCK RULLOCK
ROXANA (FATHER OF —) OXYARTES
(HUSBAND OF —) ALEXANDER
ROYAL EASY REAL RIAL ELITE
REGAL SMALT AUGUST KINGLY
REGIUS SOVRAN SUPERB BASILIC
GLORIOUS IMPERIAL IMPOSING
MAJESTIC PAVILION PRINCELY
(— MACE) SCEPTER SCEPTRE
ROYAL ANTELOPE MADOQUA
KLEENEBOC
ROYAL FERN OSMOND OSMUND
ROYALIST TORY ULTRA REGIAN
TANTIVY CAVALIER MUSCADIN
(PL.) CHOUANS
ROYALLY PURPLEY
ROYAL PALM COYAL
ROYALTY LOT ALII GALE BONUS
CROWN REGAL REALTY MAJESTY
PENALTY LORDSHIP NOBILITY
REGALITY
ROYET WILD HARSH UNRULY
ROMPING
RUB DUB BARK BILL FILE FRAY
FRET FRIG FROT RISP SHAB WIPE
CHAFE DIGHT FEEZE FRUSH
GRATE GRAZE GRIDE LABOR
SCOUR SCRUB SMEAR STONE
FRIDGE RUBBER STREAK
BEESWAX FRICACE FURBISH
MASSAGE
(— AS A ROPE) SNUG
(— AS ANIMALS) SHAB
(— AWAY) ERODE ABRADE
(— BOOT) BONE
(— DOWN) WIPE STRAP
(— ELBOWS) JOSTLE JUSTLE
(— GENTLY) STRIKE STROKE
(— HARD) SCOUR SCRUB
(— HARSHLY) GRIND
(— LIGHTLY) GRAZE
(— OFF) CROCK ABRADE ABRASE
(— OUT) ERASE EFFACE EXPUNGE
(— ROUGHLY) GRATE
(— SNUFF) DIP
(— THE SKIN OFF) SHAW
(— TOGETHER) FIDDLE
(— VELVET FROM ANTLERS)
BURNISH
(— WITH GREASE) DUB
(— WITH OIL) ANOINT
(PREF.) TRIBO
(SUFF.) TRIBE TRIPSIS
RUBBED TERSE
RUBBER BUNA FOAM PARA BUTYL
CREPE RASER ALASKA CAUCHO
DAPICO ERASER NIGGER RUNNER
BISCUIT BURUCHA EBONITE
ELASTIC GUAYULE RAMBONG
BORRACHA FRICTION NEOPRENE
SERNAMBY SERWAMBY
SOVPRENE
(— CITY) AKRON
(HARD —) EBONITE
(RECLAIMED —) SHODDY
(PL.) SHAB
RUBBERIZE FRICTION
RUBBER TREE ULE MILKER
RAMBONG
RUBBING CHAFE CARESS
ABRASION FRICTION FROTTAGE
FRICATION

(SUFF.) TRIPSIS

RUBBISH KET BUNK CRAB CRAP FLAM FLUM GEAR GWAG MULL MUSH PELF PELT PUNK RAFF ROSS TOSH TRAG BILGE BRASH BROCK CRAWM CULCH OFFAL SCOWL SLUSH STENT STUFF TRADE TRASH TRUCK WASTE COLDER DEBRIS GARBLE KELTER LITTER PALTRY PIFFLE RAFFLE RAMMEL REFUSE RUBBLE SCULCH SHRUFF SPILTH BAGGAGE BEGGARY MULLOCK RUMMAGE SLITHER TAFFIKE TRAFFIC FIRETRAP NONSENSE RIFFRAFF TRASHERY TRUMPERY CLAMJAMFRY
(VEGETABLE —) WRACK

RUBBISHY POUCY PALTRY TRASHY BAGGAGE RUMMAGY

RUBBLE BRASH STENT TALUS RAMMEL BACKING MOELLON SLITHER

RUBE JAY BOOR HICK JAKE JASPER BUMPKIN BUSHMAN HAYSEED CORNBALL

RUBELLA ROTELN

RUBELLITE SIBERITE

RUBICUND RED ROSY RUDDY FLORID FLUSHED

RUBIGINOUS RUSTY

RUBLE RO RUBLIS
(ONE-HALF —) POLTINIK

RUBRIC RED NAME CANON CLASS TITLE CONCEPT CATEGORY

RUBRICATE MINIATE

RUBY AGATE BALAS RUBIN PYROPE ANTHRAX SPARKLE VERMEIL

RUBY SPINEL BALAS ALMANDINE

RUCHING COQUILLE

RUCK RUT HEAP PILE RICK CROWD SQUAT STACK TRASH CREASE FURROW HUDDLE PUCKER RUBBISH WRINKLE

RUCKUS ADO ROW FIGHT FRACAS ROOKUS

RUCTION HURRY RUCKUS QUARREL RUPTION FRACTION

RUDABAH (FATHER OF —) MIHRAB
(HUSBAND OF —) ZAL
(SON OF —) RUSTAM

RUDD REDEYE

RUDDER HELM STEER STERN TIMON HELLIM RUTHER STEERER STEERAGE GOVERNAIL
(— BACK) TALON
(— EDGE) BEARDING
(— OF WINDMILL) TAIL
(DIVING —) HYDROVANE
(PART OF —) STOCK

RUDDERFISH CHOPA OPALEYE

RUDDINESS RUBEDITY

RUDDLE RED BOLE KEEL SMIT ROUGE

RUDDY RED RODE RUDE FRESH VIVID BLOWSY BLOWZY FLORID LIVELY GLOWING RUDDISH BLUSHFUL RUBICUND SANGUINE

RUDDY DUCK ROOK BOOBY NODDY PADDY SPRIG BOBBER DUNBIRD GREASER PINTAIL SLEEPER SPATTER BLUEBILL

BULLNECK HARDHEAD WIRETAIL

RUDE ILL RAW BOLD IRON LEWD WILD BLUFF BLUNT CRUDE GREEN GROSS PLUMP ROUGH STOUR SURLY UNORN ABRUPT BITTER BORREL BRASSY CALLOW CHUFFY CLUMSY COARSE DUDGEN GOTHIC HOMELY HOYDEN INCULT RIBALD ROBUST RUGGED RUSTIC SAVAGE SHAGGY SIMPLE STORMY UNFEEL UPLAND VULGAR ABUSIVE ARTLESS BOORISH CARLAGE CARLISH INCIVIL LOUTISH LOWBRED NATURAL UNCOUTH UNHENDE CHURLISH CLUBBISH HOMESPUN IMPOLITE INSOLENT MECHANIC PETULANT PORTERLY STUBBORN SYLVATIC UNGENTLE UNPOLITE YOKELISH
(— AND BOLD) HOIDEN HOYDEN

RUDENESS GAFF

RUDIMENT GERM ANLAGE VESTIGE BEGINNING PRIMORDIUM
(PL.) ABC ALPHABET ELEMENTS GRAMMATES

RUDIMENTARY BASIC GERMING ABORTIVE INCHOATE ABECEDARY ELEMENTAL EMBRYONIC PRIMITIVE ABECEDARIAN
(MOST —) FIRST
(PREF.) LYO PRO

RUE RU REWE MOURN CATGUT REGRET REPENT SORROW BORONIA HARMALA TENTWORT

RUEFUL SAD RUELY WOEFUL DOLEFUL PITIABLE

RUFF SET APEX FURY PAPE POPE CREST PRIDE REEVE TEASE TEAZE TRUMP COLLAR FRAISE RABATO RUFFLE TIPPET ZENITH ELATION PARTLET PASSION QUELLIO REBATER ROTONDE PICKADIL

RUFFED BUSTARD HOUBARA

RUFFED LEMUR VARI

RUFFIAN MUN LAMB PIMP PUNK THUG TORY BRAVO BULLY DEVIL ROUGH ROWDY TIGER TOUGH APACHE BRUTAL COARSE CUTTER CUTTLE MOHAWK MOHOCK NICKER PANDER TOWSER HOODLUM SWEATER TUMBLER HACKSTER HOOLIGAN

RUFFLE VEX BAIT FRET HOOP ROOL RUFF BULLY CRISP FRILL GRAZE JABOT PLEAT ROUGH ROUSE SHIRR ABRADE ATTACK GATHER NETTLE PEPLUM RIPPLE BLUSTER BRISTLE DERANGE FLOUNCE FLUTTER PANUELO STIFFEN SWAGGER TROUBLE DISHEVEL DISORDER DISTRACT FURBELOW IRRITATE QUILLING SKIRMISH
(— THE TEMPER) ROIL

RUFFLED ROUGH UNKEMPT

RUFFLING (— ON THE SURFACE OF WATER) HORROR

RUFUS (FATHER OF —) SIMON

RUG TUG BAKU COZY HAUL MAUD PULL SNUG TEAR WRAP BIJAR HERAT HEREZ JURUK KAZAK KHILA KONIA KULAH KUMEH

LADIK MECCA MELAS MOSUL NAMDA SENNA TEKKE TUZLA USHAK YURUK ZOFRA AFSHAR BALUCH KANARA KAROSS KASHAN KIRMAN MOGHAN NAMMAD PERGAM RUNNER SHIRAZ SMYRNA TABRIZ TILPAH TOUPEE WILTON BALUCHI BERGAMA BOKHARA BUFFALO DERBEND DRUGGET FERAHAN GIORDES GOREVAN HAMADAN ISPAHAN SHEERAZ SHIRVAN YARKAND AUBUSSON DOMESTIC FOOTPACE PANDERMA SARABAND SEDJADEH SERABEND WOLFSKIN
(— FOR SADDLE) PILCH
(— OF SKINS) KAROSS WOLFSKIN
(GREEK —) FLOKATI
(PLAID —) MAUD
(PRAYER —) MELAS MELES GHIORDES NAMAZLIK
(REVERSIBLE —) KILIM
(SCANDINAVIAN —) RYA

RUGA FOLD CREASE WRINKLE

RUGBY FOOTER RUGGER FOOTBALL
(— PLAY) SCRUM

RUGGED RUDE WILD HAIRY HARDY ROUGH STIFF COARSE CRAGGY HORRID JAGGED KNAGGY KNOTTY ROBUST SAVAGE STRONG STURDY UNEVEN CRABBED GNARLED OBDURATE SCRAGGED VIGOROUS

RUGGIERO (GUARDIAN OF —) ATLANTE
(SISTER OF —) MARFISA
(SLAYER OF —) TISAPHERNES
(WIFE OF —) BRADAMANTE

RUIN DO MAR POT BANE BANG COOK CRAB DAMN DASH DISH DOOM FALL FATE FELL HELL JACK KILL LOSS RASE RAZE SINK TALA BLAST BOTCH BREAK CRUSH DECAY EXILE GUBAT HUACA LEESE LEISS SHEND SHOOT SMASH SPEED SPILL SPLIT SPOIL SWAMP TRASH WRACK WRAKE WRECK BEDASH BLIGHT CANCEL COOPER DAMAGE DEFACE DEFEAT DIDDLE DISMAY FOREDO INJURY JIGGER MANGLE RAVAGE UNMAKE BOWWOWS CORRUPT DESTROY FLATTEN FORLESE FORWORK LEESING PERVERT SCUPPER SHATTER SUBVERT TORPEDO UNDOING BANKRUPT COLLAPSE DEMOLISH DESOLATE DISASTER DOWNFALL
(— AT GAMBLING) SHRUB
(SPIRITUAL —) FALL
(PL.) ASHES DEBRIS RELICS RUDERA ZIMBABWE

RUINATION DOGS

RUINED FLAT GONE LORN BROKE KAPUT BROKEN FALLEN NAUGHT NOUGHT FORLORN BANKRUPT DESOLATE

RUINER MARPLOT

RUINOUS DEADLY BANEFUL DECAYED SHENDFUL WASTEFUL CUTTHROAT

RULE LAW MAN RAJ WIN DASH KING NORM SWAY WALD WARD YARD AXIOM CANON GUIDE JUDGE MAXIM NORMA ORDER POWER REGLE REIGN RICHE RIGHT RULER SPILE STAFF SUTRA SUTTA WIELD ALIDAD CUTOFF DECIDE DECREE DITION DOMINE EMPIRE ENTAIL GNOMON GOVERN MANAGE MASTER METHOD REGNUM REGULA SQUARE VASSAL BROCARD COMMAND CONTROL COUNSEL DICTATE DIETARY FORMULA PLUMMET PRECEPT PRESIDE REGENCY PRECEPT PRESIDE DICTAMEN DOCTRINE DOMINATE FUNCTION LEGALISM MODERATE ORDINARY OVERLEAD PERSUADE REGIMENT REGNANCY STANDARD TYRANNIS OBSERVANCE
(— BY UPSTARTS) NEOCRACY
(— OUT) EXCLUDE
(— TYRANNICALLY) HORSE
(—S OF CONDUCT) ETIQUETTE
(—S OF DUELING) DUELLO
(ABSOLUTE —) AUTARCHY
(MOB —) OCHLOCRACY
(OPPOSING —) ANTINOMY
(PREF.) ARCH(AE)(AEO)(E)(EO)(I)

RULER (ALSO SEE CHIEF, TITLE, LEADER) DEY GOG JAM MIN OBA AMIR CZAR DAME DUKE EMIR INCA KING LORD OBBA RULE TSAR TZAR ALDER AMEER DECAN EMEER HAKIM MPRET MWAMI NAGID NAWAB SCALE SOPHI STEER SUBAH ZUPAN APHETA ARCHON AUTHOR CAESAR DESPOT DUARCH DYNAST EPARCH FERULE GERENT HERSIR ISWARA KABAKA KAISER MASTER NIMROD PATESI PENLOP RECTOR REGENT SAWBWA SHERIF SOLDAN SUFFEE SULTAN TYRANT ADMIRAL ALIDADE BOURBON DEMARCH FAIPULE ISHVARA KHEDIVE MONARCH MORMAER PTOLEMY RECTRIX REGULUS REIGNER TOPARCH TRIARCH WIELDER AUGUSTUS BASILEUS DRIGHTEN EXILARCH GOVERNOR HEPTARCH INTERREX OLIGARCH OVERLORD PADISHAH PENTARCH PHYLARCH REGINALD TARAFDAR WHIPKING
(— IN A NATIVITY) APHETA
(— OF ENCLOSURE) HENRY
(CURVED —) SWEEP
(ELF —) AUBREY
(INCA —) CURACA
(JEWISH —) EXILARCH
(MONGOLIAN —) HUTUKTU
(MOSLEM —) SOLDAN
(STRONG —) REGINALD
(TATAR OR MOGUL —) CHAM
(WHITE —S) SERKALI
(PREF.) ARCH(AE)(AEO)(E)(EO)(I)
(SUFF.) ARCHIC ARCHY

RULING CALL CHIEF REGENT SOVRAN CURRENT HOLDING REGITIVE HEGEMONIC

RUM ODD ROME OCUBY QUEER

RUMBO TAFIA TAFFIA BACARDI CACHACA JAMAICA PECULIAR SWITCHEL EXCELLENT

RUMBLE CROWL DICKY GROWL RUMOR SNORE BUMBLE HOTTER HUMBLE LUMBER WAMBLE GRUMBLE QUARREL
(— AS A GANG) BOP

RUMBO RUM GROG LIQUOR

RUMEN CUD PAUNCH STOMACH

RUMINANT OX COW YAK BULL DEER GOAT CAMEL LLAMA MOOSE SHEEP STEER TAKIN ALPACA MAZAME VICUNA GIRAFFE QUIDDER ANTELOPE TUBICORN
(SUFF.) MERYX

RUMINATE CHAW CHEW MULL MUSE PONDER CONCOCT REFLECT SAUNTER CONSIDER

RUMINATION MERYCISM

RUMKIN RUMMER

RUMMAGE GRUB POKE ROOT ROUT SEEK BUSTLE FORAGE POWTER TOUSLE UPROAR FOSSICK RANSACK ROMMACK DISORDER SKIRMISH UPHEAVAL
(— ABOUT FOR A PROFIT) FOSSICK
(— SALE) JUMBLE

RUMMY GIN RUM TUNK QUEER CANASTA COONCAN DRUNKARD OKLAHOMA

RUMOR CRY SAW BUZZ FAMA FAME TALK WORD BRUIT MUDGE NOISE SOUGH SOUND STORY VOGUE VOICE BREEZE CANARD FURPHY GOSSIP MURMUR POTGUN RENOWN REPORT RUMBLE CLATTER HEARING HEARSAY INKLING OPINION WHISPER NORATION GRAPEVINE SCUTTLEBUTT

RUMORED AFLOAT

RUMP ASS FUD ARSE BEAM CULE DOCK DOUP CROUP NACHE NATCH PODEX STERN BOTTOM CURPIN CROUPON CRUPPER HURDIES KEISTER PLUNDER BANKRUPT BUTTOCKS DERRIERE
(PREF.) PYG(O)
(SUFF.) PYGAL PYGE PYGIA(N) PYGOUS PYGUS

RUMPF CORE

RUMPLE FOLD MUSS WISP TOUSE TOWSE MOUSLE ROMBLE CRUMPLE SCRUNCH WRINKLE

RUMPUS RAG ROW BRAWL SHINE CLAMOR FRACAS HUBBUB RUCKUS SHINDY TOWROW UPROAR BAGARRE BOBBERY ROOKERY RUCTION ROWDYDOW

RUMSHOP BAR SALOON TAVERN BARROOM TAPROOM DRUNKERY

RUN GO BYE ERN FLY FOG GAD HOP JOG LAM LEG PLY RIN RUB URN BUNK CALL FLEE FLOW FUSE HARE HEAT HEEL HUNT IRNE KITE LEAD LEAP MELT PASS PLAY RACE RAKE RINN ROAM ROVE TEND TRIG TRIP TROT TURN WALK WEEP WORK ASSAY BLEND BREAK BRUSH CHASE COAST EXTRA GOING HURRY NOTCH POINT SCOUP SPEED SPEND STAND TABLE TRACE BICKER CAREER COURSE ELAPSE ESCAPE EXTEND GALLOP HASTEN LADDER MANAGE RESORT ROTATE SPRENT SPRINT STREAM TUMBLE VOLATA ACCURRE CONDUCT CONTAIN FLUTTER LIQUEFY OPERATE PASSAGE RETREAT SCUTTER SKELTER STRETCH FUNCTION TRANSCUR
(— ABOUT) TIG FISK DISCURRE
(— ACROSS) STRIKE
(— AGAINST) JOSTLE
(— AGROUND) BEACH GRAVEL HURTLE STRAND STRIKE
(— ALONG EDGE OF) SKIRT
(— AS STOCKING) LADDER
(— AT HIGH SPEED) SCORCH
(— AT THE NOSE) SNIVEL
(— AT TOP SPEED) SPRINT
(— AWAY) FLY GUY FLEE HIKE JINK JUMP SMUG ELOPE SCRAM SMOKE DECAMP SCAMPER SCARPER FUGITATE SKEDADDLE
(— AWAY FROM DEBTS) LEVANT
(— AWAY IN PANIC) STAMPEDE
(— BEFORE A GALE) SCUD
(— BEFORE A JUMP) FEAZE FEEZE
(— BETWEEN) INTERCUR
(— BLINDLY) SKITTLE
(— CLUMSILY) LOPPET TUMBLE
(— COUNTER) BELY BELIE CROSS
(— DOWN) SLUR TRASH OVERRUN
(— HARD) DIG
(— HIGH) FLOOD
(— IN CRICKET) BYE WIDE EXTRA NOTCH
(— IN DROPS) WEEP
(— INTO) INCUR
(— ITS COURSE) LAPSE
(— OBLIQUELY) SQUINT
(— OF CLAPBOARDING) STRAKE
(— OF MULE CARRIAGE) DRAW
(— OF SHAD) SPURT
(— OF STAIRS) GOING
(— OFF) BOLT SCADDLE
(— ON SKIS) SCHUSS
(— OUT) EXCUR ISSUE PETER
(— OVER) HEAT TRAMP OVERFLOW
(— RAPIDLY) KITE RAKE SCUR SCOUR SKIRR SPLIT CAREER
(— SOAP) FRAME
(— SPEEDILY) CHASE CAREER
(— SWIFTLY) HARE LEAP SCUD CHEVY CHIVY
(— THROUGH) PIERCE DISCURRE
(— TO) ACCURRE
(— TO EXERCISE HORSE) HEAT
(— TOGETHER) HERD MUDDY CLUTTER
(— TRAINS) BLOCK
(— WILD) GAD ESCAPE STARTLE
(— WILDLY) STARTLE
(— WITH AFFECTED PRECIPITATION) SCUTTLE
(— WITH SKIPS) SCOUP
(— WITH VELOCITY) DART
(BRIEF —) STREAK FLUTTER
(COMMON —) RUCK
(END —) SWEEP
(GLASS FURNACE —) BLAST

(MUSICAL —) TIRADE
(OBSTACLE —) GYMKHANA
(RAPID MUSICAL —) TIRADE VOLATA
(SAILING —) STRETCH
(SHEEP —) SLAIT STATION
(SHORT —) FAIL BICKER SCURRY FLUTTER RAMRACE SCUTTLE
(SKI —) PISTE SCHUSS LANGLAUF
(WILD —) LAMP
(PREF.) TRECHO TREKO

RUNAGATE APOSTATE FUGITIVE RENEGADE RUNABOUT VAGABOND WANDERER

RUNAWAY ROMP FUGIE RUNNER DECISIVE DESERTER FUGITIVE RUNAGATE
(PREF.) DRAPETO

RUNDI HUTU

RUNDLE DRUM RUNG ORBIT CIRCLE SPHERE WINDLASS

RUNDLET KEG BARREL

RUN-DOWN BAD SEEDY SHODDY SQUALID DERELICT

RUNE WEN WYN AESE WYNN CHARM OGHAM SPELL THORN SECRET MYSTERY

RUNG RIM GREE RIME STEP ROUND SCALE SPELL SPOKE STAFF STAIR STALE STAVE STEAL TREAD WRUNG DEGREE RUNDLE STOWER STREAK CROSSBAR TRAVERSE
(— OF CHAIR) SPELL
(— OF LADDER) RIME STEP RANGE SPOKE STALE RONDLE STREAK
(— OF ROPE WALK) STAKE
(PL.) STILE

RUNIC ALPHABET FUTHARK FUTHORC

RUNIC LETTER THORN

RUNLET RUSH RINDLE RUNNEL STREAM RIVELING

RUNNEL RILL BROOK RHINE RINDLE RUNLET POLLARD RIVULET STREAMLET

RUNNER SOW GOER POST SCUD SHOE SKID BLADE COBIA FLOAT RACER SABOT SCARF SKATE SLIDE SPRAY TEDGE CURSOR HEELER KANARA RENNER STOLON TOUTER CHANNEL COURIER HARRIER SARMENT CURSITOR SKIPJACK TRAILING
(— FOR GRINDING STONE) MARTIN
(— WHO SETS PACE) RABBIT
(BLUE —) HARDTAIL
(BOOKMAKER'S —) SPIV
(ERRAND —) CAD
(FLUME —) HERDER
(PAIR OF —S) SLOOP
(RACE —) SCUTTLER
(SLED —S) BOB
(SLEDGE —S) SLIPES

RUNNING RUN CARE EASY RACE FLUID QUICK COURSE LIVING COURANT CURRENT CURSIVE FLOWING HOTFOOT SCUTTER SLIDING FUGITIVE
(— ABOUT) COURANT CURSORY
(— ACROSS) DIAGONAL
(— AT SLOW PACE) JOGGING
(— OF SHIPS TOGETHER) ALLISION

(— TOWARD) APPULSE
(— VERTICALLY) DOWN
(FIRST —S) HEAD
(NOT —) DEAD
(PREF.) DROM(O)
(SUFF.) DROMOUS

RUNNING GEAR MOBILE

RUNT BOOR SCRUB SLINK STEER STUMP STUNT HEIFER PEEWEE SCRUMP TITMAN URLING BULLOCK SHARGAR SHARGER SLINKER RECKLING

RUNTY MEAN SURLY SCRUBBY SCRUNTY STUNTED DWARFISH

RUNWAY RUN TIP DUCT TRAIL TARMAC SLIPWAY AIRSTRIP DOLLYWAY
(— OF HARE) FILE

RUPEE DIB CHIP SICCA ROUPIE
(ONE-SIXTEENTH —) ANNA
(TENS OF —S) RX
(10 MILLION —S) CRORE
(100,000 —S) LAC LAKH

RUPERT'S DROP TEAR

RUPIA RUPEE ERUPTION
(HALF —) PARDO PARDAO

RUPTURE BLOW REND RENT BREAK BURST CRACK SPLIT BREACH HERNIA RHEXIS DISRUPT RUPTION FRACTION FRACTURE HERNIATE
(SUFF.) RHEXIS RRHEXIS

RUPTURED BROKEN

RURAL RUSTIC BUCOLIC COUNTRY AGRESTIC ARCADIAN LANDWARD MOFUSSIL PASTORAL PLEASANT PRAEDIAL VILLATIC

RUSE HOAX ROSE SHIFT STALL TRICK WREST ARTIFICE TRICKERY

RUSH FLY FOG RIP RIX RUB SAG BANG BENT BOLT CLAP DASH DUSH FALL FLAW GIRD HURL HUSH JUNK LASH LEAP LUSH PASH RACE RACK RASH RESE RISH ROUT SCUD SHOT SLUR SPUR SWIP TEAR TILT WHIP WIND ADRUE CARRY CHASE CHUTE DRASH DRIVE FEEZE FLASH FLUSH FNAIL FRUSH HURRY ONSET PIPES PREEL SCOUR SEAVE SHOOT SPART SPATE SPRAT SPRIT SPROT START STAVE STORM WHIRL CHARGE DELUGE FESCUE HURTLE JUNCUS POWDER RAMACK RANDOM RAVINE STREAK THRESH ASSAULT BRATTLE BULRUSH DAILIES DEBACLE JUNCITE RAMMISH RAMRACE SKELTER SMOTHER SWITHER TANTIVY TORNADO VIRETOT WHITHER CATARACT DEERHAIR SALTWEED SPLATTER VANQUISH
(— ABROAD) FLUSH
(— AGAINST) CHARGE
(— AWAY) BOLT FLEE SCUTTLE
(— DOWN) TRACE
(— FOR WEAVING) FRAIL
(— HEADLONG) BOIL RUIN SPURN STAMPEDE
(— OF LIQUID) HEAD FLUSH
(— OF WATER) FRESH SHOOT SPOUT SWASH

(— OF WORDS) SPATE
(— ON PASSER IN FOOTBALL) BLITZ
(— OUT) SALLY
(CLUMP OF —S) RASHBUSS
(COMMON —) FLOSS
(DOWNWARD —) HURL
(FLAT —) SHALDER
(FORCEFUL —) JET
(NOISY —) SCUTTER
(ONWARD —) BIRR SURGE
(PL.) REXEN
(PREF.) JUNCI THRYONO
RUSHED HECTIC
RUSHING HURL SCUD FURIOUS
HUDDLING IMPETUOUS
(— OF WIND) GUST
RUSHLIGHT SEAVE
RUSH NUT CHUFA
RUSK ZWIEBACK
RUSSELL'S VIPER DABOIA
DABOYA JESSUR KATUKA

RUSSIA

CAPITAL: MOSCOW
COIN: KOPEK RUBLE GRIVNA
KOPECK
COLLECTIVE FARM: KOLHOZ
KOLKHOZ
DISTRICT: KARELIA
FORTRESS: KREMLIN
LAKE: ARAL NEVA SEGO CHANY
ELTON ILMEN ONEGA BAYKAL
LADOGA SELETY TAYMYR
TENGIZ ZAYSAN BALKHASH
MEASURE: FUT LOF DUIM FASS
LOOF STOF FOUTE KOREC
LIGNE OSMIN PAJAK STOFF
VEDRO VERST ARSHIN CHARKA
LINIYA PALETZ SAGENE TCHAST
BOTCHKA CHKALIK GARNETZ
VERCHOC BOUTYLKA CHETVERT
KROUSHKA
MOUNTAIN: POBEDA BELUKHA
MOUNTAIN RANGE: ALAI URAL
CAUCASUS
NAME: USSR SOVIET MUSCOVY
PENINSULA: KOLA CRIMEA

KARELIA KAMCHATKA
PORT: EISK ANAPA ODESSA
PRESS AGENCY: TASS
REPUBLIC: UZBEK KAZAKH KIRGIZ
LATVIA ARMENIA ESTONIA
GEORGIA TADZHIK TURKMEN
UKRAINE MOLDAVIA LITHUANIA
BYELORUSSIA AZERBAIDZHAN
RIVER: IK OB DON ILI KET NER
OKA ROS TAZ TYM UFA USA
AMGA AMUR KARA LENA NEVA
OREL SURA SVIR URAL LOVAT
MEZEN NADYM ONEGA TEREK
TOBOL VOLGA ABAKAN DONETS
IRTYSH DNIEPER PECHORA
SEA: ARAL AZOV KARA BLACK
BAIKAL OKHOTSK
TOWN: BAKU KIEV OMSK OREL
PERM RIGA GOMEL KASAN
KAZAN KYZYL MINSK PENSA
PSKOV TOMSK FRUNZE IGARKA
KERTCH KURGAN NIZHNI
ODESSA ROSTOV SARTOV
URALSK ALMAATA BATAISK
DONETSK IRKUTSK IVANOVO
KALININ KHARKOV RYBINSK
TALLINN KOSTROMA
ORENBURG SMOLENSK
TAGANROG TASHKENT
VLADIMIR VORONEZH
YAROSLAV
VOLCANO: ALAID SHIVELUCH
TOLBACHIK

RUSSIAN IVAN RUSS SLAV VELIKA
MUSCOVITE
(— BRAID) SOUTACHE
(— HEMP) RINE
(— POOL) CARLINE
(LITTLE —) RUSSENE RUTHENE
UKRAINIAN
RUSSIAN BANK CRAPETTE
RUSSIAN CALF FUDGE
RUSSIAN OLIVE OLEASTER
RUSSIAN THISTLE SALTWORT
TUMBLEWEED
RUSSIAN TURNIP RUTABAGA

RUSSIAN WOLFHOUND BORZOI
RUST CLOWN DROSS ROOST
ROUST UREDO AERUGO CANKER
CORRODE FERRUGO OXIDIZE
(— OF PLANTS) HEMIFORM
LEPTOFORM
(KNOT OF —) TUBERCULE
RUSTAM (FATHER OF —) ZAL
(HORSE OF —) RAKSH
(MOTHER OF —) RUDAPAH
(SON OF —) SOHRAB
(WIFE OF —) TAHMINAH
RUSTIC HOB JAY PUT BOOR CARL
CHAW HICK HIND JAKE JOCK
RUBE RUDE BACON BUSHY CARLE
CHUFF CHURL COLIN DAMON
DORIC HODGE ROUGH RURAL
RURIC SILLY YOKEL AGREST
BORREL BUMKIN COARSE FARMER
GAFFER HONEST JOBSON RUSSET
SAVAGE SCOLOC SCOLOG STURDY
SYLVAN UPLAND ARTLESS
BOORISH BORRELL BUCOLIC
BUMPKIN BUSHMAN COUNTRY
DAPHNIS FIELDEN GEORGIC
HAYSEED HOBNAIL HOOSIER
LANDMAN PAISANO PEASANT
PLOWMAN THYRSIS WAYBACK
AGRESTIC ARCADIAN BACKVELD
CLOWNISH DAMOETAS GEOPONIC
LANDWARD MOSSBACK
CHAWBACON CLODHOPPER
(NOT —) CIVIL
(UNCOUTH —) JAKE
(YOUTHFUL —) SWAIN
(PL.) COUNTRYFOLK
RUSTLE FISLE STEAL FISSLE FISTLE
HIRSEL REESLE BRUSSEL BRUSTLE
CRINKLE REESTLE SKITTER
WHISTLE
(— OF SILK) SCROOP
(— UP) SNAVVLE
RUSTLER THIEF WADDY DUFFER
WADDIE HUSTLER
RUSTLING ARUSTLE CRINKLY
FROUFROU SOUGHING FRICATION
SUSURROUS

RUSTY HOARY MOROSE ROOSTY
SULLEN CANKERY OUTMODED
RUT RAT BRIM RACK RAIK RUCK
TRACK TREAD CREASE FURROW
GROOVE STRAKE UPROAR
CHANNEL OESTRUS WRINKLE
(— IN PATH) GAY
RUTABAGA BAGA SWEDE TURNIP
RUTH PITY MERCY MISERY REGRET
SORROW CRUELTY REMORSE
SADNESS SYMPATHY
(HUSBAND OF —) BOAZ MAHLON
(MOTHER-IN-LAW OF —) NAOMI
(SON OF —) OBED JESSE
RUTHENIAN RUSSENE RUSSNIAK
UKRAINIAN
RUTHLESS FELL GRIM CRUEL
BRUTAL PITILESS CUTTHROAT
RUTILE NIGRINE SAGENITE
RUTTER PLOW DRAGOON GALLANT
TROOPER
RUTTISH RANK LUSTFUL
RUY BLAS

RWANDA

CAPITAL: KIGALI
LAKE: KIVU
LANGUAGE: KIRUNDI SWAHILI
MOUNTAIN: KARISIMBI
MOUNTAIN RANGE: MITUMBA
PEOPLE: TWA HUTU TUTSI
RIVER: KAGERA AKANYARU
LUVIRONZA
TOWN: BUTARE GABIRO NYANZA
GISENYI
TRIBE: BATWA BAHUTU WATUSI
BATUTSI

RYE RAY RIE ERAY REYE SPELT
WHISKY GENTLEMAN
RYEGRASS RAY EAVER DARNEL
RYMANDRA KNIGHTIA
RYND BAIL RHIND MILRIND
RYOT RAYAT FARMER RAIYAT
TENANT TILLER PEASANT

S

S ESS SUGAR SIERRA
SABBATH SUNDAY SABAOTH
SHABBAT SHABBOS
SABER KUKRI SABRE BANCAL
BASKET TULWAR ATAGHAN
CIMETER TULWAUR YATAGAN
ACINACES SCIMITAR
SABICU JIQUE JIQUI
SABINE (BROTHER OF —) CURIACE
SABLE DWALE SAPLE OGRESS
SATURN DIAMOND ZIBELINE
(ROUNDEL —) PELLET
SABLEFISH SKIL BESHOW
COALFISH SKILFISH
SABOTAGE MASTIC DESTROY
SABRA (FATHER OF —) PTOLEMY
(HUSBAND OF —) GEORGE
(SON OF —) GUY DAVID
ALEXANDER
SABRINA (FATHER OF —) LOCRINE
(MOTHER OF —) ESTRILDIS
SABTAH (FATHER OF —) CUSH
SABTECHA (FATHER OF —) CUSH
SAC BAG GUT POD CYST SACK
ASCUS BURSA FLOAT POUCH
THECA VOLVA ACINUS AMNION
SACCUS VESICA AMPULLA
BLADDER CAPSULE CISTERN
HYGROMA UTRICLE VESICLE
BROODSAC FOLLICLE SACCULUS
SPERMARY
(PREF.) THEC(A)(I)(O)
SACAR (FATHER OF —) OBEDEDOM
(SON OF —) AHIAM
SACCHARIN SWEET STICKY
SUGARY GLUCOSE GLUSIDE
SACCHAROSE SUCROSE
SACERDOTAL HIERATIC PRIESTLY
SACHEM SAGAMORE
SACK BAG BED MAT SAC LOOT
MUID POCK POKE BAYON GOOSE
HARRY POUCH SPOIL BUDGET
POCKET RAVAGE SACKET SACQUE
DISMISS PILLAGE PLUNDER
RANSACK SACKAGE SACKBAG
DESOLATE PACKSACK PEIGNOIR
(— OF PALM LEAVES) BAYONG
(— OF WOOL) SARPLAR
(MAIL —) BUM
(PACK —) KYACK
(SAD —) BOLO
(PREF.) THYLAC(O)
SACKBUT SAMBUKE TROMBONE
SACKING SACK GUNNY CROCUS
SACKEN HESSIAN POLDAVY
SOUTAGE
SACRAMENT RITE BAPTISM
MYSTERY NAGMAAL PENANCE
SACRARIUM PISCINA
SACRED HOLY TABU HUACA PIOUS
SACRE SAINT SANCT SANTO
TABOO DIVINE SACRAL
HALLOWED HEAVENLY

NUMINOUS REVEREND
SACROSANCT
(PREF.) HAGI(O) HIER(O)
HIERATICO SACR(I)(O) SEMNO
SACRED FIG PIPAL
SACRED FISH KANNUME
SACREDNESS CHURINGA
SANCTITY TJURUNGA
SACRIFICE GIVE HOST LOSS OFFER
SPEND YAJNA CORBAN FOREGO
VICTIM EXPENSE CHILIOMB
IMMOLATE KAPPARAH LITATION
OBLATION OFFERING PASSOVER
SPHAGION PROPITIATION
(— OF CARGO) JETTISON
(— OF 100 OXEN) HECATOMB
(— OF 1000 OXEN) CHILIOMB
(PL.) HAGIGAH CHAGIGAH
SACRIFICIAL PIACULAR
SACRILEGE PROFANATION
SACRILEGIOUS IMPIOUS
SACRISTAN SEXTON SACRIST
SACRISTY SEXTRY SACRARY
VERGERY PARATORY SACRARIUM
SACROSANCT SACRED
SACRUM
(SUFF.) HIERIC
SAD LOW WAN DARK DOWY DRAM
BLACK DREAR DUSKY MESTO
MOODY SABLE SOBER SORRY
WEARY YEMER DREARY SOLEMN
SULLEN TRISTE WOEFUL BALEFUL
DOLEFUL DUMPISH FORLORN
FUNEBRE LUCTUAL MOANFUL
SOBERLY UNHAPPY DEJECTED
GROANFUL MOURNFUL
MOURNING PATHETIC PITIABLE
SUBTRIST TRISTIVE UNBLITHE
MELANCHOLY
(PREF.) TRISTI
SADDEN SAD DUMP CLOUD
GLOOM GRIEVE ATTRIST
CONTRIST DISTRESS
SADDENED BROKEN
SADDENING LUCTUAL
SADDLE PAD RIG SAG TAG LOAD
SUNK CHINE PANEL PILCH SELLE
STICK BURDEN HEADER RECADO
PIGSKIN PILLION
(— COVER) MOCHILA
(— FOR ONE-LEGGED RIDER)
SOMERSET
(— STUFFED WITH STRAW) SODS
(— WITH) STICK
(— WORKER) LORIMER
(LIGHT —) PILCH PILLION
(MOTORCYCLE —) PILLION
(PACK —) BAT
(PART OF —) HORN RING SEAT
SKIRT CANTLE FENDER JOCKEY
POMMEL STRING BINDING
LEATHER STIRRUP
(STRAW —) SUNK SUGGAN

(WITHOUT A —) ASELLATE
(PREF.) SELLI
SADDLEBACK JACK JACKBIRD
SADDLEBAG ALFORJA CANTINA
SUMPTER TEETSOOK
(PL.) JAGS JAGGS
SADDLE BLANKET CORONA
SADDLEBOW BOW ARSON
SADDLECLOTH HOUSE NAMDA
HOUSING PADCLOTH SHABRACK
SADDLEMAKER FUSTER KNACKER
SADDLE MAT FLET
SADDLE PAD PANEL NUMNAH
PILLOW
SADDLER CODDER KNACKER
LORIMER WHITTAW
SADISTIC SICK CRUEL SADIC
SADLY SAD UNWINLY
SADNESS DUMP RUTH DREAR
DUMPS GLOOM GRIEF UNWIN
SORROW
SAD SACK BOLO
SAFAWID SUFI
SAFE RUG CRIB PETE SURE WELL
AMBRY SALVA SIKER SOUND
SECURE SICCAR HEALTHY
SYKERLY COCKSURE SILVENDY
(— FOR MEAT) KEEP
(— TO DEAL WITH) CANNY
SAFEBLOWER PETEMAN
SAFEBREAKER YEGG YEGGMAN
SAFE-CONDUCT JARK COWLE
GRITH CONDUCT NAVICERT
PASSPORT
SAFECRACKER BOXMAN
PETEMAN PETERMAN TORCHMAN
SAFEGUARD SAVE WARD GUARD
HEDGE SALVE DEFEND SAFETY
SECURE BASTION BULWARK
WARRANT FREEWARD
PALLADIUM PRECAUTION
SAFEKEEPING CUSTODY STORAGE
SAFELY SAFE SICCAR SICKER
SURELY SECURELY
SAFETY REFUGE SALUTE SURETY
WARRANT SECURITY
(PREF.) SOTERIO
SAFETY ZONE ISLET ISLAND
REFUGE
SAFFLOWER KUSUM ALAZOR
SAFFRON
SAFFRON CROCUS AZAFRAN
CROCEUS
(PREF.) CROCEO CROCO
SAFROLE SHIKIMOL
SAG BAG DIP TIE SWAG CREEP
DROOP PLANK SLUMP SAGGON
CURTAIN DEFLATE
SAGA EDDA EPIC MYTH TALE
RIMUR LEGEND NJALSAGA
SAGACIOUS DEEP ACUTE CANNY
SHARP ARGUTE ASTUTE
SHREWD CORDATE POLITIC

PRUDENT SAPIENT
SAGACITY POLICY WISDOM
SMEDDUM YEPHEDE PRUDENCE
SAPIENCE
SAGAMORE SACHEM
SAGE RSI WARE WISE WITE CLARY
HAKAM IMLAC KATHA RISHI
SABIO SOLON SOPHY ABARIS
DHARMA SALVIA SAULGE
SHREWD WIZARD EYESEED
MAHATMA SAPIENT SOPHIST
TOHUNGA WISEMAN DEVARSHI
MAHARSHI WISEACRE
SAGEBRUSH SAGE HYSSOP
SAGEWOOD ARTEMISIA
SAGENESS SAPIENCE
SAGGER COFFIN SETTER CASSETTE
SAGGING DRAG SWAG PTOSIS
SAGITTA ARROW
SAGITTARIUS ARCHER
SAGO PALM CYCAD
SAGRADA CASCARA
SAGUARO SUAHARO SUWARRO
PITAHAYA
SAHIB BWANA
SAHIDIC THEBAIC
SAIBLING TORGOCH
SAID DIT QUOTH STATED RELATED
SAIL JIB LUG RAG BEAT GALE
HAUL MAIN SCUN SLAT SWAN
SWIM WING DANDY FLEET FLIER
FLOAT FLYER JUMBO RAFFE
SCALE SHEET ACCOST CANVAS
COURSE CRUISE DRIVER JIGGER
LATEEN MIZZEN MUSLIN SINGLE
ARTEMON LUGSAIL SKYSAIL
SPANKER SPENCER TRYSAIL
BACKWIND FORESAIL GAFFSAIL
HEADSAIL MAINSAIL MOONSAIL
NAVIGATE RINGSAIL STAYSAIL
STUNSAIL
(— ALONG COAST) COAST ACCOST
(— AROUND) TURN DOUBLE
(— BEFORE THE WIND) SPOON
(— BRISKLY) SPANK
(— BY THE WIND) STRETCH
(— CLOSE TO WIND) PINCH
(— DOWN) AVALE AWALE
(— FASTER) FOOT
(— IN SPECIFIED DIRECTION) STAND
(— OF WINDMILL) ARM AWE EIE
FAN VAN EIGHE FLIER FLYER
SWEEP SWIFT
(— ON COURSE) HAUL WORK
(— QUIETLY) GHOST
(— RAPIDLY) SCUR SKIRR
(— SWIFTLY) RAMP
(— TO WINDWARD) THRASH
(— WITH WIND ABEAM) LASK
(FRAGMENT OF —) HULLOCK
(LIGHT —) SHADOW
(LOWEST —) COURSE
(PART OF —) CLEW FOOT HEAD

LUFF SEAM SLAB TACK LEECH PANEL POCKET WINDOW ZIPPER CRINGLE TABLING TELLTALE HEADBOARD
(SMALL —) ROYAL
(TRIANGULAR —) RAFFE LATEEN BENTINCK
(WIND —) BADGIR
(3-CORNERED —) JIB TRINKET
(PL.) VELA CLOTH KITES LINENS SAILAGE CLOTHING
(PREF.) HISTI(O) ISTIO VELI
SAILBOAT SAIL SCOW BULLY DANDY NABBY SAPIT SCOUT SHARP SKIFF SLOOP SNIPE CANGIA DINGHY QUODDY SAILER SATTIE CATBOAT SCOOTER SHALLOP SHARPIE KEELBOAT SAILSHIP SKIPJACK TRIMARAN
(PART OF —) JIB BOOM BUNK GATE HEAD HELM KEEL MAST SINK SKEG SOLE BERTH CLEAT FRAME HATCH SALON TRUNK WHEEL WINCH ANCHOR GALLEY JIBTOP LOCKER PULPIT RUDDER SHROUD YANKEE BULWARK COAMING COCKPIT COUNTER GALLOWS PUSHPIT TOPSAIL BACKSTAY BOWSPRIT BULKHEAD FOREDECK FOREFOOT FORESTAY HEADSTAY LIFELINE MAINSAIL MASTHEAD OVERHEAD SPREADER STAYSAIL TAFFRAIL TRAVELER CUBBYHOLE MAINSHEET PORTLIGHT STANCHION STATEROOM COMPANIONWAY
(WITCH'S —) SIEVE
SAILFISH BOHO WOOHOO GUEBUCU LONGJAW VOILIER VOLADOR BILLFISH
SAILOR (ALSO SEE NAVAL OFFICER) GOB TAR JACK TOTY GUARD KLOSH LAKER LIMEY CALASH CLASHY DAYMAN DECKIE HEARTY MARINE MATLOW SEAMAN TARPOT TIERER TOPMAN COLLIER MARINAL MARINER MATELOT SHIPMAN SWABBER WARRIOR YARDMAN CANOTIER COXSWAIN DECKHAND FLATFOOT GALIONJI GUNLAYER LANDSMAN LITHSMAN MASTHEAD SHIPMATE WATERDOG WATERMAN WATERRUG YARDSMAN
(EAST INDIAN —) LASCAR
(OLD —) SALT SHELLBACK
(SCANDINAVIAN —) KLOSH
SAILORLIKE TARRISH
SAILOR'S-CHOICE BREAM PIGFISH PINFISH WHITING
SAIL YARD RAE
SAINFOIN ESPARCET
SAINT PIR RSI DADU HOLY QUTB WALI ALVAR ARHAT RISHI SANTO BHAGAT HALLOW PATRON SANTON CANONIZE MARABOUT
(CHINESE —) IMMORTAL
(PATRON —) AVOWRY
(PILLAR —) STYLITE
(PL.) SS
(PREF.) HAGI
SAINT ELMO'S FIRE HERMO CASTOR FUROLE HELENA

SAINT JOAN (AUTHOR OF —) SHAW
(CHARACTER IN —) JOAN DUNOIS ROBERT WARWICK BAUDRICOURT
ST-JOHN'S-BREAD CAROB
ST-JOHN'S-WORT AMBER TUTSAN CAMMOCK
ST REGIS RANERE
SAINTLINESS HOLINESS SANCTITY
SAINT LUCIA (CAPITAL OF —) CASTRIES
(MOUNTAIN OF —) GIMIE
(MOUNTAINS OF —) PITONS CANARIES
(VOLCANO OF —) SOUFRIERE
SAINTLY DEVOUT ANGELIC SAINTED BEATIFIC SAINTISH
(— PERSON) ZADDIK
SAINT VINCENT (CAPITAL OF —) KINGSTOWN
(PART OF —) UNION BEQUIA GRENADINES
SAITHE SILLOC SILLOCK
SAJ SAIN
SAKE SAKI SCORE ACCOUNT
SAKI BISA MONK COUXIA MONKEY YARKEE
SALA (FATHER OF —) ARPHAXAD
(SON OF —) EBER
SALABLE VENAL SELLING SELLABLE VENDIBLE
SALACIOUS LEWD SALT RUTTISH SCARLET SCABROUS
SALAD SALLET COLESLAW SILLSALLAT
(CORN —) FETTICUS
SALADA SALINA
SALAL SHALLON
SALAMANDER OLM SOW BEAR NEWT TWEEG GOPHER LIZARD TRITON AXOLOTL CRAWLER CREEPER DOGFISH MECODONT SALAMICH SHADRACH
SALAMMBO (AUTHOR OF —) FLAUBERT
(CHARACTER IN —) NARR GISCO HANNO HAVAS MATHO TAMIT HAMILCAR SALAMMBO SPENDIUS
(COMPOSER OF —) REYER
SAL AMMONIAC SPIRIT SALMIAC
SALARY PAY HIRE SCREW WAGES INCOME PACKET PENSION STIPEND
SALE FAIR VENT BREAK HEDGE TOUCH BOURSE VENDUE AUCTION MOHATRA SELLING HANDSALE KNOCKOUT PORTSALE
(— BY AUCTION) CANT ROUP BLOCK VENDUE OUTROOP
(— BY OUTCRY) ROUP ROWP HAMMER
(— OF OFFICE) BARRATRY
(— OF TOBACCO) BREAK
(PUBLIC —) AUCTION
(RUMMAGE —) JUMBLE
SALESMAN CLERK BAGMAN RUNNER SELLER BOOKMAN DRUMMER OUTRIDER PITCHMAN
(— IN FISH MARKET) BUMMAREE
SALESMANSHIP SELLING
SALESPERSON CLERK
SALESWOMAN WINSTER SHOPGIRL VENDEUSE

SALIENT SPUR BULGE CHIEF ARGINE BASTION SALTANT
SALIENTIA ANURA ANOURA ECAUDATA
SALINA SHOR SALINE
SALINE SALT SALAR SALTY MARINAL
SALIVA SPIT DROOL WATER DRIVEL SLAVER SPUTUM SPITTLE
(— FLOW) PTYALISM
(PREF.) PTYAL(O) SIAL(O)
SALIVARY SIALIC
SALIVATION PTYALISM SLOBBERS
SALLET SALADE
SALLOW WAN SALE SICK ADUST LURID MUDDY SALIX SAUCH SAUGH PALLID YELLOW
SALLY GRIP JERK PASS QUIP SAIL QUICK START ESCAPE GAMBIT SORTIE GAMBADE OUTFALL OUTLEAP DEMARCHE
SALM (BROTHER OF —) TUR IRAJ
(FATHER OF —) FARIDUN
(MOTHER OF —) SHAHRINAZ
(SLAYER OF —) MINUCHIHR
SALMAGUNDI SILLSALLAT
SALMON DOG LAX LOX SAM KETA MASU PINK AMOUT COHOE COUNT HADDO HOLIA SMOLT SMOOT SPROD TECON ALEVIN BAGGIT KIPPER LAUREL MYKISS SAMLET SAUQUI SILVER TAIMEN ANADROM ANNATTO BLUECAP BOTCHER CHINOOK DOGFISH GILLING KAHAWAI KOKANEE NEWFISH QUINNAT REDFISH RUNFISH SAWMONT SHEDDER SOCKEYE BLOBACK BRANDLIN GOLDFISH HUMPBACK LASPRING SALMONID SPRINGER OUANANICHE
(— AFTER SPAWNING) KELT BAGGIT SHEDDER
(— BEFORE SPAWNING) GILLING GIRLING
(— ENCLOSURE) YAIR
(— IN 2ND OR 3D YEAR) SMOLT
(— IN 2ND YEAR) SPROD HEPPER GILLING
(— IN 3D YEAR) PUG MORT
(— ON FIRST RETURN FROM SEA) GRILSE
(BLUEBACK —) NERKA SAUQUI SOCKEYE
(CURED —) KIPPER
(DOG —) CHUM KETA
(FATHER OF —) NAHSHON
(FEMALE —) RAUN BAGGIT
(HUMPBACK —) HADDO HOLIA
(MALE —) GIB BUCK COCK
(MILTER —) EKE
(NEWLY HATCHED —) PINK ALEVIN
(SMALL —) PEAL SKIRLING
(SON OF —) BOAZ
(SPENT —) JUDY SLAT LIGGER RUNFISH
(YOUNG —) FOG PARR PEAL GRILSE HEPPER JERKIN SAMLET BOTCHER ESSLING SKEGGER LASPRING SPARLING
SALMONELLOSIS KEEL
SALMONEUS (BROTHER OF —) SISYPHUS

(DAUGHTER OF —) TYRO
(FATHER OF —) AEOLUS
(MOTHER OF —) ENARETE
(WIFE OF —) ALCIDICE
SALOME (FATHER OF —) HEROD
(HUSBAND OF —) PHILIP ZEBEDEE ARISTOBULUS
(MOTHER OF —) HERODIAS
SALON HALL SALOON GALLERY
SALOON CAFE CUDDY DIVAN SALON SHADE BARROOM CANTINA RUMSHOP SCATTER DEADFALL DRINKERY DRUNKERY EXCHANGE BRASSERIE
SALPA SALP THALIA
SALSIFY GOATBEARD
SALT SAL CORN KERN SAWT BRINY ZIRAM AMIDOL AURATE GAMMON HALITE MALATE OLEATE OSMATE POWDER SALINE URANIN XENATE KAINITE LACTATE MALEATE NIOBATE PHYTATE TROPATE ABIETATE BRACKISH HALINOUS PIMELATE PLUMBITE
(— FISH) ROIL
(— OUT) CUT GRAIN
(DOUBLE —) ALUM
(HAIR —) ALUNOGEN
(LUMP OF —) SALTCAT
(METAL —) SILICATE
(MIXTURE OF —S) REH USAR
(ROCK —) PIG HALITE
(PREF.) HAL(I)(O) SALI SALIN(I)(O)
(SUFF.) OATE
SALTATE JUMP
SALT BOILER WELLER
SALTBUSH BLUEBUSH
SALTCELLAR SALT CELLAR SELLER SHAKER SALTFAT SALTFOOT
SALTED SALEE
SALTICID ATTID
SALT PAN PLAYA
SALTPETER NITER NITRE PETER ANATRON CALICHE PRUNELLA
SALT PIT VAT WICH WYCH
SALT PORK SOWBELLY
SALTWORKS SALINA SALTERN SALTERY SALTPANS
SALTWORT KALI BARILLA SALSOLA KELPWORT
SALTY SALT BRINY SALINE HALINOUS
SALU (SLAYER OF —) PHINEHAS
(SON OF —) ZIMRI
SALUBRIOUS HEALTHY SALUTARY
SALUTARY GOOD BENIGN HEALTHY HELPFUL BENEDICT
SALUTATION AVE HAIL ALOHA SALUS MIZPAH SALAAM SALUTE REGREET SLAINTE WELCOME DIEUGARD GREETING HAEREMAI
(DRINKING —) SKOAL PROSIT PROFACE WASSAIL
SALUTE CAP HAIL HEIL KISS MOVE YULE CHEER DRINK GREET HALCH HALSE HONOR SALUE SALVO COLORS SALAAM EMBRACE CONGREET
SALVADOR BAHIA
SALVAGE SAVE SALVE RECOVERY SCROUNGE
SALVAGER SALVOR
SALVATION BODAI MOKSHA

SAFETY NIRVANA KAIVALYA
SAVEMENT SOULHEAL
(**— APPROACH**) MARGA
SALVE SAW TAR SALVO SAUVE
NERVAL SUPPLE PLASTER
UNGUENT OINTMENT
SALVER TRAY SERVER WAITER
PLATEAU
SALVIA CHIA SAGE CLARY
MEJORANA MINTWEED
SALVO SALUTE SPREAD PROVISO
TRIBUTE STRADDLE
(**PL.**) LADDER
SAM (**FATHER OF —**) NARIMAN
(**SON OF —**) ZAL
SAMARA KEY CHAT
SAMARIA AHOLAH
SAMARITAN CUTHEAN CUTHITE
SAMBA CARIOCA
SAMBAR ELK MAHA RUSA
SAME ID EAD ILK ONE IDEM LIKE
SELF VERY DITTO EQUAL SAMEN
IDENTIC SELFSAME
(**— AS**) IQ
(**— PLACE**) IB
(**THAT —**) THILK THICKE
(**PREF.**) AUT(O) AUTH(I)
HOM(O)(OI) HOME(O) HOMOE IPSI
ISO TAUT(O)
SAMENESS ONENESS EQUALITY
IDENTITY MONOTONY
SAMLET PINK
SAMNITES SABELLI
SAMOA (**CAPITAL OF —**) APIA
PAGOPAGO
(**COIN OF —**) SENE TALA
(**ISLAND OF —**) OFU TAU ROSE
MANUA UPOLU SAVAII OLOSEGA
TUTUILA
(**MOUNTAIN OF —**) FITO SAVAII
MATAFAO
SAMOGITIAN ZHMUD
SAMOYED TUBA YURAK BELTIR
KAIBAL KOIBAL NENTSI KAMASSIN
SAMPHIRE SALTWEED
SAMPLE DIP SIP CAST PREE CHECK
ESSAY TASTE TRIAL CHANCE
COUPON FLOWER MUSTER
SWATCH TASTER EXAMPLE
EXCERPT MONSTER PATTERN
SAMPLER TASTING INSTANCE
PULLDOWN SPECIMEN
(**— OF METAL**) DIET
SAMPLING SOUNDING
SAMSON (**FATHER OF —**) MANOAH
SAMSON ET DALILA (**CHARACTER
IN —**) PRIEST SAMSON DELILAH
(**COMPOSER OF —**) SAINTSAENS
SAMUEL (**FATHER OF —**) ELKANAH
(**MOTHER OF —**) HANNAH
SAMURAI BUSHI RONIN
SAN SAMPI
SANAD SUNNUD
SANBENITO SAMARRA
SAN BLAS TULE
SAN CARLOS ARIVAIPA
SANCTIFICATION HOLINESS
SANCTIFY BLESS SACRE SACRI
DEDICATE
SANCTIMONIOUS PI DEVOUT
PECKSNIFFIAN
SANCTION AMEN FIAT ALLOW
PIETY ASSENT BISHOP RATIFY

APPROVE ENDORSE JUSTIFY
PASSAGE SUPPORT ACCREDIT
APPROVAL CANONIZE COURTESY
SUFFRAGE
SANCTIONED CANONICAL
SANCTITY SANTY HALIDOME
HOLINESS
SANCTUARY ADYT BAST BEMA
FANE HOLY SOIL ABBEY ALTAR
BAMAH FRITH GIRTH GRITH
SECOS SEKOS TOWER ADYTON
ADYTUM ASYLUM CHAPEL
HAIKAL REFUGE SENTRY SHRINE
SACRARY SHELTER ARCHEION
CABIRION DELUBRUM
HALIDOME HOLINESS
SACRARIUM
(**— FOR LAWBREAKERS**) ALSATIA
(**AUTHOR OF —**) FAULKNER
(**CHARACTER IN —**) LEE RED VAN
REBA RUBY DRAKE GOWAN
LAMAR TOMMY BENBOW HORACE
POPEYE RIVERS SNOPES TEMPLE
GOODWIN STEVENS
SANCTUM ADYT ADYTON ADYTUM
SAND DIRT GRIT ARENA GRAIL
SONDE GRAVEL ISERINE ISERITE
PARTING ASBESTIC BLINDING
(**— FOR STREWING ON FLOORS**)
BREEZE
(**— HILL**) DENE DUNE
(**— IN KIDNEYS**) ARENA
(**— MIXED WITH GRAVEL**) GARD
DOBBIN
(**— ON SEA BOTTOM**) PAAR
(**BRAIN —**) SABULUM ACERVULUS
(**COLOR —**) CHIP BEACH
(**COLORED —**) SMALT
(**DEAUVILLE —**) STUCCO
(**VOLCANIC —**) SANTORIN
(**PREF.**) AMM(O) ARENI PSAMM(O)
SANDAL TIP BAXA FLAT SOCK ZORI
TEGUA CALIGA CHARUK PATTEN
TATBEB RULLION SCUFFER
FOOTHOLD GUARACHE
HUARACHO
SANDAL TREE SANTOL
SANDALWOOD NAIO ALGUM
ALMUG MAIRE CHANDAM
SAUNDERS
SANDALWOOD TREE ILIAHI
SANDARAC TREE ARAR LIGNUM
SANDBAG CONK SANDCLUB
SAND BANK AIR CHAR MEAL
SAND BATCH HURST HYRST
KNOCK SHELF SHOAL
SANDBAR BALK LOOP SAND
BARRA SHOAL TOMBOLO
TOWHEAD
SANDBLASTER FROSTER
BLASTMAN
SAND BORER SMELT
SANDBOX TREE ASSACU
SAND COLIC SABURRA
SAND DARTER SPECK
SAND DUNE TOWAN BARCHAN
SAND EEL GRIG SANDFISH
SANDEMANIAN GLASSITE
SANDERLING OXBIRD
SAND FLEA SCREW SCROW
SANDBOY
SAND-FLY BUSH TURMERIC
SAND GROUSE GANGA ROCKER

ATTAGEN PINTAIL
SAND HOLE BUNKER
SANDIVER NATRON
SAND LAUNCE LANT SMELT
WRIGGLE AMMODYTE SANDLING
SCRIGGLE
SAND LILY SOAPROOT
SANDMAN DUSTMAN
SANDPAPER TREE CHAPARRO
SANDPIPER JACK KNOT PEEP
RUFF STIB WEET OXEYE SNIPE
STINT TEREK TIPUP WADER
DUNLIN GAMBET OXBIRD PLOVER
REDLEG TEETER TILTER TILTUP
TRINGA BROWNIE CHOROOK
CREEKER FATBIRD FIDDLER
HAYBIRD KRIEKER MONGLER
MONGREL REDBACK TATTLER
TIPTAIL GRAYBACK LEADBACK
PEETWEET REDSHANK ROCKBIRD
SANDPEEP SHADBIRD SQUATTER
SWEESWEE TELLTALE
TRIDDLER
(**FEMALE —**) REEVE
(**FLOCK OF —S**) FLING
SAND PIT BUNKER
SAND ROCKET FLIXWEED
SAND SHARK BONEDOG
SANDSTONE FAKE FLAG GRES
GRIT SAND GAIZE HAZEL ARCOSE
ARKOSE DOGGER KINGLE ARENITE
HASSOCK CARSTONE COCONINO
GANISTER PSAMMITE RUBSTONE
SANDROCK
(**BLOCK OF —**) SARSEN
SANDSTORM BURAN HABOOB
TEBBAD
SANDUST VANITY
SANDWICH BUTTY HOAGY
BURGER HOAGIE GRINDER
WESTERN
(**SUFF.**) BURGER
SANDWORT LONGROOT
SANDWEED
SANDY DEEP GINGER GRISTY
SANDED ARENOSE PSAMMOUS
SABULINE SABULOUS
SANDY BROWN LARK
SANE SAFE WISE LUCID RIGHT
FORMAL NORMAL HEALTHY
PERFECT RATIONAL SENSIBLE
SANGA-SANGA ESSANG
SANGUINARY GORY CRUEL
BLOODY CRIMSON SANGUINE
SANGUINE FOND GUZE MURREY
HEMATIC HOPEFUL SARDONYX
SANHEDRIN GEROUSIA
SANICLE ALLHEAL SELFHEAL
SANIOUS ICHOROUS
SANITARY HYGIENIC
SANITY SENSE REASON WISDOM
BALANCE MARBLES LUCIDITY
SANENESS
SAN MARINO (**CHURCH OF —**)
PIEVE
(**DISTRICTS OF —**) CASTELLI
(**MOUNTAIN OF —**) TITANO
(**SUBURB IN —**) BORGO
SANNUP SQUAW
SANSKRIT HINDU
(**— SOUND OR SIGN**) VISARGA
(**— WORK**) VEDANGA
SANS SERIF DORIC GOTHIC

SANTA MARIA TREE BIRMA
GALBA CALABA
SANTONICA WORMSEED
SAO TOME AND PRINCIPE
(**CAPITAL OF —**) SAOTOME
(**MONEY OF —**) DOBRA
(**NAME OF —**) SAOTHOME
SAINTTHOMAS
SAP MUG GOON MINE OOZE RASA
SEVE HUMBO KEEST LYMPH
SAPPER WEAKEN ALVELOZ
FLUXURE SAPHEAD
(**— COURAGE**) DAUNT
(**PALM —**) TODY TODDY
(**POISONOUS —**) UPAS
(**SUGAR MAPLE —**) HUMBO
SAPAJOU SAJOU WARINE
SAPANWOOD BOKOM BRAZIL
SIBUCAO
SAPEK DONG
SAPID SIPID FLAVORY
SAPIENT WISE SHREWD KNOWING
SAPI-UTAN ANOA
SAPLING SCOB PLANT SAPLE
SPIRE RUNNEL SPRING TILLER
STADDLE ASHPLANT SEEDLING
SHILLALA SPRINGER
(**— AMONG FELLED TREES**) WAVER
SAPODILLA GUM CHICA CHICO
DILLY ACHRAS MAMMEE SAPOTA
SAPOTE ZAPOTE NISPERO
NISBERRY NASEBERRY
SAPONIFYING KILLING
SAPONIN GITONIN SENEGIN
CYCLAMIN STRUTHIN
SAPONITE PIOTINE
SAPOTA MATASANO
SAPPHIRE SAFIR TOPAZ ADAMAS
ASTERIA ASTRION HYACINTH
SAPPHIRINE GURNARD TUB
SAPPHO (**AUTHOR OF —**) DAUDET
(**CHARACTER IN —**) JEAN ROSA
FANNY IRENE DEJOIE POTTER
CAOUDAL CESAIRE FLAMANT
GAUSSIN LEGRAND BOUCHEREAU
DECHELETTE LAGOURNERIE
SAPPY FRIM FRUM SAPFUL
SAPSAP PEPEREK
SAPUCAIA COCO COCOA
KAKARALI
SAPWOOD SAP BLEA SPLENT
SPLINT GUAYABI LISTING
ALBURNUM
SARA (**— WOMAN**) UBANGI
SARABAITES REMOBOTH
SARACEN CORSAIR
SARAH ATOSSA
(**FATHER OF —**) ASHER
(**HUSBAND OF —**) ABRAHAM
(**SON OF —**) ISAAC
SARAKOLLE WAKORE
SARASVATI VAC VACH BENTEN
SARCASM RUB GIBE WIPE FLING
IRONY TAUNT RUBBER SATIRE
BROCARD RIDICULE
SCORCHER
SARCASTIC ACID WITTY BITING
IRONIC ACERBIC CUTTING
MORDANT PUNGENT INCISIVE
SARDONIC SATIRICAL
ACRIMONIOUS
SARCASTICALLY DRILY DRYLY
ACIDLY

SARCOCARP FLESH
SARCOPHAGUS TOMB COFFIN
SARCOPSYLLA TUNGA
SARDINE BANG LOUR SARD
SILD CLUPEID PILCHARD
SARDELLE

SARDINIA

CAPITAL: CAGLIARI
CHEESE: ROMANO PECORINO
COIN: CARLINE
GREEK COLONY: OLBIA
GULF: OROSEI ASINARA CAGLIARI
ORISTANO
MOUNTAIN: RASU FERRY LINAS
GALLURA LIMBARA SERPEDDI
VITTORIA
NAME: SARDEGNA
PROVINCE: NUORO SASSARI
CAGLIARI
RIVER: MANNU TIRSO LASCIA
SAMASSI COGHINAS
FLUMENDOSA
STRAIT: BONIFACIO
TOWN: NUORO SASSARI THATARI
CAGLIARI CARBONIA IGLESIAS

SARDONIC SARCASTIC
SARGASSUM GULFWEED
SARGO ZEBRA
SARI PATOLA TAMEIN
SARONG PAU KAIN COMBOY
KIKEPA
SARPEDON (BROTHER OF —) MINOS
RHADAMANTHUS
(FATHER OF —) ZEUS JUPITER
(MOTHER OF —) LAODAMIA
SARSAPARILLA NUNNARI
SHOTBUSH
SARUCH (FATHER OF —) REU
SASH BAR BELT BENN FAJA GATE
TOBE SCARF TAPIS TOWEL VITTA
FASCIA GIRDLE BALDRIC
BURDASH CHASSIS TUBBECK
CASEMENT CORSELET
WAISTBAND
(JAPANESE —) OBI
(WINDOW —) CHESS
SASHAY WALK GLIDE STRUT
CHASSE TRAIPSE
SASH BAR MUNTIN ASTRAGAL
SASKATCHEWAN (CAPITAL OF —)
REGINA
(LAKE OF —) ROUGE REINDEER
ATHABASKA CHURCHILL
WOLLASTON
(RIVER OF —) WOOD MOOSE
SOURIS FRENCHMAN
(TOWN OF —) BIGGAR CLIMAX
ESTEVAN MOOSEJAW ROSETOWN
SASKATOON
SASQUATCH OMAH BIGFOOT
SASS LIP
SASSABY TSESSEBE
SASSAFRAS FILE SALOP SALOOP
SAXIFRAX
SASSY KICKY LIPPY
SATAN ANGEL DEVIL EBLIS FIEND
SHREW BELIAL LUCIFER SATANAS
SHAITAN DIABOLUS SATANAEL
SATANIC SABLE INFERNAL
SATCHEL SCRIP HANDBAG
KEESTER

SATE GLUT ACCLOY SATIATE
SATISFY SATURATE
SATED SAD BLASE
SATEEN VENETIAN
SATELLITE MOON ARIEL LUNET
DEIMOS MOONET OBERON
PHOBOS ACOLYTE ACOLYTH
LUNETTE ORBITER SPUTNIK
TELSTAR TRABANT
UMBRIEL COURTIER
FOLLOWER
(— OF JUPITER) IO EUROPA
CALLISTO GANYMEDE
(— OF SATURN) RHEA DIONE
MIMAS TITAN PHOEBE TETHYS
IAPETUS JAPETUS HYPERION
SATIATE CLOY FILL GLUT PALL
QUAT SADE SATE FLESH GORGE
SERVE STALL ENGLUT STODGE
RASSASY SATISFY SURFEIT
SATURATE
SATIATED SICK JADED SATED
SATIATING STODGY FULSOME
SATIETY FULNESS SURFEIT
CLOYMENT
SATIN SAY RASH ATLAS PANNE
CYPRUS MUSHRU COOTHAY
CYPRESS SATINET
(SILK —) DUCHESS
SATINFLOWER SAFFRON
SATINPOD HONESTY LUNARIA
SATINWOOD ZANTE HAREWOOD
SATIRE WIT GRIND IRONY IAMBIC
LAMPOON SARCASM SOTADIC
RIDICULE PASQUINADE
SATIRIC BITTER IRONIC ABUSIVE
CAUSTIC CUTTING POIGNANT
SLASHING
SATIRIST GRIND NIPPER SATIRE
JUVENAL PASQUIN SILLOGRAPH
AMERICAN MENCKEN
ENGLISH HONE NIGEL SWIFT
WOLCOT MARVELL
GERMAN BORNE MURNER
RABENER
GREEK LUCIAN SOTADES
ROMAN PERSIUS
SPANISH LARRA
SATIRIZE SKIN SKIT GRIND EXPOSE
IAMBIZE LAMPOON PASQUIN
RIDICULE
SATISFACTION CRO FIN PAY UTU
EASE GREE BELLY ENACH TREAT
AMENDS ASSETH CHANGE
REASON COMFORT CONTENT
DELIGHT GLADNESS PLEASURE
REPLETION
SATISFACTORILY SPROWSY
CLEVERLY
SATISFACTORY PAT FAIR GOOD
JAKE WELL DUCKY HUNKY
CLEVER DECENT NOMINAL
ADEQUATE LAUDABLE
SATISFIED SAD FAIN FULL GLAD
PAID VAIN APAID CHUFF PROUD
ASSURED CONTENT PERFECT
GRUNTLED SENSIBLE
WILCWEME
SATISFY PAY EVEN FEED FILL
MEET SAIR SATE SUIT ADEEM
AGREE APPAY QUEME SERVE
SLAKE SPEED ANSWER DEFRAY
PLEASE STODGE SUPPLY

ASSUAGE CONTENT EXPLETE
FULFILL GRATIFY GRUNTLE
RESPOND SATIATE STAUNCH
SUFFICE SATURATE
(— APPETITE) STAY
(— BY PROOF) CONVINCE
(— NEEDS) DO ADJUST
SATISFYING DUE COOL AMPLE
SQUARE PERFECT REWARDING
SATURATE SOG GLUT SATE SOAK
DRAWK IMBUE SOUSE STEEP
DRENCH IMBIBE SEETHE SODDEN
DRUNKEN INGRAIN SATIATE
SLOCKEN
(— WITH SYRUP) CANDY
SATURATED SOBBY SOGGY SOPPY
SODDEN SPONGY DRUNKEN
SATURATION CHROMA PURITY
SATURITY
SATURN (FATHER OF —) URANUS
(MOTHER OF —) GAEA
(SATELLITE OF —) RHEA DIONE
MIMAS TITAN TETHYS JAPETUS
HYPERION ENCELADUS
(SON OF —) JUPITER
SATURNINE SULLEN SATANIC
SATYAGRAHA GANDHISM
SATYR FAUN LECHER SAUMON
SALTIER WOODMAN WOODWOSE
SATYRIASIS TENTIGO
SAUCE MOLE SASS SOWL BERCY
CHILE CHILI CREAM CREME
CURRY GRAVY PESTO SALSA
CATSUP GANSEL MORNAY
PANADA ROBERT KETCHUP
MARENGO SOUBISE SUPREME
TABASCO VELOUTE BECHAMEL
CHAWDRON DRESSING DUXELLES
MATELOTE POIVRADE RAVIGOTE
REMOLADE
(CURRY —) SAMBAL
(FISH —) ALEC BAGOONG
(GARLIC —) AIOLI
(KIND OF —) MARINARA
(SALAD —) DRESSING
(SAVORY —) DIP
(THICK —) LEAR
SAUCEDISH SAUCER BIRDBATH
SAUCEPAN CHAFER GOBLET
POSNET SKILLET STEWPAN
PANNIKIN
SAUCER BIRD PATERA PHIALE
CAPSULE PANNIKIN
SAUCINESS SAUCE DICACITY
SAUCY BOG ARCH BOLD COXY
PERT BRASH DONSY DORTY
FRESH LIPPY PAWKY POKEY
SASSY SMART BANTAM COCKET
COPPED CROUSE THWART
FORWARD PAUGHTY MALAPERT
PETULANT SAUNSHACH
SAUDI ARABIA: (CAPITAL OF —)
JIDDAH RIYADH
(COIN OF —) RIYAL HALALA
HALALAH
(DESERT REGION OF —) NEFUD
DAHANA ALNAFUD
(PLATEAU OF —) NEJD
(TOWN OF —) HAIL HOFUF JIDDA
MECCA MEDINA ALHOFUF
(WEIGHT OF —) OKE
SAUL (FATHER OF —) KISH
(SON OF —) JONATHAN

SAUNTER IDLE ROAM ROVE TOIT
AMBLE RANGE SHOOL SIDLE
STRAY TRAIK BUMMEL DACKER
DANDER FAFFLE LINGER LOITER
LOUNGE POTTER PUTTER
RAMBLE SOODLE STREEL STROLL
TODDLE WANDER SNAFFLE
STAIVER STRAVAGE
SAURA MAGA
SAUREL SCAD XUREL GASCON
BLUEFISH SKIPJACK
SAURY LONGJAW SKIPPER
BILLFISH GOWDNOOK SKIPJACK
SAUSAGE POT LINK SNAG COPPA
GIGOT BANGER BOUDIN POLONY
SALAMI BOLOGNA BOLONEY
BOTARGO CHORIZO PUDDING
SAVELOY BLACKPOT CERVELAT
DRISHEEN KIELBASA LIVERING
ROLLICHE
(KIND OF —) METT
(PREF.) ALLANT(O) BOTULI
SAUTE PANFRY
SAUTERNE YQUEM
SAVAGE ILL FELL GRIM RUDE WILD
BRUTE CRUEL EAGER FELON
FERAL STERN BRUTAL FIERCE
GOTHIC IMMANE BRUTISH
FERVENT HOWLING INHUMAN
MANKEEN MANKIND ROPABLE
UNCIVIL VIOLENT WILROUN
CANNIBAL PITILESS THEREOID
WARRAGAL
(PREF.) AGRIO
SAVAGELY FELLY UNMANLY
SAVAGERY FURY FERITY FEROCITY
SAVANNA CAMPO SAHEL SABANA
(— LANDS) LALANG
SAVANT ARTIST SCIENT SCHOLAR
VIRTUOSO
SAVE BAR WIN HAIN HELP KEEP
SAFE STOP SALVE SPARE SPELL
DEFEND EXCEPT RESCUE SAVING
SCRIMP BARRING DELIVER
HUSBAND SALVAGE WARRANT
CONSERVE PRESERVE
(PREF.) SOZ(O)
SAVIN HEATH SABINE JUNIPER
SAVING FRUGAL THRIFT ECONOMY
SPARING THRIFTY PROVIDENT
SAVINGS FAT ADDLINGS
(— CLUB) MENAGE
SAVIOR LORD SAVER SOTER
REDEEMER
SAVOR EDGE SALT SAPOR SMACK
TASTE DEGUST FLAVOR RELISH
RESENT SAVOUR SEASON TASTEN
SAPIDITY
SAVORLESS FOND INSIPID
WEARISH
SAVORY GUSTY MERRY SAPID
TASTY DAINTY SMERVY GUSTFUL
GUSTABLE TASTEFUL
SAVVY SABE
SAW SAG SEY WEB BUCK REDE
ADAGE FREIT GNOME SCEAR
SPOKE JIGSAW PITSAW RIPSAW
SAYING SCRIBE BACKSAW
BUCKSAW CONVERT DRAGSAW
FRETSAW HACKSAW HANDSAW
HEADRIG HEADSAW PROVERB
SLABBER WHIPSAW CROSSCUT
SENTENCE

(— INTO LOGS) BUCK
(— LENGTHWISE OF GRAIN) RIP
(— OF SAWFISH) SERRA
(— WITH TWO BLADES) STADDA
(CIRCULAR —) BUR BURR EDGER
DAPPER TRIMMER
(CROSSCUT —) BRIAR
(CYLINDER —) CROWN TREPAN
TREPHINE
(PREF.) PRI(O) PRION(O) SERRATI
SERRATO SERRI
(SUFF.) PRION
SAWAN SRABAN SHRAVAN
SAWBILL MOTMOT
SAWDUST COOM COOMB SCOBS
SAWINGS
(PREF.) SCOBI
SAW FERN DYGAL BUNGWALL
HARDFERN
SAWFISH RAY BATOID COMBFISH
(PREF.) PRIST(O)
SAWFLY CEPHID SECURIFER
SAW GATE FRAME
SAWHORSE BUCK JACK SETTER
SAWBUCK TRESTLE
SAWING
(PREF.) PRISO
SAW KERF SKAFF
SAWMILL RASPER
(— DEVICE) KICKER
(— WORKER) PONDMAN
LEVERMAN
SAWYER WETA SAWER PITMAN
TOPMAN KNOTTER
SAXHORN ALTO TUBA ALTHORN
SAXTUBA BARITONE BARYTONE
SAXIFRAGE BAUERA BENNET
SESELI ASTILBE ROCKFOIL
SELFHEAL SENGREEN MITERWORT
PHILADELPHUS
SAXONIAN MINDEL
SAXOPHONE AX AXE SAX ALTO
TENOR SOPRANINO
SAY DEED MEAN MOVE TAKE TELL
SPEAK SPELL AUTHOR QUETHE
RELATE REMARK SAYING
REHEARSE
(— A BLESSING) BENSH
(— FOOLISHLY) BLABBER
(— FURTHER) ADD
(— GLIBLY) SCREED
(— NO TO) NAIT NICK
(— OVER AGAIN) REPEAT
(— SPITEFUL THINGS) BACKBITE
(— TOO MUCH) OVERSAY
(— UNDER OATH) DEPOSE
SAYING DIT SAW SAY TAG DICT
ITEM REDE TEXT WORD ADAGE
AXIOM CHRIA DITTY FREIT MAXIM
SPEAK BALLAD BYWORD DICTUM
DIVERB LOGION DICTION
PROVERB APOTHEGM SENTENCE
SPEAKING
(— LITTLE) DUMB
(—S OF JESUS) AGRAPHA
(—S OF RELIGIOUS TEACHER) LOGIA
(CLEVER —) QUIP
(COMMON —) CANT
(CURRENT —) DICTUM
(OBSCURE —) ENIGMA
(QUICK —) JERK
(SILLY —) FADAISE
(TERSE —) EPIGRAM

(TRUE —) SOOTHSAW
(WISE —) SCHOLIUM
(WITTY —) MOT SALLY DICTERY
WITNESS
(WITTY —S) FACETIAE
(SUFF.) LOGER LOGIA(N)
LOGIC(AL) LOGIST LOGUE LOGY
SCAB RAT ROIN SHAB SNOB CRUST
SCALD SCALL CANKER ESCHAR
RATTER GREENER RUBBERS
BLACKLEG BLACKNEB
(— ON HORSE'S HEEL) MELLIT
SCABBARD CHAPE SHEATH
PILCHER
SCABBARD FISH HIKU
SCABBLE SCAB SCALP
SCABBY MANGY SCALD ROINISH
SCABIOUS
SCABIES ITCH SCAB PSORA
SCABIOSA KNAUTIA
SCABIOUS SCABIA BLUECAP
BUNDWEED PREMORSE
SCABROUS ROUGH SULTRY
ASPEROUS
SCAD COIN AKULE XUREL DOLLAR
GOGGLER QUIAQUIA
(PL.) LOTS TONS
SCAFFOLD CAGE PEGMA STAGE
BRIDGE CATASTA HAYLOFT
STAGING HOARDING
(MOVABLE —) GANTRY
SCAFFOLDING DOCK STAGING
SCALARE ANGELFISH
SCALD BURN LEEP PLOT SCAD
BLAST PLOUT SCAUD
BLANCH SCALDER
AMBUSTION
SCALE PIP LEAF PELA PILL STEP
TAPE CLIMB FLAKE GAMUT
GENUS GULAR PALEA PELOG
PELOK PELTA POISE SCUTE SHALE
SHARD SHELL SHERD SHIVE
TRUNK ASCEND CAUDAL CINDER
COCCID FORNIX GUNTER IMBREX
KELVIN LABIAL LADDER LAMINA
LIGULE LOREAL MENTAL NUCHAL
OCULAR PERULE RAMENT
RONDLE RUSTRE SHIELD SQUAMA
STRIGA BALANCE CLINKER
ELYTRON FRONTAL FULCRUM
HUMERAL LATERAL NUCHALE
REAUMUR ROSTRUM VENTRAL
VERNIER ANALEMMA BRACHIAL
INDUSIUM LECANIUM LODICULE
MEALYBUG ODOPHONE
RAMENTUM SCRAMBLE
SQUAMULE TEMPORAL
UROSTEGE
(— DOWN) DEGRADE
(— OF CORNSTALK) SHIVE
(— OF 7 TONES) SEPTAVE
(— ON BUTTERFLY) PLUMULE
(— ON MOTH) PATAGIUM
(— USED BY TAILORS) LOG
(GRADUATED —) RETE
(GREAT —) GAMUT
(SHAD —) CENIZO
(PL.) CHAFF DANDER
(PREF.) LEPID(O) LEPO PHOLID(O)
SQUAM(ATO)(ELLI)(I)(O)(OSO)(ULI)
(MUSICAL —) CHORD(O)
(SUFF.) LEPIS PHOLIS
SCALEBOARD SCABBARD

SCALEPAN BASIN
SCALER CULLER SOOTER
SCALES TRON TRONE BALANCE
SCALETAIL SQUIRREL
SCALLION PORRET
SCALLOP DAG CLAM GIMP MUSH
CRENA QUEEN SQUIN PECTEN
COQUILLE DOUGHBOY ESCALLOP
PECTINID
SCALLOPED INVECTED
(SUFF.) CRENATE
SCALP SCAUP SKELP ATTIRE
SCALPEL BISTOURY
SCALPER PUNTER
SCALY SCABBY SQUAMY LEPROSE
PALEATE LEPIDOTE SCABROUS
SQUAMOSE
SCAMP LAD RIP LIMB SLIM ROGUE
SKEMP SKIMP THIEF BOOGER
BUGGER FRIPON NICKUM RASCAL
SINNER SORREL SORROW
HALLION HESSIAN PEASANT
RAMMACK SKELLUM SLUBBER
SNOOZER BLIGHTER SCALAWAG
SLYBOOTS SPALPEEN VAGABOND
WIDDIFOW SCALLYWAG
SCAMPER LAMP CHEVY SCOUP
SCOUR CHIVVY BRATTLE SKITHER
SKITTER
SCAN PIPE GLASS METER DEVISE
SURVEY EXAMINE
SCANDAL GUP CLASH CRACK
ECLAT SHAME CALUMNY
OFFENSE SCANMAG SLANDER
SCANDALIZE SHOCK
SCANDALMONGER CLAT
SCANDALOUS UNHOLY
SHAMEFUL
SCANDINAVIAN DANE LAPP
NORSE SWEDE VIKING LOCHLIN
NORSEMAN NORTHMAN
SCANDIAN VARANGIAN
(PL.) OSTMEN
SCANT SHY JIMP LEAN MEET POOR
THIN SCAMP SHORT SKIMP SPLAY
BARISH GEASON LITTLE MEAGER
MEAGRE SCANTY SKINNY STINGY
STINTY SLENDER SCRATCHY
(PREF.) OLIG(O)
SCANTILY BARELY FEEBLY SMALLY
SCANTLY SPARSELY
SCANTINESS PENURY PARCITY
EXIGUITY SPARSITY
SCANTLING STUD FILET JOIST
FILLET BOLSTER RIBBAND
STUDDING
SCANTY BARE JIMP LANK LEAN
POOR SLIM EXILE GNEDE SCANT
SHORT SILLY SKIMP SPARE
FRUGAL MEAGER MEASLY SCRIMP
SKIMPY SLIGHT SPARSE SCRANNY
SCRIMPY SLENDER SPARING
EXIGUOUS PENURIOUS
SCAPEGOAT STOOGE
SCAPEGRACE SCALLYWAG
SKAINSMATE
SCAPHOID NAVICULAR
SCAPOLITE DIPYRE
SCAPULA BLADE OMOPLATE
SCAPULAR CUCULLA
SCAR ARR EYE WEM SEAM SEAR
WIPE CHALK FESTER KELOID
RADDLE STIGMA TRENCH

CHELOID SCARIFY CICATRIX
SMALLPOX CICATRICE
(— ON SAWED STONE) STUN
(— ON SEED) HILUM
(— ON TREE) CATFACE
SCARAB ATEUCHUS
SCARCE DEAR RARE THIN SLACK
DAINTY GEASON CLASSIC
UNCOMMON
(PREF.) SPAN(I)(O)
SCARCELY ILL VIX JIMP SCANT
BARELY HARDLY MERELY ONETHE
SCARCE SCRIMP WENETH
SCANTLY UNEATHS UNNETHE
SCARCITY LACK WANT FAULT
SCANT DEARTH FAMINE RARITY
PAUCITY
SCARE COW BOOF BREE FAZE
FEAR FLEG FLIG FRAY GAST HUSH
SHOO ALARM APPAL GALLY GLIFF
GLOFF PSYCH SPOOK AFFRAY
FRIGHT GASTER PSYCHE SCARIFY
STARTLE TERRIFY AFFRIGHT
FRIGHTEN
(— BIRDS) KEEP
(— OFF) SCAT
SCARECROW BOGLE BUCCA
MOGGY SEWEL BOGGLE DUDMAN
MALKIN MAUMET MAWKIN
SCARER SHEWEL BOGGART
BUGABOO DEADMAN HODMADOD
SHAWFOWL
SCARED SCART SCARY AFRAID
GOOSEY STREAKED
SCAREMONGER ALARMIST
SCARF BARB HOOD SASH ABNET
ASCOT BARBE CLOUD CYMAR
FICHU LUNGI NUBIA PAGRI
SHADE STOCK STOLE TABLE
THROW CRAVAT PEPLOS REBOZO
SCREEN SQUARE TAPALO TIPPET
UPARNA BURDASH DOPATTA
FOULARD MANIPLE MUFFLER
NECKTIE ORARIUM OVERLAY
PUGGREE SAUTOIR TALLITH
CLAUDENT COINTISE DOOPUTTY
LIRIPIPE LIRIPOOP MANTILLA
MUFFETEE SLENDANG
(— ON KNIGHT'S HELMET) COINTISE
(ARABIAN —) CABAAN
(FEATHER —) BOA
(PRAYER —) TALLIS TALLITH
SCARFING GRAFTING
SCARIFY LIFT
SCARLET LAC RED PINK TULY
GRAIN KERMES
SCARLET HAW HAWTHORN
SCARLET IBIS GUARA
SCARLET LETTER (AUTHOR OF —)
HAWTHORNE
(CHARACTER IN —) PEARL ROGER
ARTHUR HESTER PRYNNE
BELLINGHAM DIMMESDALE
CHILLINGWORTH
SCARLET LYCHNIS FIREBALL
NONESUCH
SCARLET TANAGER REDBIRD
FIREBIRD
SCARLIKE ULOID
SCARP CLIFF SCARF ESCARP
SCARPLET
SCATHING MORDANT SCALDING
SCATHINGLY ROUNDLY

SCATOLOGICAL BARNYARD

SCATTER DAD SOW TED FLEE
SALT SCAT SEED SHED SPEW
VOID FLING SCALE SCHAL SEVER
SHAKE SKAIL SPRAY STREW
STROW DISPEL PEPPER SHOWER
SKIVER SPARGE SPARSE SPREAD
SPRENG WINNOW DIFFUSE
DISBAND DISJECT FRITTER
RESOLVE SCAMBLE SHATTER
SKINKLE SKITTER SLATTER
SPARKLE SPARPLE SPATTER
SWATTER DISPERSE INTERSOW
SEPARATE SPLUTTER SPRINKLE
SQUANDER SQUATTER
(— **BAIT FOR FISH**) TOLE TOLL
(— **OVER**) BESTREW
(— **WATER**) SPLASH

SCATTERED LAX OPEN STRAY
DAIMEN SPARSE DIFFUSE
SPOTTED BESPRENT FUGITIVE
SPARSILE
(PREF.) LAXI

SCATTERING SOWING DIASPORA
SCATTERY

SCAUP DUCK DOGS DIVER
DUCKER DUNBIRD POCHARD
BLUEBILL GRAYBACK SHUFFLER

SCAVAGE SCEWING

SCAVENGE CLEANSE GARBAGE

SCAVENGER BUNGY RAKER
BHANGI BHUNGI MEHTAR
REMOVER SCAFFIE CORYDORA
HALALCOR RAMSHORN

SCAZON CHOLIAMB

SCEAT SKEAT STYCA

SCENE JOG SET CODA CYKE FLAT
SITE VIEW ARENA STAGE BRIDGE
VISION EPISODE PAGEANT
COULISSE EXTERIOR INTERIOR
PROSPECT TABLETOP
(— **IN OPERA**) SCENA
(— **OF ACTION**) STAGE
(— **OF ACTIVITY**) BEEHIVE
(— **OF CONFUSION**) BABEL BEDLAM
(**CLOSING** —) FINALE
(**FINAL** —) CURTAIN EPILOGUE

SCENERY DROP FLAT DECOR
CUTOUT NATURE IMAGERY
PROFILE
(**PIECE OF** —) MASKING

SCENESHIFTER GRIP

SCENT AIR DRAG NOSE ODOR
VENT WIND CIVET FAULT FLAIR
FUMET RELES SAVOR SMACK
SMELL SNIFF SNUFF SPOOR
TASTE CHYPRE ESSENCE INCENSE
NOSEGAY ODORIZE VERDURE
FUMIGATE MARECHAL PASTILLE
REDOLENCE
(— **OF ANIMAL FOLLOWED BY**
HOUNDS) FEUTE
(— **OF COOKING**) NIDOR
(— **OF FOX**) DRAG
(**FALSE** —) RIOT
(**LOST** —) FAULT

SCENTED OLENT ODORATE
PERFUMY ESSENCED

SCEPTER ROD WAND VERGE
BAUBLE CEPTER FERULA WARDER

SCHEDULE BOOK CARD HOLD LIST
SKED TIME PANEL SCRIP SCROW
SETUP SLATE TABLE SCROLL

CATALOG TABLEAU CALENDAR
REGISTER
(— **OF DUTIES**) TARIFF
(— **OF GAMES**) SEASON

SCHEDULED DUE

SCHEDULING (**TECHNIQUE FOR** —)
PERT

SCHEELITE TUNGSTEN

SCHEHERAZADE (**HUSBAND OF** —)
SCHAHRIAH
(**SISTER OF** —) DINARZADE

SCHEMA FORM

SCHEME AIM GIN LAY WAY WEB
CAST DART GAME PLAN PLAT
PLOT REDE SWIM ANGLE BABEL
CADRE DODGE DRAFT DRIFT
KNACK PINAX REACH SCALE
SETUP SHIFT TABLE THINK TRAIN
BRIGUE BUBBLE CIPHER DESIGN
DEVICE DEVISE FIGURE HOOKUP
POLICY SCHEMA SYSTEM TAMPER
THEORY UTOPIA COUNSEL
DRAUGHT GIMMICK IMAGINE
KNAVERY NOSTRUM PROJECT
PURPOSE CONSPIRE CONTRIVE
FORECAST GIMCRACK IDEOLOGY
INTRIGUE MANEUVER PLATFORM
PRACTICE TRIPOTER WINDMILL
MACHINATE
(— **OF RANK**) LADDER
(**ABORTIVE** —) SOOTERKIN
(**BETTING** —) SYSTEM
(**DECEITFUL** —) SHIFT
(**DELUSIVE** —) BUBBLE
(**DIAGRAMMATIC** —) PINAX
(**FANCIFUL** —) WINDMILL
(**FAVORITE** —) NOSTRUM
(**VISIONARY** —) BABEL

SCHEMER ARTIST DESIGNER
ENGINEER SCHEMIST SLEEVEEN

SCHEMING SCHEMY PLANFUL
SPIDERY FETCHING PRACTICE

SCHISM RENT SCISSION SCISSURE

SCHISMATIC HERETIC

SCHIST RAG AMPELITE MICACITE
MYLONITE OLLENITE PHYLLITE

SCHIZONT MONONT AGAMONT

SCHIZOPHRENIA CATATONY

SCHNAPPER WOLLOMAI

SCHOLAR TUG DEMY GAON IMAM
CLERK PUPIL DIVINE DOCTOR
FELLOW JURIST LAMDEN MASTER
PANDIT SABORA SAVANT SCOLOG
SHEIKH BIBLIST BOOKMAN
DANTIST LATINER LEARNER
MAULANA STUDENT BOURSIER
DISCIPLE HEBRAEAN HUMANIST
ISLAMIST MASORITE TABERDAR
THAUMASTE PHILOSOPHER
(— **OF QUEENS COLLEGE**)
TABERDAR
(PL.) LITERATI
AMERICAN LOWES BLYDEN
CONANT KELSEY MILLER SARTON
BABBITT GUMMERE SEYMOUR
HAMILTON HARKNESS PERCIVAL
STERRETT LOUNSBURY
AUSTRIAN SPANN
CANADIAN MACMECHAN
CHINESE YEN
CZECH JIRACEK SAFARIK
DANISH MADVIG GULDBERG
DUTCH COBET BURMAN ERASMUS

COORNHERT BILDERDIJK
ENGLISH KER BYNG LONG BYRON
CROFT ELYOT JAMES LOWTH
MAYOR PALEY ROGET YOUNG
ALCUIN ALFORD BAXTER BRIGHT
BROOME BUTLER COWELL
DASENT FARMER GODLEY
GROCYN HARRIS JEVONS
MURRAY NECKAM NEWMAN
NICOLL YAHUDA ALDHELM
ALDRICH BUTCHER DIODATI
HOLLAND LIDDELL MACKAIL
STANLEY CHRISTIE GRIERSON
HARRISON MCKERROW PATTISON
STRACHAN TUNSTALL TYRWHITT
CONINGTON NETTLESHIP
FINNISH LONNROT PORTHAN
KOSKENNIEMI
FLEMISH BLOMMAERT
FRENCH BUDE LAMY LUCE MAURY
PARIS BAILLY BERARD GAGUIN
MAGNIN MENAGE MICHEL
BROSSES CAUMONT CHASLES
DELISLE LEFRANC LONGNON
SOURIAU DEMOGEOT JAUCOURT
BARTHELEMY TAILLANDIER
GERMAN BLEEK HEYNE KLOTZ
KROLL LEYEN STAHR KOCHLY
RAUMER CONRING GOEDEKE
GOLTHER HEUSLER LUDWICH
MOMMSEN RIBBECK RUHNKEN
AUFRECHT BERNEKER BUTTMANN
HAINISCH PFEIFFER SPANHEIM
WEINHOLD KOSCHWITZ
CAMERARIUS
GREEK DION GAZA CORAY PALLES
DIDYMUS MUSURUS RHIANUS
PORPHYRY ATHENAEUS
CAECILIUS ZENODOTUS
CALLIMACHUS CHRYSOLORAS
HUNGARIAN BEL
ICELANDIC BLONDAL SAEMUND
VIGFUSSON
INDIAN PATANJALI
IRISH BALL BUTLER MAHAFFY
KEIGHTLEY
ITALIAN DONI ZENO GNOLI
MAFFEI VARCHI ALEANDRO
MARTELLI MARSILIUS NICCOLINI
TIRABOSCHI
JAPANESE NITOBE MABUCHI
MEXICAN GAMA
PERUVIAN MENDIBURU
POLISH CIOLEK CHODZKO
RACZYNSKI OSSOLINSKI
ZDZIECHOWSKI
PORTUGUESE BRAGA
ROMAN PLINY VARRO AUSONIUS
CENSORINUS
RUSSIAN LAVROV DRAGOMANOV
SCOTTISH LANG BLACKIE
GROSART LINDSAY BELLENDEN
MACDONALD
SPANISH OCHOA CASTRO VILLENA
SWEDISH MALMSTROM
STIERNHIELM
SWISS BODMER BREITINGER
PELLICANUS

SCHOLARLY CLERKLY ACADEMIC

SCHOLARSHIP ART BOOK BURSE
BURSARY DEMYSHIP LEARNING

SCHOLASTIC PEDANTIC

SCHOOL GAM TOL EDDY PREP

AGGIE BOOKS ECOLE HEDER
NYAYA SAKHA TEACH TRADE
TRAIN TUTOR ALJAMA CAMPUS
CHEDER CHURCH KUTTAB
KYAUNG MADHAB MALIKI RABFAK
SCHOLA SCHULE SQUEEL TRIPOS
ACADEME ACADEMY CRAMMER
MADRASA PENSION STUDIUM
YESHIVA AUDITORY DOCUMENT
EXERCISE EXTERNAT PEDAGOGY
SEMINARY
(— **FOR JUDO OR KARATE**) DOJO
(— **FOR SINGERS**) MAITRISE
(— **OF BLACKFISH**) GRIND
(— **OF BUDDHISM**) CHAN RITSU
DHYANA SANRON
(— **OF FISH**) HERD SCALE SCULL
(— **OF HINDU PHILOSOPHY**) NYAYA
(— **OF PAINTING**) GENRE
(— **OF PHILOSOPHY**) SECT
ACADEMY AUDITORY
(— **OF VEDA**) SAKHA SHAKHA
(— **OF WHALES**) GAM POD
(**ART** —) BAUHAUS LUMINISM
(**AZTEC** —) CALMECAC
(**COMPARATIVE** —) FOLKLORE
(**DAY** —) EXTERNAT
(**ELEMENTARY** —) GRADES
(**HIGH** —) HIGH ACADEMY COLLEGE
(**MOSLEM** —) HANAFI KUTTAB
SHAFII HANBALI
(**REFORM** —) BORSTAL
(**RELIGIOUS** —) ALJAMA YESHIVA
(**RIDING** —) MANEGE
(**SANSKRIT** —) TOL
(**SCOTCH** —) SQUEEL
(**SECONDARY** —) LYCEE LYCEUM
COLEGIO
(**WRESTLING** —) PALESTRA

SCHOOLBOOK COCKER

SCHOOLBOY SCUG PETTY
CLERGION

SCHOOL FOR SCANDAL (**AUTHOR**
OF —) SHERIDAN
(**CHARACTER IN** —) MARIA MOSES
PETER JOSEPH OLIVER ROWLEY
TEAZLE CANDOUR CHARLES
PREMIUM SURFACE
SNEERWELL

SCHOOLHOUSE PORTABLE

SCHOOLING LEARNING

SCHOOLMASTER BEAK CAJI CAXI
AKHUN KHOJA KHODJA MASTER
PEDANT AKHOOND DOMINIE
PEDAGOG ORBILIUS

SCHOOLROOM HOMEROOM

SCHOOL SHARK TOPE TOPER

SCHOOLWORK BOOKWORK

SCHOONER JACK TERN QUART
QUINT WUINT PUNGEY
BALLAHOO

SCHORL COCKLE

SCHRADAN OMPA

SCHROTHER SHREDDER

SCHUYT SHOE SCOUT EELBOAT

SCIATICA BONESHAW

SCIENCE ART OLOGY SOPHY
MATHESIS SCIENTIA
(— **OF ALGAE**) ALGOLOGY
(— **OF ANIMALS**) ZOOLOGY
(— **OF AQUEOUS VAPOR**)
ATMOLOGY
(— **OF ATOMS**) ATOMICS

(— OF BEING OR REALITY)
ONTOLOGY
(— OF BIOLOGICAL STATISTICS)
BIOMETRY
(— OF BREEDING) GENETICS
(— OF CAUSES) ETIOLOGY
(— OF CHARACTER) ETHOLOGY
(— OF CLASSIFICATION OF
DISEASES) NOSOLOGY
(— OF DOSES) DOSOLOGY
POSOLOGY
(— OF EARTH'S FORMATION)
GEOGONY
(— OF ELECTIONS) PSEPHOLOGY
(— OF EXCHANGE) CAMBISTRY
(— OF FERMENTATION) ZYMOLOGY
(— OF FERNS) PTERIDOLOGY
(— OF FORMS OF SPEECH)
GRAMMAR
(— OF FRUIT GROWING) POMOLOGY
(— OF FUNDS MANAGEMENT)
FINANCE
(— OF GEMS) GEMMARY
GEMOLOGY
(— OF GOD) DIVINITY
(— OF GOVERNMENT) POLITICS
(— OF HEALTH MAINTENANCE)
HYGIENE
(— OF HEAT) PYROLOGY
THERMOTICS
(— OF HISTORY OF EARTH)
GEOLOGY
(— OF HUMAN SETTLEMENTS)
EKISTICS
(— OF IDEAS) IDEOLOGY
(— OF INTELLECT) NOOLOGY
(— OF LAW) NOMOLOGY
(— OF LIFE) BIOLOGY
(— OF LIFE INFLUENCES) EUGENICS
(— OF LIFE OF TREES) SILVICS
(— OF LIGHT) OPTICS
(— OF MEASURING TIME)
HOROLOGY
(— OF MEDIEVAL CHEMISTRY)
ALCHEMY
(— OF MIDWIFERY) TOKOLOGY
(— OF MORAL DUTY) ETHICS
(— OF MOSSES) BRYOLOGY
(— OF MOUNTAINS) OROLOGY
(— OF MUSCLES) MYOLOGY
(— OF NUMBERS COMBINATIONS)
ALGEBRA
(— OF PERSUADING A GOD)
THEURGY
(— OF PLANTS) BOTANY
(— OF QUANTITY) POSOLOGY
(— OF RACIAL IMPROVEMENT)
EUGENICS
(— OF REASONING) LOGIC
(— OF RECORDING GENEALOGIES)
HERALDRY
(— OF REFRIGERATION) CRYOLOGY
(— OF REMEDIES) ACOLOGY
(— OF SERUMS) SEROLOGY
(— OF SMELLS) OSMICS
(— OF SOILS) PEDOLOGY
(— OF SOUND) PHONICS
ACOUSTICS
(— OF SPATIAL MAGNITUDES)
GEOMETRY
(— OF STRUCTURE OF ANIMALS)
ANATOMY
(— OF THE EAR) OTOLOGY

(— OF TIDES) TIDOLOGY
(— OF TOUCH DATA) HAPTICS
(— OF VALUES) AXIOLOGY
(— OF VERSIFICATION) PROSODY
(— OF VIRTUE) ARETAICS
(— OF WEIGHT OR GRAVITY)
BAROLOGY
(— OF WINES) ENOLOGY
OENOLOGY
(BRANCH OF —) BIONICS
(LEGAL —) LAW
(MILITARY —) STRATEGY
(NATURAL —) STINKS PHYSICS
(PHYSICAL —) PHILOSOPHY
(RELIGIOUS —) THEOLOGY
(SUFF.) LOGER LOGIA(N)
LOGIC(AL) LOGIST LOGUE LOGY
OLOGY SOPH(ER)(IC)(IST)(Y)
(RELATING TO —) METRIC
SCIENTIST BOFFIN
SCIMITAR SAX SEAX TURK
KHEPESH TULWAUR
SCINDAPSUS POTHOS
SCINTILLATE SNAP FLASH GLEAM
GLANCE GLITTER SPARKLE
TWINKLE
SCINTILLATION SPARKLE
SPARKLET
SCION IMP ROD CION CYON ROOT
SLIP GRAFT SPRIG BRANCH
SPROUT SARMENT SETLING
SCISSORS SHEARS CLIPPER
SECATEUR
(PREF.) FORFICI
SCLERITE TORMA LABIUM PLANTA
PLAGULA AXILLARY EPIMERON
SCLERODERMA MORPHEA
SCLEROPROTEIN SPONGIN
SCLEROTIUM ERGOT SCLEROTE
TUCKAHOE
SCOFF DOR GAB GALL GECK GIBE
GIRD JEER JIBE MOCK RAIL
CURSE FLEER FLOUT GLEEK
SCORN SCOUT SNEER TAUNT
DERIDE REPROVE RIDICULE
SCOFFER MOCKER ABDERITE
SCOLD JAW MAG MOB NAG RAG
ROW WIG YAP BAWL CALL CAMP
CANT DING FLAY FRAB FUSS
HAZE JACK JOBE JOWL JUMP
RAIL RANT RATE REDD RICK
SHAW SNAG SNUB TUCK YAFF
ABUSE BARGE BASTE BOAST
CHIDE DRESS FLIRT FLITE PRATE
RANDY SCALD SCORE SHORE
SHREW SLANG STORM TARGE
VIXEN BERATE BOUNCE CALLET
CAMPLE CARPET HAMMER
HOORAY HURRAH MAGPIE
RATTLE REHETE REVILE TATTER
THREAP TONGUE YAFFLE YANKIE
CHANNER REPROVE TRIMMER
TROUNCE UPBRAID BALLYRAG
BERATTLE BETONGUE CHASTISE
CIDESTER DINGDONG RIXATRIX
SCOLDING JAW HURL JESSE
SCOLD DIRDUM JAWING RAKING
RATTLE SISERA FLITING HEARING
LECTURE RAGGING WIGGING
BLESSING CARRITCH JOBATION
SCOLEX HEAD
SCOLYTUS IPS
SCONCE SWAPE APPLIQUE

SCONE FARL FARLE
SCOOP BAIL BALE DRAG ROUT
DIDLE GOUGE KEACH SHAUL
SKEET BUCKET DIPPER DISHER
SHOVEL WIMBLE SCRAPER
SCUPPET SKIMMER SKIPPET
SCOOPFUL
(— FOR CANNON) LADLE
(— FOR DAMPENING CANVAS)
SKEET
(— FOR GRAIN) WECHT
(— UP) LAP LAVE GATHER
(CHEESE —) PALE
(GLASSMAKING —) PADDLE
(JAI ALAI —) CHISTERA
(LONG-HANDLED —) DIDLE
(SURGICAL —) CURET CURETTE
SCOOT SCOUT SKEET SKYHOOT
SCOPE AIM AREA AMBIT POWER
RANGE REACH ROUND SCALE
SCOOP SWEEP VERGE SCOUTH
SPHERE TETHER BREADTH
CIRCUIT COMPASS OPERAND
PURVIEW CONFINES DIAPASON
LATITUDE
(— OF VISION) COMMAND
(FREE —) SWING
SCOPOLINE OSCIN OSCINE
SCORBUTUS SCURVY
SCORCH BURN CHAR PLOT SCAM
SEAR ADURE ADUST BROIL
PARCH PLAUT REESE SCALD
SCAUM SINGE SWEAL SWELT
BIRSLE BISHOP DEGREE SMITCH
SOTTER SPARCH SWINGE SWITHE
BLISTER BRISTLE FRIZZLE
SCORKLE SCOWDER SWITHEN
SWITHER TORRIFY FIREFANG
SCOUTHER SCOWTHER
SCORCHED ADUST LEEPIT
SCORCHER SIZZLER
(PREF.) SIRI(O)
SCORCHING BAKING FIRING
ADURENT SCALDING
SCORE ACE CUT LAW RIT RUN
CARD DEBT DROP GAME GOAL
HAIL HOLE MAKE MARK NICK
POST RIDE SLOG CHASE CORGE
COUNT EXTRA NOTCH OPERA
TALLY COOREE FURROW SAFETY
SCOTCH SCRIVE SPADES STRING
TARGET TICKET TWENTY
CONVERT SCORING SCRATCH
SQUEEZE GAMEBALL PARTITUR
PLACEKICK
(— FOR ALE) ALESHOT
(— HEAVILY AGAINST) SHELL
(— IN BRIDGE) BOARD BONUS
SWING
(— IN CRIBBAGE) GO PEG FIFTEEN
(— IN CRICKET) BLOB CENTURY
(— IN PIQUET) CAPOT
(— OF NOTHING) DUCK
(APTITUDE —) STANINE
(BASKETBALL —) HOOP
(BOWLING —) PINFALL
(GOLF —) DEUCE EAGLE BIRDIE
BUZZARD
(PINOCHLE —) LAST
(TENNIS —) CALL FIVE LOVE
DEUCE FORTY FIFTEEN
(THREE —) SHOCK
(TIE —) HALVE DEADLOCK

(PL.) MUSIC
SCORED SULCATE SULCATED
SCOREKEEPER SCORER TALLIER
TALLYMAN
SCORER NIB MARKER NOTCHER
SCORIA SCUM SLAG CINDER
SULLAGE
SCORIFIER CAPSULE
SCORIFY SMELT
SCORN GECK LOUT HOKER SCARN
SPURN BISMER SLIGHT CONTEMN
DESPISE DESPITE DISDAIN
CONTEMPT DERISION MISPRIZE
SCORNFUL SAUCY SCORNY SNIFFY
SNIFTY HAUGHTY FRUMPISH
INSOLENT SARDONIC
SCORNFULLY ASKEW ASWASH
SCORPION NEPA ALACRAN
STINGER UROPYGI ARACHNID
PEDIPALP WHIPTAIL
SCORPION FISH LAPON SERRAN
HOGFISH SCULPIN LORICATE
RASCACIO
SCORPION FLY PANORPID
SCOT (ALSO SEE SCOTSMAN) CELT
JOCK KELT SANDY SAXON
SCOTTY BLUECAP SCOTSMAN
(PL.) SAWNY SAWNEY LALLANS
SCOTCH TRIG SCOAT SCOTS
SCOTTISH
SCOTCHMAN MAC GAUL SANDY
TARTAN SCOTCHY SCOTTIE
SCOTSMAN
SCOTER COOT FILK DIVER SCOUT
WHILK BASQUE DUCKER SURFER
PISHAUG SCOOTER SKUNKTOP
SCOTIA MOUTH
SCOTIST DUNCE
SCOTLAND ALBYN ALBANY
ALBION SCOTIA ALBAINN
ALBANIA
(NORTHERN —) PICTLAND

AUCHLET CHALDER CHOPPIN MUTCHKIN STIMPART
MOUNTAIN: HOPE ATTOW DEARG NEVIS TINTO WYVIS CHEVIOT MACDHUI
NATIVE: GAEL PICT SCOT
ORDER: THISTLE
REGION: FIFE BORDERS GRAMPIAN
RESORT: OBAN
RIVER: AYR DEE DON ESK TAY DOON GLEN NITH NORN SPEY AFTON ANNAN CLYDE FORTH GARRY TWEED YTHAN AFFRIC TEVIOT TUMMEL DEVERON FINDHORN
SEAPORT: ALLOA LEITH DUNDEE ABERDEEN
TOWN: AYR DUNS OBAN WICK ALLOA BRORA CUPAR ELLON LEITH NAIRN PERTH SALEN TROON DUNDEE GIRVAN HAWICK DUNKELD GLASGOW PAISLEY ABERDEEN DUMFRIES GREENOCK KIRKWALL STIRLING
WATERFALL: GLOMACH
WEIGHT: BOLL DROP TRONE BUSHEL

SCOTSMAN SANDY SAWNY BLUECAP
SCOTTISH SCOTCH SCOTLAND
SCOTTISH TERRIER DIEHARD SCOTTIE VERMINER
SCOUNDREL RAP PIMP SCAB VILE WARY BLECK FILTH KNAVE SHREW SMAIK SWEEP THIEF WHAUP BRIBER LIMMER SLOVEN VARLET CATAIAN GLUTTON HALLION NITHING SCROYLE SKELLUM VILIACO VILLAIN WARLOCK BEZONIAN LIDDERON MASCHANT
SCOUNDRELLY VILLAIN
SCOUR ASH BEAT RAKE SCUM SEEK SIND SKIR SCOOR SCRUB SKIRR SWEEP DRENCH SCURRY SLUICE DEGRADE FURBISH BACKWASH STONEFILE (PL.) SKIT
SCOURER BLOOMER DOLLIER PICKLER
SCOURGE EEL TAW LASH CURSE FLAIL KNOUT SLASH SWING BALEYS PLAGUE SWINGE SCORPION
SCOURGER WHIPSTER
SCOURING BEAT SCOUR HUSHING SCRUBBING
SCOUT SPY BEAR LION SKIP ROVER SPIAL VISOR ESPIAL GAYCAT DESPISE MARINER PICKEER PIONEER SCOURER WATCHER EMISSARY OUTRIDER OUTSCOUT SCURRIER SKIRMISH (BOY —) CUB BOBCAT SCOUTER WEBELOS EXPLORER
SCOW ACCON FLOAT GARVEY
SCOWL LOUR FROWN GLARE GLOOM GLOUT LOWER SKIME GLOWER VENNER GLOOMING
SCOWLING FROWNY GLARING
SCRABBLE PAW RAKE GROPE CLAMBER SCRAMBLE

SCRAGGY WEEDY
SCRAM HOP LAM BUNK BUGGER BUGOFF BUZZOFF
SCRAMBLE MUSS SPURL SCRAWM SPRAWL CLAMBER LOUSTER SCRABBLE SCRAFFLE SCRATTLE SPRACHLE
SCRAP BIT END JAG ORT PIP CRAP ITEM JAGG JUNK PICK SNAP BRAWL GRAIN PATCH SCRAN SHRED THRUM WASTE DISCARD MAMMOCK REMNANT FRACTION SCRAPPET SKERRICK SNATTOCK (— FOR PATCHING) SPETCH (— OF PAPER) SCRIP (— OF SONG) CATCH (— OF WRITING) SCRAPE (FOOD —S) BROCK (LITERARY —S) ANA (RAGGED —) SCART (PL.) ORTS SCRAN RELICS SCROFF GARBAGE GUBBINGS
SCRAPE LEG RUB CLAW COMB RAZE CLAUT CURET ERADE ERODE GRATE GRAZE GRIDE SCALP SCART SCUFF SHAVE ABRADE HOBBLE RUGINE SCREED SCROOP CORRADE CURETTE JACKPOT SCRATCH SCRABBLE (— ALONG) HARL HARLE SHOOL (— GOLF CLUB ON GROUND) SCLAFF (— OFF) SPUD (— OUT) ERASE HOLLOW (— SKINS) MOON SCUD FLESH HARASS (— TOGETHER) RAKE GLEAN MUCKER SCAMBLE (— WITH FEET) SCAUT (PREF.) RAMENTI SCAPI
SCRAPED BRIGHT
SCRAPER PAN PIG HARL SLIP CURET GLOVE HARLE QUIRL RASER SPOON DOCTOR FRESNO GRADER GRATER RASPER CURETTE FLANGER LEVELER RACLOIR SLUSHER STRIGIL GRATTOIR SCRAPPLE TERRACER UNHAIRER
SCRAPING HARL GRIDE RASURE (CRACKER —S) CUSH (METAL —S) DIET (PL.) RAMENTA
SCRAPMAN CHIPMAN
SCRAPPER BREAKER FIGHTER
SCRAPPLE PANHAS PONHAWS
SCRAPPY BITTY SNATCHY
SCRATCH RAT RIT CLAW CRAB RACE RAIN RAKE RAPE RASE RAUK RAZE RISP RIST SHAB SLUG STUN CHALK CLAUT CLAWK CURRY FRUSH GRAZE RANCH SCART SCLUM SCORE SCRAB SCRAT SCROB SCRUB SHRUB SKELP TEASE TOUCH BRUISE CANCEL CRATCH RASURE RIPPLE SCORCH SCOTCH SCRAPY SCRAWK SCRAWL SCRAWM SCRAZE SCRIVE TORACE DECLARE EMERIZE EXPUNGE SCARIFY SCRABBLE SCRATTLE SCRIBBLE (— OUT MORTAR) POINT (PREF.) RAMENTI
SCRATCHER RASER

SCRAWL SCRAWM SPRAWL SCRATCH SCRABBLE SCRIBBLE SQUIGGLE
SCRAWNY BONY LEAN SLINK SCRANK SCRAGGY SCRANKY SCRANNY SCRAGGED (— PERSON OR ANIMAL) RIBE
SCREAM CRY YAW REME WEAK YARM YAUP YAWL YAWP YOWT SKIRL SHRAME SHRIEK SHRILL SQUALL SQUAWL YAMMER SCREECH YELLOCH SKELLOCH
SCREAMER CHAJA ANHIMA
SCREECH QUAWK QUOCK SCREAM SCREEK SCRITCH SKREIGH ULULATE SKELLOCH
SCREECH OWL STRICH
SCREED BLAUD TIRADE
SCREEN TRY CAGE GOBO HARP HIDE LAWN MASK PICK REJA SCUG SEPT SIFT TENT VEIL ARRAS BLIND CHEEK CHICK CLOAK CLOSE COVER FIGHT GAUZE GRATE HOARD SHADE SHOJI SIEVE SPEER SPIER TATTY BAFFLE BASKET BORDER CANVAS DEFEND ESCORT HALLAN MEDIUM PURDAH RESEAU SCHERM SCONCE SHAKER SHIELD SHROUD THREAD VOIDER CEILING CONCEAL CRIBBLE CURTAIN FLYWIRE GOGGLES GRIZZLY REREDOS SECLUDE SHELTER SHUTTER TESTUDO TROMMEL BACKSTOP BESCREEN BLINDAGE COVERING DIFFUSER ECLIPSER EXCLUDER HOARDING OCCULTER PARAVENT PARCLOSE PAVISADE SCREENER SPLASHER STRAINER TRAVERSE UMBRELLA (— ALONGSIDE SHIP) PAVISADE (— BEHIND ALTAR) REREDOS (— FOR BATTING PRACTICE) CAGE (— FOR SHIP'S COMBATANTS) FIGHT (— FOR SIZING ORE) GRATE TROMMEL (— FOR THEATER LIGHT) JELLY MEDIUM (— IN BASKETBALL) PICK (— OF BAMBOO SLIPS) CHEEK CHICK (— OF BRUSHWOOD) SCHERM (— OF FIRE) BARRAGE (— OF SHIELDS FOR TROOPS) TESTUDO (— OF TAPESTRY) ARRAS CEILING (— ON AUTOMOBILE) GRILL GRILLE (— TO PROTECT LOOKOUTS) DODGER (— USED BY ARCHERS) PANNIER (BULLETPROOF —) MANTA MANTEL MANTELET (CHANCEL —) JUBE (FIRE —) FENDER (MECHANICALLY ACTUATED —) GRIZZLY (PAPER —) SHOJI (PL.) CANCELLI
SCREENED BLIND SECLUDED
SCREENINGS CULM SLACK SLECK
SCREENPLAY SCENARIO
SCREW HOB VISE WORM CRICK

FEEZE SCROW WREST TEMPER TOGGLE COCHLEA AIRSCREW FLATHEAD SETSCREW THUMBKIN WINDMILL (KIND OF —) ALLEN MEANTIME (PART OF —) HEAD ROOT CREST PITCH POINT SHANK THREAD
SCREWBALL KOOK ZANY FLAKE ECCENTRIC NONSENSICAL
SCREW BEAN MESQUITE SCREWPOD TORNILLA
SCREWED SQUINCH
SCREWER WORMER
SCREWMAN JACKMAN
SCREW PINE IE ARA HALA IEIE AGGAG PALMA VACOA VACONA LAUHALA PANDANUS
SCREW TREE TWISTY
SCRIBBLE SQUIB DOODLE SCRAWL SCRATCH REMARQUE SCRABBLE SQUIGGLE
SCRIBE EZRA CLERK THOTH BOOKER PENMAN SCRIVE SOPHER WRITER GRAFFER MASORET SCRIVAN NOVERINT PENCLERK SCRIPTOR SCRIVANO (PL.) SOPHERIM
SCRIMMAGE MAUL BULLY ROUGE SCRAP BICKER SPLORE SKIRMISH
SCRIMP HINCH SCREW SKIMP
SCRIPT BOOK NEUM RONDE SERTA SERTO NASKHI NESKHI SCRITE SOOLOOS THULUTH BASTARDA GURMUKHI HIRAGANA KANARESE MAGHRIBI MAITHILI MEROITIC NASTALIQ SCENARIO
SCRIPTURE WRIT AGAMA CHING SUTRA SUTTA (HINDU —) VEDA (PL.) BIBLE GRANTH GRUNTH TANACH TENACH SHASTRA
SCRIVENER PENMAN WRITER GRAFFER SCRIVER NOVERINT TABELLION
SCROFULA EVIL CRUELS STRUMA
SCROLL BEND ROLL LABEL SCRIT AMULET ESCROL LEGEND SCRAWL STEMMA VOLUME VOLUTE EVOLUTE PAPYRUS RINCEAU BANDEROL CARTOUCH MAKIMONO
SCROLL-LIKE TURBINAL
SCROPHULARIA FIGWORT
SCROTUM BAG COD PURSE (PREF.) OSCHE(O) SCROT(I)(O)
SCROUNGER SCAMBLER
SCRUB FILE SCROG COPPET MAQUIS SCODGY CLEANSE SCRUBBER YANNIGAN
SCRUBBY SHRUBBY
SCRUBLAND GARIGUE GARRIGUE
SCRUFF CUFF NAPE SCUFF SCROFF
SCRUPLE PASS DEMUR DOUBT FORCE POINT QUALM STAND STICK BOGGLE SCOTCH STRAIN STICKLE STUMBLE
SCRUPULOUS NICE SPICED TENDER CAREFUL FINICKY PRECISE DELICATE QUALMISH
SCRUTINIZE PRY SEE SPY SCAN VIEW AUDIT PROBE SIGHT SOUND VISIT PERUSE SURVEY EXAMINE INSPECT ENSEARCH TRAVERSE

SCRUTINIZING NARROW SCANNING

SCRUTINY EYE SEARCH CANVASS EXAMINE HAWKEYE PERUSAL DOCIMASY

SCRYER SEER

SCUD RACK RAMP SKID SKIM SKIP SCOOT SPOON

SCUDAMORE (LOVER OF —) AMORETTA

SCUDO FILIPPO

SCUFF SLARE SLIDE SCLAFF SCUFFER SCUFFLE SHUFFLE

SCUFFLE CUFF BUSTLE CLINCH CUFFLE TUSSLE WISTER BAGARRE BRULYIE SHAMBLE SHUFFLE SCRUFFLE

SCULL FUNNY SKULL

SCULLERY SINKROOM

SCULLION GIPPO SCULL SLUSH GALOPIN SWILLER CUSTROUN QUISTRON

SCULPIN COTTID GRUBBY JOHNNY BIGHEAD DRUMMER BULLHEAD BULLPOUT CABEZONE HARDHEAD LORICATE SCALAWAG

SCULPTOR CARVER GRAVER IMAGER MARBLER PLASTIC
AMERICAN FRY BALL HART IVES KECK LADD MEAD RUSH TAFT VOLK WARD ADAMS AKERS BEACH BROWN CLARK DOYLE EVANS GOULD HOXLE JONES KELLY KONTI MEARS MILLS PERRY PRATT STONE YOUNG AITKEN BARTHE BITTER BUFANO CALDER CLARKE COUPER CURTIS DALLIN EAKINS EBERLE ELWELL FRASER FRAZEE FRENCH GRAFLY GRIMES HARVEY HOSMER HUGHES KEMEYS KINNEY KITSON LAWRIE MOZIER NEWMAN PALMER POTTER POWERS PUTNAM RIMMER ROGERS RUMSEY WALKER WARNER ZORACH BARNARD BISSELL BORGLUM BRENNER BRIGHAM EDSTROM EZEKIEL GELLERT GODDARD GREGORY HANCOCK HARTLEY HOFFMAN JACKSON JAEGERS KENDALL LAESSLE LAURENT LONGMAN LUKEMAN MACNEIL MANSHIP MARTINY MILMORE NIEHAUS NOGUCHI OCONNOR PROCTOR ROBERTS SCHULER SCUDDER SIEVERS SIMMONS WHITNEY ALBRIGHT ATCHISON BARTLETT BREWSTER CONNELLY CRAWFORD DAVIDSON FLANAGAN LACHAISE LENTELLI MCCARTAN MULLIGAN NADELMAN ODONOVAN PARAMINO RINEHART CLEVENGER GREENOUGH HUMPHREYS MACDONALD REMINGTON RUCKSTULL VALENTINE ARCHIPENKO MACMONNIES PICCIRILLI
ARGENTINIAN ALONZO
ATHENIAN ANTENOR
AUSTRIAN DONNER NATTER TILGNER STRASSER
BELGIAN GEEFS FRAIKIN KESSELS

LALAING MEUNIER SIMONIS STAPPEN LAMBEAUX TONGERLOO
CANADIAN HEBERT MACCARTHY
CZECH STRUSA MYSLBEK
DANISH BISSEN JERICHAU WILLUMSEN THORVALDSEN
DUTCH VRIES TASSAERT DESJARDINS
ENGLISH BELL FORD GILL JOHN SWAN WARD WOOD ANGEL BACON BAILY BANKS BATES BOEHM COLIN DURST JONES MOORE RHIND STONE TWEED WATTS ARCHER DOBSON GIBSON JAGGER KENNET LANDAU EPSTEIN FLAXMAN GIBBONS GILBERT STEVENS WOOLNER ARMSTEAD CHANTREY FRAMPTON SHERIDAN MACKENNAL KENNINGTON WESTMACOTT THORNYCROFT
FLEMISH BOLOGNE
FRENCH ADAM ETEX RUDE UZES BARYE BOSIO CHAPU CRAUK DALOU DURET LEMOT PAJOU PILON PUECH RODIN DANTAN DEJOUX DUBOIS DUMONT GOUJON HOUDON ISELIN LEGROS MERCIE MILLET ROCHET ANGUIER BEGUINE BOUCHER CARRIES CHAUDET CLODION COLOMBE COUSTOU DESPIAU FREMIET LEMAIRE LEMOYNE MAILLET MAILLOL PIGALLE PRADIER PREAULT RICHIER CAFFIERI CARPEAUX CAVELIER CHAPLAIN COYSEVOX FALCONET FOYATIER GIRARDON GODEBSKI JOUFFROY LEPAUTRE SARRAZIN BARTHOLDI BEAUNEVEU BOURDELLE CLESINGER FALGUIERE INJALBERT LANDOWSKI ROUBILLAC BARTHOLOME CASSEGRAIN CHARPENTIER DELAPLANCHE
GERMAN HAHN KISS LENZ NAHL CAUER KOLBE KRAFT OESER RAUCH STOSS STUCK WOLFF BANDEL BLASER GEIGER HABICH HAHNEL HALBIG HERTER HOSAUS WAGNER AFINGER BARLACH BELLING KAUPERT KLIMSCH KLINGER KRELING SCHAPER EBERHARD EBERLEIN FERNKORN SCHLUTER ZUMBUSCH DANNECKER ENGELHARD MAGNUSSEN RIETSCHEL SIEMERING UECHTRITZ LEINBERGER SCHWANTHALER RIEMENSCHNEIDER
GREEK MYRON CHARES ONATAS SCOPAS AGASIAS BOETHUS BRYAXIS CALAMIS CRITIUS PHIDIAS SCYLLIS AGELADAS CANACHUS CRESILAS DAMOPHON LYSIPPUS PAEONIUS SOCIBIUS AGESANDER ALCAMENES ARCHERMUS BATHYCLES EUPHRANOR LEOCHARES PASITELES TAURISCUS TIMOTHEUS POLYCLITUS POLYEUCTUS PRAXITELES AGORACRITUS ATHENODORUS

CALLIMACHUS LYSISTRATUS CEPHISODOTUS
IRISH FOLEY MACDOWELL FITZGERALD
ITALIAN VELA BANCO DANTI DUPRE LEONI PORTA RIZZO VINCI CANOVA GIOTTO PISANO ROBBIA SOLARI ALGARDI BERNINI CELLINI FIESOLE LAURANA MAZZONI TRIBOLO AMMANATI ANTELAMI BARBIERE BOCCIONI CAMPAGNA CERACCHI CIVITALI LOMBARDO MARCHESI TENERANI BARTOLINI BEGARELLI BORROMINI DONATELLO SANSOVINO MODIGLIANI MONTEVERDE VERROCCHIO MICHELANGELO
NORWEGIAN VIGELAND
ROMAN COSMATI
RUMANIAN BRANCUSI
RUSSIAN ORLOVSKI ANTOKOLSKI
SPANISH CANO MENA SILOE PICASSO HERNANDEZ BERRUGUETE
SWEDISH ZORN MILLES SERGEL BYSTROM BORJESON FOGELBERG
SWISS HOERBST KISSLING

SCULPTURAL PLASTIC

SCULPTURE CAMEO DRAFT GRAVE SCULP BRONZE ENTAIL GISANT SCULPT CARVING DRAUGHT ENGRAVE GRADINO IMAGERY INSCULP STABILE MORTORIO NATIVITY PORTRAIT PREDELLA SCULLION

SCULPTURED GRAVEN GLYPHIC

SCUM BRAT FOAM GALL HEAD REAM SCUD SILT SKIM SKIN DROSS FROTH SCURF SLOAK SLOKE SLUSH SPUME FLURRY MANTLE MOTHER REFUSE RIDDAM SCRUFF BLANKET CACHAZA OFFSCUM LAITANCE PELLICLE SANDIVER SCOURING SCUMMING

SCUP BREAM PORGY SPARID SCUPPAUG

SCURF SCALD SCALL DANDER FURFUR SCRUFF DANDRUFF

SCURFY SCALD SCURVY LEPROSE SCRUFFY LEPIDOTE SCABROUS SCABERULOUS

SCURRILITY ABUSE REPROACH

SCURRILOUS LOW FOUL VILE DIRTY GROSS RIBALD VULGAR ABUSIVE SCURRIL INDECENT

SCURRY BELT CRAB SKIN CURRY HURRY SCOUR SKICE SKURRY SCUFFLE SCUTTER SCUTTLE SKELTER SKITTER

SCURRYING SKITTER

SCURVY SCALD SCUMMY SHABBY ROYNOUS SCORBUCH SCORBUTE UNLIKING

SCUT BUN

SCUTAGE ESCUAGE

SCUTATE CLYPEATE

SCUTCH SCOTCH SWINGLE

SCUTE PLATE SCUTUM SCUTELLA

SCUTELLATION SCALING

SCUTIFORM PELTATE

SCUTTLE HOD CRAB SKEP BEETLE MANHOLE SCUDDLE

SCUTTER SCRATTLE
SCUTTLEBUTT CASK RUMOR GOSSIP FOUNTAIN
SCYLLA (FATHER OF —) NISUS TYPHON
SCYLLITOL INOSITOL
SCYPHUS PYXIS
SCYTHE SY LEA HOOK MEAK CRADLE
SCYTHIAN LAMB BAROMETZ
SEA ZEE BAHR BLUE BRIM FOAM FRET GULF HOLM LAVE MAIN RACE TIDE WAVE BRINE BRINY FLOAT FLOOD LOUGH OCEAN AEQUOR PONTUS SEALET STRAND TETHYS CHANNEL HYALINE NEPTUNE BOSPORUS DEEPNESS SEAFLOOD THALASSA
(**— DIVINITY**) TRITON
(**— GOD**) PROTEUS
(**— LETTER**) PASSPORT
(**HEAVY —**) POPPLE
(**MODERATE —**) SEAWAY
(**PREF.**) HAL(I)(IO)(O) MARI MER PELAG(O) THALASS(I)(IO)(O) THALATTO
SEA ANEMONE POLYP DAHLIA OPELET ACTINIA VESTLET ACTINIAN ZOANTHID
SEA BASS HANAHILL HUMPBACK SERRANID TALLYWAG
SEA BEAR OTARIOID
SEABIRD HAGDON
SEA BISCUIT BREAD GALETTE PANTILE
SEABOARD COAST
SEA BREAD HARDTACK
SEA BREAM TAI CARP CHAD PORGY ROMAN BRAISE SARGUS SPARID TARWHINE
SEA BUTTERFLY PTEROPOD
SEACOAST BANK SEABOARD SEASHORE
SEA COW SIREN DUGONG MANATEE RHYTINA SIRENIAN
SEA CUCUMBER BALATE TREPANG CUCUMBER SYNAPTID TEATFISH
SEADOG FOGBOW
SEA DRAGON PEGASID QUAVIVER
SEA DUCK DIVER EIDER DIPPER DUCKER SCOTER
SEA EAGLE ERN ERNE PYGARG PYGARGUS
SEA-EAR ABALONE
SEAFARER SEAGOER
SEA FOX THRASHER
SEA GIRDLE CUVY CUTWEED
SEA GULL COB GOR MEW COBB ANNET COBBE POPELER
(**AUTHOR OF —**) CHEKHOV
(**CHARACTER IN —**) NINA IRINA TRIGORIN CONSTANTIN
SEA-GYPSY SELUNG
SEA HOLLY ERYNGO ERYNGIUM
SEA KALE COLE
SEAL CAN FIX FOB GUM BULL CHOP CORK HARP HOOD JARK LUTE BLANK BULLA CLOSE EAGLE PHOCA SIGIL STAMP SWILE THONG UGRUG URSUK WAFER ASSEAL BEATER CACHET COCKET

DOTARD ENSEAL ENSIGN FASTEN
GASKET MAKLUK MATKAH
OBSIGN PHOCID RANGER SEALCH
SECURE SIGNET CONFIRM
CONSIGN COWROID ENGLUTE
HOODCAP IMPRESS QUITTER
SADDLER SEALING SEALKIE
SIGNARY WEDDELL ADHESIVE
BACHELOR BEDLAMER BRELOQUE
CYLINDER MANDORLA PINNIPED
SECRETUM SEECATCH SIGILLUM
SIGNACLE TANGFISH VALIDATE
(— FOR WATCH CHAIN) ONION
BRELOQUE
(— OFF) CAP
(— OVER CORK) CAPSULE
(BEARDED —) URSUK MAKLUK
(EARED —) OTARY
(FEMALE —) MATKA
(GOLD —) BEZEL
(HARBOR —) DOTARD RANGER
TANGFISH
(HERD OF —S) PATCH
(IMMATURE —) BEDLAMER
(MALE —) WIG SADDLER
BACHELOR SEECATCH
(NEWFOUNDLAND —) SWILE
RANGER
(PAPAL —) BULL BULLA
(SHETLAND —) SILKIE
(YEARLING —) HOPPER
(YOUNG —) PUP BEATER JACKET
BLUEBACK
(3-YEAR OLD —) TURNER
(PREF.) PHOC(O) SIGILLO
SEA LACE WHIPLASH
SEA LAVENDER INKROOT STATICE
SEALED CLOSE
SEALER CAPPER GASKET
SEA LETTUCE LAVER SLAKE SLOKE
SEAWEED
SEA LILY CRINOID
SEALSKIN SKIN SCULP MATARA
SAFARI
SEALSKIN COAT NETCHA
SEALYHAM TERRIER
SEAM DRY BAND DART FASH FELL
PURL REND DEVIL PEARL SPILL
FAGGOT INSEAM STREAK SUTURE
SEAMLET JUNCTURE OVERSEAM
(— IN INGOT) SPILL
(— IN SHIP'S HULL) DEVIL
(— OF COAL) RIDER SPLIT STREAK
(IRREGULAR —) FASH
SEAMAN SALT JACKY MATLO
ARTIST CALASH LUBBER SAILOR
MARINER MASTMAN SHIPMAN
SHIPPER SMASHER WAISTER
YOUNKER DESERTER SEASONER
SEAMARK MEITH
SEAMED SEAMY RUGGED
SEA MILE NAUT
SEAMOUNT GUYOT
SEAMSTER TAILOR SEMPSTER
SEAMSTRESS SEAMER SEWSTER
NEEDLEWOMAN
SEANCE SITTING
SEA NETTLE BLUBBER
SEA OF GRASS (AUTHOR OF —)
RICHTER
(CHARACTER IN —) HAL JIM BRICE
BROCK HENRY LUTIE SARAH
JIMMIE BREWTON CAMERON

CHARLEY BREWSTER MCCURTIN
CHAMBERLAIN
SEA ONION SCILLA
SEA OTTER KID KALAN
SEA OXEYE SALTWEED SAMPHIRE
SEA PINK THRIFT SABBATIA
SEAPLANE HYDRO AIRBOAT
AEROBOAT
SEA PLANTAIN GIBBALS
SEA POACHER BULLHEAD
SEAPORT PARA PORT GROIN
NATAL HARBOR ENTREPOT
MACASSAR
SEA PUSS OFFSET
SEAR BURN FIRE SERE FLAME
FRIZZ ENSEAR SCORCH SIZZLE
FRIZZLE
SEA RAVEN SCULPIN
SEARCH FAN SPY BEAT COMB
DRAG DRAW FAND FOND GAPE
HUNT LAIT RAKE RIPE ROUT SEEK
SIFT WAIT FRISK PROBE QUEST
SNOOP VISIT DACKER DREDGE
FERRET FUMBLE RANCEL SLEUTH
ENQUIRE EXPLORE FOSSICK
INQUEST INQUIRE INSPECT
RANSACK SCRINGE ZETETIC
FINECOMB OUTREACH SCRABBLE
SCROUNGE SCRUTINY
SHAKEDOWN
(— ABOUT) GRUB PROG GROPE
(— BY FEELING) GROPE
(— DEEPLY) TENT
(— EVERYWHERE) BUSK
(— FOR) FORK HUNT LAIT SNOOK
REQUIRE
(— FOR FOX'S TRAIL) CIPHER
(— FOR GAME) DRAW GHOOM
QUEST
(— FOR GOLD) FOSSICK
(— FOR KNOWLEDGE) OUTREACH
(— FOR PARTNER) CRUISE
(— FOR PROVISIONS) FORAGE
(— FOR SMUGGLED GOODS)
DACKER JERQUE
(— FOR STOLEN GOODS) RANZEL
(— FOR WEAPONS) FRISK
(— GROPINGLY) GLAMP
(— INTO) EXQUIRE INDAGATE
(— OUT) FERRET INVENT ROOTLE
EXQUIRE INDAGATE
(— SHIP) RUMMAGE
(— SYSTEMATICALLY) COMB
(— THROUGH) TURN
(— UNDERWATER) FISH
(SYSTEMATIC —) SWEEP
SEARCHER FINDER
SEARCHING HARD CLOSE SHREWD
CURIOUS GROPING
SEARED ADUST
SEARING CAUTERY
SEA ROBIN GURNARD WINGFISH
SEA ROVER VIKING SCUMMER
SEASAN NUDE
SEASCAPE MARINE SEAPIECE
SEA SCORPION COBBLER
SEA SERPENT ELOPS
SEASHELL PROP
SEASHORE SEA RIPE CLEVE COAST
PLAYA MARINE SEASIDE
SEABEACH SEABOARD SEACOAST
SEASICKNESS HILO NAUPATHIA
SEA SNAIL LIPARIAN

SEA SNAKE CHITAL KERRIL
SEASON BEEK CORN DASH FALL
PERT SALT SEEL TIDE TIME GRASS
INURE SAUCE SAVOR SHEMU
SPICE AUTUMN EASTER FLOWER
HARDEN HAYING MASTER SPRING
STEVEN STOUND SUMMER
WINTER BUDTIME FLYTIME
HARVEST KITCHEN OATSEED
SEEDTIME
(— FOR HERRING FISHING) DRAVE
(— HIGHLY) DEVIL
(— IN THE SUN) HAZE
(— OF JOY) JUBILEE
(— OF MERRYMAKING) CARNIVAL
(CLOSED —) SHUTOFF
(DULL —) SLACK
(EGYPTIAN —) AHET PERT SHEMU
(HAYING —) HAYING HAYSEL
(LENTEN —) CAREME
(RAINLESS —) DRY
(RAINY —) KHARIF VARSHA
(REGULARLY RECURRING —) EMBER
(SPRING —) WARE APRIL GRASS
(THE RIGHT —) TID
SEASONABLE PAT TIDY TIMELY
TIDEFUL TIMEFUL VETERAN
TOWARDLY OPPORTUNE
SEASONABLY TIMELY APROPOS
BETIMES
SEASONED SAGY SALT SALTED
INDIENNE POWDERED
(MILDLY —) SWEET
SEASONER SURFACER
SEASONING SALT SPICE SEASON
SPICING OREGANUM
SEA SPIDER PYCNOGONOID
SEA SQUIRT ASCIDIAN
SEA SWALLOW TERN
SEAT BOX CAN SEE SET BANK
BOSS COSY DAIS FLOP FORM
FROG ROOM SILL SLIP SUNK TOIT
ASANA BENCH CELLE CHAIR
DICKY PERCH SELLA SELLE SETTE
SIEGE SLIDE STALL STOOL
BOUGHT DODONA EXEDRA
HUMPTY INSIDE RUMBLE SADDLE
SEATER SEGGIO SETTEE SETTLE
THWART BUTTOCK CUSHION
GRADINE GRADINO INSTALL
OTTOMAN SEATING TABORET
TRANSOM BLEACHER ENTHRONE
PULVINAR SEGGIOLA SUBSELLA
WOOLPACK
(— AT PUBLIC SPECTACLE)
PULVINAR
(— FOR CLERGY) SEDILE
(— FOR GRINDER) HORSING
(— FOR PLANE IRON) FROG
(— NEAR ALTAR) SEDILIUM
(— OF BIRTH) SIDE
(— OF CHAIR) BOTTOM
(— OF EMOTIONS) CHEST SPLEEN
(— OF FEELINGS) STOMACH
(— OF HARE) FORM
(— OF INTELLECT) HEAD
(— OF KNOWLEDGE) RUACH
(— OF ORACLE) DODONA
(— OF PITY) BOWEL
(— OF POWER) SEE
(— OF REAL LIFE) SOUL
(— OF RESPONSIBILITY) SHOULDER
(— OF RULE) OGDOAD

(— OF TURF) SUNK
(— OF UNDERSTANDING) SKULL
(— ON ELEPHANT'S BACK) TOWER
CASTLE HOWDAH
(— ONESELF) LEAN PITCH
(— SLUNG ON POLES) HORSE
(— WITH BRAZIER BELOW)
TENDOUR
(— WITHIN WINDOW OPENING)
CAROL
(AIRPLANE —) DORMETTE
(BACKLESS —) STOOL HASSOCK
(BISHOP'S —) APSE BISHOPRIC
(CANOPIED —) COSY COZY
(CARRIAGE —) DICKY
(CHIMNEY —) SCONCE
(CHURCH —) PEW DESK STALL
SEDILE
(COACH —) BOOT POOP
(COUNTRY —) TOWER GRANGE
QUINTA
(DILIGENCE —) BANQUETTE
(DRAPED —) MUSNUD
(DRIVER'S —) BOX DICKY COCKPIT
FORETOP
(ELEVATED —) PERCH
(FIXED —) DAIS
(GARDEN —) ALCOVE
(KEY —) KEYWAY
(LONG —) BANK FORM BENCH
(NIPPLE —) LUMP
(OARSMAN'S —) TAFT
(PORCH —) GLIDER
(RECLINING —) DORMEUSE
(ROWER'S —) THWART
(ROYAL —) SIEGE STEAD THRONE
(STAGECOACH —S) BASKET
(STRAW —) BOSS
(TIER OF —S) TENDIDO
(TURF —) BUNKER
(UNRESERVED —S) BLUES
(PREF.) EDRI(O)
(SUFF.) HEDRAL
SEA TANGLE FURBELOW
SEA TROUT SEWEN SMELT KIPPER
HERLING HIRLING BODIERON
(— AFTER SPAWNING) KELT
(YOUNG —) PEAL
SEA TURTLE CHELONID
SEA URCHIN WANA REPKIE
ARBACIA CIDARID ECHINID
ECHINUS RADIATE
(FOSSIL —) ECHINITE
(PREF.) ECHIN(O)
SEAWALL BULWARK
SEAWARD OFF MAKAI
SEAWEED ORE AGAR ALGA KELP
LIMU MOSS NORI OOZE REEK REIT
TANG WARE DRIFT DULSE
KOMBU LAVER SLAKE SLOKE
VAREC VRAIC WRACK DELISK
FUCOID FUNORI TANGLE HAITSAI
OARWEED OREWEED OREWOOD
REDWARE SEATANG SEAWARE
CARAGEEN GULFWEED
HEMPWEED ROCKWEED
SARGASSO SEABEARD WHIPCORD
WHIPLASH CORALLINE
NULLIPORE
(PL.) LUMUT
(PREF.) PHYC(O)
(SUFF.) PHYCEAE
SEA WOLF (AUTHOR OF —) LONDON

(CHARACTER IN —) HUMP MAUD WOLF DEATH LEACH LOUIS LARSEN JOHNSON BREWSTER HUMPHREY JOHANSEN MUGRIDGE VANWEYDEN
SEB (CONSORT OF —) NUT
(SON OF —) OSIRIS
SEBA (FATHER OF —) CUSH
SEBASTIAN (BROTHER OF —) ALONSO
(SISTER OF —) VIOLA
SEBESTEN MYXA
SECANT SEC CHORD
SECCO FRESCO
SECEDE SPLINTER
SECESSIONIST SECESH SEPARATE
SECLUDE TACKLE ENCLOSE ISOLATE RECLUSE CLOISTER SEQUESTER
SECLUDED COY SHY DEEP CLOSE QUIET HIDDEN REMOTE SECRET PRIVATE RETIRED RETRAIT SECLUSE HIDEAWAY MONASTIC SEPARATE SOLITARY UMBRATIC CLAUSTRAL
SECLUSION RECESS SHADOW PRIVACY PRIVITY RETREAT SECRECY SEQUEST SOLITUDE
(— OF WOMEN) PURDAH
SECOND AID SEC ABET BACK BETA TICK OTHER VOUCH ASSIST LATTER MOMENT TARTAN TIDDER TOTHER ANOTHER INSTANT SUPPORT SUSTAIN STICKLER
(— BASE) KEYSTONE
(— IN COMMAND) DEPUTY
(— IN HORSE RACE) PLACE
(— PERSON USE) TUISM
(MAJOR —) TONE
(1000TH OF A —) SIGMA
(60TH OF A —) THIRD
(PREF.) DEUT(O) DEUTER(O) SECUNDI
SECONDARY BY BYE SUB SLACK DONKEY SECOND CUBITAL DERIVED INFERIOR MIDDLING
(PL.) FLAGS
(PREF.) DEUT(ER)(ERO)(O) MES(O)
SECONDHAND USED
SECOND MRS TANQUERAY
(AUTHOR OF —) PINERO
(CHARACTER IN —) RAY HUGH PAULA ARDALE AUBREY ELLEAN CORTELYOU TANQUERAY
SECOND-RATE COMMON SHODDY INFERIOR
SECOND-RATER PIKER
SECRECY DERN HUSH HIDING SECRET PRIVACY PRIVITY SILENCE DARKNESS HIDLINGS SCUGGERY VELATION
SECRET SLY DARK DERN INLY BLIND CABAL CLOSE PRIVY QUIET ARCANE CLOSET COVERT HIDDEN INWARD POCKET STOLEN ARCANUM COUNSEL CRYPTIC EPOPTIC FURTIVE MYSTERY PRIVACY PRIVATE PRIVITY RECLUSE RESERVE RETIRED SECRETA UNKNOWN ESOTERIC HIDLINGS MYSTICAL SNEAKING STEALTHY

(PREF.) CRYPT(O) KRYPT(O) SUB
SECRETARY CLERK COPPY BARUCH MUNSHI RAPTOR SCRIBE FAMULUS MUNCHEE MOONSHEE
SECRETE HIDE CACHE NICHE RESET SECERN SECRET CONCEAL SECLUDE SALIVATE SEPARATE
(— MILK) LACTATE
(— ONESELF) HIVE
(— SALIVA) DROOL
(PREF.) ECCRINO
SECRETION INK LAC GOWL LAAP LERP MILT SPIT WOOL HUMOR LAARP MUCUS SEPIA SLIME SPADE CEMENT SALIVA SMEGMA CERUMEN CHALONE FLOCOON HORMONE SPITTLE AUTACOID ENDOCRIN
(THICKENED —) GUM
(WAXY —) LERP LAARP PRUINA
SECRETIVE SLY CAGY DARK SNUG CAGEY CLOSE COVERT SECRET SILENT INVOLVED
SECRETIVENESS SECRECY SLYNESS
SECRETLY CLOSE DARKLY DERNLY SECRET CLOSELY HIDLINGS INWARDLY
SECRET, THE (CHARACTER IN —) ROSE KALINA SKRIVANEK
(COMPOSER OF —) SMETANA
SECT SET ZEN BABI CLAN CULT JODO KIND SHIN ALOGI BHORA ISAWA PANTH BOHORA DONMEH HERESY SCHISM SCHOOL CATHARI DHUNDIA DOCETAE HASIDIM ISAWIYA KHALSAH RINGATU SECTARY SEQUELA SHAIKHI SHINGON SIVAISM SUBSECT AGNOETAE AHMADIYA AISSAOUA MURJIITE NAASSENE SECTUARY SHAKTISM BUCHANITES
(MEMBER OF —) KHLYST OPHITE YEZIDI MOLOKAN NUSAIRI LINGAYAT
SECTARIAN CULTIST HERETIC MAZHABI SECTARY SECTIST
SECTARY JESUIT HERETIC SECTIST SECTUARY SEPARATE
SECTION CUT END AREA PACE PART SECT UNIT CAPUT FRUST PIECE SHARE TMEMA BILLET BRANCH BRIDGE CANTON LENGTH MEMBER PASSUS SECTOR ARTICLE CUTTING HEADING SEGMENT TRANCHE ADDENDUM DIVISION FRACTION
(— AROUND HOP KILN) CURB
(— OF A BODY) LAMINA
(— OF AVICENNA'S WORK) FEN
(— OF BLOOM) STAMP
(— OF BUILDING) ENTRY
(— OF FENCE) FLAKE
(— OF FILM) EXPOSURE
(— OF FILTER) LEAF
(— OF FISHING TACKLE) TRACE
(— OF GARMENT) GORE
(— OF GLASS) SHAWL
(— OF HIGH GROUND) DIVIDE
(— OF KORAN) SURA
(— OF LADDER) FLY
(— OF LOG) BOLT FLITCH

(— OF LOOM) LAY
(— OF NET) DEEPING
(— OF NEWSPAPER) LEAD
(— OF PARLIAMENT) LAGTHING
(— OF PSALTER) CATHISMA
(— OF RHAPSODY) LASSU
(— OF ROOF) SEVERY
(— OF ROOTSTOCK) BIT
(— OF SHIP) STEERAGE
(— OF SONG) STOLLEN
(— OF THREE SHEETS) TERNION
(— OF TORAH) PARASHAH
(— OF TRENCH) BAY
(— OF VIOLIN) BOUT
(— OF WOOD) HAG
(— OF YARN) SLUB
(—S OF SCENERY) BOOK
(CONCLUDING —) ABGESANG
(CONIC —) PARABOLA
(DULL —) LONGUEUR
(LOWEST —) BOTTOM
(MINE —) BORASQUE BORRASCA
(MUSICAL —) CODA EPILOG FINALE
(NARROW —) STRIPE
(NATIVE —) KASBA CASBAH
(ONE-SIXTEENTH OF —) FORTY
(PERCUSSION —) BATTERY
(4-PAGE —) OUTSERT
(SUFF.) TOMA TOME TOMIC TOMOUS TOMY
SECTIONALISM LOCALISM
SECTOR AREA GORE HOUSE
SECULAR LAIC CIVIL COMMON EARTHLY PROFANE WORLDLY TEMPORAL
SECURE FID GET GIB KEY POT RUG SEW WIN BAIL BOLT BOND CAUK COCK COLD EASY FAST FIND FIRM FRAP GAIN GIRD HOOK LAND MOOR NAIL SAFE SEAL SHOT SNUG STAY SURE WARM BELAY BLOCK CINCH CLEAT SLOUR SOUND STRAP TIGHT TRUST ANCHOR ASSURE BECKET BUTTON CLINCH DEFEND ENSURE FASTEN OBTAIN PLEDGE SETTLE SICCAR SICKER STABLE STAPLE TRAIST ACQUIRE BULWARK CONFINE DUNNAGE FORFEND FORTIFY RAMPIRE WARRANT GARRISON PRESERVE
(— A SAIL) TRICE
(— AGAINST INTRUSION) TILE
(— AID OF) ENLIST
(— BAIT) EBB
(— FROM LEAKING) COFFER
(— WITH BARS) GRATE
SECURED BOUND SETTLED
SECURELY FAST SAFE SICCAR SICKER STRAIT SURELY SOLIDLY SOUNDLY
SECURITY PUP BAIL BAND EASE GAGE SEAL WAGE FRITH GRITH GUARD QUIET STOCK BORROW CEDULA EQUITY PLEDGE REFUGE SAFETY SCREEN SEVERE SURETY VADIUM BULWARK CAUTION CUSTODY DEFENSE DEPOSIT FLOATER HOSTAGE SHELTER SLEEPER WARRANT COLONIAL COVENANT FASTNESS GUARANTY HYPOTHEC STRENGTH VADIMONY MUNICIPAL

(BELOW AVERAGE —) LAGGARD
(PL.) PERCENTS PORTFOLIO
SEDAN SEDIA JAMPAN SALOON TONJON NORIMON TOMJOHN BROUGHAM
SEDATE CALM COOL DOUCE QUIET SOBER STAID SERENE EARNEST SERIOUS SETTLED COMPOSED DECOROUS
SEDATENESS SOBRIETY
SEDATIVE AMYTAL ACONITE CALMANT CODEINE LUPULIN BARBITAL LENITIVE QUIETIVE SOOTHING
SEDENTARY STILL SESSILE INACTIVE
SEDGE SAG LING RAIT REIT STAR CAREX CHUFA TIKUG BHABAR EHUAWA GLUMAL THATCH TOETOE TOITOI BULRUSH MONOCOT PAPYRUS SNIDDLE TUSSOCK GALANGAL JIMSEDGE
(PREF.) CARIC(O)
SEDGE FLY GRANAM GRANNOM
SEDGE WARBLER WREN MOCKBIRD REEDBIRD
SEDGY SAGGY SEGGY TWILLED
SEDIMENT CARR DREG FAEX FOOT GOBI LEES MULM SILT WARP DRAST DREGS FECES FOOTS MAGMA BOTTOM FECULA SIMMON SLUDGE DREWITE GROUNDS GRUMMEL SAPROPEL SETTLING
(— OF BEER OR ALE) CRAP
(IRON —) CAR CARR
(REDDISH —) SIMMON
SEDITION REVOLT TREASON
SEDITIOUS RIOTOUS FACTIOUS MUTINOUS
SEDUCE DRAW JAPE LOCK DECOY TEMPT WRONG ALLURE BETRAY ENTICE DEBAUCH ENSNARE MISLEAD SUGGEST TRADUCE INVEIGLE
(— WITH THE EYE) LEER
SEDUCER UNDOER LOTHARIO
SEDUCTION LURE BRIBE CHARM
SEDUCTIVE TEMPTING
SEDULOUS BUSY INTENT STUDIED DILIGENT UNTIRING
SEDULOUSNESS INDUSTRY
SEDUM MOSS ORPINE SENGREEN
SEE LO EYE KEN SPY VID ESPY LOOK MIND NOTE PIPE SEAT SEGE SPOT VIDE VIEW BESEE CATCH CHAIR SIEGE SIGHT STOOL TENEZ WATCH ATTEND BEHOLD DESCRY NOTICE QUAERE REMARK SURVEY ARCHSEE DISCERN GLIMPSE OBSERVE WITNESS CATHEDRA CONCEIVE PERCEIVE
(— ABOVE) VS
(— BELOW) VI
(— FIT) CHOOSE
(— INTO) INSEE PENETRATE
(— THROUGH) RUMBLE
(— TO) FIX
(— VISIONS) SCRY
SEED BEN MAW NIB PIP BEAN BOIL CHAT CORN DIKA GERM KOLA LIMA MOTE SETH TARE BEHEN BERRY CACAO CARAT CARVY

GRAIN LUPIN SEMEN SPAWN
SPERM SPORE STONE ABILLA
ACHENE ACINUS BONDUC
CACOON CARNEL FENNEL KERNEL
LEGUME LENTIL NICKER NUTLET
PIGNON PIPPIN TILLEY ACHIOTE
ACHUETE ALPISTE ANISEED
BUCKEYE CALINUT FRIJOLE
HARICOT HAYSEED SEEDKIN
SEEDLET SEMINAL AMBRETTE
COKERNUT CYDONIUM DILLSEED
FLAXSEED FLEASEED HEMPSEED
PIGNOLIA PRINCIPE SEEDLING
SEEDNESS PISTACHIO
PROPAGULE
(AROMATIC —S) ANISE
(COLE —) COLZA
(EDIBLE —) PEA BEAN
(FENUGREEK —) HELBEH
(GRAPE —) ACINUS
(IMMATURE —) OVULE
(MUSTARD —) SENVY SINEWY
(NUTLIKE —) PEANUT
(OILY —) ARGAN ABILLA
(PALM —) COROZO
(POPPY —) MAW MOHNSEED
(SESAME —) JINJILI GINGELLY
(PL.) ANISE COFFEE SESAME
ZERAIM IGNATIA LARKSPUR
(PREF.) COCC(O) GON(O) OVULI
SEMINI SEMINULI
SPERM(A)(ATI)(ATIO)(ATO)(I)(IO)(O)
SPOR(I)(IDI)(O)(ULI)
(BEAK-LIKE —) RYNCO
(SUFF.) COCCAL COCCIC
SPERM(A)(AE)(AL)(IA)(IC)(OUS)
(UM)(Y) SPORA SPORANGE
SPORANGIATE SPORANGIUM
SPORE SPORIC SPORIDIA
SPORIUM SPOROUS SPORY
SEEDCAKE WIG WIGG
SEEDCASE TEST TESTA THECA
SEED COAT TESTA SPIRICLE
SEEDED ARABLE
SEEDER SEEDMAN
SEEDLING FREE LINER
SEEDS
(PREF.) GRANI
SEEDY MANGY SCUFFY
SEEING SIGHT SIGHTED
(— THAT) SITH SINCE
SEEK ASK BEG SIC WOO BUSK
FAND FEEL FISH FOND FORK
HUNT LAIT LOOK SICK SIFT
COURT DELVE ESSAY FETCH
SCOUR APPETE BOTTOM FERRET
FOLLOW FRAIST PURSUE SEARCH
FORSEEK INQUIRE RANSACK
REQUIRE RUMMAGE SOLICIT
ENDEAVOR
(— AFTER) SUE SUIT ENSUE
EXPLORE
(— AIMLESSLY) PROG
(— FAVOR) WISH
(— FOR) APPETE EXPLORE
(— IN MARRIAGE) WOO PRETEND
(— OUT) COMB ENSEARCH
(— TO ATTAIN) ASPIRE
(— URGENTLY) PRESS
SEEKER TRACER PETITOR ZETETIC
SEARCHER
(— AFTER FACTS) GRADGRIND
(— OF KNOWLEDGE) PHILONIST

(JOB —) CHANCER
(PLEASURE —) FRANION
SEEKING SOKE SOKEN ZETETIC
(SUFF.) PETAL
SEEM BID EYE SEE FARE LOOK
PEER SOUND APPEAR BESEEM
REGARD
(— TO BE) LIKE
(IT —S) SEMBLE
SEEMING GUISE QUASI LIKELY
SEEMLY APPARENT SEMBLANT
(PREF.) QUASI
SEEMINGLY QUASI SEEMLY
SEEMING
SEEMLINESS GRACE DECENCY
DECORUM
SEEMLY FIT TALL CIVIL COMELY
DECENT LIKELY MODEST
BECOMING DECOROUS GRACEFUL
SEEP LEAK OOZE SIPE EXUDE
PERCOLATE
SEEPAGE SEEP SIPAGE SPRING
SEEPY WEEPY
SEER SIR SWAMI MOPSUS SCRYER
PROPHET CHALDEAN MELAMPUS
SEERBAND TURBAN
SEERESS SAGA SIBYL VOLVA
ALRUNE ALBRUNA PHOIBAD
SEESAW PUMP TILT DANDLE
TEETER TIDDLE TILTER TITTER
TOTTER
SEETHE FRY JUG BOIL CREE ITCH
STEW WALL WALM BULLER
HOTTER SIMMER BLUBBER
ELIXATE FERMENT
SEETHING ASEETHE BOILING
HUMMING ITCHING SCALDING
SEGMENT CUT LAP FALL HAND
LITH MERE PART BLANK CHORD
ELITE FEMUR FURCA SHARE SLICE
TMEMA CANTLE GLOSSA LENGTH
SAMPLE SYZYGY ARTICLE DIGITUS
EXERGUE FESTOON ISOMERE
MYOMERE MYOTOME SECTION
SETIGER ANTIMERE BRACHIUM
COLUMNAL DACTYLUS DIVISION
GONOTOME HYPOMERE INTERVAL
MESOMERE METAMERE
MYOCOMMA NARICORN
(— OF CASK) CANT
(— OF CAULIFLOWER) FLOWERET
(— OF CIRCLE) SECTION
(— OF COMMUNITY) FACIES
(— OF EARTH'S CRUST) GRABEN
(— OF FIBER) BAND
(— OF IRIS) FALL
(— OF LEAF) LACINIA
(— OF MAXILLA) STIPES SUBGALEA
(— OF RATTLESNAKE'S RATTLE)
BUTTON
(— OF SPEECH) DOMAIN
(HERALDIC —) FLANCH FLANCHE
(INSTRUCTIONAL —) LESSON
(MERE —) SNAPSHOT
(PEASANT —) HERA
(SUFF.) TMEMA TMESIS
(— OF) ILE
SEGMENTAL MERISTIC
SEGMENTATION CLEAVAGE
(SUFF.) TOMA TOME TOMIC
TOMOUS TOMY
SEGMENTED INSECTED
SEGNO SIGN

SEGREGATE SHED SEVER INTERN
ISOLATE CLASSIFY INSULATE
SEPARATE
SEGUB (FATHER OF —) HIEL HEZRON
SEIGNORAGE ROYALTY
SEIGNORY LORDSHIP
SEINE NET FARE TUCK TRAIN
POCKET SAGENE SPILLER
MADRAGUE
SEISIN VESTURE
SEIZE BAG CAP CLY GET HAP NAB
NAP BEAK BONE CLAW CLUM
FANG GALL GLOM GRAB GRIP
GRUP HAND HENT HOOK JUMP
KEEP LEVY NAIL RAMP SMUG
SNAP SPAN TAKE TIRE YOKE
CATCH CESSE CLASP CLEEK CLICK
CRIMP DRIVE GRASP GRIPE
LATCH PINCH RAVEN RAVIN
REACH REAVE SNACK ARREST
ASSUME ATTACH CLUTCH
COLLAR EXTEND FASTEN FREEZE
GOBBLE NOBBLE QUARRY SECURE
SNATCH ASSEIZE CAPTURE
ENCLASP ENCLOSE FORHENT
GRABBLE GRAPPLE IMPOUND
POSSESS PREEMPT PREHEND
SCAMBLE SWALLOW ARROGATE
COMPRISE DISTRAIN SPUILZIE
SURPRISE UNDERNIM
(— AND HOLD FIRMLY) TRUSS
(— BAIT) STRIKE
(— BY NECK) SCRAG COLLAR
SCRUFF
(— PREY) CHOP
(— SUDDENLY) NAB NIP SWOOP
SNATCH
(— UPON) ATTACK INFECT
(— WITH CLAWS) STRAIN
(— WITH TEETH) BITE
(— WITH WHOLE HAND) GLAUM
(— WITHOUT RIGHT) USURP
SEIZIN SASINE VESTURE
SEIZING FANG GRIP MARQUE
CAPTION SEIZURE
SEIZURE PIT BITE HOLD GRIPE
ICTUS SPELL ARREST EXTENT
PRISAL RAPTUS TAKING ANGARIA
CAPTION CONCEIT TELLACH
DISTRESS STOPPAGE
(SUFF.) LEPSIA LEPSIS LEPSY
LEPT(IC)
SELDOM RARE SELD RARELY
UNOFTEN
SELDOM-SEEN ANTRIN ANTERIN
SELECT ORT TAP TRY CULL PICK
SIFT SORT TAKE WALE DRAFT
ELECT ELITE PITCH TRIED ASSIGN
BALLOT CHOICE CHOOSE CLUBBY
DECIDE DESUME EXEMPT PREFER
SAMPLE SINGLE WINNOW
DRAUGHT EXCERPT EXTRACT
OUTLOOK EXIMIOUS HANDPICK
SELECTED
(— BY LOT) DRAW
(— BY PATTERN) SWATCH
(— JURY) STRIKE
SELECTED DRAFT ELECT FANCY
DRAUGHT
SELECTING DRAFT GARBLING
SELECTION BLAD CHAP CULL ITEM
PICK CHOICE CHOOSE EXCERPT
EXTRACT ELECTION

HAFTARAH PERICOPE
(— OF PSALMS) HALLEL
(VERSE —) BLAUD SINGSONG
(SUFF.) ECLEXIS
SELECTIVE CHOOSY ECLECTIC
SELED (FATHER OF —) NADAB
SELENIDE ZORGITE
SELF EGO SEL SEN JIVA SELL SOUL
DAENA NATURE PERSON PSYCHE
(INNER —) ANIMA
(OWN —) AINSELL NAINSEL
(SUPREME UNIVERSAL —) ATTA
ATMAN
(PREF.) AUT(O) AUTH(I) EGO
SELF-ACCUSATION GUILT
SELF-ACTING
(PREF.) AUT(O) AUTOMAT(O)
SELF-AGGRANDIZING IMPERIAL
SELF-ASSERTIVE BRASH PERKY
CHESTY BLUSTERY BUMPTIOUS
SELF-ASSURANCE CHEEK APLOMB
COOLNESS
SELF-ASSURED CALM PERKY
CONFIDENT
SELF-CENTERED SELFISH
SELF-CENTEREDNESS EGOTISM
SELFHOOD
SELF-COMMAND NERVE TEMPER
SELF-CONCEIT NOSISM
SELF-CONCEITED COXY PENSY
COCKSY PENCEY
SELF-CONFIDENCE CREST HUBRIS
HUTZPA CHUTZPA HUTZPAH
JOLLITY OPINION CHUTZPAH
SELF-CONFIDENT FLUSH CHESTY
SELF-CONSCIOUS GAWKY
BASHFUL
SELF-CONTAINED ABSOLUTE
SELF-CONTAINMENT CLOSURE
SELF-CONTRADICTORY ABSURD
SELF-CONTROL STAY WILL
ENCRATY MODESTY RETENUE
PATIENCE
(LOSE —) FLIP
SELF-DECEPTION FLATTERY
SELF-DEFENSE (ART OF —) KUNGFU
(ART OF-) AIKIDO
SELF-DENIAL DENIAL
SELF-DENYING ASCETIC
SELF-DESTRUCTION SUICIDE
SELF-DESTRUCTIVE SUICIDAL
SELF-DETERMINATION FREEDOM
AUTONOMY
SELF-DISCIPLINE ASCESIS
SELF-ENRICHMENT GROWTH
SELF-ESTEEM EGO PRIDE CONCEIT
SELFNESS
SELF-EVIDENT MANIFEST
SELF-EXALTATION NOSISM
ELATION
SELF-EXISTENT BEER INCREATE
UNCAUSED
SELF-FERTILIZATION AUTOGAMY
SELF-FULFILLMENT FREEDOM
SAMADHI
SELF-GENERATION AUTOGENY
SELF-GLORIFICATION VANITY
SELF-GOVERNMENT SWARAJ
SELF-HEAL ALLHEAL HOOKHEAL
HOOKWEED BLUECURLS
SELFHOOD SEITY EGOITY IPSEITY
OWNHOOD PROPRIUM SELFNESS
SELF-IDENTITY IPSEITY

SELF-IMPORTANT COXY PURDY CHESTY COCKSY BIGGETY POMPOUS BUMPTIOUS
SELF-INDULGENCE NICETY PLEASURE
SELF-INDULGENT WANTON
SELFISH PIGGISH SELFFUL DISSOCIAL
SELFISHNESS EGO SELF EGOTISM SUICISM PHILAUTY SELFHOOD SELFNESS
(MORBID —) PLEONEXIA
SELF-LOVE CONCEIT PHILAUTY
SELF-ORIGINATION ASEITY
SELF-POLLUTION ONANISM
SELF-POSSESSED COOL ASSURED COMPOSED TOGETHER
SELF-POSSESSION COOL PHLEGM POISE APLOMB COOLNESS SANGFROID
SELF-PRODUCED (PREF.) IDIO
SELF-REALIZATION FREEDOM ENERGISM
SELF-RELIANT BOLD FREE
SELF-REPROACH GUILT REGRET
SELF-RESTRAINT HO HOO ASCESIS CONTROL RESERVE RETENUE HAVLAGAH
SELF-RIGHTEOUS STUFFY
SELF-SACRIFICING HEROIC GALLANT
SELFSAME SAME VERY SELFSAID IDENTICAL
SELFSAMENESS IDENTITY
SELF-SATISFIED SMUG STODGY ASSURED
SELF-SERVICE (SUFF.) TERIA
SELF-SUFFICIENCY ASEITY ASEITAS AUTARKY AUTARCHY
SELF-SUFFICIENT ABSOLUTE
SELF-TAUGHT PRIMITIVE
SELF-WILLED SET SENSUAL STUBBLE WAYWARD CONTRARY PERVERSE
SELION BUTT
SELL DO GIVE VEND CHEAP PITCH SHAVE TRADE UTTER AFFORD BARTER MARKET AUCTION BARGAIN
(— A HORSE) CHANT
(— AT LOW PRICE) DUMP
(— BELOW COST) FOOTBALL
(— BY AUCTION) CANT ROUP
(— DRUGS ILLEGALLY) PUSH
(— FOR) BRING FETCH
(— IN SMALL QUANTITIES) RETAIL
(BUY AND —) CHOP
SELLER BOOMER BUSKER CADGER VENDOR CHANTER FLESHER CHANDLER
(WINE —) ABKAR
SELLING (SPECULATIVE —) AGIOTAGE
SELSYN SYNCHRO
SELVAGE EDGE LIST ROON GOUGE FORREL LISTING STICKING
SEMACHIAH (FATHER OF —) SHEMAIAH
SEMANTEME RHEME
SEMANTICS SEMOLOGY
SEMAPHORE FISHTAIL

SEMBLANCE FACE IDOL SHOW SIGN COLOR GHOST GLOSS GUISE IMAGE SCHEME VISAGE PRETEXT SEEMING UMBRAGE LIKENESS SEMBLANT SKERRICK SIMULACRUM
(— OF DIGNITY) FACE
(— OF REALITY) DREAM
(FALSE —) COLORING
SEME SEMY GUTTY HURTY FLEURY GOUTTE GUTTEE BEZANTE
SEME-DE-LIS FLORETTY
SEMEI (SON OF —) MATTATHIAS
SEMELE (BROTHER OF —) POLYDORUS
(FATHER OF —) CADMUS
(MOTHER OF —) HARMONIA
(SISTER OF —) INO AGAVE AUTONOE
(SON OF —) BACCHUS
SEMEN SEED SPERM
(PREF.) GON(O)
SPERM(A)(ATI)(ATIO)(ATO)(I)(IO)(O)
(SUFF.) SPERM(A)(AE)(AL)(IA)(IC)(OUS)(UM)(Y)
SEMESTER HALF
SEMIDARKNESS DUSK
SEMIDIAMETER RADIUS
SEMIDOME CONCHA
SEMIFLUID SOFT HUMOR
SEMIGLOSS EGGSHELL
SEMILIQUID SLAB
SEMINARY YESHIVA JUVENATE
SEMIOPAQUE HORNY
SEMIPORCELAIN GOMBROON
SEMIRAMIDE (CHARACTER IN —) ASSUR ARSACE SEMIRAMIS
(COMPOSER OF —) ROSSINI
SEMIRAMIS (HUSBAND OF —) NINUS
(MOTHER OF —) DERCETO
SEMITE JEW ARAB HARARI SYRIAN SEMITIC SHEMITE ARAMAEAN ASSYRIAN CHALDEAN
SEMITIC JEWISH
(— LANGUAGE) GAFAT
SEMITONE FEINT LIMMA DEMITONE HEMITONE
SEMOLINA SUJI SEMOLA
SENAPO (DAUGHTER OF —) CLORINDA
SENATE BOULE SENATO COUNCIL SENATUS GEROUSIA SENATORY
(— AND PEOPLE OF ROME) SPQR
(— DIVISION) PRYTANY
SENATOR SOLON CONSUL FATHER LAWMAKER
(PL.) ANZIANI
SENATORSHIP TOGA
SEND MIT FAST PACK SHIP ENVOY SCEND THROW RENDER ADDRESS CHANNEL COMMAND CONSIGN DELIVER FORWARD DISPATCH TRANSMIT
(— ABOUT) TROLL
(— ALOFT) CROSS
(— AWAY) MAND SHIP AMAND BANISH DISBAND DISMISS RELEGATE
(— BACK) ECHO TURN WISE REMIT REMAND REMISE RENVOY RESEND RETURN REFRACT
(— BY MAIL) DROP

(— DOWN) DEMIT DIMIT STRIKE
(— FOR) SUMMON
(— FORTH) BEAM BEAR CAST EMIT MAND DIMIT FLING EFFUSE OUTSEND
(— FORTH IN RAYS) RADIATE
(— IN) IMMIT IMMISS INTROMIT
(— MESSAGE) BLINKER
(— OFF) WING
(— OFF UNCEREMONIOUSLY) SHANK
(— OFFICIALLY) ISSUE
(— OUT) BEAM EMIT AMAND SHOOT SPEED DEDUCE DEPORT LAUNCH DIFFUSE EXPEDITE
(— TO JAIL) LAG MITTIMUS
(— TO PERDITION) CONFOUND
(SUFF.) MISE MISS MIT
SENDING SAND
(— OUT) EMISSIVE

SENILE DOLD DOTARD
SENILITY DOTAGE CADUCITY PROGERIA
SENIOR AINE DEAN SIRE DOYEN ELDER ANCIENT SUPERIOR
SENIORITY AGE ANCIENTY SIGNEURY
SENNACHERIB (FATHER OF —) SARGON
(SON OF —) ESARHADDON
SENNET SPET SIGNET
SENOR DON
SENORITA MISS SRTA SRITA
SENSATION FEEL ITCH SOUR SENSE TABET TASTE TIBBIT VEDANA FEELING ESTHESIS
(— OF COLD) RHIGOSIS
(— OF FRIGHT) FRISSON
(— OF HEAT) HOTNESS
(— OF PAIN) ALGESIS
(ANTICIPATORY —) FOREFEEL
(BURNING —) ARDOR
(DARTING —) SHOOT
(STRONG —) CREEP
(SUBJECTIVE —) AURA
(TASTE —) GUST BITTER
(TINGLING —) DIRL
(VIBRATING —) FREMITUS
(VISUAL —) PHOSE PHOTOMA
(PREF.) AESTHESIO ESTHESIO
SENSATIONAL GORY BOFFO LURID YELLOW SAFFRON SPLASHY TABLOID THRILLY STUNNING MELODRAMATIC
SENSATIONALISM BLARE SENSISM
SENSE WIT FEEL SALT SMELL LETTER MATTER REASON SCONCE WISDOM FEELING HEARING MARBLES MEANING SMEDDUM

CARRIAGE GUMPTION JUDGMENT
(— OF APPREHENSION) ANXIETY
(— OF HEARING) EAR
(— OF HUMOR) MUSIC
(— OF ONENESS) KINSHIP
(— OF OUTRAGE) SHOCK
(— OF PANIC) JITTERS
(— OF RIGHT) GRACE
(— OF SIGHT) VISION
(— OF SMELL) SCENT
(— OF SUPERIORITY) EGOTISM
(— OF TOUCH) FEEL TASTE
(— ON ONE'S WORTH) PRIDE
(— THE MEANING OF) READ
(COMMON —) NOUS SALT BALANCE GUMPTION
(DISCRIMINATING —) FLAIR
(LACKING —) INEPT
(PLAIN —) ENGLISH
(SOUND —) MATTER
SENSE AND SENSIBILITY (AUTHOR OF —) AUSTEN
(CHARACTER IN —) JOHN LUCY EDWARD ELINOR STEELE BRANDON FERRARS MARIANNE WILLOUGHBY
SENSE-DATUM SENSUM
SENSELESS MAD COLD DUMB SILLY FRIGID STUPID UNWISE WANTON FOOLISH IDIOTIC PEEVISH SOTTISH UNIDEAED POINTLESS REASONLESS
SENSIBILITY HEART SENSE FEELING DELICACY ESTHESIA JUDGMENT
(PL.) FEELINGS
SENSIBLE SANE WISE AWARE PRIVY WITTY ACTUAL FEELABLE MATERIAL PASSIBLE RATIONAL SENSICAL SENTIENT WISELIKE PERCEPTIBLE
SENSITIVE FINE KEEN SORE ALIVE MIFFY QUICK KITTLY LIABLE NIMBLE TENDER TETCHY FEELING NERVOUS PRICKLY ALLERGIC DELICATE EROGENIC SENSIBLE SENTIENT SKINLESS TOUCHOUS
(— TO PAIN) TART
(NERVOUSLY —) TOUCHY
(TOO —) OVERSTRUNG
SENSITIVENESS SENSE TOUCH ALGESIA DELICACY
SENSITIVE PEA HONEYCUP
SENSITIVE PLANT MIMOSA
SENSITIVITY FLESH DELICACY FINENESS
SENSITIZER CYANINE
SENSORY SENSUAL AFFERENT
SENSUAL LEWD BRUTE MUDDY CARNAL FLESHY SULTRY WANTON BEASTLY BESTIAL BRUTISH FLESHLY LESBIAN SWINISH PANDEMIC SENSUOUS
SENSUALITY FLESH LIKING LUXURY
SENSUOUS SOFT LYDIAN SATINY SENSAL FLESHLY SENSUAL LUSCIOUS SENSIBLE
SENTENCE BAN DIT RAP SAW DAMN DOOM TIME AWARD FUTWA JUISE TENER TROPE ARREST ASSIZE COMMIT DECREE DEPORT JUWISE REASON

ADJUDGE CENSURE CONDEMN FLOATER IMPRESA LAGGING FOREDOOM JUDGMENT VERSICLE PALINDROME
(— CONTAINING ALL LETTERS) PANGRAM
(— CONTAINING EACH LETTER) PANGRAM
(— INDICATING CHARACTER) MOTTO
(CONCISE —S) LACONICS
(IMPRISONMENT —) LAG RAP LIFE LAGGING STRETCH
(MUSICAL —) PERIOD
(SHORT —) CLAUSE
(WITTY —) ATTICISM
SENTENTIOUS CONCISE LACONIC
SENTIENCE SENSE
SENTIENT AWARE FEELING SENSILE SENSIVE SENSEFUL SENSIBLE
SENTIMENT MIND POSY ETHNOS GENIUS HOBNOB NOTION PLEDGE FEELING OPINION
(EXCESSIVE —) SCHWARMEREI
(FALSE —) FALSETTO
(SLOPPY —) DRIP
SENTIMENTAL SLAB SOFT CORNY GOOEY GUSHY MUSHY SAPPY SOBBY SOPPY SOUPY FRUITY SLUSHY SPOONY SUGARY SYRUPY INSIPID MAUDLIN MAWKISH ROMANTIC SCHMALZY SNIVELLY MOONSTRUCK NOVELETTISH
SENTIMENTALISM BATHOS SCHMALZ SCHMALTZ
SENTIMENTALIST SOFTHEAD
SENTIMENTALITY GOO HAM MUSH BLURB SIRUP SYRUP BATHOS
SENTIMENTAL TOMMY (AUTHOR OF —) BARRIE
(CHARACTER IN —) JEAN AARON LOTTA NYLES TOMMY GRIZEL ELSPETH
SENTINEL WAIT DEINO GUARD WATCH BANTAY PICKET SENTRY WARDEN PICQUET COCKATOO PEPHEDRO WATCHMAN
(MOUNTED —) VEDET VEDETTE
(PL.) GRAEAE GRAIAE
SENTINEL BOX STATION WATCHCASE
SENTRY KITE WATCH SENTINEL
SEPAL ALA LEAF HELMET LEAFLET
SEPARATE CUT TOM COMB CULL CURD DEAL FALL FRAY FREE HAZE PART REDD SERE SIFT SORT TEAR TWIN ASIDE BLEED BREAK CALVE ELONG FENCE FLAKE HEDGE PARTY SCALE SEVER SIEVE SKILL SPLIT TWAIN TWIST ABDUCT ABRUPT ASSORT AVULSE BISECT CLEAVE DECIDE DEPART DETACH DIGEST DIVIDE DIVISI FILTER PROPER REMOTE SCREEN SECERN SECRET SEJOIN SETTLE SINGLE SOLUTE SPREAD SUNDER SUNDRY SWATCH UNLUTE WINNOW ABSCISE ABSCISS BRACKET CONCERN DIALYZE DISALLY DISCERP DISJOIN DISLINK DISPAIR DISPART

DIVERSE EXPANSE FISSION ISOLATE SCATTER SCIOLTO SECTION SEJUNCT SEVERAL SWINGLE ABSTRACT BULKHEAD DETACHED DIFFRACT DISCRETE DISJOINT DISSEVER DISSOLVE DISTINCT DISTRACT DISUNITE DIVIDANT DIVIDUAL FRACTION LAMINATE LEVIGATE LIBERATE PECULIAR SEVERATE SPORADIC UNMINGLE UNSOLDER UNSTRING RESPECTIVE
(— BY BEATING) SCUTCH
(— BY CROSSWALL) ABJOINT
(— BY PICKING) LEASE LEAZE
(— COINS) JOURNEY
(— COMBATANTS) STICKLE
(— COPIES) DECOLLATE
(— FIBERS) HACKLE
(— FROM HERD) IMPRIME
(— GRAIN FROM CHAFF) FAN CAVE WINNOW
(— HAIR) BLOCK
(— INTO COMPONENTS) STRIP
(— INTO FLOCKS) DRAFT DRAUGHT
(— INTO SHREDS) TEASE
(— ONESELF) ABDICATE
(— ORE) JIG SMELT DILLUE
(— SHEEP) DRAW
(— THREADS) SLEY SLEAVE
(PREF.) APH APO CHORI(ST)(STO) ECCRINO IDIO
SEPARATED FREE ALONE BROKEN DISTANT DIVIDED ABSTRACT ISOLATED RESOLVED
(— BY INTERVAL) OPEN
(PREF.) CHORI(ST)(STO) DIALY
SEPARATELY APART SINGLY SUNDRY ASUNDER DIVISIM SEVERAL SUNDERLY ABSOLUTELY
SEPARATING BETWEEN
SEPARATION GAP GULF PART RENT SHED BREAK CHASM SPLIT SCHISM BARRIER DIVORCE ELUTION PARTING ANALYSIS AUTOTOMY AVULSION CREAMING DECISION DIALYSIS DISTANCE DISUNION DIVISION INCISION SHEDDING SOLUTION TWINNING SEQUESTER
(— OF LEAF) CHORISIS
(— OF MAN AND WIFE) ZIHAR DIVORCE
(— OF METALS) DEPART
(— OF PIGMENT) FLOATING
(— OF WORD PARTS) TMESIS
(— OF YEAST IN BEER) BREAK
(PREF.) DE
SEPARATIST ZOARITE BIMMELER
SEPARATOR RAVEL PARTER CREAMER SETTLER SEVERER SUBSIDER
SEPARATRIX SLASH DIAGONAL
SEPHESTIA (FATHER OF —) DAMOCLES
(HUSBAND OF —) MAXIMUS
(LOVER OF —) MENAPHON
(SON OF —) PLEUSIDIPPUS
SEPIA COCONUT SEPIARY
SEPOY PANDY TELINGA
SEPT KIN
SEPTEMBER 29 MICHAELMAS
SEPTET SEPTUOR

SEPTIC PURULENT
SEPTIOLITE MEERSCHAUM
SEPTIVALENT HEPTAD
SEPTUAGINT LXX
SEPTUM VITTA TABULA MYOTOME PHRAGMA MYOCOMMA
SEPULCHER BIER GRAVE TITLE CENOTAPH MONUMENT MORTUARY
SEPULCHRAL HOLLOW CHARNEL TUMULARY
SEPULTURE BURIAL
SEQUEL SUITE EFFECT SEQUENT BACKWASH SEQUENCE
SEQUENCE ROPE SUIT TRACT TRAIN DOCKET ENTAIL SEQUEL SERIES STRING CADENCE CORONET SEQUENT SUCCESS SPECTRUM STRAIGHT
(— IN MELODY) AGOGE
(— OF BEHAVIOR) ACT
(— OF BILLIARD SHOTS) BREAK
(— OF CARDS) QUART TENACE STRINGER
(— OF CHESS MOVES) DEFENCE DEFENSE
(— OF EVENTS) CYCLE SCENARIO
(— OF MELODRAMA) CHASE
(— OF ROCK UNITS) SECTION
(— OF SOUNDS) AFFIX
(ACTING —) EXTERIOR
(CUSTOMARY —) COURSE
(FILM —) INTERCUT
(LITURGICAL —) CANON
SEQUENT ENSUANT SEQUITUR
SEQUESTER SINGLE ISOLATE RECLUDE
SEQUESTERED LONELY PRIVATE RECLUSE RETIRED SECLUDED SOLITARY
SEQUIN CHICK SPANG VENTIN ZEQUIN CHEQUIN CHEQUEEN VENETIAN ZECCHINO
(PL.) GLITTER
SERAGLIO HAREM SERAI ZENANA
SERAH (FATHER OF —) ASHER
SERAIAH (BROTHER OF —) BARUCH OTHNIEL
(FATHER OF —) KENAZ NERIAH HILKIAH TANHUMETH
SERAPHIC ANGELIC BEATIFIC
SERBOCROATIAN ILLYRIAN
SERE SEAR SERULE UNGREEN HALOSERE
SERED (FATHER OF —) ZEBULUN
SERENADE AUBADE HORNING ALBORADA NOCTURNE SERENATA
(MOCK —) SHIVAREE
SERENADER WAIT
SERENE CALM EVEN CLEAR LITHE SEDATE SMOOTH HALCYON DECOROUS
SERENITY CALM PEACE REPOSE
SERF BOND THEW CHURL HELOT SLAVE THEOW THETE PENEST SERVUS THRALL BONDMAN COLONUS PEASANT ADSCRIPT PRAEDIAL YANACONA
SERFDOM BONDAGE HELOTRY SERFAGE SERVAGE HELOTISM SERFHOOD SERFSHIP
SERGE SAY SAGATHY
SERGEANT TOP SARGE CHIAUS

DESKMAN SERVANT TOPKICK HAVILDAR SERIAUNT
SERGEANT-AT-LAW COUNTOR COUNTOUR
SERGEANT FISH LING CABIO COBIA SNOOK BONITO CUBBYYEW
SERGEANT MAJOR PINTANO
SERIAL SEQUENTIAL
SERIALLY SERIATIM
SERIEMA CARIAMA GRUIFORM SCREAMER
SERIES RUN SET ECCA RANK SUIT TIRE CHAIN DRIFT DWYKA ORDER SUITE TALLY TRACE COURSE EOCENE SEQUEL STRING SYSTEM BATTERY CASCADE CATALOG BEADROLL SEQUENCE PROGRESSION
(— GATHERED TOGETHER) SORITES
(— OF ABSTRACTS) SYLLABUS
(— OF ARCHES) ARCADE
(— OF BALLET TURNS) CHAINE
(— OF BOAT RACES) REGATTA
(— OF CELLS) FILAMENT
(— OF CHARACTERS) CLINE
(— OF CHESS MOVES) COOK
(— OF CLASHES) CLATTER
(— OF COMMUNITIES) SERE
(— OF DANCE MOVEMENTS) ADAGIO
(— OF DRAIN TILES) FIELD
(— OF EVENTS) EPOS ACTION
(— OF EXTRACTS) CATENA
(— OF FORTIFICATIONS) CEINTURE
(— OF IMAGES) DREAM
(— OF LEGENDS) SAGA
(— OF LIPS) GILL
(— OF MASSES) TRENTAL
(— OF MEETINGS) SESSION
(— OF METAL DISKS) PILE
(— OF MILITARY OPERATIONS) CAMPAIGN
(— OF MOVEMENTS) DANCE
(— OF NEIGHBORING LOTS) COTE
(— OF NOTES) GAMUT GLISSADE
(— OF PASSES) FAENA
(— OF PILES) DRIFT
(— OF POEMS) DIVAN DIWAN
(— OF PRAYERS) COURSE SYNAPTE
(— OF RACES) CIRCUIT
(— OF REASONS) ARGUMENT
(— OF RINGS) COIL GIMMAL
(— OF ROOMS) SWEEP
(— OF SHOTS) BURST
(— OF SIMILAR STRUCTURES) STROBILA
(— OF SLALOM GATES) FLUSH
(— OF SLIPS) DOCK
(— OF SOILS) CECIL
(— OF STAIRS) FLIGHT
(— OF STAMPS) SET
(— OF STITCHES) STAY
(— OF STRAPS) LADDER
(— OF STRATA) KAROO
(— OF TANKS) SOAPER
(— OF THREADS) BINDER STUFFER
(— OF TONES) SCALE
(— OF TRAVELS) ODYSSEY
(— OF VERSES) ANTIPHON
(— OF WORDS) ACROSTIC ALPHABET
(CARD —) CORONET
(CONNECTED —) CATENA

(CONSECUTIVE —) STREAK
(DANCE —) DOUBLE
(GEOLOGICAL —) ECCA LIAS
DWYKA KENAI EOCENE MOLASSE
KEEWATIN
(IMPRESSIVE —) ARRAY
(RADIOACTIVE —) FAMILY
(PREF.) HIRMO

SERIOUS RUM SAD DEEP HIGH
ACUTE GRAVE HEAVY SOBER
SOLID STAID DEMURE SEDATE
SEVERE SOLEMN SOMBER
SOMBRE SULLEN AUSTERE
CAPITAL EARNEST SERIOSO
WEIGHTY GRIEVOUS
(PREF.) SERIO

SERIOUSLY BAD ILL DOWN SADLY
DEEPLY GRAVELY SOLIDLY

SERIOUSNESS EARNEST GRAVITY
SADNESS SOBRIETY

SERMON SPELL HOMILY POSTIL
ADDRESS FUNERAL KHUTBAH
SEREMENT SERMONET
PREACHMENT

SERMONIZING MORALITY

SEROPURULENT SANIOUS

SEROUS ICHOROUS

SEROW THAR JAGLA SERAU

SERPENT (ALSO SEE SNAKE) AHI
SEPS WORM ABOMA ADDER
APEPI ATHER OPHIS SIREN SNAKE
TRAIN CHITAL DIPSAS DRAGON
GERARD HYDRUS PYTHON
APOPHIS PRESTER SCYTALE
JARARACA OPHIDIAN
(— WORSHIPER) NAASSENE
(FEATHERED —) GUCUMATZ
KUKULKAN
(HERALDIC —) REMORA
(NORSE —) GOIN
(SACRED —) AVANYU AWANYU
(SKY —) AHI
(PREF.) COLUBRI OPHI(O) SERPU
VIPERI
(SUFF.) OPHIS

SERPENTINE SNAKY SPIRY OPHITE
SNAKISH BOWENITE METAXITE
SCROLLED MARMOLITE

SERPENT STAR OPHIURAN

SERRANO PERCOID GITANEMUK

SERRATE SAWED ARGUTE RAFFLE
NOTCHED SERRIED

SERRATION SERRA DENTILE

SERUG (FATHER OF —) REU

SERUM WHEY FLUID BIOLOGIC
(PREF.) ORO ORRHO SERO

SERVANT BOY FAG KID MAN PUG
TAG AMAH BATA COOK DASI
DAVY HELP HIND JACK LUCE
MATY MOZO ALILA BAGOT BOOTS
BOULT DAVUS GILLY GROOM
HAMAL MAMMY SEWER SLAVE
SOSIA SPEED USHER ABDIEL
ANDREW BATMAN BEARER
BILDAR BUTLER CHAKAR CLASHY
DORINE EWERER FEEDER FERASH
FLUNKY GILLIE GRUMIO HAIDUK
HARLOT KHAMAL MENIAL
PAMELA SIRCAR SKIVVY SLAVEY
TEABOY TEAGUE TRANIO VARLET
VASSAL VOIDER ANCILLA
BOOTBOY BOUCHAL COURIER
DUFTERY FAMULUS FEODARY

FERRASH FLUNKEY FOOTMAN
GENERAL GHILLIE MALCHUS
PANDOUR PANTLER PAPELON
PIQUEUR PISANIO WASHPOT
ASSIGNEE CHAPRASI CROMWELL
DOMESTIC FOLLOWER GRASSCUT
HENCHMAN HOUSEBOY
MANCIPLE MINISTER OUTRIDER
PANTHINO PHILOTUS PINDARUS
SERGEANT SERVITOR STANDARD
TRENCHER VADELECT WARDMAID
KITCHENER OBSERVANT
(— IN CHARGE OF BREAD) PANTLER
(— IN CHARGE OF DAIRY) DEY
(— IN OFFICE) DUFTERY
(— OF SCHOLAR OR MAGICIAN)
FAMULUS
(— WHO CARVES) TRENCHER
(— WHO CLEARS TABLE) VOIDER
(— WHO RUNS BEFORE CARRIAGE)
PIQUEUR
(— WHO SERVES TABLE) SEWER
(ARMED —) PANDOUR
(ARMY —) BATMAN LASCAR
(BENGAL —) MEHTAR SIRCAR
(BODY —) VALET SIRDAR
(BOY —) BOY KNAVE CHOKRA
BOUCHAL
(CAMP —) BILDAR
(CLOWNISH —) SPEED LAUNCE
(COLLEGE —) GYP SKIP SCOUT
(FEMALE —) AMA NAN AMAH DASI
GIRL LASS MAID MAMMY NURSE
WENCH PAMELA SKIVVY ANCILLA
HANDMAID MUCHACHA
WARDMAID
(GENERAL —) FACTOTUM
(HEAD —) BUTLER TINDAL
(HIGH PRIEST'S —) MALCHUS
(HINDU —) DAS DASI
(HOUSE —) COOK HEWE SEWER
DOMESTIC MATRANEE SCULLION
(KITCHEN —) COOK WASHPOT
(LORD OR KING'S —) THANE
(LYING —) FAG
(MAID —) NAN BONNE
(MAN —) BOY JACK MOZO SWAIN
VALET ANDREW GILLIE KNIGHT
GHILLIE KHANSAMA MUCHACHO
SERVITOR
(MISCHIEVOUS —) TEAGUE
(NON-RESIDENT —) DAILY
(PETULANT —) DORINE
(PHILIPPINE —) BATA ALILA
(SCOTTISH —) JURR
(SOLDIER'S —) PAGE
(TRUSTY —) TROUT
(PL.) FOLK VOLK STAFF FAMILIA
NETHINIM

SERVE DO KA ACT AID HOP GIVE
HELP LEAP SHEW SLAP STAY
TEND TOSS WAIT COVER FRAME
HORSE SARRA STAND ANSWER
ASSIST FRIEND INTEND SAIRVE
SARROW SETTLE SPREAD SUCCOR
ADVANCE ASSERVE BESTEAD
CONVENT FORWARD FURTHER
SERVICE FUNCTION
(— A DISH) MESS
(— AS ESCORT) SQUIRE
(— AS HOST) GIVE
(— AS SUBSTITUTE) PASS
(— AS WELL AS) AVAIL

(— DRINK) SKINK
(— FOOD) HASH KITCHEN
(— FOR PASTURE) GRAZE
(— OBSEQUIOUSLY) LACKEY
LACQUEY
(SUFF.) (— FOR) ORY

SERVER SALVER ACOLYTE
MINISTER

SERVICE AID FEE CENS DUTY HELP
RITE TIDE YOKE FAVOR MUSAF
STEAD DEVOIR EMPLOY ERRAND
FACTOR OFFICE YIZKOR BENEFIT
BONDAGE CHAKARI CORNAGE
FUNERAL LITURGY OBSEQUY
RETINUE SERVAGE SERVING
BREEDING EQUIPAGE FUNCTION
HEADWARD KINDNESS MINISTRY
ROUNDING TENDANCE SERVITIUM
(ASSIGNED —) MYSTERY
(BODYGUARD —) INWARD
(BREAKFAST —) DEJEUNER
(CHORAL —) MATIN
(CHURCH —) LAUDS CHAPEL
CHURCH HEARING STATION
SYNAXIS ASPERGES EVENSONG
(COFFEE —) CABARET
(COMPULSORY —) ANGARIA
(DOMESTIC —) CHAKARI
(FEUDAL —) BOON AVERA
ARRIAGE CORNAGE SEAWARD
HEADWARD
(MILITARY —) ARMS CAMP DUTY
ESCUAGE
(MILITIA —) COMMANDO
(RELIGIOUS —) AHA SEDER
COMMON
(SECRET —) OGPU
(TENNIS —) ACE LET

SERVICEABLE USEFUL DURABLE
THRIFTY FRIENDLY VAILABLE

SERVICEBERRY SHADBLOW
SHADBUSH SASKATOON

SERVICE TREE SORB SORBUS
CHECKER SASKATOON

SERVILE BASE BOND ABJECT
MENIAL SUPINE VASSAL CAITIFF
SLAVISH VERNILE COISTREL
CRAWLING CRINGING SERVIENT
THEWLIKE

SERVILITY CRINGE

SERVING OBED SMACK DISHFUL
HELPING SERVIENT WHIPPING
(SUFF.) ATORY
(— FOR) ORIOUS ORY

SERVITOR FAG GROOM PUNTER
SERVANT PUNTSMAN

SERVITUDE USE VIA YOKE
BONDAGE SERVICE SLAVERY
SERVITUS THEOWDOM THIRLAGE

SERVOMECHANISM SERVO
BOOSTER

SERVOMOTOR RELAY SERVO

SESAME TIL TEEL BENNE BENNI
SEMSEM VANGLO GINGILI
OILSEED WANGALA AJONJOLI
BENISEED SERGELIM

SESBANIA AGATI

SESQUITERPENE CEDROL
CLOVENE COPAENE HUMULENE

SESSION DAY BOUT DIET HOUR
SEAT COURT CLINIC SCHOOL
SEANCE ACUERDO HEARING
SEMINAR SITTING CONGRESS

SEDERUNT SEMESTER
(COURT —) HILARY
(JAM —) CLAMBAKE
(PL.) ASSIZES
(SUFF.) FEST

SESTERTIUS BRONZE

SESTINA SEXTAIN

SET DO DIP FIX GEL KIT LAY LOT
MOB PUT SIC SIT SOT CASE CREW
CUBE GAGE GANG GIVE JELL KNIT
KNOT NEST PAIR PICK PILT POSE
REST SETT SORT STEP STOW
BATCH CLASS CLOCK COVEY
CROWD FIXED GAUGE GLADE
GROUP INFIX PAVER PLACE POSIT
STACK STAID STAND STEAD
STEEK STICK SUITE ADJUST
CIRCLE CLIQUE DEFINE FASTEN
FINALE FORMAL GLAZED GROUND
HARDEN IMPOSE PARCEL SERIES
SETTLE SPREAD SQUARE STATED
BATTERY BOILING COMPANY
COMPOSE CONFIRM COTERIE
DEPOSIT DISPOSE ENCHASE
FACTION IMPLANT INSTATE
PLATOON SERVICE STATION
STIFFEN STRATUM EQUIPAGE
PANTALON SEQUENCE SOLIDIFY
STANDARD
(— A PERIOD) DATE
(— A PRICE) ASK
(— ABOUT) FALL FANG GANG
BEGIN ADDRESS
(— AFLOAT) LAUNCH
(— APART) MARK SHED DESIGN
DEVOTE EXEMPT SACRED SEPONE
SEPOSE APPOINT ISOLATE
RESERVE ALLOCATE DEDICATE
INSULATE SEPARATE SEQUESTER
(— ARROWS IN ORDER) FRUSH
(— AS ONE'S SHARE) ALLOT
(— ASIDE) BAR DISH DROP HAIN
SIDE SINK SLIP BURKE KAPUT
SEPOSE BRACKET EARMARK
PURLOIN RESERVE SUSPEND
ABROGATE DISPENSE OVERRIDE
OVERRULE REVERSED
(— AT DEFIANCE) BEARD
(— AT LIBERTY) FREE RELEASE
LIBERATE
(— BACK TO BACK) ADDORSED
ADDOSSED
(— CLOSE TOGETHER) PAVEED
(— DOG ON) SIC SLATE
(— DOWN) JOT LAY GIVE LAND
PLANK SCORE EXPONE DEPOSIT
(— DOWN UNDER NAME) TITLE
(— EDGEWISE) SURBED
(— ERECT) COCK
(— FIRMLY) FIRM STEM PLANT
POSIT
(— FORTH) DRAW ETCH SHOW
GIVEN STATE DEPART DEPICT
EXPOSE SPREAD ARTICLE
DISPLAY ENOUNCE EXHIBIT
EXPOUND PRESENT PROPONE
PROPOSE PURPOSE PROPOUND
(— FORWARD) PREFER ADVANCE
(— FREE) BAIL EASE REMIT SKILL
SOLVE ACQUIT ASSOIL ABSOLVE
DELIVER ENLARGE UNLOOSE
WINFREE ABSTRICT DISPLACE
DISSOLVE EXPEDITE UNVASSAL

(**— GOING**) INITIATE
(**— IN EARTH**) STRIKE
(**— IN FROM MARGINS**) INDENT
(**— IN MOTION**) SOW
(**— IN OPERATION**) DRIVE
(**— IN OPPOSITION**) PIT
(**— IN ORDER**) ARRAY FRUSH PITCH ADIGHT DAIKER FETTLE INFORM ADDRESS
(**— INTO**) INLAY
(**— INTO A GROOVE**) DADO
(**— LIMITS TO**) SPAN BOUND
(**— OF ACTORS**) CAST
(**— OF ARMS**) CONVEYER
(**— OF BARS**) CONCAVE
(**— OF BELLS**) RING CHIME CARILLON
(**— OF BOOKS**) PLENARY
(**— OF CARS**) DRAG
(**— OF CHIMES**) DOORBELL
(**— OF CIRCUMSTANCES**) CASE EGIS FRAME
(**— OF CORDS**) SIMPLE
(**— OF DISHES**) GARNISH SERVICE CUPBOARD
(**— OF EIGHT**) OGDOAD
(**— OF EXERCISES**) KATA
(**— OF FACTS**) BOOK
(**— OF FISH NETS**) DRIFT
(**— OF FOLDED SHEETS**) QUIRE
(**— OF FOUR**) WARP
(**— OF FURNITURE**) SUITE DINETTE
(**— OF GARMENTS**) SUIT
(**— OF GEARS**) GEARSET
(**— OF HIDES**) KIP
(**— OF HOUNDS**) VANLAY VAUNTLAY
(**— OF IDEAS**) SYSTEM
(**— OF JEWELLED ORNAMENTS**) PARURE
(**— OF LEAVES**) COROLLA
(**— OF LETTERS**) ALPHABET
(**— OF MUSICAL INSTRUMENTS**) CONSORT
(**— OF NOTES**) ACCORD
(**— OF OPINIONS**) CREDO
(**— OF ORGAN PIPES**) STOP
(**— OF ORGANS**) ARMATURE
(**— OF ORNAMENTS**) PARURE
(**— OF PINS**) KAILS KNOCKOUT
(**— OF POINTS**) INTERVAL
(**— OF PUMPS**) LIFT
(**— OF QUADRILLES**) LANCERS
(**— OF RADIATORS**) STACK
(**— OF ROOMS**) STORY
(**— OF RULES**) CODE EQUITY DECALOG
(**— OF SAILS**) CANVAS
(**— OF SHELVES**) STAGE BUFFET DRESSER WHATNOT
(**— OF SKI FASTENINGS**) BINDING
(**— OF STAVES**) SHOOK
(**— OF STEPS**) LADDER
(**— OF SYMBOLS**) KATAKANA
(**— OF TABLES**) COMPUTUS
(**— OF TEETH**) DENTURE
(**— OF TEN**) DECADE
(**— OF THREE**) BALE LEASH
(**— OF TOOLS**) STRING
(**— OF TRAMS**) JOURNEY
(**— OF TYPEFACES**) FAMILY
(**— OF VALUES**) CURRENCY
(**— OF VARIATIONS**) PARTITA

(**— OF VATS**) SOLERA
(**— OF VERSES**) STAVE
(**— OF VOWELS**) SERIES
(**— OF WARP THREADS**) LEA
(**— OF 3 ANIMALS**) LEASH
(**— OFF**) FOIL MENSE SEVER SHOOT ACCENT BUNDLE BALANCE COMMEND EMBLAZE CONTRAST DECORATE EMBLAZON
(**— OFF TO ADVANTAGE**) ADORN COMMEND
(**— ON**) TAR
(**— ON END**) UPEND
(**— ON FIRE**) SPIT TIND LIGHT ACCEND IGNIFY IGNITE KINDLE ENFLAME INFLAME ENKINDLE
(**— ONESELF**) GO
(**— OUT**) BOUN MAKE BOWNE FOUND SALLY START INTEND STARTLE
(**— OVER**) COUCH
(**— RIGHT**) REDD ADJUST SCHOOL SQUARE CORRECT REDRESS
(**— SNARE**) TAIL TILL
(**— SOLIDLY**) EMBED
(**— STRAIGHT**) DRESS
(**— THICKLY**) STUD
(**— TO MUSIC**) AIR DITTY
(**— TRAP**) TELD
(**— TYPE**) KEYBOARD
(**— UP**) AREAR ERECT RAISE INSTALL UPDRESS ACTIVATE
(**— UP IN COLUMNS**) TABULAR
(**— UPON**) BESET ATTACK AGGRESS BROWDEN
(**— UPRIGHT**) ERECT STAND ARRECT
(**— VALUE**) APPRAISE
(**— WITH BRISTLES**) STRIGOSE
(**— WITH GEMS**) CHASE
(**ANTIGEN —**) SEROTYPE
(**BECOME —**) STRIKE
(**CHESS —**) MEINY MEINIE
(**CHROMOSOME —**) GENOME COMPLEX
(**COMPLETE —**) STAND
(**INFINITE —**) FAMILY
(**MATHEMATICAL —**) MANIFOLD
(**MINIATURE —**) DIORAMA
(**RADIO —**) BLOOPER
(**SMART —**) TON
(**STAGE —**) SCENE
(**TELEVISION —**) TUBE
(**UNALTERABLY —**) STOUT
(PL.) DECOR
(SUFF.) STOLE THESIS THETE THETIC
SETA STALK WHISK CHAETA SETULA SETULE CROTCHET PODETIUM
SETBACK DASH JOLT KNOCK LURCH BLIGHT BACKSET LICKING PUTBACK REVERSE BUSINESS COMEDOWN HAYMAKER CONTRETEMPS
SETH (**BROTHER OF —**) ABEL CAIN
(**FATHER OF —**) ADAM
(**MOTHER OF —**) EVE
(**SON OF —**) ENOS
SETHUR (**FATHER OF —**) MICHAEL
SETLINE GEAR TRAWL BULTOW OUTLINE TROTLINE
SETTEE SETTLE

OTTOMAN WINDSOR
SETTER SOFA GUNDOG DROPPER FLUSHER SETTLER
SETTERWORT PIGROOTS
SETTING SET FALL PAVE VAIL CHASE MIDST SETUP CHATON MILIEU FERMAIL MONTURE SITTING INTERIOR MARQUISE MOUNTING SHOWCASE
(**— APART**) BETWEEN
(**— FREE**) SOLUTION
(**— OF GEM**) FOIL OUCH CHASE GALLERY
(**— OF REED**) CAAMING
(**— OF WHEELS**) CAMBER
(**CAMERA —**) BULB
(**FAMILIAR —**) HOME
(**MUSICAL —**) CREDO BALLAD BALLADE
(**SHUTTER —**) TIME
(**STAGE —**) SCENE
SETTLE BED FIT FIX PAY SAG SET SIT TAX BANK BIND CALM DAIS DEAS FAST FIRM HAFT LEND NEST REST ROOT SEAT SINK SNUG TOIT AGREE CLEAR COUCH ISSUE LIGHT LODGE ORDER PITCH PLACE PLANT QUIET SQUAT STATE STILL ACCORD ADJUST ALIGHT ASSIGN CLINCH DECIDE DECREE ENCAMP LOCATE NESTLE PURIFY RESIDE SCREEN SECURE SOOTHE SOPITE SQUARE ACCOUNT APPEASE APPOINT ARRANGE BALANCE CLARIFY COMPONE COMPOSE CONCERT CONFIRM DEPOSIT DERAIGN INHABIT PIONEER RESOLVE SUBSIDE COLONIZE REGULATE SQUATTLE CONJOBBLE RECONCILE
(**— A FINE**) AFFEER
(**— AMICABLY**) COMPOUND
(**— DOWN**) CAMP SLUMP STEADY DESCEND
(**— ITSELF**) INVEST
(**— LANDS ON A PERSON**) ENTAIL
(**— ON**) POINT
(**— UPON**) AFFIX AGREE TIGHT
(**— VERTICALLY**) SQUASH
SETTLED SAD SET FIRM FIXED QUIET STAID FORMED RANGED SEATED SEDATE SQUARE STAPLE STATED CERTAIN DECIDED EMPIGHT STATARY DECOROUS RESOLVED STANDING SEDENTARY
(**NOT —**) FARROW
SETTLEMENT AUL DEAL FINE FORK MISE POST BARRIO COLONY DIKTAT MOSHAV WINDUP ACCOUNT BIVOUAC FINANCE MAABARA OUTPOST STATION CLERUCHY DECISION DISPATCH JOINTURE KEVUTZAH PRESIDIO SETTLING SHOWDOWN TOWNSHIP PLANTATION
(**— OF JERRY-BUILT DWELLINGS**) BIDONVILLE
(**— OF MONKS**) SCETE SKETE
(**— OF SHACKS**) FAVELA FAVELLA
(**COLLECTIVE —**) KVUTZA MOSHAV KIBBUTZ
(**HARSH —**) DIKTAT

(**INDIAN —**) BUSTEE
(**MARRIAGE —**) MAHR ARRAS DOWNSET
(**NEW ZEALAND —**) PA PAH
(**RAPID —**) BOOM
(**UPLAND —**) BOOLEY
SETTLER METIC SAHIB LIVYER NESTER GRUELER PEOPLER PILGRIM PIONEER TRIMMER FINISHER GACHUPIN HABITANT SHAGROON SIBERSKI SIBERYAK
(**— IN AUSTRALIA**) GROPER
SETTLING SIT
(**— OF ESTATE**) ENTAIL
(PL.) LEES SEDIMENT
SET-TO BOUT TURN PLUCK FETTLE TURNUP BRANGLE
SETUP SET SITTER
SEVEN SEPT ZETA ZAYIN HEPTAD SEPTET HEBDOMAD SEPTETTE
(**— OF DIAMONDS**) POPE
(**— OF TRUMPS**) MANILLA
(**GROUP OF —**) PLEIAD
(PREF.) HEPT(A) SEPT(I) SEPTEM
SEVENFOLD SEPTUPLE
SEVENTEEN (**AUTHOR OF —**) TARKINGTON
(**CHARACTER IN —**) MAY JANE PRATT BAXTER GEORGE JOHNNY WATSON GENESIS PARCHER WILLIAM CLEMATIS
SEVEN-UP PEDRO PITCH SLEDGE
SEVER AX AXE CUT BITE DEAL HACK REND SLIT TWIN SHEAR SHRED CLEAVE DEPART DETACH DIVIDE SUNDER DISALLY DISCERP DISCIDE DISJOIN OUTRIVE DISSEVER PRESCIND SEPARATE SEVERIZE
(PREF.) TEMNO
SEVERAL ODD TEN SERE WHEEN DIVERS SUNDRY DIVERSE VARIOUS DISTINCT MULTIPLE
(PREF.) PLURI POLY
SEVERALLY APIECE SEVERAL
SEVERANCE SUNDER SOLUTION
(**— OF RELATIONSHIPS**) AIR
SEVERE BAD DRY ACID BLUE DEAR DOUR DURE FIRM HARD IRON KEEN ROID RUDE SALT SIDE SORE TART TAUT ACUTE BREME CRUEL EAGER GRUFF HARSH RETHE RIGID ROUGH SHARP SMART SNELL SOBER SOUND STARK STEER STERN STIFF STOUR TOUGH BITING BITTER BRUTAL CHASTE COARSE FROSTY HETTER SIMPLE SOLEMN STRICT TORVID UNKIND UNMILD ACERBIC ASCETIC AUSTERE CAUSTIC CHRONIC CONDIGN CRUCIAL CUTTING DRASTIC SERIOUS SPARTAN TORVOUS UNCANNY VICIOUS VIOLENT WEIGHTY ACERBATE ACULEATE CATONIAN EXACTING GRIEVOUS GRINDING HORRIBLE IRONCLAD IRONHARD RIGOROUS SCATHING STALWART STRAIGHT TERRIBLE STRINGENT
(**MOST —**) EXTREME
SEVERELY BAD HARD BADLY STARK STIFF HARDLY SORELY STRONG HEAVILY ROUGHLY

SMARTLY SOUNDLY STITHLY SHREWDLY

SEVERIAN AGNOETE AGNOITE

SEVERING (PREF.) PRISO

SEVERITY FROST RIGOR CRUELTY TORVITY TYRANNY ACRIMONY ASPERITY FERVENCY HARDNESS RIGIDITY SORENESS VIOLENCE

SEW SUE FELL SEAM SLIP PREEN STEEK NEEDLE STITCH OVERSEW THIMBLE OVERCAST OVERHAND
(— A CORPSE) SOCK
(— LOOSELY) BASTE
(— TO REINFORCE) BAR
(— UP FERRET'S MOUTH) COPE
(— WAVED PATTERN) DICE

SEWAGE SOIL WASTE SOILAGE SULLAGE AFFLUENT DRAINAGE SEWERAGE

SEWELLEL BEAVER BOOMER

SEWER SINK SIRE DRAFT DRAIN FLEET ISSUE MAKER SHORE CLOACA KILTER TACKER VENNEL BELTMAN COPYIST CULVERT DRAUGHT GULLION JAWHOLE SHIRRER PIQUIERE

SEWING TACK SUTURE SEMPSTRY (SUFF.) RHAPHY RRHAPHY

SEX KIND SECT GENDER
(FEMALE —) SMOCK
(MALE —) WEPMANKIN
(PREF.) GEN(O)

SEXLESS NEUTER EPICENE

SEXT MIDDAY

SEXTANT (PART OF —) ARC ARM DRUM LIMB MARK FRAME GLASS INDEX LEVER HANDLE MIRROR SUNSHADE TELESCOPE

SEXTET SESTET SEXTUOR SESTETTO

SEXTON SAXON SHAMUS WARDEN SACRIST SHAMASH SHAMMES VESTURER SACRISTAN

SEXTUPLE SENARY

SEXTUPLET SESTOLE SEXTOLE SESTOLET SEXTOLET

SEXUAL GAMIC CARNAL INTIMATE (PREF.) GAM(ETO)(O) GON(O)

SEXY FOXY FREUDIAN

SEYCHELLES (CAPITAL OF —) VICTORIA
(ISLAND OF —) MAHE LADIGUE PRASLIN

SGANARELLE (BROTHER OF —) ARISTE
(DAUGHTER OF —) LUCINDE
(WARD OF —) LEONORE ISABELLE
(WIFE OF —) MARTINE

SHA YASHIRO

SHAAPH (FATHER OF —) CALEB JAHDAI
(MOTHER OF —) MAACHAH

SHAB RUBBERS

SHABBINESS WAFFNESS

SHABBY BASE MEAN POKY WORN DINGY DOWDY MANGY OURIE POKEY RATTY SCALD SEEDY SORRY TACKY CHEESY FROWZY GRUBBY SCABBY SCOURY SCUFFY SCURVY SHODDY SHROVY SLEAZY TAGRAG BUNTING MESQUIN SCALLED SCRUBBY SCRUFFY

SCUFFED SHABBED SQUALID PALTERLY SLIPSHOD WAFFLIKE

SHABUOTH PENTECOST

SHACHIA (FATHER OF —) SHAHARAIM
(MOTHER OF —) HODESH

SHACK COE HUT CRIB SHAG HUMPY HUTCH SHANTY

SHACKLE COP TIE BAND BIND BOLT BOND GYVE LOCK STAY BASIL BILBO CLAMP COPSE CRAMP CRANK HUMPY TRASH TRAVE FETTER GARTER HAMPER PINION SHANGY STAYER SWATHE COTTAGE COUPLER FETLOCK MANACLE MOUSING PASTERN SHEBANG SNACKLE TRAMMEL RESTRAIN
(PL.) IRONS

SHACKLER SLOTTER

SHAD BUCK CHAD ALLIS ALOSE TRABU ALLICE TWAITE ALEWIFE ANADROM CLUPEID FLATFISH SAWBELLY

SHADBUSH DOGWOOD SERVICE SERVICEBERRY

SHADDOCK LUCBAN POMELO POMPION

SHADE EYE CAST DULL SCUG SHED TONE VEIL BLEND COLOR ENNUE GHOST GLIDE GLOOM GRAIN SCAUM SCOUG SWALE SWILL TASTE TINCT TINGE TRACE UMBER UMBRA DEGREE FRESCO SHADOW SHIELD SHROUD SPRITE STRAIN STRIPE TONING CURTAIN ECLIPSE GRADATE HACHURE KENNING PROTECT SECTION SHADING UMBRAGE BONGRACE HALFTONE UMBRELLA
(— OF COLOR) EYE CAST TONE
(— OF DIFFERENCE) NUANCE
(— OFF) GRADUATE
(— ON HAT) UGLY
(EYE —) UGLY
(OVERHANGING —) CANOPY
(WINDOW —) STORE
(PREF.) UMBRI

SHADED OMBRE SHADY DRUMLY SOMBER SOMBRE DARKLING

SHADINESS GLOOM

SHADING FLUTING LAYERING

SHADOW FOX BLOT SCUG TAIL CLOUD SCOUG SHADE UMBER UMBRA CLEEKS DARKEN FINGER SHROUD TAILER ISOGYRE PHANTOM SCARROW SUGGEST UMBRAGE UMBRATE PENUMBRA PHANTASM SHEPHERD (PREF.) SCI(A)(O) SKIA SKIO TENEBRI UMBRI

SHADOWED DARKLING

SHADOWINESS GLOOM

SHADOWLESS ASCIAN WHITEOUT

SHADOWS ON THE ROCK
(AUTHOR OF —) CATHER
(CHARACTER IN —) LAVAL CECILE HECTOR PIERRE AUCLAIR BLINKER CHARRON EUCLIDE SAINTCYR FRONTENAC

SHADOWY MISTY VAGUE GLOOMY GHOSTLY OBSCURE

SHADRACH ANANIAS HANANIAH

SHADY DARK BOSKY BOWERY CLOUDY LOUCHE SHADOW SHADOWY UMBROSE ADUMBRAL

SHAFT BAR NIB ROD BALK BOLT DART FUST HOLE PILE POLE TRAM WELL ARBOR HEUGH QUILL REACH SCAPE SHANK SHOOT SNEAD SPRAG STAFF STALE STANG STAVE STEAL STILT STING THILL TRUNK BOLTEL CANNON COLUMN GNOMON SCAPUS STAPLE TILLER TUNNEL UPRISE VAGINA BOWTELL CHIMNEY INCLINE MANDREL SPINDLE CAMSHAFT DOWNCAST ESCONSON HOISTWAY LAMPHOLE SHAFTWAY STANDARD WEIGHBAR WELLHOLE
(— CONNECTING WHEELS) AXLE
(— IN GLACIER) MOULIN
(— IN WATCH) STEM
(— OF CANDLESTICK) BALUSTER
(— OF CARRIAGE) FILL SILL THILL
(— OF CART) ROD TRAM SHARP STANG
(— OF CAVERN) DOME
(— OF CHARIOT) BEAM
(— OF CLUSTERED PIER) BOLTEL
(— OF COLUMN) FUST TIGE SCAPE VERGE
(— OF FEATHER) SCAPE SCAPUS
(— OF MINE) PIT WORK GRUFF HEUCH HEUGH RAISE SLOPE STULM WINZE GROOVE STAPLE INCLINE WINNING
(— OF PADDLE) LOOM ROUND
(— OF SPEAR OR LANCE) TREE STALE
(— OF WAGON) STAVE THILL LIMBER
(HARNESS —) HEALD
(HOLLOW —) CANNON
(MAIN —) ARBOR
(ORNAMENTAL —) VERGE
(SCYTHE —) SNEAD
(STAIRWAY —) VICE
(TWISTED —) TORSO
(VENTILATION —) UPCAST UPTAKE WINDHOLE
(PREF.) DORY SCAPI

SHAG PILE

SHAGE (SON OF —) JONATHAN

SHAGGY SHAG SWAG HARSH NAPPY ROUGH SHOCK TATTY TOUSY BRUSHY COMATE RAGGED TOOSIE HIRSUTE SHAGRAG SQUALID SWAGGED THRUMMY VILLOUS TATTERED (PREF.) DASI DASY LASI

SHAGREEN GALUCHAT

SHAGROON PILGRIM

SHAKE BOB DAD JAR JOG ROG WAG WAP JOLT JOWL PLUM QUAG RESE ROCK SHOG STIR SWAY TOZE WEVE WHAP WHOP HOTCH JAUNT KNOCK NIDGE QUASH SHOCK SWING TRILL DIDDER DITHER DODDER DODDLE EXCUSS GOGGLE HOTTER HUSTLE JOGGLE JOUNCE JUMBLE QUATCH QUAVER QUITCH QUIVER ROGGLE RUFFLE SHIMMY SHIVER TOTTER WAMBLE WANGLE

WARBLE WEAKEN WOBBLE AGITATE BRANDLE CHOUNCE CONCUSS ROULADE SHUDDER STAGGER SUCCUSS TREMBLE TWITTER WHIFFLE WHITHER BRANDISH CONVULSE ENFEEBLE
(— HERRING) SCUD
(— LIGHTLY) LIFT
(— OFF) ARISE EXCUSS
(— TO SEPARATE) HOTCH
(— UP) JABBLE JUMBLE RATTLE
(WIND —) ANEMOSIS

SHAKER DUSTER SIFTER DREDGER JUMBLER POUNCET SANDBOX

SHAKING ASPEN ASHAKE TREMOR JARRING AGITATED
(— OF AIRPLANE) BUFFET

SHAKTI TARA PRAKRITI

SHAKTIS MATRIS

SHAKUNTALA (FATHER OF —) VISHVAMITRA
(FOSTER FATHER OF —) KANVA
(HUSBAND OF —) DUSHYANTA
(MOTHER OF —) MENAKA
(SON OF —) BHARATA

SHAKY CRANK DICKY QUAKY ROCKY TIPSY TOTTY WONKY WOOZY AGUISH COGGLY CRANKY GROGGY INFIRM WAMBLY CASALTY DWAIBLE DWEEBLE PALSIED RICKETY SHOGGLY TITTUPY TOTTERY COGGLEDY INSECURE

SHALE BAT BASS BONE CLOD FLAG KOLM TILL BLAES FAKES METAL PLATE XALLE KILLAS SHILLET MUDSTONE SLIGGEEN TORBANITE

SHALL SE MAY MUN MUST SALL
(— NOT) SANNA SHANT SHANNA

SHALLOON CUBICA

SHALLOT CIBOL ALLIUM ESCHALOT SCALLION

SHALLOW EBB BANK FLAN FLAT FLUE GLIB FLEET INANE SHOAL SILLY SMALL FLIMSY FROTHY LITTLE RIFFLE SLIGHT UNDEEP CRIPPLE CURSORY TRIVIAL MAGAZINY
(PL.) FORD

SHALLOWNESS INANITY

SHALLUM (FATHER OF —) BANI KORE SHAUL JABESH JOSIAH HOLOHESH NAPHTALI
(NEPHEW OF —) JEREMIAH
(SON OF —) HOLOHESH MAASEIAH JEHIZKIAH
(WIFE OF —) HULDAH

SHALLUN (FATHER OF —) COLHOZEH

SHAM BAM FOB FOX GIG FAKE HOAX MOCK PUFF BLUFF BOGUS CHEAT DUMMY FALSE FEIGN FRAUD LETON QUEER SHUCK SNIDE ASSUME BRUMMY BUNYIP CHOUSE DECEIT DUFFER HUMBUG PSEUDO SHODDY STUMER FALSITY FORGERY GRIMACE MOCKISH PLASTER PRETEND STUMOUR POSTICHE PRETENSE SPURIOUS BRUMMAGEM PASTEBOARD SIMULACRUM
(PREF.) PSEUD(O)

SHAMAN PEAI CURER MACHI KAHUNA WABENO ANGEKOK TOHUNGA CONTRARY WITCHMAN

SHAMARIAH (FATHER OF —) REHOBOAM

SHAMASH (FATHER OF —) SIN
(SISTER OF —) ISHTAR
(WIFE OF —) AA AYA

SHAMBLE SHALE SHOOL CLOUCH BAUCHLE SCAMBLE SHACHLE SHACKLE SKEMMEL ABATTOIR SHAMMOCK
(PL.) BUTCHERY

SHAMBLING SHACKLY

SHAME SISS ABASH AIDOS SHEND SPITE ASHAME BISMER REBUKE MORTIFY PUDENCY SCANDAL SLANDER CONTEMPT DISGRACE DISHONOR REPROACH SHENDING VERGOYNE VITUPERY
(— BY CENSURE) TOUCH

SHAMED (FATHER OF —) ELPAAL

SHAMEFACED SHY

SHAMEFACEDNESS PUDENCY

SHAMEFUL BASE FOUL MEAN GROSS HONTOUS IGNOBLE FLAGRANT IMPROPER INFAMOUS

SHAMELESS HARD BRASH ARRANT BRAZEN BASHLESS BROWLESS IMMODEST IMPUDENT

SHAMELESSNESS BRASS

SHAMGAR (FATHER OF —) ANATH

SHAMIR (FATHER OF —) MICAH
(GRANDFATHER OF —) UZZIEL

SHAMMA (FATHER OF —) ZOPHAH

SHAMMAH (BROTHER OF —) DAVID
(FATHER OF —) JESSE REUEL

SHAMMAI (FATHER OF —) ONAM REKEM

SHAMMES BEADLE

SHAMMUA (FATHER OF —) DAVID ZACCUR
(MOTHER OF —) BATHSHEBA
(SON OF —) ABDA

SHAMPOO TRIPSIS

SHAMPOOING TRIPSIS

SHAMROCK SEAMROG SHAMROOT

SHANK BODY CRUS GAMB JAMB TANG FEMUR GAMBE CANNON NIBBLE TARSUS KNUCKLE
(THREAD —) STEM

SHANNY BULLY

SHANTY BOIST HUMPY HUTCH SHACK SHEBANG CHANTIER DOGHOUSE

SHAPE AX ADZ AXE CUT DIE HUE ADZE BEAT BEND CAST COLE COPE DRAW FACE FAIR FORM HACK MOLD NICK BEVEL BLOCK BOAST BUILT COLOR DRAPE DRESS FEIGN FORGE FRAME GUISE HORSE JOLLY LATHE MODEL MOULD SWAGE BROACH CHISEL CUTOUT EFFORM FIGURE FORMER FRAISE HAMMER JIGGER SQUARE CHANNEL CONFORM CONTOUR FASHION FEATURE GESTALT INCLINE OUTLINE PATTERN TONNEAU CONTRIVE LIKENESS
(— BY HAMMERING) SMITH
(— DIAMOND) BRUTE
(— GARMENTS) BOARD

(— METAL) SWAGE EXTRUDE
(— OF BUST) TAILLE
(— OF ENVELOPE FLAP) KNIFE
(— ON POTTER'S WHEEL) THROW
(— ONE'S COURSE) ETTLE
(— RIGHTLY) FIT
(— ROUGHLY) BOAST SCABBLE SCAPPLE
(— ROUGHLY WITH CHISEL) BOAST
(— STONE) BROACH SCABBLE
(CLAY —) FLOATER
(CONICAL —) BEEHIVE
(GEM —) BAGUET BAGUETTE
(GLOVE —) TRANK
(SPIRALLING —) SWIRL
(SURFACE —) GEOMETRY
(UNBLOCKED —) HOOD
(PREF.) MORPH(O)

SHAPED BUILT FITTED BLOCKED FEATURED
(— LIKE BEAN) FABIFORM
(— LIKE BERRY) BACCIFORM
(— LIKE BOAT) SCAPHOID NAVICULAR
(— LIKE BUCKLER) SCUTATE
(— LIKE CLUB) CLAVATE CLUBBED
(— LIKE COMB) CTENOID
(— LIKE CONE) CONIFORM
(— LIKE CUP) SCYPHATE
(— LIKE DOME) DOMAL
(— LIKE EAR) AURIFORM
(— LIKE FIDDLE) PANDURATE
(— LIKE HALBERD) HASTATE
(— LIKE HEART) CORDATE CORDIFORM
(— LIKE HOOK) ANKYROID
(— LIKE HORN) CORNIFORM
(— LIKE KEEL) CARINATE
(— LIKE LEAF) FOLIATE
(— LIKE LENS) LENTOID PHACOID
(— LIKE NEEDLE) ACUATE
(— LIKE ORANGE) OBLATE
(— LIKE PEAR) PYRIFORM
(— LIKE PULLEY) TROCHLEAR
(— LIKE RING) ANNULAR
(— LIKE ROD) BACILLAR
(— LIKE S) SIGMATE
(— LIKE SAUSAGE) ALLANTOID
(— LIKE SHIELD) ASPIDATE CLYPEATE
(— LIKE SICKLE) FALCULAR
(— LIKE SPINDLE) FUSOID FUSIFORM
(— LIKE SPUR) CALCARINE
(— LIKE STAR) ASTROID
(— LIKE STRAP) LIGULATE
(— LIKE SWORD) GLADIATE
(— LIKE THREAD) FILIFORM
(— LIKE TURNIP) NAPIFORM
(— LIKE WEDGE) CUNEAL CUNEATE
(— LIKE X) SALTIRE
(— WITH AX) HEWN

SHAPELESS DUMPY CLUMPY DEFORM DUMPTY INFORM FORMLESS INDIGEST UNSHAPED

SHAPELINESS DELICACY

SHAPELY GENT TIDY TRIM CLEAN TIGHT DECENT FORMAL GAINLY FEATOUS FORMFUL SHAPABLE

SHAPHAT (FATHER OF —) HORI ADLAI SHEMAIAH
(SON OF —) ELISHA

SHAPING DESCENT

SHARAI (FATHER OF —) BANI

SHARAR (SON OF —) AHIAM

SHARD SCAUR SHERD SHRED
(PL.) PITCHER

SHARE CUT END LOT RUG CANT DALE DEAL DOLE HAND PART PLOT RENT SCOT SNIP DIVVY ENTER PARTY QUOTA RATIO SHEAR SHIFT SLICE SNACK SNICK SNUCK SPLIT WHACK COMMON COPART DEPART DIVIDE FINGER IMPART RATION SHOVEL PARTAGE PARTAKE PORTION DIVIDEND DIVISION INTEREST PURPARTY PERCENTAGE PROPORTION
(— A BED) BUNK
(— EQUALLY) HALVE
(— IN ACTIVITY) PIECE
(— OF EXPENSES) LAW CLUB
(— OF LAND) DAIL DALE FREEDOM RUNDALE
(— OF PROFIT) LAY
(— OF STOCK) STOCK ACTION
(— QUARTERS) CHUM
(— SECRETS) CONFIDE
(ALLOTED —) DOLE
(ANCESTRAL —) PATTI
(FULL —) SKINFUL
(GREATER —) FECK
(LEGAL —) HAK
(ONE'S —) AFFERE
(PROPORTIONAL —) QUOTA
(SMALL —) MOIETY
(PREF.) MER(I)(O) MERISTO
(SUFF.) MER(E)(IC)(IS)(OUS)(Y)

SHARECROPPER BYWONER CROPPER

SHARED JOINT BETWEEN
(PREF.) CO

SHAREZER (BROTHER OF —) ESARHADDON ADRAMMELECH
(FATHER OF —) SENNACHERIB

SHARING (— OF EXPENSE) CLUB
(— VICARIOUSLY) ARMCHAIR

SHARK FOX GATA HAYE KULP MAKO MANO TOPE GUMMY HOMER HOUND LAMIA TIGER TOMMY TOPER BEAGLE DAGGAR GALEID PALOMA REQUIN WHALER ACRODUS BONEDOG DOGFISH FOXFISH HUNFYSH PLACOID REQUIEM SLEEPER SOUPFIN SQUALID SUNFISH TIBURON TIGRONE TUBARON BULLHEAD HYBODONT ROUSETTE SAILFISH SEAHOUND SKAAMOOG SPEAREYE SQUATINA THRASHER PORBEAGLE SELACHIAN SHOVELHEAD
(YOUNG —) CUB SHARKLET
(PREF.) SQUALI SQUALO

SHARP DRY SHY ACID ACRE CUTE EDGY FELL FINE GAIR GASH GLEG GNIB HARD HIGH KEEN PERT SALT TART ACERB ACRID ACUTE ALERT BRASH BREME BRISK CRISP DOWNY EAGER EDGED FALSE HARSH NASAL NEBBY NIPPY PEERY QUICK SMART SNELL SQUAB STEEP STIFF VIVID YAULD ACIDIC ACUATE ARGUTE ASTUTE BITING BITTER BRIGHT CRISPY

DIESIS GLASSY JAGGED PLUCKY SEVERE SHREWD SHRILL SNELLY SNITHE STINGY TOOTHY TWEAKY UNRIDE ANGULAR AUSTERE BRITTLE CAUSTIC CUTTING GINGERY NIPPING PIQUANT POINTED PUNGENT SHARPEN SLICING SPINOUS VARMINT VIOLENT HATCHETY INCISIVE POIGNANT ACRIMONIOUS
(PREF.) ACET(O) ACUT(I)(O) OXY

SHARP-EDGED VORPAL CULTRATE

SHARPEN EDGE FILE FINE HONE KEEN WHET BRISK FROST GRIND POINT RAISE SHARP SLYPE STONE STROP ACCENT AFFILE STROKE ENHANCE QUICKEN SMARTEN EXACUATE HEIGHTEN

SHARPENED ACUATE

SHARPENER SHARPER STROPPER
(SCYTHE —) RIP RIFLE

SHARPER GUE GYP BITE KITE ROOK SKIN SNAP BITER CHEAT CROOK GREEK ROGUE SHARK SHARP BESTER COGGER NICKUM PICARO ROOKER SHARPY BARNARD CATALAN GAMBLER SHARKER SPIELER BLACKLEG DECEIVER PIGEONER SWINDLER

SHARPLY DAB SHARP SNACK ACIDLY ROUNDLY SHEERLY SMARTLY STEEPLY

SHARPNESS WIT EDGE SALT WHET PLUCK ACRITY ACUITY ACUMEN ACIDITY ACERBITY ACRIDITY ACRIMONY ASPERITY EDGINESS PUNGENCY

SHARP-POINTED ACUATE ACULEATE
(PREF.) ACUT(I)(O)

SHARPSHOOTER JAGER VOLTIGEUR TIRAILLEUR BERSAGLIERE

SHARP-SIGHTED SIGHTY LYNCEAN

SHARP-TAILED GROUSE PINTAIL

SHARP-WITTED ACUTE CANNY SNELL SHREWD

SHASHAI (FATHER OF —) BANI

SHASHAK (FATHER OF —) ELPAAL

SHASTRA PURANA SASTRA
(— CLASS) SRUTI

SHATTER BLOW DASH DICE BLAST BREAK BURST CRASH CRAZE CREEM FRUSH SMASH SMOKE SPLIT WRECK SHIVER SPIDER BEGUILE CHATTER CONVELL EXPLODE SMATTER TORPEDO DEMOLISH DYNAMITE SPLINTER
(— CLAY TARGET) KILL

SHATTERED BROKEN BROOZLED DODDERED

SHAUL (FATHER OF —) SIMEON

SHAVE BARB BITE DRAW PARE RAZE GLACE GRAZE SKIVE SCHAWE SCRAPE FLATTEN UPRIGHT

SHAVED POLLED SHAVEN

SHAVEN NOT NOTT PILLED TONSURED

SHAVING SHAVE SHRED SPALE SPELL RAMENT RAMENTUM
(PL.) COOM COOMB SCOBS MOSLINGS

SHAWL MAUD WRAP LAMBA MANTA MANTO NUBIA PATTU RUMAL SCARF TOZIE AFGHAN ANGORA KAMBAL PEPLOS PEPLUM PEPLUS PUTTOO SERAPE TAPALO TOILET TONNAG ZEPHYR AMLIKAR CHUDDAR PAISLEY WHITTLE WRAPPER ALGERINE CASHMERE EPIBLEMA KAFFIYEH SLENDANG TURNOVER
(COARSE —) KAMBAL
(COTTON —) FARDA
(PLAID —) MAUD
(TASSELED —) TALLITH
SHAWM WAIT SHALM BOMBARD SCHALMEI
SHE A HE HEO HER SHU HAEC SCHO
(AUTHOR OF —) HAGGARD
(CHARACTER IN —) JOB LEO SHE HOLLY AYESHA LUDWIG USTANE VINCEY BILLALI MAHOMED KALLIKRATES
SHEAF TIE BEAT BUNG GAIT GERB OMER FLASH GAVEL GERBE GLEAN BATTEN THRAVE DORLACH HATTOCK CAPSHEAF CORNBOLE
(— LEVIED AS TAX) CORNBOLE
(— OF ARROWS) FLASH
(— OF FLAX OR HEMP) BEAT BEET GLEAN
(— OF GRAIN) GAIT GARB HOSE GARBAGE
(LAST — OF CORN) NECK
(LAST — OF HARVEST) KIRN
(PROTECTING —) HATTOCK
(UNBOUND —) REAP GAVEL
SHEAL **(FATHER OF —)** BANI
SHEALTIEL **(SON OF —)** ZERUBBABEL
SHEAR COW CUT DOD LIP NOT CLIP CROP NOTT TRIM BREAK FORCE SHARE SHEER SHIRL SLIDE STRIP FLEECE STRESS
SHEARER SNAGGER
SHEARIAH **(FATHER OF —)** AZEL
SHEARLING SHEARHOG
(PL.) ALPACA
SHEARS LEWIS SNIPS FORFEX SHEARER SNOUTER SECATEUR
(PREF.) FORFICI
SHEARWATER HAG CREW COHOW HAGDON HAGLET PETREL PUFFIN SCRABE PIMLICO SCRABER SEABIRD HACKBOLT
SHEATFISH WELS DORAD WALLER CATFISH SILURID
SHEATH COT HOT BOOT CASE CYST HOSE HOTT ARMOR CHAPE FOREL GAINE OCREA SHADE SHEAF SPILL THECA VOLVA COCOON CONDOM FORREL MYELIN OCHREA QUIVER SLOUGH VAGINA AXILEMMA EPILEMMA SCABBARD STANDARD VAGINULA NEURILEMMA
(— FOR BOOK) FOREL FORRIL
(— FOR FINGER) STALL
(— FOR GAMECOCK'S SPUR) HOT HOTT
(— OF CIGARETTE) SPILL
(— OF PLOW) STANDARD

(— OF TISSUE) PERIBLEM
(MEDULLARY —) CORONA
(PREF.) COLE(O) COLI(O) ELYTR(O)
(SUFF.) LEMMA THECA THECIUM
SHEATHBILL PADDY
SHEATHE CLAD COPPER MUZZLE IMPLATE
SHEATHED THECATE
SHEATHING SKIN ARMOR COPPER FACING SHEATH INLAYER SHIPLAP SLITWORK
SHEA TREE KARITE KARITI
SHEAVE SHEAF SHIVER HATTOCK TRUCKLE
(24 —S OF GRAIN) THRAVE THREAVE
SHEBA **(FATHER OF —)** BICHRI
SHEBANG HUT
SHEBER **(FATHER OF —)** CALEB
(MOTHER OF —) MAACHAH
SHEBUEL **(FATHER OF —)** HEMAN
SHECHANIAH **(FATHER OF —)** ARAH JEHIEL
(SON OF —) SHEMAIAH
SHED BOX CUB SOW ABRI CAST COTE DROP HELM HULL KILN MOLT PEEL POUR SHUD SKEO SLIP BOOTH HIELD HOVEL MOULT SCALE SHADE SPILL THROW VINEA ZAYAT BELFRY BROACH DINGLE EFFUSE GARAGE HANGAR HEMMEL INFUSE LINHAY MISTAL PANDAL SLOUGH CHOLTRY COTTAGE DIFFUSE DISCARD MUSCLE RADIATE SKIPPER EXUVIATE SKEELING SKILLION WOODSHED PENTHOUSE
(— BLOOD) BROACH
(— DROPS) DRIZZLE
(— FEATHERS OR HORNS) MEW
(— FOR LIVESTOCK) SHIPPEN
(— FOR SHEEP) SHEALING
(— OVER MINE SHAFT) COE
(— TEARS) GIVE
(— TO PROTECT SOLDIERS) TESTUDO
(CATTLE —) CUB HELM LAIR BELFRY
(MOVABLE —) SOW BAIL MUSCLE
(TEMPORARY —) PANDAL
(WEATHER —) DINGLE
SHEDDING FALL SPILTH ECDYSIS APOLYSIS
SHE-DEMON LAMIA
SHEDEUR **(SON OF —)** ELIZUR
SHEEN GLAZE SHINE LUSTER LUSTRE SHIMMER
SHEEP SNA TEG DOWN LAMB LONK MUGS SHIP SOAY URIN ZENU ANCON BOVID DUMBA HEDER HUNIA MUGGS OVINE SAIGA SHORN TAGGE AOUDAD ARGALI BARHAL BHARAL BIDENT CHURRO DECCAN DORPER DORSET EXMOOR HIRSEL MARKER MASHAM MERINO MUTTON NAYAUR OXFORD PANAMA PAULAR ROMNEY WETHER WOOLIE WOOLLY BIGHORN BLEATER BRAXIES CHEVIOT CRIOLLA DELAINE DISHLEY FREEZER FRONTER JUMBUCK KARAKUL LINCOLN POLLARD

SUFFOLK TARGHEE TWINTER VERMONT BIKANERI COMEBACK COTSWOLD DARTMOOR HERDWICK LONGWOOL LUGHDOAN RUMINANT SHEARHOG SHEARING TALLOWER THRINTER MONTADALE ROMELDALE SHROPSHIRE
(— DIFFICULT TO HANDLE) COBBLER
(— IN 2ND YEAR) HOB TAG TEG TAGGE TWINTER
(— THAT HAS SHED PORTION OF WOOL) ROSELLA
(— TO BE SHEARED) BOARD
(DEAD —) MORT BRAXY MORLING
(FEMALE —) EWE GIMMER SHEDER
(HORNLESS —) NOT NOTT
(LOST —) WAIF
(MALE —) RAM TUP BUCK HEDER DINMONT
(MOUNTAIN —) IBEX
(OLD —) GUMMER
(PART OF —) EAR EYE LEG RIB BACK DOCK FACE LOIN NECK RACK RUMP FLANK SHANK BREAST MUZZLE BRISKET FORELEG PASTERN WITHERS FOREHEAD SHOULDER FORESHANK
(THICK-WOOLED —) MUG
(UNSHORN —) HOG TEG
(WILD —) SHA ARGAL AUDAD RASSE URIAL AOUDAD ARGALI BHARAL SHAPOO BURRHEL MOUFLON
(YOUNG —) HOG HOGG HOGGEREL
(3-YEAR-OLD —) THRINTER
SHEEPBERRY ALISIER VIBURNUM
SHEEPCOTE SHEPPEY
SHEEPDOG KELPIE SHELTY BOBTAIL MALINOIS SHETLAND
SHEEP FLY FAG
SHEEPFOLD REE FANK KRAAL REEVE STELL BOUGHT BARKARY SHEPPEY SHEEPCOT
SHEEPHERDER SNOOZER STOCKMAN
SHEEPISH SHY
SHEEP LAUREL IVY HEATH WICKY KALMIA LAUREL CALFKILL LAMBKILL
SHEEPLIKE OVINE
SHEEPMAN HOBBER
SHEEP PLANT RAOULIA
SHEEP ROT CAW
SHEEP RUN STATION
SHEEPSHEAD JAMES JEMMY JIMMY PARGO PORGY TAUTOG FATHEAD PERCOID SPAROID
SHEEPSHEARER GUN
SHEEPSKIN ROAN SLAT MOUTON SOLDIER CAPESKIN LAMBSKIN WOOLFELL WOOLSKIN
(— TANNED WITH BARK) BASAN BASIL
(— THAT SWEATS UNEVENLY) SOLDIER
(— WITHOUT WOOL) SLAT
(ROUGH-TANNED —) CRUST
SHEEP SORREL SOURWEED
SHEEP TICK FAG KEB KED KADE
SHEEPWALK SLAIT
SHEER BOLD FINE MAIN MERE

PURE BLANK BRANT CRUDE FRANK NAKED STARK STEEP SIMPLE CLOTTED GAZETTE EVENDOWN
(MADE OF — FABRIC) PEEKABOO
SHEET FIN CARD FILM FINE FLAT FOIL LEAF SILL BLANK FLONG FOLIO NAPPE CANVAS CIRCLE DOUBLE FASCIA FENDER FLIMSY SHROUD SINDON BLANKET CHUDDAR CHUDDER FLOGGER FRISKET LEAFLET PALLIUM PAPYRUS WRAPPER AIRSHEET EIGHTEEN FOLLOWER HANDBILL INTERLAY SHEETLET
(— ADDED TO DEED) FOLLOWER
(— ATTACHED TO INVOICE) APRON
(— FOR BRIDGE SCORES) FLOGGER
(— OF CELLULOID) CEL CELL
(— OF CLOUDS) PALLIUM
(— OF DOUGH) STRUDEL
(— OF FIBER) BAT LAP BATT
(— OF ICE) GLARE GLAZE
(— OF IRON) CRAMPET CRAMPIT
(— OF LAVA) COULEE
(— OF LEAD) SOAKER
(— OF LEATHER) BUFFING
(— OF MICA) FILM
(— OF MUSCLE) PLATYSMA
(— OF PAPER) FLAT FOLIO FRISKET LEAFLET HANDBILL
(— OF PARCHMENT) SKIN FOLLOWER
(— OF RUBBER) DAM
(— OF STAMPS) PANE
(— OF STRAW) YELM
(— OF SUGAR) SLAB
(— OF TISSUE) FASCIA
(— OF TOBACCO) BINDER
(— OF WATER) NAPPE
(— USED FOR MATRIX) FLONG
(HEATED —) CAUL
(METAL —S) LATTENS
(NEWS —) GAZETTE
(ORGANIZATION —) BILL
(PERFORATED —) SIEVE
(PROTECTIVE —) CURTAIN
(THEATRICAL —) SIDE
(THIN —S OF IRON) DOUBLES
(TRANSPARENT —) GELATINE
(WINDING —) SINDON SUDARY
(PREF.) PALLIO
SHEETING PERCALE DOMESTIC AMERIKANI
SHEHARIAH **(FATHER OF —)** JEHORAM
SHEKEL **(HALF —)** BEKAH
SHEKINAH GLORY
SHELAH **(FATHER OF —)** JUDAH
SHELDRAKE SHELDER BARGOOSE BERGANDER
SHELEMIAH **(FATHER OF —)** BANI ABDEEL
(SON OF —) IRIJAH JEHUCAL HANANIAH
SHELEPH **(FATHER OF —)** JOKTAN
SHELESH **(FATHER OF —)** HELEM
SHELF BANK BERM BINK DECK DESS STEP TACK BENCH LEDGE SKELF STAGE STOOL MANTEL SCONCE SETTLE SHELVE BACKBAR BRACKET COUNTER PLATEAU CREDENCE CUPBOARD

(— BEFORE STOVE) HEARTH
(— BEHIND ALTAR) GRADINE
GRADINO RETABLE
(— IN MINE) BUNNING
(— OF ROCK) CAR LENCH
LENCHEON
(ALTAR —) BUTSUDAN
(CONTINENTAL —) PLATFORM
(FIREWORKS —) BALLOON
(RAISED —) SETTLE
SHELL ARD HUD PEN POD BAND
CASK CHOU CLAM CONE HARD
HOOF HULL HUSK MAIL OBUS
PELL PILL PIPI PUPA SKIN SWAD
UMBO UNIO BALAT CHANK CHINK
CONCH COPIS CRUMP CRUST
DRILL FRITZ GOURD MITER MITRA
MUREX ORMER SCAUP SHALE
SHARD SHEAL SHERD SHOCK
SHUCK TESTA TIARA TROCA
TURBO VALVE VENUS ANOMIA
ARCHIE BUCKIE BULLET BURGAU
CERION COCKLE CONKER COWRIE
CRUSTA DENTAL DOLIUM ECLAIR
JINGLE LORICA MAROON NOUGAT
NUCULA PULLET PURPLE SANKHA
SINGLE SLOUGH STROMB TRITON
TURBAN VANNET VENTER
VOLUTE WINKLE BALANUS
BALLOON CARACOL CARCASS
COCONUT DARIOLE DISCINA
GLADIUS LIMACEL MARINER
PAPBOAT PHILINE PROJECT
SCALLOP SPICULE SPINDLE
SPONDYL TEREBRA THIMBLE
TOHEROA TORPEDO TOXIFER
TROCHID TRUMPET UNICORN
BACULITE BACULOID CARAPACE
CONCHITE COQUILLE CYLINDER
DUCKFOOT EGGSHELL ENVELOPE
ESCALLOP FIGSHELL FOCALOID
FRUSTULE HELICINA MENINGES
OLIVELLA PUPARIUM SEASHELL
SOLARIUM STROMBUS UNIVALVE
VELUTINA VERMETID VERMETUS
WARRENER WHIZBANG
WOODCOCK
(— CONTAINING MEDICINE)
CAPSULE
(— OF DIATOM) FRUSTULE
(— OF OYSTER) HUSK SHUCK
(— OF SHIP) HULK SKIN
(— OF SLUG) LIMACEL
(— OF THE EARTH) SIAL
(— SYSTEMATICALLY) COMB
(—S FROM GUN) STUFF
(ANTIAIRCRAFT —) FLAK ARCHIE
(CARTRIDGE —S) BRASS
(CAST —S) EXUVIAE
(CUSTARD-FILLED —) ECLAIR
DARIOLE
(EMPTY —) DOP
(FOSSIL —) DOLITE AMMONITE
BACULITE BALANITE CONCHITE
(HOWITZER —) OBUS
(MATHEMATICAL —) HOMEOID
(OYSTER —S) CULCH CULTCH
(PART OF —) EAR LIP RIB TIP APEX
WING HINGE SPIRE VALVE
WHORL MUSCLE SUTURE
ADDUCTOR APERTURE
(PASTA —S) MANICOTTI
(PASTRY —) CORNET QUICHE

DARIOLE TIMBALE TALMOUSE
(PROTEIN —) CAPSID
(SNAIL —) CONKER HODMADOD
(SPIRAL —) CHANK
(TORTOISE —) HOOF
(VEGETABLE —) DOLMA
(PREF.) CHITINO CHITO CONCH(O)
LOPO OECO OSTRAC(O) TESTI
(SUFF.) OECA OECIA OSTRACA
SHELLED VINED
SHELLFISH ORM COCK BUCKY
NACRE PIROT BUCKIE LIMPET
WIGGLE MOLLUSK PERIWIG
ASTACIAN
(PART OF —) EYE FAN LEG CLAW
TAIL SHELL TOOTH FEELER
RIPPER TELSON UROPOD
ABDOMEN ANTENNA CRUSHER
CARAPACE
SHELLING RATTLES
SHELL-LESS OON
SHELL MONEY UHLLO WAKIKI
SHELOMI (FATHER OF —) ABIHUD
SHELOMITH (FATHER OF —) DIBRI
ZERUBBABEL
SHELTER CAB HUT LEE LOO ABRI
BURY EAVE GIDE GITE HERD HIDE
HIVE JOKE JOUK LOWN ROOF
SCOG SCUG BARTH BELEE BENAB
BERRY BIELD BOIST BOOTH
BOTHY BOWER CABIN CLEAD
CLOAK COVER EMBAY HAVEN
HOARD HOUSE HOVEL HOVER
HOWFF HUTCH LEWTH LITHE
RESET SCOUG SHADE SHEAL
ASYLUM AWNING BELFRY BILBIE
BOOLEY BOUGHT BURROW
COVERT CRADLE DEFEND
DUGOUT GABION GUNYAH
HANGAR HARBOR HOSTEL
PANDAL REFUGE SCONCE SCREEN
SHADOW SHIELD SHROUD
SUKKAH BOROUGH CABINET
CARPORT CHAMBER DEFENSE
EMBOSOM EMBOWER HOUSING
NACELLE QUARTER RETREAT
ROOFING TABERNA UMBRAGE
WANIGAN WICKIUP BESCREEN
DOGHOUSE ENSCONCE
LODGMENT PALLIATE SECURITY
SHIELING SNOWSHED WAYHOUSE
PESTHOUSE
(— FOR CATTLE) HELM BOOLY
STELL HEMMEL
(— FOR CROP WATCHERS) KISI
(— FOR DANCES) ENRAMADA
(— FOR SENTRY) GUERITE
(— FROM WEATHER) LEWTH
(— OVER BEEHIVE) HOOD
(BULLETPROOF —) MANTLET
MANTELET
(CONCRETE-AND-STEEL —) PILLBOX
(CRAMPED —) HUTCH
(FISH —) CROY
(LEAFY —) LEVESEL
(MINING —) TALPA
(PORTABLE —) MANTA CABANA
(ROCK —) KRAPINA
(ROUGH —) JACAL
(TEEPEELIKE —) CHUM
(TEMPORARY —) HALE HOLD
CABIN BIVOUAC
SHELTERED LEE LEW COSY COZY

LOWN SNUG BIELD LITHE SHADY
COVERT
(— SPACE) KILLOGIE
SHELTERED LIFE (AUTHOR OF —)
GLASGOW
(CHARACTER IN —) EVA BENA
CORA ETTA JOHN DELIA JENNY
WELCH BARRON GEORGE JOSEPH
PEYTON CROCKER ARCHBALD
BIRDSONG ISABELLA
SHELTERING BIELDY SHADING
SHELTERLESS HOMELESS
ROOFLESS
SHELUMIEL (FATHER OF —)
ZURISHADDAI
SHELVE DISH BURKE SHELF SHUNT
PIGEONHOLE
SHELVES STAGE ETAGERE
SHEM (BROTHER OF —) HAM
JAPHET
(FATHER OF —) NOAH
SHEMA (FATHER OF —) ELPAAL
SHEMAIAH (FATHER OF —) JOEL
HARIM DELAIAH HASSHUB
ADONIKAM OBEDEDOM
ELIZAPHAN NETHANEEL
SHECHANIAH
(SON OF —) ABDA DELAIAH
OBADIAH
SHEMARIAH (FATHER OF —) BANI
SHEMIDA (FATHER OF —) GILEAD
SHEMUEL (FATHER OF —) TOLA
SHENAZAR (FATHER OF —)
JECONIAH
SHENG SANG CHENG SHING
(ONE-HUNDREDTH —) CHAO
SHEOL HELL
SHEPHATHIAH (SON OF —)
MESHULLAM
SHEPHATIAH (FATHER OF —) DAVID
JEHOSHAPHAT
SHEPHERD HERD SHEP COLIN
CORIN GADDI GYGES SWAIN
FEEDER PASTOR TARBOX
CORYDON DAPHNIS DRAFTER
GADARIA KURUMBA THYRSIS
TITYRUS MELIBEUS MENALCAS
PASTORAL SHEEPMAN STREPHON
(GERMAN —) ALSATIAN
SHEPHERDESS DELIA MOPSA
PHEBE DORCAS BERGERE
GALATEA PASTORA PERDITA
AMARYLLIS
SHEPHERD KING, THE
(CHARACTER IN —) ELISA AMINTA
TAMIRI AGENORE ALESSANDRO
(COMPOSER OF —) MOZART
SHEPHERD'S-PURSE TOYWORT
CASEWEED COCOWORT
SHEPHI (FATHER OF —) SHOBAL
SHERAH (FATHER OF —) EPHRAIM
SHERBET ICE GLACE SHRAB
SORBET GRANITA SOUFFLE
SHERD SCARTH
SHERESH (FATHER OF —) MACHIR
(MOTHER OF —) MAACHAH
SHERIFF FOUD FOWD SCULT XERIF
DEPUTY GRIEVE SCHOUT SHIRRA
BAILIFF SHREEVE SHRIEVE
ALGUACIL HUISSIER SHIREMAN
VISCOUNT
SHERRY FINO CLOVE JEREZ XERES
DOCTOR MANCHU SOLERA

OLOROSO RANGOON SHERRIS
MONTILLA MANZANILLA
SHERRY BROWN CLOVE
SHESHAI (FATHER OF —) ANAK
SHE STOOPS TO CONQUER
(AUTHOR OF —) GOLDSMITH
(CHARACTER IN —) KATE TONY
MARLOW CHARLES LUMPKIN
NEVILLE HASTINGS PEDIGREE
CONSTANCE HARDCASTLE
SHEVA (FATHER OF —) CALEB
(MOTHER OF —) MAACHAH
SHEVRI SESBAN
SHICER DUFFER
SHIELD ECU EGIS HIDE PELT AEGIS
APRON BIELD BOARD CLOAK
COVER FENCE GUARD GULAR
MULGA PATCH PAVIS PELTA
PYGAL SCUTE SHEND TARGE
YELDE ANCILE ANGARA BLAZON
CASQUE DEFEND FENDER
GUNTUB GYROMA LINDEN
MENTAL OCULAR PAUNCH
RONDEL SCREEN SCUTUM
SECURE TARGET BUCKLER
CLIPEUS CLYPEUS CONCEAL
LOZENGE PANNIER PAVISSE
PRIDWIN PROTECT ROSTRAL
ROTELLA ROUNDEL SHELTER
SUPPORT TESTUDO CARTOUCH
CUCULLUS HIELAMEN INSULATE
MARGINAL PRESERVE RONDACHE
STERNITE SUNSHADE BREASTING
(— BELOW A DAM) APRON
(— FOR ARCHERS) PANNIER
(— FOR HORSE) BIB
(— FOR LAMP) BONNET CHIMNEY
(— OF A STIRRUP) HOOD
(— OF ABORIGINES) MULGA
HIELAMEN
(— OF CONTINENT) CORE
(— OF HIDE) SKILDFEL
(— OF SOMITE) STERNITE
(— OF TRILOBITE) CEPHALON
(— ON MAST) PAUNCH
(— ON THROAT OF FISH) GULAR
(— OVER BASE OF FAN) CANOPY
(— WITHOUT ARMS) ALBERIA
(BONY —) CARAPACE
(BULLETPROOF —) MANTA
MANTLET MANTELET
(HERALDIC —) BLAZON
(KING ARTHUR'S —) PRIWEN
PRIDWIN
(LEATHER —) CHAFE
(PART OF —) RIB BOSS ORLE UMBO
ANTIA
(SACRED —) ANCILE
(SIBERIAN —) ANGARA
(WICKERWORK —) SCIATH
(PREF.) ASPID(O) CLYPEI CLYPEO
PELTATI PELTATO SCUT(I)
SCUTATI SCUTELLI
(SUFF.) ASPIS
SHIELDBEARER SQUIRE ESQUIRE
PELTAST ESCUDERO SCUTIFER
SHIELD BUG STINKBUG
SHIELD FERN FERNGALE
SHIELDMAKER TYCHIOS
SHIELD-SHAPED PELTATE
SCUTATE THYROID
SHIFT JIB BACK CHOP CORE FEND
FLIT HAUL MOVE RUSE SHIP TACK

TOUR TURN VARY VEER WEND
BREAK BUDGE CREEP CYMAR
DRIFT HOTCH QUIRK SHIRK
SHUNT SIMAR SKIFT SLIDE
SMOCK SPELL TRICK BAFFLE
CHANGE DENIAL DEVICE DOUBLE
PALTER SKYFTE SWERVE SWITCH
CHEMISE CUTBACK EVASION
FRESHEN SHUFFLE SLEIGHT
WHIFFLE ARTIFICE DISLODGE
DISPLACE DOGWATCH DOUBLING
MUTATION RESOURCE REVIRADO
TRANSFER TRAVERSE TURNOVER
WINDLASS
(— ABOUT AS THE WIND) LARGE
(— ABRUPTLY) JUMP
(— IN DANCING) BALANCE
(— IN TACKING) JIB
(— ORDER OF BELLS) HUNT
(— RAILROAD EQUIPMENT) DRILL
(— SUDDENLY) FLY CHOP GYBE
JIBE
(— WEIGHT) WING
(MINING —) CORE
SHIFTINESS LUBRICITY
SHIFTING FLUID QUICK AMBULANT
CHOPPING DRIFTING FLOATING
SLIPPAGE VARIABLE VEERABLE
SHIFTLESS DRIFTY SOZZLY
DRIFTING FECKLESS HAVELESS
SHIFTLESSNESS SLOUCH
SHIFTY GREASY DEVIOUS EVASIVE
HANGDOG SLIDING SLIPPERY
SHIITE SHIAH SECTARY SHAIKHI
TWELVER
SHILHA SHLU CHLEUH
SHILHI (DAUGHTER OF —) AZUBAH
SHILL STICK BONNET CAPPER
BOOSTER
SHILLEM (FATHER OF —) NAPHTALI
SHILLING BOB HOG CHIP HOGG
LEVY PREST DEENER HARPER
TESTON TEVISS THIRTEEN
(20 —S) POUND
(21 —S) GUINEA
(5 —S) CROWN DECUS
SHILLY-SHALLY BACK BOGGLE
SHILSHAH (FATHER OF —) ZOPHAH
SHIM GLUT LINER SHIMMER
SHIMEA (FATHER OF —) DAVID
SHIMEATH (SON OF —) ZABAD
JOZACHAR
SHIMEI (BROTHER OF —) CONONIAH
ZERUBBABEL
(FATHER OF —) BANI GERA KISH
JAHATH GERSHON PEDAIAH
JEDUTHUN
SHIMMA (BROTHER OF —) DAVID
(FATHER OF —) JESSE
SHIMMER FLASH GLIMMER
SHIMPER SKIMMER
SHIMRI (FATHER OF —) SHEMAIAH
(SON OF —) JEDIAEL
SHIMRITH (SON OF —) JEHOZABAD
SHIMRON (FATHER OF —) ISSACHAR
SHIN SHANK SKINK SWARM
CNEMIS SHINNY
SHINBONE
(SUFF.) CNEMA CNEMIA CNEMIC
CNEMUS
SHINDIG SHINDY SHIVOO
SHINDY ROW BOBBERY
SHINE RAY SUN BEAM BUFF GLOW

LAMP LEAM LINK STAR BLARE
BLICK BLINK BLOOM EXCEL GLAIK
GLARE GLEAM GLEIT GLENT
GLINT GLISS GLORE GLORY GLOSS
GLOZE SHEEN SKYRE STARE
BEACON DAZZLE GLANCE LUSTER
LUSTRE SCANCE EFFULGE
GLIMMER GLISTEN GLITTER
RADIATE REFLECT SHIMMER
SPARKLE RUTILATE
(— BRIGHTLY) BEEK FLAME LIGHT
(— FAINTLY) SCARROW
(— UPON) SUN SMITE
SHINER CHUB DACE BREAM
REDFIN CYPRINID WINDFISH
SHINER-UP PATCHER
SHINGLE SHIM BEACH SHAKE
SHIDE SLATE ASTYLL CHESIL
KNOBBLE STARTER
SHINGLER NOBBLER
SHINGLES ZONA ZOSTER
(PREF.) ZOSTERI ZOSTERO
SHININESS GLARE GLAZE GLOSS
SHINING GLAD NEAT CLEAR GLARY
LIGHT LUCID NITID SHEER WHITE
ARDENT ARGENT ASHINE BRIGHT
FULGID GLOSSY GOLDEN LUCENT
MARBLE NITENT ORIENT SERENE
SHEENY SPUNKY STARRY
ADAZZLE BURNING FULGENT
GLARING GLIMMER LAMPING
FLASHING GLEAMING LUCULENT
LUSTRANT LUSTROUS NITIDOUS
RELUCENT RUTILANT SPLENDID
STARLIKE SUNBEAMY SUNSHINY
(PREF.) STILPNO
SHINLEAF PYROLA
SHINNY PEG SHINTY
SHINTO (— SECT) RYOBU
SHINTY CAMANACHA
SHIP (ALSO SEE BOAT AND VESSEL)
ARK CAT COG HOY NAO BARK
BOAT BOOM GRAB HAND HULK
KEEL LADE NAVY PAHI PINE PINK
SAIL SEND SNOW TREE WOOD
ZULU CHECK LAKER OILER PINTA
PRORE RAZEE SCOUT SCREW
SKIFF WHELP ANDREW ARGOSY
BARKEY BARQUE BOTTOM
CARTEL CASTLE CHASER COALER
CODMAN DECKER DIESEL GALIOT
GALLEY HOLCAD HOPPER
LANCHA LATEEN LORCHA
MASTER MISTIC MOTHER PACKET
PUFFER RUNNER SAILER SALVOR
SEALER SMOKER TONNER TRAVEL
VESSEL ADMIRAL CARRACK
CLIPPER COLLIER CONSORT
DROMOND FACTORY FELUCCA
FOREIGN FRIGATE FRUITER
GABBARD GALLEON GUNBOAT
INVOICE MACHINE MULETTA
ONERARY PATAMAR PINNACE
POLACRE SHALLOP SHIPLET
SPITKIT STEAMER BALANDRA
BALINGER BILANDER CAPITANA
CUNARDER DRUMBLER FLAGSHIP
GALLEASS GAYDIANG INDIAMAN
JAPANNER LANCHARA MAGAZINE
PESSONER PIPPINER REPEATER
SAILSHIP SCHOONER SMUGGLER
SPANIARD MERCHANTMAN

(— BUILT FROM NAILS OF DEAD)
NAGLFAR
(— FITTED AS CHURCH) BETHEL
(— IN LIQUOR TRADE) COPER
(— OF ARGONAUTS) ARGO
(— OF NORSEMEN) KEEL
(CLUMSY —) HULK
(DEPOT —) TENDER
(ESCORT —) CORVETTE
(FLEET OF —S) ARMADA
(JAPANESE —) MARU
(MALAY —) COUGNAR
(NOVA SCOTIAN —) BLUENOSE
(OBJECT SHAPED LIKE A —) NEF
(PART OF —) BOW CAP GUY RUN
BEAM BOOM GAFF JACK LIFT
MAST RAIL STAY VANG YARD
BRACE CHAIN ROYAL SHEET
TRUCK JUMPER RUDDER SHROUD
STRAKE BOBSTAY BULWARK
BUMPKIN COUNTER FORETOP
JIBSTAY MAINTOP NETTING
PENDANT RATLINE RIGGING
SKYSAIL SPANKER STIRRUP
STRIKER SWIFTER TOPMAST
BACKROPE BACKSTAY CUTWATER
FOOTROPE FOREMAST LIFELINE
MAINMAST MAINSTAY STUDDING
CROSSTREE FORESHEET
MAINSHEET NAMEBOARD
WATERLINE MARTINGALE
MIZZENMAST TOPGALLANT
(PIRATE —) GALLIVAT
(PRIZE —) CAPTURE
(QUARANTINE —) LAZARET
(RECEIVING —) GUARDO
(REMOTE-CONTROLLED —) DRONE
(SLOW —) BUCKET
(STORE —) FLUTER
(SUPPLY —) COPER COOPER
(UNTRIM —) BALLAHOO
(VIKING —) DRAKE
(PL.) NAVY MARINE SEACRAFT
SHIPPING
(PREF.) NAU(TI) NAV(I)
SHIPFITTER FITTER ERECTOR
SHIPHI (SON OF —) ZIZA
SHIPHTAN (SON OF —) KEMUEL
SHIPMASTER PADRONE
SHIPMENT CARLOT RAILING
DISPATCH SHIPPAGE
SHIPSHAPE NEAT TIDY TRIM CIVIL
ATAUNT ORDERLY
SHIP SWEEPER TOPASS
TOPIWALA
SHIPWAY BERTH
SHIPWORM ARTER BORER COBRA
TEREDO PILEWORM WOODWORM
SHIPWRECK WRACK NAUFRAGE
SHIPWRIGHT WAYMAN BUILDER
SHIRE DERBY SHEER COUNTY
SHIRK BALK FUNK GOOF MIKE
BAULK BLINK BUDGE DODGE
EVADE FEIGN FUDGE SKULK
SLACK RODNEY FINAGLE SHACKLE
SHAFFLE SOLDIER SHAMMOCK
SHIRKER FUNK PIKER SOGER
FUNKER ROTTER BLUDGER
SLACKER SLINKER SUGARER
COBERGER CUTHBERT EMBUSQUE
SCOWBANK
SHIRLEY (AUTHOR OF —) BRONTE
(CHARACTER IN —) JOE DONNE

EMILY LOUIS MOORE PRYOR
SCOTT MALONE ROBERT KEELDAR
SHIRLEY CAROLINE HELSTONE
HORTENSE SWEETING
MATTHEWSON
SHIRR SMOCK
SHIRT TOB JUPE SARK TOBE BLUEY
HAIRE JUPON KAMIS SHIFT
BANIAN BANIYA CAMISA CAMISE
PALAKA PARTLET UNDERGO
VAREUSE KAMLEIKA
(HAIR —) HAIRE CILICE
(SLEEVELESS —) FECKET
(WORKMAN'S —) FROCK
(WORNOUT —) DICKY
SHIRTING CHEVIOT HARVARD
HOLLAND SARKING
SHIRTWAIST BLOUSE GARIBALDI
SHISHA (SON OF —) AHIAH
ELIHOREPH
SHITTIMWOOD BOXWOOD
SHIVA (SON OF —) GANESHA
KARTTIKEYA
(WIFE OF —) KALI DURGA
SHIVAREE BELLING CHIVARI
HORNING SERENADE
SHIVER JAR GIRL GRUE BEVER
BREAK CHILL CREEM CREEP FRILL
GROWS QUAKE SHRUG SLICE
CHIVER DITHER DUDDER GROOSE
HOTTER NIDDER NITHER QUIVER
SHRIMP SPLINT TREMOR CHITTER
FLICKER FRISSON SHATTER
SHITHER SHUDDER TREMBLE
KAMLEIKA SPLINTER
SHIVERING AGUED CHILL OURIE
TREMOR ASHIVER
SHIZA (SON OF —) ADINA
SHOAL BAJO BANK FLAT REEF SPIT
BARRA DRAVE FLOTE SCULL
SHELF SCHOOL SHALLOW
TOWHEAD
SHOAT GURRY SHOOT SHOTT
SHOBAB (FATHER OF —) CALEB
DAVID
(MOTHER OF —) AZUBAH
BATHSHEBA
SHOBAL (FATHER OF —) SEIR CALEB
SHOBI (FATHER OF —) NAHASH
SHOCK COP JAR BLOW BUMP DINT
JOLT RACK SHOG STUN TURN
APPAL BRUNT GAVEL GLIFF
GLOFF SHAKE STOOK STOUR
DISMAY FRIGHT IMPACT JOSTLE
JUMBLE REJOLT RICKLE ROLLER
STRIKE ASTOUND CANVASS
DISGUST HATTOCK HORRIFY
STAGGER STARTLE STUPEFY
TERRIFY DISEDIFY GLIFFING
SURPRISE
(— OF CORN) STOOK STOUT
STITCH
(MENTAL —) TRAUMA
SHOCK ABSORBER SHOCK
BUFFER DASHPOT SNUBBER
SHOCKED AGHAST
SHOCKER RICKER STOOKER
SHOCKING GRIM AWFUL LURID
HORRID UNHOLY BURNING
FEARFUL FEARING GHASTLY
HIDEOUS DREADFUL ENORMOUS
HORRIBLE SCANDALOUS
SHOD CALCED

SHODDY SOFT CHEAP FOOTY
MUNGO SOFTS TACKY SLEAZY
SHOE BAL CUE PAN BOOT BROG
CLOG DRAG FLAT HALF SKID
SOCK TURN BLAKE DERBY KLOMP
MOYLE ROMEO SABOT SCRAE
SLING SPIKE STOGA STOGY STRAP
ANKLET BEAKER BROGAN
BROGUE BUSKIN CALIGA CALIGO
CHOPIN COBCAB COCKER
CRAKOW CREOLE DORSAY GAITER
GALOSH KILTIE MULLER PATTEN
PINSON POLISH SADDLE SANDAL
SECQUE BAUCHLE BLUCHER
BOTTINE CALCEUS CHOPINE
COWHIDE FLIPPER OXONIAN
RULLION SHOEPAC SLIPPER
SNEAKER BALMORAL BRODEKIN
CALCEATE COLONIAL PLATFORM
PLIMSOLL SABOTINE SANDSHOE
SKEWBACK SLIPSLOP SOLLERET
(— FOR GRINDING) MULLER
(— FOR MULE) PLANCHE
(— IN TRUSS OR FRAME)
SKEWBACK
(— NOT FASTENED ON) PUMP
(— OF A SLEDGE) HOB
(— OF AN OX) CUE
(— OF COMIC ACTOR) BAXA
(— OF SUBWAY CAR) PAN
(— REPAIRER) JACKMAN
(— TO CHECK WHEEL) DRAG SKID
(— USED AS BRAKE) SKATE
(— WORN ON EITHER FOOT)
STRAIGHT
(—S AND STOCKINGS) FEET
(ARMORED —) SABBATON
(BABY'S —) CACK
(DOWN-AT-HEEL —) SHAUCHLE
(HOBNAILED —) TACKET
(LARGE —S) GUNBOATS
(LOW-CUT —) SOCK GILLY ANKLET
BUSKIN SLIPPER COLONIAL
(MILITARY —) CALIGA
(OLD —) BAUCHLE
(PART OF —) TIP TOE ARCH FLAP
HEEL LIFT SOLE VAMP WELT
AGLET SHANK COLLAR EYELET
FOXING INSTEP LINING THROAT
TONGUE COUNTER OUTSOLE
QUARTER MUDGUARD PLATFORM
SHOELACE BREASTING
(PIKED —) BEAKER
(RAWHIDE —) HIMMING VELSKOEN
(SPORTS —S) GILLIES
(STEEL —) SOLLERET
(THIN —) PINSON SCLAFF
(WINGED —S) TALARIA
(WOODEN —) KLOMP SABOT
PATTEN RACKET RACQUET
(WORN —) SCRAE
(PL.) SHEEN SHOON SHUNE
SCHONE CASUALS FOOTGEAR
(PREF.) CALCEI
SHOEMAKER SNOB FOXER SOLER
ARCHER CHAMAR CODGER
COZIER FUDGER GOUGER SOOTER
SOUTER VAMPER COBBLER
CRISPIN CROWNER SHOEMAN
SNOBBER UPPERER CORVISER
SNOBSCAT CORDWAINER
SHOEMAKING SNOBBING
SHOGI (EXPERT LEVEL IN —) DAN

SHOGUN TYCOON
SHOHAM (FATHER OF —) JAAZIAH
SHOMER (SON OF —) JEHOZABAD
SHOO HOOSH DISPEL
SHOOK PACK BLANK SHAKE
SHOOT DAG GUN IMP PAY POT
PUT ROD TIP BANG BOLT BROD
CANE CHIT CION DRAW LEAF
PLUG SLIP WEFT ARROW BLAST
BLAZE BROWN DRILL DRIVE
EXPEL FLUSH FROND GEMMA
GLEAM LANCE LAYER PLUFF
SCION SHEET SOBOL SPEAR SPIRE
SPRAY SPRIG SPRIT SPURT SQUIB
STICK STOOL TUBER TURIO
VIMEN BRANCH FLIGHT FLOWER
GERMEN GROWTH HEADER
HURTLE LAUNCH LEADER OFFSET
RATOON SALLOW SOBOLE SPRING
SPROUT STOLON STOUND
STOVEN STRIKE SUCKER TILLER
TURION BUDLING CHIMNEY
DROPPER SCOURGE SPIRING
TENDRIL TENDRON THALLUS
ANAPHYTE APOBLAST CATAPULT
TRAILING
(— A MARBLE) LAG TAW KNUCKLE
(— A WHALE) STRIKE
(— ASIDE FROM MARK) DRIB
(— AT LONG RANGE) SNIPE
(— DOWN) SPLASH
(— DUCKS) SKAG
(— FORTH) JET GLEAM SPIRE
(— FROM DEER'S ANTLER) SPELLER
(— INDISCRIMINATELY) BROWN
(— MOOSE OR DEER) YARD
(— OF A TREE) STOW WHIP LANCE
BRANCH
(— OUT) JUT CHIT DART ERADIATE
(— SEAL) SWATCH
(— UP) SPIRE SPURT
(—S USED AS FODDER) BROWSE
(FIRST —S) BRAIRD
(FLEXIBLE —) BINE
(LATERAL —) ARM
(ORE —) BONANZA
(PAWNBROKER'S —) SPOUT
(SUGARCANE —) LALO
(TENDER —) FLUSH
(WILLOW —) SALLOW
(PREF.) BLAST(O) SOBOLI STOLONI
THALL(I)(O)
(SUFF.) BLAST(IC)(Y) SPERM(A)(AE)
(AL)(IA)(IC)(OUS)(UM)(Y)
SHOOTER SCOOT BLASTER
GUNSTER PLUFFER SHOTMAN
SKEETER
SHOOTING COCKING GUNNING
GUNPLAY HUNTING POTTING
SHOOTING STAR METEOR
COWSLIP SHOOTER PRIMWORT
SHOP CRIB TOKO BOOTH BURSE
STORE TRADE KOSHER SHOPPE
TIENDA WINKEL ALMACEN
APOTHEC BOTTEGA CABARET
MERCERY SPICERY TABERNA
TURNERY BOUTIQUE COOKSHOP
CREMERIE EMPORIUM ESPRESSO
EXCHANGE MAGAZINE
SHOWSHOP SLOPSHOP
TENDEJON WAREROOM
(BARBER —) BARBERY
(BLACKSMITH —) SMITHY

(LIQUOR —) SALOON
(OLD CLOTHES —) FLIPPERY
(PAWNBROKER'S —) LUMBER
SPROUT
(REPAIR —) GARAGE
(SUTLER'S —) CANTEEN
SHOPKEEPER CIT ARAB BAKAL
BANIAN CHETTY SOUDAGUR
SHOPLIFT BOOST
SHOPLIFTER BOOSTER
SHORE GIB TOM BANK RIPE RIVE
SAND SIDE TRIG BEACH BENCH
CLIFF COAST MARGE RAKER
RANCE SHOAR WARTH RIVAGE
STRAND BUTTRESS DOCKSIDE
LANDFALL LANDSIDE SEACOAST
SHOREBIRD TATTLER WRYBILL
SURFBIRD PHALAROPE
SANDPIPER
SHORE CRAB OCHIDORE
SHOREFISH OPALEYE
SHORER BRACER CRIBBER
SHORN NOT NOTT POLLED
TONSURED
SHORT AIM LAG LOW SHY BAIN
CURT NEAR NIGH SOON BLUFF
BRIEF BUNTY CLOSE CRISP CUTTY
FUBBY FUBSY PUNCH SQUAB
UNDER ABRUPT CRISPY SCANTY
SCARCE STUGGY STUNTY
SUDDEN ULLAGE BOBTAIL
BRUSQUE CURTATE LACONIC
SQUIDGY STUBBED SUMMARY
SNAPPISH SUCCINCT
(— AND FLAT) CAMUS
(— AND THICK) CHUNKY STOCKY
STUBBY STUMPY TRUNCH
TRUNCHED
(— AND THICKSET) NUGGETY
(— AS OF WOOL) FRIBBY
(— PERSON OR ANIMAL) PUNCH
(BRIEF —S) MONOKINI
(STOUT AND —) BUNTY CHUFFY
PLUGGY THICKSET
(PL.) BERMUDAS
(PREF.) BRACHI(O) BRACHY BREVI
(SUFF.) BRACH(ISTO)(Y)
SHORTAGE FAMINE DROUGHT
WANTAGE UNDERAGE
SHORT-BREATHED PURSY
SHORTCHANGE FLUFF SHORT
SHORTCOMING SIN DEFECT
FOIBLE
SHORT-COUPLED CHUFFY
SHORTCUT CUTOFF
SHORT-EARED OWL MOMO
SHORTEN CUT CLIP STAG ELIDE
SLASH REDUCE ABRIDGE CURTAIL
EXCERPT SCANTLE CONTRACT
DIMINISH RETRENCH ABBREVIATE
(— AND THICKEN IRON) JUMP
(— GRIP) CHOKE
SHORTENED CURTED BOBTAIL
CURTATE ABRIDGED
SHORTENING (— OF SYLLABLE)
SYSTOLE
SHORTEST LEAST
SHORTHORN DURHAM
TEESWATER
SHORT-LIVED FRAGILE
SHORTLY SOON DUMPILY
DIRECTLY PRESENTLY
SHORT-NAPPED RAS

SHORTNESS BREVITY CURTNESS
UNLENGTH
SHORT-RANGE TACTICAL
SHORT-SIGHTED SANDED
PURBLIND
SHORTSIGHTEDNESS MYOPIA
SHORT-TEMPERED CRUSTY
SNIPPY SNUFFY
SHORT-TERM FLOATING
SHORT-WINDED PURSY PURFLY
PURFLED PURSIVE
SHOT POP SET BLUE CASE JOLT
OVER PLUG SETT SLUG BLANK
FLIER FLING FLUFF FLYER OUTER
PLUFF SHOOT TOWEL WHITE
CARTON CENTER CENTRE
FOLLOW MUDCAP REBOTE
ALIIPOE BOMBARD CUTAWAY
DEADEYE GUNSHOT LANGREL
PELICAN SIGHTER BLIZZARD
BUCKSHOT HAILSHOT LANGRAGE
MARKSHOT SCORCHER
(— BEYOND TARGET) OVER
(— FOR CULVERIN) PELICAN
(— IN FIFTH CIRCLE) WHITE
(— IN FOURTH CIRCLE) BLACK
(— IN THIRD CIRCLE) BLUE
(— OF NARCOTIC) FIX
(— STRIKING BULL'S-EYE) CARTON
(— THAT HITS) CLOUT
(ARCHERY —) GREEN
(BADMINTON —) CLEAR
(BASKETBALL —) BOMB JUMPER
(BILLIARD —) DRAG STAB CAROM
MASSE SCREW FOLLOW SAFETY
SPREAD BRICOLE SCRATCH
(BOW —) DRAFT
(CAMERA —) INTERCUT
(CROQUET —) SPLIT FOLLOW
(CURLING —) INWICK OUTWICK
(FINAL —) UPSHOT
(GOOD —) SCREAMER
(PISTOL —) BARK
(POOL —) BREAK
(SIZE OF —) F T BB FF TT BBB
DUST BUCKSHOT
(SMALL —) PELLET
(SNOOKER —) POT
(TENNIS —) ACE LOB DINK SERVE
SMASH
(VOLLEY OF —S) BLIZZARD
SHOTGUN DOUBLE TUPARA
PEPPERER SCATTERSHOT
SHOULD MOW SUD WANT OUGHT
(— NOT) SHUDNA SHOULDNA
SHOULDNT
SHOULDER DOD AXLE CLOD DODD
GAIN HUMP SHIP STEP SULD
BOUGH PITCH SPALL SPULE
VERGE AXILLA EPAULE RELISH
SCOTCH SPAULD KNUCKLE
RIMBASE SHOUTHER
(— AROUND TENON) RELISH
(— OF BOLT) NAB
(— OF FIREARM STOCK) RIMBASE
(— OF FLY) CHEEK
(— OF LAMB) BANJO
(— OF PORK) HAND PICNIC
CUSHION
(— OF RABBIT OR HARE) WING
(— OF ROAD) BERM BERME
HAUNCH QUARTER
(— PAIN) OMODYNIA

(BEVELED —) GAIN
(PL.) FOREBOWS
(PREF.) OM(O)
SHOULDER BLADE SPALD SPEAL
SCAPULA OMOPLATE
(PREF.) SCAPUL(I)(O)
SHOUT BAY BOO CRY HOY HUE
BAWL CALL CROW GAPE HAIL
HOCH HOOP HOOT REME ROOT
ROUP ROUT SCRY TOOT YELL
BRAWL CHEER CLAIM CLEPE
CRACK GREDE HAVOC HOLLO
HUZZA REERE WHEWT WHOOP
ABRAID BOOHOO CLAMOR
GOLLAR GOLLER HALLOO HOLLER
HURRAH STEVEN YAMMER
ACCLAIM SHILLOO GARDYLOO
LULLILOO SCRONACH
(— AS CHILDREN) BELDER
(— DERISIVELY) BARRACK
(— FOR OR AGAINST) BARRACK
(— OF APPROVAL) BRAVO
(— OF ENCOURAGEMENT) HARK
(— OF HIGHLAND DANCER) HOOCH
(— OF JOY) IO
(HUNTING —) CHEVY
SHOUTING HUE GLAM ROUP ROUT
HOLLO CLAMOR HOLLOA JUBILEE
SHOVE JUT PUT BUNT DUSH FEND
MUCK PICK POTE PUSH SHOG
SHUN BOOST CROWD DUNCH
ELBOW HUNCH SHIVE SHUNT
HUSTLE JOSTLE JUSTLE MUSCLE
THRUST SCAMBLE
(— CARELESSLY) BUNG
(— IN MARBLES) FULK
SHOVEL FAN VAN CAST PEEL
SPUD SCOOP SHOOL SPADE
SPOON BLUNGER SCOPPET
SCUPPIT SLUDGER DUCKBILL
DUCKFOOT STROCKLE
(— FOR COIN) MAIN
(— FOR DRESSING ORE) VAN
(BRICKMAKING —) CUCKHOLD
(CASTING —) SCUTTLE
(CHARCOAL BURNER'S —) RABBLE
(FIRE —) PEEL SLICE
(GRATED —) HARP
(MINER'S —) BANJO
(PERFORATED —) SKIMMER
SHOVELER SCOOPER WHINGER
BLUEWING SHOULERD WHINYARD
SHOW DO SAY SEE WIS BOSH CALL
DASH HAVE ITEM LEAD MARK
MIEN SCAW SEEM SHEW TENT
VIEW WEAR WISE ARGUE ASSAY
EXERT FLASH GLOSS GLOZE KITHE
PRIDE PROVE SHINE SIGHT SLANG
SPORT TEACH ACCUSE ASSIGN
BETRAY BLAZON CHICHI COUTHE
DENOTE DETECT DEVICE DIRECT
ENSIGN ESCORT EVINCE EXPOSE
FIGURE FLAUNT GAIETY GAYETY
LAYOUT MUSTER OBJECT PARADE
REVEAL SCHEME SPREAD SPRUNK
VANITY ADVANCE ANALYZE
BALLOON BESPEAK BETOKEN
BRAVURA BREATHE DECLARE
DISPLAY DIVULGE EXHIBIT
EXPRESS FASHION MONSTER
PRESAGE PRODUCE PROPOSE
SELLOUT SHOWING SIGNIFY
TAMASHA TRIUMPH COLORING

CONCLUDE EVIDENCE FLOURISH
FORESHOW INDICATE MANIFEST
PRETENCE PROCLAIM SEMBLANT
SIDESHOW
(— APPROVAL) CLAP APPLAUD
(— CONTEMPT) SCOFF
(— DISCONTENT) GROUCH
(— DISPLEASURE) POUT
(— DOGS) BENCH
(— ENTHUSIASM) DROOL
(— FORTH) BLAZE CIPHER
(— IN PUBLIC CELEBRATION)
PAGEANT
(— ITSELF) APPEAR
(— MERCY) SPARE
(— OF LEARNING) SCIOLISM
(— OF LIGHT) BLINK
(— OF REASON) COLOR
(— OF VANITY) AIR
(— OFF) FLASH PRANK SPORT
SWANK HOTDOG PARADE
(— ONESELF) BE
(— POSITION OF) MEITH
(— PROMISE) FRAME SHAPE
(— RESPECT FOR) REGARD
(— REVERSE TREND) REACT
(— SIGNS OF GIVING WAY) WAVER
(— SIGNS OF ILLNESS) GRUDGE
(— THE BOTTOM) KEEL
(— THE SIGHTS) LIONIZE
(— THE TEETH) GIRN GRIN
(— THE WAY) LEAD CONDUCT
(— TO BE FALSE) BELIE DISPROVE
(— UNKINDNESS) WAIT
(— WITHOUT SUBSTANCE) FORM
(ARTFUL —) GRIMACE
(FALSE —) COLOR FUCUS BUBBLE
TINSEL ILLUSION PRETENCE
(FLOOR —) CABARET
(GAUDY —) HOOPLA BRAVERY
(MERE —) PHANTOM
(MOMENTARY —) FLASH
(ORNATE —) FLUBDUB
(OSTENTATIOUS —) SPRUNK
DISPLAY
(OUTSIDE —) VARNISH
(OUTWARD —) FUCUS VISAGE
(PUBLIC —) EXPO
(PUPPET —) DROLL MOTION
WAJANG WAYANG GUIGNOL
(RIDICULOUS —) FARCE
(RUDIMENTARY —) SATURA
(SPECIOUS —) GLOZE
(STREET —) RAREE
(SUPERFICIAL —) GLOSS VENEER
(TRAVELLING —) SLANG
(PREF.) PHAENO PHANER(O)
PHANTA PHANTO PHENO
(SUFF.) PHANY
SHOW BOAT (AUTHOR OF —)
FERBER
(CHARACTER IN —) KIM ANDY ELLY
HAWKS JULIE PARTHY GAYLORD
RAVENAL MAGNOLIA SCHULTZY
SHOWCASE ISLAND VITRINE
SHOWER WET HAIL RAIN SCAT
SUMP AUGER BLASH SKITE SOUSE
FLURRY PELTER PEPPER SHEWER
DRIBBLE SHATTER WEATHER
COMMORTH SCOUTHER
(CONCENTRATED —) BARRAGE
(HEAVY —) SUMP
(RAIN —) RASH

(SUDDEN —) SCUD SKIT BRASH
PLUMP
SHOWERY BRASHY CLASHY
SCATTY
SHOWILY GAILY BRAVELY
GAUDILY
SHOWINESS DASH GLARE PAZAZZ
PIZAZZ GLITTER PIZZAZZ
FLOURISH GEWGAWRY SPLENDOR
SHOWING SPRANK SPARKLE
(— SAME NATURE) AKIN
(SUPERFICIAL —) FACE
(PREF.) PHAEN(O) PHAINO
SHOWMANSHIP RECLAME
SHOW-ME STATE MISSOURI
SHOW-OFF CUTUP
SHOWY GAY FINE LOUD NICE
RORY VAIN DASHY FLARY FLASH
FRESH GAUDY GIDDY GRAND
JAZZY NOBBY SPICY SWANK
TOPPY VAUDY VIEWY BRANKY
BRAZEN BRUMMY CHICHI DRESSY
FLASHY FLOSSY GARISH GEWGAW
GLOSSY JAUNTY PURPLE SHANTY
SKYRIN SPANKY SPORTY TAWDRY
DASHING FLAUNTY GALLANT
GAUDFUL HOTSHOT POMPOUS
SHOWFUL SHOWISH SPLASHY
SPLURGY CLAPTRAP FASTUOUS
GIMCRACK GORGEOUS ORGULOUS
SPARKISH SPECIOUS SPLENDID
TRUMPERY CLINQUANT
OBTRUSIVE
(NOT —) CIVIL LENTEN DISCREET
SHRED DAG HOG JAG RAG ROND
ROON SNIP TEAR WISP BLYPE
CLOUT GRATE PATCH SHRAG
SHRIP CULPON SCREED SLIVER
TARGET FRAZZLE FRITTER
MAMMOCK SHATTER FILAMENT
(— FISH) SCROD
(— OF CLOTHES) TACK
(— OF FLESH) TAG AGNAIL
(— OF HAIR) TAIT
(PL.) TAVERS CADDICE TAIVERS
SHREDDED CUT
SHREDDER DEVIL
SHREW ERD JES NAG TANA PRESS
RANNY SOREX VIXEN CALLET
JUMPER MIGALE TARGER TARTAR
TUPAIA VIRAGO BLARINA
HELLCAT MUSKRAT PENTAIL
SCYTALE TUPAIID SINSRING
SORICINE SORICOID UROPSILE
XANTHIPPE
(TREE —) BANXRING
(PREF.) HYDRAC(O) SORICI
SHREWD DRY SLY ACID ARCH
CUTE FELL GASH SAGE TIDY
WARE WISE ACUTE CAGEY
CANNY HEADY LOOPY PAWKY
POKEY SHARP SMART SWACK
ARGUTE ARTFUL ASTUTE CALLID
CLEVER CRAFTY SPRACK SUBTLE
CUNNING GNOSTIC KNOWING
PARLISH PARLOUS POLITIC
PRACTIC SAPIENT SAGACIOUS
PERSPICACIOUS
(— PERSON) FILE
SHREWDLY SLILY CANNILY
ASTUTELY
SHREWDNESS NOUS SAVVY
ACUMEN POLICY SLYNESS

GUMPTION PRUDENCE SAGACITY
CALLIDITY
SHREWISH CURST CURSED
SHREWD VIXENISH
SHREWMOUSE MYGALE SCYTALE
SHRIEK CRY YIP YARM YELL CHIRK
SKIRL SCREAM SCRIKE SHRIKE
SKRIKE SPRAICH
SHRIKE POPE BATARA BOUBOU
BRUBRU FISCAL FLASHER
FLUSHER LOGHEAD MIGRANT
MINIVET TRILLER BELLBIRD
FALCONET PUFFBACK
WOODCHAT
SHRILL HIGH KEEN THIN ACUTE
PIPEY SHARP SHILL SHIRL
ARGUTE BRASSY GLASSY PIPING
SQUEAK TREBLE HAUTAIN
MINIKIN SCREAKY PIERCING
STRIDENT
(MAKE — NOISE) POTRACK
(PREF.) OXY
SHRIMP GRIT APANG CARID MYSID
PARVA PRAWN NIPPER PANDLE
SCAMPI ARTEMIA BROWNIE
CAMARON DECAPOD POLYPOD
REDTAIL SPECTER SPECTRE
CARIDEAN CRAWFISH CREVETTE
MACRURAN
(SUFF.) CARIS
SHRINE ADYT NAOS GUACA
HUACA ISEUM MAZAR SEKOS
STUPA ZIARA ADYTON ADYTUM
CHASSE DAGABA DAGOBA
DURGAH HALLOW HIERON
MEMORY SAMADH VIMANA
ZIARAT CHAITYA CHAPLET
CHORTEN EDICULE FANACLE
MARTYRY MEMORIA SACRARY
TEMENOS THESEUM AEDICULA
DELUBRUM FERETORY FERETRUM
GURDWARA LARARIUM
MARABOUT PANTHEON
VALHALLA RELIQUARY
(— STUDY) NAOLOGY
(PREF.) PASTO
SHRINK COY SHY DARE DUCK FULL
FUNK GIVE NIRL PEAK ABHOR
ARGHE CLING COWER CRINE
QUAIL RELAX RIVEL SHRAM
SHRUG SHUCK START WINCE
BLANCH BLENCH BOGGLE COTTER
CRINGE FLINCH LESSEN RECOIL
SCRUMP SETTLE SHRIMP WEAZEN
CRIMPLE CRUMPLE DWINDLE
SCUNNER SHRIVEL COLLAPSE
CONTRACT
(— FROM DRYNESS) GIZZEN
SHRINKAGE SETTLE SHRINK
SINKAGE
(— OF TYPE) SQUEEZE
SHRINKING COY SHY TIMID
BLETHE CREEPS DASTARD
FULLING LOATHFUL TIMOROUS
SHRIVE SHRIFT CONFESS SHRIEVE
SHRIVEL NIRL SEAR WELK BLAST
CLING CRINE PARCH RIVEL
SHRAM SNERP WIZEN BLIGHT
COTTER GIZZEN SCORCH SCRUMP
SHRINK WEAZEN WITHER
CROZZLE
SHRIVELED WEDE CLUNG CORKY
THIRL GIZZEN STARKY PUNGLED

SHIRPIT WIZENED WRITHEN SHRAMMED WRIZZLED

SHROPSHIRE SALOP

SHROUD HIDE SARK CLOAK CRAPE DRAPE HABIT SHEET SWIFT EMBOSK HEARSE KITTEL MUFFLE SCREEN SHADOW SINDON SUDARY BENIGHT CONCEAL CURTAIN INVOLVE SWIFTER CEREMENT
(PL.) PUTTOCK

SHROVETIDE SHROVE GUTTIDE CARNIVAL

SHROVE TUESDAY FASTENS GUTTIDE

SHRUB TI BAY HAW KAT MAY QAT TOD AKIA ALEM BUSH COCA HOYA INGA ITEA KARO KEUR KHAT MUSK ULEX AKALA AKELA ALDER ALISO ARUSA BOCCA BROOM BUAZE CEIBO CUMAY ELDER GOOMA GOUMI HAZEL HENNA IXORA LEDUM LEMON LILAC MAQUI MARIA MUDAR RETEM SALAL SHROG SUMAC TOYON ZILLA ABELIA AGRITO AKONGE AMULLA ANAGUA ANILAO ARALIA ARUSHA AUCUBA AUPAKA AZALEA BLOLLY CENIZO CHEKAN CHERRY CISTUS CORREA DAPHNE DHAURI DRIMYS FEIJOA FRUTEX JACATE JOJOBA KARAMU KOWHAI LABRUM LARREA LAUREL MATICO MYRTLE NARRAS PENAEA PITURI RAETAM SAVINE STORAX STYRAX ACEROLA AFERNAN AGARITA AMORPHA ARBORET ARRAYAN ARRIMBY AZAROLE BANKSIA BORONIA BUCKEYE BULLACE CANTUTA CHACATE CHAMISE CHANCHE DEUTZIA EHRETIA ENCELIA EPACRID EPHEDRA FUCHSIA GUMWOOD GUTWORT HOPBUSH HOPSAGE JASMINE JETBEAD JEWBUSH JOEWOOD KUMQUAT LANTANA MAHONIA NUNNARI PAVONIA PEABUSH PEARHAW PIMELEA RHODORA SPIRAEA TARBUSH THEEZAN ABELMOSK ALLTHORN BARBERRY CAMELLIA CARAGANA COMEBACK COPALCHE DRACAENA GOATBUSH GOWIDDIE GRAVILEA HARDHACK HARDTACK HAWTHORN HIBISCUS IRONWOOD KEURBOOM KOROMIKO MOORWORT NINEBARK OCOTILLO OLEASTER OSOBERRY PIPEWOOD PONDBUSH ROSEMARY SANDSTAY SANDWOOD SASANQUA SHRUBLET SNOWBALL SNOWBELL SNOWBUSH SOAPBARK STANDARD MISTLETOE POINCIANA PHILADELPHUS
(AROMATIC —) THYME CLUSIA BORONIA HOGBUSH ALLSPICE
(AUSTRALIAN —) GOOMA BUDDAH DRIMYS GEEBUNG WARATAH MILKBUSH SANDSTAY
(CHINESE —) KERRIA

(CLIMBING —) CATCLAWS SOLANDRA
(DESERT —) AFERNAN
(EVERGREEN —) BOX BAGO ILEX TITI BOLDO ERICA FURZE HEATH HOLLY KOSAM PYXIE SALAL SAVIN TOYON BAUERA DAHOON KALMIA LAUREL PEPINO PROTEA RUSCUS SAKAKI ARDISIA BARETTA JASMINE JUNIPER MADRONA MAHONIA CALFKILL CARAUNDA EVONYMUS OLEANDER SASANQUA MANZANITA
(FRAGRANT —) JASMINE HUISACHE MEJORANA MEZEREON ROSEMARY
(HAWAIIAN —) AKALA AKELA ILIMA KOKIO OLONA
(LOW —) AYAPANA
(MEXICAN —) BLUEBUSH
(NEW ZEALAND —) KARO KAWA TUTU KARAMU KIEKIE KAWAKAWA KOROMIKO
(PASTURE —) COWBERRY
(PHILIPPINE —) IPILIPIL
(POISONOUS —) GIF CUBE LITHI SUMAC GIFBLAAR LABURNUM
(PRICKLY —) CAPER COLIMA BRAMBLE CATCLAWS
(SPINY —) ULEX AROMA GORSE JUNCO ESPINO BUMELIA CARISSA CYTISUS GENISTA GOATBUSH GRANJENO GUAJILLO HUAJILLO
(STRONG-SMELLING —) SALTWORT
(STUNTED —) SCRAB SCROG SCRUB
(THORNY —) CHANAR HAWTHORN
(TREELIKE —) ARBUSCLE
(TROPICAL —) INGA MAJO HENNA CAMARA DERRIS MOMBIN OLACAD PERSEA HAMELIA JEWBUSH LANTANA SOAPBARK
(WEST INDIAN —) ANIL RATWOOD MILKWOOD
(XEROPHYTIC —) SAXAUL
(PREF.) THAMN(O)

SHRUBBERY MOGOTE ARBORET

SHRUG SHUG HURKLE SHRINK

SHRUNK WEARISH

SHRUNKEN LANK CLUNG PUNGLED SLUNKEN WIZENED CONTRACT
(— HEAD) TSANTSA

SHUAH (FATHER OF —) ABRAHAM
(MOTHER OF —) KETURAH

SHUAL (FATHER OF —) ZOPHAH

SHUBAEL (FATHER OF —) HEMAN GERSHON

SHUCK HULL HUSK SHACK SHELL SHOCK

SHUDDER GRUE CREEP GRISE HIRCH QUAKE SHRUG AGRISE GROOSE HIRTCH HOTTER HURKLE SHIVER FRISSON TREMBLE

SHUDDERING RIGOR

SHUFFLE JANK MAKE MILK SLUR MOSEY SCUFF SHALE SHIFT SHOOL JUGGLE RIFFLE RUFFLE SCLAFF SHOVEL DRAGGLE QUIBBLE SHACKLE SHAFFLE SHAMBLE SLIPPER SLUTHER
(— DISHONESTLY) PACK

SHUHAM (FATHER OF —) DAN

SHUN FIN SHY BALK FLEE TABU VOID WARE ABHOR AVOID EVADE EVITE SHUNT TABOO ASTART DEVOID ESCAPE ESCHEW REFUSE SHRINK DECLINE FORBEAR FORSAKE

SHUNI (FATHER OF —) GAD

SHUNT AYRTON BRIDGE BYPASS SWITCH

SHUSH HUSH WHISH SUPPRESS

SHUSWAP ATNAH

SHUT FAST HASP MAKE SEAL SHOT SLAM SLOT SPAR TAKE TEEN TINE CLOSE LATCH STEEK STICK CLOSED CABINET OCCLUSE UPCLOSE
(— EYES) WINK
(— IN) BAR LAP CAGE COPSE EMBAR EMBAY FORBAR PENTIT TACKLE BELOUKE ENCLAVE
(— OFF) SCREEN SECLUDE
(— OUT) BAR DEBAR REPEL SKUNK HINDER DEPRIVE EXCLUDE OCCLUDE OUTSHUT PRECLUDE
(— TOGETHER) CLASP
(— UP) BAR CUB MEW PENT STOP CHOKE FRANK STIVE STOVE CLOSET EMBOSS ENJAIL IMMURE IMPARK CONDEMN CONFINE DUNGEON ENCLOSE IMPOUND INCLUDE OCCLUDE OPPRESS PARROCK RECLUSE SECLUDE CONCLUDE PRECLUDE
(HALF —) PINK
(PREF.) OCCLUSO

SHUTDOWN LAYOFF

SHUTOUT SKUNK

SHUTTER LID DROP SHUT BLIND SHADE CUTOFF DAMPER DOUSER SLUICE AUTOMAT BUCKLER SHUTTLE JALOUSIE
(— IN ORGAN) SHADE
(— OF TRIPTYCH) VOLET

SHUTTING CLAUDENT

SHUTTLE FLY FLUTE SHUNT BROCHE LOOPER SWIVEL SHITTLE

SHUTTLECOCK BIRD PETECA VOLANT

SHVANDA THE BAGPIPER
(CHARACTER IN —) DEVIL BABINSKY ICEHEART SCHVANDA
(COMPOSER OF —) WEINBERGER

SHY COY JIB MIM SCAR SHAN SHUN SKIT UNKO WILD BLATE CAGEY CHARY DEMUR FLING PAVID SCARE SHUNT SQUAB TIMID UNCOW BOGGLE BOOGER DEMURE MODEST SHANNY SKIEGH TARTLE BASHFUL GAWKISH RABBITY STRANGE TREMBLY UPSTAGE BACKWARD COCKSHOT DAPHNEAN FAROUCHE RETIRING SHEEPISH SKITTISH SWAIMOUS VERECUND WILLYARD

SHYLOCK (DAUGHTER OF —) JESSICA

SHYNESS COYNESS MODESTY RESERVE TIMIDITY

SHYSTER PETTIFOGGER

SIALAGOGUE SALIVANT

SIAM (SEE THAILAND)

SIAMANG UNGKA GIBBON

SIB SEPT AYLLU SIBLING SIBSHIP CALPULLI

SIBERIA (GULF IN —) OB
(MOUNTAIN RANGE IN —) URAL ALTAI
(NATIVE IN —) YAKU SAGAI TATAR KIRGIZ TARTAR KIRGHIZ YUKAGIR
(RIVER IN —) OB ILI KET PUR TAZ TYM AMGA AMUR LENA MAYA ONON UCUR ALDAN ISHIM NADYM SOBOL TOBOL ANGARA IRTYSH OLEKMA VILYUY
(TOWN IN —) OMSK CHITA KYZYL TOMSK IGARKA KURGAN BARNAUL IRKUTSK LENINSK YAKUTSK

SIBERIAN SQUILL SCILLA

SIBYL SYBIL SIBYLLA VOLUSPA AMALTHEA

SIC SOOL

SICILIAN
(PREF.) SICULO

SICILIAN VESPERS, THE
(CHARACTER OF —) ELENA ARRIGO MONTFORT FREDERICK
(COMPOSER OF —) VERDI

SICILY

CAPE: BOEO FARO PASSARO
CAPITAL: PALERMO
CATHEDRAL: MONREALE
COIN: LITRA UNCIA
GULF: NOTO CATANIA
ISLAND: EGADI LIPARI USTICA
MEASURE: SALMA CAFFISO
MOUNTAIN: EREI ETNA MORO SORI IBREI NEBRODI
NATIVE: ELYMI SICEL SICANI SICULI
OLD NAME: TRINACRIA TRIQUETRA
PROVINCE: ENNA RAGUSA CATANIA MESSINA PALERMO TRAPANI SIRACUSA
RIVER: SALSO TORTO BELICE SIMETO PLATANI
SEAPORT: ACI CATANIA MARSALA MESSINA PALERMO TRAPANI
TOWN: ENNA NOTO RAGUSA CATANIA MARSALA MESSINA TRAPANI SYRACUSE
VOLCANO: ETNA AETNA

SICK BAD ILL BADLY CRONK CROOK MORBID MAWKISH SEASICK UNWHOLE CROPSICK MALADIVE PHYSICAL STREAKED

SICKEN TIRE TURN WEARY SUNDER SUNNER WEAKEN DISGUST SCUNNER SURFEIT NAUSEATE

SICKENING FELL SICKLY FULSOME MAWKISH SICKISH NAUSEOUS

SICKISH DAUNCY

SICKLE HOOK CROOK
(PREF.) DREPANI FALCI ZANCIO

SICKLY WAN FLUE FOND PALE PUKY SICK DAWNY DONCY FAINT GREEN PEAKY SILLY TEWLY WEARY WERSH WISHT AMPERY ANEMIC CLAMMY CRANKY FEEBLE

INFIRM PUKISH PULING WANKLY WEAKLY INVALID LANGUID MAWKISH PEAKING PEAKISH PIMPING QUEECHY SHILPIT SICKISH WEARISH WEERISH DELICATE DISEASED MALADIVE PINDLING

SICKLY-LOOKING SHILPIT

SICKNESS (ALSO SEE DISEASE) SICK SORE TAKING AILMENT DISEASE ILLNESS SURFEIT DISORDER
(MILK —) SLOWS TIRES
(MOTION —) KINETOSIS
(MOUNTAIN —) PUNA SOROCHE
(SUDDEN —) DWALM

SIDA ILIMA ESCOBA

SIDE CAMP COST EDGE FACE HALF HAND KANT LEAF PANE PART BOARD CHEEK FLANK LATUS PARTY PHASE SITHE BEHALF PTERON ENGLISH PENDANT FORESIDE SIDELONG
(— BY SIDE) ACCOLE ABREAST ACCOSTED PARALLEL
(— OF ATTIC) SKEELING SKILLING SKILLION
(— OF BIRD'S HEAD) LORE
(— OF BOOM JAW) HORN
(— OF BOW) BELLY
(— OF CAVITY) WALL
(— OF DECK) GANGWAY
(— OF DITCH) SCARP
(— OF DIVIDERS) LEG
(— OF FACE) CHEEK
(— OF GATE) FOLD
(— OF GEM) BEZEL
(— OF HEAD) HAFFET
(— OF HEARTH) BREAST
(— OF HILL) BRAE SCUG SLOPE
(— OF HOG) FLITCH
(— OF HORSESHOE) BRANCH
(— OF LACE) FOOTING
(— OF LAMB) CONCERTINA
(— OF LOG) RIDE
(— OF NAVE) AISLE
(— OF OPENING) JAW JAMB
(— OF PIG) BACON
(— OF QUADRANGLE) PANE
(— OF RABBET) LEDGE
(— OF RACECOURSE) STRETCH
(— OF RECTANGLE) SQUARE
(— OF ROOF) CATSLIDE
(— OF SHIP) BEAM WALE BOARD BULWARK LARBOARD SEABOARD
(— OF TENNIS RACKET) ROUGH SMOOTH
(— OF TRIANGLE) LEG
(— OF TYPE) BACK
(— OF VALLEY) COTEAU
(— PIECE) RAVE
(— SHELTERED FROM WIND) LEE LEW LEEWARD
(— WITH) SUFFRAGE
(-S OF FIREPLACE) COVING
(—S OF GALLERY) SLIPS
(BACK —) REAR BEHIND BACKSIDE
(DRESSED —) FACE
(FOR EACH —) ALL
(MOUNTAIN —) PUNA VETA SOROCHE
(OUTER — OF SKIN) GRAIN
(RIGHT —) FACE

(RIGHT — OF SWORD) INSIDE
(UNDERNEATH —) BOTTOM
(WINDWARD —) AWEATHER
(PREF.) LATER(I)(O) PLEUR(I)(O)
(— BY —) PAR(A)
(— PARTS) ALI
(BY THE — OF) JUXTA
(ON THIS —) CIS CITRA
(SUFF.) PLEURA PLEUROUS STICH(OUS)

SIDEBAR HOUND

SIDEBOARD ABACUS BUFFET SERVER COMMODE DRESSER CELLARET CREDENCE CREDENZA

SIDE-BY-SIDE ACCOLLE

SIDED
(SUFF.) MER

SIDE DISH OUTWORK

SIDEPIECE BAR BOW JAMB WING CHEEK GUSSET EARPIECE LANDSIDE

SIDES
(PREF.) (ON ALL —) CIRCUM

SIDESLIP SKID SLIP DRIFT DRILL

SIDESMAN HOGGLER QUESTMAN

SIDESTEP BEG AVOID DODGE

SIDEWALK WALKWAY PAVEMENT TROTTOIR BANQUETTE

SIDEWAYS ASKANCE

SIDEWISE ASIDE ASIDEN

SIDING CURB SLIVE SPUR GARAGE

SIDLE EDGE SLIVE PASSAGE SAUNTER

SIDRA PARASHAH

SIEGE BOUT SEDGE ASSIEGE JOURNEY LEAGUER
(— ENGINE) WARWOLF

SIEGFRIED (CHARACTER IN —) MIME WOTAN FAFNER SIEGFRIED BRUNNHILDE
(COMPOSER OF —) WAGNER
(SLAYER OF —) BRUNHILD
(WIFE OF —) KRIEMHILD

SIERRA CERO SERRA SAWBACK KINGFISH

SIERRA LEONE
CAPITAL: FREETOWN
COIN: LEONE
LANGUAGE: KRIO MENDE TEMNE
MEASURE: LOAD KETTLE
MOUNTAIN: LOMA
NATIVE: VAI KONO LOKO SUSU KISSI LIMBA MENDE TEMNE FULANI GALLINA SHERBRO MANDINGO
RIVER: MOA JONG SEWA MONGO ROKEL ROKKEL SCARCY WAANJE
SEAPORT: HEPEL BONTHE SULIMA
TOWN: BO DARU MANO KISSI LUNGI KENEMA MAKENI

SIESTA NAP MERIDIAN

SIEVE FRY TRY BOLT BUNT DRUM HARP LAWN PREE SCRY SHOE SIFT SILE SIZE TEMS GRATE RANGE SCALP TAMIS TAMMY TEMSE BOLTER RANGER RIDDER RIDDLE SEARCE SEARCH SEMMET SIFTER WEIGHT BOULTEL CHAFFER CRIBBLE DILLUER PRICKLE TIFFANY TROMMEL

COLANDER SEARCHER STRAINER
(— FOR MILK) MILSEY
(PREF.) COSCINO CRIBRI ETHMO

SIF (HUSBAND OF —) THOR

SIFT REE TRY BOLT DUST SCRY RANGE SCALP SIEVE TEMSE DREDGE GARBLE RIDDER RIDDLE SCREEN SEARCE WINNOW CANVASS CRIBBLE DRIBBLE SIFTAGE CRIBRATE
(— FLOUR) DRESS
(— IN) INFILTER
(— IN MINING) LUE
(— MEAL) BUNT
(— SHOT) TABLE
(— WHEAT) SCALP

SIFTER SIEVE BOLTER CASTER SIEVER

SIFTING DRIFT GARBLING
(PL.) BOLTING FANNINGS SIEVINGS

SIGH SOB PECH SIFE SOCK WIND MOURN SIGHT SITHE SOUGH TWANK BEMOAN BEWAIL SORROW SUTHER DEPLORE SINGULT SUSPIRE

SIGHT AIM EYE KEN RAY BONE ESPY FACE GAZE PEEP SEET VIEW FERLY RAISE SCENE SCOPE SICHT TRACK VISIE VIZZY BEHOLD DESCRY OBJECT TICKET VISION DISCERN DISPLAY EYESHOT GLIMPSE MONSTER CONSPECT DISCOVER EYESIGHT GUNSIGHT
(— FOR GUN) BEAD LEAF PEEP SCOPE VISIE VIZZY HAUSSE GUNSIGHT
(— OF COMPASS) VANE
(— ON SURVEYOR'S STAFF) TARGET
(— TO SEE IF LEVEL) BONE
(—S OF CITY) LIONS
(AMAZING —) STOUND
(IMAGINARY —) VISION
(PITIFUL —) RUTH
(SECOND —) TAISCH
(SORRY —) BYSEN
(STRANGE —) FERLY FERLIE
(SUFF.) OPSIA OPSIS OPSY OPTIC OPTICON ORAMA

SIGHTER ALINER ALIGNER

SIGHTING LANDFALL
(— DEVICE) ALIDADE

SIGHTLY VIEWLY EYEABLE

SIGHTSEE RUBBERNECK

SIGLOS DARIC

SIGN INK AYAH DASH FIRM HINT HIRE MARK NOTE OMEN TYPE BADGE COLON FRANK GHOST GUIDA HAMZA INDEX SIGIL SINGE SPOOR STAMP TOKEN TRACE ASSIGN AUGURY CARACT EFFECT EMBLEM ENGAGE ENSIGN FUGLER INDICE MOTION NOTICE PARAPH REMARK SIGLUM SIGNAL SIGNET SIGNUM SYMBOL TITTLE WITTER ALEBUSH AUSPICE CHECKER CHEQUER CONSIGN EARMARK ENDORSE INDICIA INSIGNE KNOWING PORTENT PRESAGE PRODIGY PROFFER SHINGLE SHOWING SIGNARY SURMISE SYMPTOM VESTIGE WARNING CEREMONY INDICANT INSTANCE

MONUMENT PROCLAIM SIGNACLE SYLLABIC TELLTALE
(— DOCUMENT) FIRM
(— FOR KEYNOTE) ISON
(— OF ALEHOUSE) LATTICE
(— OF AN IDEA) EMBLEM
(— OF APPROVAL) CACHET
(— OF CONTEMPT) FIG
(— OF DANGER) SEAMARK
(— OF GLOTTAL STOP) HAMZA HAMZAH
(— OF MULTIPLICATION) DOT
(— OF ZODIAC) LEO RAM BULL CRAB GOAT LION ARIES HOUSE LIBRA TWINS VIRGO ARCHER CANCER FISHES GEMINI PISCES TAURUS VIRGIN BALANCE SCORPIO AQUARIUS SCORPION
(— ON MAP) ICON
(ASTROLOGICAL —) CIPHER
(MATHEMATICAL —) NAME FUNCTOR
(MUSICAL —) GUIDA NEUME PRESA SEGNO SWELL SIMILE FERMATA
(OUTWARD —) EVIDENCE
(SANSKRIT —) ANUSVARA
(SHILLING —) SOLIDUS
(SHORTHAND —) DIPHONE
(SLIGHT —) SURMISE
(SUBSCRIPT —) SUBFIX
(SUPERSTITIOUS —) GUEST
(TAVERN —) BUSH ALEBUSH ALEPOLE CHECKER CHEQUER ALESTAKE
(TRAMP'S —) MONICA MONIKER
(VOWEL —) SEGOL SEGHOL
(PL.) INDICIA INSIGNIA
(PREF.) SEMA SEMANT(O) SEMASI(O) SEMATO SEMEIO SEMIO SEMO SYMBOLO
(SUFF.) SEME

SIGNAL OS CUE GUN PST WAG BALK BECK BELL BUZZ CALL COND FLAG GATE HASH SIGN WAFF WAFT WAVE WINK ALARM ALERT BLINK FLARE FUSEE FUZEE LIGHT SHAPE SHORT SPEAK TOKEN WHIFF ALARUM BANNER BEACON BECKON BUZZER ENSIGN HERALD MARKER OFFICE RECALL SIGNET TARGET WAVING WIGWAG BLINKER CHAMADE COMMAND EMINENT GRIFFIN NOTABLE RETREAT TURNOUT ASSEMBLY CRANTARA DIAPHONE FLAGFALL LOGOGRAM STANDARD STRIKING
(— FISHERMEN) BALK
(— FOR A PARLEY) CHAMADE
(— FOR WHALERS) WAIF
(— IN WHIST) ECHO PETER
(— OF DISTRESS) SOS
(— ON HORN) SEEK BLAST STRAKE
(— ON RADARSCOPE) BLIP
(— TO ATTACK) CHARGE
(— TO BEGIN ACTION) CUE
(— WITH FLAGS) WIGWAG
(AUDIO —) HUM
(BOAT'S —) WAFF WAFT
(DEATH —) KNELL
(FOG —) FOGHORN TORPEDO DIAPHONE

(HUNTER'S —) SEEK PRIZE GIBBET STRAKE
(MILITARY —) FLARE TURNOUT ASSEMBLY
(NAVAL —) SECURE
(RADIO —) BEAM
(RAILROAD —) BANJO BOARD FUSEE FUZEE TARGET HIGHBALL SEMAPHORE
(TRAFFIC —) ROBOT
(WARNING —) ALARM KLAXON TOCSIN
SIGNALIZE MARK
SIGNALLING TICKTACK
SIGNALMAN FLAGS BELLBOY BELLMAN
SIGNATE SENNET
SIGNATORY SIGNEE SIGNER
SIGNATURE BOLT FIRM HAND VISA FRANK SHEET SIGIL THEME SIGNUM TUGHRA SECTION HANDWRIT SIGNATOR
SIGNBOARD SIGN SHINGLE
SIGNET SIGIL
SIGNIFICANCE WIT BODY PITH SOUND AMOUNT IMPORT INTENT LETTER STRESS WEIGHT BEARING CONTENT GRAVITY MEANING SENTENCE STRENGTH
(DEVOID OF —) JEJUNE
(HIDDEN —) HYPONOIA
(LACKING —) INANE
(MORAL —) ETHOS
SIGNIFICANT REAL RICH GREAT MEATY AUGURAL EPOCHAL OMINOUS POINTED SERIOUS SENSEFUL SPEAKING PERTINENT
SIGNIFICANTLY SENSIBLY
SIGNIFICATION SENSE VALOR VALUE ETYMON IMPORT MOMENT NOTION MEANING CARRIAGE SIGNIFIE
SIGNIFICS SENSIFICS
SIGNIFY BE SAY BEAR GIVE MAKE MEAN NOTE SIGN WAVE AUGUR IMPLY SKILL SOUND SPEAK SPELL TOKEN UTTER AMOUNT ARGUFY ASSERT BEMEAN DENOTE EMPLOY IMPORT INTEND MATTER SIGNAL BESPEAK BETOKEN CONNOTE DECLARE EXPRESS PORTEND PRETEND DESCRIBE INDICATE INTIMATE MANIFEST
SIGNOR BRUSCHINO, IL
(CHARACTER IN —) SOFIA BRUSCHINO FLORVILLE GAUDENZIO
(COMPOSER OF —) ROSSINI
SIGNPOST GUIDE MERCURY WAYMARK HANDPOST
SIGURD (HORSE OF —) GRANI
(SLAIN BY —) FAFNIR
(SLAYER OF —) HOGNI
(VICTIM OF —) FAFNIR
(WIFE OF —) GUDRUN
SIGYN (HUSBAND OF —) LOKI
SIKH AKALI SINGH UDASI MAZHABI
SIKKIM (CAPITAL OF —) GANGTOK
(NATIVE OF —) RONG BHOTIA LEPCHA
(RIVER OF —) TISTA
SIKSIKA SIHASAPA

SILAS MARNER (AUTHOR OF —) ELIOT
(CHARACTER IN —) CASS AARON DOLLY EPPIE NANCY SILAS MARNER DUNSTAN GODFREY LAMMETER WINTHROP
SILENCE GAG MUM CALK CLUM HIST HUSH REST CHOKE FLOOR PEACE QUIET SHUSH SQUAT STILL CLAMOR MUFFLE SETTLE STIFLE WHISHT CONFUTE SQUELCH DUMBNESS PRECLUDE SUPPRESS
SILENCED STILL
SILENCER SOURDINE
SILENT MUM CLUM HUSH HUST MUET MUTE SNUG CLOSE MUTED STILL TACIT WHIST MUETTE SOPITE SULLEN TIPTOE WHISHT APHONIC UNWORDY ASPIRATE RESERVED RETICENT TACITURN
SILENT DON (AUTHOR OF —) SHOLOKHOV
(CHARACTER IN —) DARIA DUNIA MAURA GREGOR PIOTRA STEPAN AKSINIA DENIKIN MELEKHOV ILINICHKA PROKOFFEY PANTALEIMON
SILHOUETTE SHADE ISOTYPE OUTLINE
SILICA FLINT SILEX SINTER COESITE TRIPOLI TRIDYMITE
SILICATE MICA ALVITE CERITE EUCLASE ILVAITE LOTRITE ZEOLITE CALAMINE ERIONITE WELLSITE
SILICEOUS SHELLY
SILICLE POUCH SILICULE
SILICON (THIN SLICE OF —) WAFER
SILICOSIS CON
SILK SAY SOY CRIN ERIA LOVE MUGA ATLAS FLOSS GREGE HONAN JAPAN TABBY BLATTA CRACKS CULGEE DUCAPE FRISON MANTUA RADIUM SENDAL SHALEE SHILLA SOUPLE TUSSAH ALAMODE CHIFFON HABUTAI PERSIAN SCHAPPE SQUEEZE TIFFANY TSATLEE TUSSORE YAMAMAI ARMOZEEN ARMOZINE LUSTRINE MILANESE
(— FOR LININGS) SARSNET SARCENET
(CORDED —) PADUASOY
(HEAVY —) CRIN ARMOZINE
(RAW —) GREIGE MARABOU TAYSAAM TSATLEE MARABOUT
(REFUSE —) BUR BURR
(TWILLED —) SURAH TOBINE FOULARD LOUSINE
(UNDYED —) CORAH
(UNTWISTED —) SLEAVE
(UPHOLSTERY —) TABARET
(WASTE —) KNUB NOIL FRISON
(PREF.) SERI(CEO)(CI)(CO)
SILK COTTON KAPOK
SILK-COTTON TREE BULAK SEMUL SIMAL BOMBAX YAXCHE BENTANG MUNGUBA POCHOTE
SILKEN SILL SERIC SILKY SUAVE SEREAN
SILK GRASS KARATAS
SILK GUM SERICIN

SILK OAK LACEWOOD
SILKSMAN SCALPER
SILK TREE SIRIS
SILKWORM ERI ERIA SINA BOMBYX TUSSAH TUSSORE YAMAMAI BOMBYCID
SILKY GLOSSY SILKEN
SILKY CORNEL REDBRUSH
SILKY TAMARIN MARIKINA
SILL GIRD SOLE PLATE PATAND PATTEN SADDLE MUDSILL DOORSILL
SILLINESS BOSH FOLLY BETISE GOOSERY INANITY PORANGI SIMPLES IDLENESS NONSENSE ABSURDITY SIMPLICITY
SILLY TID BETE DAFT FOND FOOL NICE VAIN APISH BALMY BATTY BUGGY CAKEY DENSE DILLY DIZZY GOOFY INANE KOOKY LOONY SAPPY SEELY BLASHY CRANKY CUCKOO DAWISH DOTARD DOTTLE FOOTLE FRUITY GUCKED MOPOKE PAULIE SAWNEY SHANNY SIMPLE SINGLE SKIVIE SLIGHT SPOONY VACANT ASININE FATUOUS FOOLISH FOPPISH FRIBBLE GLAIKET PEEVISH PUERILE SCRANNY SHALLOW UNWITTY ANSERINE FEATLESS FOOTLING FOPPERLY
(BE —) DRIVEL
(PREF.) MORO
SILO (PART OF —) BIN DOME PIPE TANK MELON INTAKE LADDER PUMPKIN UMBRELLA PARACHUTE
SILOXANE SILICON
SILPHIUM LASER
SILT DREGS SLEECH DEPOSIT RESIDUE SULLAGE BULLDUST
SILVER LUNA MOON PINA DIANA PLATE SYCEE WEDGE WHITE ALBATA ARGENT SILLER BULLION VERMEIL ARGENTUM STERLING ARGENTINE
(— STATE) NEVADA
(DEBASED —) VELLON
(GERMAN —) ALBATA
(GILDED —) VERMEIL
(NICKEL —) PAKTONG
(PREF.) ARGENT(O) ARGYR(O)
SILVER BELL HALESIA BELLWOOD COWLICKS
SILVERFISH SHINER SLICKER FISHTAIL WOODFISH
SILVERING BACKING
SILVERSIDES IAO BRIT TINK BRITT FRIAR SMELT TAILOR TINKER GRUNION ATHERINE PEIXEREY PEJEREY SKIPJACK
SILVERSMITH SONAR
SILVERTIP BEAR
SILVER TREE IRONWOOD
SILVER TREE FERN PITAU
SILVERVINE CATVINE
SILVERWEED TANSY
SILVERWING CINDER
SILVERY WHITE ARGENT SILVER SILVERN
(PREF.) GLAUCO
SILVIA (FATHER OF —) BALLANCE
(LOVER OF —) VALENTINE
SILYBUM MARIANA

SIMAR CYMAR SYMAR ZIMARRA
SIMEON (FATHER OF —) JACOB
(MOTHER OF —) LEAH
SIMILAR LIKE SAME SUCH ALIKE EVENLY LIKELY SIMILE COGNATE KINDRED SEEMABLE SELFLIKE SUCHLIKE SUITABLE SEMBLANCE
(PREF.) HOL(O)
HOM(E)(EO)(O)(OE)(OI)
(SUFF.) (MAKE — TO) FY IFY
SIMILARITY SIMILE ANALOGY HOMOLOGY HOMOTAXY LIKENESS PARALLEL SAMENESS
SIMILARLY EQUALLY LIKEWISE
SIMILE ICON IKON IMAGE FIGURE SUIVEZ COMPARE
SIMILITUDE IMAGE FIGURE ANALOGY PARABLE PORTRAIT
SIMMER FRY CREE SILE STEW SIMPER SOTTER TOTTLE
SIMON ZELOTES
(BROTHER OF —) JESUS
(FATHER OF —) MATTATHIAS
(SON OF —) JUDAS
SIMON BOCCANEGRA
(CHARACTER IN —) MARIA PAOLO SIMON ADORNO AMELIA ANDREA FIESCO GABRIELLE BOCCANEGRA
(COMPOSER OF —) VERDI
SIMONY BARRATRY
SIMOOM SAMUM SAMIEL KHAMSIN
SIMPER MINCE SMIRK BRIDLE
SIMPLE LOW BALD BARE EASY FOND MERE NICE ONLY PURE RUDE SNAP VERY WEAK AFALD BLEAK DIZZY GREEN NAIVE NAKED PLAIN SEELY SILLY SMALL SOBER AEFALD CHASTE GLOBAL HOMELY HONEST HUMBLE NATIVE OAFISH RUSTIC SEMPLE SEVERE SINGLE STUPID VIRGIN ARTLESS ASININE AUSTERE BABYISH FATUOUS FOOLISH ONEFOLD POPULAR SIMPLEX SPECIES ARCADIAN EXPLICIT HOMEMADE INNOCENT INORNATE SACKLESS SEMPLICE SOLITARY
(PREF.) APL(O) HAPL(O) LITI
SIMPLE-MINDED SEELY SILLY INNOCENT
SIMPLETON AUF AWF COX DAW FON NUP OAF SAP SOT BOOB CAKE COOT CULL FLAT FOOL GABY GAUP GAWP GOFF GOUK GOWK GOWP GUFF PEAK ROOK SIMP SOFT TONY TOOT ZANY COKES GALAH GOOSE IDIOT IKONA JACOB LOACH NINNY NODDY PRUNE SAMMY SMELT SNIPE SPOON TOMMY BADAUD DAUKIN FONDLE GANDER GAUPUS GAWNEY GOTHAM GREENY GULPIN JOSSER NINCUM NOODLE NUPSON SAWNEY SIMKIN SIMPLE DAWPATE GOMERAL GUBBINS JUGGINS MAFFLIN MUGGINS WIDGEON ABDERITE FLATHEAD FONDLING INNOCENT JEANJEAN JOCRISSE KNOTHEAD MOONCALF MOONLING OMADHAUN PEAGOOSE SILLYTON SOFTHEAD WISEACRE

WOODCOCK NINCOMPOOP
SIMPLICITY NICETY PURITY
MODESTY NAIVETE ELEGANCE
SIMPLIFY CLARIFY EXPOUND
SIMPLY JUST ALONE FONDLY
MERELY PLATLY CRUDELY
QUIETLY NATIVELY
SIMULACRUM SHAM IMAGE
IMITATION
SIMULATE ACT FAKE MOCK FEIGN
MIMIC AFFECT ASSUME SEMBLE
SIMULE SKETCH
SIMULATED FAINT FAKED ERSATZ
FICTIOUS
SIMULATION ACTING ANALOGUE
PRETENCE PRETENSE
SIMULTANEOUS CONJOINT
CONJUGATE
SIMULTANEOUSLY ONCE
TOGETHER
SIN ERR CULP DEBT ENZU EVIL
HELL PAPA VICE BLAME CRIME
ERROR FAULT FOLLY GUILT
SLOTH WATHE WRONG AGUILT
COMMIT FELONY NANNAR
OFFEND PIACLE PLIGHT VENIAL
FRAILTY OFFENSE HAMARTIA
INIQUITY PECCANCY QUEDSHIP
TRESPASS
(DAUGHTER OF —) ISHTAR
(DEADLY —) ACEDIA
(ORIGINAL —) ADAM
(SON OF —) NESKU SHAMASH
(WIFE OF —) NINGAL
(PREF.) HAMARTIO
SINCALINE CHOLINE
SINCE AS AGO FOR FRO NOW
GONE SETH SITH SYNE BEING
WHERE FORWHY BECAUSE
SITHENS WHEREAS INASMUCH
SITHENCE
(PREF.) CIS CITRA
SINCERE GOOD REAL TRUE AFALD
FRANK CANDOR DEVOUT ENTIRE
HEARTY HONEST SIMPLE SINGLE
CORDIAL EARNEST GENUINE
ONEFOLD UPRIGHT FAITHFUL
PRAYERFUL
(NOT —) PLASTIC
SINCERELY TRULY SIMPLY SINGLY
DEVOUTLY ENTIRELY HEARTILY
SINCERITY FAITH HEART VERITY
HONESTY REALITY
SINDON CORPORAL
SINE SAGITTA
SINEW THEW BRAWN FIBER FIBRE
FORCE NERVE POWER LEADER
SINNER TENDON
SINEWY WIRY NERVY THEWY
ROBUST FIBROSE FIBROUS
NERVOUS STRINGY TENDINAL
SINFONIA SYMPHONY
SINFUL BAD EVIL VILE NEFAS
WRONG WICKED PECCANT
UNGODLY VICIOUS PIACULAR
SING HUM JIG LIP CANT CARP
GALE HYMN LILT TUNE CAROL
CARRY CHANT CHIRL CROON
DIRGE DITTY DRING FEIGN LYRIC
RAISE TOUCH TROLL YEDDE
CHAUNT CHORUS DIVIDE INTONE
MELODY RECORD RELISH STRAIN
WARBLE CHORTLE COUNTER

DESCANT GRIDDLE SINGING
TWEEDLE CHERUBIM FALDERAL
MODULATE SINGSONG VOCALIZE
(— ABOUT) BESING
(— ABOVE TRUE PITCH) SHARP
(— AS A BEGGAR) GRIDDLE
(— BRISKLY) KNACK
(— CHEERFULLY) LILT
(— FLORIDLY) DIVIDE
(— HARSHLY) SCREAM
(— IN A CRACKED VOICE) CRAKE
(— IN CHORUS) CHOIR
(— IN LOW VOICE) CROON
(— IN SWISS MANNER) YODEL
(— LOUDLY) BELT TROLL TROLLOL
(— PRAISES) LAUD
(— ROMANCES) GEST GESTE
(— SECOND PART) SURCENT
(— SOFTLY) SOWF SOWTH
(— WITH FLOURISHES) ROULADE
SINGAPORE (RIVER IN —) SUNGEI
SELETAR
(STRAIT OF —) JOHORE SEMBILAN
SINGE GAS BURN SWEAL GENAPP
SCORCH SWINGE SCOWDER
SWITHEN FIREFANG
SINGER ALTO BARD DIVA LARK
SWAN BASSO BUFFA BUFFO
SKALD VOICE BULBUL BUSKER
CANARY CANTOR LYRIST SONGER
BASSIST CHANTER CROONER
PRIMOMO SOLOIST SONGMAN
SOPRANO TROLLER WARBLER
BAYADERE CANTADOR CASTRATO
CHANTEUR FALSETTO GRIDDLER
MELODIST MONODIST THAMYRIS
VOCALIST CITYBILLY
(— OF FOLK SONGS) CANTADOR
(— OF ROCK MUSIC) ROCKER
(— OF THE GODS) GANDHARVA
(FEMALE —) SONGBIRD
(MENDICANT —) BUSKER
(PRINCIPAL —) PRIMOMO
(PROVENCAL —) MUSAR
SINGING CANT SCAT CHANT LYRIC
HYMNODY CANOROUS JONGLERY
(— CAROLS) PLYGAIN HODENING
(CANTORIAL —) HAZANUTH
HAZZANUT
(SIMULTANEOUS —) CHORUS
SINGLE ODD ONE LAST ONLY SOLE
UNAL AFALD AEFALD SIMPLE
SOLEIN SULLEN UNIQUE VERSAL
ALONELY AZYGOUS ONEFOLD
SEVERAL SIMPLEX TWOSOME
PECULIAR SEPARATE SINGULAR
SOLITARY SPORADIC PARTICULAR
(— OUT) CUT SPOT ISOLATE
SEPARATE
(PREF.) APL(O) HAPL(O) MANI
MON(O) UNI
SINGLE-FOOT RACK
SINGLEHANDEDLY SINGLY
SINGLENESS UNITY ONENESS
SINGLETON (— LEAD) SNEAK
SINGLY SINGLE SOLELY SLONELY
SINGPHO CHINGPAW
SINGSONG SOUGH CHANTING
SINGULAR ODD RARE FERLY
QUEER QUAINT SEENIL SINGLE
CURIOUS STRANGE
PECULIAR
SINGULARISM HENISM

SINGULARITY DOUBLET ONENESS
ONLINESS
SINISTER AWK CAR KAY DARK
DIRE FELL GRIM DISMAL LOUCHE
MALIGN AWKWARD OBLIQUE
OMINOUS
SINISTRAL REVERSED
SINK DIP DOP EBB LUM SAG SET
SYE BORE DRAU DRAW DROP
FADE FAIL FALL GOWT HELD KILL
LUMB SILE SWAG AVALE DRAFT
DRAIN DROOP DROWN HIELD
LAPSE LOWER MERGE POACH
SQUAT STOOP SWAMP VERGE
CLOACA DEVALL DOLINA DOLINE
DRENCH GUTTER JAWBOX
PLUNGE PUDDLE RESIDE SETTLE
COMMODE DECLINE DESCEND
DRAUGHT FOUNDER GULLION
IMMERSE RELAPSE SCUPPER
SCUTTLE SUBSIDE SWALLOW
DECREASE SINKHOLE SOAKAWAY
(— A WELL) DRILL
(— AND FALL) TWINE
(— AS IN MUD) LAIR
(— DOWN) BOG AVALE STOOP
DECLINE
(— FANGS INTO) STRIKE
(— INTO OOZE) WASEL
(— NAILHEAD) SET
(— SUDDENLY) SLUMP
(— UNDER TRIAL) QUAIL
SINKBOX BOX SINK BATTERY
SINKER BUR BURR SINK DIPSY
PLUMB BULLET
SINKHOLE SINK PONOR UVALA
CENOTE COLLECT
SINKING GONE SINKAGE
(— DOWN) FONDU
SINKIUSE COLUMBIA
SINLESS INNOCENT
SINLESSNESS HOLINESS
SINNER DEBTOR PECCANT
SINNING PECCANT
SINUATE GYROSE
SINUOSITY WRIGGLE
SINUOUS WAVY SNAKEY SINUATE
SNAKISH TORTILE WINDING
INDENTED SWANLIKE
SINUS BOSOM ANTRUM RECESS
LOCULUS TEARPIT
(PL.) ANTRA
SINUSITIS ROUP
SIOUAN ABANIC DAKOTA SANTEE
SAPONI CATAWBA DACOTAH
SIOUX (— FORCE) WAKAN WAKON
SIP BIB NIP SUP BLEB SEEP SLUP
SUCK TIFF KEACH SNACK WHIFF
TIPPLE TICKLER DELIBATE
SIPHON CRANE THIEF VALINCH
FLINCHER
SIPPING LIBANT
SIPUNCULOIDEA ACHAETA
INERMIA
SIR PO DAN DEN DON PAN AZAM
BAAS HERR MIAN STIR TUAN
BWANA SAHIB SENOR SEYID
SIEUR MESSER SAYYID SIGNOR
SIRREE DOMINUS EFFENDI
MESSIRE SIGNIOR SIGNORE
GOSPODIN GOVERNOR
(PL.) LORDINGS
SIRCAR BANIAN

SIRE BEGET THROW FATHER
GETTER
SIREN BUMMER HOOTER LIGEIA
LIGYDA ENTICER LORELEI
MERMAID SIRENIAN
SIRENIAN COWFISH MUTILATE
SIRENOMELUS SYMPUS
SYMMELUS
SIRICID UROCERID
SIRIS KOKO LEBBEK
SIRIUS SOTHIS TISHIYA CANICULA
SIRLOIN SEY BACKSEY
SIRMUELLERA BANKSIA
SIRUP WAX LICK GOLDY SYRUP
GOWDIE GREENS ORGEAT
RUNOFF ANTIQUE CLAIRCE
ECLEGMA LIQUEUR MOLASSES
QUIDDANY
SIRWASH SIDELINE
SISAL CABUYA SISALANA
SISKIN TARIN ABERDEVINE
SISSIFIED PRISSY
SISSOO TALI SHISHAM
SISSY SIS CISSIE SISTER CHICKEN
PANTYWAIST
SISTER NUN SIB SIS GIRL NURSE
SISSY TITTY WOMAN EXTERN
PERSON
(YOUNGER —) CADETTE
(PL.) SISTERN SISTREN
(PREF.) SORORI
SISTERHOOD BEGUINES SORORITY
SISTERLY SORORAL
SISYPHUS (BROTHER OF —)
ATHAMAS SALMONEUS
(FATHER OF —) AEOLUS
(MOTHER OF —) ENARETE
(SON OF —) SINON GLAUCUS
ORNYTION
(WIFE OF —) MEROPE
SIT SET LEAN SEAT BENCH PRESS
ROOST SQUAT WEIGH BESTRIDE
(— ABRUPTLY) CLAP
(— ASTRIDE) CROSS HORSE
STRADDLE
(— ERECT LIKE A DOG) BEG
(— FORCIBLY) DOSS
(— IN JUDGMENT) DEEM
(— ON) BROOD COVER
(— OVER EGGS) RUCK BROOD
CLOCK
SITA (FATHER OF —) JANAKA
(HUSBAND OF —) RAMA SOMA
SITATUNGA NAKONG
SITE AREA PLOT SEAT SITU SOLE
SPOT TOFT FIELD PLACE SITUS
STAND STANCE BIVOUAC
DAMSITE HABITAT STEADING
(— OF BIRD SEXUAL DISPLAY) LEK
(— OF HUNT) DRIVE
(— OF SMELTER) BOLE
(EXCAVATION —) DIG
(FORTIFIED —) KAME
(THRESHING —) SETTING
SITTER DOLLY DOLLIE INSESSOR
SITTING DIET SEAT ASSIS CLUTCH
SEANCE SEDENT SEJANT SESSION
CONGRESS SEDERUNT
SITUATE PLACE POSITION
SITUATED SET SEATED STATURED
(— OPPOSITE) COUNTER
SITUATION JOB LIE CASE CRIB
PASS PLOT POST SEAT SITE SPOT

BERTH SIEGE SITUS STATE STEAD ASSIZE CHANCE ESTATE OFFICE PLIGHT STATUS EPISODE PICTURE PORTENT POSTURE STATION INCIDENT INSTANCE POSITURE STANDING UBIQUITY
(— BESET BY DIFFICULTIES) SCRAPE
(— IN CRIBBAGE) GO
(— IN FARO) CATHOP
(— IN OMBRE) CODILLE
(— OF PERPLEXITY) HOBBLE STRAIT
(AMUSING —) BAR
(AWKWARD —) SCRAPE JACKPOT
(CRITICAL —) CLUTCH
(DIFFICULT —) BOX PUXY BOGGLE NINEHOLES PREDICAMENT
(DISTRESSING —) STYMIE
(EXECRABLE —) ATROCITY
(FAVORABLE —) BREAK
(FINAL — OF ACT) CURTAIN
(HIGH —) AERY AERIE
(HOPELESSLY DOOMED —) RATTRAP
(NECESSITOUS —) BREACH
(PAINFUL —) DISTRESS
(RELATIVE —) BEARING
(TIGHT —) CRUNCH
(TRYING —) COW
(UNPLEASANT —) BUMMER
(UNSATISFACTORY —) DILEMMA
(VEXATIOUS —) HEADACHE
(VILE —) DUNGHILL
(ZODIACAL —) HAYZ
SITZ BATH SITZBAD SEMICUPE
SITZMARK BATHTUB
SIVA RUDRA SHIVA ISVARA SHAMBU BHAIRAVA MAHADEVA NATARAJA
SIX VAU WAW SICE SISE HEXAD HEXADE SENARY SEXTET STIGMA DIGAMMA SIXSOME
(PREF.) HEX(A) SEX(A)(I) SEXTI
SIXFOLD SEXTUPLE
SIX-FOOTED HEXAPOD
SIXMO SEXTO
SIXPENCE HOG PIG BEND KICK ZACK SIMON SPRAT TIZZY BENDER FIDDLE TANNER TESTON CRIPPLE FIDDLER TESTRIL
SIXTEENTH ANA ANNA
SIXTH
(PREF.) SEXTI
SIXTIETH (— PART OF DAY) GHURRY
SIXTY SAMECH SAMEKH
SIZABLE SNUG HEFTY LARGE HANDSOME
SIZE WAX AREA BIND BULK MARK MASS DRESS GIRTH MOUND PLANK SCALE EXTENT FORMAT GROWTH MICKLE MOISON PICNIC SIZING BIGNESS CONTENT CORSAGE FITTING THIRTEEN TWELVEMO
(— OF BOOK) FOLIO
(— OF CARDS) TOWN LADIES
(— OF HOLE) BORE
(— OF HOSIERY) POPE
(— OF PAPERBOARD) LARGE
(— OF PARTICLE) GRIND
(— OF ROPE) GRIST
(— OF SLATE) PEGGY IMPERIAL
(— OF TYPE) GEM PICA RUBY AGATE CANON ELITE PEARL

MINION PRIMER BREVIER DIAMOND EMERALD ENGLISH PARAGON COLUMBIAN
(— YARN) SLASH
(CLOTHING —) LONG SHORT STOUT JUNIOR PETITE
(EXTRA LARGE —) SUPER
(GREAT —) MAGNITUDE
(RELATIVE —) SCALE
(UNUSUAL —) OUTSIZE
SIZING DRESSING SLASHING
(— LIQUID) GLAIR
SIZZLE FRIZZ
SKADI (FATHER OF —) THJAZI
(HUSBAND OF —) NJORD
SKANDA (BROTHER OF —) GANESHA
(FATHER OF —) SHIVA
(WIFE OF —) DEVAYANI VALLIAMMAN
SKAT CAT NULL TOURNEE
SKATE BOB RAY TUB RAJA RINK SKIT TINK TUBE FLAIR SCULL BATOID DOCTOR FLATHE PATENT PATTEN ROCKER ROLLER RUNNER SKETCH TINKER CHOPINE FLAPPER PLACOID SKETCHER
(— MARK) CUSP
(FEMALE —) MAID
(PREF.) BATO
SKATER PATTENER SKETCHER
SKEDADDLE BUNK SCOOT
SKEET KELTER KILTER PELTER
SKEIN RAP HANK HASP SCAN BOTTOM SLEAVE SELVAGE
SKEINER RANDER SLIPPER
SKELETIN SPONGIN
SKELETON CUP CAGE MORT RAME ATOMY BONES FRAME LOOFAH SICULA SKELET ANATOMY CARCASS RAWBONE ARMATURE CORALLUM MANDIBLE OSSATURE
SKELETON KEY GILT SCREW TWIRLER
SKELP SCUD
SKEPTIC DOUBTER INFIDEL ZETETIC APIKOROS APORETIC
SKEPTICAL ACADEMIC APORETIC DOUBTFUL
SKEPTICISM HUMISM UNBELIEF
SKETCH BIT DASH DRAW LIMN PLAN VIEW VITA DRAFT ENTER PAINT TRACE APERCU DESIGN DOODLE SCHEME SPLASH BOZZETO CROQUIS DRAUGHT DRAWING EBAUCHE ETCHING OUTLINE SCHIZZO ESQUISSE MONOGRAM PROFILE PROSPECT REMARQUE VIGNETTE
(— BEFOREHAND) INDICATE
(AUTOBIOGRAPHICAL —) VITA
(BIOGRAPHICAL —) ELOGY ELOGIUM
(FIRST —) ESQUISSE
(HERALDIC —) TRICK
(OUTDOORS —) LANDSKIP
(PRELIMINARY —) DRAFT ABBOZZO MAQUETTE
(ROUGH —) NOTE CROQUIS POCHADE ESQUISSE
(SATIRICAL —) SKIT
SKEW ASKEW GAUCHE
SKEWBACK SPRINGER
SKEWBALD PINTO PIEBALD

SKEWED ALOP
SKEWER PROD PROG SPIT PRICK TRUSS SKIVER TASTER BROCHETTE
SKEWERER TUBER
SKI SKEE SNOWSHOE
(— DOWN SLOPE) SCHUSS
(— DOWNHILL) WEDEL
(— METHOD) PASSGANG
(— MOVEMENT) RUADE
(— POSITION) VORLAGE
(— RACE) SLALOM
(— RACING) LANGLAUF
(— STYLE) WEDELN
(— TURN) TELEMARK
(PART OF —) TIP EDGE TAIL SHOVEL BINDING
(RELATING TO — EVENTS) NORDIC
(PL.) BOARDS
SKID DOG DRAG SLEW SLUE TRIG DRIFT DRILL SLOUGH SKIDPAN SLIPPER TRIGGER SIDESLIP
(— LOGS) SNAKE TWICH TRAVOY TWITCH
(— ON RAIL) SKATE
(AUTOMOBILE —) SPINOUT
(FENDER —) GLANCER
(IRON —) SABOT
SKIDDER SNAKER
SKIDI LOUP
SKIDWAY PIT
SKIER KANONE SNOWBIRD SCHUSSBOOMER
SKIFF CANOE SHELL SKIFT CAIQUE DINGHY SAMPAN CURRANE SKIPPET JOHNBOAT
SKIING TOURING LANGLAUF
SKIL BESHOW SKILFISH
SKILL ART CAN WIT FEAT FEEL HAND PATE TACT CRAFT DRAFT HAUNT KNACK TRICK ENGINE TECHNE ABILITY ADDRESS APTNESS CUNNING FINESSE MASTERY MYSTERY PROWESS SCIENCE SLEIGHT ARTIFICE CAPACITY CHIVALRY DEFTNESS FACILITY INDUSTRY LEARNING
(LACK OF —) INERTIA
(NAVIGATION —) SEACRAFT
(PREF.) TECHNI TECHNO
(SUFF.) ICS SHIP TECHNIC TECHNY
SKILLED OLD SEEN WISE ADEPT ASTUTE MASTER PERITE SCIENT SKILLY VERSED HOTSHOT PRACTIC EDUCATED SKILLFUL
SKILLET PRIG SPIDER
SKILLFUL APT SLY ABLE DEFT FEAT FILE FINE GOOD HEND PERT TIDY WISE ADEPT CANNY FITTY HANDY HENDE READY SLICK SWEET ADROIT ARTFUL CLEVER CRAFTY DAEDAL EXPERT HABILE SCIENT SKILLY SOLERT SUBTLE CUNNING POLITIC SKILLED DEXTROUS PRACTIVE SLEIGHTY TACTICAL PROFICIENT
SKILLFULLY DEFTLY YARELY CRAFTILY
SKILLFULNESS CRAFT
SKIM TOP RIFF SCUD SCUM SCUN SCUR SILE SKIP FLEET GRAZE SCALE SKIFF SKIRR SKIVE

BROWSE RABBLE SAMPLE DESPUME SKITTER
(— ON WATER) SCHOON
SKIMMED FLAT FLET
SKIMMER FALK LARI SKEP SCOOP LINGEL SCUMMER CUTWATER
SKIMMINGS SCRUFF
SKIMP JIMP SLUR SCAMP SKINCH
SKIMPY JIMP CHARY SPARE MEAGER MEAGRE SCANTY STINGY
SKIN KIP KIT BACK BARK CASE CAST DERM FELL FLAY FLEA HIDE HILD KITT MORT PEAU PEEL PELT RIND BALAT BLYPE BRAWN FLOAT GENET SLUFF STRIP SWARD CORIUM PELTRY SWARTH UNCASE CUTICLE DOESKIN ENDERON KIDSKIN LEATHER PELLAGE SKIMMER BUCKSKIN DRUMHEAD LAMBSKIN PARADERM PELLICLE SEALSKIN TEGUMENT VITILIGO WOOLFELL
(— FOR BOOKBINDING) BASAN
(— FOR HOLDING WATER) KIRBEH
(— OF BACON) SWARD
(— OF BOARDS) CARPET
(— OF FRUIT) PEEL
(— OF GOOSE) APRON
(— OF INSECT) CAST
(— OF POTATO) JACKET
(— OF POULTRY NECK) HELZEL
(— OF RABBIT) RACK CONEY
(— OF SEAL) SCULP
(— OF THE HEAD) SCALP
(— OF WALNUT) ZEST
(— OF YOUNG CALF) SLINK DEACON
(— WITH WOOL REMAINING ON IT) WOOLFELL
(BARE —) BUFF
(BEAVER —) PLEW
(BOAR'S —) SHIELD
(CAST —) SPOIL SLOUGH EXUVIAE
(CHAFED OR SORE —) IRE
(CHAMOIS —) FURWA
(DEEP LAYER OF THE —) CUTIS
(FAWN —) NEBRIS
(INNER PART OF THE —) DERMA
(LAMB — PREPARED LIKE FUR) BUDGE
(OUTER —) HUSK
(PENDULOUS FOLD OF —) DEWLAP
(ROUGHTANNED —) CRUST
(SHARK —) SHAGREEN
(SHEEP —) BASIL
(SQUIRREL —) VAIR
(THICKENED —) BRAWN
(THIN —) FILM PELLICLE STRIFFEN
(60 —S) TURN
(PREF.) CUT(I)(O) CUTANEO DERM(AT)(ATO)(O) DERO EPIDERM(O) SCYT(O)
(SUFF.) DERM(A)(ATOUS)(IA)(IS)(Y)
SKIN FLICK NUDIE
SKINFLINT SKIN FLINT SCREW HUDDLE PELTER SCRAPER SKEEZIX
SKINK ADDA SCINCID SCORPION
(PREF.) SCINCI SCINCO
SKINNY BONY LEAN THIN SLINK
SKIOLD (FATHER OF —) ODIN
SKIP DAP HIP BALK BOUT FOOT JUMP LEAP SLIP TRIP BOUND

CAPER DANCE FRISK SALTO SCOON SCOPE SCOUP SKITE SMOKE VAULT GAMBOL GLANCE LAUNCH SPRING GUNBOAT SALTATE SKIPPER SKITTER TRIPPLE PORPOISE RICOCHET **(— SCHOOL)** TIB
(MINING —) SLIPE
SKIPJACK SKIP BONITO ALEWIFE SKIPPER
SKIPPER IHI SKIP LAODAH LOWDAH SERANG SHIPPER
SKIRMISH FRAY BRUSH CLASH MELEE SKIRM BICKER HASSLE PICKEER RUNNING
SKIRMISHER HUSSAR TIRALLEUR
SKIRMISHING SPARRING
SKIRT CUT HUG LAP BANK BASE COAT ENGI JUPE MIDI MINI SAYA TUBE TUTU COAST JUPON LABIE PAREU PASIN STRIP TREND TWIST BASQUE DIRNDL HOBBLE JUMPER KIRTLE PEPLUM SARONG TAMEIN QUARTER BASQUINE PULLBACK SKIRTING
(ARMOR —) TASSES LAMBOYS
(DIVIDED —) CULOTTE
(HOOP —) CRINOLINE
(HOOPED —) TUBTAIL
(LONG —) MAXI
(TARTAN —) KILT ARISAID
(PL.) DOCK DOCKEN
SKIRTING DADE SKIRT PLINTH
(PL.) BROKES
SKIT BLACKOUT
SKITTAGETAN HAIDA
SKITTISH SHY CORKY GOOSY WINDY FLISKY KITTLE SKEIGH SPOOKY FLIGHTY SCADDLE SKADDLE STARTLY BOGGLISH SKITTERY STARTFUL
SKITTLES BOWLS KAYLES KITTLES SQUAILS
SKUA BONXIE JAEGER TEASER TULIAC STINKPOT WHIPTAIL
SKULDUGGERY JOUKERY PAWKERY
SKULK DERN JOUK LURK LUSK MICHE MOOCH SCOUT SHOOL
SKULL BEAN POLL CRANY MOOCH SCALP SCAUP VAULT COBBRA MAZARD PALLET SCONCE CRANIUM HARNPAN HEADMOLD PANNICLE
(— BONE) VOMER
(— POINT) TYLION
(BACK OF —) OCCIPUT
(INCOMPLETE —) CALVARIA
(UPPER HALF OF —) SINCIPUT
(PREF.) CRANI(O)
(SUFF.) CRANIA(L)
SKULLCAP COIF PIXY PIXIE SKULL VAULT BEANIE COIFFE CALOTTE CAPELINE HOODWORT
(ARABIAN —) CHECHIA
(JEWISH —) YAMILKE YARMULKE
(STEEL —) SECRET
SKUNK ANNA ATOC ATOK PUSS HURON SKINK SNIPE ZORIL CHINCHA POLECAT SEECAWK SMELLER CONEPATE CONEPATL MUSTELID PHOBYCAT ZORRILLO
(JAVANESE —) TELEDU

SKUNK CABBAGE COLLARD POCKWEED
SKY BLUE HIGH LIFT LOFT POLE TIEN AZURE CARRY DYAUS ETHER LANGI VAULT CAELUS CANOPY HEAVEN REGION WELKIN ELEMENT HEAVENS OLYMPUS TENGERE WEATHER
(ICE —) ICEBLINK
(PREF.) CAELI CAELO COELI COELO URAN(I)(O) URANOSO
SKY-BLUE
(PREF.) CERULEO
SKYLARK LARK YERK
SLAB BAT CANT CLAM LECH PARE SLAT BLADE BOARD DALLE LINER PANEL PLANK SLATE STELA STELE TABLE WADGE ABACUS FLITCH MARVER MIHRAB PAVIOR RUNNER FLAPPET PLANCHE PORPHYRY PUNCHEON SLABWOOD
(— BY SINK) BUNKER
(— OF CLAY) BAT
(— OF COAL) SKIP SLIP
(— OF ICE) SCONCE
(— OF LIMESTONE) BALATTE
(— OF MARBLE) DALLE
(— OF PEAT) SCAD
(— OF SANDSTONE) COMAL
(— OVER BROOK) CLAM
(BROKEN-OFF —) BLAUD
(GRINDING —) MULLER
(HOPSCOTCH —) PEEVER
(MEMORIAL —) LEDGER
(PAINTER'S —) SLANT
(PLASTERER'S —) HAWK
(STONE —) PLANK STELA STELE INKSTONE
SLACK DRY LAX OFF CULM DUFF LASH NESH SLOW SOFT VEER CHECK CRANK FLOWN LOOSE SLAKE TARDY ABATED FLABBY FLAPPY REMISS UNGIRT BACKING MAKINGS RELAXED SLACKEN SMEDDUM CARELESS DILATORY INACTIVE SLOBBERY NEGLIGENT
(— IN TRIGGER) CREEP
(— OF ROPE) SLATCH
(— SHEET OF SAIL) FLOW
(COAL —) COOM COOMB
(PL.) BAGS
SLACKEN LAG PAY EASE FLAG SLOW DELAY DOWSE LOOSE QUAIL RELAX SLACK SLAKE START SURGE ASLAKE EXOLVE RELENT UNBEND
(— SPEED) HANG
SLACKENING LETUP DETENTE LETDOWN SLACKAGE
SLACKER SPIV ROTTER COUCHER SLINKER EMBUSQUE
SLACKNESS LACHES LASHNESS
SLADE SOLE
SLAG SCAR DROSS CINDER DANDER SCORIA SLAKIN THOMAS QUITTER SLACKEN
SLAIN FALLEN
SLAKE ABATE SLACK LESSEN QUENCH REFRESH SATISFY
SLAKING FAT
SLAM CLAP DASH FLUB SLOG SLOT VOLE CLASH GRAND PLANK

SLOSH STRAM CHELEM FLOUNCE
SLAMMER JAIL STIR
SLANDER CANT BELIE LIBEL NOISE SMEAR BEFOUL DEFAME INJURE MALIGN MISSAY VILIFY ASPERSE CALUMNY OBTRECT SCANDAL TRADUCE TRUMPET BACKBITE DEROGATE STRUMPET ASPERSION BESPATTER
SLANDERER JUROR BLAZONER
SLANDEROUS FAMOUS VILIPEND
SLANG CANT ARGOT FLASH DIALECT
SLANT TIP CANT FLUE SKEW TILT BEVEL DRAFT SLOPE SPLAY STOOP FLANCH SKLENT DRAUGHT COLORING DIAGONAL
(PREF.) CLIN(O)
SLANTED CANTED COLORED COCKEYED
SLANTING AWRY BIAS CANT SKEW BEVEL SLOPE ASLANT ASLOPE SKLENT SQUINT LOXOTIC OBLIQUE SLOPING AVELONGE COLORING OVERWART SIDELONG
SLANTINGLY AHOO ASWASH SLANTLY
SLANT LINE VIRGULA VIRGULE
SLANTWISE
(PREF.) LECHRI(O)
SLAP BOX DAB BLIP BLOW CLAP CUFF FLAP LICK PLAT SCUD SLAT SNUB SPAT TACK BLIBE CLINK CLOUT CRACK PANDY POTCH SKEEG SKELP SKITE SMACK SPANK TWANG TWANK BLEEZE BUFFET SCLAFF SLIGHT STRIKE TINGLER WHERRET BACKSLAP
(— HARD) BLAD
(RANDOM —) FLAY
SLAPDASH BUCKEYE
SLASH CAG CUT JAG COUP GASH HASH PANE RACE RASH SLIT TOPS KNIFE MINCE SCORE SKICE SLISH RAMMEL SCORCH STREAK SLITTER DIAGONAL SLASHING
SLASHED JAGGED DECOPED TATTERED
SLASHING ABATIS
SLAT BOW LAG FLAT PALE SLOT WAND BLADE SCLAT SLOAT STAVE RIFFLE SPLINE EUPHROE BEDSTAFF
SLATE RAG SLAT FRAME KILLAS TABLET TICKET SHALDER SHINDLE SLATING
(— IN SMALL IRREGULAR PIECES) SCANTLE
(BLUE —) SHIVER SKAILLIE
(EXPOSED PART OF ROOFING —) BARI
(SIZE OF —) PEGGY DUCHESS IMPERIAL
(SURFACE —) BONE
SLATER HELER HELLIER SLATTER SKIMMITY
(TOOL OF —) STAKE
SLATTERN DAB DAW MAB FROW MAUX SLUT TRUB DOLLY FAGOT MAWKS MOGGY MOPSY BLOUSE CLATCH DOLLOP MALKIN SLOVEN STREEL TRAPES LADRONE TROLLOP HUCKMUCK SLUMMOCK

SLATTERNLY DOWDY BLOWSY DAWISH FROWZY SORDID BLOWZED TRAPISH SLATTERN SLOVENLY
SLAUGHTER WAL FELL KILL SLAM SLAY BUTCH HALAL QUELL BATTUE MURDER STRAGE BUTCHER CARNAGE KILLING SCUPPER SHAMBLE BUTCHERY MASSACRE OCCISION SHECHITA
(— ACCORDING TO MOSLEM LAW) HALAL
(— OF LARGE NUMBER) HECATOMB
(WHOLESALE —) QUELL
SLAUGHTERER KILLER SHOHET KNACKER SHOCHET
SLAUGHTERHOUSE ABATTOIR BUTCHERY MATADERO SHAMBLES
(— WORKER) LIMEMAN
SLAUGHTERING SHEHITA SHECHITA
SLAV VEND WEND CZECH HUNKS HUNKY SLAVE USKOK CROATIAN MORAVIAN POLABIAN
SLAVE BOY DAS ARDU BOND DASI DUPE ESNE MOIL SERF DAVUS HELOT SWINK THEOW ABJECT ALIPIN ALLTUD CUMHAL FORSAR GUINEA HIEROS MAMLUK SLAVEY THRALL VASSAL BONDMAN CAPTIVE CHATTEL FORSADO HACKNEY PEDAGOG SERVANT SLAVISH BONDMAID LORARIUS MAMELUKE MANCIPLE MORGIANA PRAEDIAL SLAVELET THEOWMAN ODALISQUE
(— IN TEMPLE) HIEROS
(— WHO WHIPS OTHERS) LORARIUS
(DEFORMED —) CALIBAN
(FREED —) CLIENT
(FUGITIVE —) MAROON CIMMARON
(GALLEY —) FORSAR FORSADO SFORZATO
(HAREM —) ODALISK
(HINDU —) DAS DASI
(PL.) CHIURM COFFLE HELOTRY TOXOTAE
SLAVEDRIVER RUSHER
SLAVER DROOL FROTH DRIVEL DRIBBLE SLABBER SLOBBER SALIVATE
SLAVERY YOKE THRALL BONDAGE HELOTRY MIZRAIM THRALDOM SERVITUDE
SLAVEY DRUDGE
SLAVISH MEAN MENIAL
SLAVONIC (— BEING) VILA
SLAY KILL SMITE SPILL MURDER STRIKE BUTCHER EXECUTE STRANGLE SLAUGHTER
SLAYER BANE HOGNI KILLER MURDERER
(— OF INFIDELS) GHAZI
(SUFF.) CTONUS
SLEAZY FLIMSY
SLED LUGE TODE JUMBO SCOOT SLIDE SLIPE SLOOP HURDLE JUMPER SLEDGE SLEIGH BOBSLED CLIPPER COASTER DOGBOAT DOGSLED KOMATIK MONOSKI POINTER SLIPPER TRAILER TRAVOIS HANDSLED SKELETON TOBOGGAN

SLEDGE DAN DRAG DRAY LUGE
PULK SLED GURRY PULKA SLIDE
SLIPE TRAIL TRAIN TROLL TRUNK
SLEIGH KIBITKA KOMATIK
PADDOCK TROLLEY TRAINEAU
(— FOR CRIMINALS) HURDLE
(— FOR STRAIGHTENING RAILS) GAG
(LOG —) SLOOP TIEBOY
(MINER'S —) MALLET
SLEDGEHAMMER SMASHER
SLEEK SNOD SOFT CLOSE JOLLY
SILKY SLICK TRICK SILKEN SLEEKY
SLIGHT SMARMY SMOOTH SVELTE
SLEEKIT SOIGNEE SLIPPERY
SLEEKNESS GLOSS
SLEEP BED KIP LIB LIE NAP CALK
CAMP DORM DOSS DOZE HALE
REST WINK BALMY CRASH DORSE
ROOST SWOON DROWSE SIESTA
SNOOZE SOMNUS SWEVEN
SLUMBER WINKING
(— BROKEN BY SNORING) GRUFF
(— ON A PERCH) JOUK
(DEEP —) SWOON
(LIGHT —) SLOOM
(PRETENDED —) DOGSLEEP
(PROFOUND —) SOPOR
(SHORT —) NAP SIESTA SNOOZE
(PREF.) SOPOR HYPN(O) SOMNI
(DEEP —) NARC(O)
SLEEPER TIE FENDER DORMANT
DORMEUSE ELEOTRID STRINGER
SLEEPINESS SOPITION
SLEEPING BED ASLEEP DORMANT
DORMIENT
SLEEPLESS LIDLESS WAKEFUL
RESTLESS WATCHFUL
SLEEPLESSNESS WATCH
INSOMNIA
SLEEPY DOZY HEAVY NODDY
PEEPY DROWSY GROGGY
MORPHIC SLEEPISH SLUMBERY
SOMNIFIC SLUMBEROUS
SLEET STORM
SLEEVE ARM BAND POKE ARMLET
MANCHE MOGGAN BUSHING
CATHEAD CUBITAL HOUSING
THIMBLE
(— ON A SHAFT) CANNON
(— ON GUN) BAND
(CANVAS —) DROGUE
(HANGING —) TAB
(LEG-OF-MUTTON —) GIGOT
(LONG —) POKE
(TAPERED —) SKEIN
SLEIGH SLO PUNG SLED BOOBY
SLIPE TRAIN BERLIN CUTTER
SLEDGE CARIOLE TRAINEAU
SLEIGHT ARTIFICE
SLENDER FINE HAIR JIMP LANK
LEAN PRIN SLIM THIN DELIE EXILE
FAINT LATHY REEDY SLANK
SLEEK SMALL SPIRY SWAMP
WISPY FILATE SCANTY SEMMIT
SLIGHT SPINNY SPIRED STALKY
SVELTE TENDER GRACILE
LISSOME SLIVERY SPIRLIE
SQUINNY TENUOUS THREADY
WASPISH ACICULAR ETHEREAL
HAIRLIKE PILIFORM SPINDLED
ATTENUATE
SLENDERNESS EXILITY TENUITY
SLEW LOT RAFT SLUE STROKE

SLICE CUT BITE CHIP CHOP FLAG
FLAP JERK SHED STOW CANCH
CAPER GIGOT LEACH SHARE
SHAVE SHIVE SKELB SLIPE SLIVE
CANTLE COLLOP CORNET CULPON
SHIVER SLIVER TARGET THIBLE
TRENCH SECTION SHAVING
TRANCHE COSSETTE TURNOVER
(— CUT IN PLOWING) FLAG
(— OF BACON) BARD BARDE
LARDON RASHER
(— OF BREAD) BUTTY WHANG
CROUTE TRENCHER
(— OF CHEESE) KEBBOC
(— OF COAL) SKIP
(— OF FISH) COBBIN
(— OF MEAT) STEAK COLLOP
CUTLET SCALLOP TAILZIE
(— OF MEAT OR FISH) PAUPIETTE
(— OF SMOKED SALMON) CORNET
(— OF TOAST) ROUND
(— REMOVED FROM ROADWAY)
CANCH
(— WITH MOTIONS) SAW
(—S OF APPLES) CHOPS
(LARGE —) BLAD DODGE
(THICK —) SLAB WHANG
(THIN —) CHIP WAFER SECTION
SLICED CUT
SLICK LOY GLIB SNUG SLEEK
CLASSY GLOSSY SMOOTHY
SLIDDERY
SLICKER FLOAT SLICK SMOOTH
SLEEKER SMOOTHER
SLIDE SCLY SKID SLEW SLIP SLUR
BALOP CHUTE COAST COULE
CREEP GLIDE HURRY MOUNT
SCOOT SHIRL SLADE FINDER
SLOUGH SLIDDER SLITHER
SLUTHER FADEAWAY GLISSADE
SLIDEWAY SCHLEIFER
(— A DIE) SLUR
(— CARDS) SKIN
(— DOWN) RUSE SLUMP
(— FOR LOWERING CASKS)
POLEYNE
(— ON DRUMHEAD) BRACE
(— SIDEWISE) SKID
(TENT —) EUPHROE
SLIDER REGISTER
SLIDEWAY PULLEY
SLIDING COULE
SLIGHT CUT OFF EASY FINE HURT
POOR SLAP SLIM SLUR SNUB
THIN WEAK FILMY GAUZY LIGHT
MINOR SCANT SMALL SOBER
FLIMSY FORGET LACHES LITTLE
MINUTE REMOTE TWIGGY
CONTEMN FRAGILE GRACILE
NEGLECT NOMINAL SHALLOW
SKETCHY SLENDER SLIGHTY
THREADY VILLAIN DELICATE
MISPRIZE OVERLOOK SCRANNEL
VILIPEND
SLIGHTER LESS
SLIGHTEST FIRST LEAST
SLIGHTINGLY LIGHTLY
SLIGHTLY FAINTLY SOMEWHAT
(PREF.) MI(O)
(SUFF.) ESCENT ULOUS
SLIGHTNESS DELICACY GRACILITY
SLIM THIN GAUNT WANDY SLIGHT
SLENDER TENUOUS

SLIME GLIT GORE OOZE SLAB SLIP
SLUM GLEET SLAKE SLOAK SLOKE
SLEECH SLUDGE SCHLICH
SLUBBER SLUTHER
(PREF.) MUC(I)(O) MUCOSO
MYX(O)
(SUFF.) MYXA
SLIMY OOZY SLAB MUCID GLAIRY
GLEETY GLETTY LIMOUS MUCOUS
SNOTTY SLEECHY MUCULENT
SLINE JOINT
SLING DUST LOOP FLING HONDA
SLUNG BRIDGE BRIDLE HALTER
SLACKIE
(— FOR HAULING GAME) TUMPLINE
(— OF BRAIDED FIBERS) MA
(PREF.) FUNDI
SLINGER FUNDITOR
SLINGSHOT SLING SLAPPY
TWEAKER CATAPULT SHANGHAI
SLINK SLY CAST HINT LEER LOOP
LURK PEAK MICHE SHIRK SLING
SLUNK SNEAK SLINKY
(— AWAY) SHAG SLOKE FLINCH
MIZZLE SHRINK
SLIP DIP IMP NOD SLY BALK CARD
CHIT DOCK FALL JINK LOOP RUSE
SKEW SKID SLEW SLUR SPEW
BEWET BEWIT BONER CHECK
DAGGE ERROR FLIER FLYER GLIDE
LABEL LAPSE SCAPE SCION SHIFT
SHIRL SKATE SKITE SLICK SLIDE
SLIPE SLIVE SLUMP STALK SURGE
COUPON ENGOBE LAPSUS
MISCUE SLOUGH SLURRY TICKET
UNSLIP DELAPSE FOUNDER
ILLAPSE MISSTEP MORTISE
SLIDDER SLUTHER SNAPPER
STUMBLE BOOKMARK GERTRUDE
GLISSADE HEADBAND QUICKSET
SCHEDULE SIDESLIP SLIPPAGE
SLIPPING
(— AWAY) GO BILK SKIN WISE
EVADE ELAPSE
(— BY) ELAPSE
(— FROM A PLANT) STALLON
(— OF FISH) RAND
(— OF PAPER) ALLONGE
(— OF PARCHMENT) PANEL
(— OF WOOD) SPILL REGLET
(— OFF COURSE) SLEW SLOUGH
(— ON CARELESSLY) SLIVE
(— OUT) TIB
(— SECRETLY) CREEM
(— SMOOTHLY) SWIM
(— UP) BLUNDER
(CERAMICS —) SLOP ENGOBE
(INFANT'S —) GERTRUDE
(PILLOW —) BIER
(PREF.) CLAD(O)
(SUFF.) CLADOUS
SLIPCASE CASE FOREL FORREL
SLIPKNOT BOW SNITTLE
DRAWKNOT
SLIPMAN JACKER
SLIPOVER OVERSLIP
SLIPPER FLAT MULE NEAP PUMP
SOCK TURN GLAVE MOYLE
ROMEO SCUFF BALLET BOOTEE
DORSAY JULIET PANTON PINSON
SANDAL SCLAFF SCLIFF BAUCHLE
CHINELA CRAKOWE EVERETT
SCUFFER BABOUCHE FEWTERER

PANTOFLE SCLAFFER SLIPSHOE
(PREF.) CALCEI
SLIPPERINESS SLIDDER
SLIPPERY GLEG GLIB SLID GLARY
GLINT SLAPE SLEEK SLICK SOAPY
SWACK CRAFTY GLINSE GREASY
LUBRIC SHIFTY SLIPPY ELUSIVE
EVASIVE GLIDDER SHUTTLE
SLIDDRY SLIDING SLITHER
GLIBBERY SLABBERY SLICKERY
SLIDDERY SLITHERY
(PREF.) LUBRI
SLIPPERY DICK DONCELLA
SLIPSHOD JERRY RAGGED SLOPPY
UNKEMPT SLAPDASH SLOVENLY
SLIPSTREAM RACE
SLIPUP FLUFF MISTAKE
SLIT CUT EYE JAG KIN NAG RIT
FENT GATE NICK PORT RACE
RENT SCAR SLOT VENT CRACK
SPARE BOUCHE CRANNY OSTIUM
STRENT FISSURE PERTUSE
PLACKET SLITTED SLOTTEN
WINDWAY APERTURE BOTHRIUM
(— HIND LEG) HARL
(— IN EDGE OF SHIELD) BOUCHE
(— IN ORGAN PIPE) MOUTH
(— IN STONE) GRIKE
(— MADE BY CUT) KERF
(ORNAMENTAL —) SLASH
SLITHER SLIDE HIRSEL SLIDDER
SLUTHER
SLIVER TOP SHAVE SKELF SLICE
SPELK SPELL SHIVER DELIVERY
SPLINTER
(— OF WOOL) ROLL ROVE
(SPINNING —) END RIBBON
DELIVERY
SLOB JOKER SLUDGE SLOBBER
SLOMMACK
SLOBBER SLOP SLUP SMALM
SMARM SLAVER SLABBER
SLATHER SLIVVER BESLAVER
SLOBBERY SLOBBY SMARMY
SLAVERY
SLOE SLA SNAG SLONE
SLOG SLOSH STRIKE
SLOGAN CRY CACHET CUTTER
PHRASE CATCHCRY SLUGHORN
WARDWORD CATCHWORD
SHIBBOLETH
SLOOP STAR BOYER COMET SMACK
SCHUIT HOOGAARS
SLOP SLAP SOSS SQUAB SWILL
SOSSLE SOZZLE HOGWASH
SLATTER
(— AROUND) SLAISTER
(PL.) SLIVERS SLIPSLOP
SLOPPAGE
SLOPE UP DIP LIE BAND BANK
BENT BRAE CANT CAST CURB
DROP FALL HANG HILL LEAN PALI
RAKE RAMP RISE SIDE SINK TILT
BEVEL CLIFF COAST GAMMA
HIELD PINCH PITCH SCARP SLANT
SLENT SLOOP SPLAY STEEP
TALUS VERGE YUNGA ASCENT
BAJADA BATTER BREAST BROACH
ESCARP GLACIS HADING SHELVE
TUMBLE UPBROW UPRISE
CUTBANK DESCENT DOWNSET
FORESET HANDING INCLINE
LEANING PENDANT UPGRADE

VERSANT WEATHER BANKSIDE DRIPPING GLISSADE GRADIENT SHOULDER SIDELING SNOWBANK ACCLIVITY
(— BACK) BATTER
(— DOWN) SHED
(— OF CUESTA) INFACE
(— OF ROOF) CURB
(— OF STERNPOST) RAKE
(— UPWARD) CLIMB ASCEND BATTER
(DOWNWARD —) HANG DEVALL DECLINE DESCENT HANGING DOWNHILL
(GENTLE —) GLACIS
(MARGINAL —) CESS
(MOUNTAIN —) ADRET
(SKIING —) SCHUSS
(STEEP —) BROW HEADWALL
(SUFF.) CLINAL CLINE
SLOPING CANT DEVEX SLANT SLOPE SLOPY ASLOPE SHELVY DECLIVE SCARPED DOWNHILL SIDELING
(— ABRUPTLY) BOLD
(— BACKWARD) SUPINE
SLOPPINESS BLURB
SLOPPY JUICY SOPPY SLABBY SOZZLY SPLOSHY SLABBERY SLAPDASH SLATTERN SLATTERY SLIPSHOD WATERISH
SLOSH DOWSE SLASH SLUSH SOUSE SQUDGE SPLODGE
SLOT COVE DROP SCROLL SPLINE KEYHOLE GUIDEWAY
SLOTH AI UNAU TARDO ACEDIA IGNAVY ACCIDIE IGNAVIA BRADYPOD EDENTATE PIGRITIA SLUGGING
SLOTH BEAR BHALU ASWAIL
SLOTHFUL FAT ARGH IDLE LAZY INERT LITHER THOKISH UNLUSTY DELICATE INDOLENT SLUGGISH
SLOUCH LOUCH LARRUP LOLLOP LOUNGE SLIDDER TROLLOP SHAMMOCK SLOUCHER
SLOUCH HAT SMASHER
SLOUGH CORE SHED SLEW SLUE BAYOU RAVEL SHUCK SLONK SLUFF SPOIL SWAMP ESCHAR DISCARD LAMMOCK
SLOVEN BESOM CLART SLUSH TROLLY GROBIAN HALLION TRACHLE HUDDROUN
SLOVENLY DOWDY GAUMY MESSY BLOWZY CLATTY FROWZY GRUBBY SHABBY SLOPPY SLOVEN TRAILY UNTIDY BUNTING SLIVING SLOUCHY UNSONCY CARELESS HUDDROUN SLIPSHOD SLOBBERY SLUBBERY SLUTTISH TROLLOPY
SLOW BOG LAG LAX LEK WET ARGH DREE DULL LASH LATE LAZY LENT SKID SLUG SULK BLUNT DUNCH DUNNY HEAVY HOOLY INERT POKEY SLACK SLOTH SWEER TARDE TARDO TARDY UNAPT ARREST BEHIND DRIECH DUMMEL HINDER RETARD SLOOMY SOODLY TRAILY COSTIVE DRONISH HALTING LAGGARD LANGUID SLACKEN SOAKING STRANGE TARDANT TEDIOUS

UNREADY DILATORY INACTIVE LATESOME SLUGGISH
(— DOWN) SEIZE
(— IN BURNING) SOFT
(— IN MOVEMENT) GRAVE INERT SULKY
(— OF MIND) STUPID
(— TO LEARN) BACKWARD
(— TO RESPOND) GROSS
(— UP) SLACK SLACKEN
(MODERATELY —) ANDANTE
(MUSICALLY —) LENTO
(PLEASANTLY —) SOFT
(VERY —) LARGO
(PREF.) BRADY TARDI
SLOW-BURNING PUNKY
SLOWED STIFF
SLOWER LATTER CALANDO
SLOWING
(SUFF.) STASIA STASIS
SLOW LORIS KOKAN
SLOWLY SLOW DULLY GRAVE HOOLY LENTO ADAGIO GENTLY HEAVILY
SLOW-MOVING SLEEPY DORMANT DRAWLING SLUGGISH
SLOWNESS LAG SLOTH LENTOR TARDITY LATENESS
SLOW-WITTED FAT DENSE STUPID
SLOWWORM HAGWORM
SLUDGE GUNK SLOB
SLUE SLEW SWAMP SLOUGH
SLUG BUST LINE MILL PLOW SHOT SNAG STEW ARION CLUMP LIMAX SNAIL RATTLE STRIKE SNIFTER TREPANG GEEPOUND
(PREF.) LIMACI
SLUGGARD DAW SLOW SLUG DRONE BUZZARD CAYNARD LUGGARD SWINGER SLOWBACK SLUGABED
SLUGGISH LAG DOZY DULL FOUL LATE LAZY LOGY SLOW BROSY DOPEY DRONY FAINT HEAVY INERT LOURD RESTY SULKY BOVINE DRAGGY DROWSY JACENT LEADEN SLEEPY SLOOMY SLUGGY SUPINE TORPID COSTIVE DORMANT DRONISH LAGGARD LANGUID LENTOUS LUMPISH RESTIVE DILATORY INACTIVE INDOLENT LOURDISH SLOTHFUL SLOTTERY SLUGGARD
(PREF.) BRADY
SLUGGISHNESS LEAD SLOTH APATHY LENTOR PHLEGM INERTIA LANGUOR
SLUICE CLOW GOOL GOTE GOUT SASSE SLUSH TRUNK CLOUGH FENDER LAUNDER PENSTOCK WASTWEIR
SLUICEGATE ABOIDEAU
SLUICEWAY FLASH
SLUM BUSTI BUSTEE WARREN
SLUMBER DORM DOVE DOZE JOUK REST ROUT SLEEP SLOOM DROWSE
SLUMP FALL FLOP SOSS SLOUCH LETDOWN TROLLOP
SLUR BIND SLIM COULE GLIDE SLIME SCRUFF SLIGHT SLUBBER LIGATURE
(— IN PRINTING) SHAKE

SLURRY SLIP
SLUSH MIRE POSH SIND SLOP FLUSH SLOSH SPOSH STUFF SWASH SWOSH LOPPER SLUDGE SLUTCH SLOBBER SLODDER
SLUSHY SLASHY SLOPPY SLOSHY SLUDGY STICKY SPLASHY SLOBBERY
SLUT MAUX BITCH FILTH QUEAN DOLLOP DRAZEL DRAZIL MALKIN DROSSEL PUCELLE SLAMKIN SLATTERN
SLUTTISH DRABBY SLUTTY SORDID
SLY ARCH FOXY SLEE SLID SLIM CANNY COONY LEERY LOOPY PAWKY PEERY POKEY SLOAN SNAKY ARTFUL ASTUTE CRAFTY FELINE SUBTLE SUPPLE CUNNING EVASIVE FURTIVE LEERING POLITIC SUBTILE UNFRANK GUILEFUL SLEIGHTY SNEAKING STEALTHY THIEVISH CLANDESTINE
SLYNESS CUNNING PAWKERY STEALTH ARCHNESS
SMACK BANG BARK BIFF BUSS KISS SALT SCAT SLAP TANG TROW VEIN BAWLY GOUFF SAVOR SNACK SPICE TASTE TWANG BARQUE BAWLEY FLAVOR SMATCH SMACKEE SPANKER BRAGOZZO SLAPDASH TINCTURE
(— OF) RELISH
SMACKING SKELPING
SMALL BIT SMA WEE BABY MEAN PINK SEED SLIM TINY WEAK BIJOU BITTY DAWNY DEENY DINKY ELFIN PETIT PETTY PINKY POKEY TEENY WEENY BANTAM FRIBBY GRUBBY INSECT LITTLE MIDGET MINUTE NARROW PEANUT PETITE SCANTY SLIGHT SMALLY CAPSULE NAGGISH NANITIC PICCOLO QUEECHY SCRIMPY SLENDER THRIFTY PEDDLING PILULOUS SNIPPETY MINIATURE MINISCULE
(— AND NUMEROUS) MILIARY
(— AND THICK) DUMPY DUMPTY
(— BUT TANGIBLE) CERTAIN
(— PORTION) MODICUM
(CONTEMPTIBLY —) MEASLY
(DAINTILY —) MIGNON
(EXCESSIVELY —) BOXY
(NOT —) GOOD
(VERY —) WEE FINE TINY DWARF MICRO PUSIL PYGMY TEENY MINUTE MINIKIN TIDDLEY DWARFISH
(PREF.) LEPT(O) MICR(O) OLIG(O) PARV(I) PAURO TAPIN(O)
(SUFF.) (— ONE) EL ET IUM LING OCK ULA ULE ULUM ULUS
SMALLAGE MARCH
SMALLCLOTHES SHORTS SMALLS
SMALL CRANBERRY FENBERRY
SMALLER LESS MINOR LESSER
(PREF.) MEIO MI(O) MINI
SMALLEST FIRST LEAST MINIM TITMAN MINIMUS
SMALLHOLDER TOFTMAN
SMALL-MINDED PETTY PICAYUNE

SMALLNESS NANISM EXILITY FEWNESS PAUCITY EXIGUITY SCARCITY
SMALLPOX POX VARIOLA ALASTRIM
(PREF.) VARIOLI VARIOLO
SMALT ROYAL ESCHEL SMALTZ ZAFFER ASMALTE
SMART NIP YEP BRAW FESS FLIP FOXY GNIB NICE PINK POSH RACY SNAP SPRY SWAG TRIG ACUTE BRISK CLEAN DINKY FLASH HEADY JIMMY KIPPY NIFTY NOBBY NUTTY PEERT PRANK PRIDY RITZY SASSY SAUCY SHARP SLEEK SLICK SMIRK SMOKE SMUSH SPICY SPRIG STING SWANK SWISH TIGHT TIPPY TOFFY TRICK AKAMAI BRAWLY BRIGHT CHEESY CLEVER DAPPER GIGOLO JAUNTY KITTLE PERTLY SHREWD SPANKY SPIFFY SPRINK SPRUCE STOUND SWANKY SWIDGE TIDDLY KNOWING PUNGENT SWAGGER TOFFISH VOGUISH BRUSHING SPIFFING
(— IN APPEARANCE) POSH
(— IN DRESS) GALLANT
SMART ALECK FLIP SMARTY
SMARTEN FINE PUSS SMUG GROOM PRINK SLICK TITIVATE
SMARTLY SMACK SMART SNACK YEPLY TIDELY
SMARTNESS TON SNAP SMART SPIFF SWISH
SMARTWEED CULERAGE REDKNEES
SMASH GIT BASH BUMP CAVE DASH PASH RUSH SCAT TRAP BREAK CRACK CRASH CRAZE PRANG SOCKO STAVE TRASH WRECK CRACKER SHATTER SMASHUP DEBRUISE DEMOLISH OVERHEAD STRAMASH
(— A GAP) BREACH
SMASHED BUNG KAPUT STOVEN BROOZLED
SMASHING CRACKING
SMASHUP STRAMASH
SMATTERING SMACK SMATCH SMATTER
SMEAR DAB RUB BLOT BLUR CLAM DAUB DOPE GAUM GLOB GORM MOIL CLEAM DITCH GLAIR SLAKE SLARE SMALM SMARM SULLY BEDAUB BESLAB DEFILE PLATCH SLAVER SLURRY SMIRCH SMOOCH SMUDGE SPREAD STREAK STRIKE BEPAINT BESMEAR PLASTER POLLUTE SPLOTCH SLAISTER
(— OVER) ENGLUTE
(— WITH BLOOD) GILD
(— WITH EGG WHITE) GLAIR
(— WITH MUD) CLART SLIME
(— WITH SOMETHING STICKY) GAUM GORM LIME
(— WITH TAR) PAY
(— WITH WAX) CERE
SMEAR DAB FLATFISH MARYSOLE
SMEARED FOUL BROSY MUSSY SCOVY BLOODY SMUDGY BLURRED BEGUMMED
SMEARY DAUBY GAUMY

SMEDDUM SMITHUM
SMELL FUNK FUST GUSH NOSE
ODOR VENT AROMA FETOR FLAIR
SAVOR SCENT SMACK SNIFF
SNOOK SNUFF STIFE TASTE
OLFACT RESENT SMEECH
BREATHE PERFUME REFLAIR
VERDURE
(— AFTER PREY) BREVIT
(— OFFENSIVELY) REEK
(DAMP FUSTY —) RAFT
(DISAGREEABLE —) GOO PONG
STENCH
(HAVING PLEASANT —) SNIFTY
(MUSTY —) FUST
(OFFENSIVE —) FUNK FETOR STINK
MEPHITIS
(STRONG —) HOGO
(SWEET —) SWEET
(PREF.) BROM(O) ODIO ODORI
ODORO OLFACTO OSM(O) OSMIO
OSPHRESIO OZO(NI)(NO)
(SENSE OF —) OSPHRESIO
(SUFF.) OSMA
(SENSE OF —) OSPHRESIA
SMELLY FUGGY WHIFFY SMELLFUL
SMELT DECOCT INANGA EPERLAN
ICEFISH ELIQUATE SALMONID
SPARLING SPERLING
(FRY OF —) PRIM
SMEW NUN PIED SMEE DIVER
SMETHE
SMIDGEN DAB
SMILAX LILY SARSA LILIUM
SMILE BEAM GRIN FLASH FLEER
SMEER ARRIDE SMUDGE SMIRKLE
(— AMOROUSLY) SMICKER
(AFFECTED —) SMIRK
(SELF-CONSCIOUS —) SIMPER
SMILING GOOD BONNY RIANT
SMILY BONNIE RIDENT SMIRKY
TWINKLY SMILEFUL
SMIRCH SMIT SOIL SMEAR SULLY
SLURRY SOILURE TARNISH
SMIRCHED DINGY
SMIRK DRAD YIRN SIMPER
SMICKER SMIRKLE SMURTLE
SMITE DUNT FRAP GIRD SLAY
FLING SKITE STRIKE
(— WITH LIGHTNING) LEVEN
SMITH MIMIR REGIN BOSSER
FORGER SMITHY FARRIER
GLUTTER SMITHER STEELER
WAYLAND FLOORMAN
FORGEMAN PANSMITH
SMITHSONITE CALAMINE
SMITHY FORGE SMIDDY STITHY
STUDDIE FARRIERY
SMITTEN EPRISE STRICKEN
SMOCK BRAT SLOP KAMIS SMOKE
JIBBAH JUMPER CHEMISE
SMICKET
SMOKE PEW USE BLOW FLAN
FOGO FUFF FUME FUNK HAVE
LUNT NAVE PIPE REEK ROKE
TOVE DRINK REECH SMEEK
SMORE SMUSH STIVE VAPOR
WHIFF BREATH BUCCAN POTHER
SMEECH SMUDGE INCENSE
SMOLDER SMOTHER BACONIZE
(— MARIJUANA) BLAST
(AUTHOR OF —) TURGENEV
(CHARACTER IN —) IRINA TANYA

OSININ GRIGORY POTUGIN
TATYANA BAMBAEFF SHESTOFF
BINDASOFF GUBARYOFF
LITVINOFF RATMIROFF
KAPITOLINA REISENBACH
(FROST —) BARBER
(HAZE AND —) SMAZE
(OFFENSIVE —) FUNK
(TOBACCO —) BLAST
(PREF.) ATMID(O) CAPNO
FUMAR(O) FUMI
SMOKE BROWN ASPHALT
SMOKEHOUSE FUMATORY
SMOKEJACK STACKMAN
SMOKER FUNKER NICOTIAN
(MARIJUANA —) VIPER
SMOKESTACK STACK FUNNEL
TUNNEL CHIMNEY
SMOKE TREE ZANTE FUSTET
FUSTIC SCOTINO
SMOKING ROOM DIVAN TABAGIE
SMOKY HAZY ROKY DINGY FUMID
FUMISH FUMOSE REECHY
SMUDGY SMUISTY
SMOLDER SMUSH SMOTHER
SMOLDERING PUNKY
SMOLT SMELT SMOUT SPROD
SMOOCH NECK LALLYGAG
LOLLYGAG
SMOOTH DUB FAT LAP NOT BOSS
COMB DRAG EASE EASY EVEN
FACE FAIR FILE FLAT GLAD GLEG
GLIB HONE IRON LENE NOTT
REET SLID SNOD SOFT TRIM
BLAND BRENT CLEAR COUTH
DARBY DIGHT DOLCE DRESS
EMERY FLOAT FRAZE GLARE
GOOSE HOWEL LEVEL LITHE
NAKED PLAIN PLANE PRESS
QUIET SCARF SILKY SLAPE SLEEK
SLICK SMOLT SNUFF SOAPY
SUANT SUAVE SUENT TERSE
ABRASE BUFFED CREAMY
EQUATE EVENLY FETTLE FLUENT
GLOSSY GREASE GREASY LEGATO
LIMBER MANGLE POLITE SCREED
SILKEN SLIGHT STREAK STRIKE
STROKE SVELTE UNFRET
BOULDER ERUGATE FLATTEN
SLEEKIT EXPLICIT GLABRATE
GLABROUS GLIBBERY GRAZIOSO
LEVIGATE SARSENET SLIDDERY
SQUEEGEE STRICKLE UNRUFFLE
(— BY BREAKING LUMPS) BILDER
(— MARBLE) GRIT
(— ONESELF UP) PREEN
(— OVER) GLOZE PLASTER
(— TYPE) KERN
(HYPOCRITICALLY —) SLEEK
(PHONETICALLY —) LENE LENIS
(PREF.) HOMAL(O) LEIO LEUR(O)
LIO LISS(O) LITI OXY
SMOOTHER GLAZER
SMOOTHLY SLICK EASILY EVENLY
GLIBLY SMOOTH SPROWSY
SWEETLY POLITELY
SMOOTHNESS EASE FLUENCY
SMOOTH-RUNNING SWEET
SMOOTH-TONGUED WHILLY
SMOOTH WINTERBERRY
CANHOOP
SMOTHER BURKE CHOKE SMEAR
SMOKE SMORE MOIDER SMUDGE

STIFLE FLASKER OPPRESS
QUEASON QUEAZEN SMOLDER
SMUDDER
SMOTHERED ETOUFFE STIFLED
SMUDGE BLUR GAUM SLUR SMUT
SOIL SOOT CROCK SMEAR SMOKE
SMOOCH SMUTCH SMOLDER
SMOTHER SOILURE
SMUDGED BLOTTY SMUTCHY
SMUG SLEEK SMUSH SUAVE
SMUDGE
SMUGGLE RUN STEAL BOOTLEG
SHUFFLE
SMUGGLER OWLER RUNNER
SPOTSMAN
(— OF DRUGS) MULE
SMUGGLING OWLING
SMUGLY FATLY
SMUT BUNT COOM BLACK BLECK
COLLY COOMB CROCK GRIME
SMOOT SMITCH SMUTCH
SMATTER COLBRAND
SMUTCH BLOT SMIRCH SMITCH
SMOUCH SMUDGE
SMUT GRASS TUSSOCK
SMUTTINESS RAUNCH
SMUTTY BAWDY DIRTY SOOTY
SULTRY BARNYARD FREUDIAN
SMYRNA USHAK
SNACK BIT CUT BAIT BITE NOSH
SNAP TAPA BEVER BUTTY CHACK
CHECK NACHO SHARE SNICK
TASTE GOUTER MUNGEY NACKET
SNATCH ZAKUSKA ANTOJITO
NUNCHEON
SNAFFLE GAG BRIDOON
SNAG KNAG SNUG STUB POINT
PLANTER SNAGGLE
(PL.) EMBARRAS
SNAIL HUA PILA SNAG CHINK
DRILL HELIX OLIVA PHYSA SHELL
THAIS TURBO WHELK CERION
CONKER DODMAN NATICA
NERITA NERITE PHYSID PURPLE
TRITON WINKLE RISSOID
UNICORN VERTIGO ZONITID
CASSIDID ESCARGOT HODMADOD
JANTHINA LYMNAEID MELANIAN
NERITOID RAMSHORN SOLARIUM
WALLFISH PERIWINKLE
(PREF.) STROMBI STROMBULI
(SUFF.) COCHLEI COCHLI(O)
COCHLO
SNAILFLOWER CARACOL
SNAKE (ALSO SEE SERPENT AND
REPTILE) ASP BOA BOM NAG
BOBA BOID BOMA JUBO NAGA
NAJA SEPS SNIG ABOMA ASPIC
COBRA CONGO CRIBO DRILL
JIBOA KRAIT MAMBA PTYAS
RACER SNECK TIGER VIPER
BOIGID BONGAR CANTIL CHITAL
DABOIA DIPSAS ELAPID GOPHER
HISSER JESSUR KERRIL PYTHON
ROLLER RUNNER TAIPAN
WENONA ADJIGER ANILIID
BOKADAM CAMOODI CRAWLER
CREEPER CULEBRA DIAPSID
HAGWORM LABARIA LANGAHA
PRESTER RATTLER REGULUS
REPTILE SCYTALE SERPENT
SPITTER WALPAPI ANACONDA
BONETAIL BUNGARUM CASCAVEL

CERASTES CROTALID EGGEATER
FLATHEAD HAIRWORM JARARACA
KEELBACK MOCCASIN OPHIDIAN
RINGHALS SNAKELET VIPERINE
(PREF.) OPHI(O) SERPU
(SUFF.) OPHIS
SNAKEBARK IRONBARK
SNAKEBIRD DARTER PLOTUS
ANHINGA DUCKLAR
SNAKEHEAD MURRAL
SNAKELIKE ANGUINE VIPEROUS
SNAKEMOUTH POGONIA
SNAKEPIECE POINTER
SNAKEROOT STEVIA BABROOT
BUGBANE SANGREL SANICLE
SAWWORT POOLWORT
RICHWEED WHITETOP
SNAKESKIN SPOIL HACKLE
SLOUGH
(CASTOFF —S) EXUVIAE
SNAKEWEED BISTORT
SNAP SET ZIP BARK BITE CHOP
GNAP HUFF JERK KNAP LIRP PIPE
SETT BREAK CLACK FILIP FLICK
GANCH KNACK KNICK PHOTO
SMACK SNACK BLUDGE SNAPPY
SNATCH FASTENER PUSHOVER
SNAPHEAD CREPITATE
(— AT) HANCH
(— LIGHTLY) KNICK
(— OFF) SNIP
(— TOGETHER) CRASH
(— UP) SNUP SNAFFLE
(— WITH FINGER) LIRP FILIP THRIP
FILLIP
SNAPBACK PASSBACK
SNAPDRAGON BULL SNAPS
BULLER BULLDOG DOGMOUTH
SNAPE FLINCH
SNAPPER UKU BRIM JOCU SESI
BREAM PARGO VORAZ CUBERA
HUSSAR JENOAR LAWYER NATIVE
TAMURE ULAULA COCKNEY
CRACKER BIAJAIBA CACHUCHO
FLAMENCO GNATSNAP LUTIANID
WOLLOMAI SCHNAPPER
MUTTONFISH
SNAPPING CHACK DOGGISH
SNAPPING BEETLE ELATER
SKIPPER SNAPPER ELATERID
SKIPJACK
SNAPPING TURTLE LOGHEAD
SHAGTAIL
SNAPPISH CRUP EDGY PUXY
CROSS SNACK TESTY WASPY
CUTTED SNAGGY SNAPPY SNIPPY
DOGGISH PEEVISH
SNAPPY CRISP JEMMY NIPPY
ZIPPY
SNARE GIN HAY NET PIT SET BAIT
BUKE FANG GIRN GRIN HOOK
LACE LIME TOIL TRAP WAIT WIRE
BRAKE CATCH FRAUD GNARE
LATCH LEASH SINEW SNARL
SNIRL STALE SWEEK TRAIN
COBWEB GILDER PANTER SNATCH
SPRINT TREPAN TUNNEL
ENSNARE MANTRAP OVERNET
PITFALL SETTING SNICKLE
SNIGGLE SPRINGE BIRDLIME
INVEIGLE LIMEBUSH SPRINGLE
TENDICLE MOUSETRAP
(— DEER) WITHE

(— FOR ELEPHANTS) KEDDAH
(FISH —) WEEL

SNARL ARR BITE CARL GIRN GNAR GURR HARL HURR NARR TWIT WAFF YARR GNARL GNARR GRILL KNURL RAVEL SNIRL TWINE BOWWOW BUMBLE GAUNCH MUCKER TANGLE VENNER GRIZZLE GRUMBLE

SNARLED SNAFU

SNARLER CYNIC

SNARLING LATRANT

SNATCH HAP NAB NIP RAP GRAB HINT RACE RASE SNAP SNIP WHIP WRAP SNEK BRAID CATCH CLAWK CLICK EREPT GANCH GRASP GRIPE PLUCK SNACK STRIP SWIPE SWOOP TWEAK WHIFT WREST SNITCH STRIKE TWITCH WRENCH CLAUGHT GRABBLE SCAMBLE VULTURE

SNEAK BLAB GRUB LEER LOOP LOUT LURK PEAK PIMP SHUG SNIG LURCH MEECH MOOCH SCOUT SHARK SHIRK SKULK SLIDE SLINK SLIPE SLIVE SLOKE SNEAP SNICK SNOOK BLIFIL MICHER WEASEL SLOUNGE SNIGGLE SNEAKSBY
(— AWAY) SLIPE
(— OFF) MAG SHAB MIZZLE
(PRYING —) SNOOP

SNEAKER CREEPER GUMSHOE

SNEAKING HANGDOG PEAKING SLIVING

SNEAKY FURTIVE MEECHING

SNEER SHY FLON GIBE GIRD GIRN GULE JEER JERK JIBE MOCK FLEER FLING FLOUT GLEEK JAUNT SCOFF SCOUT SLARE SLEER SNIRT GIZZEN SNEEST TWITCH WRINKLE RIDICULE

SNEERING FRUMPERY

SNEEZE NEESE NEEZE ARREST
(— AT) CONDEMN DESPISE

SNEEZEWEED ALANT ROSILLA HELENIUM

SNEEZEWOOD NIESHOUT

SNEEZEWORT HARDHEAD PTARMICA

SNEEZING PTARMIC

SNELL SNOOD TIPPET GANGING

SNICK TIP SNECK

SNICKER TITTER SMIRKLE SNIGGER SNIGGLE

SNIDE ORNERY

SNIFF NOSE TIFT VENT WIND SMELL SNAFF SNIFT SNUFF SNIVEL SNAFFLE SNIFFLE SNOTTER

SNIFTER SLUG BALLOON INHALER

SNIGGER NICKER WHICKER

SNIGGLE BRAGGLE

SNIP CUT CLIP CROP MINX NICK SHRED SNICK SCISSOR

SNIPE JACK NICK WISP SCAPE SNITE WADER WILLET BLEATER BLITTER DOWITCH HUMILITY LONGBILL SHADBIRD

SNIPER TEASER BUSHWACK

SNIVEL BUBBLE SNIFFLE SNIFTER SNOTTER SNUFFLE

SNOB SNAB SNOOT FLUNKY SHONEEN SNOBBER

SNOBBISH RITZY DICKTY SNOBBY SNOOTY UPSTAGE

SNOOK SNOOT ROBALO

SNOOP PRY PEEK PEEP SNEAK BREVIT PIROOT GUMSHOE

SNOOPER CREEP BUSYBODY

SNOOPY CURIOUS

SNOOZE DOVER SLEEP SNOOZLE

SNORE ROUT SNARK SNORK SNORT SNOCKER SNOTTER

SNORING STERTOR RHONCHUS

SNORT BLOW ROUT SNUR TOOT VENT BLURT FNESE SNARK SNEER SNIFTER SNOCKER SNORKEL SNORTLE SNOTTER

SNOUT NEB SAW BEAK BILL NOSE WROT GROIN SERRA SNOOT MUFFLE MUZZLE NOZZLE GRUNTLE ROSTRUM
(PREF.) PROBOSCI(DI) RHYNCH(O)
(SUFF.) RHYNCHUS RHYNCUS

SNOUT BEETLE CURCULIO

SNOUT MITE BDELLID

SNOW CORN DRIP GRUE COVER SPOSH STORM SUGAR WHITE POWDER COCAINE GRAUPEL RAMPART WEATHER SCOUTHER WINDSLAB
(— PELLETS) GRAUPEL
(— SLIGHTLY) SPIT
(DISSOLVING —) FLUSH
(DRIFTED —) WINDLE
(GLACIER —) FIRN NEVE BLIZZ
(HEAVY FALL OF —) PASH
(MUSHY —) SLOB
(NEW-FALLEN —) MANNA
(PARTLY MELTED —) SLUSH
(WHIRLING —) SKIRL
(PREF.) CHIO CHION(O) NIVI

SNOWBERRY MOXA WAXBERRY

SNOWBIRD JUNCO

SNOW BUNTING OATFOWL SNOWBIRD SNOWFOWL

SNOW COCK JERMONAL

SNOWDRIFT WREATH YOWDEN

SNOWDROP TREE BELLWOOD COWLICKS TISSWOOD

SNOWFALL PASH SKIFF SKIFT FLURRY ONDING

SNOWFLAKE FLAG FLAUCHT

SNOW FLEA PODURAN PODURID

SNOW GOOSE WAVY

SNOWINESS NIVOSITY

SNOW LEOPARD IRBIS

SNOWLESS GREEN

SNOW MAIDEN, THE (CHARACTER IN —) LEL BOBYL KUPAVA MIZGIR SPRING BERENDEY BOBYLIKHA SNEGUROCHKA
(COMPOSER OF —) RIMSKYKORSAKOV

SNOWMAN YETI

SNOW MOUNTAIN JOKUL

SNOWSHOE WEB PATIN PATTEN RACKET RACQUET

SNOWSTORM PURGA DRIFTER BLIZZARD

SNOWY NIVAL WHITE NIVEOUS

SNUB AIR RITZ SLAP SNIB FRUMP SNEAP SWANK REBUFF REBUTE

SIMOUS SLIGHT SNOUCH SNUBBY SETDOWN

SNUBBING MAIL

SNUBBY PUGGISH

SNUB-NOSED SIMOUS
(PREF.) SIMO

SNUFF TOP VENT MUSTY SNIFF SNUSH TABAC COHOBA PULVIL RAPPEE SNEESH STIFLE SNUFFLE BERGAMOT MACCABOY ORANGERY SMUTCHIN

SNUFFBOX MILL MULL

SNUFFBOX BEAN CACOON

SNUFFER PRICK DOUTER TOPPER PRICKER

SNUFFLE SNIVEL SNAFFLE SNIFFLE SNIFTER

SNUG LEW RUG BEIN BIEN COSH COSY COZY NEAT SNOD TAUT TEAT TOSH TOSY CANNY CLOSE COUTH POVIE QUEME TIGHT PENTIT COUTHIE SNUGGERY SNUGGISH

SNUGGLE SNUG BURROW CUDDLE SNUDGE CROODLE SNUZZLE

SNUGLY SHORT COSILY

SO SAE SUCH THAT THIS THUS THISSEN INSOMUCH SUCHWISE THUSWISE
(— AM I) LIKEWISE
(— BE IT) AMEN
(— FAR AS) QUOAD
(— TO SPEAK) FAIRLY
(NOT —) SECUS
(QUITE —) EXACTLY

SOAK RET SOB SOD SOG SOP WET BOWK BUCK SIPE BINGE DROUK DROWN SOUSE STEEP TOAST DRENCH EMBAIN IMBIBE IMBRUE SEETHE SODDEN SPONGE INSTEEP MICKERY SWELTER SATURATE
(— A CASK) GROG
(— FLAX) RET RATE
(— IN) SOP FEATHER

SOAKED SOGGY SOPPY SOBBED SODDEN WATERY DRUNKEN SOBBING DRAGGLED

SOAKING BATH SUING SOGGING INFUSION

SOAP SAPO SUDS CHIPS STOCK NIGGER CASTILE TALLATE WINDSOR SANDSOAP SAVONETTE
(CAKE OF —) TABLET TABULATE
(LIQUID —) FIT
(PREF.) SAP(O) SAPONI

SOAPBARK QUILLAI SOAPWOOD

SOAPFISH JABON

SOAP PLANT AMOLE PALMILLO SOAPROOT SOAPWEED

SOAPSTONE ALBERENE POTSTONE STEATITE

SOAPSTONER TALCER

SOAPWORT BORITH COWHERB SAPONARY SOAPROOT SOAPWEED

SOAR FLY STY KITE FLOAT MOUNT PLANE SPIRE TOWER ASCEND ASPIRE AIRPLANE

SOARING FLIGHT ICARIAN SPIRING ESSORANT

SOB YEX SIKE SNOB SNUB SOUGH BLUBBER SINGULT

SOBBING GREET

SOBER SAD CALM COOL SAGE CIVIL FRESH GRAVE QUIET STAID DOULCE SEDATE SEVERE SOLEMN SOMBER STEADY EARNEST PENSIVE REGULAR SERIOUS UNFOXED DECOROUS MODERATE ABSTEMIOUS

SOBRIETY DRYNESS GRAVITY ABSTINENCE

SOBRIQUET BYNAME HAWKEYE

SO-CALLED ALLEGED

SOCCER FOOTER FOOTBALL

SOCIABLE COSY CHUMMY CLUBBY FOLKSY SOCIAL AFFABLE AMIABLE INNERLY CLUBABLE FAMILIAR FELLOWLY INFORMAL

SOCIAL DISTAL PUBLIC SUPPER SOCIABLE SOCIETAL CONVIVIAL
(— WORKER) ALMONER

SOCIALISM ETATISM MARXISM GUESDISM

SOCIALIST FABIAN NIHILIST

SOCIALISTIC PINK

SOCIALIZE CIVILIZE

SOCIETY BUND HALL HERD SANG GUILD MONDE POLIS SABHA SAMAJ SANGH SOKOL MENAGE NANIGO PARISH SYSTEM VEREIN ACADEMY COLLEGE COLORUM COMPANY COUNCIL KINGDOM SOCIETE THIASOS EXCHANGE HETAERIA PRECINCT SOCIETAS SODALITY SORORITY
(— OF RELIGIOUS FANATICS) COLORUM
(CHORAL —) CHOIR
(CLOWN —) KOSHARE KOYEMSHI
(CRAFT —) ARTEL
(DEBATING —) POP
(GYMNASTIC —) SOKOL
(HIGH —) SWELLDOM
(LITERARY —) HALL
(POLITICAL —) TAMMANY
(RELIGIOUS —) CHURCH
(SECRET —) HUI EGBO HOEY PORO TONG LODGE MAFIA OGBONI PURRAH CAMORRA
(STUDENT —) CORPS
(UTOPIAN —) ANARCHY
(WHITE —) MAN
(PREF.) SOCIO

SOCINIAN RACOVIAN

SOCIOLOGIST AMERICAN HUNT LYND ROSS WARD BARNES DEVINE HUNTER SUMNER VEBLEN DUGDALE ELLWOOD FRAZIER NEARING STEIZLE WILLARD ZUEBLIN BOGARDUS GIDDINGS GOLDENWEISER
ENGLISH KIDD TOYNBEE
FRENCH TARDE DURKHEIM
GERMAN LANGE WEBER FREYER MICHELS SCHAFFLE THURNWALD
ITALIAN LORIA
SCOTTISH GEDDES MCLENNAN

SOCIOLOGY DEMOTICS

SOCK BOP ONE BIFF BUST HOSE VAMP ANKLET ARGYLE VAMPEY STOCKING
(— OF GOAT'S HAIR) UDO
(INFANT'S —) BOOTEE BOOTIE
(JAPANESE —) TABI

SOCKET BOX CUP PAD POD BUSH
CELL HOSE LEAD NOSE SHOE
CHAIR POINT SHANK BUCKET
BUDGET COLLET EYEPIT NOZZLE
POCKET SAUCER SCONCE
ALVEOLE COCKEYE FERRULE
FUTCHEL GUDGEON THIMBLE
TORULUS ALVEOLUS DRAWHEAD
(— FOR GEM) OUCH
(— FOR LANCE) PORT
(— FOR LENS) CELL
(— FOR MAST) TABERNACLE
(— FOR MOUTHPIECE) BIRN
(— IN GOLF CLUB HEAD) HOSE
HOSEL
(— OF BONE) POT
(— OF HINGE) PAN
(— OF MILLSTONE) INK COCKEYE
(— OF WATER PIPE) BELL
(BIT —) POD
(PREF.) GLENO TORMO
SOCKEYE NERKA KOKANEE
BLUEBACK
SOCLE ZOCCO
SOCRATES (— METHOD) MAIEUTIC
SOD HUB BEAT DELF FAIL FLAG
SCAD SONK TURF DELPH GAZON
GLEBE SCRAW SWARD CLOWER
TERRON SODDING
SODA BARILLA
SODA POP TONIC
SODDEN SAMMY SAPPY SOGGY
POACHY DRAGGLED
SODI (SON OF —) GEDDIEL
SODIUM NA SODA NATRIUM
(PREF.) NATR(O)
SODIUM BICARBONATE SODA
BICARB
SODIUM BORATE BORAX
SODIUM CARBONATE SODA
TRONA ANATRON BARILLA
SALSODA
SODIUM CHLORIDE SALT HALITE
SODIUM THIOSULFATE HYPO
SODOMITE DOG BUGGER SPINTRY
BOUGERON
SOEVER SOME
SOFA BOIST COUCH DIVAN SQUAB
CANAPE LOUNGE SETTEE
CAUSEUSE SOCIABLE
SOFFIT GATHER PLAFOND
INTRADOS PLANCIER
SOFRONIA (LOVER OF —) OLINDO
SOFT COY TID FEIL LASH LIMP
LUSH MILD MURE NASH NESH
PLUM SART TOSY WAXY WEAK
BALMY BLAND CUSHY DABBY
DOLCE DOWNY FAINT GIVEY
HOOLY LENIS LIGHT MALMY
MEALY MELCH MUSHY PADDY
PAPPY PIANO PLIFF SILKY SLACK
SMALL SOAPY SOOTH SWASH
SWEET WAXEN WETHE YAPPY
CASHIE CREAMY EFFETE FLAGGY
FLOSSY FLUFFY GENTLE LITHER
LYDIAN MEDIUM PIPING PLACID
SAMMEL SIDDER SIDDOW SILKEN
SLOPPY SMOOTH SOFTLY SPONGY
SPOONY TENDER UNDURE
CLEMENT COTTONY CRUMBLY
DUCTILE FLESHLY LENIENT
SQUASHY CUSHIONY FEMININE
FLEXIBLE HOTHOUSE LADYLIKE

SARCENET SQUELCHY TRANQUIL
(— AND FLEXIBLE) FLOPPY
(— AND LIFELESS) DOUGHY
(— IN TEXTURE) SUPPLE
(VERY —) SQUASHY
(PREF.) LENI MALAC(O) MOLLI
SOFT-COVER PAPERBACK
SOFTEN CUT CREE MELT SOAK
SOFT TAME ALLAY BATCH BREAK
FRIZZ LITHE MALAX TOUCH
WOKIE DIGEST GENTLE LENIFY
PACIFY RELENT SOOTHE SUBDUE
SUBMIT TEMPER WEAKEN
APPEASE ASSUAGE CUSHION
LENIATE MOLLIFY QUALIFY
SWEETEN UNSTEEL AMOLLISH
ATTEMPER ENFEEBLE HUMANIZE
MITIGATE MODULATE PALLIATE
PRETTIFY
(— BY BOILING) CREE
(— BY KNEADING) MALAX
MALAXATE
(— BY STEEPING) MACERATE
(— COLOR) CUT SCUMBLE
(— FIBERS) BREAK
(— GRADUALLY) SQUAT
(— JUTE) BATCH
(— LEATHER) BREY FRIZ FRIZZ
(— METAL) ALLAY
(— TONE) SURD
SOFTENED ROXY ANODYNE
MOUILLE FLEXUOUS
SOFTENING LENIENT MALACIA
BLETTING
SOFTER MANCANDO
SOFTHEARTED TENDER
SOFTLY LOW BAJO SOFT HOOLY
FAIRLY GENTLY SWEETLY
CREAMILY TENDERLY
SOFTNESS SOFT MOLLITIES
(— IN COAL SEAM) LUM LUMB
(SUFF.) MALACIA
SOFT-POINTED HEBETATE
SOFT-SHELLED TURTLE FLAPPER
FLIPPER FLAPJACK
SOFT-SOAP CON FLANNEL
SOFT-SPOKEN MEALY
SOFTWARE (COMPUTER —)
MONITOR
SOGGY SAD DUNCH SOBBY
SODDEN SPONGY WATERY
SOIGNE TRIM SLEEK MODISH
SOIL DAG DUB MUD RAY SOD BLOT
BLUR CLAY CLOD DAUB DIRT
DUST FOIL FOUL GRIT LAND MIRK
MOOL MOSS MUCK MURK MUSS
SAUR SILE SLUR SMUT SOOT
TASH BULLI CROCK EARTH GLEBE
GRIME GUMBO LAYER MUCKY
ROSEL SLUSH SMEAR SOLUM
SOULE SPARK STAIN SULLY
BARING BEDAUB BEFOUL BEMIRE
BEMOIL GROUND PODZOL SLURRY
SMIRCH SMOOCH SMUDGE
SPLASH SUDDLE BEGRIME
BENASTY BESMEAR BESMOKE
BETHUMB FEWMAND PEDOCAL
POLLUTE REGOSOL SEEDBED
SLUBBER TARNISH TRACHLE
AGROTYPE ALLUVIAL BEDABBLE
BESMIRCH BUCKSHOT FLYSPECK
LATERITE PEDALFER PLANOSOL
RENDZINA WOODCOCK

SOLONCHAK CONTAMINATE
(— ABOVE CLAY) KELLY
(— DEPOSITED BY WIND) ELUVIUM
(— FORMED BY DECAY) GEEST
(— INTERMEDIATE BETWEEN SAND
AND CLAY) ROSEL
(— PREPARED FOR SOWING) TILTH
(— REMOVED FROM ORE) BARING
(— WITH GREASE) LARD
(AGGREGATE —) PED
(ALKALINE —) SOLONETZ
(ASHLIKE —) PODSOL PODZOL
(CLAYEY —) GALT MALM MAUM
ADOBE SOLOD SOLOTH
(COTTON —) REGUR
(DRY —) GROOT
(FRIABLE —) CRUMB
(GRAVELLY —) ROACH GROWAN
(HARD —) RAMMEL
(INFERTILE —) GALL
(LEACHED —S) LATOSOL
(PEATY —) YARFA YARPHA
(PLUMBER'S —) SMUDGE
(POROUS —) SPONGE
(POTTING —) COMPOST
(PRAIRIE —) BRUNIZEM
(SILTY —) GUMBO
(SPRINGY —) WOODSERE
(ZONAL —) SEROZEM SIEROZEM
(PREF.) AGRI AGRO GE(O) PED(O)
SOLI
SOILAGE SOIL SMUDGE SOILING
SOILED FOUL BLACK DINGY DIRTY
MUSSY SOOTY TARRY SMUDGY
SMUTTY SNUFFY THUMBED
DRAGGLED SHOPWORN
SOIL-EXPOSING EROSIVE
SOIREE EVENING
SOJOURN LIE BIDE STAY STOP
ABIDE ABODE TARRY RESIDE
ALLODGE MANSION STATION
SOJOURNER PILGRIM
SOKOL FALCON
SOL SOH SOU ALCOSOL EMULSOID
HYDROSOL SOLUTION
SOLA SHOLA PAUKPAN
SOLACE CHEER CHEERER
COMFORT CONSOLE SWEETEN
SOLATION
SOLAR HELIAC SOLLER HELIACAL
SOLARIUM
(— SYSTEM APPARATUS) ORRERY
SOLAR DISK ATEN ATON
(CENTER OF —) CAZIMI
SOLAR ENERGY
(PREF.) HELI
SOLD SELT BOOKED
(ILLICITLY —) BOOTLEG
SOLDER PALE BRAZE FLOAT
SOWDER SPELTER
SOLDERER BROGUER
SOLDERING IRON COPPER
DOCTOR
SOLDIER SON TAP BLEU BOLO
GOUM GUGU KERN LEVY SHOT
SWAD TULK WART BERNE CROAT
FRITZ GUARD GUFFY KHAKI
LANCE LIMEY LINER MINER NIZAM
PERDU PIKER PIVOT POILU
PONGO SAMMY SWEAT TOLKE
TOMMY TOPAS ASKARI BONAGH
BUMMER DARTER DIGGER
EXPERT GALOOT GUNNER

GURKHA HAIDUK HEINIE HOSTER
LANCER MARKER PIETON REITER
SENTRY SKIEUR SOLDAT SWADDY
THRASO WEAPON ZOUAVE
BAYONET BILLJIM BLIGHTY
BRIGAND CARABIN CATERAN
CORSLET DARTMAN DOGFACE
DRAGOON FEDERAL FEEDMAN
FIGHTER GENETOR GOUMIER
HOBBLER INVALID JACKMAN
MATROSS ORDERLY PALIKAR
PANDOUR PAVISOR PELTAST
PIKEMAN PRIVATE REDCOAT
REGULAR REISTER SCARLET
SLINGER SOLDADO STRIKER
TROOPER VETERAN WARRIOR
ARQUEBUS BEZONIAN BLUECOAT
BUCKSKIN BUFFCOAT CAMELEER
CAVALIER DESERTER FENCIBLE
FUGLEMAN FUSILIER GALLOPER
GENDARME GRAYBACK
GRAYCOAT IRONSIDE JANIZARY
KHANDAIT LANCEMAN LINESMAN
MILITANT MIQUELET MUSTACHE
PIOUPIOU RAPPAREE SENTINEL
SERVITOR SILLADAR SPEARMAN
SWORDMAN TOLPATCH
TRANSFER TRIARIAN WARFARER
WHIFFLER YARDBIRD
CATAPHRACT
(— OF MUSCOVITE GUARD)
STRELITZ
(— WITH SIDE WHISKERS) BADGER
(ALBANIAN —) PALIKAR
(ALGERIAN —) ARBI
(ANT —) MAXIM
(AUSTRALIAN —) ANZAC DIGGER
BILLJIM
(BOMBAY —S) DUCKS
(BRITISH —) LIMEY TOMMY
BLIGHTY LOBSTER REDCOAT
ROOINEK
(BRUTAL —) PANDOUR
(CAREER —) LIFER
(COWARDLY —) CAPITANO
(FEMALE —) AMAZON
(FILE OF 6 —S) ROT
(FILIPINO —) GUGU
(FOOT —) KERN PAGE PEON
GRUNT PIETON FOOTMAN
TOLPATCH
(GERMAN —) HUN FRITZ HEINE
KRAUT HEINIE
(GREEK —) EVZONE HOPLITE
(INCOMPETENT —) BOLL
(INDIAN —) PEON JAWAN SEPOY
GURKHA
(INVALID —) FOGY FOGEY
(IRREGULAR —) CROAT CATERAN
JAYHAWK SEBUNDY MIQUELET
RAPPAREE SILLADAR
(MERCENARY —) RUTTER HESSIAN
(MOROCCAN —) ASKARI
(MOUNTED —) LANCER DRAGOON
GENETOR LOBSTER TROOPER
VEDETTE CAVALIER
(OLD —) GROGNARD
(PROFESSIONAL —) SAMURAI
(REVOLUTIONARY —) REDCOAT
BUCKSKIN
(ROMAN —S OF THIRD LINE) TRIARY
TRIARII
(RUSSIAN —) IVAN

(SCOTTISH —) JOCK
(SMALL —) BANTAM
(TURKISH —) NIZAM REDIF
(PL.) FOOT ELITE TERZO TROOP
TERTIA CATERVA ENOMOTY
MILITIA VELITES FORAGERS
INFANTRY SOLDIERY
AMERICAN DIX LEA LEE POE AMES
BELL BUTT CARR CLAY DRUM
FISK FORD HILL HOOD KNOX
LANE LEAR LONG LORD LYON
MYER OTIS RENO SHAW WOOL
YORK ALLEN BANKS BATES BEALL
BLISS BRAGG BRETT BROWN
BUELL BURNS CANBY CLARK
CORSE CRAIG CROOK DAVIS
DODGE EAKER EARLY EATON
ELIOT EWELL GATES GETTY
GRANT GREEN GREGG HAYNE
HINES HOVEY HOWZE IRWIN
LEWIS MCCOY MCRAE MEADE
MILES MOSBY MOWER OHARA
PARKE PATCH POORE PRATT
ROYCE SCOTT SHAYS SMITH
STONE SWIFT SYKES TERRY
UPTON VIELE ARNOLD BISBEE
BOWLEY BUFORD BUTLER
CULLUM CUSTER DAYTON
DEVERS EMBICK EMMONS GAINES
GIBBON GIBSON GLOVER GORDON
GORGAS GRAVES GREENE
GROVES HARDEE HARDIN
HARMON HARTLE HOOKER
HOWARD HUNTER JADWIN
JORDAN KEARNY KENNEY
LAWTON MACOMB MARION
MCCOOK MCLAWS MORGAN
MORROW NEWTON OLIVER
PATTON PHELPS PILLOW
PUTNAM RIPLEY ROGERS SCHAFF
SEVIER SHARPE SHELBY SPAATZ
STRONG STUART SUMNER
TANNER TAYLOR THAYER TWIGGS
WARNER WESSON WILCOX
ANDREWS BABCOCK BELKNAP
BINGHAM BRADLEY BUCKNER
BULLARD CARLSON CHAFFEE
CROWDER CROZIER DICKMAN
EDWARDS FERRERO FLEMING
FORREST FREMONT FUNSTON
GRANGER HALLECK HANCOCK
HARBORD HARDING HASKELL
HOUSTON INGALLS JACKSON
KRUEGER LEDYARD LEJEUNE
LIGGETT LINCOLN MAXWELL
MENOHER MERRITT NEVILLE
PARROTT PICKETT RAWLINS
SHAFTER SHERMAN SLEMMER
TORBERT TREMAIN TRIMBLE
VANDORN VENABLE WHEELER
ANDERSON BRERETON BURNSIDE
CAMPBELL DONELSON FRANKLIN
GAILLARD GRIERSON JOHNSTON
MAGRUDER MARSHALL
MCDOWELL MCNARNEY
MOULTRIE OLMSTEAD PERSHING
PRESCOTT REYNOLDS SEDGWICK
SHERIDAN SNELLING STILWELL
STODDARD SUBLETTE SULLIVAN
TOWNSEND AINSWORTH
ALEXANDER ARMISTEAD
ARMSTRONG BONESTEEL
DOOLITTLE DOUBLEDAY

FETTERMAN HARTRANFT
HUMPHREYS MACARTHUR
MCCLELLAN PEMBERTON
PETTIGREW SCHOFIELD
SUMMERALL WILKINSON
BEAUREGARD BUFFINGTON
EISENHOWER LONGSTREET
MCGLACHLIN PLEASONTON
WAINWRIGHT BUTTERFIELD
ARGENTINIAN JUSTO
AUSTRALIAN CASEY BLAMEY
MACKAY MONASH BENNETT
CHAUVEL STURDEE LAVARACK
AUSTRIAN DAUN HESS DANKL
HADIK LIGNE GALLAS GYULAI
TRENCK BENEDEK GABLENZ
ALVINCZY BEAULIEU CLERFAYT
RADETZKY PHILIPPOVIC
BOLIVIAN DAZA PANDO CAMPERO
BALLIVIAN
BRAZILIAN DUTRA FONSECA
PEIXOTO
BULGARIAN SAVOY
CANADIAN BOVEY CRERAR
HUGHES DENISON LINDSAY
CHILEAN CRUZ BULNES FREIRE
IBANEZ PRIETO OHIGGINS
COLOMBIAN REYES HERRAN
CORDOBA MOSQUERA
DANISH RANTZAU
DUTCH CHASSE KEPPEL
COEHOORN DAENDELS
ECUADORIAN ALFARO FLORES
ENGLISH COX NYE BOLS BYNG
DILL DYER GORT HAIG HEAD HILL
LACY LAKE LOWE PILE RICH ROSS
VERE WADE ANDRE BOWER
BROCK CAREW CAREY CAVAN
CLERY CLIVE CRAIG CUTTS
GOUGH HORNE JONES KIRKE
MAHON MAUDE MILNE MONCK
MOORE NEILL NIXON PLATT
SMITH STACK SYKES WARDE
AYLMER BLOUNT BROOKE
BROWNE BULFIN BURLEY
CHURCH CONWAY CREAGH
DAWSON DOBELL DUNDAS
FRENCH FULLER GORDON
GRAHAM HAKING GRANT
HOWARD INGLIS JARVIS LUGARD
MARTEL MILLER MURRAY NAPIER
NORMAN NUGENT PICTON
POPHAM SAVAGE SIDNEY SIMCOE
TEMPLE TURNER UFFORD
VYVYAN WARREN WAVELL
WEMYSS ALLENBY AMHERST
ATHLONE BARDOLF BINGHAM
BOUQUET BRANDON BRIDGES
CAVALLO CHANDOS CLAYTON
CLINTON COLLINS DOWDING
FASTOLF MACMUNN MAXWELL
METHUEN MORLAND OCONNOR
PEREIRA POWNALL ROBERTS
STEWART SWINTON TORRENS
VENNING VINCENT WANTAGE
WINGATE ALDERSON ANDERSON
AUCHMUTY BECKWITH BENTINCK
BLAKENEY BRADDOCK BRANCKER
BURGOYNE CALLWELL CAMPBELL
CARDIGAN CARLETON CATHCART
CHETWODE COLBORNE
CONGREVE FERGUSON GLEICHEN
GREVILLE HAMILTON HARDINGE

HASTINGS HAVELOCK LAWRENCE
LIGONIER LINDSELL LOCKHART
MAITLAND MONTFORT POYNINGS
STANHOPE TARLETON
ALEXANDER BEAUCHAMP
BERESFORD BROWNRIGG
CONSTABLE HARINGTON
HENDERSON KITCHENER
MACDONALD OCTERLONY
POTTINGER REPINGTON
ROBERTSON WILKINSON
WOODVILLE AUCHINLECK
CODRINGTON CORNWALLIS
DESBOROUGH MACDOUGALL
MONTGOMERY SHERBROOKE
WELLINGTON BRACKENBURY
WINTRINGHAM
FINNISH MANNERHEIM
FRENCH FAY FOY NEY BUAT FOCH
NIEL AMADE ANDRE CONTI COSSE
DOUAY DUMAS FOREY HENRY
HULIN JUNOT LALLY LEVIS LOBAU
MENOU MINIE MITRY TRACY
BELLAY BOUDET CHABOT CHANZY
CISSEY CLARKE CLOSSE DAUMAS
DAVOUT DEJEAN DROUOT
DUCROT DUNOIS FABERT FAILLY
FAVRAS FLEURY FOLARD FRIANT
GERARD GIRAUD GOBERT
JARNAC JOFFRE KLEBER LACLOS
LANNES LATUDE LAUNAY
LAUZUN MAGNAN MAISON
MANGIN MARBOT MASSUE
MONCEY MOREAU PETAIN
ROVIGO SUCHET TROCHU
BAZAINE BOICHUT BOSQUET
BOUILLE CATINAT CATROUX
CHAMILY CHARRAS CLAUSEL
CLISSON CRILLON CUSTINE
DEBENEY DREYFUS FABVIER
GAMELIN GASSION GOURAUD
GROUCHY GUIBERT JOUBERT
JOURDAN LABORDE LASALLE
LEBOEUF LECLERC LEJEUNE
LUCKNER LYAUTEY MARCEAU
MARMONT MAURICE MOLITOR
MONTLUC MORTIER NIVELLE
REYNIER TALLARD VALENCE
VENDOME WEYGAND AUGEREAU
BARATIER BOURBAKI CHAMBRUN
CHAUCHAT CHOISEUL CLUSERET
CONTADES DEGAULLE DEGOUTTE
ESTIENNE GALLIENI GOURGAUD
GOURGUES GRAZIANI HARCOURT
LAMARQUE LANGLOIS LANREZAC
LARMINAT LEFEBVRE
LORENCEZ MAUNOURY
MONTCALM PICHEGRU
TAVANNES VANDAMME
AIGUILLON ANDREOSSY
BERTHELOT BOISSOUDY
BOULANGER CANROBERT
DAMPIERRE FAIDHERBE
GROSSETTI GUEBRIANT
HUNTZIGER LAFAYETTE
LALLEMAND LAURISTON
MACDONALD MONTHOLON
NIVERNAIS PELISSIER
SCHOMBERG CHASTELLUX
GUILLAUMAT KELLERMANN
MONTGOMERY ROCHAMBEAU
WESTERMANN CHANGARNIER
JACQUEMINOT MONTMORENCY

CAULAINCOURT LESDIGUIERES
GERMAN EPP JODL ARNIM BOEHN
BULOW KLUCK KUNDT HALDER
HAUSEN HUTIER KEITEL MOLTKE
ROMMEL SEECKT BISSING
BLUCHER CAPRIVI FISCHER
FRITSCH GROENER JOCHMUS
STEUBEN BERNHARD BLOMBERG
GALLWITZ GERHARDT GUDERIAN
HAESELER HARTMANN LITZMANN
RIEDESEL SCHWERIN ZEITZLER
ALDRINGEN HAUSHOFER
HEERINGEN HINDERSIN
LINSINGEN MACKENSEN
MANSFIELD REINHARDT
RUNDSTEDT THEILMANN
WALDERSEE FRUNDSBERG
HINDENBURG KESSELRING
LUDENDORFF SCHLEICHER
SCHLIEFFEN BRAUCHITSCH
FALKENHORST FALKENHAUSEN
GREEK ARATUS KALERGES
KONDYLES PANGALOS
ALCIBIADES HIERONYMUS
GUATEMALAN CHACON ORELLANA
HAITIAN PETION RIGAUD
SALOMON GEFFRARD
HUNGARIAN GORGEY DAMJANICH
SZECHENYI
IRISH LACY WADE COLLEY
ODUFFY CADOGAN COLLINS
OREILLY OHIGGINS PAKENHAM
ITALIAN BIXIO FANTI CANEVA
COSENZ DAVILA DOUHET
CAPELLO BADOGLIO CAVIGLIA
CIALDINI COLLEONI GIARDINO
MARSIGLI RAMORINO BARATIERI
CAVALLERO DANNUNZIO
LAMARMORA PICCOLOMINI
JAPANESE ABE OKU ARAKI KOISO
NODZU SAITO TAMAI KODAMA
KUROKI DOIHARA FUSHIMI
KATSURA HASEGAWA SUGIYAMA
TERAUCHI FUKUSHIMA
HASHIMOTO HIDEYOSHI
MEXICAN MEJIA ALDAMA ARISTA
HUERTA ALMAZAN ALMONTE
ALVAREZ AMPUDIA CAMACHO
MIRAMON OBREGON VALLEJO
ZULOAGA CANALIZO CARDENAS
ESCOBEDO GONZALEZ GUERRERO
ITURBIDE VICTORIA BUSTAMANTE
NEW ZEALAND CHAYTOR
FREYBERG
PARAGUAYAN MORINIGO
ESTIGARRIBIA
PERSIAN ARTAPHERNES
PERUVIAN BALTA PRADO CACERES
GAMARRA PIEROLA CASTILLA
IGLESIAS SALAVERRY
POLISH BEM PASEK HALLER
PULASKI CHLOPICKI DEMBINSKI
KOSCIUSKO PILSUDSKI
DOMBROWSKI MALCZEWSKI
SOSNKOWSKI KRUKOWIECKI
PORTUGUESE ALMEIDA PEREIRA
SALDANHA TEIXEIRA
ROMAN AETIUS BURRUS CAEPIO
CAESAR GALLUS POLLIO ALBINUS
CAECINA CALENUS CASSIUS
CHAEREA FANNIUS LEPIDUS
PLANCUS AFRANIUS AGRICOLA
CEREATIS DENTATUS DUILLIUS

FABRICIUS FLAMINIUS PASKEVICH SERTORIUS CINCINNATUS
RUMANIAN ILIESCU ANTONESCU
RUSSIAN BERK GURKO KONEV GLINKA PLATOV ZHUKOV BLUCHER BUDENNY CHAPAEV CHUIKOV DENIKIN KALEDIN KAMENEV VATUTIN WRANGEL ALEKSEEV AVERESCU BOBRIKOV BRUSILOV GOLITSYN KAULBARS KORNILOV LINEVICH MILYUTIN SKOBELEV YUDENICH BAGRATION BENNIGSEN GORCHAKOV LECHITSKI MENSHIKOV CHERNYAIEV CHERNYSHEV DRAGOMIROV KUROPATKIN ROSTOPCHIN TIMOSHENKO VOROSHILOV SHAPOSHNIKOV
SALVADORAN REGALADO
SCOTTISH URRY BAIRD MUNRO ELIOTT RUTHVEN DRUMMOND MIDDLETON
SOUTH AFRICAN SMUTS HERTZOG PRETORIUS
SPANISH ALVA ELIO MINA MOLA RADA CROIX GARAY OSUNA ULLOA AVALOS GUZMAN ALMAGRO CORDOBA MONCADA NARVAEZ NAVARRO ODONOJU PORTOLA ALVARADO CANTERAC CARVAJAL CASTANOS CASTILLO ESPINOSA MANRIQUE MUNTANER ORELLANA VALDIVIA PEDRARIAS REQUESENS VELASQUEZ CASTELLANOS
SWEDISH HORN TOLL BANER BRAHE ARMFELT LEWENHAUPT TORSTENSON ADLERCREUTZ ADLERSPARRE
SWISS DUFOUR ERLACH JENATSCH
URUGUAYAN ORIBE FLORES
VENEZUELAN PAEZ GOMEZ CASTRO FALCON MONAGAS
YUGOSLAV ZIVKOVIC
SOLDIERLY WARLIKE
SOLDIERY HORSE MILITIA SEBUNDY MILITARY SIBBENDY
SOLE CORK FACE GADE MERE ONLY SLIP SOCK SPUR AFALD ALONE CLUMP LEMON OLEPI PELMA WHOLE GADOID INSOLE ONLEPY PLANTA SINGLE SOLEYN SULLEN THENAR TONGUE UNIQUE ANACANTH FLATFISH HOGCHOKE MARYSOLE SINGULAR SOLITARY
(— A SHOE) SPECK
(— FOR WALKING OVER SAND) BACKSTER
(— OF BIRD'S FOOT) PTERNA
(— OF FOOT) PLAT VOLA PELMA PLANT
(— OF PLANE) FACE
(— OF PLOW) SLADE
(— WITH WOOD) CLOG
(HALF —) SHOULDER
(TOWARD THE —) PLANTAD
(PREF.) PEDI(O) PELMATO
(SUFF.) PELMOUS
SOLELY SOLE ALONE SIMPLY SINGLY WHOLLY SHEERLY ENTIRELY

SOLEMN DEEP SAGE AWFUL BUDGE SOBER DEVOUT FORMAL RITUAL EARNEST SERIOUS WEIGHTY FUNEREAL
SOLEMNITY OBIT RITE SACRE GRAVITY SEVERITY
SOLEMNIZE KEEP SEAL
SOLEMNLY GRAVE HIGHLY
SOLENODONT AGOUTA ALMIQUE
SOLEPIECE SOLE GIRDER
SOL-FA SOLMIZATE
SOLICIT ASK BEG SUE WOO DRUM MOVE SEEK THIG TOUT URGE APPLY COURT CRAVE TREAT ACCOST HUSTLE INVITE INVOKE BESEECH CANVASS ENTREAT IMPLORE INSTANT PROCURE REQUEST APPROACH PETITION
SOLICITATION SUIT QUEST CANVASS INSTANT SOLICIT ENTREATY INSTANCE
SOLICITOR AVOUE LAWYER WRITER ADVOCATE ATTORNEY TRAMPLER
SOLICITOUS URGENT CAREFUL CURIOUS JEALOUS DESIROUS CONCERNED
SOLICITUDE CARE CARK FEAR HEED PAIN YEME HEART WORRY ANXIETY CONCERN BUSINESS JEALOUSY
SOLID DRY SAD CONE CUBE FAST FIRM FULL HARD CHAMP CUBIC LEVEL MASSY MEATY SOUND STIFF STOUT THICK TIGHT SECURE STABLE STODGY STRONG STURDY COMPACT CUPRENE UNIFORM CONSTANT GROUNDLY MATERIAL STERLING
(GEOMETRICAL —) CONE CUBE PRISM CONOID CUPROID FRUSTUM POLYHEDRON
(NOT —) BUBBLE
(PL.) POCHE
(PREF.) STERE(O)
SOLIDARITY CIVILITY
SOLIDIFIED SOLID HARDENED
SOLIDIFY DRY SET JELL SHOOT HARDEN COMPACT CONGEAL STIFFEN CONCRETE
SOLIDITY SADNESS FASTNESS FIRMNESS HARDNESS
SOLIDLY FIRMLY SQUARE STOUTLY GROUNDLY
SOLIDUS BEZANT NOMISMA DIAGONAL HYPERPER
(HALF —) SEMIS
SOLIPSISM EGOISM
SOLITAIRE CLARINO CANFIELD KLONDIKE NAPOLEON PATIENCE SOLITARY
SOLITARY ODD WAF LONE ONLY SOLE ALONE ELYNG LONELY ONLEPY SAVAGE SINGLE SOLEYN SULLEN DERNFAL EREMITE PRIVATE RECLUSE UNCOUTH WIDOWED DESOLATE EREMITIC ISOLATED LONESOME PEGBOARD SECLUDED SEPARATE
(PREF.) EREM(O)
SOLITUDE PRIVACY RETREAT SOLITARY
SOLLERET SABBATON

SOLO ARIA CALL ARIOSO CAVATINA SPADILLA
SOLOMON SAM KOHELETH
(BROTHER OF —) ADONIJAH
(FATHER OF —) DAVID
(MOTHER OF —) BATHSHEBA
SOLOMON ISLANDS (CAPITAL OF —) HONIARA
(ISLAND OF —) BUKA GIZO SAVO TULAGI FLORISA MALAITA RENDOVA RUSSELL CHOISEUL GUADALCANAL BOUGAINVILLE
SOLOMON'S SEAL LILY SEALWORT
SOLON SAGE GNOMIC GNOMIST SENATOR LAWMAKER
SOLPUGID TARANTULA
SOLSTICE SUNSTAY SUNSTEAD
SOLUBLE FRIM FRUM FIXED SOLUTE SOLVABLE
SOLUTION IT LYE AQUA EUSOL STAIN TINCT ACETUM ANSWER ASSOIL DOCTOR ERASER SALINE EXTRACT EYEWASH LACQUER RESOLVE SOLUTIO WORKING ANALYSIS LEACHATE TINCTURE
(— ADDED FOR GOOD MEASURE) INCAST
(— OF CHESS PROBLEM) COOK
(— OF FERMENTED BRAN) DRENCH
(— OF GUM TRAGACANTH) BED
(ALCOHOLIC —) ESSENCE
(CORROSIVE —) OLEUM
(PICKLING —) SOUSE
(PRESERVING —) BOLIN
(SALINE —) BRINE
(SOAP —) NIGRE
(STERILE —) JOHNIN
(VISCOUS —) GLUE
(WATERY —) EAU SAP
SOLVE DO FIX READ UNDO WORK BREAK CRACK LOOSE SALVE ANSWER ASSOIL CIPHER FIGURE REDUCE RIDDLE SOLUTE RESOLVE UNRAVEL DECIPHER DISSOLVE
SOLVENT ETHER SOUND ELUENT SPIRIT ACETONE ALCOHOL BENZINE COUPLER DILUENT REMOVER SPOTTER CARBITOL PICOLINE SOLVABLE STRIPPER TEREBENE TETRALIN MENSTRUUM
(UNIVERSAL —) ALKAHEST
SOMALI SOMAL SHUHALI
(PL.) ASHA
SOMALIA (CAPITAL OF —) MOGADISHU
(COIN OF —) BESA
(DIVISION OF —) HAWIYA
(MEASURE OF —) TOP CABA CHELA DARAT TABLA CUBITO
(MOUNTAIN OF —) SURUDAD
(MOUNTAIN RANGE OF —) GUBAN
(NATIVE OF —) GALLA HAWIYA ISBAAK SOMALI DANAKIL
(RIVER OF —) JUBA NOGAL SCEBELI
(TOWN OF —) MERCA BERBERA KISMAYU HARGEISA
(WEIGHT OF —) PARSALAH
SOMATIC SOMAL BODILY
SOMBER SAD DERN DULL GRAVE MORNE SOBER GLOOMY LENTEN

SOLEMN SOMBRE SULLEN AUSTERE SERIOUS DARKSOME SOMBROUS
SOME ANY ODD THIS CERTAIN
SOMEBODY QUIDAM SOMEONE
SOMEDAY ONCE
SOMEHOW HOW ONEHOW SOMEWAY SOMEGATE
SOMEONE SUCH
SOMERSAULT FLIP TOPPLE FLIFFUS SPOTTER TWISTER BACKFLIP SOMERSET
SOMETHING WHAT ALIQUID WHATNOT SOMEWHAT
(— ABNORMAL) FREAK
(— ADDED) IMP EXTRA DOCTOR
(— ATTRACTIVE) DUCK
(— BELIEVED) CREDIT
(— BIG) BOUNCER
(— BRIGHT RED) CORAL
(— CHERISHED) APPLE
(— COMMONPLACE) DROSS
(— CONSECRATED) SACRUM
(— CONTRARY TO LOGIC) ALOGISM
(— CORRUPT) CARRION
(— COUNTERFEIT) DUFFER PINCHBECK
(— DIFFICULT) STINKER
(— DISLIKED) DOGMEAT
(— DONE) GERENDUM
(— EASY) PIPE CAKEWALK
(— ELABORATE) DEVICE
(— ELUSIVE) FUGITIVE
(— EXCELLENT) DANDY
(— EXCESSIVE) LUXUS
(— EXTRAORDINARY) SNORTER
(— FALSE) HOOEY
(— FAMILIAR) KNOWN
(— FIRST-RATE) CHEESE
(— FLAWED) CRIPPLE
(— FOOLISH) IDIOCY FATUITY
(— FORGOTTEN) CORPSE
(— FORKED) CORNUTE
(— FRAUDULENT) CROSS
(— HORRIFYING) SHOCKER
(— IDENTICAL) ISOMORPH
(— ILL-DEFINED) BLOB
(— IN ADDITION TO ORDINARY) BONUS
(— INCOMPLETE) END
(— INFERIOR) DOG CULL LESS CAGMAG
(— INJURIOUS) ENEMY
(— INSIGNIFICANT) STRAW FEATHER SNICKET FRAGMENT
(— INTRICATE) KNOT
(— LARGE) GIANT SMASHER
(— MADE UP) FIGMENT
(— NOT ESSENTIAL) FRILL
(— NOT EXPLAINED) MYSTERY
(— NOTABLE) DEUCE
(— OF GREAT VALUE) EYETOOTH
(— OF LITTLE VALUE) SHUCK FOUTER FOUTRA MAKEWEIGHT
(— OF NO VALUE) HAW DAMN BAUBEE DOCKEN
(— OFFERED FOR LOAN) PREMIUM
(— OR OTHER) ANYTHING
(— OUTSTANDING) BROTH DOYEN GASSER STANDOUT
(— PAINFUL) GAFF
(— PATCHED UP) VAMP
(— POOR) FLUMMERY

(**— PRECIOUS**) DUMPLING
(**— PREJUDICIAL**) FOE
(**— PROVOKING**) DEVIL
(**— REPELLENT**) SPINACH
(**— RISKED**) HAZARD
(**— SHAPELESS**) DUMP
(**— SHOWY**) FLOSS
(**— SHRIVELED**) SCRUMP
(**— SMALL**) DOT SNIP
(**— SPECTACULAR**) DILLY
(**— STICKY**) CAB
(**— STOLEN**) CRIB
(**— STRANGE**) FANTASIA
(**— SUPERLATIVE**) DARB
(**— TAUGHT**) DOCUMENT
(**— THAT IS LIGHT**) SKIFF SKIFT
(**— THAT WHIRLS**) GIG
(**— TO BIND BARGAIN**) EARNEST
(**— TRIVIAL**) CHIP FLUFF
(**— UNDECIDED**) ACRISY
(**— UNINTELLIGIBLE**) GREEK
(**— UNPLEASANT**) GUCK SOUR
(**— UNSPECIFIED**) ITEM
(**— UNSUBSTANTIAL**) FROTH
(**— UNTRUE**) HOKUM
(**— USELESS**) CRAP BLANK
(**— VILE**) DUNG
(**— WORTHLESS**) BOTH DUST
HOKUM DUFFER AMBSACE
(**— WRITTEN**) SCRIPT
SOMETIME FORMER SOMDEL
WHILOM ANCIENT QUONDAM
SOMEDEAL SOMEPART
SOMEWHEN
SOMETIMES NOW TOO WHILE
PERDIE WHILES UMQUHILE
OCCASIONALLY
SOMEWHAT BIT POCO SOME
PRETTY RATHER SLIGHT SUMMAT
ALIQUID SOMEDEAL
(PREF.) SEMI
SOMEWHERE SOMERS SOMEGATE
SOMITE ZONITE SEGMENT TERGITE
GONOTOME MEROSOME
MESOMERE SOMATOME
SOMNIFEROUS OPIATE SOMNIFIC
SOMNUS HYPNUS
SON BEN BOY LAD ANAC FILS FITZ
ZONE CHILD KIBEI MOPSY FILIUS
JUNIOR REUBEN EPAPHUS
EPIGONUS MONSIEUR
(**— OF CHIEF**) OGTIERN
(**— OF KING OF FRANCE**) DAUPHIN
(**— OF NISEI**) SANSEI
(**— OF PEER**) MASTER
(**— OF SUDRA**) CHANDALA
(**DAVID'S FAVORITE —**) ABSALOM
(**FOURTH —**) MARTLET
(**ILLEGITIMATE —**) NEPHEW
(**YOUNG —**) MOPSY
(**YOUNGER —**) CADET
(**YOUNGEST —**) BENJAMIN
(PREF.) AP. FILI(O)
SONANT VIBRANT
SONAR ASDIC
SONCHUS DINDLE
SONG AIR DIT FIT JIG LAY UTA
CANT DUAN FOLK GATO GLEE
LEED MELE NOTE RANT RUNE
SANG TUNE BLUES CANSO CAROL
CHANT CHARM CROON DILDO
DITTY MELOS MOLPE OLDIE
PAEAN VOCAL BALLAD BRANLE

BUBBLE CANTIC CANZON
CARMEN CHANTY CHORUS
HIMENE JINGLE MELODY ORPHIC
SHANTY STRAIN VINATA WAIATA
WARBLE BACCHIC BALLATA
CANCION CANTION CHANSON
COMIQUE DESCANT MELISMA
MELODIA REQUIEM REVERDI
ROMANCE SCOLION SONGLET
THRENOS BIRDSONG BRINDISI
CANTICLE CANZONET COONJINE
FLAMENCO JUBILATE PALINODE
RHAPSODY SERVENTE SINGSONG
ZORTZICO ROUNDELAY
(**— ACCOMPANYING TOAST**)
BRINDISI
(**— FOR TWO VOICES**) GYMEL
(**— OF BASQUES**) ZORTZICO
(**— OF BIRD**) LAY KOLLER
(**— OF JOY**) CAROL PAEAN
JUBILATE
(**— OF MINSTREL**) YEDDING
(**— OF OCEANIA**) HIMENE
(**— OF PRAISE**) HYMN CAROL
ANTHEM CHORALE
(**— UNACCOMPANIED**) GLEE
(**— WITH MONOTONOUS RHYME**)
VIRELAI VIRELAY
(**—S OF BIRDS**) RAMAGE
(**ANDALUSIAN —**) SAETA
(**ART —**) LIED
(**BOAT —**) JORRAM
(**CEREMONIAL —S**) AREITO
(**CRADLE —**) HUSHO
(**CUBAN —**) GUAJIRA COMPARSA
(**DANCE —**) BALLAD BAMBUCO
(**DRINKING —**) BACCHIC SCOLION
SKOLION WASSAIL
(**EVENING —**) SERENA EVENSONG
SERENATA
(**FOLK —**) SON FADO FOLK BLUES
DOINA BYLINA CANTIGA JUBILEE
STORNELLO
(**FUNERAL —**) DIRGE MONODY
EPICEDE THRENODY
(**FUNEREAL —**) ELEGY
(**GAY —**) LILT
(**GERMAN —**) LIED
(**HAWAIIAN —**) MELE
(**HEBREW —**) ELIELI HATIKVAH
(**IMPROMPTU —**) SCOLION
(**JAPANESE —**) UTA
(**LOVE —**) ALBA CANSO CANZO
FANCY AMORET AUBADE SERENA
SERENATA
(**MELISMATIC —**) DIVISION
(**MOCKING —**) JIG
(**MORNING —**) MATIN AUBADE
(**MOURNFUL —**) DUMP PLAINT
ENDECHA
(**NEW ZEALAND —**) WAIATA
(**NIGHT —**) COMPLIN
(**NO —S**) UTAI
(**NUPTIAL —**) HYMEN
(**PART —**) CHACE TROLL CACCIA
CANZONET FROTTOLA MADRIGAL
(**PASTORAL —**) OAT
(**PLAIN —**) GROUND
(**PORTUGUESE —**) FADO
(**RELIGIOUS —**) HYMN CAROL
PSALM SHOUT ANTHEM
POLYMNY SIRVENT
(**REVOLUTIONARY —**) CARMAGNOLE

(**SACRED —**) MOTET
(**SAILOR'S —**) CHANTY SHANTY
(**SANSKRIT —**) GITA
(**SINGLE — ON RECORD**) CUT
(**STUPID —**) STROWD
(**VINTAGE —**) VINATA
(**WORK —**) HOLLER
(PL.) ZEMMI AREITO
(PREF.) MELO
(SUFF.) ODE ODIC ODIST ODY
SONGBIRD CHAT IORA LARK WREN
MAVIS ROBIN SABIA SHAMA
SIREN VEERY VIREO BULBUL
CANARY LINNET MOCKER ORIOLE
SINGER THRUSH CATBIRD
GRASSET WARBLER ACCENTOR
BENGALEE BLUEBIRD BOBOLINK
CARDINAL SONGSTER
MEADOWLARK
SONGLIKE ARIOSE
SONG OF BERNADETTE (**AUTHOR**
OF —) WERFEL
(**CHARACTER IN —**) LOUISE
THERESE FRANCOIS PEYRAMALE
SOUBIROUS BERNADETTE
SONG OF HIAWATHA (**AUTHOR OF**
—) LONGFELLOW
(**CHARACTER IN —**) KWASIND
NOKOMIS WENONAH HIAWATHA
CHIBIABOS MINNEHAHA
MUDJEKEEWIS
SONG OF ROLAND (**AUTHOR OF —**)
UNKNOWN
(**CHARACTER IN —**) ALDA ALORY
MILON OGIER BERTHA FERRAU
GERARD MEDORO MORGAN
OBERTO OLIVER ROLAND SADONE
ARGALIA CHARLOT GANELON
GODFREY MALAGIS REINOLD
ASTOLPHO KARAHEUT
BRADAMANT GLORIANDA
CHARLEMAGNE MANDRICARDO
SONGSTER SINGER WARBLER
SONG THRUSH MAVIE MAVIS
SON-IN-LAW GENER MAUGH
SONNAMBULA, LA (**CHARACTER IN**
—) LISA AMINA ELVINO TERESA
RODOLFO
(**COMPOSER OF —**) BELLINI
SONNET AMORET
SONOROUS ROUND SHILL TONOUS
OROTUND VIBRANT RESONANT
SOUNDFUL SOUNDING
RESOUNDING
SONOROUSLY DEEPLY
SONS AND LOVERS (**AUTHOR OF —**
) LAWRENCE
(**CHARACTER IN —**) LILY PAUL
ANNIE CLARA DAWES MOREL
ARTHUR BAXTER MIRIAM WALTER
LEIVERS WILLIAM GERTRUDE
SONSHIP FILIETY
SONYA (**FATHER OF —**)
MARMELADOV
SOOLOOS THULUTH
SOON ERE ANON CITO TITE EARLY
NEWLY RADLY RATHE BELIVE
SUDDEN TIMELY BETIMES
ERELONG PRESTLY SHORTLY
DIRECTLY SPEEDILY PRESENTLY
SOONER ERE ERER ERST FIRST
BEFORE TITTER
(**— STATE**) OKLAHOMA

(**— THAN**) OR ERE
SOONEST ERST RATHEST
SOOT COOM IZLE SMUT STUP SUMI
BLECK BROOK COLLY COOMB
CROCK GRIME SOTIK FULIGO
SMOUCH SMUTCH SPODIUM
(**— ON GRATE BAR**) STRANGER
SOOTHE COY DEW BALM CALM
COAX DILL EASE HUSH LULL
ACCOY ALLAY CHARM DULCE
HUMOR QUELL SALVE SLEEK
STILL BECALM PACIFY SETTLE
SMOOTH SOLACE STROKE SUPPLE
ADDULCE ASSUAGE COMFORT
COMPOSE CONSOLE DEMULCE
FLATTER GRUNTLE LULLABY
MOLLIFY PLASTER QUALIFY
ATTEMPER BLANDISH MITIGATE
UNRUFFLE
SOOTHER ANODYNE
SOOTHING MILD BALMY BLAND
DOWNY DULCE STILL SWEET
ANETIC ANIMAL DREAMY DULCET
GENTLE SMOOTH ANODYNE
BALSAMIC SEDATIVE
SOOTHSAY SORT
SOOTHSAYER SEER AUGUR
WEIRD ARIOLE DIVINE PYTHON
ARUSPEX DIVINER CHALDEAN
HARUSPEX TIRESIAS
SOOTY COLLY REECHY SMUTTY
BROOKIE COLLIED
SOOTY ALBATROSS NELLIE
QUAKER STINKER BLUEBIRD
STINKPOT
SOOTY SHEARWATER TITI
SOP BERRY SIPPET SPONGE
SUGARSOP SWEETSOP
SOPATER (**FATHER OF —**) PYRRHUS
SOPHER SCRIBE
SOPHISM FETCH ELENCH FALLACY
SOPHEME
SOPHIST SOPH DUNCE
SOPHISTICATE GARBLE
MONDAINE
SOPHISTICATED WISE BLASE
CIVIL SALTY SVELTE WORLDLY
SOPHISTICATION CHIC
SOPHISTRY DECEIT FALLACY
SOPHISM CHICANERY
SOPHONISBA (**BROTHER OF —**)
HANNIBAL
(**FATHER OF —**) HASDRUBAL
(**HUSBAND OF —**) SYPHAX
SOPORIFIC DWALE DROWSY
HYPNIC OPIATE SLEEPY
HYPNOTIC NARCOTIC SOMNIFIC
SOPPY JUICY SOAKY
SOPRANO CANARY TREBLE
DESCANT CASTRATO
SORA ORTOLAN
SORB OCCLUDE LUSATIAN
SORBIAN WENDISH
SORBOSE ACROSE
SORCERER MAGE BOYLA BRUJO
WITCH BOOLYA NAGUAL VOODOO
WIZARD KORADJI WARLOCK
WIELARE FETISHER MAGICIAN
WITCHMAN
(PL.) GOETAE
SORCERESS BRUJA CIRCE LAMIA
SIBYL WITCH ARMIDA HECATE
BABAJAGA KORRIGAN WALKYRIE

SORCERY OBI MAGIC OBEAH SPELL
MAKUTU PISHOGUE PRESTIGE
SORTIARY WIGELING WITCHERY
WITCHING NECROMANCY
(VOODOO —) OBEAH WANGA
OUANGA
SORDES SABURRA
SORDID RAW BASE GAMY MEAN
VILE DIRTY DUSTY MUCKY SEAMY
CHETIF GRUBBY SODDEN
MESQUIN SQUALID CHURLISH
SORE BUM FOX PET BUBA CHAP
DEAR GALL KIBE KYLE OUCH
SAER BLAIN BOTCH GAMMY
AGNAIL BITTER BOUBAS CANKER
FESTER MELLIT MORMAL RANKLE
TAKING CATHAIR CHANCRE
SORANCE SCALDING
(— ON HORSE'S FOOT) MELLIT
QUITTER
(ARTIFICIAL —) FOX
(SUMMER —S) CALORIS LEECHES
SO RED THE ROSE (AUTHOR OF —)
YOUNG
(CHARACTER IN —) HUGH LUCY
MARY VEAL ZACH AGNES SARAH
AMELIE DUNCAN EDWARD
BALFOUR BEDFORD CHARLES
FRANCES LUCINDA MALCOLM
MCGEHEE SHELTON VALETTE
WILLIAM HARTWELL MIDDLETON
TALIAFERRO
SORE MOUTH ORF
SORENESS FROG
SORGHUM CANE CUSH MILO
BATAD DARSO DURRA SORGO
CHOLAM HEGARI IMPHEE KAFFIR
SHALLU FETERITA KAOLIANG
SOROCHE PUNA
SORREL OCA OKA SORE CUCKOO
HEARTS OXALIS RUBICAN
SOUROCK ALLELUIA STABWORT
SORREL TREE TITI ELKWOOD
SOURWOOD
SORROW WO RUE WOE BALE
CARE DOLE HARM MOAN RUTH
SORE TEEN DOLOR GRAME GRIEF
MOURN RUING SARRA UNWIN
GRIEVE LAMENT MISERY REGRET
STOUND UNLUST ANGUISH
CONDOLE DEPLORE PENANCE
REGRATE REMORSE THOUGHT
TROUBLE WOEFARE CALAMITY
DISTRESS DOLEANCE DREARING
EGRIMONY MOURNING
(PREF.) LUCTI
SORROWFUL BAD SAD WAN
CHARY DREAR TRIST WOFUL
DISMAL DOLENT DREARY RUEFUL
BALEFUL CAREFUL DOLEFUL
LUCTUAL RUESOME UNHAPPY
WAILFUL CONTRITE DESOLATE
DOLESOME DOLOROSO GRIEFFUL
MOURNFUL PITIABLE
SORROWFULLY SADLY WRATH
DERNLY HEAVILY
SORRY BAD SAD WOE HURT
VEXED UNFAIN PITIFUL CONTRITE
WRETCHED
SORT KIN LOT BRAN COMB GERE
HUMP KIND RANK SIFT SUIT
WING WORK BRACK BREED
GENUS GRADE SAVOR SPICE

ASSORT BARREL DILLUE GARBLE
GENDER KIDNEY MANNER MISTER
NATURE STRAIN STRIPE FASHION
SPECIES SPECKLE VARIETY
CLASSIFY SEPARATE
(— COTTON BY STAPLE) STAPLE
(— MAIL) CASE
(— MERCHANDISE) BRACK
(— OF PERSON) LIKE
SORTER SHALEMAN
SORTIE ISSUE SALLY ATTACK
OUTFALL
SORTILEGE LOT
SORTING GARBLING
(— ROOM) SALLE
SORUS AECIUM TELIUM
SORVA BORRACHA
SOT LUSH SOAK DRUNK LOURD
TOPER LOURDY BLOTTER
DASTARD TOSSPOT DRUNKARD
SOTHO SUTO SESUTO
SOTIK SOOT
SOUFFLE FONDU FONDRE
SOUGHT QUESITED
SOUL BA AME EGO ALMA ANIMA
ATMAN GHOST HEART SHADE
BUDDHI DIBBUK NATURE
PNEUMA PSYCHE SPIRIT SPRITE
NEPHESH PURUSHA INTERNAL
(—S OF THE DEAD) LEMURES
(ANIMAL — IN MAN) NEPHESH
(DISEMBODIED —) KER
(EGYPTIAN IMMORTAL —) BA
(INDIVIDUAL —) JIVA
(LIBERATED —) KEVALIN
(UNIVERSAL —) HANSA
(WANDERING —) DIBBUK DYBBUK
(PREF.) PSYCH(O) THYM(O)
(SUFF.) PSYCHE
SOULFULLY GEISTLICH
SOULLESS TURNIPY
SOU MARQUE STAMPEE
SOUND GO CRY FIT BLOW DING
DRIP FAST FERE FIRM FLOG FLOW
GLUG GOOD HALE HALE KYLE
NOTE RING SAFE SANE TEST
TONE TRIG WISE AFFIX BLAST
BUGLE CHEEP DREAM FLICK
FRESH GLIFF GLUCK GRIND
GROPE HODDY NOISE PLANG
PLUMB PROBE RIGHT SLUSH
SOLID SPANG SPANK SPEAK
SWASH VALID WHOLE BICKER
BIRDIE DORSAL ENDING ENTIRE
FATHOM FAUCAL HEARTY INTACT
LABIAL LAGOON ROBUST SIGNAL
SINGLE SONANT SPLASH STABLE
STRAIN STURDY HEALTHY
HEARING HURLING PERFECT
PHONEME PLUMMET SCRATCH
SONANCE VOCABLE FLAWLESS
FOOTFALL GRINDING GROUNDLY
LAUGHTER RELIABLE SEARCHER
SYLLABIC WAKELESS
(— A BAGPIPE) DOODLE
(— AS IF BY GUN) ZAP
(— BELL) PEAL RING KNELL KNOLL
(— DRUM OR TRUMPET) TUCK
(— FORTH) BOOM
(— IN GREEK AND LATIN) AGMA
(— IN MIND) FORMAL
(— INDEPENDENTLY OF THE PLAYER)
CIPHER

(— LESS LOUD) FALL
(— LIKE THUNDER) BRONTIDE
(— LOUDLY) TANG LARUM
(— MELODIOUSLY) CHARM
(— OF BAGPIPE) DRONE
(— OF BEATING) RATAPLAN
(— OF BELL) DING PEAL RING
KNELL STROKE DINGDONG
TINGTANG
(— OF BIRD) JUG CHURR
(— OF BULLET) ZIP
(— OF CONTEMPT) HUMPH
(— OF CORK) CLOOP CLUNK
(— OF DISAPPROVAL) BOO HOOT
BAZOO
(— OF DOG) BOOK
(— OF DYING PERSON'S VOICE)
TAISCH
(— OF ENGINE) CHUG
(— OF EXPLOSION) BOUNCE
(— OF F) DIGAMMA
(— OF FLUTE) TOOTLE
(— OF GLOTTAL STOP) HAMZA
HAMZAH
(— OF HEN) CLUCK
(— OF HOG) GRUNT
(— OF HOOF) CLOP
(— OF HORN) BEEP TOOT
(— OF HORSE) BLOWING
(— OF PLUCKED STRING) TUM
(— OF POURING LIQUID) GLUG
GLUGGLUG
(— OF RAIN) SPAT
(— OF RENDING) SCAT
(— OF SHEEP) BAA BLEAT
(— OF STEAM ENGINE) CHUFF
(— OF STRAW OR LEAVES) RUSTLE
(— OF THUNDER) CLAP
(— OF TRUMPET) CLARION
(— OF WIND IN TREES) WOOSH
(— OUT) FEEL
(—S HAVING RHYTHM) MUSIC
(ABNORMAL —) BRUIT
(ADVENTITIOUS —) RALE
(BLOWING —) SOUFFLE
(BRAWLING —) CHIDE
(BUBBLING —) BLATHER
(BUZZING —) Z WHIR WHIRR
(CLICKING —) SNECK
(CONSONANT —) ALVEOLAR
(COOING —) CHIRR TURTUR
(CRACKLING —) RISK
(CRISP —) BLIP
(CRUNCHING —) CRUMP SCRUNCH
(DELICATE —) TINK TINKLE
(DISCORDANT —) JAR BRAY
JANGLE
(DISTINCTIVE —) SONG
(DULL —) BUFF THUD CLONK
CLUNK FLUMP SQUELCH
(EXPLOSIVE —) POP BARK CHUG
PUFF SNORT REPORT
(FAINT —) PEEP GLIFF WHISHT
INKLING
(FINAL —) AUSLAUT
(GULPING —) GLUCK
(GUTTURAL —) GROWL
(HARSH —) JAR BRAY BLARE
CLASH CRANK TWANG SCROOP
DISCORD STRIDOR
(HEAVY —) DUMP
(HIGH-PITCHED —) TING
(HISSING —) FIZZ SIZZ

SWISH SIZZLE
(HOLLOW —) CHOCK THUNGE
(HUMMING —) HUM BURR SUUM
DRONE SINGING
(INDISTINCT —) BLUR SURD
(INITIAL — OF WORDS) ANLAUT
(JINGLING —) SMIT
(LAPPING —) SLOOSH
(LIGHT REPEATED —) PITAPAT
(LOUD —) PEAL BLARE CLANG
CRASH CLANGOR
(LOW-PITCHED —) BASS
(MEANINGLESS —S) GABBLE
(MEDIAL —) INLAUT
(MENTALLY —) SANE WISE
(MOANING —) SUUM SOUGH
(MOURNFUL —) GROAN
(MUSICAL —) CHIME
(NASAL —) ANUSVARA
(NON-SIGNIFICANT —) GLIDE
(NONVIBRATORY —) FRICTION
(PLEASING —) EUPHONY
EUPHONIA
(RASPING —) BUZZ SKIRR SCROOP
(REPEATED —) ECHO
(RESONANT —) BONG
(REVERBERATING —) PLANG
(RINGING —) CLANG CLANK CLING
TWANG RINGLE DINGDONG
(ROARING —) BEAL
(RUSHING —) SWOOSH HURLING
(RUSTLING —) FISSLE FISTLE
(SCRAPING —) GRIDE
(SHARP —) POP PING SNAP CHINK
CRAKE KNACK SPANG SQUIRK
(SHORT, HIGH-PITCHED —) BLEEP
(SHRILL —) CHEEP KNACK SKIRL
SCREED SQUEAK STRIDOR
(SHUFFLING —) SCUFFLE
(SIBILANT —) HISS SHISH SHUSH
(SLAPPING —) CLATCH
(SLIGHT —) SWISH
(SNORING —) SNORK
(SOBBING —) YOOP
(SPEECH —) SURD DOMAL TENUE
VOWEL APICAL PHONEME
CEREBRAL
(SPLASHING —) LAP CHUNK FLURR
SPLAT SWASH
(SPOKEN —) BREATH
(SQUEAKY —) CREAK
(SQUELCHING —) SQUASH
(STRANGLED —) GLUB GLUG
(SWISHING —) SCHLOOP
(TELEPHONE —) SIDETONE
(TRAMPING —) STUMP
(TRILLING —) CHIRR CHIZZ
HIRRIENT
(TUNEFUL —) HARMONY
(UNPLEASANT —) BLOOP
(VIBRATING —) TIRL
(WARNING —) ALARM SIREN
ALARUM TOCSIN
(WHIRRING —) BIRR FLURR SKIRR
(WHISPERING —) SUSURRUS
(WHISTLING —) STRIDOR
(PREF.) AUDIO AUDIT ECHO
PHON(O) SON(I)(O) SONORI
SONORO TONICO TONO
(SUFF.) PHON(E)(IA)(Y) SONANCE
SONANT SONOUS TONE TONIA
TONIC TONOUS TONY
SOUND-ABSORBENT ACOUSTIC

SOUND AND THE FURY (AUTHOR OF —) FAULKNER
  (CHARACTER IN —) HEAD JASON DILSEY SYDNEY CANDACE COMPSON QUENTIN BENJAMIN
SOUNDBOARD BELLY
SOUNDER TICKER LEADMAN
SOUNDING RAWIN SONANT INKLING SONDAGE SONATION
  (— HARSH) BRAZEN
  (— OF BELL) CURFEW
  (— OF ORGAN PIPE) CIPHER
  (— WITH REVERBERATIONS) PLANGENT
SOUNDLY FAST TIGHT FIRMLY
SOUNDNESS HEAL SANITY FITNESS SOBRIETY STRENGTH VALIDITY
SOUP BREE KAIL KALE SOPA BROTH GUMBO POSOL BISQUE BORSCH BURGOO JOUTES POZOLE BILLIBI BORSCHT GARBURE MARMITE CONSOMME GAZPACHO MINESTRA MORTREUX MINESTRONE MULLIGATAWNEY
  (— UP) SUPE
  (BARLEY —) SMIGGINS
  (BEEFSKIN —) SKINK
  (CABBAGE —) SHCHI STCHI
  (CLEAR —) CONSOMME JULIENNE
  (COLD —) SCHAV
  (JELLIED —) GAZPACHO
  (LARGE QUANTITY OF —) SLASH
  (SHINBONE —) SKINK
  (THICK —) BISK GUMBO HOOSH PUREE BISQUE BURGOO CHOWDER GARBURE POTTAGE HOTCHPOT MORTREWES
  (THIN —) BROTH SKILLY
SOUR AWA DRY YAR ACID ASIM CRAB DOUR FOXY GRIM GRUM HARD TART TURN ACERB ACRID AIGRE EAGER GOURY GRUFF MUSTY TEART ACIDIC BITTER CRUETY CURDLE PONTIC RANCID RUGGED SULLEN TORVID ACETOSE ACIDIFY AUSTERE SUBACID ACERBATE VINEGARY
  (SLIGHTLY —) BLINK BLINKY ACESCENT
SOURCE FONS FONT HAND HEAD HIVE MINE RISE RIST ROOT SEED FOUNT RADIX SPAWN SURGE AUCTOR AUTHOR BOTTOM CENTER FATHER FONTAL ORIGIN PARENT RESORT STAPLE WHENCE EDITION FOUNTAIN WELLHEAD PROVENANCE
  (— OF AID) RECOURSE
  (— OF ANCESTRAL LINE) STOCK
  (— OF ANNOYANCE) BOGY BOGIE HARROW BUGBEAR
  (— OF ASSURANCE) FORTRESS
  (— OF CONCERN) BUGABOO
  (— OF CONFIDENCE) ANCHOR
  (— OF DISPLEASURE) DISGUST
  (— OF ENERGY) TAPAS
  (— OF HAPPINESS) SUNSHINE
  (— OF HARM) CURSE
  (— OF HONOR) CREDIT
  (— OF INCOME) TITLE REVENUE

  (— OF INFORMATION) CHECK
  (— OF INSPIRATION) CASTALIA CASTALIE
  (— OF INSTRUCTION) BOOK
  (— OF LAUGHTER) SPLEEN
  (— OF LIGHT) LAMP
  (— OF NOURISHMENT) BREAST
  (— OF POWER) STRENGTH
  (— OF REGRET) SCATH SCATHE
  (— OF STREAM OR RIVER) FILL
  (— OF STRENGTH) HORN
  (— OF SUPPLY) SHOP FEEDER ARSENAL
  (— OF TROUBLE) HEADACHE
  (— OF WATER) BRON SPRING
  (— OF WEALTH) GOLCONDA KLONDIKE
  (ENCLOSED —) FLOW
  (FROM ANOTHER —) ALIUNDE
  (MALIGNANT —) CANCER
  (PHYSICAL —) MOTHER
  (PRIMARY —) RADIX
  (RADIO —) QUASAR
SOURDOUGH LEAVEN
SOURED FOXY QUARRED
SOURING ACESCENCE
SOURNESS ACIDITY ACERBITY ACRIMONY ASPERITY TARTNESS VERJUICE
SOURSOP CORRESOL GUANABANA
SOURWOOD TITI ELKWOOD
SOUSE DIP DUCK TOSH PLUMP STOOP PLUNGE SOZZLE
SOUTANE SIMAR ZIMARRA
SOUTH MIDI AUSTER DECANI MIDDAY MERIDIAN
  (FARTHER —) BELOW
  (PREF.) AUSTR(O) NOT(O)

SOUTH AFRICA
BAY: ALGOA FALSE
CAPE: AGULHAS
CAPITAL: CAPETOWN PRETORIA
COIN: CENT RAND POUND FLORIN
LANGUAGE: BANTU HINDI TAMIL TELUGU BUJARATI
MOUNTAIN: AUX KOP KATHKIN INJASUTI
NATIVE: YOSA BANTU NAMAS PONDO DAMARA SWAHILI BECHUANA HOTTENTOT
PROVINCE: NATAL TRANSVAAL
RIVER: MODDER MOLOPO ORANGE KURUMAM LIMPOPO OLIFANTS
TOWN: AUS MARA STAD BENONI DURBAN SEVERN UMTATA KOKSTAD SPRINGS MAFEKING GERMISTON JOHANNESBURG
WATERFALL: HOWICK TUGELA AUGRABIES

SOUTH AMERICA
(ALSO SEE SPECIFIC COUNTRIES)
LAKE: MIRIM POOPO TITICACA MARACAIBO LLANQUIHUE
MOUNTAIN: BAIA ANDES GOIAZ PARIMA ACARAHY TUMUCHUMAC
NATION: PERU CHILE BRAZIL GUYANA BOLIVIA ECUADOR URUGUAY COLOMBIA PARAGUAY SURINAME

ARGENTINA NICARAGUA VENEZUELA
RIVER: NEGRO AMAZON CHUBUT PARANA SALADO ORINOCO RIONEGRO ESSEQUIBO MAGDALENA

SOUTH CAROLINA
CAPITAL: COLUMBIA
COLLEGE: COKER FURMAN LANDER CITADEL CLAFFIN CLEMSON ERSKINE WOFFORD
COUNTY: AIKEN HORRY DILLON JASPER OCONEE SALUDA
FORT: SUMTER
INDIAN: PEDEE SEWEE CUSABO SANTEE WAXHAW CATAWBA SUGEREE WATEREE CONGAREE
ISLAND: EDISTO PARRIS HILTONHEAD
LAKE: MARION MURRAY CATAWBA WATEREE HARTWELL MOULTRIE
MOUNTAIN: SASSAFRAS
NATIVE: WEASEL PALMETTO
NICKNAME: PALMETTO
PLATEAU: PIEDMONT
PRESIDENT: JACKSON
RESERVOIR: SANTEE PINOPOLIS
RIVER: BROAD EDISTO PEEDEE SALUDA SANTEE ASHEPOO TUGALOS WATEREE CONGAREE SAVANNAH
STATE BIRD: WREN
STATE FLOWER: JASMINE
STATE TREE: PALMETTO
TOWN: AIKEN GREER UNION BELTON CAMDEN CHERAW CONWAY DILLON SALUDA SENECA SUMTER BAMBERG LAURENS MANNING BEAUFORT FLORENCE NEWBERRY WALHALLA GREENVILLE SPARTANBURG

SOUTH CAROLINIAN WEASEL PALMETTO

SOUTH DAKOTA
BUTTE: MUD CROW SULLY FINGER SADDLE THUNDER DEERSEARS
CAPITAL: PIERRE
COLLEGE: HURON YANKTON
COUNTY: DAY HYDE BRULE MINER MOODY SPINK SULLY TRIPP CUSTER JERAULD YANKTON MELLETTE
INDIAN: BRULE SIOUX DAKOTA CHEYENNE
LAKE: OAHE BIGSTONE TRAVERSE
MONUMENT: RUSHMORE
MOUNTAIN: BEAR SHEEP TABLE CROOKS HARNEY MOREAU
NICKNAME: COYOTE SUNSHINE
RIVER: JAMES MOREAU CHEYENNE MISSOURI
STATE BIRD: PHEASANT
STATE FLOWER: PASQUE
STATE TREE: SPRUCE
TOWN: LEAD HAYTI HURON LEOLA ONIDA CUSTER DESMET EUREKA KADOKA LEMMON

MILLER WINNER STURGIS WEBSTER YANKTON ABERDEEN DEADWOOD SISSETON

SOUTHERLY AUSTRINE
SOUTHERN SUDIC AUSTRAL MERIDIAN SOUTHRON MERIDIONAL
  (PREF.) NOTIO
SOUTHERN CROSS CRUX CROSS CROSIER
SOUTHERNER CAVALIER SOUTHRON
SOUTHERN FRANCE MIDI
SOUTHERN ILLINOIS EGYPT
SOUTHERN INDIA DRAVIDA
SOUTHERNWOOD APPLERINGIE

SOUTH KOREA
BAY: KANGHWA
CAPITAL: SEOUL
COIN: WON HWAN
MOUNTAIN: CHIRI
PROVINCE: CHEJU CHOLLA KANGWON KYONGGI
RIVER: HAN KUM PUKHAN SOMJIN NAKTONG YONGSAN
TOWN: CHEJU MASAN MOKPO PUSAN SUWON TAEGU WONJU CHINJU CHONJU INCHON KUNSAN TAEJON CHONGJU KWANGJU CHUNCHON

SOUTHLAND AUSTER
SOUTH SEA ISLANDER KANAKA

SOUTH VIETNAM
CAPITAL: SAIGON
LANGUAGE: CHAM KHMER RHADE
MEASURE: GANG PHAN THON
MOUNTAIN: BADINH NINHHOA KNONTRAN NGOOLINH TCHEPONE
NATIVE: CHAM MALAY
PORT: DANANG SAIGON QUINHON NHATRANG
REGION: ANNAM COCHIN
RIVER: BA SONG MEKONG DONGNAI
TOWN: HUE HOIAN ANNHON DANANG GIADINH QUINHON SONGCAU TAYNINH VINHLOI PHANRANG QUANGTRI
WEIGHT: CAN YET UYEN

SOUTHWESTER SQUAM
SOUTH YEMEN (CAPITAL OF —) ADEN
  (ISLAND OF —) PERIM KAMARAN SOCOTRA
  (MONEY OF —) DINAR
  (TOWN OF —) SEIYUN MUKALLA
SOUVENIR RELIC TOKEN FAIRING NICKNACK
SOVEREIGN BEY SIR SOV BEAN CHAM CHIP FREE KHAN QUID SHAH SKIV CROWN JAMES NEGUS NIZAM QUEED CHAGAN COUTER GUINEA KAISER KINGLY MASTER PRINCE SAMORY SHINER SOLDAN SOVRAN SULTAN CROWNED MONARCH ZAMORIN AUTOCRAT DOMINANT IMPERIAL

SUFFRAIN SUZERAIN
(DIVINELY —) THEARCHIC
(FELLOW —) COUSIN
(HEAVENLY —) TENNO HEAVEN
(MOSLEM —) SOLDAN
SOVEREIGNTY SWAY CROWN
REIGN DIADEM EMPERY EMPIRE
THRONE DEMESNE DYNASTY
KINGDOM MAJESTY SCEPTER
SCEPTRE AUTARCHY DOMINION
IMPERIUM MONARCHY REGALITY
REGNANCY SOVRANTY
(— OF REASON) AUTONOMY
(JOINT —) SYNARCHY
SOVIET (ALSO SEE RUSSIA)
VOLOST COUNCIL GUBERNIA
SOW ELT HOG GILT SEED SHED
YELT YILT DRILL PLANT PLUMP
STREW CHANNEL GRUMPHY
IMPLANT OVERSOW SCATTER
ENGENDER INTERSOW SEMINATE
(PREF.) HYO SCROFUL(O)
(SUFF.) CHOERUS
SOWAR SILLADAR
SOW BUG ISOPOD SLATER
ISOPODAN
SOWENS SONS SWEENS
FLUMMERY WASHBREW
SOWER SEEDER SEEDMAN
SEEDSTER SEMINARY
SOWING SATION SEMENCE
SEEDNESS
(PREF.) SPOR(I)(IDI)(O)(ULI)
(SUFF.) SPORA SPORE SPORIC
SPORIDIA SPORIUM SPOROUS
SPORY
SOWN SEME SATIVE SEEDED
SEMEED
SOW THISTLE DINDLE GUTWEED
HOGWEED MILKWEED
SOY SHOYA SHOYU
SOYBEAN SOJA SOYA
SPA BATH CURE HYDRO
SPACE AREA BLUE CORD COSO
DENT FACE LUNG PALE RANK
ROOM SIDE VOID ABYSS BLOCK
CHINK CLEFT FIELD PLACE RANGE
CANTON HIATUS INDENT MATTER
ROOMTH ARRANGE COMPASS
FOREIGN GUNNIES LEGROOM
ROOMAGE SPACING SPATIUM
DIASTEMA DISTANCE EXOCOELE
INTERVAL
(— ABOVE EARTH) AIRSPACE
(— AMONG MUSCLES) SINUS
(— AROUND HOUSE) AMBIT
(— AT WHARF) BERTHAGE
(— BEFORE KILN) LOGIE KILLOGIE
(— BEHIND ALTAR) FERETORY
(— BETWEEN BED AND WALL)
RUELLE
(— BETWEEN BRIDGE PIERS) LOCK
(— BETWEEN CASKS) CONTLINE
(— BETWEEN COLUMNS) BAY
(— BETWEEN CONCENTRIC CIRCLES)
ANNULUS
(— BETWEEN DECKS) LAZARET
(— BETWEEN EYE AND BILL) LORE
(— BETWEEN FEATHERS) APTERYLA
(— BETWEEN FLOOR TIMBERS)
SPIRKET
(— BETWEEN FLUTINGS) FILET
FILLET GORGERIN

(— BETWEEN FURROWS) RIG
(— BETWEEN PAGES) GUTTER
(— BETWEEN RAILROAD TIES) CRIB
(— BETWEEN SAW TEETH) GULLET
**(— BETWEEN SHIP'S BOWS AND
ANCHOR)** HAWSE
(— BETWEEN STRANDS) CANTLINE
(— BETWEEN TEETH) DIASTEMA
**(— BETWEEN THUMB AND LITTLE
FINGER)** SPAN
(— BETWEEN TIMBERS) SPIRKET
(— BETWEEN TWO WIRES) DENT
(— BETWEEN VEINS OF LEAVES)
AREOLA
(— DEVOID OF MATTER) VACUUM
VACUITY
(— FOR SECRETION) BAG
(— IN CHURCH) KNEELING
(— IN COIL OF CABLE) TIER
(— IN FOREST) GLADE
(— IN MINE) GOB
(— IN THEATER) BOX
(— IN TYPE) CORE
(— OCCUPIED) VOLUME
(— OF TIME) DAY PULL STEAD
GHURRY STITCH INTERVAL
(— ON BILLIARD TABLE) BALK
BAULK
(— ON COIN) EXERGUE
(— OVER STAGE) FLIES
(— OVERHEAD) HIGH
(— UNDER STAGE) DOCK
(— USED AS LIVING-ROOM) LANAI
(— WITHIN LIMITS) CONTENT
(AIR —) CENTRUM
(ARCHITECTURAL —) METOPE
PEDIMENT SACELLUM
(BACKGAMMON —) POINT
(BARE — ON BIRD) APTERIUM
(BLANK —) GAP ALLEY LACUNA
(BOUNDLESS —) INFINITE
(BREATHING —) BARLEY
(CLEAR —) FAIRWAY HEADWAY
DAYLIGHT
(COUNTER —) BACKBAR
(CRAMPED —) CUBBY
(EMPTY —) AIR BLANK CAPACITY
(ENCLOSED —) AREA BOWL HATCH
VERGE PARVIS CHAMBER CIRCUIT
CLOSURE COMPASS PARVISE
PTEROMA CLOISTER CONFINES
(EUCLIDEAN —) FLAT
(FLAT —) HOMALOID
(LEVEL —) PLATEA PARTERRE
(NARROW —) SLOT STRAIT
(OPEN —) OUT LAWN ALLEY
COURT LAUND TAHUA MAIDAN
AREAWAY FAIRWAY LOANING
APERTURE DAYLIGHT
KNEEHOLE
(OPEN — OF WATER) WAKE
(OVERHANGING —) DOME
(POPLITEAL —) HAM HOCK
(ROOF —) CELL
(SEATING —) CAVEA
(SHELTERED —) KILLOGIE
(STORAGE —) ATTIC
(TRIANGULAR —) SPANDREL
(UNFILLED —) GAP GAPE CAVITY
HOLLOW BREAKAGE
(VAULTED —) ALCOVE
(VERTICAL —) HEADROOM
(WORKING —) COUNTER

(PREF.) SPATIO
SPACECRAFT SHIP CAPSULE
ORBITER
(PROCESS OF SLOWING DOWN —)
DEBOOST
SPACED MEATIC
SPACIOUS ROOM SIDE WIDE
AMPLE BROAD RANGY ROOMY
GOLDEN BARONIAL SCOPIOUS
SPADE DIG LOY FECK LILY PEEL
PICK SPIT SPUD DELVE DIDLE
GRAFF SLADE SLANE TRAMP
DIGGER PADDLE PATTLE SERVER
SHOVEL TUSKAR GRAFTER
SCAFFLE SCUPPIT SPADDLE
SPITTER TWISCAR
(LONG NARROW —) LOY
(PART OF —) FROG STEP BLADE
HANDLE SOCKET SHOULDER
(PEAT —) SLADE SLANE TUSKAR
(PLASTERER'S —) SERVER
(TRIANGULAR —) DIDLE
SPADEFISH POGY PORGY
MOONFISH
SPADEFUL SPIT SPITFUL
SPAGHETTI PASTA SLEEVING
SPAGNUOLO LADINO

SPAIN

CAPE: AJO NAO GATA CREUS
MORAS PALOS PENAS PRIOR
DARTUCH ORTEGAL SALINAS
TORTOSA ESPICHEL MARROQUI
SACRATIF
CAPITAL: MADRID
COIN: COB DURO PESO REAL
DOBLA CUARTO DINERO
DOBLON ESCUDO PESETA
ALFONSO CENTIMO PISTOLE
REALDOR DOUBLOON
DIALECT: BASQUE CATALAN
GALICIAN
ISLAND: IBIZA PALMA GOMERA
HIERRO ALBORAN MAJORCA
MINORCA MALLORCA
TAGOMAGO TENERIFE
ISLANDS: CANARY BALEARIC
MEASURE: PIE CODO COPA DEDO
MOYO PASO VARA ALMUD
BRAZA CAFIZ CAHIZ CARGA
LEGUA LINEA MEDIO MILLA
PALMO SESMA ARROBA CORDEL
CUARTA ESTADO FANEGA
RACION YUGADA AZUMBRE
CANTARA CELEMIN ESTADEL
PULGADA ARANZADA
FANEGADA
MOUNTAIN: GATA ANETO ROUCH
TEIDE ESTATS NETHOU TELENO
BANUELO CERREDO PERDIDO
ALMANZOR MONTSENY
MULHACEN PENALARA
MOUNTAIN RANGE: CUENCA
GREDOS MORENA TOLEDO
ALCARAZ DEMANDA MONCAYO
MALADETA MONEGROS
PYRENEES
NAME: ESPANA IBERIA HISPANIA
NATIVE: CATALAN IBERIAN
PORT: ADRA NOYA VIGO CADIZ
GADES GADIR GIJON PALOS
ABDERA CORUNA MALAGA
ALMERIA ALICANTE BARCELONA

PROVINCE: JAEN LEON LUGO
ALAVA AVILA CADIZ SORIA
BURGOS CORUNA CUENCA
GERONA HUELVA HUESCA
LERIDA MADRID MALAGA
MURCIA ORENSE OVIEDO
TERUEL TOLEDO ZAMORA
ALMERIA BADAJOZ CACERES
CORDOBA GRANADA LOGRONO
NAVARRA SEGOVIA SEVILLA
VIZCAYA ALBACETE ALICANTE
BALEARES PALENCIA VALENCIA
ZARAGOZA
REGION: LEON ARAGON BASQUE
MURCIA CASTILE GALICIA
NAVARRE ASTURIAS CASTILLA
VALENCIA
RIVER: SIL TER CEGA EBRO ESLA
LIMA MINO TAJO ULLA ADAJA
CINCA DOURO DUERO GENIL
JALON JUCAR NAVIA ODIEL
RIAZA SEGRE TAGUS TINTO
TURIA ALAGON ARAGON
ERESMA HUERVA JARAMA
ORBIGO SEGURA TOROTE
ALMERIA ALMONTE ARLANZA
BARBATE CABRIEL DURATON
GALLEGO HENARES MIJARES
PERALES GUADIANA
TOWN: ROA ASPE BAZA ELDA
HARO IRUN JAEN LEON LUGO
OLOT REUS ROTA SAMA VIGO
BAENA BEJAR CADIZ CIEZA
CUETA ECIJA EIBAR ELCHE
GIJON IBIZA JEREZ JODAR
LORCA OLIVA PALMA RONDA
SIERO UBEDA XERES YECLA
ZAFRA AVILES AZUAGA BILBAO
BURGOS DUENCA GANDIA
GERONA GETAFE GUADIX
HELLIN HUELVA HUESCA
JATIVA LERIDA LUCENA
MADRID MALAGA MATARO
MERIDA MURCIA ORENSE
OVIEDO TERMEL TOLEDO
UTRERA ZAMORA BADAJOZ
CORDOBA DAIMIEL GRANADA
JUMILLA LINARES LOGRONO
MANRESA SEGOVIA SEVILLA
TARRASA VITORIA BADALONA
FIGUERAS PAMPLONA
SABADELL SANTIAGO
TORRENTE VALENCIA
ZARAGOZA
WEIGHT: ONZA FRAIL GRANO
LIBRA MARCO TOMIN ADARME
ARROBA DINERO DRACMA
OCHAVA ARIENZO QUILATE
QUINTAL CARACTER TONELADA
WINE: RIOJA SHERRY

SPALL CHIP SCALE SPAWL GALLET
SPAN ARCH BEAM PAIR CHORD
SPANG SWING BRIDGE EXTEND
SPREAD OPENING QUARTER
BESTRIDE
(— WITH FINGERS) SPEND
(UNSUPPORTED —) BEARING
SPANDREL GROIN ALLEGE
SPANDLE
SPANGLE AGLET PRANK SPANG
SEQUIN CHEQUEEN SPANGLET
ZECCHINO PAILLETTE

SPANGLED POWDERED SPANKLED
SPANIARD DON DIEGO MULADI
(CHRISTIAN —) MOZARAB
SPANIEL TRASY COCKER SUSSEX
CLUMBER BLENHEIM PAPILLON
SPRINGER WATERRUG
SPANISH ALJAMIA
(PREF.) HISPANO
SPANISH-AMERICAN CHINO
LADINO
SPANISH BAYONET IZOTE YUCCA
SPANISH HOGFISH LADYFISH
SPANISH JACINTH SCILLA
SPANISH JASMINE MALATI
SPANISH MACKEREL SIERRA
SPANISH PLUM SIRUELAS
SPANISH STOPPER IRONWOOD
SPANK PRAT SCUD SKELP PADDLE
SLIPPER
SPANKER DRIVER MIZZEN
SPANKING SMACKING
SPANNER KEY WRENCH
SPANNING ASTRIDE
SPAR BEAM BOOM CAUK CLUB
GAFF MAST RAFT SPUR YARD
CABER SPAAD SPATH SPELK
SPRIT STODE BOUGAR RICKER
STEEVE BASTITE DERRICK
DOLPHIN JIBBOOM RIBBAND
BOWSPRIT CRYOLITE LAZULITE
OUTRIGGER MARTINGALE
(BITTER —) DOLOMITE
(HEAVY —) CAUK BARITE BARYTE
SPARE BONY FAIK GASH HAIN
LEAN NICE SAVE SLIM THIN
FAVOR LANKY SPELL LENTEN
MEAGER MEAGRE SKIMPY
RESERVE SLENDER PRESERVE
SPARGE PIPE WEEPER
SPARING CHARY GNEDE SCANT
SPARE DAINTY FRUGAL STINGY
ENVIOUS ECONOMIC SPAREFUL
PENURIOUS ABSTEMIOUS
(— OF WORDS) CURT
(NOT —) HANDSOME
(PREF.) PARCI
SPARINGNESS PARCITY SCARCITY
SPARK FUNK IZLE AIZLE GRAIN
LIGHT PURSE SPERK SPUNK
BLUETTE FLANKER FLAUGHT
SPARKLE SPUNKIE SPARKLET
SCINTILLA
(-S OF MOLTEN IRON) NILL
(VITAL —) GHOST LIGHT
(PREF.) SCINTILLO
SPARKER IGNITER
SPARKLE FUNK SNAP WINK BLINK
FLASH GLENT GLINT SHINE SPARK
GLANCE KINDLE SIMPER CRACKLE
EMICATE FLANKER GLIMMER
GLISTEN GLISTER GLITTER
RADIATE SHIMMER SKINKLE
SPANGLE TWINKLE SPRINKLE
CORUSCATE
SPARKLER TWINKLER
SPARKLING DEWY CRISP QUICK
SUNNY BRIGHT SPUNKY STARRY
CREMANT DIAMOND SHINING
TWINKLY MOUSSEUX SMIRKING
SPERLING BRILLIANT SCINTILLANT
(MAKE —) AERATE
(NOT —) STILL
SPARK PLUG (PART OF —) CAP GAP

SHELL GASKET BUSHING
TERMINAL ELECTRODE
INSULATOR
SPARLING SMELT
SPARROW SPUG DICKY DONEY
FINCH HEMPY ISAAC PADDA
PADDY SPRIG SPRUG CHIPPY
PHILIP SPRONG TOWHEE
CHANTER CHIPPIE DUNNOCK
FIELDIE HAYSUCK PINNOCK
SPADGER SPURDIE TITLENE
TITLING TITTLIN ACCENTOR
FIRETAIL HAIRBIRD WHITECAP
(PREF.) PASSERI
SPARROW HAWK MUSKET
SPARHAWK
SPARSE BALD THIN MEAGER
MEAGRE SCANTY THRIFTY
SPARTAN LACONIC
SPASM PANG CRICK QUALM
TONUS CLONUS ENTASIA
FLUTTER RAPTURE SPASMUS
MYOTONIA PAROXYSM
(— OF FOOT) PODISMUS
(— OF PAIN) GRIP
(— OF THE IRIS) HIPPUS
(—S OF WHALE) FLURRY
(TONIC —) HOLOTONY
(PREF.) CLONICO
SPASMODIC FITFUL SNATCHY
SPASMIC SPASTIC SPURTIVE
SPAT SEED BROOD JOWER GAITER
LEGGING BOOTHOSE BOOTIKIN
SPATE SLUICE
SPATHE CYMBA SHEATH
SPATHIC SPARRY SPATHOSE
SPATIAL STERIC
SPATIATE ROVE RAMBLE STROLL
SPATTER DASH JAUP BERAY SKIRP
SLART SPARK SPURT DABBLE
SPLASH SQUIRT BESPAWL
BESPETE SHATTER SMATTER
SPATTLE SPIRTLE SPLATTER
SPRINKLE
(— WITH FOAM) EMBOSS
(— WITH MUD) JAP BEMUD SPARK
SPATTERDASH SPAT BONNET
GAITER CUTIKIN LEGGING
BOOTHOSE BOOTIKIN
SPATTERDOCK DUCK CLOTE
TUCKY WOKAS NUPHAR
BONNETS CANDOCK
SPATULA SPAT SLICE THIBLE
THIVEL CESTRUM SPATTLE
SPLATTER
SPAVIN JACK SPAVIE VARISSE
SPAWN RUD BLOT RAUN REDD
RUDD SILE SPORE TODDER
(OYSTER —) CULCH CULTCH
SPAWNEATER SHINER
SPAWNING SICK MILKY SEEDING
SPAY FIX GELD ALTER DESEX
SPADE CHANGE SPEAVE
CASTRATE
SPEAK ASK CUT SAY CANT CARP
MEAN MOOT MOVE TALE TALK
TELL WORD BREAK MOUTH
NEVEN ORATE PARLE SOUND
SPELL SPIEL UTTER ACCENT
PARLEY PATTER QUETHE SERMON
SPEECH SQUEAK TONGUE
ADDRESS BESPEAK DECLAIM
DELIVER EXCLAIM PARRALL

CONVERSE REHEARSE
(— ABUSIVELY) JAW
(— AFFECTEDLY) MIMP KNACK
(— AGAINST) ACCUSE GAINSAY
FORSPEAK
(— ANGRILY) ROUSE CAMPLE
(— AT LENGTH) DISSERT ENLARGE
(— BROKENLY) FALTER
(— CAJOLINGLY) COLLOGUE
(— CONFUSEDLY) HATTER
CLUTTER SPLATHER
(— CONTEMPTUOUSLY) SCOFF
(— CRITICALLY) LAUNCH
(— CURTLY) BIRK SNAP
(— EVIL) BLACKEN
(— FAIR) PALP
(— FALSELY) ABUSE
(— FAMILIARLY) HOBNOB
(— FIRST TO) ACCOST
(— FOOLISHLY) PRATE GIBBER
(— HALTINGLY) HACK HAMMER
STAMMER
(— HOARSELY) CROAK CROUP
(— ILL OF) KNOCK DEPRAVE
DETRACT
(— IMPERFECTLY) LISP
(— IMPUDENTLY) CHEEK
(— IMPULSIVELY) BLURT
(— IN DRAWL) DRANT DRAUNT
(— IN JEST) FOOL
(— IN ONE'S EAR) HARK
(— IN POINTLESS MANNER) DROOL
(— IN STUMBLING WAY) STUTTER
(— IN UNDERTONE) WHISPER
(— IN WHINING VOICE) CANT
(— INDISTINCTLY) FUMBLE JABBER
MUFFLE MAUNDER SPLUTTER
(— INEPTLY) BUMBLE
(— INSOLENTLY) SNASH
(— LOUDLY) TANG
(— MINCINGLY) NAB MIMP
(— MONOTONOUSLY) DROLL
(— OF) CALL NEVEN MENTION
(— OUT) LEVEL SHOOT
(— PLAYFULLY) BANTER
(— POMPOUSLY) CRACK
(— PROFUSELY) PALAVER
(— QUERULOUSLY) CREAK
(— RAPIDLY) TROLL GIBBER
JABBER SQUIRT CHATTER
(— RESENTFULLY) HUFF
(— RHETORICALLY) DECLAIM
(— SARCASTICALLY) GIRD
(— SHORTLY) JERK
(— SLIGHTINGLY OF) BELITTLE
(— SLOWLY) DRAWL
(— THROUGH THE NOSE) SNAFFLE
(— TRUTH) SOOTHSAY
(— WITH EMPHASIS) DWELL
(— WITH LIPS CLOSED) MUMBLE
SPEAKEASY SHEBEEN
SPEAKER VOICE BRYTHON
LOCUTOR MOUTHER STYLIST
EPILOGUE SPEECHER
(ORATORICAL —) SPOUTER
(PUBLIC —) ORATOR STUMPER
SPEAKING STEVEN LOQUENT
PARLANCE SPELLING
(— ARTICULATELY) MEROP
MEROPIC
(— MANY LANGUAGES) POLYGLOT
(EVIL —) PRATING
(SUFF.) LOGER LOGIA(N)

LOGIC(AL) LOGIST LOGUE LOGY
LOQUENCE LOQUENT LOQUY
SPEAR GAD DART FRAM GAFF PIKE
GRAIN LANCE REJON SHAFT
STAFF VALET AMGARN BORDUN
BROACH FIZGIG FRAMEA GIDJEE
GLAIVE WASTER ASSEGAI
BOURDON HARPOON IMPALER
JAVELIN TRIDENT VERUTUM
EELSPEAR GAVELOCK LANCEGAY
STANDARD WALSPERE
(BROKEN —) TRUNCHEON
(EEL —) ELGER PILGER
(FISH —) GIG GAFF TREN POACH
FIZGIG GRAINS FISHGIG LEISTER
SNIGGER
(SALMON —) WASTER
(PREF.) DORI ENCHO HASTATO
LANCI
SPEARFISH AGUJA GOGGLE
MARLIN BILLFISH LONGJAWS
SPEAR GRASS SPANIARD
SPEARHEAD BUNT GAFF SPUD
CORONAL
SPEARMINT MENTHE LABIATE
SPEAR-SHAPED HASTATE
SPEAR THROWER ATLATL
WOMMALA WOOMERAH
SPEARWORT BANEWORT
SPECIAL VERY EXTRA KHASS
CONCRETE ESPECIAL PECULIAR
SPECIFIC
SPECIALIST SWELL EXPERT
HERALD LEGIST ALTAIST ARABIST
FAUNIST FEUDIST GRECIAN
OLOGIST SURGEON AQUINIST
ARBORIST BANTUIST BOTANIST
ETHICIST GEMARIST GEOGNOST
GEOMETER HEBRAIST HOMERIST
LATINIST URBANIST PHYSICIST
PEDIATRIST PATHOLOGIST
(SUFF.) ICIAN LOG(ER)(IA)(IAN)(IC)
(ICAL)(IST)(UE)(Y)
SPECIALTY BAG
SPECIES FOLK FORM KIND SORT
BROOD CLASS EIDOS GENRE
ESPECE MANNER MISTER
APOMICT FEATHER SPECIAL
ANALOGUE GENOTYPE INDIGENE
(— VARIANT) MORPH
(ATOMIC —) DAUGHTER
SPECIFIC EXPRESS SPECIAL
TRIVIAL CONCRETE ESPECIAL
SPECIFICALLY NAMELY
SPECIFICATION MENTION
SPECIFICITY HECCEITY
SPECIFIED SET GIVEN
SPECIFY ASSIGN DESIGN DETAIL
ARTICLE EXPRESS MENTION
INDICATE NOMINATE PRESCRIBE
SPECIMEN CAST TEST ESSAY
FACER MODEL SPICE CHANCE
SAMPLE SWATCH EXAMPLE
ICOTYPE ISOTYPE NEOTYPE
PATTERN SAMPLER ALLOTYPE
EXEMPLAR HOLOTYPE HYPOTYPE
IDEOTYPE INSTANCE
REPRESENTATIVE
(ADDITIONAL —) COTYPE
(EXTRAORDINARY —) BENDER
(FEMALE —) GYNETYPE
(FINEST —) PEARL
(LARGE —) ELEPHANT

(POOR —) APOLOGY
(SMALL —) SPRIG
SPECIOUS GAY FAIR FALSE WHITE
FACILE GLOSSY HOLLOW TINSEL
PAGEANT PLAUSIVE PROBABLE
SPURIOUS PLAUSIBLE
MERETRICIOUS
SPECIOUSNESS DISGUISE
SPECK DOT PIN PIP MOTE SPOT
TICK WHIT BLACK GLEBE PLECK
APHTHA SPECKLE FLYSPECK
NUBECULA
(— IN LINEN) SPRIT
(— ON FINGERNAIL) GIFT
(BLACK —) DARTROSE
SPECKLE FLECK GARLE SPECK
MIZZLE PECKLE STIPPLE
SPECKLED SHELD FIGGED MAILED
MENALD SANDED BLOBBED
BRACKET PECKLED SPECKED
SPECKLY FRECKLED IRONSHOT
IRRORATE JASPERED STIPPLED
SPECTACLE POMP SHOW SPEC
BYSEN SIGHT CIRCUS DEVICE
OBJECT EYEMARK PAGEANT
SPECIES TAMASHA MONUMENT
NAUMACHY STERACLE
NAUMACHIA
(ODD —) TRACK
(SORRY —) BIZEN BYSEN BYZEN
(WATER —) AQUACADE
(PL.) LUDI
(SUFF.) CADE ORAMA
SPECTACLES PAIR SPECS BRILLS
LUNETS PEEPER SIGHTS GLASSES
GOGGLES WINKERS ANAGLYPH
CHEATERS BARNACLES
SPECTACULAR VIEWY PAGEANT
SPECTATOR FAN VIEWER
WITNESS BEHOLDER OBSERVER
OVERSEER RAILBIRD VIEWSTER
SCAFFOLDER
(PL.) DEDANS
SPECTER BUG BOGY MARE BOGIE
BOGLE GHOST LARVA POOKA
SPOOK TAIPO BOGGLE EMPUSA
PHOOKA REDCAP SHADOW SPIRIT
SPOORN WRAITH BOGGARD
BOGGART BUGBEAR PHANTOM
RAWHEAD REDCOWL SPECTRE
GUYTRASH PHANTASM PRESENCE
REVENANT SPECTRUM
SPECTRAL SPOOKY GHOSTLY
SHADOWY
SPECULATE JOB BEAR STAG
GAMBLE PONDER WONDER
CONSIDER RUMINATE THEORIZE
SPECULATION THEORY THEORIC
VENTURE GAMBLING IDEOLOGY
(DISHONEST —) BUBBLE
(VAGUE —) MYSTICISM
SPECULATIVE ACADEMIC
SPECULATOR PIKER GAMBLER
PLUNGER SCALPER BOURSIER
BUMMAREE OPERATOR
SPECULUM METAL MIRROR
DILATER DIOPTER DIOPTRIC
SPEECH GOB LIP SAW SAY TAT
TOY COAX LEED REDE RUNE TALE
DUALA FRUMP GLOZE LEDEN
LINGO PARLE SERMO SPEAK
SPELL SPIEL SPOKE SQUIB VOICE
BREATH DILOGY EPILOG GAELIC

GASCON GILAKI JARGON LEDDEN
LEMOSI ORISON REASON SALUTE
STEVEN TONGUE ACCENTS
ADDRESS BROCARD EASTERN
MEITHEI ORATION PALABRA
VULGATE EPILOGUE GALICIAN
HARANGUE LANGUAGE LOCUTION
LOQUENCE MORAVIAN PARLANCE
QUESTION SONORITY SPEAKING
(— CHARACTERIZED BY SLURRING)
SLURVIAN
(— FORM) LEXEME
(— IN GREEK DRAMA) RHESIS
(— IN PLAY) SIDE
(— REDUCER) VOCODER
(AFFECTED —) CANT
(BITTER —) DIATRIBE
(BOASTFUL —) BLUSTER
(BOMBASTIC —) SQUIRT
HARANGUE
(COARSE —) HARLOTRY
(CONFUSED —) SPUTTER
(CONTEMPTUOUS —) FRUMP
(IMPUDENT —) SASS
(IRRITABLE —) SNAP
(JAVANESE —) KRAMA
(LONG —) MONOLOG
(LONG-DRAWN —) TIRADE
(MISLEADING —) PALAVER
(MOCKING —) TRIFLE
(OBSCURE —) ENIGMA
(OFFENSIVE —) INJURY
(PERT —) DICACITY
(PRETENTIOUS —) FUSTIAN
(ROUNDABOUT —) CIRCUIT
(SANCTIMONIOUS —) SNUFFLE
(SINGSONG —) CANT
(SLANDEROUS —) EVIL
(VAPID —) WASH
(PREF.) LALO LEXI LOG(O)
PHON(O)
(SUFF.) ESE LEXIA PHASIA
PHEMIA PHEMISM PHEMISTIC
PHRASEO PHRASIA PHRASIS
(— DISORDER) LALIA
SPEECHIFIER SPOUTER
SPEECHLESS DUMB MUTE SILENT
SPEECHMAKING SPOUTING
(— TO GAIN APPLAUSE) BUNKUM
BUNCOMBE
SPEED BAT HIE RIP RUN FLEE
FOOT GAIT HIGH PACE PELT PIKE
PIRR POST TILT BLAST HASTE
HURRY SMOKE WHIRL ASSIST
CAREER FOURTH HASTEN STREAK
QUICKEN WHIZZLE AIRSPEED
CELERITY DISPATCH EXPEDITE
FASTNESS MOMENTUM RAPIDITY
VELOCITY ACCELERATE
(— OF NAUTICAL MILE) KNOT
(— OF PITCH) STUFF
(— OF 100 MILES PER HOUR) TON
(— UP) HASTEN CATALYZE
EXPEDITE
(AT FULL —) AMAIN
(AUTOMOTIVE —) LOW HIGH DRIVE
FIRST THIRD FOURTH SECOND
REVERSE
(DRIVING —) SWING
(GOOD —) BONALLY
(HIGH —) CLIP MACH
(PREF.) DROM(O) TACHO
SPEEDBOAT HYDRO

SPEEDILY CITO SOON APACE
RATHE BELIVE PRESTO BETIMES
HYINGLY QUICKLY TANTIVY
SPEEDING HURTLING
SPEEDWELL CATEYE HENBIT
FLUELLEN NECKWEED NICKWELL
BROOKLIME
SPEEDY FAST SOON HASTY QUICK
RATHE SWIFT RAKING SUDDEN
POSTING TANTIVY EXPEDITE
SPEEDFUL SPINNING POSTHASTE
SPELEOLOGIST CAVEMAN
SPELL GO FIT HEX JAG HACK JINX
MOJO PULL RUNE SCAT TACK
TAKE TIFF TIME TOUR TURN
BRIEF CHARM CRAFT CRASH
MAGIC PATCH SPACE WANGA
WEIRD WHEEL ACCESS GLAMOR
GOOFER GRIGRI GUFFER MAKUTU
MANTRA PERIOD SNATCH STREAK
CANTRIP SORCERY SPELDER
CANTRAIP EXORCISM GREEGREE
MALEFICE PISHOGUE
(— OF ACTIVITY) BOUT
(— OF EXERCISE) BREATHER
(— OF LISTLESSNESS) DOLDRUMS
(— OF SHIVERING) AGUE
(— OF WEATHER) SNAP SLANT
SEASON
(BREATHING —) BLOW
(BRIEF —) SNATCH
(DRINKING —) FUDDLE
(EVIL —) JINX
(FAINTING —) DROW DWALM
(NIPPING —) SNAPE
(STORMY —) FLAW
(VOODOOISTIC —) WANGA
SPELLBIND ENCHANT
SPELLBINDING BASILISK
SPELLING GRAPH WRITING
PHONOGRAPHY
SPELT FAR EMMER FITCH SPELTZ
SPELTZ EMMER
SPENCER TRYSAIL
SPEND BIRL COST DREE DROP
LEAD PASS STOW WARE WEAR
DALLY DREIE SERVE SHOOT
TRADE BESTOW BEWARE EXPEND
LAVISH MOIDER OUTRUN
CONSUME DISPEND EXHAUST
UNPURSE CONFOUND CONTRIVE
DISBURSE
(— FRUITLESSLY) DAWDLE
(— IN IDLENESS) DRONE
(— LAVISHLY) BLUE SPORT
DEBAUCH
(— MONEY) MELT
(— RECKLESSLY) BLOW LASH
(— SUMMER) ESTIVATE
(— TIME) DREE FOOL DREIE
ENTREAT
(— TIME TEDIOUSLY) DRANT
(— WASTEFULLY) SPILL SQUANDER
SPENDTHRIFT WASTER PANURGE
ROUNDER SPENDER WASTREL
PRODIGAL PROFLIGATE
SCATTERGOOD
SPENSER IMMERITO
SPENT DONE WEARY EFFETE
OVERWORN
SPERM SEED SEMINIUM
SPERMACETI SPERM CETACEUM
SPERMOGONIUM PYCNIUM

SPERMOPHILE MARMOT SUSLIK
SPERM WHALE CACHALOT
PHYSETER
SPET SIGNET SINNET
SPEW PUKE SPUE VOMIT
SPHAERIUM CYCLAS
SPHAGION HIERA
SPHAGNUM MUSKEG
SPHALERITE JACK BLENDE
BLACKJACK
SPHENODON TUATARA HATTERIA
SPHERE ORB AREA BALL BOWL
LOKA SHOT FIELD GLOBE ORBIT
RANGE SCOPE CIRCLE CROTAL
DOMAIN HEAVEN REGION
RUNDLE COUNTRY ELEMENT
GLOBOID KINGDOM ORBICLE
PURVIEW EARTHKIN EMPYREAL
EMPYREAN MOVEABLE PROVINCE
TERRITORY
(— OF ACTION) AMBIT ARENA
WORLD DOMAIN
(— OF ACTIVITY) FIELD FRONT
(— OF AUTHORITY) DIOCESE
(— OF INFLUENCE) DOMAIN
SATRAPY
(— OF LIFE) EARTH WORLD
STATION
(— OF OPERATION) THEATER
THEATRE
(— OF WORK) TITLE
(CELESTIAL —) CYCLE ELEMENT
(ENCOMPASSING —) AMBIENT
(MAGNETIZED —) EARTHKIN
TERRELLA
(METAL —) HAMMER
(SMALL —) ORBICLE SPHERULE
(TINKLING —) CROTAL
(PREF.) GLOBO SPHAER(O)
SPHER(O)
SPHERICAL ORBIC GLOBAL
ROTUND GLOBATE GLOBOSE
ORBICAL SPHERIC GLOBULAR
ORBICULAR
(PREF.) GLOBO
SPHERULE GLOBULE VARIOLE
SPHINX MUSTANG COLOSSUS
HAWKMOTH
SPICA AZIMECH
SPICCATO PIQUE
SPICE MACE VEIN AROMA CLOVE
EPICE TASTE GINGER NUTMEG
PEPPER SEASON STACTE SPICERY
SPICING ALLSPICE CINNAMON
SEASONER
SPICEBUSH BENZOIN SNAPWOOD
SPICED SPICY POWDERED
SPICKNEL MEW SCLERE
BEARWORT
SPICULE OXEA TOXA ASTER CHELA
CYMBA DESMA DIACT SIGMA
SPINE STYLE ACTINE ANCHOR
MONACT SCLERE STYLUS TRIACT
TRIPOD TYLOTE CALTROP
DIACTIN EUASTER HEXAXON
MONAXON PINULUS RHABDUS
SPICKLE SPIRULA TETRACT
TORNOTE TRIAENE TRIAXON
TYLOTUS HEXASTER ISOCHELA
OXYASTER POLYAXON SCLERITE
SPHERULA SPICULUM STRONGYL
TETRAXON TRICHITE TYLASTER
(SUFF.) AENE

SPICY RACY SEXY GAMEY NUTTY SWEET SPICED GINGERY PEPPERY FRAGRANT SPICEFUL
SPIDER BUG COB ARAIN ATTID COBBE COPPE LOPPE NANCY TAINT ANANSI ARRAND EPEIRA HUNTER KATIPO TRIVET WEAVER ARANEID CREEPER DRASSID EPEIRID JAYHAWK KNOPPIE POKOMOO RETIARY SERPENT SKILLET SOLDIER SPINNER ARACHNID ATTERCOP CTENIZID DICTYNID ETTERCAP KARAKURT ORBITELE PHALANGE PHALANGY PHOLCOID SALTICID SOLPUGID TELARIAN ULOBORID VENANTES WANDERER TARANTULA
(PART OF —) EYE CLAW COXA FEMUR TIBIA TARSUS ABDOMEN PATELLA PEDICEL SCOPULA SPINNERET METATARSUS PEDIPALPUS TROCHANTER CEPHALOTHORAX
(PREF.) ARACHN(O)
SPIDER CRAB MAIAN MAIID
SPIDERFLOWER QUARESMA
SPIDER MONKEY SAJOU COAITA SAPAJOU
SPIDERWORT TRINITY
SPIELER BARKER
SPIGNEL MEU
SPIGOT TAP SPILE DOSSIL DOZZLE STOPCOCK
SPIKE GAD BARB BROB PICK PIKE PILE SPUR TINE PITON POINT ROUGH SPEAR SPICA SPICK MOOTER PRITCH SPADIX SPIKER TENTER ALICOLE GADLING PRICKER PRICKET TRENAIL TURNPIN SPIKELET STROBILE WHEATEAR
(— A CANNON) CLOY
(— OF CEREAL) EAR
(BRACTED —) AMENT
(DRIED —S) CANNABIS
SPIKED SPICATE SPINDLED
SPIKELET CHAT ALICOLE LOCUSTA SPICULE
SPIKENARD PHU NARD ARALIA SUMBUL ARALIAD IVYWORT SPIGNET SPIGNUT
SPILE TAP SPILL FOREPOLE
SPILL LET DRIP SHED SLOP FLOSH SCALE SKAIL SPILE SQUAB STAVE JIRBLE PURLER SLATTER SLOBBER TURNOVER
(— FOR LIGHTING PIPES) FIDIBUS
SPIN CUT BIRL DRAW GYRE HURL PIRL PURL SCREW SPONE TWIRL TWIST WEAVE WHIRL FOLLOW GYRATE VRILLE WAMBLE TWIZZLE TEETOTUM
(— AND MAKE HUM) BUM
(— AROUND) SWING
(— ON BASEBALL) STUFF
(— ON BILLIARD BALL) SIDE
(— OUT) SHOOT
(— SILK) THROW
(— SMOOTHLY) SLEEP
(— UNEVENLY) TWITTER
SPINACH SAVOY EPINARD OLITORY POTHERB
SPINAL CORD AXION

NUCHA MYELON
(WHITE MATTER OF —) ALBA NUKE
(PREF.) MYEL(O)
(SUFF.) MYELIA
SPINDLE PIN AXLE HASP PIRN SPIT STEM STUD ARBOR FLOAT QUILL SPIKE SPILL VERGE BOBBIN BROACH CANNON FUSEAU BOLSTER MANDREL SPINNEL TRENDLE WHARROW
(AXLE —) ARM
(FOURTH OF —) HASP
(ONE 24TH OF —) HEER
(PREF.) FUSI
SPINDLE TREE GAITER DOGWOOD PEGWOOD EUONYMUS
SPINDLING SPEARY SPINDLY SPIRLIE
SPINDLY LEGGY PULING
SPINE HORN PIKE PILE SETA SPUR CHINE PRICK QUILL SPEAR SPIKE SPINA THORN ACUMEN CHAETA RACHIS ACANTHA ACICULA FULCRUM GLOCHIS PAXILLA PRICKER PRICKLE ROSTRUM SPINULE STICKLE ACICULUM BACKBONE ILLICIUM PAXILLUS PELELITH SPICULUM SPINELET
(— OF SURGEON FISH) TUCK
(CURVATURE OF —) LORDOSIS
(PREF.) ACANTH(O) RACHI(O) RHACHI(O)
(SUFF.) ACANTHUS CHAETA CHAETES CHAETUS RACHIDIA RHACHIS RRHACHIS
SPINEL BALAS CANDITE ESPINEL GAHNITE VERMEIL PICOTITE SPINELLE
SPINELESS SLAVISH
SPINET ESPINET GIRAFFE OCTAVINA SOURDINE VIRGINAL
SPINNERET GALEA MAMMULA SPINNER
SPINNING STROBIC LANIFICE
(— WEB) TELARIAN
SPINNING JENNY MULE JENNY
SPINNING MULE IRONMAN
SPINNING WHEEL TURN CHARKHA CHURRUCK
(PART OF —) BAND FLYER WHEEL BOBBIN DISTAFF SPINDLE TREADLE STANDARD
SPINSTER TABBY VIRGIN
SPINULE
(PL.) CTENII
SPINY PICKED THORNY
(PREF.) ACANTH(O) CENTR(I)(O) ECHIN(O)
SPINY OYSTER SPONDYLE
SPINY RAT OCTODONT
SPIRACLE STOMA STIGMA BLOWHOLE
SPIRAEA MAY ROSACEAN MEADOWSWEET
SPIRAL COIL CURL GYRE SPIN SCREW SNARE SPIRE BUTTON GURGES LITUUS SCREWY SCROLL SPIRED TWIRLY VOLUTE HELICAL ROLLING SPIROID STROPHE WINDING WREATHY GYROIDAL HELICINE HELICOID
(LACEWORK —) PURL
(PREF.) GYR(O) HELI HELIC(O)

SPIRANT VAU WAW HISS OPEN DURATIVE
SPIRANTHES IBIDIUM
SPIRE CROWN SHAFT SIKAR SPEAR TAPER TOLLY BROACH FLECHE PRICKET SHIKARA SIKHARA SPIRALE SPIRELET
SPIRE-BEARER SPIRIFER
SPIREME SKEAN SKEIN
SPIRIT GO FLY NAG PEP VIM AITU AKUA ALMA ATUA BRIO DASH DOOK ELAN FIRE GALL GIMP HYLE JINN LIFE MARC MARE MIND MOOD SOUL TONE ZEMI ZING AGIEL ARDOR ARIEL ASURA AZOTH CHEER DEMON DHOUL DJINN DOBBY ETHOS FLING GEIST GHOST GORIC GUACA HAUNT HEART HOLDA HUACA JINNI LARVA NUMEN PLUCK POWER PRETA RALPH SAINT SHADE SHRAB SPOOK SPUNK VERVE ASTRAL ASUANG BOTTOM BREATH CHULPA COURIL DAEMON ESPRIT FAINTS FLECHE FYLGJA GENIUS GINGER INWARD KOBOLD LESHEY METTLE MORALE ORISHA PAZAZZ PECKER PIZAZZ PNEUMA PYTHON SPRAWL SPRITE TAFFIA WRAITH ALCOHOL BRAVERY CONTROL CORDIAL COURAGE ENTRAIN EUDEMON KNOCKER MANITOU PISACHI PIZZAZZ PURUSHA RAPPIST SMEDDUM STOMACH CALVADOS ERDGEIST FAMILIAR FOLLETTO PHANTASM SPIRACLE SPIRITUS
(— DWELLING IN JEWEL) AZOTH
(— DWELLING IN MINES) KNOCKER
(— HAUNTING PRINTING HOUSES) RALPH
(— OF DEAD) CHINDI CHINDEE
(— OF DEATH) CHULPA
(— OF DECEASED) AKH
(— OF FERTILITY) YAKSA YAKSHA YAKSHI
(— OF HOSTILITY) ANIMUS
(— OF LOYALTY) PIETAS
(— OF MAN) AKH
(— OF ONE WHO HAS MET VIOLENT DEATH) PISACHI
(— OF PHYSICAL HEART) AB
(— OF TRAGEDY) COTHURN
(— OF UNBAPTIZED BABE) TARAN
(— WHICH ACTUATES CUSTOMS) ETHOS
(—S OF LOWER WORLD) INFERI
(—S OF THE DEAD) MANES
(ANCESTRAL —) ANITO KATCHINA
(ARDENT —) RAK RACK ARRACK
(ASTRAL —) AGIEL ASTRAL JOPHIEL UUCHATON
(AVENGING —) FURY ALECTO ALASTOR MEGAERA
(CHARACTERISTIC —) VIBE
(COMBATIVE —) SWORD
(DISEMBODIED —) KUEI KWEI SOUL GHOST LARVA SHADE ASUANG SPECTER SPECTRE
(DIVINE —) ISVARA ISHVARA
(EARTH —) ERDGEIST
(EFFULGENT —S) ARDORS
(EMANCIPATED —) MUKTATMA

(EVIL —) DEV DIV HAG IMP OKI BAKA BENG BOKO BOLL DEVA DUSE MARA OKEE ASURA BUGAN DAEVA DEMON DEVIL JUMBY OTKON DAITYA DIBBUK DYBBUK LILITH AHRIMAN BUGGANE CASZIEL INCUBUS KANAIMA RAKSHAS SHAITAN SHEITAN SKOOKUM WINDIGO ASMODEUS BAALPEOR BEELPEOR HOBOMOCO NIGHTMARE
(FAMILIAR —) FLY GENIUS HARPIER
(FEMALE —) DUFFY DUPPY DUSIO HOLDA UNDINE BANSHEE ATAENSIC BABAJAGA BELFAGOR BELFAZOR
(FIGHTING —) DEVIL
(FOREST —) MIMING
(FULL OF —) CRANK
(FULL OF —S) BRAG
(GOOD —) DEVA EUDEMON
(GOVERNING —) ANIMUS
(GUARDIAN —) ANGEL TOTEM FYLGJA NAGUAL
(HIGH —) GINGER COURAGE
(HIGH —S) CREST GAIETY HEYDAY ELATION
(HOSTILE —S) LEMURES
(HOUSEHOLD —S) LARES PENATES
(HUMAN —) JIVATMA
(IMPISH —) PO
(IMPURE —) FAINTS
(IN VIGOROUS —S) FIERCE
(LOW —S) DUMP BLUES MEGRIM DISMALS
(MALEVOLENT —) BHUT GORIC LARVA
(MALICIOUS —) DOBBY
(MALIGNANT —) IMP KER GYRE DEMON
(MANLY —) SPLEEN
(MISCHIEVOUS —) KOBOLD TIKOLOSH
(MOUNTAIN —) RUBEZAHL
(MOVING —) SOUL
(MUSICAL —) BRIO
(NATURE —) NAT
(PARTY —) FACTION
(REFINED —) ELIXIR
(RESOLUTE —) SPRAWL
(ROVING —) RAMPLER
(SEA —) TANGIE
(SENSED —) KARMA
(SOOTHSAYING —) PYTHON
(SUPERNATURAL —) FAMILIAR
(SYLVAN —) LESHY SYLVAN
(TRICKSY —) ARIEL
(TUTELARY —S) DIS LARES
(VITAL —) TUCK
(VOLATILE —) ESSENCE
(WATER —) ARIEL KELPY UNDINE
(WICKED —) IMP THURSE
(PL.) GENII IGIGI DAUBER
(PREF.) PNEUMAT(O) PSYCH(O) THYM(O)
(SUFF.) THYMIA
SPIRITED BRAG FELL GOGO RACY TALL BEANY BIRKY CRANK EAGER FIERY FLUSH KEDGE KINKY LIFEY PEPPY PROUD SASSY SEEDY SMART SPICY VIVID AUDACE FIERCE GINGER LIVELY METTLE

PLUCKY SKEIGH SPRUCE SPUNKY
VIVACE ANIMATO DASHING
FORWARD HUMMING NERVOUS
PEPPERY SPIRITY DESIROUS
FRAMPOLD GENEROUS
PHRAMPEL SLASHING STOMACHY
VASCULAR
SPIRITEDLY GAMELY
SPIRITLESS DEAD DOWF MEAN
MEEK POOR TAME AMORT FAINT
MILKY MUSTY SEEDY SOGGY
VAPID ABJECT ANEMIC CRAVEN
DREEPY FLASHY JEJUNE LEADEN
SODDEN SOFTLY WOODEN
HILDING INSIPID LANGUID
FECKLESS FLAGGING LISTLESS
THEWLESS
SPIRITLESSLY DAVIELY
SPIRITLESSNESS LANGUOR
SPIRITLIKE ETHEREAL
SPIRITS LACE RAKI HOOCH MANES
FETTLE PECKER FEATHER
LEMURES SAMSHOO WAIPIRO
SPIRITUAL ABOVE DEVOUT
INWARD MISTLY GHOSTLY
CHURCHLY INTERNAL NUMINOUS
SUPERIOR PNEUMATIC
(— LEADER) ZADDIK
SPIRITUALISM SPOOKISM
SPIRITUALITY HEAVEN
SPIRITUALIZE REFINE
SPIRITUOUS HARD
SPIROCHETE BORRELIA
SPIT YEX FUFF RACK FROTH REACH
SPAWL BROACH SPITTLE
SANDSPIT SPITTING
(— AND POLISH) BULL
(SUFF.) PTYSIS
SPITE ENVY ONDE DEPIT LIVOR
PIQUE VENOM MALICE MAUGRE
RANCOR SPLEEN DESPITE
AMBITION
SPITEFUL MEAN CATTY NASTY
NEBBY PETTY SNAKY ELVISH
MALIGN SULLEN WANTON
WICKED CATTISH ENVIOUS
PEEVISH SNAKISH VICIOUS
WASPISH CANKERED KNAPPISH
VENOMOUS
SPITFIRE CACAFOGO PEPPERBOX
SPITTING FUFF EMPTYSIS
SPITTING SNAKE RINGHALS
SPITTLE SPIT SPAWL SPUTUM
SLOBBER
(PREF.) PTYAL(O)
SPITTOON GABOON PIGDAN
SPITBOX CRACHOIR CUSPIDOR
SPIV RORTER
SPLAKE MENDIGO
SPLANCHNIC VISCERAL
SPLASH JAW LAP DASH GLOB
GOUT JAUP LOSH LUSH SKIT
SOSS SPAT WASH BLASH FLASH
FLICK FLOOD FLOSH PLASH
PLOUT QUASH SKIRP SLART
SLASH SLOSH SLUSH SQUAT
SWILK BEDASH DABBLE DOLLOP
FLOUSE JABBLE LABBER PLATCH
SLUNGE SOZZLE SPLOSH SPRENT
SQUIRT PLOUTER SPATTER
SPIRTLE SPLODGE SPLURGE
SWATTER SPLAIRGE SPLAtHER
SPLATTER SPLOTHER

SPLUTHER SPLUTTER
(— OF COLOR) GOUT
(SLIGHT —) GILP
SPLASHBOARD FENDER
SPLASHER
SPLASHING SWASH FLASHY
JABBLE DASHING SPATTER
SPLUTTER SWASHING
SPLASHY BLASHY SLOPPY
SPRAWLY
SPLATTER DASH BLASH SPLAIRGE
SPLAY FLAN
SPLAYED FLEW FLUE
SPLAYFOOT FLATFOOT
SPLEEN IRE PIP BILE LIEN MELT
MILT RHEUM MALICE STOMACH
(PREF.) LIEN(O) SPLEN(I)(O)
(SUFF.) SPLENIA
SPLEENY PEEVISH
SPLENDID GAY BRAW FINE NEAT
RIAL BRAVE GRAND JOLLY NOBLE
PROUD REGAL ROYAL SHEEN
SHOWY STOUT TOUGH WALLY
WLONK CANDID COSTLY SIGHTY
SOLEMN SPIFFY SUPERB ELEGANT
GALLANT SHINING SUBLIME
TEARING BARONIAL CHAMPION
CLINKING COLOSSAL GLORIOUS
GORGEOUS MAJESTIC ORGULOUS
RATTLING SLASHING SPANKING
STUNNING TERRIFIC
(CHEAPLY —) TINNY
SPLENDIDLY FINE FINELY
SPROWSY
SPLENDOR SUN UMA GITE LUXE
POMP BLAZE GLARE GLEAM
GLORY SHEEN SHINE FULGOR
LUSTER LUSTRE PARADE RUFFLE
CLARITY DISPLAY JOLLITY
PANACHE GRANDEUR RADIANCE
SUMPTURE
SPLENETIC SULLEN VAPORY
PEEVISH
SPLENIC LIENAL
SPLICE FOOT JOIN SCAB PIECE
SCARE SKELB CROTCH PIECEN
SPLICING
SPLICER STRAPPER
SPLINE FIN FEATHER
SPLINT SCOB FANON MATCH
SPELK SPELL TASSE SPLENT
THOMAS CALIPER SPLINTER
(— FOR FRACTURE) JUNK
SPLINTER BROOM BURST PURSE
SHAKE SHIDE SHIVE SKELB SKELF
SLICE SPAIL SPALE SPALL SPALT
SPEEL SPELK SPELL SPILE SPILL
SPLIT SPOON SLIVER SPLEET
SPLINT FLINDER SHATTER
SLITHER SPLITTER
SPLINTERY SKELVY
SPLINTWOOD ALBURNUM
SPLIT AX AXE CUT RIT BUCK CHAP
CONE DUNT GAIG MALL MAUL
RASH REND RENT RIFT RIVE SKAG
SLAT TEAR BLAST BREAK BURST
CHECK CHINE SHAKE SHEAR
SKIVE SLENT SLIVE SMASH SPALD
SPALL SPLAT CLEAVE CLOVEN
CREASE DIVIDE FLAGGY FLERRY
SCHISM SPRING SUNDER BIVALVE
SHATTER SLITHER CREVASSE
SCISSION SCISSURE SPLINTER

(— FISH) SCROD
(— IN BOWLING) BEDPOSTS
(— OFF) SPALL SPAWL SCREEVED
(— TICKET) SCRATCH
(PREF.) SCHISTO SCHIZ(O)
SPLITTERMAN BOLTER
SPLITTING FLAGGY FISSION
SCISSION
(PL.) FILMS
(SUFF.) RHEXIS RRHEXIS
SPLOTCH DAB BLOB DASH HALO
SPOT FLICK SMUDGE SPECKLE
SPLATCH SPLURGE
SPLURGE BINGE SPRAY SPREE
SPLASH
SPLUTTER FUFF GLUTTER
SPATTER SPUTTER SPLOTHER
SPODOPTERA LAPHYGMA
SPODUMENE KUNZITE TRIPHANE
SPOIL MAR MUX ROT BLOT BOOT
COOK DAZE FANG FOIL FRAB
GAIN KILL MANK PELF PREY
ADDLE BITCH BLEND BLUNK
BOOTY BOTCH CROSS DECAY
LOUSE QUAIL QUEER SHEND
SPILL STAIN STRIP TOUCH TRASH
WALLY BOODLE BUGGER COOPER
CORPSE COSSET CURDLE DEFACE
DEFORM FORAGE INJURE
MANGLE PERISH RAVAGE TIDDLE
BAUCHLE BEDEVIL BLEMISH
CONNACH CORRUMP CORRUPT
ESTREPE INDULGE MULLOCK
PILLAGE PLUNDER SPOLIUM
TARNISH VIOLATE BANKRUPT
CONFOUND DISGRACE MISGUIDE
SPOLIATE
SPOILED BAD BLOWN DAZED
MUSTY CADISH STICKIT BRATTISH
(EASILY —) GINGER
SPOILER HARROWER
SPOILERS (AUTHOR OF —) BEACH
(CHARACTER IN —) ROY BILL
HELEN CHERRY DEXTRY STRUVE
CHESTER MALOTTE MCNAMARA
STILLMAN GLENISTER
SPOILFIVE MAW
SPOILS BAG LOOT SKIN SWAG
BOOTY FORAY SPOLIA PILLAGE
PLUNDER PICKINGS
SPOILSPORT NARK LETGAME
SPOILT MARDY
SPOKE RUNG QUOTH SPACK SPAKE
LOWDER SPONDIL SPONDYL
SPOKEN ORAL SAID VERBAL
SPOKESMAN MOUTH HERALD
PROPHET SPEAKER TRUMPET
MOUTHPIECE
SPOLIATION REIF SPOIL RAPINE
PILLAGE PLUNDER SPOILING
SPONGE BOT FORM MUMP POLE
SILK SORN SWAB ASCON CADGE
GRASS LUFFA SCAFF SHARK
SHIRK SHOOL SYCON ASCULA
BUMMER COSHER LEUCON
LOOFAH MALKIN MOPPET
RHAGON ROLLER YELLOW
BADIAGA BLEEDER GELFOAM
RADIATE SCOURER SCRUNGE
SYCONID ZIMOCCA DEADBEAT
HARDHEAD HEDGEHOG
MANDRUKA OLYNTHUS
REDBEARD SCROUNGE SILICEAN

SPHERIDA SUBERITE ZOOPHYTE
PORIFERAN
(YOUNG —) SEEDLING
(SUFF.) AENE
SPONGER BOT BUM TRAMP
BUMMER CADGER SPONGE
SCAMBLER SMOOTHER
SPONGINESS FOZINESS
SPONGING TRENCHER
SPONGY FOZY FUZZY QUAGGY
BIBULOUS
SPONSOR COACH GOSSIP SURETY
WITNESS
(— AT BAPTISM) HEAVE
SPONSORSHIP EGIS AEGIS
SPONTANEOUS FREE CARELESS
FREEWILL UNTAUGHT
SPONTANEOUSLY KINDLY SELFLY
SPOOK GYRE GHOST HAUNT
SCARE
SPOOL COB COP PIRN REEL QUILL
SPILL SPULE TWEEL TWILL
BOBBIN BROACH CHEESE COPPIN
CARRIER
(— FOR NETS) GURDY
SPOON HORN CUTTY LABIS SHELL
COCHLEA JUMBLER MUDDLER
SKIMMER SPINNER STIRRER
BARSPOON COCHLEAR GOBSTICK
(EUCHARISTIC —) LABIS
(FISHING —) TROLL
(LONG-HANDLED —) LADLE
(SKIMMING —) LINGEL SKIMMER
(SNUFF —) PEN
(PREF.) COCHLEARI LIGUL(I)
SPOONBILL AJAJA SPOONY
POPELER CICONIID
(PREF.) PLATALEI
SPOONFUL COCHLEARE
SPOON-SHAPED COCHLEAR
SPATULAR
SPOOR SIGN SPUR PISTE
SPORADIC POPPING ISOLATED
SPORANGIUM THECA OOTHECA
SPORE CYST SEED SPORID
AGAMETE AKINETE BISPORE
ISOLANT ISOLATE OOSPORE
SPORULE SWARMER CONIDIUM
EXOSPORE GONIDIUM
PROPAGULE
SPORES
(PREF.) CONI(DI)
SPOROCYST ZOOCYST SPOROSAC
SPORT FUN GIG KID MUM RIE RUX
SEE TOY ALSO GAME GAUD GLEE
JEST JOKE LAKE LARK PLAY PLOY
RAGE TAIT BOURD BREAK DALLY
DROLL FREAK MIRTH FROLIC
LAUGHS POPJOY RACING SHIKAR
SKIING BOATING CAMOGIE
DISPORT DUCKING FOWLING
MARLOCK PASTIME ROLLICK
ROUNDER SAILING SPANIEL
FALCONRY PLEASURE SKYDIVING
MOUNTAINEERING
(— OF HAWKING) RIVER
(BOISTEROUS —) HIJINKS
(JAPANESE —) KENDO AIKIDO
(ROUGH —) ROMP
(WATER —S) NAUTICS AQUATICS
(WINTER —) SKIJORING
(PREF.) LUDI
SPORTING VARMINT SPORTIVE

SPORTIVE GAY TAIT LARKY MERRY
FRISKY JOCUND LIVELY LUSORY
TOYFUL TOYING WANTON
COLTISH FESTIVE GAMEFUL
JESTING JOCULAR PLAYFUL
TOYSOME TRICKSY WAGGISH
FROLICKY GAMESOME PLAYSOME
PLEASANT SPORTFUL
SPORTIVENESS HELL KNAVERY
SPORTSMAN SPORT ATHLETE
SHIKARI
SPORTSMANLIKE CLEAN SPORTY
SPORTY FLASH RORTY FLASHY
RAKISH
SPORULE GRANULE
SPOT BIT DAB PIP WEM BLOT BLUR
CHUB DIRT DRAB FLAW GALL
MAIL MOIL MOLE PLOT SCAM SITE
SKIP SLUR SMUT SOIL SPAT TICK
AMPER BLACK CLOUD FLECK
GARLE GOODY GUTTA HATCH
JIMMY MACLE PATCH PLACE
PLECK POINT ROACH SMEAR
SPLAT STAIN SULLY TACHE TAINT
WHERE BLANCH BLOTCH DAPPLE
FOGDOG GERATE MACULE
MAZUCA MOTTLE SMUDGE
SMUTCH SPLECK STIGMA
BLEMISH CHARBON CHECKER
FLECKER FRECKLE GUTTULA
MASOOKA OCELLUS OLDWIFE
SMATTER SMITTER SPATTER
SPECKLE SPLOTCH SPOTTLE
STATION STIPPLE TERRAIN
FENESTRA LOCALITY MACULATE
PUNCTULE SPARKLET SPRINKLE
(— A SHIELD) GERATE
(— IN CLOTH) YAW
(— IN MINERAL) MACLE
(— IN PAPER) SHINER
(— IN SAW BLADE) BLOB
(— IN STEEL) STAR
(— IN WOOD) WEM
(— IN YARN) MOTE
(— OF INK) MONK
(— OF PAINT) DAUB
(— OF QUICKSAND) SUCKHOLE
(— ON CAT) BUTTON
(— ON CAT'S FACE) LAVALIER
(— ON EGG) EYE
(— ON FINGERNAIL) GIFT
(— ON FOREHEAD) TILAK TILAKA
(— ON HAWK) GOUT
(— ON HORSE) RACE SNIP STAR
RACHE
(— ON HORSE'S TOOTH) CHARBON
(— ON INSECT WINGS) BULLA
(— ON MOTH'S WINGS) FENESTRA
(— ON PLAYING CARD) PIP
(— ON SUN) FACULA GRANULE
SUNSPOT
(—S IN BOOKS) FOXING
(BARREN —) GALL
(BLIND —) SCOTOMA SCOTOSIS
(BROWN —) SPRAIN SPRAING
(CRUSTY —) SCAB
(ESSENTIAL —) EYE
(FERTILE —) OASIS
(FIRM —) HAG
(GREEN — IN VALLEY) HAW
(HALLOWED —) BETHEL
(INFLAMED —) AMPER
(LEAF —) TIKKA BLACKARM

(LIVER —S) CHLOASMA
(LIVID —) TOKEN
(LOW —) DIP SWAMP HOLLOW
(RED —) FLEABITE
(RETIRED —) SHADE
(ROUGH — IN WOVEN GOODS) FAG
(ROUND —) BLOB
(SCABBY —) SCALD
(SECLUDED —) ALCOVE CLOISTER
(SHADY —) SWALE
(SKIN —) MOLE BLISTER FRECKLE
LENTIGO PETECHIA
(SMALL —) DOT PLECK STIGMA
LUNULET SPARKLET
(SOILED —) SLOP
(SORE —) BUBU BOTCH
(SWAMPY —) FLAM
(TIGHT —) JAM JACKPOT
(WEAK —) GALL HOLE CHINK
NERVE
(WORN —) FRAY FRET
(PL.) MOONING
(PREF.) MACUL(I)(O) SPIL(O)
SPOTLESS FAIR PURE WEMLESS
INNOCENT
SPOTLIGHT ARC SPOT DEUCE
SPOTTED PIED MARLY SCOVY
SHELD CALICO FIGGED HAWKED
MACLED MAILED MARLED MIRLED
PARDED SPOTTY TICKED
BRACKET BROOKED FINCHED
GUTTATE MOTTLED PARDINE
PIEBALD PINTADO SPARKED
SPECKED SPECKLY TIGROID
FRECKLED LITURATE MACULOSE
SPECKLED STIPPLED
(SUFF.) MACULATE
SPOTTED EAGLE RAY MILLER
OBISPO
SPOTTED FLYCATCHER COBWEB
RAFTER WALLBIRD
SPOTTED GUM EUCALYPT
SPOTTED JEWFISH GUASA
SPOTTED SANDPIPER TIPUP
TILTUP CREEKER TIPTAIL
PEETWEET
SPOTTED SPURGE DOVEWEED
SPOTTED WINTERGREEN
RATSBANE
SPOTTED WOODPECKER PICUS
WITWALL
SPOTTER DOTTER
SPOTTY MEALY PATCHY PLATTY
SCABBY SPOTTED
SPOUSE EX FERE MAKE WIFE
BRIDE MATCH PARTY FELLOW
MARROW CONSORT ESPOUSE
HUSBAND
SPOUT JET LIP BEAK DALE GEAT
GUSH NOSE SHOE ORATE SPILE
SPUME SPURT NOZZLE RIGGOT
SPLOIT SPROUT STRONE STROUP
BUBBLER FOUNTAIN GARGOYLE
(RAIN —) RONE
SPOUTER VAPORER
SPOUTING BLOW SALIENT
SPRAG TRAILER
SPRAGGER SCOTCHER
SPRAIN RICK CHINK STAVE THRAW
THROW WRAMP WREST WRICK
STRAIN WRENCH STREMMA
SPRAT SMY BLAY BRIT BRITT
SPRET SPRIT GARVIE ALFIONE

GARVOCK BRISLING
(—S CAUGHT EARLY IN SEASON)
DROVE
SPRAWL LOLL TAVE SPURL
SCRAWL GRABBLE SCAMBLE
SPARTLE SPELDER SCRAMBLE
SPRADDLE SPRANGLE STRADDLE
SPRAWLING SPRANGLY
SPRAY FOG HOSE SCUD SPRY
STEW SPREE STOUR SWISH TRAIL
TWIST SHOWER SPARGE SPLASH
SPRANG SPRITZ CURTAIN
SPAIRGE SYRINGE INHALANT
SPRANGLE
(— FROM SMALL WAVES) LIPPER
(— MASH) SPARGE
(— OF GEMS) AIGRETTE
(REDUCE TO —) NEBULIZE
SPREAD BED FAN LAY RUN COAT
DRAW FLUE SPAN TEER TELD
TUCK VEIN WALK APPLY CLEAM
CREEP FLARE KILIM PASTE SCALE
SLICE SPEND SPLAT SPLAY STALK
STREW WIDEN BUTTER EXTEND
FLANGE LARDER LAYOUT MANTLE
SETOUT THRUST UNFOLD
UNFURL BROADEN CANVASS
DIFFUSE DISPLAY DISTEND
EXPANSE EXPLAIN FEATHER
OPENING SCATTER STRETCH
DIASPORA DISPENSE DISPERSE
HUMIFUSE INCREASE MULTIPLY
SPLATHER STRAGGLE
(— ABROAD) TOOT BLAZE DELATE
SPRING DIVULGE EMANATE
(— APART) GAPE
(— AS GOSSIP) BUZZ
(— BY REPORT) BLOW NOISE
NORATE
(— DEFAMATION) LIBEL
(— FOR DRYING) TED
(— INTO) INVADE
(— LIKE GRAIN) FLOOR
(— NEWS) HORN
(— ON THICK) COUCH SLATHER
(— OUT) FAN FLOW OPEN ROLL
SPAN ASPAR BREDE SPLAT SPLAY
SPRAY EXPAND FLANGE FRINGE
MANTLE OUTLAY SPRAWL
UNLOCK DIFFUSE DISPAND
DISTENT EXPLAIN FEATHER
DIFFUSED SPRADDLE SPRANGLE
STRAGGLY
(— OUTWARD) FLARE
(— OVER) LAP DASH COVER
SUFFUSE
(— PAINT) KNIFE
(— THINLY) BRAY DRIVE TOUCH
SCANTY
(— TO) CATCH
(— TO THE WIND) SET
(EVENLY —) SUANT
(TAPESTRY-WOVEN —) KILIM
(PREF.) STRATO
(SUFF.) CHORE
SPREADER PLOW PLOUGH
SANDER
SPREADING FLAN BUSHY FLANGE
PATENT ASPREAD DIFFUSE
FLARING SPRAYEY PATULENT
PATULOUS SPRANGLY
(— OF LIGHT) HALATION
(— RAPIDLY) RUNNING

(NOT —) ERECT
(SLOW —) CREEPAGE
SPREE BAT BUM JAG BLOW BUST
GELL LARK RANT SOAK TEAR
TIME TOOT BEANO BINGE BOOZE
BURST DRINK DRUNK SOUSE
SPRAY BENDER BUSTER HOORAY
HURRAH JUNKET RANDAN
RANTAN RAZZLE SPLORE
BLOWOFF JAMBOREE WINGDING
SPRIG POINT
(—S FOR MOURNING) CYPRESS
SPRIGGER STRIPPER
SPRIGHTLINESS GAIETY AIRINESS
ALACRITY BUOYANCY VIVACITY
SPRIGHTLY GAY TID AIRY GNIB
PERT WARM ALIVE BRISK CANTY
CRISP DESTO MERRY PERKY
QUICK ALEGER BLITHE BREEZY
JAUNTY LIVELY SPANKY SPRACK
WIMBLE CHIPPER DELIVER
JOCULAR SPARKLY LIFESOME
PLEASANT
SPRING EN AIN BUG EYE FLY HOP
JET OJO URN VER WAX BATH
BOLT BOUT BUCK BUNT DART
FLOW FONT GEON HAIR HEAD
JUMP KELD LEAP PERT RISE SEEP
SKIP SOAK STEM URNA WALM
WARE WELL WIND YOAR ARISE
BOUND DANCE FLIRT FOUNT
FRESH GIHON GLENT GRASS
ISSUE LYMPH PRIME QUELL SALLY
SOURD SPEND SPOUT START
STEND SURGE THROW VAULT
BOUNCE CHARCO DERIVE
GAMBOL GEYSER JUMPER LOCKET
ORIGIN PIRENE RESORT RESULT
SILOAM SOURCE SPRINT VENERO
BUDTIME EMANATE ESTUARY
FLOUNCE GAMBADO PROCEED
REBOUND WRAPPER BACKSTAY
BANDUSIA CASTALIA FOUNTAIN
SPANGHEW ORIGINATE
(— AWKWARDLY) KEVEL
(— BACK) RECOIL RESULT RETORT
REBOUND
(— DOWN) ALIGHT
(— FORWARD) LAUNCH
(— FROM) DESCEND
(— OF THE YEAR) VER VOAR
(— ON SHEARS) BACKSTAY
(— SEASON) APRIL GRASS
BUDTIME
(— SUDDENLY) FLY BOUNCE
(— TO FASTEN NECKLACE) LOCKET
(— UP) ARISE SHOOT SPROUT
BURGEON UPSPRING
(BOILING —) TUBIG
(CARRIAGE —) ROBBIN
(ERUPTIVE —) WALM GEYSER
(GUSHING —) CHARCO
(HOT —) SPRUDEL
(INTERMITTENT —) NAILBOURN
(INTERMITTENT —S) GIPSIES
GYPSIES
(LAND —) LAVANT
(MECHANICAL —) RESORT
RESSORT
(MINERAL —) SPA BALNEARY
(SALT —) LICK SALINE
(WARM —S) THERMAE
(WATCH —) SLEEVE

(PREF.) CREN(O) CROUNO PEGO
(SUFF.) CRENE
SPRING BEAUTY LETTUCE
SPRINGBOARD BATULE TREMPLIN
SPRINGBOK GAZELLE SPRINGER
SPRING CHAPLET JAMMER
SPRINGE TRAP NOOSE SNARE
SPRINGILY BOUNCILY SPONGILY
SPRINGINESS GIVE LIFE
SPRINGING LAUNCH SALIENT
  (— BACK) RESULT ELASTIC
  (— FROM STEPS) GRADY
SPRINGLIKE VERNAL
SPRING ORANGE STYRAX
SPRINGTAIL PODURA FURCULA
  PODURID SKIPTAIL
SPRINGTIME VER WARE
  GERMINAL
SPRINGY WHIPPY ELASTIC
  FLEXIBLE
SPRINKLE ASH DAG DEG BLOW
  DAMP SHED SPIT FLASH SHAKE
  SPURT WATER BEDROP DABBLE
  POUNCE SPARGE SPRENT SPRINK
  SQUIRT ARROUSE ASPERGE
  ASPERSE DRIZZLE RANTIZE
  SCATTER SKINKLE SKITTER
  SPAIRGE SPARKLE SPARPLE
  SPATTER SPATTLE SPERPLE
  SPURTLE DISPUNGE INTERSOW
  SPITTING SPRINGLE STRINKLE
  (— IN BAPTISM) RANTIZE
  (— OF RAIN) SPIT
  (— SEED) SPRAIN
  (— TOBACCO) BLOW
  (— WITH FLOUR) DREDGE
  (— WITH POWDER) DUST
  (— WITH SALT) CORN
  (— WITH SAND) SAND
SPRINKLED SEEDED SPRENT
  (— OVER) BESPRENT
SPRINKLER SPARGER SPRAYER
  WATERER DAMPENER STRINKLE
  (HOLY WATER —) HYSSOP
SPRINKLING SEME LACING
  SPARGE STRANK RANTISM
  STIPPLE STOURING
  (— OF PEOPLE) SALT
SPRINT BICKER SPRENT SPRUNT
SPRITE ELF HOB PUG PIXY PUCK
  BUCCA DOBBY FAIRY HOLDA
  PIXIE GOBLIN PILWIZ SPIRIT
  SPOORN UMBRIEL COLTPIXY
  GLAISTIG WATERMAN
  (WATER —) NIX NECK NIXIE
  NICKER
SPRITELY WIMBLE
SPROCKET WHELP
SPROUT BUD LAD PUT BROD CHIT
  CHUN CION DRAW TOOT CATCH
  CHICK SCUTE SHOOT SPEAR
  SPIRE SPRIT SPURT BRAIRD
  GERMEN RATOON SIRING STOVEN
  TELLER TILLER BURGEON
  COPPICE SPURTER TENDRON
  BOURGEON PULLULATE
  (— OF BARLEY) TAIL
  (FIRST —S) BREER BRAIRD BREIRD
  (STUMP —) TILLER
  (PREF.) BLAST(O) CLAD(O)
  CYM(I)(O)
  (SUFF.) BLAST(IC)(Y) CLADOUS
  SPERM(A)(AE)(AL)(IA)(IC)(OUS)

(UM)(Y)
SPRUCE GIM DEFT JIMP NEAT
  POSH SMUG SPRY TRIG TRIM
  BRISK COMPT CRISP DINKY FRESH
  JEMMY JIMMY NATTY NIFTY
  SLICK SMART SMIRK SPIFF SPRIG
  DAPPER PICKED SPONGE SPRUNT
  SPRUSH FINICAL FOPPISH
  SMARTEN SMICKER SPRUNNY
  EPINETTE SPIFFING TITIVATE
  (TRIMMED —) LOBSTICK
SPRUE RUNNER PSILOSIS
SPRUER GATER
SPRY AGILE BRISK QUICK NIMBLE
  BOBBISH
SPUD SPADE TATER BARKER
  PADDLE POTATO SPUDDER
SPUME EST BEES FOAM FROTH
  YEAST
SPUNK GETUP SPRAWL SMEDDUM
SPUR ARM GAD GIG EDGE GAFF
  GOAD KNAG MOVE STUD TANG
  ARETE DRIVE PRICK PRONG
  ROWEL SPICA SPURN BROACH
  CALCAR DIGGER EXCITE FILLIP
  FOMENT GAFFLE GRIFFE INCITE
  MOTIVE OFFSET RIPPON SICKLE
  SPERON WEAPON BICYCLE
  GABLOCK INCITER LORMERY
  SCRATCH COCKSPUR GAVELOCK
  (— OF COCK) HEEL
  (— ON HORSESHOE) CALK
  (— TO ACTION) GOOSE
  (—S OF COCK) WEAPON
  (PART OF —) BAND CHAIN ROWEL
  BUTTON
  (PREF.) CALCARI
SPURGE BALSAM INTISY RICINUS
  SUNWEED CATEPUCE DOVEWEED
  FLUXWEED MILKBUSH MILKWEED
  TITHYMAL WARTWEED
  WARTWORT POINSETTIA
SPURIOUS BAD DOG FAKE SHAM
  BOGUS FUNNY PHONY QUEER
  SHICE SNIDE NOTHAL PSEUDO
  BASTARD NOTHOUS POSTICHE
  PINCHBECK SYNDIETIC
  (PREF.) NOTH(O) PSEUD(O)
SPURN FOOT TACK SCORN REJECT
  CONSPUE CONTEMN DECLINE
  DESPISE DISDAIN
SPURRY YARR FRANK COWQUAKE
  SANDWEED
SPURT JET GILP GIRD GOUT JAUP
  SPAR SPIN BURST CHIRT FLASH
  PULSE SALLY SPOUT GEYSER
  RANDOM SPLURT SPRING
  SPROUT SQUIRT SPATTER
SPUTTER SPIT FIZZLE SOTTER
  SPATTER SPLUTTER
SPUTUM SPIT
SPY FLY PRY ESPY NARK NOSE
  STAG TOOT TOUT WAIT WORM
  LOWER PERDU PLANT SCOUT
  SNEAP SPIAL SPION SPOOK
  WATCH BEAGLE BEHOLD DESCRY
  GAYCAT MOUTON PEEPER
  PERDUE SEARCH SHADOW SPIRAL
  TOUTER WAITER EXAMINE
  LURCHER OTACUST SMELLER
  SPOTTER WATCHER DISCOVER
  EMISSARY HIRCARRA MOUCHARD
  (— ON RACEHORSES) TOUT

(— UPON) LAY
(AUTHOR OF —) COOPER
(CHARACTER IN —) JACK BIRCH
  HENRY SARAH CAESAR HARPER
  HARVEY LAWTON PEYTON
  FRANCES WHARTON ISABELLA
  JEANETTE THOMPSON
  DUNWOODIE SINGLETON
  WELLEMERE
(PLANTED —) STOOGE
(POLICE —) SETTER
SPYBOAT VEDET VEDETTE
SQUAB PIPER SQUABBY SQUEAKER
  SQUEALER SQUILGEE
SQUABBLE MUSS TIFF BRAWL
  SCRAP BICKER JANGLE SQUALL
  BOBBERY BRABBLE BRANGLE
  CONTEND PRABBLE QUARREL
  SWABBLE
SQUAD CREW DECURY TWENTY
  PLATOON
  (— OF DETECTIVES) HOMICIDE
SQUADRON BLUE SOTNIA
  SQUADER
  (CAVALRY —) RESSALAH
SQUALID DINGY DIRTY MANGY
  SEEDY FILTHY FROWZY SORDID
  SCABROUS SLOTTERY
SQUALL DROW FRET GUST MEWL
  ROAR SCAT WAUL BARAT FRESH
  PERRY SKELP BAYAMO FLURRY
  SQUAWK BORASCA SUMATRA
  TORNADO BLIZZARD BORASQUE
  CHUBASCO
SQUALOR DIRT
SQUAMA ALULA TEGULA
SQUANDER SOT BLOW BLUE BURN
  GAME LASH WARE SPEND SPILL
  SPORT WASTE BEZZLE LAVISH
  MAFFLE MUDDLE PADDLE PALTER
  PERISH PLUNGE TIPPLE BRANGLE
  CONSUME DEBAUCH DEBOISE
  DISPEND PROFUSE SCAMBLE
  SCATTER SKITTLE SLATHER
  SWATTER EMBEZZLE MISSPEND
  SQUATTER
SQUANDERER PRODIGAL
SQUANDERING WASTEFUL
SQUARE FIX EDGE EVEN FOUR
  FULL LAME POST QUAD SUIT
  AGREE CHECK CROSS FRAME
  HUNKY PLACE PLAIN PLAZA
  SUPER BLOCKY DINKUM ISAGON
  MICKEY PIAZZA QUARRY ZENZIC
  ZOCALO CARREAU CHECKER
  COMMONS EMERALD UPRIGHT
  QUADRANT QUADRATE
  SQUADRON TETRAGON
  (— A STONE) PITCH
  (— FOR BOWLING SCORE) FRAME
  (— OF CANVAS) SKATE
  (— OF CLOTH) PANE
  (— OF DOUGH) KNISH
  (— OF FRAMING) PAN
  (— OF GLASS) QUARREL
  (— OF LINEN) PALL
  (— OF TURF) DIVOT QUADREL
  (— OFF) BUTT
  (— ON BILLIARD TABLE) CROTCH
  (— ON CHESSBOARD) HOUSE
  POINT
  (BUILDINGS FORMING —) INSULA
  (CARPENTER'S —) NORMA

(CHURCH —) PARVIS
(LINEN —) SUDARIUM
(ONE-MILE —) SECTION
(PATTERN OF —S) DAMIER
(WOVEN —) SINKER
(PREF.) QUADR(ATO)(I)(U)
SQUARED HEWN QUARTO SQUARE
SQUARE DANCE TUCKER
SQUARE-DEALING WHITE
SQUARELY BUNG FAIR FULL
  FLUSH SPANG FAIRLY DIRECTLY
  SMACKDAB
  (— AND SHARPLY) SMACK
SQUARISH BOXY
SQUASH PEPO QUAT GOURD
  SQUAB CASHAW CUCURB
  CUSHAW MARROW SIMNEL
  SQUISH SQUUSH TURBAN
  HUBBARD PUMPKIN CUCURBIT
  CYMBLING PEPONIUM ZUCCHINI
SQUASH BUG STINKBUG
SQUASHY SWASHY SQUUSHY
SQUAT QUAT RUCK STUB SWAT
  SWOT COWER DUMPY FUBSY
  HUNCH PUDGY SQUAB FODGEL
  HUNKER HURKLE QUATCH
  STOCKY STUBBY SQUATTY
  TAPPISH SQUATTLE THICKSET
SQUATINA RHINA
SQUATTER NESTER BYWONER
SQUAW JACK WEBB HOUND
  WENCH MAHALA SQUARK
SQUAWBUSH SHOVAL
SQUAWFISH CHUB BOXHEAD
  BIGMOUTH CHAPPAUL
SQUAWK SCRAWK SQUALL
  SQUARK SQUAWL COMPLAIN
SQUAWROOT CLAPWORT
  ELOTILLO
SQUEAK GIKE PEEP WEAK CHEEP
  CHIRK QUEAK SCRAWK SCROOP
  SQUEAL
SQUEAKING SCRANNEL
SQUEAKY CREAKY
SQUEAL PIP RAT FINK HOWL
  SWEEL SCREAK WHISTLE
SQUEALER FINK CANARY
SQUEAMISH HELO NICE NAISH
  PAWKY PENSY DAINTY DAUNCH
  PENCEY QUAINT QUEASY SPICED
  TICKLE WAIRCH WAMBLY FINICAL
  MAWKISH WEARISH NAUSEOUS
  OVERNICE
SQUEAMISHNESS NICETY
  DISGUST MALAISE DELICACY
SQUEEZE EKE HUG JAM NIP CLAM
  MULL MURE VISE ZEST BIRSE
  BUNCH CHIRT CREEM CROWD
  CRUSH PINCH PRESS SQUAB
  SQUAT WRING GRUDGE QUEASE
  SCRUMP SCRUZE SQUASH STRAIN
  THRIMP THRING THRONG TWEEZE
  TWITCH SCRINGE SCROOGE
  SCROUGE SCRUNCH SCRUNGE
  SQUEEGE SQUINCH COMPRESS
  CONTRACT PRESSURE SHOEHORN
  THRIMBLE THRUMBLE
  (— FROM) SPONGE
  (— IN) FUDGE
  (— INTO) THRIMBLE
  (— OUT) PINCH STRAIN
  (ECONOMIC —) CRUNCH
  (PREF.) PRESSI

SQUEEZED STRETTA STRETTO
SQUEEZER REAMER ALLIGATOR
SQUELCH QUELCH SQUASH
SQUISH SQUIDGE
SQUELCHER BLIZZARD
SQUETEAGUE DRUM DRUMMER
SQUETEE BLUEFISH CHICKWIT
WEAKFISH
SQUIB MOTE SKIT FILLER
EXPLODER
SQUID PLUG CALAMARY
SQUIFFED DRUNK BLOTTO
STONED
SQUIGGLE SCRIGGLE
SQUILL SCILLA SLANGKOP
(PREF.) SCILLI
SQUINT AWRY GLEE GLEG SKEN
SKEW BAGGE GLENT GLEDGE
GOGGLE SHEYLE SKELLY SQUINCH
SQUINNY
SQUINT-EYED GLEE GLEED
SQUINTING LOUCHE
SQUIRE SWAIN DONZEL JUNKER
TIMIAS ARMIGER ESQUIRE
SQUIRET YOUNKER HENCHMAN
SCUTIGER SERVITOR SQUARSON
SQUIREEN
SQUIRM CURL WIND TWINE
WRING WRITHE WRESTLE
WRIGGLE SCRIGGLE SQUIGGLE
SQUIRREL BUN CON BUNT LEAD
SCUG BUNNY XERUS BOOMER
CHIPPY GOPHER RODENT
TAGUAN ARDILLA SCHILLU
SCIURID CHIPMUNK EGGEATER
GRAYBACK JELERANG RATATOSK
CHICKAREE
(— SKIN) VAIR
(FLYING —) ASSAPAN
(PREF.) SCIURO
SQUIRRELFISH ALAIHI MARIAN
MOJARRA SERRANO SOLDIER
SANDFISH WELSHMAN
SQUIRREL SHREW TANA TUPAIA
PENTAIL
SQUIRT CHIRT SCOOT SKITE SLIRT
SPIRT SPOUT SPURT SQUIB SQUIT
SPLOIT SPRENT SPRITZ SCOOTER
SQUITTER

SRI LANKA
CAPITAL: COLOMBO
COIN: CENT RUPEE
FORMER NAME: CEYLON
GULF: MANNAR
MEASURE: PARA PARAH AMUNAM
PARRAH
POINT: PEDRO
STRAIT: PALK
TOWN: GALLE KANDY JAFFNA
MANNAR MATARA BADULLA
COLOMBO PUTTALAM
TREE: HORA PALU

S-SHAPED
(PREF.) SIGMO SIGMOID(O)
STAB DAB DAG JAB JAG JOB DIRK
GORE PINK POKE PROB SHIV
STOB STOG STUG YERK CHIVE
KNIFE POACH PRICK PRONG
STICK STOKE BROACH DAGGER
PIERCE POUNCE SLIVER STITCH
THRUST BAYONET STAGGER

PRICKADO STILETTO STOCCADO
STOCCATA
(— IN MIDBREAST) SLOT
STABBING THORNY JABBING
PUNGENT STICKING
(SUFF.) NYXIS
STABILITY POISE FIXURE BALANCE
SADNESS FIRMNESS SECURITY
CONSTANCY
STABILIZE FIX SET EVEN TRIM
POISE SCHOOL STEADY BALANCE
BALLAST STIFFEN
STABILIZER ACARDITE
STABLE BYRE FAST FIRM SURE
HARAS HEMEL SOLID SOUND
STALL STIFF STOUT TAMBO
LINTER LIVERY SECURE SICKER
STATIC STEADY STRONG STURDY
DURABLE EQUERRY LASTING
OXHOUSE SETTLED SHIPPEN
STABILE BALANCED IMMOBILE
RESIDENT STANDING PERMANENT
(ROYAL —S) MEWS
(PREF.) MONIMO
STABLEBOY LAD MAFU MAFOO
JACKBOY
STABLEMAN OSTLER HOSTLER
STACCATO TUT SECCO DETACHE
SALTATO RICOCHET SALTANDO
(NOT —) TENUTO
STACK COB MOW SOW BIKE DESS
LEET PACK PILE POKE RICK
CANCH CLAMP GOAVE POAKE
SCROO SHOCK STAKE STALK
STOCK COLUMN FUNNEL RICKLE
CALENDER STACKAGE
(— BRICKS) CLAMP SCINTLE
(— IN KILN) BOX
(— LUMBER) STICK
(— OF ARMS) PILE
(— OF BRICK) LIFT
(— OF CERAMICS) BŰNG
(— OF CORN) SHOCK
(— OF FISH) BULK
(— OF GRAIN) RICK
(— OF HIDES) BED
(— OF PANS) SWEATER
(— OF SHEETS) BOOK
(HAY OR CORN —) HOVEL
(SMALL —) COB CANCH RICKLE
(TILE —) WELL
STACKER CROWDER PITCHER
STACKMAN
STACKYARD MOWIE MOWHAY
HAGGARD
STADIUM BOWL STADE STAGE
FURLONG STADION COLISEUM
STAFF PIN ROD TAU TAW CANE
CLUB KENT LIMB MACE MALL
MAUL PIKE POLE RUNG TREE
VARE YARD BATON CROOK CROSS
KEVEL NIBBY PEDUM PERCH
STAVE STICK SUITE VERGE
BASTON CADUCE CEPTER CLEEKY
CROCHE CRUTCH FAMILY FERULE
GROUND LITUUS MULETA
POTENT PRITCH RADIUS RISSLE
TAIAHA THYRSE WARDER
BACULUS BOURDON CAMBUCA
CROSIER CRUMMIE DISTAFF
FESTUCA PALSTER SCEPTER
SCEPTRE STADDLE THYRSUS
CADUCEUS CRUMMOCK

PARTISAN PASTORAL PLOWFOOT
TIPSTAFF
(— AT END OF NET) BRAIL
(— OF AUTHORITY) VARE VERGE
(— OF COOKS) BOUCHE
(— OF OFFICIALS) OMLAH
(— WITH CROSSPIECE) POTENT
(BISHOP'S —) BAGLE BACULUS
CROSIER CROZIER PASTORAL
(FIELD MARSHAL'S —) BATON
(FORKED —) LINSTOCK
(GRADUATED —) LIMB
(HOTTENTOT —) KIRVI
(MAGICIAN'S —) RHABDOS
(NEWSPAPER —) DAYSIDE
(NUBIAN —) KUERR
(PILGRIM'S —) BURDEN
(PLASTERER'S —) BEATER
(SHEPHERD'S —) KENT CROOK
(SPARTAN —) SCYTALE
(TEACHING —) FACULTY
(THIEVES' —) FILCH
(PREF.) LITUI SCEPTRO
STAG HART ROYAL SPADE STAIG
WAPITI BULLOCK KNOBBER
POINTER KNOBBLER
(— OF THE 3D YEAR) SPIRE
(— OF 2ND YEAR) BROCKET
(— OF 8 YEARS OR MORE) ROYAL
(— THAT HAS CAST HIS ANTLERS)
POLLARD
(DEAD —) MORT
(HORNLESS —) HUMMEL
(TURNED TO —) ACTAEON
(3-YEAR OLD —) SPADE
(PREF.) ELAPH(O)
STAG BEETLE LUCANID
STAGE LEG BANK GEST POST STEP
TREK APRON DUMMY ETAGE
FLAKE GRADE PEGME PHASE
POINT SCENE STAIR STATE
BOARDS DEGREE HEMMEL
PERIOD PHASIS STRIDE CATASTA
MANSION ROSTRUM STADIUM
INSTANCE PLATFORM SCAFFOLD
PROSCENIUM
(— FOR DRYING FISH) FLAKE
(— FOR HAY) HEMMEL
(— IN DELIRIUM) TILMUS
(— IN FEVER) FLUSH
(— IN PORCELAIN FURNACE)
HOWELL
(— IN TRAVELING) GEST
(— MANAGER) REGISSEUR
(— OF CUPOLA) LANTERN
(— OF DEVELOPMENT) ERA
BLOSSOM
(— OF FUNGUS) OIDIUM
(— OF GLACIATION) RISS WURM
ACHEN MINDEL
(— OF INSECT) INSTAR
(— OF LIFE) AGE ASRAMA
ASHRAMA
(— OF MITOSIS) ANAPHASE
PROPHASE
(— OF PERSONALITY) LATENCY
(— OF ROCKET) BOOSTER
(— OF THEATER) SCAENA
THEATRON
(— WHERE SLAVES WERE SOLD)
CATASTA
(BOTTOMMOST —) CELLAR
(COMIC —) SOCK

(EARLIEST —) PRIME
(FINAL —) CLOSE FINISH STRETCH
(FIRST —) YOUTH SPRING
(FLOATING —) DUMMY
(FLOOD —) CREST
(GEOLOGICAL —) GUNZ GLACIAL
SENONIAN
(GLACIATION —) WURM
(INITIAL —) INFANCY
(LANDING —) STAIR BRIDGE
STAITH STELLING
(MOVING —) PEGMA PEGME
(PART OF —) FLY ARCH DROP FLAT
WING APRON DRAPE BATTEN
BORDER BRIDGE CENTER RETURN
TEASER CURTAIN ENTRANCE
TORMENTOR PROSCENIUM
(RADIO —) STEP
(THIRD —) AUTUMN
(PREF.) SCENO
STAGECOACH DILLY STAGE
STAGEHAND GRIP DAYMAN
GAFFER
STAGER SOAKER
STAGGER REEL ROLL STOT DAVER
DODGE HODGE LURCH PITCH
STITE STOIT DACKER DAIDLE
FALTER GOGGLE STAVER STIVER
SWAVER TOTTER WALTER
WAMBLE WELTER WIGGLE
WINTLE MEGRIMS STACHER
STACKER STAMMER STOITER
STOTTER STUMBLE SWAGGER
VANDYKE WAUCHLE TITUBATE
STAGGERBUSH LAMBKILL
STAGGERED STURTAN STURTIN
STAGGERS DUNT GOGGLES
MEGRIMS STAVERS VERTIGO
STAGHEAD SPIKETOP
STAGING STAGE CRIPPLE DERRICK
HURRIES
STAGNANCY STASIS
STAGNANT DEAD DULL INERT
STILL STATIC COBWEBBY
SLUGGISH STAGNATE STANDING
STAGNATION STASIS TORPOR
LANGUOR
STAID SET CIVIL GRAVE SOBER
DEMURE STEADY EARNEST
SERIOUS DECOROUS
STAIN DYE LIT WEM BLOT BLUR
BUFF DIRT DRAB FILE FOIL HURT
MEAL MOLE RUST SCAM SLUR
SMAD SMIT SMUT SOIL SPOT
TASH BLACK BLEND BRAND
CLOUD DIRTY HATCH PAINT
PLECK SMEAR SPECK SULLY
TACHE TAINT TINGE WEMMY
BREATH GIEMSA IMBRUE INFAMY
INFECT MACULA SMIRCH SMUDGE
SMUTCH SPLASH STIGMA SUDDLE
ATTAINT BESTAIN BLEMISH
DEPAINT DISTAIN SLUBBER
SOILURE SPATTER SPLOTCH
STADDLE TARNISH BESMIRCH
CARMALAN DISCOLOR DISGRACE
DISHONOR FLYSPECK MACULATE
PYRONINE TAINTURE
(— BLACK) EBONIZE
(— IN LINEN) MELL
(— ON BRICK) SCUMMING
(— WITH BLOOD) ENGORE
(PREF.) MACUL(I)(O) SPIL(O)

STAINED FOXY RUSTY SMUDGY
SMUTCHY
(— BY DECAY) DOATY
(— WITH BLOOD) BLOODY
IMBRUED
STAINED GLASS VITRAIL
STAINER TRACER
STAINLESS PURE CHASTE
INNOCENT
STAIR STY GREE RUNG STEP
DEGREE COCHLEA ESCALIER
(MINING —) LOB
(WINDING —) VICE CARACOL
CARACOLE
(PL.) PAIR PITCH FLIGHT
DANCERS ESCALIER
STAIRCASE SCALE ESCALIER
(PART OF —) MOLD POST RAIL
NEWEL RISER TREAD NOSING
LANDING BALUSTER BANISTER
HANDRAIL BALUSTRADE
(SPIRAL —) SPIRAL CARACOLE
STAIRWAY STOOP GREESE
PERRON DESCENT ESCALIER
(— ON RIVER BANK) GHAT
(CURVED —) SWEEP
(SHIP'S —) LADDER
(WINDING —) VICE TURNPIKE
STAITH TIP
STAKE BET HOB LAY SET TAW VIE
WAD WED ANTE BENT GAGE
MAIN PALE PAWN PEEL POOL
PUNT RISK STAB STOB TREE
WAGE PITCH SPILE SPOKE SPRAG
STOCK STOOP STOUR WAGER
BAIKIE CAULIS CHANCE CORNER
CROTCH ENGAGE GAMBLE
HAZARD IMPONE LOGGAT
LOGGET PALING PICKET STOWER
TRUNCH WEDFEE STOATER
STUCKEN VENTURE INTEREST
PALISADE PEASTICK STUCKING
(CART —) RUNG
(COMPULSORY — IN POKER) BLIND
(GAMBLING —) MISE
(POINTED —) SOULE SOWEL
PICKET
(SURVEYORS' —) HUB
(TETHERING —) PUTTO
(TINSMITH'S —) TEEST
(PL.) JACKPOT
STAKE-SHAPED SUDIFORM
STALACE COLUMELLA
STALE OLD COLD FLAT HOAR PALL
SICK WORN BLOWN DUSTY
FROWY HOARY MOLDY MUSTY
RAFTY SANDY TRITE FROWZY
MOULDY STUFFY EXOLETE
FROUGHY INSIPID OVERWORN
STAGNANT
(DAMP AND —) WAUGH
STALEMATE PATT STALE
STALK BUN RAY CORN HAFT MOTE
POLE RISP STAM STEG STEM TIGE
QUILL SCAPE SHANK SPEAR SPIRE
STAKE STALE STEAL STIPE STUMP
WRIDE COULIS RATOON STIPES
CASTOCK FUNICLE PEDICEL
PETIOLE SPINDLE CAUDICLE
FILAMENT PEDUNCLE PODETIUM
STALKLET STERIGMA PETIOLULE
(— OF BUCKWHEAT) STRAW
(— OF CRINOID) COLUMN

(— OF GRAIN) RESSUM RIZZOM
(— OF GRASS) BENT SPEAR
(— OF HAY) RISP
(— OF PLANT) SPINDLE TENACLE
(— OF SPOROGONIUM) SETA
(— OF STAMEN) FILAMENT
(— OF SUGAR CANE) RATOON
(— OF UMBEL) RAY
(—S OF GRAIN) KARBI STRAW
(CABBAGE —) CASTOCK
(CROSSBOW —) TILLER
(DRY —) KEX KECK BENNET
(FLOWER —) SCAPE
(HOLLOW —) BUN KEX KECK
(PL.) HAULM STRAW WRIDE
IWAIWA
(PREF.) CAUL(I)(O) CULMI
STALKLESS SESSILE
**STALKY AND COMPANY (AUTHOR
OF —)** KIPLING
(CHARACTER IN —) JOHN MTURK
ARTHUR BEETLE STALKY
CORKRAN GILBERT
STALL BAY BIN BOX CUB PEW
BULK CRIB SPAR STAW BOOSE
BOOSY BOOTH CRAME PITCH
STAND STASH CARCER CARREL
STANCE TRAVIS WICKET
BALAGAN CABINET SHAMBLE
SHIPPEN BUTCHERY STANDING
TRAVERSE
(— FOR TIME) HAVER STRETCH
(— IN CLOISTER) CAROL
(— IN COAL MINE) BREAST WICKET
(— IN MUD) STOG
(— IN ROMAN CIRCUS) CARCER
(BISHOP'S —) TRIBUNE
(CHURCH —) PEW
(THEATER —) LOGE FAUTEUIL
STALLED STOODED
STALLION SIRE STAG STUD ENTRE
HORSE COOSER ENTIRE
STALLAND
STALWART RUDE STARK STIFF
WIGHT STRONG STURDY BUIRDLY
VALIANT
STAMEN TAMIN STAMMEL
(PREF.) ANDR(O)
(SUFF.) STEMONOUS
STAMINA GUTS SAND BOTTOM
STAMMER FAM HACK MANT STOT
STUT GANCH WLAFF FAFFLE
FALTER FAMBLE HACKER HAFFLE
HAMMER HOCKER HOTTER
MAFFLE MAMMER YAMMER
FRIBBLE STUMBLE STUTTER
HESITATE SPLUTTER TITUBATE
STAMMERING HACK PSELLISM
TRAULISM BALBUTIES
STAMP CHOP COIL DRUB FAKE
MARK NIXY PAUT POSS RUFF
SEAL SNAP TYPE APPEL BLOCK
DOLLY ERROR FRANK LABEL
LOCAL NIXIE PRINT PUNCH
STOCK STOMP STUNT TENOR
TOUCH WRITE ACCENT CACHET
CLICHE DOCKER FULLER INCUSE
INCUTE INDENT LOCKUP PASTER
POUNCE SCRIBE SHAPER SIGNET
STRAMP STRIKE CARRIER
CHARACT EDITION IMPRESS
IMPRINT MINTAGE POUNDER
REPRINT SEEBECK SPECIAL

SQUELCH STICKER TAXPAID
WRAPPER HALLMARK ORIGINAL
PRESSURE PUNCHEON
(— AFTER ASSAY) TOUCH
(— BOOK COVER) BLIND
(— FOR CUTTING DOUGH) DOCKER
(— HERRING BARREL) DUNT
(— HIDES) STOCK
(— HOLES) STOACH
(— OUT) SCOTCH
(— WITH DIE) DINK
(BOOKBINDING —) BLOCK FILLET
(CANCELLING —) KILLER
(HALF OF —) BISECT
(HAND —) CANCELER
(OFFICIAL —) CHOP
(POSTAGE —) AIR DUE CAPE FAKE
HEAD ERROR LABEL LOCAL
BUREAU INVERT AIRMAIL
BICOLOR CHARITY CLASSIC
REPRINT STICKER ADHESIVE
COLONIAL ORIGINAL SPECIMEN
PRECANCEL
(REVENUE —) FISCAL TAXPAID
(SMART —) APPEL
(PL.) MIXTURE KILOWARE
(PREF.) TIMBRO
STAMP-COLLECTING PHILATELY
TIMBROLOGY
STAMPEDE RUSH BLITZ CHUTE
DEBACLE STAMPEDO
STAMPER FANCIER STOMPER
STAMPING TITLING
STANCE STATION STANDING
(— OF GOLFER) ADDRESS
(— OF HORSE) GATHER
STANCH FIRM STEM STIFF STOUT
HEARTY TRUSTY STAUNCH
FAITHFUL RESOLUTE
STANCHION BAIL PITON CROTCH
CRUTCH STENCIL STANCHEL
STANCHER
STAND GO JIB SET BANK BEAR
BIER DESK HALT RACK RANK
REST STAY STEL ZARF BIPOD
BLOCK ERECT FRAME FRONT
KIOSK STALL STICK STONE STOOL
CASTER COLORS ENDURE HASTER
INSIST PATTEN PILLAR SMOKER
STANCE STANZA STOUND STRIKE
TEAPOY TRIPOD TRIVET CONSIST
DIOPTER EPERGNE FOURBLE
LECTERN STATION TABORET
TRESTLE TROLLEY ATTITUDE
BLEACHER COATRACK CROWFOOT
FRIPPERY GUERIDON HASTENER
INKSTAND POSITION SCAFFOLD
STALLAGE STANDING STANDISH
STILLAGE STILLING STILLION
(— AS SPONSOR) FANG HEAVE
CHRISTEN
(— AT AN ANGLE) CATER
(— AT ATTENTION) BACK
(— BACK) BACCARE BACKARE
(— BEFORE A FIRE) FOOTMAN
(— BEHIND) COVER
(— BY) SERVE
(— CLOSE) CROWD ENVIRON
(— FASTENED TO MESS TABLE)
CROWFOOT
(— FIRM) STAY
(— FOR) DENOTE
(— FOR AUCTIONING) BLOCK

(— FOR BARRELS) JIB THRALL
(— FOR COFFIN) BIER
(— FOR COMPASS) BINNACLE
(— FOR CONFINING HEAT) HASTER
HASTENER
(— FOR DRESSES) FRIPPERY
(— FOR DRILL PIPE) FOURBLE
(— FOR FINJAN) ZARF
(— FOR TILES) CRISS
(— FOR WRITING MATERIALS)
STANDISH
(— GUARD) COVER
(— IN AWE) FEAR
(— OF FOREST) GROWTH
(— OF PLANTS) STOOL
(— OFF) AROINT
(— ON AND OFF SHORE) BUSK
(— ON END) STARE UPEND
(— ON TWO FEET) BIPOD DUOPOD
(— OUT) CUT TOOT FLAUNT
(— READY) ABIDE
(— STILL) HO HOO HALT STAY
(— TO SHOOT) ADDRESS
(— TREAT) MUG SHOUT
(— UNSTEADILY) STAGGER
(— UP STIFF) STIVER
(— UP TO) CONFRONT
(— WITH LEGS APART) STRIDE
(CAKE —) CURATE
(CONCESSION —) JOINT
(FIRECLAY —) CRANK
(ONE-NIGHT —) GIG
(PRINTER'S —) BANK FRAME
(PULPIT-LIKE —) AMBO
(RAISED —) PERGOLA
(SCULPTOR'S —) CHASSIS
(SHOOTING —) BUTT
(THREE-LEGGED —) TRIVET
STANDARD ALEM DICK FIAR FLAG
GAGE IDEA MARK NORM SIGN
TEST TOUG ALLOY BOGEY CANON
CHECK DOLLY DRAKE EAGLE
GAUGE IDEAL JEDGE MODEL
NORMA SCALE STAND STOOL
AQUILA ASSIZE BANNER CORNET
DOLLIE FILLER NORMAL SOCKET
SQUARE STAPLE TIPONI TRIPOD
VIOLLE ANCIENT CLASSIC
DECORUM DRAPEAU LABARUM
MODULUS STANDER BRATTACH
GONFALON MOUNTING ORIFLAMB
ORTHODOX VEXILLUM
(— IN GATE) STRIKE
(— OF ACCURACY) COCKER
(— OF CONDUCT) LINE GNOMON
(— OF PERFECTION) IDEAL
(— OF PERFORMANCE) BOGY
BOGEY BOGIE
(— OF PITCH) DIAPASON
(— OF QUALITY) GRADE
(—S OF BEHAVIOR) ETHICS
(CONVENTIONAL —) PIETY
(LIGHT —) CARCEL
(NOT —) BASTARD
(TURKISH —) ALEM TOUG
(PL.) LIGHTS HOLSTERS
STANDARD-BEARER CORNET
ENSIGN ALFEREZ ANCIENT
STALLER SIGNIFER STANDARD
VEXILLARY
STANDARDIZE FORDIZE MACHINE
CALIBRATE
STANDEL STORER

STANDING BEING ERECT STATE CREDIT ESTEEM REGULAR RESPECT PRESTIGE STAGNANT PERPENDICULAR
(**— ALONE**) SEPARATE
(**— BY ITSELF**) ABSOLUTE DETACHED
(**— ERECT**) HORRENT
(**— INCOORDINATION**) ASTASIA
(**— ON STEPS**) DEGRADED
(**— OUT**) BOLD EXTANT SALIENT
(**— OUT CLEARLY**) EMINENT
(**— POSITION**) OFFHAND
(**HIGH —**) WORSHIP
(**MODE OF —**) STANCE
(**SOCIAL —**) LEVEL ESTATE FASHION STATION
(**PREF.**) STAT(O)
(**— IN SECOND PLACE BEYOND**) DVI EKA
(**SUFF.**) STASIA STASIS STAT STATIC STATICS
STANDPATTISM TORYISM
STANDPOINT STANCE
STANDSTILL JIB SET HALT REST STAY STAND STANCE
STANZA CALL RANN ENVOI ENVOY STAFF STAND STAVE VERSE BASTON DIXAIN DIZAIN OCTAVE SEPTET SESTET SEXTET SIXAIN STANCE STANZO HUITAIN SEXTAIN STROPHE TRIOLET TROILUS CINQUAIN OCTONARY QUATRAIN QUINTAIN RISPETTO SETTAINE TRISTICH TROPARION
(**SUFF.**) STICH
STAPES STIRRUP
STAPLE LOOP FLOSS STITCH SHACKLE STEEPLE VERVELLE
(**PL.**) BROKES
STAR COR SUN BEID FIRE LAMP ASTER COMES DWARF EXCEL GIANT MOLET RISHI SHINE STARN ALNATH ASTRAL BINARY COUPLE DOUBLE ETOILE LUCIDA MULLET NITHAM SHINER SPHERE STELLA BENEFIC DINGBAT ESTOILE GEMINID STARLET STARNIE ASTERISK ASTEROID HEXAGRAM MALEFICE PENTACLE SUBDWARF SUBGIANT VARIABLE
(**COMPANION —**) COMES
(**DOG —**) SEPT SOPT SEPTI SIRIUS
(**EVENING —**) VENUS HESPER VESPER EVESTAR HESPERUS
(**FEATHER —**) COMATULA
(**FILM —**) VEDETTE
(**GUIDING —**) LOADSTAR LODESTAR
(**MORNING —**) VENUS DAYSTAR PHOSPHOR
(**NEW —**) NOVA
(**OFFICER'S —**) PIP
(**PULSATING —**) CEPHEID
(**SHOOTING —**) BOLIDE LEONID METEOR COWSLIP SHOOTER
(**SPECIFIC —**) YED ADIB ALYA ATIK CAPH ENIF ENIR IZAR KIED MAIA NAOS PHAD SADR VEGA WEGA ACRAB ACRUX AGENA ALCOR ALGOL ALKES ANCHA ARNEB CHARA DABIH DELTA DENEB DUBHE GIEDI GUIAM GUYAM HAMAL HAMUL JUGUM MERAK MIZAR NIBAL NIHAI PHACD PHAET RIGEL SAIPH SPICA TEJAT WASAT WEZEN ZOSMA ADHARA ALHENA ALIOTH ALKAID ALMACH ALTAIR ALUDRA APOLLO ARIDED CASTOR CELENO CHELEB DIPHDA ELNATH ETAMIN GIENAH HYADES KOCHAB LESUTH MAASYM MARKAB MARKEB MARSIC MEGREZ MENKAR MENKIB MEROPE MIRACH MIRFAK MIRZAM NEKKAR PHECDA POLLUX PROPUS RANICH SCHEAT SHEDIR SIRIUS THABIT THUBAN ACUBENS ALBIREO ALCHIBA ALCYONE ALGENIB ALGIEBA ALGORAH ALMAACK ALNILAM ALNITAK ALPHARD ALPHIRK ALSHAIN ANTARES AZIMECH BUNGULA CANOPUS CAPELLA ELECTRA GIANSAR GOMELZA GRUMIUM MEBSUTA MELUCTA MENCHIB MINTAKA MUFRIDE POLARIS PROCYON REGULUS ROTANIM RUCHBAR SCHEDAR SEGINUS SHELLAK STEROPE TARAZED TAYGETA TEGMINE THEENIM ACHERNAR ALPHECCA ARCTURUS ASTERION DENEBOLA GRAFFIAS HERCULES MULIPHEN PRAESEPE SCALOOIN SCHEMALI SHERATAN
(**THREE —S**) KIDS ELLWAND TRIANGLE
(**7 —S OF GREAT BEAR**) CAR
(**PREF.**) ASTER(O) ASTR(I)(O) SIDERO STELLI
(**SUFF.**) ASTER ID
STAR APPLE CAIMITO
STARCH AMYL ARUM SAGO STIFF TIKOR AMYDON AMYLUM CONJEE FARINA FECULA CASSAVA CURCUMA FAECULA MARANTA TALIPOT AMIDULIN DRESSING FIXATURE GLUCOSAN
(**— IN SOLUTION**) AMIDIN
(**ANIMAL —**) GLYCOGEN
(**PREF.**) AMYL(I)(O)
STARCHED FORMAL
STARE EYE BORE DARE GAPE GAUM GAUP GAWK GAWP GAZE GOVE GYPE KIKE LOOK PORE GLARE GLORE GLOWER GOGGLE EYEBALL
(**— IDLY**) GOVE GOAVE
(**— VACANTLY**) GOWK
(**COLD —**) FISHEYE
STARFISH PAD STAR ASTERID RADIATE ASTEROID OPHIURAN
(**PART OF —**) ARM ANUS DISC SPINE EYESPOT TENTACLE MADREPORITE
STARING STEEP ASTARE GOGGLE GOOGLY HAGGARD
STAR JELLY STARSHOT
STARK BUCK CARK FAIR HARD CRUDE HARSH NAKED STIFF STARCH DESOLATE METALLIC
STARLIKE ASTRAL SPHERY
STARLING SALI STARE BEAVER PASTOR TILYER SPREEUW STARNEL STAYNIL CHEPSTER CUTWATER SHEPSTER
STARRED LIZARD HARDIM

STARRING FEATURED
STARRY ASTRAL STARNY STELLED SIDEREAL
STAR SAPPHIRE ASTERIA ASTRION ASTROITE
STAR-SHAPED ASTROID
START DIG SET BOLT BOUN DART DASH HEAD JERK JUMP OPEN TURN WHIP ARISE BEGIN BIRTH BRAID BREAK BUDGE ENTER FLIRT GLENT ONSET RAISE ROUSE STORT THROW ABRADE BOGGLE BROACH FLINCH INTEND OFFSET OUTSET SETOFF SETOUT STRIKE TWITCH GETAWAY OPENERS OPENING STARTLE SUNRISE COMMENCE CONCEIVE INCHOATE OUTSTART
(**— A HORSE**) WINCE
(**— ASIDE**) SHY SKIT DODGE
(**— BACK**) RESILE
(**— BURNING**) SPIT KINDLE
(**— FERMENTATION**) PITCH
(**— OF BIRD'S FLIGHT**) SOUSE
(**— OUT**) FRAME INTEND
(**— UP**) JUMP ASTART ASTERT
(**SUDDEN —**) SHY SQUIRT
STARTER KOJI
(**BUNG —**) FLOGGER
STAR THISTLE CALTROP CALTHROP
STARTING INCOMING
STARTLE SOHO ALARM SCARE SHOCK START STURT AFFRAY BOGGLE BOOGER FRIGHT FRIGHTEN SURPRISE
STARTLING ALARMING SHOCKING
STARVATION LACK PINE FAMINE
STARVE CLEM FAST FAMINE FAMISH AFFAMISH
STARVED MEAGER MEAGRE STARVEN
STARVED-LOOKING SLINK
STARVELING SHARGAR SHARGER
STARVING CLUNG
STARWORT ASTROFEL ASTROPHEL
STATE WU LAY PUT SAY CASE MODE NAME POMP PORT TERM TIFF COVIN ESTER ESTRE POLIS SPEAK STADE TERMS TUATH WHACK AFFIRM AGENCY ASSERT ASSURE CAESAR EFFEIR EMPIRE ESTATE IMPORT NATION PLIGHT POLICY POLITY RENDER RIALTY SOVIET STATUS STEVEN CIVITAS DECLARE DESERET DUKEDOM ENOUNCE EXPOUND EXPRESS KINSHIP PROPOSE SPECIFY STATION TERMINE CEREMONY DEVACHAN DOMINION FRANKLIN HEGEMONY INDICATE KINGSHIP REPUBLIC STATELET PREDICAMENT
(**— EXPLICITLY**) DEFINE
(**— FORMALLY**) ENOUNCE
(**— IN NORTH CAROLINA**) FRANKLIN
(**— OF AFFAIRS**) CASE ARRAY STATUS
(**— OF ALARM**) GAST FEEZE SCARE
(**— OF AMAZEMENT**) STOUND
(**— OF ANGER**) FUME
(**— OF APATHY**) STUPOR
(**— OF BEING CUT**) SCISSION

(**— OF BEING DRAWN**) TRACTION
(**— OF BEING OVERFULL**) PLETHORA
(**— OF BEING POISONOUS**) TOXICITY
(**— OF BEING WORSE**) PEJORITY
(**— OF CONCENTRATION**) DHARANA SAMADHI
(**— OF CONFUSION**) FOG FLAP HACK MUSS CHAOS SWIRL HASSLE HUBBUB FLUMMOX TROYTOWN
(**— OF CONSECRATION**) IHRAM
(**— OF COOPERATION**) HOOKUP
(**— OF DISASTER**) SMASH
(**— OF DISORDER**) HELL MUSS FANTAD ANARCHY
(**— OF DISSENSION**) SCISSION
(**— OF DISTURBANCE**) GARBOIL
(**— OF DOUBT**) MIST
(**— OF EAGERNESS**) HURRY
(**— OF ECSTASY**) SWOON
(**— OF ENCHANTMENT**) SPELL
(**— OF ENLIGHTENMENT**) BODHI
(**— OF EXALTATION**) FURY ECSTASY
(**— OF EXCITATION**) FOMENT
(**— OF EXCITEMENT**) FRY FLAP GALE HIGH SNIT STEW FEEZE HOIGH DITHER DOODAH HUBBUB FANTEEG FLUSTER KIPPAGE SWELTER FANTIGUE
(**— OF EXHAUSTION**) GONENESS
(**— OF FEAR**) FUNK JELLY SCARE
(**— OF HAPPINESS**) ELYSIUM PARADISE
(**— OF HEALTH**) EUCRASIA
(**— OF HUMILIATION**) DUST
(**— OF IDEAL PERFECTION**) UTOPIA
(**— OF IMPERFECTION**) SCARCITY
(**— OF INACTION**) DEADLOCK
(**— OF INCIPIENCE**) EMBRYO
(**— OF INTENSITY**) BUILD
(**— OF IRRITABILITY**) FUME GALL FANTAD
(**— OF JOY**) JUBILEE
(**— OF MELANCHOLY**) GLOOM
(**— OF MENTAL INACTIVITY**) TORPOR
(**— OF MENTAL READINESS**) ATTITUDE
(**— OF MIND**) CUE HIP CASE MOOD HUMOR FETTLE CARAPACE
(**— OF MISERY**) HELL GEHENNA
(**— OF NEGLECT**) LIMBO
(**— OF OPPOSITION**) DEFIANCE
(**— OF OSTRACISM**) COVENTRY
(**— OF PERFECTION**) SIDDHI
(**— OF PERTURBATION**) CRISE
(**— OF PREOCCUPATION**) CARE
(**— OF READINESS**) GUARD
(**— OF REALITY**) ACT
(**— OF REJECTION**) GATE
(**— OF REPOSE**) KEF CALM
(**— OF RETIREMENT**) GRASS
(**— OF REVERIE**) DUMP
(**— OF SENSITIVITY**) NERVES
(**— OF SLUGGISHNESS**) COMA
(**— OF SUSPENSE**) TRANCE
(**— OF SUSPENSION**) ABEYANCE
(**— OF TENSION**) FANTEEG STRETCH FANTIGUE
(**— OF THE SOUL**) BARDO
(**— OF THINGS**) FARE PASS
(**— OF TRANQUILLITY**) KEF KIF PEACE

(— OF UNCERTAINTY) FOG FLUX
(— OF UNREST) FERMENT
(— OF WEATHER) FREEZE
(— OF WORRY) TEW SWEAT
FANTAD
(— POSITIVELY) AFFIRM
(— UNDER OATH) ALLEGE
(AGITATED —) FUSS SNIT STIR
CHURN STORM LATHER SWIVET
(BLISSFUL —) NIRVANA
(BUFFER —) GLACIS
(CHINESE —) WU SHU WEI
(DAZED —) DAMP
(DEPRESSED —) GLOOM WALLOW
(DISTURBED —) STIR STORM
UNREST
(DOMINANT —) SUZERAIN
(DROWSY —) DOVER
(EMOTIONAL —) FEVER FEELING
(FEUDAL —) WEI
(FICTITIOUS —) FABLE
(FILTHY —) DIRT
(FREE —) SAORSTAT
(GLOOMY —) DUMP
(HIGHEST —) SUPREME
(HOLY —) IHRAM
(HORIZONTAL —) LEVEL
(INDONESIAN —) NEGARA
(IRISH —) TUATH
(LIQUID —) FLUOR FLUIDITY
(LOWEST —) BEDROCK
(MARRIED —) SPOUSAL
(MENTAL —) EARNEST DELUSION
(MORBID —) HIP IODISM
(MORMON —) DESERET
(NEUTRAL —) BUFFER
(PECUNIARY —) FACULTY
(PERTURBED —) DEVIL
(PROFOUND —) DEPTH
(SWISS —) CANTON
(ULTIMATE —) END
(UNCULTIVATED —) FERITY
(UNFAVORABLE —) FOULNESS
(VERIFIED —) FACT
(PREF.) CRATO TYP(I)(O)
(SUFF.) ANCE ANCY ANDRA
ANDRIA ATE ATION CY DOM ENCE
ENCY ERY HEAD HOOD ION
ISATION ISM ITY IZATION MENT
NESS OSIS SHIP TH
(CHARACTERIZED BY —) SOME
(DISEASED —) SIS
(MORBID —) IASIS
STATED GIVEN CERTAIN
(DIRECTLY —) EXPRESS
STATE FAIR (AUTHOR OF —) STONG
(CHARACTER IN —) PAT ABEL
WARE EMILY FRAKE HARRY
MARGY WAYNE ELEANOR
GILBERT MELISSA
STATEHOUSE CAPITOL
STATELINESS STATE DIGNITY
MAJESTY GRANDEUR
STATELY DATE BURLY GRAND
LARGO LOFTY NOBLE PROUD
REGAL STATE STOUT AUGUST
COUPON PORTLY SOLEMN
SUPERB TOGATE GALLANT
BARONIAL IMPOSING MAESTOSO
MAJESTIC STATEFUL
STATEMENT SAY BILL VOTE WORD
AXIOM BRIEF COUNT DIXIT LIBEL
STATE STORY BELIEF DICTUM

DOCKET EXPOSE FACTUM
RETURN SAYING SPEECH
ACCOUNT ADDRESS ANALOGY
DISSENT EPITAPH EPITOME
FORMULA INVOICE MENTION
SHOWING ABSTRACT ANTINOMY
ARGUMENT AVERMENT BULLETIN
DELIVERY EQUATION EXPLICIT
JUDGMENT PROPOSAL SCHEDULE
SENTENCE SPEAKING SYNGRAPH
SYNOPSIS
(— AS PRECEDENT) AUTHORITY
(— OF OPINION) CHANT
(— OF RELATIONS) THEOREM
(— ON DRUG LABEL) LEGEND
(AUTHORITATIVE —) DICTUM
(CASUAL —) REMARK
(CONCISE —) SCHEME APHORISM
(CONDENSED —) RESUME
SYNOPSIS
(DEFAMATORY —) LIBEL
(EXAGGERATED —) STRETCH
(FABRICATED —) CANARD
(FINAL — OF ACCOUNT) AUDIT
(FINANCIAL —) BUDGET
(FOOLISH —) INANITY
(FORMAL —) CITATION
(IRRATIONAL —) ALOGISM
(OBSCURE —) ENIGMA
(PLAINTIFF'S —) BODY
(POMPOUS —) BRAG
(PUBLIC —) OUTGIVING
(SELF-CONTRADICTORY —)
PARADOX
(SOOTHING —) SALVE
(UNTRUE —) LIE
STATER COLT TURTLE PEGASUS
CYZICENE
STATEROOM BIBBY CABIN
STATESMAN GENRO SOLON
FATHER STATIST WARWICK
JACOBEAN WEALSMAN
AMERICAN HAY JAY LEE AMES
BURR CLAY FISH HALE HULL OTIS
POLK REED ROOT RUSK BAKER
BLAND BORAH CHASE GERRY
HENRY MARCY OLNEY WYTHE
BARUCH BLAINE BOWLES BROOKE
BUNCHE CARTER EVARTS FOSTER
GORHAM HURLEY MCKEAN
MORRIS NORRIS RODNEY
SEWARD SUMNER TOOMBS
ACHESON ALDRICH BARBOUR
CLINTON CUMMINS DANIELS
EVERETT KELLOGG LANSING
LAURENS LINCOLN MORRILL
SHERMAN STIMSON WEBSTER
FRANKLIN GALLATIN HAMILTON
MILLEDGE PINCKNEY RANDOLPH
RUTLEDGE SCHUYLER TRUMBULL
DICKINSON ELLSWORTH
FULBRIGHT PICKERING
WASHINGTON SCHUSCHNIGG
BRECKENRIDGE
ARGENTINIAN MITRE ALBERDI
CARCANO DORREGO FRONDIZI
RIVADAVIA
AUSTRALIAN SEE COOK BRUCE
EVATT LYONS PRICE BARTON
DEAKIN FISHER HOLDER HUGHES
ISSACS LAWSON PARKES SCULLIN
NICHOLSON
AUSTRIAN BACH BRUCK KHESL

RAMEK UNGER BADENI GLASER
PLENER RENNER SEIPEL TAAFFE
BURESCH FIRMIAN HELFERT
KAUNITZ KOERBER SCHOBER
STADION BELCREDI DOLLFUSS
HAYMERLE HUSSAREK
LAMMASCH EGGENBERG
BELLEGARDE METTERNICH
SCHMERLING BARTENSTEIN
GOLUCHOWSKI PILLERSDORF
STARHEMBERG
BELGIAN SPAAK DEVAUX HYMANS
JACOBS JASPAR MERODE ROGIER
ANETHAN NOTHOMB THEUNIS
ZEELAND DECHAMPS BEERNAERT
DELACROIX SCHOLLAERT
VANDERVELDE
BOLIVIAN FRIAS MONTES
BALDIVIESO
BRAZILIAN ABREU FEIJO CAXIAS
BERNARDES MAGALHAES
BULGARIAN DANEV SAVOY
MALINOV TSANKOV LIAPCHEV
KARAVELOV STAMBOLOV
RADOSLAVOV STAMBOLISKI
CANADIAN KING GOUIN JETTE
SCOTT TACHE VIGER BORDEN
BOWELL FISHER FOSTER HUGHES
MANION SIFTON TUPPER
BENNETT BRODEUR CARTIER
DOHERTY LAURIER MEIGHEN
PEARSON RALSTON TRUDEAU
MICHENER THOMPSON
MACDONALD MACKENZIE
PELLETIER CARTWRIGHT
LAFONTAINE DIEFENBAKER
FITZPATRICK
CHILEAN CRUZ RIOS EGANA
MONTT FREIRE CRUCHAGA
OHIGGINS BALMACEDA
ALESSANDRI
CHINESE WU KOO YEN KUNG
COLOMBIAN ZEA HERRAN
COSTA RICAN CASTRO
CUBAN PALMA
CZECH BENES HACHA HODZA
KRAMAR RIEGER SVEHLA UDRZAL
MASARYK
DANISH HALL ZAHLE BLUHME
ESTRUP MONRAD RANTZAU
GULDBERG STAUNING
NEERGAARD GRIFFENFELD
DUTCH CATS FOCK ASSER DOUSA
FAGEL HAREN COLIJN DEWITT
KUYPER GROTIUS HEINSIUS
KLEFFENS HEEMSKERK
KARNEBEEK VANDIEMEN
BARNEVELDT BEEREENBROUCK
ECUADORIAN FLORES
EGYPTIAN SADAT ZIWAR
ENGLISH FOX LAW PYM EDEN
HOPE HYDE LAMB LONG MORE
PEEL PITT VANE WEBB WOOD
AMERY BEVAN BURKE ELIOT
HEATH HOARE JUXON LEWIS
NIGEL PAGET BLOUNT BRIGHT
COBDEN CRIPPS CURZON GEDDES
GIBSON GRAHAM HARLEY
HATTON HEATON HOLLES
MORELY MORTON SAVILE SELDEN
SIDNEY SOMERS TEMPLE WOLSEY
ASQUITH BALDWIN BALFOUR
CANNING GIFFARD GOSCHEN

HALDANE HAMPDEN HERRIES
LAMBTON OSBORNE READING
RUSSELL STANLEY STEWART
SWINTON WALPOLE WINDHAM
WYKEHAM WYNDHAM ADDERLEY
ANNESLEY BEAUFORT CARTERET
COURTNEY CROMWELL DISRAELI
GARDINER GOULBURN HAMILTON
HARCOURT HASTINGS MACAULAY
MONTFORT ROBINSON STANHOPE
VILLIERS ADDINGTON BLEDISLOE
CHURCHILL CUSHENDUN
FITZNEALE FITZPETER FORTESCUE
GAITSKELL GLADSTONE
GLANVILLE GODOLPHIN
GREENWOOD GRENVILLE
HUSKISSON KIMBERLEY
LANSDOWNE LIVERPOOL
MACDONALD NORTHCOTE
STRAFFORD WAKEFIELD
BIRKENHEAD PALMERSTON
ROCKINGHAM WALSINGHAM
WELLINGTON WHITELOCKE
WILLINGDON BOLINGBROKE
CHAMBERLAIN FITZWILLIAM
SHAFTESBURY SOUTHAMPTON
CHESTERFIELD
ESTONIAN PATS STRANDMAN
FINNISH KALLIO CAJANDER
MECHELIN RELANDER STAHLBERG
MANNERHEIM
FRENCH DARU MOLE DUPUY
FAURE FAVRE FERRY FOULD
MARET MONIS PASSY RIBOT
SIMON SUGER SULLY AVENOL
BARROT BERNIS BIGNON BRIAND
CARNOT CASSIN DOUMER
DUPRAT FLEURY FOUCHE GUIZOT
LOUBET MELINE NECKER PERIER
ROUHER THIERS TURGOT
COLBERT DECAZES GRAMONT
HERRIOT MAISTRE MARIGNY
MAUPEOU MAZARIN MOLLIEN
NOGARET REGNIER ROUVIER
SEGUIER VILLELE VIVIANI
CHOISEUL CONSTANS DALADIER
DELCASSE FONTANES FRANCOIS
GAMBETTA HANOTAUX PAINLEVE
POINCARE POMPIDOU PORTALIS
BOURGEOIS CHAMPAGNY
CLEMENTEL DOUMERGUE
FALLIERES LAFAYETTE
MILLERAND RICHELIEU
VERGENNES BARTHELEMY
CLEMENCEAU TALLEYRAND
WADDINGTON BASSOMPIERRE
CHATEAUBRIAND
GERMAN BLOS CUNO FALK MARX
SOLF BEUST JAGOW NOSKE
PAPEN BRANDT GERBER KRANTZ
LUTHER MAURER MIQUEL
BRUNING CAPRIVI CURTIUS
FABRICE GESSLER STEPHAN
ADENAUER BISMARCK HAINISCH
HERTLING HOLSTEIN KUHLMANN
SEVERING SPANHEIM BENNIGSEN
ERZBERGER MICHAELIS
BERNSTORFF FEHRENBACH
HILFERDING RICHTHOFEN
SCHLEICHER STRESEMANN
WINDTHORST ZIMMERMANN
SECKENDORFF
GREEK ZAIMES KANARES KORIZES

RANGABE RHALLES BULGARIS
GOUNARES KONDYLES PANGALOS
PERICLES TIMOLEON DINARCHUS
DRAGOUMES PERIANDER
TIMOTHEUS TRIKOUPES
TSALDARES TSOUDEROS
VENIZELOS SKOULOUDES
THEMISTIUS THERAMENES
DEMOSTHENES THRASYBULUS
THEMISTOCLES
KOUMOUNDOUROS
MAVROKORDATOS
MICHALAKOPOULOS
HUNGARIAN DEAK VASS CSAKY
SZELL TISZA BANFFY BAROSS
EOTVOS GOMBOS HORTHY
LONYAY TELEKI BETHLEN
HORVATH HUNYADI KOSSUTH
WEKERLE ANDRASSY SZECHENYI
MARTINUZZI
ICELANDIC HAFSTEIN SIGURDSSON
INDIAN NOON GUPTA NEHRU
SINHA BAJPAI GANDHI SASTRI
IRISH HYDE ANDREWS GRATTAN
MCNEILL COSGRAVE CRAIGAVON
ISRAELI DAYAN
ITALIAN BALBO BERTI CIANO
CROCE FACTA LANZA MANIN
NITTI ROCCO ROSSI SELLA VOLPI
BONGHI CAVOUR CRISPI FEDELE
GRANDI PEPOLI RUDINI SFORZA
ADRIANI ALFIERI AZEGLIO
CADORNA CAIROLI DURANDO
GRAVINA MAMIANI MANCINI
ORLANDO PELLOUX PONTANO
SONNINO TANUCCI TITTONI
VILLARI ALBERONI CIBRARIO
CORRENTI DEPRETIS GIOLITTI
LAFARINA LUZZATTI MATTIOLI
MENABREA NICOTERA RATTAZZI
RICASOLI SALANDRA SCIALOIA
FEDERZONI GARIBALDI
GUERRAZZI LAMARMORA
MINGHETTI MONTANELLI
ZANARDELLI MACHIAVELLI
LAMBRUSCHINI
JAPANESE ITO GOTO HARA KATO
SATO MUTSU OKUBO OKUMA
INOUYE KANEKO KOMURA
MAKINO TANAKA HAYASHI
ITAGAKI IWAKURA IYEYASU
KATSURA SAIONJI HIRANUMA
KIYOMORI MATSUOKA
NOBUNAGA TERAUCHI
YAMAGATA YAMAMOTO
HAMAGUCHI HIDEYOSHI
MATSUKATA WAKATSUKI
LATVIAN KVIESIS ULMANIS
MEIEROVICS
LIBERIAN TUBMAN TOLBERT
LITHUANIAN SMETONA
VOLDEMARAS
MEXICAN DIAZ ALAMAN ZULOAGA
IGLESIAS
NEW ZEALAND FOX HALL WARD
ALLEN VOGEL COATES FORBES
FRASER MASSEY SEDDON
ATKINSON STAFFORD
NORWEGIAN KOHT FALSEN
HAMBRO HAGERUP KNUDSEN
SVERDRUP MICHELSEN
MOWINCKEL NYGAARDSVOLD
PERUVIAN CORNEJO CADLERON

BENAVIDES MENDIBURU
PHILIPPINE ROXAS OSMENA
QUEZON
POLISH BECK WITOS DMOWSKI
ZALESKI ZALUSKI SIKORSKI
SKRYNSKI KOSCIUSKO PILSUDSKI
PADEREWSKI WOJCIECHOWSKI
PORTUGUESE PAES COSTA
POMBAL ALMEIDA ARRIAGA
CARMONA MACHADO SALAZAR
CARVALHO SALDANHA
SANTAREM
PRUSSIAN BULOW
ROMAN CATO CINNA CAESAR
CICERO LAELIUS RUFINUS
CAMILLUS MAECENAS STILICHO
FABRICIUS FLAMINIUS SERTORIUS
SYMMACHUS CASSIDORUS
HORTENSIUS
ROMANIAN CARP MANIU IONESCU
CATARGIU MIRONESCU
TITULESCU MARGHILOMAN
KOGALNICEANU
RUSSIAN BIRON GIERS WITTE
BLUDOV CANCRIN KALININ
MOLOTOV MUNNICH SIEVERS
TOLSTOI AVERESCU CHICHKOV
DMITRIEV GOLITSYN IZVOLSKI
LAMSDORF POTMEKIN STOLYPIN
CALINESCU CHICHERIN
GORCHAKOV GOREMYKIN
GRIBOEDOV MENSHIKOV
SPERANSKI NESSELRODE
PROTOPOPOV
SOUTH AFRICAN BOTHA BRAND
REITZ SMUTS STEYN KRUGER
SPRIGG COGHLAN HERTZOG
MERRIMAN
SCOTTISH HUME KNOX BEATON
GORDON MURRAY JAMESON
MAITLAND RANDOLPH
WARRISTON ELPHINSTONE
SERBIAN GRUIC
SPANISH LUNA ALAVA GODOY
OSUNA PEREZ GALVEZ MANUEL
TORENO ABASCAL ALARCON
ISTURIZ MENDOZA NARVAEZ
SAGASTA SILVELA ENSENADA
ESCOSURA MANRIQUE OLIVARES
QUINTANA ZORRILLA
CALOMARDE ESCOIQUIZ
ESPARTERO REQUESENS
JOVELLANOS MIRAFLORES
SWEDISH EDEN GEER HORN TOLL
BRAHE ESSEN UNDEN HANSSON
LINDMAN SANDLER BRANTING
FORSSELL EHRENSVARD
GYLLENBORG WENNERBERG
OXENSTIERNA OXENSTJERNA
HAMMARSKJOLD
SWISS ADOR DROZ FAZY KERN
MUSY FURER GOBAT MEYER
MOTTA BLUMER ESCHER MINGER
MULLER DEUCHER BLUNTSCHLI
SCHULTHESS
TURKISH INONU SARACOGLU
URUGUAYAN RIVERA
VENEZUELAN VARGAS BOLIVAR
MONAGAS BETANCOURT
YUGOSLAV PASIC PROTIC
ZIVKOVIC DAVIDOVIC
MARINKOVIC PRIBICEVIC
STATICE ARMERIA LIMONIUM

STATION BY BYE FIX ORB RUN SET
BASE GARE POST RANK ROOM
SEAT STOP BEING BERTH CHOKY
DEPOT PLACE POSTE SIEGE
STAGE STALL STAND STATE
DEGREE LOCATE STANCE
CONTROL CUARTEL DIGNITY
HABITAT OUTPOST GARRISON
PILTDOWN POSITION STANDING
TERMINAL TERMINUS TRANSFER
(— IN BASEBALL) BASE
(— IN LIFE) BEING CALLING
(— OF HERON) SEDGE SIEGE
(CONCEALED —) AMBUSH
(CUSTOMS —) CHOKEY
(EXALTED —) PURPLE
(POLICE —) TANA TANNA THANAH
KOTWALEE
(POST —) DAK
(RADIO —S) CHAIN NETWORK
(RAILWAY —) GARE CABIN
(SIGNALLING —) BANTAY BEACON
(SURVEYING —) STADIA
(TRADING —) FACTORY
(WAY —) TAMBO
STATIONARY SET FAST FIXED
STILL LEDGER STATIC DORMANT
SITFAST STABILE STATARY
IMMOBILE
STATIONERY PAPER PAPETERIE
STATISTICIAN ANALYST STATIST
STATOBLAST SPORE
STATUARY IMAGERY
STATUE HERM ICON IDOL IKON
TERM BUSTO HERMA IMAGE
MOSES AGALMA BRONZE HERMES
MEMNON STATUA WEEPER
XOANON ILISSUS PASQUIN
PICTURE STATURE STATUTE
ACROLITH CARYATID MARFORIO
MONUMENT PANTHEUM
PORTRAIT VICTORIA
(— ENDOWED WITH LIFE) GALATEA
(— OF ATHENA) PALLADIUM
(— OF GIGANTIC SIZE) COLOSSUS
(COLOSSAL —) GOG MAGOG
STATUETTE WAX EMMY OSCAR
WINNIE TANAGRA FIGULINE
FIGURINE SIGILLUM
(AWARD —) GRAMMY
STATURE PITCH GROWTH HEIGHT
INCHES WASTME CAPACITY
STATUS RANK SEAT PLACE STATE
ASPECT FOOTING STATURE
POSITION STANDING SITUATION
(— OF YOUNGER SON) CADENCY
(HIGH —) CACHET
(LEGAL —) CAPUT
(SECONDARY —) BACKSEAT
STATUTE ACT LAW LEX DOOM
EDICT ASSIZE DECREE SETNESS
SITTING STATUTUM TANZIMAT
(— FAIR) MOP
STATUTORY LEGAL
STAUNCH FAST STOUT TRUSTY
FAITHFUL STALWART
STAVE LAG SLAT STAP SHAKE
STAFF STOVE VERSE BASTON
STANZA WATTLE
(— IN) BILGE BULGE
(SET OF —S) SHOOK
(PL.) LAGGEN LAGGIN STICKS
STAVING

STAY DAY GET LIE BASE HOLD
LEND PROP REST SIST STOP WAIT
ABIDE ABODE APPUI DEFER
DELAY DEMUR DWELL LEAVE
STINT TARRY THOLE ARREST
ATTEND BIDING DETAIN EXPECT
GUSSET POTENT REMAIN TIMBER
UPHOLD EMBASSY JIBSTAY
LAYOVER MANSION SOJOURN
SUSPEND BACKSTAY CONTINUE
FORESTAY HORNSTAY MAINSTAY
MARTINGALE
(— AWAY) SKIP
(— BEHIND) LAG
(— CLEAR) AVOID
(— FOR) AWAIT
(— THE NIGHT) BUNK HOSTLE
(— WITH) STICK
(PRIEST'S —) STATION
(TAILORING —) BRIDLE
(PL.) JUMPS JUPES BODICE
STAY-AT-HOME HOMEBODY
HOMESTER
STAYER BONER
STAYLACE AGLET AIGLET
STAYSAIL JUMBO
STEAD LIEU ROOM VICE PLACE
BEHALF
STEADFAST PAT SAD FAST FIRM
SURE TRUE ROCKY STAID STEER
STABLE STANCH STEADY CERTAIN
EXPRESS SETTLED STAUNCH
VALIANT CONSTANT FAITHFUL
RESOLUTE STALWART
STEADFASTLY FIRM FIRMLY
INTENTLY
STEADILY SAD FAST STEADY
STEADINESS NERVE BALANCE
STEADING ONSET ONSTEAD
STEADY GUY SAD BEAU EVEN
FIRM SURE TRIG TRUE CANNY
FRANK LEVEL SOBER STUDY
SUANT TIGHT SICCAR SMOOTH
STABLE STANCH BALLAST
EQUABLE STABILE STATARY
STAUNCH CONSTANT DECOROUS
DILIGENT FAITHFUL RESOLUTE
TRANQUIL UNSHAKEN
(— AT ANCHOR) HOLSOM
STEAK BROIL SHELL FLITCH
TUCKET GRISKIN PORTERHOUSE
STEAL BAG CAB CLY COP FOX GYP
LAG MAG NAP NIM NIP RAP RIG
BONE CHON COON CRIB FAKE
GLOM HOOK KNAP LIFT LURK
MAGG MAKE MILL NAIL NICK
PEAK PICK PRIG SLIP SMUG
ANNEX BOOST BRIBE CLOUT
CREEP FETCH FILCH FLIMP FRISK
GLIDE HARRY HEIST HOIST LURCH
MOOCH MOUCH PINCH PLUCK
POACH SCOFF SHAKE SHARP
SHAVE SLIDE SNAKE SNARE
SNEAK STALK SWIPE TOUCH
TRUFF COLLAR CONVEY FINGER
HIJACK MOOTCH NOBBLE PILFER
RIPOFF SNITCH STRIKE THIEVE
TWITCH BESTEAL CABBAGE
PLUNDER PURLOIN SCHLEPP
SKYUGLE SNABBLE SNAFFLE
SURREPT ABSTRACT CRIBBAGE
EMBEZZLE LIBERATE MANARVEL
PECULATE SCROUNGE

SHOPLIFT PLAGIARIZE
(**— A GLANCE**) GLIME
(**— A WATCH**) FLIMP
(**— ALONG**) SLIME SLINK
(**— AWAY**) LOOP SLINK
(**— BY ALTERING BRANDS**) DUFF
(**— CALVES**) NUGGET
(**— CATTLE**) DUFF RUSTLE
(**— COPPER FROM VESSEL'S BOTTOM**) TOSH
(**— OFF**) RUN
(**— SLYLY**) SCROUNGE
STEALER (**CATTLE —**) DUFFER
ABACTOR
STEALING STALE
(PREF.) KLEPT(O)
STEALTHILY SIDLINS THIEFLY
SIDELINS
STEALTHY CATTY PRIVY ARTFUL
FELINE TIPTOE CATLIKE FURTIVE
SNEAKING THIEVISH
STEAM OAM ROKE STEM BLAST
SMOKE SWEAT VAPOR BREATH
POTHER CUSHION
(PREF.) ATM(O) ATMID(O)
STEAMBOAT KICKUP STEAMER
STEAMER CLAM LINER TENDER
CUNARDER
STEAMER DUCK RACER LOGHEAD
STEAMSHIP SCREW STEAM
STEAMER SEATRAIN SHOWBOAT
STEAM SHOVEL NAVVY NAVVIE
STEATIN MULL
STEATITE LARDITE POTSTONE
SOAPROCK
STEATOPYGOUS RUMPY
STEED NAG ROIL HORSE MOUNT
STEAD PEGASUS SLEIPNER
STEEL RAIL BLOOM BRACE FUSIL
TERNE WEAPON WHITTLE
FLEERISH
(**— FOR STRIKING FIRE**) ESLABON
(**— FOR USE WITH FLINT**) FUSIL
FURISON FLEERISH
(**— INLAID WITH GOLD**) KOFT
KOFTGARI
(**DAMASCUS —**) DAMASK
(**INDIAN —**) WOOTZ
(**MOLTEN —**) HEAT
STEELER BONER
STEELING ACIERAGE
STEELWORKER HOOKER
STICKMAN STRANDER STRANNER
STEELYARD BISMAR BISMER
DESEMER DOTCHIN STATERA
STEENBRAS BISKOP
STEEP SOP BATE BOLD BOWK
BUCK DEAR DRAW DUNG ELIX
LIME MASH MASK SOAK STAY
STEW STEY BLUFF BRANT BRENT
HATCH HEAVY HILLY QUICK
SHARP SHEER SOUSE STIFF
ABRUPT BLUFFY CLIFFY CLIFTY
DECOCT IMBIBE INFUSE SPRUNT
STEEPY ARDUOUS BRASQUE
CLIVOSE INSTEEP PRERUPT
STICKLE HEADLONG MACERATE
SATURATE SIDELING STIFFISH
STRAIGHT PRECIPITOUS
STEEPED SODDEN
STEEPING SOUSE INFUSION
STEEPLE SPEAR SPIRE
STEEPLECHASE CHASE GRIND

STEER COX PLY AIRT BEEF BULL
HELM LEAD STEM STOT GUIDE
SPADE SPADO STERN TOLLY
CANNER RUDDER BULLOCK
STOCKER COWBRUTE MOSSHORN
NAVIGATE
(**— VEHICLE**) DRIVE
(**FAT —**) BEAST
(**HORNLESS —**) NOT NOTT
(**VICIOUS —**) LADINO
(**WILD —**) YAW YEW COWBRUTE
(**YOUNG —**) STOT STOTT
STEERAGE STERN
STEERER SLUER CAPPER
STEERSMAN PILOT WHEEL
PATRON SLEWER CANOPUS
SHIPMAN STEERER COXSWAIN
HELMSMAN SEACUNNY
STERNMAN WHEELMAN
COCKSWAIN
STEGOMYIA AEDES
STEIN SHANT
STEINBOCK BOUQUETIN
STELE SHAFT EUSTELE
STELLAR STARRY
STELLATE ASTROSE
STEM BUN BASE BEAK BEAM BINE
BIRN CANE CULM CURB NOSE
PIPE PROW RISP ROOT RUNT
SHAW STUD ARISE FILUM HAULM
SCAPE SCREW SHAFT SHANK
SHOOT SPIRE STALE STALK STEAL
STICK STIPE STOCK STRAW
THEME TRUNK TUBER BRANCH
CAUDEX CAULIS DERIVE SCAPUS
SPRING CAULOME CONTAIN
FULCRUM HOPBINE HOPVINE
PEDICEL PETIOLE PLASHER
SARMENT SPINDLE STEMLET
TIGELLA CAULICLE ENGENDER
EPICOTYL FORESTEM PEDUNCLE
PIPESTEM TIGELLUM
(**— OF ARROW**) SHAFT
(**— OF BANANAS**) COUNT
(**— OF GLASS**) BALUSTER
(**— OF GRAPES**) RAPE
(**— OF HOOKAH**) SNAKE
(**— OF MATCH**) SHAFT
(**— OF MUSHROOM**) STIPE
(**— OF MUSICAL NOTE**) TAIL FILUM
VIRGULA
(**— OF PIPE**) STAPPLE
(**— OF PLANT**) AXIS RUNT CAULIS
(**— OF SHIP**) PROW STEMPOST
(**— OF TREE**) BOLE CAUDEX
(**—S OF CULTIVATED PLANTS**)
HAULM
(**BULBLIKE —**) CORM
(**DRY WITHERED —**) BIRN
(**EDIBLE —**) EDDO
(**GRIEF —**) KELLY
(**MAIN — OF DEER'S ANTLERS**) BEAM
(**ORNAMENTAL —**) STAVE
(**PITHY JOINTED —**) CANE
(**THORNY —**) LAWYER
(**TWINING —**) BINE
(PREF.) CAUL(I) CORM(O) CULMI
SCAPI STIRPI
(SUFF.) DENDRON OME
STEMLESS ACAULINE
STEMMA OCELLUS OCELLANA
PEDIGREE
STEMMER STRIPPER

STENCH FOGO HOGO FETOR SMELL
STINK WHIFF FOETOR MEPHITIS
STENCIL (**— PROCESS**) POCHOIR
STENCILED COFFERED
STENOGRAPHY SHORTHAND
STENOSIS SMALLING
STEP CUT FIT JOG PEG PIP BEMA
DESS FOOT GREE LINK PACE PEEP
RUNG STAP BRASS CORTE DODGE
FLIER FLYER GRECE NOTCH POINT
STAGE STAIR TOOTH TRACE
TREAD DEGREE GRADIN RUNDLE
STRIDE WINDER CURTAIL
DESCENT FOOTING GRADINE
GRADING COONJINE DEMARCHE
DOORSTEP FOOTPACE FOOTSTEP
FORESTEP PREDELLA STRATLIN
(**— ASIDE**) DIGRESS
(**— BACKWARD**) DODGE
(**— BY STEP**) GRADATIM
(**— DOWNWARD**) DESCENT
(**— FOR GEM MOUNTING**) KITE
(**— FORWARD**) ADVANCE
(**— IN A BEARING**) BRASS
(**— IN BELL RINGING**) DODGE
(**— IN DOCK**) ALTAR
(**— IN SELF-ESTEEM**) PEG
(**— IN SEQUENCE**) PLACE
(**— IN SOCIAL SCALE**) CUT
(**— IN TRENCH**) BANQUETTE
(**— LIVELY**) SKELP
(**— OF LADDER**) RIME RUNG
ROUND RUNDLE
(**— OF TUSK**) TOOTH
(**— PERFORMED BY COMPUTER**)
OPERATION
(**— SUPPORTING MILLSTONE**)
TRAMPOT
(**—S OF BOWLER**) APPROACH
(**ALTAR —S**) GRADUAL
(**BALLET —**) PLIE FOUETTE
SISSONE SISSONNE
(**BALLET —S**) ALLEGRO
(**BOUNDING —**) SKIP
(**CLUMSY —**) STAUP
(**DANCE —**) DIP PAS SET BUZZ
DRAG DRAW FLAT SHAG SKIP
BRAWL CHASS COULE GLIDE
IRISH STOMP BRANLE CANTER
CHASSE DOUBLE INTURN STRIDE
BRANSLE BUFFALO FISHTAIL
GLISSADE PIGEONWING
(**FALSE —**) HOB SLIP SPHALM
SNAPPER SPHALMA STUMBLE
(**FIRST —**) STARTER RUDIMENT
(**FLIGHT OF —S**) GRECE GRICE
PERRON GEMONIES
(**HALF —**) HALFTONE SEMITONE
(**LIGHT —**) PITAPAT
(**MINING —**) LOB STEMPEL
STEMPLE
(**POMPOUS —**) STRUT
(**PRIM —**) MINCE
(**SET OF —S**) STILE
(**STATELY —**) STALK
(PL.) STY GHAT GHAUT STILE
LADDER
STEPFATHER FATHER STEPSIRE
STEPLADDER TRAP STEPS
(**PART OF —**) RAIL REST RUNG
SHOE STEP BRACE SPREADER
STEPMOTHER MOTHER HANGNAIL
STEPDAME

(**RELATING TO —**) NOVERCAL
STEPPE PUSZTA
(**— REGION**) SAHEL
(**ARID REGION OF —**) POECHORE
STEPPED STOPEN
STEPPENWOLF (**AUTHOR OF —**)
HESSE
(**CHARACTER IN —**) HARRY MARIA
HALLER HERMINE
STEPPING
(SUFF.) GRADE
STEREOISOMER ANOMER EPIMER
STEREOTYPE CAST CLICHE
STEREO
STEREOTYPED CHAIN STAGE
TRITE USUAL STEREO
STERILE DRY DEAD DEAF GELD
POOR AXENIC BARREN GALLED
MEAGER MULISH OTIOSE ASEPTIC
ACARPOUS BANKRUPT IMPOTENT
(PREF.) STEIRO
STERILITY ATOCIA APHORIA
STERILIZE INSULATE
STERILIZING BURNING
STERLING SOUND
(**100,000 POUNDS —**) PLUM
STERN GRIL GRIM HARD POOP
ASPER CRUEL GRUFF HARSH
RIGID ROUGH ROUND STARK
STOUR FLINTY GLOOMY GRIMLY
SHREWD STRICT SULLEN TORVID
UNKIND WICKED AUSTERE
TORVOUS STEERAGE STERNFUL
STRAIGHT
(**— OF SHIP**) DOCK APLUSTRE
STERNFAST PROVISO
STERNNESS RIGOR TORVITY
SEVERITY
STERNPOST POST STEM
MAINPOST
STERNUTATIVE ERRHINE PTARMIC
STERNUTATOR ERRHINE
STEROL AMYRIN STERIN AMBRAIN
STEROPE (**FATHER OF —**) ATLAS
(**MOTHER OF —**) PLEIONE
(**SON OF —**) OENOMAUS
STEVEDORE STOWER TRIMMER
WHARFIE CARGADOR DOCKHAND
STEVENSON, R.L. TUSITALA
STEW JUG FRET ITCH SLUM SNIT
SWOT BREDI CIVET CURRY DAUBE
SALMI STIVE STOVE SWEAT
BRAISE BURGOO HODDLE
MUDDLE PAELLA SEETHE SIMMER
BROTHEL CALDERA GOULASH
HARICOT NAVARIN PUCHERO
STOVIES TERRINE FRIJOADA
HOTCHPOT MORTREUX
MULLIGAN STEWPOND STUFFATA
SLUMGULLION
(**— A HARE**) JUG
(**— IN A SAUCE**) DAUBE
(**— MADE IN FORECASTLE**) HODDLE
(**— OF TRAMPS**) MULLIGAN
(**FISH —**) STODGE CHOWDER
MATELOTE
(**IRISH —**) STOVIES
(**MUTTON —**) NAVARIN
STEWARD HIND VOGT DEWAN
DIWAN GRAFF GRAVE REEVE
COMMIS FACTOR FARMER GRIEVE
LOOKER SIRCAR SIRDAR BAILIFF
CURATOR DAPIFER FLUNKEY

GRANGER HUSBAND MAORMOR
MORMAOR PESHKAR PROCTOR
PROVOST SPENCER SPENDER
APPROVER BHANDARI CELLARER
CONSUMAH GASTALDO
HERENACH KHANSAMA LARDINER
MALVOLIO MANCIPLE PROVISOR
STEADMAN VILLICUS
MAJORDOMO
(JOCKEY CLUB —) STIPE
STEWED SODDEN
STEWING ITCHING
STEWPAN STEW COCOTTE SKILLET
STHENELUS (FATHER OF —)
PERSEUS CAPANEUS ANDROGEOS
(MOTHER OF —) EVADNE
ANDROMEDA
(SON OF —) EURYSTHEUS
(WIFE OF —) NICIPPE
STHENOBOEA (FATHER OF —)
IOBATES
(HUSBAND OF —) PROETUS
STIBNITE SURMA STIBIUM
ANTIMONY
STIBOPHEN FUADIN
STICHIC SERIAL
STICK CAT CLA DIP GAD HEW LUG
WAN BROG BUFF CHOP CLAG
CLAM CLUB CRAB GLUE HANG
HURL PALE PALO PICK POLE POTE
RICE RUNG STAY TREE YARD
BATON BRAIL CAMAN CLAME
CLAVE CLEAM CLING CROME
DEMUR HURLY PASTE PRICK
SPELK STAFF STAKE STANG
STAVE STEND STING STOCK
STOKE VALET VERGE WADDY
ADHERE ATLATL BALLOW BATLER
BATLET BATTLE BILLET BROACH
BULGER CEMENT CLEAVE CLEEKY
COHERE CUDGEL FESCUE HOCKEY
INHERE KIERIE KIPPIN LIBBET
MALLET RADDLE RAMMER RISSLE
STRIKE STRING THIVEL TWITCH
BACKSET BATLING CAMMOCK
CUMMOCK GAMBREL HURLBAT
KILNRIB KIPPEEN MOLINET
NOBBLER SHANGAN SPURTLE
WOOLDER ASHPLANT BLUDGEON
BRINGSEL BRINSELL CATPIECE
CATSTICK CRUMMOCK DIPSTICK
DUTCHMAN GIBSTAFF GOBSTICK
KILNTREE POTSTICK SPREADER
(— AS ARCHERY MARK) WAND
(— FAST) JAM JAMB SEIZE
FITCHER
(— FASTENED TO DOG'S TAIL)
SHANGAN
(— FOR ADMITTING TENANTS)
VERGE
(— FOR FIRING CANNON) LINSTOCK
(— FOR KILLING FISH) NOBBLER
(— FOR MAKING FENCE) RADDLE
(— FOR MIXING CHOCOLATE)
MOLINET
(— FOR MIXING MORTAR) RAB
(— FOR SNUFF) DIP
(— FOR THATCHING) SPAR GROOM
SPELK SPRINGLE
(— IN MUD) STODGE
(— IN OPERATION) FREEZE
(— IT OUT) LAST
(— OF A FAN) BRIN

(— OF CANDY) GIBBY
(— OF CHALK) CRAYON
(— OF ORCHESTRA LEADER) BATON
(— OUT) BUG POKE BULGE SHOOT
EXSERT EXTEND EXTRUDE
PROTEND
(— REGULATING SLUICEWAY)
CATPIECE
(— SEPARATING LUMBER PILES)
STICKER
(— TO BEAT CLOTHES) BATLER
BATLET
(— TO DISTEND CARCASS) STEND
BACKSET
(— TO HOLD BOW) TILLER
(— TO HOLD LOG LOAD)
DUTCHMAN
(— TO KEEP ANIMAL QUIET)
TWITCH
(— TO MARK CROSSING) BROG
(— TO POKE WITH) POTE
(— TO REMOVE HOOK FROM FISH)
GOBSTICK
(— TO STRETCH NET) BRAIL
(— TO STUFF DOLLS) RAMMER
(— TO THROW AT BIRDS) SQUAIL
(— TO TIGHTEN KNOT) WOOLDER
(— TOGETHER) CLOT BLOCK CLING
BALTER CEMENT COHERE
COAGMENT
(— UP) COCK
(— USED AS POINTER) FESCUE
(BAMBOO —) LATHI LATHEE
(BASKETRY —) LEAGUE
(BENT —) RIFLE
(FIELD HOCKEY —) BULGER
CAMMOCK
(FISHING —) GAD
(FORKED —) GROM GROOM
(HOCKEY —) CAMAN HURLY
HOCKEY HURLEY SHINNY
CAMMOCK CUMMOCK DODDART
(IRON-POINTED —) VALET
(KNOBBED —) BILLET
(LACROSSE —) CROSSE
(LARGE —) MOCK
(MARKING —) LEAD
(ODD —) JAY
(POLISHING —) BUFF
(PRAYER —) PAHO
(PRINTER'S —) SHOOTER
(RANGE-FINDING —) STADIA
(ROUND —) DOWEL SPINDLE
(STIRRING —) MUNDLE POOLER
SPURTLE POTSTICK SWIZZLER
(STOUT —) BAT COSH LOWDER
(TALLY —) TAIL
(THROWING —) ATLATL HORNERAH
(TOBACCO —) LATH
(WALKING —) CANE KEBBY WADDY
JAMBEE JOCKEY KEBBIE
WHANGEE ASHPLANT GIBSTAFF
(PREF.) RHABD(O)
STICKER HINGE LABEL STRIP
WAFER HOPPER PASTER BLEEDER
CROSSER MOPSTICK STICKLER
STICK-IN STRANDER
STICKINESS GAUM TACK
ROPINESS
STICKING ADHERENT ADHESION
COHESION COHESIVE
STICKLE DEMUR BOGGLE HAGGLE
HIGGLE

STICKLEBACK BAGGIE BANDIE
HACKLE GHOSTER PINFISH
STICKLER (— FOR FORMALITY)
TAPIST
STICKMAN DEALER
STICKS BOONIES
STICKUM GLUE
STICKY CAB CLAM CLIT ICKY
DABBY FATTY GAUMY GLUEY
GOOEY GUMMY JAMMY MALMY
PUGGY SHORT TACKY TOUGH
CLAGGY CLAMMY CLARTY CLINGY
CLOGGY PLUCKY SMEARY VISCID
VISCOUS ADHESIVE TENACIOUS
(PREF.) GLOEO GLOIO
STIFF BUM SAD CARK HARD NASH
TRIG BUDGE CLUNG RIGID SOLID
STARK STEER STITH STOUR
THARF TOUGH BOARDY CLEDGY
CLUMSY CLUNCH FORMAL
FROZEN PLUGGY STARKY STEEVE
STICKY STILTY STOCKY STURDY
UNEASY WOODEN ANGULAR
BUCKRAM COSTIVE STARCHY
STILTED RAMRODDY RIGOROUS
STAFFISH
(SOMEWHAT —) CARKLED
(PREF.) ANKYL(O) TORPI TORPORI
STIFFELIO (CHARACTER IN —) LINA
STANKAR RAFFAELE STIFFELIO
(COMPOSER OF —) VERDI
STIFFEN GUM SET SIZE BRACE
STARK STIFF STRUT TRUSS
HARDEN STARCH STOVER
CONGEAL STARKEN
(— PRICE) HARDEN
STIFFENED FUSED CARKLED
STIFFENER KNEE COUNTER
STIFFENING PUFF DRESS
STIFFNESS KINK RIGOR STARCH
BUCKRAM PRIMNESS RIGIDITY
SEVERITY
STIFLE DAMP FUNK SLAY CHOKE
CRUSH STIVE STUFF MUFFLE
QUENCH FLASKER QUERKEN
SMOTHER SCOMFISH STRANGLE
SUPPRESS THROTTLE
STIFLED DEAF ETOUFFE
STIFLING CLOSE STIVY SMUDGY
POTHERY SMOTHERY
STIGMA BLOT FOIL NOTE SLUR
SPOT BRAND ODIUM STAIN TAINT
BLOTCH BLEMISH
STIGMATIZE BLOT BRAND
DENOUNCE
STILBITE DESMINE
STILE STY STICK TIMBER
STILETTO BODKIN STYLET PIERCER
POINTEL
STILL BUT COY LAY YET BODY
CALM COSH HUSH LOWN LULL
WORM ACCOY CHECK QUIET
WHIST HOWEER HUSHED PACIFY
QUENCH SETTLE SILENT SOOTHE
STATIC SUBDUE WITHAL ALEMBIC
CORNUTE HOWEVER PELICAN
SILENCE CUCURBIT RECEIVER
RESTRAIN STAGNANT STILLERY
SUPPRESS
(— PART) KELD
(PART OF —) HEAD TUBE RETORT
CONDENSER
STILLAGE SLOP STILLING STILLION

STILL-HUNT STALK
STILLNESS CALM HUSH REST
PEACE LANGUOR SILENCE
STATION
STILT KAKI POGO TILT LAWYER
PATTEN SCATCH YEGUITA
LONGLEGS STILTIFY TRIANGLE
STILTED LOFTY STIFF FORMAL
POETIC STILTY POMPOUS
STIMULANT COCA STIM INULA
BRACER CINDER FILLIP GINGER
HARMAL PHYTIN CAMPHOR
CARDIAC OUABAIN REVIVER
ADONIDIN AMMONIAC EXCITANT
INCITANT PEMOLINE STIMULUS
STIMULATE FAN HOP KEY PEP
FUEL GOAD HYPO MOVE SEED
SPUR STIR URGE WHET FILIP
IMPEL PIQUE PRIME ROUSE
SPARK STING AROUSE BESTIR
EXCITE FILLIP INCITE SPIRIT
TICKLE UPSTIR ANIMATE ENLIVEN
INNERVE INSPIRE PROVOKE
QUICKEN ACTIVATE FARADIZE
IRRITATE MOTIVATE TITILLATE
(FAIL TO —) UNDERWHELM
STIMULATING PERT SEXY BRISK
BRACING PUNGENT EROGENIC
EXCITING GENEROUS INCITANT
POIGNANT STIRRING
(— ANGER) ADRENAL
(PREF.) AUXO EXCITO
STIMULATION GINGER IMPETUS
(MENTAL —) SPRITE
STIMULUS CUE AURA BROD EDGE
GOAD HYPO SPUR STIM STING
FILLIP MOTIVE SOURCE BAHNUNG
IMPETUS OESTRUS
STING NIP BARB BITE BURN FOIN
GOAD TANG ATTER DEVIL PIQUE
PRICK STANG TOUCH NETTLE
ACULEUS BUGBITE PIERCER
IRRITATE STIMULUS
STINGILY STRAIT SCARCELY
STINGINESS PARSIMONY
STINGING KEEN SMART PEPPERY
PIQUANT POINTED PRICKLY
PUNGENT ACRIMONY ACULEATE
NETTLING POIGNANT SCALDING
URTICANT
STINGING ANT KELEP
STINGRAY ANGLER OBISPO
SEPHEN TRYGON BATFISH
LOPHIID STINGER WAIREPO
STINGY DRY DREE GAIN GAIR
HARD MEAN NEAR NIGH CLOSE
MINGY SCALY TIGHT DRIECH
GRIPPY HUNGRY MEASLY
NARROW SCABBY SCARCE
SCRIMY SKIMPY SKINNY SNIPPY
STRAIT CHINCHY CHINTZY
MISERLY NIGGARD PENURIOUS
PARSIMONIOUS
STINK FOGO GOAD NIFF PONG
STEW SMELL SMEECH STENCH
MEPHITIS
(PREF.) BROM(O)
STINKBIRD HOACIN HOATZIN
STINKING FOUL HIGH FETID PUTID
STINKY MALODOROUS
STINKWOOD DOGWOOD
STINT TASK GRIST PINCH SCANT
SNAPE SCRIMP SKINCH STINGY

TANTUM SCANTLE
(SHORT —) SNATCH
(WITHOUT —) FREELY
STIPE STEM STALK
STIPEND ANN HIRE ANNAT WAGES
SALARY PENSION PREBEND
PROVEND COMMENDA
STIPENDIARY BEAK
STIPPLE SPONGE
STIPPLED DOTTED
STIPULATE ARTICLE PROTEST
PROVIDE COVENANT
STIPULATION IF ANNEX CLAUSE
ARTICLE PREMISE PROVISO
COVENANT
(PL.) TERMS
STIPULE SPINE SHEATH STIPEL
STIPULA TENDRIL
STIR DO ADO FAN GOG JEE PUG
WAG BEET BUZZ CARD FUSS
MOVE PEAL POKE RAUK ROKE
WAKE AMOVE BUDGE CHURN
CREEP ERECT FUROR HURRY
MUDGE POACH QUICH RAISE
ROUST SLICE SPARK STING
STOOR STURT TEASE TOUCH
AROUSE AWAKEN BUBBLE
BUSTLE CRUTCH EXCITE FLURRY
GINGER HUBBUB JUMBLE KIAUGH
MUDDLE PADDLE POUTER
QUINCH QUITCH REMBLE REMOVE
ROUNCE STODGE SUMMON
TATTER ACTUATE ANIMATE
BLATHER CLUTTER COMMOVE
FLUTTER PROVOKE STARKLE
SWIZZLE TROUBLE SPLUTTER
(— ABOUT) KNOCK
(— CALICO COLORS) TEER
(— DRINK) MUDDLE SWIZZLE
(— LIQUID) ROG
(— SOIL) CHISEL
(— UP) FAN MIX BUZZ DRUM FUSS
MOVE PROG ROIL TOSS AMOVE
AREAR AWAKE ERECT QUICK
ROUSE SNURL SPOOK STOKE
TARRY BESTIR BOTHER CHOUSE
EXCITE INCITE JOSTLE KINDLE
PUDDLE RUMBLE TICKLE UPSTIR
AGITATE ANIMATE COMMOVE
DISTURB PRODDLE PROVOKE
STUDDLE TORMENT UNQUEME
DISTRACT
(— UP WITH YEAST) BARM
STIRRER HOG DOLLY ROUSER
RUMMAGER
STIRRING RACY ASTIR DEEDFUL
ROUSING THRILLY EXCITING
PATHETIC
STIRRUP IRON CHAPELET
STEELBOW
(PART OF —) EYE PAD TREAD
BRANCH
(PREF.) STAPED(I)(IO)
STITCH BAR RUN SEW KNIT LOOP
PURL WHIP CABLE CLOSE POINT
PREEN PUNTO STEEK ACCRUE
FESTON SUTURE TRICOT
CROCHET POPCORN FAGOTING
(— OF CLOTHES) TACK
(NEEDLEPOINT —) BARGELLO
(PL.) JOURS FILLING PINWORK
STITCHBIRD IHI
STITCHDOWN SEWROUND

STITCHED BROCHE
STITCHER WHIPPER
STITCHING SERGING FAGOTING
STOATING WHIPPING
(SUFF.) RHAPHY RRHAPHY
STITCHWORT PAIGLE ALLBONE
SNAPPER HEADACHE SNAPJACK
SNAPWORT
STITHY STUDY SMITHY STIDDY
STUDDY
STOAT VAIR ERMINE WEASEL
CLUBSTER FUTTERET WHITRACK
STOCK COP DOG KIN ROD CANT
CROP FILL FOND FUND SEED SELL
STEM TRIP BLOND BLOOD BROTH
CASTE CREAM FLESH HOARD
ISSUE PLANT STALE STIRP STORE
STUFF TALON BUDGET CHOKER
COMMON FUTURE KAFFIR
SHARES STOVEN STRAIN SUPPLY
CAPITAL DESCENT PILLORY
PROSAPY PROVIDE REPLETE
RESERVE BONEYARD BOUTIQUE
CROSSBAR DIESTOCK GILLIVER
GUNSTOCK MAGAZINE
MERCHANT ORDINARY SECURITY
PROVISIONS
(— OF ANCHOR) CROSS
(— OF BREEDING MARES) STRUDE
(— OF FOOD) FARE
(— OF GRAIN) COP
(— OF INDIVIDUALS) CLONE
(— OF MORPHEMES) LEXICON
(— OF WEAPONS) ARSENAL
(— OF WHIP) CROP
(— OF WINE) CELLAR
(— SOLD SHORT) BEAR
(FARM —) BOW
(LANGUAGE —) SALISH SIOUAN
BOROTUKE
(MEAT —) BLOND BOUILLON
(PLASTIC —) BISCUIT
(RAILROAD —) GRANGER
(PL.) FOODS CIPPUS HARMAN
TIMBER CATASTA KAFFIRS
(PREF.) STIPI(T)(TI) STIPULI STIRPI
(SUFF.) STIPULAR STIPULATE
STOCKADE BOMA PEEL ETAPE
ZAREBA BARRIER TAMBOUR
STOCKADO
STOCK EXCHANGE BOURSE
COULISSE
STOCKFISH STOCK LUTFISK
TITLING SPELDING SPELDRON
(PREF.) SALPI
STOCKING HOSE SOCK SHANK
STOCK CALIGA MOGGAN
SCOGGER SHINNER BOOTHOSE
(FOOTLESS —) HOGGER HUSHION
(SOLELESS —) TRAHEEN
(PL.) HOSE NYLONS BUSKINS
BOOTHOSE
STOCKJOBBING AGIOTAGE
STOCKWORK CARBONA
STOCKY FAT COBBY DUMPY
GROSS SQUAT STOUT CHUMPY
CHUNKY DUMPTY STUBBY
STUGGY STUNTY BUNTING
COMPACT HEAVYSET STOCKISH
THICKSET
STODGY STUFFY STUGGY
BOURGEOIS
STOIC IMPASSIVE

STOKEHOLD FIREROOM
STOKER FIREMAN BLOCKMAN
STOLE STAW ARMIL ORARY
ARMILLA ORARION PALATINE
STOLEN HOT BENT INOME STOUN
FURTIVE
(— GOODS) MAINOUR
STOLID BEEFY BOVINE CLUMSE
STUPID WOODEN CLUMPST
DEADPAN PASSIVE
STOLIDITY MORGUE
STOLON WIRE SOBOL SOBOLE
SOLENIUM
STOMA PORE OPENING OSTIOLE
STOMACH MAW CROP GUTS KYTE
MARY POKE READ TANK WAME
WOMB BINGY BROOK GORGE
GROUF HEART TUMMY BINGEE
BINGEY BONNET CROPPY GEBBIE
PECHAN VENTER CONCOCT
CRAPPIN GIZZARD ABOMASUM
(— OF ANIMAL) CRAW
(— OF CALF) VELL
(— OF RUMINANT) READ RUMEN
BONNET OMASUM PAUNCH
ABOMASUM MANIFOLD RODDIKIN
(PIG'S —) JAUDIE
(PREF.) GASTER(O) GASTR(I)(O)
RUMENO
(SUFF.) GASTER GASTRIA
STOMACHACHE FANTAD GULLION
STOMACHER GIMP TRUSS
ECHELLE PLACARD POITREL
FOREPART
STOMACHIC COTO CORNUS
BITTERS CALUMBA GENTIAN
LUPULIN ANTHEMIS
STOMATITIS NOMA
STONE DAM GEM RAG BOND DUCK
FLAG HERD KLIP KNAR MARK
PELT ROCK STEN TRIG BAUTA
CAPEL CHUCK DRAKE GUARD
LAPIS PAVER PITCH SCRAE SCREE
SNECK STANE ASHLAR BEDDER
BENBEN CEPHAS CHATON CLOSER
COBBLE GAMAHE GIBBER HEADER
JUMPER LEDGER MARVER
METATE MULLER NUTLET PEEVER
PINNER RUNNER SUMMER
TORSEL ANGRITE CALLAIS
DINGBAT DONNOCK DORNICK
GLIDDER KNEELER KNICKER
PERPEND PITCHER PUTAMEN
RATCHEL STANNER SURFACE
THROUGH BAETULUS CABOCHON
DENDRITE EBENEZER HAGSTONE
LAPIDATE LAPILLUS LAPSTONE
MACEHEAD MONOLITH NAKHLITE
SKEWBACK TOPSTONE
(— ADHERING TO LEAD ORE) KEVEL
(— AS AMULET) HAGSTONE
(— AS IT COMES FROM QUARRY)
RUBBLE
(— AS ROAD MARKER) LEAGUE
(— AT DOOR) RYBAT
(— BLOCK) ASSIZE
(— FOR GLASS-ROLLING) MARVER
(— FOR MOUNTING HORSE)
MONTOIR
(— FORMING CAP OF PIER)
SUMMER CUSHION
(— HARD TO MOVE) SITFAST
(— HEAP) MAN

(— IN BLAST FURNACE) DAM
(— IN MEMORY OF DEAD)
MONUMENT
(— IN SMALL FRAGMENTS)
RATCHEL
(— IN WALL) PARPEN
(— MARKING CENTER OF WORLD)
OMPHALOS
(— OF FRUIT) COB PIT PAIP COBBE
NUTLET PYRENE PUTAMEN
(— OF PYRAMID SHAPE) BENBEN
**(— PROVIDING CHANGE OF
DIRECTION)** KNEELER
(— SET IN RING) CHATON
(— SHAPED BY WIND) VENTIFACT
(— SHOT FROM STONE-BOW) JALET
(— TO DEATH) LAPIDATE
(— USED AS MONUMENT)
MEGALITH
(— USED IN GAME) DUCK DRAKE
(— WITH INTERNAL CAVITY) GEODE
(—S FROM CRUSHER) TAILINGS
(—S IN WATER) STANNERS
(ARTIFICIAL —) ALBOLITE
(BINDING —) PERPEND THROUGH
PIERPONT
(BOND —) GIRDER KEYSTONE
(BOUNDARY —) TERM TERMINUS
(BROKEN —) RIPRAP
(BROKEN — USED FOR ROADS)
BALLAST MACADAM
(BUILDING —) SUMMER MITCHEL
SPERONE
(CARVED —) CAMEO CUVETTE
(CASTING —) TYMP
(CHINA —) PETUNSE
(CLAY —) LECH
(COPING —) SKEW TABLET
TABLING CAPSTONE
(CURLING —) HOG HERD GUARD
LOOFIE POTLID
(CYLINDRICAL —) TAMBOUR
(DESERT —) GIBBER
(DRUID —) SARSEN
(DRYING —) STILLAGE
(EDGING —) SETTER
(FLAT —) PLAT DRAKE LEDGER
(FOUNDATION —) BEDDER
(GLITTERING —) DAZE
(GRAVE —) BAUTA STELE
(GREEN —) CALLAIS
(GRINDING —) METATE MULLER
(HOLY —) BEAR BAETYL
(HOPSCOTCH —) PEEVER PALLALL
(IMAGINARY —) ADAMANT
(KIDNEY —) NEPHRITE
(LAST — IN COURSE) CLOSER
(LOOSE —) GLIDDER
(MAGICAL —) BAETYL
(MEMORIAL —) BAUTA EBENEZER
(METEORIC —) ANGRITE AEROLITE
AEROLITH NAKHLITE
(MIDDLE —) HONEY
(MIDDLE — OF ARCH) KEY
(MONUMENTAL —) LECH
(PAVING —) PAVER REBATE
PITCHER
(PHILOSOPHER'S —) ADROP
MAGISTERY
(PRECIOUS —) GEM OPAL RUBY
EWAGE JEWEL TOPAZ ADAMAS
LIGURE SHAMIR ASTERIA
ASTRION CRAPAUD CUVETTE

DIAMOND DIONISE EMERALD
GELATIA JACINTH OLIVINE
SARDINE SARDIUS AMETHYST
ASTROITE HYACINTH PANTARBE
SAPPHIRE YDRIADES
(PRECIOUS —S) PERRIE
(REFUSE —) ROACH
(ROCKING —) LOGAN
(SACRED —) BAETYL BAETULUS
(SEMIPRECIOUS —) ONYX SARD
MURRA GARNET CITRINE
TIGEREYE
(SHARPENING —) HONE WHET
(SHOEMAKER'S —) LAPSTONE
(SMALL ROUND —) JACK
(SOFTENED —) SAP
(STEPPING —) GOAT SARN
(STRATIFIED —) FLAG SLAB
(TALISMANIC —) GAMAHE
(TRANSPARENT —) PHENGITE
(UNSQUARED —) BACKING
(UPRIGHT —) BAUTA MENHIR
MASSEBAH
(PL.) LAPIDES LAPILLI
(PREF.) LITH(O) LAPIDI LAPILLI
(— OF FRUIT) PYREN(O)
(SUFF.) LITE LITH(IC) LITIC
STONEBASS BAFARO WHAPUKU
STONEBOAT DRAY
STONEBOW RODD
STONECHAT CHAT SMICH
SAXICOLA WHEATEAR
STONECROP SEDUM ORPINE
PRICKET WALLWORT
STONE CURLEW BUSTARD
STONECUTTER MASON JADDER
LAPICIDE SCABBLER SCAPPLER
SQUAREMAN
STONEFLY NAIAD
STONEHAND LOCKUP
STONELIKE LITHOID
STONEMAN IMPOSER
STONE MARTEN FOIN
STONEMASON DORBIE
STONE PARSLEY HONEWORT
STONE PINE PINON AROLLA
CEMBRA
STONE ROLLER MAMMY MOMMY
TOTER
STONE TOTER CUTLIPS
STONEWALLER STICKER
STONEWARE GRES BASALT
JASPER BASALTES CANEWARE
CHIENYAO
STONINESS LAPIDITY PETREITY
STONY RIGID COBBLY PETROUS
LAPIDOSE PETROSAL
STOOL FORM MORA SEAT STAB
COPPY CROCK HORSE STOLE
TREST BUFFET CREEPY CURRIE
TRIPOD TUFFET COMMODE
CREEPIE KNEELER SHAMBLE
TABORET TRESTLE TUMBREL
BARSTOOL STILLAGE
(CLOSE —) TOM
(CUCKING —) THEW
(LOW —) COPPY SUNKIE CREEPIE
CRICKET
(3-LEGGED —) BUFFET THRESTLE
STOOLBALL TUTBALL
STOOL PIGEON NARK SNITCH
STOOGE STOOLIE
STOOP BOW BEND CURB LEAN

LOUT POKE SINK COUCH COURB
DEIGN STOPE STULP COORIE
CROUCH HUCKLE BALCONY
DECLINE DESCEND RUCKSEY
SUCCUMB
(— OF HAWK) SOUSE
STOOPING DUCK ASTOOP
DESCENT
(PREF.) CYPH(O)
STOP HO BAS COG CUT DAM DIE
DIT DOG END HOO KEP LIN MAR
NIX SET BALK BODE BUNG CALK
CALL COOL DROP EASE HALT
HELP HOLD HOOK KILL QUIT REED
REST SIST SNUB SOFT STAP STAY
STEM STOW TEAT TENT TOHO
TRIG VIOL WEAR WHOA ABIDE
ABORT AVAST BASTA BELAY
BLOCK BRAKE BREAK CAULK
CEASE CHECK CHOKE CHUCK
CLAMP CLOSE DELAY EMBAR
HITCH LEAVE MEDIA PAUSE
PEACE POINT QUINT REEST
SCOTE SLAKE SPARE SPRAG
STAND STASH STEEK STICK STINT
VIOLA AEOLIN ANCHOR ARREST
ASTINT BIFARA BOGGLE BORROW
CHEESE CLAMOR COLLAR DESIST
DETAIN DEVALL GRAVEL INSTOP
MONTRE NASARD PERIOD
SCOTCH SQUASH STANCE
STANCH STIFLE TENUIS TROMBA
BASSOON CAESURA MELODIA
MUSETTE OPPRESS SOJOURN
STATION TERTIAN TWELFTH
ASPIRATA BACKSTOP BOMBARDE
PRECLUDE RECORDER STOPOVER
STOPPAGE SUPPRESS SURCEASE
TENOROON WALDHORN
WITHSPAR
(— AS IF FRIGHTENED) BOGGLE
(— BLAST) DAMP
(— FLOW) BAFFLE STANCH
(— FOR FOOD) BAIT
(— FOR HORSE) BLOW
(— FROM FERMENTING) STUM
(— GROWTH) BLAST
(— GUN BREECH) OBTURATE
(— IN EARLY STAGES) ABORT
(— IN SPEAKING) HAW
(— LEAK) CALK CAULK FOTHER
(— ROWING) EASY
(— SHORT) JIB
(— SWINGING) SET
(— UNDESIREDLY) STALL
(— UP) DAM CALK CLOG CLOY FILL
PLUG CHINK ESTOP STUFF
STANCH OCCLUDE STAUNCH
OPPILATE
(— USING) SINK
(— WITH CLAY) PUG
(— WORK) SECURE
(BRIEF —) CALL
(GLOTTAL —) STOD CATCH STOSS
PLOSIVE STOSSTON
(HARPSICHORD —) LUTE
(ROUGH —) ASPIRATA
(SUCTION —) CLICK
(TEMPORARY —) PAUSE SUSPEND
(VOICELESS —) TENUIS
(PL.) REEDWORK
(PREF.) ISCH(O)
STOPCOCK BIB BIBB BIBCOCK

BALLCOCK TURNCOCK
STOPGAP RESOURCE
STOPLIGHT IMPEDER
STOPOVER LAYOVER
STOPPAGE JAM BLIN ALLAY
CHECK HITCH LEATH STICK STINT
ARREST DEVALL STASIS
EMBARGO GASLOCK REFUSAL
SHUTOFF STOPPLE ASTYLLEN
SHUTDOWN STOPWORK
CESSATION
(— OF BLOOD) REMORA
(— OF DEVELOPMENT) ATROPHY
(WORK —) BUND HARTAL LOWSIN
STRIKE
(PREF.) ISCH(O) STASI
(SUFF.) STASIA STASIS
STOPPED PILEATA
(— WITH HAND) BOUCHE
STOPPER WAD BUNG CORK STOP
VICE CHECK FIPPLE STANCH
BOUCHON CLOSURE SHUTOFF
STOPGAP STOPPLE TAMPION
STOPCOCK
STOPPERED BOUCHE
STOPPING STAY HOLDUP
PHASEOUT STOPPAGE
(GRADUAL — OF OPERATIONS)
PHASEOUT
STORAGE STORE STOWAGE
BESTOWAL
STORAX COPALM STACTE STYRAX
LORDWOOD
STORE CAVE CRIB DECK FOND
FUND HOLD KEEP MASS SAVE
SHOP STOW TOKO CACHE DEPOT
HOUSE HUTCH STASH STOCK
UPLAY BAZAAR CELLAR GARNER
GIRNEL RECOND STEEVE SUPPLY
TIENDA WINKEL ARSENAL
BHANDAR BOOTERY GROCERY
HARVEST HUSBAND IMBURSE
REPOSIT RESTORE SHEBANG
BOUTIQUE EMPORIUM EXCHANGE
GARRISON MAGAZINE TENDEJON
WAREROOM WARNISON
(— BEER) AGE LAGER
(— CROP) BARN
(— FODDER) ENSILE
(— IN A MOW) GOVE
(— IN LUMBER CAMP) VAN
(— KEPT BY CHINESE) TOKO
(— OF FOOD) LARDER
(— OF WEALTH) FORTUNE
(— POTATOES) HOG
(— UP) FUND POWDER IMBURSE
SQUIRREL
(ABUNDANT —) MINE
(BREAD —) PANARY
(HIDDEN —) BIKE
(LARGE —) RAFF
(LIQUOR —) GROGGERY
(MILITARY —) DUMP
(READY-TO-EAT FOOD —) DELI
DELLY
(RESERVE —) SLUICE
(RICH —) ARGOSY
(SMALL —S) SLOPS
(PL.) SAMAN SUPPLY
STOREHOUSE BIKE GOLA CACHE
DEPOT ETAPE STORE ARGOSY
ARMORY BODEGA GODOWN
PALACE PANARY STAPLE VINTRY

ARSENAL BHANDAR CAMALIG
CAMARIN GRANARY STORAGE
ENTREPOT MAGAZINE SADDLERY
TREASURE
(— FOR BREAD) PANARY
(RAISED —) WHATA FUTTAH
PATAKA
(UNDERGROUND —) PALACE
MATTAMORE
STOREKEEPER MERCHANT
STOREMAN
STOREROOM CAVE GOLA WARD
GOLAH BODEGA CELLAR DINGLE
BOXROOM BUTTERY GENIZAH
LAZARET POULTRY THALAMUS
(PAWNBROKER'S —) LUMBER
STORESHIP FLUTE
STOREY ETAGE ENTRESOL
STORK WADER ARGALA JABIRU
SIMBIL HURGILA MAGUARI
MARABOU ADJUTANT CICONIID
MARABOUT OPENBEAK OPENBILL
(PREF.) CICONI PELARGO
STORKLIKE PELARGIC
STORKSBILL ERODIUM
STORM RIG WAP BLOW HAIL HUFF
RAGE RAMP RAND RAVE WIND
BLIZZ BLOUT BRASH DEVIL DRIFT
FORCE ORAGE STOUR ATTACK
BARBER EASTER EXPUGN WESTER
BLUSTER BRAVADO CYCLONE
DUSTING EQUINOX GAUSTER
PISACHI SHAITAN SNIFTER
TEMPEST TORMENT WEATHER
BLOWDOWN CALAMITY
ERUPTION UPHEAVAL WILLIWAW
(— OF BLOWS) STOUR
(DUST —) DEVIL DUSTER HABOOB
KHAMSIN PEESASH SHAITAN
(FURIOUS —) TEMPEST
(HAWAIIAN —) KONA
(SEVERE —) PEELER SNIFTER
(VIOLENT —) FLAW TUFAN
CYCLONE SNORTER
STORM DOOR DINGLE
STORMY FOUL GURL RUDE WILD
DIRTY DUSTY GURLY GUSTY
STARK WINDY WROTH COARSE
RUGGED UNFINE WINTRY
FURIOUS NIMBOSE RIOTOUS
SQUALLY TROUBLE VIOLENT
AGITATED BLUSTERY CLUTTERY
ORAGIOUS TEMPESTY
BOISTEROUS
STORMY PETREL MITTY WITCH
SPENCY
STORY GAG SAW DECK DIDO FLAT
LORE REDE TALE TEXT YARN
ATTIC CRACK ETAGE FABLE
FLOOR KATHA PITCH PROSE
RECIT SOLAR SPELL SPIEL STAGE
STORE CUFFER FABULA FLIGHT
PISTLE SCREED SOLLAR ADVANCE
HAGGADA HISTORY MANSARD
MARCHEN PROCESS RECITAL
ANECDOTE DREADFUL ENTRESOL
TREATISE NARRATIVE
(— FROM THE PAST) LEGEND
(— OF BEEHIVE) SUPER
(— OF BUILDING) DECK FLAT ATTIC
CHESS ETAGE FLOOR PIANO
SOLAR STAGE FLIGHT SOLLAR
MANSARD ENTRESOL MEZZANINE

(— OF HEROES) SAGA
(ABSURD —) CANARD
(ADVENTURE —) YARN
(AMUSING —) BAR DROLLERY
(BIRTH —) JATAKA
(DOLEFUL —) JEREMIAD
(EERIE —) CHILLER
(FAKE —) STRING
(FALSE —) SHAVE CANARD
WHOPPER
(LONG, INVOLVED —) MEGILLA
MEGILLAH
(MADE-UP —) FUDGE
(MONSTROUS —) BANGER
(MORBIDLY SENSATIONAL —)
DREADFUL
(MYSTERY —) WHODUNIT
(NEWS —) SIDEBAR
(NEWSPAPER —) LEAD FEATURE
(OLD —) DIDO
(POMPOUS —) BRAG
(PREPOSTEROUS —) CUFFER
(RIBALD —) HARLOTRY
(SATIRICAL —) SKIT
(SHORT —) CONTE NOVELLA
(STALE —) CHESTNUT
(UPPER —) ATTIC GARRET
BARBECUE HYPEROON
(PL.) LEGENDA
STORY BOOK TALEBOOK
**STORY OF A BAD BOY (AUTHOR
OF —)** ALDRICH
(CHARACTER IN —) BEN TOM BILL
EZRA PHIL SETH ADAMS BINNY
KITTY MEEKS NELLY SILAS
CONWAY MARDEN NUTTER
PEPPER ROGERS ABIGAIL
ALDRICH CHARLEY COLLINS
WALLACE WINGATE GRIMSHAW
WHITCOMB TREFETHEN
GLENTWORTH
**STORY OF AN AFRICAN FARM
(AUTHOR OF —)** SCHREINER
(CHARACTER IN —) EM ROSE TANT
WALDO SANNIE GREGORY
LYNDALL BLENKINS
BONAPARTE
STORYTELLER CONTEUR DISCOUR
DISSOUR
STOUP STOOP BENITIER
STOUT FAT SAD FIRM STUT TRIM
BONNY BROSY BULKY BUNTY
BURLY COBBY FRACK FRECK
GREAT HARDY KEDGE OBESE
PLUMP PODDY PUNCH STARK
STERN BONNIE FLESHY PORTER
PORTLY PRETTY PYKNIC ROTUND
SQUARE STRONG STUFFY STURDY
BOWERLY REPLETE FORCIBLE
PLUMPISH POWERFUL ROBOREAN
STALWART THICKSET
(— PERSON) GURK
STOUTHEARTED GOOD VALIANT
STOUTLY FAST HARDILY
STOUTNESS STRENGTH
CORPULENCE
STOVE HOD STOW BOGEY CHULA
PEACH PLATE CHULHA COCKLE
COOKER HEATER PRIMUS
BRASERO CHAUFFER FRANKLIN
POTBELLY SALAMANDER
(— FOR DRYING GUNPOWDER)
GLOOM

(— ON SHIP) GALLEY
(RUSSIAN —) PEACH
(WARMING —) KANGRI
STOVER OVENSMAN
STOW BIN BOX SET CRAM LADE
MASS CROWD DOUSE STORE
BESTOW COOPER STEEVE
DUNNAGE RUMMAGE
STOWAGE BURTON REMBLAI
RUMMAGE
STOWED IN
STOWER TOPPER
STOWING BINNING GOBBING
STP DOM
STRABISMUS CAST CROSS SQUINT
TROPIA ANOPSIA COCKEYE
WALLEYE
STRADDLE SADDLE SPREAD
STRIDE BESTRIDE SPRADDLE
STRIDDLE
STRAGGLE GAD ROVE TRAIL
RAMBLE RANGLE SPRAWL STREEL
TAGGLE WANDER DRAGGLE
MEANDER SCRAMBLE SPRANGLE
STRAGGLER STRAY BUMMER
STRAGGLING RAGGED RAGGLED
SPRAYEY SCRATCHY VAGULOUS
STRAIGHT BOLT FAIR FULL GAIN
BRANT CLEAN DOGGY FLUSH
RIGHT SHORT SPANG ARIGHT
DIRECT HONEST STRAIT STRICT
BOBTAIL REGULAR UPRIGHT
DIRECTLY SEQUENCE
(— AHEAD) ANON PLUMP
OUTRIGHT
(— UP AND DOWN) SHEER CLEVER
EVENDOWN
(NOT —) CRAZY
(PREF.) EUTHY ITHO ITHY
ORTH(O) RECT(I)
STRAIGHTEDGE LUTE RULE RULER
STRICKLE
STRAIGHTEN GAG ORDER STENT
EXTEND SQUARE UNKINK
COMPOSE RECTIFY STRETCH
(— BY HEATING) SET
(— NEEDLE) RUB
(— RAILS) GAG
STRAIGHT-FIBERED BROAD
STRAIGHTFORWARD EVEN PLAT
APERT FRANK LEVEL NAKED
PLAIN ROUND CANDID DEXTER
DIRECT HONEST SIMPLE SQUARE
JANNOCK SINCERE EVENDOWN
HOMESPUN OUTRIGHT STRAIGHT
OPENHEARTED
(NOT —) CROOKED PLAITED
(PREF.) LITI
STRAIGHTFORWARDLY SINGLY
SQUARE STRAIGHT
STRAIGHT-THINKING CLEAR
STRAIGHTWAY ANON AWAY
RIGHT ARIGHT BEDEEN BEDENE
DIRECTLY
STRAIN FIT LAG RAX SIE TAX TRY
TUG ACHE BEND CALL DASH
DRAG HEAT HEFT LAWN NOTE
PULL RACK RANN RICK SILE SINE
SOLO SONG VEIN WORK BRUNT
CHAFE DEMUR DRAIN FORCE
HEAVE PRESS RETCH SHADE
SHEAR STOCK SURGE TAMMY
TOUCH WREST WRICK CLENCH

EFFORT EXTEND EXTORT FILTER
INTEND KVETCH SPRAIN SPRING
STREAK STRESS STRIND THRONG
DESCANT DISCANT EUPLOID
FATIGUE STRAINT STRETCH
STROPHE TENSION TORMENT
COLANDER DIAPASON DIATRIBE
DIHYBRID SUBBREED
(— MILK) SIE SYE
(— OF AN ARCH) THRUST
(— OF CHICKENS) ANCOBAR
(— OF RAILING LANGUAGE)
DIATRIBE
(— ON BUGLE) MOT
(— ON HORN) RECHASE RECHEAT
(— THROUGH COLANDER) COIL
(CONCLUDING —) CADENCE
(MELANCHOLY —) DUMP
(MUSICAL —) FIT SOLO POINT
(MUSICAL —S) TOUCH
(MUTANT —) SALTANT
(PREF.) STREMMATO
STRAINED PENT TENSE INTENSE
LABORED INTENDED
STRAINER CAGE ROSE SILE RENGE
SIEVE STRUM TAMIS TAMMY
THEAD SEARCE SEARCH CRIBBLE
COLATORY COLATURE SEARCHER
(— OF TWIGS) HUCKMUCK
(COFFEE —) GRECQUE
(MILK —) SAY MILSEY MILSIE
(WICKER —) THEAD THEDE
(PREF.) COLI ETHMO
STRAINING CUTE COILED ASTRAIN
INTENSE COLATURE
STRAIT CUT GUT BAND BELT FRET
KYLE NECK PACE BRAKE CANAL
PHARE PINCH SHARD SOUND
ANGUST FRETUM NARROW
PLUNGE CHANNEL EURIPUS
BOSPORUS JUNCTURE
(IN —S) SET
(LAST —) EXIGENT
(NEWFOUNDLAND —) TICKLER
(PL.) CHOPS PRESS EXTREMES
STRAITEN PINCH SCANT STRAIT
STRAITENED CRIMP NARROW
CRIMPED
STRAITJACKET CAMISOLE
STRAITLACED STIFF STUFFY
BLUENOSED
STRAKE SHEER COURSE RISING
STREAK COAMING SAXBOARD
(PL.) TIRE
STRAMONIUM DEWTRY
STRAND PLY TOP BANK CORE
FLAT TOWT WISP BEACH BRAID
CLIFF PRAYA READY SHORE
LISSOM SINGLE SLIVER STRAIN
STRIKE SUTURE HAIRLINE
(— OF FIBERS) ROVING
(— OF HAIR) LICK SWITCH
(— OF PROTOPLASM) BRIDGE
(— OF TEXTILE) ROVE
(PREF.) CROCO
STRANDED AGROUND ISOLATED
STRANDER EDGER
STRANGE ODD RUM EERY FELL
FREM NICE RARE UNCO ALIEN
EERIE FREMT FUNNY KINKY
NOVEL QUEER UNKET UNKID
WOOZY ALANGE FERLIE QUAINT
UNIQUE UNKENT UNKIND

CURIOUS ERRATIC HEATHEN
ODDBALL UNHEARD UNKNOWN
UNUSUAL FANCIFUL INSOLENT
INSOLITE PECULIAR SELCOUTH
SINGULAR UNCOLIKE UNCOMMON
UNKENNED UNKINDLY
MONSTROUS
(PREF.) XEN(O)
STRANGENESS ODDITY
STRANGER COME UNCO UNKO
ALIEN GUEST FRENNE GANGER
INCOME INMATE FUIDHIR
INCOMER UNCOUTH MALIHINI
OUTCOMER PEREGRIN
OUTLANDER
(SUFF.) XENE XENOUS XENY
STRANGLE CHOKE GRAIN GRANE
SNARL WORRY STIFLE GARROTE
QUACKLE GARROTTE JUGULATE
THROTTLE
STRANGLEHOLD CHANCERY
STRANGUL
STRANIERA, LA (CHARACTER IN —)
ALAIDE ARTURO ISOLETTA
VALDEBURGO
(COMPOSER OF —) BELLINI
STRAP BAR TUG BAND CLIP CURB
GIRD HASP RIDE RIEM BRACE
CHEEK GIRTH GUIGE PATTE RIDER
RISER SABOT SLING STROP
THONG TRACE VITTA ANKLET
BACKER BILLET COLLAR ENARME
GARTER HALTER HANGER LAINER
LATIGO SANDAL TOGGLE
WARROK BABICHE BOWYANG
CRIBBER DOLPHIN LANYARD
LATCHET LEATHER RIEMPIE
STIRRUP TICKLER WEBBING
BACKSTAY BRETELLE SQUILGEE
TURNBACK WRISTLET
(— AROUND HORSE'S THROAT)
CRIBBER
(— AROUND MAST) DOLPHIN
(— FOR SHIELD) GUIGE ENARME
BRETELLE
(— IN FLAIL) TAPLING
(— OF BRIDLE) REIN
(— OF SENNIT) BACKER
(— ON HAWK'S LEAD) JESS JESSE
SENDAL
(— WITH SLIT END) TAWS TAWSE
(ANKLE —) BRACELET
(CARRYING —) METUMP TUMPLINE
(DOOR —) HASP
(MINER'S —) BYARD
(SHOE —) BAR
(STIRRUP —S) CHAPELET
(TIE —) SHANK
(U-SHAPED —) STIRRUP
(PL.) LADDER
(PREF.) LIGUL(I)
STRAP FERN LONGLEAF
STRAPHANGER COMMUTER
STRAPPER SPLICER
STRAPPING SWANK BOUNCING
CHOPPING SLAPPING SWANKING
STRAP-SHAPED LORATE LIGULAR
LIGULATE
STRATA EOCENE TERRANE
UNDERAIR
(— OF COAL) MEASURES
STRATAGEM JIG COUP LOCK RUSE
TRAM TURN WILE ANGLE DRAFT

FETCH FRAUD GUILE JOKER
KNACK TRAIN TRICK WREST
BLENCH DECEIT DEVICE HUMBUG
POLICY TRAPAN TREPAN WOIDRE
WRENCH FINESSE SLEIGHT
ARTIFICE CONTOISE FARFETCH
INTRIGUE LIRIPIPE LIRIPOOP
PRACTICE PRACTISE QUENTISE
STRATEGY TRICKERY MOUSETRAP
STRATEGY GAME FINESSE
STRATIFICATION BEDDING
STRATIFIED BEDDED VARVED
STRATONICE (FATHER OF —)
DEMETRIUS
(HUSBAND OF —) SELEUCUS
(MOTHER OF —) PHILA
STRATUM BED CAP CUT LAY RIB
FAST LAIN SEAM COUCH ELITE
FLOOR LAYER LEDGE SHELF
TABLE COUCHE GIRDLE GRAVEL
LAYING LISSOM PINNEL AQUAFER
AQUIFER ENTIRIS FISHBED
SUBSOIL UPRIGHT AQUIFUGE
FAHLBAND SUBGRADE
(— OF COAL) BENCH
(— OF FIRECLAY) THILL
(— OF PALE COLOR) FAHLBAND
(— OF SANDSTONE) PINNEL
(— OF SOIL) SOD
(— OF STONE) GIRDLE
(SOCIAL —) CUT
(THIN —) SEAM LENTIL
STRAW BAKU GLOY MOTE REED
RUSH TOYO WASE HAULM PEDAL
SHILF STALK STREW YEDDA
FESCUE FETTLE PANAMA RIZZOM
SIPPER TUSCAN BANGKOK
SABUTAN STUBBLE WINDLIN
STRAMMEL
(— CUT FINE) CHAFF
(— FOR MAKING HATS) SENNIT
BANGKOK LEGHORN SABUTAN
(— FOR THATCHING) YELM
(— MEASURE) KEMPLE
(— TO PROTECT PLANTS) MULCH
(BROKEN —) BHUSA BHOOSA
(COOKERY —S) PAILLES
(PLAITED —) SENNIT
(WAXED —) STRASS
(PREF.) CARPHO
STRAWBERRY BERRY DUNLAP
FRAISE RUNNER HAUTBOY
FRUTILLA HAUTBOIS KLONDIKE
ROSACEAN
STRAWBERRY BUSH WAHOO
EUONYMUS EVONYMUS
FISHWOOD
STRAWBERRY FINCH AMADAVAT
AVADAVAT
STRAWBERRY SHRUB BUBBY
COWBERRY
STRAWBERRY TOMATO
PHYSALIS
STRAY ERR ODD FALL RAVE ROVE
WAFF WAIF WALK DRIFT RANGE
TRAIK VAGUE WAVER ESTRAY
RANGLE SWERVE VAGARY
WANDER WILDER DEVIATE
FORLORN STRAYER DIVAGATE
MAVERICK STRAGGLE
STRAYING ASTRAY ERRANT
ABERRANT VAGATION
STREAK PAY RAY BAND SEAM

VEIN WALE FLAKE FLECK FLICK
FREAK GARLE GLADE SLASH
FACULA SMUDGE STRAIN STRAKE
STREAM STRIPE FLECKER
SPRAING STIPPLE DISCOLOR
TRAVERSE
(— CAUSED BY BLOOD) VIBEX
(— IN FABRIC) CRACK SHINER
(— IN GLASS) SKIM
(— IN HAIR) BLAZE
(— IN SKY) ICEBLINK
(— IN WOOD) ROE
(— OF BLUBBER) BLANKET
(— OF LIGHT) STREAM
(— ON BEAST'S FACE) RACE
(— ON SURFACE OF SUN) FACULA
(— WITH FINE STRIPES) LACE
(—S FROM PLANE) CONTRAIL
(BACTERIOLOGICAL —) STROKE
(LOSING —) SLUMP
(THEATRICAL —) HAM
(WHITE —) SHIM
STREAKED ROWY LACED HAWKED
SMEARY BRINDLE BROCKED
BROOKED FINCHED SPARKED
STRIPED WHIPPED BRINDLED
IRONSHOT PINROWED
STREAKY ROWY SCOVY STREAKED
STREAM EA PUP RIO RUN BECK
BURN FLOW FLUX FORD GILL
GOTE KHAL KILL LAKE OOZE PUIT
PURL RILL SICK SIKE SILE SPIN
TIDE BACHE BATCH BAYOU
BOGUE BOURN BROOK CREEK
DRILL DRINK FLARE FLASH FLEAM
FLOOD FLOSS FLUOR FRESH
GHYLL NYMPH PRILL RITHE RIVER
SWAMP TCHAI TRAIN ARROYO
BANKER BOURNE BRANCH
BURNIE CANADA COULEE FILLER
FLUENT GUZZLE OUTLET PIRATE
RANDOM RUNDLE RUNNEL
SLUICE SPRUIT STRAND STRONE
CHANNEL CURRENT DRIBBLE
FLUENCE FRESHET RIVULET
TRICKLE AFFLUENT INFLUENT
MILLSTREAM
(— ALONG) SLIDE
(— FULL TO TOP) BANKER
(— OF AIR OR SMOKE) PEW
(— OF ELECTRODES) BEAM
(— OF LAVA) COULEE
(— OF SIRUP) THREAD
(— OF SPEECH) STRAIN
(— OUT) BREAK
(FLOWING —) NYMPH
(HIGH-SPEED —) JET
(MYTHOLOGICAL —S) ELIVAGAR
(SLOW —) OOZE
(SLOW-MOVING —) POW
(SLUGGISH —) LANE
(SMALL —) BECK LAKE SIKE DRAFT
RITHE COULEE SICKET SQUIRT
STRIPE DRAUGHT GRINDLE
(THIN —) TRICKLE TRICKLET
(TIDAL —) COVE SEAPOOSE
(TRANSIENT —) RILL
(TRICKLING —) DRILL
(TURBID —) DRUVE
(UNDERGROUND —) AAR SWALLET
(VIOLENT —) TORRENT
(WEAK —) DRIP
(PREF.) AMNI FLUVI

(— OF LAVA) RHYACO
STREAMER FLAG VANE FALLAL
GARTER GUIDON LAPPET PENCEL
PENNON PINNET SCROLL SIMPLE
WIMPLE BANDEROL FILAMENT
(— OF MOSS) WEEPER
(— ON HEADDRESS) LIRIPIPE
(PAPER —S) CONFETTI
STREAMING SLUICY ASTREAM
CRINITE CYCLOSIS DOWNPOUR
STREAMLET RILL RILLET RUNDLE
RUNLET RUNNEL RIVULET
STREAMLINE SIMPLIFY
(— FLOW) LAMINAR
STREAMLINED CLEAN SLEEK
STREET ROW RUE WAY CHAR
DRUM GATE PAVE STEM TOBY
BLOCK BORGO CALLE CANON
CHAWK CORSO DRIVE PASEO
AVENUE BOWERY CANYON
CAUSEY RAMBLA POULTRY
TERRACE THROUGH ARTERIAL
BROADWAY BYSTREET CHAUSSEE
CONTRADA PROSPECT
(— IN BARCELONA) RAMBLA
(— IN FLORENCE) BORGO
(MAIN —) CHAWK CHOWK
TOWNGATE
(NARROW —) CHAR ALLEY CHARE
(PRINCIPAL —) ARTERY
(SIDE —) HUTUNG
STREETCAR TRAMCAR TRAMWAY
ELECTRIC
STREET CLEANER ORDERLY
CLEANSER
STREET CLEANING SLOPPING
STREET SCENE (AUTHOR OF —)
RICE
(CHARACTER IN —) SAM ROSE
FRANK STEVE KAPLIN SANKEY
WILLIAM MAURRANT
STREETWALKER BULKER CRUISER
STRENGTH EL ARM VIR BEEF
DRAW GRIP GUTS HEAD HORN
IRON MAIN THEW BRAWN CRAFT
ETHAN FIBER FIBRE FORCE HEART
JUICE MIGHT NERVE POWER
SINEW VIGOR ENERGY FOISON
MAUGHT MUSCLE STARCH
VIRTUE ABILITY AFFORCE
COURAGE STAMINA STHENIA
CAPACITY FIRMNESS VALIDITY
PUISSANCE
(— OF ACID OR BASE) AVIDITY
(— OF ALE) STRIKE
(— OF CARD HAND) BODY
(— OF CHARACTER) GRISTLE
(— OF CURRENT) AMPERAGE
(— OF SOLUTION) TITER TITRE
(— OF SPIRITS) PROOF
(— OF TEA) DRAW
(— OF WILL) BACKBONE
(— OF WINE) SEVE
(PREF.) CRATO DYNAM(I)(O)
ISCHY(O)
(SUFF.) DYNAMIA DYNAMOUS
STRENGTHEN IMP ABLE BACK
BIND FIRM FRAP HELP PROP
SOUD STAY BRACE CLEAT FORCE
SINEW STEEL THRAP TONIC
TRUSS ANNEAL ASSURE DEEPEN
ENDURE ENFIRM ENFORT GABION
HARDEN INTEND MUNIFY MUNITE

NEEDLE SETTLE STRING STRONG
AFFORCE BUCKRAM COMFORT
CONFIRM ENFORCE FASCINE
FORTIFY NERVATE QUICKEN
RAMPIRE SUPPORT THICKEN
BUTTRESS ENERGIZE ENTRENCH
HEIGHTEN ROBORATE
STRENGTHENED BULLED
BRANDIED
STRENGTHENING BRACING
ROBORANT
STRENGTHLESS DOWLESS
STRENUOUS HARD EAGER
ARDUOUS WILLING VIGOROUS
STREPHON (BELOVED OF —) CHLOE
STREPSIPTERON STYLOPS
STRESS HIT BIRR BRUNT ICTUS
PINCH SHEAR ACCENT STRAIN
THRONG CENTROID DOWNBEAT
EMPHASIS PRESSURE
(— OF SOUND) LENGTH
STRESSED TONIC STRONG
STRETCH EKE LAG LIE RAX RUN
BEAT DRAW LAST MAIN PASS
RACK REAM ROLL RYKE SPAN
TEND BOARD BURST FETCH
RATCH RETCH SIGHT SPELL
STENT SWAGE VERGE EXTEND
LENGTH SMOOTH STRAIN STRAKE
STREEK DISPLAY DISTEND
EXPANSE SPELDER ELONGATE
LENGTHEN STRAIGHT
(— CLOTH) TENTER
(— FORTH) PORRECT
(— INJURIOUSLY) SPRAIN
(— IRREGULARLY) TRAIL
(— LEATHER) DRAFT STAKE
DRAUGHT
(— METAL) FORM
(— OF ARMS) FATHOM
(— OF GROUND) BRECK
(— OF INTERVAL) CARSE
(— OF LAND) SWALE COMMON
GALLOP PARCEL COMMONS
(— OF ROAD) SIGHT
(— OF SEA) CHOP
(— OF TIME) TIFF
(— OF WALL) CURTAIN
(— OF WATER) GLIDE LEVEL LOGIN
FAIRWAY
(— OUT) GROW SPIN REACH
STENT STRUT TWINE INTEND
OUTLIE SPRAWL SPREAD SPRING
DISTEND OUTSPAN PORTEND
ELONGATE
(— THE NECK) CRANE
(GRASSY —) DRINN
(LEVEL —) LAWN
(PREF.) TANY TASI TEN(O)
TENONT(O) TETANI TETANO TINO
(SUFF.) EURYSIS
STRETCHED PROSTRATE
(— OUT) PORRECT PROJECT
PROLATE ELONGATE EXTENDED
(TENSELY —) TAUT TORT STIFF
STRETCHER COT STENT GURNEY
LITTER ANGAREP TROLLEY
ANGAREEB BRANCARD STRAINER
STRETCHING
(SUFF.) ECTASIA ECTASIS
STREW BED SOW CLOT DUST LARD
SPEW BESET STRAW STRAY
STROW CARPET LITTER SPREAD

BESTREW SCATTER SKINKLE SPARKLE
(— WITH BULLETS) SPRAY
STREWED BESPRENT
STREWING SEME
STREWN DOTTED BESPRENT
STRIA CORD STRIOLA DRAGLINE STRIOLET
STRIATE VEIN
STRIATION STREAK STRIGA
STRICKEN STREAKED
STRICKER TIPPLER
STRICKLE SWEEP STRIKER
STRICT HARD TAUT TRUE CLOSE EXACT HARSH RIGID STARK STERN TIGHT GIUSTO SEVERE STRAIT STRONG ASCETIC AUSTERE PRECISE REGULAR DISTRICT RESTRICT RIGOROUS STRINGENT
(NOT —) LAX SCIOLTO
STRICTLY NARROW STRAIT CLOSELY PROPERLY
STRICTNESS RIGOR RIGIDITY RIGORISM SEVERITY
STRIDE LAMP SAIL STEP FLOAT SKELP SPANG STEND STRUT LAMPER STROAM STROKE STROME BESTRIDE POINTING STRIDDLE
(— LOFTILY) STALK
(— PURPOSEFULLY) SLING
STRIDENT HARD HARSH BRASSY GLASSY SHRILL RAUCOUS YELLING GRINDING
STRIDULATE PITTER
STRIFE TUG WAR WIN BATE FEUD HOLD PLEA BRIGE CHEST FLITE JEHAD JIHAD NOISE STOUR STROW STRUT STURT BARRAT BICKER BRIGUE DEBATE ESTRIF MUTINY STRIVE BARGAIN CONTECK CONTEST DISCORD DISPUTE HURLING QUARREL CONFLICT CONTRAST DISPEACE STRUGGLE CONTENTION
(AUTHOR OF —) GALSWORTHY
(CHARACTER IN —) ENID JOHN ANNIE DAVID EDGAR SIMON ANTHONY FRANCIS HARNESS ROBERTS UNDERWOOD
(CIVIL —) STASIS
STRIGIL COMB SCRAPER
STRIKE GO BAT BOB BOP BOX BUM COB CUE DAD DUB GET HAB HIT JOB JOW LAM LAY PUG RAP WAP ABRE BAFF BEAK BEAT BELT BIFF BILL BLAD BLIP BUFF BUMP CHAP CLUB COIN COPE COSH CUFF DING DINT DONG DUNT FALL FANG FIRK FLAP FLOG FRAP GIRD GOWF HACK HURT JOWL KILL KNEE LASH LILT LUSH MARK NAIL PAIK PASH PLAT PUCK ROUT SLAM SLAP SLAT SLAY SLOG SLUG SOCK SPAR SPAT SWAP SWAT SWIP TAKE WHAP WHOP WIPE ANGLE BATON CATCH CHECK CHIME CHINK CLOUT CLUNK CRACK CRUNT DEVEL DOUSE DOWSE DRIVE DUNCH FETCH FILCH FILIP FLAIL KNOCK PANDY PASTE POKER POTCH

SABER SKELP SKITE SLOSH SMACK SMITE SNICK SOUND SPANK SQUAP STAMP STEEK SWACK SWEEP SWIPE SWISH THROW WHALE WHANG ACOUPE AFFECT AFFRAP ALIGHT ATTAIN BATTER BOUNCE BUFFET COURSE DUNDER FETTLE FILLIP HAMMER INCUSE INCUTE KEEPER SLOUGH STOUSH STRICK STRIPE SWITCH THRASH WALLOP BEARING FLYFLAP IMPINGE KNUCKLE PERCUSS STRIKER TURNOUT WHAMPLE WILDCAT STOPPAGE STOPWORK STRAMASH STRICKLE
(— A WICKET) BREAK
(— ABOUT) FLOP
(— AGAINST) RAM BANG STUMP ASSAULT COLLIDE
(— AND REBOUND) CAROM
(— CRICKET BALL) EDGE
(— DOWN) LAY FALL SLAY WEND FLASH FLOOR AFFLICT SIDERATE
(— DUMB) DUMFOUND
(— FEET TOGETHER) HITCH
(— FORCIBLY) GET CLOUT DEVEL SLASH
(— GENTLY) PAT
(— GOLF BALL) HOOK DRIVE SCLAFF
(— HEAVILY) BASH DUNT DUSH FLOP SLUG CLUMP SLOUGH CLOBBER
(— IN CURLING) WICK
(— LIGHTLY) BOB DAB SPAT FLICK
(— OF LOCK) KEEPER STRIKE
(— ON HEAD) COP NOBBLE
(— OUT) FAN DELE POKE TAKE CROSS ELIDE CANCEL DELETE EXPUNGE OUTLASH EXCUDATE
(— REPEATEDLY) DRUM LICK
(— SHARPLY) CUT SNICK
(— SMARTLY) NAP RAP KNAP
(— TEETH TOGETHER) GNASH
(— TOGETHER) CLASH KNACK
(— UP) LILT YERK RAISE
(— VIOLENTLY) RIP BASH DING PASH SOUSE BENSEL
(— WITH AMAZEMENT) CONFOUND
(— WITH BAT) DRIVE
(— WITH FEAR) ALARM ASTONISH
(— WITH FIST) PLUG NODDLE
(— WITH FOOT) KICK BUNCH SPURN STAMP
(— WITH HAMMER) CHAP JOWL MELL
(— WITH HORNS) BUNT BUTT HOOK
(— WITH SHAME) ABASH
(— WITH SPEAR) STICK
(— WITH STICK) SQUAIL
(— WITH WHIP) JERK LASH QUIRK
(— WITH WONDER) SURPRISE
(BOWLING —S) DOUBLE
(HUNGER —) ENDURA
(LABOR —) STEEK STICK TURNOUT WALKOUT
(LUCKY —) BONANZA
(MINING —) TREND
(THREE —S) TURKEY
(PREF.) PLESSI PLEXI TYPTO
STRIKEBREAKER FINK BLACKLEG
STRIKER BATMAN DRUMMER

TURNOUT PULSATOR
STRIKER-OUT SETTER
STRIKING FITTY FRESH SHOWY VIVID DARING SIGNAL STRONG SALIENT SKELPIN TELLING COLORFUL CONFLICT DRAMATIC FRAPPANT KNOCKOUT SENSIBLE SPEAKING NOTICEABLE PERCUSSION
STRING LAG BAND BEND CORD FILE LACE MEAN PAIR SLIP TAPE TAUM BRAID BRIDE CHORD POINT SINEW SNEAD STRAP CORDON STRAND TREBLE MINIKIN LIGATURE RHAPSODY
(— IN BIRD'S EGG) CHALAZA
(— OF BEADS) ROSARY CHAPLET NECKLACE
(— OF CASH) QUAN TIAO
(— OF DRUM) SNARE
(— OF FIDDLE) THARM
(— OF FLAGS) HOIST
(— OF LOCK) KEEPER
(— OF LYRE) MESE NETE TRITE HYPATE PARAMESE PARAMETE
(— OF MUSICAL INSTRUMENT) WIRE CHORD DRONE THAIRM CATLING MINIKIN LICHANOSE
(— OF ONIONS) REEVE TRACE
(— OF PHRASES) CENTO
(— OF RAILWAY CARS) SET
(— OF SUGAR CRYSTALS) COB
(— OF VEGETABLES) STRAP
(— OF VERSES) LAISSE
(— OF VIOL) MEAN
(— OF WAGONS) RAKE
(— TOBACCO) SEW
(— UP) KILT
(BONNET —) BRIDE
(E —) QUINT
(LEADING —) BAND
(OAKUM —) PLEDGET
(ORNAMENTAL —) CORDON
(SURGICAL —) LIGATURE
(VIOLIN —) THAIRM VIBRATOR
(WEAVING —) LEASH
(SUFF.) CHORD(AL)
STRING BEAN SNAP HARICOT SNAPPER
STRINGCOURSE LEDGE TABLE CORDON STRING
STRINGENT HARD RIGID TIGHT SEVERE STRICT EXTREME
STRINGER BALK BAULK
STRINGHALTED CRAMPY
STRINGY ROPY WOOLY SINEWY THONGY WOOLLY GARGETY SINEWED THREADY
STRIP BAR LAG TAG BAND BARE BEAD BELT BEND BUSK DRIP FUSE GAGE GAIR HILD HUSK LIST MALL NAKE NUDE PEEL RAND ROLL SACK SHIM SKIN TIRL TIRR WELT CLEAN DRIVE EXUTE FILET FLAKE FLYPE GAUGE GLEAN GUARD HARRY LABEL LINER LYNCH PANEL PLUME REEVE SHEAR SHRED SKELP SLIPE SPEEL SPOIL STRAP STROP STRUB SWATH UNGUM UNRIG BORDER BOXING BRIDGE COLLAR CULPON DENUDE DEVEST DIVEST FEELER FILLET FLEECE LIBBET MATRIX

PANUNG REGLET SCROLL SPLINE STREAK STRIPE TARGET UNBARE UNBARK UNCASE BANDAGE BEREAVE CHANNEL DEPLUME DEPRIVE DESPOIL DISROBE FEATHER FLOUNCE LAMBEAU LANGUET NAILROD PINRAIL PLUNDER UNCLOAK UNCOVER UNDRESS BOOKMARK COSSETTE DISARRAY DISENDOW DISTRUSS FOOTBAND SEPARATE
(— A PLANT) SPRIG
(— BARK) PILL
(— BINDING STALKS TO WALL) TACK
(— BLUBBER FROM WHALE) FLENSE
(— EAR OF CORN) SILK
(— FOR DRAWING CURVED LINES) SPLINE
(— FOR GUIDING PLASTER) BEAD
(— FOR MAKING TUBE) SKELP
(— HANGING AROUND SKIRT) FLOUNCE
(— IN BASKETMAKING) INSIDES
(— IN BEEHIVE) STARTER
(— IN CANING) SPLENT SPLINT
(— IN TYPEWRITER) DRAWBAND
(— OF CANVAS) FOOTBAND
(— OF CLOTH) LIST PATA RIND ROON GUARD BANNER DUTCHMAN
(— OF CORK) SPREADER
(— OF FABRIC) FLIPPER
(— OF FAT) FATBACK LARDOON
(— OF FIELD HOCKEY AREA) ALLEY
(— OF FUR) GROTZEN
(— OF GRASS) VERGE
(— OF HIDE) SPECK DEWLAP
(— OF LAND) BUTT LAND RAIK RAIN RAKE TANG BREAK CREEK SLANG SLIPE SPONG SCREED SELION STRAKE STRIPE FURLONG ISTHMUS CORRIDOR SIDELING
(— OF LEATHER) LAY RAND WELT APRON RANGE THONG BACKSTAY
(— OF LEAVES) TWIST
(— OF LINEN) SETON
(— OF MASONRY) ARCHBAND
(— OF OFFICE) BREAK
(— OF OSIER) SKEIN
(— OF PALM LEAF) CADJAN CAJANG
(— OF PASTRY) STRAW
(— OF PLANKING) APRON
(— OF PLASTER) SCREED
(— OF PRAIRIE) COVE
(— OF PROVISIONS) FORAGE
(— OF RANK) DEGRADE
(— OF RED CLOTH) COXCOMB
(— OF ROADWAY) LANE
(— OF RUBBER) CUSHION
(— OF TURF) PARKING
(— OF UNPLOWED LAND) GAIR HADE HEADLAND
(— OF WATER) INLET
(— OF WOOD) LAG LAT LATH LIST SHAW SLAT WELT CHINK CLEAT STAVE BATTEN INWALE RADDLE REEPER REGLET FOOTING FURRING STICKER TRACKER FOOTLING
(— OFF) TIRL FLIPE FLYPE SLIPE
(— OFF SKIN) CASE FLAY

(— ON FOLDING DOORS) ASTRAGAL
(— ON PRINTER'S GALLEY) LEDGE
(— ON SQUASH COURT) TELLTALE
(— ON TIRE) CHAFER
(— SEPARATING LINES OF TYPE)
LEAD REGLET
(BOUNDARY —) PERIMETER
(CAMOUFLAGING —) GARLAND
(COMIC —) FUNNY
(CONSTRUCTION —S) LAGGING
(CORSET —) BUSK
(DEPENDENT —) LAMBEAU
(DIVIDING —) CLOISON
(HORSESHOE-SHAPED —) BAIL BALE
(IRON IN —S) NAILROD
(MEDIAN —) MALL
(NARROW —) SEAM SLAT SLIP
TAPE REEVE STRAKE
(PAPER —) ORIHON
(PROJECTING —) FEATHER
(RAISED —) RIDGE
(STRENGTHENING —) BEND
(THATCHING —) LEDGER
(UNPLOWED —) BALK
STRIPE BAR RAY BAND BEND LIST
PALE SLAT TRIM WALE WEAL
WELT ZONE FLECK PLAGA STRIA
STRIP SWATH VITTA WHEAL
BORDER CLAVUS COTICE FRENUM
LADDER RIBBON STRAKE STREAK
STREAM COTTISE SPRAING
MUSTACHE TRAVERSE
(— OF CHEVRON) ARC
(— OF COLOR ON CHEEK) FRENUM
FRAENUM
(— ON ANIMAL'S FACE) SNIP BLAZE
(— ON FABRIC) CROSSBAR
(— ON MILITARY SLEEVE) SLASH
(— ON SHIELD) ENDORSE
(ENCIRCLING —) ZONE
(PURPLE —) CLAVUS
(SET OF —S) BAR
STRIPED BANDY PALED PIRNY
RAWED RAYED ROWED WALED
ZONED BARRED CORDED LISTED
PIRNED BROCKED TIGROID
VITTATE FASCIATE STRIPPED
(— CROSSWISE) BAYADERE
STRIPED BASS ROCKFISH
SERRANID
STRIPED MAPLE DOGWOOD
STRIPING HAIRLINE
STRIPLIGHT BORDER
STRIPLING LAD SLIP STIRRA
YONKER SPAUGHT YOUNKER
SKIPJACK SPRINGAL SHAVELING
STRIPPED BARE NUDE NAKED
HUSKED PICKED PLUMED
UNPEELED
STRIPPER STEMMER SPRIGGER
STRIPPING STROKINGS
(PL.) JIBBINGS
STRIPTEASE (RELATING TO —)
EXOTIC
STRIPTEASER STRIPPER
ECDYSIAST
STRIVE AIM HIE TEW TRY TUG
DEAL FEND PAIN TOIL WORK
BANDY DRIVE EXERT FIGHT
FORCE LABOR PRESS BRIGUE
BUCKLE BUFFET DEBATE INTEND
PINGLE STRAIN STRIKE AGONIZE
BARGAIN CONTEND CONTEST

DISPUTE ENFORCE SCUFFLE
CONTRAST ENDEAVOR PURCHASE
STRUGGLE
(— AFTER) SEEK FOLLOW
CANVASS
(— FOR SUPERIORITY) VIE KEMP
(— IN OPPOSITION) RIVAL
CONTEND
(— TO EQUAL) EMULATE
(— TO OVERTAKE) ENSUE
STRIVING NISUS HORMIC STRIFT
CONATUS CONATION
STRIX SYRNIUM
STROBILE BUR BELL BURR CHAT
CONE BRUSH
STROKE BAT COY CUT DAB FIT
JOW ODD PAT PET POP RUB
BAFF BEAT BLOW CHAP CHOP
CLAP COUP CUFF DASH DENT
DING DINT DIRD DRAW DUNT
EDGE FIRK FLAP FLEG FLIP FLOP
FUNG GOWF HAND HURT JERK
JOWL KERF LASH LICK NACK PAIK
PEAL PECK SHOT SMIT SWAP TILT
TIRE TUCK WELT WHAP WIPE
BRUSH CHASE DOUSE DOWSE
DRAFT FLACK FLICK FORCE
HATCH ICTUS MINIM PANDY
PULSE SHOCK SLASH SLING SLIVE
SLOSH STRIP SWEEP SWING
SWIPE THROW TOUCH TRAIT
TRICE WHACK CARESS CENTER
FONDLE FOOZLE GENTLE GLANCE
PLAGUE PLUNGE SMOOTH STRAIK
STRAKE STRIKE STRIPE DRAUGHT
OUTLASH SOLIDUS VIRGULE
APOPLEXY BACKHAND
DRUMBEAT FOREHAND INSTROKE
SCORCHER
(— IN PAINTING) HAND
(— IN PENMANSHIP) MINIM
(— IN TENNIS) LET LOB BOAST
CHASE SMASH BRICOLE
BACKHAND FOREHAND
OVERHAND
(— OF A LETTER) DUCT STEM SERIF
POTHOOK CROSSBAR
(— OF BAD FORTUNE) CLAP
(— OF BELL) JOW BELL JOWL
KNELL TELLER
(— OF FORTUNE) CAST BREAK
BONZER FELICITY
(— OF LUCK) HIT FLUKE STRIKE
TURNUP CAPTION
(— OF MISFORTUNE) SISERARY
(— OF SCYTHE) SWATH SWATHE
(— OF SHEARS) SNIP
(— OF WIT) FLIRT
(— OF WORK) BAT CHAR
(— ON THE PALM) LOOFIE
(— WITH CLAW) CLOYE
(BILLIARDS —) SPOT STUN FLUKE
FORCE MASSE HAZARD
(CONNECTING —) LIGATURE
(CRICKET —) CUT GLANCE
(CROQUET —) ROQUET
(CURLING —) INWICK
(CUTTING —) GIRD
(DOUBLE SPINNING —) DRAW
(DRUM —) DRAG
(FINISHING —) NOBBLER
(GOLF —) ODD BAFF BISK HOOK
LIKE BLAST SLICE BISQUE FOOZLE

SCLAFF APPROACH
(HOCKEY —) JOB SCOOP
(JERKY —) STAB
(LIGHTNING —) BOLT
(MEDICAL —) ICTUS APOPLEXY
(MUSICAL —) TACT
(ORNAMENTAL —) FLOURISH
(QUICK —) FLIP
(SKATING —) EDGE MOHAWK
CHOCTAW
(SMART —) FIRK
(SOOTHING —) COY
(SWIMMING —) CRAWL TRUDGEN
SIDESTROKE
(SWINGING —) HEW
(SWORD —) MONTANTO
(PREF.) BOLO PLEGA PLEGO
(SUFF.) BOLA BOLE BOLIC BOLISM
BOLIST PLEGIA PLEGY PLEXIA
STROLL JET IDLE ROAM ROVE
ANTER JAUNT RANGE STRAY
TRAIK BUMMEL DACKER DANDER
GANDER LOUNGE PALMER
RAMBLE SOODLE STROAM
STROME TODDLE WANDER
SAUNTER TURNOUT SPATIATE
STRAVAGE STRAVAIG
PERAMBULATE
STROLLER SULKY TRAMP SHULER
FLANEUR SHUILER VAGRANT
BOHEMIAN PUSHCHAIR
STROLLING FLANERIE FUGITIVE
STROMA ECOID OECOID
STRONG FAT FIT HOT FELL FERE
FIRM FORT HALE HANG HARD
HIGH IRON KEEN RANK SURE
TRIG TRIM ACRID BONNY FORCY
FRECK FRESH HARDY HEAVY
HOGEN HUSKY JOLLY LUSTY
NAPPY NERVY ORPED PITHY
SHARP SMART SOLID SOUND
STARK STEER STERN STIFF STOUR
STOUT SWITH THEWY VALID
VIVID WIGHT YAULD ARDENT
BRAWNY BUCKRA BUNKUM
FEIRIE FIERCE MIGHTY POTENT
PRETTY ROBUST RUGGED SECURE
SEVERE SINEWY STABLE STANCH
STARCH STURDY WIELDY
BOARDLY BUIRDLY DOUGHTY
DURABLE EXALTED FECKFUL
HUFFCAP HUMMING INTENSE
LUSTFUL NERVOUS POLLENT
SKOOKUM STHENIC ATHLETIC
BIDDABLE MUSCULAR REVERENT
ROBOREAN SPANKING STALWART
STIFFISH VIGOROUS MERACIOUS
(PREF.) TRACHY VALE
STRONGBOX PETE COFFER
DEEDBOX
STRONGEST EXTREME
STRONGHOLD HOLD KEEP PEEL
PIECE PLACE TOWER CASTLE
WARDER CITADEL KREMLIN
REDOUBT FASTHOLD FASTNESS
FORTRESS FRONTIER MUNIMENT
STRENGTH
STRONGLY BUT SAD BADLY SWITH
FIRMLY STRONG DURABLY
FRESHLY HEFTILY SOLIDLY
STITHLY STOUTLY HEARTILY
STRONG-SCENTED HIGH RANK
STRONG-SMELLING FOXY

STRONTIUM SULPHATE
ACANTHIN
STROP RIP STRAP
STROPHE ALCAIC LAISSE STANZA
SAPPHIC
STROPHIC MELIC
STROPHIUS (FATHER OF —)
CRISSUS
(MOTHER OF —) ANTIPHATIA
(SON OF —) PYLADES
(WIFE OF —) ANAXIBIA ASTYOCHIA
CYDRAGORA
STRUCK (— SHARPLY) SMITTEN
(— WITH AMAZEMENT) AGAZED
AGHAST
STRUCTURAL ORGANIC
ANATOMIC TECTONIC
(— UNIT) IDANT
STRUCTURE CAGE FALX FORM
MAKE ANNEX BOOTH CABIN
FLOAT FRAME GETUP HOUSE
KIOSK PEGMA SETUP SHAPE
STOCK BRIDGE CAGEOT FABRIC
GANTRY GIRDER ISOGEN KELSON
PREFAB TIMBER COTTAGE
EDIFICE FAIRING FEATURE
GATEWAY GESTALT KEELSON
MANSION NURAGHE OUTCAST
PAGEANT STADIUM TURNOUT
ZEUGITE AEDICULA AIRCRAFT
AIRFRAME BUILDING BUTTRESS
COMPAGES CRIBWORK
DOMATIUM ENDOCONE ESCORIAL
HEADWORK MOUNTURE
NEOMORPH SKELETON
STANDARD
(— BUILT IN WATER) PIER
(— CONTAINING KILN) HOVEL
(— EXTENDED INTO SEA) JETTY
(— FOR PIGEONS) COTE
(— FRAMING SHIP) KEELSON
(— IN ROCKS) FLASER
(— OF CARTRIDGE) ANVIL
(— OF PRETENSION) PERRON
(— ON ROOF) CUPOLA FEMERELL
(— ON SHIP) BLISTER
(— ON STEAMER) TEXAS
(— PRODUCING SMOOTH OUTLINE)
FAIRING
(— SHELTERING INSECTS)
DOMATIUM
(— SUPPORTING AIRSHIP
PROPELLER) PYLON
(— WITHIN SHELL) ENDOCONE
(ANATOMICAL —) BUD APRON
CARINA CRESCENT
(ANTICLINAL —) SWELL
(ARCHED —) FORNIX
(BODILY —) FRAME PHYSIQUE
(BRICK —) KANG HOVEL
(BRISTLELIKE —) ARISTA
(BRONZE AGE —) HENGE
(CABINLIKE —) CABANA
(CLIMBING —) LADDER
(COMPLEX —) EMBOLUS
(CONELIKE —) PYRAMID
(CONICAL —) BULLET
(CREMATION —) DARGA
(CROWNLIKE —) CORONA
(CRYSTAL —) POLYTYPE
(CYLINDRICAL —) SILO
(DEADENING —) BAFFLE
(DEFENSIVE —) CAT

(FORTIFIED —) CAVALIER
(GENERAL —) GETUP
(GEOLOGICAL —) CAMBER
(HIGH —) TOWER
(HOLLOW —) SHELL
(KNEE-LIKE —) GENU
(LENS-SHAPED —) LENTOID
(LOFTY —) BABEL STEEPLE
(LOGICAL —) EIDOS
(MEGALITHIC —) HENGE
(ORGANIZED —) BULK
(ORIENTAL STORIED —) PAGODA
(ORNAMENTAL —) KIOSK
(PLANT —) DISC DISK
(POINTED —) BEAK
(PUEBLO —) KIVA
(RAISED —) CIMBORIO
(RAMSHACKLE —) COOP
(RINGLIKE —) ANNULUS
(RUDE STONE —S) SPECCHIE
(SACRIFICIAL —) ALTAR
(SENTENCE —) SYNTAX
(SHELTERING —) COT
(SICKLE-SHAPED —) FALX
(SLENDER —) HAIR
(STONE —) TAULA
(TEMPORARY —) HUT
(THEATER —) SKENE
(UNDERLYING —) BOTTOM
(UNSTABLE —) COBHOUSE
(WATERTIGHT —) CAMEL
(WHITE —) ALBEDO
(PREF.) MORPH(O)
(RADIATED —) ACTIN(O)
(SUFF.) (— OF A KIND) ID
(— UNIT) EME
STRUGGLE IT TEW TUG VIE WIN
AGON CAMP COPE DEAL FEND
FICK FRAB GAME PULL TAVE TOIL
AGONY FIGHT FLING HEAVE
LABOR STRAY SWORD TEAVE
TWEIL WORRY WRELE BATTLE
BUCKLE BUFFET BUSTLE COMBAT
EFFORT HASSLE JOSTLE JUSTLE
PINGLE RELUCT SEESAW SPRAWL
SPRUNT STIVER STRIFE STRIVE
TERVEE TUSSLE WARSLE WIDDLE
AGONIZE CLAMBER CONTEND
CONTEST DISPUTE FLOUNCE
GRAPPLE SCUFFLE TUILYIE
WARFARE WAUCHLE WRESTLE
CONFLICT ENDEAVOR FLOUNDER
SCRAFFLE SCRAMBLE SLUGFEST
SPRANGLE SPRATTLE
(— ALONG) HOBBLE
(— CONVULSIVELY) SPRAWL
(— FOR LARGESS) SCAMBLE
(— FORTH) ELUCTATE
(— TO GAIN FOOTING) SCRABBLE
SPROTTLE
(AGONIZED —) THROE
(CONFUSED —) MUSS
(DEATH —) AGONY
(HAND-TO-HAND —) GRAPPLE
(HAPHAZARD —) SCUFFLE
(SPIRITUAL —) PENIEL
(UNCEREMONIOUS —) SCRAMBLE
STRUGGLER LAOCOON
STRUM THRUM
STRUMA GOITER GOITRE
STRUMPET BRIM PUNK TRULL
WENCH WHORE BLOWEN BULKER
STIVER TOMBOY TOMRIG

COCOTTE SUCCUBA DOLLYMOP
PUNKLING SUCCUBUS VENTURER
(WORN-OUT —) HARRIDAN
STRUT JET BRAG COCK POMP
SPUR BRANK CORSO MAJOR
PRINK RANCE SWANK SASHAY
SCOTCH STROKE STROOT STRUNT
NAUNTLE PEACOCK STEMPLE
SWAGGER TRANSOM
STRUTTER HAM
STRUTTING COCKING
STUB BUTT SNAG SPUD STOB
STUD CHECK ERGOT GUARD
HINGE STUMP SPRUNT
STUBBLE BUN ETCH MANE SHACK
ARRISH EDDISH STOVER STUMPS
EEGRASS GRATTEN STIBBLE
STUBBORN SOT BALKY ROWDY
RUSTY STIFF STOUT STUNT
THRAW TOUGH MULISH STURDY
THWART BULLDOG PEEVISH
PIGGISH RESTIVE WAYWARD
WILLFUL OBDURATE PERVERSE
STUNKARD THRAWART
OBSTINATE PIGHEADED
TENACIOUS REFRACTORY
STUBBORNNESS STOMACH
ADAMANCY
STUBBY STUB CUTTY SQUAT
STOCKY STUMPY STUBBED
STUCCO ALBARIUM
STUCK FAST MASHED STICKIT
STOODED
STUCK-UP BUG FROSTED
STUD SET BOLT BOSS KNOB KNOP
KNOT NAIL RACE SLUG SPOT
BESET BULLA CLOUT HARAS
JOIST WRIST ASHLAR ENSTAR
INSTAR STOOTH STRING
CONTACT POTENCE QUARTER
STUDDLE PUNCHEON STANDARD
STUDDERY
(— FARM) HARAS
(— IN BOOT SOLE) SLUG
(— IN WATCH) POTENCE
(— SHOES) HOBNAIL
(— WITH NAILS) CLOUT
(INTERMEDIATE —) PUNCHEON
(ORNAMENTED —) AGLET AIGLET
STUDDED BOSSY BILLETY STELLED
BILLETTE
STUDDLE POST ROIL
STUDENT BOY DIG WIT COED
PLUG PREP SMUG SOPH AGGIE
BAHUR BEJAN FUCHS GRIND
MEDIC PUPIL SIZAR SPOON
BOCHER BURSAR BURSCH INTERN
JUNIOR JURIST MEDICO OPTIME
PREMED PRIMAR PRIMER PUISNE
SCOLOG SENIOR ADVISEE
CHRONIC CLASSIC DANTEAN
EDUCAND ETONIAN FAILURE
GOLIARD GRECIAN INTERNE
INTRANT LEARNER MIDDLER
MOOTMAN OPPIDAN PASSMAN
PHARMIC PLUGGER SCHOLAR
STUDIER TEMPLAR THEOLOG
BOTANIST CABALIST COLLEGER
DEMOTIST DISCIPLE EDUCATOR
FEMINIST HOMERIST HOSTELER
ISLAMIST PREMEDIC REPEATER
SECONDAR SUBSIZAR TRANSFER
(— IN TALMUDIC ACADEMY) BAHUR

(— LAST IN CLASS) SPOON
(— OF LOW RANK) TERNAR TERNER
(— WHO LIVES IN TOWN) OPPIDAN
(ABNORMALLY ABSORBED —) SAP
(DAY —) EXTERN EXTERNE
(DIVINITY —) STIBBLER
(DRUDGING —) PLUG
(ENGLISH SCHOOL —) BLUE SWOT
ETONIAN OXONIAN SWOTTER
BATTELER
(GRADUATE —) FELLOW
(LAW —) PUNEE JURIST LEGIST
PUISNE TEMPLAR STAGIARY
(MILITARY —) CADET
(MOSLEM —) SOFTA
(NON-COLLEGIATE —) TOSHER
(PLODDING —) DIG SMUG
(WANDERING —) GOLIARD
(1ST-YEAR —) FUCHS
(3RD-YEAR —) JUNIOR TERTIAN
(PL.) GOWN CLASS HOUSE SEMI-
NAR
(SUFF.) LOG(ER)(IA)(IAN)(IC)(ICAL)
(IST)(UE)(Y)
STUDIED COOL VOULU STUDIOUS
STUDIO LOT SHOT ATELIER
BOTTEGA GALLERY
STUDIOUS BOOKY BOOKISH
CLERKLY DILIGENT SEDULOUS
STUDY CON BEAT BONE BOOK
CASE MUZZ ROOM SIFT STUD
GRIND ESTUDY EXAMEN LESSON
MUSEUM SCOLEY SURVEY
ABBOZZO ACCOUNT ANALYZE
CANVASS CROQUIS POCHADE
REVOLVE SANCTUM ANALYSIS
BOOKWORK CONSIDER EXERCISE
MEDITATE SCRUTINY TYPOLOGY
(— HARD) DIG MUG SAP BONE
SMUG STEW SWOT
(— OF BRAMBLES) BATOLOGY
(— OF ONESELF) AUTOLOGY
(— OF PUNISHMENT) PENOLOGY
(— OF SACRED EDIFICES) NAOLOGY
(— OF SNOW AND ICE) CRYOLOGY
(— OF VALUES) AXIOLOGY
(— UNDER PRESSURE) CRAM
(ART —) ABBOZZO CROQUIS
POCHADE
(BROWN —) REVERIE
(CLAY —) BOZZETTO
(MUSICAL —) ETUDE
(PRELIMINARY —) SKETCH
(UNINTERESTING —) GRIND
(SUFF.) ICS SOPH(ER)(IC)(IST)(Y)
STUDY IN SCARLET (AUTHOR OF —
) DOYLE
(CHARACTER IN —) HOPE JOHN
LUCY HOLMES TOBIAS WATSON
FERRIER GREGSON LESTRADE
SHERLOCK STAMFORD
JEFFERSON STANGERSON
STUFF PAD RAM WAD CRAM CRAP
GAUM GEAR JAZZ PANG STOP
TACK TRIG TUCK WHAT CROWD
DUROY FARCE FORCE KEDGE
METAL PASTE SQUAB TRADE
FABRIC GRAITH KIBOSH MATTER
PAUNCH STEEVE STODGE TACKLE
TIMBER BOMBARD BOMBAST
DRUGGET ELEMENT ENFARCE
DIAPHANE MARINATE MATERIAL
SPLUTTER WHIPPING

(— AND NONSENSE) HAVERS
PICKLE PIFFLE
(— FILLET OF VEAL) BOMBARD
(— FULL) STODGE
(— OF POOR QUALITY SILK) RASH
(— ONESELF) MAST
(— POULTRY) FARCE MARINATE
(— WITH DRESSING) QUILT
(COTTON —) CALICO
(HOUSEHOLD —) GEAR
(INFERIOR —) MOCKADO
(SILKEN —) TARS TARSE DIAPHANE
(STICKY —) GOOK
(TASTELESS —) GLOP
(THIN —) CRAPE
(THIN SILK —) LOVE
(WATERY —) BLASH
(WISHY-WASHY —) BLASH
(WOOLEN —) SAY DUROY TWILLY
DRUGGET SAGATHY SHALLOON
(WORTHLESS —) GEAR GLOP
HOGWASH
STUFFED PANG TRIG BLOAT FARCI
STODGY BLOATED BOMBAST
STUFFING PAD TAR FARCE STECH
STUFF BOMBAST FARCING
SAWDUST SALPICON STUFFAGE
(— FOR MATTRESS) PULU
STUFFY POKY CLOSE FUBBY FUBSY
FUGGY STIVY WOOLY WOOLLY
AIRLESS FROUSTY
STULTIFY SOT PUPPIFY
STUMBLE CHIP FALL HAMP PECK
STOT TRIP HAMEL LURCH SPURN
STOIT STUMP BUMBLE CHANCE
FALTER HALPER HAMBLE HAPPEN
LUMPER OFFEND STEVEL TUMBLE
WAGGER BLUNDER FOUNDER
SCAMBLE SNAPPER STAMMER
STAMPLE STOITER STOTTER
STUMMER FLOUNDER THRUMBLE
STUMBLING HACK HURTING
OFFENCE OFFENSE
STUMP CAG GET JOB NOG SET
BUTT DOCK GRUB LUMP MORE
RUNT SNAG STAB STAM STOB
STUB STUD CHUNK SCRAB SCRAG
STICK STOCK STOMP STOOL
STOOP STOWL DOTARD NUBBIN
SCRUNT SPRONG STOVEN
WICKET DODDARD RAMPICK
RAMPIKE SLEEPER STUMMEL
BALDHEAD HUSTINGS STUBBLES
(— AND ROOT) MOCK
(— OF TAIL) STRUNT
(CIGAR —) TOPPER
(CRICKET —) STICKS
(DEAD —) RUNT
(TREE —) MOCK STOW STOCK
STOOP ZUCHE DOTARD NUBBIN
STOVEN DODDARD
(WALNUT —) BUTT
STUMPY SNUB BUNTY SNUBBED
STUN DIN DAZE ROCK
DAUNT DAVER DEAVE DOVER
DOZEN DROWN STONY ASTONY
BEDAZE BENUMB DEADEN
DEAFEN DEVVEL NOBBLE
STOUND WITHER ASTOUND
DAMMISH SANDBAG SILENCE
STUPEFY STUPEND ASTONISH
PARALYZE
(— BY A SHOT) CREASE

STUNNED SILLY STUPENT ASTONIED

STUNNER KNOCKER THUMPER TRIMMER

STUNNING CRASHING SHOCKING

STUNT GAG KIP FEAT NIRL BLAST CANOE CROWL DWARF STINT STOCK BARANI BARONI CRADDY DOLPHIN BACKBEND CATALINA CRUCIFIX PORPOISE SUPPRESS **(SWIMMING —)** SHARK SPIRAL

STUNTED URLED GRUBBY RUNTISH SCROGGY SCRUBBY SCRUFFY SCRUNTY WANTHRIVEN

STUPA TOPE CHORTEN

STUPEFACTION STOUND STUPOR

STUPEFIED MAD DAMP DAZED DRUNK MAZED SILLY SOTTED BEMAZED BEMUSED DONNERT DOZENED DOZZLED STUPENT BESOTTED DATELESS MINDLESS

STUPEFIER OPIUM

STUPEFY FOX BAZE DAMP DAZE DOZE DRUG DULL GOOF MAZE MULL STUN BESOT DAUNT DAVER DEAVE DIZZY DOZEN SHEND SMOKE STONY ASTONE ASWEVE BEMUSE BENUMB DUDDLE FUDDLE MOIDER MUDDLE STOUND ASTOUND CONFUSE FORDULL SLUMBER STUPEND ASTONISH BEFUDDLE BEMUDDLE BEWILDER CONFOUND MORPHINE PARALYZE SOMNIATE SOPORATE

STUPEFYING STONY

STUPENDOUS GREAT IMMENSE ENORMOUS MONSTROUS

STUPID FAT JAY BETE DOWF DULL DUMB DUNT FOOL HAZY LEWD NICE NUMB SLOW BLUNT BOOBY BRUTE CRASS DENSE DOTED DUNNY GLAKY GOOSY GROSS HEAVY INERT MOSSY MUZZY SILLY THICK ASSISH BARREN BOVINE CUCKOO DAWKIN DOITED DROWSY DUMMEL HEBETE LOGGER LURDAN OBTUSE OPAQUE SIMPLE SODDEN STOLID STULTY STURDY SUMPHY URLUCH WOODEN ASININE BRUTISH CHUCKLE DOLTISH DOWFART DUFFING DUMPISH FATUOUS FOOLISH FOPPISH GAWKISH GLAIKIT GULLISH INSULSE LUMPISH LURDANE PEAKISH PINHEAD PROSAIC SOTTISH TAIVERT TOMFOOL VACUOUS WITLESS ANSERINE BAYARDLY BESOTTED BLOCKISH BOBBYISH BOEOTIAN CLODDISH DONNERED DUNCICAL FOOTLESS GAUMLESS HEADLESS IMBECILE STOCKISH PINHEADED SENSELESS **(— PERSON)** HOIT JUKES SUMPH LUMMOX TUMFIE KALLIKAK (PREF.) MORO

STUPIDITY BETISE TORPOR BOBBERY DENSITY DUNCERY FATUITY DULLNESS DUMBNESS HEBETUDE STOLIDITY

STUPOR FOG SOG DAMP DOTE SOPOR SWARF STOUND TORPOR TRANCE NARCOMA LETHARGY NARCOSIS (PREF.) NARC(O) TYPH(O)

STURDILY BUFF TOUGH

STURDY GID BUFF DUNT RUDE TALL THRO BURLY CRANK FELON HARDY HUSKY LUSTY SOLID SOUND STARK STERN STIFF STOUT VAUDY WALLY FEERIE PLUGGY ROBUST RUGGED RUSTIC SQUARE STABLE STEADY STEEVE STOCKY STRONG STUGGY VIRILE FECKFUL UPRIGHT VALIANT STALWART STUBBORN VIGOROUS YEOMANLY

STURGEON HUSO ELOPS BELUGA GANOID MAMMOSE OSSETER STERLET

STUTTER FAM BUFF HACK MANT STOT STUT GANCH FAMBLE HABBER HABBLE STAMMER

STUTTERER RATTLER

STUTTERING TRAULISM BALBUTIENT

STY PEN QUAT STYE WEST FRANK CRUIVE PIGPEN STITHE HORDEOLUM

STYLE AIR CUT DUB PEN SAY TON WAY CHIC FACE FORM GARB HAND KIND MODE MOLD NAME PILE RATE TWIG VEIN GENRE GETUP GUISE SHAPE STATE SWANK TASTE FESCUE FORMAT GNOMON GOTHIC PHRASE STEELE STRAIN STYLUS UMBONE COSTUME DIALECT DICTION FASHION INSTYLE QUALITY EQUIPAGE LANGUAGE MARINISM NARRANTE PULLBACK PHRASEOLOGY **(— HAIR)** CORNROW **(— OF ARCHITECTURE)** ORDER DRAVIDA GEORGIAN **(— OF COOKING)** CUISINE **(— OF DRESS)** GUISE **(— OF GEM SETTING)** BOX **(— OF HANDWRITING)** CHANCERY SCRIPTION **(— OF HAT)** BLOCK **(— OF MOUNTING)** SETTING **(— OF MUSIC)** BOOGIE **(— OF PAINTING)** GENRE **(— OF PENMANSHIP)** HAND **(— OF PRINTING)** CAMAIEU **(— OF SPEAKING)** ADDRESS **(— OF WRESTLING)** SAMBO **(AFFECTED —)** EUPHUISM **(ARTISTIC —)** GUSTO GOTHIC ARTIFICE DANDYISM MANNERISM **(BOOKBINDING —)** ALDINE MAIOLI MAJOLI FANFARE GROLIER ETRUSCAN HARLEIAN ROXBURGH **(CUSTOMARY —)** GATE **(DECORATIVE —)** ARTDECO **(DISTINCTIVE —)** CLOTHES **(FAVORED —)** GROOVE **(HAIR —)** CROP TETE **(INFLATED —)** FUSTIAN **(LATEST —)** KICK **(PRETENTIOUS —)** BOMBAST **(PROPER —)** WEAR **(THEATRICAL —)** LYCEUM **(WRITING —)** MINUSCULE

(SUFF.) **(IN THE — OF)** ESQUE

STYLET SPEAR STILET STYLUS TROCAR MANDRIN STILETTE

STYLIDIUM CANDOLEA

STYLISH CHIC DOSS POSH TONY DOGGY NIFTY NOBBY RITZY SASSY SHARP SMART SWELL TIPPY TOPPY CHEESY CLASSY DAPPER FLOSSY JAUNTY SWANKY TONISH DASHING DOGGISH GENTEEL KNOWING SWAGGER TOFFISH

STYLOBATE PODIUM

STYLOID BELONOID

STYLUS GAD PEN STYLE CUTTER GREFFE TRACER HARPAGO POINTEL PYROPEN

STYMPHALUS (FATHER OF —) ELATUS **(MOTHER OF —)** LAODICE

STYPTIC ALUM AMADOU MATICO BAROMETZ STANCHER

STYRENE STYROL CINNAMOL

STYX (FATHER OF —) OCEANUS **(HUSBAND OF —)** PALLAS **(MOTHER OF —)** TETHYS

SUAEDA DONDIA

SUAH (FATHER OF —) ZOPHAH

SUAN PAN SOROBAN

SUAVE OILY SMUG SOFT BLAND SOAPY SVELT GLOSSY SILKEN SMOOTH URBANE FULSOME POLITIC UNCTUOUS

SUAVELY CREAMILY

SUAVITY COMITY URBANITY

SUB GRASS

SUBALTERN WART

SUBBASE PLINTH

SUBCINCTORIUM BALTEUS BALTHEUS

SUBCLASS GENDER BRYALES CESTODA CYCLIAE DIGENEA SPECIES AMOEBAEA ANAPSIDA CESTODES COPEPODA GANOIDEI SELACHII

SUBCOMPACT MINICAR

SUBCUTANEOUS DEEP

SUBDEACON MINISTER

SUBDIVIDE CARVE MINCE

SUBDIVISION DEN OBE SEX BEAT CAZA DHER HAPU ITEM TASU BUNDA CORPS CURIA DEKAN DHERI FERAE FORTY HSIEN IOWAN NAHIE OKRUG PHYLE SITIO STAGE TALUK TARAF TURMA UINTA ALBIAN ARENIG BANNER BRANCH BUREAU CERCLE CIRCLE CLAUSE COHORT COLUMN COMMOT DAKOTA DANIAN DOGGER FACIES GUELPH HEMERA IMBREX LENGTH LUDLOW MARKAZ NAHIYE OBLAST ONEIDA SANJAK SECTOR SERIAL SHIRAZ STRAIN SUBAGE TAHSIL TASSOO TEHSIL BUKEYEF CENTURY CHEMUNG CHIRIPA COCHITI COMARCA ECOTYPE ELEMENT EPARCHY EPISODE GENESEE MANIPLE MONTANA ORBITAL PHRATRY RONDOUT SASTEAN SECTION SEEDBED SUBAREA SUBLINE SUBPLAT SUBPLOT SUBRACE SUBZONE

SUPPORT TRENTON TRINITY WASATCH WASHITA WENLOCK WICHITA BANOVINA DISTRICT DIVISION DJAGATAY ENDBRAIN FLOTILLA GUBERNIA LOCATION MONTEREY NAUCRARY PARTICLE PRECINCT STOCKTON SUBCASTE SUBORDER SUBSTAGE SUBTRIBE TOWNSHIP PARAGRAPH **(— OF SCOUTS)** CREW **(EGYPTIAN —)** KISM **(SPARTAN —)** ENOMOTY

SUBDOMINANT FOURTH

SUBDUE BOW COW ADAW BEAT BEND QUAY TAME ACCOY ALLAY AMATE CHARM CRUSH DAUNT DOMPT QUAIL QUASH QUELL SOBER STILL ADAUNT BRIDLE CHASTE DEBELL DISMAY EVINCE GENTLE MASTER QUENCH REDUCE SUBACT SUBMIT UNWILD ABANDON AFFAITE CAPTURE CHASTEN CONQUER DAUNTON OVERAWE REPRESS REPRIME SUCCUMB CONVINCE OVERCOME SUPPEDIT SUPPRESS SURMOUNT VANQUISH

SUBDUED MAK SOFT TAME MUTED SOBER STILL UNDER BROKEN CHASTE GENTLE ASHAMED SUBMISS SOURDINE

SUBFAMILY KHOISAN CUSHITIC ACRAEINAE

SUBGROUP BAND FAMILY

SUBHEAD BOXHEAD SIDEHEAD

SUBIMAGO DUN

SUBINDEX SUFFIX

SUBIRRIGATE SUB SUBWATER

SUBIRRIGATION SUBBING

SUBJECT DUX PUT ABLE ALLY BODY BONE ITEM OPEN TEXT HOBBY PLACE STOOP STUDY TESTO THEMA THEME TOPIC GROUND IMPOSE LIABLE PATHIC REDUCE SACOPE SUBDIT SUBMIT THRALL VASSAL CAITIVE CITIZEN FEODARY FEUDARY OBVIOUS PROBAND SERVILE AMENABLE ELECTIVE INCIDENT INFERIOR OBEDIENT OCCASION SENTENCE SUBJUGAL **(— OF DISCOURSE)** NOUN **(— OF FUGUE)** GUIDA **(— OF PROPOSITION)** EXTREME **(— TO ABUSE)** REVILE **(— TO ARGUMENT)** MOOT **(— TO BAD TEMPER)** MOODY **(— TO CHANGE)** MUTABLE FUGITIVE **(— TO CRITICISM)** SCOURGE **(— TO FATE)** FIE **(— TO PERCOLATION)** DISPLACE **(— TO SOME ACTION)** TREAT **(CONTROVERTED —)** ISSUE **(LOYAL —)** LIEGE (PL.) FOLK

SUBJECTION SLAVERY SERVITUS THIRLING

SUBJECTIVE IMMANENT INSEEING INTERNAL PECTORAL EPISTEMIC

SUBJOIN AFFIX

SUBJUGATION BONDAGE SERVITUDE

SUBKINGDOM PHYLUM ANNULOSA CHORDATA

SUBLEADER HEADMAN

SUBLEASE FARMOUT SUBTACK

SUBLET JOB SUBSET CONACRE SUBLEASE

SUB-LIEUTENANT CORNET

SUBLIMATE FLOWER ALCOHOL SUBLIME

SUBLIME BIG FUME GRAND LOFTY NOBLE AUGUST REFINE SOLEMN WINGED DANTEAN ELEVATO EXALTED EMPYREAL EMPYREAN MAGNIFIC MAJESTIC SERAPHIC SPLENDID MAGNIFICENT (— IN STYLE) MILTONIC

SUBLIMITY GRANDEUR

SUBLUNARY EARTHLY

SUBMARINE SUB BOAT DIVER FRITZ GUPPY SUBSEA PIGBOAT TIDDLER (PART OF —) DECK SAIL PLANE TOWER BRIDGE RUDDER PROPELLER SAILPLANE TURTLEBACK FAIRWEATHER

SUBMEDIANT SIXTH

SUBMERGE BOG DIP BURY DIVE DUNK HIDE SINK SOAK TAKE DROWN SOUSE SWAMP WHELM DELUGE DRENCH ENGULF DEMERGE IMPLUNGE INUNDATE SUBMERSE SURROUND OVERWHELM

SUBMERGENCE ONLAP

SUBMISSION VAIL STOOP PATIENCE

SUBMISSIVE MEEK BUXOM DEMISS DOCILE DUTIFUL PASSIVE SERVILE SLAVISH SUBJECT SUBMISS UNERECT OBEDIENT RESIGNED YIELDING (— TO WIFE) UXORIOUS

SUBMISSIVENESS SLAVERY

SUBMIT BOW EAT ABOW BEND CAVE LEAN OBEY TAKE VAIL AVALE DEFER HIELD STAND STOOP YIELD ASSENT CRINGE DELATE RESIGN CONSIGN KNUCKLE SUBJECT SUBMISE SUCCUMB TRUCKLE PROPOUND (— FOR CONSIDERATION) REMIT (— TAMELY) EAT (— TO) ABIDE STAND SUFFER

SUBNORMAL OFF SICK ABNORMAL

SUBORDER LARI ALCAE APODA APODI GALLI GRUES ARDEAE COHORT CUCULI SAURIA AGLOSSA ANSERES ARCACEA ASCONES CORACII COSTATA SARCURA SYCONES ACRASIDA ADEPHAGA BATOIDEI COLUMBAE CORACIAE CURSORIA ENOPLINA EUSUCHIA FALCONES FREGATAE SELACHII

SUBORDINARY ENDORSE ROUNDEL

SUBORDINATE SUB SINK PETTY SCRUB UNDER EXEMPT MINION PUISNE SECOND YEOMAN PARTIAL SERVANT SERVILE SUBJECT HENCHMAN INFERIOR MYRMIDON PARERGAL POSTPONE

SERVIENT ANCILLARY SUBALTERN (PREF.) (— TO) VICE

SUBORN HAVE BRIBE

SUBOVAL PETALOID

SUBPHYLUM EUCHORDA

SUBPOENA SUMMONS

SUBRACE STOCK

SUB ROSA COVERTLY SECRETLY PROVATELY

SUBSCRIBE SIGN ASSENT ASCRIBE CONSIGN SUBSIGN

SUBSCRIBER RAILBIRD

SUBSCRIPT INFERIOR

SUBSCRIPTION APPROVAL SIGNATURE ABONNEMENT

SUBSEQUENT AFTER LATER FUTURE PUISNE ENSUING POSTNATE (PREF.) POST (— TO) CIS

SUBSEQUENTLY SO LATER SINCE

SUBSERVIENT OILY VASSAL DUTEOUS SERVILE SLAVISH OFFICIAL

SUBSHRUB STOCK GUAYULE COLUMNEA PERIWINKLE

SUBSIDE DIE EBB LAY LIE ADAW CALM FALL LULL SILE SINK VAIL ABATE ALLAY LAPSE RESIDE SETTLE ASSUAGE RELAPSE UNSWELL WITHDRAW

SUBSIDENCE FALL SETTLING

SUBSIDIARY CHILD DONKEY SUBSIDY ACCESSORY

SUBSIDIZE BONUS

SUBSIDY AID BONUS BOUNTY POUNDAGE

SUBSILICIC BASIC

SUBSIST BE LIVE RELY

SUBSISTENCE BEING LIVING

SUBSISTENT ENTITY

SUBSOIL PAN LECK SOLE SHRAVE RATCHEL

SUBSTAGE CARY GUNZ IOWAN MANKATO STADIAL TAZEWELL

SUBSTANCE FAT SUM BODY CORE FECK GIST GITE TACK WHAT ADROP AGENT ALLOY ARCHE BEING FOMES GREAT KEEST METAL MOYEN OUSIA PROOF SENSE STUFF THING BOTTOM GADUIN GETTER IMPORT MATTER STAPLE WEALTH AEROSOL AGAROID ANTIGEN COLICIN COLLOID CONTENT ELEIDIN EMANIUM ERGUSIA ESSENCE HYALINE MEANING PURPORT REAGENT SUBJECT SUPTION ACCEPTOR ADDITIVE ADHESIVE ALLERGEN AMBEROID ANTIFOAM BASSORIN HARDNESS MATERIAL (— CAPABLE OF EXPANSION) DILATANT (— FORMED IN VINEGAR) MOTHER (— FROM CRUSHED APPLES) POMACE (— IN BLOOD) ALEXINE ABLASTIN (— IN LIGHT BULBS) GETTER (— IN WOODY TISSUE) LIGNIN (— OF DENTINE) IVORY (— OF EXTREME HARDNESS) ADAMANT DIAMOND (— PRODUCING POISONOUS

ATMOSPHERE) GAS (— SURROUNDED BY FOREIGN TISSUE) ENCLAVE (— THAT STOPS LOCOMOTION) ARRESTANT (— TO ADD STABILITY) BALLAST (— TRANSPORTING GERMS) FOMES (— USED AS HYPNOTIC) URAL (— USED IN DETECTING OTHERS) REAGENT (— WITH MOLDY ODOR) CHARACIN (ADHESIVE —) GLUE GLOEA PASTE CEMENT STICKER (AMORPHOUS —) GLASS RESIN LIGNIN PECTIN FERRITE SAPONIN (AROMATIC —) BALSAM (ASTRINGENT —) ALUM CATECHU (BITTER —) ALOIN LININ ILICIN (BLACK —) SOOT BLECK (CLEANSING —) LYE (COLLOIDAL —) ALGIN EXPANDER (COMBUSTIBLE —) COAL (CORROSIVE —) CAUSTIC (CRYSTALLINE —) LAURIN ALANINE HELENIN ELATERIN (DARK —) ATRAMENT (DISSOLVED —) SOLUTE (ETERNAL —) DHARMA ADHARMA (FATLIKE —) DEGRAS LIPOID ERGUSIA (FATTY —) SMEAR SUBERIN (FERMENTATION —) LEAVEN (FIBROUS —) COTTON (FILAMENTOUS —) HARL (FILMY —) GOSSAMER (FIRST —) YLEM (GRINDING —) ABRASIVE (GROWTH-PROMOTING —) AUXIN (GUMMY —) GUM GURRY AMYLOID GLACTAN (HARD ANIMAL —) BONE ENAMEL (HORNY —) BALEEN CHITIN CHONDRIN (HYPOTHETICAL —) FLUID INOGEN PROTYL (IDEAL —) CONTINUUM (INFLAMMABLE —) BITUMEN (INSOLUBLE —) CARRIER HYALOGEN (LIVERLIKE —) HEPAR (NARCOTIC —) DRUG (NITROGENOUS —) LACTENIN (POISONOUS —) ARSENIC PHRYNIN EXOTOXIN (POWDER OF ANY —) FLOUR (POWDERY —) STOUR (PREDOMINATING —) BASE (RESINOUS —) LAC COPAL CARANNA CARAUNA COPALINE COPALITE (SELF-DEFENSIVE —) ACRAEIN (SEMISOLID —) GEL (SOUR —) ACID (STICKY —) GOO GOOP SIZE STICK GLUTEN BIRDLIME (SUBTLE —) SPIRIT (SWEET —) SUGAR (SYNTHETIC —) HORMONE (TRANSLUCENT —) HYALINE CHONDRIN (UNBREAKABLE —) ADAMANT (UNCREATED —) ADHARMA (VISCOUS —) GLAIR

GREASE SLUBBER (VITAL —) KEEST (WAXY —) CERIN PARAFFIN SUBERINE (PREF.) HYL(O) (SUFF.) (— HAVING FORM) PHANE (— PRODUCED THRU PROCESS) STATE

SUBSTANDARD BAD BAUCH

SUBSTANTIAL FAT FIRM MEATY PUKKA STOUT ACTUAL BODILY HEARTY SQUARE STABLE STANCH STUFFY STURDY MASSIVE MATERIAL SUBSTANT TANGIBLE

SUBSTANTIATE BACK CONFIRM SUPPORT VALIDATE

SUBSTANTIVE DIRECT

SUBSTITUTE SUB MOCK VICE AKORI EXTRA PINCH PROXY VICAR BACKUP BEWITH CHANGE DEPUTY DOUBLE ERSATZ STOOGE COMMUTE REPLACE RESERVE STANDBY STOPGAP SUBDEAN SUFFECT SUPPOSE DISPLACE EMERGENT MAKESHIFT (— FOR TEA) TIA FAHAM (NOT —) FULL (POOR —) APOLOGY (PREF.) PSEUD(O) (SUFF.) ETTE

SUBSTITUTING (PREF.) (— FOR) PRO

SUBSTITUTION SHIFT CHANGE ERSATZ ENALLAGE EXCHANGE NOVATION REPLACEMENT (— OF SOUNDS) LALLATION

SUBSTRATUM SUB GROUND SUBBING SUBJECT

SUBSTREAM MATTER

SUBSTRUCTURE PODIUM FOOTING CENTERING

SUBSUME COVER EXPLAIN INCLUDE

SUBSUMING GENERIC

SUBTENANT VAVASOUR

SUBTERFUGE MASK BLIND CROOK QUIRK SHIFT TRICK WRINK AMBAGE CHICANE ARTIFICE PRETENCE TRAVERSE VOIDANCE

SUBTILE SUBTLE TENUOUS

SUBTILIZE EXALT

SUBTITLE TITLE LEADER CAPTION

SUBTLE SLY FINE NICE WILY WISE ACUTE ARGUTE ASTUTE CRAFTY SHREWD CUNNING FRAGILE SUBTILE CLERGIAL (TOO —) FINESPUN

SUBTLETY NICE FRAUD DECEIT NUANCE EXILITY FINESSE QUILLET DELICACY FINENESS QUIDDITY QUODLIBET REFINEMENT

SUBTLY FINE SLILY SLYLY

SUBTRACT BATE PULL TAKE SHAVE DEDUCE DEDUCT DETRACT SUBDUCE SUBDUCT SUBTRAY DIMINISH

SUBTRIBE HAPU SENAAH SEMNONES

SUBURB ANNEX BORGO BARRIO PETTAH BANLIEU ENDSHIP FAUBOURG (PL.) SKIRTS ENVIRONS

OUTPARTS SUBURBIA
SUBURBIA VILLADOM
SUBVERSION FALL SABOTAGE
SUBVERSIVE RUINOUS
SUBVERT SAP KILL RAZE RUIN
EVERT UPSET GAINSAY OVERSET
REVERSE RUINATE OVERTURN
SUBVERTED LOST
SUBWAY DIVE METRO
SUCCEED GO FAY HIT FARE RISE
WORK CLICK ENSUE FADGE
PROVE SCORE SPEED COTTON
FOLLOW OBTAIN SECOND THRIVE
ACHIEVE INHERIT PREVAIL
PROSPER THROUGH FLOURISH
SUPPLANT
(— TO THRONE) ACCEDE ASCEND
SUCCEEDING VICE AFTER CHANGE
ULTERIOR
SUCCESS DO GO HIT MAX WIN
WOW BANG CESS LUCK SMASH
SPEED THRIFT EXPLOIT FORTUNE
FURTHER PROWESS THEEDOM
FELICITY GODSPEED
(— IN A MATCH) GAME
(ACCIDENTAL —) FLUKE
(BRILLIANT —) ECLAT
(SUDDEN —) KILLING
(UNEXPECTED —) JACKPOT
(WORLDLY —) ARTHA
SUCCESSFUL HOT MADE SOCK
BOFFO LUCKY SPEEDFUL
THRIVING
(BARELY —) NARROW
SUCCESSFULLY GREAT HAPPILY
PROUDLY
SUCCESSION RUN SUIT ROUND
SUITE TRACK ASSISE COURSE
SEQUEL SERIES STREAM STRING
HEIRDOM SUCCESS ANCESTRY
DIADOCHE MUTATION SEQUENCE
(— OF CHANGES) FLUX
(— OF CHORDS) CADENCE
(— OF CRUSTS) CALICHE
(— OF STAGES) CASCADE
(— OF WAVES) CRIMP
(— RULERS) DYNASTY
SUCCESSIVELY AROW
SUCCESSOR HEIR CALIF HERES
CALIPH HAERES EPIGONUS
(— OF CHIEFTAIN) TANIST
(— OF MUHAMMAD) CALIF CALIPH
(ECCLESIASTICAL —) COARB
(PL.) DIADOCHI
SUCCINCT BRIEF SHORT TERSE
CONCISE LACONIC SUMMARY
SUCCINIC DIACETIC
SUCCOR AID HELP RESET SERVE
SPEED ASSIST RELIEF RESCUE
SUPPLY UPTAKE COMFORT
DELIVER PRESIDY RELIEVE
SECOURS SUSTAIN BEFRIEND
SUCCORY CHICORY
SUCCULENT FRIM FRUM LUSH
JUICY LUSHY PAPPY PULPY
SAPPY YOUNG CASHIE FLESHY
TENDER WATERISH
SUCCUMB BREAK QUAIL STOOP
TRAIK YIELD
SUCH SIC SICK THAT SWICH
SUCHNESS TATHATA
SUCK SOUK SWIG SWOOP SUCKLE
(— DRY) SOAK

(— UP) DRINK ABSORB TIPPLE
(SUFF.) MYZA MYZON
SUCKEN THIRL
SUCKER CHUB FISH GULL PATSY
SOBOL THIEF CHUPON CUPULE
MULLET RATOON REDFIN SOBOLE
SPROUT SQUARE STOLON SUPPER
TILLER CUTLIPS GONOTYL
LOCULUS OSCULUM PEDICEL
SCOURGE BOTHRIUM HUMPBACK
LOLLIPOP PUSHOVER REDHORSE
SURCULUS QUILLBACK
(PREF.) BDELL(O) BOTHR(I)(IO)(O)
MYZO STOLONI SURCULI
(SUFF.) BDELLA
SUCKLE FEED MILK SUCK LACTATE
NOURISH
SUCKLING SUCKER LACTANT
SUCKLER TEATLING
SUCTION INTAKE
(SUFF.) MYZA MYZON
SUCTORIA ACINETAE

SUDAN
CAPITAL: KHARTOUM
DESERT: NUBIAN
LANGUAGE: GA EWE IBO KRU EFIK
MOLE TSHI YORUBA MANDINGO
MEASURE: UD
MOUNTAIN: KINYETI
NATIVE: DAZA GOLO NUER SERE
DINKA FULAH HAUSA MOSSI
NUBIYIN
PROVINCE: DARFUR KASSALA
KORDOFAN
REGION: DARFUR KASSALA
KORDOFAN
RIVER: NILE
TOWN: WAU JUBA KOSTI MEROE
ATBARA ALUBAYD KASSALA
MALAKAL OMDURMAN
WEIGHT: HABBA

SUDANESE FULA FULAH
SUDAN GRASS GARAVA GARAWI
SUDDEN BRASH FERLY HASTY
ICTIC SWIFT ABRUPT FIERCE
SNAPPY SPEEDY PRERUPT
HEADLONG SPURTIVE SUBITANY
SUBITOUS OVERNIGHT
PRECIPITATE
SUDDENLY BOB POP BOLT FLOP
SLAP AMAIN SHORT SKELP SOUSE
ASTART BOUNCE PRESTO SUBITO
ASUDDEN UNAWARES
SUDDENNESS ATTACK SUDDENTY
SUDORIFIC SWEAT SWEATER
HIDROTIC SUDATORY
SUDRA VELLALA
SUDS BUCK FOAM SAPPLES
SOAPSUDS
SUE LAW WOO SUIT IMPLEAD
TROUNCE
SUET TALLOW
(PREF.) STEAR(I)(O) STEAT(O)
(SUFF.) STEARIN
SUFFER BYE GET LET BEAR BIDE
DREE FIND GAIN HURT PAIN PINE
ALLOW DREIE INCUR LABOR
PROVE SMART SMOKE STAND
THOLE ABEGGE BETEEM ENDURE
PERMIT AGONIZE SUPPORT
SUSTAIN UNDERGO TOLERATE

(— AGONY) THROE
(— AT STAKE) SMOKE
(— DEFEAT) BOW
(— FOR) ABY ABYE ABIDE
(— FROM TIME) AGE
(— GREAT AFFLICTION) GROAN
(— HUNGER) CLEM STARVE
AFFAMISH
(— LOSS OF) GIVE
(— PAIN) STOUND ANGUISH
(— PENALTY) SWEAT
(— REMORSE) RUE
(— RUIN) WRECK
(— SYNCOPE) FAINT
(— THROUGH) PASS
(— TO ENTER) ADMIT
SUFFERABLE PATIBLE
SUFFERANCE PAIN MISERY
PATIENCE THOLANCE
SUFFERER MARTYR AMNESIC
DOORMAT PATIENT
(SUFF.) PATH(IA)(IC)(Y)
SUFFERING BALE COST DREE
HURT PAIN PINE RACK AGONY
DOLOR GRIEF SMART WRAKE
PATHIC PATHOS THRALL INVALID
LANGUOR PASSION PASSIVE
TRAVAIL DISTRESS HARDSHIP
MARTYRDOM
(— FROM HANGOVER) CHIPPY
(— FROM ILL HEALTH) DOWN
(— OF MIND) CARE
(—S OF CHRIST) AGONY
(SUFF.) PATH(IA)(IC)(Y)
(— OF) ITIS
SUFFICE DO LAST COVER REACH
SERVE SATISFY
SUFFICIENCY ENOUGH PLENTY
ADEQUACY ABUNDANCE
PLENITUDE
SUFFICIENT DUE FAIR GOOD
AMPLE DECENT ENOUGH PRETTY
BASTANT ABUNDANT ADEQUATE
RELEVANT COMPETENT
(BARELY —) SCANT SKIMP
NARROW SCRIMPY
(BE — FOR) COVER
SUFFICIENTLY DULY WELL
ENOUGH
SUFFIX POSTFIX
SUFFOCATE CHOKE DROWN
SMOOR STIVE STUFF SWELT
SLOKEN STIFLE OVERLIE QUACKLE
SMOLDER SMOTHER SCUMFISH
STRANGLE THROTTLE
SUFFRAGE VOTE VOICE TONGUE
VERSICLE
SUFFUSE DIP FILL BATHE EMBAY
TINGE INFUSE MANTLE
SUFFUSION COLOR
SUGAR CANDY DIOSE IDOSE MELIS
PIECE SUCRE THIRD ACROSE
ALDOSE ALLOSE FUCOSE GULOSE
HEXOSE INVERT KETOSE LYXOSE
OCTOSE PANELA TALOSE TRIOSE
XYLOSE AGAVOSE ALTROSE
BASTARD CHITOSE GLUCOSE
GLUTOSE GLYCOSE LACTOSE
MALTOSE MANNOSE PAPELON
PENOCHI PENTOSE PENUCHE
SORBOSE SUCROSE SWEETEN
TETROSE THREOSE BROWNING
CONCRETE CYMAROSE DEXTROSE

FRUCTOSE FURANOSE LEVULOSE
PYRANOSE RHAMNOSE
RHODEOSE SECALOSE TURANOSE
(BROWN —) CARAIBE JAGGARY
DEMERARA JAGGHERY
(COARSE —) RAAB PANOCHA
(CRUDE —) GUR HEAD MELADA
CONCRETE
(INFERIOR —) BASTARD
(SIMPLE —) OSE
(UNREFINED —) CASSONADE
(PREF.) GLUC(O) GLYC(O) LYXO
SACCHAR(I)(O) SUCR(O) THREO
(SUFF.) ULOSE
SUGARCANE CANE GRAIN
GLUMAL RATOON MATTRESS
(— SAP) LIQUOR
SUGARHOUSE (PART OF —)
PURGERY
SUGARLESS DRY
SUGARPLUM KISS
SUGARY FAT SUGAR SWEET
OVERRIPE
SUGGEST JOG BEAR GIVE HINT
MINT IMPLY OFFER SPEAK ADVISE
ALLUDE INDITE INFUSE MOTION
PROMPT RESENT SUBMIT
CONNOTE DICTATE INSPIRE
INDICATE INTIMATE PROPOUND
(— DRINKING) PROPOSE
(— INSIDIOUSLY) INFUSE
(— STRONGLY) ARGUE
SUGGESTIBLE SOFT
SUGGESTION CUE CAST HINT
TANG WIND GLIFF TWANG
ADVICE BREATH MOTION SMATCH
INKLING LEADING POINTER
PROFFER REMNANT SOUPCON
WRINKLE INNUENDO INSTANCE
PROPOSAL
SUGGESTIVE ANICONIC
PREGNANT REDOLENT
(— OF MELODY) CANOROUS
SUICIDAL KAMIKAZE
SUIT DO GO APT DOW FIT GEE HIT
SET SIT ACTO LIKE LIST PAIR
SEEM SORT ADAPT AGREE APPLY
BEFIT BESIT CLUBS COLOR DRAPE
DRESS FADGE FANCY FRAME
HABIT LEVEL MATCH PLEAD
QUEME SAVOR SERVE SHAPE
STAND SUING TALLY AFFEIR
ANSWER BECOME COHERE
COMPLY DITTOS EFFEIR HEARTS
PRAYER SPADES SPEECH SQUARE
BEHOOVE COMPORT COSTUME
COULEUR FASHION PURSUIT
REQUEST SEERPAW DIAMONDS
INSTANCE QUADRATE SKELETON
STANDARD TAILLEUR TROPICAL
PINSTRIPE
(— AT LAW) ACTO CASE LAWSUIT
(— OF ARMOR) PANOPLY
(— OF MAIL) CATAPHRACT
(DIVER'S —) SCAPHANDER
(SWIMMING —) BATHER BIKINI
MAILLOT
SUITABILITY (MUTUAL —) DECENCY
IDONEITY SYMPATHY
SUITABLE APT FIT PAT ABLE FEAT
GAIN GOOD JUMP JUST MEET
TALL WELL WEME DIGNE EQUAL
FITTY QUEME RIGHT SUITY

COMELY FITTEN GAINLY GIUSTO
HABILE HONEST LIABLE LIKELY
PROPER SUITLY AVENANT
COMMODE CONDIGN CONGRUE
FITTING IDONEAL PLIABLE
SEEMING BECOMING DECOROUS
ELIGIBLE FEASIBLE HANDSOME
IDONEOUS SORTABLE ACCORDING
OPPORTUNE
(— FOR MALE AND FEMALE) UNISEX
(— FOR STAGE PERFORMANCE)
ACTING
(EXACTLY —) VERY
SUITABLENESS APTNESS
HONESTY APTITUDE PROPERTY
SUITABLY FITLY MEETLY TIDELY
APROPOS GRADELY
SUITCASE BAG CAP GRIP CAPCASE
DORLACH KEESTER
SUITE SET SUIT TAIL SWEEP
SWEET TRAIN SERIES PARTITA
RETINUE ENSEMBLE EQUIPAGE
(— OF MOLDINGS) LEDGMENT
(— OF ROOMS) FLAT CHAMBER
SUITED FIT ADAPT SEEMLY
ADAPTED ASSORTED CONGENIAL
(POORLY —) CROOK
(SUFF.) **(— FOR)** ILE
SUITING COVERT CHEVIOT
SHARKSKIN
SUITOR MAN BEAU SUER SWAIN
WOOER GALLANT SERVANT
SUKU WASUKUMA
SULFATE DEX
SULFIDE GLANCE CUBANITE
SULFURET
SULFUR BRIMSTONE
(PREF.) THI(O)
SULK DOD PET CHAW CRAB DORT
GLUM POUT SULL BOODY FRUMP
GLUMP GROUT GRUMP GROUCH
SNUDGE THURMUS
(PL.) GEE HUMP GLOUT MUMPS
FRUMPS SULLENS BOUDERIE
SULKER MUMPER
SULKINESS DORT GRUMP
SULKING PET BOUDERIE
SULKY CART CHUFF DODDY DORTY
GOURY HUFFY HUMPY CHUFFY
GLUMPY GROUTY JINKER SNUFFY
STUFFY SULLEN SUMPHY
DOGGISH HUFFISH MUMPISH
(NOT —) GOOD
SULLEN DOUR FOUL GLUM GRIM
SOUR BLACK CHUFF CROSS
DUMPY FELON GRUFF HARSH
MOODY RUSTY STERN SULKY
SURLY WEMOD CRUSTY DOGGED
GLOOMY GLUMMY GLUMPY
GLUNCH GROUTY MOROSE
MULISH SOMBER SOMBRE STUFFY
AUSTERE CRABBED CYNICAL
FRETFUL LOURING LUMPISH
MUMPISH PEEVISH CHUMPISH
CHURLISH FAROUCHE LOWERING
PETULANT SPITEFUL STUNKARD
SULLENNESS GEE DORT GLUM
MUMPS STOMACH
SULLIED DIRTY SPOTTED
SULLY BLOT BLUR DASH FOUL
SLUR SMIT SMUT SOIL CLOUD
DIRTY GRIME SMEAR SMOKE
STAIN TAINT BEFOUL DARKEN

DEFILE SMIRCH SMUTCH ATTAINT
BEGRIME BESMEAR BLEMISH
CORRUPT DISTAIN ECLIPSE
POLLUTE SLUBBER TARNISH
BESMIRCH BESPATTER
SULPHATE ALUM BARITE ILESITE
LOWEITE SULFATE VITRIOL
KRAUSITE
SULPHIDE HEPAR GLANCE ZARNEC
SULFIDE ZARNICH CUBANITE
(PL.) MATTE
SULPHUR ORE SPIRIT SULFUR
YELLOW QUEBRITH BRIMSTONE
SULPHURIC ACID VITRIOL
SULTAN SOLDAN
SULTANATE SULTANY ZANZIBAR
SULTANESS SOWDONES
SULTRY CLOSE FLUSH FAINTY
SMUDGY POTHERY PUTHERY
SWELTRY FEVERISH
SUM ALL GOB AGIO CASH DRAB
DUMP FARM FINE FOOT FUND
MASS TALE DEDIT GROSS KITTY
SUMMA TOTAL WHOLE AMOUNT
DEMAND DYADIC FIGURE
NUMBER DECUPLE INGOING
MANBOTE SUBSIDY SUMMARY
SUMMATE ENTIRETY OCTONION
QUANTITY MOUNTANCE
OVERDRAFT POLYNOMIAL
(— AND SUBSTANCE) TOUR SHORT
UPSHOT
**(— AS COMPENSATION FOR
KILLING)** MANBOTE
(— FOR REENLISTMENT) GRATUITY
(— FOR SCHOLARSHIP) BURSARY
(— IN BASSET) SEPTLEVA
(— OF) SIGMA
(— OF DETERMINANTS) STIRP
(— OF EXPONENTS) DEGREE
(— OF FACTORS) COMPLEX
(— OF GOOD QUALITIES) ARETE
(— OF MONEY) POT BANK COVER
STOCK BUNDLE ACCOUNT
STIPEND
(— OF 25 POUNDS) PONY PONEY
(— OF 3 FARTHINGS) GILL
(— OF 500 POUNDS) MONKEY
(— PAYABLE AT FIXED INTERVALS)
FARM
(— RISKED) STAKE
(— UP) ADD TOT FOOT RECKON
SUBSUME SUMMATE COMPRISE
CONCLUDE PERORATE
(ENTIRE —) SOLIDUM
(EXCESS —) BONUS
(FORFEITED —) DEDIT
(GREAT —) PLUNK SIGHT MICKLE
(LARGE —) GOB SCREAMER
(PETTY —) CENT DIME DRAB
(SMALL — OF MONEY) SPILL
DRIBBLE DRIBLET SHOESTRING
(TRIFLING —) HAY GROAT
(UNEXPENDED —S) SAVINGS
(VECTOR —) GRADIENT
(PL.) BATTELS
SUMAC FUSTET KARREE SUMACH
ANACARD BURTREE SCOTINO
SHOEMAKE
SUMATRA (LANGUAGE IN —) NIAS
(MEASURE OF —) PAAL
(MOUNTAIN IN —) LEUSER
KERINTJI

(RIVER IN —) HARI MUSI ROKAN
DJAMBI
(TOWN IN —) ACHIN KUALA
MEDAN NATAL SOLOK DJAMBI
LANGSA PADANG RENGAT
BENKULEN
SUMBUL SAMBUL MUSKROOT
SUMERIAN ACCADIAN AKKADIAN
SUMITRA (HUSBAND OF —)
DASHARATHA
(SON OF —) LAKSHMANA
SHATRUGHNA
SUMMARIZE PRECIS RESUME
ABSTRACT
SUMMARY SUM CURT LEAD BRIEF
CHART RECAP SCORE SHORT
SUMMA TOTAL APERCU PRECIS
RESUME SUMMAR CHAPTER
CONCISE EPITOME EXTRACT
MEDULLA OUTLINE RUNDOWN
VIDIMUS ABSTRACT ARGUMENT
BREVIARY BREVIATE DRUMHEAD
HEADNOTE OVERVIEW SUCCINCT
SYNOPSIS
(— OF FAITH) SYMBOL
(— OF PRINCIPLES) CREED
SUMMATION SUM DIGEST
SUMMARY
SUMMER SHEMU SOMER AESTAS
SIMMER DORMANT
(OF —) ESTIVAL
(PREF.) ESTIVO
SUMMER CYPRESS KOCHIA
SUMMER FLOUNDER PLAICE
SUMMERHOUSE FOLLY KIOSK
MAHAL TUPEK ALCOVE CASINO
GAZEBO PAGODA CABINET
BELVEDERE
SUMMER HYACINTH GALTONIA
SUMMER TANAGER REDBIRD
SUMMERWOOD LATEWOOD
SUMMIT DOD SUM TIP TOP VAN
ACME APEX BALD CRAP DODD
HELM KNAP KNOT PEAK ROOF
CREST CROWN SPIRE COMBLE
CULMEN HEIGHT VERTEX ZENITH
CALOTTE SUMMARY SUMMITY
PINNACLE MOUNTAINTOP
(— OF TUBE) MOUTH
(— WITHOUT FOREST) BALD
(ROCKY —) KNOT
(ROUND —) DOD DODD
(SNOW-CAPPED —) CALOTTE
(PREF.) APICO CORY(PH)(PHO)
(SUFF.) ACE
SUMMON BAN CRY BUZZ CALL
CITE DRUM HAIL SIST BUGLE
CHARM CLEPE EVOKE HIGHT
KNELL SOUND VOUCH ACCITE
ADVOKE BECALL COMPEL
DEMAND SOMPNE VOCATE
ACCERSE COMMAND CONJURE
CONVENE CONVENT CONVOKE
PROVOKE SUMMONS WHISTLE
ASSUMMON EXORCISE
(— FOR HIRING) YARD
(— INTO COURT) DEMAND
(— TOGETHER) BAND MUSTER
ASSEMBLE
(— UP) FIND GATHER COLLECT
SUMMONER SUMNER LOCKMAN
SOMPNER OUTRIDER
SUMMONING CALL ARRAY

(— OF KING'S VASSALS) BAN
SUMMONS CRY CALL BREVE CITAL
TICKET BIDDING CALLING STICKER
WARNING WARRANT CITATION
MONITION VOCATION
(FALCONER'S —) WO
SUMP SINK STANDAGE
SUMPTUOUS RICH GRAND SHOWY
WLONK COSTLY DELUXE SOLEMN
SUPERB COSTLEW ELEGANT
MAGNIFIC SPLENDID
MAGNIFICENT
SUMPTUOUSNESS LUXE DAINTY
SUMPTURE
SUN SOL ATEN ATON BASK INTI
LAMP STAR SENGE SURYA TITAN
SUNLET DAYSTAR IOSKEHA
PHOEBUS SAVITAR JOUSKEHA
(— MOON AND STARS) HOST
(RISING —) HERAKHTI
(PREF.) HELI(O) SOLARO SOLI
(SUFF.) HELION
SUN ALSO RISES (AUTHOR OF —)
HEMINGWAY
(CHARACTER IN —) BILL COHN
JAKE MIKE BRETT CLYNE PEDRO
ASHLEY BARNES GORTON ROBERT
ROMERO FRANCES MICHAEL
MONTOYA CAMPBELL GEORGETTE
SUNAPEE TROUT SAIBLING
SUNBATHE APRICATE
SUNBEAM BANANA
SUN BEAR BRUANG
SUNBIRD MAMO CADET FINFOOT
SUN BITTERN CARLE CAURALE
SUNBIRD
SUN BLIND CHICK UMRELLA
SUNBONNET TILT UGLY CRESIE
KAPPIE SHAKER
SUNBURN GREENING HELIOSIS
SUNBURNT ADUST BROWN
TANNED
SUNBURST SUNRAY SUNBREAK
SUNSHINE
SUNDAE GEDUNK
SUNDAY EXAUDI JUDICA GAUDETE
TRINITY
(FOURTH — IN LENT) LAETARE
(THIRD — AFTER EASTER) JUBILATE
SUNDER PART RIVE TWIN BREAK
SEVER TWAIN TWINE DEPART
DIVIDE SINDER ASUNDER DISALLY
DISJOIN DIVORCE DISSEVER
SEJUGATE SEPARATE UNSOLDER
SUNDEW DROSERA EYEBRIGHT
SUNDIAL DIAL GHURRY HOROLOGE
SCAPHION SOLARIUM
(PART OF —) DIAL LINE PLATE
GNOMON DIAGRAM
SUN DISK ATEN ATON CAKRA
CHAKRA
SUNDOG WINDGALL PARHELION
SUNDOWNER WHALER
TUSSOCKER
SUN-DRIED TILED
SUNDROPS SCABISH
SUNDRY DIVERS DIVERSE SEVERAL
SUNFISH SUN HURO MOLA OPAH
RUFF BREAM FLIER FLYER ROACH
SUNNY KIVVER MOLOID REDEAR
REDEYE CRAPPIE CROPPIE
PANFISH PERCOID BLUEGILL
FLATFISH FLOUNDER HEADFISH

MOONFISH PONDFISH WARMOUTH REDBREAST PUMPKINSEED

SUNFLOWER GOLD HELIO CANADA GOLDEN SUNFOIL GIRASOLE TURNSOLE
(— STATE) KANSAS

SUNGLASSES SHADES

SUN-GREBE FINFOOT SUNBIRD GRUIFORM

SUNK SUNKEN
(— TO LOW STATE) ABJECT

SUNKEN SUNK LAIGH HOLLOW

SUNKEN BELL (CHARACTER IN —) MAGDA HEINRICH RAUTENDELEIN
(COMPOSER OF —) RESPIGHI

SUNLESS BLAE

SUNLIGHT GLARE

SUNN SAN SANN DAGGA SANAI JANAPA MADRAS JANAPAN SANNHEMP

SUNNITE IHLAT SUNNI SUNNIAH

SUNNY GOOD SUNSHINE

SUN PARLOR SOLARIUM

SUNRISE ARIST SUNUP ORIENT

SUNSET SUNFALL
(— STATE) OREGON ARIZONA

SUNSHADE PARASOL ROUNDEL TIRESOL SOMBRERO

SUNSHINE SUN SHINE SUNLIGHT
(— STATE) FLORIDA

SUNSPOT SPOT FACULA MACULA

SUNSPURGE SUNWEED TURNSOLE WARTWEED WARTWORT

SUNSTROKE HELIOSIS SIRIASIS

SUNTAN MERIDA

SUN TREE HINOKI

SUNWISE DEASIL DESSIL

SUNYATA VOID

SUP EAT DINE SOWP FEAST CONSUME SWALLOW

SUPAWN MUSH

SUPER-
(PREF.) HYPER

SUPERABOUND OVERFLOW

SUPERABUNDANCE FLOOD EXCESS CATARACT PLEONASM PLETHORA PLEURISY PLURISIE

SUPERABUNDANT RANK LAVISH PROFUSE

SUPERALTAR PREDELLA

SUPERANNUATE OVERYEAR

SUPERB GRAND GOLDEN CLIPPING GORGEOUS SPLENDID

SUPERCARGO MERCHANT

SUPERCILIOUS GRAND POTTY PROUD OVERLY SNIFFY SNIPPY SNOOTY SNOTTY SNUFFY HAUGHTY ARROGANT CAVALIER SNIFFISH SUPERIOR

SUPERCLASS AGNATHA

SUPERCONSCIOUSNESS SAMADHI

SUPERCOOL SUBCOOL SURFUSE

SUPERFAMILY APINA APOIDEA BOVOIDEA
(SUFF.) OIDA OIDEA OIDEI

SUPERFICIAL GLIB ECTAL SUPER FACIAL FACILE FLIMSY FORMAL FROTHY GLASSY OVERLY SLIGHT CURSORY OUTSIDE OUTWARD PASSING SHALLOW SKETCHY SLIGHTY SURFACE SURFACY

COSMETIC EXTERNAL MAGAZINY SMATTERY DEPTHLESS

SUPERFICIALLY FLEET

SUPERFICIES TERM EXTENT

SUPERFLUITY FAT FRILL LUXUS EXCESS OVERSET SURFEIT PLETHORA REDUNDANCY
(CONFUSING —) FLUTHER

SUPERFLUOUS SPARE OTIOSE USELESS NEEDLESS REDUNDANT

SUPERFRONTAL FRONTLET

SUPERHEATED GASEOUS

SUPERHIGHWAY MOTORWAY
(AVOID —) SHUNPIKE

SUPERHUMAN DEMON DAEMON DIVINE INHUMAN UNHUMAN

SUPERIMPOSE LAY OVERLAY SURPRINT

SUPERIMPOSING DISSOLVE

SUPERINTEND CON CONN GUIDE OVERSEE PRESIDE

SUPERINTENDENCE CARE CONTROL EPISCOPY GUIDANCE

SUPERINTENDENCY EDILITY AEDILITY

SUPERINTENDENT BOSS SUPE EPHOR SUPER EDITOR VENEUR VIEWER WARDEN CAPTAIN CURATOR EPHORUS MANAGER DIRECTOR OVERSEER SURVEYOR SWINGMAN

SUPERIOR JOE AYNE COOL FINE MORE OVER TRIE ABBOT ABOVE CHIEF CREAM EIGNE ELDER ELITE EXTRA FANCY FRANK GREAT LIEGE PRIOR PUKKA SWANK UPPER ABBESS BETTER COCKUP CUSTOS DOMINA FATHER FORBYE MAHANT SELECT SENIOR STRONG FORTHBY PALMARY RANKING ABNORMAL DOMINANT GUARDIAN SINGULAR SPLENDID SUPERIAL MARVELOUS PARAMOUNT
(— OF CONVENT) HEGUMEN
(— TO) BEFORE
(PREF.) SUPER

SUPERIORITY DROP GREE PRICE HEIGHT MASTERY PROWESS EMINENCE PRIORITY
(MENTAL —) GENIUS

SUPERLATIVE RAVING CURIOUS ROUSING CRASHING OLYMPIAN PEERLESS SWINGING
(ABSOLUTE —) ELATIVE
(SUFF.) EST

SUPERLATIVELY CRACKING SWINGING

SUPERMAN OVERMAN OBERMENSCH

SUPERNATURAL FEY DIVINE NUMINOUS DIVINER MARVELOUS PARANORMAL
(— FORCE) WAKANDA

SUPERNUMERARY ORRA
(PREF.) POLY

SUPERORDER GLIRES

SUPERPOSE APPLY

SUPERSCRIBE DIRECT

SUPERSCRIPT SUPERIOR

SUPERSEDE REPLACE OVERRIDE SUPPLANT

SUPERSTITION FREIT

IDOLATRY ABERGLAUBE

SUPERSTITIOUS FREITY

SUPERTONIC SECOND

SUPERVENE BEFALL FOLLOW

SUPERVISE BOSS GUIDE DIRECT GOVERN HANDLE SURVEY FOREMAN OVERSEE PROCTOR ENGINEER OVERLOOK CHAPERONE

SUPERVISION EYE CARE DUTY HAND CHECK CHARGE OVERSIGHT

SUPERVISOR BOSS BULL EPHOR GUIDE SUPER CENSOR GASMAN RUNMAN SOURER WARDEN DESKMAN PROCTOR ALYTARCH CHAIRMAN FLOORMAN FOREHAND KNIFEMAN LEACHMAN MASHGIAH OVERSEER

SUPINE INERT DROWSY LANGUID SERVILE UPRIGHT CARELESS INACTIVE INDOLENT LISTLESS SLUGGISH

SUPPER CENA MEAL CUDDY HOCKEY PASCHAL
(HARVEST-HOME —) HOCKEY
(LAST —) MAUNDY
(LORD'S —) NAGMAAL

SUPPING CENATION

SUPPLANT FOLLOW REMOVE REPLACE DISPLACE DISPLANT

SUPPLE BAIN FLIP OILY SOFT LINGY LITHE SLAMP SWACK AJOINT LIMBER LITHER LUTHER SUMPLE SVELTE SWANKY WANDLE LISSOME PLIABLE SPRINGE FLEXIBLE

SUPPLEJACK SOAPWORT

SUPPLEMENT ARM EKE MEND TACK ANNEX SUPPLY BOLSTER CODICIL ADDENDUM APPENDIX BOUNTITH
(PL.) FIXINGS

SUPPLEMENTAL SPECIAL

SUPPLEMENTARY ADDED SECOND RIPIENO REMANENT PERIPHERAL

SUPPLENESS WHIP

SUPPLIANT ASKER PLEADING

SUPPLICATE BEG PRAY CRAVE PLEAD INVOKE OBTEST SUPPLY BESEECH ENTREAT IMPLORE REQUEST SOLICIT PETITION

SUPPLICATION CRY VOW BEAD BILL LIBEL VENIE APPEAL LITANY PRAYER CRAVING SYNAPTE ENTREATY PETITION PLEADING ROGATION ROGATIVE SUFFRAGE

SUPPLICATORY EUCTICAL

SUPPLIED (— WITH FOOD) THORN
(AMPLY —) ABUNDANT
(SCANTILY —) BARE

SUPPLIER SOURCE

SUPPLIES STOCK STUFF DUFFEL STORES VICTUAL ESTOVERS ORDNANCE

SUPPLY FEED FILL FIND FRET FUND GIVE HEEL LEND LINE ARRAY CATER ENDUE EQUIP INDUE OFFER SERVE STOCK STORE STUFF YIELD BUDGET DONATE EMPLOY FOISON LAYOUT POCKET RENDER SUBMIT

ADVANCE FORTIFY FRAUGHT FURNISH LISSOME PROVIDE ACCOMMODATE
(— ABUNDANTLY) SWILL
(— ARRANGED BEFOREHAND) RELAY
(— FOR AN OCCASION) GRIST
(— OF MONEY) BANKROLL
(— OF POTENTIAL JURORS) TALES
(— OF REMOUNTS) REMUDA
(— OF TIN) SERVING
(— PROVISIONS) PURVEY
(— THE NEED) FOR
(— WITH CLOTHES) INFIT
(— WITH FUEL) STOKE
(— WITH MONEY) GILD
(— WITH OXYGEN) AERATE
(— WITH WATER) FANG
(CACHED —) CAVE
(CONSTANT —) STREAM
(EXTRA —) RESERVE
(FRESH —) RECRUIT
(HIDDEN —) HOARD
(INADEQUATE —) DEARTH
(OVERABUNDANT —) SURFEIT
(PLENTIFUL —) CHOICE
(RESERVE —) CUSHION
(RICH —) ARGOSY
(SCANTY —) SCANT

SUPPORT AID ARM BAY BED BOW KAI LEG PEG RIB TIE TOM ABET ABUT AXIS BACK BASE BEAM BEAR BUOY CRIB DADE FEND FIND FIRM FORK FUEL HAVE HELP HOLD KEEP KILP LIFT POST PROP RACK REST ROCK SALT SIDE STAY STEM STUD TRIG ADOPT ANGEL APPUI ATLAS BIPOD BLOCK BRACE BROOK CARRY CHAIR CHEER CHOCK CLEAT CRANK FAVOR FLOAT FRAME OXTER PLUNK POISE RANCE SALVE SHORE SPURN STAFF STAKE STEAD STELL STIPE STOCK STOOP STRUT STULL TOWER VOUCH WEIGH ANCHOR ASSERT ASSIST BARROW BEHALF CHEVAL COLUMN CORSET CRADLE CRUTCH DEFEND DONKEY DUOPOD GARTER PATTEN PILLAR POTENT PULPIT PUTLOG SADDLE SECOND SHIELD SOCKET SPLINT STAYER STEADY SUFFER TASSEL TIMBER TINGLE TORSEL UPHAND UPHOLD UPKEEP UPTAKE WHIMSY ALIMENT ARMREST BACKING BOLSTER COMFORT CONFIRM CRIPPLE DEADMAN ENDORSE FINDING FULCRUM GROMMET HOUSING JACKLEG JUSTIFY KEEPING KNUCKLE NOURISH NURTURE PABULUM PROTECT RADICAL SPIRALE SPONSOR SQUINCH STADDLE STANDER STIFFEN STIRRUP SUBSIST SUSTAIN THICKEN TRESTLE ADJUMENT ADVOCATE BALUSTER BEFRIEND BESTRIDE BOOKREST BUTTRESS CAPSHORE FAIRLEAD FOOTREST FORESTAY FORTRESS HANDREST HOLDFAST JACKSTAY KEYSTONE MAINSTAY MAINTAIN MOUNTING NEEDLING

OVERCAST PEDESTAL PEDIMENT STANDARD STILLAGE STOCKING STRENGTH SYMPATHY UNDERLIE UNDERPIN UNDERSET PATRONAGE MAINTENANCE
(— FOR ANVIL) STOCK
(— FOR BELL CLAPPER) BALDRIC
(— FOR CANOPY) BAIL
(— FOR CATALYST) CARRIER
(— FOR CORSET) BUSK
(— FOR HEAVY MACHINERY) BUNTING
(— FOR LAUNCHING SHIP) POPPET
(— FOR LEVER) BAIT
(— FOR LIFE-CAR) BAIL
(— FOR MILL) LOWDER
(— FOR MINE PASSAGE) OVERCAST
(— FOR OARLOCK) OUTRIGGER
(— FOR PICTURE HOOKS) CORNICE
(— FOR PIPE) CHAPLET
(— FOR PLATFORM) STEMPEL STEMPLE
(— IN A LATHE) DOCTOR
(— IN PAPERMAKING TUB) DONKEY
(— OF COPING) KNEELER
(— OF MOLD CORE) ARBOR ARBOUR
(— OF RAIL) CHAIR BALUSTER
(— THROUGH BIT AND BRIDLE) APPUI
(CRUTCHLIKE —) DEADMAN
(ELBOW-SHAPED —) CRANK
(EMBEDDED —) SPURN
(FIREPLACE —) ANDIRON
(GIVE —) FEED
(INCLINED —) RIDER
(MINING —) CAP FRAME
(PORTABLE —) STOOL
(PRINCIPAL —) BACKBONE
(TEMPORARY —) NEEDLING
(UPRIGHT —) POPPET BANISTER
(WHEELED —) CARRIAGE
(PL.) SHIPWAY
SUPPORTED BASED BLOCKED ACCOSTED SUCCINCT
(— BY EVIDENCE) PROBABLE
SUPPORTER ALLY JOCK ATLAS STOOP COHORT DRAGON SATRAP APOSTLE BOOSTER DEVOTEE FAVORER FOUNDER LAUDIAN PATROON PROPPER SUPPORT ADHERENT ASSERTER ERASTIAN ESPOUSER FAVORITE HENCHMAN STALWART UPHOLDER CHURCHITE
(ATHLETIC —) CUP JOCK
(CHIEF —) STOOP PILLAR
(PL.) SECOND
(SUFF.) CRAT ITE
SUPPORTING BEHIND BEARING
SUPPORTIVE ENGAGE
SUPPOSE SAY SEE SET WIS WIT DEEM POSE READ TAKE TROW WEEN ALLOW COUNT ETTLE FANCY GUESS JUDGE OPINE SEPAD THINK ASSUME DEVISE DIVINE EXPECT RECKON BELIEVE CONCEIT DARESAY IMAGINE PRESUME PROPOSE SUPPONE SURMISE CONCEIVE CONCLUDE CONSIDER OPINIATE
SUPPOSED ALLEGED ASSUMED PUTATIVE

SUPPOSING IF
SUPPOSITION IDEA FICTION SURMISE WEENING
SUPPOSITORY BOUGIE CANDLE PESSARY
SUPPRESS LAY DOWN GULP HIDE HUSH SINK SLAY SNUB STOP BLACK BURKE CHOKE CRUSH ELIDE QUASH QUELL SHUSH SMORE SPIKE STILL CANCEL QUENCH SQUASH STIFLE CONTAIN CUSHION INHIBIT OPPRESS REPRESS SILENCE SMOLDER SMOTHER SQUELCH RESTRAIN STRANGLE SUPPRIME VANQUISH
SUPPRESSED BLIND CENSORED
SUPPRESSION ABEYANCE AMEIOSIS BLACKOUT
(— OF VOWEL) ELISION
(— OF WORD SOUNDS) SYNCOPE ECLIPSIS
(PREF.) ISCH(O)
(SUFF.) SCHESIS SCHETIC
SUPPURATE RUN BEAL WHEAL DIGEST MATTER QUITTER MATURATE
SUPPURATING
(PREF.) EMPYO
SUPPURATION PYOSIS BEALING COCTION
SUPPURATIVE DIGERENT
SUPRACLAVICLE SCAPULA
SUPREMACY PALM PRIMACY DOMINION OVERRULE
SUPREME HIGH LAST CHIEF VITAL SUBLIME SUMMARY TOPLESS FOREMOST GREATEST PEERLESS
SURA FATIHA FATIHAH
SURCHARGE PACK
SURCINGLE WANTY ROLLER
SURCOAT JUPON CYCLAS KABAYA
SURD SHARP ATONIC FLATED
SURE COLD SAFE BOUND SECURE SICCAR SICKER STEADY WITTER ASSURED CERTAIN PERFECT COCKSURE POSITIVE UNERRING
SURELY WIS FINE SURE PARDY REDLY ATWEEL PARDIE
SURENESS SURETY SECURITY
SURETY VAS ANDI BAIL BAND BORROW CAUTION ENGAGER SOVERTY SPONSOR BAILSMAN SECURITY
SURETYSHIP SPONSION
SURF BREACH KALEMA
(— NOISE) RUT ROTE
SURFACE DAY AREA FACE ORLO PLAT RYME SIDE BOSOM FLOOR STONE SWARF CHROME FINISH GROUND SCRUFF ASPHALT BLANKET COUNTER ENVELOP OUTFACE OUTSIDE STRETCH ADHEREND CONCRETE EXTERIOR PLATFORM
(— BETWEEN FLUTES OF SHAFT) ORLO
(— BETWEEN TRIGLYPH CHANNELS) MEROS
(— IN BEATER) BACKFALL
(— OF BEAM) BACK
(— OF BODY) FLESH HABIT
(— OF COAL) BUTT

(— OF CRICKET FIELD) CARPET
(— OF DIAMOND) SPREAD
(— OF EARTH) DUST GROUND TERRENE PENEPLAIN PENEPLANE
(— OF ESCUTCHEON) FIELD
(— OF GROUND OVER MINE) DAY
(— OF PARACHUTE) CANOPY
(— OF RIFLE BARREL) LAND
(— OF SAWED LUMBER) FUR
(— OF TOOTH) TRITOR
(— OF VAULT) GROIN
(— OF WATER) RYME SCRUFF
(— WITHIN EARTH) GEOID
(CONCAVE —) LAP
(CURVED —) BELLY
(DULL —) MAT MATTING
(EXTERNAL —) PERIPHERY
(FLAT —) BED FLAT AEQUOR PAGINA
(FLOOR —) BOWL
(GEOMETRIC —) TORE CONOID SPHERE QUARTIC CONICOID CYLINDER HELICOID PARABOLOID
(GLOSSY —) GLAZE
(GROOVED —) DROVE
(HAIRY —) NAP
(HORIZONTAL —) LEVEL
(INCLINED —) CANT DESCENT
(MINERAL —) DRUSE
(PAVED —) FOOTWALK
(PILE —) FRIEZE
(PLANE —) AREA FACET
(PRINCIPAL —) FACE
(PRINTING —) CUT
(PROTECTIVE —) LAGGING
(ROAD —) MACADAM CORDUROY
(ROUGH —) KEY CRIZZLE STUBBLE
(ROUGHENED —) MAT FOOTGRIP
(SLIPPERY —) GLARE
(SLOPING —) SHELVING
(STRIKING —) BLADE
(UNDER — OF SKI) PALM
(UNGLOSSY PAINT —) FLAT
(UPPER —) NOTAEUM
(UPRIGHT —) JAMB
(PREF.) **(BENT —)** SINU SINUATO
SURFACER SEASONER
SURFBOARD GUN
SURF DUCK COOT SCOTER
SURFEIT CLOY FILL GLUT SATE STAW STALL STUFF AGROTE ENGLUT SICKEN SATIATE SATIETY SURCLOY SATURATE REPLETION SATURATION
SURFEITED SAD SICK BLASE JADED WEARY REPLETE SATIATED
SURFER **(GIRL —)** WAHINE
(INEXPERIENCED —) GREMMY GREMMIE
SURF FISH PERCH ALFIONA
SURF SCOTER COOT SCOTER SURFER PISHAUG SKUNKTOP
SURF SHINER SPARADA
SURGE JAW GUST TIDE WASH DRIVE GURGE LUNGE SPURT SWELL BILLOW BREACH COURSE SEETHE WALLOW WALTER ESTUATE REDOUND AESTUATE UNDULATE
(— OF ELECTRIC POWER) GLITCH
(SHOREWARD —) SUFF
SURGEON (ALSO SEE PHYSICIAN

AND DOCTOR) LEECH ARTIST INTERN MEDICO OPERATOR SAWBONES
(TREE —) TREEMAN
AMERICAN EVE BULL LONG MOTT REED AGNEW COLEY FLINT GROSS FINNEY MORRIS MORTON SHRADY ASHFORD CUSHING HALSTED HARTLEY KELLOGG LAPLACE BEAUMONT MCBURNEY MCDOWELL METTAUER
CANADIAN BIRKETT
ENGLISH POTT REID BRAID HADEN BARKER BEDDOE BOWMAN CHEYNE COOPER FAYRER ERICHSEN MOYNIHAN ABERNETHY BRIFFAULT CHESELDEN PARKINSON
FRENCH ANEL PARE BOYER BROCA PETIT BECHAMP CHOPART CIVIALE DESAULT NELATON CHAULIAC CHASSAIGNAC
GERMAN GRAEFE ESMARCH BILLROTH
GREEK AMMONIUS
IRISH MADDEN OMEARA
SCOTTISH SYME BANKS LISTON MACEWEN
SOUTH AFRICAN BARNARD
SWISS KOCHER
SURGEONFISH TANG TANGE DOCTOR MEDICO BARBERO SURGEON SAWBONES
SURGERY KNIFE
(VETERINARY —) ZOIATRIA
(SUFF.) CHIRURGIA
SURGING WALE ESTURE ESTUOUS
SURICATE ZENICK MEERKAT
SURINAM (CAPITAL OF —) PARAMARIBO
(RIVER OF —) ITANY MARONI COPPENAME SARAMACCA COURANTYNE
(TOWN OF —) ALBINA KWATTA TOTNESS LELYDORP
SURINAMINE ANDIRINE ANGELINE
SURINAM TOAD PIPA PIPAL
SURLINESS CYNICISM MOROSITY
SURLY BAD ILL GRUM LUNT BLUFF CHUFF CYNIC GRUFF GURLY PURDY ROUGH RUNTY RUSTY CHUFFY CRUSTY GRUFFY GRUMPY MOROSE RUGGED SNARLY SULLEN CHURLISH
SURMISE DEEM REDE GUESS INFER TWANG SURMIT JALOUSE SUSPECT WEENING MISTRUST
SURMOUNT TOP BEAT TIDE CROWN ENSIGN HURDLE MASTER OUTTOP OVERGO SUBDUE CONQUER SURPASS OVERCOME SUPERATE
(— DIFFICULTIES) SWIM
SURMOUNTING BROCHANT
SURNAME BYNAME SURNOUN COGNOMEN OVERNAME SURSTYLE
SURPASS CAP COB TOP WAR BANG BEAT CAMP COTE DING FLOG FOIL HEAD PASS SHED WHAP WHOP EXCEL OUTDO OUTGO TRUMP ATREDE BETTER EXCEED OUTRAY OUTRUN

OUTVIE OUTWIT OVERDO PRECEL ECLIPSE FORPASS OUTPEER OVERTOP PARAGON PRECEDE ANTECEDE DISTANCE DOMINATE OUTCLASS OUTMATCH OUTRANGE OUTREACH OUTSHINE OUTSTRIP OUTWRITE SURMOUNT

SURPASSING BEST FINE ABOVE PASSANT PASSING DOMINANT FRABJOUS TOWERING (PREF.) PRETER SUPER

SURPLICE SARK COTTA EPHOD STOLA CHRISOM (PL.) WHITES

SURPLUS OVER PLUS REST EXCESS LUMBER SPILTH VELVET OVERAGE OVERRUN OVERSUM ARISINGS LEFTOVER OVERCOME OVERFLOW OVERMUCH OVERPLUS

SURPRISE CAP SHED SWAN YACH AMAZE SHOCK SNEAK FERLIE WAYLAY WONDER ASTOUND GLOPPEN PERPLEX STARTLE ASTONISH BEWILDER CONFOUND DUMFOUND (BY —) ABACK (EXCLAMATION OF —) QUOTHA (EXPRESS —) MIRATE (SUDDEN —) KICK

SURPRISING FERLIE STRIKING

SURRA MBORI

SURREJOINDER TRIPLY

SURRENDER HEM LET PUT CEDE CESS DING FALL QUIT TAKE REMIT YIELD ADDICT REMISE RENDER RESIGN SUBMIT ABANDON CONCEDE DELIVER FORSAKE KAMERAD ABDICATE ABNEGATE EDITION DELIVERY RENOUNCE UNDERLIE (— BY DEED) REMISE

SURREPTITIOUS SECRET BOOTLEG FURTIVE SNEAKING

SURROUND HEM LAP ORB BELT DIKE DYKE FOLD GIRD GIRT HOOP WRAP BESET BRACE CLASP EMBAY EMBED FENCE HEDGE IMBED INARM ROUND BECLIP BEGIRD BEGIRT CIRCLE COLLET CORRAL ENFOLD ENWRAP FORSET GIRDLE IMPALE INCASE INVEST SPHERE SWATHE ARROUND BESIEGE BESTAND COMPASS EMBOSOM ENCLAVE ENCLOSE ENFEOFF ENROUND ENVELOP ENVIRON INVOLVE WREATHE CLOISTER ENCIRCLE ENTRENCH STOCKADE (— WITH BOOM) CRIB (— WITH CORD) GIRT (— WITH MORTAR) GROUT

SURROUNDED AMID AMONG AMIDST AMONGST BETWEEN

SURROUNDING MIDST ROUND CIRCUM AMBIENT (PL.) SCENE HARNESS ENVIRONS (PREF.) CIRCUM PERI

SURROYALS CROWN

SURVEILLANCE WATCH SCRUTINY STAKEOUT OVERSIGHT

SURVEY SEE DIAL SCAN VIEW AVIEW STOCK STUDY PERUSE

REGARD REVIEW SEARCH CANVASS CAPSULE OVERSEE SURVIEW TERRIER THEORIC EPISCOPY LUSTRATE OVERLOOK OVERVIEW PROSPECT SURVEYAL TRAVERSE RECONNAISANCE (— RAPIDLY) GLANCE (— TIMBER) SKYLOOK (BRIEF —) APERCU

SURVEYING GEODESY GROMATICS (MINE —) LATCHING

SURVEYOR BOLO ARTIST DIALER DIALLER NOTEMAN CHAINMAN GROMATIC LEVELMAN

SURVIVAL ECHO RELIC RELICT (ANACHRONISTIC —) LEFTOVER (USELESS —) SNUFF

SURVIVE LAST BILEVE OUTLAST OUTLIVE

SURVIVOR RELICT

SURYA (FATHER OF —) ADITI DYAUS (MESSENGER OF —) PUSHAN (WIFE OF —) USHAS

SUSCEPTIBILITY CAVIL SENSE EMOTION FEELING FRAILTY (— TO ILL-HEALTH) DELICACY

SUSCEPTIBLE EASY SOFT LIABLE FEELING PATIENT SENSIBLE TOLERANT (— TO CHANGE) CASALTY

SUSIAN ELAMITE

SUSLIK SISEL ZIZEL MARMOT

SUSPECT FEAR DOUBT FANCY GUESS SMOKE THINK BELIEVE ENDOUTE JALOUSE MISDEEM SUPPOSE DISTRUST JEALOUSE MISDOUBT MISTRUST (NOT —) COLD

SUSPECTED SPOTTED SUSPECT

SUSPEND CALL HALT HANG OUST SHUT SIST STAY BREAK CLOSE DEBAR DEFER DEMUR EXPEL POISE REMIT SLING SWING APPEND DANGLE ADJOURN EXCLUDE FLUIDIZE INTERMIT OVERHANG PROROGUE REPRIEVE SCAFFOLD SUSPENSE PRETERMIT (— ANCHOR) COCKBILL

SUSPENDED SWING AFLOAT LATENT HANGING PENDANT PENDENT PENSILE HOVERING SUSPENSE

SUSPENDER GALLUS GARTER BRETELLE (PL.) BRACES GALLOWS GALLUSES

SUSPENSE DEMUR POISE

SUSPENSION FOG BREI FUME SIST STAY STOP DELAY DOUBT MAGMA SMOKE BREACH CUTOFF SLURRY AEROSOL FAILURE RESPITE ABEYANCE BACTERIN EMULSION INFUSION SHUTDOWN SUSPENSE WISHBONE (— OF JUDGMENT) EPOCHE (— OF NOISE) HUSH (— OF RESPIRATION) SYNCOPE

SUSPENSIVENESS DRIVE

SUSPENSORY SUPPORT

SUSPICION HINT DOUBT SOUPCON SURMISE SUSPECT UMBRAGE DISTRUST JEALOUSY MISDOUBT MISTRUST TINCTURE

SUSPICIOUS SHY FISHY LEERY PEERY QUEER SMOKY SHODDY JEALOUS SOUPCON SUSPECT DOUBTFUL WAFFLIKE

SUSPICIOUSLY ASKANCE

SUSQUEHANNA CONESTOGA

SUSTAIN ABET BACK BEAR BUOY DURE HELP HOLD LAST PROP STAY ABIDE CARRY FAVOR SINEW SPRAG STAND ASSIST CONVEY ENDURE FOSTER SECOND SUCCOR SUFFER UPHOLD UPSTAY ALIMENT BOLSTER CONTAIN NOURISH OUTBEAR PROLONG SUPPORT UNDERFO BEFRIEND BUTTRESS CONTINUE MAINTAIN PRESERVE SCAFFOLD (PREF.) CO

SUSTAINED TENUTO SOUTENU

SUSTENANCE GEAR SALT BREAD FOISON LIVING RELIEF ALIMENT PABULUM TABLING

SUSU GERIP SOOSOO DOLPHIN

SUSURRUS WHISPER

SUTLER PROVANT VIVANDIER

SUTTEE SATI

SUTURE SEAM RAPHE SETON HARMONY PTERION (SUFF.) RHAPHY RRHAPHY

SVANTOVIT TRIGLAV

SVELTE CHIC TRIM LITHE SLEEK SUAVE SMOOTH URBANE SLENDER

SVENO (SLAYER OF —) SOLIMANO

SWAB GOB MOP BOSH SWOB PATCH DOSSIL SPONGE EPAULET SWABBER SQUILGEE

SWADDLE SWEEL SWATHE

SWAG DRUM GAME LOOT BOOTY LUCRE MONEY BOODLE FESTOON MATILDA

SWAGE BOSS MOUTH UPSET FULLER JUMPER SHAPER SWAGER SWEDGE FLATTER (PL.) OLIVER

SWAGGER JET ROY BRAG COCK FACE ROLL BOAST BRANK BRAVE NUTTY STRUT SWANK SWASH BLAGUE BOUNCE GOSTER HECTOR PARADO PRANCE RENOWN RUFFLE SPROSE BLUSTER BRAVADO GAUSTER PANACHE ROISTER SOLDIER DOMINEER TIGERISM

SWAGGERER HUFF SWAG BUCKO FACER TIGER CUTTLE JETTER PISTOL BRAVADO HUFFCAP RUFFLER FANFARON WHIFFLER

SWAGGERING HUFFY FACING GASCON HUFFCAP TEARCAT BLUSTERY TIGERISH

SWAGMAN WHALER DRUMMER TRAVELER

SWAIN COLIN CUDDY RUSTIC STREPHON

SWAINSONA INDIGO

SWALE SLASH

SWALLOW OFF SUP BOLT DOWN DROP GAUP GLUP GLUT GULP SINK TAKE CLUNK DRINK GORGE GURGE POUCH QUILT SLOCK SWOOP ABSORB ENGLUT ENGULF GLUTCH GOBBET GOBBLE

GODOWN GUZZLE IMBIBE INGEST MARTIN POCKET PROGNE SWELLY CONSUME ENGORGE ARUNDELL WITCHUCK (— GREEDILY) BEND SLUP GORGE GULCH SWILL WORRY INHALE (— HASTILY) SWAP SWOP GLOUP SLUMMOCK (— IN AGAIN) RESORB (— UP) GULF SWAMP ABSORB DEVOUR (— WITH GREEDINESS) ENGORGE (LOSS OF ABILITY TO —) APHAGIA (NOISY —) SLURP (WOMAN TURNED INTO —) PROCNE (PREF.) CHELID(O)

SWALLOWTAIL TROILUS

SWALLOWWORT CELANDINE

SWAMP BOG FEN FLAT FLOW MIRE MOSS SLEW SLUE SOAK SUMP VLEI VLEY WHAM WHIN FLUSH LERNA LETCH MARSH SWALE SWANG URMAN DELUGE DISMAL ENGULF MORASS SLOUGH CIENAGA POCOSIN GREENING INUNDATE QUAGMIRE

SWAMP COTTONWOOD LIAR

SWAMPER BUSHER GOPHER

SWAMPHEN COOT

SWAMP LOOSESTRIFE PEATWEED PEATWOOD

SWAMP MAHOGANY GUNNUNG

SWAMP MILKWEED DAGGA

SWAMPY PUXY BOGGY POOLY CALLOW POACHY QUASHY QUEASY SLUMPY MOORISH PALUDAL ULIGINOUS

SWAMPY CREE MASKEGON

SWAN COB ELK PEN OLOR CYGNET HOOPER SWANNET WHOOPER (FLOCK OF —S) GAME MARK

SWANFLOWER SWANWORT

SWANHILD (FATHER OF —) SIGURD (MOTHER OF —) GUDRUN

SWANK CHIC

SWANKY SWASH

SWAP CHOP SWOP TRADE TRUCK DICKER EXCHANGE

SWARD SOD TURF SPINE SWARF SWATH SWARTH

SWARM FRY SNY BIKE CAST FARE HOST KNIT NEST SORT SWIM TEEM CLOUD CROWD FLOCK FLUSH FRACK HORDE SNARL FLIGHT HOTTER RABBLE SWARVE THRONG OVERRUN SUBCAST PULLULATE (— IN) FILL (— OF BEES) BIKE HIVE (— OF INSECTS) BAND FLIGHT (— OF PEOPLE) BIKE DRIFT (THIRD — OF BEES) COLT

SWARMING ALIVE ASWARM SWARMY

SWARTBACK SWARBIE

SWARTHY DUN DARK BLACK BROWN DUSKY GRIMY MOORY SWART MORIAN SWARTH BISTRED BISTERED

SWASH SWIG SWILL SWATCH SWABBLE SWASHWAY

SWASHBUCKLER SWASH GASCON SLASHER SWASHER

SWASTIKA FYLFOT GAMMADION
SWAT SWOT DEHGAN STRIKE
SWATH SWIPE STADDLE
SWATHE LAP BIND WRAP SWARF
SWADDLE WINDROW
SWATTER FLYSWAT
SWAY NOD WAG BEAR BEND BIAS
FLAP HIKE LILT ROCK ROLL RULE
SHOG SWAB SWAG SWIG TILT
TOSS WALD WAVE CARRY CHARM
LURCH POWER REIGN SHAKE
SWALE SWING WAVER WHEEL
AFFECT ALLURE CAREEN DIRECT
EMPIRE TOTTER WAGGLE
COMMAND SHOGGIE STAGGER
SWABBLE SWIGGLE
(SUFF.) CRACY CRAT(IC)
SWAYBACK WARFA LORDOSIS
RENGUERA
SWAYING ASWAY ROLLING
SWAZILAND (CAPITAL OF —)
MBABANE
(COIN OF —) RAND
(LANGUAGE OF —) SISWATI
(MONEY OF —) LILANGENI
(RIVER IN —) USUTU KOMATI
MHLATUZE UMBULUZI
(TOWN OF —) STEGI GOLLEL
MANZINI PIGGSPEAK
SWEAR VOW VUM DAMN SINK
SNUM SWAN SWOW TAKE CURSE
ADJURE AFFIRM BEDAMN
DEPONE DEPOSE OBJURE
CONJURE DEJERATE EXECRATE
FORSWEAR
(— FALSELY) RAP MOUNT
FORSWEAR MANSWEAR
SWEARING JURANT JURATION
(FALSE —) PERJURY
SWEARWORD CUSS
SWEAT DEW WET STEW WASH
BREAN MADOR SUDOR SUDATE
LAUNDER PARBOIL SWELTER
SWIVVET TRANSUDE
PERSPIRATION
(— SKINS) STALE
(DYNAMITE —) LEAK
(PREF.) HIDR(O) HYDR(O) SUDORI
(SUFF.) IDROSIS
SWEATBOX HOTBOX
SWEATER FROCK GANSEY JUMPER
WOOLLY CARDIGAN SLIPOVER
(CLOSE-FITTING —) POORBOY
(WOMAN'S SHORT —) SHRINK
SWEATHOUSE TEMESCAL
SWEATING TUB ASWEAT SWELTRY
SUDATION SUDATORY
SWEATY PUGGY ASWEAT
PERSPIRY SUDOROUS SWEATFUL

SWEDEN

CAPITAL: STOCKHOLM
COIN: ORE KRONA SKILLING
COUNTY: KALMAR OREBRO
UPPSALA
DIVISION: AMT LAEN SKANE
OREBRO UPPSALA GOTALAND
JAMTLAND SWEALAND
GULF: BOTHNIA
ISLAND: OLAND GOTALAND
LAKE: SILJA VANERN MALAREN
VATTERN DALALVEN
STORAVAN HJALMAREN

MEASURE: AM ALN FOT MIL REF
TUM FAMN STOP FODER
KANNA KAPPE LINJE NYMIL
SPANN STANG TUNNA FATHOM
JUMFRU KOLLAST OXHUVUD
TUNLAND FJARDING KAPPLAND
KOLTUNNA
MOUNTAIN: SARV AMMAR OVIKS
HELAGS SARJEK
PROVINCE: KALMAR OREBRO
GOTLAND HALLAND UPPSALA
ALVSBORG BLEKINGE ELFSBORG
JAMTLAND MALMOHUS
WERMLAND
RIVER: DAL UME GOTA KLAR LULE
KALIX PITEA RANEA LAINIO
LJUSNE TORNEA WINDEL
ANGERMAN
TOWN: UMEA BODEN BORAS
EDANE FALUN GAVLE LULEA
MALMO PITEA VISBY YSTAD
ARVIKA OREBRO LUDVIKA
UPPSALA GOTEBORG NYKOPING
VASTERAS
WATERFALL: HANDOL
TANNFORSEN
WEIGHT: ASS LOD ORT MARK
PUND STEN UNTZ NYLAST
LISPUND SKEPPUND

SWEDISH CLOVER ALSIKE
SWEEP BUCK DUST RAFF SOOP
SWAY TILT BESOM BROOM DIGHT
DRIFT FETCH SCOPE SKIRL SWIPE
SWOOP BREADTH CLEANSE
PICOTAH SHADOOF STRICKLE
(— A NET) BEAT
(— MAJESTICALLY) SWAN
(— OF SCYTHE) SWATH SWATHE
(— OFF) SLIPE
(— ON CULTIVATOR) SKIN
(CHIMNEY —) CHUMMY SWEEPY
RAMONEUR
(HAY —) BUCK
SWEEPBOARD STRICKLE
SWEEPER BUNGY SWEEP TOPAZ
BHANGI BHUNGI MEHTAR PRYLER
ROADER SOOPER TOPASS
BROOMER TUBEMAN BHUNGINI
MATRANEE SCRUBBER
SWEEPING SURGE RASANT
SWEEPY
(— FOR FISH) DRAFT DRAUGHT
(PL.) DUST FULVIE FULZIE
RIFFRAFF
SWEET DOUX DUMP FOOL SOOT
SUCK CREAM DILIS DOUCE DULCE
FRESH HONEY MERRY SOOTH
SPICY SPLIT BREEZE DULCET
FRUITY GENTLE SILKEN SILVER
SIRUPY SUGARY DARLING
FAIRING HONEYED INSIPID
MUSICAL PANDROP SUGARED
SWEETLY WINNING WINSOME
AROMATIC ENGAGING FLUMMERY
LIEBLICH LUSCIOUS NECTARED
PLEASANT
(SLIGHTLY —) SEC
(PREF.) DULCI GLYCERO GLYCO
HEDY SUAVI
SWEET BAY BREWSTER MAGNOLIA
SWEETBREAD BUR BURR
PANCREAS

(— OF DEER) INCHPIN
SWEETBRIER BEDEGUAR
EGLANTINE
SWEET CALABASH KURUBA
SWEET CASSAVA AIPI AIPIM
SWEET CHERRY MAZZARD
SWEET CICELY MYRRH
SWEET CLOVER LOTUS MELILOT
SWEET COLTSFOOT LAGWORT
SWEETEN CANDY HONEY SUGAR
SWEET PURIFY ADDULCE
CLEANSE DULCIFY FRESHEN
MOLLIFY PERFUME MITIGATE
SWEETENER SACCHARIN
SWEET FENNEL FINOCHIO
FLORENCE
SWEET FERN FERNGALE
SWEETFISH AYU
SWEET FLAG SEDGE BEEWORT
CALAMUS
SWEET GALE GOLD GAGEL
BAYBUSH FLEAWOOD GALEWORT
GALLBUSH
SWEET GUM AMBER COPALM
STORAX BILSTED
SWEETHEART JO BOY GRA HON
JOE LAD PUG SIS AGRA BABY
BEAU DEAR DOLL DOXY DUCK
FAIR GILL GIRL JILL LADY LASS
LIEF LOVE MASH MORT POUT
AGRAH BULLY BUSSY CHERI
COOKY DOLLY DONAH DONEY
DONNA DRURY FLAME LEMAN
LOVER PUGGY SPARK SWEET
COOKIE EMILIA FELLOW FRIEND
MOPSEY PIGEON STEADY WAHINE
AMOROSA BELOVED PHYLLIS
PIGSNEY QUERIDA SPRUNNY
SWEETIE TOOTSIE DOWSABEL
DULCINEA FOLLOWER LADYBIRD
LADYLOVE LIEBCHEN LOVELASS
MISTRESS SWEETING TRUELOVE
SWEETLEAF DYELEAVES
SYMPLOCOS
SWEET MARJORAM OREGANO
SWEETMEAT DROP DUMP KISS
DULCE FUDGE GOODY PASTE
PLATE SPICE TOFFY BONBON
BUCAYO COMFIT DRAGEE
DREDGE JUNKET ALCORZA
BANQUET CARAMEL CARAWAY
CLAGGUM CONFECT LOUKOUM
PENUCHE SUCCADE CONSERVE
HARDBAKE MARZIPAN PASTILLE
(PL.) BALUSHAI CONFETTI
SWEETNESS DULCE HONEY SIRUP
SYRUP DULCOR DOUCEUR
DULCITY SUAVITY FLORIMEL
WORDNESS
SWEET ORANGE CHINA CHINO
SWEET PEA CATGUT LATHYRUS
SWEET PEPPERBUSH CLETHRA
SOAPBUSH
SWEET POTATO YAM SWEET
BATATA CAMOTE KUMARA
OCARINA
SWEET RUSH SQUINANT
SWEET-SMELLING AROMATIC
SWEETSOP ANON ATES ATIS ATTA
CORAZON SWEETING
SWEET-SOUNDING MERRY
SWEET VIOLET FINELEAF
SWEET WILLIAM DIANTHUS

SWELL BAG DON NIB NOB BEAL
BELL BLAB BLOW BLUB BOLL
BULB BULK BUMP BUOY DOME
FILL GROW HOVE HUFF HUSH
PINK PLIM RISE SWAG TOFF TONY
WAVE BELLY BERRY BLAST BLOAT
BULGE BUNCH FLASH PLUFF
PREEN SMART STOCK STRUT
SURGE TULIP BILLOW BOWDEN
DILATE EXPAND GROWTH LOVELY
SPRING STROUT TUMEFY UPRISE
AUGMENT BLUBBER BURGEON
DISTEND INFLATE REGULAR
SWAGGER OVERBLOW TURGESCE
(— OF GUN MUZZLE) TULIP
(— OF WATER) HUSH SURF FLOOD
SURGE
(— OUT) BAG POD BUNT DRAW
POUT BOSOM BILLOW SPONGE
BALLOON BLADDER
(HEAVY —) RUN SEA
(PREF.) OEDE OEDI TUME
SWELLDOODLE EGGFISH
SWELLED BIAS BLOWN
SWELLFISH BLOWER PUFFER
TAMBOR
SWELLING BIG BUR NOB PAP PIN
BLAB BOLL BUBO BUMP BURR
CLAP COWL CURB FROG FULL
GALL KNOB KNOT NODE POKE
PONE PUFF AMPER BLAIN BOTCH
BOUGE BULGE BUNCH BUNNY
CLOUR EDEMA JETTY MOUSE
PROUD SURGE SWELL TUBER
TUMOR ANCOME ASWELL
BOSOMY BUNCHY CALLUS
FLATUS GIBBER GROWTH KERNEL
PIMPLE RANULA STRUMA
SWELTH WARBLE AMPULLA
BOSSING CAPELET CHAGOMA
CUSHION GOUNDOU HAPTERE
PUSTULE SURGENT TURGENT
UREDEMA UROCELE APOSTEME
BULLNECK CHEMOSIS DACRYOMA
FURUNCLE GLANDULE GOURDING
HAPTERON HEMATOMA
MUCOCELE NODOSITY PULVINUS
PUMPKNOT QUELLUNG SCIRRHUS
STYLOPOD VESSICNON
(— IN HORSE'S CHEST) ANTICOR
(— IN HORSE'S MOUTH) LAMPAS
(— IN PLASTER) BLUB
(— OF PLANT TISSUE) GALL
(— OF THE CHEEK) HONE
(— ON ANIMAL'S JOINTS) BUNNY
CAPELLET
(— ON HEAD) COWL
(EYE —) STY STYE
(PREF.) GANGLI GANGLO STRUMI
(SUFF.) EMATOMA PHYMA
SWELTER STEW SWELT
SWELTERING STEWY SULTRY
SWELTRY
SWERVE BOW CUT LUG YAW BIAS
FADE JOUK SKEW VARY VEER
WARP SHEER STRAY DEPART
DEVIATE DIGRESS DIVERGE
INSWING
SWIDDEN CAINGIN KAINGIN
SWIFT CRAN FAST FLIT MAIN VITE
FLEET HASTY LIGHT QUICK RAPID
SNELL SWITH WIGHT WINDY
ARROWY MARLET NIMBLE

RAKING SOUPLE SPEEDY STRICT SUDDEN SWIFTY TOTTER WINGED COLLIER DEVELIN FLIGHTY POSTING SWALLOW TANTIVY DEVELING HEPIALID PEGASEAN SCREAMER SCUTTLER SQUEALER SWIFTLET SALANGANE (PREF.) CITI CYPSELO OCY TACHEO TACHISTO TACHO TACHY
SWIFTLY FAST SWAP APACE SNELL SNELLY LIGHTLY STEEPLY TANTIVY
SWIFTNESS FOOT HASTE SPEED CELERITY FASTNESS VELOCITY
SWIG SCOUR SWILL SWING SWIGGLE
SWILL SOSS BROCK SLOSH SLUICE HOGWASH PIGWASH SWILLING
SWIM DIP COWD SAIL SOOM SPAN TEEM BATHE CRAWL FLEET FLOAT GLIDE SWARM PLUNGE OVERFLOW
(— IN NEW DIRECTION) MILL
(— IN NUDE) SKINNYDIP
(— TOGETHER) SCHOOL
(PREF.) NECT(O)
(SUFF.) NECTAE NECTES
SWIMMER BATHER NATATOR
SWIMMERET PLEOPOD
SWIMMING ASWIM NATANT FLOTANT NATATION
(— STUNT) MARLIN WALKOVER
SWIMMING POOL POOL THERM PLUNGE THERME PISCINA NATATORY
(— ON LINER) LIDO
SWINDLE CON GIP GYP JOB RIG BILK FAKE FLAP HAVE MACE PULL RAMP ROOK ROPE SCAM SWIZ BUNCO BUNKO CHEAT FLING FOIST GOUGE LURCH PLANT ROGUE SHARK SHARP SHAVE SHUCK SLANG SPOOF STING SWIZZ UNCLE BOODLE BUBBLE BUCKET CHOUSE DIDDLE FIDDLE GAZUMP HUSTLE INTAKE NOBBLE SUCKER TREPAN FINAGLE SKELDER THIMBLE VERNEUK FLIMFLAM BAMBOOZLE
SWINDLER DO FOB GYP LEG BILK FYNK HAWK ROOK SKIN CHEAT CROOK ESROC FAKER GREEK HARPY KNAVE MACER ROGUE CHIAUS GOUGER INTAKE RINGER ROOKER SALTER SHAVER VERSER BUBBLER HUSTLER MACEMAN MAGSMAN NOBBLER SHARPER SKELDER SLICKER SPIELER BARNACLE BLACKLEG FINAGLER GILENYER LUMBERER PIGEONER SHELLMAN TRAMPOSO
(DECOY —) BARNARD
SWINDLING MACE BUNCO BUNKO ROOKY SHARK GYPPERY JOUKERY CHEATERY JOOKERIE
SWINE HOG OIC PIG SOW BOAR GALT GILT PORK SUID YILT DUROC ESSEX SWIPE WHITE GUSSIE POLAND PORKER PORKET BUSHPIG LACOMBE PECCARY SUFFOLK SUIDIAN CHESHIRE HYOTHERE LANDRACE TAMWORTH

(— AND FOOD) PANNAGE
(— AND MAN) OMNIVORA
(PREF.) HYO
SWINEHERD GURTH HOGMAN EUMAEUS HOGHERD HOGWARD
SWINE-LIKE GADARENE
SWING GO HIKE JUMP LILT SCUP SHOG STOT SWAY SWEE TURN SHAKE SHOWD SLING SWALE TREND DANGLE GYRATE HANDLE SWINGE SWITCH SWIVEL TOTTER JUMPING SHOGGIE SWINGEL WAMPISH BRANDISH FLOURISH OSCILLATE
(— A SHIP) SPRING
(— AROUND) JIB SLEW SLUE SLOUGH
(— BY BATTER) CUT
(— FROM POSITION) CANT
(— FROM SIDE TO SIDE) JOW
(— FROM THE TIDE) TEND
(— OF PENDULUM) BEAT
(— OF SAIL) GYBE JIBE
(— OF SWORD) MOULINET
(— OUT OF LINE) SWAG
(— THE FOREFEET) DISH
(RHYTHMICAL —) LILT
(WILD —) HAYMAKER
(PREF.) OSCILLO
SWINGING BANK ASWING SWINGY
SWINGLE SWORD SCUTCH SWIPPLE
SWING SEAT TRANSOM
SWINISH SOWISH HOGGISH PORCINE SUILLINE
SWIPE COP CHOP GLOM SLOG WIPE SNAKE STEAL VULTURE
SWIRL BOIL EDDY GULF HURL PURL WALM GURGE SWALE SWEEL SWORL SWOOSH WREATHE TOURBILLION
(— OF SALMON) BULGE
SWIRLING VORTICAL
SWISH HISH WHIP SMART SWILL WHISH
SWISS SWISSER HELVETIC
(— PINE) MUGHO
SWISS FAMILY ROBINSON
(AUTHOR OF —) WYSS
(CHARACTER IN —) JACK EMILY FRITZ ERNEST FRANCIS MONTROSE ROBINSON
SWITCH GAD TAN LASH TWIG WAND AZOTE BIRCH BREAK SHUNT SWISH CHANGE CUTOUT DERAIL DIPPER FERULA FERULE LARRUP RATTAN SCUTCH SILENT SPRING HICKORY KIPPEEN SCOURGE SQUITCH CRYOTRON HAIRWORK POSTICHE
(— FOCUS) FADE
(ELECTRIC —) KEY
(RAILROAD —) GATE POINT
SWITCH ENGINE GOAT
SWITCHMAN SHUNTER SWITCHER

FRIBOURG OBWALDEN
CAPITAL: BERN BERNE
COIN: FRANC RAPPE RAPPEN ANGSTER DUPLONE BLAFFERT
LAKE: URI ZUG THUN AGERI LEMAN MORAT BIENNE BRIENZ GENEVA LUGANO SARNEN WALLEN ZURICH HALLWIL LUCERNE LUNGERN VIERWALD
MEASURE: IMI POT AUNE ELLE FUSS IMMI MUID PIED SAUM ZOLL LIEVE LIGNE LINIE MAASS MOULE POUCE SCHUH STAAB TOISE PERCHE SETIER STRICH JUCHART KLAFTER VIERTEL
MOUNTAIN: JURA RIGI ROSA BLANC CENIS KARPF LINARD PIZELA BERNINA BEVERIN GRIMSEL PILATUS ROTONDO BALMHORN JUNGFRAU
MOUNTAIN PASS: CENIS FURKA ALBERG MALOJA BRENNER GRIMSEL SIMPLON SPLUGEN LOTSCHEN
NAME: HELVETIA
RIVER: AAR INN AARE THUR BROYE DOUBS LINTH REUSS RHINE RHONE MAGGIA SARINE TICINO PRATIGAU
TOWN: BALE BERN BIEL BRIG CHUR SION BASEL VEVEY GENEVA GLARUS LUZERN SCHWYZ ZURICH FYZABAD HERISAU LUCERNE LAUSANNE MONTREUX
VALLEY: AAR ZERMATT ENGADINE
WATERFALL: SIMMEN HANDEGG IFFIGEN DIESBACH GIESSBACH STAUBBACH TRUMMELBACH
WEIGHT: PFUND CENTNER QUINTAL

SWIVEL LOPER SWAPE SWIPE CASTER FIDDLE TIRRET TOGGLE TONGUE TRAVERSE TRUNNION
SWOLLEN BLUB FULL PLIM RANK BLOWN CHUFF GOUTY GREAT GUMMY POBBY PROUD PUFFY TUMID BOLLEN BRAWNY BULLED GOURDY TURGID BESTRUT BLOATED BLUBBER BULBOUS GIBBOSE GIBBOUS GOURDED GOUTISH STICKLE TURGENT BEPUFFED BLADDERY TUMOROUS
(PREF.) PHYS(O)
SWOON KEEL SWEB SWIM DOVER DROWN DWALM FAINT SLOOM SOUND SWARF SWELT STOUND SWOUND TRANCE ECSTASY SWITHER SYNCOPE SWOONING
SWOONING ASWOON SYNCOPE
SWOOP CHOP DIVE JOUK SWAP SWOP SOUSE STOOP SWOPE POUNCE SOURCE DESCEND
SWOOPING SOUSE
SWORD FOX SAX BILL DIRK FALX GRAM IRON PATA SAEX SEAX SPIT TOOL TUCK TURK BILBO BLADE BRAND DEGEN DEGO ESTOC GULLY KNIFE KUKRI PRICK RIPON SABER SABRE SHARP STEEL ANDREW BARONG BILBOA CATTAN DAMASK DUSACK

FLORET GLAIVE HANGER KHANDA KUKERI MIMING PARANG PINKER PORKER RAPIER SMITER SPATHA TILTER TIZONA TOLEDO WAFTER BALMUNG BRANDON CURTANA CUTLASH CUTLASS ESPADON ESTOQUE FERRARA FLEURET IMPALER JOYEUSE MALCHUS MORGLAY SHABBLE SLASHER SNICKER SPURTLE TOASTER WHIFFLE WHINGER ACINACES BASELARD CAMPILAN CLAYMORE DAMASCUS DURENDAL FALCHION FLAMBERG SCHLAGER SPADROON SPITFROG WACADASH WHINYARD
(— OF CHARLEMAGNE) JOYEUSE
(— OF CID) TIZONA
(— OF HERMES) HARPE
(— OF LANCELOT) ARONDIGHT
(— OF ROLAND) DURENDAL
(— OF SIEGFRIED) GRAM BALMUNG
(— OF SIR BEVIS) MORGLAY
(— OF ST. GEORGE) ASCALON ASKELON
(— USED BY ST. PETER) MALCHUS
(BLUNT —) WAFTER SCHLAGER
(CELTIC —) SAX SAEX
(DOUBLE-EDGED —) KEN PATA KHANDA SPATHA
(DUELLING —) EPEE SHARP
(DYAK —) PARANG
(FENCING —) EPEE FOIL SABER SABRE RAPIER
(HALF OF —) FORTE
(JAPANESE —) CATAN CATTAN KATANA WACADASH
(LONG —) SPATHA WHIFFLE
(MATADOR'S —) ESTOQUE
(MORO —) BARONG CAMPILAN
(NARROW —) TUCK
(NORMAN —) SPATHA
(PERSIAN —) ACINACES
(POINTLESS —) CURTANA CURTEIN
(RUSTY —) SHABBLE
(SHORT —) DIRK ESTOC KUKRI SKEAN CREESE CURTAXE WHINGER WHINYARD
(THRUSTING —) ESTOC STOCK
(TWO-HANDED —) ESPADON SPADONE CLAYMORE
(WOODEN —) WASTER STRICKLE
SWORD-BEARER VERGER SELICTAR PORTGLAVE
(PL.) ENSIFERI
SWORD DANCER MATACHIN
SWORDFISH AU ESPADA ESPADON XIPHIAS ALBACORA BILLFISH BOATBILL FORKTAIL XIPHIOID SCOMBROID
(PREF.) XIPH(O)
SWORD-LIKE
(PREF.) XIPH(I)(O)
SWORDPLAY SPADROON
(STYLIZED —) KENDO
SWORD-SHAPED ENSATE ENSIFORM GLADIATE
SWORDSMAN BLADE BLADER FENCER SLASHER SWORDER THRUSTER
SWORDTAIL HELLERI
SWORN AVOWED
SWOT GRI MUG
SYAGUSH SHARGOSS

SWITZERLAND
BAY: URI
CANTON: ZUG BERN JURA VAUD BASEL AARGAU GENEVA GLARUS LUZERN SCHWYZ TICINO VALAIS ZURICH GRISONS THURGAU

SYBARITE EPICURE
SYBARITIC SENSUOUS
SYCAMORE MAY DAROO
COTONIER LACEWOOD PLANTAIN
SYCEE SHOE
SYCOPHANCY FAWNERY
SYCOPHANT TOADY COGGER
FAWNER GNATHO HANGBY
TAGTAIL CLAWBACK PARASITE
PICKTHANK SATELLITE
SYCOPHANTIC FAWNING SERVILE
SLAVISH OBEDIENT TRENCHER
SYCORAX (SON OF —) CALIBAN
SYCOSIS MENTAGRA
SYENITE APPINITE TRACHYTE
SYLLABARY KANA IROFA IROHA
KATAKANA
SYLLABIC SONANT CENTROID
SONANTIC
SYLLABLE ARSIS BREVE GROUP
SHORT DISEME SYLLAB THESIS
TRISEME ASSONANT
(— DENOTING ASSENT) OM
(BOBIZATION —) BO CE DI GA GE
LO MA NI
(LAST —) ULTIMA
(LAST — BUT ONE) PENULT
(LONG —) LONG
(MUSICAL —) DI DO FA FI LA LE LI
ME MI RA RE RI SE SI SO TA TE TI
TO UT SOL
(REFRAIN —) DILDO
(SHORT —) MORA SHORT
(STRONG —) STRESS
(UNACCENTED —S) THESIS
(UNSTRESSED —) OUTRIDE
SYLLABUS PROGRAM VIDIMUS
HEADNOTE SYNOPSIS
PROGRAMME
SYLLOGISM BARBARA ABDUCTION
ENTHYMEME
(SERIES OF —S) SORITES
SYLPH ARIEL SYLPHID
SYLVAN WOODY FOREST SILVAN
WOODEN WOODISH SYLVATIC
SYLVITE HARDSALT
SYMBIOSIS LICHENISM
MUTUALISM NUTRICISM
SYMBOL KEY CODE FISH FOUR
ICON IDOL IKON MARK NEUM
SEAL SIGN BADGE CREST
CROSS EAGLE IMAGE INDEX
PRIME TOKEN CARACT CIPHER
EMBLEM ENSIGN FIGURE LETTER
PNEUME SHADOW SIGNAL
FACIEND MANDALA PALATAL
CEREMONY CONSTANT DIRECTOR
EXPONENT GUTTURAL IDEOGRAM
LIGATURE LOGOGRAM OPERATOR
SWASTIKA SYMBOLUM TRISKELE
ORIFLAMME PHRASEOGRAM
(— AS ROAD SIGN) GLYPH
(— FOR WAVELENGTH) LAMBDA
(— OF DEATH) CYPRESS
(— OF DISTINCTION) BELT HONOR
(— OF FAITHFUL DEAD) ORANT
(— OF FRANCE) LILY
(— OF LIFE) ANKH
(— OF MONK) COWL
(— OF PHYSICIAN) CADUCEUS
(— OF RAILROAD) HERALD
(— OF SPRING) KARPAS

(— OF STRENGTH) HORN
(— OF SUN) DISC DISK
(— OF UNIVERSE) MANDALA
(— ON UNCHANGEABLENESS)
LEOPARD
(— REPRESENTING THE ABSOLUTE)
TAIKIH
(ALGEBRAIC —) EXPONENT
(CRICKET —) ASHES
(CRUSADERS' —) CROSS
(CURVED —) HOOK
(KOREAN —) TAHGOOK
(MAGIC —) CARACT
(MATHEMATICAL —) KNOWN
FACTOR FACIEND OPERAND
PLACEHOLDER
(PHALLIC —) LINGA LINGAM
(PICTOGRAPHIC —) ISOTYPE
(PRINTING —) DIAGONAL
(PRONUNCIATION —) ENG
(RELIGIOUS —) LABRYS
(PL.) KATAKANA
SYMBOLIC GRAPHIC SHADOWY
ANICONIC
SYMBOLICAL ALLUSIVE MYSTICAL
SYMBOLISM ICONOLOGY
SYMBOLIZE BODY SIGN TOKEN
FIGURE SAMPLE SHADOW
SYMBOL TYPIFY BETOKEN
EXPRESS PORTEND SIGNIFY
RESEMBLE
SYMMETRICAL FORMAL DIMERIC
REGULAR SHAPELY SPHERAL
BALANCED
(NOT —) SKEW
SYMMETRY MEASURE
SYMPATHETIC AKIN FERE SOFT
WARM HUMAN FELLOW KINDLY
TENDER PIETOSO SIMPATICO
SYMPATHIZER FABIAN BLACKNEB
SHAYSITE
SYMPATHY PITY RUTH FLESH
PHILIA CONSENT EMPATHY
RAPPORT AFFINITY KINDNESS
SYMPHONY SINFONIA
SYMPOSIUM POTATION
SYMPTOM MARK NOTE SIGN
SHOWER STIGMA INSTANCE
PRODROME
SYNAGOGUE SHUL SCHUL
ALJAMA PROSEUCHA
SYNAPSIS PAIRING
SYNAPTE ECTENE EKTENE
SYNARTHROSIS SUTURE
SYNCHRO SELSYN
SYNCHRONIZER SPEEDGUN
SYNCLINE DOWNFOLD ISOCLINE
SYNCOPATED ZOPPA ABRIDGED
SYNCOPE SWOON COTYPE
FAINTING
SYNDICATE HUI GROUP COMBINE
SYNDICATED CANNED
SYNECDOCHE MERISM
SYNERGIST BOOSTER SESAMIN
SYNOD SOBOR
SYNODAL SENAGE
SYNONYM ANTONYM HOMONYM
EUPHONYM POLYONYM
SYNOPSIS BRIEF TABLE EPITOME
OUTLINE SUMMARY ABSTRACT
ANALYSIS SCENARIO SYLLABUS
ABRIDGMENT

SYNSACRUM SACRARY
SYNTACTICAL FORMAL
SYNTHESIS SUMMA FUSION
SYSTASIS
SYNTHETIC ERSATZ PLASTIC
SYSTATIC ARTIFICER
SYPHAX (WIFE OF —) SOPHENISBA
SYPHILIS PIP POX LUES SYPH
CRINKUM GRINCOME

SYRIA

CAPITAL: DAMASCUS
COIN: POUND TALENT PIASTER
DISTRICT: ALEPPO HAURAN
LAKE: DJEBOID TIBERIAS
MEASURE: MAKUK GARAVA
MOUNTAIN: HERMON LIBANUS
NAME: ARAM
NATIVE: DRUSE ANSARIE SARACEN
ANSARIEH
RIVER: ASI BALIKH BARADA
JORDAN KNABUR ORONTES
EUPHRATES
TOWN: ALEP HAMA HOMS NAWA
BUSRA CALNO DERRA HALAB
HAMAH IDLIB JERUD RAQQA
ALEPPO BALBEL LATAKIA
SELEUCIA
WEIGHT: COLA ROTL ARTAL ARTEL
RATEL TALENT

SYRINGA PHILADELPHUS
SYRINGE GUN HYPO ENEMA
SCOOT DOUCHE FILLER SQUIRT
SCOOTER SERRING
SYRINGIN LILACIN
SYRINX PANPIPE
SYRNIUM STRIX
SYRUP DIBS LICK SIRUP ORGEAT
ANTIQUE ECLEGMA FALERNUM
QUIDDANY
(FRUIT —) ROB
(STARCH —) GLUCOSE
SYRUPY FRUITY
SYRYENIAN SYRYAN ZYRIAN
(PL.) KAMI KOMI
SYSTEM ISM AREA CREDO FRAME
ORDER CIRCLE METHOD SCHEME
STEREO SYNTAX COMPLEX
DUALISM ECONOMY FAGGERY
NAVARHO REGIMEN ENSEMBLE
GALENISM OVERRIDE RELIGION
UNIVERSE
(— OF BARS) LATTICE
(— OF BELIEFS) FAITH
(— OF BELL CHANGES) CATERS
QUATERS STEDMAN
(— OF CORDS) BRIDLE
(— OF CROSSING THREADS) LEASE
(— OF DIET) BANTING
(— OF ETHICS) SELFISM
(— OF EXCHANGE) KULA
(— OF EXERCISES) AEROBICS
(— OF FAITH) CREED
(— OF GEARS) COMPOUND
(— OF JOINTS) CLEAT
(— OF LANGUAGE SIGNS) SIGNARY
(— OF LAW) EQUITY
(— OF LINES IN EYEPIECE) RETICLE
RETICULE
(— OF LOGIC) RAMISM

(— OF MANUAL TRAINING) SLOJD
SLOYD
(— OF MARKETING) ADMASS
(— OF MEANING) SEMANTIC
(— OF MEDICINE) AYURVEDA
(— OF NUMERALS) ALGORISM
(— OF OCCULT THEOSOPHY)
CABALA
(— OF PHILOSOPHY) HUMISM
COMTISM HOBBISM SAMKHYA
SANKHYA STOICISM
(— OF PHONETIC NOTATION) ROMIC
(— OF PRINCIPLES) CODE
(— OF RAYS) ASTER
(— OF ROCKS) CENOZOIC
DEVONIAN SILURIAN
(— OF RULE) REGIME
(— OF RULES) ART
(— OF SOLMIZATION) FASOLA
(— OF SPACES) LACUNOME
(— OF SYMBOLS) CODE
(— OF TENANCY) CROFTING
(— OF TRANSPORTATION) AIRLINE
AIRMAIL
(— OF TRUSSING) CABANE
(— OF VALUES) ETHOS
(— OF WEIGHTS) TROY
(— OF WIRES) HARNESS
(— OF WORSHIP) CULT CULTUS
(— OF WRITING) KANJI BRAILLE
ALPHABET
(— TO LOCATE AN OBJECT) LIDAR
(ACOUSTICAL —) SODAR
(AGRICULTURAL —) KOLKOZ
KOLKHOS
(ALARM —) BUG
(BANKING —) GIRO
(BETTING —) ALEMBERT PERFECTA
QUINELLA MARTINGALE
(COLLOIDAL —) SOL
(COMMUNICATION —) BLOWER
CIRCUIT
(COMPUTER —) KLUGE KLUDGE
(CULTURAL —) ISLAM
(DEFENSE —) SAGE
(DISPERSE —) GEL
(ELECTRICAL —) SELSYN
(GEOLOGICAL —) EOCENE
CAMBRIAN DEVONIAN KEEWATIN
TERTIARY
(HAULING —) DILLY
(IRRIGATION —) KAREZ
(LANGUAGE —) LATINXUA
(NAVIGATION —) GEE LANAC
TACAN NAVAID SHORAN
NAVARHO OMNIRANGE
(RELIGIOUS —) LAW CULT CULTUS
SHIISM SUNNISM DRUIDISM
(RHYTHMIC —) STROPHE
GLYCONIC
(SOCIAL —) CASTE
(STAR —) GALAXY
(TECHNOLOGICAL —) FORDISM
(TELEVISION —) SCOPHONY
(TRIANGULATION —) SOFAR
(TRUCK —) TOMMY
SYSTEMATIC ORDERLY REGULAR
METHODIC
SYSTEMATIZE ORDER CODIFY
ORGANIZE METHODIZE
SYSTEMATIZED ORGANIC
SYSTEMIC DEMETON

T

T TEE TARE TANGO

TAAL AFRIKAANS

TAB JAG PAN TAG BILL COST CHECK FLASH PRICE TALLY WATCH EARTAB EARTAG SIGNAL TOEPLATE

TABANID GADFLY

TABARD CHIMER CHIMERE

TABARRO, IL (CHARACTER IN —) LUIGI MICHELE GIORGETTA

(COMPOSER OF —) PUCCINI

TABERNACLE PIX PYX HOVEL SACRARY

TABES WASTING

TABETIC MARCID

TABLATURE LYRAWAY PICTURE PAINTING

TABLE KEY PIE PYE RUN BANK BUCK DAIS DESK FORM MESS BELLY BENCH BOARD CANON CHART PINAX PLANK SCALE STALL STAND STONE WAGON COMMON SCHEME TABLET TABULA TARIFF TEAPOY TRIPOD VANNER CABARET CAMBIST CONSOLE COUNTER DIAGRAM DIPTYCH DRESSER PROJECT SHAMBLE TABLEAU TESSERA TROLLEY WHIRLER CALENDAR CREDENCE GUERIDON PEDIGREE PEMBROKE REGIMENT SPECULUM STILLAGE TOILETTE VANITORY NIGHTSTAND

(— FOR BOWING HAT-BODY) HURL

(— FOR GLAZING LEATHER) BANK

(— FOR ORNAMENT) CARTOUCH

(— FOR PHOTOGRAPHIC PLATES) WHIRLER

(— FURNISHED WITH MEAL) SPREAD

(— IN STORE) COUNTER

(— OF ANCESTORS) PEDIGREE

(— OF CONTENTS) INDEX METHOD

(— OF DECLINATIONS) REGIMENT

(— TOP) AMOEBA

(— USED IN FELTING A HAT) BASON

(— WITH BRAZIER BENEATH) TENDOOR TENDOUR

(ARITHMETIC —) TARIFF

(ASTROLOGICAL —) SPECULUM

(BOTANIC —) KEY

(CIRCULAR —) ROUNDEL

(COMMUNION —) ALTAR CREDENCE

(DINING —) MAHOGANY

(DRESSING —) TOILET VANITY TOILETTE

(FOLDING —) SERVETTE

(INNER —) HOME

(MASSAGE —) PLINTH

(MUSICAL —) DIAGRAM

(NIGHT —) SOMNO

(PRINCIPAL —) DAIS

(PROFUSELY ORNAMENTED —) PEMBROKE

(SERVING —) WAGON

(SHAKING —) SLIMER

(SMALL —) KURSI STAND TABORET TABOURET

(STONE —) DOLMEN

(TEA —) TEAPOY

(WRITING —) DESK

TABLEAU LAYOUT PAGEANT PICTURE

TABLECLOTH CLOTH COVER CARPET

TABLE D'HOTE DINNER

TABLELAND PLAT PUNA PUNO KAROO TABLE KARROO PLATEAU BALAGHAT

TABLET PAX BRED ALBUM FACIA PIECE PINAX SLATE TABLE ABACUS TABULA TABULE TROCHE ASPIRIN CODICIL DIPTYCH PALETTE PREFORM TABLING CARTOUCH CHURINGA TABULATE TRIPTYCH MEDALLION

(— BEARING SYMBOL OF CHRIST) PAX

(— FOR PUBLISHING LAWS) PARAPEGM

(— OVER SHOP FRONT) FACIA FASCIA

(MEDICATED —) ASPIRIN JELLOID TABELLA

(MEDICINAL —) DISC DISK TROCHE

(MEMORIAL —) BRASS TABUT

(PAINTER'S —) PALETTE

(SQUARE —) ABACK

(UPRIGHT —) STELA STELE

(VOTIVE —) PINAX

(WRITING —) CODICIL TRIPTYCH

(PREF.) PINA PINAC(O) PLAC(O)

TABLEWARE CHINA FLATWARE HAVILAND

TABOO KAPU TABU TAPU FORBIDDEN INEFFABLE

TABOR ATABAL TABRET TIMBRE TABORIN TIMBREL

TABULATION SCALE SCHEME TABLING

TABUT TAZIA TAZEEA

TACHOMETER CUTMETER

TACHYGLOSSUS ECHIDNA

TACIT SILENT IMPLICIT

TACITURN DUMB STILL SILENT RESERVED RETICENT

TACK LAY BEAT CAST STAY BASTE BOARD FETCH ENTAIL LAVEER TACKET TINGLE SADDLERY

(GLAZIERS' —) BRAD

TACKER GUN SPREADER

TACKLE CAT RIG TAW SWIG TACK YOKE ANGLE FALLS ATTACK BURTON COLLAR GARNET JIGGER LEDGER RUNNER STEEVE TAGLIA

TEAGLE DERRICK HALYARD HARNESS RIGGING FISHFALL PURCHASE TACKLING

(— FOR RAISING BOAT) FALLS

(— TO HOIST ANCHOR) CAT

(COMBINATION OF —S) JEER JEERS

(FISHING —) TEW LEGER OTTER LEDGER

TACO FLAUTA TAQUITO

TACT TOUCH ADDRESS CONDUCT DELICACY

TACTFUL POLITIC DISCREET GRACEFUL

TACTFULLY HAPPILY

TACTIC GAME

TACTLESS BRASH GAUCHE

TADPOLE POWHEAD BULLHEAD POLEHEAD POLLIWOG PORWIGLE

TAEL LIANG

TAENNIN KOSIN KOUSIN

TAFFETA TABBY ARMOZEEN FLORENCE

TAFFY GUNDY TOFFY TOFFEE CLAGGUM

TAG HE DAG EAR TAB TIG TAIL TICK AGLET DAGGE LABEL TALLY TOUCH AIGLET EARTAB EARTAG FOLLOW SWATCH TAGGLE TAGRAG TICKET TIGTAG HANGTAG

(— OF A LACE) AGLET AIGLET

(ANGLING —) TOUCH

(ORNAMENTED —S) FANCY

TAGALOG PULAHAN

TAGETES MARIGOLD

TAGRAG SHAGRAG

TAHATH (FATHER OF —) BERED

TAHITI (CAPITAL OF —) PAPEETE

(FORMER NAME OF —) OTAHEITE

(MOUNTAIN IN —) OROHENA

TAHMURATH (BROTHER OF —) YIMA

(FATHER OF —) VIVANGHAO

(SLAYER OF —) AHRIMAN

TAHR KRAS JHARAL

TAHSILDAR TALUKDAR

TAI LI AHOM SHAM THAI PORGY KHAMTI

TAIGA URMAN

TAIL BOB BUN CUE BUNT BUSH CLUB FLAG POLE SCUT BRUSH CAUDA SNAKE START STERN TRAIN TWIST FLIGHT FOLLOW RUMPLE SWITCH TAILET TAILLE FANTAIL FOXTAIL RATTAIL

(— OF ARTIFICIAL FLY) TOPPING

(— OF BELL CLAPPER) FLIGHT

(— OF BIRD) FAN

(— OF BIRD OR ANIMAL) CUE POLE START

(— OF BOAR) WREATH

(— OF CART) ARSE

(— OF COAT) DOCK

(— OF COMET) BEARD STREAM STREAMER CHEVELURE

(— OF DEER) FLAG SINGLE SHINGLE

(— OF DOG) FLAG STERN

(— OF FISH) UROSOME

(— OF FLY) WHISK

(— OF FOX) BUSH BRUSH FOXTAIL

(— OF HARE OR RABBIT) BUN FUD BUNT SCUT

(— OF HOOD) LIRIPIPE

(— OF HORSE) BOB

(— OF MAN'S TIED HAIR) CLUB

(— OF METEOR) TRAIN

(— OF MUSICAL NOTE) QUEUE

(— OF PUG DOG) TWIST

(— OF SQUIRREL) BUN

(— OF STANZA) CODA

(DRAGON'S —) KETU

(STUMP OF —) STRUNT

(TIP OF —) TAG

(PREF.) CAUD(I)(O) CERC(O) ONCHO UR(O)

(SUFF.) CERCAL CERCY URA URE UROUS URUS

TAILBAND FOOTBAND

TAILBOARD ENDGATE ENDBOARD ENDPIECE

TAILED CAUDATE CAUDATED

(PREF.) UR(O)

(SUFF.) URA URE UROUS URUS

TAILING CHAT

(PL.) SAND TAIL GRUFFS

TAILLE TALLY

TAILLESS ACAUDAL ANUROUS ACAUDATE ECAUDATE

TAILOR SLOP SNIP BUILD DARZI GORER SHRED CUTTER DARZEE FULLER SARTOR SNYDER STITCH BOTCHER CABBAGE SNIPPER TIREMAN CLOTHIER SEAMSTER SEMPSTER SHEPSTER

(ITINERANT —) CARDOOER

TAILORBIRD DARZEE

TAILPIECE QUEUE ANQUERA

TAILRACE AFTERBAY

TAILSPIN FLICKER

TAILSTOCK DEADHEAD

TAINO HAITIAN

(— BELIEFS) ZEMIISM

TAINT HAUL HOGO MOIL SMUT SPOT VICE CLOUD STAIN TOUCH DARKEN INFECT REMORD SMIRCH SMUTCH ATTAINT BLEMISH CORRUPT DEBAUCH ENVENOM FLYBLOW FORRUMP POLLUTE TARNISH VITIATE EMPOISON TAINTURE CONTAMINATE

TAINTED OFF GAMY HIGH BLOWN PINDY SAPPY TAINT WEMMY RANCID ROTTEN SINFUL SMUTTY CORRUPT FOUGHTY FLYBLOWN

TAIWAN (CAPITAL OF —) TAIPEI

(ISLAND GROUP OF —) MATSU PENGHU QUEMOY
(MOUNTAIN IN —) TZUKAO YUSHAN HSINKAO
(OTHER NAME OF —) FORMOSA
(RIVER IN —) WUCHI TACHIA CHOSHUI HUALIEN TANSHUI
(TOWN IN —) CHIAL TAINAN TAIPEI CHILUNG KEELUNG PINGTUNG TAICHUNG
TAJIN TOTONAC
TAJ MAHAL (SITE OF —) AGRA
TAKE COP HIT NIM NIP NOB BEAR BONE DRAW FANG GLOM HAVE LEAD TACK TEEM TOLL ADOPT AFONG BRING CARRY CATCH CREEL FETCH GRASP GRIPE LATCH SEIZE SNAKE ACCEPT CLUTCH COTTON DERIVE EXTEND FERRET FINGER RECIPE SNATCH TAKING ATTRACT CABBAGE CAPTURE RECEIVE UNPURSE UNDERNIM
(— A BATH) TOSH
(— A CERTAIN POSITION) SIT
(— A DIRECTION) STEER
(— A DRINK) PULL SMILE
(— A LITTLE) DELIBATE
(— A NAP) DOSS
(— A STAND) ASSERT
(— ACTION) ACT
(— ADVANTAGE) DO ABUSE BLUDGE CLUTCH EXPLOIT
(— AFTER) BRAID FOLLOW
(— AIM) BEAD
(— AS ONE'S OWN) ADOPT
(— AWAY) BATE EASE HENT LIFT TOLL WISP BENIM BLEED HEAVE REAVE STEAL ABDUCT CONVEY DEDUCE DEDUCT DEMISE DEPOSE DEVEST DIVEST ELOIGN EXEMPT REMOVE UNVEST ABJUDGE BEREAVE DEPRIVE DETRACT FORTAKE RETRACT SUBDUCE SUBLATE ABSTRACT DEROGATE DIMINISH SUBTRACT
(— BACK) RECALL RECANT REVOKE RETRACT
(— BACK TO ONESELF) RESUME
(— BY FRAUD) BOB
(— BY LEVY) ESTREAT
(— BY STEALTH) HOOK SNITCH
(— BY STORM) EXPUGN INVADE SURPRISE
(— CARE) FIX SEE GARE KEEP MIND TEND WARD YEME NURSE BEWARE GOVERN INTEND CUIDADO HUSBAND CHAPERON
(— CENSUS OF) MUSTER
(— CHANCE) DICE RISK
(— CHARGE) ATTEND
(— CHARGE OF) CURE SOLICIT
(— COVER) COOK
(— DAMAGE) BANGE
(— DINNER) DINE
(— DOWN) STOOP STRIKE
(— EXCEPTION) DEMUR STRAIN
(— FOOD) EAT DINE GRUB
(— FOR GRANTED) BEG ASSUME PRESUME
(— FOR ONESELF) CAB
(— FOR RESALE) FLOG
(— FORM) FORM INFORM

(— FRAUDULENTLY) STEAL STRIKE
(— FRIGHT) BOOGER
(— FROM) DETRACT
(— FROM DEPOSIT) DRAW
(— GOLFING STANCE) ADDRESS
(— GREAT DELIGHT) REVEL
(— HEART) BRACE
(— HEED) RECK TENT
(— HOLD) GET BITE GRAB PINCH SEIZE ARREST BEGRIPE
(— HOLIDAY) LAKE
(— IN) IN EAT SUP BITE HOAX KEEP DOWSE DRINK ABSORB DEVOUR ENFOLD GATHER HARBOR INCEPT INGEST INSORB INSUME INTAKE MUZZLE BEGRIPE EMBRACE INCLUDE
(— IN BY LEAKING) LADE
(— IN LIVESTOCK) AGIST
(— IN SAIL) BRAIL
(— INTO HANDS) TOUCH EMBRACE
(— LEGALLY) ATTACH
(— LEVEL OF) BONE
(— LUNCH) TIFFIN
(— MEALS) BOARD
(— NOTE OF) NB COUNT SMOKE NOTICE WITNESS
(— OATH) ABJURE
(— OFF) OFF DOFF LIFT VAIL DOUSE SHUCK STRIP DEDUCT
(— OFFENSE) DORT HUFF
(— ON) HIRE MOUNT START
(— ONE'S LEAVE) CONGEE
(— ONESELF) BETAKE
(— OUT) DELE KILL EXCERPT AIRBRUSH
(— OUT OF EARTH) EXTER
(— OVER) ABSORB
(— PAINS) BOTHER
(— PART) LEAD FIGHT ENGAGE
(— PLACE) BE DO GO COME GIVE PASS ARISE BEFALL HAPPEN
(— PLEASURE IN) ENJOY ADMIRE
(— PORTION OF) PARTAKE
(— POSSESSION) GRIP ANNEX BESET SEIZE SPOIL EXTEND CONQUER INHERIT DISTRAIN
(— REFUGE) HIDE SOIL EVADE HAVEN WATCH
(— ROOT) MARE MORE ENROOT STRIKE
(— SHAPE) JELL
(— SHELTER) HOWF NESTLE SHROUD
(— SUPPER) SUP
(— THE PLACE OF) ENSUE SECOND SUPPLY DISPLACE SUPPLANT
(— THOUGHT) ADVISE
(— TO BE TRUE WITHOUT PROOF) PRESUME
(— TO TASK) JACK CARPET CHAPTER
(— TO WING) FLUSH
(— UNAWARE) DECEIVE
(— UP) ENTER MOUNT ADSORB ASSUME GATHER HANDLE STRIKE
(— UP AGAIN) RESUME
(— UP WITH) ALL
(— WELL OR ILL) RESENT
(— WIND ON OPPOSITE QUARTER) JIBE
TAKEN TON TAIN
(— ABACK) BLANK

(— AWAY) ADEMPT
TAKEOFF JATO SPOOF SCRAMBLE
TAKEOUT STACK
TAKER PERNOR
TAKING HOT TAKY CAPTION ADOPTION PERNANCY PREEMPTION
(— EVERYTHING INTO ACCOUNT) OVERALL
(— LIBERTIES) PRESUMPTUOUS
(— OF LIFE) BLOOD
(— PLACE) AGATE
(PREF.) **(— IN)** END(O)
(SUFF.) LEPSIA LEPSIS LEPSY LEPT(IC)
TALAK AHSAN
TALARI PATACA PATACOON
TALAUS (FATHER OF —) BIAS
(MOTHER OF —) PERO
(SON OF —) ADRASTUS
(WIFE OF —) LYSIMACHE
TALC SPAAD TALCUM AGALITE STEATITE
TALE SAW DIDO JEST LEED REDE TELL BOURD CRACK FABLE RECIT SPELL SPOKE STORY WINDY AITION FABULA LEGEND PISTLE PURANA FABLIAU FICTION HISTORY MARCHEN ROMANCE ANECDOTE FOLKTALE SPELLING TREATISE
(— OF ACHIEVEMENTS) GEST GESTE
(— OF FOUR) WARP
(— OF GOLD COAST NEGROS) NANCY
(COMIC COARSE —) FABLIAU
(DEVISED —) AITION
(EPIC —) TAIN
(FALSE —) BAM VANITY SLANDER
(FATEFUL —) WEIRD
(FOLK —) NANCY THRENE
(HUMOROUS —S) FACETIAE
(MERRY —) BOURD
(POETIC NARRATIVE —) SAGA
(SENSATIONAL —) BLOOD
(SHORT —) LAI CONTE
(PREF.) STORIO
TALEBEARER BUZZER GOSSIP TATTLER TALEPYET TELLTALE
TALEBEARING TALEWISE
TALENT GIFT HEAD NOUS VEIN DOWER DOWRY VERVE CICHAR GENIUS ABILITY CHARISM FACULTY CAPACITY CHARISMA
TALENTED ABLE CLEVER GIFTED
TALE OF TWO CITIES (AUTHOR OF —) DICKENS
(CHARACTER IN —) JOHN JERRY LORRY LUCIE PROSS BARSAD CARTON DARNAY JARVIS SYDNEY CHARLES DEFARGE GASPARD MANETTE STRYVER CRUNCHER EVREMONDE
TALER ORT THALER
TALES OF HOFFMANN
(CHARACTER IN —) ANDRES LUTHER STELLA ANTONIA CRESPEL LINDORF MIRACLE OLYMPIA HOFFMANN SCHLEMIL COPPELIUS GIULIETTA NICALUSSE DAPERTUTTO SPALANZANI PITICHINACCHIO

(COMPOSER OF —) OFFENBACH
TALIPES CLUBFOOT
TALISMAN ANGLE CHARM IMAGE OBEAH SAFFI AMULET GRIGRI SAPHIE SCARAB TELESM ICHTHUS ICHTHYS GREEGREE
(AUTHOR OF —) SCOTT
(CHARACTER IN —) DAVID EDITH PHILIP KENNETH RICHARD SALADIN BERENGARIA MONTFERRAT PLANTAGENET
TALK GAB JAW JIB RAP SAW SAY YAP BLAT BUCK BUKH CANT CARP CHAT CHIN GAFF GIVE GUFF KNAP MEAN TALE TOVE WORD CRACK FABLE MOUTH PARLE PITCH SPEAK SPELL SPIEL SPOKE TUTEL COMMON GAMMON INDABA KORERO PATTER SERMON SPEECH STEVEN TONGUE YABBER ADDRESS CHINWAG DISCUSS LIPWORK PALABRA PALAVER PARRALL PURPOSE WINDJAM CAUSERIE COLLOQUY CONVERSE LANGUAGE PARLANCE QUESTION
(— ABOUT) HASH
(— BACK) SASS
(— BIG) SWANK BOUNCE
(— BOASTFULLY) GAS BLATTER
(— BOMBASTICALLY) BEMOUTH
(— CASUALLY) DISH
(— CONFIDENTIALLY) CUTTER
(— CONFUSEDLY) HOTTER
(— DISMALLY) CROAK
(— EMPTILY) BLOW
(— FAMILIARLY) TOVE CONFAB
(— FATUOUSLY) BABBLE
(— FONDLY) COO
(— FOOLISHLY) YAK BLAT FLAP YACK HAVER BABBLE DRIVEL FOOTER FOOTLE GABBLE GIBBER SAWNEY TOOTLE BLATHER BLETHER
(— GLIBLY) PATTER SCREED
(— IDLY) GAB BLAB CHIN GASH FABLE GABBLE JANGLE TATTLE CHATTER GNATTER PRATTLE
(— IMPUDENTLY) SASS
(— INACCURATELY) BLAGUE
(— INARTICULATELY) CHUNNER CHUNTER
(— INCESSANTLY) YANK BURBLE WAFFLE CHATTER
(— INCOHERENTLY) BABBLE BURBLE HOTTER MITHER MOIDER
(— INCONSIDERATELY) BLAT
(— INDECISIVELY) WAFFLE
(— INFORMALLY) HOBNOB
(— INSOLENTLY) SNASH
(— INTENDED TO DECEIVE) GAMMON PALAVER
(— IRRATIONALLY) RAVE
(— MONOTONOUSLY) DRONE
(— NEEDLESSLY) PALAVER
(— NOISILY) CLAP BLATTER BRABBLE
(— NONSENSE) GAS ROT BLEAT DROOL FUDGE HAVER
(— OFFICIOUSLY) BLEEZE
(— PERTLY) CHELP

(— PRIVATELY) COLLOGUE
(— RAPIDLY) GABBLE JABBER GNATTER
(— SCANDAL) HORN
(— SNAPPISHLY) KNAP
(— SPORTIVELY) DAFF
(— SUPERFICIALLY) SMATTER
(— TEDIOUSLY) DINGDONG
(— THOUGHTLESSLY) BLAB
(— TOGETHER) DEVISE
(— VAGUELY) WOOZLE
(— VOLUBLY) CHIN PATTER
(— WEAKLY) DRIVEL
(— WITH) CONTACT
(— WITHOUT MEANING) GABBLE
(ABSURD —) BOSH
(ABUSIVE —) HOKER JAWING
(ARROGANT —) GUM BRAG
(BOASTFUL —) BULL GAFF
(BOMBASTIC —) FLASH
(COMMON —) FAME FABLE NOISE HEARSAY
(CONCEITED —) BLAGUE
(CONTINUAL —) CLACK
(COUNTRY —) CLASH
(DECEPTIVE —) GAMMON
(EMPTY —) GAS BOSH GASH FRASE GLOZE FRAISE BLAFLUM GASSING PRATTLE BALLYHOO GALBANUM MOONSHINE POPPYCOCK
(ENTHUSIASTIC —) JAZZ
(FALSE —) BALLYHOO
(FAMILIAR —) CONFAB CHITCHAT
(FANTASTIC —) GUYVER
(FOOLISH —) GUP GAFF JIVE BLEAT CLACK FABLE BLETHERS COBBLERS
(FORMAL —) ADDRESS
(FRIVOLOUS —) PERSIFLAGE
(GLIB —) JIVE
(IDLE —) GAB BLAB BUFF CHAT GAFF GEST GUFF FABLE GESTE BABBLE CLAVER GOSSIP JANGLE CHATTER CLATTER PALAVER TWATTLE BABBLING BATTOLOGY
(IMPUDENT —) PRATE SLACK
(INCOHERENT —) GABBER JABBER
(INFORMAL —) CAUSERIE
(INSINCERE —) JAZZ CROCK BUNKUM MALARKEY
(JESTING —) CHAFF JAPERY
(LIGHT —) TRIFLING
(MEANINGLESS —) SLIPSLOP
(NONSENSICAL —) BLABBER BLATHER FOLDEROL
(PIOUS OR SANCTIMONIOUS —) PI
(RAPID —) GABBLE JABBER CHATTER CLATTER
(SALES —) PITCH
(SCOLDING —) HARANGUE
(SILLY —) BLAH BUFF CLART CACKLE FOOTLE TWADDLE
(SMALL —) CHAT BACKCHAT CHITCHAT
(SMOOTH —) GLOZE BLARNEY
(STUPID —) MOROLOGY
(TRIFLING —) PRATTLE CHITCHAT
(USELESS —) WASTE
(VIOLENT —) BLUSTER
(WEAK —) SLIPSLOP
(WHINING —) BLEAT
(SUFF.) LALIA LOG(ER)(IA)(IAN)(IC) (ICAL)(IST)(UE)(Y)

TALKATIVE COSY GASH GLIB NAWY BUZZY TALKY CHATTY CLASHY CRACKY FLUENT FUTILE SOCIAL VOLUBLE BIGMOUTH FLIPPANT TELLSOME
TALKATIVENESS FUTILITY
TALKER YENTA CAMPER POTGUN CAUSEUR SPIELER
(IDLE —) WHIFFLER
(NOISY —) BLELLUM
(PROFESSIONAL —) JAWSMITH
(SENSELESS —) RATTLE
TALKING (LOUD —) NORATION
TALKING-TO EARFUL LECTURE
TALKY GABBY
TALL HIGH LANKY LOFTY STEEP WANDY CRANEY PROCERE
(— AND FEEBLE) TANGLE
(VERY —) TAUNT
TALLAGE CUTTING
TALLER DOMINANT
TALLNESS PROCERITY
TALLOW SUET SEVUM ARMING TAULCH CHERVICE
(PREF.) SEBI SEBO STEAR(O) STEAT(O)
(SUFF.) STEARIN
TALLY TAB JUMP NICK SUIT AGREE CHECK COUNT SCORE STICK STOCK CENSUS STRING SWATCH TAILYE COMPORT TAILZIE
TALMAI (FATHER OF —) AMMIHUD
TALMUD GEMARA
TALON FANG SERE UNCE CLUTCH POUNCE UNGUIS WEAPON
(— OF TOOTH) HEEL
TALONID HEEL
TALPA TESTUDO
TALTHIB GLAGA GLAGAH
TALUS SCREE RUBBLE ASTRAGAL
TAMANDUA ANTEATER
TAMAR (AUTHOR OF —) JEFFERS
(CHARACTER IN —) LEE WILL DAVID JINNY TAMAR STELLA ANDREWS MORELAND CAULDWELL
(FATHER OF —) DAVID ABSALOM
(HUSBAND OF —) ER ONAN
(MOTHER OF —) MAACHAH
(SON OF —) ZARAH PHAREZ
TAMARACK LARCH LARIX EPINETTE
TAMARIN PINCHE JACCHUS LEONCITO MARIKINA MARMOSET
TAMARIND SAMPALOC
TAMARISK ATLE JHOW HEATH MYRICA
TAMASHEK TUAREG
TAMBOURINE RIKK TAAR DAIRA TAMBO TABOUR TIMBER TABORIN TIMBREL
(PART OF —) HEAD TACK SHELL JINGLE
TAMBURLAINE THE GREAT
(AUTHOR OF —) MARLOWE
(CHARACTER IN —) ALMEDA AMYRAS COSROE ZABINA MEANDER MYCETES ORCANES BAJAZETH CALYPHAS MENAPHON CALLAPINE CELEBINUS SIGISMUND TECHELLES ZENOCRATE THERIDAMAS USUMCASANE TAMBURLAINE

TAME MAN CADE DEAD MEEK MILD PACK ACCOY ATAME BREAK DAUNT MILKY SPAKE CADISH ENTAME GENTLE INWARD MEEKEN UNWIFE AFFAITE AMENAGE CORRECT INSIPID SUBDUED CICURATE DOMESTIC MANSUETE
(— FALCON) MAN RECLAIM
TAMED BROKE GENTLE
TAMENESS MANSUETUDE
TAMIL VELLALA
TAMING OF THE SHREW (AUTHOR OF —) SHAKESPEARE
(CHARACTER IN —) SLY BIANCA CURTIS GREMIO GRUMIO TRANIO BAPTISTA LUCENTIO BIONDELLO HORTENSIO KATHARINA PETRUCHIO VINCENTIO CHRISTOPHER
TAMMUZ (FATHER OF —) NINGISHZIDA
TAMMY TAMIS STAMIN
TAMONEA MICONIA
TAM-O-SHANTER TAM TAMMY
TAMP PUG STEM
TAMPER FIX COOK FAKE FOOL GAFF TOUCH DABBLE FIDDLE MEDDLE MONKEY POTTER PUDDLE PUTTER TEMPER FALSIFY TRINKLE
(— WITH HORSE'S TEETH) BISHOP
TAMPION TOMKIN TAMPOON
TAM-TAM GONG
TAN FAN ARAB BARK ADUST ASCOT DRESS TANKA TAWNY ORIOLE COCONUT EMBROWN LEATHER SUNBURN
(BEACH —) SEDGE
(TROTTEUR —) BAY
(PREF.) TANN(I)(O)
TANACETYL THUJYL
TANAGER YENI LINDO REDBIRD WARBIRD CARDINAL EUPHONIA FIREBIRD ORGANIST
TANBARK BARK TAWN AVARAM TURWAR ALGERIAN ALGERINE
TANCRED (FATHER OF —) OTHO
(LOVER OF —) ERMINIA CLORINDA
(MOTHER OF —) EMMA
TANDAN EELFISH
TANEKAHA TOATOA
TANG NIP FANG TING VEIN SHANK STING STRAP TASTE TWANG RELISH TANGLE TONGUE SEATANG FAREWELL
TANGELO UGLI
TANGENCY CONTACT
TANGENT SLOPE
TANGERINE NAARTJE MANDARIN
TANGIBLE ACTUAL TACTILE CONCRETE MATERIAL PALPABLE
TANGLE COT ELF ORE TAT FANK FOUL HARL SHAG TAUT HARLE KNURL SKEIN SNARL SNIRL THRUM TWINE WOPSE BALTER BURBLE ENTRAP FANKLE HANGER JUNGLE MOMBLE MUCKER RAFFLE SLEAVE TAFFLE TARDLE TAUGHT TEIHTE BRANGLE TAISSLE THICKET FURBELOW SCROBBLE
(PL.) COBWEB

TANGLED AFOUL TOUSY MESHED SNARLY TAUTED IMPLICIT INTORTED INVOLVED CESPITOSE
(— UP) HAYWIRE
TANGLEHEAD PILI
TANGUE TENREC
TANGY BRISK
TANHA TRISHNA
TANK DAM DIP TAL VAT BOSH SUMP BASIN MIXER STANK STEEP TRUNK BLOWUP BOILER HOPPER PANZER TROUGH BATTERY BLOWPIT BREAKER CISTERN FLUSHER PISCINA PLUNGER POACHER SETTLER STEEPER BLEACHER DIGESTOR LANDSHIP SUBSIDER
(— FOR DYE OR SOAP) BECK
(— FOR FISH) STEW TRUNK PISCINA AQUARIUM STEWPOND
(— IN SHIP) FOREPEAK
(ARMORED —) FLAIL PANZER WHIPPET LANDSHIP
(PAPER MANUFACTURING —) POACHER
(PHOTOGRAPHIC —) CUVETTE
(POTTER'S —) PLUNGER
(RECTANGULAR —) BOWLY
(SALT MANUFACTURING —) GRAINER
(STORAGE —) CHEST
(SUGAR REFINING —) TIGER BLOWUP
(TANNING —) FLOATER
(PL.) HEAVIES
(PREF.) LACO
TANKAGE AMMONATE
TANKARD GUN JACK FACER STOOP STOUP PEWTER POTTLE TANKER GODDARD
TANKER BOWSER
TANNED BROWN RUDDY TAWNY REECHY BRONZED
(NOT —) RAW
TANNER EGGER SAMAR BARKER STAKER PERCHER
TANNHAUSER (CHARACTER IN —) VENUS HERMANN WOLFRAM ELISABETH TANNHAUSER
(COMPOSER OF —) WAGNER
TANNING PASTING
(— SOLUTION) PLUMPER
TANSY COSTMARY
TANSY MUSTARD FLIXWEED FLUXWEED
TANSY RAGWORT RAGWEED
TANTALIZE GRIG JADE MOCK TEASE HARASS
TANTALUS (DAUGHTER OF —) NIOBE
(FATHER OF —) AMPHION JUPITER THYESTES
(MOTHER OF —) NIOBE PLUTO
(SON OF —) PELOPS
(WIFE OF —) DIONE CLYTIA EUPRYTO TAYGETE
TANTAMOUNT SAME
TANTRA AGAMA
TANTRUM HISSY TIRRIVEE WINGDING

TANZANIA
CAPITAL: DARESSALAAM

COIN: SENTI SHILINGI
ISLAND: MAFIA PEMBA ZANZIBAR
LAKE: RUKWA
NATIVE: BANTU SUKUMA
MAKONDE SWAHILI
REGION: MARA MBEYA PEMBA
PWANI TANGA MWANZA
RUVUMA TABORA SINGIDA
RIVER: RUVU WAMI RUAHA
KAGERA RUFIJI RUVUMA
PANGANI MBENKURU
TOWN: WETE KILWA MBEYA
MOSHI TANGA ARUSHA
DODOMA IRINGA KIGOMA
MTWARA MWANZA TABORA
MTAWARA MOROGORO
ZANZIBAR
VOLCANO: KIBO KILIMANJARO
WATERFALL: KALAMBO
WEIGHT: FARSALAH

TAO MAN PEASANT
(— PRACTICE) WUWEI
TAP BOB DAB PAT TAT TIP TIT TOP
BEAT COCK DRUB FLIP JOWL
PENK TICK TIRL TUCK TUNK
APPEL FLIRT QUILL SNOCK START
TOUCH ALETAP BROACH CANNEL
DABBLE FAUCET NATTLE TAPLET
BIBCOCK BLENDER DRAWOFF
HEELTAP PERCUSS
(— A CASK) QUILL STRIKE
(— A DRUM) TUCK
(— FOR A LOAN) TIG
(— ON SHOE) CLUMP UNDERLAY
(— ON THE SHOULDER) FOB
(— REPEATEDLY) DRUM
(— THE GROUND) BEAT
(FENCING —) BEAT
(MASTER —) HOB HUB
(SMART — OF THE FOOT) APPEL
TAPA KAPA SIAPO KIKEPA
TAPACOLO TURCO
TAPE LEAR FERRET GARTER
SCOTCH TAPERY YNKELL BINDING
MEASURE TAPELINE TELETAPE
(— CARTRIDGE) CASSETTE
(DEMONSTRATION —) DEMO
(FISH —) SNAKE
(LAMP —) WICK
(LINEN —) INKLE
(METALLIC —) GALLOON
(NARROW —) TASTE
(RED —) WIGGERY
TAPE GRASS EELGRASS
TAPEMAN CHAINMAN
TAPER DRAW RISE RUSH DRAFT
GAUDY PINCH SCARF SNAPE
SWAGE CIERGE DRAUGHT
LIGHTER PRICKET SHAMMES
TRINDLE DIMINISH ACUMINATE
(— OF A SPRING) DRAW
(— OF PATTERN) STRIP
(— OFF) CEASE TONGUE
TAPERED BARRELED BOATTAIL
GRADUATED
TAPERING SHARP SPIRY SPIRAL
SPIRED TERETE SPIRING
FUSIFORM SUBULATE ATTENUATE
TAPER ROD PODGER
TAPESTRY ARRAS TAPET TAPIS
COSTER DORSER DOSSER CEILING
GOBELIN HANGING SUSANEE

VERDURE AUBUSSON MORTLAKE
TAPEWORM TAPE LIGULA TAENIA
CESTODE CESTOID COENURE
HYDATID PLATODE BANDWORM
COENURUS DAVAINEA
FLATWORM HELMINTH STROBILA
(— LARVA) MEASLE
(PL.) CYSTICA
(PREF.) TAENI(A)(O)
TAPHATH (FATHER OF —) SOLOMON
TAPHOLE TAP FLOSS MOUTH
TAPIOCA CASSAVA
TAPIR ANTA KUDA DANTA TENNU
TAPIROID
TAPPED ABROACH
TAPPET CAM WIPER
TAPROOM TAP SALOON BARROOM
BUVETTE TAPHOUSE
TAPSTER NICKPOT SKINKER
TAPUYAN GE GES GHES BUGRE
GESAN JUYAS CAYAPO GOYANA
CAMACAN CARAHOS COROADO
TIMBIRA APINAGES BOTOCUDO
CAINGANG CHAVANTE
TAR PAY BREA BINDER ALKITRAN
(BIRCH —) DAGGETT
(MINERAL —) MALTHA
TARA DOLMA
TARANTULA HUNTER JAYHAWK
MYGALID
TARAS BULBA (AUTHOR OF —)
GOGOL
(CHARACTER IN —) BULBA OSTAP
TARAS ANDRII YANKEL KIRDYAGA
TARBOOSH FEZ
TARDIGRADA ARCTISCA
TARDILY SLOWLY
TARDINESS SLOTH TARDITY
TARDY LAG LAX DREE LATE SLOW
SLACK DREIGH LAGGED REMISS
LAGGING OVERDUE DILATORY
LATESOME
TARE TINE VETCH LEAKAGE
(PL.) FILTH
TAREA (FATHER OF —) MICAH
TARES ZIZANY
TARGE BUCKLER
TARGET AIM MOT BUTT MARK
WAND CLOUT LEVEL PRICK
ROVER SCOOP SCOPE TARGE
WHITE BANNER NIVEAU OBJECT
SLEEVE COCKSHY INCOMER
OUTGOER SARACEN POPINJAY
(— OF KNEELING FIGURE) SQUAW
(— OF LEVELING STAFF) VANE
(— OF RIDICULE) GAME
(— RING) SOUS
(EASY —) SITTER
(PIECE OF —) SCAB
(RAILROAD SWITCH —) BANNER
(STRIKE A —) KEYHOLE
(THROWN —) COCKSHY COCKSHUT
(TOWED —) DROGUE
(UNIDENTIFIED —) SKUNK
TARHEEL STATE NORTHCAROLINA
TARIFF ZABETA AVERAGE TRIBUTE
TARNISH DIM BLOT SMIT SOIL
CLOUD DIRTY STAIN SULLY
TACHE BREATH DARKEN DEFILE
INJURE SMIRCH ASPERSE
BEGRIME BESMEAR BLEMISH
OBSCURE BESMIRCH DISCOLOR
TARO COCO DALO EDDO GABE

KALO MASI TALO COCCO KAROU
TANIA TANYA COCKER TARROW
YAUTIA DASHEEN MALANGA
COCOROOT EDDYROOT
TAROT NAIB TAROCCO
TARPON SABALO
TARRAGON TARCHON ESTRAGON
TARRY BIDE LENG STAY STOP
ABIDE DALLY DEMUR PAUSE
ARREST LINGER PITCHY REMAIN
SOJOURN
TARSIER LEMUR MALMAG
TARSOMETATARSUS SHANK
TARSUS HAND ANKLE DIGITAL
(BIRD'S —) SHANK
TART ACID FLAN SOUR BOWLA
CUPID EAGER SHARP SNIPPY
SUNKET PIQUANT POLYNEE
PUNGENT SUBACID TARTLET
TURNOVER
TARTAN PLAID
(— PATTERN) SETT
TARTAR ARGAL ARGOL CALCULUS
TARTARIN OF TARASCON
(AUTHOR OF —) DAUDET
(CHARACTER IN —) BAIA BRAVIDA
GREGORY BEZUQUET TARTARIN
BARBASSOU
TARTNESS ACRITY ACIDITY
VERDURE ACERBITY ASPERITY
VERJUICE
TARTUFFE (AUTHOR OF —) MOLIERE
(CHARACTER IN —) ARGAS DAMIS
ORGON DORINE ELMIRE VALERE
CLEANTE MARIANE PERNELLE
TARTUFFE
TASHMET (HUSBAND OF —) NEBO
TASK FAG JOB TAX CHAR DARG
TOIL CHARE CHORE GRIND KNACK
LABOR NULLO STINT CHARGE
DEVOIR NIYOGA PENSUM
RAMSCH TOURNE FATIGUE
SWEATER TRAVAIL BUSINESS
EXERCISE TRAUCHLE
(— AS PSYCHOLOGICAL TEST)
AUFGABE
(ASSIGNED —) STENT STINT
DEVOIR
(DIFFICULT —) BUGGER
(EASY —) PIPE SNAP SETUP
(ONE WHO PERFORMS MENIAL —S)
DOGSBODY
(ONEROUS —) CORVEE
(ROUTINE —) DRUDGE
TASKMASTER DRIVER TASKER
RAWHIDER
TASMANIA (CAPITAL OF —)
HOBART
(LAKE IN —) ECHO SORELL
(MOUNTAIN IN —) DROME NEVIS
BARRON CRADLE LOMOND
HUMBOLDT
(RIVER IN —) ESK HUDN TAMAR
GORDON JORDAN PIEMAN
DERWENT
(TOWN IN —) BURNIE HOBART
TASMANIAN DEVIL DASYURID
TASMANIAN WOLF HYENA
THYLACINE
TASSEL TAG TUFT LABEL THRUM
TARCEL TARGET TOORIE
CORDELLE
(PL.) ZIZITH

(PREF.) THYSAN(O)
TASTABLE GUSTABLE
TASTE EAT GAB GOO LAP SIP CAST
DASH GOUT GUST HINT PREE
RASA SALT TANG TEST TINT
WAFT ASSAY DRINK FANCY
GUSTO HEART PROVE RELES
SAPOR SAVOR SHADE SKILL
SMACK SNACK SPICE TOOTH
TOUCH DEGUST FLAVOR GENIUS
LIKING PALATE RELISH SAMPLE
SMATCH ATTASTE PREGUST
SOUPCON THOUGHT APPETITE
JUDGMENT PENCHANT SAPIDITY
(— COMBINED WITH APTITUDE)
FLAIR
(— IN MATTERS OF ART) FANCY
(BAD —) GOTHISM
(DECIDED —) PENCHANT
(DELICATE —) BREED
(DISCRIMINATING —) SKILL
(GOOD —) DECORUM
(STRONG —) GOO
(PL.) MERIDIAN
(PREF.) SAPORI
(SUFF.) GEUSIA
TASTEFUL NEAT ELEGANT
GUSTOSO
TASTELESS DEAF FLAT FLASH
MALMY VAPID WERSH WALLON
FATUOUS INSIPID INSULSE
WEARISH UNSAVORY
TASTER TRIER
TASTING ASSAY
(— OF MALT) CORNY
TASTY SAPID GUSTABLE TASTEFUL
PALATABLE
TATAR KIN JUNG KITAN SOYOT
CHAZAR KHAZAR KHITAN KHOZAR
SHORTZY MELETSKI
(PL.) HU
TATER SPUD POTATO
TATOUAY CABASSOU
TATTER JAG RAG TAG SHRED
FITTER LIBBET TAGRAG TARGET
FLITTER TROLLOP
(PL.) DUDS TAVERS FITTERS
RIBBONS TAIVERS FLITTERS
TATTERED DUDDY BEATEN
TAGGED FORWORN TATTERY
TOTTERED
TATTING LACE
TATTLE BLAB GASH CHEEP CLASH
CLYPE PEACH SNEAK TUTEL
GOSSIP QUATCH SNITCH TATTER
TITTLE CLATTER
TATTLER LAB CLASH SNIPE FABLER
GAMBET GOSSIP TUTLER YELPER
TITTLER TELLTALE
TATTLING LEAKY FUTILE
TATTOO TAT MOKO PINK POUNCE
RATAPLAN
TATTOOED PINKED
(— MAN) YUN
TATTOOING MOKO
TAUGHT MAK TEACHED INSTRUCT
(EASILY —) DOCIBLE
TAUNT BOB DIG MOB CHIP GIBE
GIRD JAPE JEER JEST MOCK
PROG SKIT TWIT CHECK FRUMP
GLAIK JAUNT SCOFF SCORN
SLANT SLARE SLART DERIDE
SNEEST UPCAST SARCASM

TWITTER RIDICULE
TAUNTING RAIL SARCASTIC
TAUPE MOLESKIN
TAUROTRAGUS OREAS ORIAS
TA-URT THOUERIS
TAUT SNUG TORT STIFF TIGHT
CORDED
TAUTEN SNUB STIFFEN SWIFTER
TENSION
TAUTOG CHUB MOLL LABROID
TAVERN BAR INN BUSH HOWF
VENT FONDA MITER MITRE
TAMBO BISTRO CABACK KNEIPE
BUVETTE CABARET CANTEEN
OSTERIA TABERNA GASTHAUS
ORDINARY POTHOUSE TAPHOUSE
TAW TER ALLY ALLEY SCORE
MARBLE GLASSIE SHOOTER
TAWDRY CHEAP GAUDY NASTY
GILDED TINSEL RAFFISH
TAWNY FUSC BRUSK DUSKY
FULVID TANNED FULVOUS
JACINTH MUSTELINE
(PREF.) CIRRO FUSCO PYRR(O)
PYRRH(O)
TAWNY BROWN TENNE CHAMOIS
TAW-SUG SULU
TAX LAY LOT CAST CESS DUTY
GELD GELT GILD KAIN LEVY POLL
RATE SCAT SCOT SESS TAIL TASK
TOLL ABUSE AGIST DONUM FINTA
HANSA HANSE LEKIN MAILL
OBROK QUINT SCATT STENT
TOUST VERGI WATCH ZAKAH
ZAKAT ABKARI ASSESS AVANIA
BURDEN CEDULA DEMAND
EXCISE EXTENT HIDAGE IMPOST
JEZIAH KHARAJ MURAGE OCTROI
OCTROY PAVAGE PURVEY SENSUS
STRAIN SURTAX VINAGE
BOOMAGE BOSCAGE CHANCER
CHEVAGE CHIVAGE CONDUCT
FINANCE GABELLE LASTAGE
PATENTE PENSION POLLAGE
PONTAGE SCUTAGE STIPEND
TAILAGE TERRAGE TRIBUTE
ALCABALA AUXILIUM BONAUGHT
CARUCAGE CORNBOLE DANEGELD
EXACTION EXERCISE KERNETTY
MALTOLTE OBLATION PESHKASH
ROMESCOT ROMESHOT
STACKAGE SUPERTAX TAXATION
WHEELAGE CAPITATION
(— AT HARVESTTIME) CORNBOLE
(— FOR STORING LOGS) BOOMAGE
(— OF ONE-FIFTH) QUINT
(— ON EVERY PLOW) CARUCAGE
(— ON HERRING CATCH) LASTAGE
(— ON LIQUOR) ABKARI
(— ON SALT) GABELLE
(— ON UNBELIEVERS) KHARAJ
(— ON WALLS) MURAGE
(— ON WOOD) BOSCAGE
(— ON WOOL) MALETOTE
MALTOLTE
(— TO PETTY PRINCES) KERNETTY
(— TO SYNAGOGUE) FINTA
(— TO TENTH AMOUNT) TITHE
(— UNDULY) STRAIN
(CAPITATION —) JIZYA JIZYAH
(CHINESE —) LEKIN LIKEN LIKIN
(EXTRAORDINARY —) AUXILIUM
(FEUDAL —) AID

(IRISH —) BONAGHT
(MOHAMMEDAN —) JEZIAH
(PARISH —) PURVEY
(PHILIPPINES —) CEDULA
(POLL —) TOLL CENSUS
(RUSSIAN —) OBROK
(SPANISH —) ALCABALA
ALCAVALA
(TURKISH —) VERGI AVANIA
TAXABLE LISTABLE
TAX COLLECTOR TITHER
GABELLER
TAXGATHERER POLLER TAXMAN
TAXI JIXIE CRAWLER
(3-WHEELED —) CYCLO
TAXICAB CAB HACK CRUISER
MOTORCAB
TAXIDERMY NASSOLOGY
TAXING SEVERE GRUELING
TAXON MONERA
TAXONOMIC
(SUFF.) (— DIVISION) IA
TAXONOMIST LUMPER SPLITTER
TAYASSU PECARI
TAYGETE (FATHER OF —) ATLAS
(MOTHER OF —) PLEIONE
(SON OF —) EUROTAS
LACEDAEMON
TAYRA GALERA
TCHAMBULI CHAMBERI
TEA CHA CHAR CHIA TCHA THAM
TSIA ASSAM CAPER CHAIS CONGO
FAHAM HYSON MIANG PEKOE
STEEP CONGOU KEEMUN OOLONG
PTISAN SUNGLO LAPSANG
REDROOT TWANKAY AUTUMNAL
GOWIDDIE SOUCHONG
WORMSEED
(AFRICAN —) CAT KAT QAT KHAT
QUAT
(BLACK —) BOHEA CONGO OOPAK
CONGOU OOPACK SYCHEE
(COARSE —) BANCHA
(HIGH-GRADE —) GYOKURO
(INFERIOR —) BOHEA
(MEDICINAL —) TISANE
(MEXICAN —) BASOTE APASOTE
(POOR —) BLASH
(PREF.) THEI
TEA BOWL CHAWAN
TEACAKE LUNN SCONE
TEACH ARAL LEAR READ SHOW
TECH TENT BREED CARRY COACH
EDIFY ENDUE LEARN SPELL TRAIN
TUTOR WISSE INFORM PREACH
SCHOOL BITECHE EDUCATE
EXAMPLE EXPOUND GRAMMAR
AMAISTER DISCIPLE DOCUMENT
INSTRUCT PUPILIZE
(— TO FIGHT) SPAR
TEACHABLE APT DOCILE DOCIBLE
TEACHABLENESS DOCITY
DOSSETY
TEACHER RAB ALIM GURU AKHUN
BIDDY CADET GUIDE MOLLA
RABBI REBBE TUTOR USHER
AKHUND AMAUTA DOCENT
DOCTOR DOZENT FATHER
MADRIH MAULVI MENTOR
MULLAH PANDIT PUNDIT RABBAN
READER REGENT RHETOR SUPPLY
ACHARYA ALFAQUI DOMINIE
MAESTRA MAESTRO MOOLVIE

MUNCHEE MURSHID PEDAGOG
SHASTRI SOPHIST SPONSOR
STARETS TRAINER ALFAQUIN
AYUDANTE DIRECTOR EDUCATOR
EXTENDER GAMALIEL MAGISTER
MELAMMED MISTRESS
MOONSHEE MUJTAHID
MAHARISHI PEDAGOGUE
PRECEPTOR ABECEDARIAN
PRIVATDOCENT
(— OF ELOQUENCE) RHETOR
(— OF EMINENCE) MAESTRO
(— OF HIGH LEARNING) SOPHIST
(— OF KORAN) ALFAKI ALFAQUIN
(— OF PAUL) GAMALIEL
(INCA —) AMAUTA
(MOHAMMEDAN —) COJA HODJA
KHOJA KHOJAH
TEACHING LAW DHARMA DOCENT
LESSON LORING ACROAMA
TUITION BUDDHISM DIDACTIC
DOCTRINE DOCUMENT TUTELAGE
(PL.) ACOUSMA BROWNISM
CACODOXY DIDACTICS
TEAK SAJ DJATI EBONY
TEAKETTLE SUKE SUKEY CHAFER
KETTLE POURIE CRESSET
TEAL CRICK BLUEWING GARGANEY
SARCELLE
TEAM SET FIVE PLOW SIDE SPAN
YOKE DRAFT SWING EQUIPE
PLOUGH SEXTET DRAUGHT
CARTWARE
(— HARNESSED ONE BEFORE
ANOTHER) TANDEM
(— OF CARS) ECURIE
(— OF GLASSWORKERS) SHOP
CHAIR
(— OF 3 HORSES ABREAST) TROIKA
(— THAT FINISHES LAST) DOORMAT
(— 2 ABREAST, 1 LEADING) SPIKE
UNICORN
(ATHLETIC —) CLUB
(BASEBALL —) NINE
(BASKETBALL —) FIVE
(FOOTBALL —) ELEVEN
(2-HORSE —) PODANGER
(3-HORSE —) RANDEM
TEAMSTER CARTER TEAMEO
CARTMAN SKINNER TEAMMAN
TEAPOT TRACK TRACKPOT
TEAR RIP RIT RUG TUT CLAW PILL
PULL RACE RASE RASH RAVE
REND RIVE RUGG SKAG SNAG
STUN BREAK CLAUT LARME
PEARL RANCH SHARK SLENT
SPALT SPLIT TOUSE CLEAVE
HARROW RANCHE RIPPLE SCHISM
SCREED WRENCH CHATTER
CONVELL DISCIND EYEDROP
SCRATCH DISTRAIN FRACTURE
LACERATE LACHRYMA TEARDROP
(— APART) REND TEASE DISCERP
DIVULSE
(— ASUNDER) DIVEL
(— AWAY) AVULSE
(— DOWN) UNPILE DESTROY
DEMOLISH
(— IN NEGATIVE) SLUG
(— INTO) LAMBAST LAMBASTE
(— INTO PIECES) DRAW TOLE
DEVIL SHRED TEASE LANIATE
MAMMOCK

(— INTO SHREDS) HOG DEVIL
TATTER
(— OFF) STRIP ABRUPT DISCERP
(— OPEN) PROSCIND
(— UP BY THE ROOTS) ARACHE
(PL.) DEW BRINE RHEUM
EYEWATER
(PREF.) DACRY(O) LACHRYMI
LACHRYMO SPARASSO
TEARDROP EYEWATER
TEARFUL SOFT TEARY WEEPY
LIQUID WATERY WEEPLY FLEBILE
MAUDLIN SHOWERY SNIVELY
SNIVELLY
TEARING SCREED
(— AWAY) AVULSION
TEARPIT CRUMEN LARMIER
TEASE COD FUN MAD RAG RIB ROT
TAR TRY TUM VEX BAIT CHIP
DRAG FASH FRET GRIG HARE
HOCK JADE JIVE JOSH LARK
NARK RAZZ SOOL TARR TOUT
WORK CHAFF CHEEK CHEVY
CHIAK CHYAK DEVIL FEEZE RALLY
TARIE TAUNT TOOSE WRACK
BANTER BOTHER CADDLE CHIVVY
HARASS HOORAY HURRAH
MOLEST MURDER NEEDLE PESTER
PLAGUE HATCHEL TERRIFY
TORMENT WHERRET
TEASEL KING TASSEL TEASLE
MANWEED
TEASELER GIGGER TEASER
TEASELING MOZING
TEASER TIZEUR
TEASING CHAFF MERRY BANTER
DEVILING QUIZZING
TEAT DUG PAP TIT DIDDY SPEAN
NIPPLE SUCKLE
TEA TREE TI MANUKA
TEBAH (FATHER OF —) NAHOR
TEBALIAH (FATHER OF —) HOSAH
TECHNICIAN SWITCHER
TECHNIQUE FEAT GATE WRINKLE
COQUILLE INDUSTRY SPICCATO
(BILLIARD —) FOLLOW
(DANCE —) HEELWORK
(DECORATION —) IKAT
(DRAMATIC —) METHOD
(JUMPING —) SCISSORS
(WRESTLING —) GLIMA
(WRITING —) CUBISM
(SUFF.) URGE URGIC URGY
TECHNOLOGY FISHERY TECHNIC
CERAMICS
TECMESSA (FATHER OF —)
TELEUTAS
(HUSBAND OF —) AJAX
(SON OF —) EURYSACES
TECOMIN LAPACHOL
TECTRIX COVERT
TEDDER KICKER
TEDIOUS DEAD DREE DULL LATE
POKY PROSY WEARY ALENGE
BORING DREECH DREIGH ELENGE
MORTAL PROLIX STODGY
IRKSOME OPEROSE PREACHY
PROSAIC VERBOSE BORESOME
DRAGGING TIRESOME WEARIFUL
TEDIUM IRK YAWN ENNUI
BOREDOM
TEE COCK TIGHT TOZEE WITTER
BULLHEAD

TEEM SNY FLOW SWIM SWARM ABOUND BUSTLE SCRAWL PULLULATE
TEEMER SHOOTMAN
TEEMING BIG ALIVE TUMID FERTILE GUSHING TEEMFUL ABUNDANT BRAWLING PREGNANT SWARMING
TEENAGER TEENY TEENYBOPPER
TEENY SMALL
TEESWATER MUGS MUGGS
TEETER ROCK WAVER JIGGLE QUIVER SEESAW WOBBLE TREMBLE
TEETH CTENII CHOPPERS CRACKERS GRINDERS
(HAVING —) IVORIED
(PETRIFIED —) BUFONITE
(SET OF —) DENTURE
(PREF.) DENT(ATO)(I)(INO)(O)
(SUFF.) ODON
TEETHRIDGE ALVEOLE ALVEOLUS
TEETOTUM TOTUM WHIRLIGIG
TEGETICULA PRONUBA
TEGMENTUM ROOF
TEGULA SQUAMA EPAULET SCAPULA PATAGIUM SQUAMULA
TEGUMENT COAT TEGMEN
TEHUELCHE PATAGON
TEJU TEIOID JACUARU TEGUEXIN
TELAMON ATLAS
(BROTHER OF —) PELEUS
(FATHER OF —) AEACUS
(MOTHER OF —) ENDEIS
(SON OF —) AJAX TEUCER
(WIFE OF —) GLAUCE HESIONE
TELAMONES ATLANTES
TELEDU BADGER STINKARD
TELEGONUS (FATHER OF —) ULYSSES
(MOTHER OF —) CIRCE
(SON OF —) ITALUS
(WIFE OF —) PENELOPE
TELEGRAM TAR WIRE FLASH FLIMSY
TELEGRAPH WIRE CABLE BUZZER TELEGRAM TELOTYPE
TELEMACHUS (FATHER OF —) ULYSSES
(MOTHER OF —) PENELOPE
(SON OF —) LATINUS
TELENCEPHALON ENDBRAIN
TELEOLOGICAL TELIC FINALIST
TELEOLOGY FINALITY
TELEPHASSA (DAUGHTER OF —) EUROPA
(HUSBAND OF —) AGENOR
(SON OF —) CADMUS PHOENIX
TELEPHONE RING PHONE HANDSET
(PART OF —) PAD BASE CORD DIAL HOLE STOP PLATE CRADLE HANDLE HANDSET PLUNGER SPEAKER EARPIECE RECEIVER MOUTHPIECE TRANSMITTER
TELEPHOTE DIAPHOTE
TELEPHUS (FATHER OF —) HERCULES
(MOTHER OF —) AUGE
(WIFE OF —) ARGIOPE LAODICE ASTYOCHE
TELEPRINTER CREED
TELESCOPE TUBE COUDE GLASS

SCOPE TRUNK ALINER FINDER SECTOR ALIGNER BINOCLE TRANSIT PROSPECT SPYGLASS REFRACTOR PERSPECTIVE
(PART OF —) LEG CELL LENS TUBE CLAMP GUIDE MOUNT SCOPE CRADLE DEWCAP SLEEVE TRIPOD DIAGONAL DRAWTUBE EYEPIECE MOUNTING SUNSHADE VIEWFINDER
(SURVEYOR'S —) LEVEL
TELEVISION TV AIR TELLY
(— SET) BOX TUBE BOOBTUBE
TELIOSPORE TELEUTO
TELL SAY DEEM MAKE MEAN MOOT READ SHOW TALE AREAD AREED BREAK BREVE COUNT NEVEN PITCH SPELL STORY TEACH UTTER AUTHOR DEVISE IMPART INFORM MUSTER QUETHE RECITE RELATE REPEAT REPORT REVEAL CONFESS DIVULGE NARRATE PARTAKE RECOUNT ACQUAINT REHEARSE
(— CONFIDENTIALLY) CONFIDE
(— CONFUSEDLY) SPLATHER
(— EARNESTLY) ASSURE
(— IN ADVANCE) FORESAY
(— LIES) BELY LIGE BELIE
(— OFF) JAR
(— ROMANCES) GEST GESTE
(— SECRETS) CHEEP CLYPE SPILL BABBLE
(— STRIKINGLY) CRACK
(— TALES) BLAB CANT PEACH
TELLER SPINNER STORIER TALLIER FABLEIST FABULIST SENACHIE
TELLING REDE PUNGENT POWERFUL STINGING
(— OF SECRETS) BLAB
TELLTALE CLASH TATTLER TITTLER REGISTER
TELLURIDE ALTAITE
TELSON PLEON
TELUGU GENTU GENTOO TELINGA
TEM TUM ATMU ATUM
TEMA (FATHER OF —) ISHMAEL
TEMAN (FATHER OF —) ELIPHAZ
(MOTHER OF —) ADAH
TEMENI (FATHER OF —) ASHUR
(MOTHER OF —) NAARAH
TEMERITY GALL CHEEK NERVE AUDACITY RASHNESS
TEMPER CUE MAD BAIT BATE COOL DASH DRAW MOOD MULL NEAL PADD SCOT TONE ALLOY BIRSE BLOOD CREST DELAY FRAME GRAIN HUMOR IRISH SAUCE SOBER TRAMP ADJUST ANIMUS ANNEAL DANDER MASTER MONKEY SEASON SPIRIT SPLEEN STRAIN SUBMIT CHASTEN CLIMATE COURAGE HACKLES QUALIFY STOMACH EBENEZER GRADUATE MITIGATE MODERATE MOORBURN
(— CLAY) TAMPER
(— METAL) ALLAY
(— OF MIND) CUE SPIRIT
(CAPRICIOUS —) SPLEEN
TEMPERAMENT BLOOD GEMUT HEART HUMOR CRASIS KIDNEY NATURE TEMPER

STOMACH SANGUINE
TEMPERAMENTAL FITIFIED
TEMPERANCE MEDIETY SOBRIETY
TEMPERATE CALM COOL MILD SOFT GREEN SOBER STEADY TEMPRE MODERATE ORDINATE ABSTINENT CONTINENT ABSTEMIOUS
TEMPERATURE SUN HEAT TEMP HOTNESS DEWPOINT
(— FACTOR) WINDCHILL
(— UNIT) KELVIN
TEMPERED HARD MILD SOBER SARCENET
TEMPERING MODULATION
TEMPEST GALE THUD WIND ORAGE STORM TUMULT TORMENT TURMOIL WEATHER
(AUTHOR OF —) SHAKESPEARE
(CHARACTER IN —) IRIS JUNO ARIEL CERES ADRIAN ALONSO ANTONIO CALIBAN GONZALO MIRANDA TINCULO PROSPERO STEPHANO FERDINAND FRANCISCO SEBASTIAN
TEMPESTUOUS WILD GUSTY STERN WINDY RUGGED STORMY VIOLENT STALWART
TEMPLATE CURB NORMA TEMPLET PADSTONE STRICKLE
TEMPLE VAT WAT DEUL FANE NAOS RATH CANDI GUACA HUACA KIACK KOVIL MARAE RATHA CHANDI HAFFET HERION MANDIR SACRUM SHRINE TEOPAN TJANDI VIHARA HERAEUM HERAION TEMPLET TEMPLUM VARELLA OLYMPIUM PANTHEON RAMESEUM TEOCALLI VALHALLA PARTHENON
(— AREA) MANDAPA
(CAVE —) SPEOS
(FIJI —) BURE
(HAWAIIAN —) HEIAU
(PART OF —) PRONAOS
(SHINTO —) SHA JINJA JINSHA YASHIRO
(STUDY OF —S) NAOLOGY
(TOWERLIKE —) ZIGGURAT
(PREF.) NAO
TEMPLES
(PREF.) TEMPORO
TEMPLET FORMER STRICKLE
TEMPO TAKT TIME AGOGE MOVEMENT
TEMPORAL CIVIL CARNAL TIMELY EARTHLY PROFANE SECULAR
TEMPORARY FLYING INTERIM STOPGAP WHILEND EPISODAL EPISODIC TEMPORAL PROVISIONAL
(PREF.) PSEUD(O)
TEMPORIZER DRIFTER POLITIC
TEMPT EGG FAND FOND LURE TEMP TENT ASSAY COURT ALLURE ASSAIL ENTICE INVITE SEDUCE ASSAULT ATTEMPT SOLICIT SUGGEST
TEMPTATION TRIAL ATTEMPT TESTING SEDUCTION
TEMPTER DEVIL
TEMPTING ALLURING INVITING
TEMPTRESS SIREN DELILAH

TEN ICRE IOTA CHANG DIKER CHEUNG DECADE DENARY DICKER ARTICLE BRISQUE
(— OF TRUMPS) GAME
(PREF.) DEC(A)(I)(U) DECEM DEK(A)
(SUFF.) TY
TEN'A KOYUKON
TENACE FORK
TENACIOUS FAST ROPEY STIFF TOUGH CLAGGY CLEDGY DOGGED GRIPPY PLUGGY STICKY STRONG VISCID GRIPPLE ADHESIVE GRASPING HOLDFAST PERTINACIOUS
TENACIOUSNESS TENACY FASTNESS
TENACITY LENTOR COURAGE
TENACULUM CLASP
TENANCY CONACRE JOINTURE
TENANT KMET LEUD SAER BARON CEILE DRENG LAIRD BORDAR COTTAR COTTER DRENGH GENEAT HOLDER INMATE LESSEE MOLMAN RADMAN RENTER SOCMAN VASSAL CHAKDAR COTTIER FEODARY FEUDARY GAVELER HOMAGER SOCAGER SOKEMAN VAVASOR COLIBERT CUSTOMER SERGEANT SUCKENER
(LIFE —) LIVIER LIVEYER
(NEW —) INCOME INCOMER
TENCH CYPRINID
TEN COMMANDMENTS DECALOG
TEND HOP NOD RUN SET WRY BABY BEND DRAW GROW KEEP MAKE MIND MOVE TENT DRESS GROOM NURSE TENOR SOUND TREND VERGE WATCH AFFECT GOVERN INTEND CHERISH CONDUCE DECLINE INCLINE PROPEND
(— A FIRE) STOKE
(— IN A CERTAIN DIRECTION) LEAD
(— TO ONE POINT) CONVERGE
(— TOWARD) AFFECT
(— WHILE AT PASTURE) GRAZE
TENDENCY SET BENT BIAS HAND TONE VEIN DRAFT DRIFT DRIVE HABIT KNACK TENOR TREND TWIST ANIMUS COURSE EONISM GENIUS MOTION APTNESS CONATUS DRAUGHT IMPULSE LEANING NITENCY SAMKARA APTITUDE INSTINCT STEERING VERGENCY
(— IN NATURE) KIND
(— TO APPROACH) ADIENCE
(— TO STICK TOGETHER) CLANSHIP
(— TO WITHDRAW) ABIENCE
(— TO WRATH) TIDE
(SUFF.) (— TOWARD) PHIL(A)(AE) (E)(IA)(ISM)(IST)(OUS)(US)(Y)
TENDER RAW TID BEAR COCK FINE FOND FRIM FRUM KIND NESH SOFT SORE TAKE TART TENT WARM CAGER OFFER DEFER FRAIL GREEN MUSHY OFFER PAPPY DELATE DRIVER GENTLE GIMPER GINGER HUMANE LOVELY RAISER SILKEN ADVANCE AMABILE AMOROSO AMOROUS CONCHER CRAMPER FLESHLY MASHMAN

OBLATIO PATACHE PINNACE
PITEOUS PITIFUL PORRECT
PROFFER RUTHFUL STENTER
CAMELEER COCKBOAT EFFETMAN
FEMININE HEATSMAN HERDSMAN
LADYLIKE MERCIFUL MORTISER
SPREADER
(PREF.) ABRO HABRO
TENDERFOOT DUDE INNOCENT
TENDERHEARTED HUMAN PITIFUL
TENDERIZER PAPAIN
TENDERLOIN FILET PSOAS FILLET
UNDERCUT
TENDERLY FONDLY GENTLY
AMOROSO
TENDERNESS CHERTE TENDER
DELICACY FONDNESS KINDNESS
SYMPATHY TENERITY YEARNING
(— OF FEELING) FLESH
TENDING
(SUFF.) CLINIC CLINOUS
(— TO) ABLE ATIVE ATORY BOND
BUND CUND FUL IBLE
TENDINOUS SINEWY
TENDON CORD TAIL CHORD NERVE
SINEW TENON LEADER PAXWAX
STRING
(PREF.) TENO
TENDRIL CURL CLASP CROOK
TWIST CIRRUS WINDER CAPREOL
CIRRHUS CLASPER TENTACLE
(PREF.) PAMPINI PAMPINO
TENEMENT LAND RENT TACK
CHAWL DECKER LIVING WARREN
HOLDING LETTING ROOKERY
BUILDING PRAEDIUM
TENES (FATHER OF —) CYNCUS
(MOTHER OF —) PROCLEA
PHILONOME
(SISTER OF —) HEMITHEA
(SLAYER OF —) ACHILLES
TENET ADOXY CREDO CREED
DOGMA BELIEF GNOMON
HOLDING MISHNAH PARADOX
DOCTRINE
(PL.) FAITH FAMILISM
TENFOLD DENARY DECUPLE
TENNANTITE FAHLERZ FAHLORE
TENNE TAWNY ORANGE HYACINTH

TENNESSEE

CAPITAL: NASHVILLE
COLLEGE: FISK LANE SIENA
BETHEL BELMONT LAMBUTH
LEMOYNE MILLIGAN TUSCULUM
VANDERBILT
COUNTY: DYER KNOX RHEA COCKE
GILES HENRY MEIGS OBION
COFFEE GRUNDY MCMINN
SEVIER UNICOI BLEDSOE
FENTRESS
DAM: WILSON WHEELER
INDIAN: SHAWNEE CHEROKEE
CHICKASAW
LAKE: DOUGLAS CHEROKEE
REELFOOT WATTSBAR
MOUNTAIN: GUYOT LOOKOUT
MOUNTAIN RANGE: SMOKY
NATIONAL PARK: SHILOH
NATIVE: WHELP
NICKNAME: VOLUNTEER
PRESIDENT: POLK JACKSON
RIVER: ELK DUCK CANEY HOLSTON

HIWASSEE CUMBERLAND
STATE BIRD: MOCKINGBIRD
STATE FLOWER: IRIS
STATE TREE: POPLAR
TOWN: ERIN ALAMO ALCOA
ERWIN PARIS CAMDEN CELINA
JASPER SELMER SPARTA
BOLIVAR DICKSON JACKSON
MEMPHIS PULASKI GALLATIN
KNOXVILLE CHATTANOOGA

TENNIS (— SHOT) LET LOB DINK
(ANCIENT —) BANDY
TENON COG PIN COAK STUB TUSK
LEWIS TOOTH TABLING DOVETAIL
LEWISSON
TENOR PES FECK TONE VEIN
COURSE EFFECT TAILLE TENURE
CURRENT PURPORT STRENGTH
TENDENCY TENORINO
TENOROON FAGOTTINO
TENOR VIOL VIOLET
TENOR VIOLIN ALTO
TENPINS BOWLS NEWPORT
TENPOUNDER AWA CHIRO
MACABI BONEFISH BONYFISH
LADYFISH SKIPJACK SPRINGER
TENREC TANGUE CENTETES
CENTETID HEDGEHOG HEDGEPIG
TENSE EDGY RAPT TAUT STIFF
AORIST CORDED FLINCH FUTURE
INTENT NARROW STRAIT STRICT
BRITTLE INTENSE PRIMARY
FRENETIC PRETERIT SYNTONIC
TENSION BENT HEAT DRIVE STEAM
SATTVA SPRING STRAIN STRESS
TROPPO BALANCE STRAINT
TENSURE ISOTONIA
TENT AUL TOP HALE PAWL TAWN
TELD TILT CABIN CRAME LODGE
TOPEK TUPIK CANNAT CANVAS
DOSSIL SEARCH WIGWAM
BALAGAN CABINET KIBITKA
MARQUEE SPARVER TABERNA
TENTLET TENTORY ZDARSKY
PAVILION SHAMIANA TENTICLE
TENTWORK SHOOLDARRY
(— FOR WOUNDS) PENICIL
(— WHERE GOODS ARE SOLD)
CRAME
(CIRCULAR —) YURT YOURT YURTA
KIBITKA
(INDIAN —) TEPEE WIGWAM
(SAMOYED —) CHUM
(SOUTH AMERICAN —) TOLDO
TENTACLE HORN SAIL PACLE
FEELER BRACHIUM
TENTATIVE GINGERLY
TENT CATERPILLAR WEBWORM
TENTERER RACKER RATCHER
TENTH DIME DISME TITHE DECIMA
(— OF CENT) MILL
(— OF LINE) GRY
(PREF.) DECI
TEN THOUSAND
(PREF.) MYRIA MYRIO
TENUITY EXILITY DELICACY
TENUOUS FILMY FOGGY FRAIL
SUBTLE TENDER FRAGILE
GASEOUS SLENDER SUBTILE
ETHEREAL GOSSAMER
(TOO —) FINESPUN
TENUOUSNESS FRAILTY

TENURE FEU SORN TACK TAKE
TERM GAVEL JAGIR BARONY
CAPITE JAGHIR RUNRIG SOCAGE
SORREN ALMOIGN BONDAGE
BORDAGE BURGAGE CENSIVE
CORNAGE CURTESY FARMAGE
JAGHEER SOCCAGE SOREHON
COPYHOLD DRENGAGE FREEHOLD
OVERLAND SOCMANRY SUITHOLD
VAVASORY VENVILLE
TEPEE CHUM TENT TIPI HOGAN
LODGE TEEPEE WICKIUP
TEPHROSIA CRACCA
TEPID LEW WARM WLACH WLECH
LUKEWARM
TEQUISLATEC CHONTAL
TERAH (SON OF —) HARAN NAHOR
ABRAHAM
TERATOMA EMBRYOMA
TERCET TRISTICH
TEREBINTH TEIL TURPENTINE
TEREDO BORER WOODWORM
TERENTIA (HUSBAND OF —) CICERO
TERETE CENTRIC
TEREUS (FATHER OF —) MARS
(SON OF —) ITYS
(WIFE OF —) PROCNE
TERGITE TERGUM PYGIDIUM
TERGIVERSATION DECEIT
TERGUM PYGIDIUM
TERM HALF NAME NOME WORD
LEASE RHEMA SPEAK STYLE
TRYST ABBACY GNOMON HILARY
NOTION PARODY EPITHET
EXTREME SESSION SUBJECT
SUMMAND TERMINE VOCABLE
EQUIVOKE HEADWORD
MAHALATH POCHISMO SEMESTER
TERMTIME
(— IN JAIL) JOLT
(— IN LOGIC) CONSTANT
(— OF ABUSE) CUSSWORD
(— OF ADDRESS) SIRRAH
MADONNA
(— OF CONTEMPT) SLIPE PILCHER
TITIVIL
(— OF DEFERENCE) AHUNG
(— OF ENDEARMENT) ASTOR
CHUCK COCKY HONEY MOPSY
ASTHORE MACHREE STOREEN
POSSODIE POWSOWDY
(— OF IMPRISONMENT) LAG
LAGGING STRETCH
(— OF PUNISHMENT) JOB
(— OF RATIO) EXTREME
(— OF REPROACH) GIB BESOM
MINGO RONYON
(— OF SYLLOGISM) EXTREME
ARGUMENT
(ARITHMETICAL —) NOME
GNOMON
(HYPHENED —) COMPOUND
(LITERAL —S) LETTER
(SOCIAL —S) FOOTING
(UNIVERSAL —) CONCEPT
(PL.) LAY MEANS
(PREF.) HORO
TERMAGANT JADE RUDAS SHREW
VIXEN VIRAGO
TERMINABLE FINITE
TERMINAL JACK LAST POLE
ANODE DEPOT IMPUT INPUT
MUCRO CATHODE

POTHEAD DESINENT
TERMINATE CUT END ABUT CALL
HALT KILL ABORT BLEED CEASE
CLOSE ISSUE LAPSE EXPIRE
FINISH FOREDO RESULT INCLUDE
TERMINE COMPLETE CONCLUDE
DISSOLVE
(— A SESSION) PROROGUE
TERMINATED EXPIATE
TERMINATING FINAL
(— ABRUPTLY) BLIND
(SUDDENLY —) ABRUPT
TERMINATION END ISH DATE
TERM ABORT CLOSE EVENT ISSUE
ENDING EXITUS EXPIRY FINALE
PERIOD UPSHOT TERMINUS
(— OF CHURCH CHOIR) CHEVET
(— OF FURNITURE LEGS) FOOT
(— OF RIGHT) LAPSE
TERMINATIVE FINITIVE
TERMINOLOGY JARGON
TERMINUS END FLAT
(— IN FINGERPRINT) DELTA
(— OF PERIOD) TIME
TERMITE ANAI ANAY KING NASUTE
WORKER POLILLA
TERMITOPHILE SYMPHILE
TERN KIP DARR INCA LARI NOIO
PIRL PIRR RIXY LARID NODDY
PEARL SCRAY SKEER SKIRR STERN
CHIRRE KERMEW PICKET
GOELAND MEDRICK PIRRMAW
RITTOCK SCURRIT SEAFOWL
STRIKER TARRACK TERNLET
MANUSINA SPARLING TIRRACKE
TERPENE CARENE PINENE
BORNANE SANTENE THUJENE
CAMPHENE FENCHENE LIMONENE
NOPINENE
TERRA GE GAEA TELLUS
(DAUGHTER OF —) RHEA THEA
PHOEBE TETHYS THEMIS
MNEMOSYNE
(HUSBAND OF —) URANUS
(SON OF —) OCEANUS
TERRACE POY DAIS PNYX STEP
XYST BEACH BENCH HEIAU LINCH
OFFSET PERRON LINCHET
BARBETTE CHABUTRA
(LOUNGING —) LANAI
(NATURAL —) MESA
TERRA JAPONICA GAMBIR
GAMBIER
TERRAPENE CISTUDO
TERRAPIN EMYD COUNT COODLE
POTTER SLIDER TURPIN TURTLE
EMYDIAN FEUILLE SKILPOT
REDBELLY TORTOISE
(FEMALE —) HEIFER
(MALE —) BULL
TERRARIUM VIVARIUM
TERRELLA EARTHKIN
TERRENE EARTHLY
TERRESTRIAL EARTHY EARTHLY
TERRENE PLANETAL SUBLUNAR
SUBSOLAR TELLURIC PLANETARY
SUBASTRAL
TERRET CRINGLE
TERRIBLE DIRE UGLY AWFUL
GHAST LURID DEADLY PRETTY
TARBLE TRAGIC TURBLE CHRONIC
DIREFUL FEARFUL FERDFUL
GHASTLY HIDEOUS ALMIGHTY

BHAIRAVA FLEYSOME HORRIBLE TERRIFIC TIMOROUS TRAGICAL (PREF.) DEIN(O) DIN(O)

TERRIBLY FELLY FIERCE GRISLY CONSARN

TERRIER SKYE LHASA SILKY BOSTON DANDIE RATTER SCOTTY DIEHARD SCOTTIE ABERDEEN AIREDALE RATTONER SEALYHAM VERMINER WIREHAIR

TERRIFIC FINE SWEET GORGON FEARFUL GORGEOUS

TERRIFIED AFRAID AGHAST GHASTLY

TERRIFY AWE COW HAG BREE DARE FEAR FLAY FLEY APPAL DREAD GALLY SCARE ADREAD AFFRAY AGRISE AWHAPE DISMAY FLIGHT FREEZE FRIGHTEN

TERRIFYING GHASTLY HIDEOUS FLEYSOME TERRIBLE

TERRITORIALISM ITOISM

TERRITORY FEE GOA HAN SOC AREA MARK PALE SOKE BANAT DUCHY FIELD MARCH STATE TUATH BORDER COLONY DOMAIN EMPERY EMPIRE GROUND APANAGE CONFINE COUNTRY DEMESNE DUKEDOM EARLDOM ENCLAVE EPARCHY REGENCY SATRAPY APPANAGE CASTLERY CONFINES CONQUEST DISTRICT DOMINION IMPERIUM LIGEANCE LUCUMONY PARMESAN PASHALIK REGALITY SEIGNORY (MONASTIC —) ABTHANE

TERROR AWE FEAR FRAY ALARM APPAL DREAD PANIC AFFRAY ALARUM APPALL FRIGHT HORROR DRIDDER AFFRIGHT DREDDOUR SURPRISE

TERRORISM NIHILISM

TERRORIST GOONDA ALARMIST SICARIUS

TERRORIZE FRIGHTEN

TERROR-STRICKEN AWFUL

TERSE CURT SINEWY COMPACT CONCISE LACONIC POINTED SUMMARY UNWORDY SUCCINCT

TERSENESS BREVITY LACONISM

TERTIARY NEOZOIC PALAEIC

TESSELLATED MOSAIC

TESSELLATION AREOLE

TESSERA TILETTE ABACULUS TESSELLA

TESS OF DURBERVILLES (AUTHOR OF —) HARDY
(CHARACTER IN —) ALEC JACK TESS ANGEL CLARE DURBERVILLE DURBEYFIELD

TEST CON SAY TRY FAND FEEL FOND TASK TENT ASSAY AVENA CANON CHECK ESSAY GROPE ISSUE PROBE PROOF PROVE SENSE SOUND TASTE TEMPT TESTA TOUCH TRIAL SAMPLE TIENTA APPROOF APPROVE AUSSAGE CONTROL EXAMINE GANTLET PLUMMET TESTATE BIOASSAY EXERCISE GAUNTLET SEROLOGY STANDARD
(— CHEESE) PALE
(— EGGS) CANDLE

(— FOR WEIGHT AND FINENESS) PYX
(— GROUND) BOSE
(— OF COURAGE) SCRATCH
(— OF CRINOID) CALYX
(— OF GUILT) CORSNED
(— OF ORE) VAN
(SEVERE —) CRUCIBLE
(SYPHILIS —) KOLMER
(PREF.) DOCIMO OECO
(SUFF.) OECA OECIA

TESTA TEST LORICA EPISPERM

TESTACEOUS SHELLY

TESTAMENT TEST QUETHE WITWORD COVENANT

TESTAR TETARD

TESTATOR LEGATOR

TESTED FIRED TRIED WEIGHED

TESTER TRIER CONNER PROVER SPARVER DENIERER TESTIERE
(BUTTER —) SEARCHER

TESTES (SUFF.) ORCHISM

TESTICLE STONE BALLOCK DIDYMUS GENITOR
(PREF.) ORCHI(O) ORCHID(O) ORCHO

TESTICLES (SUFF.) ORCHISM

TESTIFY SPEAK SWEAR AFFIRM DEPONE DEPOSE WITTEN WITNESS EVIDENCE
(— FALSELY) MOUNT
(— TO) BESPEAK

TESTIMONIAL CHIT SCROLL CHARACTER

TESTIMONY TEST ATTEST AVOUCH PROBATE TESTATE TESTIFY WITNESS EVIDENCE

TESTING ASSAY CRUCIAL SHAKEDOWN

TESTIS BALL GONAD STONE BALLOCK CULLION KNOCKER SPERMARY
(PL.) COBS CODS COJONES DOWSETS

TEST TUBE PROOF TESTER PROBATE

TESTUDINATA CHELONIA

TESTUDO SNAIL GALAPAGO TORTOISE

TESTY DONCY MUSTY TUTTY DONSIE PATCHY SPUNKY PEEVISH TETTISH TOUSTIE WASPISH SNAPPISH

TETANIC SPASTIC

TETANUS LOCKJAW HOLOTONY

TETE-A-TETE TWOSOME CAUSEUSE

TETHER BAND LEASH STAKE PICKET TEDDER TOGGLE PASTERN CABESTRO
(— A HAWK) WEATHER

TETHYS APLYSIA
(DAUGHTERS OF —) OCEANIDES
(FATHER OF —) URANUS
(HUSBAND OF —) OCEANUS
(MOTHER OF —) TERRA

TETHYUM CYNTHIA

TETRA- (PREF.) QUATER

TETRACHORD GENUS HYPATON LICHANOS

TETRACTYS TETRAD

TETRAD FOURFOLD

TETRADRACHMA OWL

TETRAGONAL DIMETRIC

TETRAHEDRITE FAHLERZ FAHLORE PANABASE

TETRAHEXAHEDRON FLUOROID

TETRAHYDRIDE GERMANE STANNANE

TETRASACCHARIDE LUPEOSE

TETTER DARTRE

TETTIX ACRYDIUM

TEUCER (DAUGHTER OF —) ASTERIA
(FATHER OF —) TELAMON SCAMANDER
(HALF-BROTHER OF —) AJAX
(MOTHER OF —) IDAEA HESIONE
(WIFE OF —) EUNE

TEUTON GOTH LOMBARD

TEUTONIC GOTHIC GERMANIC GOTHONIC

TEXAS

CAPITAL: AUSTIN
COLLEGE: SMU TCU RICE WILEY BAYLOR
COUNTY: BEE CASS COKE JACK REAL RUSK VEGA WEBB WISE BEXAR DELTA ECTOR ERATH GARZA RAINS FANNIN GOLIAD YOAKUM ZAPATA ZAVALA HIDALGO REFUGIO ATASCOSA
FORTRESS: ALAMO
INDIAN: LIPAN BILOXI KICHAI SHUMAN HASINAI COMANCHE TONKAWAN
LAKE: FALCON TEXOMA AMISTAD
MOUNTAIN: GUADALUPE
NATIVE: TEJANO
NICKNAME: LONESTAR
PRESIDENT: JOHNSON EISENHOWER
RIVER: RED PECOS BRAZOS NUECES TRINITY
STATE BIRD: MOCKINGBIRD
STATE FLOWER: BLUEBONNET
STATE TREE: PECAN
TOWN: GAIL VEGA WACO BRYAN MARFA OZONA PAMPA TYLER BORGER DALLAS DENTON ELPASO KILEEN LAREDO ODESSA QUANAH SONORA ABILENE HOUSTON LUBBOCK AMARILLO BEAUMONT FLOYDADA GALVESTON

TEXAS BUCKTHORN LOTEBUSH

TEXAS FEVER TRISTEZA

TEXT BODY MIQRA PLACE SAKHA TESTO PURANA SCRIPT SHAKHA TEXTUS TEXTLET ANTETHEM PERICOPE VARIORUM
(— OF ADVERTISEMENT) COPY
(— OF OPERA) LIBRETTO
(— SET TO MUSIC) ORATORIO
(REVISED —) RECENSION
(SHASTRA —) SRUTI SHRUTI

TEXTBOOK DUNCE TUTOR GENETICS

TEXTILE (ALSO SEE FABRIC) SABA STUFF GREIGE MOCKADO SAGURAN SINAMAY TEXTURE TIFFANY
(— MACHINE) WILLOW

(PL.) DRAPE

TEXTURE WEB BONE HAND KNIT WALE WOOF GRAIN COBWEB FABRIC WEFTAGE FRACTURE
(— OF SOAP) FIT

THADDEUS OF WARSAW
(AUTHOR OF —) PORTER
(CHARACTER IN —) MARY ROSS SARA DIANA BUTZOU ROBSON VINCENT BEAUFORT EUPHEMIA PEMBROKE SOBIESKI SOMERSET THADDEUS CAVENDISH KOSCIUSKO SACKVILLE TINEMOUTH CONSTANTINE

THAHASH (FATHER OF —) NAHOR
(MOTHER OF —) REUMAH

THAI LAO SIAMESE

THAILAND

CAPITAL: BANKOK BANGKOK
COIN: AT ATT BAHT FUANG TICAL PYNUNG SALUNG SATANG
FORMER NAME: SIAM
ISLAND: PHUKET
ISTHMUS: KRA
MEASURE: WA KEN NIV NMU RAI SAT SEN SOK WAH YOT KEUP NGAN TANG YOTE KWIEN LAANG SESTI TANAN KABIET KAMMEU CHAIMEU ROENENG CHANGAWN
MOUNTAIN: KHIEO MAELAMUN
MOUNTAIN RANGE: DAWNA BILAUKTAUNG
NATIVE: LAO THAI
PLAIN: KHORAT
RIVER: CHI NAN PING MENAM MEKONG MEPING
TOWN: UBON PUKET RANONG AYUDHYA AYUTHIA BANGKOK LOPBURI RAHAENG SINGORA SONGKLA KHONKAEN KIANGMAI THONBURI
WEIGHT: HAP PAI SEN SOK BAHT HAPH KLAM KLOM CATTY CHANG COYAN PILUL FLUANG SALUNG SOMPAY TAMLUNG

THAIS (CHARACTER IN —) THAIS ATHANAEL
(COMPOSER OF —) MASSENET

THAISA (FATHER OF —) SIMONIDES
(HUSBAND OF —) PERICLES

THALABA (WIFE OF —) ONEIZA

THALER DALER

THALLOGEN AMPHIGEN

THALLOID FRONDOSE

THALLUS FROND THALAMUS THAMNIUM

THAMNOPHIS EUTAENIA

THAMYRAS (FATHER OF —) PHILAMMON
(MOTHER OF —) ARGIOPE

THAN AS NA NE OR TO AND BUT NOR THEN TILL

THANE THEGN BANQUO GESITH ABTHAIN MACDUFF

THANK GRACE MERCY AGGRATE REGRACY REMERCY

THANKFUL GRATEFUL

THANKLESS INGRATE SLOWFUL

THANKS TA GRACE MERCI MERCY GRAMERCY

THANKSGIVING GLORY
DOXOLOGY
THANK-YOU-MA'AM CAHOT
THAT AS AT SE BUT HOW THE THO
WHO YAT LEST THAM THIK THON
WHAT YOND THICK THILK
THOUGH BECAUSE
(— IS TO SAY) NAMELY
(— ONE) ILLE
(— WHICH HAS TO BE PROVED)
IQED
(— YONDER) THON
THATCH NIPA DATCH SIRKI SIRKY
STING THRUM CADJAN
(— OVER BEEHIVE) HOOD
THATCHED THACK REEDED
THATCHER HELER CROWDER
HELLIER THACKER
THAUMAS (DAUGHTER OF —) IRIS
AELLO HARPY OCYPETE
(FATHER OF —) PONTUS NEPTUNE
(MOTHER OF —) GAEA TERRA
(WIFE OF —) ELECTRA
THAUMATURGIST
(PL.) GOETAE
THAUMATURGY MAGIC
THAW GIVE MELT FRESH UNTHAW
DEFROST
THE LA LE SE TA THI THAM THEY
YARE THERE
(PREF.) AL
THEA CAMELLIA
(FATHER OF —) URANUS
(HUSBAND OF —) HYPERION
(MOTHER OF —) TERRA
THEANO (FATHER OF —) CISSEUS
(HUSBAND OF —) ANTENOR
METAPONTUS
(MOTHER OF —) TELECLIA
(SISTER OF —) HECUBA
(SON OF —) ACAMAS AGENOR
POLYBUS HELICAON IPHIDAMAS
ARCHELOCHUS
THEATER CINE GAFF KINO CAVEA
HOUSE LEGIT ODEUM SCENE
STAGE CINEMA OZONER ADELPHI
COCKPIT GUIGNOL ORPHEUM
THEATRE BIOSCOPE COLISEUM
PANTHEON SHOWSHOP SPELLKEN
STRAWHAT THEATRON
PLAYHOUSE NICKELODEON
(NEIGHBORHOOD —) NABE
(PUPPET —) BUNRAKU
THEATRICAL CAMP HAMMY
STAGY DRAMATIC SCENICAL
SINGSONG
THEATRICALITY HAM PANACHE
THEBAN LAIUS NIOBE AMPHION
CADMEAN JOCASTA OEDIPUS
PENTHEUS
THEBE (FATHER OF —) ASOPUS
(HUSBAND OF —) ZETHUS
(MOTHER OF —) METOPE
(SISTER OF —) AEGINA
THECA CUP URN CELL VAGINA
CAPSULE PYXIDIUM VAGINULE
THEELIN ESTRONE FEMININ
OESTRIN
THEFT CRIB LIFT HEIST PINCH
SCORE STALE STEAL FURTUM
RIPOFF STOUTH BRIBERY
LARCENY MICHERY PICKING
PILFERY ROBBERY STEALTH

BURGLARY STEALAGE STEALING
(LITERARY —) PIRACY
(PETTY —) CRIB PICKERY
(PREF.) KLEPT(O)
(SUFF.) KLEPT
THEINE CAFFEINE
THEIR ARE HER ORE HORE YARE
THEIRS HERN THEIRN
THEM A EM HI UM HEM MUN
HEMEN
THEME DUX BASE IDEA TEMA TEXT
DITTY HOBBY LEMMA MOTIF
PLACE SCOPE TESTO THEMA
TOPIC URLAR MATTER MYTHOS
SUBJECT ANTETHEM
(— OF FUGUE) DUX
(HACKNEYED —) CLICHE
(MAIN —) BURDEN
(RECURRING —) BURDEN
(STOCK —) TOPOS
THEMIS (DAUGHTER OF —) DICE
IRENE EUNOMIA
(FATHER OF —) URANUS
(HUSBAND OF —) JUPITER
(MOTHER OF —) TERRA
THEMSELVES HEM HEMSELF
THEN SO AND POI THO ANON SYNE
THENCE AWAY THEN THEREFRO
THEOCRACY KHALSA
THEODELINDE (FATHER OF —)
GARIBALD
(HUSBAND OF —) AGO AUTHARI
THEODOLITE TAIPO DIOPTER
TRANSIT TRANSEPT
THEOLOGIAN FAQIH ULEMA
DIVINE MUJTAHID
AMERICAN BROWN HATCH NEVIN
SMITH TYLER WOODS BURTON
FOSTER MACHEN STUART
TAYLOR EDWARDS EVERETT
HOPKINS MCCLURE MOFFATT
NIEBUHR PEABODY VINCENT
MCGIFFERT WORCESTER
AUSTRIAN MOHR BRUNNER
DENIFLE JELLINEK
BELGIAN BAIUS
CZECH COMENIUS
DANISH MONRAD MULLER
MYNSTER PEDERSEN GRUNDTVIG
PONTOPPIDAN
DUTCH HAAR VOET WITS BEKKER
JANSEN KUENEN KUYPER
GOMARUS BOGERMAN LIMBORCH
SCHOLTEN EPISCOPIUS
ENGLISH BEDE BULL HORT OWEN
WARD BLUNT COLET HATCH
PALEY PUSEY SWETE WATTS
BUTLER FERRAR HARRIS HOOKER
NEWMAN PECOCK WESLEY
LANGTON MARBECK MAURICE
PEARSON WHATELY WHISTON
CARDWELL DRUMMOND
PELAGIUS WYCLIFFE CHADERTON
GUILLAUME LIGHTFOOT
STAPLETON WARBURTON
GROSSETESTE CHILLINWORTH
FRENCH BEZE GURY AILLY FAVRE
PAJON SIMON CALVIN GERSON
GLAIRE GOGUEL JURIEU PORREE
RICHER SORBON ABELARD
AMYRAUT BASNAGE BAUTAIN
BOCHART CHARRON QUESNEL
CASAUBON COURAYER SABATIER

CASTELLIO BOURDALOUE
LICHTENBERGER
LABERTHONNIERE
GERMAN ECK ESS ADAM ARND
BAUR DUHM EBER GASS HEIM
MERX RUPP ZAHN AMMON
BAUER BUDDE CALOV EMSER
FRANK GOEZE HAUCK HENKE
KNAPP KRAUS LANGE MAJOR
ROTHE STORR WALCH WEBER
WEISS ALSTED ANDREA BAHRDT
BENGEL CRAMER DALMAN DIPPEL
DORNER EBRARD FICKER GEIGER
HEILER HERMES HERZOG HEUSSI
HIRSCH MOHLER NATORP PEUCER
PLANCK REUSCH SEMLER SPENER
UHLICH ZELLER ZIMMER AGRIPPA
AMSDORF BOUSSET CASPARI
CRUSIUS ECKHART EHRHARD
ERNESTI FORSTER GERHARD
HAERING HARNACK HOFMANN
KOSTLIN LECHLER MOSHEIM
MUNSTER NAUMANN NEANDER
NIPPOLD RITSCHL STRAUSS
TILLICH ULLMANN URSINUS
WILHELM BULTMANN CALIXTUS
CANISIUS CHEMNITZ COCCEIUS
CRUCIGER DIBELIUS DILLMANN
EBERHARD EICHHORN FLIEDNER
GESENIUS HAUSRATH KAUTZSCH
KLIEFOTH MICHELIS MYCONIUS
OETINGER OSIANDER REIMARUS
SCHENKEL AURIFABER
BEYSCHLAG BUSEMBAUM
DELITZSCH DOLLINGER FABRICIUS
FREIDRICH JABLONSKI MICHAELIS
NIEMOLLER OLEVIANUS
OLSHAUSEN PFEIDERER
BAUMGARTEN MARHEINEKE
NEUMEISTER WISLICENUS
TISCHENDORF FROHSCHAMMER
BRETSCHNEIDER
SCHLEIERMACHER
GREEK ALLACCI CLEMENT
EUSEBIUS
HUNGARIAN BALLAGI
IRISH DODWELL PLUNKET
TYRRELL
ITALIAN OCHINO LOMBARD
PERRONE SOCINUS PASSAGLIA
JEWISH HIRSCH
NORWEGIAN MOE
SCOTTISH CAIRD EADIE ALESIUS
CAMERON ROLLOCK TULLOCH
CAMPBELL CHALMERS FAIRBAIRN
CUNNINGHAM RUTHERFORD
SPANISH CANO MOLINA SUAREZ
VALDES ENZINAS CARRANZA
EYMERICO SERVETUS
MALDONADO SEPULVEDA
SWEDISH FRYXELL SODERBLOM
FAHLCRANTZ
SWISS BARTH GODET VINET
ISELIN DIODATI ERASTUS
LECLERC BUCHMANN HEIDEGGER
SYRIAN AETIUS
THEOLOGY KALAM IRENICS
DIVINITY POIMENIC POLEMICS
THEONOE (BROTHER OF —)
CALCHAS
(FATHER OF —) PROTEUS THESTOR
(MOTHER OF —) LEUCIPPE
PSAMATHE

THEORBO ARCHLUTE
THEOREM DUAL LEMMA
CONVERSE
THEORETIC PURE
THEORETICAL BOOK PURE CLOSET
THEORIC ABSTRACT ACADEMIC
ARMCHAIR NOTIONAL PLATONIC
THEORIST OPINATOR
THEORIZE SUGGEST
THEORIZING IDEOLOGY
THEORY ISM OVISM EROTIC ETHICS
HOLISM LAXISM SYSTEM AGOGICS
ANIMISM ATOMISM BAASKAP
BIGBANG CAMBISM DUALISM
FORMISM HOBBISM PEELISM
PLENISM THEORIC TYCHISM
ACOSMISM AXIOLOGY DITHEISM
DYNAMISM ENERGISM ESTHETIC
ETIOLOGY FEMINISM FINITISM
GHOSTISM GOBINISM HEDONICS
IDEALISM IDEOLOGY MOLINISM
MONADISM ONTOLOGY PROGRESS
SEMANTIC SEMIOTIC SPERMISM
(SUFF.) ISM LOGER LOGIA(N)
LOGIC(AL) LOGIST LOGUE LOGY
OLOGY
THEOW SERF THRALL THEOWMAN
THERAPEUTICS ACEOLOGY
THERAPY PHYSIATRICS
(SUFF.) PATH(IA)(IC)(Y)
THERAVADA HINAYANA
THERE ERE YARE ALONG VOILA
WHERE YONDER THEASUM
THITHER
THEREABOUTS NEARBY
THEREAFTER UPON THENCE
THEREFORE SO ERGO THEN ARGAL
HENCE FORTHY IGITUR THENCE
THEREON UPON
THEREUPON SO SINCE WITHAL
THEREON THEREUP
THEREWITH MIT WITH
THERIACA GALENA
THERMOMETER GLASS HYDRA
CELSIUS REAUMUR
(PART OF —) BORE BULB LENS
SCALE COLUMN GRADUATIONS
CONSTRICTION
THERMOPLASTIC SARAN
THERMOSTAT DETECTOR
PYROSTAT
THERSANDER (FATHER OF —)
POLYNICES
(MOTHER OF —) ARGIA
(SLAYER OF —) TELEPHUS
THESAURUS TREASURE
THESE THIR THIS THEASUM
THESEUS (FATHER OF —) AEGEUS
(MOTHER OF —) AETHRA
(SON OF —) HIPPOLYTUS
(WIFE OF —) PHAEDRA
THESIS ACT THEMA DOWNBEAT
LOGICISM THESICLE
THESTIUS (DAUGHTER OF —)
ALTHAEA
(FATHER OF —) PARTHAON
(MOTHER OF —) EURYTE
(SON OF —) TOXEUS PLEXIPPUS
THESTOR (DAUGHTER OF —)
THEONOE LEUCIPPE
(FATHER OF —) IDMON APOLLO
(MOTHER OF —) LAOTHOE
(SON OF —) CALCHAS

THETIS (FATHER OF —) NEREUS
(HUSBAND OF —) PELEUS
(MOTHER OF —) DORIS
(SON OF —) ACHILLES
THEY A HI THO THEI
(— READ) LEG
THIAMINE ANEURIN
THICK FAT SAD HAZY SLAB BLIND
BROAD BURLY BUSHY CLOSE
CRASS DENSE FOGGY GREAT
GROSS MURKY SOLID SQUAB
STIFF STOUT CHUMPY COARSE
GREASY LUBBER SLABBY SPISSY
STOCKY STODGY TURBID
BLUBBER GRUMOUS FAMILIAR
LUTULENT MOTHERED
(— WITH SMOKE) SMUDGY
(SHORT AND —) SQUAT
(11 POINTS —) HEAVY
(PREF.) CRASSI DASI DASY
HADR(O) PACHY ULO
(— WITH HAIR) DASI DASY
THICKEN GEL BODY CLOT FULL
BREAK KEECH LITHE DEEPEN
HARDEN ENGROSS STIFFEN
(— HEDGE) PLASH
THICKENED BODIED BULLED
FURRED CALLOUS CLUBBED
SPISSATED
THICKENER NAPALM
THICKENING FALX LEAR ROUX
SWELL CALLUS CLAVATE LIAISON
PLACODE ATHEROMA CLUBBING
CRASSULA PYCNOSIS EPHIPPIUM
(— OF COAL SEAM) SWELLY
(— OF LETTER STROKE) STRESS
THICKET COP BOSK RONE SHAG
SHAW BLUFF BRAKE CLUMP
COPSE COVER DROKE HEDGE
QUICK SHOLA SLICK THICK
BOSKET BUSHET COVERT GREAVE
JUNGLE MALLEE QUEACH SPINNY
BOSCAGE BOSQUET BRUSHET
COPPICE CORYLET SPINNEY
WOODRIS CHAMISAL FERNSHAW
QUICKSET SHINNERY THICKSET
SALICETUM
THICKHEADED DULL DENSE
THICKHEADED FLY CONOPID
THICK-KNEE CURLEW DIKKOP
BUSTARD
THICKLY STEFLY
THICKNESS PLY BODY LAYER
DIAMETER
(— OF CHIP) CUT FEED
(— OF CLOTH) LAY
(— OF METAL) GRIP
(— OF PAPER) BULK CALLIPER
UNDERLAY
(ONE — OVER ANOTHER) LAYER
(SECOND —) DOUBLING
THICKSET STUB BEEFY PUNCH
SQUAT STOUT THICK CHUMPY
CHUNKY HUMPTY PLUGGY
ROBUST STOCKY STUBBY STUGGY
NUGGETY SQUATTY
THIEF GUN NIP PAD CHOR GILT
LIFT MILL PRIG BUDGE CREEP
CROOK FAKER GANEF PIKER
SNEAK TAKER TILER ANGLER
BULKER CANNON CLOYER DISMAS
GONOPH HOOKER KALLAN LIFTER
MICHER NIMMER NIPPER PICKER

PIRATE RATERO ROBBER SNATCH
TOSHER WASTER BOOSTER
COLLERY FOOTMAN GORILLA
GRIFTER HARRIER HEISTER
LADRONE LURCHER MEECHER
MERCURY PRIGGER PRIGMAN
PROLLER PROWLER SNAPPER
SPOTTER STEALER THIEVER
CLYFAKER CONVEYER CUTPURSE
FINGERER HARROWER LARCENER
PETERMAN PICAROON PICKLOCK
PILFERER PRIGSTER SNATCHER
(— AT A MINE) CAVER
(CATTLE —) ABACTOR BLOTTER
PLANTER RUSTLER
(CLEVER —) KID CANNON
(CRUCIFIED —) DISMAS
(FLASHY —) KIDDY
(MOUNTAIN —) CHOAR
(NIGHT —) SCOURER
(PETTY —) HOOKER SLOCKER
(RIVER —) ACKMAN LUMPER
(SNEAK —) LURCHER
(VAGABOND —) WASTER
(WHARF —) TOSHER
(PREF.) KLEPT(O)
(SUFF.) KLEPT
THIEVE MAG NIM
THIEVERY PRIGGERY
THIEVING LAW SHARK PUGGING
PROGGERY STEALING
THIEVING MAGPIE, THE
(CHARACTER IN —) NINETTA
PODESTA GIANETTO
(COMPOSER OF —) ROSSINI
THIEVISH STEALY FURTIVE
KLEPTIC SCADDLE PRIGGISH
THIEVISHNESS PRIGGISM
THIGH HAM HOCK FEMUR FLANK
GAMMON
(— PAIN) MERALGIA
(PREF.) CRURO FEMORO MER(O)
(SUFF.) MERUS
THILL FILL SILL BLADE SHAFT
LIMBER
THIMBLE SKEIN BUSHEL GOBLET
SLEEVE CRINGLE
THIMBLEBERRY MULBERRY
THIN HOE LEW BONY FINE FLUE
FUSE LANK LEAN LIMP PRIN RARE
SLIM WEAK WHEY EXILE FRAIL
GAUNT GAUZY LATHY PEAKY
SHEER SLINK SMALL SPARE
SWAMP THIRL WASHY WIZEN
AERIAL BLASHY DILUTE FLUTED
HOLLOW MAUGER MEAGER
MEAGRE PEAKED SCRANK SEROSE
SEROUS SHELLY SKINNY SLEAZY
SLIGHT SPINNY SUBTLE TENDER
TWIGGY WATERY WEAKEN
COVERED FOLIOUS FRAGILE
GRACILE HAGGARD SANIOUS
SCRAGGY SCRAILY SCRANKY
SCRAWNY SHALLOW SHILPIT
SLENDER SPIDERY SPINDLY
TENUOUS THREADY ARANEOUS
CACHETIC EGGSHELL HAIRLINE
ICHOROUS MACILENT SCRAGGED
SCRANNEL SKINKING VAPORISH
WATERISH ATTENUATE
SPINDLING
(— AND PINCHED) CHITTY
(— LEATHER) DOLE

(— OUT) HOE CHOP DISBUD
FEATHER
(— SEEDLINGS) SINGLE
(— THE WALLS) IRON
(PREF.) AREO LEPT(O) MANO
TENUI
THINE TUUM
THING JOB RES BABY ITEM SORT
WHAT CHEAT CHOSE AFFAIR
ANIMAL DINGUS FELLOW GILGUY
MATTER ARTICLE DINGBAT
MINIKIN SHEBANG WHATNOT
THINGLET
(— DONE) FACT ACTUS
(— FOUND) TROVE
(— OF LITTLE ACCOUNT) GEWGAW
(— OF LITTLE VALUE) NIFLE TRIFLE
TRINKET
(— OF LITTLE WORTH) STIVER
(— TO BE REGRETTED) DAMAGE
(— TO EXHIBIT) BRAVERY
(—S PROHIBITED) VETANDA
(ANOTHER —) ALIUD
(CONSECRATED —) ANATHEMA
(CORRECT —) CHEESE
(ENORMOUS —) MONSTER
(ENTIRE —) INTEGRAL
(EXTRAORDINARY —) ONER
(FAIR —) POTATO
(FIT —) CHECKER
(GOOD —) WELFARE
(HOLY —S) HAGIA KODASHIM
(IMPORTANT —) ACE
(INSIGNIFICANT —) SCRAT
(INSIGNIFICANT —S) SMATTER
(JEWISH —S) JUDAICA
(LITTLE —S) FEWTRILS
(LIVING —S) BIOTA
(MISSHAPEN —) ABORTION
(NEW —) NEWEL
(OUTMODED —) SNUFF
(PETTY —) SHABBLE
(PRECIOUS —) JEWEL
(PRECISE —) POINT
(RIDICULOUS —) MONUMENT
(RIGHT —) POTATO
(ROTTEN —) ROTTOCK
(SAD —) RUTH
(SILLY —) TRIMTRAM
(SINGLE —) UNIT
(SMALL —) SNIPPET
(STRAY —) WAIF
(STUNTED —) SCRUNT SNEESHIN
(SURE —) CERT SNIP
(TERRIFYING —) BOGEYMAN
(UNEXPECTED —) GODSEND
(UNIQUE —) ONER UNICUM
(UNREAL —) NOMINAL
(UNSPECIFIED —S) JAZZ
(UNSUBSTANTIAL —) PUFF
(WORLDLY —S) EARTH
(WORNOUT —) SNUFF HUSHEL
(PL.) GEAR REALIA SQUARES
(PREF.) REI
(SUFF.) ORIUM ORY SOME
(— USED) ANT
(— USED FOR) ORIUM
THINGAMY DOODAD
THING-IN-ITSELF THINGY
NOUMENON
THINGS
(SUFF.) IA
THINGUMBOB DODAD DOODAD

JIGGER THINGUM
THINK LET SEE WIS WIT DEEM
FEEL HOLD MAKE MEAN MINT
MULL MUSE READ TROW WEEN
ALLOW CENSE FANCY GUESS
JUDGE LOUSE OPINE PANSE
SEPAD ESTEEM EXPECT FIGURE
IDEATE RECKON REPUTE BELIEVE
CONCEIT IMAGINE REFLECT
SUPPOSE COGITATE CONSIDER
ENVISAGE
(— BEST) SEEM
(— HARD) YERK
(— OF) MIND PURPENSE
(— OF AS) ACCOUNT
(— OVER) BETHINK
(— UP) INVENT
(— UPON) BROOD
(— WELL OF) APPROVE
THINKER SOPHIST PHILOSOPH
PHILOSOPHER
(CHINESE —) LEGALIST
THINKING CONCEIT THOUGHT
(CLEVER —) HEADWORK
THINLY AIRILY SPARSE SPARSELY
THINNESS RARITY EXILITY FINESSE
TENUITY EXIGUITY
THINNING BALK BAULK PINCH
CLEANING
THIOL MERCAPTAN
THIRD FACE GAMMA TERCE THREE
DITONE TERTIA TIERCE
(PREF.) TRIT(O)
THIRDLY TERTIO
THIRD-RATE C3 HEDGE
THIRD-RATER PIKER
THIRST DRY ADRY CLEM DRYTH
APOSIA DROUTH THRIST
DROUGHT DIPSOSIS POLYDIPSIA
(PREF.) DIPS(O)
THIRSTING SITIENT
THIRSTY DRY ADRY ATHIRST
DROUGHTY
THIS HE SO THIK THILK
THIS ABOVE ALL (AUTHOR OF —)
KNIGHT
(CHARACTER IN —) PRUE CLIVE
MONTY BRIGGS CATHAWAY
PRUDENCE
THISTLE PUHA HOYLE CARDON
DASHEL DINDLE FISTLE TEASEL
CALTROP CARDUUS CARLINA
GUTWEED RAURIKI WARATAH
BEDEGUAR CALTHROP COMPOSIT
ECHINOPS MILKWEED
(PREF.) CARDO
THITHER TO YON YOND THERE
YONDER ULTERIOR YONDWARD
THOAS (BROTHER OF —) EUNEUS
(DAUGHTER OF —) HYPSIPYLE
(FATHER OF —) BACCHUS
ANDRAEMON
(MOTHER OF —) GORGE ARIADNE
HYPSIPYLE
(SON OF —) SICINUS
(WIFE OF —) MYRINE
THOMIST AQUINIST
THOMSONITE MESOLE MESOTYPE
OZARKITE
THONG LORE RIEM BRAIL GIRTH
LASSO LEASH ROMAL STRAP
THUNK WHANG WHANK LACING
LINGEL STRING TWITCH

AMENTUM BABICHE LANIARD
LANYARD LATCHET RIEMPIE
(— ON JAVELIN) AMENTUM
(HAWK'S —) BRAIL
(PREF.) HIMANTO
THOR THUNAR THUNOR
(FATHER OF —) ODIN
(HAMMER OF —) MJOLLNIR
(MOTHER OF —) JORDH
THORACIC DORSAL
THORAX CHEST TRUNK BREAST
PEREION ALITRUNK CORSELET
FOREBODY
THORITE ENALITE ORANGITE
THORN BROD BUSH GOAD PIKE
STOB STUG BRIAR BRIER DOORN
PRICK SPIKE SPINE FUSTIC
JAGGER ACANTHA PRICKER
STICKER COCKSPUR THORNLET
(PL.) SPEAR HAYBOTE
(PREF.) ACANTH(O) SPINI
SPINO(SO) SPINULI SPINULOSO
(SUFF.) ACANTHUS SPINOSE
THORN APPLE HAW METEL
STAMONY
THORNBACK RAY DORN ROKER
THORNBILL TOMTIT
THORNY HARD SPINY PRICKLY
SCROGGY SPINOUS THISTLY
THORNED
THORON RADON
THOROUGH RUN DEEP FIRM FULL
SOUND ERRANT HOLLOW STRICT
HOTSHOT INGOING REGULAR
COMPLETE GROUNDLY INTIMATE
PRECIOUS
THOROUGHBRED HOTBLOOD
THOROUGHFARE BUND DRUM
ROAD ALLEY AVENUE STREET
BIKEWAY HIGHWAY PARKWAY
WHITEHALL
THOROUGHGOING PAKKA
ARRANT ERRANT HEARTY
PROPER PUREDEE RADICAL
ABSOLUTE PROFOUND TRUEBRED
THOROUGHLY BUT FULL GOOD
INLY CLEAN FULLY PROOF
DEEPLY GAINLY KINDLY PROPER
RICHLY RIPELY WHOLLY ROUNDLY
SOAKING SOBBING SOGGING
SOUNDLY DRIPPING GROUNDLY
HEARTILY INWARDLY
(PREF.) E
THOROUGHWORT BONESET
THOSE THEM THEY YOND
THOTH DHOUTI
THOUGH AS AND SET YET ALTHO
ALTHOUGH
THOUGHT CARE IDEA MOOD VIEW
FANCY TASTE TRACE NOTION
PENSEE CONCEIT CONCEPT
COUNSEL OPINION SURMISE
PEMMICAN RUMINATE
(— OUT) ADVISED
(CAREFUL —) ADVICE ACCOUNT
(FANCIFUL —) CONCEIT
(HIGHEST —) IDEE
(REASONED —) STUDY
(UNCLEAN —) SEWERAGE
(WELL-EXPRESSED —) STROKE
(PREF.) LOG(O)
THOUGHTFUL EARNEST PENSIVE
SERIOUS STUDIED

STUDIOUS THOUGHTY
THOUGHTFULNESS GRACE
COUNSEL
THOUGHTLESS RASH VAIN DIZZY
GLAKY SUPINE VACANT ETOURDI
GLAIKET RAMSTAM HEEDLESS
RECKLESS
THOUSAND CHI MIL GRAND MILLE
CHILIAD
(FIVE —) EPSILON
(SIX —) DIGAMMA
(TEN —) TOMAN
(10 —) MYRIAD
(100 —) LAC LAKH
(PREF.) CHILI(A) KILO MILLE MILLI
(TEN —) MYRIA MYRIO
**THOUSANDTH (— OF CUBIC
CENTIMETER)** LAMBDA
(— OF INCH) MIL
(HUNDRED —) SSU
(PREF.) MILLI
THRACIAN GETE GETAN GETIC
THRAX
THRALL SERF GURTH SLAVE
CAPTIVE
THRALLDOM BONDAGE SLAVERY
THIRLAGE
THRASH DAD LAM PAY TAN BANG
BEAT BELT COMB DING DRUB
DUST FLAX JERK LACE LICK LOUK
MILL PAIL SOCK SOLE SOWL
SWAP SWOP TOSE TRIM WALK
WHAP WHIP WHOP YERK BASTE
BELAM BLESS CURRY DRASH
FLAIL FRAIL LINCH LINGE NOINT
PASTE SLATE SLOSH SWACK
SWING TABOR TARGE THUMP
TOWEL TWINK WHALE WHANG
ANOINT BUMFEG CUDGEL FETTLE
JACKET LARRUP LATHER MUZZLE
RADDLE STOUSH SWINGE TANCEL
THREAP THRESH THWACK
WALLOP LAMBACK LEATHER
SWADDLE TROLLOP TROUNCE
BETHWACK BUMBASTE
LAMBASTE LAMBSKIN RIBROAST
SPIFLICATE
THRASHER THREAPER THRESHER
SICKLEBILL
THRASHING TOCO WIPING
BELTING LAMMING LICKING
WARMING WHALING DRUBBING
THRASYMEDES (FATHER OF —)
NESTOR
(MOTHER OF —) ANAXIBIA
THREAD BAR END BAVE CHIP
CLEW CLUE CORD DOUP FILE
FILM GIMP GOLD LACE LINE POIL
PURL ROON SILK TRAM WIRE
WORM BRIDE CHIVE FIBER FIBRE
FLOAT FLOSS HYPHA INKLE
REEVE SCREW SETON SHIVE
SHOOT SHUTE STEEK THRUM
TWEER TWIRE TWIST WATAP
BOTTOM COBWEB COTTON
ENFILE FIBRIL INFILE SINGLE
STAMEN STITCH STRAIN STRAND
STRING TISSUE BABICHE BASTING
DOUPING SLUBBER SPIREME
TWITTER WARPING ACONTIUM
FILAMENT GOSSAMER LIGATURE
PICKOVER RAVELING SPINNING
SPIRICLE

(— AROUND BOWSTRING) SERVING
(— IN SEED COATING) SPIRICLE
(— LEGS OF RABBIT) HARL HARLE
(— OF SCREW) WORM
(— OF WAX) SWARF
(— USED FOR COCOON) BAVE
(—S THAT CROSS WARP) WEFT
WOOF
(BADLY TWINED —) SLUBBER
(BALL OF —) CLEW CLUE CLOWE
GLOME
(BUTTONHOLE —S) BAR
(COARSE —) GIRD
(COARSEST — IN LACE) GIMP
(COILED —) COP
(FILLING —) PICK
(FLOATING —) PICKOVER
(HARD —) LISLE
(LINEN —) LINE INCLE INKLE
(LOOSELY TWISTED —S) BUMP
(METAL —) LAME WIRE
(OAKUM —) PLEDGET
(PULLED —) SNAG
(REFUSE —S) BUR BURR
(SHOEMAKER'S —) END LINGEL
LINGLE
(SILK —) TRAM TRAME DOUPIONI
(SOFT SHORT —) THRUM
(STRONG —) GOUNAU
(SURGICAL —) SETON
(WARP —) END STAMEN
(WAXED —) TACKER
(WEFT —) PICK SHOT
(40 —S) BEER BIER
(PL.) FLOSS
(PREF.) FILI(CI) MIT(O) NEM(A)(O)
NEMAT(O) STAMIN(I)
(SUFF.) NEMA NEME STEMONOUS
THREADBARE BARE SEAR SERE
TRITE PILLED SHABBY NAPLESS
THREADFIN SEER SEIR SULEA
BARBUDO KINGFISH SEERFISH
THREADFISH COBBLER SUNFISH
THREADING SCREW STRINGING
THREADLIKE FILATE FILOSE
THREADWORK MACRAME
THREAT ATTACK MENACE
THUNDER
(PL.) MINES
THREATEN BRAG FACE MINT
BOAST SHORE ATTACK IMPEND
MENACE ENDANGER MINATORY
OVERHANG
(— TO RAIN) SCOUTHER
THREATENED FRAUGHT
THREATENING BIG GLUM UGLY
ANGRY BOAST SABLE GREASY
BANEFUL BODEFUL OMINOUS
RAMPANT MINATORY MINITANT
MINACIOUS
(— TO RAIN) HEAVY
THREE TREY GIMEL LEASH TRIAS
TERNARY TERNION
(— CENT PIECE) TRIME
(— IN ONE) TRIUNE
(— MILES) LEAGUE
(— OF A KIND) GLEEK BRELAN
TRIPLET
(GROUP OF —) TRIO TRIAD TRIPLE
TROIKA
(SET OF —) PAIRIAL
(PREF.) TER TERNATI TERNATO
TRE TRI(S)

(— DIMENSIONS) STERE(O)
(SUFF.) TERNATE
**THREE BLACK PENNIES (AUTHOR
OF —)** HERGESHEIMER
(CHARACTER IN —) HOWAT JAMES
PENNY SUSAN EUNICE JANNAN
JASPER POLDER BRUNDON
MARIANA LUDOWIKA
WINSCOMBE
**THREE-CORNERED HAT (AUTHOR
OF —)** ALARCON
(CHARACTER IN —) LUCAS WEASEL
EUGENIO MERCEDES FRASQUITA
THREE-DIMENSIONAL CUBIC
CUBICAL
THREEFOLD TERN TRINE TERNAL
TREBLE TRINAL TRIPLE TERNARY
TRIFOLD TRIPLEX
THRIBBLE
THREE-FORKED TRISULC
**THREE MUSKETEERS (AUTHOR OF
—)** DUMAS
(CHARACTER IN —) ATHOS ARAMIS
WARDES PORTHOS DEWINTER
PLANCHET BONACIEUX
CONSTANCE DARTAGNAN
RICHELIEU
THREEPENCE JOEY TREY THRIP
THRUM TICKEY TICKIE
THREE SISTERS (AUTHOR OF —)
CHEKHOV
(CHARACTER IN —) OLGA IRINA
MASHA ANDREY SOLENI KULIGIN
NATASHA PROSOROV
VERSHININ
THREE SOLDIERS (AUTHOR OF —)
DOSPASSOS
(CHARACTER IN —) DAN RED ANDY
JOHN MABE YVONNE ANDREWS
FUSELLI ANDERSON GENEVIEVE
CHRISTFIELD
THRENODY DIRGE HEARSE
THRENE
THRESH COB BEAT CAVE LUMP
WHIP BERRY FLAIL FRAIL SPELT
STAMP THRASH
THRESHEL DRASHEL
THRESHER TASKER
THRESHER SHARK FOX FOXFISH
WHIPTAIL
THRESHOLD HEAD SILL SOLE
DEARN LIMEN DRASHEL
DOORSILL
THRIFT SAVING VIRTUE ECONOMY
STATICE THEEDOM PARSIMONY
THRIFTILY NEAR
THRIFTLESS WASTEFUL
THRIFTY CANNY FENDY PUIST
FRUGAL SAVING CAREFUL
SPARING
THRILL JAG BANG DIRL GIRL KICK
FLUSH SHOOT THIRL DINDLE
STOUND TICKLE TINGLE TREMOR
ENCHANT FRISSON VIBRATE
FREMITUS
(PROVIDING A —) KICKY
(SHARP —) ZING
THRILLING TINGLY VIBRANT
PLANGENT TINGLING
THRINTER FRONTER
THRIPID PHYSOPOD
THRIPS BLACKFLY PHYSOPOD
THRIVE DOW GROW LIKE RISE

THEE ADDLE FADGE MOISE PROVE THRAM BATTEN BATTLE CATTER CHIEVE PROSPER STORKEN SUCCEED WELFARE FLOURISH THRODDEN
(— IN) LOVE

THRIVING BIEN GRUSHIE ROARING THRIFTY BLOOMING TOWARDLY

THRIVINGLY GAILY GAYLY BRAVELY

THROAT MAW CRAG CROP GOWL GULA HALS HASS LANE GORGE HALSE SWIRE FAUCES GARGET GULLET GUTTUR GUZZLE RICTUS CHANNEL JUGULUM STOMACH SWALLOW WEASAND THRAPPLE THROPPLE THROTTLE
(— OF ANCHOR) CLUTCH
(— OF COROLLA) FAUCES
(— OF FROG) KNEE
(MOUTH AND —) WHISTLE
(SORE —) HOUSTY PRUNELLA
(PREF.) BRONCH(I)(IO)(O) DER(O) GUTTERO

THROATLATCH FIADOR

THROATY THICK GUTTURAL

THROB ACHE BEAT BELK DRUM DUNT LEAP PANT QUOP WARK FLACK PULSE STANG WARCH STOUND STRIKE STROKE TINGLE WALLOP FLACKER PULSATE VIBRATE FLICHTER PALPITATE
(— IN PAIN) SHOOT
(RAPID —S) FRIMITTS

THROBBING DUNT ATHROB THRILL BEATING PITAPAT VIBRANT PULSATORY

THROE PANG PULL STOUR SHOWER PAROXYSM
(—S OF DEATH) AGONY

THROMBIN PLASMASE

THROMBOPLASTIN COAGULIN CYTOZYME

THROMBOSIS SHOCK CORONARY

THRONE GADI SEAT ASANA GADDI GADHI SELLE SIEGE STALL STATE STEAD STOOL MUSNUD SEGGIO SHINZA TRIBUNE CATHEDRA SEGGIOLA SINHASAN
(BISHOP'S —) SEE APSE CATHEDRA

THRONE ROOM AIWAN

THRONG CREW HEAP HOST ROUT CHIRT CROWD FLOCK FRACK POSSE PRESS SHOAL SWARM RESORT THRAVE THREAT THRIMP THRUST COMPANY TEMPEST THRUTCH SURROUND
(— OF SEAFOWL) SAVSSAT
(CONFUSED —) LURRY

THRONGED ALIVE FREQUENT NUMEROUS

THROTTLE GUN CHOKE SCRAG STIFLE GARROTE STRANGLE THROPPLE

THROUGH BY PER DONE THRU WITH ROUND AROUND
(RIGHT —) TILL
(PREF.) DIA PER

THROUGHOUT OVER ABOUT ROUND ABROAD BEDENE BIDENE DURING ENTIRE PASSIM SEMPRE OVERALL THRUOUT
(PREF.) HOL(O)

THROW GO DAB DAD HIP HIT PAT PEG PUT SHY ACES BIFF BUCK BUNG CALE CAST CHIP CLOD COOK CUCK DART DASH DROW HAIL HANK HIPE HULL HURL HYPE JERK LACE MILL PECK PICK PURL SEND SKIM SLAT SOSS TOSS TURF VANG WARP WURP YEND CHUCK CHUNK DOUSE FLICK FLING FLIRT FLURR HEAVE PITCH SLING SPANG DEVEST ELANCE HAUNCH HURTLE INJECT LAUNCH SLIGHT THRILL BLUNDER BUTTOCK COCKSHY MANGANA UPTHROW VIBRATE CATAPULT JACULATE
(— A BASEBALL PITCH) HANG
(— ABOUT) BOUNCE
(— ASIDE) DEVEST
(— AWAY) DICE DOFF BANDY WAIVE PROJECT JETTISON SQUANDER
(— BASEBALL) BURN
(— BY KICKING) WINCE
(— CARELESSLY) COB
(— DICE) JEFF
(— DOWN) DUSH EVEN PILE FLUMP LODGE ABJECT DETURB THRING FLATTEN
(— FORTH) EJECT
(— FORWARD) LAUNCH
(— HEAVILY) LOB
(— HEEDLESSLY) SLIGHT
(— IN CRAPS) CRAP PASS CRABS BOXCARS NATURAL
(— INTO CONFUSION) CLUB FLUTTER CONFOUND CONVULSE
(— INTO DISORDER) PIE ADDLE BOLLIX DERANGE DISRANK DISRUPT EMBROIL DISARRAY
(— INTO PERPLEXITY) FLUMMOX
(— INTO WASTE) BACK
(— JERKILY) FLIRT
(— LIGHT UPON) ILLUME
(— LIQUID) JAW
(— OF A STEER) DOGFALL
(— OF SHUTTLE) SHOT SHOOT SHUTE
(— OF THREES) COCKEYES
(— OFF) CANT CAST SLIRT SPILL SLOUGH CONFUSE UNBURDEN
(— OFF COURSE) EMIT SHED DERAIL
(— ONESELF) CLAP
(— OPEN) DISPARK
(— OUT) FIRE HOOF LADE BELCH EJECT ERUPT SPOUT DETURB IGNORE EXTRUDE
(— QUICKLY) LASH
(— SIDEWISE) SHY
(— SILK) THROWST
(— SMARTLY) SLAT
(— STEER) BUST
(— STICKS) SQUAIL
(— STONES) ROCK
(— TOGETHER) HUDDLE
(— UNDER) SUBJECT
(— UP) BARF CAVE PICK VOMIT
(— VIOLENTLY) BUZZ DING PASH SOCK WHAP WHOP SMASH HURTLE WUTHER WHITHER SPANGHEW PRECIPITATE
(— WITH A JERK) JET CANT

SQUIRR FLOUNCE
(— WITH GREAT FORCE) BUZZ SWACK
(— WITHOUT VIOLENCE) HURL
(CHEATING — OF DICE) KNAP
(FOOTBALL —) GROUND
(FREE —) FOUL
(LARIAT —) HOOLIAN
(LOWEST — AT DICE) AMBSACE AMESACE
(WRESTLING —) HANK HIPE HYPE BUTTOCK BACKHEEL
(SUFF.) JECT

THROWAWAY DODGER

THROWBACK ATAVISM

THROWER TRAMMER THROWSTER
(SPEAR —) ATLATL

THROWING DARTING

THROWING-STICK ATLATL WOMMERA WOOMERA HORNERAH TROMBASH TRUMBASH

THROWN (— AWAY) CASTAWAY
(— DOWN) DEJECTED
(PREF.) (— OUT) RHIPTO

THROWSTER TWISTER

THRUM FUM STRUM THUMB

THRUSH POP OMAO SOOR APTHA BREVE FRUSH GRIVE MAVIS OUZEL PITTA SABIA SHAMA SHIRL SPREW UZZLE VEERY APHTHA DRAINE JAYPIE KICKUP MISSEL OLOMAO PULISH SHRITE JAYPIET REDWING WAGTAIL BELLBIRD CHERCOCK FORKTAIL PRUNELLA SHAGBARK THRASHER THROSTLE THRUSHEL THRUSTLE URTICATE WOODCHAT SOLITAIRE MONILIASIS NIGHTINGALE

THRUSHLIKE TURDOID

THRUST DAB DEG DIG DUB JAB JAG JAM JOB POP PUG BANG BEAR BIRR BOKE BORE BUCK BUTT CANT CHOP CRAM DART DASH DUSH FOIN HURL KICK LICK MURE PASS PICK PILT POKE PORR POSS POTE PROD PUSH SEND SINK SPAR STAB STOP TILT VENY WHAP WHOP BREAK DRIFT DRIVE EXERT HUNCH LUNGE POACH POINT PROKE PUNCH SHOOT SPANK STAVE STICK STOKE STUFF THROW DARTLE PLUNGE POUNCE STITCH STRAIN STRESS STRIKE STRIPE BEARING IMPULSE PRESSURE SHOULDER STOCCADO
(— A LANCE) AVENTRE
(— ASIDE) DAFF SHUFFLE
(— AWAY) DOFF SHOVE DETRUDE ABSTRUDE
(— DOWN) THRING DEPULSE DETRUDE
(— IN) INSERT STRIKE INTRUDE
(— OF ARCH) DRIFT
(— OF EXPLOSION) BLOWOUT
(— ONESELF) CHISEL
(— OUT) POUT REACH STRUT EXSERT DETRUDE EXTRUDE OBTRUDE PROTRUDE OBTRUSIVE
(— SUDDENLY) STRIKE
(— THROUGH) ENFILED

(— WITH ELBOW) HUNCH
(— WITH GREAT FORCE) BUZZ
(— WITH NOSE) NUDDLE
(— WITH WEAPON) FOIN SHOVE
(DAGGER —) DAG
(FENCING —) PASS VENY BOTTE PUNTO VENUE REPOST TIMING PASSADO RIPOSTE STOCCADO STOCCATA
(HOME —) HAI HAY
(MATADOR'S —) ESTOCADA
(SARCASTIC —) GIRD

THUD BAFF DUMP PHUT PLOD SWAG DOYST FLUMP POUND BOUNCE SQUELCH

THUG MUG GOON GOONDA RODMAN GORILLA HOODLUM GANGSTER

THUJA BIOTA

THUJONE SALVIOL

THULUTH SOOLOOS

THUMB THOOM POLLEX THENAR
(BALL OF —) THENAR

THUMBSTALL POUCER POUSÉR

THUMP COB DAD DUB BANG BEAT BLOW BUMP DING DIRD DRUB DUNT KNUB LUMP PAIK PAKE POLT SOSS THUD TUND TUNK YARK YERK BLAFF BLIBE BUNCH CLOUR CLUNK CRUMP KNOCK POUND TABOR THACK WHELK BOUNCE HAMMER PUMMEL THUNGE

THUMPING WHAPPING WHOPPING

THUNDER SULFUR BRATTLE FOULDRE SULPHUR INTONATE
(PREF.) BRONT(E)(O) CERAUN(O) KERAUN(O)

THUNDERBOLT BOLT FIRE VAJRA FULMEN FOULDRE ARTIFACT FIREBOLT
(PREF.) CERAUN(O) KERAUN(O)

THUNDERING TONANT

THUNDERSQUALL BAYAMO VENDAVAL

THUNDERSTONE ARTIFACT

THUNDERSTORM HOUVARI TEMPEST TORNADO

THURIBLE CENSER

THUS AS SIC DYCE THUSLY THISWISE THUSGATE

THWACK BLOW DUNT CRUMP SOUSE

THWART BALK WART BENCH CROOK CROSS SPITE THRAW THROW ZYGON BAFFLE SCOTCH STYMIE SNOOKER CONTRAIR CONTRARY TRAVERSE

THWARTING CROSS CROSSING

THYESTES (BROTHER OF —) ATREUS
(FATHER OF —) PELOPS
(MOTHER OF —) HIPPODAMIA

THYIA (FATHER OF —) CASTALIUS CEPHISSEUS
(SON OF —) DELPHUS

THYINE THUGA THUYA

THYLACINE YABBI

THYME MARUM PELETRE HILLWORT SERPOLET

TI KI TOI TITI

TIAMAT (HUSBAND OF —) APSU
(SLAYER OF —) MARDUK

TIARA MITER REGNUM

CIDARIS TIARELLA
TIBBU DAZA TEDA

TIBET
CAPITAL: LASSA LHASA
COIN: TANGA
LAKE: ARU BAM BUM NAM MEMA
TOSU JAGOK TABIA DAGTSE
GARHUR KASHUN SELING
TANGRA YAMDOK KYARING
TERINAM TSARING ZILLING
JIGGITAI
LANGUAGE: BODSKAD
MOUNTAIN: KAMET SAJUM KAILAS
BANDALA
MOUNTAIN RANGE: KAILAS
KUNLUN HIMALAYA
NATIVE: BHOTIA BHOTIYA
RIVER: NAK NAU SAK SONG INDUS
SUTLEJ MATSANG SALWEEN
TOWN: NOH KARAK LHASA
GARTOK TOTLING GYANGTSE
SHIGATSE

TIBETAN BALTI DRUPA BHOTIA
BHUTIA CHAMPA DROKPA
KHAMBA KHAMBU PANAKA
SHERPA TANGUT BHOTIYA
BHUTANI GYARUNG
TIBIA SHIN SHANK CNEMIS
SHINBONE
(SUFF.) CNEMA CNEMIA CNEMIC
CNEMUS
TIBOURBOU CORTEZ
TIC FIXATION
(ONE SUBJECT TO —) TIQUEUR
TICAL BAHT
TICK FAG JAR KEB KED BEAT KADE
NICK PEAK PICK PIKE CHALK
CHICK CRIKE PIQUE STRAP
ACARID IXODID PALLET TALAJE
TAMPAN ACARIAN ARGASID
BEDTICK IXODIAN PINOLIA
ARACHNID CARAPATO GARAPATA
GARAPATO TURICATA
(PREF.) ACAR(I)(O) CROTO
TICKED MACKEREL
TICKET LOT TAG BLANK CHECK
DUCAT FICHE TOKEN BALLOT
BILLET COUPON DOCKET PIGEON
POLICY RETURN BENEFIT ETIQUET
CONTRACT DEADHEAD STOPOVER
TRANSFER PASTEBOARD
(COMMISSION —) SPIFF
(FREE —) PASS
(LOTTERY —) BLANK HORSE
BENEFIT
(SALES —) TRAVELER
(SEASON —) IVORY
(PL.) PAPER
TICKET WINDOW GUICHET
TICKING KISS TICK BEDTICK
TICKLE AMUSE TEASE EXCITE
KITTLE PLEASE THRILL TIDDLE
CUITTLE
TICKLISH GOOSEY KITTLE KITTLY
QUEASY TENDER TOUCHY TRICKY
KITTLISH
TICKSEED COREOPSIS
TICK TREFOIL BEDSTRAW
SAINFOIN TICKSEED
TIDBIT NOSH SAYNETE BEATILLE
KICKSHAW

TIDDLEYWINK SQUAIL
TIDE FLOW NEAP WAVE AGGER
ROUST SPRING OVERTIDE
SEAFLOOD
(— MOVEMENT) LAKIE
(PREF.) (HIGH —) PLEMYRA
TIDINGS NEWS WORD RUMOR
SOUND UNCOW ADVICE MESSAGE
(GLAD —) GOSPEL
TIDY RID COSH MACK NEAT SIDE
SMUG SNOD SNUG TAUT TOSH
TRIG WEME CHART DONCY
DONSY DOUCE NATTY NIFTY
QUEME TIGHT DONSIE FETTLE
POLITE SPOONY ORDERLY
ALLIGATE MACKLIKE MENSEFUL
SHIPSHAPE
TIE BOW LAP TYE BAND BEND BIND
BOND CAST DRAW KILT KNOT
LACE LOCK ROOT WISP YOKE
ASCOT BRACE CADGE LEASH
NEXUS POINT THRAP THROW
TRICE TRUSS ATTACH BUNDLE
CONNEX COPULA COUPLE
FASTEN LIGATE SECURE DOGFALL
FOULARD JAZZBOW NECKTIE
SHACKLE SLEEPER SPANCEL
TABLEAU CROSSTIE INTERTIE
LIGATURE STANDOFF STRINGER
VINCULUM
(— BENEATH) SUBNECT
(— IN TENNIS) DEUCE
(— IN WRESTLING) DOGFALL
(— KNOT) CAST
(— LEGS) HOBBLE
(— ONIONS) TRACE
(— SCORE) PEELS
(— THE SCORE) EQUALIZE
(— TOGETHER) KNIT LEASH
HARNESS
(— UP) SNUB TRAMMEL LIGATURE
TWITCHEL
(— UP SHORT) SNUB
(LEATHER —) WANTY
(MADE-UP —) TECK
(NEEDLEWORK —) BRIDE
(PL.) GILLIES
TIED EVEN FAST KNIT SQUARE
TIEPIN PROP SCARFPIN STICKPIN
TIE PLATE TURTLE
TIER ROW BANK DECK RANK CHESS
STORY WITHE DEGREE PINAFORE
(— OF CASKS) RIDER
(— OF SEATS) CIRCLE
(— OF SHELVES) STAGE
TIERCE LEASH THIRD UNDERSONG
TIFF MIFF SPAT TIFT
TIFFIN CONDOR
TIGER SHER SHIR TIGRE TIGERKIN
(PREF.) TIGRO
TIGER CAT CHATI MARGAY
TIGERFOOT IPOMOEA
TIGER SNAKE ELAPID ELAPOID
TIGHT WET FULL HARD PANG
SNUG TAUT TIDY TRIG CLOSE
DENSE DRUNK STENT TENSE
STINGY STRAIT STRICT AIRTIGHT
TIGHTEN JAM CALK FIRM FRAP
BRACE CAULK CINCH CLOSE
FEEZE SCREW THRAP WRENCH
STRAITEN
TIGHTFISTED NARROW STINGY
TIGHT-LIPPED SILENT

TIGHTLY FAST HARD SHORT
STRAIT CLOSELY
TIGHTS MAILLOT LEOTARDS
TIGHTWAD FIST PIKER STIFF
TIKVAH (SON OF —) SHALLUM
JAHAZIAH
TILDE TIL WAVE TITTLE
(HAVING A —) CURLY
TILE LUMP SLAT FAVUS KASHI
LATER SLATE IMBREX LAPPET
PAMENT QUARRY SLATER
TEGULA AZULEJO CARREAU
CONDUIT PANTILE QUARREL
STARTER MAINTILE
(— USED IN MOSAIC) ABACULUS
(HEXAGONAL —) FAVUS
(HOLLOW —) BACKING
(HOPSCOTCH —) PEEVER
(LARGE —) DALLE QUARL QUARLE
(MAH JONG —) HONOR SEASON
(ONE-HALF —) HEAD
(PERSIAN —) KASHI
(ROUNDED —) CREASE
(SMALL —) TILETTE
(SQUARE —) QUADREL QUARREL
(PREF.) OSTRAC(O) PLINTHI
TILER HELER HELLIER
TILL TO EAR FIT LOB CASH FARM
PLOW TEAL TOIL DRESS LABOR
UNTIL WHILE FURROW MANURE
PLOUGH TILLER WHILST
HUSBAND SHUTTLE DUCKFOOT
OXHARROW
TILLABLE EARABLE
TILLAGE GAINOR MANURE
ARATION CULTURE TILTURE
TILLED GEOM TOILED
TILLER HELM STERN STOOL
HUSBAND KILLIFER
TILLING EARTH FALLOW
TILON (FATHER OF —) SHIMON
TILT DIP TIP TOP BANK CANT CAVE
COCK HEEL LIST PEAK SWAG
TRAP BRASH HEELD HIELD JOUST
STOOP TIPUP CASTER TILTER
TOPPLE CURRENT TOURNEY
ATTITUDE COCKBILL QUINTAIN
(— BRICK) HACK
(— IN WATER) DABBLE
(— OF BOWSPRIT) STAVE
(— OF NOSE) KIP KIPP
TILTED ACOCK ASTOOP
TILT HAMMER OLIVER
TILTING DIP JOUSTING
TIMANDRA (FATHER OF —)
TYNDAREUS
(HUSBAND OF —) ECHEMUS
PHYLEUS
(MOTHER OF —) LEDA
(SISTER OF —) HELEN
CLYTEMNESTRA
TIMBAL DRUM TYMBALON
TIMBER CAP LOG RIB BEAM BIBB
BUNK BUNT CLOG DRAM FELL
FISH FROG GIRT PUMP RAFF SKID
SPAR SPUR TREE WOOD CAHUY
CAVEL CRUCK FLOOR GRIPE JOIST
KEVEL LEDGE ORGUE PLATE
RIDER SISSU SPALE STICK BEARER
BRIDGE BUMPER CAMBER CORBEL
DAGGER FENDER FOREST KNIGHT
LIZARD ROOFER SISSOO SUMMER
TIMMER BOLSTER CARLING

DEADMAN DIVIDER FALLAGE
FUTCHEL FUTTOCK GROUSER
PARTNER PITWOOD RIBBAND
TRANSOM CORDWOOD COULISSE
DOGSHORE FOREHOOK STRINGER
STUMPAGE TRIPSILL WOODFALL
(— BETWEEN TRIMMERS) HEADER
(— CUT TO LENGTH) JUGGLE
(— IN MINE) COG STULL LIFTER
DIVIDER JUGGLER
(— KEPT DRY) BRIGHT
(— ON SCAFFOLD) LIGGER PUTLOG
(— ON SLED) BUNK
(— PIECE) PUTLOG
(— SAWED AND SPLIT) LUMBER
(— SUPPORTING CAP) LEGPIECE
(— SUSTAINING YARDS) MAST
(— TO PROP COAL) BROB
(CONVEX —) CAMBER
(CURVED —) CRUCK
(CUT —) FELL
(FELLED —) HAG
(FLOOR —) JOIST SUMMER
(FLOORING —) BATTEN
(FOUNDATION —) PILE
(FRAMING —) PUNCHEON
(HORIZONTAL —) REASON
(NORWEGIAN —) DRAM
(PHILIPPINE —) LAUAN
(PRINCIPAL — OF VESSEL) KEEL
(ROOF —) LEVER RAFTER
(ROOFING —S) SILE
(SHIPBUILDING —S) STOCKS
DEADWOOD HARPINGS
(SHIP'S —) CANT KEEL KNEE RUNG
SPUR APRON LEDGE WRONG
DAGGER HARPIN LACING SCROLL
BRACKET FUTTOCK STEMSON
DOGSHORE STANDARD
(SLABBED —) CANT
(SQUARED —) BALK
(SUPPORT —) SILL GIRDER LEDGER
PUNCHEON STRINGER
(SYSTEM OF —S) BOND
(UNCUT —) STUMPAGE
(WEATHERBEATEN —) DRIKI
TIMBERLAND STICKS WOODLAND
TIMBERMAN BRACER
TIMBO CUBE AJARI
TIMBRE CLANG COLOR KLANG
COLORING
TIMBREL TABOR TABOUR
TIME DAY ELD BELL BOUT HINT
HOUR SELE SITH TIDE WHET
ABYSS CHARE EPOCH FLASH
FRIST KALPA SITHE SPACE STOUN
STOUR TEMPO TEMPS VOLTA
WHACK WHILE COURSE KAIROS
PERIOD SEASON STOUND
TEMPUS CADENCE DEWFALL
SESSION MOVEMENT
(— AFTER) POST
(— ALLOWED FOR PAYMENT)
USANCE
(— FOR PAYING) KIST
(— FOR PAYMENT) CREDIT
(— GRANTED) FRIST
(— IN SERVICE) AGE
(— INTERVAL) WINDOW
(— INTERVENING) INTERIM
MEANTIME
(— LONG SINCE PAST) YORE
(— OF BEAUTY) BLOOM

(— OF CRISIS) EXIGENT
(— OF DYING) LAST
(— OF EXPIRY) ISH
(— OF EXUBERANCE) CARNIVAL
(— OF FEASTING) GUTTIDE
(— OF HIGHEST STRENGTH) HEYDAY
(— OF LIGHT) DAY
(— OF MATURITY OR DECLINE) AUTUMN
(— OF NEWS STORY) BREAK
(— OF OLD AGE) SUNSET
(— OF QUIET) DEAD
(— OF REST) BREATH SABBATH
(— OF WOE) WOSITH
(— TO COME) FUTURITY
(ANOTHER —) AGAIN
(AT ANOTHER —) ALIAS
(BRIEF —) TINE FLASH THROW
(BY THE —) AGAINST
(EACH —) ONCE
(ENDLESS —) PERPETUITY
(EXTENDED —) TRAIN
(FIXED —) HOUR STEVEN
(FUTURE —) MANANA
(GAY —) FRISK WHOOPEE
(GOOD —) BALL BASH BEANO JOLLY BARNEY FROLIC HOLIDAY
(HARD —) GYP BUSINESS
(IMMEASURABLY LONG PERIOD OF —) EON AEON
(INFINITE —) ABYSS
(LONG —) AGE
(OLD —S) ELD
(PAST —) FORETIME
(POINT OF —) MOMENT
(QUIET —) SLACK
(RIGHT —) TID
(SECOND —) YET EFTSOON EFTSOONS
(SET —) TRYST
(SHORT —) TIFF SPACE START MINUTE STOUND
(SPARE —) TOOM LEISURE
(TRIPLE —) TRIPLA
(UNENGAGED —) LEISURE
(UNIT OF —) AEON
(WORKING —) CORE
(PL.) SYSE
(PREF.) CHRON(O) HORO
(SUFF.) AD CHRONE CHRONOUS SEMIC
TIMEAUS (SON OF —) BARTIMAEUS
TIME CLOCK BUNDY TELLTALE
TIME-HONORED VINTAGE
TIMELESS AGELESS ETERNAL DATELESS
TIMELESSNESS ETERNITY
TIMELY PAT DULY TIDY COGENT TIMEFUL TIMEOUS TOWARDLY SEASONABLE
TIME OF YOUR LIFE (AUTHOR OF —) SAROYAN
(CHARACTER IN —) JOE TOM NICK KITTY MCCARTHY
TIMEPIECE DIAL CLOCK TIMER VERGE WATCH GHURRY PENDULE HOROLOGE HOROLOGY
TIMETABLE BRADSHAW SCHEDULE
TIMID SHY ARGH EERY NESH SELY SHAN BAUCH BLATE EERIE FAINT PAVID SCARE SCARY AFRAID COWARD ASHAMED BASHFUL CHICKEN FEARFUL FRIGHTY

NERVOUS RABBITY SCADDLE STRANGE TREMBLY COWARDLY FEARSOME GHASTFUL RETIRING TIMOROSO TIMOROUS PIGEONHEARTED
TIMIDITY SHYNESS TIMERITY FUNKINESS
TIMIDLY SMALL
TIMNA (BROTHER OF —) LOTAN
(LOVER OF —) ELIPHAZ
(SON OF —) AMALEK
TIMOLEON (FATHER OF —) TIMODEMUS
(MOTHER OF —) DEMARISTE
TIMON OF ATHENS (AUTHOR OF —) SHAKESPEARE
(CHARACTER IN —) CUPID TIMON TITUS CAPHIS LUCIUS FLAVIUS PHRYNIA LUCILIUS LUCULLUS PHILOTUS TIMANDRA APEMANTUS FLAMINIUS SERVILIUS VENTIDIUS ALCIBIADES HORTENSIUS SEMPRONIUS
TIMOR (CAPITAL OF —) DILI
(COIN OF —) AVO PATACA
(ISLAND OF —) MOA LETI LAKOR
(LANGUAGE OF —) TETUM
(TOWN IN —) KUPANG ATAMBUA
TIMOROUS ASPEN FAINT MILKY TIMID AFRAID COWISH TREPID FEARFUL FERDFUL MEACOCK NERVOUS FEARSOME SHEEPISH TEMEROUS TIMOROSO
TIMOTHY (COMPANION OF —) PAUL
(WIFE OF —) SIF
TIN SN DIXY JOVE DIXIE KATIN SWELL TINNY KHATIN JUPITER PILLION STANNUM PRILLION TINGLASS
(MESS —) DIXY DIXIE
(ROOFING —) TERNE
(SHEET —) LATTEN LATTIN
(TIE — CAN TO TAIL) TAILPIPE
(PREF.) STANN(I)(O)
TINAMOU YUTU MACUCA YNAMBU TATAUPA MARTINET
TINCAL ALTINCAR
TINCTURE BUFO DRUG COLOR IMBUE SMACK STAIN TAINT TENNE TINCT ARGENT ARNICA ELIXIR SATURN DIAMOND SERICON ARAMAIZE INFUSION LAUDANUM TAINTURE PAREGORIC
TINDER SPUNK AMADOU TENDRE FIREBOX
TINE BAY KNAG SNAG TANG GRAIN OFFER POINT PRONG RIGHT TOOTH GRAINING TINETARE TINEWEED
(ANTLER'S —) RIGHT CROCKET SURROYAL
TIN FOIL TAIN
TINGE DYE EYE HUE CAST DASH TANG TINT WOAD COLOR FLUSH IMBUE PAINT SAVOR SHADE STAIN TAINT TINCT TOUCH SEASON SMUTCH BEPAINT DISTAIN GLIMPSE DISCOLOR TINCTION TINCTURE
TINGED FLORID GILDED
TINGGIAN ITNEG ITANEG
TINGLE SOO BURN DIRL GELL GIRL

THIRL DINDLE SWIDGE TINKLE PRINGLE PRINKLE TRINKLE VIBRATE
TINKER PRIG TINK CAIRD FIDDLE FIDGET MUGGER KETTLER PROJECT TRAVELER
TINKLE TINK DINDLE DINGLE TINGLE TRINKLE TWINKLE
TINKLING THIN
TINNER TINKER
TINSEL GAUDY TINSY TINNET CLINQUANT
TINT DYE EYE COLOR ENNUE GRAIN TINCT TINGE SPRAING
(— IN HORSE'S COAT) BLOSSOM
(— WITH COSMETICS) SURFLE
(CLANG —) TIMBRE
TINTED TINCT
TINWORKS STANNARY
TINY TINE BITSY BITTY DEENY SMALL TEENY TIDDY WEENY ATOMIC BITTIE WEESHY MINIKIN ATOMICAL
TIP CAP DIP END FEE NEB TOP APEX CANT CAVE COCK DUMP HEEL HELD HORN KEEL LEAD LIST PALM PIKE PILE SWAG TILT TYPE VAIL GRIFF HEELD MUCRO POINT POUCH SPIRE SPURE STEER CAREEN CENTER CENTRE TICKLE TIPLET TIPPLE TOPPLE WHEEZE APICULA CUMSHAW DERTRUM DOUCEUR GRIFFIN POINTER PROPINE WRINKLE APICULUS BONAMANO ENTOMION FOOTHOLD GRATUITY PERQUISITE
(— OF ANTENNA) ARISTA
(— OF BILLIARD CUE) LEATHER
(— OF BIRD'S BILL) DERTRUM
(— OF ELBOW) NOOP
(— OF FOX'S BRUSH) CHAPE
(— OF SKI) SHOVEL
(— OF SPIDER) BULB
(— OF STAMP) SHOE
(— OF TOE) POINTE
(— OF TONGUE) CORONA
(— OF UMBO) BEAK
(— OF WHEAT KERNEL) BRUSH
(— OF WHIP) SNAPPER
(— ON ORGAN PIPE) TOE
(— OVER) TOP PURL OVERSET
(— UP) CANT COUP COWP
(ABRUPT —) MUCRO
(BOW —) HORN
(INWARD —) BANK
(LARGE —S) LARGESS LARGESSE
(RUBBISH —) TOOM
(PREF.) ACR(O) APIC(O)
TIPCART COUPE COCOPAN
TIPCAT CAT PIGGY PUSSY KITCAT PIGGIE
TIPPED BANKED
(EASILY —) CRANK
TIPPER DUMPER THROWER TIPPLER
TIPPET FUR AMICE SCARF ALMUCE SINDON LIRIPIPE LIRIPOOP PELERINE VICTORINE
TIPPLE BIB NIP POT SOT DRAM GILL BIBBER BIBBLE FUDDLE PUDDLE SIPPLE TIPPLER TOOTHFUL
TIPPLER SOUSE TOAST WINER

BIBBER BOLLER BOOZER BUBBER DRAMMER PANURGE POTATOR TUMBLER WHETTER ALESTAKE MALTWORM
TIPPLING POTTING BIBACITY BIBATION
TIPSTER PROPHET
TIPSY CUT BOSKY DRUNK FRESH MUSED MUZZY NAPPY TIGHT TOTTY TOZIE BUMPSY GROGGY SLEWED SPRUNG EBRIOSE EBRIOUS EXALTED ELEVATED MUCKIBUS OVERSEEN PLEASANT
TIP-TOP SWELL TIPPY REGULAR TOPPING
TIRADE LAISSE SCREED STOUSH JEREMIAD PHILIPPIC
TIRAS (FATHER OF —) JAPHETH
TIRE DO FAG HAG LAG SAG BORE CORD FLAT FLOG JADE KILL MOIL SHOE LABOR SPARE WEARY CASING HAGGLE HARASS SICKEN TIRING TUCKER BALLOON EXHAUST FATIGUE FRAZZLE TRACHLE CLINCHER FORSPEND
(— OUT) HAG FLOG THEAD BEJADE HARASS OVERWEARY
(WORN —) CARCASS
TIRED SAD TAM BEAT BOEG DEAD TIRY BLOWN WEARY AWEARY BLEARY BUSHED PLAYED TAVERT FORWORN SHAGGED TAIVERT FATIGUE FORWAKED
TIREDNESS FATIGUE
TIRESIAS (FATHER OF —) EVERES
(MOTHER OF —) CHARICLO
TIRESOME DRY DREE FAGGY ALANGE BORING DREICH PROLIX IRKSOME PROSAIC TEDIOUS BORESOME BROMIDIC ENNUYANT LONGSOME
TIRHANAH (FATHER OF —) CALEB
(MOTHER OF —) MAACHAH
TIRIA (FATHER OF —) JEHALELEEL
TIRING DRUDGING
TIRL RISP
TIRTHANKARA JINA
TIRZAH (FATHER OF —) ZELOPHEHAD
TISAMENUS (FATHER OF —) ORESTES THERSANDER
(MOTHER OF —) HERMIONE
TISANE PTISAN TILLEUL
TISSUE FAT WEB CORK FOIL PITH TELA TEXT FACIA GLEBA GRAFT SUBER TRAMA CALLUS DARTOS DIPLOE FABRIC FASCIA LIGNUM PANNUS PHLOEM SHEATH TEXTUS ADENOID ALBUMEN BINDWEB CAMBIUM CLYPEUS EPITELA EXPLANT HYDROME KLEENEX MESTOME NEURINE PHLOEM TEXTURE TWITTER ADHESION BLASTEMA DESMOGEN ECTODERM ENDODERM EPIPLOON HISTOGEN HYPODERM ISOGRAFT MERISTEM OSTEOGEN PERIDERM PERIDESM POLYPARY STEREOME
(— OF FUNGUS) CENTRUM
(— SURROUNDING TEETH) GUM
(BLACK —) CLYPEUS
(CONNECTING —) WEB STROMA

TENDON LIGAMENT MESENCHYME
(CORK —) SUBER
(FATTY —) LARD GREASE
(HARD —) BONE
(HYPOTHETICAL —) COAGULIN
(LYMPHOID —) TONSIL
(NERVE —) GANGLION
(SOFT —) FLAB
(VEGETABLE —) ARMOR
(WOOD —) LIGNUM VITRAIN
(PL.) CHIRATA CHIRETTA MESODERM
(PREF.) FASCIO HIST(I)(IO)(O) HYPHO
(FATTY —) ADIP(O)
(FIBROUS —) FIBR(I)(ILLI)(INO)(O)(OSO) IN(O)
TISWIN TESVINO TEXGUINO
TIT TID MESIA TITTY BLUECAP COLETIT MUFFLIN PINNOCK
TITAN BANA LETO MAIA ASURA ATLAS COEUS CREUS CRIOS DIONE THEIA CRONOS CRONUS PALLAS PHOEBE TETHYS THEMIS IAPETUS OCEANUS HYPERION
(AUTHOR OF —) DREISER
(CHARACTER IN —) FRANK PETER AILEEN BUTLER PLATOW FLEMING BERENICE LAUGHLIN STEPHANIE COWPERWOOD
TITANIA (HUSBAND OF —) OBERON
TITANIC HUGE GREAT TITAN IMMENSE COLOSSAL GIGANTIC
TITANITE SPHENE GROTHITE LEDERITE LIGURITE
TITANIUM DIOXIDE ANATASE
TITA ROOT MISHMI MISHMEE
TITHE DIME DISME TEIND TENTH DECIMA PREBEND TITHING
TITHING BORGH BORROW DECIME DENARY DECENARY
TITHINGMAN DEAN DECURION TUTTIMAN
TITHONUS (FATHER OF —) LAOMEDON
(MOTHER OF —) STRYMO
TITI ORA TEETEE WISTIT SAIMIRI WISTITI IRONWOOD MARMOSET ORABASSU OUISTITI
TITILLATE AMUSE KITTLE TICKLE
TITILLATING GAMY GAMEY
TITIVATE PRIMP
TITLARK PIPIT TEETING
TITLE (ALSO SEE LEADER, CHIEF, GOVERNOR, RULER) AGA AYA BAN BEG BEY DAN DOM DUE FRA JAM LAR MIR PAN SAG SIR ABBA ABBE AGHA AMIR ANBA BABU DAME DEVI EMIR FRAY GAON GRAF HAJI HERR KHAN KNEZ LARS NAME PANI SIDI SLUG ABGAR ABUNA AMEER BABOO BEGUM CCOYA CLAIM CROWN EMEER FRATE GHAZI GOODY GRACE HADJI HAJJI HAKAM HANUM HONOR KNIAZ KNYAZ LEMMA MIRZA MPRET NAWAB NEGUS NIZAM PANNA RABBI RIGHT SINGH SOPHI SOPHY UNWAN BASHAW BEGANI COUSIN DEGREE DEMAND DESPOT DOMINE EPONYM EXARCH HANDLE HUZOOR

LEGEND MADAME MASTER MEHTAR MISTER PESHWA PREFIX SHERIF SQUIRE SUFFEE TITULE VIDAME ALFEREZ ALTESSE ALTEZZA BAHADUR CANDACE CAPTION CONVITO CRAWLER DIGNITY EFFENDI EPITHET ESQUIRE FIDALGO GAEKWAR GRAVITY HEADING HIDALGO INFANTE KHEDIVE MAHARAO MESSIRE RABBONI SHAREEF TITULUS VOIVODE BANNERET BASILEUS COMMENDA CONVIVIO EMINENCE GOSPODIN HIGHNESS HOLINESS HOSPODAR INTEREST LOKINDRA MAGISTER MAHARAJA MAHARANA MAHARSHI MISTRESS MONSIEUR PADISHAH PRINCIPE RAUGRAVE SUBTITLE TAMBURAN TITULADO
(— ACQUISITION) USUCAPT
(— OF BOOK) QUARE
(— OF MEMBER OF PRIMROSE LEAGUE) KNIGHT
(— OF RESPECT) SIR SRI COJA LIEF MIAN SHRI SIDI BURRA HODJA KHAJA KHOJA MADAM SAHIB SIEUR KHOJAH MADAME MILADY
(BENEDICTINE —) DOM
(MOCK —) IDLESHIP
TITMOUSE MAG NUN TIT MAGG OXEYE PARUS SPICK FUFFIT HEFFEL PUFFER TOMTIT VERDIN BLUECAP BUSHTIT COLETIT COLMOSE GOLDTIT GRIGNET HAGMALL JACKSAW MUFFLIN PINCHEM PINNOCK TINNOCK TITMALL TOMNOUP CHICADEE HACKMALL OVENBIRD REEDLING SHABROON SHARPSAW
TITTER GIGGLE SNICKER TWITTER WHICKER
TITTLE JOT IOTA TITLE MINUTE
TITUBATE REEL STAGGER
TITULAR LEGAL NOMINAL HONORARY
TITUS ANDRONICUS (AUTHOR OF —) SHAKESPEARE
(CHARACTER IN —) AARON CAIUS TITUS CHIRON LUCIUS MARCUS MUTIUS TAMORA ALARBUS LAVINIA MARTIUS PUBLIUS QUINTUS AEMILIUS BASSIANUS DEMETRIUS VALENTINE SATURNINUS SEMPRONIUS
TITYUS (FATHER OF —) TERRA JUPITER
(MOTHER OF —) ELARA
TIU ER EAR TIW TYR ZIO ZIU TIWAZ SAXNOT
TIV MUNCHI
TIZZY SNIT STEW PUCKER SWIVET SWIVVET
TLAKLUIT ECHE LOOT WISHRAM
TLEPOLEMUS (FATHER OF —) HERCULES
(MOTHER OF —) ASTYOCHIA
(SLAYER OF —) SARPEDON
TLINGIT SITKA KOLUSH SUMDUM CHILCAT CHILKAT STIKINE
TMESIS DIACOPE
TNT TROTYL
TO A AD FOR INTO TILL

UNTO UPON
(— A CONCLUSION) OUT
(— BE) IBE
(— BE SURE) EVEN
(— COME) BEHIND
(— COMPLETION) DOWN
(— IT) TOOT SESSA
(— PRESS) DOWN
(— SUCH DEGREE) EVEN
(— THAT TIME) UNTIL
(— THE END) AF
(— THE OPPOSITE SIDE) ACROSS
(— THE REAR) ABAFT ASTERN
(— THIS) HERETO
(— THIS PLACE) HERE HITHER
(— VICTORY) ABU ABOO
(— WHAT) WHERETO
(— WIT) NAMELY INNUENDO SCILICET
(PREF.) AC AD AF AG AL AP AS AT INTRO OB
TOAD PAD AGUA BUFO FROG HYLA PIPA PODE HYLID PADDO PADDY PIPAL PIPID TOADY ANURAN CRAPON PEEPER BUFONID CHARLIE CRAPAUD CRAWLER CREEPER FROGLET GANGREL HOPTOAD PADDOCK PODDOCK PUDDOCK QUILKIN REPTILE SERPENT GANGEREL
(PREF.) BATRACH(O) PHRYN(O)
(SUFF.) BATRACH(O)(US)
TOADFISH SAPO SARPO GRUBBY SLIMER CABEZON FROGFISH LORICATE SCORPION
TOADFLAX FLAX FLAXWEED FLAXWORT FLUELLEN GALLWEED GALLWORT RAMSTEAD
TOAD RUSH SALTWEED
TOADSTONE BUFONITE
TOADSTOOL CANKER FUNGUS
TOADY FAWN SUCK TOAD ZANY COTTON EARWIG FAWNER FLUNKY GREASE LACKEY MUCKER FLUNKEY JENKINS LACQUEY PLACEBO SHONEEN TRUCKLE BOOTLICK CLAWBACK LICKSPIT PARASITE SYCOPHANT
TOADYING GNATHONIC
TOADYISM FLUNKYISM
TOAST WET TOSS BREDE ROUSE SKOAL TRINQ BIRSLE BUMPER CHEERS HEALTH PLEDGE PROSIT BRISTLE CAROUSE CHEERIO FRIZZLE LEHAYIM PROFACE PROPINE RESPECT SLAINTE WASSAIL BRINDISI SCOUTHER
(— AND ALE) SWIG
(— ONESELF) LEEP
(JACOBITE —) LIMP
TOBACCO CANE CAPA HAND LEAF LUGS NAVY POAK POKE QUID ROLL SHAG WEED BACCO BACCY BACKY BROKE CUBAN DARKS FOGUS PETUN REGIE SMOKE SNOUT TABAC TWIST BACKER BRIGHT BURLEY COLORY COWPEN FILLER HAVANA RETURN TOMBAC TUMBAK CAPORAL CRACCUS GAGROOT GORACCO KNASTER LATAKIA NAILROD NICOTIA ORONOKO PERIQUE PIGTAIL SOTWEED UPPOWOC CANASTER

HONEYDEW MAKHORKA MARYLAND NICOTIAN ORONOOKO SEEDLEAF VIRGINIA MUNDUNGUS NICOTIANA
(— AND PAPER) MAKINGS
(— CAKED IN PIPE BOWL) DOTTEL DOTTLE TOPPER
(— HAVING OFFENSIVE SMELL) MUNDUNGO
(— IN ROPES) BOGIE
(— JUICE) AMBEER PRAISS
(— MOISTENED WITH MOLASSES) HONEYDEW
(— MOSAIC) WALLOON
(— PASTE) GORACCO
(— ROOM) PRIZERY
(— WORKER) LOOPER LEAFBOY LEAFGIRL
(CAKED —) HEEL
(COARSE —) SHAG SCRAP CAPORAL
(CUT —) CANASTER PICADURA
(DRIED —) TABACUM
(HARD-PRESSED —) NAILROD
(HATING —) MISOCAPNIC
(INDIAN —) GAGROOT PUKEWEED EYEBRIGHT
(INFERIOR —) LUGS
(LADIES' —) CUDWEED
(LOWER LEAVES OF —) FLYING
(MILD —) RETURN
(PERSIAN —) SHIRAZ TUMBEK TUMBEKI
(PERUVIAN —) SANA
(POOR QUALITY —) DOGLEG
(PULVERIZED —) SNUFF
(QUID OF —) CUD
(RAW —) LEAF
(ROLLED —) CARROT
(SMALL PIECE OF —) FIG
(VIRGINIA —) COWPEN VIRGINIA
TOBACCO BROWN TABAC
TOBACCO ROAD (AUTHOR OF —) CALDWELL
(CHARACTER IN —) ADA LOV DUDE RICE ELLIE PEARL BENSEY BESSIE JEETER LESTER
TOBACCO WORM HORNWORM
TOBOGGAN COAST CARIOLE CARRIOLE
TOCHARIAN A AGNEAN
TOCHARIAN B KUCHEAN
TOCSIN ALARUM
TODAY DAY NOW NOWADAYS
TODDLE TOT FADGE DADDLE DIDDLE DODDLE PADDLE TOTTLE WADDLE
TODDLER TROT GANGREL TROTTIE
TODDY TOD TUBA TERRY SAGWIRE
TO-DO ADO FUSS STIR WORK STINK DOMENT HOOPLA FLUSTER FOOSTER FOOFARAW TRAVALLY
TODY ROBIN
TOE TER DIGIT DACTYL HALLUX MINIMUS TOENAIL TRIPPET POULAINE
(— OF BIRD) HEEL
(LITTLE —) MINIMUS
(PL.) TUN TAIS TOON
(PREF.) DACTYL(O) DACTYLIO DIGITI DIGITO
TOENAIL
(SUFF.) ONYCHA ONYCHES

ONYCHIA ONYCHIUM
ONYCHUS ONYX
TOEPLATE SHOD
TOFF NOB
TOGA GOWN ROBE TOGUE TRABEA
TOGETHER ONCE SAME ATONE
YFERE BEDENE INSAME JOINTLY
ENSEMBLE
(— WITH) AND INTO
(PREF.) CO COL COM CON COR
SYM SYN
TOGGLE COTTAR COTTER TOGGEL
NETSUKE
TOGO (CAPITAL OF —) LOME
(LANGUAGE OF —) EWE TWI MINA
HAUSA KABRAIS LOTOCOLI
(MOUNTAIN IN —) AGOU
(NATIVE OF —) EWE MINA CABRAI
KABRAI OUATCHI
(RIVER IN —) OTI ANIE HAHO
MONO
(TOWN IN —) KANDE ANECHO
PALIME SOKODE TSEVIE
ATAKPAME
TOHUBOHU RIOT CHAOS
DISORDER CONFUSION
TOI (SON OF —) JORAM
TOIL FAG TUG DARG GRUB HACK
MOIL MUCK PLOD TASK WORK
LABOR SCRAT SLAVE SWINK
TWEIL YAKKA BILDER DRUDGE
EFFORT HAMMER KIAUGH
MITHER MOIDER STRIVE UNRUFE
YACKER FATIGUE TRAVAIL
TURMOIL DRUDGERY INDUSTRY
TOILER SLAVE MOILER WORKER
TOILET CAN LOO HEAD JOHN BIFFY
CRAPPER BASEMENT BATHROOM
LAVATORY PLUMBING
TOILSOME HARD SWEATY
ARDUOUS TOILFUL MOILSOME
SWEATFUL
TOJOLABAL CHANABAL
TOKAY TUCKTOO
TOKEN BUCK CENT HARP SIGN
TYPE BADGE CHECK INDEX SCRIP
BEAVER CASTOR COLLAR COPPER
COUPON DOLLAR EMBLEM
JETTON MARKER OSTENT
REMARK SIGNAL TICKET WITTER
AUSPICE COUNTER EARNEST
INDICIA MEMENTO PRESAGE
SYMPTOM TESSERA BUNGTOWN
COINTISE EVIDENCE FOOTSTEP
FORBYSEN INSTANCE KEEPSAKE
MONUMENT SHILLING SIGNACLE
(— OF LUCK) HANSEL HANDSEL
(— OF RESPECT) SALUTE
(— OF SUPERIORITY) PALM
(— OF VICTORY) LAUREL
(CANADIAN —) HARP
(LOVE —) DRURY AMORET
(PORCELAIN —S) PI
TOKHARI KUCHEAN
TOKYO (— STREET) GINZA
(FORMER NAME OF —) EDO YEDO
TOLA (FATHER OF —) ISSACHAR
TOLERABLE GAY SOSO PRETTY
TARBLE LIVABLE PATIBLE
BEARABLE PASSABLE PORTABLE
TOLERABLY GAIN GEYAN FAIRLY
MEETLY MEETERLY MIDDLING
TOLERANCE MERCY SHERE

LEEWAY REMEDY
TOLERANT SOFT BROAD BENIGN
PATIENT PLACABLE PERMISSIVE
TOLERATE GO BEAR BIDE HACK
HAVE ABEAR ABIDE ALLOW
BROOK SPARE STAND STICK
THOLE ACCEPT ENDURE PARDON
PERMIT SUFFER COMPORT
STOMACH SUPPORT SUSTAIN
TOLERATION WITHGANG
TOLL JOW TAX JOWL PIKE RENT
KNELL PEAGE CAPHAR EXCISE
OCTROI PEDAGE PESAGE
BOOMAGE KEELAGE LASTAGE
LOCKAGE MULTURE PASSAGE
PICCAGE PIERAGE PONTAGE
SCAVAGE SUMMAGE TERRAGE
TOLLAGE TRONAGE BERTHAGE
STALLAGE WEIGHAGE WHEELAGE
(PL.) CUSTOMS RAHDARI
RATTAREE
TOLLHOUSE TOLLERY
TOLLIKER DUMMY
TOLSEN FOOTSTEP
TOLUENE DILUENT
TOLYL CRESYL
TOMAHAWK HATCHET NEOLITH
TOMATO TOM BERRY BURBANK
TOMB PIR BIER CIST MOLE GRAVE
GUACA HUACA MAZAR SPEOS
TABUT THOLE TURBE BURIAL
CHULPA DARGAH DURGAH
GALGAL HEARSE HEROON
SAMADH SHRINE SYRINX THOLOS
TROUGH TURBEH CHULLPA
MASTABA OSSUARY TOMBLET
TRITAPH CENOTAPH CISTVAEN
CUBICULO HALLCIST HYPOGEUM
KISTVAEN MARABOUT MASTABAH
MONUMENT TREASURY
MAUSOLEUM SEPULCHER
(— IN CHURCH) SACELLUM
(— OF MOSLEM SAINT) ZIARA
ZIARAT
(CAVE —) SPEOS
(PREHISTORIC —) KURGAN
TOMBAC ORSEDE ORSEDUE
TOMBOY HEMP RAMP GAMINE
HOYDEN MADCAP TOMRIG
TOMBSTONE SLAT TITLE
THROUGH
TOMCAT GIB TOMMY PODGER
THOMAS
TOMCOD GADE GADID SMELT
GADOID WHITING TOMMYCOD
TOMENTUM WOOL
TOMFOOLERY HELL HORSE
TOM JONES (AUTHOR OF —)
FIELDING
(CHARACTER IN —) TOM BETTY
JENNY JONES NANCY BLIFIL
GEORGE SOPHIA SQUARE
WATERS BRIDGET WESTERN
THWACKUM ALLWORTHY
BELLASTON PARTRIDGE
FITZPATRICK NIGHTINGALE
TOMMY FOOL PODGER REQUIN
TOMMYROT WAHOO
TOMMY TALKER KAZOO
TOMORROW MANANA MORROW
TOMORN
TOM SAWYER (AUTHOR OF —)
TWAIN CLEMENS

(CHARACTER IN —) AMY JOE SID
TOM FINN HUCK MARY MUFF
BECKY POLLY HARPER POTTER
SAWYER DOUGLAS LAWRENCE
ROBINSON THATCHER
TOMTATE CAESAR
TON TUN TOUN STYLE
TONALAMATL TZOLKIN
TONALITY KEY
TONE A F DO FA LA MI RE SI SO TI
DOH KEY SOH SOL CALL FLAT
NOTE COLOR COUAC DRONE
FIFTH FORTE PRIME SHARP SIXTH
SOUND STYLE TONUS ACCENT
DEGREE FOURTH SECOND
FORMANT MEDIANT PARTIAL
DEMITINT ELEVENTH FORENOTE
HARMONIC HEADNOTE
PARAMESE PARANETE SONORITY
(— A DRAWING) STUMP
(— DOWN) DRAB TAME SOFTEN
SUBDUE
(— UP) BRACE
(ACCENTED —) SFORZANDO
(BROKEN —) CRACK
(COMPLEX —) KLANG
(DEEP —) BASS
(DOMINANT —) ANIMUS
(DRAWLING —) DRANT DRAUNT
(HIGH-PITCHED —) PIP
(KEY —) KEYNOTE
(LOUD —) FORTE
(LOW —) SEMISOUN
(MONOTONOUS —) DRONE
(SHARP NASAL —) TWANG
(SIGNIFICANT —) ACCENT
(SINGLE UNVARIED —) MONOTONE
(STRIDENT —) COUAC
(WHINING —) GIRN
(PREF.) PHON(O)
TONGA (CAPITAL OF —)
NUKUALOFA
(COIN OF —) PAANGA SENITI
(ISLAND GROUP OF —) TOFUA
VAVAU HAAPAI NIUAFOO
TONGATAPU NIUATOBUTABU
(ISLAND OF —) ONO TOFUA VAVAU
HAAPAI
(TOWN OF —) NEIAFU
TONGS SNAPS SERVER FORCEPS
GRAMPUS TUEIRON SCISSORS
TONGUE COG GAB CHIB CLAP KALI
NEAP PAWL POLE REED CLACK
IDIOM LADIN VOICE GADABA
GLOSSA KABYLE KALIKA LADINO
LANGUE LINGUA SPEECH
CLAPPER DIALECT FEATHER
ILOKANO LANGUET DOVETAIL
LANGUAGE LORRIKER PLECTRUM
(— IN FLOORING) SPLINE
(— OF BELL) CLAPPER
(— OF JEW'S-HARP) TANG
(— OF LAND) DOAB REACH
LANGUE LANGUET
(— OF MOLLUSC) RADULA
(— OF OXCART) COPE
(— OF SHOE) FLAP KILTY KILTIE
(— OF VEHICLE) NEAP SHAFT
(BELLOWS —) GUSSET
(GIVE —) PRATE
(GOSSIPING —) CLACK CLACKER
(PART OF —) BUD UVULA FAUCES
LINGUA SEPTUM

(PIVOTED —) PAWL
(ROMANY —) ROMANES
(PL.) GAURA
(PREF.) GLOSS(O) GLOTT(I)(O)
LIGUL(I) LINGU(I)(LI)(O)
(SUFF.) GLOSSA GLOSSIA GLOT
TONGUEFISH SOLE
TONGUE-LASH SCOLD
TONGUE-LASHING RAT TOCO
BUSINESS
TONGUELESS AGLOSSAL
TONGUE-TIED SILENT
TONIC DO DOH ALOE KEEP PICHI
PRIME BRACER SAMBUL SONANT
SUMBUL BONESET CALAMUS
CALOMBO CHIRATA COLOMBA
DAMIANA FUMARIA GENTIAN
KEYNOTE NERVINE SALICIN
TONICAL ANTHEMIS BARBERRY
BERBERRY HELONIAS ROBORANT
TRILLIUM PIPSISSEWA
TONICITY MYOTONIA
TONKA BEAN GAIAC CUMARU
GUAIAC COUMAROU
TONNA DOLIUM
TONNAGE PORTAGE
TONO-BUNGAY (AUTHOR OF —)
WELLS
(CHARACTER IN —) RINK EFFIE
FRAPP GROVE MOGGS SUSAN
ARCHIE EDWARD GEORGE
MANTEL MARION OSPREY
GARVELL RAMBOAT BEATRICE
NORMANDY NICODEMUS
PONDEREVO
TONSIL ALMOND KERNEL ADENOID
AMYGDAL AMYGDALA
(PREF.) AMYGDAL(O)
TONSILITIS QUINSY
TONSURE CROWN SHAVE SHEAR
CORONA DIKSHA RASURE
TONSURED PEELED PILLED
SHAVED
TOO SO ALSO OVER TROP LUCKY
OVERLY LIKEWISE
(PREF.) OVER
TOOL (ALSO SEE IMPLEMENT AND
INSTRUMENT) AX ADZ AWL AXE
BIT BUR DIE DIG GIN GUN HOB
KEY LAP LOY RIP SAW SAX TAP
TIT VOL ZAX ADZE BORE BRAY
BURR CLAW COMB DADO DISC
DISK DUPE EDGE FILE FLAY FROE
FROG FROW GAGE HACK HAWK
HONE LEAF LOOM MILL PICK ROLL
SATE SEAX SLED SNAP SPID SPUD
STOP TAMP TIER VISE AUGER
BLADE BORAL BORER BRAKE
BRAND BREAK BRUSH BURIN
CROZE DARBY DOLLY DRIFT DRILL
DUMMY EDGER FLAKE FLOAT
FLUTE GAUGE GOUGE GUIDE
HARDY HOBBY HOWEL KNIFE
KNURL LEVEL MAKER MISER
MODEL PLANE POINT PRUNT
PUNCH QUIRK SABER SABRE
SCREW SHAVE SHELL SLICE SLICK
SNIPE SPADE SPEAR SPLIT STAKE
STAMP STING STOCK STRIG STYLE
SWAGE TEWEL TOYLE UPSET
VALET WAGON BEADER BEATER
BIDENT BIFACE BLADER BODKIN
BROACH BUDGER BUFFER CALKER

CHASER CHISEL CLEAVE COGGLE
COLTER CRADLE CRANNY CUTTER
DEVICE DIBBLE DIGGER DOCTOR
DRIVER ENGINE FASCET FERRET
FILLET FLANGE FLORET FLUTER
FORMER FRAISE FILLER GIMLET
GLAZER GOFFER GRAVER
GUMMER HACKER HAMMER
HEMMER HOGGER HOLDER
HULLER JIGGER JUMPER LADKIN
LASTER LIFTER NIBBER PALLET
PARTER PICKAX PICKER PLENCH
PLIERS PROPER PUPPET REAMER
RIPPER ROCKER RUNNER SAPPER
SCRIBE SCUTCH SEATER SHAPER
SHAVER SHEARS SHOVEL SKIVER
SLATER SOCKET SQUARE STYLET
STYLUS SWIVEL TAGGER TASTER
TONGUE TREPAN TURNER
TURREL TWILLY VEINER WAGGON
WIGWAG WIMBLE WORDLE
WORMER YANKEE ABRADER
BLOCKER BRADAWL CALIPER
CAULKER CHAMFER CHIPPER
CHOPPER CLEANER CLEAVER
COULTER CREASER DIAMOND
DOLABRA DRESSER FISTUCA
FLANGER FREEZER FROTTON
GRAINER GROOVER GRUBBER
GUDGEON JOINTER KNOTTER
LOGHEAD MITERER OUSTITI
POINTEL POINTER PROFILE
RIVETER ROUGHER ROUNDER
SCAUPER SCORPER SCRIBER
SCRIVER SCURFER SLASHER
SLEEKER SLICKER SPLAYER
SPUDDER STEMMER STRIKER
STROKER TICKLER TREBLET
TWIBILL UPRIGHT WRAITHE
AIGUILLE BIFACIAL BILLHOOK
BOOTJACK BURGOYNE CALLIPER
CREATURE CRIPPLER CROSSCUT
CROWFOOT DUCKFOOT
ELEVATOR EXPANDER FLOUNDER
GRAVETTE GRIFFAUN POLISHER
PRITCHEL PROPERTY PUNCHEON
RAVEHOOK RECAPPER SCRAPPLE
SCULPTOR SPLITTER STIPPLER
STRICKLE STRINGER SURFACER
THWACKER TOLLIKER WARKLOOM
WORKLOOM SCRATCHER **(— A BOOK)** FINISH
(PL.) TEW FISH GEAR TRADE
CUTLERY GIBBLES PIONERY
ENGINERY
TOOLED GOFFERED
(— WITHOUT GILDING) BLIND
TOOLHOLDER TURRET MONITOR
TOOLHOUSE COPHOUSE
TOOLSHED DOGHOUSE
TOON LIM CEDAR TOONWOOD
TOOT BLOW TOWT BLAST SOUND
TRUMPET
TOOTH BIT COG GAM JAG PEG
DENS DENT FANG LEAF RASP
SNAG TIND TINE TUSH TUSK
CRENA IVORY MOLAR PEARL
PRONG RAKER TENON BROACH
CANINE CUSPID CUTTER DENTAL
INDENT JOGGLE TRIGON TRITOR
DENTILE DIVIDER GRINDER
INCISOR LATERAL SURDENT
UNCINUS ABUTMENT BICUSPID

BLEPHARA DENTICLE EYETOOTH
GAGTOOTH MARGINAL
PREMOLAR SAWTOOTH
SPROCKET TOOTHLET TRIGONID
CARNASSIAL
(— OF A MOSS) BLEPHARA
(— OF HORSE) DIVIDER
(— OF MOLLUSC) MARGINAL
(— OF PINION) LEAF
(— OF RADULA) UNCINUS
(— ON ROTATING PIECE) WIPER
(ARTIFICIAL —) DUMMY PONTIL
(CANINE —) CUSPID HOLDER
LANIARY CYNODONT DOGTOOTH
EYETOOTH
(GEAR —) COG GUB DENT
ADDENDUM SPROCKET
(HARROW —) TINE
(MOLAR —) WANG
(PART OF —) GUM NECK PULP
ROOT CROWN DENTIN ENAMEL
CEMENTUM
(UPPER SURFACE OF —) TABLE
(PREF.) DENT(ATO)(I)(INO)(O)(ODO)
ODONT(O)
(SUFF.) DENT(ATE)
ODON(T)(TA)(TES)(TIA)(TY) ODUS
TOOTHACHE WORM DENTAGRA
TOOTHED SERRATE VIRGATE
SERRATED PECTINATE
(SUFF.) ODON ODUS
TOOTHLESS GUMMY
TOOTHPICK QUILL ARKANSAN
TOOTHSOME PALATABLE
TOOTHWORT CROWTOE
COOLWORT
TOP CAP COP GIG NUN TAP TIP
ACME APEX BEAT COCK CULM
HEAD HELM ROOF SKIM STOP
BLOOM CHIEF COVER CREST
CROWN FANCY GIGGE PITCH
RIDGE SPIRE STRIP TOTUM
TRUMP UPPER CALASH CAPOTE
CULMEN SUMMIT UPWARD
VERTEX CACUMEN SPINNER
ROUNDTOP SURMOUNT
TEETOTUM CULMINATION
(— FOR CHIMNEY OR PIPE) COWL
HOOD
(— OF ALTAR) MENSA
(— OF AUTOMOBILE) HEAD HOOD
(— OF CAPSTAN) DRUMHEAD
(— OF FURNACE) ARCH
(— OF GLASS) PRETTY
(— OF HEAD) MOLD PATE MOULD
SCALP VERTEX
(— OF HELMET) SKULL
(— OF HILL) KNAG KNAP KNOLL
(— OF INGOT) CROPHEAD
(— OF MINING SHAFT) PITHEAD
(— OF MOUNTAIN) MAN
(— OF PLANT OR TREE) CROP
(— OF ROOF) DECK
(— OF SPINDLE) COCKHEAD
(— OF THUNDERCLOUD) INCUS
(— OF WAVE) COMB
(— OF WOODEN STAND) CRISS
(—S OF CROP) SHAW
(BOOT —) RUFF
(BOX —) COUPON
(CARRIAGE —) CALASH
(PEG —) PEERIE
(RESEMBLING A —) STROBIC

(SPINNING —) PEERY PEERIE
(PREF.) ACR(O)
(SPINNING —) RHOMB(O)
TOPAZ PYCNITE PYCNIUM
PHSALITE
TOPCOAT OVERCOAT SIPHONIA
TOPE DHER DHERI STUPA DAGOBA
SOUPFIN
TOPER BOUSER CUPMAN POTMAN
POTTER SIPPER SOAKER SUPPER
TROUGH BOMBARD POTLING
SWILLER TOSSPOT BLACKPOT
DRUNKARD MALTWORM
TOPI TIANG
TOPIC HARE ITEM TEXT HOBBY
THEMA THEME BURDEN GAMBIT
GROUND MATTER SUBJECT
OCCASION
(STOCK —) TOPOS
TOPKNOT ONKOS TOPPING
TOPMAN COB
TOPMINNOW GUPPY LIMIA
GULARIS HELLERI SAILFIN
GAMBUSIA MOLLIENSIA
TOPOGRAPHIC TERRAIN
TOPPLE TIP TOP TILT LEVEL
TOTTLE
TOPSAIL RAFFE RAFFEE
TOPSOIL KELLY
TOPSTONE CAPSTONE
TOPSWARM TOPCAST
TOPSY-TURVY COCKEYED
REELRALL
TOQUE ZATI MUNGA MACACO
RILAWA MACAQUE
TOQUILLA JIPIJAPA
TORCEL BURN BERNE BORNE
TORCH DUCK JACK LAMP LINK
LUNT PINE TEAD WASE WISP
BLAZE BRAND FLARE MATCH
FOCKLE LAMPAD MASHAL
MUSSAL BRANDON CRESSET
GRIDDLE LUCIGEN ROUGHIE
TORCHET FLAMBEAU
(PREF.) DAD(O) LAMPADE
TORCHBEARER KERYX LINKBOY
LINKMAN DADUCHUS TORCHMAN
TOREADOR TORERO CAPEADOR
TORII (PART OF —) NYKI DAIWA
KASAGI KUSABI LINTEL
GAKUZUKA CROSSPIECE
TORIL CHIQUERO
TORMENT WO RAG TAW TRY WOE
BAIT BALE FRET MOIL PAIN PANG
PINE RACK SOOL TEAR TUCK
CHEVY CURSE DEVIL GRILL HARRY
SCALD TEASE TWIST WRING
CHIVVY HARASS HARROW
HECTOR INFEST NEEDLE PLAGUE
TRAVEL AFFLICT ANGUISH
BEDEVIL CRUCIFY HAGRIDE
HATCHEL MALISON PERPLEX
PINDING TERRIFY TORTURE
TRAVAIL CRUCIATE DISTRAIN
LACERATE MACERATE
(EXTREME —) AGONY
TORMENTED CRUCIATE
TORMENTIL SEPTFOIL
TORMENTING PLAGUY
TORMINA TORSION
TORN RENT BROKEN BLASTED
TORNADO VORTEX CYCLONE
TRAVADO TWISTER

TORPEDO FISH SHELL SQUIB
BATOID HOAGIE
TORPID FOUL NUMB BROSY INERT
SODDEN STUPID TOGGER
LANGUID TORPENT COMATOSE
COMATOUS SLUGGISH
TORPIFY DAZE ETHERIZE
TORPOR COMA SLEEP SWOON
ACEDIA ACCIDIE SLUMBER
LETHARGY
(PREF.) NARC(O)
TORQUE BEE SARPE TWIST
TORREFY PARCH
TORRENT FLOW RUSH FLOOD
SPATE STREAM NIAGARA
CATARACT
(— OF WORDS) BLATTER
TORREYA SAVIN TUMION
TORRID HOT SULTRY AUSTRAL
BOILING
TORSALO BERNE
TORSION STRESS DIDROMY
TORSK CUSK
TORT LIBEL WRONG
TORTE DOBOS
TORT-FEASOR ACTOR
TORTICOLLIS WRYNECK
TORTILLA TACO BREAD BURRITO
TOSTADO ENCHILADA
QUESADILLA
TORTOISE EMYD BEKKO GAPER
COOTER GOPHER TURTLE
EMYDIAN HICATEE MUNGOFA
TESTUDO GALAPAGO KASHYAPA
SHELLPAD SHELLPOT TERRAPIN
(PREF.) CHEL(O)(Y)
TORTOISESHELL CAREY
TORTUOUS CRANKY SCREWY
SINUATE WRIGGLY SINUATED
TORTURE GYP TAW BOOT CARD
FIRE PAIN PANG PINE RACK
AGONY SCREW TWIST ENGINE
EXTORT IMPALE MARTYR AFFLICT
AGONIZE ANGUISH BOOTING
CRUCIFY PERPLEX TORMENT
MARTYRDOM
TORTURER BOURREAU
TORUS CORK TORE BASTON
BOLTEL BOUTELL BOWTELL
THALAMUS
TORY BANDIT OUTLAW ROBBER
PEELITE TANTIVY ABHORRER
LOYALIST
TOSS BUM COB LAB SHY BUNG
CANT CAST CAVE DOSS FLAP FLIP
HIKE PASS SHAG SLAT TOUT
CHAFE CHUCK FLICK FLING FLIRT
FLURR HEAVE PITCH TEAVE
THROW BETOSS BOUNCE DANDLE
TOTTER WALTER WELTER
WENTLE BLANKET TURMOIL
WAMPISH WHEMMEL
(— A COIN) SKY
(— A JACK) LAG
(— ABOUT) SWAB TAVE POPPLE
THRASH THRESH TORFLE
WAMPISH
(— ASIDE) BANDY
(— AWAY) BLOW
(— HEAD) CAVE GECK BRANK
(— OF HORSE'S HEAD) CHACK
(— OF THE HEAD) HEEZE
(— OFF) SWAP SWOP

(**— ON WAVES**) SURGE
(**— TO AND FRO**) WALK
(**— TOGETHER CONFUSEDLY**) SCRAMBLE
(**— WITH THE HORNS**) DOSS HIKE
TOSSING SURGING
(**— OF BULLFIGHTER**) COGIDA
TOSTAO TESTON
TOTAL SUM TAB TOT DEAD MERE TALE COUNT GROSS MOUNT SLUMP SUMMA UTTER WHOLE ENTIRE GLOBAL OMNIUM SUMMED TOTTLE EMBRACE FOOTING GENERAL PERFECT ABSOLUTE COMPLETE ENTIRETY SURMOUNT TEETOTAL
(**PREF.**) HOL(O)
TOTALITY ALL BODY HEAP BEING ALLNESS ECOLOGY ETERNITY HUMANITY INTEGRAL INTERVAL OMNITUDE
TOTALLY COLD GOOD QUITE WHOLLY
TOTEM HUACA
TO THE LIGHTHOUSE (**AUTHOR OF —**) WOOLF
(**CHARACTER IN —**) LILY PRUE JAMES MCNAB ANDREW BANKES RAMSAY BRISCOE CAMILLA CHARLES TANSLEY WILLIAM CARMICHAEL
TOTTER TOT ROCK TOIT WALT SHAKE WAVER COGGLE DADDLE DODDER DOTTER FALTER HOTTER JOGGLE STAVER SWERVE TITTER TOTTLE WAMBLE WANGLE WAPPER BRANDLE FRIBBLE STAGGER TREMBLE WHITHER TITUBATE VACILLATE
(**PREF.**) LABE
TOTTERING LURCH SHAKY GROGGY CRAMBLY PALSIED RICKETY TOTTERY TITUBANT WAMBLING
TOU (**SON OF —**) HAMATH
TOUCAN TOCO TUCANA ARACARI
TOUCH GET RAP TAG TIG TIP ABUT BILL DASH FEEL HAND KISS KNEE MEET PALP PEAL PLAY RAKE RINE TACT TAKE GLISK GRAZE GROPE SPICE TAINT TASTE TATTO TINGE TRAIT TREAT AFFECT ATTAIN CARESS FINGER GLANCE HANDLE REGARD SCRUFF SMUTCH STRAIN TACTUS TWITCH ATTAINT ATTINGE CONTACT FEELING PALPATE SOUPCON TACTION FLOURISH TINCTURE
(**— A KEY**) STRIKE
(**— BRIEFLY**) GLANCE
(**— CARESSINGLY**) FLATTER
(**— CLOSELY**) IMPINGE
(**— GENTLY**) DAB TAT TICK BRUSH
(**— LIGHTLY**) GRAZE SCUFF SKIFF
(**— OF BRUSH**) HAND
(**— OF COLOR**) EYE
(**— OF PAINT**) GLOB
(**— OF PLEASURE**) GLISK
(**— RIGHTLY**) NICK
(**DELICATE —**) STROKE
(**FINISHING —**) HOODER COPESTONE
(**PAINTING —**) ACCENT

(**SLIGHT —**) SKIFF SMATCH
(**PREF.**) TAC TACTO TANGO THIGMO THIXO
(**SUFF.**) APHIA
(**HAVING A — OF**) ISH ISTIC
TOUCHDOWN ROUGE
TOUCHED FEY DOTTY
TOUCHING ABOUT LIBANT TENDER AGAINST CONTACT TANGENT ADJACENT PATHETIC POIGNANT AFFECTING CONTINUOUS
(**— LIGHTLY**) LAMBENT
TOUCHSTONE TEST TOUCH LYDITE BASANITE STANDARD
TOUCHWOOD FUNK MONK PUNK SPUNK PUNKWOOD
TOUCHY HUFFY MIFFY SNAKY TESTY FEISTY KITTLE SNAKEY SNUFFY SPUNKY TENDER TETCHY GROUCHY NERVOUS PEEVISH PEPPERY TEMPERY TICKLISH
TOUGH RUM BHOY HARD TAUT WIRY BUTCH CLUNG HARDY STIFF STOUT WITHY BALLSY KNOTTY SINEWY STARCH STRONG HICKORY BULLYBOY LEATHERY UNTENDER ROUGHNECK TENACIOUS
TOUGHEN TAW ANNEAL ENDURE HARDEN TEMPER
(**— METAL**) PLANISH
TOUGHENED CLUNG
TOUGHNESS TUCK FIBER FIBRE STRENGTH TENACITY
TOUPEE RUG HOLD SCALP POSTICHE TOPPIECE
TOUR GIRO TURN SWING TOWER TURUS JUNKET SAFARI JOURNEY INVASION PROGRESS TOURETTE
(**— OF DUTY**) HERD STATION
(**CANARY —**) GLUCK GLUCKE
TOURACO LORY LOURIE TURAKOO
TOURBILLON KARRUSEL
TOUR DE FORCE STUNT
TOURIST TOURER TRIPPER VISITANT RUBBERNECK
TOURMALINE SHORL SCHORL DRAVITE ACHROITE SIBERITE
TOURNAMENT TILT JERID JOUSTS TOURNEY BONSPIEL CAROUSEL
TOURNEUR DEALER
TOURNEY PLAY
TOURNIQUET GARROT STANCH TWISTER STANCHER TORCULAR
TOUSLE SOOL SOWL RUMPLE TOOZLE
TOUSLED TAUTED TOWZIE TUMBLED UNKEMPT
TOUT SKIV BRUIT PLIER BARKER STEERER
TOW CRIB HAUL PULL HURDS STUPE TRACK TRACT CODILLA CORDELLE
TOWAGE TRACKAGE
TOWAI BIRCH KAMAHI
TOWARD AD INTO TORT ANENT ANENST AGAINST FORNENT ADVERSUS GAINWARD
(**— CENTER**) CENTRAD
(**— CENTER OF EARTH**) DOWN
(**— ONE SIDE**) ASLANT
(**— THE END**) SF
(**— THE HEAD**) ANTERIOR

(**— THE REAR**) ABACK DORSAD BACKWARD
(**— THE RIGHT**) DEXTRAD
(**— THE SIDE**) LATERAD
(**— THE STERN**) AFTER
(**PREF.**) AC AD AF AG AL AP AS AT IL IM IN INTRO IR OB PROS
(**SUFF.**) AD
(**GOING —**) PETAL
TOWEL CLOUT WIPER DIAPER LAVABO RUBBER
TOWER TOR PEEL PIKE REAR RISE SOAR SPUR TOUR BABEL BROCH HEAVE MINAR MOUNT PYLON SIKAR SPIRE STUPA TEXAS ASCEND ASPIRE BELFRY CASTLE CHULPA DOKHMA DONJON GOPURA ROLLER RONDEL SPRING TURRET BASTIDE CHULLPA DERRICK GIRALDA LANTERN MIRADOR NURAGHE SHIKARA SIKHARA STEEPLE TALAYOT TORREON TOURNEL TRACKER TURRION BARBICAN BASTILLE CLOGHEAD DOMINEER RONDELLE SCRUBBER TOURELLE TOWERLET PEPPERBOX
(**— CONTAINING COKE**) SCRUBBER
(**— FOR SENTINEL**) GUERITE
(**— OF FORT**) SPUR
(**— OF MOSQUE**) MINARET
(**— OF SILENCE**) DAKHMA
(**— ON SUMMIT**) PIKE
(**— OVER**) DROWN BESTRIDE
(**ATTACHED —**) DETAIL
(**BELL —**) CARILLON
(**CONNING —**) SAIL
(**FRACTIONATING —**) STILL
(**PYRAMIDAL —**) SIKAR VIMANA SHIKARA SIKHARA
(**SIEGE —**) BRATTICE
(**SIGNAL —**) BANTAYAN
(**WIND —**) BADGIR
(**PREF.**) PYRGO TURRI
TOWERING EMINENT SUPERNAL AMBITIOUS
TOWERMAN LEVERMAN
TOWER MUSTARD CRUCIFER
TOWHEE JOREE CHEWINK CHEEWINK
TOWING TRACKAGE
TOWLINE CORDELLE
TOWN BY BYE HAM WON CAMP CITY STAD TOON WENE WICK BAYAN BORGO BOURH BRUGH BURGH DERBY MACHI PLACE PLECK SIEGE STAND STEAD VILLE CIUDAD HAMMON ORANGE PUEBLO STAPLE BASTIDE BOROUGH CHESTER OPPIDUM QUIVIRA TOWNLET BOOMTOWN BOURGADE ENCEINTE HOMETOWN TOWNSHIP
(**DESOLATED —**) GUBAT
(**FORTIFIED —**) BURG BURGH ENCEINTE
(**MYTHICAL —**) QUIVIRA
(**SMALL —**) SHTETL SHTETEL
(**UNFORTIFIED —**) BOURGADE
(**UNIMPORTANT —**) PODUNK
(**WALLED —**) CHESTER
(**PL.**) PARGANA
(**SUFF.**) GRAD

TOWN HALL HALL CABILDO RATHAUS TOLBOOTH STADHOUSE
TOWNSHIP DEME DORP VILL BAYAN TREEN BOROUGH
TOWNSMAN CAD CIT DUDE SNOB TOWNY TOWNEE BURGHER CITIZEN COCKNEY OPPIDAN
(**PL.**) BURGWARE
TOWROPE TOW CABLET GUNLINE TOWLINE CORDELLE
TOXALBUMIN ROBIN PHALLIN
TOXEMIA BLACKLEG ECLAMPSIA
TOXIC VENOMOUS
TOXIN BOTULIN EXOTOXIN
TOY ARK DIE GAY TOP COCK DOLL FOOL MOVE PLAY BLOCK CORAL DALLY FLIRT HAPPY KNACK LAKIN PLAID SPORT TRICK WALLY BAUBLE DANDLE DOODLE FADDLE FINGER FIZGIG GEWGAW LAKING PRETTY PUPPET RATTLE SUCKER BLOWOUT CRICKET DREIDEL PLAYOCK TANGRAM TRINKET TUMBLER WHIZZER GIMCRACK KICKSHAW PINWHEEL SQUAWKER SQUEAKER TEETOTUM WINDMILL ZOETROPE
(**— AMOROUSLY**) MIRD
(**— WITH**) PADDLE
(**FLYING —**) PIGEON
TOYON TOLLON CHAMISO
TRACE RUN TUG WAD CAST ECHO HINT LICK MARK RACK SHOW SIGN STEP TANG TINT TROD BRING GHOST GLEAM GLIFF GRAIN PRINT SHADE SPICE SPOOR STAMP STEAD THEAT TINGE TOUCH TRACK TRACT TRAIL TRAIN TRESS DERIVE ENGRAM HARBOR LACING RESENT SHADOW SKETCH SMUTCH STRAIN STREAK SWATHE COCKEYE GLIMPSE KENNING MENTION REMNANT SOUPCON SURMISE SYMPTOM THOUGHT UMBRAGE VESTIGE WHISPER DESCRIBE ENGRAMME FOOTSTEP SKERRICK TINCTURE WAINROPE SIMULACRUM
(**— A BEE**) COURSE
(**— A CURVE**) SWEEP
(**— A DESIGN**) CALK
(**— MATHEMATICALLY**) GENERATE
(**— OF A HARE**) FARE
(**— ON CHART**) PRICK
(**— THE COURSE OF**) DEDUCE
(**HARNESS —**) TUG THEAT TREAT
(**HAVE A —**) SMACK
(**MEMORY —**) ENGRAM ENGRAMME
(**SLIGHT —**) GHOST STAIN SMATCH SPARKLE
(**SLIGHTEST —**) SCINTIL
(**PL.**) FEUTE
(**SUFF.**) (**HAVING A —**) ISH ISTIC
TRACER SEEKER OUTLINER SEARCHER
TRACERY FANWORK FROSTING TRAILERY
TRACHEA ARTERY WINDPIPE
(**— OF CRANE**) TRUMP
TRACHEID HYDROID
TRACHYANDESITE ARSOITE VULSINITE

TRACHYTE PIPERNO
TRACING BAROGRAM POLYGRAM
TRAILING
TRACK DOG PUG RAT RUT TAN
WAD WAY CLEW CLUE DRAW
FARE FOIL FOOT HUNT LANE
MARK PAGE PATH PIST RACE
RACK RAIK RAIL ROAD SHOE SLOT
SPUR TROD VENT BLOCK CHUTE
DRIFT FEUTE HOUND LODGE
PISTE PLANE SLIDE SPACE SPOOR
STEAD SWATH TRACE TRACT
TRADE TRAIL TRASH TREAD
BEARER COURSE GROOVE
HARBOR LADDER RETURN
RUNWAY SIDING SLEUTH STRAIN
STREAM SWATHE CHANNEL
FOILING FOOTING PATHWAY
TANGENT TRAFFIC VESTIGE
BACKBONE FOOTSTEP GUIDEWAY
TRANSFER TRECKPOT TREKPATH
WAGONWAY
(— FOR ROPE) CHANNEL
(— GAME) DRAW
(— OF DEER) SLOT STRAIN
(— OF GAME IN GRASS) FOILING
(— OF HARE) FILE
(— OF WOUNDED BEAST) PERSUE
(— ON PRINTING PRESS) BANK
BEARER
(RAILROAD —) LEAD SPUR STUB
SIDING TANGENT APPROACH
BACKBONE
(RUNNING —) FLAT CINDERS
(SHORT BRANCH —) RETURN
(SIDE —) LIE HOLE
(SKATER'S —) FLAT
(TEMPORARY —) SHOOFLY
(WORM —) NEREITE
(PREF.) ICHN(O)
TRACKER PUGGI PUGGY TRAILER
TRAILMAN
TRACKLESS INVIOUS PATHLESS
TRACKMAN SPIKER
TRACT AREA BEAT DUAR FLAT
ZONE CAMPO CLIME COAST
DRIVE ESSAY FIELD GRABE HORST
PATCH SWEEP TRACK BARONY
BUNDLE EXTENT REGION
ENCLAVE EURIPUS QUARTER
ROYALTY TERRAIN TRACTUS
BROCHURE CAMPAGNA
CAMPAIGN CINGULUM DISTRICT
FARMHOLD FORESTRY PAMPHLET
PROVINCE TOWNSITE TREATISE
(— KEPT IN NATURAL STATE) PARK
(— OF BARREN LAND) BARREN
DERELICT
(— OF BRAIN FIBERS) PEDUNCLE
(— OF GRASSLAND) PRAIRIE
(— OF LAND) CRU DOAB DUAB
DUAR GORE MARK BLOCK CHASE
CLAIM EJIDO FRITH GRANT LAINE
SCOPE SWELL TALUK EIGHTY
ESTATE FOREST GARDEN ISLAND
POLDER STRATH AIRPORT
QUILLET RESERVE TERRAIN
BOUNDARY CLEARING DERELICT
FARMHOLD INTERVAL SCABLAND
SLASHING
(— OF MUDDY GROUND) SLOB
(— OF OPEN UPLAND) DOWN
DOWNS

(— OF UNCOVERED ICE) GLADE
(— OF WASTE LAND) HEATH
(BOGGY —) RUNN MORASS
(CLAYEY —) TAKYR
(CLEARED —) JUM JHUM JOOM
(DRY —) SEARING
(FORESTLESS —) STEPPE
(GENITAL —) BEARING
(IRREGULAR —) GORE
(OPEN —) VEGA SLASH
(SANDY —) DEN DENE LANDE
(SHRUBBY —) MONTE
(SWAMPY —) FLOW BAYGALL
**(UNOCCUPIED AND UNCULTIVATED
—)** DESERT
(WATERLESS —) THIRST
TRACTABLE EASY SOFT TAME
BUXOM TAWIE DOCILE GENTLE
TOWARD DUCTILE FLEXILE
PLIABLE AMENABLE FLEXIBLE
GUIDABLE OBEDIENT TOWARDLY
YIELDING MALLEABLE
TRACTARIANISM PUSEYISM
TRACTION DRAFT DRAUGHT
TRACTOR CAT MULE DRAGON
BOBTAIL CRAWLER PEDRAIL
AGRIMOTOR
(TRAILER —) RIG
TRADE CHAP CHOP COUP DEAL
SELL SWAP CHEAP CRAFT GRAFT
PRICE TREAD TROKE TRUCK
BAKERY BARTER CHANGE
EMPLOY HANDLE METIER MISTER
NIFFER OCCUPY SCORCE SCORSE
BARGAIN CALLING CHAFFER
FACULTY MYSTERY SCIENCE
BUSINESS CABOTAGE EXCHANGE
PLUMBING MERCHANDISE
(SUFF.) ERY
TRADEMARK CHOP MARK BRAND
COUPON
TRADER SART BANYA PLIER
BALIJA BANIAN BANYAN CHETTY
DEALER MONGER NEPMAN
TROKER CHAPMAN MARWARI
SANGLEY TRUCKER ASTORIAN
CHANDLER KURVEYOR
MERCHANT OPERATOR
(HORSE —) JOCKEY
(INEXPERIENCED —) LAMB
TRADESMAN CIT BAKAL COOPER
EGGLER SELLER TENSOR FRUITER
GOLADAR OCCUPIER UPHOLDER
TRADESWOMAN WINSTER
TRADING CABOTAGE
TRADITION CABAL STORY SUNNA
CABALA SMRITI SUNNAH THREAP
HALACHA HALAKAH HEREDITY
HERITAGE TRANSFER
(PL.) LEGEND
TRADITIONAL CLASSIC POMPIER
TRADUCE ILL SLUR ABUSE
DEFAME MALIGN REVILE VILIFY
ASPERSE DETRACT SCANDAL
SLANDER
TRAFFIC COUP DEAL MANG MART
MONG BROKE TRADE BARTER
PALTER TRAVEL CHAFFER
DEALING PASSAGE BUSINESS
CHAFFERY COMMERCE
EXCHANGE NAVIGATION
(— IN SACRED THINGS) SIMONY
(— IN SLAVES) MAGONIZE

TRAFFICKER COUPER DEALER
TRAGEDY BUSKIN TRAGIC
TROIADES
TRAGIC DIRE DREADFUL THESPIAN
TRAGICOMEDY DRAME
TRAGOPAN MONAL
TRAGUS EARLET
TRAIL PAD PUG DRAG FOIL HARL
HUNT NECK PATH PIST SIGN
SLOT BLAZE CRAWL DRAIL PISTE
ROUTE SPOOR STOCK SWEEP
TRACE TRADE TRAIN COMING
DAGGLE FOLLOW RUNWAY
SHADOW SLEUTH STRAIN TAIGLE
TRAPES DRAGGLE TRACHLE
TRAFFIC OUTTRAIL STRIGGLE
TRAILERY
(— ALONG) STREEL TRAPES
(— OF A FISH) LOOM
(— OF STAG) ABATURE
(— OUT) STREAM
(— THROUGH MUD) DAGGLE
(DESCENDING —) BAHADA BAJADA
(MOUNTAIN —) CLIMB
(WAGON —) RUDLOFF
TRAILBLAZER HARBINGER
TRAILER SEMI COACH BOXCAR
CARAVAN FLATBED FROGGER
GONDOLA ARTMOBILE
TRAILING (— ON GROUND)
PROSTRATE
TRAIN SET DRAG GAIT SECT TILL
TIRE TURN ZULU BEARD BREED
COACH DRESS DRILL ENTER
FOCUS LOCAL RANGE TRACE
TRACT TRADE TRAIL TRYNE
CONVOY DIRECT GENTLE
GROUND INFORM MANURE
NUZZLE RAPIDE REPAIR SCHOOL
SEASON STRING SUBWAY
AFFAITE BRIGADE CARAVAN
EDUCATE FREIGHT GEARING
LIMITED PEDDLER RATTLER
RETINUE SHUTTLE VARNISH
CIVILIZE DISCIPLE ELECTRIC
EQUIPAGE EXERCISE HIGHBALL
INSTRUCT MANIFEST REHEARSE
(— AN ANIMAL) BREAK
(— FINE) GAUNT
(— FOR CONTEST) POINT
(— FOR FIGHTING) SPAR
(— OF ANIMALS) COFFLE
(— OF ATTENDANTS) CORTEGE
(— OF COMET) TAIL
(— OF EXPLOSIVE) FUSE
(— OF MINING CARS) JAG RUN
TRIP
(CAMEL —) KAFILA
(FUNERAL —) CONVOY
(PACK —) CONDUCTA
(RAILROAD —) DRAG HOOK LOCAL
PICKUP EXPRESS FREIGHT
LIMITED RATTLER
TRAINED GOOD MADE ADEPT
BROKE BROKEN
TRAINEE BOOT CADET
TRAINER FEEDER JINETE LANISTA
TRAINING DRILL THEAT ASCESIS
ASKESIS CULTURE NURTURE
PAIDEIA BREEDING
(— IN HUMANITIES) CIVILITY
(— OF HORSE) DRESSAGE
(RELIGIOUS —) SADHANA

TRAIPSE GAD WALK TRAMP
SASHAY WANDER
TRAIT ITEM LEAD MARK VEIN
ANGLE CHARM KNACK TRACT
TRICK AMENITY ELEMENT
HALLMARK JAPANISM
(CULTURE —) SURVIVAL
(FOREIGN —) EXOTISM
(GOOD —) THEW
(UNDESIRABLE —) DEMON
DAEMON
(WELL-DEFINED —) STREAK
(PL.) CORNERS
TRAITOR RAT JUDAS RUSTY
NITHING WARLOCK APOSTATE
ISCARIOT PRODITOR QUISLING
SQUEALER TRADITOR TREACHER
TRAITOROUS FALSE FELON
APOSTATE RENEGADE
TRAJECTORY SPORABOLA
TRA-LA-LA TRALIRA
TRAM TUB DRAM TRAMCAR
TRAMMEL TRANVIA
(COAL —) TIP
(SET OF —S) JOURNEY
TRAMCAR TRAM DUMMY PICKUP
TRAMMEL TRAM HAMPER STIFLE
COTTEREL
TRAMMER PUTTER
TRAMONTANE ALIEN FOREIGN
OVERBERG
TRAMP BO BUM PAD BOOM HAKE
HIKE HOBO HUMP PUNK SLOG
SWAG VAMP WALK YEGG BURLY
CAIRD CLAMP JAVEL PIKER
ROGUE SHACK STIFF STRAG
TRAIK TRAIL TRASH TROMP
TROUT BAGMAN GAYCAT JOCKER
PICARO STODGE STRAMP STROLL
TINKER TRANCE TRAPES TRUANT
TRUDGE DRUMMER FLOATER
RUFFLER SWAGGER SWAGMAN
TRAIPSE TRAMPLE TROUNCE
TROWANE VAGRANT YEGGMAN
CLOCHARD FOOTSLOG GANGEREL
STROLLER TRAVELER VAGABOND
SUNDOWNER
(— ABOUT) WAG
(LONG —) HUMP
(PL.) MONKERY
TRAMPING MONKERY
TRAMPLE HOX JAM PUG FARE
FOIL FULL HOOF CHAMP POACH
SCAUT SPURN TRAMP TRASH
TREAD DEFOIL DEFOUL PADDLE
SAVAGE STOACH STRAMP
WADDLE OPPRESS OVERRUN
SCAMBLE FORTREAD OVERRIDE
TRANCE RAPTUS AMENTIA
ECSTASY SAMADHI CATALEPSY
TRANQUIL CALM COOL EASY
LOWN MILD SOFT EQUAL QUIET
STILL GENTLE PACATE PIPING
SERENE CALMATO EQUABLE
PACIFIC RESTFUL
PEACEFUL
TRANQUILIZE CALM LULL QUIET
STILL BECALM PACIFY SERENE
SETTLE SOFTEN SOOTHE APPEASE
COMPOSE
TRANQUILIZING ATARAXIC
SOOTHING
TRANQUILLITY KEF LEE EASE

TRANQUILLITY REST PEACE QUIET SATTVA SERENE HARMONY QUIETAGE QUIETUDE SERENITY
TRANS ANTI
TRANSACT DO PASS AGITATE CONDUCT PERFORM
TRANSACTION DEAL DEED GAGE GAGER ACTION AFFAIR FIDDLE MARGIN SPREAD BARGAIN MOHABAT PASSAGE CONTRACT KNOCKOUT OPERATION PROCEEDING
(— AT LOWER PRICE) DOWNTICK
(PL.) ACTA BUSINESS
TRANSCEND PASS SOAR EXCEED OVERTOP SURPASS
TRANSCENDENTAL ACOSMIC
TRANSCENDING EXQUISITE
(PREF.) SUPRA
TRANSCRIBE COPY BRAILLE DESCRIBE EXSCRIBE
TRANSCRIBED CANNED
TRANSCRIBER COPIER COPYIST
TRANSCRIPT COPY SCORE TENOR DOUBLE APOGRAPH EXSCRIPT
TRANSCRIPTION
(PL.) PAZAND PAZEND
TRANSEPT PLAGE PORCH
TRANSFER CEDE DEED FLIT GIVE JUMP PASS SALE SELL TURN ALIEN CABLE CARRY CROSS DROGH REFER REMIT SHIFT ASSIGN ATTORN CHANGE DECANT DELATE DONATE REMOVE SWITCH CESSION CONNECT CONSIGN DELIVER DEVOLVE DISPONE MIGRATE TRADUCE ALIENATE ANTEDATE CROCKING DELEGATE DELIVERY DONATION EXCHANGE TRANSACT TRANSUME VIREMENT NEGOTIATE
(— A RECORDING) OVERDUB
(— DYE) EXHAUST
(— HEAT) CONVECT
(— HOMAGE) ATTORN
(— MOLTEN GLASS) LADE
(— OF ENERGY) FLOW
(— OF PROPERTY) DEED GIFT GRANT DISPOSAL
(— PIGMENT) FLUSH
TRANSFERENCE DEMISE EMOTION REMOVAL DELATION DISPOSAL TRANSFER
TRANSFIGURE DEIFY CLARIFY
TRANSFIX FIX DART PITCH STAKE STICK SKEWER THRILL BESTICK
TRANSFORM TURN SHIFT TOUCH CHANGE STRIKE CONVERT FASHION PERMUTE CATALYZE DISGUISE HETERIZE
(— ENERGY) ABSORB
TRANSFORMATION CHANGE HAIRWORK
TRANSFORMER SET DIMMER JIGGER TEASER TOROID VARIAC BALANCE BOOSTER HEDGEHOG
TRANSFUSE ENDUE INDUE
TRANSGRESS ERR SIN BREAK OFFEND OVERGO DIGRESS DISOBEY VIOLATE INFRINGE OVERPASS OVERSLIP OVERSTEP TRESPASS

TRANSGRESSION SIN SLIP CRIME FAULT SCAPE BREACH DELICT ESCAPE MISDEED OFFENSE DELICTUM OVERLOUP TRESPASS
TRANSGRESSOR SINNER OFFENDER
TRANSIENCE FUGACITY
TRANSIENT FLEET BUBBLE FLIGHTY PASSING FLEETING FUGITIVE MOMENTARY
TRANSIENTLY HOVERLY
TRANSISTOR FET
TRANSIT BINOCLE PASSAGE TRANSEPT
TRANSITION CUT JUMP LEAP SEGUE SHIFT FERMENT PASSAGE
TRANSITIVE ACTIVE
TRANSITORINESS CADUCITY
TRANSITORY FLEET CADUCE FLYING BRITTLE PASSANT PASSING SLIDING VOLATIC WHILEND CADUCOUS FLEETING FLITTING TEMPORAL VOLATILE MOMENTARY
TRANSKEI (CAPITAL OF —) UMTATA
(TOWN OF —) BUTTERWORTH
TRANSLATE PUT DRAW MAKE TURN WEND RENDER CONVERT ENGLISH EXPOUND TRADUCE CONSTRUE INTERPRET
TRANSLATION CAB KEY CRIB PONY STEP TROT GLOSS HORSE TARGUM UNSEEN BICYCLE CABBAGE ENGLISH THARGUM TRADUCT VERSION SUBTITLE VERBATIM
(— OF BIBLE) PESHITO
(— OF THE CLASSICS) JACK
(LOAN —) CALQUE
TRANSLATOR TURNER
TRANSLUCENT CLEAR LUCID LIMPID LUCENT HYALINE
(PREF.) HYAL(O)
TRANSMIGRATION SAMARA SAMSARA SANSARA
TRANSMISSION ENTAIL DESCENT GEARBOX PASSAGE SENDING TRANSFER
(— OF SOUND) AUDIO
(— TO OFFSPRING) HEREDITY
(SUFF.) PHORESIS
TRANSMIT AIR BEAM EMIT SEND CARRY CONVEY DEMISE DERIVE ENTAIL EXPORT IMPACT IMPART RENDER CONDUCT CONSIGN FORWARD TRADUCE TRADUCT TRAJECT BEQUEATH DESCRIBE PROPAGATE
(PREF.) DIAGO
TRANSMITTER TUBA SLAVE SPARK BEACON JAMMER PINGER SENDER VEHICLE RADIATOR
TRANSMITTING ALIVE
TRANSMUTE CHEMIC CHEMICK ENNOBLE PERMUTE EXCHANGE TRANSMUE TRANSUME
TRANSOM PATIBLE TRAVERSE
TRANSPARENCY SLIDE
TRANSPARENT THIN CLEAR FILMY LUCID BRIGHT LIMPID LUCENT CRYSTAL FRAGILE HYALINE HYALOID TIFFANY DIOPTRIC LUCULENT LUMINOUS

LUSTROUS PELLUCID
(PREF.) DIAPHAN(O) HYAL(O)
TRANSPIRE HAPPEN
TRANSPLANT SPOT SHIFT DEPLANT
TRANSPORT DAK JOY ROB BEAR BOAT BUSS DAWK DRAY HAUL PASS PORT RAPE RAPT RIDE SEND SHIP BLISS CANOE CARRY DROGH FERRY FLUTE GILLY BANISH BARREL CONVEY DEPORT GALLOP KURVEY WAFTER ECSTASY EXPRESS FRAUGHT ONERARY RAPTURE TRADUCE TROOPER CABOTAGE CARRIAGE DAYDREAM ENRAVISH PALANDER
(— BY PACKHORSE) JAG
(— FOR CRIME) LAG
(— LOGS) BOB
(— ORE) SLUSH
(PREF.) PEREIO
TRANSPORTATION AIR DAK FARE AIRLIFT BOATAGE FREIGHT TRAJECT TRANSPORT
(AIRPORT —) LIMO
TRANSPORTED RAPT
(— BY GLACIER) ERRATIC
TRANSPOSE ADJOINT CONVERT REVERSE
TRANSPOSITION SHIFT ANSWER ANAGRAM
TRANSUBSTANTIATION METUSIA
TRANSVAAL DAISY GERBERA
TRANSVAALER TAKHAAR
TRANSVERSE CROSS FACING THWART OBLIQUE
TRANSVERSELY ATHWART
TRANSVESTISM EONISM
TRANSVESTITE BERDACHE
TRAP COY GET GIN PIT SET FALL GIRN GRIN HOOK LACE LIME NAIL PUTT TIPE TOIL WAIT WEEL BRAKE BRIKE CATCH LEASH PLANT POUND SNARE SPELL STALE SWICK SWIKE TRAIN COBWEB CRUIVE EELPOT ENGINE KEDDAH POCKET QUILEZ SNATCH STAYER WILLOW FLYTRAP PITFALL PITFOLD PUTCHEN PUTCHER RATTRAP SETTING SPRINGE TRAMMEL BIRDLIME COALHOLE DEADFALL DOWNFALL TRAPROCK
(— FOR BIRDS) SCRAPE
(— FOR LARGE GAME) HOPO
(— FOR RABBITS, MICE, ETC) TIPE TYPE
(— FOR RATS) CLAM
(— FOR SALMON) PUTT
(— FOR SMALL ANIMALS) HATCH
(— FOR THE FEET) CALTROPS
(— IN POKER) SANDBAG
(— IN THEATER) SCRUTO
(— INTO SERVICE) CRIMP
(FISH —) FYKE KILL LEAP WEEL WEIR CREEL WILLY CORRAL CRUIVE WILLOW
(SAND —) BUNKER
TRAPDOOR DROP SLOT TRAP SCRUTO VAMPIRE TRAPFALL
TRAPPED CORNERED
TRAPPER WIRER VOYAGEUR
TRAPPINGS GEAR JHOOL ARMORY

TOGGERY BARDINGS EQUIPAGE HOUSINGS CAPARISON
TRAPSHOOTING SKEET
TRASH ROT BOSH GEAR GOOK JUNK PELF RAFF TOSH TRAG CLART DRECK DRUSH STUFF SWASH THROW TRADE TROKE WASTE WRACK BUSHWA CULTCH KELTER KITSCH PALTRY RAMMEL REFUSE RUBBLE SCULCH TROUSE BAGGAGE BEGGARY FULLAGE GARBAGE PEDLARY RUBBISH TOSHERY TRAFFIC BLATHERY CLAPTRAP FLUMMERY MUCKMENT PEDDLERY SKITTLES SMACHRIE TRASHERY TRUMPERY
TRASHY CHEAP FLASH TOSHY TRIPY PALTRY SHODDY SLUSHY BAGGAGE RUBBISH RIFFRAFF RUBBISHY SIXPENNY TRUMPERY
TRAUMA WOUND INJURY STRESS
TRAVAIL PAIN TASK TOIL AGONY LABOR TORMENT
TRAVEL GO BAT BUS FLY GIG WAG FARE GANG HIKE PASS PATH RIVE TOTE TRIP VAMP WEND COVER KNOCK SLOPE THROW TRACK CRUISE TRANCE VOYAGE EXPRESS JOURNEY TRAVAIL TRUNDLE WAYFARE PROGRESS TRAVERSE
(— ACROSS SNOW) MUSH
(— AIMLESSLY) SAUNTER
(— ALONG GROUND) TAXI
(— AROUND) TURN COAST CIRCLE GIRDLE COMPASS
(— AT GOOD SPEED) CRACK
(— AT HIGH SPEED) HELL BARREL SCORCH
(— AT RANDOM) DRIFT
(— AT SPEED OF) DO
(— BACK AND FORTH) SHUNT COMMUTE
(— BY AIRCRAFT) AIR FLY AIRPLANE
(— BY OX WAGON) TREK
(— FAST) STREAK
(— IN A VEHICLE) TOOL
(— ON FOOT) HIKE SHANK KNAPSACK PERAMBULATE PEREGRINE
(— ON WATER) SAIL
(— OVER) TRANCE TRAVERSE
(— THROUGH) GO
(— THROUGH WOODS) BUSHWACK
(— WITHOUT EQUIPMENT) SIWASH
(DAY'S —) JORNADA JOURNAL JOURNEY
TRAVELER GOER CRAWL FARER GUEST HORSE BAGMAN GANGER KILROY POSTER SAILOR VIATOR CRUISER DRUMMER FOOTMAN HOWADJI LEEFANG PILGRIM SWAGGIE TRAILER TREKKER TRIPPER WAYGOER ARGONAUT EXPLORER MAGELLAN OUTRIDER VOYAGEUR WAYFARER PASSENGER
(COMPANY OF —S) CARAVAN
TRAVELER'S JOY HAGROPE BINDWITH CLEMATIS
TRAVELING ERRANT PEREGRINE

TRAVELING SALESMAN RIDER DRUMMER

TRAVERSE DO GO SEE BURN DENY KNEE LIFT MAKE PASS SPAN WALK COAST COVER CROSS SHEAR SWEEP THIRL TRACE TRACK CIRCLE COURSE DENIAL OVERGO PERCUR TRAVEL VOYAGE WANDER CHANNEL JOURNEY MEASURE OVERRUN PARADOS PERVADE DESCRIBE NAVIGATE OVERPASS OVERWEND SCRAMBLE UNTHREAD PERAMBULATE

TRAVERTINE TOPHUS

TRAVESTY EXODE PARODY SATIRE EXODIUM TRAVEST BURLESQUE

TRAVIATA, LA (CHARACTER IN —) FLORA VALERY ALFREDO BERVOIX DOUPHOL GERMONT GIORGIO VIOLETTA

(COMPOSER OF —) VERDI

TRAVOIS DRAY TRAVOY ALLIGATOR

TRAWL SEINE BOULTER DRAGNET STOWNET TRAWLNET TROTLINE

TRAWLER PAREJA BRAGOZZO

TRAY HOD CASE TILL TRUG BATEA BOARD FLOAT SCALE SLICE SUSAN GALLEY MONKEY SALVER SERVER SERVET VOIDER WAITER BALANCE CABARET COASTER CONSOLE SHALLOW DEJEUNER

(— FOR CRUMBS) VOIDER

(— FOR DRYING FISH) FLAKE

(— FOR MATCH SPLINTS) CAUL MONKEY

(— FOR SHELLFISH) FLOAT

(— FOR TYPE) GALLEY

(— TO CATCH OVERFLOW) SAFE

(CIRCULAR —) ROUNDEL

TREACHEROUS FOUL CATTY DIRTY FALSE PUNIC SNAKY SWACK FELINE FICKLE HOLLOW ROTTEN YELLOW SNAKISH FRAUDFUL IMPOSING PLOTTING SLIDDERY

TREACHERY GUILE SWICK TRAIN DECEIT FELONY PERFIDY TREASON UNTRUTH DASTARDY DISTRUST TRAHISON TRAITORY

TREACLE DIBS CLAGGUM THERIAC

TREAD FIT PAD BEAT FOOT PATH POST RUNG STEP VOLT CLAMP TRACK TRADE DEFOIL DEFOUL PADDLE CRAWLER FEATHER FOOTING RETREAD TREADER FOOTSTEP

(— CLUMSILY) CLUMP BALTER

(— DOWN SHOE HEEL) CAM

(— HEAVILY) SPURN TRAMPLE

(— OF FOWL'S EGG) GRANDO

(— ON) FOIL

(— TO MUSIC) FOOT

(— WARILY) PUSSYFOOT

(TIRE —) COVER

TREADLE PEDAL CHALAZA

TREASON SEDITION

TREASURE POSE ROON HOARD PRIZE STORE TROVE VALUE BURSAR COFFER FINDAL GERSUM WEALTH ASTHORE FINANCE THESAUR WARISON

GARRISON TREASURY

(— STATE) MONTANA

(LITTLE —) STOREEN

(PL.) CIMELIA

TREASURE BOX HANAPER

TREASURED DEAR CHARY PRECIOUS

TREASURE ISLAND (AUTHOR OF —) STEVENSON

(CHARACTER IN —) BEN JIM PEW GUNN JOHN BONES HANDS ISRAEL SILVER HAWKINS LIVESEY SMOLLETT TRELAWNEY

TREASURER FISC BOWSER BURSAR FISCAL GABBAI BOUCHER HOARDER SPENDER BHANDARI COFFERER HAZNADAR PROVISOR QUAESTOR RECEIVER

TREASURY FISC FISK KIST CHEST HOARD PURSE COFFER CORBAN FISCAL FISCUS BOWSERY BURSARY CHAMBER CHECKER CHEQUER HORDARY AERARIUM THESAURY TREASURE

(PAPAL —) CAMERA

TREAT RUN USE DEAL DOSE HOCK LEAD PLAY BEANO BESEE COVER DIGHT GUIDE LEECH SERVE SETUP SHOUT TRACT TRAIT WRITE DEMEAN DOCTOR GOVERN HANDLE LIQUOR PADDLE REGALO CONDUCT ENTREAT GARNISH ACTIVATE AIRBRUSH

(— A HIDE) DRUM

(— AS EQUAL) EVEN

(— BADLY) ILLGUIDE

(— CARELESSLY) BANG BANDY

(— CLOUDS) SEED

(— CONFIDENTIALLY) HUSH

(— CRUELLY) CRUCIFY

(— DAINTILY) PAMPER

(— DIABOLICALLY) BEDEVIL

(— DISCOURTEOUSLY) DISGRACE

(— FIBERS) GILL

(— FLOUR) AGENIZE

(— FONDLY) DANDLE

(— FUR) CARROT

(— GENTLY) FAVOR

(— HAIR) CONK

(— ILLNESS) POMSTER

(— IMPROPERLY) MISUSE

(— IMPUDENTLY) NOSE

(— LIGHTLY) SCRUFF

(— LOVINGLY) COAX

(— MALICIOUSLY) SPITE

(— MASH) LAUTER

(— OF) DISCOURSE

(— OF DRINKS) SETUP

(— ROUGHLY) BANG MUMBLE GRABBLE MALTREAT

(— SILK TO RUSTLE) SCROOP

(— SLIGHTINGLY) LIGHTLY

(— STEEL) HARVEY

(— UNFAIRLY) DO

(— UNSKILLFULLY) FOOZLE

(— WITH ACID) SOUR

(— WITH CARE) CODDLE

(— WITH CONTEMPT) HUFF SNUB BLURT FLIRT FLOCK FLOUT FLAUNT BAUCHLE

(— WITH HEAT) FOMENT

(— WITH HONOR) RESPECT

(— WITH INATTENTION) FORGET

(— WITH INDULGENCE) FONDLE

(— WITH PARTIALITY) ACCEPT

(— WITH RESPECT) HONOR

(— WITH RIDICULE) SCOUT

(— WITH RUDENESS) FRUMP

(— WITH TAR) BLACK

(— WITH TENDERNESS) CODDLE

(NEW YEAR'S EVE —) HAGMENA HOGMANAY

TREATISE AGAMA DONET FAUNA FLORA LIBEL SILVA SUMMA SYLVA TRACT TREAT BOTANY POETRY POMONA SERTUM SYSTEM ALGEBRA ANATOMY BIOLOGY COMMENT DIETARY GEOLOGY GRAMMAR HISTORY PANDECT PHYSICS PINETUM POETICS ZOOLOGY ALMAGEST BROCHURE CALCULUS DIDACTIC ECTHESIS EXERCISE GENETICS GEOMANCY GEOMETRY GERMANIA HORNBOOK LAPIDARY MONUMENT PANTHEON PASTORAL PRACTICE SITOLOGY SPECULUM TRACTATE MONOGRAPH

(SUFF.) ICS LOGER LOGIA(N) LOGIC(AL) LOGIST LOGUE LOGY OLOGY

TREATMENT CURE WORK TREAT USAGE ANIMUS DETAIL FACIAL QUARTER BEHAVIOR DEMEANOR ENTREATY

(— BY MASSAGE) SEANCE

(— FOR WOOLLENS) SPONGING

(BAD —) MISUSAGE

(COLD —) FREEZE

(COMPASSIONATE —) MERCY

(CONTEMPTUOUS —) SPURN

(CRUEL —) SEVERITY

(DIRE —) DOLE

(HARMFUL —) ABUSE

(HARSH —) SHAFT

(INHUMAN —) CRUELTY

(LUXURIOUS —) DELICACY

(SEVERE —) ROUGH

(PREF.) **(MEDICAL —)** IATR(O)

(SUFF.) PRAXIS

(MEDICAL —) IATRIA IATRIC(S) IATRIST IATRY

TREATY MISE ACCORD CARTEL CONCORD ENTENTE LOCARNO ALLIANCE ASSIENTO TREATISE CONCORDAT

TREBLE TRIPLE DESCANT MINIKIN SOPRANO TRIPLUM

TREBUCHET DONDINE DONDAINE

TREE TI ACH ADY AMA APA ARN ASH BAY BEL BEN BUR DAK DAR EBO ELM FIG FIR GUM HAW KOA KOU LIN OAK SAJ SAL TAL TUI ULE YEW ACLE AGBA AKEE AMLA ANAM ANAN ANDA ARAR ASAK ASOK ATIS ATLE ATTA AULU AUSU BAEL BAKU BITO BOGO BOOM BREA BURI BURR CADE COLA CRAB DATE DHAK DILO DITA DOON EBOE IPIL JACK KINO KOKO LIME MABI MORA OHIA OMBU PALA PINE POLE POON SADR SORB SUPA TALA TAWA TCHE TEAK TEIL TITI TOON TREW TUNG TUNO UPAS VERA WOOD YATE YAYA AALII ABETO ABURA ACANA ACAPU ACOMA AFARA AGATI AGOHO AKEKI ALAMO ALANI ALDER ALGUM ALISO ALMON ALMUG AMAGA AMAPA AMBAK ANABO ANJAN APPLE ARACA ARBOR ARECA ARJAN ARJUN ARTAR ASOKA ASPEN ATLEE BABUL BALAO BALSA BALTA BANAK BEECH BEHEN BETIS BIRCH BONGO BOREE BOSSE BUMBO CACAO CARAP CAROB CEBIL CEDAR CEIBO DADAP DHAVA DHAWA DILLY DRYAD DURIO ELDER GABUN GAIAC GENIP GINEP GINKO HAZEL ICICA IXORA JAMBO JIQUE JIQUI KAPOR KAPUR KEENA KOKAN KOKIO KOKUM KONGU KUSAM LANSA LARCH LARIX LEHUA LEMON LICCA LIMBA LINDE LINER LINGO MAHOE MAHUA MAMIE MAPLE MAQUI NARRA NIEPA NURSE OADAL OSAGE OSIER PACAY PAPAW PECAN PIPER RAULI ROBLE ROHAN ROWAN SALAI SAMAN SASSY SCRAG SIMAL SIRIS SISSU STICK SUMAC TABOG TARFA TENIO TERAP TIKUR TIMBO TINGI TOONA TUART ULMUS UMIRI URUCA URUCU UVITO WAHOO YACAL YACCA YULAN ZAMAN ACAJOU AHKROT AKEAKE ALAGAO ALERCE ALERSE ALFAJE ALMOND ALUPAG AMAMAU AMBASH AMUGIS AMUYON ANAGAP ANAGUA ANAQUA ANGICO ANILAO ARALIA ARANGA ARBUTE AUSUBO AZALEA BABOEN BACURY BAHERA BAKULA BALSAM BANABA BANAGO BANANA BANCAL BANIAN BANYAN BARBAS BATAAN BIRIBA BOMBAX BONDUC BONETE BOTONG BRAUNA BUCARE BUSTIC CALABA CAMARA CANELA CANELO CAPUMO CARAPA CASSIA CATIVO CAUCHO CEDRON CHALTA CHERRY CHICHA CHINAR CHOGAK CITRON COBOLA COCUYO CUMBER DATURA DHAMAN DHAURA DHAURI DRIMYS DURIAN ELCAJA EMBLIC EMBUIA FEIJOA FILLER FUSTIC GABOON GINGKO GUAIAC GURJAN GURJUN IDESIA IDIGBO ILIAHI ILLIPE ILLUPI JAGUEY JUJUBE KAMALA KEMPAS KINDAL KITTUL LANSAT LANSEH LAUREL LIGNUM LINDEN LITCHI LOCUST LONGAN MAFURA MALLET MAYTEN MEDLAR MILKER MIMOSA ORANGE PANAMA PAWPAW PIQUIA POPLAR RAMBEH ROHUNA RUNNEL SABICU SABINO SANDAN SANTOL SAPELE SAPOTA SAPOTE SATINE SAWYER SERAYA SINTOC SISSOO SOUARI STYRAX SUMACH SUNDRI TALUTO TAMANU TARATA TEETEE TIKOOR TIMBER TINGUY TOATOA TOTARA TUPELO URUCUM URUSHI UVALHA

WABAYO WABOOM WAHAHE
WALNUT WAMARA WAMPEE
WANDOO WATTLE YACHAN
YAGHAN YAMBAN ZAMANG
ACHIOTE ACHUETE AILANTO
AKEPIRO AMBATCH AMBOINA
AMUGUIS AMUYONG ANABONG
ANNATTO ANONANG APITONG
APRICOT ARARIBA ARAROBA
ARBORET ARBUTUS AROEIRA
ASSAGAI AVOCADO AVODIRE
BANILAD BANKSIA BECUIBA
BENZOIN BILLIAN BOLLING
BUBINGA BUCKEYE BUISSON
CADAMBA CAJAPUT CAJUPUT
CANELLA CARAIPE CASTANA
CATALPA CAUTIVO CERILLO
CHAMPAC CHECHEM CHECKER
CHENGAL COCULLO CONIFER
CURUPAY CYPRESS DEADMAN
DESCENT DETERMA DHAMNOO
EPACRID FRUITER GONDANG
GRIBBLE GUMIHAN HICKORY
HOLLONG HOPBUSH HORMIGO
KAMASSI KAMBALA KICKXIA
KITTOOL KOKOONA KOOMBAR
KUMQUAT LOGWOOD MADRONA
MANJACK MARGOSA NAARTJE
PARAIBA PEREIRA PIMENTO
PULASAN PYRAMID RATWOOD
REDWOOD SERINGA SERVICE
SHITTAH SPINDLE STOPPER
SUNDARI SURETTE TANGELO
TANGHIN TARAIRI TARATAH
TARWOOD TINDALO TREELET
TWISTER URUNDAY VETERAN
WALAHEE WALLABA WEENONG
WONGSHY WONGSKY YAMANAI
YOHIMBE YOHIMBI ACEITUNA
ALGAROBA ALLSPICE ALMACIGA
ALMANDER ALMENDRO
ALOEWOOD AMARILLO
ARAGUANE ARBOLOCO ARBUSCLE
AVELLANO BAKUPARI BASSWOOD
BAYBERRY BELLWOOD BINDOREE
BITANHOL BLACKBOX BOARWOOD
BORRACHA BREADNUT
CABREUVA CAMELLIA CAMUNING
CARAGANA CARAUNDA
CHAMPACA CHESTNUT
CHINCONA CHINOTTO CINNAMON
COCOPLUM COPALCHE
COUMAROU CRABWOOD
CUCUMBOL DEADFALL
DOMINANT DOTTEREL
DOVEWOOD DRACAENA
DRUMWOOD ETABALLI FIREFALL
FORESTER GAMDEBOO GEELHOUT
GENISARO GUACACOA GUAYROTO
HALAPEPE HARDTACK
HARDWOOD HOLDOVER
HORNBEAM HOROPITO
IRONWOOD ISHPINGO ITCHWOOD
JELOTONG JELUTONG KAJUGARU
KINGWOOD KNOBWOOD
LACEBARK LEADWOOD
LORDWOOD MAHOGANY
MANDARIN MILKWOOD
MOKIHANA OITICICA OLEASTER
ONEBERRY PEDIGREE PICHURIM
PINKWOOD RAMBUTAN
RASAMALA SANDARAC
SANDWOOD SAPUCAIA

SASSWOOD SEBESTEN SHAGBARK
SHAVINGS SILKWOOD SLOGWOOD
SOAPBARK STANDARD SUCUPIRA
SWEETSOP SYCAMORE
TAMARACK TAMARIND
TANEKAHA TREELING TURMERIC
ZAPATERO PERSIMMON
PISTACHIO SASSAFRAS
SATINWOOD SANDALWOOD
(— CUT BACK) DOTARD POLLARD
(— FURNISHING SUPPORT TO VINE)
HUSBAND
(— IN STREAM) SAWYER
(— LEFT IN CUTTING) HOLDOVER
(— OF HEAVEN) AILANTO
AILANTHUS
(— ON WALL) RIDER
(— OVER 2 FT. DIAMETER) VETERAN
(— SYMBOLIZING UNIVERSE)
YGDRASIL
(— WITH BRANCHES TRIMMED) LOP
LOPSTICK
(—S IN FOREST) STAND
(AROMATIC —) CLUSIA LABIATE
(AUSTRALIAN —) ASH GUM TOON
BELAH BELAR BOREE BUNDY
BUNYA GIDIA HAZEL KARRI
NONDA PENDA SALLY WILGA
BAOBAB DRIMYS GIDGEE GIMLET
GYMPIE JARRAH KOWHAI
MARARA PEROBA SALLEE
DOGWOOD GEEBUNG PEEBEEN
BEEFWOOD CARABEEN
COOLABAH FLINDOSA GRAVILEA
IRONBARK LACEBARK QUANDONG
ROSEBUSH SANDSTAY
SOAPWOOD TILESEED
(BIG —) SEQUOIA
(BORNEO —) BILIAN
(BURMESE —) PADOUK
(CEYLON —) HORA
(CITRUS —) SHADDOCK
(CLOTHES —) COSTUMER
(CLUMP OF —S) TOLL TUMP STELL
(CONTORTED —) SAXAUL
(CUBAN —) JIQUE JIQUI
GUACACOA
(CURSED —) WARYTREE
(DEAD —) RUNT SNAG RAMPIKE
(DEAD —S) DRIKI
(DECAYED —) DOTTEREL
(DWARF —) SCRUB ARBUSCLE
(EVERGREEN —) FIR YEW PINE
SUGI TAWA ABIES ATHEL CAROB
CEDAR CLOVE HOLLY LARCH
LEMON OLIVE THUJA BALSAM
BIBIRU COIGUE COIHUE KANAGI
KAPUKA LOQUAT ORANGE
SPRUCE ARDISIA BEBEERU
BILIMBI CONIFER HEMLOCK
JUNIPER MADRONA MADRONO
EUCALYPT EUONYMUS
SAPODILLA SANDORICUM
(FAMILY —) STEMMA DESCENT
PEDIGREE
(FRUIT —) CORDON
(GENEALOGICAL —) ARBOR JESSE
(GROWTH OF —S) SYLVAGE
(GUM —) KARI KINO BABUL BALTA
BUMBO ICICA KARRI KIKAR
GIMLET MALLET STORAX TEWART
WANDOO GOMMIER COOLIBAH
(HAWAIIAN —) KOA LEHUA ILIAHI

(INFERNAL —) ZAQQUM
(JAPANESE —) KAYA KIAKI KEYAKI
KADSURA KATSURA SATSUMA
ZELKOVA
(MANDARIN —) SATSUMA
(MEXICAN —) ULE AMAPA DRAGO
EBANO SERON CAPULI CATENA
CHILTE CAPULIN COPALCHE
(MYTHICAL —) TUBA
(NEW ZEALAND —) AKE KARO
KAWA MIRO PUKA RATA RIMU
TAWA TORU WHAU HINAU KAORI
KAURI MAIRE MANGI MAPAU
MATAI TOWAI AKEAKE KAMAHI
KANUKA KAPUKA KARAKA
KARAMU KAWAKA KONINI
MANUKA PURIRI TARATA TITOKI
TOATOA TOTARA WAHAHE
AKEPIRO MANGEAO PUKATEA
TARAIRI TARWOOD KAWAKAWA
KOHEKOHE MAKOMAKO
(ORNAMENTAL —) KABIKI
LABURNUM POINCIANA
(PHILIPPINES —) DAO IBA TUA TUI
BOGO DITA IFIL IPIL AGOHO
AGOJO ALMON AMAGA ANABO
BAYOG BAYOK BETIS DANLI
GUIJO LAUAN LIGAS TABOG
YACAL ALAGAO ALUPAG AMUYON
ANAGAP ANUBIN ARANGA
BANUYO BATAAN BATETE BATINO
BOTONG DUNGON KATMON
LANETE MABOLO MARANG
MOLAVE SAGING TALUTO
AMUGUIS AMUYONG ANABONG
ANOBING ANONANG APITONG
BINUKAU CAMAGON DANGLIN
MANCONO MAYAPIS TINDALO
ALMACIGA BITANHOL KALIPAYA
KALUMPIT LUMBAYAO MACAASIM
MALAPAHO TANGUILE
(POISONOUS —) GUAO UPAS LIGAS
TANGHIN TANQUEN MANCHINEEL
(POLYNESIAN —) MACUDA
(SACRED —) CHAMPAC CHAMPAK
(SALT —) ATLE
(SHADE —) ELM DILLY GUAMA
HEVEA CATALPA HALESIA
INKWOOD JOEWOOD SYCAMORE
(SHOWY —) ASAK ASOK ASOKA
(SMALL —) AKE BOX TCHE ALDER
CUMAY DWARF HENNA NGAIO
SERON AKEAKE BLOLLY CHANAR
JOJOBA KOWHAI ARBORET
INKWOOD JOEWOOD KADAMBA
STADDLE TREELET EMAJAGUA
HARDTACK HUISACHE OLEASTER
SNOWBELL SOURWOOD TREELING
(SPINY —) LIME AROMA AROMO
HONEY BOOGUM BUCARE
BUMELIA CATECHU COLORIN
LAVANGA COCKSPUR
(STANDING —) FILLER
(STUNTED —) SCRAB SCRUB
SCRUNT
(THORNY —) BEL BAEL BREA
LEMON AMBACH SAMOHU
AMBATCH
(TIMBER —) ASH DAR ENG FIR SAL
ACLE ANDA BAKU COCO CUYA
EKKI IPIL PELU PINE TALA TEAK
YANG ACAPU ALMON AMAPA
AMATE AMBAY ANJAN ARACA

ARGAN BANAK BIRCH CAROB
CEDAR COCOA CULLA EBONY
ERIZO FOTUI HALDU ICICA IROKO
KAURI KHAYA KIAKI KOKAN
MANIU MAPLE MVULE NARRA
ROBLE TIMBO ALERCE ALUPAG
BABOEN BACURY BANABA
BANCAL CARBON CHUPON
CORTEZ DAGAME DEGAME
DUKUMA ESPAVE FREIJO GAMARI
GUMHAR IMBUIA JACANA LEBBEK
MUERMO PADAUK SANDAN
SATINE SISSOO AMUGUIS
AROEIRA BECUIBA BILLIAN
CARAIPI CYPRESS ESPAVEL
GATEADO GOMAVEL GUARABU
GUAYABI HARPULA HOLLONG
KOOMBAR LAPACHO REDWOOD
AMARILLO BOARWOOD
CABREUVA CARACOLI COCOBOLO
CRABWOOD DONCELLA
GUATAMBU GUAYACAN
MAHOGANY SLOGWOOD
SUCUPIRA
(TRAINED —) ESPALIER
(TROPICAL —) AKEE AULU DALI
DIKA EBOE EKKI GUAO INGA
MABA MAHO MAJO PALM SHEA
ACKEE BALSA BONGO COUMA
DALLI FOTUI GUAMA GUARA
ICICA ILAMA JIGUA MARIA NEPAL
NJAVE POOLI TARFA ANUBIN
BAKULA BALATA BANANA
CASHEW CEDRON CHUPON
GENIPA HACKIA ITAUBA LEBBEK
LECYTH MAMMEE OBECHE
PERSEA ANGELIN ANNATTO
CAULOTE COPAIBA DATTOCK
EHRETIA EUGENIA GATEADO
GUACIMO LAPACHO MAJAGUA
MOMBINI SANDBOX SOURSOP
SURETTE BEEFWOOD CALABASH
CAMUNING CORKWOOD
FUNTUMIA MUSKWOOD
PATASHTE SWEETSOP TAMARIND
MONKEYPOD MANGOSTEEN
(UNARMED —) ALBIZZIA
(VARNISH —) DOON THEETSEE
(XEROPHYTIC —) SAXAUL
(YOUNG —) RUNNEL SPRING
TILLER SAPLING SEEDLING
SPRINGER
(PL.) BLUFF RINDS SILVA
OVERSTORY
(PREF.) ARBORI DENDR(O)
(SUFF.) DENDRON
TREE CREEPER TOMTIT
TREE CYPRESS GILIA
TREE DUCK FIDDLER YAGUAZA
TREE FROG FERREIRO
TREE MOSS USNEA
TREENAIL NOG GUTTA MOOTER
TRUNNEL
TREE PEONY MOUTAN
TREE TOAD HYLA HYLID ANURAN
TREETOP LAP LOP
TREFOIL CANCH LOTUS CLAVER
CROWTOE BEDSTRAW SAINFOIN
TICKSEED
TREHALOSE MYCOSE
TRELLIS TRAIL PERGOLA TARLIES
ESPALIER
TREMATODE FLUKE

MARITA STRIGEID

TREMBLE DARE DIRL RESE BEVER QUAKE SHAKE SLOWS WIVER AGRISE DIDDER DINGLE DITHER DODDER FALTER HOTTER HOTTLE NITHER QUAVER QUIVER SHIMMY THRILL TITTER TOTTER TREMOR TRYMLE WABBLE WOBBLE WUTHER FLICKER SHUDDER STAGGER TWIDDLE WHITHER THRIMBLE
(PL.) TIRE TIRES
(PREF.) TREMELLI TROMO

TREMBLER BUZZER HAMMER VIBRATOR

TREMBLING BEVER SHAKY DITHER TREMOR TREPID AQUIVER DODDERY PALSIED QUAKING QUAVERY QUIVERY TREMBLY TWITTER

TREMBLY WOOZY

TREMENDOUS BIG AWFUL GIANT GREAT LARGE HOWLING TEARING ENORMOUS HORRIBLE TERRIBLE TERRIFIC MONSTROUS

TREMOLO HURRY TRILLO

TREMOR RIGOR SHAKE DINDLE QUIVER THRILL SHUDDER TREMBLE

TREMULOUS ASPEN QUAKY SHAKY PALSIED SHIVERY TREMBLY SHIMMERY TINGLING

TRENCH GAW SAP FOSS GRIP GURT LINE MOAT RILL SICK SIKE TAJO TRIG BOYAU CHASE DITCH DRAIN DRILL FLOAT FOSSE GRAFF GRAFT GRAVE GROOP SEUCH TRINK COFFER FURROW GULLET GUTTER SHEUGH ACEQUIA CUNETTE CUVETTE OPENCUT SLIDDER ENCROACH LOCKSPIT PARALLEL SPREADER THOROUGH TRESPASS
(— BELOW FOREST FIRE) GUTTER
(— FOR BURYING POTATOES) CAMP
(— FOR DRAIN TILES) CHASE
(— FORMED BY BANKING VEGETABLES) GRAVE
(ARTIFICIAL —) LEAT
(IRRIGATION —) FLOAT SUGSLOOT
(PREF.) BOTHR(O) BOTHRI(O)

TRENCHANT ACID KEEN EDGED SHARP TUANT INCISIVE

TRENCHER PLATTER ROUNDEL

TREND BEND BIAS HAND TONE TURN BULGE CURVE DRIFT SENSE SLANT SWING TENOR SQUINT STRIKE CURRENT DOWNSIDE MOVEMENT TENDENCY
(LOWERING PRICE —) EASE

TREPANG BALATE SWALLO SWALLOW TITFISH TEATFISH

TREPIDATION FEAR ALARM DISMAY

TRESPASS DEBT GILUT POACH BREACH FURTUM INVADE INTRUDE OFFENSE ENCROACH ENTRENCH INFRINGE INTRENCH OVERLOUP

TRESS CURL LOCK TAIL BRAID SWITCH RINGLET WIMPLER

TRES-TINE TRAY ROYAL

TRESTLE MARE HORSE INRUN

CHEVALET SAWHORSE

TREVALLY TURRUM

TREWS TROUSERS

TRIACETATE ACETIN EUROBIN

TRIAD MAJOR TRIAS TRINE TRIUNE TERNARY TERNION TRILOGY TRINARY TRINITY TRIMURTI TRIRATNA

TRIAL SAY SHY TRY BOUT DOOM FIRE HACK OYER STAB TEST TURN ASSAY CROSS ESSAY GRIEF ISSUE POINT PROOF TASTE TOUCH WHACK ASSIZE EFFORT EQUITY TRINAL APPROOF ATTEMPT CALVARY DISGUST HEARING PROVING SCRATCH CRUCIBLE EXERCISE JUDGMENT QUAESTIO TENTAMEN PROLUSION
(— BY BATTLE) WAGER
(— BY ORDEAL) ORDALIUM
(— FOR HOUNDS) DERBY
(— OF SPEED) DASH
(— OF STRENGTH) CRUNCH
(AUTHOR OF —) KAFKA
(CHARACTER IN —) LENI JOSEPH ADVOCATE BURSTNER TITORELLI
(EXPERIMENTAL —) TENTAMEN
(RACING —) PREP
(SEVERE —) ORDEAL CRUCIBLE
(PREF.) PEIRA

TRIANGLE APEX CYMBAL OXYGON TRIGON PYRAMID SCALENE TRINITY TRIQUET DINGDONG ISOSCELE

TRIANGULAR HEATER CUNEATE HASTATE
(— AREA) QUIRK
(— CLOTH) GORE
(— INSET) GODET
(PREF.) TRIGON(O)

TRIBAL GENTILE GENTLIC TRIBULAR

TRIBE (ALSO SEE NATIVE AND PEOPLE) AO GI ATI AUS BOH EVE EWE GOG KHA KIN KRA ROD SUK YAO ADAI AKAN AKHA AKIM AKKA BAYA BONI CLAN DAGO GUHA PURU QUNG RACE RAVI REKI SAHO SEID SHIK SHOR SIOL SOGA SUKU SUSU TOBA TURI TUSH UBII VEPS VILI VIRA YANA AEQUI ANGKA APTAL ARAWA BASSI BATAK BESSI BONGO BROOD CHANG CINEL DADJO DEDAN DIERI FIRCA GIBBI HORDE HOUSE ICENI KAJAR KANDH KEDAR KHOND KIWAI KONGO KOTAR KREPI LANGO MAGOG MARSI MBUBA MENDE MENDI MOSSI MUTER NANDI PHYLE PONDO QUADI SERER SOTIK STAMM SUEVI TAIPI TAULI TCAWI TEKKE TELEI TUATH VEPSE VOLOF WAKHI WARRI WASHO WAYAO YOMUD ADIGHE AGAWAM AMHARA ANAMIM ANTEVA APAYAO ARAINS BANYAI BASOGA BUDUMA BUSAOS CHAMPA CHAWIA CHORAI DOROBO FAMILY HERULI KARLUK KEREWA KHAMTI KONYAK KORANA LOBALE MANGAR

MOLALA NATION NERVII PAHARI PHYLON POKOMO RAMNES SHAGIA SICULI SIMEON SUKUMA TAINUI TAMOYO TCHIAM TELEUT THUSHI TUSHIN TYPEES VENETI WABENA WABUMA WAGOMA WAGUHA WAHEHE WARORI WASOGA WAVIRA ZARAMO ZEGUHA ZENAGA ABABDEH ABANTES AIAWONG AKWAPIM AMAKOSA ANOMURA ANTAIVA ARVERNI BAGIRMI BAKATAN BAKONGO BAKUNDA BAMBARA BASONGO CABINDA CHAOUIA CHAUWIA CHONTAL CHUKCHI COLLERY DADAYAG DADSCHO ILLANUN JAZYGES KABINDA KABONGA KHOKANI KOLDAJI KONIAGA KOREISH KUBACHI KURUMBA LLANERO NAIADES PALAUNG PARISII PIMENTO RAURACI SAMBALA SAMBARA SEKHWAN SENONES SEQUANI SHAMMAR SHERANI SHERPAS SHUKRIA SILIPAN SUIONES SUKKIIM TAKELMA TARKANI TURKANA VIDDHAL WAGWENO WAICURI WAMBUGU WAREGGA WASANGO ZONGORA AMAFINGO ANDOROBO ASHANGOS ASSHURIM AWABAKAL BARKINJI BATETELA BOANBURA CHERUSCI CHITRALI GEZRITES JICAQUES KUKURUKU LANDUMAN NEBAIOTH ORUNCHUN PALLIYAN PHASIRON PUPULUCA PUPURURU RAHANWIN SAKALAVA SHINWARI SINGSING SINTSINK TCHUKCHI TENGGRIS USTARANA WANGATTA WAPOGORO WAPOKOMO
(— OF ISRAEL) DAN GAD ASHER REUBEN EPHRAIM ISSACHAR MANASSEH
(CHINESE —S) HU
(PRIVILEGED —) MAGHZEN MAKHZAN
(SEA GYPSY —) SELUNG
(PREF.) PHYL(O)
(SUFF.) INI

TRIBROMOETHANOL AVERTIN

TRIBULATION AGONY CROSS MISERY SORROW DISTRESS

TRIBUNAL BAR FEME ROTA VEHM BENCH COURT FEHME FORUM JUNTA VEHME MAJLIS ACUERDO ESGUARD MEJLISS RIGSRET AREOPAGY KANGAROO

TRIBUNE BEMA VELUTUS

TRIBUTARY ARM BOGAN BRANCH FEEDER TYBURN AFFLUENT ANABRANCH

TRIBUTE AID FEE TAX CAIN GELT KUDO LEVY PORT RENT SCAT CANON GAVEL HANSE MAILL SALVO SCATT CHAUTH HERIOT HIDAGE HOMAGE IMPOST CARATCH CHEVAGE CHIEFRY OVATION PENSION SYNODAL TREWAGE AUXILIUM BRENNAGE HEREGELD PESHKASH ROMESCOT ROMESHOT

TRICE GIRD BLINK THROW INSTANT

TRICHECHUS MANATUS

TRICHINA NEMATODE

TRICHINIZED MEASLY

TRICHION CRINION

TRICHOME SCALE

TRICHOMONIASIS CANKER ABORTION

TRICK DO BAM BOB COG CON CUN DAP DOR FOB FOX FUB FUN GIN GUM JIG JOB PAW RIG BILK BITE BORE CHAW CHIP DIDO DIRT DUPE FAKE FIRK FLAM FLUM FOOL GAFF GAME GAUD GECK GULL HAVE HOAX JAPE JEST JINK JOUK JUNT LOCK LURK PASS PAWK PRAT PULL RORT RUSE SELL SKIT SLUR TURN WILE WIPE WOOL ANTIC BLEAR BLINK CATCH CHEAT CONNU CRAFT CREEK CROOK CULLY CURVE DODGE DORRE ELUDE FEINT FETCH FOURB FRAUD GLEEK GRIFT GUILE KNACK PAVIE PLANT PRANK SHIFT SHINE SKITE SLICK STUNT TRAIN TRUFF TWIST WHEEL WREST WRINK BAFFLE BANTER BEGUNK BEJAPE BLENCH BROGUE CAUTEL CHOUSE CRADDY DECEIT DELUDE DOUBLE EUCHRE FOURBE HOCKET HUMBUG ILLUDE JOCKEY JUGGLE MANNER PLISKY POLICY SCONCE SHAVIE SPRING TREPAN VAGARY WHEEZE WINNER CANTRIP CHICANE CONCEIT FICELLE FINESSE FORWARD GUILERY KNAVERY MARLOCK PAGEANT SHUFFLE SLEIGHT WHIZZER ARTIFICE CHALDESE CLAPTRAP CLOWNADE CONTOISE CROTCHET DELUSION DOUBLING FLAGARIE FLIMFLAM GILENYIE INTRIGUE JEOPARDY PRACTICE PRANCOME PRESTIGE QUENTISE SLAMPAMP TRAVERSE TRICKING BAMBOOZLE STRATAGEM
(— OUT) FARD FANGLE FINIFY
(BEGUILING —) WILE
(CARD —) CLUB HEART SPADE STICH DIAMOND WEAVING
(FRAUDULENT —) RIG TOP
(JUGGLING —) FOIST
(KNAVISH —) DOGTRICK
(LOVE —) AMORETTO
(MEAN —) TOUCH
(MONKEY —) SINGERIE
(OLD —) CONNU
(PETTY —S) CRANS
(SIX —S) BOOK
(SMART —) LIRIPIPE LIRIPOOP
(STUPID —) SHINE
(VEXING —) CHAW
(WRESTLING —) CHIP CLICK FAULX FORWARD
(PL.) DAGS

TRICKER TRUMPER

TRICKERY DOLE GAFF SHAM TRAP TRAY WILE COVIN FRAUD HOCUS SHARK TRAIN CAUTEL COVINE DECEIT JAPERY JUGGLE TREGET DODGERY FALLACY GULLERY JOUKERY KNAVERY PAWKERY SLEIGHT ARTIFICE CHEATING

COZENAGE JOOKERIE JUGGLERY
PRACTICE TRICKING TRUMPERY
TRICKILY FOXILY
TRICKINESS PAWKERY
TRICKISH KNAVISH FRAUDFUL
TRICKLE DRIB DRIP DRILL STILL
TRILL DISTIL DRIVEL GUTTER
SICKER SIGGER STRAIN ZIGGER
DISTILL DRIBBLE DRIZZLE
DROPPLE TRINTLE
TRICKSTER GULL SHAM RASCAL
TRAPAN SLICKER TRICKER
SLEEVEEN TRAMPOSO
TREGETOUR
TRICKSY ELFISH QUIRKSEY
TRICKY SLY DEEP BRAID DODGY
FIKIE GAUDY ROWDY SNIDE
ARTFUL CATCHY LUBRIC QUIRKY
SHIFTY SMARTY TWISTY DEVIOUS
SLANTER TRICKLE WINDING
FLIMFLAM JUGGLING LUBRICAL
SHIFTFUL SKITTISH SLIDDERY
SLIPPERY TORTUOUS TRICKING
TRICLINIC ANORTHIC
TRICOT JERSEY
TRICYCLE VELO CYCLE TRIKE
WHEEL TANDEM TRICAR
RANTOON ROADSTER SOCIABLE
TRIDENT VAJRA TRISUL TRISULA
TRIED TESTED PROBATE WEIGHED
RELIABLE
TRIFECTA TRIPLE
TRIFLE ACE BOB DAB HAW PIN
SOU TOY BEAN COOT DOIT FICO
FOOL HAIR HOOT JAUK MESS
MOCK MOTE PLAY RUSE WHIT
DALLY FLIRT FLUKE GLAIK ITEMY
NIFLE PLACK POINT SCRAT SPORT
TRICK TRUFF BAWBEE BREATH
DABBLE DANDLE DAWDLE
DELUDE DIBBLE DOODAD
DOODLE FADDLE FESCUE FIDDLE
FOOTER FOOTLE FRIVOL
GEWGAW MONKEY NIDDLE
NIGGLE NIGNAY PADDLE PALTER
PETTLE PICKLE PIDDLE PIGGLE
PINGLE POTTER PUTTER STIVER
TIFFLE VANITY WANTON
FEATHER FLAMFEW FRIBBLE
NOTHING QUIDDLE THOUGHT
TRANEEN TRINKET TRIVIAL
WHIFFLE COQUETTE FALDERAL
FLIMFLAM FOLDEROL GIMCRACK
KICKSHAW MOLEHILL NIFFNAFF
NIHILITY NUGAMENT RIGMAREE
TRANTLUM BAGATELLE
(— WITH) JANK DANDLE DELUDE
NIGGLE
(ATTRACTIVE —) CONCEIT
(LITERARY —) TOY
(MERE —) SONG STRAW
(MEREST —) FIG
(SHOWY —) WALLY
(PL.) NUGAE TRIVIA GIBLETS
FEWTRILS NONSENSE
TRIFLER DOODLE PLAYER WANTON
FLANEUR FOOTLER FRIBBLE
NUGATOR PINGLER TWIDDLER
WHIFFLER
TRIFLES
(PREF.) NUGI
TRIFLING AIRY FOND IDLE FUNNY
INANE LIGHT PETTY POTTY SILLY

SMALL FADDLE FLIMSY FUTILE
LEVITY LIMUTE LITTLE PALTRY
SIMPLE STRAWY TOYISH FOOLISH
FRIBBLE ITEMING NOMINAL
TRIVIAL TWATTLE COQUETRY
FIDDLING FLIMFLAM FRIPPERY
IMMOMENT NUGATORY PIDDLING
SNIPPING WHIFFLERY NEGLIGIBLE
TRIFOLIUM CLOVER TREFOIL
TRIG SNOD TRIM CHIPPER
TRIGGER VERGE TRICKER
TRIGGERFISH COCUYO TURBOT
OLDWIFE BALISTID FILEFISH
OLDWENCH
TRIGON TRINE SABBEKA SACKBUT
SAMBUCA TRIGONON
TRIGONOMETRY SPHERICS
TRILBY (AUTHOR OF —) DUMAURIER
(CHARACTER IN —) ALICE GECKO
SANDY TAFFY BILLEE TRILBY
OFERRALL SVENGALI
TRILL BURR FLAP ROLL SHAKE
QUAVER THRILL TRILLO WARBLE
ROULADE TRILLET
TRILLED HIRRIENT
TRILLION
(PREF.) TERA TREG(A)
TRILLIONTH
(PREF.) PICO
TRILLIUM SARA TRUE SARAH
TRUMP BENJAMIN TRUELOVE
TRILOBITE EODISCID
TRIM AX AXE CUT DUB GIM LIP
LOP NET BARB BEAD BUTT CLIP
CROP DEFT DINK FEAT FUSS
GASH GIMP HACK JIMP LACE
NEAT PICK SNAG SNOD SNUG
SPUR STOW TACK TOSH TRIG
BRAID BRUSH CLEAN COPSE
DRESS FITTY GENTY HEDGE
KEMPT KNIFE NATTY PREEN
PRIME PRUNE PURGE SAUCY
SHAVE SHEAR SHRAG SHRIP
SLEEK SMART SMIRK SPRIG
STUMP TIGHT TRICK VERGE
BARBER DAPPER DONSIE DOUBLE
FETTLE PICKED REFORM SHROUD
SOIGNE SPRUCE SVELTE SWITCH
TRIMLY CHIPPER FEATHER
FLOUNCE SCISSOR MANICURE
ORNAMENT TRIMMING
SHIPSHAPE
(— A BOAT) SIT
(— ENDS OF HAIR) SHIRL
(— HEDGE) DUB
(— HIDES) ROUND
(— MEAT) CONDITION
(— SAIL) FILL
(— SEAMS) FETTLE
(— SHOE) FOX
(— TREES) PRIME SWAMP
(— WITH EMBROIDERY) GIMP
PANEL
TRIMLY SMARTLY SPRUCELY
TRIMMED PEEKABOO
TRIMMER FINER BRIDLE TACKER
VOLANT ROUNDER SMOCKER
SCRATTER
TRIMMING COQ FUR GIMP LACE
BRAID CHAPE COQUE FRILL
GUARD INKLE JABOT ROBIN
RUCHE ERMINE LACING OSPREY
PURFLE ROBING BEADING

CASCADE FALBALA FURRING
GALLOON MARABOU PUFFING
ROULEAU BRAIDING EAVESING
FALDERAL FOLDEROL FROSTING
FROUFROU FURBELOW JEWELING
PAILETTE PEARLING PICKADIL
PLASTRON SOUTACHE PAILLETTE
SPAGHETTI STRAPPING
(PL.) LOP FLOTS SHORTS FIXINGS
LOPPING BRAIDING FRILLIES
TRIMURTI TRINITY
TRINE TRENE TRIGON
**TRINIDAD-TOBAGO (CAPITAL
OF —)** PORTOFSPAIN
(POINT OF —) GALERA
(RIVER OF —) ORTOIRE
(TOWN OF —) TOCO ARIMA COUVA
LABREA MORUGA SIPARIA
TRINITARIAN MATHURIN
TRINITROTOLUENE TOLITE
TRITON
TRINITY TRIAD TRIAS TRINE
TRIUNE GODHEAD TERNARY
TRIMURTI TRINUNITY
TRINKET TOY DIDO GAUD MERE
BIJOU HEART KNACK TAHLI
BAUBLE CHARME DEVICE
DOODAD GEWGAW BIBELOT
TRANGAM TRANKUM GIMCRACK
KICKSHAW TRANTLUM TRINKLET
WHIMWHAM
(PL.) TRINKUMS
TRINKETRY KNAVERY
TRIO GLEEK TERZET TRIUNE
TERZETTO
TRIOLEFIN TRIENE
TRIONYX AMYDA
TRIOPAS (DAUGHTER OF —)
IPHIMEDIA
(FATHER OF —) NEPTUNE
(MOTHER OF —) CANACE
(SON OF —) ERYSICHTHON
TRIOPS APUS
TRIP HOP JAG JET JOG TIP BOUT
CHIP FOOT GAIT GATE KILT LINK
RAKE SKIP TOUR TROT TURN
BROAD DANCE DRIVE HITCH
JAUNT SALLY CRUISE ERRAND
FLIGHT HEGIRA OFFEND OUTING
RAMBLE SAFARI SASHAY VOYAGE
JOURNEY SAILING SETDOWN
STUMBLE TRIPPER CAMPAIGN
PERIPLUS
(— ALONG) CHIP LINK
(— BY DOG TEAM) MUSH
(— IN WRESTLING) CHIP CLICK
(— INTO COUNTRY) CAMPAIGN
(— UP) SUPPLANT
(HUNTING —) SHOOT
(PLEASURE —) JUNKET
TRIPE PAUNCH ROLPENS
TRILLIBUB
TRIPLE TRINE TREBLE TERNARY
TRIFOLD TRIPLEX THRIBBLE
TRIFECTA
TRIPLE BOND
(SUFF.) (CONTAINING —) OLIC
TRIPLET TRIN BRELAN PARIAL
TERCET TRIOLE TRIPLE TERZINA
TRIOLET HEMIOLIA TRILLING
TRIPLING TRISTICH
(— OF BASES) CODON
TRIPLETAIL SAMA CHOBIE

FLASHER GROUPER
TRIPLICITY TRIGON
TRIPOD CAT TRIP SPIDER TEAPOY
TRIPOS TRIVET TRESTLE
TRIPODY HEMIEPES
TRIPOLI SILEX TRIPEL
TRIPPER DECKMAN
TRIPTOLEMUS (FATHER OF —)
CELEUS
(MOTHER OF —) METANIRA
TRISHAW CYCLO
TRISMUS LOCKJAW TETANUS
**TRISTAN UND ISOLDE
(CHARACTER IN —)** MARK MELOT
ISOLDE TRISTAN BRANGANE
KURWENAL
(COMPOSER OF —) WAGNER
**TRISTRAM SHANDY (AUTHOR OF
—)** STERNE
(CHARACTER IN —) SLOP TOBY
TRIM BOBBY SHANDY WADMAN
WALTER YORICK SUSANNAH
TRISTRAM
TRITE FADE HACK WORN BANAL
CONNU CORNY HOARY MUSTY
STALE VAPID BEATEN COMMON
MODERN HACKNEY PERCOCT
TRIVIAL BROMIDIC SHOPWORN
TRITENESS BATHOS
TRITERPENOID CERIN
TRITON NEWT TRUMPET
(FATHER OF —) NEPTUNE
(MOTHER OF —) AMPHITRITE
TRITURATE POUND POWDER
TRITURATION TRIPSIS
TRITURUS MOLGE
TRIUMPH WIN CROW PALM
INSULT PREVAIL VICTORY
CONQUEST
(— OVER) SCALP
TRIUMPHANT VICTOR JUBILANT
TRIUMPHING OVANT
TRIUNGULIN CRAWLER
TRIVET SPIDER TRIPOD TRESTLE
TRIPPER BRANDISE
TRIVIAL BALD JERK NICE VAIN
BANAL LEGER LIGHT PETTY SILLY
SMALL TIDDY FIDFAD FOOTLE
PALTRY SLIGHT TOYISH COMICAL
PIPERLY PUERILE SHALLOW
TIDDLEY DOGGEREL FEATHERY
FOOTLING GIMCRACK PIDDLING
PILULOUS TRIFLING TRINKETY
(NOT —) SOLID EARNEST
TRIVIALITY FOLLY NIGNAY TRIFLE
INANITY IDLENESS NONSENSE
NUGACITY
TROCHANTER SCAPULA
TROCHE ROTULA TABLET
CACHUNDE PASTILLE
TROCHEE CHOREE CHOREUS
TROCHEUS
TROCHLEA PULLEY
TROCTOLITE GABBRO
TRODDEN TRADED
(MUCH —) BEATEN
TROGLODYTIC SPELEAN
TROGON QUEZAL QUETZAL
TOCORORO
TROILUS (BELOVED OF —) CRESSIDA
(FATHER OF —) PRIAM
(MOTHER OF —) HECUBA
(SLAYER OF —) ACHILLES

TROILUS AND CRESSIDA
(AUTHOR OF —) SHAKESPEARE
(CHARACTER IN —) AJAX HELEN
PARIS PRIAM AENEAS HECTOR
NESTOR ANTENOR CALCHAS
HELENUS TROILUS ULYSSES
ACHILLES CRESSIDA DIOMEDES
MENELAUS PANDARUS
AGAMEMNON ALEXANDER
CASSANDRA DEIPHOBUS
PATROCLUS THERSITES
ANDROMACHE MARGARELON
TROJAN TROIC DARDAN ANTENOR
(PL.) TEUCRI
TROLL DROW HARL SPIN TROW
ANGLE HARLE MOOCH TRAWL
TROLLOL
TROLLER MOOCHER
TROLLEY BOGEY BOGIE TRUCK
PANTOGRAPH
TROLLOP CUT DOXY BITCH DOXIE
TROLL TRULL DOLLOP
TROMBONE BONE TRAM BUSINE
POSAUNE SACKBUT SLIPHORN
(PART OF —) BOW CUP KEY RIM
BELL CROOK FLARE SHANK SLIDE
BUMPER FLANGE BALANCER
MOUTHPIECE
TRONA URAO
TROOP FARE GING ROUT TURM
ROUTE SOLAK STAND TURMA
WERED CORNET RISALA ROUGHT
SCHOOL THREAT TICHEL TROUPE
COMPANY COMITIVA
(— OF ARMED MEN) CREW
(— OF FOXES) SKULK
(— OF WORSHIPPERS) THIASUS
(—S ATTACHED TO SOVEREIGN)
GUARDS
(—S IN BATTLE ARRAY) SHELTRON
(—S ON WING OF ARMY) ALARES
(ASSAULTING —S) WAVE
(BOMBAY —S) DUCKS
(CAVALRY —) CORNET
(GIRL SCOUT —) SHIP
(LIGHT-ARMED —) PSILOI
(MOUNTAIN —) ALPINI
(SCOTTISH —S) JOCKS
(PL.) PARADE
TROOPER BARGIR REITER RUTTER
BARGEER
TROPARION HIRMOS HEIRMOS
TROPARY KATABASIS
TROPE IMAGE EVOVAE
TROPHONEMA VILLUS
TROPHONIUS (BROTHER OF —)
AGAMEDES
(FATHER OF —) APOLLO ERGINUS
TROPHOZOITE CEPHALIN
SPORADIN
TROPHY BAG EMMY PALM PRIZE
SCALP REWARD LAURELS
(WRITING —) HUGO
TROPIC SOLAR TROPHIC
TROPINE HYOSCINE
TROS (FATHER OF —) ERICTHONIUS
ERICHTHONIUS
(MOTHER OF —) CALLIRRHOE
(SON OF —) ILUS GANYMEDE
ASSARACUS
TROT JOG SPUD TRIG FADGE
HURRY PIAFFE
TROTH CERTY TROGS

TRUTH CERTIE
TROTTER DRIVER CRUBEEN
SPANKER
TROUBADOR MINSTREL SORDELLO
TROUBLE ADO AIL DIK HOE ILL IRK
MAR VEX WOE BEAT BUSY CAIN
CARK EARN FASH FIKE GRAM
JEEL MASH MOIL PAIN PINE ROUT
SORE STIR TEEN TINE TRAY UNRO
WORK ANNOY BESET CROSS
DROVE DUTCH GRIEF HAUNT
LABOR ROWEL SMITE SPITE
STEER STURT SUSSY THRIE
TWEAK WHILE WORRY BARRAT
BOTHER BURBLE CADDLE
CUMBER DITHER EFFORT GRIEVE
GRUDGE HARASS HATTER
KIAUGH MOLEST POTHER RATTLE
RUBBER SORROW SQUALL
TAKING THREAT UNEASE UNRUFE
WORRIT AFFLICT AGITATE
ANXIETY CHAGRIN CONCERN
DISEASE DISTURB DRUBBLE
EMBROIL FASHERY INFLICT
PERTURB PILIKIA SCRUPLE
SPUTTER THOUGHT TRACHLE
TRAVAIL TRIBBLE TURMOIL
BUSINESS DARKNESS DISORDER
DISQUIET DISTRESS NOISANCE
VEXATION WANDRETH
(— ONE'S SELF) PASS
(PL.) CHAGRINS
TROUBLED DRUBLY DRUMLY
GRUMLY QUEASY CAREFUL
FRETFUL HAUNTED AGITATED
HARASSED
TROUBLESHOOTER FIXER
TROUBLESOME DIK ILL SAD BUSY
HARD FIKIE PESKY ROWDY TIGHT
PLAGUY SHREWD STICKY THORNY
UNEASY BRICKLE HARMFUL
PESTFUL PLAGUEY TEWSOME
ANNOYING FASHIOUS SPITEFUL
UNTOWARD
TROUBLESOMENESS BOTHER
TROUBLING CHRONIC
TROU-DE-LOUP TRAPHOLE
TROUGH BOX CUP HOD RUN TOM
BACK BOSH BUNK COVE DAIL
DALE DISH DORR SHOE SINK
TRAY TROW VALE BAKIE CHUTE
DITCH LAVER SHOOT SHUTE
SLIDE SPOUT STRIP ALVEUS
BACKET BUDDLE GUTTER
HARBOR HOPPER LAVABO
MANGER RUNNER SALTER SINKER
SLUICE STRAKE TROGUE VALLEY
WALLOW CHENEAU CONDUIT
LAUNDER RIFFLER TRENDLE
TROFFER LAVATORY PENSTOCK
(— FOR ASHES) BAKIE
(— FOR COOLING INGOTS) BOSH
(— FOR PAPER PULP) RIFFLER
(— FOR WASHING ORE) TOM
HUTCH STRIP BUDDLE STRAKE
(— IN MONASTERY) LAVABO
(— OF A WAVE) SULK
(— OF CIDER MILL) CHASE
(— OF ROCK) SYNCLINE
(— OF THE SEA) ALVEUS
(ANNULAR —) CUP
(BAKER'S —) HUTCH
(EAVES —) CANAL CHENEAU

(GLACIAL —) DORR
(ORE —) TYE
(SHEEP-DIPPING —) DUP
(WOODEN —) TRUG BAKIE TROGUE
(PREF.) BOTHR(O) BOTHRI(O)
PYEL(O)
(SUFF.) SCAPH
TROUNCE MOP FLOG TRAMP
WHOMP COURSE CUDGEL
CANVASS SHELLAC
TROUNCING LACING WARMING
TROUPE BALLET SERVANTS
CUADRILLA
TROUSER STROSSER
TROUSERING CASINET
TROUSERS BAGS CORDS DUCKS
JEANS KICKS PANTS SLOPS
TONGS TREWS BRAIES CHINOS
DENIMS FLARES SHORTS SKILTS
SLACKS WHITES BOTTOMS
BRACCAE BROGUES KERSEYS
NANKINS SHALWAR SLIVERS
STRIDES BLOOMERS BREECHES
FLANNELS KICKSEYS MOLESKIN
NANKEENS OVERALLS SHINTYAN
PANTALOONS
TROUT CHAR KELT PEAL POGY
BROOK BROWN CHARR LAKER
LUNGE SCURF SEWEN SEWIN
SHARD SQUET SQUIT TRUFF
FINNOC KIPPER MYKISS QUASKY
SALTER TAIMEN TRUCHA TULADI
BOREGAT BROOKIE BROWNIE
COASTER HERLING OQUASSA
POUNDER RAINBOW SQUETEE
AUREOLUS BODIERON GILLAROO
HARDHEAD KAMLOOPS SAIBLING
SALMONID SISCOWET
(SMALL —) SCURLING SKIRLING
(YOUNG —) WHITLING
TROUVERE BLONDEL
TROVATORE, IL (CHARACTER IN —)
INEZ RUIZ DILUNA AZUCENA
LEONORA MANRICO FERRANDO
(COMPOSER OF —) VERDI
TROW DROW TRUE FAITH BELIEF
COVENANT
TROWEL HAWK LEAF PIPE DARBY
DERBY FLOAT TAPER TREWEL
(HEARTSHAPED —) HEART
DOGTAIL
(MOLDER'S —) LEAF TAPER
(PLASTERER'S —) FLOAT
TROY ILION TROIA TROJA
(FOUNDER OF —) ILUS TROS
(INHABITANT OF —) ILIAN
TROYENS, LES (CHARACTER IN —)
ANNA DIDO IOPAS PRIAM AENEAS
HECTOR NARBAL ASCANIUS
PANTHEUS CASSANDRA
CHOROEBUS
(COMPOSER OF —) BERLIOZ
TRUANT HOOKY TRONE TROUT
MICHER MEECHER TRIVANT
VAGRANT
TRUCE PAX BARLEY TREAGUE
INDUCIAE
TRUCK DAN UTE BUNK CORF DRAB
DRAG DUCK DUMP GUNK RACK
WYNN BOGIE BUGGY DILLY DOLLY
GILLY LORRY TROKE BARTER
BUMMER CAMION DIESEL
DROGUE DRUGGE DUMPER

JITNEY PICKUP SLOVEN TIPPER
TURTLE CARAVAN FOURGON
GONDOLA SKIDDER SLEEPER
TROLLEY TRUCKLE TRUNDLE
DELIVERY HAULAWAY TRANSFER
(COAL —) DAN
(FIRE —) PUMPER
(LOGGING —) BUNK BUMMER
(MINING —) CORF SKIP BARNEY
(PART OF —) DECK HOOD STEP
TANK TIRE GUARD LIGHT STAKE
WHEEL BUMPER GRILLE MIRROR
AIRHORN CARRIER EXHAUST
MUDFLAP BULKHEAD HEADLIGHT
TAILLIGHT COMPRESSOR
WINDSHIELD
(TIMBER —) DRUG WYNN
TRUCKLE FAWN TOADY SLAVER
TRUCKLING SERVILE
TRUCULENCE BRAG
TRUCULENT MEAN CRUEL HARSH
FIERCE SAVAGE SCATHING
TRUDGE JOG PAD HAKE PLOD
STOG JAUNT TRACE TRAIK
TRAMP TRASH STODGE TAIGLE
TRAIPSE
TRUE SO GOOD JUST LEAL PURE
REAL VERY VRAI PLUMB RIGHT
SOOTH SOUND VERAY ACTUAL
FIDELE LAWFUL DEVOTED
GENUINE GERMANE PRECISE
SINCERE STAUNCH FAITHFUL
RELIABLE RIGHTFUL SOOTHFUL
UNERRING
(— TO THE FACT) LITERAL
(QUESTIONABLY —) ALLEGED
(PREF.) ALETHO ETYMO EU
ORTH(O) VERI
TRUFFLE TRUB TRUFF EARTHNUT
TRUISM SOOTH
TRULL DELL BLOWZE CALLET
TRULY YEA AWAT EVEN FEGS IWIS
JUST QUITE SOOTH SYKER TIGHT
ATWEEL DINKUM INDEED SIMPLY
VERILY INSOOTH SOOTHLY
VERAMENT WITTERLY
TRUMP DIS DIX LOW PAM LILY
RUFF BASTA BASTO DEECE
TROMBE MANILLA MATADOR
TRIUMPH SPADILLE
(NOT —S) LAY
(2ND HIGHEST —) MANILLE
TRUMPERY MOCKADO RUBBISH
GIMCRACK PEDDLERY
TRUMPET BEME LURE TUBA SHELL
TRUMP BOZINE BUCCIN CORNET
KERANA LITUUS TROMBA TULNIC
ALCHEMY BUCCINA CLARINO
CLARION KERRANA SALPINX
NARSINGA SLUGHORN SOURDINE
WATERCUP
(— OF DAFFODIL) CORONA
(PREF.) SALPING(O)
(SUFF.) SALPINX
TRUMPET BELL CODON PAVILON
TRUMPET CALL DIAN DIANA
SENNET
TRUMPET CREEPER TECOMA
COWHAGE CREEPER FOXGLOVE
HELLVINE
TRUMPETER MOKI AGAMI TRUMP
TOOTER JACAMIN TUBICEN
YAKAMIK

TRUMPETER FISH MOKI MOKIHI
TRUMPETER PERCH MADO
TRUMPETS WATERCUP
TRUMPET-SHAPED BUCCINAL
TRUMPETWOOD IMBAUBA
TRUNCATED ABRUPT STUBBED
TRUNKED
TRUNCHEON BATON BILLY
WARDER SPONTON PARTISAN
SPONTOON
TRUNDLE HURL RUNG TRILL TROLL
RUNDLE TRUCKLE WALLOWER
TRUNK BOX BODY BOLE BOOT
BULK KIST LICH RUNT STAM
STEM STUD CABER PETER SHAFT
STICK STOCK TORSO ARIGUE
BARREL CAUDEX COFFER LOCKER
CARCASS CORSAGE STOWAGE
TRUNCUS SARATOGA
(ARTERIAL —) AORTA
(ELEPHANT'S —) SNOUT
(FOSSIL —) CYCAD
(SMALL —) HATBOX
(SPLIT —) PUNCHEON
(SWIM —S) JAMS
(TREE —) BOLE BUTT STICK RICKER
**(TREE — OVER 8 INCHES IN
DIAMETER)** MAST
(TRIMMED TREE —) LOG
(WORSHIPPED TREE —S) IRMINSUL
(PREF.) CORM(O) PROBOSCI(DI)
TRUNKFISH CHAPIN BOXFISH
COWFISH
TRUSS SPAN WARREN DORLACH
(— OF STRAW) WAP
(— UP) KILT
TRUST AFFY HOPE LITE POOL RELY
REST TICK TREW TROW FAITH
FRIST GROUP TRUTH BELIEF
CARTEL CHARGE CORNER CREDIT
DEPEND FIANCE LIPPEN OFFICE
TICKET BELIEVE BETRUST
COMBINE CONFIDE CREANCE
CRIANCE JAWBONE SECRECY
VENTURE AFFIANCE COMMENDA
CREDENCE MONOPOLY RELIANCE
TRUSTED FIDUCIAL
TRUSTEE CURATOR FEOFFEE
SINDICO VISITOR ASSIGNEE
MUTWALLI
TRUSTWORTHINESS HONOR
TRUST CREDIT HONESTY
CREDENCE AXIOPISTY
TRUSTWORTHY SAFE SURE TRIG
SOOTH SOUND SYKER TRIED
HONEST SECRET SECURE SICKER
STABLE TRUSTY COCKSURE
CREDIBLE FIDUCIAL RELIABLE
TRUSTFUL
TRUSTY TRIG FECKFUL STAUNCH
FAITHFUL RELIABLE
TRUTH TAO UNA SOOTH TROTH
WHITE SATTVA SOOTH
LOWDOWN VERITAS VERACITY
VERIDITY VERIMENT
(— TABLE) MATRIX
(IDEAL —) CHRIST DHARMA
(IN —) CERTES
(RELATING TO —) ALETHIC
(ULTIMATE —) LIGHT SUNYATA
**TRUTH AND JUSTICE (AUTHOR OF
—)** TAMMSAARE
(CHARACTER IN —) MARI PAAS

KARIN TIINA ANDRES INDREK
TRUTHFUL TRUE VERY SOOTH
HONEST VERIDIC
TRUTHFULLY GOSPELLY
TRUTHFULNESS HONESTY
VERACITY SINCERITY
TRY GO SAY SHY BURL FAND HACK
PASS PENK PREE SEEK SLAP TEST
TIRL TURN AFOND ASSAY CRACK
ESSAY ETTLE FLING GROPE
JUDGE OFFER PROVE SENSE
SOUND TASTE TEMPT TOUCH
WHACK WHIRL APPOSE ASSAIL
FRAIST GRIEVE STRIVE AFFLICT
AFFORCE APPROVE ATTEMPT
DISCUSS ESPROVE IMITATE
STAGGER ENDEAVOR STRUGGLE
(— DESPERATELY) AGONIZE
(— FOR GOAL) SHOT
(— HARD) STRIVE
(— OUT) SAMPLE AUDITION
(— TO ATTAIN) AFFECT
(CASUAL —) FLING
(QUICK —) SLAP
TRYING NASTY ARDUOUS CRUCIAL
GRUELING
TRYSAIL SPENCER
TSAR SALTAN (CHARACTER IN —)
GUIDON SALTAN MILITRISA
POVARIKHA TKACHIKHA
(COMPOSER OF —)
RIMSKYKORSAKOV
**TSAR'S BRIDE, THE (CHARACTER IN
—)** IVAN LYKOV MARFA
LYUBASHA GRYANZNOY
(COMPOSER OF —)
RIMSKYKORSAKOV
TSETSE FLY KIVU GANDI
DIPTERAN GLOSSINA
T-SHAPED TAU
TSILTADEN CHILION
TSUBO BU
TSWANA CHUANA SECHUANA
TUAREG IMOHAGH IMOSHAGH
TUATARA GUANA GUANO IGUANA
HATTERIA
TUB FAT HOD KID KIT SOE SOW
TUN VAT BACK BOWK COOL CORF
COWL GAWN KNOP MEAL TYND
TYNE BOWIE ESHIN KEEVE KIVER
SKEEL STAND BUCKET KEELER
KILLER KIMNEL TROUGH TURNEL
BATHTUB BREAKER SALTFAT
TANKARD TRUNDLE KOOLIMAN
LAVATORY
(— FOR ALEWIVES) HOD
(— FOR AMALGAMATING ORES)
TINA
(— FOR BREAD) BARGE
(— OF BUTTER) COOL
(— OF HOGWASH) SWILLTUB
(— USED AS DIPPER) HANDY
PIGGIN
(— WITH SLOPING SIDES) SHAUL
(BREWER'S —) BACK KEEVE
(LAUNDRY —) WASHTRAY
(MESS —) KID KIT
(MINING —) CORF
(TANNING —) LEACH
(WATER —) DAN JAILER
(WOODEN —) KIT SOE KIMNEL
TRINDLE
TUBA BASS HELICON BOMBARDON

TUBE TAG BEAK BODY BOOT CANE
CASE CAST CORE CURL DRUM
DUCT HORN HOSE PIPE REED
WORM BATON CANAL CORER
CROOK CRYPT DRAIN GLAND
HEART LI_R QUILL SIGHT SKELP
SLIDE SPILE SPOUT THECA THIEF
TRUMP TUBAL VALVE AUDION
BARREL CALCAR CANNEL
CANNON COLUMN CORNET
DEWCAP FILTER GULLET HEADER
NOZZLE OCTODE SLEEVE SUCKER
SYRINX THROAT TRIODE TUBING
TUBULE TUNNEL UPTAKE VESSEL
BLOWGUN CHIMNEY CONDUIT
CUVETTE DROPPER FERRULE
FISTULA HOUSING OOBLAST
OVIDUCT QUILLET ROSTRUM
SALPINX SHALLOT SNORTER
SNUFFER SOXHLET STOPPLE
THIMBLE TUBULUS VENTURI
ADJUTAGE BOMBILLA CORNICLE
DIATREME DRAWTUBE FAIRLEAD
GRADUATE ORTHICON OVARIOLE
PENSTOCK PIPESTEM SAUCISSE
SIPHONET SLEEVING URCEOLUS
ZOOECIUM
(— AT BASE OF PETAL) CALCAR
**(— CARRYING BASSOON
MOUTHPIECE)** CROOK
(— COVERING TRACE CHAIN) PIPING
(— FOR DEPOSITING CONCRETE)
TREMIE
(— FOR DRINKING MATE) BOMBILLA
(— FOR LINING WELL) WELLRING
(— FOR STIFFENING STRING) TAG
(— FOR TRANSFERRING LIQUID)
SIPHON SYPHON
(— FOR WINDING THREAD) COP
(— FROM SHIP'S PUMP) DALE
(— IN ENGINE CYLINDER) LINER
(— OF BALLOON) APPENDIX
(— OF GUN) BORE BARREL
(— OF RETORT) BEAK ROSTRUM
(— OF SPIRIT LEVEL) BUBBLE
(— OF TOBACCO) CIGARET
(— TO LINE A VENT) BOUCHE
(— TWISTED IN COILS) WORM
(— USED IN WHALING) LULL
(AMPLIFIER —) STAGE
(BONE —) SNUFFER
(CAMERA —) ORTHICON
(DISTILLING —) TOWER
(ELECTRO —) BULB
(ELECTRODE —) AUDION PENTODE
(ELECTRON —) DIODE DRIVER
TETRODE KENOTRON KLYSTRON
PLIOTRON TRINISCOPE
(FIREWORKS —) LEADER
(GLANDULAR —) CRYPT
(GLASS —) SIGHT MATRASS
(GLASSBLOWER'S —) BLOWPIPE
(HONEY —) NECTARY SIPHONET
(KNITTED —) STOCKING
(PAPER —) LEADER PASTILLE
(PASTRY —) CORNET
(POLLEN —) SPERMARY
(PRIMING —) AUGET
(RECTIFIER —) IGNITRON
(SILK — OF SPIDER) SPIGOT
(SPEAKING —) GOSPORT
(SUCKING —) STRAW
(SURGICAL —) CANNULA

(THERMOMETER —) STEM
(VACUUM —) DIODE KEYER
HEXODE HEPTODE DYNATRON
MAGNETRON
(PREF.) FISTULI SIPHON(O)
SOLEN(O) SYRING(O)
TUBELET CIRCLET
TUBER ANU SET ANYU BULB CLOG
COCO ROOT SEED SETT YAMP
COCCO SALEP JICAMA PIGNUT
POTATO WAPATA WINDER
YAUTIA EARTHNUT MURRNONG
TUBERCLE PEARL NODULE
STEMMA CUSPULE VERRUCA
TUBERCULAR PHTHISIC
TUBERCULOSIS CON LUPUS
CLYERS DECLINE PHTHISIS
SCROFULA
TUBING HOSE TUBAGE
TUBMAN DUCKER
TUBULAR PIPY PIPED TUBATE
QUILLED CANNULAR
(NOT —) FARCTATE
(PREF.) SOLEN(O)
TUBULE TRACHEA TUBULET
TUBULUS
TUCANO BETOYAN
TUCK TOKE STUFF TRUSS FLANGE
(— IN) TRUSS TROUSS
(— UP) FAKE KILT
TUCKER CORDER KILTER PLEATER
(— OUT) TIRE
**TUESDAY (SECOND — AFTER
EASTER)** HOCKDAY HOKEDAY
TUFA TOPHUS
TUFF TRASS PEPERINO PORODITE
SANTORIN
TUFT COP EAR FAG FOB NOB SOP
TOP COMA DOWN KNOB KNOP
MOCK TAIT TATE TUFF TUSK
TUZZ WISP BEARD BUNCH CREST
FLOCK STUPA THRUM WHISK
CATKIN CIRRUS DOLLOP PAPPUS
PENCIL TASSEL TUFFET CIRRHUS
FEATHER FLOCCUS HOBNAIL
PANACHE SCOPULA TOPKNOT
TOPPING TUSSOCK AIGRETTE
FLOCCULE ARBUSCULE
(— OF BRISTLES) BIRSE
(— OF CLOTH) FAG
(— OF DIRTY WOOL) DAG
(— OF DOWN) FRIEZE
(— OF FEATHERS) EAR HORN HULU
EGRET
(— OF FILAMENTS) BYSSUS
(— OF GRASS) FAG SOP MOCK
HASSOCK TUSSOCK
(— OF HAIR) TOP COMA TUZZ
BRUSH SWITCH COWLICK
FEATHER FLOCCUS SCOPULA
TOPKNOT IMPERIAL KROBYLOS
(— OF HAIR ON HORSE'S HOOF)
FETLOCK
(— OF HAY) SOP
(— OF MALE TURKEY) BEARD
(— OF WOOL) FOB TUSK TUZZ
FLOCK
(— ON BIRD'S HEAD) COP CUCK
EGRET
(— ON BONNET) TOORIE
(— ON PINEAPPLE) CROWN
(— ON SEED PLANT) PAPPUS
(— ON SPIDER'S FEET) SCOPULA

(—S OF ROPE YARN) THRUM
(VASCULAR —) GLOMUS
(PREF.) LOPH(O) LOPHI(O)
TUFTED COMOSE TAPPET TAPPIT
CRISTATE
TUG LUG PUG RUG TIT TOG CHUG
DRAG HALE HAUL PULL TOIL
TUCK CHUFF HITCH PLUCK
SHRUG TRACE JIGGER RUGGLE
TOWBOAT TUGBOAT
TUGBOAT TOW TUG TOWBOAT
TRACKER
TUI POE TUA KOKO TUWI POEBIRD
TUITION CUSTODY
TULIP LILY LILIUM BIZARRE
BREEDER PICOTEE TURNSOLE
TULIP TREE POPLAR BASSWOOD
CUCUMBER
TULIPWOOD AUBURN
TULLE ILLUSION
TUMATAKURU IRISHMAN
MATAGORY
TUMBLE TOP COUP WALT LATCH
SPILL THROW TIFLE TRACE
COTTON GROVEL PURLER TIFFLE
TOPPLE WALTER WAMBLE
WELTER STUMBLE WHEMMEL
(— OVER) TIPPLE WALLOP
TUMBLE-DOWN RUINOUS
TUMBLER NUT CLICK GLASS LEVER
WIPER ROLLER ACROBAT
DRUMMER TIPPLER TOPPLER
VOLTIGEUR
TUMID TURGID BLOATED BULGING
FUSTIAN TURGENT INFLATED
TUMOROUS
TUMOR PAP WEN BEAL PIAN
WART AMPER BOTCH GUMMA
MYOMA NEVUS PHYMA SWELL
TALPA AMBURY ANBURY EPULIS
GLIOMA GYROMA INCOME KELOID
LIPOMA MYXOMA NUROMA
RISING WARBLE ADENOMA
ANGIOMA CYSTOMA DERMOID
DESMOID FIBROID FIBROMA
LUTEOMA MYELOMA NEUROMA
OSTEOMA OSTEOME SARCOMA
TESTUDO THYMOMA ULONCUS
ATHEROMA BLASTOMA
CHLOROMA CHORIOMA
EMBRYOMA GANGLION
GLANDULE HEMATOMA
HEPATOMA HOLDFAST
LYMPHOMA MELANOMA
MELICERA NEOPLASM
ODONTOMA PHLEGMON
PLASMOMA PSAMMOMA
SCIRRHUS SEMINOMA TERATOID
TERATOMA WINDGALL
CHALAZION PAPILLOMA
(— OF EYELID) GRANDO
(— ON HORSE'S LEGS) JARDE
(PUSTULAR —) BLAIN
(SKIN —) OUCH
(STUDY OF —S) ONCOLOGY
(PREF.) GANGLI(O) GANGLO
MYOM(O) ONCO SCIRRH(O)
(SUFF.) CELE COELE COELUS OMA
ONCUS SCIRRHUS
TUMULT DIN COIL FARE FLAW
FRAY FUSS HURL MUSS REEL
RIOT ROUT VISE BRAWL BROIL
HURLY HURRY LURRY NOISE

ROUST STOOR STOUR WHIRL
AFFRAY BUSTLE CLAMOR DIRDUM
EMEUTE FRACAS HUBBUB
MUTINY PUDDER RABBLE RIPPET
ROMAGE RUFFLE SHINDY STEERY
UPROAR UPSTIR BLUSTER
BOBBERY BRATTLE FACTION
FERMENT GARBOIL TEMPEST
TURMOIL DISORDER SEDITION
STIRRING STRAMASH
COMMOTION PANDEMONIUM
TUMULTUOUS HIGH LOUD RUDE
NOISY ROUGH STORMY FURIOUS
HURRIED LAWLESS RIOTOUS
VIOLENT AGITATED CONFUSED
DRAWLING HURTLING
TUMULUS LOW MOTE TUMP
MOUND BARROW BURIAN
COTERELL
TUN CASK HAAB
(ONE-THIRD —) TERTIAN
(20 —S) KATUN
TUNA AHI ATUN TUNNY BLUEFIN
PELAMYD ALBACORE KAWAKAWA
TUNE AIR ARIA DUMP FADO LEED
NOTE PORT RANT SONG CHARM
CHORD DRANT POINT ATTUNE
GROUND MAGGOT STRAIN
STRING TEMPER GUAJIRA
HALLING MEASURE MELISMA
SONANCE ANGLAISE FANDANGO
GUARACHA HABANERA
QUICKSTEP
(— A HARP) WREST
(— AN INSTRUMENT) STRING
(DANCE —) FURIANT ANGLAISE
GALLIARD
(FOLK —) FADO
(HILLBILLY —) HOEDOWN
(LIGHT —) TOY
(LITTLE —) CATCH
(LIVELY —) LILT SPRING HORNPIPE
(MELANCHOLY —) DUMP
(SACRED —) CHORAL CHORALE
(TRADITIONAL —) TONE
TUNEBO TAME GUACICO
TUNEFUL TUNY CHANTANT
TUNESOME
TUNEFULNESS MELODY
TUNGST-
(PREF.) WOLFRAM
TUNGSTEN W WOLFRAM SCHEELIN
TUNGUS EVENK LAMUT
TUNIC COAT JAMA JUPE VEST
COTTE FROCK GIPPO JAMAH
JUPON PALLA ACHKAN BLIAUT
CAMISE CHITON CYCLAS FECKET
HARDIE KABAYA KIRTLE TABARD
ARISARD BLEAUNT CAMISIA
PALTOCK SURCOAT TUNICLE
COLOBIUM GANDOURA
SUBTUNIC SUBUCULA
SUKKENYE
(— OF MAIL) HAUBERK
(HOODED FUR —) SOVIK
TUNICATE SALP SALPA SALPID
ASCIDIAN TUNICARY
UROCHORD
TUNICLE SACCOS
TUNING ANESIS
TUNING FORK EVEL EVIL FORK
TUNER DIAPASE DIAPASON
MODULANT

TUNING HAMMER KEY

TUNNEL ADIT BORE CAVE CURL
PUKA SINK TUBE DRIFT DRIVE
KAREZ STALL BURROW PIERCE
(— INTO AN IGLOO) TOSSUT
(PROPOSED —) CHUNNEL
TUNNY TUNA ALBACORE
SCOMBRID
(YOUNG —) PELAMYD
TUP TIP TRIP MONKEY BLISSOM
TUR (BROTHER OF —) IRAJ SALM
(FATHER OF —) FARIDUN
(MOTHER OF —) SHAHRINAZ
TURACO LORY
TURANDOT (CHARACTER IN —) LIU
CALAF TURANDOT
(COMPOSER OF —) PUCCINI
TURBAN PAT MOAB PATA SASH
TUFT LUNGI MITER MITRE PAGRI
PATTI TOWEL TUFFE MANDIL
WRAPPER KAFFIYEH PUGGAREE
SEERBAND TOLIPANE TULIPANT
TURBANTO
TURBELLARIA APROCTA
TURBELLARIAN FLATWORM
TURBID FAT RILY DROVY GUMLY
MUDDY RILEY ROILY DRUMLY
GRUMLY QUALLY FECULENT
LUTULENT
TURBIDITY RILE
TURBOT BRET BRILL WHIFF
FLATFISH
TURBULENCE FURY UPROAR
FERMENT RIOTING
(— IN WATER) BULLER
TURBULENT GURL HIGH LOUD
RUDE WILD ROILY ROUGH
WROTH RUGGED STORMY
UNRULY YEASTY FURIOUS
RABBISH RACKETY TROUBLE
VIOLENT MUTINOUS SCAMBLING
BOISTEROUS
TURCO IN ITALIA, IL (CHARACTER
IN —) DAMELEC GERONIO
FIORILLA PROSDOCIMO
(COMPOSER OF —) ROSSINI
TURDUS MERULA
TUREEN DISH TERRINE
TURF SOD VAG CESS DELF FAIL
FALE FEAL FLAG FLAT FLAW
PONE SUNK DELFT SCRAW SPINE
SWARD TRUFF FLAUGHT

SHIRREL SODDING
(— CUT BY GOLF STROKE) DIVOT
(— FOR LINING PARAPET) GAZON
(DRIED — FOR FUEL) VAG
(PARED —) BEAT
(ROUGH —) GOR
(SMALL PIECE OF —) TAB
(THIN LAYER OF —) FLAW
TURF SPADE SLANE
TURGID ERECT TUMID BLOATED
INFLATED PLETHORIC
TURGIDNESS TYMPANY
TURK TURCO TURKO SELJUK
CORSAIR OSMANLI OTTOMAN
TURQUET KONARIOT
TURKANA ELKUMA
TURKEY BUST FLOP STAG STEG
BUSTARD ERECTER ERECTOR
GOBBLER ALDERMAN
(BRUSH —) VULTURN TALEGALLA
(MALE —) TOM
(YOUNG —) POULT

TURKEY BUZZARD AURA
BROMVOEL BROMVOGEL
GALLINAZO
TURKEY-COCK STAG
TURKEY OAK CERRIS
TURKI KAZAK QAZAQ KAZAKH

TURKISH TURK TURCIC OSMANLI OTTOMAN
TURKISH DELIGHT LOUKOUM
TURKOMAN SEID ERSAR
TURK'S CAP LILY MARTAGON
TURMERIC REA ANGO HALDI OLENA HULDEE AZAFRAN CURCUMA
TURMIT TURNIP
TURMOIL ADO DIN COIL DUST MOIL TOIL TOSS BURLE HURLY HURRY STROW TOUSE WHIRL HASSLE JABBLE POTHER ROMAGE UPROAR WELTER CLUTTER EMOTION FERMENT GARBOIL HURLING MAKADOO RUMMAGE TEMPEST DISPEACE DISQUIET
TURN GO BOW CUT GEE JAR RUN TON WIN AIRT BEND BOUT BOWL CALE CAST CHAR CHOP COCK EDDY GIRO HACK HEAD HINT HURL JAMB KINK PULL PURL QUIP ROLL ROVE SLEW TIRL TOUR VEER VERT VICE WAFT WELT WIND AIRTH ANGLE BLANK CHARE CRANK CRASH CREEK CRICK CROOK ELBOW FEEZE GLINT PIVOT PLUCK PRICK QUIRK SHIFT SPELL SWING SWIRL TARVE TERVE TREND TRILL TROLL TWINE TWIST VERSE VOLTI WHEEL WREST ATTURN BOUGHT CIRCLE COURSE DEPEND DIRECT DOUBLE GRUPPO GYRATE INDENT INTEND INTURN POSSET QUEEVE RESORT RETURN ROTATE SPIRAL STRAIN SWIVEL TOURNE TURKEN VOLUME VOLUTE WIMPLE CONVERT CRANKLE CRINKLE DEFLECT DISTURB FLEXION FLEXURE FLOUNCE INCLINE INFLECT PASSADE REVERSE REVOLVE SERPENT SINUATE TWINGLE TWISTER VERSATE WREATHE CLINAMEN DOUBLING FLECTION TOURNURE TRAVERSE VOLUTION
(— ABOUT) SLEW SLUE SLOUGH WINDLASS
(— AGAINST) CROSS
(— AROUND) GYRE WELT WEND RATCH BEWEND SPHERE
(— ASIDE) ERR WRY DAFF SKEW WARD ABHOR AVERT BLENK DETER EVADE FENCE GLENT SHEER WAIVE BLENCH DEPART DETURN DIVERT SWERVE SWITCH CRINKLE DECLINE DEFLECT DEVIATE DIGRESS DIVERGE PERVERT SCRITHE
(— AT DRINKING) TIRL
(— ATTENTION) ADVERT ADDRESS
(— AWAY) DOFF AVERT CHARE HIELD REPEL AVERSE DESERT DETURN DIVERT REVOLT ABANDON DECLINE REVERSE OVERTURN WITHTURN
(— AWRY) CONTORT
(— BACK) KEP ABORT FLIPE FLYPE RETORT RETURN REVERT REFLECT UNTWIST RENVERSE
(— BACK ON) RUMP
(— BROWN) AUGUST

(— BY TOSSING) FLAP
(— CARD FACE UP) BURN
(— DOWN) DIP DENY VETO
(— FOR BETTER) CRISIS
(— IN ARCHERY) END
(— IN CROQUET) BISK BISQUE
(— IN ROPE) NIP RIDER
(— INSIDE OUT) EVERT FLYPE INVERT
(— INTO ICE) CONGEAL
(— INTO STEEL) ACIERATE
(— INTO VINEGAR) ACETIFY
(— LEAVES OF BOOK) LEAF TOSS
(— OF AFFAIRS) GO JOB KICK
(— OF CABLE) BITTER
(— OF DUTY) TOUR SHIFT TRICK
(— OF EVENTS) WENT
(— OF EXPRESSION) CONCETTO
(— OF FANCY) GUST
(— OF MIND) FREAK
(— OF STRING) WAP
(— OF TIDE) PINCH
(— OF WIT) FLIRT
(— OF YARN) MOUSING
(— OFF) SHUNT DIVERT
(— ON) HIT
(— ON LATHE) THROW
(— OUT) GO USH BEAR FALL FARE OUST SORT TAKE CHIVE FUDGE OUTPUT SUCCEED
(— OUT TO BE) PROVE EXFLECT
(— OUTWARD) EVERT SPLAY
(— OVER) CANT FLAP FLIP KEEL VETTE VOLVE CLINCH DESIGN AGITATE CAPSIZE OVERSET
(— POINT OF) ABATE
(— RAPIDLY) SPIN TIRL GIDDY
(— RIGHT) HAP HUP
(— SAIL YARD) BRACE
(— SKIS) STEM
(— SOUR) FOX BLINK PRILL BLEEZE CHANGE SOUREN
(— SUDDENLY) FLOP SLUE
(— TO NEAR SIDE) HAW
(— TO OFF SIDE) GEE
(— TO ONE SIDE) CORNER GOGGLE
(— TO THE LEFT) HAW PORT WIND WYND
(— UP) FACE HAPPEN
(— UP NOSE) FLIRT SNURL
(— UPSIDE DOWN) CANT COUP WHELM INVERT QUELME WHELVE WHEMMLE
(— VESSEL IN CIRCLE) CHAPEL
(— WHEELS) CRAMP
(— YELLOW) FIRE
(BALLET —) PIROUETTE
(COMPLETE —) LAP
(DOWNWARD —) SLIDE
(ECCENTRIC —) CRANKUM
(FORTUNATE —) BREAK
(GOOD —) BOON
(HALF —) CARACOLE
(IN —) AROUND
(SERIES OF TIGHT —S) CHICANE
(SHARP —) DOUBLE WRENCH ZIGZAG HAIRPIN
(SKI —) SWING CHRISTIE TELEMARK
(SUDDEN —) CURL
(PL.) ALLEGRO
(PREF.) STREPHO STREPSI STREPT(O) TREPO TROP(IDO)(O)

VERSI VERTEBR(I)(O) VERTI
(SUFF.) TROPAL TROPE TROPIA TROPIC TROPY
TURNBUCKLE TURNEL TURNBOUT
TURNCOAT APOSTATE RENEGADE
TURNED SOUR VERSED COCKEYED INFLEXED
(— ABOUT) CONVERSE
(— BACK) EVOLUTE
(— DOWNWARD) ABASED DEFLEXED
(— EDGEWISE) BLIND
(— INWARD) VARUS
(— OUTWARD) EXTRORSE
(— TOWARD) ANODIC
(— TOWARD ONE SIDE) AWRY
(— UP) ACOCK URVED
(— WRONG WAY) AWK
(PREF.) STREPSI
TURNER SLICE BODGER SLIDER TWIRLER
TURNING HEAD WIND TWIST VOLTA WRINK DETOUR ROTARY FLEXION FLEXURE VERSION VOLVENT FLECTION STREPSIS WHEELERY ACESCENCE
(— OF EYE) CAST
(— SOUR) ACESCENT
(— TO RIGHT) DEXTRO
(— TOWARD STEM) ADVERSE
(METAL —S) SWARF
(PL.) SCULL
(PREF.) STROPH(O) TROPIDO TROPO
(SUFF.) TROPAL TROPE TROPIA TROPIC(AL) TROPISM TROPOUS TROPY
TURNIP BAGA NAPE NEEP RAPE NAVEW SWEDE RAPEYE TURMUT CRUCIFER RUTABAGA
(PL.) KRAUT RAPPINI
(PREF.) NAPI
TURNIP-SHAPED NAPIFORM RAPACEUS
TURNIX QUAIL HEMIPOD ORTYGAN HEMIPODE
TURNKEY SCREW LOCKSMAN
TURN OF THE SCREW (AUTHOR OF —) JAMES
(CHARACTER IN —) FLORA MILES PETER QUINT JESSEL
TURNOUT RIG TEAM SETOUT EQUIPAGE TRANSFER
TURNOVER PASTY BRIDIE BRAMBLE EMPANADA FLAPJACK
(PL.) PIROJKI PIROSHKI
TURNPIN TAMPION
TURNSOLE HELIO
TURNSPIT HASTLER
TURNSTILE TIRL STILE MOULINE TURNGATE TURNPIKE TOURNIQUET
TURNSTONE PLOVER REDLEG CHICARIC CREDDOCK
TURNTABLE DECK RACER ROTARY NONSYNC PLAYBACK
TURNUS (FATHER OF —) DAUNUS
(MOTHER OF —) VENILIA
(SLAYER OF —) AENEAS
TURPENTINE THUS TURPS SCRAPE THINNER OLEORESIN
(BORDEAUX —) GALIPOT
TURPENTINE TREE PEEBEEN

TURPITUDE FEDITY
TURQUOISE TURKEY TURKIS CALAITE CALLAIS
TURRET ROUND BELFRY CUPOLA GARRET GAZEBO LOUVER TOURET BARMKIN GUERITE MIRADOR MONITOR BARBETTE BARTIZAN GUNHOUSE TURRICLE PEPPERBOX
TURTLE EMYD ARRAU CARET CAREY TORUP COODLE COOTER JURARA SLIDER THURGI TURKLE CRAWLER CREEPER EMYDIAN JUNIATA LOGHEAD SNAPPER TORTUGA CHELONID FLAPJACK HAWKBILL MATAMATA SHAGTAIL STINKPOT TERRAPIN TORTOISE THALASSIAN
(— HAVING COMMERCIAL SHELL) CHICKEN
(OLD —) MOSSBACK
(PART OF —) EAR BEAK CLAW SHELL SHIELD CARAPACE PLASTRON
TURTLEHEAD BALMONY CHELONE CODHEAD
TUSCAN BROWN MECCA MOHAWK
TUSCANY COLCOTHAR
TUSK GAM CUSK HORN TUSH IVORY TOOTH ELEPHANT
(— OF WILD BOAR) RAZOR
(ELEPHANT'S —) SCRIVELLO
TUSSLE TUG SCRAP BICKER TASSEL TOUSLE WARSLE TUILYIE
TUSSOCK HASSOCK
TUT HOOT TOOT HOOTS
TUTELAGE TUTELE YEMSEL NURTURE TEACHING
TUTELARY GENIUS
TUTOR DON ABBE TUTE COACH TRACH DOCENT FEEDER GROUND MASTER PEDANT SCHOOL GRINDER TEACHER CRANSIER CREANCER GOVERNOR PANGLOSS PUPILIZE PRECEPTOR
TUTTI RIPIENO
TUTU TOOT TUPAKIHI
TUVALU (CAPITAL OF —) FUNAFUTI
(FORMER NAME OF —) ELLICEISLANDS LAGOONISLANDS
(ISLAND OF —) NANUMEA NUKUFETAU NUKULAILAI
TUXEDO TUX SOFA TUCK
TVASHTRI (DAUGHTER OF —) SARANYU
TWADDLE ROT BOSH TOSH FUDGE HAVER BABBLE DRIVEL FOOTLE PIFFLE TOOTLE FADAISE TWATTLE NONSENSE SLIPSLOP TOMMYROT
TWANA COLCINE
TWANG TANG PLUCK PLUNK SNUFFLE TWANGLE TWANKLE
TWAYBLADE DUFOIL TWIFOIL
(PL.) LISTERA
TWEAK FEAK TWIG
TWEED PATTU PATTOO
TWEEZERS TIT TWIRK TWINGE TWITCH MULLETS PINCERS PINCETTE VOLSELLA
TWELFTH TWALT DOZENTH
(— OF INCH) SECOND
(— OF LIGHT PERIOD) INCH

(— PART) UNCIA
TWELFTH NIGHT (AUTHOR OF —)
SHAKESPEARE
(CHARACTER IN —) TOBY BELCH
CURIO FESTE MARIA VIOLA
ANDREW FABIAN OLIVIA ORSINO
ANTONIO MALVOLIO AGUECHEEK
SEBASTIAN VALENTINE
TWELVE TWAL DOZEN DICKER
DODECADE
(PREF.) DODEC(A) DUODECIM
TWELVEMONTH TOWMONT
TWELVER IMAMI
TWELVE-TONE SERIAL
TWELVE-TONE-ROW SET
TWENTIETH VIGESIMAL VINGTIEME
TWENTY KAPH CORGE KAPPA
SCORE COOREE
(PREF.) ICOS(A) VIGINTI
TWENTY-FIVE QUARTERN
TWENTY-FOURTH CARAT
TWENTY-ONE PONTOON VANJOHN
BLACKJACK
**20,000 LEAGUES UNDER THE
SEA (AUTHOR OF —)** VERNE
(CHARACTER IN —) NED LAND
NEMO PIERRE ARONNAX CONSEIL
TWERP DRONGO
TWICE BIS DOPPIO
(— A DAY) BID
(PREF.) BI BIS DI DIS
TWIDDLE TWEEDLE TWITTER
(— FEET) CUT
TWIG COW CHAT RICE RISP SLIP
WAND YARD BIRCH BRIAR BRIER
SHRAG SHRED SPRAY SPRIG
STICK TWIST VIRGA WAVER
WITHE BALEYS BROWSE FESCUE
GREAVE SALLOW SPRING SWITCH
WATTLE WICKER SCOLLOP
TWIGLET ANAPHYTE
(— FOR SNUFF) DIP
(— GROWING FROM STUMP)
WAVER
(— IN BIRD SNARE) SWEEK
(— WORN AT SACRIFICES)
INARCULUM
(—S FOR BURNING) CHATWOOD
(—S FOR WATTLING) FRITLES
(—S MADE INTO BROOM) BESOM
(BARE —) COW
(BROKEN —S) BRUSH
(CUT —) SARMENT
(DRIED —) CHAD
(LITTLE —) SURCLE
(THATCHING —) SCOLLOP
(WILLOW —) SALLOW ANAPHYTE
(SUFF.) CLEMA
TWIGGED VIRGATE
TWIGGY SPRAYEY
TWILIGHT EVE DIMPS DUMPS
GLOAM TWALE DIMMET DIMMIT
UGHTEN DUCKISH COCKSHUT
EVENFALL EVENGLOW GLOAMING
GRISPING CREPUSCLE
(— OF THE GODS) RAGNAROK
(DARKER PART OF —) DUSK
(MORNING —) DAWN
TWILL WALE CHINO CADDIS
RUSSEL CADDICE DUNGAREE
TWILLED CORDED
TWIN DUAL GEMEL SOSIE DIDYMUS
JUMELLE SIAMESE TWINDLE

DIDYMATE DIDYMOID DIDYMOUS
PARASITE TWINLING
(PL.) GEMEL COUPLET
(PREF.) DIDYM(O) GEMINI
(SUFF.) DIDYMUS
TWINE MAT COIL DUNE LACE PIRL
WIND WRAP TWIRL TWIST
INFOLD INTORT ANAMITE
ENTWINE SKEENYIE
(HANK OF —) RAN
(PITCHED —) WHIPPING
(PREF.) PLEC(O)
TWINEBUSH PINBUSH
TWINFLOWER LINNAEA
TWINGE GIRD PANG PULL SHOOT
TOUCH TWANG STOUND
(— OF CONSCIENCE) SCRUPLE
(— OF PAIN) GLISK
TWINING VOLUBLE AMPLECTANT
TWINKLE WINK BLINK TWEER
TWINK TWIRE BICKER SIMPER
WINKLE SPARKLE
TWINKLING MOMENT TWINKLY
TWINLEAF HELMETPOD
TWIRL SPIN TIRL DRILL QUERL
TRILL TWIRK TWIST WHIRL
TRUNDLE TWIDDLE TWIZZLE
(— OF BAGPIPE) WARBLER
TWIST BOB CUE MAT PLY WIN WIP
CAST COIL CURL DRAW HURL
KICK KINK PIRL RICK SKEW SLEW
SLUB SLUE TURN WARP WIND
WISP WORK CHINK CRANK CRICK
CRINK CROOK CURVE FEEZE
GNARL KINCH PLAIT QUIRK QUIRL
REEVE SCREW SKELL SNAKE
SNIRL SNURL SPIRE SWIRL
THRAW THROW TWEAK TWIND
TWINE TWIRE TWIRL WINCE
WITHE WREST WRICK BOUGHT
DETORT EXTORT HANKLE INTORT
QUEEVE SLOUGH SQUIRM SQUIRL
SQUIRM STRAND TWEEZE
WAMBLE WARPLE WASHIN
WICKER WIMBLE WRABBE
WRITHE CHIGNON CONTORT
CRANKLE CRINKLE CROOKLE
CRUMPLE DISTORT ENTWINE
ENTWIST FLOUNCE GIMMICK
SQUINCH TORTURE TWISTER
TWISTLE TWIZZLE WREATHE
WRIGGLE CLINAMEN CONVOLVE
ENTANGLE FOREHARD FORETURN
SPRINKLE SQUIGGLE VOLUTION
(— A ROPE) DALLY
(— AWAY) WAIVE
(— BACK) RETORT
(— FORCIBLY) WRING
(— IN A ROPE) GRIND SQUIRM
(— IN GRAIN OF A BOW) BOUGHT
(— IN ONE'S NATURE) KINK
(— OF FACE) STITCH
(— OF HAY) HAYBRAND
(— OF PAPER) SPILL
(— OF PEN IN WRITING) QUIRK
(— OF SPEECH) CRANK
(— OF THE MOUTH) DRAD
(— OF TOBACCO) ROLL PIGTAIL
(— OF YARNS) FORETURN
(— OUT OF SHAPE) BUCKLE
CONTORT
(— SHARPLY) FEAK
(— TOGETHER) CABLE RADDLE

(CAUSE TO —) TORQUE
(PREF.) SPIR(I)(O) STREMMATO
STREPHO STREPSI STREPT(O)
TORSO TORTI
TWISTED CAM KAM WRY AWRY
TORT KINKY SCREW TORSE
WELKT WRONG ATWIST GAUCHE
HURLED KNOTTY SCREWY
SKEWED SWIRLY THRAWN
THROWN TURKEN TWISTY
WARPED WRITHE CRISPED
CROOKED GNARLED KNOTTED
SCREWED TORQUED TORTILE
TORTIVE WHELKED WREATHY
COCKEYED IMPLICIT INTORTED
INVOLVED NONPLANE THRAWART
WREATHEN
(PREF.) PLEC(O) PLECT(O) STREPSI
STREPT(O)
TWISTING DALLY KNECK AJOINT
TWIRLY WIGWAG ENTRAIL
TWIDDLY SQUIGGLY STREPSIS
TORTUOUS
(PREF.) STROPH(O)
TWIT TIT CHECK TAUNT ETWITE
TWITTER RIDICULE
TWITCH TIC TIT FEAK FIRK JERK
JUMP PIRN TWIG WINK YANK
PLUCK START THRIP TWEAK
TWICK TWIRK QUATCH QUETCH
QUITCH TWINGE TWITCHEL
VELLICATE
TWITCHING TIC JERKS PALMUS
WORKING SACCADIC
TWITTER TWIT CHIRM CHIRP
GARRE TWINK JARGON WARBLE
CHIPPER CHIRRUP CHITTER
QUITTER TWITTLE WHITTER
TWO TWA BOTH TWAY TWIN
TWAIN BINARY COUPLE DOUBLE
(— LINES) LONGWAYS
(— OF A KIND) BRACE
(IN —) ATWO
(US —) UNC
(PREF.) BI BIS DUO DY(O) TWI
(— EACH) BINI
(IN —) DICH(O)
(MORE THAN —) MULTI
TWO-COLORED BICHROME
(PREF.) DICHRO(O)
TWO-FACED JANUS JANIFORM
(PREF.) JANI
TWO-FIFTEEN PM TIME
TWOFOLD DUAL BINAL DUPLE
BACKED BIFOLD DOUBLE DUPLEX
DIGONAL DIPLOID TWIFOLD
DIDYMATE DIDYMOID DIDYMOUS
DIPLASIC TWEYFOLD BIFARIOUS
(PREF.) DI DIPHY DIPL(O)
TWO-FOOTED BIPED
TWO-FORKED BIFURCAL
**TWO GENTLEMEN OF VERONA
(AUTHOR OF —)** SHAKESPEARE
(CHARACTER IN —) JULIA MILAN
SPEED LAUNCE SILVIA THURIO
ANTONIO LUCETTA PROTEUS
EGLAMOUR PANTHINO
VALENTINE
TWO-HANDED BIMANAL
BIMANOUS
TWO-HEADED
(PREF.) DICRANO JANI
TWO-HORNED BICORN BICORNED

TWOPENCE TUPPENCE
TWOS POT DEUCE
TWO-UP SWY
**TWO WIDOWS, THE (CHARACTER
IN —)** ANEZKA MUMLAL KAROLINA
LADISLAV
(COMPOSER OF —) SMETANA
TWO-WINGED
(PREF.) DIPTER(O)
TYCHICUS (COMPANION OF —)
PAUL
TYCOON SHOGUN TAIKUN
TYDEUS (FATHER OF —) EONEUS
OENEUS
(MOTHER OF —) PERIBOEA
(SON OF —) DIOMEDES
TYMPANUM DRUM TYMPAN
EARDRUM EPIPHRAGM
TYNDAREUS (BROTHER OF —)
ICARIUS
(DAUGHTER OF —) PHILOPOE
TIMANDRA CLYTEMNESTRA
(FATHER OF —) OEBALUS PERIERES
(MOTHER OF —) BATIA
GORGOPHONE
(WIFE OF —) LEDA
TYPE CUT ILK CAST KIND MAKE
MOLD NORM SORT TAKE BOGUS
BROOD IMAGE MOULD PRINT
STAMP EMBLEM KICKER KIDNEY
LETTER NATURE SHADOW STRIPE
SYMBOL TAKING TIMBER
BATARDE FASHION PARABLE
ANTETYPE EXEMPLAR
(— BLOCK) QUAD
(— OF EXCELLENCE) PARAGON
(— PLACED BOTTOM UP) TURN
(— SET UP) MATTER
(ASSORTMENT OF —) FONT
(DANCE —) LASYA
(DISARRANGED —) PI PIE
(GERMAN —) FRAKTUR
(HEAVY-FACED —) IONIC
(HIGHEST —) PINK
(IDEAL —) CHRIST
(OPPOSITE —) ANTITYPE
(PART OF —) BACK BALL BODY
FACE FOOT NICK SIZE STEM
BEARD BELLY BEVEL SERIF SHANK
GROOVE COUNTER ASCENDER
CROSSBAR SHOULDER
DESCENDER
(PHYSICAL —) HABIT
(RACIAL —) DEHWAR
(REPRESENTATIVE —) GENIUS
(SET —) STICK
(SIZE OF —) (SEE SIZE)
(STYLE OF —) CANON DORIC ELITE
GOUDY GREEK IONIC KABEL
ROMAN BODONI CASLON CICERO
GOTHIC HEBREW ITALIC JENSON
MODERN BOOKMAN BREVIER
CENTURY ELZEVIR EMERALD
FULLFACE GARAMOND
(PREF.) MORPH(O)
TYPEBAR
(PL.) BASKET
TYPEE (AUTHOR OF —) MELVILLE
(CHARACTER IN —) TOM TOBY
MARNOO MEHEVI FAYAWAY
KORYKORY
TYPEFACE FACE FRAKTUR
BOLDFACE SANSERIF

TYPEHOLDER PALLET
TYPESETTER MONO
TYPESETTING FAT PHAT
TYPEWRITER MILL TYPER TYPIST
PORTABLE
(PART OF —) BAR KEY BAIL KNOB
LOOP STOP GUIDE LEVER PLATE
SCALE SHIFT HOLDER MARGIN
PLATEN RETURN ROLLER SPACER
CONTROL RELEASE SUPPORT
CARRIAGE KEYBOARD
REGULATOR BACKSPACER
TYPHON (FATHER OF —) TARTARUS
(MOTHER OF —) TERRA

TYPHOON WIND CYCLONE
TUFFOON
TYPICAL FAIR TYPAL TYPIC USUAL
AVERAGE CLASSIC PATTERN
PERFECT REGULAR
(PREF.) EU
(SUFF.) (— OF) ISH ISTIC
TYPIFY TYPE IMAGE SHADOW
ADUMBRATE EPITOMIZE
PERSONIFY REPRESENT
SYMBOLIZE
TYPIFYING GENERIC
TYR ER EAR TIU TYRR
(BROTHER OF —) THOR

(FATHER OF —) ODIN
TYRANNICAL LORDLY SLAVISH
ABSOLUTE DESPOTIC
TYRANNIZE OPPRESS DOMINEER
OVERLORD
TYRANNOUS ABSOLUTE
TYRANNY ROD DESPOTISM
TYRANT ANARCH DESPOT NIMROD
FUEHRER PHARAOH PHALARIS
TYRANT FLYCATCHER PEWEE
TYRO HAM BABE COLT PUPIL
NOVICE RABBIT TYRONE
BEGINNER NEOPHYTE
(FATHER OF —) SALMONEUS

(HUSBAND OF —) CRETHEUS
(MOTHER OF —) ALCIDICE
(SON OF —) AESON NELEUS PELIAS
PHERES AMYTHAON
TYRRHENIAN ETRUSCAN
TYRRHENUS (BROTHER OF —)
LYDUD TARCHON
(FATHER OF —) ATYS HERCULES
TELEPHUS
(MOTHER OF —) HIERA OMPHALE
CALLITHEA
TYTO ALUCO STRIX

U

U UNCLE UNION
(PREF.) (— SHAPED) HY(O)
UDDER BAG DUG TID EWER ELDER
SUMEN VESSEL
UFO (STUDY OF —S) UFOLOGY

UGANDA

CAPITAL: KAMPALA
COLLEGE: MAKERERE
FORMER CAPITAL: ENTEBBE
LAKE: KYOGA ALBERT EDWARD
GEORGE VICTORIA
LANGUAGE: ATESO GANDA
LUGANDA SWAHILI
MOUNTAIN: ELGON MARGHERITA
MOUNTAIN RANGE: RUWENZORI
NATIVE: ATESO BANTU LANGO
ACHOLI ANKOLE BAGISU
BAKIGA BASOGA BATORO
BAGANDA BUNYORO LUGBARA
NILOTIC SUDANIC
PLATEAU: ANKOLE
PROVINCE: BUGANDA
RIVER: ASWA KAFU PAGER
KATONGA
SEAPORT: MOMBASA
TOWN: ARUA JINJA MBALE
KITGUM MOROTO TORORO
ENTEBBE MOMBASA
WATERFALL: KABALEGA

UGLY FOUL AWFUL OUGLE SNIVY
UNKED CRANKY DREEPY GORGON
GROTTY HOMELY LAIDLY ORNERY
CRABBED GRIZZLY HIDEOUS
HOUGHLY VICIOUS GRUESOME
UGLISOME UNLOVELY
MONSTROUS
UGLY-TEMPERED SNARLISH
UGNI BLANC TREBBIANO
UIGHUR JAGATAI
UITOTAN KAIMO WITOTAN
UKE JARANA
UKRAINIAN RUSSNIAK
UKULELE UKE TAROPATCH
ULAM (FATHER OF —) ESHEK
ULCER FRET KYLE SORE WOLF
BOTCH ISSUE RUPIA ULCUS
APHTHA MORMAL TETTER
BEDSORE CHANCRE EGILOPS
ENCAUMA FISTULA AEGILOPS
FONTANEL FOSSETTE ULCUSCLE
(ARTIFICIAL —) ISSUE
(PREF.) CHANCRI HELC(O)
ULCERATING EXEDENT
ULCERATION NOMA CANKER
CARIES BEDSORE HELCOSIS
ULCEROUS HELCOID
ULEX LING
ULEXITE TIZA
ULLIKUMMI (FATHER OF —)
KUMARBI
ULNA CUBIT CUBITAL CUBITUS

ULTIMATE IT NTH DIRE LAST
FINAL ULTIME SUPREME
ABSOLUTE EVENTUAL FARTHEST
ULTIMITY
ULTIMATELY FINALLY
ULTIMO PAST
ULTRA EXTREME FANATIC
FORWARD
ULTRACONSERVATISM TORYISM
ULTRACONSERVATIVE WHITE
ULTRAFASHIONABLE RITZY
SWELL SWAGGER
ULTRAMONTANISM CURIALISM
ULUA PAPIO PAPIOPIO
ULYSSES (AUTHOR OF —) JOYCE
(CHARACTER IN —) BUCK RUDY
BLOOM BREEN MOLLY BLAZES
BOYLAN COFFEY GERTIE HAINES
MARION DEDALUS LEOPOLD
PUREFOY STEPHEN MULLIGAN
MACDOWELL
(FATHER OF —) LAERTES
(MOTHER OF —) ANTICLEA
(SLAYER OF —) TELEGONUS
(SON OF —) TELEMACHUS
(WIFE OF —) PENELOPE
UMBEL RAY RADIUS SERTULE
UMBELLA SERTULUM UMBELLET
UMBELLIFERONE CUMARIN
COUMARIN
UMBER OMER OMBER PARTRIDGE
UMBILICUS NAVEL
(PREF.) OMPHAL(O)
UMBO BEAK UMBONULE
UMBONES NATES
UMBRA DOGFISH MUDFISH
NUCLEUS UMBRINE
UMBRAGE PIQUE SNUFF OFFENSE
UMBRELLA BELL GAMP MUSH
DUMPY BROLLY CHATTA PAYONG
PILEUS CHATTAH GINGHAM
ROUNDEL FITTISOL KITTYSOL
MUSHROOM TYRASOLE
(PART OF —) CAP RIB ROD TIP
GORE JOINT PANEL SHAFT
BULLET HANDLE RUNNER SPRING
CLOSURE FERRULE STRETCHER
UMBRELLA BIRD COTINGA
COTINGID
UMBRELLA BUSH MILJEE
UMBRELLA PALM KENTIA
UMBRELLA PLANT SEDGE
GLUMAL
UMBRELLA TREE WAHOO
ELKWOOD MAGNOLIA
UMBRETTE UMBRE HOMBRE
UMBRET CICONIID
UMBRIAN IGUVINE
UMBURANA ROBLE
UMLAUT MUTATION METAPHONY
UMPIRE UMP JUDGE TRIER
ARBITER DAYSMAN ODDSMAN
STICKLER

UNABASHED BROWLESS
UNABBREVIATED FULL
UNABLE UNHABILE POWERLESS
UNACCENTED GRAVE LIGHT
ATONIC
UNACCEPTABLE DREADFUL
UNACCOMPANIED BARE SOLO
ALONE SECCO SINGLE
UNACCOUNTABLE STRANGE
UNACCUSTOMED UNUSED
STRANGE INSOLITE WONTLESS
UNACQUAINTED STRANGE
UNCOUTH
UNADORNED DRY BALD PLAIN
SECCO STARK RUSTIC SEVERE
SIMPLE AUSTERE LITERAL
INORNATE
UNADULTERATED NET FRANK
HONEST VIRGIN GENUINE
SINCERE ABSOLUTE
UNADVANTAGEOUSLY ILL
UNAFFECTED EASY REAL PLAIN
HOMELY NATIVE RUSTIC SIMPLE
ARTLESS BUCOLIC SINCERE
SEMPLICE
UNAFRAID BOLD BRAVE DEFIANT
UNAGGRESSIVE AMIABLE
UNALERT SUPINE
UNALLOYED DEEP SOLID VIRGIN
GENUINE
UNALTERABLE IMMUTABLE
UNAMBIGUOUS EXPLICIT
UNANIMATED FLAT VAPID INSIPID
UNANIMITY ATTACK CONSENT
UNANIMOUS SOLID WHOLE
UNANIME UNIVOCAL
UNAPPROACHABLE STATELY
UNARMED BARE INERM
UNBARBED
(PREF.) ANOPL(O)
UNASSAILABLE SECURE
UNASSUMED NATURAL
UNASSUMING SHY HUMBLE
MODEST SIMPLE NATURAL
RETIRING
UNATTACHED FREE LOOSE SINGLE
UNATTENDED SINGLE
UNATTRACTIVE BLAH UGLY PLAIN
WORSE HOMELY FRUMPISH
UNLIKELY
UNAVAILING VAIN FUTILE
BOOTLESS GAINLESS NUGATORY
UNAVOIDABLE SHUNLESS
NECESSARY
UNAVOWED SECRET
UNAWARE UNWARE WITLESS
HEEDLESS INNOCENT UNBEWARE
WARELESS OBLIVIOUS
UNAWARES ABACK SHORT
UNBALANCED HITE DOTTY NUTTY
FRUITY UNEVEN FANATIC
DERANGED LOPSIDED PIXILATED
MOONSTRUCK

UNBAR UNSLOT
UNBARRED UNSTOKEN
UNBEARDED CALLOW
UNBECOMING RUDE INEPT PLAIN
INDIGN UNMEET BENEATH
IMPROPER INDECENT UNSEEMLY
UNWORTHY
UNBEFITTING BENEATH
UNBELIEF UNFAITH
UNBELIEVABLE HOT THIN
UNBELIEVER PAGAN GIAOUR
ATHEIST DOUBTER INFIDEL
SCOFFER SKEPTIC
UNBELIEVING MISCREANT
UNBEND REST THAW FRESE RELAX
UNTIE EXTEND DISBEND
UNCROOK
UNBENDING RIGID STARK STERN
STIFF THARF CATONIAN
OBDURATE RAMRODDY
RESOLUTE
UNBIASED FAIR JUST DETACHED
UNBIND FREE UNDO UNTIE
UNGIRD UNDRESS
UNBLAMABLE INNOCENT
UNBLEACHED BLAE BLAY ECRU
BEIGE BROWN
UNBLEMISHED FAIR PURE SOUND
WHITE ENTIRE SPOTLESS
UNBLOCK REDD
UNBLOODY INCRUENT
UNBOLT OPEN UNBAR UNPIN
UNBOSOM OPEN
UNBOUGHT UNCOFT
UNBOUND FREE LOOSE
UNBOUNDED HUGE
UNBRANDED SLICK NATIVE
UNBROKEN DEAD FLAT FERAL
FLUSH SHEER SOLID SOUND
SINGLE CERRERO REGULAR
UNRACED STRAIGHT UNBACKED
WAKELESS
UNBUILD DESTROY
UNBUILT UNBIGGED
UNBURDEN EMPTY UNLOAD
UNSHIP
UNBURNISHED WHITE MATTED
UNCANNY EERY UNCO EERIE
SCARY UNCOW UNKID WEIRD
WISHT CREEPY SPOOKY
UNCOUTH ELDRITCH
POKERISH
UNCASTRATED INTACT
UNCAUGHT UNHENT
UNCEASING ENDLESS ETERNAL
EASELESS MINUTELY
UNCEREMONIOUS CURT BLUFF
BLUNT SHORT ABRUPT CASUAL
FAMILIAR INFORMAL
UNCERTAIN WAW DARK HAZY
WILD FLUKY SHADY SHAKY
WAUGH CASUAL CLOUDY
CRANKY FITFUL FLUKEY GLEAMY

QUEASY CASALTY CHANCEY
COMICAL DUBIOUS TRICKSY
VAGRANT VARIOUS WILSOME
CATCHING DELICATE FLICKERY
FUGITIVE HOVERING INSECURE
SLIPPERY TECHNOUS TICKLISH
UNCERTAINTY MIST WERE DEMUR
DOUBT MAYBE BAFFLE BALANCE
DUBIETY CASUALTY MISTRUST
SUSPENSE UNSURETY SKEPTICISM
UNCHALLENGED ACCEPTED
UNCHANGEABLE FAST STABLE
DURABLE ETERNAL
UNCHANGING STATIC ETERNAL
UNIFORM CONSTANT STATICAL
UNCHASTE LEWD BAWDY FRAIL
LIGHT LOOSE IMPURE WANTON
FORLAIN HAGGARD SCARLET
IMMODEST
UNCHASTITY BAWDRY STUPRUM
ADULTERY
UNCHECKED LIBERAL RAMPANT
REINLESS
UNCIFORM HAMATUM
UNCINARIA NECATOR
UNCIVIL RUDE BLUFF ROUGH
RUSTY SURLY COARSE CRUSTY
RUGGED UNFEEL IMPOLITE
UNCIVILIZED RUDE WILD MYALL
INCULT SAVAGE UNCIVIL
BARBARIC IGNORANT SYLVATIC
UNCLAD LOOSE UNDRESSED
UNCLE EME OOM TIO YEME BUNKS
NUNKY NUNCLE
UNCLEAN FOUL TREF VILE BLACK
TARRY TERFA TREFA COMMON
FILTHY IMMUND IMPURE DEFILED
UNCLEANLINESS
(PREF.) MYS(O)
UNCLEANNESS DIRT FOULNESS
UNCLEAR DIM HAZY SHAGGY
UNCLEARLY DIMLY
UNCLENCH UNDOUBLE
**UNCLE TOM'S CABIN (AUTHOR OF
—)** STOWE
(CHARACTER IN —) EVA TOM BIRD
CASSY CHLOE ELIZA HALEY
HARRY LOKER MARKS SIMON
TOPSY GEORGE HARRIS LEGREE
RACHEL SHELBY SIMEON OPHELIA
STCLAIR EMMELINE HALLIDAY
UNCLOSE OPE OPEN UNHASP
DISCLOSE
UNCLOTHE TIRL SPOIL UNRIG
DEVEST DESPOIL
UNCLOTHED STARKERS
UNCLOUDED CLEAR SERENE
UNCOIL UNLINK
UNCOLORED FAIR
UNCOMBED UNKAMED UNTEWED
UNCOMBINED FREE FRANK LOOSE
UNCOMELY INDECENT
UNCOMFORTABLE HOT EVIL
POOR HARSH UNKET UNKID
QUEASY STICKY UNFELE
UNCOMMON MUCH NICE RARE
SELD UNCO BYOUS FORBY
UNCOW VAUDY DAINTY FORBYE
SCARCE SPECIAL STRANGE
UNUSUAL SINGULAR UNWONTED
UNCOMMONLY UNCO BYOUS
EXTRA JOLLY UNCOW UNCOLY
UNCOMMONNESS SCARCITY

UNCOMMUNICATIVE DUMB
SILENT PRIVATE RESERVED
UNCOMPLICATED RURAL HONEST
SIMPLE
UNCOMPOUNDED SIMPLEX
UNCOMPROMISING ACID FIRM
GRIM RIGID STERN STOUT ULTRA
SEVERE STRICT STRONG EXTREME
BRASSBOUND
UNCONCEALED BARE OPEN
OUVERT APPARENT
UNCONCERN APATHY EASINESS
UNCONCERNED COOL EASY
BLAND CASUAL CARELESS
UNCONCERNEDLY LIGHTLY
UNCONDITIONAL FREE FRANK
UTTER SIMPLE ABSOLUTE
EXPLICIT TERMLESS
UNCONDITIONED POSITIVE
UNCONFINED LAX FREE LOOSE
UNCONGENIAL HATEFUL INGRATE
KINDLESS
UNCONNECTED GAPPY REMOTE
DETACHED
UNCONQUERED INVICT INVICTED
UNCONSCIOUS OUT COLD BRUTE
ASLEEP BLOTTO CUCKOO TORPID
UNAWARE WITLESS COMATOSE
IGNORANT SENSELESS
UNCONSIDERED WILD
UNCONSTRAINED FREE UNNET
SIMPLE FAMILIAR
UNCONTROLLABLE WILD
UNCONTROLLED FREE MADCAP
LIBERAL ABSOLUTE UNBITTED
UNCONVENTIONAL FLAKY GYPSY
LOOSE CASUAL FLAKE DEVIOUS
ODDBALL OFFBEAT BOHEMIAN
INFORMAL
(— IN STYLE) MOD
UNCONVINCING FALSE FISHY
UNCOOKED RAW
UNCOOPERATIVE (TO BE —)
STONEWALL
UNCOUNTABLE SUMLESS
UNCOUPLE CUT UNDOCK DISLINK
UNCOUTH RUDE CRUDE DORIC
GURLY ROUGH UNKED UNKID
GOTHIC JUNGLY QUAINT RENISH
AWKWARD BOORISH CUBBISH
HIRSUTE LOUTISH AGRESTIC
UNGAINLY YOKELISH
(— PERSON) TUG
UNCOVER BARE DOFF HUNT ROOT
ROUT TIRL TIRR BREAK STRIP
TIRVE UNLAP UNLID UNWRY
DETECT EXHUME SEARCH
UNBARE UNCASE UNHALE UNVEIL
UNDRAPE UNEARTH DISCLOSE
DISCOVER UNMANTLE UNMUFFLE
UNCOVERED BARE OVERT
(PREF.) GYMN(O)
UNCTION CHRISM OINTMENT
UNCTUOUS FAT OILY SALVY SLEEK
SOAPY SUAVE GREASY SMARMY
COURTLY PINGUID OLEAGINOUS
UNCULTIVATED RAW BRUT FERAL
DESERT FALLOW INCULT SAVAGE
SLOVEN WILDERN
UNCULTURED RUDE INCULT
ARTLESS
UNCUT RASPED
UNDAMAGED WHOLE

UNDARKENED CLEAR
UNDAUNTED BOLD BRAVE MANLY
SPARTAN FEARLESS INTREPID
UNDE WAVY UNDEE
UNDECAYED GREEN
UNDECEIVE DISABUSE
UNDECIDED MOOT DUBIOUS
PENDING DOUBTFUL WAVERING
UNDECIDEDLY HUMDRUM
UNDECLARED SECRET
UNDEFENDED UNKEPT
UNDEFILED PURE CHASTE INTACT
VIRGIN
UNDEFINED OBSCURE
UNDELIVERABLE DEAD
UNDEMONSTRATIVE COLD
ASEPTIC LACONIC RESERVED
UNDENIABLE BRUTAL
UNDENIABLY INDEED
UNDEPENDABLE CASUAL FLUFFY
UNDER SUB BAJO BELOW INFRA
NEATH SOTTO ANEATH ANUNDER
BENEATH
(— ORDERS) SUPPOSED
(— THE WORD) IV
(— THE YEAR) SA
(— THIS TITLE) HT
(— THIS WORD) SV SHV
(— WAY) AFOOT
(PREF.) HYPO SUB
UNDERBODICE JUMP BASQUINE
CAMISOLE
UNDERBRUSH FILTH COVERT
GARSIL MAQUIS RAMMEL
ABATURE
UNDERBURNED SOFT SAMEL
UNDERBUTLER WASHPOT
UNDERCARRIAGE BOGY BOGEY
BOGIE
UNDERCLAY THILL WARRANT
UNDERCLOTHES LININGS
UNDERCOAT PILE ALPACA
SURFACER
(WOOL OF — OF MUSK-OX) QIVIUT
UNDERCOVER SECRET
UNDERCRUST ABAISSE
UNDERCURRENT UNDERLAY
UNDERRUN UNDERSET
UNDERCUT JAD HOLE LAME POOL
SUMP KIRVE NOTCH
UNDERDONE RARE REAR
UNDERDRAWERS FLANNELS
UNDERESTIMATE DISPRIZE
MINIMIZE
UNDERFLEECE PASHM
UNDERFRAME SOLE
UNDERGARMENT BAND SLIP
CYMAR SIMAR SKIRT SMOCK
TUNIC WAIST BANIAN BANYAN
BODICE CAMISE CILICE CORSET
GIRDLE STAMIN CHEMISE
DOUBLET DRAWERS STAMMEL
TALLITH BLOOMERS KNICKERS
(WOMAN'S —) PANTIHOSE
(PL.) SMALLS FLANNELS FLIMSIES
SNUGGIES
UNDERGO PASS SERVE ENDURE
SUFFER SUSTAIN
UNDERGOER
(SUFF.) EE
UNDERGRADUATE MAN TASSEL
SERVITOR
UNDERGROWTH RUSH COVER

RAMMEL SPRING BUSHWOOD
UNDERHAND SLY DERN SHADY
BYHAND SECRET CROOKED
OBLIQUE INVOLVED SINISTER
SNEAKING
UNDERHANDED DERN FUNNY
FILTHY SECRET SINISTER
UNDERIVED ORIGINAL
UNDER JAW
(PREF.) GENYO
UNDERLAYER SLASHING
UNDERLIE SUBTEND
UNDERLING MENIAL SEQUEL
UNDERER HENCHMAN INFERIOR
UNDERLYING COVERT IMPLICIT
UNDERMINE SAP CAVE HOLE POOL
ERODE KNIFE WEAKEN FOSSICK
FOUNDER SUBVERT ENFEEBLE
SUPPLANT
UNDERMINED ROTTEN
UNDERNEATH BELOW BENEATH
UNNEATH
(PREF.) INTRA
UNDERNSONG TIERCE
UNDERPANTS BRIEFS BLOOMERS
KNICKERS
UNDERPART BELLY
UNDERPASS DIVE SUBWAY
UNDERRATE DECRY DISCOUNT
UNDERRUN BOTTOM
UNDERSACRISTAN CUSTOS
UNDERSHIRT VEST SHIFT SHIRT
CAMISA JERSEY LINDER SEMMIT
SINGLET WRAPPER
UNDERSHRUB HEATH PINKEYE
SEEPWEED SUBSHRUB
SAGEBRUSH SANTOLINA
UNDERSIDE BOTTOM BREAST
(— OF CLOUD) BASE
(— OF FINGER) BALL
(— OF FLOOR) CEILING
(— OF STAIRCASE) SOFFIT
(PREF.) **(ON THE —)** INFERO
UNDERSIZED DEENY SCRUB
STUNT
UNDERSKIRT QUILT CRINOLINE
PETTICOAT
UNDERSONG FABURDEN
UNDERSTAND CAN CON DIG GET
KEN SEE GAUM HAVE MAKE TAKE
TWIG BRAIN ENTER GRASP
REACH SAVVY SEIZE SENSE SKILL
SPELL ACCEPT COTTON FIGURE
FOLLOW INTAKE INTEND SUBAUD
UPTAKE CONCEIT DISCERN
COMPRISE CONCEIVE CONSTRUE
CONTRIVE FORSTAND PERCEIVE
PERSTAND UNDERNIM
UNDERSTANDABLE PLAIN
UNDERSTANDING KEN WIT GAUM
HEAD BRAIN CLASP HEART INWIT
SENSE SKILL ACCORD INTENT
NOTION REASON TREATY UPTAKE
COMPACT CONCEIT CONCEPT
ENTENTE INSIGHT MEANING
WITNESS DAYLIGHT PREHENSION
(IMPERFECT —) DARKNESS
(PREF.) NOEMA
UNDERSTATEMENT LITOTES
MEIOSIS
UNDERSTOOD LUCID SUPPOSED
(— ONLY BY SPECIALLY INITIATED)
ESOTERIC

(EASILY —) EASY CLEAR EXTANT
(NOT —) DARKSOME
UNDERSTUDY DOUBLE
UNDERSURFACE SOLE
UNDERTAKE GO TRY DARE FANG
FOND GRANT OFFER ASSUME
INCEPT PLEDGE ATTEMPT
EMBRACE EMPRISE PRETEND
UNDERFO CONTRACT PRESTATE
(— RESPONSIBILITY) ACCEPT
ANSWER
UNDERTAKER UPHOLDER
MORTICIAN
UNDERTAKING JOB AVAL TASK
CAUTIO EFFORT SCHEME VOYAGE
ATTEMPT CALLING PROJECT
VENTURE COVENANT
(— IN CARDS) CONTRACT
(UNPROFITABLE —) FOLLY
UNDERTEACHER USHER
UNDERTONE INKLING SUBTONE
UNDERTOW SEAPOOSE
UNDER TWO FLAGS (AUTHOR OF —
) OUIDA
(CHARACTER IN —) RAKE CECIL
AMAGUE BERTIE CORONA
BERKELEY CIGARETTE
GUENEVERE ROYALLIEU
CHATEAUROY ROCKINGHAM
UNDERVALUE DECRY DISABLE
DISPRIZE DISVALUE MISPRISE
MISPRIZE
UNDERVEST BODICE SEMMIT
SINGLET
UNDERWAIST CAMISOLE
UNDERWATER (— DEVICE) OTTER
PARAVANE
UNDERWEAR BRIEFS SHORTS
SKIVVY UNDIES DESSOUS
HEAVIES LONGIES LINGERIE
PRETTIES SCANTIES
(PL.) SMALLS
UNDERWING CATOCALA
UNDERWOOD FRITH BOSCAGE
COPPICE
UNDERWORLD DUAT DEWAT
HADES ORCUS SHEOL MICTLAN
XIBALBA GANGLAND
UNDERWRITE SIGN INSURE
ENDORSE
UNDERWRITER INSURER
UNDESERVED INDIGN
UNDETERMINED UNSET DUBIOUS
PENDENT AORISTIC DOUBTFUL
INFINITE
UNDEVELOPED CRUDE MORON
LATENT SLOVEN GERMING
IMMATURE JUVENILE
UNDEVIATINGLY SMACK
UNDIFFERENCED ENTIRE
UNDIFFERENTIATED GLOBAL
AMERISTIC
UNDIGESTED CRUDE
UNDIGNIFIED DOGGREL DOGGEREL
UNDILUTED MERE NEAT PURE
NAKED SHEER SHORT STRAIGHT
UNDIMINISHED ENTIRE
UNDIMMED CLEAR
UNDINE NIX
(CHARACTER IN —) HUGO VEIT
TOBIAS UNDINE BERTHALDA
KUHLEBORN
(COMPOSER OF —) LORTZING

UNDISCIPLINED WANTON
COLTISH
UNDISCLOSED HIDDEN SEALED
UNDISCRIMINATING GROSS
UNDISGUISED BALD NAKED PLAIN
UNDISMAYED ONFLEMED
UNDISPUTED LIQUID
UNDISTINGUISHED GROSS
COMMON UNNOBLE FAMELESS
NAMELESS NOTELESS
UNDISTORTED CLEAR
UNDISTURBED CALM SOUND
SERENE VIRGIN TRANQUIL
UNDIVIDED WHOLE ENTIRE SINGLE
UNDO DUP COOK POOP SLIP
FORDO SPEED UNPAY DEFEAT
DIDDLE FOREDO UNBIND UNKNIT
UNLOCK UNTUCK UNWORK
DEFEISE DESTROY NULLIFY
UNRAVEL UNRIVET UNTWIRL
UNWEAVE UNWREST DECIPHER
DISSOLVE DISTRUSS UNFASTEN
UNDOER ACHAN
UNDOGMATIC AGNOSTIC
UNDOING DEFEAT DOWNFALL
(PREF.) DE DIS
UNDOMESTICATED WILD FERAL
FERINE
UNDOUBTEDLY SURELY FRANKLY
UNDRESS MOB DOFF FLAY PEEL
TIRR STRIP UNRAY UNRIG DEVEST
DIVEST UNBUSK UNCASE UNLACE
UNRIND UNROBE UNTIRE
DISCASE UNARRAY UNREADY
UNSPOIL UNTRUSS NEGLIGEE
UNATTIRE
UNDRESSED UNDIGHT
UNDUE EXTREME
UNDULATE WAVE WAVY FLOAT
SWING BILLOW GYROSE KELTER
UNDATE UNDOSE FLICKER
UNDATED
UNDULATING SURGING FLEXUOUS
INDENTED
UNDULATION FOLD ROLL WAVE
CRIMP TEETER WAVING
CRIMPING
UNDULATORY WAVY
UNDUTIFULNESS IMPIETY
UNDYED CORAH
UNDYING IMMORTAL
UNEARTH DIG MOOT EXPOSE
UNCOVER DISCOVER
UNEARTHLY EERY EERIE WEIRD
AWESOME UNCANNY UNGODLY
UNEASINESS ENVY GENE FIDGET
NETTLE SORROW UNEASE
AILMENT ANXIETY DISEASE
MISEASE TROUBLE DISQUIET
DISTASTE
UNEASY SICKLY FIDGETY INQUIET
NERVOUS RESTIVE UNQUIET
WORRIED RESTLESS
UNEDUCATED RUDE SIMPLE
IGNORANT
UNEMBELLISHED DRY PROSE
STARK AUSTERE
UNEMOTIONAL DRY COLD COOL
STOIC STONY STOICAL
UNEMOTIONALLY EVENLY
UNEMPLOYED IDLE ORRA VOID
OTIANT OTIOSE VACANT IDLESET
LEISURE UNBUSIED

UNEMPLOYMENT IDLENESS
UNENCUMBERED VACANT
EXPEDITE
UNENDING ABYSMAL AGELONG
CHRONIC ENDLESS UNDYING
TERMLESS TIMELESS
UNENJOYABLE JOYLESS
UNENLIGHTENED MISTY HEATHEN
IGNORANT
UNENTHUSIASTIC COLD
UNEQUAL IMPAR DISPAR UNEGAL
UNEVEN INEQUAL INFERIOR
(— TO STRAIN) FEEBLE
(PREF.) ANIS(O) IMPARI INEQUI
UNEQUALED UNIQUE NONESUCH
UNEQUIVOCAL DIRECT SQUARE
PERFECT DEFINITE DISTINCT
EXPLICIT RESOUNDING
UNERRING DEAD TRUE DEADLY
INERRANT
UNERRINGLY CLEAN
UNEVEN RUDE EROSE GOBBY
HAGGY JAGGY MEALY ROUGH
HOBBLY PLATTY RAGGED
RUGGED SPOTTY TWITTY UNFAIR
UNLIKE DIURNAL ERRATIC
HOTTERY INEQUAL SCALENE
STREAKY UNEQUAL HUMMOCKY
SCRAGGED SCRATCHY SNAGGLED
ACCIDENTED
(— IN COLOR) CLOUDY
UNEVENLY AWRY
UNEVENNESS BUMP WAVE FRAZE
ANOMALY WRINKLE ACCIDENT
ASPERITY
UNEVENTFUL STILL UNDATED
UNEXCITED LEVEL
UNEXCITING DEAD DULL TAME
BORING PROSAIC
UNEXPECTED EERY EERIE ABRUPT
SUDDEN UNWARY INOPINE
UNLOOKED
UNEXPECTEDLY UNWARES
UNAWARES
UNEXPIRED ALIVE
UNEXPLAINED HIDDEN
UNEXPOSED RAW
UNFADABLE FAST
UNFADED FRESH BRIGHT
UNFAILING SURE DEADLY
INFALLID UNERRING
UNFAIR FOUL CROOK WRONG
BIASED SHABBY UNEVEN UNJUST
DEVIOUS PARTIAL SLANTER
UNEQUAL UNSEEMLY WRONGFUL
UNFAIRLY HARDLY
UNFAIRNESS CROSS INEQUITY
UNFAITHFUL INFIDEL TRAITOR
DISLOYAL RECREANT
UNFALTERING SURE TRUE STEADY
UNERRING
UNFAMILIAR NEW FREMD
HEATHER STRANGE UNKNOWN
UNFASTEN FREE OPEN UNDO
LOOSE UNPIN UNBIND UNHASP
UNLIME UNLINK UNLOCK
UNMAKE UNTINE UNDIGHT
UNHITCH UNSTECK UNTRUSS
UNFATHOMABLE ABYSMAL
ABYSSAL PROFOUND
UNFATHOMED COSMIC
UNFAVORABLE BAD ILL FOUL
HARD POOR CRONK SHREWD

UNFAIR UNKIND ADVERSE
AWKWARD FROWARD HOSTILE
UNHAPPY BACKWARD CONTRARY
INIMICAL SINISTER UNKINDLY
(PREF.) DYS
UNFAVORABLY BADLY CROSS
UNFEATHERED SQUAB
UNFEELING COLD DULL HARD
CRASS CRUEL HARSH ROCKY
STERN STONY BRUTAL LEADEN
MARBLE STOLID CALLOUS
OBDURATE
UNFEELINGLY HARSHLY
UNFEELINGNESS APATHY
UNFEIGNED OPEN TRUE HEARTY
CORDIAL NATURAL SINCERE
UNFERMENTED AZYMOUS
UNFERTILE BARREN
UNFETTERED FREE UNGYVED
UNFILLED BLANK EMPTY VACANT
VACUOUS
UNFINISHED RAW GRAY GREY
CRUDE KACHA ROUGH KUTCHA
RAGGED KACHCHA STICKIT
IMMATURE INCHOATE
UNFIRED GREEN
UNFIRM UNFAST
UNFIT BAD SICK UNAPT WISHT
WRONG COMMON FAULTY
NOUGHT UNTIDY DISABLE
UNFITTY IMPROPER UNFITTEN
UNLIKELY UNLIKING
UNFITTING UNMEETLY
UNFIXED AFLOAT
UNFLEDGED SQUAB CALLOW
UNFLINCHING LEVEL STAUNCH
UNFOLD OPEN BREAK BURST
SOLVE UNLAP UNTIE DEPLOY
EVOLVE EXPAND EXPLAT FLOWER
SPREAD UNFURL UNPLAT
UNROLL UNTUCK BLOSSOM
DEVELOP DISPLAY DIVULGE
EXPLAIN UNPLAIT UNRAVEL
UNWEAVE UNDOUBLE UNPLIGHT
UNFOLDED OPEN EVOLUTE
EXPANDED
UNFOLDING DISPLAY
(— OF EVENTS) ACTION
(— TO VIEW) BURST
UNFORCED EASY GLIB WILLING
UNFORESEEN CASUAL SUDDEN
IMPREVU UNAWARE
UNFORMED CALLOW INFORM
UNFORTUNATE ILL EVIL POOR
DONCY TOUGH WEARY SHREWD
HAPLESS UNHAPPY UNLUCKY
LUCKLESS UNTOWARD
WANHAPPY
UNFREQUENTED LONE EMPTY
UNCOUTH SOLITARY
UNFRIENDLY ILL COLD FOUL CHILL
BITTER CHILLY FIERCE FROSTY
UNSOME HOSTILE INGRATE
STRANGE INIMICAL
UNFROCK DEFROCK DEGRADE
DISFROCK UNPRIEST
UNFRUITFUL BLUNT ADDLED
BARREN EFFETE WASTED STERILE
USELESS INFECUND
UNFULFILLMENT BREACH
UNFURL BREAK SPREAD UNFOLD
DEVELOP OUTROOL
UNFURNISHED BARE VACANT

UNGAINLY LANKY SPLAY WEEDY CLUMSY UNGAIN AWKWARD BOORISH NUNTING UNHEPPEN UNLICKED UNWIELDY

UNGENEROUS MEAN SHABBY STINGY GRUDGING

UNGENIAL CHILLY

UNGIRDED DISCINCT

UNGODLINESS ATHEISM IMPIETY

UNGODLY SINFUL WICKED GODLESS IMPIOUS PROFANE

UNGOVERNABLE WILD UNRULY FROWARD IMPOTENT

UNGRACEFUL HARD CLUMSY ANGULAR AWKWARD HALTING UNTOWARD

UNGRACEFULLY HARSHLY

UNGRACIOUS GRUFF UNFEEL UNFELE CHURLISH SNAPPISH

UNGRATEFUL UNKIND INGRATE

UNGROOMED UNDRESSED

UNGUARDED STIFF

UNGUENT CEROMA CHRISM PIMENT POMADE SMEGMA POMATUM UNCTION OINTMENT (PREF.) MYRO

UNGULATE HOG PIG DEER HORSE TAKIN TAPIR HOOFED AMBLYPOD ELEPHANT

UNGUMMED BRIGHT

UNHALLOWED IMPURE UNHOLY PROFANE

UNHAMPERED FREE DIRECT EXPEDITE

UNHAPPINESS MISERY SORROW ILLFARE SADNESS UNBLISS

UNHAPPY SAD POOR DISMAL UNLUCKY UNLUSTY WANSOME DEJECTED DOWNBEAT DOWNGONE WOBEGONE WRETCHED

UNHARMED SAFE UNSHENT

UNHARNESS UNGEAR OUTSHUT OUTSPAN UNHORSE UNTACKLE

UNHEALED GREEN

UNHEALTHY BAD MORBID QUEASY SICKLY UNHALE NAUGHTY PECCANT EPINOSIC MALADIVE

UNHEATED COLD

UNHEEDED IGNORED UNTENTED

UNHEEDING DEAF CARELESS

UNHESITATING READY UNPOISED

UNHITCH OUTSPAN

UNHOLY IMPURE WICKED IMPIOUS PROFANE

UNHORSE PURL THROW UNCOLT DISMOUNT UNSADDLE

UNHURRIED EASY SLOW SOFT SOBER

UNHURT SAFE HARMLESS HURTLESS UNHARMED

UNIAT MALKITE MELCHITE

UNICORN LIN REEM KILIN LICORN LICORNE NARWHAL HOWITZER

UNICORN FISH LIJA UNIE

UNICORN PLANT MARTINOE

UNICUM UNION

UNIDENTIFIED FACELESS INCOGNITO

UNIFICATION SYSTEM ENSEMBLE

UNIFIED GLOBAL

UNIFIER UMBRELLA

UNIFORM KIT DEAD EVEN FLAT JUST LIKE SAME SELF SUIT ALIKE BLUES CLOTH KHAKI SOLID SUITY GLOBAL GREENS LIVERY SINGLE STEADY EQUABLE REGULAR SIMILAR SUNTANS CONSTANT EQUIFORM EQUIPAGE MEASURED STANDARD UNIVOCAL
(— IN HUE) FLAT
(LEATHER —) BUFF
(NOT —) SQUALLY
(PRISONER'S —) STRIPES
(PREF.) IS ISO

UNIFORMITY ONENESS EQUALITY EVENNESS MONOTONY SAMENESS

UNIFORMLY EVENLY EQUALLY

UNIFY MERGE UNITE CEMENT COMPACT UNITIZE COALESCE

UNILATERAL SECUND

UNIMAGINATIVE DULL SODDEN STUPID LIMITED LITERAL PROSAIC UNIDEAL PEDANTIC PEDESTRIAN

UNIMPAIRED FRESH SOUND ENTIRE INTACT
(— BY) DEVOID

UNIMPASSIONED SOBER WHOLE STEADY

UNIMPEDED FREE EXPEDITE

UNIMPORTANT VAIN PETTY SMALL CASUAL SIMPLE TRIVIAL IMMOMENT PIDDLING TRINKETY JERKWATER

UNINFLECTED APTOTIC

UNINFORMED GREEN UNTOLD IGNORANT

UNINHABITED WILD EMPTY DESERT VACANT DESOLATE WASTEFUL

UNINHIBITED LARGE

UNINJURED INTACT SINCERE

UNINSPIRED HACK STODGY POMPIER DRYASDUST

UNINSPIRING TAME

UNINSTRUCTED NAIVE IGNORANT

UNINTELLIGENT DUMB OBTUSE OPAQUE STUPID ASININE FOOLISH VACUOUS WITLESS

UNINTELLIGIBLE BLIND MISTY OPAQUE MYSTICAL

UNINTENTIONAL UNMEANT

UNINTERESTING DRY ARID COLD DRAB DREE DULL FADE FLAT TAME DREAR SANDY STALE BORING DREICH JEJUNE INSIPID BROMIDIC FRUMPISH

UNINTERMITTENT ITHAND

UNINTERRUPTED SMOOTH STEADY ENDLESS ETERNAL STRAIGHT

UNINTERRUPTEDLY AWAY

UNIO MUSSEL

UNION SUM ZYG BLOC DUAD JOIN ALLOY GROUP JOINT NONOP UNITY ENOSIS FUSION GREMIO TAWHID VEREIN COMPACT CONCERT CONTACT MEETING ONENESS SOCIETY ADHESION ALLIANCE COHESION ESPOUSAL JOINTURE JUNCTION JUNCTURE SODALITY SYSTASIS TRIALISM VINCULUM ZOLLVEREIN
(— OF TWO SETS) CUP
(— OF TWO VOWELS) CRASIS
(MARITAL —) BED
(POLITICAL —) ANSCHLUSS
(SEXUAL —) COPULA COUPLING
(TURKISH —) JETTRU
(PREF.) ZYG(O)(OTO)
(SEXUAL —) GAMO
(SUFF.) APSIS
GAM(AE)(IST)(OUS)(Y) GAMETE

UNIONIST REFUGEE

UNION OF SOVIET SOCIALIST REPUBLICS (SEE RUSSIA)

UNIQUE ODD RARE SOLE UNIC ALONE UNION SINGLE SULLEN UNICUM ALONELY SOLEYNE SPECIAL STRANGE ISOLATED SINGULAR

UNIQUENESS SOLITUDE

UNISON FIRST CONCORD HOMOPHONY

UNIT (ALSO SEE MEASURE AND WEIGHT) (ALSO SEE MEASURE) ACE ONE ATOM BARN KLAN FLOOR HUMIT MONAD NEPER ADDRESS DIOPTER ELEMENT ENERGID KLAVERN
(— IN COUNTING FISH) MEASE
(— IN EARTHWORK) FLOAT FLOOR
(— OF ABSORPTION) SABIN
(— OF ACCELERATION) GAL MILLIGAL
(— OF ACTION) EPISODE
(— OF ANGULAR MEASURE) CENTRAD
(— OF ARCHEOLOGICAL CLASSIFICATION) ASPECT
(— OF BINARY DIGITS) BYTE
(— OF BRIGHTNESS) NIT STILB LAMBERT
(— OF CAPACITANCE) JAR FARAD
(— OF CAPACITY) LAST PIPE ARDAB ARDEB TIERCE AMPHORA
(— OF COMIC STRIP) BOX
(— OF CONDUCTANCE) SIEMENS
(— OF COUNTING) POINT
(— OF DATA TRANSMISSION SPEED) BAUD
(— OF DESIGN) LARME
(— OF DISTANCE) DAY VERST PARSEC MEGAPARSEC
(— OF ELASTANCE) DARAF
(— OF ELECTRIC CAPACITY) FARAD
(— OF ELECTRIC CONDUCTANCE) MHO
(— OF ELECTRIC FORCE) VOLT KILOVOLT STATVOLT
(— OF ELECTRIC INDUCTANCE) HENRY
(— OF ELECTRIC INTENSITY) AMPERE OERSTED
(— OF ELECTRIC RELUCTANCE) REL STATOHM
(— OF ELECTRIC RESISTANCE) BEGOHM
(— OF ELECTRICAL RESISTANCE) ABOHM
(— OF ELECTRICITY) ES COULOMB
(— OF ENERGY) ERG RAD JOULE ATOMERG QUANTUM
(— OF FINENESS) CARAT KARAT
(— OF FLOW) CUSEC
(— OF FLUIDITY) RHE
(— OF FLUX DENSITY) GAUSS
(— OF FORCE) G DYNE STAPP

NEWTON STHENE POUNDAL
(— OF FREQUENCY) HERTZ FRESNEL MEGAHERTZ
(— OF GEOLOGIC TIME) AEON
(— OF GOVERNMENT) DEME LAND KREIS GEMEINDE
(— OF HEAT) BTU THERM CALORIE
(— OF ILLUMINANCE) LUX NIT PHOT MICROLUX
(— OF ILLUMINATION) PHOT
(— OF INFORMATION) NIT
(— OF INSTRUCTION) FRAME
(— OF INTERSTELLAR SPACE) PARSEC
(— OF LAND AREA) ARE SULUNG
(— OF LANGUAGE) SYLLABLE
(— OF LENGTH) FERMI MICRON MICROMETER
(— OF LIGHT) LUMEN
(— OF LIGHT INTENSITY) PYR PHOTON
(— OF LOUDNESS) PHON SONE DECIBEL
(— OF MACHINERY) STAND
(— OF MAGNETIC FLUX) WEBER
(— OF MAGNETIC FORCE) KAPP GILBERT
(— OF MAGNETIC INTENSITY) GAMMA OERSTED MAGNETON
(— OF MAGNIFICATION) DIAMETER
(— OF MASS) AMU SLUG CRITH DALTON AVOGRAM
(— OF MEMORY) BIT MNEMON
(— OF METRICAL QUANTITY) MATRA
(— OF MOMENT) DEBYE
(— OF MOMENTUM) BOLE
(— OF NARCOTIC) JOLT
(— OF NYLON FINENESS) DENIER
(— OF ONE INCH) BUTTON
(— OF PAIN INTENSITY) DOL
(— OF PERMEABILITY) DARCY
(— OF PIPE) FOURBLE
(— OF POWER) WATT DYNAM KILOWATT PONCELET
(— OF PRESSURE) BAR TORR BARAD BARIE BARYE GWELY OSMOL PASCAL MEGABAR CENTIBAR MILLIBAR
(— OF PRESSWORK) TOKEN
(— OF RADIATION) RAD REM REP LANGLEY
(— OF RADIOACTIVITY) CURIE
(— OF RESISTANCE) OHM
(— OF ROCKET) STAGE
(— OF SATURATION) SATRON
(— OF SOCIETY) CLAN HORDE CHAPTER
(— OF SPACE AND CIRCULATION) MILLINE
(— OF SPEECH) WORD
(— OF SPEED) BAUD KNOT
(— OF STRUCTURE) MICELLE
(— OF THICKNESS) POINT
(— OF TIME) BEAT SVEDBERG
(— OF TRADING) CONTRACT
(— OF VELOCITY) VELO
(— OF VERSE METER) FOOT
(— OF VISCOSITY) POISE STOKE SECONDS
(— OF WAVELENGTH) ANGSTROM
(— OF WEIGHT) SSU TON GERA GRAM CARAT GRAIN OUNCE

POUND STEIN ARROBA GRAMME
(— OF WIRE MEASUREMENT) MIL
(— OF WORK) ERG CROP HOUR
ERGON JOULE KILERG DINAMODE
(— OF YARN) LEA
(— OF YARN SIZE) CUT
(— OF 20) CORGE
(— OF 100 MEN) CENTURY
(ADMINISTRATIVE —) BLOCK HSIEN
AGENCY BUREAU CIRCLE
DISTRICT
(ARBITRARY —) OLFACTY
(ARCHERY —) END
(ARMY —) LEGION BRIGADE
COMPANY MAHALLA
(ARTILLERY —) BATTERY
(AVAILABLE AS —) MARRIED
(BOWLING —) ALLEY
(BOY SCOUT —) SHIP
(BUILDER'S —) SQUARE
(CIGAR-MANUFACTURING —)
BUCKEYE
(COLLECTIVE —) COMMUNE
(COMBAT —) ARMAMENT
(DISCRETE —) FRACTION
(EDUCATIONAL —) COURSE
(ELECTROMAGNETIC —) ABFARAD
ABHENRY MAXWELL ABAMPERE
(FUNDAMENTAL —) BASE
(GRAMMATICAL —) JUNCTION
(HARMONIC —) CELL
(HOUSING —) HUTMENT
(HYPOTHETICAL —) ID IDANT
MICELLE
(INDIVIDUALLY OWNED LIVING —)
CONDO
(LIFE —) BIOPHORE
(LIVING —) BIONT BIOGEN
(LOGARITHMIC —) BEL
(LOGGING —) CHANCE
(MILITARY —) ARMY GOUM CORPS
GROUP LANCE SQUAD BRIGADE
PLATOON SECTION COMMANDO
DIVISION REGIMENT SQUADRON
(NAZI —) FEHME
(ORGANIZATIONAL —) CELL
ACTIVITY
(PHOTOMETRIC —) VIOLLE
(POLITICAL —) POLITY SOVIET
MUNICIPALITY
(RHYTHMIC —) BASIS COLON
(SELF-PERPETUATING —) BIOSOME
(SOCIAL —) SEPT GROUP KRAAL
SOCIUS
(STORAGE —) BUFFER
(TELEGRAPHIC —) BAUD
(TEMPERATURE —) KELVIN
(TERRITORIAL —) STAKE STATE
COMMOT CANTRED CANTREF
KINGDOM
(THERMAL —) THERM CALORY
CALORIE
(TRIBAL —) TOWNSHIP
(VOTING —) CENTURY
(SUFF.) MONAS ON
UNITARIAN ARIAN SOCINIAN
UNITE ADD MIX ONE OOP PAN SAM
SEW UNE UNY ALLY BAND BIND
CLUB COAK FUSE HASP JOIN KNIT
KNOT LINK SAMM SEAM SOUD
UNIT BANDY CLOSE GRADE
GRAFT INONE JACOB JOINT
MERGE NITCH UNIFY WHOLE

ATTACH CEMENT CONCUR
COUPLE EMBODY ENTIRE GATHER
LAUREL LEAGUE SOLDER SPLICE
STRIKE SUTURE ACCRETE
AMALGAM CLUSTER COALITE
COMBINE CONJOIN CONNECT
CONSORT JACOBUS SIAMESE
ALLIGATE ANCYLOSE ANKYLOSE
ASSEMBLE COALESCE COMPOUND
CONCRETE CONSPIRE COPULATE
FEDERATE LAMINATE
COLLIGATE
(— BY INTERWEAVING) PLEACH
SPLICE
(— BY THREADS) SEW STITCH
(— CLOSELY) FAY YOT WELD
CEMENT COTTON
(— FOR INTRIGUE) CABAL
(— HOSE) COLLECT
(— IN MARRIAGE) WED SACRE
SACRI SPLICE SPOUSE
(— METALS) WELD SWEAT
(— TIMBERS) SCARF
(PREF.) GAMETO GAMO
UNITED ONE TIED ADDED FUSED
JOINT ALLIED CONNATE ENDLESS
UNIONED COMBINED CONCRETE
CONJOINT CONJUNCT FEDERATE
COADUNATE
(PREF.) GAM(ETO)(O)
UNITED ARAB EMIRATES
(CAPITAL OF —) ABUDHABI
(FORMER NAME OF —)
TRUCIALOMAN TRUCIALCOAST
TRUCIALSTATES
(MONEY OF —) DIRHAM
(MOUNTAINS OF —) HAJAR
(STATE OF —) AJMAN DUBAI
SHARJAH FUJAIRAH
(TOWN OF —) DUBAI JEBEL
BURAIMI SHARJAH
UNITED KINGDOM (SEE ENGLAND)

UNITED STATES (ALSO SEE
SPECIFIC STATES)
LAKE: ERIE MEAD SALT HURON
TAHOE CRATER ONTARIO
MICHIGAN SUPERIOR
CHAMPLAIN OKEECHOBEE
MOUNTAIN: BEAR BONA SILL
GREEN OZARK ROCKY UINTA
WHITE ANTERO ELBERT
SHASTA SIERRA BELFORD
FORAKER HARVARD MASSIVE
RAINIER SANFORD WASATCH
WHITNEY CATSKILL MCKINLEY
WRANGELL BLACKBURN
ADIRONDACK BITTERROOT
APPALACHIAN
PRESIDENT: ABE CAL DDE FDR IKE
JFK LBJ FORD POLK TAFT
ADAMS GRANT HARRY HAYES
JIMMY NIXON TEDDY TYLER
ARTHUR CARTER HOOVER
MONROE PIERCE REAGAN
TAYLOR TRUMAN WILSON
HARDING JACKSON JOHNSON
KENNEDY LINCOLN MADISON
BUCHANAN COOLIDGE
FILLMORE GARFIELD HARRISON
MCKINLEY VANBUREN
JEFFERSON ROOSEVELT
EISENHOWER WASHINGTON

VICE PRESIDENT: BURR BUSH FORD
KING ADAMS AGNEW DAWES
GERRY NIXON TYLER ARTHUR
COLFAX CURTIS DALLAS
GARNER HAMLIN HOBART
MORTON TRUMAN WILSON
BARKLEY CALHOUN CLINTON
JOHNSON MONDALE SHERMAN
WALLACE WHEELER COOLIDGE
FILLMORE HUMPHREY
MARSHALL TOMPKINS
VANBUREN FAIRBANKS
HENDRICKS JEFFERSON
ROOSEVELT STEVENSON
ROCKEFELLER BRECKINRIDGE
WATERFALL: TWIN AKAKA SEVEN
NARADA RIBBON FEATHER
PALOUSE PASSAIC SLUISKIN
YOSEMITE BRIDALVEIL
YELLOWSTONE

UNITING SUTURE
UNITS
(SUFF.) (HAVING TIME —) SEMIC
UNITY UNION SYSTEM ONENESS
UNITUDE IDENTITY SODALITY
SYMPATHY TOTALITY
(— OF SPIRIT AND NATURE)
ABSOLUTE
UNIVALENT MONATOMIC
UNIVERSAL ALL LOCAL QUALE
TOTAL WHOLE WORLD COMMON
GLOBAL PUBLIC VERSAL GENERAL
GENERIC CATHOLIC ECUMENIC
PANDEMIC
(TRANSCENDENT —) IDEA
UNIVERSALITY ALLNESS
OMNITUDE
UNIVERSE ALL LOKA MASS OLAM
WORLD COSMOS SYSTEM
CREATURE EXEMPLAR
(SIDEREAL —) SPACE
(PREF.) COSM(O) COSMETO
COSMICO
UNIVERSITY STUDY CAMPUS
SCHOOL ACADEMY COLLEGE
MADRASA STUDIUM VARSITY
MADRASAH REDBRICK
(RELATING TO BRITISH —)
OXBRIDGE REDBRICK PLATEGLASS
UNJUST HARD UNFAIR WANTON
WICKED UNEQUAL UNRICHT
UNRIGHT WRONGFUL
UNJUSTIFIED INVALID
UNJUSTLY UNDULY FALSELY
UNKEELED RATITE
UNKEMPT ROUGH FROWZY
RUGGED SHAGGY INCOMPT
RAFFISH RUFFLED SCRUFFY
SHAGRAG TOUSLED DRAGGLED
SCRAGGLY SLIPSHOD STRUBBLY
UNCOMBED
UNKIND BAD ILL MEAN VILE CRUEL
HARSH STERN SEVERE UNMEEK
UNKINDNESS DISFAVOR
UNKNOWABLE SEALED
UNKNOWN IGN UNCO UNKET
UNKID IGNOTE MUNKAR SEALED
SECRET UNWARE UNWIST
FARAWAY OBSCURE UNCOUTH
UNHEARD IGNORANT UNAWARES
UNKENNED UNWITTING
UNLADEN LEAR LEER

UNLATCH UNSNECK
UNLAWFUL ILLEGAL ILLICIT
NONLICET UNLEEFUL UNLEISUM
UNLEARNED LEWD GROSS PLAIN
BOOKLESS IGNORANT UNLEARED
UNLEAVENED AZYMOUS
UNLESS BUT NIF LESS NISI SAVE
BINNA NOBUT LESSEN ONLESS
WITHOUT
(— BEFORE) NIPR NIPRI
(— OTHERWISE NOTED) NAN
UNLETTERED LEWD BORREL
IGNORANT
UNLIGHTED BLIND LAMPLESS
UNLIKE DIFFORM DISLIKE DIVERSE
(MOST —) OTHEREST
UNLIKELY REMOTE DUBIOUS
(MOST —) LAST
UNLIMITED VAST SOVRAN
ABSOLUTE UNTERMED
(— IN POWER) ALMIGHTY
UNLINED SINGLE
UNLOAD TIP DROP DUMP HOVEL
DECANT STRIKE UNLADE UNSHIP
UNSTOW DELIVER DEPLETE
DETRUCK DISLOAD UNTRUSS
DISCHARGE
UNLOCK UNMAKE RESERATE
UNLOUKEN
UNLOOSE OUTWIND UNRIVET
UNLUCKY BAD FAY ILL EVIL FOUL
DONSY DISMAL DONSIE HOODOO
WICKED HAPLESS INFAUST
UNHAPPY UNCHANCY
UNTOWARD WANCHANCY
(— THING) AMBSACE
UNMAN UNDO CRUSH UNNERVE
UNMANAGEABLE ROID DONSY
RANDY WANTON RESTIVE
CHURLISH STAFFISH CAMSTAIRY
REFRACTORY
UNMANLY SOFT MANLESS
UNLUSTY
UNMANNERLY RUDE BOORISH
UNCIVIL IMPOLITE UNGENTLE
MISLEARED
UNMARKED MAVERICK NOTELESS
UNMARRIED ONE LONE SOLE
OLEPI YOUNG ONLEPY SINGLE
UNMASK EXPOSE UNFACE
DISMASK UNCLOAK
UNMASKING EXPOSURE
UNMEASURED UNMEET
MODELESS
UNMELODIOUS SCRANNEL
UNMERCHANTABLE SALABLE
SALEABLE
UNMERCIFUL CRUEL PITILESS
RUTHLESS
UNMETHODICAL CURSORY
UNMINDFUL SLOWFUL CARELESS
HEEDLESS MINDLESS
UNMISTAKABLE FLAT OPEN
BROAD CLEAR FRANK PLAIN
PATENT DECIDED EXPRESS
APPARENT DECISIVE MANIFEST
UNIVOCAL
UNMISTAKABLY SIGNALLY
UNMITIGATED PURE GROSS
RUDDY ARRANT DAMNED
SOVRAN PERFECT PUREDEE
REGULAR ABSOLUTE OUTRIGHT
UNMIX EXSOLVE

UNMIXED NET DEEP MERE PURE SELF SOLE BLANK SHEER UTTER IMMIXT SIMPLE STRAIGHT
UNMODIFIED BRUTE STRAIGHT
UNMOLESTED SACKLESS
UNMOVED CALM COOL FIRM STONY TIGHT IMMOTE SERENE ADAMANT IMMOVED
UNMOVING INERT IMMOBILE IMMOTIVE
UNMUSICAL NOTELESS SCABROUS
UNNATURAL EERY EERIE STIFF CLAMMY CREEPY UNKIND STRANGE UNCANNY VIOLENT ABNORMAL ABSONANT FARCICAL KINDLESS UNKINDLY MONSTROUS
UNNECESSARY USELESS NEEDLESS
UNNEEDED WASTE
UNNERVE UNMAN UNMAKE WEAKEN ENERVATE PARALYZE
UNNERVED SHOOK
UNNOTICED SILENT
UNOBJECTIONABLE VENIAL
UNOBSERVANT HEEDLESS
UNOBSTRUCTED FAIR FREE OPEN PATENT THROUGH APPARENT
UNOBTRUSIVE SHY QUIET MODEST SEDATE DISCREET RETIRING
UNOCCUPIED IDLE VOID BLANK EMPTY WASTE OTIOSE VACANT LEISURE UNSEATED WASTEFUL
UNORGANIZED ACOSMIC INCHOATE
UNORTHODOX HERETIC
UNOSTENTATIOUS SHY QUIET LENTEN MODEST
UNPACK UNFARDLE
UNPAID DUE UNQUIT UNWAGED HONORARY WAGELESS OUTSTANDING
UNPAIRED IMPAR AZYGOUS
UNPALATABLE SOD HARD BITTER BRACKISH
UNPARALLELED ALONE UNIQUE EPOCHAL PEERLESS SINGULAR UNPEERED
UNPERTURBED BLAND STILL
UNPLEASANT BAD ACID EVIL HARD NICE SOUR UGLY VILE AWFUL CRUDE GRIMY GUMMY HAIRY HARSH MUCKY NASTY ROUGH TOUGH BRUTAL CRIMPY RANCID STICKY THRAWN UNFELE UNGAIN UNLIEF BEASTLY BILIOUS GHASTLY INGRATE SPINOUS UNLUSTY UNQUEME UNSONCY CHISELLY DREADFUL HORRIBLE INDECENT SCABROUS UNLOVELY ABOMINABLE (PREF.) CAC(O) CACH
UNPLEASANTLY QUEER HARDLY UNWINLY
UNPLEASANTNESS ILLNESS
UNPLOWED LEA
UNPOETICAL MUSELESS
UNPOLISHED ILL RUDE BLIND CRUDE ROUGH COARSE INCULT RUGGED RUSTIC SAVAGE SHAGGY UPLAND INCOMPT UNKEMPT AGRESTIC
UNPOPULARITY ENVY

UNPRACTICED RAW FRESH UNTRADED
UNPREDICTABLE CHANCY CRANKY ERRATIC
UNPREJUDICED FAIR
UNPREMEDITATED CASUAL
UNPREPARED TARDY
UNPREPOSSESSING SEEDY
UNPRETENDING LOWLY HOMELY HUMBLE
UNPRETENTIOUS HOMY HOMEY PLAIN SOBER COMMON HOMELY HUMBLE MODEST SIMPLE DISCREET HOMESPUN
UNPRINCIPLED LEWD LIMMER
UNPRODUCTIVE DRY SHY ARID DEAD DEAF LEAN POOR VAIN YELD YELL ADDLE DUSTY WASTE BARREN GEASON SAPLESS STERILE WOODSERE
UNPRODUCTIVENESS BORASCO BORASQUE BORRASCA
UNPROFESSIONAL LAY BUSH LAICAL JACKLEG
UNPROFITABLE BAD DRY DEAD LEAN SECK BARREN BOOTLESS GAINLESS UNGAINLY
UNPROGRESSIVE SLOW DORMANT BACKWARD
UNPROMISING BLUE DUBIOUS
UNPRONOUNCED MUTE
UNPROPITIOUS ILL EVIL FOUL THRAW MALIGN SULLEN ADVERSE AVERTED INFAUST OMINOUS THRAWART
UNPROTECTED NAKED EXPOSED HELPLESS
UNPROVOKED WANTON
UNPUBLISHED INED INEDITED
UNQUALIFIED NET BARE FULL MERE PURE VERY BLACK PLUMP SHEER UNFIT DIRECT ENTIRE UNABLE CLOTTED PLENARY IMPLICIT INHABILE POSITIVE
UNQUESTIONABLE ASSURED CERTAIN DECIDED ABSOLUTE DECISIVE DISTINCT
UNQUESTIONED CLEAR
UNQUESTIONING IMPLICIT
UNRAVEL REDD UNDO BREAK ENODE FEAZE RAVEL RETEX SOLVE EVOLVE TIFFLE UNFOLD UNKNIT UNLACE ENODATE RESOLVE
UNREAL VAIN AERIAL GOTHIC CHEMICK FANCIED SHADOWY AERIFORM CHIMERIC FARCICAL ILLUSORY NOTIONAL SCENICAL VISIONAL (PREF.) PSEUD(O)
UNREALISTIC CHIMERIC
UNREALIZED BEHIND
UNREASONABLE ABSURD FANATIC ABSONANT
UNREASONABLENESS ALOGY INSANITY
UNREASONABLY SINFULLY
UNREASONING BRUTE RABID
UNRECOGNIZED UNSUNG CRYPTIC UNWITTED
UNRECOVERABLE DEAD
UNRECTIFIED IMPURE
UNREDEEMED CHEAP

UNREFINED RAW DARK LOUD BRUTE CRUDE DORIC GROSS COARSE COMMON EARTHY JUNGLY VULGAR BOORISH UNCOUTH UNKEMPT DREADFUL SWAINISH
UNREFLECTING GLIB VACANT
UNREGENERACY ADAM
UNREGENERATE NATURAL
UNREGENERATELY MANLY
UNREHEARSED IMPROMPTU
UNRELATED FREMD STRAY UNAKIN UNTOLD EXTREME FRAMMIT POSITIVE
UNRELAXED UNSLAKED
UNRELAXING TONIC
UNRELENTING GRIM HARD IRON CRUEL STERN BRASSY SEVERE RIGOROUS
UNRELIABLE FISHY SHADY FICKLE GREASY UNSAFE CASALTY STREAKY WILDCAT FECKLESS GLIBBERY SLIPPERY TICKLISH
UNRELIEVED DEAD BRUTE ABJECT EXQUISITE
UNREMITTING BUSY FAST HARD DOGGED
UNREMUNERATIVE HONORARY
UNRESERVED FREE CLEAN FRANK ROUND COMMON UNCLOSE EXPLICIT
UNRESERVEDNESS FREEDOM
UNRESISTING BUXOM
UNRESPONSIVE DEAD DUMB BARREN SILENT STUBBORN
UNREST MOTION AILMENT DISREST WANREST DISQUIET CHEMISTRY PSYCHOSIS
UNRESTRAINED LAX MAD FREE WILD BROAD FANTI FRANK LARGE LOOSE FACILE FANTEE LAVISH UNTIED WANTON FLYAWAY RAMPANT RIOTOUS BARBARIC FAMILIAR FREEHAND LAXATIVE PINDARIC ABANDONED LIBERTINE
UNRESTRAINT LICENSE IMMUNITY
UNRESTRICTED FREE GLOBAL SOVRAN UNZONED ABSOLUTE
UNRETURNED UNYOLDEN
UNREVEALED UNTOLD
UNRHYMED BLANK
UNRIG STRIP
UNRIGHTEOUSNESS ADHARMA
UNRIPE RAW CRUDE GREEN CALLOW UNCURED IMMATURE
UNROBE DISROBE UNDRESS DISARRAY
UNROLL EVOLVE UNCURL DEVELOP OUTROLL TRINDLE UNTREND
UNROOF TIRL TIRR TIRVE DISROOF
UNRUFFLE SMOOTH SOOTHE MOLLIFY
UNRUFFLED CALM COOL EASY EVEN QUIET SOBER STILL ASLEEP PLACID SEDATE SERENE SMOOTH DECOROUS
UNRULY HIGH RAMP ROYT TOUGH HAUNTY WANTON LAWLESS RAMMAGE ROPABLE UNRULED VICIOUS WANRULY WAYWARD INDOCILE MUTINOUS CAMSTAIRY

REFRACTORY OBSTREPEROUS RAMBUNCTIOUS
UNSADDLE OUTSPAN UNPANEL
UNSAFE HOT FISHY EXPOSED INSECURE PERILOUS
UNSANCTIFIED PROFANE
UNSATISFACTORY BAD ILL EVIL POOR CROOK LOUSY SHREWD WRETCHED
UNSATISFYING DUSTY HOLLOW
UNSATURATED (PREF.) EN
UNSAVORY WERSH INSIPID WEARISH
UNSAY WITHDRAW
UNSCHOLARLY BOOKLESS
UNSCRUPULOUS SKIN CROOK BRAZEN DEVIOUS JACKLEG DEXTROUS RASCALLY
UNSEASONABLE LAT UNRIPE UNTIDY UNCHANCY UNTIMELY
UNSEASONED RAW GREEN
UNSEAT ADDRESS DISSEAT
UNSEEING BLIND GAZELESS
UNSEEMLY HOIDEN UNFAIR IMPROPER INDECENT SEEMLESS UNMEETLY UNWORTHY
UNSEEN SECRET UNEYED CRYPTIC VIEWLESS
UNSERRIED LOOSE
UNSETTLE JAR TURN UNFIX UNSET UPSET COMMOVE DERANGE DISTURB STAGGER UNHINGE UNQUEME DISORDER DISQUIET DISTRACT
UNSETTLED MOOT LIGHT SHAKY UNSAD VAGUE BROKEN FICKLE QUEASY VAGOUS DUBIOUS NOMADIC SHUTTLE UNSTAID RESTLESS UNSTABLE VAGABOND
UNSETTLING NASTY
UNSHAKABLE DOGGED ADAMANT IRONCLAD
UNSHAKEN FIRM STEADY UNMOVED UNSHOOK CONSTANT RESOLUTE
UNSHAPELY DEFORMED UNMACKLY
UNSHARED SOLE
UNSHEATHE DISCASE
UNSHEATHED BARE
UNSHELTERED BLEAK
UNSHOD BAREFOOT DISCALCED
UNSHORN UNPOLLED
UNSIGHTLY UGLY AWFUL MESSY HOMELY INDECENT
UNSKILLED JAY PUNY GREEN PUISNE UNGAIN UNSEEN STRANGE FECKLESS
UNSKILLFUL ILL EVIL RUDE ARTLESS AWKWARD UNFEATY BUNGLING TINKERLY UNHEPPEN
UNSMILING GLUM AUSTERE
UNSOCIABLE SULLEN FAROUCHE INSOCIAL
UNSOILED CLEAN
UNSOPHISTICATE SQUARE
UNSOPHISTICATED JAY NAIF PURE FRANK GREEN NAIVE SILLY CALLOW SIMPLE BUCOLIC NATURAL VERDANT HOMEBRED HOMESPUN INNOCENT PROVINCIAL

UNSOUND BAD ILL EVIL SICK
ADDLE BARMY CRAZY CRONK
DICKY DOTTY DOZED SANDY
SHAKY WONKY ABSURD FAULTY
FLAWED HOLLOW INFIRM INSANE
ROTTEN UNHALE INVALID
RICKETY UNWHOLE
UNSOUNDNESS CRACK INSANITY
UNSPARING DRASTIC SCATHING
UNSPIRITUAL CARNAL
UNSPOILED RACY UNSHENT
PRISTINE
UNSPOKEN TACIT SILENT
UNSPORTSMANLIKE DIRTY
UNSPOTTED CLEAR SPOTLESS
UNSPUN RAW
UNSTABLE FLUX BATTY LOOSE
SANDY BROTEL CHOPPY FICKLE
FITFUL FLITTY LABILE LUBRIC
ROTTEN SHIFTY TICKLE UNFIRM
WANKLE WANKLY DWAIBLE
DWAIBLY DWEEBLE RICKETY
SLIDDER SLIDDRY VOLUBLE
FEVERISH FIRMLESS FUGITIVE
INSECURE LUBRICAL REMUABLE
SKITTISH SLIPPERY TICKLISH
TOTTLISH VARIABLE
(MENTALLY —) BRAINISH
UNSTEADILY GROGGILY
UNSTEADINESS FALTER
UNSTEADY WALT CRANK CRONK
DOTTY FLUKY LIGHT NERVY
SLACK TIPPY TIPSY TOTTY UNSAD
WALTY WONKY COGGLY FICKLE
FLICKY FLUFFY GROGGY JIGGLY
JOGGLY SWIMMY TOTTIE WAFFLY
WAGGLY WAMBLY WANKLE
WEEWAW WEEWOW DODDERY
GLAIKIT JIGGETY QUAVERY
QUEACHY TITTUPY TOTTERY
WAYWARD SKITTISH STAGGERY
TICKLISH TITUBANT UNSTABLE
VARIABLE VERSATILE
UNSTINTED LAVISH ENDLESS
UNSTRESS SLACK
UNSTRESSED SHORT
UNSTRING DISSOLVE
UNSTUDIED GLIB CASUAL
CARELESS GLANCING
UNSUBDUED VIRGIN UNBOWED
UNSUBSTANTIAL TOY AIRY LIMP
THIN WINDY AERIAL BUBBLE
CHAFFY FLIMSY SLEAZY SLEEZY
SLIGHT UNREAL FOLIOUS FRAGILE
INSOLID SHADOWY TENUOUS
FILIGREE FINESPUN FOOTLESS
GIMCRACK VAPOROUS
PASTEBOARD
UNSUCCESSFUL BAD MANQUE
UNSPED STICKIT UNHAPPY
ABORTIVE
UNSUITABLE INEPT UNAPT
UNDUE UNFIT UNKIND UNMETE
UNCOMELY UNGAINLY UNLIKELY
UNSUITABLENESS IMPOLICY
UNSUITED BAD
UNSULLIED FAIR PURE CLEAR
VIRGIN INNOCENT SPOTLESS
VIRGINAL
UNSUPPLIED HELPLESS
UNSUPPORTED BLIND NAKED
BACKWARD STAYLESS
UNSURE TIMID INFIRM DOUBTFUL

INSECURE UNSICKER
UNSURPASSED CHAMPION
UNSUSPECTING INNOCENT
UNSWEET UNSOOT
UNSWERVING FIXED FLUSH LOYAL
DIRECT STEADY STRICT STURDY
STAUNCH
UNSWERVINGLY HEADLONG
UNSYMMETRICAL LOPSIDED
UNSYMPATHETIC DRY HARD
STONY FROZEN GLASSY HOSTILE
KINDLESS
UNTAINTED FREE GOOD PURE
INNOCENT
UNTAMED WILD FERAL RAMAGE
SAVAGE HAGGARD RAMMISH
WARRAGAL
UNTANGLE FREE SLEAVE UNLACE
UNTARNISHED PURE
UNTAUGHT WASTE UNLERED
IGNORANT
UNTHINKABLE PUERILE
UNTHINKING GLIB BRUTE CASUAL
FECKLESS HEEDLESS
UNTHINKINGLY STUPID
UNTIDINESS JAKES LITTER
UNTIDY DOWDY GAUMY MESSY
ROOKY BUNTING DRAGGLY
LITTERY RUMMAGY SCRUFFY
UNSIDED DRAGGLED SLOVENLY
STRUBBLY UNHEPPEN
UNTIE UNDO UNBIND UNLASH
UNLATCH UNTRUSS UNTWINE
UNFASTEN
UNTIL AD OR TO GIN HENT INTO
UNTO FORTO TWELL WHILE
WHILES WHILST PENDING
(— THEN) BEFORE
UNTILLED INCULT UNEARED
UNTIMELY UNTIDY IMMATURE
PREVIOUS TIMELESS
UNTIRING BUSY SEDULOUS
TIRELESS
UNTITLED (— MEN) AUMAGA
UNTO TILL
UNTOLD VAST UNQUOD
UNTOUCHABLE DOM HARIJAN
CHANDALA
(PL.) PANCHAMA
UNTOUCHED FREE INTACT
PRISTINE
(PREF.) INTEGRI
UNTOWARD ILL UNRULY
FROWARD WAYWARD
UNTRAINED RAW RUDE GREEN
HAGGARD
UNTRAMMELED FREE
UNTRIED MAIDEN UNSOUGHT
UNTRIMMED UNTEWED
UNTRODDEN PATHLESS
UNFOOTED
UNTROUBLED CHEERY
UNTRUE FLAM FALSE LEASE
WRONG UNFAST DISLOYAL
MENDACIOUS
(PREF.) PSEUD(O)
UNTRUSTWORTHINESS FALSITY
UNTRUSTWORTHY PUNIC SHAKY
LIMBER TRICKY UNSURE
SLIDDERY SLIPPERY
UNTRUTH LIE FABLE LEASE
SKLENT FALSITY UNTROTH
MENDACITY

UNTRUTHFUL SLANTER
UNTUNABLE ABSONANT
UNTUTORED NATURAL IGNORANT
PRIMITIVE
UNTWILLED PLAIN
UNTWINE FRESE UNTWIST
UNTWIST FAG FEAZE UNLAY
UNSPIN UNTWIRL
UNTWISTED SLEIDED
UNUSABLE WASTE INUTILE
UNUSED IDLE FRESH WASTE
INURED MAIDEN VACANT
DERELICT INITIATE UNWONTED
UNUSUAL ODD EERY RARE SELD
TALL CRAZY EERIE FORBY NOVEL
UTTER WEIRD EXEMPT FORBYE
SCREWY SINGLE UNIQUE
STRANGE ABNORMAL DISTINCT
ESPECIAL INSOLENT KNOCKOUT
SELCOUTH SINGULAR SPANKING
UNCOMMON UNTRADED
UNWONTED PRODIGIOUS
(PREF.) ANOM(O)
UNUSUALLY EXTRA
UNVARIED SAMELY
UNVARNISHED EVERYDAY
UNVARYING FLAT SAME FRANK
LEVEL STABLE UNIFORM
UNVEIL REVEAL UNCOVER
UNCROWN UNDRAPE UNSCREEN
UNWIMPLE
UNVENTILATED CLOSE
UNVERSED STRANGE
UNWANTED STRAY TRAMP
FAULTY
UNWARRANTED UNDUE
UNWARY RASH UNAWARE
CARELESS HEEDLESS WARELESS
UNWASHED SOAPLESS
UNWASTEFUL FRUGAL
UNWAVERING FIRM CLEAN LEVEL
SOLID GLASSY STABLE EXPRESS
STAUNCH
UNWAVERINGLY FAST
UNWEAKENED CLEAR
UNWELL BAD ILL EVIL PUNK SICK
BADLY CROOK SEEDY AILING
CHIPPY WICKED COMICAL
UNWHOLESOME ILL EVIL SICK
CAGMAG IMPURE MORBID SICKLY
CORRUPT NOISOME NOXIOUS
UNCLEAN DISEASED EPINOSIC
UNWIELDY BULKY CLUMSY
UNRIDE AWKWARD HULKING
CUMBROUS UNGAINLY
UNWILLING CHARY LOATH SWEER
WERSE AVERSE ESCHEW
BACKWARD GRUDGING
UNWILLINGLY MAUGER MAUGRE
UNWILLINGNESS GRUDGE
NOLITION
UNWIND UNCLEW UNREEL
UNREAVE UNTWINE
UNWISE FALSE INANE SILLY
SIMPLE FOOLISH WITLESS
UNWITTING UNWIST WEETLESS
UNWOMANLY MANKIND
UNWORLDLY WEIRD ASTRAL
SPIRITUAL
UNWORTHY BASE INDIGN
BENEATH UNDIGNE WANWORDY
UNWOUNDED COLD
UNWREATHE UNPLAT

UNWRINKLED BRANT BRENT
UNWROUGHT RAW LIVE
UNYIELDING PAT SET ACID DOUR
FAST FIRM GRIM HARD RIGID
STARK STEEL STIFF STITH STONY
TOUGH FLINTY FROZEN GLASSY
KNOBBY MARBLE STEELY STURDY
ADAMANT AUSTERE COSTIVE
FROWARD CHURLISH OBDURATE
OBEDIENT STUBBORN
PERTINACIOUS
UNYOKE LOWSE UNTEAM
OUTSHUT OUTSPAN
UNYOKED
(PREF.) AZYGO
UP ON ONE OOP ABOUT ASTIR
DORMY DORMIE
(— AND ABOUT) AFOOT
(— TO) INTO
(— TO THE TIME) UNTIL
(— YONDER) UPBY UPBYE
(FARTHER —) ABOVE
(HIGH —) ALOFT
(PREF.) ANA ANO SUR
UPANISHAD ISHA KATHA
UPAS DITA ANTIAR CHETTIK
UPBEAT ARSIS AUFTAKT
ANACRUSIS
UP-BOW POUSSE
UPBRAID CHEW RAIL SNUB TUCK
TWIT ABUSE ROUSE SCOLD
TAUNT UPBRAY EMBRAID
REPROVE DISGRACE OUTBRAID
UPCARD STARTER
UPFOLD SADDLE ANTICLINE
UPHEAVAL BOIL STORM UPLIFT
RUMMAGE UPTHROW
UPHILL UPBANK UPWITH
UPHOLD AID TOM ABET BACK
FAVOR AFFIRM ASSERT DEFEND
SOOTHE BOLSTER SUPPORT
SUSTAIN CHAMPION MAINTAIN
PRESERVE
UPHOLDER DEFENDER ERASTIAN
FEUDALIST
UPHOLDING BEHIND
UPHOLSTER SQUAB
UPHOLSTERER TAPISER
UPHOLDER
UPKEEP MAINTENANCE
UPLAND DOWN DOWNS MAUKA
COTEAU FASTLAND
(PL.) BRAES DOWNS
UPLAND PLOVER QUAILY
HILLBIRD PAPABOTE
UPLIFT TOSS BOOST TOWER
UPTHRUST
UPLIFTED ERECT EXALTEE
UPON ON PON SUR INTO OVER
ABOVE AGAINST
(— THAT) THEREAT
(PREF.) EP EPH EPI OB
UPPER OVER VAMP SKIVE VAMPEY
SUPERIOR
(PL.) FINISH
(PREF.) ANO HYPER SUPERO
(SITUATED ON — SIDE) SUPRA
UPPERCUT BOLO
UPPER HURONIAN LAWSON
UPPERMOST UMEST UPMOST
OVEREST BUNEMOST OVERMOST
UPPER VOLTA (CAPITAL OF —)
OUAGADOUGOU

(LANGUAGE OF —) BOBO LOBI SAMO MANDE MOSSI
(MOUNTAIN IN —) TEMA
(NATIVE OF —) BOBO LOBI SAMO BISSA HAUSA MANDE MARKA MOSSI PUEHL TUAREG SENOUFO VOLTAIC YATENGA MANDINGO
(RIVER IN —) VOLTA SOUROU
(TOWN OF —) PO LEO DORI PAMA YAKO DJIBO GAOUA LAWRA HOUNDE TOUGAN BANFORA
UPRAISED SUBLIME
UPRIGHT FAIR GOOD HARR JUST PROP STUD TIDY TRUE ANEND CHEEK ERECT GUIDE JELLY MORAL RIGHT ROMAN SETUP STALE STALK STILE ARRECT DIRECT ENTIRE HONEST SQUARE FRIZZEN HOUSING JANNOCK PITPROP SINCERE INNOCENT RIGHTFUL STANDARD STANDING STRAIGHT VERTICAL VIRTUOUS
(NOT —) ATILT BEVEL
(PL.) STUDDING
(PREF.) ORTH(O)
UPRIGHTNESS HONOR TRUTH APLOMB EQUITY HONESTY PROBITY JUSTNESS SINCERITY
UPRISING RIOT EMEUTE MUTINY PUTSCH REVOLT TUMULT UPRISE UPRISAL REBELLION
UPROAR DIN RUT CAIN FLAW GILD HELL MOIL RIOT ROUT BABEL BURLE CHANG FUROR HURLY RUMOR STOUN STOUR CLAMOR DIRDUM EMEUTE FRACAS HABBLE HUBBLE HUBBUB RANDAN RATTLE RIPPET RUCKUS RUMBLE RUMPUS SHINDY STEVEN STOUND TUMULT CATOUSE FERMENT GARBOIL GAUSTER ORATION OUTROAR RUCTION STASHIE TURMOIL BALLYHOO BROUHAHA SCOUTHER STIRRING STRAMASH TINTAMAR CHARIVARI SHEMOZZLE PANDEMONIUM
UPROARIOUS FURIOUS ROUTOUS
UPROOT HACK LOUK MORE UNROUT UNPLANT DISPLANT ROOTWALT SUPPLANT
UPROOTED LUMPEN
UPSET ILL TIP TOP TUP CAVE COUP COWP FUSS JUMP PURL ROCK TILT TURN WELT EVERT KNOCK ROUSE SHAKE SKAIL SKELL SPILL WHELM BOTHER DISMAY QUELME TIPPLE TOPPLE UPCAST WALTER CAPSIZE DERANGE DISTURB FRAZZLE HAYWIRE OVERSET PERVERT REVERSE SLATTER SUBVERT TEMPEST TURMOIL CAPSIZAL DISTRAIT OVERTILT OVERTURN STREAKED SUPPLANT TURNOVER OVERTHROW
(EASILY —) FUSSY FLAPPABLE
UPSHOT ISSUE SHORT UPSET EFFECT SEQUEL UPPING OUTCOME UPSHOOT UPSTROKE
UPSIDE-DOWN CRAZY REVERSE OVERHAND UPSEDOUN
UPSILON
(PREF.) YPSILI

UPSTAIRS ABOVE
UPSTANDING GRADELY
UPSTART KIP QUAT SNIP SNOB SQUIRT UPSKIP DALTEEN PARVENU ARRIVIST MUSHROOM SKIPJACK UPSPRING
UP-TO-DATE MOD MODERN TRENDY ABREAST TODAYISH
UPWARD ALOFT UPLONG UPWAYS UPWITH SKYWARD UPALONG UPWARDS
(PREF.) ANO
UPWARD-MOVING ANABATIC
URAEUS ASP
URAMIL MUREXAN
URANUS OURANOS HERSCHEL
(WIFE OF —) GAEA
URAO TRONA
URARTAEAN KHALDIAN
URARTU VAN
URATE LITHATE
URBAN TOWN URBIC URBANE BURGHAL OPPIDAN
URBANE CIVIL SUAVE POLITE SVELTE AMIABLE GRACIOUS
URBANITY COMITY SUAVITY COURTESY ELEGANCE
URCHIN IMP WAIF ELFIN GAMIN KEELIE NIPPER HURCHEON
(PREF.) (SEA —) ECHIN(O)
URD MUNGO
URDEE MATELEY
URDU REKHTA REKHTI MOORISH
URDUR (SISTER OF —) SKULD VERTHANDI
URGE ART DUN EGG HIE PLY PUT SIC SUE TAR YEN BROD COAX CRAM EDGE FIRK GOAD MOVE PING POKE PUSH SICK SPUR WHIP CROWD DRIVE FILIP FORCE HOOSH IMPEL LABOR PRESS PRICK SPANK TREAT COMPEL DEHORT DESIRE ENGAGE EXCITE FILLIP HARDEN HOICKS HUSTLE INCITE INDUCE INVITE MOTION PROMPT PROPEL STRAIN THREAP THREAT ANIMATE COMMOVE ENFORCE INSTANT OPPRESS PERSIST SOLICIT SUGGEST URGENCY ADMONISH INSTANCE PERSUADE
(— IMPORTUNATELY) DUN PRESS
(— ON) EGG ERT HAG SOOL WHIG ALARM CHIRK CROWD DRIVE FILIP HASTE HURRY IMPEL ROWEL YOICK ALARUM FILLIP HARDEN HASTEN INCITE
(— ON A HORSE) HUP CRAM CHUCK
(— STRONGLY) EXHORT SOLICIT
(— WITH VEHEMENCE) DING
URGENCY NEED PRESS STRESS COGENCE COGENCY URGENCE EXIGENCY INSTANCE INSTANCY PRESSURE
URGENT HOT DIRE LOUD RASH ACUTE HASTY STRONG BURNING CLAMANT EXIGENT INSTANT URGEFUL CRITICAL PRESSING PRESSIVE NECESSITOUS
URGING QUEST
URI (SON OF —) GEBER BEZALEEL
URIAH (WIFE OF —) BATHSHEBA

URIAL SHA OORIAL
URIEL (DAUGHTER OF —) MAACHAH
(FATHER OF —) TAHATH
URIJAH (FATHER OF —) SHEMAIAH
URINAL DUCK PISSOIR SANITARY
URINATE WET LEAK EMPTY STALE PIDDLE EVACUATE MICTURATE
URINATION MICTION NOCTURIA
URINE MIG SIG LAGE LANT WASH STALE WATER NETTING EMICTION
(— USED AS COSMETIC) LOTIUM
(PREF.) UR(O) URIC(O) URIN(I)(O)
(SUFF.) URIA URIC
URN JAR EWER KIST URNA VASE CAPANNA
(— FOR MAKING TEA) KITCHEN SAMOVAR
(— IN KENO) GOOSE
(BURIAL —) OSSUARY
(CINERARY —) DINOS DEINOS
(STONE —) STEEN
URN-SHAPED URCEOLAR
UROCHORDA ASCIDIA TUNICATA
UROPYGIUM RUMP
UROSTYLE COCCYX
URSA MAJOR OKNARI CHARIOT WAGONER WAGGONER
URSINE ARCTOID
URTICARIA HIVES UREDO CNIDOSIS
URTICASTRUM LAPORTEA
URUBU ZOPILOTE

URUGUAY
CAPITAL: MONTEVIDEO
DEPARTMENT: ROCHA SALTO FLORES RIVERA ARTIGAS COLONIA DURAZNO FLORIDA SORIANO
ESTUARY: PLATA
LAKE: MERIN MIRIM DIFUNTOS
MEASURE: VARA LEGUA CUADRA SUERTE
RIVER: MALO MIRIM NEGRO ULIMAR CUAREIM QUEGUAY YAGUARON CEBOLLATI
TOWN: MELO AIGUA MINAS PANDO ROCHA SALTO VERAS RIVERA DURAZNO FLORIDA MERCEDES PAYSANDU
WEIGHT: QUINTAL

URUGUAYAN ORIENTAL
URUS TUR URE AUROCHS
US HIS HIZ HUZ
U.S.A. (AUTHOR OF —) DOSPASSOS
(CHARACTER IN —) ANN BEN JOE MAC MARY WARD DELLA FAINY JANEY MARGO TRENT FRENCH MAISIE SAVAGE STAPLE STRANG CHARLEY COMPTON DOWLING ELEANOR EVELINE RICHARD SPENCER ANDERSON GERTRUDE HUTCHINS MCCREARY STODDARD WILLIAMS ANNABELLE MOOREHOUSE
USABLE FIT UTILE SERVABLE
USAGE USE ASAL FORM WONE HABIT HAUNT SUNNA USURE CUSTOM MANNER FASHION HALACHA HALAKAH USATION PRACTICE
(BAD —) ABUSAGE

(HARD —) GRIEF
(ILL —) ABUSE
(RELIGIOUS —) RITUS
(PL.) CEREMONY
(PREF.) NOM(O)
(SUFF.) NOMY
USE URE BOOT CALL DUTY HAVE NAIT NOTE USUS WISE APPLY AVAIL GUIDE HABIT SPEND STEAD TREAT USAGE WASTE BEHOOF EMPLOY FINISH HANDLE OCCUPY USANCE ACCOUNT ADHIBIT ENTREAT IMPROVE PURPOSE SERVICE UTILITY ACCUSTOM EXERCISE FUNCTION PRACTICE
(— AS WONTED) ADOPT
(— EXPERIMENTALLY) TRY
(— FIGURE OF SPEECH) TROPE
(— IMPROPERLY) ABUSE
(— INDISCRIMINATELY) HACK
(— OF MORE WORDS THAN NECESSARY) PLEONASM
(— OF NEW WORD) NEOLOGY
(— OF SUBTERFUGE) CHICANE
(— UP) EAT TIRE WEAR SHOOT ABSORB DEVOUR EXPEND GUZZLE PERUSE CONSUME EXHAUST OVERWEAR
(— WASTEFULLY) SPILL
(— WITH FULL COMMAND) WIELD
(EXCESSIVE — OF FACE AND HANDS) ABHINAYA
(FOR TEMPORARY —) JURY
(FRUGAL —) SPARE
(GENERAL —) CURRENCY
(LITURGICAL —) RITE
(MUCH IN —) GREAT
(UNRESTRICTED —) FREEDOM
(WRONG —) ABUSE
(PREF.) USU
USED WONT
(— CONTINUOUSLY) HOT
(— IN FLIGHT) VOLAR
(— UP) ALL BEAT SHOT SPENT FOREWORN
(MUCH —) GREAT HACKNEY
USEFUL GAIN GOOD UTILE UTIBLE HELPFUL THRIFTY BEHOVELY UTENSILE BEHOVEFUL
(— FOR LONG TIME) HARD
(SUFF.) CHRESIS CHRESTIC CHRESTO
USEFULNESS USE AVAIL VALUE WORTH PROFIT MILEAGE UTILITY
USELESS IDLE LEWD VAIN VOID WIDE EMPTY DOLESS GROTTY NOUGHT OTIOSE SCREWY TRASHY INUTILE STERILE VAINFUL BOOTLESS FOOTLESS FOOTLING WASTEFUL
USELESSNESS FUTILITY IDLENESS
USER USUS
(SUFF.) STER STRESS
USHABTI SHAWABTI
USHER BOW USH SHOW CRIER HERALD ISCHAR SEATER VERGER CHOBDAR HUISHER JANITOR MARSHAL STEWARD
USSR (SEE RUSSIA)
USUAL RIFE NOMIC COMMON FAMOUS NORMAL SOLEMN VULGAR WONTED AVERAGE

GENERAL NATURAL REGULAR TYPICAL USITATE EVERYDAY FREQUENT HABITUAL ORDINARY ORTHODOX ACCUSTOMED

USURER SHARK GAVELER HARPAGON

USURP ASSUME INVADE PRESUME ACCROACH ARROGATE

USURY GAVEL OCKER USURE USANCE GOMBEEN

UTAH

CAPITAL: SALTLAKECITY
COLLEGE: WEBER
COUNTY: IRON JUAB CACHE PIUTE CARBON SEVIER TOOELE UINTAH SANPETE
INDIAN: UTE
LAKE: SALT SWAN SEVIER
MOTTO: INDUSTRY
MOUNTAIN: LENA LION WAAS KINGS PEALE TRAIL FRISCO NAVAJO SWASEY GRANITE GRIFFIN HAWKINS PENNELL LINNAEUS
MOUNTAIN RANGE: CEDAR HENRY HOGUP UINTA WAHWAH TERRACE CONFUSION
NATIONAL PARK: ZION
NICKNAME: MORMON BEEHIVE
RIVER: WEBER JORDAN SEVIER
STATE BIRD: SEAGULL
STATE FLOWER: SEGOLILY
STATE TREE: SPRUCE
TOWN: LOA MOAB OREM DELTA HEBER KANAB LOGAN MAGNA MANTI NEPHI OGDEN PRICE PROVO KEARNS TOOELE VERNAL BRIGHAM BOUNTIFUL COALVILLE

UTENSIL (ALSO SEE IMPLEMENT AND TOOL) HOD BOAT IRON MOLD PECK STEW BAKER FRIER FRYER GRILL KNIFE MOULD RICER SCOOP SHEET SHELL SIEVE SLICE ULLER BEATER BEETLE BREWER COOKER DABBER FUNNEL GRATER GRILLE KETTLE LINGEL MASKER POPPER PUSHER SHAKER SIFTER BRAZIER BROILER DUSTPAN FLIPPER GLUEPOT MUDDLER SCUMMER SKIMMER STEAMER STIRRER TOASTER CALABASH GRIDIRON SAUCEPAN SAUCEPOT SHREDDER SPOUCHER STRAINER
(— FOR COVERING FIRE) CURFEW
(COOKING —) WOK
(LITURGICAL —) ASTERISK
(PL.) BATTERY COOKWARE IRONWARE

UTERUS WOMB BELLY METRA MATRIX BEARING
(PREF.) METR(O)

UTHAI (FATHER OF —) BIGVAI AMMIHUD

UTILITARIAN USEFUL ECONOMIC

UTILITY USE AVAIL USAGE PROFIT BENEFIT SERVICE

UTILIZE USE EMPLOY ENLIST CONSUME EXPLOIT HARNESS HUSBAND

UTILIZING
(SUFF.) IC(AL)

UTMOST END NTH BEST LAST MOST FINAL EXTREME OUTMOST SUPREME DAMNDEST POSSIBLE UTTEREST

UTOPIA ZION

UTOPIAN IDEAL

UTOPIANISM FUTURISM

UTRAQUIST CALIXTIN

UTRICULUS ALVEUS

UTTER ASK OUT SAY BARK BLOW BOOM DEAD DRIB EMIT FAIR GASP GIVE HURL MAIN MOOT MOVE PASS PURE RANK SEND TELL VENT VERY BLACK COUGH CRUDE FETCH FRAME FRANK GROSS ISSUE MOUTH RAISE SHEER SOUND SPEAK SPELL STARK THICK TOTAL VOICE ACCENT ARRANT BROACH

DAMNED DIRECT INTONE PARLEY PROFER PROPER TONGUE BLUSTER BREATHE DELIVER ENOUNCE EXCLAIM EXPRESS OUTMOST OUTTELL PERFECT PROLATE UPBRAID ABSOLUTE BLINKING COMPLETE CRASHING INTONATE BLITHERING
(— ABRUPTLY) BLURT
(— AFFECTEDLY) KNAP MINCE
(— ARGUMENTS) BLAZE
(— CASUALLY) DROP
(— EXPLOSIVELY) BOLT
(— FALSEHOODS) FABLE
(— FOOLISHLY) BLABBER
(— GLIBLY) SCREED
(— HALTINGLY) BLUBBER
(— HURRIEDLY) CHOP
(— IN HARSH VOICE) GRIT GRATE
(— INADVERTENTLY) SLIP
(— INDISTINCTLY) CHEW
(— LOUD CRY) BRAY BLARE
(— LOUDLY) CRY BLAT CALL HALLO HALLOO HULLOO PRABBLE
(— LOW SOUNDS) MURMUR WHISPER
(— MEANINGLESS SOUNDS) BABBLE
(— RAPIDLY) FIRE CHATTER
(— RAUCOUSLY) BLAT
(— REPETITIVELY) CHIME
(— RHETORICALLY) DECLAIM
(— SOLEMNLY) SWEAR
(— STUPIDLY) BLUNDER
(— SUDDENLY) CRACK
(— UNCTUOUSLY) DROOL
(— VIGOROUSLY) FLING
(— WITH EFFORT) HEAVE

UTTERANCE CRY GAB CALL OSSE BLURT DITTY PAROL VOICE ACCENT ACTION BREATH CHORUS DRIVEL GIBBER ORACLE PAROLE TONGUE EXPRESS INKLING LALLING STATUTE DELIVERY FOOTNOTE HOMESPUN JUDGMENT LOCUTION SYLLABIC
(— FROM A DIVINITY) ORACLE
(— OF PRAISE) MAGNIFICAT

(— OF VOCAL SOUNDS) PHONESIS
(CONDEMNATORY —) INFAMY
(DEFECTIVE —) STAMMER
(FAINT —) INKLING
(FOOLISH —) DRIVEL
(FOOLISH —S) GUFF
(GUSHING —) EFFUSION
(IMPULSIVE —) BLURT
(INDISTINCT —) BUMBLE
(MALICIOUS —) SLANDER
(OFFENSIVE —) AFFRONT
(PROPHETIC —) OSSE
(PUBLIC —) AIR OUTGIVING
(SHORT —) DITTY
(SOLEMN —) EFFATE EFFATUM
(TRADITIONAL —) AGRAPHON
(VAPID —) CUCKOO
(PL.) BYRONICS

UTTERED SPOKEN

UTTERLY DOG BONE DEAD BLACK OUTLY PLUMB PROOF HOLLOW MERELY BLANKLY OUTERLY SHEERLY PROPERLY

UTU (FATHER OF —) NANNA

UVULA CION UVULE PLECTRUM STAPHYLE
(PREF.) CION(O) STAPHYL(O)

UVULARIA OAKESIA

UZ (FATHER OF —) ARAM NAHOR DISHAN
(GRANDFATHER OF —) SEIR SHEM

UZAI (SON OF —) PALAL

UZAL (FATHER OF —) JOKTAN

UZBEK JAGATAI

UZZAH (BROTHER OF —) AHIO
(FATHER OF —) ABINADAB

UZZI (FATHER OF —) BANI BELA TOLA BUKKI
(SON OF —) ZERAHIAH

UZZIAH (FATHER OF —) AMAZIAH
(SON OF —) ATHAIAH JEHONATHAN

UZZIEL (FATHER OF —) ISHI KOHATH HARHAIAH
(SON OF —) ZITHRI MISHAEL ELIZAPHAN

V

V VEE FIVE VICTOR
  (INVERTED —) CARET
VACANCY HOLE WANT VACUIT
  VACUITY VACATION
VACANT IDLE OPEN VOID BLANK
  EMPTY FISHY INANE WASTE
  DEVOID HOLLOW DORMANT
  UNFILLED
  (BECOME —) FALL
  (PREF.) VACUO
VACATE QUIT TOLL VOID AVOID
  EMPTY WAIVE VACANT ABANDON
  RESCIND ABROGATE EVACUATE
VACATION OUT REST LEAVE
  OUTING RECESS HOLIDAY
  NONTERM VACANCY
  (SUMMER —) LONG
VACCINE LYMPH BACTERIN
  BIOLOGIC
VACCINIA COWPOX
VACILLATE HALT SWAG WAVE
  DACKER DITHER HALPER TEETER
  WABBLE WAFFLE WOBBLE
  SHAFFLE STICKLE SWITHER
  WHIFFLE HESITATE
VACILLATING INFIRM MOBILE
  HALTING
VACILLATION SEESAW WAVERING
VACUITY BLOW VACANCY
  FONTANEL
VACUOLE GUTTA
VACUOUS DULL BLANK EMPTY
  SILLY VACANT
VACUUM GAPE VOID VACANCY
  VACUITY VACATION
VACUUM TUBE
  (SUFF.) TRON
VAGABOND BUM VAG HOBO KERN
  JAVEL ROGUE SHACK STIFF
  BRIBER CANTER HARLOT JOCKEY
  PICARA PICARO RODNEY RUNNER
  TAGRAG TRUANT WAFFIE
  COASTER ERRATIC FAITOUR
  GADLING GANGREL OUTCAST
  SCOURER SKELDER SWAGMAN
  SWINGER TINKLER TRUCKER
  VAGRANT VAURIEN WASTREL
  BOHEMIAN BRODYAGA CURSITOR
  CUSTROUN FUGITIVE GLASSMAN
  PALLIARD RAPPAREE RUNABOUT
  RUNAGATE WHIPJACK
VAGARY WHIM FANCY FREAK
  VAGUE CAPRICE CONCEIT
  CRANKUM FLAGARIE VAGRANCY
  (PL.) HUMORS
VAGINA
  (PREF.) COLP(O) ELYTR(O)
VAGINATE SHEATHED
VAGRANCY MOPERY ROGUING
VAGRANT BUM WAFF WAIF CAIRD
  PIKER PIKEY ROGUE SKELB STRAG
  TRAMP VAGUE ARRANT CASUAL
  SHAKER SHULER TINKER TRUANT

VAGROM VAGUER WAFFIE
  DEVIOUS DRIFTER ERRATIC
  FLOATER GANGREL ROGUISH
  SKILDER SWAGMAN TINKLER
  TRAMPER TROGGER BRODYAGA
  PLANETIC STROLLER VAGABOND
  SHACKLING
  (PL.) FLOTSAM
VAGUE LAX DARK HAZY FOGGY
  FUZZY GROSS LOOSE MISTY
  MUDDY WOOZY CLOUDY DREAMY
  MYSTIC SHAGGY BLURRED
  EVASIVE OBSCURE SHADOWY
  UNFIXED CONFUSED INFINITE
  NEBULOUS NUBILOUS
VAGUELY DIMLY DARKLY DUMBLY
  DREAMILY
VAIN MAD IDLE NULL PUFF VOID
  WANE COCKY EMPTY FLORY
  PROUD SAUCY VOGIE WASTE
  FLIMSY FUTILE HOLLOW OTIOSE
  VAUNTY BIGGITY CARRIED
  TRIVIAL VAINFUL BOOTLESS
  CONCEITY NUGATORY PEACOCKY
  VAPOROUS WASTEFUL
  (NOT —) SOLID
VAINGLORY POMP RUFF GLORY
  VANITY ELATION
VAINLY IDLY TOOMLY
VAIR POTENT
VAISRAVANA BISHAMON
VAISYA BAIS BICE
VAJEZATHA (FATHER OF —)
  HAMAN
VAJRA DORJE
VAKULA THE SMITH (CHARACTER
  IN —) CHUB DEVIL OXANA PANAS
  VAKULA SOLOKHA
  (COMPOSER OF —) TCHAIKOVSKY
VAL LACE
VALANCE PAND PELMET
  FRONTLET PALMETTE
VALE DALE DEAN DELL BACHE
  BATCH ENNIS
VALEDICTORY FAREWELL
VALENCE ADICITY ATOMISM
VALENTINE (SISTER OF —)
  GRETCHEN
  (SLAYER OF —) FAUST
VALERIAN HELIO BENNET SUMBUL
  ALLHEAL CUTHEAL SETWALL
  CETEWALE
VALERIC PENTOIC
VALET MAN ANDREW SIRDAR
  TARTAR WALLIE CRISPIN
  TIREMAN
VALIANT SAD BOLD BRAG PREU
  PROW WILD BRAVE LUSTY ORPED
  PROUD STOUT WIGHT FIERCE
  HEROIC DOUGHTY GAILLARD
  GALLIARD INTREPID STALWART
  VIRTUOUS
VALID FAIR GOOD JUST LEGAL

SOUND COGENT LAWFUL
  BINDING ETERNAL WEIGHTY
  FORCIBLE VAILABLE VALIDOUS
  VALUABLE
  (PREF.) RATI
VALIDATE FIRM SEAL VALID
  AFFIRM CONFIRM
VALIDITY FORCE VIGOR STRENGTH
VALISE BAG GRIP MAIL DORLACH
  SATCHEL VALLIES SUITCASE
VALKYRIE SHIELDMAY
VALLECULA VALLEY
VALLEY DIB GUT COMB COOM
  COVE DALE DELL DENE GILL HOLE
  HOPE HOWE HOYA PARK VALE
  WADI WADY ATRIO BACHE BREAK
  CHASM COMBE COOMB DHOON
  GHYLL GLACK GOYAL GOYLE
  HEUGH SLACK SLADE SWALE
  TEMPE YUNGA BOLSON BOTTOM
  CANADA CLOUGH COULEE
  DINGLE HOLLOW LAAGTE LEEGTE
  RINCON STRATH AIJALON
  BLOWOUT GEHENNA VAALITE
  (— BETWEEN CONES OF VOLCANO)
  ATRIO
  (— IN THESSALY) TEMPE
  (— ON MOON'S SURFACE) RILL
  CLEFT RILLE
  (— ON MT BLANC) NANT
  (CIRCULAR —) RINCON
  (DEEP —) CANON GRIKE CANYON
  (DROWNED —) VIA
  (FLAT-FLOORED DESERT —) BOLSON
  (GRASSY MOUNTAIN —) HOLE
  (LOWEST PART OF —) SOLE
  (MINIATURE —) GULLY GULLEY
  (NARROW —) DEAN DENE GLEN
  GLACK GOYLE GRIFF KLOOF
  CLOUGH
  (RIVER —) WATER
  (SECLUDED —) GLEN DINGLE
  (TRENCHLIKE —) COULEE
VALOR ARETE MERIT VALUE
  BOUNTY VALOUR BRAVERY
  COURAGE PROWESS STOMACH
  CHIVALRY VALIANCY
VALOROUS BOLD BRAVE
  VIRTUOUS
VALUABLE DEAR COSTLY PRIZED
  WORTHY EMINENT WEALTHY
  PRECIOUS PRIZABLE SINGULAR
VALUATION PRIZE VALOR VALUE
  ESTEEM EXTENT ESTIMATE
  TAXATION
VALUE SET COST FECK FOOT HOLD
  RATE TELL AVAIL CARAT CHEAP
  COUNT FORCE PRICE PRIZE
  STAMP STENT STOCK VALOR
  WORTH ASSESS ASSIZE EQUITY
  ESTEEM EXTENT FIGURE HIDAGE
  MATTER MOMENT PRAISE
  REGARD VALURE VALUTA VIRTUE

ACCOUNT ADVANCE APPRIZE
  CAPITAL CHERISH COMPUTE
  PRETIUM RESPECT VALENCY
  WERGILD ESTIMATE EVALUATE
  GOODWILL SPLENDOR TREASURE
  VALIDITY VALLIDOM
  (— HIGHLY) PRIZE ENDEAR
  (— OF ANGLE) EPOCH
  (— OF COW) SET
  (— OF TIMBER) STUMPAGE
  (ABSOLUTE —) MODULUS
  (AESTHETIC —) AMENITY
  (ESTABLISHED —) PAR
  (GOOD —) SNIP
  (MATHEMATICAL —) EXTREMUM
  (NEGATIVE —) DISVALUE
  (STUDY OF —) AXIOLOGY
  (TESTED —) ASSAY
  (PREF.) AXIO TIMO
VALUED DEAR
VALUELESS BAFF STRAWY
  NAUGHTY
VALVE TAP COCK DISC DISK GATE
  ORAL STOP CHOKE CLACK MIXER
  VALVA WAFER BINODE BOTTLE
  CUTOUT DAMPER KICKER PALLET
  POPPET POTLID SCUTUM SLUICE
  SUCKER VENTIL WASHER CLICKET
  DRAWOFF PETCOCK REDUCER
  SCALLOP SCOLLOP SHUTOFF
  VALVULA VALVULE DRAWGATE
  EPITHECA EPIVALVE STOPCOCK
  THROTTLE
  (— OF BARNACLE) SCUTUM
  (— OF MUSICAL INSTRUMENT)
  PISTON VENTIL
  (— OF PUMP BOX) FANG
  (ANATOMICAL —) TRICUSPID
  (THIN —) WAFER
  (TRIPLE —) KICKER
  (PREF.) THYRE(O) THYRO
  (SUFF.) THYRIS
VAMBRACE BRACELET
VAMOOSE SCRAM CHEESE
  DECAMP SKIDDOO
VAMPIRE LAMIA ALUKAH
VAN WAN FORE LEAD SAIL FRONT
  TRUCK VAUNT WAGON VAWARD
  CARAVAN FOURGON FOREWARD
  KHALDIAN
VANADATE UVANITE TURANITE
VANDAL HUN HUNLIKE SARACEN
  HOOLIGAN
VANDALIZE TRASH
VANE FAN TEE WEB COCK TAIL
  WING FAINE BUCKET TARGET
  DOGVANE FLIGHTER VEXILLUM
  (— OF ARROW) FEATHER
  (— OF CONVEYOR BELT) FLIGHT
  (— OF FEATHER) WEB FLUE
  VEXILLUM
  (— OF SURVEYING STAFF)
  TRANSOM

(— OF WINDMILL) FAN FANE TAIL FAINE
(COOLING — IN BREWING) FLIGHTER
VANESSA PYRAMEIS
VANGUARD FORLORN
VANIAH (FATHER OF —) BANI
VANISH DIE FLY DROP FADE FLEE MELT PASS SANT WEDE WEND CLEAR FLEET SAUNT SLIDE EXHALE EVANISH SCATTER CONQUEST DISSOLVE EVANESCE
(— BY DEGREES) DRILL
VANISHED LAPSED EXTINCT
VANITY ABEL POMP VAIN FOLLY PRIDE EGOISM CONCEIT FEATHER FOPPERY INANITY SANDUST IDLENESS IDLESHIP PRETENSION
VANITY FAIR (AUTHOR OF —) THACKERAY
(CHARACTER IN —) JOS PITT BECKY SHARP AMELIA DOBBIN GEORGE JOSEPH RAWDON SEDLEY STEYNE CRAWLEY OSBORNE WILLIAM
VANNER SLIMER
VANNIC KHALDIAN
VANQUISH GET WIN BEAT LICK MILL UTTER EXPUGN MASTER OUTRAY SUBDUE THRASH CONQUER OVERWIN SMOTHER CONQUEST OVERCOME SURMOUNT VENKISEN
VANQUISHED CRAVEN
VANUATU (CAPITAL OF —) VILA
(FORMER NAME OF —) NEWHEBRIDES
(ISLAND OF —) EPI EFATE MALEKULA PENTECOST ESPIRITUSANTO
(MONEY OF —) VATU
(VOLCANO OF —) TANNA AMBRYN LOPEVI
VAPID DRY DULL FADE FLAT STALE TRITE JEJUNE INSIPID WATERISH
VAPOR FOG FUME REEK ROKE STEW BOAST BRUME EWDER HUMOR SMOKE STEAM STIFE BREATH VAPOUR EXHAUST HALITUS
(HOT —) LUNT
(NOXIOUS —) DAMP
(PL.) BRUME
(PREF.) ATM(O) ATMID(O) MANO PNEUMAT(O) TYPH(O)
VAPORIZATION BURNUP BOILOFF
VAPORIZE DRIVE FLASH STEAM AERATE AERIFY VAPORATE
VAPOROUS FUMY FUMID HUMID FUMISH FUMOSE STEAMY VOLATILE
VARANGIAN VARIAG WARING
(PL.) ROS
VARIABILITY HETERISM
VARIABLE FLUX FREE CHOPPY FICKLE FITFUL KITTLE WRAIST CEPHEID FACIENT FLUXILE MUTABLE ROLLING STREAKY UNEQUAL VARIANT VARIOUS ARGUMENT FLOATING FLUXIBLE SHIFTING SKITTISH UNSTABLE VEERABLE
(EXCEEDINGLY —) PROTEAN
(RANDOM —) STATISTIC

VARIANCE ODDS DISCORD DISPUTE
VARIANT STATE VERSION
(— IN WHEAT) SPELTOID
(POSITIONAL —) ALLOPHONE
(PL.) DIAPHONE
VARIATION REX TURN ERROR ROGUE SHADE CHANGE DOUBLE JITTER SWITCH CYCLING DESCANT EXTREME SHADING VARIETY WINDING DIVISION DYNAMICS HETERISM MUTATION
(— IN AIR PRESSURE) ROBBING
(— IN CURRENT) SURGE
(— IN FREQUENCY) SWINGING
(— IN SPEED) HUNTING
(— OF COLOR) ABRASH
(— OF PUPIL OF EYE) HIPPUS
(— OF SHOE) SPRING
(— OF VOWELS) ABLAUT
(ALLOWABLE —) LEEWAY
(BALLET —) ATTITUDE
(TOPOGRAPHICAL —) BREAK
(PL.) PIBROCH
VARICOCELE RAMEX
VARIED SORTY DAEDAL SEVERAL VARIANT VARIOUS MANIFOLD
VARIED BUNTING PRUSIANO
VARIEGATE DROP FRET FLECK FREAK SHOOT AUMAIL DAPPLE STRIPE VARIFY CHECKER
VARIEGATED FAW PIED SHOT JASPE LYART SHELD DAEDAL MARLED MENALD MOSAIC SKEWED BROCKED BROCKIT CHECKED CLOUDED DAPPLED FREAKED FRETTED PECKLED SPARKED VARIOUS DISCOLOR FRECKLED OVERSHOT PANACHED SKEWBALD
(PREF.) POECIL(O)
VARIEGATION COLOR
VARIETY BREW FORM KIND MODE SORT BRAND BREED CLASS COLOR SPICE CHANGE NATURE STIRPS STRAIN STRIPE SPECIES VARIENS
VARIOLA HORSEPOX SMALLPOX
VARIOUS MANY SERE DIVERS SUNDER SUNDRY VARIED DIVERSE SEVERAL VARIANT MANIFOLD
(PREF.) PARTI POECIL(O) POEKIL(O)
VARISCITE UTAHITE
VARIX
(PREF.) CIRS(O)
VARLET BOY LAD GIPPO JIPPO PAVISER COISTREL VARLETTO
VARNISH DOPE JAPAN LACKER MEDIUM PUNDUM FIXATIF LACQUER VEHICLE VERMEIL FIXATIVE OVERGILD THEETSEE
VARY HUNT ALTER BREAK DRIFT SHIFT SPORT CHANGE DIFFER RECEDE VARIFY CHECKER DEVIATE DISSENT DIVERGE VARIATE DISAGREE OSCILLATE
VARYING CURRENT
VASE PYX URN OLLA VASA VASO ASKOS CYLIX DINOS DIOTA KYLIX PYXIS BASKET BOWPOT COTULA COTYLA CRATER DEINOS DOLIUM

FILLER HYDRIA KALPIS KOTYLE KRATER LEKANE SITULA AMPHORA AMPULLA CANOPUS PATELLA POTICHE PSYKTER SCYPHUS SKYPHOS STAMNOS URCEOLE BOUGHPOT LECYTHUS LEKYTHOS MURRHINE PROCHOOS
(— FOR PERFUME) CONCH
(— ON PEDESTAL) TAZZA
(—S UNDER THEATER SEATS) SCHEA
(PREF.) POTICHO VAS(I)(O) VASCUL(I)(O)
VASHNI (FATHER OF —) SAMUEL
VASHTI (HUSBAND OF —) AHASUERUS
VASODILATOR KELLIN KHELLIN
VASSAL MAN WER BOND LEUD SERF CEILE LIEGE SLAVE CLIENT GENEAT SACOPE BONDMAN FEEDMAN FEODARY HOMAGER RUDIGER SAMURAI SERVANT SUBJECT VAVASOR PALATINE
(PL.) MANRED
VASSALAGE MANRENT
VAST HUGE BROAD ENORM GREAT LARGE STOUR VASTY COSMIC IMMANE MIGHTY UNTOLD ABYSMAL IMMENSE OCEANIC VASTITY ENORMOUS INFINITE MOUNTAIN SPACIOUS
VASTNESS IMMANE GRANDEUR WIDENESS
VAT ARK BAC DIP FAT PIT TAP TUN BACK BECK COOM FATE GAAL GAIL GYLE KEEL KIER TINE APRON COOMB FETTE FLOAT KEEVE KIEVE ROUND STAND STEEP KIMNEL MOTHER BLUNGER DRAINER GRAINER KEELVAT STEEPER PRESSFAT
(— USED IN MEASURING SLIPS) ARK
(BREWER'S —) BACK FLOAT KEEVE UNION CUMMING
(CHEESE —) CHESSEL CHESSET CHESSART
(COOLING —) KELDER
(DYER'S —) JIG LEAD DYEBECK
(EVAPORATING —) APRON GRAINER
(FERMENTING —) TUN COMB COOM GYLE KEEL COOMB FLOAT
(TANNER'S —) TAP HANGER SPENDER
(TEXTILE —) KIER
(WINE —) LAKE CUVEE
(PREF.) PYEL(O)
VATICAN CITY (BASILICA OF —) STPETERS
(WALL OF —) LEONINE
VAU DIGAMMA
VAUDEVILLE ZARZUELA
VAULT BOUT COPE JUMP LEAP PEND SKIP TOMB VOLT WOWT AZURE CROFT CRYPT EMBOW VOLTO CELLAR CUPOLA FORNIX SHROUD CONCAVE DUNGEON TESTUDO VALTAGE CATACOMB LEAPFROG MONUMENT
(— IN CEILING) LACUNAR
(— OF HEAVEN) WELKIN
(— OF SKY) CONVEX ZENITH CONCAVE
(PART OF —) PENDENTIVE

VAULTED CONCAVE CRYPTED EMBOWED
VAULTER VOLTIGEUR
VAULTING POMADA POMMADO
VAUNT GAB BRAG BOAST ROOSE VOUST AVAUNT INSULT BLUSTER GLORIFY FLOURISH
(— ONESELF) WIND
VAUNTMURE MANURE
VEAL VEAU SLINK FRICANDO
(LIKE —) VITULINE
VECTOR I K PHASOR GRADIENT
VEDA SHASTER
VEDDOID PANYAN
VEDIC (— PRINCIPLE) RTA RITA
VEER CUT DIP FLY CAST CHOP SLEW SLUE SWAY TACK WYRE FETCH SHIFT SWOOP BROACH CHANGE SLOUGH SWERVE TUMBLE BOXHAUL DEVIATE WHIFFLE
VEERING DRIFT CHOPPY
VEGETABLE PEA YAM BEAN BEET CORN KALE LEEK OKRA CHARD GRASS ONION SABZI SALAD CARROT CELERY LEGUME LENTIL POTATO RADISH SQUASH TOMATO TOPEPO TURNIP BLOATER CABBAGE CELTUCE LETTUCE PARSNIP PEASCOD RHUBARB SPINACH VEGETAL BROCCOLI EGGPLANT RUTABAGA
(— MATTER) SUDD
(—S FOR MARKET) TRUCK
(EARLY —) PRIMEUR
(EARLY —S) HASTINGS
(GARDEN —S) SASS SAUCE
(HYBRID —) GARLION
(PREF.) PHYT(I)(O)
VEGETARIAN VEGAN
VEGETATION HERB COVER GREEN SCRUB GROWTH HERBAGE COVERAGE PLANTAGE PLEUSTON SMELLAGE
(DECOMPOSED —) STAPLE
(SCRUB —) BRUSH
(UNWANTED —) FILTH
(PREF.) PHYT(I)(O)
VEGETATIVE ASEXUAL PLANTAL
VEHEMENCE FURY GLOW HEAT RAGE WARMTH STRENGTH VIOLENCE
VEHEMENT HOT HIGH KEEN LOUD ANGRY EAGER FIERY HEFTY YEDER ARDENT BITTER FERVID FIERCE FLASHY HEARTY HEATED RAGING STRONG ANIMOSE ANIMOUS FURIOSO INTENSE JEALOUS VIOLENT
VEHEMENTLY AMAIN PELLMELL
VEHICLE BUS CAB CAR FLY VAN ARBA AUTO CART DUKE FLAT GOER JEEP SLED TAXI TEAM WAIN ARABA BRAKE BREAK BUGGY CARRY DILLY FLAIL GUIDE HANSA NODDY STAGE WAGON BLADER CAMPER CHARET CISIUM DIESEL HEARSE JITNEY MEDIUM RANDEM SLEDGE SLEIGH SURREY TRISHA TROIKA CARRIER CHARIOT CRUISER HOTSHOT ICEBOAT KIBITKA MACHINE MINIBUS OMNIBUS PEDICAB PEDRAIL

SHEBANG SHUTTLE SPEEDER
SPRAYER STEAMER STEERER
TARTANA TAXICAB TRAVOIS
TURNOUT UTILITY AUTORAIL
AUTOSLED CARRIAGE CHARETTE
CYCLECAR DEADHEAD DELIVERY
ELECTRIC FILMOGEN SHOWCASE
SOCIABLE UNICYCLE
MOTORCYCLE SNOWMOBILE
(— DRAWN BY BULLOCK) EKKA
(— FOR COLORS) MEGILP
(— FOR HAULING) TRACTOR
(— ON RUNNERS) SLED CARRO
SLEDGE SLEIGH ICEBOAT
AUTOSLED
(— ON SINGLE RAIL) AEROTRAIN
(— PULLED BY MAN) BROUETTE
RICKSHAW
(— RUNNING ON RAILS) LORRY
TRAIN
(— WITH 3 HORSES ABREAST)
TROIKA
(— WITH 3 HORSES BEHIND EACH
OTHER) RANDEM
(AIRPORT —) SKYLOUNGE
(AMMUNITION —) CAISSON
(AMPHIBIOUS —) BUFFALO
(AWKWARD —) ARK
(CHILD'S —) PRAM WALKER
SCOOTER STROLLER
(COVERED —) SEDAN LANDAU
CARAVAN KIBITKA
(EARTH-MOVING —) SCOOP
(LITTLE —) HINAYANA
(LUMBERING —) TUG TODE
(MILITARY —) AMTRACK
(MOTOR —) WHEELS
(OBSOLETE —) CRATE
(POOR-QUALITY —) DOG
SHANDRYPAN
(RUDE —) KIBITKA
(RUSSIAN —) TARANTAS
(SATELLITE —) SLV
(SLEDGE-LIKE —) GAMBO
(SNOW —) SKIBOB
(SPACE —) LANDER
(WHEELLESS —) DRAY
(2-WHEELED —) GIG CART SULKY
TONGA CISIUM JINGLE LIMBER
BICYCLE CALECHE CROYDON
RICKSHAW
(PL.) PARK
(SUFF.) MOBILE
VEIL WRY FALL FILM HIDE MASK
WRAP COVER GLOSS RUMAL
SHADE VELUM VIMPA VOLET
WREIL BUMBLE CHRISM FAILLE
SHADOW SHROUD VEILER
WEEPER WIMPLE CORTINA
CURTAIN ENDOTYS PARANJA
VEILING CALYPTRA ENDOTHYS
HEADRAIL KALYPTRA MAHARMAH
MANTILLA TELEBLEM
(— IN CHURCH) AER ENDOTYS
ENDOTHYS
(— ON FUNGI) CORTINA
(DOUBLE —) YASHMAK
(HUMERAL —) SUDARY
(WIDOW'S —) WEEPER
VEILED COVERT LATENT VELATED
SHROUDED
VEILING PURDAH GOSSAMER
VEIN BAR LOB RIB CAVA LODE

MOOD RAKE REEF VENA AMPER
CLOUD COMES COSTA LEDGE
MEDIA NERVE RIDER SCRIN VARIX
LEADER MEDIAL STRAIN STREAK
VENULA VENULE AXILLAR
AZYGOUS CUBITAL DROPPER
JUGULAR NERVURE PRECAVA
PRESTER SAPHENA VEINLET
AXILLARY EMULGENT PREMEDIA
PROFUNDA SUBCOSTA
(— IN MARBLE) CLOUD
(— OF LEAF) RIB COSTA MIDRIB
(— OF MINERAL) STREAK STRINGER
(— OF ORE) LODE ROKE BUNCH
LEDGE RIDER SCRIN LEADER
STRING DROPPER UNDERSET
(— OF WING) CUBIT RADIUS
CUBITAL CUBITUS SUBCOSTA
SUBCOSTAL
(GRANITIC —) ELVAN
(QUARTZ —) SADDLE
(VARICOSE —) AMPER
(PREF.) CIRS(O) PHLEB(O) PYL(E)(O)
VENI VENO
(SWOLLEN —) CIRS(O)
VEINED MARBLED NERVOSE
VELA SAILS
VELAR GUTTURAL
VELD BUSHVELD SOURVELD
VELELLA SALLYMAN
VELLEITY DESIRE WOULDING
VELLINCH FLINCHER
VELLUM ORIHON
VELOCIPEDE HOBBY STEED
TRICAR BICYCLE DICYCLE
RANTOON SPEEDER DRAISINE
TRICYCLE
VELOCITY DRIFT CELERITY
RAPIDITY STRENGTH
(— OF FLOW) CURRENT
(— OF 1 FOOT PER SECOND) VELO
VELOUR SOLEIL
VELOUTE POULETTE
VELUM VEIL VELAMEN VELARIUM
VELVET PILE PANNE YUZEN
BIRODO VELURE FRAYING
VELLUTE
VELVETEEN TRIPE
VELVET GRASS FOG
VELVETLEAF DAGGA PAREIRA
VENAL CORRUPT SALABLE
HIRELING SALEABLE VENDIBLE
VEND HAWK SELL UTTER MARKET
PEDDLE
VENDA (CAPITAL OF —)
THOHOYANDOU
(TOWN OF —) SIBASA MAKWARELA
VENDIBLE VENAL SALABLE
SALEABLE
VENDOR FAKER SELLER VENDER
ALIENOR BUTCHER HUSTLER
PITCHER PURLMAN VIANDER
PITCHMAN SAUCEMAN VENDITOR
VENEER BURL BURR JAPAN SHOOK
OVERLAY SKILLET
VENEERER DUSTER
VENERABLE OLD HOAR SAGE
AWFUL HOARY AUGUST SACRED
VETUST ANCIENT VENERAL
VINTAGE
(PREF.) SEBASTO
VENERATE FEAR DREAD HALLOW
REVERE VENERE

RESPECT WORSHIP
VENERATED HOLY SACRED
HALLOWED
VENERATION AWE CULT DULIA
CULTISM RESPECT DEVOTION
VENESECTION PHLEBOTOMY
VENETIAN RED SIENA SIERRA
VENETIAN SUMAC SCOTINO

VENEZUELA

CAPITAL: CARACAS
COIN: REAL MEDIO FUERTE
  BOLIVAR CENTIMO MOROCOTA
GULF: PARIA
MEASURE: GALON MILLA FANEGA
  ESTADEL
MOUNTAIN: PAVA YAVI DUIDA
  ICUTU CONCHA CUNEVA
  PARIMA IMUTACA MASAITI
  RORAIMA
NATIVE: CARIB TIMOTE
  GUARAUNO
RIVER: META APURE CAURA
  ARAUCA CARONI CUYUNI
  GUANARE ORINOCO ORITUCO
  PARAGUA SUAPURE VICHADA
  GUAVIARE VENTUARI
STATE: LARA APURE SUCRE ZULIA
  ARAGUA FALCON MERIDA
  BOLIVAR COJEDES GUARICO
  MONAGAS TACHIRA YARACUY
  CARABOBO TRUJILLO
TOWN: AROA CORO ATURES
  CUMANA MERIDA BARINAS
  CABELLO GUAWARE MARACAY
  MATURIN CARUPANO
  TACUPITA VALENCIA
WATERFALL: ANGEL CUQUENAN
WEIGHT: BAG LIBRA

VENGEANCE WRACK WREAK
WRECK AVENGE ULTION WANION
ALASTOR REVENGE VINDICT
REQUITAL VINDICTA
VENILIA (HUSBAND OF —) DAUNUS
(SISTER OF —) AMATA
(SON OF —) TURNUS
VENISON BILTONG
VENOM GALL ATTER VIRUS
POISON SWELTER CROTALIN
CROTALUS
VENOMOUS TOXIC ATTERN
DEADLY SNAKEY VENOMY
BANEFUL NOXIOUS SMITTLE
SNAKISH POISONED VIPERINE
VIPEROUS VIRULENT POISONOUS
VENT EMIT HOLE REEK BELCH
DRAIN FROTH ISSUE TEWEL
OUTAGE OUTLET CHIMNEY
EXPRESS OPENING ORIFICE
OUTCAST OUTFALL OUTTAKE
RELEASE VENTAGE APERTURE
BREATHER DIATREME FONTANEL
MOFFETTE SESPERAL SPIRACLE
SUSPIRAL VENTHOLE VOMITORY
(— IN EARTH'S CRUST) VOLCANO
(VOLCANIC —) BOCCA DIATREME
SOLFATARA
VENTILATE AIR WIND AERATE
EXPRESS
VENTILATION AERAGE AIRING
VENTILATOR BADGIR LOUVER
FEMERELL

VENTING GUST
VENTRAL BELLY HEMAL STERNAL
ANTERIOR INFERIOR
(PREF.) (— AREA) GASTER(O)
GASTR(I)(O)
VENTRICLE HEART TRICORN
DIACOELE
(SUFF.) CELE COELE COELUS
VENTURE HAB RUN SET CAST
DARE JUMP KITE LUCK MINT
REST RISK WAGE ETTLE FLIER
FLYER FROST RISCO SALLY STAKE
TEMPT WAGER CHANCE DANGER
HAZARD SASHAY FLUTTER
IMPERIL JEOPARD PRESUME
PRETEND ENDANGER GETPENNY
(— AT DICE) THROW
(— TO SAY) DARESAY
VENTURESOME BOLD RASH RISKY
DARING PARLOUS TEMEROUS
VENTURESOMELY CHANCILY
VENUS LOVE VESPER LUCIFER
HESPERUS PHOSPHOR
(FATHER OF —) JUPITER
(HUSBAND OF —) VULCAN
(MOTHER OF —) DIONE
(SON OF —) AMOR CUPID AENEAS
VENUSIAN VENEREAN
VERACIOUS TRUE VERY TRUTHY
SINCERE VERIDIC FAITHFUL
TRUTHFUL
VERACITY HSIN TROTH TRUTH
VERITY FIDELITY
VERANDA PYAL LANAI PORCH
STOEP STOOP PIAZZA BALCONY
GALERIE GALLERY
VERB RHEMA ACTIVE NOMINAL
DEPONENT
(AUXILIARY —) BE DO CAN MAY
HAVE MUST WILL SHALL
VERBAL ORAL WORDY
VERBATIM DIRECT VERBAL
LITERAL DIRECTLY
VERBENA ALOYSIA VERVAIN
VERBENALIN CORNIN
VERBIAGE TALK
VERBOSE WINDY WORDY PROLIX
VERBAL DIFFUSE WORDISH
(NOT —) LEAN
VERBOSITY MACROLOGY
VERDANT BOSKY GREEN VIRID
VERDICT WORD VARDI ASSIZE
FINDING OPINION DECISION
JUDGMENT VEREDICT
VERDIGRIS AERUGO CANKER
VERDET
VERDIN GOLDTIT
VERDURE GREENTH GREENERY
VIRIDITY
(PREF.) CHLO
VERGE TOP EDGE WAND YARD
BRINK POINT TOUCH BORDER
TRENCH TRIGGER
VERGER WANDSMAN
VERGILIAN MARONIAN MARONIST
VERIFICATION AUDIT AVERRAL
CHECKUP AVERMENT
VERIFY AVER TRUE AUDIT CHECK
PROVE ATTEST RATIFY COLLATE
CONFIRM CONTROL JUSTIFY
SUPPORT CONSTATE
VERILY YEA AMEN FAITH PARDY
CERTES INDEED PARDIE FAITHLY

VERITABLE REAL TRUE VERY
ACTUAL HONEST PROPER
GENUINE VERIMENT
VERITY TROTH TRUTH VERIDITY
VERJUICE VARGE
VERMICELLI FEDELINI
VERMICULE VAALITE
VERMICULITE KERRITE MACONITE
VERMIFUGE KOSIN HARMAL
HARMEL KAMALA KAMELA
KOOSIN COWHAGE HELONIAS
WORMWOOD
VERMILION RED GOYA MINIUM
MINIATE PAPRIKA PIMENTO
VERMEIL ZINOBER CARMETTA
CINNABAR TOREADOR
VERMIN FILTH CARRION VARMINT
VERMIS WORM

VERMONT
CAPITAL: MONTPELIER
COLLEGE: BENNINGTON
MIDDLEBURY
COUNTY: ESSEX ORANGE ADDISON
ORLEANS WINDSOR LAMOILLE
LAKE: CASPIAN DUNMORE
SEYMOUR CHAMPLAIN
MOUNTAIN: BROMLEY HOGBACK
ASCUTNEY PROSPECT
MANSFIELD
MOUNTAIN RANGE: GREEN
TACONIC
NICKNAME: GREENMOUNTAIN
PRESIDENT: ARTHUR COOLIDGE
RIVER: SAXTONS LAMOILLE
NULHEGAN POULTNEY
WINOOSKI
STATE BIRD: THRUSH
STATE FLOWER: CLOVER
STATE TREE: MAPLE
TOWN: BARRE STOWE CHELSEA
GRAFTON NEWFANE RUTLAND
BENNINGTON BURLINGTON
UNIVERSITY: NORWICH

VERMOUTH CINZANO CHAMBERY
VERNACULAR LINGO COMMON
JARGON PATOIS ROMAIC TONGUE
VULGAR CHALDEE DIALECT
TRIVIAL SCOTTISH
VERNALIZE IAROVIZE JAROVIZE
YAROVIZE
VERNIER NONIUS
VERONICA HEBE SUDARIUM
VERNICLE BROOKLIME
VERRUCOSE WARTY WARTED
VERSATILE HANDY FICKLE MOBILE
FLEXILE
VERSE FIT EPIC LINE POSE RANN
RICH RIME SONG BLANK IONIC
METER METRE RHYME STAVE
STICH TANKA ADONIC ALCAIC
BURDEN CHIAVE CYWYDD
DIPODY HEROIC JINGLE PANTUN
SCAZON STANZA VERSET
ANAPEST DICOLON DOGGREL
ELEGIAC PAEONIC PANTOUM
PENNILL SAPPHIC SAVITRI
SOTADIC STICHOS TRIPODY
TROILUS CHOLIAMB DACTYLIC
DINGDONG DOGGEREL GLYCONIC
LEONINES PRIAPEAN RESPONSE
SENTENCE SINGSONG TERETISM

TRIMETER VERSICLE MACARONIC
(— FORM) VIRELAY KYRIELLE
(— OF 14 LINES) SONNET
(— OF 2 FEET) DIPODY DIMETER
(— OF 6 FEET) CHOLIAMB
SENARIAN SENARIUS
(— WITH LIMPING MOVEMENT)
SCAZON
(DEVOTIONAL —) ANTIPHON
OFFERTORY
(HINDU —) SLOKA
(JAPANESE —) HAIKAI
(MEDIEVAL —) SIRVENTE
(NONSENSE —S) AMPHIGORY
(UNMELODIOUS —) TERETISM
(PL.) TRIPOS PINDARICS
VERSED SEEN WITTY BESEEN
TRADED STUDIED FREQUENT
OVERSEEN SCIENCED
(WELL —) SKILLFUL
VERSICLE VERSE VERSET STICHOS
SUFFRAGE
VERSIFIER BARD POET RHYMER
VERSER METERER
VERSIFY METER
VERSION DRAM DRAUGHT EDITION
READING TURNING REDACTION
(SHORT —) BRIEF
(SIMPLIFIED —) KEY
(TRANSLATED —) CONSTRUE
VERSO REVERSE
VERT VERD POMME VENUS
PRASINE SINOPLE GREENHEW
VERTEBRA AXIS RACK ATLAS
DORSAL LUMBAR SACRAL
ACANTHA CENTRUM CERVICAL
METAMERE PROATLAS RACKBONE
SPONDYLE
(PREF.) ASTRAGAL(O) SPONDYL(O)
(SUFF.) SPONDYLI SPONDYLUS
VERTEBRATA CRANIATA
CRANIOTA
VERTEBRATE CRANIATE
SAUROPSID
VERTEX APEX COPE NODE POLE
CROWN PITCH SUMMIT VERTICAL
VERTICAL APEAK ERECT PLUMB
SHEER WHIRL ORTHAL UPRIGHT
COLUMNAR SHEERING STRAIGHT
(PREF.) ORTH(O)
VERTICALLY PLUMP ENDLONG
SHEERLY DIRECTLY PALEWISE
VERTICIL WHORL
VERTIGINOUS DIZZY
VERTIGO DINUS TIEGO MEGRIM
MIRLIGO SWIMMING WHIRLING
VERUMONTANUM COLLICLE
VERVAIN GERVAO FROGFOOT
IRONWEED
VERVE DARE DASH ELAN BOUNCE
ENERGY PANACHE VITALITY
VIVACITY
VERY SO ALL BIG DOG GAY GEY
MUY TOO BRAW DEAD FELL FULL
JUST MAIN MUCH PURE RARE
REAL SAME SELF SUCH TRES
UNCO WELL ASSAI AWFUL BLAME
BULLY CRAZY DOOMS JOLLY
MOLTO PESKY RIGHT SOWAN
SUPER SWITH UNCOW VERRA
BITTER BLAMED DAMNED
DEUCED FREELY GAINLY LIVING
MAINLY MASTER MIGHTY NATION

POISON PROPER SORELY STRONG
TARNAL THRICE VERRAY
WONDER AWFULLY BOILING
GALLOWS GREATLY PARLOUS
PASSING PRECISE SOPPING
STRANGE DEUCEDLY DREADFUL
ENORMOUS FAMOUSLY
POWERFUL PRECIOUS SPANKING
SWINGING WHACKING
ABSOLUTELY
(PREF.) ERI MALLO
VESICANT LEWISITE MESEREUM
VESICA PISCIS MANDORLA
VESICATORY BLISTER
VESICLE BLEB CYST APTHA BULLA
BURSE FLOAT APHTHA AMPULLA
BLADDER BLISTER HYDATID
OTOCYST POMPHUS UTRICLE
VACUOLE AEROCYST MIDBRAIN
VESICULA PHAGOSOME
(SUFF.) YDATIS
VESICULAR BULLOSE BULLOUS
VESPERAL TOWEL
VESPERS LYCHNIC PLACEBO
EVENSONG
VESSEL (ALSO SEE BOAT AND SHIP)
GO CAN CAT COG CUP FAT GUM
HOY NEF PIG POT TUB VAS VAT
VIA BARK BOAT BODY BOMB
BOOT BOSS BOWL BRIG BUSH
BUSS CASK CELL COWL DISH DRIP
DUCT GAWN GRAB HORN HULK
JACK JUNK KOFF LOTA PINK PINT
POST PROW SAIL SHIP SNOW
TING YAWL AMULA BAKIE BARGE
BASIN BIDET BIKIE BOCAL BOYER
CADUS CANNE CHURN COGUE
CRACK CRAER CRAFT CRARE
CRUET CRUSE DANDY DIOTA
DUBBA FLASK GLOBE GUIDE
JUBBE KETCH LADLE LAKER
LAVER LINER PIECE PYKAR SCOOP
SMACK STEAM STILL XEBEC
YANKY ZABRA BANKER BARQUE
BARREL BILALO BOILER BOTTLE
BOUTRE BUCKET BURNER CAIQUE
CANNER CAPPIE CHARGE
CODMAN COFFIN CONCHA
COOLER COPPER CRATER CRAYER
CRUISE CUTTER DECKER DEINOS
DOGGER DUBBAH ELUTOR FESSEL
FIRKIN FLAGON HOLCAD HOOKER
JAGGER KERNOS KETTLE KRATER
LANCHA LATEEN LEKANE LORCHA
MASLIN MONKEY MULLER PACKET
PANKIN PATERA PICARD PITHOS
POURIE ROLLER SALTER SATTIE
SEALER SERVER SETTEE SHIBAR
SITULA SMOKER TARTAN TENDER
TOPMAN VESICA WHALER
BAGGALA BALLOEN BALLOON
BLICKEY BLICKIE CARAVEL
CARRIER CISTERN CLIPPER
CORSAIR COUGNAR CRAGGAN
CRESSET CRISSET CRUISER
CUVETTE DRIFTER DRINKER
DROGHER FELUCCA FLYBOAT
FRIGATE GABBARD GABBART
GAIASSA GALASSA GUNBOAT
ORANGER PATAMAR PINNACE
POACHER POLACRE PSYKTER
REDUCER SALTFAT SCALDER
SEEDLIP SETTLER SPARGER

SPOUTER STEAMER STEEPER
TRACHEA TRENDLE UTENSIL
BELANDER BENITIER BILANDER
BILLYBOY BIRDBATH BLEACHER
BUGGALOW CORVETTE CRUCIBLE
CRUISKEN CUCURBIT DECANTER
DIGESTER DUTCHMAN EFFERENT
EMISSARY FIREBOAT FLESHPOT
GALLIPOT GALLIVAT GAROOKUH
GAYDIANG HELLSHIP HONEYPOT
INKSTAND INRIGGER IRONCLAD
IRONSIDE KEELBOAT LATEENER
LAVATORY NITRATOR PICAROON
SCHOONER SMUGGLER SPITTOON
WATERPOT
(— CUT FROM BLOCK OF WOOD)
BAMBOOS
(— FOR COAL) GEORDIE
(— FOR DYE) TOBY
(— FOR HEATING LIQUIDS) ETNA
(— FOR HOLY WATER) FAT FONT
STOCK STOOP STOUP AMPULLA
BENITIER
(— FOR HYPODERMIC USE) AMPUL
AMPULE AMPOULE
(— FOR LIQUID WASTE) DRIP
(— FOR MEASURING ORE) HOPPET
(— FOR MOLTEN METAL) LADLE
(— FOR ORE WASHINGS) LOOL
(— FOR PERFUMES) CENSER
(— FOR PORRIDGE) BICKER
(— FOR SOLDIER'S FOOD) MESSTIN
(— FOR WINE SAMPLING) TASTER
(— HOLDING CONDIMENTS) CRUET
CASTER
(— IN MINE) CORB
(— MADE OF HOLLOW LOG) GUM
(— OF BARK) COOLAMAN
COOLAMON COOLIMAN
(— OF HORN) BUGLE
(— ON TRIPOD) HOLMOS
(— ROWED BY OARS) CATUR
GALLEY
**(— STATIONED IN ENGLISH
CHANNEL)** GROPER
(— USED IN MAKING GLAZE) HILLER
(ABANDONED —) DERELICT
(ARMORED —) CRUISER IRONCLAD
IRONSIDE
(BAPTISMAL —) FONT
(BARGELIKE —) PANGARA
(BLOOD —) AORTA ARTERY
BLEEDER EFFERENT
(BREWER'S —) ROUND
(CANDLEMAKING —) JACK
(CHEMIST'S —) BATH FLASK STILL
BEAKER RETORT
(CHINESE —) JUNK SAMPAN
(CIRCULAR —) KIT
(CLUMSY —) CRAY CRARE
HAGBOAT
(COASTING —) DHOW DONI GRAB
PONTIN SHEBAR SHIBAR TRADER
COASTER GRIBANE MISTICO
BILLYBOY HOVELLER
(CODFISHING —) BANKER CODMAN
(DECORATIVE —) AIGUIERE
(DISTILLING —) BODY STILL
RETORT MATRASS CUCURBIT
(DRINKING —) CAP CUP TIN BOOT
PECE FOUNT GLASS GOURD
JORUM POKAL SCALE BICKER
CAPPIE CHOPIN COOPER COOTIE

DIPPER DUBBER FIRLOT GOBLET KITTIE QUAICH QUAIGH RABBIT RUMKIN BIBERON CANAKIN CANIKIN GALLIOT SCYPHUS SKINKER SKYPHOS TANKARD CANNIKIN CYLINDER

(DUTCH —) KOFF YANKY HOOKER SCHUIT SCHUYT

(EARTHEN —) PIG BAYAN PANKIN TINAGE CRAGGAN

(ELECTROPLATING —) TROUGH

(EUCHARISTIC —) AMA PYX AMULA PYXIS FLAGON COLUMBA CHRISMAL CIBORIUM MONSTRANCE

(GLASS —) VERRE UNDINE BALLOON

(HERRING-FISHING —) BUSS

(HOLLOW METALLIC —) BELL

(INVERTED —) BELL

(LADLING —) GAUN

(LARGE-NECKED —) JORDAN

(LATEEN-RIGGED —) DHOW LATEEN LATEENER

(LEATHER —) BOOT JACK OLPE GIRBA DUBBER

(LEVANTINE —) JERM SAIC

(LONG-NECKED —) GOGLET GUGLET

(LYMPHATIC —) LACTEAL

(MALAYAN —) PROA COUGNAR

(MELTING —) GRISSET

(OPEN —) LOOM

(PERFORATED —) LEACH

(PINECONE-SHAPED —) THYRSE

(PORTUGUESE —) MULET

(RARE —) SNOW

(SEED —) POD BUTTON BIVALVE

(SERVING —) ARGYLE ARGYLL SERVER

(SHALLOW —) KIVER SKEEL BEDPAN PANCHION

(SMALL —) CAG HOY VIAL PHIAL VEDET JIGGER LIEPOT PICARD TINLET YETLIN FLIVVER VEDETTE YETLING GALLIPOT

(TOP-HEAVY —) CRANK

(TURKISH —) MAHONE

(WHALING —) WHALER SPOUTER

(WICKER —) POT

(WINE —) AMA AMULA TINAGE

(WOODEN —) COG KIT BOSS BAKIE KIVER BICKER CAPPIE COOTIE DUDDIE FIRKIN STOUND

(PL.) CRAFT WAFTAGE

(PREF.) ANGI(O) ARTERI VAS(I)(O) VASCUL(I)(O)

(HOLLOW —) CYT(O)

(SUFF.) ANGE ANGIUM

VEST GARB GOWN ROBE GILET ACCRUE ATTACH FECKET INVEST JACKET JELICK LINDER WESKIT ENFEOFF CLOTHING

(— IN) STATE

VESTA WAX

(FATHER OF —) SATURN

(MOTHER OF —) RHEA

(SISTER OF —) JUNO CERES

VESTED BESTEAD DONATIVE

VESTIBULE HALL ENTRY FOYER PORCH ATRIUM EXEDRA EPINAOS NARTHEX PASSAGE PRONAOS TAMNOUR ANTEROOM VESTIARY

VESTIGE TAG DREG MARK RACK

SIGN PRINT RELIC SPARK TRACE TRACK TRACT UMBRA SHADOW MENTION LEFTOVER RUDIMENT TINCTURE

VESTIGIAL REDUCED OBSOLETE

VESTING ADITIO

VESTITURE TIRE RAIMENT TUNICLE

VESTMENT ALB CAP ALBE COPE PALL VEST AMICE COTTA EPHOD FANON RABAT RASON STOLE RHASON ROCHET SACCOS SAKKOS VAKASS MANIPLE ORARION PALLIUM PILLION PLUVIAL TUNICLE VESTURE CHASUBLE DALMATIC PHRYGIUM RATIONAL SCAPULAR SURPLICE VESTIARY

(PL.) GARB GEAR DRESS CLOTHING

VESTRY SACRISTY VESTIARY

VESTURE COAT

VESUVIANITE EGERAN CYPRINE IDOCRASE VESUVIAN XANTHITE

VETCH DAL ERS AKRA LUCK TARE TINE ERVIL FITCH AXSEED FECCHE THETCH ARVEJON TINETARE TINEWEED

VETERAN VET CHAUVIN EMERITUS HARDENED SEASONED

VETERINARIAN VET LEECH FARRIER

VETERINARY VET FARRIERY

VETIVER BEN KHUS CUSCUS KUSKUS KHASGHAS KHUSKHUS

VETO NIX KILL DISALLOW NEGATIVE

VEUGLAIRE FOWLER

VEX FRY NOY TEW CARK CHAW FASH FAZE FRET FYKE GALL HALE HUMP ITCH RILE ROIL RUCK TEEN TOUT YOKE ANGER ANNOY CHAFE FRUMP GRAME GRILL GRIND GRIPE HARRY SCALD SPITE STURT TARRY TEASE WORRY WRACK WRATH YEARN BOTHER BURDEN CORSIE COTTER CUMBER GRIEVE GRUDGE HARASS HARROW INFEST NETTLE OFFEND PLAGUE POTHER RUFFLE THREAT WORRIT AFFLICT BEDEVIL CHAGRIN DESPITE PERPLEX PROVOKE TORMENT ACERBATE BEPESTER BULLYRAG EXERCISE IRRITATE MACERATE

VEXATION VEX CHAW FASH MOIL TEEN TRAY CHAFE CROSS ERROR GRIEF HARRY PIQUE SPITE STEAM THORN WORRY BOTHER REPINE CHAGRIN DISGUST NOISANCE SORENESS

VEXATIOUS MEAN SORE TEEN NASTY PESKY ACHING FIERCE SHREWD THORNY VEXFUL IRKSOME PEEVISH PRICKLY TARSOME ANNOYING CUMBROUS FRAMPOLD PHRAMPEL UNTOWARD VEXATORY WEARIFUL PESTILENT

VEXATIOUSLY PLAGUY

VEXED DIK MAD RILY SORE TEEN WAXY WILD WRAW ANGRY NARKY RAGGY ROILY MIFFED

MUFFED SHIRTY SNUFFY FRABOUS GRIEVED IRKSOME OUTDONE

(EASILY —) CROSS

VEXILLUM WEB VEXIL BANNER STANDARD

VEXING CHRONIC TECHING WAYWARD ANNOYING NETTLING TEACHING

V-GOUGE VEINER

VIABLE VITAL HEALTHY

VIAL AMPUL CRUET PHIAL AMPULE CASTER CASTOR AMPOULE

VIANDS CATE DIET FOOD CHEER VIANDRY VICTUALS

VIBRANT RINGY BRAWLING RESONANT SONOROUS VIGOROUS

VIBRATE JAR WAG BEAT CAST DIRL PLAY ROCK TIRL WHIR PULSE QUAKE SWING THIRL THROB TRILL WAVER DINDLE HOTTER JUDDER QUAVER QUIVER SHIMMY SHIVER THRILL TINGLE WARBLE CHATTER FLUTTER LIBRATE STAGGER TREMBLE TWIDDLE EVIBRATE FLICHTER RESONATE UNDULATE

(— ABNORMALLY) SHIMMY

VIBRATING PLANGENT

(— OF AIRPLANE) BUFFET

VIBRATION BUZZ DIRL FLIP TIRL SWING TRILL DINDLE JUDDER QUAVER QUIVER THRILL TREMOR DANCING FLUTTER TEMBLOR DIADROME FREMITUS VIBRANCY OSCILLATION

(— OF SAW) CUPPING

(RATTLING —) JAR

VIBRATIONS KARMA

VIBRATO TRILL WHINE TREMOLO

VIBRATOR TREMBLER

VIBRISSA FEELER SMELLER

VIBURNUM MAE MAY SNOWBALL ARROWWOOD SHEEPBERRY

VICAR PROXY DEPUTY STALLAR ALTARIST STALLARY

VICAR OF WAKEFIELD (AUTHOR OF —) GOLDSMITH

(CHARACTER IN —) MOSES GEORGE OLIVIA SOPHIA WILMOT DEBORAH ARABELLA BURCHELL PRIMROSE THORNHILL

VICE SIN EVIL CRIME FAULT TAINT ULCER DEFECT DEPUTY BUGGERY OFFENSE INIQUITY

VICE-GERENT EPHOR

VICE-PRESIDENT CROUPIER

(— OF SANHEDRIN) ABBETDIN

VICEREGENT VICAR SUBPRIOR

VICEROY EARL VALI NABOB NAWAB NAZIM SUBAH EXARCH KEHAYA PROREX PROVES SATRAP WARDEN PROVOST TSUNGTU SUBAHDAR

VICIA FABA

VICINITY HERE SHADOW ENVIRONS

(— OF MINE SHAFT) COLLAR

(NEAR —) SUBURBS

VICIOUS BAD ILL EVIL LAZY LEWD MEAN UGLY VILE ROWDY TOUGH SINFUL STRONG VITIAL WICKED CORRUPT IMMORAL NAUGHTY

SKAITHY DEPRAVED DEVILISH FRATCHED INFAMOUS THEWLESS MONSTROUS NEFARIOUS

VICIOUSNESS VICE

VICISSITUDE CHANGE MUTATION

(— OF FORTUNE) WEATHER

VICTIM BUTT DUPE GOAT GULL PREY PATHIC QUARRY CASUALTY

(— FOR SHARPERS) JAY

(INTENDED —) CHUMP

(SACRIFICIAL —) HOST MERIAH

(UNFORTUNATE —) BASTARD

VICTIMIZATION RIDE

VICTIMIZE HOAX BUNCO BUNKO COZEN

VICTOR COCK CAPTOR MASTER WINNER BANGSTER

VICTORFISH AKU

VICTORIA (FATHER OF —) PALLAS

(MOTHER OF —) STYX

VICTORIA LAKE PUCE

VICTORIAN GENTEEL

VICTORIOUS VICTOR WINNING

VICTORY WIN PALM PRICE BETTER SUBDUE VICTOR MASTERY SACKING TRIUMPH WINNING CONQUEST DECISION WALKOVER

(AUTHOR OF —) CONRAD

(CHARACTER IN —) AXEL LENA WANG HEYST JONES PEDRO MARTIN RICARDO DAVIDSON MORRISON SCHOMBERG

(EASY —) BREEZE

(OVERWHELMING —) SWEEP

VICTUAL BIT VITE VITTLE

(BROKEN —S) SCRAN

(PL.) KAI BITE CHOW FOOD GRUB PROG SAND VIVERS PROVENDER PROVISIONS

VICTUALER PURVEYOR

VIDELICET NAMELY SCILICET

VIE ENVY JOSTLE STRIVE COMPARE COMPETE CONTEND CONTEST EMULATE

VIETNAM (SEE NORTH VIETNAM AND SOUTH VIETNAM)

VIETNAMESE ANNAMESE

VIEW EYE KEN FACE GLOM MAKE VISE ADVEW AVIEW BLUSH CATCH MOUTH SCAPE SCENE SIGHT VISTA VIZZY ADVICE ADVISE ASPECT DEVICE GLANCE REGARD SURVEY ALOGISM CONCEIT FEELING GLIMPSE KENNING LOOKOUT OFFLOOK OPINION RESPECT SCENERY SURVIEW THOUGHT AIRSCAPE CONSPECT EYESIGHT OFFSCAPE PROSPECT SEASCAPE SENTENCE SENTIMENT

(— ATTENTIVELY) GAZE

(— CLOSELY) INSPECT

(— FROM AFAR) DESCRY

(— FROM ANGLE) SLANT

(— OF MAN) DUALISM

(— WITH SURPRISE) ADMIRE

(BRIEF —) SNAPSHOT

(COMPREHENSIVE —) PANORAMA

(GENERAL —) LANDSKIP

(OPEN —) LIGHT

(PHYSICAL —) INSIGHT

(SATISFYING —) EYEFUL

(SUFF.) ORAMA SCOPE SCOPIC

SCOPUS SCOPY

VIEWING
(SUFF.) SCOPE SCOPIC SCOPUS
SCOPY

VIEWPOINT SIGHT LAXISM

VIGIL WAKE WATCH WAKING
AGRYPNIA

VIGILANCE WATCH JEALOUSY

VIGILANT AGOG WARE WARY
ALERT AWAKE AWARE CHARY
SHARP JEALOUS LIDLESS
WAKEFUL CAUTIOUS WATCHFUL

VIGOR GO PEP SAP VIM VIR VIS
BIRR DASH EDGE ELAN LUST PITH
SEVE SNAP SOUL TUCK ARDOR
DRIVE FLUSH FORCE GREEN
JUICE NERVE OOMPH POWER
PUNCH VERVE ENERGY ESPRIT
FOISON GINGER SPRAWL SPRING
STARCH STINGO VIGOUR VIRTUS
FREEDOM SMEDDUM STAMINA
STHENIA FLOURISH STRENGTH
TONICITY VITALITY
(FULL OF —) LIFESOME
(MENTAL —) DOCITY SPIRIT
(RENEWED —) REST

VIGOROUS YEP ABLE CANT FRIM
HALE LIVE RUDE SPRY YEPE
ALIVE CRANK EAGER FRACK
FRANK HEFTY JUICY LUSTY NIPPY
PEPPY PITHY PROUD SASSY SOLID
STARK STIFF STOUT TOUGH VIVID
FLORID GOLDEN HEARTY LIVELY
MANFUL POTENT PRETTY RAUCLE
ROBUST RUGGED SINEWY
SQUARE STRONG STURDY
BUCKISH CHIPPER CORDIAL
DRASTIC FECKFUL FURIOUS
HEALTHY LUSTFUL NERVOSE
NERVOUS VALIANT VIBRANT
ZEALOUS ATHLETIC BOUNCING
CHOPPING FORCEFUL MUSCULAR
SLAMBANG SLASHING STUBBORN
VEHEMENT VIGOROSO YOUTHFUL
TRENCHANT
(NOT —) GENTEEL

VIGOROUSLY DOWN FELL HARD
VERN CRANK SNELL TIGHT VERNE
HARDLY SNELLY FRESHLY
SMARTLY STOUTLY WIGHTLY
HEARTILY

VIGOROUSNESS ENERGY
FREEDOM

VIKING DANE WIKING NORSEMAN

VIKRAMADITYA BIKRAM

VILE BAD BASE CLAM FOUL RANK
CHEAP MUCKY POCKY RUSTY
SLIMY WILLE ABJECT CRUSTY
DRAFTY DRASTY FILTHY LECHER
NOUGHT PALTRY SORDID TURPID
UNKIND BEASTLY BENEATH
CAITIFF CORRUPT DEBASED
HATEFUL IGNOBLE SCABBED
SLAVISH VICIOUS BASEBORN
DEPRAVED UNKINDLY

VILENESS FEDITY VILITY
TURPITUDE

VILIFICATION REPROACH

VILIFY ILL VILE ABUSE LIBEL STAIN
DEFAME MALIGN REVILE SLIGHT
ASPERSE BLACKEN DEBAUCH
DETRACT SLANDER TRADUCE
REPROACH STRUMPET

VILIPEND BELITTLE

VILL HAM TOWN TOWNSHIP

VILLA ALDEA DACHA LODGE
CHALET DATCHA QUINTA
TRIANON

VILLAGE BY AUL BYE GAV HAM
KOM PAH REW BOMA BURG DORP
HOME MURA TOWN VILL WICK
ALDEA BOURG CASAL PLACE
THORP VICUS ALDEIA BARRIO
BUSTEE CASTLE GOTHAM
HAMLET HAMMON MOUZAH
PETTAH PUEBLO AMBALAM
BOROUGH CAMPODY CASERIO
CLACHAN ENDSHIP MAABARA
MISSION OUTPORT BEREWICK
BOURGADE CAMPOODY
CRANFORD TOLDERIA VILLACHE
VILLAGET VILLAKIN
(— IN WHICH BARLEY IS GROWN)
BEREWICK
(— OUTSIDE OF FORT) PETTAH
(AFRICAN —) STAD KRAAL
(ARABIAN —) DOUAR
(ARGENTINE —) TOLDERIA
(FRENCH —) BASTIDE
(IMAGINARY —) CRANFORD
(INDIAN —) CASTLE PUEBLO
CAMPODY CAMPOODY
(JAPANESE —) MURA BUSTI
BUSTEE
(JAVANESE —) DESSA
(JEWISH —) SHTETL SHTETEL
(MALAY —) CAMPONG KAMPONG
(MAORI —) KAIK KAIKA KAINGA
(MEXICAN —) EJIDO
(NEW ZEALAND FORTIFIED —) PA
PAH
(NEWFOUNDLAND —) OUTPORT
(RUSSIAN —) MIR STANITSA
STANITZA

VILLAIN IAGO LOUT SERF BADDY
BRAVO CHURL DEMON DEVIL
FAGIN FELON HEAVY KNAVE
ROGUE SCAMP SHREW BADDIE
VILIACO SCELERAT SCOUNDREL

VILLAINOUS BAD EVIL GALLUS
GALLOWS KNAVISH RAFFISH
VILEYNS FLAGRANT RASCALLY
MISCREANT

VILLAINY CRIME KNAVERY

VILLEIN SERF CHURL BORDAR
COTTER VILLAR BONDMAN
TOWNMAN VILLAIN COTARIUS

VILLI (HAVING —) ZONARY

VILLOUS SHAGGY

VIM ZIP GIMP ZING FORCE VIGOR
ENERGY GINGER SPIRIT STARCH
VINEGAR RAZZMATAZZ

VINA BEN BIN BINA

VINCENTIAN LAZARIST

VINDICATE FREE CLEAR RIGHT
SALVE WREAK ACQUIT ASSERT
AVENGE EXCUSE UPHOLD
ABSOLVE DERAIGN JUSTIFY
PROPUGN REVENGE SUSTAIN
DARRAIGN MAINTAIN

VINDICATION BEHALF APOLOGY
THEODICY SATISFACTION

VINDICATOR VINDEX ASSERTER
DEFENDER

VINDICTIVE HOSTILE PUNITIVE
SPITEFUL VENGEFUL

VINE AKA FIG HOP IVY IYO BINE
CARO GOGO ODAL SOMA TINE
AKEBI BUAZE BWAZI CAAPI
CACUR GUACO KAIWI KUDZU
LIANA MAILE PALAY PRIVY TACSO
TIMBO TRAIL TWINE WITHE
WONGA BEJUCO CISSUS COBAEA
COWAGE DERRIS DODDER
ECANDA GERKIN IPOMEA JICAMA
LABLAB PIKAKE RUNNER TURURI
TWINER ULLUCO WINDER
APRICOT BIGROOT BONESET
BRAMBLE CALAMUS CATVINE
CERIMAN CLIMBER COWHAGE
COWITCH CUPSEED EPACRID
GHERKIN IPOMOEA LAVANGA
PAREIRA PUMPKIN TRAILER
VINELET YANGTAO ATRAGENE
BINDWEED BOXTHORN CLEMATIS
COMEBACK CUCUMBER CUCURBIT
DECUMARY DOLICHOS EARDROPS
EARTHPEA EVONYMUS
GULANCHA HEARTPEA
HEMPWEED MUSCATEL
REDWITHE TINETARE TINEWEED
TRAILERY TRAILING TREEBINE
VINIFERA WINETREE WISTARIA
WISTERIA OLOLIUQUI
(PREF.) AMPEL(O) VITI

VINEGAR VIM EISEL ESILL ACETUM
ALEGAR ASCILL SOURING
BEEREGAR VINAIGRE
(— AND HONEY) OXYMEL
(PREF.) ACET(O)

VINEGAR EEL EELWORM

VINEGARY ACETOSE ACETOUS

VINEGROWER VINITOR

VINEYARD CRU CLOS COTE VINER
VINERY WINEYARD

VINGT-ET-UN MACAO MACCO

VINOUS WINY

VINTAGE OLD VINT WINE CUVEE
ARCHAIC CLASSIC VENDAGE
OUTMODED

VIOL GUE GIGA LIRA TURR GIGUE
GUDOK TARAU VOYAL VOYOL
CHELYS FIDDLE VIELLE VIOLET
MINIKIN QUINTON SARINDA
SULTANA VIHUELA VIOLONE
BARBITON BASSETTE SERINGHI
VIOLETTE

VIOLA ALTO QUINT TENOR TENORE
VIOLET
(BROTHER OF —) SEBASTIAN
(HUSBAND OF —) ORSINO

VIOLA BASTARDA BARITONE
BARYTONE

VIOLA DA BRACCIO QUINT

VIOLA DA GAMBA GAMBA

VIOLA D'AMORE VIOLET

VIOLATE ERR SIN FLAW ABUSE
BREAK CRACK FORCE FRACT
HARRY LOOSE VIOLE WRONG
BREACH BROACH DEFILE INVADE
OFFEND RAVISH DEBAUCH
DISOBEY FALSIFY INFRACT
OUTRAGE POLLUTE PROFANE
VITIATE DEFLOWER DISHONOR
FORSWEAR FRACTURE INFRINGE
MISTREAT STUPRATE SURPRISE
TEMERATE TRESPASS VIOLENCE

VIOLATED FRACTED INFRACT

VIOLATION SIN DEBT ABUSE
CRIME ERROR FAULT SALLY
BREACH INJURY MISCONDUCT
(HOCKEY —) STICKS
(TRIVIAL —) MOPERY

VIOLATOR WRONGER

VIOLENCE FURY NEED RAGE RUFF
BRUNT FORCE RIGOR STORM
BENSIL ESTURE HUBRIS RANDOM
RAPINE STOUSH STRESS BENSAIL
BENSALL OUTRAGE FEROCITY
SEVERITY SORENESS
ROUGHHOUSE
(LETHAL —) DEATH

VIOLENT BIG HOT TEZ DERF HARD
HIGH MAIN RANK RUDE WILD
WOOD ACUTE FIERY HEADY
HEAVY HEFTY RABID SHARP
SMART STARK STERN STIFF
STOOR STOUR STOUT WROTH
BROTHE FIERCE HEARTY MANIAC
MIGHTY SAVAGE SEVERE STORMY
STRONG STURDY SUDDEN
CRIMSON DRASTIC FURIOUS
HOTSPUR RAMMISH RAMPANT
RAPEFUL RUFFIAN TEARING
VIOLOUS WILSOME CHURLISH
DIABOLIC FLAGRANT FORCEFUL
IMPOTENT MANIACAL PERACUTE
RIGOROUS SEETHING SLAMBANG
STALWART VEHEMENT

VIOLENTLY HARD AMAIN HOTLY
HARDLY SORELY HOPPING
SOUNDLY

VIOLET CANON GRAPE MAUVE
VIOLA BLAVER CANYON DAHLIA
DAMSON EVEQUE JOHNNY
HOOKERS LOBELIA OPHELIA
PRELATE PRIMULA PUREAYN
CLEMATIS DAMEWORT FINELEAF
IANTHINE ROOSTERS WISTERIA
(PREF.) IO

VIOLIN GUE KIT ALTO GIGA AMATI
CROWD CRWTH GEIGE GIGUE
REBAB REBEC STRAD TARAU
VIOLA CATGUT CHORUS CROUTH
FIDDLE FITHEL REBECK TAILLE
VIOLON CATLING CHROTTA
CREMONA THEYAOU VIOLAND
VIOLINO GUARNERI KEMANCHA
VIOLOTTA
(PART OF —) NUT PEG TOP FROG
HEAD HEEL HOLE NECK BELLY
TABLE BRIDGE BUTTON PEGBOX
SCROLL STRING PURFLING
SOUNDBOARD FINGERBOARD

VIPER ASP HABU ADDER ASPIC
ATHER URUTU WYVER ASPIDE
DABOIA DABOYA JESSUR KATUKA
KUPPER HAGWORM MAMUSHI
VIPERID AMMODYTE CERASTES
JARARACA VIPERINE

VIRAGO RANDY AMAZON BELDAM
CALLET BELDAME TRIMMER
VIRAGIN RIXATRIX

VIREO REDEYE GRASSET TEACHER
GREENLET PREACHER

VIRGATE YOKE VERGE YARDLAND
(HALF —) MANTAL

VIRGILIAN MARONIAN

VIRGIN NEW LIVE MAID PURE
FRESH CHASTE MAIDEN VESTAL
INITIAL PUCELLE DOROTHEA
PARAMOUR

(— OF PARADISE) HURI HOURI
(PREF.) PARTHEN(O)
VIRGINAL CHERRY INTACT
SYMPHONY TRIANGLE

VIRGINIA

CAPITAL: RICHMOND
COLLEGE: AVERETT HOLLINS
MADISON RADFORD
LONGWOOD
COUNTY: LEE BATH PAGE WISE
BLAND CRAIG FLOYD SMYTH
SURRY WYTHE AMELIA LOUISA
ACCOMAC HENRICO PATRICK
PULASKI ROANOKE CULPEPER
FLUVANNA TAZEWELL
INDIAN: SAPONI TUTELO
MONACAN MANAHOAC
MEHERRIN NOTTAWAY
POWHATAN
LAKE: KERR SMITH
MOUNTAIN: CEDAR ELLIOT
ROGERS BALDKNOB
MOUNTAIN RANGE: CLINCH
ALLEGHENY BLUERIDGE
NICKNAME: OLDDOMINION
MOTHEROFSTATES
MOTHEROFPRESIDENTS
PRESIDENT: TYLER MONROE
TAYLOR WILSON MADISON
HARRISON JEFFERSON
WASHINGTON
RIVER: DAN JAMES POTOMAC
RAPIDAN
STATE BIRD: CARDINAL
STATE FLOWER: DOGWOOD
STATE TREE: DOGWOOD
TOWN: GALAX LURAY SALEM
MARION BEDFORD BRISTOL
EMPORIA NORFOLK PULASKI
ROANOKE DANVILLE HOPEWELL
MANASSAS STAUNTON
TAZEWELL

VIRGINIA COWSLIP LUNGWORT
VIRGINIA CREEPER CREEPER
WOODBIND WOODBINE
VIRGINIA KNOTWEED JUMPSEED
VIRGINIAN BEAGLE COOHEE
CAVALIER TUCKAHOE
(AUTHOR OF —) WISTER
(CHARACTER IN —) WOOD HENRY
MOLLY STEVE SHORTY TRAMPAS
VIRGINIANS (AUTHOR OF —)
THACKERAY
(CHARACTER IN —) THEO WILL
FANNY HARRY HETTY MARIA
MILES ESMOND GEORGE RACHEL
LAMBERT MOUNTAIN BERNSTEIN
CASTLEWOOD WARRINGTON
WASHINGTON
VIRGINIA SNAKEROOT SANGREL
SNAGREL
VIRGINIA STICKSEED SOLDIERS
VIRGINIA WATERLEAF SHAWNY
VIRGINIA WILLOW ITEA
VIRGINITY HONOR CHASTITY
PUCELAGE
VIRGIN MARY DESPOINA
THEOTOCOS
VIRGIN'S-BOWER LOVE
HONESTY CLEMATIS
MOONWORT

VIRGIN SOIL (AUTHOR OF —)
TURGENEV
(CHARACTER IN —) KOLYA
PAHKLIN SOLOMIN MARIANNA
MASHURIN SIPYAGIN MARKELOFF
VALENTINA NEZHDANOFF
OSTRODUMOFF
VIRGULE SLANT VIRGULA
DIAGONAL
VIRIDIAN EMERAUDE
VIRILE MALE MACHO MANLY
(AGGRESSIVELY —) MACHO
VIRILITY LUST GREEN MANHEAD
MANHOOD
VIRTUAL IMPLICIT PRACTICAL
VIRTUALLY BUT NEARLY MORALLY
VIRTUE JEN HSIN THEW ARETE
FAITH GRACE POWER VALOR
VERTU WORTH BOUNTY DHARMA
FOISON CHARISM CHARITY
JUSTICE PROBITY QUALITY
CHARISMA CHASTITY EFFICACY
GOODNESS MORALITY PARAMITA
PROPERTY
(CONFUCIAN —) LI
(PL.) CIVISM
(PREF.) ARETO
VIRTUOSO EXPERT SAVANT
ESTHETE LAPIDARY
VIRTUOUS GOOD PURE BRAVE
CIVIL MORAL PIOUS CHASTE
HONEST MODEST GODDARD
SAINTED SINCERE UPRIGHT
VIRTUAL STRAIGHT
VIRULENCE VIRUS
VIRULENT RANK ACRID RABID
DEADLY MALIGN VIROSE
NOXIOUS VIRIFIC WASPISH
VENOMOUS
(LESS THAN —) MITIS
VIRUS VENOM POISON PATHOGEN
SPECIFIC
VIS PEIKTHA
VISAGE FACE PHIZ CHEER IMAGE
VISOR ASPECT FASHION
VISCERA GUTS HASLET INSIDE
UMBLES GARBAGE GIBLETS
HASSLET INMEATS INNARDS
INSIDES NUMBLES ENTRAILS
HARIGALS
(PREF.) SPLANCHNO
VISCERAL GUT
VISCID SLAB WAXY GOOEY GLAIRY
STICKY LENTOUS STRINGY
VISCOUS MOTHERED
VISCIDITY LENTOR
VISCOSITY BODY ROPINESS
(— UNIT) POISE
VISCOUS LIMY ROPY SIZY SLAB
GOBBY GUMMY MUCIC ROPEY
SLIMY STIFF TARRY SIRUPY
SLABBY SMEARY SNOTTY STICKY
THONGY VISCID LENTOUS
SQUISHY VISCOSE MUCULENT
VISE GEE CHAP JACK SHOP VICE
CHEEK CLAMP CRAMP WINCH
(PART OF —) JAW BASE BOLT
ANVIL SCREW SLIDE HANDLE
SWIVEL
VISHNU RAMA VASU KALKI
KRISHNA BALARAMA BHAGAVAT
(AVATAR OF —) KALKI KURMA
BUDDHA MATSYA VAMANA

VARAHA KRISHNA NARASINHA
PARASHURAMA RAMACHANDRA
(BREAST JEWEL OF —) KAUSTUBHA
(BREASTMARK OF —) SHRIVATSA
(VEHICLE OF —) GARUDA
(WIFE OF —) SHRI LAKSHMI
(WRIST JEWEL OF —) SYAMANTAKA
VISIBLE OUT FAIR SEEN CLEAR
GROSS EXTANT SIGHTY EVIDENT
GLARING OBVIOUS OPTICAL
SIGHTLY APPARENT DIOPTRIC
EXPLICIT EXTERNAL MANIFEST
PROSPECT
(BARELY —) DARK
(SCARCELY —) DIM
(PREF.) DELO PHANER(O) PHANTA
PHANTASMO PHANTO
VISION EYE RAY DREAM FANCY
SIGHT FANTAD SEEING SWEVEN
AISLING SHOWING SPECTER
SPECTRE EYESIGHT PHOTOPIA
PROSPECT
(— IN DIM LIGHT) SCOTOPIA
(BLURRED —) SWIMMING
(DEFECTIVE —) ANOPIA
(DOUBLE —) DIPLOPIA
(IMAGINARY —) SHADOW
(IMPERFECT —) CALIGO DARKNESS
(MULTIPLE —) POLYOPIA
(PREF.) OPTI(CO) OPTO VISUO
(RANGE OF —) METROPIA
(SUFF.) OPSIA OPSIS OPSY OPTIC
OPTICON
(— DEVIATION) TROPIA
VISIONARY FEY AERY AIRY WILD
BIGOT IDEAL VIEWY ASTRAL
INSANE SHANDY UNREAL
DREAMER FANTAST LAPUTAN
UTOPIAN ACADEMIC DELUSIVE
FANCIFUL FINESPUN IDEALIST
NOTIONAL PHANTAST QUIXOTIC
ROMANTIC UTOPIAST VISIONER
VISIT DO GAM SEE VIS CALL CHAT
STAY APPLY HAUNT TRYST VIZZY
COSHER RESORT RETURN CEILIDH
CEILIDHE FREQUENT INVASION
(— BETWEEN WHALERS) GAM
(— PERSISTENTLY) INFEST
(— PROFESSIONALLY) ATTEND
(— RELATIVES) COUSIN
(— WRETCHED NEIGHBORHOODS)
SLUM
(CEREMONIAL —) SELAMLIK
VISITATION SENE VISIT SENDING
VISITING ACTIVE SOCIAL
VISITOR GUEST LAKER CALLER
VISITANT
(MEALTIME —) SCAMBLER
(PL.) COMPANY
VISOR BILL SIGHT UMBER UMBRE
VIZOR BEAVER MESAIL UMBRIL
VIZARD EYESHADE UMBRIERE
VISTA VIEW SCENE OUTLOOK
PERSPECTIVE
VISUAL OPTIC OCULAR SCOPIC
VISORY VISIBLE
VISUALIZE SEE FANCY IDEATE
SYMBOL IMAGINE PICTURE
CONCEIVE ENVISAGE
VITAL KEY LIVE BASIC CHIEF FRESH
SAPPY LIVELY MOVING VIABLE
ZOETIC ANIMATE CAPITAL
CORDIAL EXIGENT

NEEDFUL ESSENTIAL
VITALITY SAP VIM LIFE COLOR
GUSTO JUICE OOMPH PULSE
PUNCH BIOSIS BREATH ENERGY
FOISON HEALTH MARROW
PAZAZZ PIZAZZ STARCH PIZZAZZ
VIVENCY STRENGTH
(DEFICIENT —) ASTHENIA
(LACKING —) STUFFY TURNIPY
VITALIZE ACTIVATE ENERGIZE
VITAMIN BIOTIN CITRIN NIACIN
ADERMIN ANEURIN CHOLINE
THIAMIN TORULIN ADVITANT
INOSITOL NUTRAMIN ORYZANIN
VITAMINE
VITAMIN A RETINOL
VITIATE BEAT BLEND SPOIL TAINT
CANCEL DEBASE POISON
CORRUPT DEBAUCH DEPRAVE
VITIATED PICAL CORRUPT
(PREF.) CAC(O) CACH
(SUFF.) CACE
VITICULTURIST VIGNERON
VITREOUS GLASSY GLAIZIE
VITREAN VITROUS
VITRIFY GLAZE
VITRIOL BLUEJACK COPPERAS
(PL.) SORY
VITRIOLIC SHARP BITING BITTER
CAUSTIC MORDANT SCATHING
VITUPERATE RAIL ABUSE CURSE
SCOLD SLANG BERATE REVILE
VITUPERATION ABUSE VITUPER
VITUPERATIVE ABUSIVE REVILING
SHAMEFUL
VIVACE VIVO LEBHAFT
VIVACIOUS GAY AIRY PERT BRISK
CRISP MERRY SUNNY ACTIVE
BRIGHT LIVELY LIVING SPARKY
VIVACE ANIMATE JOCULAR
ANIMATED SPIRITED SPORTIVE
VIVACITY BRIO FIRE LIFE ZEAL
ARDOR VERVE VIGOR ESPRIT
GAIETY GAYETY SPIRIT SPRAWL
SPARKLE
VIVARIUM STEW VIVARY
STEWPOND
VIVAT HOCH
VIVERRINE CIVET GENET FOUSSA
MUSANG LINSANG FALANAKA
MONGOOSE SURICATE
VIVIANO (BROTHER OF —) MALAGIGI
ALDIGIERI
(SISTER OF —) BRADAMANTE
VIVID DEEP HARD KEEN LIVE RICH
VIVE BRISK FRESH GREEN LURID
QUICK RUDDY SHARP GARISH
LIVELY LIVING STRONG VISUAL
EIDETIC FLAMING FREAKED
GLARING GLOWING GRAPHIC
INTENSE PEPPERY VIOLENT
COLORFUL DISTINCT DRAMATIC
SLASHING STRIKING VIGOROUS
PICTURESQUE
VIVIDNESS COLOR EMPHASIS
VIVIFY LIFE FOMENT ANIMATE
QUICKEN SPARKLE
VIVIPARUS PALUDINA
VIXEN BARD FURY RANDY SCOLD
SHREW VIRAGO TAGSTER
TRIMMER
VIZIER WAZIR ATABEG ATABEK
VISIER

VLACH WALLACH
V-MAIL AIRGRAPH
VOCABULARY CANT LEXIS SLANG
JARGON DICTION LEXICON
POCHISMO WORDBOOK
(FAULTY —) CACOLOGY
(UNDERWORLD —) ARGOT
(PREF.) LEXICO
VOCAL GLIB ORAL VOWEL FLUENT
TONGUED VOCULAR ELOQUENT
VOCALIST BOPPER SINGER
BOPPIST BOPSTER SONGSTER
VOCALLER
VOCATION CALL HOBBY METIER
CALLING SCIENCE
VOCATIONAL BANAUSIC
VOCIFERATION CLAMOR OUTCRY
VOCIFEROUS LOUD NOISY
BAWLING BLATANT BRAWLING
STRIDENT
VODKA SAMOGON SAMOGONKA
VOGUE CUT FAD TON CHIC MODE
RAGE TURN STYLE CUSTOM
FASHION RECLAME PRACTICE
VOGUL MANSI
VOICE SAY VOX EMIT GIVE HARP
PIPE TONE TURN WISH FROTH
LEDEN RAISE RUMOR SOUND
UTTER ACTIVE CHOICE STEVEN
TAISCH THROAT TONGUE
EXPRESS OPINION SONORIZE
DIATHESIS
(— PRAISE) SLAVER
(ARTIFICIAL —) FALSETTO
(FIFTH —) QUINTUS
(HOARSE —) FOGHORN
(LOWEST —) BASS BASSO
(MIDDLE —) MOTETUS
(PRINCIPAL —) CANTUS
(PUBLIC —) CRY
(SINGING —) ALTO BASS TENOR
BREAST SOPRANO BARITONE
FALSETTO
(TENOR —) TAILLE
(UPPER —) DESCANT DISCANT
(PREF.) PHON(O) PHTHONGO VOCI
(LOUD —) STENTORO
(SUFF.) PHON(E)(IA)(Y)
VOICED SOFT WEAK TONIC MEDIAL
SONANT VIBRANT PHTHONGAL
VOICELESS MUM DUMB HARD
MUTE SURD SHARP ATONIC
FLATED SILENT ANAUDIA
APHONIC SPIRATE APHONOUS
BREATHED NOTELESS
VOID NO BAD FREE KORE LEAR
LEER MUTE NULL PASS TOOM
ABYSS AVOID BLANK EGEST
EJECT EMPTY INEPT LAPSE
PURGE SLICE SPACE WASTE
DEVOID HOLLOW VACANT
VACUUM CONCAVE INVALID
VACANCY VACUITY EVACUATE

INDIGENT NONBEING
(— OF FEELING) BLATE
(— OF SENSE) INANE
(— OF SUBSTANCE) JEJUNE
VOIDED FALSE CLECHE CLECHY
CLECHEE
VOILE NINON ETAMINE
VOLATILE LIGHT FIGENT LIVELY
VOLAGE BUOYANT DARTING
ELASTIC FLIGHTY FLYAWAY
GASEOUS FUGITIVE SKITTISH
VAPOROSE VAPOROUS
FUGACIOUS
(PREF.) PTENO
VOLATILITY LEVITY
VOLCANO APO DOME ETNA ASKJA
PELEE SHASTA VULCAN FURNACE
VULCANO FUMAROLE KRAKATOA
SPITFIRE VESUVIUS
(MUD —) SALSE SALINELLE
VOLE CRABER CRICETID
CAMPAGNOL
VOLITATION FLIGHT VOLATION
VOLITION WILL CHOICE INTENT
VOLENCY VELLEITY
VOLLEY TIRE CROWD DRIFT VOLEE
FLIGHT BARRAGE PLATOON
BLIZZARD
VOLPLANE GLIDE
VOLPONE (AUTHOR OF —) JONSON
(CHARACTER IN —) CELIA MOSCA
BONARIO CORVINO VOLPONE
VOLTORE POLITICK CORBACCIO
PEREGRINE
VOLSUNG WAELS
VOLT VOLTA REPOLON
(— AMPERE UNIT) VAR
VOLTAGE KICKBACK
VOLTAIC GUR GALVANIC
VOLTE-FACE BACKFLIP
VOLUBILITY FLUENCY
VOLUBLE GLIB WORDY FLUENT
VOLUME MO PEN BAND BOOK
BULK CODE SIZE TOME CODEX
SPACE CUBAGE CONTENT
DIURNAL MENAION VOLUMEN
CAPACITY CUBATURE SOLIDITY
STRENGTH
(— OF SOUND) STRESS
(— OF WORT) LENGTH
(PATTERN —) DUMMY
VOLUMINOUS FULL AMPLE BULKY
LARGE BOUFFANT
VOLUMNIA (SON OF —)
CORIOLANUS
VOLUNTARILY WILLES WILLICHE
VOLUNTARY FREE WILLY SORTIE
WILFUL PRELUDE SORTITA
WILLFUL WILLING ELECTIVE
FREEWILL HONORARY OPTIONAL
POSTLUDE UNFORCED
VOLUNTEER OFFER ENLIST
PROFFER FENCIBLE STRANGER

(— STATE) TENNESSEE
VOLUPTUARY SYBARITE
VOLUPTUOUS ADIN LUXIVE
LYDIAN SULTRY WANTON
SENSUAL DELICATE LUSCIOUS
SENSUOUS
VOLUPTUOUSNESS DELICE
LUXURY
VOLUTE TURN HELIX SCROLL
VOLUTA CILLERY VOLUTION
VOLUTION COIL TWIST WHORL
VERTICIL
VOLVA CUP WRAPPER
VOMIT CAT PUT BALK BARF BOCK
BOKE CACK CAST PICK PUKE SICK
SPEW SPUE VOME WOOM BRAKE
EVOME HEAVE REACH RETCH
SHOOT POSSET REJECT VOMITO
CASCADE CASTING REGORGE
DISGORGE PARBREAK SICKNESS
VOMITING
VOMITING BOKE EMESIS PYEMESIS
(PREF.) EMET(O)
VOMITUS SPEW SPUE
VOODOO HEX OBI CHARM OBEAH
HOODOO SORCERER
(— DESIGN) VERVER
(— PRIEST) BOCOR BOKOR
(— SPELL) MOJO
VOODOOISM VODUN WANGA
VOPHSI (SON OF —) NAHBI
VORACIOUS GORB GREEDY
BULIMIC ESURINE GLUTTON
THROATY EDACIOUS ESURIENT
RAVENING RAVENOUS
VORACITY BULIMIA EDACITY
VORTEX APEX EDDY GYRE SWIRL
WHIRL
VOTARESS NUN
VOTARY PALMER ZEALOT
DEVOTEE SECTARY ADHERENT
DEVOTARY FOLLOWER
VOTE AYE CON NAY PRO ELECT
FAGOT GRACE VOICE BALLOT
DIVIDE FAGGOT TONGUE
APPROVE PLUMPER SUFFRAGE
(— AGAINST) NAY KNIFE NEGATIVE
(— APPROVAL) CONFIRM
(— FOR) AY AYE PRO SUPPORT
(— OF ASSENT) PLACET
VOTER BOLTER POLLER CHOOSER
ELECTOR FLOATER ASSENTOR
VOTIVE VOWED
VOTYAK UDMURT
VOUCH ABLE ASSURE ATTEST
AVOUCH ENDORSE ACCREDIT
VOUCHER CHIT CHALAN COUPON
POLICY TICKET WARRANT
VOUCHSAFE GIVE SEND DEIGN
GRANT VOUCH BETEEM
PLEASE WITSAFE
VOUSSOIR QUOIN WEDGE
KEYSTONE SPRINGER

VOW LAY VUM AVOW OATH SNUM
VOTE SWEAR VOUCH BEHEST
PLEDGE BEHIGHT PROMISE
PROTEST
(PREF.) EUCHO
VOWEL SHWA WIDE GLIDE SCHWA
VOCOID AUGMENT PALATAL
GEMINATE ORINASAL
(— POINT) SERE
(BACK —) VELAR
(CHANGE OF —) UMLAUT
(GROUP OF 2 —S) BROAD DIGRAM
DIGRAPH
(PREFIXED —) AUGMENT
(SHORT —) MATRA
VOYAGE SAIL TRIP VIAGE COURSE
CRUISE FLIGHT TRAVEL CARAVAN
JOURNEY PASSAGE SAILING
STEAMER PERIPLUS SHIPPING
VOYAGING SEA NAVIGANT
VOYEUR PEEPER
VULCAN MULCIBER
VULCANITE EBONITE
VULCANIZATION BURNING
VULCANIZE BURN CURE METALIZE
VULCANIZER CEMENTER
VULGAR LOW LEWD LOUD RUDE
BANAL CHEAP FLASH GROSS
SLANG SLIMY TOUGH COARSE
COMMON PORTER RABBLE
VULGUS WOOLEN BLATANT
BOORISH GENERAL KNAVISH
LOWBRED MOBBISH OBSCENE
POPULAR PROFANE RAFFISH
SECULAR TABLOID VILLAIN
WOOLLEN BANAUSIC CHURLISH
MECHANIC PANDEMIC PLEBEIAN
PORTERLY POTHOUSE SOUTERLY
VULGARIAN CAD SLOB TIGER
KEELIE RAFFISH
VULGARITY RAUNCH SHODDY
FOULNESS HARLOTRY
VULGARIZE PLEBIFY PROFANE
VULGARIZED DEGRADED
VULGARLY CHEAPLY
VULNERABILITY GAP EXPOSURE
VULNERABLE NAKED LIABLE
EXPOSED PREGNABLE
VULPINE SLY FOXY ALOPECOID
VULTURE AURA GEIR PAPA AREND
GRAAP GRAPE GRIPE SWIPE
URUBU CONDOR CORBIE FALCON
GRIPHE RAPTOR SNATCH TORGOS
GRIFFIN GRIFFON GRYPHON
NEKHEBT AASVOGEL DIRTBIRD
GEREAGLE NEKHEBET ZOPILOTE
GALLINAZO
VULVA DOCK PUDENDUM
(PREF.) EPISIO
VUM SNUM

W WAW WHISKEY WILLIAM
WA VU KAWA LAWA
WABBLE COCKLE COGGLE HOBBLE
WAGGLE WARBLE WAUBLE
WOBBLE
WABBLY COGGLE WAGGLY
WOBBLY
WABBY LOON WHABBY
WABRON WAYBERRY
WACKY CRAZY INSANE MENTAL
ERRATIC
WAD BAT BET BOB PAD COLF LINE
POKE SWAB SWOB WISP WAGER
PLEDGE SCOURER GRAPHITE
WADDING BOMBAST
WADDLE WAG DAIDLE HODDLE
PODDLE TODDLE WALLOP
WIDDLE WAUCHLE
WADDY PEG STICK COWBOY
RUSTLER WHADDIE
WADE FORD WYDE SLOSH PLODGE
PLOUTER PLUTTER
(— IN MUD) LAIR
WADI OUED WASH GULLY RAVINE
WADSET PAWN PLEDGE
MORTGAGE
WAFER HOST ABRET OBLEY
CACHET GAUFRE LAVASH
MATZOH OFLETE POPADAM
FLATBROD PARTICLE
WAFF WAG FLAP GUST ODOR
PUFF WAVE WHIFF PALTRY
FLUTTER GLIMPSE LOWBORN
WAFFENSCHMEID, DER
(CHARACTER IN —) GEORG MARIE
CONRAD LIEBENAU STADINGER
(COMPOSER OF —) LORTZING
WAFFIE VAGRANT VAGABOND
WAFFLE GOFER WAFER GAUFRE
BLATHER
WAFT PUFF WING WHEFT WHIFF
BECKON WINNOW
WAG LUG NOD WIG WIT WOG
CARD CHAP FLAG WAFF WALK
DROLL JOKER ROGUE SHAKE
TROLL FARCER JESTER NICKUM
WADDLE WAGGLE WAGWIT
WIGWAG FARCEUR HUMORIST
SLYBOOTS
WAGE FEE PAY WAR HIRE LEVY
FIGHT WADGE WEDGE EMPLOY
ENGAGE PACKET OVERTIME
(— BATTLE) STRIKE
WAGER GO BET LAY PUT SET VIE
WED GAGE HOLD PAWN TOSS
WOID BOUND PRIZE RAISE REVIE
SPORT STAKE STOOP WADGE
DEPONE GAMBLE IMPONE
LEVANT WEDFEE STOATER
QUINELLA
WAGES FEE PAY UTU GAGE HIRE
MEED GAGES TUNCA REWARD
SALARY PENSION SERVICE

STIPEND GRATUITY LABORAGE
PAYCHECK REQUITAL
WAGGISH ARCH DROLL JOKEY
JOCOSE JESTING JOCULAR
PARLOUS ROGUISH WAGSOME
HUMOROUS SPORTIVE
WAGGLE WAG WIGGLE WOBBLE
WOGGLE
WAGON CAR FLY VAN CART CHAR
DRAG DRAY PLOW RACK TEAM
TRAM WAIN WANE BUGGY DILLY
JERKY RULLY TRUCK CAMION
ROLLEY SPIDER TELEGA CAISSON
CHARIOT COASTER FOURGON
SHELVER TUMBREL TUMBRIL
DEMOCRAT LANDSHIP RUNABOUT
WHITETOP
(— WITHOUT SPRINGS) JERKY
TELEGA
(BAGGAGE —) FOURGON
(COVERED —) VAN CARAVAN
TARTANA LANDSHIP CONESTOGA
(LUMBER —) GILLY
(MINING —) TRAM HUTCH RULLY
ROLLEY
(ROUNDUP —) HOODLUM
(RUSSIAN —) TELEGA KIBITKA
(SCREENED —) ARABA
(STATION —) MICROBUS
SUBURBAN
(TEA —) SERVER
WAGONER AURIGA TREKKER
WAINMAN
WAGONETTE BREAK
WAGONLOAD FODDER FOTHER
WAGONMAN FOOTMAN
WAGTAIL MOLLY OATEAR WAGGIE
WASHER MOTACIL WATERIE
SEEDBIRD WASHDISH WASHTAIL
WAHINE WIFE WOMAN FEMALE
VAHINE FEMININE MISTRESS
WAHOO ONO PETO BASSWOOD
EUONYMUS GUARAPUCU
WAIF WEFT STRAY FEEBLE PALTRY
STRAFE CURRENT IGNOBLE
WASTREL
WAIL CRY WOW BAWL GURL
HOWL KEEN MOAN RAME YARM
CROON MOURN ULULU LAMENT
PLAINT YAMMER EJULATE
PLANGOR ULULATE ULLAGONE
WAILING WO WOE LAMENT
ULULANT
WAIN CART WAGON WEYNE
CHARIOT
WAINSCOT CEIL CARDIGAN
WAINSCOTING CEILING PANELING
WAIST JOSIE BASQUE BLOUSE
BODICE HALTER MIDDLE TAILLE
CORSAGE PIERROT
WAISTCOAT VEST BENJY GILET
FECKET JERKIN VESKIT WESKIT
SINGLET CAMISOLE

WAISTER TROUNCER
WAIT BIDE HOLD KEEP LITE PARK
STAY TEND WHET ABIDE ABODE
DEFER HOVER LURCH TARRY
WATCH ATTEND DEPEND EXPECT
HARKEN LAYOUT LINGER
(— A WHILE) TAIHOA
(— FOR) KEEP ABIDE AWAIT
ATTEND EXPECT
(— ON) HOP SEE SERVE INTEND
LACKEY
(— TABLE) HASH SERVE
WAITER MOZO CARHOP COMMIS
DRAWER FLUNKY GARCON
HASHER KIDNEY SALVER TENDER
THOMAS DAPIFER FLUNKEY
KELLNER PANNIER PICCOLO
SERVITOR KITMUDGAR
WAITING DORMANT
WAITRESS NIPPY HASHER
MOUSMEE PHYLLIS
WAIVE ABEY DEFER EVADE FORGO
ABANDON DECLINE FORSAKE
POSTPONE RENOUNCE
RELINQUISH
WAKA CANOE
WAKE WAK CROW NECK PLAY STIR
ALERT REVEL ROUSE TANGI TRAIL
VIGIL WATCH AROUSE AWAKEN
EXCITE FEATHER
WAKEFUL ALERT WACKER
RESTLESS VIGILANT WALKRIFE
WATCHFUL
WAKEFULNESS VIGIL WATCH
INSOMNIA
WAKE-ROBIN ARUM SARA SARAH
TRILLIUM
WAKF WAQF VAKUF VACOUF
WALACHIAN RUMAN VLACH
ROMANESE
WALAHEE ALAHEE
WALAPAI HUALPAI
WALDENSIAN LEONIST PATARIN
VAUDOIS SABOTIER
WALE RIB BEND PICK WEAL WELT
RIDGE WHELP CHOICE HARPIN
STROKE
(PL.) BEND HARPINS
WALES CYMRU CAMBRIA
(PREF.) CAMBRO

WALES		
BAY: SWANSEA CARDIGAN TREMADOC		
CAPITAL: CARDIFF		
COUNTY: FLINT RADNOR DENBIGH ANGLESEY CARDIGAN MONMOUTH PEMBROKE		
LAKE: BALA VYRNWY		
LANGUAGE: CYMRAEG		
MEASURE: COVER CANTRED CANTREF LESTRAD LISTRED CRANNOCK		

MOUNTAIN: SNOWDON		
MOUNTAIN RANGE: BERWYN CAMBRIAN		
PEOPLE: CYMRY KYMRY WELSH		
PORT: CARDIFF		
RIVER: DEE USK WYE TAFF TEME TOWY TEIFI SEVERN VYRNWY		
TOWN: MOLD RHYL ROSS FLINT TOWYN AMLWCH BANGOR BRECON RUTHIN CARDIFF NEWPORT RHONDDA SWANSEA HEREFORD HOLYHEAD PEMBROKE BRECKNOCK		
WATERFALL: CAIN RHAIADR		

WALK GO JET MOG FOOT GAIT
GANG HIKE HOOF LAMP PACE
PAUT REEL STEP TROD ALLEE
ALLEY ARBOR LEAVE MARCH
PORCH SHANK SLOPE SPACE
STALK TRACE TRACK TRADE
TRAMP TREAD TROOP ATTEND
AVENUE BEHAVE BOUNCE BRIDGE
BROGUE DANDER PASEAR
SASHAY STROKE TODDLE TRAVEL
TRUDGE BALTEUS BERCEAU
CRAMBLE FOOTING GALLERY
SHUFFLE STRETCH TRACHLE
TRAIPSE TURNOUT AMBULATE
ARBORWAY FLAGGING FRESCADE
NAVIGATE TRAVERSE
PROMENADE PEREGRINATE
(— ABOUT) SLOSH
(— AFFECTEDLY) PRINK
(— AIMLESSLY) PAUP POAP
(— AWKWARDLY) STAUP SHAMBLE
(— BEFORE) PREAMBLE
(— BEHIND BATTLEMENTS) ALURE
(— BRISKLY) LEG SKELP
(— CARELESSLY) JAYWALK
(— CAUTIOUSLY) STALK
(— CLUMSILY) JOLL STUMP
LOPPET
(— FOR CATTLE) GANG
(— FOR EXAMINING ENGINE)
GALLERY
(— FOR EXERCISE) HIKE GRIND
(— HEAVILY) PLOD CLUMP
STUMP TRAMP LAMPER
PLODGE
(— IDLY) DANDER POTTER
SAUNTER
(— IN AFFECTED MANNER) MINCE
(— LAME) LIMP HIRPLE HOBBLE
CRIPPLE
(— LEISURELY) AMBLE DANDER
STROLL
(— ON) BEAT TREAD
(— OUT) FLOUNCE
(— RAPIDLY) LAMP LINK STAVE
(— SHAKILY) DOTTER
(— SLOWLY) JET LAG
(— SMARTLY) LINK

595

(**— STEADILY**) SNOVE SNOOVE
(**— UNSTEADILY**) REEL DADDLE
FALTER STAVER STAGGER
STUMBLE
(**— WAVERINGLY**) SHEVEL WARPLE
(**— WITH DIFFICULTY**) CRAMBLE
CRAMMEL LOUTHER
(**— WITH JERK**) HIRCH
(**— WITH LOFTY GAIT**) JET
(**— WITH OSTENTATION**) PRANCE
(**— WITH SHUFFLE**) COONJINE
(**— WITH STRIDES**) STAG
(**— WITH TREES**) XYST XYSTUS
ALAMEDA
(**— WITHOUT LIFTING FEET**) SCUFF
(**BACKSTAGE —**) BRIDGE
(**COOL —**) FRESCADE
(**COVERED —**) PAWN PORCH
CLOISTER
(**FOLIAGE-COVERED —**) BERCEAU
(**HARD —**) STRAM SWINGE
(**LIMPING —**) GIMP
(**LONG —**) STRAM
(**POMPOUS —**) STRUT
(**PUBLIC —**) XYST XYSTUS
ALAMEDA
(**RAISED —**) GALLERY
(**SHADED —**) MALL ARBOR XYSTUS
(**TEDIOUS —**) TRAIL
(PL.) BALTEI
(PREF.) AMBULO GRADIO GRADO
WALKER GOER FOOTER FULLER
GANGER FOOTMAN TODDLER
PEDESTRIAN
(PL.) FEET
WALKING HOTFOOT PASSANT
AMBULANT GRADIENT TRIPPING
(PREF.) BASI BASO
(SUFF.) BAT(ES)(IC) GRADE
WALKING STICK BAT CANE GIBBY
KEBBY STICK WADDY KEBBIE
PHASMID SPECTER ASHPLANT
GIBSTAFF WOODHORSE
WALKOUT STRIKE
WALKURE, DIE (**CHARACTER IN —**)
MIME WOTAN FRICKA HUNDING
SIEGMUND SIEGLINDE
BRUNNHILDE
(**COMPOSER OF —**) WAGNER
WALKWAY CATWALK SIDEWALK
WALL WA DAM FIN MUR WAW
BAIL BELT CELL CORE CRIB CURB
DICK DIKE DRUM DYKE FACE
HEAD MURE PACK SKIN SPUR
WING WOGE ATTIC BOARD CHEEK
CRUST DIGUE EMURE FENCE
HEDGE MEURE MURAL PIRCA
SHOJI WOGHE WOUGH BAFFLE
BAILEY BATTER CUTOFF DOKHMA
IMMURE LEADER PARIES PARPEN
PRETIL REBOTE RIPRAP SCREEN
SEPTUM SHIELD VALLUM
CHEMISE CURTAIN ENCLOSE
MIZRACH PARAPET PERPEND
PLUTEUS REREDOS TAMBOUR
FIREBACK SPANDREL TRAVERSE
(**— ABOVE FACADE**) ATTIC
(**— AROUND**) IMMURE
(**— BEHIND ALTAR**) REREDOS
(**— BETWEEN TWO OPENINGS**) PIER
(**— CARRYING CUPOLA**) DRUM
(**— CARRYING ROOF**) BAHUT
(**— CROSSING RAMPART**) SPUR

(**— IN HOCKEY RINK**) BOARD
(**— IN ROMAN ARENA**) SPINA
(**— IN TRUCK**) HEADER
(**— OF BLAST FURNACE**) DAM
INWALL FIREBACK
(**— OF CASTLE**) BARMKIN
(**— OF CLAY**) COTTLE
(**— OF HOOF**) CRUST
(**— OF MINE**) FACE
(**— OF MOUTH**) CHEEK
(**— OF TENT**) KANAT CANAUT
(**BODY —**) MANTLE
(**CIRCULAR —**) CASHEL
(**CORE —**) HEARTING
(**CURVED —**) SWEEP
(**DIVIDING —**) SEPTUM
(**END — OF BUILDING**) GABLE
(**FISH —**) LEADER
(**HIGHEST PART OF —**) CRAPWA
(**INNER SLOPE OF —**) BATTER
(**LOG —**) CRIB
(**LOW —**) BAHUT PODIUM
PLUTEUS
(**LOWER PART OF —**) DADO
(**OUTER — OF CASTLE**) BAIL BAILEY
(**PEAT —**) COP
(**PUDDLE —**) HEARTING
(**RETAINING —**) CRIB BULKHEAD
(**SCARPED —**) GHAT
(**SECONDARY —**) CHEMISE
(**SUSTAINING —**) RIPRAP
(**THINNED PART OF —**) ALLEGE
(**VENTRAL —**) STERNUM
(**WING —**) AILERON
(PL.) PERICARP
(PREF.) MURI PARIETO TICHO
(SUFF.) (**COAT OF SPORE —**)
SPORIUM
WALLABA APA
WALLABY WURRUP BRUSHER
TOOLACH WURRUNG BOONGARY
KANGAROO PADMELON WHIPTAIL
WALLACHIAN RUMAN
WALLAROO EURO
WALLBOARD GOBO
WALLET JAG JAGG MAIL POKE
BOGET BOUGE BULCH BULGE
SCRIP BUDGET READER SACKET
ALFARGA ALFORJA LEATHER
BILLFOLD NOTECASE POCHETTE
(PREF.) PERO
WALLEYE WHALL SAUGER
LEUCOMA WATCHEYE EXOTROPIA
WALLEYED PIKE DORE DORY
JACK PERCID SALMON WALLEYE
PICKEREL
WALLFLOWER CUBA CHEIR GILLY
JACKS KEIRI GELOFER WARRIOR
GILLIVER
WALL HAWKWEED LUNGWORT
WALLOP BEAT BEER FLOP SLUG
SOCK PASTE POUND VALOP
GALLOP IMPACT WALLOW
FLUTTER TROUNCE FLOUNDER
LAMBASTE
WALLOW FADE LAIR ROLL SOIL
SLOSH WALWE GROVEL MUDDLE
WALTER WELTER WITHER
SLUDDER SWELTER FLOUNDER
KOMMETJE VOLUTATE
WALLOWISH FLAT WELSH INSIPID
WALLPAPER GROUND SCENIC
HANGING TENTURE TAPESTRY

WALL PEPPER SEDUM
STONECROP
WALL PLATE PAN RASEN
WALL RUE TENTWORT
WALLY TOY FINE SPOIL PAMPER
ROBUST STRONG STURDY
SPLENDID VIGOROUS
WALLY, LA (**CHARACTER IN —**)
WALLY GELLNER HAGENBACH
(**COMPOSER OF —**) CATALANI
WALNUT ACAPU NOGAL TRYMA
AKHROT BANNUT HEARTNUT
(**BRAZILIAN —**) EMBOYA IMBUIA
(PL.) JUGLANS
WALNUT BROWN TAFFY
WALNUT SHELL BOLSTER
WALPI HUALPI
WALRUS MORSE WALTRON
PELAGIAN PINNIPED ROSMARINE
WALT CRANK UNSTEADY
WALTZ LUG CARRY MARCH VALSE
BOSTON BREEZE FLOUNCE
WAMARA CLUBWOOD IRONWOOD
PANOCOCO
WAMBLE ROLL SPIN WAMEL
NAUSEA REVOLVE
WAMBLY FAINT SHAKY
WAME WEM WAMB WYME BELLY
WAMPUM PEAG FADME HAWOK
MONEY PAAGE SEWAN FATHOM
SEAWAN ROANOKE
WAMUS JACKET WAMPUS
WARMUS
WAN DIM HAW FADE PALE PALY
SICK BLAKE FAINT WHITE FEEBLE
PALLID SALLOW GHASTLY
LANGUID
WANAPUM SOKULK
WAND ROD VARE YARD BATON
STAFF STICK VERGE VIRGA
FERULA THYRSE WATTLE
RHABDOS THYRSUS CADUCEUS
(**JESTER'S —**) BAUBLE
(PREF.) RHABD(O)
WANDER BAT BUM ERR GAD WAG
HAAK HAIK HAKE MAZE MUCK
RAKE RAVE ROAM ROIL ROLL
ROVE WALK WILL WORE DAVER
DRIFT GLAIK KNOCK RANGE
ROGUE SHACK SLOSH STRAY
TAVER TRAIK VAGUE WAIVE
WAVER CANDER CRUISE DANDER
DAUNER FORAGE LOITER MITHER
MOIDER MUCKER PALMER
PERUSE RAMBLE RANGLE STRAKE
STROLL SWERVE WILDER
MEANDER TRAFFIC TRAIPSE
VAGRATE VANDYKE ABERRATE
CUTICULA SQUANDER STRAGGLE
STRAVAGE STRAVAIG
(**— ABOUT**) DIVAGATE
(**— ABSTRACTEDLY**) MOON
(**— AIMLESSLY**) SWAN SLOSH
TRACE MEANDER
(**— AS A VAGABOND**) SHACK
(**— AS A VAGRANT**) LOITER
(**— AT RANDOM**) SQUANDER
(**— ERRATICALLY**) SWASH
(**— FROM DIRECT COURSE**)
STRAGGLE
(**— FROM PLACE TO PLACE**) WAG
(**— IDLY**) HAKE LOUT MAUNDER
SHACKLE

(**— IN DELIRIUM**) DWALE DWALL
(**— IN MIND**) DAVER DANDER
DELIRE
(**— LEISURELY**) BUMMEL
(**— RESTLESSLY**) FEEK
WANDERER WAIF ROVER VAGUE
RANGER PILGRIM RAMBLER
FUGITIVE RUNAGATE TRAVELER
VAGABOND
(**AUTHOR OF —**) FOURNIER
(**CHARACTER IN —**) FRANTZ GALAIS
MILLIE SEUREL YVONNE
AUGUSTIN BLONDEAU FRANCOIS
MEAULNES VALENTINE
CHARPENTIER
WANDERING GAD ROAM WAFF
ERROR STRAY VAGUE ARRANT
ASTRAY ERRANT MOBILE ROVING
VAGANT VAGOUS DEVIOUS
NOMADIC ODYSSEY VAGANCY
VAGRANT WINDING ABERRANT
FLOATING FUGITIVE PELAGSIC
PLANETAL PLANETIC RAMBLING
RESTLESS TRAILING VAGABOND
WINDRING MIGRATORY
PEREGRINE
(PREF.) PLAN(O) VAGO
(SUFF.) PLANIA
WANDERING JEW (**AUTHOR OF —**)
SUE
(**CHARACTER IN —**) ROSE HARDY
RODIN SIMON DJALMA SAMUEL
BAUDOIN GABRIEL JACQUES
ADRIENNE AGRICOLA AIGRIGNY
DAGOBERT FRANCOIS HERODIAS
RENNEPONT CARDOVILLE
WANDFLOWER GALAX SPARAXIS
WANDOROBO WAASI
WAND-SHAPED VIRGATE
WANE GO EBB SET WELK WILK
ABATE DECAY UNWAX WANZE
REPINE DECLINE DWINDLE
DECREASE
(**— OF MOON**) WADDLE
WANGA CHARM SPELL OUANGA
WONGAH SORCERY
WANGLE FAKE SHAKE WIGGLE
FINAGLE
WANIGAN ARK CHEST COFFER
WANGUN
WANT HURT LACK LIKE MISS NEED
OONT PINE VOID WANE WONT
CRAVE FAULT FORGO BESOIN
CHOOSE DEARTH DEFECT DESIRE
MISTER PENURY PLIGHT ABSENCE
BEGGARY BLEMISH BORASCA
DEFAULT MISEASE NEEDHAM
POVERTY REQUIRE VACANCY
MISCHIEF WANTROKE
(**— EXCEEDINGLY**) DIE
(**— OF CONTROL**) ACRASY
(**— OF ENERGY**) ATONY
(**— OF GOOD SENSE**) FOLLY
(**— OF REST**) UNRO
(**— OF SUCCESS**) FAILURE
(**— OF VIGOR**) DELICACY
WANTAGE ULLAGE
WANTING LACK VOID WANE
ALACK MINUS ABSENT LACKING
MISSING INDIGENT
(**— ORIGINALITY**) BANAL
WANTON JAY NAG RIG DAFT GOLE
IDLE LEWD NICE RAGE SKIT

CADGY DALLY LIGHT SAUCY GIGLET GIGLOT HARLOT HAUNTY LACHES LUBRIC RAKISH RIGSBY TICKLE TOYING TOYISH UNRULY COLTISH FULSOME GIGGISH HAGGARD IMMORAL KITTOCK LUSTFUL PAPHIAN RIGGISH RIOTOUS SMICKER WAYWARD FLAGRANT LUSCIOUS MISTRESS PETULANT PLAYSOME RUMBELOW SKITTISH SLIPPERY SPITEFUL SPORTIVE UNCHASTE

WANTONNESS FOLLY PRIDE SPORT RAGERY SUCCUDRY SURQUIDY

WAP BIND BLOW WHOP WRAP BLAST FIGHT KNOCK STORM TRUSS BUNDLE STRIKE

WAPITI ELK ALCE DEER LOSH LUSH STAG MARAL MOOSE CERVID WAMPOOSE

WAR WIN CAMP FEUD MART FIGHT SWORD WORSE WORST BATTLE CONTEND CRUSADE CONFLICT GUERILLA OVERCOME **(RELIGIOUS —)** JEHAD JIHAD **(PREF.)** BELLI MACHO POLEMO

WAR AND PEACE (AUTHOR OF —) TOLSTOY **(CHARACTER IN —)** LISE ELLEN MARYA ANDREY PIERRE ROSTOV ANATOLE BEZUHOV KURAGIN KUTUZOV NATASHA NIKOLAY VASSILY NAPOLEON BOLKONSKY NIKOLUSHKA

WARBLE SING CAROL CHANT CHIRL CHIRM SHAKE TRILL YODEL JARGON RALISH RELISH WARNEL WORMIL DESCANT VIBRATE WOURNIL

WARBLE FLY OXFLY BOTFLY GADFLY OESTRID OESTRIAN

WARBLER CUT KIT CHAT SMEU WREN FITTE PEGGY CANARY EYSOGE REELER SMEUTH SYLVIA TITIEN CREEPER CROMBEC FANTAIL HAYBIRD HAYSUCK PITBIRD REDPOLL SYLVIID TROCHIL BEAMBIRD BLACKCAP FAUVETTE MALURINE MOCKBIRD OVENBIRD PINCPINC REDSTART REEDBIRD RIRORIRO TROCHILUS

WAR CLUB MAR MER MERE MERAI MARREE

WAR CRY ALALA BANZAI SLOGAN

WARD CARE GUARD MAHAL VICUS WAIRD WATCH ALUMNA BARRIO CALPUL DEFEND ROWENA KEEPING NATUARY CALPOLLI CONTRADA **(— OFF)** FEND WEAR WERE AVERT AWARD FENCE PARRY REPEL STAVE SHIELD BUCKLER EXPIATE FORFEND

WARDAGE WARTH

WARDEN ALCADE DIZDAR PORTER RANGER REGENT ROLAND WARNER ALCAIDE HOGMACE LEATMAN ROWLAND BEARWARD CLAVIGER **(AUTHOR OF —)** TROLLOPE **(CHARACTER IN —)** TOM BOLD JOHN SUSAN FINNEY TOWERS

ABRAHAM ELEANOR GRANTLY HARDING SEPTIMUS HAPHAZARD QUIVERFUL THEOPHILUS

WARDER PORTER GUARDER HEIMDAL TURNKEY WATCHMAN BEEFEATER

WARDROBE KAS CLOSET VESTRY ALMIRAH ARMOIRE VESTUARY

WARE CLOTH GOODS SPEND FABRICS SEAWEED SQUANDER **(CERAMIC —)** SPODE **(CLOISONNE —)** SHIPPO **(ENAMELED —)** BILSTON COALPORT **(INFERIOR —S)** SLUM **(JAPANESE —)** IMARI YAYOI **(JAPANESE CERAMIC —)** SETO BIZEN KARATSU **(KIND OF —)** RAKU MINTON WHIELDON **(KIND OF JAPANESE POTTERY —)** SANDA **(MAJOLICA —)** DERUTA **(PORCELAIN —)** CHINA IMARI BERLIN **(UNGLAZED —)** BISQUE **(PL.)** TROKE CHAFFER TROGGIN

WAREHOUSE GOLA HONG ETAPE GOLAH STORE BODEGA FONDUK GODOWN STAITH ALMACEN FUNDUCK SPICERY STOWAGE ENTREPOT MAGAZINE SERAGLIO

WARFARE WAR ARMS IRON ARMOR BATTLE PSYWAR MILITIA CONFLICT **(NONAGGRESSIVE —)** SITZKRIEG **(SUFF.)** MACHIA MACHY

WAR-HORSE CHARGER COURSER DESTRER TROOPER DESTRIER

WARILY TIPTOE GINGERLY

WARINESS CAUTEL CAUTION DISTRUST WARESHIP WARIMENT

WARKLOOM TOOL WARKLUME

WARLIKE WARLY MARTIAL CAVALIER FIGHTING MILITARY BELLICOSE **(NOT —)** IMBELLIC

WARLOCK IMP WITCH SPRITE WARLOW WIZARD CONJUROR SORCERER

WARLORD TUCHUN

WARM HOT LEW LOO RUG BASK BEEK KEEN LEWD MILD CALID CHAFE EAGER FRESH MALMY MUNGY SLACK TEPID TOAST ACHAFE ARDENT BIRSLE DEVOUT DIGEST FOSTER GENIAL HEARTY HEATED RIZZLE TENDER CHERISH CLEMENT CORDIAL GLOWING THERMAL ZEALOUS FRIENDLY PRESSING SANGUINE **(— UP)** SCORE **(MODERATELY —)** LEW SLACK TEPID **(PREF.)** CAL(E)(I)(ORI)

WARMHEARTED KIND TENDER FRIENDLY GENEROUS

WARMING FOVENT

WARMOUTH BIGMOUTH FLATFISH SACALAIT

WARMTH GLOW HEAT LIFE ZEAL ARDOR LEWTH ENERGY FERVOR ARDENCY PASSION

CALIDITY FERVENCY **(INNER —)** JUICE

WARN REDE WARD WERN ALERT AREAD WEIRD ADVERT ADVISE EXHORT INFORM CAUTION COMMAND COUNSEL GARNISH PREVISE ADMONISH THREATEN **(— OFF)** FORBID

WARNING AHEM ITEM ALARM CHECK KNELL BEACON CAVEAT LESSON NOTICE OFFICE SAMPLE SIGNAL TIPOFF AVISION CALLING CAUTION EXAMPLE GRIFFIN JIGGERS MEMENTO MONITOR PRESAGE SUMMONS DOCUMENT GARDYLOO MONITION PREMONITION **(— OF DISASTER)** DIRE **(ARCHERY —)** FAST **(DANGER —)** VIGIA

WARP CUP WEB BIAS CANE CAST LIFT WARF WERP WIND ANGLE CHAIN CHOKE CRAWL CROOK GEYZE KEDGE PORRY THRAW TWINE WEAVE BUCKLE CHEESE DEFORM WASHIN DEFLECT DISTORT SKELLER **(— IN WEAVING)** CRAM **(PREF.)** HIST(O)

WARPED WRY BUCKLED GNARLED HOUSING

WARPER BALLER

WARPING BOW PANDATION

WARRAGAL WILD DINGO HORSE OUTLAW

WARRANT ABLE WARN AMRIT BERAT FIANT PRESS SANAD VOUCH AMRITA ASSERT BRANCH BREVET COUPON DOCKET ENSURE INSURE PARDON PERMIT PLEVIN POLICY POTENT SUNNUD TICKET WARDOG BEHIGHT CAPTION JUSTIFY PRECEPT PROMISE GUARANTY MITTIMUS

WARRANTED VALID

WARRAU GUARANO

WARREN SLUM CONYGER WARRANT

WARRIOR TOA WER EARL HERO KEMP RINK WEER BERNE FREIK FREKE HAGEN LLUDD SEPAD SINGH THANE THEGN OSSIAN WARMAN WEAPON FIGHTER SOLDIER STARKAD WARWOLF ZERBINO CHAMPION RODOMONT SHARDANA STARKATH SWORDMAN WARFARER **(— CLASS)** MAGANI **(— OF NOBLE RANK)** EARL **(AMERICAN INDIAN —)** BRAVE SANNUP **(BOASTFUL —)** RODOMONT **(BRYTHONIC —)** LLUDD **(BURGUNDIAN —)** HAGEN **(FEMALE —)** AMAZON SHIELDMAY **(IRISH —)** FENIAN **(KAFFIR —S)** IMPI **(MUSLIM —)** GAZI GHAZI **(NOTED —)** THANE THEGN **(SCANDINAVIAN —)** BERSERK **(SCOTTISH —)** ZERBINO **(TROJAN —)** AGENOR **(VALIANT —)** TOA

(VIRGIN —) CAMILLA **(PL.)** IMPI CHIVALRY GAMMADIM

WARSHIP GUIDE WAFTER CRUISER MONITOR SULTANA SULTANE CORVETTE

WART RAT WRAT AMBURY ANBURY SYCOMA PUSTULE VERRUCA VERRUGA EPIDERMA PAPILLOMA **(POTATO —)** CANKER **(PREF.)** VERRUCI

WART HOG EMGALLA

WARTLIKE PYRENOID

WART SNAKE XENODERM

WARTY MURICATE

WARY SHY CAGY WISE AWARE CAGEY CANNY DOWNY HOOLY LEERY TENDER CAREFUL GUARDED PRUDENT WAREFUL CAUTIOUS SKITTISH VIGILANT WATCHFUL

WAS VAS WIS WUZ WYS PAST WISSHE **(— ABLE)** COULD **(— NOT)** NAS **(I —)** CHWAS

WASH DO BOG FEN LAG LAP NET TUB BEER BUCK EDDY HOSE HUSH LAVE SILT SUDS WADI BATHE CLEAN CLEAR DOLLY DRAFF ERODE MARSH RINSE SCRUB SLOSH SOUSE SWILL BUDDLE CRADLE DOLLIE LOTION PURIFY SLOOSH SLUICE SOZZLE STREAM ALLUVIO CLEANSE LAUNDER SHAMPOO ALLUVIUM EYEWATER LAVAMENT LAVATORY **(— A GAS)** SCRUB **(— AWAY)** GULL **(— BY TREADING IN WATER)** TRAMP **(— DOWN)** SIND SOOGEE **(— FOR GOLD)** PAN **(— GIVEN TO SWINE)** DRAFF **(— GRAVEL)** ROCK **(— IN LYE)** BUCK **(— LIGHTLY)** RINSE **(— OFF)** DETERGE **(— ORE)** TYE HUTCH BUDDLE CRADLE STRAKE **(— OUT)** SIND ELUTE FLUSH LAVAGE **(— ROUGHLY)** SLUSH **(— THOROUGHLY)** SCOUR **(— VIGOROUSLY)** SLOSH **(— WITH BROOM)** TYE **(— WITH COSMETIC)** SURFLE SURPHUL **(DRY —)** ARROYA ARROYO

WASHBASIN LAVER LAVABO LAVATORY ALJOFAINA

WASHCLOTH FLANNEL

WASHED ABLUTED **(— UP)** SHOT THROUGH

WASHER BUR BURR DRUM ROVE CLOUT BUTTON RONDEL SOURER GROMMET LEATHER RACCOON COTTEREL LAVENDER RONDELLE SCRUBBER

WASHERMAN DHOBI DHOBIE LAVANDERO

WASHERWOMAN LAUNDER

WASHING LAG BATH LAVAGE SLOOSH LAUNDRY ABLUTION

LAVAMENT LAVATION
(PL.) ELUATE
WASHING MACHINE DASHWHEEL

WASHINGTON
CAPITAL: OLYMPIA
COLLEGE: WHITMAN
COUNTY: ASOTIN KITSAP SKAGIT
YAKIMA CLALLAM KITTITAS
DAM: COULEE
INDIAN: HOH LUMMI MAKAH
TWANA SAMISH SKAGIT
YAKIMA CHINOOK CLALLAM
COWLITZ SANPOIL CHIMAKUM
OKANAGON
LAKE: CHELAN
MOUNTAIN: JACK TUNK ADAMS
LEMEI LOGAN MOSES SLOAN
QUARTZ SIMCOE STUART
OLYMPUS RAINIER SHUKSAN
MOUNTAIN RANGE: KETTLE
CASCADE OLYMPIC
NICKNAME: CHINOOK EVERGREEN
RIVER: SNAKE YAKIMA COLUMBIA
SOUND: PUGET
STATE BIRD: GOLDFINCH
STATE TREE: HEMLOCK
TOWN: OMAK PASCO TACOMA
YAKIMA EPHRATA EVERETT
OTHELLO SEATTLE SPOKANE
LONGVIEW

WASHOUT FLOP STUMOR FAILURE
WASHROOM BASEMENT
LAVATORY
WASHSTAND COMMODE
WASHTUB FLASKET
WASHY SOFT WEAK LOOSE MOIST
FEEBLE PALLID WATERY DILUTED
SHILPIT
WASP MASON SPHEX WHAMP
WOPSE BEMBEX DAUBER DIGGER
HORNET TIPHIA TREMEX VESPID
CYNIPID DRYINID EUMENID
MASARID SCOLIID SERPHID
SIRICID SPHECID STINGER
ACULEATE MUTILLID POMPILID
WASPISH TESTY FRETFUL PEEVISH
CHOLERIC SNAPPISH
WASSAIL TOAST PLEDGE
CAROUSE REVELRY CAROUSAL
WASTE EAT FUD GOB TED BURN
GNAW JUNK LOSS PASS PEAK
ROSS SACK TEAR TINE WEAR
WILD DROSS EXILE HAVOC SCRAP
SLOOM SLOTH SLOUM SPILL
TABID THRUM BANGLE BEZZLE
COMMON DEBRIS DESERT
DEVOUR DIDDLE DRAFFY DRIVEL
ELAPSE EXPEND FOREST GARBLE
GOUSTY LAVISH MOLDER
MUDDLE PADDLE PERISH RAVAGE
REFUSE SCATHE SPILTH WESTEN
CONNACH CONSUME EXHAUST
FRITTER GARBAGE MULLOCK
RUBBISH SLATTER CONFOUND
DEMOLISH SLATTERN SQUANDER
(— AWAY) BATE MELT DECAY
DWINE SWAIN SWEAL TRAIK
WANZE TABEFY WINDLE
DWINDLE FORPINE MISLIKE
DISSOLVE EMACIATE FORSPEND
MACERATE

(— GRADUALLY) WEAR ABSUME
(— IN DRUNKENNESS) SOT
(— IN RIOT) BEZZLE
(— OF INK) INKSHED
(— OF SILK COCOONS) KNUB
(— TIME) FOOL FRIG IDLE DALLY
DEFER DRILL DAWDLE DIDDLE
FOOTER FOOTLE LOITER DRINGLE
FOOSTER GAUSTER
(COAL —) SLUDGE
(COTTON —) FLUKE SLASHER
SPOOLER
(FOOD —) SLOP
(LIQUID —) DRIPPING EFFLUENT
(MINING —) GOB GOAF
(WOOL —) FUD MUNGO GARNETT
(YARN —) THRUM EYEBROW
WASTEBASKET HELL HELLBOX
WASTED IDLE FORWORN
RAVAGED DECREPIT
WASTEFUL LAVISH PROFUSE
DESOLATE PRODIGAL SPENDFUL
WASTEFULNESS WAIT UNTHRIFT
WASTELAND CURAGH CURRACH
WASTER THIEF LEISTER WASTREL
PRODIGAL
WASTING FRET DECAY LIGHT
AWASTE ATROPHY CACHEXY
EXEDENT MISLIKE PREYING
TABIFIC CACHEXIA PHTHISIS
SYNTEXIS
(— AWAY) MARASMUS SYNTECTIC
(PREF.) PHTHISIO TABE TABI
TABO
(PROGRESSIVE —) TABO
WASTREL WAIF LOSEL REFUSE
WASTER ROUNDER VAGABOND
STROYGOOD
WATCH EYE FOB NIT SEE SPY TAB
DIAL ESPY GLIM GLOM HACK
HEED KEEP LOOK MARK MIND
PIPE TOUT TWIG VACH WAIK
WAKE WARD YARD CLOCK
GUARD SCOUT SPIAL SPIER
TIMER VERGE VIGIL VIRGE WAKEN
WHEEL BEHOLD DEFEND DIACLE
FOLLOW HUNTER PERDUE
SENTRY SHADOW TICKER TICTIC
TURNIP WAKING YEMING
OBSERVE OVERSEE ROSKOPF
STRIKER THIMBLE TOMPION
HOROLOGE MEDITATE SENTINEL
SPECTATE TICKTICK
(— FOR) TENT ABIDE AWAIT
(— OF ARMY) BIVOUAC
(— ON THE SLY) FOX
(— OVER) HOLD KEEP TEND TENT
GUARD ATTEND OVERLOOK
(— PEOPLE EATING) GROAK
(— QUIETLY) HINT
(— THAT STRIKES) STRIKER
REPEATER
(— UNIT) LIGNE
(— WITH HINGED COVER) HUNTER
(ALARM —) TATLER TATTLER
(CLOSE —) SCRUTINY
(NAUTICAL —) HACK DOGWATCH
(NIGHT —) LICHWAKE LYKEWAKE
(PART OF —) BOW FOB CASE DIAL
FACE HAND STEM BEZEL COVER
CROWN FRAME CHAPTER
CRYSTAL DISPLAY NUMERAL
SHOULDER

(SUFF.) SCOPE SCOPIC SCOPUS
SCOPY
WATCHBAND WRISTER WRISTLET
WATCH CRYSTAL LUNET
LUNETTE
WATCHDOG CUR GARM GARMR
MATIN BANDOG KRATIM
CERBERUS
WATCHER VEIL ARGUS WAKER
VIEWER WAITER MUSAHAR
SPOTTER WATCHMAN
WATCHFUL IRA ALERT AWARE
CANNY CHARY ERECT TENTY
WAKER TENTIE WACKER ANXIOUS
GUARDED JEALOUS LIDLESS
WAKEFUL VIGILANT WAKERIFE
WAUKRIFE OBSERVANT
WATCHFULNESS OUTLOOK
JEALOUSY
WATCHMAN FLAG MINA WAIT
GUARD SCOUT VIGIL WATCH
ASKARI BANTAY GHAFIR SERENO
SHOMER TOOTER WAITER
WARDEN WARDER BELLMAN
CHARLEY GUARDER TALLIAR
WAKEMAN CHOKIDAR SENTINEL
(NIGHT —) SERENO CHARLIE
WATCHTOWER WARD BEACON
GARRET MIZPAH SENTRY
ATALAYA LOOKOUT MIRADOR
BARBICAN SENTINEL SPECCHIE
WATCHWORD CRY MAXIM
ALERTA ENSIGN PAROLE SIGNAL
NAYWORD PASSWORD
WATCH WORKS MOVEABLE
WATER EAU TJI AGUA AQUA BATH
BRIM BROO BURN LAGE LAKE
POND POOL TIDE WAVE ABYSS
BILGE FLUME LOUGH LYMPH
RIVER TABBY TEARS TUBIG
BALLOW BAREGE CAMLET
CONGEE CONJEE PAWNEE
PHLEGM SALIVA STREAM VADOSE
WATHER AQUATIC CRYSTAL
JAVELLE IRRIGATE SNOWMELT
(— AFTER BOILING RICE) CONGEE
CONJEE
(— AS REFUGE FOR GAME) SOIL
(— AT THE MOUTH) DROOL
(— BY CALENDERING) TABBY
(— FOR BREWING) BURN
(— IN SOIL) HOLARD
(— IN WEIR) LASHER
(— REDDISH WITH IRON) RIDDAM
**(— RUNNING AGAINST MAIN
CURRENT)** EDDY
(— SPIRIT) KELPIE
(— SURROUNDED BY ICE) WAKE
(— UNDER PRESSURE) HUSH
(BAPTISMAL —) LAVER
(BARLEY —) PTISAN
(BOTTOM — OF SEA) ABYSS
(BOUNDARY —) SHARD
(BUBBLING —) SPRUDEL
(DEEP —) BALLOW
(DIRTY —) SAUR PUDDLE
(FAST-MOVING —) SOUP
(FEN —) SUDS
(FROZEN —) ICE FROST
(HOLY —) HYSSOP
(HOT —) SOUP
(LIVING —) RASA
(MINERAL —) VICHY SELTER

SELTZER APOLLINARIS
(OPEN —) POLYNYA
(QUININE —) TONIC
(RED —) RESP RIDDAM
(ROUGH —) SEA
(RUNNING —) SEA
(SALT —) BRACK BRINE SEAWATER
(SOAPY —) SUDS GRAITH
(SPLASH OF —) FLASH
(STILL —) KELD LOGIN
(SULPHUR —) BAREGE
(SURFACE OF —) RYME
(SWEETENED —) AMRIT AMRITA
(WASHING —) LAVATION
(PL.) APSU
(PREF.) AQUA AQUEO AQUI AQUO
HIDRO HYDAT(O) HYDR(O)
(GO THROUGH —) SILLO
(STAGNANT —) TELMAT(O)
(SUFF.) LIMNION YDATIS
WATER ARUM DRAGON
WATER BAG CHAGUL MATARA
MUSSUK
WATERBIRD ALCATRAS
WATERBRAIN GID
WATERBUCK COB CHUZWI
DEFASSA WATERDOE
WATER BUFFALO KERBAU
WATER CARRIER BHISTI
AGUADOR BHEESTY
WATER CART DILLY
WATER CASK WINGER
WATER CHESTNUT LING CALTROP
SALIGOT SINGHARA
WATER CHINQUAPIN BONNET
NELUMBO WANKAPIN YONCOPIN
RATTLENUT
WATER CLOCK GHURRY
CLEPSYDRA
WATER CLOSET PETTY PRIVY
STOOL SANITARY NECESSARY
WATER COCK KORA
WATERCOLOR GRAPHIC
WATERCOURSE (ALSO SEE
STREAM AND RIVER) RUN URN
AGOS DIKE DYKE GOTE HAHR
KHOR LADE LEAT REAN WADI
WADY YORA AUWAI BAYOU
BROOK CANAL CANEL COWAL
DITCH DRAIN RHINE ARROYO
CANNEL COURSE FURROW
GUTTER KENNEL NULLAH
CHANNEL TRINKET
WATERCRESS EKER KERS CARSE
KERSE BILDERS NOSESMART
WATER DOG OTTER WATERRUG
WATER DRINKER HYDROPOT
WATERED MOIRE TABBY
WATERFALL LIN LYN FALL FOSS
LINN SALT CHUTE FORCE SAULT
SHOOT SPOUT LASHER CASCADE
CATADUPE CATARACT OVERFALL
(FROZEN —) ICEFALL
WATER FENNEL EDGEWEED
WATER FLEA CYCLOPS DAPHNID
WATERFOWL WADER SWIMMER
WATERFRONT PRAYA
WATERGALL WINDDOG WINDGALL
JELLYFISH
WATER GERMANDER SCORDIUM
WATER HEMLOCK CICUTA
COWBANE DEATHIN JELLICA
WATER HOG BUSHPIG CAPYBARA

WATER HOLE DUB CHARCO TINAJA ALBERCA
WATER ICE SHERBET
WATERINESS AQUEITY AQUOSITY
WATERING EPIPHORA RIGATION
WATER JUG GAMLA GOMLAH GOOLAH
WATERLEAF SHAWNY NEMOPHILA
WATERLESS
(PREF.) ANHYDR(O)
WATER LETTUCE QUIAPO
WATER LILY DUCK LOTOS LOTUS WOCAS WOKAS BOBBIN CANDOCK NELUMBO CAMALOTE NENUPHAR
WATERLOGGED SOGGY SWAMPY EDEMATOUS
WATERMAN MERMAN QUENCH OARSMAN
WATERMARK CROWN TIDEMARK
WATERMARKED LAID
WATERMELON PEPO GOURD MELON TSAMA CITRUL SANDIA ANGURIA MILLION CUCURBIT PEPONIDA PEPONIUM SKIPJACK
WATER MOCCASIN CONGO
WATER NEWT ASK TRITON
WATER OPOSSUM YAPOK YAPOCK
WATER OUZEL PIET OOZEL OWZEL DIPPER DUCKER
WATER PEPPER LAKEWEED
WATER PLANT LIMU AQUATIC
WATER PLANTAIN ALISMA THRUMWORT
WATERPOT FONTAL
WATERPROOF RAINCOAT (— MATERIAL) KERATOL
WATER RAIL RUNNER BILCOCK MOORHEN OARCOCK
WATER RAT VOLE CRABER MUSKRAT WATERRUG
WATER SCORPION NEPID
WATERSHED BROW DIVIDE DIVORT SNOWSHED
WATER SHIELD FANWORT DEERFOOD FROGLEAF
WATERSKIN MASHAK MATARA MUSSUK MUSSACK MUSSICK
WATER SOLDIER PONDWORT
WATER SPIRIT ARIEL KELPY KELPIE UNDINE
WATERSPOUT RONE CANAL SPATE SPOUT VORTEX PRESTER TWISTER CATARACT GARGOYLE
WATER STRIDER SKATER SKIMMER SKIPPER SKETCHER
WATER THRUSH KICKUP WAGTAIL
WATER TIGER DYTISCID
WATERTIGHT THEAT THEET TIGHT STANCH THIGHT STAUNCH
WATER WALLY BATAMOTE
WATERWAY GUT CASH DOCK HOLE LODE DITCH INLET ARTERY SEAWAY CULVERT FAIRWAY HIGHWAY IGARAPE (ARTIFICIAL —) LEAD CANAL (PL.) SCUPPERS
WATERWHEEL NORIA SAKIA SAGEER SAKIEH DANAIDE SAKIYEH TYMPANUM
WATERY WET LASH PALE SICK THIN WHEY BOGGY MOIST

SAMMY WASHY BLASHY FLASHY LIQUID PALLID SEROSE SEROUS SWASHY AQUATIC AQUEOUS CHOROUS HYDROUS PHLEGMY SANIOUS HUMOROUS HYDATOID ICHOROUS SKINKING
WATT (ONE BILLION —S) GIGAWATT
WATTLE GILL JOWL PLAT SALY TWIG WAND BOREE COOBA FRITH MULGA SALLY SALWE STAVE STICK HURDLE JEWING JOLLOP LAPPET SALLOW BLUEBUSH CARUNCLE
WATTLEBIRD IAO MOHO MINER MANUAO MAOMAO GILLBIRD
WATTLE CROW KOKAKO
WAVE FAN FLY JAW SEA WAW BECK FLAG FLAP GUST LUMP SUFF SULK SWAY WAFF WAFT WAWE YTHE BLESS CRIMP FLASH FLOAT FLOTE PULSE SHAKE SURGE SWELL SWING BILLOW COMBER FLAUNT MARCEL RIPPLE ROLLER WAFFLE WINNOW BREAKER BRIMMER CRIMPLE DECUMAN FEATHER FLICKER FLUTTER TSUNAMI WHIFFLE ARTEFACT BRANDISH FLOURISH GRAYBACK UNDULATE UNIPULSE WHISTLER WHITECAP (— ABOUT) WAMPISH (— OF EXCITATION) IMPULSE (— OF FLAG) DOT DASH (— OF SHIP) BONE (ARCH OF —) CURL (ELECTRIC —) STRAY CARRIER (HAIR —) PERMANENT (LARGE —) HEAVY (TIDAL —) EAGER (PL.) SURF (PREF.) CUMA CYM(I)(O) CYMATO KYM(I)(O) KYMATO ONDA ONDO UNDI
WAVER HALT REEL SWAG SWAY VARY CHECK DAKER DOUBT FLOAT SWALE SWING WIVER DACKER DAIKER DITHER FALTER MAMMER QUIVER SWERVE TEETER TOTTER WABBLE WAFFLE WOBBLE BALANCE FLICKER FLITTER FLUTTER STAGGER SWITHER VIBRATE HESITATE VACILLATE
WAVERING WAW WAVY WEAK WAUCH WAUGH FICKLE GROGGY WAVERY WIGGLY DUBIOUS LAMBENT SHUTTLE DOUBTFUL FLEXUOSE FLEXUOUS FLICKERY HOVERING WAVEROUS PENDULOUS
WAVERLEY (AUTHOR OF —) SCOTT (CHARACTER IN —) EVAN LEAN ROSE VOHR ALICE COSMO DAVIE FLORA DONALD FERGUS STUART CHARLES EVERARD MACIVOR GARDINER PEMBROKE WAVERLEY GELLATLEY MACCOMBICH BRADWARDINE
WAVINESS CRIMP
WAVING UNDE WAFT AWAVE OUNDY UNDEE WAFTURE FLOURISH
WAVY ONDE UNDE UNDY CRISP

MOIRE SNAKY UNDEE CRIMPY FLECKY REPAND SNAKEY UNDATE WIGGLY BUCKLED CRINKLY CURVING ENDATED ROLLING SINUATE UNDULAR ENRIDGED FLEXUOUS ONDOYANT SQUIGGLY UNDULATE (PEOPLE WITH — HAIR) VEDDOID
WAWL HOWL WAIL WOWL SQUALL
WAX WOX CERE CODE GROW RAGE WACE WOXE SCALE BECOME CAPPING CERESIN KLISTER CARNAUBA CERESINE CEROXYLE COCCERIN EPILATOR INCREASE (— FAINT) APPAL (— FROM INSECT) PELA (— IN HONEYCOMB) CAPPING (— STRONG) PREVAIL (CHINESE —) PELA (COBBLER'S —) CODE (EAR —) CERUMEN (KIND OF —) PINSANG (SKI —) KLISTER (PREF.) CER(I)(O) KERO
WAXBILL ASTRILD REDBILL
WAXEN WAX PALLID CEREOUS
WAXER GLAZER WAXMAN
WAXFLOWER EPIPHYTE
WAX MYRTLE ARRAYAN
WAX PLANT HOYA
WAXWING WAXBIRD RECOLLET SILKTAIL
WAXY ANGRY VEXED CEREOUS PLIABLE YIELDING
WAY LAW PAD TAO VIA WON WYE FARE FORE FORM GAIT GANG GATE KIND LANE LARK PACE PATH PAWK RAKE ROAD SORT TOBY WISE ALLEY CHANT FORTH GOING GUISE HABIT MOYEN ROUTE SHEAR STEPS STYLE TRACT TRADE ACCESS AVENUE CAREER CHEMIN COURSE MANNER METHOD PHASIS STREET TRAJET CHANNEL FASHION HIGHWAY PASSAGE SKIDWAY APPROACH CONTRADA DISTRICT FOOTPATH THOROUGH VICINITY LAUNCHING (— OF DEPARTURE) EXIT (— OF ESCAPE) BOLTHOLE (— OF LIFE) LARK TRACE HEDONISM (— OF SPEAKING) AMBAGE (— OF THINKING) DIET (— OF WALKING) JET (— OUT) IT EXIT SALVO (— THROUGH MINEFIELD) BREACH (CLEVER —) KNACK (COVERED —) CORRIDOR (INDIRECT —) AMBAGES (LONG —) FAR (MAJOR —) STEM (NARROW —) DRANG (ODD —S) JIMJAMS (PLANK —) BRIDGE (RAISED —) BANQUETTE (ROUNDABOUT —) DETOUR CIRCUIT (ROUNDABOUT —S) AMBAGES (SETTLED —) BIAS (SIDE —) BRANCH

(SLOPING —) RAMP (UNDEVIATING —) GROOVE (PL.) DAPS (PREF.) HODO ODO VIA (SUFF.) ODE OID WISE
WAYBILL CHALAN WILLIE CHALLAN
WAYFARER SHULER VIATOR PILGRIM SHUILER TRAVELER PASSENGER
WAYFARING TREE WHITTEN COTTONER VIBURNUM
WAYLAY BELAY BESET BLOCK BRACE AMBUSH FORLAY FORSET FORELAY OBSTRUCT SURPRISE
WAYLAYER WAIT
WAYMARK AHU
WAY OF ALL FLESH (AUTHOR OF —) BUTLER (CHARACTER IN —) JOHN ELIZA ELLEN MARIA PRYER ALLABY ALTHEA ERNEST GEORGE JOSEPH OVERTON SKINNER MAITLAND PONTIFEX THEOBALD CHARLOTTE CHRISTINA
WAY OF THE WORLD (AUTHOR OF —) CONGREVE (CHARACTER IN —) FOIBLE FAINALL MARWOOD ROWLAND WILFULL WITWOOD MIRABELL WAITWELL WISHFORT MILLAMANT
WAYSIDE HEDGE
WAYWARD PEEVISH
WEAK DIM LEW COOL DOWY FOND LAME NESH NICE PALE PUNY SELI SELY SOFT THIN WASH WAUF WOKE BAUCH BAUGH CRIMP DICKY FAINT FLASH FRAIL JERKY LIGHT NAISH REEDY ROCKY SEELY SILLY SLACK STANK WASHY WAUGH WEARY WERSH YOUNG CADUKE DEBILE DILUTE DOTISH FEEBLE FLABBY FLAGGY FLIMSY FOIBLE GROGGY INFIRM LIMBER LITTLE MARCID SEMMIT SICKLY SINGLE SWASHY TENDER UNSURE UNWISE WAIRCH WATERY BRICKLE DWAIBLY DWEEBLE FLACCID FOOLISH FRAGILE INSIPID INVALID LANGUID PIMPING PUERILE REGULAR RICKETY SAUGHEN SHALLOW SHILPIT SLENDER SPINDLY TOTTERY UNHARDY UNLUSTY WEARISH ASTHENIC CHILDISH DECREPIT DEFINITE FECKLESS FEMININE FLAGGING GRIPLESS HELPLESS IMBECILE IMPOTENT LADYLIKE LANGUENT PHTHISIC RESOLUTE RUSHLIKE SACKLESS SCRANNEL THEWLESS UNMIGHTY UNWIELDY SPINELESS (— FROM FATIGUE) TANGLE (— FROM HUNGER) LEER (— IN RESOLUTION) FRAIL (MENTALLY —) TOTTY (PREF.) ASTHEN(O) LEPT(O)
WEAKEN GO LAG SAP DAMP FAIL HURT MELT PALL SINK THIN ALLAY BLUNT BREAK CRAZE DELAY QUAIL SHAKE SPEND WATER APPALL ATTRIT DEACON DEADEN DEFEAT DEJECT DENUDE

DILUTE FALTER IMPAIR INFIRM
LABEFY LESSEN PERISH REBATE
REDUCE SICKEN SOFTEN
CORRODE CORRUPT CRIPPLE
DECLINE DEPRESS DISABLE
MOLLIFY QUALIFY RESOLVE
THREADY UNBRACE UNNERVE
CASTRATE DIMINISH EMBEZZLE
ENERVATE ENFEEBLE ETIOLATE
INFRINGE LABEFACT UNSTRENG

WEAKENED GROGGY ANODYNE
INVALID SHOTTEN DECREPIT
LABEFACT STRAINED

WEAKENING CHRONIC FAILURE
FLAGGING

WEAKEST RECKLING

WEAKFISH DRUM TROUT ACOUPA
SALMON CORBINA CORVINA
DRUMMER SQUETEE TOTOABA
TOTUAVA BLUEFISH CHICKWIT

WEAKLING TOY WRIG DUGON
PULER SLINK SOFTIE DILLING
RECKLING SOFTLING

WEAKLY FEEBLY FEMALE SIMPLY

WEAK-MINDED DAFT DOTY
DOTED FOOLISH

WEAKNESS ATONY CRACK CRAZE
FAULT FOLLY TOUCH ATONIA
DEFECT FOIBLE ACRATIA FAILING
FISSURE FRAILTY LANGUOR
ASTHENIA DEBILITY DELICACY
FONDNESS
(CARNAL —) FLESH
(SUFF.) (— FOR) ITIS

WEAL WHEAL RICHES STRIPE
WEALTH WELFARE

WEALTH WAD WON DHAN GEAR
GOLD GOOD MUCK WONE MEANS
THING WORTH GRAITH MAMMON
POCKET PURPLE RICHES TALENT
CASHBOX FORTUNE RICHDOM
WARISON WELFARE CATALLUM
OPULENCE OPULENCY PROPERTY
TREASURE WARRISON
MONEYBAGS
(— OF NATION) STOCK
(PATRON OF —) YAKSHA
(PREF.) APHNO PLUT(O)

WEALTHY FAT BEIN BIEN FULL
OOFY RICH WELI AMPLE PURSY
TINNY LOADED OOFIER COUTHIE
MONEYED PURSIVE ABUNDANT
AFFLUENT

WEAN CHILD SPAIN SPANE WAYNE
INFANT ESTRANGE

WEANING ABLACTATION

WEAPON (ALSO SEE SPECIFIC TYPE
OF WEAPON) ARM BOW GUN
BILL BOLA BOLO CLUB COSH
DART EDGE EPEE FALX FOIL IRON
MACE PATU PIKE TOOL WIWI
ADAGA ARROW BILLY CAKRA
DEATH FLAIL KNIFE LANCE ONCIN
ORGUE SHARP SPEAR SQUID
STEEL SWORD VOUGE WAPIN
CANNON CHAKRA DAGGER
GLAIVE MACANA TOMBOC
ARCHERY BAZOOKA FIREARM
GISARME HALBERD HARPOON
HURLBAT JAVELIN LIANGLE
POUNAMU SHOTGUN SLASHER
STICKER TICKLER WHIFFLE
ARBALEST BLOWBACK BLUDGEON

CROSSBOW FAUCHARD
HEDGEHOG LEEANGLE PARTISAN
TROMBASH
(CELTIC —) PALSTAFF
(DEADLY —) DEATH
(LINE OF —S) RIDGE
(PREHISTORIC —) CELT
(PL.) WAR TACKLE ARCHERY
WEAPONRY
(PREF.) ARMI HOPL(O)

WEAR KIT BEAR FRAY FRET GROW
HAVE PASS CHAFE GUARD SPEND
VOGUE WEARY ABRADE BATTER
BECOME BETHUMB CONSUME
DEFENSE DEGRADE FASHION
FATIGUE FRAZZLE PROCEED
WEATHER PROGRESS
(— AN OPENING) BREACH
(— AND TEAR) GAFF SLITE
GRUELING
(— AWAY) EAT FADE FRET GALL
GNAW GULL PINE ERODE GULLY
SCOUR SPEND ABRADE CORRADE
CORRODE CONTRIVE
(— CLOTHES) DRESS
(— DOWN) BRAY GRIND ABRADE
ABRASE GRAVEL
(— FURROWS) GUTTER
(— IN PUBLIC) SPORT
(— OFF) FRAY ABRADE
(— OUT) DO BURN COOK FLOG
JADE MUSH TIRE TUCK BREAK
SLAVE SLITE SPEND TRASH
BUGGER HATTER MAGGLE
PERUSE EXHAUST FORWEAR
FORWORK HACKNEY INVALID
SHACHLE OVERFRET OVERWEAR
(— SHIP) CAST
(— SHOES OUT OF SHAPE) SHACHLE
SHACKLE
(— TIGHT CORSETS) LACE

WEARIED AWEARY FORGONE
FATIGUED WEARIFUL

WEARINESS TIRE FATIGUE
BRAINFAG SICKNESS VEXATION

WEARING DECAY SCUFF BURNING
CLOTHES ABRASION GARMENTS
GRINDING

WEARISOME DRY DULL HARD
SLOW WEARY BORING MORTAL
PROLIX SODDEN IRKSOME
TEDIOUS SAWDUSTY TIRESOME
TOILSOME

WEARISOMENESS TEDIUM

WEARY FAG IRK SAD BOEG BORE
CLOY MOIL PALL POOP PUNY
SADE TIRE TIRY WEAK WORE
WORN BORED BREAK CURSE
SPENT ABRADE BETOIL HARASS
PLAGUE SICKLY SQUEAL TUCKER
EXHAUST FATIGUE IRKSOME
SWINKED FATIGATE FORCHASE
GRIEVOUS TIRESOME WRETCHED
FORJASKIT
(BECOME —) JADE

WEARY WILLIE TRAMP

WEASAND WISEN GULLET THROAT
WIZZEN TRACHEA WINDPIPE

WEASEL CANE VAIR VARE WARE
HULDA HURON SNEAK STOAT
TAIRA TAYRA ERMINE FERRET
HULDAH VERMIN ARCTOID
VORMELA FUTTERET MUISHOND

MUSTELIN WHITRACK
(PREF.) GALEO

WEASEL CAT LINSANG

WEATHER SKY DIRT RAIN TIME
COLLA STORM WINDWARD
(— CONDITION) WHITEOUT
(FAIR —) SHINE
(HOT AND HUMID —) SIZZARD
(INCLEMENT —) SEASON
(INTERVAL OF FAIR —) SLATCH
(UNDER THE —) SEEDY
(VIOLENT —) ELEMENTS
(PREF.) EUDIO METEOR(O)

WEATHERBEATEN GNARLED
SEAGOING

WEATHERCOCK COCK FANE VANE
FAINE FANACLE

WEAVE CANE HABI HUCK JOIN
LACE LENO LOOM REED ROCK
SPIN WALE WARP WIND WOOF
DOBBY DRAPE PLAIT TWINE
UNITE BROCHE DAMASK DEVISE
DIAPER DOBBIE FABRIC CANILLE
ENTWINE FASHION INDRAPE
SATINET SHUTTLE VANDYKE
DIAGONAL DUCHESSE OVERSHOT
(— PATTERNS INTO) BROCADE
(BASKET —) BARLEYCORN
(CARPET —) FLOSSA
(HERRINGBONE —) SUMAK
SOUMAK SHEMAKA
(LATTICE —) TEE
(OPEN —) LENO BAREGE

WEAVER KORI TANTI WEBBE
DRAWBOY WEBSTER WOBSTER
PENELOPE TAPESTER

WEAVERBIRD NUN BAYA MAYA
TAHA FINCH MUNIA VIDUA
WEBBE BISHOP CANARY OXBIRD
WHIDAH WHYDAH BENGALI
AMADAVAT AVADAVAT
CARDINAL MANNIKIN

WEAVING TANIKO TEXTURE
WEBBING
(— OF WORDS) CONTEXT
(— TOGETHER) PLEXURE

WEAZEN WIZEN SHRINK WIZENED

WEB PLY WOB CAUL FELT MAZE
TENT TOIL VANE WARP WEFT
SKEIN SNARE THROW TWIST
FLEECE TISSUE ENSNARE
FEATHER LAYETTE TEXTURE
SNOWSHOE VEXILLUM
(— IN EYE) HAW
(CRANK —) THROW
(PREF.) HIST(O) HISTI(O) HYPHO

WEBBED RINGED PALMATE

WEBBING MAT WEB PALAMA

WEB-FOOTED PALMATE
PALAMATE PALMIPED

WEB SPINNER EMBIID WEBWORM

WED GET BEWED BRIDE MARRY
STAKE WAGER ENGAGE PLEDGE
SPOUSE ESPOUSE WEDLOCK

WEDDING BRIDAL SPLICE NUPTIAL
WEDLOCK ESPOUSAL MARRIAGE

WEDGE KEY COIN FROE FROW
GLUT HORN KYLE PLUG STOB
TRIG TRIP WAGE CHOCK CHUCK
CLEAT COIGN HACEK HORSE
QUINE QUOIN SCOTE SLICE
THROW COTTER CUNEUS QUINET
SCOTCH EMBOLUS QUINNET

SCHOCHE VOUSSOIR
(— BETWEEN TWO FEATHERS) KEY
(— IN) JAM JAMB
(— OF OATMEAL) FARL FARLE
(— TO PREVENT MOTION) CHOCK
(CURVED —) CAM
(WOODEN —) COW GLUT JACK
(PREF.) CUNEI CUNEO EMBOL(O)
SPHEN(O)

WEDGER SPRINGER

WEDGE-SHAPED CUNEAL SPHENIC
CUNEATED SPHENOID
(PREF.) CUNEO SPHEN(O)

WEDLOCK WIFE SPOUSAL
MARRIAGE SPOUSAGE

WEDNESDAY MIDWEEK

WEE TINY EARLY SMALL TEENY
YOUNG LITTLE

WEED BUR HOE BURR CHOP CULL
DOCK FORB LOUK SHIM SIDA
TARE WEID CIGAR DRANK DRAWK
DRESS DROKE FLESH BLINKS
CASUAL COCKLE DARNEL JIMSON
KNAWEL RIPGUT SARCLE SPURGE
SPURRY STROIL ASHWORT
BUGLOSS COHITRE CUCKOLD
EGILOPS GARMENT GOSMORE
HOGWORT RAGWEED RAGWORT
SANDBUR TOBACCO VERVAIN
VERVINE CHADLOCK COCKSPUR
COWWHEAT PIRIPIRI PLANTAIN
PURSLANE TOADFLAX ALFILERIA
MARIJUANA
(— OUT) ROGUE
(MEXICAN —) BIRDEYE
(ROADSIDE —) PLANTAGO
(TROUBLESOME —) KEX TITTER
(WATER —) ANACHARIS
(PL.) FILTH WRACK DISMAL
SPRING WEEDAGE TRUMPERY

WEEDER SARCLER

WEEDY FOUL LANKY

WEEK OOK WOK OULK WOKE
SENNET STANZA HEBDOMAD
SENNIGHT
(TWO —S) FORTNIGHT

WEEKDAY FERIA WARDAY

WEEKLY AWEEK HEBDOMADARY

WEEL LEAP POOL TRAP RIGHT
WHIRLPOOL

WEEN MEAN VENE WEND FANCY
GUESS EXPECT BELIEVE IMAGINE
SUPPOSE CONCEIVE

WEENY TINY SMALL WEESHY

WEEP CRY ORP SOB BAWL BEND
GIVE LEAK OOZE PIPE TEAR WAIL
GREET BEWAIL BEWEEP BOOHOO
BUBBLE LAMENT SHOWER
BLUBBER LAPWING SQUINNY
COMPLAIN

WEEPER GREETER MOURNER
CAPUCHIN
(PL.) FLENTES

WEEPING WOP GREET MILCH
RAINY BOOHOO LAMENT OOZING
PIPING BLUBBER MAUDLIN
TEARFUL DRIPPING LACRIMAL
MADIDANS PLORATION

WEEPING SINEW GANGLION

WEEVER JUGULAR STINGBULL

WEEVIL MAX BOUD POPE WHULE
PICUDO WEEBLE BILLBUG
BRUCHUS VAQUITA

CURCULIO WOODWORM
(PLUM —) TURK
WEFT WEB PICK WOOF BLAST
FABRIC FILLING
WEIGH GO SIT HEFT PEIS TARE
TELL COUNT HEAVE HOIST PEIZE
POISE RAISE SCALE BURDEN
PONDER ANALYZE BALANCE
DEPRESS LIBRATE CONSIDER
EVALUATE MEDITATE MILITATE
(— DOWN) LADE SWAY SWEE
BESET HEAVY PEISE CADDLE
CHARGE CUMBER PESTER
DEPRESS FREIGHT INGRATE
OPPRESS OVERLAY ENCUMBER
(— UPON) SIT GRIEVE
WEIGHER BOXMAN PEISER SCALER
WEIGHING METAGE
(— MACHINE) TRON SCALE TRONE
WEIGHT (ALSO SEE MEASURE AND
UNIT) BOB FEN FOB KIN MAN
NET OKE RAM SER SIR TOM TUP
ABAS ATOM BEEF CLOG DROP
GRAM HEFT IRON KITE LEAD
LOAD MACE MEAL NAIL ONUS
PEIS POND PORT ROTL SEAM
SEER SINK WAIT ABBAS CLOVE
CRITH GARCE LIVRE MAUND
PEASE PEISE PICUL POISE POIZE
PRESS RIDER SCALE STAMP
AUNCEL BURDEN CHARGE
DIRHEM HAMMER IMPORT
MOMENT MONKEY PASSIR
PONDER PONDUS SINKER STRESS
BALLAST DOLPHIN GRAVITY
MILLIER PLATINE PLUMMET
POSIURE CHALDRON DEMIMARK
DUMBBELL ENCUMBER FARASULA
LISPOUND PRESSURE PRESTIGE
QUINCUNX STANDARD STRENGTH
(— AFTER TARE DEDUCTION)
SUTTLE
(— CARRIED BY HORSE) IMPOST
(— CLOTH) FLOCK
(— FOR HURLING) HAMMER
(— FOR LEAD) FOTHER FOTMAL
(— FOR PRECIOUS STONE) CARAT
(— FOR WOOL) TOD SARPLER
(— FOR WOOL, CHEESE, ETC.) CLOVE
(— OF BROADSIDE) GUNPOWER
(— OF COAL) KEEL
(— OF COFFEE) MAT
(— OF HYDROGEN) CRITH
(— OF METAL) JOURNEY
(— OF ONE 10TH TAEL) MACE
(— OF ONE 100TH TAEL) FEN
(— OF PENDULUM) BOB
(— OF PILE DRIVER) TUP
(— OF RAW SILK) PARI
(— OF SILK OR RAYON) DRAMMAGE
(— OF 100 LBS.) CENTAL CENTENA
CENTNER
(— OF 1000 LIVRES) MILLIER
(— OF 20 OR 21 LBS.) SCORE
(— OF 40 BUSHELS) WEY
(— OF 5 UNCIAE) QUINCUNX
(— ON MINE SWEEPER) KITE
(— ON STEELYARD) PEA
(— ON WATCH CHAIN) FOB
(— TO BEND HOT METAL) DUMPER
(— TO DETECT FALSE COINS)
PASSIR
(— TO HINDER MOTION) CLOG

(— WHICH VESSEL CAN CARRY)
TONNAGE
(ABYSSINIAN —) FARASULA
(CARAT —) SILIQUA
(CLOCK —) PEISE
(COUNTERFEIT —) SLANG
(FALSE —) SLANG
(GREATLY VARYING —) MAN
MAUND
(HEAVY —) MONKEY
(LIGHT —) SUTTLE
(MONEYER'S —) DROIT
(ORIENTAL —) TAEL CATTY
(SASHCORD —) MOUSE
(SHUFFLEBOARD —) SHIP
(SMALL —) MITE GERAH RIDER
(SPLINE —) DOLPHIN
(UNIT OF —) SER VIS WEY GERA
LAST ROTL SEER LIANG LIBRA
LINGO MINAL PECUL PERIT PIKOL
KANTAR LINGOE MISKAL POCKET
LISPUND PRICKLE QUINTAL
ZOLOTNIK
(PREF.) BAR(I)(O)(Y) PONDERO
(SUFF.) BAR(IC)
WEIGHTED BIAS LOADED
WEIGHTER FULLER
WEIGHT-PRODUCING GRAVIFIC
WEIGHTY GRAVE GREAT HEAVY
HEFTY MASSY SOLID VALID
COGENT SOLEMN EARNEST
MASSIVE ONEROUS PEISANT
PESANTE SERIOUS TELLING
GRIEVOUS MATERIAL POWERFUL
PREGNANT PORTENTOUS
SIGNIFICANT
WEIR DAM PEN CRIB KEEP LEAP
STOP CAULD DOACH GARTH
GORCE HATCH HEDGE SASSE
STANK LASHER BURROCK
WEIRD ODD EERY UNCO UNKO
EERIE UNCOW UNKID CREEPY
ELDRICH ELRITCH UNCANNY
UNUSUAL WIZARDLY
(— SISTERS) FATES
WEITSPEKAN YUROK
WEKA RAIL WOODHEN RAILBIRD
WELCOME SEE FAIN GOOD HAIL
ADOPT CHEER GREET RESET
TREAT ACCOIL INVITE SALUTE
ACCLAIM ACCUEIL EMBRACE
GRATIFY BIENVENU GREETING
HAEREMAI PLEASANT
ACCEPTABLE
WELD SHUT WELL SWAGE UNITE
WOALD ACACIA
WELDED SHOT
WELDING FUSION SHUTTING
WELFARE SEL GOOD HALE HEAL
SELE WEALTH BENISON BLESSING
WELKIN SKY HEAVENS WALKENE
WELL AIN EYE GAY PIT WEL BENE
FINE FLOW GOOD PANT PUIT
PURE RITE SAFE SINK WINK
AWEEL BOOLY BOWLY GREAT
MUSHA OILER QUELL WALLY
WISHA ATWEEL BUCKET CENOTE
ENOUGH FAIRLY GASSER NICELY
OFFSET PUMPER TUNNEL
FALLWAY GRADELY HEALTHY
WILDCAT BOREHOLE FOUNTAIN
GRAITHLY POSTHOLE WATERPIT
WEALSOME

(— AND STRONG) BUNKUM
(— IN GLACIER) MOULIN
**(— THROUGH FLOORS OF
WAREHOUSE)** FALLWAY
(— UP) WALL WALM DIGHT
(AS —) ALSO
(NONPRODUCTIVE —) DUSTER
(NOT —) DONNY SOBER INVALID
(OIL —) OILER GASSER GUSHER
SPOUTER WILDCAT STRIPPER
(RECTANGULAR —) BOOLY BOWLY
(SACRED — AT MECCA) ZEMZEM
(TOLERABLY —) GAYLIES GEYLIES
(VERY —) BRAWLY CLEVER
(PREF.) BENE EU
WELL-BALANCED SOBER
WELL-BEHAVED GOOD NICE
MODEST MANNERED
WELL-BEING HEAL SKIN WEAL
HEALTH WEALTH COMFORT
EUCRASY WELFARE EUCRASIA
PROSPERITY
WELLBORN GENTLE EUGENIC
WELL-BRED GENTIL POLITE
GENTEEL REFINED CULTURED
LADYLIKE
WELL-BUILT TIGHT
WELL CASING STEANING
WELL-CHOSEN CHOICE
WELL-CONDITIONED SONSY
WELL-CONSIDERED THRIFTY
WELL CURB PUTEAL
WELL-DEFINED STRICT
WELL-DISPOSED SIB FAIN GOOD
VAIN
WELL DONE SHABASH
WELL-DRESSED BRAW GASH
SMART BRAWLY
WELL-FED BLOWSY BLOWZY
CHUBBY GAWCEY GAWSIE
WELL-FINISHED SOIGNE
WELL-FORMED TIGHT DECENT
PROPER SEEMLY SHAPELY
WELL-FOUNDED FIRM GOOD JUST
SOUND WORTHY
WELL-GROOMED SMUG CRISP
SOIGNE SOIGNEE
WELL-GROUNDED JUST VALID
WELL-GROWN THRODDY
WELL-HUSBANDED THRIFTY
WELL-INFORMED KNOWING
PERFECT
WELL-INTENTIONED AMIABLE
WELL-KEPT SMUG POLITE
WELL-KNIT WIRY
WELL-KNOWN BREEM BREME
BEATEN FAMOUS KENNED PUBLIC
FAMILIAR PROMINENT
WELL-LIKED FANCIED POPULAR
WELL-MADE CLEVER FEATOUS
WELL-MANNERED POLITE
COURTEOUS
WELL-NIGH WELLY ALMOST
NEARLY WELLMOST
WELL-ORDERED
(PREF.) COSM(ETO)(ICO)(O)
WELL-ORGANIZED SNOD
WELL-PLEASED FAIN VAIN
WELL-PROPORTIONED SUING
TRETIS HANDSOME
WELL-READ STUDIED LITERARY
WELL-ROUNDED CHUBBY
WELL-SHAPED CLEVER FEATOUS

WELL-TILLED NOT NOTT
WELL-TO-DO ABLE BEIN BIEN EASY
WARM PODDED
WELL-TRODDEN TRITE
WELL-WISHER FRIEND FAVORER
WELS WALLER SHEATFISH
WELSH (ALSO SEE WALES) CYMRY
FUDGE TAFFY CYMRIC KYMRIC
CAMBRIAN
WELSHER SHICER QUITTER
WELSHMAN CELT KELT TAFFY
BRYTHON CAMBRIAN
WELSH ONION CIBOL CIBOULE
CHESBOLL
WELT WALE RIDGE STRIP WHELP
WELTING BANDELET TURNOVER
(SHOE —S) WATTIS
WELTANSCHAUUNG FAITH
IDEOLOGY
WELTER REEL RIOT TOSS WILT
GROVEL TUMBLE WALLOW
WRITHE SMOTHER STAGGER
SWELTER
(— OF SOUNDS) DIN
WELWITSCHIA TUMBOA
WEM FLAW SCAR SPOT STAIN
WEN CYST WYNN CLIER CLYER
TALPA TUMOR GOITER
WENCH DELL DILL DOXY DRAB
GILL GIRL JADE MAID MOLL PRIM
TRUG GOUGE KITTY MADAM
QUEAN TRULL WHORE AUDREY
BLOUSE BLOWEN BLOWZE
DRAZEL JILLET KITTIE MOTHER
POPLET WOTLINK POPLOLLY
(CLUMSY —) MODER MODDER
MOTHER MAUTHER
WENCHER DRABBER STRIKER
WEND BOW END SORB VEND
STEER BETAKE DEPART DIRECT
TRAVEL PROCEED SORBIAN
LUSATIAN
(— ONE'S WAY) MARK
WENT GODE LANE ROAD YEDE
ALLEY PASSAGE
(— ABOUT) WOLK
WENTLETRAP SCALA
WENZEL JACK
WERE **(— IT NOT)** SAVE
WEREWOLF TURNSKIN VERSIPEL
WERTHER (BELOVED OF —) LOTTE
WEST STY BEWEST PONENT
OCCIDENT
WESTERN PONENT SCAEAN
HESPERIC SANDWICH
(PREF.) HESPER(O)
WESTERN SAMOA (CAPITAL OF —)
APIA
(ISLAND OF —) UPOLU MANONO
SAVAII APOLIMA
(MONEY OF —) TALA
WEST HIGHLAND KYLOE

WEST INDIES
ISLAND: CAT CUBA LONG ABACO
EXUMA HAITI NEVIS PELEE
TURKS ANDROS BAHAMA
CAICOS CAYMAN INAGUA
TOBAGO VIRGIN ACKLINS
ANTIGUA BONAIRE CROOKED
CURACAO GRENADA JAMAICA
LEEWARD STKITTS STLUCIA
TORTOLA ANGUILLA BARBADOS

DOMINICA STTHOMAS
TRINIDAD WINDWARD
ELEUTHERA MARGARITA
MAYAGUANA STVINCENT
GUADELOUPE HISPANIOLA
MARTINIQUE MONTSERRAT
PUERTORICO
NATION: BARBADOS

WEST VIRGINIA
CAPITAL: CHARLESTON
COLLEGE: SALEM BETHANY
CONCORD MARSHALL
BLUEFIELD
COUNTY: CLAY WIRT BOONE
HARDY MINGO ROANE TUCKER
UPSHUR BARBOUR KANAWHA
INDIAN: MONETON
LAKE: LYNN
NICKNAME: MOUNTAIN
RIVER: ELK OHIO KANAWHA
POTOMAC GUYANDOT
STATE BIRD: CARDINAL
STATE FLOWER: RHODODENDRON
STATE TREE: MAPLE
TOWN: ELKINS KEYSER RIPLEY
VIENNA WESTON BECKLEY
GRAFTON SPENCER WEIRTON
FAIRMONT WHEELING

WESTWARD WESSEL OCCASIVE
WESTLINS
WESTWARD HO (AUTHOR OF —)
KINGSLEY
(CHARACTER IN —) YEO JOHN
LUCY ROSE AMYAS FRANK LEIGH
DESOTO GUZMAN EUSTACE
OXENHAM RICHARD GRENVILE
SALTERNE AYACANORA
WET DEW DIP SOP WAT DAMP
DANK LASH MOIL SLOW SOAK
SOFT UVID BATHE DABBY DROOK
DRUNK HUMID JUICE JUICY
LEACH MADID MOIST MOOTH
RAINY SLAKE SNAPY SOBBY
SOPPY SPEWY STEEP TIGHT
WEAKY CLASHY DABBLE DAGGLE
DAMPEN HUMECT IMBRUE
JARBLE LABBER MADEFY MARSHY
MOISTY QUASHY SHOWER
SLABBY SOBBED SPONGY SPOUTY
SWASHY WATERY ARROUSE
BLUBBER DRABBLE FLOTTER
MOISTEN SLOPPED SOBBING
SPEWING SPRINGY IRRIGATE
SATURATE SLATTERY SLOBBERY
SLOTTERY WATERISH
(— AND STORMY) FOUL
(— LIGHTLY) SPRINKLE
(— THOROUGHLY) SOUSE DRENCH
(SOFTLY —) SQUASHY
(VERY —) SOPPY
(PREF.) HYGR(O) UDO
WETHER PUR RAM HAMEL
DINMAN DINMONT
WETNESS DANK
WETTING SOUCE SOUSE SOWSE
MOILING
WHACK DAD LAM TRY BANG BELT
BIFF DEAL HACK SWAK TIME
DRIVE SHARE STATE SWACK
WHANG CHANCE DEFEAT STROKE

THWACK BARGAIN LAMBACK
PORTION
WHACKING VERY WHALING
WHOPPING EXTREMELY
WHALE SEI CETE HUEL HULL LASH
ORCA WALL KOGIA POGGY SCRAG
SPERM STUNT BALEEN BELUGA
BLOWER FINNER GIBBAR KILLER
THRASH BOWHEAD DOLPHIN
FINBACK FINFISH GIBBERT
GRAMPUS MARSOON RIPSACK
RORQUAL SPOUTER ZIPHIAN
BALAENID CACHALOT CETACEAN
DOEGLING GREYBACK HARDHEAD
HUMPBACK JUBARTES MUTILATE
PHYSETER THRASHER ZIPHIOID
(— BUTCHER) LEMMER
(— REFUSE) GURRY
(FINBACK —) GRASO
(SCHOOL OF —S) GAM POD
(PREF.) BALAENI BALAENO CET(O)
WHALEBONE BALEEN
WHALER HEADER BUSHMAN
SPOUTER SWAGMAN WHACKER
WHOPPER CETICIDE
WHALESKIN MUKTUK
WHANG BEAT BLOW FLOG CHUNK
THONG WHACK THRASH
RAWHIDE
WHARF KEY POW DOCK GARE PIER
QUAY SLIP BERTH JETTY LEVEE
STADE STAITH STRAND LANDING
PANTALAN STELLING
WHARVE WARVE WHIRL WHORL
WHAT FAT HOT HOW WET WHO
HOOT HOTE WHEN STUFF WHICH
MATTER PARTLY
WHATA FUTTAH FUTTER
WHAT EVERY WOMAN KNOWS
(AUTHOR OF —) BARRIE
(CHARACTER IN —) JOHN ALICK
DAVID JAMES SHAND SYBIL
WYLIE BRIERE MAGGIE CHARLES
VENABLES TENTERDEN
WHATNOT OMNIUM ETAGERE
WHAT PRICE GLORY (AUTHOR OF
—) ANDERSON
(CHARACTER IN —) FLAGG QUIRT
CHARMAINE
WHAT'S-ITS-NAME TIMENOGUY
WHATSOEVER MORTAL
WHEAL HIVE HUEL WALE WELT
URTICA POMPHUS
WHEAT WIT CORN CONES EMMER
FULTZ GRAIN SPELT SPICA TRIGO
BULGUR BURGUL CEREAL
KANRED STAPLE TURKEY
EINKORN FORMITY FRUMETY
KUBANKA MARQUIS POLLARD
FRUMENTY SPELTOID
(— BOILED IN MILK) FURMITY
(— MEASURE) TRUG
(BEARDED —) RIVETS
(CRACKED —) GROATS
(GRANULATED —) SUJI SUJEE
(HARD —) DURUM
(PARCHED —) BULGUR
(PREF.) TRITICO
WHEATCAKE PURI
WHEATEAR CHACK ARLING
WITTOL CHACKER ORTOLAN
SNORTER WITTALL CHICKELL
SAXICOLA

WHEATGRASS BLUESTEM
WHEATLIKE VULGARE
WHEEDLE COG CANT CLAW COAX
CARNY FLUFF GLOSE GLOZE
INGLE JOLLY BANTER CAJOLE
CUITER FLEECH GLAVER RADDLE
SMOOGE WHILLY BLARNEY
CUITTLE PALAVER SMOODGE
TWEEDLE BLANDISH COLLOGUE
SCROUNGE
WHEEDLING BUTTERY COMETHER
WHEEL BOB BUR COG FAN NUT
ORB BEAD BUFF GEAR HELM
HURL PURL ROLL ROTA RULL
STAR TIRL WYLE ATHEY FLIER
FLUFF FLYER IDLER NORIA REWET
RHOMB ROWEL SWING TRUCK
BILOBE CASTER CASTOR CIRCLE
DRIVEN DRIVER FANNER HORRAL
JAGGER KURUMA LEADER PINION
ROLLER ROTATE RUNDLE
RUNNER TRACER BALANCE
BICYCLE CHUKKER GUDGEON
LANTERN PEDRAIL PRICKER
REVOLVE STEPNEY TRAILER
TRILOBE TRINDLE TROCHUS
TRUCKLE TRUNDLE UNILOBE
WILDCAT CARACOLE FOLLOWER
ODOMETER SPROCKET
(— A SKIN) FLUFF
(— CHARGED WITH DIAMOND DUST)
SLITTER
(— CONTROLLING RUDDER) HELM
(— FOR EXECUTIONS) RAT
(— IN KNITTING MACHINE) BUR
BURR
(— IN TIMEPIECE) BALANCE
(— OF LIFE) ZOETROPE
(BUCKET —) LIFTER
(DIAMOND —) SKIVE
(GEAR —) DRIVEN HELICAL
(GRINDING —) SHELL
(GROOVED —) PULLEY SHEAVE
SHIVER
(INTERRUPTER —) TICKER TIKKER
(LOCOMOTIVE —) DRIVER
(METAL —) FILET FILLET
(MILL —) PIRN
(PAIR OF LOGGING —S) CATYDID
KATYDID
(POINTED —) TRACER
(POLISHING —) BOB BUFF SKAIF
SKEIF BUFFER SCAIFE
(POTTER'S —) LATHE THROW
(SPARE —) STEPNEY
(SPINNING —) TURN CHARKA
CHARKHA
(SPUR —) ROWEL
(TANK —) BOGY BOGEY BOGIE
(TOOTHED —) GEAR PINION
ROULETTE
(TURBINE —) ROTOR
(TWO PAIRS OF —S) CUTS CUTTS
(VANED —) FLIER FLYER
(WATER —) NORIA SAKIA SAKIEH
SAKIYEH TYMPANUM
(PL.) KATYDID
(PREF.) CYCL(O) ROTA ROTATO
ROTI ROTO TROCH(I)(LEI)(O)
(SUFF.) TROCH(A)(AL)(OUS)(US)
WHEELBARROW GURRY BARROW
CARRIAGE
(PART OF —) BED LEG GRIP TIRE

TRAY BRACE FRAME WHEEL
HANDLE BRACKET SUPPORT
WHEELER POLER PUSHER
WHEEL-SHAPED ROTATE TROCHAL
ROTIFORM
WHEELWORK MOTION
WHEELWRIGHT WHEELER
WOODMAN WHEELMAN
WHEEZE JOKE HOOSE HOOZE
TRICK COGHLE
WHELK FILK GRUB WELT BUCKIE
MAGGOT PAPULE PIMPLE WINKLE
PUSTULE
WHELP CUB PUP SON CHIT FAWN
PUPPY YELPER KITLING
SPROCKET
WHEMMEL UPSET FUMMEL
FUMMLE WHAMBLE OVERTURN
WHEN AS BUT FAN FRO GIN THO
WON THAN THEN THOA TILL
SINCE UNTIL ENOUGH ALTHOUGH
WHENEVER ONCE
WHERE AS FAR FUR FAUR FEAR
FERRE PLACE QUAIR THERE
WHITHER LOCATION
(— ABOVE MENTIONED) US
WHEREFORE WHY CAUSE
FORWHY REASON
WHERENESS UBIETY
WHEREVER THERE
WHEREWITHAL MEANS MONEY
RESOURCES
WHERRET BOX CUFF SLAP HURRY
TEASE WORRY TROUBLE
WHIRRICK
WHERRY BARGE ROWBOAT
WHIRREY
WHET WET GOAD HONE TIME
TURN GRIND POINT RIFLE ROUSE
SLITE WHILE EXCITE INCITE
STROKE QUICKEN SHARPEN
APERITIF EXACUATE
WHETHER IF GIF GIN WHAR
WHERE EITHER
WHETSTONE BUR RIP RUB BUHR
BURR SLIP STONE RUBBER STRAIK
SHARPER WASHITA WHITTLE
OILSTONE RUBSTONE STRICKLE
WHEY PALE QUAY WHIG SERUM
THRUST WATERY
(PREF.) ORO
WHIBA UEBA
WHICH AS THE WHO THAT QUILK
WHILK
(— SEE) QV QQV
WHICKER NEIGH WHINNY WIGHER
WHIDAH BIRD VEUVE WEAVER
WHYDAH REDBILL
WHIFF FAN GUF BLOW GUFF GUST
HINT PUFF TIFT WAFT WIFT
FLUFF QUIFF SMOKE EXHALE
MAGRIM MEGRIM WHIFFET
WHIFFLE FIFE SWAY FLICKER
FLUTTER
WHIFFLETREE HEELTREE
SWINGLEBAR
WHIG JOG QUIG WHEY
WHILE AS BIT GAM THO YET FILE
FYLE TIDE TILL WHEN WHET
WOLE FILIE PIECE SPACE STEAD
STOUN THROW UNTIL STOUND
WHENAS WHILOM BEGUILE
TROUBLE EXERTION OCCASION

(— AWAY) AMUSE FLEET DIVERT BEGUILE DECEIVE

(LITTLE —) AWEE DRASS WHILEY WHILEEN WHILOCK

WHILES UNTIL SOMETIMES

WHILLY GULL CAJOLE WHEEDLE

WHILST TILL UNTIL

WHIM BEE FAD GIG GIN TOY FIKE FLAM KINK CRANK FANCY FLISK FOLLY FREAK HUMOR MEINY QUIRK THRUM FEGARY FITTEN MAGGOT MEGRIM SPLEEN VAGARY WHIMSY BOUTADE CAPRICE CONCEIT WRINKLE CROTCHET

WHIMBREL JACK SPOW SPOWE CURLEW MAYBIRD MAYFOWL TITTEREL

WHIMPER GIRN MEWL PULE WAIL WEAK BLEAT WHINE SIMPER WHINGE YAMMER GRIZZLE SNIFFLE SNUFFLE WHINDLE WHINNEL WHITTER WHINNOCK

WHIMSICAL FAIRY FANCY BAROCK COCKLE FLISKY NOTION QUAINT BAROQUE BIZARRE GIGGISH PUCKISH BIZZARRO FANCIFUL FREAKISH HUMOROUS NOTIONAL SINGULAR VAPOROUS PIXILATED

WHIMSY WHIM FREAK VAGARY CAPRICE WHIMWHAM

WHIN FUN ULEX FURZE WHINCOW WOODWAX

WHINCHAT TICK UTICK WHEATEAR

WHINE WOW GIRN GOWL MEWL PULE TIRM TOOT YARM YIRN BLEAT CROON MEECH QUINE TWINE WHAUP WHEWT PEENGE SNIVEL TREBLE WHINGE WINNEL YAMMER WHIMPER WHINDLE

WHINING QUERULOUS

WHINNY HINNY NEIGH PLAIN SNICKER WHICKER

WHINSTONE TRAP WHIN SCURDY

WHINYARD SWORD HANGER POCHARD WHINGER SHOVELER

WHIP CAT EEL FAN GAD ROD TAW BEAT CAST COIL DICK DUST FIRK FLOG FOAM GOAD HIDE JEHU JERK LASH LICK LOUK PLET TAWS URGE WHUP ABUSE AZOTE BIRCH CRACK FLAIL FLICK FLISK IMPEL KNOUT LEASH PLETE QUILT ROMAL SLASH STRAP SWEPE SWING SWISH TAWSE THONG THUMP AROUSE BREECH CHABUK DEFEAT FEAGUE INCITE LAINER LARRUP LICKER MAIDEN NETTLE PIZZLE QUIPPE SCUTCH SNATCH SWINGE SWITCH THRASH TICKLE CHABOUK CHICOTE COWHIDE COWSKIN CURBASH KURBASH LAMBAST LAYOVER NAGAIKA RAWHIDE SCOURGE SHINGLE SJAMBOK SLASHER TICKLER CHAWBUCK COACHMAN CONFOUND FLAGELLA KOURBASH PEPPERER

(— EGGS) CAST

(— HANDLE) CROP

(— IN PIANO ACTION) WIPPEN

(— WITH 3 LASHES) PLET PLETE

(HORSE —) WAND CHABOUK

(JOCKEY'S —) BAT

(RIDING —) CROP DICK QUIRT

(RUSSIAN —) KNOUT

(PREF.) FLAGELLI MASTIG(O)

(SUFF.) MASTIX

WHIPLASH THONG COSAQUE CRACKER

WHIPPED BEATEN BROKEN DEFEATED FOUETTEE CHANTILLY

WHIPPER TICKLER THONGMAN THRASHER THREAPER

WHIPPER-IN PRICKER

WHIPPERSNAPPER SQUIRT WHIFFET WHIPSTER

WHIPPING LICK TOCO TOKO HIDING CLANKER FANNING SERVING BIRCHING BROWSING SKELPING

WHIPPING POST FORK PILLAR

WHIP SCORPION GRAMPUS PHRYNID PEDIPALP WHIPTAIL

WHIPSOCKET SNEAD

WHIPSTITCH MINUTE INSTANT OVERCAST

WHIR BIRR ZIZZ WHIRRY

WHIRL BIRL EDDY FURL GYRE HURL PURL REEL RUSH SPIN TIRL DRILL GIDDY SKIRL SQUIR SWIRL THIRL THROW TWIRL TWIST WALTZ WHORL BUSTLE CIRCLE GYRATE HURTLE SWINGE VORTEX WHORLE WINDLE WIRBLE MIZMAZE REVOLVE TRUNDLE TURMOIL VERTICIL

(— ABOUT) DOZE GURGE

(— IN THE AIR) WARP

WHIRLIGIG GIG SPIN TURN WHEEL FIZGIG FISHGIG

WHIRLING GIDDY WHEELY STROBIC GYRATION GYRATORY VORTICAL PIROUETTE

(PREF.) STROBO

WHIRLPOOL EDDY GULF SUCK WEEL WELL WIEL GORCE GOURD GURGE BULLER GORGES SWELTH VORTEX GURGLET SWALLOW SWILKIE SUCKHOLE MAELSTROM

(PREF.) DINO

WHIRLWIND OE DEVIL VORTEX PRESTER TORNADO TOURBILLION

WHISHT HUSH SILENCE

WHISK ZIP FISK TUFT WHID WHIP WISP CAURI FLICK FLISK HURRY SPEED SWISH CHAURI CHOWRY SWITCH COWTAIL WHISKER

WHISKER HAIRLINE VIBRISSA

(PL.) BEARD ZIFFS WEEPER GALWAYS VIBRISSA MOUSTACHE SIDEBURNS

WHISKY RYE BOND CORN CIDER IRISH USQUE POTEEN REDEYE SCOTCH BOURBON BLOCKADE BUSTHEAD CREATURE POPSKULL USQUABAE MOONSHINE TANGLEFOOT

(GLASS OF —) RUBDOWN

(RAW —) DRUDGE

WHISPER BUZZ HARK HINT ROUN RUNE ROUND RUMOR TRACE TUTEL BREATH BREEZE HARKEN MURMUR SUSURR TITTLE WHISHT HEARKEN SUSURRUS

WHIST MORT VINT QUIET BOSTON SILENT WHEESHT

WHISTLE BLOW CALL FLUTE PIPE WHEW QUILL WHAUP WHEEP WHUTE BUMMER BUZZER CUCKOO FUSSLE HOOTER SIFFLE SISTLE SQUEAL WARBLE YELPER CATCALL TWEEDLE BIRDCALL

(— FEEBLY) WHEEDLE

WHISTLE FLUTE SIFFLOT

WHISTLER PIPER MARMOT ROARER FLUTIST LAPWING SIFFLEUR

WHISTLING PIPY PIPEY ROARING SIFFLET RHONCHUS SUSSURANT

WHIT BIT JOT RAP ATOM DOIT HATE HOOT IOTA QUAT QUIT AUGHT BODLE GROAT POINT QUITE SPECK CIVITE PARTICLE TWOPENNY

WHITE CUT WAN BAWN FITE HOAR LILY PALE QUAT QUIT ASHEN BLOND HAOLE HOARY LABAN LINEN SNOWY ALBINO ARGENT BLANCH BRIGHT BUCKRA CANDID CIVITE ERMINE SILVER WINTRY CANDENT LEUCOUS NIVEOUS WHITTLE FAVORITE INNOCENT LACTEOUS

(— AND SMOOTH) IVORINE

(— OF EGG) GLAIR ALBUMEN

(— PERSON) OFAY

(POOR —) YAHOO CRACKER

(PREF.) ALB(I)(O) CALI CALLI LEUC(O) LEUK(O)

WHITE ALDER CLETHRA

WHITE ANT ANAY NASUTE TERMITE

WHITEBAIT SMELT ICEFISH SALANGID SALMONID

WHITEBEAM ARIA SERVICE MULBERRY

WHITEBOY PET LEVELER

WHITE BRYONY COWBIND MANDRAKE

WHITE CEDAR JUNIPER

WHITE CLOVER LADINO SHAMROCK

WHITE COMPANY (AUTHOR OF —) DOYLE

(CHARACTER IN —) JOHN MAUDE NIGEL HORDLE LORING SAMKIN ALLEYNE AYLWARD EDRICSON

WHITEFISH BLOAT CISCO PILOT POWAN BELUGA CHIVEY POLLAN TULIPI VENDIS BLOATER BOWBACK GWYNIAD LAVARET VENDACE BLACKFIN GREYBACK HUMPBACK MENOMINI SALMONID SCHNABEL TULLIBEE

WHITEFLY HOMOPTER MEALYWING

WHITE GUM TUART

WHITE-HEADED GOLDEN FAVORED FORTUNATE

WHITE HELLEBORE ITCHREED ITCHWEED

WHITE IPECAC ITOUBOU

WHITE LEAD CERUSE

WHITE MAPAN PIRIPIRI

WHITE MUSTARD KEDLOCK SINAPIS CRUCIFER

WHITEN CAM CAUM SCURF ALBIFY

BLANCH BLANCO BLEACH BLENCH DEALBATE EMBLANCH ETIOLATE PIPECLAY

WHITENED DEALBATE

WHITENESS IVORY ALBEDO ARGENT CANDOR PURITY CANITIES PALENESS

WHITE OAK ROBLE

WHITE POPLAR ABELE ABELTREE

WHITE SNAKEROOT STEVIA POOLWORT RICHWEED WHITETOP

WHITE STURGEON BELUGA

WHITETHROAT JACK MUFF MUFTY MUGGY PEGGY EYSOGE MILLER MUFFET WHISKY WINNEL HAYSUCK WHEYBIRD

WHITEWASH LIME GLASS BLANCH PARGET CHICAGO LIMEWASH PALLIATE

WHITEWEED DAISY

WHITE WHALE BELUGA

WHITHER GUST HURL RUSH WHIZ HURRY SHAKE WHERE FLURRY BLUSTER WHERETO

WHITING BARB HAKE CORBINA CORVINA MERLING KINGFISH MOONFISH

WHITING-POUT BIB KLEG BLENS

WHITISH BAWN PALE DILUTE SUBALBID

WHITLOW FELON AGNAIL ANCOME FETLOW BREEDER PANARIS BREDSORE RUNROUND

WHITLOW GRASS DRABA NAILWORT SHADBLOW

WHITRACK WEASEL FUTTERET WHITTRET

WHITSUNDAY TERM

WHITSUNTIDE PINXTER PINGSTER PINKSTER

WHITTLE CUT PARE CARVE KNIFE STEEL TWITE EXCITE MANTLE THWITE BLANKET

WHIZ BUZZ DEAL GIRL PIRR QUIZ SING WHIR ZIZZ SOUGH WHISH WHIZZ WIZARD BARGAIN SWITHER WHIDDER WHINNER

WHIZ-BANG EXPERT NOTABLE

WHO AS HOW THE WHA WHAT WHICH

WHOA WO WAY WHO STOP

WHOEVER WHATSO EVERWHO

WHOLE ALL HOW SUM BODY COOL EVEN HALE HALF HOLY HULL BLOCK GREAT GROSS HAILL SOLID SOUND TOTAL TOTUM TUTTA UNCUT CORPSE ENTIRE HEALED INTACT VERSAL GENERAL INFRACT INTEGER PERFECT SINCERE SOLIDUM COMPLETE ENSEMBLE ENTIRETY GLOBULAR INTEGRAL LIVELONG OUTRIGHT UNBROKEN

(— OF ANY ORGANISM) SOMA

(— OF REALITY) ABSOLUTE

(ORGANIC —) SYSTEM

(PREF.) ALL HOL(O) INTEGRI PAN TOTI TOTO

WHOLEHEARTED HEARTY SINCERE ZESTFUL COMPLETE IMPLICIT

WHOLESALE MASSIVE SWEEPING

WHOLESALER JOBBER EXPORTER
WHOLESOME GOOD CLEAN
SOUND SWEET BENIGN SAVORY
HEALTHY PRUDENT CURATIVE
HALESOME HEALSOME HOMELIKE
REMEDIAL SALUTARY HEALTHFUL
WHOLE-SOULED SINCERE
WHOLLY ALL FAIR FLAT HALE
ONLY BLACK CLEAR FULLY QUITE
STARK ALGATE BODILY FLATLY
HOLLOW PURELY SOLELY
ALGATES ROUNDLY SOLIDLY
TOTALLY DIRECTLY ENTIRELY
(PREF.) TOTI
WHOOP BOOM HOOP HOOT BOOST
RAISE SHOUT EXCITE HALLOO
HOOPOE
WHOOPING COUGH KINKHOST
CHINCOUGH PERTUSSIS
WHOP WAP BEAT THUD THUMP
STRIKE THRASH
WHOPPER LIE SIZER BOUNCER
CRUMPER SLAPPER SNAPPER
SWAPPER SWINGER SCROUGER
STRAPPER WALLOPER
WHOPPING VERY LARGE BANGING
RAPPING WAPPING WHALING
SWINGING THUMPING WHACKING
WALLOPING
WHORE DRAB JILT FILTH QUAIL
WENCH HARLOT PUTAIN
DEBAUCH PINNACE STRUMPET
SUCCUBUS PROSTITUTE
WHOREMONGER HOLOUR
WHORL TURN CYCLE SPIRE SWIRL
WHIRL THWORL VOLUTE WHARVE
WREATH ANNULUS CALYCLE
CALYCULE GYRATION VERTICIL
VOLUTION
(PREF.) SPONDYL(O) VERTICILL(I)
WHORLED (NOT —) ACYCLIC
WHORTLEBERRY HOT HURT
FRAWN HOOTE FRAGHAN
BILBERRY COWBERRY
WHY HOW QUI ENIGMA FORWHY
WICK BAD EVIL FARM TOWN
ANGLE CREEK DAIRY MATCH
QUICK SEAVE SNAST CORNER
LIVING WICKED VILLAGE
FARMSTEAD
(— CLOGGED WITH TALLOW)
ROUGHIE
(LONG WAXED —) TAPER
WICKED BAD SAD DARK EVIL FAST
FOUL IRON LAZY LEWD MEAN
PIKY VILE BLACK CURST FELON
SHREW SORRY WRONG WROTH
CURSED GUILTY LITHER LUTHER
NEFAST PERDIT PITCHY SEVERE
SHREWD SINFUL UNHOLY
UNJUST UNLEAD UNLEDE
UNWELL CAITIFF DARKSUM
GODLESS HEINOUS HELLISH
IMMORAL NAUGHTY NINETED
NOXIOUS PRAVOUS PROFANE
ROGUISH UNGODLY UNSEELY
UNSOUND UNWREST VICIOUS
VILLAIN ACCURSED CRIMINAL
DARKSOME DEPRAVED DEVILISH
DIABOLIC ENORMOUS FELONOUS
FIENDISH FLAGRANT MESCHANT
OBDURATE PERVERSE TERRIBLE
UNKINDLY ABANDONED

NEFARIOUS PERNICIOUS
(PREF.) PONERO
WICKEDNESS ILL SIN EVIL HARM
VICE CRIME FOLLY GUILT BELIAL
FELONY NOUGHT UNGOOD
ATHEISM DEVILRY ILLNESS
PRAVITY DARKNESS DEVILTRY
INIQUITY MISCHIEF SATANISM
WANGRACE
WICKER SALE
WICKERWORK WEB WEEL
TWIGGEN BASKETRY
WICKET GATE HOOP HATCH PITCH
STUMP GUICHET
(FALLING OF —S) ROT
WICKETKEEPER STUMP STUMPER
WICKFORD POINT (AUTHOR OF —)
MARQUAND
(CHARACTER IN —) JIM JOE BERG
MARY ALLEN AVERY BELLA BRILL
HARRY STOWE ARCHIE CALDER
HOWARD WRIGHT GIFFORD
SOUTHBY LEIGHTON PATRICIA
CLOTHILDE
WICKIUP HUT WAKIUP SHELTER
WIDDRIM FIT FURY
WIDDY NOOSE WIDOW WITHY
HALTER
WIDE FAR LAX DEEP ROOM SIDE
AMPLE BROAD LARGE ROOMY
SHARP SLACK WRONG ASTRAY
ROOMWARD SPACEFUL SPACIOUS
(— OF) BESIDE
(— OF THE MARK) AWRY WILD
ABROAD
(LONG AND —) SIDE
(PREF.) EURY LATI
WIDE-AWAKE FLY FOXY KEEN LIVE
ALERT FLASH LEERY CADDIE
SLIPPY KNOWING WAKEFUL
WATCHFUL
WIDELY FAR BROAD ABROAD
GREATLY LARGELY
WIDEN FLAN REAM DILATE
EXPAND EXTEND FLANCH
FLANGE FUNNEL BROADEN
WIDENESS WIDTH BREADTH
WIDESPREAD RIFE DIFFUSE
GENERAL POPULAR PROLATE
CATHOLIC EXTENDED PANDEMIC
SWEEPING
WIDGEON SMEE WHIM GOOSE
WHEWER ZUISIN POACHER
POTCHER BALDPATE BLUEBILL
WHISTLER
WIDOW VID BALO DAME SKAT
BLIND KITTY VEUVE WEEDA
WIDDY MATRON RELICT TERCER
DOWAGER EMPRESS BARONESS
DOWERESS
(PL.) VIDUAGE
WIDOWED VIDUOUS
WIDOWHOOD VIDUAGE VIDUITY
WIDTH GAPE SIDE RANGE SCOPE
BREADTH OPENING FRONTAGE
FULLNESS LARGEOUR LATITUDE
WIDENESS
(— OF CUT) KERF
(— OF HORSESHOE) COVER
(— OF PALM) HAND
(— OF PAPER) FILL
(— OF PULLEY) FACE
(— OF SHIP) BEAM

(— OF SHIP'S BAND) STRAKE
(— OF TYPE) SET
(— OF WEB) DECKLE
WIELD PLY RUN BEAR WALT WIND
APPLY EXERT SWING VELDE
EMPLOY GOVERN HANDLE
MANAGE STRAIN CONTROL
WIFE UX FEM HEN MRS RIB WYF
BABY BIBI DAME DORA ENID
FEME FERE FRAU FROW JAEL
LADY MAKE MAMA MATE RANI
UXOR DIRCE DONNA DUTCH
FEMME LUCKY MAMMA MATCH
MUJER SQUAW WOMAN ELMIRE
EMILIA GAMMER KEEPER
MATRON MISSIS MISSUS MULIER
SPOUSE VENDER WAHINE
BEDMATE DIONYZA EMPRESS
PARTNER WEDLOCK DEIANIRA
DEIDAMIA ERIPHYLE HELPMATE
HELPMEET MISTRESS PECULIAR
(— OF COTTER) COTQUEAN
(— OF KNIGHT OR BARONET) DAME
(— OF MOHAMMEDAN) KHADIJA
(AFFIANCED —) FUTURE
(INDIAN'S —) WEBB
(OLD —) GAMMER
(PL.) PUNALUA
(PREF.) UXOR(I)
WIG BOB JIZ RUG TIE FRIZ GIZZ
JANE JIZZ LOCK TETE TOUR
BUSBY CAXON FLASH JASEY
MAJOR SCALP SCOLD ADONIS
BRUTUS FROWZE MERKIN
PERUKE REBUKE TOUPEE TOUPET
COMBING RAMILIE SCRATCH
SHEITEL SPENCER BOBJEROM
CHEDREUX CHEWELER
DALMAHOY NIGHTCAP PERUKERY
POSTICHE ROGERIAN VALLANCY
(— WITH ROUGHLY CROPPED HAIR)
BRUTUS
(BUSHY —) BUSBY
(GRAY —) GRIZZLE
(WORSTED —) JASEY
(18TH CENTURY —) ADONIS
GEORGE
WIGGLE JET HOTCH JIGGLE
WABBLE WANGLE
WIGGLER PUPA LARVA WRYER
WIGHT MAN SWIFT STRONG
VALIANT CREATURE STALWART
WIGMAKER WIGGER PERUKER
PERUKIER
WIGWAG SIGNAL
WIGWAM TIPI LODGE TEPEE
WEEKWAM WICKIUP
WIKENO NIKENO HEILTSUK
WILD APE MAD REE SHY FAST
RUDE SCAR WOWF CRAZY FANTI
FELON FERAL GIDDY MYALL
RANDY RANTY ROUGH ROYET
SKEER WASTE DESERT FANTEE
FERINE FIERCE LAVISH MADCAP
NATIVE RAMAGE RANDOM
RENISH SAVAGE SHANDY STORMY
UNRULY BERSERK BREACHY
ERRATIC FRANTIC GALLOUS
GALLOWS HAGGARD HOWLING
MADDING NATURAL OUTWARD
RIOTOUS SKADDLE SKEERED
WILDING ABERRANT AGRESTAL
BARBARIC CHIMERIC DESOLATE

FAROUCHE FRENETIC HALUCKET
HELLICAT RECKLESS UNTILLED
WARRAGAL WILLYARD
BOISTEROUS
(— CARD) FREAK
(PREF.) AGRIO
WILD ASS GOUR KIANG KULAN
COTULA KOULAN ONAGER
QUAGGA CHIGETAI
WILD BALSAM APPLE CREEPER
WILD BEE KARBI
WILD BOAR APER SUID TUSKER
SOUNDER SUIDIAN WILRONE
SANGLIER
WILD BUFFALO ARNA ARNEE
WILD BUSH BEAN PHASEMY
WILD CABBAGE YELLOWS
WILD CARDAMOM RUEWORT
KNOBWOOD
WILD CARROT DILL ELTROT
FIDDLE BIRDNEST HILLTROT
WILDCAT CAT BALU EYRA CHATI
CHAUS MANUL TIGER MARGAY
SERVAL WAGATI COLOCOLA
WILD CELERY ACHE ECHE
EELGRASS SMALLAGE
WILD CHERRY GEAN MERRY
MAZZARD
WILD CHERVIL KECK COWWEED
HONEWORT MILKWEED
WILD CYCLAMEN SOWBREAD
WILD DOG ADJAG DHOLE DINGO
GUARA AGUARA AGOUARA
CIMARRON WARRAGAL
WILD DUCK (AUTHOR OF —) IBSEN
(CHARACTER IN —) GINA EKDAL
SORBY WERLE HANSEN HEDVIG
GREGERS HJALMAR RELLING
WILDEBEEST GNU
WILDERNESS BUSH WILD WASTE
DESERT FOREST WESTERN
SOLITUDE
WILD-EYED HAGGARD RADICAL
WILDFOWL VOLATILE
WILD GARLIC MOLY
WILD GERANIUM ALUMROOT
DOVEFOOT FLUXWEED
WILD GOAT TUR IBEX TAHR
EVECK PASAN MAZAME
MARKHOR AEGAGRUS MARKHOOR
WILD HORSE BRUMBY KUMRAH
TARPAN BRUMBIE WARRAGAL
WARRIGAL
WILD HYACINTH CUCKOO
CROWTOE GREGGLE BRODIAEA
CROWFOOT
WILD INDIGO SHOOFLY
WILD LETTUCE FIREWEED
WILD MAN SAVAGE WOODMAN
WOODSMAN
WILD MANGOSTEEN SANTOL
WILD MARJORAM ORGAN
ORGAMY ORGANY ORIGAN
ORGAMENT
WILD MULBERRY YAWWEED
WILD MUSTARD RUNCH
CHARLOCK
WILDNESS FERITY HEYDAY
HEYDEY FEROCITY SAVAGERY
SAVAGISM
WILD OAT DRANK DRAWK DROKE
HAVER HEVER EGILOPS
WILD ONION UMBEL UMBELLA

WILD OX BUF YAK ANOA BUFF
REEM UNICORN
WILD PARSLEY ELTROT HILLTROT
WILD PEAR DOGBERRY
WILD PLUM SLOE ISLAY
WILD POTATO MANROOT
WAPATOO
WILD RADISH RUNCH
WILD RICE MANOMIN
WILD SAGE EYESEED
WILD SARSAPARILLA SHOTBUSH
**WILDSCHUTZ, DER (CHARACTER IN
—)** BACULUS NANETTE EBERBACH
FREIMANN GRETCHEN KRONTHAL
(COMPOSER OF —) LORTZING
WILD SERVICE TREE SORB
SORBUS
WILD SHEEP SHA AUDAD URIAL
AOUDAD ARGALI BHARAL
NAYAUR BIGHORN MOUFLON
WILD SWAN ELK
WILD THYME HILLWORT
SERPOLET
WILD TOBACCO GAGROOT
SOURBUSH MARIJUANA
SALVADORA
WILD TURNIP NAVEW
WILD VANILLA LIATRIS
WILE ART PAUK PAWK RUSE
FRAUD GUILE TRICK ALLURE
BLENCH DECEIT ENGINE ENTICE
BEGUILE ARTIFICE TRICKERY
WILGA WILLOW
WILL EGO MAY ULL WAY FATE LIST
TEST WISH LEAVE OUGHT SHALL
WORST ANIMUS CHOICE CHOOSE
DESIRE DEVICE DEVISE LEGATE
LIKING QUETHE SCRIPT APPETITE
CODICIL PASSION WITWORD
AMBITION BEQUEATH PLEASING
PLEASURE VOLITION
(— NOT) WONT WINNA WONNA
WUNNA WONNOT
(— OF DEITY) DECREE
(— OF GOD) LAW
(— OF LEGISLATURE) ACT
(— TO LIVE) TANGHA
(FREE —) ACCORD
(GOOD —) GREE
(I —) CHILL
(ILL —) ARR ENVY HEST ANIMUS
ENMITY UNTHANK AMBITION
(SUFF.) (CONDITION OF —) THYMIA
(STATE OF —) BOULIA BULIA BULIC
WILLET TATLER TATTLER
WILLFUL HEADY WILLY FEISTY
UNRULY HAGGARD WAYWARD
WILSOME CAMSTRARY
WILLFULLY WOLDES SCIENTER
WILLIAM TELL (AUTHOR OF —)
SCHILLER
(CHARACTER IN —) JOHN TELL
FURST HENRY ARNOLD BERTHA
ULRICH WALTER WERNER
GESSLER WILLIAM MATHILDE
BAUMGARTEN
(COMPOSER OF —) ROSSINI
WILLIES JUMPS CREEPS
WILLING BAIN FAIN FREE GLAD
LIEF RATH PRONE READY MINDED
TOWARD CONTENT UNFORCED
WILLINGLY LIEF SOON FREELY
GLADLY LIEFLY FRANKLY READILY

WILLINGNESS HEART FREEDOM
FAINNESS
(— TO FIGHT) DEFIANCE
WILLIWAW STORM WOOLLY
TEMPEST
WILLOW DULY ITEA SALE WYLW
OSIER SALEW SALIX SAUGH
WIDDY WITHY WOODY DUSTER
SALLOW TEASER TWILLY WITHEN
WUDDIE
(— FOR THATCHING) SPRAYS
(— IN TEXTILES) WOLF
(NATIVE —) COOBA COOBAH
(SIMPLE —) WHIPPER
(PREF.) (— TWIG) LYGO
WILLOWER DULER DUSTER
TEASER WILLIER
WILLOW HERB WICOPY EPILOBE
FIRETOP PIGWEED ROSEBAY
BURNWEED FIREWEED
WILLOW WARBLER SMEU
SMEUTH MUDDLER TROCHIL
OVENBIRD
WILLOW WREN PEGGY
WILLOWY SUPPLE SLIPPER
DELICATE
WILLY-NILLY PERFORCE
WILSON'S PLOVER COLLIER
WILSON'S SNIPE JACK SHADBIRD
WILSON'S TERN MEDRICK
WILSON'S THRUSH VEERY
WILT EBB SAG DROP FADE FLAG
WELK DROOP SUCCUMB
COLLAPSE
WILTED EMARCID
WILY SLY FOXY CANNY SLICK
ARTFUL ASTUTE CLEVER CRAFTY
QUAINT SHREWD STALKY SUBTLE
TRICKY CUNNING POLITIC
VERSUTE WINDING SERPENTINE
WIMBLE BORE BRISK ACTIVE
GIMLET LIVELY NIMBLE WIBBLE
WUMMEL
WIMPLE BEND WIND CURVE
TWIST GORGET RIPPLE MEANDER
WIMLUNGE
WIN BAG COP HIT DRAW GAIN
HAVE LAND LICK FORCE SCORE
ATTACH CLINCH OBTAIN ACHIEVE
ACQUIRE CONQUER DESERVE
HARVEST POSSESS TRIUMPH
DECISION OVERCOME STRAIGHT
(— AGAINST) BREAK SCOOP
(— AWAY) STEAL DEBAUCH
(— BACK) RECOVER
(— BY GUILE) GET POT BEAR
CARRY RAISE TRAIN GATHER
CAPTURE INVEIGLE PROMERIT
(— EASILY) ROMP
(— NARROWLY) SQUEEZE
(— OVER) DEFEAT DISARM
(— OVERWHELMINGLY) SWEEP
WINCE KICK CHECK QUECH CRINGE
FLINCH QUATCH QUINCH QUITCH
RECOIL SHRINK
WINCH CRAB JACK REEL WINK
GIPSY WINZE ROLLER WHIMSY
WINDLE CATHEAD TRAVELER
VARIABLE WINDLASS
WIND AIR COP LAP BALL BIRR BISE
BIZE COIL CONE CURL EAST FIST
FLAW FOHN GALE GUST KINK
PUFF PUNO ROLL WEST WRAP

BATCH BLAST BLORE CRANK
CREEK CROOK FOEHN QUILL
SPOOL STORM TRADE TREND
TWINE TWIST WEAVE WITHE
BOTTOM BOUGHT BREEZE
BUSTER CAURUS COLLAR KECKLE
SANSAR SHAMAL SPIRAL SPIRIT
SQUALL WAMPLE WESTER
ZEPHYR BREATHE CRANKLE
CRINKLE CYCLONE ENTWINE
EQUINOX ETESIAN GREGALE
INVOLVE MEANDER MISTRAL
SERPENT SINUATE TEMPEST
TWINGLE TWISTER WEATHER
WHIRLER WINDILL ARGESTES
DOWNWARD EASTERLY
FAVONIUS
(— ABEAM) LASK
(— ABOUT) WIRE SNAKE
(— AFTER DYEING) BATCH
(— FROM THE ANDES) ZONDA
PAMPERO
(— IN AND OUT) INDENT WINGLE
(— MAGNETS) COMPOUND
(— OF ARGENTINA) ZONDA
PAMPERO
(— OF CUBA) BAYAMO
(— OF HAWAII) KONA
(— OF OREGON AND WASHINGTON)
CHINOOK
(— OF TUNISIA) CHILE CHILI CHILLI
(— ROPE) WORM WOOLD
(— THREAD OR YARN) QUILL
CHEESE
(— TO PREVENT CHAFING) KECKLE
(— WOOL) TREND
(— YARN) BEAM SERVE WINDLE
(—S OF CHILE AND PERU) SURES
(ADRIATIC —) BORA
(BREAKING —) FIST
(BROKEN —) HEAVES
(COLD —) BISE BIZE BORA SARSAR
BLIZZARD
(COOLING —) IMBAT
(DEAD —) NOSER
(DESERT —) SAMUM GIBLEH
SAMIEL SIMOOM SIMOON
KHAMSIN SIROCCO
(DRYING —) TRADE
(EASTERLY —) LEVANT LEVANTER
(FIERCE —) BUSTER
(GUST OF —) FLAN FLAW
(HEAD —) NOSER MUZZLE
(HIGH —) RIG
(HOT —) CHILI GIBLEH SAMIEL
SOLANO CHAMSIN KHAMSIN
SIROCCO
(LIGHT GENTLE —) BREEZE
(MOUNTAIN —) PUNA
(NORTH —) BISE AQUILO BOREAS
AQUILON MISTRAL
(NORTHEAST —) BURAN GREGALE
(NORTHWEST —) CAURUS
MAESTRO ARGESTES
(PERIODICAL —) ETESIAN
MONSOON
(PERSIAN GULF —) SHAMAL SHARKI
SHIMAL
(PERUVIAN —) PUNA PUNO
(ROARING —) BLORE
(SEVERE —) SNIFTER
(SOUTH —) NOTUS AUSTER
(SOUTHEAST —) EURUS SOLANO

(SOUTHEASTERLY —) SHARKI
SHURGEE
(SOUTHWEST —) CHINOOK
LIBECCIO
(STRONG —) BIRR
(VIOLENT —) BUSTER SQUALL
SNORTER
(WARM —) FOHN FOEHN CHINOOK
SANTANA
(WEST —) ZEPHYR FAVONIUS
ZEPHYRUS
(PREF.) ANEM(O) AURO VENTI
VENTO
(SOUTH —) AUSTRO
WINDAGE DRIFT
WINDER REEL WINCH DRUMMER
PLUGGER SKEINER SPOOLER
TENDRIL
WINDFALL VAIL GRAVY MANNA
CADUAC FALLING BLOWDOWN
BUCKSHEE
WINDGALL PUFF WINDDOG
WINDING LINK MAZY CRANK
LACET SPIRE CREEKY DETOUR
GYRATE SCREWY SPIRAL TWISTY
WANLAS CRANKLE CRINKLE
DEVIOUS MEANDER SINUOUS
SNAKING WRIGGLY WRINKLE
(PL.) AMBAGES RADDLINGS
WINDING-SHEET SHROUD SUDARY
CEREMENT
WINDING STAIR COCKLE COCLEA
WINDER COCHLEA
**WIND INSTRUMENT
(PREF.)** AEOLO
WINDLASS CRAB WINK FEARN
WINCH STOWCE STOWSE TACKLE
TURNEL WINDAS WINDLE
TWISTER WILDCAT ARTIFICE
DRAWBEAM MANEUVER
WINDMILL JUMBO MOTOR COPTER
PINWHEEL
(— BAR) UPLONG
(— SAIL) AWE EIE EIGHE FLIER
FLYER SWEEP SWIFT
(PART OF —) BAR CAP FAN AXLE
CORD HEEL LINE SAIL WHIP
BLADE ROTOR STOCK SWEEP
TOWER FANTAIL HELMATH
CANNISTER WINDSHAFT
WINDOW BAY EYE LOOP ROSE
SASH SLIT SLOT CHAFF GLAZE
GRILL INLET LIGHT OGIVE SIGHT
THURL AWNING DORMER GRILLE
LANCET PEEPER ROSACE SPLITE
THURLE WICKET BALCONE
COUPLET DORMANT FENSTER
GUICHET LUTHERN MIRADOR
ORIFICE TRANSOM VENTANA
WINDOCK WINNOCK CASEMENT
FANLIGHT FENESTER FENESTRA
JALOUSIE VENETIAN
(— OF TWO LIGHTS) COUPLET
(BAY —) ORIEL MIRADOR
(BLANK —) ORB
(DORMER —) OXEYE DORMANT
LUCARNE LUTHERN
(HIGH NARROW —) LANCET
(OVAL —) OXEYE
(PART OF —) BEAD JAMB LOCK
PANE RAIL SASH STOP YOKE
APRON FRAME SKIRT STILE
STOOL STRIP CASING MUNTIN

BRICKMOLD WINDOWPANE COUNTERWEIGHT
(ROUND —) OXEYE OCULUS ROUNDEL
(SEMICIRCULAR —) FANLIGHT
(TICKET —) GRILLE GUICHET
(TWIN —) AJIMEZ
(PL.) STORMS
WINDOW DRESSING TRIM FRONT FACADE
WINDOW FRAME SASH REVEAL
WINDOW OYSTER COPIS
WINDOWPANE LIGHT LOZEN QUIRK LOZENGE
WINDOWSILL SOLE
WINDPIPE HALS ARBER ARBOR ERBER HALSE WIZEN ARTERY GUGGLE STROUP WEEZLE KEACORN TRACHEA WEASAND THRAPPLE THROPPLE THROTTLE
(PREF.) BRONCH(I)(IO)(O) TRACHE(O) TRACHO TRACHY
WINDROW BANK HEAP RIDGE SWATH SWATHE
WINDSOR CHAIR FANBACK
WINDSTORM BLOW BURA THUD BURAN BOURRAN
WINDWARD ALOOF WEATHER AWEATHER
(— SIDE) KOOLAU
WINDY BLOWY EMPTY GASSY GUSTY HUFFY PROUD STARK SWALE FLIMSY STORMY WONDIE BREATHY FEARFUL GUSTFUL NERVOUS VENTOSE VIOLENT BOISTEROUS
(— CITY) CHICAGO
WINE CUP VIN BOIS BUAL CUIT CUTE DEAL PALM PORT RAPE ROSE ROSY TENT TYRE CAPRI GRAPE KRAMA LUNEL PETER PLONK PORTO SCIAN SHRAB SOAVE TINTO TOKAY VINUM WHITE BAROLO BARSAC CORTON COUTET GRAVES KIJAFA LISBON MASDEU PIMENT ROCHET SAUMUR SHIRAZ SOLERA TIVOLI ALICANT AMBONNA BACCHUS BANYULS BARBERA BASTARD CATAWBA CHACOLI CHATEAU DEZALEY FALERNO MARSALA MISSION MOSELLE ORVIETO PALERMO PIGMENT RHENISH ROSOLIO SERCIAL SILLERY VERNAGE VIDONIA VINTAGE APERITIF BORDEAUX BURGUNDY CHARNECO DELAWARE LACHRYMA LIBATION MALVASIA MARSALLA MOUNTAIN RIESLING ROCHELLE RULANDER RUMBOOZE SPARKLER BARDOLINO
(— BOILED WITH HONEY) MULSE
(— CHEST) TANTALUS
(— FROM VINEGAR) ESILL
(— MIXED WITH WATER) KRASIS
(— OF EXCELLENT QUALITY) VINTAGE
(— OF SACRAMENT) BLOOD
(— SELLER) ABKAR BISTRO WINARE
(— SERVING) VOIDEE
(AROMATIZED —) DUBONNET
(BANANA —) MARAMBA

(BULK —) CUVEE
(CONSECRATED —) CUP
(FIRST-GROWTH —) LAFITE LAFITTE
(FRANCONIAN —) STEIN LEISTEN
(GREEK —) RUMNEY RETSINA RESINATA
(HEATED —) WHITEPOT
(INFERIOR —) PLONK
(JAPANESE —) SAKI
(LIGHT —) BUAL CAPRI BAROLO CANARY
(MULLED —) GLUHWEIN
(NEW —) MUST
(NEW — BOILED DOWN) CUIT CUTE
(PALM —) SAGWIRE
(RED —) MACON TINTA BEAUNE CLARET CHIANTI HOLLOCK POMMARD ALICANTE BURGUNDY CABERNET FLORENCE
(REVIVED —) STUM
(RHINE —) HOCK SYLVANER
(SPANISH —) SACK TENT DULCE OPORTO SHERRY ALICANT ALIKANT BASTARD TARRAGONA
(STILL —) PONTAC PONTACQ
(SWEET —) TYRE DULCE MULSE CANARY BASTARD MALMSEY CHARNECO MUSCATEL
(TENT —) TINTO
(TOKAY —) ESSENCE
(TUSCAN —) VERDEA CHIANTI FLORENCE
(WHITE —) HOCK SACK CAPRI CASEL FORST BARSAC MALAGA BROMIAN CATAWBA CHABLIS CONTHEY LANGOON ANGELICA BUCELLAS RIESLING SAUTERNE VERMOUTH
(PL.) PALUS
(PREF.) ENO OEN(O) OINO VINI VINO
WINEBERRY MAKO MAKOMAKO
WINEGLASS FLUTE
WINEGROWER WINER VIGNERON
WINESBURG OHIO (AUTHOR OF —) ANDERSON
(CHARACTER IN —) JOHN KATE WING DAVID HARDY HELEN JESSE REEFY SWIFT WHITE CURTIS GEORGE LOUISE BENTLEY HARTMAN WILLARD TRUNNION ELIZABETH BIDDLEBAUM
WINESHOP BISTRO BODEGA
WINE-VAULT SHADE
WING ALA ARM ELL FAN FLY OAR RIB VAN FORE JAMB SAIL TAIL ALULA ANNEX BLOCK FLANK JAMBE PINNA POINT SHEAR VOLET BRANCH FLETCH FLIGHT HALTER PENNON PINION POISER DEMIVOL ELYTRON ELYTRUM AEROFOIL BALANCER DISPATCH TORMENTOR
(— OF ARMY) HORN
(— OF BUILDING) ELL JAMB JAMBE ALETTE ALLETTE FLANKER
(— OF SHELL) AURICLE
(— OF THEATER) COULISSE TORMENTOR
(— OF TRIPTYCH) VOLET
(—S DISPLAYED) VOL
(BASTARD —) ALULA
(BIRD'S —) FLAG

(FLY'S —S) HALTERES
(PL.) PENS FEATHERS
(PREF.) ALI PTER(O) PTERIDO PTERYG(O) PTERYLO PTIL(O)
(SUFF.) PTERA PTERIS PTEROUS PTERUS PTERYX
WINGED AILE ALATE LOFTY RAPID SWIFT ALATED PENNED PENNATE ELEVATED
(PREF.) PTENO
(SUFF.) PTENE
WINGED DISK FEROHER
WING-FOOTED FLEET SWIFT ALIPED
WINGLESS APTERAL
WING-LIKE ALARY ALIFORM PTEROID PTERTGOID
WING SHELL STROMB ELYTRON STROMBUS
WINGS OF THE DOVE (AUTHOR OF —) JAMES
(CHARACTER IN —) CROY KATE MARK MILLY MERTON THEALE DENSHER
WINK BAT NAP PINK BLINK DEATH FLASH PRINK SLEEP TWINK CONNIVE FLICKER INSTANT NICTATE SPARKLE TWINKLE NICTITATE
WINKER EYE BLINKER EYELASH
WINKING BLINK
WINKLE PERIWIG TWINKLE
WINNER VICTOR FACEMAN BANGSTER
(SURE —) SNIP
WINNIE-THE-POOH (AUTHOR OF —) MILNE
(CHARACTER IN —) ROO KANGA ROBIN EEYORE PIGLET RABBIT HEFFALUMP CHRISTOPHER
WINNING GAIN SWEET PROFIT GAINING VICTORY WINSOME CHARMING
(— OF ALL TRICKS) CAPOT SCHWARZ
(PL.) WIN VELVET
WINNOW FAN WIM CHAR SIFT WIND DIGHT SIEVE DELETE REMOVE SELECT WINDER SEPARATE
WINNOWER VAN WINDER DIGHTER
WINSOME GAY BUXOM SWEET CHARMING CHEERFUL PLEASANT
WINTER BISE SNOW YEAR HIEMS DECEMBER HIBERNATE
(— OVER) HOG
WINTERBERRY PRINOS HOOPWOOD
WINTERBLOOM AZALEA
WINTERGREEN JINKS CHINKS PYROLA DRUNKER BOXBERRY DRUNKARD EYEBERRY GAYWINGS IVYBERRY LIMONIUM RATSBANE SHINLEAF TEABERRY PINEDROPS PIPSISSEWA
WINTERLIKE BRUMAL
WINTERSET (AUTHOR OF —) ANDERSON
(CHARACTER IN —) MIO CARR GARTH GAUNT TROCK ESDRAS SHADOW ROMAGNA MIRIAMNE BARTOLOMEO

WINTER'S TALE (AUTHOR OF —) SHAKESPEARE
(CHARACTER IN —) DION MOPSA DORCAS EMILIA CAMILLO LEONTES PAULINA PERDITA FLORIZEL HERMIONE ANTIGONUS AUTOLYCUS CLEOMENES MAMILLIUS POLIXENES ARCHIDAMUS
WINTRY AGED COLD WHITE BOREAL HIEMAL STORMY BRUMOUS CHILLING HIBERNAL
WINTUN COPEHAN
WINY VINOUS DRUNKEN
WINZE CURSE RAISE OPENING PASSAGEWAY
WIPE BEAT BLOW DRUB DUST GIBE DICHT DIGHT SWIPE CANCEL SPONGE SPUNGE STRIKE ABOLISH CLEANSE ABSTERGE SQUEEGEE
(— BEAK OF HAWK) FEAK
(— NOSE) SNITE
(— OFF) SCUFF
(— OUT) ERASE SCRUB SWEEP EFFACE DESTROY
(— UP) SWAB SWOB
WIPER DUSTER TRIPPET
WIRE GUY TAP BINE CORE DENT DRAG FILE FUSE PURL CABLE OUTER RISER SNAKE SWEEP TAPER BRIDGE FESCUE FINGER HEATER JUMPER NEEDLE STAPLE STOLON STRAND DROPPER HAYWIRE LAMETTA LASHING PRICKER SHIFTER SNUFFER FILAMENT LIGATURE PALISADE PULLDOWN STRINGER TELEGRAM
(— BETWEEN TWO VESSELS) SWEEP
(— FASTENED TO TEETH) BRACES
(— FOR CUTTING CLAY) SLING
(— FOR SUSTAINING HAIR) PALISADE
(— IN BLASTING CAP) BRIDGE
(— IN CATHETER) STYLET
(— IN WEAVING LOOM) DENT
(— OF GOLD,SILVER OR BRASS) LAMETTA
(— TO ADJUST WICK) SNUFFER
(— TO CLOSE A BREAK) JUMPER
(— TO REMOVE TUMORS) LIGATURE
(— USED AS POINTER) FESCUE
(— USED IN SPLICING CABLES) TAPER
(—S BOUND TOGETHER) SELVAGE
(ENAMELED —) LITZ
(FENCE —) DROPPER
(FRAYED —) JAGGER
(GOLD —) KINSEN
(LOOPED —) OESE
(PALLET —) PULLDOWN
(PRIMING —) PICKER EPINGLETTE
(SURGICAL —) STYLET
(TWISTED —) HEALD HEADLE HEDDLE
(VENT —) PRICKER
(4 —S TWISTED TOGETHER) QUAD
WIRE CUTTER SECATEUR
WIREDRAW WREST OUTWIT DEFRAUD DISTORT ELONGATE
WIREGLASS FLUTE
WIRE GRASS POA
WIRELESS RADIO
WIRE ROPE JACKSTAY

WIRETAP BUG
(REMOVE —) DEBUG
WIREWORM ELATER ELATERID
MILLIPEDE
WIRY THIN HARDY STIFF WITHY
FEEBLE KNOTTY SINEWY STRINGY
THREADY
WIS KNOW THINK SURELY
SUPPOSE

WISCONSIN
CAPITAL: MADISON
COLLEGE: RIPON BELOIT ALVERNO
CARROLL VITERBO CARTHAGE
COUNTY: DOOR VILAS JUNEAU
CALUMET SHAWANO
WAUSHARA
INDIAN: FOX SAUK KICKAPOO
WINNEBAGO
LAKE: POYGAN MENDOTA
WISSOTA WINNEBAGO
MOUNTAIN: TIMSHILL SUGARBUSH
NATIVE: BADGER
NICKNAME: BADGER
RIVER: FOX BLACK STCROIX
CHIPPEWA MENOMINEE
STATE BIRD: ROBIN
STATE FLOWER: VIOLET
STATE TREE: MAPLE
TOWN: ANTIGO BELOIT RACINE
WAUSAU ASHLAND BARABOO
KENOSHA MADISON OSHKOSH
PORTAGE SHAWANO LACROSSE
SUPERIOR WAUKESHA

WISDOM WIT LORE SABE SABBY
SAVEY SENSE SOPHY ADVICE
GNOSIS HOKMAH POLICY SATTVA
SOPHIA WISURE CUNNING
MINERVA SAGESSE SLEIGHT
AFTERWIT JUDGMENT PRUDENCE
SAPIENCE
(DIVINE —) WORD THEOMAGY
(ESOTERIC —) GNOSIS
(SUPREME —) PRAJNA
(UNIVERSAL —) PANSOPHY
(PREF.) SOPH(O) SOPHI(O)
(SUFF.) SOPH(ER)(IC)(IST)(Y)
WISE HEP SLY DEEP GASH GOOD
KIND SAGE SANE SEND TURN
CANNY FRESH GUIDE SMART
SOUND WITTY ADVISE CRAFTY
DIRECT QUAINT WITFUL WITTER
ANCIENT ERUDITE GNOSTIC
KNOWING LEARNED POLITIC
PRUDENT SAPIENT THRIVEN
PERSUADE PROFOUND SENSIBLE
SPACIOUS
(— MAN) AMAUTA
(PREF.) SOPH(O) SOPHI(O)
(SUFF.) SOPH(ER)(IC)(IST)(Y)
WISEACRE SAGE DUNCE GOTHAM
SOLONIST WISEHEAD WISELING
WISECRACK JOKE QUIP
WISENT BISON AUROCH UROCHS
BONASUS
WISH CARE GIVE GOAL HOPE LIST
LUST MIND VOTE WANT WILL
BOSOM COVET CRAVE DREAM
HEART TASTE VOICE DESIRE
UTINAM FAREWELL GODSPEED
PLEASURE
(DEATH —) DESTRUDO

(SLIGHT —) VELLEITY
WISHBONE FURCULA FOURCHET
FURCULUM MERRYTHOUGHT
WISHFUL EAGER HOPEFUL
LONGING ALLURING
WISHING ANXIOUS DESIROUS
WISHY-WASHY PALE THIN WEAK
BLAND VAPID FEEBLE DILUTED
INSIPID SLIPSLOP
WISKET BASKET WHISKET
WISP TATE WUSP SCRAP SHRED
SKIFF SKIFT TWIST RUMPLE
CRUMPLE MASSAGE
(— OF HAY) RISP
(— OF STRAW) WAP WASE DOSSIL
(— OF THATCH) TIPPET
WISPY FRAIL NEBULOUS
WISTERIA FUJI KRAUNHIA
WISTFUL INTENT PENSIVE
WISHFUL MOURNFUL YEARNING
WISTITI WISTIT MARMOSET
WIT VAT VYT WAG KNOW NOUS
SALT BRAIN HUMOR IRONY SENSE
THINK WHITE WOTTE ACUMEN
ESPRIT POLICY SANITY SATIRE
WISDOM CONCEIT CUNNING
PICADOR SARCASM SUPPOSE
THINKER WITWORM BADINAGE
REPARTEE
(BITING —) DICACITY
(PL.) SCONCE BUTTONS
WITCH ALP ANI HAG HEG HEX
MARE SAGA TRAT WYCH BRUJA
BUTCH GREBE LAMIA SIBYL
WEIRD WIGHT ASUANG CARLEY
CARLIN CUMMER DOWSER
DUESSA HECATE KIMMER PILWIZ
WIZARD AGANICE CANIDIA
CARLINE HAGGARD HELLCAT
SYCORAX BABAJAGA CAROLINE
ERICHTHO SORCERER SPAEWIFE
VERSIERA WALKYRIE
(PL.) COVEN
WITCHCRAFT CHARM GOETY
OBEAH WICCA CUNNING HEXEREI
MYALISM SORCERY BRUJERIA
DEVILTRY PISHOGUE WIZARDRY
WITCH DOCTOR BOCOR BOKOR
GOOFER GUFFER
WITCHERY CHARM SPELL
SORCERY SORTIARY
WITCHES'-BROOM STAGHEAD
WITCHGRASS COUCH PANIC
PANICLE
WITE WAT BLAME FAULT WAYTE
CENSURE REPROACH HAMESOKEN
WITH BY CUM MID MIT WUD AVEC
CHEZ DOWN AMONG ANENT
WIGHT AGAINST
(— HAND ON HIP) AKIMBO
(— REGARD TO) ABOUT
(— SPEED) TIVY
(PREF.) CO COL COM CON COR
META SYM SYN
WITHDRAW GO COY DROP TAKE
AVOID DEMIT LOOSE REVEL SHIFT
START UNSAY CHANGE DECEDE
DESERT DETACH DETRAY DEVOID
EFFACE FLINCH MINISH RECALL
RECANT RECEDE RETIRE REVOKE
ROGATE SECEDE SHRINK SINGLE
SYPHON ABSCOND CONCEAL
DESCEND DETRACT FORSAKE

INVEIGH RETRACT RETREAT
SCRATCH SCUTTLE SECLUDE
SUBDUCE SUBDUCT UNSCREW
SEPARATE SUBTRACT SEGREGATE
SEQUESTER
(— FROM) VAIK ABANDON
(— FROM POKER POT) DROP
(— SUPPORT) ABANDON
WITHDRAWAL DRAIN FLIGHT
HIDING OFFLAP RETIRE SHRINK
ABSENCE DUNKIRK PULLOUT
REGRESS RETIRAL RETREAT
SCUTTLE RECESSION REVULSION
(— FROM WORLDLY THINGS)
ABSTRACTION
(— OF BUILDING FACE) SETBACK
(— OF PROMISE) BACKWORD
(— OF SUIT) RETRAXIT
WITHDRAWN SHY ASOCIAL
INGROWN SECLUSE DISTRAIT
ISOLATED SECLUDED RECESSIVE
ABSTRACTED
WITHE HANK ROPE TIER TWIG
WITHY WATTLE WICKER CRINGLE
WITHER BURN DAZE FADE MIFF
PINE RUST SEAR STUN WARP
WELK WELT BLAST CLING DAVER
DECAY QUAIL WIZEN COTTER
GIZZEN SHRINK WALLOW WELTER
WILTER WINDER AREFACT
DECLINE FORWELK SENESCE
SHRIVEL LANGUISH PARALYZE
WITHERED DRY ARID SEAR SERE
CORKY SCRAM MARCID BLASTED
UNGREEN WEARISH WIZENED
AUTUMNAL
WITHERING SCATHING
WITHHELD DEFERRED SUSPENSE
WITHHOLD CURB DENY HIDE KEEP
STOP CHECK SCANT ABSENT
DEPORT DETAIN REFUSE RETAIN
ABSTAIN BOYCOTT DEFORCE
FORBEAR OUTHOLD REPRESS
RESERVE SUSPEND RESTRAIN
SUBTRACT
(— CONSENT) DECLINE
WITHHOLDING DETAINER
(— OF DUES) CHECKOFF
WITHIN IN ON BEN BIN INBY INLY
INTRA ABOARD HEREIN INSIDE
INWITH INDOORS ENCLOSED
INCLUDED INWARDLY
(PREF.) END(O) ENT(O) ESO IL IM
IN INFRA INTER INTRA INTRO
(ARISING —) IDIO
WITHOUT EX BUT OUT SEN BOUT
FREE OHNE SANS SINE MINUS
SENZA FAILING OUTSIDE
WANTING INNOCENT OUTDOORS
(— A FLANGE) BALD
(— A MATE) ODD
(— ACTION) DEEDLESS
(— BEGINNING OR END) ETERNAL
(— BLEMISH) CHOICE
(— CONTENTS) INANE
(— DELAY) AWAY FOOTHOT .
SUMMARY
(— DELIBERATION) HEADLONG
(— EMOTION) DRYLY DULLY
(— EXCEPTION) ALWAYS
(— FEET) APOD
(— FUNDS) CLEAN
(— HORNS) ACEROUS

(— INTEREST) BARREN
(— LIFE) AZOIC
(— LIGHT) APHOTIC
(— LIMITS OF DURATION) AGELESS
(— ORDER) ANYHOW
(— POWER) ADRIFT
(— QUESTION) EASILY SECURELY
(— REALITY) AIRY
(— REASON) BLINDLY
(— REMEDY) BOOTLESS
(— ROADS) INVIOUS
(— RULE OR LAW) ANARCHIC
(— SADDLES) ASELLATE
(— TEETH, TONGUE OR CLAWS)
MORNE
(— WINGS) APTEROUS
(PREF.) A ECT(O) LIPO
(— GOVERNMENT) ANARCH(O)
(SUFF.) LESS
WITHSTAND BIDE DEFY TAKE
ABIDE OPPOSE OPPUGN RESIST
CONTAIN CONTEST FORBEAR
SUSTAIN CONFRONT WITHSTAY
WITHY WIRY AGILE OSIER WOODY
WILLOW WOODIE WINDING
WITLESS MAD GROSS SILLY
INSANE STUPID FATUOUS
FOOLISH UNWITTY HEEDLESS
SLAPHAPPY
WITLOOF ENDIVE CHICORY
WITNESS SEE TAKE TEST PROOF
ATTEST BEHOLD MARTYR
RECORD TESTIS TESTOR
CURATOR TESTATE TESTIFY
EVIDENCE RECORDER SUFFRAGE
(FALSE —) JUROR
(PL.) SECTA
(PREF.) TESTI
WITNESS-BOX STAND
WITOTO HUITOTE
WITTICISM WIT JEER JEST JOKE
QUIP SALLY SLENT WHEEZE
WITTING NEWS TIDINGS
WITTINGLY SCIENTER
WITTOL FOOL CUCKOLD WITTALL
WITTY GASH WILY WISE DROLL
LEPID PAWKY SHARP SMART
CLEVER FACETE JOCOSE JOCULAR
KNOWING CONCEITY HUMOROUS
(NOT —) INFICETE
WIVERN DRAGON WYVERN
WIZARD MAGE SEER SHIZ FIEND
WITCH DOCTOR EXPERT PELLAR
WARLOW CHARMED MAGICAL
SPAEMAN WARLOCK WISEMAN
CONJUROR MAGICIAN SORCERER
TROLLMAN WITCHMAN
ARCHIMAGE
(PL.) GOETAE
WIZARDRY SORCERY
WIZEN DRY WITHER SHRIVEL
WIZENED SERE GIZZEN WEAZEN
WOAD DYE NIL ODE ANIL KERS
NILL OADE CRESS ANILLA INDICO
INDIGO PASTEL
(PREF.) ISAT(O)
WOADWAXEN ALLELUIA
ALLELUJA
WOBBLE COCKLE COGGLE HOBBLE
QUAVER SHIMMY TEETER TITTER
WABBLE WIGGLE TREMBLE
NUTATION
WOBBLY LOOSE SHAKY COGGLY

DRUNKEN DOUBTFUL

WOE WA WEI BALE BANE DULE PAIN PINE WAWE GRIEF MISERY SORROW TROUBLE WILLAWA CALAMITY DISTRESS WELLADAY WELLAWAY

WOEBEGONE WAFF UNHAPPY DEJECTED DESOLATE DOWNCAST

WOEFUL MEAN DISMAL PALTRY RUEFUL DIREFUL DOLEFUL RUTHFUL DOLOROUS PITIABLE WRETCHED

WOLF GLUT LOBO CANID FREKI YABBI CHANCO COYOTE FAMINE FENRIR ISGRIN KABERU LOAFER MASHER SIGRIM THOOID POVERTY ISENGRIM

(FOX —) ZORRO

(PREF.) LUPI LYC(O) VULPI

WOLFBERRY BUCKBUSH

WOLFHOUND ALAN BORZOI PSOVIE

WOLFISH LUPINE RAVENOUS

WOLFLIKE THOOID

WOLFRAMITE CAL TUNGSTEN

WOLFSBANE ACONITE DOGBANE FOXBANE

WOLF SPIDER HUNT JAGER HUNTER JAEGER JAYHAWK LYCOSID TARANTULA

WOLVERINE PIG GLUT GORB MIKER GLOTUM HELLUO GLUTTON GUTLING LURCHER MOOCHER RAVENER SWILLER CARCAJOU DRAFFMAN GOURMAND GULLYGUT

(— STATE) MICHIGAN

WOMAN BIM BIT DAM EVE HEN HER JUG MEG SHE TEG TIT BABE BABY BINT BOSS CONY DAME FAIR FEME FLAG FROW JADE JANE LADY MAMA MARY MORT PERI SLUT WIFE BIDDY BIMBO BLADE BROAD CHINA DONAH FEMME FRAIL JATNI LUBRA LUCKY MAMMA MUJER QUEAN SKIRT SMOCK SQUAW TAGGE TOOTS TWIST UMMAN VROUW BURDIE CALICO CARLIN CUMMER FEMALE GIMMER HEIFER KIMMER LUCKIE MANESS MULIER SISTER TOMATO VIRAGO WAHINE CARLING CHANGAR DISTAFF PARTLET PINNACE PLACKET QUAEDAM MISTRESS PETTICOAT

(— DESERTED BY HUSBAND) AGUNAH

(— OF CONSEQUENCE) HERSELF

(— OF LOW CASTE) DASI

(— OF RANK) DOMINA

(— OF UNSTEADY CHARACTER) FLAP CALLET

(— OF WEALTH) FORTUNE

(— WHO ACTS AS ADVISER) EGERIA

(— WITH ONE CHILD) UNIPARA

(— WITH 3 CHILDREN) TRIPARA

(ABORIGINAL —) GIN LUBRA

(ABUSIVE —) FISHWIFE

(ALLURING —) DISH

(ATHENIAN — OF HIGH RANK) GERARA GERAERA

(ATTRACTIVE —) DOLLY SHEBA DOLLIE LOOKER CHARMER

(AUSTRALIAN —) BINT

(AWKWARD —) ROIL

(BEAUTIFUL —) HURI PERI BELLE HOURI SIREN SPARK CHERUB EYEFUL MUSIDORA

(BOISTEROUS —) HOYDEN

(BOLD —) RAMP

(CLEANING —) CHAR

(COARSE —) BEAST RUDAS BLOWZE RULLION

(COOLIE —) CHANGAR

(COY —) HAGGARD

(CREMATED —) SATI SUTTEE

(DEAR —) PEAT

(DUTCH OR GERMAN —) FRAU FROW FROKIN FRAULEIN

(ENGAGED —) BONDAGER

(ENTICING —) SIREN

(EVIL OLD —) HAG HELLHAG

(EXCITED —) MAENAD

(FASHIONABLE —) MILADY GALLANT ELEGANTE

(FAT —) BOSS FUSTILUGS

(FINE —) SCREAMER

(FIRST —) EMBLA PANDORA

(FLIRTING —) CHIPPY FIZGIG

(FOOLISH —) TAWPIE

(FORWARD —) STRAP

(GAUDY —) JAY

(GENTLE —) DOVE

(GOSSIPY —) HAIK HAKE BIDDY TABBY

(GOSSIPY, TALKATIVE —) YENTA

(GROSS —) SOW

(GYPSY —) ROMI ROMNI GITANA

(ILL-TEMPERED —) VIXEN CATAMARAN

(IMMORAL —) RIG GITCH FLAPPER HARLOTRY

(IMPUDENT —) YANKIE

(INDIAN —) SQUAW WENCH KLOOCH BUCKEEN

(INSPIRED —) PHOEBAD

(ITALIAN —) DONNA

(LASCIVIOUS —) GIGLET

(LEARNED —) PUNDITA CLERGESS

(LEWD —) REP SLUT BITCH HUSSY HUZZY MALKIN BROTHEL CYPRIAN

(LOOSE —) BAG BIM KIT MOB TIB DRAB FLAP BIMBO TROLL GILLOT HARLOT LIMMER BAGGAGE COCOTTE FRANION TROLLOP

(LOUD-SPOKEN —) RANDY

(LOW OR WORTHLESS —) JADE JURR BUNTER SLINGDUST

(MARRIED — OF LOWLY STATION) GOODY

(MASCULINE —) AMAZON RULLION COTQUEAN

(MEEK —) GRIZEL

(MYTHOLOGICAL —) HEROINE

(NON-JEWISH —) SHIKSA

(OLD —) GIB HEN BABA TROT CRONE FAGOT FRUMP TROUT BELDAM CARLIN GAMMER GEEZER GRANNY CARLINE GRANDAM HARRIDAN

(OLD SHRIVELED —) FAGOT FAGGOT

(PEDANTIC —) BLUE

(PERT —) CHIT

(PORTUGUESE —) SENHORA

(PREGNANT —) GRAVIDA

(PRIGGISH —) PRUDE

(RUSTIC —) JOAN

(SCOLDING —) RANDY SHREW COTQUEAN RIXATRIX

(SHORT OR STUMPY —) CUTTY

(SHOWY —) ANONYMA

(SHREWISH —) JADE HARPY SKELLAT

(SLATTERNLY —) DRAB FLEABAG SLAMKIN

(SLENDER GRACEFUL —) SYLPH

(SLIPSHOD —) MAUX CLATCH TROLLIMOG

(SLOVENLY —) BAG DAW SOW SLUT BESOM TAWPY TROLL TROLLOP SLATTERN

(SPANISH —) DONA GITANA

(SPANISH-INDIAN —) CHOLA

(SPITEFUL —) CAT FURY BITCH

(SQUAT —) TRUB

(SQUEAMISH —) COCKNEY

(STAID —) MATRON

(STATELY —) JUNO

(STORMY VIOLENT —) FURY

(TRACTABLE —) SHEEP

(UGLY —) HAG GORGON

(UNCHASTE —) JILT

(UNMARRIED —) DAME GIRL SPINSTER MADEMOISELLE

(VIXENISH —) HARRIDAN

(WANTON —) MINX TRUB PARNEL

(WICKED —) JEZEBEL

(WISE —) VOLVA ALRUNA ALRUNE

(WITHERED —) CRONE

(YOUNG —) BIT BIRD BURD CHIT DAME DELL DOLL GIRL LASS PUSS BEAST CHICK FILLY FLUFF TOAST DAMSEL HEIFER PIGEON SHEILA SUBDEB BAGGAGE CHICKEN DAMOZEL FLAPPER WINKLOT DAUGHTER GRISETTE

(PREF.) FEMINO GYN(AE)(AECO) (AEO)(ANDRO)(E)(EO)(O)

(SUFF.) GYN(E)(IST)(OUS)

WOMAN HATER MISOGYNIST

WOMANHOOD MULIEBRITY

WOMAN IN WHITE (AUTHOR OF —) COLLINS

(CHARACTER IN —) ANNE FOSCO GLYDE LAURA PESCA MARIAN WALTER FAIRLIE HALCOMBE PERCIVAL CATHERICK HARTRIGHT

WOMANISH FEMALE FEMININE LADYLIKE PETTICOAT

WOMANKIND WOMEN CALICO MUSLIN FEMINIE

WOMAN'S TONGUE LEBBEK

WOMB BELLY CRADLE UTERUS VENTER

(PREF.) COLP(O) HYSTER(O) METRO UTER(O) VULVI VULVO

(SUFF.) COLPOS METRA METRIUM

WOMBAT KOALA BADGER DIDELPH VOMBATID

WOMEN DISTAFF

(— OF EARLY CHURCH) SETTERS AGAPETAE

WON CITY LIVE ROOM ABIDE DWELL REGION

WONDER AWE MUSE SELI SIGN TROW UNCO UNKO VERY FARLY FERLY SELLE SELLY UNCOW

ADMIRE MARVEL MIRATE MAGNALE MIRABLE MIRACLE PORTENT PRODIGY STRANGE UNCOUTH AMERVEIL SELCOUTH SURPRISE

(PREF.) TERAT(O) THAUMA(TO) THAUMO

WONDERFUL KEEN NEAT SELI FERLY GRAND GREAT SELLE SWELL WAKON GEASON MIGHTY AMAZING EPATANT GALLANT MIRABLE MIRIFIC STRANGE GLORIOUS MIRABILE TERRIFIC WONDROUS

WONDERFULLY AMAZING

WONDER-WORKER THEURGIC THEURGIST

WONDER-WORKING MIRIFIC

WONG FIELD GROVE PLAIN MEADOW

WONKY AWRY SHAKY WRONG UNSTEADY

WONT APT USE FAIN USED VAIN HABIT USAGE CUSTOM INCLINED

WONTED TAME USUAL HAUNTED

WOO SUE LOVE SEEK SUIT WALE COURT SPARK SPOON ASSAIL SPLUNT SUITOR ADDRESS

WOOD (ALSO SEE TREE AND TIMBER) HAG KIP BOIS BOSK BOWL EKKI HOLT HYLE KIRI MASS MOCK PALO SHAW SUPA TREE WOLE CAHUY CHARK CROWD EDDER FLOUR GROVE HURST HYRST KOKRA RESAK SHOLA STICK STUFF WEALD ALMOND ANGILI AUSUBO BRAZIL EKHIMI FOREST ITAUBA JARANA LUMBER PALING SPINNY TIMBER APITONG AVODIRE BOSCAGE BOSKAGE COPPICE DADDOCK DUDGEON HAYBOTE SATINAY VENESIA BAGTIKAN CRANTARA FIREBOOT CALAMANDER

(— BURNT AS PERFUME) AGALLOCH

(— FOR CARPENTRY) STUFF

(— FOR REPAIRING HEDGE) TINING HAYBOTE

(— OF SMALL EXTENT) GROVE

(— OF THE VERA) VENESIA

(— ON RAFTER) FUR

(— ROTATED ON STRING) ROMBOS RHOMBOS

(— USEFUL FOR TINDER) PUNK SPONK TOUCHWOOD

(— YIELDING PERFUME) LINALOA

(BABUL —) SUNT

(BLACK —) EBONY

(CONE-SHAPED PIECE OF —) ACORN

(DARK RED —) RATA

(DEAD —) RAMMEL

(DENSIFIED —) STAYPAK

(ELASTIC —) SYCAMORE

(FLAT ROUND PIECE OF —) TRENCHER

(FLEXIBLE —) EDDER

(FOSSIL —) PINITE PEUCITES

(FRAGRANT —) CEDAR SANDALWOOD

(FUEL —) ESTOVERS

(HARD —) ASH DAO ELM SAL BAKU IPIL KARI LANA POON ANJAN EBONY GIDYA KARRI

KOKRA MAPLE MAZER ZANTE
BANUYO CAMARA FREIJO GIDGEE
KEMPAS SABICU SAPELE WALNUT
CURUPAY DATTOCK HICKORY
GUAIACUM IRONBARK
MAHOGANY
(HEAVY —) DAO EBON EBONY
CHENGAL GUAYABI SUCUPIRA
(LIGHT —) POON BALSA HEMLOCK
(LIMBA —) KORINA
(LOGGED —) CHIP
(LOST —) CHIPPAGE
(LUSTROUS —) LEZA BOARWOOD
(MATCHBOX —) SKILLET
(MOTTLED —) AMBOINA
CALAMBOUR
(NARROW BAR OF —) SLAT
(NUMBER 1 —) DRIVER
(NUMBER 2 —) BRASSIE
(NUMBER 3 —) SPOON
(NUMBER 4 —) CLEEK
(OILY —) BATETE
(OLIVE —) COLLIE
(PETRIFIED —) LITHOXYL
ROCKWOOD
(PINKISH —) BOSSE
(POINTED PIECE OF —) TRIPPET
(REDDISH —) KOA KARI KARRI
ARANGA BANABA CHERRY
DUNGON SATINE KAMBALA
(REDDISH-YELLOW —) GUYO
(ROTTEN —) DADDOCK
(SANDARAC —) ALERCE
(SMALL —) SHAW
(SOFT —) KIRI GABUN GABOON
ELKWOOD AGALLOCH ALBURNUM
GUATAMBU
(SQUARE LOG OF —) NOG
(STICK OF —) BILLET
(STRIP OF —) LATH STAVE BATTEN
REEPER REGLET
(WATER-RESISTING —) AMUGIS
(YELLOWISH —) HALDU FUSTIC
IDIGBO KADAMBA KAMASSI
GUATAMBU
(PREF.) HYL(O) LIGN(I)(O) XYL(O)
(SUFF.) XYLON XYLUM
WOOD ANEMONE CYME EMONY
BOWBELLA SNOWDROP
WOODBARK SABLE BLONDINE
WOODBINE BIND WIDBIN
EGLATERE
WOODCARVER BODGER
WOODCHUCK CHUG CHUCK
MONAX MARMOT SUSLIK WEJACK
MOONACK GROUNDHOG
WOODCOCK QUIS PEWEE PEWIT
SNIPE SNITE SHRUPS BECASSE
SIMPLETON
WOODCUT BLOCK
WOODCUTTER AXEMAN LOGGER
WOODMAN WOODSMAN
WOOD DUCK SQUEALER
BRANCHIER
WOODED BOSKY TREEY HYLEAN
SYLVAN FORESTED NEMOROUS
WOODEN DRY DULL STIFF TREEN
CLUMSY STICKY STOLID TIMBER
AWKWARD DEADPAN TIMBERN
LIFELESS
WOOD GUM XYLAN
WOOD HEN WEKA
WOODHEWER PICUCULE

WOOD HOOPOE WHOOP WHOOPE
IRRISOR DUNGBIRD PICARIAN
WOOD HYACINTH SCILLA
CROWTOE GREGGLE HAREBELL
WOOD IBIS STORK GANNET
JABIRU IRONHEAD
WOODLAND DESERT MIOMBO
SPRING BOSCAGE
(WASTE —) WEALD
WOODPECKER AWL CHAB JYNX
KATE PEEK ECCLE HECCO HEWEL
ICKLE PICUS SPEKT HECKLE
NICKER NICKLE PECKER PIANET
PICULE SPRITE TAPPER YAFFLE
YUCKER YUKKEL CLIMBER
CREEPER FLICKER HEWHOLE
HICKWAY LOGCOCK REDHEAD
SAPSUCK SNAPPER SPEIGHT
WHETILE WITWALL WRYNECK
DIRTBIRD HICKWALL PICARIAN
PICUCULE POPINJAY RAINBIRD
RAINFOWL WALLHICK SAPSUCKER
(LIKE A —) PICIFORM
(PREF.) PICI
WOOD PIGEON CUSHAT ZOOZOO
WOODPILE STRAN STRAND
WOODRICK
WOOD ROBIN MIRO TOMTIT
WOODRUFF HAIROF MUGGET
MUGWET WOODROW HAIRHOOF
WOODS BOSK BUSH BOSQUE
(PREF.) NEMO SILVI SYLVI
WOODSMAN BUSHY SILVAN
SYLVAN BUSHMAN BUSHWACK
WOOD SORREL OCA COCKOO
HEARTS LUJULA OXALIS TREFOIL
ALLELUIA ALLELUJA SHAMROCK
STABWORT
WOOD THRUSH MAYBIRD
WOODTURNER BODGER
WOODWIND OBOE FLUTE CORNET
BASSOON PIBGORN PICCOLO
CLARINET
WOODWORK CEILING
WOODWORKER JOINER TURNER
MILLMAN
WOODWORM GRIBBLE
(PREF.) TERMITO
WOODY BOSKY WITHY FRITHY
STICKY SYLVAN XYLOID LIGNOSE
LIGNEOUS
WOOER BEAU LOVER WOWER
SUITOR COURTER WOOSTER
COURTIER PARAMOUR
WOOF WEFT WOUGH FILLING
TEXTURE
WOOING SUIT WOHLAC
WOOL OO COT DAG HOG VOL
WOW BEAT BLUE FRIB PILE PULU
ROCK FADGE LAINE MUNGO
STUFF TIPPY ALPACA ARGALI
BOTANY BREECH FLEECE GREASE
JACKET JERSEY KERSEY LUSTER
SLIVER WETHER COMBING
HASLOCK KASHMIR MORLING
STUBBLE WIGGING CASHMERE
CLOTHING COMEBACK MORTLING
PICKLOCK TOMENTUM
(— AS IT COMES FROM SHEEP)
GREASE
(— FROM DEAD SHEEP) MORLING
MORTLING
(— FROM LEOMINSTER) ORE

(— FROM RAGS) EXTRACT
(— OF UNDERCOAT OF MUSK-OX)
QIVIUT
(— ON SHEEP'S LEG) GARE BREECH
(— ON SHEEP'S THROAT) HASLOCK
(— WEIGHT) TOD
(COARSE —) ABB SHAG BRAID
COWTAIL
(COTTON —) CADDIS CADDICE
(DUNGY BIT OF —) FRIB
(FINE GRADE OF —) PICKLOCK
SPINNERS
(GREASY —) TIPPY
(INFERIOR GRADE OF —) HEAD
(KNOT OF —) NOIL
(LAMB'S —) WASSAIL
(LOCK OF —) FLOCK STAPLE
(LONG —) BLUE
(LOW GRADE OF —) LIVERY
(MATTED —) DAG KET SHAG
(PULLED —) SLIPE
(RECLAIMED —) MUNGO SHODDY
(REFUSE —) COT COTT FLOCK
PINION
(ROLL OF —) CARDING
(RUSSIAN —) DONSKY
(SMALL PIECE OF —) TATE
(SPUN —) YARN
(WOUND —) TREND
(PREF.) ERIO LAN(I)(O) MALLO
(SUFF.) LAN
WOOLCLOTH HODDEN
WOOLEN (ALSO SEE FABRIC)
CADDIS CAMLET SUCLAT
CADDICE PASHMINA
(PL.) LAINAGE
WOOL FAT LANOLIN
WOOLLY SHEEP WOOZY LANATE
LANOSE COTTONY FLOCCOSE
PERONATE
WOOLLY BEAR WOUBIT
WOOLLY CROTON HOGWORT
WOOLY
(PREF.) DASI DASY ULO
WOOZY SICK DRUNK TIGHT VAGUE
BLURRY WOOLLY
WORD GIG MOT EZEL GULE HAIT
NEWS RAFF TERM VERB WHID
WHUD ADNEX CHEEP COUCH
DERRY DILLY FITCH GLOSS HAPAX
HOKEY HYNDE LEMMA MAXIM
ORDER PAROL RHEMA RUMOR
SPELL ACCENT ADVERB AVOWAL
BREATH COPULA ETYMON KIBBER
LATIVE ONEYER PAROLE PLEDGE
QUATCH REMARK REPORT
SAYING ACCOUNT ADJUNCT
BICCHED COMMAND COMMENT
DICTION DUCDAME GENTILE
GITTITH HOMONYM INCIPIT
MESSAGE PALABRA PARONYM
PRAYFUL PRENZIE PROMISE
PROVERB SYNONYM VOCABLE
ACROSTIC CATCHCRY CHEVILLE
COMPOUND ENCLITIC EQUIVOKE
FRABJOUS FRINGENT IDEOGRAM
ILLATIVE LATINISM SYLLABLE
SYNTAGMA NEOLOGISM
PALINDROME PARTICIPLE
MONOSYLLABLE
(— AS CALL TO DUCK) DILLY
(— EXPRESSING COMMAND)
JUSSIVE

(— FORMED FROM VOWELS)
EUOUAE
(— FROM INITIAL LETTERS)
ACRONYM
(— IN A PUZZLE) LIGHT
(— MISPRONOUNCED) BEARD
(— OF CONCLUSION) AMEN
EXPLICIT
(— OF HONOR) PAROLE
(— OF MOUTH) FIDELITY
(— OF OPPOSITE MEANING)
ANTONYM
(— OF SECONDARY RANK) ADNEX
(— OF UNCERTAIN MEANING)
FRINGENT
(— OF UNKNOWN MEANING) KIBBER
ONEYER PRAYFUL PRENZIE
(—S IN LOW TONE) ASIDE
(—S OF OPERA) LIBRETTO
(BIBLICAL — OF DOUBTFUL
MEANING) EZEL FITCH GITTITH
(CALL —) JINGO
(CHARACTERIZING —) EPITHET
(CODE —) DOG FOX JIG ABLE EASY
ECHO GOLF ITEM KING BRAVO
DELTA HOTEL INDIA SUGAR
GEORGE CHARLIE
(EMPTY —S) WAFFLE
(FINE —S) DICK
(GATHERING —) SLOGAN
(HONEYED —S) MANNA
(HYPHENATED —) SOLID
(IDENTIFYING —) LABEL
(LAST — OF SPEECH) CUE
(MAGIC —) ABRACADABRA
(MEANINGLESS —) DERRY
(MEANINGLESS —S) NOISE
(METAPHORICAL —) KENNING
(MNEMONIC —) VIBGYOR
(MYSTIC —) ABRAXAS
(NONSENSE —) RAFF RAFFE
FRABJOUS RUNCIBLE
(ORIGINAL —) STEM
(PARTING —) ENVOI
(QUOTED —) CITATION
(REDUNDANT —) CHEVILLE
(ROOT —) ETYMON PRIMITIVE
(SIGNAL —) NAYWORD SECURITY
(SIGNIFICANT —) ACCENT
(SINGLE —) PHRASE
(SOURCE —) ETYMON
(THIEVES' SLANG —) TWAG WHID
(UNEXPLAINED —) DUCDAME
(UTTERED —S) SPEECH
(PL.) LIP TALK SPEECH
LANGUAGE DISCOURSE
(PREF.) LEXI LEXICO LOG(O)
ONOMATO RHEMATO VERBI
VERBO
(SUFF.) EPY LEXIA ONYM
WORD-BLINDNESS ALEXIA
WORDBOOK LEXICON SPELLER
LIBRETTO
WORDINESS VERBIAGE
WORDING LEGEND DICTION
PHRASING
WORDLESS DUMB TACIT SILENT
TACITURN
WORDMAKING RHEMATIC
WORDPLAY EQUIVOKE
WORDY PROLIX VERBAL DIFFUSE
VERBOSE WORDISH
REDUNDANT

WORK DO GO ACT FAG JOB DIKE DYKE FEND FRET NOTE OPUS TASK TEND TOIL ERGON GRAFT GRIND KARMA KNEAD LABOR PRESS YAKKA ARBEIT BONNET EFFECT HUSTLE OEUVRE REDUIT RESULT STRIVE THRIFT CALLING EXECUTE EXPLOIT FERMENT HEXAPLA LOUSTER MISSION OPERATE OPIFICE OPUSCLE OUVRAGE OVERAGE PICHERY PURSUIT TRAVAIL ADVOCACY AGENTING BUSINESS CAPONIER DEMILUNE DRUDGERY ENDEAVOR FUNCTION INDUSTRY LABORAGE OPUSCULE PARERGON RETRENCH EXECUTION
(— ACROSS GRAIN) THURM
(— ACTIVELY) LOUSTER
(— AGAINST) KNIFE ATTACK COMBAT
(— AIMLESSLY) FIDDLE
(— AS REPORTER) HEEL
(— BEYOND ONE'S POWERS) OVERDO
(— CARELESSLY) RABBLE
(— DILIGENTLY) PEG PLUG STRIKE BELABOR
(— DONE) WRIHTE
(— FOR) LABOR SERVE BESWINK
(— FREE) START
(— HARD) TEW MOIL SLOG SWOT BULLOCK LEATHER
(— HIDES) BEAM
(— INSIDUOUSLY) WORM
(— INTO A MASS) KNEAD
(— LAND) FLOAT
(— LEISURELY) DAKER DAIKER
(— OCCASIONALLY) SMOOT SMOUT
(— OF ACKNOWLEDGED EXCELLENCE) CLASSIC
(— OF ART) GEM CRAFT ANTIQUE CAPRICE CREATION EPIPHANY EXERCISE MANDORLA
(— OF FICTION) SHOCKER
(— OF HISTORY) STORY
(— OF MENIAL KIND) DRUDGE
(— ONE'S WAY) WISE
(— OUT) BLOCK FUDGE SOLVE DESIGN EVOLVE
(— OUT IN ADVANCE) FOREPLOT
(— OVER) DIGEST
(— PAID FOR IN ADVANCE) HORSE
(— PERSISTENTLY) HAMMER
(— RESEMBLING PATCHWORK) CENTO
(— SLIPSHOD) MULLOCK
(— STEADILY) PLY
(— TO EXHAUSTION) FAG
(— TO WINDWARD) CLAW
(— TOGETHER) COACT
(— TRIFLINGLY) PIDDLE
(— UNDER ANOTHER NAME) ALLONYM
(— UNFAIRLY OR CRUELLY) HORSE
(— UP) SPUNK
(— UPON) TILL LABOR
(— UPWARD) HIKE
(— VIGOROUSLY) BEND
(ALLEGORICAL —) BESTIARY
(ANONYMOUS —) ADESPOTA
(BUNGLED —) BOTCH
(CANVAS —) POINT

(CHASED —) CISELURE
(CLEANING —) CHAR
(CLUMSY —) BOTCH
(COMPLETED —) TRAVAIL
(CONTRACT —) GYPPO
(DAMASCENE —) KOFTGARI
(DAY'S —) DARG DARGUE
(DECORATIVE —) FLOCKING MARQUETRY
(DIVINE —) THEURGY
(DULL —) DRUDGERY
(EMBOSSED —) CELATURE
(FRAUDULENT —) JERRY
(HAND —) CAMAY
(HARD —) TEW MOIL MUCK SWOT TWIG YERK SWEAT EFFORT MOIDER LEATHER SLAVERY SLOGGING
(INLAY —) INTARSIA
(JOINER —) FINISH
(LITERARY —) STUDY CHASER SEQUEL SERIAL CLASSIC DIPTYCH PRODUCTION
(LURID —) BLOOD
(MANUAL —) FATIGUE
(METAL —) NIELLO
(MINOR —) OPUSCULE OPUSCULUM
(MOSAIC —) EMBLEM
(ORNAMENTAL —) BEADWORK FILIGREE LEAFWORK
(PIECE OF —) JOB
(REFERENCE —) BIBLE SOURCE
(SACRED —) HIERURGY
(SCHOLASTIC —) SUMMA
(SKILLED MECHANICAL —) SLOJD SLOYD
(SOCIAL —) ALMONING
(USELESS —) BOONDOGGLE
(WOMAN'S —) DISTAFF
(PL.) CANON PLANT STODGE FACTORY BUSINESS
(PREF.) ERG(O) ERGAT(O) OPERA
(EMBOSSED —) TOREUMATO
(SUFF.) ERGATE ERGY
WORKABLE YOUNG PLIANT VIABLE FEASIBLE
(EASILY —) SWEET
WORKADAY HUMDRUM PROSAIC ORDINARY
WORKBASKET CABA CABAS CALATHUS
WORKBENCH SIEGE DONKEY TEMPLATE
WORKED INWROUGHT
(— OUT) DEAD
(— UP) ANGRY EXCITED
WORKER (ALSO SEE WORKMAN AND LABORER) AGER CARL DOER HAND HIND ICER SCAB AXMAN BOXER BUTTY DEMAS DRIER EDGER ENDER FILER FIRER FIXER FLYER FOXER GLUER GORER HOLER INKER JERRY LINER LURER MAXIM MINIM NURSE TAPER TOWER ASHMAN BACKER BAILER BALLER BANDER BEADER BENDER BINDER BINMAN BLADER BLOWER BOILER BONDER BOOKER BOSHER BRACER BUFFER BUMPER BURNER BURRER CAPPER CARMAN CASTER CASUAL CHASER COMBER COOKER

DAYMAN DIPPER DOCKER DOGGER DOTTER DUMPER ETCHER FACTOR FAGGER FANMAN FASHER FEEDER FELLER FILLER FITTER FLAKER FLAMER FLUTER FLUXER FOILER FOLDER FORCER FORMER FRAMER GASSER GOFFER GRADER GUMMER GUTTER HASHER HEADER HEELER HELPER HEMMER HOLDER HOOKER HOOPER HOPPER HUNKIE INKMAN JOGGER JOINER LEAFER LEASER LEGGER NOILER PUGGER READER REEDER SCORER SEAMAN SEAMER SHAKER SKIVER SLAKER SLICER SLIDER SLOPER STAVER STAYER TOILER TOPPER BUILDER CREATOR EMPLOYE FIELDER LABORER OUVRIER
(— IN LEATHER) BEAMER CHUMAR JACKER BLACKER CHUCKLER
(— IN METALS) SMITH FLAPPER
(ADDITIONAL —) EXTRA
(AGRICULTURAL —) ARKIE KISAN
(AIRCRAFT —) BOOTMAN
(ANT —) MAXIM ERGATES REPLETE
(ASBESTOS —) COBBER
(AUTO —) DISKER
(BAKERY —) BRAKER COOLER DIVIDER BENCHMAN SPREADER
(BLUE-COLLAR —) STIFF
(BREWERY —) HOPPER STEEPER STILLMAN
(BRICK —) DAUBER CROWDER
(CANNERY —) SLIMER SCALDER SHEDMAN
(CLOCK —) STAKER
(CLUMSY —) BODGE BODGER
(COAL —) SUMPER GEORDIE SPRAGGER
(CONSTRUCTION —) HARDHAT
(DOCK —) BUNGS HOLDMAN SHENANGO
(DOMESTIC —) HELP
(FELLOW —) CONFRERE
(FOUNDRY —) FLOGGER SNAGGER
(GARMENT —) FACER SLEEVER ASSORTER INSEAMER
(GUN —) BLUER
(HARD —) SLOGGER
(HAT —) CURLER BRIMMER
(HIDE —) HEFTER COLORER
(HOSPITAL —) ALMONER
(HOTEL —) SCRUB
(ICEHOUSE —) AIRMAN
(JEWELRY —) ARBORER
(LOGGING —) SNIPER SKIDDER
(MATTRESS —) BEATER
(MIGRATORY —) HOBO OKIE
(MILL —) BILLER SPOUTER
(MINE —) BYEMAN FOOTER GOPHER LANDER DROPPER FACEMAN SLEDGER SWAMPER DRIFTMAN
(OIL WELL —) ROUGHNECK
(ORCHARD —) SMUDGER
(PACKINGHOUSE —) COOK
(PAPERMILL —) SIZER SIZEMAN
(PIANO —) BELLYMAN
(PLODDING —) GRUBBER
(POTTERY —) CASER BATTER BEDDER FETTLER

JOLLIER JUSTLER
(PRINTING —) FLY FLYBOY
(PUERTO RICAN —) GIBARO JIBARO
(QUARRY —) BREAKER
(RAILROAD —) JERRY HERDER BRAKEMAN
(SAWMILL —) BOLTER SETTER BOATMAN DECKMAN CHAINMAN
(SHOE —) CASER FOXER ARCHER FUDGER HEELER CHALKER BOTTOMER
(SKILLED —) ARTISTE
(SLAUGHTERHOUSE —) FATTER SHOVER SINGER SLIMER CHEEKER CHOPPER KNOCKER LIMEMAN SCALPER SCRIBER STICKER SNATCHER
(SOCIAL —) ALMONER
(TANNERY —) GATER STONER CROPPER CURRIER DELIMER BEAMSMAN SEASONER
(TEXTILE —) DOFFER DOUPER DRAWER GIGGER LAPPER LEASER SINGER CREELER DOUBLER JACKMAN KETTLER SKEINER SPINNER SHUTTLER SOFTENER SPLITTER TEASELER
(THEATER —) FLYMAN STAGEMAN
(TOBACCO —) BULKER SIFTER STEMMER SCRAPMAN SPRIGGER STICKMAN STRIPPER
(UNSKILLED —) HELPER DILUTEE GREENER
(USELESS —) TOOL
(WHITE-COLLAR —) EFFENDI
(YARN —) SOURER CHAINER
(PL.) LABOR
(PREF.) ERG(O) ERGAT(O)
(SUFF.) ERGAT(E) URGE URGIC URGY
WORKHORSE AVER AIVER TRESTLE SAWHORSE
WORKHOUSE UNION FACTORY WORKSHOP
WORKING PLAY GOING OPENCUT FUNCTION LABORAGE OPENCAST OPENWORK OPERATIC OPERATIVE
(— ALONE) HATTING
(— HARD) HOPPING
(— OF MINE) GWAG CROSSCUT
(— ON) PRACTICE
(MINE —S) SPLIT
(NOT —) DUFF
WORKMAN (ALSO SEE WORKER AND LABORER) BOSS HAND MATE ROTO CAGER CONER EXTRA FINER FLINT FLUER FROCK LAYER MAJOR MIXER POLER TONER TRIER TUBER BEAMER BLOUSE BOOMER BOWLER BUCKER BUMMER COATER DIPPER DRIVER FORKER GAGGER HANGER LASTER LATHER MASTER NIPPER OILMAN PUFFER RUNNER SAMMER SCORER SHAKER SKIVER SLICER SLIDER SOAKER SPIKER STAGER STAVER TAPPER TARRER TEEMER TILTER TIPMAN TIPPER TOPMAN WARMER WASHER WETTER WRIGHT ARTISAN DRUMMER HOTSHOT LUDDITE SHOPMAN
(CHIEF —) BOSS

(CLUMSY —) BUNGLER COBBLER
(FELLOW —) BULLY BUTTY
(PROFICIENT —) DEACON
(UNSKILLFUL —) HUNKY BUTCHER
(PL.) VOLK
WORKMANLIKE DEFT ADEPT
SKILLFUL
WORKMANSHIP HAND FABRIC
FACTURE OVERAGE ARTIFICE
ARTISANRY
WORKROOM DEN STUDY ATELIER
WORKS HACIENDA
(— OF CLOCK) WATCH
(SALT —) SALINA
WORKSHOP LAB SHED SHOP
FORGE LODGE SMIDDY SMITHY
ATELIER BOTTEGA HOSPITAL
OFFICINA PLUMBERY SKINNERY
WORKTABLE BENCH
WORLD ORB LOKA VALE WARD
EARTH WADRU WARDE CAREER
PUBLIC KINGDOM MONDIAL
CREATION CREATURE UNIVERSE
(— OF BOXING) FISTIANA
(— OF DARKNESS) SHEOL
(— OF DOGS) DOGDOM
(— OF FASHION) STYLEDOM
SWELLDOM
(— OF GODS) DEVALOKA
(— OF THE DEAD) DEEP
(— OF WOMEN) FEMINIE
(ACADEMIC —) CAMPUS
(EXTERNAL —) NONEGO
(GREAT —) MACROCOSM
(LITTLE —) MICROCOSM
(LOWER —) ORCUS
(PRIVATE —) AUTOCOSM
(THE —) FOLD
(TWO-DIMENSIONAL —) FLATLAND
(PREF.) COSM(O) MUNDI
(SUFF.) COSM
WORLDLINESS MAMMON
WORLDLING DIVES
WORLDLY LAY WARLY CARNAL
EARTHY MUNDAL EARTHLY
FLESHLY MUNDANE PROFANE
SECULAR SENSUAL TERRENE
(NOT —) INTERIOR
**WORLD'S ILLUSION (AUTHOR
OF —)** WASSERMANN
(CHARACTER IN —) EVA LAY IVAN
VOSS CYRIL DENIS KAREN SOREL
BECKER AMADEUS BERNARD
CRAMMON CHRISTIAN
ENGELSCHALL WAHNSCHAFFE
WORLD-WEARY BLASE
WORLDWIDE GLOBAL ECUMENIC
GLOBULAR PLANETAL PLANETARY
(PREF.) GLOBO
WORLD-WISE KNOWING PRUDENT
WORM BOB EEL ESS LOA MAD
LURG NAIS NEMA ARTER CADEW
FLUKE LYTTA PIPER SCREW
SNAKE DRAGON NEREID NEREIS
PALMER PALOLO SHAMIR SYLLID
SYLLIS TEREDO VERMIS WRETCH
ANNELID ASCARID CARBORA
ENOPLAN SABELLA SAGITTA
SERPENT SERPULA SETARID
SHUFFLE SPIONID TAGTAIL
TRICLAD WRIGGLE BRANDLIN
CEPHALOB CERCARIA CHETOPOD
GILTTAIL HELMINTH LEODICID

MEASURER NEMATODE
POLYCLAD STRONGYL TRICHINA
VERMICLE NEMERTEAN
TOOTHACHE SCHISTOSOME
(— IN HAWKS) FILANDER
(— USED FOR BAIT) TAGTAIL
(AQUATIC —) TUBIFEX
(BLOODSUCKING —) LEECH
(CADDIS —) CADEW PIPER
CADBAIT
(FLUKE —) PLAICE
(MEASURING —) LOOPER
(MUD —) IPO LOA
(SHIP —) BROMA COBRA
(PL.) APODA ENTOZOA
(PREF.) HELMINTH(O) LUMBRICI
SCOLEC(I)(O) VERMI
(SUFF.) SCOLEX
WORM-EATEN PITTED DECAYED
VERMOULU WERMETHE
WORMER JAG
WORMHOLE PIQURE
WORMLIKE VERMIAN
WORMSEED AMBROSIA
WORMWOOD MOXA ABSINTH
CUDWEED MUGWORT ABSINTHE
COMPOSIT MINGWORT
SANTONICA
WORMY EARTHY
WORN SEAR SERE USED PASSE
TRITE MAGGED MIZPAH SHABBY
ATTRITE CONTRITE
(— NEXT TO SKIN) INTIMATE
(— OUT) SHOT BANAL JADED
SEELY SPENT STALE STANK
BEATEN BEDRID BLEARY EFFETE
EPUISE SCREWY SHABBY CRIPPLE
FORWORN DECREPID FOUGHTEN
HARASSED OBSOLETE STRICKEN
(— SMOOTH) BEATEN
WORRICOW DEVIL BUGABOO
BUGBEAR HOBGOBLIN
WORRIED TOEY UNEASY ANXIOUS
FRETTED STREAKED CONCERNED
WORRIT VEX WORRY DISTRESS
WORRY DOG HOE HOW HOX LUG
NAG RUX TEW VEX BAIT BITE
CARE CARK FAZE FIKE FRAB FRET
FUSS HARE MOIL SOOL STEW
ANNOY CHEVY CHOKE DEAVE
FEEZE GALLY HARRY HURRY
LURRY PHASE SCALD SHAKE
TEASE TOUSE TOWSE BOTHER
CADDLE CHIVVY COTTER CUMBER
FERRET FIDGET GALLOW HARASS
HATTER HECTOR INFEST SCAUD
MOIDER PESTER PINGLE PLAGUE
POTHER ANXIETY CHAGRIN
HATCHEL TROUBLE TURMOIL
WHERRET FASHERIE STRANGLE
WORRYING ANXIOUS
WORSE VER WAR SEAMY
WORSEN DESCEND
WORSHIP GOD CULT HERY PUJA
RANK ADORE DULIA HONOR
NAMAZ WURTH YAJNA CREDIT
PRAISE REPUTE REVERE BAALISM
ELOHISM ICONISM IDOLISM
IDOLIZE IMAGERY OBSERVE
BLESSING HIERURGY VENERATE
(— OF ALL GODS) PANTHEISM
(— OF SHAKESPEARE) BARDOLATRY
(ANCESTOR —) SCIOTHEISM

(FORM OF —) RITUAL
(HIGHEST KIND OF —) LATRIA
(INFERIOR KIND OF —) DULIA
(SERPENT —) OPHISM
(STAR —) SABAISM
(PREF.) LITURGIO THRESKI
(SUFF.) LATER LATRIA LATROUS
LATRY
WORSHIPER ISIAC BHAKTA
PRAISER IDOLATER
(— OF STARS) AKKUM SABIAN
(FIRE —) PARSI GHEBER GUEBER
PARSEE
(SERPENT —) SETHIAN SETHITE
WORSHIPFUL GOOD PROUD
NOTABLE
WORST ACE GET BEST LAST
OUTDO SHEND WREST DEFEAT
(PREF.) KAKISTO
WORSTED GARN JERRY SERGE
CUBICA VESSES WHIPCORD
WORT GAIL GYLE SWAT PLANT
LENGTH TUTSAN FILLING
KRAUSEN POTHERB
(FERMENTED —) FEED WASH
(UNFERMENTED —) GROUT
WORTH FECK MEED CARAT MERIT
PRICE VALOR VALUE BECOME
BOUNTY DESERT ESTEEM REGARD
RICHES VALENT VIRTUE WEALTH
DIGNITY PRETIUM VALIANT
WORSHIP SPLENDOR TREASURE
VALIDITY VALLIDOM
(NET —) CAPITAL
(OF LITTLE —) SHLOCK SCHLOCK
(PREF.) AXIO TIMO
WORTHINESS DESERT WORSHIP
WORTHLESS BAD BUM LOW WAF
BAFF BALD BARE BASE EVIL IDLE
LEWD ORRA PUNK RACA SLIM
VAIN VILE WAFF BLANK BLOWN
DUSTY FLASH FOUTY LOSEL
LOUSY PUTID SLINK SORRY
STRAW WASHY ABJECT CHAFFY
CHEESY CRUMMY DRAFFY
DRASTY DROSSY HOLLOW
LIMMER LITHER LUTHER MEASLY
NAUGHT PALTRY RASCAL ROTTEN
TRASHY WOODEN BAGGAGE
FUSTIAN MAUVAIS NAUGHTY
NOTHING PIPERLY RAFFISH
RUBBISH SCABBED SHILPIT
USELESS FECKLESS HARLOTRY
NUGATORY PRECIOUS RASCALLY
RUBBISHY TRUMPERY VAGABOND
WANWORDY WRETCHED
(— THING) AMBSACE
WORTHLESSNESS BELIAL
UNTHRIFT
WORTHWHILE TANTI
WORTHY BIG DEAR FAIR GOOD
HOLY TIDY AUGHT CANNY DIGNE
EXALT HONOR JELLY NOBLE
PIOUS GENTLE CONDIGN
GRADELY PAREGAL THRIFTY
ELIGIBLE VALUABLE WAUREGAN
(— OF BELIEF) CREDIBLE
(— OF DEVOTION) HOLY
(— OF PRAISE) LAUDABLE
(SUFF.) ABLE IBLE
WOULD WAD WID WANT WISH
COULD SHOULD
(— NOT) NOLD WADNA WADDENT

(I —) CHUD CHOLD
WOULD-BE MANQUE
WOUND ARR CUT HEW PIP WIN
BITE CALK CLAW DUNT FAKE
FOIN GALL GORE HARM HURT
MAIM PAIN PINK RASE RAZE RIST
SCAR SKAG SORE STAB TEAR
VULN WING BLESS BROKE GANCH
GRIEF KNIFE KNOCK SHOOT STICK
STING SUGAT THIRL TOUCH
BREACH BRUISE CREASE ENTAME
GRIEVE HARROW INJURE LAUNCH
LESION MARTYR OFFEND PIERCE
PLAGUE SCOTCH TRAUMA
AFFLICT ATTAINT BATTERY
BLIGHTY DIACOPE GUNSHOT
SCRATCH DISTRESS FLANKARD
FLEABITE INCISION LACERATE
SPURGALL VULNERATE
(— FROM BOAR'S TUSK) GANCH
GAUNCH
(— FROM BULL'S HORN) CORNADA
(— FROM RUBBING) GALL
(— IN DEER'S SIDE) FLANKARD
(— MADE BY THRUST) FOIN
(— ON FOOT) FIKE
(— ON HORSE'S ANKLE) CREPANCE
(— WITH POINTED WEAPON) STAB
SWORD
(DEEP —) DIACOPE
(MINUTE —) PRICK SCART
(TRIFLING —) FLEABITE
(PL.) NOUNS
(PREF.) HELC(O) TRAUMAT(O)
VULNI
WOUNDED HURT WUND VULNED
WINGED VULNOSE STRICKEN
WOUNDWORT BETONY ALLHEAL
HERCULES
WOU-WOU WAWA WAWAH
CAMPER GIBBON
WOVEN BROCHE BROWDEN
DAMASSE
(— FULL WIDTH) SEAMLESS
(— WIDE) BROAD
(— WITH RIB) SOLEIL
WOW HIT MEW BARK HOWL RAVE
WAIL WHINE SUCCESS
WOZZECK (CHARACTER IN —)
MARIE ANDRES WOZZECK
(COMPOSER OF —) BERG
WRACK KELP RACK RUIN VAREC
CUTWEED DESTROY DOWNFALL
EELGRASS WRECKAGE
WRAITH WAFT FETCH GHOST
SPOOK DOUBLE SHADOW
SWARTH SPECTRE
WRANGLE RAG YED CAMP MOIL
SPAR TIFT ARGLE ARGUE BRAWL
CHIDE DAFER FLITE JOWER
PLEAD STRUT ARGUFY BICKER
CAFFLE CAMPLE CANGLE DACKER
FRAPLE FRATCH HAGGLE HASSLE
JANGLE RAGGLE THREAP
BRABBLE BRANGLE DISPUTE
PICKEER QUARREL SCRAFFLE
SQUABBLE TIRRWIRR
WRANGLER CAMPER COWBOY
GRATER HAFTER WRAGER
DEBATER DEFENDER OPPONENT
WRANGLING JANGLE
WRAP HAP LAP LOT WAP BIND
FURL ROLL WHIP AMICE CLASP

CLOAK LAMBA MANTA NUBIA
SERVE TWINE WOOLD AFGHAN
BURLAP CLOTHE COCOON
COOLER DOLMAN EMBALE
MOIDER MUFFLE PATTOO
SACQUE SWATHE WRIXLE
ENVELOP INVOLVE SWADDLE
UMBELAP BARRACAN
(— CABLE) KECKLE
(— DEAD BODY) CERE
(— ONESELF) HUDDLE
(— UP) HAP MAIL ENROL IMPLY
(— UP HEAD) MOB MOP MOBLE
(— WIRE AROUND FISHING LINE)
GANGE
(— WITH BANDAGE) SWATHE
(PL.) SECRECY RESTRAINT
WRAPPER APRON COVER MOTTO
PILCH SHAWL SMOCK COUPON
FARDEL JACKET ENVELOP
OVERALL SARPLER COVERING
MAHARMAH WOOLPACK
(— FOR BOOK) JACKET
(— FOR CUTLET) PAPILLOTE
(— WORN IN EGYPT) GALABIA
GALABEAH
(COOKING —) PAPILLOTE
WRAPPING WAP PACK GELILAH
LAPPING COVERING MANTLING
(— FOR DEAD) CEREMENT
(— OF HEBREW SCROLL) GELILAH
(— OF ROPE) SERVICE
WRASSE COOK BALLAN COMBER
CONNER CUNNER LABRID
HOGFISH PIGFISH SEAWIFE
CORKWING DONCELLA JANIZARY
LADYFISH SENORITA
WRATH IRE FURY GRIM ANGER
WROTH CHOLER FELONY PASSION
VIOLENCE
WRATHFUL IRY EVIL HIGH ANGRY
IRATE WROTH IREFUL RAGING
FURIOUS JEALOUS CHOLERIC
WREAK CAUSE AVENGE EXPEND
GRATIFY INDULGE INFLICT
REVENGE
(— DESTRUCTION) ESTREPE
WREATH LEI ORLE PLAY CROWN
GREEN LAURE LORRE OLIVE
TORSE WHORL WRASE ANADEM
CRANTS CREASE LAUREL POTONG
TORTIL CHAPLET CORONAL
CORONET CROWNAL DOLPHIN
FESTOON GARLAND WRINKLE
KELYPHYTE
(SPIRAL —) VOLUTION
WREATHE BIND WIND CRISP
TWINE TWIST WRING INTORT
WRITHE CONTORT ENTWINE
INTWIST INVOLVE
WREATHED SPIRY TORTILE
TORTIVE WRITHED INTORTED
TORTILLE
WRECK CRAB HULK RUIN BLAST
CRACK PRANG SHOOT SMASH
TRASH WRACK DESPOIL DESTROY
FOUNDER GODSEND SHATTER
TORPEDO DEMOLISH SABOTAGE
SHAMBLES
(— COMPLETELY) TOTAL
(HUMAN —) DERELICT
WRECKAGE WRACK FINDAL
FLOTSAM GODSEND

WAVESON SHAMBLES
WRECKED NOUGHT
**WRECKERS, THE (CHARACTER
IN —)** AVIS MARK PASCOE THRIZA
(COMPOSER OF —) SMYTH
WREN GIRL STAG TOPE CUTTY
JENNY KITTY PEGGY SALLY STAID
TYDIE SCUTTY TIDIFE TIDLEY
TINTIE TOMTIT WRANNY
BLUECAP REGULUS MALURINE
WRANNOCK
WRENCH KEY PIN RUG PULL RACK
RICK RUGG TEAR YERK CRICK
CRINK FORCE THRAW THROW
TWIST WRAMP WREST BEDKEY
SPRAIN STRAIN TWEEZE DISTORT
SPANNER SPANULE SQUINCH
TORTURE TWISTLE
WREST REAR REND EXACT FORCE
TWIST ARREST EXTORT WRENCH
WRITHE ABSTORT WIREDRAW
(— AWAY) STRIP DESPOIL
WRESTLE PRAY RASSLE SQUIRM
TUSSLE WRAXLE WRITHE
GRAPPLE SCUFFLE THRIMBLE
THRUMBLE
WRESTLER MATMAN WELTER
CLICKER MATSTER GRAPPLER
WRESTLING SUMO SAMBO
PALESTRA WRAXLING
(— TECHNIQUE) GLIMA
(STYLE OF —) SAMBO
WRETCH DOG MIX FILE WARY
MISER SLAVE THING BUGGER
PERSON SQUALL BRETHEL
CAITIFF CAMOOCH CHINCHE
CULLION GLUTTON HILDING
SCROYLE BEZONIAN CREATURE
MESCHANT POLTROON RECREANT
SCULLION
WRETCHED EVIL FOUL LORN
MEAN POOR DAWNY DEENY
GAUNT SORRY WISHT WOFUL
YEMER ABJECT CAITIF DISMAL
MEAGER PALTRY RASCAL SHABBY
SICKLY SORDID UNLEAD UNLEDE
WOEFUL ABYSMAL BENEATH
FORLORN OUTWORN PITIFUL
SQUALID UNSEELY MESCHANT
MISERABLE
(— PERSON OR ANIMAL) MISERY
WRIGGLE EEL REG RIG FRIG LASH
WIND WRIG SLIDE WRELE WRING
SQUIRM WAMBLE WANGLE
WARPLE WIDDLE WIMPLE
WINTLE WRITHE EYEBROW
SNIGGLE TWIDDLE TWINGLE
WRABILL WRESTLE SCRIGGLE
SQUIGGLE
WRIGGLING EELY SCRIGGLE
SQUIGGLY
WRIGGLY SNAKY SNAKISH
SQUIRMING
WRING RACK DRAIN EXACT SCREW
TWIST WREST EXTORT OPPRESS
SQUEEZE TORMENT TORTURE
(— THE NECK) SCRAG
WRINGER RUNG WRUNG
SQUEEZER
WRINKLE RUT DRAW FOLD FURL
HINT KNIT LIRK RUCK RUGA
SEAM BREAK CRIMP CRISP DELVE
FAULT FRILL REEVE RIVEL SNIRL

BUCKLE COCKLE CRAVAT CREASE
FURROW METHOD PUCKER
RIMPLE RUMPLE RUNKLE SCRIMP
WREATH BLEMISH CRANKLE
CRINKLE CRUMPLE CRUNKLE
FROUNCE FRUMPLE CONTRACT
IRRUGATE RUGOSITY
(— OF FLESH) CRAVAT
(PREF.) RUTI RUTID(O)
WRINKLED CRUMP PURFLY
RUGATE RUGGED RUGOSE
RUGOUS SEAMED COCKLED
ROUCHED SAVOYED CRUMPLED
FURROWED PUCKERED WRITHLED
WRIZZLED
WRINKLING KNIT KNOT FROWN
WRIST CARPUS SHACKLE
(PREF.) CARP(O)
WRISTER MUFFETEE
WRISTLET WRISTER MUFFETEE
WRISTWATCH BAGUET BAGUETTE
WRIT AIEL CAPE MISE PONE TOLT
ALIAS BREVE BRIEF ERROR RECTO
UTRUM BRIEVE CAPIAS ELEGIT
EXTENT PLAINT VENIRE ACCOUNT
DEDIMUS DETINUE EXIGENT
LATITAT PLURIES PRECEPT
PROCESS SUMMONS WARRANT
CESSAVIT COINAGE DETAINER
DOCUMENT FORMEDON
MANDAMUS MITTIMUS NOVERINT
PRAECIPE QUOMINUS REPLEVIN
SISERARY SUBPOENA TESTATUM
WARRANTY
(— FOR SUMMONING EXTRA
JURORS) TALES
WRITE INK PEN BACK BOOK DITE
DRAW READ CLERK DRAFT STYLE
AUTHOR ENFACE INDITE SCRIBE
SCRIVE ADDRESS COMPILE
COMPOSE DICTATE EMPAPER
EXARATE SCREEVE BIOGRAPH
INSCRIBE
(— ADDRESS) BACK
(— BRIEFLY) JOT
(— CARELESSLY) DASH SCRAWL
SCRIBBLE
(— DOWN) SIGN BREVE DENOTE
RECORD AMORTIZE DESCRIBE
(— FURTHER) ADD
(— HASTILY) SCRATCH SCRIBBLE
SQUIGGLE
(— IN A LARGE HAND) ENGROSS
(— IN LARGE CHARACTERS) TEXT
(— ON FRONT OF BILL) ENFACE
(— PASTORAL POEMS) PHILLIS
(— WHAT IS NOT TRUE) FABLE
(SUFF.) GRAPH(ER)(IA)(IC)(Y)
WRITER (ALSO SEE AUTHOR) PEN
BARD HACK PUFF ALVAR GHOST
ODIST SQUIB AUTHOR FATHER
GLOZER HEROIC LAWYER LETTER
MUNSHI NOTARY PENMAN
PRABHU PROSER PURVOE SCRIBE
TRAGIC YEOMAN ADAPTER
ADSMITH ANALYST DIARIST
ELOHIST ESSAYER GLOSSER
GNOMIST HYMNIST IAMBIST
JUVENAL LAUDIST MUNCHEE
PENSTER PROPHET PROSAIC
REVUIST SCRIVER STYLIST
SUMMIST TEXTMAN AUGUSTAN
BLURBIST COMEDIAN COMPOSER

DECADENT DECADIST DIDACTIC
EMBOSSER EPISTLER ESSAYIST
FABLEIST FABULIST GROMATIC
HUMORIST IDYLLIST MONODIST
MOONSHEE NOVELIST PARODIST
PENWOMAN PREFACER
PRESSMAN PROSAIST PROSEMAN
PSALMIST REVIEWER SCRIPTER
VERSEMAN PROSATEUR
PAMPHLETEER
(— OF BURLESQUE) GABBER
(FREE-LANCE —) CREEPER
(HACK —) PENSTER
(INCOMPETENT —) BOTCHER
(SATIRICAL —) SILLOGRAPH
WRITHE WRY WIND THROW TWIRL
TWIST WRING SQUIRM TERVEE
WAMBLE WRABBE WRENCH
AGONIZE WRESTLE
WRIGGLE WRINGLE
CONVOLVE
WRITHING EELY WRING WRITHY
WRITING BOOK DITE FAIT PAGE
POEM KANJI LIBEL SCROW
CADJAN GOSSIP LEGEND LETTER
PAGINE SCRIPT SCRITE SCRIVE
UNCIAL ARTICLE AUTONYM
DIPLOMA ESCRIPT SCREEVE
APOCRYPH CONTRACT
DOCUMENT GRAVAMEN
HARANGUE KAKEMONO
LETTRURE LIPOGRAM
PAMPHLET SCRIBING
SONNETRY
(— OF LITTLE VALUE) STUFF
SCRIBBLE
(— ON PAPER SCROLL) MAKIMONO
(— ON SILK) KAKEMONO
(— UNDER SEAL) BOND
(BITTER —) DIATRIBE
(CARELESS —) SCRAWL
(CRAMPED —) NIGGLE
(CURSIVE —) JOINHAND
(HINDU —) VEDA
(HUMOROUS —S) FACETIAE
(ILLUMINATED —) FRACTUR
(MUSICAL —) GIMEL GYMEL
(NORSE —) EDDA
(PRETENTIOUS —) FUSTIAN
(SACRED —) ARANYAKA
BRAHMANA SCRIPTURE
(SATIRICAL —) PASQUINADE
(SECRET —) SCYTALE
(SHORT —) SCRIP
(SHORTHAND —) PHONOGRAPHY
(STYLE OF —) ACADEMESE
(SYLLABIC —) KANA
(VAPID —) WASH
(VERBOSE —) TOOTLE
(WORTHLESS —) TRIPE
(PL.) LEGENDA ARANYAKA
POSTHUMA
(PREF.) GRAMO GRAPHI GRAPHO
(SUFF.) GRAM GRAPH(ER)(IA)(IC)(Y)
WRITING CASE STANDISH
SCRUTOIRE
WRITTEN KETIB KETHIB
KTHIBH GRAPHIC
LITERAL
(— ABOVE) SS
(— AFTER) ADSCRIPT
(— HASTILY) STRAY
(PREF.) GRAPTO

WROCLAW BRESLAU
WRONG BAD CAR ILL MIS OUT
WET AWRY HARM HURT SORE
SOUR TORT WITE AGATE AGLEE
AGLEY AMISS CRIME DUTCH
FALSE GLEED GRIEF MALUM
UNFIT WATHE WOUGH AGUILT
ASTRAY BLOOEY FAULTY INJURE
INJURY NOUGHT OFFEND
SARAAD SINFUL UNTRUE WICKED
WONDER ABUSION ABUSIVE
DAMNIFY DEFRAUD IMMORAL
INJURIA MISBEDE NAUGHTY
UNRIGHT VIOLATE AGGRIEVE
COCKEYED MISTAKEN PERVERSE
UNLEEFUL
(CIVIL —) TORT
(IMAGINARY —) WINDMILL
(SHOCKINGLY —) MONSTROUS
(PREF.) MIS

WRONGDOER ACTOR SINNER
FAULTER MISDOER OFFENDER
WRONGDOING MISS CRIME FAULT
DEFAULT MISCONDUCT
MALFEASANCE
WRONGFUL UNFAIR UNJUST
TORTIOUS TORTUOUS UNLAWFUL
WRONGHEADED WRY PERVERSE
WRONGLY AMISS BADLY FALSE
NOUGHT UNRICHT UNRIGHT
OVERWART
WROTH ANGRY IRATE IREFUL
WROUGHT BEATEN CARVEN
FORMED SHAPED VROCHT
CREATED HAMMERED
(ELABORATELY —) LABORED
WRY ASKEW AVERT TWIST WRING
WRONG WRITHE DEFLECT
DISTORT TWISTED WRITHEN
SATURNINE

WRYNECK IYNX JYNX SLAB WEET
LOXIA PEABIRD WEETBIRD
TORTICOLLIS
**WUTHERING HEIGHTS (AUTHOR
OF —)** BRONTE
(CHARACTER IN —) DEAN EDGAR
ELLEN JOSEPH LINTON ZILLAH
FRANCES HARETON HINDLEY
EARNSHAW ISABELLA LOCKWOOD
CATHERINE HEATHCLIFF
WYCH ELM WITCH WITCHEN
WYLIECOAT WALYCOAT
NIGHTGOWN PETTICOAT
WYND HAW ALLEY CLOSE

WYOMING
CAPITAL: CHEYENNE
COUNTY: TETON UINTA GOSHEN
BIGHORN LARAMIE NIOBRARA
INDIAN: ARAPAHO

LAKE: JACKSON
MOUNTAIN: ELK CLOUD GANNET
HOBACK FREMONT ATLANTIC
SHERIDAN
MOUNTAIN RANGE: TETON ABSARO
BIGHORN LARAMIE
RATTLESNAKE
NICKNAME: EQUALITY
RIVER: GREEN SNAKE PLATTE
POWDER BIGHORN
STATE BIRD: MEADOWLARK
STATE FLOWER: PAINTBRUSH
STATE TREE: COTTONWOOD
TOWN: CODY LUSK CASPER
BUFFALO LARAMIE RAWLINS
WORLAND GREYBULL
KEMMERER SHERIDAN
SUNDANCE

X EX XRAY ERROR MISTAKE
XANTHIC YELLOW
XANTHIPPE NAG SHREW
  (HUSBAND OF —) SOCRATES
XANTHIPPUS (SON OF —) PERICLES
XEBEC SHIP CHEBEC CHEBECK
  SHABEQUE
XENIUM GIFT DAINTY DELICACY
XERES JEREZ SHERRY

XERIC DRY
XHOSA KAFIR KAFFIR
  (PL.) AMAKOSA AMAXOSA
XIPHARES (FATHER OF —)
  MITHRIDATE
XIPHISTERNUM XIFOID
XIPHOSURUS LIMULUS
X-RAY UROGRAM

XUREL SCAD SAUREL
XUTHUS (ADOPTED SON OF —) ION
  (BROTHER OF —) DORUS AEOLUS
  (FATHER OF —) HELLEN
  (MOTHER OF —) ORSEIS
  (SON OF —) ION DURUS ACHAEUS
  (WIFE OF —) CREUSA
XYLEM WOOD HADROM

HADROME XYLOGEN
XYLOID WOODY LIGNEOUS
XYLOPHONE REGAL SARON
  BALAFO GAMBANG GAMELAN
  MARIMBA BALAPHON GAMELANG
  GIGELIRA STICCADO
XYSTUS WALK XYST PORTICO
  TERRACE

Y

Y WY YA WYE YOD YOKE YANKEE
(— CONNECTION) SIAMESE
(— COORDINATE) SINE
(PREF.) (LETTER —) YPSILI
YABBER TALK JABBER LANGUAGE
YABBY CRAWLIE
YACARE CAIMAN CAYMAN JACARE
YACHT SAIL SCOW BRUTE YATCH
DINGHY SONDER YEAGHE
CRUISER KEELBOAT
YAFF YAP BARK YELP
YAFFLE ARMFUL YAFFIL
YAHOO BRUTE CLOWN ROWDY
BUMPKIN
YAHWEH GOD JAVE JAHVAH
YAHWIST JEHOVIST
YAK GAG JOKE LAUGH BULBUL
SARLAK SARLYK YAMMER
CHATTER
YAKALA JAGA
YAKKA WORK LABOR
YAKUT SAKHA
YAM HOI UBE UBI UVE JAMB LIMA
RAIL TUGUI IGNAME INAMIA
INHAME POTATO BONIATA
(TARO —) KOKO
YAMA (FATHER OF —) VIVASVANT
(SISTER OF —) YAMI
YAM BEAN KAMAS JICAMA
WAYAKA SINCAMAS
YAMEN COURT YAMUN OFFICE
YAMEO LLAMEO
YAMMER CRY WAIL SCOLD WHINE
YEARN YOMER GRUMBLE
WHIMPER
YAMP YAMPA SQUAWROOT
YANAN NOZI
YANG HONK GURJUN
YANK FLOG JERK SLAP HOICK
SNAKE BUFFET
YAP BARK YAWP YELP MOUTH
SCOLD WAFFLE BUMPKIN
CHATTER KYOODLE
YAPOK YAPOCK OPOSSUM
OYAPOCK
YAQUI YAKI HIAQUI
YARD HAW HOF YED CREW CROW
DUMP FOLD SKID SPAR TILT
COURT GARTH PATIO STICK
CANCHA HOPPET LOANIN
CURTAIN GARSTON KNACKERY
OUTGARTH
(— OF SAWMILL) DUMP
(— WHERE COWS ARE MILKED)
LOANIN LOANING
(FINAL —) FELL
(GRASSY —) GARSTON
(PAVED —) CAUSEY
(POULTRY —) BARTON
(SAIL —) RAE
(1-16TH OF A —) NAIL
(1-3RD OF CUBIC —) CARTLOAD
(20 —S) SCORE

(5 AND A HALF —S) ROD
YARD GRASS ELEUSINE
MANGRASS
YARDLAND VERGE VIRGATE
YARDMASTER DINGER
YARDSTICK VERGE YAIRD METRIC
MEASURE METWAND METEWAND
STANDARD
YARE YAR AYRE YORE BRISK
READY LIVELY NIMBLE PROMPT
YARETA LLARETA
YARM WAIL NOISE OUTCRY SHRIEK
YARN ABB END FOX CORD GARN
GIMP PIRN SILK SLIP WEFT WHIP
DYNEL FLOSS GRAIN INKLE PITCH
SPIEL ALASKA ANGORA BERLIN
BROACH CADDIS COTTON
CREWEL CUFFER DACRON
ESTRON FLORET FRIEZE MERINO
MOTTLE PEELER RATINE SAXONY
SINGLE STRAND THREAD VINYON
WOOLEN ZEPHYR ACETATE
CADDICE FILLING GENAPPE
INGRAIN MELANGE RACKING
SCHAPPE VIGOGNE WORSTED
ASBESTOS BOURETTE CHENILLE
FORTISAN ROUNDING SPINNING
WHEELING ORGANZINE
VIGOUREUX
(— FOR WARP) ABB
(— FROM FLOSS SILK) FLORET
(— SIZE) TYPP
(BALL OF —) CLEW CLUE
(BITS OF ROPE —) THRUMS
(BUNDLE OF —) PAD
(CONICAL MASS OF —) COP
(ELASTIC —) LASTEX
(EXAGGERATED —) STRETCHER
(FINE SOFT —) ZEPHYR KASHMIR
CASHMERE
(LINEN —) SPINEL
(ROLL OF —) PRICK CHEESE
(ROPE —S) SOOGEE
(SILK —) TRAM
(SMALL PIECE OF SPUN —) RABAND
ROBBIN ROPEBAND
(UNEVEN —) BOUCLE
(PL.) FOX MENDINGS
YARRAN GIDYA MYALL GIDGEA
GIDGEE
YARROW ALLHEAL CAMMOCK
MAUDLIN MILFOIL PELLITORY
YASHIRO SHA
YASHMAK VEIL ASMACK YAKMAK
YATAGHAN SABER ATAGHAN
SIMITAR
YATTER CHATTER PRATTLE
YAUD MARE YADE
YAUPON ASSI HOLLY YUPON
CASINA CASSINE
YAUTIA COCO TARO TANIA
COCKER TANIER MALANGA
YAW GAPE YAWN LURCH SHEER

BROACH SWERVE
YAWL HOWL DANDY MIZZEN
SCREAM SCHOKKER
YAWN GAP GALP GANE GANT
GAPE YANE ABYSM CHAUM
CAVITY TEDIUM DULLNESS
OSCITATE
YAWNING HIANT CHASMA GAPING
OSCITANT
YAWP BAWL GAPE RANT STARE
SQUAWK YAMMER COMPLAIN
YAWS PIAN TUBBA TUBBOE
YAWWEED RHUBARB
YAYA COPA
YEA YA YES YOY YIGH TRULY
ASSENT REALLY VERILY
YEAN EAN LAMB
YEANLING KID LAMB EANLING
YEAR EAR SUN AYRE HAAB TIME
ANNUS VAGUE WINTER ZODIAC
TOWMOND TZOLKIN BIRTHDAY
(— OF EMANCIPATION) JUBILEE
(ACADEMIC —) SESSION
(IN THIS —) HA
(LAST —) FERNYEAR
(MANY —S) AGE
(MAYAN —) TUN HAAB
(ONE BILLION —S) AEON
(SABBATICAL —) JUBILE JUBILEE
(1000 —S) MILLENARY
MILLENNIUM
(4320 MILLION —S) KALPA
(PL.) SEASONS
(SUFF.) ENNIAL ENNIUM
YEARBOOK ANNUAL SERIAL
ANNUARY
YEARLING COLT HORNOTINE
(AUTHOR OF —) RAWLINGS
(CHARACTER IN —) LEM ORA JODY
HUTTO PENNY TWINK BAXTER
NELLIE OLIVER WILSON GINRIGHT
FORRESTER WEATHERBY
FODDERWING
YEARLY ANNUAL SOLEMN
YEARN HO YEN ACHE BURN EARN
GAPE HONE IRNE LONG PANT
PINE SIGH CRAVE GREEN GRIEN
ASPIRE CURDLE GRIEVE HANKER
YAMMER
YEARNING EROS DESIRE HANKER
RENNET CRAVING EARNFUL
HOMESICK
YEAST BEE EST BARM BEES EAST
KOJI SOTS FROTH SPUME LEAVEN
NEWING RISING SIZING TORULA
FERMENT SIZZING EMPTINGS
(FILM —) FLOR
YEASTY LIGHT FROTHY TRIVIAL
RESTLESS
YEGG ROBBER BURGLAR
YELL CRY CALL GOWL HOWL ROAR
YARM YAUP YOWL YOWT GOLLY
SHOUT TIGER BELLOW GOLLAR

HOLLER SCREAM YAMMER
YELLOCH SCRONACH SKELLOCH
YELLOW (ALSO SEE COLOR) OR
GULL AMBER BLAKE BLOND
FAVEL FLAVE JAUNE PALEW
SHELL YELWE ALMOND BANANA
FLAVID MELINE MIMOSA NUGGET
OXGALL BISCUIT JASMINE
JONQUIL LEGHORN LUTEOUS
MEXICAN MUSTARD NANKEEN
OATMEAL POPCORN SAFFRON
TILLEUL WHEATEN YUCATAN
AUREOLIN GENERALL ICTEROID
LUMINOUS MARIGOLD ORPIMENT
PRIMROSE
(— AS BUTTER) BLAKE
(BROWNISH —) FULVID FULVOUS
(GOLDEN —) FLAVID
(GREENISH —) ACACIA
(INDIAN —) PURI PURREE
(LEMON —) GENERALL
(PREF.) CHLOR(O) CHRYS(O)
FLAV(I)(O) OCHRO XANTH(O)
XANTIN(O)
YELLOW ALDER SAGEROSE
YELLOW BEDSTRAW CRUDWORT
CURDWORT FLEAWEED
YELLOW BUGLE IVA IVE IVY
YELLOW CLINTONIA DOGBERRY
YELLOW FEVER VOMITO
YELLOW FOXTAIL STICKERS
YELLOW GENTIAN FELWORT
YELLOW GREEN PISTACHE
YELLOWHAMMER SKYT YITE
AMMER GOWDY SKITE GLADDY
GOLDIE VERDIN YORLIN FLICKER
GLADEYE YELDRIN YOLDRING
(— STATE) ALABAMA
YELLOW IRIS SEDGE LEVERS
DAGGERS
YELLOWISH SALLOW ICTERINE
SAFFRONY
(— GREEN) GLAUCOUS
(— RED) FALLOW
(PREF.) LUTEO
YELLOW JACKET VESPA VESPID
YELLOW JASMINE WOODBINE
YELLOWLEGS KILLCU TATLER
WINTER YELPER TATTLER
YELLOW MACKEREL CREVALLE
YELLOWNESS FLAVEDO
YELLOW POND LILY DUCK CLOTE
CLOTS NUPHAR
YELLOW PRICKLE RUBIA
YELLOW RATTLE RATEL
COCKSCOMB LOUSEWORT
YELLOW TOADFLAX RAMSTEAD
YELLOW WAGTAIL OATEAR
YELLOW WATER LILY KELP
WOKAS
YELLOWWOOD FUSTIC FUSTOC
GOPHER MANGWE VIRGILIA
YELP CRY YAP YIP BAFF BARK KIYI

WAFF YAFF YAUP YAWP BOAST YAMPH AVOCET SQUEAL YAFFLE YELLOW
YELPING CRY

YEMEN

ANCIENT KINGDOM: SABA SHEBA
CAPITAL: SANA SANAA
COIN: RIYAL
MUSLIM SECT: SHIA SUNNI
OFFICIAL NAME: YEMENARABREPUBLIC
PEOPLE: ZAIDI SHAFAI
PORT: MOKA MOCHA
REGION: TIHAMA
RULER: IMAM
TOWN: MOKA DAMAR MOCHA TAIZZ HODEIDA

YEN EYES LONG URGE YEARN DESIRE SUCKER LONGING
YENTA GOSSIP TALKER
YEOMAN CHURL CLERK WRITER GOODMAN GUIDMAN GRAYCOAT RETAINER BEEFEATER
YERBA SANTA TARBUSH
YERK BEAT GOAD HURL JERK KICK STAB YARK THUMP EXCITE THRASH LASHING
YES AY DA IS JA OC SI YA AYE ISS YAS YAW YEA YEP YIS YUH YUS YEAH JOKOL TRULY
YESTERDAY YESTER YESTREEN
(OF —) PRIDIAN
YET AND BUT YIT EVEN STILL ALGATE HOWEER THOUGH FINALLY HOWEVER HITHERTO
YETT GATE
YEUK EWK YUK ITCH YUCK ITCHING
YEW YO HEW UGH YOE YOW VIEW TAXUS TOPIARY CHINWOOD
YEX YOLK
YIDDISH JEWISH
YIELD GO BOW CUT ILD PAN PLY BEAR BEND CAST CEDE CESS COME CROP DRAG DUCK FOLD GIVE HEAR HELD LOUT QUIT SELL VAIL WAGE AGREE ALLOW AMAIN AVALE AWALE BRING BUDGE CARRY CAUSE DEFER GRANT HEALD HIELD LEAVE OFFER SLAKE STOOP ACCEDE AFFORD BOUNTY BUCKLE COMPLY CONFER FOLLOW IMPART OUTPUT RELENT RENDER RETURN SUBMIT SUPPLY SWERVE UNGIVE UPGIVE ABANDON ANALYZE BEARING CONCEDE DELIVER FURNISH HARVEST KNUCKLE OUTTURN PRODUCE PROVIDE REDOUND RUCKSEY SUCCUMB BEGRUDGE FRUITAGE OVERGIVE PICKINGS UNDERLIE RELINQUISH
(— FRUIT) ADDLE GRAIN
(— GRASS) GRAZE
(— OF FIELD) BURDEN
(— OF MINE) BONANZA

(— ON BOND) BASIS
(— TO) INDULGE
(— TO TEMPTATION) FALL
(— UP) LET FORLET FORLEIT
(— WELL) HIT BLEED
(MINERAL —) PROSPECT
(SUFF.) FER(ENCE)(ENT)(OUS)
YIELDED
(SUFF.) GENETIC
YIELDING ABLE MEEK NESH SOFT TALL WAXY NAISH WAXEN BONAIR CAVING FACILE FEEBLE FLABBY LIMBER LITHER OUTPUT PLIANT QUAGGY SUPPLE BEARING CESSION FINGENT FLACCID DEDITION LADYLIKE RECREANT
(— IRREGULARLY) BUNCHY
(— OF HORSE) FLEXION
(— STAGE) SEAR
(— TO IMPULSES) ABANDON
YIN SHANG
YIRMILIK METALLIK
YODEL SONG JODEL WARBLE REFRAIN
YODH IOD JOD
YOGA JOG
YOGI JOGI FAKIR FAKEER
YOKE BOW YOK BAIL CROW DRAG FORK HOOP PAIR POKE SOLE BANGY FURCA SHEBA SPANG BANGHY COUPLE INSPAN DRAGBAR HARNESS OPPRESS ADJUGATE
(— BAR) SKEY
(— TO HOLD DRILL) CROW
(— TO RAISE CANNON) BAIL
(PREF.) ZYG(O)(OTO)
(SUFF.) ZYGOMATIC ZYGOSIS ZYGOTE
YOKEFELLOW MATE FELLOW PARTNER YOKEMATE
YOKEL YOB BOOR CLUB JAKE JOCK FARMER JOSKIN BUMPKIN HAYSEED WAYBACK ABDERITE CHAWBACON
YOKING BOUT CONTEST MUGGING
YOLANTA (CHARACTER IN —) RENE ROBERT YOLANTA VAUDEMONT
(COMPOSER OF —) TCHAIKOVSKY
YOLDRING YOWLEY
YOLK CENTER YELLOW ESSENCE LATEBRA VITELLUS PARABLAST
(HAVING A —) LECITHAL
(PREF.) LECITH(O) VITELLI VITELLO
(SUFF.) LECITHAL
YON YONDER THITHER BACKWARD
YONDER THAT THERE THOSE THITHER
YORE PAST YARE YEARS
(OF —) OLDEN
YORKER TICE
YORKSHIREMAN TIKE TYKE LEAROYD
YORUBA NAGO
YOU DU HE IT OW TA TU WE YA YO ONE OWE SHE SIE YOW YUH THOU YOUSE YOURSELF

YOU CAN'T GO HOME AGAIN
(AUTHOR OF —) WOLFE
(CHARACTER IN —) ELSE JACK LLOYD ESTHER GEORGE KOHLER MCHARG WEBBER EDWARDS FOXHALL
YOU NEVER CAN TELL (AUTHOR OF —) SHAW
(CHARACTER IN —) BOON BOHUM DOLLY GLORIA PHILIP CLANDON MCCOMAS WILLIAM GRAMPTON VALENTINE
YOUNG FRY JUV BIRD CALF DROP BIRTH BROOD FETUS YOUR GREEN SMALL UNOLD JUNIOR KINDLE JUVENAL IMMATURE YEANLING YOUTHFUL
(— OF ANY ANIMAL) FRY BABY CALF FOAL JOEY LAMB TOTO
(— OF BEAST) SLINK
(— OF BIRD) CHICK
(— OF CAMEL) COLT
(— OF DOG) WHELP
(— OF FISH) FRY
(— OF SEA TROUT) HERLING
(VERY —) SUCKING NEPHIONIC SHIRTTAIL
(PREF.) FETI FETO FOETI FOETO
(SUFF.) (— ONE) LING
(MODE OF HATCHING —) PAEDES
YOUNGER KID LESS PUNEE JUNIOR PUISNE OFFSPRING
YOUNGEST (— OF BROOD) WALLYDRAG
YOUNGSTER KID BIRD COLT CHILD YOUTH BUTTON SHAVER URCHIN YONKER YOUNKER SPALPEEN
YOUNKER DUPE CHILD KNIGHT NOVICE SQUIRE YUNKER
YOUR OR YO THY YAR YER OURE OWRE YOURN
YOURSELF ITSELF HERSELF HIMSELF ONESELF
YOUTH BOY BUD IMP LAD CHAP COLT PAGE BAHUR CHABO GROOM HYLAS POULT PRIME SPRIG SWAIN WHELP BOCHUR BURSCH EPHEBE HOYDEN INFANT JUVENT KOUROS MASTER SPRING SQUIRT YONKER CALLANT EPHEBOS GOSSOON JUVENAL PUBERTY SAPLING YOUDITH YOUNGTH ENDYMION JUVENILE SPRINGAL
(— WHO SERVES LIQUORS) GANYMEDE
(DELINQUENT —) BODGIE
(GODDESS OF —) HEBE
(IMPUDENT —) SQUIRT
(INEXPERIENCED —) GUNSEL
(NON-JEWISH —) SHEGETZ
(PERT —) PRINCOX
(RUDE —) HOYDEN
(RUSSIAN — ORGANIZATION) KOMSOMOL
(SILLY —) CALF SLENDER
(WELLBORN —) CHILD
(PREF.) HEBE
YOUTHFUL RATH FRESH GREEN

YOUNG BOYISH GOLDEN JUNIOR MAIDEN NEANIC VIRGIN YOUTHY LADDISH PUERILE YOUNGLY IMMATURE JUVENILE SPRINGAL VIGOROUS
YOUTHFULNESS JEUNESSE
YOWL GOWL HOWL WAIL YELL YELP
YUAN DOLLAR
YUAPIN YARURA
YUCATEC MAYA
YUCCA LILY PITA YUCA DATIL IZOTE PALMA JOSHUA LILIAL LILIUM PALMITO SOAPWEED
YUGA KALI

YUGOSLAVIA

CAPITAL: BEOGRAD BELGRADE
COIN: PARA DINAR
GULF: KVARNER
LAKE: OHRID PRESPA SCUTARI
MEASURE: RIF AKOV RALO DONUM KHVAT LANAZ STOPA MOTYKA PALAZE RALICO
MOUNTAIN: TRIGLAV DURMITOR
MOUNTAIN RANGE: DINARIC
PEOPLE: SERB CROAT SLOVENE
PORT: KOTOR SPLIT RIJEKA NOVISAD BELGRADE DUBROVNIK
PRESS AGENCY: TANYUG
REGION: BANAT BOSNIA SRBIJA
REPUBLIC: SERBIA CROATIA SLOVENIA
RIVER: UNA DRIM IBAR KRKA SAVA BOSNA CAZMA DRAVA DRINA RASKA TAMIS TISZA VRBAS DANUBE MORAVA VARDAR VELIKA NERETVA
TOWN: NIS AGRAM BUDVA RTANJ SPLIT TUZLA USKUB BITOLJ MORAVA MOSTAR OSIJEK PRILEP RAGUSA RIJEKA TETOVO VARDAR ZAGREB CATTARO NOVISAD PRIZREN SKOPLJE MONASTIR SARAJEVO SUBOTICA LJUBLJANA
WEIGHT: OKA OKE DRAMM TOVAR WAGON SATLIJK

YUKON TERRITORY (CAPITAL OF —) WHITEHORSE
(LAKE OF —) KLUANE
(MOUNTAIN OF —) LOGAN
(MOUNTAIN RANGE OF —) OGILVIE STIKINE MACKENZIE
(RIVER OF —) PEEL LEWES LIARD PELLY WHITE KLONDIKE PORCUPINE
(TOWN OF —) ELSA MAYO BARLOW DAWSON
YULE NOEL CHRISTMAS
YUMA CUCHAN
YUMAN PATAYAN
YUNX WRYNECK
YURT TENT

Z

Z ZAD ZED ZEE ZETA ZULU IZARD
ZEBRA IZZARD
(SHAPED LIKE A —) OPENBAND
ZAAVAN (FATHER OF —) EZER
ZABAD (FATHER OF —) NEBO ZATTU
NATHAN
(MOTHER OF —) SHIMEATH
ZABAGLIONE SABAYON
ZABBAI (SON OF —) BARUCH
ZABBUD (FATHER OF —) BIGVAI
ZABDI (FATHER OF —) ASAPH ZERAH
ZABDIEL (SON OF —) JASHOBEAM
ZABUD (FATHER OF —) NATHAN
ZACCUR (FATHER OF —) IMRI
ASAPH JAAZIAH
(SON OF —) HANAN SHAMMUA
ZACHARIAH (DAUGHTER OF —)
ABIJAH
(FATHER OF —) JEROBOAM
ZACHARIAS (FATHER OF —)
BARACHIAS
(SON OF —) JOHN
(WIFE OF —) ELISABETH
ZACHER (FATHER OF —) JEHIEL
(MOTHER OF —) MAACHAH
ZADOK (DAUGHTER OF —)
JERUSHAH
(FATHER OF —) BAANA IMMER
AHITUB MERAIOTH
ZAFFER SMALT SAFFIOR ZAPHARA
ZAGREUS (FATHER OF —) JUPITER
(MOTHER OF —) PROSERPINE
ZAHAM (FATHER OF —) REHOBOAM
(MOTHER OF —) ABIHAIL

ZAIRE
ALTERNATE NAME: CONGO
CAPITAL: KINSHASA
COIN: SENGI LIKUTA
COINS: MAKUTA
LAKE: KIVU MWERU
LANGUAGE: KIKONGO LINGALA
SWAHILI TSHILUBA
MONEY: ZAIRE
MOUNTAIN RANGE: MITUMBA
VIRUNGA RUWENZORI
PROVINCE: KIVU KASAI SHABA
EQUATOR KATANGA
BANDUNDU EQUATEUR
ORIENTAL
RIVER: RUKI CONGO DENGU IBINA
KASAI LINDI ZAIRE LIKATI
LOMAMI LUKUGA UBANGI
ARUWIMI LUALABA
LULONGA
TOWN: BAYA BOMA LEBO AKETI
BUKAVU KAMINA KIKWIT
MATADI BUTEMBO
KANANGA KOLWEZI
BAKWANGA YANGAMBI
KISANGANI

ZALAPH (SON OF —) HANUN

ZAMBIA
CAPITAL: LUSAKA
COIN: NGWEE KWACHA
FALLS: VICTORIA
LAKE: MWERU BANGWEULU
TANGANYIKA
LANGUAGE: LOZI BEMBA TONGA
LUVALE NYANJA AFRIKAANS
MOUNTAIN RANGE: MUCHINGA
RIVER: KAFUE LUANGWA
LUAPULA ZAMBEZI
TOWN: KITWE NDOLA LUAPULA
LUANSHYA MUFULIRA
WATERFALL: VICTORIA

ZAMBO CHINO SAMBO CAFUSO
CURIBOCA
ZAMIA BANGA CICAD CYCAD
COONTIE
ZAMINDAR MALIK
ZAMOUSE GAMOUS
ZAMPOGNA BAGPIPE PANPIPE
ZANDER ZANT PERCID SANDER
SANDRA
ZANTHOXYLUM FAGARA
ZANY FOOL CRAZY TOADY
SAWNEY BUFFOON IDIOTIC
CLOWNISH SCREWBALL
ZANZIBAR (SEE TANZANIA)
ZAPARO IQUITO
ZAPATERO LIMA BOXWOOD
CERILLO
ZARA (FATHER OF —) JUDAH
ZARAH KAZOO
ZARPANIT (HUSBAND OF —)
MERODACH
ZAZA (FATHER OF —) JONATHAN
ZEAL FIRE MOOD ARDOR FLAME
HEART FERVOR WARMTH
DEVOTION GOODWILL JEALOUSY
(WITH —) DINGDONG
(PREF.) ZELO
ZEALOT BIGOT VOTARY VOTEEN
ZELANT DEVOTEE FANATIC
CANANEAN SERAPHIC SICARIUS
VOTARESS VOTARIST
ZEALOUS HOT HIGH ARDENT
FERVID STRING CORDIAL
DEVOTED EARNEST EMULOUS
FERVENT FORWARD JEALOUS
PUSHFUL VIGOROUS PERFERVID
RELIGIOUS
(— ABOUT BEAUTY) ESTHETIC
ZEALOUSLY FAST INNERLY
HEARTILY
ZEBADIAH (FATHER OF —) ASAHEL
ISHMAEL JEROHAM MICHAEL
MESHELEMIAH
ZEBAH (SLAYER OF —) GIDEON
ZEBEDEE (SON OF —) JOHN JAMES
(WIFE OF —) SALOME
ZEBINA (FATHER OF —) NEBO

ZEBRA DAUW EQUID HORSE
QUAGGA SOLIPED
ZEBRAWOOD ARAROBA ZINGANA
ZEBU BRAMIN BRAGMAN BRAHMIN
(HYBRID OF — AND CATTLE)
CATTABU
(HYBRID OF — AND YAK) ZOBO
ZEBUDAH (HUSBAND OF —) JOSIAH
(SON OF —) JEHOIAKIM
ZEBULUN (FATHER OF —) JACOB
ZECCHINO SEQUIN
ZECHARIAH (DAUGHTER OF —) ABI
ABIJAH
(FATHER OF —) IDDO BEBAI HOSAH
JEHIEL PASHUR ISSHIAH
PHAROSH JEHOIADA JONATHAN
BERECHIAH JEBERECHIAH
JEHOSHAPHAT MESHELEMIAH
(SON OF —) JAHAZIEL
ZEDEKIAH (BROTHER OF —)
JEHOAHAZ
(FATHER OF —) JOSIAH HANANIAH
MAASEIAH CHENAANAH
(MOTHER OF —) HAMUTAL
ZEDOARY SETWALL
ZELOPHEHAD (FATHER OF —)
HEPHER
ZELUS (FATHER OF —) PALLAS
(MOTHER OF —) STYX
(SISTER OF —) NIKE
ZEMIRA (FATHER OF —) BECHER
ZEN (— PARADOX) KOAN
(— QUESTIONS) MONDO
ZENANA HAREM HARIM SERAGLIO
ZEND AVESTAN
ZENICK SURICATE
ZENITH ACME PEAK HIGHT PITCH
HEIGHT SUMMIT VERTEX
ZENOBIA (HUSBAND OF —)
ODENATHUS
ZEOLITE ANALCIME ANALCITE
ZEPHANIAH (FATHER OF —)
MAASEIAH
(SON OF —) JOSIAH
ZEPHO (FATHER OF —) ELIPHAZ
ZEPHON (FATHER OF —) GAD
ZEPHYR FINE SOFT BERLIN BREEZE
ZEPHYRUS FAVONIUS
(FATHER OF —) AEOLUS ASTRAEUS
(MOTHER OF —) EOS
(SON OF —) CARPOS
(WIFE OF —) CHLORIS
ZEPPELIN ZEP ZEPP AIRSHIP
ZERAH (FATHER OF —) IDDO REUEL
SIMEON
ZERBINETTE (FATHER OF —)
ARGANTE
ZERBINO (BELOVED OF —) ISABELLA
(COMPANION OF —) ORLANDO
(SISTER OF —) GINEVRA
(SLAYER OF —) MANDRICARDO
ZERESH (HUSBAND OF —) HAMAN
ZERETH (FATHER OF —) ASHUR

(MOTHER OF —) HELAH
ZERI (FATHER OF —) JEDUTHUN
ZERO OH NIL NUL BLOB DUCK
NULL AUGHT CLOSE EMPTY
OUGHT TRAIN ZILCH ABSENT
CIPHER NAUGHT LACKING
NOTHING NULLITY SCRATCH
NINETEEN
(EQUAL TO —) NILPOTENT
(HAVING — AS LIMIT) NULL
(HAVING VARIABLES EQUAL TO —)
TRIVIAL
ZERUAH (FATHER OF —) NEBAT
(SON OF —) JEROBOAM
ZERUIAH (SON OF —) JOAB ASAHEL
ABISHAI
ZEST EDGE ELAN JASM GUSTO
FLAVOR RELISH STINGO
PIQUANCY
ZESTFUL RACY SPICY BREEZY
ZETES (BROTHER OF —) CALAIS
(FATHER OF —) BOREAS
(MOTHER OF —) ORITHYIA
ZETHAM (FATHER OF —) LAADAN
ZETHUS (BROTHER OF —) AMPHION
(FATHER OF —) JUPITER
(MOTHER OF —) ANTIOPE
ZEUS ZAN SOTER ALASTOR
CRONION KRONION POLIEUS
CRONIDES
(BROTHER OF —) HADES POSEIDON
(FATHER OF —) KRONOS
(MOTHER OF —) RHEA
(SISTER OF —) HERA HESTIA
DEMETER
(SON OF —) ARES ARCAS ARGUS
AEACUS AGACUS APOLLO
HERMES TITYUS PERSEUS
DARDANUS DIONYSUS HERCULES
TANTALUS
(WIFE OF —) HERA JUNO METIS
THEMIS EURYNOME
(PREF.) ZENO
ZEUXIS UNDERLAY
ZIBEON (SON OF —) ANAH
ZIBIA (FATHER OF —) SHAHARAIM
(MOTHER OF —) HODESH
ZIBIAH (SON OF —) JOASH
ZICHRI (FATHER OF —) ASAPH
IZHAR
(SON OF —) JOEL AMASIAH
ELIEZER ELISHAPHAT
ZIGZAG BOYAU CRANK BROKEN
INDENT CRANKLE CHEVRONY
FLEXUOSE TRAVERSE
(PREF.) ZYZZO
ZILIANTE (BROTHER OF —)
ORRIGILLE
(FATHER OF —) MONODANTE
(SISTER OF —) BRANDIMARTE
ZILPAH (SON OF —) GAD ASHER
ZIMARRA CYMAR SIMAR CASSOCK
ZIMB FLY ZEBUB

617

ZIMBABWE

CAPITAL: HARARE SALISBURY
DIVISION: RHODESIA
LANGUAGE: ILA BANTU SHONA
NDEBELE
PEOPLE: BANTU MASHOMA
MATABELE BALOKWAKWA
RIVER: SABI GWAII LUNDI
LIMPOPO SANYATI ZAMBEZI
TOWN: GWELO UMTALI
BULAWAYO
WATERFALL: VICTORIA

ZIMMAH (FATHER OF —) SHIMEI
ZIMRAN (MOTHER OF —) KETURAH
ZIMRI (FATHER OF —) SALU ZERAH
ZINA (FATHER OF —) SHIMEI
ZINC FAR SPELT ZINCUM SPELTER
TUTENAG EXCLUDER
ZING PEP VIM ZIP DASH SNAP
ENERGY SPIRIT RAZZMATAZZ
ZINGEL PERCID
ZINKE CORNET
ZINNIA CRASSINA
ZION SION ISRAEL UTOPIA
ZIONIST IRGUNIST
ZIP VIM DASH SNAP FORCE WHISK
BUTTON ENERGY STINGO
ZIPHAH (FATHER OF —) JEHALELEEL
ZIPHION (FATHER OF —) GAD
ZIPPER FASTENER
(PART OF —) TAB FACE PULL STOP
TAPE CHAIN SLIDE TOOTH
ZIPPOR (SON OF —) BALAK
ZIPPORAH (FATHER OF —) REUEL
JETHRO
(HUSBAND OF —) MOSES
(SON OF —) ELIEZER GERSHOM
ZIRCON JARGON AZORITE

MALACON HYACINTH STARLITE
ZITHER KIN QIN CANON CANUN
GUSLI KANOON CITHARA GITERNE
GITTERN AUTOHARP GALEMPONG
(JAPANESE —) KOTO
ZITHER HARP KOTO
ZIZA (FATHER OF —) SHIPHI
REHOBOAM
(MOTHER OF —) MAACHAH
ZIZITH SISITH FRINGES TASSELS
TSITSITH
ZO DZO ZOH ZOBO
ZOARITE BIMMELER
ZOBEBAH (FATHER OF —) COZ
ZOBO ZO DZO ZOH ZOBU
ZODIAC GIRDLE BALDRIC
BAWDRICK SIGNIFIER
(SECTION OF —) TRIGON
(SIGN OF —) LEO RAM BULL CRAB
FISH GOAT LION ARIES LIBRA
SCALE TWINS VIRGO ARCHER
CANCER GEMINI PISCES TAURUS
SCORPIO AQUARIUS CAPRICORN
ZOHAR (FATHER OF —) SIMEON
(SON OF —) EPHRON
ZOHETH (FATHER OF —) ISHI
ZOISITE THULITE
ZONA ZOSTER
ZONE BED AREA BAND BEAM BELT
HALO PLAGE TRACT CIRCLE
REGION ZODIAC CLIMATE
HORIZON ZONULET CINCTURE
CINGULUM FRONTIER HABENULA
HISTOGEN STRINGER
(— OF CONFLICT) FRONT
(— OF FLAME) MANTLE
(— OF MINERALS) CORONA
(— OF VENUS) CEST CESTUS
(ABYSSAL —) BASSALIA
(PALEONTOLOGIC —S) ASSISE

(SAFETY —) ISLET ISLAND REFUGE
(STRATOGRAPHIC —) HEMERA
(WELDING —) ROOT
ZOOECIUM AUTOPORE
ZOOID PERSON SIPHON BRYOZOAN
HYDRANTH POLYPIDE ZOOTHOME
ZOOLOGIST AMERICAN DEAN GILL
ADAMS ALLEN BAIRD BAKER
BIRGE CLARK GOULD GUYER
MORSE SHULL BINNEY BROOKS
BUTLER CASTLE ELLIOT FISHER
GARMAN HOLMES KOFOID
MORGAN NEWMAN PARKER
RIDDLE STILES WILDER WILSON
AGASSIZ BARTSCH FERNALD
KELLOGG MCCLUNG NUTTING
VERRILL WHITMAN CRAMPTON
GRINNELL HORNADAY KIRTLAND
MELANDER SHELFORD
COCKERELL DAVENPORT
PETRUNKEVITCH
AUSTRIAN FRISCH
BELGIAN BENEDEN
CANADIAN ANDERSON
DANISH STEENSTRUP
ENGLISH BUSK GRAY OWEN
FLOWER GROGAN LISTER
MORGAN MURRAY NEWTON
PARKER BEDDARD GUNTHER
HASWELL POULTON YARRELL
GOODRICH MACBRIDE MITCHELL
FRENCH DELAGE PERRIER
DUJARDIN BLAINVILLE
VALENCIENNES
GERMAN VOGT BREHM BRONN
CARUS CLAUS DOHRN BOVERI
LEYDIG MOBIUS MULLER
HERTWIG SIEBOLD SPEMANN
BUTSCHLI GUENTHER BECHSTEIN
LEUCKHART SCHAUDINN

BLUMENBACH GOLDSCHMIDT
REICHENBACH LICHTENSTEIN
ITALIAN GRASSI
NORWEGIAN SARS NANSEN
RUSSIAN PANDER KOVALEVSKI
METCHNIKOFF
SWEDISH LOVEN
ZOOPHYTE CORAL SPONGE
HYDROID
ZOOSPORE MONAD SWARMER
ZOOCARP
ZOPHAH (FATHER OF —) HELEM
HOTHAM
ZOPHAI (FATHER OF —) ELKANAH
ZORIL SKUNK POWCAT CHINCHE
POLECAT MUISHOND
ZOROASTRIAN GABAR PARSI
GUEBRE PARSEE
ZOROASTRIANISM MAZDAISM
ZOUAVE ZUZU SCALER ZOUZOU
ZOUNDS OONS WAUNS ZOONS
ZUAR (SON OF —) NETHANEEL
ZUCCHETTO CALOTTE SOLIDEO
SKULLCAP
ZUCCHINI COURGETTE
ZULU CAR TRAIN LUGGER
MATABELE
ZUNI CIBOLAN SHALAKO
ZUR (FATHER OF —) JEHIEL
(SON OF —) COZBI
ZURIEL (FATHER OF —) ABIHAIL
ZWINGLIAN TIGURINE
ZYGOMATIC JUGAL
ZYGOSPORE COPULA
ZYGOTE OOCYST OOSPERM
OOSPORE SPORONT OOKINETE
ZYME YEAST ZYMIN ENZYME
FERMENT
ZYMOGEN PEPSINOGEN
ZYRIAN KOMI SYRYAN